This awesome tome entitled

THE N. I. V. EXHAUSTIVE CONCORDANCE

is hereby presented by Messrs.

Bernard Bowers B.A. Esq.,
Andrew Philip M.A. (Hons) Esq.,
Gordon J. Jones M.A. (Hons) Esq.

to their friend and flatmate, Mr.

Glyn J. Hackett M.A. (Hons) Esq.

on the occasion of his 24th birthday,
on this 27th day of September
in the year of our Lord 1998.

Bernard Andy Gordon

A Regency Reference Library Book

The NIV *Exhaustive Concordance*

Edward W. Goodrick &
John R. Kohlenberger III
Donald L. Potts & James A. Swanson,
Associate Editors

Hodder & Stoughton
LONDON SYDNEY AUCKLAND TORONTO

The NIV Exhaustive Concordance

A Subsidiary of Harper Collins Publishers

First published in Great Britain 1990

A CIP record for this title is available from the British Library

ISBN 0-340-53777-9

CONTENTS

PREFACE

A Brief History of the NIV Concordance Project

The King James Version was published in 1611. Its first multilingual concordance, Robert Young's *Analytical Concordance to the Bible*, appeared 268 years later. It took forty years of manual labor—including three years of typesetting! In 1894, James Strong's *Exhaustive Concordance to the Bible* joined Young's. It too involved nearly three decades of labor. The Revised Standard Version was completed in 1952, and its first multilingual concordance was issued in 1988: *Eerdmans' Analytical Concordance to the Revised Standard Version*, edited by Richard E. Whitaker. The New American Standard was published in 1971. *The New American Standard Exhaustive Concordance of the Bible* (Holman) appeared in 1981, a project that involved more than ten years and seventy contributors under the general editorship of Robert L. Thomas. *The NIV Exhaustive Concordance* now joins these multilingual concordances after seven years of labor on the part of two full-time editors, two part-time associate editors, and two consulting computer analysts.

The NIV Exhaustive Concordance is in fact the fourth to be produced by The NIV Concordance Project. Within two years of its inception in October of 1979, and just three years after the release of the New International Version itself, the Project created *The NIV Complete Concordance* (Zondervan, 1981). The following year, 1982, saw the release of *The NIV Handy Concordance*, which is also printed in millions of NIV Bibles as the NIV "Mini" or "Standard" Concordance. (Anglicized Editions of these two *Concordances* were prepared and published by Hodder and Stoughton in 1983 and 1985, respectively.) A further abridgement, known in-house as the NIV "Micro" Concordance, was also made in 1982 and is published only in NIV Bibles.

Work on *The NIV Exhaustive Concordance* began in 1983, pairing editors Edward W. Goodrick and John R. Kohlenberger III with computer analysts Dennis B. Thomas and Barbara Perz. Proofreaders James Swanson and Donald Potts put in so many hours on the project that they were named associate editors. The analysts developed software that would assist the editors to manually interrelate or "match up" the NIV to the Hebrew, Aramaic, and Greek originals. The primary focus of this "match-up" process was on the identification of the lexical or root form of each Hebrew, Aramaic, and Greek word and describing the interrelation of each word of the original with each word of the NIV. The "match-up" process and its several levels of proofreading took six years—from 1983 through 1989.

The database that resulted from this process contains nearly 900,000 lines, each of which has five fields of data. Thus, the database contains nearly 4,500,000 items of information that required at least 10 million editorial decisions. This database, dubbed the "Portland Index" after its place of origin, can be read in either the order of the NIV or the order of the original languages. It serves as the basis for this concordance, for the computer program the **NIV**[PC] (Zondervan Electronic Publishing, 1989), and for all future concordances and indexes to the NIV planned by Zondervan and The NIV Concordance Project.

The *Concordance* was typeset by John R. Kohlenberger III, using Xerox Ventura Publisher 2.0 and WordPerfect 5.0, and is perhaps the largest and most complex book yet produced by desktop publishing technology. The typesetting process, from first proofs to camera-ready copy, took only ten weeks.

ACKNOWLEDGMENTS

So many people have encouraged us by word and with prayer over the past decade that we cannot possibly begin to thank you all. But the authors do want to specially acknowledge those who have had direct involvement in the planning, shaping and production of this concordance.

Bob De Vries, former publisher of Zondervan, entrusted this project to two unknown educators from Oregon and never wavered in his support. Paul Hillman, former president of Zondervan Publishing House, was also supportive and sensitive to our needs.

Stan Gundry, General Manager, Zondervan Publishing House, and Publisher, Academic and Professional Books, was directly in charge of this project throughout its history. He was always there to make decisions and to provide encouragement and support. Editor Ed van der Maas was close to the project for its last three years and personally worked through its final marathon typesetting sessions. The corporate management at Zondervan, especially Jim Buick and Bruce Ryskamp, showed great interest and support.

John Van Diest, publisher of Multnomah Press, saw the value of the project from the beginning and encouraged us to pursue it.

Bob Lind and Dennis Thomas, formerly of Control Data, were introduced to us by Dale Benoit and helped get the project underway. Rolf Engelbrecht provided creative input for the design of the original software. Dennis Thomas and Barbara Perz developed original software for all phases of the concordance project.

Jim Swanson began as a proofreader for both the New and Old Testament materials but developed into an associate editor greatly responsible for the integrity of the concordance database. He also did the lion's share of the work on the KJV cross-references and on the indexes to Strong's numbering system. Don Potts, also an associate editor, spent many long hours helping to correct the New Testament data and was instrumental in the design of the concordance.

Drs. Ronald Youngblood and Walter Wessel of Bethel Seminary West interacted with our text-critical questions. The authors assume full responsibility for the text represented in the concordance.

Jan Goodrick graciously tolerated the invasion of her home by the disruptive activities of the concordance gang.

Rex Koivisto of Multnomah School of the Bible helped significantly with the Greek vocabulary lists. Hodder and Stoughton provided preliminary materials comparing the North American and Anglicized editions of the NIV. Carolyn Kohlenberger compared the two editions in their entirety to develop the exhaustive lists of spelling and word differences. She also helped complete the NIV related-word list and the KJV cross-references.

Ed Smith provided technical proofreading and helped complete the Hebrew transliterations. Laura Weller read every heading and context line of the main concordance and with amazingly good humor found many intentional and unintentional errors.

Larry and Cyndi Stone and Aaron Jarrard of OmniTek Computers in Portland, Oregon provided invaluable technical assistance and allowed us to experiment endlessly with their hardware and software. Bob Palioca, chief executive officer of Kethiv Technologies, also of Portland, provided counsel and the use of equipment without reserve.

Mark Hunt, John J. Hughes, and Jeffrey William Gillette of Zondervan Electronic Publishing supplied us with an early release of their Scripture Fonts software, designed by Ronald Allen Simkins, which was used to produce the Hebrew, Aramaic, and Greek characters in the biblical-language index-lexicons.

The staff of Multnomah Graphics, particularly its director Eric Weber and typesetter Brian Davis, provided us 24-hour access to their offices and equipment for two long weeks in June.

DEDICATION

This concordance is dedicated to our wives and children
who for so many years endured so much with love, patience, and support.

To the memory of Gwen Goodrick.
To Janet Goodrick, John Goodrick, Cynthia Goodrick Parkhurst,
Lynda Goodrick Bock, and James Goodrick.

To Carolyn Kohlenberger.
To Sarah Kohlenberger and Joshua Kohlenberger.

INTRODUCTION

A concordance is an index to a book. It is usually arranged in alphabetical order and shows the location of each word in the book. In addition, it often supplies several words of the context in which each word is found.

There are two kinds of Bible concordances for the nonspecialist: those that deal only with the English text of the Bible version on which they are based, and those that also deal with the Hebrew, Aramaic, and Greek texts from which the Bible version was translated.

Examples of English-only concordances are *Cruden's Complete Concordance* for the King James Version and the *NIV Complete Concordance*. The best-known examples of multilingual concordances are Young's *Analytical Concordance* and Strong's *Exhaustive Concordance*, both based on the King James Version.

An *analytical* concordance is organized in English alphabetical order and shows a complete index of all the different words of a given translation (with the exception of the most common articles, conjunctions, prepositions, and pronouns, such as *a, and, to,* and *he*). Each entry is subdivided according to the Hebrew, Aramaic, or Greek words that underlie the English. Each reference in these subdivisions is listed with a brief context. The analytical concordance also contains index-lexicons of biblical-language vocabulary, showing the various English words that translate them.

An *exhaustive* concordance by definition should contain every reference to every word of the Bible version on which it is based. This is true of Strong's *Exhaustive Concordance to the Bible* (but not of Thomas's *New American Standard Exhaustive Concordance of the Bible*, which did not index the most common articles, conjunctions, prepositions, and pronouns). An exhaustive concordance is organized in English alphabetical order, indexes every word of the Bible, and lists every single biblical reference in which that word appears. For all but the most common words, a context is also given with each reference. (In Strong's work, the more common words are exhaustively indexed but without contexts.) Unlike the analytical concordance, an exhaustive concordance lists the references for each English word in biblical order, from Genesis to Revelation.

In Strong's *Concordance* and the NAS *Concordance*, the relationship of the English to the originals is indicated by a numbering system that was originally devised for Strong's concordance. Strong made a list of the Hebrew and "Chaldee" (Aramaic) words used in the Old Testament and of the Greek words used in the New. To each word he assigned a number. This number appears at the end of each context line to indicate the word the English translates. By consulting the dictionaries in the back of these exhaustive concordances, the user can match numbers in order to identify the biblical word, to see its "root" definition, and to find its range of translation in the English Bible.

The *NIVEC* adopts the simple format of the exhaustive concordance for the main concordance. Like Strong's, it is truly exhaustive, indexing even the most frequent articles, conjunctions, prepositions, and pronouns in their own special section. Like Strong's, the *NIVEC* uses a numbering system but, for reasons explained below (p. xvi), it is an entirely new system. Two indexes cross-reference Strong's numbers to the new numbers and vice versa. For its biblical-language indexes, the *NIVEC* adopts the format of the analytical concordance. It has three separate indexes—Hebrew, Aramaic, and Greek—that list every word in the original-language texts and every word and phrase used to translate them in the NIV. Thus the *NIVEC* combines the best features of Young's and Strong's concordances.

FEATURES OF THE NIV EXHAUSTIVE CONCORDANCE

The *NIVEC* is divided into four major sections: (1) the Main Concordance, (2) the Index of Articles, Conjunctions,

Particles, Prepositions, and Pronouns, (3) the Biblical Language Indexes, and (4) the Numbering System Indexes.

THE MAIN CONCORDANCE

Below is a typical entry from the Main Concordance:

AARON (318) [AARON'S, AARONIC]
Ex 4:14 "What about your brother, **A** the Levite? 195
4:27 The LORD said to **A**, "Go into the desert 195

The heading consists of:
(1) the indexed word (AARON);
(2) the frequency count in parentheses (318);
(3) the list of related words (AARON'S, AARONIC).

The context lines consist of:
(1) the book-chapter-verse reference;
(2) the context for the indexed word;
(3) the number key to the index-lexicon.

Headings

There are four kinds of headings: (1) NIV word headings, (2) NIV "See" references, (3) NIV Anglicized "See" references, and (4) KJV "See" references.

NIV Word Headings

The North American Edition of the NIV contains 726,109 total words, with a unique vocabulary of 14,462. The *NIVEC* is an exhaustive alphabetic index to every word and numeral of the NIV.

The simplest heading is composed of the NIV word and its frequency count, for example:

ABBA (3)

The frequency count lists the total number of times the word appears in the NIV, which is also the number of contexts listed in the concordance. The *NIVEC* is the first exhaustive concordance to provide this information.

The headings show the indexed words exactly as they are spelled in the NIV. If the word occurs in other forms or spellings, these words appear in square brackets following the frequency count:

ABANDON (13) [ABANDONED, ABANDONS]

ABANDONED (36) [ABANDON]

ABANDONS (1) [ABANDON]

Rather than listing all related words after each indexed word, the editors chose one indexed word to act as the "group heading." All related words are listed after the group heading, and each of the related word headings points back to the group heading. In the example above, ABANDON serves as the group heading for ABANDONED and ABANDONS.

The headings also group together words that share common elements. For example:

ABLE (133) [ABILITY, ABLE-BODIED, DISABLED, ENABLE, ENABLED, ENABLES, ENABLING]

Place names composed of more than one word have a single, multiple-word heading:

BAAL GAD (3) [BAAL, GAD]

If the second or third term of a multiple-word place name is not indexed as an NIV word in its own right, it still appears in the Main Concordance as a heading that refers to the multiple-word heading:

AMMONI See KEPHAR AMMONI

(Multiple-word headings appear only for place names generated by transliteration. They are not used for place names that combine a geographic term and a proper noun, such as the Jordan River, the Sea of Galilee, or Mount Sinai.)

NIV "See" References

78 words occur a total of 364,004 times—more than half the bulk of the NIV! These words are exhaustively indexed in their own section: the Index of Articles, Conjunctions, Particles, Prepositions, and Pronouns (see p. xiv). These words are also represented by headings in the Main Concordance, with a message referring to this special index:

A (9144) [AN] See Index of Articles Etc.

Eight of these 78 words have a selected listing of contexts in the Main Concordance.

HAD, HAS, and HAVE are usually used as auxiliary verbs to indicate the English perfect tense, as in the clause "everything I **have** commanded you." As auxiliary verbs, these words are not indexed in the Main Concordance. But these words also occur as verbs in their own right, expressing the idea of ownership, "He **had** so many flocks," or causing action, "God **had** me wander." In these latter cases, the words are indexed in the Main Concordance: HAD 533 of 2791 occurrences, HAS 266 of 2407, HAVE 827 of 4313.

Neither I nor AM is indexed in the Main Concordance, but many important passages containing the self-revelation of

God contain the phrase I AM, such as Exodus 3:14, "**I AM** WHO **I AM**," and John 8:58, "before Abraham was born, **I am**!" 61 highly significant verses have been selected from the 1036 occurrences of the phrase I AM for the Main Concordance.

When ON is used as a proper name (4 of 4658 occurrences), it is indexed in the Main Concordance, as is SO (1 of 3003). When WILL is used in the sense of volition, as in the will of God or will of man (166 of 10,192 occurrences), it is indexed in the Main Concordance.

NIV Anglicized "See" References

The Anglicized Edition of the NIV was published in the United Kingdom in 1979. Anglicization "in Bible translation has come to mean the adoption of the English spelling, vocabulary, and usages common to British, as distinct from American, readers" (*The NIV: The Making of a Contemporary Translation*, p. 137 [Zondervan, 1986]).

Most of the differences between the North American and Anglicized editions are matters of spelling. At the end of this introduction is a list of the 288 words that are consistently spelled differently between the two editions, words such as "centre" and "center," "honour" and "honor," "pasture-land" and "pastureland."

In 227 verses, however, the differences between the two editions go beyond spelling. These more major differences are handled in two ways. First, at the end of the introduction, there is a complete, alphabetical listing of verbal differences involving indexed words. Second, "See" references for 65 key word differences have been included in the Main Concordance. They appear in headings such as:

EARS OF CORN (Anglicized) See HEADS OF GRAIN

The editors hope that these features will make the *NIVEC* fully useful to readers of both the North American and Anglicized editions of the NIV.

KJV "See" References

The King James or Authorized Version has been the dominant English Bible translation from the early seventeenth century to the latter half of the twentieth century. Because of this, the KJV has had profound impact on the language of both the Church and English-speaking society. To help users familiar with KJV vocabulary find the proper NIV terms, more than 2000 KJV words appear in 1600 KJV "See" references. These include such headings as:

COMFORTER (KJV) See COUNSELOR

[GIVE UP THE] GHOST (KJV) See BREATHED HIS LAST, DIE, DIED, DYING GASP, GAVE UP HIS SPIRIT, PERISHED

[HOLY] GHOST (KJV) See [HOLY] SPIRIT

Context Lines

Concordances are word indexes. At the very least, they index the book, chapter, and verse in which these words are located. Most concordances also show each word within a brief phrase or clause: a context. This gives the user a better idea of the use of the word and helps to locate a specific verse that contains that word.

Most concordances limit their contexts to a single line. This is generally true of the *NIVEC*; however, it has many two-line and several three-line contexts. These longer contexts help give a better glimpse into a word's function within the English text and give a better idea of the relationship of the English to the original languages.

The purpose of context lines in a concordance is merely to help the reader recognize or find a specific verse in the Bible. For word study—or any kind of Bible study—the context offered by a concordance is rarely enough to go on. Nevertheless, sometimes a short sentence or a whole verse fits on one line, as in the case of John 11:35: "Jesus wept." Under the heading PRAISE, the *NIVEC* was able to present the entirety of Psalm 150 on thirteen consecutive lines!

Taken by themselves, context lines can and do misrepresent the teaching of Scripture by omitting key words. "There is no God" is a context taken straight from Psalm 14:1. Of course the Bible does not teach this; it is what "the fool says in his heart"! Similarly, a context for Leviticus 24:16 might read "the LORD must be put to death" while the text actually says "anyone who blasphemes the name of the LORD must be put to death."

Great care has been taken by the editors, programmers, and proofreaders of the *NIVEC* to create contexts that are informative and accurate. But the reader should always check word contexts by looking them up in the NIV itself. "The Wicked Bible," a KJV edition of 1631, accidentally omitted the word "not" from the seventh commandment, for which the printers were fined 300 pounds sterling! Though there are no such fines for misleading contexts, the editors are still deeply concerned that the *NIVEC* be used discerningly.

Bible Translating and Concordance Making

Traduttore traditore, "the translator is a traitor," is an ancient proverb oft quoted in books about Bible translations. To a degree this proverb is true, for no translation can perfectly bring over all the meaning and nuances of one language into another. Because no two languages share identical grammar and an identical range of word meanings, not even the best-intentioned word-for-word translation can claim to perfectly represent the original.

If the translator is a traitor, the concordance maker must be his partner in crime. For no multilingual concordance can perfectly represent both the English and biblical-language texts it indexes. It can perfectly represent the vocabulary of the English text, for it needs only to list the location of each of its words. In this respect a concordance is either absolutely right or absolutely wrong. But when a concordance attempts to display the relationship between the English text and the biblical languages, it falls heir to the same difficulties that face the Bible translator.

Much of Bible translation involves one-to-one relationships. More often than not, אֱלֹהִים is translated "God," Ἰησοῦς "Jesus," and ἀγαπάω "love." This part of translating and concordance making is easy.

Often, however, more than one word is needed in English to render a word in the originals. For example, the Greek word τεκνίον is regularly translated "little children" in the KJV and NAS and "dear children" in the NIV. Conversely, one English word can translate several words from the originals. Thus the infamous number "666" of Revelation 13:18 translates three Greek words.

Sometimes, because of differences in idiom, it takes several English words to translate two or more words from the original languages. This is called "dynamic equivalence" or "functional equivalence." For example, the famous KJV expletive "God forbid!" translates one word in Hebrew and two words in Greek—neither of which has either "God" or "forbid" as part of its "literal" meaning! Nevertheless, "God forbid!" is the *functional* equivalent of the Greek and Hebrew phrases.

Multilingual concordances of the past have tended to display the relationship between English and the original languages as if it were almost always one-to-one. Scan a few columns of Strong's *Concordance*, and you see context after context presenting one indexed word followed by one number. Over the years, this has lent support to the misconception that the KJV is an absolutely "literal," word-for-word translation. However, the original preface to the KJV stated, "We have not tied our selves to an uniformity of phrasing, or to an identity of words, as some peradventure would wish that we had done. . . ." Young's *Analytical Concordance*, and more so *Eerdmans' Analytical Concordance to the RSV* that followed it, attempt to show multiple-word translation by means of multiple-word headings. However, nothing within the context itself shows how the indexed word relates to the original Greek or Hebrew.

The *NIVEC*, by means of three different typefaces in the context line and a more nuanced use of its entirely new numbering system, shows more fully than any previous concordance the interrelation of the English text and the biblical languages.

Context Lines: Word-for-Word Translation

The simplest context line presents four items of information. First, the location of the indexed word by book, chapter, and verse. Second, the context line. Third, within the context line, the indexed word is abbreviated by its first letter and is *usually* in bold type. Fourth, a number at the right margin indicates the Hebrew, Aramaic, or Greek word the indexed word translates. For example, under the heading AARON on page 1:

Ex 4:14 "What about your brother, **A** the Levite? 195
4:27 The LORD said to **A,** "Go into the desert 195

Note that the book abbreviation is not repeated in the second reference. Book abbreviations are repeated at the top of new columns (see columns 2 and 3, page 1). A complete list of NIV book abbreviations appears at the beginning of the Main Concordance.

The numbering system indicates which biblical language is translated. Hebrew words are represented by numbers in normal "roman" type, from 1 through 9597. Aramaic word numbers are also in roman type, from 10001 through 10779. Greek word numbers are in italics, from *1* through *6068*. This "Goodrick/Kohlenberger numbering system," named after its editors, is hereafter referred to as "G/K numbers."

Context Lines: Multiple-Word Translation

One English Word—Multiple Original Words. When the indexed word translates more than one word from the original, this is indicated by an appropriate number of G/K numbers at the end of the line. This is especially true of numerals, for example:

Rev 7:5 From the tribe of Judah **12,000** *1577+5942*

Nu 1:46 The total number was **603,550.**
547+547+2256+2256+2256
+2822+2822+4395+4395+8993+9252

The second example is a very rare occurrence of a string of G/K numbers too long to fit on one line. In this case, the string of numbers is broken to fit on two lines; the second line begins with a plus (+) to show that it is a continuation of the previous line. Strings of G/K numbers are always organized in numerical order.

In some cases, multiple English words are needed to define a Hebrew, Aramaic, or Greek word or phrase. We will refer to this as "multiple-word translation." In other cases, multiple English words are needed to translate the inflection of the original, to express, for example, the tense of a verb or the number and gender of a noun. We will refer to this as "assisting in translation." These two concepts are explained below.

Multiple-word Translation. As mentioned above, the Greek word τεκνίον is regularly translated "little children" in the KJV and NAS and "dear children" in the NIV. If you were to look up the word "little" in either Strong's or the NAS *Concordance* and look at the context for 1 John 2:1, you would find the word abbreviated by its first letter with the number *5040* at the end of the line. However, if you looked up the word "children" you would find the same thing:

1Jo 2: 1 My *l* children, these things write *5040*

1Jo 2: 1 My little *c*, these things write I *5040*

In these examples (reproduced from Strong's *Concordance*), it would appear that the Greek word number *5040* meant only "little" or "children," depending on which entry you looked up first. Nothing in the context line would inform you that Greek word *5040* actually means "little children." Young's *Concordance*, on the other hand, does not list 1 John 2:1 under the word "little," but has a heading "CHILD or children, little—" under which our verse is indexed.

The *NIVEC* has solved the problem of indicating such multiple-word translations by putting *all* the words in bold type. Using the same example of 1 John 2:1, under the headings "dear" and "children":

1Jn 2: 1 My **d children,** I write this to you so *5448*

1Jn 2: 1 My **dear c,** I write this to you so *5448*

If more than one English word is used to render several words from the original, the typefaces and the G/K numbers show all the words involved in this multiple-word translation. Such is the case with "have children" in Mark 12:19, as indexed under both words:

Mk 12:19 must marry the widow and **have c** *1985+5065*

Mk 12:19 widow and **h children** for his brother. *1985+5065*

This unique convention shows at a glance all the words involved in a multiple-word translation, the English words as well as the original-language words.

Assist in Translation. The biblical languages use spelling or "inflection" to indicate such things as the subject and tense of a verb, or the number and gender of a noun. Such inflections are not part of the definition of a word, but are necessary to reflect in translation.

English does not inflect to the same degree as the biblical languages. Thus translators have to use auxiliary or "assisting" words to render these inflections. Common assisting words are pronouns such as "he" and "she," auxiliary verbs such as "shall" and "will," and quantifying words such as "many," "some," and even "two."

If you were to look up the word "will" in either Strong's or the NAS *Concordance*, you would notice that for most of the several thousand references to the word, there is no number at the end of the context line. Some might take this to mean that the word does not represent any word in the original but was simply supplied by the translators. But for the most part this is not true. The word "will" was used to translate the inflection of a Hebrew, Aramaic, or Greek verb, not the verb itself. But the editors did not put the number of that verb at the end of the context line lest the user misinterpret "will" as the *definition* of that number.

The *NIVEC* has solved this problem by means of different typefaces and a code. If an indexed word is a word that "assists in translation," the context line displays it in three ways, as shown in the following example, found under the heading LET:

Ge 1:26 God said, *"L us* **make** man in our image, AIT

First, the abbreviation of the indexed word is in italics, because it is not the main word but a word that assists in the translation of "make." Second, the word it assists ("make") is in bold. Third, the code AIT ("Assisting In Translation") appears at the end of the line in the place of a G/K number.

On the other hand, if the indexed word is assisted by other NIV words, the indexed word is abbreviated and in bold type, but the assisting words are in italics. Using the same example, but looking now under the heading MAKE:

Ge 1:26 God said, *"Let us* **m** man in our image, 6913

In both examples, the auxiliary verb "Let" and the pronoun "us" are marked as assisting words by the italic typeface. In both contexts, the verb "make" is shown to be the main, "defining" word by the bold typeface. Under their own headings, the code AIT also marks the assisting word, while the G/K number identifies the defining word.

By using these conventions to identify multiple-word translations and to distinguish between defining words and assisting words, the *NIVEC* more thoroughly displays the relationship between the English and the biblical languages than any concordance that has preceded it.

Context Lines: "Substitution" Translation

For stylistic reasons, Bible translators often substitute nouns for pronouns and pronouns for nouns. For example, John 8:1 in the KJV reads "Jesus went unto the mount of Olives." Strong tells us that here "Jesus" translates Greek word *846*, which is not the proper name Ἰησοῦς (Strong's word *2424*), but the pronoun αὐτός, "he." Such "substitutionary" translations are common and acceptable in Bible translations, but other concordances treat them as if they were one-to-one translations.

The *NIVEC* indicates substitutionary translation by attaching a raised "S" to the G/K number or numbers at the end of the context line. For example, under AARON:

Ex 30:21 This is to be a lasting ordinance for **A** 2257[S]

Ex 10:11 Then **Moses and A** were driven out 4392[S]

In the first example, "Aaron" substitutes for the masculine singular pronominal suffix ךָ, normally translated "he," "him," or "his." In the second example, the phrase "Moses and Aaron" substitutes for the masculine plural pronominal suffix םָ, normally translated "they," "their," or "them."

Similarly, the NIV often uses forms of the verb "do" to substitute for a more specific verb repeated in the context. For example, Deuteronomy 6:16 reads "Do not test the LORD your God as you **did** at Massah" rather than "Do not test the LORD your God as you **tested** him at Massah." This substitutionary translation is indicated under DID:

Dt 6:16 Do not test the LORD your God as *you* **d** 5814[S]

The NIV is not unique in using substitutionary translation. The *NIVEC* is unique in displaying it.

Context Lines: "Not in Hebrew" and "Not in Greek"

Because modern English and ancient Hebrew, Aramaic, and Greek do not have identical rules of grammar and style, translators must often add words for the sake of clarity. For example, Mark 16:9 in the KJV begins "Now when Jesus was risen early. . . ." Strong has no number at the end of this context line because there is no Greek word for "Jesus" in this verse; it was supplied by the translators to give a subject to the verb.

The *NIVEC* follows this practice of indicating NIV words that are not in the originals by using the code NIH, "Not In Hebrew," for both the Hebrew and Aramaic of the Old Testament and *NIG*, "Not In Greek," for the New. Under the heading ABRAHAM, for example, we find:

Ge 21:33 **A** planted a tamarisk tree in Beersheba, NIH

Heb 6:15 **A** received what was promised. *NIG*

As in the case of the KJV in Mark 16:9, these proper names were supplied for clarity, for the benefit of the reader.

A Note on NIV Typefaces

In the NIV text itself, italics are used when a Hebrew, Aramaic, or Greek word is not translated, but merely spelled out in English letters. These "transliterated" words include *Selah* in the Psalms and *"Eloi, eloi, lama sabachthani?"* in Matthew 27:46 and Mark 15:34. However, the NIV italic typeface could be confused with the italics used in the concordance for words that assist in translation (AIT). Therefore, all italics used in the NIV text are printed as normal "roman" type in context lines.

The NIV uses half brackets (⌊ ⌋) to indicate words supplied for clarity. The KJV, NAS and other translations use italics for the same purpose. (Compare 1 Samuel 13:1 in the NIV, KJV, and NAS.) The *NIVEC* uses regular brackets ([ ]) instead.

The NIV uses a typographical convention to distinguish between two different Hebrew words, both of which are usually translated "Lord" in English versions. For the proper name of God, יהוה ("Yahweh"), the NIV uses "LORD." For the title אֲדֹנָי, it uses "Lord." The *NIVEC* also distinguishes these two words under two separate headings. "Lord" and its possessive form "Lord's" are indexed under the headings *LORD and *LORD'S (pages 683-86). "LORD" and "LORD's" are indexed under the headings †LORD and †LORD'S (pages 686-708). In context lines, these words appear as in the NIV text.

THE INDEX OF ARTICLES, CONJUNCTIONS, PARTICLES, PREPOSITIONS, AND PRONOUNS

The Main Concordance indexes 363,965 references to 14,452 NIV words, numerals, and compound proper names. The Index of Articles, Conjunctions, Particles, Prepositions, and Pronouns indexes 364,004 references to 78 NIV words. These include 55 words that appear more than 1000 times each, such as "I," "me," and "my," and 23 less frequent words that are related to them, such as "myself," "I'll," and "I'm." This index makes the *NIVEC* the first truly exhaustive concordance since Strong's.

The format of the Index of Articles Etc. is very simple. Each of the 78 words has its own heading, followed by a frequency count. For example:

A (9144)

The eight words that are partially indexed in the Main Concordance (AM, HAD, HAS, HAVE, I, ON, SO, and WILL, see above pages x-xi) also have the message "See also selected list in the Main Concordance."

The 78 words of this section are indexed without contexts, since providing contexts would be of little benefit to the reader and would double the size of the *NIVEC*! Book, chapter, and verse references appear in biblical order. Books and chapters are set in bold print for easy location. If the indexed word occurs more than once in a verse, the total number of occurrences is indicated by a raised number:

Lev 1:3^2, 9, 10^2, 13, 14^3, 17; **2:**1, 2^2, 3, 4, 5, 6, 7,

This example from the indefinite article "A" shows that the article appears twice in Leviticus 1:3, 1:10, and 2:2, and three times in 1:14. Note too that book and chapter references appear just once. Verses within the same chapter are set off by commas. The final verse of the chapter is followed by a semicolon. The final verse of the entry is followed by a period.

THE BIBLICAL-LANGUAGE INDEX-LEXICONS

At the end of each context line in the Main Concordance is a code or a G/K number, describing the relationship of the NIV to the original languages. The three Biblical-Language Index-Lexicons list all of the words that are found in the Hebrew, Aramaic, and Greek texts from which the NIV was translated. These lists are in the alphabetical order of each of the three languages, which is also the order of the G/K numbering system.

The Index-Lexicon follows the pattern of Young's *Analytical Concordance* rather than that of Strong's dictionaries. This system more accurately interrelates the original languages to the NIV and is easier to read. The entry for Greek word *27* can serve as an example for most features of all three Index-Lexicons:

27 ἀγάπη *agapē* (116)
love (109)
love (2) *+26*
love (2) *+2400*
it^{S} (1) *+3836*
love feasts (1)
loves (1)

The heading begins with the G/K number, in bold type for easy location. Next is the lexical form or dictionary form of the word, followed by its transliteration, and the total number of occurrences in the biblical text. (The transliteration follows the system used in Zondervan's *Expositor's Bible Commentary*. A complete transliteration and pronunication guide appears before each index.)

The heading is followed by a list of all the ways in which the word is translated in the NIV, in descending order of frequency. If two words (or phrases) have the same frequency, they are listed in alphabetical order. Following the NIV word is its frequency count, in parentheses.

One-to-one translations are indicated by one NIV word, as in the case of the first and last NIV words in the example above. Multiple-word translations are indicated in two ways: by multiple NIV words and/or multiple G/K numbers. The next-to-the-last line, "love feasts (1)," indicates a multiple-word NIV translation. If you look up "love" and "feasts" in the Main Concordance, you will find the following contexts under Jude 1:12:

Jude 1:12 These men are blemishes at your l **feasts,** *27*
Jude 1:12 These men are blemishes at your **love f,** *27*

Under both headings, the phrase "love feasts" is shown to be the definition of Greek word *27*. (Multiple-word translation is described above on page xiii.)

When an NIV word or phrase translates more than one word of the original, the G/K number of the additional word (or words) follows the frequency count. That is why there are three separate lines for "love" in the example above. The first is a one-to-one translation. The second shows that in two cases "love" translates two Greek words: *27* and *26*. Similarly, the third shows that "love" translates Greek words *27* and *2400*.

Words that "assist in translation" (see above, page xiii) do not appear in the Index-Lexicons. This is because they do not *define* words. Rather, they assist words in translating tense, number, gender, and mood.

"Substitution" translation (see above, pages xiii-xiv) is noted with a raised "S," as in the Main Concordance. The fourth indexed word in the example above indicates that "it" is a substitution translation for Greek words *27+3836*. Because "it" is not indexed in the Main Concordance, you cannot locate this reference. (No other multilingual concordance allows the user to do this either.) By reading through the rest of the index, however, you see that the normal translation of the word is "love."

Untranslated Words

There is one other category of words in the Index-Lexicons that cannot be looked up in the Main Concordance. If a word in the originals is not translated in the NIV, either directly or in multiple-word translation, this is noted by the word "untranslated." This word is always last in the index list and includes a frequency count.

For example, the Hebrew word שָׁנָה (G/K 9102, Strong 8141) is normally translated "year(s)" in English versions. But its use with numbers is so repetitious in the Hebrew text that no English version translates it every time it appears. A word-for-word translation of Genesis 23:1 would be: "And the life of Sarah was one hundred **year** and twenty **year** and seven **years**—the **years** of the life of Sarah." Though שָׁנָה appears four times in this verse, "year(s)" appears only twice in the KJV and NAS, and once in the NIV.

According to the Hebrew Index-Lexicon to Young's *Analytical Concordance*, שָׁנָה is translated 805 times in the KJV. The Hebrew-Aramaic Dictionary of the NAS *Concordance* has a total of 789 occurrences. Actually, the word appears 880 times in the Hebrew text. The Hebrew Index-Lexicon of the *NIVEC* lists this word (9102) as translated 780 times and untranslated 100 times. Although all Bible translations leave words untranslated, the *NIVEC* is the first multilingual concordance to indicate this.

"Variant; not used"

The Index-Lexicons of the *NIVEC* list several hundred words that are alternate spellings of Hebrew, Aramaic, and Greek words, or words not found in the original-language texts translated by the NIV. The three word lists were compiled from several standard lexicons and grammars in the hope that the G/K numbering system could be used in a multitude of reference works, describing the textual base of most of the Bible translations currently in print.

Because these words are not translated by the NIV, they have no NIV words to index. Rather, on the line following the heading is the message "Variant; not used." The first word in each of the three Index-Lexicons (each of which is the first letter of its respective alphabet) is an example of this convention.

The Index-Lexicons to the *NIVEC* have three features not found in the indexes or dictionaries of any other concordance. First, the *NIVEC* provides frequency statistics of both the biblical languages and the English, including untranslated words. Second, each entry lists exhaustively all the NIV words and phrases that translate each word of the original, showing multiple-word translation and substitution translation. Third, the NIV words and phrases indexed are in their exact textual spelling, so the user can locate its heading in the Main Concordance without any further cross-referencing.

Index-Lexicon Versus Dictionary Format

The index-lexicon format was chosen over the dictionary format used in Strong's *Concordance* and the NAS *Concordance* for two reasons. First, it is the best and most readable format to show the relationship between the English text and the biblical languages. Second, it avoids a major problem inherent in the traditional dictionary format.

The dictionaries in Strong's *Concordance* and the NAS *Concordance* usually give a single "root" definition for each word. This is often misunderstood as the *only* definition or the "literal" meaning of the word and can be misused to criticize other valid translations of the word—even in the KJV and NAS themselves! For example, Young's Index-Lexicon to the New Testament lists 57 different KJV translations of the Greek word ποιέω (POIEŌ). Strong's dictionary defines this word as "to *make* or *do*." Either the KJV translators were wrong in 96% of their definitions or there is more to the meaning of ποιέω than "to *make* or *do*"!

The lists of NIV translations in the Index-Lexicons do in fact constitute a dictionary. The best definition of a biblical word is its range of meaning throughout the Bible.

THE NUMBERING SYSTEM INDEXES

You may have noticed in the examples above that the "Goodrick/Kohlenberger" numbering system differs from that of Strong. Advances in biblical scholarship have made it difficult, if not impossible, to use Strong's century-old system. In the first place, Strong's system indexes only the vocabulary of the original-language texts that underlie the KJV. Second, modern analysis of the biblical languages divides many words of identical spelling into two or three or more unique "homographs"—words with the same spelling but different meanings (such as the English word "bow"). This is especially true of biblical Hebrew. Third, Strong mixed the Hebrew and Aramaic ("Chaldee") vocabularies together into one numbering scheme, whereas all modern lexicons and grammars treat them as different languages. Fourth, even after a century and dozens of corrected editions, Strong's system still suffers from numerous typographical and factual errors. These factors demand both expansion and revision of Strong's system.

The general editor of the NAS *Concordance* opted to retain Strong's numbers. Typographical and factual errors were corrected while indexing the dictionaries to the NAS. To overcome the need for additional words and numbers, letters of the alphabet were added to Strong's existing numbers. For example, to number a word not included in Strong's original list that should be alphabetized between words 112 and 113, the NAS altered Strong's numbers to 112a, 112b, and 113.

Rather than attempt to similarly patch up Strong's well-worn system, the editors of the *NIVEC* decided to make a clean break and develop a new standard for use in up-to-date biblical-language reference works. But for the benefit of those who want to cross-reference to Strong's system, the editors also created two sets of indexes to show the relationship of these two numbering schemes.

Index of Strong to Goodrick/Kohlenberger Numbers

The first index is organized according to Strong's numbering system. It first indexes Strong's Hebrew and Aramaic ("Chaldee") numbers, then his Greek numbers.

Most of the index involves a one-to-one correspondence:

Strong	G/K
1	3
2	10003
3	4
4	10004

The first four words of Strong's Hebrew/Aramaic numbering system consist of two Hebrew and two Aramaic words. This is immediately apparent by the five-digit (Aramaic) G/K numbers.

Sometimes a single Strong's number corresponds to more than one G/K number, due to spelling variations. In this case, each corresponding G/K number is listed on its own line, but Strong's is replaced by a ditto mark (").

11 10
" 11

Sometimes Strong assigned a number to a compound name that the NIV treats as two separate words. The plus sign (+) marks this relationship:

25 . . . . 3+1500

Index of Goodrick/Kohlenberger to Strong Numbers

This set of indexes has one for each of the biblical languages: Hebrew, Aramaic, and Greek. Each index is organized according to the G/K numbering system.

As in the case of the previous set, most relationships are one-to-one:

G/K . . . . Strong
1 . . . . *1*
2 . . . . *2*
3 . . . . *3*
4 . . . . *4*

Sometimes a G/K number corresponds to more than one Strong number. In this case, each corresponding Strong number is listed on its own line, but the G/K number is replaced by a ditto mark (").

41 . . . . *39*
" *40*

Sometimes a G/K number is assigned to a compound word that Strong treated only as two separate words. The plus sign (+) marks this relationship:

15 . . 18 + 2041

In many cases, a G/K number has no corresponding Strong number. In this case, the G/K number is simply followed by blank space, as is the case with Greek numbers *122* and *207*.

In Conclusion

To Ralph Waldo Emerson, "A foolish consistency is the hobgoblin of little minds." To the editors of the *NIVEC*, there is no such thing as a foolish consistency in a biblical reference book. Every effort has been made by the editors, programmers, and proofreaders to make the *NIVEC* consistent and error-free. Strong's and Young's *Concordances* have each been through more than two dozen revisions, and we realize that our work has not been perfect either.

If you find anything that appears to be an error, write to The NIV Concordance Project, c/o Zondervan Publishing House, 1415 Lake Drive, S.E., Grand Rapids, MI 49506.

List of Spelling Differences between the Anglicized and North American Editions

Anglicized	*North American*
Abel Karamim	Abel Keramim
afterwards	afterward
ageing	aging
almug-wood	almugwood
any more	anymore
armour-bearer	armor-bearer
armour-bearers	armor-bearers
armour	armor
armoury	armory
authorisation	authorization
authorised	authorized
axe	ax
axe-head	axhead
backwards	backward
baptise	baptize
baptised	baptized
baptising	baptizing
battering-rams	battering rams
battle-bow	battle bow
behaviour	behavior
Berakiah	Berekiah
birth-pains	birth pains
blood-relative	blood relative
blood-relatives	blood relatives
broken-hearted	brokenhearted
burnt-out	burned-out
cauldron	caldron
cauldrons	caldrons
cancelled	canceled
cancelling	canceling
centre	center
centres	centers
channelled	channeled
chiselled	chiseled
chiselling	chiseling
clamour	clamor
coloured	colored
colourful	colorful
colours	colors
commander-in-chief	commander in chief
conies	coneys
counselled	counseled
counsellor	counselor
counsellors	counselors
criticised	criticized
Chuza	Cuza
defence	defense
defences	defenses
dishonour	dishonor
dishonoured	dishonored
dishonours	dishonors
distil	distill
door-frame	doorframe
door-frames	doorframes
door-keeper	doorkeeper
door-post	doorpost
drag-net	dragnet
dwelling-place	dwelling place
dwelling-places	dwelling places
ear-rings	earrings
enquire	inquire
enquiring	inquiring
enrol	enroll
enrolment	enrollment
equalled	equaled
ever-flowing	ever flowing
eye-witnesses	eyewitnesses
face down	facedown
faint-hearted	fainthearted
fault-finders	faultfinders

favour	favor
favourable	favorable
favourably	favorably
favoured	favored
favouritism	favoritism
favours	favors
fellow-citizens	fellow citizens
fellow-elder	fellow elder
fellow-man	fellowman
fellow-men	fellow men
fellow-prisoner	fellow prisoner
fellow-prisoners	fellow prisoners
fellow-servant	fellow servant
fellow-servants	fellow servants
fellow-soldier	fellow soldier
fellow-worker	fellow worker
fellow-workers	fellow workers
fertilise	fertilize
fervour	fervor
fig-tree	fig tree
fig-trees	fig trees
fish-hooks	fishhooks
flavour	flavor
for ever	forever
for evermore	forevermore
fulfil	fulfill
fulfilment	fulfillment
fulfils	fulfills
fulness	fullness
good-bye	good-by
grape-pickers	grape pickers
grey	gray
grey-haired	gray-haired
half-dead	half dead
half-tribe	half tribe
hand mill	handmill
harbour	harbor
harboured	harbored
harbours	harbors
hard-hearted	hardhearted
head-dresses	headdresses
heavenwards	heavenward
hiding-place	hiding place
hiding-places	hiding places
home town	hometown
honour	honor
honourable	honorable
honourably	honorably
honoured	honored
honouring	honoring
jaw-bone	jawbone
Joash	Jehoash
jewellery	jewelry
Joshbakashah	Joshbekashah
kind-hearted	kindhearted
labour	labor
laboured	labored
labourer	laborer
labourer's	laborer's
labourers	laborers
labouring	laboring
labours	labors
laughing-stock	laughingstock
law-breaker	lawbreaker
law-breakers	lawbreakers
levelled	leveled
licence	license
life-time	lifetime
lustre	luster
market-place	marketplace
market-places	marketplaces
marshalled	marshaled
marvelled	marveled
marvelling	marveling
marvellous	marvelous
Michmash	Micmash
mid-air	midair
misdemeanour	misdemeanor
mobilised	mobilized
moulded	molded
moulding	molding
moulds	molds
mouldy	moldy
money-lender	moneylender
multicoloured	multicolored
moustache	mustache
naiive	naive
near by	nearby
near-sighted	nearsighted
neighbour	neighbor
neighbour's	neighbor's
neighbouring	neighboring
neighbours	neighbors
neighbours'	neighbors'
newly-built	newly built
night-time	nighttime
no-one	no one
north-easter	northeaster
north-west	northwest
odour	odor
offence	offense
offences	offenses
open-handed	openhanded
over-righteous	overrighteous
panelled	paneled
panelling	paneling
paralysed	paralyzed
parcelled	parceled
pasture-land	pastureland
pasture-lands	pasturelands
plough	plow
ploughed	plowed
ploughing	plowing
ploughman	plowman
ploughs	plows
ploughshares	plowshares
plumb-line	plumb line
practise	practice
practised	practiced
practises	practices
pre-eminent	preeminent
pretence	pretense
quarrelled	quarreled
quarrelling	quarreling
realise	realize
realised	realized
realising	realizing
recognise	recognize
recognised	recognized
recognises	recognizes
recognising	recognizing
re-entered	reentered
re-established	reestablished
resting-place	resting place
revelled	reveled
revellers	revelers
revelling	reveling
river bed	riverbed
rumour	rumor
rumours	rumors
sandalled	sandaled
sand-bar	sandbar
sand-bars	sandbars
Saviour	Savior
sawn	sawed
sceptre	scepter
sceptres	scepters
Shammau	Shammua
sheep-shearers	sheepshearers
shield-bearer	shield bearer
shrine-prostitute	shrine prostitute
shrine-prostitutes	shrine prostitutes
shrivelled	shriveled
sick-bed	sickbed
side walls	sidewalls
signalled	signaled
signalling	signaling
simple-hearted	simplehearted
skilful	skillful
skilfully	skillfully
smoulder	smolder
smouldering	smoldering
smoulders	smolders
sombre	somber
south-east	southeast
south-west	southwest
splendour	splendor
storey	story
stout-hearted	stouthearted
stumbling-block	stumbling block
stumbling-stone	stumbling stone
sub-division	subdivision
sub-divisions	subdivisions
sulphur	sulfur
symbolises	symbolizes
sympathise	sympathize
sympathised	sympathized
thank-offering	thank offering
thank-offerings	thank offerings
theatre	theater
threshing-cart	threshing cart
threshing-floor	threshing floor
threshing-floors	threshing floors
threshing-sledge	threshing sledge
threshing-sledges	threshing sledges
tight-fisted	tightfisted
totalled	totaled
towards	toward
travelled	traveled
traveller	traveler
travellers	travelers
travelling	traveling
treasure-house	treasure house
tumble-weed	tumbleweed
tumours	tumors
unauthorised	unauthorized
unequalled	unequaled
unfavourable	unfavorable
unploughed	unplowed
unsandalled	unsandaled
untravelled	untraveled
upside-down	upside down
upwards	upward
vapour	vapor
vigour	vigor
water-carrier	water carrier
water-carriers	water carriers

wilful	willful
wilfully	willfully
wind-blown	windblown
wing-span	wingspan
woollen	woolen
worshipped	worshiped
worshipper	worshiper
worshippers	worshipers
worshipping	worshiping
worth while	worthwhile
yoke-fellow	yokefellow

Index of Word Differences Between the Anglicized and North American Editions

Anglicized	*North American*	*Verse Reference*
360	three hundred and sixty	2Sa 2:31
a man	anyone	Jn 7:51
ankles do not turn over	ankles do not turn	2Sa 22:37
ankles do not turn over	ankles do not turn	Ps 18:36
assistant	aide	Ex 24:13
assistant	aide	Ex 33:11
assistant	aide	Nu 11:28
assistant	aide	Jos 1:1
assistant	aide	Ne 6:5
become	be	1Ki 1:17
bind	obligate	Nu 30:2
binds	obligates	Nu 30:3
binds	obligates	Nu 30:6
binds	obligates	Nu 30:8
binds	obligates	Nu 30:8
binds	obligates	Nu 30:10
bitumen	tar	Ge 11:3
bound	obligated	Nu 30:4
bound	obligated	Nu 30:5
bound	obligated	Nu 30:7
bound	obligated	Nu 30:11
bound	obligated	Ro 1:14
brazier	fire pot	Ge 15:17
brazier	fire pot	Jer 36:22
brazier	fire pot	Jer 36:23
brazier	fire pot	Zec 12:6
bring up	rear	Hos 9:12
bringing them up	rearing them	2Ki 10:6
brought	took	Lk 10:34
brought up	reared	Isa 51:18
bruises	welts	Isa 1:6
burnt-out	burned-out	Jer 51:25
call	get	Nu 20:25
camp	encamp	Ex 14:2 [twice]
caused	raised	Ac 9:21
Chuza	Cuza	Lk 8:3
cock	rooster	Pr 30:31
cock	rooster	Mt 26:34
cock	rooster	Mt 26:74
cock	rooster	Mt 26:75
cock	rooster	Mk 13:35
cock	rooster	Mk 14:30
cock	rooster	Lk 22:34
cock	rooster	Lk 22:60
cock	rooster	Lk 22:61
cock	rooster	Jn 13:38
cock	rooster	Jn 18:27
corn	grain	Ge 37:7
corn	grain	Ex 22:6
corn	grain	Dt 16:9
corn	grain	Dt 23:25
corn	grain	Jdg 15:5 [twice]
corn	grain	2Ki 4:42
corn	grain	Ps 65:13
corn	grain	Ps 65:9
corn	grain	Ps 72:16
corn	grain	Isa 17:5
corn	grain	Isa 36:17
corn	grain	Jer 50:11
corn	grain	Jer 9:22
corn	grain	Eze 36:29
corn	grain	Hos 14:7
corn	grain	Mk 4:28
corn in the ear	kernel in the head	Mk 4:28
cornfield	grainfield	Dt 23:25
cornfields	grainfields	Mt 12:1
cornfields	grainfields	Mk 2:23
cornfields	grainfields	Lk 6:1
dishes	basins	1Ki 7:50
ears	kernels	Dt 23:25
ears	heads	Mt 13:26
ears of corn	heads of grain	Ge 41:5
ears of corn	heads of grain	Ge 41:6
ears of corn	heads of grain	Ge 41:7
ears of corn	heads of grain	Ge 41:22
ears of corn	heads of grain	Ge 41:24
ears of corn	heads of grain	Ge 41:26
ears of corn	heads of grain	Ge 41:27
ears of corn	heads of grain	Job 24:24
ears of corn	heads of grain	Isa 17:5
ears of corn	heads of grain	Mt 12:1
ears of corn	heads of grain	Mk 2:23
ears of corn	heads of grain	Lk 6:1
edge	ledge	Eze 43:14
elder	older	1Sa 18:17
eldest	oldest	1Ch 24:31
entrance	entryway	2Ki 16:18
entrance	entryway	Mk 14:68
expend	spend	Dt 32:23
feigned insanity	pretended to be insane	1Sa 21:13
fishing nets	fishnets	Eze 26:14
fourth	quarter	2Ki 6:25
further	farther	Lk 24:28
gave	delivered	1Sa 24:10
gave	delivered	1Sa 24:18
gave	delivered	1Sa 26:23
give	turn	Nu 27:7
give	turn	Nu 27:8
given	delivered	1Sa 26:8
go	get away	1Sa 20:29
grain	kernels	Lk 6:1
grain	kernel	Jn 12:24
grains	kernels	Dt 32:14
hand	turn	Ps 27:12
handcrafted	crafted	Nu 31:51
handed	turned	Jer 39:14
have just seen	just saw	2Sa 18:10
heap	pile	Lk 14:35
I am	I'm	2Sa 18:14
ill-treat	mistreat	Ge 31:50
ill-treat	mistreat	Ex 22:21
ill-treat	mistreat	Lev 19:33
ill-treat	mistreat	1Sa 25:7
ill-treat	mistreat	1Sa 25:15
ill-treat	mistreat	Jer 38:19
ill-treat	mistreated	Eze 22:7
ill-treat	mistreat	Eze 22:29
ill-treat	mistreat	Lk 6:28
ill-treat	mistreat	Ac 14:5
ill-treated	mistreated	Ge 15:13

ill-treated	mistreated	Ge 16:6
ill-treated	mistreated	Nu 20:15
ill-treated	mistreated	Dt 26:6
ill-treated	mistreated	Jer 13:22
ill-treated	mistreated	Mt 22:6
ill-treated	mistreated	Ac 7:6
ill-treated	mistreated	Ac 7:24
ill-treated	mistreated	Heb 11:25
ill-treated	mistreated	Heb 11:37
ill-treated	mistreated	Heb 13:3
ill-treating	mistreating	Ac 7:27
in back	behind	Rev 4:6
in flood	at flood stage	Jos 3:15
in flood	at flood stage	Jos 4:18
legally made over	deeded	Ge 23:17
legally made over	deeded	Ge 23:20
let	have	Ex 10:11
light to the other	light to the other side	Ex 14:20
made	had	Ge 24:11
made	had	Lev 23:43
made	had	Nu 5:18
made	had	Nu 11:24
made	had	Nu 27:22
made	had	1Sa 16:8
made	had	1Sa 16:9
made	had	1Sa 16:10
made	had	1Sa 20:17
made	had	2Ch 34:32
made	had	2Ch 34:33
make	have	Ge 45:1
make	have	Ex 19:10
make	have	Ex 28:5
make	have	Nu 5:16
make	have	Nu 5:24
make	have	Nu 5:26
make	have	Nu 5:30
make	have	Nu 8:7
make	have	Nu 8:8
make	have	Nu 8:13
make	have	Nu 9:2
make	have	Nu 11:16
make	have	Nu 27:19
make	have	Dt 21:12
make	have	Dt 31:19
make	have	Jos 6:4
make	have	Jos 6:5
make	have	Jos 6:6
make	have	2Ki 5:8
make	have	2Ki 7:13
make	have	2Ki 17:27
make	have	2Ki 22:4
make	have	2Ki 22:5
make	have	2Ki 22:6
make	have	Ne 7:3
make	have	Lk 9:14
make	have	Jn 6:10
nowhere	no place	Lk 9:58
nowhere	no place	Mt 8:20
offence	stench	1Sa 13:4
offence	stench	2Sa 10:6
offence	stench	1Ch 19:6
on fire	afire	Dt 32:22
onto	on	2Ki 4:35
pushes	shoves	Nu 35:20
pushes	shoves	Nu 35:22
put...on bail	made...post bond	Ac 17:9
quietened	quieted	Ps 131:2
quietened	quieted	Ac 19:35
raped	violated	Ge 34:2
receives	gets	2Sa 15:4
required	obligated	Gal 5:3
round	around	Ge 37:7
round	around	Lev 25:31
round	around	Eph 6:14
sank	melted	Jos 2:11
sawn	sawed	Heb 11:37
scrawny	rawboned	Ge 49:14
shall	will	Nu 17:12
short-sighted	nearsighted	2Pe 1:9
sink	melt with fear	Jos 14:8
slaughtered	butchered	1Sa 28:24
slaughtered	butchered	Mt 22:4
spat	spit	Nu 12:14
spat	spit	Mt 26:67
spat	spit	Mt 27:30
spat	spit	Mk 7:33
spat	spit	Mk 15:19
spat	spit	Jn 9:6
standing corn	standing grain	Isa 17:5
stones from the field	fieldstones	Dt 27:6
supple	limber	Ge 49:24
tidy up	take care of	Ac 9:34
timber	lumber	2Ch 2:9
to and fro	back and forth	Est 2:11
to and fro	back and forth	Job 1:7
to and fro	back and forth	Job 2:2
to and fro	back and forth	Eze 37:2
to hand	on hand	1Sa 21:3
to hand	on hand	1Sa 21:4
turn him over	hand him over	Mk 15:1
turned over	handed over	Lk 18:32
two thousand seven hundred	twenty-seven hundred	1Ch 26:32
two thousand six hundred	twenty-six hundred	2Ch 35:8
until	through	Ex 12:15
warder	warden	Ge 39:21
was in the ear	headed	Ex 9:31
young plant	sprout	Isa 61:11

THE NIV EXHAUSTIVE CONCORDANCE

FEATURES OF THE MAIN CONCORDANCE

NIV WORD HEADING
The indexed word as spelled in the NIV (see the introduction, pages x, xi).

FREQUENCY COUNT
Total number of occurrences in the NIV (see the introduction, page x).

RELATED WORD LIST
Other spellings and related words in the NIV (see the introduction, page x).

ABLE (133) [ABILITY, ABLE-BODIED, DISABLED, ENABLE, ENABLED, ENABLES, ENABLING]

Ge 13: 6 that *they were* not **a** to stay together. 3523

G/K NUMBER
Refers to the biblical-language index-lexicons; one- to four-digit "roman" type is Hebrew; five-digit is Aramaic; *italic* is Greek (see the introduction, pages xii, xv, xvi). For the explanation of a superscript "S" after a G/K number (for example, 3523[S]), see the introduction, pages xiii, xiv.

INDEXED WORD
Abbreviated by its first letter, usually in **bold** type.

ITALIC TYPEFACE
Indicates words that "assist in translation" (see the introduction, page xiii).

BIBLICAL REFERENCE
See the abbreviations table below.

1Ch 9: 13 They were **a men,** 1475+2657

ADDITIONAL G/K NUMBER(S)
Indicates more than one Hebrew, Aramaic, or Greek word is represented by the NIV translation (introduction, page xiii).

BOLD TYPEFACE
In addition to the indexed word, indicates multiple-word translation (intro., p. xiii).

2Ch 1: 10 for who *is a to* **govern** this great people AIT

AIT
Indicates the indexed word "assists in translation"; the indexed word abbreviation in *italics*, the word it assists is in **bold** (see the introduction, page xiii).

Rev 5: 5 He is **a** to open the scroll *NIG*

***NIG* or NIH**
"Not in Greek" and "Not in Hebrew/Aramaic" indicates the indexed word was supplied for clarity in translation (see the introduction, page xiv).

A (9144) [AN] See Index of Articles Etc.

NIV "See" REFERENCES
Refers to an index in another location (see the introduction, page x).

ABATED (KJV) See RECEDED, GONE

KJV "See" REFERENCES
Cross-references key words to NIV vocabulary (introduction, p. xi).

ASSISTANT (Anglicized) See also AIDE

ANGLICIZED "See" REFERENCES
Cross-references Anglicized and North American editions of the NIV (see the introduction, page xi, and word lists, pages xvii-xx).

ABBREVIATIONS FOR THE BOOKS OF THE BIBLE

Book	Abbr.	Book	Abbr.	Book	Abbr.	Book	Abbr.	Book	Abbr.	Book	Abbr.
Genesis	Ge	2 Kings	2Ki	Isaiah	Isa	Nahum	Na	Romans	Ro	Titus	Tit
Exodus	Ex	1 Chronicles	1Ch	Jeremiah	Jer	Habakkuk	Hab	1 Corinthians	1Co	Philemon	Phm
Leviticus	Lev	2 Chronicles	2Ch	Lamentations	La	Zephaniah	Zep	2 Corinthians	2Co	Hebrews	Heb
Numbers	Nu	Ezra	Ezr	Ezekiel	Eze	Haggai	Hag	Galatians	Gal	James	Jas
Deuteronomy	Dt	Nehemiah	Ne	Daniel	Da	Zechariah	Zec	Ephesians	Eph	1 Peter	1Pe
Joshua	Jos	Esther	Est	Hosea	Hos	Malachi	Mal	Philippians	Php	2 Peter	2Pe
Judges	Jdg	Job	Job	Joel	Joel	Matthew	Mt	Colossians	Col	1 John	1Jn
Ruth	Ru	Psalms	Ps	Amos	Am	Mark	Mk	1 Thessalonians	1Th	2 John	2Jn
1 Samuel	1Sa	Proverbs	Pr	Obadiah	Ob	Luke	Lk	2 Thessalonians	2Th	3 John	3Jn
2 Samuel	2Sa	Ecclesiastes	Ecc	Jonah	Jnh	John	Jn	1 Timothy	1Ti	Jude	Jude
1 Kings	1Ki	Song of Songs	SS	Micah	Mic	Acts	Ac	2 Timothy	2Ti	Revelation	Rev

NIV EXHAUSTIVE CONCORDANCE

A

A (9144) [AN] See Index of Articles Etc.

AARON (318) [AARON'S, AARONIC]

Ex 4:14 "What about your brother, A the Levite? 195
4:27 The LORD said to A, "Go into the desert 195
4:28 Then Moses told A everything 195
4:29 Moses and A brought together all the elders 195
4:30 and A told them everything 195
5: 1 Afterward Moses and A went to Pharaoh 195
5: 4 But the king of Egypt said, "Moses and A, 195
5:20 they found Moses and A waiting 195
6:13 and A about the Israelites and Pharaoh king 195
6:20 who bore him A and Moses. 195
6:23 A married Elisheba, daughter 195
6:25 of A married one of the daughters of Putiel, 195
6:26 It was this same A and Moses to whom 195
6:27 It was the same Moses and A. 195
7: 1 and your brother A will be your prophet. 195
7: 2 and your brother A is to tell Pharaoh to let 195
7: 6 Moses and A did just as the LORD commanded them. 195
7: 7 and A eighty-three when they spoke 195
7: 8 The LORD said to Moses and A, 195
7: 9 'Perform a miracle,' then say to A, 195
7:10 and A went to Pharaoh and did just as 195
7:10 A threw his staff down in front of Pharaoh 195
7:19 The LORD said to Moses, "Tell A, 195
7:20 Moses and A did just as the LORD had commanded. 195
7:22 he would not listen to **Moses and A,** 2157[S]
8: 5 Then the LORD said to Moses, "Tell A, 195
8: 6 So A stretched out his hand over the waters 195
8: 8 Pharaoh summoned Moses and A and said, 195
8:12 After Moses and A left Pharaoh, 195
8:15 and would not listen to **Moses and A,** 2157[S]
8:16 Then the LORD said to Moses, "Tell A, 195
8:17 and when A stretched out his hand with 195
8:25 Pharaoh summoned Moses and A and said, 195
9: 8 Then the LORD said to Moses and A, 195
9:12 and he would not listen to **Moses and A,** 2157[S]
9:27 Then Pharaoh summoned Moses and A. 195
10: 3 So Moses and A went to Pharaoh and said 195
10: 8 Then Moses and A were brought back 195
10:11 Then **Moses and** A were driven out 4392[S]
10:16 Pharaoh quickly summoned Moses and A 195
11:10 Moses and A performed all these wonders 195
12: 1 The LORD said to Moses and A in Egypt, 195
12:28 the LORD commanded Moses and A. 195
12:31 the night Pharaoh summoned Moses and A 195
12:43 The LORD said to Moses and A, 195
12:50 the LORD had commanded Moses and A. 195
16: 2 community grumbled against Moses and A. 195
16: 6 So Moses and A said to all the Israelites, 195
16: 9 Then Moses told A, 195
16:10 While A was speaking to the whole Israelite 195
16:33 So Moses said to A, 195
16:34 A put the manna in front of the Testimony, 195
17:10 A and Hur went to the top of the hill. 195
17:12 A and Hur held his hands up— 195
18:12 and A came with all the elders of Israel 195
19:24 "Go down and bring A up with you. 195

Ex 24: 1 "Come up to the LORD, you and A, 195
24: 9 Moses and A, Nadab and Abihu, 195
24:14 A and Hur are with you, 195
27:21 A and his sons are to keep 195
28: 1 "Have A your brother brought to you from 195
28: 2 Make sacred garments for your brother A, 195
28: 3 that they are to make garments for A, 195
28: 4 for your brother A and his sons, 195
28:12 A is to bear the names on his shoulders as 195
28:29 "Whenever A enters the Holy Place, 195
28:30 Thus A will always bear the means 195
28:35 A must wear it when he ministers. 195
28:41 on your brother A and his sons, 195
28:43 A and his sons must wear them 195
28:43 "This is to be a lasting ordinance for A 2257[S]
29: 4 Then bring A and his sons to the entrance 195
29: 5 the garments and dress A with the tunic, 195
29: 9 Then tie sashes on A and his sons. 195
29: 9 In this way you shall ordain A and his sons. 195
29:10 and A and his sons shall lay their hands 195
29:15 and A and his sons shall lay their hands 195
29:19 and A and his sons shall lay their hands 195
29:20 the lobes of the right ears of A and his sons, 195
29:21 and sprinkle it on A and his garments and 195
29:24 the hands of A and his sons and wave them 195
29:27 of the ordination ram that belong to A 195
29:28 the regular share from the Israelites for A 195
29:32 A and his sons are to eat the meat of 195
29:35 "Do for A and his sons everything I have commanded you, 195
29:44 the altar and will consecrate A and his sons 195
30: 7 "A must burn fragrant incense on 195
30:10 a year A shall make atonement on its horns. 195
30:19 A and his sons are to wash their hands 195
30:21 This is to be a lasting ordinance for A 2257[S]
30:30 "Anoint A and his sons 195
31:10 both the sacred garments for A the priest 195
32: 1 they gathered around A and said, "Come, 195
32: 2 A answered them, "Take off the gold earrings 195
32: 3 and brought them to A. 195
32: 5 When A saw this, he built an altar 195
32:21 He said to A, "What did these people do 195
32:22 "Do not be angry, my lord," A answered. 195
32:25 that A had let them get out of control and 195
32:35 of what they did with the calf A had made. 195
34:30 When A and all the Israelites saw Moses, 195
34:31 so A and all the leaders of the community 195
35:19 both the sacred garments for A the priest 195
38:21 under the direction of Ithamar son of A, 195
39: 1 They also made sacred garments for A, 195
39:27 For A and his sons, 195
39:41 both the sacred garments for A the priest 195
40:12 "Bring A and his sons to the entrance to 195
40:13 Then dress A in the sacred garments, 195
40:31 and Moses and A and his sons used it 195

Lev 1: 7 The sons of A the priest are to put fire on 195
2: 3 The rest of the grain offering belongs to A 195
2:10 The rest of the grain offering belongs to A 195
6: 9 "Give A and his sons this command: 195
6:16 A and his sons shall eat the rest of it, 195
6:18 Any male descendant of A may eat it. 195
6:20 the offering A and his sons are to bring to 195
6:25 "Say to A and his sons: 195
7:10 belongs equally to all the sons of A. 195
7:31 but the breast belongs to A and his sons. 195
7:33 of A who offers the blood and the fat of 195
7:34 that is presented and have given them to A 195
7:35 by fire that were allotted to A and his sons 195
8: 2 "Bring A and his sons, 195
8: 6 Then Moses brought A 195
8: 7 He put the tunic on A, 2257[S]

Lev 8:14 A and his sons laid their hands on its head. 195
8:18 A and his sons laid their hands on its head. 195
8:22 A and his sons laid their hands on its head. 195
8:27 of A and his sons and waved them before 195
8:30 and sprinkled them on A and his garments 195
8:30 So he consecrated A and his garments 195
8:31 Moses then said to A and his sons, 195
8:31 saying, 'A and his sons are to eat it.' 195
8:36 So A and his sons did everything 195
9: 1 On the eighth day Moses summoned A 195
9: 2 He said to A, "Take a bull calf 195
9: 7 Moses said to A, "Come to the altar 195
9: 8 So A came to the altar and slaughtered 195
9:15 A then brought the offering that was for NIH
9:20 and then A burned the fat on the altar. NIH
9:21 A waved the breasts and the right thigh 195
9:22 Then A lifted his hands toward the people 195
9:23 and A then went into the Tent of Meeting. 195
10: 3 Moses then said to A, 195
10: 3 A remained silent. 195
10: 6 Then Moses said to A and his sons Eleazar 195
10: 8 Then the LORD said to A, 195
10:12 Moses said to A and his remaining sons, 195
10:19 A replied to Moses, 195
11: 1 The LORD said to Moses and A, 195
13: 1 The LORD said to Moses and A, 195
13: 2 he must be brought to A the priest or to one 195
14:33 The LORD said to Moses and A, 195
15: 1 The LORD said to Moses and A, 195
16: 1 the death of the two sons of A who died 195
16: 2 "Tell your brother A not to come 195
16: 3 how A is to enter the sanctuary area: 195
16: 6 "A is to offer the bull 195
16: 9 A shall bring the goat whose lot falls to 195
16:11 "A shall bring the bull 195
16:17 from the time A goes in to make atonement 2257[S]
16:20 "When A has finished making atonement NIH
16:23 "Then A is to go into the Tent of Meeting 195
17: 2 to A and his sons and to all the Israelites 195
21: 1 "Speak to the priests, the sons of A, 195
21:17 "Say to A: 'For the generations to come 195
21:21 of A the priest who has any defect is 195
21:24 to A and his sons and to all the Israelites. 195
22: 2 "Tell A and his sons to treat with respect 195
22: 4 of A has an infectious skin disease or 195
22:18 to A and his sons and to all the Israelites 195
24: 3 A is to tend the lamps before the LORD 195
24: 9 It belongs to A and his sons, 195

Nu 1: 3 and A are to number by their divisions all 195
1:17 A took these men whose names had been given, 195
1:44 by Moses and A and the twelve leaders 195
2: 1 The LORD said to Moses and A: 195
3: 1 the account of the family of A and Moses at 195
3: 2 of A were Nadab the firstborn and Abihu, 195
3: 4 during the lifetime of their father A. 195
3: 6 of Levi and present them to A the priest 195
3: 9 Give the Levites to A and his sons; 195
3:10 Appoint A and his sons to serve as priests; 195
3:32 of the Levites was Eleazar son of A, 195
3:38 and A and his sons were to camp to the east 195
3:39 at the LORD's command by Moses and A 195
3:48 the additional Israelites to A and his sons." 195
3:51 the redemption money to A and his sons, 195
4: 1 The LORD said to Moses and A: 195
4: 5 A and his sons are to go in and take down 195
4:15 "After A and his sons have finished 195
4:16 "Eleazar son of A, the priest, 195
4:17 The LORD said to Moses and A, 195
4:19 A and his sons are to go into the sanctuary 195
4:27 under the direction of A and his sons. 195
4:28 be under the direction of Ithamar son of A, 195

Nu 4:33 under the direction of Ithamar son of A, 195
4:34 A and the leaders of the community 195
4:37 Moses and A counted them according to 195
4:41 Moses and A counted them according to 195
4:45 Moses and A counted them according to 195
4:46 A and the leaders of Israel counted all 195
6:23 "Tell A and his sons, 195
7: 8 under the direction of Ithamar son of A, 195
8: 2 "Speak to A and say to him, 195
8: 3 A did so; he set up the lamps 195
8:11 A is to present the Levites before 195
8:13 the Levites stand in front of A and his sons 195
8:19 to A and his sons to do the work at the Tent 195
8:20 A and the whole Israelite community did 195
8:21 Then A presented them as a wave offering 195
8:22 under the supervision of A and his sons. 195
9: 6 they came to Moses and A that same day 195
10: 8 "The sons of A, the priests, 195
12: 1 and A began to talk against Moses because 195
12: 4 the LORD said to Moses, A and Miriam, 195
12: 5 to the Tent and summoned A and Miriam. 195
12:10 A turned toward her and saw 195
13:26 and A and the whole Israelite community 195
14: 2 Israelites grumbled against Moses and A, 195
14: 5 Then Moses and A fell facedown in front of 195
14:26 The LORD said to Moses and A: 195
15:33 to Moses and A and the whole assembly, 195
16: 3 as a group to oppose Moses and A and said 195
16:11 Who is A that you should grumble 195
16:16 you and they and A. 195
16:17 and A are to present your censers also." 195
16:18 and stood with Moses and A at the entrance 195
16:20 The LORD said to Moses and A, 195
16:22 Moses and A fell facedown and cried out, NIH
16:37 of A, the priest, to take the censers out of 195
16:40 of A should come to burn incense before 195
16:41 community grumbled against Moses and A. 195
16:42 to Moses and A and turned toward the Tent 195
16:43 Then Moses and A went to the front 195
16:46 Then Moses said to A, 195
16:47 So A did as Moses said, 195
16:47 but A offered the incense NIH
16:50 Then A returned to Moses at the entrance to 195
18: 1 The LORD said to A, 195
18: 8 Then the LORD said to A, 195
18:20 The LORD said to A, 195
18:28 the LORD's portion to A the priest. 195
19: 1 The LORD said to Moses and A: 195
20: 2 in opposition to Moses and A. 195
20: 6 Moses and A went from the assembly to 195
20: 8 and you and your brother A gather 195
20:10 He and A gathered the assembly together 195
20:12 But the LORD said to Moses and A, 195
20:23 the LORD said to Moses and A, 195
20:24 "A will be gathered to his people. 195
20:25 Get A and his son Eleazar and take them 195
20:26 for A will be gathered to his people; 195
20:28 And A died there on top of the mountain. 195
20:29 whole community learned that A had died, 195
25: 7 Phinehas son of Eleazar, the son of A, 195
25:11 the son of A, the priest, 195
26: 1 to Moses and Eleazar son of A, 195
26: 9 and A and were among Korah's followers 195
26:59 To Amram she bore A, 195
26:60 A was the father of Nadab and Abihu, 195
26:64 among those counted by Moses and A 195
27:13 as your brother A was, 195
33: 1 under the leadership of Moses and A. 195
33:38 the LORD's command A the priest went 195
33:39 A was a hundred and twenty-three years old 195
Dt 9:20 And the LORD was angry enough with A 195
9:20 but at that time I prayed for A too. 195
10: 6 There A died and was buried, 195
32:50 just as your brother A died on Mount Hor 195
Jos 21: 4 of A the priest were allotted thirteen towns 195
21:10 of A who were from the Kohathite clans of 195
21:13 of A the priest they gave Hebron (a city 195
21:19 the descendants of A, were thirteen, 195
24: 5 " 'Then I sent Moses and A, 195
24:33 And Eleazar son of A died and was buried 195
Jdg 20:28 the son of A, ministering before it.) 195
1Sa 12: 6 and A and brought your forefathers up out 195
12: 8 and the LORD sent Moses and A, 195
1Ch 6: 3 A, Moses and Miriam. 195
6: 3 The sons of A: Nadab, Abihu, Eleazar and 195
6:49 But A and his descendants were 195
6:50 These were the descendants of A: 195
6:54 of A who were from the Kohathite clan, 195
6:57 So the descendants of A were given Hebron 195
12:27 leader of the **family of A**, with 3,700 men, 195
15: 4 He called together the descendants of A 195
23:13 The sons of Amram: A and Moses. 195
23:13 A was set apart, 195
23:32 under their brothers the descendants of A, 195
24: 1 These were the divisions of the sons of A: 195
24: 1 The sons of A were Nadab, Abihu, 195
24:19 for them by their forefather A, 195
24:31 as their brothers the descendants of A did, 195
27:17 Hashabiah son of Kemuel; over A: 195
2Ch 13: 9 the sons of A, and the Levites, 195
13:10 the LORD are sons of A, 195
26:18 the descendants of A, 195
29:21 the descendants of A, 195
31:19 As for the priests, the descendants of A, 195
35:14 because the priests, the descendants of A, 195
Ezr 7: 5 the son of A the chief priest— 195
Ne 10:38 A priest descended from A is to accompany 195
Ne 12:47 the portion for the descendants of A. 195
Ps 77:20 like a flock by the hand of Moses and A. 195
99: 6 Moses and A were among his priests, 195
105:26 He sent Moses his servant, and A, 195
106:16 grew envious of Moses and of A, 195
115:10 O house of A, trust in the LORD— 195
115:12 he will bless the house of A, 195
118: 3 Let the house of A say: 195
135:19 O house of A, praise the LORD; 195
Mic 6: 4 also A and Miriam. 195
Lk 1: 5 also a descendant *of* A. *2*
Ac 7:40 They told A, 'Make us gods who will go *2*
Heb 5: 4 he must be called by God, just as A was. *2*
7:11 not in the order *of* A? *2*

AARON'S (35) [AARON]

Ex 7:12 But A staff swallowed up their staffs. 195
15:20 Then Miriam the prophetess, A sister, 195
28:30 be over A heart whenever he enters 195
28:38 It will be on A forehead, 195
28:38 on A forehead continually so that they will 2257S
28:40 sashes and headbands for A sons, 195
29:26 the breast of the ram for A ordination, 195
29:29 "A sacred garments will belong 195+4200
Lev 1: 5 then A sons the priests shall bring the blood 195
1: 8 A sons the priests shall arrange the pieces, 195
1:11 of the altar before the LORD, and A sons 195
2: 2 and take it to A sons the priests. 195
3: 2 Then A sons the priests shall sprinkle 195
3: 5 Then A sons are to burn it on the altar 195
3: 8 Then A sons shall sprinkle its blood against 195
3:13 Then A sons shall sprinkle its blood against 195
6:14 A sons are to bring it before the LORD, 195
8: 9 the turban on A head and set the gold plate, 2257S
8:12 of the anointing oil on A head 195
8:13 Then he brought A sons forward, 195
8:23 and put it on the lobe of A right ear, 195
8:24 also brought A sons forward and put some 195
10: 1 A sons Nadab and Abihu took their censers, 195
10: 4 sons of A uncle Uzziel, and said to them, 195
10:16 A remaining sons, and asked, 195
Nu 3: 3 Those were the names of A sons, 195
17: 3 On the staff of Levi write A name, 195
17: 6 and A staff was among them. 195
17: 8 of the Testimony and saw that A staff, 195
17:10 "Put back A staff in front of the Testimony, 195
20:26 Remove A garments and put them 195
20:28 Moses removed A garments and put them 195
1Ch 23:28 of the Levites was to help A descendants in 195
Ps 133: 2 running down on A beard, 195
Heb 9: 4 A staff that had budded, *2*

AARONIC (1) [AARON]

2Ch 35:14 for themselves and for the A priests. 195+1201

AARONITES (KJV) See AARON

ABADDON (1)

Rev 9:11 whose name in Hebrew is A, and in Greek, *3*

ABAGTHA (1)

Est 1:10 Mehuman, Biztha, Harbona, Bigtha, A, 5

ABANA (1)

2Ki 5:12 Are not A and Pharpar, 76

ABANDON (13) [ABANDONED, ABANDONS]

Dt 4:31 not **a** or destroy you or forget the covenant 8332
Jos 10: 6 "*Do* not **a** your servants. 3338+4946+8332
1Ki 6:13 and *will* not **a** my people Israel." 6440
2Ch 12: 5 therefore, I now **a** you to Shishak.' " 6440
Ne 9:19 not **a** them in the desert. 6440
9:31 not put an end to them or **a** them, 6440
Ps 16:10 because *you will* not **a** me to the grave, 6440
138: 8 *do* not **a** the works of your hands. 8332
Jer 12: 7 "I will forsake my house, **a** my inheritance; 5759
48:28 **A** your towns and dwell among the rocks, 6440
Eze 27:29 All who handle the oars *will* **a** their ships; 3718+4946
Ac 2:27 because *you will* not **a** me to the grave, *1593*
1Ti 4: 1 that in later times some *will* **a** the faith *923*

ABANDONED (36) [ABANDON]

Ge 24:27 who *has* not **a** his kindness and faithfulness 6440
Dt 29:25 "It is because this people **a** the covenant of 6440
32:15 *He* **a** the God who made him and rejected 5759
Jdg 4:15 and Sisera **a** his chariot and fled on foot. 3718
5: 6 in the days of Jael, the roads *were* **a**; 2532
6:13 now the LORD *has* **a** us and put us into 5759
1Sa 30:13 My master **a** me 6440
31: 7 *they* **a** their towns and fled. 6440
2Sa 5:21 The Philistines **a** their idols there, 6440
1Ki 18:18 You *have* **a** the LORD's commands 6440
2Ki 7: 7 the dusk and **a** their tents and their horses 6440
1Ch 10: 7 *they* **a** their towns and fled. 6440
14:12 The Philistines *had* **a** their gods there, 6440
2Ch 11:14 even **a** their pasturelands and property, 6440
12: 1 *he* and all Israel with him **a** the law of 6440
12: 5 'You *have* **a** me; 6440
16: 5 he stopped building Ramah and **a** his work. 8697
2Ch 24:18 *They* **a** the temple of the LORD, 6440
Ne 9:28 Then *you* **a** them to the hand 6440
Job 18: 4 *is* the earth *to* **be a** for your sake? 6440
Ps 78:60 *He* **a** the tabernacle of Shiloh, 5759
Isa 2: 6 *You have* **a** your people, the house of Jacob. 5759
10:14 as men gather **a** eggs, 6440
17: 9 like *places* **a** *to* thickets and undergrowth. 6440
27:10 an **a** settlement, forsaken like the desert; 8938
32:14 The fortress *will* **be a**, 5759
54: 7 "For a brief moment *I* **a** you, 6440
Jer 7:29 and **a** this generation that is 5759
49:25 Why *has* the city of renown not **been a**, 6440
La 2: 7 and **a** his sanctuary. 5545
Mic 5: 3 Therefore Israel *will be* **a** until the time 5989
Zep 2: 4 Gaza will be **a** and Ashkelon left in ruins. 6440
Ac 2:31 that *he was* not **a** to the grave, *1593*
Ro 1:27 also **a** natural relations with women *918*
2Co 4: 9 but not **a**; struck down, but not destroyed. *1593*
Jude 1: 6 of authority but **a** their own home— *657*

ABANDONS (1) [ABANDON]

Jn 10:12 *he* **a** the sheep and runs away. *918*

ABARIM (5) [IYE ABARIM]

Nu 27:12 in the A range and see the land I have given 6305
33:47 and camped in the mountains of A, 6305
33:48 of A and camped on the plains of Moab by 6305
Dt 32:49 into the A Range to Mount Nebo in Moab, 6305
Jer 22:20 cry out from A, 6305

ABASE, ABASED, ABASING (KJV) See FRIGHTENED, LOW, LOWER, HUMBLE, IN NEED

ABASHED (1)

Isa 24:23 The moon *will be* **a**, the sun ashamed; 2917

ABATED (KJV) See RECEDED, GONE

ABBA (3)

Mk 14:36 "**A**, Father," he said, "everything is possible *5*
Ro 8:15 And by him we cry, "**A**, Father." *5*
Gal 4: 6 the Spirit who calls out, "**A**, Father." *5*

ABDA (2)

1Ki 4: 6 Adoniram son of A— 6272
Ne 11:17 and A son of Shammua, the son of Galal, 6272

ABDEEL (1)

Jer 36:26 and Shelemiah son of A to arrest Baruch 6274

ABDI (3)

1Ch 6:44 Ethan son of Kishi, the son of A, 6279
2Ch 29:12 of A and Azariah son of Jehallelel; 6279
Ezr 10:26 Mattaniah, Zechariah, Jehiel, A, 6279

ABDIEL (1)

1Ch 5:15 Ahi son of A, the son of Guni, 6280

ABDOMEN (3)

Nu 5:21 to waste away and your **a** to swell. 1061
5:22 so that your **a** swells 1061
5:27 her **a** will swell and her thigh waste away, 1061

ABDON (9)

Jos 19:28 It went to A, Rehob, Hammon and Kanah, 6278
21:30 from the tribe of Asher, Mishal, A, 6278
Jdg 12:13 After him, A son of Hillel, from Pirathon, 6277
12:15 Then A son of Hillel died, 6277
1Ch 6:74 the tribe of Asher they received Mashal, A, 6278
8:23 A, Zicri, Hanan, 6277
8:30 and his firstborn son was A, 6277
9:36 and his firstborn son was A, 6277
2Ch 34:20 Ahikam son of Shaphan, A son of Micah, 6277

ABEDNEGO (14)

Da 1: 7 and to Azariah, A. 6284
2:49 and A administrators over the province 10524
3:12 Shadrach, Meshach and A— 10524
3:13 Nebuchadnezzar summoned Shadrach, Meshach and A. 10524
3:14 "Is it true, Shadrach, Meshach and A, 10524
3:16 Meshach and A replied to the king, 10524
3:19 Meshach and A, and his attitude 10524
3:20 Meshach and A and throw them into 10524
3:22 up Shadrach, Meshach and A, 10524
3:26 "Shadrach, Meshach and A, 10524
3:26 Meshach and A came out of the fire, 10524
3:28 be to the God of Shadrach, Meshach and A, 10524
3:29 and A be cut into pieces and their houses 10524
3:30 Meshach and A in the province of Babylon. 10524

ABEL (13)

Ge 4: 2 Later she gave birth to his brother A. 2040
4: 2 A kept flocks, and Cain worked the soil. 2040
4: 4 But A brought fat portions from some of 2040
4: 4 The LORD looked with favor on A 2040

Ge 4: 8 Now Cain said to his brother A, 2040
4: 8 Cain attacked his brother A and killed him. 2040
4: 9 "Where is your brother A?" 2040
4:25 another child in place of A, 2040
2Sa 20:18 'Get your answer at A,' and that settled it. 64
Mt 23:35 from the blood of righteous A to the blood 6
Lk 11:51 the blood *of* A to the blood of Zechariah, 6
Heb 11: 4 By faith A offered God 6
12:24 a better word than the blood *of* A. 6

ABEL BETH MAACAH (4)

2Sa 20:14 the tribes of Israel to A and 68
20:15 and besieged Sheba in A. 68
1Ki 15:20 A and all Kinnereth 68
2Ki 15:29 Assyria came and took Ijon, A, Janoah, 68

ABEL KERAMIM (1)

Jdg 11:33 vicinity of Minnith, as far as A. 70

ABEL MAIM (1)

2Ch 16: 4 A and all the store cities of Naphtali. 72

ABEL MEHOLAH (3) [MEHOLAH]

Jdg 7:22 as the border of A near Tabbath. 71
1Ki 4:12 from Beth Shan to A across 71
19:16 from A to succeed you as prophet. 71

ABEL MIZRAIM (1) [MIZRAIM]

Ge 50:11 near the Jordan is called A. 73

ABEL SHITTIM (1) [SHITTIM]

Nu 33:49 from Beth Jeshimoth to A. 69

ABEZ (KJV) See EBEZ

ABHOR (12) [ABHORRED, ABHORRENT, ABHORS]

Lev 26:11 and I *will* not a you. 1718
26:15 and if you reject my decrees and **a** my laws 1718
26:30 and I *will* a you. 1718
26:44 or a them so as to destroy them completely, 1718
Dt 7:26 **Utterly** a and detest it, 9210+9210
23: 7 *Do* not a an Edomite, for he is your brother. 9493
23: 7 *Do* not a an Egyptian, 9493
Ps 26: 5 *I* a the assembly of evildoers and refuse 8533
119:163 I hate and a falsehood but I love your law. 9493
139:21 and a those who rise up against you? 7752
Am 6: 8 "I a the pride of Jacob 9290
Ro 2:22 You who a idols, do you rob temples? *1009*

ABHORRED (4) [ABHOR]

Lev 20:23 they did all these things, *I* a them. 7762
26:43 and a my decrees. 1718
Ps 106:40 with his people and a his inheritance. 9493
Isa 49: 7 and a *by* the nation, to the servant of rulers: 9493

ABHORRENT (4) [ABHOR]

Jer 15: 4 I will make them a to all the kingdoms of 2317
24: 9 I will make them a and an offense to all 2317
29:18 and will make them a to all the kingdoms 2317
34:17 I will make you a to all the kingdoms of 2317

ABHORS (2) [ABHOR]

Ps 5: 6 and deceitful men the LORD **a**. 9493
Pr 11: 1 The LORD **a** dishonest scales, 9359

ABI-ALBON (1)

2Sa 23:31 A the Arbathite, Azmaveth the Barhumite, 50

ABIA, ABIAH (KJV) See ABIJAH

ABIASAPH (1)

Ex 6:24 of Korah were Assir, Elkanah and A. 25

ABIATHAR (30)

1Sa 22:20 But A, a son of Ahimelech son of Ahitub, 59
22:22 Then David said to A: 59
23: 6 (Now A son of Ahimelech had brought 59
23: 9 he said to A the priest, "Bring the ephod." 59
30: 7 Then David said to A the priest, 59
30: 7 A brought it to him, 59
2Sa 8:17 and Ahimelech son of A were priests; 59
15:24 and A offered sacrifices until all 59
15:27 and Jonathan son of A. 59
15:27 You and A take your two sons with you. NIH
15:29 So Zadok and A took the ark of God back 59
15:35 the priests Zadok and A be there with you? 59
15:36 of Zadok and Jonathan son of A, 59
17:15 Hushai told Zadok and A, the priests, 59
19:11 to Zadok and A, the priests: 59
20:25 Zadok and A were priests; 59
1Ki 1: 7 with Joab son of Zeruiah and with A 59
1:19 A the priest and Joab the commander of 59
1:25 the commanders of the army and A 59
1:42 Jonathan son of A the priest arrived. 59
2:22 for A the priest and Joab son of Zeruiah!" 59
2:26 To A the priest the king said, 59
1Ki 2:27 So Solomon removed A from 59
2:35 the army in Joab's position and replaced A 59
4: 4 Zadok and A—priests; 59
1Ch 15:11 David summoned Zadok and A the priests, 59
18:16 and Ahimelech son of A were priests; 59
24: 6 of A and the heads of families of the priests 59
27:34 by Jehoiada son of Benaiah and by A. 59
Mk 2:26 In the days of A the high priest, 8

ABIB (5)

Ex 13: 4 Today, in the month of A, you are leaving. 26
23:15 at the appointed time in the month of A, 26
34:18 at the appointed time in the month of A, 26
Dt 16: 1 the month of A and celebrate the Passover 26
16: 1 of A he brought you out of Egypt by night. 26

ABIDA (2)

Ge 25: 4 Epher, Hanoch, A and Eldaah. 30
1Ch 1:33 Ephah, Epher, Hanoch, A and Eldaah. 30

ABIDAH (KJV) See ABIDA

ABIDAN (5)

Nu 1:11 from Benjamin, A son of Gideoni; 29
2:22 of the people of Benjamin is A son 29
7:60 On the ninth day A son of Gideoni, 29
7:65 This was the offering of A son of Gideoni. 29
10:24 and A son of Gideoni was over the division 29

ABIDE, ABIDETH, ABIDING (KJV) See LIVE, REMAIN, SURVIVE

ABIEL (3)

1Sa 9: 1 whose name was Kish son of A, 24
14:51 and Abner's father Ner were sons of A. 24
1Ch 11:32 from the ravines of Gaash, A the Arbathite, 24

ABIEZER (6) [ABIEZRITE, ABIEZRITES]

Jos 17: 2 the clans of A, Helek, Asriel, Shechem, 48
Jdg 8: 2 the full grape harvest of A? 48
2Sa 23:27 A from Anathoth, Mebunnai 48
1Ch 7:18 to Ishhod, A and Mahlah. 48
11:28 of Ikkesh from Tekoa, A from Anathoth, 48
27:12 for the ninth month, was A the Anathothite, 48

ABIEZRITE (1) [ABIEZER]

Jdg 6:11 in Ophrah that belonged to Joash the A, 49

ABIEZRITES (3) [ABIEZER]

Jdg 6:24 To this day it stands in Ophrah of the A. 49
6:34 summoning the A to follow him. 48
8:32 of his father Joash in Ophrah of the A. 49

ABIGAIL (17)

1Sa 25: 3 and his wife's name was A. 28
25:14 One of the servants told Nabal's wife A: 28
25:18 A lost no time. 28
25:23 When A saw David, she quickly got off 28
25:32 David said to A, "Praise be to the LORD, 28
25:36 When A went to Nabal, 28
25:39 Then David sent word to A, 28
25:40 His servants went to Carmel and said to A, 28
25:42 A quickly got on a donkey and, 28
27: 3 Ahinoam of Jezreel and A of Carmel, 28
30: 5 Ahinoam of Jezreel and A, 28
2Sa 2: 2 Ahinoam of Jezreel and A, 28
3: 3 Kileab the son of A the widow of Nabal 28
17:25 an Israelite who had married A, 28
1Ch 2:16 Their sisters were Zeruiah and A. 28
2:17 A was the mother of Amasa, 28
3: 1 the second, Daniel the son of A of Carmel; 28

ABIHAIL (6)

Nu 3:35 of the Merarite clans was Zuriel son of A; 38
1Ch 2:29 Abishur's wife was named A, 35
5:14 These were the sons of A son of Huri, 38
2Ch 11:18 of David's son Jerimoth and of A, 35
Est 2:15 the daughter of his uncle A) to go to 38
9:29 So Queen Esther, daughter of A, 38

ABIHU (12)

Ex 6:23 and she bore him Nadab and A, 33
24: 1 you and Aaron, Nadab and A, 33
24: 9 Moses and Aaron, Nadab and A, 33
28: 1 along with his sons Nadab and A, 33
Lev 10: 1 and A took their censers, put fire in them 33
Nu 3: 2 of Aaron were Nadab the firstborn and A, 33
3: 4 Nadab and A, however, fell dead before 33
26:60 Aaron was the father of Nadab and A, 33
26:61 and A died when they made an offering 33
1Ch 6: 3 Nadab, A, Eleazar and Ithamar. 33
24: 1 The sons of Aaron were Nadab, A, 33
24: 2 Nadab and A died before their father did, 33

ABIHUD (1)

1Ch 8: 3 The sons of Bela were: Addar, Gera, A, 34

ABIJAH (31) [ABIJAH'S]

1Sa 8: 2 and the name of his second was A, 31
1Ki 14: 1 At that time A son of Jeroboam became ill, 31
14:31 And A his son succeeded him as king. 31
15: 1 A became king of Judah, 31
15: 7 There was war between A and Jeroboam. 31
15: 8 And A rested with his fathers 31
2Ki 18: 2 His mother's name was A daughter 23
1Ch 2:24 A the wife of Hezron bore him Ashhur 31
3:10 Solomon's son was Rehoboam, A his son, 31
6:28 Joel the firstborn and A the second son. 31
7: 8 Omri, Jeremoth, A, Anathoth and Alemeth. 31
24:10 the seventh to Hakkoz, the eighth to A, 31
2Ch 11:20 who bore him A, Attai, 31
11:22 Rehoboam appointed A son of Maacah to 31
12:16 And A his son succeeded him as king. 31
13: 1 A became king of Judah, 31
13: 2 There was war between A and Jeroboam. 31
13: 3 A went into battle with a force 31
13: 4 A stood on Mount Zemaraim, 31
13:15 and all Israel before A and Judah. 31
13:17 A and his men inflicted heavy losses 31
13:19 A pursued Jeroboam and took from him 31
13:20 not regain power during the time of A. 32
13:21 But A grew in strength. 32
14: 1 And A rested with his fathers 31
29: 1 His mother's name was A daughter 31
Ne 10: 7 Meshullam, A, Mijamin, 31
12: 4 Iddo, Ginnethon, A, 31
Mt 1: 7 Rehoboam the father of A, *7*
1: 7 A the father of Asa, *7*
Lk 1: 5 to the priestly division *of* A; *7*

ABIJAH'S (4) [ABIJAH]

1Ki 15: 6 and Jeroboam throughout [A] lifetime. 2257S
15: 7 As for the other events of A reign, 31
2Ch 13:22 The other events of A reign, 31
Ne 12:17 of A, Zicri; of Miniamin's 31

ABILENE (1)

Lk 3: 1 and Lysanias tetrarch *of* A— *9*

ABILITY (14) [ABLE]

Ge 47: 6 of any among them with **special a**, 2657
Ex 31: 3 **a** and knowledge in all kinds of crafts— 9312
35:31 **a** and knowledge in all kinds of crafts— 9312
35:34 of the tribe of Dan, the **a** to teach others. 4213
36: 1 to whom the LORD has given skill and **a** 9312
36: 2 to whom the LORD had given **a** 928+2683+4213
Dt 8:18 for it is he who gives you the **a** 3946
Ezr 2:69 to their **a** they gave to the treasury 3946
Da 5:12 and also the *a to* **interpret** dreams, AIT
Mt 25:15 each according to his **a**. *1539*
Ac 8:19 "Give me also this **a** so that everyone *2026*
11:29 The disciples, each according to his **a**, *2344*
2Co 1: 8 far beyond our **a** to endure, *1539*
8: 3 and even beyond their **a**. *1539*

ABIMAEL (2)

Ge 10:28 Obal, A, Sheba, 42
1Ch 1:22 Obal, A, Sheba, 42

ABIMELECH (61) [ABIMELECH'S]

Ge 20: 2 Then A king of Gerar sent for Sarah 43
20: 3 to A in a dream one night and said to him, 43
20: 4 Now A had not gone near her, so he said, 43
20: 8 next morning A summoned all his officials, 43
20: 9 Then A called Abraham in and said, 43
20:10 And A asked Abraham, 43
20:14 Then A brought sheep and cattle and male 43
20:15 And A said, "My land is before you; 43
20:17 and God healed A, 43
21:22 At that time A and Phicol the commander 43
21:25 Then Abraham complained to A about 43
21:26 A said, "I don't know who has done this. 43
21:27 and cattle and gave them to A, 43
21:29 and A asked Abraham, 43
21:32 A and Phicol the commander 43
26: 1 and Isaac went to A king of the Philistines 43
26: 8 A king of the Philistines looked down from 43
26: 9 So A summoned Isaac and said, 43
26:10 A said, "What is this you have done to us? 43
26:11 So A gave orders to all the people: 43
26:16 Then A said to Isaac, "Move away from us; 43
26:26 A had come to him from Gerar, 43
Jdg 8:31 also bore him a son, whom he named A. 43
9: 1 A son of Jerub-Baal went 43
9: 3 they were inclined to follow A, 43
9: 4 and A used it to hire reckless adventurers, 43
9: 6 at the pillar in Shechem to crown A king. 43
9:16 in good faith when you made A king, and 43
9:18 and made A, the son of his slave girl, 43
9:19 may A be your joy, and may you be his, 43
9:20 let fire come out from A and consume you, 43
9:20 and Beth Millo, and consume A!" 43
9:21 because he was afraid of his brother A. 43
9:22 After A had governed Israel three years, 43
9:23 an evil spirit between A and the citizens 43
9:23 who acted treacherously against A. 43
9:24 might be avenged on their brother A and on 43
9:25 and this was reported to A. 43
9:27 and drinking, they cursed A. 43
9:28 Then Gaal son of Ebed said, "Who is A, 43

Jdg 9:28 Why should we serve A? 5647[S]
9:29 I would say to A, 'Call out your whole army 43
9:31 Under cover he sent messengers to A, 43
9:34 So A and all his troops set out by night 43
9:35 at the entrance to the city gate just as A 43
9:38 'Who is A that we should be subject 43
9:39 the citizens of Shechem and fought A. 43
9:40 A chased him, and many fell wounded 43
9:41 A stayed in Arumah, 43
9:42 and this was reported to A. 43
9:44 A and the companies with him rushed 43
9:45 All that day A pressed his attack against 43
9:47 A heard that they had assembled there, 43
9:49 all the men cut branches and followed A. 43
9:50 Next A went to Thebez and besieged it 43
9:52 A went to the tower and stormed it. 43
9:55 When the Israelites saw that A was dead, 43
9:56 the wickedness that A had done 43
10:1 After the time of A a man of Issachar, 43
2Sa 11:21 Who killed A son of Jerub-Besheth? 43
Ps 34:T When he pretended to be insane before A, 43

ABIMELECH'S (2) [ABIMELECH]

Ge 20:18 closed up every womb in A household 43
21:25 a well of water that A servants had seized. 43

ABINADAB (9) [ABINADAB'S]

1Sa 16:8 Then Jesse called A and had him pass 44
17:13 the second, A; and the third, Shammah. 44
31:2 and they killed his sons Jonathan, A 44
2Sa 6:3 and brought it from the house of A, 44
6:3 Uzzah and Ahio, sons of A, 44
1Ch 2:13 the second son was A, the third Shimea, 44
8:33 Malki-Shua, A and Esh-Baal. 44
9:39 Malki-Shua, A and Esh-Baal. 44
10:2 and they killed his sons Jonathan, A 44

ABINADAB'S (2) [ABINADAB]

1Sa 7:1 They took it to A house on the hill 44
1Ch 13:7 the ark of God from A house on a new cart, 44

ABINOAM (4)

Jdg 4:6 She sent for Barak son of A from Kedesh 45
4:12 of A had gone up to Mount Tabor, 45
5:1 and Barak son of A sang this song: 45
5:12 Take captive your captives, O son of A.' 45

ABIRAM (11)

Nu 16:1 Dathan and A, sons of Eliab, 53
16:12 Then Moses summoned Dathan and A, 53
16:24 from the tents of Korah, Dathan and A.'" 53
16:25 Moses got up and went to Dathan and A, 53
16:27 from the tents of Korah, Dathan and A. 53
16:27 and A had come out and were standing 53
26:9 of Eliab were Nemuel, Dathan and A. 53
26:9 The same Dathan and A were 53
Dt 11:6 and what he did to Dathan and A, 53
1Ki 16:34 at the cost of his firstborn son A, 53
Ps 106:17 it buried the company of A. 53

ABISHAG (5)

1Ki 1:3 for a beautiful girl and found A, 54
1:15 to see the aged king in his room, where A 54
2:17 to give me A the Shunammite as my wife." 54
2:21 "Let A the Shunammite be given in marriage 54
2:22 "Why do you request A the Shunammite 54

ABISHAI (26)

1Sa 26:6 then asked Ahimelech the Hittite and A son 57
26:6 "I'll go with you," said A. 57
26:7 So David and A went to the army by night, 57
26:8 A said to David, 57
26:9 But David said to A, "Don't destroy him! 57
2Sa 2:18 Joab, A and Asahel. 57
2:24 But Joab and A pursued Abner, 57
3:30 (Joab and his brother A murdered Abner 57
10:10 of A his brother and deployed them against 93
10:14 they fled before A and went inside the city. 57
16:9 Then A son of Zeruiah said to the king, 57
16:11 David then said to A and all his officials, 57
18:2 of Joab, a third under Joab's brother A son 57
18:5 The king commanded Joab, A and Ittai, 57
18:12 the king commanded you and A and Ittai, 57
19:21 Then A son of Zeruiah said, 57
20:6 David said to A, 57
20:7 under the command of A, 2257[S]
20:10 and his brother A pursued Sheba son 57
21:17 A son of Zeruiah came to David's rescue; 57
23:18 A the brother of Joab son 57
1Ch 2:16 Zeruiah's three sons were A, 93
11:20 A the brother of Joab was chief of 93
18:12 A son of Zeruiah struck 93
19:11 under the command of A his brother, 93
19:15 they too fled before his brother A and went 93

ABISHALOM (2)

1Ki 15:2 mother's name was Maacah daughter of A. 58
15:10 His grandmother's name was Maacah daughter of A. 58

ABISHUA (5)

1Ch 6:4 Phinehas the father of A, 55
6:5 A the father of Bukki, 55
6:50 Phinehas his son, A his son, 55
8:4 A, Naaman, Ahoah, 55
Ezr 7:5 the son of A, the son of Phinehas, the son 55

ABISHUR (1) [ABISHUR'S]

1Ch 2:28 The sons of Shammai: Nadab and A. 56

ABISHUR'S (1) [ABISHUR]

1Ch 2:29 A wife was named Abihail, 56

ABITAL (2)

2Sa 3:4 the fifth, Shephatiah the son of A; 40
1Ch 3:3 Shephatiah the son of A; 40

ABITUB (1)

1Ch 8:11 By Hushim he had A and Elpaal. 39

ABIUD (2)

Mt 1:13 Zerubbabel the father of A, *10*
1:13 A the father of Eliakim, *10*

ABJECTS (KJV) See ATTACKERS

ABLAZE (12)

Dt 5:23 while the mountain *was* a with fire, 1277
9:15 from the mountain while it *was* a with fire. 1277
Job 41:21 His breath sets coals a, 4265
Ps 83:14 the forest or a flame sets the mountains a, 4265
Isa 9:18 sets the forest thickets a, 3675
30:33 like a stream of burning sulfur, sets it a. 1277
33:12 like cut thornbushes *they will be* set a." 836+928+2021+3675
43:2 the flames *will* not set you a. 1277
50:11 and of the torches *you have* set a. 1277
64:2 fire sets twigs a and causes water to boil, 7706
Da 7:9 and its wheels were all a. 10178+10471
Rev 8:8 all a, was thrown into the sea. *2794+4786*

ABLE (133) [ABILITY, ABLE-BODIED, DISABLED, ENABLE, ENABLED, ENABLES, ENABLING]

Ge 13:6 that *they were* not a to stay together. 3523
14:23 so that *you will* never *be a to* say, AIT
45:3 But his brothers *were* not a to answer him, 3523
Ex 7:18 the Egyptians *will* not be a to drink 4206
18:23 *you will be* a to stand the strain, 3523
Lev 26:26 ten women *will be a to* bake your bread AIT
26:37 not be a to stand before your enemies. 9538
Nu 1:3 or more *who are a to* serve *in* the army. AIT
1:20 or more *who were a to* serve *in* the army AIT
1:22 or more *who were a to* serve *in* the army AIT
1:24 or more *who were a to* serve *in* the army AIT
1:26 or more *who were a to* serve *in* the army AIT
1:28 or more *who were a to* serve *in* the army AIT
1:30 or more *who were a to* serve *in* the army AIT
1:32 or more *who were a to* serve *in* the army AIT
1:34 or more *who were a to* serve *in* the army AIT
1:36 or more *who were a to* serve *in* the army AIT
1:38 or more *who were a to* serve *in* the army AIT
1:40 or more *who were a to* serve *in* the army AIT
1:42 or more *who were a to* serve *in* the army AIT
1:45 or more *who were a to* serve in Israel's army AIT
5:28 be a to have children. 2445+2446
14:16 not a to bring these people into 3523
22:6 *be* a to defeat them and drive them out of 3523
22:11 *be* a to fight them and drive them away.'" 3523
22:37 *Am I* really not a to reward you?" 3523
26:2 or more *who are a to* serve in the army AIT
Dt 7:24 No one *will be a to* stand up against you; AIT
9:28 the LORD *was* not a to take them into 3523
11:25 No man *will be a to* stand against you. AIT
31:2 and twenty years old and *I am* no longer a 3523
Jos 1:5 *be a to* stand up against you all the days AIT
10:8 one of them *will be a to* withstand you." AIT
17:12 Yet the Manassites *were* not a to occupy 3523
22:27 not *be a to* say to ours, AIT
23:9 this day no one *has been a to* withstand you. AIT
24:19 *"You are* not a to serve the LORD. 3523
Jdg 2:14 whom *they were* no longer a to resist. 3523
8:3 What *was I* a to do compared to you?" 3523
1Sa 17:9 If *he is* a to fight and kill me, 3523
17:33 not a to go out against this Philistine 3523
1Ki 3:9 For who *is* a to govern this great people 3523
2Ki 2:16 "we your servants have fifty a men. 1201+2657
9:37 so that no *one will be a to* say, AIT
18:35 gods of these countries *has been a to* save his land AIT
1Ch 9:13 They were a men, 1475+2657
12:2 with bows and were a to shoot arrows or NIH
12:8 ready for battle and *a to* handle the shield AIT
26:7 and Semakiah were also a men. 1201+2657
26:9 who were a men— 18 in all. 1201+2657
26:30 seventeen hundred a men— 1201+2657
26:32 were a men and heads of families, 1201+2657
29:14 *we should be* a to give as generously 3946+6806
2Ch 1:10 for who *is a to* govern this great people AIT
2:6 But who *is* a to build a temple for him, 3946+6806
13:3 of four hundred thousand a fighting men, 1033
13:3 with eight hundred thousand a troops. 1033
13:17 among Israel's a men. 1033
20:37 The ships were wrecked and *were* not a 6806
25:5 *a to* handle the spear and shield. AIT
30:3 not *been* a to celebrate it at the regular time 3523
32:13 the gods of those nations ever a to deliver their land 3523+3523
32:14 that my fathers destroyed *has been* a 3523
32:15 or kingdom *has been* a to deliver his people 3523
Ne 8:2 up of men and women and all *who were* a 1067
10:28 and all their sons and daughters *who are* a 3359
11:6 in Jerusalem totaled 468 a men. 2657
11:14 who were a men—128. 1475+2657
Job 41:10 Who then *is a to* stand against me? AIT
Ps 36:12 thrown down, not a to rise! 3523
Isa 36:20 gods of these countries *has been a to* save his land AIT
Eze 7:19 and gold *will* not *be* a to save them in 3523
Da 2:26 "Are you a to tell me what I saw 10346
2:47 for *you were* a to reveal this mystery." 10321
3:15 Then what god *will be a to* rescue you AIT
3:17 the God we serve *is* a to save us from it, 10321
4:37 those who walk in pride *he is* a to humble. 10321
5:16 that *you are* a to give interpretations and 10321
6:20 *been* a to rescue you from the lions?" 10321
11:16 no *one will be a to* stand against him. AIT
11:25 *be a to* stand because of the plots devised AIT
Hos 5:13 But he *is* not a to cure you, 3523
5:13 not a to heal your sores. NIH
Zep 1:18 Neither their silver nor their gold *will be* a 3523
Mt 9:28 "Do you believe that *I am* a to do this?" *1538*
18:25 *Since* he *was* not a to pay, *2400*
26:61 *'I am* a to destroy the temple of God *1538*
Mk 3:20 he and his disciples *were* not even a to eat. *1538*
6:19 But *she was* not a to, *1538*
Lk 1:20 now you will be silent and not a to speak *1538*
8:19 but *they were* not a to get near him because *1538*
13:24 will try to enter and *will* not *be* a to. *2710*
14:29 For if he lays the foundation and *is* not a *2710*
14:30 'This fellow began to build and *was* not a *2710*
14:31 down and consider whether he is a *1543*
14:32 If he is not a, *NIG*
21:15 that none of your adversaries *will be* a *1538*
21:36 that *you may* be a to escape all that is about *2996*
21:36 that *you may be a to* stand before the Son *AIT*
Jn 18:28 *they wanted to be a to* eat the Passover. *AIT*
Ac 5:39 *you will* not be a to stop these men; *1538*
15:10 that neither we nor our fathers *have been* a *2710*
19:40 In that case we *would* not *be* a to account *1538*
22:13 And at that very moment I *was* a to see him. *329*
24:8 By examining him yourself *you will be* a *1538*
27:16 *we were* hardly a to make the lifeboat *2710*
Ro 8:39 *be* a to separate us from the love of God *1538*
11:23 for God *is* a to graft them in again. *1543*
12:2 Then you will be a to test and *1650+3836*
14:4 for the Lord *is* a to make him stand. *1542*
16:25 Now to him who *is* a to establish you *1538*
1Co 12:28 those a to help others, *516*
2Co 8:3 they gave as much as they were a, *1539+2848*
9:8 God *is* a to make all grace abound to you, *1542*
Eph 3:4 *you will be* a to understand my insight *1538*
3:20 Now to him who *is* a to do immeasurably *1538*
6:13 *you may be* a to stand your ground, *1538*
Php 1:10 so that you *may be a to* discern what is best *AIT*
1Ti 3:2 respectable, hospitable, a to teach, *1434*
2Ti 1:12 that he is a to guard what I have entrusted *1543*
2:24 he must be kind to everyone, a to teach, *1434*
3:7 but never a to acknowledge the truth. *1538*
3:15 which *are* a to make you wise for salvation *1538*
Heb 2:18 when he was tempted, *he is* a *1538*
3:19 So we see that *they were* not a to enter, *1538*
5:2 *He is* a to deal gently with those who are ignorant *1538*
7:25 Therefore *he is* a to save completely *1538*
9:9 and sacrifices being offered *were* not a *1538*
Jas 3:2 a to keep his whole body in check. *1543*
4:12 the one who *is* a to save and destroy. *1538*
2Pe 1:15 after my departure you *will* always *be* a *2400*
Jude 1:24 *To* him who *is* a to keep you from falling *1538*
Rev 5:5 He is a to open the scroll *NIG*

ABLE-BODIED (3) [ABLE]

Dt 3:18 But all your a men, armed for battle, 2657
2Sa 24:9 In Israel there were eight hundred thousand a men who could handle 2657
1Ch 5:18 a men who could handle shield and sword, 1201+2657

ABNER (56) [ABNER'S]

1Sa 14:50 the commander of Saul's army was A son 46
17:55 he said to A, commander of the army, 79
17:55 "A, whose son is that young man?" 79
17:55 A replied, "As surely as you live, O king, 79
17:57 A took him and brought him before Saul, 79
20:25 opposite Jonathan, and A sat next to Saul, 79
26:5 He saw where Saul and A son of Ner, 79
26:7 A and the soldiers were lying around him. 79
26:14 He called out to the army and to A son 79
26:14 "Aren't you going to answer me, A?" 79
26:14 A replied, "Who are you who calls to 79
2Sa 2:8 Meanwhile, A son of Ner, the commander 79
2:12 A son of Ner, together with the men 79
2:14 Then A said to Joab, 79
2:17 and A and the men of Israel were defeated 79

2Sa 2:19 He chased A, turning neither to the right 79
2:20 A looked behind him and asked, 79
2:21 Then A said to him, 79
2:22 Again A warned Asahel, "Stop chasing me! 79
2:23 so A thrust the butt of his spear 79
2:24 But Joab and Abishai pursued A, 79
2:25 the men of Benjamin rallied behind A. 79
2:26 A called out to Joab, 79
2:29 that night A and his men marched through 79
2:30 Then Joab returned from pursuing A 79
2:31 and sixty Benjamites who were with A. 79
3: 6 A had been strengthening his own position 79
3: 7 And Ish-Bosheth said to A, 79
3: 8 A was very angry because 79
3: 9 May God deal with A, 79
3:11 not dare to say another word to A, 79
3:12 Then A sent messengers on his behalf 79
3:16 Then A said to him, "Go back home!" 79
3:17 A conferred with the elders of Israel 79
3:19 A also spoke to the Benjamites in person. 79
3:20 When A, who had twenty men with him, 79
3:21 Then A said to David, 79
3:21 David sent A away, and he went in peace. 79
3:22 But A was no longer with David in Hebron, 79
3:23 that A son of Ner had come to the king and 79
3:24 Look, A came to you. 79
3:25 You know A son of Ner; 79
3:26 and sent messengers after A, 79
3:27 Now when A returned to Hebron, 79
3:28 the LORD concerning the blood of A son 79
3:30 (Joab and his brother Abishai murdered A 79
3:31 and walk in mourning in front of A." 79
3:32 They buried A in Hebron, 79
3:33 The king sang this lament for A: 79
3:33 "Should A have died as the lawless die? 79
3:37 the king had no part in the murder of A son 79
4: 1 of Saul heard that A had died in Hebron, 79
1Ki 2: 5 A son of Ner and Amasa son of Jether. 79
2:32 A son of Ner, commander of Israel's army, 79
1Ch 26:28 A son of Ner and Joab son of Zeruiah, 79
27:21 Jaasiel son of A; 79

ABNER'S (3) [ABNER]

1Sa 14:51 and A father Ner were sons of Abiel. 79
2Sa 3:32 and the king wept aloud at A tomb. 79
4:12 of Ish-Bosheth and buried it in A tomb 79

ABNORMALLY (1) [NORMALLY]

1Co 15: 8 he appeared to me also, as to one a born. *1765*

ABOARD (7) [BOARD]

Eze 27: 8 O Tyre, were a as your seamen. 928
Jnh 1: 3 he went a and sailed for Tarshish to flee 928+3718
Jn 21:11 Simon Peter climbed a and dragged *326*
Ac 20:13 where we were going to take Paul a. *377*
20:14 we took him a and went on to Mitylene. *377*
21: 6 we went a the ship, *1650*
27:17 When the men had hoisted it a, *149*

ABODE (2)

Job 38:19 "What is the way to the a of light? 8905
Isa 33:20 your eyes will see Jerusalem, a peaceful a, 5659

ABODEST (KJV) See STAY

ABOLISH (4) [ABOLISHED, ABOLISHING]

Da 11:31 and will a the daily sacrifice. 6073
Hos 2:18 Bow and sword and battle I will a from 8689
Mt 5:17 not think that I have come to a the Law or *2907*
5:17 not come to a them but to fulfill them. *2907*

ABOLISHED (2) [ABOLISH]

Da 12:11 the daily sacrifice is a and the abomination 6073
Gal 5:11 the offense of the cross has been a. *2934*

ABOLISHING (1) [ABOLISH]

Eph 2:15 by a in his flesh the law *2934*

ABOMINABLE (3) [ABOMINATION]

Isa 66:17 the flesh of pigs and rats and other a things— 9211
Jer 32:34 They set up their a idols in the house 9199
Rev 17: 4 with a things and the filth of her adulteries. *1007*

ABOMINATION (5) [ABOMINABLE, ABOMINATIONS]

Da 9:27 a wing [of the temple] he will set up an a 9199
11:31 up the a that causes desolation. 9199
12:11 and the a that causes desolation is set up, 9199
Mt 24:15 'the a that causes desolation,' spoken of *1007*
Mk 13:14 'the a that causes desolation' standing *1007*

ABOMINATIONS (3) [ABOMINATION]

Pr 26:25 for seven a fill his heart. 9359
Isa 66: 3 and their souls delight in their a; 9199
Rev 17: 5 BABYLON THE GREAT THE MOTHER OF PROSTITUTES AND OF THE A OF THE EARTH. *1007*

ABOUND (7) [ABOUNDING, ABOUNDS]

2Ki 9:22 all the idolatry and witchcraft of your mother Jezebel a?" 8041
Ps 4: 7 when their grain and new wine a. 8045
72: 7 prosperity will a till the moon is no more. 8044
72:16 Let grain a throughout the land; 2118+7172
2Co 9: 8 And God is able to make all grace a to you, *4355*
9: 8 you will a in every good work. *4355*
Php 1: 9 that your love may a more and more *4355*

ABOUNDED, ABOUNDETH (KJV) See also ENHANCE, INCREASE, OVERFLOW

ABOUNDING (10) [ABOUND]

Ex 34: 6 slow to anger, a in love and faithfulness, 8041
Nu 14:18 a in love and forgiving sin and rebellion. 8041
Dt 33:23 "Naphtali is a with the favor of the LORD 8428
Ne 9:17 slow to anger and a in love. 8041
Ps 86: 5 O Lord, a in love to all who call to you. 8041
86:15 slow to anger, a in love and faithfulness. 8041
103: 8 slow to anger, a in love. 8041
Pr 8:24 when there were no springs a with water; 3877
Joel 2:13 slow to anger and a in love, 8041
Jnh 4: 2 slow to anger and a in love, 8041

ABOUNDS (1) [ABOUND]

Hab 1: 3 there is strife, and conflict a. 5951

ABOUT (873)

Ge 3:17 from the tree a which I commanded you, AIT
12:11 As he was a to enter Egypt, 7928
12:20 Pharaoh gave orders a Abram to his men, 6584
13: 5 Now Lot, who was moving a with Abram, 2143
18:10 surely return to you a this time next year, 3869
18:17 from Abraham what I am a to do? AIT
18:19 so that the LORD will bring a 995
19:14 the LORD is a to destroy the city!" AIT
21: 6 and everyone who hears a this will laugh AIT
21:12 "Do not be so distressed a the boy 6584
21:16 a a bowshot away, for she thought, 3869
21:25 Abraham complained to Abimelech a 128+6584
21:26 and I heard a it only today." AIT
22: 2 of the mountains I will tell you a." AIT
22: 3 for the place God had told him a. AIT
22: 9 they reached the place God had told him a, AIT
24:28 and told her mother's household a 3869
24:57 "Let's call the girl and ask her a it." AIT
25:32 "Look, I am a to die," Esau said. 2143
26: 7 the men of that place asked him a his wife, 4200
26:32 and told him a the well they had dug. 128+6584
29:13 As soon as Laban heard the news a Jacob, AIT
31:43 Yet what can I do today a these daughters 4200
31:43 or a the children they have borne? 4200
34: 5 so he kept quiet a it until they came home. AIT
37: 2 he brought their father a bad report a them. AIT
38:24 A three months later Judah was told, 3869
41:25 to Pharaoh what he is a to do. AIT
41:28 God has shown Pharaoh what he is a to do. AIT
42: 9 Then he remembered his dreams a them 4200
43: 7 "The man questioned us closely a 4200
43:27 "How is your aged father you told me a? AIT
43:29 he looked a and saw his brother Benjamin, 5951+6524
43:29 the one you told me a?" AIT
45: 2 and Pharaoh's household heard a it. AIT
45:13 Tell my father a all AIT
45:13 in Egypt and a everything you have seen. NIH
45:20 Never mind a your belongings, 6584
48:21 Then Israel said to Joseph, "I am a to die, AIT
49:29 "I am a to be gathered to my people. AIT
50: 5 "I am a to die; AIT
50:24 Joseph said to his brothers, "I am a to die. AIT
Ex 1: 8 a new king, who did not know a Joseph, 3359
2:25 on the Israelites and was concerned a them. 3359
3: 7 and I am concerned a their suffering. 3359
4:14 "What a your brother, Aaron the Levite? 2022+4202
4:24 the LORD met [Moses] and was a to 1335
4:28 told Aaron everything the LORD had sent him to say, and also a AIT
4:31 that the LORD was concerned a them 7212
6:13 and Aaron a the Israelites and Pharaoh king 448
6:27 spoke to Pharaoh king of Egypt a AIT
8:12 to the LORD a the frogs he had brought 1821+6584
11: 4 'A midnight I will go throughout Egypt. 3869
12:37 There were a six hundred thousand men 3869
14: 5 and his officials changed their minds a 448
18: 8 told his father-in-law a AIT
18: 8 and the Egyptians for Israel's sake and a all NIH
18: 9 Jethro was delighted to hear a all 6584
22: 9 other lost property a which somebody says, AIT
32:28 and that day a three thousand of 3869
Lev 5: 1 something he has seen or learned a, 3359
5: 4 any matter one might carelessly swear a— NIH
6: 2 to the LORD by deceiving his neighbor a 928
6: 3 or if he finds lost property and lies a it, or 928
6: 5 or whatever it was he swore falsely a. 6584
10:16 When Moses inquired a the goat of 2011+2011
11:29 the animals that move a on the ground, 9237
11:41 that moves a on the ground is detestable; 9237
11:42 You are not to eat any creature that moves a 9237
11:44 by any creature that moves a on the ground. 8253
11:46 in the water and every creature that moves a 9237
Lev 15: 3 This is how his discharge will bring a 928+2118
19:16 " 'Do not go a spreading slander 2143
Nu 10:29 "We are setting out for the place a which AIT
11: 1 the people complained a their hardships in AIT
11:31 the camp to a three feet above the ground, 3869
13:32 a bad report a the land they had explored. AIT
14:10 the whole assembly talked a stoning them. AIT
14:13 "Then the Egyptians will hear a it! AIT
14:14 tell the inhabitants of this land a AIT
14:15 the nations who have heard this report a AIT
14:36 against him by spreading a bad report a 6584
14:37 spreading the bad report a the land AIT
16:30 the LORD brings a something totally new, 1343
20:14 You know a all the hardships 3359
21:17 O well! Sing a it, 4200
21:18 a the well that the princes dug, that NIH
30: 4 and her father hears a her vow or pledge AIT
30: 5 if her father forbids her when he hears a it, AIT
30: 7 and her husband hears a it but says nothing AIT
30: 8 her husband forbids her when he hears a it, AIT
30:11 and her husband hears a it but says nothing AIT
30:12 when he hears a them, AIT
30:14 says nothing to her a AIT
30:14 by saying nothing to her when he hears a AIT
30:15 he nullifies them some time after he hears a AIT
32:28 Then Moses gave orders a them to Eleazar 4200
Dt 1:22 and bring back a report a the route we are AIT
2: 4 'You are a to pass through the territory AIT
3:26 "Do not speak to me anymore a this matter. 928
4: 1 the decrees and laws I am a to teach you. AIT
4: 6 who will hear a all these decrees and say, AIT
4:22 but you are a to cross over AIT
4:32 Ask now a the former days, 4200
6: 7 Talk a them when you sit at home and 928
9: 1 You are now a to cross the Jordan to go in AIT
9: 2 You know a them and have heard it said: 3359
11:19 talking a them when you sit at home and 928
11:31 You are a to cross the Jordan to enter AIT
12:29 before you the nations you are a to invade AIT
12:30 be careful not to be ensnared by inquiring a 4200
13:12 If you hear it said a one of the towns 928
20: 2 When you are a to go into battle, AIT
23:14 the LORD your God moves a in your camp 2143
24: 1 because he finds something indecent a her, 928
28:29 At midday you will grope a like 5491
33: 7 And this he said a Judah: 4200
33: 8 A Levi he said: 4200
33:12 A Benjamin he said: 4200
33:13 A Joseph he said: 4200
33:18 A Zebulun he said: 4200
33:20 A Gad he said: 4200
33:22 A Dan he said: 4200
33:23 A Naphtali he said: 4200
33:24 A Asher he said: 4200
Jos 1: 2 into the land I am a to give to them— AIT
3: 4 But keep a distance of a a thousand yards 3869
4:13 A forty thousand armed for battle crossed 3869
5: 6 The Israelites had moved a in 2143
6:18 bring a your own destruction 3049
7: 4 So a three thousand men went up; 3869
7: 5 who killed a thirty-six of them. 3869
7: 9 the other people of the country will hear a AIT
8:12 Joshua had taken a five thousand men 3869
9: 1 of the Jordan heard a these things— AIT
10:13 and delayed going down a a full day. 3869
14: 6 the man of God at Kadesh Barnea a you 128+6584
14:10 while Israel moved a in the desert. 2143
22:33 And they talked no more a going to war AIT
23:14 "Now I am a to go the way of all the earth. AIT
Jdg 3:16 sword a a foot and a half long, 1688
3:29 down a ten thousand Moabites, all vigorous 3869
4: 9 because of the way you are going a this, 2143
6:13 that our fathers told us a when they said, AIT
8:10 of a fifteen thousand men, all that were left 3869
8:15 a whom you taunted me by saying, AIT
9: 7 When Jotham was told a this, AIT
9:49 a a thousand men and women, also died. 3869
16:27 and on the roof were a three thousand men 3869
17: 2 of silver that were taken from you and a NIH
19:30 Think a it! 6584
20:12 "What a this awful crime AIT
20:31 that a thirty men fell in the open field and 3869
20:39 casualties on the men of Israel (a thirty), 3869
Ru 1: 4 After they had lived there a ten years, 3869
2:11 "I've been told all a what you have done 5583+5583
2:17 and it amounted to a an ephah. 3869
2:19 told her mother-in-law a AIT
1Sa 2:22 heard a everything his sons were doing AIT
2:23 hear from all the people a AIT
3:11 "See, I am a to do something in Israel AIT
3:13 because of the sin he knew a; 3359
4: 2 who killed a four thousand of them on 3869
9: 5 or my father will stop thinking a 4946
9: 5 about the donkeys and start worrying a us." 4200
9:13 you should find him a this time." 3869
9:16 "A this time tomorrow I will send you 3869
9:17 "This is the man I spoke to you a; AIT
9:20 do not worry a them; they have been found. 4200
9:22 invited—a thirty in number. 3869
9:26 They rose a daybreak and Samuel called 3869
10: 2 your father has stopped thinking a them AIT
10: 2 about them and is worried a you. 4200
10: 2 He is asking, "What shall I do a my son?" 4200
10:16 not tell his uncle what Samuel had said a AIT
12:16 the LORD is a to do before your eyes! AIT
13: 3 and the Philistines heard a it. AIT

1Sa 13:15 They numbered **a** six hundred. 3869
14: 2 With him were **a** six hundred men, 3869
14:14 in an area of **a** half an acre. 3869
14:45 *he* who *has* **brought a** this great deliverance 6913
16: 2 Saul *will* **hear** *a* it and kill me." AIT
18:20 and when *they* **told** Saul *a* it, AIT
19: 3 I'll speak to him **a** you 928
19:21 Saul *was* **told** *a* it, and he sent more men, AIT
20:23 And **a** the matter you and I discussed— NIH
21: 2 *to* **know** anything **a** your mission 3359
21:11 Isn't he the one they sing **a** in their dances: 4200
22: 1 and his father's household **heard** *a* it, AIT
22: 2 **A** four hundred men were with him. 3869
22: 8 None of you is concerned **a** me or tells me 6584
22:15 for your servant knows nothing at all **a** 928
23:13 **a** six hundred in number, 3869
23:23 Find out **a** all the hiding places he uses 4946
23:25 and when David *was* **told** *a* it, AIT
25:13 **A** four hundred men went up with David, 3869
25:38 **A** ten days later, 3869
26:12 No one saw or **knew a** it, 3359
28: 9 a trap for my life to **bring a** my **death?"** 4637
29: 3 **"What a** these Hebrews?" 4537
29: 5 the David they sang **a** in their dances: 4200
2Sa 3:28 Later, when David **heard** *a* this, he said, AIT
4: 4 He was five years old when the **news** *a* Saul AIT
5:17 but David **heard** *a* it and went down to AIT
7:19 also spoken **a** the future of the house 4200
10: 5 When David **was told** *a* this, AIT
11: 3 and David sent someone to find out **a** her. 4200
13:13 **What a** me? 2256
13:13 **And what a** you? 2256
13:33 not *be* **concerned a** the report that all 448+4213+8492
15:11 **knowing** nothing **a** the matter. 3359
15:20 today *shall I* **make** you **wander a** with us, 5675
17: 9 whoever **hears** *a* it will say, AIT
17:19 No *one* **knew** anything **a** it. 3359
18: 3 *they* won't **care a** us. 448+4213+8492
18:29 "I saw great confusion just as Joab was **a** NIH
19:10 So why *do* you **say nothing** *a* bringing AIT
19:42 Why are you angry **a** it? 6584
22: 5 "The waves of death **swirled a** me; 705
23:10 The LORD **brought a** a great victory 6913
23:12 and the LORD **brought a** a great victory. 6913
1Ki 1:18 and *you,* my lord the king, *do* not **know a** it. 3359
2: 2 "I *am a to* go the way of all the earth," AIT
2:27 the LORD had spoken at Shiloh **a** 6584
4:33 He also taught **a** animals and birds, 6584
8: 5 of Israel that had gathered **a** him were 6584
10: 1 When the queen of Sheba **heard** *a* the fame AIT
10: 2 and **talked** with him *a* all that she had AIT
10: 6 "The report I heard in my own country **a** 6584
11: 2 from nations *a* **which** the LORD had told AIT
11:29 **A** that time Jeroboam was going out 928
14: 5 "Jeroboam's wife is coming to ask you **a** 448
16: 3 So I *am a to* **consume** Baasha and his house, AIT
19:11 for the LORD *is a to* **pass by."** AIT
20: 6 But **a** this time tomorrow I am going 3869
22: 6 **a** four hundred men— 3869
22: 8 he never prophesies anything good **a** 6584
22:18 that he never prophesies anything good **a** 6584
2Ki 2: 1 *a to* **take** Elijah **up** AIT
3:20 **a** the time for offering the sacrifice, 3869
4:16 **"A** this time next year," Elisha said, 4200
4:17 and the next year **a** that same time 4200
7: 1 **A** this time tomorrow, 3869
7:18 **"A** this time tomorrow, 3869
8: 4 **"Tell** me *a* all the great things Elisha AIT
8: 6 The king **asked** the woman *a* it, AIT
9:23 Joram **turned a** and fled, 2200+3338
9:25 when the LORD made this prophecy **a** 6584
9:30 When Jezebel **heard** *a* it, AIT
11: 2 who *were a to* **be murdered.** AIT
12:17 **A this time** Hazael king of Aram went up 255
14:13 a section **a six hundred feet** long. 564+752+4395
22:13 for all Judah **a** what is written in this book 6584
23:27 *a* **which** I said, 'There shall my Name be.' " AIT
1Ch 11:14 the LORD **brought a** a great **victory.** 3828+9591
14: 8 David **heard** *a* it and went out to meet them. AIT
15:13 *We did* not **inquire of** him *a* how to do it in AIT
17:17 you have spoken **a** the future of the house 4200
19: 5 someone came and told David **a** the men, 6584
2Ch 2: 4 Now I *am a to* **build** a temple for the Name AIT
5: 6 of Israel that had gathered **a** him were 6584
9: 1 to Solomon and **talked** with him *a* AIT
9: 5 "The report I heard in my own country **a** 6584
15: 5 In those days it was not safe to **travel a,** 995+2256+3655
15:15 All Judah rejoiced **a** the oath 6584
18: 7 he never prophesies anything good **a** 6584
18:17 that he never prophesies anything good **a** 6584
21:14 now the LORD *is a to* **strike** your people, AIT
22: 7 God **brought a** Ahaziah's downfall. 2118+4946
22:11 royal princes who *were a to* **be murdered** AIT
24:27 the many prophecies **a** him, 6584
25: 9 "But what **a** the hundred talents I paid 4200
25:23 a section **a six hundred feet** long. 564+752+4395
29:36 at what God *had* **brought a** for his people, 3922
31: 9 Hezekiah asked the priests and Levites **a** 6584
32: 3 and military staff **a** blocking off the water 4200
32:19 They spoke **a** the God of Jerusalem 448
32:19 the God of Jerusalem as they did **a** the gods 6584
32:20 of Amoz cried out in prayer to heaven **a** 6584
32:31 of Babylon to **ask** him *a* the miraculous sign AIT
34:21 and for the remnant in Israel and Judah **a** 6584
35: 3 It is not to be **carried a** on your shoulders. 5362
Ezr 7:14 the king and his seven advisers to inquire **a** 10542
8:23 So we fasted and petitioned our God **a** this, 6584
Ne 1: 2 and I questioned them **a** the Jewish remnant 6584
1: 2 and also **a** Jerusalem. 6584
2:10 and Tobiah the Ammonite official **heard** *a* AIT
2:18 *I* also **told** them *a* the gracious hand AIT
2:19 and Geshem the Arab **heard** *a* it, AIT
6: 6 reports you *are a to* **become** their king AIT
6: 7 to make this proclamation **a** you 6584
6:16 When all our enemies **heard** *a* this, AIT
13: 7 Here I learned **a** the evil thing 928
Est 1:18 of the nobility who *have* **heard** *a* AIT
2: 1 and what he had decreed **a** her. 6584
2:22 But Mordecai **found out** *a* the plot AIT
3: 4 Therefore *they* **told** Haman *a* it AIT
4: 4 and eunuchs came and **told** her *a* AIT
5:11 Haman **boasted** to them *a* his vast wealth, AIT
6: 4 **speak** to the king *a* hanging Mordecai AIT
9:32 Esther's decree confirmed these **regulations** *a* AIT
Job 2:11 **heard** *a* all the troubles that had come AIT
3: 4 *may* God above not **care a** it; 2011
11:18 *you will* **look a** you and take your rest 2916
15:23 He **wanders a**—food for vultures; 5610
21: 6 When *I* **think a** this, I am terrified; 2349
21:11 their little ones **dance a.** 8376
21:21 For what does he care **a** 928
22:14 as *he* **goes a** *in* the vaulted heavens.' 2143
24: 5 the poor **go a** their labor of foraging food; 3655
24:10 Lacking clothes, *they* **go a** naked; 2143
27:11 "I will teach you **a** the power of God; 928
30:22 *you* **toss** me **a** in the storm. 4570
30:28 *I* **go a** blackened, but not by the sun; 2143
33: 2 *I am a to* **open** my mouth; AIT
36:30 See how he scatters his lightning **a** him, 6584
38:41 its young cry out to God and **wander a** 9494
41:14 **ringed a** *with* his fearsome teeth? 6017
Ps 12: 8 The wicked freely strut **a** 6017
22:30 future generations will be told **a** the Lord. 4200
26: 6 and **go a** your altar, O LORD, 6015
35:11 on things *I* **know** nothing **a.** 3359
35:14 *I* **went a** mourning as though for my friend 2143
38: 6 all day long *I* **go a** mourning. 2143
38:17 I *am* **a** to fall, and my pain is ever with me. 3922
39: 6 *He* **bustles a,** but only in vain; 2159
40: 7 it is written **a** me in the scroll. 6584
42: 9 Why *must I* **go a** mourning, 2143
43: 2 Why *must I* **go a** mourning, 2143
48:12 **Walk a** Zion, go around her, 6015
55:10 Day and night *they* **prowl a** on its walls; 6015
59: 6 snarling like dogs, and **prowl a** the city. 6015
59:11 In your might **make** them **wander a,** 5675
59:14 snarling like dogs, and **prowl a** the city. 6015
59:15 They **wander a** for food and howl if 5675
64: 5 *they* **talk** *a* hiding their snares; AIT
69:26 and talk **a** the pain of those you hurt. 448
77: 5 *I* **thought** *a* the former days, AIT
82: 5 *They* **walk a** in darkness; 2143
109:19 May it be like a cloak wrapped **a** him, 4200
118:13 I was pushed back and *a to* **fall,** AIT
119:45 *I will* **walk a** in freedom, 2143
142: 7 the righteous *will* **gather a** me because 4193
Pr 6:12 *who* **goes a** with a corrupt mouth, 2143
20:14 then off he goes and **boasts** *a* his purchase. AIT
23: 7 of man who is always thinking **a** the cost. 928
24: 2 and their lips **talk** *a* making trouble. AIT
24:12 If you say, "But *we* **knew** nothing **a** this," 3359
27: 1 Do not boast **a** tomorrow, 928
29: 7 The righteous **care a** justice for the poor, 3359
31:17 *She* **sets a** her **work** vigorously; 2520+5516
Ecc 7:14 a man cannot **discover** anything *a* AIT
12: 5 to his eternal home and mourners **go a** 6015
SS 3: 2 I will get up now and **go a** the city, 6015
Isa 3: 1 *is a to* **take** from Jerusalem and Judah AIT
5: 1 for the one I love a song **a** his vineyard: 4200
8: 7 the Lord *is a to* **bring** against them AIT
13:21 and there the wild goats *will* **leap a.** 8376
22:17 *a to* **take firm hold** AIT
26:17 and **a** to give birth writhes and cries out 7928
27: 2 In that day—"Sing **a** a fruitful vineyard: 4200
35: 8 wicked fools *will* not **go a** on it. 9494
38:19 fathers tell their children **a** 448
45:11 do you question me **a** my children, 6584
45:11 or give me orders **a** the work of my hands? 6584
45:20 Ignorant are those *who* **carry a** idols 5951
46: 1 **images that are carried a** 5953
46:11 What I have said, that *will I* **bring a;** 995
60: 4 "Lift up your eyes and look **a** you: 6017
66:18 *am a to* **come** and gather all nations AIT
Jer 1:15 *I am a to* **summon** all the peoples of AIT
2:36 Why *do you* **go a** so much, 261
5:12 They have lied **a** the LORD; 928
6:20 **What do I care a** 2296+3276+4200+4200+4537
6:24 We have heard **reports** *a* them, AIT
6:28 **going a** to slander. 2143
7:22 I did not just give them commands **a** 1821+6584
9:24 but let him who boasts boast **a** this: 928
11:21 "Therefore this is what the LORD says **a** 6584
12: 1 Yet I would speak with you **a** your justice: NIH
12: 3 you see me and test my thoughts **a** you. 907
14:10 This is what the LORD says **a** this people: 4200
14:15 this is what the LORD says **a** 6584
16: 3 For this is what the LORD says **a** the sons 6584
16: 3 and **a** the women who are their mothers 6584
21: 4 *I am a to* **turn against** you the weapons AIT
22: 6 the LORD says **a** the palace of the king 6584
22:11 the LORD says **a** Shallum son of Josiah, 448
22:18 Therefore this is what the LORD says **a** 448
26:10 the officials of Judah **heard** *a* these things, AIT
26:19 We *are a to* **bring** a terrible disaster AIT
27:19 the LORD Almighty says **a** the pillars, 448
27:21 says **a** the things that are left in the house 6584
28:16 'I *am a to* **remove** you from the face of AIT
29:16 the LORD says **a** the king who sits 448
29:21 says **a** Ahab son of Kolaiah 448
29:31 'This is what the LORD says **a** Shemaiah 448
31:24 and *those who* **move a** with their flocks. 5825
32: 3 *a to* **hand** this city **over** AIT
32:28 *a to* **hand** this city **over** AIT
32:36 "You are saying **a** this city, 'By the sword, 448
33: 4 says **a** the houses in this city and 6584
33:10 'You say **a** this place, 928
34: 2 *a to* **hand** this city **over** AIT
36: 3 Perhaps *when* the people of Judah **hear** *a* AIT
36:30 the LORD says **a** Jehoiakim king 6584
37: 5 the **report** *a* them, AIT
38:24 not let anyone know **a** this conversation, 928
39:11 of Babylon had given these orders **a** 6584
39:16 I *am a to* **fulfill** my words AIT
40: 3 And now the LORD *has* **brought** it **a;** 995
40:16 What you are saying **a** Ishmael is not true." 448
41: 4 before anyone **knew a** it, 3359
41:11 with him **heard** *a* all the crimes Ishmael son AIT
44:21 and **think a** the incense burned in the towns 4213+6584+6590
46:13 **spoke** to Jeremiah the prophet *a* AIT
46:25 "I *am a to* **bring punishment** on Amon god AIT
47: 4 The LORD *is a to* **destroy** the Philistines, AIT
50:43 king of Babylon has heard **reports** *a* them, AIT
51:60 **written** on a scroll *a* AIT
La 3:54 *a to* **be cut off.** AIT
4:15 When they flee and **wander a,** 5675
Eze 1:17 wheels *did* not **turn a** as the creatures went. 6015
6: 3 I *am a to* **bring** a sword against you, AIT
7: 8 I am **a to** pour out my wrath on you 4946+6964+7940
8:16 were **a** twenty-five men. 3869
10:11 not **turn a** as the cherubim went. 6015
12:19 'This is what the Sovereign LORD says **a** 4200
12:27 and he prophesies **a** the distant future.' 4200
16: 6 " 'Then I passed by and saw you **kicking a** 1008
16:22 **kicking a** in your blood. 1008
16:44 " 'Everyone who quotes proverbs will quote this proverb **a** 6584
18: 2 by quoting this proverb **a** the land of Israel: 6584
19: 4 The nations heard **a** him, 448
19: 8 those from regions **round a.** 6017
20:47 I *am a to* **set fire** to you, AIT
21:28 'This is what the Sovereign LORD says **a** 448
21:29 concerning you and lying divinations **a** 4200
23:28 *a to* **hand** you **over** AIT
23:43 Then I said **a** the one worn out by adultery, 4200
24:16 with one blow I *am a to* **take away** from you AIT
24:21 I *am a to* **desecrate** my sanctuary— AIT
25:16 I *am a to* **stretch out** my hand against AIT
32: 2 in the seas **thrashing a** in your streams, 1631
32: 9 the hearts of many peoples when I **bring a** 995
33:30 your countrymen are talking together **a** you 928
38: 7 you and all the hordes gathered **a** you, 6584
Da 1:20 of wisdom and understanding *a* **which** AIT
2:27 to the king the mystery he *has* **asked** *a,* AIT
4: 2 to **tell** you *a* the miraculous signs AIT
4:33 Immediately what had been said **a** 10542
6:12 and spoke to him **a** his royal decree: 10542
7: 8 "While I was thinking **a** the horns, 10089
7:20 to know **a** the ten horns on its head and 10542
7:20 on its head and **a** the other horn that came NIH
8: 5 As I was thinking **a** this, NIH
8:27 I got up and **went a** the king's business. 6913
9:21 came to me in swift flight **a** the time of 3869
10:11 consider carefully the words I *am a to* **speak** AIT
Hos 3: 2 for fifteen shekels of silver and **a** a homer NIH
5: 3 **I know all a** Ephraim; 3359
Joel 1:18 The herds **mill a** 1003
Am 4: 5 and **brag** *a* your freewill offerings— AIT
4: 5 **boast** *a* them, you Israelites, AIT
Ob 1: 1 This is what the Sovereign LORD says **a** 4200
Jnh 2: 3 and the currents **swirled a** me; 6015
4: 6 and Jonah was very happy **a** the vine. 6584
4: 9 "Do you have a right to be angry **a** 6584
4:10 "You have been concerned **a** this vine, 6584
4:11 not be concerned **a** that great city?" 6584
Mic 1: 8 *I will* **go a** barefoot and naked. 2143
2: 6 "Do not prophesy **a** these things; 4200
Na 2: 4 *they* **dart a** like lightning. 8132
3:19 the **news** *a* you claps his hands at your fall, AIT
Hab 3:14 though **a** to devour the wretched who were NIH
Zec 8:10 No one *could* **go a** *his* **business** safely 995+2256+3655
Mal 3:14 and **going a** like mourners before 2143
Mt 1:18 how the birth of Jesus Christ **came a:** *1639*
4:24 News *a* **him** spread all over Syria, *AIT*
6:25 I tell you, *do* not **worry a** your life, *3534*
6:25 or **a** your body, what you will wear. *NIG*
6:28 "And why do you worry **a** clothes? *4309*
6:34 Therefore do not worry **a** tomorrow, *1650*
6:34 for tomorrow *will* **worry a** itself. *3534*
9:30 "See that no one **knows a** this." *1182*
9:31 But they went out and **spread the news a** *1424*
10:19 *do* not **worry a** what to say or how to say it. *3534*
11: 7 Jesus began to speak to the crowd **a** John: *4309*
11:10 This is the one **a** whom it is written: *4309*
13:19 the message *a* **the kingdom** and does *AIT*
13:52 law who has been instructed *a* **the kingdom** *AIT*

Mt 14: 1 the tetrarch heard the reports *a* **Jesus,** *AIT*
14:21 of those who ate was **a** five thousand men, *6059*
15: 7 Isaiah was right when he prophesied **a** you: *4309*
16: 8 why are you talking among yourselves **a** *4022*
16:11 that I was not talking to you **a** bread? *4309*
16:15 "But what **a** you?" *NIG*
17:13 that he was talking to them **a** John *4309*
18:13 he is happier **a** that one sheep than about *2093*
18:13 about that one sheep than **a** the ninety-nine *2093*
18:19 I tell you that if two of you on earth agree **a** *4309*
19:17 "Why do you ask me **a** what is good?" *4309*
20: 3 "**A** the third hour he went out *4309*
20: 5 "He went out again **a** the sixth hour and *4309*
20: 6 **A** the eleventh hour he went out *4309*
20: 9 "The workers who were hired **a** the eleventh *4309*
20:24 *When* the ten **heard a** this, *201*
21:45 they knew he was talking **a** them. *4309*
22:31 But **a** the resurrection of the dead— *4309*
22:42 "What do you think **a** the Christ? *4309*
24:36 "No one knows **a** that day or hour, *4309*
24:39 and they **knew** nothing **a** what would happen *1182*
26:24 of Man will go just as it is written **a** him. *4309*
26:70 "I don't know what *you're* **talking a,"** *3306*
27:46 **A** the ninth hour Jesus cried out in *4309*
Mk 1: 1 the gospel *a* **Jesus Christ,** the **Son** of God *AIT*
1:28 News *a* **him** spread quickly over *AIT*
1:30 and they told Jesus **a** her. *4309*
3:21 *When* his family **heard a** this, *201*
4:10 others around him asked him *a* the **parables.** *AIT*
5:13 The herd, **a** two thousand in number, *6055*
5:16 and told **a** the pigs as well. *4309*
5:27 When she heard **a** Jesus, *4309*
5:43 not to let anyone **know a** this, *1182*
6:14 King Herod **heard a** this, *201*
6:48 **A** the fourth watch of the night he went out *4309*
6:48 He was **a** to pass by them, *NIG*
6:52 for they had not understood **a** the loaves; *2093*
7: 6 "Isaiah was right when he prophesied **a** *4309*
7:17 his disciples **asked** him **a** this parable. *2089*
7:25 In fact, as soon as she heard **a** him, *4309*
7:36 the more they *kept* **talking a** it. *3062*
8: 9 **A** four thousand men were present. *6055*
8:17 "Why *are you* **talking a** having no bread? *1368*
8:29 "But what **a** you?" *NIG*
8:30 Jesus warned them not to tell anyone **a** *4309*
8:32 *He* **spoke** plainly **a** this, *3281*
9:13 just as it is written **a** him." *2093*
9:16 **arguing** with them **a?"** *5184*
9:32 and were afraid *to* **ask** him **a** it. *2089*
9:33 "What *were you* **arguing a** on the road?" *1368*
9:34 on the way *they had* **argued a** who was *1363*
9:39 in the next moment **say** anything **bad a** me, *2800*
10:10 the disciples asked Jesus **a** this. *4309*
10:41 *When* the ten **heard a** this, *201*
12:26 Now **a** the dead rising— *4309*
13: 4 the sign that they *are* all **a to** be fulfilled?" *3516*
13:11 *do* not **worry beforehand a** what to say. *4628*
13:32 "No one knows **a** that day or hour, *4309*
14:21 of Man will go just as it is written **a** him. *4309*
14:68 or understand what you're **talking a,"** *3306*
14:71 "I don't know this man *you're* **talking a."** *3306*
Lk 1:56 for **a** three months and then returned home. *6055*
1:65 of Judea *people were* **talking a** *1362*
1:66 Everyone who heard this **wondered a** it,
1877+2840+3836+5502
2:15 which the Lord *has* **told us a."** *1192*
2:17 concerning what had been told them **a** *4309*
2:33 and mother marveled at what was said **a** *4309*
2:38 she gave thanks to God and spoke **a** *4309*
3:23 Now Jesus himself was **a** thirty years old *6059*
4:14 and news **a** him spread through *4309*
4:37 And the news **a** him spread throughout *4309*
5:15 Yet the news **a** him spread all the more, *4309*
7: 2 was sick and **a to** die. *3516*
7:17 This news **a** Jesus spread throughout Judea *4309*
7:18 John's disciples told him **a** all these things. *4309*
7:24 Jesus began to speak to the crowd **a** John: *4309*
7:27 This is the one **a** whom it is written: *4309*
8: 1 Jesus **traveled a** from one town *1476*
8:42 a girl of **a** twelve, was dying. *6055*
9: 7 the tetrarch **heard a** all that was going on. *201*
9: 9 Who, then, is this I hear such things **a?** *4005+4309*
9:11 the crowds **learned a** it and followed him. *1182*
9:11 and spoke to them **a** the kingdom of God, *4309*
9:14 (**A** five thousand men were there.) *6059*
9:14 "Have them sit down in groups of **a** fifty *6059*
9:20 "But what **a** you?" *NIG*
9:28 **A** eight days after Jesus said this, *6059*
9:31 *They* **spoke a** his departure, *3306*
9:31 which *he was* **a to** bring to fulfillment *3516*
9:44 to what **I am a to tell** *you:* *3364+3836+4047*
9:45 and they were afraid to ask him **a** it. *4309*
10: 1 to every town and place where he *was* **a to** *3516*
10:41 "you are worried and upset **a** many things, *4309*
12:11 not **worry a** how you will defend yourselves *3534*
12:22 *do* not **worry a** your life, what you will eat; *3534*
12:22 or **a** your body, what you will wear. *NIG*
12:26 why do you worry **a** the rest? *4309*
12:29 *do* not **worry a** it. *3577*
13: 1 at that time who told Jesus **a** *4309*
14:31 "Or suppose a king *is* **a** to go to war *4513*
16: 2 'What is this I hear **a** you? *4309*
18: 2 a judge who neither feared God nor **cared a** *1956*
18: 4 though I don't fear God or **care a** men, *1956*
18: 7 not God **bring a** justice for his chosen ones, *4472*
18:11 Pharisee stood up and prayed **a** himself: *4639*
18:31 *a* **the Son** *of* **Man** will be fulfilled. *AIT*
Lk 18:34 they did not know what *he was* **talking a.** *3306*
21: 5 Some of his disciples were remarking **a** *4309*
21: 7 And what will be the sign that they *are* **a to** *3516*
21:36 be able to escape all that *is* **a to** happen, *3516*
22:37 what is written **a** me *4309*
22:41 He withdrew **a** a stone's throw *6059*
22:59 **A** an hour later another asserted, *6059*
22:60 I don't know what *you're* **talking a!"** *3306*
23: 8 From what he had heard **a** him, *4309*
23:44 It was now **a** the sixth hour, *6059*
23:54 and the Sabbath *was* **a to begin.** *2216*
24: 4 While they were wondering **a** this, *4309*
24:13 **a** seven miles **from** Jerusalem. *600*
24:14 They were talking with each other **a** *4309*
24:19 "**A** Jesus of Nazareth," they replied. *4309*
24:36 *While* they *were still* **talking a** this, *3281*
24:44 be fulfilled that is written **a** me in the Law *4309*
Jn 1:22 What do you say **a** yourself?" *4309*
1:39 It was **a** the tenth hour. *6055*
1:45 "We have found the one Moses **wrote a** in *1211*
1:45 and **a** whom the prophets also wrote— *NIG*
2:25 He did not need man's testimony **a** man, *4309*
3:26 the one you **testified a—** *3455*
4: 6 It was **a** the sixth hour. *6055*
4:32 to eat that you know nothing **a."** *NIG*
5:31 "If I testify **a** myself, *4309*
5:32 and I know that his testimony **a** me is valid. *4309*
5:39 These are the Scriptures that testify **a** me, *4309*
5:46 you would believe me, for he wrote **a** me. *4309*
6:10 **a** five thousand of them. *6055*
6:41 At this the Jews began to grumble **a** him *4309*
6:61 Aware that his disciples were grumbling **a** *4309*
7:12 crowds there was widespread whispering **a** *4309*
7:13 But no one would say anything publicly **a** *4309*
7:18 there is nothing false **a** him. *1877*
7:32 the crowd whispering such things **a** him. *4309*
8:27 not understand that *he was* **telling** them **a** *3306*
9:17 "What have you to say **a** him? *4309*
10:36 what **a** the one whom the Father set apart *NIG*
10:41 all that John said **a** this man was true." *4309*
11:54 Therefore Jesus no longer **moved a** publicly *4344*
12: 3 Then Mary took **a a pint** of pure nard, *3354*
12: 6 not say this because he cared **a** the poor but *4309*
12:16 that these things had been written **a** him *2093*
12:41 because he saw Jesus' glory and spoke **a** *4309*
13:27 "What *you are* **a to do,** do quickly," *AIT*
15:26 he will testify **a** me. *4309*
16:19 Jesus saw that they wanted to ask him **a** *NIG*
16:25 of language but will tell you plainly **a** *4309*
18:19 the high priest questioned Jesus **a** *4309*
18:34 "or did others talk to you **a** me?" *4309*
19:14 Passover Week, **a** the sixth hour. *6055*
19:39 **a** seventy-five pounds. *6055*
21: 8 **a** a hundred yards. *6055*
21:21 he asked, "Lord, what **a** him?" *NIG*
Ac 1: 1 I wrote **a** all that Jesus began to do and *4309*
1: 3 over a period of forty days and spoke **a** *4309*
1: 4 which you have heard me speak **a.** *NIG*
1:15 group **numbering a** a hundred and twenty) *6059*
1:19 Everyone in Jerusalem **heard a** this, *1181+1196*
2:25 David said **a** him: *1650*
2:41 and **a** three thousand were added *6059*
3: 3 When he saw Peter and John **a to** enter, *3516*
4: 4 the number of men grew to **a** five thousand. *6055*
4:20 For we cannot **help speaking a** *3281+3590*
5: 7 **A** three hours later his wife came in, *6055*
5:11 the whole church and all who **heard a** *201*
5:36 and **a** four hundred men rallied to him. *6055*
7:13 Pharaoh **learned a** Joseph's family. *1181+5745*
7:18 another king, who **knew** nothing **a** Joseph, *3857*
8:34 please, who is the prophet talking **a,** *4309*
8:35 **told** him **the good news a** *2294*
8:40 appeared at Azotus and **traveled a,** *1451*
9:13 "I have heard many reports **a** this man *4309*
9:28 **moved a freely** in Jerusalem, *1660+1744+2779*
9:32 **traveled a the country,** *1328+1451+4246*
9:37 **A** that time she became sick and died, *1877*
10: 3 at **a** three in the afternoon he had a vision.
4309+6059
10: 9 **A** noon the following day as they were *4309*
10:17 While Peter *was* **wondering a** the meaning *1389*
10:19 While Peter was still thinking **a** the vision, *4309*
10:43 All the prophets testify *a* **him** *AIT*
11:12 The Spirit told me to have no hesitation **a** *NIG*
11:20 **telling** them **the good news a** *2294*
12: 1 It was **a** this time *2848*
12:17 "**Tell** James and the brothers **a** *550*
13:11 darkness came over him, and he **groped a,** *4310*
13:12 he was amazed at the teaching *a* **the Lord.** *AIT*
13:18 he endured their conduct for **a** forty years *6055*
13:20 All this took **a** 450 years. *6055*
13:29 that was written **a** him, *4309*
13:42 the people invited them *to* **speak** further **a** *3281*
14: 6 But *they* **found out a** it and fled to *5328*
15: 2 **see** the apostles and elders **a** *4309*
15:12 and Paul **telling a** the miraculous signs *2007*
16:25 **A** midnight Paul and Silas were praying *2848*
16:27 he drew his sword and *was* **a to** kill himself *3516*
17:18 the good news *a* **Jesus** and the resurrection. *AIT*
17:21 but **talking a** and listening to *3306*
17:32 When they **heard a** the resurrection of *201*
18:14 Just as Paul **was a to** speak, *3516*
18:14 "If you Jews were **making a complaint a** *1639S*
18:15 But since it involves questions **a** words *4309*
18:25 and he spoke with great fervor and taught **a** *4309*
19: 7 There were **a** twelve men in all. *6059*
19: 8 arguing persuasively **a** the kingdom *4309*
Ac 19:15 and *I* **know a** Paul, but who are you?" *2179*
19:23 **A** that time there arose a great disturbance *2848*
19:23 that time there arose a great disturbance **a** *4309*
19:34 they all shouted in unison for **a** two hours: *6055*
20: 3 a plot against him just *as he was* **a to** sail *3516*
20:25 among whom *I have* **gone a** preaching *1451*
21:24 in these reports **a** you, *4309*
21:37 *As* the soldiers *were* **a to** take Paul into *3516*
22: 6 "**A** noon as I came near Damascus, *4309*
22:18 they will not accept your testimony **a** me.' *4309*
22:29 Those who *were* **a to** question him *3516*
23: 5 not **speak** evil **a** the ruler of your people.' " *3306*
23:11 As you have testified **a** me in Jerusalem, *4309*
23:15 of wanting more accurate information **a** *4309*
23:20 of wanting more accurate information **a** *4309*
23:27 by the Jews and they *were* **a to** kill him, *3516*
23:29 to do with questions *a* their **law,** *AIT*
24: 2 and your foresight *has* **brought a** reforms *1181*
24: 8 the truth **a** all these charges we are bringing *4309*
24:24 for Paul and listened to him as he spoke **a** *4309*
25:19 they had some points of dispute with him **a** *4309*
25:19 with him about their own religion and **a** *4309*
25:24 Jewish community has petitioned me **a** *4309*
25:26 to write to His Majesty **a** him. *4309*
26:13 **A** noon, O king, as I was on the road, *NIG*
27: 2 a ship from Adramyttium **a to** sail for ports *3516*
27:27 across the Adriatic Sea, when **a** midnight *2848*
28:21 or said anything bad **a** you. *4309*
28:23 of God and tried to convince them **a** Jesus *4309*
28:31 of God and taught **a** the Lord Jesus Christ. *4309*
Ro 1:19 what may be known *a* **God** is plain to them, *AIT*
2:17 on the law and **brag a** your relationship *3016*
2:23 You who brag **a** the law, *1877*
4: 2 he had **something to boast a—** *3017*
4:19 since he was **a** a hundred years old— *4543*
10: 2 I can testify *a* **them** that they are zealous *AIT*
11: 2 the Scripture says in the passage **a** Elijah— *NIG*
13:14 *do* not **think a** how to gratify the desires of
the sinful nature. *4472+4630*
14:22 So whatever you believe **a** *NIG*
15:21 "Those who were not told **a** him will see, *4309*
16:19 Everyone *has* **heard a** your obedience, *919*
16:19 but I want you to be wise **a** what is good, *1650*
16:19 and innocent **a** what is evil. *1650*
1Co 1: 6 our testimony *a* **Christ** was confirmed *AIT*
2: 1 as I proclaimed to you the testimony *a* **God.** *AIT*
2:15 The spiritual man **makes judgments a** *373*
3:21 So then, no more boasting **a** men! *1877*
6: 4 if you have disputes **a** such matters, *NIG*
7: 1 Now for the matters you wrote **a:** *4309*
7:25 Now **a** virgins: I have no command from the *4309*
7:32 An unmarried man *is* **concerned a** *3534*
7:33 a married man *is* **concerned a** the affairs *3534*
7:34 or virgin *is* **concerned a** the Lord's affairs: *3534*
7:34 a married woman *is* **concerned a** the affairs *3534*
8: 1 Now **a** food sacrificed to idols: *4309*
8: 4 So then, **a** eating food sacrificed to idols: *4309*
9: 9 Is it *a* **oxen** that God is concerned? *AIT*
11:16 If anyone wants to be contentious **a** this, *NIG*
12: 1 Now **a** spiritual gifts, brothers, *4309*
14:35 If they want *to* **inquire a** something, *3443*
15:15 we are then found to be false witnesses **a** *NIG*
15:15 for we have testified **a** God *2848*
16: 1 Now **a** the collection for God's people: *4309*
16:12 Now **a** our brother Apollos: *4309*
2Co 1: 8 **a** the hardships we suffered in the province *5642*
7: 7 He told us **a** your longing for me, *NIG*
7:14 I had boasted to him **a** you, *5642*
7:14 so our **boasting a** you to Titus has proved *3018*
8: 1 *to* **know a** the grace that God has given *1192*
8:10 And here is my advice **a** what is best *NIG*
9: 1 to write to you **a** this service to the saints. *4309*
9: 2 and *I have been* **boasting a** it to *3016*
9: 3 the brothers in order that our boasting **a** *5642*
9: 4 not *to* **say** anything **a** you— *3306*
10: 8 if I boast somewhat freely **a** the authority *4309*
10:16 not *want to* **boast a** work already done *3016*
11:12 with us in the things *they* **boast a.** *3016*
11:21 What anyone else dares to boast **a—** *NIG*
11:21 I also dare to boast **a.** *NIG*
12: 5 I will boast **a** a man like that, *5642*
12: 5 but I will not boast **a** myself, *5642*
12: 5 except **a** my weaknesses. *1877*
12: 9 Therefore I will boast all the more gladly **a** *1877*
Gal 4:20 because I am perplexed **a** you! *1877*
6:13 to be circumcised that they may boast **a** *1877*
Eph 1:15 *since* I **heard a** your faith in the Lord Jesus *201*
3: 2 Surely *you have* **heard a** the administration *201*
5:32 but I am talking **a** Christ and the church. *1650*
Php 1: 7 It is right for me to feel this way **a** all *5642*
1:27 whether I come and see you or only hear **a** *4309*
2:19 also may be cheered when I receive news **a** *4309*
4: 6 *Do* not *be* **anxious a** anything, *3534*
4: 8 **think a** such things. *3357*
Col 1: 5 that *you have* **already heard a** in the word *4578*
1: 9 since the day we **heard a** you, *201*
2:18 **goes into great detail a** what he has seen, *1836*
4: 7 Tychicus will tell you all the news **a** me. *2848*
4: 8 the express purpose that you may know **a** *4309*
4:10 (You have received instructions **a** him; *4309*
1Th 1: 8 we do not need to **say** anything **a** it, *3281*
3: 5 I sent to **find out a** your faith. *1182*
3: 6 *has* **brought good news a** your faith *2294*
3: 7 and persecution we were encouraged **a** you *2093*
4: 9 Now **a** brotherly love we do not need *4309*
4:13 to be ignorant **a** those who fall asleep, *4309*
5: 1 **a** times and dates we do not need to write *4309*

2Th 1: 4 among God's churches we boast **a** *5642*
1Ti 1: 7 not know what *they are* **talking a** *3306*
1:18 with the prophecies once made **a** you, *2093*
5:13 into the habit of being idle and **going a** *4320*
6: 4 and **quarrels a words** that result in envy, *3363*
6:15 which God *will* **bring a** in his own time— *1259*
2Ti 1: 8 do not be ashamed to testify *a* our **Lord,** *AIT*
2:14 before God against **quarreling a words;** *3362*
3:10 You, however, **know all a** my teaching, *4158*
Tit 2: 8 because they have nothing bad to say **a** us. *4309*
2:10 the teaching *a* **God** our **Savior** attractive. *AIT*
3: 9 and arguments and quarrels **a the law,** *3788*
Phm 1: 5 because I hear *a* your **faith** in the Lord *AIT*
Heb 1: 8 But **a** the Son he says, "Your throne, *4639*
2: 5 **a** which we are speaking. *4309*
4: 4 For somewhere he has spoken **a** *4309*
4: 8 not have spoken later **a** another day. *4309*
5:11 We have much to say **a** this, *4309*
5:13 with the teaching *a* **righteousness.** *AIT*
6: 1 the elementary teachings *a* **Christ** and go on *AIT*
6: 2 instruction *a* **baptisms,** *AIT*
7:14 in regard to that tribe Moses said nothing **a** *4309*
8: 5 *when he was* **a to** build the tabernacle: *3516*
10: 7 it is written **a** me in the scroll— *4309*
10:15 The Holy Spirit also **testifies** to us **a** this. *3455*
11: 7 when warned **a** things not yet seen, *4309*
11:17 the promises *was a to* **sacrifice** his one *AIT*
11:22 spoke **a** the exodus of the Israelites *4309*
11:22 from Egypt and gave instructions **a** *4309*
11:32 I do not have time to tell **a** Gideon, Barak, *4309*
11:37 *They* **went a** in sheepskins and goatskins, *4320*
12:17 *He could* **bring a** no change of mind, *2351*
Jas 1:11 even while he **goes a his business.** *4512*
1:20 for man's anger *does* not **bring a** *2237*
2:16 but does nothing *a* **his** physical needs, *AIT*
3:14 do not boast **a** it or deny the truth. *NIG*
5:11 the Lord finally brought **a.** *NIG*
2Pe 1:16 when *we* **told** you **a** the power *1192*
1:20 that no prophecy of Scripture **came a** by *1181*
3:12 That day will **bring a** the destruction of *1328*
1Jn 2:26 I am writing these things to you **a** *4309*
2:27 as his anointing teaches you **a** all things *4309*
5: 9 which he has given **a** his Son. *4309*
5:10 not believed the testimony God has given **a** *4309*
5:16 I am not saying that he should pray **a** that. *4309*
3Jn 1: 3 and **tell a** your faithfulness to the truth *3455*
1: 6 They *have* **told** the church **a** your love. *3455*
1:10 **gossiping** maliciously **a** about us. *5826*
Jude 1: 3 although I was very eager to write to you **a** *4309*
1: 4 men whose condemnation **was written a** *4592*
1: 9 when he was disputing with the devil **a** *4309*
1:14 prophesied *a* **these** *men:* *AIT*
1:16 they boast **a** themselves and flatter others *NIG*
Rev 2:10 not be afraid of what *you are* **a** to suffer. *3516*
3: 2 Strengthen what remains and *is* **a to** die, *3516*
3:16 *I am* **a to** spit you out of my mouth. *3516*
8: 1 there was silence in heaven for **a** half *6055*
8:13 of the trumpet blasts **a to** be sounded by *3516*
10: 4 the seven thunders spoke, *I was* **a to** write; *3516*
10: 7 in the days when the seventh angel *is* **a to** *3516*
10:11 "You must prophesy again **a** many peoples, *2093*
12: 2 in pain *as she was a to* **give birth.** *AIT*
12: 4 of the woman who *was* **a to** give birth, *3516*
16:21 From the sky huge hailstones of **a** *6055*

ABOVE (147)

Ge 1: 7 under the expanse from the water **a** it. 4946+6584
1:20 and let birds fly **a** the earth across 6584
3:14 "Cursed are you **a** all the livestock and all 4946
7:17 the ark high **a** the earth. 4946+6584
27:39 away from the dew of heaven **a.** 4946+6584
28:13 There **a** it stood the LORD, and he said: 6584
32:31 The sun rose **a** him as he passed Peniel, 4200
49:25 with blessings of the heavens **a,** 4946+6584
Ex 20: 4 an idol in the form of anything in heaven **a** 4946+5087
25:22 **a** the cover between the two cherubim 4946+6584
28:27 close to the seam **just a** the waistband 4946+5087
39:20 close to the seam **just a** the waistband 4946+5087
40:36 from **a** the tabernacle, they would set out; 6584
Lev 16:13 the atonement cover **a** the Testimony, 6584
26:19 and make the **sky** *a* you like iron and AIT
Nu 7:89 two cherubim **a** the atonement cover 4946+6584
9:15 the cloud **a** the tabernacle looked like fire. 6584
9:17 Whenever the cloud lifted from **a** the Tent, 6584
10:11 the cloud lifted from **a** the tabernacle of 6584
11:31 camp to about three feet **a** the ground, 6584+7156
12:10 When the cloud lifted from **a** the Tent, 6584
16: 3 Why then do you set yourselves **a** 6584
Dt 4:39 the LORD is God in heaven **a** and on 4946+5087
5: 8 an idol in the form of anything in heaven **a** 4946+5087
10:15 their descendants, **a** all the nations, 4946
11:21 as the days that the heavens are **a** the earth. 6584
26:19 fame and honor high **a** all 6584
28: 1 the LORD your God will set you high **a** 6584
28:43 The alien who lives among you will rise **a** 6584
33:13 the precious dew **from** heaven *a* and with AIT
Jos 2:11 the LORD your God is God in heaven **a** 4946+5087
2Sa 22:49 You exalted me **a** my foes; 4946
1Ki 7: 3 with cedar **a** the beams that rested on 4946+5087+6584
7:11 **A** were high-grade stones, cut to size, 2025+4200+4946+5087
7:20 **a** the bowl-shaped part next to the network, 4200+4946+4946+5087+6645
7:29 **A** and below the lions 4946+5087
8:23 like you in heaven **a** or on earth below 4946+5087
2Ki 19:30 and bear fruit **a.** 2025+4200+5087
1Ch 4:38 The men listed **a** by name were leaders NIH
11:21 He was doubly honored **a** the Three 4946
16:25 he is to be feared **a** all gods. 6584
29: 3 **over and a** everything I have provided 2025+4200+5087
2Ch 7: 3 and the glory of the LORD **a** the temple, 6584
34: 4 to pieces the incense altars that were **a** 2025+4200+5087
Ne 3:28 **A** the Horse Gate, the priests made repairs, 4946+6584
3:31 and as far as the **room a** the corner; 6608
3:32 the **room a** the corner and the Sheep Gate 6608
8: 5 because he was standing **a** them; 4946+6584
9: 5 may it be exalted **a** all blessing and praise. 6584
12:37 and passed **a** the house of David to 4946+6584
Est 5:11 how he had elevated him **a** the other nobles 6584
Job 3: 4 may God **a** not care about it; 4946+5087
18:16 up below and his branches wither **a.** 4946+5087
19: 5 If indeed you would exalt yourselves **a** me 6584
31: 2 For what is man's lot from God **a,** 4946+5087
35: 5 gaze at the clouds so high **a** you. 4946
Ps 8: 1 You have set your glory **a** the heavens. 6584
18:48 You exalted me **a** my foes; 4946
27: 6 be exalted **a** the enemies who surround me; 6584
45: 7 therefore God, your God, has set you **a** 4946
50: 4 He summons the heavens **a,** 4946+6584
57: 5 Be exalted, O God, **a** the heavens; 6584
57:11 Be exalted, O God, **a** the heavens; 6584
68:33 to him who rides the ancient **skies a,** 9028+9028
78:23 Yet he gave a command to the skies **a** 4946+5087
89: 6 in the **skies a** can compare with the LORD? 8836
95: 3 the great King **a** all gods. 6584
96: 4 he is to be feared **a** all gods. 6584
97: 9 you are exalted far **a** all gods. 6584
103:11 For as high as the heavens are **a** the earth, 6584
104: 6 the waters stood **a** the mountains. 6584
108: 5 Be exalted, O God, **a** the heavens, 6584
113: 4 his glory **a** the heavens. 6584
138: 2 for you have exalted **a** all things your name 6584
148: 1 praise him in the **heights a.** 5294
148: 4 you highest heavens and you waters **a** 4946+6584
148:13 his splendor is **a** the earth and the heavens. 6584
Pr 4:23 **A** all else, guard your heart, 4946
8:28 when he established the clouds **a** 4946+5087
Isa 2: 2 it will be raised **a** the hills, 4946
6: 2 **A** him were seraphs, each with six wings: 4946+5087
10:15 the ax raise itself **a** him who swings it, 6584
14:13 I will raise my throne **a** the stars of God; 4946+5087
14:14 I will ascend **a** the tops of the clouds; 6584
24:21 the powers in the heavens **a** 928+2021+5294
37:31 and bear fruit **a.** 2025+4200+5087
40:22 He sits enthroned **a** the circle of the earth, 6584
45: 8 "You heavens **a,** rain down righteousness; 4946+5087
Jer 4:28 the earth will mourn and the heavens **a** 4946+5087
17: 9 The heart is deceitful **a** all things and 4946
21:13 you *who* **live** *a* this valley *on* AIT
31:37 "Only if the heavens **a** can be measured 2025+4200+4946+5087
43:10 he will spread his royal canopy **a** them. 6584
52:23 the total number of pomegranates **a** 6584
Eze 1:22 Spread out **a** the heads of 6584
1:25 a voice from the expanse over their heads 6584
1:26 **A** the expanse over their 4946+5087
1:26 and **high a** on the throne was a figure like that of a man. 2025+4200+4946+5087
9: 3 of Israel went up from **a** the cherubim, 6584
10: 1 a throne of sapphire **a** the expanse that was 448
10: 4 Then the glory of the LORD rose from **a** 6584
10:18 of the temple and stopped **a** the cherubim. 6584
10:19 the glory of the God of Israel was **a** them. 2025+4200+4946+5087
11:22 the glory of the God of Israel was **a** them. 2025+4200+4946+5087
11:23 the city and stopped **a** the mountain east 6584
19:11 It towered **high a** the thick foliage, 1068+6584
29:15 and will never again exalt itself **a** 6584
31: 3 its top **a** the thick foliage. 1068
31:10 lifting its top **a** the thick foliage, 448+1068
31:14 lifting their tops **a** the thick foliage. 448+1068
41: 6 one **a** another, thirty on each level. 448
41:17 In the space **a** the outside of the entrance 4946+6584
41:20 the floor to the area **a** the entrance, 4946+6584
Da 11:36 He will exalt and magnify himself **a** 6584
11:37 but will exalt himself **a** them all. 6584
12: 6 who was **a** the waters of the river, 4946+5087
12: 7 who was **a** the waters of the river, 4946+5087
Am 2: 9 I destroyed his fruit **a** and his roots below. 4946+5087
Mic 4: 1 it will be raised **a** the hills, 4946
Mt 10:24 "A student is not **a** his teacher, *5642*
10:24 nor a servant **a** his master. *5642*
27:37 **A** his head they placed the written charge *2062*
Mk 2: 4 they made an opening in the roof **a** Jesus *3963*
Lk 6:40 A student is not **a** his teacher, *5642*
23:38 There was a written notice **a** him, *2093*
Jn 3:31 "The one who comes **from a** is above all; *540*
3:31 "The one who comes from above is **a** all; *2062*
3:31 The one who comes from heaven is **a** all. *2062*
8:23 "You are from below; I am from **a.** *539*
19:11 over me if it were not given to you **from a.** *540*
Ac 2:19 the heaven **a** and signs on the earth below, *539*
Ro 12:10 Honor one another **a** *yourselves.* *4605*
Gal 4:26 But the Jerusalem that is **a** is free, *539*
Eph 1:21 **far a** all rule and authority, *5645*
Php 2: 9 and gave him the name that is **a** *5642*
Col 3: 1 set your hearts on things **a,** *539*
3: 2 Set your minds on things **a,** *539*
1Ti 3: 2 Now the overseer must be **a reproach,** *455*
Heb 1: 9 therefore God, your God, has set you **a** *4123*
4: 5 And again in **the passage a** he says, *4047*
7:26 **exalted a** the heavens. *5734*
9: 5 **A** the ark were the cherubim of the Glory, *5645*
Jas 1:17 Every good and perfect gift is **from a,** *540*
5:12 **A** all, my brothers, do not swear— *4574*
1Pe 4: 8 **A** all, love each other deeply, *4574*
2Pe 1:20 **A all,** you must understand *4047+4754*
Rev 10: 1 with a rainbow **a** his head; *2093*

ABRAHAM (230) [ABRAHAM'S, ABRAM, ABRAM'S]

Ge 17: 5 your name will be **A,** 90
17: 9 Then God said to **A,** "As for you, 90
17:15 God also said to **A,** 90
17:17 **A** fell facedown; he laughed 90
17:18 And **A** said to God, 90
17:22 When he had finished speaking with **A,** 90
17:23 On that very day **A** took his son Ishmael 90
17:24 **A** was ninety-nine years old 90
17:26 **A** and his son Ishmael were both circumcised 90
18: 1 to **A** near the great trees of Mamre 2257[S]
18: 2 **A** looked up and saw three men 2257[S]
18: 6 So **A** hurried into the tent to Sarah. 90
18:11 **A** and Sarah were already old 90
18:13 Then the LORD said to **A,** 90
18:16 and **A** walked along with them to see them 90
18:17 "Shall I hide from **A** what I am about 90
18:18 **A** will surely become a great 90
18:19 about for **A** what he has promised him." 90
18:22 **A** remained standing before the LORD. 90
18:23 Then **A** approached him and said: 90
18:27 Then **A** spoke up again: 90
18:31 **A** said, "Now that I have been so bold as NIH
18:33 the LORD had finished speaking with **A,** 90
18:33 he left, and **A** returned home. 90
19:27 the next morning **A** got up and returned to 90
19:29 he remembered **A,** and he brought Lot out 90
20: 1 Now **A** moved on from there into 90
20: 2 and there **A** said of his wife Sarah, 90
20: 9 Then Abimelech called **A** in and said, 90
20:10 And Abimelech asked **A,** 90
20:11 **A** replied, "I said to myself, 90
20:14 and female slaves and gave them to **A,** 90
20:17 Then **A** prayed to God, 90
21: 2 Sarah became pregnant and bore a son to **A** 90
21: 3 **A** gave the name Isaac to the son 90
21: 4 When his son Isaac was eight days old, **A** circumcised him, 90
21: 5 **A** was a hundred years old 90
21: 7 to **A** that Sarah would nurse children? 90
21: 8 and on the day Isaac was weaned **A** held 90
21: 9 the Egyptian had borne to **A** was mocking, 90
21:10 and she said to **A,** 90
21:11 The matter distressed **A** greatly 90
21:14 Early the next morning **A** took some food 90
21:22 the commander of his forces said to **A,** 90
21:24 **A** said, "I swear it." 90
21:25 Then **A** complained to Abimelech about 90
21:27 So **A** brought sheep and cattle 90
21:28 **A** set apart seven ewe lambs from the flock, 90
21:29 and Abimelech asked **A,** 90
21:33 **A** planted a tamarisk tree in Beersheba, NIH
21:34 And **A** stayed in the land of the Philistines 90
22: 1 Some time later God tested **A.** 90
22: 1 He said to him, **"A!"** 90
22: 3 Early the next morning **A** got up 90
22: 4 the third day **A** looked up and saw the place 90
22: 6 **A** took the wood for the burnt offering 90
22: 7 Isaac spoke up and said to his father **A,** 90
22: 7 "Yes, my son?" **A** replied. NIH
22: 8 **A** answered, "God himself will provide 90
22: 9 **A** built an altar there and arranged 90
22:11 to him from heaven, **"A! Abraham!"** 90
22:11 to him from heaven, "Abraham! **A!"** 90
22:13 **A** looked up and there in a thicket he saw 90
22:14 **A** called that place The LORD Will Provide. 90
22:15 of the LORD called to **A** from heaven 90
22:19 Then **A** returned to his servants, 90
22:19 And **A** stayed in Beersheba. 90
22:20 Some time later **A** was told, 90
23: 2 and **A** went to mourn for Sarah and to weep 90
23: 3 Then **A** rose from beside his dead wife 90
23: 5 The Hittites replied to **A,** 90
23: 7 Then **A** rose and bowed down before 90
23:10 among his people and he replied to **A** in 90
23:12 Again **A** bowed down before the people of 90
23:14 Ephron answered **A,** 90
23:16 **A** agreed to Ephron's terms 90
23:18 to **A** as his property in the presence of all 90
23:19 Afterward **A** buried his wife Sarah in 90
23:20 in it were deeded to **A** by the Hittites as 90
24: 1 **A** was now old and well advanced in years, 90
24: 6 not take my son back there," **A** said. 90
24: 9 the thigh of his master **A** and swore an oath 90
24:12 "O LORD, God of my master **A,** 90
24:12 and show kindness to my master **A.** 90
24:27 the God of my master **A,** 90

Ge 24:42 I said, 'O LORD, God of my master A, 90
24:48 the God of my master A, 90
25: 1 A took another wife, 90
25: 5 A left everything he owned to Isaac. 90
25: 7 A lived a hundred and seventy-five years. 90
25: 8 Then A breathed his last and died at 90
25:10 the field A had bought from the Hittites. 90
25:10 There A was buried with his wife Sarah. 90
25:12 Hagar the Egyptian, bore to A. 90
25:19 A became the father of Isaac, 90
26: 3 the oath I swore to your father A. 90
26: 5 A obeyed me and kept my requirements, 90
26:15 in the time of his father A, 90
26:18 in the time of his father A, 90
26:18 the Philistines had stopped up after A died, 90
26:24 "I am the God of your father A. 90
26:24 for the sake of my servant A." 90
28: 4 the blessing given to A, 90
28: 4 the land God gave to A." 90
28: 9 and daughter of Ishmael son of A, 90
28:13 God of your father A and the God of Isaac. 90
31:42 the God of A and the Fear of Isaac, 90
31:53 May the God of A and the God of Nahor, 90
32: 9 Jacob prayed, "O God of my father A, 90
35:12 The land I gave to A and Isaac I also give 90
35:27 Hebron), where A and Isaac had stayed. 90
48:15 "May the God before whom my fathers A 90
48:16 by my name and the names of my fathers A 90
49:30 which A bought as a burial place 90
49:31 There A and his wife Sarah were buried, 90
50:13 which A had bought as a burial place 90
50:24 to the land he promised on oath to A, 90
Ex 2:24 and he remembered his covenant with A, 90
3: 6 "I am the God of your father, the God of A, 90
3:15 the God of A, the God of Isaac and the God 90
3:16 the God of A, Isaac and Jacob— 90
4: 5 the God of A, the God of Isaac and the God 90
6: 3 I appeared to A, to Isaac and to Jacob 90
6: 8 with uplifted hand to give to A, 90
32:13 Remember your servants A, 90
33: 1 go up to the land I promised on oath to A, 90
Lev 26:42 with Isaac and my covenant with A, 90
Nu 32:11 the land I promised on oath to A, Isaac 90
Dt 1: 8 to A, Isaac and Jacob— 90
6:10 to A, Isaac and Jacob, to give you— 90
9: 5 to A, Isaac and Jacob. 90
9:27 Remember your servants A, 90
29:13 and as he swore to your fathers, A, Isaac 90
30:20 to give to your fathers, A, Isaac 90
34: 4 "This is the land I promised on oath to A, 90
Jos 24: 2 including Terah the father of A and Nahor, 90
24: 3 But I took your father A from the land 90
1Ki 18:36 "O LORD, God of A, Isaac and Israel, 90
2Ki 13:23 for them because of his covenant with A, 90
1Ch 1:27 and Abram (that is, A). 90
1:28 The sons of A: Isaac and Ishmael. 90
1:34 A was the father of Isaac. 90
16:16 the covenant he made with A, 90
29:18 O LORD, God of our fathers A, 90
2Ch 20: 7 to the descendants of A your friend? 90
30: 6 return to the LORD, the God of A, 90
Ne 9: 7 of Ur of the Chaldeans and named him A. 90
Ps 47: 9 the people of the God of A, for the kings of 90
105: 6 O descendants of A his servant, 90
105: 9 the covenant he made with A, 90
105:42 holy promise given to his servant A. 90
Isa 29:22 who redeemed A, says to the house 90
41: 8 you descendants of A my friend, 90
51: 2 look to A, your father, and 90
63:16 though A does not know us 90
Jer 33:26 to rule over the descendants of A, 90
Eze 33:24 'A was only one man, 90
Mic 7:20 and show mercy to A, 90
Mt 1: 1 Jesus Christ the son of David, the son *of* A: 11
1: 2 A was the father of Isaac, 11
1:17 in all from A to David, 11
3: 9 'We have A as our father.' 11
3: 9 God can raise up children *for* A. 11
8:11 will take their places at the feast with A, 11
22:32 'I am the God *of* A, 11
Mk 12:26 how God said to him, 'I am the God *of* A, 11
Lk 1:55 *to* A and his descendants forever, 11
1:73 the oath he swore to our father A: 11
3: 8 'We have A as our father.' 11
3: 8 God can raise up children *for* A. 11
3:34 the son *of* A, the son of Terah, 11
13:16 should not this woman, a daughter *of* A, 11
13:28 and gnashing of teeth, when you see A, 11
16:23 he looked up and saw A far away, 11
16:24 So he called to him, 'Father A, 11
16:25 "But A replied, 'Son, remember that 11
16:29 "A replied, 'They have Moses and 11
16:30 " 'No, father A,' he said, 11
19: 9 because this man, too, is a son *of* A. 11
20:37 for he calls the Lord 'the God *of* A, 11
Jn 8:39 "A is our father," they answered. 11
8:39 "then you would do the things A did. 11
8:40 A did not do such things. 11
8:52 A died and so did the prophets, 11
8:53 Are you greater than our father A? 11
8:56 Your father A rejoiced at the thought 11
8:57 "and you have seen A!" 11
8:58 Jesus answered, "before A was born, I am!" 11
Ac 3:13 The God *of* A, Isaac and Jacob, 11
3:25 He said to A, "Through your offspring 11
7: 2 The God of glory appeared to our father A 11
7: 5 even though at that time A had no child. 899S
7: 8 he gave A the covenant of circumcision. 899S
7: 8 And A became the father of Isaac NIG
7:16 that A had bought from the sons of Hamor 11
7:17 near for God to fulfill his promise *to* A. 11
7:32 the God *of* A, Isaac and Jacob.' 11
13:26 "Brothers, children *of* A, 11
Ro 4: 1 What then shall we say that A, 11
4: 2 If, in fact, A was justified by works, 11
4: 3 "A believed God, and it was credited 11
4:12 of the faith that our father A *had* 11
4:13 that A and his offspring received 11
4:16 but also to those who are of the faith *of* A. 11
4:18 A in hope believed and so became 4005S
11: 1 I am an Israelite myself, a descendant of A, 11
Gal 3: 6 Consider A: "He believed God, 11
3: 7 that those who believe are children *of* A. 11
3: 8 and announced the gospel in advance *to* A: 11
3: 9 along with A, the man of faith. 11
3:14 that the blessing given *to* A might come to 11
3:16 The promises were spoken *to* A and 11
3:18 in his grace gave it *to* A through a promise. 11
4:22 For it is written that A had two sons, 11
Heb 6:13 When God made his promise *to* A, 11
6:15 A received what was promised. NIG
7: 1 He met A returning from the defeat of 11
7: 2 and A gave him a tenth of everything. 11
7: 4 patriarch A gave him a tenth of the plunder! 11
7: 5 their brothers are descended from A. 11
7: 6 a tenth *from* A and blessed him who had 11
7: 9 paid the tenth through A, 11
7:10 because when Melchizedek met A, 899S
11: 8 By faith A, when called to go to 11
11:11 By faith A, even though he was past age— NIG
11:17 By faith A, when God tested him, 11
11:19 A reasoned that God could raise the dead, NIG
Jas 2:21 not our ancestor A considered righteous 11
2:23 "A believed God, and it was credited 11
1Pe 3: 6 who obeyed A and called him her master. 11

ABRAHAM'S (23) [ABRAHAM]

Ge 17:27 And every male in A household, 2257S
20:18 because of A wife Sarah. 90
22:23 to A brother Nahor. 90
24:15 who was the wife of A brother Nahor. 90
24:34 So he said, "I am A servant. 90
24:52 When A servant heard what they said, 90
24:59 with her nurse and A servant and his men. 90
25:11 After A death, God blessed his son Isaac, 90
25:12 This is the account of A son Ishmael, 90
25:19 This is the account of A son Isaac. 90
26: 1 besides the earlier famine of A time— 90
1Ch 1:32 The sons born to Keturah, A concubine: 90
Lk 16:22 and the angels carried him to A side. 11
Jn 8:33 "We are A descendants 11
8:37 I know you are A descendants. 11
8:39 "If you were A children," said Jesus, 11
Ro 4: 9 that A faith was credited to him 11
4:16 and may be guaranteed to all A offspring— NIG
9: 7 Nor because they are his descendants are they all A children. 11
9: 8 children of the promise who are regarded as A offspring. NIG
2Co 11:22 Are they A descendants? 11
Gal 3:29 then you are A seed, 11
Heb 2:16 it is not angels he helps, but A descendants. 11

ABRAM (60) [ABRAHAM]

Ge 11:26 he became the father of A, 92
11:27 Terah became the father of A, 92
11:29 A and Nahor both married. 92
11:31 Terah took his son A, 92
11:31 Sarai, the wife of his son A, 92
12: 1 The LORD had said to A, 92
12: 4 So A left, as the LORD had told him; 92
12: 4 A was seventy-five years old 92
12: 6 A traveled through the land as far as 92
12: 7 The LORD appeared to A and said, 92
12: 9 A set out and continued toward the Negev. 92
12:10 and A went down to Egypt to live there for 92
12:14 When A came to Egypt, 92
12:16 He treated A well for her sake, 92
12:16 and A acquired sheep and cattle, 2257S
12:18 So Pharaoh summoned A. 92
12:20 Pharaoh gave orders about A to his men, 2257S
13: 1 So A went up from Egypt to the Negev, 92
13: 2 A had become very wealthy in livestock 92
13: 4 There A called on the name of the LORD. 92
13: 5 Now Lot, who was moving about with A, 92
13: 8 So A said to Lot, 92
13:12 A lived in the land of Canaan, 92
13:14 The LORD said to A after Lot had parted 92
13:18 So A moved his tents and went to live near 92
14:13 and reported this to A the Hebrew. 92
14:13 Now A was living near the great trees 2085S
14:13 all of whom were allied with A. 92
14:14 When A heard that his relative had been taken captive, 92
14:15 the night A divided his men to attack them 2085S
14:17 After A returned from defeating 2257S
14:19 and he blessed A, 2084S
14:19 saying, "Blessed be A by God Most High, 92
14:20 Then A gave him a tenth of everything. NIH
14:21 The king of Sodom said to A, 92
14:22 But A said to the king of Sodom, 92
14:23 'I made A rich.' 92
15: 1 the word of the LORD came to A in 92
15: 1 "Do not be afraid, A. 92
15: 2 But A said, "O Sovereign LORD, 92
15: 3 A said, "You have given me no children; 92
15: 6 A believed the LORD, and he credited it NIH
15: 8 But A said, "O Sovereign LORD, NIH
15:10 A brought all these to him, NIH
15:11 but A drove them away. 92
15:12 A fell into a deep sleep, 92
15:18 the LORD made a covenant with A 92
16: 2 so she said to A, 92
16: 2 A agreed to what Sarai said. 92
16: 3 after A had been living in Canaan ten years, 92
16: 5 Then Sarai said to A, 92
16: 6 "Your servant is in your hands," A said. 92
16:15 So Hagar bore A a son, 92
16:15 and A gave the name Ishmael to 92
16:16 A was eighty-six years old 92
17: 1 When A was ninety-nine years old, 92
17: 3 A fell facedown, and God said to him, 92
17: 5 No longer will you be called A; 92
1Ch 1:27 and A (that is, Abraham). 92
Ne 9: 7 who chose A and brought him out of Ur of 92

ABRAM'S (5) [ABRAHAM]

Ge 11:29 The name of A wife was Sarai, 92
12:17 and his household because of A wife Sarai. 92
13: 7 And quarreling arose between A herdsmen 92
14:12 They also carried off A nephew Lot 92
16: 1 Sarai, A wife, had borne him no children. 92

ABROAD (4)

Ps 41: 6 he goes out and spreads it **a.** 2021+2575+4200
112: 9 *He has* **scattered a** his gifts to the poor, 7061
SS 4:16 that its fragrance *may* **spread a.** 5688
2Co 9: 9 *"He has* **scattered a** his gifts to the poor; *5025*

ABRONAH (2)

Nu 33:34 They left Jotbathah and camped at A. 6307
33:35 They left A and camped at Ezion Geber. 6307

ABSALOM (92) [ABSALOM'S]

2Sa 3: 3 the third, A the son of Maacah daughter 94
13: 1 the beautiful sister of A son of David. 94
13:20 Her brother A said to her, 94
13:22 A never said a word to Amnon, 94
13:24 A went to the king and said, 94
13:25 Although A urged him, NIH
13:26 Then A said, "If not, 94
13:27 But A urged him, 94
13:28 A ordered his men, "Listen! 94
13:29 to Amnon what A had ordered. 94
13:30 "A has struck down all the king's sons; 94
13:34 Meanwhile, A had fled. 94
13:37 A fled and went to Talmai son 94
13:38 After A fled and went to Geshur, 94
13:39 the spirit of the king longed to go to A, 94
14: 1 that the king's heart longed for A. 94
14:21 Go, bring back the young man A." 94
14:23 and brought A back to Jerusalem. 94
14:24 So A went to his own house and did not see 94
14:25 for his handsome appearance as A. 94
14:27 Three sons and a daughter were born to A. 94
14:28 A lived two years in Jerusalem 94
14:29 Then A sent for Joab in order to send him 94
14:32 A said to Joab, "Look, 94
14:33 Then the king summoned A, 94
14:33 And the king kissed A. 94
15: 1 A provided himself with a chariot 94
15: 2 A would call out to him, 94
15: 3 Then A would say to him, "Look, 94
15: 4 And A would add, 94
15: 5 A would reach out his hand, NIH
15: 6 A behaved in this way toward all 94
15: 7 At the end of four years, A said to the king, 94
15:10 Then A sent secret messengers throughout 94
15:10 then say, 'A is king in Hebron.' " 94
15:11 from Jerusalem had accompanied A. 94
15:12 While A was offering sacrifices, 94
15:13 "The hearts of the men of Israel are with A." 94
15:14 or none of us will escape from A. 94
15:19 Go back and stay with King A. NIH
15:31 among the conspirators with A." 94
15:34 But if you return to the city and say to A, 94
15:37 at Jerusalem as A was entering the city. 94
16: 8 the kingdom over to your son A. 94
16:15 A and all the men of Israel came 94
16:16 David's friend, went to A and said to him, 94
16:17 A asked Hushai, "Is this the love you show 94
16:18 Hushai said to A, "No, 94
16:20 A said to Ahithophel, "Give us your advice. 94
16:22 So they pitched a tent for A on the roof, 94
16:23 and A regarded all of Ahithophel's advice. 94
17: 1 Ahithophel said to A, 94
17: 4 This plan seemed good to A and to all 94
17: 5 But A said, "Summon also Hushai 94
17: 6 When Hushai came to him, A said, 94
17: 7 Hushai replied to A, 94
17: 9 among the troops who follow A.' 94
17:14 A and all the men of Israel said, 94
17:14 in order to bring disaster on A. 94
17:15 "Ahithophel has advised A and the elders 94
17:18 But a young man saw them and told A. 94
17:24 and A crossed the Jordan with all the men 94

2Sa 17:25 A had appointed Amasa over the army 94
17:26 The Israelites and A camped in the land 94
18: 5 with the young man A for my sake." 94
18: 5 the king giving orders concerning A to each 94
18: 9 Now A happened to meet David's men. 94
18:10 "I just saw A hanging in an oak tree." 94
18:12 'Protect the young man A for my sake.' 94
18:14 into Absalom's heart while A was still alive 5647S
18:15 ten of Joab's armor-bearers surrounded A, 94
18:17 They took A, threw him into a big pit in 94
18:18 During his lifetime A had taken a pillar 94
18:29 "Is the young man A safe?" 94
18:32 "Is the young man A safe?" 94
18:33 As he went, he said: "O my son **A**! 94
18:33 My son, my son **A**! 94
18:33 O **A**, my son, my son!" 94
19: 1 "The king is weeping and mourning for **A**." 94
19: 4 "O my son **A**! 94
19: 4 O **A**, my son, my son!" 94
19: 6 be pleased if A were alive today and all 94
19: 9 now he has fled the country because of **A**; 94
19:10 and **A**, whom we anointed to rule 94
20: 6 of Bicri will do us more harm than A did. 94
1Ki 1: 6 and was born next after **A**.) 94
2: 7 by me when I fled from your brother **A**. 94
2:28 with Adonijah though not with **A**, 94
1Ch 3: 2 A the son of Maacah daughter 94
2Ch 11:20 Then he married Maacah daughter of **A**, 94
11:21 of A more than any of his other wives 94
Ps 3: T When he fled from his son **A**. 94

ABSALOM'S (12) [ABSALOM]

2Sa 13: 4 Tamar, my brother A sister." 94
13:20 And Tamar lived in her brother A house, 94
13:23 A sheepshearers were at Baal Hazor 94+4200
13:29 So A men did 94
13:32 This has been A expressed intention ever 94
14:30 So A servants set the field on fire. 94
14:31 Joab did go to A house and he said to him, 94
15:12 and A following kept on increasing. 94
17:20 A men came to the woman at the house, 94
18: 9 A head got caught in the tree. 2257S
18:14 into A heart while Absalom was still alive 94
18:18 and it is called A Monument to this day. 94

ABSENCE (3) [ABSENT]

Ac 24:17 "After an a of several years, *NIG*
Php 1:27 and see you or only hear about you **in** *my* **a**, *582*
2:12 but now much more in my **a**— *707*

ABSENT (5) [ABSENCE]

Pr 10:19 When words are many, sin *is* not **a**, 2532
2Co 10:11 in our letters *when we are* **a**, *582*
13: 2 I now repeat it *while* **a**: *582*
13:10 *when I am* **a**, that when I come I may *582*
Col 2: 5 For though *I am* **a from** you in body, *582*

ABSOLUTE (1) [ABSOLUTELY]

1Ti 5: 2 as sisters, with a purity. *4246*

ABSOLUTELY (3) [ABSOLUTE]

Ex 22:17 her father **a refuses** to give her to him, 4412+4412
Gal 2:17 that Christ promotes sin? **A not!** *1181+3590*
3:21 opposed to the promises of God? **A not!** *1181+3590*

ABSTAIN (7) [ABSTAINED, ABSTAINS]

Ex 19:15 **A from sexual relations."** 440+448+851+5602
Nu 6: 3 *he must* **a** from wine 5693
Ac 15:20 telling them *to* **a from** food polluted *600*
15:29 *You are to* **a from** food sacrificed to idols, *600*
21:25 that they *should* **a from** food sacrificed *5875*
1Ti 4: 3 and order them *to* **a from** certain foods, *600*
1Pe 2:11 *to* **a from** sinful desires, *600*

ABSTAINED (1) [ABSTAIN]

Ex 31:17 and on the seventh day *he* **a from work** 8697

ABSTAINS (1) [ABSTAIN]

Ro 14: 6 and he who **a**, does so to the Lord *2266+3590*

ABSTINENCE (KJV) See FAST, FASTING

ABUNDANCE (33) [ABUNDANT]

Ge 27:28 an **a** *of* grain and new wine. 8044
41:29 of great **a** are coming throughout the land 8426
41:30 Then all the **a** in Egypt will be forgotten, 8426
41:31 The **a** in the land will not be remembered, 8426
41:34 of Egypt during the seven years of **a**. 8426
41:47 of **a** the land produced plentifully. 8426
41:48 the food produced in those seven years of **a** NIH
41:53 The seven years of **a** in Egypt came to 8426
Dt 33:19 they will feast on the **a** *of* the seas, 9179
1Ch 29:16 as for all this **a** that we have provided 2162
29:21 and other sacrifices **in a** for all Israel. 4200+8044
2Ch 29:35 There were burnt offerings **in a**, 4200+8044
Ne 9:25 olive groves and fruit trees **in a**. 4200+8044
Job 36:31 the nations and provides food in **a**. 3892
Ps 36: 8 They feast on the **a** *of* your house; 2016
65:11 and your carts overflow with **a**. 2016
66:12 but you brought us to a **place of a**. 8122
73:10 to them and drink up waters in **a**. 4849
Pr 20:15 Gold there is, and rubies **in a**, 8044
Ecc 5:12 the **a** of a rich man permits him no sleep. 8426
Isa 7:22 And because of the **a** of the milk they give, 8044
30:33 with an **a** of fire and wood; 2221
33:23 Then an **a** *of* spoils will be divided and 5269
66:11 and delight in her overflowing **a**." 3883
Jer 2:22 with soda and **use an a** *of* soap, 8049
31:14 I will satisfy the priests with **a**, 2016
40:12 And they harvested an **a** of wine 2221+4394
Mt 13:12 and *he will* **have an a**. *4355*
25:29 and *he will* **have an a**. *4355*
Lk 12:15 not consist in the **a** of his possessions." *4355*
1Pe 1: 2 Grace and peace *be* yours *in* **a**. *4437*
2Pe 1: 2 *in* **a** through the knowledge of God and *4437*
Jude 1: 2 Mercy, peace and love *be* yours *in* **a**. *4437*

ABUNDANT (31) [ABUNDANCE, ABUNDANTLY]

Nu 24: 7 their seed will have **a** water. 8041
Dt 28:11 The LORD *will* **grant** you **a** prosperity— 3855
32: 2 like **a rain** on tender plants. 8053
2Ch 11:23 He gave them **a** provisions 4200+8044
Ne 5:18 and every ten days an **a supply** of wine 2221
9:37 its **a** harvest goes to 8049
Est 1: 7 and the royal wine was **a**, 8041
Job 36:28 down their moisture and **a** showers fall 8041
Ps 68: 9 You gave **a** showers, O God; 5607
78:15 in the desert and gave them water as **a** as 8041
132:15 *I will* **bless** her *with* **a** provisions; 1385+1385
145: 7 They will celebrate your **a** goodness 8041
Pr 12:11 He who works his land *will* **have a** food, 8425
13:23 A poor man's field may produce **a** food, 8044
14: 4 the strength of an ox comes an **a** harvest. 8044
28:19 He who works his land *will* **have a** food, 8425
Isa 23:18 for **a** food and fine clothes. 8429
Jer 33: 6 and will let them enjoy **a** peace 6988
33: 9 the **a** prosperity and peace I provide for it.' 3972
Eze 17: 5 He planted it like a willow by **a** water, 8041
17: 8 It had been planted in good soil by **a** water 8041
19:10 and full of branches because of **a** water. 8041
31: 5 spreading because of **a** waters. 8041
31: 7 for its roots went down to **a** waters. 8041
31: 9 I made it beautiful with **a** branches, 8044
31:15 and its **a** waters were restrained. 8041
32:13 from beside **a** waters no longer to be stirred 8041
Da 4:12 Its leaves were beautiful, its fruit **a**, 10678
4:21 with beautiful leaves and **a** fruit, 10678
Joel 2:23 He sends you **a showers**, 1773
Ro 5:17 much more will those who receive God's **a provision** *4353*

ABUNDANTLY (5) [ABUNDANT]

Ge 24:35 The LORD has blessed my master **a**, 4394
Jos 17:14 and the LORD has blessed us **a**." 889+3907+6330+6330
Ps 65: 9 you enrich it **a**. 8041
78:20 water gushed out, and streams **flowed a**. 8851
1Ti 1:14 **poured out** on me **a**, *5670*

ABUSE (5) [ABUSED, ABUSIVE, ABUSIVELY]

1Sa 31: 4 and run me through and **a** me." 6618
1Ch 10: 4 uncircumcised fellows will come and **a** me." 6618
Ps 55:10 malice and **a** are within it. 6662
Pr 9: 7 whoever rebukes a wicked man incurs **a**. 4583
1Pe 4: 4 and *they* **heap a on** you. *1059*

ABUSED (1) [ABUSE]

Jdg 19:25 and they raped her and **a** her throughout 6618

ABUSIVE (2) [ABUSE]

Ac 18: 6 when the Jews opposed Paul and *became* **a**, *1059*
2Ti 3: 2 **a**, disobedient to their parents, ungrateful, *1061*

ABUSIVELY (2) [ABUSE]

Ac 13:45 and talked **a** against what Paul was saying. *1059*
Jude 1:10 Yet these men **speak a against** *1059*

ABUTTED (1)

Eze 40:18 It **a** the sides of the gateways and was 448

ABYSS (9)

Lk 8:31 not to order them to go into the **A**. *12*
Rev 9: 1 star was given the key to the shaft *of* the **A**. *12*
9: 2 When he opened the **A**, *12*
9: 2 by the smoke *from* the **A**. *5853*
9:11 as king over them the angel *of* the **A**, *12*
11: 7 that comes up from the **A** will attack them, *12*
17: 8 up out of the **A** and go to his destruction. *12*
20: 1 the **A** and holding in his hand a great chain. *12*
20: 3 He threw him into the **A**, *12*

ACACIA (28) [ACACIAS]

Ex 25: 5 of sea cows; **a** wood; 8847
25:10 "Have them make a chest of **a** wood— 8847
25:13 of **a** wood and overlay them with gold. 8847
25:23 "Make a table of **a** wood— 8847
25:28 Make the poles of **a** wood, 8847
26:15 "Make upright frames of **a** wood for 8847
26:26 "Also make crossbars of **a** wood: 8847
26:32 on four posts of **a wood** overlaid with gold 8847
26:37 and five posts of **a wood** overlaid with gold. 8847
27: 1 "Build an altar of **a** wood, 8847
27: 6 of **a** wood for the altar and overlay them 8847
30: 1 an altar of **a** wood for burning incense. 8847
30: 5 of **a** wood and overlay them with gold. 8847
35: 7 of sea cows; **a** wood; 8847
35:24 and everyone who had **a** wood for any part 8847
36:20 They made upright frames of **a** wood for 8847
36:31 They also made crossbars of **a** wood: 8847
36:36 They made four posts of **a wood** for it 8847
37: 1 Bezalel made the ark of **a** wood— 8847
37: 4 of **a** wood and overlaid them with gold. 8847
37:10 They made the table of **a** wood— 8847
37:15 for carrying the table were made of **a** wood 8847
37:25 the altar of incense out of **a** wood. 8847
37:28 of **a** wood and overlaid them with gold. 8847
38: 1 the altar of burnt offering of **a** wood, 8847
38: 6 of **a** wood and overlaid them with bronze. 8847
Dt 10: 3 So I made the ark out of **a** wood 8847
Isa 41:19 I will put in the desert the cedar and the **a**, 8847

ACACIAS (1) [ACACIA]

Joel 3:18 and will water the valley of **a**. 8847

ACBOR (7)

Ge 36:38 Baal-Hanan son of A succeeded him 6570
36:39 When Baal-Hanan son of A died, 6570
2Ki 22:12 Ahikam son of Shaphan, A son of Micaiah, 6570
22:14 Hilkiah the priest, Ahikam, **A**, 6570
1Ch 1:49 Baal-Hanan son of A succeeded him 6570
Jer 26:22 however, sent Elnathan son of A to Egypt, 6570
36:12 of Shemaiah, Elnathan son of **A**, 6570

ACCAD (KJV) See AKKAD

ACCENT (1)

Mt 26:73 for your **a** gives you away." *3282*

ACCEPT (77) [ACCEPTABLE, ACCEPTABLY, ACCEPTANCE, ACCEPTED, ACCEPTING, ACCEPTS]

Ge 14:23 that *I will* **a** nothing belonging to you, 4374
14:24 I will **a** nothing but what my men have eaten NIH
21:30 **"A** these seven lambs from my hand as 4374
23:13 **A** it from me so I can bury my dead there." 4374
33:10 **a** this gift from me. 4374
33:11 Please **a** the present that was brought 4374
Ex 22:11 The owner *is to* **a** this, 4374
23: 8 *"Do* not **a** a bribe, 4374
Lev 22:25 and you must not **a** such animals from NIH
26:23 of these things *you do* not **a** my **correction** 3579
Nu 7: 5 **"A** these from them, 4374
16:15 *"Do* not **a** their offering. 7155
32:30 *they must* **a** *their* **possession** with you 296
35:31 not **a** a ransom for the life of a murderer, 4374
35:32 not **a** a ransom for anyone who has fled to 4374
Dt 16:19 *Do* not **a** a bribe, 4374
20:11 If *they* **a** and open their gates, 6699
21: 8 **A** *this* **atonement** for your people Israel, 4105
1Sa 2:15 *he* won't **a** boiled meat from you, 4374
10: 4 which *you will* **a** from them. 4374
26:19 then *may he* **a** an offering. 8193
2Sa 24:23 *"May* the LORD your God **a** you." 8354
2Ki 5:15 Please now **a** a gift from your servant." 4374
5:16 whom I serve, *I will* not **a** a thing." 4374
5:23 He urged Gehazi to **a** them, NIH
5:26 or to **a** clothes, olive groves, vineyards, 4374
Est 4: 4 but *he would* not **a** them. 7691
Job 2:10 *Shall we* **a** good from God, 7691
22:22 **A** instruction from his mouth and lay 4374
42: 8 and *I will* **a** his prayer and not deal 5951+7156
Ps 15: 5 and *does* not **a** a bribe against the innocent. 4374
20: 3 and **a** your burnt offerings. 2014
119:108 **A**, O LORD, the willing praise 8354
Pr 1:25 and *would* not **a** my rebuke, 14
1:30 not **a** my advice and spurned my rebuke, 14
2: 1 if *you* **a** my words and store 4374
4:10 Listen, my son, **a** what I say, 4374
6:35 *He will* not **a** any compensation; 5951+7156
10: 8 The wise in heart **a** commands, 4374
19:20 Listen to advice and **a** instruction, 7691
Ecc 5:19 to **a** his lot and be happy in his work— 5951
Isa 29:24 those who complain *will* **a** instruction." 4340
Jer 14:10 So the LORD *does* not **a** them; 8354
14:12 I *will* not **a** them. 8354
Eze 20:40 and there *I will* **a** them. 8354
20:41 *I will* **a** you as fragrant incense 8354
22:12 In you *men* **a** bribes to shed blood; 4374
43:27 Then *I will* **a** you, 8354
Da 4:27 O king, be pleased to **a** my advice: NIH
Am 5:22 *I will* not **a** them. 8354
Zep 3: 7 'Surely you will fear me and **a** correction!' 4374
Mal 1: 8 *Would he* **a** you?" 5951+7156
1: 9 *will he* **a** you?"— 5951+7156
1:10 *I will* **a** no offering from your hands. 8354
1:13 *should I* **a** them from your hands?" 8354
Mt 11:14 And if you are willing *to* **a** it, *1312*
19:11 "Not everyone can **a** this word, *6003*
19:12 The one who can **a** this should accept it." *6003*
19:12 The one who can accept this *should* **a** it." *6003*

Mk 4:20 hear the word, a it, and produce a crop— 4138
Jn 3:11 but still *you people do* not a our testimony. 3284
5:34 Not that I a human testimony; 3284
5:41 *"I do* not a praise from men, 3284
5:43 and *you do* not a me; 3284
5:43 in his own name, *you will* a him. 3284
5:44 How can you believe *if you* a praise 3284
6:60 Who can a it?" 201
12:48 and *does* not a my words; 3284
14:17 The world cannot a him, 3284
Ac 16:21 for us Romans *to* a or practice." 4138
22:18 *they will* not a your testimony about me.' 4138
Ro 14:1 A him whose faith is weak, 4689
15:7 A one another, then, just 4689
1Co 2:14 not a the things that come from the Spirit 1312
16:11 No one, then, *should* **refuse to a** him. 2024
Jas 1:21 the evil that is so prevalent and humbly a 1312
1Jn 5:9 *We* a man's testimony, 3284

ACCEPTABLE (17) [ACCEPT]
Ex 28:38 so that they will be a to the LORD. 8356
Lev 1:3 to the Tent of Meeting so that it will be a to 8356
22:21 be without defect or blemish to be **a.** 8356
22:27 *it will* **be a** as an offering made to 8354
27:9 " 'If what he vowed is an animal that *is* a 7928
27:11 not a as an offering to the LORD— 7928
Jdg 14:3 an a woman among your relatives or NIH
Pr 21:3 To do what is right and just *is* more a to 1047
Isa 58:5 a day a to the LORD? 8356
Jer 6:20 Your burnt offerings are not **a;** 8356
Mal 1:14 an a male in his flock and vows to give it, NIH
3:4 and Jerusalem *will be* a to the LORD, 6844
Ro 15:16 the Gentiles might become an offering a 2347
15:31 and that my service in Jerusalem may be a 2347
2Co 8:12 the gift is a according to what one has, 2347
Php 4:18 They are a fragrant offering, an a sacrifice, 1283
1Pe 2:5 offering spiritual sacrifices a to God 2347

ACCEPTABLY (1) [ACCEPT]
Heb 12:28 so worship God a with reverence and awe, 2299

ACCEPTANCE (3) [ACCEPT]
Ro 11:15 what will their a be but life from the dead? 4691
1Ti 1:15 a trustworthy saying that deserves full **a:** 628
4:9 a trustworthy saying that deserves full a 628

ACCEPTED (34) [ACCEPT]
Ge 4:7 If you do what is right, will you not be **a?** 8420
33:11 And because Jacob insisted, Esau a it. 4374
Lev 1:4 and *it will* **be a** on his behalf 8354
7:18 *it will* not **be a**, 8354
19:5 sacrifice it in such a way that it will be a 8356
19:7 it is impure and *will* not **be a.** 8354
22:19 in order that it may be a *on* your *behalf.* 8356
22:20 because it will not be a on your behalf. 8356
22:23 *it will* not **be a** in fulfillment of a vow. 8354
22:25 *They will* not **be a** on your behalf, 8354
22:29 sacrifice it in such a way that it will be a 8356
23:11 the LORD so it will be a *on* your *behalf;* 8356
Nu 31:51 Moses and Eleazar the priest a from them 4374
31:54 the priest a the gold from the commanders 4374
Jdg 13:23 *he would* not *have* a a burnt offering 4374
1Sa 8:3 and a bribes and perverted justice. 4374
12:3 From whose hand *have I* a a bribe 4374
25:35 Then David a from her hand 4374
Job 42:9 and the LORD a Job's prayer. 906+5951+7156
Isa 56:7 and sacrifices *will be* a on my altar; 8356
60:7 they will be a as offerings on my altar, 8356
Lk 4:24 "no prophet is a in his hometown. 1283
Jn 3:33 The man who *has* a it has certified 3284
17:8 the words you gave me and they a them. 3284
Ac 2:41 Those who a his message were baptized, 622
8:14 in Jerusalem heard that Samaria *had* a 1312
15:8 that he a them by giving the Holy Spirit NIG
Ro 10:16 But not all the Israelites a the good news. 5634
14:3 for God *has* a him. 4689
15:7 then, just as Christ a you, 4689
2Co 11:4 or a different gospel from the one *you* **a,** 1312
Gal 1:9 to you a gospel other than what *you* **a,** 4161
1Th 2:13 *you* a it not as the word of men, 1312
Heb 10:34 in prison and joyfully a the confiscation 4657

ACCEPTING (2) [ACCEPT]
2Ki 5:20 by not a from him what he brought. 4374
Isa 33:15 and keeps his hand from a bribes, 9461

ACCEPTS (15) [ACCEPT]
Dt 10:17 who shows no partiality and a no bribes. 4374
27:25 "Cursed is the man *who* a a bribe to kill 4374
Ps 6:9 the LORD a my prayer. 4374
Pr 17:23 A wicked man a a bribe in secret to pervert 4374
Mic 7:3 the ruler demands gifts, the judge a bribes, NIH
Zep 3:2 She obeys no one, *she* a no correction. 4374
Mal 2:13 or a them with pleasure from your hands. 4374
Jn 3:32 but no one a his testimony. 3284
13:20 whoever a anyone I send accepts me; 3284
13:20 whoever accepts anyone I send a me; 3284
13:20 and whoever a me accepts 3284
13:20 and whoever accepts me a 3284
Ac 10:35 a men from every nation who fear him 1283+1639
Heb 12:6 and he punishes everyone *he* a as a son." 4138
Jas 1:27 Religion that God our Father a as pure NIG

ACCESS (3)
Est 1:14 Persia and Media *who* **had special a to** 7156+8011
Ro 5:2 through whom we have gained a by faith 4643
Eph 2:18 through him we both have a to the Father 4643

ACCESSORIES (7)
Ex 25:39 be used for the lampstand and all these **a.** 3998
30:27 the lampstand and its **a,** 3998
31:8 the pure gold lampstand and all its **a,** 3998
35:14 that is for light with its **a,** lamps and oil for 3998
37:24 the lampstand and all its a from one talent 3998
39:37 with its row of lamps and all its **a,** and 3998
Nu 4:10 Then they are to wrap it and all its a in 3998

ACCHO (KJV) See ACCO

ACCIDENTALLY (4)
Nu 35:11 who has killed someone a may flee. 928+8705
35:15 who has killed another a can flee there. 928+8705
Jos 20:3 so that anyone who kills a person a 928+8705
20:9 who killed someone a could flee 928+8705

ACCLAIM (2) [ACCLAMATION]
Ps 89:15 to a you, who walk in the light 9558
Isa 24:14 from the west *they* a the LORD's majesty. 7412

ACCLAMATION (1) [ACCLAIM]
2Ch 15:14 an oath to the LORD with loud **a,** 7754

ACCO (1)
Jdg 1:31 in A or Sidon or Ahlab or Aczib or Helbah 6573

ACCOMPANIED (25) [ACCOMPANY]
Ge 50:7 All Pharaoh's officials a him— 907+6590
Ru 1:22 So Naomi returned from Moab **a by** Ruth 6640
1Sa 10:26 also went to his home in Gibeah, **a by** 2143+6640
2Sa 15:11 from Jerusalem *had* a Absalom. 907+2143
15:18 the six hundred Gittites who *had* a him 995+8079
1Ki 20:1 **A by** thirty-two kings with their horses 907
1Ch 15:16 **a by** musical instruments: 928
25:1 **a by** harps, lyres and cymbals. 928
2Ch 5:12 They were **a by** 120 priests 6640
5:13 **A by** trumpets, cymbals 928
29:27 **a by** trumpets and the instruments 3338+6584
29:35 and the drink offerings that a 4200
30:21 **a by** the LORD's instruments of praise. 928
Jer 17:25 **a by** the men of Judah and those living NIH
22:4 **a by** their officials and their people. 2256
Mk 6:1 **a by** his disciples. 199
16:20 by the signs that a it. 2051
Jn 19:39 *He was* **a by** Nicodemus, 2262+2779
Ac 18:18 **a by** Priscilla and Aquila. 5250
20:4 He *was* **a by** Sopater son of Pyrrhus 5299
20:38 Then *they* a him to the ship. 4636
21:5 and their wives and children a us out of 4636
21:16 Some of the disciples from Caesarea a us 5250+5302
1Co 10:4 from the spiritual rock *that* a them, 199
Jas 2:17 faith by itself, if *it is* not **a by** action, 2400

ACCOMPANIES (3) [ACCOMPANY]
Isa 40:10 and his recompense a him. 4200+7156
62:11 and his recompense a him.' " 4200+7156
2Co 9:13 for the obedience that *a* your **confession** of AIT

ACCOMPANY (10) [ACCOMPANIED, ACCOMPANIES, ACCOMPANYING]
Ge 33:12 on our way; *I'll* a you." 2143+4200+5584
Dt 28:2 upon you and a you if you obey 5952
1Sa 28:1 and your men *will* a me in the army." 907+3655
Ne 10:38 A priest descended from Aaron is to a 6640
Est 5:12 the only person Queen Esther invited to **a** 6640
Ecc 8:15 Then joy *will* a him in his work all 4277
Mk 16:17 And these signs *will* a those who believe: 4158
1Co 16:4 *they will* a me. 4513+5250
2Co 8:19 he was chosen by the churches to a us 5292
Heb 6:9 things **that** a salvation. 2400

ACCOMPANYING (1) [ACCOMPANY]
Nu 28:7 The a drink offering is to be a quarter of NIH

ACCOMPLICE (1)
Pr 29:24 The a *of* a thief is his own enemy; 2745+6640

ACCOMPLISH (11) [ACCOMPLISHED, ACCOMPLISHES, ACCOMPLISHING]
Ge 50:20 but God intended it for good to a what is 6913
Dt 9:5 to a what he swore to your fathers, 7756
2Ki 8:13 a mere dog, a such a feat?" 6913
19:31 zeal of the LORD Almighty *will* a this. 6913
Ecc 2:2 And what *does* pleasure **a?"** 6913
Isa 9:7 zeal of the LORD Almighty *will* a this. 6913
37:32 zeal of the LORD Almighty *will* a this. 6913
44:28 'He is my shepherd and *will* a all 8966
55:11 to me empty, but *will* a what I desire 6913
Jer 48:30 "and her boasts a nothing. 6913
Rev 17:17 *to* a his purpose by agreeing to give 4472

ACCOMPLISHED (7) [ACCOMPLISH]
Jdg 8:2 "What *have I* a compared to you? 6913
Isa 26:12 all *that* we have a you have done for us. 5126
Mt 5:18 from the Law until everything *is* **a.** 1181
Lk 1:45 what the Lord has said to her will be **a!"** 5459
Ro 15:18 of anything except what Christ *has* a 2981
Eph 3:11 according to his eternal purpose which *he* a 4472
Rev 10:7 the mystery of God *will be* **a,** 5464

ACCOMPLISHES (2) [ACCOMPLISH]
Jer 23:20 until he **fully** a the purposes of his heart. 2256+6913+7756
30:24 until he **fully** a the purposes of his heart. 2256+6913+7756

ACCOMPLISHING (2) [ACCOMPLISH]
2Ki 10:30 in a what is right in my eyes and have done 6913
Jn 11:47 "What *are we* **a?"** 4472

ACCORD (6) [ACCORDED, ACCORDANCE, ACCORDING, ACCORDINGLY]
Nu 24:13 I could not do anything of my own **a,** 4213
2Ki 10:15 "Are you **in a with** me, as I am with you?" 3838+4222
Jer 5:5 But **with one a** they too had broken off 3481
Jn 10:18 but I lay it down of **my own a.** 1831
12:49 For I did not speak of **my own a,** 1831
Tit 2:1 You must teach what *is* **in a** 4560

ACCORDANCE (59) [ACCORD]
Ex 12:4 the amount of lamb needed **in a with** 4200+7023
24:8 the LORD has made with you **in a with** 6584
34:27 for **in a with** these words I have made 6584+7023
Nu 6:21 to the LORD **in a with** his separation, 6584
9:3 **in a with** all its rules and regulations." 3869
9:14 the LORD's Passover must do so **in a with** 3869
9:23 **in a with** his command through Moses. 6584
14:19 **In a with** your great love, 3869
Dt 2:37 But **in a with** the command of 889+3972
Jos 6:22 **in a with** your oath to her." 889+3869
15:13 **In a with** the LORD's command to him, 448
22:9 which they had acquired **in a with** 6584
1Ki 16:12 **in a with** the word of the LORD spoken 3869
16:34 **in a with** the word of the LORD spoken 3869
2Ki 9:26 **in a with** the word of the LORD." 3869
14:6 **in a with** what is written in the Book of 3869
14:25 **in a with** the word of the LORD, 3869
16:11 So Uriah the priest built an altar **in a with** 3869
17:13 **in a with** the entire Law 3869
17:33 also served their own gods **in a with** 3869
22:13 not acted **in a with** all that is written there 3869
23:16 **in a with** the word of 3869
23:25 **in a with** all the Law of Moses. 3869
24:2 **in a with** the word of 3869
1Ch 5:1 in the genealogical record **in a with** 4200
6:49 **in a with** all that Moses the servant 3869
15:15 as Moses had commanded **in a with** 3869
16:40 **in a with** everything written in the Law of 4200
2Ch 25:4 but acted **in a with** what is written in 3869
34:21 not acted **in a with** all that is written 3869
34:32 of Jerusalem did this **in a with** the covenant 3869
Ezr 3:2 **in a with** what is written in the Law 3869
3:4 Then **in a with** what is written, 3869
7:18 **in a with** the will of your God. 10341
7:25 Ezra, **in a with** the wisdom of your God, 10341
10:3 **in a with** the counsel of my lord and 928
10:8 **in a with** the decision of the officials 3869
Ne 8:18 **in a with** the regulation, 3869
Ps 109:26 save me **in a with** your love. 3869
119:149 Hear my voice **in a with** your love; 3869
Jer 42:5 If we do not act **in a with** everything 3869+4027
Eze 7:9 I will repay you **in a with** your conduct and 3869
25:14 and they will deal with Edom **in a with** 3869
35:11 I will treat you **in a with** the anger 3869
Da 1:13 treat your servants **in a with** what you see." 3869
6:8 **in a with** the laws of the Medes 10341
6:12 **in a with** the laws of the Medes 10341
Mt 2:16 **in a with** the time he had learned from 2848
22:16 and that you teach the way of God **in a with** 1877
Mk 12:14 but you teach the way of God **in a with** 2093
Lk 20:21 teach the way of God **in a with** the truth. 2093
Jn 19:40 This was **in a with** Jewish burial customs. 2777
Ro 8:5 but those who live **in a with** 2848
8:27 the Spirit intercedes for the saints **in a with** 2848
12:3 with sober judgment, **in a with** the measure 6055
Eph 1:5 **in a with** his pleasure and will— 2848
1:7 **in a with** the riches of God's grace 2848
4:21 and were taught in him **in a with** the truth 2777
2Th 2:9 the lawless one will be **in a with** the work 2848

ACCORDED (1) [ACCORD]
Ge 45:13 Tell my father about all the **honor** *a* me AIT

ACCORDING (297) [ACCORD]
Ge 1:11 **a to** their various kinds." 4200
1:12 plants bearing seed **a to** their kinds 4200
1:12 and trees bearing fruit with seed in it **a to** 4200
1:21 **a to** their kinds, 4200
1:21 and every winged bird **a to** its kind. 4200
1:24 "Let the land produce living creatures **a to** 4200
1:24 and wild animals, each **a to** its kind." 4200

Ge 1:25 the wild animals **a to** their kinds, 4200
1:25 the livestock **a to** their kinds, 4200
1:25 along the ground **a to** their kinds. 4200
7:14 They had with them every wild animal **a to** 4200
7:14 all livestock **a to** their kinds, 4200
7:14 that moves along the ground **a to** its kind 4200
7:14 and every bird **a to** its kind, 4200
10:32 **a to** their lines of descent, 4200
23:16 **a to the weight current** among merchants. 6296
25:16 the names of the twelve tribal rulers **a to** 928
36:30 **a to** their divisions, in the land of Seir. 4200
36:40 by name, **a to** their clans and regions: 4200
36:43 **a to** their settlements in 4200
47:12 **a to** the number of their children. 4200
Ex 6:16 of the sons of Levi **a to** their records: 4200
6:19 the clans of Levi **a to** their records. 4200
25:40 See that you make them **a to** 928
26:30 the tabernacle **a to** the plan shown you on 3869
30:13 **a to** the sanctuary shekel, 928
30:24 all **a to** the sanctuary shekel— 928
38:24 **a to** the sanctuary shekel. 928
38:25 shekels, **a to** the sanctuary shekel— 928
38:26 half a shekel, **a to** the sanctuary shekel, 928
Lev 5:15 **a to** the sanctuary shekel. 928
20:23 You must not live **a to** the customs of 928
27: 3 **a to** the sanctuary shekel; 928
27: 8 will set the value for him **a to** what 6584+7023
27:16 to be set **a to** the amount of seed required 4200
27:18 the priest will determine the value **a to** 6584
27:25 to be set **a to** the sanctuary shekel, 928
Nu 1:20 **a to** the records of their clans and families. 4200
1:22 **a to** the records of their clans and families. 4200
1:24 **a to** the records of their clans and families. 4200
1:26 **a to** the records of their clans and families. 4200
1:28 **a to** the records of their clans and families. 4200
1:30 **a to** the records of their clans and families. 4200
1:32 **a to** the records of their clans and families. 4200
1:34 **a to** the records of their clans and families. 4200
1:36 **a to** the records of their clans and families. 4200
1:38 **a to** the records of their clans and families. 4200
1:40 **a to** the records of their clans and families. 4200
1:42 **a to** the records of their clans and families. 4200
1:45 to serve in Israel's army were counted **a to** 4200
2: 9 **a to** their divisions, number 186,400. 4200
2:16 **a to** their divisions, number 151,450. 4200
2:24 **a to** their divisions, number 108,100. 4200
2:32 counted **a to** their families. 4200
3:20 **a to** their families. 4200
3:39 by Moses and Aaron **a to** their clans, 4200
3:47 **a to** the sanctuary shekel, 928
3:50 shekels, **a to** the sanctuary shekel. 928
4:37 Moses and Aaron counted them **a to** 6584
4:41 Moses and Aaron counted them **a to** 6584
4:45 Moses and Aaron counted them **a to** 6584
6:21 **a to** the law of the Nazirite.'" 6584
7:13 both **a to** the sanctuary shekel, 928
7:19 both **a to** the sanctuary shekel, 928
7:25 both **a to** the sanctuary shekel, 928
7:31 both **a to** the sanctuary shekel, 928
7:37 both **a to** the sanctuary shekel, 928
7:43 both **a to** the sanctuary shekel, 928
7:49 both **a to** the sanctuary shekel, 928
7:55 both **a to** the sanctuary shekel, 928
7:61 both **a to** the sanctuary shekel, 928
7:67 both **a to** the sanctuary shekel, 928
7:73 both **a to** the sanctuary shekel, 928
7:79 both **a to** the sanctuary shekel, 928
7:85 **a to** the sanctuary shekel. 928
7:86 **a to** the sanctuary shekel. 928
18:16 **a to** the sanctuary shekel, 928
26:54 to receive its inheritance **a to** the number 4200
26:55 be **a to** the names for its ancestral tribe. 4200
29:18 and drink offerings **a to** 928
29:21 and drink offerings **a to** 928
29:24 and drink offerings **a to** 928
29:27 and drink offerings **a to** 928
29:30 and drink offerings **a to** 928
29:33 and drink offerings **a to** 928
29:37 and drink offerings **a to** 928
33:54 Distribute the land by lot, **a to** your clans. 4200
33:54 Distribute it **a to** your ancestral tribes. 4200
35:24 the avenger of blood **a to** these regulations. 6584
Dt 12:15 **a to** the blessing the LORD your God gives 3869
17:10 You must act **a to** the decisions 6584+7023
17:11 Act **a to** the law they teach you and 6584+7023
26:13 **a to** all you commanded. 3869
29:21 **a to** all the curses of the covenant written 3869
30: 2 and with all your soul **a to** 3869
32: 8 for the peoples **a to** the number of the sons 4200
Jos 4: 5 **a to** the number of the tribes of 4200
4: 8 **a to** the number of the tribes of 4200
8:31 He built it **a to** what is written in the Book 3869
11:23 to Israel **a to** their tribal divisions. 3869
12: 7 as an inheritance to the tribes of Israel **a to** 3869
14: 7 And I brought him back a report **a to** 889+3869
17: 4 **a to** the LORD's command. 448
18: 4 **a to** the inheritance of each. 4200+7023
18:10 to the Israelites **a to** their tribal divisions. 3869
1Sa 2:35 who will do **a to** what is in my heart 3869
6: 4 a to the number of the Philistine rulers, NIH
6:18 And the number of the gold rats was a to NIH
2Sa 3:39 May the LORD repay the evildoer **a to** 3869
7:21 the sake of your word and **a to** your will, 3869
22:21 "The LORD has dealt with me **a to** 3869
22:21 **a to** the cleanness of my hands 3869
22:25 The LORD has rewarded me **a to** 3869
22:25 **a to** my cleanness in his sight. 3869
1Ki 2: 6 Deal with him **a to** your wisdom, 3869
3: 3 for the LORD by walking **a to** the statutes 928
6:38 in all its details **a to** its specifications. 4200
8:39 deal with each man **a to** all he does, 3869
8:59 of his people Israel **a to** each day's need, 928
13: 5 and its ashes poured out **a to** the sign given 3869
15:29 **a to** the word of the LORD given 3869
2Ki 1:17 **a to** the word of the LORD 3869
2:22 **a to** the word Elisha had spoken. 3869
4:44 **a to** the word of the LORD. 3869
10:17 **a to** the word of the LORD spoken 3869
22:16 and its people, **a to** everything written in 907
23:35 and gold from the people of the land **a to** 3869
24: 3 Surely these things happened to Judah **a to** 6584
1Ch 5: 7 listed **a to** their genealogical records: 4200
6:19 of the Levites listed **a to** their fathers: 4200
6:32 They performed their duties **a to** 3869
7: 4 **A to** their family genealogy, 4200
15:20 and Benaiah were to play the lyres **a to** 6584
15:21 directing **a to** sheminith. 6584
16:37 **a to** each day's requirements. 4200
17:19 the sake of your servant and **a to** your will, 3869
23:27 **A to** the last instructions of David, 928
24:19 **a to** the regulations prescribed for them 3869
24:30 These were the Levites, **a to** their families. 4200
26:13 **a to** their families, young and old alike. 4200
26:31 Jeriah was their chief **a to** 4200
28:15 **a to** the use of each lampstand; 3869
2Ch 4: 7 He made ten gold lampstands **a to** 3869
6:16 in all they do to walk before me **a to** 928
6:30 and deal with each man **a to** all he does, 3869
8:13 **a to** the daily requirement 928
8:14 the priests **a to** each day's requirement. 4200
24:13 the temple of God **a to** its original design 6584
25: 5 of Judah together and assigned them **a to** 4200
26:11 to go out by divisions **a to** their numbers 928
30: 5 not been celebrated in large numbers **a to** 3869
30:19 not clean **a to the rules** *of* the sanctuary." 3869
31: 2 them **a to** their duties as priests 3869+7023
31:15 to their fellow priests **a to** their divisions, 928
31:16 the daily duties of their various tasks, **a to** 928
31:17 **a to** their responsibilities 928
35: 4 **a to** the directions written by David king 928
35:26 **a to** what is written in the Law of 3869
Ezr 2:69 **A to** their ability they gave to the treasury 3869
6:14 the temple **a to** the command of the God 10427
6:18 **a to** what is written in the Book of Moses. 10341
10: 3 Let it be done **a to** the Law. 3869
Ne 6: 6 **a to** these reports you are about 3869
12:45 **a to** the commands of David 3869
13:22 show mercy to me **a to** your great love. 3869
Est 1:15 "**A to** law, what must be done 3869
Job 42: 8 and not deal with you **a to** your folly. NIH
Ps 6: T **A to** sheminith. 6584
7: 8 O LORD, **a to** my righteousness, 3869
7: 8 **a to** my integrity, O Most High. 3869
8: T **A to** gittith. 6584
12: T **A to** sheminith. 6584
18:20 The LORD has dealt with me **a to** 3869
18:20 **a to** the cleanness of my hands 3869
18:24 The LORD has rewarded me **a to** 3869
18:24 **a to** the cleanness of my hands in his sight. 3869
25: 7 **a to** your love remember me, 3869
46: T **A to** alamoth. 6584
51: 1 O God, **a to** your unfailing love; 3869
51: 1 **a to** your great compassion blot out my transgressions. 3869
53: T **A to** mahalath. 6584
62:12 Surely you will reward each person **a to** 3869
81: T **A to** gittith. 6584
84: T **A to** gittith. 6584
88: T **A to** mahalath leannoth. 6584
103:10 as our sins deserve or repay us **a to** 3869
119: 1 who walk **a to** the law of the LORD. 928
119: 9 By living **a to** your word. 3869
119:25 preserve my life **a to** your word. 3869
119:28 strengthen me **a to** your word. 3869
119:37 preserve my life **a to** your word. 928
119:41 your salvation **a to** your promise; 3869
119:58 be gracious to me **a to** your promise. 3869
119:65 Do good to your servant **a to** your word, 3869
119:76 **a to** your promise to your servant. 3869
119:88 Preserve my life **a to** your love, 3869
119:107 O LORD, **a to** your word. 3869
119:116 Sustain me **a to** your promise, 3869
119:124 Deal with your servant **a to** your love 3869
119:133 Direct my footsteps **a to** your word; 928
119:149 O LORD, **a to** your laws. 3869
119:154 preserve my life **a to** your promise. 4200
119:156 preserve my life **a to** your laws. 3869
119:159 O LORD, **a to** your love. 3869
119:169 give me understanding **a to** your word. 3869
119:170 deliver me **a to** your promise. 3869
122: 4 the LORD **a to** the statute given to Israel. NIH
Pr 12: 8 A man is praised **a to** his wisdom, 4200+7023
24:12 Will he not repay each person **a to** 3869
26: 4 Do not answer a fool **a to** his folly, 3869
26: 5 Answer a fool **a to** his folly, 3869
Isa 8:20 If they do not speak **a to** this word, 3869
59:18 **A to** what they have done, 3869+6584
63: 7 **a to** all the LORD has done for us— 3869+6584
63: 7 **a to** his compassion and many kindnesses. 3869
Jer 17:10 to reward a man **a to** his conduct, 3869
17:10 **a to** what his deeds deserve." 3869
25:14 I will repay them **a to** their deeds and 3869
32:19 you reward everyone **a to** his conduct and 3869
Eze 7: 3 I will judge you **a to** your conduct 3869
Eze 7: 8 I will judge you **a to** your conduct 3869
7:27 I will deal with them **a to** their conduct, 4946
18:30 I will judge you, each one **a to** his ways, 3869
20:44 with you for my name's sake and not **a to** 3869
23:24 they will punish you **a to** their standards. 928
24:14 You will be judged **a to** your conduct 3869
31:11 for him to deal with **a to** its wickedness. 3869
33:20 But I will judge each of you **a to** 3869
36:19 I judged them **a to** their conduct 3869
39:24 I dealt with them **a to** their uncleanness 3869
44:24 as judges and decide it **a to** my ordinances. 928
45: 8 the house of Israel to possess the land **a to** 4200
47:21 among yourselves **a to** the tribes of Israel. 4200
Da 6:15 that a to the law of the Medes NIH
9: 2 **a to** the word of the LORD given 889
Hos 12: 2 he will punish Jacob **a to** his ways 3869
12: 2 to his ways and repay him **a to** his deeds. 3869
Zec 5: 3 for **a to** what it says on one side, 4017
5: 3 and **a to** what it says on the other, 4017
Mt 9:29 "**A to** your faith will it be done to you"; *2848*
16:27 and then he will reward each person **a to** *2848*
25:15 each **a to** his ability. *2848*
Mk 7: 5 "Why don't your disciples live **a to** *2848*
Lk 1: 9 **a to** the custom of the priesthood, *2848*
2:22 the time of their purification **a to** the Law *2848*
2:42 they went up to the Feast, **a to** the custom. *2848*
Jn 19: 7 and **a to** that law he must die, *2848*
Ac 7:44 **a to** the pattern he had seen. *2848*
11:29 The disciples, each **a to** his ability, *2777*
15: 1 *a to* **the custom** taught *by* **Moses,** *AIT*
21:21 or live *a to* **our customs.** *AIT*
23: 3 You sit there to judge me **a to** the law, *2848*
26: 5 that **a to** the strictest sect of our religion, *2848*
Ro 2: 6 to each person **a to** what he has done." *2848*
8: 4 not live **a to** the sinful nature but according *2848*
8: 4 to the sinful nature but **a to** the Spirit. *2848*
8: 5 Those who live **a to** the sinful nature *2848*
8:12 not to the sinful nature, to live **a to** it. *2848*
8:13 For if you live **a to** the sinful nature, *2848*
8:28 who have been called **a to** his purpose. *2848*
12: 6 **a to** the grace given us. *2848*
16:25 **a to** the revelation of the mystery hidden *2848*
1Co 3: 8 each will be rewarded **a to** his own labor. *2848*
15: 3 Christ died for our sins **a to** the Scriptures, *2848*
15: 4 that he was raised on the third day **a to** *2848*
2Co 1:12 We have done so not **a to** worldly wisdom *1877*
1:12 not according to worldly wisdom but **a to** *1877*
8:11 **a to** *your* **means.** *1666+2400+3836*
8:12 the gift is acceptable **a to** what one has, *2848*
8:12 not **a to** what he does not have. *2848*
Gal 1: 4 **a to** the will of our God and Father, *2848*
3:29 and heirs **a to** the promise. *2848*
Eph 1: 9 of his will **a to** his good pleasure, *2848*
1:11 having been predestined **a to** the plan *2848*
3:11 **a to** his eternal purpose which he accomplished *2848*
3:20 **a to** his power that is at work within us, *2848*
4:29 for building others up **a to** their needs, *NIG*
Php 2:13 to will and to act **a to** his good purpose. *5642*
3:17 and take note of those who live **a to** *4048*
4:19 And my God will meet all your needs **a to** *2848*
Col 1:11 with all power **a to** his glorious might so *2848*
1Th 4:15 **A to** the Lord's own word, *1877*
2Th 1:12 **a to** the grace of our God and *2848*
3: 6 not live **a to** the teaching you received *2848*
2Ti 1: 1 **a to** the promise of life that is *2848*
2: 5 unless he competes **a to the rules.** *3789*
Heb 2: 4 and gifts of the Holy Spirit distributed **a to** *2848*
8: 5 "See to it that you make everything **a to** *2848*
1Pe 1: 2 who have been chosen **a to** *2848*
4: 6 be judged **a to** men in regard to the body, *2848*
4: 6 but live **a to** God in regard to the spirit. *2848*
4:19 those who suffer **a to** *2848*
1Jn 5:14 we ask anything **a to** his will, he hears us. *2848*
Rev 2:23 I will repay each of you **a to** your deeds. *2848*
20:12 The dead were judged **a to** *2848*
20:13 and each person was judged **a to** *2848*
22:12 to everyone **a to** what he has done. *6055*

ACCORDINGLY (3) [ACCORD]

Lev 25:52 that and pay for his redemption **a.** 3869+7023
1Ki 20:25 He agreed with them and acted **a.** 4027
1Ch 24: 4 and they *were* **divided** *a:* AIT

ACCOUNT (75) [ACCOUNTABLE, ACCOUNTED, ACCOUNTING, ACCOUNTS]

Ge 2: 4 This is the **a** *of* the heavens and the earth 9352
5: 1 This is the written **a of** Adam's **line.** 9352
6: 9 This is the **a** *of* Noah. 9352
10: 1 This is the **a** *of* Shem, Ham and Japheth, 9352
11:10 This is the **a** *of* Shem. 9352
11:27 This is the **a** *of* Terah. 9352
25:12 This is the **a** *of* Abraham's son Ishmael, 9352
25:19 This is the **a** *of* Abraham's son Isaac. 9352
26: 7 of this place might kill me **on a of** 6584
26: 9 I thought I might lose my life **on a of** her." 6584
36: 1 This is the **a** *of* Esau (that is, Edom). 9352
36: 9 the **a** *of* Esau the father of the Edomites in 9352
37: 2 This is the **a** *of* Jacob. 9352
Ex 12: 4 having **taken into** a the number 928
Nu 3: 1 the **a of the family** *of* Aaron and Moses at 9352
6: 7 make himself ceremonially unclean **on a of** 4200
9: 6 they were ceremonially unclean **on a of** 4200
13:27 *They* **gave** Moses *this* **a:** 6218

Dt 9: 4 it is **on a of** the wickedness 928
9: 5 **on a of** the wickedness of these nations, 928
18:19 *I* myself *will* **call** him **to a.** 2011+4946+6640
Jos 22:23 *may* the LORD himself **call** us **to a.** 1335
1Sa 17:32 "Let no one lose heart **on a of** 6584
20:16 **call** David's enemies **to a."** 1335+3338+4946
23:10 to Keilah and destroy the town **on a of** me. 6288
2Sa 11:18 Joab sent David a full **a** *of* the battle. 1821
11:19 the king this **a** *of* the battle, 1821
13: 2 of illness **on a of** his sister Tamar, 6288
21: 1 "It is **on a of** Saul 448
1Ki 9:15 Here is the **a** *of* the forced labor 1821
11:27 the **a** of how he rebelled against the king: 1821
2Ki 22: 7 not **a for** the money entrusted to them, 907+3108
1Ch 27:24 on Israel **on a of** this numbering, 928
2Ch 24:22 the LORD see this and **call** you **to a."** 2011
24:27 The **a** of his sons, NIH
Est 10: 2 together with a **full a** *of* the greatness 7308
Job 31:14 What will I answer when **called to a?** 7212
31:37 I would give him an **a** *of* my every step; 5031
Ps 10:13 *"He* won't **call** me **to a"?** 2011
10:15 **call** him **to a** *for* his wickedness 2011
56: 7 **On no a** let them escape; 224+6584
Ecc 3:15 **call** the past **to a.** 1335
Isa 2:22 Of what **a** is he? 3108
23:13 this people that is now **of no a!** 4202
Eze 16:14 among the nations **on a of** your beauty, 928
28:17 Your heart became proud **on a of** 928
Mt 10:18 **On** my **a** you will be brought *1915*
11: 6 the man who does not fall away **on a of** *1877*
12:36 **give a** on the day of judgment **for** *625*
26:31 you will all fall away **on a of** me, *1877*
26:33 "Even if all fall away **on a of** you, *1877*
Mk 12:26 **in the a** of the bush, *2093*
13: 9 **On a** of me you will stand before governors *1915*
Lk 1: 1 Many have undertaken to draw up an **a** of *1456*
1: 3 also to me *to* **write an** orderly **a** for you, *1211*
7:23 the man who does not fall away **on a of** *1877*
16: 2 Give an **a** of your management, *3364*
20:37 But **in the a** of the bush, *2093*
21:12 and all **on a** of my name. *1915*
Jn 12:11 for **on a of** him many of *1328*
Ac 4: 9 If we *are being* **called to a** today for *373*
19:40 In that case we would not be able *to* **a** *625+3364*
Ro 5:13 not **taken into a** when there is no law. *1824*
11:28 they are enemies **on** your **a;** *1328*
11:28 they are loved **on a of** the patriarchs, *1328*
14:12 each of us will give an **a** of himself to God. *3364*
1Co 6: 4 appoint as judges even men of **little a** in *2024*
2Co 7:12 not **on a** of the one who did the wrong or *1915*
Php 1:26 in Christ Jesus will overflow **on a of** me. *1877*
4:17 for what may be credited to your **a.** *3364*
Heb 4:13 the eyes of him to whom we must give **a.** *3364*
13:17 over you as men who must give an **a.** *3364*
1Pe 4: 5 to give **a** to him who is ready to judge *3364*
1Jn 2:12 your sins have been forgiven **on a of** *1328*
Rev 16:21 they cursed God **on a of** the plague of hail, *1666*

ACCOUNTABLE (8) [ACCOUNT]

Eze 3:18 *I will* **hold** you **a** *for* his blood. 1335+3338+4946
3:20 *I will* **hold** you **a** *for* his blood. 1335+3338+4946
33: 6 *I will* **hold** the watchman **a** 2011+3338+4946
33: 8 *I will* **hold** you **a** *for* his blood. 1335+3338+4946
34:10 shepherds and *will* **hold** them **a** 2011+3338+4946
Da 6: 2 The satraps were made **a** to them so that 10302
Jnh 1:14 not **hold** us **a** *for* killing an innocent man, 5989+6584
Ro 3:19 silenced and the whole world **held a** *1181+5688*

ACCOUNTED (1) [ACCOUNT]

Ezr 8:34 Everything was **a** for by number NIH

ACCOUNTING (5) [ACCOUNT]

Ge 9: 5 your lifeblood *I will* surely **demand an a.** 2011
9: 5 *I will* **demand an a** from every animal. 2011
9: 5 *I will* **demand an a** *for* the life 2011
42:22 Now *we must* **give an a** *for* his blood." 2011
2Ki 12:15 *They did* not **require an a** *from* those 3108

ACCOUNTS (3) [ACCOUNT]

Job 21:29 Have you paid no regard to their **a**— 253
Mt 18:23 like a king who wanted to settle **a** *3364*
25:19 those servants returned and **settled a** *3364+5256*

ACCREDITED (1) [CREDIT]

Ac 2:22 of Nazareth was a man **a** by God to you *617*

ACCUMULATE (1) [ACCUMULATED]

Dt 17:17 not **a large amounts** *of* silver and gold 4394+8049

ACCUMULATED (4) [ACCUMULATE]

Ge 12: 5 all the possessions *they had* **a** and 8223
31:18 with all the goods *he had* **a** in Paddan Aram, 8223
1Ki 10:26 Solomon **a** chariots and horses; 665
2Ch 1:14 Solomon **a** chariots and horses; 665

ACCURATE (7) [ACCURATELY]

Dt 25:15 You must have **a** and honest weights 8969
Pr 11: 1 but **a** weights are his delight. 8969
Eze 45:10 You are to use **a** scales, 7406
45:10 an **a** ephah and an accurate bath. 7406
45:10 an accurate ephah and an **a** bath. 7406

Ac 23:15 the pretext of wanting *more* **a** information *209*
23:20 of wanting *more* **a** information about him. *209*

ACCURATELY (1) [ACCURATE]

Ac 18:25 with great fervor and taught about Jesus **a,** *209*

ACCURSED (5) [CURSE]

Nu 5:27 and she will become **a** among her people. 460
2Ki 22:19 that they would become **a** and laid waste, 7839
Isa 65:20 to reach a hundred *will* **be considered a.** 7837
Mic 6:10 and the short ephah, which *is* **a?** 2404
2Pe 2:14 in greed—**an a** brood! *2932*

ACCUSATION (7) [ACCUSE]

Ezr 4: 6 they lodged an **a** against the people 8478
Mic 6: 2 Hear, O mountains, the LORD's **a;** 8190
Ac 23:29 I found that the **a** had to do with questions *1592*
24: 9 The Jews **joined in the a,** *5298*
Col 1:22 without blemish and **free from a**— *441*
1Ti 5:19 an **a** against an elder unless it is brought *2990*
Jude 1: 9 to bring a slanderous **a** against him, *3213*

ACCUSATIONS (3) [ACCUSE]

Ps 35:20 but devise false **a** against those who live 1821
Ac 26: 2 as I make my defense against all the **a** of *1592*
2Pe 2:11 not bring slanderous **a** against such beings *3213*

ACCUSE (18) [ACCUSATION, ACCUSATIONS, ACCUSED, ACCUSER, ACCUSERS, ACCUSES, ACCUSING]

Dt 19:16 If a malicious witness takes the stand to **a** 6699
1Sa 22:15 *Let* not the king **a** your servant 928+1821+8492
2Sa 3: 8 Yet now *you* **a** me *of* an offense 6584+7212
Ps 50:21 I will rebuke you and **a** you to your face. 6885
103: 9 *He will* not always **a,** 8189
109: 4 In return for my friendship *they* **a** me, 8476
Pr 3:30 *Do* not **a** a man for no reason— 8189
Isa 57:16 *I will* not **a** forever, 8189
Hos 4: 4 *let* no man **a** another, 3519
Zec 3: 1 Satan standing at his right side to **a** him. 8476
Mt 12:10 Looking for a reason to **a** Jesus, *2989*
Mk 3: 2 for a reason to **a** Jesus, *2989*
Lk 3:14 and don't **a** people **falsely**— *5193*
6: 7 for a reason *to* **a** Jesus, *2989*
23: 2 And they began *to* **a** him, saying, *2989*
Jn 5:45 do not think I *will* **a** you before the Father. *2989*
10:36 Why then *do* you **a** me of blasphemy *3306*
1Pe 2:12 *though they* **a** you of doing wrong, *2895*

ACCUSED (10) [ACCUSE]

Nu 35:12 so that a *person* **a of murder** may not die 8357
35:25 the *one* **a of murder** from the avenger 8357
35:26 the **a** ever goes outside the limits of the city 8357
35:27 of blood may kill the **a** without being guilty 8357
35:28 The **a** must stay in his city of refuge until NIH
Dt 19:15 not enough to convict a man **a of** 4200
Jos 20: 5 they must not surrender the *one* **a,** 8357
21:13 (a city of refuge for *one* **a of murder),** 8357
21:21 (a city of refuge for *one* **a of murder)** 8357
21:27 (a city of refuge for *one* **a of murder)** 8357
21:32 (a city of refuge for *one* **a of murder),** 8357
21:38 (a city of refuge for *one* **a of murder),** 8357
Ne 5: 7 I pondered them in my mind and then **a** 8189
Da 6:24 the men who *had* **falsely a** Daniel were brought 10030+10642
Mt 27:12 When he *was* **a** by the chief priests and *2989*
Mk 15: 3 The chief priests **a** him of many things. *2989*
Lk 16: 1 a rich man whose manager *was* **a** *1330*
Ac 22:30 to find out exactly why Paul *was being* **a** by *2989*

ACCUSER (5) [ACCUSE]

Job 31:35 let my **a** put his indictment in writing. 408+8190
Ps 109: 6 let an **a** stand at his right hand. 8477
Isa 50: 8 Who is my **a?** 1251+5477
Jn 5:45 Your **a** is Moses, *2989*
Rev 12:10 For the **a** of our brothers, *2992*

ACCUSERS (10) [ACCUSE]

Ps 71:13 May my **a** perish in shame; 8476
109:20 be the LORD's payment to my **a,** 8476
109:25 I am an object of scorn to **my a;** 2157S
109:29 My **a** will be clothed with disgrace 8476
Jer 18:19 hear what my **a** are saying! 3742
Ac 23:30 I also ordered his **a** to present *2991*
23:35 when your **a** get here." *2991*
24:12 My **a** did not find me arguing with anyone *NIG*
25:16 any man before he has faced his **a** *2400+2991*
25:18 When his **a** got up to speak, *2991*

ACCUSES (3) [ACCUSE]

Job 40: 2 Let him *who* **a** God answer him!" 3519
Isa 54:17 you will refute every tongue *that* **a** you. 2021+4200+5477+7756
Rev 12:10 who **a** them before our God day and night, *2989*

ACCUSING (7) [ACCUSE]

Ps 31:20 you keep them safe from **a** tongues. 8190
Mk 15: 4 See how many things *they are* **a** you **of."** *2989*
Lk 23:10 standing there, vehemently **a** him. *2989*
Jn 8: 6 in order to have a basis *for* **a** him. *2989*

Ac 23:28 I wanted to know why *they were* **a** him, *1592*
26: 7 because of this hope that the Jews *are* **a** *me.* *1592*
Ro 2:15 and their thoughts now **a,** *2989*

ACCUSTOMED (3) [CUSTOM]

Jer 2:24 a wild donkey **a to** the desert, sniffing 4341
13:23 Neither can you do good *who* are **a to** 4341
1Co 8: 7 Some people are still so **a to** idols that *5311*

ACELDAMA (KJV) See AKELDAMA

ACHAIA (10)

Ac 18:12 While Gallio was proconsul *of* **A,** *938*
18:27 When Apollos wanted to go to **A,** *938*
19:21 passing through Macedonia and **A.** *938*
Ro 15:26 and **A** were pleased to make a contribution *938*
1Co 16:15 of Stephanas were the first converts *in* **A,** *938*
2Co 1: 1 together with all the saints throughout **A:** *938*
9: 2 since last year you in **A** were ready to give; *938*
11:10 in the regions *of* **A** will stop this boasting *938*
1Th 1: 7 to all the believers in Macedonia and **A.** *938*
1: 8 from you not only in Macedonia and **A**— *938*

ACHAICUS (1)

1Co 16:17 Fortunatus and **A** arrived, *939*

ACHAN (7)

Jos 7: 1 **A** son of Carmi, the son of Zimri, 6575
7:18 and **A** son of Carmi, the son of Zimri, 6575
7:19 Then Joshua said to **A,** "My son, 6575
7:20 **A** replied, "It is true! 6575
7:24 took **A** son of Zerah, the silver, the robe, 6575
7:26 Over **A** they heaped up a large pile 2257S
22:20 When **A** son of Zerah 6575

ACHAR (1)

1Ch 2: 7 The son of Carmi: **A,** 6580

ACHAZ (KJV) See AHAZ

ACHBOR (KJV) See ACBOR

ACHE (1)

Pr 14:13 Even in laughter the heart *may* **a,** 3872

ACHIEVE (4) [ACHIEVED, ACHIEVEMENT, ACHIEVEMENTS, ACHIEVING]

Job 5:12 so that their hands **a** no success. 6913
Ecc 2:11 to **a,** everything was meaningless, 6913
Isa 55:11 and **a** *the* **purpose** for which I sent it. 7503
Da 11:24 and *will* **a** what neither his fathers 6913

ACHIEVED (3) [ACHIEVE]

1Ki 9: 1 and had **a** all he had desired to do, NIH
16:27 what he did and the things *he* **a,** 6913
22:45 the things he **a** and his military exploits, 6913

ACHIEVEMENT (1) [ACHIEVE]

Ecc 4: 4 I saw that all labor and all **a** spring 4179+5126

ACHIEVEMENTS (10) [ACHIEVE]

1Ki 10: 6 about your **a** and your wisdom is true. 1821
15:23 all the other events of Asa's reign, all his **a,** 1476
16: 5 what he did and his **a,** 1476
2Ki 10:34 all he did, and all his **a,** 1476
13: 8 all he did and his **a,** 1476
13:12 all he did and his **a,** 1476
14:15 what he did and his **a,** 1476
14:28 all he did, and his military **a,** 1476
20:20 all his **a** and how he made the pool and 1476
2Ch 9: 5 about your **a** and your wisdom is true. 1821

ACHIEVING (1) [ACHIEVE]

2Co 4:17 For our light and momentary troubles *are* **a** *2981*

ACHIM (KJV) See AKIM

ACHISH (19)

1Sa 21:10 from Saul and went to **A** king of Gath. 429
21:11 But the servants of **A** said to him, 429
21:12 and was very much afraid of **A** king 429
21:14 **A** said to his servants, "Look at the man! 429
27: 2 and went over to **A** son of Maoch king 429
27: 3 David and his men settled in Gath with **A.** 429
27: 5 Then David said to **A,** 429
27: 6 So on that day **A** gave him Ziklag, 429
27: 9 Then he returned to **A.** 429
27:10 When **A** asked, 429
27:12 **A** trusted David and said to himself, 429
28: 1 **A** said to David, 429
28: 2 **A** replied, "Very well, 429
29: 2 at the rear with **A.** 429
29: 3 **A** replied, "Is this not David, 429
29: 6 So **A** called David and said to him, 429
29: 9 **A** answered, "I know that you have been 429
1Ki 2:39 two of Shimei's slaves ran off to **A** son 429

1Ki 2:40 he saddled his donkey and went to A 429

ACHMETHA (KJV) See ECBATANA

ACHOR (5)
Jos 7:24 to the Valley of **A.** 6574
7:26 the Valley of A ever since. 6574
15: 7 then went up to Debir from the Valley of A 6574
Isa 65:10 the Valley of A a resting place for herds, 6574
Hos 2:15 will make the Valley of A a door of hope. 6574

ACHSA, ACHSAH (KJV) See ACSAH

ACHSHAPH (KJV) See ACSHAPH

ACHZIB (KJV) See ACZIB

ACKNOWLEDGE (40) [ACKNOWLEDGED, ACKNOWLEDGES, ACKNOWLEDGMENT]
Dt 4:39 A and take to heart this day that 3359
21:17 *He must* **a** the son of his unloved wife as 5795
33: 9 or **a** his own children, 3359
1Ch 28: 9 my son Solomon, **a** the God of your father, 3359
Ps 79: 6 not **a** you, on the kingdoms that do not call 3359
87: 4 and Babylon among *those who* **a** me— 3359
Pr 3: 6 in all your ways **a** him, 3359
Isa 19:21 and in that day they *will* **a** the LORD. 3359
29:23 *they will* **a** *the* **holiness** *of* the Holy One 7727
33:13 you who are near, **a** my power! 3359
45: 4 though *you do* not **a** me. 3359
59:12 and *we* **a** our iniquities: 3359
61: 9 All who see them *will* **a** that they are 5795
63:16 Abraham does not know us or Israel **a** us; 5795
Jer 3:13 Only **a** your guilt— 3359
9: 3 *they do* not **a** me," declares the LORD. 3359
9: 6 in their deceit they refuse *to* **a** me," 3359
10:25 on the nations that *do* not **a** you, 3359
14:20 *we* **a** our wickedness and the guilt 3359
Eze 12:16 *they may* **a** all their detestable practices. 6218
Da 4:25 until *you* **a** that the Most High is sovereign 10313
4:26 to you when *you* **a** that Heaven rules. 10313
4:32 until *you* **a** that the Most High is sovereign 10313
11:39 and will greatly honor *those who* **a** him. 5795
Hos 2:20 and *you will* **a** the LORD. 3359
5: 4 *they do* not **a** the LORD. 3359
6: 3 *Let us* **a** the LORD; 3359
6: 3 let us press on to **a** him. 3359
8: 2 'O our God, *we* **a** you!' 3359
13: 4 *You shall* **a** no God but me, 3359
Mt 10:32 also **a** him before my Father in heaven. *3933*
Lk 12: 8 of Man *will* also **a** him before the angels *3933*
Ac 23: 8 but the Pharisees **a** them all.) *3933*
24: 3 *we* **a** this with profound gratitude. *622*
1Co 14:37 *let him* **a** that what I am writing to you is *2105*
2Ti 3: 7 always learning but never able *to* **a** *2106+2262*
1Jn 4: 3 but every spirit that *does* not **a** Jesus is not *3933*
2Jn 1: 7 not **a** Jesus Christ as coming in the flesh, *3933*
Rev 3: 5 but *will* **a** his name before my Father *3933*
3: 9 at your feet and **a** that I have loved you. *1182*

ACKNOWLEDGED (8) [ACKNOWLEDGE]
Lev 22:32 *I must* **be a as holy** by the Israelites. 7727
1Ch 29:22 **a** Solomon son of David **as king** 4887
Ps 32: 5 Then *I* **a** my sin *to* you and did not cover 3359
Isa 45: 5 though *you have* not **a** me, 3359
Da 5:21 with the dew of heaven, until *he* **a** that 10313
Hos 2: 8 not **a** that I was the one who gave her 3359
Lk 7:29 **a that** God's way *was* **right,** *1467*
Jn 9:22 that anyone who **a that** Jesus was *3933*

ACKNOWLEDGES (6) [ACKNOWLEDGE]
Ps 91:14 I will protect him, for *he* **a** my name. 3359
Mt 10:32 "Whoever **a** me before men, *3933*
Lk 12: 8 "I tell you, whoever **a** me before men, *3933*
1Jn 2:23 whoever **a** the Son has the Father also. *3933*
4: 2 that **a that** Jesus Christ has come in *3933*
4:15 If anyone **a** that Jesus is the Son of God, *3933*

ACKNOWLEDGMENT (2) [ACKNOWLEDGE]
Hos 4: 1 no love, no **a** *of* God in the land. 1981
6: 6 and **a** *of* God rather than burnt offerings. 1981

ACQUAINTANCE (1) [ACQUAINTANCES, ACQUAINTED]
Php 4:15 in the early days of your **a** with the gospel, *NIG*

ACQUAINTANCES (1) [ACQUAINTANCE]
Job 19:13 my **a** are completely estranged from me. 3359

ACQUAINTED (4) [ACQUAINTANCE]
Ac 24:22 Then Felix, *who was* well **a with** the Way, *3857*
26: 3 so because you are **well a with** all *1195*
Gal 1:18 to Jerusalem *to* **get a with** Peter and stayed *2707*
Heb 5:13 **is not a with** the teaching *586*

ACQUIRE (5) [ACQUIRED, ACQUIRES, ACQUIRING]
Ge 34:10 Live in it, trade in it, and **a property** in it." 296
Lev 25:28 if he *does* not **a** the means to repay him, 5162
Dt 17:16 not **a great numbers** *of* horses for himself 8049
Ru 4: 5 *you* **a** the dead man's widow, 7864
Ne 5:16 *we did* not **a** any land. 7864

ACQUIRED (13) [ACQUIRE]
Ge 12: 5 and the people *they had* **a** in Haran, 6913
12:16 and Abram **a** sheep and cattle, 2118+4200
36: 6 and all the goods *he had* **a** in Canaan, 8223
46: 6 and the possessions *they had* **a** in Canaan, 8223
47:27 *They* **a property** there and were fruitful 296
Nu 31:50 to the LORD the gold articles each of us **a—** 5162
Jos 22: 9 which *they had* **a** in accordance with 296
Ru 4:10 *I have* also **a** Ruth the Moabitess, 7864
2Ch 32:29 and **a** great numbers of flocks and herds, 5238
Ecc 2: 8 *I* **a** men and women singers, 6913
Isa 15: 7 So the wealth *they have* **a** and stored 6913
Jer 48:36 The wealth *they* **a** is gone. 6913
Rev 3:17 *I have* **a wealth** and do not need a thing.' *4456*

ACQUIRES (2) [ACQUIRE]
Lev 25:26 and **a** a sufficient means to redeem it, 5162
Pr 18:15 The heart of the discerning **a** knowledge; 7864

ACQUIRING (1) [ACQUIRE]
Pr 1: 3 for **a** a disciplined and prudent life, 4374

ACQUIT (3) [ACQUITTED, ACQUITTING]
Ex 23: 7 for *I will* not **a** the guilty. 7405
Isa 5:23 *who* **a** the guilty for a bribe, 7405
Mic 6:11 *Shall I* **a** a man with dishonest scales, 2342

ACQUITTED (1) [ACQUIT]
Mt 12:37 For by your words *you will be* **a,** *1467*

ACQUITTING (2) [ACQUIT]
Dt 25: 1 **a** the innocent and condemning the guilty. 7405
Pr 17:15 **A** the guilty and condemning 7405

ACRE (1) [TEN-ACRE]
1Sa 14:14 in an area of about half an **a.** 5103+7538

ACROSS (52) [CROSS]
Ge 1:20 above the earth **a** the expanse of the sky." 6584+7156
9:23 and Japheth took a garment and laid it **a** 6584
32:23 After *he had* **sent** them **a** the stream, 6296
Ex 10:13 and the LORD made an east wind blow **a** 928
23: 4 "If *you* **come a** your enemy's ox 7003
Nu 22: 1 and camped along the Jordan **a from** 4946+6298
26: 3 So on the plains of Moab by the **Jordan** *a* AIT
26:63 of Moab by the **Jordan** *a from* Jericho. AIT
31:12 by the **Jordan** *a from* Jericho. AIT
33:48 of Moab by the **Jordan** *a from* Jericho. AIT
33:50 the **Jordan** *a from* Jericho the LORD said AIT
35: 1 On the plains of Moab by the **Jordan** *a* AIT
36:13 of Moab by the **Jordan** *a from* Jericho. AIT
Dt 3:20 the LORD your God is giving them, **a** 928+6298
3:28 for he *will* **lead** this people **a** 4200+6296+7156
9: 3 the LORD your God is the *one who* **goes a** 6296
11:30 these mountains are **a** the Jordan, 928+6298
22: 6 If you **come a** a bird's nest beside the road, 4200+7156+7925
32:49 **a from** Jericho, and view Canaan, 6584+7156
34: 1 of Moab to the top of Pisgah, **a from** 6584+7156
Jos 7: 7 why *did you ever* **bring** this people **a** 6296+6296
13:32 in the plains of Moab **a** the Jordan east 4946+6298
Jdg 20:48 All the towns they **came a** they set on fire. 5162
1Sa 31: 7 and those **a** the Jordan saw 928+6298
2Sa 19:15 the king and **bring** him **a** the Jordan. 6296
19:41 **bring** him and his household **a** 6296
1Ki 4:12 from Beth Shan to Abel Meholah **a** 4946+6298
6:21 and he extended gold chains **a** the front of 4200
7:38 and measuring four cubits **a,** NIH
2Ki 3:22 To the Moabites **a the way,** 4946+5584
1Ch 6:78 from the tribe of Reuben **a** the Jordan 4946+6298
2Ch 3: 4 of the temple was twenty cubits long **a** 6584+7156
Job 38: 5 Who stretched a measuring line **a** it? 6584
SS 2: 8 Here he comes, leaping **a** the mountains, 6584
Isa 9: 4 the **bar** *a* their shoulders, AIT
16: 1 from Sela, **a** the desert, 2025
Jer 25:22 the kings of the coastlands **a** the sea; 928+6298
Eze 41: 4 and its width was twenty cubits **a** the end 448
Joel 2: 2 Like dawn spreading **a** the mountains 6584
Hab 1: 6 who sweep **a** the whole earth 4200
Mt 4:25 and the **region a** the Jordan followed him. *4305*
16: 5 When they went **a** the lake, *1650+3836+4305*
Mk 3: 8 the **regions a** the Jordan and around Tyre *4305*
5: 1 They went **a** the lake to the region of *4305*
10: 1 into the region of Judea and **a** the Jordan. *4305*
Lk 8:26 which is **a** the lake from Galilee. *527*
Jn 6:17 a boat and set off **a** the lake for Capernaum. *4305*
10:40 Then Jesus went back **a** the Jordan to *4305*
11:38 a cave with a stone **laid a** the entrance. *2130*
Ac 27: 5 *When we had* **sailed a** the open sea off *1386*
27:27 fourteenth night we were still being driven **a** *1877*
Rev 20: 9 They marched **a** the breadth of the earth *2093*

ACSAH (5)
Jos 15:16 "I will give my daughter A in marriage to 6578
15:17 so Caleb gave his daughter A to him 6578
Jdg 1:12 "I will give my daughter A in marriage to 6578
1:13 so Caleb gave his daughter A to him 6578
1Ch 2:49 Caleb's daughter was **A.** 6578

ACSHAPH (3)
Jos 11: 1 to the kings of Shimron and **A,** 439
12:20 the king of A one 439
19:25 Helkath, Hali, Beten, **A,** 439

ACT (41) [ACTED, ACTING, ACTION, ACTIONS, ACTIVE, ACTIVITY, ACTS]
Ex 8:29 not **a deceitfully** again by not letting 9438
Lev 20:21 it is an **a of impurity;** 5614
Nu 5:13 **been caught in the a),** 9530
23:19 Does he speak and then not **a?** 6913
Dt 17:10 *You must* **a** according to 6913
17:11 A according to the law they teach you and 6913
24:13 be regarded as a **righteous a** in the sight of 7407
Jdg 20: 6 **lewd** and disgraceful **a** 2365
1Sa 14: 6 Perhaps the LORD *will* **a** in our behalf. 6913
2Sa 6: 7 against Uzzah because of his **irreverent a;** 8915
14: 2 A like a woman who has spent many days grieving 2118
1Ki 8:32 then hear from heaven and **a.** 6913
8:39 your dwelling place. Forgive and **a;** 6913
21: 7 "Is this how you **a** as king over Israel? 6913
2Ch 6:23 then hear from heaven and **a.** 6913
19:11 A with courage, and may the LORD be 6913
24: 5 But the Levites *did* not **a at once.** 4554
Ezr 10:14 *Let* our officials **a** for the whole assembly. 6641
Ne 5:15 of reverence for God I *did* not **a** like that. 6913
Ps 119:126 It is time for you to **a,** O LORD; 6913
Pr 3:27 when it is in your power to **a.** 6913
Isa 43:13 *When I* **a,** who can reverse it?" 7188
52:13 See, my servant *will* **a wisely;** 8505
Jer 6:28 they all **a corruptly.** 8845
42: 5 against us if we *do* not **a** in accordance 6913
Eze 24:14 The time has come *for me to* **a.** 6913
Da 9:19 O Lord, hear and **a!** 6913
11:23 *he will* **a** deceitfully, 6913
Mic 6: 8 *To* **a** justly and to love mercy and 6913
Zep 3: 7 But they were still eager *to* **a corruptly** 8845
Jn 8: 4 this woman *was* **caught in the a** of adultery. *900+2093+2898*
Ac 4: 9 **a of kindness shown to** a cripple *2307*
Ro 5:18 of one **a of righteousness** was justification *1468*
12: 1 this is your spiritual **a of worship.** *3301*
2Co 8: 6 to completion this **a of grace** on your part. *5921*
10: 6 be ready to punish every **a of disobedience,** *4157*
12:18 *Did we* not **a** in the same spirit and follow *4344*
Php 2:13 and *to* **a** according to his good purpose. *1919*
Col 4: 5 in the way *you* **a** toward outsiders; *4344*
2Th 1:11 and every **a** prompted by your faith. *2240*
Jas 2:12 and **a** as those who are going to be judged *4472*

ACTED (29) [ACT]
Dt 32: 5 *They have* **a corruptly** toward him; 8845
Jos 7: 1 Israelites **a unfaithfully** in regard to 5085+5086
22:20 of Zerah **a unfaithfully** regarding 5085+5086
22:31 not **a unfaithfully** toward the LORD 5085
Jdg 9:16 if *you have* **a** honorably and in good faith 6913
9:19 if then *you have* **a** honorably and 6913
9:23 who **a treacherously** against Abimelech. 953
15: 7 "Since *you've* **a** like this, 6913
1Sa 13:13 *"You* **a foolishly,"** Samuel said. 6118
21:13 he was in their hands *he* **a like a madman,** 2147
26:21 Surely *I have* **a like a fool** 6118
1Ki 8:47 we have done wrong, *we have* **a wickedly';** 8399
20:25 He agreed with them and **a** accordingly. 6913
2Ki 12:15 because they **a** with complete honesty. 6913
22:13 they *have* not **a** in accordance with all 6913
2Ch 6:37 we have done wrong and **a wickedly';** 8399
11:23 *He* **a wisely,** dispersing some of his sons 1067
25: 4 but **a** in accordance with what is written in NIH
34:21 not **a** in accordance with all that is written 6913
Ne 1: 7 *We have* **a very wickedly** toward you. 2472+2472
9:33 *you have* **a** faithfully, while we did wrong. 6913
Ps 106: 6 we have done wrong and **a wickedly.** 8399
Isa 48: 3 then suddenly *I* **a,** and they came to pass. 6913
Jer 38: 9 these men *have* **a wickedly** 8317
Eze 25:15 'Because the Philistines **a** in vengeance 6913
Lk 16: 8 because *he had* **a** shrewdly. *4472*
24:28 Jesus **a as if** he were going farther. *4701*
Ac 3:17 brothers, I know that *you* **a** in ignorance, *4556*
1Ti 1:13 because *I* **a** in ignorance and unbelief. *4472*

ACTING (9) [ACT]
2Sa 12:21 "Why *are you* **a** this way? 6913
2Ki 10:19 But Jehu *was* **a** deceptively in order 6913
22: 7 because they *are* **a** faithfully." 6913
Eze 16:30 **a** *like* a brazen prostitute! 5126
Mal 2:14 the LORD *is* **a as** *the* **witness** between you 6386
Ro 14:15 *you are* no longer **a** in love. *4344*
1Co 3: 3 *Are you* not **a** like mere men? *4344*
7:36 If anyone thinks *he is* **a improperly** toward *858*
Gal 2:14 that *they were* not **a in line** with the truth *3980*

ACTION (7) [ACT]
Jer 32:39 I will give them singleness of heart and **a,** 2006
Da 11:28 *He will* **take a** against it and then return 6913

Lk 23:51 not consented to their decision and a. 4552
Ac 7:22 and was powerful in speech and a. 2240
2Co 9: 2 stirred most of them to a. 2241
Jas 2:17 if it is not accompanied by a, is dead. 2240
1Pe 1:13 prepare your minds for a; 350+3836+4019

ACTIONS (24) [ACT]

Pr 20:11 Even a child is known by his a, 5095
Isa 66:18 I, because of their a and their imaginations, 5126
Jer 4:18 "Your own conduct and a have brought this 5095
7: 3 Reform your ways and your a, 5095
7: 5 and your a and deal with each other justly, 5095
18:11 and reform your ways and your a.' 5095
26:13 and your a and obey the LORD your God. 5095
35:15 from your wicked ways and reform your a; 5095
44:22 LORD could no longer endure your wicked a 5095
44:25 by your a what you promised 3338
Eze 14:22 and when you see their conduct and their a, 6613
14:23 when you see their conduct and their a, 6613
20:43 and all the a by which you have defiled 6613
24:14 according to your conduct and your a, 6613
36:17 they defiled it by their conduct and their a. 6613
36:19 according to their conduct and their a. 6613
Mt 11:19 But wisdom is proved right by her a." 2240
2Co 10:11 we will be in our a when we are present. 2240
11:15 Their end will be what their a deserve 2240+2848
Gal 6: 4 Each one should test his own a. 2240
Tit 1:16 but by their a they deny him. 2240
Jas 2:22 and his a were working together, 2240
1Jn 3:12 Because his own a were evil 2240
3:18 not love with words or tongue but with a 2240

ACTIVE (2) [ACT]

Phm 1: 6 that you may be a in sharing your faith, 1921
Heb 4:12 For the word of God is living and a. 1921

ACTIVITY (5) [ACT]

Ne 11:23 which regulated their daily a. 1821
Ecc 3: 1 and a season for every a under heaven: 2914
3:17 for there will be a time for every a, 2914
Ac 5:38 For if their purpose or a is of human origin, 2240
2Co 10:15 our area of a among you 2834

ACTS (36) [ACT]

Ex 6: 6 and with mighty a of judgment. 9150
7: 4 with mighty a of judgment I will bring out my divisions, 9150
Jdg 5:11 They recite the righteous a of the LORD, 7407
5:11 the righteous a of his warriors in Israel. 7407
1Sa 12: 7 the righteous a performed by the LORD 7407
1Ch 16: 9 tell of all his wonderful a. AIT
2Ch 32:32 and his a of devotion are written in 2876
35:26 of Josiah's reign and his a of devotion, 2876
Est 10: 2 And all his a of power and might, 5126
Ps 71:16 I will come and proclaim your mighty a, 1476
71:24 of your righteous a all day long, 7407
105: 2 tell of all his wonderful a. AIT
106: 2 Who can proclaim the mighty a of 1476
145: 4 they will tell of your mighty a. 1476
145:12 that all men may know of your mighty a 1476
150: 2 Praise him for his a of power; 1476
Pr 12:10 but the kindest a of the wicked are cruel. 8171
13:16 Every prudent man a out of knowledge, 6913
Isa 59: 6 and a of violence are in their hands. 7189
64: 4 who a on behalf of those who wait for him. 6913
64: 6 and all our righteous a are like filthy rags; 7407
Jer 13:27 I have seen your detestable a on the hills 9199
29:26 you should put any madman who a like a prophet into the stocks 5547
Eze 22: 9 the mountain shrines and commit lewd a. 2365
Da 9:16 in keeping with all your righteous a, 7407
Mic 6: 5 that you may know the righteous a of 7407
Mt 6: 1 to do your 'a of righteousness' before men, 1466
Jn 7: 4 to become a public figure a in secret. 4472
Ro 1:27 Men committed indecent a with other men, 859
Gal 5:19 The a of the sinful nature are obvious: 2240
Heb 6: 1 of repentance from a that lead to death, 2240
9:14 cleanse our consciences from a that lead 2240
10:17 and lawless a I will remember no more." 490
Jude 1:15 of all the ungodly a they have done in 2240
Rev 15: 4 for your righteous a have been revealed." 1468
19: 8 (Fine linen stands for the righteous a of 1468

ACTUAL (1) [ACTUALLY]

Dt 21:16 in preference to his a firstborn, NIH

ACTUALLY (8) [ACTUAL]

Ge 37: 8 Will you a rule us?" 5440+5440
37:10 your brothers a come and bow down to 995+995
Jos 9:22 while a you live near us? NIH
Jer 8: 8 when a the lying pen of 434
Jn 7:22 because Moses gave you circumcision (though a it did not come from Moses, 4022
Ro 7:10 to bring life a brought death. NIG
1Co 5: 1 is a reported that there is sexual immorality 3914
1Th 2:13 but as it a is, the word of God, 242

ACZIB (4)

Jos 15:44 Keilah, A and Mareshah— 424
19:29 and came out at the sea in the region of A, 424
Jdg 1:31 or Sidon or Ahlab or A or Helbah or Aphek 424
Mic 1:14 The town of A will prove deceptive to 424

ADADAH (1)

Jos 15:22 Kinah, Dimonah, A, 6368

ADAH (8)

Ge 4:19 one named A and the other Zillah. 6336
4:20 A gave birth to Jabal; 6336
4:23 Lamech said to his wives, "A and Zillah, 6336
36: 2 A daughter of Elon the Hittite, 6336
36: 4 A bore Eliphaz to Esau, 6336
36:10 Eliphaz, the son of Esau's wife A, 6336
36:12 These were grandsons of Esau's wife A. 6336
36:16 they were grandsons of A. 6336

ADAIAH (9)

2Ki 22: 1 mother's name was Jedidah daughter of A; 6347
1Ch 6:41 the son of Zerah, the son of A, 6347
8:21 A, Beraiah and Shimrath were the sons 6347
9:12 A son of Jeroham, the son of Pashhur, 6347
2Ch 23: 1 Azariah son of Obed, Maaseiah son of A, 6348
Ezr 10:29 Meshullam, Malluch, A, Jashub, 6347
10:39 Shelemiah, Nathan, A, 6347
Ne 11: 5 the son of Hazaiah, the son of A, 6347
11:12 A son of Jeroham, the son of Pelaliah, 6347

ADALIA (1)

Est 9: 8 Poratha, A, Aridatha, 130

ADAM (21) [ADAM'S]

Ge 2:20 But for A no suitable helper was found. 134
3:17 To A he said, "Because you listened 134
3:20 A named his wife Eve, 134
3:21 for A and his wife and clothed them. 134
4: 1 A lay with his wife Eve, 134
4:25 A lay with his wife again, 134
5: 3 When A had lived 130 years, 134
5: 4 A lived 800 years and had other sons 134
5: 5 Altogether, A lived 930 years, 134
Jos 3:16 a town called A in the vicinity of Zarethan, 136
1Ch 1: 1 A, Seth, Enosh, 134
Hos 6: 7 Like A, they have broken the covenant— 134
Lk 3:38 the son of Seth, the son of A, 77
Ro 5:14 from the time of A to the time of Moses, 77
5:14 by breaking a command, as did A, who was 77
1Co 15:22 For as in A all die, 77
15:45 "The first man A became a living being"; 77
15:45 the last A, a life-giving spirit. 77
1Ti 2:13 For A was formed first, then Eve. 77
2:14 And A was not the one deceived; 77
Jude 1:14 Enoch, the seventh from A, 77

ADAM'S (1) [ADAM]

Ge 5: 1 This is the written account of A line. 134

ADAMAH (1)

Jos 19:36 A, Ramah, Hazor, 142

ADAMANT (KJV) See FLINT

ADAMI NEKEB (1)

Jos 19:33 passing A and Jabneel to Lakkum 146

ADAR (9)

Ezr 6:15 on the third day of the month A, 10009
Est 3: 7 the month of A. 160
3:13 the month of A, and to plunder their goods. 160
8:12 the month of A. 160
9: 1 the month of A, 160
9:15 on the fourteenth day of the month of A, 160
9:17 on the thirteenth day of the month of A, 160
9:19 the month of A as a day of joy and feasting, 160
9:21 and fifteenth days of the month of A 160

ADBEEL (2)

Ge 25:13 the firstborn of Ishmael, Kedar, A, 118
1Ch 1:29 the firstborn of Ishmael, Kedar, A, 118

ADD (32) [ADDED, ADDING, ADDITION, ADDITIONAL, ADDS]

Ge 30:24 "May the LORD a to me another son." 3578
Lev 2:13 a salt to all your offerings. 7928
5:16 a a fifth of the value to that and give it all 3578
6: 5 a a fifth of the value to it and give it all to 3578
6:12 Every morning the priest is to a firewood 6584
22:14 to the priest for the offering and a a fifth of 3578
27:13 he must a a fifth to its value. 3578
27:15 he must a a fifth to its value, 3578
27:19 he must a a fifth to its value, 3578
27:31 he must a a fifth of the value to it. 3578
Nu 5: 7 a one fifth to it and give it all to 3578
Dt 4: 2 Do not a to what I command you and do 3578
12:32 do not a to it or take away from it. 3578
20: 8 Then the officers shall a, 3578
2Sa 15: 4 And Absalom would a, 606
2Ki 20: 6 I will a fifteen years to your life. 3578
1Ch 22:14 And you may a to them. 3578
2Ch 28:13 Do you intend to a to our sin and guilt? 3578
Pr 1: 5 let the wise listen and a to their learning, 3578
9: 9 teach a righteous man and he will a 3578
30: 6 Do not a to his words, 3578
Isa 5: 8 to you who a house to house and join field 5595
29: 1 A year to year and let your cycle 3578
38: 5 I will a fifteen years to your life. 3578
Jer 7:21 Go ahead, a your burnt offerings 3578
30:19 I will a to their numbers, 8049
Eze 16:43 Did you not a lewdness 6913
Mt 6:27 by worrying can a a single hour to his life? 4707
Lk 12:25 by worrying can a a single hour to his life? 4707
Gal 3:15 Just as no one can set aside or a to 2112
2Pe 1: 5 to a to your faith goodness; 2220
Rev 22:18 God will a to him the plagues described 2202

ADDAN (KJV) See ADDON

ADDAR (2) [HAZAR ADDAR, ATAROTH ADDAR]

Jos 15: 3 Then it ran past Hezron up to A and curved 162
1Ch 8: 3 The sons of Bela were: A, Gera, Abihud, 161

ADDED (39) [ADD]

Ge 16:10 The angel a, "I will so increase 606
21: 7 And she a, "Who would have said 606
24:25 And she a, "We have plenty of straw 606
30:28 He a, "Name your wages, 606
38:25 she said. And she a, "See 606
Ex 12:34 before the yeast was a, 2806
Lev 10: 1 put fire in them and a incense; 8492
Nu 36: 3 from our ancestral inheritance and a to that 3578
36: 4 their inheritance will be a to that of 3578
Dt 5:22 and he a nothing more. 3578
Jdg 19:13 He a, "Come, let's try to reach Gibeah 606
Ru 2:20 She a, "That man is our close relative; 606
3:17 and a, "He gave me these six measures 606
1Sa 12:19 for we have a to all our other sins the evil 3578
26:18 he a, "Why is my lord pursuing his servant? 606
2Sa 19:35 Why should your servant be an a burden 6388
1Ki 2:14 he a, "I have something to say to you." 606
22:28 he a, "Mark my words, all you people!" 606
2Ch 2:12 And Hiram a: "Praise be to 606
18:27 he a, "Mark my words, all you people!" 606
Est 5:12 "And that's not all," Haman a. 606
Pr 9:11 and years will be a to your life. 3578
Ecc 3:14 nothing can be a to it and nothing taken 3578
Jer 36:32 many similar words were a to them. 3578+6388
40: 5 Jeremiah turned to go, Nebuzaradan a, NIH
44:19 The women a, "When we burned incense NIH
45: 3 The LORD has a sorrow to my pain; 3578
Zec 1:15 but they a to the calamity.' 6468
5: 6 And he a, "This is the iniquity of the people 606
Lk 3:20 Herod a this to them all. 4707
Jn 1:51 He then a, "I tell you the truth, 3306
Ac 1:26 so he was a to the eleven apostles. 5164
2:41 about three thousand were a to their number 4707
2:47 And the Lord a to their number daily 4707
5:14 in the Lord and were a to their number. 4707
Ro 5:20 The law was a so that 4209
Gal 2: 6 those men a nothing to my message. 4707
3:19 It was a because of transgressions until 4707
Rev 19: 9 he a, "These are the true words of God." 3306

ADDER (2) [ADDERS]

Job 20:16 the fangs of an a will kill him. 704
Isa 59: 5 and when one is broken, an a is hatched. 704

ADDERS (1) [ADDER]

Isa 30: 6 of a and darting snakes, 704

ADDERS (KJV) See also VIPER

ADDI (1)

Lk 3:28 the son of A, the son of Cosam, 79

ADDICTED (1)

Tit 2: 3 not to be slanderers or a to much wine, 1530

ADDING (5) [ADD]

Lev 27:27 a a fifth of the value to it. 3578
2Sa 14:11 to prevent the avenger of blood from a to 8049
1Ki 11:25 a to the trouble caused by Hadad. 907+2256
Ezr 10:10 you have married foreign women, a 3578
Ecc 7:27 "A one thing to another to discover NIH

ADDITION (38) [ADD]

Ge 28: 9 in a to the wives he already had. 6584
Lev 9:17 burned it on the altar in a to 963+4200+4946
23:38 These offerings are in a to those 963+4200+4946
23:38 and in a to your gifts 963+4200+4946
Nu 6:21 in a to whatever else he can afford. 963+4200+4946
16:49 in a to those who had died 963+4200+4946
28:10 in a to the regular burnt offering 6584
28:23 Prepare these in a to 963+4200+4946
28:24 it is to be prepared in a to 6584
28:31 in a to the regular burnt offering 963+4200+4946
29: 6 These are in a to the monthly 963+4200+4946
29:11 in a to the sin offering 963+4200+4946
29:16 in a to the regular burnt offering 963+4200+4946
29:19 in a to the regular burnt offering 963+4200+4946
29:22 in a to the regular burnt offering 963+4200+4946
29:25 in a to the regular burnt offering 963+4200+4946

Nu 29:28 **in a to** the regular burnt offering 963+4200+4946
29:31 **in a to** the regular burnt offering 963+4200+4946
29:34 **in a to** the regular burnt offering 963+4200+4946
29:38 **in a to** the regular burnt offering 963+4200+4946
29:39 " '**In a to** what you vow 963+4200
35: 6 **In a,** give them forty-two other towns. 2256
Dt 29: 1 **in a to** the covenant he had made 963+4200+4946
Jos 13:22 **In a to** those slain in battle, 448
Jdg 20:15 **in a to** seven hundred chosen men 963+4200
1Ki 5:11 **in a to** twenty thousand baths 2256
15:20 and all Kinnereth **in a to** Naphtali. 6584
2Ch 31:16 **In a,** they distributed to 963+4200+4946
Ezr 1: 6 **in a to** all the freewill offerings. 963+4200
Ne 5:15 of silver from them **in a to** food and wine. 339
Ecc 12:12 my son, of **anything in a** to them. 3463
Eze 16:23 **In a to** all your other wickedness, 339
39:14 **in a to** them, 907
44: 7 **In a to** all your other detestable practices, 448
Lk 24:22 **In a,** some of our women amazed us. *247+2779*
2Co 7:13 **In a** to our own encouragement, *1254+2093*
8:22 **In a,** we are sending *1254*
Eph 6:16 In **a** to all this, take up the shield of faith, *NIG*

ADDITIONAL (3) [ADD]
Ge 43:22 also brought **a** silver with us to buy food. 337
Ex 26:12 As for the **a** length of the tent curtains, 6369
Nu 3:48 the redemption of the **a** Israelites to Aaron 6369

ADDON (2)
Ezr 2:59 Tel Harsha, Kerub, **A** and Immer, 150
Ne 7:61 Tel Harsha, Kerub, **A** and Immer, 124

ADDRESS (3) [ADDRESSED, ADDRESSES]
Dt 20: 2 the priest shall come forward and **a** 1819
Ac 12:21 **delivered a public a** to his people. *1319*
1Co 3: 1 not **a** you as spiritual but as worldly— *3281*

ADDRESSED (3) [ADDRESS]
Ac 2:14 raised his voice and **a** the crowd: *710*
5:35 Then *he* **a** them: *3306*
15: 7 Peter got up and **a** them: *3306+4639*

ADDRESSES (1) [ADDRESS]
Heb 12: 5 that word of encouragement that **a** you *1363*

ADDS (5) [ADD]
Job 34:37 To his sin *he* **a** rebellion; 3578
Pr 10:22 and *he* **a** no trouble to it. 3578
10:27 The fear of the LORD **a length** *to* life, 3578
Heb 10:17 Then *he* **a**: "Their sins *3306*
Rev 22:18 If anyone **a** anything **to** them, *2202*

ADEQUATELY (1)
Ac 18:26 to him the way of God **more a.** *209*

ADER (KJV) See EDER

ADHERE (1)
2Ki 17:34 neither worship the LORD nor **a to** 3869+6913

ADIEL (3)
1Ch 4:36 Jaakobah, Jeshohaiah, Asaiah, **A,** Jesimiel, 6346
9:12 and Maasai son of **A,** the son of Jahzerah, 6346
27:25 of **A** was in charge of the royal storehouses. 6346

ADIN (4)
Ezr 2:15 of **A** 454 6350
8: 6 of the descendants of **A,** Ebed son 6350
Ne 7:20 of **A** 655 6350
10:16 Adonijah, Bigvai, **A,** 6350

ADINA (1)
1Ch 11:42 **A** son of Shiza the Reubenite, 6351

ADITHAIM (1)
Jos 15:36 **A** and Gederah (or Gederothaim)— 6353

ADJOINING (5) [JOIN]
Ne 3: 2 The men of Jericho built the **a section,** 3338+6584
3:10 **A** this, Jedaiah son of Harumaph 3338+6584
Eze 41:11 and the **base** *a* the open area AIT
42:10 **a** the temple courtyard and opposite 448+7156
45: 6 cubits long, **a** the sacred portion; 4200+6645

ADJOURNED (1)
Ac 24:22 with the Way, **a the proceedings.** *327*

ADJURE (KJV) See CHARGE, COMMAND, SWEAR

ADLAI (1)
1Ch 27:29 Shaphat son of **A** was in charge of 6354

ADMAH (5)
Ge 10:19 Gomorrah, **A** and Zeboiim, as far as Lasha. 144
14: 2 Shinab king of **A,** 144
14: 8 the king of Gomorrah, the king of **A,** 144
Dt 29:23 the destruction of Sodom and Gomorrah, **A** 144
Hos 11: 8 How can I treat you like **A?** 144

ADMATHA (1)
Est 1:14 Carshena, Shethar, **A,** Tarshish, Meres, 148

ADMINISTER (7) [ADMINISTERED, ADMINISTERING, ADMINISTRATION, ADMINISTRATOR, ADMINISTRATORS]
1Ki 3:28 that he had wisdom from God to **a** justice. 6913
2Ch 19: 8 and heads of Israelite families to **a** the law NIH
Ezr 7:25 appoint magistrates and judges to **a justice** 10169
Jer 21:12 " '**A** justice every morning; 1906
Zec 7: 9 "This is what the LORD Almighty says: '**A** true justice; 9149
2Co 8:19 which we **a** in order to honor *1354*
8:20 of the way we **a** this liberal gift. *1354*

ADMINISTERED (1) [ADMINISTER]
Heb 11:33 **a** justice, and gained what was promised; *2237*

ADMINISTERING (2) [ADMINISTER]
1Ki 3:11 but for discernment in **a** justice, 9048
1Pe 4:10 faithfully **a** God's grace *3874*

ADMINISTRATION (3) [ADMINISTER]
1Co 12:28 **those with gifts of a,** *3236*
Eph 3: 2 the **a** of God's grace that was given to me *3873*
3: 9 and to make plain to everyone the **a** *3873*

ADMINISTRATOR (7) [ADMINISTER]
2Ki 10: 5 So the palace **a,** the city governor, 889+6584^{S}
18:18 Eliakim son of Hilkiah the palace **a,** 889+6584^{S}
18:37 Eliakim son of Hilkiah the palace **a,** 889+6584^{S}
19: 2 He sent Eliakim the palace **a,** 889+6584^{S}
Isa 36: 3 Eliakim son of Hilkiah the palace **a,** 889+6584^{S}
36:22 Eliakim son of Hilkiah the palace **a,** 889+6584^{S}
37: 2 He sent Eliakim the palace **a,** 889+6584^{S}

ADMINISTRATORS (8) [ADMINISTER]
2Ch 35: 8 the **a** *of* God's temple, 5592
Est 9: 3 the governors and the king's **a** helped 4856+6913
Da 2:49 and Abednego **a** over the province 10525
6: 2 with three **a** over them, 10518
6: 3 so distinguished himself among the **a** and 10518
6: 4 the **a** and the satraps tried to find grounds 10518
6: 6 So the **a** and the satraps went as a group to 10518
6: 7 The royal **a,** prefects, satraps, 10518

ADMIRABLE (1)
Php 4: 8 whatever is lovely, whatever is **a**— *2368*

ADMIT (7) [ADMITTED]
Jos 20: 4 Then *they are to* **a** him into their city 665
Job 27: 5 **a** you are **in the right;** 7405
40:14 Then *I* myself *will* **a** *to* you 3344
Isa 48: 6 *Will* you not **a** them? 5583
Hos 5:15 to my place until *they* **a** *their* **guilt.** 870
Ac 24:14 *I* **a** that I worship the God of our fathers as *3933*
2Co 11:21 To my shame *I* **a** that we were too weak *3306*

ADMITTED (2) [ADMIT]
Ne 13: 1 or Moabite *should* ever *be* **a** into 995
Heb 11:13 And *they* **a** that they were aliens *3933*

ADMONISH (2) [ADMONISHED, ADMONISHING, ADMONITION]
Col 3:16 and **a** one another with all wisdom, *3805*
1Th 5:12 over you in the Lord and who **a** you. *3805*

ADMONISHED (2) [ADMONISH]
Ne 9:26 who *had* **a** them in order to turn them back 6386
9:30 By your Spirit *you* **a** them 6386

ADMONISHING (1) [ADMONISH]
Col 1:28 **a** and teaching everyone with all wisdom, *3805*

ADMONITION (2) [ADMONISH]
Mal 2: 1 "And now this **a** is for you, O priests. 5184
2: 4 that I have sent you this **a** so 5184

ADNA (2)
Ezr 10:30 From the descendants of Pahath-Moab: **A,** 6363
Ne 12:15 of Harim's, **A;** of Meremoth's, Helkai; 6363

ADNAH (2)
1Ch 12:20 **A,** Jozabad, Jediael, Michael, Jozabad, 6367
2Ch 17:14 **A** the commander, with 300,000 6365

ADO (KJV) See COMMOTION

ADONI-BEZEK (3) [BEZEK]
Jdg 1: 5 that they found **A** and fought against him, 152
1: 6 **A** fled, but they chased him 152
1: 7 Then **A** said, "Seventy kings 152

ADONI-ZEDEK (2)
Jos 10: 1 Now **A** king of Jerusalem heard 155
10: 3 So **A** king of Jerusalem appealed 155

ADONIJAH (26) [ADONIJAH'S]
2Sa 3: 4 **A** the son of Haggith; 153
1Ki 1: 5 Now **A,** whose mother was Haggith, 153
1: 7 **A** conferred with Joab son of Zeruiah and 153
1: 8 and David's special guard did not join **A.** 154
1: 9 **A** then sacrificed sheep, 154
1:11 "Have you not heard that **A,** 154
1:13 Why then has **A** become king?' 154
1:18 But now **A** has become king, and you, 153
1:24 declared that **A** shall be king after you, 154
1:25 'Long live King **A!'** 154
1:41 **A** and all the guests who were 154
1:42 **A** said, "Come in. 154
1:50 But **A,** in fear of Solomon, 154
1:51 "**A** is afraid of King Solomon 154
1:53 **A** came and bowed down to King Solomon, NIH
2:13 Now **A,** the son of Haggith, 154
2:19 to King Solomon to speak to him for **A,** 154
2:21 be given in marriage to your brother **A."** 154
2:22 the Shunammite for **A?** 154
2:23 so severely, if **A** does not pay with his life 154
2:24 **A** shall be put to death today!" 154
2:25 and he struck down **A** and he died. 2257^{S}
2:28 who had conspired with **A** though not 153
1Ch 3: 2 the fourth, **A** the son of Haggith; 153
2Ch 17: 8 Asahel, Shemiramoth, Jehonathan, **A,** 154
Ne 10:16 **A,** Bigvai, Adin, 153

ADONIJAH'S (1) [ADONIJAH]
1Ki 1:49 all **A** guests rose in alarm and dispersed. 154+4200

ADONIKAM (3)
Ezr 2:13 of **A** 666 156
8:13 of the descendants of **A,** 156
Ne 7:18 of **A** 667 156

ADONIRAM (5)
2Sa 20:24 **A** was in charge of forced labor; 157
1Ki 4: 6 **A** son of Abda—in charge of forced labor. 157
5:14 **A** was in charge of the forced labor. 157
12:18 King Rehoboam sent out **A,** 157
2Ch 10:18 King Rehoboam sent out **A,** 2067

ADOPT (1) [ADOPTED, ADOPTION]
Job 15: 5 *you* **a** the tongue of the crafty. 1047

ADOPTED (3) [ADOPT]
Est 2:15 Esther (the girl Mordecai *had* **a,** 1426+4200+4374
Ps 106:35 with the nations and **a** their customs. 4340
Eph 1: 5 to be **a as** his **sons** through Jesus Christ, *5625*

ADOPTION (2) [ADOPT]
Ro 8:23 as we wait eagerly for our **a as sons,** *5625*
9: 4 Theirs is the **a as sons;** *5625*

ADORAIM (1)
2Ch 11: 9 **A,** Lachish, Azekah, 126

ADORE (1)
SS 1: 4 How right *they are to* **a** you! 170

ADORN (7) [ADORNED, ADORNMENT, ADORNS]
Job 40:10 Then **a** *yourself with* glory and splendor, 6335
Ps 144:12 be like pillars carved to **a** a palace. 9322
Pr 1: 9 and a chain to **a** your neck. NIH
Isa 60: 7 and *I will* **a** my glorious temple. 6995
60:13 to **a** the place of my sanctuary; 6995
Jer 4:30 *You* **a yourself** in vain. 3636
10: 4 *They* **a** it with silver and gold; 3636

ADORNED (9) [ADORN]
2Sa 1:24 who **a** your garments *with* ornaments 6584+6590
2Ch 3: 6 *He* **a** the temple *with* precious stones. 4200+7596+9514
Ps 45: 8 from **palaces** *a with* ivory the music of AIT
Eze 16:11 *I* **a** you *with* jewelry: 6335
16:13 So *you were* **a** *with* gold and silver; 6335
28:13 every precious stone **a** you: 5010
Hos 10: 1 his land prospered, *he* **a** his sacred stones. 3512
Am 3:15 the **houses** *a with* ivory will be destroyed AIT
Lk 21: 5 how the temple *was* **a** with beautiful stones *3175*

ADORNMENT (1) [ADORN]
1Pe 3: 3 not come from outward **a,** *3180*

ADORNS (3) [ADORN]
Ps 93: 5 holiness a your house for endless days, 5533
Isa 61:10 as a bridegroom a his head like a priest, 6996
61:10 and as a bride a herself with her jewels. 6335

ADRAMMELECH (3)
2Ki 17:31 the fire as sacrifices to A and Anammelech, 165
19:37 his sons A and Sharezer cut him down with 166
Isa 37:38 his sons A and Sharezer cut him down with 166

ADRAMYTTIUM (1)
Ac 27: 2 a ship from A about to sail for ports along *101*

ADRIATIC (1)
Ac 27:27 across the A Sea, *102*

ADRIEL (2)
1Sa 18:19 she was given in marriage to A of Meholah. 6377
2Sa 21: 8 whom she had borne to A son of Barzillai 6377

ADULLAM (9) [ADULLAMITE]
Ge 38: 1 to stay with a man of A named Hirah. 6356
Jos 12:15 the king of A one 6355
15:35 Jarmuth, A, Socoh, Azekah, 6355
1Sa 22: 1 and escaped to the cave of A. 6355
2Sa 23:13 down to David at the cave of A, 6355
1Ch 11:15 down to David to the rock at the cave of A, 6355
2Ch 11: 7 Beth Zur, Soco, A, 6355
Ne 11:30 A and their villages, 6355
Mic 1:15 the glory of Israel will come to A. 6355

ADULLAMITE (2) [ADULLAM]
Ge 38:12 and his friend Hirah the A went with him. 6356
38:20 the young goat by his friend the A in order 6356

ADULTERER (3) [ADULTERY]
Lev 20:10 a and the adulteress must be put to death. 5537
Job 24:15 The eye of the a watches for dusk; 5537
Heb 13: 4 the a and all the sexually immoral. *3659*

ADULTERERS (9) [ADULTERY]
Ps 50:18 you throw in your lot with a. 5537
Isa 57: 3 you offspring of a and prostitutes! 5537
Jer 9: 2 they *are* all a, a crowd of unfaithful people. 5537
23:10 The land is full of a; 5537
Hos 7: 4 They *are* all a, 5537
Mal 3: 5 to testify against sorcerers, a and perjurers, 5537
Lk 18:11 evildoers, a—or even like this tax collector. *3659*
1Co 6: 9 the sexually immoral nor idolaters nor a *3659*
1Ti 1:10 *for* a and perverts, for slave traders *4521*

ADULTERESS (12) [ADULTERY]
Lev 20:10 adulterer and the a must be put to death. 5537
Pr 2:16 It will save you also from the a, 851+2424
5: 3 For the lips of an a drip honey, 2424
5:20 Why be captivated, my son, by an a? 2424
6:26 and the a preys upon your very life. 408+851
7: 5 they will keep you from the a, 851+2424
22:14 The mouth of an a is a deep pit; 2424
30:20 "This is the way of an a: 5537
Hos 3: 1 though she is loved by another and *is an* a. 5537
Mt 5:32 causes her *to* become an a, *3658*
Ro 7: 3 she is called an a. *3655*
7: 3 from that law and is not an a, *3655*

ADULTERESSES (KJV) See WOMEN WHO COMMIT ADULTERY

ADULTERIES (7) [ADULTERY]
Jer 3: 8 and sent her away because of all *her* a. 5537
13:27 your a and lustful neighings, 5539
Rev 14: 8 the maddening wine *of* her a." *4518*
17: 2 intoxicated with the wine *of* her a." *4518*
17: 4 and the filth *of* her a. *4518*
18: 3 the maddening wine *of* her a. *4518*
19: 2 corrupted the earth by her a. *4518*

ADULTEROUS (9) [ADULTERY]
Eze 6: 9 how I have been grieved by their a hearts, 2388
16:32 " 'You a wife! 5537
23:45 they *are* a and blood is on their hands. 5537
Hos 1: 2 an a wife and children of unfaithfulness, 2393
2: 2 Let her remove the a look from her face 2393
Mt 12:39 "A wicked and a generation asks for *3655*
16: 4 A wicked and a generation looks for *3655*
Mk 8:38 in this a and sinful generation, *3655*
Jas 4: 4 *You* a *people,* don't you know *3655*

ADULTERY (48) [ADULTERER, ADULTERERS, ADULTERESS, ADULTERIES, ADULTEROUS]
Ex 20:14 *"You shall* not commit a. 5537
Lev 20:10 a man commits a with another man's wife 5537
Dt 5:18 *"You shall* not commit a. 5537
Ps 51: T David *had* committed a with Bathsheba. 448+995
Pr 6:32 But *a man who* commits a lacks judgment; 5537
Jer 3: 6 and *has* committed a there. 2388
3: 8 she also went out and committed a. 2388
3: 9 and committed a with stone and wood. 5537
5: 7 yet *they* committed a and thronged to 5537
7: 9 commit a and perjury, 5537
23:14 They commit a and live a lie. 5537
29:23 *they have* committed a 5537
Eze 16:38 *women who* commit a and who shed blood; 5537
23:37 for *they have* committed a and blood is 5537
23:37 *They* committed a with their idols; 5537
23:43 Then I said about the one worn out by a, 5539
23:45 to the punishment of *women who* commit a 5537
Hos 1: 2 guilty of the vilest a 2388+2388
2: 4 because they are the children of a. 2393
4: 2 lying and murder, stealing and a; 5537
4:13 and your daughters-in-law *to* a. 5537
4:14 your daughters-in-law when *they* commit a, 5537
4:15 "Though you commit a, O Israel, 2388
Mt 5:27 *'Do* not commit a.' *3658*
5:28 who looks at a woman lustfully *has* already committed a with her *3658*
5:32 the divorced woman commits a. *3656*
15:19 a, sexual immorality, theft, false testimony, *3657*
19: 9 and marries another woman commits a." *3656*
19:18 " 'Do not murder, *do* not commit a, *3658*
Mk 7:21 sexual immorality, theft, murder, a, *3657*
10:11 and marries another woman commits a *3656*
10:12 and marries another man, *she* commits a." *3656*
10:19 'Do not murder, *do* not commit a, *3658*
Lk 16:18 and marries another woman commits a, *3658*
16:18 a divorced woman commits a. *3658*
18:20 *'Do* not commit a, do not murder, *3658*
Jn 8: 3 in a woman caught in a. *3657*
8: 4 this woman was caught in the act *of* a. *3658*
Ro 2:22 that people *should* not commit a, *3658*
2:22 *do you* commit a? *3658*
13: 9 The commandments, *"Do* not commit a," *3658*
Jas 2:11 For he who said, *"Do* not commit a," *3658*
2:11 not commit a but do commit murder, *3658*
2Pe 2:14 With eyes full *of* a, *3655*
Rev 2:22 and I will make those who commit a *3658*
17: 2 the earth committed a and the inhabitants *4519*
18: 3 The kings of the earth committed a *4519*
18: 9 the kings of the earth who committed a *4519*

ADULTS (1)
1Co 14:20 but in your thinking be a. *5455*

ADUMMIM (2)
Jos 15: 7 which faces the Pass of A south of 147
18:17 which faces the Pass of A, 147

ADVANCE (20) [ADVANCED, ADVANCES, ADVANCING]
Dt 1: 7 Break camp and a *into* the hill country of 5825
Jos 6: 7 And he ordered the people, "A! 6296
8: 5 I and all those with me *will* a on the city, 7928
Jdg 4:15 At Barak's a, the LORD routed Sisera 4200+7156
9:33 a against the city. 7320
2Sa 22:30 With your help *I can* a *against* a troop; 8132
Job 19:12 His troops a in force; 995
30:14 *They* a as *through* a gaping breach; 910
Ps 18:29 With your help *I can* a *against* a troop; 8132
27: 2 evil men a against me to devour my flesh, 7928
Pr 30:27 yet they a together in ranks; 3655
Eze 38:16 *You will* a against my people Israel like 6590
Da 11:13 *he will* a with a huge army fully equipped. 995
Joel 3:12 *let them* a into the Valley of Jehoshaphat, 6590
Hab 1: 9 Their hordes a like a desert wind 2025+7156
Ro 9:23 whom *he* prepared in a for glory— *4602*
2Co 9: 5 to urge the brothers to visit you in a *1650+4616*
Gal 3: 8 announced the gospel in a *4603*
Eph 2:10 which God prepared in a for us to do. *4602*
Php 1:12 to me has really served to a the gospel *4620*

ADVANCED (18) [ADVANCE]
Ge 18:11 and Sarah were already old and well a 995
24: 1 Abraham was now old and well a 995
Jos 13: 1 When Joshua was old and well a in years, 995
23: 1 Joshua, by then old and well a in years, 995
23: 2 "I am old and well a in years. 995
Jdg 1:10 They a against the Canaanites living 2143
1:11 From there *they* a against the people living 2143
11:29 from there *he* a *against* the Ammonites. 6296
1Sa 17:12 and in Saul's time he was old and well a 995
2Sa 10:13 Then Joab and the troops with him a 5602
1Ki 1: 1 King David was old and well a in years, 995
20:21 of Israel a and overpowered the horses 3655
2Ki 24:10 of Babylon a *on* Jerusalem and laid siege 6590
1Ch 19:14 Then Joab and the troops with him a 5602
19:17 *he* a against them 995
Job 32: 7 a years should teach wisdom.' 8044
Ps 18:12 of the brightness of his presence clouds a, 6296
48: 4 when *they* a together, 6296

ADVANCES (3) [ADVANCE]
Jer 4:13 *He* a like the clouds, 6590
46:22 a fleeing serpent as the enemy a in force; 2143
Na 2: 1 An attacker a against you, [Nineveh]. 6590

ADVANCING (4) [ADVANCE]
1Ki 20:17 who reported, "Men *are* a from Samaria." 3655
Eze 38: 9 a like a storm; 995
Mt 11:12 of heaven *has been* forcefully a, *1041*
Gal 1:14 *I was* a in Judaism beyond many Jews *4621*

ADVANTAGE (13)
Ex 22:22 *"Do* not take a of a widow or an orphan. 6700
Lev 25:14 *do* not take a of each other. 3561
25:17 *Do* not take a of each other, 3561
Dt 24:14 *Do* not take a of a hired man who is poor 6943
Ecc 3:19 man has no a over the animal. 4639
6: 8 What a has a wise man over a fool? 3463
7:12 but the a *of* knowledge is this: 3862
Isa 30: 5 who bring neither help nor a, 3603
Ro 3: 1 What a, then, is there in being a Jew, *4356*
2Co 11:20 or takes a of you or pushes himself forward *3284*
1Th 4: 6 or take a of him. *4430*
Heb 13:17 for that would be of no a to you. *269*
Jude 1:16 and flatter others for their own a. *6066*

ADVENTURERS (2)
Jdg 9: 4 and Abimelech used it to hire reckless a, 7069
11: 3 where a group of a gathered around him 8199

ADVERSARIES (14) [ADVERSARY]
Dt 32:41 on my a and repay those who hate me. 7640
2Sa 19:22 This day you have become my a! 8477
22:40 you made my a bow at my feet. 7756
Job 27: 7 my a like the unjust! 7756
Ps 18:39 you made my a bow at my feet. 7756
44: 7 you put our a to shame. 8533
44:10 and our a have plundered us. 8533
74:23 Do not ignore the clamor of your a, 7675
89:23 before him and strike down his a. 8533
92:11 My eyes have seen the defeat of my a; 8806
106:11 The waters covered their a; 7640
139:20 your a misuse your name. 6839
Da 4:19 to your enemies and its meaning to your a! 10568
Lk 21:15 that none of your a will be able to resist *512*

ADVERSARY (9) [ADVERSARIES, ADVERSITY]
Dt 32:27 lest the a misunderstand and say, 7640
1Ki 5: 4 and there is no a or disaster. 8477
11:14 LORD raised up against Solomon an a, 8477
11:23 God raised up against Solomon another a, 8477
11:25 Rezon was Israel's a as long 8477
Est 7: 6 "The a and enemy is this vile Haman." 7640
Mt 5:25 a who is taking you to court. *508*
Lk 12:58 As you are going with your a to *508*
18: 3 'Grant me justice against my a.' *508*

ADVERSITIES (KJV) See ANXIETY, CALAMITY, TROUBLE

ADVERSITY (2) [ADVERSARY]
Pr 17:17 and a brother is born for a. 7650
Isa 30:20 Although the Lord gives you the bread of a 7639

ADVERTISE (KJV) See WARN, BRING TO ATTENTION

ADVICE (37) [ADVISE]
Ex 18:19 now to me and *I will* give you *some* a, 3619
Nu 31:16 the ones who followed Balaam's a 1821
2Sa 15:34 by frustrating Ahithophel's a. 6783
16:20 "Give us your a. 6783
16:23 in those days the a Ahithophel gave 3619+6783
16:23 and Absalom regarded all of Ahithophel's a. 6783
17: 6 "Ahithophel has given this a. 1821
17: 7 a Ahithophel *has* given 3619+6783
17:14 "The a *of* Hushai the Arkite is better than 6783
17:14 to frustrate the good a *of* Ahithophel 6783
17:23 When Ahithophel saw that his a had 6783
20:22 to all the people with her wise a, 2683
1Ki 12: 8 rejected the a the elders gave him 3619+6783
12: 9 He asked them, "What *is* your a? 3619
12:13 Rejecting the a given him by the elders, 3619+6783
12:14 he followed the a *of* the young men 6783
12:28 seeking a, the king made two golden calves. 3619
2Ch 10: 8 rejected the a the elders gave him 3619+6783
10: 9 He asked them, "What *is* your a? 3619
10:13 Rejecting the a *of* the elders, 6783
10:14 he followed the a *of* the young men 6783
Est 1:21 and his nobles were pleased with this a, 1821
2: 4 This appealed to the king, 1821
Job 26: 3 What a *you have* offered to one 3619
Pr 1:25 since you ignored all my a and would 6783
1:30 not accept my a and spurned my rebuke, 6783
12: 5 but the a *of* the wicked is deceitful. 9374
12:15 but a wise man listens to a. 6783
13:10 but wisdom is found in *those who* take a. 3619
19:20 Listen to a and accept instruction, 6783
20:18 Make plans by seeking a; 6783
Isa 19:11 of Pharaoh give senseless a. 6783
Eze 11: 2 and giving wicked a in this city. 3619+6783
Da 4:27 O king, be pleased to accept my a: 10422
Ac 27:11 followed the a of the pilot and of the owner *NIG*
27:21 "Men, you should *have* taken my a not *4272*
2Co 8:10 And here is my a about what is best for you *1191*

ADVISABLE (1) [ADVISE]
1Co 16: 4 If *it seems* a for me to go also, *545+1639*

ADVISE (5) [ADVICE, ADVISABLE, ADVISED, ADVISER, ADVISERS]
2Sa 17:11 "So *I* a you: Let all Israel, 3619
1Ki 1:12 *let me* a you how you can save 3619+6783
12: 6 *would* you a me to answer these people?" 3619
2Ch 10: 6 "How *would* you a me 3619
Ac 5:38 Therefore, in the present case *I* a you: *3306*

ADVISED (5) [ADVISE]
2Sa 17:15 "Ahithophel *has* a Absalom and the elders 3619
17:15 but I *have* a them to do so and so. 3619
17:21 Ahithophel *has* a such and such 3619
1Ki 20:23 the officials of the king of Aram a him, 606
Jn 18:14 Caiaphas was the one who *had* a the Jews *5205*

ADVISER (3) [ADVISE]
Ge 26:26 with Ahuzzath his **personal a** and Phicol 5335
1Ki 4: 5 a priest and **personal** a *to* the king; 8291
2Ch 25:16 "Have we appointed you an a to the king? 3446

ADVISERS (20) [ADVISE]
2Sa 8:18 and David's sons were **royal a.** 3913
2Ki 25:19 of the fighting men and five royal **a.** 7156+8011
2Ch 22: 4 after his father's death they became his **a,** 3446
25:17 Amaziah king of Judah **consulted** *his* **a,** 3619
Ezr 7:14 You are sent by the king and his seven a 10325
7:15 that the king and his a have freely given to 10325
7:28 to me before the king and his a and all 3446
8:25 the articles that the king, his a, his officials 3446
Est 6:13 His a and his wife Zeresh said to him, 2682
Job 12:20 the lips of **trusted** a and takes away 586
Pr 11:14 but many a make victory sure. 3446
15:22 but with many a they succeed. 3446
24: 6 and for victory many a. 3446
Jer 52:25 and seven royal **a.** 7156+8011
Da 3: 2 prefects, governors, **a,** treasurers, judges, 10011
3: 3 So the satraps, prefects, governors, **a,** 10011
3:24 to his feet in amazement and asked his **a,** 10196
3:27 and royal a crowded around them. 10196
4:36 My a and nobles sought me out, 10196
6: 7 a and governors have all agreed that 10196

ADVOCATE (1) [ADVOCATING]
Job 16:19 my witness is in heaven; my a is on high. 8446

ADVOCATING (2) [ADVOCATE]
Ac 16:21 by a customs unlawful for us Romans *2859*
17:18 "He seems to be a foreign gods." *2858*

AENEAS (3)
Ac 9:33 There he found a man named A, *138*
9:34 "A," Peter said to him, *138*
9:34 Immediately A got up. *NIG*

AENON (1)
Jn 3:23 John also was baptizing at A near Salim, *143*

AFAR (16) [FAR]
Job 36: 3 I get my knowledge from **a;** 8158
36:25 men gaze on it from **a.** 8158
39:25 He catches the scent of battle from **a,** 8158
39:29 his eyes detect it from **a.** 8158
Ps 138: 6 but the proud he knows from **a.** 5305
139: 2 you perceive my thoughts from **a.** 8158
Pr 31:14 bringing her food from **a.** 5305
Isa 10: 3 when disaster comes from **a?** 5305
30:27 the Name of the LORD comes from **a,** 5305
33:17 and view a land that **stretches a.** 5305
43: 6 from a and my daughters from the ends of 8158
49:12 See, they will come from **a—** 8158
60: 4 your sons come from **a,** 8158
60: 9 bringing your sons from **a,** 8158
Jer 50:26 Come against her from **a.** 7891
Hab 1: 8 their horsemen come from **a.** 8158

AFFAIR (2) [AFFAIRS]
Nu 25:18 when they deceived you in the a *of* Peor 1821
1Sa 22:15 at all about this whole **a."** 1821

AFFAIRS (12) [AFFAIR]
1Ch 26:32 to God and for the a *of* the king. 1821
Ne 11:24 was the king's agent in all a relating to 1821
Ps 112: 5 who conducts his a with justice. 1821
Pr 31:27 She watches over the a *of* her household 2142
Da 3:12 over the a *of* the province of Babylon— 10525
6: 4 in his conduct of **government a,** 10424
1Co 7:32 concerned about the Lord's **a—** *3836*
7:33 But a married man is concerned about **the a** *3836*
7:34 or virgin is concerned about the Lord's **a:** *3836*
7:34 a married woman is concerned about **the a** *3836*
1Ti 5:17 the a of the church well are worthy *NIG*
2Ti 2: 4 as a soldier gets involved in **civilian a** *1050+4548*

AFFECT (1) [AFFECTED, AFFECTS]
Job 35: 6 If you sin, how *does that* a him? 7188

AFFECTED (3) [AFFECT]
Lev 13:50 and isolate the **a article** for seven days. 5596
13:55 After the **a article** has been washed, 5596
13:55 the mildew has a one side or the other. 928

AFFECTION (6)
Dt 7: 7 The LORD *did* not **set** *his* a on you 3137
10:15 the LORD **set** *his* a on your forefathers 3137
Eze 24:21 delight of your eyes, the object of your **a.** 5883
2Co 6:12 We are not withholding our a from you, *5073*
7:15 And his a for you is all the greater *5073*
Php 1: 8 for all of you with the a of Christ Jesus. *5073*

AFFECTS (1) [AFFECT]
Job 35: 8 Your wickedness a only a man 4200

AFFINITY (KJV) See ALLIANCE, ALLIED BY MARRIAGE, INTERMARRY

AFFIRM (1) [REAFFIRM]
1Ti 1: 7 about or what *they* so **confidently a.** *1331*

AFFIXING (1) [FIX]
Ne 9:38 our Levites and our priests *are* a their **seals** 3159

AFFLICT (6) [AFFLICTED, AFFLICTING, AFFLICTION, AFFLICTIONS]
Lev 26:24 be hostile toward you and *will* a you 5782
Dt 28:27 The LORD *will* a you with the boils 5782
28:28 The LORD *will* a you with madness, 5782
28:35 The LORD *will* a your knees and legs 5782
Ps 55:19 will hear them and a them— 6700
Na 1:12 [O Judah,] *I will* a you no more. 6700

AFFLICTED (45) [AFFLICT]
Dt 29:22 with which the LORD *has* a it. 2703
Jos 24: 5 and *I* a the Egyptians by what I did there, 5597
Jdg 2:18 under those who oppressed and a them. 1895
Ru 1:21 The LORD *has* a me; 6700
1Sa 5: 6 upon them and a them with tumors. 5782
5: 9 *He* a the people of the city, 5782
5:12 Those who did not die **were** a with tumors, 5782
1Ki 8:35 from their sin because *you have* a them, 6700
2Ki 15: 5 The LORD a the king *with* leprosy until 5595
17:20 *he* a them and gave them into the hands 6700
2Ch 6:26 from their sin because *you have* a them, 6700
16:12 of his reign Asa *was* **a with a disease** 2688
21:18 the LORD a Jehoram with 5597
26:20 because the LORD *had* a him. 5595
Job 2: 7 and a Job with painful sores from the soles 5782
30:11 that God has unstrung my bow and a me, 6700
36: 6 the wicked alive but gives the a their rights. 6714
Ps 9:12 he does not ignore the cry of the **a.** 6705
9:18 nor the hope of the a ever perish. 6705+6714
10:17 You hear, O LORD, the desire of the **a;** 6705
22:24 or disdained the suffering of the a *one;* 6714
25:16 for I am lonely and **a.** 6714
34: 2 let the a hear and rejoice. 6705
72: 2 your a *ones* with justice. 6714
72: 4 He will defend the a *among* the people 6714
72:12 the a who have no one to help. 6714
74:19 the lives of your a *people* forever. 6714
76: 9 to save all the a *of* the land. 6705
88:15 From my youth I have been a and close 6714
90:15 for as many days as *you have* a us, 6700
102: T A prayer of an a *man.* 6714
116:10 I believed; therefore I said, "I *am* greatly **a."** 6700
119:67 Before *I was* a I went astray, 6700
119:71 *to* **be a** so that I might learn your decrees. 6700
119:75 and *in* faithfulness *you have* a me. 6700
Isa 1: 5 your whole heart **a.** 1868
14:32 and in her his a people will find refuge." 6714
49:13 and will have compassion on his a *ones.* 6714
51:21 Therefore hear this, you a *one,* 6714
53: 4 smitten by him, and **a.** 6700
53: 7 He was oppressed and **a,** 6700
54:11 "O a city, lashed by storms and 6714
Jer 14:19 Why *have you* a us so that we cannot 5782
Na 1:12 Although *I have* a you, [O Judah,] 6700
Zec 11:11 and so the a *of* the flock 6714

AFFLICTING (1) [AFFLICT]
2Sa 24:16 and said to the angel who *was* a the people, 8845

AFFLICTION (21) [AFFLICT]
Dt 16: 3 of **a,** because you left Egypt in haste— 6715
Job 10:15 I am full of shame and drowned in my **a.** 6715
36: 8 held fast by cords of **a,** 6715
36:15 he speaks to them in their **a.** 4316
36:21 which you seem to prefer to **a.** 6715
Ps 25:18 Look upon my a and my distress 6715
31: 7 for you saw my a and knew the anguish 6715
31:10 my strength fails because of my **a,** 6411
107:17 and **suffered** a because of their iniquities. 6700
107:41 of their a and increased their families 6715
119:92 I would have perished in my **a.** 6715
Ecc 5:17 with great frustration, a and anger. 2716
Isa 30:20 of **a,** your teachers will be hidden no more; 4316
48:10 I have tested you in the furnace of **a.** 6715
La 1: 3 After a and harsh labor, 6715
1: 7 In the days of her a 6715
1: 9 "Look, O LORD, on my **a,** 6715
3: 1 I am the man who has seen a by the rod 6715
3:19 I remember my a and my wandering, 6715
3:33 not willingly **bring** a or grief to the children 6700
Ro 12:12 Be joyful in hope, patient *in* **a,** *2568*

AFFLICTIONS (5) [AFFLICT]
Lev 26:21 I will multiply your a seven times over, 4804
1Ki 8:38 each one aware of the a *of* his own heart, 5596
2Ch 6:29 each one aware of his a and pains, 5596
Col 1:24 in regard to Christ's **a,** *2568*
Rev 2: 9 I know your a and your poverty— *2568*

AFFORD (9) [AFFORDED]
Lev 5: 7 " 'If he cannot a a lamb, 1896+3338+5595
5:11 he cannot a two doves 3338+5952
12: 8 If she cannot a a lamb, 1896+3338+5162
14:21 "If, however, he is poor and cannot a these, 3338+5952
14:22 which he *can* **a,** 3338+5952
14:30 which the person *can* **a,** 3338+5952
14:32 an infectious skin disease and who cannot a 3338+5952
27: 8 what the man making the vow *can* **a.** 3338+5952
Nu 6:21 in addition to whatever else he *can* **a.** 3338+5952

AFFORDED (2) [AFFORD]
Ro 7: 8 the opportunity **a by** the commandment, *1328*
7:11 the opportunity **a by** the commandment, *1328*

AFFRIGHT (KJV) See TERRIFY

AFIRE (1) [FIRE]
Dt 32:22 and its harvests and **set a** the foundations of 4265

AFLAME (1) [FLAME]
Isa 13: 8 at each other, their faces **a.** 4258

AFOOT (1) [FOOT]
Ac 14: 5 There was a **plot** a among the Gentiles *3995*

AFOREHAND (KJV) See BEFOREHAND

AFORETHOUGHT (5) [THINK]
Nu 35:20 If anyone with **malice** a shoves another 8534
Dt 4:42 if he had unintentionally killed his neighbor without **malice a.** 4946+8533+8997+9453
19: 4 one who kills his neighbor unintentionally, without **malice a.** 4946+8533+8997+9453
19: 6 he did it to his neighbor without **malice a.** 4946+8533+8997+9453
Jos 20: 5 and without **malice a.** 4946+8533+8997+9453

AFRAID (211) [FEAR]
Ge 3:10 and *I was* a because I was naked; so I hid." 3707
15: 1 *"Do* not *be* **a,** Abram. 3707
18:15 Sarah *was* **a,** so she lied and said, 3707
19:30 for *he was* a to stay in Zoar. 3707
20: 8 they *were* very much **a.** 3707
21:17 *Do* not *be* **a;** 3707
26: 7 "She is my sister," because *he was* a to say, 3707
26:24 *Do* not *be* **a,** for I am with you; 3707
28:17 *He was* a and said, 3707
31:31 Jacob answered Laban, *"I was* **a,** 3707
32:11 for I *am* a he will come and attack me, 3707
35:17 "Don't *be* **a,** for you have another son." 3707
42: 4 *he was* a that harm might come to him. 606[S]
43:23 "Don't *be* **a.** 3707
46: 3 *"Do* not *be* a to go down to Egypt, 3707
50:19 But Joseph said to them, "Don't *be* **a.** 3707
50:21 So then, don't *be* **a.** 3707
Ex 2:14 Then Moses *was* a and thought, 3707
3: 6 because *he was* a to look at God. 3707
14:13 Moses answered the people, *"Do* not *be* **a.** 3707
20:20 Moses said to the people, *"Do* not *be* **a.** 3707
34:30 and *they were* a to come near him. 3707
Lev 26: 6 down and no *one will* **make** you **a.** 3006
Nu 12: 8 not a to speak against my servant Moses?" 3707
14: 9 And *do* not *be* a *of* the people of the land, 3707
14: 9 *Do* not *be* a *of* them." 3707
21:34 *"Do* not *be* a *of* him, 3707
Dt 1:17 *Do* not *be* a of any man, 1593
1:21 *Do* not *be* **a;** do not be discouraged." 3707
1:29 *do* not *be* a of them. 3707
2: 4 *They will be* a of you, but be very careful. 3707
3: 2 *"Do* not *be* a *of* him, 3707
3:22 *Do* not *be* a *of* them; 3707
5: 5 because *you were* a of the fire and did 3707
7:18 But *do* not *be* a of them; 3707
13:11 Then all Israel will hear and *be* **a,** 3707
17:13 All the people will hear and *be* **a,** 3707
18:22 *Do* not *be* a of him. 1593
19:20 of the people will hear of this and *be* **a,** 3707
20: 1 *do* not *be* a of them, 3707
20: 3 Do not be fainthearted or **a;** 3707
20: 8 "Is any man a or fainthearted? 3710
21:21 All Israel will hear of it and *be* **a.** 3707
31: 6 *Do* not *be* a or terrified because of them, 3707
31: 8 *Do* not *be* **a;** do not be discouraged." 3707

Jos 8: 1 the LORD said to Joshua, "Do not be a; 3707
10: 8 "Do not be a of them; 3707
10:25 Joshua said to them, "Do not be a; 3707
11: 6 "Do not be a of them, 3707
Jdg 4:18 Don't be a." 3707
6:23 Do not be a. 3707
6:27 because he was a of his family and the men 3707
7:10 If you are a to attack, 3710
8:20 because he was only a boy and was a. 3707
9:21 because he was a of his brother Abimelech. NIH
Ru 3:11 And now, my daughter, don't be a. 3707
1Sa 3:15 He was a to tell Eli the vision, 3707
4: 7 the Philistines were a. 3707
7: 7 they were a because of the Philistines. 3707
12:20 "Do not be a," Samuel replied. 3707
15:24 I was a of the people and so I gave in 3707
18:12 Saul was a of David, 3707
18:15 he was a of him. 1593
18:29 Saul became still more a of him, 3707
21:12 and was very much a of Achish king 3707
22:23 Stay with me; don't be a; 3707
23: 3 "Here in Judah we are a. 3710
23:17 "Don't be a," he said. 3707
28: 5 Saul saw the Philistine army, he was a; 3707
28:13 The king said to her, "Don't be a. 3707
2Sa 1:14 "Why were you not a to lift your hand 3707
3:11 because he was a of him. 3707
6: 9 David was a of the LORD that day 3707
9: 7 "Don't be a," David said to him, 3707
10:19 So the Arameans were a to help 3707
12:18 David's servants were a to tell him that 3707
13:28 Don't be a. 3707
14:15 because the people have made me a. 3707
1Ki 1:51 "Adonijah is a of King Solomon 3707
17:13 Elijah said to her, "Don't be a. 3707
19: 3 Elijah was a and ran for his life. 3707
2Ki 1:15 do not be a of him." 3707
6:16 "Don't be a," the prophet answered. 3707
19: 6 Do not be a of what you have heard— 3707
25:24 "Do not be a of the Babylonian officials," 3707
1Ch 13:12 David was a of God that day and asked, 3707
21:30 because he was a of the sword of the angel 1286
22:13 Do not be a or discouraged. 3707
28:20 Do not be a or discouraged, 3707
2Ch 20:15 'Do not be a or discouraged because 3707
20:17 Do not be a; do not be discouraged. 3707
32: 7 not be a or discouraged because of the king 3707
32:18 make them a in order to capture the city. 987
Ezr 4: 4 and make them a to go on building. 987
Ne 2: 2 I was very much a, 3707
4:14 "Don't be a of them. 3707
6:16 all the surrounding nations were a 3707
Est 9: 2 of all the other nationalities were a of them. 5877+6584+7065
Job 6:21 you see something dreadful and are a. 3707
11:19 with no one to make you a, 3006
39:22 He laughs at fear, a of nothing; 3169
Ps 27: 1 of whom shall I be a? 7064
56: 3 When I am a, I will trust in you. 3707
56: 4 I will not be a. 3707
56:11 I will not be a. 3707
118: 6 The LORD is with me; I will not be a. 3707
Pr 3:24 you will not be a; 7064
Ecc 9: 2 so with those who are a to take them. 3707
12: 5 when men are a of heights and of dangers in 3707
Isa 7: 4 'Be careful, keep calm and don't be a. 3707
10:24 do not be a of the Assyrians, 3707
12: 2 I will trust and not be a. 7064
17: 2 with no one to make them a. 3006
20: 5 in Cush and boasted in Egypt will be a 3169
37: 6 Do not be a of what you have heard— 3707
40: 9 lift it up, do not be a; 3707
41:14 Do not be a, O worm Jacob, O little Israel, 3707
43: 5 Do not be a, for I am with you; 3707
44: 2 Do not be a, O Jacob, my servant, 3707
44: 8 Do not tremble, do not be a. 3724
54: 4 "Do not be a; you will not suffer shame. 3707
Jer 1: 8 Do not be a of them, 3707
23: 4 and they will no longer be a or terrified, 3707
30:10 and no one will make him a. 3006
38:19 "I am a of the Jews who have gone over to 1793
40: 9 "Do not be a to serve the Babylonians," 3707
41:18 They were a of them because Ishmael son 3707
42:11 Do not be a of the king of Babylon, 3707
42:11 Do not be a of him, declares the LORD, 3707
46:27 and no one will make him a. 3006
51:46 or be a when rumors are heard in the land; 3707
Eze 2: 6 do not be a of them or their words. 3707
2: 6 Do not be a, 3707
2: 6 be a of what they say or terrified by them, 3707
3: 9 Do not be a of them or terrified by them, 3707
34:28 and no one will make them a. 3006
39:26 in their land with no one to make them a. 3006
Da 1:10 "I am a of my lord the king, 3710
4: 5 I had a dream that made me a. 10167
10:12 Then he continued, "Do not be a, Daniel. 3707
10:19 "Do not be a, O man highly esteemed," 3707
Joel 2:21 Be not a, O land; be glad and rejoice. 3707
2:22 Be not a, O wild animals, 3707
Jnh 1: 5 All the sailors were a and each cried out 3707
Mic 4: 4 and no one will make them a, 3006
7:17 the LORD our God and will be a of you. 3707
Zep 3:13 lie down and no one will make them a." 3006
Zec 8:13 Do not be a, but let your hands be strong." 3707
8:15 Do not be a. 3707
Mt 1:20 not be a to take Mary home as your wife, 5828
2:22 he was a to go there. 5828
Mt 8:26 "You of little faith, why are you so a?" 1264
10:26 "So do not be a of them. 5828
10:28 Do not be a of those who kill the body 5828
10:28 be a of the One who can destroy both soul 5828
10:31 So don't be a; 5828
14: 5 but he was a of the people, 5828
14:27 Don't be a." 5828
14:30 But when he saw the wind, he was a and, 5828
17: 7 "Don't be a." 5828
21:26 we are a of the people, 5828
21:46 but they were a of the crowd because 5828
25:25 So I was a and went out 5828
28: 4 so a of him that they shook and became 5832
28: 5 The angel said to the women, "Do not be a, 5828
28: 8 a yet filled with joy, 3552+5832
28:10 Then Jesus said to them, "Do not be a. 5828
Mk 4:40 "Why are you so a? 1264
5:15 and they were a. 5828
5:36 "Don't be a; just believe." 5828
6:50 Don't be a." 5828
9:32 not understand what he meant and were a 5828
10:32 while those who followed were a. 5828
12:12 But they were a of the crowd; 5828
16: 8 because they were a. 5828
Lk 1:13 "Do not be a, Zechariah; 5828
1:30 But the angel said to her, "Do not be a, 5828
2:10 But the angel said to them, "Do not be a. 5828
5:10 Then Jesus said to Simon, "Don't be a; 5828
8:35 and they were a. 5828
8:50 Jesus said to Jairus, "Don't be a; 5828
9:34 and they were a as they entered the cloud. 5828
9:45 and they were a to ask him about it. 5828
12: 4 do not be a of those who kill the body and 5828
12: 7 of your head are all numbered. Don't be a; 5828
12:32 "Do not be a, little flock, 5828
19:21 I was a of you, 5828
20:19 But they were a of the people. 5828
22: 2 for they were a of the people. 5828
Jn 6:20 But he said to them, "It is I; don't be a." 5828
9:22 His parents said this because they were a of 5828
12:15 "Do not be a, O Daughter of Zion; 5828
14:27 be troubled and do not be a. 1262
19: 8 he was even more a, 5828
Ac 9:26 but they were all a of him, 5828
18: 9 "Do not be a; 5828
23:10 the commander was a Paul would be torn 5828
24:25 Felix was a and said, 1873
27:24 'Do not be a, Paul. 5828
Ro 11:20 Do not be arrogant, but be a. 5828
13: 4 But if you do wrong, be a, 5828
2Co 11: 3 But I am a that just as Eve was deceived 5828
12:20 For I am a that when I come I may 5828
12:21 I am a that when I come again NIG
Gal 2:12 because he was a of those who belonged 5828
1Th 3: 5 I was a that in some way NIG
Heb 11:23 and they were not a of the king's edict. 5828
13: 6 I will not be a. 5828
2Pe 2:10 not a to slander celestial beings; 5554
Rev 1:17 "Do not be a. 5828
2:10 not be a of what you are about to suffer. 5828

AFRESH (KJV) See ALL OVER AGAIN

AFTER (723) [AFTERWARD]

Ge 3:24 A he drove the man out, 2256
4:17 and he named it a his son Enoch. 3869
5: 4 A Seth was born, 339
5: 7 And a he became the father of Enosh, 339
5:10 And a he became the father of Kenan, 339
5:13 And a he became the father of Mahalalel, 339
5:16 And a he became the father of Jared, 339
5:19 And a he became the father of Enoch, 339
5:22 And a he became the father of Methuselah, 339
5:26 And a he became the father of Lamech, 339
5:30 A Noah was born, 339
5:32 A Noah was 500 years old, 2256
7:10 And a the seven days the floodwaters came 4200
8: 6 A forty days Noah opened 4946+7891
8:19 came out of the ark, one kind a another. 2157+4200+5476
9: 9 with you and with your descendants a you 339
9:28 A the flood Noah lived 350 years. 339
10: 1 who themselves had sons a the flood. 339
10:32 the nations spread out over the earth a 339
11:10 Two years a the flood, 339
11:11 And a he became the father of Arphaxad, 339
11:13 And a he became the father of Shelah, 339
11:15 And a he became the father of Eber, 339
11:17 And a he became the father of Peleg, 339
11:19 And a he became the father of Reu, 339
11:21 And a he became the father of Serug, 339
11:23 And a he became the father of Nahor, 339
11:25 And a he became the father of Terah, 339
11:26 A Terah had lived 70 years, 2256
13:14 to Abram a Lot had parted from him, 339
14:17 A Abram returned from defeating 339
15: 1 A this, the word of the LORD came 339
16: 3 So a Abram had been living 4946+7891
17: 7 and you and your descendants a you for 339
17: 7 and the God of your descendants a you. 339
17: 8 to you and your descendants a you; 339
17: 9 you and your descendants a you for 339
17:10 with you and your descendants a you, 339
17:19 for his descendants a him. 339
18:12 "A I am worn out and my master is old, 339
Ge 18:19 and his household a him to keep the way of 339
21:32 A the treaty had been made at Beersheba, 2256
24:19 A she had given him a drink, she said, 3983
24:67 Isaac was comforted a his mother's death. 339
25:11 A Abraham's death, God blessed his son 339
25:26 A this, his brother came out, 339
26:18 which the Philistines had stopped up a 339
27:30 A Isaac finished blessing him 889+3869
29:14 A Jacob had stayed with him for 2256
30:25 A Rachel gave birth to Joseph, 889+3869
31:33 A he came out of Leah's tent, 2256
31:54 A they had eaten, 2256
32:23 A he had sent them across the stream, 2256
33:18 A Jacob came from Paddan Aram, 928
35: 9 A Jacob returned from Paddan Aram, 928
35:12 to your descendants a you." 339
37:17 So Joseph went a his brothers 339
37:27 a all, he is our brother, 3954
38:12 A a long time Judah's wife, 2256
38:19 A she left, she took off her veil and put 2256
38:23 A all, I did send her this young goat, 2180
39: 7 and a a while his master's wife took notice 339+465+1821+2021+2021
39:10 And though she spoke to Joseph day a day, AIT
40: 4 A they had been in custody for some time, 2256
41: 3 A them, seven other cows, ugly and gaunt, 339
41: 6 A them, seven other heads 339
41:19 A them, seven other cows came up— 339
41:21 But even a they ate them, 2256
41:23 A them, seven other heads sprouted— 339
42:25 A this was done for them, 2256
43:31 A he had washed his face, he came out and, 2256
44: 4 "Go a those men at once, 339
47: 7 A Jacob blessed Pharaoh, 2256
48: 4 to your descendants a you.' 339
48: 6 Any children born to you a them will 339
50:14 A burying his father, 339
50:26 And a they embalmed him, 2256
Ex 2:11 One day, a Moses had grown up, 2256
3:20 A that, he will let you go. 339
7:25 Seven days passed a the LORD struck 339
8:12 A Moses and Aaron left Pharaoh, 2256
10: 5 They will devour what little you have left a 4946
10:15 They devoured all that was left a the hail— NIH
11: 1 A that, he will let you go from here, 339
11: 8 A that I will leave." 339
12:44 Any slave you have bought may eat of it a 255
13:10 at the appointed time year a year. 2025
13:11 "A the LORD brings you into the land of 3954
13:20 A leaving Succoth they camped at Etham 2256
14:10 and there were the Egyptians, marching a 339
14:17 of the Egyptians so that they will go in a 339
16: 1 on the fifteenth day of the second month a NIH
18: 2 A Moses had sent away his wife Zipporah, 339
19: 1 the third month a the Israelites left Egypt— NIH
19: 2 A they set out from Rephidim, 2256
19:14 A Moses had gone down the mountain to 2256
21:21 to be punished if the slave gets up a a day NIH
22: 3 but if it happens a sunrise, AIT
28:41 A you put these clothes 2256
29:26 A you take the breast of the ram 2256
36: 3 to bring freewill offerings morning a 928
Lev 13: 7 But if the rash does spread in his skin a 339
13:35 But if the itch does spread in the skin a 339
13:55 A the affected article has been washed, 339
13:56 the mildew has faded a 339
14: 8 A this he may come into the camp, 339
14:19 A that, the priest shall slaughter 339
14:36 A this the priest is to go in and inspect 339
14:43 in the house a the stones have been torn out 339
14:48 not spread a the house has been plastered, 339
15:28 and a that she will be ceremonially clean. 339
16: 1 The LORD spoke to Moses a the death of 339
22: 7 and a that he may eat the sacred offerings, 339
23:11 to wave it on the day a the Sabbath. 4740
23:15 " 'From the day a the Sabbath, 4740
23:16 up to the day a the seventh Sabbath, 4740
23:39 a you have gathered the crops of the land, 928
24: 8 the LORD regularly, Sabbath a Sabbath, 928+928+2021+2021+3427+3427+8701+8701
25:29 the right of redemption a full year a 6330
25:48 of redemption a he has sold himself. 339
26:18 " 'If a all this you will not listen to me, 6330
27:18 But if he dedicates his field a the Jubilee, 339
Nu 1: 1 of the second year a the Israelites came out 4200
4:15 "A Aaron and his sons have finished 339+4027
5:18 A the priest has had the woman stand 2256
5:26 a that, he is to have the woman drink 339
6:19 " 'A the Nazirite has shaved off the hair 339
6:20 A that, the Nazirite may drink wine. 339
7:88 the dedication of the altar a it was anointed. 339
8:12 "A the Levites lay their hands on the heads 2256
8:15 "A you have purified the Levites 339+4027
8:22 A that, the Levites came to do their work at 339
9: 1 the second year a they came out of Egypt. 4200
12:14 a that she can be brought back." 339
12:16 A that, the people left Hazeroth 339
15: 2 'A you enter the land I am giving you as 3954
15:39 and not prostitute yourselves by going a 339
19: 7 A that, the priest must wash his clothes 2256
21:32 A Moses had sent spies to Jazer, 2256
26: 1 A the plague the LORD said to Moses 339
27:13 A you have seen it, 2256
30: 6 "If she marries a she makes a vow or 2256
30: 6 "If she marries after she makes a vow or a NIH
30:15 he nullifies them some time a he hears 339
31: 2 A that, you will be gathered 339

Nu 32: 9 A they went up to the Valley of Eshcol 2256
32:42 and called it Nobah a himself. 928
33: 3 the **day a** the Passover. 4740
33:38 of the fortieth year a the Israelites came out 4200
35:28 only a the death of the high priest 339
Dt 1: 4 This was a he had defeated Sihon king of 339
1: 8 and to their descendants a them." 339
3:14 it was named a him, 6584
3:20 **A that,** each of you may go back to 2256
4: 9 to your children and to their children a NIH
4:25 A you have had children and grandchildren 3954
4:37 and chose their descendants a them, 339
4:40 with you and your children a you and 339
6: 2 and their children a them may fear NIH
9: 4 A the LORD your God has driven them out 928
12:25 with you and your children a you, 339
12:28 with you and your children a you, 339
12:30 and a they have been destroyed before you, 339
16:13 the Feast of Tabernacles for seven days a 928
21:13 A she has lived in your house 339+4027
22:13 If a man takes a wife and, a lying with her, 2256
24: 2 **and if a** she leaves his house she becomes 2256
24: 4 to marry her again a she has been defiled. 339
24: 9 to Miriam along the way a you came out 928
28:29 **day a day** you will be oppressed 2021+3427+3972
28:32 watching for them **day a day,** 2021+3427+3972
31:24 A Moses finished writing in a book 3869
31:27 how much more will you rebel a I die! 339
31:29 For I know that a my death you are sure 339
Jos 1: 1 A the death of Moses the servant of 339
1:15 **A that,** you may go back 2256
2: 5 Go a them quickly. 339
3: 2 A three days the officers went 4946+7895
5: 4 in the desert on the way a leaving Egypt. 928
5: 8 a the whole nation had been circumcised, 889+3869
5:11 The **day a** the Passover, that very day, 4740
5:12 the **day a** they ate this food from the land; 4740
7:25 and a they had stoned the rest, 2256
8:17 in Ai or Bethel who did not go a Israel. 339
9:16 Three days a they made the treaty with 339
10: 9 A an all-night march from Gilgal, 2256
14:15 (Hebron used to be called Kiriath Arba a NIH
18: 6 A you have written descriptions of 2256
19:47 settled in Leshem and named it Dan a 3869+9005
23: 1 A a long time had passed and 339
24:20 a he has been good to you." 339
24:29 A these things, Joshua son of Nun, 339
Jdg 1: 1 A the death of Joshua, 339
1: 9 **A that,** the men of Judah went down 339
2: 6 A Joshua had dismissed the Israelites, 2256
2:10 A that whole generation had been gathered 1685+2256
3:18 A Ehud had presented the tribute, 889+3869
3:22 Even the handle sank in a the blade, 339
3:24 A he had gone, 2256
3:31 A Ehud came Shamgar son of Anath, 339
4: 1 A Ehud died, the Israelites once again did evil in the eyes of the LORD 2256
5:15 rushing a him into the valley. 928+8079
7:19 **just a** they had changed the guard. 421
9:22 A Abimelech had governed Israel three years, 2256
9:27 A they had gone out into the fields 2256
10: 1 **A the time of** Abimelech a man of Issachar, 339
11:39 A the two months, 4946+7891
12: 8 A him, Ibzan of Bethlehem led Israel. 339
12:11 A him, Elon the Zebulunite led Israel 339
12:13 A him, Abdon son of Hillel, from Pirathon, 339
16:16 With such nagging she prodded him **day a day** 2021+3427+3972
16:22 the hair on his head began to grow again a it had been shaved. 889+3869
18:23 As they shouted a them, 448
18:29 named it Dan a their forefather Dan, 928+9005
19: 2 A she had been there four months, 2256
19:21 A they had washed their feet, 2256
20: 5 During the night the men of Gibeah came a 6584
20:45 They kept pressing a the Benjamites as far 339
Ru 1: 4 A they had lived there about ten years, 2256
2: 9 and follow along a the girls. 339
2:18 and gave her what she had left over a 4946
3:10 You have not run a the younger men, 339
1Sa 1: 3 Year a year this man went up 2025
1: 7 This went on year a year. 928
1:22 "A the boy is weaned, 6330
1:24 A he was weaned, 889+3869
5: 1 A the Philistines had captured the ark 2256
5: 9 But a they had moved it, 339
7: 2 of Israel mourned and sought a the LORD. 339
8: 3 They turned aside a dishonest gain 339
9:25 A they came down from the high place to 2256
10: 5 "A that you will go to Gibeah of God, 339
10:13 A Saul stopped prophesying, 2256
12: 8 "A Jacob entered Egypt, 889+3869
12:21 Do not turn away a useless idols. 339
13:14 the LORD has sought out a man a 3869
14:12 "Climb up a me; 339
14:31 a the Israelites had struck down 2256
14:36 "Let us go down a the Philistines by night 339
14:37 "Shall I go down a the Philistines? 339
14:47 A Saul had assumed rule over Israel, 2256
17:35 I went a it, struck it and rescued the sheep 339
17:51 A he killed him, 2256
18: 1 A David had finished talking with Saul, 3869
18: 6 When the men were returning home a 928
20: 5 until the evening of the **day a tomorrow.** 8958
1Sa 20:12 by this time the **day a** tomorrow! 8958
20:19 The **day a tomorrow,** toward evening, 8992
20:37 Jonathan called out a him, 339
20:41 A the boy had gone, NIH
23:14 **Day a day** Saul searched for him, 2021+3427+3972
24: 1 A Saul returned from pursuing 889+3869
31: 2 The Philistines **pressed hard a** Saul 1815
2Sa 1: 1 A the death of Saul, David returned 339
1:10 that a he had fallen he could not survive. 339
3:26 Joab then left David and sent messengers a 339
4: 7 A they stabbed and killed him, 2256
5:13 A he left Hebron, 339
6:18 A he had finished sacrificing 2256
7: 1 A the king was settled in his palace and 3954
8:13 And David became famous a he returned 928
10:15 A the Arameans saw 2256
11: 8 and a gift from the king was sent a him. 339
11:27 A the time of mourning was over, 2256
12:15 A Nathan had gone home, 2256
12:20 A he had washed, 2256
12:28 and it will be named a me." 6584
13: 4 look so haggard morning a morning? 928
13:17 of here and bolt the door a her." 339
13:18 and bolted the door a her. 339
13:38 A Absalom fled and went to Geshur, 2256
17:21 A the men had gone, 339
18:18 He named the pillar a himself, 6584
20:13 A Amasa had been removed from the road, 889+3869
21:12 where the Philistines had hung them a 928+3427
21:14 A that, God answered prayer in behalf of 339
23: 4 the brightness a rain that brings the grass 4946
24: 5 A crossing the Jordan, 2256
24: 8 A they had gone through the entire land, 2256
24:10 David was conscience-stricken a 339+4027
1Ki 1: 6 also very handsome and was born **next a** 339
1:13 "Surely Solomon your son shall be king a 339
1:17 'Solomon your son shall be king a me, 339
1:20 on the throne of my lord the king a him. 339
1:24 declared that Adonijah shall be king a you, 339
1:27 on the throne of my lord the king a him?" 339
1:30 Solomon your son shall be king a me, 339
1:40 And all the people went up a him, 339
2:22 **a all,** he is my older brother— 3954
3:18 The third day a my child was born, 4200
5:11 to do this for Hiram year a year. 928
6: 1 In the four hundred and eightieth year a 4200
8: 9 the Israelites a they came out of Egypt. 928
9:24 A Pharaoh's daughter had come up from 421
10:25 Year a year, everyone who came 928+1821
11: 2 because they will surely turn your hearts a 339
11: 4 his wives turned his heart a other gods, 339
12:16 **Look a** your own house, O David!" 8011
12:28 A seeking advice, the king made two golden calves. 2256
13:14 and rode a the man of God. 339
13:31 A burying him, he said to his sons, 339
13:33 Even a this, Jeroboam did 339
16:24 calling it Samaria, a Shemer, 6584
18: 1 A a long time, in the third year, 2256
19:11 A the wind there was an earthquake, 339
19:12 A the earthquake came a fire, 339
19:12 And a the fire came a gentle whisper. 339
19:20 Elisha then left his oxen and ran a Elijah. 339
20:36 **And a** the man went away, 2256
21:26 He behaved in the vilest manner by going a 339
22:46 male shrine prostitutes who remained there **even a** the reign of his father Asa. 928
2Ki 1: 1 A Ahab's death, Moab rebelled 339
3: 5 But a Ahab died, the king of Moab rebelled 3869
3: 9 A a roundabout march of seven days, 2256
4:20 A the servant had lifted him up 2256
5:19 A Naaman had traveled some distance, 2256
5:20 I will run a him and get something 339
5:21 So Gehazi hurried a Naaman. 339
6: 8 A conferring with his officers, he said, 2256
6:20 A they entered the city, Elisha said, 3869
6:23 **and a** they had finished eating 2256
7:14 the king sent them a the Aramean army. 339
10:15 A he left there, 2256
14: 5 A the kingdom was firmly in his grasp, 889+3869
14:17 for fifteen years a the death of Jehoash son 339
14:19 but they sent men a him to Lachish 339
14:22 to Judah a Amaziah rested with his fathers. 339
18: 5 either before him or a him. 339
23:25 Neither before nor a Josiah was there 339
1Ch 2:24 A Hezron died in Caleb Ephrathah, 339
6:31 of the LORD a the ark came to rest there. 4946
8: 8 Sons were born to Shaharaim in Moab a 4946
10: 2 The Philistines pressed hard a Saul 339
12:19 a consultation, their rulers sent him away. 928
12:22 Day a day men came to help David, 928
15: 1 A David had constructed buildings 2256
16: 2 A David had finished sacrificing 2256
16:23 proclaim his salvation day a day. 448
17: 1 A David was settled in his palace, 889+3869
19:16 A the Arameans saw that they had been 2256
2Ch 1:12 before you ever had and none a 339
2:17 a the census his father David had taken; 339
5:10 the Israelites a they came out of Egypt. 928
9:24 Year a year, everyone who came 928+1821
10:16 **Look a** your own house, O David!" 8011
12: 1 A Rehoboam's position 3869
20: 1 A this, the Moabites and Ammonites 339
20:21 A consulting the people, 2256
20:23 A they finished slaughtering the men 3869
2Ch 20:36 A these were built at Ezion Geber, 2256
21:18 A all this, the LORD afflicted Jehoram 339
22: 4 as the house of Ahab had done, for a 339
24:17 A the death of Jehoiada, 339
25: 3 A the kingdom was firmly in his control 889+3869
25:17 A Amaziah king of Judah 2256
25:25 for fifteen years a the death of Jehoash son 339
25:27 but they sent men a him to Lachish 339
26: 2 to Judah a Amaziah rested with his fathers. 339
26:16 But a Uzziah became powerful, 3869
31: 1 A they had destroyed all of them, 6330
32: 1 A all that Hezekiah had so faithfully done, 339
35:14 **A this,** they made preparations 339
35:20 A all this, when Josiah had set the temple 339
Ezr 3: 5 A that, they presented the regular burnt offerings, 339
3: 8 the second year a their arrival at the house 4200
7: 1 A these things, during the reign 339
9: 1 A these things had been done, 3869
9:10 now, O our God, what can we say a this? 339
Ne 2:11 **and a** staying there three days 2256
4:14 A I looked things over, 2256
7: 1 A the wall had been rebuilt 889+3869
8:18 Day a day, from the first day to the last, 928
9:28 in your compassion you delivered them **time a time.** 6961+8041
Est 3: 1 A these events, King Xerxes honored Haman son of Hammedatha, 339
3: 4 Day a day they spoke to him but he refused 2256
Job 3: 1 A this, Job opened his mouth and cursed 339
5: 5 and the thirsty **pant** *a* his wealth. AIT
10: 6 and probe a my sin— 4200
13:25 *Will you* **chase** a dry chaff? 8103
19:26 And a my skin has been destroyed, 339
21: 3 and a I have spoken, mock on. 339
21:33 all men follow a him, 339
29:22 A I had spoken, they spoke no more; 339
31: 5 in falsehood or my foot has hurried a 6584
37: 4 A that comes the sound of his roar; 339
37:21 the skies a the wind has swept them clean. 2256
42: 7 A the LORD had said these things to Job, 339
42:10 A Job had prayed for his friends, 928
42:16 A this, Job lived a hundred and forty years; 339
Ps 16: 4 of those will increase *who* **run a** other gods. 4554
19: 2 Day a day they pour forth speech; 4200
19: 2 night a night they display knowledge. 4200
49:11 though they had named lands a themselves. 928
51: T the prophet Nathan came to him a 889+3869
61: 8 to your name and fulfill my vows **day** *a* AIT
68:25 a them the musicians; 339
78:38 **Time a time** he restrained his anger and did 8049
96: 2 proclaim his salvation day a day. 4200
Pr 1:19 all who **go a ill-gotten gain;** 1298+1299
6:25 **lust** in your heart a 2773
8:30 I was filled with delight **day** *a* day, AIT
20: 7 blessed are his children a him. 339
24:27 **a that,** build your house. 339
27:18 *he who* **looks** a his master will be honored. 9068
29: 1 A man who remains stiff-necked a NIH
Ecc 1:14 a **chasing** a the wind. 8296
1:17 too, is a **chasing** a the wind. 8301
2:11 a **chasing** a the wind; 8296
2:17 a **chasing** a the wind. 8296
2:18 to the one who comes a me. 339
2:26 a **chasing** a the wind. 8296
3:22 to see what will happen a him? 339
4: 4 a **chasing** a the wind. 8296
4: 6 with toil and **chasing** a the wind. 8296
4:16 a **chasing** a the wind. 8301
6: 9 a **chasing** a the wind. 8296
6:12 under the sun a he is gone? 339
10:14 can tell him what will happen a him? 339+4946
11: 1 for a many days you will find it again. 928
12: 2 and the clouds return a the rain; 339
Isa 1:23 they all love bribes and **chase a** gifts. 8103
5:11 in the morning *to* **run a** their drinks, 8103
21: 8 And the lookout shouted, **"Day a day,** 3429+9458
24:13 gleanings are left a the grape harvest. 561+3983
24:22 up in prison and be punished a many days. 4946
28:19 morning a morning, by day and by night, 928
38: 9 of Hezekiah king of Judah a his illness 928
43:10 nor will there be one a me. 339
53:11 A the suffering of his soul, 4946
58: 2 For **day** *a* day they seek me out; AIT
62:12 and you will be called **Sought A,** 2011
64:12 A all this, O LORD, 6584
Jer 2:23 I have not run a the Baals'? 339
2:25 I love foreign gods, and I must go a them.' 339
3: 7 I thought that a she had done all this 339
3:15 I will give you shepherds a my own heart, 3869
7:25 until now, **day a day,** again 3427
12:15 But a I uproot them, 339
13:10 of their hearts and go a other gods to serve 339
16:16 A that I will send for many hunters, 339
21: 7 A that, declares the LORD, 339
24: 1 A Jehoiachin son of Jehoiakim king 339
25:26 near and far, one a the other— 448
25:26 And a all of them, 339
28:12 **Shortly** a the prophet Hananiah had broken the yoke off the neck of the prophet 339
29: 2 (This was a King Jehoiachin and 339
31:19 A I strayed, I repented; 339
31:19 a I came to understand, I beat my breast. 339
31:33 with the house of Israel a that time," 339
32:16 "A I had given the deed of purchase 339
32:18 into the laps of their children a them. 339
32:39 and the good of their children a them. 339

Jer 34: 8 the LORD a King Zedekiah had made 339
34:14 A he has served you six years, 2256
36:13 A Micaiah told them everything he had heard 2256
36:20 A they put the scroll in the room 2256
36:27 A the king burned the scroll containing 339
37:11 A the Babylonian army had withdrawn 928
39:12 "Take him and **look a** him; 6524+6584+8492
40: 1 the LORD a Nebuzaradan commander of 339
40: 4 if you like, and I *will* **look a** you 6524+6584+8492
41: 4 The day a Gedaliah's assassination, 9108
41:16 from Ishmael son of Nethaniah a 339
45: 1 a Baruch had written on a scroll 928
La 1: 3 A affliction and harsh labor, 4946
Eze 4: 6 "A you have finished this, lie down again, 2256
6: 9 which *have* **lusted a** their idols. 339+2388
15: 4 And a it is thrown on the fire as fuel and NIH
16:28 **and even a** that, you still were not satisfied. 2256
16:34 **runs a** you **for** your **favors.** 339+2388
20:24 and their eyes [lusted] a their fathers' idols. 339
20:30 the way your fathers did and **lust a** 339+2388
23: 5 *she* **lusted a** her lovers, the Assyrians 6311+6584
23: 7 with all the idols of everyone *she* **lusted a.** 6311
23:12 *She* too **lusted a** the Assyrians— 448+6311
23:16 *she* **lusted a** them and sent messengers 6311+6584
23:17 A she had been defiled by them, 2256
23:20 There *she* **lusted a** her lovers, 6311+6584
23:30 because you **lusted a** the nations 339+2388
34:11 for my sheep and **look a** them. 1329
34:12 As a shepherd **looks a** his scattered flock 1333
34:12 so *will I* **look a** my sheep. 1329
38: 8 A many days you will be called to arms. 4946
40: 1 the fourteenth year a the fall of the city— 339
44:10 from me a their idols must bear 339
44:26 A he is cleansed, he must wait seven days. 339
46:12 he shall go out, and a he has gone out, 339
48:31 the city will be named a the tribes of Israel. 6584
Da 1: 5 a that they were to enter the king's service. 4946+7921
2:39 "A you, another kingdom will rise, 10092
4: 8 a the name of my god, 10341
7: 6 "A that, I looked, and there 10092
7: 7 "A that, in my vision at night I looked, 10092
7:24 A them another king will arise, 10021
8: 1 a the one that had already appeared to me. 339
9:26 A the sixty-two 'sevens,' 339
11: 4 A he has appeared, 3869
11: 6 A some years, they will become allies. 4200+7891
11:13 and a several years, 4200+7891
11:19 **A this,** he will turn back toward 2256
11:23 A coming to an agreement with him, 4946
Hos 1: 8 A she had weaned Lo-Ruhamah, 2256
2: 5 She said, 'I will go a my lovers, 339
2: 7 *She will* **chase a** her lovers but 8103
2:13 and went a her lovers, but me she forgot," 339
6: 2 A two days he will revive us; 4946
Am 7: 1 He was preparing swarms of locusts a 339
Jnh 1: 3 A paying the fare, 2256
Zec 2: 8 "A he has honored me and has sent me 339
14:16 go up year a year to worship the King, 928+1896+4946
Mt 1:12 A the exile to Babylon: *3552*
1:20 But *a* he *had* **considered** this, *AIT*
2: 1 *A* Jesus *was* **born** in Bethlehem in Judea, *AIT*
2: 9 *A* they *had* **heard** the king, *AIT*
2:19 *A* Herod **died,** an angel of *AIT*
3:11 **a** me will come one who is more powerful *3958*
4: 2 *A* **fasting** forty days and forty nights, *AIT*
6:32 For the pagans **run a** all these things, *2118*
9:25 A the crowd had been put outside, *4021*
11: 1 A Jesus had finished instructing his twelve disciples, *4021*
14:23 *A he had* **dismissed** them, *AIT*
15:23 for she keeps crying out a us." *3957*
15:39 *A* Jesus *had* **sent** the crowd **away,** *AIT*
16:24 "If anyone would come a me, *3958*
17: 1 A six days Jesus took with him Peter, *3552*
17:24 *A* Jesus and his disciples **arrived** *AIT*
21:32 And even *a* you **saw** this, *AIT*
24:29 "Immediately a the distress of those days *3552*
25:19 "A a long time the master *3552*
25:36 I was sick and *you* **looked a** me, *2170*
25:43 and in prison and *you did* not **look a** me.' *2170*
26:22 began to say to him **one a the other,** *1651+1667*
26:32 But a I have risen, I will go ahead of you *3552*
26:73 A a little while, those standing there went *3552*
27:31 A they had mocked him, *4021*
27:34 but *a* **tasting** it, he refused to drink it. *AIT*
27:53 and a Jesus' resurrection they went into *3552*
27:62 The next day, the one a Preparation Day, *3552*
27:63 'A three days I will rise again.' *3552*
28: 1 **A the Sabbath,** at dawn on the first day of the week, *4067+4879*
Mk 1: 7 "A me will come one more powerful than I, *3958*
1:14 A John was put in prison, *3552*
1:32 That evening a sunset the people brought *4021*
2: 4 *a* **digging through** it, *AIT*
5:40 *A* he **put** them all **out,** *AIT*
6:46 *A* **leaving** them, he went up on *AIT*
7:17 A he had left the crowd and entered *4021*
7:33 *A he* **took** him aside, **away from** *AIT*
8:31 be killed and a three days rise again. *3552*
8:34 "If anyone would come a me, *3958*
9: 2 A six days Jesus took Peter, *3552*
9:28 *A* Jesus *had* **gone** indoors, *AIT*
9:31 and a three days he will rise." *3552*
14:28 But a I have risen, I will go ahead of you *3552*
14:70 A a little while, those standing near said *3552*
Mk 16: 2 on the first day of the week, **just a sunrise,** *422+2463+3836*
16:14 those who had seen him *a he had* **risen.** *AIT*
16:19 A the Lord Jesus had spoken to them, *3552*
Lk 1:24 A this his wife Elizabeth became pregnant *3552*
1:59 to name him a his father Zechariah, *2093*
2:36 with her husband seven years a *608*
2:43 *A* the Feast *was* **over,** *AIT*
2:46 A three days they found him in *3552*
5:27 A this, Jesus went out and saw *3552*
5:39 no one *a* **drinking** old wine wants the new, *AIT*
7:24 *A* John's messengers **left,** *AIT*
8: 1 **A this,** Jesus traveled about *1877+2759+3836*
8: 4 to Jesus **from** town **a town,** *2848*
9:23 "If anyone would come a me, *3958*
9:28 About eight days a Jesus said this, *3552*
10: 1 A this the Lord appointed seventy-two *3552*
10:35 '**Look a** him,' he said, 'and when I return, *2150*
12: 4 be afraid of those who kill the body and a *3552*
12: 5 Fear him who, a the killing of the body, *3552*
12:30 For the pagan world **runs a** all such things, *2118*
15: 4 in the open country and go a the lost sheep *2093*
15:13 "Not long a that, the younger son *3552*
15:14 *A he had* **spent** everything, *AIT*
17: 7 a servant plowing or **looking a the sheep.** *4477*
17: 8 a that you may eat and drink'? *3552*
17:23 *Do* not **go running off a** them. *599+1503+3593*
19:14 and sent a delegation a him to say, *3958*
19:28 *A* Jesus *had* **said** this, he went on ahead, *AIT*
22:17 *A* **taking** the cup, he gave thanks and said, *AIT*
22:20 a the supper he took the cup, saying, *3552*
Jn 1:15 'He who comes a me has surpassed me *3958*
1:16 of his grace we have all received one blessing a another. *505*
1:27 He is the one who comes a me, *3958*
1:30 'A man who comes a me has surpassed me *3958*
2:10 and then the cheaper wine a *4020*
2:12 A this he went down to Capernaum *3552*
2:22 A he was raised from the dead, *4021*
3:22 A this, Jesus and his disciples went out into *3552*
4:43 A the two days he left for Galilee. *3552*
6: 1 **Some time a** this, Jesus crossed to *3552*
6:14 *A* the people **saw** the miraculous sign *AIT*
6:23 *a* the Lord *had* **given thanks.** *AIT*
7: 1 A this, Jesus went around in Galilee, *3552*
7:10 a his brothers had left for the Feast, *6055*
11:11 A he had said this, he went on to tell them, *3552*
11:28 And *a she had* **said** this, *AIT*
12:16 Only a Jesus was glorified did they realize *4021+5538*
12:19 how the whole world has gone a him!" *3958*
12:37 *a* Jesus *had* **done** all these miraculous signs *AIT*
13: 5 **A that,** he poured water into a basin *1663*
13:21 *A he had* **said** this, Jesus was troubled *AIT*
14: 9 a I have been among you such a long time? *NIG*
16:16 and **then a** a little while you will see me." *4099*
16:17 and **then a** a little while you will see me,' *4099*
16:19 and **then a** a little while you will see me'? *4099*
17: 1 A Jesus said this, he looked toward heaven *NIG*
20:20 *A he* **said** this, he showed them his hands *AIT*
21:14 to his disciples *a he was* **raised** from *AIT*
Ac 1: 2 *a* **giving instructions** through *AIT*
1: 3 A his suffering, he showed himself *3552*
1: 9 *A he* **said** this, he was taken up *AIT*
4:21 *A* **further threats** they let them go. *AIT*
4:31 *A* they **prayed,** the place *AIT*
5: 4 And *a it was* **sold,** *AIT*
5:37 A him, Judas the Galilean appeared in *3552*
5:42 **Day a day,** in the temple courts and *2465+4246*
7: 4 A the death of his father, *3552*
7: 5 and his descendants a him would possess *3552*
7: 8 and circumcised him eight days a his birth. *NIG*
7:14 **A this,** Joseph sent for his father Jacob *1254*
7:30 "A forty years **had passed,** *4444*
9:19 and *a* **taking** some food, *AIT*
9:23 A many days had gone by, *6055*
10:37 beginning in Galilee a the baptism *3552*
10:41 by us who ate and drank with him a he rose *3552*
12: 4 *A* **arresting** him, he put him in prison, *AIT*
12: 4 to bring him out for public trial a *3552*
12:19 *A* Herod *had* **a thorough search made for** *AIT*
13: 3 *a they had* **fasted** and **prayed,** *AIT*
13:15 A the reading from the Law and *3552*
13:20 "A this, God gave them judges until *3552*
13:22 *A* **removing** Saul, he made David their king. *AIT*
13:22 'I have found David son of Jesse a man a *2848*
13:25 No, but he is coming a me, *3552*
14:20 *a* the disciples *had* **gathered around** *AIT*
14:24 *A* **going through** Pisidia, *AIT*
15: 7 A much discussion, Peter got up *NIG*
15:16 " 'A this I will return *3552*
15:33 *A* **spending** some time there, *AIT*
16:10 A Paul had seen the vision, *6055*
16:23 *A they had been* severely **flogged,** *AIT*
16:40 *A* Paul and Silas **came out** *AIT*
18: 1 A this, Paul left Athens and went *3552*
18:23 *A* **spending** some time in Antioch, *AIT*
19: 4 the people to believe in the one coming a *3552*
19:21 A all this had happened, *6055*
19:21 "A I have been there," he said, *3552*
19:41 *A he had* **said** this, *AIT*
20: 1 for the disciples and, *a* **encouraging** them, *AIT*
20: 6 But we sailed from Philippi a the Feast *3552*
20:11 *A* **talking** until daylight, he left. *AIT*
20:15 The **day a** that we crossed over to Samos, *2283*
20:29 I know that a I leave, *3552*
20:30 the truth in order to draw away disciples a *3958*
Ac 21: 1 *A we had* **torn** *ourselves* **away** *AIT*
21: 3 *A* **sighting** Cyprus and passing to the south *AIT*
21: 6 *A* **saying good-by** to each other, *AIT*
21:10 *A we had* **been there** a number of days *AIT*
21:15 A this, we got ready and went up *3552*
24:17 "A an absence of several years, *1328*
25: 1 Three days a arriving in the province, *3552*
25: 6 *A* **spending** eight or ten days with them, *AIT*
25:12 *A* Festus *had* **conferred with** *AIT*
27: 9 because by now *it was* a the Fast. *4216*
27:21 *A* the men *had* **gone** *AIT*
27:35 *A he* **said** this, he took some bread *AIT*
28: 6 but *a* **waiting** a long time *AIT*
28: 8 Paul went in to see him and, *a* **prayer,** *AIT*
28:11 A three months we put out to sea in a ship *3552*
28:25 *a* Paul *had* **made** this final **statement:** *AIT*
Ro 4:10 Was it **a he was circumcised,** *1639+1877+4364*
4:10 It was not **a,** but before! *NIG*
11:24 **A all,** if you were cut out of an olive tree *1142*
15:24 **a** I have enjoyed your company for a while. *4754*
15:28 So *a I have* **completed** this task *AIT*
1Co 3: 5 What, **a all,** is Apollos? *4036*
9:27 so that *a I have* **preached** to others, *AIT*
11:25 same way, a supper he took the cup, *3552+3836*
15: 6 **A that,** he appeared to more *2083*
15:24 the Father a he has destroyed all dominion, *4020*
15:46 but the natural, **and a** that the spiritual. *2083*
16: 5 A I go through Macedonia, *4020*
2Co 12:14 **A all,** children should not have to save *1142*
Gal 1:18 Then a three years, I went up to Jerusalem *3552*
3: 3 *A* **beginning** with the Spirit, *AIT*
Eph 5:29 **A all,** no one ever hated his own body, *1142*
6:13 and *a you have* **done** everything, to stand. *AIT*
Col 4:16 A this letter has been read to you, *4020*
1Th 4:17 **A that,** we who are still alive *2083*
Tit 3:10 A that, have nothing to do with him. *3552*
Heb 1: 3 *A he had* **provided** purification for sins, *AIT*
6:15 And so *a* **waiting patiently,** *AIT*
7:27 not need to offer sacrifices **day a day,** *2465+2848*
7:28 but the oath, which came a the law, *3552*
8:10 with the house of Israel a that time, *3552*
9:27 and a that to face judgment, *3552*
10: 1 same sacrifices repeated endlessly **year a year,** *1929+2848*
10:11 **Day a day** every priest stands *2465+2848*
10:16 the covenant I will make with them a *3552*
10:26 If we deliberately keep on sinning a *3552+3836*
10:32 *a you had* **received** the **light,** *AIT*
11:23 for three months *a he was* **born,** *AIT*
11:30 *a* the people *had* **marched around** *AIT*
Jas 1:15 *a* desire *has* **conceived,** it gives birth to sin; *AIT*
1:24 *a* **looking at** himself, goes away *AIT*
1:27 *to* **look a** orphans and widows *2170*
1Pe 5:10 *a you have* **suffered** a little while, *AIT*
2Pe 1:15 that a my departure you will always be able *3552*
2: 8 living among them day a day, *1666*
Rev 4: 1 A this I looked, and there before me *3552*
4: 1 and I will show you what must take place a *3552*
7: 1 A this I saw four angels standing at *3552*
7: 9 A this I looked and there before me was *3552*
11:11 But a the three and a half days a breath *3552*
15: 5 A this I looked and in heaven the temple, *3552*
18: 1 A this I saw another angel coming down *3552*
19: 1 A this I heard what sounded like the roar of *3552*
20: 3 A that, he must be set free for a short time. *3552*

AFTERBIRTH (1)

Dt 28:57 the a from her womb and 8953

AFTERNOON (5)

Jdg 19: 8 Wait till **a!"** 2021+3427+5742
Lk 9:12 **Late in** the a the Twelve came *806+2465+3111*
Ac 3: 1 the time of prayer—at **three in the a,** *1888*
10: 3 at about **three in the a** he had a vision. *1888+2465+3836+6052*
10:30 at **three in the a.** *1888*

AFTERWARD (36) [AFTER]

Ge 6: 4 in those days—and also **a—** 339+4027
15:14 and a they will come out 339+4027
23:19 A Abraham buried his wife Sarah in 339+4027
41:27 ugly cows that came up a are seven years, 339
45:15 A his brothers talked with him. 339+4027
Ex 5: 1 A Moses and Aaron went to Pharaoh 339
32: 6 A they sat down to eat and drink and got up 2256
34:32 A all the Israelites came near him, 339+4027
Lev 16:26 **a** he may come into the camp. 339+4027
16:28 **a** he may come into the camp. 339+4026
Jos 8:34 **A,** Joshua read all the words of the law 339+4027
Jdg 7:11 **A,** you will be encouraged to attack 339
19: 6 A the girl's father said, 2256
1Sa 9:13 **a,** those who are invited will eat. 339+4027
24: 5 **A,** David was conscience-stricken 339+4027
1Ki 14:28 **and a** they returned them to the guardroom. 2256
20:22 **A,** the prophet came to the king of Israel 2256
2Ki 4: 5 She left him **and a** shut the door behind her 2256
2Ch 12:11 **and a** they returned them to the guardroom. 2256
33:14 A he rebuilt the outer wall of the City 339+4027
Est 6:12 A Mordecai returned to the king's gate. 2256
Ps 73:24 and a you will take me into glory. 339
Ecc 9: 3 and a they join the dead. 339
Isa 1:26 A you will be called the City 339+4027
Jer 34:11 But a they changed their minds 339+4027
49: 6 "Yet **a,** I will restore the fortunes of 339+4027
Eze 20:39 But a you will surely listen to me 339

Hos 3: 5 **A** the Israelites will return and seek 339
Joel 2:28 **a,** I will pour out my Spirit on all people. 339+4027
Mt 15:37 **A** the disciples picked up seven basketfuls *2779*
Mk 8: 8 **A** the disciples picked up seven basketfuls *2779*
16:12 **A** Jesus appeared in a different form to two *3552+4047*
Lk 7:11 **Soon a,** Jesus went to a town called Nain, *1877+2009+3836*
Jn 21: 1 **A** Jesus appeared again to his disciples *3552+4047*
Ac 7: 7 **a** they will come out of that country *3552+4047*
Heb 12:17 **A,** as you know, when he wanted *3575*

AGABUS (2)

Ac 11:28 One of them, named **A,** *13*
21:10 a prophet named **A** came down from Judea. *13*

AGAG (7) [AGAGITE]

Nu 24: 7 "Their king will be greater than **A;** 97
1Sa 15: 8 He took **A** king of the Amalekites alive, 97
15: 9 the army spared **A** and the best of the sheep 97
15:20 and brought back **A** their king. 97
15:32 "Bring me **A** king of the Amalekites." 97
15:32 **A** came to him confidently, thinking, 97
15:33 And Samuel put **A** to death before 97

AGAGITE (5) [AGAG]

Est 3: 1 the **A,** elevating him and giving him a seat 98
3:10 the **A,** the enemy of the Jews. 98
8: 3 an end to the evil plan of Haman the **A,** 98
8: 5 of Hammedatha, the **A,** devised and wrote 98
9:24 For Haman son of Hammedatha, the **A,** 98

AGAIN (459)

Ge 4:25 Adam lay with his wife **a,** 6388
8:10 He waited seven more days and **a** sent out 3578
8:12 and sent the dove out **a,** 6388
8:21 "Never **a** will I curse the ground 3578+6388
8:21 And never **a** will I destroy all living creatures, 3578+6388
9:11 Never **a** will all life be cut off by the waters 6388
9:11 never **a** will there be a flood to destroy 6388
9:15 Never **a** will the waters become a flood 6388
18:27 Then Abraham spoke up **a:** NIH
18:29 **Once a** he spoke to him, 3578+6388
19:34 Let's get him to drink wine **a** tonight, 1685
19:35 **A** he was not aware of it when she lay 2256
20:17 so they could have children **a,** NIH
23:12 **A** Abraham bowed down before the people 2256
24:16 filled her jar **and** came up *a.* AIT
29:33 She conceived **a,** and when she gave birth 6388
29:34 **A** she conceived, and when she gave birth 6388
29:35 She conceived **a,** and when she gave birth 6388
30: 7 Rachel's servant Bilhah conceived **a** 6388
30:19 Leah conceived **a** and bore Jacob 6388
35: 9 God appeared to him **a** and blessed him. 6388
35:21 Israel moved on **a** and pitched his tent 2256
38: 4 She conceived **a** and gave birth to a son 6388
38:19 and put on her widow's clothes **a.** 2256
38:26 And he did not sleep with her **a.** 3578+6388
40:21 *he once a* **put** the cup into Pharaoh's hand, AIT
41: 5 He fell asleep **a** and had a second dream: 2256
42:24 but then turned back and spoke to them **a.** NIH
43: 3 not see my face **a** unless your brother is NIH
43: 5 not see my face **a** unless your brother is NIH
44:23 you will not see my face **a.'** 3578
46: 4 and I will surely bring you back **a.** 1685
48:11 "I never expected to see your face **a,** NIH
Ex 8:29 that Pharaoh does not act deceitfully **a** by 3578
9:34 and thunder had stopped, he sinned **a:** 3578
10:14 nor will there ever be **a.** 339
10:28 Make sure you do not appear before me **a!** 3578
10:29 "I will never appear before you **a."** 3578+6388
11: 6 has ever been or *ever will be* **a.** 3578
14:13 The Egyptians you see today you will never see **a.** 3578+6388
30: 8 He must burn incense **a** when he lights 2256
Lev 13: 6 to examine him **a,** and if the sore has faded 9108
13: 7 he must appear before the priest **a.** 9108
13:58 must be washed **a,** and it will be clean." 9108
27:15 and the house *will a* **become** his. AIT
27:19 and the field *will a* **become** his. AIT
Nu 11: 4 and **a** the Israelites started wailing and said, 8740
11:25 they prophesied, but *they did* not **do** *so* **a.** 3578
18: 5 that wrath will not fall on the Israelites **a.** 6388
20:20 **A** they answered: "You may 2256
22:25 So he beat her **a.** 3578
32:15 he *will* **a** leave all this people in 3578+6388
Dt 9:18 **once a** I fell prostrate before 2021+3869+8037
9:19 But **a** the LORD listened to me. 928+1685+2021+2021+2085+7193
13:11 among you will do such an evil thing **a.** 3578
17:13 and will not be contemptuous **a.** 6388
17:16 "You are not to go back that way **a."** 3578+6388
19:20 and never **a** will such an evil thing be done 3578+6388
24: 4 to marry her **a** after she has been defiled. 8740
24:21 **go over the vines a.** 339+6618
28:68 a journey I said you *should* never **make a.** 3578+6388
30: 3 and gather you **a** from all the nations 8740
30: 8 You will **a** obey the LORD 8740
30: 9 The LORD will **a** delight in you 8740
Jos 5: 2 and circumcise the Israelites **a."** 8740+9108
24:10 **blessed** you **a and again,** 1385+1385
24:10 **blessed** you **again and a,** 1385+1385
Jdg 3:12 **Once a** the Israelites did evil in the eyes of 3578
3:15 **A** the Israelites cried out to the LORD, 2256
4: 1 the Israelites **once a** did evil in the eyes of 3578
6: 1 **A** the Israelites did evil in the eyes of 2256
8:28 the Israelites and did not raise its head **a.** 3578
8:33 the Israelites **a** prostituted themselves to 8740
9:37 But Gaal spoke up **a:** 3578+6388
10: 6 **A** the Israelites did evil in the eyes of 3578
13: 1 **A** the Israelites did evil in the eyes of 3578
13: 8 let the man of God you sent to us come **a** 6388
13: 9 and the angel of God came **a** to the woman 6388
13:21 of the LORD *did* not show himself **a** 3578+6388
16:14 **A** she called to him, "Samson, 2256
16:22 But the hair on his head **began** to grow *a* AIT
20:22 and **a** took up their positions 3578
20:23 up **a** to battle against the Benjamites, 3578
20:28 **a** to battle with Benjamin our brother, 3578+6388
Ru 1:14 At this they wept **a.** 6388
1Sa 3: 6 **A** the LORD called, "Samuel!" 3578+6388
7:13 and did not invade Israelite territory **a.** 3578+6388
9: 8 The servant answered him **a.** 3578
15:35 he did not go to see Saul **a,** 3578
20:27 David's place was empty **a.** 2256
23: 4 **Once a** David inquired of the LORD, 3578+6388
23:12 **A** David asked, "Will the citizens 2256
26:21 I will not try to harm you **a.** 6388
2Sa 2:22 **A** Abner warned Asahel, "Stop chasing me! 3578+6388
3:34 And all the people wept over him **a.** 3578
6: 1 David **a** brought together out 6388
12:23 Can I bring him back **a?** 6388
14:10 and he will not bother you **a."** 3578+6388
15:25 and let me see it and his dwelling place **a.** NIH
18:22 Ahimaaz son of Zadok **a** said to Joab, 3578+6388
20:10 Without being stabbed **a,** Amasa died. 9101
21:15 **Once a** there was a battle between 6388
21:17 "Never **a** will you go out with us to battle, 6388
24: 1 **A** the anger of the LORD burned 3578
1Ki 10:10 Never **a** were so many spices brought in 6388
12:24 the word of the LORD and went home **a,** 8740
12:27 they will **a give** their **allegiance** 4213+8740
18:34 **"Do** *it* **a,"** he said, and they did it again. 9101
18:34 "Do it again," he said, and *they* **did** *it* **a.** 9101
18:37 that you are turning their hearts back **a."** NIH
19: 6 He ate and drank and then lay down **a.** 8740
20: 5 The messengers **came a** and said, 8740
20:22 the king of Aram will attack you **a."** NIH
2Ki 2:21 Never **a** will it cause death or make 6388
5:17 servant will never **a** make burnt offerings 6388
6:10 **Time and a** Elisha warned the king, 285+2256+4202+4202+9109
19: 9 So *he* **a** sent messengers to Hezekiah 8740
21: 8 not **a** make the feet of the Israelites wander 3578
24: 7 not march out from his own country **a,** 3578+6388
1Ch 7:23 Then he lay with his wife **a,** NIH
14:14 so David inquired of God **a,** 6388
2Ch 19: 4 and he went out **a** among the people 8740
28:17 The Edomites had **a** come 6388
33: 8 not **a** make the feet of the Israelites leave 3578
36:15 through his messengers **a and again,** 2256+8899+8938
36:15 through his messengers **again and a,** 2256+8899+8938
Ezr 9:14 *Shall we* **a** break your commands 8740
Ne 9:28 *they* **a** did what was evil in your sight. 8740
9:28 And when they cried out to you **a,** 8740
13:21 If *you* **do** *this* **a,** I will lay hands on you." 9101
Est 1:19 that Vashti is never **a** to enter the presence NIH
5: 6 the king **a** asked Esther, 2256
7: 2 the king **a** asked, "Queen Esther, 1685
8: 3 Esther **a** pleaded with the king, 3578
Job 7: 7 my eyes will never see happiness **a.** 8740
7:10 He will never come to his house **a;** 6388
10: 9 **turn** me to dust **a?** 8740
10:16 a lion and **a** display your awesome power 8740
14: 7 If it is cut down, it will sprout **a,** 6388
14:14 If a man dies, *will he* **live a?** 2649
16:14 **A and again** *he* **bursts** upon me 7287+7288+7288
16:14 **Again and a** *he* **bursts** upon me 7287+7288+7288
17:10 "But come on, all of you, **try a!** 8740
20: 9 The eye that saw him *will* not see him **a;** 3578
34:32 if I have done wrong, *I will* not **do** so **a.'** 3578
41: 8 the struggle and never **do** *it* **a!** 3578
42:10 the LORD **made** him **prosperous a** 8654+8740
Ps 3: 5 I wake **a,** because the LORD sustains me. NIH
28: 5 down and never **build** them **up** *a.* AIT
39:13 that *I may* **rejoice** *a* before I depart AIT
71:20 many and bitter, you will restore my life **a;** 8740
71:20 of the earth *you will* **a** bring me up. 8740
71:21 and comfort me **once a.** 6015
77: 7 Will he never show his favor **a?** 3578+6388
78:34 *they* eagerly **turned** *to* him **a.** 8740
78:41 **A and again** they put God to the test; 8740
78:41 **Again and a** they put God to the test; 8740
85: 4 **Restore** us **a,** O God our Savior, 8740
85: 6 Will you not revive us **a,** 8740
94:15 Judgment *will* **a** be founded 8740
104: 9 never **a** will they cover the earth. 8740
Pr 19:19 *you will have to* **do** it **a.** 3578+6388
24:16 he rises **a,** but the wicked are brought 2256
Ecc 1: 7 there they return **a.** 8740
1: 9 What has been *will* **be** *a,* AIT
1: 9 what has been done *will* **be done** *a;* AIT
4: 1 **A** I looked and saw all the oppression 8740
4: 7 **A** I saw something meaningless under 8740
9: 6 never **a** will they have a part in anything 6388
11: 1 for after many days *you will* **find** it *a.* AIT
SS 5: 3 must I put it on **a?** NIH
5: 3 must I soil them **a?** NIH
Isa 6:13 *it will* **a** be laid waste. 8740
7:10 **A** the LORD spoke to Ahaz, 3578
8: 5 The LORD spoke to me **a:** 3578+6388
14: 1 **once a** he will choose Israel 6388
14:20 wicked will never be mentioned **a.** 4200+6409
21:12 and come **back** yet **a."** 8740
24:20 never to rise **a.** 3578
34:10 **ever** pass through it **a.** 4200+5905+5905
38:11 I said, "I will not **a** see the LORD, NIH
43:17 and they lay there, never *to* **rise** *a,* AIT
51:22 you will never drink **a.** 6388
52: 1 and defiled will not enter you **a.** 3578+6388
54: 9 the waters of Noah would never **a** cover 6388
54: 9 never to rebuke you **a.** NIH
60:20 Your sun will never set **a,** 6388
62: 8 "Never **a** will I give your grain as food 6388
62: 8 and never **a** will foreigners drink NIH
65:20 "Never **a** will there be in it 6388
Jer 1:13 The word of the LORD came to me **a:** 9108
2: 9 "Therefore I bring charges against you **a,"** 6388
3: 1 should he return to her **a?** 6388
6: 9 **pass** your hand over the branches **a,** 8740
7:13 I spoke to you **a and again,** 8899
7:13 I spoke to you **again and a,** 8899
7:25 **a and again** I sent you my servants 8899
7:25 **again and a** I sent you my servants 8899
11: 7 I warned them **a and again,** saying, 8899
11: 7 I warned them **again and a,** saying, 8899
12:15 *I will* **a** have compassion 8740
22:10 nor see his native land **a.** NIH
22:12 he will not see this land **a."** 6388
23:36 not mention 'the oracle of the LORD' **a,** 6388
25: 3 and I have spoken to you **a and again,** 8899
25: 3 and I have spoken to you **again and a,** 8899
25: 4 the prophets to you **a and again,** 8899
25: 4 the prophets to you **again and a,** 8899
26: 5 whom I have sent to you **a and again** 8899
26: 5 whom I have sent to you **again and a** 8899
29:19 "words that I sent to them **a and again** 8899
29:19 "words that I sent to them **again and a** 8899
30:10 Jacob *will* **a** have peace and security, 8740
31: 4 I will build you up **a** and you will 6388
31: 4 **A** you will take up your tambourines 6388
31: 5 **A** you will plant vineyards on the hills 6388
31:23 in its towns will **once a** use these words: 6388
31:40 The city will never **a** be uprooted 6388
32:15 fields and vineyards will **a** be bought 6388
32:33 though I taught them **a and again,** 8899
32:33 though I taught them **again and a,** 8899
33:12 in all its towns there will **a** be pastures 6388
33:13 flocks will **a** pass under the hand of 6388
34:11 and enslaved them **a.** NIH
34:16 to become your slaves **a.** NIH
35:14 But I have spoken to you **a and again,** 8899
35:14 But I have spoken to you **again and a,** 8899
35:15 **A and again** I sent all my servants 8899
35:15 **Again and a** I sent all my servants 8899
42:18 you will never see this place **a.'** 6388
44: 4 **A and again** I sent my servants 8899
44: 4 **Again and a** I sent my servants 8899
44:26 in Egypt will **ever a** invoke my name 6388
46:27 Jacob *will* **a** have peace and security, 8740
50:39 It will never **a** be inhabited or lived in 6388
La 3: 3 against me **a and again,** 8740
3: 3 against me **again and a,** 8740
Eze 3:20 **"A,** when a righteous man turns 2256
4: 6 "After you have finished this, lie down **a,** 2256
5: 4 **A,** take a few of these and throw them into 6388
5: 9 before and will never do **a.** 6388
8:13 **A,** he said, "You will see them doing things 2256
11:17 the land of Israel **a.'** NIH
16:63 be ashamed and never **a** open your mouth 6388
17:14 brought low, unable *to* **rise a,** 5951
21: 5 it will not return **a.'** 6388
22:23 **A** the word of the LORD came to me: 2256
24:13 you will not be clean **a** until my wrath 6388
26:21 but you will never **a** be found, 6388
29:15 of kingdoms and will never **a** exalt itself 6388
29:15 that it will **never** *a* rule over the nations. AIT
36:12 *you will* never **a** deprive them 3578+6388
36:16 **A** the word of the LORD came to me: 2256
36:37 Once **a** I will yield to the plea of the house 6388
37:22 and they will never **a** be two nations or 6388
43: 7 of Israel will never **a** defile my holy name— 6388
Da 10:18 **A** the one who looked like 3578
11:29 the South **a,** but this time the outcome will 8740
Hos 1: 6 Gomer conceived **a** and gave birth to 6388
3: 1 "Go, show your love to your wife **a,** 6388
12: 9 I will make you live in tents **a,** 6388
14: 3 We will never **a** say 'Our gods' 6388
14: 7 Men will dwell **a** in his shade. 8740
Joel 2:19 never **a** will I make you an object of scorn 6388
2:26 **never a** will my people be shamed. 4200+4202+6409
2:27 **never a** will my people be shamed. 4200+4202+6409
3:17 never **a** will foreigners invade her. 6388
Am 5: 2 never to rise **a,** deserted in her own land, 3578
8:14 they will fall, never to rise **a."** 6388
9:15 never **a** to be uprooted from 6388
Jnh 2: 4 *I will* look **a** toward your holy temple.' 3578
Mic 1: 7 of prostitutes *they will* **a be used."** 8740
7:19 *You will* **a** have compassion on us; 8740

Zep 3:11 Never a will you be haughty 3578+6388
3:15 never a will you fear any harm. 6388
Zec 1:17 'My towns will a overflow with prosperity, 6388
1:17 and the LORD will a comfort Zion 6388
2:12 the holy land and will a choose Jerusalem. 6388
4:12 A I asked him, 9108
5: 1 I looked a—and there before me 8740
6: 1 I looked up a—and there before me 8740
7: 8 word of the LORD came a to Zechariah: NIH
8: 1 A the word of the LORD Almighty came 2256
8: 4 "Once a men and women 6388
8:15 "so now I have determined to do good a 8740
8:18 A the word of the LORD Almighty came 2256
9: 8 Never a will an oppressor overrun my people, 6388
11:15 Take a the equipment of a foolish shepherd. 6388
14:11 never a will it be destroyed. 6388
Mal 3:18 And you will a see the distinction between 8740
Mt 4: 8 A, the devil took him to 4099
5:13 how can it be made salty a? NIG
5:22 A, anyone who says to his brother, 'Raca,' 1254
5:33 "A, you have heard that it was said to 4099
12:29 "Or a, how can anyone enter NIG
13:44 When a man found it, he hid it a, NIG
13:45 "A, the kingdom of heaven is like 4099
13:47 "Once a, the kingdom of heaven is like 4099
18:19 "A, I tell you that if two of you 4099
19:24 A I tell you, it is easier for a camel to go 4099
20: 5 "He went out a about the sixth hour and 4099
21:19 "May you never bear fruit a!" 172+1650+3836
22: 1 Jesus spoke to them a in parables, saying: 4099
23:39 you will not see me a until you say, 608+785
24:21 never to be equaled a. 3590+4024
25:14 "A, it will be like a man going on NIG
26:43 he a found them sleeping, 4099
26:72 He denied it a, with an oath: 4099
27:30 and struck him on the head a and again. NIG
27:30 and struck him on the head again and a. NIG
27:50 when Jesus had cried out a in a loud voice, 4099
27:63 'After three days I will rise a.' 1586
Mk 2: 1 when Jesus a entered Capernaum, 4099
2:13 Once a Jesus went out beside the lake. 4099
3:20 and a a crowd gathered, 4099
4: 1 A Jesus began to teach by the lake. 4099
4:30 A he said, "What shall we say the kingdom 2779
5:10 And he begged Jesus a and again not 4498
5:10 And he begged Jesus again and a not 4498
5:21 When Jesus had a crossed over by boat to 4099
7:14 A Jesus called the crowd to him and said, 4099
8:31 he must be killed and after three days rise a. 482
9:25 come out of him and never enter him a." 3600
9:50 how can you make it salty a? NIG
10: 1 A crowds of people came to him, 4099
10:10 When they were in the house a, 4099
10:24 But Jesus said a, "Children, 4099
10:32 A he took the Twelve aside 4099
11:14 "May no one ever eat fruit from you a." 3600
11:27 They arrived a in Jerusalem, 4099
13:19 and never to be equaled a. NIG
14:25 I will not drink a of the fruit of the vine 4033
14:40 he a found them sleeping, 4099
14:61 A the high priest asked him, 4099
14:69 she said a to those standing around, 4099
14:70 A he denied it. 4099
15: 4 So a Pilate asked him, 4099
15:19 A and again they struck him on the head AIT
15:19 a they struck him on the head with a staff AIT
Lk 13:20 A he asked, "What shall I compare 4099
13:35 you will not see me a until you say, NIG
14:34 how can it be made salty a? NIG
15:24 this son of mine was dead and is alive a; 348
15:32 of yours was dead and is alive a; 348
18:33 On the third day he will rise a." 482
22:16 I will not eat it a until it finds fulfillment in NIG
22:18 For I tell you I will not drink a of the fruit 608+3814+3836
23:20 Pilate appealed to them a. 4099
24: 7 and on the third day be raised a.' " 482
Jn 1:35 The next day John was there a with two 4099
2:19 and I will raise it a in three days." 1586
3: 3 the kingdom of God unless he is born a." 540
3: 7 'You must be born a.' 540
4:13 "Everyone who drinks this water will be thirsty a, 4099
5:14 "See, you are well a. NIG
6:15 withdrew a to a mountain by himself. 4099
8: 2 At dawn he appeared a in 4099
8: 8 A he stooped down and wrote on 4099
8:12 When Jesus spoke a to the people, he said, 4099
9:17 Finally they turned a to the blind man, 4099
9:27 Why do you want to hear it a? 4099
10: 7 Therefore Jesus said a, "I tell you the truth, 4099
10:17 only to take it up a. 4099
10:18 to lay it down and authority to take it up a. 4099
10:19 At these words the Jews were a divided. 4099
10:31 A the Jews picked up stones to stone him, 4099
10:39 A they tried to seize him, 4099
11:23 Jesus said to her, "Your brother will rise a." 482
11:24 "I know he will rise a in the resurrection at 482
12:28 "I have glorified it, and will glorify it a." 4099
16:22 but I will see you a and you will rejoice, 4099
18: 7 A he asked them, "Who is it you want?" 4099
18:27 A Peter denied it, 4099
18:38 With this he went out a to the Jews 4099
19: 3 went up to him a and again, AIT
19: 3 went up to him again and a, AIT
20:21 A Jesus said, "Peace be with you! 4099
20:26 his disciples were in the house a, 4099
21: 1 Afterward Jesus appeared a to his disciples, 4099
21:16 A Jesus said, "Simon son of John, 1309+4099
Ac 4:18 in a and commanded them not to speak NIG
8:39 and the eunuch did not see him a, 4033
9:17 so that you may see a and be filled with 329
9:18 and he could see a. 329
11:10 and then it was all pulled up to heaven a. 4099
17:32 "We want to hear you a on this subject." 4099
20:11 he went upstairs a and broke bread and ate. NIG
20:25 the kingdom will ever see me a. 4033
20:38 never see his face a. 4033
27: 4 From there we put out to sea a and passed NIG
27:28 A short time later they took soundings a 4099
Ro 5:16 A, the gift of God is not like the result of 2779
6: 9 he cannot die a; 4033
8:15 not receive a spirit that makes you a slave a 4099
10:19 A I ask: Did Israel not understand? 247
11:11 A I ask: Did they stumble 4036
11:23 for God is able to graft them in a. 4099
15:10 A, it says, "Rejoice, O Gentiles, 4099
15:11 And a, "Praise the Lord, all you Gentiles, 4099
15:12 And a, Isaiah says, "The Root 4099
15:15 remind you of them a, 2057
1Co 3:20 and a, "The Lord knows that the thoughts 4099
7: 5 Then come together a so that Satan will 4099
8:13 I will never eat meat a, 172+1650+3590+3836+4024
14: 8 A, if the trumpet does not sound 2779
2Co 3: 1 to commend ourselves a? 4099
5:12 not trying to commend ourselves to you a, 4099
5:15 him who died for them and was raised a. 1586
10: 7 he should consider a that we belong 4099
11:23 and been exposed to death a and again. 4490
11:23 and been exposed to death again and a. 4490
12:21 when I come a my God will humble me 4099
Gal 1: 9 As we have already said, so now I say a: 4099
2: 1 Fourteen years later I went up a 4099
4: 9 to be enslaved by them all over a? 540+4099
4:19 for whom I am a in the pains of childbirth 4099
5: 1 and do not let yourselves be burdened a by 4099
5: 3 A I declare to every man who lets himself 4099
Php 1:26 that through my being with you a your joy 4099
2:28 that when you see him a you may be glad 4099
3: 1 for me to write the same things to you a, NIG
3:18 before and now say a even with tears, NIG
4: 4 I will say it a: Rejoice! 4099
4:16 you sent me aid a and again when I was 562
4:16 you sent me aid again and a when I was 1489
1Th 2:18 certainly I, Paul, did, a and again— 562
2:18 certainly I, Paul, did, again and a— 1489
3:10 that we may see you a NIG
4:14 that Jesus died and rose a and so we believe 482
Heb 1: 5 Or a, "I will be his Father, 4099
1: 6 And a, when God brings his firstborn into 4099
2:13 And a, "I will put my trust in him." 4099
2:13 And a he says, "Here am I, 4099
4: 5 And a in the passage above he says, 4099
4: 7 Therefore God a set a certain day, 4099
5:12 of God's word all over a. 4099
6: 1 not laying a the foundation of repentance 4099
6: 6 crucifying the Son of God all over a 416
9:25 to offer himself a and again, 4490
9:25 to offer himself again and a, 4490
10:11 a and again he offers the same sacrifices, 4490
10:11 again and a he offers the same sacrifices, 4490
10:30 I will repay," and a, 4099
11:35 received back their dead, raised to life a. 414
Jas 5:18 A he prayed, and the heavens gave rain, 4099
1Pe 1:23 For you have been born a, 335
2Pe 2:20 and Savior Jesus Christ and are a entangled 4099
Rev 2: 8 who died and came to life a. NIG
3:12 Never a will he leave it. 2285
7:16 Never a will they hunger; 2285+4024
7:16 never a will they thirst. 2285+4028
10:11 "You must prophesy a about many peoples, 4099
18:21 never to be found a. 2285
18:22 will never be heard in you a. 2285
18:22 of any trade will ever be found in you a. 2285
18:22 of a millstone will never be heard in you a. 2285
18:23 of a lamp will never shine in you a. 2285
18:23 and bride will never be heard in you a. 2285
19: 3 And a they shouted: "Hallelujah! 1309

AGAINST (1303)

Ge 13:13 and were sinning greatly a the LORD. 4200
14: 2 went to war a Bera king of Sodom, AIT
14: 9 a Kedorlaomer king of Elam, Tidal king 907
14: 9 four kings a five. 907
16:12 be a everyone and everyone's hand 928
16:12 be against everyone and everyone's hand a 928
18:20 "The outcry a Sodom and Gomorrah is AIT
19:13 outcry to the LORD a AIT
20: 6 and so I have kept you from sinning a me. 4200
20:16 the offense a you before all who are 4200
27:41 Esau held a grudge a Jacob because of 8475
34:30 and if they join forces a me and attack me, 6584
39: 9 a wicked thing and sin a God?" 4200
42:22 "Didn't I tell you not to sin a the boy? 928
42:36 Everything is a me!" 6584
50:15 "What if Joseph holds a grudge a us 8475
Ex 1:10 fight a us and leave the country." 928
4:14 Then the LORD's anger burned a Moses 928
7: 5 the LORD when I stretch out my hand a 6584
9:14 the full force of my plagues a you and 448
9:14 and a your officials and your people, 928
9:17 You still set yourself a my people and will 928
10:16 "I have sinned a the LORD your God and 4200
10:16 against the LORD your God and a you. 4200
14:25 The LORD is fighting for them a Egypt." 928
14:31 the great power the LORD displayed a 928
15:24 So the people grumbled a Moses, saying, 6584
16: 2 the whole community grumbled a Moses 6584
16: 7 he has heard your grumbling a him. 6584
16: 7 that you should grumble a us?" 6584
16: 8 he has heard your grumbling a him. 6584
16: 8 You are not grumbling a us, 6584
16: 8 but a the LORD." 6584
17: 3 and they grumbled a Moses. 6584
17:16 be at war a the Amalekites from generation 928
19:22 or the LORD will break out a them." 928
19:24 or he will break out a them." 928
20:16 not give false testimony a your neighbor. 928
23:21 Do not rebel a him; 928
23:33 or they will cause you to sin a me, 4200
24:11 not raise his hand a these leaders of 448
29:16 and sprinkle it a the altar on all sides. 6584
29:20 Then sprinkle blood a the altar on all sides. 6584
32:10 so that my anger may burn a them and 928
32:11 "why should your anger burn a 928
32:29 for you were a your own sons and brothers, 928
32:33 "Whoever has sinned a me I will blot out 4200
Lev 1: 5 and sprinkle it a the altar on all sides at 6584
1:11 the priests shall sprinkle its blood a 6584
3: 2 the priests shall sprinkle the blood a 6584
3: 8 Aaron's sons shall sprinkle its blood a 6584
3:13 Aaron's sons shall sprinkle its blood a 6584
5: 9 of the blood of the sin offering a the side of 6584
5:19 he has been guilty of wrongdoing a 4200
7: 2 and its blood is to be sprinkled a the altar 6584
8:19 the ram and sprinkled the blood a the altar 6584
8:24 he sprinkled blood a the altar on all sides. 6584
9:12 and he sprinkled it a the altar on all sides. 6584
9:18 and he sprinkled it a the altar on all sides. 6584
17: 6 the blood a the altar of the LORD at 6584
17:10 I will set my face a that person 928
19:18 " 'Do not seek revenge or bear a grudge a 5757
20: 3 I will set my face a that man 928
20: 5 I will set my face a that man and his family 928
20: 6 " 'I will set my face a the person who turns 928
26:17 I will set my face a you so that you will 928
26:22 I will send wild animals a you, 928
26:40 their treachery a me and their hostility 928
Nu 5:13 (since there is no witness a her and she has 928
10: 9 When you go into battle in your own land a 6584
11:33 of the LORD burned a the people, 928
12: 1 and Aaron began to talk a Moses because 928
12: 8 not afraid to speak a my servant Moses?" 928
12: 9 The anger of the LORD burned a them, 928
12:11 do not hold a us the sin we have 6584
14: 2 the Israelites grumbled a Moses and Aaron, 6584
14: 9 Only do not rebel a the LORD. 928
14:27 "How long will this wicked community grumble a me? 6584
14:29 in the census and who has grumbled a me. 6584
14:34 and know what it is like to have me a you.' 9481
14:35 which has banded together a me. 6584
14:36 and made the whole community grumble a 6584
16: 2 and rose up a Moses. 4200+7156
16:11 It is a the LORD that you 6584
16:11 Who is Aaron that you should grumble a 6584
16:41 the whole Israelite community grumbled a 6584
17: 5 of this constant grumbling a you by 6584
17:10 will put an end to their grumbling a 4946+6584
18: 1 responsibility for offenses a AIT
18: 1 responsibility for offenses a AIT
18:23 responsibility for offenses a it. AIT
20:20 Then Edom came out a them with a large 7925
20:24 both of you rebelled a my command at 907
21: 5 they spoke a God and against Moses, 928
21: 5 they spoke against God and a Moses, 928
21: 7 "We sinned when we spoke a the LORD 928
21: 7 when we spoke against the LORD and a 928
21:23 and marched out into the desert a Israel. 7925
21:26 who had fought a the former king of Moab 928
22:25 crushing Balaam's foot a it. 448
23:23 There is no sorcery a Jacob, 928
23:23 no divination a Israel. 928
24:10 Then Balak's anger burned a Balaam. 448
25: 3 And the LORD's anger burned a them. 928
25: 8 the plague a the Israelites was stopped 4946+6584
26: 9 the community officials who rebelled a 6584
26: 9 when they rebelled a the LORD. 6584
27: 3 who banded together a the LORD, 6584
31: 3 of your men to go to war a the Midianites 6584
31: 7 They fought a Midian, 6584
32:13 The LORD's anger burned a Israel 928
32:23 you will be sinning a the LORD; 4200
Dt 1:26 you rebelled a the command of 907
1:41 "We have sinned a the LORD. 4200
1:43 You rebelled a the LORD's command and 907
1:44 in those hills came out a you; 7925
2:15 The LORD's hand was a them 928
4:26 I call heaven and earth as witnesses a 928
5:20 not give false testimony a your neighbor. 928
6:15 is a jealous God and his anger will burn a 928
7: 4 and the LORD's anger will burn a you 928
7:24 No one will be able to stand up a you; 928+7156
8:19 I testify a you today that you will surely 928
9: 2 "Who can stand up a the Anakites?" 4200+7156
9: 7 you have been rebellious a the LORD. 6640
9:16 I saw that you had sinned a the LORD 4200
9:23 But you rebelled a the command of 907

Dt 9:24 You have been rebellious a the LORD 6640
11:17 Then the LORD's anger will burn a you, 928
11:25 No man will be able to stand a you. 928+7156
13: 5 because he preached rebellion a the LORD 6584
15: 9 He may then appeal to the LORD a you, 6584
19:18 giving false testimony a his brother, 928
20: 1 to war a your enemies and see horses 6584
20: 3 today you are going into battle a 6584
20: 4 with you to fight for you a your enemies 6640
20:18 and you will sin a the LORD your God. 4200
20:19 fighting a it to capture it, 6584
21:10 When you go to war a your enemies and 6584
23: 9 When you are encamped a your enemies, 6584
24:15 Otherwise he may cry to the LORD a you, 6584
28: 7 that the enemies who rise up a you will 6584
28:48 the enemies the LORD sends a you. 928
28:49 The LORD will bring a nation a you 6584
29: 7 and Og king of Bashan came out to fight a 7925
29:20 his wrath and zeal will burn a that man. 928
29:27 the LORD's anger burned a this land, 928
30:19 and earth as witnesses a you that I have set 928
31:19 so that it may be a witness for me a them. 928
31:21 this song will testify a them, 4200+7156
31:26 There it will remain as a witness a you. 928
31:27 If you have been rebellious a the LORD 6640
31:28 and call heaven and earth to testify a them. 928
32:23 upon them and spend my arrows a them. 928
32:24 I will send wasting famine a them, 928
32:24 I will send a them the fangs of wild beasts, NIH
33: 7 Oh, be his help a his foes!" 4946
33:11 Smite the loins of *those who* **rise up** *a* him; AIT
Jos 1: 5 stand up a you all the days of your life. 4200+7156
1:18 Whoever rebels a your word and does 907
7: 1 So the LORD's anger burned a Israel. 928
7: 3 "Not all the people *will have to* **go up** *a* AIT
7:12 Israelites cannot stand a their enemies 4200+7156
7:13 You cannot stand a your enemies 4200+7156
7:20 I have sinned a the LORD, 4200
8: 5 and when the men come out a us, 7925
8:14 that an ambush had been set a him behind 4200
8:20 and saw the smoke of the city rising a 2025
8:20 the desert had turned back a their pursuers. 448
8:22 of the ambush also came out of the city a 7925
9: 2 they came together to make war a Joshua 6640
9:18 The whole assembly grumbled a the leaders 6584
10: 5 with all their troops and took up positions a 6584
10: 6 from the hill country have joined forces a 448
10:21 and no one uttered a word a the Israelites. 4200
10:31 he took up positions a it and attacked it. 6584
10:34 they took up positions a it and attacked it. 6584
11: 5 to fight a Israel. 6640
11: 7 and his whole army came a them suddenly 6584
11:18 Joshua waged war a all these kings for 907
11:20 to **wage** war *a* Israel, AIT
15:15 From there he marched a the people living 448
22:12 of Israel gathered at Shiloh to go to war a 6584
22:16 and build yourselves an altar in rebellion a 928
22:18 " 'If you rebel a the LORD today, 928
22:19 But do not rebel a the LORD or against us 928
22:19 But do not rebel against the LORD or a us 907
22:29 "Far be it from us to rebel a the LORD 928
22:33 about going to war a them to devastate 6584
23:16 the LORD's anger will burn a you, 928
24: 8 They fought a you, 907
24: 9 prepared to fight a Israel, 928
24:11 The citizens *of* Jericho fought a you, 928
24:22 "You are witnesses a yourselves 928
24:27 "This stone will be a witness a us. 928
24:27 It will be a witness a you if you are untrue 928
Jdg 1: 1 to go up and fight for us a the Canaanites?" 448
1: 3 to fight a the Canaanites. 928
1: 5 that they found Adoni-Bezek and fought a 928
1: 9 down to fight a the Canaanites living in 928
1:10 They advanced a the Canaanites living 448
1:11 From there they advanced a the people 448
2:14 In his anger a Israel the LORD handed them 928
2:15 of the LORD was a them to defeat them, 928
3: 8 The anger of the LORD burned a Israel so 928
4:24 the Israelites grew stronger and stronger a 6584
5:20 from their courses they fought a Sisera. 6640
5:23 to help the LORD a the mighty.' 928
7: 2 In order that Israel may not boast a me 6584
7: 9 "Get up, go down a the camp, 928
7:24 down a the Midianites and seize the waters 7925
8: 3 their resentment a him subsided. 4946+6584
9:18 (but today you have revolted a 6584
9:23 who acted treacherously a Abimelech. 928
9:24 that the **crime** *a* Jerub-Baal's seventy sons, AIT
9:31 to Shechem and are stirring up the city a 6584
9:33 advance a the city. 6584
9:33 When Gaal and his men come out a you, 448
9:45 All that day Abimelech pressed his attack a 928
9:49 They piled them a the stronghold and set it 6584
10: 9 the Jordan to fight a Judah, Benjamin and 928
10:10 "We have sinned a you, 4200
10:18 the attack a the Ammonites will be 928
11:12 "What do you have a us 4200
11:27 by waging war a me. 928
11:29 from there *he* **advanced** *a* the Ammonites. AIT
12: 4 the men of Gilead and fought a Ephraim. 907
16:26 so that I may lean a them." 6584
16:29 Bracing himself a them, 6584
18:27 a a peaceful and unsuspecting people. 6584
20: 9 We'll go up a it as the lot directs. 6584
20:11 and united as one man a the city. 448
20:14 at Gibeah to fight a the Israelites. 6640
20:18 "Who of us shall go first to fight a 6640
Jdg 20:20 up battle positions a them at Gibeah. 907
20:23 up again to battle a the Benjamites, 6640
20:23 The LORD answered, "Go up a them." 448
20:30 up a the Benjamites on the third day 448
20:30 on the third day and took up positions a 448
Ru 1:13 the LORD's hand has gone out a me!" 928
1Sa 2:10 He will thunder a them from heaven; 6584
2:25 If a man sins a another man, 4200
2:25 but if a man sins a the LORD, 4200
3:12 At that time I will carry out a 448
3:12 against Eli everything I spoke a 448
4: 1 Israelites went out to fight a the Philistines. 7925
5: 9 the LORD's hand was a that city, 928
7: 6 "We have sinned a the LORD." 4200
7:10 the LORD thundered with loud thunder a 6584
7:13 hand of the LORD was a the Philistines. 928
12: 3 Testify a me in the presence of the LORD 928
12: 5 "The LORD is witness a you, 928
12: 9 and the king of Moab, who fought a them. 928
12:12 of the Ammonites was moving a you, 6584
12:14 and serve and obey him and do not rebel a 907
12:15 and if you rebel a his commands, 907
12:15 his hand will be a you, 928
12:15 as it was a your fathers. 928
12:23 that I should sin a the LORD by failing 4200
13:12 Philistines will come down a me at Gilgal, 448
14:33 the men are sinning a the LORD 4200
14:34 Do not sin a the LORD by eating meat 4200
14:47 he fought a their enemies on every side: 928
17:19 fighting a the Philistines." 6640
17:33 "You are not able to go out a this Philistine 448
17:45 "You come a me with sword and spear 448
17:45 but I come a you in the name of 448
18:17 "I will not raise a hand a him. 928
18:21 so that the hand of the Philistines may be a 928
22: 8 Is that why you have all conspired a me? 6584
22:13 "Why have you conspired a me, 6584
22:13 so that he has rebelled a me and lies in wait 448
23: 1 the Philistines are fighting a Keilah 928
23: 3 if we go to Keilah a the Philistine forces!" 448
23: 9 David learned that Saul was plotting a him, 6584
24: 6 or lift my hand a him; 928
24:10 I said, 'I will not lift my hand a my master, 928
24:14 "A whom has the king of Israel come out? 339
25:39 who has upheld my cause a Nabal 3338+4946
26:19 If the LORD has incited you a me, 928
27:10 "A the Negev of Judah" or "Against 6584
27:10 of Judah" or "A the Negev of Jerahmeel" or 6584
27:10 or "Against the Negev of Jerahmeel" or "A 448
28: 1 to fight a Israel. 928
28:15 "The Philistines are fighting a me, 928
28:18 the LORD or carry out his fierce wrath a 928
29: 4 or *he will* **turn** a us during the fighting. 2118+4200+8477
29: 8 "What have you found a your servant from 928
29: 8 Why can't I go and fight a the enemies 928
30:23 over to us the forces that came a us. 6584
31: 1 Now the Philistines fought a Israel; 928
2Sa 1:16 Your own mouth testified a you 928
4: 8 the LORD has avenged my lord the king a 4946
5:20 the LORD *has* **broken out** *a* my enemies AIT
6: 7 The LORD's anger burned a Uzzah 928
6: 8 the LORD's wrath had broken out a 928
10: 9 and deployed them a the Arameans. 7925
10:10 of Abishai his brother and deployed them a 7925
10:17 to meet David and fought a him. 6640
11:17 the city came out and fought a Joab, some 907
11:23 "The men overpowered us and came out a 448
11:25 Press the attack a the city and destroy it.' 448
12: 5 with anger a the man and said to Nathan, 928
12:13 "I have sinned a the LORD." 4200
12:26 Meanwhile Joab fought a Rabbah of 928
12:27 "I have fought a Rabbah 928
14: 7 the whole clan has risen up a your servant; 6584
14:13 then have you devised a thing like this a 6584
17:21 Ahithophel has advised such and such a 6584
18:12 I would not lift my hand a the king's son. 448
18:28 the men who lifted their hands a my lord 928
18:31 from all who rose up a you." 6584
20:10 Amasa was not on his guard a the dagger 928
20:15 and it stood a the outer fortifications. 928
20:21 has lifted up his hand a the king, 928
20:21 up his hand against the king, a David. 928
21: 5 for the man who destroyed us and plotted a 4200
21:15 David went down with his men *to* **fight** *a* AIT
22:30 With your help *I can* **advance** *a* a troop; AIT
23: 8 he raised his spear a eight hundred men, 6584
23:18 He raised his spear a three hundred men, 6584
23:21 Benaiah went a him with a club. 448
24: 1 the anger of the LORD burned a Israel, 928
24: 1 and he incited David a them, saying, 928
24:12 Choose one of them for me to carry out a 4200
1Ki 5: 3 **waged** a my father David **from all sides,** 6015
6: 5 A the walls of the main hall 6584
8:33 an enemy because they have sinned a you, 4200
8:35 because your people have sinned a you, 4200
8:44 your people go to war a their enemies, 6584
8:46 "When they sin a you— 4200
8:50 who have sinned a you; 4200
8:50 the offenses they have committed a you, 928
11:14 LORD raised up a Solomon an adversary, 4200
11:23 up a Solomon another adversary, 4200
11:26 Jeroboam son of Nebat rebelled a the king. 928
11:27 the account of how he rebelled a the king: 928
12:19 So Israel has been in rebellion a the house 928
12:21 to make war a the house of Israel and 6640
12:24 Do not go up to fight a your brothers, 6640
1Ki 13: 2 He cried out a the altar by the word of 6584
13: 4 of God cried out a the altar at Bethel, 6584
13:32 of the LORD a the altar in Bethel and 6584
13:32 the LORD against the altar in Bethel and a 6584
15:17 Baasha king of Israel went up a Judah 6584
15:20 the commanders of his forces a the towns 6584
15:27 of Ahijah of the house of Issachar plotted a 6584
16: 1 the LORD came to Jehu son of Hanani a 6584
16: 9 of half his chariots, plotted a him. 6584
16:12 the word of the LORD spoken a Baasha 448
16:16 in the camp heard that Zimri *had* **plotted** *a* AIT
17:18 "What do you have a me, man of God? 4200
20:26 and went up to Aphek to fight a Israel. 6640
21:13 sat opposite him and **brought charges a** 6386
22: 4 with me to fight a Ramoth Gilead?" NIH
22: 6 "Shall I go to war a Ramoth Gilead, 6584
22:15 shall we go to war a Ramoth Gilead, 448
2Ki 1: 1 After Ahab's death, Moab rebelled a Israel. 928
3: 5 of Moab rebelled a the king of Israel. 928
3: 7 "The king of Moab has rebelled a me. 928
3: 7 Will you go with me to fight a Moab?" 448
3:21 that the kings had come to fight a them; 928
3:26 of Moab saw that the battle had gone a 4946
3:27 The fury a Israel was great; 6584
6:32 shut the door and **hold** it **shut** *a* him. AIT
8:20 Edom rebelled a Judah and set 3338+4946+9393
8:22 To this day Edom has been in rebellion a Judah. 3338+4946+9393
8:28 of Ahab to war a Hazael king of Aram 6640
9:14 the son of Nimshi, conspired a Joram. 448
9:14 all Israel had been defending Ramoth Gilead a Hazael 4946+7156
10: 9 It was I who conspired a my master 6584
10:10 a word the LORD has spoken a the house 6584
12:20 His officials **conspired** *a* him AIT
13: 3 So the LORD's anger burned a Israel, 928
13:12 including his war a Amaziah king of Judah, 6640
14:15 including his war a Amaziah king of Judah, 6640
14:19 They conspired a him in Jerusalem, 6584
15:10 Shallum son of Jabesh conspired a 6584
15:25 Pekah son of Remaliah, conspired a him. 6584
15:30 Then Hoshea son of Elah conspired a 6584
15:37 of Aram and Pekah son of Remaliah a 928
16: 5 **marched up** to fight *a* Jerusalem AIT
17: 5 **marched** *a* Samaria and laid siege to it AIT
17: 7 because the Israelites had sinned a 4200
17: 9 The Israelites secretly did things a 6584
18: 7 He rebelled a the king of Assyria and did 928
18: 9 Shalmaneser king of Assyria marched a 6584
18:20 that you rebel a me? 928
18:25 to march a this country and destroy it.' " 6584
19: 8 he withdrew and found the king fighting a 6584
19: 9 was marching out to fight a him. 907
19:21 the word that the LORD has spoken a 6584
19:22 A whom have you raised your voice 6584
19:22 A the Holy One of Israel! 6584
19:27 when you come and go and how you rage a 448
19:28 Because you rage a me 448
19:32 before it with shield or build a siege ramp a 6584
21:13 **measuring line** *used a* AIT
21:13 the **plumb line** *used a* the house of Ahab. AIT
21:23 Amon's officials conspired a him 6584
21:24 of the land killed all who had plotted a 6584
22:13 Great is the LORD's anger that burns a us 928
22:17 my anger will burn a this place and will not 928
22:19 when you heard what I have spoken a 6584
23:17 from Judah and pronounced a the altar 6584
23:26 which burned a Judah because of all 928
24: 1 then he changed his mind and rebelled a 928
24: 2 Moabite and Ammonite raiders a him. 928
24:20 Zedekiah rebelled a the king of Babylon. 928
25: 1 of Babylon marched a Jerusalem 6584
1Ch 5:10 During Saul's reign they waged war a 6640
5:19 They waged war a the Hagrites, Jetur, 6640
10: 1 Now the Philistines fought a Israel; 928
11:11 he raised his spear a three hundred men, 6584
11:20 He raised his spear a three hundred men, 6584
11:23 Benaiah went a him with a club. 448
12:19 when he went with the Philistines to fight a 6584
12:21 They helped David a raiding bands, 6584
13:10 The LORD's anger burned a Uzzah, 928
13:11 the LORD's wrath had broken out a 928
14:11 God *has* **broken out** *a* my enemies AIT
15:13 the LORD our God broke out in anger a 928
19:10 and deployed them a the Arameans. 7925
19:11 and they were deployed a the Ammonites. 7925
19:17 he advanced a them 448
19:17 and they fought a him. 6640
21: 1 Satan rose up a Israel and incited David 6584
21:10 Choose one of them for me to carry out a 4200
2Ch 6:24 an enemy because they have sinned a you 4200
6:26 because your people have sinned a you, 4200
6:34 your people go to war a their enemies, 6584
6:36 "When they sin a you— 4200
6:39 who have sinned a you. 4200
10:19 So Israel has been in rebellion a the house 928
11: 1 to make war a Israel and to regain 6640
11: 4 Do not go up to fight a your brothers. 6640
11: 4 and turned back from marching a 448
13: 3 and Jeroboam drew up a battle line a him 6640
13: 6 rebelled a his master. 6584
13:12 the battle cry a you. 6584
13:12 Men of Israel, do not fight a the LORD, 6640
14: 9 Zerah the Cushite marched out a them with 448
14:11 like you to help the powerless a the mighty. 1068
14:11 and in your name we have come a 6584
14:11 do not let man prevail a you." 6640

2Ch 16: 1 went up a Judah and fortified Ramah 6584
16: 4 the commanders of his forces a the towns 448
17: 1 as king and strengthened himself a Israel. 6584
18: 3 *"Will you* **go** with me *a* Ramoth Gilead?" AIT
18: 5 "Shall we go to war a Ramoth Gilead, 448
18:14 shall we go to war a Ramoth Gilead, 448
19:10 to warn them not to sin a the LORD; 4200
20: 2 "A vast army is coming a you from Edom, 6584
20:16 Tomorrow march down a them. 6584
20:22 the LORD set ambushes a the men 6584
20:23 up a the men from Mount Seir to destroy 6584
20:29 how the LORD had fought a the enemies 6640
20:37 of Dodavahu of Mareshah prophesied a 6584
21: 8 Edom rebelled a Judah and set 3338+4946+9393
21:10 To this day Edom has been in rebellion a Judah. 3338+4946+9393
21:16 The LORD aroused a Jehoram 6584
22: 5 of Ahab king of Israel to war a Hazael king 6584
24:19 and though they testified a them, 928
24:21 But they plotted a him, 6584
24:23 the army of Aram marched a Joash; 6584
24:25 His officials conspired a him for murdering 6584
24:26 Those who conspired a him were Zabad, 6584
25:15 The anger of the LORD burned a 928
25:27 they conspired a him in Jerusalem 6584
26: 6 He went to war a the Philistines and broke 928
26: 7 God helped him a the Philistines and 6584
26: 7 and a the Arabs who lived in Gur Baal and 6584
26: 7 the Arabs who lived in Gur Baal and a NIH
26:13 a powerful force to support the king a 6584
28:10 also guilty of sins a the LORD your God? 4200
32:16 Sennacherib's officers spoke further a 6584
32:16 against the LORD God and a 6584
32:17 the God of Israel, and saying this a him: 6584
33:11 So the LORD brought a them 6584
33:24 Amon's officials conspired a him 6584
33:25 of the land killed all who had plotted a 6584
34:27 when you heard what he spoke a this place 6584
36: 8 and all that was found a him, 6584
36:13 He also rebelled a King Nebuchadnezzar, 928
36:16 of the LORD was aroused a his people 928
36:17 up a them the king of the Babylonians, 6584
Ezr 4: 5 to work a them and frustrate their plans 6584
4: 6 they lodged an accusation a the people 6584
4: 8 and Shimshai the secretary wrote a letter a 10542
4:19 that this city has a long history of revolt a 10542
7:23 Why should there be wrath a the realm of 10542
8:22 his great anger is a all who forsake him." 6584
Ne 1: 6 have committed a you. 4200
2:19 "Are you rebelling a the king?" 6584
4: 8 and fight a Jerusalem and stir up trouble 928
4: 8 against Jerusalem and stir up trouble a it. 4200
5: 1 and their wives raised a great outcry a 448
6:12 but that he had prophesied a me 6584
9:10 You sent miraculous signs and wonders a 928
9:10 a all his officials and all the people 928
9:26 they were disobedient and rebelled a you; 928
9:29 They sinned a your ordinances, 928
13:15 *I* **warned** them *a* selling food on that day. AIT
13:18 Now you are stirring up more wrath a 6584
Est 1:16 not only a the king but also against all 6584
1:16 also a all the nobles and the peoples of all 6584
4:16 even though it is a the law. 3869+4202
5: 9 he was filled with rage a Mordecai. 6584
6:13 you cannot stand a him— 4200
8: 3 which he had devised a the Jews. 6584
9: 2 No one could stand a them, 4200+7156
9:24 had plotted a the Jews to destroy them 6584
9:25 that the evil scheme Haman had devised a 6584
Job 2: 3 though you incited me a him to ruin him 928
6: 4 God's terrors *are* **marshaled** *a* me. AIT
8: 4 When your children sinned a him, 4200
10: 2 but tell me what **charges** *you have a* me. AIT
10:16 and again display your awesome power a 928
10:17 You bring new witnesses a me 5584
10:17 your forces come a me wave upon wave. 6640
11: 5 that he would open his lips a you 6640
13:19 Can anyone bring charges a me? 6643
13:26 For you write down bitter things a me 6584
15: 6 your own lips testify a you. 928
15:13 so that you vent your rage a God 448
15:25 at God and vaunts himself a the Almighty, 448
15:26 defiantly charging a him with a thick, 448
16: 4 I could make fine speeches a you 6584
16: 8 my gauntness rises up and testifies a me 928+7156
16:10 in scorn and unite together a me. 6584
17: 8 the innocent are aroused a the ungodly. 6584
19: 5 above me and use my humiliation a me, 6584
19:11 His anger burns a me; 6584
19:12 they build a siege ramp a me and encamp 6584
19:19 those I love have turned a me. 928
20:23 God will vent his burning anger a him 928
20:27 the earth will rise up a him. 4200
22: 4 that he rebukes you and brings charges a 6640
23: 6 No, he would not press charges a me. 928
23:14 He carries out his **decree** *a* me, AIT
24:13 "There are those *who* **rebel** *a* the light, AIT
27:22 It hurls itself a him without mercy 6584
30:12 they build their siege ramps a me. 6584
31:13 when they had a grievance a me, 6643
31:21 if I have raised my hand a the fatherless, 6584
31:30 to sin by **invoking** a curse *a* his life— AIT
31:38 "if my land cries out a me 6584
32:14 But Job has not marshaled his words a me, 448
34:37 among us and multiplies his words a God." 4200
39:23 The quiver rattles a his **side,** 6584
40:23 the Jordan should surge a his mouth. 448
Job 41:10 Who then is able to stand a me? 4200+7156
41:11 Who **has a claim** a me that I must pay? 7709
Ps 2: 2 the rulers gather together a the LORD and 6584
2: 2 the LORD and a his Anointed One. 6584
3: 1 How many rise up a me! 6584
3: 6 of thousands drawn up a me on every side. 6584
5:10 for they have rebelled a you. 928
7: 6 rise up a the rage of my enemies. 928
11: 2 they set their arrows a the strings to shoot 6584
15: 5 without usury and does not accept a bribe a 6584
18:29 With your help *I can* **advance** *a* a troop; AIT
21:11 Though they plot evil a you 6584
22:13 Roaring lions tearing their prey open their mouths wide a me. 6584
27: 2 evil men advance a me to devour my flesh, 6584
27: 3 though war break out a me, 6584
27:12 for false witnesses rise up a me, 928
31:13 they conspire a me and plot to take my life. 6584
31:18 and contempt they speak arrogantly a 6584
32: 2 the LORD does not count a him and 4200
34:16 face of the LORD is a those who do evil, 928
35: 1 fight a those who fight against me. 907
35: 1 fight against *those who* **fight** *a* me. AIT
35: 3 and javelin a those who pursue me. 7925
35:15 attackers gathered a me 6584
35:20 but devise false accusations a 6584
36:11 *May* the foot of the proud not **come** *a* me, AIT
37:12 The wicked plot a the righteous 4200
41: 4 heal me, for I have sinned a you." 4200
41: 7 All my enemies whisper together a me; 6584
41: 9 has lifted up his heel a me. 6584
43: 1 and plead my cause a an ungodly nation; 4946
50: 7 O Israel, and I will testify a you: 928
50:20 You speak continually a your brother 928
51: 4 A you, you only, have I sinned 4200
55:12 if a foe were raising himself a me, 6584
55:18 from the battle waged a me, 4200
59: 1 protect me from *those who* **rise up** *a* me. AIT
59: 3 Fierce men conspire a me for no offense 6584
60: 4 a banner to be unfurled a the bow. 4946+7156
60:11 Give us aid a the enemy, 4946
61: 3 a strong tower a the foe. 4946+7156
64: 8 He will turn their own tongues a them 6584
66: 7 let not the rebellious rise up a him. 4200
71:10 For my enemies speak a me; 4200
74: 1 Why does your anger smolder a the sheep 928
75: 5 Do not lift your horns a heaven; 4200
76:10 Surely your **wrath** *a* men brings you praise, AIT
78:17 But they continued to sin a him, 4200
78:17 **rebelling** in the desert *a* the Most High. AIT
78:19 They spoke a God, saying, 928
78:21 his fire broke out a Jacob, 928
78:21 and his wrath rose a Israel, 928
78:31 God's anger rose a them; 928
78:40 How often *they* **rebelled** *a* him in AIT
78:49 He unleashed a them his hot anger, 928
78:56 But they put God to the test and rebelled a 907
79: 8 Do not hold a us the sins of the fathers; 4200
80: 4 how long will your anger smolder a 928
81: 5 statute for Joseph when he went out a Egypt 6584
81:14 and turn my hand a their foes! 6584
83: 3 With cunning they conspire a your people; 6584
83: 3 they plot a those you cherish. 6584
83: 5 they form an alliance a you— 6584
91:12 that you will not strike your foot a a stone. 928
94:16 Who will rise up for me a the wicked? 6640
94:16 Who will take a stand for me a evildoers? 6640
94:21 They band together a the righteous 6584
102: 8 *those who* **rail** *a* me use my name as AIT
105:25 to conspire a his servants. 928
105:28 for had they not rebelled a his words? 907
106:33 for they rebelled a the Spirit of God, 907
107:11 for *they had* **rebelled** *a* the words of God AIT
108:12 Give us aid a the enemy, 4946
109: 2 deceitful men have opened their mouths a 6584
109: 2 they have spoken a me with lying tongues. 907
119:11 in my heart that I might not sin a you. 4200
124: 3 when their anger flared a us, 928
135: 9 O Egypt, a Pharaoh and all his servants. 928
137: 9 and dashes them a the rocks. 448
138: 7 you stretch out your hand a the anger 6584
139:21 and abhor *those who* **rise up** *a* you? AIT
141: 5 my prayer is ever a the deeds of evildoers; 928
149: 9 to carry out the sentence written a them. 928
Pr 3:29 Do not plot harm a your neighbor, 6584
17:11 a merciless official will be sent a him. 928
19: 3 yet his heart rages a the LORD. 6584
21:30 no plan that can **succeed** a the LORD. 4200+5584
23:11 he will take up their case a you. 907
24:15 like an outlaw a a righteous man's house, 4200
24:28 not testify a your neighbor without cause, 928
25:18 the man who gives false testimony a 928
Ecc 9:14 And a powerful king came a it, 448
9:14 surrounded it and built huge siegeworks a 6584
10: 4 If a ruler's anger rises a you, 6584
Isa 1: 2 but they have rebelled a me. 928
1:25 I will turn my hand a you; 6584
2: 4 Nation will not take up sword a nation, 448
3: 5 man a man, neighbor against neighbor. 928
3: 5 man against man, neighbor a neighbor. 928
3: 5 The young will rise up a the old, 928
3: 5 the base a the honorable. 928
3: 8 their words and deeds are a the LORD, 448
3: 9 The look on their faces testifies a them; 928
3:14 into judgment a the elders and leaders 6640
5:25 the LORD's anger burns a his people; 928
7: 1 of Israel marched up to fight a Jerusalem, 6584
Isa 8: 7 therefore the Lord is about to bring a them 6584
9: 8 The Lord has sent a message a Jacob; 928
9:11 the LORD has strengthened Rezin's foes a 6584
9:21 together they will turn a Judah. 6584
10: 6 I send him a a godless nation, 928
10: 6 I dispatch him a a people who anger me, 6584
10:12 When the Lord has finished all his work a 928
10:15 or the saw boast a him who uses it? 6584
10:24 who beat you with a rod and lift up a club a 6584
10:25 Very soon my anger a you will end NIH
13:17 See, I will stir up a them the Medes, 6584
14: 4 you will take up this taunt a the king 6584
14:22 "I will rise up a them," 6584
19: 2 "I will stir up Egyptian a Egyptian— 928
19: 2 brother will fight a brother, 928
19: 2 neighbor a neighbor, city against city, 928
19: 2 city a city, kingdom against kingdom. 928
19: 2 city against city, kingdom a kingdom. 928
19:12 the LORD Almighty has planned a Egypt. 6584
19:16 that the LORD Almighty raises a them. 6584
19:17 of what the LORD Almighty is planning a 6584
20: 3 as a sign and portent a Egypt and Cush, 6584
23: 8 Who planned this a Tyre, 6584
25: 4 the ruthless is like a **storm** *driving a* a wall AIT
27: 4 I would march a them in battle; 928
28:22 of the destruction decreed a the whole land. 6584
29: 3 I will encamp a you all around; 6584
29: 3 with towers and set up my siege works a 6584
29: 7 hordes of all the nations that fight a Ariel, 6584
29: 8 of all the nations that fight a Mount Zion. 6584
31: 2 He will rise up a the house of the wicked, 6584
31: 2 a those who help evildoers. 6584
31: 4 of shepherds is called together a him, he is 6584
31: 6 to him you have so greatly **revolted a,** 6240
33:15 who stops his ears a plots of murder 4946
33:15 against plots of murder and shuts his eyes a 4946
36: 5 that you rebel a me? 928
36:10 to march a this country and destroy it.' " 448
37: 8 he withdrew and found the king fighting a 6584
37: 9 was marching out to fight a him. 907
37:22 this is the word the LORD has spoken a 6584
37:23 A whom have you raised your voice 6584
37:23 A the Holy One of Israel! 448
37:28 when you come and go and how you rage a 448
37:29 Because you rage a me and 448
37:33 before it with shield or build a siege ramp a 6584
41:11 "All who rage a you will surely 928
41:12 Those who wage **war** *a* you will be AIT
42:24 a whom we have sinned? 4200
43:27 your spokesmen rebelled a me. 928
45:24 All who have raged a him will come to him 928
48:14 LORD's chosen ally will carry out his purpose a Babylon; 928
48:14 his arm will be a the Babylonians. NIH
50: 8 Who then will bring charges a me? 907
54:17 no weapon forged a you will prevail, 6584
59:12 and our sins testify a us. 928
59:13 rebellion and treachery a the LORD, 928
63:10 and he himself fought a them. 928
64: 5 But when we continued to sin a them, 928
66:24 the dead bodies of those who rebelled a 928
Jer 1:15 they will come a all her surrounding walls 6584
1:15 against all her surrounding walls and a all 6584
1:18 a bronze wall to stand a the whole land— 6584
1:18 a the kings of Judah, its officials, 4200
1:19 They will fight a you but will 448
2: 8 the leaders rebelled a me. 928
2: 9 "Therefore I bring charges a you again," 907
2: 9 "And I will bring charges a 907
2:21 did you turn a me into a corrupt, wild vine? 4200
2:29 "Why do you bring charges a me? 448
2:29 You have all rebelled a me," 928
3:13 you have rebelled a the LORD your God, 928
3:25 We have sinned a the LORD our God, 4200
4:12 Now I pronounce my judgments a them." 907
4:16 raising a war cry a the cities of Judah. 6584
4:17 because she has rebelled a me,' " 907
5:15 "I am bringing a distant nation a you— 6584
6: 3 Shepherds with their flocks will come a 448
6: 4 "Prepare for battle a her! 6584
6: 6 down the trees and build siege ramps a 6584
6:12 when I stretch out my hand a 6584
8:14 because we have sinned a him. 4200
11:19 I did not realize that they had plotted a me, 6584
12: 6 they have raised a loud cry a you. 339
13:14 I will smash them one a the other, 448
14: 7 Although our sins testify a us, O LORD, 928
14: 7 we have sinned a you. 4200
14:20 we have indeed sinned a you. 4200
15: 3 "I will send four kinds of destroyers a 6584
15: 8 At midday I will bring a destroyer a 6584
15:14 a fire that will burn a you." 6584
15:20 they will fight a you but will 448
16:10 the LORD decreed such a great disaster a 6584
16:10 What sin have we committed a 4200
18:11 a disaster for you and devising a plan a 6584
18:18 "Come, let's make plans a Jeremiah; 6584
18:22 when you suddenly bring invaders a them, 6584
19:15 around it every disaster I pronounced a 6584
21: 4 *to* **turn** a you the weapons of war that are 6015
21: 5 I myself will fight a you with 907
21:13 I am a you, [Jerusalem,] 448
21:13 you who say, "Who can come a us? 6584
22: 7 I will send destroyers a you, 6584
23:30 "I am a the prophets who steal 6584
23:31 the LORD, "I am a the prophets who wag 6584
23:32 I am a those who prophesy false dreams," 6584

Jer 24:10 and plague a them until they are destroyed 928
25: 9 "and I will bring them a this land 6584
25: 9 against this land and its inhabitants and a 6584
25:13 that land all the things I have spoken a it, 6584
25:13 in this book and prophesied by Jeremiah a 6584
25:30 "Now prophesy all these words a them 448
25:30 from his holy dwelling and roar mightily a 6584
25:30 shout a all who live on the earth. 448
25:31 for the LORD will bring charges a 928
26:11 because he has prophesied a this city. 448
26:12 to prophesy a this house and this city all 448
26:13 not bring the disaster he has pronounced a 6584
26:19 not bring the disaster he pronounced a 6584
26:20 he prophesied the same things a this city 6584
28: 8 disaster and plague a many countries 448
28:16 because you have preached rebellion a 448
29:17 "I will send the sword, famine and plague a 928
29:32 because he has preached rebellion a me.' " 6584
31:20 I often speak a him, I still remember him. 928
32: 5 If you fight a the Babylonians, 907
33: 4 to be used a the siege ramps and the sword 448
33: 8 from all the sin they have committed a me 4200
33: 8 and will forgive all their sins of rebellion a 928
34: 1 in the empire he ruled were fighting a 6584
34: 7 of Babylon was fighting a Jerusalem and 6584
34:22 They will fight a it, 6584
35:17 in Jerusalem every disaster I pronounced a 6584
36: 7 and wrath pronounced a this people by 448
36:31 of Judah every disaster I pronounced a 448
37:18 "What crime have I committed a you 4200
39: 1 of Babylon marched a Jerusalem 448
39:16 I am about to fulfill my words a this city 448
40: 3 because you people sinned a the LORD 4200
41: 9 of his **defense** a Baasha king of Israel. 4946+7156
42: 5 the LORD be a true and faithful witness a 928
43: 3 But Baruch son of Neriah is inciting you a 928
44: 6 it raged a the towns of Judah and the streets 928
44:23 and have sinned a the LORD and have 4200
44:29 that my threats of harm a you will 6584
46: 2 This is the message a the army 6584
46:20 but a gadfly is coming a her from the north. 928
46:22 they will come a her with axes, 4200
48: 8 The destroyer will come a every town, 448
48:18 for he who destroys Moab will come up a 928
49: 2 "when I will sound the battle cry a Rabbah 448
49:19 And what shepherd can stand a me?" 4200+7156
49:20 hear what the LORD has planned a Edom, 448
49:20 what he has purposed a those who live 448
49:30 of Babylon has plotted a you; 6584
49:30 he has devised a plan a you. 6584
49:36 I will bring a Elam the four winds from 448
50: 7 for they sinned a the LORD, 4200
50: 9 For I will stir up and bring a Babylon 6584
50: 9 They will take up their positions a her, 4200
50:14 for she has sinned a the LORD. 4200
50:15 Shout a her on every side! 6584
50:26 Come a her from afar. 4200
50:29 "Summon archers a Babylon, 448
50:31 "See, I am a you, O arrogant one," 448
50:35 "A sword a the Babylonians!" 6584
50:35 "a those who live in Babylon and 448
50:35 "against those who live in Babylon and a 448
50:36 A sword a her false prophets! 448
50:36 A sword a her warriors! 448
50:37 A sword a her horses and chariots and all 448
50:37 A sword a her treasures! 448
50:44 And what shepherd can stand a me?" 4200+7156
50:45 hear what the LORD has planned a 448
50:45 what he has purposed a the land of 448
51: 1 up the spirit of a destroyer a Babylon and 6584
51:12 Lift up a banner a the walls of Babylon! 448
51:12 his decree a the people of Babylon. 448
51:25 "I am a you, O destroying mountain, 448
51:25 "I will stretch out my hand a you, 6584
51:27 Prepare the nations for battle a her; 6584
51:27 summon a her these kingdoms: 6584
51:27 Appoint a commander a her; 6584
51:28 Prepare the nations for battle a her— 6584
51:29 the LORD's purposes a Babylon stand— 6584
51:46 of violence in the land and of ruler a ruler. 6584
51:53 I will send destroyers a her," 4200
51:56 A destroyer will come a Babylon; 6584
52: 3 Zedekiah rebelled a the king of Babylon. 928
52: 4 of Babylon marched a Jerusalem 6584
La 1:15 an army a me to crush my young men. 6584
1:18 yet *I* **rebelled** *a* his command. AIT
2:16 All your enemies open their mouths wide a 6584
2:22 you summoned *a* me **terrors** on every side. AIT
3: 3 he has turned his hand a me again 928
3:46 "All our enemies have opened their mouths wide a us. 6584
3:60 all their plots a me. 4200
3:61 all their plots a me— 6584
3:62 what my enemies whisper and mutter a 6584
Eze 2: 3 a rebellious nation that has rebelled a me; 928
2: 3 they and their fathers have been in revolt a 928
3:13 the wings of the living creatures brushing a 448
4: 2 Then lay siege to it: Erect siege works a it, 6584
4: 2 set up camps a it and put battering rams 6584
4: 7 and with bared arm prophesy a her. 6584
5: 6 Yet in her wickedness she has rebelled a 907
5: 8 I myself am a you, Jerusalem, 6584
5:13 "Then my anger will cease and my wrath a 928
5:17 I will send famine and wild beasts a you, 6584
5:17 and I will bring the sword a you. 6584
6: 2 set your face a the mountains of Israel; 448
6: 2 mountains of Israel; prophesy a them 448
Eze 6: 3 I am about to bring a sword a you, 6584
6:14 And I will stretch out my hand a them 6584
7: 3 upon you and I will unleash my anger a 928
7: 6 It has roused itself a you. 448
7: 8 on you and spend my anger a you; 928
11: 4 Therefore prophesy a them; 6584
11: 8 and the sword is what I will bring a you, 6584
13: 2 prophesy a the prophets of Israel who are 448
13: 8 I am a you, declares the Sovereign LORD. 448
13: 9 be a the prophets who see false visions 448
13:15 So I will spend my wrath a the wall and 928
13:15 against the wall and a those who covered it 928
13:17 set your face a the daughters 448
13:17 their own imagination. Prophesy a them 6584
13:20 I am a your magic charms 448
14: 8 I will set my face a that man and make him 928
14: 9 and I will stretch out my hand a him 6584
14:13 if a country sins a me by being unfaithful 4200
14:13 and I stretch out my hand a it 6584
14:17 if I bring a sword a that country and say, 6584
14:21 How much worse will it be when I send a 448
15: 7 I will set my face a them. 928
15: 7 And when I set my face a them, 928
16:27 So I stretched out my hand a you 6584
16:37 I will gather them a you from all around 6584
16:40 They will bring a mob a you, 6584
16:42 Then my wrath a you will subside 928
17:15 But the king rebelled a him 928
18:20 of the wicked will be **charged** a him. 6584
18:22 be remembered a him. 4200
19: 8 Then the nations came a him, 6584
20: 8 " 'But they rebelled a me and would 928
20: 8 and spend my anger a them in Egypt. 928
20:13 people of Israel rebelled a me in the desert. 928
20:21 " 'But the children rebelled a me: 928
20:21 and spend my anger a them in the desert. 928
20:38 of those who revolt and rebel a me. 928
20:46 preach a the south and prophesy against 448
20:46 against the south and prophesy a the forest 448
21: 2 set your face a Jerusalem and preach 448
21: 2 and preach a the sanctuary. 448
21: 2 Prophesy a the land of Israel 448
21: 3 I am a you. 448
21: 4 my sword will be unsheathed a everyone 448
21:12 son of man, for it is a my people; 928
21:12 it is a all the princes of Israel. 928
21:20 Mark out one road for the sword to come a 907
21:20 of the Ammonites and another a Judah 907
21:22 to set battering rams a the gates, 6584
21:31 upon you and breathe out my fiery anger a 6584
23:22 I will stir up your lovers a you, 6584
23:22 from in disgust, and I will bring them a you 6584
23:24 They will come a you with weapons, 6584
23:24 up positions a you on every side with large 6584
23:25 I will direct my jealous anger a you, 928
23:46 a mob a them and give them over to terror 6584
24:13 not be clean again until my wrath a 928
25: 2 set your face a the Ammonites 448
25: 2 against the Ammonites and prophesy a 6584
25: 6 the malice of your heart a the land of Israel, 448
25: 7 therefore I will stretch out my hand a you 6584
25:13 I will stretch out my hand a Edom 6584
25:16 to stretch out my hand a the Philistines, 6584
26: 3 I am a you, O Tyre, 6584
26: 3 and I will bring many nations a you, 6584
26: 7 to bring a Tyre Nebuchadnezzar king 448
26: 8 he will set up siege works a you, 6584
26: 8 up to your walls and raise his shields a you. 6584
26: 9 of his battering rams a your walls 928
28: 7 to bring foreigners a you, the most ruthless 6584
28: 7 they will draw their swords a your beauty 6584
28:21 set your face a Sidon; 448
28:21 face against Sidon; prophesy a her 6584
28:22 " 'I am a you, O Sidon, 6584
28:23 with the sword a her on every side. 6584
29: 2 set your face a Pharaoh king of Egypt 6584
29: 2 and prophesy a him and against all Egypt. 6584
29: 2 and prophesy against him and a all Egypt. 6584
29: 3 " 'I am a you, Pharaoh king of Egypt, 6584
29: 8 a sword a you and kill your men 6584
29:10 therefore I am a you and 448
29:10 therefore I am against you and a 448
29:18 in a hard campaign a Tyre; 448
29:18 from the campaign he led a Tyre. 6584
30: 4 A sword will come a Egypt, 928
30:11 They will draw their swords a Egypt 6584
30:22 I am a Pharaoh king of Egypt. 448
30:25 the king of Babylon and he brandishes it a 448
32:11 of the king of Babylon *will* **come** *a* you. AIT
33: 2 'When I bring the sword a a land, 6584
33: 3 and he sees the sword coming a the land 6584
33:16 be remembered a him. 4200
34: 2 prophesy a the shepherds of Israel; 6584
34:10 I am a the shepherds 448
35: 2 set your face a Mount Seir; 6584
35: 2 against Mount Seir; prophesy a it 6584
35: 3 I am a you, Mount Seir, 448
35: 3 and I will stretch out my hand a you 6584
35:12 the contemptible things you have said a 6584
35:13 You boasted a me and spoke against me 6584
35:13 You boasted against me and spoke a me 6584
36: 5 In my burning zeal I have spoken a the rest 6584
36: 5 the rest of the nations, and a all Edom, 6584
38: 2 set your face a Gog, of the land of Magog, 448
38: 2 Meshech and Tubal; prophesy a him 6584
38: 3 I am a you, O Gog, 448
38:12 I will plunder and loot and turn my hand a 6584
Eze 38:16 You will advance a my people Israel like 6584
38:16 O Gog, I will bring you a my land, 6584
38:17 for years that I would bring you a them. 6584
38:21 a sword a Gog on all my mountains, 6584
38:21 Every man's sword will be a his brother. 928
39: 1 "Son of man, prophesy a Gog and say: 6584
39: 1 I am a you, O Gog, 448
39: 2 the far north and send you a the mountains 6584
Da 3:29 or language who say anything a the God 10542
4:24 the decree the Most High has issued a 10542
5:23 you have set yourself up a the Lord 10542
6: 4 to find grounds for charges a Daniel 10378
6: 5 "We will never find any basis for charges a 10378
7:21 this horn was waging war a the saints 10554
7:25 He will speak a the Most High 10378+10608
8: 4 No animal could stand a him, 4200+7156
8: 7 The ram was powerless to stand a him; 4200+7156
8:25 and take his stand a the Prince of princes. 6584
9: 8 with shame because we have sinned a you. 4200
9: 9 even though we have rebelled a him; 928
9:11 because we have sinned a you. 4200
9:12 You have fulfilled the words spoken a us 6584
9:12 against us and a our rulers by bringing 6584
10:20 Soon I will return to fight a the prince 6640
10:21 (No one supports me a them except Michael 6584
11: 2 he will stir up everyone a the kingdom 907
11: 7 he will fight a them and be victorious. 928
11:11 in a rage and fight a the king of the North, 6640
11:14 "In those times many will rise a the king of 6584
11:16 no one will be able to stand a him. 4200+7156
11:25 up his strength and courage a the king of 6584
11:25 to stand because of the plots devised a him. 6584
11:28 his heart will be set a the holy covenant. 6584
11:28 He will take action a it and then return NIH
11:30 Then he will turn back and vent his fury a 6584
11:36 and will say unheard-of things a the God 6584
11:40 the king of the North will storm out a him 6584
Hos 4: 1 because the LORD has a charge to bring a 6640
4: 4 like *those who* **bring charges** *a* a priest. AIT
4: 7 the more they sinned a me; 4200
5: 1 This judgment is a you: 4200
5: 5 Israel's arrogance testifies a them; 928+7156
7:10 Israel's arrogance testifies a him, 928+7156
7:13 because they have rebelled a me! 928
7:13 I long to redeem them but they speak lies a 6584
7:15 but they plot evil a me. 448
8: 1 and rebelled a my law. 6584
8: 5 My anger burns a them. 928+6330
10:10 nations will be gathered a them to put them 6584
10:14 the roar of battle will rise a your people, so 928
11:12 And Judah is unruly a God, 6640
11:12 even a the faithful Holy One. 6640
12: 2 The LORD has a charge to bring a Judah; 6640
13: 9 because you are a me, against your helper. 928
13: 9 because you are against me, a your helper. 928
13:16 because they have rebelled a their God. 928
Joel 3: 2 There I will enter into judgment a them 6640
3: 4 "Now what have you a me, 4200
Am 1: 8 I will turn my hand a Ekron, 6584
3: 1 Hear this word the LORD has spoken a 6584
3: 1 a the whole family I brought up out 6584
3:13 "Hear this and testify a the house 928
6:14 "I will stir up a nation a you, 6584
7: 9 with my sword I will rise a the house 6584
7:10 "Amos is raising a conspiracy a you in 6584
7:16 You say, " 'Do not prophesy a Israel, 6584
7:16 and stop preaching a the house of Isaac.' 6584
Ob 1: 1 "Rise, and let us go a her for battle"— 6584
1:10 of the **violence** *a* your brother Jacob, AIT
Jnh 1: 2 to the great city of Nineveh and preach a it, 6584
Mic 1: 2 the Sovereign LORD may witness a you, 928
1:15 a conqueror a you who live in Mareshah. 4200
2: 3 "I am planning disaster a this people, 6584
3: 5 they prepare to wage war a him. 6584
4: 3 Nation will not take up sword a nation, 448
4:11 But now many nations are gathered a you. 6584
5: 1 O city of troops, for a siege is laid a us. 6584
5: 5 we will raise a him seven shepherds, 6584
6: 2 For the LORD has a case a his people; 6640
6: 2 he is lodging a charge a Israel. 6640
7: 6 a daughter rises up a her mother, 928
7: 6 a daughter-in-law a her mother-in-law— 928
7: 9 Because I have sinned a him, 4200
Na 1: 2 and maintains his wrath a his enemies. 4200
1: 9 Whatever they plot a 448
1:11 has one come forth who plots evil a 6584
2: 1 attacker advances a you, [Nineveh]. 6584+7156
2:13 "I am a you," 448
3: 5 "I am a you," 448
Hab 3: 8 Was your wrath a the streams? 928
3: 8 Did you rage a the sea when you rode 928
Zep 1: 4 "I will stretch out my hand a Judah and 6584
1: 4 against Judah and a all who live 6584
1:16 and battle cry a the fortified cities and 6584
1:16 the fortified cities and a the corner towers. 6584
1:17 because they have sinned a the LORD. 4200
2: 5 the word of the LORD is a you, 6584
2: 8 who insulted my people and made threats a 6584
2:13 He will stretch out his hand a the north 6584
Zec 1:21 of the nations who lifted up their horns a 448
2: 8 and has sent me a the nations 448
2: 9 I will surely raise my hand a them so 6584
8:10 for I had turned every man a his neighbor. 928
8:17 *do* not **plot** evil a your neighbor, 928+3108+4222
9: 1 The word of the LORD is a the land of 928
9: 8 I will defend my house a marauding forces. 4946
9:13 I will rouse your sons, O Zion, a your sons, 6584

Zec 10: 3 "My anger burns **a** the shepherds, 6584
12: 3 the nations of the earth are gathered **a** her, 6584
13: 7 "Awake, O sword, **a** my shepherd, 6584
13: 7 **a** the man who is close to me!" 6584
13: 7 and I will turn my hand **a** the little ones. 6584
14: 2 the nations to Jerusalem to fight **a** it; NIH
14: 3 Then the LORD will go out and fight **a** 928
14:12 the nations that fought **a** Jerusalem: 6584
Mal 3: 5 I will be quick to testify **a** sorcerers, 928
3: 5 **a** those who defraud laborers 928
3:13 "You have said harsh things **a** me," 6584
3:13 "Yet you ask, 'What have we said **a** you?' 6584
Mt 4: 6 you will not strike your foot **a** a stone.' " *4639*
5:11 and falsely say all kinds of evil **a** you *2848*
5:23 that your brother has something **a** you, *2848*
6:14 if you forgive men when they **sin a** you, *4183*
7:25 and the winds blew and **beat a** that house; *4700*
7:27 and the winds blew and **beat a** that house, *4684*
10:17 "Be on your guard **a** men; *608*
10:21 children *will* **rebel a** their parents *2060*
10:35 I have come to turn " 'a man **a** his father, *2848*
10:35 a daughter **a** her mother, *2848*
10:35 a daughter-in-law **a** her mother-in-law— *2848*
12:25 "Every kingdom divided **a** itself will *2848*
12:25 or household divided **a** itself will not stand. *2848*
12:26 he is divided **a** himself. *2093*
12:30 "He who is not with me is **a** me, *2848*
12:31 **blasphemy a** the Spirit will not be forgiven. *1060*
12:32 a word **a** the Son of Man will be forgiven, *2848*
12:32 but anyone who speaks **a** the Holy Spirit *2848*
14:24 by the waves because the wind was **a** it. *1885*
16: 6 on your guard **a** the yeast of the Pharisees *608*
16:11 on your guard **a** the yeast of the Pharisees *608*
16:12 not telling them to guard **a** the yeast used *608*
16:12 but **a** the teaching of the Pharisees *608*
18:15 "If your brother sins **a** you, *1650*
18:21 when he sins **a** me? *1650*
20:11 they began to grumble **a** the landowner. *2848*
23:31 So you testify *a* **yourselves** that you are *AIT*
24: 7 Nation will rise **a** nation, *2093*
24: 7 and kingdom **a** kingdom. *2093*
26:59 for false evidence **a** Jesus so *2848*
26:62 **testimony** that these men *are* **bringing a** *2909*
27: 6 "It is **a** the law to put this into the treasury, *4024*
27:13 **testimony** *they are* **bringing a** *2909*
27:37 the written **charge a** him: *162*
Mk 3:24 If a kingdom is divided **a** itself, *2093*
3:25 If a house is divided **a** itself, *2093*
3:29 But whoever blasphemes **a** *1650*
5:31 "You see the people **crowding a** you," *5315*
6:11 as a testimony *a* **them."** *AIT*
6:19 So Herodias **nursed a grudge a** John *1923*
6:48 because the wind was **a** them. *1885*
9:40 for whoever is not **a** us is for us. *2848*
10:11 marries another woman commits adultery **a** *2093*
11:25 if you hold anything **a** anyone, forgive him, *2848*
12:12 the parable **a** them. *4639*
13: 8 Nation will rise **a** nation, *2093*
13: 8 and kingdom **a** kingdom. *2093*
13:12 Children *will* **rebel a** their parents *2060*
14:55 for evidence **a** Jesus so *2848*
14:56 Many testified falsely **a** him, *2848*
14:57 up and gave this false testimony **a** him: *2848*
14:60 What *is* this **testimony** *that* these men *are* **bringing a** you?" *2909*
15:26 The written notice of the charge *a* **him** read: *AIT*
15:46 Then he rolled a stone **a** the entrance of *2093*
Lk 2:34 and to be a sign *that will be* **spoken a,** *515*
4:11 you will not strike your foot **a** a stone.' " *4639*
8:45 **crowding** and pressing **a** *5309*
9: 5 as a testimony **a** them." *2093*
9:50 "for whoever is not **a** you is for you." *2848*
10:11 that sticks to our feet *we* **wipe off a** you. *669*
11: 4 for we also forgive everyone who sins *a* **us.** *AIT*
11:17 "Any kingdom divided **a** itself will *2093*
11:17 and a house divided **a** itself will fall. *2093*
11:18 If Satan is divided **a** himself, *2093*
11:23 "He who is not with me is **a** me, *2848*
12: 1 on your guard **a** the yeast of the Pharisees, *608*
12:10 a word **a** the Son of Man will be forgiven, *1650*
12:10 but anyone who blasphemes **a** *1650*
12:15 Be on your guard **a** all kinds of greed; *608*
12:52 be five in one family divided **a** each other, *NIG*
12:52 three **a** two and two against three. *2093*
12:52 three against two and two **a** three. *2093*
12:53 father **a** son and son against father, *2093*
12:53 father against son and son **a** father, *2093*
12:53 mother **a** daughter and daughter *2093*
12:53 against daughter and daughter **a** mother, *2093*
12:53 mother-in-law **a** daughter-in-law *2093*
12:53 and daughter-in-law **a** mother-in-law." *2093*
14:31 a king is about to go to war *a* **another king.** *AIT*
14:31 to oppose the one coming **a** him *2093*
15:18 I have sinned **a** heaven and against you. *1650*
15:18 I have sinned against heaven and **a** you. *1967*
15:21 I have sinned **a** heaven and against you. *1650*
15:21 I have sinned against heaven and **a** you. *1967*
17: 4 If he sins **a** you seven times in a day, *1650*
18: 3 'Grant me justice **a** my adversary.' *608*
19:43 an embankment *a* **you** and encircle you *AIT*
20:19 they knew he had spoken this parable **a** *4639*
21:10 "Nation will rise **a** nation, *2093*
21:10 and kingdom **a** kingdom. *2093*
21:23 in the land and wrath *a* **this people.** *AIT*
23: 4 "I find no basis for a charge **a** this man." *1877*
23:14 and have found no basis for your charges **a** *2848*
Jn 13:18 has lifted up his heel **a** me.' *2093*
Jn 13:25 Leaning back **a** Jesus, he asked him, "Lord, *2093*
18:29 "What charges are you bringing **a** *2848*
18:38 "I find no basis for a charge **a** him. *1877*
19: 4 that I find no basis for a charge **a** him." *1877*
19: 6 I find no basis for a charge **a** him." *1877*
21:20 (This was the one who had leaned back **a** *2093*
Ac 4:26 the rulers gather together **a** the Lord and *2848*
4:26 against the Lord and **a** his Anointed One.' *2848*
4:27 to conspire **a** your holy servant Jesus, *2093*
5:39 you will only find yourselves **fighting a God."** *2534*
6: 1 among them complained **a** *4639*
6:10 but they could not **stand up a** his wisdom *468*
6:11 of blasphemy **a** Moses and against God." *1650*
6:11 of blasphemy against Moses and **a** God." *NIG*
6:13 "This fellow never stops speaking **a** *2848*
6:13 against this holy place and **a** the law. *NIG*
7:60 "Lord, do not hold this sin *a* **them."** *AIT*
8: 1 On that day a great persecution broke out **a** *2093*
9: 1 Saul was still breathing out murderous threats **a** the Lord's disciples. *1650*
10:28 "You are well aware that it is **a** our **law** for *116*
13:11 Now the hand of the Lord is **a** you. *2093*
13:45 with jealousy and **talked** abusively **a** *515*
13:50 **stirred up** persecution **a** Paul and Barnabbas *2074*
13:51 from their feet in protest **a** them and went *2093*
14: 2 up the Gentiles and poisoned their minds **a** *2848*
16:22 The crowd joined in the attack **a** Paul *2848*
19:38 a grievance **a** anybody, *4639*
20: 3 the Jews made a plot *a* **him** just as he was *AIT*
21:28 the man who teaches all men everywhere **a** *2848*
23:29 but there was no charge **a** him *NIG*
23:30 of a plot to be carried out **a** the man, *1650*
23:30 to present to you their case **a** him. *4639*
24: 1 and they brought their charges **a** Paul *2848*
24: 8 **charges** we *are* **bringing a** him." *2989*
24:13 **charges** *they are* now **making a** me. *2989*
24:19 bring charges if they have anything **a** me. *4639*
25: 2 and presented the charges **a** Paul. *2848*
25: 5 with me and **press charges a** the man there, *2989*
25: 7 **bringing** many serious charges **a** him, *2965*
25: 8 "I have done nothing wrong **a** the law of *1650*
25: 8 the Jews or **a** the temple or against Caesar." *1650*
25: 8 the Jews or against the temple or **a** Caesar." *1650*
25:11 the **charges brought a** me by these Jews *2989*
25:15 the Jews brought charges **a** him and asked *2848*
25:16 an opportunity to defend himself **a** *4309*
25:27 a prisoner without specifying the charges **a** *2848*
26: 2 as I make my defense **a** all the accusations *4309*
26:10 *I* **cast** *my* vote **a** them. *2965*
26:11 In my obsession **a** them, *NIG*
26:14 It is hard for you to kick **a** the goads.' *4639*
27: 4 the lee of Cyprus because the winds were **a** *1885*
27:29 that we would be dashed **a** the rocks, *2848*
28:17 although I have done nothing **a** our people *1883*
28:17 against our people or **a** the customs *NIG*
28:19 had any **charge to bring a** my own people. *2989*
28:22 that people everywhere *are* **talking a** *515*
Ro 1:18 of God is being revealed from heaven **a** all *2093*
2: 2 Now we know that God's judgment **a** *2093*
2: 5 you are storing up wrath *a* **yourself** for *AIT*
2:21 You who preach **a** stealing, do you steal? *3590*
4: 8 the Lord will never count **a** him." *NIG*
4:18 **A** all hope, Abraham in hope believed and *4123*
7:23 **waging war a** the law of my mind *529*
8:31 If God is for us, who can be **a** us? *2848*
8:33 Who will bring any charge **a** *2848*
11: 2 how he appealed to God **a** Israel: *2848*
13: 2 he who **rebels a** the authority is rebelling *530*
13: 2 against the authority *is* **rebelling a** *468*
1Co 4: 6 not take pride in one man **over a** another. *2848*
6: 6 one brother goes to law **a** another— *3552*
6:18 he who sins sexually sins **a** his own body. *1650*
8:12 When you sin **a** your brothers in this way *1650*
8:12 you sin **a** Christ. *1650*
11:27 be **guilty of sinning a** the body and blood *1944*
2Co 5:19 not counting men's sins *a* **them.** *AIT*
10: 5 that sets itself up **a** the knowledge of God, *2848*
13: 8 For we cannot do anything **a** the truth, *2848*
Gal 5:23 **A** such things there is no law. *2848*
Eph 6:11 of God so that you can take your stand **a** *4639*
6:12 For our struggle is not **a** flesh and blood, *4639*
6:12 but **a** the rulers, against the authorities, *4639*
6:12 but against the rulers, **a** the authorities, *4639*
6:12 **a** the powers of this dark world and against *4639*
6:12 against the powers of this dark world and **a** *4639*
Col 2:14 that was **a** us and that stood opposed to us; *2848*
3:13 forgive whatever grievances you may have **a** one another. *4639*
1Ti 3:10 and then if there is **nothing a them,** *441*
5:19 an accusation **a** an elder unless it is brought *2848*
2Ti 2:14 before God **a** quarreling about words; *3590*
4:15 You too *should be* **on** *your* **guard a** him, *5875*
4:16 May it not be held **a them.** *AIT*
Heb 12: 4 In your struggle **a** sin, *4639*
Jas 4:11 Anyone who **speaks a** his brother *2895*
4:11 judges him **speaks a** the law and judges it. *2895*
5: 3 Their corrosion will testify *a* **you** *AIT*
5: 4 workmen who mowed your fields are crying out **a** you. *608*
5: 9 Don't grumble **a** each other, brothers, *2848*
1Pe 2:11 which war **a** your soul. *2848*
3:12 face of the Lord is **a** those who do evil." *2093*
3:16 so that those who **speak maliciously a** *2092*
2Pe 2:11 do not bring slanderous accusations **a** *2848*
Jude 1: 9 **bring** a slanderous accusation **a** *2214*
1:10 Yet these men **speak abusively a** *1059*
Jude 1:15 harsh words ungodly sinners have spoken **a** *2848*
Rev 2: 4 Yet I hold this **a** you: *2848*
2:14 Nevertheless, I have a few things **a** you: *2848*
2:16 to you and will fight **a** them with the sword *3552*
2:20 Nevertheless, I have this **a** you: *2848*
12: 7 and his angels fought **a** the dragon, *3552*
12:17 at the woman and went off to make war **a** *3552*
13: 4 Who can make war **a** him?" *3552*
13: 7 He was given power to make war **a** *3552*
17:14 They will make war **a** the Lamb, *3552*
19:19 to make war **a** the rider on the horse *3552*

AGAR (KJV) See HAGAR

AGATE (2)

Ex 28:19 an **a** and an amethyst; 8648
39:12 an **a** and an amethyst; 8648

AGATES (KJV) See RUBY

AGE (67) [AGE-OLD, AGED, AGES, AGING]

Ge 15:15 in peace and be buried at a good **old a.** 8484
17:17 Will Sarah bear a child *at* the **a** *of* ninety?" 1426+9102
18:11 and Sarah was past the **a of childbearing.** 784+851+2021+3869
21: 2 and bore a son to Abraham in his **old a,** 2421
21: 7 Yet I have borne him a son in his **old a."** 2421
24:36 a son in her **old a,** 2420
25: 8 a good **old a,** an old man and full of years; 8484
37: 3 he had been born to him in his **old a;** 2421
44:20 a young son born to him in his **old a.** 2421
48:10 because of **old a,** 2419
50:26 Joseph died at the **a** *of* a hundred and ten. 1201+9102
Nu 4: 3 from thirty to fifty years *of* **a** who come 1201
4:23 from thirty to fifty years *of* **a** who come 1201
4:30 from thirty to fifty years *of* **a** who come 1201
4:35 from thirty to fifty years *of* **a** who came 1201
4:39 from thirty to fifty years *of* **a** who came 1201
4:43 from thirty to fifty years *of* **a** who came 1201
4:47 to fifty years *of* **a** who came to do the work 1201
8:25 but at the **a** *of* fifty, 1201
Jos 5: 4 all the men of **military a—** 4878
5: 6 until all the men who were of **military a** 4878
24:29 died at the **a** *of* a hundred and ten. 1201+9102
Jdg 2: 8 died at the **a** *of* a hundred and ten. 1201+9102
8:32 at a good **old a** and was buried in the tomb 8484
Ru 4:15 and sustain you in your **old a.** 8484
2Sa 19:32 a very old man, eighty years *of* **a.** 1201
1Ki 14: 4 his sight was gone because of his **a.** 8483
15:23 In his **old a,** however, 2420
1Ch 29:28 He died at a good **old a,** 8484
2Ch 24:15 he died at the **a** *of* a hundred and thirty 1201+9102
Ezr 3: 8 Levites twenty years *of* **a** and older 1201
Job 32: 7 I thought, '**A** should speak; 3427
Ps 92:14 They will still bear fruit in **old a,** 8484
Isa 46: 4 Even to your **old a** and gray hairs I am he, 2420
Da 1:10 the other young men your **a?** 1636
5:31 at the **a** of sixty-two. 10120+10732
Zec 8: 4 and women **of ripe old a** will sit in 2418
8: 4 with cane in hand because of his **a.** 3427+8044
Mt 12:32 either in this **a** or in the age to come. *172*
12:32 either in this age or in the **a** to come. *NIG*
13:39 The harvest is the end *of* the **a,** *172*
13:40 so it will be at the end *of* the **a.** *172*
13:49 This is how it will be at the end *of* the **a.** *172*
24: 3 of your coming and of the end *of* the **a?"** *172*
28:20 to the very end of the **a."** *172*
Mk 10:30 a hundred times as much in this present **a** *2789*
10:30 and in the **a** to come, eternal life. *172*
Lk 1:36 to have a child in her **old a,** *1179*
18:30 to receive many times as much in this **a** *2789*
18:30 in the **a** to come, eternal life." *172*
20:34 "The people *of* this **a** marry and are given *172*
20:35 *in* that **a** and in the resurrection from *172*
Jn 9:21 He is **of a;** he will speak for himself." *2461*
9:23 "He is **of a;** ask him." *2461*
1Co 1:20 Where is the philosopher *of* this **a?** *172*
2: 6 not the wisdom *of* this **a** or of the rulers *172*
2: 6 of this age or of the rulers *of* this **a,** *172*
2: 8 None of the rulers *of* this **a** understood it, *172*
3:18 by the standards of this **a,** *172*
2Co 4: 4 The god *of* this **a** has blinded the minds *172*
Gal 1: 4 to rescue us from the present evil **a,** *172*
1:14 in Judaism beyond many Jews **of** my **own a** *5312*
Eph 1:21 in the present **a** but also in the one to come. *172*
1Ti 6:19 as a firm foundation for the coming **a,** *NIG*
Tit 2:12 upright and godly lives in this present **a,** *172*
Heb 6: 5 of God and the powers *of* the coming **a,** *172*
11:11 Abraham, even though he was past **a—** *2461*

AGE-OLD (4) [AGE]

Ge 49:26 than the bounty of the **a** hills. 6409
Jdg 5:21 river Kishon swept them away, the **a** river, 7704
Isa 58:12 will raise up the **a** foundations; 1887+1887+2256
Hab 3: 6 and the **a** hills collapsed. 6409

AGED (11) [AGE]

Ge 43:27 "How is your **a** father you told me about? 2418
44:20 And we answered, 'We have an **a** father, 2418
Lev 19:32 " 'Rise in the presence of the **a,** 8484
1Ki 1:15 So Bathsheba went to see the **a** king 2416+4394

2Ch 36:17 nor young woman, old man or a. 3844
Job 12:12 Is not wisdom found among the a? 3813
15:10 The gray-haired and the a are on our side, 3813
32: 9 the a who understand what is right. 2418
Pr 17: 6 Children's children are a crown to the a, 2418
Isa 25: 6 a banquet of a wine— 9069
47: 6 Even on the a you laid a very heavy yoke. 2418

AGEE (1)

2Sa 23:11 to him was Shammah son of A the Hararite. 96

AGENT (2)

Ne 11:24 the king's a in all affairs relating to 3338+4200
Ro 13: 4 a of wrath to bring punishment *1690*

AGES (14) [AGE]

Ge 43:33 order of their a, from the firstborn to 1148+7584
Lev 27: 3 between the a of twenty and sixty 1201+9102
27: 5 between the a of five and twenty, 1201+9102
Isa 45:17 to shame or disgraced, to a everlasting. 6409
Joel 2: 2 as never was of old nor ever will be in a 9102
Ac 15:18 that have been known for a. *172*
Ro 16:25 of the mystery hidden for long a past, *173*
1Co 10:11 on whom the fulfillment of the a has come. *172*
Eph 2: 7 in order that in the coming a he might show *172*
3: 9 which for a past was kept hidden in God, *172*
Col 1:26 the mystery that has been kept hidden for a *172*
Heb 9:26 at the end of the a to do away with sin by *172*
Jude 1:25 through Jesus Christ our Lord, before all a, *172*
Rev 15: 3 Just and true are your ways, King of the a. *172*

AGGRESSION (1) [AGGRESSIVE, AGGRESSOR]

Isa 14: 6 in fury subdued nations with relentless a. 5284

AGGRESSIVE (2) [AGGRESSION]

Isa 18: 2 an a nation of strange speech, 4431
18: 7 an a nation of strange speech, 4431

AGGRESSOR (1) [AGGRESSION]

Isa 16: 4 the a will vanish from the land. 8252

AGHAST (2)

Job 26:11 pillars of the heavens quake, a at his rebuke. 9449
Isa 13: 8 They will look a at each other, 9449

AGING (1) [AGE]

Heb 8:13 what is obsolete and a will soon disappear. *1180*

AGITATING (1) [AGITATORS]

Ac 17:13 a the crowds and stirring them up. *4888*

AGITATORS (1) [AGITATING]

Gal 5:12 As for those a, *415*

AGO (48)

Jos 24: 2 'Long a your forefathers, 4946+6409
1Sa 9:20 the donkeys you lost three days a, 2021+3427
30:13 when I became ill three days a. AIT
2Sa 20:18 "Long a they used to say, 928+2021+8037
2Ki 19:25 Long a I ordained it. 4200+4946+8158
Ezr 5:11 the temple that was built many years a, 10180+10427+10622
Ne 12:46 For long a, in the days of David 4946+7710
Ps 44: 1 in their days, in days long a. 7710
77: 5 the years of long a; 6409
77:11 I will remember your miracles of long a. 7710
93: 2 Your throne was established long a; 255+4946
119:152 Long a I learned from your statutes 7710
143: 5 I remember the days of long a; 7710
Ecc 1:10 It was here already, long a; 4200+6409
Isa 22:11 for the One who planned it long a. 4946+8158
25: 1 things planned long a. 4946+8158
37:26 Long a I ordained it. 4200+4946+8158
44: 8 not proclaim this and foretell it long a? 255+4946
45:21 Who foretold this long a, 4946+7710
46: 9 the former things, those of long a; 6409
48: 3 I foretold the former things long a, 255+4946
48: 5 I told you these things long a; 255+4946
48: 7 They are created now, and not long a; 255+4946
Jer 2:20 "Long a you broke off your yoke 4946+6409
La 2:17 which he decreed long a. 3427+4946+7710
Eze 26:20 go down to the pit, to the people of long a. 6409
Mic 7:14 in Bashan and Gilead as in days long a. 6409
7:20 on oath to our fathers in days long a. 7710
Mt 5:21 that it was said to the people long a, *792*
5:33 that it was said to the people long a, *792*
11:21 they would have repented long a *4093*
Mk 6:15 like one of the prophets of long a." *NIG*
Lk 1:70 through his holy prophets of long a), *172*
9: 8 of the prophets of long a had come back *792*
9:19 of the prophets of long a has come back *792*
10:13 they would have repented long a, *4093*
Jn 11: 8 "a short while a the Jews tried to stone you, *3814*
Ac 1:16 the Holy Spirit spoke long a through *4625*
3:21 as he promised long a *172+608*
5:36 Some time a Theudas appeared, *2465+3836+4047+4574*
10:30 "Four days a I was in my house praying *NIG*
15: 7 some time a God made a choice *608+792+2465*
21:38 the desert some time a?" *2465+3836+4047+4574*
24:11 no more than twelve days a I went up *608+4005*
2Co 12: 2 in Christ who fourteen years a was caught *4574*
1Pe 3:20 who disobeyed long a when God waited *4537*
2Pe 3: 5 But they deliberately forget that long a *1732*
Jude 1: 4 about long a have secretly slipped in *4093*

AGONE (KJV) See AGO

AGONY (11)

Ps 6: 2 O LORD, heal me, for my bones are in a. 987
42:10 My bones suffer mortal a 8358
Jer 4:19 Oh, the a of my heart! 7815
Eze 30:16 Pelusium will writhe in a. 2655+2655
Mic 4:10 Writhe in a, O Daughter of Zion, 1631
Zec 9: 5 Gaza will writhe in a, and Ekron too, 2655+4394
Lk 16:24 because I am in a in this fire.' *3849*
16:25 now he is comforted here and you are in a. *3849*
Ac 2:24 freeing him from the a of death, *6047*
Rev 9: 5 the a they suffered was like that of the sting *990*
16:10 Men gnawed their tongues in a *4506*

AGREE (14) [AGREED, AGREEING, AGREEMENT, AGREEMENTS, AGREES, DISAGREE, DISAGREEMENT]

Ge 34:17 But if you will not a to be circumcised, 9048
2Sa 14:16 the king will a to deliver his servant from 9048
1Ki 20: 8 "Don't listen to him or a to his demands." 14
22:13 Let your word a with theirs, 285+2118+3869
2Ch 18:12 Let your word a with theirs, 285+2118+3869
Mt 18:19 of you on earth a about anything you ask *5244*
20:13 Didn't you a to work for a denarius? *5244*
Mk 14:56 but their statements did not a. *2698*
14:59 Yet even then their testimony did not a. *2698*
Ac 5: 9 could you a to test the Spirit of the Lord? *5244*
Ro 7:16 I a that the law is good. *5238*
1Co 1:10 that all of you a with one another *899+3306+3836*
Php 4: 2 with Syntyche to a with each other in *5858*
1Ti 6: 3 and does not a to the sound instruction *4665*

AGREED (27) [AGREE]

Ge 16: 2 Abram a to what Sarai said. 9048
23:16 Abraham a to Ephron's terms 9048
30:34 "A," said Laban. 2176
34:24 All the men who went out of the city gate a 9048
37:27 His brothers a. 9048
Ex 2:21 Moses a to stay with the man, 3283
Jos 2:21 "A," she replied. 4026
Jdg 15:13 "A," they answered. 4202
17:11 So the Levite a to live with him, 3283
1Ki 15:20 Ben-Hadad a with King Asa and sent 9048
20:25 He a with them and acted accordingly. 4200+7754+9048
2Ki 12: 8 The priests a that they would 252
1Ch 13: 4 The whole assembly a to do this, 606
2Ch 16: 4 Ben-Hadad a with King Asa and sent 9048
20:36 He a with him to construct a fleet 2489
30:23 The whole assembly then a to celebrate 3619
Est 9:23 So the Jews a to continue 7691
Jer 34:10 into this covenant a 9048
34:10 They a, and set them free. 9048
Da 1:14 So he a to this and tested them for ten days. 9048
6: 7 advisers and governors have all a that 10324
Am 3: 3 Do two walk together unless they have a 3359
Mt 20: 2 He a to pay them a denarius for the day *5244*
Lk 22: 5 They were delighted and a *5338*
Ac 15:25 So we all a to choose some men *1181+3924*
23:20 "The Jews have a to ask you to bring Paul *5338*
Gal 2: 9 They a that we should go to the Gentiles, *NIG*

AGREEING (1) [AGREE]

Rev 17:17 by a to give the beast their power to rule, *1191+1651+4472*

AGREEMENT (12) [AGREE]

Ge 26:28 'There ought to be a sworn a between us'— 460
2Sa 3:12 Make an a with me, 1382
3:13 "I will make an a with you. 1382
Ne 9:38 we are making a binding a, 591
Job 2:11 and met together by a to go and sympathize 3585
41: 4 Will he make an a with you for you 1382
Isa 28:15 with the grave we have made an a. 2603
28:18 your a with the grave will not stand. 2607
Da 11:23 After coming to an a with him, 2489
Ac 15:15 words of the prophets are in a with this, *5244*
2Co 6:16 What a is there between the temple of God *5161*
1Jn 5: 8 and the three are in a. *1650+1651+3836*

AGREEMENTS (1) [AGREE]

Hos 10: 4 take false oaths and make a; 1382

AGREES (3) [AGREE]

Ac 7:42 This a with what is written in the book of *2777*
24:14 I believe everything that a with the Law and *2848*
1Co 4:17 which a with what I teach everywhere *2777*

AGRIPPA (11)

Ac 25:13 A few days later King A and Bernice *68*
25:22 Then A said to Festus, "I would like to hear *68*
25:23 The next day A and Bernice came *68*
25:24 "King A, and all who are present with us, *68*
25:26 and especially before you, King A, *68*
26: 1 Then A said to Paul, "You have permission *68*
26: 2 "King A, I consider myself fortunate *68*
26:19 King A, I was not disobedient to the vision *68*
26:27 King A, do you believe the prophets? *68*
26:28 Then A said to Paul, "Do you think *68*
26:32 A said to Festus, "This man could have been *68*

AGROUND (4) [GROUND]

Ac 27:17 that they would run a on the sandbars *1738*
27:26 we must run a on some island." *1738*
27:39 where they decided to run the ship a *2034*
27:41 But the ship struck a sandbar and ran a. *2131*

AGUE (KJV) See FEVER

AGUR (1)

Pr 30: 1 The sayings of A son of Jakeh— 101

AH (15) [AHA]

Ge 27:27 he blessed him and said, "A, 8011
Nu 24:23 "A, who can live when God does this? 208
Jos 7: 7 And Joshua said, "A, Sovereign LORD, 177
Jdg 6:22 he exclaimed, "A, Sovereign LORD! 177
Isa 1: 4 A, sinful nation, a people loaded with guilt, 2098
1:24 "A, I will get relief from my foes 2098
44:16 He also warms himself and says, "A! 2027
Jer 1: 6 "A, Sovereign LORD," I said, 177
4:10 Then I said, "A, Sovereign LORD, 177
14:13 But I said, "A, Sovereign LORD, 177
32:17 "A, Sovereign LORD, you have made 177
47: 6 " 'A, sword of the LORD,' [you cry,] 2098
Eze 9: 8 crying out, "A, Sovereign LORD! 177
11:13 "A, Sovereign LORD! 177
20:49 Then I said, "A, Sovereign LORD! 177

AHA (11) [AH]

Job 39:25 At the blast of the trumpet he snorts, 'A!' 2027
Ps 35:21 They gape at me and say, "A! 2027
35:21 at me and say, "Aha! A! 2027
35:25 Do not let them think, "A, 2027
40:15 May those who say to me, "A! 2027
40:15 May those who say to me, "Aha! A!" 2027
70: 3 May those who say to me, "A! 2027
70: 3 May those who say to me, "Aha! A!" 2027
Eze 25: 3 Because you said "A!" 2027
26: 2 because Tyre has said of Jerusalem, 'A! 2027
36: 2 The enemy said of you, "A! 2027

AHAB (85) [AHAB'S]

1Ki 16:28 And A his son succeeded him as king. 281
16:29 A son of Omri became king of Israel, 281
16:30 A son of Omri did more evil in the eyes of 281
16:33 A also made an Asherah pole and did more 281
17: 1 from Tishbe in Gilead, said to A, 281
18: 1 "Go and present yourself to A, 281
18: 2 So Elijah went to present himself to A. 281
18: 3 and A had summoned Obadiah, 281
18: 5 A had said to Obadiah, 281
18: 6 A going in one direction and Obadiah 281
18: 9 over to A to be put to death? 281
18:12 If I go and tell A and he doesn't find you, 281
18:15 I will surely present myself to A today." 2257S
18:16 So Obadiah went to meet A and told him, 281
18:16 and A went to meet Elijah. 281
18:20 So A sent word throughout all Israel 281
18:41 And Elijah said to A, "Go, eat and drink, 281
18:42 So A went off to eat and drink, 281
18:44 So Elijah said, "Go and tell A, 281
18:45 a heavy rain came on and A rode off 281
18:46 he ran ahead of A all the way to Jezreel. 281
19: 1 A told Jezebel everything Elijah had done 281
20: 2 He sent messengers into the city to A king 281
20:10 Ben-Hadad sent another message to A: 2257S
20:13 Meanwhile a prophet came to A king 281
20:14 "But who will do this?" asked A. 281
20:15 So A summoned the young officers of NIH
20:33 A had him come up into his chariot. NIH
20:34 [A said,] "On the basis of NIH
21: 1 close to the palace of A king of Samaria. 281
21: 2 A said to Naboth, "Let me have your vineyard 281
21: 4 So A went home, sullen and angry 281
21:15 she said to A, "Get up and take possession 281
21:16 When A heard that Naboth was dead, 281
21:18 "Go down to meet A king of Israel, 281
21:20 A said to Elijah, "So you have found me, 281
21:21 and cut off from A every last male 281
21:24 to A who die in the city, 281
21:25 (There was never a man like A, 281
21:27 When A heard these words, 281
21:29 how A has humbled himself before me? 281
22:20 'Who will entice A into attacking 281
22:40 A rested with his fathers. 281
22:41 in the fourth year of A king of Israel. 281
22:49 At that time Ahaziah son of A said 281
22:51 of A became king of Israel in Samaria in 281
2Ki 3: 1 of A became king of Israel in Samaria in 281
3: 5 But after A died, the king of Moab rebelled 281
8:16 In the fifth year of Joram son of A king 281

2Ki 8:18 as the house of A had done, 281
8:18 for he married a daughter of A. 281
8:25 In the twelfth year of Joram son of A king 281
8:27 of the house of A and did evil in the eyes of 281
8:27 as the house of A had done, 281
8:28 Ahaziah went with Joram son of A to war 281
8:29 down to Jezreel to see Joram son of A, 281
9:7 to destroy the house of A your master, 281
9:8 The whole house of A will perish. 281
9:8 I will cut off from A every last male 281
9:9 I will make the house of A like the house 281
9:25 in chariots behind A his father when 281
9:29 (In the eleventh year of Joram son of A, 281
10:1 in Samaria seventy sons of the house of A. 281
10:10 against the house of A will fail. 281
10:11 in Jezreel who remained of the house of A, 281
10:18 "A served Baal a little; 281
10:30 and have done to the house of A all I had 281
21:3 as A king of Israel had done. 281
21:13 the plumb line used against the house of A. 281
2Ch 18:1 and he allied himself with A by marriage. 281
18:2 Some years later he went down to visit A 281
18:2 A slaughtered many sheep and cattle 281
18:3 A king of Israel asked Jehoshaphat king 281
18:19 'Who will entice A king of Israel 281
21:6 as the house of A had done, 281
21:6 for he married a daughter of A. 281
21:13 just as the house of A did. 281
22:3 in the ways of the house of A, 281
22:4 as the house of A had done, 281
22:5 with Joram son of A king of Israel to war 281
22:6 down to Jezreel to see Joram son of A 281
22:7 to destroy the house of A. 281
22:8 executing judgment on the house of A, 281
Jer 29:21 about A son of Kolaiah and Zedekiah son 281
29:22 like Zedekiah and A, 282

AHAB'S (8) [AHAB]

1Ki 16:34 In A time, Hiel of Bethel rebuilt Jericho. 2257S
21:8 So she wrote letters in A name, 281
22:39 As for the other events of A reign, 281
2Ki 1:1 After A death, Moab rebelled against Israel. 281
8:27 for he was related by marriage to A family. 281
10:1 and to the guardians of A children. 281
10:17 killed all who were left there of A family; 281
Mic 6:16 of Omri and all the practices of A house, 281

AHARAH (1)

1Ch 8:1 Ashbel the second son, A the third, 341

AHARHEL (1)

1Ch 4:8 and Hazzobebah and of the clans of A son 342

AHASAI (KJV) See AHZAI

AHASBAI (1)

2Sa 23:34 Eliphelet son of A the Maacathite, 335

AHASUERUS' (KJV) See XERXES

AHAVA (3)

Ezr 8:15 at the canal that flows toward A, 178
8:21 There, by the A Canal, I proclaimed a fast, 178
8:31 the first month we set out from the A Canal 178

AHAZ (44)

2Ki 15:38 And A his son succeeded him as king. 298
16:1 A son of Jotham king of Judah began 298
16:2 A was twenty years old 298
16:5 to fight against Jerusalem and besieged A, 298
16:7 A sent messengers to say 298
16:8 And A took the silver and gold found in 298
16:10 Then King A went to Damascus 298
16:11 with all the plans that King A had sent 298
16:11 and finished it before King A returned. 298
16:15 King A then gave these orders to Uriah 298
16:16 the priest did just as King A had ordered. 298
16:17 King A took away the side panels 298
16:19 As for the other events of the reign of A, 298
16:20 A rested with his fathers and was buried 298
17:1 In the twelfth year of A king of Judah, 298
18:1 Hezekiah son of A king of Judah began 298
20:11 down on the stairway of A. 298
23:12 on the roof near the upper room of A, 298
1Ch 3:13 A his son, Hezekiah his son, 298
8:35 Pithon, Melech, Tarea and A. 298
8:36 A was the father of Jehoaddah, 298
9:41 Pithon, Melech, Tahrea and A. 298
9:42 A was the father of Jadah, 298
2Ch 27:9 And A his son succeeded him as king. 298
28:1 A was twenty years old 298
28:16 that time King A sent to the king of Assyria 298
28:19 because of A king of Israel, 298
28:21 A took some of the things from the temple 298
28:22 In his time of trouble King A became 298
28:24 A gathered together the furnishings from 298
28:27 A rested with his fathers and was buried in 298
29:19 that King A removed in his unfaithfulness 298
Isa 1:1 Jotham, A and Hezekiah, kings of Judah. 298
7:1 When A son of Jotham, the son of Uzziah, 298
7:2 the hearts of A and his people were shaken, 2257S
7:3 to meet A at the end of the aqueduct of 298
7:10 Again the LORD spoke to A, 298
7:12 But A said, "I will not ask; 298
14:28 This oracle came in the year King A died: 298
38:8 down on the stairway of A.' " 298
Hos 1:1 Jotham, A and Hezekiah, kings of Judah, 298
Mic 1:1 A and Hezekiah, kings of Judah— 298
Mt 1:9 Jotham the father of A, *937*
1:9 A the father of Hezekiah, *937*

AHAZIAH (39) [AHAZIAH'S]

1Ki 22:40 And A his son succeeded him as king. 302
22:49 At that time A son of Ahab said 302
22:51 A son of Ahab became king of Israel 302
2Ki 1:2 Now A had fallen through the lattice 301
1:17 Because A had no son, 2257S
8:24 And A his son succeeded him as king. 302
8:25 A son of Jehoram king of Judah began 302
8:26 A was twenty-two years old 302
8:28 A went with Joram son of Ahab to war NIH
8:29 Then A son of Jehoram king of Judah went 302
9:16 because Joram was resting there and A king 301
9:21 of Israel and A king of Judah rode out, 302
9:23 calling out to A, "Treachery, Ahaziah!" 302
9:23 calling out to Ahaziah, "Treachery, A!" 301
9:27 A king of Judah saw what had happened, 301
9:29 A had become king of Judah.) 301
10:13 he met some relatives of A king of Judah 302
10:13 They said, "We are relatives of A, 302
11:1 the mother of A saw that her son was dead, 302
11:2 daughter of King Jehoram and sister of A, 302
11:2 took Joash son of A and stole him away 301
12:18 Jehoshaphat, Jehoram and A, 302
13:1 of Joash son of A king of Judah, 302
14:13 the son of A, at Beth Shemesh. 302
1Ch 3:11 Jehoram his son, A his son, Joash his son, 302
2Ch 20:35 of Judah made an alliance with A king 301
20:37 you have made an alliance with A, 302
21:17 Not a son was left to him except A, 3370
22:1 The people of Jerusalem made A, 302
22:1 So A son of Jehoram king of Judah began 302
22:2 A was twenty-two years old 302
22:6 Then A son of Jehoram king of Judah went 302
22:7 When A arrived, he went out with Joram 2257S
22:8 who had been attending A, 302
22:9 He then went in search of A, 302
22:9 in the house of A powerful enough to retain 302
22:10 the mother of A saw that her son was dead, 302
22:11 took Joash son of A and stole him away 302
25:23 the son of A, at Beth Shemesh 3370

AHAZIAH'S (5) [AHAZIAH]

2Ki 1:18 As for all the other events of A reign, 302
2Ch 22:7 Through A visit to Joram, NIH
22:7 God brought about A downfall. 302
22:8 of Judah and the sons of A relatives, 302
22:11 of the priest Jehoiada, was A sister, she hid 302

AHBAN (1)

1Ch 2:29 who bore him A and Molid. 283

AHEAD (97) [HEAD]

Ge 31:18 **drove** all his livestock **a** 5627
32:3 Jacob sent messengers **a** *of* him 4200+7156
32:16 and said to his servants, "Go **a** *of* me, 4200+7156
32:20 with these gifts I am sending on **a**; 4200+7156
32:21 So Jacob's gifts went on **a** *of* him, 6584+7156
33:3 He himself went on **a** and bowed down 4200+7156
33:14 So let my lord go on **a** *of* his servant, 4200+7156
45:5 to save lives that God sent me **a** *of* you 4200+7156
45:7 But God sent me **a** *of* you to preserve 4200+7156
46:28 Jacob sent Judah **a** *of* him to Joseph 4200+7156
48:20 So he put Ephraim **a** *of* Manasseh. 4200+7156
Ex 13:21 By day the LORD went **a** *of* them in 4200+7156
17:5 "Walk on **a** *of* the people. 4200+7156
23:20 an angel **a** *of* you to guard you along 4200+7156
23:23 My angel will go **a** *of* you and bring 4200+7156
23:27 "I will send my terror **a** *of* you 4200+7156
23:28 hornet **a** *of* you to drive the Hivites, 4200+7156
Nu 22:26 Then the angel of the LORD **moved on a** 6296
32:17 we are ready to arm ourselves and go **a** 4200+7156
Dt 1:22 "Let us send men **a** to spy out the land 4200+7156
1:33 who went **a** *of* you on your journey, 4200+7156
3:18 over **a** *of* your brother Israelites. 4200+7156
9:3 the one who goes across **a** *of* you like 4200+7156
31:3 God himself will cross over **a** *of* you. 4200+7156
31:3 Joshua also will cross over **a** *of* you, 4200+7156
Jos 1:14 must cross over **a** *of* your brothers. 4200+7156
3:6 ark of the covenant and pass on **a** *of* 4200+7156
3:6 So they took it up and went **a** *of* them. 4200+7156
3:11 will go into the Jordan **a** *of* you. 4200+7156
3:14 the ark of the covenant went **a** *of* them 4200+7156
6:7 the armed guard going **a** *of* the ark 4200+7156
6:9 The armed guard marched **a** *of* 4200+7156
6:13 The armed men went **a** *of* them and 4200+7156
24:12 I sent the hornet **a** *of* you, 4200+7156
Jdg 4:14 Has not the LORD gone **a** *of* you?" 4200+7156
7:24 the Jordan **a** *of* them as far as Beth Barah." 4200
Ru 2:2 Naomi said to her, **"Go a,** my daughter." 2143
1Sa 9:12 "He's **a** *of* you. 4200+7156
9:19 "Go up **a** *of* me to the high place, 4200+7156
9:27 "Tell the servant to go on **a** *of* us"— 4200+7156
10:8 "Go down **a** *of* me to Gilgal. 4200+7156
14:7 **"Go a;** I am with you heart and soul." 5742
17:7 His shield bearer went **a** *of* him. 4200+7156
23:24 set out and went to Ziph **a** *of* Saul. 4200+7156
25:19 Then she told her servants, "Go on **a;** 4200+7156
30:20 and his men drove them **a** *of* 4200+7156
2Sa 7:3 **go a** and do it, for the LORD is with you." 2143
15:1 and horses and with fifty men to run **a** 4200+7156
15:22 David said to Ittai, **"Go a,** march on." 2143
1Ki 1:5 with fifty men to run **a** *of* him. 4200+7156
18:46 he ran **a** *of* Ahab all the way to Jezreel. 4200+7156
2Ki 4:31 went on **a** and laid the staff on the boy's face, 4200+7156
5:23 and they carried them **a** *of* Gehazi. 4200+7156
6:32 The king sent a messenger **a,** 4200+4946+7156
Ne 4:7 the repairs to Jerusalem's walls *had* **gone a** 6590
Pr 4:25 Let your eyes look **straight a,** 4200+5790
Jer 7:21 *Go a,* **add** your burnt offerings AIT
44:25 *"Go a* then, **do** what you promised! AIT
Eze 1:9 Each one went **straight a;** 448+6298+7156
1:12 Each one went **straight a.** 448+6298+7156
10:22 Each one went **straight a.** 448+6298+7156
Joel 2:8 each marches **straight a.** 5019
Mt 2:9 the star they had seen in the east **went a of** *4575*
11:10 " 'I will send my messenger **a** of you, *4574+4725*
14:22 and **go on a of** him to the other side, *4575*
21:2 "Go to the village **a** of you, *2978*
21:9 The crowds that **went a of** him and those *4575*
21:31 **entering** the kingdom of God **a of** you. *4575*
24:25 See, *I have* **told** you **a of time.** *4625*
26:32 *I will* **go a of** you into Galilee." *4575*
28:7 from the dead and *is* **going a of** you *4575*
Mk 1:2 "I will send my messenger **a** of you, *4574+4725*
6:33 from all the towns and **got there a of** them. *4601*
6:45 the boat and **go on a of** him to Bethsaida, *4575*
11:2 "Go to the village **a** of you, *2978*
11:9 Those who **went a** and those who followed *4575*
13:23 **told** you everything **a of time.** *4625*
14:28 *I will* **go a of** you into Galilee." *4575*
16:7 *'He is* **going a of** you into Galilee. *4575*
Lk 7:27 " 'I will send my messenger **a** of you, *4574+4725*
9:52 And he sent messengers **on a,** *4574+4725*
10:1 two by two **a** of him to every town *4574+4725*
19:4 So he ran **a** and climbed *1869*
19:28 After Jesus had said this, he went on **a,** *1869*
19:30 "Go to the village **a** of you, *2978*
19:32 Those who were sent **a** went *NIG*
Jn 3:28 'I am not the Christ but am sent **a** of him.' *1869*
5:7 someone else goes down **a** of me." *4574*
10:4 he goes **on a** of them, *1869*
Ac 2:31 **Seeing what was a,** he spoke *4632*
20:5 These men **went on a** and waited for us *4601*
20:13 We **went on a** to the ship and sailed *4601*
1Co 11:21 each of you **goes a** without waiting *4624*
Php 3:13 behind and straining toward what is **a,** *1869*
1Ti 5:24 **reaching** the place of judgment **a** of them; *4575*
Heb 11:26 because *he was* **looking a** to his reward. *611*
2Jn 1:9 Anyone who **runs a** and does not continue *4575*

AHER (1)

1Ch 7:12 and the Hushites the descendants of A. 338

AHI (2)

1Ch 5:15 A son of Abdiel, the son of Guni, 306
7:34 A, Rohgah, Hubbah and Aram. 306

AHIAH (1)

Ne 10:26 A, Hanan, Anan, 308

AHIAM (2)

2Sa 23:33 A son of Sharar the Hararite, 307
1Ch 11:35 A son of Sacar the Hararite, 307

AHIAN (1)

1Ch 7:19 A, Shechem, Likhi and Aniam. 319

AHIEZER (6)

Nu 1:12 from Dan, A son of Ammishaddai; 323
2:25 The leader of the people of Dan is A son 323
7:66 On the tenth day A son of Ammishaddai, 323
7:71 the offering of A son of Ammishaddai. 323
10:25 A son of Ammishaddai was in command. 323
1Ch 12:3 A their chief and Joash the sons 323

AHIHUD (2)

Nu 34:27 A son of Shelomi, the leader from the tribe 310
1Ch 8:7 and who was the father of Uzza and A. 312

AHIJAH (21) [AHIJAH'S]

1Sa 14:3 among whom was A, 308
14:18 Saul said to A, "Bring the ark of God." 308
1Ki 4:3 Elihoreph and A, sons of Shisha— 308
11:29 and A the prophet of Shiloh met him on 308
11:30 and A took hold of the new cloak 308
12:15 to Jeroboam son of Nebat through A 308
14:2 A the prophet is there— 308
14:4 Now A could not see; 309
14:5 But the LORD had told A, 309
14:6 So when A heard the sound of her footsteps 309
14:18 through his servant the prophet A. 309
15:27 of A of the house of Issachar plotted 308
15:29 of the LORD given through his servant A 308
15:33 Baasha son of A became king of all Israel 308
21:22 of Nebat and that of Baasha son of A, 308
2Ki 9:9 and like the house of Baasha son of A. 308

1Ch 2:25 Bunah, Oren, Ozem and A. 308
8: 7 A, and Gera, who deported them 308
11:36 Hepher the Mekerathite, A the Pelonite, 308
2Ch 9:29 of A the Shilonite and in the visions of Iddo 308
10:15 to Jeroboam son of Nebat through A 309

AHIJAH'S (1) [AHIJAH]
1Ki 14: 4 and went to A house in Shiloh. 308

AHIKAM (20)
2Ki 22:12 A son of Shaphan, Acbor son of Micaiah, 324
22:14 Hilkiah the priest, A, Acbor, 324
25:22 of Babylon appointed Gedaliah son of A, 324
2Ch 34:20 A son of Shaphan, Abdon son of Micah, 324
Jer 26:24 A son of Shaphan supported Jeremiah, 324
39:14 over to Gedaliah son of A, 324
40: 5 "Go back to Gedaliah son of A, 324
40: 6 of A at Mizpah and stayed with him among 324
40: 7 of A as governor over the land 324
40: 9 Gedaliah son of A, the son of Shaphan, 324
40:11 and had appointed Gedaliah son of A, 324
40:14 Gedaliah son of A did not believe them. 324
40:16 But Gedaliah son of A said to Johanan son 324
41: 1 came with ten men to Gedaliah son of A 324
41: 2 up and struck down Gedaliah son of A, 324
41: 6 he said, "Come to Gedaliah son of A." 324
41:10 of the imperial guard had appointed Gedaliah son of A. 324
41:16 after he had assassinated Gedaliah son of A: 324
41:18 of Nethaniah had killed Gedaliah son of A, 324
43: 6 with Gedaliah son of A, 324

AHILUD (5)
2Sa 8:16 Jehoshaphat son of A was recorder; 314
20:24 Jehoshaphat son of A was recorder; 314
1Ki 4: 3 Jehoshaphat son of A— 314
4:12 Baana son of A— 314
1Ch 18:15 Jehoshaphat son of A was recorder; 314

AHIMAAZ (15)
1Sa 14:50 wife's name was Ahinoam daughter of A. 318
2Sa 15:27 with your son A and Jonathan son 318
15:36 A son of Zadok and Jonathan son 318
17:17 Jonathan and A were staying at En Rogel. 318
17:20 they asked, "Where are A and Jonathan?" 318
18:19 Now A son of Zadok said, 318
18:22 A son of Zadok again said to Joab, 318
18:23 Then A ran by way of the plain and outran 318
18:27 that the first one runs like A son of Zadok." 318
18:28 A called out to the king, "All is well!" 318
18:29 A answered, "I saw great confusion just 318
1Ki 4:15 A—in Naphtali (he had married Basemath 318
1Ch 6: 8 Zadok the father of A, 318
6: 9 A the father of Azariah, 318
6:53 Zadok his son and A his son. 318

AHIMAN (4)
Nu 13:22 where A, Sheshai and Talmai, 317
Jos 15:14 Sheshai, A and Talmai— 317
Jdg 1:10 and defeated Sheshai, A and Talmai. 317
1Ch 9:17 Akkub, Talmon, A and their brothers, 317

AHIMELECH (19)
1Sa 21: 1 David went to Nob, to A the priest. 316
21: 1 A trembled when he met him, and asked, 316
21: 2 David answered A the priest, 316
21: 8 David asked A, "Don't you have a spear or 316
22: 9 of Jesse come to A son of Ahitub at Nob. 316
22:10 A inquired of the LORD for him; NIH
22:11 the king sent for the priest A son of Ahitub 316
22:14 A answered the king, "Who of all 316
22:16 But the king said, "You will surely die, A, 316
22:20 But Abiathar, a son of A son of Ahitub, 316
23: 6 of A had brought the ephod down with him 316
26: 6 then asked A the Hittite and Abishai son 316
30: 7 the son of A, "Bring me the ephod." 316
2Sa 8:17 and A son of Abiathar were priests; 316
1Ch 18:16 and A son of Abiathar were priests; 316
24: 3 a descendant of Eleazar and A a descendant 316
24: 6 A son of Abiathar and the heads of families 316
24:31 and of Zadok, A, and the heads of families 316
Ps 52: T "David has gone to the house of A." 316

AHIMOTH (1)
1Ch 6:25 The descendants of Elkanah: Amasai, A, 315

AHINADAB (1)
1Ki 4:14 A son of Iddo—in Mahanaim; 320

AHINOAM (7)
1Sa 14:50 His wife's name was A daughter 321
25:43 David had also married A of Jezreel, 321
27: 3 A of Jezreel and Abigail of Carmel, 321
30: 5 A of Jezreel and Abigail, 321
2Sa 2: 2 A of Jezreel and Abigail, 321
3: 2 His firstborn was Amnon the son of A 321
1Ch 3: 1 The firstborn was Amnon the son of A 321

AHIO (6)
2Sa 6: 3 Uzzah and A, sons of Abinadab, 311
6: 4 and A was walking in front of it. 311
1Ch 8:14 A, Shashak, Jeremoth, 311
8:31 Gedor, A, Zeker 311
9:37 Gedor, A, Zechariah and Mikloth. 311
13: 7 with Uzzah and A guiding it. 311

AHIRA (5)
Nu 1:15 from Naphtali, A son of Enan." 327
2:29 of the people of Naphtali is A son of Enan. 327
7:78 On the twelfth day A son of Enan, 327
7:83 This was the offering of A son of Enan. 327
10:27 and A son of Enan was over the division of 327

AHIRAM (1) [AHIRAMITE]
Nu 26:38 through A, the Ahiramite clan; 325

AHIRAMITE (1) [AHIRAM]
Nu 26:38 through Ahiram, the A clan; 326

AHISAMACH (3)
Ex 31: 6 I have appointed Oholiab son of A, 322
35:34 both him and Oholiab son of A, 322
38:23 with him was Oholiab son of A, of the tribe 322

AHISHAHAR (1)
1Ch 7:10 Ehud, Kenaanah, Zethan, Tarshish and A. 328

AHISHAR (1)
1Ki 4: 6 A—in charge of the palace; 329

AHITHOPHEL (17) [AHITHOPHEL'S]
2Sa 15:12 he also sent for A the Gilonite, 330
15:31 "A is among the conspirators 330
16:15 and A was with him. 330
16:20 Absalom said to A, "Give us your advice. 330
16:21 A answered, "Lie with your father's 330
16:23 Now in those days the advice A gave was 330
17: 1 A said to Absalom, "I would choose 330
17: 6 Absalom said, "A has given this advice. 330
17: 7 advice A has given is not good this time. 330
17:14 the Arkite is better than that of A." 330
17:14 of A in order to bring disaster on Absalom. 330
17:15 "A has advised Absalom and the elders 330
17:21 A has advised such and such against you." 330
17:23 When A saw that his advice had 330
23:34 Eliam son of A the Gilonite, 330
1Ch 27:33 A was the king's counselor. 330
27:34 A was succeeded by Jehoiada son 330

AHITHOPHEL'S (3) [AHITHOPHEL]
2Sa 15:31 turn A counsel into foolishness." 330
15:34 you can help me by frustrating A advice. 330
16:23 and Absalom regarded all of A advice. 330

AHITUB (15)
1Sa 14: 3 He was a son of Ichabod's brother A son 313
22: 9 of Jesse come to Ahimelech son of A 313
22:11 of A and his father's whole family, 313
22:12 Saul said, "Listen now, son of A." 313
22:20 But Abiathar, a son of Ahimelech son of A, 313
2Sa 8:17 Zadok son of A and Ahimelech son 313
1Ch 6: 7 Amariah the father of A, 313
6: 8 A the father of Zadok, 313
6:11 Amariah the father of A, 313
6:12 A the father of Zadok, 313
6:52 Amariah his son, A his son, 313
9:11 the son of Meraioth, the son of A, 313
18:16 Zadok son of A and Ahimelech son 313
Ezr 7: 2 the son of Zadok, the son of A, 313
Ne 11:11 the son of Meraioth, the son of A, 313

AHLAB (1)
Jdg 1:31 or Sidon or A or Aczib or Helbah or Aphek 331

AHLAI (2)
1Ch 2:31 Sheshan was the father of A. 333
11:41 Uriah the Hittite, Zabad son of A, 333

AHOAH (1)
1Ch 8: 4 Abishua, Naaman, A, 291

AHOHITE (5)
2Sa 23: 9 to him was Eleazar son of Dodai the A. 292+1201
23:28 Zalmon the A, Maharai the Netophathite, 292
1Ch 11:12 to him was Eleazar son of Dodai the A, 292
11:29 Sibbecai the Hushathite, Ilai the A, 292
27: 4 for the second month was Dodai the A; 292

AHOLAH (KJV) See OHOLAH

AHOLIAB (KJV) See OHOLIAB

AHOLIBAH (KJV) See OHOLAH

AHOLIBAMAH (KJV) See OHOLIBAMAH

AHUMAI (1)
1Ch 4: 2 and Jahath the father of A and Lahad. 293

AHUZZAM (1)
1Ch 4: 6 Naarah bore him A, Hepher, 303

AHUZZATH (1)
Ge 26:26 with A his personal adviser and Phicol 304

AHZAI (1)
Ne 11:13 Amashsai son of Azarel, the son of A, 300

AI (37)
Ge 12: 8 with Bethel on the west and A on the east. 6504
13: 3 and A where his tent had been earlier 6504
Jos 7: 2 Now Joshua sent men from Jericho to A, 6504
7: 2 So the men went up and spied out A. 6504
7: 3 the people will have to go up against A. 6504
7: 4 but they were routed by the men of A, 6504
8: 1 and go up and attack A. 6504
8: 1 into your hands the king of A, 6504
8: 2 You shall do to A and its king as you did 6504
8: 3 and the whole army moved out to attack A. 6504
8: 9 between Bethel and A, to the west of Ai— 6504
8: 9 between Bethel and Ai, to the west of A— 6504
8:10 of Israel marched before them to A. 6504
8:11 They set up camp north of A, 6504
8:12 in ambush between Bethel and A, 6504
8:14 When the king of A saw this, 6504
8:16 the men of A were called to pursue them, 6504
8:17 Not a man remained in A or Bethel who did 6504
8:18 toward A the javelin that is in your hand, 6504
8:18 Joshua held out his javelin toward A. 2021+6551[S]
8:20 of A looked back and saw the smoke of 6504
8:21 around and attacked the men of A. 6504
8:23 of A alive and brought him to Joshua. 6504
8:24 the men of A in the fields and in the desert 6504
8:24 to A and killed those who were in it. 6504
8:25 fell that day—all the people of A. 6504
8:26 until he had destroyed all who lived in A. 6504
8:28 So Joshua burned A and made it 6504
8:29 the king of A on a tree and left him there 6504
9: 3 to Jericho and A, 6504
10: 1 of Jerusalem heard that Joshua had taken A 6504
10: 1 to A and its king as he had done to Jericho 6504
10: 2 it was larger than A, 6504
12: 9 the king of Jericho one the king of A 6504
Ezr 2:28 of Bethel and A 223 6504
Ne 7:32 of Bethel and A 123 6504
Jer 49: 3 "Wail, O Heshbon, for A is destroyed! 6504

AIAH (4) [AIAH'S]
Ge 36:24 The sons of Zibeon: A and Anah. 371
2Sa 3: 7 a concubine named Rizpah daughter of A. 371
21:10 of A took sackcloth and spread it out 371
1Ch 1:40 The sons of Zibeon: A and Anah. 371

AIAH'S (2) [AIAH]
2Sa 21: 8 the two sons of A daughter Rizpah, 371
21:11 David was told what A daughter Rizpah, 371

AIATH (1)
Isa 10:28 They enter A; they pass 6569

AID (10) [AIDE]
Ge 50:24 But God will **surely come to** your a 7212+7212
50:25 "God will **surely come to** your a, 7212+7212
Ex 13:19 "God will **surely come to** your a, 7212+7212
Ru 1: 6 the LORD had **come to the a of** his people 7212
Ps 35: 2 arise and come to my a. 6476
60:11 Give us a against the enemy, 6476
106: 4 **come to** my a when you save them, 7212
108:12 Give us a against the enemy, 6476
Isa 38:14 I am troubled; O Lord, **come to** my a!" 6842
Php 4:16 you sent me a again and again when I was *NIG*

AIDE (5) [AID]
Ex 24:13 Then Moses set out with Joshua his a, 9250
33:11 but his young a Joshua son of Nun did 9250
Nu 11:28 *who had been* Moses' a since youth, 9250
Jos 1: 1 to Joshua son of Nun, Moses' a: 9250
Ne 6: 5 Sanballat sent his a to me with 5853

AIJA (1)
Ne 11:31 A, Bethel and its settlements, 6509

AIJALON (10)
Jos 10:12 O moon, over the Valley of A." 389
19:42 Shaalabbin, A, Ithlah, 389

Jos 21:24 A and Gath Rimmon, together 389
Jdg 1:35 in Mount Heres, A and Shaalbim, but when 389
12:12 and was buried in A in the land of Zebulun. 389
1Sa 14:31 down the Philistines from Micmash to A, 389
1Ch 6:69 A and Gath Rimmon, 389
8:13 in A and who drove out the inhabitants 389
2Ch 11:10 Zorah, A and Hebron. These were fortified cities in Judah 389
28:18 A and Gederoth, as well as Soco, 389

AILS (1)
Job 16: 3 What **a** you that you keep on arguing? 5344

AIM (4) [AIMLESSLY]
Ps 21:12 when *you* **a** at them with drawn bow. 3922
64: 3 and **a** their words like deadly arrows. 2005
1Co 7:34 Her **a is to** be devoted to the Lord in *2671*
2Co 13:11 **A for perfection,** listen to my appeal, *2936*

AIMLESSLY (1) [AIM]
1Co 9:26 I do not run like a man running **a;** *85*

AIN (5)
Nu 34:11 to Riblah on the east side of A and continue 6526
Jos 15:32 Shilhim, A and Rimmon— 6526
19: 7 A, Rimmon, Ether and Ashan— 6526
21:16 A, Juttah and Beth Shemesh, together 6526
1Ch 4:32 Their surrounding villages were Etam, A, 6526

AIR (59) [AIRING, MIDAIR]
Ge 1:26 the fish of the sea and the birds of the **a,** 9028
1:28 the fish of the sea and the birds of the **a** and 9028
1:30 of the earth and all the birds of the **a** and all 9028
2:19 of the field and all the birds of the **a.** 9028
2:20 of the **a** and all the beasts of the field. 9028
6: 7 and birds of the **a—** 9028
7:23 and the birds of the **a** were wiped from 9028
9: 2 of the **a,** upon every creature that moves 9028
Ex 9: 8 a furnace and have Moses toss it into the **a** 9028
9:10 Moses tossed it into the **a,** 9028
Dt 4:17 on earth or any bird that flies in the **a,** 9028
28:26 for all the birds of the **a** and the beasts of 9028
1Sa 17:44 to the birds of the **a** and the beasts of 9028
17:46 the Philistine army to the birds of the **a** and 9028
2Sa 21:10 she did not let the birds of the **a** touch them 9028
1Ki 14:11 of the **a** will feed on those who die in 9028
16: 4 of the **a** will feed on those who die in 9028
21:24 of the **a** will feed on those who die in 9028
Job 12: 7 or the birds of the **a,** and they will tell you; 9028
28:21 concealed even from the birds of the **a.** 9028
35:11 the birds of the **a?'** 9028
41:16 to the next that no **a** can pass between. 8120
Ps 8: 8 the birds of the **a,** 9028
79: 2 as food to the birds of the **a,** 9028
104:12 The birds of the **a** nest by the waters; 9028
Ecc 10:20 a bird of the **a** may carry your words, 9028
Jer 7:33 for the birds of the **a** and the beasts of 9028
9:10 of the **a** have fled and the animals are gone. 9028
15: 3 the dogs to drag away and the birds of the **a** 9028
16: 4 for the birds of the **a** and the beasts of 9028
19: 7 as food to the birds of the **a** and the beasts 9028
34:20 for the birds of the **a** and the beasts of 9028
Eze 29: 5 of the earth and the birds of the **a.** 9028
31: 6 All the birds of the **a** nested in its boughs, 9028
31:13 the birds of the **a** settled on the fallen tree, 9028
32: 4 I will let all the birds of the **a** settle on you 9028
38:20 The fish of the sea, the birds of the **a,** 9028
Da 2:38 of the field and the birds of the **a.** 10723
4:12 and the birds of the **a** lived in its branches; 10723
4:21 in its branches for the birds of the **a—** 10723
Hos 2:18 the beasts of the field and the birds of the **a** 9028
4: 3 the beasts of the field and the birds of the **a** 9028
7:12 I will pull them down like birds of the **a.** 9028
Zep 1: 3 the birds of the **a** and the fish of the sea. 9028
Mt 6:26 Look at the birds *of* the **a;** *4041*
8:20 and birds *of* the **a** have nests, *4041*
13:32 *of* the **a** come and perch in its branches." *4041*
Mk 4:32 the birds *of* the **a** can perch in its shade." *4041*
Lk 8: 5 and the birds *of* the **a** ate it up. *4041*
9:58 and birds *of* the **a** have nests, *4041*
13:19 the birds *of* the **a** perched in its branches." *4041*
Ac 10:12 as reptiles of the earth and birds *of* the **a.** *4041*
11: 6 wild beasts, reptiles, and birds *of* the **a** *4041*
22:23 and flinging dust into the **a,** *113*
1Co 9:26 I do not fight like a man beating the **a.** *113*
14: 9 You will just be speaking into the **a.** *113*
Eph 2: 2 and of the ruler of the kingdom *of* the **a,** *113*
1Th 4:17 in the clouds to meet the Lord in the **a.** *113*
Rev 16:17 into the **a,** and out of the temple came *113*

AIRING (1) [AIR]
Pr 18: 2 but delights in **a** his own opinions. 1655

AJAH (KJV) See AIAH

AJALON (KJV) See AIJALON

AKAN (2)
Ge 36:27 The sons of Ezer: Bilhan, Zaavan and **A.** 6826
1Ch 1:42 The sons of Ezer: Bilhan, Zaavan and **A.** 6826

AKELDAMA (1) [BLOOD, FIELD]
Ac 1:19 they called that field in their language **A,** *192*

AKIM (2)
Mt 1:14 Zadok the father of **A,** *943*
1:14 **A** the father of Eliud, *943*

AKKAD (1)
Ge 10:10 Erech, **A** and Calneh, in Shinar. 422

AKKUB (8)
1Ch 3:24 Hodaviah, Eliashib, Pelaiah, **A,** Johanan, 6822
9:17 The gatekeepers: Shallum, **A,** Talmon, 6822
Ezr 2:42 descendants of Shallum, Ater, Talmon, **A,** 6822
2:45 Lebanah, Hagabah, **A,** 6822
Ne 7:45 descendants of Shallum, Ater, Talmon, **A,** 6822
8: 7 Jeshua, Bani, Sherebiah, Jamin, **A,** 6822
11:19 **A,** Talmon and their associates, 6822
12:25 and **A** were gatekeepers who guarded 6822

ALABASTER (3)
Mt 26: 7 with an **a jar** of very expensive perfume, *223*
Mk 14: 3 with an **a jar** of very expensive perfume, *223*
Lk 7:37 she brought an **a jar** of perfume, *223*

ALAMETH (KJV) See ALEMETH

ALAMMELECH (KJV) See ALLAMMELECH

ALAMOTH (2)
1Ch 15:20 to play the lyres according to **a,** 6628
Ps 46: T According to **a.** 6628

ALARM (7) [ALARMED]
1Ki 1:49 all Adonijah's guests rose *in* **a** 3006
Job 33: 7 No fear of me *should* **a** you, 1286
Ps 31:22 In my **a** I said, 2905
Da 4:19 *do* not *let* the dream or its meaning **a** you." 10097
11:44 from the east and the north *will* **a** him, 987
Joel 2: 1 **sound** *the* **a** on my holy hill. 8131
2Co 7:11 what indignation, what **a,** what longing, *5832*

ALARMED (13) [ALARM]
Jos 10: 2 *He and his people were* very much **a** at this, 3707
2Sa 4: 1 he lost courage, and all Israel *became* **a.** 987
2Ch 20: 3 **A,** Jehoshaphat resolved to inquire of 3707
Job 40:23 When the river rages, *he is* not **a;** 2905
Da 5:10 "Don't *be* **a!** 10097
Mt 24: 6 but see to it that *you are* not **a.** *2583*
Mk 13: 7 *do* not *be* **a.** *2583*
16: 5 and *they were* **a.** *1701*
16: 6 "Don't *be* **a,"** he said. *1701*
Ac 16:38 and Silas were Roman citizens, *they were* **a.** *5828*
20:10 "Don't *be* **a,"** he said. *2572*
22:29 The commander himself *was* **a** *5828*
2Th 2: 2 not to become easily unsettled or **a** *2583*

ALAS (11)
Jer 4:31 stretching out her hands and saying, **"A!** 208
6: 4 But, **a,** the daylight is fading, 208
15:10 **A,** my mother, that you gave me birth, 208
22:18 not mourn for him: **'A,** 2098
22:18 **A,** my sister!' 2098
22:18 They will not mourn for him: **'A,** 2098
22:18 **A,** his splendor!' 2098
34: 5 a fire in your honor and lament, **"A,** 2098
Eze 6:11 and stamp your feet and cry out **"A!"** 277
30: 2 " 'Wail and say, **"A** for that day!" 2081
Joel 1:15 **A** for that day! 177

ALCOVE (2) [ALCOVES]
Eze 40:12 of each **a** was a wall one cubit high, 9288
40:13 the top of the rear wall of one **a** to the top 9288

ALCOVES (9) [ALCOVE]
Eze 40: 7 The **a for the guards** were one rod long 9288
40: 7 between the **a** were five cubits thick, 9288
40:10 the east gate were three **a** on each side; 9288
40:12 and the **a** were six cubits square. 9288
40:16 The **a** and the projecting walls inside 9288
40:21 Its **a—**three on each 9288
40:29 Its **a,** its projecting walls 9288
40:33 Its **a,** its projecting walls 9288
40:36 as did its **a,** its projecting walls 9288

ALEMETH (4)
1Ch 6:60 Geba, **A** and Anathoth, 6630
7: 8 Omri, Jeremoth, Abijah, Anathoth and **A.** 6631
8:36 Jehoaddah was the father of **A,** 6631
9:42 Jadah was the father of **A,** 6631

ALERT (8)
Jos 8: 4 All of you be **on the a.** 3922
Ps 17:11 with eyes **a,** to throw me to the ground. 8883
Isa 21: 7 *let him be* **a,** fully alert." 7992+7993
21: 7 let him be alert, fully **a."** 7993
Mk 13:33 on guard! *Be* **a!** You do not know *1063*
Eph 6:18 be **a** and always keep on praying for all *70*
1Th 5: 6 but *let us be* **a** and self-controlled. *1213*
1Pe 5: 8 *Be* self-controlled and **a.** *1213*

ALEXANDER (5)
Mk 15:21 Simon, the father *of* **A** and Rufus, *235*
Ac 4: 6 **A** and the other men of *235*
19:33 The Jews pushed **A** to the front, *235*
1Ti 1:20 Among them are Hymenaeus and **A,** *235*
2Ti 4:14 **A** the metalworker did me a great deal *235*

ALEXANDRIA (2) [ALEXANDRIAN]
Ac 6: 9 of Cyrene and **A** as well as the provinces *233*
18:24 a native **of A,** came to Ephesus. *233*

ALEXANDRIAN (2) [ALEXANDRIA]
Ac 27: 6 There the centurion found an **A** ship sailing *234*
28:11 It was an **A** ship with the figurehead of *234*

ALGUM (1) [ALGUMWOOD, ALMUGWOOD]
2Ch 2: 8 pine and **a** logs from Lebanon, 454

ALGUMWOOD (2) [ALGUM]
2Ch 9:10 they also brought **a** and precious stones 454+6770
9:11 The king used the **a** to make steps for 454+6770

ALIAH (KJV) See ALVAH

ALIEN (73) [ALIEN'S, ALIENATE, ALIENATED, ALIENS]
Ge 17: 8 where you are now an **a,** 4472
19: 9 they said, "This fellow came here *as an* **a,** 1591
21:23 the country where *you are* **living as an a** 1591
23: 4 "I am an **a** and a stranger among you. 1731
28: 4 of the land where you now **live as an a,** 4472
Ex 2:22 "I have become an **a** in a foreign land." 1731
12:19 whether he is an **a** or native-born. 1731
12:48 "An **a** living among you who wants 1731
12:49 to the native-born and to the **a** living 1731
18: 3 "I have become an **a** in a foreign land"; 1731
20:10 nor the **a** within your gates. 1731
22:21 "Do not mistreat an **a** or oppress him, 1731
23: 9 "Do not oppress an **a;** 1731
23:12 and the **a** as well, may be refreshed. 1731
Lev 16:29 whether native-born or an **a** living 1731
17: 8 or any **a** living among them who offers 1731
17:10 " 'Any Israelite or any **a** living 1731
17:12 nor may an **a** living among you eat blood." 1731
17:13 " 'Any Israelite or any **a** living 1731
17:15 " 'Anyone, whether native-born or **a,** 1731
19:10 Leave them for the poor and the **a.** 1731
19:33 " 'When an **a** lives with you in your land, 1731
19:34 The **a** living with you must be treated 1731
20: 2 or any **a** living in Israel who gives any 1731
22:18 either an Israelite or an **a** living in Israel— 1731
23:22 Leave them for the poor and the **a.** 1731
24:16 Whether an **a** or native-born, 1731
24:22 You are to have the same law for the **a** and 1731
25:35 as you would an **a** or a temporary resident, 1731
25:47 " 'If an **a** or a temporary resident 1731
25:47 and sells himself to the **a** living among you 1731
Nu 9:14 " 'An **a** living among you who wants 1731
9:14 the same regulations for the **a** and 1731
15:14 whenever an **a** or anyone else living 1731
15:15 the same rules for you and for the **a** living 1731
15:15 the **a** shall be the same before the LORD: 1731
15:16 to you and to the **a** living among you.' " 1731
15:29 a native-born Israelite or an **a.** 1731
15:30 whether native-born or **a,** 1731
Dt 1:16 or between one of them and an **a.** 1731
5:14 nor the **a** within your gates, 1731
10:18 and loves the **a,** giving him food 1731
14:21 You may give it to an **a** living in any 1731
23: 7 because you lived as an **a** in his country. 1731
24:14 a brother Israelite or an **a** living in one 1731
24:17 Do not deprive the **a** or the fatherless 1731
24:19 Leave it for the **a,** 1731
24:20 Leave what remains for the **a,** 1731
24:21 Leave what remains for the **a,** 1731
26:12 you shall give it to the Levite, the **a,** 1731
26:13 the **a,** the fatherless and the widow, 1731
27:19 the man who withholds justice from the **a,** 1731
28:43 The **a** who lives among you will rise 1731
Jos 20: 9 Any of the Israelites or any **a** living 1731
Jdg 19:12 We won't go into an **a** city, 5799
2Sa 1:13 "I am the son of an **a,** an Amalekite," 1731
Job 15:19 the land was given when no **a** passed 2424
19:15 they look upon me as an **a.** 5799
Ps 39:12 For I dwell with you as an **a,** a stranger, 1731
69: 8 an **a** to my own mother's sons; 5799
81: 9 you shall not bow down to an **a** god. 5797
94: 6 They slay the widow and the **a;** 1731
105:23 Jacob **lived as an a** in the land of Ham. 1591
146: 9 over the **a** and sustains the fatherless and 1731
Isa 28:21 and perform his task, his **a** task. 5799
Jer 7: 6 if you do not oppress the **a,** 1731
22: 3 Do no wrong or violence to the **a,** 1731
Eze 14: 7 or any **a** living in Israel separates himself 1731
22: 7 the **a** and mistreated the fatherless and 1731
22:29 the poor and needy and mistreat the **a,** 1731
47:23 In whatever tribe the **a** settles, 1731
Hos 8:12 but they regarded them as *something* **a.** 2424
Zec 7:10 the fatherless, the **a** or the poor. 1731

ALIEN'S (1) [ALIEN]

Lev 25:47 among you or to a member of the **a** clan, 1731

ALIENATE (1) [ALIEN]

Gal 4:17 What they want is *to* **a** you [from us], *1710*

ALIENATED (3) [ALIEN]

Job 19:13 *"He has* **a** my brothers from me; 8178
Gal 5: 4 to be justified by law *have been* **a** *2934*
Col 1:21 Once you were **a from** God *558*

ALIENS (33) [ALIEN]

Ex 6: 4 where they lived *as* **a.** 1591
22:21 for you were **a** in Egypt. 1731
23: 9 you yourselves know how it feels to be **a,** 1731
23: 9 because you were **a** in Egypt. 1731
Lev 18:26 the **a** living among you must not do any 1731
19:34 for you were **a** in Egypt. 1731
25:23 because the land is mine and you are but **a** 1731
Nu 15:26 the **a** living among them will be forgiven, 1731
19:10 both for the Israelites and for the **a** living 1731
35:15 **a** and any other people living among them, 1731
Dt 10:19 And you are to love those who are **a,** 1731
10:19 for you yourselves were **a** in Egypt. 1731
14:29 or inheritance of their own) and the **a,** 1731
16:11 the Levites in your towns, and the **a,** 1731
16:14 and the Levites, the **a,** 1731
26:11 and the **a** among you shall rejoice in all 1731
29:11 and the **a** living 1731
31:12 and the **a** living in your towns— 1731
Jos 8:33 All Israel, **a** and citizens alike, 1731
8:35 and the **a** who lived among them. 1731
2Sa 4: 3 and have lived there *as* **a** to this day. 1591
1Ch 22: 2 to assemble the **a** living in Israel, 1731
29:15 We are **a** and strangers in your sight, 1731
2Ch 2:17 a census of all the **a** who were in Israel, 1731
30:25 including the **a** who had come from Israel 1731
Isa 14: 1 **A** will join them and unite with the house 1731
61: 5 **A** will shepherd your flocks; 2424
La 5: 2 Our inheritance has been turned over to **a,** 2424
Eze 47:22 and for the **a** who have settled among you 1731
Mal 3: 5 and deprive **a** of justice, 1731
Eph 2:19 you are no longer foreigners and **a,** *4230*
Heb 11:13 that they were **a** and strangers on earth. *3828*
1Pe 2:11 I urge you, as **a** and strangers in the world, *4230*

ALIKE (26) [LIKE]

Ge 18:25 treating the righteous and the wicked **a.** 3869
Ex 11: 2 Tell the people that men **and** women **a** are 2256
35:22 All who were willing, men **and** women **a,** 6584
36:29 both were made **a.** 4027
Nu 5: 3 Send away male **and** female **a;** 6330
Dt 1:17 **both** small *and* great **a.** 3869
Jos 8:33 All Israel, aliens and citizens **a,** 3869
1Sa 30:24 All will share **a."** 3481
1Ch 25: 8 Young and old **a,** 4200+6645
26:13 young and old **a,** 3869
2Ch 31:15 old and young **a.** 3869
Job 34:29 Yet he is over man and nation **a,** 3480
Ps 49: 2 both low and high, rich and poor **a:** 3480
49:10 the foolish and the senseless **a** perish 3480
115:13 small **and** great **a.** 6640
Jer 6:13 prophets **and** priests **a,** all practice deceit. 6330
6:21 Fathers and sons **a** will stumble over them; 3481
8:10 prophets **and** priests **a,** all practice deceit. 6330
13:14 fathers and sons **a,** declares the LORD. 3481
Eze 1:16 and all four looked **a.** 285
10:10 the four of them looked **a;** 285
18: 4 **both** *a* belong to me. AIT
Lk 14:18 "But they all **a** began to make excuses. *608+1651*
Ac 26:22 and testify to small and great **a.** *NIG*
Ro 3: 9 the charge that Jews **and** Gentiles **a** are all under sin. *2779+5445*
14: 5 another man considers every day **a.** *NIG*

ALIVE (85) [LIVE]

Ge 6:19 male and female, to **keep** them **a** with you. 2649
6:20 the ground will come to you to *be* **kept a.** 2649
7: 3 **keep** their various kinds **a** 2649
11:28 **While** his father Terah was **still a,** 6584+7156
43:28 "Your servant our father is still **a** 2645
45:26 They told him, "Joseph is still **a!** 2645
45:28 My son Joseph is still **a.** 2645
46:30 I have seen for myself that you are still **a."** 2645
Ex 4:18 in Egypt to see if any of them are still **a."** 2645
22: 4 "If the stolen animal is found **a** 2645
Lev 16:10 as the scapegoat shall be presented **a** before 2645
Nu 16:30 and they go down **a** into the grave, 2645
16:33 They went down **a** into the grave, 2645
Dt 4: 4 to the LORD your God are still **a** today. 2645
5: 3 with all of us who are **a** here today. 2645
6:24 we might always prosper and *be* **kept a,** 2649
20:16 *do* not **leave a** anything that breathes. 2649
31:27 the LORD while I am still **a** and with you, 2645
Jos 8:23 the king of Ai **a** and brought him to Joshua. 2645
14:10 *he has* **kept** me **a** for forty-five years since 2649
1Sa 2: 6 "The LORD brings death and **makes a;** 2649
14:36 **leave** one of them **a."** 8636
15: 8 He took Agag king of the Amalekites **a,** 2645
25:22 if by morning *I* **leave a** one male 8636
25:34 to Nabal *would have* **been left a** 3855
27: 9 **leave** a man or woman **a,** 2649
27:11 **leave** a man or woman **a** 2649
2Sa 1: 9 in the throes of death, but I'm still **a.'** 928+5883
12:21 While the child was **a,** 2645
12:22 He answered, "While the child was still **a,** 2645
17:12 nor any of his men *will* **be left a.** 3855
18:14 while Absalom was still **a** in the oak tree. 2645
19: 6 be pleased if Absalom were **a** today and all 2645
1Ki 3:23 'My son is **a** and your son is dead,' 2645
3:23 Your son is dead and mine is **a.' "** 2645
3:26 The woman whose son was **a** was filled 2645
17:23 "Look, your son is **a!"** 2645
18: 5 **keep** the horses and mules **a** 2649
20:18 for peace, take them **a;** 2645
20:18 if they have come out for war, take them **a."** 2645
20:32 The king answered, "Is he still **a?** 2645
21:15 He is no longer **a,** but dead." 2645
2Ki 7:12 and then we will take them **a** and get into 2645
10:14 "Take them **a!"** 2645
10:14 So they took them **a** and slaughtered them 2645
2Ch 25:12 of Judah also captured ten thousand *men* **a,** 2645
Ne 5: 2 in order for us to eat and **stay a,** 2649
Job 36: 6 *He does* not **keep** the wicked **a** but gives 2649
Ps 22:29 *those who* cannot **keep** themselves **a.** 2649
33:19 to deliver them from death and **keep** them **a** 2649
55:15 let them go down **a** to the grave, 2645
124: 3 they would have swallowed us **a;** 2645
Pr 1:12 let's swallow them **a,** like the grave, 2645
Ecc 4: 2 are happier than the living, who are still **a.** 2645
Isa 7:21 a man *will* **keep a** a young cow 2649
La 1:11 for food to **keep themselves a.** 5883+8740
1:19 for food *to* **keep themselves a.** 906+4392+5883+8740
Mt 27:63 that while *he was* still **a** that deceiver said, *2409*
Mk 16:11 that Jesus *was* **a** and that she had seen him, *2409*
Lk 15:24 this son of mine was dead and *is* **a again;** *348*
15:32 of yours was dead and *is* **a again;** *348*
20:38 but of the living, for to him all *are* **a."** *2409*
24:23 who said he *was* **a.** *2409*
Jn 21:22 "If I want him to remain **a** until I return, *NIG*
21:23 "If I want him to remain **a** until I return, *NIG*
Ac 1: 3 that *he was* **a.** *2409*
9:41 the widows and presented her to them **a.** *2409*
20:10 be alarmed," he said. "He's **a!"** *899+1877*
20:12 The people took the young man home **a** *2409*
25:19 dead man named Jesus who Paul claimed *was* **a.** *2409*
Ro 6:11 count yourselves dead to sin but **a** to God *2409*
7: 2 to her husband *as long as he is* **a,** *2409*
7: 3 *while* her husband *is still* **a,** *2409*
7: 9 Once I *was* **a** apart from law; *2409*
8:10 your spirit is **a** because of righteousness. *2437*
1Co 15:22 so in Christ all *will be* **made a.** *2443*
2Co 4:11 For we who *are* **a** are always being given *2409*
Eph 2: 5 **made** us **a with** Christ even *5188*
Col 2:13 God **made** you **a with** Christ. *5188*
1Th 4:15 we tell you that we who *are still* **a,** *2409*
4:17 we who *are still* **a** and are left will *2409*
1Pe 3:18 He was put to death in the body but **made a** *2443*
Rev 1:18 and behold I am **a** for ever and ever! *2409*
3: 1 you have a reputation of *being* **a,** *2409*
19:20 of them were thrown **a** into the fiery lake *2409*

ALL (4660)

Ge 1:25 and **a** the creatures that move along 3972
1:26 over the livestock, over **a** the earth, 3972
1:26 and over **a** the creatures that move along 3972
1:30 to **a** the beasts of the earth and all the birds 3972
1:30 of the earth and **a** the birds of the air and all 3972
1:30 of the earth and all the birds of the air and **a** 3972
1:31 God saw **a** that he had made, 3972
2: 1 in **a** their vast array. 3972
2: 2 the seventh day he rested from **a** his work. 3972
2: 3 on it he rested from **a** the work of creating 3972
2: 9 And the LORD God made **a** *kinds* 3972
2:19 the ground **a** the beasts of the field and all 3972
2:19 the ground all the beasts of the field and **a** 3972
2:20 So the man gave names to **a** the livestock, 3972
2:20 of the air and **a** the beasts of the field. 3972
3:14 "Cursed are you above **a** the livestock 3972
3:14 the livestock and **a** the wild animals! 3972
3:14 on your belly and you will eat dust **a** 3972
3:17 through painful toil you will eat of it **a** 3972
3:20 because she would become the mother of **a** 3972
4:21 the father of **a** who play the harp and flute. 3972
4:22 who forged **a** *kinds of* tools out of bronze 3972
6: 5 of the thoughts of his heart was only evil **a** 3972
6:12 for **a** the people on earth had corrupted 3972
6:13 "I am going to put an end to **a** people, 3972
6:17 to destroy **a** life under the heavens, 3972
6:19 into the ark two of **a** living creatures, 3972
7: 5 And Noah did **a** that the LORD commanded 3972
7: 8 of birds and of **a** creatures that move along 3972
7:11 on that day **a** the springs of 3972
7:14 **a** livestock according to their kinds, 3972
7:15 of **a** creatures that have the breath of life 3972
7:19 and **a** the high mountains under 3972
7:21 **a** the creatures that swarm over the earth, 3972
7:21 that swarm over the earth, and **a** mankind. 3972
8: 1 and **a** the wild animals and the livestock 3972
8: 9 because there was water over **a** the surface 3972
8:17 the animals, and **a** the creatures that move 3972
8:19 **A** the animals and all the creatures 3972
8:19 the animals and **a** the creatures that move 3972
8:19 along the ground and **a** the birds— 3972
8:20 of **a** the clean animals and clean birds, 3972
8:21 never again will I destroy **a** living creatures, 3972
9: 2 and dread of you will fall upon **a** the beasts 3972
Ge 9: 2 the beasts of the earth and **a** the birds of 3972
9: 2 and upon **a** the fish of the sea; 3972
9:10 the livestock and **a** the wild animals, 3972
9:10 **a** those that came out of the ark with you— 3972
9:11 Never again will **a** life be cut off by 3972
9:12 a covenant for **a** generations to come: NIH
9:15 between me and you and **a** living creatures 3972
9:15 the waters become a flood to destroy **a** life. 3972
9:16 and **a** living creatures of every kind on 3972
9:17 between me and **a** life on the earth." 3972
10:21 Shem was the ancestor of **a** the sons 3972
10:29 **A** these were sons of Joktan. 3972
11: 8 from there over **a** the earth, 3972
12: 3 and **a** peoples on earth will be blessed 3972
12: 5 **a** the possessions they had accumulated 3972
13:15 **A** the land that you see I will give to you 3972
14: 3 **A** these latter kings joined forces in 3972
14:11 The four kings seized **a** the goods 3972
14:11 of Sodom and Gomorrah and **a** their food; 3972
14:13 **a** *of whom* were allied with Abram. 2156[S]
14:16 He recovered **a** the goods 3972
15:10 Abram brought **a** these to him, 3972
16:12 in hostility toward **a** his brothers." 3972
17:23 and **a** those born in his household 3972
18: 4 and then *you may a* **wash** your feet and rest AIT
18:18 and **a** nations on earth will be blessed 3972
18:25 Will not the Judge of **a** the earth do right?" 3972
19: 4 **a** the men from every part of the city 3972
19:25 including **a** those living in the cities— 3972
19:28 toward **a** the land of the plain, 3972
19:31 as is the custom **a** *over* the earth. 3972
20: 7 be sure that you and **a** yours will die." 3972
20: 8 next morning Abimelech summoned **a** his officials, 3972
20: 8 when he told them **a** that had happened, 3972
20:16 the offense against you before **a** who are 3972
22:18 and through your offspring **a** nations 3972
23:10 the hearing of **a** the Hittites who had come 3972
23:17 **a** the trees within the borders of the field— 3972
23:18 the presence of **a** the Hittites who had come 3972
24: 2 the one in charge of **a** that he had, 3972
24:10 taking with him **a** *kinds of* good things 3972
24:20 and drew enough for **a** his camels. 3972
24:66 Then the servant told Isaac **a** he had done. 3972
25: 4 **A** these were descendants of Keturah. 3972
25:18 in hostility toward **a** their brothers. 3972
26: 3 your descendants I will give **a** these lands 3972
26: 4 in the sky and will give them **a** these lands, 3972
26: 4 and through your offspring **a** nations 3972
26:11 So Abimelech gave orders to **a** the people: 3972
26:15 **a** the wells that his father's servants had dug 3972
27:37 and have made **a** his relatives his servants, 3972
28:14 **A** peoples on earth will be blessed 3972
28:22 and of **a** that you give me I will give you 3972
29: 3 When **a** the flocks were gathered there, 3972
29: 8 "until **a** the flocks are gathered and 3972
29:13 and there Jacob told him **a** these things. 3972
29:22 So Laban brought together **a** the people of 3972
30:32 through **a** your flocks today and remove 3972
30:35 That same day he removed **a** the male goats NIH
30:35 and **a** the speckled or spotted female goats 3972
30:35 or spotted female goats (**a** that had white 3972
30:35 on them) and **a** the dark-colored lambs, 3972
30:38 Then he placed the peeled branches in **a** NIH
31: 1 and has gained **a** this wealth 3972
31: 6 for your father with **a** my strength, 3972
31: 8 **a** the flocks gave birth to speckled young; 3972
31: 8 then **a** the flocks bore streaked young. 3972
31:12 and see that **a** the male goats mating with 3972
31:12 for I have seen **a** that Laban has been doing 3972
31:16 Surely **a** the wealth that God took away 3972
31:18 and he drove **a** his livestock ahead of him, 3972
31:18 along with **a** the goods he had accumulated 3972
31:21 So he fled with **a** he had, 3972
31:37 you have searched through **a** my goods, 3972
31:43 **A** you see is mine. 3972
32:10 I am unworthy of **a** the kindness 3972
32:17 who owns **a** these animals in front of you?' NIH
32:19 and **a** the others who followed the herds: 3972
32:23 he sent over **a** his possessions. NIH
33: 7 **Last of a** came Joseph and Rachel, 339
33: 8 by **a** these droves I met?" 3972
33:11 to me and I have **a** I *need."* 3972
33:13 **a** the animals will die. 3972
34:15 like us by circumcising **a** your males. 3972
34:19 of **a** his father's household, 3972
34:23 and **a** their other animals become ours? 3972
34:24 **A** the men who went out of 3972
34:25 while **a** of them were still in pain, NIH
34:29 They carried off **a** their wealth 3972
34:29 and **a** their women and children, 3972
35: 2 to his household and to **a** who were 3972
35: 4 So they gave Jacob **a** the foreign gods 3972
35: 5 of God fell upon the towns **a around** them 6017
35: 6 and **a** the people with him came to Luz 3972
36: 6 and sons and daughters and **a** the members 3972
36: 6 as his livestock and **a** his other animals 3972
36: 6 and **a** the goods he had acquired in Canaan, 3972
37: 5 they hated him **a the more.** 3578+6388
37: 8 they hated him **a the more** because 3578+6388
37:14 "Go and see if **a** is well with your brothers NIH
37:27 **after a,** he is our brother, 3954
37:35 **A** his sons and daughters came 3972
38:23 **After a,** I did send her this young goat, 2180
39: 5 of his household and of **a** that he owned, 3972
39:22 in charge of **a** those held in the prison, 3972
39:22 and he was made responsible for **a** 3972

Ge	40:14	But when *a* **goes well** with you,	AIT
	40:17	In the top basket were **a kinds** *of* baked goods	3972+4946
	40:20	and he gave a feast for **a** his officials.	3972
	41: 8	for **a** the magicians and wise men of Egypt.	3972
	41:19	I had never seen such ugly cows in **a**	3972
	41:30	**a** the abundance in Egypt will be forgotten,	3972
	41:35	They should collect **a** the food	3972
	41:37	to Pharaoh and to **a** his officials.	3972
	41:39	"Since God has made **a** this known to you,	3972
	41:40	**a** my people are to submit to your orders.	3972
	41:44	or foot in **a** Egypt."	3972
	41:48	Joseph collected **a** the food produced	3972
	41:51	God has made me forget **a** my trouble	3972
	41:51	and **a** my father's household."	3972
	41:54	There was famine in **a** the other lands,	3972
	41:55	When **a** Egypt began to feel the famine,	3972
	41:55	Then Pharaoh told **a** the Egyptians,	3972
	41:57	And **a** the countries came to Egypt	3972
	41:57	the famine was severe in **a** the world.	3972
	42: 6	the one who sold grain to **a** its people.	3972
	42:11	We are **a** the sons of one man.	3972
	42:17	And he put **them** *a* in custody for three days.	AIT
	42:29	they told him **a** that had happened to them.	3972
	43: 2	So when they had eaten **a**	3983
	43: 9	I will bear the blame before you **a** my life.	3972
	43:23	"It's **a right,"** he said.	8934
	44:13	Then they **a** loaded their donkeys	408
	44:32	before you, my father, **a** my life!'	3972
	45: 1	before **a** his attendants,	3972
	45: 8	and ruler of **a** Egypt.	3972
	45: 9	God has made me lord of **a** Egypt.	3972
	45:10	your flocks and herds, and **a** you have.	3972
	45:11	and your household and **a** who belong	3972
	45:13	about **a** the honor accorded me in Egypt	3972
	45:15	And he kissed **a** his brothers and wept	3972
	45:16	Pharaoh and **a** his officials were pleased.	NIH
	45:20	the best of **a** Egypt will be yours.' "	3972
	45:26	In fact, he is ruler of **a** Egypt."	3972
	46: 1	So Israel set out with **a** that was his,	3972
	46: 6	Jacob and **a** his offspring went to Egypt.	3972
	46: 7	and granddaughters—**a** his offspring.	3972
	46:15	and daughters of his were thirty-three *in* **a.**	3972
	46:18	to his daughter Leah—sixteen *in* **a.**	5883
	46:22	born to Jacob—fourteen *in* **a.**	3972
	46:25	to his daughter Rachel—seven *in* **a.**	3972
	46:26	**A** those who went to Egypt with Jacob—	3972
	46:27	which went to Egypt, were seventy *in* **a.**	3972
	46:34	for **a** shepherds are detestable to	3972
	47:12	and **a** his father's household with food,	3972
	47:14	Joseph collected **a** the money that was to	3972
	47:15	**a** Egypt came to Joseph and said,	3972
	47:17	with food in exchange for **a** their livestock.	3972
	47:20	So Joseph bought **a** the land in Egypt	3972
	47:20	The Egyptians, **one and a,** sold their fields,	408
	48:15	God who has been my shepherd **a** my **life**	4946+6388
	48:16	Angel who has delivered me from **a** harm	3972
	49:26	*Let a these* **rest** on the head of Joseph,	AIT
	49:28	**A** these are the twelve tribes of Israel,	3972
	50: 7	**A** Pharaoh's officials accompanied him—	3972
	50: 7	the dignitaries of his court and **a**	3972
	50: 8	besides **a** *the members*	3972
	50:14	and **a** the others who had gone with him	3972
	50:15	a grudge against us and pays us back for **a**	3972
	50:22	along with **a** his father's family.	NIH
Ex	1: 5	of Jacob numbered seventy *in* **a;**	3972
	1: 6	Now Joseph and **a** his brothers and all	3972
	1: 6	Now Joseph and all his brothers and **a**	3972
	1:14	and mortar and with **a** *kinds of* work in	3972
	1:14	in **a** their hard labor	3972
	1:22	Pharaoh gave this order to **a** his people:	3972
	3:20	and strike the Egyptians with **a** the wonders	3972
	4:19	for **a** the men who wanted	3972
	4:21	see that you perform before Pharaoh **a**	3972
	4:28	and also about **a**	3972
	4:29	and Aaron brought together **a** the elders of	3972
	5:11	but your work will not be reduced **at a.' "**	1821
	5:12	So the people scattered **a** over Egypt	3972
	5:23	**rescued** your people **at a."**	5911+5911
	7:19	over the ponds and **a** the reservoirs'—	3972
	7:20	and **a** the water was changed into blood.	3972
	7:24	And **a** the Egyptians dug along the Nile	3972
	8: 4	and your people and **a** your officials.' "	3972
	8:17	**A** the dust throughout the land	3972
	9: 6	**A** the livestock of the Egyptians died,	3972
	9:11	that were on them and on **a** the Egyptians.	3972
	9:14	that there is no one like me in **a** the earth.	3972
	9:16	and that my name might be proclaimed in **a**	3972
	9:22	the sky so that hail will fall **a** over Egypt—	3972
	9:24	in **a** the land of Egypt since it had become	3972
	10: 6	of **a** your officials and all the Egyptians—	3972
	10: 6	of all your officials and **a** the Egyptians—	3972
	10:13	across the land **a** that day and all that night.	3972
	10:13	across the land all that day and **a** that night.	3972
	10:14	they invaded **a** Egypt and settled down	3972
	10:15	They covered **a** the ground	3972
	10:15	They devoured **a** that was left after	3972
	10:15	on tree or plant in **a** the land of Egypt.	3972
	10:22	and total darkness covered **a** Egypt	3972
	10:23	Yet **a** the Israelites had light in the places	3972
	11: 5	and **a** the firstborn of the cattle as well.	3972
	11: 8	**A** these officials of yours will come to me,	3972
	11: 8	you and **a** the people who follow you!'	3972
	11:10	and Aaron performed **a** these wonders	3972
	12: 6	when **a** the people of the community	3972
	12:12	and I will bring judgment on **a** the gods	3972
Ex	12:16	Do no work **at a** on these days,	3972
	12:16	that is **a** you may do.	963+4200
	12:21	Then Moses summoned **a** the elders	3972
	12:29	the LORD struck down **a** the firstborn	3972
	12:29	and the firstborn of **a** the livestock as well.	3972
	12:30	and **a** his officials and all the Egyptians got	3972
	12:30	and all his officials and **a** the Egyptians got	3972
	12:33	"For otherwise," they said, "we will **a** die!"	3972
	12:41	**a** the LORD's divisions left Egypt.	3972
	12:42	on this night **a** the Israelites are	3972
	12:48	the LORD's Passover must have **a**	3972
	12:50	**A** the Israelites did just what	3972
	13:12	**A** the firstborn males	3972
	14: 4	for myself through Pharaoh and **a** his army,	3972
	14: 7	along with **a** the other chariots of Egypt,	3972
	14: 7	with officers over **a** *of* them.	3972
	14: 9	**a** Pharaoh's horses and chariots,	3972
	14:17	through Pharaoh and **a** his army,	3972
	14:20	so neither went near the other **a** night *long.*	3972
	14:21	and **a** that night the LORD drove	3972
	14:23	and **a** Pharaoh's horses and chariots	3972
	15:20	and **a** the women followed her,	3972
	15:26	to his commands and keep **a** his decrees,	3972
	16: 3	and ate **a** the food we **wanted,**	8427
	16: 6	Moses and Aaron said to **a** the Israelites,	3972
	16: 8	**a** the bread you **want** in the morning,	8425
	18: 8	the Egyptians for Israel's sake and about **a**	3972
	18: 9	Jethro was delighted to hear about **a**	3972
	18:11	the LORD is greater than **a** other gods,	3972
	18:12	and Aaron came with **a** the elders of Israel	3972
	18:14	When his father-in-law saw **a**	3972
	18:14	while **a** these people stand around you	3972
	18:21	select capable men from **a** the people—	3972
	18:22	as judges for the people at **a** times,	3972
	18:23	and **a** these people will go home satisfied."	3972
	18:25	from **a** Israel and made them leaders of	3972
	18:26	as judges for the people at **a** times.	3972
	19: 5	then out of **a** nations you will	3972
	19: 7	the people and set before them **a** the words	3972
	19: 8	The people **a** responded together,	3972
	19:11	on Mount Sinai in the sight of **a** the people.	3972
	20: 1	And God spoke **a** these words:	3972
	20: 9	and do **a** your work,	3972
	20:11	the sea, and **a** that is in them,	3972
	22: 9	In **a** cases of illegal possession of an ox,	3972
	23:17	"Three times a year **a** the men are to appear	3972
	23:22	to what he says and do **a** that I say,	3972
	23:27	I will make **a** your enemies turn their backs	3972
	24: 3	the people **a** the LORD's words and laws,	3972
	24: 8	in accordance with **a** these words."	3972
	25: 9	and **a** its furnishings exactly like	3972
	25:22	with you and give you **a** my commands for	3972
	25:30	on this table to be before me **at a times.**	9458
	25:33	the same for **a** six branches extending from	NIH
	25:35	six branches in **a.**	NIH
	25:36	and branches shall **a** be of one piece with	3972
	25:39	for the lampstand and **a** these accessories.	3972
	26: 2	**A** the curtains are to be the same size—	3972
	26: 8	**A** eleven curtains are to be the same size—	NIH
	26:17	Make **a** the frames of the tabernacle	3972
	26:24	the bottom **a the way to** the top, and fitted	6584
	27: 3	Make **a** its utensils of bronze—	3972
	27:17	**A** the posts around the courtyard are	3972
	27:19	**A** the other articles used in the service of	3972
	27:19	including **a** the tent pegs for it and those for	3972
	28: 3	Tell **a** the skilled men	3972
	29:13	Then take **a** the fat around the inner parts,	3972
	29:16	and sprinkle it against the altar **on a sides.**	6017
	29:20	sprinkle blood against the altar **on a sides.**	6017
	29:24	Put **a** these in the hands of Aaron	3972
	30: 3	the top and **a** the sides and the horns	6017
	30:14	**A** who cross over, those twenty years old or	3972
	30:24	**a** according to the sanctuary shekel—	NIH
	30:27	the table and **a** its articles,	3972
	30:28	the altar of burnt offering and **a** its utensils,	3972
	30:34	and pure frankincense, **a** in equal amounts,	NIH
	31: 3	and knowledge in **a** *kinds of* crafts—	3972
	31: 5	to engage in **a** *kinds of* craftsmanship.	3972
	31: 6	Also I have given skill to **a** the craftsmen	3972
	31: 7	and **a** the other furnishings of the tent—	3972
	31: 8	pure gold lampstand and **a** its accessories,	3972
	31: 9	and **a** its utensils, the basin with its stand—	3972
	32: 3	So **a** the people took off their earrings	3972
	32:13	I will give your descendants **a** this land I promised them,	3972
	32:26	And **a** the Levites rallied to him.	3972
	33: 8	**a** the people rose and stood at the entrances	3972
	33:10	they **a** stood and worshiped,	3972
	33:16	and your people from **a** the other people on	3972
	33:19	"I will cause **a** my goodness to pass in front	3972
	34:10	**a** your people I will do wonders never	3972
	34:10	before done in any nation in **a** the world.	3972
	34:19	including **a** the firstborn males	3972
	34:20	Redeem **a** your firstborn sons.	3972
	34:23	a year **a** your men are to appear before	3972
	34:30	Aaron and **a** the Israelites saw Moses,	3972
	34:31	so Aaron and **a** the leaders of	3972
	34:32	Afterward **a** the Israelites came near him,	3972
	34:32	and he gave them **a** the commands	3972
	35:10	**"A** who are skilled among you are to come	3972
	35:13	the table with its poles and **a** its articles and	3972
	35:16	its poles and **a** its utensils;	3972
	35:21	Tent of Meeting, for **a** its service,	3972
	35:22	**A** *who* were willing, men and women alike,	3972
	35:22	and brought gold jewelry of **a** *kinds:*	3972
	35:22	They **a** presented their gold as	3972
	35:26	And **a** the women who were willing	3972
Ex	35:29	**A** the Israelite men and women	3972
	35:29	to the LORD freewill offerings for **a**	3972
	35:31	and knowledge in **a** *kinds of* crafts—	3972
	35:33	to work in wood and to engage in **a** kinds	3972
	35:35	He has filled them with skill to do **a** *kinds*	3972
	35:35	**a** *of* them master craftsmen and designers.	3972
	36: 1	how to carry out **a** the work of constructing	3972
	36: 3	They received from Moses **a** the offerings	3972
	36: 4	So **a** the skilled craftsmen who were doing	3972
	36: 4	craftsmen who were doing **a** the work	3972
	36: 7	more than enough to do **a** the work.	3972
	36: 8	**A** the skilled men among	3972
	36: 9	**A** the curtains were the same size—	285
	36:15	**A** eleven curtains were the same size—	285
	36:22	They made **a** the frames of the tabernacle	3972
	36:29	the bottom **a the way to** the top and fitted	448
	37:19	the same for **a** six branches extending from	NIH
	37:21	six branches in **a.**	NIH
	37:22	and the branches were **a** of one piece with	3972
	37:24	and **a** its accessories from one talent	3972
	37:26	They overlaid the top and **a** the sides and	6017
	38: 3	They made **a** its utensils of bronze—	3972
	38:16	**A** the curtains around the courtyard were	3972
	38:17	so **a** the posts of the courtyard	3972
	38:20	**A** the tent pegs of the tabernacle and of	3972
	38:24	from the wave offering used for **a** the work	3972
	38:30	with its bronze grating and **a** its utensils,	3972
	38:31	for its entrance and **a** the tent pegs for	3972
	39:32	So **a** the work on the tabernacle,	3972
	39:33	the tent and **a** its furnishings, its clasps,	3972
	39:36	the table with **a** its articles and the bread of	3972
	39:37	with its row of lamps and **a** its accessories,	3972
	39:39	its poles and **a** its utensils;	3972
	39:40	**a** the furnishings for the tabernacle,	3972
	39:42	The Israelites had done **a** the work just as	3972
	40: 9	consecrate it and **a** its furnishings,	3972
	40:10	the altar of burnt offering and **a** its utensils;	3972
	40:15	that will continue for **a** generations	4392[S]
	40:36	In **a** the travels of the Israelites,	3972
	40:38	in the sight of **a** the house of Israel	3972
	40:38	the house of Israel during **a** their travels.	3972
Lev	1: 5	against the altar **on a sides** at the entrance to	6017
	1: 9	and the priest is to burn **a** *of* it on the altar.	3972
	1:11	against the altar **on a sides.**	6017
	1:13	and the priest is to bring **a** *of* it and burn it	3972
	2: 2	together with **a** the incense,	3972
	2:13	Season **a** your grain offerings with salt.	3972
	2:13	add salt to **a** your offerings.	3972
	2:16	together with **a** the incense,	3972
	3: 2	the blood against the altar **on a sides.**	6017
	3: 3	**a** the fat that covers the inner parts	3972
	3: 8	against the altar **on a sides.**	6017
	3: 9	to the backbone, **a** the fat that covers	3972
	3:13	against the altar **on a sides.**	6017
	3:14	**a** the fat that covers the inner parts	3972
	3:16	**A** the fat is the LORD's.	3972
	4: 8	He shall remove **a** the fat from the bull of	3972
	4:11	But the hide of the bull and **a** its flesh,	3972
	4:12	**a** *the rest of* the bull—	3972
	4:19	He shall remove **a** the fat from it	3972
	4:26	He shall burn **a** the fat on the altar	3972
	4:31	He shall remove **a** the fat,	3972
	4:35	He shall remove **a** the fat,	3972
	5:16	add a fifth of the value to that and give it **a**	NIH
	6: 5	the value to it and give it **a** to the owner on	NIH
	6:15	with **a** the incense on the grain offering,	3972
	7: 2	to be sprinkled against the altar **on a sides.**	6017
	7: 3	**A** its fat shall be offered:	3972
	7:10	belongs equally to **a** the sons of Aaron.	3972
	8:11	anointing the altar and **a** its utensils and	3972
	8:15	and with his finger he put it on **a** the horns	6017
	8:16	also took **a** the fat around the inner parts,	3972
	8:19	the blood against the altar **on a sides.**	6017
	8:24	against the altar **on a sides.**	6017
	8:25	the fat tail, **a** the fat around the inner parts,	3972
	8:27	He put **a** these in the hands of Aaron	3972
	9:12	he sprinkled it against the altar **on a sides.**	6017
	9:18	he sprinkled it against the altar **on a sides.**	6017
	9:23	and the glory of the LORD appeared to **a**	3972
	9:24	And when **a** the people saw it,	3972
	10: 3	of **a** the people I will be honored.' "	3972
	10: 6	But your relatives, **a** the house of Israel,	3972
	10:11	and you must teach the Israelites **a**	3972
	11: 2	'Of **a** the animals that live on land,	3972
	11: 9	" 'Of **a** the creatures living in the water of	3972
	11:10	But **a** creatures in the seas or streams	3972
	11:10	among **a** the swarming things or among all	3972
	11:10	among all the swarming things or among **a**	3972
	11:20	**" 'A** flying insects that walk	3972
	11:20	that walk on **a fours** are to be detestable	752
	11:21	some winged creatures that walk on **a fours**	752
	11:23	But **a** other winged creatures	3972
	11:27	Of **a** the animals that walk on all fours,	3972
	11:27	Of all the animals that walk on **a fours,**	752
	11:31	Of **a** those that move along the ground,	3972
	11:42	or walks on **a fours** or on many feet;	752
	13:12	the disease **breaks out a over** his skin	7255+7255
	13:12	it covers **a** the skin of the infected person	3972
	13:13	Since it has **a** turned white, he is clean.	3972
	14: 8	shave off **a** his hair and bathe with water;	3972
	14: 9	seventh day he must shave off **a** his hair;	3972
	14:41	He must have **a** the inside walls of	6017
	14:45	its stones, timbers and **a** the plaster—	3972
	16:18	the goat's blood and put it on **a** the horns of	6017
	16:21	over it **a** the wickedness and rebellion of	3972
	16:21	rebellion of the Israelites—**a** their sins—	3972
	16:22	The goat will carry on itself **a** their sins to	3972

Lev 16:30 you will be clean from a your sins. 3972
16:33 and for the priests and a the people of 3972
16:34 Atonement is to be made once a year for a 3972
17: 2 to Aaron and his sons and to a the Israelites 3972
18:27 for a these things were done by 3972
19:24 In the fourth year a its fruit will be holy, 3972
19:37 " 'Keep a my decrees and all my laws 3972
19:37 " 'Keep all my decrees and a my laws 3972
20: 5 both him and a who follow him 3972
20:22 " 'Keep a my decrees and laws 3972
20:23 they did a these things, I abhorred them. 3972
21:24 and his sons and to a the Israelites. 3972
22:18 to Aaron and his sons and to a the Israelites 3972
23:31 You shall do no work at a. 3972
23:38 and a the freewill offerings you give to 3972
23:42 A native-born Israelites are to live 3972
24:14 A those who heard him are 3972
25:10 throughout the land to a its inhabitants. 3972
26: 5 a the food you **want** 8427
26:14 to me and carry out a these commands, 3972
26:15 and fail to carry out a my commands and 3972
26:18 " 'If after a **this** you will not listen to me, 465
26:34 Then the land will enjoy its sabbath years a 3972
26:35 A the time that it lies desolate, 3972
Nu 1: 3 to number by their divisions a the men 3972
1:20 A the men twenty years old 3972
1:22 A the men twenty years old 3972
1:24 A the men twenty years old 3972
1:26 A the men twenty years old NIH
1:28 A the men twenty years old 3972
1:30 A the men twenty years old 3972
1:32 A the men twenty years old 3972
1:34 A the men twenty years old 3972
1:36 A the men twenty years old 3972
1:38 A the men twenty years old 3972
1:40 A the men twenty years old 3972
1:42 A the men twenty years old 3972
1:45 A the Israelites twenty years old 3972
1:50 over a its furnishings 3972
1:50 the tabernacle and a its furnishings; 3972
1:54 The Israelites did a this just as 3972
2: 9 A the men assigned to the camp of Judah, 3972
2:16 A the men assigned to the camp of Reuben, 3972
2:24 A the men assigned to the camp of Ephraim, 3972
2:31 A the men assigned to the camp of Dan 3972
2:32 A *those in* the camps, by their divisions, 3972
3: 8 They are to take care of a the furnishings of 3972
3:13 for a the firstborn are mine. 3972
3:13 I struck down a the firstborn in Egypt, 3972
3:22 The number of a the males a month old 3972
3:28 The number of a the males a month old 3972
3:34 The number of a the males a month old 3972
3:36 its crossbars, posts, bases, a its equipment, 3972
3:40 The LORD said to Moses, "Count a 3972
3:41 in place of a the firstborn of the Israelites, 3972
3:41 of the Levites in place of a the firstborn of 3972
3:42 So Moses counted a the firstborn of 3972
3:45 "Take the Levites in place of a the firstborn 3972
4: 3 Count a the men from thirty to fifty years 3972
4: 9 and a its jars for the oil used to supply it. 3972
4:10 and a its accessories in a covering of hides 3972
4:12 to take a the articles used for ministering in 3972
4:14 on it a the utensils used for ministering at 3972
4:15 the holy furnishings and a the holy articles, 3972
4:23 Count a the men from thirty to fifty years 3972
4:26 and a the equipment used in its service. 3972
4:26 The Gershonites are to do a that needs to 3972
4:27 A their service, whether carrying 3972
4:27 as their responsibility a they are to carry. 3972
4:30 Count a the men from thirty to fifty years 3972
4:32 a their equipment and everything related 3972
4:35 A the men from thirty to fifty years 3972
4:37 This was the total of a *those in* 3972
4:39 A the men from thirty to fifty years 3972
4:43 A the men from thirty to fifty years 3972
4:46 the leaders of Israel counted a the Levites 3972
4:47 A the men from thirty to fifty years 3972
5: 7 and give it a to the person he has wronged. NIH
5: 9 A the sacred contributions 3972
7: 1 and consecrated it and a its furnishings. 3972
7: 1 and consecrated the altar and a its utensils. 3972
7: 8 They were a under the direction NIH
8:17 I struck down a the firstborn in Egypt, 3972
8:18 the Levites in place of a the firstborn sons 3972
8:19 **Of a** the Israelites, 4946+9348
9: 3 with a its rules and regulations." 3972
9:12 they must follow a the regulations. 3972
10:25 Finally, as the rear guard for a the units, 3972
11:11 that you put the burden of a these people 3972
11:12 Did I conceive a these people? 3972
11:13 Where can I get meat for a these people? 3972
11:14 I cannot carry a these people by myself; 3972
11:22 Would they have enough if a the fish in 3972
11:29 that a the LORD's people were prophets 3972
11:31 It brought them down a **around** the camp to 6017
11:32 A that day and night and all the next day 3972
11:32 All that day and night and a the next day 3972
11:32 they spread them out a **around** the camp. 6017
12: 4 *a* **three** *of* you." AIT
12: 7 he is faithful in a my house. 3972
13: 3 A *of* them were leaders of the Israelites. 3972
13:32 A the people we saw there are of great size. 3972
14: 1 That night a the people *of* 3972
14: 2 A the Israelites grumbled against Moses 3972
14:10 at the Tent of Meeting to a the Israelites. 3972
14:11 of a the miraculous signs I have performed 3972
14:15 you put these people to death a at one time, 408

Nu 14:39 Moses reported this to a the Israelites, 3972
14:45 and beat them down **a the way to** Hormah. 6330
15:26 because a the people were involved in 3972
15:39 and so you will remember a the commands 3972
15:40 to obey a my commands and will 3972
16: 5 Then he said to Korah and a his followers: 3972
16: 6 Korah, and a your followers are to do this: 3972
16:10 and a your fellow Levites near himself, 3972
16:11 and a your followers have banded together. 3972
16:16 and a your followers are to appear before 3972
16:17 250 censers in **a—** NIH
16:19 When Korah had gathered a his followers 3972
16:22 "O God, God of the spirits of a mankind, 3972
16:26 be swept away because of a their sins." 3972
16:28 the LORD has sent me to do a these things 3972
16:31 As soon as he finished saying a this, 3972
16:32 with their households and a Korah's men 3972
16:32 and a their possessions. 3972
16:34 a the Israelites around them fled, shouting, 3972
17: 9 Then Moses brought out a the staffs from 3972
17: 9 the staffs from the LORD's presence to a 3972
17:12 We are lost, we are a lost! 3972
17:13 *Are we* a going to die?" 9462
18: 3 and are to perform a the duties of the Tent, 3972
18: 4 a the work at the Tent— 3972
18: 8 a the holy offerings the Israelites give me 3972
18: 9 From a the gifts they bring me 3972
18:11 from the gifts of a the wave offerings of 3972
18:12 "I give you a the finest olive oil and all 3972
18:12 "I give you all the finest olive oil and a 3972
18:13 A the land's firstfruits that they bring to 3972
18:21 "I give to the Levites a the tithes in Israel 3972
18:28 to the LORD from a the tithes you receive 3972
19:18 and sprinkle the tent and a the furnishings 3972
20:14 about a the hardships that have come 3972
21:25 Israel captured a the cities of the Amorites 3972
21:25 and a its surrounding settlements. 3972
21:26 of Moab and had taken from him a his land 3972
21:30 Heshbon is destroyed **a the way to** Dibon. 6330
22: 2 of Zippor saw a that Israel had done to 3972
23: 6 with a the princes of Moab. 3972
23:13 you will see only a part but not a *of* them. 3972
23:25 "Neither **curse** them **at a** nor bless 7686+7686
23:25 at all nor **bless** them **at a!"** 1385+1385
24:17 the skulls of a the sons of Sheth. 3972
25: 4 "Take a the leaders of these people, 3972
26: 2 a *those* twenty years old 3972
26:43 A *of* them were Shuhamite clans; 3972
26:62 A the male Levites a month old 3972
27:16 the God of the spirits of a mankind, 3972
28:11 a year old, *a* **without defect.** AIT
28:19 a year old, *a* **without defect.** AIT
29: 2 a year old, *a* **without defect.** AIT
29: 8 a year old, *a* **without defect.** AIT
29:13 a year old, *a* **without defect.** AIT
29:17 a year old, *a* **without defect.** AIT
29:20 a year old, *a* **without defect.** AIT
29:23 a year old, *a* **without defect.** AIT
29:26 a year old, *a* **without defect.** AIT
29:29 a year old, *a* **without defect.** AIT
29:32 a year old, *a* **without defect.** AIT
29:36 a year old, *a* **without defect.** AIT
29:40 Moses told the Israelites a that 3972
30: 4 then a her vows and every pledge 3972
30:11 then a her vows or the pledges 3972
30:14 then he confirms a her vows or 3972
31: 9 and took a the Midianite herds, 3972
31:10 They burned a the towns where 3972
31:10 as well as a their camps. 3972
31:11 They took a the plunder and spoils, 3972
31:13 and a the leaders of the community went 3972
31:15 "Have you allowed a the women to live?" 3972
31:17 Now kill a the boys. 3972
31:19 "A *of* you who have killed anyone 3972
31:26 of the community are to count a the people 4917[S]
31:51 a the crafted articles. 3972
31:52 A the gold from the commanders 3972
32:15 he will again leave a this people in 3972
32:21 if a of you will go armed over the Jordan 3972
33: 3 They marched out boldly in full view of a 3972
33: 4 who were burying a their firstborn, whom 3972
33:52 drive out a the inhabitants of the land 3972
33:52 Destroy a their carved images 3972
33:52 and demolish a their high places. 3972
35: 3 flocks and a their other livestock. 3972
35: 7 *In* a you must give 3972
Dt 1: 1 to a Israel in the desert east of the Jordan— 3972
1: 3 Moses proclaimed to the Israelites a that 3972
1: 7 to a the neighboring peoples in the Arabah, 3972
1:12 and your disputes **a by myself?** 963+3276+4200
1:19 the hill country of the Amorites through a 3972
1:22 Then a *of* you came to me and said, 3972
1:31 a the way you went until you reached this 3972
1:44 and beat you down from Seir **a the way to** 6330
1:46 a the time you spent there. 3869
2: 7 The LORD your God has blessed you in a 3972
2:25 the terror and fear of you on a the nations 3972
2:32 When Sihon and a his army came out 3972
2:34 At that time we took a his towns 3972
2:36 The LORD our God gave us a of them. 3972
3: 3 of Bashan and a his army. 3972
3: 4 At that time we took a his cities. 3972
3: 5 A these cities were fortified with high walls 3972
3: 7 But a the livestock and the plunder 3972
3:10 We took a the towns on the plateau, 3972
3:10 the plateau, and a Gilead, and all Bashan 3972
3:10 and a Bashan as far as Salecah and Edrei, 3972

Dt 3:13 The rest of Gilead and also a *of* Bashan, 3972
3:18 But a your able-bodied men, 3972
3:21 "You have seen with your own eyes a that 3972
3:21 the same to a the kingdoms over there 3972
4: 4 but a *of* you who held fast to 3972
4: 6 who will hear about a these decrees 3972
4:19 a the heavenly array— 3972
4:19 the LORD your God has apportioned to a 3972
4:29 if you look for him with a your heart and 3972
4:29 with all your heart and with a your soul. 3972
4:30 and a these things have happened to you, 3972
4:34 like a the things the LORD your God did 3972
4:40 the LORD your God gives you for a time. 3972
4:49 included a the Arabah east of the Jordan, 3972
5: 1 Moses summoned a Israel and said: 3972
5: 3 with a *of* us who are alive here today. 3972
5:13 and do a your work, 3972
5:23 a the leading men of your tribes 3972
5:27 to a that the LORD our God says. 3972
5:29 and keep a my commands always, 3972
5:31 so that I may give you a the commands, 3972
5:33 Walk in a the way that the LORD your God 3972
6: 2 as long as you live by keeping a his decrees 3972
6: 5 with a your heart and with all your soul and 3972
6: 5 with all your heart and with a your soul and 3972
6: 5 with all your soul and with a your strength. 3972
6:11 with a *kinds of* good things you did 3972
6:19 thrusting out a your enemies before you, 3972
6:24 to obey a these decrees and to fear 3972
6:25 if we are careful to obey a this law before 3972
7: 6 of a the peoples on the face of the earth to 3972
7: 7 for you were the fewest of a peoples. 3972
7:15 but he will inflict them on a who hate you. 3972
7:16 You must destroy a the peoples 3972
7:18 to Pharaoh and to a Egypt. 3972
7:19 the same to a the peoples you now fear. 3972
7:22 be allowed to eliminate them **a at once,** 4554
8: 2 the LORD your God led you a the way in 3972
8:13 and a you have is multiplied, 3972
9:10 On them were a the commandments 3972
9:18 because of a the sin you had committed, 3972
10:12 to walk in a his ways, to love him, 3972
10:12 the LORD your God with a your heart and 3972
10:12 with all your heart and with a your soul, 3972
10:15 their descendants, above a the nations, 3972
10:22 down into Egypt were seventy **in a,** 5883[S]
11: 6 the middle of a Israel and swallowed them 3972
11: 7 that saw a these great things 3972
11: 8 Observe therefore a the commands I am giving you today, 3972
11:13 with a your heart and with all your soul— 3972
11:13 with all your heart and with a your soul— 3972
11:22 If you carefully observe a these commands 3972
11:22 walk in a his ways and to hold fast to him— 3972
11:23 the LORD will drive out a these nations 3972
11:32 be sure that you obey a the decrees 3972
12: 2 Destroy completely a the places on 3972
12: 5 among a your tribes to put his Name there 3972
12:10 from a your enemies around you so 3972
12:11 special gifts, and a the choice possessions 3972
12:28 to obey a these regulations I am giving you, 3972
12:31 they do a *kinds of* detestable things 3972
12:32 See that you do a I command you; 3972
13: 3 with a your heart and with all your soul. 3972
13: 3 with all your heart and with a your soul. 3972
13: 9 and then the hands of a the people. 3972
13:11 Then a Israel will hear and be afraid, 3972
13:15 to the sword a who live in that town. NIH
13:16 Gather a the plunder of the town into 3972
13:16 and a its plunder as a whole burnt offering 3972
13:18 keeping a his commands 3972
14: 2 of a the peoples on the face of the earth, 3972
14: 9 Of a the creatures living in the water, 3972
14:19 A flying insects that swarm are unclean 3972
14:22 of a that your fields produce each year. 3972
14:28 bring a the tithes of that year's produce 3972
14:29 the LORD your God may bless you in a 3972
15: 5 to follow a these commands I am giving you today. 3972
15:10 your God will bless you in a your work 3972
16: 3 so that a the days 3972
16: 4 be found in your possession in a your land 3972
16:15 in a your harvest and in all the work 3972
16:15 in all your harvest and in a the work 3972
16:16 Three times a year a your men must appear 3972
17: 7 and then the hands of a the people. 3972
17:13 A the people will hear and be afraid, 3972
17:14 "Let us set a king over us like a the nations 3972
17:19 and he is to read it a the days of his life so 3972
17:19 and follow carefully a the words of this law 3972
18: 5 and their descendants out of a your tribes 3972
18: 6 and comes in a earnestness to the place 3972
18: 7 like a his fellow Levites who serve there in 3972
19: 9 because you carefully follow a these laws 3972
20:11 a the people in it shall be subject 3972
20:13 put to the sword a the men in it. 3972
20:15 how you are to treat a the cities that are at 3972
20:18 to follow a the detestable things they do 3972
21: 5 the LORD and to decide a cases of dispute 3972
21: 6 Then a the elders of the town nearest 3972
21:17 by giving him a double share of a he has. 3972
21:21 Then a the men of his town shall stone him 3972
21:21 A Israel will hear of it and be afraid. 3972
23:24 a the grapes you **want,** 8427
24:19 the LORD your God may bless you in a 3972
25:18 and cut off a who were lagging behind; 3972
25:19 the LORD your God gives you rest from a 3972

Dt 26: 2 of the firstfruits of a that you produce from 3972
26:11 and the aliens among you shall rejoice in a 3972
26:12 a tenth of a your produce in the third year, 3972
26:13 according to a you commanded. 3972
26:16 carefully observe them with a your heart 3972
26:16 with all your heart and with a your soul. 3972
26:18 and that you are to keep a his commands. 3972
26:19 above a the nations he has made and 3972
27: 1 "Keep a these commands 3972
27: 3 Write on them a the words of this law 3972
27: 8 And you shall write very clearly a 3972
27: 9 who are Levites, said to a Israel, "Be silent, 3972
27:14 to a the people of Israel in a loud voice: 3972
27:15 Then a the people shall say, "Amen!" 3972
27:16 Then a the people shall say, "Amen!" 3972
27:17 Then a the people shall say, "Amen!" 3972
27:18 Then a the people shall say, "Amen!" 3972
27:19 Then a the people shall say, "Amen!" 3972
27:20 Then a the people shall say, "Amen!" 3972
27:21 Then a the people shall say, "Amen!" 3972
27:22 Then a the people shall say, "Amen!" 3972
27:23 Then a the people shall say, "Amen!" 3972
27:24 Then a the people shall say, "Amen!" 3972
27:25 Then a the people shall say, "Amen!" 3972
27:26 Then a the people shall say, "Amen!" 3972
28: 1 carefully follow a his commands I give you 3972
28: 1 above a the nations on earth. 3972
28: 2 A these blessings will come upon you 3972
28:10 Then a the peoples on earth will see 3972
28:12 and to bless a the work of your hands. 3972
28:15 not carefully follow a his commands 3972
28:15 a these curses will come upon you 3972
28:25 and you will become a thing of horror to a 3972
28:26 Your carcasses will be food for a the birds 3972
28:33 but cruel oppression a your days. 3972
28:37 of scorn and ridicule to a the nations where 3972
28:42 of locusts will take over a your trees and 3972
28:45 A these curses will come upon you. 3972
28:52 to a the cities throughout your land until 3972
28:52 They will besiege a the cities throughout 3972
28:55 It will be a he has left because of 3972
28:55 on you during the siege of a your cities. 3972
28:58 If you do not carefully follow a the words 3972
28:60 He will bring upon you a the diseases 3972
28:64 LORD will scatter you among a nations, 3972
29: 2 Moses summoned a the Israelites and said 3972
29: 2 Your eyes have seen a that the LORD did 3972
29: 2 to a his officials and to all his land. 3972
29: 2 to all his officials and to a his land. 3972
29:10 A *of* you are standing today in the presence 3972
29:10 and a the other men of Israel, 3972
29:20 A the curses written in this book will fall 3972
29:21 The LORD will single him out from a 3972
29:21 to a the curses of the covenant written 3972
29:24 A the nations will ask: 3972
29:27 so that he brought on it a the curses written 3972
29:29 that we may follow a the words of this law. 3972
30: 1 When a these blessings 3972
30: 2 with a your heart and with all your soul 3972
30: 2 with all your heart and with a your soul 3972
30: 3 from a the nations where he scattered you. 3972
30: 6 so that you may love him with a your heart 3972
30: 6 with all your heart and with a your soul, 3972
30: 7 The LORD your God will put a these curses 3972
30: 8 follow a his commands I am giving you 3972
30: 9 in a the work of your hands and in the fruit 3972
30:10 the LORD your God with a your heart and 3972
30:10 with all your heart and with a your soul. 3972
31: 1 and spoke these words to a Israel: 3972
31: 5 to them a that I have commanded you. 3972
31: 7 and said to him in the presence of a Israel, 3972
31: 9 and to a the elders of Israel. 3972
31:11 when a Israel comes to appear before 3972
31:12 and follow carefully a the words 3972
31:18 on that day because of a their wickedness 3972
31:28 before me a the elders of your tribes 3972
31:28 of your tribes and a your officials, NIH
32: 4 and a his ways are just. 3972
32: 8 when he divided a mankind, NIH
32:27 the LORD has not done a this.' " 3972
32:44 of Nun and spoke a the words of this song 3972
32:45 Moses finished reciting a these words 3972
32:45 When Moses finished reciting all these words to a Israel, 3972
32:46 "Take to heart a the words 3972
32:46 to obey carefully a the words of this law. 3972
33: 3 a the holy ones are in your hand. 3972
33: 3 At your feet they a bow down, NIH
33:11 Bless a his skills, O LORD, NIH
33:12 for he shields him a day long, 3972
33:16 *Let a these* rest on the head of Joseph, AIT
34: 2 a *of* Naphtali, the territory of Ephraim 3972
34: 2 a the land of Judah as far as 3972
34:11 who did a those miraculous signs 3972
34:11 and to a his officials and to his whole land. 3972
34:12 that Moses did in the sight of a Israel. 3972
Jos 1: 2 Now then, you and a these people, 3972
1: 4 a the Hittite country— 3972
1: 5 be able to stand up against you a the days 3972
1: 7 Be careful to obey a the law 3972
1:14 but a your fighting men, fully armed, 3972
2: 9 that a who live in this country are melting 3972
2:13 and a who belong to them, 3972
2:18 and a your family into your house. 3972
2:22 the pursuers had searched a along the road 3972
2:24 a the people are melting in fear because 3972
3: 1 and a the Israelites set out from Shittim 3972
Jos 3: 7 to exalt you in the eyes of a Israel, 3972
3:11 of a the earth will go into the Jordan ahead 3972
3:13 the Lord of a the earth— 3972
3:15 Jordan is at flood stage a during harvest. 3972
3:17 while a Israel passed by until 3972
4:11 and as soon as a *of* them had crossed, 3972
4:14 in the sight of a Israel; 3972
4:14 and they revered him a the days of his life, 3972
4:24 that a the peoples of the earth might know 3972
5: 1 Now when a the Amorite kings west of 3972
5: 1 the Amorite kings west of the Jordan and a 3972
5: 4 A those who came out of Egypt— 3972
5: 4 a the men of military age— 3972
5: 5 A the people that came out had been circumcised, 3972
5: 5 but a the people born in the desert during 3972
5: 6 until a the men who were of military age 3972
6: 3 around the city once with a the armed men. 3972
6: 5 have a the people give a loud shout; 3972
6: 9 **A this time** the trumpets were sounding. 2143
6:17 The city and a that is in it are to be devoted 3972
6:17 and a who are with her in her house shall 3972
6:19 A the silver and gold and the articles 3972
6:22 and bring her out and a who belong to her, 3972
6:23 and brothers and a who belonged to her. 3972
6:25 with her family and a who belonged to her, 3972
7: 3 "Not a the people will have to go up 3972
7: 3 to take it and do not weary a the people, 3972
7:15 along with a that belongs to him. 3972
7:23 brought them to Joshua and a the Israelites 3972
7:24 Then Joshua, together with a Israel, 3972
7:24 his tent and a that he had, 3972
7:25 Then a Israel stoned him, 3972
8: 4 A *of* you be on the alert. 3972
8: 5 I and a those with me will advance on 3972
8:13 a *those in* the camp to the north of the city 3972
8:14 and a the men of the city hurried out early 3972
8:15 and a Israel let themselves be driven back 3972
8:16 A the men of Ai were called 3972
8:21 and a Israel saw that the ambush had taken 3972
8:24 When Israel had finished killing a the men 3972
8:24 a the Israelites returned to Ai 3972
8:25 fell that day—a the people of Ai. 3972
8:26 until he had destroyed a who lived in Ai. 3972
8:33 A Israel, aliens and citizens alike, 3972
8:34 Joshua read a the words of the law— 3972
8:35 a word of a that Moses had commanded 3972
9: 1 when a the kings west of the Jordan heard 3972
9: 5 A the bread of their food supply was dry 3972
9: 9 a that he did in Egypt, 3972
9:10 and a that he did to the two kings of 3972
9:11 and a those living in our country said to us, 3972
9:19 but a the leaders answered, 3972
9:24 and to wipe out a its inhabitants from 3972
10: 2 and a its men were good fighters 3972
10: 5 up with a their troops and took up positions 3972
10: 6 because a the Amorite kings from 3972
10: 7 including a the best fighting men. 3972
10:10 down **a the way to** Azekah and Makkedah. 6330
10:15 Then Joshua returned with a Israel to 3972
10:24 he summoned a the men of Israel and said 3972
10:25 to a the enemies you are going to fight." 3972
10:29 Then Joshua and a Israel with him moved 3972
10:31 Then Joshua and a Israel with him moved 3972
10:34 Then Joshua and a Israel with him moved 3972
10:36 Then Joshua and a Israel with him went up 3972
10:38 Then Joshua and a Israel with him turned 3972
10:40 together with a their kings. 3972
10:40 He totally destroyed a who breathed, 3972
10:42 A these kings and their lands Joshua conquered in one campaign, 3972
10:43 Then Joshua returned with a Israel to 3972
11: 4 with a their troops and a large number 3972
11: 5 A these kings joined forces 3972
11: 6 by this time tomorrow I will hand a 3972
11: 8 and pursued them **a the way to** 6330
11:10 the head of a these kingdoms.) 3972
11:12 Joshua took a these royal cities 3972
11:14 for themselves a the plunder and livestock 3972
11:14 but a the people they put to the sword 3972
11:15 of a that the LORD commanded Moses. 3972
11:16 the hill country, a the Negev, 3972
11:17 He captured a their kings and struck them 3972
11:18 Joshua waged war against a these kings for 3972
11:19 who took them a in battle. 3972
11:21 from a the hill country of Judah, 3972
11:21 and from a the hill country of Israel. 3972
12: 1 including a the eastern side of the Arabah: 3972
12: 5 a *of* Bashan to the border of the people 3972
12:24 king of Tirzah one thirty-one kings *in* a. 3972
13: 2 a the regions of the Philistines 3972
13: 3 a of it counted as Canaanite (the territory of NIH
13: 4 a the land of the Canaanites, 3972
13: 5 and a Lebanon to the east, 3972
13: 6 "As for a the inhabitants of 3972
13: 6 that is, a the Sidonians, 3972
13:10 a the towns of Sihon king of the Amorites, 3972
13:11 a *of* Mount Hermon and all Bashan as far 3972
13:11 all of Mount Hermon and a Bashan as far 3972
13:17 to Heshbon and a its towns on the plateau, 3972
13:21 —a the towns on the plateau and 3972
13:25 a the towns of Gilead and half 3972
13:30 and including a *of* Bashan, the entire realm 3972
13:30 a the settlements of Jair in Bashan, 3972
15:46 a that were in the vicinity of Ashdod, 3972
16: 9 also included a the towns and their villages 3972
17:16 and a the Canaanites who live in 3972
Jos 18:20 of the clans of Benjamin **on a sides.** 6017
19: 8 and a the villages around these towns as far 3972
21:19 A the towns for the priests, 3972
21:26 A these ten towns 3972
21:33 A the towns of the Gershonite clans 3972
21:39 four towns *in* a. 3972
21:40 A the towns allotted to the Merarite clans, 3972
21:41 by the Israelites were forty-eight *in* a, 3972
21:42 this was true for a these towns. 3972
21:43 So the LORD gave Israel a the land 3972
21:44 the LORD handed a their enemies over 3972
21:45 Not one of a the LORD's good promises 3972
22: 2 "You have done a that Moses the servant 3972
22: 5 to walk in a his ways, 3972
22: 5 to him and to serve him with a your heart 3972
22: 5 with all your heart and a your soul." 3972
23: 1 from a their enemies around them, 3972
23: 2 summoned a Israel—their elders, 3972
23: 3 to a these nations for your sake; 3972
23: 4 an inheritance for your tribes a the land of 3972
23: 6 to obey a that is written in the Book of 3972
23:14 "Now I am about to go the way of a 3972
23:14 You know with a your heart and soul that 3972
23:14 that not one of a the good promises 3972
23:15 on you a the evil he has threatened, 3972
24: 1 Then Joshua assembled a the tribes 3972
24: 2 Joshua said to a the people, 3972
24:14 and serve him with a faithfulness. 9459
24:17 on our entire journey and among a 3972
24:18 LORD drove out before us a the nations, 3972
24:27 he said to a the people. 3972
24:27 It has heard a the words 3972
Jdg 2: 4 of the LORD had spoken these things to a 3972
2: 7 and who had seen a the great things 3972
2:14 sold them to their enemies **a around,** 4946+6017
3: 1 to test a *those* Israelites who had 3972
3: 3 a the Canaanites, the Sidonians, 3972
3:19 And a his attendants left him. 3972
3:29 a vigorous and strong; not a man escaped. 3972
4:13 and a the men with him, 3972
4:15 the LORD routed Sisera and a his chariots 3972
4:16 A the troops of Sisera fell by the sword; 3972
5:30 a this as plunder?' NIH
5:31 "So may a your enemies perish, O LORD! 3972
6: 4 the land and ruined the crops **a the way to** 6330
6: 9 and from the hand of a your oppressors. 3972
6:13 why has a this happened to us? 3972
6:13 Where are a his wonders 3972
6:16 a the Midianites **together."** 285+408+3869
6:33 Now a the Midianites, 3972
6:37 If there is dew only on the fleece and a 3972
6:40 a the ground was covered with dew. 3972
7: 1 and a his men camped at the spring 3972
7: 6 A the rest got down on their knees to drink. 3972
7: 7 Let a the other men go, 3972
7:12 and a the other eastern peoples had settled 3972
7:16 and empty jars in the hands of a *of* them, 3972
7:18 and a who are with me blow our trumpets, 3972
7:18 then from a around the camp blow yours 3972
7:21 a the Midianites ran, 3972
7:23 Asher and a Manasseh were called out, 3972
7:24 So a the men of Ephraim were called out 3972
8:10 a that were left of the armies of 3972
8:27 A Israel prostituted themselves 3972
8:34 the hands of a their enemies on every side. 3972
8:35 for a the good things he had done for them. 3972
9: 1 and said to them and to a his mother's clan, 3972
9: 2 "Ask a the citizens of Shechem, 3972
9: 2 to have a seventy of Jerub-Baal's sons rule 3972
9: 3 the brothers repeated a this to the citizens 3972
9: 6 Then a the citizens of Shechem 3972
9:14 "Finally a the trees said to the thornbush, 3972
9:34 and a his troops set out by night and took 3972
9:40 **a the way to** the entrance to the gate. 6330
9:45 A that day Abimelech pressed his attack 3972
9:48 he and a his men went up Mount Zalmon. 3972
9:49 So a the men cut branches 3972
9:49 So a the people in the tower of Shechem, 3972
9:51 to which a the men and women— 3972
9:51 a the people of the city—fled. 3972
9:57 of Shechem pay for a their wickedness. 3972
10: 8 For eighteen years they oppressed a 3972
10:18 be the head of a those living in Gilead." 3972
11: 8 and you will be our head over a who live 3972
11:11 And he repeated a his words before 3972
11:13 **a the way to** the Jordan. 6330
11:20 He mustered a his men and encamped 3972
11:21 and a his men into Israel's hands, 3972
11:21 over a the land of the Amorites who lived 3972
11:22 capturing a *of* it from the Arnon to 3972
11:26 the surrounding settlements and a 3972
12: 6 **"A right,** say 'Shibboleth.' " 5528
13:13 "Your wife must do a that I have told her. 3972
13:23 nor shown us a these things or 3972
14: 3 or among a our people? 3972
16: 2 the place and lay in wait for him a night at 3972
16: 3 and tore them loose, bar **and a.** 6640
16:27 a the rulers of the Philistines were there, 3972
16:30 Then he pushed with a his might, NIH
16:30 down came the temple on the rulers and a 3972
18: 2 These men represented a their clans. 7896
18:31 a the time the house of God was in Shiloh. 3972
19:29 and sent them into a the areas of Israel. 3972
20: 1 Then a the Israelites from Dan 3972
20: 2 The leaders of a the people of the tribes 3972
20: 7 Now, a you Israelites, speak up 3972
20: 8 A the people rose as one man, saying, 3972

Jdg 20:10 of every hundred from **a** the tribes of Israel, 3972
20:10 for **a** this vileness done in Israel." 3972
20:11 So **a** the men of Israel got together 3972
20:16 Among **a** these soldiers there were 3972
20:17 **a** *of* them fighting men. 3972
20:25 **a** *of* them armed with swords. 3972
20:26 Then the Israelites, **a** the people, 3972
20:33 **A** the men of Israel moved 3972
20:35 Benjamites, **a** armed with swords. 3972
20:44 **a** *of* them valiant fighters. 3972
20:46 **a** *of* them valiant fighters. 3972
20:48 went back to Benjamin and put **a** the towns 5507
20:48 **A** the towns they came across they set 3972
21: 5 "Who from **a** the tribes of Israel has failed 3972
21:14 But there were not enough for **a** of them. NIH
Ru 2:11 "I've been told **a** about what you have done 3972
2:14 She ate **a** *she* **wanted** 8425
2:21 until they finish harvesting **a** my grain.' " 3972
3:11 I will do for you **a** you ask. 3972
3:11 **A** my fellow townsmen know that you are 3972
4: 9 Then Boaz announced to the elders and **a** 3972
4: 9 from Naomi **a** the property of Elimelech, 3972
4:11 Then the elders and **a** those at the gate said, 3972
1Sa 1: 4 to his wife Peninnah and to **a** her sons 3972
1:11 then I will give him to the LORD for **a** 3972
1:21 the man Elkanah went up with **a** his family 3972
2:14 how they treated **a** the Israelites who came 3972
2:22 to **a** Israel and how they slept with 3972
2:23 from **a** the people about these wicked deeds 3972
2:28 of **a** the tribes of Israel to be my priest, 3972
2:28 I also gave your father's house **a** 3972
2:33 and **a** your descendants will die in 3972
3:20 And **a** Israel from Dan 3972
4: 1 And Samuel's word came to **a** Israel. 3972
4: 5 **a** Israel raised such a great shout that 3972
4: 6 "What's **a** this shouting in 1524
4: 8 the Egyptians with **a** *kinds of* plagues in 3972
5: 8 So they called together **a** the rulers of 3972
5:11 So they called together **a** the rulers of 3972
6: 3 but **by a means send** a guilt offering to him. 8740+8740
6:12 **keeping** on the road and lowing **a the way;** 2143+2143
6:16 the Philistines saw **a** this and then returned NIH
7: 2 It was a long time, twenty years in **a,** NIH
7: 2 and **a** the people of Israel mourned 3972
7: 3 to the LORD with **a** your hearts, 3972
7: 5 "Assemble **a** Israel at Mizpah 3972
7:15 as judge over Israel **a** the days of his life. 3972
7:16 judging Israel in **a** those places. 3972
8: 4 So **a** the elders of Israel gathered together 3972
8: 5 such as **a** the other nations have." 3972
8: 7 "Listen to **a** that the people are saying 3972
8:10 Samuel told **a** the words of the LORD to 3972
8:20 Then we will be like **a** the other nations, 3972
8:21 When Samuel heard **a** that the people said, 3972
9:19 and will tell you **a** that is in your heart. 3972
9:20 to whom is **a** the desire of Israel turned, 3972
9:20 if not to you and **a** your father's family?" 3972
9:21 and is not my clan the least of **a** the clans 3972
10: 9 and **a** these signs were fulfilled that day. 3972
10:11 When **a** those who had formerly known him saw him prophesying 3972
10:18 and **a** the kingdoms that oppressed you.' 3972
10:19 who saves you out of **a** your calamities 3972
10:20 Samuel brought **a** the tribes of Israel near, 3972
10:24 Samuel said to **a** the people, 3972
10:24 There is no one like him among **a** 3972
11: 1 And **a** the men of Jabesh said to him, 3972
11: 2 of you and so bring disgrace on **a** Israel." 3972
11: 4 they **a** wept aloud. 3972
11:15 So **a** the people went to Gilgal 3972
11:15 and **a** the Israelites held a great celebration. 3972
12: 1 Samuel said to **a** Israel, 3972
12: 7 with evidence before the LORD as to **a** 3972
12:18 So **a** the people stood in awe of the LORD 3972
12:19 The people **a** said to Samuel, 3972
12:19 to **a** our other sins the evil of asking for 3972
12:20 "You have done **a** this evil; 3972
12:20 but serve the LORD with **a** your heart. 3972
12:24 and serve him faithfully with **a** your heart; 3972
13: 4 So **a** Israel heard the news: 3972
13: 7 and **a** the troops with him were quaking 3972
13:13 over Israel for **a time.** 6409
13:20 So **a** Israel went down to the Philistines 3972
14: 7 "Do **a** that you have in mind," 3972
14:16 the army melting away **in a directions.** 2151
14:20 and **a** his men assembled and went to 3972
14:22 When **a** the Israelites who had hidden in 3972
14:38 **a** you who are leaders of the army, 3972
14:40 Saul then said to **a** the Israelites, 3972
14:52 **A** the days of Saul there was bitter war with 3972
15: 6 for you showed kindness to **a** the Israelites 3972
15: 7 **a the way** from Havilah **to** Shur, 995
15: 8 and **a** his people he totally destroyed with 3972
15:11 and he cried out to the LORD **a** that night. 3972
16:11 *"Are these* **a** the sons you have?" 9462
17:11 Saul and **a** the Israelites were dismayed 3972
17:19 They are with Saul and **a** the men of Israel 3972
17:24 they **a** ran from him in great fear. 3972
17:47 **A** those gathered here will know that it is 3972
17:47 and he will give **a** of you into our hands." NIH
18: 5 This pleased **a** the people, 3972
18: 6 the women came out from **a** the towns 3972
18:16 But **a** Israel and Judah loved David, 3972
18:22 and his attendants **a** like you; 3972
19: 1 and **a** the attendants to kill David. 3972
1Sa 19: 5 a great victory for **a** Israel, 3972
19:18 at Ramah and told him **a** that Saul had done 3972
19:24 He lay that way **a** that day and night. 3972
20: 6 If your father **misses** me **at a,** tell him, 7212+7212
20:39 (The boy knew nothing of **a** this; 4399
22: 2 **A** those who were in distress or in debt 3972
22: 6 with **a** his officials standing around him. 3972
22: 7 Will the son of Jesse give **a** *of* you fields 3972
22: 7 Will he make **a** *of* you commanders 3972
22: 8 that why you have **a** conspired against me? 3972
22:11 and they **a** came to the king. 3972
22:14 of **a** your servants is as loyal as David, 3972
22:15 your servant knows nothing **at a** 196+1524+7785
23: 8 And Saul called up **a** his forces for battle, 3972
23:23 Find out about **a** the hiding places he uses 3972
23:23 in the area, I will track him down among **a** 3972
24: 2 from **a** Israel and set out to look for David 3972
25: 1 **a** Israel assembled and mourned for him; 3972
25: 6 And good health to **a** that is yours! 3972
25:16 Night and day they were a wall around us **a** 3972
25:21 **a** my watching over this fellow's property 3972
25:22 of **a** who belong to him!" 3972
25:26 and **a** who intend to harm my master be NIH
25:37 his wife told him **a** these things, NIH
26:12 They were **a** sleeping, 3972
26:24 and deliver me from **a** trouble." 3972
28: 3 and **a** Israel had mourned for him 3972
28: 4 while Saul gathered **a** the Israelites and set 3972
28:20 for he had eaten nothing **a** that day 3972
29: 1 The Philistines gathered **a** their forces 3972
30: 2 the women and **a** who were in it, NIH
30:20 He took **a** the flocks and herds, 3972
30:22 But **a** the evil men and troublemakers 3972
30:24 *A will* **share** alike." AIT
30:31 to those in **a** the other places where David 3972
31: 6 and **a** his men died together that same day. 3972
31:12 **a** their valiant men journeyed through 3972
2Sa 1:11 and **a** the men with him took hold 3972
2: 9 Benjamin and **a** Israel. 3972
2:14 **"A right,** *let them* **do it,"** 7756[S]
2:28 and **a** the men came to a halt; 3972
2:29 **A** that night Abner and his men marched 3972
2:30 and assembled **a** his men. 3972
2:32 and his men marched **a** night and arrived 3972
3:12 I will help you bring **a** Israel over to you." 3972
3:16 weeping behind her **a the way** to Bahurim. 2143
3:18 and from the hand of **a** their enemies.' " 3972
3:21 and assemble **a** Israel for my lord the king, 3972
3:21 over **a** that your heart desires." 3972
3:23 Joab and **a** the soldiers with him arrived, 3972
3:29 of Joab and upon **a** his father's house! 3972
3:31 Then David said to Joab and **a** the people 3972
3:32 **A** the people wept also. 3972
3:34 And **a** the people wept over him again. 3972
3:35 Then they **a** came and urged David 3972
3:36 **A** the people took note and were pleased; 3972
3:37 on that day **a** the people and all Israel knew 3972
3:37 on that day all the people and **a** Israel knew 3972
4: 1 and **a** Israel became alarmed. 3972
4: 7 they traveled **a** night by way of the Arabah. 3972
4: 9 who has delivered me out of **a** trouble, 3972
5: 1 **A** the tribes of Israel came to David 3972
5: 3 When **a** the elders of Israel had come 3972
5: 5 over **a** Israel and Judah thirty-three years. 3972
5:25 **a the way** from Gibeon **to** Gezer. 995+6330
6: 1 thirty thousand *in* **a.** 3972
6: 2 and **a** his men set out from Baalah of Judah 3972
6: 5 with **a** their might before the LORD, 3972
6:14 danced before the LORD with **a** his might, 3972
6:19 And **a** the people went to their homes. 3972
7: 1 from **a** his enemies around him, 3972
7: 7 Wherever I have moved with **a** 3972
7: 9 and I have cut off **a** your enemies from 3972
7:11 also give you rest from **a** your enemies. 3972
7:17 Nathan reported to David **a** the words 3972
8: 4 He hamstrung **a** but a hundred of 3972
8:11 from **a** the nations he had subdued: 3972
8:14 and **a** the Edomites became subject 3972
8:15 David reigned over **a** Israel, 3972
8:15 and right for **a** his people. 3972
9: 7 to you **a** the land that belonged 3972
9:12 and **a** the members 3972
10:17 David was told of this, he gathered **a** Israel, 3972
10:19 When **a** the kings who were vassals 3972
11: 9 with **a** his master's servants and did not go 3972
12: 8 And if **a** this had been too little, NIH
12:12 in broad daylight before **a** Israel.' " 3972
12:31 He did this to **a** the Ammonite towns. 3972
13:21 King David heard **a** this, he was furious. 3972
13:23 he invited **a** the king's sons to come there. 3972
13:25 **"A** *of* us should not go; 3972
13:29 Then **a** the king's sons got up, 3972
13:30 "Absalom has struck down **a** 3972
13:31 and **a** his servants stood by 3972
13:32 "My lord should not think that they killed **a** 3972
13:33 the report that **a** the king's sons are dead. 3972
13:36 too, and **a** his servants wept very bitterly. 3972
14:19 "Isn't the hand of Joab with you in **a** this?" 3972
14:19 and who put **a** these words into the mouth 3972
14:25 In **a** Israel there was not a man 3972
15: 6 Absalom behaved in this way toward **a** 3972
15:14 Then David said to **a** his officials who were 3972
15:17 with **a** the people following him, 3972
15:18 **A** his men marched past him, 3972
15:18 along with **a** the Kerethites and Pelethites; 3972
15:18 with all the Kerethites and Pelethites; and **a** 3972
15:22 the Gittite marched on with **a** his men and 3972
2Sa 15:23 The whole countryside wept aloud as **a** 3972
15:23 **a** the people moved on toward the desert. 3972
15:24 and **a** the Levites who were 3972
15:24 until **a** the people had finished leaving 3972
15:30 **A** the people with him covered their heads 3972
16: 4 "**A** that belonged to Mephibosheth is 3972
16: 6 He pelted David and **a** the king's officials 3972
16: 6 though **a** the troops and 3972
16: 8 for **a** the blood you shed in the household 3972
16:11 then said to Abishai and **a** his officials, 3972
16:14 The king and **a** the people with him arrived 3972
16:15 and **a** the men of Israel came to Jerusalem, 3972
16:18 and by **a** the men of Israel— 3972
16:21 Then **a** Israel will hear 3972
16:22 in the sight of **a** Israel. 3972
16:23 how both David and Absalom regarded **a** 3972
17: 2 and then **a** the people with him will flee. 3972
17: 3 and bring **a** the people back to you. 3972
17: 3 will mean the return of **a;** 3972
17: 3 **a** the people will be unharmed." 3972
17: 4 to Absalom and to **a** the elders of Israel. 3972
17:10 for **a** Israel knows that your father is 3972
17:11 Let **a** Israel, from Dan to Beersheba— 3972
17:13 then **a** Israel will bring ropes to that city, 3972
17:14 Absalom and **a** the men of Israel said, 3972
17:16 or the king and **a** the people with him will 3972
17:22 So David and **a** the people with him set out 3972
17:24 and Absalom crossed the Jordan with **a** 3972
18: 4 So the king stood beside the gate while **a** 3972
18: 5 And **a** the troops heard the king 3972
18:17 **a** the Israelites fled to their homes. 3972
18:28 to the king, **"A is well!"** 8934
18:31 from **a** who rose up against you." 3972
18:32 the king and **a** who rise up to harm you be 3972
19: 5 "Today you have humiliated **a** your men, 3972
19: 6 if Absalom were alive today and **a** 3972
19: 7 be worse for you than **a** the calamities 3972
19: 8 they **a** came before him. 3972
19: 9 the people were **a** arguing with each other, 3972
19:14 over the hearts of **a** the men of Judah as 3972
19:14 "Return, you and **a** your men." 3972
19:28 **A** my grandfather's descendants deserved nothing 3972
19:39 So **a** the people crossed the Jordan, 3972
19:40 **A** the troops of Judah and half the troops 3972
19:41 Soon **a** the men of Israel were coming to 3972
19:41 together with **a** his men?" 3972
19:42 **A** the men of Judah answered the men 3972
20: 2 So **a** the men of Israel deserted David 3972
20: 2 stayed by their king **a the way from** the Jordan 4946
20: 7 and **a** the mighty warriors went out under 3972
20:12 and the man saw that **a** the troops came to 3972
20:13 **a** the men went on with Joab 3972
20:14 Sheba passed through **a** the tribes of Israel 3972
20:15 **A** the troops with Joab came 3972
20:22 Then the woman went to **a** the people 3972
21: 9 *A* **seven** *of* them fell together; AIT
21:20 on each foot—twenty-four **in a.** 5031
22: 1 of **a** his enemies and from the hand of Saul. 3972
22:23 **A** his laws are before me; 3972
22:31 He is a shield for **a** who take refuge in him. 3972
22:46 **They** *a* lose heart; AIT
23: 6 evil men are **a** to be cast aside like thorns, 3972
23:39 There were thirty-seven *in* **a.** 3972
24: 7 toward the fortress of Tyre and **a** the towns 3972
24:23 O king, Araunah gives **a** this to the king." 3972
1Ki 1: 9 He invited **a** his brothers, the king's sons, 3972
1: 9 and **a** the men 3972
1:19 and has invited **a** the king's sons, 3972
1:20 the eyes of **a** Israel are on you, 3972
1:25 He has invited **a** the king's sons, 3972
1:39 the trumpet and **a** the people shouted, 3972
1:40 And **a** the people went up after him, 3972
1:41 Adonijah and **a** the guests who were 3972
1:41 the meaning of **a** the noise in the city?" NIH
1:43 **"Not at a!"** Jonathan answered. 66
1:49 **a** Adonijah's guests rose in alarm 3972
2: 2 "I am about to go the way of **a** the earth," 3972
2: 3 so that you may prosper in **a** you do 3972
2: 4 before me with **a** their heart and soul, 3972
2:15 **A** Israel looked to me as their king. 3972
2:22 **after a,** he is my older brother— 3954
2:26 and shared **a** my father's hardships." 3972
2:44 in your heart **a** the wrong you did 3972
3:15 Then he gave a feast for **a** his court. 3972
3:28 When **a** Israel heard the verdict 3972
4: 1 So King Solomon ruled over **a** Israel. 3972
4: 7 over **a** Israel, who supplied provisions for 3972
4:10 and **a** the land of Hepher were his); 3972
4:12 and Megiddo, and in **a** *of* Beth Shan next 3972
4:21 And Solomon ruled over **a** the kingdoms 3972
4:21 and were Solomon's subjects **a** his life. 3972
4:24 For he ruled over **a** the kingdoms west of 3972
4:24 and had peace on **a** sides. 3972
4:27 for King Solomon and **a** who came to 3972
4:30 the wisdom of **a** the men of the East, 3972
4:30 and greater than **a** the wisdom of Egypt. 3972
4:31 to **a** the surrounding nations. 3972
4:34 Men of **a** nations came to listen 3972
4:34 sent by **a** the kings of the world, 3972
5: 3 **waged against** my father David **from a sides,** 6015
5: 8 and will do **a** you want in providing 3972
5:10 with **a** the cedar and pine logs he wanted, 3972
5:13 King Solomon conscripted laborers from **a** Israel— 3972

1Ki 6:10	he built the side rooms **a** along the temple.	3972
6:12	and keep **a** my commands and obey them,	3972
6:29	On the walls **a** around the temple,	3972
6:38	the temple was finished in **a** its details	3972
7: 5	**A** the doorways had rectangular frames;	3972
7: 9	**A** these structures, from the outside to	3972
7:14	experienced in **a** *kinds of* bronze work.	3972
7:14	He came to King Solomon and did **a**	3972
7:20	pomegranates in rows **a around.**	6017
7:33	spokes and hubs were **a** *of* cast metal.	3972
7:36	with wreaths **a around.**	6017
7:37	They were **a** cast in the same molds	3972
7:40	So Huram finished **a**	3972
7:45	**A** these objects that Huram made	3972
7:47	Solomon left **a** these things unweighed,	3972
7:48	also made **a** the furnishings that were in	3972
7:51	When **a** the work King Solomon had done	3972
8: 1	**a** the heads of the tribes and the chiefs of	3972
8: 2	**A** the men of Israel came together	3972
8: 3	When **a** the elders of Israel had arrived,	3972
8: 4	the LORD and the Tent of Meeting and **a**	3972
8:25	if only your sons are careful in **a** they **do**	2006
8:39	deal with each man according to **a** he does,	3972
8:39	(for you alone know the hearts of **a** men),	3972
8:40	that they will fear you **a** the time they live	3972
8:43	so that **a** the peoples of the earth may know	3972
8:48	if they turn back to you with **a** their heart	3972
8:50	forgive **a** the offenses they have committed	3972
8:53	from **a** the nations of the world to	3972
8:54	When Solomon had finished **a** these prayers	3972
8:56	of **a** the good promises he gave	3972
8:58	in **a** his ways and to keep the commands,	3972
8:60	so that **a** the peoples of the earth may know	3972
8:62	and **a** Israel with him offered sacrifices	3972
8:63	and **a** the Israelites dedicated the temple of	3972
8:65	and **a** Israel with him—	3972
8:65	fourteen days in **a.**	NIH
8:66	for **a** the good things the LORD had done	3972
9: 1	and had achieved **a** he had desired to do,	3972
9: 4	and do **a** I command	3972
9: 7	and an object of ridicule among **a** peoples.	3972
9: 8	**a** who pass by will be appalled	3972
9: 9	the LORD brought **a** this disaster	3972
9:11	because Hiram had supplied him with **a**	3972
9:19	as well as **a** his store cities and the towns	3972
9:19	in Jerusalem, in Lebanon and throughout **a**	3972
9:20	**A** the people left from the Amorites,	3972
10: 2	with him about **a** that she had on her mind.	3972
10: 3	Solomon answered **a** her questions;	3972
10: 4	of Sheba saw **a** the wisdom of Solomon	3972
10:13	the queen of Sheba **a** she desired and asked	3972
10:15	from **a** the Arabian kings and the governors	3972
10:21	**A** King Solomon's goblets were gold,	3972
10:21	and **a** the household articles in the Palace	3972
10:23	in riches and wisdom than **a** the other kings	3972
10:29	They also exported them to **a** the kings of	3972
11: 8	He did the same for **a** his foreign wives,	3972
11:15	had struck down **a** the men in Edom.	3972
11:16	Joab and **a** the Israelites stayed there	3972
11:16	until they had destroyed **a** the men	3972
11:32	which I have chosen out of **a** the tribes	3972
11:34	I have made him ruler **a** the days of his life	3972
11:37	you will rule over **a** that your heart desires;	3972
11:41	**a** he did and the wisdom he displayed—	3972
11:42	in Jerusalem over **a** Israel forty years.	3972
12: 1	for **a** the Israelites had gone there	3972
12:12	and **a** the people returned to Rehoboam,	3972
12:16	When **a** Israel saw that the king refused	3972
12:18	but **a** Israel stoned him to death.	3972
12:20	When **a** the Israelites heard	3972
12:20	and made him king over **a** Israel.	3972
12:31	and appointed priests from **a sorts**	7896
13:11	whose sons came and told him **a** that	3972
13:32	and against **a** the shrines on the high places	3972
13:33	for the high places from **a sorts** *of* people.	7896
14: 8	and followed me with **a** his heart,	3972
14: 9	You have done more evil than **a** who lived	3972
14:10	until it *is* **a gone.**	9462
14:13	**A** Israel will mourn for him and bury him.	3972
14:18	and **a** Israel mourned for him,	3972
14:21	the LORD had chosen out of **a** the tribes	3972
14:24	in **a** the detestable practices of the nations	3972
14:26	He took everything, including **a**	3972
14:29	and **a** he did,	3972
15: 3	He committed **a** the sins his father had done	3972
15: 5	to keep any of the LORD's commands **a**	3972
15: 7	and **a** he did,	3972
15:12	of **a** the idols his fathers had made.	3972
15:14	to the LORD **a** his life.	3972
15:18	then took **a** the silver and gold that was left	3972
15:20	and **a** Kinnereth in addition to Naphtali.	3972
15:22	King Asa issued an order to **a** Judah—	3972
15:23	As for **a** the other events of Asa's reign,	3972
15:23	of Asa's reign, **a** his achievements,	3972
15:23	**a** he did and the cities he built,	3972
15:27	while Nadab and **a** Israel were besieging it.	3972
15:29	but destroyed them **a**, according to	NIH
15:31	other events of Nadab's reign, and **a** he did,	3972
15:33	of Ahijah became king of **a** Israel	3972
16: 7	of **a** the evil he had done in the eyes of	3972
16:13	because of **a** the sins Baasha	3972
16:14	other events of Elah's reign, and **a** he did,	3972
16:17	and **a** the Israelites with him withdrew	3972
16:25	and sinned more than **a** those before him.	3972
16:26	He walked in **a** the ways of Jeroboam son	3972
16:33	to anger than did **a** the kings of Israel	3972
18: 5	"Go through the land to **a** the springs	3972
1Ki 18:19	the people from **a** over Israel to meet me	3972
18:20	So Ahab sent word throughout **a** Israel	3972
18:24	**a** the people said, "What you say is good."	3972
18:30	Then Elijah said to **a** the people,	3972
18:36	and have done **a** these things	3972
18:39	When **a** the people saw this,	3972
18:46	he ran ahead of Ahab **a the way to** Jezreel.	995+3870+6330
19: 1	and how he had killed **a** the prophets with	3972
19: 5	**A at once** an angel touched him and said,	2180+2296
19:18	**a** whose knees have not bowed down	3972
19:18	and **a** whose mouths have not kissed him."	3972
20: 4	I and **a** I have are yours."	3972
20: 7	of Israel summoned **a** the elders of the land	3972
20: 8	The elders and the people **a** answered,	3972
20: 9	'Your servant will do **a** you demanded	3972
20:15	the rest of the Israelites, 7,000 **in a.**	3972
20:24	Remove **a** the kings from their commands	408
22:10	with **a** the prophets prophesying	3972
22:12	**A** the other prophets were prophesying	3972
22:17	"I saw **a** Israel scattered on the hills	3972
22:19	the LORD sitting on his throne with **a**	3972
22:22	in the mouths of **a** his prophets,'	3972
22:23	in the mouths of **a** these prophets of yours.	3972
22:28	he added, "Mark my words, **a** you people!"	3972
22:35	**A day long** the battle raged,	928+2021+2021+2085+3427
22:39	including **a** he did,	3972
2Ki 1:14	the first two captains and *a* their **men.**	AIT
1:18	for *a* the **other** events of Ahaziah's reign,	AIT
3: 6	from Samaria and mobilized **a** Israel.	3972
3:19	stop up **a** the springs,	3972
3:21	Now **a** the Moabites had heard that	3972
3:25	They stopped up **a** the springs and cut	3972
4: 2	"Your servant has nothing there **at a,"**	3972
4: 3	and ask **a** your neighbors for empty jars.	3972
4: 4	Pour oil into **a** the jars,	3972
4: 6	When **a** the jars were full,	NIH
4:13	'You have gone to **a** this trouble for us.	3972
4:23	"It's **a right,"** she said.	8934
4:26	'Are you **a right?**	8934
4:26	Is your husband **a right?**	8934
4:26	Is your child **a right?'** "	8934
4:26	"Everything is **a right,"** she said.	8934
5: 5	**"By a means, go,"** the king of Aram replied.	995+2143
5:15	and **a** his attendants went back to the man	3972
5:15	that there is no God in **a** the world except	3972
5:21	"Is everything **a right?"**	8934
5:22	"Everything is **a right,"** Gehazi answered.	8934
5:23	**"By a means,** take two talents,"	3283
6:17	of horses and chariots of fire **a around**	6017
7:13	like that of **a** the Israelites left here—	2162+3972
7:13	like **a** these Israelites who are doomed.	2162+3972
8: 4	about **a** the great things Elisha has done."	3972
8: 6	including **a** the income from her land from	3972
8: 7	"The man of God has come **a the way up**	6330
8: 9	with him as a gift forty camel-loads of **a**	3972
8:21	Jehoram went to Zair with **a** his chariots.	3972
8:23	Jehoram's reign, and **a** he did,	3972
9: 7	of **a** the LORD's servants shed by Jezebel.	3972
9:11	"Is everything **a right?**	8934
9:14	**a** Israel had been defending Ramoth Gilead	3972
9:22	**a** the idolatry and witchcraft of your mother Jezebel **abound?"**	8041
10: 7	the princes and slaughtered **a** seventy	NIH
10: 9	He stood before **a** the people and said,	3972
10: 9	but who killed **a** these?	3972
10:11	as well as **a** his chief men,	3972
10:17	he killed **a** who were left there	3972
10:18	Then Jehu brought **a** the people together	3972
10:19	Now summon **a** the prophets of Baal,	3972
10:19	**a** his ministers and all his priests.	3972
10:19	all his ministers and **a** his priests.	3972
10:21	and **a** the ministers of Baal came;	3972
10:22	"Bring robes for **a** the ministers of Baal."	3972
10:30	and have done to the house of Ahab **a** I had	3972
10:31	the God of Israel, with **a** his heart.	3972
10:33	in **a** the land of Gilead (the region of Gad,	3972
10:34	the other events of Jehu's reign, **a** he did,	3972
10:34	all he did, and **a** his achievements,	3972
11: 7	that normally go off Sabbath duty are **a**	3972
11:14	and **a** the people of the land were rejoicing	3972
11:18	**A** the people of the land went to the temple	3972
11:19	the guards and **a** the people of the land,	3972
11:20	and **a** the people of the land rejoiced.	3972
12: 2	the eyes of the LORD **a** the years Jehoiada	3972
12: 4	"Collect **a** the money that is brought	3972
12: 9	into the chest **a** the money that was brought	3972
12:12	and met **a** the other expenses of restoring	3972
12:18	But Joash king of Judah took **a**	3972
12:18	and **a** the gold found in the treasuries of	3972
12:19	reign of Joash, and **a** he did,	3972
13: 8	**a** he did and his achievements,	3972
13:12	**a** he did and his achievements,	3972
14:14	He took **a** the gold and silver and all	3972
14:14	the gold and silver and **a** the articles found	3972
14:21	Then **a** the people of Judah took Azariah,	3972
14:28	other events of Jeroboam's reign, **a** he did,	3972
15: 6	Azariah's reign, and **a** he did,	3972
15:16	and ripped open **a** the pregnant women.	3972
15:21	Menahem's reign, and **a** he did,	3972
15:26	Pekahiah's reign, and **a** he did,	3972
15:29	including **a** the land of Naphtali,	3972
15:31	other events of Pekah's reign, and **a** he did,	3972
16:11	the priest built an altar in accordance with **a**	3972
2Ki 16:15	burnt offering of **a** the people of the land,	3972
16:15	the altar **a** the blood of the burnt offerings	3972
17: 7	*A this* **took place** because	AIT
17: 9	high places in **a** their towns.	3972
17:13	and Judah through **a** his prophets and seers:	3972
17:16	They forsook **a** the commands of	3972
17:16	They bowed down to **a** the starry hosts,	3972
17:20	the LORD rejected **a** the people of Israel;	3972
17:22	The Israelites persisted in **a** the sins	3972
17:23	as he had warned through **a** his servants	3972
17:32	appointed **a sorts** *of* their own *people*	4946+7896
17:39	from the hand of **a** your enemies."	3972
18: 5	like him among **a** the kings of Judah,	3972
18:12	**a** that Moses the servant of	3972
18:13	of Assyria attacked **a** the fortified cities	3972
18:15	So Hezekiah gave him **a** the silver	3972
18:21	of Egypt to **a** who depend on him.	3972
18:35	Who of **a** the gods of these countries	3972
19: 2	the leading priests, *a* **wearing** sackcloth,	AIT
19: 4	the LORD your God will hear **a** the words	3972
19:11	of Assyria have done to **a** the countries,	3972
19:15	you alone are God over **a** the kingdoms of	3972
19:19	so that **a** kingdoms on earth may know	3972
19:24	With the soles of my feet I have dried up **a**	3972
19:35	there were **a** the dead bodies!	3972
20:13	the messengers and showed them **a**	3972
20:13	or in **a** his kingdom that Hezekiah did	3972
20:17	and **a** that your fathers have stored up	NIH
20:20	**a** his achievements and how he made	3972
21: 3	to **a** the starry hosts and worshiped them.	3972
21: 5	he built altars to **a** the starry hosts.	3972
21: 7	which I have chosen out of **a** the tribes	3972
21:14	be looted and plundered by **a** their foes,	3972
21:17	Manasseh's reign, and **a** he did,	3972
21:21	He walked in **a** the ways of his father;	3972
21:24	of the land killed **a** who had plotted	3972
22: 2	in the eyes of the LORD and walked in **a**	3972
22:13	for me and for the people and for **a** Judah	3972
22:13	with **a** that is written there concerning us."	3972
22:17	by **a** the idols their hands have made,	3972
22:20	not see **a** the disaster I am going to bring	3972
23: 1	Then the king called together **a** the elders	3972
23: 2	**a** the people from the least to the greatest.	3972
23: 2	in their hearing **a** the words of the Book of	3972
23: 3	regulations and decrees with **a** his heart	3972
23: 3	with all his heart and **a** his soul,	3972
23: 3	Then **a** the people pledged themselves to	3972
23: 4	to remove from the temple of the LORD **a**	3972
23: 4	for Baal and Asherah and **a** the starry hosts.	3972
23: 5	the constellations and to **a** the starry hosts.	3972
23: 8	Josiah brought **a** the priests from the towns	3972
23:19	Josiah removed and defiled **a** the shrines at	3972
23:20	Josiah slaughtered **a** the priests	3972
23:21	The king gave this order to **a** the people:	3972
23:24	and **a** the other detestable things seen	3972
23:25	with **a** his heart and with all his soul and	3972
23:25	with all his heart and with **a** his soul and	3972
23:25	with all his soul and with **a** his strength,	3972
23:25	in accordance with **a** the Law of Moses.	3972
23:26	which burned against Judah because of **a**	3972
23:28	other events of Josiah's reign, and **a** he did,	3972
24: 3	of the sins of Manasseh and **a** he had done,	3972
24: 5	Jehoiakim's reign, and **a** he did,	3972
24: 7	of Babylon had taken **a** his territory,	3972
24:12	his nobles and his officials *a* **surrendered**	AIT
24:13	Nebuchadnezzar removed **a** the treasures	3972
24:13	and took away **a** the gold articles	3972
24:14	He carried into exile **a** Jerusalem:	3972
24:14	**a** the officers and fighting men,	3972
24:14	and **a** the craftsmen and artisans—	3972
24:20	of the LORD's anger that *a this* **happened**	AIT
25: 1	the city and built siege works **a around** it.	6017
25: 5	**A** his soldiers were separated from him	3972
25: 9	the royal palace and **a** the houses	3972
25:14	dishes and **a** the bronze articles used in	3972
25:15	**a** that were made of pure gold or silver.	NIH
25:17	and pomegranates of bronze **a** around.	3972
25:20	Nebuzaradan the commander took **them** *a*	AIT
25:23	When **a** the army officers	3972
25:26	**a** the people from the least to the greatest,	3972
1Ch 1:23	**A** these were sons of Joktan.	3972
1:33	**A** these were descendants of Keturah.	3972
2: 4	Judah had five sons *in* **a.**	3972
2: 6	and Darda—five *in* **a.**	3972
2:23	**A** these were descendants of Makir	3972
3: 8	Elishama, Eliada and Eliphelet—nine in **a.**	NIH
3: 9	**A** *these* were the sons of David,	3972
3:22	and Shaphat—six in **a.**	NIH
3:23	and Azrikam—three in **a.**	NIH
3:24	and Anani—seven in **a.**	NIH
4:33	and **a** the villages around these towns as far	3972
5:13	and Eber—seven in **a.**	NIH
5:16	and on **a** the pasturelands of Sharon as far	3972
5:17	**A** these were entered in	3972
5:20	the Hagrites and **a** their allies over to them,	3972
6:48	Their fellow Levites were assigned to **a**	3972
6:49	on the altar of incense in connection with **a**	3972
6:49	in accordance with **a** that Moses the servant	3972
6:60	were thirteen *in* **a.**	3972
7: 1	and Shimron—four in **a.**	NIH
7: 3	**A** five *of* them were chiefs.	3972
7: 5	to **a** the clans of Issachar,	3972
7: 5	in their genealogy, were 87,000 in **a.**	3972
7: 7	of families—five in **a.**	NIH
7: 8	**A** these were the sons of Beker.	3972
7:11	**A** these sons of Jediael were heads	3972
7:28	and Shechem and its villages **a the way to**	6330

1Ch 7:40 A these were descendants of Asher— 3972
8:28 A these were heads of families, AIT
8:38 A these were the sons of Azel. 3972
8:40 and grandsons—150 in a. NIH
8:40 A these were the descendants of Benjamin. 3972
9: 1 A Israel was listed in 3972
9: 9 A these men were heads of their families. 3972
9:29 of the furnishings and a the other articles of 3972
9:34 A these were heads of Levite families, AIT
10: 6 and a his house died together. 3972
10: 7 When a the Israelites in the valley saw that 3972
10:11 When a the inhabitants of Jabesh Gilead 3972
10:12 a their valiant men went and took 3972
11: 1 A Israel came together to David at Hebron 3972
11: 3 When a the elders of Israel had come 3972
11: 4 and a the Israelites marched to Jerusalem 3972
11:10 they, together with a Israel, 3972
12:15 when it was overflowing a its banks, 3972
12:21 for a of them were brave warriors, 3972
12:32 with a their relatives under their command; 3972
12:38 A these were fighting men who volunteered 3972
12:38 to make David king over a Israel. 3972
12:38 A the rest of the Israelites were also 3972
13: 4 because it seemed right to a the people. 3972
13: 5 So David assembled a the Israelites, 3972
13: 6 David and a the Israelites with him went 3972
13: 8 David and a the Israelites were celebrating 3972
13: 8 with a their might before God, 3972
14: 8 over a Israel, they went up in full force 3972
14:16 a the way from Gibeon to Gezer. 6330
14:17 the LORD made a the nations fear him. 3972
15: 3 David assembled a Israel in Jerusalem 3972
15:27 as were a the Levites who were carrying 3972
15:28 So a Israel brought up the ark of 3972
16: 9 tell of a his wonderful acts. 3972
16:14 his judgments are in a the earth. 3972
16:23 Sing to the LORD, a the earth; 3972
16:24 his marvelous deeds among a peoples. 3972
16:25 he is to be feared above a gods. 3972
16:26 For a the gods of the nations are idols, 3972
16:30 Tremble before him, a the earth! 3972
16:32 Let the sea resound, and a that is in it; 4850
16:36 Then a the people said "Amen" and "Praise 3972
16:43 Then a the people left, 3972
17: 6 Wherever I have moved with a 3972
17: 8 and I have cut off a your enemies from 3972
17:10 I will also subdue a your enemies. 3972
17:15 Nathan reported to David a the words 3972
17:19 and made known a these great promises. 3972
18: 4 He hamstrung a but a hundred of 3972
18:10 Hadoram brought a kinds of articles 3972
18:11 and gold he had taken from a these nations: 3972
18:13 a the Edomites became subject to David. 3972
18:14 David reigned over a Israel, 3972
18:14 and right for a his people. 3972
19:17 he gathered a Israel and crossed the Jordan; 3972
20: 3 David did this to a the Ammonite towns. 3972
20: 6 on each foot—twenty-four in a. NIH
21: 3 are they not a my lord's subjects? 3972
21: 5 In a Israel there were one million one hundred thousand men who could handle 3972
21:23 I will give a this." 3972
22: 5 and splendor in the sight of a the nations. 3972
22: 9 and I will give him rest from a his enemies 3972
22:17 Then David ordered a the leaders of Israel 3972
23: 2 He also gathered together a the leaders 3972
23: 8 and Joel—three in a. NIH
23: 9 and Haran—three in a. NIH
23:10 These were the sons of Shimei—four in a. NIH
23:12 and Uzziel—four in a. NIH
23:23 and Jerimoth—three in a. NIH
23:28 of a sacred things and the performance 3972
23:29 and a measurements of quantity and size. 3972
25: 3 Shimei, Hashabiah and Mattithiah, six in a, NIH
25: 5 A these were sons of Heman 3972
25: 6 A these men were under the supervision 3972
25: 7 a of them trained and skilled in music for 3972
26: 8 A these were descendants of Obed-Edom; 3972
26: 8 descendants of Obed-Edom, 62 in a. NIH
26: 9 who were able men—18 in a. NIH
26:11 sons and relatives of Hosah were 13 in a. 3972
26:26 of a the treasuries for the things dedicated 3972
26:28 and a the other dedicated things were in 3972
26:30 of the Jordan for a the work of the LORD 3972
27: 1 and their officers, who served the king in a 3972
27: 3 of a the army officers for the first month. 3972
27:31 A these were the officials in charge 3972
28: 1 David summoned a the officials of Israel 3972
28: 1 of a the property and livestock belonging to 3972
28: 1 the mighty men and a the brave warriors. 3972
28: 4 to make me king over a Israel. 3972
28: 5 Of a my sons— 3972
28: 8 the sight of a Israel and of the assembly of 3972
28: 8 Be careful to follow a the commands of 3972
28:12 of a that the Spirit had put in his mind for 3972
28:12 the LORD and a the surrounding rooms, 3972
28:13 and for a the work of serving in the temple 3972
28:13 as for a the articles to be used in its service. 3972
28:14 the weight of gold for a the gold articles to 3972
28:14 the weight of silver for a the silver articles 3972
28:19 "A this," David said, "I have in writing 3972
28:19 and he gave me understanding in a 3972
28:20 not fail you or forsake you until a the work 3972
28:21 of the priests and Levites are ready for a 3972
28:21 in any craft will help you in a the work. 3972
28:21 The officials and a the people will obey 3972
29: 2 With a my resources I have provided for 3972

1Ch 29: 2 and a kinds of fine stone and marble— 3972
29: 2 a of these in large quantities. NIH
29: 5 for a the work to be done by the craftsmen. 3972
29:11 you are exalted as head over a. 3972
29:12 you are the ruler of a things. 3972
29:12 and power to exalt and give strength to a. 3972
29:15 as were a our forefathers. 3972
29:16 for a this abundance that we have provided 3972
29:16 and a of it belongs to you. 3972
29:17 A these things have I given willingly and 3972
29:20 So they a praised the LORD, 3972
29:21 other sacrifices in abundance for a Israel. 3972
29:23 He prospered and a Israel obeyed him. 3972
29:24 A the officers and mighty men, 3972
29:24 as well as a of King David's sons, 3972
29:25 in the sight of a Israel and bestowed 3972
29:26 David son of Jesse was king over a Israel. 3972
29:30 and the kingdoms of a the other lands. 3972
2Ch 1: 2 Then Solomon spoke to a Israel— 3972
1: 2 to the judges and to a the leaders in Israel, 3972
1:17 They also exported them to a the kings of 3972
2: 5 our God is greater than a other gods. 3972
2:14 He is experienced in a kinds of engraving 3972
2:16 and we will cut a the logs from Lebanon 3972
2:17 a census of a the aliens who were in Israel, 3972
4:16 shovels, meat forks and a related articles. 3972
4:16 A the objects that Huram-Abi made NIH
4:18 A these things that Solomon made 3972
4:19 also made a the furnishings that were 3972
5: 1 When a the work Solomon had done for 3972
5: 1 the silver and gold and a the furnishings— 3972
5: 2 a the heads of the tribes and the chiefs of 3972
5: 3 And a the men of Israel came together to 3972
5: 4 When a the elders of Israel had arrived, 3972
5: 5 up the ark and the Tent of Meeting and a 3972
5:11 A the priests who were there had consecrated themselves, 3972
5:12 A the Levites who were musicians— 3972
6:16 in a they do to walk before me according 2006
6:30 deal with each man according to a he does, 3972
6:31 and walk in your ways a the time they live 3972
6:33 so that a the peoples of 3972
6:38 if they turn back to you with a their heart 3972
7: 3 When a the Israelites saw the fire coming 3972
7: 4 the king and a the people offered sacrifices 3972
7: 5 So the king and a the people dedicated 3972
7: 6 and a the Israelites were standing. 3972
7: 8 and a Israel with him— 3972
7:11 and had succeeded in carrying out a he had in mind 3972
7:17 and do a I command, 3972
7:20 and an object of ridicule among a peoples. 3972
7:21 a who pass by will be appalled and say, 3972
7:22 that is why he brought a this disaster 3972
8: 4 He also built up Tadmor in the desert and a 3972
8: 6 as well as Baalath and a his store cities, 3972
8: 6 and a the cities for his chariots and 3972
8: 6 in Jerusalem, in Lebanon and throughout a 3972
8: 7 A the people left from the Hittites, 3972
8:16 A Solomon's work was carried out, 3972
9: 1 with him about a she had on her mind. 3972
9: 2 Solomon answered a her questions; 3972
9:12 of Sheba a she desired and asked for; 3972
9:14 Also a the kings of Arabia and 3972
9:20 A King Solomon's goblets were gold, 3972
9:20 and a the household articles in the Palace 3972
9:22 in riches and wisdom than a the other kings 3972
9:23 A the kings of the earth sought audience 3972
9:26 He ruled over a the kings from the River to 3972
9:28 from Egypt and from a other countries. 3972
9:30 in Jerusalem over a Israel forty years. 3972
10: 1 for a the Israelites had gone there 3972
10: 3 and a Israel went to Rehoboam and said 3972
10:12 and a the people returned to Rehoboam, 3972
10:16 When a Israel saw that the king refused 3972
10:16 So a the Israelites went home. 3972
11: 3 to a the Israelites in Judah and Benjamin, 3972
11:12 He put shields and spears in a the cities, 3972
11:13 and Levites from a their districts 3972
11:21 In a, he had eighteen wives 3954
11:23 and to a the fortified cities. 3972
12: 1 he and a Israel with him abandoned the law 3972
12:13 the LORD had chosen out of a the tribes 3972
13: 4 "Jeroboam and a Israel, listen to me! 3972
13:15 and a Israel before Abijah and Judah. 3972
14: 8 A these were brave fighting men. 3972
14:14 They destroyed a the villages 3972
14:14 They plundered a these villages, 3972
15: 2 Asa and a Judah and Benjamin. 3972
15: 5 for a the inhabitants of the lands were 3972
15: 9 Then he assembled a Judah and Benjamin 3972
15:12 with a their heart and soul. 3972
15:13 A who would not seek the LORD, 3972
15:15 A Judah rejoiced about the oath 3972
15:17 fully committed [to the LORD] a his life. 3972
16: 4 and a the store cities of Naphtali. 3972
16: 6 King Asa brought a the men of Judah, 3972
17: 2 He stationed troops in a the fortified cities 3972
17: 5 and a Judah brought gifts to Jehoshaphat, 3972
17: 9 around to a the towns of Judah and taught 3972
17:10 of the LORD fell on a the kingdoms of 3972
18: 9 with a the prophets prophesying 3972
18:11 A the other prophets were prophesying 3972
18:16 "I saw a Israel scattered on the hills 3972
18:18 the LORD sitting on his throne with a 3972
18:21 in the mouths of a his prophets,' 3972
18:27 he added, "Mark my words, a you people!" 3972

2Ch 18:34 A day long the battle raged, 928+2021+2021+2085+3427
20: 3 and he proclaimed a fast for a Judah. 3972
20: 6 over a the kingdoms of the nations. 3972
20:13 A the men of Judah, 3972
20:15 King Jehoshaphat and a who live in Judah 3972
20:18 and a the people of Judah 3972
20:27 a the men of Judah 3972
20:29 The fear of God came upon a the kingdoms 3972
21: 2 A these were sons of Jehoshaphat king 3972
21: 4 he put a his brothers to the sword along 3972
21: 9 with his officers and a his chariots. 3972
21:17 and carried off a the goods found in 3972
21:18 After a this, the LORD afflicted Jehoram 3972
22: 1 had killed a the older sons. 3972
22: 9 who sought the LORD with a his heart." 3972
23: 2 and the heads of Israelite families from a 3972
23: 5 and a the other men are to be in 3972
23: 6 but a the other men are to guard what 3972
23: 8 The Levites and a the men of Judah did just 3972
23:10 He stationed a the men, 3972
23:13 and a the people of the land were rejoicing 3972
23:17 A the people went to the temple of Baal 3972
23:20 the rulers of the people and a the people of 3972
23:21 and a the people of the land rejoiced. 3972
24: 2 of the LORD a the years of Jehoiada 3972
24: 5 the money due annually from a Israel, 3972
24:10 A the officials and all the people 3972
24:10 All the officials and a the people 3972
24:23 it invaded Judah and Jerusalem and killed a 3972
24:23 They sent a the plunder to their king 3972
25: 5 and commanders of hundreds for a Judah 3972
25:12 down so that a were dashed to pieces. 3972
25:24 He took a the gold and silver and all 3972
25:24 the gold and silver and a the articles found 3972
26: 1 Then a the people of Judah took Uzziah, 3972
26:20 and a the other priests looked at him, 3972
27: 7 including a his wars and 3972
28:14 in the presence of the officials and a 3972
28:15 the plunder they clothed a who were naked. 3972
28:15 A those who were weak they put 3972
28:23 and the downfall of a Israel. 3972
28:26 of his reign and a his ways, 3972
29: 5 Remove a defilement from the sanctuary. AIT
29:18 of burnt offering with a its utensils, 3972
29:18 the consecrated bread, with a its articles. 3972
29:19 We have prepared and consecrated a 3972
29:24 for a sin offering to atone for a Israel, 3972
29:24 and the sin offering for a Israel. 3972
29:28 A this continued until the sacrifice of 3972
29:31 a whose hearts were willing brought burnt offerings. 3972
29:32 a of them for burnt offerings to 3972
29:34 were too few to skin a the burnt offerings; 3972
29:36 Hezekiah and a the people rejoiced 3972
30: 1 to a Israel and Judah and also wrote letters 3972
30:17 the Passover lambs for a those who were 3972
30:22 Hezekiah spoke encouragingly to a 3972
30:25 and a who had assembled from Israel, 3972
31: 1 When a this had ended, 3972
31: 1 After they had destroyed a of them, NIH
31: 5 and honey and a that the fields produced. 3972
31:16 a who would enter the temple of 3972
31:18 They included a the little ones, the wives, 3972
31:19 among them and to a who were recorded in 3972
32: 1 a that Hezekiah had so faithfully done, AIT
32: 4 and they blocked a the springs and 3972
32: 5 Then he worked hard repairing a 3972
32: 9 and a his forces were laying siege 3972
32: 9 for a the people of Judah who were there: 3972
32:13 and my fathers have done to a the peoples 3972
32:14 Who of a the gods of these nations 3972
32:21 who annihilated a the fighting men and 3972
32:22 of Assyria and from the hand of a others. 3972
32:23 on he was highly regarded by a the nations. 3972
32:27 spices, shields and a kinds of valuables. 3972
32:33 A Judah and the people 3972
33: 3 to a the starry hosts and worshiped them. 3972
33: 5 he built altars to a the starry hosts. 3972
33: 7 which I have chosen out of a the tribes 3972
33: 8 concerning a the laws, 3972
33:14 He stationed military commanders in a 3972
33:15 as well as a the altars he had built on 3972
33:19 as well as a his sins and unfaithfulness, 3972
33:19 a are written in the records of the seers. 4392S
33:22 Amon worshiped and offered sacrifices to a 3972
33:25 of the land killed a who had plotted 3972
34: 7 the idols to powder and cut to pieces a 3972
34: 9 and the entire remnant of Israel and from a 3972
34:12 a who were skilled 3972
34:13 had charge of the laborers and supervised a 3972
34:21 they have not acted in accordance with a 3972
34:24 a the curses written in the book 3972
34:25 to anger by a that their hands have made, 3972
34:28 not see a the disaster I am going to bring 3972
34:29 Then the king called together a the elders 3972
34:30 a the people from the least to the greatest. 3972
34:30 in their hearing a the words of the Book of 3972
34:31 regulations and decrees with a his heart 3972
34:31 with all his heart and a his soul, 3972
34:33 Josiah removed a the detestable idols 3972
34:33 from a the territory belonging to 3972
34:33 and he had a who were present 3972
35: 3 who instructed a Israel 3972
35: 7 for a the lay people who were there a total 3972
35: 7 a from the king's own possessions. 465S
35:13 and served them quickly to a the people. 3972

2Ch 35:18 and a Judah and Israel who were there with 3972
35:20 After a this, when Josiah had set the temple 3972
35:24 a Judah and Jerusalem mourned for him. 3972
35:25 and to this day a the men 3972
35:27 a the events, from beginning NIH
36: 8 and a that was found against him, NIH
36:14 a the leaders of the priests and 3972
36:14 following a the detestable practices of 3972
36:17 God handed a of them over 3972
36:18 to Babylon a the articles from the temple 3972
36:19 they burned a the palaces 3972
36:21 a the time of its desolation it rested, 3972
36:23 of heaven, has given me a the kingdoms of 3972
Ezr 1: 2 of heaven, has given me a the kingdoms of 3972
1: 6 A their neighbors assisted them 3972
1: 6 in addition to a the freewill offerings. 3972
1:11 *In a,* there were 5,400 articles of gold and 3972
1:11 Sheshbazzar brought a these along when 3972
3: 5 for a the appointed sacred feasts of 3972
3: 8 and a who had returned from the captivity 3972
3: 9 and brothers—a Levites— NIH
3:11 And a the people gave a great shout 3972
6:17 as a sin offering for a Israel, 10353
6:20 and were a ceremonially clean. 3972
6:20 the Passover lamb for a the exiles, 3972
6:21 with a who had separated themselves from 3972
7:16 with a the silver and gold you may obtain 10353
7:19 of Jerusalem *a* the **articles** entrusted AIT
7:21 order a the treasurers of Trans-Euphrates 10353
7:25 to a the people of Trans-Euphrates— 10353
7:25 a who know the laws of your God. 10353
7:28 before the king and his advisers and a 3972
8:20 A were registered by name. 3972
8:21 with a our possessions. 3972
8:22 against a who forsake him." 3972
8:25 and a Israel present there had donated for 3972
8:35 twelve bulls for a Israel, ninety-six rams, 3972
8:35 A this was a burnt offering to the LORD. 3972
10: 3 to send away a these women 3972
10: 5 the leading priests and Levites and a Israel 3972
10: 7 and Jerusalem for a the exiles to assemble 3972
10: 8 failed to appear within three days would forfeit a his property, 3972
10: 9 a the men of Judah 3972
10: 9 a the people were sitting in the square 3972
10:16 and a *of* them designated by name. 3972
10:17 the first month they finished dealing with a 3972
10:19 *a* **gave** their hands **in pledge** AIT
10:44 A these had married foreign women, 3972
Ne 4: 6 the wall till a *of* it reached half its height, 3972
4: 6 for the people worked *with a* their **heart.** AIT
4: 8 They a plotted together to come and fight 3972
4:15 we a returned to the wall, 3972
4:16 The officers posted themselves behind a 3972
5:16 A my men were assembled there for 3972
5:18 an abundant supply of wine of a *kinds.* 3972
5:18 In spite of a this, NIH
5:19 for a I have done for these people. 3972
6: 9 They were a trying to frighten us, thinking, 3972
6:16 When a our enemies heard about this, 3972
6:16 a the surrounding nations were afraid 3972
8: 1 a the people assembled as one man in 3972
8: 2 up of men and women and a who were able 3972
8: 3 And a the people listened attentively to 3972
8: 5 A the people could see him 3972
8: 5 and as he opened it, the people a stood up. 3972
8: 6 and a the people lifted their hands 3972
8: 9 the people said to them a, 3972
8: 9 For a the people had been weeping 3972
8:11 The Levites calmed a the people, saying, 3972
8:12 a the people went away to eat and drink, 3972
8:13 the heads of a the families, 3972
9: 2 Those of Israelite descent had separated themselves from a foreigners. 3972
9: 5 be exalted above a blessing and praise. 3972
9: 6 and a their starry host, 3972
9: 6 the earth and a that is on it, 3972
9: 6 the seas and a that is in them. 3972
9:10 against a his officials and all the people 3972
9:10 against all his officials and a the people 3972
9:25 with a *kinds of* good things, 3972
9:32 do not let a this hardship seem trifling 3972
9:32 upon our fathers and a your people, 3972
9:33 In a that has happened to us, 3972
9:38 "In view of a this, 3972
10:28 and a who separated themselves from 3972
10:28 and a their sons and daughters who are able 3972
10:29 a these now join their brothers the nobles, NIH
10:29 the servant of God and to obey carefully a 3972
10:31 the land and will cancel a debts. 3972
10:33 for a the duties of the house of our God. 3972
10:37 the fruit of a our trees and of our new wine 3972
10:37 the tithes in a the towns where we work. 3972
11: 2 The people commended a the men 3972
11:20 were in a the towns of Judah, 3972
11:24 was the king's agent in a affairs relating to 3972
11:30 **a the way** from Beersheba **to** 6330
12:47 a Israel contributed the daily portions for 3972
13: 3 from Israel a who were of foreign descent. 3972
13: 6 But while a this was going on, 3972
13: 8 and threw a Tobiah's household goods out 3972
13:10 that a the Levites and singers responsible 408
13:12 A Judah brought the tithes of grain, 3972
13:15 grapes, figs and a *other kinds of* loads. 3972
13:15 And they were bringing a this NIH
13:16 in fish and a *kinds of* merchandise 3972
13:18 so that our God brought a this calamity 3972
Ne 13:20 and sellers of a *kinds of* goods spent 3972
13:26 and God made him king over a Israel, 3972
13:27 you too are doing a this terrible wickedness 3972
Est 1: 3 a banquet for a his nobles and officials. 3972
1: 5 a the people from the least to the greatest, 3972
1: 8 for the king instructed a the wine stewards 3972
1:16 not only against the king but also against a 3972
1:16 against all the nobles and the peoples of a 3972
1:17 to a the women, 3972
1:18 about the queen's conduct will respond to a 3972
1:20 throughout a his vast realm, 3972
1:20 a the women will respect their husbands, 3972
1:22 He sent dispatches to a parts of 3972
2: 3 of his realm to bring a these beautiful girls 3972
2:18 for a his nobles and officials. 3972
2:23 *A this* **was recorded** in the book of AIT
3: 1 a seat of honor higher than that of a 3972
3: 2 A the royal officials at the king's gate knelt 3972
3: 6 for a way to destroy a Mordecai's people, 3972
3: 8 among the peoples in a the provinces 3972
3: 8 from those of a other people and who do 3972
3:12 of each people a Haman's orders to 3972
3:13 by couriers to a the king's provinces with 3972
3:13 kill and annihilate a the Jews— 3972
4: 1 Mordecai learned of a that had been done, 3972
4:11 "A the king's officials and the people of 3972
4:13 in the king's house you alone of a 3972
4:16 gather together a the Jews who are in Susa, 3972
4:17 and carried out a *of* Esther's instructions. 3972
5:11 and a the ways the king had honored him 3972
5:12 "And that's not a," Haman added. 677
5:13 But a this gives me no satisfaction as long 3972
5:14 His wife Zeresh and a his friends said 3972
6:13 and a his friends everything 3972
8: 5 devised and wrote to destroy the Jews in a 3972
8: 9 They wrote out a Mordecai's orders to 3972
8:12 for the Jews to do this in a the provinces 3972
9: 2 The Jews assembled in their cities in a 3972
9: 2 of a the other nationalities were afraid 3972
9: 3 And a the nobles of the provinces, 3972
9: 5 The Jews struck down a their enemies with 3972
9:20 and he sent letters to a the Jews throughout 3972
9:24 the Agagite, the enemy of a the Jews, 3972
9:27 and a who join them should without fail 3972
9:30 And Mordecai sent letters to a the Jews in 3972
10: 2 And a his acts of power and might, 3972
10: 3 and spoke up for the welfare of a the Jews. 3972
Job 1: 3 the greatest man among a the people of 3972
1:22 In a this, Job did not sin by charging God 3972
2: 4 "A man will give a he has for his own life. 3972
2:10 In a this, Job did not sin in what he said. 3972
2:11 heard about a the troubles that had come 3972
4:14 and made a my bones shake. 8044
6: 2 be weighed and a my misery be placed on 3480
8:13 Such is the destiny of a who forget God; 3972
9:22 It is **a the same,** 285
9:28 I still dread a my sufferings, 3972
11: 2 "Are a these words to go unanswered? 8044
12: 3 Who does not know a these things? 4017
12: 9 of a these does not know that the hand of 3972
12:10 and the breath of a mankind. 3972
13: 1 "My eyes have seen a *this,* 3972
13: 4 you are worthless physicians, a *of* you! 3972
13:27 you keep close watch on a my paths 3972
14:14 A the days of my hard service I will wait 3972
14:20 You overpower him **once for a,** 4200+5905
15:20 A his days the wicked man suffers torment, 3972
15:20 the ruthless through a the years stored up 5031
15:21 when a seems well, marauders attack him. NIH
16: 2 miserable comforters are you **a!** 3972
16:12 A was **well** with me, but he shattered me; AIT
17:10 "But come on, a *of* you, try again! 3972
19:19 A my intimate friends detest me; 3972
21:33 a men follow after him, 3972
22:10 That is why snares are **a around** you, 6017
23:15 when I think of a this, I fear him. NIH
24: 4 and force a the poor of the land into hiding. 3480
24:17 For a of them, 3481
24:24 and gathered up like a *others;* 3972
26: 5 those beneath the waters and *a that* **live in** AIT
27:10 Will he call upon God at a times? 3972
27:12 You have a seen this yourselves. 3972
27:19 when he opens his eyes, a is gone. 5647S
28:10 his eyes see a its treasures. 3972
29:19 the dew *will* **lie a night** on my branches. 4328
30:23 to the place appointed for a the living. 3972
31:38 against me and a its furrows are wet 3480
33:11 he keeps close watch on a my paths.' 3972
33:29 "God does a these things to a man— 3972
34:15 a mankind would perish together 3972
34:19 for they are a the work of his hands? 3972
36:19 or even a your mighty efforts sustain you 3972
36:25 A mankind has seen it; 3972
37: 7 a men he has made may know his work, 3972
37:24 for does he not have regard for a the wise 3972
38: 7 and a the angels shouted for joy? 3972
38:18 Tell me, if you know a this. 3972
40:13 Bury **them** *a* in the dust together; AIT
40:20 and a the wild animals play nearby. 3972
41:34 He looks down on a that are haughty; 3972
41:34 he is king over a that are proud." 3972
42: 2 "I know that you can do a *things;* 3972
42:11 A his brothers and sisters 3972
42:11 over a the trouble the LORD had brought 3972
42:15 in a the land were there found women 3972
Ps 2:12 Blessed are a who take refuge in him. 3972
3: 7 Strike a my enemies on the jaw; 3972
Ps 5: 5 you hate a who do wrong. 3972
5:11 But let a who take refuge in you be glad; 3972
6: 6 a night *long* I flood my bed with weeping 3972
6: 7 they fail because of a my foes. 3972
6: 8 Away from me, a you who do evil, 3972
6:10 A my enemies will be ashamed 3972
7: 1 save and deliver me from a who pursue me, 3972
8: 1 how majestic is your name in a the earth! 3972
8: 7 a flocks and herds, 3972
8: 8 a that swim the paths of the seas. NIH
8: 9 how majestic is your name in a the earth! 3972
9: 1 O LORD, with a my heart; 3972
9: 1 I will tell of a your wonders. 3972
9:17 a the nations that forget God. 3972
10: 4 in a his thoughts there is no room for God. 3972
10: 5 he sneers at a his enemies. 3972
12: 3 May the LORD cut off a flattering lips 3972
14: 3 A have turned aside, 3972
16: 3 the glorious ones in whom is a my delight. 3972
18: T of a his enemies and from the hand of Saul. 3972
18:22 A his laws are before me; 3972
18:30 He is a shield for a who take refuge in him. 3972
18:45 **They** *a* lose heart; AIT
19: 4 Their voice goes out into a the earth, 3972
20: 3 May he remember a your sacrifices 3972
20: 4 and make a your plans succeed. 3972
20: 5 May the LORD grant a your requests. 3972
21: 8 Your hand will lay hold on a your enemies; 3972
22: 7 A who see me mock me; 3972
22:14 and a my bones are out of joint. 3972
22:17 I can count a my bones; 3972
22:23 A you descendants of Jacob, honor him! 3972
22:23 Revere him, a you descendants of Israel! 3972
22:27 A the ends of the earth will remember 3972
22:27 and a the families of the nations will bow 3972
22:29 A the rich of the earth will feast 3972
22:29 a who go down to the dust will kneel 3972
23: 6 Surely goodness and love will follow me a 3972
24: 1 the world, and *a* who **live** in it; AIT
25: 5 and my hope is in you a day long. 3972
25:10 A the ways of the LORD are loving 3972
25:18 and my distress and take away a my sins. 3972
25:22 O God, from a their troubles! 3972
26: 7 and telling of a your wonderful deeds. 3972
27: 4 in the house of the LORD a the days 3972
29: 9 And in his temple a cry, "Glory!" 3972
31:11 Because of a my enemies, 3972
31:23 Love the LORD, a his saints! 3972
31:24 a you who hope in the LORD. 3972
32: 3 through my groaning a day long. 3972
32:11 sing, a you who are upright in heart! 3972
33: 4 he is faithful in a he does. 3972
33: 8 Let a the earth fear the LORD; 3972
33: 8 let a the people of the world revere him. 3972
33:11 his heart through **a generations.** 1887+1887+2256
33:13 down and sees a mankind; 3972
33:14 from his dwelling place he watches a who live 3972
33:15 he who forms the hearts of a, 3480
33:17 despite *a* its **great** strength it cannot save. AIT
34: 1 I will extol the LORD at a times; 3972
34: 4 he delivered me from a my fears. 3972
34: 6 he saved him out of a his troubles. 3972
34:17 he delivers them from a their troubles. 3972
34:19 but the LORD delivers him from them a; 3972
34:20 he protects a his bones, 3972
35:26 May a who gloat over my distress be put 3481
35:26 may *a* who **exalt** *themselves* over me AIT
35:28 and of your praises a day long. 3972
37:38 But a sinners will be destroyed; 3481
38: 6 a day long I go about mourning. 3972
38: 9 A my longings lie open before you, 3972
38:12 a day long they plot deception. 3972
39: 8 Save me from a my transgressions; 3972
39:12 a stranger, as a my fathers were. 3972
40:14 May a who seek to take my life be put 3480
40:14 may *a who* **desire** my ruin be turned back AIT
40:16 But may a who seek you rejoice and 3972
41: 7 A my enemies whisper together against me; 3972
42: 3 while men say to me a day long, 3972
42: 7 a your waves and breakers have swept 3972
42:10 saying to me a day long, 3972
44: 8 In God we make our boast a day long, 3972
44:15 My disgrace is before me a day long, 3972
44:17 A this happened to us, 3972
44:22 Yet for your sake we face death a day long; 3972
45: 8 A your robes are fragrant with myrrh 3972
45:13 A glorious is the princess 3972
45:17 through a generations; 3972
47: 1 Clap your hands, a you nations; 3972
47: 2 the great King over a the earth! 3972
47: 7 For God is the King of a the earth; 3972
49: 1 Hear this, a you peoples; 3972
49: 1 listen, a who live in this world, 3972
49:10 For *a can* **see** that wise men die; AIT
50:12 for the world is mine, and **a that** is **in** it. 4850
51: 2 Wash away a my iniquity and cleanse me 2221
51: 9 from my sins and blot out a my iniquity. 3972
52: 1 Why do you boast a day long, 3972
54: 7 he has delivered me from a my troubles, 3972
56: 1 a day long they press their attack. 3972
56: 2 My slanderers pursue me a day long; 3972
56: 5 A day long they twist my words; 3972
57: 5 let your glory be over a the earth. 3972
57:11 let your glory be over a the earth. 3972
59: 5 rouse yourself to punish a the nations; 3972
59: 8 you scoff at a those nations. 3972

Ps 62: 3 Would **a** *of* you throw him down— 3972
62: 8 Trust in him at **a** times, O people; 3972
63:11 **a** who swear by God's name will praise him, 3972
64: 8 **a** who see them will shake their heads 3972
64: 9 **A** mankind will fear; 3972
64:10 let **a** the upright in heart praise him! 3972
65: 2 to you **a** men will come. 3972
65: 5 the hope of **a** the ends of the earth and of 3972
66: 1 Shout with joy to God, **a** the earth! 3972
66: 4 **A** the earth bows down to you; 3972
66:16 **a** you who fear God; 3972
67: 2 your salvation among **a** nations. 3972
67: 3 may **a** the peoples praise you. 3972
67: 5 may **a** the peoples praise you. 3972
67: 7 and **a** the ends of the earth will fear him. 3972
69:19 **a** my enemies are before you. 3972
69:34 the seas and **a** that move in them, 3972
70: 2 may *a who* **desire** my ruin be turned back AIT
70: 4 But may **a** who seek you rejoice and 3972
71: 8 declaring your splendor **a** day long. 3972
71:15 of your salvation **a** day long, 3972
71:18 your might to **a** who are to come. 3972
71:24 of your righteous acts **a** day long, 3972
72: 5 **through a generations.** 1887+1887
72:11 **A** kings will bow down to him 3972
72:11 down to him and **a** nations will serve him. 3972
72:15 for him and bless him **a** day long. 3972
72:17 **A** nations will be blessed through him, 3972
73:14 **A** day long I have been plagued; 3972
73:16 When I tried to understand *a* **this,** AIT
73:27 you destroy **a** who are unfaithful to you. 3972
73:28 I will tell of **a** your deeds. 3972
74: 3 **a** this destruction the enemy has brought on 3972
74: 6 They smashed **a** the carved paneling 3480
74:17 It was you who set **a** the boundaries of 3972
74:22 remember how fools mock you **a** day long. 3972
75: 3 When the earth and **a** its people quake, 3972
75: 8 and **a** the wicked of the earth drink it down 3972
75:10 I will cut off the horns of **a** the wicked, 3972
76: 9 to save **a** the afflicted of the land. 3972
76:11 let **a** the neighboring lands bring gifts to 3972
77: 8 his promise failed for **a time?** 1887+1887+2256
77:12 I will meditate on **a** your works 3972
77:12 and consider **a** your mighty deeds. NIH
78:14 by day and with light from the fire **a** night. 3972
78:25 **a** the food they **could eat.** 8427
78:28 **a around** their tents. 6017
78:32 In spite of **a** this, they kept on sinning; 3972
78:51 He struck down **a** the firstborn of Egypt, 3972
79: 3 like water **a around** Jerusalem, 6017
80:12 so that **a** who pass by pick its grapes? 3972
82: 5 **a** the foundations of the earth are shaken. 3972
82: 6 you are **a** sons of the Most High.' 3972
82: 8 for **a** the nations are your inheritance. 3972
83:11 **a** their princes like Zebah and Zalmunna, 3972
83:18 that you alone are the Most High over **a** 3972
85: 2 of your people and covered **a** their sins. 3972
85: 3 You set aside **a** your wrath and turned 3972
85: 5 through **a generations?** 1887+1887+2256
86: 3 O Lord, for I call to you **a** day long. 3972
86: 5 abounding in love to **a** who call to you. 3972
86: 9 **A** the nations you have made will come 3972
86:12 O Lord my God, with **a** my heart; 3972
87: 2 of Zion more than **a** the dwellings of Jacob. 3972
87: 7 **"A** my fountains are in you." 3972
88: 7 with **a** your waves. 3972
88:17 **A** day long they surround me like a flood; 3972
89: 1 through **a generations.** 1887+1887+2256
89: 4 through **a generations.'** " 1887+1887+2256
89: 7 he is more awesome than **a** who surround him. 3972
89:11 you founded the world and **a that is in** it. 4850
89:16 They rejoice in your name **a** day long; 3972
89:35 **Once for a,** I have sworn by my holiness— 285
89:40 You have broken through **a** his walls 3972
89:41 **A** who pass by have plundered him; 3972
89:42 you have made **a** his enemies rejoice. 3972
89:47 For what futility you have created **a** men! 3972
89:50 in my heart the taunts of **a** the nations, 3972
90: 1 throughout **a generations.** 1887+1887+2256
90: 9 **A** our days pass away under your wrath; 3972
90:14 we may sing for joy and be glad **a** our days. 3972
91:11 to guard you in **a** your ways; 3972
92: 7 up like grass and **a** evildoers flourish, 3972
92: 9 **a** evildoers will be scattered. 3972
93: 2 you are from **a eternity.** 6409
94: 4 **a** the evildoers are full of boasting. 3972
94:15 and **a** the upright in heart will follow it. 3972
95: 3 the great King above **a** gods. 3972
96: 1 sing to the LORD, **a** the earth. 3972
96: 3 his marvelous deeds among **a** peoples. 3972
96: 4 he is to be feared above **a** gods. 3972
96: 5 For **a** the gods of the nations are idols, 3972
96: 9 tremble before him, **a** the earth. 3972
96:11 let the sea resound, and **a that is in** it; 4850
96:12 **a** the trees of the forest will sing for joy; 3972
97: 5 before the Lord of **a** the earth. 3972
97: 6 and **a** the peoples see his glory. 3972
97: 7 **A** who worship images are put to shame, 3972
97: 7 worship him, **a** you gods! 3972
97: 9 are the Most High over **a** the earth; 3972
97: 9 you are exalted far above **a** gods. 3972
98: 3 **a** the ends of the earth have seen 3972
98: 4 Shout for joy to the LORD, **a** the earth, 3972
98: 7 the world, and *a who* **live** in it. AIT
99: 2 he is exalted over **a** the nations. 3972

Ps 100: 1 Shout for joy to the LORD, **a** the earth. 3972
100: 5 through **a generations.** 1887+1887+2256
101: 8 Every morning I will put to silence **a** 3972
102: 8 **A** day long my enemies taunt me; 3972
102:12 through **a generations.** 1887+1887+2256
102:15 **a** the kings of 3972
102:24 years go on through **a generations.** 1887+1887
102:26 they will **a** wear out like a garment. 3972
103: 1 **a** my inmost being, praise his holy name. 3972
103: 2 O my soul, and forget not **a** his benefits— 3972
103: 3 who forgives **a** your sins 3972
103: 3 and heals **a** your diseases, 3972
103: 6 and justice for **a** the oppressed. 3972
103:19 and his kingdom rules over **a.** 3972
103:21 Praise the LORD, **a** his heavenly hosts, 3972
103:22 **a** his works everywhere in his dominion. 3972
104:11 They give water to **a** the beasts of the field; 3972
104:20 and **a** the beasts of the forest prowl. 3972
104:24 In wisdom you made them **a;** 3972
104:27 These **a** look to you to give them their food 3972
104:33 I will sing to the LORD **a** my life; 928
105: 2 tell of **a** his wonderful acts. 3972
105: 7 his judgments are in **a** the earth. 3972
105:16 on the land and destroyed **a** their supplies 3972
105:21 ruler over **a** he possessed, 3972
105:36 he struck down **a** the firstborn in their land, 3972
105:36 the firstfruits of **a** their manhood. 3972
106:46 to be pitied by **a** who held them captive. 3972
106:48 Let **a** the people say, "Amen!" 3972
107:18 They loathed **a** food and drew near 3972
107:42 but **a** the wicked shut their mouths. 3972
108: 1 I will sing and make music with **a** my soul. 677
108: 5 and let your glory be over **a** the earth. 3972
109:11 May a creditor seize **a** he has; 3972
111: 1 the LORD with **a** my heart in the council 3972
111: 2 they are pondered by **a** who delight 3972
111: 7 **a** his precepts are trustworthy. 3972
111:10 **a** who follow his precepts have good understanding. 3972
113: 4 The LORD is exalted over **a** the nations, 3972
115: 8 and so will **a** who trust in them. 3972
116:11 in my dismay I said, **"A** men are liars." 3972
116:12 the LORD for **a** his goodness to me? 3972
116:14 the LORD in the presence of **a** his people. 3972
116:18 the LORD in the presence of **a** his people, 3972
117: 1 Praise the LORD, **a** you nations; 3972
117: 1 extol him, **a** you peoples. 3972
118:10 **A** the nations surrounded me, 3972
119: 2 and seek him with **a** their heart. 3972
119: 6 when I consider **a** your commands. 3972
119:10 I seek you with **a** my heart; 3972
119:13 With my lips I recount **a** the laws that come 3972
119:20 with longing for your laws at **a** times. 3972
119:34 and obey it with **a** my heart. 3972
119:58 I have sought your face with **a** my heart; 3972
119:63 I am a friend to **a** who fear you, 3972
119:63 to *a who* **follow** your precepts. AIT
119:69 I keep your precepts with **a** my heart. 3972
119:86 **A** your commands are trustworthy; 3972
119:90 through **a generations;** 1887+1887+2256
119:91 for **a** *things* serve you. 3972
119:96 To **a** perfection I see a limit; 3972
119:97 I meditate on it **a** day long. 3972
119:99 I have more insight than **a** my teachers, 3972
119:118 You reject **a** who stray from your decrees, 3972
119:119 **A** the wicked of the earth you discard 3972
119:128 because I consider **a** your precepts right, 3972
119:145 I call with **a** my heart; 3972
119:151 O LORD, and **a** your commands are true. 3972
119:160 **A** your words are true; 8031
119:160 **a** your righteous laws are eternal. 3972
119:168 for **a** my ways are known to you. 3972
119:172 for **a** your commands are righteous. 3972
121: 7 The LORD will keep you from **a** harm— 3972
128: 1 Blessed are **a** who fear the LORD, 3972
128: 5 the LORD bless you from Zion **a** the days 3972
129: 5 May **a** who hate Zion be turned back 3972
130: 8 from **a** their sins. 3972
132: 1 and **a** the hardships he endured. 3972
134: 1 **a** you servants of the LORD who minister 3972
135: 5 that our Lord is greater than **a** gods. 3972
135: 6 in the seas and **a** their depths. 3972
135: 9 against Pharaoh and **a** his servants. 3972
135:11 of Bashan and **a** the kings of Canaan— 3972
135:13 O LORD, through **a generations.** 1887+1887+2256
135:18 and so will **a** who trust in them. 3972
138: 1 O LORD, with **a** my heart; 3972
138: 2 above **a** *things* your name and your word. 3972
138: 4 May **a** the kings of the earth praise you, 3972
139: 3 you are familiar with **a** my ways. 3972
139:16 **A** the days ordained for me were written 3972
143: 5 I meditate on **a** your works 3972
143:12 destroy **a** my foes, for I am your servant. 3972
145: 9 The LORD is good to **a;** 3972
145: 9 he has compassion on **a** he has made. 3972
145:10 **A** you have made will praise you, 3972
145:12 so that **a men** may know of your mighty acts 132+1201+2021
145:13 through **a** generations. 3972
145:13 The LORD is faithful to **a** his promises 3972
145:13 and loving toward **a** he has made. 3972
145:14 The LORD upholds **a** those who fall 3972
145:14 and lifts up **a** who are bowed down. 3972
145:15 The eyes of **a** look to you, 3972
145:17 The LORD is righteous in **a** his ways 3972
145:17 and loving toward **a** he has made. 3972
145:18 The LORD is near to **a** who call on him, 3972

Ps 145:18 to **a** who call on him in truth. 3972
145:20 The LORD watches over **a** who love him, 3972
145:20 but **a** the wicked he will destroy. 3972
146: 2 I will praise the LORD **a** my life; 928
146:10 reigns forever, your God, O Zion, for **a generations.** 1887+1887+2256
148: 2 Praise him, **a** his angels, praise him, 3972
148: 2 praise him, **a** his heavenly hosts. 3972
148: 3 praise him, **a** you shining stars. 3972
148: 7 you great sea creatures and **a** ocean depths, 3972
148: 9 you mountains and **a** hills, 3972
148: 9 fruit trees and **a** cedars, 3972
148:10 wild animals and **a** cattle, 3972
148:11 kings of the earth and **a** nations, 3972
148:11 you princes and **a** rulers on earth, 3972
148:14 the praise of **a** his saints, of Israel, 3972
149: 9 This is the glory of **a** his saints. 3972
Pr 1:13 we will get **a** *sorts of* valuable things 3972
1:17 to spread a net in full view of **a** the birds! 3972
1:19 the end of **a** who go after ill-gotten gain; 3972
1:25 since you ignored **a** my advice and would 3972
3: 5 the LORD with **a** your heart and lean not 3972
3: 6 in **a** your ways acknowledge him, 3972
3: 9 with the firstfruits of **a** your crops; 3972
3:17 and **a** her paths are peace. 3972
4: 4 "Lay hold of my words with **a** your heart; NIH
4: 7 it cost **a** you have, get understanding. 3972
4:23 Above **a** else, guard your heart, 3972
5:21 and he examines **a** his paths. 3972
6:31 it costs him **a** the wealth of his house. 3972
7:22 **A at once** he followed her like an ox going 7328
8: 4 I raise my voice to **a mankind.** 132+1201
8: 8 **A** the words of my mouth are just; 3972
8: 9 To the discerning **a** *of* them are right; 3972
8:16 and **a** nobles who rule on earth. 3972
8:36 **a** who hate me love death." 3972
9: 4 *a* who are simple **come in** AIT
9:16 *a* who are simple **come in** AIT
10:12 but love covers over **a** wrongs. 3972
11: 7 *a* he **expected** *from* his power comes AIT
14:23 **A** hard work brings a profit, 3972
15:15 **A** the days of the oppressed are wretched, 3972
16: 2 **A** a man's ways seem innocent to him, 3972
16: 5 The LORD detests **a** the proud of heart. 3972
16:11 **a** the weights in the bag are of his making. 3972
17:17 A friend loves at **a** times, 3972
18: 1 he defies **a** sound judgment. 3972
19: 7 A poor man is shunned by **a** his relatives— 3972
20: 8 he winnows out **a** evil with his eyes. 3972
21: 2 **A** a man's ways seem right to him, 3972
21:20 but a foolish man devours **a he has.** 5647[S]
21:26 **A** day long he craves for more, 3972
22: 2 The LORD is the Maker of them **a.** 3972
22:18 in your heart and have **a** *of them* ready 3481
27:24 and a crown is not secure for **a generations.** 1887+1887+2256
29:12 **a** his officials become wicked. 3972
30: 4 Who has established **a** the ends of 3972
31: 5 and deprive **a** the oppressed of their rights. 3972
31: 8 for the rights of **a** who are destitute. 3972
31:12 not harm, **a** the days of her life. 3972
31:21 for **a** *of* them are clothed in scarlet. 3972
31:29 but you surpass them **a."** 3972
Ecc 1: 3 from **a** his labor at which he toils under 3972
1: 7 **A** streams flow into the sea, 3972
1: 8 **A** things are wearisome, 3972
1:13 and to explore by wisdom **a** that is done 3972
1:14 I have seen **a** the things that are done under 3972
1:14 **a** of them are meaningless, 3972
2: 5 and planted **a** *kinds of* fruit trees in them. 3972
2: 9 **In a this** my wisdom stayed with me. 677
2:10 My heart took delight in **a** my work, 3972
2:10 and this was the reward for **a** my labor. 3972
2:11 when I surveyed **a** that my hands had done 3972
2:17 **A** of it is meaningless, 3972
2:18 I hated **a** the things I had toiled for under 3972
2:19 Yet he will have control over **a** the work 3972
2:20 to despair over **a** my toilsome labor under 3972
2:21 and then he must leave *a* he **owns** AIT
2:22 a man get for **a** the toil and anxious striving 3972
2:23 **A** his days his work is pain and grief; 3972
3:13 and find satisfaction in **a** his toil— 3972
3:19 **A** have the same breath; 3972
3:20 **A** go to the same place; 3972
3:20 **a** come from dust, and to dust all return. 3972
3:20 all come from dust, and to dust **a** return. 3972
4: 1 Again I looked and saw **a** the oppression 3972
4: 4 that **a** labor and all achievement spring 3972
4: 4 and **a** achievement spring from man's envy 3972
4: 8 There was a man **a alone;** 401+9108
4:15 I saw that **a** who lived and walked under 3972
4:16 There was no end to **a** the people who were 3972
5: 9 The increase from the land is taken by **a;** 3972
5:17 **A** his days he eats in darkness, 3972
6: 6 Do not **a** go to the same place? 3972
6: 7 **A** man's efforts are for his mouth, 3972
7:18 man who fears God will avoid **a** [extremes]. 3972
7:23 **A** this I tested by wisdom and I said, 3972
7:28 not one [upright] woman among them **a.** 3972
8: 9 **A** this I saw, 3972
8:15 Then joy will accompany him in his work **a** NIH
8:17 then I saw **a** that God has done. 3972
8:17 Despite *a his* **efforts** to search it out, AIT
9: 1 So I reflected on **a** this and concluded that 3972
9: 2 **A** share a common destiny— 3972
9: 3 The same destiny overtakes **a.** 3972
9: 9 **a** the days of this meaningless life 3972

Ecc	9: 9	a your meaningless days.	3972
	9:10	do it with a your might, for in the grave,	NIH
	9:11	but time and chance happen to them a.	3972
	11: 5	the Maker of a *things.*	3972
	11: 8	let him enjoy them a.	3972
	11: 9	that for a these things God will bring you	3972
	12: 4	but a their songs grow faint;	3972
	12:13	Now a has been heard;	3972
SS	3: 1	A **night long** on my bed I looked for	928+2021+4326
	3: 6	and incense made from a the spices of	3972
	3: 8	a *of* them wearing the sword,	3972
	3: 8	a experienced in battle,	NIH
	4: 4	a *of* them shields of warriors.	3972
	4: 7	A beautiful you are, my darling;	3972
	4:14	and aloes and a the finest spices.	3972
	8: 7	to give a the wealth of his house for love,	3972
Isa	1:23	they a love bribes and chase after gifts.	3972
	1:25	and remove a your impurities.	3972
	2: 2	and a nations will stream to it.	3972
	2:12	a day in store for a the proud and lofty,	3972
	2:12	for a that is exalted (and they will	3972
	2:13	for a the cedars of Lebanon,	3972
	2:13	tall and lofty, and a the oaks of Bashan,	3972
	2:14	for a the towering mountains and all	3972
	2:14	for all the towering mountains and a	3972
	3: 1	a supplies of food and all supplies of water,	3972
	3: 1	all supplies of food and a supplies of water,	3972
	4: 3	a who are recorded among the living	3972
	4: 5	Then the LORD will create over a	3972
	4: 5	over a the glory will be a canopy.	3972
	5:14	with a their brawlers and revelers.	NIH
	5:25	Yet for a this, his anger is not turned away,	3972
	5:28	a their bows are strung;	3972
	7: 9	you will not stand **at a.'** "	3954
	7:19	They will a come and settle in	3972
	7:19	on a the thornbushes and at all	3972
	7:19	the thornbushes and at a the water holes.	3972
	7:22	A who remain in the land will eat curds	3972
	7:25	for a the hills once cultivated by the hoe,	3972
	8: 7	the king of Assyria with a his pomp.	3972
	8: 7	It will overflow a its channels,	3972
	8: 7	run over a its banks	3972
	8: 9	Listen, a you distant lands.	3972
	9: 9	A the people will know it—	3972
	9:12	Yet for a this, his anger is not turned away,	3972
	9:17	Yet for a this, his anger is not turned away,	3972
	9:21	Yet for a this, his anger is not turned away,	3972
	10: 4	Yet for a this, his anger is not turned away,	3972
	10: 8	'Are not my commanders a kings?'	3481
	10:12	When the Lord has finished a his work	3972
	10:14	so I gathered a the countries;	3972
	11: 9	nor destroy on a my holy mountain,	3972
	12: 5	let this be known to a the world.	3972
	13: 7	Because of this, a hands will go limp,	3972
	13:15	a who are caught will fall by the sword.	3972
	13:20	lived in through **a generations;**	1887+1887+2256
	14: 7	A the lands are at rest and at peace;	3972
	14: 9	The grave below *is* **a astir** to meet you	8074
	14: 9	a those who were leaders in the world;	3972
	14: 9	a those who were kings over the nations.	3972
	14:10	They will a respond, they will say to you,	3972
	14:11	A your pomp has been brought down to	NIH
	14:18	A the kings of the nations lie in state,	3972
	14:26	the hand stretched out over a nations.	3972
	14:29	a you Philistines, that the rod	3972
	14:31	Melt away, a you Philistines!	3972
	15: 3	and in the public squares they a wail,	3972
	15: 4	their voices are heard **a the way to** Jahaz.	6330
	16:14	and a her many people will be despised,	3972
	17: 9	And *a will* **be** desolation.	AIT
	18: 3	A you people of the world,	3972
	18: 6	They will a be left to the mountain birds	3481
	18: 6	the birds *will* feed on them **a summer,**	7810
	18: 6	the wild animals **a winter.**	3069
	19: 8	a who cast hooks into the Nile;	3972
	19:10	and a the wage earners will be sick at heart.	3972
	19:14	they make Egypt stagger in a that she does,	3972
	21: 2	to an end a the groaning she caused.	3972
	21: 9	A the images of its gods lie shattered on	3972
	21:16	a the pomp of Kedar will come to an end.	3972
	22: 1	that you have a gone up on the roofs,	3972
	22: 3	A your leaders have fled together;	3972
	22: 3	A you who were caught were taken prisoner together,	3972
	22:24	A the glory of his family will hang on him:	3972
	22:24	a its lesser vessels,	3972
	22:24	from the bowls to a the jars.	3972
	23: 9	to bring low the pride of a glory and	3972
	23: 9	and to humble a who are renowned on	3972
	23:17	as a prostitute and will ply her trade with a	3972
	24: 7	a the merrymakers groan.	3972
	24:11	a joy turns to gloom,	3972
	24:11	a gaiety is banished from the earth.	NIH
	25: 6	a feast of rich food for a peoples, a banquet	3972
	25: 7	the shroud that enfolds a peoples, the sheet	3972
	25: 7	the sheet that covers a nations;	3972
	25: 8	the tears from a faces;	3972
	25: 8	the disgrace of his people from a the earth.	3972
	26:12	a that we have accomplished you have done for	3972
	26:14	you wiped out a memory of them.	3972
	26:15	you have extended a the borders of	3972
	27: 4	I would set them a on fire.	3480
	27: 6	and blossom and fill a the world with fruit.	7156
	27: 9	When he makes a the altar stones to be	3972
	28: 8	A the tables are covered with vomit	3972
Isa	28:29	*A* **this** also comes from the LORD	AIT
	29: 3	I will encamp against you **a around;**	1885+2021+3869
	29: 7	Then the hordes of a the nations that fight	3972
	29: 8	with the hordes of a the nations that fight	3972
	29:20	and a who have an eye for evil will	3972
	30:17	at the threat of five *you will a* **flee away,**	AIT
	30:18	Blessed are a who wait for him!	3972
	32:13	for a houses of merriment and for this city	3972
	34: 1	Let the earth hear, and **a that is in** it,	4850
	34: 1	the world, and a that comes out of it!	3972
	34: 2	The LORD is angry with a nations;	3972
	34: 2	his wrath is upon a their armies.	3972
	34: 4	A the stars of the heavens will be dissolved	3972
	34: 4	a the starry host will fall	3972
	34:12	a her princes will vanish away.	3972
	36: 1	of Assyria attacked a the fortified cities	3972
	36: 6	of Egypt to a who depend on him.	3972
	36:20	Who of a the gods of these countries	3972
	37: 2	the leading priests, *a* **wearing** sackcloth,	AIT
	37:11	of Assyria have done to a the countries,	3972
	37:16	you alone are God over a the kingdoms of	3972
	37:17	listen to a the words Sennacherib has sent	3972
	37:18	Assyrian kings have laid waste a these peoples	3972
	37:20	so that a kingdoms on earth may know	3972
	37:25	With the soles of my feet I have dried up a	3972
	37:36	there were a the dead bodies!	3972
	38:13	but like a lion he broke a my bones;	3972
	38:15	I will walk humbly a my years because	3972
	38:17	you have put a my sins behind your back.	3972
	38:20	with stringed instruments a the days	3972
	39: 2	or in a his kingdom that Hezekiah did	3972
	39: 6	and a that your fathers have stored up	NIH
	40: 2	the LORD's hand double for a her sins.	3972
	40: 5	and a mankind together will see it.	3972
	40: 6	"A men are like grass,	3972
	40: 6	a their glory is like the flowers of the field.	3972
	40:17	Before him a the nations are as nothing;	3972
	40:26	Who created *a* **these?**	AIT
	41:11	"A who rage against you will surely	3972
	41:12	who wage war against you will be as **nothing at a.**	401+700+2256
	41:29	See, they are a false!	3972
	42: 5	the earth and **a that comes out** *of* it,	7368
	42:10	and **a that is in** it, you islands,	4850
	42:10	you islands, and *a who* **live in** them.	AIT
	42:15	and hills and dry up a their vegetation;	3972
	42:22	a *of* them trapped in pits or hidden away	3972
	43: 9	A the nations gather together and	3972
	43:14	to Babylon and bring down as fugitives a	3972
	44: 9	A who make idols are nothing,	3972
	44:11	Let them a come together	3972
	44:13	of man in a his glory,	NIH
	44:23	you forests and a your trees,	3972
	44:24	I am the LORD, who has made a *things,*	3972
	44:28	'He is my shepherd and will accomplish a	3972
	45: 7	I, the LORD, do a these things.	3972
	45:13	I will make a his ways straight.	3972
	45:16	A the makers of idols will be put to shame	3972
	45:22	a you ends of the earth;	3972
	45:23	my mouth has uttered *in a* **integrity**	AIT
	45:24	A who have raged against him will come	3972
	45:25	the LORD a the descendants of Israel will	3972
	46: 3	a you who remain of the house of Israel,	3972
	46:10	and I will do a that I please.	3972
	47: 9	and a your potent spells.	4394
	47:13	A the counsel you have received has only worn you out!	8044
	47:15	**That** is *a* they can do for you—	AIT
	48: 6	look at them a.	3972
	48:13	I summon them, *they a* **stand up** together.	AIT
	48:14	"Come together, a *of* you, and listen:	3972
	49:11	I will turn a my mountains into roads,	3972
	49:18	a your sons gather and come to you.	3972
	49:18	"you will wear them a as ornaments;	3972
	49:21	I was left **a alone,** but these—	963+4200
	49:26	Then a mankind will know that I,	3972
	50: 9	They will a wear out like a garment;	3972
	50:11	a you who light fires	3972
	51: 3	with compassion on a her ruins;	3972
	51: 8	my salvation through **a generations."**	1887+1887
	51:18	Of a the sons she bore there was none	3972
	51:18	of a the sons she reared there was none	3972
	52: 5	a day long my name is constantly blasphemed.	3972
	52:10	in the sight of a the nations,	3972
	52:10	and a the ends of the earth will see	3972
	53: 6	We a, like sheep, have gone astray,	3972
	53: 6	on him the iniquity of us a.	3972
	54: 5	he is called the God of a the earth.	3972
	54:12	and a your walls of precious stones.	3972
	54:13	A your sons will be taught by the LORD,	3972
	55: 1	"Come, a you who are thirsty,	3972
	55:12	a the trees of the field will clap their hands.	3972
	56: 6	a who keep the Sabbath	3972
	56: 7	be called a house of prayer for a nations."	3972
	56: 9	Come, a you beasts of the field,	3972
	56: 9	a you beasts of the forest!	3972
	56:10	they a lack knowledge;	3972
	56:10	they are a mute dogs, they cannot bark;	3972
	56:11	they a turn to their own way,	3972
	57:10	You were wearied by a your ways,	8044
	57:13	The wind will carry a *of* them off,	3972
	58: 3	as you please and exploit a your workers.	3972
	59: 9	We look for light, but a is darkness;	NIH
	59:11	We a growl like bears;	3972
Isa	60: 4	A assemble and come to you;	3972
	60: 6	And a from Sheba will come,	3972
	60: 7	A Kedar's flocks will be gathered to you,	3972
	60:14	a who despise you will bow down	3972
	60:15	and the joy of **a generations.**	1887+1887+2256
	60:21	Then will a your people be righteous	3972
	61: 2	to comfort a who mourn,	3972
	61: 9	A who see them will acknowledge	3972
	61:11	and praise spring up before a nations.	3972
	62: 2	and a kings your glory;	3972
	63: 3	and I stained a my clothing.	3972
	63: 7	according to a the LORD has done	3972
	63: 9	In a their distress he too was distressed,	3972
	63: 9	up and carried them a the days of old.	3972
	64: 6	A *of* us have become like one who is unclean,	3972
	64: 6	and a our righteous acts are like filthy rags;	3972
	64: 6	we a shrivel up like a leaf,	3972
	64: 8	we are a the work of your hand.	3972
	64: 9	we pray, for we are a your people.	3972
	64:11	and a that we treasured lies in ruins.	3972
	64:12	After *a* **this,** O LORD,	AIT
	65: 2	A day long I have held out my hands to	3972
	65: 5	a fire that keeps burning a day.	3972
	65: 8	I will not destroy them a.	3972
	65:12	and you will a bend down for the slaughter;	3972
	65:25	nor destroy on a my holy mountain,"	3972
	66: 2	Has not my hand made a these things,	3972
	66: 6	LORD repaying his enemies *a* they **deserve.**	AIT
	66:10	a you who love her;	3972
	66:10	a you who mourn over her.	3972
	66:16	upon a men, and many will be those slain	3972
	66:18	to come and gather a nations and tongues,	3972
	66:20	And they will bring a your brothers,	3972
	66:20	from a the nations, to my holy mountain	3972
	66:23	a mankind will come and bow down	3972
	66:24	and they will be loathsome to a mankind."	3972
Jer	1:14	be poured out on a who live in the land.	3972
	1:15	I am about to summon a the peoples of	3972
	1:15	against a her surrounding walls and	3972
	1:15	and against a the towns of Judah.	3972
	2: 3	a who devoured her were held guilty,	3972
	2: 4	a you clans of the house of Israel.	3972
	2:11	(Yet they are **not** gods *at a.*)	AIT
	2:29	You have a rebelled against me,"	3972
	2:34	Yet in spite of a this	3972
	3: 5	but you do *a* the **evil** you can."	AIT
	3: 7	after she had done a this she would return	3972
	3: 8	because of a her adulteries,	3972
	3:10	In spite of a this,	3972
	3:10	not return to me with a her heart,	3972
	3:17	and a nations will gather in Jerusalem	3972
	4:24	a the hills were swaying.	3972
	4:26	a its towns lay in ruins before the LORD,	3972
	4:29	A the towns are deserted;	3972
	5: 7	**supplied** a their **needs,**	8425
	5:16	a *of* them are mighty warriors.	3972
	5:19	'Why has the LORD our God done a this	3972
	6:13	a are greedy for gain;	3972
	6:13	prophets and priests alike, a practice deceit.	3972
	6:15	**have** no **shame at a;**	1017+1017
	6:28	They are a hardened rebels,	3972
	6:28	they a act corruptly.	3972
	7: 2	the word of the LORD, a you people	3972
	7:10	safe to do a these detestable things?	3972
	7:13	While you were doing a these things,	3972
	7:15	just as I did a your brothers,	3972
	7:23	Walk in a the ways I command you,	3972
	7:27	"When you tell them a this,	3972
	8: 2	be exposed to the sun and the moon and a	3972
	8: 3	Wherever I banish them, a the survivors	3972
	8:10	a are greedy for gain;	3972
	8:10	prophets and priests alike, a practice deceit.	3972
	8:12	they **have** no **shame at a;**	1017+1017
	8:16	the city and *a who* **live** there."	AIT
	9: 2	for they are a adulterers,	3972
	9:25	I will punish a who are circumcised only	3972
	9:26	Moab and a who live in the desert	3972
	9:26	a these nations are really uncircumcised,	3972
	10: 7	Among a the wise men of the nations and	3972
	10: 7	of the nations and in a their kingdoms,	3972
	10: 8	They are a senseless and foolish;	285+928
	10: 9	a made by skilled workers.	3972
	10:16	for he is the Maker of a *things,*	3972
	10:20	a its ropes are snapped.	3972
	10:21	not prosper and a their flock is scattered.	3972
	11: 6	"Proclaim a these words in the towns	3972
	11: 8	So I brought on them a the curses of	3972
	11:12	they will not **help** them **at a** when disaster strikes.	3828+3828
	12: 1	Why do a the faithless live at ease?	3972
	12: 9	Go and gather a the wild beasts;	3972
	12:12	Over a the barren heights in	3972
	12:14	"As for a my wicked neighbors who seize	3972
	13:13	with drunkenness a who live in this land,	3972
	13:13	the priests, the prophets and a those living	3972
	13:19	A Judah will be carried into exile,	3972
	14:22	for you are the one who does a this.	3972
	15: 4	to a the kingdoms of the earth because	3972
	15:13	of a your sins throughout your country.	3972
	16:10	"When you tell these people a this	3972
	16:15	up out of the land of the north and out of a	3972
	16:17	My eyes are on a their ways;	3972
	17: 3	and a your treasures I will give away	3972
	17: 9	The heart is deceitful above a *things* and	3972
	17:13	a who forsake you will be put to shame.	3972
	17:19	stand also at a the other gates of Jerusalem.	3972

Jer	17:20	and a people of Judah and everyone living	3972
	18:16	a who pass by will be appalled	3972
	18:23	O LORD, a their plots to kill me.	3972
	19: 8	a who pass by will be appalled	3972
	19: 8	and will scoff because of a its wounds.	3972
	19:13	a the houses where they burned incense on	3972
	19:13	where they burned incense on the roofs to a	3972
	19:14	of the LORD's temple and said to a	3972
	20: 4	a terror to yourself and to a your friends;	3972
	20: 4	I will hand a Judah over to the king	3972
	20: 5	to their enemies a the wealth of this city—	3972
	20: 5	a its products, all its valuables and all	3972
	20: 5	all its products, a its valuables and all	3972
	20: 5	and a the treasures of the kings of Judah.	3972
	20: 6	and a who live in your house will go	3972
	20: 6	you and a your friends	3972
	20: 7	I am ridiculed a day long;	3972
	20: 8	and reproach a day long.	3972
	20:10	A my friends are waiting for me to slip,	3972
	22:15	so a went well with him.	NIH
	22:16	and so a went well.	NIH
	22:20	for a your allies are crushed.	3972
	22:22	wind will drive a your shepherds away,	3972
	22:22	because of a your wickedness.	3972
	23: 3	of a the countries where I have driven them	3972
	23: 8	up out of the land of the north and out of a	3972
	23: 9	a my bones tremble.	3972
	23:14	They are a like Sodom to me;	3972
	23:17	And to a who follow the stubbornness	3972
	24: 7	for they will return to me with a their heart.	3972
	24: 9	an offense to a the kingdoms of the earth,	3972
	25: 1	The word came to Jeremiah concerning a	3972
	25: 2	the prophet said to a the people of Judah	3972
	25: 2	of Judah and to a those living in Jerusalem:	3972
	25: 4	though the LORD has sent a his servants	3972
	25: 9	I will summon a the peoples of the north	3972
	25: 9	and against a the surrounding nations.	3972
	25:13	upon that land a the things I have spoken	3972
	25:13	a that are written in this book	3972
	25:13	and prophesied by Jeremiah against a	3972
	25:15	with the wine of my wrath and make a	3972
	25:17	the LORD's hand and made a the nations	3972
	25:19	his officials and a his people,	3972
	25:20	and a the foreign people there;	3972
	25:20	a the kings of Uz;	3972
	25:20	a the kings of the Philistines (those	3972
	25:22	a the kings of Tyre and Sidon;	3972
	25:23	Tema, Buz and a who are in distant places;	3972
	25:24	a the kings of Arabia and all the kings of	3972
	25:24	all the kings of Arabia and a the kings of	3972
	25:25	a the kings of Zimri, Elam and Media;	3972
	25:26	and a the kings of the north, near	3972
	25:26	a the kingdoms on the face of the earth.	3972
	25:26	And after a of them,	NIH
	25:29	a sword upon a who live on the earth,	3972
	25:30	"Now prophesy a these words against them	3972
	25:30	shout against a who live on the earth.	3972
	25:31	he will bring judgment on a mankind	3972
	26: 2	and speak to a the people of the towns	3972
	26: 6	an object of cursing among a the nations of	3972
	26: 7	the prophets and a the people heard	3972
	26: 8	But as soon as Jeremiah finished telling a	3972
	26: 8	the prophets and a the people seized him	3972
	26: 9	And a the people crowded around Jeremiah	3972
	26:11	and the prophets said to the officials and a	3972
	26:12	Then Jeremiah said to a the officials and all	3972
	26:12	Then Jeremiah said to all the officials and a	3972
	26:12	and this city a the things you have heard.	3972
	26:15	to speak a these words in your hearing."	3972
	26:16	Then the officials and a the people said to	3972
	26:18	He told a the people of Judah,	3972
	26:21	When King Jehoiakim and a his officers	3972
	27: 6	Now I will hand a your countries over	3972
	27: 7	A nations will serve him and his son	3972
	27:16	I said to the priests and a these people,	3972
	27:20	with a the nobles of Judah and Jerusalem—	3972
	28: 1	the presence of the priests and a the people:	3972
	28: 3	to this place a the articles of	3972
	28: 4	and a the other exiles from Judah who went	3972
	28: 5	and a the people who were standing in	3972
	28: 6	the LORD's house and a the exiles back	3972
	28: 7	in your hearing and in the hearing of a	3972
	28:11	before a the people, "This is what	3972
	28:11	of Babylon off the neck of a the nations	3972
	28:14	an iron yoke on the necks of a these nations	3972
	29: 1	the prophets and a	3972
	29: 4	says to a those I carried into exile	3972
	29:13	when you seek me with a your heart.	3972
	29:14	I will gather you from a the nations	3972
	29:16	the king who sits on David's throne and a	3972
	29:18	and will make them abhorrent to a	3972
	29:18	among a the nations where I drive them.	3972
	29:20	a you exiles whom I have sent away	3972
	29:22	a the exiles from Judah who are	3972
	29:25	You sent letters in your own name to a	3972
	29:25	and to a the other priests.	3972
	29:31	"Send this message to a the exiles:	3972
	30: 2	in a book a the words I have spoken to you.	3972
	30:11	'Though I completely destroy a the nations	3972
	30:14	A your allies have forgotten you;	3972
	30:16	" 'But a who devour you will be devoured;	3972
	30:16	a your enemies will go into exile.	3972
	30:16	a who make spoil of you I will despoil.	3972
	30:20	I will punish a who oppress them.	3972
	31: 1	"I will be the God of a the clans of Israel,	3972
	31:24	in Judah and a its towns—	3972
	31:34	because they will a know me,	3972
Jer	31:37	be searched out will I reject a	3972
	31:37	of Israel because of a they have done,"	3972
	31:40	and a the terraces out to the Kidron Valley	3972
	32:12	and of a the Jews sitting in the courtyard of	3972
	32:19	Your eyes are open to a the ways of men;	3972
	32:20	both in Israel and among a mankind,	NIH
	32:23	So you brought a this disaster upon them.	3972
	32:27	the God of a mankind.	3972
	32:32	of Israel and Judah have provoked me by a	3972
	32:37	I will surely gather them from a the lands	3972
	32:41	in this land with a my heart and soul.	3972
	32:42	As I have brought a this great calamity	3972
	32:42	on this people, so I will give them a	3972
	33: 5	from this city because of a its wickedness.	3972
	33: 8	from a the sin they have committed	3972
	33: 8	and will forgive a their sins of rebellion	3972
	33: 9	praise and honor before a nations on earth	3972
	33: 9	on earth that hear of a the good things I do	3972
	33:12	in a its towns there will again be pastures	3972
	34: 1	and a his army and all the kingdoms	3972
	34: 1	and all his army and a the kingdoms	3972
	34: 1	and a its surrounding towns,	3972
	34: 6	the prophet told a this to Zedekiah king	3972
	34: 8	a covenant with a the people in Jerusalem	3972
	34:10	So a the officials and people who entered	3972
	34:17	to a the kingdoms of the earth.	3972
	34:19	and a the people of the land who walked	3972
	35: 3	and his brothers and a his sons—	3972
	35:15	and again I sent a my servants the prophets	3972
	35:18	and have followed a his instructions	3972
	36: 2	and write on it a the words I have spoken	3972
	36: 2	Judah and a the other nations from	3972
	36: 4	and while Jeremiah dictated a the words	3972
	36: 6	to a *the people of* Judah who come in	3972
	36: 9	before the LORD was proclaimed for a	3972
	36:10	to a the people at the LORD's temple	3972
	36:11	heard a the words of the LORD from	3972
	36:12	where a the officials were sitting:	3972
	36:12	and a the other officials.	3972
	36:14	a the officials sent Jehudi son	3972
	36:16	When they heard a these words,	3972
	36:16	"We must report a these words to	3972
	36:17	"Tell us, how did you come to write a this?	3972
	36:18	"he dictated a these words to me,	3972
	36:21	the secretary and read it to the king and a	3972
	36:24	a his attendants who heard all these words	3972
	36:24	who heard a these words showed no fear,	3972
	36:28	and write on it a the words that were on	3972
	36:32	Baruch wrote on it a the words of the scroll	3972
	37:21	of the bakers each day until a the bread in	3972
	38: 1	heard what Jeremiah was telling a the people	3972
	38: 4	as well as a the people,	3972
	38: 9	*in* a they have done to Jeremiah	3972
	38:22	A the women left in the palace of the king	3972
	38:23	"A your wives and children will	3972
	38:27	A the officials did come to Jeremiah	3972
	39: 3	Then a the officials of the king	3972
	39: 3	a high official and a the other officials of	3972
	39: 4	and a the soldiers saw them, they fled;	3972
	39: 6	before his eyes and also killed a the nobles	3972
	39:13	a high official and a the other officers of	3972
	40: 1	among a the captives from Jerusalem	3972
	40: 3	*A* **this** happened because you people sinned	AIT
	40: 7	When a the army officers	3972
	40:11	When a the Jews in Moab, Ammon,	3972
	40:11	Edom and a the other countries heard that	3972
	40:12	they a came back to the land of Judah,	3972
	40:12	from a the countries	3972
	40:13	of Kareah and a the army officers still in	3972
	40:15	Why should he take your life and cause a	3972
	41: 3	Ishmael also killed a the Jews who were	3972
	41: 9	the cistern where he threw a the bodies of	3972
	41:10	Ishmael made captives of a the rest of	3972
	41:10	along with a the others who were left there,	3972
	41:11	When Johanan son of Kareah and a	3972
	41:11	about a the crimes Ishmael son	3972
	41:12	they took a their men and went	3972
	41:13	When a the people Ishmael had	3972
	41:14	A the people Ishmael had taken captive	3972
	41:16	Then Johanan son of Kareah and a	3972
	41:16	with him led away a the survivors	3972
	42: 1	Then a the army officers,	3972
	42: 1	and a the people from the least to	3972
	42: 8	and a the army officers who were with him	3972
	42: 8	the army officers who were with him and a	3972
	42:17	a who are determined to go to Egypt	3972
	42:21	the LORD your God in a he sent me	3972
	43: 1	the people a the words of the LORD	3972
	43: 2	and a the arrogant men said to Jeremiah,	3972
	43: 4	of Kareah and a the army officers and all	3972
	43: 4	of Kareah and all the army officers and a	3972
	43: 5	and a the army officers led away all	3972
	43: 5	the army officers led away a the remnant	3972
	43: 5	in the land of Judah from a the nations	3972
	43: 6	They also led away a the men,	3972
	44: 1	This word came to Jeremiah concerning a	3972
	44: 2	on Jerusalem and on a the towns of Judah.	3972
	44: 8	and reproach among a the nations on earth.	3972
	44:11	on you and to destroy a Judah.	3972
	44:12	They will a perish in Egypt;	3972
	44:15	Then a the men who knew	3972
	44:15	with a the women who were present—	3972
	44:15	and a the people living in Lower	3972
	44:20	Then Jeremiah said to a the people,	3972
	44:24	Then Jeremiah said to a the people,	3972
	44:24	a you people of Judah in Egypt.	3972
	44:26	a Jews living in Egypt:	3972
Jer	44:27	and famine until they are a destroyed.	3972
	45: 5	For I will bring disaster on a people,	3972
	46:28	"Though I completely destroy a the nations	3972
	47: 2	a who dwell in the land will wail	3972
	47: 4	For the day has come to destroy a	3972
	47: 4	to cut off a survivors who could help Tyre	3972
	48:17	Mourn for her, a who live around her,	3972
	48:17	a who know her fame;	3972
	48:24	to a the towns of Moab, far and near.	3972
	48:31	for a Moab I cry out,	3972
	48:38	On a the roofs in Moab and in	3972
	48:39	an object of horror to a those around her."	3972
	49: 5	I will bring terror on you from a those	3972
	49:13	and a its towns will be in ruins forever."	3972
	49:17	a who pass by will be appalled	3972
	49:17	and will scoff because of a its wounds.	3972
	49:26	a her soldiers will be silenced in that day,"	3972
	49:29	be carried off with a their goods	3972
	50:10	a who plunder her will have their fill,"	3972
	50:13	A who pass Babylon will be horrified	3972
	50:13	and scoff because of a her wounds.	3972
	50:14	a you who draw the bow.	3972
	50:27	Kill a her young bulls;	3972
	50:29	a those who draw the bow.	3972
	50:29	Encamp a **around** her; let no one escape.	6017
	50:30	a her soldiers will be silenced in that day,"	3972
	50:32	that will consume a who are around her."	3972
	50:33	A their captors hold them fast,	3972
	50:37	against her horses and chariots and a	3972
	51:19	for he is the Maker of a *things,*	3972
	51:24	and a who live in Babylonia for all	3972
	51:24	for a the wrong they have done in Zion,"	3972
	51:28	their governors and a their officials,	3972
	51:28	and a the countries they rule.	3972
	51:38	Her people a roar like young lions,	3481
	51:47	be disgraced and her slain will a lie fallen	3972
	51:48	and earth and a that is in them will shout	3972
	51:49	the slain in a the earth have fallen because	3972
	51:60	Jeremiah had written on a scroll about a	3972
	51:60	a that had been recorded	3972
	51:61	see that you read a these words aloud.	3972
	52: 3	of the LORD's anger that *a this* **happened**	AIT
	52: 4	the city and built siege works a **around** it.	6017
	52: 8	A his soldiers were separated from him	3972
	52:10	he also killed a the officials of Judah.	3972
	52:13	the royal palace and a the houses	3972
	52:14	the imperial guard broke down a the walls	3972
	52:17	the temple of the LORD and they carried a	3972
	52:18	dishes and a the bronze articles used in	3972
	52:19	*a* **that** were made of pure gold or silver.	AIT
	52:22	and pomegranates of bronze a around.	3972
	52:26	Nebuzaradan the commander took **them** *a*	AIT
	52:30	There were 4,600 people *in* a.	3972
La	1: 2	Among a her lovers there is none	3972
	1: 2	A her friends have betrayed her;	3972
	1: 3	A who pursue her have overtaken her in	3972
	1: 4	A her gateways are desolate,	3972
	1: 6	A the splendor has departed from	3972
	1: 7	and wandering Jerusalem remembers a	3972
	1: 8	A who honored her despise her,	3972
	1:10	The enemy laid hands on a her treasures;	3972
	1:11	A her people groan as they search	3972
	1:12	"Is it nothing to you, a you who pass by?	3972
	1:13	He made me desolate, faint a the day long.	3972
	1:15	"The Lord has rejected a the warriors	3972
	1:18	Listen, a you peoples;	3972
	1:21	A my enemies have heard of my distress;	3972
	1:22	"Let a their wickedness come before you;	3972
	1:22	with me because of a my sins.	3972
	2: 2	the Lord has swallowed up a the dwellings	3972
	2: 4	Like a foe he has slain a who were pleasing	3972
	2: 5	He has swallowed up a her palaces	3972
	2:15	A who pass your way clap their hands	3972
	2:16	A your enemies open their mouths wide	3972
	3: 3	against me again and again, a day long.	3972
	3:14	I became the laughingstock of a my people;	3972
	3:14	they mock me in song a day long.	3972
	3:18	*a that* I had **hoped**	AIT
	3:34	To crush underfoot a prisoners in the land,	3972
	3:46	"A our enemies have opened their mouths	3972
	3:51	because of a the women of my city.	3972
	3:60	a their plots against me.	3972
	3:61	a their plots against me—	3972
	3:62	and mutter against me a day long.	3972
Eze	1: 8	*A* **four** *of* them had faces and wings,	AIT
	1:16	and *a* **four** looked alike.	AIT
	1:18	and *a* **four** rims were full	AIT
	1:18	of eyes a **around.**	6017
	2: 6	though briers and thorns are a **around** you	907
	3:10	and take to heart a the words I speak	3972
	5: 2	and strike it with the sword a **around**	6017
	5: 5	with countries a **around** her.	6017
	5: 9	Because of a your detestable idols,	3972
	5:10	on you and will scatter a your survivors to	3972
	5:11	with a your vile images	3972
	5:14	in the sight of a who pass by.	3972
	6: 9	and for a their detestable practices.	3972
	6:11	of a the wicked and detestable practices of	3972
	6:13	and on a the mountaintops,	3972
	6:13	to a their idols.	3972
	7: 3	for a your detestable practices.	3972
	7: 8	for a your detestable practices.	3972
	7:16	A who survive and escape will be in	3972
	7:21	I will hand **it** *a* over as plunder	AIT
	8:10	and I saw portrayed a **over**	6017+6017+6584
	8:10	over the walls a kinds of crawling things	3972
	8:10	and detestable animals and a the idols	3972

Eze	9: 4	over a the detestable things that are done	3972
	11:18	to it and remove a its vile images	3972
	12:14	to the winds a those around him—	3972
	12:14	his staff and a his troops—	3972
	12:16	they go they may acknowledge a their	
		detestable practices.	3972
	12:19	because of the violence of a who live there.	3972
	13:18	on a their wrists and make veils	3972
	14: 3	**let them inquire of *me* at a?**	2011+2011+4200
	14: 5	who have a deserted me for their idols.'	3972
	14: 6	and renounce a your detestable practices!	3972
	14:11	with a their sins.	3972
	16:22	In a your detestable practices	3972
	16:23	In addition to a your other wickedness,	3972
	16:30	when you do a these things,	3972
	16:33	but you give gifts to a your lovers,	3972
	16:36	and because of a your detestable idols,	3972
	16:37	to gather a your lovers,	3972
	16:37	from **a around** and will strip you in front	6017
	16:37	and they will see a your nakedness.	3972
	16:43	but enraged me with a these things,	3972
	16:43	to a your other detestable practices?	3972
	16:47	in a your ways you soon became more	
		depraved than they.	3972
	16:51	by a these things you have done.	3972
	16:54	of a you have done in giving them comfort.	3972
	16:57	the daughters of Edom and a her neighbors	3972
	16:57	a those around you who despise you.	NIH
	16:63	for you for a you have done,	3972
	17: 9	A its new growth will wither.	3972
	17:18	in pledge and yet did a these things,	3972
	17:21	A his fleeing troops will fall by the sword,	3972
	17:24	A the trees of the field will know that I	3972
	18:13	he has done a these detestable things,	3972
	18:14	"But suppose this son has a son who sees a	3972
	18:19	and has been careful to keep a my decrees,	3972
	18:21	"But if a wicked man turns away from a	3972
	18:21	and keeps a my decrees	3972
	18:28	Because he considers a the offenses	3972
	18:30	Turn away from a your offenses;	3972
	18:31	of a the offenses you have committed,	3972
	19: 7	The land and **a who were in** it were terrified	4850
	20: 6	the most beautiful of a lands.	3972
	20:15	most beautiful of a lands—	3972
	20:31	to defile yourselves with a your idols	3972
	20:40	along with a your holy sacrifices.	3972
	20:43	your conduct and a the actions	3972
	20:43	and you will loathe yourselves for a	3972
	20:47	and it will consume a your trees,	3972
	21: 5	Then a people will know that I	3972
	21:12	it is against a the princes of Israel.	3972
	21:15	the sword for slaughter at a their gates.	3972
	21:24	revealing your sins in a that you do—	3972
	22: 2	confront her with a her detestable practices	3972
	22: 4	to the nations and a laughingstock to a	3972
	22:18	a *of* them are the copper, tin,	3972
	22:19	'Because you have a become dross,	3972
	22:31	down on their own heads *a* they have **done,**	AIT
	23: 6	a *of* them handsome young men,	3972
	23: 7	as a prostitute to a the elite of the Assyrians	3972
	23: 7	of the Assyrians and defiled herself with a	3972
	23:12	a handsome young men.	3972
	23:15	a *of* them looked like Babylonian	3972
	23:23	the Babylonians and a the Chaldeans,	3972
	23:23	and a the Assyrians with them,	3972
	23:23	a *of* them governors and commanders,	3972
	23:23	a mounted on horses.	3972
	23:43	for that is a she is.'	NIH
	23:48	that a women may take warning and	3972
	24: 4	a the choice pieces—	3972
	24:12	It has frustrated *a* **efforts;**	AIT
	25: 6	rejoicing with a the malice of your heart	3972
	25: 8	the house of Judah has become like a	3972
	26:11	of his horses will trample a your streets;	3972
	26:16	Then a the princes of the coast will step	3972
	26:17	you put your terror on a who lived there.	3972
	27: 5	They made a your timbers of pine trees	3972
	27: 9	A the ships of the sea	3972
	27:21	" 'Arabia and a the princes	3972
	27:22	of a *kinds of* spices and precious stones,	3972
	27:27	your merchants and a your soldiers,	3972
	27:29	A who handle the oars will abandon their	
		ships;	3972
	27:29	and a the seamen will stand on the shore.	3972
	27:34	your wares and a your company have gone	3972
	27:35	A who live in the coastlands are appalled	3972
	28:18	in the sight of a who were watching.	3972
	28:19	A the nations who knew you are appalled	3972
	28:26	on a their neighbors who maligned them.	3972
	29: 2	against him and against a Egypt.	3972
	29: 4	with a the fish sticking to your scales.	3972
	29: 5	you and a the fish of your streams.	3972
	29: 6	Then a who live in Egypt will know	3972
	30: 5	Cush and Put, Lydia and a Arabia,	3972
	30: 8	to Egypt and a her helpers are crushed.	3972
	31: 4	their streams flowed **a around** its base	6017
	31: 4	around its base and sent their channels to a	3972
	31: 5	So it towered higher than a the trees of	3972
	31: 6	A the birds of the air nested in its boughs,	3972
	31: 6	a the beasts of the field gave birth	3972
	31: 6	a the great nations lived in its shade.	3972
	31: 9	of a the trees of Eden in the garden of God.	3972
	31:12	Its boughs fell on the mountains and in a	3972
	31:12	its branches lay broken in a the ravines of	3972
	31:12	A the nations of the earth came out from	3972
	31:13	A the birds of the air settled on	3972
	31:13	and a the beasts of the field were	3972
Eze	31:14	they are a destined for death,	3972
	31:15	and a the trees of the field withered away.	3972
	31:16	Then a the trees of Eden,	3972
	31:16	a the trees that were well-watered,	3972
	31:18	" 'This is Pharaoh and a his hordes,	3972
	32: 4	I will let a the birds of the air settle on you	3972
	32: 4	of the air settle on you and a the beasts of	3972
	32: 6	with your flowing blood **a the way to**	448
	32: 8	A the shining lights in the heavens	3972
	32:12	the most ruthless of a nations.	3972
	32:12	and a her hordes will be overthrown.	3972
	32:13	I will destroy a her cattle from	3972
	32:15	when I strike down a who live there,	3972
	32:16	Egypt and a her hordes they will chant it,	3972
	32:20	let her be dragged off with a her hordes.	3972
	32:22	by the graves of a her slain,	3972
	32:22	a who have fallen by the sword.	NIH
	32:23	A who had spread terror in the land of	3972
	32:24	with a her hordes around her grave.	3972
	32:24	A *of* them are slain, fallen by the sword.	3972
	32:24	A who had spread terror in the land of	NIH
	32:25	with a her hordes around her grave.	3972
	32:25	A *of* them are uncircumcised,	3972
	32:26	with a their hordes around their graves.	3972
	32:26	A *of* them are uncircumcised,	3972
	32:29	her kings and a her princes;	3972
	32:30	"A the princes of the north and all	3972
	32:30	of the north and a the Sidonians are there;	3972
	32:31	"Pharaoh—he and a his army—	3972
	32:31	and he will be consoled for a his hordes	3972
	32:32	Pharaoh and a his hordes will be laid	3972
	33:29	of a the detestable things they have done.'	3972
	33:33	"When **a this** comes true—	2023[S]
	34: 5	for a the wild animals.	3972
	34: 6	My sheep wandered over a the mountains	3972
	34: 8	and has become food for a	3972
	34:12	I will rescue them from a the places	3972
	34:13	in the ravines and in a the settlements in	3972
	34:21	butting a the weak sheep with your horns	3972
	35: 7	and cut off from it *a who* **come** and go.	AIT
	35: 8	and in your valleys and in a your ravines.	3972
	35:12	that I the LORD have heard a	3972
	35:15	O Mount Seir, you and a *of* Edom.	3972
	36: 5	the rest of the nations, and against a Edom,	3972
	36:24	from a the countries and bring you back	3972
	36:25	I will cleanse you from a your impurities	3972
	36:25	and from a your idols.	3972
	36:29	I will save you from a your uncleanness.	3972
	36:33	On the day I cleanse you from a your sins,	3972
	36:34	of lying desolate in the sight of a who pass	3972
	37:16	belonging to Joseph and a the house	3972
	37:21	from **a around** and bring them back	6017
	37:22	over a *of* them and they will never again	3972
	37:23	from a their sinful backsliding,	3972
	37:24	and they will a have one shepherd.	3972
	38: 4	a *of* them brandishing their swords.	3972
	38: 5	a with shields and helmets,	3972
	38: 6	with a its troops, and Beth Togarmah from	3972
	38: 6	from the far north with a its troops—	3972
	38: 7	you and a the hordes gathered about you,	3972
	38: 8	and now a *of* them live in safety.	3972
	38: 9	and a your troops and the many nations	3972
	38:11	a *of* them living without walls and	3972
	38:13	of Tarshish and a her villages will say	3972
	38:15	a *of* them riding on horses, a great horde,	3972
	38:20	and a the people on the face of	3972
	38:21	a sword against Gog on a my mountains,	3972
	39: 4	and a your troops and the nations with you.	3972
	39: 4	as food to a kinds of carrion birds and to	3972
	39:11	Gog and a his hordes will be buried there.	3972
	39:13	A the people of the land will bury them,	3972
	39:17	Call out to every kind of bird and a	3972
	39:17	and come together from **a around** to	6017
	39:18	a *of* them fattened animals from Bashan.	3972
	39:21	and a the nations will see	3972
	39:23	and they a fell by the sword.	3972
	39:25	and will have compassion on a the people	3972
	39:26	and a the unfaithfulness they showed	3972
	40:14	projecting walls **a around** the inside	6017+6017
	40:16	by narrow parapet openings **a around,**	6017+6017
	40:16	the openings **a around** faced inward.	6017+6017
	40:17	that had been constructed **a around**	6017+6017
	40:25	portico had narrow openings **a around**	6017+6017
	40:29	and its portico had openings **a around.**	6017+6017
	40:33	and its portico had openings **a around.**	6017+6017
	40:36	and it had openings **a around.**	6017+6017
	40:41	eight tables in **a—**	NIH
	40:43	were attached to the wall **a around.**	6017+6017
	41: 6	There were ledges **a around** the wall	6017+6017
	41: 7	The side rooms **a around**	6015
	41: 8	the temple had a raised base **a around**	6017+6017
	41:10	was twenty cubits wide **a around**	6017+6017
	41:11	area was five cubits wide **a around.**	6017+6017
	41:12	was five cubits thick **a around,**	6017+6017
	41:17	walls at regular intervals **a around**	6017+6017
	41:19	They were carved **a around**	6017+6017
	42:15	and measured the area **a around:**	6017+6017
	42:20	So he measured the area on *a* **four** sides.	AIT
	43:11	of a they have done, make known to them	3972
	43:11	its whole design and a its regulations	3972
	43:11	to its design and follow a its regulations.	3972
	43:12	A the surrounding area on top of	3972
	43:17	a cubit and a gutter of a cubit **a around.**	6017
	43:20	of the upper ledge and **a around** the rim,	6017
	44: 5	concerning a the regulations regarding	3972
	44: 5	the entrance of the temple and a the exits of	3972
	44: 7	to a your other detestable practices,	3972
Eze	44:14	the temple and a the work that is to be done	3972
	44:24	and my decrees for a my appointed feasts,	3972
	44:30	The best of a the firstfruits and	3972
	44:30	and of a your special gifts will belong to	3972
	45:16	A the people of the land will participate	3972
	45:17	at a the appointed feasts of the house	3972
	45:22	for himself and for a the people of the land.	3972
	46: 4	and a ram, *a* **without defect.**	AIT
	46: 6	six lambs and a ram, *a* **without defect.**	AIT
	46:23	with places for fire built **a around** under	6017
	47:12	of a *kinds* will grow on both banks of	3972
	48:19	from the city who farm it will come from a	3972
	48:35	distance **a around** will be 18,000 cubits.	6017
Da	1:17	and understanding of a *kinds of* literature	3972
	1:17	and dreams of a *kinds.*	3972
	1:20	he found them ten times better than a	3972
	2:12	that he ordered the execution of a	10353
	2:38	he has made you ruler over them a.	10353
	2:40	so it will crush and break a the others.	10353
	2:44	It will crush a those kingdoms	10353
	2:48	and placed him in charge of a its wise men.	10353
	3: 2	and a the other provincial officials to come	10353
	3: 3	judges, magistrates and a the other	10353
	3: 5	lyre, harp, pipes and a kinds of music,	10353
	3: 7	harp and a kinds of music, all the peoples,	10353
	3: 7	harp and all kinds of music, a the peoples,	10353
	3:10	pipes and a kinds of music must fall down	10353
	3:15	lyre, harp, pipes and a kinds of music,	10353
	4: 1	who live in a the world:	10353
	4: 6	that a the wise men of Babylon be brought	10353
	4:12	its fruit abundant, and on it was food for a.	10353
	4:21	providing food for a, giving shelter to	10353
	4:28	A this happened to King Nebuchadnezzar.	10353
	4:35	A the peoples of the earth are regarded	10353
	4:37	and a his ways are just.	NIH
	5: 8	Then a the king's wise men came in,	10353
	5:19	a the peoples and nations and men	10353
	5:22	though you knew a this.	10353
	5:23	in his hand your life and a your ways.	10353
	6: 7	advisers and governors have a agreed that	10353
	6:24	and crushed a their bones.	10353
	6:25	Then King Darius wrote to a the peoples,	10353
	7: 7	It was different from a the former beasts,	10353
	7: 9	and its wheels were **a ablaze.**	10178+10471
	7:14	a peoples, nations and men	10353
	7:16	and asked him the true meaning of a this.	10353
	7:19	which was different from a the others	10353
	7:23	from a the other kingdoms and will devour	10353
	7:27	and a rulers will worship and obey him.'	10353
	9: 4	of love with *a who* **love** him	AIT
	9: 6	and to a the people of the land.	3972
	9: 7	and people of Jerusalem and a Israel,	3972
	9: 7	and all Israel, both near and far, in a	3972
	9:11	A Israel has transgressed your law	3972
	9:13	a this disaster has come upon us,	3972
	9:16	in keeping with a your righteous acts,	3972
	9:16	an object of scorn to a those around us.	3972
	10: 3	**used no lotions at a**	6057+6057
	11: 2	who will be far richer than a *the others.*	3972
	11:37	but will exalt himself above *them* a.	3972
	11:43	of the treasures of gold and silver and a	3972
	12: 7	a these things will be completed."	3972
	12: 8	what will the outcome of *a* **this** be?"	AIT
Hos	1: 6	that *I should* **at a forgive** them.	5951+5951
	2:11	I will stop a her celebrations:	3972
	2:11	a her appointed feasts.	3972
	2:18	so that a may lie down in safety.	4392[S]
	4: 2	*they* **break a bounds,**	7287
	4: 3	and a who live in it waste away;	3972
	5: 2	I will discipline a *of* them.	3972
	5: 3	**I know a about** Ephraim;	3359
	7: 2	that I remember a their evil deeds.	3972
	7: 4	They are a adulterers,	3972
	7: 6	Their passion smolders a night;	3972
	7: 7	A *of* them are hot as an oven;	3972
	7: 7	A their kings fall,	3972
	7:10	but despite a this he does not return to	3972
	9: 4	a who eat them will be unclean.	3972
	9: 8	yet snares await him on a his paths,	3972
	9:15	"Because of a their wickedness in Gilgal,	3972
	9:15	a their leaders are rebellious.	3972
	10:14	that a your fortresses will be devastated—	3972
	11: 8	a my compassion is aroused.	3480
	12: 1	the east wind a day and multiplies lies	3972
	12: 8	With a my wealth they will not find	3972
	13: 2	a *of* them the work of craftsmen.	3972
	13:10	Where are your rulers in a your towns,	3972
	13:15	be plundered of a its treasures.	3972
	14: 2	"Forgive a our sins	3972
Joel	1: 2	listen, a who live in the land.	3972
	1: 5	Wail, a you drinkers of wine;	3972
	1:12	a the trees of the field—are dried up.	3972
	1:14	and a who live in the land to the house of	3972
	1:19	and flames have burned up a the trees of	3972
	2: 1	Let a who live in the land tremble,	3972
	2: 7	**They** *a* march in line,	AIT
	2:12	"return to me with a your heart,	3972
	2:28	I will pour out my Spirit on a people.	3972
	3: 2	I will gather a nations and bring them	3972
	3: 4	and Sidon and a you regions of Philistia?	3972
	3: 9	Let a the fighting men draw near	3972
	3:11	a you nations from every side,	3972
	3:12	for there I will sit to judge a the nations	3972
	3:18	a the ravines of Judah will run with water.	3972
	3:20	and Jerusalem through **a generations.**	
			1887+1887+2256
Am	1:11	with a sword, stifling *a* **compassion,**	AIT

Am 2: 3 and kill **a** her officials with him," 3972
3: 2 "You only have I chosen of **a** the families 3972
3: 2 therefore I will punish you for **a** your sins." 3972
5:16 "There will be wailing in **a** the streets 3972
5:17 There will be wailing in **a** the vineyards, 3972
6:14 that will oppress you **a** the way NIH
7:10 The land cannot bear **a** his words. 3972
8: 8 and **a** who live in it mourn? 3972
8:10 into mourning and **a** your singing 3972
8:10 I will make **a** *of* you wear sackcloth 3972
9: 1 Bring them down on the heads of **a** 3972
9: 5 and **a** who live in it mourn— 3972
9: 9 among **a** the nations as grain is shaken in 3972
9:10 **A** the sinners among my people will die by 3972
9:10 will die by the sword, **a** those who say, NIH
9:12 the remnant of Edom and **a** the nations 3972
9:13 the mountains and flow from **a** the hills. 3972
Ob 1: 7 **A** your allies will force you to the border; 3972
1:15 of the LORD is near for **a** nations. 3972
1:16 so **a** the nations will drink continually; 3972
Jnh 1: 5 **A** the sailors were afraid and each cried out NIH
1: 8 for making **a** this trouble for us? NIH
2: 3 **a** your waves and breakers swept over me. 3972
3: 5 They declared a fast, and **a** of them, NIH
Mic 1: 2 Hear, O peoples, **a** *of* you, listen, 3972
1: 2 listen, O earth and **a who are in** it, 4850
1: 5 **A** this is because of Jacob's transgression, 3972
1: 7 **A** her idols will be broken to pieces; 3972
1: 7 **a** her temple gifts will be burned with fire; 3972
1: 7 I will destroy **a** her images. 3972
1:10 Tell it not in Gath; **weep** not **at a.** 1134+1134
2:10 it is ruined, **beyond a remedy.** 5344
2:12 "I will surely gather **a** *of* you, O Jacob; 3972
3: 7 They will **a** cover their faces 3972
3: 9 who despise justice and distort **a** 3972
4: 5 **A** the nations may walk in the name 3972
4:13 their wealth to the Lord of **a** the earth. 3972
5: 9 and **a** your foes will be destroyed. 3972
5:11 and tear down **a** your strongholds. 3972
6:16 the statutes of Omri and **a** the practices 3972
7: 2 **A** men lie in wait to shed blood; 3972
7: 3 *they* **a conspire** *together.* AIT
7:16 deprived of **a** their power. 3972
7:19 and hurl **a** our iniquities into the depths of 3972
Na 1: 4 he makes **a** the rivers run dry. 3972
1: 5 the world and **a** who live in it. 3972
2: 1 brace yourselves, marshal **a** your strength! 4394
2: 9 the wealth from **a** its treasures! 3972
3: 4 **a** because of the wanton lust of a harlot, 8044
3: 7 **A** who see you will flee from you and say, 3972
3:10 and **a** her great men were put in chains. 3972
3:12 **A** your fortresses are like fig trees 3972
3:13 Look at your troops—they are **a** women! NIH
Hab 1: 9 they **a** come bent on violence. 3972
1:10 They laugh at **a** fortified cities; 3972
1:15 wicked foe pulls **a** *of* them up with hooks, 3972
2: 5 he gathers to himself **a** the nations 3972
2: 5 the nations and takes captive **a** the peoples. 3972
2: 6 "Will not **a** *of* them taunt him with ridicule 3972
2:20 let **a** the earth be silent before him." 3972
Zep 1: 4 against Judah and against **a** who live 3972
1: 8 and the king's sons and **a** those clad 3972
1: 9 that day I will punish **a** who avoid stepping 3972
1:11 **a** your merchants will be wiped out, 3972
1:11 **a** who trade with silver will be ruined. 3972
1:18 a sudden end of **a** who live in the earth." 3972
2: 3 Seek the LORD, **a** you humble of the land, 3972
2:11 be awesome to them when he destroys **a** 3972
2:15 **A** who pass by her scoff 3972
3: 6 no one will be left—no one at **a.** NIH
3: 7 nor **a** my punishments come upon her. 3972
3: 7 to act corruptly in **a** they did. 3972
3: 8 **a** my fierce anger. 3972
3: 9 that **a** *of* them may call on the name of 3972
3:11 that day you will not be put to shame for **a** 3972
3:14 Be glad and rejoice with **a** your heart, 3972
3:19 with **a** who oppressed you; 3972
3:20 and praise among **a** the peoples of the earth 3972
Hag 2: 4 Be strong, **a** you people of the land,' 3972
2: 7 I will shake **a** nations, 3972
2: 7 and the desired of **a** nations will come, 3972
2:17 I struck **a** the work of your hands 3972
Zec 2:13 Be still before the LORD, **a** mankind, 3972
4:14 to serve the Lord of **a** the earth." 3972
6: 3 *a of them* **powerful.** AIT
7: 5 "Ask **a** the people of the land and 3972
7:14 'I scattered them with a whirlwind among **a** 3972
8:12 I will give **a** these things as an inheritance 3972
8:17 I hate **a** this," declares the LORD. 3972
8:23 "In those days ten men from **a** languages 3972
9: 1 of men and **a** the tribes of Israel are on 3972
10:11 and **a** the depths of the Nile will dry up. 3972
11:10 the covenant I had made with **a** the nations. 3972
12: 2 to make Jerusalem a cup that sends **a** 3972
12: 3 when **a** the nations of the earth are gathered 3972
12: 3 an immovable rock for **a** the nations. 3972
12: 3 **A** who try to move it will injure themselves. 3972
12: 4 but I will blind **a** the horses of the nations. 3972
12: 6 and left **a** the surrounding peoples, 3972
12: 9 On that day I will set out to destroy **a** 3972
12:14 and **a** the rest of the clans and their wives. 3972
14: 2 I will gather **a** the nations to Jerusalem 3972
14: 5 and **a** the holy ones with him. 3972
14:12 with which the LORD will strike **a** 3972
14:14 of **a** the surrounding nations will 3972
14:15 and **a** the animals in those camps. 3972
14:16 Then the survivors from **a** the nations 3972
Zec 14:19 and the punishment of **a** the nations that do 3972
14:21 and **a** who come to sacrifice will take some 3972
Mal 2: 9 to be despised and humiliated before **a** 3972
2:10 Have we not **a** one Father? 3972
2:17 "**A** who do evil are good in the eyes of 3972
3:12 "Then **a** the nations will call you blessed, 3972
4: 1 **A** the arrogant and every evildoer will 3972
4: 4 and laws I gave him at Horeb for **a** Israel. 3972
Mt 1:17 Thus there were fourteen generations *in* **a** 4246
1:22 **A** this took place to fulfill what 3910
2: 3 and **a** Jerusalem with him. 4246
2: 4 When he had called together **a** 4246
2:16 and he gave orders to kill **a** the boys 4246
3: 5 to him from Jerusalem and **a** Judea and 4246
3:15 for us to do this to fulfill **a** righteousness." 4246
4: 8 to a very high mountain and showed him **a** 4246
4: 9 "**A** this I will give you," he said, 4246
4:24 News about him spread **a over** Syria, 1650+3910
4:24 and people brought to him **a** who were ill 4246
5:11 and falsely say **a** *kinds* of evil against you 4246
5:34 But I tell you, Do not swear **at a:** 3914
6:29 in **a** his splendor was dressed like one 4246
6:32 For the pagans run after **a** these things, 4246
6:33 **a** these things will be given to you as well. 4246
7: 4 when **a** the time there is a plank NIG
8:16 the spirits with a word and healed **a** 4246
8:33 went into the town and reported **a** *this,* 4246
9:26 News of this spread through **a** that region. 3910
9:31 the news about him **a over** that region. 3910
9:35 through **a** the towns and villages, 4246
10:22 **A** *men* will hate you because of me, 4246
10:30 the very hairs of your head are **a** numbered. 4246
11:13 For **a** the Prophets and the Law prophesied 4246
11:27 "**A** *things* have been committed to me 4246
11:28 **a** you who are weary and burdened, 4246
12:15 and he healed **a** their sick, 4246
12:23 **A** the people were astonished and said, 4246
13: 2 while **a** the people stood on the shore. 4246
13:32 Though it is the smallest *of* **a** your seeds, 4246
13:33 a large amount of flour until it worked **a** 3910
13:34 Jesus spoke **a** these things to the crowd 4246
13:41 that causes sin and **a** who do evil. NIG
13:44 then in his joy went and sold **a** he had 4012+4246
13:47 into the lake and caught **a** kinds of fish. 4246
13:51 "Have you understood **a** these things?" 4246
13:56 Aren't **a** his sisters with us? 4246
13:56 then did this man get **a** these things?" 4246
14:20 They **a** ate and were satisfied, 4246
14:35 to **a** the surrounding country. 3910
14:35 People brought **a** their sick to him 4246
14:36 and **a who** touched him were healed. 4012
15:37 They **a** ate and were satisfied. 4246
17:11 Elijah comes and will restore **a** *things.* 4246
18:25 and **a** that he had be sold to repay the debt. 4012+4246
18:32 'I canceled **a** that debt of yours 4246
18:34 until he should pay back **a** he owed. 4246
19:20 "**A** these I have kept," the young man said. 4246
19:26 but with God **a** *things* are possible." 4246
19:28 at the renewal of **a** things, NIG
20: 6 'Why have you been standing here **a** day long doing nothing?' 3910
20:31 but they shouted **a the louder,** "Lord, 3505
21:12 and drove out **a** who were buying 4246
21:26 for they **a** hold that John was a prophet." 4246
21:37 **Last of a,** he sent his son to them. 5731
22:10 and gathered **a** the people they could find, 4246
22:28 since **a** *of them* were married to her?" 4246
22:37 with **a** your heart and with all your soul and 3910
22:37 with all your heart and with **a** your soul and 3910
22:37 with all your soul and with **a** your mind.' 3910
22:40 **A** the Law and the Prophets hang 3910
23: 8 and you are **a** brothers. 4246
23:35 upon you will come **a** the righteous blood 4246
23:36 **a** this will come upon this generation. 4246
24: 2 "Do you see **a** these things?" 4246
24: 8 **A** these are the beginning of birth pains. 4246
24: 9 and you will be hated by **a** nations because 4246
24:14 as a testimony *to* **a** nations, 4246
24:30 and **a** the nations of the earth will mourn. 4246
24:33 Even so, when you see **a** these things, 4246
24:34 until **a** these things have happened. 4246
24:39 until the flood came and took *them* **a** away. 570
24:47 in charge of **a** his possessions. 4246
25: 5 and they **a** became drowsy and fell asleep. 4246
25: 7 "Then **a** the virgins woke up 4246
25:31 and **a** the angels with him, 4246
25:32 **A** the nations will be gathered before him, 4246
26: 1 Jesus had finished saying **a** these things, 4246
26:27 saying, "Drink from it, **a** of you. 4246
26:31 "This very night you will **a** fall away 4246
26:33 "Even if **a** fall away on account of you, 4246
26:35 And **a** the other disciples said the same. 4246
26:52 "for **a** who draw the sword will die by 4246
26:56 But this has **a** taken place that the writings 3910
26:56 Then **a** the disciples deserted him and fled. 4246
26:64 "But I say to **a** of you: NIG
26:70 But he denied it before *them* **a.** 4246
27: 1 **a** the chief priests and the elders of 4246
27:22 They **a** answered, "Crucify him!" 4246
27:23 But they shouted **a the louder,** 4360
27:25 **A** the people answered, 4246
27:45 until the ninth hour darkness came over **a** 4246
27:54 the earthquake and **a** that had happened, NIG
28:18 "**A** authority in heaven and on earth 4246
28:19 go and make disciples of **a** nations, 4246
Mk 1: 5 and **a** the people of Jerusalem went out 4246
Mk 1:27 The people were **a** so amazed 570
1:32 after sunset the people brought to Jesus **a** 4246
2:12 and walked out in full view of *them* **a.** 4246
3: 8 When they heard **a** he was doing, 4012
3:28 **a** the sins and blasphemies of men will 4246
4: 1 while **a** the people were along the shore at 4246
4:28 **A by itself** the soil produces grain— 897
4:32 and becomes the largest *of* **a** garden plants, 4246
5:20 And **a** the *people* were amazed. 4246
5:26 of many doctors and had spent **a** she had, 4246
5:39 "Why **a** this commotion and wailing? NIG
5:40 After he put *them* **a** out, 4246
6:30 and reported to him **a** they had done 4246
6:33 on foot from **a** the towns and got there 4246
6:39 to have **a** the *people* sit down in groups on 4246
6:41 He also divided the two fish among them **a.** 4246
6:42 They **a** ate and were satisfied, 4246
6:50 because they **a** saw him and were terrified. 4246
6:56 and **a who** touched him were healed. 323+4012
7: 3 (The Pharisees and **a** the Jews do not eat 4246
7:19 Jesus declared **a** foods "clean.") 4246
7:23 **A** these evils come from inside and make 4246
7:27 "First let the children **eat a they want,"** 5963
9: 2 where they were **a** alone. 3668
9:12 and restores **a** *things.* 4246
9:15 As soon as **a** the people saw Jesus, 4246
9:35 and the servant *of* **a."** 4246
10:20 "**a** these I have kept since I was a boy." 4246
10:27 **a** *things* are possible with God." 4246
10:44 to be first must be slave *of* **a.** 4246
10:48 but he **shouted a the more,** "Son of David, 3189+3437+4498
11:17 be called a house of prayer *for* **a** nations'? 4246
12: 6 He sent him **last of a,** saying, 2274
12:22 Last *of* **a,** the woman died too. 4246
12:28 he asked him, *"Of* **a** the commandments, 4246
12:30 with **a** your heart and with all your soul and 3910
12:30 with all your heart and with **a** your soul and 3910
12:30 with all your soul and with **a** your mind 3910
12:30 and with **a** your strength.' 3910
12:33 To love him with **a** your heart, 3910
12:33 with **a** your understanding and 3910
12:33 and with **a** your strength, 3910
12:33 is more important than **a** burnt offerings 4246
12:43 into the treasury than **a** the others. 4246
12:44 They **a** gave out of their wealth; 4246
12:44 **a** she had to live on." 3910+4012
13: 2 "Do you see **a** these great buildings?" NIG
13: 4 And what will be the sign that they are **a** 4246
13:10 gospel must first be preached to **a** nations. 4246
13:13 **A** *men* will hate you because of me, 4246
13:30 until **a** these things have happened. 4246
14:23 and they **a** drank from it. 4246
14:27 "You will **a** fall away," Jesus told them, 4246
14:29 Peter declared, "Even if **a** fall away, 4246
14:31 And **a** the others said the same. 4246
14:53 and **a** the chief priests, 4246
14:64 They **a** condemned him as worthy of death. 4246
15:14 But they shouted **a the louder,** 4360
16:15 into **a** the world and preach the good news 570
16:15 and preach the good news *to* **a** creation. 4246
16:18 it will **not** hurt them **at a;** 3590+4024
Lk 1: 6 observing **a** the Lord's commandments 4246
1:10 the time for the burning of incense came, **a** 4246
1:48 now on **a** generations will call me blessed, 4246
1:65 The neighbors were **a** filled with awe, 4246
1:65 about **a** these things. 4246
1:71 and from the hand *of* **a** who hate us— 4246
1:75 and righteousness before him **a** our days. 4246
2:10 of great joy that will be *for* **a** the people. 4246
2:18 and **a** who heard it were amazed at what 4246
2:19 But Mary treasured up **a** these things 4246
2:20 for **a** the *things* they had heard and seen, 4246
2:31 in the sight *of* **a** people, 4246
2:38 the child *to* **a** who were looking forward to 4246
2:51 But his mother treasured **a** these things 4246
3: 3 into **a** the country around the Jordan, 4246
3: 6 And **a** mankind will see God's salvation.' " 4246
3:15 and were **a** wondering in their hearts 4246
3:16 John answered *them* **a,** 4246
3:19 and **a** the other evil things he had done, 4246
3:20 Herod added this to *them* **a:** 4246
3:21 When **a** the people were being baptized, 570
4: 5 a high place and showed him in an instant **a** 4246
4: 6 "I will give you **a** their authority 570
4: 7 So if you worship me, it will **a** be yours." 4246
4:13 the devil had finished **a** this tempting, 4246
4:22 **A** spoke well of him and were amazed at 4246
4:28 **A** the *people* in the synagogue were furious 4246
4:35 the man down before them **a** and came out NIG
4:36 **A** the *people* were amazed and said 4246
4:40 to Jesus **a** who had various kinds 570
5: 5 we've worked hard **a** night 3910
5: 9 and **a** his companions were astonished at 4246
5:15 Yet the news about him spread **a the more,** 3437
6:10 He looked around at them **a,** 4246
6:17 and a great number of people from **a over** 4246
6:19 and the people **a** tried to touch him, 4246
6:19 from him and healing *them* **a.** 4246
6:26 Woe to you when **a** men speak well of you, 4246
7: 1 When Jesus had finished saying **a** *this* in 4246
7:16 They were **a** filled with awe 4246
7:18 about **a** these things. 4246
7:29 (**A** the people, even the tax collectors, 4246
7:35 wisdom is proved right by **a** her children." 4246
8:24 the storm subsided, and **a** was calm. NIG
8:37 Then **a** the people of the region of 570

Lk 8:39 man went away and told **a over** town *2848+3910*
8:40 for they were **a** expecting him. *4246*
8:45 When they **a** denied it, Peter said, "Master, *4246*
8:47 In the presence *of* **a** the people, *4246*
8:52 **a** the *people* were wailing and mourning *4246*
9: 1 to drive out **a** demons and to cure diseases, *4246*
9: 7 Now Herod the tetrarch heard about **a** *4246*
9:13 we go and buy food for **a** this crowd." *4246*
9:17 They **a** ate and were satisfied, *4246*
9:23 Then he said to *them* **a:** *4246*
9:43 And they were **a** amazed at the greatness *4246*
9:43 While everyone was marveling at **a** *4246*
9:48 For he who is least among you **a—** *4246*
10:19 and scorpions and to overcome **a** the power *4246*
10:22 **"A** *things* have been committed to me *4246*
10:27 with **a** your heart and with all your soul and *3910*
10:27 with all your heart and with **a** your soul and *3910*
10:27 with all your soul and with **a** your strength *3910*
10:27 and with **a** your mind'; *3910*
10:40 by **a** the preparations that had to be made. *4498*
11:42 rue and **a** other *kinds* of garden herbs, *4246*
11:50 *of* **a** the prophets that has been shed since *4246*
11:51 be held responsible for it **a.** *NIG*
12: 7 the very hairs of your head are **a** numbered. *4246*
12:15 Be on your guard against **a** *kinds* of greed; *4246*
12:18 there I will store **a** my grain and my goods. *4246*
12:27 in **a** his splendor was dressed like one *4246*
12:30 the pagan world runs after **a** such things, *4246*
12:44 in charge of **a** his possessions. *4246*
13: 2 these Galileans were worse sinners than **a** *4246*
13: 3 unless you repent, you too will **a** perish. *4246*
13: 4 do you think they were more guilty than **a** *4246*
13: 5 unless you repent, you too will **a** perish." *4246*
13:11 could not straighten up **at a.** *1650+3836+4117*
13:17 **a** his opponents were humiliated, *4246*
13:17 with **a** the wonderful things he was doing. *4246*
13:21 a large amount of flour until it worked **a** *3910*
13:27 Away from me, **a** you evildoers!' *4246*
13:28 and **a** the prophets in the kingdom of God, *4246*
14:10 in the presence *of* **a** your fellow guests. *4246*
14:18 "But they **a** alike began to make excuses. *4246*
15: 1 and "sinners" were **a** gathering around *4246*
15:13 the younger son got together **a** he had, *4246*
15:29 *A* **these years** I've been slaving for you *AIT*
16:14 heard **a** this and were sneering at Jesus. *4246*
16:26 And besides **a** this, between us and you *4246*
17:17 Jesus asked, "Were not **a** ten cleansed? *3836*
17:27 Then the flood came and destroyed *them* **a.** *4246*
17:29 down from heaven and destroyed *them* **a.** *4246*
18:12 a week and give a tenth of **a** I get.' *4012+4246*
18:21 **"A** these I have kept since I was a boy," *4246*
18:28 We have left **a** *we* **had** to follow you!" *2625+3836*
18:39 but he shouted **a the more,** "Son of David, *3437+4498*
18:43 **a** the people saw it, they also praised God. *4246*
19: 7 **A** *the people* saw this and began to mutter, *4246*
19:37 to praise God in loud voices for **a** *4246*
19:48 because **a** the people hung on his words. *570*
20: 6 'From men,' **a** the people will stone us, *570*
20:38 but of the living, for to him **a** are alive." *4246*
20:45 While **a** the people were listening, *4246*
21: 3 "this poor widow has put in more than **a** *4246*
21: 4 **A** these people gave their gifts out *4246*
21: 4 of her poverty put in **a** she had to live on." *4246*
21:12 But before **a** this, they will lay hands on you *4246*
21:12 and **a** on account of my name. *NIG*
21:17 **A** *men* will hate you because of me. *4246*
21:22 the time of punishment in fulfillment of **a** *4246*
21:24 be taken as prisoners to **a** the nations. *4246*
21:29 "Look at the fig tree and **a** the trees. *4246*
21:32 until **a** these *things* have happened. *4246*
21:35 For it will come upon **a** those who live on *4246*
21:36 be able to escape **a** that is about to happen, *4246*
21:38 and **a** the people came early in the morning *4246*
22:12 a large upper room, **a** furnished. *NIG*
22:70 They **a** asked, "Are you then the Son *4246*
23: 5 up the people **a** over Judea by his teaching. *3910*
23: 5 in Galilee and has come **a** the way here." *NIG*
23:48 When **a** the people who had gathered *4246*
23:49 But **a** those who knew him, *4246*
24: 9 they told **a** these things to the Eleven and *4246*
24: 9 to the Eleven and *to* **a** the others. *4246*
24:19 and deed before God and **a** the people. *4246*
24:21 it is the third day since **a** this took place. *NIG*
24:25 to believe **a** that the prophets have spoken! *4246*
24:27 beginning with Moses and **a** the Prophets, *4246*
24:27 to them what was said in **a** the Scriptures *4246*
24:47 be preached in his name to **a** nations, *4246*
Jn 1: 3 Through him **a** *things* were made; *4246*
1: 7 so that through him **a** *men* might believe. *4246*
1:12 Yet to **a who** received him, *4012*
1:16 of his grace we have **a** received one blessing *4246*
1:28 This **a** happened at Bethany on *NIG*
2:15 and drove **a** from the temple area, *4246*
2:18 to prove your authority to do **a** this?" *NIG*
2:24 for he knew **a** *men.* *4246*
3:31 one who comes from above is above **a;** *4246*
3:31 one who comes from heaven is above **a.** *4246*
4:45 They had seen **a** that he had done *4246*
4:53 So he and **a** his household believed. *3910*
5:18 For this reason the Jews tried **a the harder** *3437*
5:20 the Son and shows him **a** he does. *4246*
5:22 but has entrusted **a** judgment to the Son, *4246*
5:23 that **a** may honor the Son just as they honor *4246*
5:28 for a time is coming when **a** who are *4246*
6:12 When they had **a** had enough to eat, *NIG*
6:37 **A** that the Father gives me will come to me, *4246*
Jn 6:39 I shall lose none of **a** that he has given me, *4246*
6:45 'They will **a** be taught by God.' *4246*
7:21 and you are **a** astonished. *4246*
8: 2 where **a** the people gathered around him, *4246*
8:25 Just what I have been claiming **a along** *794+3836*
10: 4 When he has brought out **a** his own, *4246*
10: 8 **A** who ever came before me were thieves *4246*
10:29 is greater than **a;** *4246*
10:41 **a** that John said about this man was true." *4246*
11:49 spoke up, "You know **nothing at a!** *4024+4029*
11:56 **Isn't** he coming to the Feast **at a?"** *3590+4024*
12:16 not understand *a* **this.** *AIT*
12:32 will draw **a** *men* to myself." *4246*
12:37 Jesus had done **a these** miraculous signs *5537*
13: 3 Jesus knew that the Father had put **a** *things* *4246*
13:18 "I am not referring to **a** of you; *4246*
13:35 By this **a** *men* will know *4246*
14:25 "*A* **this** I have spoken while still with you. *AIT*
14:26 will teach you **a** *things* *4246*
16: 1 **"A this** I have told you so that you will *AIT*
16:13 comes, he will guide you into **a** truth. *4246*
16:15 **A** that belongs to the Father is mine. *4246*
16:30 that you know **a** *things* and that you do not *4246*
16:32 You will leave me **a alone.** *3667*
17: 2 over **a** people that he might give eternal life *4246*
17: 2 to **a** those you have given him. *4246*
17:10 **A** I have is yours, and all you have is mine. *4246*
17:10 All I have is yours, and **a** you have is mine. *NIG*
17:21 that **a** *of them* may be one, *4246*
18: 4 knowing **a** that was going to happen *4246*
18:20 where **a** the Jews come together. *4246*
19:28 Later, knowing that **a** was now completed, *4246*
21:17 He said, "Lord, you know **a** *things;* *4246*
Ac 1: 1 about **a** that Jesus began to do and to teach *4246*
1: 8 and in **a** Judea and Samaria, *4246*
1:14 They **a** joined together constantly in prayer, *4246*
1:18 and **a** his intestines spilled out. *4246*
2: 1 they were **a** together in one place. *4246*
2: 4 **A** *of them* were filled with the Holy Spirit *4246*
2: 7 **a** these men who are speaking Galileans? *570*
2:14 "Fellow Jews and **a** *of you* who live *4246*
2:17 I will pour out my Spirit on **a** people. *4246*
2:32 and we are **a** witnesses of the fact. *4246*
2:36 "Therefore let **a** Israel be assured of this: *4246*
2:39 and *for* **a** who are far off— *4246*
2:39 for **a whom** the Lord our God will call. *323+4012*
2:44 **A** the believers were together *4246*
2:47 praising God and enjoying the favor of **a** *3910*
3: 9 When **a** the people saw him walking *4246*
3:11 **a** the people were astonished *4246*
3:16 as you can **a** see. *4246*
3:18 through **a** the prophets, *4246*
3:24 "Indeed, **a** the prophets from Samuel on, *4246*
3:25 'Through your offspring **a** peoples *4246*
4:10 you and **a** the people of Israel; *4246*
4:18 to speak or teach **at a** in the name of Jesus. *2773*
4:21 because **a** the people were praising God *4246*
4:23 to their own people and reported **a that** *4012*
4:31 And they were **a** filled with the Holy Spirit *570*
4:32 **A** the believers were one in heart and mind. *4436*
4:33 and much grace was upon them **a.** *4246*
5: 5 great fear seized **a** who heard what had happened. *4246*
5:11 and **a** who heard about these events. *4246*
5:12 And **a** the believers used to meet together *570*
5:16 and **a** of them were healed. *570*
5:17 Then the high priest and **a** his associates, *4246*
5:34 who was honored *by* **a** the people, *4246*
5:36 **a** his followers were dispersed, *4246*
5:36 and it **a** came to nothing. *NIG*
5:37 and **a** his followers were scattered. *4246*
6: 2 So the Twelve gathered **a** the disciples together *4436*
6:15 **A** who were sitting in the Sanhedrin *4246*
7:10 and rescued him from **a** his troubles. *4246*
7:10 over Egypt and **a** his palace. *3910*
7:11 "Then a famine struck **a** Egypt and Canaan, *3910*
7:14 and his whole family, seventy-five in **a.** *6034*
7:22 Moses was educated in **a** the wisdom of *4246*
7:50 Has not my hand made **a** these things?' *4246*
7:57 they **a** rushed at him, *3924*
8: 1 and **a** except the apostles were scattered *4246*
8: 6 they **a** paid close attention to what he said. *3924*
8: 9 and amazed **a** the people of Samaria. *NIG*
8:10 and **a** the *people,* *4246*
8:27 in charge of **a** the treasury of Candace, *4246*
8:40 in **a** the towns until he reached Caesarea. *4246*
9:13 about this man and **a** the harm he has done *4012*
9:14 from the chief priests to arrest **a** who call *4246*
9:21 **A** those who heard him were astonished *4246*
9:26 but they were **a** afraid of him, *4246*
9:35 **A** those who lived in Lydda *4246*
9:39 **A** the widows stood around him, *4246*
9:40 Peter sent *them* **a** out of the room; *4246*
9:42 This became known **a** over Joppa, *3910*
10: 2 He and **a** his family were devout *4246*
10:12 It contained **a** *kinds* *4246*
10:22 who is respected by **a** the Jewish people. *3910*
10:33 Now we are **a** here in the presence of God *4246*
10:36 who is Lord *of* **a.** *4246*
10:38 and healing **a** who were under the power of *4246*
10:41 He was not seen *by* **a** the people, *4246*
10:43 **A** the prophets testify about him *4246*
10:44 the Holy Spirit came on **a** who heard *4246*
11:10 then it was **a** pulled up to heaven again. *570*
11:14 and **a** your household will be saved.' *4246*
11:23 and encouraged *them* **a** to remain true to *4246*
Ac 11:23 to the Lord with **a** their hearts. *NIG*
13:10 *of* **a** *kinds of* deceit and trickery. *4246*
13:20 **A** this took about 450 years. *NIG*
13:24 John preached repentance and baptism *to* **a** *4246*
13:29 When they had carried out **a** *4246*
13:48 and **a who** were appointed *4012*
14:16 he let **a** nations go their own way. *4246*
14:27 the church together and reported **a that** *4012*
15: 3 This news made **a** the brothers very glad. *4246*
15:17 and **a** the Gentiles who bear my name, *4246*
15:25 So we **a** agreed to choose some men *NIG*
15:36 in **a** the towns where we preached the word *4246*
16: 3 for they **a** knew that his father was a Greek. *570*
16:26 At once **a** the prison doors flew open, *4246*
16:28 We are **a** here!" *570*
16:32 to him and to **a** the others in his house. *4246*
16:33 and **a** his family were baptized. *4246*
17: 6 "These men who have caused trouble **a** *NIG*
17: 7 They are **a** defying Caesar's decrees, *4246*
17:21 (**A** the Athenians and *4246*
17:25 because he himself gives **a** *men* life *4246*
17:30 now he commands **a** people everywhere *4246*
17:31 *to* **a** *men* by raising him from the dead." *4246*
18: 2 because Claudius had ordered **a** the Jews *4246*
18:17 Then they **a** turned on Sosthenes *4246*
18:23 strengthening **a** the disciples. *4246*
19: 7 There were about twelve men **in a.** *4246*
19:10 so that **a** the Jews and Greeks who lived in *4246*
19:16 on them and overpowered *them* **a.** *317*
19:17 they were **a** seized with fear, *4246*
19:21 After **a** this had happened, *NIG*
19:26 that man-made gods are **no** gods **at a.** *4024*
19:34 they **a** shouted in unison for *4246*
19:35 doesn't **a the world** know that the city *476+1639+4005+5515*
20:26 that I am innocent of the blood *of* **a** *men.* *4246*
20:28 Keep watch over yourselves and **a** the flock *4246*
20:32 among **a** those who are sanctified. *4246*
20:36 he knelt down with **a** of them and prayed. *4246*
20:37 They **a** wept as they embraced him *4246*
21: 5 **A** the disciples and their wives *4246*
21:18 and **a** the elders were present. *4246*
21:20 and **a** *of them* are zealous for the law. *4246*
21:21 They have been informed that you teach **a** *4246*
21:28 the man who teaches **a** *men* everywhere *4246*
21:30 the people came running from **a** directions. *NIG*
21:40 When they were **a silent,** *4498+4968*
22: 5 high priest and **a** the Council can testify. *4246*
22:10 be told **a** that you have been assigned *4246*
22:12 of the law and highly respected by **a** *4246*
22:15 to **a** men of what you have seen and heard. *4246*
22:30 the chief priests and **a** the Sanhedrin *4246*
23: 1 to God *in* **a** good conscience to this day." *4246*
23: 8 but the Pharisees acknowledge them **a.**) *317*
24: 5 up riots *among* the Jews **a** over the world. *4246*
24: 8 about **a** these charges we are bringing *4246*
25:24 and **a** who are present with us, *4246*
25:26 I have brought him before **a** of you, *NIG*
26: 2 against **a** the accusations of the Jews, *4246*
26: 3 so because you are well acquainted with **a** *4246*
26: 4 "The Jews **a** know *4246*
26: 9 "I too was convinced that I ought to do **a** *4498*
26:14 We **a** fell to the ground, *4246*
26:20 then to those in Jerusalem and in **a** Judea, *4246*
26:29 that not only you but **a** who are listening *4246*
27:20 we finally gave up **a** hope of being saved. *4246*
27:24 the lives of **a** who sail with you.' *4246*
27:33 Just before dawn Paul urged *them* **a** to eat. *570*
27:35 and gave thanks to God in front of *them* **a.** *4246*
27:36 They were **a** encouraged *4246*
28: 2 and welcomed us **a** because it was raining *4246*
28:30 and welcomed **a** who came to see him. *4246*
Ro 1: 5 from among **a** the Gentiles to the obedience *4246*
1: 7 *To* **a** in Rome who are loved by God *4246*
1: 8 I thank my God through Jesus Christ for **a** *4246*
1: 8 because your faith is being reported **a** over *3910*
1:10 in my prayers **at a times;** *4121*
1:18 against **a** the godlessness and wickedness *4246*
2:12 **A who** sin apart from the law will *4012*
2:12 and **a who** sin under the law will be judged *4012*
3: 2 **First of a,** they have been entrusted with *4754*
3: 4 **Not at a!** Let God be true, *1181+3590*
3: 9 Are we any better? Not **at a!** *4122*
3: 9 and Gentiles alike are **a** under sin. *4246*
3:12 **A** have turned away, *4246*
3:22 in Jesus Christ to **a** who believe. *4246*
3:23 for **a** have sinned and fall short of the glory *4246*
3:31 nullify the law by this faith? **Not at a!** *1181+3590*
4:11 he is the father *of* **a** who believe but have *4246*
4:16 be guaranteed *to* **a** Abraham's offspring— *4246*
4:16 He is the father *of* us **a.** *4246*
4:18 Against **a hope,** Abraham in hope believed *1828*
5:12 and in this way death came to **a** men, *4246*
5:12 to all men, because **a** sinned— *4246*
5:18 for **a** men, so also the result of one act *4246*
5:18 that brings life for **a** men. *4246*
5:20 sin increased, grace **increased a the more,** *5668*
6: 3 that **a** of us who were baptized *4012*
6:10 he died to sin **once for a;** *2384*
8:24 But hope that is seen is no hope at **a.** *NIG*
8:28 And we know that in **a** *things* God works *4246*
8:32 but gave him up for us **a—** *4246*
8:32 graciously give us **a** *things?* *4246*
8:36 "For your sake we face death **a** day long; *3910*
8:37 in **a** these things we are more than conquerors *4246*
8:39 nor anything else in **a** creation, *NIG*

Ro 9: 5 who is God over **a,** forever praised! 4246
9: 6 **a** who are descended from Israel are Israel. 4246
9: 7 they are his descendants are they **a** Abraham's children. 4246
9:14 Is God unjust? **Not at a!** 1181+3590
9:17 and that my name might be proclaimed in **a** 4246
10:12 *of* **a** and richly blesses all who call on him, 4246
10:12 of all and richly blesses **a** who call on him, 4246
10:16 not **a** the Israelites accepted the good news. 4246
10:18 "Their voice has gone out into **a** the earth, 4246
10:21 "**A** day **long** I have held out my hands to 3910
11:11 to fall beyond recovery? **Not at a!** 1181+3590
11:24 **After a,** if you were cut out of an olive tree 1142
11:26 so **a** Israel will be saved, as it is written: 4246
11:32 For God has bound **a** *men* over 4246
11:32 so that he may have mercy on them **a.** 4246
11:36 through him and to him are **a things.** 3836+4246
12: 4 and these members do not **a** have 4246
12: 5 and each member belongs to **a the others.** 253
14:10 we will **a** stand before God's judgment seat 4246
14:20 **A** food is clean, 4246
15:11 again, "Praise the Lord, **a** you Gentiles, 4246
15:11 and sing praises to him, **a** you peoples." 4246
15:13 *with* **a** joy and peace as you trust in him, 4246
15:19 **a the way** around **to** 3588
15:33 The God of peace be with you **a.** Amen. 4246
16: 4 Not only I but **a** the churches of 4246
16:15 and Olympas and **a** the saints with them. 4246
16:16 **A** the churches of Christ send greetings. 4246
16:26 **a** nations might believe and obey him— 4246
1Co 1: 2 together with **a** those everywhere who call 4246
1: 5 in **a** your speaking and 4246
1: 5 and in **a** your knowledge— 4246
1:10 that **a** of you agree with one another so 4246
2:10 The Spirit searches **a** *things,* 4246
2:15 about **a** *things,* but he himself is not subject 4246
3: 5 What, **after a,** is Apollos? 4036
3:21 **A** *things* are yours, 4246
3:22 or the future—**a** are yours, 4246
4: 8 Already *you* **have a you want!** 1639+3170
5:10 not **at a** meaning the people 4122
6:18 **A** other sins a man commits are outside his body, 4246
7: 7 I wish that **a** men were as I am. 4246
7:17 the rule I lay down in **a** the churches. 4246
8: 1 We know that we **a** possess knowledge. 4246
8: 4 that an idol is nothing at **a** in the world and NIG
8: 6 from whom **a things** came and 3836+4246
8: 6 through whom **a** *things* came and 4246
9:12 shouldn't we have it **a the more?** 3437
9:22 I have become **a** *things* to all men so that 4246
9:22 I have become all things *to* **a** *men* so that 4246
9:22 that **by a possible means** I might save some. 4122
9:23 I do **a** this for the sake of the gospel, 4246
9:24 not know that in a race **a** the runners run, 4246
10: 1 that our forefathers were **a** under the cloud 4246
10: 1 the cloud and that they **a** passed through 4246
10: 2 They were **a** baptized into Moses in 4246
10: 3 They **a** ate the same spiritual food 4246
10:17 for we **a** partake of the one loaf. 4246
10:31 do it **a** for the glory of God. 4246
12: 6 the same God works **a** *of them* in all men. 4246
12: 6 the same God works all of them in **a** *men.* 4246
12:11 **A** these are the work of one and 4246
12:12 **a** its parts are many, they form one body. 4246
12:13 For we were **a** baptized by one Spirit 4246
12:13 we were **a** given the one Spirit to drink. 4246
12:19 If they were **a** one part, 4246
12:28 God has appointed **first of a** apostles, 4754
12:29 Are **a** apostles? 4246
12:29 Are **a** prophets? 4246
12:29 Are **a** teachers? 4246
12:29 Do **a** work miracles? 4246
12:30 Do **a** have gifts of healing? 4246
12:30 Do **a** speak in tongues? 4246
12:30 Do **a** interpret? 4246
13: 2 of prophecy and can fathom **a** mysteries 4246
13: 2 and **a** knowledge, and if I have a faith 4246
13: 3 If I give **a** I possess to the poor 4246
14:10 Undoubtedly there are **a** sorts of languages 5537
14:18 that I speak in tongues more than **a** of you. 4246
14:24 by **a** that he is a sinner and will be judged 4246
14:24 that he is a sinner and will be judged by **a,** 4246
14:26 **A** *of these* must be done for 4246
14:31 For you can **a** prophesy in turn so 4246
14:33 As in **a** the congregations of the saints, 4246
15: 7 then *to* **a** the apostles, 4246
15: 8 and last *of* **a** he appeared to me also, 4246
15:10 No, I worked harder than **a** of them— 4246
15:19 we are to be pitied more than **a** men. 4246
15:22 For as in Adam **a** die, 4246
15:22 so in Christ **a** will be made alive. 4246
15:24 after he has destroyed **a** dominion, 4246
15:25 until he has put **a** his enemies 4246
15:28 so that God may be **a** in all. 4246
15:28 so that God may be all in **a.** 4246
15:29 If the dead are not raised **at a,** 3914
15:39 **A** flesh is not the same: 4246
15:51 We will not **a** sleep, 4246
15:51 but we will **a** be changed— 4246
16:20 **A** the brothers here send you greetings. 4246
16:24 My love to **a** of you in Christ Jesus. Amen. 4246
2Co 1: 1 with **a** the saints throughout Achaia: 4246
1: 3 of compassion and the God *of* **a** comfort, 4246
1: 4 who comforts us in **a** our troubles, 4246
2: 3 I had confidence in **a** of you, 4246
2: 3 that you would **a** share my joy. 4246
2: 5 not so much grieved me as he has grieved **a** 4246
3:18 who with unveiled faces **a** reflect 4246
4:15 **A** this is for your benefit, 4246
4:17 glory **that far outweighs them a.** 983+1650+2848+5651+5651
5:10 For we must **a** appear before 4246
5:14 we are convinced that one died for **a,** 4246
5:14 and therefore **a** died. 4246
5:15 And he died for **a,** 4246
5:18 **A** *this* is from God, 4246
7: 4 in **a** our troubles my joy knows no bounds. 4246
7:13 **By a this** we are encouraged. 1328+4047
7:13 his spirit has been refreshed by **a** of you. 4246
7:15 for you is **a** the greater when he remembers NIG
7:15 that you were **a** obedient, 4246
8:18 with him the brother who is praised by **a** 4246
9: 8 God is able to make **a** grace abound to you, 4246
9: 8 so that in **a** *things* at all times, 4246
9: 8 so that in all things **at a times,** 4121
9: 8 having **a** that you need, 4246
11:28 of my concern *for* **a** the churches. 4246
12: 9 Therefore I will boast **a the more** gladly 3437
12:14 **After a,** children should not have to save 1142
12:19 Have you been thinking **a along** 4093
13:13 **A** the saints send their greetings. 4246
13:14 fellowship of the Holy Spirit be with you **a.** 4246
Gal 1: 2 and **a** the brothers with me, To 4246
1: 7 which is really **no** gospel **at a.** 4024
2:10 **A they asked was** that we should continue 3667
2:14 I said to Peter in front of *them* **a,** 4246
3: 8 "**A** nations will be blessed through you." 4246
3:10 **A who** rely on observing the law are under 4012
3:26 You are **a** sons of God through faith 4246
3:27 for **a** *of you* **who** were baptized 4012
3:28 for you are **a** one in Christ Jesus. 4246
4: 9 to be enslaved by them **a over again?** 540+4099
4:15 What has happened to **a** your joy? NIG
5: 2 **no** value to you **at a.** 4029
6: 6 in the word must share **a** good things 4246
6:10 let us do good to **a** *people,* 4246
6:16 Peace and mercy to **a who** follow this rule, 4012
Eph 1: 8 on us with **a** wisdom and understanding. 4246
1:10 to bring **a things** in heaven and 3836+4246
1:15 in the Lord Jesus and your love for **a** 4246
1:21 far above **a** rule and authority, 4246
1:22 And God placed **a** *things* under his feet 4246
2: 3 **A** of us also lived among them at one time, 4246
3: 8 I am less than the least *of* **a** God's people, 4246
3: 9 who created **a things.** 3836+4246
3:18 together with **a** the saints, 4246
3:19 that you may be filled to the measure of **a** 4246
3:20 to do immeasurably more than **a** we ask 4246
3:21 in Christ Jesus throughout **a** generations, 4246
4: 6 one God and Father *of* **a,** 4246
4: 6 who is over **a** and through all and in all. 4246
4: 6 who is over all and through **a** and in all. 4246
4: 6 who is over all and through all and in **a.** 4246
4:10 the very one who ascended higher *than* **a** 4246
4:13 until we **a** reach unity in the faith and in 4246
4:15 in **a** *things* grow up into him who is 4246
4:19 *Having* **lost a sensitivity,** 556
4:25 for we are **a** members of one body. NIG
4:31 Get rid of **a** bitterness, rage and anger, 4246
5: 9 the fruit of the light consists in **a** goodness, 4246
5:29 **After a,** no one ever hated his own body, 1142
6:16 In addition to **a** *this,* 4246
6:16 with which you can extinguish **a** 4246
6:18 in the Spirit on **a** occasions with all kinds 4246
6:18 in the Spirit on all occasions with **a** *kinds* 4246
6:18 be alert and always keep on praying for **a** 4246
6:24 Grace to **a** who love our Lord Jesus Christ 4246
Php 1: 1 *To* **a** the saints in Christ Jesus at Philippi, 4246
1: 4 In **a** my prayers for all of you, 4246
1: 4 In all my prayers for **a** of you, 4246
1: 7 It is right for me to feel this way about **a** 4246
1: 7 **a** of you share in God's grace with me. 4246
1: 8 how I long for **a** of you with the affection 4246
1:25 with **a** of you for your progress and joy in 4246
2:17 I am glad and rejoice with **a** of you. 4246
2:26 For he longs for **a** of you and is distressed 4246
2:28 I am **a the more eager** to send him, 5081
3: 8 for whose sake I have lost **a** *things.* 4246
3:12 Not that I have already obtained **a** this, NIG
3:15 **A of** us who are mature should take such 4012
4: 5 Let your gentleness be evident *to* **a.** 476+4246
4: 7 which transcends **a** understanding, 4246
4:19 And my God will meet **a** your needs 4246
4:21 Greet **a** the saints in Christ Jesus. 4246
4:22 **A** the saints send you greetings, 4246
Col 1: 4 and of the love you have for **a** the saints— 4246
1: 6 **A over** the world this gospel is bearing fruit 4246
1: 6 and understood God's grace in **a** its truth. NIG
1: 9 of his will through **a** spiritual wisdom 4246
1:11 being strengthened with **a** power according 4246
1:15 the firstborn *over* **a** creation. 4246
1:16 For by him **a things** were created: 3836+4246
1:16 **a** *things* were created by him and for him. 4246
1:17 He is before **a** *things,* 4246
1:17 and in him **a things** hold together. 3836+4246
1:19 to have **a** his fullness dwell in him, 4246
1:20 him to reconcile to himself **a things,** 3836+4246
1:28 and teaching everyone with **a** wisdom, 4246
1:29 struggling with **a** his energy, NIG
2: 1 and for **a who** have not met me personally. 4012
2: 3 in whom are hidden **a** the treasures 4246
2: 9 in Christ **a** the fullness of the Deity lives 4246
2:13 He forgave us **a** our sins, 4246
2:22 These are **a** destined to perish with use, 4246
3: 8 of **a** such *things* as these: 4246
3:11 slave or free, but Christ is **a,** and is in all. 4246
3:11 slave or free, but Christ is all, and is in **a.** 4246
3:14 And over **a** these virtues put on love, 4246
3:14 which binds them **a** together NIG
3:16 and admonish one another with **a** wisdom, 4246
3:17 do it **a** in the name of the Lord Jesus, 4246
3:23 work at it with **a** your heart, NIG
4: 7 Tychicus will tell you **a** the news about me. 4246
4:12 you may stand firm in **a** the will of God, 4246
1Th 1: 2 We always thank God for **a** of you, 4246
1: 7 so you became a model *to* **a** the believers 4246
2:15 and are hostile *to* **a** men 4246
3: 7 in **a** our distress and persecution 4246
3: 9 for you in return for **a** the joy we have in 4246
3:13 with **a** his holy ones. 4246
4: 6 The Lord will punish men for **a** such sins, 4246
4:10 you do love **a** the brothers 4246
5: 5 You are **a** sons of the light and sons of 4246
5:18 give thanks in **a** *circumstances,* 4246
5:26 Greet **a** the brothers with a holy kiss. 4246
5:27 before the Lord to have this letter read *to* **a** 4246
2Th 1: 4 about your perseverance and faith in **a** 4246
1: 5 **A** this is evidence NIG
1:10 at among **a** those who have believed. 4246
2: 9 the work of Satan displayed in **a** *kinds* 4246
2:12 and so that **a** will be condemned who have 4246
3:16 of peace himself give you peace at **a** *times* 4246
3:16 The Lord be with **a** of you. 4246
3:17 the distinguishing mark in **a** my letters. 4246
3:18 of our Lord Jesus Christ be with you **a.** 4246
1Ti 2: 1 I urge, then, first *of* **a,** that requests, 4246
2: 2 for kings and **a** those in authority, 4246
2: 2 and quiet lives in **a** godliness and holiness. 4246
2: 4 who wants **a** men to be saved and to come 4246
2: 6 who gave himself as a ransom for **a** *men*— 4246
3:16 **Beyond a question,** the mystery 3935
4: 8 but godliness has value for **a** *things,* 4246
4:10 who is the Savior *of* **a** men, 4246
5: 4 these should learn **first of a** 4754
5: 5 in need and **left a alone** puts her hope 3670
5:10 in trouble and devoting herself *to* **a** *kinds* 4246
6: 1 **A who** are under the yoke 4012
6:10 love of money is a root *of* **a** *kinds* of evil. 4246
6:11 But you, man of God, flee from *a* **this,** AIT
2Ti 2: 7 the Lord will give you insight into **a** this. 4246
3: 6 and are swayed *by* **a kinds** of evil desires, 4476
3:10 You, however, **know a about** my teaching, 4158
3:11 Yet the Lord rescued me from **a** *of them.* 4246
3:16 **A** Scripture is God-breathed and is useful 4246
4: 5 But you, keep your head in **a** *situations,* 4246
4: 5 **discharge a** the duties of your ministry. 4442
4: 8 *to* **a** who have longed for his appearing. 4246
4:17 and **a** the Gentiles might hear it. 4246
4:21 Linus, Claudia and **a** the brothers. 4246
Tit 1:15 To the pure, **a** *things* are pure, 4246
2:11 that brings salvation has appeared *to* **a** men. 4246
2:14 for us to redeem us from **a** wickedness and 4246
2:15 Encourage and rebuke with **a** authority. 4246
3: 2 and to show true humility toward **a** men. 4246
3: 3 *by* **a kinds of** passions and pleasures. 4476
3:15 Grace be with you **a.** 4246
Phm 1: 5 in the Lord Jesus and your love for **a** 4246
Heb 1: 2 whom he appointed heir *of* **a** *things,* 4246
1: 3 sustaining **a things** by his powerful word. 3836+4246
1: 6 he says, "Let **a** God's angels worship him." 4246
1:11 they will **a** wear out like a garment. 4246
1:14 Are not **a** angels ministering spirits sent 4246
2:15 and free those who **a** their lives were held 4246
3: 2 as Moses was faithful in **a** God's house. 3910
3: 5 as a servant in **a** God's house, 3910
3:16 Were they not **a** those Moses led out 4246
4: 4 God rested from **a** his work." 4246
4:13 Nothing in **a** creation is hidden NIG
5: 9 of eternal salvation *for* **a** who obey him 4246
5:12 the elementary truths of God's word **a** NIG
6: 6 **crucifying** the Son of God **a over again** 416
6:16 and puts an end *to* **a** argument. 4246
7:27 He sacrificed for their sins **once for a** 2384
8:11 because they will **a** know me, 4246
9:12 the Most Holy Place **once for a** 2384
9:19 of the law *to* **a** the people, 4246
9:19 and sprinkled the scroll and **a** the people. 4246
9:26 now he has appeared **once for a** at the end 562
10: 2 worshipers would have been cleansed **once for a,** 562
10:10 of the body of Jesus Christ **once for a.** 2384
10:12 this priest had offered **for a time** one sacrifice 1457+1650+3836
10:25 **a the more** as you see the Day approaching. 3437+5537
11:13 **A** these people were still living by faith 4246
11:39 These were **a** commended for their faith, 4246
12: 9 we have **a** had human fathers who disciplined us NIG
12:14 to live in peace with **a** *men* and to be holy; 4246
12:23 You have come to God, the judge *of* **a** *men,* 4246
13: 4 Marriage should be honored by **a,** 4246
13: 4 the adulterer and **a** the sexually immoral. NIG
13: 9 Do not be carried away *by* **a kinds of** 4476
13:24 Greet **a** your leaders and all God's people. 4246
13:24 Greet all your leaders and **a** God's people. 4246
13:25 Grace be with you **a.** 4246
Jas 1: 5 who gives generously *to* **a** 4246

Jas 1: 8 unstable in **a** he does. *4246*
1:18 be a kind of firstfruits of **a** he created. *NIG*
1:21 get rid of **a** moral filth and the evil that is *4246*
2:10 at just one point is guilty *of* breaking **a** *4246*
3: 2 We **a** stumble in many ways. *570*
3: 7 **A** kinds of animals, birds, *4246*
3:17 that comes from heaven is **first of a** pure; *4754*
4:16 **A** such boasting is evil. *4246*
5:12 Above **a**, my brothers, do not swear— *4246*
1Pe 1: 6 to suffer grief in **a kinds of** trials. *4476*
1:15 so be holy in **a** you do; *4246*
1:24 For, "**A** men are like grass, *4246*
1:24 **a** their glory is like the flowers of the field; *4246*
2: 1 rid yourselves of **a** malice and all deceit, *4246*
2: 1 rid yourselves of all malice and **a** deceit, *4246*
2:18 to your masters with **a** respect, *4246*
3: 8 **a** of you, live in harmony with one another; *4246*
3:18 For Christ died for sins **once for a,** *562*
3:20 In it only a few people, eight in **a,** *NIG*
4: 7 The end *of* **a** *things* is near. *4246*
4: 8 Above **a,** love each other deeply, *4246*
4:11 so that in **a** *things* God may be praised *4246*
5: 5 **A** of you, clothe yourselves with humility *4246*
5: 7 Cast **a** your anxiety on him *4246*
5:10 And the God *of* **a** grace, *4246*
5:14 Peace *to* **a** of you who are in Christ. *4246*
2Pe 1:10 be **a the more** eager to make your calling *3437*
1:20 **Above a,** you must understand *4047+4754*
3: 3 **First of a,** you must understand that in *4047+4754*
3:16 He writes the same way in **a** his letters, *4246*
1Jn 1: 5 in him there is no darkness **at a.** *4029*
1: 7 his Son, purifies us from **a** sin. *4246*
1: 9 and purify us from **a** unrighteousness. *4246*
2:20 and **a** of you know the truth. *4246*
2:27 as his anointing teaches you about **a** *things* *4246*
5:17 **A** wrongdoing is sin, *4246*
2Jn 1: 1 not I only, but also **a** who know the truth— *4246*
3Jn 1: 2 and that **a** may go well with you, *4246*
Jude 1: 3 that was **once for a** entrusted to the saints. *562*
1: 5 Though you already know **a** *this,* *4246*
1:15 and to convict **a** the ungodly of all *4246*
1:15 of **a** the ungodly acts they have done in *4246*
1:15 in the ungodly way, and of **a** *4246*
1:25 before **a** ages, now and forevermore! *4246*
Rev 1: 7 and **a** the peoples of the earth will mourn *4246*
1:16 like the sun shining in **a** its brilliance. *NIG*
2:11 **not** be hurt **at a** *3590+4024*
2:23 Then **a** the churches will know *4246*
4: 8 and was covered with eyes **a around,** *3239*
4:11 for you created **a things,** *3836+4246*
5: 6 the seven spirits of God sent out into **a** *4246*
5:13 and **a** that is in them, singing: *4246*
7: 4 144,000 from **a** the tribes of Israel. *4246*
7:11 **A** the angels were standing around *4246*
8: 3 with the prayers *of* **a** the saints, *4246*
8: 7 and **a** the green grass was burned up. *4246*
8: 8 **a ablaze,** was thrown into the sea. *2794+4786*
10: 6 who created the heavens and **a** that is *NIG*
10: 6 the earth and **a** that is in it, *NIG*
10: 6 and the sea and **a** that is in it, and said, *NIG*
12: 5 who will rule **a** the nations with *4246*
13: 8 **A** inhabitants of the earth will worship *4246*
13: 8 **a** whose names have not been written in *NIG*
13:12 He exercised **a** the authority of *4246*
13:15 and cause **a who** refused to worship *1569+4012*
14: 8 which made **a** the nations drink *4246*
15: 4 **A** nations will come and worship *4246*
18: 3 For **a** the nations have drunk *4246*
18:14 **A** your riches and splendor have vanished, *4246*
18:17 and **a** who travel by ship, the sailors, *4246*
18:17 and **a who** earn their living from the sea, *4012*
18:19 where **a** who had ships on the sea *4246*
18:23 By your magic spell **a** the nations *4246*
18:24 *of* **a** who have been killed on the earth." *4246*
19: 5 "Praise our God, **a** you his servants, *4246*
19:17 a loud voice *to* **a** the birds flying in midair, *4246*
19:18 and the flesh *of* **a** *people,* free and slave, *4246*
19:21 and **a** the birds gorged themselves *4246*
21: 7 He who overcomes will inherit **a** this, *NIG*
21: 8 the idolaters and **a** liars— *4246*
22: 9 and *of* **a who** keep the words of this book. *3836*

ALL-NIGHT (1) [NIGHT]

Jos 10: 9 After an **a** march from Gilgal, 2021+3972+4326

ALL-SURPASSING (1) [SURPASS]

2Co 4: 7 to show that this **a** power is from God and *5651*

ALLAMMELECH (1)

Jos 19:26 **A,** Amad and Mishal. On the 526

ALLEGIANCE (3) [ALLY]

1Ki 12:27 they *will* **again give** their **a** to their lord, 4213+8740
Isa 19:18 and **swear a** to the LORD Almighty. 8678
Eze 21:23 like a false omen to those *who have* **sworn a** 8652+8678

ALLEGING (KJV) See PROVING

ALLEGORY (1)

Eze 17: 2 an **a** and tell the house of Israel a parable. 2648

ALLELUIA (KJV) See HALLELUIA

ALLEYS (1)

Lk 14:21 into the streets and **a** of the town and bring *4860*

ALLIANCE (8) [ALLY]

1Ki 3: 1 Solomon **made an a** with Pharaoh king 3161
2Ch 20:35 of Judah **made an a** with Ahaziah king 2489
20:37 Because you *have* **made an a** with Ahaziah, 2489
Ps 83: 5 they form an **a** against you— 1382
Isa 30: 1 **forming an a,** but not by my Spirit, 5011+5818
Jer 50: 9 against Babylon an **a** *of* great nations from 7736
Da 11: 6 to the king of the North to make an **a,** 4797
11:17 of his entire kingdom and will make an **a** 3838

ALLIED (8) [ALLY]

Ge 14: 5 the kings **a with** him went out and defeated 907
14:13 all of whom were **a** *with* Abram. 1251+1382
14:17 and the kings **a with** him, 907
Jos 13:21 **princes** *a with* Sihon— AIT
1Ki 20:16 while Ben-Hadad and the 32 kings **a with** 6468
2Ch 18: 1 **a himself** with Ahab **by marriage.** 3161
Ps 94:20 *Can* a corrupt throne *be* **a with** you— 2489
Isa 7: 2 "Aram *has* **a** *itself* with Ephraim"; 5663

ALLIES (13) [ALLY]

1Ch 5:20 handed the Hagrites and all their **a** 6640+8611S
Jer 13:21 as your special **a?** 476
22:20 for all your **a** are crushed. 170
22:22 and your **a** will go into exile. 170
30:14 All your **a** have forgotten you; 170
La 1:19 "I called to my **a** but they betrayed me. 170
Eze 30: 6 " 'The **a** *of* Egypt will fall 6164
31:17 its **a** among the nations, 2432
32:21 of Egypt and her **a,** 6468
Da 11: 6 After some years, *they will become* **a.** 2489
Ob 1: 7 All your **a** will force you to the border; 408+1382
Na 1:12 "Although *they have* **a** and are numerous, 8969
3: 9 Put and Libya were among her **a.** 6476

ALLOCATE (1)

Jos 13: 6 *to* **a** this land to Israel for an inheritance, 5877

ALLON (1)

1Ch 4:37 the son of **A,** the son of Jedaiah, 474

ALLON BACUTH (1)

Ge 35: 8 So it was named **A.** 475

ALLOT (3) [ALLOTMENT, ALLOTS, ALLOTTED, ALLOTTING]

Eze 45: 1 " 'When you **a** the land as an inheritance, 5877
47:22 *to* **a** it as an inheritance for yourselves and 5877
48:29 *to* **a** as an inheritance to the tribes of Israel, 5877

ALLOTMENT (13) [ALLOT]

Ge 47:22 because they received a **regular a** 2976
47:22 from the **a** Pharaoh gave them. 2976
Dt 12:12 who have no **a** or inheritance of their own. 2750
14:27 they have no **a** or inheritance of their own. 2750
14:29 the Levites (who have no **a** or inheritance 2750
18: 1 are to have no **a** or inheritance with Israel. 2750
Jos 15: 1 The **a** for the tribe of Judah, clan by clan, 1598
16: 1 The **a** for Joseph began at the Jordan 1598
17: 1 This was the **a** for the tribe of Manasseh 1598
17: 2 So this **a** was for the rest of the people NIH
17:14 "Why have you given us only one **a** 1598
17:17 You will have not only one **a** 1598
Eze 48:13 the Levites will have an **a** 25,000 NIH

ALLOTS (4) [ALLOT]

Job 20:29 Such is the fate God **a** the wicked, 4946
21:17 the fate God **a** in his anger? 2745
27:13 "Here is the fate God **a to** the wicked, 6640
Isa 34:17 He **a** their portions; 5877

ALLOTTED (32) [ALLOT]

Lev 7:35 **portion** of the offerings made to the LORD by fire that were *a* AIT
Nu 26:53 *to* **be a** to them as an inheritance based on 2745
34: 2 the land that *will be* **a** to you as 5877
36: 3 the inheritance **a** to us will be taken away. 1598
Dt 32: 9 Jacob his **a** inheritance. 2475
Jos 14: 1 and the heads of the tribal clans of Israel **a** 5706
18:11 Their **a** territory lay between the tribes 1598
19:49 the land into its **a portions,** 1473
21: 4 of Aaron the priest *were* **a** thirteen towns 928+1598+2021+2118
21: 5 of Kohath's descendants were **a** ten towns 928+1598+2021
21: 6 of Gershon were **a** thirteen towns from 928+1598+2021
21: 8 the Israelites **a** to the Levites these towns 928+1598+2021+5989
21: 9 From the tribes of Judah and Simeon *they* **a** 5989
21:20 Levites *were* **a** towns from the tribe 1598+2118
21:40 All the towns **a** to the Merarite clans, 1598+2118
23: 4 Remember how *I have* **a** as an inheritance 5877
24:33 which *had* **been a** to his son Phinehas in 5989
Jdg 1: 3 "Come up with us into the **territory a** 1598
1Sa 18:26 So before the **a time** elapsed, 3427
1Ch 6:54 of their settlements **a** as their **territory** 1473
6:61 of Kohath's descendants were **a** ten towns 928+1598+2021
6:62 were **a** thirteen towns from the tribes 4200
6:63 were **a** twelve towns from the tribes 928+1598+2021
6:65 Simeon and Benjamin *they* **a** 928+1598+2021+5989
Ne 5:14 neither I nor my brothers ate the **food** *a to* AIT
5:18 I never demanded the **food** *a to* AIT
Job 7: 3 so I *have* **been a** months of futility, 5706
21:21 behind when his **a** months come to an end? 5031
Ps 78:55 and **a** their lands *to* them as an inheritance; 5877
125: 3 not remain over the *land* **a** *to* the righteous, 1598
Eze 47:22 with you *they are to be* **a** an inheritance 5877
Da 12:13 to receive your **a inheritance."** 1598

ALLOTTING (1) [ALLOT]

Ne 9:22 **a** *to* them even the remotest frontiers. 2745

ALLOW (19) [ALLOWANCE, ALLOWED, ALLOWING, ALLOWS]

Ex 10:25 "You *must* **a** us to have sacrifices 5989
22:18 *"Do* not **a** a sorceress **to live.** 2649
Nu 33:55 those *you* **a to remain** will become barbs 3855
35:32 *a* him *to* **go back** AIT
Jdg 6:39 *A me* one more **test** AIT
1Sa 16:22 saying, *"A* David *to* **remain** in my service, AIT
24: 7 and *did* not **a** them to attack Saul. 5989
2Ch 20:10 whose territory *you would* not **a** Israel 5989
Job 11:14 **a** no evil **to dwell** 8905
Ps 132: 4 *I will* **a** no sleep to my eyes, 5989
Pr 6: 4 **A** no sleep to your eyes, 5989
Jer 13:14 *I will* **a** no **pity** or mercy or compassion 2798
Eze 45: 8 **a** the house of Israel **to possess** 5989
Mk 5:12 **a** us to go into them." *NIG*
11:16 not **a** anyone to carry merchandise through *918*
Lk 4:41 But *he* rebuked them and *would* not **a** them *1572*
Ac 16: 7 but the Spirit of Jesus *would* not **a** them to. *1572*
27: 7 **a** us **to hold** our **course,** *4661*
Ro 14:16 Do not *a* what you consider good *to be* **spoken of as evil.** *AIT*

ALLOWANCE (3) [ALLOW]

2Ki 25:30 by day the king gave Jehoiachin a regular **a** 786
Jer 52:34 of Babylon gave Jehoiachin a regular **a** 786
Lk 12:42 of his servants to give them their **food a** at *4991*

ALLOWED (25) [ALLOW]

Ge 3:22 He must **not be a** to reach out his hand 7153
31: 7 However, God *has* not **a** him to harm me. 5989
46:34 *be a to* **settle** in the region of Goshen, AIT
48:11 God *has* **a** me **to see** your children too." 8011
Lev 11:39 " 'If an animal that you are **a** to eat dies, 4200
Nu 31:15 **a** all the women **to live?"** 2649
Dt 7:22 *You will* not *be* **a to** eliminate them all 3523
24: 4 *is* not **a** to marry her again 3523
Jdg 2:23 **a** those nations **to remain;** 5663
3:28 *they* **a** no one to cross over. 5989
2Sa 8: 2 and the third length *was* **a to live.** 2649
1Ki 1:48 who *has* **a** my eyes to see a successor 5989
1Ch 16:21 *He* **a** no man to oppress them; 5663
2Ch 25:13 and *had* not *a to* **take part** in AIT
34:11 had **a to fall into ruin.** 8845
Est 1: 8 By the king's command each guest *was* **a** 401+646
4: 2 because no one clothed in sackcloth was **a** NIH
Job 31:30 not **a** my mouth to sin by invoking a curse 5989
Ps 105:14 *He* **a** no one to oppress them; 5663
Eze 33:12 *will* not *be* **a** to live because 3523
Da 7:12 but **were a** to live for a period of time.) 10314
Ac 27: 3 and Julius, in kindness to Paul, **a** him to go *2205*
28: 4 Justice *has* not **a** him to live." *1572*
28:16 Paul *was* **a** to live by himself, *2205*
1Co 14:34 They *are* not **a** to speak, *2205*

ALLOWING (2) [ALLOW]

Lev 22:16 by *a* them *to* **eat** the sacred offerings and AIT
Jdg 1:34 not **a** them to come down into the plain. 5989

ALLOWS (2) [ALLOW]

Ex 21:22 woman's husband demands and the court **a.** 5989
Ro 14: 2 One man's faith **a** him to eat everything, *NIG*

ALLURE (1) [ALLURING]

Hos 2:14 "Therefore I *am* now *going to* **a** her; 7331

ALLURING (1) [ALLURE]

Na 3: 4 **a,** the mistress of sorceries, 2834+3202

ALLY (2) [ALLEGIANCE, ALLIANCE, ALLIED, ALLIES]

Jos 23:12 "But if you turn away and **a** *yourselves* 1815
Isa 48:14 LORD's **chosen a** will carry out his purpose 170

ALMIGHTY (345) [MIGHT]

Ge 17: 1 "I am God **A;** 8724
28: 3 May God **A** bless you 8724
35:11 And God said to him, "I am God **A;** 8724

Ge 43:14 And may God A grant you mercy before 8724
48: 3 "God A appeared to me at Luz in the land 8724
49:25 who helps you, because of the A, 8724
Ex 6: 3 to Isaac and to Jacob as God A, 8724
Nu 24: 4 who sees a vision from the A, 8724
24:16 who sees a vision from the A, 8724
Ru 1:20 because the A has made my life very bitter. 8724
1:21 the A has brought misfortune upon me." 8724
1Sa 1: 3 to worship and sacrifice to the LORD A 7372
1:11 she made a vow, saying, "O LORD A, 7372
4: 4 the ark of the covenant of the LORD A, 7372
15: 2 This is what the LORD A says: 7372
17:45 against you in the name of the LORD A, 7372
2Sa 5:10 because the LORD God A was with him. 7372
6: 2 the name of the LORD A, 7372
6:18 the people in the name of the LORD A. 7372
7: 8 'This is what the LORD A says: 7372
7:26 'The LORD A is God over Israel!' 7372
7:27 "O LORD A, God of Israel, 7372
1Ki 18:15 Elijah said, "As the LORD A lives, 7372
19:10 very zealous for the LORD God A. 7372
19:14 very zealous for the LORD God A. 7372
2Ki 3:14 "As surely as the LORD A lives, 7372
19:31 zeal of the LORD A will accomplish this. 7372
1Ch 11: 9 because the LORD A was with him. 7372
17: 7 'This is what the LORD A says: 7372
17:24 Then men will say, 'The LORD A, 7372
Job 5:17 so do not despise the discipline of the A. 8724
6: 4 The arrows of the A are in me, 8724
6:14 even though he forsakes the fear of the A. 8724
8: 3 Does the A pervert what is right? 8724
8: 5 you will look to God and plead with the A, 8724
11: 7 Can you probe the limits of the A? 8724
13: 3 to the A and to argue my case with God. 8724
15:25 at God and vaunts himself against the A, 8724
21:15 Who is the A, that we should serve him? 8724
21:20 let him drink of the wrath of the A. 8724
22: 3 What pleasure would it give the A 8724
22:17 What can the A do to us?' 8724
22:23 If you return to the A, you will be restored: 8724
22:25 then the A will be your gold, 8724
22:26 in the A and will lift up your face to God. 8724
23:16 the A has terrified me. 8724
24: 1 the A not set times for judgment? 8724
27: 2 who has denied me justice, the A, 8724
27:10 Will he find delight in the A? 8724
27:11 the ways of the A I will not conceal. 8724
27:13 a ruthless man receives from the A: 8724
29: 5 when the A was still with me 8724
31: 2 his heritage from the A on high? 8724
31:35 let the A answer me; 8724
32: 8 it is the spirit in a man, the breath of the A, 8724
33: 4 the breath of the A gives me life. 8724
34:10 from the A to do wrong. 8724
34:12 that the A would pervert justice. 8724
35:13 the A pays no attention to it. 8724
37:23 The A is beyond our reach and exalted 8724
40: 2 with the A correct him? 8724
Ps 24:10 The LORD A— he is the King of glory. 7372
46: 7 The LORD A is with us; 7372
46:11 The LORD A is with us; 7372
48: 8 have we seen in the city of the LORD A, 7372
59: 5 O LORD God A, the God of Israel, 7372
68:14 When the A scattered the kings in the land, 8724
69: 6 O Lord, the LORD A; 7372
80: 4 O LORD God A, 7372
80: 7 Restore us, O God A; 7372
80:14 Return to us, O God A! 7372
80:19 Restore us, O LORD God A; 7372
84: 1 lovely is your dwelling place, O LORD A! 7372
84: 3 a place near your altar, O LORD A, 7372
84: 8 Hear my prayer, O LORD God A; 7372
84:12 O LORD A, blessed is the man who trusts 7372
89: 8 O LORD God A, who is like you? 7372
91: 1 in the shadow of the A. 8724
Isa 1: 9 the LORD A had left us some survivors, 7372
1:24 Therefore the Lord, the LORD A, 7372
2:12 The LORD A has a day in store for all 7372
3: 1 See now, the Lord, the LORD A, 7372
3:15 declares the Lord, the LORD A. 7372
5: 7 The vineyard of the LORD A is the house 7372
5: 9 The LORD A has declared in my hearing: 7372
5:16 the LORD A will be exalted by his justice, 7372
5:24 of the LORD A and spurned the word of 7372
6: 3 "Holy, holy, holy is the LORD A; 7372
6: 5 the King, the LORD A." 7372
8:13 The LORD A is the one you are to regard 7372
8:18 and symbols in Israel from the LORD A, 7372
9: 7 zeal of the LORD A will accomplish this. 7372
9:13 nor have they sought the LORD A. 7372
9:19 the LORD A the land will be scorched and 7372
10:16 Therefore, the Lord, the LORD A, 7372
10:23 The Lord, the LORD A, 7372
10:24 this is what the Lord, the LORD A, says: 7372
10:26 The LORD A will lash them with a whip, 7372
10:33 See, the Lord, the LORD A, 7372
13: 4 LORD A is mustering an army for war. 7372
13: 6 it will come like destruction from the A. 8724
13:13 at the wrath of the LORD A, 7372
14:22 declares the LORD A. 7372
14:23 declares the LORD A. 7372
14:24 The LORD A has sworn, "Surely, 7372
14:27 For the LORD A has purposed, 7372
17: 3 declares the LORD A. 7372
18: 7 to the LORD A from a people tall 7372
18: 7 the place of the Name of the LORD A. 7372
19: 4 declares the Lord, the LORD A. 7372
19:12 the LORD A has planned against Egypt. 7372
19:16 the uplifted hand that the LORD A raises 7372
19:17 because of what the LORD A is planning 7372
19:18 and swear allegiance to the LORD A. 7372
19:20 be a sign and witness to the LORD A in 7372
19:25 The LORD A will bless them, saying, 7372
21:10 what I have heard from the LORD A, 7372
22: 5 The Lord, the LORD A, 7372
22:12 The Lord, the LORD A, 7372
22:14 The LORD A has revealed this 7372
22:14 says the Lord, the LORD A. 7372
22:15 This is what the Lord, the LORD A, says: 7372
22:25 "In that day," declares the LORD A, 7372
23: 9 The LORD A planned it, 7372
24:23 for the LORD A will reign on Mount Zion 7372
25: 6 the LORD A will prepare a feast 7372
28: 5 the LORD A will be a glorious crown, 7372
28:22 the Lord, the LORD A, 7372
28:29 All this also comes from the LORD A, 7372
29: 6 the LORD A will come with thunder 7372
31: 4 the LORD A will come down to do battle 7372
31: 5 the LORD A will shield Jerusalem; 7372
37:16 "O LORD A, God of Israel, enthroned 7372
37:32 zeal of the LORD A will accomplish this. 7372
39: 5 "Hear the word of the LORD A: 7372
44: 6 Israel's King and Redeemer, the LORD A: 7372
45:13 says the LORD A." 7372
47: 4 the LORD A is his name— 7372
48: 2 the LORD A is his name: 7372
51:15 the LORD A is his name. 7372
54: 5 the LORD A is his name— 7372
Jer 2:19 declares the Lord, the LORD A. 7372
5:14 the LORD God A says: 7372
6: 6 This is what the LORD A says: 7372
6: 9 This is what the LORD A says: 7372
7: 3 This is what the LORD A, 7372
7:21 " 'This is what the LORD A, 7372
8: 3 declares the LORD A.' 7372
9: 7 Therefore this is what the LORD A says: 7372
9:15 Therefore, this is what the LORD A, 7372
9:17 This is what the LORD A says: 7372
10:16 the LORD A is his name. 7372
11:17 The LORD A, who planted you, 7372
11:20 O LORD A, you who judge righteously 7372
11:22 therefore this is what the LORD A says: 7372
15:16 for I bear your name, O LORD God A. 7372
16: 9 For this is what the LORD A, 7372
19: 3 This is what the LORD A, 7372
19:11 'This is what the LORD A says: 7372
19:15 the LORD A, the God of Israel, says: 7372
20:12 O LORD A, you who examine 7372
23:15 this is what the LORD A says concerning 7372
23:16 This is what the LORD A says: 7372
23:36 the LORD A, our God. 7372
25: 8 Therefore the LORD A says this: 7372
25:27 tell them, 'This is what the LORD A, 7372
25:28 tell them, 'This is what the LORD A says: 7372
25:29 declares the LORD A.' 7372
25:32 This is what the LORD A says: "Look! 7372
26:18 'This is what the LORD A says: 7372
27: 4 'This is what the LORD A, 7372
27:18 let them plead with the LORD A that 7372
27:19 For this is what the LORD A says about 7372
27:21 this is what the LORD A, 7372
28: 2 the LORD A, the God of Israel, says: 7372
28:14 This is what the LORD A, 7372
29: 4 the LORD A, the God of Israel, says 7372
29: 8 Yes, this is what the LORD A, 7372
29:17 this is what the LORD A says: 7372
29:21 This is what the LORD A, 7372
29:25 the LORD A, the God of Israel, says: 7372
30: 8 " 'In that day,' declares the LORD A, 7372
31:23 This is what the LORD A, 7372
31:35 the LORD A is his name: 7372
32:14 the LORD A, the God of Israel, says: 7372
32:15 For this is what the LORD A, 7372
32:18 whose name is the LORD A, 7372
33:11 saying, "Give thanks to the LORD A, 7372
33:12 "This is what the LORD A says: 7372
35:13 the LORD A, the God of Israel, says: 7372
35:17 "Therefore, this is what the LORD God A, 7372
35:18 "This is what the LORD A, 7372
35:19 Therefore, this is what the LORD A, 7372
38:17 "This is what the LORD God A, 7372
39:16 'This is what the LORD A, 7372
42:15 This is what the LORD A, 7372
42:18 This is what the LORD A, 7372
43:10 say to them, 'This is what the LORD A, 7372
44: 2 the LORD A, the God of Israel, says: 7372
44: 7 "Now this is what the LORD God A, 7372
44:11 "Therefore, this is what the LORD A, 7372
44:25 This is what the LORD A, 7372
46:10 that day belongs to the Lord, the LORD A— 7372
46:10 For the Lord, the LORD A, 7372
46:18 whose name is the LORD A, 7372
46:25 The LORD A, the God of Israel, says: 7372
48: 1 This is what the LORD A, 7372
48:15 whose name is the LORD A. 7372
49: 5 declares the Lord, the LORD A. 7372
49: 7 This is what the LORD A says: 7372
49:26 declares the LORD A. 7372
49:35 This is what the LORD A says: 7372
50:18 Therefore this is what the LORD A, 7372
50:25 for the Sovereign LORD A has work to do 7372
50:31 the LORD A, "for your day has come, 7372
50:33 This is what the LORD A says: 7372
50:34 the LORD A is his name. 7372
Jer 51: 5 the LORD A, though their land is full 7372
51:14 The LORD A has sworn by himself: 7372
51:19 the LORD A is his name. 7372
51:33 This is what the LORD A, 7372
51:57 whose name is the LORD A. 7372
51:58 This is what the LORD A says: 7372
Eze 1:24 like the voice of the A, 8724
10: 5 like the voice of God A when he speaks. 8724
Hos 12: 5 the LORD God A, 7372
Joel 1:15 it will come like destruction from the A. 8724
Am 3:13 declares the Lord, the LORD God A. 7372
4:13 the LORD God A is his name. 7372
5:14 Then the LORD God A will be with you, 7372
5:15 the LORD God A will have mercy on 7372
5:16 the LORD God A, says: 7372
5:27 says the LORD, whose name is God A. 7372
6: 8 the LORD God A declares: 7372
6:14 For the LORD God A declares, 7372
9: 5 The Lord, the LORD A, 7372
Mic 4: 4 for the LORD A has spoken. 7372
Na 2:13 "I am against you," declares the LORD A. 7372
3: 5 "I am against you," declares the LORD A. 7372
Hab 2:13 Has not the LORD A determined that 7372
Zep 2: 9 as surely as I live," declares the LORD A, 7372
2:10 and mocking the people of the LORD A. 7372
Hag 1: 2 This is what the LORD A says: 7372
1: 5 Now this is what the LORD A says: 7372
1: 7 This is what the LORD A says: 7372
1: 9 declares the LORD A. 7372
1:14 to work on the house of the LORD A, 7372
2: 4 For I am with you,' declares the LORD A. 7372
2: 6 "This is what the LORD A says: 7372
2: 7 says the LORD A. 7372
2: 8 declares the LORD A. 7372
2: 9 says the LORD A. 7372
2: 9 declares the LORD A." 7372
2:11 "This is what the LORD A says: 7372
2:23 " 'On that day,' declares the LORD A, 7372
2:23 declares the LORD A." 7372
Zec 1: 3 This is what the LORD A says: 7372
1: 3 'Return to me,' declares the LORD A, 7372
1: 3 to you,' says the LORD A. 7372
1: 4 This is what the LORD A says: 7372
1: 6 'The LORD A has done 7372
1:12 the angel of the LORD said, "LORD A, 7372
1:14 This is what the LORD A says: 7372
1:16 declares the LORD A. 7372
1:17 This is what the LORD A says: 7372
2: 8 For this is what the LORD A says: 7372
2: 9 that the LORD A has sent me. 7372
2:11 that the LORD A has sent me to you. 7372
3: 7 "This is what the LORD A says: 7372
3: 9 says the LORD A, 7372
3:10 declares the LORD A." 7372
4: 6 but by my Spirit,' says the LORD A. 7372
4: 9 that the LORD A has sent me to you. 7372
5: 4 The LORD A declares, 'I will send it out, 7372
6:12 Tell him this is what the LORD A says: 7372
6:15 that the LORD A has sent me to you. 7372
7: 3 the priests of the house of the LORD A 7372
7: 4 the word of the LORD A came to me: 7372
7: 9 "This is what the LORD A says: 7372
7:12 the LORD A had sent by his Spirit through 7372
7:12 So the LORD A was very angry. 7372
7:13 I would not listen,' says the LORD A. 7372
8: 1 the word of the LORD A came to me. 7372
8: 2 This is what the LORD A says: 7372
8: 3 and the mountain of the LORD A will 7372
8: 4 This is what the LORD A says: 7372
8: 6 This is what the LORD A says: 7372
8: 6 declares the LORD A. 7372
8: 7 This is what the LORD A says: 7372
8: 9 This is what the LORD A says: 7372
8: 9 for the house of the LORD A, 7372
8:11 declares the LORD A. 7372
8:14 This is what the LORD A says: 7372
8:14 says the LORD A, 7372
8:18 the word of the LORD A came to me. 7372
8:19 This is what the LORD A says: 7372
8:20 This is what the LORD A says: 7372
8:21 the LORD and seek the LORD A. 7372
8:22 to seek the LORD A and to entreat him." 7372
8:23 This is what the LORD A says: 7372
9:15 and the LORD A will shield them. 7372
10: 3 for the LORD A will care for his flock, 7372
12: 5 because the LORD A is their God.' 7372
13: 2 declares the LORD A. 7372
13: 7 declares the LORD A. 7372
14:16 the King, the LORD A, and to celebrate 7372
14:17 the LORD A, they will have no rain. 7372
14:21 and Judah will be holy to the LORD A, 7372
14:21 a Canaanite in the house of the LORD A. 7372
Mal 1: 4 But this is what the LORD A says: 7372
1: 6 says the LORD A. 7372
1: 8 says the LORD A. 7372
1: 9 says the LORD A. 7372
1:10 says the LORD A, 7372
1:11 says the LORD A. 7372
1:13 says the LORD A. 7372
1:14 For I am a great king," says the LORD A, 7372
2: 2 says the LORD A, 7372
2: 4 says the LORD A. 7372
2: 7 he is the messenger of the LORD A. 7372
2: 8 with Levi," says the LORD A. 7372
2:12 he brings offerings to the LORD A. 7372
2:16 says the LORD A. 7372
3: 1 will come," says the LORD A. 7372

Mal 3: 5 but do not fear me," says the LORD **A.** 7372
3: 7 says the LORD **A.** 7372
3:10 Test me in this," says the LORD **A,** 7372
3:11 says the LORD **A.** 7372
3:12 says the LORD **A.** 7372
3:14 about like mourners before the LORD **A?** 7372
3:17 "They will be mine," says the LORD **A,** 7372
4: 1 says the LORD **A.** 7372
4: 3 says the LORD **A.** 7372
Ro 9:29 "Unless the Lord **A** had left us descendants, *4877*
2Co 6:18 says the Lord **A.**" *4120*
Jas 5: 4 the ears *of* the Lord **A.** *4877*
Rev 1: 8 and who was, and who is to come, the **A.**" *4120*
4: 8 "Holy, holy, holy is the Lord God **A,** *4120*
11:17 "We give thanks to you, Lord God **A,** *4120*
15: 3 and marvelous are your deeds, Lord God **A.** *4120*
16: 7 "Yes, Lord God **A,** *4120*
16:14 for the battle on the great day *of* God **A.** *4120*
19: 6 For our Lord God **A** reigns. *4120*
19:15 of the fury of the wrath of God **A.** *4120*
21:22 Lord God **A** and the Lamb are its temple. *4120*

ALMODAD (2)

Ge 10:26 Joktan was the father of **A,** Sheleph, 525
1Ch 1:20 Joktan was the father of **A,** Sheleph, 525

ALMON (1)

Jos 21:18 and **A,** together with their pasturelands— 6626

ALMON DIBLATHAIM (2) [BETH DIBLATHAIM]

Nu 33:46 and camped at **A.** 6627
33:47 They left **A** and camped in 6627

ALMOND (7) [ALMONDS]

Ge 30:37 **a** and plane trees and made white stripes 4280
Ex 25:33 Three cups **shaped like a flowers** with buds 5481
25:34 to be four cups **shaped like a flowers** 5481
37:19 Three cups **shaped like a flowers** with buds 5481
37:20 lampstand were four cups **shaped like a flowers** 5481
Ecc 12: 5 when the **a tree** blossoms and 9196
Jer 1:11 "I see the branch of an **a tree,**" I replied. 9196

ALMONDS (2) [ALMOND]

Ge 43:11 some pistachio nuts and **a.** 9196
Nu 17: 8 blossomed and produced **a.** 9196

ALMOST (16)

Ex 17: 4 They are **a** ready to stone me." 5071+6388
Jos 10:20 **a to a man—** 4392+6330+9462
Jdg 19: 9 said, "Now look, it's **a** evening. 8332
19:11 near Jebus and the day was **a** gone, 4394
2Sa 1: 6 with the chariots and riders **a upon** him. 1815
Job 10:20 *Are* not my few days *a* **over?** AIT
Ps 73: 2 But as for me, my feet had **a** slipped; 3869+5071
119:87 They **a** wiped me from the earth, 3869+5071
Lk 8:42 the crowds *a* **crushed** him. *AIT*
24:29 the day *is* **a over.**" *3111*
Jn 2:13 it was **a time** for the Jewish Passover, *1584*
11:55 When it was **a time** for the Jewish Passover, *1584*
Ac 13:44 the next Sabbath **a** the whole city gathered *3585*
Ro 13:12 The night is nearly over; the day *is* **a here.** *1581*
Php 2:27 Indeed he was ill, and **a** died. *4180*
2:30 because *he* **a** died for the work of Christ, *1581*

ALMS (KJV) See ACTS OF RIGHTEOUSNESS, GIVE TO NEEDY, TO THE POOR

ALMSDEEDS (KJV) See HELPING THE POOR

ALMUGWOOD (3) [ALGUM]

1Ki 10:11 they brought great cargoes of **a** 523+6770
10:12 The king used the **a** to make supports 523+6770
10:12 So much **a** has never been imported 523+6770

ALOES (5)

Nu 24: 6 like **a** planted by the LORD, 193
Ps 45: 8 with myrrh and **a** and cassia; 189
Pr 7:17 with myrrh, **a** and cinnamon. 193
SS 4:14 with myrrh and **a** and all the finest spices. 189
Jn 19:39 a mixture *of* myrrh and **a,** *264*

ALONE (123) [LONELY]

Ge 2:18 "It is not good for the man to be **a.** 963+4200
32:24 So Jacob was left **a,** 963+4200
Ex 4:26 So the LORD **let** him **a.** 8332
14:12 **Leave** us **a;** let us serve the Egyptians 2532+4946
18:14 Why do you **a** sit as judge, 963+4200
18:18 you cannot handle it **a.** 963+4200
21: 3 If he comes **a,** he is to go free alone; 928+1727+2257
21: 3 If he comes alone, he is to go free **a;** 928+1727+2257
24: 2 but Moses **a** is to approach the LORD; 963+4200
32:10 Now **leave** me **a** so that my anger may burn 5663
Lev 13:46 He must live **a;** 970
Nu 11:17 so that you will not have to carry it **a.** 963+4200
18: 1 and you and your sons **a** are to bear NIH
Dt 1: 9 a burden *for* me to carry **a.** 963+4200
8: 3 not live on bread **a** but on every word 963+4200
9:14 **Let** me **a,** so that I may destroy them 8332
16:20 Follow justice and **justice** *a,* AIT
32:12 The LORD **a** led him; 970
33:28 So Israel will live in safety **a;** 970
Jdg 3:20 approached him while he was sitting **a** 963+4200
1Sa 21: 1 and asked, "Why are you **a?** 963+4200
25:24 "My lord, let the blame be on **me a.** 638+3276
2Sa 16:11 this Benjamite! **Leave** him **a;** 5663
18:24 he looked out, he saw a man running **a.** 963+4200
18:25 The king said, "If he is **a,** 963+4200
18:26 "Look, another man running **a!**" 963+4200
1Ki 3:18 also had a baby. We were **a;** 3481
8:39 you know his heart (for you **a** know 963+4200
11:29 two of them were **a** out in the country, 963+4200
2Ki 4:27 but the man of God said, **"Leave** her **a!** 8332
19:15 you **a** are God over all the kingdoms of 963+4200
19:19 on earth may know that you **a,** 963+4200
23:18 **"Leave** it **a,"** he said. 5663
2Ch 6:30 you know his heart (for you **a** know 963+4200
Ezr 4: 3 We **a** will build it for the LORD, 3480
Ne 9: 6 You **a** are the LORD. 963+4200
Est 4:13 because you are in the king's house you **a** NIH
Job 7:16 **Let** me **a;** my days have no meaning. 2532
7:19 or **let** me **a** even for an instant? 8332
9: 8 He **a** stretches out the heavens 963+4200
14: 6 So look away from him and **let** him **a,** 2532
15:19 (to whom **a** the land was given 963+4200
19: 4 my error remains **my** concern *a.* AIT
21:14 Yet they say to God, **'Leave us a!** 4946+6073
22:17 They said to God, **'Leave us a!** 4946+6073
23:13 he stands **a,** and who can oppose him? 285+928
28:23 to it and **he a** knows where it dwells, 2085
Ps 4: 8 for you **a,** O LORD, 970+4200
62: 1 My soul finds rest in God **a;** 421
62: 2 He **a** is my rock and my salvation; 421
62: 5 in God **a;** my hope comes from him. 421
62: 6 He **a** is my rock and my salvation; 421
71:16 I will proclaim your righteousness, yours **a.** 963+4200
72:18 who **a** does marvelous deeds. 963+4200
76: 7 **You a** are to be feared. 911+911
83:18 you **a** are the Most High over all the earth. 963+4200
86:10 you **a** are God. 963+4200
102: 7 I have become like a bird **a** on a roof. 969
136: 4 to him who **a** does great wonders, 963+4200
148:13 for his name **a** is exalted; 963+4200
Pr 5:17 Let them be yours **a,** 963+4200
9:12 if you are a mocker, you **a** will suffer." 963+4200
Ecc 4: 8 There was a man **all a;** 401+9108
4:11 But how can **one** keep warm *a?* AIT
SS 4: 2 Each has its twin; not one of them is **a.** 8891
6: 6 Each has its twin, not one of them is **a.** 8891
Isa 2:11 the LORD **a** will be exalted in that day. 963+4200
2:17 the LORD **a** will be exalted in that day, 963+4200
5: 8 till no space is left and you live **a** in 963+4200
26:13 but your name **a** do we honor. 963+4200
37:16 you **a** are God over all the kingdoms of 963+4200
37:20 on earth may know that you **a,** 963+4200
44:24 who **a** stretched out the heavens, 963+4200
45:24 'In the LORD **a** are righteousness NIH
49:21 I was left **all a,** but these— 963+4200
63: 3 "I have trodden the winepress **a;** 963+4200
Jer 15:17 I sat **a** because your hand was on me 970
41: 8 So *he* **let** them **a** and did not kill them 2532
49:31 its people live **a.** 970
La 3:28 Let him sit **a** in silence, 970
Eze 9: 8 While they were killing and I *was* **left a,** 8636
14:16 They **a** would be saved, 963+4200
14:18 They **a** would be saved. 963+4200
37: 3 I said, "O Sovereign LORD, **you** *a* know." AIT
44:16 **They** *a* are to enter my sanctuary; AIT
44:16 **they** *a* are to come near my table to minister AIT
Da 10: 8 I was left **a,** gazing at this great vision; 963+4200
11: 8 **leave** the king of the North **a.** 4946+6641
Hos 4:17 Ephraim is joined to idols; **leave** him **a!** 5663
8: 9 to Assyria like a wild donkey **wandering a.** 969
Mt 4: 4 'Man does not live on bread **a,** *3668*
14:23 When evening came, he was there **a,** *3668*
27:49 The rest said, "Now **leave** him **a.** *918*
Mk 2: 7 Who can forgive sins but God **a?"** *1651*
4:10 When he was **a,** *2848+3668*
4:34 when he was **a** with his own disciples, *2625+2848*
6:47 and he was **a** on land. *3668*
9: 2 where they were all **a.** *2625*
10:18 "No one is good—except God **a.** *1651*
14: 6 **"Leave her a,"** said Jesus. *918*
15:36 "Now **leave** him **a.** *918*
Lk 4: 4 'Man does not live on bread **a.'** " *3668*
5:21 Who can forgive sins but God **a?"** *3668*
9:36 they found that Jesus was **a.** *3668*
13: 8 **'leave** it **a** for one more year, *918*
18:19 "No one is good—except God **a.** *1651*
Jn 6:22 but that they had gone away **a.** *3668*
8:16 my decisions are right, because I am not **a.** *3668*
8:29 he has not left me **a,** *3667*
12: 7 **"Leave her a,"** Jesus replied. *918*
16:32 You will leave me **all a.** *3667*
16:32 Yet I am not **a,** for my Father is with me. *3668*
17:20 "My prayer is not for them **a.** *3667*
Ac 5:38 **Leave** these men **a!** *923*
Ro 4:23 credited to him" were written not for him **a,** *3668*
14: 7 of us lives to himself **a** and none of us dies *NIG*
14: 7 and none of us dies to himself **a.** *NIG*
1Co 7: 4 not belong to her **a** but also to her husband. *NIG*
7: 4 not belong to him **a** but also to his wife. *NIG*
1Ti 5: 5 in need and **left all a** puts her hope *3670*
6:16 who **a** is immortal and who lives *3668*
Jas 2:24 by what he does and not by faith **a.** *3667*
Rev 15: 4 For you **a** are holy. *3668*

ALONG (307) [ALONGSIDE]

Ge 1:24 livestock, creatures that move **a** the ground, NIH
1:25 the **creatures that move** *a* the ground AIT
1:26 the creatures that move **a** the ground." 6584
2:14 it **runs a** the east side of Asshur. 2143
6: 7 **creatures that move a the ground,** 8254
6:20 and of every kind of **creature that moves** *a* AIT
7: 8 and of all creatures that move **a** the ground, 6584
7:14 every creature that moves **a** the ground 6584
7:23 and animals and the creatures that move **a** NIH
8:17 all the creatures that move **a** the ground— 6584
8:19 that move **a** the ground and all the birds— NIH
9: 2 *that* **moves a** the ground, and upon all 8253
15: 9 **a with** a dove and a young pigeon." 2256
18:16 and Abraham **walked a** with them 2143
24:59 **a with** her nurse and Abraham's servant 2256
31:18 **a with** all the goods he had accumulated 2256
33:14 while I **move a** slowly at the pace of 5633
43: 4 If you will send our brother **a with** us, 907
43: 8 the boy **a with** me and we will go at once, 907
44: 2 **a with** the silver for his grain." 2256
46:32 tend livestock, and *they have* **brought** *a* AIT
48: 1 and Ephraim **a with** him. 6640
49:17 a viper **a** the path, 6584
49:30 **a** with the field. NIH
50:13 **a with** the field. 907
50:22 **a with** all his father's family. 2256
Ex 2: 3 the child in it and put it among the reeds **a** 6584
2: 5 and her attendants were walking **a** 6584
2:17 Some shepherds **came a** 995
7:24 And all the Egyptians dug **a** the Nile 6017
10:10 **a with** your women and children! 2256
12: 8 **a with** bitter herbs, 6584
14: 7 **a with** all the other chariots of Egypt, 2256
18: 8 and about all the hardships they had met **a** 928
23:18 to me **a with** anything containing yeast. 6584
23:20 to guard you **a** the way and to bring you to 928
26: 4 Make loops of blue material **a** the edge of 6584
26:10 Make fifty loops **a** the edge of 6584
26:10 and also **a** the edge of the end curtain in 6584
28: 1 **a with** his sons Nadab and Abihu, 907
29: 3 **a with** the bull and the two rams. 2256
29:25 on the altar **a with** the burnt offering for 6584
34:25 to me **a with** anything containing yeast, 6584
36:11 Then they made loops of blue material **a** 6584
36:17 Then they made fifty loops **a** the edge of 6584
36:17 and also **a** the edge of the end curtain in 6584
Lev 5: 2 **creatures that move a the ground—** 9238
7:12 then **a with** this thank offering he is 6584
7:13 **A with** his fellowship offering 6584
11:31 Of all those *that* **move a** the ground, 9238
14:10 **a with** three-tenths of an ephah 2256
14:12 **a with** the log of oil; 2256
20:25 or anything that **moves a** the ground— 8253
24: 7 **A** each row put some pure incense as 6584
Nu 1:47 were not counted **a with** the others. 928+9348
2:33 were not counted **a with** the other Israelites, 928+9348
5: 8 to the priest, **a with** the ram 963+4200+4946
13:23 **a with** some pomegranates and figs. 2256
13:29 Canaanites live near the sea and **a** the 3338+6584
14:25 and set out toward the desert *a* the **route** *to* AIT
15:24 **a with** its prescribed grain offering 2256
16:46 **a with** fire from the altar, 2256
20:17 *We will* **travel a** the king's highway and 2143
20:19 "We will go **a** the main road, 928
21: 1 heard that Israel *was* **coming** *a* the road AIT
21: 4 **traveled** from Mount Hor *a* AIT
21:15 of Ar and lie **a** the border of Moab." 4200
21:22 We will travel **a** the king's highway 928
21:33 Then they turned and **went up** *a* the road AIT
22: 1 of Moab and camped **a** the Jordan across 4200
26:10 and swallowed them **a with** Korah, 2256
26:62 not counted **a with** the other Israelites 928+9348
28: 8 **a** with the same kind of grain offering NIH
31: 6 **a with** Phinehas son of Eleazar, the priest, 2256
33:49 There on the plains of Moab they camped **a** 6584
34: 3 of the Desert of Zin **a** the border of Edom. 6584
34:11 and continue **a** the slopes east of the Sea 6584
34:12 down **a** the Jordan and end at the Salt Sea. 2025
Dt 1: 7 in the Negev and **a** the coast, 928
1:40 **set out** toward the desert *a* the route AIT
2: 1 **set out** toward the desert *a* the route AIT
2: 8 and **traveled a** the desert road of Moab. 6296
2:37 the land **a** the course of the Jabbok nor that 3338
3: 1 and **went up** *a* the road toward Bashan, AIT
4:18 like any creature that moves **a** the ground 928
6: 7 when you sit at home and when you walk **a** 928
11:19 when you sit at home and when you walk **a** 928
24: 9 to Miriam **a** the way after you came out 928
25:17 to you **a** the way when you came out 928
31: 4 whom he destroyed **a with** their land. 2256
33: 5 **a with** the tribes of Israel. 3480
Jos 2:22 the pursuers had searched all **a** the road 928
5: 1 of the Jordan and all the Canaanite kings **a** 6584
6: 2 **a with** its king and its fighting men. 2256
7:15 **a with** all that belongs to him. 2256

Jos 9: 1 the western foothills, and **a** the entire coast 928
10:10 Israel **pursued** them *a* the road going up AIT
15: 4 *It* then **passed a** to Azmon and joined 6296
15: 7 It **continued a** to the waters of En Shemesh 6296
15: 8 Then it ran up the Valley of Ben Hinnom **a** 448
15:10 ran **a** the northern slope of Mount Jearim 448
15:11 **passed a** *to* Mount Baalah 6296
17: 4 Joshua gave them an inheritance **a with** 928+9348
18:14 on the south the boundary turned south **a** 4200
18:16 the Hinnom Valley **a** the southern slope of 448
Jdg 5:10 and you who walk **a** the road, 6584
11:18 passed **a** the eastern side of the country 4946
11:26 and all the towns **a** the Arnon. 3338+6584
14: 9 with his hands and ate as *he* **went a.** 2143+2143
18:20 and the carved image and went **a with** 928+7931
20:45 the Israelites cut down five thousand men **a** 928
Ru 2: 9 and **follow a** after the girls. 2143
4: 1 the kinsman-redeemer he had mentioned **came a,** 6296
1Sa 1:24 **a with** a three-year-old bull, 928
6:11 the cart and **a** with it the chest containing NIH
7:11 slaughtering them **a** the way to NIH
15: 6 so that I do not destroy you **a with** them; 6640
17:18 **Take a** these ten cheeses to the commander 995
17:52 Their dead were strewn **a** 928
18: 4 **a with** his tunic, and even his sword, 2256
19:23 and *he* **walked a** prophesying until 2143+2143
23:26 Saul was going **a** one side of the mountain, 4946
24: 3 He came to the sheep pens **a** the way; 6584
29:10 Now get up early, **a with** 2256
31: 7 Israelites **a** the valley and those across 928+6298
2Sa 5:11 **a with** cedar logs and carpenters 2256
8: 3 to restore his control **a** the Euphrates River. 928
15:18 **a with** all the Kerethites and Pelethites; 2256
15:19 "Why should you come **a with** us? 907
16:13 So David and his men continued **a** the road 928
16:13 along the road while Shimei was going **a** 928
19:17 a thousand Benjamites, **a with** Ziba, 2256
1Ki 6:10 he built the side rooms all **a** the temple. 6584
9:25 burning incense before the LORD **a with** 907
10:22 of trading ships at sea **a with** the ships 6640
18: 7 Obadiah was **walking a,** Elijah met him. 928+2006+2021
2Ki 2:11 were **walking a** and talking *together,* 2143+2143
2:23 As he was walking **a** the road, 928
4:42 **a with** some heads of new grain. 2256
6:30 As he went **a** the wall, the people looked, 6584
10:16 Then *he* **had** him **ride a** in his chariot. 8206
14: 9 Then a wild beast in Lebanon **came a** 6296
15:25 **a with** Argob and Arieh, 907
25:11 **a with** the rest of the populace 2256
1Ch 7:29 **A** the borders of Manasseh were Beth Shan, 6584
14: 1 **a with** cedar logs, 2256
18: 3 when he went to establish his control **a** 928
25: 7 **A with** their relatives— 6640
2Ch 21: 4 put all his brothers to the sword **a with** 1685+2256
25:18 Then a wild beast in Lebanon **came a** 6296
30:25 **a with** the priests and Levites 2256
35: 9 Conaniah **a with** Shemaiah and Nethanel, 2256
Ezr 1:11 Sheshbazzar **brought** all these **a** when 6590
2:70 **a with** some of the other people, 2256
8:31 from enemies and bandits **a** the way. 6584
10:14 **a with** the elders and judges of each town, 6640
Ne 4:19 from each other **a** the wall. 6584
7: 2 **a with** Hananiah the commander of 2256
7:73 **a with** certain of the people and the rest of 2256
8:13 **a** with the priests and the Levites, NIH
9:24 to them, **a with** their kings and the peoples 2256
12:33 **a with** Azariah, Ezra, Meshullam, 2256
Est 5:12 And she has invited me **a with** 6640
9:29 **a with** Mordecai the Jew, 2256
Job 11:10 "If *he* **comes a** and confines you in prison 2736
39:23 **a** with the flashing spear and lance. NIH
40:15 which I made **a with** you and which feeds 6640
42:15 an inheritance **a with** their brothers. 928+9348
Ps 26: 9 Do not take away my soul **a with** sinners, 6640
58: 8 Like a slug melting away *as it* **moves a,** 2143
87: 4 Philistia too, and Tyre, **a with** Cush— 6640
140: 5 of their net and have set traps for me **a** 3338+4200
Pr 1:11 If they say, "Come **a with** us; 907
1:15 do not go **a with** them, 907
4:11 of wisdom and lead you **a** straight paths. 928
7: 8 **walking a** *in* the direction of her house 7575
8: 2 On the heights **a** the way, 6584
8:20 **a** the paths of justice, 928+9348
12:28 **a** that path is immortality. 2006
28:10 the upright **a** an evil path will fall 928
Ecc 10: 3 Even as he walks **a** the road, 928
12: 5 and the grasshopper **drags himself a** 6022
Isa 3:16 **walking a** with outstretched necks, 2143
3:16 **tripping a with mincing steps,** 2143+2256+3262
5:18 *those who* **draw** sin **a** with cords of deceit, 5432
9: 1 by the way of the sea, **a** the Jordan— 6298
14:11 **a** with the noise of your harps; NIH
15: 8 Their outcry **echoes a** the border of Moab; 5938
18: 1 the land of whirring wings **a** the rivers 4946+6298
19: 7 also the plants **a** the Nile, 6584
19: 7 Every **sown field** *a* the Nile, AIT
19:24 **a with** Egypt and Assyria, 4200
23:10 Till your land as **a** the Nile, NIH
42:16 **a** unfamiliar paths I will guide them; 928
59:10 Like the blind *we* **grope a** the wall, 1779
59:19 that the breath of the LORD **drives a.** 5674
60: 8 "Who are these *that* **fly a** like clouds, 6414
Jer 19: 1 Take **a** some of the elders of the people and NIH
23:39 of my presence **a with** the city I gave to you 2256
26:22 **a with** some other men. 907
27:20 **a with** all the nobles of Judah 2256
32:29 they will burn it down, **a with** the houses 2256
39: 9 **a with** those who had gone over to him, 2256
41: 9 the men he had killed **a with** Gedaliah 928+3338
41:10 the king's daughters **a with** all 2256
44:15 **a with** all the women who were present— 2256
49:18 **a with** their neighboring towns," 2256
50:40 and Gomorrah **a with** 2256
52:15 **a with** the rest of the craftsmen 2256
Eze 1:20 the wheels would rise **a with** them, 4200+6645
1:21 the wheels rose **a with** them, 4200+6645
16:53 and your fortunes **a with** them, 928+9348
20:40 **a with** all your holy sacrifices. 928
21:12 They are thrown to the sword **a with** 907
23:42 from the desert **a with** men from the rabble, 448
25:10 I will give Moab **a with** the Ammonites to 6584
25:16 and destroy those **remaining** *a* the coast. AIT
30: 5 by the sword **a with** Egypt. 907
38:20 every creature that moves **a** the ground, 6584
39: 2 I will turn you around and **drag** you **a.** 9255
40:14 *He* **measured** *a* the faces of AIT
40:17 there were thirty rooms **a** the pavement. 448
42:10 On the south side **a** the length of the wall 928
45:24 **a with** a hin of oil for each ephah. 2256
46: 5 **a with** a hin of oil for each ephah. 2256
46: 7 **a with** a hin of oil with each ephah. 2256
46:11 **a with** a hin of oil for each ephah. 2256
47:10 Fishermen will stand **a** the shore; 6584
47:17 **a** the northern border of Damascus, NIH
47:18 **a** the Jordan between Gilead and the land NIH
47:19 then **a** the Wadi [of Egypt] to NIH
47:22 **a with** you they are to be allotted 907
48:20 **a with** the property of the city. 448
48:28 then **a** the Wadi [of Egypt] to NIH
Da 1: 2 **a with** some of the articles from the temple 2256
6:24 **a** with their wives and children. NIH
Hos 2:18 and the **creatures that move** *a* the ground. AIT
9: 8 The prophet, **a with** my God, 6640
Joel 2: 4 *they* **gallop a** like cavalry. 8132
2: 9 they run **a** the wall. 928
Am 3:15 the winter house **a with** the summer house; 6584
4:10 **a with** your captured horses. 6640
Mt 4:15 **a** the Jordan, Galilee of the Gentiles— *4305*
10: 9 *Do* not **take a** any gold or silver or copper *3227*
13: 4 some fell **a** the path, *4123*
13:19 This is the seed sown **a** the path. *4123*
15:29 Jesus left there and went **a** the Sea *4123*
18:16 he will not listen, take one or two others **a,** *3552*
22:16 They sent their disciples to him **a with** *3552*
25: 4 however, took oil in jars **a with** their lamps. *3552*
26:37 **took** Peter and the two sons of Zebedee **a** *4161*
Mk 2:14 *As he* **walked a,** *4135*
2:23 and as his disciples **walked a,** *3847+4472*
4: 1 while all the people were **a** the shore at *2093*
4: 4 some fell **a** the path, *4123*
4:15 Some people are like seed **a** the path, *4123*
4:36 *they* **took** him **a,** just as he was, in the boat. *4161*
8:34 Then he called the crowd to him **a with** *5250*
10:52 and followed Jesus **a** the road. *1877*
11:20 In the morning, *as they* **went a,** *4182*
14:33 He took Peter, James and John **a with** him, *3552*
Lk 1: 7 and they were both **well a** in years. *4581*
1:18 I am an old man and my wife is **well a** *4581*
5:12 a man came **a** who was covered *NIG*
7:11 and a large crowd **went a with** him. *5233*
8: 5 some fell **a** the path; *4123*
8:12 Those **a** the path are the ones who hear, *4123*
9:57 As they were walking **a** the road, *1877*
17: 7 **'Come a** now and sit down to eat'? *4216*
17:11 Jesus **traveled a** the border *1451*
19:36 *As* he **went a,** *4513*
23:33 **a with** the criminals— *2779*
24:15 Jesus himself came up and **walked a with** *5233*
24:17 *as you* **walk a?"** *4344*
Jn 8:25 "Just what I have been claiming **all a,"** *794+3836*
9: 1 *As he* **went a,** he saw a man blind from birth *4135*
11:33 Jews who *had* **come a with** her also weeping, *5302*
Ac 1:14 **a with** the women and Mary the mother *5250*
8:36 As they traveled **a** the road, *2848*
10:23 some of the brothers from Joppa **went a.** *5302*
15: 2 **a with** some other believers, *2779*
16: 3 Paul wanted to take him **a** on the journey, *899+5250*
19:25 **a with** the workmen in related trades, *2779*
21:26 the men and purified himself **a with** them. *5250*
25: 3 an ambush to kill him **a** the way. *2848*
27: 2 from Adramyttium about to sail for ports **a** *2848*
27: 8 We **moved a** the coast with difficulty *4162*
27:13 and sailed **a the shore** of Crete. *839*
27:15 so *we* gave way to it and *were* **driven a.** *5770*
27:17 **let** the ship *be* **driven a.** *5770*
Ro 8:32 how will he not also, **a with** him, *5250*
1Co 7:36 and if she is **getting a in years** *5644*
9: 5 **take** a believing wife **a** *4310*
16:11 I am expecting him **a with** the brothers. *3552*
2Co 8:18 And we are sending **a with** him *3552*
12:19 Have you been thinking **all a** *4093*
Gal 2: 1 *I* **took** Titus **a** also. *5221*
3: 9 So those who have faith are blessed **a with** *5250*
Eph 4:31 **a with** every form of malice. *5250*
Php 4: 3 **a with** Clement and the rest *3552*
1Ti 1:14 **a with** the faith and love that are *3552*
2Ti 2:22 **a with** those who call on the Lord out of *3552*
Heb 11:25 He chose *to be* **mistreated a with** the people *5156*
2Pe 1:21 *as they were* **carried** *a* by the Holy Spirit. *AIT*
3Jn 1: 2 even as your soul **is getting a well.** *2338*
Jude 1:12 **blown a** by the wind; *4195*
Rev 17:12 as kings **a with** the beast. *3552*

ALONGSIDE (5) [ALONG]

Ex 20:23 Do not make any gods to be **a** me; 907
Nu 21:13 They set out from there and camped **a** 4946+6298
1Ch 26:16 Guard was **a of** guard: 4200+6645
Eze 27: 9 the ships of the sea and their sailors came **a** 928
48:13 **"A** the territory of the priests, 4200+6645

ALOOF (3)

Job 21:16 I **stand a** from the counsel of the wicked. 8178
22:18 I **stand a** from the counsel of the wicked. 8178
Ob 1:11 On the day you stood **a** 4946+5584

ALOTH (1)

1Ki 4:16 Baana son of Hushai—in Asher and in **A;** 6599

ALOUD (33) [LOUD]

Ge 27:38 Then Esau wept **a.** 5951+7754
29:11 Jacob kissed Rachel and began to weep **a.** 906+5951+7754
Nu 14: 1 community raised their voices and **wept a.** 1134
Jdg 2: 4 the people wept **a,** 906+5951+7754
Ru 1: 9 Then she kissed them and they wept **a** 5951+7754
1Sa 11: 4 they all wept **a.** 906+5951+7754
24:16 And he wept **a.** 5951+7754
30: 4 So David and his men wept **a** 906+5951+7754
2Sa 3:32 the king wept **a** at Abner's tomb. 906+5951+7754
13:19 **weeping a** as she went. 2410
15:23 The whole countryside wept **a** as all 1524+7754
19: 4 The king covered his face and cried **a,** 1524+7754
Ezr 3:12 wept **a** when they saw the foundation 928+1524+7754
Ne 8: 3 *He* **read** it **a** from daybreak till noon 7924
13: 1 Book of Moses **was read a** in the hearing 7924
Job 2:12 they began to weep **a,** 5951+7754
Ps 3: 4 To the LORD I cry **a,** 7754
26: 7 proclaiming **a** your praise and telling 928+7754
81: 1 **shout a** to the God of Jacob! 8131
95: 1 *let us* **shout a** to the Rock 8131
142: 1 I cry **a** to the LORD; 7754
Pr 1:20 Wisdom **calls a** in the street, 8264
2: 3 for insight and **cry a** for understanding, 5989+7754
8: 3 at the entrances, *she* **cries a:** 8264
Isa 12: 6 **Shout a** and sing for joy, people of Zion, 7412
33: 7 Look, their brave men **cry a** in the streets; 7590
44:23 **shout a,** O earth beneath. 8131
58: 1 **"Shout it a,** do not hold back. 928+1744+7924
Jer 4: 5 Cry **a** and say: 'Gather together! 4848
51:61 **read** all these words **a.** 7924
Mic 4: 9 Why *do you* now **cry a—** 8131+8275
Zep 3:14 Sing, O Daughter of Zion; **shout a,** 8131
Gal 4:27 break forth and **cry a,** *1066*

ALPHA (3)

Rev 1: 8 "I am the **A** and the Omega," *270*
21: 6 I am the **A** and the Omega, *270*
22:13 I am the **A** and the Omega, *270*

ALPHAEUS (5)

Mt 10: 3 James son *of* **A,** and Thaddaeus; *271*
Mk 2:14 *of* **A** sitting at the tax collector's booth. *271*
3:18 Thomas, James son *of* **A,** Thaddaeus, *271*
Lk 6:15 Thomas, James *son of* **A,** *271*
Ac 1:13 James *son of* **A** and Simon the Zealot, *271*

ALREADY (89) [READY]

Ge 18:11 and Sarah were **a** old and well advanced NIH
28: 9 in addition to the wives **he** *a had.* AIT
33: 9 But Esau said, "I **a have** plenty, my brother. AIT
Ex 1: 5 Joseph **was** *a* in Egypt. AIT
4:14 He is **a** on his way to meet you, 2180
30:13 to those **a counted** is to give a half shekel, AIT
36: 7 what *they a* **had** was more than enough AIT
Lev 13:11 because he is **a** unclean. NIH
27:26 since the firstborn **a** belongs to the LORD; NIH
Nu 14:14 *They have a* **heard** that you, O LORD, AIT
16:47 The plague *had a* **started** among the people, AIT
Dt 14:21 Do not eat anything you find **a dead.** 5577
Jos 18: 7 Manasseh *have a* **received** their inheritance AIT
Jdg 8: 6 "Do you **a** have the hands of Zebah 6964
8:15 'Do you **a** have the hands of Zebah 6964
1Sa 29: 3 He *has a* **been** with me for over a year, AIT
2Sa 13:16 a greater wrong than what *you have a* **done** AIT
2Ch 20: 2 It is **a** in Hazazon Tamar" (that is, En Gedi). 2180
28:13 For our guilt is **a** great, NIH
Ne 5: 5 of our daughters *have a* **been enslaved,** AIT
9:25 wells *a* **dug,** vineyards, AIT
Est 7: 7 realizing that the king *had a* **decided** his fate, AIT
Job 9:29 Since I *am a found* **guilty,** AIT
38:21 Surely you know, for you were **a** born! 255
Ecc 1:10 It was here **a,** long ago; 3893
2:12 What more can the king's successor do than what has **a** been done? 3893
3:15 Whatever is has **a** been, 3893
4: 2 I declared that the dead, who had **a** died, 3893
6:10 Whatever exists has **a** been named, 3893
Isa 16:13 the LORD has **a** spoken concerning Moab. 255+4946

Isa 56: 8 to them besides *those* **a** **gathered."** *AIT*
Da 8: 1 after the one that had **a** appeared to me. 928+2021+9378
Jnh 1:10 because *he had* **a** **told** them so.) *AIT*
Mal 2: 2 Yes, *I have* **a** **cursed** them, *AIT*
Mt 3:10 The ax is **a** at the root of the trees, *2453*
5:28 woman lustfully has **a** committed adultery *2453*
14:15 and it's **a** getting late. *2453*
14:24 but the boat was **a** a considerable distance *2453*
15:32 they have **a** been with me three days *2453*
17:12 But I tell you, Elijah has **a** come, *2453*
Mk 6:35 they said, "and it's **a** very late. *2453*
8: 2 they have **a** been with me three days *2453*
11:11 but since it was **a** late, *2453*
15:44 to hear that he was **a** dead. *2453*
15:44 he asked him if Jesus had **a** died. *4093*
Lk 3: 9 The ax is **a** at the root of the trees, *2453*
6:24 for *you have* **a** **received** your comfort. *AIT*
11: 7 The door is **a** locked, *2453*
12:49 and how I wish it were **a** kindled! *2453*
19:25 " 'Sir,' they said, *'he* **a** **has** ten!' *AIT*
Jn 3:18 not believe stands condemned **a** *2453*
6: 6 he **a** *had* **in mind** what he was going to do. *AIT*
9:22 for **a** the Jews had decided *2453*
9:27 "I have told you **a** and you did not listen. *2453*
11:17 Jesus found that Lazarus had **a** been in *2453*
13: 2 the devil had **a** prompted Judas Iscariot, *2453*
15: 3 You are **a** clean because of *2453*
19:33 to Jesus and found that he was **a** dead, *2453*
Ac 10:41 *by* witnesses whom God *had* **a** **chosen—** *4742*
27: 9 and sailing had **a** become dangerous *2453*
Ro 3: 9 *We have* **a** **made the charge** that Jews *4577*
8:24 Who hopes for what *he* **a** **has?** *AIT*
1Co 3:11 the one *a* **laid,** *AIT*
4: 8 **A** you have all you want! *2453*
4: 8 **A** you have become rich! *2453*
5: 3 And I have **a** passed judgment on *2453*
6: 7 you have been completely defeated **a.** *2453*
7:18 a man *a* **circumcised** when he was called? *AIT*
2Co 10:16 not want to boast about **work a done** *2289*
11: 1 but *you are a* **doing that.** *AIT*
13: 2 **a gave** you a **warning** *4625*
Gal 1: 9 As *we have* **a said,** so now I say again: *4625*
Eph 3: 3 as *I have* **a written** briefly. *4592*
Php 3:12 Not that I have **a** obtained all this, *2453*
3:12 or have **a** been made perfect, *2453*
3:16 up to what *we have a* **attained.** *AIT*
Col 1: 5 in heaven and that *you have* **a heard about** *4578*
1Th 4: 6 as *we have* **a told** you and warned you. *4625*
2Th 2: 2 saying that the day of the Lord *has a* **come.** *AIT*
2: 7 secret power of lawlessness is **a** at work; *2453*
1Ti 5:15 in fact **a** turned away to follow Satan. *2453*
2Ti 2:18 that the resurrection has **a** taken place, *2453*
4: 6 For I am **a** being poured out like *2453*
Heb 8: 4 *for there* **are** *a* men who offer *AIT*
9:11 *of* the good things **that are** *a here,* *AIT*
2Pe 3:17 dear friends, *since* you **a know** this, *4589*
1Jn 2: 8 and the true light is **a** shining. *2453*
4: 3 and even now is **a** in the world. *2453*
Jude 1: 5 Though you **a** know all this, *562*

ALSO (813)

Ge 1:16 He **a** made the stars. 2256
2:12 aromatic resin and onyx are **a** there.) NIH
3: 6 **and a** desirable for gaining wisdom, 2256
3: 6 She **a** gave some to her husband, 1685
3:22 be allowed to reach out his hand and take **a** 1685
4:22 Zillah **a** had a son, Tubal-Cain, 1685
4:26 Seth **a** had a son, and he named him Enosh. 1685
6: 4 in those days—and **a** afterward— 1685
7: 3 **and a** seven of every kind of bird, 1685
9:26 He **a** said, "Blessed be the LORD, 2256
10:21 Sons were **a** born to Shem, 1685
13: 5 **a** had flocks and herds and tents. 1685
13: 7 The Canaanites and Perizzites were **a** living 2256
14:12 They **a** carried off Abram's nephew Lot 2256
15: 7 He **a** said to him, "I am the LORD, 2256
16:11 The angel of the LORD **a** said to her: 2256
17:15 God **a** said to Abraham, 2256
19:25 **and a** the vegetation in the land. 2256
19:35 to drink wine that night **a,** 1685
19:38 The younger daughter **a** had a son, 1685
20: 5 and didn't she **a** say, 'He is my brother'? 1685
21:13 son of the maidservant into a nation **a,** 1685+2256
22:20 "Milcah is **a** a mother; 1685
22:24 whose name was Reumah, **a** had sons: 1685
24:46 So I drank, and she watered the camels **a.** 1685
24:53 he **a** gave costly gifts to her brother and 2256
24:64 Rebekah **a** looked up and saw Isaac. 2256
25:30 (That is why he was **a** called Edom.) NIH
26:21 but they quarreled over that one **a;** 1685
26:34 **and a** Basemath daughter of Elon 2256
27:16 She **a** covered his hands and 2256
29:27 then we will give you the younger one **a,** 1685
29:30 Jacob lay with Rachel **a,** 1685
31:49 It was **a** called Mizpah, because he said, 2256
31:51 Laban **a** said to Jacob, "Here is this heap, 2256
32: 1 Jacob **a** went on his way, 2256
32:11 and **a** the mothers with their children. NIH
32:19 He **a** instructed the second, 1685
35:12 The land I gave to Abraham and Isaac I **a** NIH
35:14 he **a** poured oil on it. 2256
36: 3 **a** Basemath daughter of Ishmael and sister 2256
36:12 Esau's son Eliphaz **a** had 2256
38:10 so he put him to death **a.** 1685
41:22 "In my dreams I **a** saw seven heads 2256
42: 5 for the famine was in the land of Canaan **a.** NIH
43:13 Take your brother **a** and go back to the man 2256
43:15 the amount of silver, **and** Benjamin **a.** 2256
43:22 We have **a** brought additional silver with us 2256
44: 5 the cup my master drinks from **and a** uses 2256
45:19 "You are **a** directed to tell them, 'Do this: 2256
45:21 **and** he **a** gave them provisions 2256
46: 6 They **a** took with them their livestock and 2256
47: 4 They **a** said to him, 2256
47:12 Joseph **a** provided his father 2256
50: 9 Chariots and horsemen **a** went up with him. 1685
50:23 **A** the children of Makir son 1685
Ex 3:15 God **a** said to Moses, "Say to the Israelites, 6388
4:28 **and a** about all 2256
4:30 He **a** performed the signs before the people, 2256
6: 2 God **a** said to Moses, "I am the LORD. 2256
6: 4 I **a** established my covenant with them 1685+2256
7:11 and the Egyptian magicians **a** did 1685
8: 7 they **a** made frogs come up on the land 2256
8:32 But this time **a** Pharaoh hardened his heart 1685
12:32 And **a** bless me." 1685
14:19 The pillar of cloud **a** moved from in front 2256
16: 8 Moses **a** said, "You will know that it was 2256
21:29 the bull must be stoned and the owner **a** 1685
21:31 This law **a** applies if the bull gores a son NIH
25:25 **A** make around it a rim a handbreadth wide 2256
26:10 the edge of the end curtain in one set **and a** 2256
26:26 **"A** make crossbars of acacia wood: 2256
26:29 **A** overlay the crossbars with gold. 2256
27:11 The north side shall **a** be 4027
27:13 the courtyard shall **a** be fifty cubits wide. 2256
28:30 **A** put the Urim and the Thummim in 2256
29:43 there **a** I will meet with the Israelites, 2256
30:20 **A,** when they approach the altar to minister 196
31: 6 **A** I have given skill to all the craftsmen 2256
31:10 **and a** the woven garments, 2256
35:28 They **a** brought spices and olive oil for 2256
36:12 They **a** made fifty loops on one curtain NIH
36:17 the edge of the end curtain in one set **and a** 2256
36:31 They **a** made crossbars of acacia wood: 2256
36:34 They **a** overlaid the crossbars with gold. 2256
37:12 They **a** made around it a rim 2256
37:29 They **a** made the sacred anointing oil and 2256
38:11 The north side was **a** a hundred cubits long 2256
38:13 toward the sunrise, was **a** fifty cubits wide. 2256
39: 1 They **a** made sacred garments for Aaron, 2256
Lev 6:19 The LORD **a** said to Moses, 2256
8: 7 He **a** tied the ephod to him 2256
8:16 Moses **a** took all the fat around 2256
8:24 Moses **a** brought Aaron's sons forward 2256
8:29 He **a** took the breast— 2256
9:17 He **a** brought the grain offering, 2256
16:25 He shall **a** burn the fat of the sin offering 2256
20:18 **and** she has **a** uncovered it. 2256
22: 4 He will **a** be unclean 2256
23:39 **and** the eighth day **a** 2256
25:45 You may **a** buy some of 1685+2256
26:39 **a** because of their fathers' sins they will waste away. 677+2256
Nu 3:11 The LORD **a** said to Moses, 2256
3:44 The LORD **a** said to Moses, 2256
4:22 "Take a census **a** of the Gershonites 1685
5:15 He must **a** take an offering of a tenth of 2256
7: 1 He **a** anointed and consecrated the altar 2256
10:10 **A** at your times of rejoicing— 2256
11: 5 **a** the cucumbers, melons, leeks, NIH
11: 9 the manna **a** came down. NIH
11:26 **Yet** the Spirit **a** rested on them, 2256
12: 2 "Hasn't he **a** spoken through us?" 1685
15:10 **A** bring half a hin of wine as 2256
16: 8 Moses **a** said to Korah, "Now listen, 2256
16:13 **And** now you **a** want to lord it over us? 1685
16:17 and Aaron are to present your censers **a."** 2256
18:11 "This **a** is yours: 2256
18:28 In this way you **a** will present an offering 1685
19: 8 The man who burns it must **a** 2256
19:10 of the heifer must **a** wash his clothes, 2256
19:18 must **a** sprinkle anyone who has touched 2256
19:21 of cleansing must **a** wash his clothes, 2256
26:58 These **a** were Levite clans: NIH
31: 8 They **a** killed Balaam son of Beor with 2256
31:23 **But** it must **a** be purified with the water 421
Dt 1:37 of you the LORD became angry with me **a** 1685
3: 3 So the LORD our God **a** gave 1685
3: 5 and there were **a** a great many 963+4200
3:13 The rest of Gilead **and a** all of Bashan, 2256
9:21 **A** I took that sinful thing of yours, 2256
9:22 You **a** made the LORD angry at Taberah, 2256
10: 1 **A** make a wooden chest. 2256
10:10 the LORD listened to me at this time **a.** 1685
14: 8 The pig is **a** unclean; 2256
22: 9 not only the crops you plant **but a** the fruit 2256
28:61 The LORD will **a** bring on you every kind 1685
29:15 the presence of the LORD our God **but a** 2256
31: 3 Joshua **a** will cross over ahead of you, NIH
Jos 8:22 The men of the ambush **a** came out of 2256
10:30 The LORD **a** gave that city and its king 1685
12: 3 He **a** ruled over the eastern Arabah from 2256
13:11 It **a included** Gilead, the territory of 2256
15:19 give me **a** springs of water." 2256
16: 9 It **a** included all the towns 2256
17:11 Manasseh **a** had Beth Shan, 2256
21:23 **A** from the tribe of Dan 2256
24:11 as did **a** the Amorites, Perizzites, 2256
24:12 **a** the two Amorite kings. NIH
Jdg 1: 8 of Judah attacked Jerusalem **a** and took it. 2256
1:15 give me **a** springs of water." 2256
1:18 The men of Judah **a** took Gaza, 2256
1:35 **And** the Amorites were determined **a** 2256
4:10 **and** Deborah **a** went with him. 2256
6:35 and **a** into Asher, Zebulun and Naphtali, 1685
7:25 They **a** captured two of 2256
8:17 He **a** pulled down the tower of Peniel 2256
8:31 who lived in Shechem, **a** bore him a son, 1685
8:35 They **a** failed to show kindness to 2256
9:49 about a thousand men and women, **a** died. 1685
9:57 God **a** made the men of Shechem pay 2256
10: 9 The Ammonites **a** crossed the Jordan 1685
11: 2 Gilead's wife **a** bore him sons, 2256
11:17 They sent **a** to the king of Moab, 1685
18: 7 **A,** they lived a long way from 2256
Ru 1: 5 both Mahlon and Kilion **a** died, 1685
2:18 Ruth **a** brought out 2256
3:15 He **a** said, "Bring me 2256
4:10 I have **a** acquired Ruth the Moabitess, 1685
1Sa 2:28 I **a** gave your father's house all 2256
4:17 **A** your two sons, Hophni and Phinehas, 1685+2256
7:17 **and** there he **a** judged Israel. 2256
10:11 Is Saul **a** among the prophets?" 1685
10:12 "Is Saul **a** among the prophets?" 1685
10:26 Saul **a** went to his home in Gibeah, 1685
12: 5 **and a** his anointed is witness this day, 2256
17:25 He will **a** give him his daughter in marriage 2256
19:20 of God came upon Saul's men and they **a** 1685
19:21 and they **a** prophesied. 1685
19:24 He stripped off his robes and **a** prophesied 1685
19:24 "Is Saul **a** among the prophets?" 1685
22:10 he **a** gave him provisions and the sword 2256
22:19 He **a** put to the sword Nob, 2256
22:23 the man who is seeking your life is seeking mine **a.** NIH
25:43 David had **a** married Ahinoam of Jezreel, 2256
28:19 The LORD will **a** hand over the army 1685
2Sa 2: 3 David **a** took the men who were with him, 2256
2: 9 Ashuri and Jezreel, **and a** over Ephraim, 2256
3:19 Abner **a** spoke to the Benjamites in person. 1685
3:32 All the people wept **a.** 2256
7:11 I will **a** give you rest 2256
7:19 you have **a** spoken about the future of 1685
8: 2 David **a** defeated the Moabites. 2256
8:12 He **a** dedicated the plunder taken 2256
10: 6 **and a** twelve thousand men from Tob. 2256
10:18 He **a** struck down Shobach the commander 2256
11:21 If he asks you this, then say to him, **'A,** 1685
15: 5 **A,** whenever anyone approached him 2256
15:12 he **a** sent for Ahithophel the Gilonite, 2256
15:23 The king **a** crossed the Kidron Valley, 2256
15:27 The king **a** said to Zadok the priest, 2256
17: 5 "Summon **a** Hushai the Arkite, 1685
17:28 They **a** brought wheat and barley, 2256
19:24 **a** went down to meet the king. 2256
19:31 the Gileadite **a** came down from Rogelim 2256
21:20 He **a** was descended from Rapha 1685
23:20 He **a** went down into a pit on a snowy day 2256
24:23 Araunah **a** said to him, 2256
1Ki 1: 6 He was **a** very handsome 1685
1:47 **A,** the royal officials have come 1685+2256
2:44 The king **a** said to Shimei, 2256
3:18 this woman **a** had a baby. 1685
4: 7 Solomon **a** had twelve district governors 2256
4:28 They **a** brought to 2256
4:33 He **a** taught about animals and birds, 2256
6:20 **and** he **a** overlaid the altar of cedar. 2256
6:22 He **a** overlaid with gold the altar 2256
6:25 The second cherub **a** measured ten cubits, 2256
6:30 He **a** covered the floors of both the inner 2256
6:34 He **a** made two pine doors, 2256
7: 8 Solomon **a** made a palace like this hall 2256
7:16 He **a** made two capitals of cast bronze 2256
7:27 He **a** made ten movable stands of bronze; 2256
7:40 He **a** made the basins and shovels 2256
7:48 Solomon **a** made all the furnishings 2256
7:50 the Most Holy Place, and **a** for the doors of NIH
9:23 They were **a** the chief officials in charge NIH
9:26 King Solomon **a** built ships at Ezion Geber, 2256
10:17 He **a** made three hundred small shields 2256
10:26 which he kept in the chariot cities **and a** 2256
10:29 They **a** exported them to all the kings of 2256
11:21 **and** that Joab the commander of the army was **a** dead. 2256
11:26 **A,** Jeroboam son of Nebat rebelled against 2256
12:32 **And** at Bethel he **a** 2256
13: 5 **A,** the altar was split apart 2256
13:11 They **a** told their father what he had said to 2256
14:23 They **a** set up for themselves high places, 1685
15:22 up Geba in Benjamin, **and a** Mizpah. 2256
16: 7 **and a** because he destroyed it. 2256
16:31 **but** he **a** married Jezebel daughter 2256
16:33 Ahab **a** made an Asherah pole 2256
17:20 have you brought tragedy **a** 1685
18:38 **and a** licked up the water in the trench. 2256
19:16 **A,** anoint Jehu son of Nimshi king 2256
20:25 You must **a** raise an army like 2256
20:27 **When** the Israelites were **a** 2256
21:23 **a** concerning Jezebel the LORD says: 1685
22: 5 **But** Jehoshaphat **a** said to the king 2256
22:44 Jehoshaphat was **a** at peace with the king 2256
2Ki 3: 7 He **a** sent this message to Jehoshaphat king 2256
3:18 he will **a** hand Moab over to you. 2256
5:18 **and** I bow there **a—** 2256
7: 8 from it and hid them **a.** 2256
11:17 He **a** made a covenant between the king 2256
13: 6 **A,** the Asherah pole remained standing 1685+2256
14:10 and that of Judah **a?"** 6640

2Ki 14:14 He **a** took hostages and returned 2256
17:32 **but** they **a** appointed all sorts 2256
17:33 **but** they **a** served their own gods 2256
21: 3 he **a** erected altars to Baal and made 2256
21:16 Manasseh **a** shed so much innocent blood 2256
22: 6 **A** have them purchase timber 2256
23: 7 He **a** tore down the quarters of 2256
23:13 The king **a** desecrated the high places 2256
23:15 **and** burned the Asherah pole **a.** 2256
23:27 "I will remove Judah **a** from my presence 1685
24:15 He **a** took from Jerusalem to Babylon 2256
24:16 The king of Babylon **a** deported to Babylon 2256
25:14 They **a** took away the pots, shovels, 2256
25:19 He **a** took the secretary who was chief 2256
25:25 and assassinated Gedaliah **and a** the men 2256
1Ch 1:51 Hadad **a** died. 2256
2:49 She **a** gave birth to Shaaph the father 2256
3: 6 There were **a** Ibhar, Elishua, Eliphelet, 2256
3:20 There were **a** five others: 2256
4:36 **a** Elioenai, Jaakobah, Jeshohaiah, 2256
4:41 the Hamites in their dwellings **and a** 2256
5:21 **a** took one hundred thousand people captive 2256
6:71 in Bashan **and a** Ashtaroth, together 2256
11:22 He **a** went down into a pit on a snowy day 2256
12:16 and some men from Judah **a** came to David 2256
12:38 the rest of the Israelites were **a** of one mind 1685
12:40 **A,** their neighbors from as far away 1685+2256
13: 2 **and a** to the priests and Levites who are 2256
15:24 and Jehiah were **a** to be doorkeepers for 2256
15:27 David **a** wore a linen ephod. 2256
16:38 He **a** left Obed-Edom 2256
16:38 Obed-Edom son of Jeduthun, **and a** Hosah, 2256
17:10 I will **a** subdue all your enemies. 2256
18: 2 David **a** defeated the Moabites, 2256
19:18 He **a** killed Shophach the commander 2256
20: 6 He **a** was descended from Rapha. 1685
21: 7 This command was **a** evil in the sight 2256
22: 1 **and a** the altar of burnt offering for Israel." 2256
22: 4 He **a** provided more cedar logs than could 2256
23: 2 He **a** gathered together all the leaders 2256
23:30 They were **a** to stand every morning 2256
24:31 They **a** cast lots, 1685
26: 4 Obed-Edom **a** had sons: 2256
26: 6 His son Shemaiah **a** had sons, 2256
26: 7 his relatives Elihu and Semakiah were **a** NIH
28:18 He **a** gave him the plan for the chariot, 2256
28:20 David **a** said to Solomon his son, 2256
29: 9 David the king **a** rejoiced greatly. 1685+2256
2Ch 1:12 **And** I will **a** give you wealth, 2256
1:14 which he kept in the chariot cities **and a** 2256
1:17 They **a** exported them to all the kings of 2256
2: 8 "Send me **a** cedar, 2256
3: 9 He **a** overlaid the upper parts with gold. 2256
3:11 while its other wing, **a** five cubits long, NIH
3:12 and its other wing, **a** five cubits long, NIH
3:16 He **a** made a hundred pomegranates 2256
4: 8 **a** made a hundred gold sprinkling bowls. 2256
4:11 He **a** made the pots and shovels 2256
4:19 Solomon **a** made all the furnishings 2256
8: 4 He **a** built up Tadmor in the desert and all 2256
8:10 They were **a** King Solomon's chief officials 2256
8:14 He **a** appointed the gatekeepers 2256
9:10 they **a** brought algumwood 1685+2256
9:14 **A** all the kings of Arabia and the governors 2256
9:16 He **a** made three hundred small shields 2256
9:25 which he kept in the chariot cities **and a** 2256
14:15 They **a** attacked the camps of the herdsmen 1685+2256
15:16 King Asa **a** deposed his grandmother 1685+2256
17:13 He **a** kept experienced fighting men 2256
18: 4 **But** Jehoshaphat **a** said to the king 2256
19: 8 In Jerusalem **a,** Jehoshaphat appointed 1685+2256
20:25 of equipment and clothing **and a** articles 2256
21:11 He had **a** built high places on the hills 1685
21:13 have **a** murdered your own brothers, 1685+2256
22: 5 He **a** followed their counsel when he went 1685
23:19 He **a** stationed doorkeepers at the gates of 2256
24:12 and **a** workers in iron and bronze to repair 1685
24:14 and for the burnt offerings, **and a** dishes 2256
25: 6 He **a** hired a hundred thousand fighting men from Israel 2256
25:12 The army of Judah **a** 2256
25:19 and that of Judah **a?"** 6640
26:10 He **a** built towers in the desert 2256
27: 5 the same amount **a** in the second 2256
28: 2 of the kings of Israel and **a** made cast idols 1685
28: 5 was **a** given into the hands of the king 1685+2256
28: 8 They **a** took a great deal of plunder, 1685+2256
28:10 **But** aren't you **a** guilty of sins against 8370
29: 7 They **a** shut the doors of the portico 1685
29:27 singing to the LORD began **a,** 2256
30: 1 to all Israel and Judah and **a** wrote letters 1685
30:12 **A** in Judah the hand of God was on 1685
31: 6 of Judah **a** brought a tithe of their herds 1685
31:14 the contributions made to the LORD **and a** 2256
32: 5 He **a** made large numbers of weapons 2256
32:17 king **a** wrote letters insulting the LORD, 2256
32:28 He **a** made buildings to store the harvest 2256
33: 3 he **a** erected altars to the Baals 2256
33:14 he **a** made it much higher. 2256
34:11 They **a** gave money to the carpenters 2256
35: 7 **and a** three thousand cattle— 2256
35: 8 His officials **a** contributed voluntarily to 2256
35: 9 **A** Conaniah along with Shemaiah 2256
36: 7 Nebuchadnezzar **a** took to Babylon articles 2256
36:13 He **a** rebelled against King Nebuchadnezzar, 1685+2256

Ezr 2:65 **and** they **a** had 200 men 2256
5: 4 They **a** asked, "What are the names 10008+10358
5:10 We **a** asked them their names, 10059+10221
6: 5 **A,** the gold and silver articles 10059+10221
7: 7 **a** came up to Jerusalem in the seventh year 2256
7:24 You are **a** to know 10221
8:20 They **a** brought 220 of 2256
8:36 They **a** delivered the king's orders to 2256
Ne 1: 2 **and a** about Jerusalem. 2256
2: 7 I **a** said to him, "If it pleases the king, 2256
2: 9 The king had **a** sent army officers 2256
2:18 I **a** told them about the gracious hand 2256
3: 4 **and** next to him Zadok son of Baana **a** 2256
3:13 They **a** repaired five hundred yards of 2256
3:15 He **a** repaired the wall of the Pool 2256
4:11 **A** our enemies said, 2256
4:22 At that time I **a** said to the people, 1685
5:10 my brothers and my men are **a** lending 1685+2256
5:11 **and a** the usury you are charging them— 2256
5:13 I **a** shook out the folds of my robe and said, 1685
5:15 Their assistants **a** lorded it over the people. 1685
6:14 remember **a** the prophetess Noadiah 1685+2256
6:17 **A,** in those days the nobles 1685
7: 3 **A** appoint residents of Jerusalem as guards, 2256
7:67 **and** they **a** had 245 men 2256
10:35 "We **a** assume responsibility for bringing 2256
10:36 "As it is **a** written in the Law, 2256
12: 8 Sherebiah, Judah, and **a** Mattaniah, who, NIH
12:28 The singers **a** were brought together from 2256
12:31 I **a** assigned two large choirs 2256
12:35 and **a** Zechariah son of Jonathan, NIH
12:42 **and a** Maaseiah, Shemaiah, 2256
12:43 The women and children **a** rejoiced. 1685+2256
12:45 as did **a** the singers and gatekeepers, 2256
12:47 They **a** set aside the portion for 2256
13: 5 **and a** the tithes of grain, 2256
13:10 I **a** learned that the portions assigned to 2256
13:22 Remember me for this **a,** O my God, 1685
13:31 I **a** made provision for contributions 2256
Est 1: 9 Queen Vashti **a** gave a banquet for 1685
1:16 against the king but **a** against all the nobles NIH
1:19 **A** let the king give her royal position 2256
2: 7 This girl, who was **a** known as Esther, NIH
2: 8 Esther **a** was taken to the king's palace 2256
4: 8 He **a** gave him a copy of the text of 2256
8: 9 and the language of each people **and a** to 2256
8:14 **And** the edict was **a** 2256
9: 7 They **a** killed Parshandatha, Dalphon, 2256
9:12 It will **a** be granted." 6388
9:13 to carry out this day's edict tomorrow **a,** 1685
9:16 in the king's provinces **a** assembled 2256
Job 1: 6 and Satan **a** came with them. 1685
2: 1 and Satan **a** came with them 1685
3:18 Captives **a** enjoy their ease; 3480
5:18 For he wounds, **but** he **a** binds up; 2256
5:18 he injures, **but** his hands **a** heal. 2256
13: 2 What you know, I **a** know; 1685
16: 4 I **a** could speak like you, 1685
31:28 then these **a** would be sins to be judged, 1685
32: 3 He was **a** angry with the three friends, 2256
42:13 **And** he **a** had seven sons 2256
Ps 16: 9 my body **a** will rest secure, 677
19:13 Keep your servant **a** from willful sins; 1685
74:16 The day is yours, **and** yours **a** the night; 677
78:20 **But** can he **a** give us food? 1685
84: 6 the autumn rains **a** cover it with pools. 1685
89:11 heavens are yours, **and** yours **a** the earth; 677
89:27 I will **a** appoint him my firstborn, 677
Pr 2:16 It will save you **a** from the adulteress, NIH
9: 2 she has **a** set her table. 677
24:14 **a** that wisdom is **sweet** 4027[S]
24:23 These **a** are sayings of the wise: 1685
31:28 her husband **a,** and he praises her: NIH
Ecc 1:17 **and a** of madness and folly, 2256
2: 1 But that **a** proved to be meaningless. 1685
2: 7 I **a** owned more herds 1685
2:12 **and a** madness and folly. 2256
2:15 "The fate of the fool will overtake me **a.** 1685
3:11 He has **a** set eternity in the hearts of men; 1685
3:18 I **a** thought, "As for men, NIH
4:11 **A,** if two lie down together, 1685
9:13 I **a** saw under the sun this example 1685
12: 9 **but a** he imparted knowledge to the people. 6388
Isa 7:13 Will you try the patience of my God **a?** 1685
7:20 and to take off your beards **a.** 1685
14:10 "You **a** have become weak, as we are; 1685
16: 8 the vines of Sibmah **a.** NIH
19: 7 **a** the plants along the Nile, NIH
21:12 "Morning is coming, but **a** the night. 1685
28: 7 And these **a** stagger from wine and reel 1685
28:29 All this **a** comes from 1685
30:23 He will **a** send you rain for 2256
34:14 the night creatures will **a** repose and find 421
34:15 there **a** the falcons will gather, 421
44:15 **But** he **a** fashions a god and worships it; 677
44:16 He **a** warms himself and says, "Ah! 677
49: 6 I will **a** make you a light for the Gentiles, 2256
57:15 **but a** with him who is contrite and lowly 2256
66: 4 so I **a** will choose harsh treatment for them 1685
66:21 of them **a** to be priests and Levites," 1685
Jer 2:16 **A,** the men of Memphis 1685
2:37 You will **a** leave that place with your hands 1685
3: 8 she **a** went out and committed adultery. 1685
17:19 stand **a** at all the other gates of Jerusalem. 2256
28: 4 I will **a** bring back 2256
29: 7 **A,** seek the peace and prosperity of the city 2256
35: 7 **A** you must never build houses, 2256

Jer 36:29 **A** tell Jehoiakim king of Judah, 2256
39: 6 of Zedekiah before his eyes **and a** killed all 2256
41: 3 Ishmael **a** killed all the Jews who were 2256
43: 6 They **a** led away all the men, 2256
46:14 proclaim it **a** in Memphis and Tahpanhes: 2256
52:10 he **a** killed all the officials of Judah. 1685+2256
52:18 They **a** took away the pots, shovels, 2256
52:25 He **a** took the secretary who was chief 2256
La 4:21 **But** to you **a** the cup will be passed; 1685
Eze 1:10 each **a** had the face of an eagle. 2256
1:19 from the ground, the wheels **a** rose. NIH
1:21 When the creatures moved, they **a** moved; NIH
1:21 the creatures stood still, they **a** stood still; NIH
4:11 **A** measure out a sixth of a hin of water 2256
8:17 Must they **a** fill the land with violence NIH
10:17 the cherubim stood still, they **a** stood still; NIH
16:17 You **a** took the fine jewelry I gave you, 2256
16:19 **A** the food I provided for you— 2256
17:13 He **a** carried away the leading men of 2256
20:12 **A** I gave them my Sabbaths as a sign 1685+2256
20:15 **A** with uplifted hand I swore to them 1685+2256
20:23 **A** with uplifted hand I swore to them 1685
20:25 I **a** gave them over to statutes that were 1685+2256
20:27 In this **a** your fathers blasphemed me 6388
23:26 They will **a** strip you of your clothes 2256
23:38 They have **a** done this to me: 6388
31:17 had **a** gone down to the grave with it, 1685
34:18 Must you **a** trample the rest of your pasture 2256
34:18 Must you **a** muddy the rest with your feet? 2256
36: 7 the nations around you will **a** suffer scorn. NIH
38: 6 **a** Gomer with all its troops, NIH
39:16 (**A** a town called Hamonah will be 1685+2256
40:27 The inner court **a** had a gate facing south, 2256
40:42 There were **a** four tables of dressed stone 2256
41: 2 He **a** measured the outer sanctuary; 2256
41:13 with its walls were **a** a hundred cubits long. NIH
41:26 The side rooms of the temple **a** 2256
43:17 The upper ledge **a** is square, 2256
43:25 you are **a** to provide a young bull and a ram 2256
45:15 **A** one sheep is to be taken from every flock 2256
46:14 You are **a** to provide with it morning 2256
46:16 it will **a** belong to his descendants; NIH
Da 2:26 king asked Daniel (**a** called Belteshazzar), NIH
4:19 Then Daniel (**a** called Belteshazzar) NIH
5:12 and **a** the ability to interpret dreams, NIH
7:20 I **a** wanted to know about the ten horns 10221
11: 8 He will **a** seize their gods, 1685+2256
11:41 He will **a** invade the Beautiful Land. 2256
Hos 4: 6 I **a** reject you as my priests; 2256
4: 6 I **a** will ignore your children. 1685
5: 5 Judah **a** stumbles with them. 1685
6:11 **"A** for you, Judah, a harvest is appointed. 1685
Am 2:11 I **a** raised up prophets from 2256
4: 7 "I **a** withheld rain from you when 1685+2256
7:14 **and** I **a** took care of sycamore-fig trees. 2256
Mic 6: 4 **a** Aaron and Miriam. NIH
Zep 1: 5 and swear by the LORD **and** who **a** swear 2256
Zec 4: 3 **A** there are two olive trees by it, 2256
4: 9 his hands will **a** complete it. 2256
Mt 4: 7 Jesus answered him, "It is **a** written: *4099*
5:39 turn to him the other **a.** *2779*
6:12 as we **a** have forgiven our debtors. *2779*
6:14 your heavenly Father will **a** forgive you. *2779*
6:21 your treasure is, there your heart will be **a.** *2779*
10:32 I will **a** acknowledge him before my Father *2779*
13:26 then the weeds **a** appeared. *2779*
19:28 you who have followed me will **a** sit *2779*
20: 4 'You **a** go and work in my vineyard, *2779*
20: 7 'You **a** go and work in my vineyard.' *2779*
20:10 But each one of them **a** received a denarius. *2779*
21:21 but **a** you can say to this mountain, 'Go, *2779*
21:24 "I will **a** ask you one question. *2779*
23:18 You **a** say, 'If anyone swears by the altar, *2779*
23:26 and then the outside **a** will be clean. *2779*
24:44 So you **a** must be ready, *2779*
25:11 "Later the others **a** came. *2779*
25:17 **So a,** the one with *6058*
25:22 "The man with the two talents **a** came. *2779*
25:44 "They **a** will answer, 'Lord, *2779*
26:13 what she has done will **a** be told, *2779*
26:69 "You **a** were with Jesus of Galilee," *2779*
27:44 the robbers who were crucified with him **a** *2779*
Mk 1:34 He **a** drove out many demons, *2779*
1:38 so I can preach there **a.** *2779*
2:26 And he **a** gave some to his companions." *2779*
4:26 He **a** said, "This is what the kingdom *2779*
4:36 There were **a** other boats with him. *2779*
6:41 He **a** divided the two fish among them all. *2779*
8: 7 he gave thanks for them **a** and told *NIG*
12:21 but he **a** died, leaving no child. *2779*
14: 9 what she has done will **a** be told, *2779*
14:67 "You **a** were with that Nazarene, Jesus," *2779*
15:32 Those crucified with him **a** heaped insults *2779*
15:41 up with him to Jerusalem were **a** there. *NIG*
Lk 1: 3 it seemed good **a** to me to write *2779*
1: 5 his wife Elizabeth was **a** a descendant *NIG*
2: 4 So Joseph **a** went up from the town *2779*
2:36 There was **a** a prophetess, Anna, *2779*
3:12 Tax collectors **a** came to be baptized. *2779*
4:43 the kingdom of God to the other towns **a,** *2779*
6: 4 And he **a** gave some to his companions." *2779*
6:13 whom he **a** designated apostles: *2779*
6:29 turn to him the other **a.** *2779*
6:39 He **a** told them this parable: *2779*
8: 2 **and a** some women who had been cured *2779*
11: 4 we **a** forgive everyone who sins against us. *2779*
11:30 **a** will the Son of Man be to this generation. *2779*

Lk 11:34 your whole body a is full of light. 2779
11:34 your body a is full of darkness. 2779
11:40 the outside make the inside a? 2779
11:45 when you say these things, you insult us a." 2779
12: 8 the Son of Man will a acknowledge him 2779
12:34 your treasure is, there your heart will be a. 2779
12:40 You a must be ready, 2779
16:10 with very little can a be trusted with much, 2779
16:10 with very little will a be dishonest 2779
16:22 The rich man a died and was buried. 2779
16:28 so that they will not a come to this place 2779
17:10 So you a, when you have done everything you were told to do, 2779
17:26 a will it be in the days of the Son of Man. 2779
18:15 People were a bringing babies to Jesus 2779
18:43 all the people saw it, they a praised God. 2779
20: 3 He replied, "I will a ask you a question. 2779
20:11 but that one a they beat 2779
21: 2 He a saw a poor widow put 1254
22:24 A a dispute arose among them as to which 2779
22:36 take it, and a a bag; 3931
22:58 "You a are one of them." 2779
23: 7 who was a in Jerusalem at that time. 2779
23:32 were a led out with him to be executed. 2779
23:36 The soldiers a came up and mocked him. 2779
Jn 1:45 and about whom the prophets a wrote— NIG
2: 2 and his disciples had a been invited to 2779
3:23 John a was baptizing at Aenon near Salim, 2779
4:12 as did a his sons and his flocks and herds?" 2779
4:45 for they a had been there. 2779
5:19 whatever the Father does the Son a does. 2779
7:10 he went a, not publicly, but in secret. 2779
7:47 "You mean he has deceived you a?" 2779
8:19 you would know my Father a." 2779
9:15 Therefore the Pharisees a asked him 2779
10:16 I must bring them a. 2779
11:16 "Let us a go, that we may die with him." 2779
11:33 the Jews who had come along with her a NIG
11:52 that nation but a for the scattered children 2779
12: 9 only because of him but a to see Lazarus, 2779
12:26 and where I am, my servant a will be. 2779
13:14 you a should wash one another's feet. 2779
14: 1 Trust in God; trust a in me. 2779
14: 3 and take you to be with me that you a may 2779
14:19 Because I live, you a will live. 2779
15:20 they will persecute you a. 2779
15:20 they will obey yours a. 2779
15:27 And you a must testify, 2779
17:20 I pray a for those who will believe in me 2779
17:21 May they a be in us so that 2779
18:18 Peter a was standing with them, 2779
19:35 and he testifies so that you a may believe. 2779
20: 8 the tomb first, a went inside. 2779
Ac 1:23 Joseph called Barsabbas (a known 4005
2:26 my body a will live in hope, 2779
5: 1 a sold a piece of property. NIG
5: 9 and they will carry you out a." NIG
5:16 Crowds gathered a from the towns 2779
6: 5 a Philip, Procorus, Nicanor, Timon, 2779
8:19 "Give me a this ability so that everyone 2779
11: 1 throughout Judea heard that the Gentiles a 2779
11:12 These six brothers a went with me, 2779
11:20 to Antioch and began to speak to Greeks a, 2779
12: 3 he proceeded to seize Peter a. 2779
12:12 of Mary the mother of John, a called Mark, NIG
12:25 taking with them John, a called Mark. NIG
13: 9 Then Saul, who was a called Paul, 2779
15:37 a called Mark, with them, 2779
17:12 as did a a number 2779
17:34 a a woman named Damaris, 2779
19:21 he said, "I must visit Rome a." 2779
19:27 but a that the temple of 2779
20: 4 Gaius from Derbe, Timothy a, 2779
21:13 but a to die in Jerusalem for the name of 2779
22: 5 as a the high priest and all 2779
23:11 so you must a testify in Rome." 2779
23:30 I a ordered his accusers to present 2779
26: 4 and a in Jerusalem. 5445
26:20 and to the Gentiles a, 2779
27:10 and to our own lives a." 2779
Ro 1: 6 And you a are among those who are called 2779
1:15 to preach the gospel a to you who are 2779
1:27 the men a abandoned natural relations 2779
1:32 but a approve of those who practice them. 2779
2:12 the law will a perish apart from the law, 2779
2:15 their consciences a bearing witness, 2779
4: 9 or a for the uncircumcised? 2779
4:12 And he is a the father of 2779
4:12 not only are circumcised but who a walk in 2779
4:16 not only to those who are of the law but a 2779
4:19 and that Sarah's womb was a dead. NIG
4:24 but a for us, 2779
5: 3 but we a rejoice in our sufferings, 2779
5:11 but we a rejoice in God 2779
5:18 so a the result of one act 2779
5:19 so a through the obedience of the one man 2779
5:21 so a grace might reign 2779
6: 5 we will certainly a be united with him 2779
6: 8 we believe that we will a live with him. 2779
7: 4 you a died to the law through the body 2779
8:11 he who raised Christ from the dead will a 2779
8:17 in order that we may a share in his glory. 2779
8:29 For those God foreknew he a predestined 2779
8:30 And those he predestined, he a called; 2779
8:30 those he called, he a justified; 2779
8:30 those he justified, he a glorified. 2779
8:32 how will he not a, along with him, 2779

Ro 8:34 the right hand of God and is a interceding 2779
9:24 whom he a called, 2779
9:24 from the Jews but a from the Gentiles? 2779
11:22 Otherwise, you a will be cut off. 2779
13: 5 of possible punishment but a because 2779
13: 6 This is a why you pay taxes, 2779
16: 5 Greet a the church that meets 2779
1Co 1:16 I a baptized the household of Stephanas; 2779
6:14 and he will raise us a. 2779
7: 4 to her alone but a to her husband. NIG
7: 4 not belong to him alone but a to his wife. NIG
7:37 this man a does the right thing. NIG
10:13 he will a provide a way out so 2779
11:12 so a man is born of woman. 2779
11:23 from the Lord what I a passed on to you: 2779
12:28 a those having gifts of healing, 2083
14:15 but I will a pray with my mind; 2779
14:15 but I will a sing with my mind. 2779
15: 8 and last of all he appeared to me a, 2779
15:18 Then those a who have fallen asleep 2779
15:21 the resurrection of the dead comes a 2779
15:40 There are a heavenly bodies 2779
15:44 there is a a spiritual body. 2779
15:48 so a are those who are of heaven. 2779
16: 4 If it seems advisable for me to go a, 2779
16:18 For they refreshed my spirit and yours a. 2779
2Co 1: 5 so a through Christ our comfort overflows. 2779
1: 7 so a you share in our comfort. 2779
2:10 If you forgive anyone, I a forgive him. 2779
4:10 life of Jesus may a be revealed in our body. 2779
4:13 With that same spirit of faith we a believe 2779
4:14 the Lord Jesus from the dead will a raise us 2779
5:11 and I hope it is a plain to your conscience. 2779
6:13 open wide your hearts a. 2779
7: 7 but a by the comfort you had given him. 2779
8: 6 to bring a to completion this act of grace 2779
8: 7 see that you a excel in this grace of giving. 2779
8:10 to give but a to have the desire to do so. 2779
8:21 not only in the eyes of the Lord but a in 2779
9: 6 Whoever sows sparingly will a 2779
9: 6 and whoever sows generously will a 2779
9:10 the sower and bread for food will a supply NIG
9:12 but is a overflowing in many expressions 2779
11:21 I a dare to boast about. 2779
Gal 2: 1 I took Titus along a. 2779
2: 8 was a at work in my ministry as an apostle 2779
4: 3 So a, when we were children, 2779
4: 7 you are a son, God has made you a an heir. 2779
6: 1 watch yourself, or you a may be tempted. 2779
Eph 1:11 In him we were a chosen, 2779
1:13 And you a were included in Christ NIG
1:18 I pray a that the eyes of your heart may NIG
1:21 in the present age but a in the one to come. 2779
2: 3 All of us a lived among them at one time, 2779
4: 9 that he a descended to the lower, 2779
5:24 so a wives should submit to their husbands 2779
5:33 each one of you a must love his wife 2779
6:19 Pray a for me, 2779
6:21 so that you a may know how I am 2779
Php 1:29 but a to suffer for him, 2779
2: 4 but a to the interests of others. 2779
2:19 that I a may be cheered 2779
2:25 who is a your messenger, 1254
2:27 and not on him only but a on me, 2779
Col 1: 8 and who a told us of your love in the Spirit. 2779
2:11 In him you were a circumcised, 2779
3: 4 then you a will appear with him in glory. 2779
4: 1 because you know that you a have a Master 2779
4:11 who is called Justus, a sends greetings. NIG
4:16 see that it is a read in the church of 2779
1Th 1: 5 but a with power, 2779
2:13 And we a thank God continually because, 2779
2:15 the Lord Jesus and the prophets and a 2779
3: 6 just as we a long to see you. 2779
1Ti 1: 9 We a know that law is made not for NIG
2: 9 I a want women to dress modestly, 6058
3: 7 He must a have a good reputation 2779
5:13 but a gossips and busybodies, 2779
2Ti 1: 5 I am persuaded, now lives in you a. 2779
2: 2 to reliable men who will a be qualified 2779
2:11 we will a live with him; 2779
2:12 we will a reign with him. 2779
2:12 If we disown him, he will a disown us; 2779
2:20 but a of wood and clay; 2779
3: 8 so a these men oppose the truth— 2779
4: 8 a to all who have longed for his appearing. 2779
Phm 1: 9 and now a a prisoner of Christ Jesus— 2779
Heb 1:10 He a says, "In the beginning, O Lord, 2779
2: 4 God a testified to it by signs, 5296
4: 2 we a have had the gospel preached to us, 2779
4:10 for anyone who enters God's rest a rests 2779
5: 5 So Christ a did not take upon himself 2779
7: 2 then a, "king of Salem" means "king 2779
7:12 there must a be a change of the law. 2779
8: 3 for this one a to have something to offer. 2779
9: 1 for worship and a an earthly sanctuary. 5445
10:15 The Holy Spirit a testifies to us about this. 2779
12:26 not only the earth but a the heavens." 2779
13:12 so Jesus a suffered outside the city gate 2779
Jas 2: 2 a poor man in shabby clothes a comes in. 2779
2:11 "Do not commit adultery," a said, 2779
3: 6 The tongue a is a fire, 2779
1Pe 2: 5 you a, like living stones, are being built 2779
2: 8 which is a what they were destined for. 2779
2:18 but a to those who are harsh. 2779
3:19 through whom a he went and preached to 2779
3:21 that now saves you a— 2779

1Pe 4: 1 arm yourselves a with the same attitude, 2779
5: 1 of Christ's sufferings and one who a 2779
2Pe 2: 1 But there were a false prophets among 2779
3: 6 By these waters a the world of NIG
3:15 as our dear brother Paul a wrote you with NIG
1Jn 1: 3 so that you a may have fellowship with us. 2779
2: 2 and not only for ours but a for the sins of 2779
2:23 the Son has the Father a. 2779
2:24 you a will remain in the Son and in 2779
4:11 we a ought to love one another. 2779
4:21 Whoever loves God must a 2779
5:20 We know a that the Son of God has come 1254
2Jn 1: 1 not I only, but a all who know the truth— 2779
3Jn 1:10 He a stops those who want to do so 2779
1:12 We a speak well of him, 2779
Rev 2: 6 the practices of the Nicolaitans, which I a 2779
2:15 Likewise you a have those who hold to 2779
2:17 I will a give him a white stone with 2779
2:28 I will a give him the morning star. 2779
3:10 I will a keep you from the hour of trial 2779
3:12 and I will a write on him my new name. 2779
4: 6 A before the throne there was what looked 2779
8:12 and a a third of the night. 3931
11: 8 where a their Lord was crucified. 2779
13: 4 and they a worshiped the beast and asked, 2779
13:16 He a forced everyone, small and great, 2779
17:10 They are a seven kings. 2779

ALTAR (381) [ALTARS]

Ge 8:20 Then Noah built an a to the LORD and, 4640
12: 7 So he built an a there to the LORD, 4640
12: 8 an a to the LORD and called on the name 4640
13: 4 and where he had first built an a. 4640
13:18 where he built an a to the LORD. 4640
22: 9 an a there and arranged the wood on it. 4640
22: 9 and laid him on the a, 4640
26:25 an a there and called on the name of 4640
33:20 up an a and called it El Elohe Israel. 4640
35: 1 and build an a there to God, 4640
35: 3 where I will build an a to God, 4640
35: 7 There he built an a, 4640
Ex 17:15 Moses built an a and called it 4640
20:24 " 'Make an a of earth for me and sacrifice 4640
20:25 If you make an a of stones for me, 4640
20:26 And do not go up to my a on steps, 4640
21:14 take him away from my a and put him 4640
24: 4 up early the next morning and built an a at 4640
24: 6 and the other half he sprinkled on the a. 4640
27: 1 "Build an a of acacia wood, 4640
27: 2 so that the horns and the a are of one piece, 5647[S]
27: 2 and overlay the a with bronze. 2257[S]
27: 5 the ledge of the a so that it is halfway up 4640
27: 5 of the altar so that it is halfway up the a 4640
27: 6 of acacia wood for the a and overlay them 4640
27: 7 be on two sides of the a when it is carried. 4640
27: 8 Make the a hollow, out of boards. 2257[S]
28:43 of Meeting or approach the a to minister in 4640
29:12 on the horns of the a with your finger, 4640
29:12 pour out the rest of it at the base of the a. 4640
29:13 and burn them on the a. 4640
29:16 and sprinkle it against the a on all sides. 4640
29:18 Then burn the entire ram on the a. 4640
29:20 sprinkle blood against the a on all sides. 4640
29:21 on the a and some of the anointing oil 4640
29:25 on the a along with the burnt offering for 4640
29:36 Purify the a by making atonement for it, 4640
29:37 For seven days make atonement for the a 4640
29:37 Then the a will be most holy, 4640
29:38 to offer on the a regularly each day: 4640
29:44 and the a and will consecrate Aaron 4640
30: 1 an a of acacia wood for burning incense. 4640
30: 4 Make two gold rings for the a below 2257[S]
30: 6 Put the a in front of the curtain that is 2257[S]
30: 7 on the a every morning when he tends 2257[S]
30: 9 Do not offer on this a any other incense 2257[S]
30:18 between the Tent of Meeting and the a, 4640
30:20 when they approach the a to minister 4640
30:27 the a of incense, 4640
30:28 the a of burnt offering and all its utensils, 4640
31: 8 the a of incense, 4640
31: 9 the a of burnt offering and all its utensils, 4640
32: 5 an a in front of the calf and announced, 4640
35:15 the a of incense with its poles, 4640
35:16 the a of burnt offering 4640
37:25 the a of incense out of acacia wood. 4640
38: 1 the a of burnt offering of acacia wood, 4640
38: 2 that the horns and the a were of one piece, 5647[S]
38: 2 and they overlaid the a with bronze. 2257[S]
38: 4 They made a grating for the a, 4640
38: 4 to be under its ledge, halfway up the a. 2257[S]
38: 7 be on the sides of the a for carrying it. 4640
38:30 the bronze a with its bronze grating 4640
39:38 the gold a, the anointing oil, 4640
39:39 the bronze a with its bronze grating, 4640
40: 5 the gold a of incense in front of the ark of 4640
40: 6 "Place the a of burnt offering in front of 4640
40: 7 of Meeting and the a and put water in it. 4640
40:10 the a of burnt offering and all its utensils; 4640
40:10 consecrate the a, and it will be most holy. 4640
40:26 the gold a in the Tent of Meeting in front 4640
40:29 the a of burnt offering near the entrance to 4640
40:30 and the a and put water in it for washing, 4640
40:32 the Tent of Meeting or approached the a, 4640
40:33 and a and put up the curtain at the entrance 4640
Lev 1: 5 the a on all sides at the entrance to the Tent 4640
1: 7 of Aaron the priest are to put fire on the a 4640

Lev 1: 8 on the burning wood that is on the a. 4640
1: 9 and the priest is to burn all of it on the a. 4640
1:11 the north side of the a before the LORD, 4640
1:11 against the a on all sides. 4640
1:12 on the burning wood that is on the a. 4640
1:13 to bring all of it and burn it on the a. 4640
1:15 The priest shall bring it to the a, 4640
1:15 wring off the head and burn it on the a; 4640
1:15 be drained out on the side of the a. 4640
1:16 and throw it to the east side of the a, 4640
1:17 on the wood that is on the fire on the a. 4640
2: 2 burn this as a memorial portion on the a, 4640
2: 8 who shall take it to the a. 4640
2: 9 from the grain offering and burn it on the a 4640
2:12 to be offered on the a as a pleasing aroma. 4640
3: 2 the blood against the a on all sides. 4640
3: 5 the a on top of the burnt offering that is on 4640
3: 8 against the a on all sides. 4640
3:11 The priest shall burn them on the a as food, 4640
3:13 against the a on all sides. 4640
3:16 The priest shall burn them on the a as food, 4640
4: 7 of the a of fragrant incense that is before 4640
4: 7 of the a of burnt offering at the entrance to 4640
4:10 Then the priest shall burn them on the a 4640
4:18 the horns of the a that is before the LORD 4640
4:18 of the a of burnt offering at the entrance to 4640
4:19 the fat from it and burn it on the a, 4640
4:25 the a of burnt offering and pour out the rest 4640
4:25 the rest of the blood at the base of the a. 4640
4:26 the fat on the a as he burned the fat of 4640
4:30 the a of burnt offering and pour out the rest 4640
4:30 the rest of the blood at the base of the a. 4640
4:31 the a as an aroma pleasing to the LORD. 4640
4:34 the a of burnt offering and pour out the rest 4640
4:34 the rest of the blood at the base of the a. 4640
4:35 and the priest shall burn it on the a on top 4640
5: 9 of the sin offering against the side of the a; 4640
5: 9 be drained out at the base of the a. 4640
5:12 as a memorial portion and burn it on the a 4640
6: 9 to remain on the a hearth throughout 4640
6: 9 and the fire must be kept burning on the a. 4640
6:10 on the a and place them beside the altar. 4640
6:10 on the altar and place them beside the a. 4640
6:12 The fire on the a must be kept burning; 4640
6:13 be kept burning on the a continuously; 4640
6:14 in front of the a. 4640
6:15 and burn the memorial portion on the a as 4640
7: 2 to be sprinkled against the a on all sides. 4640
7: 5 on the a as an offering made to the LORD 4640
7:31 The priest shall burn the fat on the a, 4640
8:11 of the oil on the a seven times, 4640
8:11 anointing the a and all its utensils and 4640
8:15 on all the horns of the a to purify the altar. 4640
8:15 on all the horns of the altar to purify the a. 4640
8:15 the rest of the blood at the base of the a. 4640
8:16 and burned it on the a. 4640
8:19 and sprinkled the blood against the a 4640
8:21 the whole ram on the a as a burnt offering, 4640
8:24 Then he sprinkled blood against the a 4640
8:28 from their hands and burned them on the a 4640
8:30 of the blood from the a and sprinkled them 4640
9: 7 to the a and sacrifice your sin offering 4640
9: 8 So Aaron came to the a and slaughtered 4640
9: 9 the blood and put it on the horns of the a; 4640
9: 9 at the base of the a. 4640
9:10 On the a he burned the fat, 4640
9:12 he sprinkled it against the a on all sides. 4640
9:13 and he burned them on the a. 4640
9:14 on top of the burnt offering on the a. 4640
9:17 took a handful of it and burned it on the a 4640
9:18 he sprinkled it against the a on all sides. 4640
9:20 and then Aaron burned the fat on the a. 4640
9:24 and the fat portions on the a. 4640
10:12 without yeast beside the a, 4640
14:20 and offer it on the a, 4640
16:12 the a before the LORD and two handfuls 4640
16:18 "Then he shall come out to the a that is 4640
16:18 and put it on all the horns of the a. 4640
16:20 the Tent of Meeting and the a, 4640
16:25 the fat of the sin offering on the a. 4640
16:33 for the Tent of Meeting and the a, 4640
17: 6 against the a of the LORD at the entrance 4640
17:11 for yourselves on the a; 4640
21:23 not go near the curtain or approach the a, 4640
22:22 on the a as an offering made to the LORD 4640
Nu 3:26 the tabernacle and a, and the ropes— 4640
4:11 the gold a they are to spread a blue cloth 4640
4:13 from the bronze a and spread a purple cloth 4640
4:14 the utensils used for ministering at the a, 2257S
4:26 the tabernacle and a, 4640
5:25 before the LORD and bring it to the a. 4640
5:26 a memorial offering and burn it on the a; 4640
7: 1 and consecrated the a and all its utensils. 4640
7:10 When the a was anointed, 4640
7:10 and presented them before the a. 4640
7:11 for the dedication of the a." 4640
7:84 of the a when it was anointed: 4640
7:88 the offerings for the dedication of the a 4640
16:38 the censers into sheets to overlay the a, 4640
16:39 to overlay the a, 4640
16:46 along with fire from the a, 4640
18: 3 the furnishings of the sanctuary or the a, 4640
18: 5 for the care of the sanctuary and the a, 4640
18: 7 in connection with everything at the a and 4640
18:17 the a and burn their fat as an offering made 4640
23: 2 of them offered a bull and a ram on each a. 4640
23: 4 on each a I have offered a bull and a ram." 4640
Nu 23:14 and offered a bull and a ram on each a. 4640
23:30 and offered a bull and a ram on each a. 4640
Dt 12:27 Present your burnt offerings on the a of 4640
12:27 beside the a of the LORD your God, 4640
16:21 the a you build to the LORD your God, 4640
26: 4 in front of the a of the LORD your God. 4640
27: 5 Build there an a to the LORD your God, 4640
27: 5 to the LORD your God, an a of stones. 4640
27: 6 Build the a of the LORD your God 4640
33:10 and whole burnt offerings on your a. 4640
Jos 8:30 Then Joshua built on Mount Ebal an a to 4640
8:31 an a of uncut stones, 4640
9:27 the community and for the a of the LORD 4640
22:10 of Manasseh built an imposing a there by 4640
22:11 the Israelites heard that they had built the a 4640
22:16 from the LORD and build yourselves an a 4640
22:19 against us by building an a for yourselves, 4640
22:19 other than the a of the LORD our God. 4640
22:23 If we have built our own a to turn away 4640
22:26 'Let us get ready and build an a— 4640
22:28 Look at the replica of the LORD's a, 4640
22:29 by building an a for burnt offerings, 4640
22:29 the a of the LORD our God that stands 4640
22:34 and the Gadites gave the a this name: 4640
Jdg 6:24 So Gideon built an a to the LORD there 4640
6:25 down your father's a to Baal and cut down 4640
6:26 a proper kind of a to the LORD your God 4640
6:28 there was Baal's a, demolished, 4640
6:28 on the newly built a! 4640
6:30 because he has broken down Baal's a 4640
6:31 when someone breaks down his a." 4640
6:32 because he broke down Baal's a. 4640
13:20 As the flame blazed up from the a 4640
21: 4 Early the next day the people built an a 4640
1Sa 2:28 to go up to my a, to burn incense, 4640
2:33 of you that I do not cut off from my a will 4640
7:17 And he built an a there to the LORD. 4640
14:35 Then Saul built an a to the LORD; 4640
2Sa 24:18 an a to the LORD on the threshing floor 4640
24:21 "so I can build an a to the LORD, 4640
24:25 David built an a to the LORD there 4640
1Ki 1:50 went and took hold of the horns of the a. 4640
1:51 and is clinging to the horns of the a. 4640
1:53 and they brought him down from the a. 4640
2:28 and took hold of the horns of the a. 4640
2:29 of the LORD and was beside the a. 4640
3: 4 a thousand burnt offerings on that a. 4640
6:20 and he also overlaid the a of cedar. 4640
6:22 also overlaid with gold the a that belonged 4640
7:48 in the LORD's temple: the golden a; 4640
8:22 before the a of the LORD in front of 4640
8:31 the oath before your a in this temple, 4640
8:54 he rose from before the a of the LORD, 4640
8:64 because the bronze a before 4640
9:25 on the a he had built for the LORD, 4640
12:32 and offered sacrifices on the a. 4640
12:33 he offered sacrifices on the a he had built 4640
12:33 and went up to the a to make offerings. 4640
13: 1 as Jeroboam was standing by the a to make 4640
13: 2 He cried out against the a by the word of 4640
13: 2 of the LORD: "O a, altar! 4640
13: 2 of the LORD: "O altar, a! 4640
13: 3 The a will be split apart and the ashes 4640
13: 4 of God cried out against the a at Bethel, 4640
13: 4 he stretched out his hand from the a 4640
13: 5 the a was split apart 4640
13:32 of the LORD against the a in Bethel and 4640
16:32 up an a for Baal in the temple of Baal 4640
18:26 they danced around the a they had made. 4640
18:30 and he repaired the a of the LORD, 4640
18:32 With the stones he built an a in the name of 4640
18:35 around the a and even filled the trench. 4640
2Ki 11:11 near the a and the temple, 4640
12: 9 He placed it beside the a, 4640
16:10 He saw an a in Damascus and sent to Uriah 4640
16:10 to Uriah the priest a sketch of the a, 4640
16:11 So Uriah the priest built an a in accordance 4640
16:12 from Damascus and saw the a, 4640
16:13 of his fellowship offerings on the a. 4640
16:14 The bronze a that stood before 4640
16:14 the new a and the temple of the LORD— 4640
16:14 and put it on the north side of the new a. 4640
16:15 "On the large new a, 4640
16:15 on the a all the blood of the burnt offerings 2257S
16:15 the bronze a for seeking guidance." 4640
18:22 "You must worship before this a 4640
23: 9 of the high places did not serve at the a of 4640
23:15 Even the a at Bethel, 4640
23:15 even that a and high place he demolished. 4640
23:16 from them and burned on the a to defile it, 4640
23:17 from Judah and pronounced against the a 4640
1Ch 6:49 on the a of burnt offering and on the altar 4640
6:49 on the a of incense in connection with all 4640
16:40 on the a of burnt offering regularly, 4640
21:18 an a to the LORD on the threshing floor 4640
21:22 of your threshing floor so I can build an a 4640
21:26 David built an a to the LORD there 4640
21:26 from heaven on the a of burnt offering. 4640
21:29 the a of burnt offering were at that time on 4640
22: 1 and also the a of burnt offering for Israel." 4640
28:18 and the weight of the refined gold for the a 4640
2Ch 1: 5 But the bronze a that Bezalel son of Uri, 4640
1: 6 the bronze a before the LORD in the Tent 4640
4: 1 He made a bronze a twenty cubits long, 4640
4:19 in God's temple: the golden a; 4640
5:12 stood on the east side of the a, 4640
6:12 before the a of the LORD in front of 4640
2Ch 6:22 the oath before your a in this temple, 4640
7: 7 the bronze a he had made could not hold 4640
7: 9 the dedication of the a for seven days and 4640
8:12 On the a of the LORD that he had built 4640
15: 8 He repaired the a of the LORD that was 4640
23:10 near the a and the temple, 4640
26:16 of the LORD to burn incense on the a 4640
26:19 in their presence before the incense a in 4640
29:18 the a of burnt offering with all its utensils, 4640
29:19 They are now in front of the LORD's a." 4640
29:21 to offer these on the a of the LORD. 4640
29:22 the blood and sprinkled it on the a; 4640
29:22 and sprinkled their blood on the a; 4640
29:22 and sprinkled their blood on the a. 4640
29:24 the goats and presented their blood on the a 4640
29:27 to sacrifice the burnt offering on the a. 4640
32:12 before one a and burn sacrifices on it'? 4640
33:16 Then he restored the a of the LORD 4640
35:16 and the offering of burnt offerings on the a 4640
Ezr 3: 2 and his associates began to build the a of 4640
3: 3 they built the a on its foundation 4640
7:17 and sacrifice them on the a of the temple 10401
Ne 10:34 a contribution of wood to burn on the a of 4640
Ps 26: 6 and go about your a, O LORD, 4640
43: 4 Then will I go to the a of God, to God, 4640
51:19 then bulls will be offered on your a. 4640
84: 3 a place near your a, O LORD Almighty, 4640
118:27 up to the horns of the a. 4640
Isa 6: 6 which he had taken with tongs from the a. 4640
19:19 be an a to the LORD in the heart of Egypt, 4640
27: 9 the a stones to be like chalk stones crushed 4640
29: 2 she will be to me like an a hearth. 789
36: 7 "You must worship before this a"? 4640
40:16 Lebanon is not sufficient for a fires, AIT
56: 7 and sacrifices will be accepted on my a; 4640
60: 7 they will be accepted as offerings on my a, 4640
La 2: 7 The Lord has rejected his a 4640
Eze 8: 5 the gate of the a I saw this idol of jealousy. 4640
8:16 between the portico and the a, 4640
9: 2 in and stood beside the bronze a. 4640
40:46 for the priests who have charge of the a. 4640
40:47 And the a was in front of the temple. 4640
41:22 There was a wooden a three cubits high 4640
43:13 the a in long cubits, that cubit being a cubit 4640
43:13 And this is the height of the a: 4640
43:15 The a hearth is four cubits high, 2219
43:16 The a hearth is square, 789
43:17 The steps of the a face east." 2084S
43:18 and sprinkling blood upon the a 4640
43:20 and put it on the four horns of the a and on 2257S
43:20 so purify the a and make atonement for it. 2257S
43:22 and the a is to be purified as it was purified 4640
43:26 to make atonement for the a and cleanse it; 4640
43:27 and fellowship offerings on the a. 4640
45:19 the four corners of the upper ledge of the a 4640
47: 1 south of the a. 4640
Joel 1:13 wail, you who minister before the a. 4640
2:17 weep between the temple porch and the a. 4640
Am 2: 8 down beside every a on garments taken 4640
3:14 the horns of the a will be cut off and fall to 4640
9: 1 I saw the Lord standing by the a, 4640
Zec 9:15 for sprinkling the corners of the a. 4640
14:20 be like the sacred bowls in front of the a. 4640
Mal 1: 7 "You place defiled food on my a. 4640
1:10 you would not light useless fires on my a! 4640
2:13 You flood the LORD's a with tears. 4640
Mt 5:23 if you are offering your gift at the a 2603
5:24 leave your gift there in front of the a. 2603
23:18 You also say, 'If anyone swears by the a, 2603
23:19 the gift, or the a that makes the gift sacred? 2603
23:20 the a swears by it and by everything on it. 2603
23:35 between the temple and the a. 2603
Lk 1:11 at the right side of the a of incense. 2603
11:51 who was killed between the a and 2603
Ac 17:23 I even found an a with this inscription: 1117
1Co 9:13 the a share in what is offered on the altar? 2603
9:13 the altar share in what is offered on the a? 2603
10:18 the sacrifices participate in the a? 2603
Heb 7:13 from that tribe has ever served at the a. 2603
9: 4 which had the golden a of incense and 2593
13:10 an a from which those who minister at 2603
Jas 2:21 when he offered his son Isaac on the a? 2603
Rev 6: 9 the a the souls of those who had been slain 2603
8: 3 came and stood at the a. 2603
8: 3 on the golden a before the throne. 2603
8: 5 filled it with fire from the a, 2603
9:13 from the horns of the golden a that is 2603
11: 1 and measure the temple of God and the a, 2603
14:18 came from the a and called in a loud voice 2603
16: 7 And I heard the a respond: 2603

ALTARS (61) [ALTAR]

Ex 34:13 Break down their a, 4640
Lev 26:30 cut down your incense a 2802
Nu 3:31 the table, the lampstand, the a, 4640
23: 1 Balaam said, "Build me seven a here, 4640
23: 4 and Balaam said, "I have prepared seven a, 4640
23:14 and there he built seven a and offered 4640
23:29 Balaam said, "Build me seven a here, 4640
Dt 7: 5 Break down their a, 4640
12: 3 down their a, smash their sacred stones 4640
Jdg 2: 2 but you shall break down their a.' 4640
1Ki 19:10 broken down your a, 4640
19:14 broken down your a, 4640
2Ki 11:18 the a and idols to pieces and killed Mattan 4640
11:18 the priest of Baal in front of the a. 4640

2Ki 18:22 high places and a Hezekiah removed, 4640
21: 3 he also erected a to Baal and made 4640
21: 4 He built a in the temple of the LORD, 4640
21: 5 he built a to all the starry hosts. 4640
23:12 down the a the kings of Judah had erected 4640
23:12 the a Manasseh had built in the two courts 4640
23:20 on the a and burned human bones on them. 4640
2Ch 14: 3 the foreign a and the high places, 4640
14: 5 the high places and incense a in every town 2802
23:17 the a and idols and killed Mattan the priest 4640
23:17 the priest of Baal in front of the a. 4640
28:24 up a at every street corner in Jerusalem. 4640
30:14 the a in Jerusalem and cleared away 4640
30:14 in Jerusalem and cleared away the incense a 5232
31: 1 the high places and the a throughout Judah 4640
32:12 and a, saying to Judah 4640
33: 3 he also erected a to the Baals 4640
33: 4 He built a in the temple of the LORD, 4640
33: 5 he built a to all the starry hosts. 4640
33:15 as all the a he had built on the temple hill 4640
34: 4 the a *of* the Baals were torn down; 4640
34: 4 he cut to pieces the incense a that were 2802
34: 5 the bones of the priests on their a, 4640
34: 7 he tore down the a and the Asherah poles 4640
34: 7 to powder and cut to pieces all the incense a 2802
Isa 17: 8 They will not look to the a, 4640
17: 8 and the incense a their fingers have made. 2802
27: 9 no Asherah poles or incense a will 2802
36: 7 and a Hezekiah removed, 4640
65: 3 and burning incense on a of brick; 4246
Jer 11:13 and the a you have set up to burn incense 4640
17: 1 of their hearts and on the horns of their a. 4640
17: 2 Even their children remember their a 4640
Eze 6: 4 Your a will be demolished 4640
6: 4 be demolished and your incense a will 2802
6: 5 and I will scatter your bones around your a. 4640
6: 6 your a will be laid waste and devastated, 4640
6: 6 your incense a broken down, 2802
6:13 around their a, on every high hill and on all 4640
Hos 8:11 Ephraim built many a for sin offerings, 4640
8:11 these have become a for sinning. 4640
10: 1 As his fruit increased, he built more a; 4640
10: 2 The LORD will demolish their a 4640
10: 8 and thistles will grow up and cover their a. 4640
12:11 Their a will be like piles of stones on 4640
Am 3:14 I will destroy the a *of* Bethel; 4640
Ro 11: 3 and torn down your a; *2603*

ALTER (1) [ALTERED]

Ps 89:34 or a what my lips have uttered. 9101

ALTERED (1) [ALTER]

Da 6: 8 and put it in writing so that *it* cannot *be* a— 10731

ALTERNATE (1) [ALTERNATED]

Ex 28:34 the pomegranates *are to* a around the hem 2256+2298+7194+8232[S]

ALTERNATED (2) [ALTERNATE]

Ex 39:26 and pomegranates a around the hem of 2256+7194+8232[S]
Eze 41:18 Palm trees a with cherubim. 1068

ALTHOUGH (65) [THOUGH]

Ge 42: 8 A Joseph recognized his brothers, 2256
Ex 19: 5 A the whole earth is mine, 3954
34: 9 A this is a stiff-necked people, 3954
Dt 14: 7 A they chew the cud, 3954
14: 8 a it has a split hoof, 3954
Jdg 12: 2 and *a I* called, AIT
Ru 3:12 A it is true that I am near of kin, 3954
1Sa 2:32 A good will be done to Israel, 889+928+3972
15:17 "A you were once small in your own eyes, 561
2Sa 13:25 A Absalom urged him, 2256
23:21 A the Egyptian had a spear in his hand, 2256
1Ki 11:10 A he had forbidden Solomon 2256
15:14 A he did not remove the high places, 2256
2Ki 17:15 They imitated the nations around them a 889
23: 9 A the priests of the high places did 421
1Ch 11:23 A the Egyptian had a spear like 2256
26:10 Shimri the first (a he was not the firstborn, 3954
2Ch 15:17 A he did not remove the high places 8370
24:19 A the LORD sent prophets to the people 2256
24:24 A the Aramean army had come with only 3954
30:18 A most of the many people who came 3954
Ne 5: 5 A we are of the same flesh and blood 6964
Job 9:21 "A I am blameless, I have no concern NIH
34: 6 A I am right, I am considered a liar; 6584
34: 6 a I am guiltless, NIH
Ecc 8:12 A a wicked man commits a hundred crimes 889
Isa 12: 1 A you were angry with me, 3954
17:13 A the peoples roar like the roar NIH
30:20 A the Lord gives you the bread of adversity 2256
60:15 "A you have been forsaken and hated, 9393
Jer 2:22 A you wash yourself with soda and use 561+3954
5: 2 A they say, 'As surely as the LORD lives,' 561
11:11 A they cry out to me, 2256
14: 7 A our sins testify against us, O LORD, 561
14:12 A they fast, I will not listen to their cry; 3954
23:38 A you claim, 'This is the oracle of 561
48:33 A there are shouts, NIH
Eze 8:18 A they shout in my ears, 2256
11:16 A I sent them far away among the nations 3954
15: 7 A they have come out of the fire, NIH
Eze 20:13 a the man who obeys them will live NIH
20:21 a the man who obeys them will live NIH
20:38 A I will bring them out of the land NIH
32:32 A I had him spread terror in the land of 3954
Hos 8:10 A they have sold themselves among 1685+3954
Na 1:12 "A they have allies and are numerous, 561
1:12 A I have afflicted you, [O Judah,] 2256
Lk 14:14 A they cannot repay you, *4022*
Jn 4: 2 a in fact it was not Jesus who baptized, *2793*
Ac 20:19 *a I was severely* tested *AIT*
28:17 *a I have* done nothing against our people or *AIT*
Ro 1:21 For *a they* knew God, *AIT*
1:22 *A they* claimed to be wise, *AIT*
1:32 *A* they know God's righteous decree *AIT*
1Co 7:21 a if you can gain your freedom, do so. *247*
2Co 12: 1 *A* there is nothing *to be* gained, *AIT*
Gal 4: 1 *a he* owns the whole estate. *AIT*
Eph 3: 8 A I am less than the least of all God's people *NIG*
1Ti 3:14 *A I* hope to come to you soon, *AIT*
Phm 1: 8 *a* in Christ I could be bold *AIT*
Heb 5: 8 A he was a son, he learned obedience *2788*
10: 8 (a the law required them to be made). *NIG*
Jas 3: 4 *A they* are so large and are driven *AIT*
2Pe 2:11 *a they* are stronger and more powerful, *AIT*
Jude 1: 3 a I was very eager to write to you about *NIG*

ALTOGETHER (22) [TOGETHER]

Ge 5: 5 A, Adam lived 930 years, and then he died. 3972
5: 8 A, Seth lived 912 years, and then he died. 3972
5:11 A, Enosh lived 905 years, and then he died. 3972
5:14 A, Kenan lived 910 years, 3972
5:17 A, Mahalalel lived 895 years, 3972
5:20 A, Jared lived 962 years, and then he died. 3972
5:23 A, Enoch lived 365 years. 3972
5:27 A, Methuselah lived 969 years, 3972
5:31 A, Lamech lived 777 years, 3972
9:29 A, Noah lived 950 years, and then he died. 3972
25: 7 A, Abraham lived a hundred 465+2256
25:17 A, Ishmael lived a hundred 465+2256
Ex 26: 7 over the tabernacle—eleven a. NIH
36:14 over the tabernacle—eleven a. NIH
Nu 7:85 A, the silver dishes weighed two thousand 3972
7:86 A, the gold dishes weighed a hundred 3972
1Ch 9:22 A, those chosen to be gatekeepers at 3972
Job 13: 5 If only *you would be* a silent! 3087+3087
Ps 19: 9 of the LORD are sure and a righteous. 3481
50:21 you thought *I* was a like you. 2118+2118
SS 5:16 he is a lovely. 3972
Ac 27:37 A there were 276 of us on board. *3836+4246*

ALUSH (2)

Nu 33:13 They left Dophkah and camped at A. 478
33:14 They left A and camped at Rephidim, 478

ALVAH (2)

Ge 36:40 and regions: Timna, A, 6595
1Ch 1:51 The chiefs of Edom were: Timna, A, 6595

ALVAN (2)

Ge 36:23 A, Manahath, Ebal, Shepho and Onam. 6597
1Ch 1:40 A, Manahath, Ebal, Shepho and Onam. 6597

ALWAYS (135)

Ge 26:29 but a treated you well and sent you away 8370
Ex 19: 9 and will a put their trust in you." 4200+6409
28:30 Thus Aaron will a bear the means 9458
29:28 This is a to be the regular share from 6409
Lev 25:32 " 'The Levites a have the right 6409
Nu 22:30 which you have a ridden, to this day? 4946+6388
Dt 5:29 and keep all my commands a, 2021+3427+3972
6:24 that we might a prosper and be kept alive, 2021+3427+3972
11: 1 his laws and his commands a. 2021+3427+3972
12:28 so that it may a go well with you 6330+6409
14:23 to revere the LORD your God a. 2021+3427+3972
15:11 *There will* a be poor people in the land 2532+4202
18: 5 minister in the LORD's name a. 2021+3427+3972
19: 9 to love the LORD your God and to walk a in his ways— 2021+3427+3972
28:13 you will a be at the top, 8370
Jos 4:24 and so that you might a fear 2021+3427+3972
1Sa 1:22 and he will live there a." 6330+6409
2:35 he will minister before my anointed one a. 2021+3427+3972
7:17 But he a went back to Ramah, NIH
2Sa 9: 7 and you will a eat at my table." 9458
9:10 will a eat at my table." 9458
9:13 because he a ate at the king's table, 9458
1Ki 5: 1 because he had a been on friendly terms 2021+3427+3972
9: 3 My eyes and my heart will a be there. 2021+3427+3972
11:36 that David my servant may a have a lamp 2021+3427+3972
12: 7 they will a be your servants." 2021+3427+3972
22: 8 about me, but a bad. NIH
2Ki 17:37 You must a be careful to keep the decrees 2021+3427+3972
1Ch 16:11 seek his face a. 9458
2Ch 7:16 My eyes and my heart will a be there. 2021+3427+3972
10: 7 they will a be your servants." 2021+3427+3972
18: 7 about me, but a bad. 3427+3972
Job 31:32 for my door *was* a open to the traveler— AIT
Ps 9:18 But the needy will not a be forgotten, 4200+5905
10: 5 His ways are a prosperous; 928+3972+6961
10: 6 I'll a be happy and never have trouble." 1887+1887+2256+4200
16: 8 I have set the LORD a before me. 9458
34: 1 his praise will a be on my lips. 9458
35:27 may they a say, "The LORD be exalted, 9458
37:26 They are a generous and lend freely; 2021+3427+3972
40:11 may your love and your truth a protect me. 9458
40:16 may those who love your salvation a say, 9458
51: 3 and my sin is a before me. 9458
56: 5 they are a plotting to harm me. 3972
70: 4 may those who love your salvation a say, 9458
71: 3 Be my rock of refuge, to which I can a go; 9458
71:14 But as for me, I will a have hope; 9458
73:12 a carefree, they increase in wealth. 6409
73:23 Yet I am a with you; 9458
103: 9 He will not a accuse, 4200+5905
105: 4 seek his face a. 9458
109:15 May their sins a remain before the LORD, 9458
119:44 I will a obey your law, for ever and ever. 9458
119:117 I will a have regard for your decrees. 9458
119:132 as you a do to those who love your name. 5477
Pr 5:19 may her breasts satisfy you a, 928+3972+6961
6:14 he a stirs up dissension. 928+3972+6961
8:30 rejoicing a in his presence, 928+3972+6961
23: 7 for he is the kind of *man who is a* thinking AIT
23:17 but a be zealous for the fear of the LORD. 2021+3427+3972
28:14 Blessed is the man who a fears the LORD, 9458
29:14 his throne will a be secure. 4200+6329
Ecc 9: 8 A be clothed in white, 928+3972+6961
9: 8 and a anoint your head with oil. 440+2893
Isa 57:16 nor will I a be angry, 4200+5905
58:11 The LORD will guide you a; 9458
60:11 Your gates will a stand open, 9458
Jer 3: 5 will you a be angry? 4200+6409
8: 5 Why does Jerusalem a turn away? 5904
12: 1 You are a righteous, O LORD, NIH
12: 2 You are a on their lips but far 7940
17: 8 its leaves are *a* green. AIT
32:39 that they will a fear me for their own good 2021+3427+3972
35: 7 but must a live in tents. 3427+3972
La 5:20 Why do you a forget us? 4200+5905
Hos 7: 2 they are a before me. 6964
12: 6 and wait for your God a. 9458
Mal 1: 4 people a under the wrath of the LORD. 6330+6409
Mt 18:10 their angels in heaven a see the face *1328+4246*
26:11 The poor you will a have with you, *4121*
26:11 but you will not a have me. *4121*
28:20 And surely I am with you a, *2465+3836+4246*
Mk 14: 7 The poor you will a have with you, *4121*
14: 7 But you will not a have me. *4121*
Lk 15:31 the father said, 'you are a with me, *4121*
18: 1 to show them that they should a pray and *4121*
21:36 Be a on the watch, *1877+2789+4246*
Jn 5:17 *a* at his work to this *AIT*
8:29 for I a do what pleases him." *4121*
11:42 I knew that you a hear me, *4121*
12: 8 You will a have the poor among you, *4121*
12: 8 but you will not a have me." *4121*
18:20 "I a taught in synagogues or at the temple, *4121*
Ac 2:25 " 'I saw the Lord a before me. *1328+4246*
7:51 You a resist the Holy Spirit! *107*
9:36 who was a doing good and helping *4441*
24:16 So I strive a to keep my conscience clear *1328+4246*
Ro 15:20 It *has a been my* ambition to preach *AIT*
1Co 1: 4 I a thank God for you because *4121*
13: 7 It a protects, always trusts, always hopes, *4246*
13: 7 It always protects, a trusts, always hopes, *4246*
13: 7 It always protects, always trusts, a hopes, *4246*
13: 7 always trusts, always hopes, a perseveres. *4246*
15:58 A give yourselves fully to the work of *4121*
2Co 1:19 but in him *it has a* been "Yes." *AIT*
2:14 who a leads us in triumphal procession *4121*
4:10 We a carry around in our body the death *4121*
4:11 For we who are alive are a being given *107*
5: 6 Therefore we are a confident and know that *4121*
6:10 sorrowful, yet a rejoicing; *107*
Gal 4:18 to be so a and not just when I am with you. *4121*
Eph 5:20 a giving thanks to God the Father *4121*
6:18 and a keep on praying for all the saints. *4246*
Php 1: 4 I a pray with joy *4121*
1:20 now as a Christ will be exalted in my body, *4121*
2:12 my dear friends, as you have a obeyed— *4121*
4: 4 Rejoice in the Lord a. *4121*
Col 1: 3 We a thank God, *4121*
4: 6 Let your conversation be a full of grace, *4121*
4:12 He is a wrestling in prayer for you, *4121*
1Th 1: 2 We a thank God for all of you, *4121*
2:16 In this way they a heap up their sins to *4121*
3: 6 that you a have pleasant memories of us *4121*
5:15 but a try to be kind to each other and *4121*
5:16 Be joyful a; *4121*
2Th 1: 3 We ought a to thank God for you, brothers, *4121*
2:13 But we ought a to thank God for you, *4121*
2Ti 3: 7 a learning but never able to acknowledge *4121*
Tit 1:12 "Cretans are a liars, evil brutes, *107*
Phm 1: 4 I a thank my God as I remember you *4121*
Heb 3:10 and I said, 'Their hearts are a going astray, *107*
7:25 because he a lives to intercede for them. *4121*
1Pe 3:15 A be prepared to give an answer *107*
2Pe 1:12 So I will a remind you of these things, *107*
1:15 that after my departure you will a be able *1668*

AM (1125) [BE] See Index of Articles Etc.— See also selected listing under I AM

AMAD (1)
Jos 19:26 Allammelech, A and Mishal. 6675

AMAL (1)
1Ch 7:35 Zophah, Imna, Shelesh and A. 6663

AMALEK (12) [AMALEKITE, AMALEKITES]
Ge 36:12 Timna, who bore him A. 6667
36:16 Korah, Gatam and A. These were the chiefs descended from Eliphaz 6667
Ex 17:14 the memory of A from under heaven." 6667
Nu 24:20 Then Balaam saw A and uttered his oracle: 6667
24:20 "A was first among the nations, 6667
Dt 25:19 you shall blot out the memory of A from 6667
Jdg 5:14 whose roots were in A; 6667
1Sa 15: 5 of A and set an ambush in the ravine. 6667
2Sa 8:12 the Ammonites and the Philistines, and A. 6667
1Ch 1:36 and Kenaz; by Timna: A. 6667
18:11 the Ammonites and the Philistines, and A. 6667
Ps 83: 7 Ammon and A, Philistia, 6667

AMALEKITE (4) [AMALEK]
Ex 17:13 So Joshua overcame the A army with 6667
1Sa 30:13 "I am an Egyptian, the slave of an A. 6668
2Sa 1: 8 " 'An A,' I answered. 6668
1:13 "I am the son of an alien, an A," 6668

AMALEKITES (34) [AMALEK]
Ge 14: 7 the whole territory of the A, 6668
Ex 17: 8 The A came and attacked the Israelites 6667
17: 9 of our men and go out to fight the A. 6667
17:10 Joshua fought the A as Moses had ordered, 6667
17:11 the A were winning. 6667
17:16 The LORD will be at war against the A 6667
Nu 13:29 The A live in the Negev; 6667
14:25 A and Canaanites are living in the valleys, 6668
14:43 the A and Canaanites will face you there. 6668
14:45 Then the A and Canaanites who lived in 6668
Dt 25:17 Remember what the A did to you along 6667
Jdg 3:13 Getting the Ammonites and A to join him, 6667
6: 3 A and other eastern peoples invaded 6667
6:33 A and other eastern peoples joined forces 6667
7:12 the A and all the other eastern peoples 6667
10:12 the A and the Maonites oppressed you 6667
12:15 in the hill country of the A. 6668
1Sa 14:48 He fought valiantly and defeated the A, 6667
15: 2 'I will punish the A for what they did 6667
15: 3 attack the A and totally destroy everything 6667
15: 6 the A so that I do not destroy you along 6668
15: 6 So the Kenites moved away from the A. 6667
15: 7 the A all the way from Havilah to Shur, 6667
15: 8 He took Agag king of the A alive, 6667
15:15 "The soldiers brought them from the A; 6668
15:18 and completely destroy those wicked people, the A; 6667
15:20 the A and brought back Agag their king. 6667
15:32 "Bring me Agag king of the A." 6667
27: 8 the Girzites and the A. 6668
28:18 or carry out his fierce wrath against the A, 6667
30: 1 the A had raided the Negev and Ziklag. 6668
30:18 David recovered everything the A had taken 6667
2Sa 1: 1 the A and stayed in Ziklag two days. 6667
1Ch 4:43 the remaining A who had escaped, 6667

AMAM (1)
Jos 15:26 A, Shema, Moladah, 585

AMANA (1)
SS 4: 8 Descend from the crest of A, 592

AMARIAH (15) [AMARIAH'S]
1Ch 6: 7 Meraioth the father of A, 618
6: 7 A the father of Ahitub, 618
6:11 Azariah the father of A, 618
6:11 A the father of Ahitub, 618
6:52 Meraioth his son, A his son, Ahitub his son, 618
23:19 Jeriah the first, A the second, 618
24:23 Jeriah the first, A the second, 619
2Ch 19:11 "A the chief priest will be over you 619
31:15 A and Shecaniah assisted him faithfully in 619
Ezr 7: 3 the son of A, the son of Azariah, 618
10:42 Shallum, A and Joseph. 618
Ne 10: 3 Pashhur, A, Malkijah, 618
11: 4 the son of A, the son of Shephatiah, 618
12: 2 A, Malluch, Hattush, 618
Zep 1: 1 the son of A, the son of Hezekiah, 618

AMARIAH'S (1) [AMARIAH]
Ne 12:13 of Ezra's, Meshullam; of A, Jehohanan; 618

AMASA (18)
2Sa 17:25 Absalom had appointed A over the army 6690
17:25 A was the son of a man named Jether, 6690
19:13 And say to A, 6690
20: 4 Then the king said to A, 6690
20: 5 But when A went to summon Judah, 6690
20: 8 A came to meet them. 6690
20: 9 Joab said to A, "How are you, 6690
20: 9 Then Joab took A by the beard 6690
20:10 A was not on his guard against the dagger 6690
20:10 Without being stabbed again, A died. NIH
20:11 One of Joab's men stood beside A and said, 2257[S]
20:12 A lay wallowing in his blood in the middle 6690
20:12 that everyone who came up to A stopped, 6690
20:13 After A had been removed from the road, NIH
1Ki 2: 5 Abner son of Ner and A son of Jether. 6690
2:32 and A son of Jether, 6690
1Ch 2:17 Abigail was the mother of A, 6690
2Ch 28:12 and A son of Hadlai— 6690

AMASAI (5)
1Ch 6:25 The descendants of Elkanah: A, Ahimoth, 6691
6:35 the son of Mahath, the son of A, 6691
12:18 Then the Spirit came upon A, 6691
15:24 Shebaniah, Joshaphat, Nethanel, A, 6691
2Ch 29:12 Mahath son of A and Joel son of Azariah; 6691

AMASHSAI (1)
Ne 11:13 A son of Azarel, the son of Ahzai, 6692

AMASIAH (1)
2Ch 17:16 A son of Zicri, 6674

AMASSED (2) [AMASSES]
Ecc 2: 8 *I* a silver and gold for myself, 4043
Eze 28: 4 and a gold and silver in your treasuries. 6913

AMASSES (1) [AMASSED]
Pr 28: 8 by exorbitant interest a it for another, 7695

AMAZED (39) [AMAZEMENT]
Isa 29: 9 and a, blind yourselves and be sightless; 9449
Hab 1: 5 and *be* **utterly a.** 9449+9449
Mt 7:28 the crowds *were* a at his teaching, *1742*
8:27 The men *were* a and asked, *2513*
9:33 The crowd *was* a and said, *2513*
13:54 and they *were* a. *1742*
15:31 The people *were* a when they saw *2513*
21:20 When the disciples saw this, *they were* a. *2513*
22:22 When they heard this, *they were* a. *2513*
Mk 1:22 The *people were* a at his teaching, *1742*
1:27 so a that they asked each other, *2501*
2:12 This a everyone and they praised God, *2014*
5:20 And all the people *were* a. *2513*
6: 2 and many who heard him *were* a. *1742*
6: 6 And *he was* a at their lack of faith. *2513*
6:51 *They were* completely a, *2014*
10:24 The disciples *were* a at his words. *2501*
10:26 The disciples *were* even more a, *1742*
11:18 the whole crowd *was* a at his teaching. *1742*
12:17 And *they were* a at him. *1703*
15: 5 Jesus still made no reply, and Pilate **was a.** *2513*
Lk 2:18 and all who heard it *were* a at what *2513*
2:47 Everyone who heard him *was* a *2014*
4:22 and *were* a at the gracious words that came *2513*
4:32 *They were* a at his teaching, *1742*
4:36 the people were a and said to each other, *2502*
5:26 Everyone *was* a and gave praise to God. *1749+3284*
7: 9 When Jesus heard this, *he was* **a at** him, *2513*
9:43 And *they were* all a at the greatness of God. *1742*
11:14 and the crowd *was* a. *2513*
24:22 In addition, some of our women a us. *2014*
Jn 5:28 "*Do* not *be* **a at** this, *2513*
7:15 The Jews *were* a and asked, *2513*
Ac 2: 7 **Utterly a,** they asked: *2014+2513*
2:12 A and perplexed, they asked one another, *2014*
7:31 When he saw this, he *was* **a at** the sight. *2513*
8: 9 in the city and a all the people of Samaria. *2014*
8:11 They followed him because *he had* a them *2014*
13:12 *for he was* a at the teaching about the Lord. *1742*

AMAZEMENT (7) [AMAZED, AMAZING]
Da 3:24 leaped to his feet in a and asked 10097+10755
Mt 27:14 to the great a of the governor. *2513*
Mk 7:37 *People were* **overwhelmed with a.** *1742+5669*
Lk 8:25 In fear and a they asked one another, *2513*
24:41 not believe it because of joy and a, *2513*
Jn 5:20 to your a he will show him *2513*
Ac 3:10 with wonder and a at what had happened *1749*

AMAZIAH (40) [AMAZIAH'S]
2Ki 12:21 And A his son succeeded him as king. 604
13:12 including his war against A king of Judah, 604
14: 1 A son of Joash king of Judah began 605
14: 8 Then A sent messengers to Jehoash son 604
14: 9 But Jehoash king of Israel replied to A king 605
14:11 A, however, would not listen, 605
14:11 He and A king of Judah faced each other 605
14:13 Jehoash king of Israel captured A king 605
14:15 including his war against A king of Judah, 605
14:17 A son of Joash king of Judah lived 605
14:21 and made him king in place of his father A. 605
14:22 after A rested with his fathers. 2021+4889[S]
14:23 In the fifteenth year of A son of Joash king 605
15: 1 Azariah son of A king of Judah began 604
15: 3 just as his father A had done. 605
1Ch 3:12 A his son, Azariah his son, Jotham his son, 605
4:34 Meshobab, Jamlech, Joshah son of A, 604
6:45 the son of A, the son of Hilkiah, 604
2Ch 24:27 And A his son succeeded him as king. 605
25: 1 A was twenty-five years old 605
25: 5 A called the people of Judah together 605
25: 9 A asked the man of God, 605
25:10 So A dismissed the troops who had come 605
25:11 A then marshaled his strength 605
25:13 Meanwhile the troops that A had sent back 605
25:14 When A returned from slaughtering 605
25:15 The anger of the LORD burned against A, 605
25:17 A king of Judah consulted his advisers, 605
25:18 But Jehoash king of Israel replied to A king 605
25:20 A, however, would not listen, 605
25:21 He and A king of Judah faced each other 605
25:23 Jehoash king of Israel captured A king 605
25:25 A son of Joash king of Judah lived 605
25:27 the time that A turned away from following 605
26: 1 and made him king in place of his father A. 605
26: 2 after A rested with his fathers. 2021+4889[S]
26: 4 just as his father A had done. 605
Am 7:10 Then A the priest of Bethel sent a message 604
7:12 Then A said to Amos, "Get out, you seer! 604
7:14 Amos answered A, "I was neither a prophet 604

AMAZIAH'S (2) [AMAZIAH]
2Ki 14:18 As for the other events of A reign, 605
2Ch 25:26 As for the other events of A reign, 605

AMAZING (3) [AMAZEMENT]
Jos 3: 5 for tomorrow the LORD will do a *things* 7098
Jdg 13:19 the LORD did an a *thing* while Manoah 7098
Pr 30:18 "There are three things *that are* too a 7098

AMBASSADOR (1) [AMBASSADORS]
Eph 6:20 for which *I am an* a in chains. *4563*

AMBASSADORS (2) [AMBASSADOR]
Isa 57: 9 You sent your a far away; 7495
2Co 5:20 *We are* therefore Christ's a, *4563*

AMBASSAGE (KJV) See DELEGATION

AMBER (KJV) See GLOWING METAL

AMBITION (7)
Ro 15:20 It *has always been my* a to preach *5818*
Gal 5:20 jealousy, fits of rage, **selfish a,** dissensions, *2249*
Php 1:17 The former preach Christ out of **selfish a,** *2249*
2: 3 Do nothing out of **selfish a** or vain conceit, *2249*
1Th 4:11 **Make it** *your* a to lead a quiet life, *5818*
Jas 3:14 But if you harbor bitter envy and **selfish a** *2249*
3:16 For where you have envy and **selfish a,** *2249*

AMBUSH (25) [AMBUSHES]
Jos 8: 2 Set an a behind the city." 741
8: 4 You *are to* **set an a** behind the city. 741
8: 7 you are to rise up from a and take the city. 741
8: 9 and they went to the **place of a** and lay 4422
8:12 about five thousand men and set them **in a** 741
8:13 to the north of the city and the a to the west 6811
8:14 not know that an a *had been* **set** against him 741
8:19 the *men* **in** *the* a rose quickly 741
8:21 and all Israel saw that the a had taken 741
8:22 **The men of the a** also came out 465[S]
Jdg 9:25 of Shechem set men on the hilltops *to* a 741
9:43 into three companies and **set an a** in 741
20:29 Then Israel set an a around Gibeah. 741
20:33 and the Israelite a charged out of its place 741
20:36 because they relied on the a they had set 741
20:37 *been* **in** a made a sudden dash into Gibeah, 741
20:38 the a that they should send up a great cloud 741
1Sa 15: 5 of Amalek and **set an a** in the ravine. 741
2Ch 13:13 in front of Judah the a was behind them. 4422
Ps 10: 8 from a he murders the innocent, 5041
64: 4 They shoot from a at the innocent man; 5041
Jer 51:12 station the watchmen, prepare an a! 741
Hos 6: 9 As marauders **lie in a** *for* a man, 2675
Ac 23:21 of them *are* **waiting in a for** him. *1910*
25: 3 for they were preparing an a to kill him *1909*

AMBUSHES (1) [AMBUSH]
2Ch 20:22 the LORD set a against the men 741

AMEN (57)
Nu 5:22 Then the woman is to say, "**A. So be it.**" 589+589
Dt 27:15 Then all the people shall say, "A!" 589
27:16 Then all the people shall say, "A!" 589
27:17 Then all the people shall say, "A!" 589
27:18 Then all the people shall say, "A!" 589
27:19 Then all the people shall say, "A!" 589
27:20 Then all the people shall say, "A!" 589
27:21 Then all the people shall say, "A!" 589
27:22 Then all the people shall say, "A!" 589
27:23 Then all the people shall say, "A!" 589
27:24 Then all the people shall say, "A!" 589
27:25 Then all the people shall say, "A!" 589
27:26 Then all the people shall say, "A!" 589
1Ki 1:36 of Jehoiada answered the king, "A! 589
1Ch 16:36 Then all the people said "A" and "Praise 589
Ne 5:13 At this the whole assembly said, "A," 589

Ne 8: 6 people lifted their hands and responded, "A! 589
8: 6 and responded, "Amen! A!" 589
Ps 41:13 A and Amen. 589
41:13 Amen and A. 589
72:19 A and Amen. 589
72:19 Amen and A. 589
89:52 A and Amen. 589
89:52 Amen and A. 589
106:48 Let all the people say, "A!" 589
Jer 11: 5 I answered, "A, LORD." 589
28: 6 He said, "A! 589
Ro 1:25 who is forever praised. A. 297
9: 5 over all, forever praised! A. 297
11:36 be the glory forever! A. 297
15:33 The God of peace be with you all. A. 297
16:27 through Jesus Christ! A. 297
1Co 14:16 those who do not understand say "A" 297
16:24 My love to all of you in Christ Jesus. A. 297
2Co 1:20 And so through him the "A" is spoken by us 297
Gal 1: 5 to whom be glory for ever and ever. A. 297
6:18 with your spirit, brothers. A. 297
Eph 3:21 for ever and ever! A. 297
Php 4:20 for ever and ever. A. 297
4:23 the Lord Jesus Christ be with your spirit. A. 297
1Ti 1:17 for ever and ever. A. 297
6:16 be honor and might forever. A. 297
2Ti 4:18 for ever and ever. A. 297
Heb 13:21 for ever and ever. A. 297
1Pe 4:11 for ever and ever. A. 297
5:11 To him be the power for ever and ever. A. 297
2Pe 3:18 both now and forever! A. 297
Jude 1:25 now and forevermore! A. 297
Rev 1: 6 for ever and ever! A. 297
1: 7 So shall it be! A. 297
3:14 These are the words of the A, 297
5:14 The four living creatures said, "A," 297
7:12 "A! Praise and glory 297
7:12 for ever and ever. A!" 297
19: 4 And they cried: "A, Hallelujah!" 297
22:20 I am coming soon." A. 297
22:21 grace of Lord Jesus be with God's people. A. 297

AMENDS (3)

2Sa 21: 3 How *shall I* **make a** so that you will bless 4105
Job 20:10 His children *must* **make a** *to* the poor; 8355
Pr 14: 9 Fools mock at **making a for sin,** 871

AMERCE (KJV) See FINE

AMETHYST (3)

Ex 28:19 an agate and an **a**; 334
39:12 an agate and an **a**; 334
Rev 21:20 the eleventh jacinth, and the twelfth **a**. 287

AMI (1)

Ezr 2:57 Pokereth-Hazzebaim and A 577

AMIABLE (KJV) See LOVELY

AMID (7) [MIDDLE]

Job 4:13 **A** disquieting dreams in the night, 928
30:14 **a** the ruins they come rolling in. 9393
Ps 47: 5 God has ascended **a** shouts of joy, 928
47: 5 the LORD **a** the sounding of trumpets. 928
Am 1:14 that will consume her fortresses **a** war cries 928
1:14 **a** violent winds on a stormy day. 928
2: 2 in great tumult **a** war cries and the blast of 928

AMINADAB (KJV) See AMMINADAB

AMISS (KJV) See WRONG

AMITTAI (2)

2Ki 14:25 spoken through his servant Jonah son of A, 624
Jnh 1: 1 of the LORD came to Jonah son of A: 624

AMMAH (1) [METHEG AMMAH]

2Sa 2:24 they came to the hill of A, 565

AMMI (KJV) See MY PEOPLE

AMMINADIB (KJV) See PEOPLE

AMMIEL (6)

Nu 13:12 from the tribe of Dan, A son of Gemalli; 6653
2Sa 9: 4 the house of Makir son of A in Lo Debar." 6653
9: 5 from the house of Makir son of A. 6653
17:27 and Makir son of A from Lo Debar, 6653
1Ch 3: 5 by Bathsheba daughter of A. 6653
26: 5 A the sixth, Issachar the seventh 6653

AMMIHUD (10)

Nu 1:10 from Ephraim, Elishama son of A; 6654
2:18 of Ephraim is Elishama son of A. 6654
7:48 On the seventh day Elishama son of A, 6654
7:53 This was the offering of Elishama son of A. 6654
10:22 Elishama son of A was in command. 6654
34:20 Shemuel son of A, from the tribe 6654
Nu 34:28 Pedahel son of A, 6654
2Sa 13:37 Absalom fled and went to Talmai son of A, 6654
1Ch 7:26 Ladan his son, A his son, Elishama his son, 6654
9: 4 Uthai son of A, 6654

AMMINADAB (16)

Ex 6:23 daughter of A and sister of Nahshon, 6657
Nu 1: 7 from Judah, Nahshon son of A; 6657
2: 3 of the people of Judah is Nahshon son of A. 6657
7:12 on the first day was Nahshon son of A of 6657
7:17 This was the offering of Nahshon son of A. 6657
10:14 Nahshon son of A was in command. 6657
Ru 4:19 Ram the father of A, 6657
4:20 A the father of Nahshon, 6657
1Ch 2:10 Ram was the father of A, 6657
2:10 and A the father of Nahshon, 6657
6:22 A his son, Korah his son, Assir his son, 6657
15:10 A the leader and 112 relatives. 6657
15:11 Joel, Shemaiah, Eliel and A the Levites. 6657
Mt 1: 4 Ram the father of A, *300*
1: 4 A the father of Nahshon, *300*
Lk 3:33 the son *of* A, *300*

AMMISHADDAI (5)

Nu 1:12 from Dan, Ahiezer son of A; 6659
2:25 of the people of Dan is Ahiezer son of A. 6659
7:66 On the tenth day Ahiezer son of A, 6659
7:71 This was the offering of Ahiezer son of A. 6659
10:25 Ahiezer son of A was in command. 6659

AMMIZABAD (1)

1Ch 27: 6 His son A was in charge of his division. 6655

AMMON (15) [AMMONITE, AMMONITES]

Jdg 11:28 The king of A, however, 1201+6648
11:33 Thus Israel subdued A. 1201+6648
2Ki 23:13 the detestable god of the people of A. 6648
2Ch 20:10 "But now here are men from A, 6648
20:22 against the men of A and Moab 6648
20:23 The men of A and Moab rose up against 6648
Ne 13:23 from Ashdod, A and Moab. 6649
Ps 83: 7 A and Amalek, Philistia, 6648
Jer 9:26 A, Moab and all who live in the desert 1201+6648
25:21 Edom, Moab and A; 1201+6648
27: 3 word to the kings of Edom, Moab, A, 1201+6648
40:11 When all the Jews in Moab, A, 1201+6648
Eze 25: 5 for camels and A into a resting place 1201+6648
Da 11:41 the leaders of A will be delivered 1201+6648
Am 1:13 "For three sins of A, even for four, 1201+6648

AMMONI See KEPHAR AMMONI

AMMONITE (21) [AMMON]

Dt 23: 3 No A or Moabite or any 6649
Jos 13:25 the A country as far as Aroer, 1201+6648
Jdg 11:12 to the A king with the question: 1201+6648
11:14 messengers to the A king, 1201+6648
1Sa 11: 1 the A went up and besieged Jabesh Gilead. 6649
11: 2 But Nahash the A replied, 6649
2Sa 10: 3 the A nobles said to Hanun their lord, 1201+6648
12:31 He did this to all the A towns. 1201+6648
23:37 Zelek the A, Naharai the Beerothite, 6649
1Ki 14:21 Naamah; she was an A. 6649
14:31 Naamah; she was an A. 6649
2Ki 24: 2 Moabite and A raiders against him. 1201+6648
1Ch 11:39 Zelek the A, Naharai the Berothite, 6649
19: 3 the A nobles said to Hanun, 1201+6648
20: 3 David did this to all the A towns. 1201+6648
2Ch 12:13 Naamah; she was an A. 6649
24:26 son of Shimeath an A *woman*, 6649
Ne 2:10 and Tobiah the A official heard about this, 6649
2:19 the A official and Geshem the Arab heard 6649
4: 3 Tobiah the A, who was at his side, said, 6649
13: 1 and there it was found written that no A 6649

AMMONITES (88) [AMMON]

Ge 19:38 he is the father of the A of today. 1201+6648
Nu 21:24 but only as far as the A, 1201+6648
Dt 2:19 When you come to the A, 1201+6648
2:19 of any land belonging to the A. 1201+6648
2:20 but the A called them Zamzummites. 6649
2:21 from before **the A**, 2157[S]
2:37 not encroach on any of the land of the A, 1201+6648
3:11 It is still in Rabbah of the A.) 1201+6648
3:16 which is the border of the A. 1201+6648
Jos 12: 2 which is the border of the A. 1201+6648
13:10 out to the border of the A. 1201+6648
Jdg 3:13 Getting the A and Amalekites to join him, 1201+6648
10: 6 the A and the gods of the Philistines. 1201+6648
10: 7 the hands of the Philistines and the A, 1201+6648
10: 9 The A also crossed the Jordan to fight 1201+6648
10:11 the Egyptians, the Amorites, the A, 1201+6648
10:17 the A were called to arms and camped 1201+6648
10:18 the A will be the head of all those 1201+6648
11: 4 when the A made war on Israel, 1201+6648
11: 6 "be our commander, so we can fight the A." 1201+6648
11: 8 come with us to fight the A, 1201+6648
11: 9 the A and the LORD gives them to me 1201+6648
11:13 the A answered Jephthah's messengers 1201+6648
Jdg 11:15 the land of Moab or the land of the A. 1201+6648
11:27 between the Israelites and the A." 1201+6648
11:29 from there he advanced against the A. 1201+6648
11:30 "If you give the A into my hands, 1201+6648
11:31 when I return in triumph from the A 1201+6648
11:32 Jephthah went over to fight the A, 1201+6648
11:36 of your enemies, the A. 1201+6648
12: 1 go to fight the A without calling us 1201+6648
12: 2 in a great struggle with the A, 1201+6648
12: 3 and crossed over to fight the A, 1201+6648
1Sa 11:10 They said to the A, NIH
11:11 the A and slaughtered them until the heat of 6648
12:12 of the A was moving against you, 1201+6648
14:47 the A, Edom, the kings of Zobah, 1201+6648
2Sa 8:12 the A and the Philistines, and Amalek. 1201+6648
10: 1 the king of the A died, 1201+6648
10: 2 David's men came to the land of the A 1201+6648
10: 6 the A realized that they had become 1201+6648
10: 8 The A came out and drew up 1201+6648
10:10 and deployed them against the A. 1201+6648
10:11 but if the A are too strong for you, 1201+6648
10:14 A saw that the Arameans were fleeing, 1201+6648
10:14 from fighting the A and came 1201+6648
10:19 to help the A anymore. 1201+6648
11: 1 the A and besieged Rabbah. 1201+6648
12: 9 killed him with the sword of the A. 1201+6648
12:26 of the A and captured the royal citadel. 1201+6648
17:27 of Nahash from Rabbah of the A, 1201+6648
1Ki 11: 1 Moabites, A, Edomites, 6649
11: 5 and Molech the detestable god of the A. 6649
11: 7 Molech the detestable god of the A. 1201+6648
11:33 and Molech the god of the A, 1201+6648
1Ch 18:11 Moab, the A and the Philistines, 1201+6648
19: 1 Nahash king of the A died, 1201+6648
19: 2 the land of the A to express sympathy 1201+6648
19: 6 the A realized that they had become 1201+6648
19: 6 the A sent a thousand talents of silver 1201+6648
19: 7 the A were mustered from their towns 1201+6648
19: 9 The A came out and drew up 1201+6648
19:11 and they were deployed against the A. 1201+6648
19:12 but if the A are too strong for you, 1201+6648
19:15 A saw that the Arameans were fleeing, 1201+6648
19:19 not willing to help the A anymore. 1201+6648
20: 1 the A and went to Rabbah and besieged it, 1201+6648
2Ch 20: 1 A with some of the Meunites came 1201+6648
26: 8 The A brought tribute to Uzziah, 6649
27: 5 the king of the A and conquered them. 1201+6648
27: 5 the A paid him a hundred talents 1201+6648
27: 5 The A brought him the same amount 1201+6648
Ezr 9: 1 Hittites, Perizzites, Jebusites, A, Moabites, 6649
Ne 4: 7 the A and the men of Ashdod heard that 6649
Isa 11:14 and the A will be subject to them. 1201+6648
Jer 40:14 Baalis king of the A has sent Ishmael 1201+6648
41:10 and set out to cross over to the A. 1201+6648
41:15 from Johanan and fled to the A. 1201+6648
49: 1 Concerning the A: This is what the LORD says: 1201+6648
49: 2 the battle cry against Rabbah of the A; 1201+6648
49: 6 I will restore the fortunes of the A," 1201+6648
Eze 21:20 the sword to come against Rabbah of the A 1201+6648
21:28 the Sovereign LORD says about the A 1201+6648
25: 2 the A and prophesy against them. 1201+6648
25:10 with the A to the people of the East 1201+6648
25:10 the A will not be remembered among 1201+6648
Zep 2: 8 insults of Moab and the taunts of the A 1201+6648
2: 9 the A like Gomorrah— 1201+6648

AMNON (28) [AMNON'S]

2Sa 3: 2 His firstborn was A the son of Ahinoam 596
13: 1 A son of David fell in love with Tamar, 596
13: 2 A became frustrated to the point of illness 596
13: 3 Now A had a friend named Jonadab son 596
13: 4 He asked A, "Why do you, the king's son, 2257[S]
13: 4 A said to him, "I'm in love with Tamar, 596
13: 6 So A lay down and pretended to be ill. 596
13: 6 the king came to see him, A said to him, 596
13: 7 of your brother A and prepare some food 596
13: 8 Tamar went to the house of her brother A, 596
13: 9 "Send everyone out of here," A said. 596
13:10 Then A said to Tamar, 596
13:10 to her brother A in his bedroom. 596
13:15 Then A hated her with intense hatred. 596
13:15 A said to her, "Get up and get out!" 596
13:20 "Has that A, your brother, been with you? 578
13:22 Absalom never said a word to A, 596
13:22 he hated A because he had disgraced his sister 596
13:26 please let my brother A come with us." 596
13:27 with him A and the rest of the king's sons. 596
13:28 When A is in high spirits 596
13:28 'Strike A down,' then kill him. 596
13:29 to A what Absalom had ordered. 596
13:32 only A is dead. 596
13:32 since the day A raped his sister Tamar. 2257[S]
13:33 Only A is dead." 596
1Ch 3: 1 The firstborn was A the son of Ahinoam 596
4:20 A, Rinnah, Ben-Hanan and Tilon. 596

AMNON'S (1) [AMNON]

2Sa 13:39 for he was consoled concerning A death. 596

AMOK (1) [AMOK'S]

Ne 12: 7 A, Hilkiah and Jedaiah. 6651

AMOK'S (1) [AMOK]

Ne 12:20 of Sallu's, Kallai; of A, Eber; 6651

AMON (18) [AMON'S]

1Ki 22:26 and send him back to A the ruler of the city 571
2Ki 21:18 And A his son succeeded him as king. 571
21:19 A was twenty-two years old 571
21:24 of the land killed all who had plotted against King A, 571
1Ch 3:14 A his son, Josiah his son. 571
2Ch 18:25 and send him back to A the ruler of the city 571
33:20 And A his son succeeded him as king. 571
33:21 A was twenty-two years old 571
33:22 A worshiped and offered sacrifices to all 571
33:23 A increased his guilt. 571
33:25 of the land killed all who had plotted against King A, 571
Ne 7:59 Pokereth-Hazzebaim and A 571
Jer 1:2 the reign of Josiah son of A king of Judah, 571
25:3 the thirteenth year of Josiah son of A king 571
46:25 "I am about to bring punishment on A god 572
Zep 1:1 the reign of Josiah son of A king of Judah: 571
Mt 1:10 Manasseh the father of A, *321*
1:10 A the father of Josiah, *321*

AMON'S (3) [AMON]

2Ki 21:23 A officials conspired against him 571
21:25 As for the other events of A reign, 571
2Ch 33:24 A officials conspired against him 2257S

AMONG (812)

Ge 3:8 the LORD God a the trees of the garden. 928+9348
6:9 blameless a the people of his time, 928
13:12 while Lot lived a the cities of the plain 928
17:10 Every male a you shall be circumcised. 4200
17:12 For the generations to come every male a 4200
23:4 "I am an alien and a stranger a you. 6640
23:6 You are a mighty prince a us. 928+9348
23:9 to me for the full price as a burial site a 928+9348
23:10 Ephron the Hittite was sitting a his people 928+9348
23:16 the weight current a the merchants. 4200
24:3 a whom I am living, 928+7931
25:27 **staying** *a* the tents. AIT
27:46 If Jacob takes a wife **from a** the women 4946
28:2 **from a** the daughters of Laban, 4946
33:1 so he divided the children a Leah, 6584
34:10 You can settle a us; the land is open to you. 907
34:16 We'll settle a you and become one people 907
34:23 and they will settle a us." 907
36:15 These were the **chiefs** *a* Esau's descendants: AIT
41:2 sleek and fat, and they grazed a the reeds. 928
41:18 fat and sleek, and they grazed a the reeds. 928
42:5 So Israel's sons were a those who went 928+9348
47:6 of any a them with special ability, 928
49:26 on the brow of the **prince** *a* his brothers. AIT
Ex 2:3 in it and put it a the reeds along the bank of 928
2:5 She saw the basket a the reeds 928+9348
3:20 all the wonders that I will perform a 928+7931
10:1 miraculous signs of mine a them 928+7931
10:2 and how I performed my signs a them, 928
11:7 But a the Israelites not a dog will bark 3972+4200
12:48 "An alien living a you who wants 907
12:49 the native-born and to the alien living a 928+9348
13:2 of every womb a the Israelites belongs 928
13:7 nothing with yeast in it is to be seen a you, 4200
13:13 Redeem every firstborn a your sons. 928
15:11 "Who a the gods is like you, O LORD? 928
17:7 "Is the LORD a us or not?" 928+7931
22:25 of my people a you who is needy, do not be 6640
23:11 Then the **poor** *a* your people may get food AIT
23:25 I will take away sickness from a you, 7931
25:8 and I will dwell a them. 928+9348
27:21 a lasting ordinance a the Israelites 907+4946
28:1 to you from a the Israelites, 9348
29:45 Then I will dwell a the Israelites and 928+9348
29:46 of Egypt so that I might dwell a them. 928+9348
34:10 The people you live a will see 928+7931
34:12 or they will be a snare a you. 928+7931
35:10 "All who are skilled a you are to come 928
36:8 All the skilled men a the workmen made 928
Lev 10:3 " 'A those who approach me I will show myself holy; 928
11:10 whether a all the swarming things or 4946
11:10 among all the swarming things or a all 4946
15:31 which is a them.' " 928+9348
16:16 which *is* a them in the midst 907+8905
16:29 whether native-born or an alien living a 928+9348
17:8 or any alien living a them who offers 928+9348
17:10 " 'Any Israelite or any alien living a 928+9348
17:12 nor may an alien living a you eat blood.' 928+9348
17:13 " 'Any Israelite or any alien living a 928+9348
18:26 the aliens living a you must not do any 928+9348
19:16 " 'Do not go about spreading slander a 928
20:14 so that no wickedness will be a you. 928+9348
20:27 or woman who is a medium or spiritist a 928
21:10 the one a his brothers who has had 4946
21:15 he will not defile his offspring a his people. 928
23:30 I will destroy from a his people anyone who 7931
24:10 father went out a the Israelites, 928+9348
25:6 and temporary resident who live a you, 6640
25:33 towns of the Levites are their property a 928+9348
25:35 and is unable to support himself a you, 6640
25:35 so he can continue to live a you. 6640
Lev 25:36 to live a you. 6640
25:39 of your countrymen becomes poor a you 6640
25:40 as a hired worker or a temporary resident a 6640
25:45 of the temporary residents living a you 6640
25:47 or a temporary resident a you becomes rich 6640
25:47 to the alien living a you or to a member of 6640
26:11 I will put my dwelling place a you, 928+9348
26:12 I will walk a you and be your God, 928+9348
26:25 I will send a plague a you, 928+9348
26:33 I will scatter you a the nations 928
26:38 You will perish a the nations; 928
Nu 3:12 the Levites from a the Israelites in place of 9348
5:3 where I dwell a them." 928+9348
5:27 she will become accursed a her people. 928+7931
8:6 the Levites from a the other Israelites 9348
9:14 " 'An alien living a you who wants 907
11:1 Then fire from the LORD burned a them 928
11:3 fire from the LORD had burned a them. 928
11:16 as leaders and **officials** *a* the people. AIT
11:20 who is a you, and have wailed before him, 928+7931
11:21 "Here I am a six hundred thousand men 928+7931
11:26 They were listed a the elders, 928
12:6 **prophet** *of* the LORD is *a* AIT
13:32 And they spread a the Israelites 448
14:6 who were a those who had explored 4946
14:11 miraculous signs I have performed a 928+7931
14:13 brought these people up from a them. 7931
15:14 whenever an alien or anyone else living a 907
15:15 for you and for the alien living a you; NIH
15:16 both to you and to the alien living a you.' " 907
15:26 aliens living a them will be forgiven, 928+9348
16:47 The plague had already started a 928
17:6 and Aaron's staff was a them. 928+9348
18:6 from a the Israelites as a gift to you, 9348
18:20 nor will you have any share a them; 928+9348
18:20 I am your share and your inheritance a 928+9348
18:23 They will receive no inheritance a 928+9348
18:24 'They will have no inheritance a 928+9348
19:10 the Israelites and for the aliens living a 928+9348
20:13 and where he showed himself holy a them. 928
21:6 the LORD sent venomous snakes a them; 928
23:21 the shout of the King is a them. 928
24:20 "Amalek was **first** *a* the nations, AIT
25:11 as zealous as I am for my honor a them, 928+9348
26:9 and Aaron and were a Korah's followers 928
26:56 by lot a the larger and smaller groups." 1068
26:62 because they received no inheritance a 928+9348
26:64 of them was a those counted by Moses 4946
27:3 He was not a Korah's followers, 928+9348
27:4 Give us property a our father's relatives 928+9348
27:7 an inheritance a their father's relatives 928+9348
31:8 A their victims were Evi, Rekem, Zur, 6584
33:4 whom the LORD had struck down a them; 928
35:15 and any other people living a them, 928+9348
35:34 for I, the LORD, dwell a the Israelites.' 928+9348
Dt 2:16 when the last of these fighting men a 4946+7931
4:3 The LORD your God destroyed from a 7931
4:27 The LORD will scatter you a the peoples, 928
4:27 of you will survive a the nations to which 928
6:15 the LORD your God, who is a you, 928+7931
7:20 the LORD your God will send the hornet a 928
7:21 is a you, is a great and awesome God. 928+7931
10:9 the Levites have no share or inheritance a 6640
12:5 the LORD your God will choose **from a** 4946
13:1 appears a you and announces to you 928+7931
13:5 You must purge the evil from a you. 7931
13:11 and no one a you will do such 928+7931
13:13 that wicked men have arisen a you 4946+7931
13:14 this detestable thing has been done a 928+7931
15:4 However, there should be no poor a you, 928
15:7 If there is a poor man a your brothers 928
16:11 fatherless and the widows living a you. 928+7931
17:2 woman living a you in one of the towns 928+7931
17:7 You must purge the evil from a you. 7931
17:15 He must be from a your own brothers. 7931
18:2 They shall have no inheritance a 928+7931
18:10 be found a you who sacrifices his son 928
18:15 up for you a prophet like me from a 7931
18:18 a prophet like you from a their brothers; 7931
19:19 You must purge the evil from a you. 7931
19:20 an evil thing be done a you. 928+7931
21:11 if you notice a the captives 928
21:21 You must purge the evil from a you. 7931
22:21 You must purge the evil from a you. 7931
22:24 You must purge the evil from a you. 7931
23:14 that he will not see a you anything indecent 928
23:16 Let him live a you wherever he likes 928+7931
24:7 You must purge the evil from a you. 7931
26:11 you and the Levites and the aliens a 928+7931
28:43 The alien who lives a you will rise 928+7931
28:54 Even the most gentle and sensitive man a 928
28:56 most gentle and sensitive woman a you— 928
28:64 the LORD will scatter you a all nations, 928
28:65 A those nations you will find no repose, 928
29:17 You saw a them their detestable images 6640
29:18 clan or tribe a you today 928
29:18 make sure there is no root a you 928
30:1 the LORD your God disperses you a 928
31:7 **divide** *it a* them as their **inheritance.** AIT
32:51 you did not uphold my holiness a 928+9348
33:16 on the brow of the **prince** *a* his brothers. AIT
Jos 3:5 the LORD will do amazing things a you. 928+7931
3:10 you will know that the living God is a 928+7931
4:2 "Choose twelve men **from a** the people, 4946
4:6 to serve as a sign a you. 928+7931
6:25 and she lives a the Israelites to this day. 928+7931
Jos 7:12 unless you destroy whatever a 4946+7931
7:13 which is devoted is a you, O Israel. 928+7931
8:35 and the aliens who lived a them. 928+7931
13:7 an inheritance a the nine tribes and half of 4200
13:13 so they continue to live a the Israelites 928+7931
14:3 not granted the Levites an inheritance a 928+9348
14:15 who was the greatest man a the Anakites.) 928
16:10 Canaanites live a the people of Ephraim 928+7931
17:4 to give us an inheritance a our brothers 928+9348
17:6 of Manasseh received an inheritance a 928+9348
17:9 Ephraim lying a the towns of Manasseh 928+9348
18:7 however, do not get a portion a you, 928+7931
19:49 of Nun an inheritance a them, 928+9348
20:9 of the Israelites or any alien living a 928+9348
22:14 of a family division a the Israelite clans. 4200
23:7 with these nations that remain a you; 907
23:12 the survivors of these nations that remain a 907
24:17 He protected us on our entire journey and a 928
24:23 "throw away the foreign gods that are a 928+7931
Jdg 1:16 with the men of Judah to live a the people 907
1:29 Canaanites continued to live there a them. 928+7931
1:30 who remained a them; 928+7931
1:32 the people of Asher lived a 928+7931
1:33 but the Naphtalites too lived a 928+7931
3:5 The Israelites lived a the Canaanites, 928+7931
5:8 a shield or spear was seen a forty thousand 928
5:9 with the willing volunteers a the people. 928
5:16 Why did you stay a the campfires to hear 1068
10:16 Then they got rid of the foreign gods a 4946+7931
14:3 an acceptable woman a your relatives or 928
14:3 among your relatives or a all our people? 928
16:25 When they stood him a the pillars, 1068
18:1 yet come into an inheritance a the tribes 928+9348
20:12 that was committed a you? 928
20:16 A all these soldiers there were seven 4946
21:12 They found a the people living 4946
Ru 2:7 'Please let me glean and gather a 928
2:15 "Even if she gathers a the sheaves, 1068
4:10 from a his family or from the town records. 6640
1Sa 2:24 not a good report that I hear **spreading a** 6296
9:2 an impressive young man without equal a 4946
10:11 Is Saul also a the prophets?" 928
10:12 "Is Saul also a the prophets?" 928
10:22 he has hidden himself a the baggage." 448
10:23 and as he stood a the people he was 928+9348
10:24 There is no one like him a all the people." 928
13:6 they hid in caves and thickets, a the rocks, 928
14:3 a whom was Ahijah, NIH
14:34 he said, "Go out a the men and tell them, 928
15:33 so will your mother be childless a women." 4946
19:24 "Is Saul also a the prophets?" 928
23:19 "Is not David hiding a us in the strongholds 6640
23:23 if he is in the area, I will track him down a 928
30:22 But all the evil men and troublemakers a 4946
31:9 the temple of their idols and a their people. 907
2Sa 11:13 to sleep on his mat a his master's servants; 6640
12:19 servants were **whispering a themselves** 4317
15:31 "Ahithophel is a the conspirators 928
17:9 'There has been a slaughter a 928
19:28 a place a those who sat at your table. 928
22:50 O LORD, a the nations; 928
23:19 even though he was not included a them. 6330
23:23 but he was not included a the Three. 448
23:24 A the Thirty were: 928
1Ki 2:7 of Gilead and let them be a those who eat 928
3:8 Your servant is here a 928+9348
3:13 in your lifetime you will have no equal a 928
6:13 And I will live a the Israelites and will 928+9348
9:7 and an object of ridicule a all peoples. 928
14:7 from a the people and made you a leader 9348
21:9 and seat Naboth in a **prominent place** *a* AIT
21:12 and seated Naboth in a **prominent place** *a* AIT
2Ki 4:13 "I have a home a my own people." 928+9348
11:2 of Ahaziah and stole him away from a 9348
17:25 so he sent lions a them 928
17:26 He has sent lions a them, 928
18:5 There was no one like him a all the kings 928
20:13 and everything found a his treasures. 928
20:15 "There is nothing a my treasures that I did 928
1Ch 6:60 which were **distributed a** 928
7:15 a wife **from a** the Huppites and Shuppites. 4200
10:9 of the Philistines to **proclaim the news** *a* AIT
11:21 even though he was not included a them. 6330
11:25 but he was not included a the Three. 448
12:1 of Saul son of Kish (they were a 928
12:4 a mighty man a the Thirty, 928
16:8 known a the nations what he has done. 928
16:24 Declare his glory a the nations, 928
16:24 his marvelous deeds a all peoples. 928
16:31 let them say a the nations, 928
22:2 and from a them he appointed stonecutters NIH
24:4 A larger number of leaders **were found** *a* AIT
24:4 among Eleazar's descendants than a NIH
24:5 of God a the descendants of both Eleazar 4946
26:31 and capable men a the Hebronites 928
27:6 a **mighty man** *a* the Thirty and was over AIT
2Ch 7:13 the land or send a plague a my people, 928
7:20 and an object of ridicule a all peoples. 928
11:22 to be the chief prince a his brothers, 928
13:17 five hundred thousand casualties a Israel's 4946
15:9 Manasseh and Simeon who had settled a 6640
19:4 and he went out again a the people 928
20:25 and they found a them a great amount 928
22:11 from a the royal princes who were about to 9348
26:6 and elsewhere a the Philistines. 928
31:19 to distribute portions to every male a them 928

2Ch 36:23 Anyone of his people a you— 928
Ezr 1: 3 Anyone of his people a you— 928
2:61 And **from a** the priests: 4946
8:15 I checked a the people and the priests, 928
10:18 A the descendants of the priests, 4946
10:23 A the Levites: Jozabad, 4946
10:25 And a the other Israelites: 4946
Ne 1: 8 I will scatter you a the nations, 928
4:11 be right there a them and will kill them 448+9348
6: 6 "It is reported a the nations— 928
7:63 And **from a** the priests: 4946
9:17 to remember the miracles you performed a 6640
11:17 Bakbukiah, second a his associates; 4946
12:23 The family heads a the descendants of Levi NIH
13:26 A the many nations there was no king 928
Est 2: 6 a those taken captive with Jehoiachin king 6640
3: 8 a certain people dispersed and scattered a 1068
4: 3 there was great mourning a the Jews, 4200
8:17 there was joy and gladness a the Jews, 4200
9:28 nor should the memory of them die out a 4946
10: 3 preeminent a the Jews, 4200
Job 1: 3 He was the greatest man a all the people of 4946
2: 8 and scraped himself with it as he sat a 928+9348
3: 6 not be included a the days of the year nor 928
5: 5 taking it even from a thorns, 448
8:17 of rocks and looks for a *place* a the stones. 1075
12:12 Is not wisdom found a the aged? 928
15:19 land was given when no alien passed a 928+9348
17:10 I will not find a wise man a you. 928
18:19 He has no offspring or descendants a 928
19:11 he counts me a his enemies. 3869
24:11 They crush olives a the terraces; 1068
29:25 I dwelt as a king a his troops; 928
30: 6 a the rocks and in holes in the ground. NIH
30: 7 They brayed a the bushes and huddled in 1068
30: 9 I have become a byword a them. 4200
34:37 scornfully he claps his hands a us 1068
36:14 a male prostitutes of the shrines. 928
40:19 He ranks **first** *a* the works of God, AIT
40:21 **hidden** *a* the reeds in the marsh. AIT
41: 6 Will they divide him up a the merchants? 1068
Ps 9:11 proclaim a the nations what he has done. 928
12: 1 the faithful have vanished **from a** men. 4946
12: 8 about when what is vile is honored a men. 4200
18:49 Therefore I will praise you a the nations, 928
22:18 They divide my garments a them 4200
35:18 a throngs of people I will praise you. 928
36: 7 **low a men** find refuge in the shadow 132+1201
42: 4 and thanksgiving a the festive throng. NIH
44:11 and have scattered us a the nations. 928
44:14 You have made us a byword a the nations; 928
45: 9 of kings are a your honored women; 928
46:10 I will be exalted a the nations, 928
54: T "Is not David hiding a us?" 6640
55:15 for evil finds lodging a them. 928+7931
57: 4 I lie a ravenous beasts— NIH
57: 9 I will praise you, O Lord, a the nations; 928
57: 9 I will sing of you a the peoples. 928
58: 1 Do you judge uprightly a men? NIH
67: 2 your salvation a all nations. 928
68:13 Even while you sleep a the campfires, 1068
68:30 Rebuke the **beast** *a* the reeds, AIT
68:30 the herd of bulls a the calves of the nations. 928
72: 4 He will defend the **afflicted** *a* the people AIT
77:14 you display your power a the peoples. 928
78:31 he put to death the sturdiest a them, 928
78:60 the tent he had set up a men. 928
79:10 make known a the nations that you avenge 928
81: 9 You shall have no foreign god a you; 928
82: 1 he gives judgment a the "gods": 928+7931
86: 8 A the gods there is none like you, O Lord; 928
87: 4 "I will record Rahab and Babylon a 4200
88: 4 I am counted a those who go down to 6640
89: 6 like the LORD a the heavenly beings? 928
89:19 I have exalted a young man **from a** 4946
94: 8 you senseless ones a the people; 928
96: 3 Declare his glory a the nations, 928
96: 3 his marvelous deeds a all peoples. 928
96:10 Say a the nations, "The LORD reigns." 928
99: 6 Moses and Aaron were a his priests, 928
99: 6 Samuel was a those who called 928
102: 6 like an **owl** *a* the ruins. AIT
104:12 they sing a the branches. 1068+4946
105: 1 known a the nations what he has done. 928
105:27 They performed his miraculous signs a 928
105:37 and from a their tribes no one faltered. 928
106:18 Fire blazed a their followers; 928
106:27 make their descendants fall a the nations 928
106:29 and a plague broke out a them. 928
108: 3 I will praise you, O LORD, a the nations; 928
108: 3 I will sing of you a the peoples. 928
120: 5 that I live a the tents of Kedar! 6640
120: 6 Too long have I lived a 6640
126: 2 Then it was said a the nations, 928
136:11 from a them His love endures forever. 9348
Pr 6:19 a man who stirs up dissension a brothers. 1068
7: 7 I saw a the simple, 928
7: 7 I noticed a the young men, 928
14: 9 but goodwill is found a the upright. 1068
14:33 even a fools she lets herself be known. 928+7931
15:31 a life-giving rebuke will be at home a 928+7931
16:19 be lowly in spirit and a the oppressed than 907
23:28 and multiplies the unfaithful a men. 928
25: 6 and do not claim a place a great men; 928
30:14 the needy **from a** mankind. 4946
30:30 mighty a beasts, who retreats 928
31:23 he takes his seat a the elders of the land. 6640
Ecc 7:28 I found one [upright] man a a thousand, 4946
7:28 but not one [upright] woman a them all. 928
9: 4 Anyone who *is* a the living has hope— 2489
SS 2: 2 Like a lily a thorns is my darling among 1068
2: 2 among thorns is my darling a the maidens. 1068
2: 3 Like an apple tree a the trees of 928
2: 3 among the trees of the forest is my lover a 1068
2:16 he browses a the lilies. 928
4: 5 like twin fawns of a gazelle that browse a 928
5:10 outstanding a ten thousand. 4946
6: 3 he browses a the lilies. 928
6:12 my desire **set** me *a* the royal chariots AIT
Isa 2: 2 be established as **chief** *a* the mountains; AIT
4: 3 all who are recorded a the living 4200
5:17 lambs *will* **feed** *a* the ruins of the rich. AIT
6: 5 and I live a a people of unclean lips, 928+9348
7: 6 let us tear it apart and divide it a ourselves, 448
8:16 Bind up the testimony and seal up the law a 928
10: 4 but to cringe a the captives or fall among 9393
10: 4 but to cringe among the captives or fall a 9393
12: 4 known a the nations what he has done, 928
12: 6 great is the Holy One of Israel a you." 928+7931
13: 4 Listen, an **uproar** *a* the kingdoms, AIT
24:13 will it be on the earth and a the nations, 928+9348
29:23 When they see a them their children, 928+7931
30:14 shattered so mercilessly that a its pieces not 928
39: 2 his entire armory and everything found a 928
39: 4 "There is nothing a my treasures that I did 928
41:28 no one a them to give counsel, 4946
43:12 I, and not some foreign god a you. 928
44:14 He let it grow a the trees of the forest, 928
45: 9 a potsherd a the potsherds on the ground. 907
50:10 Who a you fears the LORD and obeys 928
53:12 Therefore I will give him a portion a 928
57: 5 You burn with lust a the oaks and 928
57: 6 [The idols] a the smooth stones of 928
59:10 a the strong, we are like the dead. 928
61: 9 be known a the nations and their offspring 928
61: 9 among the nations and their offspring a 928+9348
63:11 he who set his Holy Spirit a them, 928+7931
65: 4 who sit a the graves 928
66:19 "I will set a sign a them, 928
66:19 They will proclaim my glory a the nations. 928
Jer 4: 3 up your unplowed ground and do not sow a 448
4:29 some climb up a the rocks. 928
5:26 "A my people are wicked men who lie 928
6:15 So they will fall a the fallen; 928
8:12 So they will fall a the fallen; 928
8:17 "See, I will send venomous snakes a you, 928
9:16 I will scatter them a nations 928
10: 7 A all the wise men of the nations and 928
11: 9 "There is a conspiracy a the people 928
12:14 and I will uproot the house of Judah from a 9348
12:16 they will be established a my people. 928+9348
14: 9 You are a us, O LORD, 928+7931
18:13 "Inquire a the nations: 928
23:13 "A the prophets of Samaria 928
23:14 And a the prophets 928
25:16 because of the sword I will send a them." 1068
25:27 because of the sword I will send a you.' 1068
26: 6 of cursing a all the nations of the earth.' " 4200
29: 1 to the surviving **elders** *a* the exiles and to AIT
29: 8 "Do not let the prophets and diviners a 928+7931
29:18 a all the nations where I drive them. 928
29:27 who poses as a prophet a you? 4200
29:32 He will have no one left a this people, 928+9348
30:11 the nations a **which** I scatter you, 9004[S]
30:21 their ruler will arise from a them. 7931
31: 8 A them will be the blind and the lame, 928
32:20 both in Israel and a all mankind, 928
37: 4 Jeremiah was free to come and go a 928+9348
37:12 of the property a the people there. 928+9348
39:14 So he remained a his own people. 928+9348
40: 1 in chains a all the captives from Jerusalem 928+9348
40: 5 and live with him a the people, 928+9348
40: 6 him a the people who were left behind 928+9348
44: 8 of cursing and reproach a all the nations 928
46:18 "one will come who is like Tabor a 928
46:28 the nations a which I scatter you, 2025
48:27 Was she caught a thieves, 928
48:28 Abandon your towns and dwell a the rocks, 928
49:15 "Now I will make you small a the nations, 928
49:15 among the nations, despised a men. 928
50: 2 and proclaim a the nations, lift up a banner 928
50:23 How desolate is Babylon a the nations! 928
50:46 its cry will resound a the nations. 928
51:27 Blow the trumpet a the nations! 928
51:41 a horror Babylon will be a the nations! 928
La 1: 1 who once was great a the nations! 928
1: 1 She who was queen a the provinces has 928
1: 2 A all her lovers there is none 4946
1: 3 She dwells a the nations; 928
1:17 Jerusalem has become an unclean thing a 1068
2: 9 and her princes are exiled a the nations, 928
3:45 You have made us scum and refuse a 928+7931
4:15 people a the nations say, 928
4:20 that under his shadow we would live a 928
Eze 1: 1 I was a the exiles by the Kebar River, 928+9348
1:13 Fire moved back and forth a the creatures; 1068
2: 5 will know that a prophet has been a 928+9348
2: 6 around you and you live a scorpions. 448
3:15 I sat a them for seven days— 928+9348
3:25 so that you cannot go out a the people. 928+9348
4:13 of Israel will eat defiled food a the nations 928
5:14 and a reproach a the nations around you, 928
6: 7 Your people will fall slain a you, 928+9348
6: 8 the sword when you are scattered a 928
6:13 when their people lie slain a their idols 928+9348
7: 4 and the detestable practices a you. 928+9348
7: 9 and the detestable practices a you. 928+9348
8:11 of Shaphan was standing a them. 928+9348
10: 2 "Go in a the wheels beneath the cherubim. 1068
10: 2 from a the cherubim and scatter them over 1068
10: 6 "Take fire from a the wheels, 1068
10: 6 from a the cherubim," 1068
10: 7 to the fire that was a them. 1068
11: 1 I saw a them Jaazaniah son of Azzur 928+9348
11:16 Although I sent them far away a 928
11:16 among the nations and scattered them a 928
12: 2 you are living a a rebellious people. 928+9348
12:12 "The prince a them will put his things 928+9348
12:15 when I disperse them a the nations 928
12:24 or flattering divinations a the people 928+9348
13: 4 O Israel, are like jackals a ruins. 928
13:19 You have profaned me a my people for 448
14: 9 and destroy him from a my people Israel. 9348
15: 6 the vine a the trees of the forest as fuel for 928
16:14 And your fame spread a the nations 928
18:18 and did what was wrong a his people. 928+9348
19: 2 a lioness was your mother a the lions! 1068
19: 2 She lay down a the young lions 928+9348
19: 6 He prowled a the lions, 928+9348
20: 9 in the eyes of the nations they lived a 928+9348
20:23 in the desert that I would disperse them a 928
20:41 and I will show myself holy a you in 928
22:15 I will disperse you a the nations 928
22:26 so that I am profaned a them. 928+9348
22:30 a man a them who would build up the wall 4946
23:10 She became a byword a women, 4200
24:23 your sins and groan a **yourselves.** 278+408+448
25: 4 up their camps and pitch their tents a you; 928
25:10 the Ammonites will not be remembered a 928
27:36 The merchants a the nations hiss at you; 928
28:14 you walked a the fiery stones. 928+9348
28:16 O guardian cherub, from a the fiery stones. 9348
28:25 I will show myself holy a them in the sight 928
29: 3 you great monster lying a your streams. 928+9348
29: 4 I will pull you out from a your streams, 9348
29:12 I will make the land of Egypt desolate a 928+9348
29:12 her cities will lie desolate forty years a 928+9348
29:12 And I will disperse the Egyptians a 928
29:21 and I will open your mouth a them. 928+9348
30: 7 'They will be desolate a desolate lands, 928+9348
30: 7 and their cities will lie a ruined cities. 928+9348
30:23 I will disperse the Egyptians a the nations 928
30:26 I will disperse the Egyptians a the nations 928
31:13 the beasts of the field were a its branches. 448
31:14 for the earth below, a mortal men, 928+9348
31:17 its allies a the nations, 928+9348
31:18 you will lie a the uncircumcised 928+9348
32: 2 " 'You are like a **lion** *a* the nations; AIT
32: 9 when I bring about your destruction a 928
32: 9 a lands you have not known. 6584
32:19 Go down and be laid a the uncircumcised.' 907
32:20 will fall a those killed by the sword. 928+9348
32:25 A bed is made for her a the slain, 928+9348
32:25 they are laid a the slain. 928+9348
32:28 broken and will lie a the uncircumcised 928+9348
32:32 Pharaoh and all his hordes will be laid a 928+9348
33:33 that a prophet has been a them." 928+9348
34:24 my servant David will be prince a them 928+9348
35:11 of them and I will make myself known a 928
36:19 I dispersed them a the nations, 928
36:20 And wherever they went a 448
36:21 the house of Israel profaned a the nations 928
36:22 which you have profaned a the nations 928
36:23 which has been profaned a the nations, 928
36:23 the name you have profaned a them. 928+9348
36:30 so that you will no longer suffer disgrace a 928
37: 2 He led me back and forth a them, 6584
37:26 I will put my sanctuary a them forever. 928+9348
37:28 when my sanctuary is a them forever.' 928+9348
39: 7 " 'I will make known my holy name a 928+9348
39:21 "I will display my glory a the nations, 928
39:28 though I sent them into exile a the nations, 448
43: 7 where I will live a the Israelites forever. 928+9348
43: 9 and I will live a them forever. 928+9348
44: 9 the foreigners who live a the Israelites. 928+9348
46:10 The prince is to be a them, 928+9348
47:13 an inheritance a the twelve tribes of Israel, 4200
47:14 You are to divide it **equally a them.** 278+408+2257+3869
47:21 to distribute this land a yourselves 4200
47:22 for the aliens who have settled a you 928+9348
47:22 to be allotted an inheritance a the tribes 928+9348
Da 1: 6 A these were some from Judah: 928
2:11 and they do not live a men." 10554
2:25 a man a the exiles from Judah who can tell 10427
4:15 with the animals a the plants of the earth. 10089
6: 3 Now Daniel so distinguished himself a 10542
7: 8 a little one, which came up a them; 10099
11:14 The **violent** men *a* your own people AIT
11:24 loot and wealth a his followers. 4200
Hos 5: 9 A the tribes of Israel I proclaim what is certain. 928
8: 8 she is a the nations like a worthless thing. 928
8:10 Although they have sold themselves a 928
9:17 they will be wanderers a the nations. 928
11: 9 the Holy One a you. 928+7931
13:15 even though he thrives a his brothers. 1068
Joel 2:17 a byword a the nations. 928
2:17 Why should they say a the peoples, 928
2:25 my great army that I sent a you. 928

Joel 2:32 a the survivors whom the LORD calls. 928
3: 2 for they scattered my people a the nations 928
3: 9 Proclaim this a the nations: 928
Am 2:11 up prophets from a your sons and Nazirites 4946
2:11 from among your sons and Nazirites from a 4946
3: 9 and the oppression a her people." 928+7931
4:10 "I sent plagues a you as I did to Egypt. 928
6: 7 Therefore you will be a the first to go 928
7: 8 a plumb line a my people Israel; 928+7931
9: 9 of Israel a all the nations as grain is shaken 928
9:10 All the sinners a my people will die by AIT
Ob 1: 2 I will make you small a the nations; 928
1: 4 the eagle and make your nest a the stars, 1068
Mic 3:11 "Is not the LORD a us? 928+7931
4: 1 be established as chief a the mountains; AIT
5: 2 though you are small a the clans of Judah, 928
5: 8 The remnant of Jacob will be a the nations, 928
5: 8 like a lion a the beasts of the forest, 928
5: 8 like a young lion a flocks of sheep, 928
5:10 from a you and demolish your chariots. 7931
5:13 and your sacred stones from a you; 7931
5:14 from a you your Asherah poles 7931
Na 1:10 They will be entangled a thorns and drunk 6330
3: 9 Put and Libya were a her allies. 928
Zep 3:20 and praise a all the peoples of the earth 928
Hag 2: 5 And my Spirit remains a you. 928+9348
Zec 1: 8 He was standing a the myrtle trees in 1068
1:10 man standing a the myrtle trees explained, 1068
1:11 who was standing a the myrtle trees, 1068
2:10 For I am coming, and I will live a you," 928+9348
2:11 I will live a you and you will know that 928+9348
3: 7 of my courts, and I will give you a place a 1068
7:14 'I scattered them with a whirlwind a all 6584
8:13 As you have been an object of cursing a 928
10: 9 Though I scatter them a the peoples, 928
12: 6 like a flaming torch a sheaves. 928
12: 8 that the feeblest a them will be like David, 928
14: 1 your plunder will be divided a you. 928+7931
Mal 1:11 My name will be great a the nations, 928
1:11 my name will be great a the nations," 928
1:14 "and my name is to be feared a the nations. 928
Mt 2: 6 are by no means least a the rulers of Judah; 1877
4:23 and healing every disease and sickness a 1877
10: 5 "Do not go a the Gentiles or enter any town 1650
10:16 sending you out like sheep a wolves. 1877+3545
11:11 A those born of women there has 1877
13: 7 Other seed fell a thorns, 2093
13:22 that fell a the thorns is the man who hears 1650
13:25 his enemy came and sowed weeds a 324+3545
16: 7 They discussed this a themselves and said, 1877
16: 8 why are you talking a yourselves 1877
18: 2 little child and had him stand a them. 1877+3545
20:26 whoever wants to become great a you must 1877
21:25 They discussed it a themselves and said, 1877
22:25 Now there were seven brothers a us. 4123
23:11 The greatest a you will be your servant. AIT
26: 5 "or there may be a riot a the people." 1877
27:56 A them were Mary Magdalene, 1877
28:15 And this story has been widely circulated a 4123
Mk 4: 7 Other seed fell a thorns, 1650
4:18 Still others, like seed sown a thorns, 1650
5: 5 Night and day a the tombs and in 1877
5:12 "Send us a the pigs; 1650
6: 4 a his relatives and in his own house is 1877
6:41 He also divided the two fish a them all. NIG
9:36 took a little child and had him stand a 1877+3545
10:43 whoever wants to become great a you must 1877
11:31 They discussed it a themselves and said, 4639
15:31 and the teachers of the law mocked him a 4639
15:40 A them were Mary Magdalene, 1877
Lk 1: 1 of the things that have been fulfilled a us, 1877
1:25 and taken away my disgrace a the people." 1877
1:42 "Blessed are you a women, 1877
1:61 "There is no one a your relatives who has 1666
2:44 for him a their relatives and friends. 1877
2:46 sitting a the teachers, 1877+3545
7:16 "A great prophet has appeared a us," 1877
7:28 I tell you, a those born 1877
7:49 The other guests began to say a 1877
8: 7 Other seed fell a thorns, 1877+3545
8:14 that fell a thorns stands for those who hear, 1650
9:46 An argument started a the disciples as 1877
9:48 For he who is least a you all— 1877
10: 3 I am sending you out like lambs a wolves. 1877+3545
16:15 What is highly valued a men is detestable 1877
19:47 and the leaders a the people were trying AIT
20: 5 They discussed it a themselves and said, 4639
22:17 "Take this and divide it a you. 1650
22:23 They began to question a themselves which 4639
22:24 Also a dispute arose a them as to which 1877
22:26 greatest a you should be like the youngest, 1877
22:27 But I am a you as one who serves. 1877+3545
24: 5 "Why do you look for the living a 3552
24:36 Jesus himself stood a them and said 1877+3545
Jn 1:14 and made his dwelling a us. 1877
1:26 "but a you stands one you do not know. 3545
6: 9 but how far will they go a so many?" 1650
6:43 "Stop grumbling a yourselves," 3552
6:52 Jews began to argue sharply a themselves, 4639
7:12 A the crowds there was widespread whispering about him. 1877
7:35 people live scattered a the Greeks, 1402+3836
11:54 about publicly a the Jews. 1877
12: 2 while Lazarus was a those reclining at 1651+1666
12: 8 You will always have the poor a you, 3552
12:20 Now there were some Greeks a 1666
Jn 12:42 even a the leaders believed in him. 1666
14: 9 after I have been a you such a long time? 3552
15:24 I had not done a them what no one else did, 1877
19:24 divided my garments a 1374
20:19 Jesus came and stood a them 1650+3545+3836
20:26 Jesus came and stood a them 1650+3545+3836
21:23 the rumor spread a the brothers 1650
Ac 1:15 Peter stood up a the believers 1877+3545
1:21 the Lord Jesus went in and out a us, 2093
2:22 which God did a you through him, 1877+3545
3:22 a prophet like me from a your own people; 1666
3:23 be completely cut off from a his people.' NIG
4:17 from spreading any further a the people, 1650
4:34 There were no needy persons a them. 1877
5:12 and wonders a the people. 1877
6: 1 the Grecian Jews a them complained NIG
6: 3 choose seven men from a 1666
6: 8 did great wonders and miraculous signs a 1877
9:21 the man who raised havoc in Jerusalem a NIG
12:18 there was no small commotion a 1877
14: 5 a the Gentiles and Jews, AIT
15: 7 a choice a you that the Gentiles might hear 1877
15:12 and wonders God had done a the Gentiles 1877
15:22 two men who were leaders a the brothers. 1877
17:34 A them was Dionysius, 1877
20:25 that none of you a whom I have gone 1877
20:29 savage wolves will come in a you and will 1656
20:32 up and give you an inheritance a 1877
21:19 and reported in detail what God had done a 1877
21:21 that you teach all the Jews who live a 2848
24: 5 up riots a the Jews all over the world. AIT
26:18 a place a those who are sanctified by faith 1877
28:25 They disagreed a themselves and began 4639
Ro 1: 5 and apostleship to call people from a all 1877
1: 6 also are a those who are called to belong 1877
1:13 now) in order that I might have a harvest a 1877
1:13 just as I have had a the other Gentiles. 1877
2:24 "God's name is blasphemed a the Gentiles 1877
8:29 be the firstborn a many brothers. 1877
11:17 have been grafted in a the others and 1596
15: 5 a spirit of unity a yourselves 1877
15: 9 "Therefore I will praise you a the Gentiles; 1877
15:26 a contribution for the poor a the saints AIT
16: 7 They are outstanding a the apostles, 1877
1Co 1:10 so that there may be no divisions a you and 1877
1:11 that there are quarrels a you. 1877
2: 6 speak a message of wisdom a the mature, 1877
2:11 For who a men knows the thoughts of AIT
3: 3 there is jealousy and quarreling a you, 1877
5: 1 that there is sexual immorality a you, and 1877
5: 1 a kind that does not occur even a pagans: 1877
5:13 "Expel the wicked man from a you." 1666
6: 5 that there is nobody a you wise enough 1877
6: 7 The very fact that you have lawsuits a 3552
9:11 If we have sown spiritual seed a you, AIT
11:18 there are divisions a you, 1877
11:19 No doubt there have to be differences a you 1877
11:30 That is why many a you are weak and sick, 1877
14:16 how can one who finds himself a 5536
14:25 exclaiming, "God is really a you!" 1877
2Co 1:19 who was preached a you by me and Silas 1877
2:15 For we are to God the aroma of Christ a 1877
6:16 "I will live with them and walk a them, 1853
8:23 he is my partner and fellow worker a you; 1650
10:15 of activity a you will greatly expand, 1877
12:12 were done a you with great perseverance. 1877
13: 3 but is powerful a you. 1877
Gal 1:16 so that I might preach him a the Gentiles, 1877
2: 2 the gospel that I preach a the Gentiles. 1877
3: 5 and work miracles a you 1919
Eph 2: 3 All of us also lived a them at one time, 1877
5: 3 But a you there must not be even a hint 1877
Col 1: 6 just as it has been doing a you since 1877
1:18 he is the beginning and the firstborn from a 1666
1:27 To them God has chosen to make known a 1877
4:11 the only Jews a my fellow workers for NIG
1Th 1: 5 how we lived a you for your sake. 1877
2: 7 but we were gentle a you, 1877+3545
2:10 and blameless we were a you who believed. AIT
5:12 to respect those who work hard a you, 1877
2Th 1: 4 a God's churches we boast 1877
1:10 in his holy people and to be marveled at a 1877
3:11 We hear that some a you are idle. 1877
1Ti 1:20 A them are Hymenaeus and Alexander, AIT
3:16 was preached a the nations, 1877
2Ti 2:17 A them are Hymenaeus and Philetus, AIT
Heb 5: 1 Every high priest is selected from a men 1666
Jas 1: 1 To the twelve tribes scattered a the nations: 1877
2: 4 have you not discriminated a yourselves 1877
3: 6 a world of evil a the parts of the body. 1877
3:13 Who is wise and understanding a you? 1877
4: 1 What causes fights and quarrels a you? 1877
1Pe 2:12 Live such good lives a the pagans that, 1877
2:13 to every authority instituted a men: 474
5: 1 To the elders a you, 1877
2Pe 2: 1 there were also false prophets a the people, 1877
2: 1 just as there will be false teachers a you. 1877
2: 8 living a them day after day, 1594
1Jn 4: 9 This is how God showed his love a us: 1877
4:17 love is made complete a us so 3552
Jude 1: 4 about long ago have secretly slipped in a NIG
Rev 1:13 and a the lampstands was someone "like a son of man," 1877+3545
2: 1 walks a the seven golden lampstands: 1877+3545
6: 6 I heard what sounded like a voice a 1877+3545
6:15 in caves and a the rocks of the mountains. 1650
14: 4 They were purchased from a men 608

AMORITE (10) [AMORITES]

Ge 14:13 near the great trees of Mamre the A, 616
Nu 21:13 in the desert extending into A territory. 616
Dt 2:24 I have given into your hand Sihon the A, 616
4:47 the two A kings east of the Jordan. 616
Jos 5: 1 when all the A kings west of the Jordan 616
10: 6 because all the A kings from 616
24:12 also the two A kings. 616
Eze 16: 3 your father was an A and your mother 616
16:45 a Hittite and your father an A. 616
Am 2: 9 "I destroyed the A before them, 616

AMORITES (76) [AMORITE]

Ge 10:16 Jebusites, A, Girgashites, 616
14: 7 the A who were living in Hazazon Tamar. 616
15:16 the A has not yet reached its full measure." 616
15:21 A, Canaanites, Girgashites and Jebusites." 616
48:22 from the A with my sword and my bow." 616
Ex 3: 8 the home of the Canaanites, Hittites, A, 616
3:17 A, Perizzites, Hivites and Jebusites— 616
13: 5 Hittites, A, Hivites and Jebusites— 616
23:23 of you and bring you into the land of the A, 616
33: 2 A, Hittites, Perizzites, 616
34:11 I will drive out before you the A, 616
Nu 13:29 Jebusites and A live in the hill country; 616
21:13 between Moab and the A. 616
21:21 to say to Sihon king of the A: 616
21:25 the cities of the A and occupied them, 616
21:26 the city of Sihon king of the A, 616
21:29 as captives to Sihon king of the A. 616
21:31 So Israel settled in the land of the A. 616
21:32 and drove out the A who were there. 616
21:34 to him what you did to Sihon king of the A, 616
22: 2 that Israel had done to the A, 616
32:33 of Sihon king of the A and the kingdom 616
32:39 and drove out the A who were there. 616
Dt 1: 4 after he had defeated Sihon king of the A, 616
1: 7 and advance into the hill country of the A; 616
1:19 toward the hill country of the A through all 616
1:20 the hill country of the A, 616
1:27 into the hands of the A to destroy us. 616
1:44 The A who lived in those hills came out 616
3: 2 to him what you did to Sihon king of the A, 616
3: 8 of the A the territory east of the Jordan, 616
3: 9 the A call it Senir.) 616
4:46 in the land of Sihon king of the A, 616
7: 1 the Hittites, Girgashites, A, Canaanites, 616
20:17 Completely destroy them—the Hittites, A, 616
31: 4 the kings of the A, 616
Jos 2:10 the two kings of the A east of the Jordan, 616
3:10 Perizzites, Girgashites, A and Jebusites. 616
7: 7 into the hands of the A to destroy us? 616
9: 1 A, Canaanites, Perizzites, 616
9:10 that he did to the two kings of the A east of 616
10: 5 Then the five kings of the A— 616
10:12 On the day the LORD gave the A over 616
11: 3 to the A, Hittites, Perizzites and Jebusites 616
12: 2 Sihon king of the A, 616
12: 8 the lands of the Hittites, A, Canaanites, 616
13: 4 the region of the A, 616
13:10 and all the towns of Sihon king of the A, 616
13:21 and the entire realm of Sihon king of the A, 616
24: 8 of the A who lived east of the Jordan. 616
24:11 as did also the A, Perizzites, Canaanites, 616
24:15 or the gods of the A, 616
24:18 including the A, who lived in the land. 616
Jdg 1:34 The A confined the Danites to 616
1:35 And the A were determined also to hold out 616
1:36 of the A was from Scorpion Pass to Sela 616
3: 5 A, Perizzites, Hivites and Jebusites. 616
6:10 do not worship the gods of the A, 616
10: 8 the land of the A. 616
10:11 the A, the Ammonites, the Philistines, 616
11:19 to Sihon king of the A, 616
11:21 the land of the A who lived in that country, 616
11:23 the A out before his people Israel, 616
1Sa 7:14 there was peace between Israel and the A. 616
2Sa 21: 2 a part of Israel but were survivors of the A; 616
1Ki 4:19 (the country of Sihon king of the A and 616
9:20 All the people left from the A, Hittites, 616
21:26 the A the LORD drove out before Israel.) 616
2Ki 21:11 the A who preceded him and has led Judah 616
1Ch 1:14 Jebusites, A, Girgashites, 616
2Ch 8: 7 All the people left from the Hittites, A, 616
Ezr 9: 1 Ammonites, Moabites, Egyptians and A. 616
Ne 9: 8 A, Perizzites, Jebusites and Girgashites. 616
Ps 135:11 the A, Og king of Bashan and all the kings 616
136:19 of the A His love endures forever. 616
Am 2:10 in the desert to give you the land of the A. 616

AMOS (8)

Am 1: 1 of A, one of the shepherds of Tekoa— 6650
7: 8 LORD asked me, "What do you see, A?" 6650
7:10 "A is raising a conspiracy against you in 6650
7:11 For this is what A is saying: 6650
7:12 Amaziah said to A, "Get out, you seer! 6650
7:14 A answered Amaziah, 6650
8: 2 "What do you see, A?" 6650
Lk 3:25 the son of A, the son of Nahum, 322

AMOUNT (24) [AMOUNTED, AMOUNTS]

Ge 43:12 Take double the a of silver with you, AIT
43:15 So the men took the gifts and double the a AIT
Ex 12: 4 determine the a of lamb needed 4082

Ex 38:24 The **total** *a of* the gold from AIT
Lev 25: 8 of years **a to** a period of forty-nine years. 2118
27: 8 the vow is too poor to pay the **specified a,** 6886
27:16 according to the **a** *of* seed required for it— 7023
1Sa 30:16 the **great a** of plunder they had taken from 1524
2Ki 12:10 that there was a **large a** *of* money in 8041
12:11 When the **a** *had* **been determined,** 9419
1Ch 22: 3 a **large a** of iron to make nails for 4200+8044
2Ch 14:13 Judah carried off a **large a** of plunder. 2221+4394
20:25 a **great a** of equipment and clothing 4200+8044
24:11 and they saw that there was a **large a** 8041
24:11 and collected a **great a** of money. 4200+8044
27: 5 The Ammonites brought him the **same a** 2296S
31: 5 They brought a **great a,** 4200+8044
31:10 and this **great a** is left over." 2162
Est 4: 7 including the **exact a** 7308
Isa 41:29 Their deeds **a to nothing;** 700
Da 1: 5 The king assigned them a daily **a** of food 1821
Mt 13:33 a large **a** of flour until it worked all through *4929*
Lk 13:21 mixed into a **large a of flour** *236+4929+5552*
19: 8 I will pay back four times the **a."** *NIG*

AMOUNTED (3) [AMOUNT]

Ru 2:17 and *it* **a to** about an ephah. 2118
2Ch 4:18 All these things that Solomon made **a** to NIH
29:33 The animals consecrated as sacrifices **a** NIH

AMOUNTS (5) [AMOUNT]

Ex 30:34 pure frankincense, all **in equal a,** 928+963+963
38:21 These are the **a** *of* the materials used for 7217
Dt 17:17 *He must* not **accumulate large a** *of* silver 4394+8049
Mk 12:41 Many rich people threw in **large** *a.* *AIT*
2Co 10:10 and his speaking **a to nothing."** *2024*

AMOZ (13)

2Ki 19: 2 to the prophet Isaiah son of **A.** 576
19:20 Isaiah son of **A** sent a message to Hezekiah: 576
20: 1 of **A** went to him and said, "This is what 576
2Ch 26:22 are recorded by the prophet Isaiah son of **A.** 576
32:20 and the prophet Isaiah son of **A** cried out 576
32:32 the vision of the prophet Isaiah son of **A** in 576
Isa 1: 1 that Isaiah son of **A** saw during the reigns 576
2: 1 of **A** saw concerning Judah and Jerusalem: 576
13: 1 that Isaiah son of **A** saw: 576
20: 2 the LORD spoke through Isaiah son of **A.** 576
37: 2 to the prophet Isaiah son of **A.** 576
37:21 Isaiah son of **A** sent a message to Hezekiah: 576
38: 1 of **A** went to him and said, "This is what 576

AMPHIPOLIS (1)

Ac 17: 1 When they had passed through **A** *315*

AMPLIATUS (1)

Ro 16: 8 Greet **A,** whom I love in the Lord. *309*

AMPLY (1)

Php 4:18 *I am* **a supplied,** *4444*

AMRAM (13) [AMRAM'S, AMRAMITES]

Ex 6:18 The sons of Kohath were **A,** Izhar, 6688
6:20 **A** married his father's sister Jochebed, 6688
6:20 **A** lived 137 years. 6688
Nu 3:19 **A,** Izhar, Hebron and Uzziel. 6688
26:58 (Kohath was the forefather of **A;** 6688
26:59 To **A** she bore Aaron, 6688
1Ch 6: 2 **A,** Izhar, Hebron and Uzziel. 6688
6: 3 The children of **A:** 6688
6:18 **A,** Izhar, Hebron and Uzziel. 6688
23:12 **A,** Izhar, Hebron and Uzziel—four in all. 6688
23:13 The sons of **A:** Aaron and Moses. 6688
24:20 from the sons of **A:** 6688
Ezr 10:34 From the descendants of Bani: Maadai, **A,** 6688

AMRAM'S (1) [AMRAM]

Nu 26:59 the name of **A** wife was Jochebed, 6688

AMRAMITES (2) [AMRAM]

Nu 3:27 To Kohath belonged the clans of the **A,** 6689
1Ch 26:23 From the **A,** the Izharites, 6689

AMRAPHEL (2)

Ge 14: 1 At this time **A** king of Shinar, 620
14: 9 **A** king of Shinar and Arioch king 620

AMZI (2)

1Ch 6:46 the son of **A,** 603
Ne 11:12 the son of **A,** the son of Zechariah, 603

AN (1185) [A] See Index of Articles Etc.

ANAB (2)

Jos 11:21 from Hebron, Debir and **A,** 6693
15:50 **A,** Eshtemoh, Anim, 6693

ANAH (12)

Ge 36: 2 the Hittite, and Oholibamah daughter of **A** 6704
36:14 of Esau's wife Oholibamah daughter of **A** 6704
36:18 Esau's wife Oholibamah daughter of **A.** 6704
36:20 Lotan, Shobal, Zibeon, **A,** 6704
36:24 The sons of Zibeon: Aiah and **A.** 6704
36:24 the **A** who discovered the hot springs in 6704
36:25 The children of **A:** 6704
36:25 Dishon and Oholibamah daughter of **A.** 6704
36:29 Lotan, Shobal, Zibeon, **A,** 6704
1Ch 1:38 The sons of Seir: Lotan, Shobal, Zibeon, **A,** 6704
1:40 The sons of Zibeon: Aiah and **A.** 6704
1:41 The son of **A:** Dishon. 6704

ANAHARATH (1)

Jos 19:19 Hapharaim, Shion, **A,** 637

ANAIAH (2)

Ne 8: 4 Shema, **A,** Uriah, Hilkiah and Maaseiah; 6717
10:22 Pelatiah, Hanan, **A,** 6717

ANAK (7) [ANAKITES]

Nu 13:22 Sheshai and Talmai, the descendants of **A,** 6737
13:28 We even saw descendants of **A** there. 6737
13:33 (the descendants of **A** come from 6737
Jos 15:13 (Arba was the forefather of **A.**) 6737
15:14 and Talmai—descendants of **A.** 6737
21:11 (Arba was the forefather of **A.**) 6710
Jdg 1:20 who drove from it the three sons of **A.** 6737

ANAKIMS (KJV) See ANAKITE

ANAKITES (11) [ANAK]

Dt 1:28 We even saw the **A** there.' " 1201+6737
2:10 and as tall as the **A.** 6737
2:11 the **A,** they too were considered Rephaites, 6737
2:21 and as tall as the **A.** 6737
9: 2 The people are strong and tall—**A!** 1201+6737
9: 2 "Who can stand up against the **A?"** 1201+6737
Jos 11:21 that time Joshua went and destroyed the **A** 6737
11:22 No **A** were left in Israelite territory; 6737
14:12 the **A** were there and their cities were large 6737
14:15 who was the greatest man among the **A.**) 6737
15:14 Hebron Caleb drove out the three **A**— 1201+6737

ANAMIM (KJV) See ANAMITES

ANAMITES (2)

Ge 10:13 Mizraim was the father of the Ludites, **A,** 6723
1Ch 1:11 Mizraim was the father of the Ludites, **A,** 6723

ANAMMELECH (1)

2Ki 17:31 as sacrifices to Adrammelech and **A,** 6724

ANAN (1)

Ne 10:26 Ahiah, Hanan, **A,** 6728

ANANI (1)

1Ch 3:24 Pelaiah, Akkub, Johanan, Delaiah and **A**— 6730

ANANIAH (2)

Ne 3:23 Azariah son of Maaseiah, the son of **A,** 6731
11:32 in Anathoth, Nob and **A,** 6732

ANANIAS (13)

Ac 5: 1 Now a man named **A,** *393*
5: 3 Then Peter said, **"A,** how is it *393*
5: 5 When **A** heard this, he fell down and died. *393*
5: 8 the price you and **A** got for the land?" *NIG*
9:10 In Damascus there was a disciple named **A.** *393*
9:10 The Lord called to him in a vision, **"A!"** *393*
9:12 a vision he has seen a man named **A** come *393*
9:13 **A** answered, "I have heard many reports *393*
9:15 But the Lord said to **A,** "Go! *899S*
9:17 Then **A** went to the house and entered it. *393*
22:12 "A man named **A** came to see me. *393*
23: 2 the high priest **A** ordered those standing *393*
24: 1 Five days later the high priest **A** went down *393*

ANATH (2)

Jdg 3:31 After Ehud came Shamgar son of **A,** 6742
5: 6 "In the days of Shamgar son of **A,** 6742

ANATHEMA (KJV) See CURSE

ANATHOTH (18) [ANATHOTHITE]

Jos 21:18 **A** and Almon, together 6743
2Sa 23:27 Abiezer **from A,** Mebunnai the Hushathite, 6745
1Ki 2:26 "Go back to your fields in **A.** 6743
1Ch 6:60 Geba, Alemeth and **A,** 6743
7: 8 Omri, Jeremoth, Abijah, **A** and Alemeth. 6744
11:28 of Ikkesh from Tekoa, Abiezer **from A,** 6745
Ezr 2:23 of **A** 128 6743
Ne 7:27 of **A** 128 6743
10:19 Hariph, **A,** Nebai, 6744
11:32 in **A,** Nob and Ananiah, 6743
Isa 10:30 Listen, O Laishah! Poor **A!** 6743
Jer 1: 1 the priests at **A** in the territory of Benjamin. 6743
11:21 of **A** who are seeking your life and saying, 6743
11:23 of **A** in the year of their punishment.' " 6743
29:27 not reprimanded Jeremiah **from A,** 6745
32: 7 'Buy my field at **A,** 6743
32: 8 'Buy my field at **A** in the territory 6743
32: 9 the field at **A** from my cousin Hanamel 6743

ANATHOTHITE (2) [ANATHOTH]

1Ch 12: 3 Beracah, Jehu the **A,** 6745
27:12 for the ninth month, was Abiezer the **A,** 6745

ANCESTOR (4) [ANCESTORS, ANCESTRAL, ANCESTRY]

Ge 10:21 Shem was the **a** *of* all the sons of Eber. 3
Jos 17: 1 Makir was the **a** *of* the Gileadites, 3
Heb 7:10 Levi was still in the body *of* his **a.** *4252*
Jas 2:21 not our **a** Abraham considered righteous *4252*

ANCESTORS (4) [ANCESTOR]

Lev 26:45 with their **a** whom I brought out of Egypt 8037
1Ki 19: 4 "Take my life; I am no better than my **a."** 3
Am 2: 4 the gods their **a** followed, 3
Ac 28:17 or against the customs of our **a,** *4262*

ANCESTRAL (10) [ANCESTOR]

Nu 1:16 the leaders of their **a** tribes. 3
13: 2 From each **a** tribe send one of its leaders." 3
17: 2 from the leader of each of their **a** tribes. 3
17: 3 be one staff for the head of each **a** tribe. 3
17: 6 one for the leader of each of their **a** tribes, 3
18: 2 Bring your fellow Levites from your **a** tribe 3
26:55 be according to the names for its **a** tribe. 3
33:54 Distribute it according to your **a** tribes. 3
36: 3 from our **a** inheritance and added to that of 3
Ne 11:20 each on his **a property.** 5709

ANCESTRY (6) [ANCESTOR]

Nu 1:18 The people **indicated** *their* **a** by their clans 3528
Eze 16: 3 Your **a** and birth were in the land of 4808
21:30 in the land of your **a,** I will judge you. 4808
29:14 the land of their **a.** 4808
Ro 9: 5 from them is traced the **human a** of Christ, *4922*
Heb 7:16 as to his **a** but on the basis of the power of *4921*

ANCHOR (3) [ANCHORED, ANCHORS]

Ac 27:13 they **weighed a** and sailed along the shore *149*
27:17 the **sea a** and let the ship be driven along. *5007*
Heb 6:19 We have this hope as an **a** for the soul, *46*

ANCHORED (1) [ANCHOR]

Mk 6:53 they landed at Gennesaret and **a** there. *4694*

ANCHORS (3) [ANCHOR]

Ac 27:29 they dropped four **a** from the stern *46*
27:30 to lower some **a** from the bow. *46*
27:40 Cutting loose the **a,** *46*

ANCIENT (33) [ANCIENTS]

Ge 49:26 the blessings of the **a** mountains, 6329
Dt 33:15 with the choicest gifts of the **a** mountains 7710
1Sa 27: 8 (From **a times** these peoples had lived in 6409
1Ch 4:22 (These records are **from a times.**) 6972
Ezr 4:15 a place of rebellion from **a** times. 10550
Ps 24: 7 be lifted up, you **a** doors, 6409
24: 9 lift them up, you **a** doors, 6409
68:33 to him who rides the **a** skies above, 7710
119:52 I remember your **a** laws, O LORD, 4946+6409
Pr 22:28 Do not move an **a** boundary stone set up 6409
23:10 not move an **a** boundary stone or encroach 6409
Isa 19:11 a disciple of the **a** kings"? 7710
43:13 Yes, and from **a** days I am he. NIH
44: 7 since I established my **a** people, 6409
46:10 from **a times,** what is still to come. 7710
58:12 Your people will rebuild the **a** ruins 6409
61: 4 They will rebuild the **a** ruins and restore 6409
64: 4 Since **a times** no one has heard, 6409
Jer 5:15 an **a** and enduring nation, 4946+6409
6:16 ask for the **a** paths, 6409
18:15 in their ways and in the **a** paths. 6409
Eze 25:15 with **a** hostility sought to destroy Judah, 6409
26:20 as in **a** ruins, 4946+6409
35: 5 an **a** hostility and delivered the Israelites 6409
36: 2 The **a** heights have become our possession.' " 6409
Da 7: 9 and the **A** *of* Days took his seat. 10578
7:13 He approached the **A** *of* Days and was led 10578
7:22 until the **A** *of* Days came 10578
Mic 5: 2 from of old, from **a** times." 6409
Hab 3: 6 The **a** mountains crumbled and 6329
2Pe 2: 5 not spare the **a** world when he brought *792*
Rev 12: 9 that **a** serpent called the devil, or Satan, *792*
20: 2 He seized the dragon, that **a** serpent, *792*

ANCIENTS (1) [ANCIENT]

Heb 11: 2 This is what the **a** were commended for. *4565*

ANCLE (KJV) See ANKLE, ANKLES

AND (29600) See Index of Articles Etc.

ANDREW (14)

Mt 4:18 Simon called Peter and his brother **A.** *436*
10: 2 and his brother **A;** *436*
Mk 1:16 he saw Simon and his brother **A** casting *436*
1:29 and John to the home of Simon and **A.** *436*
3:18 **A,** Philip, Bartholomew, *436*
13: 3 James, John and **A** asked him privately, *436*
Lk 6:14 his brother **A,** James, John, Philip, *436*
Jn 1:40 **A,** Simon Peter's brother, *436*
1:41 The first thing **A** did was *4047S*
1:44 Philip, like **A** and Peter, *436*
6: 8 Another of his disciples, **A,** *436*
12:22 Philip went to tell **A;** *436*
12:22 **A** and Philip in turn told Jesus. *436*
Ac 1:13 present were Peter, John, James and **A;** *436*

ANDRONICUS (1)

Ro 16: 7 Greet **A** and Junias, *438*

ANEM (1)

1Ch 6:73 and **A,** together with their pasturelands; 6722

ANER (3)

Ge 14:13 a brother of Eshcol and **A,** 6738
14:24 to **A,** Eshcol and Mamre. 6738
1Ch 6:70 the tribe of Manasseh the Israelites gave **A** 6739

ANETHOTHITE, ANETOTHITE (KJV)
See ANATHOTH, ANATHOTHITE

ANEW (2) [NEW]

Mt 26:29 on until that day when I drink it **a** with you *2785*
Mk 14:25 when I drink it **a** in the kingdom of God." *2785*

ANGEL (207) [ANGEL'S, ANGELS, ARCHANGEL]

Ge 16: 7 The **a** *of* the LORD found Hagar near 4855
16: 9 Then the **a** *of* the LORD told her, 4855
16:10 The **a** added, "I will 3378+4855
16:11 The **a** *of* the LORD also said to her: 4855
21:17 the **a** *of* God called to Hagar from heaven 4855
22:11 But the **a** *of* the LORD called out to him 4855
22:15 The **a** *of* the LORD called to Abraham 4855
24: 7 he will send his **a** before you so 4855
24:40 will send his **a** with you 4855
31:11 The **a** *of* God said to me in the dream, 4855
48:16 **A** who has delivered me from all harm— 4855
Ex 3: 2 There the **a** *of* the LORD appeared to him 4855
14:19 Then the **a** *of* God, 4855
23:20 an **a** ahead of you to guard you along 4855
23:23 My **a** will go ahead of you and bring you 4855
32:34 and my **a** will go before you. 4855
33: 2 I will send an **a** before you and drive out 4855
Nu 20:16 and sent an **a** and brought us out of Egypt. 4855
22:22 and the **a** *of* the LORD stood in the road 4855
22:23 the **a** *of* the LORD standing in the road 4855
22:24 the **a** *of* the LORD stood in a narrow path 4855
22:25 When the donkey saw the **a** *of* the LORD, 4855
22:26 Then the **a** *of* the LORD moved on ahead 4855
22:27 When the donkey saw the **a** *of* the LORD, 4855
22:31 and he saw the **a** *of* the LORD standing in 4855
22:32 The **a** *of* the LORD asked him, 4855
22:34 Balaam said to the **a** *of* the LORD, 4855
22:35 The **a** *of* the LORD said to Balaam, 4855
Jdg 2: 1 The **a** *of* the LORD went up from Gilgal 4855
2: 4 When the **a** *of* the LORD had spoken these 4855
5:23 'Curse Meroz,' said the **a** *of* the LORD. 4855
6:11 The **a** *of* the LORD came and sat down 4855
6:12 the **a** *of* the LORD appeared to Gideon, 4855
6:20 The **a** *of* God said to him, 4855
6:21 the **a** *of* the LORD touched the meat and 4855
6:21 And the **a** *of* the LORD disappeared. 4855
6:22 When Gideon realized that it was the **a** *of* 4855
6:22 I have seen the **a** *of* the LORD face 4855
13: 3 The **a** *of* the LORD appeared to her 4855
13: 6 He looked like an **a** *of* God, 4855
13: 9 and the **a** *of* God came again to the woman 4855
13:13 The **a** *of* the LORD answered, 4855
13:15 Manoah said to the **a** *of* the LORD, 4855
13:16 The **a** *of* the LORD replied, 4855
13:16 not realize that it was the **a** *of* the LORD.) 4855
13:17 Manoah inquired of the **a** *of* the LORD, 4855
13:20 the **a** *of* the LORD ascended in the flame. 4855
13:21 When the **a** *of* the LORD did 4855
13:21 Manoah realized that it was the **a** *of* 4855
1Sa 29: 9 as pleasing in my eyes as an **a** *of* God; 4855
2Sa 14:17 an **a** *of* God in discerning good and evil. 4855
14:20 My lord has wisdom like that of an **a** 4855
19:27 My lord the king is like an **a** *of* God; 4855
24:16 When the **a** stretched out his hand 4855
24:16 to the **a** who was afflicting the people, 4855
24:16 The **a** *of* the LORD was then at 4855
24:17 When David saw the **a** who was striking 4855
1Ki 13:18 an **a** said to me by the word of the LORD: 4855
19: 5 All at once an **a** touched him and said, 4855
19: 7 The **a** *of* the LORD came back 4855
2Ki 1: 3 **a** *of* the LORD said to Elijah the Tishbite, 4855
1:15 The **a** *of* the LORD said to Elijah, 4855
19:35 That night the **a** *of* the LORD went out 4855
1Ch 21:12 the **a** *of* the LORD ravaging every part 4855
21:15 And God sent an **a** to destroy Jerusalem. 4855
21:15 But as the **a** was doing so, NIH
21:15 to the **a** who was destroying the people, 4855
21:15 The **a** *of* the LORD was then standing at 4855
21:16 up and saw the **a** *of* the LORD standing 4855
21:18 Then the **a** *of* the LORD ordered Gad 4855
21:20 he turned and saw the **a;** 4855
21:27 Then the LORD spoke to the **a,** 4855
21:30 because he was afraid of the sword of the **a** 4855
2Ch 32:21 And the LORD sent an **a,** 4855
Job 33:23 if there is an **a** on his side as a mediator, 4855
Ps 34: 7 The **a** *of* the LORD encamps 4855
35: 5 the **a** *of* the LORD driving them away; 4855
35: 6 with the **a** *of* the LORD pursuing them. 4855
Isa 37:36 Then the **a** *of* the LORD went out and put 4855
63: 9 and the **a** *of* his presence saved them. 4855
Da 3:28 who has sent his **a** 10417
6:22 My God sent his **a,** 10417
Hos 12: 4 He struggled with the **a** and overcame him; 4855
Zec 1: 9 The **a** who was talking with me answered, 4855
1:11 And they reported to the **a** *of* the LORD, 4855
1:12 Then the **a** *of* the LORD said, 4855
1:13 and comforting words to the **a** who talked 4855
1:14 Then the **a** who was speaking to me said, 4855
1:19 I asked the **a** who was speaking to me, 4855
2: 3 Then the **a** who was speaking to me left, 4855
2: 3 and another **a** came to meet him 4855
3: 1 the high priest standing before the **a** *of* 4855
3: 3 in filthy clothes as he stood before the **a.** 4855
3: 4 The **a** said to those who were standing NIH
3: 5 while the **a** *of* the LORD stood by. 4855
3: 6 The **a** *of* the LORD gave this charge 4855
4: 1 Then the **a** who talked with me returned 4855
4: 4 I asked the **a** who talked with me, 4855
4:11 Then I asked **the a,** 2257S
5: 5 Then the **a** who was speaking 4855
5:10 I asked the **a** who was speaking to me. 4855
6: 4 I asked the **a** who was speaking to me, 4855
6: 5 The **a** answered me, 4855
12: 8 the **A** *of* the LORD going before them. 4855
Mt 1:20 an **a** of the Lord appeared to him in *34*
1:24 the **a** of the Lord had commanded him *34*
2:13 an **a** of the Lord appeared to Joseph in *34*
2:19 an **a** of the Lord appeared in a dream *34*
28: 2 **a** of the Lord came down from heaven and, *34*
28: 5 The **a** said to the women, *34*
Lk 1:11 Then an **a** of the Lord appeared to him, *34*
1:13 But the **a** said to him: *34*
1:18 Zechariah asked the **a,** *34*
1:19 The **a** answered, "I am Gabriel. *34*
1:26 God sent the **a** Gabriel to Nazareth, *34*
1:28 The **a** went to her and said, "Greetings, *34*
1:30 But the **a** said to her, "Do not be afraid, *34*
1:34 "How will this be," Mary asked the **a,** *34*
1:35 The **a** answered, "The Holy Spirit will come upon you, *34*
1:38 Then the **a** left her. *34*
2: 9 An **a** of the Lord appeared to them, *34*
2:10 But the **a** said to them, "Do not be afraid. *34*
2:13 of the heavenly host appeared with the **a,** *34*
2:21 the name the **a** had given him *34*
22:43 An **a** from heaven appeared to him *34*
Jn 12:29 others said an **a** had spoken to him. *34*
Ac 5:19 the night an **a** of the Lord opened the doors *34*
6:15 that his face was like the face *of* an **a.** *34*
7:30 an **a** appeared to Moses in the flames of *34*
7:35 the **a** who appeared to him in the bush. *34*
7:38 the **a** who spoke to him on Mount Sinai, *34*
8:26 Now an **a** of the Lord said to Philip, *34*
10: 3 He distinctly saw an **a** of God, *34*
10: 4 The **a** answered, "Your prayers and gifts to *NIG*
10: 7 When the **a** who spoke to him had gone, *34*
10:22 A holy **a** told him to have you come *34*
11:13 how he had seen an **a** appear in his house *34*
12: 7 an **a** of the Lord appeared and a light shone *34*
12: 8 Then the **a** said to him, *34*
12: 8 the **a** told him. *NIG*
12: 9 the **a** was doing was really happening; *34*
12:10 suddenly the **a** left him. *34*
12:11 without a doubt that the Lord sent his **a** *34*
12:15 they said, "It must be his **a.**" *34*
12:23 an **a** of the Lord struck him down, *34*
23: 9 if a spirit or an **a** has spoken to him?" *34*
27:23 Last night an **a** of the God whose I am *34*
1Co 10:10 and were killed by the destroying **a.** *NIG*
2Co 11:14 Satan himself masquerades as an **a** of light. *34*
Gal 1: 8 if we or an **a** from heaven should preach *34*
4:14 you welcomed me as if I were an **a** of God, *34*
Rev 1: 1 by sending his **a** to his servant John, *34*
2: 1 *"To* the **a** of the church in Ephesus write: *34*
2: 8 *"To* the **a** of the church in Smyrna write: *34*
2:12 *"To* the **a** of the church in Pergamum write: *34*
2:18 *"To* the **a** of the church in Thyatira write: *34*
3: 1 *"To* the **a** of the church in Sardis write: *34*
3: 7 the **a** of the church in Philadelphia write: *34*
3:14 *"To* the **a** of the church in Laodicea write: *34*
5: 2 a mighty **a** proclaiming in a loud voice, *34*
7: 2 I saw another **a** coming up from the east, *34*
8: 3 Another **a,** who had a golden censer, *34*
8: 5 Then the **a** took the censer, *34*
8: 7 The first **a** sounded his trumpet, *NIG*
8: 8 The second **a** sounded his trumpet, *34*
8:10 The third **a** sounded his trumpet, *34*
Rev 8:12 The fourth **a** sounded his trumpet, *34*
9: 1 The fifth **a** sounded his trumpet, *34*
9:11 as king over them the **a** of the Abyss, *34*
9:13 The sixth **a** sounded his trumpet, *34*
9:14 It said *to* the sixth **a** who had the trumpet, *34*
10: 1 Then I saw another mighty **a** coming down *34*
10: 5 the **a** I had seen standing on the sea and on *34*
10: 7 the seventh **a** is about to sound his trumpet, *34*
10: 8 *of* the **a** who is standing on the sea and on *34*
10: 9 to the **a** and asked him to give me *34*
11:15 The seventh **a** sounded his trumpet, *34*
14: 6 Then I saw another **a** flying in midair, *34*
14: 8 A second **a** followed and said, "Fallen! *34*
14: 9 A third **a** followed them and said in *34*
14:15 Then another **a** came out of the temple *34*
14:17 Another **a** came out of the temple *34*
14:18 Still another **a,** who had charge of the fire, *34*
14:19 The **a** swung his sickle on the earth, *34*
16: 2 The first **a** went and poured out his bowl on *NIG*
16: 3 The second **a** poured out his bowl on *NIG*
16: 4 The third **a** poured out his bowl on *NIG*
16: 5 I heard the **a** in charge of the waters say: *34*
16: 8 The fourth **a** poured out his bowl on *NIG*
16:10 The fifth **a** poured out his bowl on *NIG*
16:12 The sixth **a** poured out his bowl on *NIG*
16:17 The seventh **a** poured out his bowl into *NIG*
17: 3 Then the **a** carried me away in the Spirit *NIG*
17: 7 the **a** said to me: "Why are you astonished? *34*
17:15 Then the **a** said to me, *NIG*
18: 1 After this I saw another **a** coming down *34*
18:21 a mighty **a** picked up a boulder the size of *34*
19: 9 Then the **a** said to me, "Write: *NIG*
19:17 And I saw an **a** standing in the sun, *34*
20: 1 I saw an **a** coming down out of heaven, *34*
21:15 The **a** who talked with me had *NIG*
21:17 which the **a** was using. *34*
22: 1 **a** showed me the river of the water of life, *NIG*
22: 6 The **a** said to me, *NIG*
22: 6 sent his **a** to show his servants the things *34*
22: 8 the **a** who had been showing them to me. *34*
22:16 have sent my **a** to give you this testimony *34*

ANGEL'S (2) [ANGEL]

Rev 8: 4 went up before God from the **a** hand. *34*
10:10 the little scroll from the **a** hand and ate it. *34*

ANGELS (96) [ANGEL]

Ge 19: 1 The two **a** arrived at Sodom in the evening, 4855
19:15 With the coming of dawn, the **a** urged Lot, 4855
28:12 and the **a** *of* God were ascending 4855
32: 1 and the **a** *of* God met him. 4855
Job 1: 6 One day the **a** came to present themselves 466+1201+2021
2: 1 the **a** came to present themselves before 466+1201+2021
4:18 if he charges his **a** with error, 4855
38: 7 and all the **a** shouted for joy? 466+1201
Ps 78:25 Men ate the bread of **a;** 52
78:49 a band of destroying **a.** 4855
91:11 For he will command his **a** concerning you 4855
103:20 Praise the LORD, you his **a,** 4855
148: 2 Praise him, all his **a,** praise him, 4855
Mt 4: 6 " 'He will command his **a** concerning you, *34*
4:11 and **a** came and attended him. *34*
13:39 and the harvesters are **a.** *34*
13:41 The Son of Man will send out his **a,** *34*
13:49 The **a** will come and separate the wicked *34*
16:27 to come in his Father's glory with his **a,** *34*
18:10 that their **a** in heaven always see the face *34*
22:30 they will be like the **a** in heaven. *34*
24:31 he will send his **a** with a loud trumpet call, *34*
24:36 not even the **a** in heaven, nor the Son, *34*
25:31 and all the **a** with him, *34*
25:41 *for* the devil and his **a.** *34*
26:53 put at my disposal more than twelve legions *of* **a?** *34*
Mk 1:13 and **a** attended him. *34*
8:38 in his Father's glory with the holy **a.**" *34*
12:25 they will be like the **a** in heaven. *34*
13:27 And he will send his **a** and gather his elect *34*
13:32 not even the **a** in heaven, nor the Son, *34*
Lk 2:15 the **a** had left them and gone into heaven, *34*
4:10 " 'He will command his **a** concerning you *34*
9:26 in the glory of the Father and *of* the holy **a.** *34*
12: 8 also acknowledge him before the **a** of God. *34*
12: 9 before men will be disowned before the **a** *34*
15:10 the **a** of God over one sinner who repents." *34*
16:22 when the beggar died and the **a** carried him *34*
20:36 for they are **like the a.** *2694*
24:23 that they had seen a vision *of* **a,** *34*
Jn 1:51 and the **a** of God ascending and descending *34*
20:12 and saw two **a** in white, *34*
Ac 7:53 that was put into effect through **a** but have *34*
23: 8 and that there are neither **a** nor spirits, *34*
Ro 8:38 neither **a** nor demons, *34*
1Co 4: 9 *to* **a** as well as to men. *34*
6: 3 Do you not know that we will judge **a?** *34*
11:10 For this reason, and because of the **a,** *34*
13: 1 If I speak in the tongues of men and *of* **a,** *34*
Gal 3:19 The law was put into effect through **a** by *34*
Col 2:18 and the worship *of* **a** disqualify you for *34*
2Th 1: 7 in blazing fire with his powerful **a.** *34*
1Ti 3:16 by the Spirit, was seen *by* **a,** *34*
5:21 of God and Christ Jesus and the elect **a,** *34*
Heb 1: 4 So he became as much superior to the **a** as *34*

Heb 1: 5 For to which of the a did God ever say, 34
1: 6 he says, "Let all God's a worship him." 34
1: 7 In speaking of the a he says, 34
1: 7 "He makes his a winds, 34
1:13 To which of the a did God ever say, 34
1:14 Are not all a ministering spirits sent NIG
2: 2 if the message spoken by a was binding, 34
2: 5 not to a that he has subjected the world 34
2: 7 You made him a little lower than the a; 34
2: 9 who was made a little lower than the a, 34
2:16 For surely it is not a he helps, 34
12:22 upon thousands of a in joyful assembly, 34
13: 2 by so doing some people have entertained a 34
1Pe 1:12 Even a long to look into these things. 34
3:22 with a, authorities and powers 34
2Pe 2: 4 if God did not spare a when they sinned, 34
2:11 yet even a, although they are stronger 34
Jude 1: 6 And the a who did not keep their positions 34
Rev 1:20 seven stars are the a of the seven churches, 34
3: 5 before my Father and his a. 34
5:11 I looked and heard the voice of many a, 34
7: 1 After this I saw four a standing at 34
7: 2 to the four a who had been given power 34
7:11 the a were standing around the throne and 34
8: 2 I saw the seven a who stand before God, 34
8: 6 Then the seven a who had 34
8:13 about to be sounded by the other three a!" 34
9:14 "Release the four a who are bound at 34
9:15 And the four a who had been kept ready 34
12: 7 and his a fought against the dragon, 34
12: 7 and the dragon and his a fought back. 34
12: 9 and his a with him. 34
14:10 the presence of the holy a and of the Lamb. 34
15: 1 seven a with the seven last plagues— 34
15: 6 Out of the temple came the seven a with 34
15: 7 the seven a seven golden bowls filled with 34
15: 8 of the seven a were completed. 34
16: 1 from the temple saying to the seven a, 34
17: 1 the seven a who had the seven bowls came 34
21: 9 the seven a who had the seven bowls full of 34
21:12 and with twelve a at the gates. 34

ANGER (262) [ANGERED, ANGERS, ANGRY]

Ge 39:19 he burned with a. 678
49: 6 for they have killed men in their a 678
49: 7 Cursed be their a, so fierce, and their fury, 678
Ex 4:14 Then the LORD's a burned against Moses 678
11: 8 Then Moses, hot with a, left Pharaoh. 678
15: 7 You unleashed your **burning a**; 3019
22:24 My a will be aroused, 678
32:10 Now leave me alone so that my a may burn 678
32:11 "why should your a burn 678
32:12 Turn from your fierce a; 678
32:19 his a burned and he threw the tablets out 678
34: 6 and gracious God, slow to a, abounding 678
Lev 26:28 then in my a I will be hostile toward you, 2779
Nu 11: 1 and when he heard them his a was aroused. 678
11:33 the a of the LORD burned against 678
12: 9 The a of the LORD burned against them, 678
14:18 'The LORD is slow to a, 678
24:10 Then Balak's a burned against Balaam. 678
25: 3 And the LORD's a burned against them. 678
25: 4 that the LORD's fierce a may turn away 678
25:11 has turned my a away from the Israelites; 2779
32:10 The LORD's a was aroused that day 678
32:13 The LORD's a burned against Israel 678
Dt 4:25 and **provoking** him **to a**, 4087
6:15 is a jealous God and his a will burn 678
7: 4 and the LORD's a will burn against you 678
9: 7 **provoked** the LORD your God **to a** 7911
9:18 and so **provoking** him **to a**. 4087
9:19 I feared the a and wrath of the LORD, 678
11:17 Then the LORD's a will burn against you, 678
13:17 that the LORD will turn from his fierce a; 678
29:23 which the LORD overthrew in fierce a. 678
29:24 Why this fierce, burning a?" 678
29:27 the LORD's a burned against this land, 678
29:28 In furious a and in great wrath 678
31:29 of the LORD and **provoke** him **to a** 4087
Jos 7: 1 So the LORD's a burned against Israel. 678
7:26 Then the LORD turned from his fierce a. 678
23:16 the LORD's a will burn against you, 678
Jdg 2:12 **provoked** the LORD **to a** 4087
2:14 In his a against Israel 678+3013
3: 8 The a of the LORD burned against Israel 678
14:19 Burning with a, he went up 678
1Sa 11: 6 and he burned with a. 678
17:28 he burned with a at him and asked, 678
20:30 Saul's a flared up at Jonathan and he said 678
20:34 Jonathan got up from the table in fierce a; 678
2Sa 6: 7 The LORD's a burned against Uzzah 678
11:20 the king's a may flare up, 2779
12: 5 with a against the man and said to Nathan, 678
24: 1 the a of the LORD burned against Israel, 678
1Ki 14: 9 you have **provoked** me **to a** and thrust me 4087
14:15 **provoked** the LORD **to a** 4087
14:22 **stirred up** his **jealous a** 7861
15:30 **provoked** the LORD, the God of Israel, **to a.** 4087+4088
16: 2 to sin and to **provoke** me **to a** by their sins. 4087
16: 7 **provoking** him **to a** by the things he did, 4087
16:13 **provoked** the LORD, the God of Israel, **to a** 4087
16:26 **provoked** the LORD, the God of Israel, **to a** 4087
16:33 **provoke** the LORD, the God of Israel, **to a** 4087
21:22 because you have **provoked** me **to a** 4087+4088
1Ki 22:53 **provoked** the LORD, the God of Israel, **to a**, 4087
2Ki 13: 3 So the LORD's a burned against Israel, 678
17:11 **provoked** the LORD **to a.** 4087
17:17 **provoking** him **to a.** 4087
21: 6 **provoking** him **to a.** 4087
21:15 in my eyes and have **provoked** me **to a** 4087
22:13 the LORD's a that burns against us 2779
22:17 to other gods and **provoked** me **to a** by all 4087
22:17 my a will burn against this place and will 2779
23:19 **provoked** the LORD **to a.** 4087
23:26 not turn away from the heat of his fierce a, 678
23:26 to **provoke** him **to a.** 4087+4088
24:20 of the LORD's a that all this happened 678
1Ch 13:10 The LORD's a burned against Uzzah, 678
15:13 that the LORD our God **broke out in a** 7287
2Ch 12:12 the LORD's a turned from him, 678
24:18 God's a came upon Judah and Jerusalem. 7912
25:15 The a of the LORD burned 678
28:11 for the LORD's fierce a rests on you." 678
28:13 and his fierce a rests on Israel." 678
28:25 **provoked** the LORD, the God of his fathers, **to a.** 4087
29: 8 the a of the LORD has fallen on Judah 7912
29:10 so that his fierce a will turn away from us. 678
30: 8 that his fierce a will turn away from you. 678
33: 6 **provoking** him **to a.** 4087
34:21 Great is the LORD's a that is poured out 2779
34:25 to other gods and **provoked** me **to a** by all 4087
34:25 my a will be poured out on this place 2779
Ezr 8:22 his great a is against all who forsake him." 678
10:14 until the fierce a of our God 678
Ne 9:17 slow to a and abounding in love. 678
Est 1:12 the king became furious and burned with a. 2779
2: 1 when the a of King Xerxes had subsided, 2779
Job 4: 9 at the blast of his a they perish. 678
9: 5 and overturns them in his a. 678
9:13 God does not restrain his a; 678
10:17 against me and increase your a toward me; 4089
14:13 and conceal me till your a has passed! 678
16: 9 and tears me in his a and gnashes his teeth 678
18: 4 You who tear yourself to pieces in your a, 678
19:11 His a burns against me; 678
20:23 God will vent his burning a against him 678
21:17 the fate God allots in his a? 678
32: 5 his a was aroused. 678
35:15 that his a never punishes and he does 678
Ps 2: 5 in his a and terrifies them in his wrath, 678
4: 4 In your a do not sin; 8074
6: 1 do not rebuke me in your a or discipline me 678
7: 6 O LORD, in your a; 678
27: 9 do not turn your servant away in a; 678
30: 5 For his a lasts only a moment, 678
37: 8 Refrain from a and turn from wrath; 678
38: 1 do not rebuke me in your a or discipline me 7912
55: 3 upon me and revile me in their a. 678
56: 7 in your a, O God, bring down the nations. 678
69:24 let your fierce a overtake them. 678
74: 1 Why does your a smolder against the sheep 678
77: 9 Has he in a withheld his compassion?" 678
78:31 God's a rose against them; 678
78:38 Time after time he restrained his a and did 678
78:49 He unleashed against them his hot a, 678
78:50 He prepared a path for his a; 678
80: 4 how long will your a **smolder** against 6939
85: 3 and turned from your fierce a. 678
85: 5 Will you prolong your a 678
86:15 and gracious God, slow to a, abounding 678
90: 7 by your a and terrified by your indignation. 678
90:11 Who knows the power of your a? 678
95:11 So I declared on oath in my a, 678
103: 8 slow to a, abounding in love. 678
103: 9 nor will he **harbor** his a forever; 5757
106:29 **provoked** the LORD **to a** 4087
124: 3 when their a flared against us, 678
138: 7 you stretch out your hand against the a 678
145: 8 slow to a and rich in love. 678
Pr 15: 1 but a harsh word stirs up a. 678
21:14 A gift given in secret soothes a, 678
27: 4 A is cruel and fury overwhelming, 2779
29: 8 but wise men turn away a. 678
29:11 A fool gives full vent to his a, 8120
30:33 so stirring up a produces strife." 678
Ecc 5:17 with great frustration, affliction and a. 7912
7: 9 for a resides in the lap of fools. 4088
10: 4 If a ruler's a rises against you, 8120
Isa 5:25 the LORD's a burns against his people; 678
5:25 Yet for all this, his a is not turned away, 678
7: 4 because of the fierce a of Rezin and Aram 678
9:12 Yet for all this, his a is not turned away, 678
9:17 Yet for all this, his a is not turned away, 678
9:21 Yet for all this, his a is not turned away, 678
10: 4 Yet for all this, his a is not turned away, 678
10: 5 "Woe to the Assyrian, the rod of my a, 678
10: 6 I dispatch him against a people who a me, 6301
10:25 Very soon my a against you will end 2405
12: 1 your a has turned away 678
13: 9 a cruel day, with wrath and fierce a— 678
13:13 in the day of his burning a. 678
14: 6 which in a struck down peoples 6301
30:27 with burning a and dense clouds of smoke; 678
30:30 down with raging a and consuming fire, 678
42:25 So he poured out on them his burning a, 678
54: 8 of a I hid my face from you for a moment, 7912
57:17 I punished him, and hid my face in a, 7911
60:10 Though in a I struck you, 7912
63: 3 in my a and trod them down in my wrath; 678
63: 6 I trampled the nations in my a; 678
Isa 66:15 he will bring down his a with fury, 678
Jer 4: 8 for the fierce a of the LORD has 678
4:26 before the LORD, before his fierce a. 678
7:18 to other gods to **provoke** me **to a.** 4087
7:20 My a and my wrath will be poured out 678
8:19 "Why have they **provoked** me **to a** 4087
10:24 in your a, lest you reduce me to nothing. 678
11:17 and **provoked** me **to a** by burning incense 4087
12:13 because of the LORD's fierce a." 678
15:14 for my a will kindle a fire that will burn 678
17: 4 for you have kindled my a, 678
18:23 deal with them in the time of your a. 678
21: 5 a mighty arm in a and fury and great wrath. 678
23:20 The a of the LORD will not turn back 678
25: 6 do not **provoke** me **to a** 4087
25:37 be laid waste because of the fierce a of 678
25:38 and because of the LORD's fierce a. 678
30:24 The fierce a of the LORD will 678
32:29 where the people **provoked** me **to a** 4087
32:31 this city has so aroused my a and wrath 678
32:37 where I banish them in my furious a 678
33: 5 of the men I will slay in my a and wrath. 678
36: 7 for the a and wrath pronounced 678
42:18 'As my a and wrath have been poured out 678
44: 3 They **provoked** me **to a** by burning incense 4087
44: 6 Therefore, my fierce a was poured out; 678
44: 8 Why **provoke** me **to a** 4087
49:37 even my fierce a," declares the LORD. 678
50:13 of the LORD's a she will not be inhabited 7912
51:45 Run from the fierce a of the LORD. 678
52: 3 of the LORD's a that all this happened 678
La 1:12 on me in the day of his fierce a? 678
2: 1 of Zion with the cloud of his a! 678
2: 1 in the day of his a. 678
2: 3 In fierce a he has cut off every horn 678
2: 6 in his fierce a he has spurned both king 678
2:21 You have slain them in the day of your a; 678
2:22 the day of the LORD's a no one escaped 678
3:43 "You have covered yourself with a 678
3:66 Pursue them in a and destroy them from 678
4:11 he has poured out his fierce a. 678
Eze 3:14 in bitterness and in the a of my spirit, 2779
5:13 "Then my a will cease and my wrath 678
5:15 in a and in wrath and with stinging rebuke. 678
7: 3 now upon you and I will unleash my a 678
7: 8 on you and spend my a against you; 678
8:17 and continually **provoke** me **to a?** 4087
8:18 Therefore I will deal with them in a; 2779
13:13 a violent wind, and in my a hailstones 678
16:26 and **provoked** me **to a** 4087
16:38 of my wrath and **jealous a.** 7863
16:42 and my **jealous a** will turn away 7863
20: 8 and spend my a against them in Egypt. 678
20:21 and spend my a against them in the desert. 678
20:28 made offerings that **provoked** me **to a**, 4088
21:31 and breathe out my fiery a against you; 6301
22:20 so will I gather you in my a and my wrath 678
22:31 and consume them with my fiery a, 6301
23:25 I will direct my **jealous a** against you, 7863
25:14 in accordance with my a and my wrath; 678
35:11 I will treat you in accordance with the a 678
38:18 my hot a will be aroused, 678
43: 8 So I destroyed them in my a. 678
Da 9:16 turn away your a and your wrath 678
11:20 yet not in a or in battle. 678
Hos 8: 5 My a burns against them. 678
11: 9 I will not carry out my fierce a, 678
12:14 Ephraim has bitterly **provoked** him **to a**; 4087
13:11 So in my a I gave you a king, 678
14: 4 for my a has turned away from them. 678
Joel 2:13 slow to a and abounding in love, 678
Am 1:11 because his a raged continually 678
Jnh 3: 9 and with compassion turn from his fierce a 678
4: 2 slow to a and abounding in love, 678
Mic 5:15 I will take vengeance in a and wrath upon 678
Na 1: 3 LORD is slow to a and great in power; 678
1: 6 Who can endure his fierce a? 678
Hab 3:12 the earth and in a you threshed the nations. 678
Zep 2: 2 before the fierce a of the LORD comes 678
2: 3 be sheltered on the day of the LORD's a. 678
3: 8 all my fierce a. 678
3: 8 be consumed by the fire of my **jealous a.** 7863
Zec 10: 3 "My a burns against the shepherds, 678
Mt 18:34 In a his master turned him over to 3974
Mk 3: 5 He looked around at them in a and, 3973
Ro 2: 8 there will be wrath and a. 2596
2Co 12:20 jealousy, **outbursts of a**, factions, slander, 2596
Eph 4:26 "In your a do not sin": 3974
4:31 Get rid of all bitterness, rage and a, 3973
Col 3: 8 a, rage, malice, slander, 3973
1Ti 2: 8 without a or disputing. 3973
Heb 3:11 So I declared on oath in my a, 3973
4: 3 "So I declared on oath in my a, 3973
11:27 not fearing the king's a; 2596
Jas 1:20 for man's a does not bring about 3973

ANGERED (9) [ANGER]

Dt 32:16 and a him with their detestable idols. 4087
32:19 and rejected them because he was a 4088
32:21 and a me with their worthless idols. 4087
Ezr 5:12 because our fathers a the God of heaven, 10653
Ps 78:58 They a him with their high places; 4087
106:32 the waters of Meribah they a the LORD, 7911
Pr 22:24 do not associate with one **easily a**, 2779
Zec 8:14 when your fathers a me," 7911
1Co 13: 5 it is not self-seeking, it is not **easily a**, 4236

ANGERS (1) [ANGER]

Pr 20: 2 *he who* **a** him forfeits his life. 6297

ANGLE (5)

2Ch 26: 9 the Valley Gate and at the **a of the wall,** 5243
Ne 3:19 the ascent to the armory as far as the **a.** 5243
3:20 from the a to the entrance of the house 5243
3:24 from Azariah's house to the **a** and 5243
3:25 the **a** and the tower projecting from 5243

ANGRY (118) [ANGER]

Ge 4: 5 So Cain *was* very **a,** 3013
4: 6 the LORD said to Cain, "Why *are* you **a?** 3013
18:30 Then he said, "*May* the Lord not *be* **a,** 3013
18:32 Then he said, "*May* the Lord not *be* **a,** 3013
27:45 When your brother is no longer **a** with you 678
30: 2 Jacob *became* **a** with her and said, 678+3013
31:35 Rachel said to her father, "Don't *be* **a,** 928+3013+6524
31:36 Jacob *was* **a** and took Laban to task. 3013
40: 2 Pharaoh *was* **a** with his two officials, 7911
41:10 Pharaoh *was once* **a** with his servants, 7911
44:18 *Do* not *be* **a** with your servant, 678+3013
45: 5 *be* **a** with yourselves for selling me here, 3013
Ex 16:20 So Moses *was* **a** with them. 7911
32:22 "*Do* not *be* **a,** my lord," Aaron answered. 678+3013
Lev 10: 6 or you will die and the LORD *will be* **a** 7911
10:16 *he was* **a** with Eleazar and Ithamar, 7911
Nu 11:10 The LORD *became* exceedingly **a,** 678+3013
16:15 Then Moses *became* very **a** and said to 3013
16:22 *will you be* **a** with the entire assembly 7911
22:22 But God *was* **very a** when he went, 678+3013
22:27 *he was* **a** and beat her with his staff. 678+3013
31:14 Moses *was* **a** with the officers of 7911
32:14 and making the LORD even more **a** 678+3019
Dt 1:34 *he was* **a** and solemnly swore: 7911
1:37 of you the LORD *became* **a** with me also 647
3:26 because of you the LORD *was* **a** with me 6297
4:21 The LORD *was* **a** with me because of you, 647
9: 8 the LORD's wrath so that he *was* **a** *enough* 647
9:19 *he was* **a** *enough* with you to destroy you. 7911
9:20 And the LORD *was* **a** enough with Aaron 647
9:22 *You* also **made** the LORD **a** at Taberah, 2118+7911
31:17 On that day I *will become* **a** with them 678+3013
32:21 *I will* **make** them **a** by a nation 4087
Jos 22:18 *be* **a** with the whole community of Israel. 7911
Jdg 2:20 the LORD *was* **very a** with Israel 678+3013
6:39 Gideon said to God, "*Do* not *be* **a** with me. 678+3013
9:30 he *was* **very a.** 678+3013
10: 7 he *became* **a** with them. 678+3013
1Sa 18: 8 Saul *was* very **a;** this refrain galled him. 3013
29: 4 the Philistine commanders *were* **a** with him 7911
2Sa 3: 8 Abner *was* very **a** because 3013
6: 8 Then David *was* **a** because 3013
19:42 Why *are* you **a** about it? 3013
22: 8 they trembled because he *was* **a.** 3013
1Ki 8:46 and *you become* **a** with them and give them 647
11: 9 The LORD *became* **a** with Solomon 647
20:43 and **a,** the king of Israel went to his palace 2409
21: 4 sullen and **a** because Naboth 2409
2Ki 5:11 But Naaman went away **a** and said, 7911
13:19 The man of God *was* **a** with him and said, 7911
17:18 So the LORD *was* very **a** with Israel 647
1Ch 13:11 Then David *was* **a** because 3013
2Ch 6:36 and *you become* **a** with them and give them 647
16:10 Asa *was* **a** with the seer because of this; 4087
26:19 to burn incense, *became* **a.** 2406
28: 9 the God of your fathers, was **a** with Judah, 2779
Ezr 9:14 not *be* **a** enough with us to destroy us, 647
Ne 4: 1 he *became* **a** and was greatly incensed. 3013
4: 7 they *were* very **a.** 3013
5: 6 I *was* very **a.** 3013
Est 2:21 *became* **a** and conspired 7911
Job 32: 2 *became* **very a** with Job 678+3013
32: 3 He *was* also **a** with the three friends, 678+3013
42: 7 "I *am* **a** with you and your two friends, 678+3013
Ps 2:12 *be* **a** and you be destroyed in your way, 647
18: 7 they trembled because he *was* **a.** 3013
60: 1 *you have been* **a**— now restore us! 647
76: 7 before you when you are **a?** 678
78:21 *he was* **very a;** 6297
78:59 When God heard them, *he was* **very a;** 6297
78:62 *he was* **very a** with his inheritance. 6297
79: 5 *Will you be* **a** forever? 647
85: 5 *Will you be* **a** with us forever? 647
89:38 *you have been* **very a** 6297
95:10 forty years *I was* **a** with that generation; 7752
106:40 the LORD *was* **a** with his people 678+3013
Pr 25:23 so a sly tongue brings **a** looks. 2404
29:22 An **a** man stirs up dissension, 678
Ecc 5: 6 *be* **a** at what you say and destroy the work 7911
SS 1: 6 My mother's sons *were* **a** with me 5723
Isa 12: 1 Although *you were* **a** with me, 647
27: 4 I am not **a.** 2779
34: 2 The LORD is **a** with all nations; 7912
47: 6 *I was* **a** with my people 7911
54: 9 So now I have sworn not *to be* **a** with you, 7911
57:16 nor *will I* always *be* **a,** 7911
64: 5 to sin against them, you *were* **a.** 7911
64: 9 *Do* not *be* **a** beyond measure, O LORD; 7911
Jer 2:35 he *is* **not a** with me.' 678+8740
3: 5 *will you* always *be* **a?** 5757
3:12 '*I will* not *be* **a** forever. 5757
Jer 10:10 When he is **a,** the earth trembles; 7912
37:15 They *were* **a** with Jeremiah 7911
La 5:22 and *are* **a** with us beyond measure. 7911
Eze 16:42 I will be calm and no longer **a.** 4087
Da 2:12 the king so **a** and furious that he ordered 10113
Jnh 4: 1 Jonah was greatly displeased and *became* **a.** 3013
4: 4 "Have you any right *to be* **a?"** 3013
4: 9 "Do you have a right *to be* **a** about 3013
4: 9 "I *am* **a** enough to die." 3013
Mic 2: 7 "*Is* the Spirit of the LORD **a?** 7918
7:18 You do not stay **a** forever but delight 678
Hab 3: 8 *Were you* **a** with the rivers, O LORD? 3013
Zec 1: 2 LORD *was* **very a** with your forefathers 7911+7912
1:12 which *you have been* **a** 2404
1:15 I *am* very **a** with the nations that feel secure. 7911+7912
1:15 I *was* only a little **a,** 7911
7:12 So the LORD Almighty was very **a.** 7912
Mt 5:22 that anyone who *is* **a** with his brother will *3974*
Lk 14:21 *became* **a** and ordered his servant, *3974*
15:28 "The older brother *became* **a** and refused *3974*
Jn 7:23 why *are you* **a** with me for healing *5957*
Ro 10:19 *I will* **make** you **a** by a nation *4239*
Eph 4:26 the sun go down while you are still **a,** *4240*
Heb 3:10 That is why *I was* **a** with that generation, *4696*
3:17 And with whom *was he* **a** for forty years? *4696*
Jas 1:19 slow to speak and slow to become **a,** *3973*
Rev 11:18 The nations *were* **a;** *3974*

ANGUISH (42) [ANGUISHED]

Ex 15:14 **a** will grip the people of Philistia. 2659
Dt 2:25 of you and will tremble and *be* **in a** because 2655
1Sa 1:16 I have been praying here out of my great **a** 8490
Job 6: 2 "If only my **a** could be weighed 4089
7:11 I will speak out in the **a** *of* my spirit, 7639
15:24 Distress and **a** fill him with terror; 5188
26: 5 "The dead *are* **in deep a,** 2655
Ps 6: 3 My soul *is* **in a.** 987+4394
25:17 free me from my **a.** 5188
31: 7 for you saw my affliction and knew the **a** 7650
31:10 My life is consumed by **a** and my years 3326
38: 8 I groan in **a** *of* heart. 5639
39: 2 even saying anything good, my **a** increased. 3873
55: 4 My heart *is* **in a** within me; 2655
116: 3 the **a** *of* the grave came upon me; 5210
118: 5 In my **a** I cried to the LORD, 5210
Pr 31: 6 wine to *those who* are **in a;** 5253+5883
Isa 13: 8 pain and **a** will grip them; 2477
23: 5 *they will be* **in a** at the report from Tyre. 2655
38:15 because of this **a** *of* my soul. 5253
38:17 it was for my benefit that I suffered *such* **a.** 5253
65:14 from **a** *of* heart and wail in brokenness 3873
Jer 4:19 Oh, my **a,** my anguish! 5055
4:19 Oh, my anguish, my **a!** 5055
6:24 **A** has gripped us, 7650
15: 8 suddenly I will bring down on them **a** 6552
49:24 **a** and pain have seized her, 7650
50:43 **A** has gripped him, 7650
La 1: 4 her maidens grieve, and she is in **bitter a.** 5253
Eze 27:31 with **a** *of* soul and with bitter mourning. 5253
30: 4 and **a** will come upon Cush. 2714
30: 9 **A** will take hold of them on the day 2714
Da 10:16 "I am overcome with **a** because of 7496
Joel 2: 6 At the sight of them, nations *are* **in a;** 2655
Am 5:16 wailing in all the streets and cries of **a** 2082+2082
Hab 3: 7 the dwellings of Midian **in a.** 8074
Zep 1:15 a day of distress and **a,** 5188
Lk 21:25 nations will be in **a** and perplexity at *5330*
22:44 And being in **a,** he prayed more earnestly, *75*
Jn 16:21 but when her baby is born she forgets the **a** *2568*
Ro 9: 2 I have great sorrow and unceasing **a** *3850*
2Co 2: 4 For I wrote you out of great distress and **a** *5330*

ANGUISHED (2) [ANGUISH]

Jer 48: 5 on the road down to Horonaim **a** cries over 7639
Da 6:20 he called to Daniel in an **a** voice, "Daniel, 10565

ANIAM (1)

1Ch 7:19 Ahian, Shechem, Likhi and **A.** 642

ANIM (1)

Jos 15:50 Anab, Eshtemoh, **A,** 6719

ANIMAL (85) [ANIMALS]

Ge 6:20 of every kind of **a** and of every kind 989
7: 2 with you seven of every kind of clean **a,** 989
7: 2 and two of every kind of unclean **a,** 989
7:14 with them every **wild a** according 2651
9: 5 I will demand an accounting from every **a.** 2651
37:20 and say that a ferocious **a** devoured him. 2651
37:33 Some ferocious **a** has devoured him. 2651
43:16 slaughter an **a** and prepare dinner; 3181
Ex 9: 4 no **a** belonging to the Israelites will die.' " 1821[S]
9: 6 not one **a** belonging to the Israelites died. 5238
9:19 the hail will fall on every man and **a** 989
11: 7 not a dog will bark at any man or **a.'** 989
13: 2 whether man or **a."** 989
13:15 both man and **a.** 989
19:13 Whether man or **a,** 989
21:34 and the **dead a** will be his. AIT
21:35 both the money and the **dead** *a* equally. AIT
21:36 the owner must pay, **a** for animal, 8802
21:36 the owner must pay, animal for **a,** 8802
21:36 and the **dead** *a* will be his. AIT
Ex 22: 4 **stolen** *a* is found alive in his possession— AIT
22:10 a sheep or any other **a** to his neighbor 989
22:12 But if the **a** was stolen from the neighbor, NIH
22:13 **was torn to pieces by a wild a,** 3271+3271
22:13 not be required to pay for the torn **a.** NIH
22:14 "If a man borrows an **a** from his neighbor NIH
22:15 But if the owner is with **the a,** 2257[S]
22:15 If **the a** was hired, 2085[S]
22:19 with an **a** must be put to death. 989
22:31 **a torn by** wild **beasts;** 3274
Lev 1: 2 to the LORD, bring as your offering an **a** 989
3: 1 and he offers an **a** from the herd, NIH
3: 1 he is to present before the LORD an **a** 5647[S]
3: 6 an **a** from the flock as a fellowship offering NIH
7:21 or an unclean **a** or any unclean, 989
7:24 The fat of an **a found dead** or torn 5577
7:25 of an **a** from which an offering by fire may 989
7:26 you must not eat the blood of any bird or **a.** 989
11: 3 You may eat any **a** that has 989
11:26 " 'Every **a** that has a split hoof 989
11:39 " 'If an **a** that you are allowed to eat dies, 989
17:13 among you who hunts any **a** or bird 2651+7473
18:23 " 'Do not have sexual relations with an **a** 989
18:23 A woman must not present herself to an **a** 989
20:15 " 'If a man has sexual relations with an **a,** 989
20:15 and you must kill the **a.** 989
20:16 an **a** to have sexual relations with it, 989
20:16 kill both the woman and the **a.** 989
20:25 Do not defile yourselves by any **a** or bird 989
22:24 an **a** whose testicles are bruised, NIH
24:18 of someone's **a** must make restitution— 989
24:21 Whoever kills an **a** must make restitution, 989
27: 9 an **a** that is acceptable as an offering to 989
27: 9 an **a** given to the LORD becomes holy. 5647[S]
27:10 if he should substitute *one* **a** for another, 989
27:11 a ceremonially unclean **a**— 989
27:11 the **a** must be presented to the priest, 989
27:13 If the owner wishes to redeem **the a,** 5626[S]
27:26 may dedicate the firstborn of an **a,** 989
27:28 whether man or **a** or family land— 989
27:32 every tenth **a** that passes under NIH
27:33 both **the a** and its substitute become holy 2085[S]
Nu 3:13 whether man or **a.** 989
8:17 whether man or **a,** is mine. 989
18:15 both man and **a,** 989
Dt 4:17 or like any **a** on earth or any bird that flies 989
14: 6 You may eat any **a** that has 989
15:21 If an **a** has a defect, is lame or blind, 2257[S]
16: 2 an **a from** your **flock** or herd at the place 7366
27:21 "Cursed is the man who has sexual relations with any **a."** 989
Job 39:15 that some wild **a** may trample them. 2651
Ps 50:10 for every **a** *of* the forest is mine, 2651
Pr 12:10 righteous man cares for the needs of his **a,** 989
Ecc 3:19 man has no advantage over the **a.** 989
3:21 and if the spirit of the **a** goes down into 989
Jer 51:62 so that neither man nor **a** will live in it; 989
Eze 29:11 No foot of man or **a** will pass through it; 989
44:31 priests must not eat anything, bird or **a,** 989
Da 4:16 and let him be given the mind of an **a,** 10263
5:21 from people and given the mind of an **a;** 10263
8: 4 No **a** could stand against him, 2651
Hos 13: 8 a wild **a** will tear them apart. 2651
Mal 1:14 then sacrifices a **blemished** *a* to the Lord. AIT
Heb 12:20 "If even an **a** touches the mountain, *2563*
Jas 3: 3 we can turn the whole **a.** *NIG*

ANIMALS (145) [ANIMAL]

Ge 1:24 and wild **a,** each according to its kind." 2651
1:25 the wild **a** according to their kinds, 2651
3: 1 of the wild **a** the LORD God had made. 2651
3:14 above all the livestock and all the wild **a!** 2651
6: 7 men and **a,** and creatures that move along 989
7: 8 Pairs of clean and unclean **a,** 989
7:16 The *a* **going in** were male and female AIT
7:21 birds, livestock, **wild a,** 2651
7:23 and **a** and the creatures that move along 989
8: 1 the **wild a** and the livestock that were 2651
8:17 the **a,** and all the creatures that move along 989
8:19 the **a** and all the creatures that move along 2651
8:20 of all the clean **a** and clean birds, 989
9:10 the birds, the livestock and all the wild **a,** 2651
30:40 and dark-colored **a** *that belonged* 7366
30:40 and did not put them with Laban's **a.** 7366
30:41 the **a** so they would mate near the branches, 7366
30:42 but if the **a** were weak, 7366
30:42 So the weak **a** went to Laban and NIH
31:39 **a torn by wild beasts;** 3274
32:17 and who owns all these **a** in front of you?' NIH
33:13 all the **a** will die. 7366
34:23 and all their *other* **a** become ours? 989
36: 6 as well as his livestock and all his *other* **a** 989
45:17 Load your **a** and return to the land 1248
Ex 8:17 gnats came upon men and **a.** 989
8:18 And the gnats were on men and **a.** 989
9: 7 even one of the **a** *of* the Israelites had died. 5238
9: 9 on men and **a** throughout the land." 989
9:10 and festering boils broke out on men and **a.** 989
9:22 on men and **a** and on everything growing in 989
9:25 both men and **a;** 989
12: 5 The **a** you choose must be year-old males 8445
12:12 both men and **a**— 989
12:21 at once and select the **a** for your families 7366
20:10 nor your **a,** nor the alien within your gates. 989
23:11 and the wild **a** may eat what they leave. 2651
23:29 and the wild **a** too numerous for you. 2651

Lev 5: 2 whether the carcasses of unclean **wild a** or 2651
7:24 or **torn by wild a** may be used 3274
11: 2 'Of all the **a** that live on land, 989
11:27 Of all the **a** that walk on all fours, 2651
11:29 " 'Of the **a** that move about on the ground, 9238
11:46 " 'These are the regulations concerning **a**, 989
17:15 or **torn by wild a** must wash his clothes 3274
19:19 " 'Do not mate different kinds of **a**. 989
20:25 a distinction between clean and unclean **a** 989
22: 8 or **torn by wild a**, 3274
22:25 and you must not accept such **a** from 465[S]
25: 7 as well as for your livestock and the **wild a** 2651
26:22 I will send **wild a** against you, 2651
27:27 If it is one of the unclean **a**, 989
Nu 7:87 of **a** for the burnt offering came 1330
7:88 The total number of **a** *for* the sacrifice of 1330
18:15 and every firstborn male of unclean **a**. 989
28:31 Be sure the **a** are without defect. NIH
31:11 including the people and **a**, 989
31:26 the people and **a** that were captured. 989
31:30 cattle, donkeys, sheep, goats or other **a**. 989
31:47 of every fifty persons and **a**, 989
Dt 5:14 nor your ox, your donkey or any of your **a**, 989
7:22 or the **wild a** will multiply around you. 2651
12:15 you may slaughter your **a** in any NIH
12:21 you may slaughter **a** from the herds NIH
14: 4 These are the **a** you may eat: 989
Jdg 20:48 the **a** and everything else they found. 989
2Sa 21:10 of the air touch them by day or the **wild a** 2651
1Ki 4:33 He also taught about **a** and birds, 989
18: 5 so we will not have to kill any of our **a**." 989
2Ki 3: 9 for themselves or for the **a** with them. 989
3:17 your cattle and your other **a** will drink. 989
2Ch 29:33 The *a* **consecrated** as sacrifices amounted AIT
35:11 while the Levites skinned the **a**. NIH
35:13 the **Passover a** over the fire as prescribed, 7175
Job 5:23 and the **wild a** will be at peace with you. 2651
12: 7 "But ask the **a**, and they will teach you, 989
37: 8 The **a** take cover; they remain in their dens. 2651
40:20 and all the **wild a** play nearby. 2651
Ps 66:15 I will sacrifice **fat a** to you and an offering 4671
135: 8 the firstborn of men and **a**. 989
148:10 **wild a** and all cattle, 2651
Ecc 3:18 that they may see that they are like the **a**. 989
3:19 Man's fate is like that of the **a**; 989
Isa 1:11 of rams and the fat of **fattened a**; 5309
18: 6 of prey and to the **wild a**; 989
18: 6 the **wild a** all winter. 989
30: 6 An oracle concerning the **a** *of* the Negev: 989
40:16 nor its **a** enough for burnt offerings. 2651
43:20 The **wild a** honor me, 2651
Jer 9:10 of the air have fled and the **a** are gone. 989
12: 4 the **a** and birds have perished. 989
21: 6 both men and **a**— 989
27: 5 the earth and its people and the **a** that are 989
27: 6 I will make even the **wild a** subject to him. 2651
28:14 even give him control over the **wild a**.' " 2651
31:27 with the offspring of men and of **a**. 989
32:43 'It is a desolate waste, without men or **a**, 989
33:10 "It is a desolate waste, without men or **a**." 989
33:10 inhabited by neither men nor **a**, 989
33:12 desolate and without men or **a**— 989
36:29 and cut off both men and **a** from it?" 989
50: 3 both men and **a** will flee away. 989
Eze 4:14 or **torn by wild a**. 3274
8:10 of crawling things and detestable **a** and all 989
14:13 upon it and kill its men and their **a**, 989
14:17 and I kill its men and their **a**, 989
14:19 killing its men and their **a**, 989
14:21 to kill its men and their **a**! 989
25:13 against Edom and kill its men and their **a**. 989
29: 8 against you and kill your men and their **a**. 989
33:27 in the country I will give to the **wild a** to 2651
34: 3 with the wool and slaughter the **choice** *a*, AIT
34: 5 for all the **wild a**. 2651
34: 8 and has become food for all the **wild a**, 2651
34:28 nor will **wild a** devour them. 2651
36:11 I will increase the number of men and **a** 989
39: 4 of carrion birds and to the **wild a**. 2651
39:17 to every kind of bird and all the **wild a**: 2651
39:18 all of them **fattened a** *from* Bashan. 5309
44:31 found dead or **torn by wild a**. 3274
Da 4:14 Let the **a** flee from under it and the birds 10263
4:15 with the **a** among the plants of the earth. 10263
4:23 let him live like the **wild a**, 10263
4:25 from people and will live with the **wild a**; 10263
4:32 from people and will live with the **wild a**; 10263
Hos 2:12 and **wild a** will devour them. 2651
Joel 1:20 Even the **wild a** pant for you; 989
2:22 Be not afraid, O **wild a**, 989
Hab 2:17 and your destruction of **a** will terrify you. 989
Zep 1: 3 "I will sweep away both men and **a**; 989
Zec 14:15 and all the **a** in those camps. 989
Mal 1: 8 When you bring **blind** *a* for sacrifice, AIT
1: 8 When you sacrifice crippled or **diseased** *a*, AIT
1:13 or **diseased** *a* and offer them as sacrifices, AIT
Mk 1:13 He was with the **wild a**, *2563*
Ac 10:12 It contained all kinds of **four-footed a**, *5488*
11: 6 into it and saw **four-footed a** of the earth, *5488*
15:20 the **meat of strangled a** and from blood. *4465*
15:29 the **meat of strangled a** *4465*
21:25 from the **meat of strangled a** and *4465*
Ro 1:23 to look like mortal man and birds and **a** *5488*
1Co 15:39 of flesh, **a** have another, *3229*
Heb 13:11 the blood *of* **a** into the Most Holy Place as *2442*
Jas 3: 7 All kinds *of* **a**, birds, *2563*
Jude 1:10 by instinct, like unreasoning **a**— *2442*

ANISE (KJV) See DILL

ANKLE (1) [ANKLE-DEEP, ANKLES]

Isa 3:20 the headdresses and **a chains** and sashes, 7578

ANKLE-DEEP (1) [ANKLE, DEEP]

Eze 47: 3 and then led me through water that was **a**. 701

ANKLES (4) [ANKLE]

2Sa 22:37 so that my **a** do not turn. 7972
Ps 18:36 so that my **a** do not turn. 7972
Isa 3:16 with ornaments jingling on their **a**. 8079
Ac 3: 7 the man's feet and **a** became strong. *5383*

ANNA (1)

Lk 2:36 There was also a prophetess, **A**, *483*

ANNALS (40)

1Ki 11:41 are they not written in the book of the **a** 1821
14:19 in the book of the **a** of the kings 1821+3427
14:29 in the book of the **a** of the kings 1821+3427
15: 7 in the book of the **a** of the kings 1821+3427
15:23 in the book of the **a** of the kings 1821+3427
15:31 in the book of the **a** of the kings 1821+3427
16: 5 in the book of the **a** of the kings 1821+3427
16:14 in the book of the **a** of the kings 1821+3427
16:20 in the book of the **a** of the kings 1821+3427
16:27 in the book of the **a** of the kings 1821+3427
22:39 in the book of the **a** of the kings 1821+3427
22:45 in the book of the **a** of the kings 1821+3427
2Ki 1:18 in the book of the **a** of the kings 1821+3427
8:23 in the book of the **a** of the kings 1821+3427
10:34 in the book of the **a** of the kings 1821+3427
12:19 in the book of the **a** of the kings 1821+3427
13: 8 in the book of the **a** of the kings 1821+3427
13:12 in the book of the **a** of the kings 1821+3427
14:15 in the book of the **a** of the kings 1821+3427
14:18 in the book of the **a** of the kings 1821+3427
14:28 in the book of the **a** of the kings 1821+3427
15: 6 in the book of the **a** of the kings 1821+3427
15:11 in the book of the **a** of the kings 1821+3427
15:15 in the book of the **a** of the kings 1821+3427
15:21 in the book of the **a** of the kings 1821+3427
15:26 in the book of the **a** of the kings 1821+3427
15:31 in the book of the **a** of the kings 1821+3427
15:36 in the book of the **a** of the kings 1821+3427
16:19 in the book of the **a** of the kings 1821+3427
20:20 in the book of the **a** of the kings 1821+3427
21:17 in the book of the **a** of the kings 1821+3427
21:25 in the book of the **a** of the kings 1821+3427
23:28 in the book of the **a** of the kings 1821+3427
24: 5 in the book of the **a** of the kings 1821+3427
1Ch 27:24 in the book of the **a** of King David. 1821+3427
2Ch 20:34 are written in the **a** *of* Jehu son of Hanani, 1821
33:18 are written in the **a** *of* the kings of Israel. 1821
Ne 12:23 in the book of the **a**. 1821+3427
Est 2:23 All this was recorded in the book of the **a** 1821+3427
10: 2 in the book of the **a** of the kings 1821+3427

ANNAS (4)

Lk 3: 2 the high priesthood *of* **A** and Caiaphas, *483*
Jn 18:13 and brought him first to **A**, *484*
18:24 Then **A** sent him, still bound, *484*
Ac 4: 6 **A** the high priest was there, *484*

ANNIHILATE (6) [ANNIHILATED, ANNIHILATION]

Dt 9: 3 and **a** them quickly, 6
2Sa 21: 2 for Israel and Judah had tried to **a** them.) 5782
2Ch 20:23 from Mount Seir to destroy and **a** them. 9012
Est 3:13 kill and **a** all the Jews— 6
8:11 and **a** any armed force of any nationality 6
Da 11:44 in a great rage to destroy and **a** many. 3049

ANNIHILATED (1) [ANNIHILATE]

2Ch 32:21 *who* **a** all the fighting men and the leaders 3948

ANNIHILATION (2) [ANNIHILATE]

Est 4: 8 a copy of the text of the edict for their **a**, 9012
7: 4 for destruction and slaughter and **a**. 6

ANNIVERSARY (1)

Dt 16: 6 on the **a** *of* your departure from Egypt. 4595

ANNOTATIONS (2) [NOTE]

2Ch 13:22 are written in the **a** *of* the prophet Iddo. 4535
24:27 of the temple of God are written in the **a** *on* 4535

ANNOUNCE (13) [ANNOUNCED, ANNOUNCEMENT, ANNOUNCES, ANNOUNCING]

Jdg 7: 3 **a** now to the people, 7924
Isa 42: 9 before they spring into being *I* **a** them 9048
48:20 **A** this with shouts of joy and proclaim it. 5583
Jer 4: 5 "**A** in Judah and proclaim in Jerusalem 5583
5:20 "**A** this to the house of Jacob 5583
18: 7 at any time *I* **a** that a nation or kingdom is 1819
18: 9 And if at another time *I* **a** that a nation 1819
46:14 "**A** this in Egypt, and proclaim it in Migdol; 5583
48:20 **A** by the Arnon that Moab is destroyed. 5583
50: 2 "**A** and proclaim among the nations, lift up 5583
51:31 and messenger follows messenger to **a** to 5583
Zec 9:12 now I **a** that I will restore twice as much 5583
Mt 6: 2 *do* not **a** it **with trumpets,** *4895*

ANNOUNCED (13) [ANNOUNCE]

Ex 32: 5 he built an altar in front of the calf and **a**, 7924
Lev 23:44 So Moses **a** to the Israelites 1819
Ru 4: 9 Boaz **a** to the elders and all the people, 606
1Ki 20:13 to Ahab king of Israel and **a**, "This is what 606
Ps 68:11 The Lord **a** the word, 5989
Isa 48: 3 my mouth **a** them and I made them known; 3655
48: 5 before they happened *I* **a** them *to* you so 9048
La 1:21 the day *you have* **a** so they may become 7924
Da 4:17 " 'The decision is **a** *by* messengers, 10141
Lk 23: 4 Pilate **a** to the chief priests and the crowd, *3306*
Gal 3: 8 **a the gospel in advance** *4603*
Heb 2: 3 which *was* first **a** by the Lord, *3281*
Rev 10: 7 just as *he* **a** to his servants the prophets." *2294*

ANNOUNCEMENT (1) [ANNOUNCE]

Isa 48:16 the first **a** I have not spoken in secret; NIH

ANNOUNCES (2) [ANNOUNCE]

Dt 13: 1 among you and **a** to you a miraculous sign 5989
Job 36:33 His thunder **a** the coming storm; 5583

ANNOUNCING (1) [ANNOUNCE]

Jer 4:15 A voice *is* **a** from Dan, 5583

ANNOYANCE (1)

Pr 12:16 A fool shows his **a** at once, 4088

ANNUAL (7) [ANNUALLY]

Ex 30:10 This **a** atonement must be made 285+928+2021+9102
Jdg 21:19 the **a** festival of the LORD in Shiloh, 2025+3427+3427+4946
1Sa 1:21 with all his family to offer the **a** sacrifice to 3427
2:19 up with her husband to offer the **a** sacrifice. 3427
20: 6 because an **a** sacrifice is being made there 3427
2Ch 8:13 New Moons and the three **a** feasts— 928+2021+7193+9102
Heb 10: 3 those sacrifices are an **a** reminder of sins, *1929+2848*

ANNUALLY (2) [ANNUAL]

2Ch 24: 5 and collect the money **due a** from all Israel, 928+1896+4946+9102+9102
Est 9:21 to have them celebrate **a** the fourteenth 928+2256+3972+9102+9102

ANNULLED (1) [NULLIFY]

Isa 28:18 Your covenant with death *will* **be a**; 4105

ANOINT (28) [ANOINTED, ANOINTING]

Ex 28:41 **a** and ordain them. 5417
29: 7 the anointing oil and **a** him by pouring it 5417
29:36 and **a** it to consecrate it. 5417
30:26 Then use it *to* **a** the Tent of Meeting, 5417
30:30 "**A** Aaron and his sons and consecrate them 5417
40: 9 "Take the anointing oil and **a** the tabernacle 5417
40:10 Then **a** the altar of burnt offering 5417
40:11 **A** the basin and its stand 5417
40:13 **a** him and consecrate him 5417
40:15 **A** them just as you anointed their father, 5417
Jdg 9: 8 One day the trees went out to **a** a king 5417
9:15 'If you really *want to* **a** me king over you, 5417
1Sa 9:16 **A** him leader over my people Israel; 5417
15: 1 the one the LORD sent to **a** you king 5417
16: 3 *You are to* **a** for me the one I indicate." 5417
16:12 Then the LORD said, "Rise and **a** him; 5417
1Ki 1:34 and Nathan the prophet **a** him king 5417
19:15 you get there, **a** Hazael king over Aram. 5417
19:16 **a** Jehu son of Nimshi king over Israel, 5417
19:16 and **a** Elisha son of Shaphat 5417
2Ki 9: 3 *I* **a** you king over Israel.' 5417
9: 6 '*I* **a** you king over the LORD's people 5417
9:12 *I* **a** you king over Israel.' " 5417
Ps 23: 5 *You* **a** my head with oil; my cup overflows. 2014
Ecc 9: 8 and always **a** your head *with* oil. 6584
Da 9:24 to seal up vision and prophecy and to **a** 5417
Mk 16: 1 so that *they might* go to **a** Jesus' body. *230*
Jas 5:14 and **a** him with oil in the name of the Lord. *230*

ANOINTED (83) [ANOINT]

Ge 31:13 where *you* **a** a pillar and where you made 5417
Ex 29:29 so that they *can be* **a** and ordained in them. 5417
40:15 Anoint them just as *you* **a** their father, 5417
Lev 4: 3 " 'If the **a** priest sins, 5431
4: 5 Then the **a** priest shall take some of 5431
4:16 Then the **a** priest is to take some of 5431
6:20 to bring to the LORD on the day he *is* **a**: 5417
6:22 to succeed him as **a** priest shall prepare it. 5431
7:36 On the day they *were* **a**, 5417
8:10 and **a** the tabernacle and everything in it, 5417
8:12 and **a** him to consecrate him. 5417

Lev 16:32 The priest who *is* a and ordained 5417
Nu 3: 3 the a priests, who were ordained to serve 5417
7: 1 *he* a it and consecrated it 5417
7: 1 *He* also a and consecrated the altar 5417
7:10 When the altar *was* a, 5417
7:84 for the dedication of the altar when it was a: 5417
7:88 for the dedication of the altar after it was a. 5417
35:25 who *was* a with the holy oil. 5417
1Sa 2:10 to his king and exalt the horn of his a." 5431
2:35 he will minister before my a *one* always. 5431
10: 1 *"Has* not the LORD a you leader 5417
12: 3 in the presence of the LORD and his a. 5431
12: 5 and also his a is witness this day, 5431
15:17 The LORD a you king over Israel. 5417
16: 6 "Surely the LORD's a stands here before 5431
16:13 So Samuel took the horn of oil and a him 5417
24: 6 the LORD's a, or lift my hand 5431
24: 6 for he is the a *of* the LORD." 5431
24:10 because he is the LORD's a.' 5431
26: 9 Who can lay a hand on the LORD's a and 5431
26:11 that I should lay a hand on the LORD's a. 5431
26:16 not guard your master, the LORD's a. 5431
26:23 I would not lay a hand on the LORD's a. 5431
2Sa 1:14 to destroy the LORD's a?" 5431
1:16 'I killed the LORD's a.' " 5431
2: 4 to Hebron and there *they* a David king over 5417
2: 7 and the house of Judah *has* a me king 5417
3:39 And today, though I *am* the a king, 5417
5: 3 and *they* a David king over Israel. 5417
5:17 that David *had been* a king over Israel, 5417
12: 7 'I a you king over Israel, 5417
19:10 whom *we* a to rule over us, 5417
19:21 He cursed the LORD's a." 5431
22:51 he shows unfailing kindness to his a, 5431
23: 1 the man a *by* the God of Jacob, 5431
1Ki 1:39 of oil from the sacred tent and a Solomon. 5417
1:45 and Nathan the prophet *have* a him king 5417
5: 1 of Tyre heard that Solomon *had been* a king 5417
2Ki 11:12 *They* a him, and the people clapped their hands 5417
23:30 of Josiah and a him and made him king 5417
1Ch 11: 3 and *they* a David king over Israel, 5417
14: 8 that David *had* been a king over all Israel, 5417
16:22 "Do not touch my a *ones;* 5431
2Ch 6:42 O LORD God, do not reject your a *one.* 5431
22: 7 the LORD *had* a to destroy the house 5417
23:11 *They* a him and shouted, 5417
Ps 2: 2 against the LORD and against his A *One.* 5431
18:50 he shows unfailing kindness to his a, 5431
20: 6 Now I know that the LORD saves his a; 5431
28: 8 a fortress of salvation for his a *one.* 5431
45: 2 and your lips *have* been a *with* grace, 3668
84: 9 look with favor on your a *one.* 5431
89:20 with my sacred oil *I have* a him. 5417
89:38 you have been very angry with your a *one.* 5431
89:51 of your a *one.* 5431
105:15 "Do not touch my a *ones;* 5431
132:10 do not reject your a *one.* 5431
132:17 for David and set up a lamp for my a *one.* 5431
Isa 45: 1 "This is what the LORD says to his a, 5431
61: 1 the LORD *has* a me to preach good news 5417
La 4:20 The LORD's a, our very life breath, 5431
Eze 28:14 You were a as a guardian cherub, 4937
Da 9:25 and rebuild Jerusalem until the A *One,* 5431
9:26 the A *One* will be cut off 5431
Hab 3:13 to save your a *one.* 5431
Zec 4:14 the two *who are* a to serve the Lord of all the earth." 1201+2021+3658
Mk 6:13 and a many sick people with oil *230*
Lk 4:18 because *he has* a me to preach good news to *5987*
Ac 4:26 against the Lord and against his A One.' *5986*
4:27 against your holy servant Jesus, whom *you* a *5987*
10:38 how God a Jesus of Nazareth with *5987*
2Co 1:21 you stand firm in Christ. *He* a us, *5987*

ANOINTING (30) [ANOINT]

Ex 25: 6 for the a oil and for the fragrant incense; 5418
29: 7 Take the a oil and anoint him by pouring it 5418
29:21 the blood on the altar and some of the a oil 5418
30:25 Make these into a sacred a oil, 5418
30:25 It will be the sacred a oil. 5418
30:31 to be my sacred a oil for the generations 5418
31:11 and the a oil and fragrant incense for 5418
35: 8 for the a oil and for the fragrant incense; 5418
35:15 the a oil and the fragrant incense; 5418
35:28 and olive oil for the light and for the a oil 5418
37:29 also made the sacred a oil and the pure, 5418
39:38 the a oil, the fragrant incense, 5418
40: 9 "Take the a oil and anoint the tabernacle 5418
40:15 Their a will be to a priesthood 5420
Lev 8: 2 the a oil, the bull for the sin offering, 5418
8:10 Then Moses took the a oil and anointed 5418
8:11 a the altar and all its utensils and the basin 5417
8:12 the a oil on Aaron's head and anointed him 5418
8:30 of the a oil and some of the blood from 5418
10: 7 because the LORD's a oil is on you." 5418
21:10 the a oil poured on his head 5418
21:12 because he has been dedicated by the a oil 5418
Nu 4:16 the regular grain offering and the a oil. 5418
1Ch 29:22 a him before the LORD to be ruler 5417
Ps 45: 7 above your companions by a you with 5417
Heb 1: 9 above your companions by a you with *5987*
1Jn 2:20 But you have an a from the Holy One, *5984*
2:27 a you received from him remains in you, *5984*
2:27 as his a teaches you about all things and as *5984*
2:27 and as that a is real, not counterfeit— *NIG*

ANON (KJV) See AT ONCE

ANOTH See BETH ANOTH

ANOTHER (359) [ANOTHER'S]

Ge 4:25 "God has granted me a child in place 337
8:19 came out of the ark, one kind after a. 2157+4200+5476
25: 1 Abraham took a wife, 3578
26:21 Then they dug a well, 337
26:22 He moved on from there and dug a well, 337
29:27 in return for a seven years of work." 337+6388
29:30 And he worked for Laban a seven years. 337+6388
30:24 "May the LORD add to me a son." 337
35:17 "Don't be afraid, for you have a son." 1685
37: 9 Then he had a dream, 337+6388
37: 9 "Listen," he said, "I had a dream, 6388
38: 5 to still a son and named him Shelah. 3578+6388
42:21 They said to one a, 278[S]
43: 6 by telling the man you had a brother?" 6388
43: 7 'Do you have a brother?' NIH
Ex 12:16 and a *one* on the seventh day. 5246+7731[S]
21:10 If he marries a *woman,* 337
21:14 a man schemes and kills a *man* deliberately, 8276[S]
21:16 "Anyone who kidnaps a and 408[S]
21:35 "If a man's bull injures the bull of a 8276[S]
22: 5 and they graze in a *man's* field, 337
26: 9 into one set and the other six into a set. 963+4200
36:16 into one set and the other six into *a* set. AIT
Lev 13: 5 he is to keep him in isolation a seven days. 9108
13:33 to keep him in isolation a seven days. 9108
13:54 Then he is to isolate it for a seven days. 9108
19:11 " 'Do not deceive one a. 6660[S]
19:20 a slave girl promised to a man but who has NIH
20:10 man commits adultery with a man's wife— NIH
26:37 over one a as though fleeing from 278[S]
27:10 if he should substitute one animal for a, 989[S]
Nu 5: 6 a man or woman wrongs a in any way 132+2021[S]
5:13 by sleeping with a man, NIH
23:13 with me to a place where you can see them; 337
23:27 "Come, let me take you to a place. 337
35:15 anyone who has killed a accidentally can flee there. 5883[S]
35:20 with malice aforethought shoves a 5647[S]
35:22 'But if without hostility someone suddenly shoves a 2257[S]
Dt 4:34 for himself one nation out of a nation, NIH
19: 4 the rule concerning the *man who* kills a 8357
22:22 a man is found sleeping with a man's wife, NIH
22:24 the man because he violated a man's wife. 8276
24: 2 she becomes the wife of a man, 337
28:30 but a will take her and ravish her. 337
28:32 and daughters will be given to a nation, 337
29:28 from their land and thrust them into a land, 337
Jdg 2:10 a generation grew up, 337
11: 2 "because you are the son of a woman." 337
19:10 But, unwilling to stay a night, NIH
20:22 the men of Israel encouraged one a 2021+6639
20:25 down a eighteen thousand Israelites, 6388
Ru 1: 9 in the home of a husband." 2023[S]
1:12 I am too old to have a husband. NIH
2: 8 in a field and don't go away from here. 337
1Sa 2:25 If a man sins against a man, NIH
10: 3 a three loaves of bread, 285[S]
10: 3 and a a skin of wine. 285[S]
13:18 a toward Beth Horon, 285[S]
17: 3 and the Israelites a, 2021+2215+2296+4946[S]
2Sa 3:11 Ish-Bosheth did not dare to say a word 6388
11:25 the sword devours one as well as a. 2296[S]
18:20 "You may take the news a time, 337
18:26 Then the watchman saw a man running, 337
18:26 "Look, a man running alone!" NIH
21:18 there was a battle with the Philistines, 6388
21:19 In a battle with the Philistines at Gob, 6388
21:20 In still a battle, which took place 6388
1Ki 11:23 up against Solomon a adversary, NIH
13:10 So he took a road and did not return by 337
18: 6 in one direction and Obadiah in a. 285[S]
20:10 Then Ben-Hadad sent a message to Ahab: NIH
20:37 The prophet found a man and said, 337
21: 6 I will give you a vineyard in its place.' NIH
22:20 "One suggested this, and a that. 2296[S]
2Ki 1:11 At this the king sent to Elijah a captain 337
4: 6 she said to her son, "Bring me a one." 6388
7: 6 so that they said to one a, "Look, 278[S]
7: 8 and entered a tent and took some things 337
1Ch 2:26 Jerahmeel had a wife, 337
7:15 A descendant was named Zelophehad, 9108
16:20 from one kingdom to a. 337
17: 5 I have moved from one tent site to a, 185[S]
17: 5 from one dwelling place to a. NIH
20: 5 In a battle with the Philistines, 6388
20: 6 In still a battle, which took place 6388
2Ch 15: 6 One nation was being crushed by a 1580[S]
15: 6 by another and one city by a, 6551[S]
18:19 "One suggested this, and a that. 2296[S]
20:23 they helped to destroy one a. 8276[S]
30:23 for a seven days they celebrated joyfully. NIH
32: 5 He built a wall outside that one 337
Ne 3:11 of Pahath-Moab repaired a section and 9108
3:19 ruler of Mizpah, repaired a section, 9108
3:20 of Zabbai zealously repaired a section, 9108
3:21 the son of Hakkoz, repaired a section, 9108
3:24 Binnui son of Henadad repaired a section, 9108
3:27 the men of Tekoa repaired a section, 9108
Ne 3:30 the sixth son of Zalaph, repaired a section. 9108
9: 3 and spent a quarter in confession and NIH
Est 2:14 the morning return to a part *of* the harem 9108
4:14 for the Jews will arise from a place, 337
8: 8 Now write a decree in the king's name NIH
9:22 of food to one a and gifts to the poor. 8276[S]
Job 1:16 a messenger came and said, 2296[S]
1:17 a messenger came and said, 2296
1:18 yet a messenger came and said, 2296[S]
2: 1 On a day the angels came 2021[S]
19:27 I, and not a. 2424
21:25 *A* man dies in bitterness of soul, AIT
31:10 then may my wife grind a *man's* grain, 337
33:14 God does speak—now one way, now a— 9109
41:17 They are joined fast to one a; 278[S]
Ps 49: 7 No man can redeem the life of a or give 278[S]
75: 7 He brings one down, he exalts a. 2296[S]
105:13 from one kingdom to a. 337
109: 8 may a take his place of leadership. 337
145: 4 One generation will commend your works to a; 1887[S]
Pr 5:10 and your toil enrich a man's house. 5799
5:20 Why embrace the bosom of a *man's wife?* 5799
6: 1 if you have struck hands in pledge for a, 2424
6:29 So is he who sleeps with a man's wife; 8276
11:15 up security for a will surely suffer, 2424
11:24 *a* withholds unduly, but comes to poverty. AIT
13: 7 *a* pretends to be poor, AIT
18:17 till a comes forward and questions him. 8276[S]
23:35 will I wake up so I can find a drink?" 3578+6388
25: 9 do not betray a *man's* confidence, 337
27: 2 Let a praise you, and not your own mouth; 2424
27:17 iron sharpens iron, so one man sharpens a. 8276[S]
28: 8 *a, who will be* kind AIT
Ecc 6: 1 I have seen a evil under the sun, NIH
7:27 to a to discover the scheme of things— 285[S]
Isa 6: 3 And they were calling to one a: 2296[S]
42: 8 I will not give my glory to a or my praise 337
44: 5 a will call himself by the name of Jacob; 2296[S]
44: 5 still a will write on his hand, 2296[S]
48:11 I will not yield my glory to a. 337
65:15 but to his servants he will give a name. 337
66:23 to a and from one Sabbath to another, 2544[S]
66:23 to another and from one Sabbath to a, 8701[S]
Jer 3: 1 and she leaves him and marries a man, 337
3:16 nor will a one be made. 6388
5: 8 each neighing for a *man's* wife. 8276[S]
9: 3 They go from one sin to a; 8288[S]
9:20 teach one a a lament. 8295[S]
18: 4 so the potter formed it into a pot, 337
18: 9 And if at a time I announce that a nation 8092
22: 8 by this city and will ask one a, 8276[S]
22:26 into a country, where neither 337
23:27 dreams they tell one a will make my people forget my name, 8276[S]
23:30 from one a words supposedly from me. 8276[S]
26:20 from Kiriath Jearim was a man who prophesied 1685
36:28 "Take a scroll and write on it all the words 337
36:32 So Jeremiah took a scroll and gave it to 337
46:12 One warrior will stumble over a; 1475[S]
48:11 not poured from one jar to a— 3998[S]
51:31 One courier follows a 8132[S]
51:46 one rumor comes this year, a the next 2021+9019[S]
Eze 1: 9 and their wings touched one a. 295[S]
1:11 one touching the wing of a creature on 408[S]
12: 3 and go from where you are to a place. 337
17: 7 " 'But there was a great eagle 285
19: 5 she took a of her cubs and made him 285[S]
21:20 against Rabbah of the Ammonites and a NIH
22:11 a shamefully defiles his daughter-in-law, 408[S]
22:11 and a violates his sister, 408[S]
34:17 I will judge between one sheep and a, 8445[S]
34:22 I will judge between one sheep and a. 8445[S]
37:16 Then take a stick of wood, and write on it, 285[S]
40:44 and a at the side of the south gate NIH
41: 6 one above a, thirty on each level. 7521[S]
41:11 one on the north and a on the south; 285[S]
46:21 and I saw in each corner a court. NIH
47: 4 He measured off a thousand cubits NIH
47: 4 He measured off a thousand and led me NIH
47: 5 He measured off a thousand, NIH
Da 2:39 "After you, a kingdom will rise, 10023
2:44 nor will it be left to a people. 10025
7: 6 I looked, and there before me was a beast, 10023
7: 8 there before me was a horn, a little one, 10023
7:24 After them a king will arise, 10025
8: 9 Out of one of them came a horn, 285[S]
8:13 and a holy one said to him, 285[S]
11:13 the king of the North will muster a army, 8740
Hos 1: 8 Gomer had a son. NIH
3: 1 she is loved by a and is an adulteress. 8276[S]
4: 4 let no man accuse a, NIH
Am 4: 7 but withheld it from a. 285[S]
4: 7 a had none and dried up. 2754[S]
Hag 2:15 before one stone was laid on a in 74[S]
Zec 2: 3 and a angel came to meet him 337
7: 9 show mercy and compassion to one a. 278[S]
8:21 inhabitants of one city will go to a and say, 285[S]
14:13 Each man will seize the hand of a, 8276[S]
Mal 2:10 by breaking faith with one a? 278[S]
2:13 A thing you do: You flood the LORD's 9108
Mt 2:12 they returned to their country by a route. *257*
8:21 A disciple said to him, "Lord, *2283*
10:23 in one place, flee to a. *2283*
13:24 Jesus told them a parable: *257*
13:31 He told them a parable: *257*

Mt 13:33 He told them **still a** parable: *257*
19: 9 and marries a *woman* commits adultery." *257*
21:33 "Listen to a parable: *257*
21:35 they beat one, killed **a,** and stoned a third. *4005*
22: 5 one to his field, **a** to his business. *1254+4005*
24: 2 not *one* stone here will be left on **a;** *3345S*
25:15 *to* **a** two talents, and to another one *1254+4005*
25:15 two talents, and *to* **a** one talent, *1254+4005*
25:32 and he will separate the people **one** from **a** *253*
26:71 **a** *girl* saw him and said to the people there, *257*
Mk 3: 1 **A time** he went into the synagogue, *4099*
8: 1 During those days **a** large crowd gathered. *4099*
8:16 They discussed this with **one a** and said, *253*
10:11 and marries **a** *woman* commits adultery *257*
10:12 and marries **a** *man,* *257*
12: 4 Then he sent **a** servant to them; *257*
12: 5 He sent **still a,** and that one they killed. *257*
12: 7 the tenants said to **one a,** 'This is the heir. *1571*
13: 2 "Not one stone here will be left on **a;** *3345S*
14: 4 to **one a,** "Why this waste *1571*
14:58 and in three days will build **a,** *257*
Lk 2:15 the shepherds said to **one a,** *253*
6: 6 On **a** Sabbath he went into the synagogue *2283*
6:11 to discuss with **one a** what they might do *253*
8: 1 **from one** town and village **to a,** *2848*
8:25 In fear and amazement they asked **one a,** *253*
9:56 and they went to **a** village. *2283*
9:59 He said to **a** *man,* "Follow me." *2283*
9:61 Still **a** said, "I will follow you, Lord; *2283*
12: 1 so that they were trampling on **one a,** *253*
14:19 "**A** said, 'I have just bought five yoke *2283*
14:20 "Still **a** said, 'I just got married, *2283*
14:31 a king is about to go to war *against* **a** king. *2283*
16:18 and marries **a** *woman* commits adultery, *2283*
19:20 "Then **a** servant came and said, 'Sir, *2283*
19:44 They will not leave one stone on **a,** *3345S*
20:11 He sent **a** servant, *2283*
21: 6 when not one stone will be left on **a;** *3345S*
22:59 About an hour later **a** asserted, *257+5516*
Jn 1:16 of his grace we have all received one blessing after **a.** *5921S*
4:37 the saying 'One sows and **a** reaps' is true. *257*
5:32 There is **a** who testifies in my favor, *257*
5:44 if you accept praise from **one a,** *253*
6: 8 **A** of his disciples, Andrew, *1651*
7:35 The Jews said to **one a,** *1571*
11:56 in the temple area they asked **one a,** *253*
12:19 So the Pharisees said to **one a,** "See, *1571*
13:22 His disciples stared at **one a,** *253*
13:34 "A new command I give you: Love **one a.** *253*
13:34 I have loved you, so you must love **one a.** *253*
13:35 you are my disciples, if you love **one a."** *253*
14:16 and he will give you **a** Counselor to be *257*
16:17 Some of his disciples said to **one a,** *253*
16:19 "Are you asking **one a** what I meant *253*
18:15 and **a** disciple were following Jesus. *257*
18:36 But now my kingdom is **from a place."** *1949*
19:24 "Let's not tear it," they said to **one a.** *253*
19:37 as **a** scripture says, *2283*
Ac 1:20 and, " 'May **a** take his place of leadership.' *2283*
2:12 Amazed and perplexed, they asked **one a,** *257+257+4639*
7:18 Then **a** king, who knew nothing *2283*
12:17 he said, and then he left for **a** place. *2283*
17: 7 saying that there is **a** king, *2283*
19:32 Some were shouting one thing, some **a.** *257*
21:34 in the crowd shouted one thing and some **a,** *257*
22:19 **from one** synagogue **to a** *2848*
26:11 **from one synagogue to a** *2848+4246+5252*
26:31 and while talking with **one a,** they said, *253*
Ro 1:24 the degrading of their bodies with **one a.** *899*
1:27 and were inflamed with lust for **one a.** *253*
7: 3 if she marries **a** man *2283*
7: 3 even though she marries **a** man. *2283*
7: 4 that you might belong *to* **a,** *2283*
7:23 but I see **a** law at work in the members *2283*
12:10 Be devoted to **one a** in brotherly love. *253*
12:10 Honor **one a** above yourselves. *253*
12:16 Live in harmony with **one a.** *253*
13: 8 except the continuing debt to love **one a,** *253*
14: 2 but **a** man, whose faith is weak, *NIG*
14: 5 One man considers one day more sacred than **a;** *2465S*
14: 5 **a man** considers every day alike. *1254+4005*
14:13 let us stop passing judgment on **one a.** *253*
15: 7 Accept **one a,** then, just *253*
15:14 and competent to instruct **one a.** *253*
16:12 **a** *woman* **who** has worked very hard in *4015*
16:16 Greet **one a** with a holy kiss. *253*
1Co 1:10 of you agree with one **a** so that there may *NIG*
1:12 **a,** "I follow Apollos"; *1254*
1:12 **a,** "I follow Cephas"; *1254*
1:12 **still a,** "I follow Christ." *1254*
3: 4 For when one says, "I follow Paul," and **a,** *2283*
4: 6 you will not take pride in one man over against **a.** *2283+3836*
6: 1 If any of you has a dispute with **a,** *2283*
6: 6 instead, one brother goes to law against **a—** *81S*
7: 7 one has this gift, **a** has that. *1254+3836*
11:21 One remains hungry, **a** gets drunk. *1254+4005*
12: 8 *to* **a** the message of knowledge by means *257*
12: 9 *to* **a** faith by the same Spirit, *2283*
12: 9 *to* **a** gifts of healing by that one Spirit, *257*
12:10 *to* **a** miraculous powers, *257*
12:10 *to* **a** prophecy, to another distinguishing *257*
12:10 *to* **a** distinguishing between spirits, *257*
12:10 *to* **a** speaking in different kinds of tongues, *2283*
1Co 12:10 and *to* still **a** the interpretation of tongues. *257*
15:39 of flesh, animals have **a,** *257*
15:39 birds **a** and fish another. *257*
15:39 birds another and fish **a.** *257*
15:40 and the splendor of the earthly bodies is **a.** *2283*
15:41 the moon **a** and the stars another; *257*
15:41 the moon another and the stars **a;** *257*
16:20 Greet **one a** with a holy kiss. *253*
2Co 2: 1 that I would not make **a** painful visit *4099*
10:16 in **a** *man's* territory. *259*
13:12 Greet **one a** with a holy kiss. *253*
Gal 5:13 rather, serve **one a** in love. *253*
Eph 4: 2 be patient, bearing with **one a** in love. *253*
4:32 Be kind and compassionate to **one a,** *253*
5:19 Speak *to* **one a** with psalms, *4932*
5:21 *to* **one a** out of reverence for Christ. *253*
Col 3:13 forgive whatever grievances you may have against one **a.** *NIG*
3:16 and admonish **one a** with all wisdom, *4932*
1Th 5:11 encourage **one a** and build each other up, *253*
Tit 3: 3 being hated and hating **one a.** *253*
Heb 3:13 But encourage **one a** daily, *4932*
4: 8 not have spoken later about **a** day. *2283*
5: 6 And he says in **a** *place,* *2283*
7:11 why was there still need for **a** priest *2283*
7:15 if **a** priest like Melchizedek appears, *2283*
8: 7 no place would have been sought for **a.** *1311*
10:24 And let us consider how we may spur **one a** *253*
10:25 but let us encourage one **a—** *NIG*
Jas 4:11 Brothers, do not slander **one a.** *253*
1Pe 1:22 love **one a** deeply, from the heart. *253*
3: 8 all of you, live in harmony with one **a;** *NIG*
4: 9 to **one a** without grumbling. *253*
5: 5 with humility *toward* **one a,** *253*
5:14 Greet **one a** with a kiss of love. *253*
1Jn 1: 7 we have fellowship with **one a,** *253*
3:11 We should love **one a.** *253*
3:23 and to love **one a** as he commanded us. *253*
4: 7 Dear friends, let us love **one a,** *253*
4:11 we also ought to love **one a.** *253*
4:12 but if we love **one a,** God lives in us *253*
2Jn 1: 5 I ask that we love **one a.** *253*
Rev 6: 4 Then **a** horse came out, a fiery red one. *257*
7: 2 I saw **a** angel coming up from the east, *257*
8: 3 **A** angel, who had a golden censer, *257*
10: 1 Then I saw a mighty angel coming down *257*
12: 3 Then **a** sign appeared in heaven: *257*
13:11 I saw **a** beast, coming out of the earth. *257*
14: 6 Then I saw **a** angel flying in midair, *257*
14:15 Then **a** angel came out of the temple *257*
14:17 **A** angel came out of the temple in heaven, *257*
14:18 Still **a** angel, who had charge of the fire, *257*
15: 1 in heaven **a** great and marvelous sign: *257*
18: 1 After this I saw **a** angel coming down *257*
18: 4 Then I heard **a** voice from heaven say: *257*
20:12 **A** book was opened, *257*

ANOTHER'S (4) [ANOTHER]

Jer 19: 9 and they will eat one **a** flesh during 8276S
Zec 11: 9 Let those who are left eat one **a** flesh." 8295S
Jn 13:14 you also should wash **one a** feet. *253*
1Co 10:29 be judged by **a** conscience? *257*

ANSWER (158) [ANSWERABLE, ANSWERED, ANSWERING, ANSWERS]

Ge 41:16 but God *will* **give** Pharaoh *the* **a** he desires." 6699
45: 3 But his brothers were not able to **a** him, 6699
46:34 *you should* **a,** 'Your servants have tended 606
Ex 19: 8 Moses brought their **a** back to the LORD. 1821
Nu 22: 8 "and I will bring you back the **a** 1821
Dt 29:25 And *the* **a** *will be:* 606
Jos 22:28 or to our descendants, *we will* **a:** 606
Jdg 5:29 The wisest of her ladies **a** her; 6699
14:12 "If *you can* **give** me *the* **a** within 5583+5583
14:13 If you can't **tell** me *the* **a,** 5583
14:14 For three days they could not give the **a.** 2648
14:16 but *you* haven't **told** me *the* **a."** 5583
19:28 But there was no **a.** 6699
1Sa 2:16 the servant *would* then **a,** "No, 606
8:18 the LORD *will* not **a** you in that day." 6699
14:37 But God *did* not **a** him that day. 6699
14:41 the God of Israel, "Give me the **right a."** 9459
26:14 "Aren't *you going to* **a** me, Abner?" 6699
28: 6 not **a** him by dreams or Urim or prophets. 6699
2Sa 14:18 not keep from me the **a** to what I am going 1821
15: 2 *He would* **a,** "Your servant is from one of 606
20:18 **Get** *your* **a** at Abel,' and that settled it. 8626+8626
22:42 to the LORD, but *he did* not **a.** 6699
24:13 think it over and decide how *I should* **a** 1821+8740
1Ki 9: 9 *People will* **a,** 'Because they have forsaken 606
12: 6 you advise me to **a** these people?" 1821+8740
12: 7 **give** them a favorable **a,** 1819+1821
12: 9 How *should we* **a** these people 1821+8740
14: 5 **give** her such and such **an a.** 1819
18:26 "O Baal, **a** us!" 6699
18:37 **A** me, O LORD, answer me, 6699
18:37 Answer me, O LORD, **a** me, 6699
20: 9 and took the **a** back to Ben-Hadad. 1821
2Ki 4:29 and if anyone greets you, *do* not **a.** 6699
18:36 *"Do* not **a** him." 6699
22:20 So they took her **a** back to the king. 1821
1Ch 21:12 how *I should* **a** the one who sent me." 1821+8740
2Ch 7:22 *People will* **a,** 'Because they have forsaken 606
10: 6 to **a** these people?" 1821+8740
10: 7 **give** them a favorable **a,** 1819+1821
2Ch 10: 9 How *should we* **a** these people 1821+8740
34:28 So they took her **a** back to the king. 1821
Ezr 5:11 This is the **a** they gave us: 10601
Ne 6: 4 and each time I gave them the same **a.** 1821
Est 4:13 he sent back *this* **a:** 606
5: 8 Then *I will* **a** the king's question." 6913
Job 5: 1 "Call if you will, but *who will* **a** you? 6699
9: 3 not **a** him one time out of a thousand. 6699
9:15 *I could* not **a** him; 6699
9:32 not a man like me that *I might* **a** him, 6699
13:22 Then summon me and I *will* **a,** 6699
14:15 You will call and I *will* **a** you; 6699
15: 2 *"Would* a wise man **a** *with* empty notions 6699
19:16 I summon my servant, but *he does* not **a,** 6699
20: 2 "My troubled thoughts **prompt** me **to a** 8740
23: 5 I would find out what *he would* **a** me, 6699
30:20 "I cry out to you, O God, but *you do* not **a;** 6699
31:14 What *will I* **a** when called to account? 8740
31:35 *let* the Almighty **a** me; 6699
32:14 and *I will* not **a** him with your arguments. 8740
33: 5 **A** me then, if you can; 8740
33:32 If you have anything to say, **a** me; 8740
35:12 *He does* not **a** when men cry out because of 6699
38: 3 I will question you, and *you shall* **a** me. 3359
40: 2 *Let him* who accuses God **a** him!" 6699
40: 5 I spoke once, but *I* **have** no **a—** 6699
40: 7 I will question you, and *you shall* **a** me. 3359
42: 4 I will question you, and *you shall* **a** me.' 3359
Ps 4: 1 **A** me when I call to you, 6699
13: 3 Look on me and **a,** O LORD my God. 6699
17: 6 I call on you, O God, for *you will* **a** me; 6699
18:41 to the LORD, but *he did* not **a.** 6699
20: 1 the LORD **a** you when you are in distress; 6699
20: 9 **A** us when we call! 6699
22: 2 I cry out by day, but *you do* not **a,** 6699
27: 7 be merciful to me and **a** me. 6699
38:15 you *will* **a,** O Lord my God. 6699
55: 2 hear me and **a** me. 6699
65: 5 *You* **a** us with awesome deeds 6699
69:13 O God, **a** me with your sure salvation. 6699
69:16 **A** me, O LORD, out of the goodness 6699
69:17 **a** me quickly, for I am in trouble. 6699
86: 1 Hear, O LORD, and **a** me, 6699
86: 7 for *you will* **a** me. 6699
91:15 He will call upon me, and *I will* **a** him; 6699
102: 2 when I call, **a** me quickly. 6699
119:42 then *I will* **a** the one who taunts me, 1821+6699
119:145 I call with all my heart; **a** me, O LORD, 6699
143: 7 **A** me quickly, O LORD; 6699
Pr 1:28 they will call to me but *I will* not **a;** 6699
15: 1 A gentle **a** turns away wrath, 5101
24:26 An honest **a** is like a kiss on the lips, 1821+8740
26: 4 *Do* not **a** a fool according to his folly, 6699
26: 5 **A** a fool according to his folly, 6699
26:16 than seven *men who* **a** discreetly 8740
27:11 then *I can* **a** anyone who treats me 1821+8740
Ecc 10:19 but money *is the* **a** *for* everything. 6699
SS 5: 6 I called him but *he did* not **a.** 6699
Isa 14:32 What **a** *shall be* **given** *to* the envoys of 6699
21: 9 And *he* **gives back** *the* **a:** 6699
29:11 please," *he will* **a,** "I can't; it is sealed." 606
29:12 and say, "Read this, please," *he will* **a,** 606
30:19 As soon as he hears, *he will* **a** you. 6699
36:21 *"Do* not **a** him." 6699
41:17 But I the LORD *will* **a** them; 6699
41:28 no one to give **a** when I ask them. 1821
46: 7 Though one cries out to it, *it does* not **a;** 6699
49: 8 "In the time of my favor *I will* **a** you, 6699
50: 2 I called, why was there no *one to* **a?** 6699
58: 9 you will call, and the LORD *will* **a;** 6699
65:12 for I called but *you did* not **a,** 6699
65:24 Before they call I *will* **a;** 6699
Jer 7:13 I called you, but *you did* not **a.** 6699
7:27 when you call to them, *they will* not **a.** 6699
22: 9 And *the* **a** *will be:* 'Because they have 606
23:35 'What *is* the LORD's **a?'** 6699
23:37 'What *is* the LORD's **a** *to* you?' 6699
33: 3 to me and *I will* **a** you and tell you great 6699
35:17 I called to them, but *they did* not **a.' "** 6699
38:15 "If *I* **give** you **an a,** will you not kill me? 5583
Eze 14: 4 I the LORD *will* **a** him myself in keeping 6699
14: 7 I the LORD *will* **a** him myself. 6699
Da 9:23 soon as you began to pray, an **a** was given, 1821
Hos 14: 8 I *will* **a** him and care for him. 6699
Mic 3: 4 but *he will* not **a** them. 6699
3: 7 because there is no **a** *from* God." 5101
6: 3 How have I burdened you? **A** me. 6699
Hab 2: 1 **a** *I am to* **give** 8740
Zec 10: 6 the LORD their God and *I will* **a** them. 6699
13: 6 *he will* **a,** 'The wounds I was given at 606
13: 9 on my name and I *will* **a** them; 6699
Mt 15:23 Jesus *did* not **a** a word. *646*
21:24 If *you* **a** me, *3306*
25:37 "Then the righteous *will* **a** him, 'Lord, *646*
25:44 "They also *will* **a,** 'Lord, *646*
26:62 *"Are you* not *going to* **a?** *646*
27:12 *he* **gave** no **a.** *646*
Mk 11:29 **A** me, and I will tell you *646*
12:28 **given** them a good **a,** *646*
14:60 *"Are you* not **going to a?** *646*
14:61 But Jesus remained silent and **gave** no **a.** *646*
15: 4 "Aren't *you* **going to a?** *646*
Lk 13:25 "But *he will* **a,** *646*
20:26 astonished by his **a,** they became silent. *647*
22:68 and if I asked you, *you would* not **a.** *646*
23: 9 but Jesus **gave** him no **a.** *646*
Jn 1:22 an **a** to take back to those who sent us. *647*

Jn 5:19 Jesus **gave** them this **a:** *646*
18:22 "Is this the way *you* **a** the high priest?" *646*
19:9 he asked Jesus, but Jesus gave him no **a.** *647*
Ac 12:13 and a servant girl named Rhoda came *to* **a** *5634*
Ro 11:4 And what *was* God's **a** to him? *3306*
1Co 4:13 when we are slandered, *we* **a kindly.** *4151*
2Co 1:11 for the gracious favor granted us **in a to** *1666*
5:12 so that you can **a** those who take pride *NIG*
Col 4:6 so that you may know how *to* **a** everyone. *646*
Phm 1:22 because I hope to be restored to you **in a to** *1328*
1Pe 3:15 an **a** to everyone who asks you to give *665*

ANSWERABLE (1) [ANSWER]

Mt 5:22 'Raca,' is **a** to the Sanhedrin. *1944*

ANSWERED (397) [ANSWER]

Ge 3:10 *He* **a,** "I heard you in the garden, 606
16:8 from my mistress Sarai," *she* **a.** 606
18:5 "Very well," *they* **a,** "do as you say." 606
18:30 *He* **a,** "I will not do it if I find thirty there." 606
18:32 *He* **a,** "For the sake of ten, 606
19:2 *they* **a,** "we will spend the night in 606
22:8 Abraham **a,** "God himself will provide 606
23:14 Ephron **a** Abraham, 6699
24:24 *She* **a** him, "I am the daughter of Bethuel, 606
24:50 and Bethuel **a,** "This is from the LORD; 6699
24:65 "He is my master," the servant **a.** 606
25:21 The LORD **a** his **prayer,** 6983
26:9 'She is my sister'?" Isaac **a** him, 606
26:28 *They* **a,** "We saw clearly that 606
27:1 "Here I am," *he* **a.** 606
27:18 "Yes, my son," *he* **a.** 606
27:32 "I am your son," *he* **a,** "your firstborn, 606
27:37 Isaac **a** Esau, "I have made him lord 6699
27:39 His father Isaac **a** him, 6699
29:5 "Yes, we know him," *they* **a.** 606
31:11 *I* **a,** 'Here I am.' 606
31:31 Jacob **a** Laban, "I was afraid, 6699
31:43 Laban **a** Jacob, "The women are my daughters, 6699
32:27 "Jacob," *he* **a.** 606
33:5 Jacob **a,** "They are the children God has graciously given your servant." 606
35:3 who **a** me in the day of my distress 6699
37:17 on from here," the man **a.** 606
38:18 and the staff in your hand," *she* **a.** 606
40:8 "We both had dreams," *they* **a,** 606
42:10 "No, my lord," *they* **a.** 606
43:7 *We* simply **a** his questions. 5583
44:20 And *we* **a,** 'We have an aged father, 606
Ex 1:19 The midwives **a** Pharaoh, 606
2:8 "Yes, go," she **a.** 606
2:19 *They* **a,** "An Egyptian rescued us from 606
4:1 Moses **a,** "What if they do not believe me 6699
8:29 Moses **a,** "As soon as I leave you, 606
10:9 Moses **a,** "We will go with our young 606
14:13 Moses **a** the people, "Do not be afraid. 606
17:5 The LORD **a** Moses, 606
18:15 Moses **a** him, "Because the people come 606
19:19 and the voice of God **a** him. 6699
32:2 Aaron **a** them, "Take off the gold earrings 606
32:22 "Do not be angry, my lord," Aaron **a.** 606
Nu 9:8 Moses **a** them, "Wait until I find out what 606
10:30 *He* **a,** "No, I will not go; 606
11:23 The LORD **a** Moses, 606
20:18 But Edom **a:** "You may 606
20:20 Again *they* **a:** "You may not pass through." 606
22:18 But Balaam **a** them, 6699
22:29 Balaam **a** the donkey, 606
23:12 *He* **a,** "Must I not speak what 6699
23:26 Balaam **a,** "Did I not tell you 6699
24:12 Balaam **a** Balak, "Did I not tell 606
32:31 The Gadites and Reubenites **a,** 6699
Dt 1:14 *You* **a** me, "What you propose 6699
Jos 1:16 Then *they* **a** Joshua, 6699
9:9 *They* **a:** "Your servants have come from a 606
9:19 but all the leaders **a,** 606
9:24 *They* **a** Joshua, "Your servants were clearly 6699
17:15 "If you are so numerous," Joshua **a,** 606
24:16 Then the people **a,** 6699
Jdg 1:2 The LORD **a,** "Judah is to go; 606
6:16 The LORD **a,** "I will be with you, 606
8:2 But *he* **a** them, 606
8:8 but they **a** as the men of Succoth had. 6699
8:18 "Men like you," *they* **a,** 606
8:25 *They* **a,** "We'll be glad to give them." 606
9:9 "But the olive tree **a,** 606
9:13 "But the vine **a,** 606
11:9 Jephthah **a,** "Suppose you take me back 606
11:13 the Ammonites **a** Jephthah's messengers, 606
12:2 Jephthah **a,** "I and my people were engaged 606
13:13 The angel of the LORD **a,** 606
13:23 But his wife **a,** 606
15:10 *they* **a,** "to do to him as he did to us." 606
15:11 *He* **a,** "I merely did to them what they did 606
15:13 "Agreed," *they* **a.** 606
16:7 Samson **a** her, "If anyone ties me 606
18:6 The priest **a** them, "Go in peace. 606
18:9 *They* **a,** "Come on, let's attack them! 606
18:19 *They* **a** him, "Be quiet! 606
18:25 The Danites **a,** "Don't argue with us, 606
19:18 *He* **a,** "We are on our way from Bethlehem 606
20:23 The LORD **a,** "Go up against them." 606
Ru 3:5 "I will do whatever you say," Ruth **a.** 606
1Sa 1:17 Eli **a,** "Go in peace, 6699
1Sa 3:4 Samuel **a,** "Here I am." 606
3:16 Samuel **a,** "Here I am." 606
5:8 *They* **a,** "Have the ark of the god 606
6:3 *They* **a,** "If you return the ark of the god 606
7:9 and the LORD **a** him. 6699
8:22 The LORD **a,** "Listen to them 606
9:8 The servant **a** him again. 6699
9:12 "He is," *they* **a.** 6699
9:21 Saul **a,** "But am I not a Benjamite, 6699
10:12 A man who lived there **a,** 6699
15:15 Saul **a,** "The soldiers brought them from 606
16:11 "There is still the youngest," Jesse **a,** 606
16:18 One of the servants **a,** 6699
17:30 and the men **a** him as before. 1821+8740
20:28 Jonathan **a,** "David earnestly asked me 6699
21:2 David **a** Ahimelech the priest, 606
21:4 But the priest **a** David, 6699
22:12 "Yes, my lord," *he* **a.** 606
22:14 Ahimelech **a** the king, 6699
23:2 The LORD **a** him, "Go, 606
23:4 and the LORD **a** him, "Go down to Keilah, 6699
25:10 Nabal **a** David's servants, 6699
26:22 "Here is the king's spear," David **a.** 6699
29:9 Achish **a,** "I know that you have been 6699
30:8 "Pursue them," *he* **a.** 606
30:15 *He* **a,** "Swear to me before God 606
2Sa 1:3 *He* **a,** "I have escaped from 606
1:8 " 'An Amalekite,' *I* **a.** 606
1:13 the son of an alien, an Amalekite," *he* **a.** 606
2:1 "To Hebron," the LORD **a.** 606
2:20 "It is," *he* **a.** 606
2:27 Joab **a,** "As surely as God lives, 606
3:8 because of what Ish-Bosheth said and *he* **a,** 606
4:9 David **a** Recab and his brother Baanah, 6699
5:19 The LORD **a** him, "Go, 606
5:23 and *he* **a,** "Do not go straight up, 606
9:3 Ziba **a** the king, "There is still a son 606
9:4 Ziba **a,** "He is at the house of Makir son 606
12:22 *He* **a,** "While the child was still alive, 606
14:19 The woman **a,** "As surely as you live, 6699
15:15 The king's officials **a** him, 606
16:2 Ziba **a,** "The donkeys are for 606
16:21 Ahithophel **a,** "Lie with 606
17:20 The woman **a** them, 606
18:4 The king **a,** "I will do whatever seems best 606
18:29 Ahimaaz **a,** "I saw great confusion just 606
19:34 But Barzillai **a** the king, 606
19:42 All the men of Judah **a** the men of Israel, 6699
19:43 Then the men of Israel **a** the men of Judah, 6699
20:17 "I am," *he* **a.** 606
21:4 The Gibeonites **a** him, 606
21:5 *They* **a** the king, 606
21:14 God **a prayer** in behalf of the land. 6983
24:21 "To buy your threshing floor," David **a,** 606
24:25 the LORD **a prayer** in behalf of the land, 6983
1Ki 1:36 Benaiah son of Jehoiada **a** the king, 6699
1:43 "Not at all!" Jonathan **a.** 6699
2:13 *He* **a,** "Yes, peacefully." 606
2:22 King Solomon **a** his mother, 6699
2:30 But *he* **a,** "No, I will die here." 606
2:30 "This is how Joab **a** me." 6699
2:38 Shimei **a** the king, "What you say is good. 606
3:6 Solomon **a,** "You have shown great kindness 606
10:3 Solomon **a** all her questions; 5583
12:5 Rehoboam **a,** "Go away for three days and 606
12:13 The king **a** the people harshly. 6699
12:16 they **a** the king: 1821+8740
13:8 But the man of God **a** the king, 606
13:18 The old prophet **a,** "I too am a prophet, 606
18:26 But there was no response; no *one* **a.** 6699
18:29 But there was no response, no *one* **a,** 6699
20:4 The king of Israel **a,** "Just as you say, 6699
20:8 The elders and the people all **a,** 606
20:11 The king of Israel **a,** "Tell him: 6699
20:14 The prophet **a,** "You will." 606
20:32 The king **a,** "Is he still alive? 606
21:6 *He* **a** her, "Because I said to Naboth 1819
21:20 "I have found you," *he* **a,** 606
22:6 *they* **a,** "for the Lord will give it into 606
22:8 The king of Israel **a** Jehoshaphat, 606
22:15 "Attack and be victorious," *he* **a,** 606
22:17 Then Micaiah **a,** "I saw all Israel scattered 606
2Ki 1:10 Elijah **a** the captain, "If I am a man of God, 6699
3:8 "Through the Desert of Edom," *he* **a.** 606
3:11 An officer of the king of Israel **a,** 6699
3:13 "No," the king of Israel **a,** 606
4:43 But Elisha **a,** "Give it to the people to eat. 606
5:16 The prophet **a,** "As surely as 606
5:22 "Everything is all right," Gehazi **a.** 606
5:25 Your servant didn't go anywhere," Gehazi **a.** 606
6:16 "Don't be afraid," the prophet **a.** 606
6:22 "Do not kill them," *he* **a.** 606
6:28 *She* **a,** "This woman said to me, 606
7:2 **a** Elisha, "but you will not eat any of it!" 606
7:13 One of his officers **a,** 6699
8:10 Elisha **a,** "Go and say to him, 606
8:12 the harm you will do to the Israelites," *he* **a.** 606
8:13 you will become king of Aram," **a** Elisha. 606
10:15 "I am," Jehonadab **a.** 606
20:9 Isaiah **a,** "This is the LORD's sign to you 606
1Ch 5:20 He **a** their **prayers,** 6983
14:10 The LORD **a** him, "Go, 606
14:14 and God **a** him, "Do not go straight up, 606
21:26 the LORD **a** him with fire from heaven on 6699
21:28 the LORD *had* **a** him on the threshing floor 6699
2Ch 1:8 Solomon **a** God, "You have shown great kindness to David 606
2Ch 9:2 Solomon **a** all her questions; 5583
10:5 Rehoboam **a,** "Come back to me 606
10:13 The king **a** them harshly. 6699
10:16 they **a** the king: 8740
18:5 *they* **a,** "for God will give it into 606
18:7 The king of Israel **a** Jehoshaphat, 606
18:14 "Attack and be victorious," *he* **a,** 606
18:16 Then Micaiah **a,** "I saw all Israel scattered 606
31:10 from the family of Zadok, **a,** 606
32:24 *who* **a** him and gave him a miraculous sign. 606
Ezr 4:3 of the heads of the families of Israel **a,** 606
8:23 and *he* **a** our **prayer.** 6983
Ne 2:5 and *I* **a** the king, 606
2:20 *I* **a** them by saying, 1821+8740
Est 6:3 for him," his attendants **a.** 606
6:5 His attendants **a,** "Haman is standing in 606
6:7 So he **a** the king, 606
7:3 Then Queen Esther **a,** 6699
9:13 "If it pleases the king," Esther **a,** 606
Job 1:7 Satan **a** the LORD, 6699
2:2 Satan **a** the LORD, 6699
12:4 though I called upon God and *he* **a—** 6699
32:12 none of you *has* **a** his arguments. 6699
38:1 Then the LORD **a** Job out of the storm. 6699
40:3 Then Job **a** the LORD: 6699
Ps 34:4 I sought the LORD, and *he* **a** me; 6699
81:7 *I* **a** you out of a thundercloud; 6699
99:6 they called on the LORD and he **a** them. 6699
99:8 O LORD our God, you **a** them; 6699
118:5 and he **a** by setting me free. 6699
118:21 I will give you thanks, for *you* **a** me; 6699
119:26 I recounted my ways and *you* **a** me; 6699
138:3 When I called, *you* **a** me; 6699
Pr 21:13 he too will cry out and not **be a.** 6699
Isa 6:11 O Lord?" And *he* **a:** 606
66:4 For when I called, no *one* **a,** when I spoke, 6699
Jer 1:13 tilting away from the north," *I* **a.** 606
11:5 *I* **a,** "Amen, LORD." 6699
21:3 But Jeremiah **a** them, "Tell Zedekiah, 606
24:3 "Figs," *I* **a.** 606
38:5 "He is in your hands," King Zedekiah **a.** 606
Eze 9:9 *He* **a** me, "The sin of the house of Israel 606
Da 2:4 Then the astrologers **a** the king in Aramaic, 1819
2:8 the king, "I am certain that you are trying 10558
2:10 The astrologers **a** the king, 10558
4:19 Belteshazzar **a,** "My lord, 10558
5:17 Then Daniel **a** the king, 10558
6:12 The king **a,** "The decree stands— 10558
6:21 Daniel **a,** "O king, live forever! 10425
Hos 4:12 a wooden idol and *are* **a** *by* a stick of wood. 5583
Am 7:14 Amos **a** Amaziah, "I was neither a prophet 6699
8:2 "A basket of ripe fruit," *I* **a.** 606
Jnh 1:9 *He* **a,** "I am a Hebrew and I worship 606
2:2 to the LORD, and he **a** me. 6699
Mic 6:5 and what Balaam son of Beor **a.** 6699
Hag 2:12 The priests **a,** "No." 6699
Zec 1:9 The angel who was talking with me **a,** 606
1:19 *He* **a** me, "These are the horns 606
1:21 *He* **a,** "These are the horns 606
2:2 *He* **a** me, "To measure Jerusalem, 606
4:2 *I* **a,** "I see a solid gold lampstand with 606
4:5 He **a,** "Do you not know what these are?" 6699
5:2 *I* **a,** "I see a flying scroll, 606
6:5 The angel **a** me, 6699
Mt 4:4 Jesus **a,** "It is written: *646*
4:7 Jesus **a** him, "It is also written: *5774*
9:15 Jesus **a,** "How can the guests of *3306*
12:3 He **a,** "Haven't you read what David did *3306*
12:39 He **a,** "A wicked and adulterous *646*
13:29 he **a,** 'because while you are pulling *5774*
13:37 He **a,** "The one who sowed *646*
14:17 of bread and two fish," they **a.** *3306*
15:24 He **a,** "I was sent only to the lost sheep *646*
15:28 Jesus **a,** "Woman, you have great faith! *646*
15:33 His disciples **a,** "Where could we get *3306*
16:16 Simon Peter **a,** "You are the Christ, *646*
17:26 "From others," Peter **a.** *3306*
18:22 Jesus **a,** "I tell you, not seven times, *3306*
19:21 Jesus **a,** "If you want to be perfect, go, *5774*
19:27 Peter **a** him, "We have left everything *646*
20:7 " 'Because no one has hired us,' *they* **a.** *3306*
20:13 "But he **a** one of them, 'Friend, *646*
20:22 "We can," *they* **a.** *3306*
20:33 "Lord," *they* **a,** "we want our sight." *3306*
21:11 The crowds **a,** "This is Jesus, *3306*
21:27 So *they* **a** Jesus, "We don't know." *646*
21:29 " 'I will not,' he **a,** *646*
21:30 He **a,** 'I will, sir,' but he did not go. *646*
21:31 "The first," *they* **a.** *3306*
24:4 Jesus **a:** "Watch out *646*
26:25 Jesus **a,** "Yes, it is you." *3306*
26:34 "I tell you the truth," Jesus **a,** *5774*
26:66 "He is worthy of death," they **a.** *646*
27:21 "Barabbas," they **a.** *3306*
27:22 *They* all **a,** "Crucify him!" *3306*
27:25 All the people **a,** *646*
27:65 "Take a guard," Pilate **a.** *5774*
Mk 2:19 Jesus **a,** "How can the guests of *3306*
2:25 *He* **a,** "Have you never read what David did *3306*
5:31 his disciples **a,** "and yet you can ask, *3306*
6:24 "The head of John the Baptist," she **a.** *3306*
6:37 *he* **a,** "You give them something to eat." *646*
8:4 His disciples **a,** "But where *646*
8:20 *They* **a,** "Seven." *3306*
8:29 Peter **a,** "You are the Christ." *646*
9:17 A man in the crowd **a,** "Teacher, *646*
9:21 "From childhood," he **a.** *3306*

Mk 10:11 He a, "Anyone who divorces his wife 3306
10:18 "Why do you call me good?" Jesus a. 3306
10:39 "We can," they a. 3306
11: 6 They a as Jesus had told them to, 3306
11:22 "Have faith in God," Jesus a. 646
11:33 So they a Jesus, "We don't know." 646
12:29 "The most important one," a Jesus, "is this: 646
12:34 When Jesus saw that he had a wisely, 646
14:30 "I tell you the truth," Jesus a, "today— 3306
Lk 1:19 The angel a, "I am Gabriel. 646
1:35 The angel a, "The Holy Spirit will come 646
1:38 "I am the Lord's servant," Mary a. 3306
3:11 John a, "The man with two 646
3:16 John a them all, "I baptize you with water. 646
4: 4 Jesus a, "It is written: 646
4: 8 Jesus a, "It is written: 646
4:12 Jesus a, "It says: 646
5: 5 Simon a, "Master, we've worked hard all night 646
5:31 Jesus a them, "It is not 646
5:34 Jesus a, "Can you make the guests of 3306
6: 3 Jesus a them, "Have you never read what David did 646
7:40 Jesus a him, "Simon, I have something 646
9:13 They a, "We have only five loaves of bread 3306
9:20 Peter a, "The Christ of God." 646
10:27 He a: " 'Love the Lord your God with all 646
10:28 "You have a correctly," Jesus replied. 3306
10:41 "Martha, Martha," the Lord a, 646
11:45 One of the experts in the law a him, 646
12:42 The Lord a, "Who then is the faithful 3306
13: 2 Jesus a, "Do you think 646
13:15 The Lord a him, "You hypocrites! 646
15:29 But he a his father, 'Look! 646
16:27 "He a, 'Then I beg you, father, 3306
18:19 "Why do you call me good?" Jesus a. 3306
19:19 "His master a, 'You take charge 3306
20: 7 So they a, "We don't know 646
22:34 Jesus a, "I tell you, Peter, 3306
22:35 "Nothing," they a. 3306
22:51 But Jesus a, "No more of this!" 646
22:67 Jesus a, "If I tell you, 3306
23:43 Jesus a him, "I tell you the truth, 3306
Jn 1:21 He a, "No." 646
1:48 Jesus a, "I saw you while you were still 646
2:19 Jesus a them, "Destroy this temple, 646
3: 5 Jesus a, "I tell you the truth, 646
4:10 Jesus a her, "If you knew the gift of God 646
4:13 Jesus a, "Everyone who drinks this water will be thirsty again, 646
6: 7 Philip a him, "Eight months' wages would 646
6:26 Jesus a, "I tell you the truth, 646
6:29 Jesus a, "The work of God is this: 646
6:43 among yourselves," Jesus a. 646
6:68 Simon Peter a him, "Lord, 646
7:16 Jesus a, "My teaching is not my own. 646
7:20 "You are demon-possessed," the crowd a. 646
8:14 Jesus a, "Even if I testify 646
8:33 They a him, "We are Abraham's descendants 646
8:39 "Abraham is our father," they a. 646
8:48 The Jews a him, 646
8:58 "I tell you the truth," Jesus a, 3306
9:20 "We know he is our son," the parents a, 646
9:27 He a, "I have told you already and you did 646
9:30 The man a, "Now that is remarkable! 646
10:25 Jesus a, "I did tell you, 646
10:34 Jesus a them, "Is it not written 646
11: 9 Jesus a, "Are there not twelve hours 646
11:24 Martha a, "I know he will rise again in 3306
13: 8 Jesus a, "Unless I wash you, 646
13:10 Jesus a, "A person who has had 3306
13:26 Jesus a, "It is the one 646
13:38 Then Jesus a, "Will you really lay 646
14: 6 Jesus a, "I am the way and the truth and 3306
14: 9 Jesus a: "Don't you know me, 3306
16:31 "You believe at last!" Jesus a. 646
18: 8 "I told you that I am he," Jesus a. 646
18:37 Jesus a, "You are right in saying I am 646
19: 6 But Pilate a, "You take him 3306
19:11 Jesus a, "You would have no power 646
19:15 the chief priests a. 646
19:22 Pilate a, "What I have written, 646
21: 5 "No," they a. 646
21:16 He a, "Yes, Lord, you know 3306
21:22 Jesus a, "If I want him to remain alive 3306
Ac 8:20 Peter a: "May your money perish with you, 3306
8:24 Then Simon a, "Pray to the Lord for me so 646
9:10 "Yes, Lord," he a. 3306
9:13 Ananias a, "I have heard many reports 646
10: 4 The angel a, "Your prayers and gifts to 3306
10:30 Cornelius a: "Four days ago I was in my 5774
13:46 Then Paul and Barnabas a them boldly: 3306
19: 2 They a, "No, we have not even heard NIG
19:15 [One day] the evil spirit a them, 646
21:13 Then Paul a, "Why are you weeping 646
21:39 Paul a, "I am a Jew, from Tarsus in Cilicia, 3306
22:27 "Yes, I am," he a. 5774
25: 4 Festus a, "Paul is being held at Caesarea, 646
25:10 Paul a: "I am now standing before Caesar's 3306
Rev 7:14 I a, "Sir, you know." 3306

ANSWERING (3) [ANSWER]

Job 32: 1 So these three men stopped a Job, 6699
34:36 that Job might be tested to the utmost for a 9588
Jer 44:20 both men and women, who were a him, 6699

ANSWERS (14) [ANSWER]

1Sa 20:10 if your father a you harshly?" 6699
28:15 He no longer a me, 6699
1Ki 18:24 The god who a by fire—he is God." 6699
Job 21:34 Nothing is left of your a but falsehood!" 9588
33:13 Why do you complain to him that he a none 6699
Ps 3: 4 and he a me from his holy hill. 6699
20: 6 he a him from his holy heaven with 6699
120: 1 the LORD in my distress, and he a me. 6699
Pr 15:28 The heart of the righteous weighs its a, 6699
18:13 He who a before listening— 1821+8740
18:23 but a rich man a harshly. 6699
22:21 you can give sound a to him who sent you? 609
Lk 2:47 at his understanding and his a. 647
11: 7 "Then the one inside a, 'Don't bother me. 646

ANT (1) [ANTS]

Pr 6: 6 Go to the a, you sluggard; 5805

ANTELOPE (2)

Dt 14: 5 the ibex, the a and the mountain sheep. 9293
Isa 51:20 like a caught in a net. 9293

ANTHOTHIJAH (1)

1Ch 8:24 Hananiah, Elam, A, 6746

ANTICHRIST (4) [ANTICHRISTS]

1Jn 2:18 and as you have heard that the a is coming, 532
2:22 Such a man is the a— 532
4: 3 This is the spirit of the a, 532
2Jn 1: 7 Any such person is the deceiver and the a. 532

ANTICHRISTS (1) [ANTICHRIST]

1Jn 2:18 even now many a have come. 532

ANTICIPATING (1)

Ac 12:11 from everything the Jewish people were a." 4660

ANTIOCH (21)

Ac 6: 5 and Nicolas from A, a convert to Judaism. 523
11:19 as far as Phoenicia, Cyprus and A, telling 522
11:20 went to A and began to speak to Greeks 522
11:22 and they sent Barnabas to A. 522
11:26 he brought him to A. 522
11:26 disciples were called Christians first at A. 522
11:27 down from Jerusalem to A. 522
13: 1 In the church at A there were prophets 522
13:14 From Perga they went on to Pisidian A. 522
14:19 Then some Jews came from A and Iconium 522
14:21 they returned to Lystra, Iconium and A, 522
14:26 From Attalia they sailed back to A, 522
15: 1 down from Judea to A and were teaching NIG
15:22 of their own men and send them to A 522
15:23 To the Gentile believers in A, 522
15:30 and went down to A, 522
15:35 But Paul and Barnabas remained in A, 522
18:22 the church and then went down to A. 522
18:23 After spending some time in A, NIG
Gal 2:11 When Peter came to A, 522
2Ti 3:11 what kinds of things happened to me in A, 522

ANTIPAS (1)

Rev 2:13 even in the days of A, my faithful witness, 525

ANTIPATRIS (1)

Ac 23:31 the night and brought him as far as A. 526

ANTIQUITY (KJV) See OLD

ANTOTHIJAH (KJV) See ANTHOTHIJAH

ANTOTHITE (KJV) See ANATHOTHITE

ANTS (1) [ANT]

Pr 30:25 A are creatures of little strength, 5805

ANUB (1)

1Ch 4: 8 who was the father of A and Hazzobebah 6707

ANVIL (1)

Isa 41: 7 the hammer spurs on him who strikes the a. 7193

ANXIETIES (1) [ANXIOUS]

Lk 21:34 drunkenness and the a of life, 3533

ANXIETY (6) [ANXIOUS]

Ps 94:19 When a was great within me, 8595
Ecc 11:10 banish a from your heart and cast off 4088
Eze 4:16 in a and drink rationed water in despair, 1796
12:19 in a and drink their water in despair, 1796
Php 2:28 be glad and I may have less a. 267
1Pe 5: 7 Cast all your a on him because he cares 3533

ANXIOUS (5) [ANXIETIES, ANXIETY, ANXIOUSLY]

Dt 28:65 There the LORD will give you an a mind, 8076
Ps 139:23 test me and know my a thoughts. 8595
Pr 12:25 An a heart weighs a man down, 1796
Ecc 2:22 a striving with which he labors under 4213+8301
Php 4: 6 Do not be a about anything, 3534

ANXIOUSLY (1) [ANXIOUS]

Lk 2:48 Your father and I have been a searching 3849

ANY (582) [ANYBODY, ANYMORE, ANYONE, ANYONE'S, ANYTHING, ANYWHERE]

Ge 2:16 "You are free to eat from a tree in 3972
3: 1 Now the serpent was more crafty than a of 3972
3: 1 not eat from a tree in the garden'?" 3972
6: 2 and they married a of them they chose. 3972
13: 8 not have a quarreling between you and me, NIH
17:14 A uncircumcised male, NIH
27:36 "Haven't you reserved a blessing for me?" NIH
30: 1 that she was not bearing Jacob a children, NIH
30:33 A goat in my possession that is 3972
30:33 or a lamb that is not dark-colored, 928
31:14 "Do we still have a share in the inheritance NIH
31:50 if you take a wives besides my daughters, NIH
36:31 in Edom before a Israelite king reigned: NIH
37: 3 Now Israel loved Joseph more than a 3972
37: 4 that their father loved him more than a 3972
37:22 "Don't shed a blood. NIH
38:21 "There hasn't been a shrine prostitute here," NIH
38:22 'There hasn't been a shrine prostitute here.' NIH
44: 9 If a of your servants is found to have it, 889
47: 6 of a among them with special ability, 408
48: 6 A children born to you after them will NIH
Ex 3: 5 "Do not come a closer," God said. AIT
3:22 to ask her neighbor and a woman living AIT
4:18 in Egypt to see if a of them are still alive." AIT
5:10 'I will not give you a more straw. NIH
5:18 You will not be given a straw, NIH
9:28 you don't have to stay a longer." 3578
11: 7 not a dog will bark at a man 4946
12: 4 If a household is too small for 2021
12:10 Do not leave a of it till morning; 4946
12:44 A slave you have bought may eat of it 3972
12:46 Do not break a of the bones. NIH
13: 7 to be seen among you, nor shall a yeast AIT
15:26 on you a of the diseases I brought on 3972
16:19 "No one is to keep a of it until morning." 4946
16:25 not find a of it on the ground today. AIT
16:26 the Sabbath, there will not be a." 928
20:10 On it you shall not do a work, neither you, 3972
20:23 Do not make a gods to be alongside me; NIH
21:11 without a payment of money. 401+2855
22: 9 or a other lost property 3972
22:10 a sheep or a other animal to his neighbor 3972
22:20 "Whoever sacrifices to a god other than 2021
29:34 And if a of the meat of the ordination ram 4946
29:34 of the ordination ram or a bread is left over 4946
30: 9 Do not offer on this altar a other incense NIH
30: 9 or a burnt offering or grain offering, NIH
30:32 on men's bodies and do not make a oil with NIH
30:37 Do not make a incense with this formula 2021
30:38 Whoever makes a like it NIH
31:14 whoever does a work on that day must NIH
31:15 Whoever does a work on NIH
32:24 I told them, 'Whoever has a gold jewelry, NIH
33: 4 to mourn and no one put on a ornaments. 2257S
34:10 before done in a nation in all the world. 3972
34:14 Do not worship a other god, AIT
34:25 and do not let a of the sacrifice from NIH
35: 2 Whoever does a work on it must be put NIH
35: 3 Do not light a fire in a of your dwellings 3972
35:24 for a part of the work brought it. 3972
Lev 1: 2 a of you brings an offering to the LORD, 132
2:11 for you are not to burn a yeast or honey in 3972
3:17 You must not eat a fat or any blood.' " 3972
3:17 You must not eat any fat or a blood.' " 3972
4: 2 in a of the LORD's commands— 3972
4:13 and does what is forbidden in a of 285+3972
4:22 and does what is forbidden in a of 285+3972
4:27 and does what is forbidden in a of 285
5: 4 in a matter one might carelessly swear about 3972
5: 4 of it, in a case when he learns of it he will 285
5: 5 " 'When anyone is guilty in a 285
5:13 for a of these sins he has committed, 285
5:15 in regard to a of the LORD's holy things, NIH
5:17 and does what is forbidden in a of 285+3972
6: 3 or if he commits a such sin 3972
6: 7 be forgiven for a of these things he did 285
6:18 A male descendant of Aaron may eat it. 3972
6:27 Whatever touches a of NIH
6:27 if a of the blood is spattered on a garment, 4946
6:29 A male in a priest's family may eat it; 3972
6:30 But a sin offering whose blood is brought 3972
7: 6 A male in a priest's family may eat it, 3972
7:17 A meat of the sacrifice left over till 4946
7:18 If a meat of the fellowship offering is eaten 4946
7:18 the person who eats a of it will 4946
7:20 But if anyone who is unclean eats a meat of NIH
7:21 or an unclean animal or a unclean, 3972
7:21 and then eats a of the meat of 4946
7:23 'Do not eat a of the fat of cattle, 3972
7:24 be used for a other purpose, 3972
7:26 not eat the blood of a bird or animal. 3972

Lev 11: 3 You may eat **a** animal that has 3972
11: 9 you may eat **a** that have fins and scales. 3972
11:14 the red kite, **a** kind of black kite, NIH
11:15 **a** kind of raven, 3972
11:16 the screech owl, the gull, **a** kind of hawk, NIH
11:19 **a** kind of heron, the hoopoe and the bat. NIH
11:22 Of these you may eat **a** kind of locust, NIH
11:26 [the carcass of] **a** of them will be unclean. NIH
11:29 the weasel, the rat, **a** kind of great lizard, NIH
11:34 **A** food that could be eaten but has water 3972
11:34 and **a** liquid that could be drunk 3972
11:37 If a carcass falls on **a** seeds that are to 3972
11:42 not to eat **a** creature that moves about on 3972
11:43 Do not defile yourselves by **a** of these 3972
11:44 not make yourselves unclean by **a** creature 3972
13:47 "If **a** clothing is contaminated 2021
13:47 **a** woolen or linen clothing, NIH
13:48 **a** woven or knitted material of linen NIH
13:48 **a** leather or anything made of leather— NIH
13:49 or **a** leather article, is greenish or reddish, 3972
13:52 or **a** leather article that has 3972
13:58 or **a** leather article that has been washed 3972
13:59 or **a** leather article, 3972
14:54 for **a** infectious skin disease, 3972
15: 2 'When **a man** has a bodily discharge, 408+408
15: 4 " '**A** bed the man with a discharge lies 3972
15:10 and whoever touches **a** *of the things* 3972
15:12 **a** wooden article is to be rinsed with water. 3972
15:17 **A** clothing or leather that has semen 3972
15:24 **a** bed he lies on will be unclean. 3972
15:26 **A** bed she lies on 3972
16:29 and not do **a** work— 3972
17: 3 **A** Israelite who sacrifices an ox, 408
17: 7 They must no longer offer **a** NIH
17: 8 '**A** Israelite or any alien living 408
17: 8 or **a** alien living among them who offers 4946
17:10 " '**A** Israelite or any alien living 408
17:10 " 'Any Israelite or **a** alien living 4946
17:10 among them who eats **a** blood— 3972
17:13 " '**A** Israelite or any alien living 408
17:13 " 'Any Israelite or **a** alien living 4946
17:13 among you who hunts **a** animal or bird NIH
17:14 "You must not eat the blood of **a** creature, 3972
18: 6 " 'No one is to approach **a** close relative 3972
18:21 not give **a** *of* your children to be sacrificed 4946
18:24 not defile yourselves in **a** *of* these ways, 3972
18:26 the aliens living among you must not do **a** 3972
18:29 " 'Everyone who does **a** 3972
18:30 Keep my requirements and do not follow **a** 4946
19: 7 *a of it* **is eaten** on the third day, AIT
19:23 the land and plant **a** *kind of* fruit tree, 3972
19:26 " 'Do not eat **a** meat with the blood still NIH
20: 2 '**A** Israelite or any alien living 408
20: 2 or **a** alien living in Israel who gives any 4946
20: 2 or any alien living in Israel who gives **a** 4946
20:25 by **a** animal or bird or anything that moves 2021
21: 1 for **a** of his people who die, NIH
21:18 No man who has **a** defect may come near: NIH
21:20 or who has **a** eye defect, NIH
21:21 the priest who has **a** defect is to come near NIH
22: 3 'For the generations to come, if **a** 408+3972
22: 5 or if he touches **a** crawling thing 3972
22: 5 or *a* **person** who makes him unclean, AIT
22: 6 The one who touches **a such thing** will 2257[S]
22: 6 He must not eat **a** *of* the sacred offerings 4946
22:12 not eat **a** *of* the sacred contributions. 928
22:13 however, may eat **a** *of* it. 928
22:18 'If **a** of you—either and Israelite 408
22:22 Do not place **a** *of* these on the altar as 4946
23: 3 You are not to do **a** work; 3972
23:14 You must not eat **a** bread, NIH
23:30 among his people anyone who does **a** work 3972
25:14 of your countrymen or buy **a** from him, NIH
25:33 that is, a house sold in **a** town they hold— NIH
25:36 Do not take **interest of a kind** from him, 2256+5968+9552
25:49 An uncle or a cousin or **a** blood relative 4946
25:54 if he is not redeemed in **a** of these ways, NIH
27:31 If a man redeems **a** *of* his tithe, 4946
27:33 from the bad or make **a** substitution. 5647[S]
Nu 5: 2 or **a** discharge *of* **a** *kind,* 3972
5: 6 in **a** *way* and so is unfaithful to the LORD, 3972
5:31 be innocent of **a** wrongdoing, NIH
7: 9 But Moses did not give **a** to the Kohathites, NIH
9:10 'When **a** of you or your descendants 408+408
9:12 not leave **a** *of* it till morning or break any 4946
9:12 not leave any of it till morning or break **a** NIH
11:31 as far as a day's walk **in a direction.** 2256+3907+3907
15:22 " 'Now if you unintentionally fail to keep **a** 3972
15:23 **a** *of* the LORD's commands to you 3972
16:15 nor have I wronged **a** of them." 285
18:20 nor will you have **a** share among them; NIH
20:17 We will not go through **a** field or vineyard, NIH
20:17 or drink water from **a** well. NIH
20:19 if we or our livestock drink **a** of your water, NIH
21:22 not turn aside into **a** field or vineyard, NIH
21:22 or drink water from **a** well. NIH
30: 9 "**A** vow or obligation taken by a widow 3972
30:13 or nullify **a** vow she makes 3972
30:13 or **a** sworn pledge to deny herself. 3972
32:19 not **receive** *a* **inheritance** with them on AIT
35:15 and **a** other people living among them, 2021
36: 8 in **a** Israelite tribe must marry someone NIH
Dt 1:17 Do not be afraid of **a** man, NIH
1:17 Bring me **a** case too hard for you, 2021
2: 5 for I will not give you **a** *of* their land, 4946
Dt 2: 9 for I will not give you **a** part *of* their land. 4946
2:19 of **a** land belonging to the Ammonites. 4946
2:37 you did not encroach on **a** *of* the land of 3972
4:15 *of* **a** *kind* the day the LORD spoke to you 3972
4:16 an image of **a** shape, 3972
4:17 like **a** animal on earth or any bird that flies 3972
4:17 like any animal on earth or **a** bird that flies 3972
4:18 like **a** creature that moves along the ground 3972
4:18 the ground or **a** fish in the waters below. 3972
4:25 then become corrupt and make **a** kind 3972
4:33 Has **a** other people heard the voice NIH
4:34 Has **a** god ever tried to take NIH
5:14 On it you shall not do **a** work, neither you, 3972
5:14 your donkey or **a** *of* your animals, 3972
5:25 voice of the LORD our God **a longer.** 3578+6388
7:14 be blessed more than **a** other people; 3972
7:14 nor **a** of your livestock without young. NIH
10:16 and do not be stiff-necked **a longer.** 6388
12:15 in **a** *of* your towns and eat as much of 3972
14: 3 Do not eat **a** detestable thing. 3972
14: 6 You may eat **a** animal that has 3972
14: 9 you may eat **a** that has fins and scales. 3972
14:11 You may eat **a** clean bird. 3972
14:13 the red kite, the black kite, **a** kind of falcon, NIH
14:14 **a** kind of raven, 3972
14:15 the screech owl, the gull, **a** kind of hawk, NIH
14:18 **a** kind of heron, the hoopoe and the bat. NIH
14:20 But **a** winged creature 3972
14:21 You may give it to an alien living in **a** NIH
15: 3 you *must* **cancel** *a* **debt** your brother owes AIT
15: 7 among your brothers in **a** *of* the towns of 285
15:21 is lame or blind, or has **a** serious flaw, 3972
16: 4 Do not let **a** *of* the meat you sacrifice on 4946
16: 5 in **a** town the LORD your God gives you 285
16:21 not set up **a** wooden Asherah pole beside 3972
17: 1 an ox or a sheep that has **a** defect or flaw 3972
19:15 to convict a man accused of **a** crime 3972
20: 8 "Is **a man** afraid or fainthearted? 408+2021+4769
23: 2 No one born of a forbidden marriage nor **a** 4200
23: 3 or **a** *of* his descendants may enter 4200
23:18 of the LORD your God to pay **a** vow, 3972
23:24 but do not put **a** in your basket. NIH
24: 5 not be sent to war or have **a** other duty laid 3972
24:10 you make a loan of **a kind** to your neighbor, 4399
26:13 nor have I forgotten **a** of them. NIH
26:14 I have not eaten **a** *of* the sacred portion 4946
26:14 nor have I removed **a** *of* it 4946
26:14 nor have I offered **a** *of* it to the dead. 4946
27: 5 Do not use **a** iron tool upon them. NIH
27:21 "Cursed is the man who has sexual relations with **a** animal." 3972
28:14 from **a** *of* the commands I give you today, 3972
28:51 nor **a** calves of your herds or lambs NIH
28:55 to one of them **a** *of* the flesh of his children 4946
Jos 5:12 there was no longer **a** manna for NIH
6:18 about your own destruction by taking **a** 4946
8:20 to escape **in a direction,** 2178+2178+2256
11:13 Yet Israel did not burn **a** *of* the cities built 3972
11:22 Gath and Ashdod *did a* **survive.** AIT
20: 9 **A** *of* the Israelites or any alien living 3972
20: 9 Any of the Israelites or **a** alien living 3972
Jdg 2:21 I will no longer drive out before them **a** of 408
3: 1 not experienced **a** *of* the wars in Canaan 3972
11: 2 *"You are* not *going to* **get** *a* **inheritance** AIT
13:14 nor drink **a** wine or other fermented drink NIH
13:16 I will not eat **a** *of* your food. 928
16: 7 I'll become as weak as **a** other man." 285
16:11 I'll become as weak as **a** other man." 285
16:13 I'll become as weak as **a** other man." 285
16:17 I would become as weak as **a** other man." 3972
21: 7 an oath by the LORD not to give them **a** 4946
Ru 1:11 Am I going to have **a more** sons, 6388
1Sa 4:20 she did not respond or pay **a attention.** AIT
5: 5 nor **a** others who enter Dagon's temple 3972
9: 2 a head taller than **a** *of* the others. 3972
10:23 the people he was a head taller than **a** *of* 3972
12: 3 If I have done **a** of these, NIH
14:24 "Cursed be **a** man who eats food 2021
14:28 'Cursed be **a** man who eats food today!' 2021
21: 4 "I don't have **a** ordinary bread on hand; NIH
21: 8 my sword or **a** other weapon, NIH
22:15 Let not the king accuse your servant or **a** 3972
30:12 not eaten *a* **food** or drunk any water AIT
30:12 not eaten any food or drunk *a* **water** AIT
2Sa 6:20 of his servants as **a** vulgar fellow would!" 285
7: 7 to **a** *of* their rulers whom I commanded 285
12:17 and he would not eat **a** food with them. NIH
14: 2 and don't use **a** cosmetic lotions. NIH
17:12 nor **a** *of* his men will be left alive. 3972
18:22 You don't have **a** news that will bring you NIH
19:28 to make **a more** appeals to the king?" 6388
19:42 Have we eaten **a** *of* the king's provisions? 4946
23:23 He was held in greater honor than **a** of NIH
1Ki 4:31 He was wiser than **a** other man, 3972
6: 7 chisel or **a** other iron tool was heard at 3972
8:16 not chosen a city in **a** tribe of Israel to have 3972
8:37 an enemy besieges them in **a** of their cities, NIH
8:38 and when a prayer or plea is made by **a** 3972
9:22 But Solomon did not make slaves of **a** of NIH
10:20 for **a** other kingdom. 3972
15: 5 the LORD and had not failed to keep **a** *of* 3972
16:30 of the LORD than **a** *of* those before him. 3972
17:12 she replied, "I don't have **a** bread— NIH
18: 5 not have to kill **a** *of* our animals." 4946
19:17 to death **a** who escape the sword of Hazael, 2021
19:17 and Elisha will put to death **a** who escape 2021
2Ki 5:12 better than **a** *of* the waters of Israel? 3972
2Ki 5:17 sacrifices to *a* **other** god but the LORD. AIT
6:33 for the LORD **a longer?"** 6388
7: 2 "but you will not eat **a** *of* it!" 4946
7:19 but you will not eat **a** *of* it!" 4946
10:24 of you lets **a** of the men I am placing 408
12: 8 not collect **a** more money from the people NIH
12:13 trumpets or **a** other articles of gold or silver 3972
13:11 the LORD and did not turn away from **a** 3972
14:24 the LORD and did not turn away from **a** 3972
17:35 "Do not worship *a* **other** gods or bow down AIT
18:33 the god of **a** nation ever delivered his land 2021
23:22 had **a** such Passover been observed. 2021
1Ch 1:43 in Edom before **a** Israelite king reigned: NIH
11:25 He was held in greater honor than **a** of NIH
17: 6 to **a** *of* their leaders whom I commanded 285
23:26 or **a** *of* the articles used in its service." 3972
28:21 in **a** craft will help you in all the work. 3972
29: 8 **A** who had precious stones gave them to 2257[S]
2Ch 2:14 and can execute **a** design given to him. 3972
6: 5 not chosen a city in **a** tribe of Israel to have 3972
6:28 or when enemies besiege them in **a** NIH
6:29 and when a prayer or plea is made by **a** 3972
8:15 to the priests or to the Levites in **a** matter, 3972
9:19 for **a** other kingdom. 3972
11:21 of Absalom more than **a** *of* his other wives 3972
19:11 the chief priest will be over you in **a** matter 3972
19:11 over you in **a** matter concerning the king, 3972
23: 8 for Jehoiada the priest had not released **a** of NIH
23:19 in **a** way unclean might enter. 3972
25: 7 not with **a** *of* the people of Ephraim. 3972
29: 7 or present **a** burnt offerings at the sanctuary NIH
31:19 around their towns or in **a** *other* towns, 3972
32:15 of **a** nation or kingdom has been able 3972
Ezr 1: 4 the people of **a** place where survivors may 3972
2:63 The governor ordered them not to eat **a** *of* 4946
6:12 overthrow **a** king or people who lifts 10353
7:13 that **a** of the Israelites in my kingdom, 10353
7:24 tribute or duty on **a** *of* the priests, Levites, 10353
7:25 you are to teach *a* **who** do not know them. AIT
9:12 a treaty of friendship with them at **a time,** 6409
Ne 2:16 or nobles or officials or *a* **others** who would AIT
2:20 you have no share in Jerusalem or **a** claim NIH
5:16 we did not acquire *a* **land.** AIT
7:65 not to eat **a** *of* the most sacred food 4946
10:31 from them on the Sabbath or on **a** holy day. NIH
Est 2:17 to Esther more than to **a** *of* 3972
2:17 and approval more than **a** *of* 3972
4:11 of the royal provinces know that for **a** man 3972
8:11 to destroy, kill and annihilate **a** armed force 3972
8:11 of **a** nationality or province NIH
Job 2: 3 against him to ruin him **without a reason."** 2855
3: 6 the year nor be entered in **a** *of* the months. 5031
6:13 Do I have **a** power to help myself, 401[S]
6:30 Is there **a** wickedness on my lips? NIH
10:18 I wish I had died before **a** eye saw me. NIH
17:15 Who can see **a** hope for me? NIH
32:21 nor will I flatter *a* **man;** AIT
34:27 from following him and had no regard for **a** 3972
37:20 Would **a** man ask to be swallowed up? NIH
39: 8 and searches for **a** green thing. 3972
41: 9 **A** hope of subduing him is false; NIH
Ps 4: 6 "Who can show us **a** good?" NIH
14: 2 to see if there are *a who* **understand,** AIT
14: 2 *a who* **seek** God. AIT
53: 2 to see if there are *a who* **understand,** AIT
53: 2 *a who* **seek** God. AIT
139:24 See if there is **a** offensive way in me, NIH
Pr 3:31 a violent man or choose **a** *of* his ways, 3972
6:35 He will not accept **a** compensation; 3972
8:26 before he made the earth or its fields or **a** 8031
14:34 but sin is a disgrace to **a** people. NIH
26:10 a fool or **a** passer-by. NIH
Ecc 5:19 God gives **a** man wealth and possessions, 3972
SS 4:10 the fragrance of your perfume than **a** spice! 3972
Isa 7:17 on the house of your father a time unlike **a** NIH
33:20 nor **a** *of* its ropes broken. 3972
35: 9 nor will *a* ferocious **beast** get up on it; AIT
36:18 the god of **a** nation ever delivered his land 2021
41:26 no one heard *a* **words** *from* you. AIT
43:24 You have not bought *a* **fragrant calamus** AIT
44: 8 Is there **a** God besides me? NIH
52:14 beyond that of *a* **man** and his form marred AIT
53: 9 nor was **a** deceit in his mouth. NIH
56: 2 and keeps his hand from doing **a** evil." 3972
56: 3 And let not **a** eunuch complain, 2021
64: 4 no eye has seen **a** God besides you, NIH
Jer 2:24 **A** males that pursue her need 3972
3: 2 Is there *a place* **where** you have AIT
3:19 the most beautiful inheritance of *a* **nation.'** AIT
5: 6 to tear to pieces **a** who venture out, 3972
7:16 for this people nor offer **a** plea or petition NIH
10: 5 nor *can* they **do** *a* **good."** AIT
11:14 for this people nor offer **a** plea or petition NIH
12:17 But if **a** nation does not listen, 2085[S]
14:22 Do **a** *of* the worthless idols of 928
17:22 a load out of your houses or do **a** work on 3972
17:24 the Sabbath day holy by not doing **a** work 3972
17:27 the Sabbath day holy by not carrying **a** load NIH
18: 7 If **at a time** I announce that a nation 8092
20: 9 "I will not mention him or speak **a more** 6388
23: 4 nor *will a* **be missing,"** declares the LORD. AIT
25: 4 you have not listened or **paid a attention.** 265+4200+5742+9048
27: 8 **a** nation or kingdom will 2021
27:11 if **a** nation will bow its neck under the yoke 2021
27:13 the LORD has threatened **a** nation 2021
29:26 you should put **a** madman who acts like 3972

Jer 34:14 you must free **a** fellow Hebrew who has sold himself 2257S
35: 7 you must never have **a** of these things, NIH
37: 2 nor the people of the land **paid** *a* **attention** AIT
37:17 "Is there **a** word from the LORD?" NIH
38: 9 to death when there is no longer **a** bread in 2021
51:26 nor **a** stone for a foundation, NIH
La 1:12 Is **a** suffering like my suffering NIH
3:39 Why should **a** living man complain 1505S
4:12 nor did **a** *of* the world's people, 3972
Eze 1:17 in **a** one of the four directions NIH
10:11 in **a** one of the four directions NIH
12:28 of my words will be delayed **a longer;** 6388
14: 4 When **a** Israelite sets up idols in his heart 408
14: 7 " 'When **a** Israelite or any alien living 408
14: 7 or **a** alien living in Israel separates himself 2021
15: 2 of a branch on **a** of the trees in the forest? 3972
16: 5 or had compassion enough to do **a** 285
18:10 or does **a** of these other things 285
18:23 *Do I* **take a pleasure in** the death of 2911+2911
20:28 and they saw **a** high hill or any leafy tree, 3972
20:28 and they saw any high hill or **a** leafy tree, 3972
24:16 Yet do not lament or weep or shed **a** tears. 3870S
37:23 and vile images or with **a** *of* their offenses, 3972
39:28 not leaving **a** behind. 4946+6388
44:13 as priests or come near **a** *of* my holy things 3972
44:17 they must not wear **a** woolen garment NIH
44:24 " 'In **a** dispute, the priests are to serve NIH
46:18 not take **a** *of* the inheritance of the people, 4946
48:14 They must not sell or exchange **a** *of* it. 4946
Da 1: 4 young men without **a** physical defect, 3972
1:15 and better nourished than **a** *of* 3972
2:10 has ever asked such a thing of **a** magician 10353
2:43 **a more than** iron mixes with clay. 10168+10195+10341
3:28 or worship **a** god except their own God. 10353
3:29 of **a** nation or language who say anything 10353
6: 5 "We will never find **a** basis for charges 10353
6: 7 to **a** god or man during the next thirty days, 10353
6:12 to **a** god or man except to you, 10353
6:18 and without **a** entertainment being brought NIH
6:22 Nor have I ever done **a** wrong before you, NIH
11:37 nor will he regard **a** god, 3972
Hos 3: 3 be a prostitute or be intimate with **a** man, NIH
12: 8 not find in me **a** iniquity or sin." NIH
Jnh 3: 7 Do not let **a** man or beast, herd or flock, 2021
4: 4 **"Have** you **a right** to be angry?" 3512
Zep 3:15 never again will you fear **a** harm. NIH
Hag 2:19 Is there yet **a** seed left in the barn? NIH
Zec 14:17 If **a of** the peoples of the earth do not go 907+4946
Mt 5:18 will by **a** means disappear from the Law *NIG*
10: 5 not go among the Gentiles or enter **a** town *NIG*
10: 9 Do not take along **a** gold or silver or copper *NIG*
12:11 "If **a** of you has a sheep and it falls into *5515*
16: 7 "It is because we didn't bring **a** bread." *NIG*
18:14 not willing that **a** of these little ones should *1651*
19: 3 to divorce his wife for **a and every** reason?" *4246*
22:46 to ask him **a more** questions. *4033*
25: 3 but did not take **a** oil with them. *NIG*
26:60 But they did not find **a,** *NIG*
26:65 Why do we need **a more** witnesses? *2285*
Mk 4:13 How then will you understand **a** parable? *4246*
5: 3 and no one could bind him **a more,** *4033*
5:35 "Why bother the teacher **a more?"** *2285*
6: 5 He could not do **a** miracles there, *4029*
6:11 And **if a** place will not welcome you *323+4005*
11:13 he went to find out if it had **a** fruit. *5516*
12:20 and died without leaving **a** children. *NIG*
12:22 In fact, none of the seven left **a** children. *NIG*
12:34 no one dared ask him **a** more questions. *NIG*
14: 7 and you can help them **a time** you want. *4020*
14:55 but they did not find **a.** *NIG*
14:63 "Why do we need **a more** witnesses?" *2285*
Lk 3:13 "Don't collect **a more** *than* you are required *4123+4498*
4:26 Yet Elijah was **not** sent to **a** of them, *4029*
7:44 You did not give me **a** water for my feet, *NIG*
8:49 **"Don't** bother the teacher **a more."** *3600*
10:35 **a** extra expense you may have.' *323+4005+5516*
11:17 **"A** kingdom divided against itself will *4246*
13: 6 to look for fruit on it, but did not find **a.** *NIG*
13: 7 on this fig tree and haven't found **a.** *NIG*
13:33 **In a case,** I must keep going today *4440*
14:33 **a** of you who does not give *4246*
16: 2 because you cannot be manager **a longer.'** *2285*
18:34 The disciples did **not** understand **a** of this. *4029*
19:48 Yet they could not find **a way** to do it, *3836+5515*
20:40 **no** one dared to ask him **a more** *4033*
22:71 "Why do we need **a more** testimony? *2285*
Jn 7: 6 for you **a** time is right. *4121*
7:48 "Has **a** of the rulers or of *5516*
8: 7 "If **a** one of you is without sin, *NIG*
8:46 Can **a** of you prove me guilty of sin? *5515*
10:33 "We are not stoning you for **a** of these," *NIG*
17:14 world **a more than** I am of the world. *2777+4024*
21: 5 "Friends, haven't you **a** fish?" *5516*
Ac 4:17 to stop this thing from spreading **a further** *2093+4498*
4:32 that **a** of his possessions was his own, *5516*
8:16 the Holy Spirit had not yet come upon **a** *4029*
9: 2 he found **a** there who belonged to the Way, *5516*
10:28 that I should **not** call **a** man impure *3594*
10:29 **without raising a objection.** *395*
22: 3 as zealous for God as **a** of you are today. *4246*
24:18 nor was I involved in **a** disturbance. *NIG*
25:10 I have **not** done **a** wrong to the Jews, *4029*
25:16 over **a** man before he has faced his accusers *5516*
Ac 25:18 **not** charge him with **a** of the crimes *4029*
25:24 shouting that he ought not to live **a longer.** *3600*
26: 8 Why should **a** of you consider it incredible *NIG*
27:42 to prevent **a** of them from swimming away *5516*
28:18 because I was **not** guilty of **a** crime deserving death. *3594*
28:19 not that I had **a** charge to bring *5516*
28:21 "We have **not** received **a** letters from Judea *4046*
Ro 3: 9 Are we **a** better? *NIG*
6: 2 how can we live in it **a longer?** *2285*
8:33 Who *will* **bring a charge** *1592*
8:38 the present nor the future, nor **a** powers, *NIG*
12: 2 **conform** *a longer* **to the pattern of** *AIT*
14:13 up your mind not to put **a** stumbling block *NIG*
16: 2 to give her **a** help she may need from you, *323*
1Co 1: 7 not lack **a** spiritual gift as you eagerly wait *3594*
1:14 I am thankful that I did **not** baptize **a** *4029*
2:15 is **not** subject to **a** *man's* judgment: *4029*
3:11 For no one can lay **a** foundation other than *NIG*
3:12 If **a** *man* builds on this foundation using *5516*
3:18 If **a one** of you thinks he is wise by *5516*
4: 3 if I am judged by you or by **a** human court; *NIG*
6: 1 If **a** of you has a dispute with another, *5516*
7:12 If **a** brother has a wife who is not a believer *5516*
9:15 But I have not used **a** of these rights. *4029*
2Co 1: 4 that we can comfort those in **a** trouble with *4246*
7: 9 **not** harmed in **a way** *3594*
8:20 We want to avoid **a** criticism of *5516*
9: 4 For if **a** Macedonians come with me *NIG*
11: 9 from being a burden to you in **a** *way,* *4246*
12:17 through **a** of the men I sent you? *5516*
13: 2 not spare those who sinned earlier or **a** of *4246*
Gal 1:12 I did not receive it from **a** man, *NIG*
1:16 I did not consult **a** man, *NIG*
5: 6 nor uncircumcision has **a** value. *5516*
Eph 4:29 Do not let **a** unwholesome talk come out *4246*
5: 3 or of **a** *kind* of impurity, or of greed, *4246*
5: 5 has **a** inheritance in the kingdom of Christ *NIG*
5:27 without stain or wrinkle or **a other** blemish, *5516*
Php 1:28 in **a way** by those who oppose you. *3594*
2: 1 If you have **a** encouragement *5516*
2: 1 if **a** comfort from his love, *5516*
2: 1 if **a** fellowship with the Spirit, *5516*
2: 1 if **a** tenderness and compassion, *5516*
4:12 of being content in **a** and every situation, *4246*
Col 2:23 but they lack **a** value *5516*
2Th 2: 3 Don't let anyone deceive you **in a way,** *2848+3594+5573*
3: 8 that we would not be a burden to **a** of you. *5516*
1Ti 1: 3 not to teach false doctrines **a** longer *NIG*
5:16 If **a** *woman* who is a believer has widows *5516*
2Ti 2:21 the Master and prepared to do **a** good work. *4246*
Phm 1:14 that a favor you do will be spontaneous and *3836*
1:18 If he has done you **a** wrong *5516*
Heb 4:12 Sharper than **a** double-edged sword, *4246*
7:20 Others became priests without **a** oath, *NIG*
10:18 there is no longer **a** sacrifice for sin. *NIG*
Jas 1: 5 If **a** of you lacks wisdom, *5516*
5:13 Is **a** *one* of you in trouble? *5516*
5:14 Is **a** one of you sick? *5516*
1Pe 3: 1 if **a** *of them* do not believe the word, *5516*
4:15 not be as a murderer or thief or **a** other kind *NIG*
2Jn 1: 7 **A such person** is the deceiver and *4047*
Rev 2:24 not impose **a** other burden on you): *NIG*
7: 1 to prevent **a** wind from blowing on the land *NIG*
7: 1 on the land or on the sea or on **a** tree. *4246*
7:16 nor **a** scorching heat. *4246*
9: 4 not to harm the grass of the earth or **a** plant *4246*
18: 4 that you will not receive **a** of her plagues; *NIG*
18:11 because no one buys their cargoes **a more—** *4033*
18:22 No workman *of* **a** trade will ever be found *4246*
21: 1 and there was no longer **a** sea. *NIG*
22: 3 No longer will there be **a** curse. *4246*

ANYBODY (7) [ANY]

Lk 19: 8 and if I have cheated **a** out of anything, *5516*
Ac 19:38 a grievance against **a,** *5516*
1Co 11:21 ahead without waiting for **a** else. *NIG*
14:37 **a** thinks he is a prophet or spiritually gifted, *5516*
Gal 1: 9 If **a** is preaching to you *5516*
1Th 4:12 **not** be dependent on **a.** *3594*
1Jn 2: 1 But if **a** does sin, we have one who speaks *5516*

ANYMORE (17) [ANY]

Dt 3:26 Do not speak to me **a** about this matter 3578+6388
18:16 nor see this great fire **a,** 3578+6388
Jos 7:12 be with you **a** unless you destroy whatever 3578
2Sa 2:28 nor *did they* fight **a.** 3578+6388
7:10 Wicked people will not oppress them **a,** 3578
10:19 to help the Ammonites **a.** 6388
1Ch 17: 9 Wicked people will not oppress them **a,** 3578
19:19 not willing to help the Ammonites **a.** 6388
Isa 1: 5 Why should you be beaten **a?** 6388
2: 4 nor will they train for war **a.** 6388
Jer 22:30 on the throne of David or rule **a** in Judah." 6388
Eze 14:11 nor will they defile themselves **a** 6388
23:27 with longing or remember Egypt **a.** 6388
Am 7:13 Don't prophesy **a** at Bethel, 3578+6388
Mic 4: 3 nor will they train for war **a.** 6388
Jn 14:19 Before long, the world will **not** see me **a,** *4033*
Rev 20: 3 to keep him from deceiving the nations **a** *2285*

ANYONE (403) [ANY]

Ge 4:15 if **a** kills Cain, he will suffer vengeance 3972
13:16 so that if **a** could count the dust, 408
19:12 "Do you have **a** else here— 4769
19:12 or **a** else in the city who belongs to you? 3972
26:11 **"A** who molests this man or his wife shall 2021
31:32 But if you find *a* **who** has your gods, AIT
41:38 "Can we find **a** like this man, NIH
43:34 as much as **a** else's. 3972
Ex 10:23 No one could see **a else** or leave his place 278S
20: 7 not hold *a* guiltless **who** misuses his name. AIT
21:12 *"A who* **strikes** a man and kills him shall AIT
21:15 *"A who* **attacks** his father or his mother AIT
21:16 *"A who* **kidnaps** another and either sells AIT
21:17 *"A who* **curses** his father or mother must AIT
22:19 **"A** who has sexual relations with 3972
24:14 **a** involved in a dispute can go to them." 4769
30:33 **a other than a priest** 2424
31:14 *A who* **desecrates** it must be put to death; AIT
33: 7 **A** inquiring of the LORD would go to 3972
33:16 How *will a* **know** that you are pleased AIT
Lev 4: 2 'When **a** sins unintentionally 5883
5: 5 " 'When *a is* **guilty** in any of these ways, AIT
6: 2 "If **a** sins and is unfaithful to the LORD 5883
7: 8 a burnt offering for **a** may keep its hide 408
7:19 **a** ceremonially clean may eat it. 3972
7:20 But if **a** who is unclean eats any meat of 5883
7:21 If **a** touches something unclean— 5883
7:25 **A** who eats the fat of an animal from which 3972
7:27 If **a** eats blood, 3972+5883
7:29 **'A** who brings a fellowship offering to 2021
11:28 **A** who picks up their carcasses must wash his clothes, 2021
11:36 but *a who* **touches** one AIT
11:39 **a** who touches the carcass will be unclean 2021
11:40 **A** who eats some of the carcass 2021
11:40 **A** who picks up the carcass 2021
13: 2 "When **a** has a swelling or a rash or 132
13: 9 "When **a** has an infectious skin disease, 132
14:32 for **a** who has an infectious skin disease 2257
14:46 **"A** who goes into the house 2021
14:47 **A** who sleeps or eats in 2021
15: 5 **A** who touches his bed must wash his clothes 408
15:11 **" 'A** the man with a discharge touches 3972
15:19 and **a** who touches her will be unclean 3972
15:23 when **a** touches it, he will be unclean 2257
15:32 for *a made* **unclean** by an emission AIT
17:14 **a** who eats it must be cut off." 3972
17:15 **" 'A,** whether native-born or alien, 3972+5883
20: 9 " 'If **a** curses his father or mother, 408+408
22: 4 by a corpse or by **a** who has an emission 408
22:12 **a other than a priest,** 2424
22:14 " 'If **a** eats a sacred offering by mistake, 408
22:21 When **a** brings from the herd or flock 408
23:29 **A** who does not deny himself on 2021+3972+5883
23:30 **a** who does any work on 2021+3972+5883
24:15 Say to the Israelites: 'If **a** curses his God, 408+408
24:16 *a who* **blasphemes** the name of AIT
24:17 " 'If **a** takes the life of a human being, 408
24:18 *A who* **takes the life** of someone's animal AIT
24:19 If **a** injures his neighbor, 408
27: 2 'If **a** makes a special vow 408
27: 8 If **a** making the vow is too poor to pay 2085
Nu 1:51 **A else** who goes near it shall be put 2424
3:10 **a else** who approaches the sanctuary must 2424
3:38 **A else** who approached the sanctuary was 2424
5: 2 to send away from the camp **a** who has 3972
12: 3 more humble than **a** else on the face of 3972
15:14 or **a** *else* living among you presents 889
15:30 " 'But **a** who sins defiantly, 5883
17:13 **A** who even comes near the tabernacle of 3972
18: 7 **A else** who comes near the sanctuary must 2424
19:11 "Whoever touches the dead body of **a** 132+3972
19:13 of **a** and fails to purify himself defiles 132
19:14 **A** who enters the tent and anyone who is 3972
19:14 the tent and **a** who is in it will be unclean 3972
19:16 **"A** out in the open who touches someone who has been killed 3972
19:16 or **a** who touches a human bone or a grave, NIH
19:18 He must also sprinkle **a** who has touched 2021
19:21 and **a** who touches the water 2021
19:22 and **a** who touches it becomes unclean 5883
21: 8 **a** who is bitten can look at it and live." 3972
21: 9 when **a** was bitten by a snake and looked at 408
31:19 "All of you who have killed **a** 5883
31:19 touched **a** who was killed must stay outside 2021
35:15 **a** who has killed another accidentally can flee there. 3972
35:17 if **a** has a stone in his hand that could kill, NIH
35:18 Or if **a** has a wooden object in his hand NIH
35:20 *a* with malice aforethought **shoves** AIT
35:30 **" 'A** who kills a person is to be put to death 3972
35:32 not accept a ransom for *a who has* **fled** to AIT
36: 6 They may marry **a** they please as long 2021
Dt 4:42 *a who had* **killed a person** AIT
5:11 not hold a guiltless **a** who misuses his name. 889
18:12 **A** who does these things is detestable to 3972
18:19 If **a** does not listen to my words that 408+2021
19: 3 so that **a** who kills a man may flee there. 3972
20: 5 "Has **a** built a new house and 408+2021+4769
20: 6 Has **a** planted a vineyard 408+2021+4769
20: 7 Has **a** become pledged to a woman and 408+2021+4769
21:23 *a who* **is hung** on a tree is under God's curse AIT
22: 5 LORD your God detests **a** who does this. 3972
25:16 LORD your God detests **a** who does these 3972
25:16 **a** who deals dishonestly. 3972
Jos 2:19 If **a** goes outside your house into the street, 3972
2:19 As for **a** who is in the house with you, 3972
11:14 not sparing **a** that breathed. 3972

Jos 20: 3 so that a who kills a person accidentally 8357S
Jdg 4:20 by and asks you, 'Is a here?' 408
7: 3 'A who trembles with fear may turn back 4769
16: 7 "If *a* **ties** me with seven fresh thongs AIT
16:11 "If *a* **ties** me **securely** with new ropes AIT
18: 7 and had no relationship with a else. 132
18:28 and had no relationship with a else. 132
21: 5 a solemn oath that *a* **who** failed to assemble AIT
21:18 be *a who* **gives** a wife to a Benjamite.' AIT
Ru 2: 2 and pick up the leftover grain behind a 889
3:14 but got up before a could be recognized; 408
1Sa 2:13 with the people that whenever a offered 408+3972
11: 7 to the oxen of a who does not follow Saul 2257
26:12 nor *did a* **wake up.** AIT
2Sa 5: 8 "A who conquers the Jebusites will have 3972
6:21 who chose me rather than your father or a 3972
9: 1 "Is there a still left of the house of Saul 889
14:10 "If a says anything to you, bring him to me, 2021
15: 2 Whenever a came with a complaint 408+2021+3972
15: 5 whenever a approached him to bow down 408
19:22 Should a be put to death in Israel today? 408
21: 4 nor do we have the right to put a in Israel 408
1Ki 3:12 that there will never have been a like you, NIH
13:33 A who wanted to become 2021
15:17 to prevent *a* from **leaving** or entering AIT
15:29 He did not leave Jeroboam a that breathed, 3972
18:40 Don't let a get away!" 408
22:31 "Do not fight with a, small or great, 963+4200
2Ki 4:29 If you meet a, do not greet him, 408
4:29 do not greet him, and if a greets you, 408
7:10 not a sound of a— 132
9:15 don't let a slip out of the city to go and tell 7127S
10: 5 We will not appoint a as king; 408
10:19 A who fails to come will no longer live." 3972
11: 8 A who approaches your ranks must be put 2021
11:15 and put to the sword a who follows her." 2021
23:18 "Don't let a disturb his bones." 408
2Ch 6: 5 nor have I chosen a to be the leader 408
16: 1 to prevent *a* from **leaving** or entering AIT
18:30 "Do not fight with a, small or great, NIH
23: 7 A who enters the temple must be put 2021
23:14 and put to the sword a who follows her." 2021
36:23 A of his people among you— 4769
Ezr 1: 3 A of his people among you— 4769
6:11 I decree that if a changes this edict, 10050+10353
10: 8 A who failed to appear 3972
Ne 2:12 I had not told a what my God had put 132
Job 13:19 Can a bring charges against me? 4769
21:22 "*Can a* **teach** knowledge to God, AIT
31:19 I have seen *a* **perishing** for lack of clothing, AIT
40:24 *Can a* **capture** him by the eyes, AIT
Pr 20:24 How then can a understand his own way? 132
27:11 *a who* **treats** me **with contempt.** AIT
28: 9 If *a* **turns** a deaf ear to the law, AIT
Ecc 1:16 in wisdom more than a who has ruled 3972
2: 7 I also owned more herds and flocks than a 3972
2: 9 I became greater by far than a in Jerusalem 3972
6:11 and how does that profit a? 132
9: 4 A who is among the living has hope— 4769
Isa 47:14 Here are no coals to warm a; NIH
54:15 *a does* **attack** you, it will not be my doing; AIT
Jer 16: 7 *a* **give** them *a* **drink** AIT
23:24 Can a hide in secret places so 408
23:34 If a prophet or a priest or a else claims, 6639S
26:19 "Did Hezekiah king of Judah or a *else* 3972
27: 5 and I give it to a I please. 889
36:19 Don't let a know where you are." 408
38:24 "Do not let a know about this conversation, 408
41: 4 before a knew about it, 408
Eze 9: 6 but do not touch a who has the mark. 408+3972
16:15 You lavished your favors on a who passed 3972
16:25 to a who passed by. 3972
18: 7 He does not oppress a, 408
18:16 not oppress a or require a pledge for a loan. 408
18:32 I take no pleasure in the death of a, 2021+4637S
33: 4 then if *a* **hears** the trumpet but does AIT
45:20 the month for a who sins unintentionally or 408
Da 4:17 gives them to a he wishes and sets 10168+10426
4:25 and gives them to a he wishes. 10168+10426
4:32 and gives them to a he wishes." 10168+10426
5:21 and sets over them a he wishes. 10168+10426
6: 7 that a who prays to any god or man during 10353
6:12 during the next thirty days a who prays 10050+10353
Am 6:10 of the house and asks a still hiding there, 889
6:10 "Is a with you?" NIH
Na 3: 7 Where can I find *a to* **comfort** you?" AIT
Hag 2:16 a came to a heap of twenty measures, 4392
2:16 *a* **went** to a wine vat to draw fifty measures, AIT
Zec 13: 3 And if a still prophesies, 408
Mt 5:19 A who breaks one of the least *1569*
5:21 and a who murders will be subject *323*
5:22 that a who is angry with his brother will *4246*
5:22 a who says to his brother, 'Raca,' *323+4005*
5:22 But a who says, 'You fool!' *323+4005*
5:28 But I tell you that a who looks at *4246*
5:31 'A who divorces his wife must give her *323+4005*
5:32 But I tell you that a who divorces his wife, *4246*
5:32 and a who marries *1569+4005*
8: 4 "See that you **don't** tell a. *3594*
8:10 I have **not** found a in Israel *4029*
10:14 If a will not welcome you or listen *4005*
10:37 "A who loves his father *3836*
10:37 a who loves his son *3836*
10:38 and a who does not take his cross *4005*
10:41 A who receives a prophet because he is *3836*
Mt 10:41 and a who receives a righteous man *3836*
10:42 if a gives even a cup of cold water to one *4005*
11:11 not risen a greater than John the Baptist; *NIG*
12:29 how can a enter a strong man's house *5516*
12:32 A who speaks a word against the Son *1569*
12:32 but a who speaks against *323*
13:19 When a hears the message about *4246*
15: 4 'A who curses his father or mother must *3836*
16:20 Then he warned his disciples **not** to tell a *3594*
16:24 "If a would come after me, *5516*
17: 9 "**Don't** tell a what you have seen, *3594*
18: 6 But if a causes one of these little ones *4005*
19: 9 I tell you that a who divorces his wife, *323*
21: 3 If a says anything to you, *5516*
22: 9 and invite to the banquet a you find.' *1569+4012*
23: 9 And do not call a on earth 'father,' *NIG*
23:16 You say, 'If a swears by the temple, *4005*
23:16 but if a swears by the gold of the temple, *4005*
23:18 You also say, 'If a swears by the altar, *4005*
23:18 but if a swears by the gift on it, *4005*
24:23 At that time if a says to you, 'Look, *5516*
24:26 "So if a tells you, 'There he is, *NIG*
Mk 1:44 "See that you don't tell this *to* a. *3594*
4:23 If a has ears to hear, let him hear." *5516*
5:37 He did not let a follow him except Peter, *4029*
5:43 He gave strict orders not to let a know *3594*
7:10 'A who curses his father or mother must *3836*
7:24 He entered a house and did **not** want a *4029*
7:36 Jesus commanded them **not** to tell a. *3594*
8: 4 in this remote place can a get enough bread *5516*
8:30 Jesus warned them **not** to tell a about him. *3594*
8:34 "If a would come after me, *5516*
8:38 If a is ashamed of me and my words *4005*
9: 3 whiter than a in the world could bleach *NIG*
9: 8 they no longer saw a *4029*
9: 9 Jesus gave them orders **not** to tell a what they had seen *3594*
9:30 not want a to know where they were, *5516*
9:35 "If a wants to be first, he must be the very last, and the servant of all." *5516*
9:41 a who gives you a cup of water in my name *323*
9:42 "And if a causes one of these little ones *4005*
10:11 "A who divorces his wife *323*
10:15 a who will not receive the kingdom of God *323*
11: 3 If a asks you, 'Why are you doing this?' *5516*
11:16 not allow a to carry merchandise through *5516*
11:23 if a says to this mountain, 'Go, *4005*
11:25 if you hold anything against a, forgive him, *5516*
13:21 At that time if a says to you, 'Look, *5516*
16: 8 They said nothing *to* a, *4029*
Lk 4: 6 and I can give it *to* a I want to. *1569+4005*
5:14 Then Jesus ordered him, "**Don't** tell a, *3594*
6:30 and if a takes what belongs to you, *3836*
8:51 he did not let a go in with him except Peter, *5516*
8:56 but he ordered them **not** to tell a what had happened. *3594*
9:21 **not** to tell this *to* a. *3594*
9:23 "If a would come after me, *5516*
9:26 If a is ashamed of me and my words, *4005*
10: 4 and do **not** greet a on the road. *3594*
12:10 but a who blasphemes against *3836*
12:21 be with a who stores up things for himself *3836*
14:26 "If a comes to me and does *5516*
14:27 And a who does not carry his cross *4015*
16:18 "A who divorces his wife *4246*
16:26 nor can a cross over from there to us.' *NIG*
18:17 a who will not receive the kingdom of God *323*
19:31 If a asks you, 'Why are you untying it?' *5516*
Jn 6:51 If a eats of this bread, he will live forever. *5516*
7:17 If a chooses to do God's will, *5516*
7:37 "If a is thirsty, let him come to me *5516*
7:51 "Does our law condemn a *476+3836S*
8:33 and have never been slaves *of* a. *4029*
8:51 I tell you the truth, if a keeps my word, *5516*
8:52 yet you say that if a keeps your word, *5516*
9:22 a who acknowledged that Jesus was *1569+5516*
11:57 that if a found out where Jesus was, *5516*
13:20 whoever accepts a I send accepts me; *5516*
14: 9 A who has seen me has seen the Father. *3836*
14:12 a who has faith in me will do what I *3836*
14:23 Jesus replied, "If a loves me, *5516*
15: 6 If a does not remain in me, *5516*
16: 2 a who kills you will think he is offering *4246*
16:30 not even need to have a ask you questions. *5516*
18:31 "But we have no right to execute a," *4029*
19:12 A who claims to be a king opposes Caesar." *4246*
20:23 If you forgive a his sins, they are forgiven; *5516*
Ac 2:45 they gave *to* a as he had need. *4246*
3:23 A who does not listen to him *1569+4246+6034*
4:17 to speak no longer *to* a in this name." *3594*
4:35 and it was distributed *to* a as he had need. *1667*
9: 7 they heard the sound but did **not** see a. *3594*
10:47 "Can a keep these people from being *5516*
23:22 "**Don't** tell a that you have reported this *3594*
24:12 My accusers did not find me arguing with a *5516*
Ro 5: 7 Very rarely will a die for a righteous man, *5516*
6: 7 *a* who has died has been freed from sin. *AIT*
8: 9 And if a does not have the Spirit of Christ, *5516*
10:11 "A who trusts in him will never be put *4246*
12:17 Do **not** repay a evil for evil. *3594*
14:14 But if a regards something as unclean, *3836*
14:18 because a who serves Christ *3836*
1Co 1:16 I don't remember if I baptized a else.) *5516*
3:17 If a destroys God's temple, *5516*
4: 7 For who makes you different from a else? *NIG*
5:11 not associate with a who calls himself *1569+5516*
7:36 If a thinks he is acting improperly toward *5516*
1Co 7:39 she is free to marry a she wishes, *4005*
8:10 For if a with a weak conscience sees you *5516*
9:15 I would rather die than have a deprive me *4029*
10:28 But if a says to you, *5516*
10:32 Do not cause a to stumble, whether Jews, *NIG*
11:16 If a wants to be contentious about this, *5516*
11:29 For a who eats and drinks *3836*
11:34 If a is hungry, he should eat at home, *5516*
14: 2 For a who speaks in a tongue does not speak to men but to God. *3836*
14: 7 how will a know what tune is being played *NIG*
14: 9 how will a know what you are saying? *NIG*
14:13 For this reason a who speaks in *3836*
14:27 If a speaks in a tongue, two— *5516*
16:22 If a does not love the Lord— *5516*
2Co 2: 5 If a has caused grief, *5516*
2:10 If you forgive a, I also forgive him. *4005*
3:16 But whenever *a* **turns** to the Lord, *AIT*
5:17 if a is in Christ, he is a new creation; *5516*
10: 7 If a is confident that he belongs to Christ, *5516*
11: 9 I was not a burden to a, *4029*
11:20 up with a who enslaves you or exploits you *5516*
11:21 What a else dares to boast about— *5516*
Gal 6: 3 If a thinks he is something *5516*
6: 6 A who receives instruction in *3836*
Php 3: 4 If a else thinks he has reasons *5516*
Col 2:16 not let a judge you by what you eat *5516*
2:18 Do **not** let a who delights in false humility *3594*
3:25 A who does wrong will be repaid *3836*
1Th 2: 6 not from you or a **else.** *257*
2: 9 a burden to a while we preached the gospel *5516*
2Th 2: 3 Don't let a deceive you in any way, *5516*
3:14 If a does not obey our instruction *5516*
1Ti 3: 1 If a sets his heart on being an overseer, *5516*
3: 5 (If a does not know how *5516*
4:12 **Don't** let a look down on you *3594*
5: 8 If a does not provide for his relatives, *5516*
6: 3 If a teaches false doctrines and does *5516*
2Ti 2: 5 Similarly, if a competes as an athlete, *5516*
Tit 2:15 Do **not** let a despise you. *3594*
Heb 4:10 for a who enters God's rest also rests *3836*
5:13 A who lives on milk, being still an infant, *4246*
10:28 A who rejected the law of Moses died *5516*
11: 6 because a who comes to him must believe *3836*
Jas 1:13 **nor** does he tempt **a;** *1254+4029*
1:23 A who listens to the word but does *5516*
1:26 If a considers himself religious and *5516*
2:13 without mercy will be shown *to* a who has *3836*
3: 2 If a is never at fault in what he says, *5516*
4: 4 A who chooses to be a friend of *1569*
4:11 A who speaks against his brother *3836*
4:17 A, then, who knows the good he ought *NIG*
5:13 Is a happy? Let him sing songs of praise. *5516*
1Pe 4:11 If a speaks, he should do it as one speaking *5516*
4:11 If a serves, he should do it with *5516*
2Pe 1: 9 But if a does not have them, *4005*
3: 9 not wanting a to perish, *5516*
1Jn 2: 5 But if a obeys his word, *4005*
2: 9 A who claims to be in the light *3836*
2:15 If a loves the world, *5516*
2:27 and you do not need a to teach you. *5516*
3: 7 Dear children, do **not** let a lead you astray. *3594*
3:10 A who does not do what is right is not *4246*
3:10 nor is a who does not love his brother. *NIG*
3:14 A who does not love remains in death. *3836*
3:15 A who hates his brother is a murderer, *4246*
3:17 If a has material possessions *4005*
4:15 If a acknowledges that Jesus is the Son *4005*
4:20 If a says, "I love God," *5516*
4:20 For a who does not love his brother, *3836*
5:10 A who believes in the Son *3836*
5:10 A who does not believe God has made him out to be a liar, *3836*
5:16 If a sees his brother commit a sin that does *5516*
5:18 that a born of God does not continue to sin; *4246*
2Jn 1: 9 A who runs ahead and does not continue in *4246*
1:10 If a comes to you and does *5516*
1:11 A who welcomes him shares *3836*
3Jn 1:11 A who does what is good is from God. *3836*
1:11 A who does what is evil has not seen God. *3836*
Rev 3:20 If a hears my voice and opens the door, *5516*
11: 5 If a tries to harm them, fire comes *5516*
11: 5 how a who wants to harm them must die. *5516*
13:10 If a is to go into captivity, *5516*
13:10 If a is to be killed with the sword, *5516*
13:18 If a has insight, let him calculate the number *3836S*
14: 9 "If a worships the beast and his image *5516*
14:11 for a who receives the mark of his name." *5516*
21:27 nor will a who does what is shameful *4246*
22:18 If a adds anything to them, *5516*
22:19 And if a takes words away from this book *5516*

ANYONE'S (6) [ANY]

1Sa 12: 4 not taken anything from a hand." 408
Job 30:13 without *a* **helping** them. AIT
Ac 20:33 I have **not** coveted a silver or gold *4029*
2Co 6: 3 We put no stumbling block in a path, *3594*
2Th 3: 8 nor did we eat a food without paying for it. *5515*
Rev 20:15 If a name was not found written in *5516*

ANYTHING (203) [ANY]

Ge 18:14 Is a too hard for the LORD? 1821
19: 8 But don't do a to these men, 1821
19:22 because I cannot do a until you reach it." 1821
22:12 "Do not do a to him. 4399

Ge 30:31 "Don't give me **a**," Jacob replied. 4399
31:24 "Be careful not *to* **say** *a* to Jacob, AIT
31:29 'Be careful not to say **a** to Jacob, NIH
31:32 see for yourself whether there is **a** NIH
39: 6 he did not concern himself with **a** except 4399
39: 8 not concern himself with **a** in the house; 4537
39:23 The warden paid no attention to **a** 3972+4399
44: 7 be it from your servants to do **a** like that! 1821
Ex 12:15 whoever eats **a with yeast in it** 2809
12:19 whoever eats **a with yeast in it** 4721
20: 4 an idol in the form *of* **a** in heaven above or 3972
20:17 or **a** that belongs to your neighbor." 3972
21: 2 he shall go free, **without paying a.** 2855
23:18 to me along with **a containing yeast.** 2809
34:25 to me along with **a containing yeast,** 2809
36: 6 or woman is to make **a** else as an offering 4856
Lev 5: 2 touches **a** ceremonially unclean— 1821+3972
5: 3 **a** that would make him unclean— 3972
5: 4 person thoughtlessly takes an oath to do **a,** NIH
7:16 but **a** left over may be eaten on 2021
7:19 that touches **a** ceremonially unclean must 3972
11:12 **A** living in the water that does not have fins 3972
11:35 **A** that one of their carcasses falls 3972
12: 4 not touch **a** sacred or go to the sanctuary 3972
13:48 any leather or **a** made of leather— 3972
15: 4 and **a** he sits on will be unclean. 2021+3972+3998
15: 6 on **a** that the man with a discharge sat 3998
15:20 " '**A** she lies on during her period will 3972
15:20 and **a** she sits on will be unclean. 3972
15:22 Whoever touches **a** she sits 3972+3998
15:23 Whether it is the bed or **a** she was sitting 3998
15:26 **a** she sits on will be unclean, 2021+3972+3998
17:15 who eats **a found dead** or torn 5577
19: 6 **a** left over until the third day must 2021
19:16 Do not **do a that endangers** your neighbor's **life.** 1947+6584+6641
20:25 by any animal or bird or **a** that moves along 3972
22: 8 He must not eat **a found dead** or torn 5577
22:20 Do not bring **a** with a defect, 3972
22:22 **a with warts** or festering or running sores. 3301
Nu 6: 4 not eat **a** that comes from the grapevine, 3972
11: 6 we never see **a** but this manna!" 3972
16:26 Do not touch **a** belonging to them, 3972
19:22 **A** that an unclean person touches becomes unclean, 3972
22:16 *Do* not *let* **a keep** *you* from coming to me, AIT
22:18 not do *a* **great** or small to go beyond AIT
22:38 "But can I say just **a?** 4399
24:13 *a* of my own accord, **good** AIT
31:23 and **a** else that can withstand fire must 1821+3972
Dt 2: 7 and you have not lacked **a.** 1821
4:23 of **a** the LORD your God has forbidden. 3972
4:32 Has **a** so great as this ever happened, 1821
4:32 or has **a** like it ever been heard of? NIH
5: 8 an idol in the form of **a** in heaven above or 3972
5:21 or **a** that belongs to your neighbor." 3972
14:10 But **a** that does not have fins 3972
14:21 Do not eat **a** you find already dead. 3972
14:26 or other fermented drink, or **a** you wish. 3972
18:20 in my name **a** I have not commanded him 1821
20:16 do not leave alive **a** that breathes. 3972
22: 3 or his cloak or **a** he loses. 3972
23:14 that he will not see among you **a** indecent 1821
23:19 or food or **a** else that may earn interest. 1821+3972
Jos 11:11 not sparing **a** that breathed, 3972
Jdg 13: 4 and that you do not eat **a** unclean, 3972
13: 7 and do not eat **a** unclean, 3972
13:14 not eat **a** that comes from the grapevine, 3972
13:14 or other fermented drink nor eat **a** unclean. 3972
19:19 We don't need **a.**" 1821+3972
Ru 1:17 **if a but** death separates you and me." 3954
1Sa 3:17 if you hide from me **a** he told you." 1821+1821+2021+3972+4946
12: 4 not taken **a** from anyone's hand." 4399
12: 5 that you have not found **a** in my hand." 4399
20: 2 Look, my father doesn't do **a,** 1821
21: 2 'No one is to know **a** about your mission 4399
30:19 plunder or **a** *else* they had taken. 3972
2Sa 3:35 so severely, if I taste bread or **a** *else* 3972+4399
13: 2 it seemed impossible for him to do **a** to her. 4399
14:10 The king replied, "If anyone says **a** to you, NIH
14:19 or to the left from **a** my lord the king says. 3972
14:32 and if I am guilty of **a,** NIH
15:35 Tell them **a** you hear in the king's palace. 1821+2021+3972
15:36 Send them to me with **a** you hear." 1821+3972
17:19 No one knew **a** about it. 1821
19:38 **a** you desire from me I will do for you." 3972
19:42 *Have we* **taken a** for ourselves?" 5951+5951
1Ki 14:13 the God of Israel, has found **a** good. 1821
22: 8 because he never prophesies *a* **good** AIT
22:18 that he never prophesies *a* **good** about me, AIT
2Ki 10: 5 and we will do **a** you say. 3972
2Ch 18: 7 because he never prophesies *a* **good** AIT
18:17 that he never prophesies *a* **good** about me, AIT
Ezr 7:20 And **a else** needed for the temple 10692
Ne 5:12 we will not demand **a** more from them. NIH
Est 2:13 **A** she wanted was given her to take 889+3972
6:10 Do not neglect **a** you have recommended." 1821+3972+4946
Job 21:25 never having enjoyed **a** good. 2021[S]
33:32 If you have **a to say,** answer me; 4863
Ps 39: 2 not even saying *a* **good,** AIT
Pr 14:15 A simple man believes **a,** 1821+3972
Ecc 1:10 Is there **a** of which one can say, "Look! 1821
5: 2 do not be hasty in your heart to utter **a** 1821
6: 5 Though it never saw the sun or knew **a,** 4202[S]
Ecc 7:14 a man cannot discover **a** about his future. 4399
9: 6 a part in **a** that happens under the sun. 3972
12:12 my son, of **a in addition** to them. 3463
Jer 2:10 see if there has ever been **a** like this: NIH
18:13 Who has ever heard **a** like this? NIH
18:18 and pay no attention to **a** he says." 3972
32:27 Is **a** too hard for me? 1821+3972
38:14 "Do not hide **a** from me." 1821
Eze 4:14 until now I have never eaten **a found dead** 5577
15: 3 from it to make **a useful?** 4856
15: 4 is it then useful for **a?** 4856
15: 5 it was not useful for **a** when it was whole, 4856
44:18 not wear **a** that makes them perspire. NIH
44:31 The priests must not eat **a,** bird or animal, 3972
Da 3:29 or language who say **a** against the God 10712
Joel 1: 2 Has **a** like this ever happened in your days NIH
Am 8: 7 "I will never forget **a** they have done. 3972
Jnh 3: 7 taste **a;** do not let them eat or drink. 4399
Mt 5:13 **no** longer good for **a,** *4029*
5:37 **a** beyond this comes from the evil one. *3836*
12:34 how can you who are evil say **a** good? *NIG*
13:34 he did **not** say **a** to them without using *4029*
18:19 if two of you on earth agree about **a** you ask for, *1569+4005+4246+4547*
21: 3 If anyone says **a** to you, *5516*
24:17 the roof of his house go down to take **a** out *3836*
27:19 **"Don't** have **a** to do with *3594*
Mk 2:12 saying, "We have never seen **a** like this!" *NIG*
4:34 not say **a** to them without using a parable. *NIG*
6:22 "Ask me for **a** you want, *1569+4005*
7:12 then you no longer let him do **a** *4029*
8:23 Jesus asked, "Do you see **a?**" *5516*
9:22 you can do **a,** take pity on us and help us." *5516*
9:39 in the next moment say **a** bad about me, *NIG*
11:25 if you hold **a** against anyone, forgive him, *5516*
13:15 down or enter the house to take **a** out. *5516*
Lk 5: 5 and **haven't** caught **a.** *4029*
6:35 **without** expecting to get **a** *3594*
11: 7 I can't get up and give you **a.**' *NIG*
15:16 but no one gave him **a.** *NIG*
17:31 no one in the field should go back for **a.** *NIG*
19: 8 and if I have cheated anybody out of **a,** *5516*
22:35 bag or sandals, did you lack **a?**" *5516*
24:41 "Do you have **a** here to eat?" *5516*
Jn 1:46 Can **a** good come from there?" *5516*
7:13 But no one would say **a** publicly about him *NIG*
14:14 You may ask me for **a** in my name, *1569+5516*
16:23 In that day you will no longer ask me **a.** *4029*
16:24 now you have not asked for **a** in my name. *4029*
Ac 9: 9 and did not eat or drink **a.** *NIG*
10:14 "I have never eaten **a** impure or unclean." *4246*
10:15 "Do not call **a** impure *NIG*
11: 9 'Do not call **a** impure **that** *4005*
15:28 **not** to burden you with **a** *3594*
17:25 as if he needed **a,** *5516*
19:36 you ought to be quiet and **not** do **a** rash. *3594*
19:39 If there is **a** further you want to bring up, *5516*
20:20 to preach **a** that would be helpful to you *NIG*
23:14 "We have taken a solemn oath **not** to eat **a** *3594*
24:19 before you and bring charges if they have **a** *5516*
25: 5 if he has done **a** wrong." *5516*
25:11 I am guilty of doing **a** deserving death, *5516*
26:31 "This man is **not** doing **a** *4029*
27:33 you **haven't** eaten **a.** *3594*
28:21 from there has reported or said **a** bad *5516*
Ro 8:39 nor **a** else in all creation, *5516*
9:11 the twins were born or had done **a** good *5516*
14:20 for a man to eat **a** that causes someone else *NIG*
14:21 not to eat meat or drink wine or to do **a** else *NIG*
15:18 of **a** except what Christ has accomplished *5516*
1Co 3: 7 nor he who waters is **a,** *5516*
6:12 but I will not be mastered by **a.** *5516*
9:12 up with **a** rather than hinder the gospel *4246*
10:19 then that a sacrifice offered to an idol is **a,** *5516*
10:19 or that an idol is **a?** *5516*
10:25 Eat **a** sold in the meat market *4246*
2Co 1:13 For we do not write you **a** you cannot read *257*
2:10 if there was **a** to forgive— *5516*
3: 5 in ourselves to claim **a** for ourselves, *5516*
9: 4 not to say **a** about you— *NIG*
13: 7 to God that you will **not** do **a** wrong. *3590+3594*
13: 8 For we cannot do **a** against the truth, *5516*
Gal 6:15 nor uncircumcision means **a;** *5516*
Php 4: 6 **not** be anxious about **a,** *3594*
4: 8 if **a** is excellent or praiseworthy— *5516*
1Th 1: 8 Therefore we do not need to say **a** about it, *5516*
2Ti 1: 9 not because of **a** we have done but because *NIG*
2:23 **Don't have a to do with** *4148*
Tit 1:16 disobedient and unfit for doing **a** good. *4246*
Phm 1:14 **not** want to do **a** without your consent, *4029*
1:18 or owes you **a,** charge it to me. *NIG*
Jas 1: 4 be mature and complete, **not** lacking **a.** *3594*
1: 7 That man should not think he will receive **a** *5516*
5:12 not by heaven or by earth or by **a** else. *5516*
1Jn 2:15 not love the world **or a** in the world. *3593+3836*
3:22 and receive from him **a** we ask, *1569+4005*
5:14 we ask **a** according to his will, he hears us. *5516*
Rev 22:18 If anyone adds **a** to them, God will add *NIG*

ANYWHERE (15) [ANY]

Ge 19:17 and don't stop **a** in the plain! 3972
Ex 10:19 Not a locust was left **a** in Egypt. 3972
13: 7 among you, nor shall any yeast be seen **a** 3972
34: 3 No one is to come with you or be seen **a** on 3972
Nu 18:31 You and your households may eat the rest of it **a,** 928+3972+5226
Dt 12:13 sacrifice your burnt offerings **a** you please. 928+3972+5226
18: 6 If a Levite moves from one of your towns **a** 3972
1Sa 27: 1 Saul will give up searching for me **a** 1473+3972
2Sa 21: 5 and have no place **a in** Israel, 928+1473+3972
1Ki 2:36 but do not go **a else.** 625+625+2025+2025+2256
2:42 'On the day you leave to go **a else,** 625+625+2025+2025+2256
2Ki 5:25 "Your servant didn't go **a,**" 625+625+2025+2025+2256
Jer 40: 5 or go **a** *else* you please." 3972
44:26 'that no one from Judah living **a** 3972
Ac 24:12 up a crowd in the synagogues or **a else in** *2848*

APACE (KJV) See HASTE

APART (62) [PART]

Ge 21:28 Abraham set **a** seven ewe lambs from 963+4200
21:29 these seven ewe lambs you have set **a** 963+4200
30:40 **set a** the young of the flock **by themselves,** 7233
Ex 19:23 **set** it **a as holy.'** " 7727
32:29 "You *have been* **set a** to the LORD today, 3338+4848
Lev 20:24 who *has* **set** you **a** from the nations. 976
20:25 those which *I have* **set a** as unclean 976
20:26 and *I have* **set** you **a** from the nations to 976
Nu 3:13 *I* **set a** for myself every firstborn in Israel, 7727
8:14 In this way *you are to* **set** the Levites **a** 976
8:17 *I* **set** them **a** for myself. 7727
16:31 the ground under them **split a** 1324
23: 9 I see a people who live **a** and do 970+4200
31:28 **set a** as tribute for the LORD one out 8123
31:42 which Moses **set a** from that of 2936
Dt 7:26 like it, will be **set a for destruction.** 3051
7:26 for it is **set a for destruction.** 3051
10: 8 that time the LORD **set a** the tribe of Levi 976
15:19 **Set a** for the LORD your God every firstborn male 7727
Jos 20: 7 So *they* **set a** Kedesh in Galilee in 7727
Jdg 13: 5 to be a **Nazirite,** *set a to* God from birth, AIT
14: 6 upon him in power so that *he* **tore** the lion **a** 9117
16:17 "because I have been a **Nazirite** *set a* AIT
20:17 Israel, **a** from Benjamin, 963+4200
1Ki 13: 3 The altar *will* **be split a** and the ashes 7973
13: 5 the altar **was split a** 7973
19:11 and powerful wind **tore** the mountains **a** 7293
2Ki 2:12 his own clothes and **tore** them **a.** 4200+7973+7974+9109
1Ch 23:13 Aaron **was set a,** 976
25: 1 **set a** some of the sons of Asaph, 976
Ezr 8:24 Then *I* **set a** twelve of the leading priests, 976
Ps 4: 3 the LORD *has* **set a** the godly for himself; 7111
16: 2 **a from** you I have no good thing." 6584
88: 5 I am **set a** with the dead, 2930
Pr 18:18 **keeps** strong opponents **a.** 7233
Isa 7: 6 *let us* **tear** it **a** and divide it 7763
23:18 Yet her profit and her earnings will be **set a** 7731
43:11 and **a from** me there is no savior. 1187+4946
44: 6 **a from** me there is no God. 1187+4946
45: 5 **a from** me there is no God. 2314
45:21 And there is no God **a from** me, 1187+4946
Jer 1: 5 before you were born *I* **set** you **a;** 7727
12: 3 **Set** them **a** for the day of slaughter! 7727
Hos 13: 8 a wild animal *will* **tear** them **a.** 1324
Mic 1: 4 and the valleys **split a,** 1324
Mt 10:29 the ground **a from** the will of your Father. *459*
Mk 5: 4 but he **tore** the chains **a** and broke the irons *1400*
Jn 10:36 what about the one whom the Father **set a** *39*
15: 5 **a from** me you can do nothing. *6006*
Ac 13: 2 **"Set a** for me Barnabas and Saul for *928*
Ro 1: 1 to be an apostle and **set a** for the gospel *928*
2:12 All who sin **a from the law** will *492*
2:12 the law will also perish **a from the law,** *492*
3:21 now a righteousness from God, **a from** law, *6006*
3:28 a man is justified by faith **a from** observing *6006*
4: 6 to whom God credits righteousness **a from** *6006*
7: 8 For **a from** law, sin is dead. *6006*
7: 9 Once I was alive **a from** law; *6006*
2Co 12: 3 whether in the body or **a from** the body I do *6006*
Gal 1:15 who **set** me **a** from birth and called me *928*
Heb 7:26 blameless, pure, **set a** from sinners, *6004*
1Pe 3:15 But in your hearts **set a** Christ as Lord. *39*

APARTMENT (1)

Jer 36:22 and the king was sitting in the winter **a,** 1074

APELLES (1)

Ro 16:10 Greet **A,** tested and approved in Christ. *593*

APES (2)

1Ki 10:22 silver and ivory, and **a** and baboons. 7761
2Ch 9:21 silver and ivory, and **a** and baboons. 7761

APHARSACHITES, APHARSITES (KJV) See PERSIAN

APHARSATHCHITES (KJV) See OFFICIALS

APHEK (9)

Jos 12:18 the king of **A** one the king of Lasharon one 707

Jos 13: 4 from Arah of the Sidonians as far as A, 707
19:30 Ummah, A and Rehob. 707
Jdg 1:31 or Sidon or Ahlab or Aczib or Helbah or A 707
1Sa 4: 1 and the Philistines at A. 707
29: 1 at A, and Israel camped by the spring 707
1Ki 20:26 and went up to A to fight against Israel. 707
20:30 The rest of them escaped to the city of A, 707
2Ki 13:17 the Arameans at A." 707

APHEKAH (1)
Jos 15:53 Janim, Beth Tappuah, A, 708

APHIAH (1)
1Sa 9: 1 the son of A *of* Benjamin. 688

APHIK (KJV) See APHEK

APHRAH (KJV) See BETH OPHRAH

APHSES (KJV) See HAPPIZZEZ

APOLLONIA (1)
Ac 17: 1 through Amphipolis and A, *662*

APOLLOS (11)
Ac 18:24 Meanwhile a Jew named A, *663*
18:27 When A wanted to go to Achaia, *899S*
19: 1 While A was at Corinth, *663*
1Co 1:12 another, "I follow A"; *663*
3: 4 "I follow Paul," and another, "I follow A," *663*
3: 5 What, after all, is A? *663*
3: 6 I planted the seed, A watered it, *663*
3:22 or A or Cephas or the world or life or death *663*
4: 6 I have applied these things to myself and A *663*
16:12 Now about our brother A: *663*
Tit 3:13 the lawyer and A on their way and see *663*

APOLLYON (1)
Rev 9:11 in Hebrew is Abaddon, and in Greek, A. *661*

APOSTLE (21) [APOSTLES, APOSTLES', APOSTLESHIP, APOSTOLIC, SUPER-APOSTLES]
Ro 1: 1 an a and set apart for the gospel of God— *693*
11:13 Inasmuch as I am the a to the Gentiles, *693*
1Co 1: 1 called to be an a of Christ Jesus by the will *693*
9: 1 Am I not an a? *693*
9: 2 Even though I may not be an a to others, *693*
15: 9 and do not even deserve to be called an a, *693*
2Co 1: 1 Paul, an a of Christ Jesus by the will of God, *693*
12:12 The things that mark an a— *693*
Gal 1: 1 Paul, an a— sent not from men *693*
2: 8 **ministry of** Peter as an a *692*
2: 8 was also at work in my ministry as an a to *NIG*
Eph 1: 1 Paul, an a of Christ Jesus by the will of God, *693*
Col 1: 1 Paul, an a of Christ Jesus by the will of God, *693*
1Ti 1: 1 Paul, an a of Christ Jesus by the command *693*
2: 7 a herald and an a— *693*
2Ti 1: 1 Paul, an a of Christ Jesus by the will of God, *693*
1:11 a herald and an a and a teacher. *693*
Tit 1: 1 Paul, a servant of God and an a of Jesus *693*
Heb 3: 1 the a and high priest whom we confess. *693*
1Pe 1: 1 Peter, an a of Jesus Christ, To God's elect, *693*
2Pe 1: 1 Simon Peter, a servant and a of Jesus Christ, *693*

APOSTLES (57) [APOSTLE]
Mt 10: 2 These are the names *of* the twelve a: *693*
Mk 3:14 He appointed twelve—designating them a *693*
6:30 The a gathered around Jesus and reported *693*
Lk 6:13 whom he also designated a: *693*
9:10 When the a returned, *693*
11:49 'I will send them prophets and a, *693*
17: 5 The a said to the Lord, *693*
22:14 Jesus and his a reclined at the table. *693*
24:10 the others with them who told this to the a. *693*
Ac 1: 2 the Holy Spirit *to* the a he had chosen. *693*
1:26 so he was added to the eleven a. *693*
2:37 the heart and said to Peter and the other a, *693*
2:43 and miraculous signs were done by the a. *693*
4: 2 because **the a** were teaching the people *899S*
4:33 the a continued to testify to the resurrection *693*
4:36 the a called Barnabas (which means Son *693*
5:12 The a performed many miraculous signs *693*
5:18 the a and put them in the public jail. *693*
5:21 and sent to the jail for **the a.** *899S*
5:26 with his officers and brought **the a.** *899S*
5:27 Having brought **the a,** *899S*
5:29 Peter and the other a replied: *693*
5:40 They called the a in and had them flogged. *693*
5:41 **The a** left the Sanhedrin, *3525+3836S*
6: 6 They presented these men to the a, *693*
8: 1 the a were scattered throughout Judea *693*
8:14 When the a in Jerusalem heard *693*
9:27 and brought him to the a. *693*
11: 1 The a and the brothers *693*
14: 4 with the Jews, others with the a. *693*
14:14 the a Barnabas and Paul heard of this, *693*
15: 2 to see the a and elders about this question. *693*
15: 4 by the church and the a and elders, *693*
15: 6 The a and elders met to consider this *693*
15:22 Then the a and elders, *693*
15:23 The a and elders, your brothers, *693*
16: 4 the a and elders in Jerusalem for the people *693*
Ro 16: 7 They are outstanding among the a, *693*
1Co 4: 9 that God has put us a on display at the end *693*
9: 5 as do the other a and the Lord's brothers *693*
12:28 the church God has appointed first of all a, *693*
12:29 Are all a? *693*
15: 7 he appeared to James, then *to* all the a, *693*
15: 9 the a and do not even deserve to be called *693*
2Co 11:13 For such men are **false a,** *6013*
11:13 masquerading as a of Christ. *693*
Gal 1:17 up to Jerusalem to see those who were a *693*
1:19 I saw none *of* the other a— *693*
Eph 2:20 on the foundation *of* the a and prophets, *693*
3: 5 by the Spirit to God's holy a and prophets. *693*
4:11 It was he who gave some to be a, *693*
1Th 2: 6 As a of Christ we could have been a burden *693*
2Pe 3: 2 by our Lord and Savior *through* your a. *693*
Jude 1:17 the a of our Lord Jesus Christ foretold. *693*
Rev 2: 2 tested those who claim to be a but are not, *693*
18:20 Rejoice, saints and a and prophets! *693*
21:14 on them were the names *of* the twelve a of *693*

APOSTLES' (5) [APOSTLE]
Ac 2:42 They devoted themselves to the a' teaching *693*
4:35 and put it at the a' feet, *693*
4:37 the money and put it at the a' feet. *693*
5: 2 but brought the rest and put it at the a' feet. *693*
8:18 at the laying on *of* the a' hands, *693*

APOSTLESHIP (2) [APOSTLE]
Ro 1: 5 we received grace and a to call people from *692*
1Co 9: 2 For you are the seal *of* my a in the Lord. *692*

APOSTOLIC (1) [APOSTLE]
Ac 1:25 to take over this a ministry, *692*

APOTHECARIES (KJV) See BLENDED, PERFUME-MAKERS

APOTHECARY (KJV) See PERFUMER

APPAIM (2)
1Ch 2:30 The sons of Nadab: Seled and A. 691
2:31 The son of A: 691

APPALLED (22)
Lev 26:32 your enemies who live there *will be* a. 9037
1Ki 9: 8 all who pass by *will be* a and will scoff 9037
2Ch 7:21 all who pass by *will be* a and say, 9037
Ezr 9: 3 from my head and beard and sat down a. 9037
9: 4 And I sat there a until the evening sacrifice. 9037
Job 17: 8 Upright men *are* a at this; 9037
18:20 Men of the west are a at his fate; 9037
Ps 40:15 *be* a at their own shame. 9037
Isa 52:14 as there were many *who were* a at him— 9037
59:16 *he was* a that there was no one to intervene; 9037
63: 5 *I was* a that no one gave support; 9037
Jer 2:12 *Be* a at this, O heavens, 9037
4: 9 and the prophets *will be* a." 9449
18:16 *will be* a and will shake their heads. 9037
19: 8 all who pass by *will be* a and will scoff 9037
49:17 all who pass by *will be* a and will scoff 9037
Eze 4:17 *They will be* a at the sight of each other 9037
26:16 trembling every moment, a at you. 9037
27:35 All who live in the coastlands *are* a at you; 9037
28:19 All the nations who knew you *are* a at you; 9037
32:10 **cause** many peoples **to be a** 9037
Da 8:27 *I was* a by the vision; 9037

APPAREL (KJV) See CLOTHES, GARMENTS, ROBES

APPARENTLY (KJV) See CLEARLY

APPEAL (16) [APPEALED, APPEALING, APPEALS]
Dt 15: 9 *He may* then a to the LORD against you, 7924
Job 5: 8 "But if it were I, *I would* a to God; 2011
Ps 77:10 Then I thought, *"To* this I *will* a: 2704
Ac 25:11 *I* a to Caesar!" *2126*
25:21 *When* Paul **made** his a to be held over for *2126*
25:25 but *because* he **made** his a to *2126*
28:19 I was compelled *to* a to Caesar— *2126*
1Co 1:10 *I* a to you, brothers, *4151*
2Co 5:20 though God *were* **making** *his* a through us. *4151*
8:17 For Titus not only welcomed our a, *4155*
10: 1 I a to you—I, Paul, *4151*
13:11 Aim for perfection, **listen to** my a, *4151*
1Th 2: 3 the a we make does not spring from error *4155*
Phm 1: 9 yet *I* a to you on the basis of love. *4151*
1:10 *I* a to you for my son Onesimus, *4151*
1Pe 5: 1 To the elders among you, *I* a *4151*

APPEALED (7) [APPEAL]
Ex 5:15 Israelite foremen went and a to Pharaoh: 7590
Jos 10: 3 of Jerusalem a to Hoham king of Hebron, 8938
Est 2: 4 This advice a **to** the king, 928+3512+6524
Lk 23:20 Pilate a to them again. *4715*
Ac 25:12 *"You have* a to Caesar. *2126*
26:32 if *he had* not a to Caesar." *2126*
Ro 11: 2 how *he* a to God against Israel: *1961*

APPEALING (1) [APPEAL]
2Pe 2:18 by a to the lustful desires *NIG*

APPEALS (1) [APPEAL]
2Sa 19:28 So what right do I have to **make** any more a 2410

APPEAR (50) [APPEARANCE, APPEARANCES, APPEARED, APPEARING, APPEARS, REAPPEARS]
Ge 1: 9 and *let* dry ground a." 8011
27:12 *I would* a to be tricking 928+2118+3869+6524
Ex 4: 1 'The LORD *did* not a to you'?" 8011
10:28 Make sure *you do* not a before me again! 8011
10:29 *"I will* never a before you again." 8011
22: 8 of the house *must* a before the judges 7928
23:15 "No *one is to* a before me empty-handed. 8011
23:17 "Three times a year all the men *are to* a 8011
34:20 "No *one is to* a before me empty-handed. 8011
34:23 Three times a year all your men *are to* a 8011
34:24 when you go up three times each year to a 8011
Lev 9: 4 For today the LORD *will* a to you.' " 8011
9: 6 that the glory of the LORD *may* a to you." 8011
13: 4 the spot on his skin is white but does not a 5260
13: 7 *he must* a before the priest again. 8011
13:32 and it does not a to be more than skin deep, 5260
14:37 that a to be deeper than the surface of 5260
16: 2 *I* a in the cloud over the atonement cover. 8011
Nu 16:16 "You and all your followers *are to* a before 2118
Dt 16:16 Three times a year all your men *must* a 8011
16:16 No man *should* a before the LORD empty-handed: 8011
31:11 to a before the LORD your God at 8011
1Sa 3:21 The LORD continued to a at Shiloh, 8011
2Sa 9: 2 They called him to a before David, NIH
Ezr 10: 8 Anyone who failed *to* a 995
Job 19:18 *when I* a, they ridicule me. 7756
Ps 102:16 For the LORD will rebuild Zion and a 8011
SS 2:12 Flowers a on the earth; 8011
Isa 1:12 When you come to a **before** me, 7156+8011
58: 8 and your healing *will* a quickly a; 7541
Eze 16:52 *they* a more **righteous** than you. 7405
16:52 **made** your sisters **a righteous.** 7405
Da 7:23 a fourth kingdom *that will* a on earth. 10201
11: 2 Three more kings *will* a in Persia, 6641
11: 3 Then a mighty king *will* a, 6641
Hos 6: 3 As surely as the sun rises, he *will* a; 3922+4604
Zec 9:14 Then the LORD *will* a over them; 8011
Mt 23:28 the outside you a to people **as** righteous but *5743*
24:11 and many false prophets *will* a *1586*
24:24 For false Christs and false prophets *will* a *1586*
24:30 that time the sign of the Son of Man *will* a *5743*
Mk 13:22 For false Christs and false prophets *will* a *1586*
Lk 19:11 that the kingdom of God was going to a *428*
Ac 5:27 *they made* them a before the Sanhedrin to *2705*
11:13 how he had seen an angel a in his house *2705*
19:30 Paul wanted to a before the crowd, *NIG*
2Co 5:10 For we must all a before the judgment seat *5746*
Col 3: 4 then you also *will* a with him in glory. *5746*
Heb 9:24 now *to* a for us in God's presence. *1872*
9:28 and *he will* a a second time, *3972*

APPEARANCE (30) [APPEAR]
Lev 13:55 and if the mildew has not changed its a, 6524
1Sa 16: 7 "Do not consider his a or his height, 5260
16: 7 Man looks at the **outward a,** 6524
16:12 with a fine a and handsome features. 6524
2Sa 14:25 a man so highly praised for his **handsome a** 3637
Ecc 8: 1 a man's face and changes its hard a. 7156
SS 5:15 His a is like Lebanon, choice as its cedars. 5260
Isa 52:14 his a was so disfigured beyond that 5260
53: 2 nothing in his a that we should desire him. 5260
La 4: 7 their a like sapphires. 1619
Eze 1: 5 *In* a their form was that of a man, 5260
1:13 The a *of* the living creatures was 5260
1:16 This was the a and structure of the wheels: 5260
1:28 Like the a *of* a rainbow in the clouds on 5260
1:28 This was the a *of* the likeness of the glory 5260
8: 2 up his a was as bright as glowing metal. 5260
10:10 for their a, the four of them looked alike; 5260
10:22 the same a as those I had seen by 1952
40: 3 and I saw a man whose a was like bronze; 5260
Da 1:13 Then compare our a with that of 5260
2:31 enormous, dazzling statue, awesome in a. 10657
Joel 2: 4 They have the a *of* horses; 5260
Mt 16: 3 You know how to interpret the a of the sky, *4725*
28: 3 His a was like lightning, *1624*
Lk 9:29 he was praying, the a of his face changed, *1626*
12:56 to interpret the a of the earth and the sky. *4725*
Gal 2: 6 God *does* not **judge by external a**— *476+3284+4725*
Php 2: 8 And being found **in a** as a man, *5386*
Col 2:23 Such regulations indeed have an a *3364*
Rev 4: 3 the one who sat there had the a of jasper *3970*

APPEARANCES (1) [APPEAR]
Jn 7:24 Stop judging by mere a, *4071*

APPEARED (97) [APPEAR]

Ge 2: 5 the field *had* yet **a** on the earth and no plant 2118
12: 7 The LORD **a** to Abram and said, 8011
12: 7 the LORD, who *had* **a** to him. 8011
15:17 with a blazing torch **a** and passed between 2180
17: 1 the LORD **a** to him and said, 8011
18: 1 The LORD **a** to Abraham near 8011
26: 2 The LORD **a** to Isaac and said, 8011
26:24 That night the LORD **a** to him and said, 8011
35: 1 who **a** to you when you were fleeing 8011
35: 9 God **a** to him again and blessed him. 8011
46:29 As soon as Joseph **a** before him, 8011
48: 3 "God Almighty **a** to me at Luz in the land 8011
Ex 3: 2 the angel of the LORD **a** to him in flames 8011
3:16 God of Abraham, Isaac and Jacob—**a** to me 8011
4: 5 the God of Jacob—*has* **a** to you." 8011
6: 3 *I* **a** to Abraham, to Isaac and to Jacob 8011
16:14 thin flakes like frost on the ground **a** on 2180
Lev 9:23 the glory of the LORD **a** to all the people. 8011
Nu 14:10 Then the glory of the LORD **a** at the Tent 8011
16:19 of the LORD **a** to the entire assembly. 8011
16:42 and the glory of the LORD **a.** 8011
20: 6 and the glory of the LORD **a** to them. 8011
Dt 31:15 LORD **a** at the Tent in a pillar of cloud, 8011
32:17 not known, gods that recently **a,** 995
Jdg 6:12 When the angel of the LORD **a** to Gideon, 8011
13: 3 The angel of the LORD **a** to her and said, 8011
13:10 The man who **a** to me the other day!" 8011
14:11 When he **a,** he was given thirty companions. 8011
1Ki 3: 5 At Gibeon the LORD **a** to Solomon during 8011
9: 2 the LORD **a** to him a second time, 8011
9: 2 as *he had* **a** to him at Gibeon. 8011
11: 9 the God of Israel, who *had* **a** to him twice. 8011
2Ki 2:11 **suddenly** a chariot of fire and horses of fire
a and separated the two of them, 2180
2Ch 1: 7 That night God **a** to Solomon and said 8011
3: 1 where the LORD *had* **a** to his father David. 8011
7:12 the LORD **a** to him at night and said: 8011
Jer 31: 3 The LORD **a** to us in the past, saying: 8011
Eze 1:16 Each **a** to be made like a wheel intersecting 5260
1:27 from *what* **a** to be his waist up he looked 5260
8: 2 From *what* **a** to be his waist down he was 5260
37: 8 and flesh **a** on them and skin covered them, 6590
Da 5: 5 the fingers of a human hand **a** and wrote on 10485
8: 1 after the *one that had* already **a** to me. 8011
11: 4 After he *has* **a,** his empire will be broken up 6641
Mt 1:20 of the Lord **a** to him in a dream and said, *5743*
2: 7 from them the exact time the star *had* **a.** *5743*
2:13 of the Lord **a** to Joseph in a dream. *5743*
2:19 of the Lord **a** in a dream to Joseph in Egypt *5743*
13:26 then the weeds also **a.** *5743*
17: 3 then *there* **a** before them Moses and Elijah, *3972*
27:53 into the holy city and **a** to many people. *1872*
Mk 9: 4 And *there* **a** before them Elijah and Moses, *3972*
9: 7 Then a cloud **a** and enveloped them, *1181*
14:43 Judas, one of the Twelve, **a.** *4134*
16: 9 *he* **a** first to Mary Magdalene, *5743*
16:12 Afterward Jesus **a** in a different form *5746*
16:14 Later Jesus **a** to the Eleven *5746*
Lk 1:11 Then an angel of the Lord **a** to him, *3972*
1:80 in the desert until he **a publicly** to Israel. *345*
2: 9 An angel of the Lord **a** to them, *2392*
2:13 a great company of the heavenly host **a** *1181*
7:16 "A great prophet *has* **a** among us," *1586*
9: 8 others that Elijah *had* **a,** *5743*
9:31 **a** in glorious splendor, *3972*
9:34 a cloud **a** and enveloped them, *1181*
22:43 An angel from heaven **a** to him *3972*
24:34 The Lord has risen and *has* **a** to Simon." *3972*
Jn 8: 2 At dawn *he* **a** again in the temple courts, *4134*
21: 1 Jesus **a** again to his disciples, *1571+5746*
21:14 now the third time Jesus **a** to his disciples *5746*
Ac 1: 3 *He* **a** to them over a period of forty days *3964*
5:36 Some time ago Theudas **a,** *482*
5:37 the Galilean **a** in the days of the census *482*
7: 2 The God of glory **a** to our father Abraham *3972*
7:30 an angel **a** to Moses in the flames of *3972*
7:35 through the angel who **a** to him in the bush. *3972*
8:40 however, **a** at Azotus and traveled about, *2351*
9:17 Jesus, who **a** to you on the road *3972*
12: 7 an angel of the Lord **a** and a light shone in *2392*
25: 2 **a** before him **and presented the charges** *1872*
25: 7 *When* Paul **a,** the Jews who had come down *4134*
26:16 *I have* **a** to you to appoint you as a servant *3972*
27:20 *When* neither sun nor stars **a** for many days *2210*
1Co 15: 5 and that *he* **a** to Peter, *3972*
15: 6 *he* **a** to more than five hundred of *3972*
15: 7 Then *he* **a** to James, then to all the apostles, *3972*
15: 8 and last of all *he* **a** to me also, *3972*
1Ti 3:16 He **a** in a body, was vindicated by the Spirit, *5746*
Tit 2:11 the grace of God that brings salvation *has* **a** *2210*
3: 4 the kindness and love of God our Savior **a,** *2210*
Heb 9:26 But now *he has* **a** once for all at the end of *5746*
1Jn 1: 2 The life **a;** we have seen it *5746*
1: 2 which was with the Father and *has* **a** to us. *5746*
3: 5 But you know that he **a** so *5746*
3: 8 The reason the Son of God **a** was to destroy *5746*
Rev 12: 1 A great and wondrous sign **a** in heaven: *3972*
12: 3 Then another sign **a** in heaven: *3972*

APPEARING (9) [APPEAR]

Ex 16:10 and there was the glory of the LORD **a** in 8011
Ps 21: 9 the time of your **a** you will make them like 7156
Zec 5: 5 "Look up and see what this is that *is* **a.**" 3655
Jn 8:13 **a** as your own **witness;** *3455*
1Ti 6:14 until the **a** of our Lord Jesus Christ, *2211*
2Ti 1:10 but it has now been revealed through the **a** *2211*
4: 1 and in view of his **a** and his kingdom, *2211*
4: 8 but also to all who have longed for his **a.** *2211*
Tit 2:13 the glorious **a** of our great God and Savior, *2211*

APPEARS (24) [APPEAR]

Ge 9:14 the earth and the rainbow **a** in the clouds, 8011
9:16 Whenever the rainbow **a** in the clouds, 2118
Lev 13: 3 the sore has turned white and the sore **a** to 5260
13:14 But whenever raw flesh **a** on him, 8011
13:19 a white swelling or reddish-white spot **a,** 2118
13:20 and if it **a** to be more than skin deep and 5260
13:24 or white spot **a** in the raw flesh of the burn, 2118
13:25 and it **a** to be more than skin deep, 5260
13:30 and if it **a** to be more than skin deep and 5260
13:34 and if it has not spread in the skin and **a** to 5260
Dt 13: 1 **a** among you and announces to you 7756
Ps 84: 7 till *each* **a** before God in Zion. 8011
Pr 27:25 the hay is removed and new growth **a** and 8011
SS 6:10 Who is this that **a** like the dawn, 9207
Isa 16:12 When Moab **a** at her high place, 8011
60: 2 the LORD rises upon you and his glory **a** 8011
Na 3:17 but when the sun **a** they fly away, 2436
Mal 3: 2 Who can stand when he **a?** 8011
Col 3: 4 When Christ, who is your life, **a,** *5746*
Heb 7:15 if another priest like Melchizedek **a,** *482*
Jas 4:14 You are a mist that **a** for a little while and *5743*
1Pe 5: 4 And *when* the Chief Shepherd **a,** *5746*
1Jn 2:28 so that when *he* **a** we may be confident *5746*
3: 2 But we know that when *he* **a,** *5746*

APPEASE (2)

Pr 16:14 but a wise man *will* **a** it. 4105
Ac 16:39 They came *to* **a** them and escorted them *4151*

APPERTAIN (KJV) See DUE

APPETITE (6) [APPETITES]

Nu 11: 6 But now we have lost our **a;** 5883
Pr 16:26 The laborer's **a** works for him; 5883
Ecc 6: 7 yet his **a** is never satisfied. 5883
6: 9 the eye sees than the roving of the **a.** 5883
Isa 5:14 the grave enlarges its **a** and opens its mouth 5883
Jer 50:19 his **a** will be satisfied on the hills 5883

APPETITES (2) [APPETITE]

Isa 56:11 They are dogs with mighty **a;** 5883
Ro 16:18 but their own **a.** *3120*

APPHIA (1)

Phm 1: 2 *to* **A** our sister, *722*

APPII (KJV) See APPIUS

APPIUS (1)

Ac 28:15 and they traveled as far as the Forum *of* **A** *716*

APPLE (7) [APPLES]

Dt 32:10 he guarded him as the **a** *of* his eye, 413
Ps 17: 8 Keep me as the **a** *of* your eye; 413+1426
Pr 7: 2 guard my teachings as the **a** *of* your eye. 413
SS 2: 3 Like an **a tree** among the trees of 9515
8: 5 Under the **a tree** I roused you; 9515
Joel 1:12 the pomegranate, the palm and the **a tree—** 9515
Zec 2: 8 for whoever touches you touches the **a** 949

APPLES (3) [APPLE]

Pr 25:11 A word aptly spoken is like **a** *of* gold 9515
SS 2: 5 refresh me with **a,** for I am faint with love. 9515
7: 8 the fragrance of your breath like **a,** 9515

APPLIED (7) [APPLY]

2Ki 20: 7 They did so and **a** it to the boil, 8492
Pr 24:32 I **a** my heart *to* what I observed 8883
Ecc 1:17 Then *I* **a** myself to the understanding 5989
8: 9 as I **a** my mind to everything done under 5989
8:16 When *I* **a** my mind to know wisdom and 5989
Da 4:19 if only the dream **a to** your enemies 10378
1Co 4: 6 *I have* **a** these things to myself *3571*

APPLIES (6) [APPLY]

Ex 12:49 The same law **a** to the native-born and to 2118
21:31 also **a** if the bull gores a son or daughter. 6913
Lev 7: 7 " 'The same law **a to** both the sin offering 4200
Nu 8:24 "This **a to** the Levites: 4200
15:29 One and the same law **a** 2118
19:14 the law that **a** when a person dies in a tent: NIH

APPLY (6) [APPLIED, APPLIES, APPLYING]

Nu 5:30 the LORD and *is to* **a** this entire law 6913
15:16 The same laws and regulations *will* **a** both 2118
Job 5:27 So hear it and **a** it to yourself." 3359
Pr 22:17 **a** your heart to what I teach, 8883
23:12 **A** your heart to instruction and your ears 995
Isa 38:21 "Prepare a poultice of figs and **a** it to 5302

APPLYING (2) [APPLY]

Pr 2: 2 and **a** your heart to understanding, 5742
Heb 9:10 external regulations **a** until the time of *2130*

APPOINT (31) [APPOINTED, APPOINTING, APPOINTMENT, APPOINTS]

Ge 41:34 *Let* Pharaoh **a** commissioners over 7212
Ex 18:21 and **a** them as officials over thousands, 8492
Nu 1:50 **a** the Levites to be in charge of 7212
3:10 **A** Aaron and his sons to serve as priests; 7212
27:16 **a** a man over this community 7212
34:18 And **a** one leader from each tribe 4374
Dt 16:18 **A** judges and officials for each 5989
17:15 **be sure to a** over you the king 8492+8492
20: 9 *they shall* **a** commanders over it. 7212
Jos 18: 4 **A** three men from each tribe. 2035
1Sa 2:36 "**A** me to some priestly office 6202
8: 5 now **a** a king to lead us, 8492
2Ki 10: 5 *We will* not **a** anyone **as king;** 4887
1Ch 15:16 the leaders of the Levites to **a** their brothers 6641
Ezr 7:25 **a** magistrates and judges 10431
Ne 7: 3 Also **a** residents of Jerusalem as guards, 6641
Est 2: 3 the king **a** commissioners in every province 7212
Ps 61: 7 **a** your love and faithfulness to protect him. 4948
89:27 I *will* also **a** him my firstborn, 5989
109: 6 **A** an evil man to oppose him; 7212
Jer 1:10 today *I* **a** you over nations and kingdoms 7212
23:32 yet I did not send or **a** them. 7422
49:19 Who is the chosen one *I will* **a** for this? 7212
50:44 Who is the chosen one *I will* **a** for this? 7212
51:27 **A** a commander against her; 7212
Da 6: 1 It pleased Darius *to* **a** 120 satraps to rule 10624
Hos 1:11 and *they will* **a** one leader and will come 8492
Ac 26:16 I have appeared to you to **a** you as a servant *4741*
1Co 6: 4 **a as judges** even men of little account in *2767*
1Th 5: 9 For God *did* not **a** us to suffer wrath but *5502*
Tit 1: 5 and **a** elders in every town, *2770*

APPOINTED (150) [APPOINT]

Ge 18:14 at the **a** time next year and Sarah will have 4595
Ex 5:14 The Israelite foremen **a** by Pharaoh's slave 8492
13:10 at the **a time** year after year. 4595
23:15 Do this at the **a time** in the month of Abib, 4595
31: 6 I *have* **a** Oholiab son of Ahisamach, 5989
34:18 Do this at the **a time** *in* the month of Abib, 4595
Lev 16:21 in the care of a man **a for the task.** 6967
23: 2 'These are my **a feasts,** 4595
23: 2 the **a feasts** *of* the LORD, 4595
23: 4 " 'These are the LORD's **a feasts,** 4595
23: 4 to proclaim at their **a times:** 4595
23:37 (" 'These are the LORD's **a feasts,** 4595
23:44 to the Israelites the **a feasts** *of* the LORD. 4595
Nu 1:16 These were the *men* **a** *from* the community, 7924
3:32 He was **a** *over* those who were responsible 7213
3:36 The Merarites were **a** *to* take care of 7213
9: 2 the Passover at the **a time.** 4595
9: 3 Celebrate it at the **a time,** 4595
9: 7 with the other Israelites at the **a time?"** 4595
9:13 the LORD's offering at the **a time.** 4595
10:10 your **a feasts** and New Moon festivals— 4595
16: 2 well-known community leaders *who* had
been **a** *members* 7951
28: 2 that you present to me at the **a time** the food 4595
29:39 for the LORD at your **a feasts:** 4595
Dt 1:15 and **a** them to have authority over you— 5989
Jos 4: 4 the twelve men *he had* **a** from the Israelites, 3922
1Sa 8: 1 *he* **a** his sons as judges for Israel. 8492
12: 6 "It is the LORD who **a** Moses and Aaron 6913
13:14 a man after his own heart and **a** him leader 7422
25:30 concerning him and *has* **a** him leader 7422
2Sa 6:21 from his house when he **a** me ruler over 7422
7:11 the time *I* **a** leaders over my people Israel. 7422
15: 4 "If only I *were* **a** judge in the land! 8492
17:25 Absalom *had* **a** Amasa over the army 8492
18: 1 and **a** over them commanders of thousands 8492
1Ki 1:35 *I have* **a** him ruler over Israel and Judah." 7422
12:31 on high places and **a** priests from all sorts 6913
13:33 but once more **a** priests for the high places 6913
2Ki 12:11 to the *men* **a** to supervise the work on 7212
17:32 but *they* also **a** all sorts of their own people 6913
22: 5 to the *men* **a** to supervise the work on 7212
23: 5 the pagan priests **a** *by* the kings of Judah 5989
25:22 of Babylon **a** Gedaliah son of Ahikam, 7212
25:23 **a** Gedaliah **as governor,** 7212
1Ch 15:17 So the Levites **a** Heman son of Joel; 6641
16: 4 *He* **a** some of the Levites to minister before 5989
17:10 the time *I* **a** leaders over my people Israel. 7422
22: 2 and from among them *he* **a** stonecutters 6641
23:31 and at New Moon festivals and at **a feasts.** 4595
24: 3 for their **a order** of ministering. 7213
24:19 This was their **a order** of ministering 7213
26:10 his father *had* **a** him the first), 8492
2Ch 2: 4 and at the **a feasts** *of* the LORD our God. 4595
8:14 *he* **a** the divisions of the priests 6641
8:14 He also **a** the gatekeepers by divisions for NIH
11:15 And *he* **a** his own priests for the high places 6641
11:22 Rehoboam **a** Abijah son of Maacah to be 6641
19: 5 *He* **a** judges in the land, 6641
19: 8 Jehoshaphat **a** some of the Levites, 6641
20:21 Jehoshaphat **a** men to sing to the LORD 6641
25:16 *"Have we* **a** you an adviser to the king? 5989
31: 3 New Moons and **a feasts** as written in 4595
32: 6 *He* **a** military officers over the people 5989
34:10 to the *men* **a** to supervise the work on 7212

2Ch 35: 2 *He* **a** the priests to their duties 6641
36:23 the earth and he *has* **a** me to build a temple 7212
Ezr 1: 2 the earth and he *has* **a** me to build a temple 7212
3: 5 and the sacrifices for all the **a** sacred **feasts** 4595
5:14 whom *he had* **a** governor, 10682
Ne 5:14 when I *was* **a** to be their governor in 7422
6: 7 even **a** prophets to make this proclamation 6641
7: 1 and the singers and the Levites **were a.** 7212
9:17 and in their rebellion **a** a leader in order 5989
10:33 New Moon festivals and **a feasts;** 4595
12:44 At that time men **were a** to be in charge of 7212
Est 8: 2 And Esther **a** him over Haman's estate. 8492
8:12 The day **a** for the Jews to do this in all 285
9:27 in the way prescribed and at the **time a.** 2375
Job 20:29 the heritage **a** *for* them by God." 609
30:23 to the place **a** for all the living. 4595
34:13 Who **a** him over the earth? 7212
Ps 75: 2 You say, "I choose the **a time;** 4595
102:13 the **a time** has come. 4595
Pr 8:23 *I* **was a** from eternity, 5820
Isa 1:14 and your **a feasts** my soul hates. 4595
Jer 1: 5 *I* **a** you as a prophet to the nations." 5989
6:17 *I* **a** watchmen over you and said, 7756
8: 7 the stork in the sky knows her **a seasons,** 4595
14:14 not sent them or **a** them or spoken to them. 7422
29:26 'The LORD *has* **a** you priest in place 5989
33:20 and night no longer come at their **a time,** 6961
40: 5 of Babylon *has* **a** over the towns of Judah, 7212
40: 7 **a** Gedaliah son of Ahikam **as governor** 7212
40:11 **a** Gedaliah son of Ahikam, the son of Shaphan, **as governor** 7212
41: 2 king of Babylon *had* **a as governor** over 7212
41:10 of the imperial guard *had* **a** Gedaliah son 7212
41:18 king of Babylon *had* **a as governor** over 7212
La 1: 4 for no one comes to her **a feasts.** 4595
2: 6 LORD has made Zion forget her **a feasts** 4595
2: 7 of the LORD as on the day of an **a feast.** 4595
Eze 21:11 " 'The sword *is* **a** to be polished, 5989
36:38 at Jerusalem during her **a feasts.** 4595
44:24 and my decrees for all my **a feasts,** 4595
45:17 at all the **a feasts** *of* the house of Israel. 4595
46: 9 the LORD at the **a feasts,** whoever enters 4595
46:11 " 'At the festivals and the **a feasts,** 4595
Da 1:11 to the guard whom the chief official *had* **a** 4948
2:24 the king *had* **a** to execute the wise men 10431
2:49 at Daniel's request the king **a** Shadrach, 10431
5:11 **a** him chief of the magicians, enchanters, 10624
8:19 the vision concerns the **a time** *of* the end. 4595
11:27 because an end will still come at the **a time.** 4595
11:29 the **a time** he will invade the South again, 4595
11:35 for it will still come at the **a time.** 4595
Hos 2:11 her Sabbath days—all her **a feasts.** 4595
6:11 "Also for you, Judah, a harvest *is* **a.** 8883
9: 5 on the day of your **a feasts,** 4595
12: 9 as in the days of your **a feasts.** 4595
Mic 6: 9 "Heed the rod and the One who **a** it. 3585
Hab 1:12 *you have* **a** them to execute judgment; 8492
2: 3 For the revelation awaits an **a time;** 4595
Zep 2: 2 the **a time** arrives and that day sweeps on 2976
3:18 "The sorrows for the **a feasts** I will remove 4595
Mt 8:29 to torture us before the **a** time?" *NIG*
26:18 My **a** time is near. *NIG*
Mk 3:14 *He* **a** twelve—designating them apostles— *4472*
3:16 These are the twelve *he* **a**: *4472*
Lk 10: 1 After this the Lord **a** seventy-two others *344*
12:14 who **a** me a judge or an arbiter *2770*
19:12 to a distant country *to have* himself **a** king *3284*
Jn 15:16 and **a** you to go and bear fruit— *5502*
Ac 3:20 *who has been* **a** for you—even Jesus. *4741*
10:42 the one whom God **a** as judge of the living *3988*
12:21 *On* the **a** day Herod, *5414*
13:48 and all who were **a** for eternal life believed. *5435*
14:23 Paul and Barnabas **a** elders for them *5936*
15: 2 So Paul and Barnabas *were* **a**, *5435*
17:31 the world with justice by the man *he has* **a.** *3988*
Ro 9: 9 "At the **a** time I will return, *4047*
1Co 4: 5 Therefore judge nothing before the **a** time; *NIG*
12:28 in the church God *has* **a** first of all apostles, *5502*
Eph 1:22 and **a** him *to be* head over everything for *1443*
1Ti 2: 7 And for this purpose I *was* **a** a herald and *5502*
2Ti 1:11 And of this gospel I *was* **a** a herald and *5502*
Tit 1: 3 at his **a season** he brought his word to light *2789*
Heb 1: 2 whom *he* **a** heir of all things, *5502*
3: 2 He was faithful *to* the one who **a** him, *4472*
5: 1 among men and *is* **a** to represent them *2770*
7:28 which came after the law, **a** the Son, *NIG*
8: 3 Every high priest *is* **a** to offer both gifts *2770*

APPOINTING (2) [APPOINT]

Ezr 3: 8 **a** Levites twenty years of age and older 6641
1Ti 1:12 considered me faithful, **a** me to his service. *5502*

APPOINTMENT (1) [APPOINT]

2Ch 31:13 by **a** *of* King Hezekiah and Azariah 5152

APPOINTS (2) [APPOINT]

Jer 31:35 *he who* **a** the sun to shine by day, 5989
Heb 7:28 law **a** as high priests men who are weak; *2770*

APPORTIONED (2) [PORTION]

Dt 4:19 the LORD your God *has* **a** to all 2745
Eph 4: 7 of us grace has been given as Christ **a** it. *3586*

APPRAISED (1)

Job 28:27 then he looked at wisdom and **a** it; 6218

APPREHEND (KJV) See ARREST, TAKE, TOOK

APPREHENSIVE (1)

Lk 21:26 **a** of what is coming on the world, *4660*

APPROACH (21) [APPROACHED, APPROACHES, APPROACHING]

Ex 19:22 Even the priests, who **a** the LORD, 5602
24: 2 but Moses alone *is to* **a** the LORD; 5602
28:43 or **a** the altar to minister in the Holy Place, 5602
30:20 when they **a** the altar to minister 5602
Lev 10: 3 " 'Among *those who* **a** me I will show myself holy; 7940
18: 6 " 'No one *is to* **a** any close relative 7928
18:19 not **a** a woman to have sexual relations 7928
21:23 not go near the curtain or **a** the altar, 5602
1Sa 10: 5 As you **a** the town, 995
Job 31:37 like a prince *I would* **a** him.)— 7928
36:33 even the cattle make known *its* **a.** 6590
40:19 yet his Maker *can* **a** him with his sword. 5602
41:13 Who *would* **a** him with a bridle? 995
Ecc 12: 1 the days of trouble come and the years **a** 5595
Isa 5:19 *Let it* **a**, let the plan of the Holy One 7928
41: 5 *They* **a** and come forward; 7928
La 2: 3 He has withdrawn his right hand at the **a** *of* 7156
Eze 42:13 where the priests who **a** the LORD will eat 7940
Hos 7: 6 *they* **a** him with intrigue. 7928
Eph 3:12 through faith in him *we may* **a** God *2400+4643*
Heb 4:16 then **a** the throne of grace with confidence, *4665*

APPROACHED (45) [APPROACH]

Ge 18:23 Then Abraham **a** him and said: 5602
33: 3 the ground seven times as he **a** his brother. 5602
33: 6 Then the maidservants and their children **a** 5602
Ex 14:10 As Pharaoh **a**, the Israelites looked up, 7928
20:21 while Moses **a** the thick darkness 5602
32:19 When Moses **a** the camp and saw the calf 7928
40:32 the Tent of Meeting or **a** the altar, 7928
Lev 16: 1 two sons of Aaron who died when they **a** 7928
Nu 3:38 Anyone else who **a** the sanctuary was to 7929
27: 1 Milcah and Tirzah. *They* **a** 7928
Dt 22:14 "I married this woman, but when *I* **a** her, 7928
Jos 8:11 up and **a** the city and arrived in front of it. 5602
14: 6 Now the men of Judah **a** Joshua at Gilgal, 5602
21: 1 the family heads of the Levites **a** Eleazar 5602
Jdg 3:20 Ehud then **a** him while he was sitting alone 448+995
9:52 *as he* **a** the entrance to the tower to set it 5602
14: 5 As *they* **a** the vineyards of Timnah, 995+6330
15:14 As *he* **a** Lehi, the Philistines came 995+6330
Ru 3: 7 Ruth **a** quietly, uncovered his feet 995
1Sa 9:18 Saul **a** Samuel in the gateway and asked, 5602
17:40 with his sling in his hand, **a** the Philistine. 5602
30:21 As David and his men **a**, he greeted them. 5602
2Sa 15: 5 whenever anyone **a** him to bow down 7928
16: 5 As King David **a** Bahurim, 995+6330
2Ki 16:12 he **a** it and presented offerings on it. 7928
1Ch 21:21 David **a**, and when Araunah looked 995+6330
Est 5: 2 Esther **a** and touched the tip of the scepter. 7928
Jer 42: 1 the people from the least to the greatest **a** 5602
Da 3:26 then **a** the opening of the blazing furnace 10638
7:13 *He* **a** the Ancient of Days and was led 10413
7:16 *I* **a** one of those standing there 10638
Mt 14:15 *As* evening **a**, the disciples came to him *1181*
17:14 a man **a** Jesus and knelt before him. *4665*
21: 1 As *they* **a** Jerusalem and came *1581*
21:34 When the harvest time **a**, *1581*
27:57 *As* evening **a**, there came a rich man *1181*
Mk 11: 1 As *they* **a** Jerusalem and came *1581*
15:42 So *as* evening **a**, *1181*
Lk 7:12 As *he* **a** the town gate, *1581*
9:51 the time **a** for him to be taken up to heaven, *5230*
18:35 As Jesus **a** Jericho, a blind man was sitting *1581*
19:29 As *he* **a** Bethphage and Bethany at *1581*
19:41 As *he* **a** Jerusalem and saw the city, *1581*
22:47 *He* **a** Jesus to kiss him, *1581*
24:28 As *they* **a** the village *1581*

APPROACHES (5) [APPROACH]

Lev 20:16 " 'If a woman **a** an animal 7928
Nu 3:10 anyone else who **a** the sanctuary must 7929
Dt 23:11 But as evening **a** he is to wash himself, 7155
2Ki 11: 8 Anyone *who* **a** your ranks must be put 448+995
Est 4:11 woman who **a** the king in the inner court 448+995

APPROACHING (10) [APPROACH]

Ge 24:63 and as he looked up, he saw camels **a.** 995
Lev 18:14 by **a** his wife to have sexual relations; 7928
2Ki 9:17 on the tower in Jezreel saw Jehu's troops **a,** 995
Lk 22: 1 called the Passover, *was* **a,** *1581*
Jn 1:47 *When* Jesus saw Nathanael **a,** *2262+4639*
6:19 they saw Jesus **a** the boat, *1181+1584*
Ac 10: 9 as they were on their journey and **a** *1581*
27:27 the sailors sensed they *were* **a** land. *4642*
Heb 10:25 and all the more as you see the Day **a.** *1581*
1Jn 5:14 This is the confidence we have **in a** God: *4639*

APPROPRIATE (2)

Ge 49:28 giving each the blessing **a** *to* him. 3869
1Ti 2:10 **a** for women who profess to worship God. *4560*

APPROVAL (8) [APPROVE]

Jdg 18: 6 Your journey has the LORD's **a."** 5790
Est 2:17 and she won his favor and **a** more than any 2876
Hos 8: 4 they choose princes without *my* **a.** 3359
Jn 6:27 the Father has placed his seal of **a."** *NIG*
Ac 8: 1 And Saul was there, **giving a** to his death. *5306*
22:20 I stood there **giving** my **a** and guarding *5306*
1Co 11:19 to show which of you have God's **a.** *1511*
Gal 1:10 **trying to win the a of** *4275*

APPROVE (7) [APPROVAL, APPROVED, APPROVES]

1Sa 29: 6 but the rulers don't **a of** you. 928+3202+6524
Ps 49:13 and of their followers, *who* **a** their sayings. 8354
Lk 11:48 that *you* **a of** what your forefathers did; *5306*
Ro 1:32 but also **a of** those who practice them. *5306*
2:18 if you know his will and **a of** *1507*
12: 2 be able *to* **test and a** what God's will is— *1507*
1Co 16: 3 of introduction to the men *you* **a** *1507*

APPROVED (5) [APPROVE]

Ro 14:18 in this way is pleasing to God and **a** *1511*
16:10 Greet Apelles, **tested and a** in Christ. *1511*
2Co 10:18 the one who commends himself who is **a,** *1511*
1Th 2: 4 we speak as men **a** by God to be entrusted *1507*
2Ti 2:15 to present yourself to God as one **a,** *1511*

APPROVES (1) [APPROVE]

Ro 14:22 not condemn himself by what *he* **a.** *1507*

APRONS (1)

Ac 19:12 and **a** that had touched him were taken to *4980*

APT (1) [APTITUDE, APTLY]

Pr 15:23 A man finds joy in **giving an a reply** 5101+7023

APTITUDE (1) [APT]

Da 1: 4 **showing a** for every kind of learning, 8505

APTLY (1) [APT]

Pr 25:11 A word **a** spoken is like apples of gold 698+6584

AQUEDUCT (3)

2Ki 18:17 and stopped at the **a** *of* the Upper Pool, 9498
Isa 7: 3 at the end of the **a** *of* the Upper Pool, 9498
36: 2 When the commander stopped at the **a** *of* 9498

AQUILA (7)

Ac 18: 2 There he met a Jew named **A,** *217*
18:18 accompanied by Priscilla and **A.** *217*
18:19 where Paul left **Priscilla and A.** *1697S*
18:26 When Priscilla and **A** heard him, *217*
Ro 16: 3 Greet Priscilla and **A,** *217*
1Co 16:19 **A** and Priscilla greet you warmly in *217*
2Ti 4:19 and **A** and the household of Onesiphorus. *217*

AR (6)

Nu 21:15 the ravines that lead to the site of **A** and lie 6840
21:28 It consumed **A** *of* Moab, 6840
Dt 2: 9 I have given **A** to the descendants of Lot as 6840
2:18 to pass by the region of Moab at **A.** 6840
2:29 and the Moabites, who live in **A,** 6840
Isa 15: 1 **A** *in* Moab is ruined, destroyed in a night! 6840

ARA (1)

1Ch 7:38 Jephunneh, Pispah and **A.** 736

ARAB (4) [ARABIA, ARABIAN, ARABS]

Jos 15:52 **A,** Dumah, Eshan, 742
Ne 2:19 and Geshem the **A** heard about it, 6861
6: 1 Geshem the **A** and the rest of our enemies 6861
Isa 13:20 no **A** will pitch his tent there, 6862

ARABAH (28) [BETH ARABAH]

Dt 1: 1 east of the Jordan—that is, in the **A**— 6858
1: 7 go to all the neighboring peoples in the **A,** 6858
2: 8 We turned from the **A** road, 6858
3:17 Its western border was the Jordan in the **A,** 6858
3:17 from Kinnereth to the Sea of the **A** 6858
4:49 and included all the **A** east of the Jordan, 6858
4:49 as far as the Sea of the **A,** 6858
11:30 of those Canaanites living in the **A** in 6858
Jos 3:16 the **A** (the Salt Sea) was completely cut off. 6858
8:14 at a certain place overlooking the **A.** 6858
11: 2 in the **A** south of Kinnereth, 6858
11:16 of Goshen, the western foothills, the **A** and 6858
12: 1 including all the eastern side of the **A**: 6858
12: 3 the eastern **A** from the Sea of Kinnereth to 6858
12: 3 the Sea of Kinnereth to the Sea of the **A** 6858
12: 8 the western foothills, the **A,** 6858
18:18 of Beth Arabah and on down into the **A.** 6858
1Sa 23:24 in the **A** south of Jeshimon. 6858
2Sa 2:29 and his men marched through the **A.** 6858

2Sa 4: 7 they traveled all night by way of the **A.** 6858
2Ki 14:25 from Lebo Hamath to the Sea of the **A,** 6858
25: 4 They fled toward the **A,** 6858
Isa 33: 9 Sharon is like the **A,** 6858
Jer 39: 4 and headed toward the **A.** 6858
52: 7 They fled toward the **A,** 6858
Eze 47: 8 and goes down into the **A,** 6858
Am 6:14 from Lebo Hamath to the valley of the **A.**" 6858
Zec 14:10 south of Jerusalem, will become like the **A.** 6858

ARABIA (8) [ARAB]

2Ch 9:14 Also all the kings of **A** and the governors of 6851
Isa 21:13 An oracle concerning **A:** 6851
21:13 who camp in the thickets of **A,** 6851
Jer 25:24 all the kings of **A** and all the kings of 6851
Eze 27:21 " '**A** and all the princes 6851
30: 5 Cush and Put, Lydia and all **A,** 6851
Gal 1:17 into **A** and later returned to Damascus. *728*
4:25 for Mount Sinai in **A** and corresponds to *728*

ARABIAN (1) [ARAB]

1Ki 10:15 and from all the **A** kings and the governors 6851

ARABS (6) [ARAB]

2Ch 17:11 and the **A** brought him flocks: 6861
21:16 the Philistines and of the **A** who lived near 6861
22: 1 who came with the **A** into the camp, 6861
26: 7 the Philistines and against the **A** who lived 6861
Ne 4: 7 But when Sanballat, Tobiah, the **A,** 6861
Ac 2:11 to Judaism); Cretans and **A**— *732*

ARAD (5)

Nu 21: 1 When the Canaanite king of **A,** 6866
33:40 The Canaanite king of **A,** 6866
Jos 12:14 the king of Hormah one the king of **A** one 6866
Jdg 1:16 of the Desert of Judah in the Negev near **A.** 6866
1Ch 8:15 Zebadiah, **A,** Eder, 6865

ARAH (5)

Jos 13: 4 from **A** of the Sidonians as far as Aphek, 6869
1Ch 7:39 The sons of Ulla: **A,** Hanniel and Rizia. 783
Ezr 2: 5 of **A** 775 783
Ne 6:18 he was son-in-law to Shecaniah son of **A,** 783
7:10 of **A** 652 783

ARAM (69) [ARAM MAACAH, ARAM NAHARAIM, ARAM ZOBAH, ARAMAIC, ARAMEAN, ARAMEANS, PADDAN ARAM]

Ge 10:22 Elam, Asshur, Arphaxad, Lud and **A.** 806
10:23 The sons of **A:** Uz, Hul, Gether and 806
22:21 Buz his brother, Kemuel (the father of **A**), 806
Nu 23: 7 "Balak brought me from **A,** 806
Jdg 3:10 of **A** into the hands of Othniel, 806
10: 6 and the gods of **A,** the gods of Sidon, 806
2Sa 15: 8 at Geshur in **A,** I made this vow: 806
1Ki 11:25 So Rezon ruled in **A** and was hostile 806
15:18 the son of Hezion, the king of **A,** 806
19:15 you get there, anoint Hazael king over **A.** 806
20: 1 of **A** mustered his entire army. 806
20:20 of **A** escaped on horseback with some 806
20:22 the king of **A** will attack you again." 806
20:23 the officials of the king of **A** advised him, 806
22: 1 For three years there was no war between **A** 806
22: 3 to retake it from the king of **A?**" 806
22:31 the king of **A** had ordered his thirty-two chariot commanders, 806
2Ki 5: 1 of the army of the king of **A.** 806
5: 1 the LORD had given victory to **A.** 806
5: 2 from **A** had gone out and had taken captive 806
5: 5 "By all means, go," the king of **A** replied. 806
6: 8 Now the king of **A** was at war with Israel. 806
6:11 This enraged the king of **A.** 806
6:23 from **A** stopped raiding Israel's territory. 806
6:24 of **A** mobilized his entire army 806
8: 7 and Ben-Hadad king of **A** was ill. 806
8: 9 of **A** has sent me to ask, 806
8:13 that you will become king of **A,**" 806
8:28 against Hazael king of **A** at Ramoth Gilead. 806
8:29 in his battle with Hazael king of **A.** 806
9:14 against Hazael king of **A,** 806
9:15 in the battle with Hazael king of **A.**) 806
12:17 About this time Hazael king of **A** went up 806
12:18 and he sent them to Hazael king of **A,** 806
13: 3 under the power of Hazael king of **A** 806
13: 4 the king of **A** was oppressing Israel. 806
13: 5 and they escaped from the power of **A.** 806
13: 7 of **A** had destroyed the rest and made them 806
13:17 the arrow of victory over **A!**" 806
13:19 then you would have defeated **A** 806
13:22 of **A** oppressed Israel throughout the reign 806
13:24 Hazael king of **A** died, 806
15:37 the LORD began to send Rezin king of **A** 806
16: 5 of **A** and Pekah son of Remaliah king 806
16: 6 Rezin king of **A** recovered Elath for Aram 806
16: 6 Rezin king of Aram recovered Elath for **A** 806
16: 7 of the hand of the king of **A** and of the king 806
1Ch 1:17 Elam, Asshur, Arphaxad, Lud and **A.** 806
1:17 The sons of **A:** 806
2:23 (But Geshur and **A** captured Havvoth Jair, 806
7:34 Ahi, Rohgah, Hubbah and **A.** 806
2Ch 16: 2 and sent it to Ben-Hadad king of **A,** 806
16: 7 "Because you relied on the king of **A** and 806
16: 7 the king of **A** has escaped from your hand. 806
18:30 of **A** had ordered his chariot commanders, 806
22: 5 against Hazael king of **A** at Ramoth Gilead. 806
22: 6 in his battle with Hazael king of **A.** 806
24:23 the army of **A** marched against Joash; 806
28: 5 over to the king of **A.** 806
28:23 gods of the kings of **A** have helped them, 806
Isa 7: 1 of **A** and Pekah son of Remaliah king 806
7: 2 "**A** has allied itself with Ephraim"; 806
7: 4 of Rezin and **A** and of the son of Remaliah. 806
7: 5 **A,** Ephraim and Remaliah's son have plotted your ruin, 806
7: 8 for the head of **A** is Damascus, 806
17: 3 of **A** will be like the glory of the Israelites," 806
Eze 27:16 " '**A** did business with you because 806
Hos 12:12 Jacob fled to the country of **A;** 806
Am 1: 5 The people of **A** will go into exile to Kir," 806

ARAM MAACAH (1) [ABEL BETH MAACAH, ARAM, MAACAH]

1Ch 19: 6 Aram Naharaim, **A** and Zobah. 807

ARAM NAHARAIM (5) [ARAM]

Ge 24:10 for **A** and made his way to 808
Dt 23: 4 from Pethor in **A** to pronounce 808
Jdg 3: 8 Cushan-Rishathaim king of **A,** to whom 808
1Ch 19: 6 chariots and charioteers from **A,** 808
Ps 60: T he fought **A** and Aram Zobah, 808

ARAM ZOBAH (1) [ARAM, ZOBAH]

Ps 60: T he fought Aram Naharaim and **A,** 809

ARAMAIC (13) [ARAM]

2Ki 18:26 "Please speak to your servants **in A,** 811
Ezr 4: 7 The letter was written **in A** script and in 811
4: 7 in Aramaic script and **in** the **A** language. 811
Isa 36:11 "Please speak to your servants **in A,** 811
Da 2: 4 the astrologers answered the king **in A,** 811
Jn 5: 2 which **in A** is called Bethesda *1580*
19:13 Stone Pavement (which **in A** is Gabbatha). *1580*
19:17 the Skull (which **in A** is called Golgotha). *1580*
19:20 and the sign was written **in A,** *1580*
20:16 She turned toward him and cried out **in A,** *1580*
Ac 21:40 he said to them **in A:** *1365+1579*
22: 2 they heard him speak to them **in A,** *1365+1579*
26:14 and I heard a voice saying to me **in A,** *1365+1579*

ARAMEAN (17) [ARAM]

Ge 25:20 of Bethuel the **A** from Paddan Aram 812
25:20 and sister of Laban the **A.** 812
28: 5 to Laban son of Bethuel the **A,** 812
31:20 Jacob deceived Laban the **A** by 812
31:24 to Laban the **A** in a dream at night and said 812
Dt 26: 5 "My father was a wandering **A,** 812
2Sa 8: 6 He put garrisons in the **A kingdom** 806
10: 6 they hired twenty thousand **A** foot soldiers 806
1Ki 20:29 on the **A** foot soldiers in one day. 806
2Ki 5:20 on Naaman, this **A,** by not accepting 812
7:10 into the **A** camp and not a man was there— 806
7:14 and the king sent them after the **A** army. 806
24: 2 The LORD sent Babylonian, **A,** 806
1Ch 7:14 through his **A** concubine. 812
18: 6 He put garrisons in the **A kingdom** 806
2Ch 24:24 the **A** army had come with only a few men, 806
Jer 35:11 to escape the Babylonian and **A** armies.' 806

ARAMEANS (48) [ARAM]

2Sa 8: 5 When the **A** *of* Damascus came 806
8: 6 and the **A** became subject to him 806
10: 8 the **A** *of* Zobah and Rehob and the men 806
10: 9 in Israel and deployed them against the **A.** 806
10:11 Joab said, "If the **A** are too strong for me, 806
10:13 with him advanced to fight the **A,** 806
10:14 the Ammonites saw that the **A** were fleeing, 806
10:15 **A** saw that they had been routed by Israel, 806
10:16 Hadadezer had **A** brought from beyond 806
10:17 The **A** formed their battle lines 806
10:19 So the **A** were afraid to help 806
1Ki 10:29 to all the kings of the Hittites and of the **A.** 806
20:20 At that, the **A** fled, 806
20:21 and inflicted heavy losses on the **A.** 806
20:26 The next spring Ben-Hadad mustered the **A** 806
20:27 while the **A** covered the countryside. 806
20:28 the **A** think the LORD is a god of the hills 806
22:11 the **A** until they are destroyed.' " 806
22:35 up in his chariot facing the **A.** 806
2Ki 6: 9 because the **A** are going down there." 806
7: 4 over to the camp of the **A** and surrender. 806
7: 5 up and went to the camp of the **A.** 806
7: 6 for the Lord had caused the **A** to hear 806
7:12 "I will tell you what the **A** have done to us. 806
7:15 and equipment the **A** had thrown away 806
7:16 and plundered the camp of the **A.** 806
8:28 The **A** wounded Joram; 812
8:29 from the wounds the **A** had inflicted on him 812
9:15 from the wounds the **A** had inflicted on him 812
13:17 "You will completely destroy the **A** 806
1Ch 18: 5 When the **A** *of* Damascus came 806
18: 6 and the **A** became subject to him 806
19:10 in Israel and deployed them against the **A.** 806
19:12 Joab said, "If the **A** are too strong for me, 806
19:14 with him advanced to fight the **A,** 806
19:15 the Ammonites saw that the **A** were fleeing, 806
19:16 **A** saw that they had been routed by Israel, 806
19:16 and had **A** brought from beyond the River, 806
19:17 David formed his lines to meet the **A** 806
19:19 So the **A** were not willing to help 806
2Ch 1:17 to all the kings of the Hittites and of the **A.** 806
18:10 the **A** until they are destroyed.' " 806
18:34 up in his chariot facing the **A** until evening. 806
22: 5 The **A** wounded Joram; 812
24:25 When **the A** withdrew, 4392S
28: 5 The **A** defeated him and took many NIH
Isa 9:12 **A** from the east and Philistines from 806
Am 9: 7 the Philistines from Caphtor and the **A** 806

ARAMITESS (KJV) See ARAMEAN

ARAN (2)

Ge 36:28 The sons of Dishan: Uz and **A.** 814
1Ch 1:42 The sons of Dishan: Uz and **A.** 814

ARARAT (4)

Ge 8: 4 the ark came to rest on the mountains of **A.** 827
2Ki 19:37 and they escaped to the land of **A.** 827
Isa 37:38 and they escaped to the land of **A.** 827
Jer 51:27 **A,** Minni and Ashkenaz. 827

ARAUNAH (17)

2Sa 24:16 then at the threshing floor of **A** the Jebusite. 779
24:18 to the LORD on the threshing floor of **A** 779
24:20 When **A** looked and saw the king 779
24:21 **A** said, "Why has my lord the king come 779
24:22 **A** said to David, "Let my lord the king take 779
24:23 O king, **A** gives all this to the king." 779
24:23 **A** also said to him, "May the LORD 779
24:24 But the king replied to **A,** "No, 779
1Ch 21:15 then standing at the threshing floor of **A** 821
21:18 to the LORD on the threshing floor of **A** 821
21:20 While **A** was threshing wheat, 821
21:21 and when **A** looked and saw him, 821
21:23 **A** said to David, "Take it! 821
21:24 But King David replied to **A,** "No, 821
21:25 So David paid **A** six hundred shekels 821
21:28 on the threshing floor of **A** the Jebusite, 821
2Ch 3: 1 on the threshing floor of **A** the Jebusite, 821

ARBA (3) [KIRIATH ARBA]

Jos 14:15 to be called Kiriath Arba after **A,** NIH
15:13 (**A** was the forefather of Anak.) NIH
21:11 (**A** was the forefather of Anak.) NIH

ARBAH (KJV) See KIRIATH ARBA

ARBATHITE (2)

2Sa 23:31 Abi-Albon the **A,** Azmaveth 6863
1Ch 11:32 from the ravines of Gaash, Abiel the **A,** 6863

ARBEL See BETH ARBEL

ARBITE (1)

2Sa 23:35 Hezro the Carmelite, Paarai the **A,** 750

ARBITER (1) [ARBITRATE]

Lk 12:14 who appointed me a judge or an **a** *3537*

ARBITRATE (1) [ARBITER]

Job 9:33 only there were *someone to* **a** between us, 3519

ARCHANGEL (2) [ANGEL]

1Th 4:16 the voice *of* the **a** and with the trumpet call *791*
Jude 1: 9 But even the **a** Michael, *791*

ARCHELAUS (1)

Mt 2:22 when he heard that **A** was reigning in Judea *793*

ARCHER (4) [ARCHERS]

Ge 21:20 He lived in the desert and became an **a** 8009+8050
Pr 26:10 Like an **a** who wounds 8043
Jer 51: 3 Let not the **a** string his bow, 2005
Am 2:15 The **a** will not stand his ground, 8008+9530

ARCHERS (9) [ARCHER]

Ge 49:23 With bitterness **a** attacked him; 1251+2932
1Sa 31: 3 and when the **a** overtook him, 408+928+2021+4619+8008
2Sa 11:24 Then the **a** shot arrows at your servants 4619
1Ch 10: 3 and when the **a** overtook him, 928+2021+4619+8008
2Ch 35:23 **A** shot King Josiah, and he told his officers, 3452
Job 16:13 his **a** surround me. 8043
Isa 66:19 Libyans and Lydians (famous as **a**), 5432+8008
Jer 4:29 of horsemen and **a** every town takes 8008+8227
50:29 "Summon **a** against Babylon, 8043

ARCHES (KJV) See PORTICO

ARCHEVITES (KJV) See ERECH

ARCHI, ARCHITE (KJV) See ARKITES

ARCHIPPUS (2)
Col 4:17 Tell **A**: "See to it that you complete *800*
Phm 1: 2 *to* **A** our fellow soldier and to the church *800*

ARCHITECT (1)
Heb 11:10 whose **a** and builder is God. *5493*

ARCHIVES (3)
Ezr 4:15 made in the **a** of your predecessors. 10177+10515
5:17 a search be made in the royal **a** of Babylon 10103+10148
6: 1 in the **a** stored in the treasury at Babylon. 10103+10515

ARCTURUS (KJV) See BEAR

ARD (3) [ARDITE]
Ge 46:21 Ehi, Rosh, Muppim, Huppim and **A**. 764
Nu 26:40 of Bela through **A** and Naaman were: 764
26:40 through **A**, the Ardite clan; 764

ARDENT (1)
2Co 7: 7 your deep sorrow, your **a concern** for me, *2419*

ARDITE (1) [ARD]
Nu 26:40 through Ard, the **A** clan; 766

ARDON (1)
1Ch 2:18 These were her sons: Jesher, Shobab and **A**. 765

ARE (3890) [BE] See Index of Articles Etc.

AREA (55) [AREAS]
Ge 25:18 His descendants settled in the **a** NIH
34: 2 the ruler of that **a**, saw her, 824
Ex 10:14 in every **a** *of* the country in great numbers. 1473
Lev 10:17 the sin offering in the sanctuary **a**? 5226
10:18 the goat in the sanctuary **a**, NIH
13:33 must be shaved except for the **diseased a**, 5999
16: 3 how Aaron is to enter the **sanctuary a**: 7731
Nu 8: 2 to light the **a** in front of the lampstand.' " NIH
35: 5 They will have **this** *a* as pastureland for AIT
Jos 13: 5 the **a** *of* the Gebalites; 824
19:46 with the **a** facing Joppa. 1473
Jdg 19: 1 Now a Levite who lived in a **remote a** *in* 3752
19:18 to a **remote a** *in* the hill country of Ephraim 3752
1Sa 9: 4 and through the **a** *around* Shalisha, 824
14:14 in an **a** of about half an acre. 8441
23:23 Then I will go with you; if he is in the **a**, 824
27: 9 Whenever David attacked an **a**, 824
2Sa 5: 9 He built up the **a around** it, 6017
1Ch 5: 8 the **a** from Aroer to Nebo and Baal Meon. NIH
Ne 12:29 and from the **a** *of* Geba and Azmaveth, 8441
Eze 40: 5 I saw a wall completely surrounding the temple **a**. 2575+4946
41: 9 The **open a** between the side rooms of 4965
41:11 the **open a**, one on the north and another on 4965
41:11 the **open a** was five cubits wide all around. 4965
41:20 From the floor to the **a** above the entrance, NIH
42:15 inside the **temple a**, he led me out by 1074
42:15 the east gate and measured **the a** all around: 2257^{S}
42:20 So he measured **the a** on all four sides. 2257^{S}
43:12 All the surrounding **a** on top of 1473
43:21 the designated part of the **temple a** outside 1074
45: 1 the entire **a** will be holy. 1473
45: 5 An **a** 25,000 cubits long and 10,000 NIH
45: 6 to give the city as its property an **a** 5,000 NIH
45: 7 of the **a** formed by the sacred district and NIH
48:15 "The **remaining** *a*, 5,000 AIT
48:18 What remains of the **a**, NIH
48:21 of the **a** formed by the sacred portion and NIH
48:22 of the city will lie in the center of the **a** NIH
48:22 The **a** belonging to the prince will lie NIH
Mt 4:13 the lake in the **a** of Zebulun and Naphtali— *3990*
21:12 Jesus entered the **temple a** *2639*
21:15 and the children shouting in the **temple a**, *2639*
Mk 5:10 and again not to send them out *of* the **a**. *6001*
11:15 Jesus entered the **temple a** *2639*
Lk 4:37 throughout the surrounding **a**. *5536*
19:45 Then he entered the **temple a** *2639*
Jn 2:15 and drove all from the **temple a**, *2639*
8:20 in the **temple a** near the place where *2639*
10:23 and Jesus was in the **temple a** walking *2639*
11:56 in the **temple a** they asked one another, *2639*
Ac 16: 3 because of the Jews who lived in that **a**, *5536*
20: 2 He traveled through that **a**, *3538*
21:28 the **temple a** and defiled this holy place." *2639*
21:29 Paul had brought him into the **temple a**.) *2639*
2Co 10:15 our **a of activity** among you *2834*

AREAS (6) [AREA]
Jos 13: 1 and there are still very large **a of land** to 824
14: 1 Now these are **the a** the Israelites received 889^{S}
Jdg 19:29 and sent them into all the **a** *of* Israel. 1473
1Ki 20:34 "You may set up your own **market a** 2575
2Ch 27: 4 and forts and towers in the **wooded a**. 3091
Eze 48:21 Both these **a** running the length of NIH

ARELI (2) [ARELITE]
Ge 46:16 Haggi, Shuni, Ezbon, Eri, Arodi and **A**. 739
Nu 26:17 through **A**, the Arelite clan. 739

ARELITE (1) [ARELI]
Nu 26:17 through Areli, the **A** clan. 740

AREN'T (17) [BE, NOT]
Jdg 8: 2 **A** the gleanings of Ephraim's grapes better than the full grape harvest of Abiezer? 4202
9:38 **A** these the men you ridiculed? 4202
18: 9 **A** you *going to* **do something?** 3120
1Sa 26:14 "**A** you going to answer me, Abner?" 4202
26:15 David said, "You're a man, **a** you? 4202
2Sa 15:27 said to Zadok the priest, "**A** you a seer? 2022
2Ki 12: 7 "Why **a** you repairing the damage done to 401
2Ch 28:10 But **a** you also guilty of sins against 4202
Mt 13:55 and **a** his brothers James, Joseph, *NIG*
13:56 **A** all his sisters with us? *1639+4049*
22:16 You **a** swayed by men, *4024*
Mk 6: 3 **A** his sisters here with us?" *1639+4024*
12:14 You **a** swayed by men, *4024*
15: 4 "**A** you going to answer? *4024*
Lk 23:39 "**A** you the Christ? *1639+4049*
Jn 8:48 "**A** we right in saying that you are a Samaritan and demon-possessed?" *4024*
Ac 21:38 "**A** you the Egyptian who started a revolt *1639+4024*

ARENA (1)
1Co 4: 9 like men condemned to die in the **a**. *NIG*

AREOPAGITE (KJV) See AREOPAGUS

AREOPAGUS (3)
Ac 17:19 and brought him to a **meeting of the A**, *740*
17:22 Paul then stood up in the **meeting of the A** *740*
17:34 a **member of the A**, *741*

ARETAS (1)
2Co 11:32 the governor *under* King **A** had the city of *745*

ARGOB (5)
Dt 3: 4 the whole region of **A**, 758
3:13 of **A** in Bashan used to be known as a land 758
3:14 of **A** as far as the border of the Geshurites 758
1Ki 4:13 as well as the district of **A** in Bashan 758
2Ki 15:25 along with **A** and Arieh, 759

ARGUE (10) [ARGUED, ARGUING, ARGUMENT, ARGUMENTS]
Jdg 18:25 Danites answered, "Don't **a** with us, 7754+9048
Job 9:14 How can I find words to **a** with him? NIH
13: 3 to speak to the Almighty and *to* **a** my **case** 3519
13: 8 *Will you* **a the case** for God? 8189
15: 3 *Would* he **a** with useless words, 3519
Pr 25: 9 If you **a** your case with a neighbor, 8189
Isa 43:26 *let us* **a** *the matter* together; 9149
Jn 6:52 Then the Jews *began to* **a sharply** *3481*
Ac 6: 9 *These men* began *to* **a with** Stephen, *5184*
Ro 3: 7 Someone might **a**, "If my falsehood enhances God's truthfulness *NIG*

ARGUED (3) [ARGUE]
1Ki 3:22 And so *they* **a** before the king. 1819
Mk 9:34 on the way *they had* **a about** who was *1363*
Ac 23: 9 Pharisees stood up and **a vigorously**. *1372*

ARGUING (8) [ARGUE]
2Sa 19: 9 the people *were* all **a with each other**, 1906
Job 16: 3 What ails you that *you keep on* **a**? 6699
Mk 9:14 around them and the teachers of the law **a** *5184*
9:16 "What *are you* **a** with them **about?"** *5184*
9:33 "What *were you* **a about** on the road?" *1368*
Ac 19: 8 **a** persuasively about the kingdom of God. *1363*
24:12 My accusers did not find me **a** with anyone *1363*
Php 2:14 Do everything without complaining or **a**, *1369*

ARGUMENT (5) [ARGUE]
Job 13: 6 Hear now my **a**; 9350
Lk 9:46 An **a** started among the disciples as *1369*
Jn 3:25 An **a** developed between some *2428*
Ro 3: 5 (*I am* **using** a human **a**.) *3306*
Heb 6:16 and puts an end *to* all **a**. *517*

ARGUMENTS (10) [ARGUE]
Job 6:25 But what do your **a** prove? 3519
23: 4 before him and fill my mouth with **a**. 9350
32:12 none of you has answered his **a**. 609
32:14 and I will not answer him with your **a**. 609
Isa 41:21 "Set forth your **a**," says Jacob's King. 6802
59: 4 They rely on empty **a** and speak lies; NIH
2Co 10: 5 We demolish **a** and every pretension *3361*
Col 2: 4 that no one may deceive you by **fine-sounding a**. *4391*
2Ti 2:23 to do with foolish and stupid **a**, *2428*
Tit 3: 9 and genealogies and **a** and quarrels about *2251*

ARID (2)
Mt 12:43 through **a** places seeking rest and does *536*
Lk 11:24 through **a** places seeking rest and does *536*

ARIDAI (1)
Est 9: 9 Parmashta, Arisai, **A** and Vaizatha, 767

ARIDATHA (1)
Est 9: 8 Poratha, Adalia, **A**, 792

ARIEH (1)
2Ki 15:25 along with Argob and **A**, 794

ARIEL (5)
Ezr 8:16 So I summoned Eliezer, **A**, Shemaiah, 791
Isa 29: 1 Woe to you, **A**, Ariel, 790
29: 1 Woe to you, Ariel, **A**, 790
29: 2 Yet I will besiege **A**; 790
29: 7 against **A**, that attack her and her fortress 790

ARIGHT (1) [RIGHT]
Ps 90:12 Teach us to number our days **a**, 4026

ARIMATHEA (4)
Mt 27:57 there came a rich man from **A**, *751*
Mk 15:43 Joseph of **A**, a prominent member of *751*
Lk 23:51 the Judean town *of* **A** and he was waiting *751*
Jn 19:38 of **A** asked Pilate for the body of Jesus. *751*

ARIOCH (6)
Ge 14: 1 **A** king of Ellasar, 796
14: 9 Amraphel king of Shinar and **A** king 796
Da 2:14 When **A**, the commander of 10070
2:15 **A** then explained the matter to Daniel. 10070
2:24 Then Daniel went to **A**, 10070
2:25 **A** took Daniel to the king at once and said, 10070

ARISAI (1)
Est 9: 9 Parmashta, **A**, Aridai and Vaizatha, 798

ARISE (33) [RISE]
Nu 23:18 Then he uttered his oracle: "**A**, Balak, 7756
Jdg 5:12 **A**, O Barak! 7756
2Ch 6:41 "Now **a**, O LORD God, 7756
Est 4:14 relief and deliverance for the Jews *will* **a** 6641
Ps 3: 7 **A**, O LORD! Deliver me, O my God! 7756
7: 6 **A**, O LORD, in your anger; 7756
9:19 **A**, O LORD, let not man triumph; 7756
10:12 **A**, LORD! Lift up your hand, O God. 7756
12: 5 *I will* now **a**," says the LORD. 7756
35: 2 **a and come** to my aid. 7756
59: 4 **A** to help me; look on my plight! 6424
68: 1 *May* God **a**, may his enemies be scattered; 7756
73:20 a dream when one awakes, so when you **a**, 6424
102:13 You *will* **a** and have compassion on Zion, 7756
132: 8 **a**, O LORD, and come 7756
Pr 31:28 Her children **a** and call her blessed; 7756
SS 2:10 My lover spoke and said to me, "**A**, 7756
2:13 **A**, come, my darling; 7756
Isa 33:10 "Now *will I* **a**," says the LORD. 7756
60: 1 "**A**, shine, for your light has come, 7756
Jer 6: 4 **A**, let us attack at noon! 7756
6: 5 So **a**, let us attack at night 7756
30:21 their ruler *will* **a** from among them. 3655
49:28 "**A**, and attack Kedar and destroy 7756
49:31 "**A** and attack a nation at ease, 7756
La 2:19 **A**, cry out in the night, 7756
Da 7:24 After them another king *will* **a**, 10624
8:23 a master of intrigue, *will* **a**. 6641
11: 7 *"One* from her family line *will* **a** 6641
12: 1 Michael, the great prince who protects your people, *will* **a**. 6641
Hab 2: 7 *Will* not your debtors suddenly **a**? 7756
Ac 20:30 Even from your own number men *will* **a** *482*
Ro 15:12 one who *will* **a** to rule over the nations; *482*

ARISEN (1) [RISE]
Dt 13:13 that wicked men *have* **a** among you 3655

ARISES (1) [RISE]
Ecc 10: 5 the sort of error that **a** from a ruler: 3655

ARISTARCHUS (5)
Ac 19:29 The people seized Gaius and **A**, *752*
20: 4 **A** and Secundus from Thessalonica, *752*
27: 2 **A**, a Macedonian from Thessalonica, *752*
Col 4:10 fellow prisoner **A** sends you his greetings, *752*
Phm 1:24 And so do Mark, **A**, Demas and Luke, *752*

ARISTOBULUS (1)
Ro 16:10 to the household *of* **A**. *755*

ARK (219)

Ge 6:14 So make yourself an a of cypress wood; 9310
6:15 The a is to be 450 feet long, 9310
6:16 for it and finish the a to within 18 inches of 9310
6:16 a door in the side of the a and make lower, 9310
6:18 and you will enter the a— 9310
6:19 into the a two of all living creatures, 9310
7: 1 LORD then said to Noah, "Go into the a, 9310
7: 7 and his sons' wives entered the a to escape 9310
7: 9 came to Noah and entered the a, 9310
7:13 the wives of his three sons, entered the a. 9310
7:15 in them came to Noah and entered the a. 9310
7:17 the waters increased they lifted the a high 9310
7:18 the a floated on the surface of the water. 9310
7:23 and those with him in the a. 9310
8: 1 the livestock that were with him in the a, 9310
8: 4 of the seventh month the a came to rest on 9310
8: 6 the window he had made in the a 9310
8: 9 so it returned to Noah in the a. 9310
8: 9 and brought it back to himself in the a. 9310
8:10 and again sent out the dove from the a. 9310
8:13 Noah then removed the covering from the a 9310
8:16 "Come out of the a, you and your wife 9310
8:19 came out of the a, one kind after another. 9310
9:10 all those that came out of the a with you— 9310
9:18 of Noah who came out of the a were Shem, 9310
Ex 25:15 poles are to remain in the rings of this a; 778
25:16 Then put in the a the Testimony, 778
25:21 the cover on top of the a and put in the ark 778
25:21 the cover on top of the ark and put in the a 778
25:22 the two cherubim that are over the a of 778
26:33 the clasps and place the a of the Testimony 778
26:34 Put the atonement cover on the a of 778
30: 6 in front of the curtain that is before the a of 778
30:26 the a of the Testimony, 778
31: 7 the a of the Testimony with 778
35:12 the a with its poles and 778
37: 1 Bezalel made the a of acacia wood— 778
37: 5 the poles into the rings on the sides of the a 778
39:35 the a of the Testimony with its poles and 778
40: 3 the a of the Testimony in it and shield 778
40: 3 of the Testimony in it and shield the a with 778
40: 5 the gold altar of incense in front of the a of 778
40:20 the Testimony and placed it in the a, 778
40:20 the a and put the atonement cover over it. 778
40:21 Then he brought the a into the tabernacle 778
40:21 the shielding curtain and shielded the a of 778
Lev 16: 2 in front of the atonement cover on the a, 778
Nu 3:31 They were responsible for the care of the a, 778
4: 5 down the shielding curtain and cover the a 778
7:89 above the atonement cover on the a of 778
10:33 The a of the covenant of the LORD went 778
10:35 Whenever the a set out, Moses said, 778
14:44 nor the a of the LORD's covenant moved 778
Dt 10: 3 So I made the a out of acacia wood 778
10: 5 and put the tablets in the a I had made, 778
10: 8 of Levi to carry the a of the covenant of 778
31: 9 the a of the covenant of the LORD, 778
31:25 the a of the covenant of the LORD: 778
31:26 and place it beside the a of the covenant of 778
Jos 3: 3 "When you see the a of the covenant of 778
3: 4 a thousand yards between you and the a; 2257^S
3: 6 "Take up the a of the covenant and pass on 778
3: 8 the priests who carry the a of the covenant: 778
3:11 the a of the covenant of the Lord of all 778
3:13 And as soon as the priests who carry the a 778
3:14 the a of the covenant went ahead of them. 778
3:15 as the priests who carried the a reached 778
3:17 The priests who carried the a of 778
4: 5 over before the a of the LORD your God 778
4: 7 before the a of the covenant of the LORD. 778
4: 9 the spot where the priests who carried the a 778
4:10 the a remained standing in the middle of 778
4:11 the a of the LORD and the priests came to 778
4:16 the priests carrying the a of the Testimony 778
4:18 the river carrying the a of the covenant of 778
6: 4 of rams' horns in front of the a. 778
6: 6 up the a of the covenant of the LORD 778
6: 7 with the armed guard going ahead of the a 778
6: 8 and the a of the LORD's covenant 778
6: 9 and the rear guard followed the a. 778
6:11 So he had the a of the LORD carried 778
6:12 the priests took up the a of the LORD. 778
6:13 before the a of the LORD and blowing 778
6:13 of them and the rear guard followed the a 778
7: 6 to the ground before the a of the LORD, 778
8:33 on both sides of the a of the covenant of 778
Jdg 20:27 the a of the covenant of God was there, 778
1Sa 3: 3 where the a of God was. 778
4: 3 the a of the LORD's covenant 778
4: 4 and they brought back the a of 778
4: 4 were there with the a of the covenant 778
4: 5 the a of the LORD's covenant came into 778
4: 6 that the a of the LORD had come into 778
4:11 The a of God was captured, 778
4:13 because his heart feared for the a of God. 778
4:17 and the a of God has been captured." 778
4:18 When he mentioned the a of God, 778
4:19 that the a of God had been captured and 778
4:21 because of the capture of the a of God and 778
4:22 for the a of God has been captured." 778
5: 1 the Philistines had captured the a of God, 778
5: 2 the a into Dagon's temple and set it 778
5: 3 on the ground before the a of the LORD! 778
5: 4 on the ground before the a of the LORD! 778
5: 7 "The a of the god of Israel must 778

1Sa 5: 8 "What shall we do with the a of the god 778
5: 8 the a of the god of Israel moved to Gath." 778
5: 8 So they moved the a of the God of Israel. 778
5:10 So they sent the a of God to Ekron. 778
5:10 As the a of God was entering Ekron, 778
5:10 the a of the god of Israel around to us 778
5:11 "Send the a of the god of Israel away; 778
6: 1 When the a of the LORD had been 778
6: 2 "What shall we do with the a of the LORD? 778
6: 3 "If you return the a of the god of Israel, 778
6: 8 the a of the LORD and put it on the cart, 778
6:11 the a of the LORD on the cart and along 778
6:13 and when they looked up and saw the a, 778
6:15 The Levites took down the a of 778
6:18 on which they set the a of the LORD, 778
6:19 to death because they had looked into the a 778
6:20 To whom will the a go up from here?" NIH
6:21 "The Philistines have returned the a of 778
7: 1 of Kiriath Jearim came and took up the a 778
7: 1 to guard the a of the LORD. 778
7: 2 that the a remained at Kiriath Jearim, 778
14:18 Saul said to Ahijah, "Bring the a of God." 778
2Sa 6: 2 of Judah to bring up from there the a 778
6: 2 between the cherubim that are on the a. 2257^S
6: 3 the a of God on a new cart and brought it 778
6: 4 with the a of God on it, 778
6: 6 Uzzah reached out and took hold of the a 778
6: 7 and he died there beside the a of God. 778
6: 9 can the a of the LORD ever come to me?" 778
6:10 to take the a of the LORD to be with him 778
6:11 The a of the LORD remained in the house 778
6:12 because of the a of God." 778
6:12 So David went down and brought up the a 778
6:13 the a of the LORD had taken six steps, 778
6:15 the entire house of Israel brought up the a 778
6:16 the a of the LORD was entering the City 778
6:17 the a of the LORD and set it in its place 778
7: 2 while the a of God remains in a tent." 778
11:11 a and Israel and Judah are staying in tents, 778
15:24 with him were carrying the a of 778
15:24 They set down the a of God, 778
15:25 "Take the a of God back into the city. 778
15:29 and Abiathar took the a of God back 778
1Ki 2:26 the a of the Sovereign LORD 778
3:15 stood before the a of the Lord's covenant 778
6:19 the a of the covenant of the LORD there. 778
8: 1 to bring up the a of the LORD's covenant 778
8: 3 the priests took up the a, 778
8: 4 and they brought up the a of the LORD 778
8: 5 about him were before the a, 778
8: 6 the a of the LORD's covenant to its place 778
8: 7 over the place of the a and overshadowed 778
8: 7 of the ark and overshadowed the a 778
8: 9 in the a except the two stone tablets 778
8:21 I have provided a place there for the a, 778
1Ch 6:31 of the LORD after the a came to rest there. 778
13: 3 Let us bring the a of our God back to us, 778
13: 5 to bring the a of God from Kiriath Jearim. 778
13: 6 the a of God the LORD, who is enthroned 778
13: 6 the a that is called by the Name. NIH
13: 7 the a of God from Abinadab's house on 778
13: 9 Uzzah reached out his hand to steady the a, 778
13:10 down because he had put his hand on the a. 778
13:12 can I ever bring the a of God to me?" 778
13:13 the a to be with him in the City of David. 778
13:14 The a of God remained with the family 778
15: 1 a place for the a of God and pitched a tent 778
15: 2 "No one but the Levites may carry the a 778
15: 2 the LORD chose them to carry the a of 778
15: 3 to bring up the a of the LORD to 778
15:12 to consecrate yourselves and bring up the a 778
15:14 in order to bring up the a of the LORD, 778
15:15 And the Levites carried the a of God with 778
15:23 to be doorkeepers for the a. 778
15:24 to blow trumpets before the a of God. 778
15:24 also to be doorkeepers for the a. 778
15:25 the a of the covenant of the LORD from 778
15:26 the Levites who were carrying the a of 778
15:27 the Levites who were carrying the a, 778
15:28 up the a of the covenant of the LORD 778
15:29 As the a of the covenant of the LORD 778
16: 1 They brought the a of God and set it inside 778
16: 4 of the Levites to minister before the a of 778
16: 6 to blow the trumpets regularly before the a 778
16:37 before the a of the covenant of the LORD 778
17: 1 the a of the covenant of the LORD is 778
22:19 so that you may bring the a of the covenant 778
28: 2 to build a house as a place of rest for the a 778
28:18 that spread their wings and shelter the a of 778
2Ch 1: 4 Now David had brought up the a of God 778
5: 2 to bring up the a of the LORD's covenant 778
5: 4 the Levites took up the a, 778
5: 5 up the a and the Tent of Meeting and all 778
5: 6 about him were before the a, 778
5: 7 the a of the LORD's covenant to its place 778
5: 8 over the place of the a and covered the ark 778
5: 8 over the place of the ark and covered the a 778
5: 9 from the a, could be seen from in front of 778
5:10 There was nothing in the a except 778
6:11 There I have placed the a, 778
6:41 you and the a of your might. 778
8:11 the a of the LORD has entered are holy." 778
35: 3 the sacred a in the temple that Solomon son 778
Ps 78:61 He sent [the a of] his might into captivity, NIH
132: 8 you and the a of your might. 778
Jer 3:16 'The a of the covenant of the LORD.' 778
Mt 24:38 up to the day Noah entered the a; 3066

Lk 17:27 up to the day Noah entered the a. 3066
Heb 9: 4 and the gold-covered a of the covenant. 3066
9: 4 This a contained the gold jar of manna, 4005^S
9: 5 Above the a were the cherubim of 899^S
11: 7 in holy fear built an a to save his family. 3066
1Pe 3:20 of Noah while the a was being built. 3066
Rev 11:19 and within his temple was seen the a 3066

ARKITE (5) [ARKITES]

2Sa 15:32 Hushai the A was there to meet him, 805
16:16 Then Hushai the A, David's friend, 805
17: 5 "Summon also Hushai the A, 805
17:14 "The advice of Hushai the A is better than 805
1Ch 27:33 Hushai the A was the king's friend. 805

ARKITES (3) [ARKITE]

Ge 10:17 Hivites, A, Sinites, 6909
Jos 16: 2 over to the territory of the A in Ataroth, 805
1Ch 1:15 Hivites, A, Sinites, 6909

ARM (77) [ARMED, ARMIES, ARMLETS, ARMOR, ARMOR-BEARER, ARMOR-BEARERS, ARMORY, ARMRESTS, ARMS, ARMY]

Ex 6: 6 with an outstretched a and with mighty acts 2432
15:16 By the power of your a they will be as still 2432
Nu 11:23 "Is the LORD's a too short? 3338
20:11 Then Moses raised his a and struck 3338
31: 3 "A some of your men to go to war against 2741
32:17 But we are ready to a ourselves and go 2741
32:20 if you will a yourselves before 2741
Dt 4:34 by a mighty hand and an outstretched a, 2432
5:15 with a mighty hand and an outstretched a. 2432
7:19 the mighty hand and outstretched a, 2432
9:29 great power and your outstretched a." 2432
11: 2 his mighty hand, his outstretched a; 2432
26: 8 with a mighty hand and an outstretched a, 2432
33:20 tearing at a or head. 2432
2Sa 1:10 that was on his head and the band on his a 2432
1Ki 8:42 mighty hand and your outstretched a— 2432
2Ki 5:18 to bow down and he is leaning on my a 3338
7: 2 on whose a the king was leaning said to 3338
7:17 on whose a he leaned in charge of the gate, 3338
17:36 with mighty power and outstretched a, 2432
2Ch 6:32 and your outstretched a— 2432
32: 8 With him is only the a of flesh, 2432
Job 26: 2 How you have saved the a that is feeble! 2432
31:22 then let my a fall from the shoulder, 4190
35: 9 for relief from the a of the powerful. 2432
38:15 and their upraised a is broken. 2432
40: 9 Do you have an a like God's, 2432
Ps 10:15 Break the a of the wicked and evil man; 2432
44: 3 nor did their a bring them victory; 2432
44: 3 it was your right hand, your a, 2432
77:15 With your mighty a you redeemed your people, 2432
79:11 of your a preserve those condemned to die. 2432
89:10 with your strong a you scattered your enemies. 2432
89:13 Your a is endued with power; 2432
89:21 surely my a will strengthen him. 2432
98: 1 and his holy a have worked salvation 2432
136:12 with a mighty hand and outstretched a; 2432
SS 2: 6 His left a is under my head, NIH
2: 6 and his right a embraces me. NIH
8: 3 His left a is under my head NIH
8: 3 and his right a embraces me. NIH
8: 6 like a seal on your a; 2432
Isa 17: 5 and harvests the grain with his a— 2432
30:30 and will make them see his a coming down 2432
30:32 in battle with the blows of his a. NIH
40:10 and his a rules for him. 2432
44:12 he forges it with the might of his a. 2432
48:14 his a will be against the Babylonians. 2432
50: 2 Was my a too short to ransom you? 3338
51: 5 and my a will bring justice to the nations. 2432
51: 5 to me and wait in hope for my a. 2432
51: 9 O a of the LORD; 2432
52:10 The LORD will lay bare his holy a in 2432
53: 1 the a of the LORD been revealed? 2432
59: 1 a of the LORD is not too short to save, 3338
59:16 so his own a worked salvation for him, 2432
60: 4 and your daughters are carried on the a. 7396
62: 8 by his right hand and by his mighty a: 2432
63: 5 so my own a worked salvation for me, 2432
63:12 who sent his glorious a of power to be 2432
66:12 you will nurse and be carried on her a 7396
Jer 21: 5 with an outstretched hand and a mighty a 2432
27: 5 and outstretched a I made the earth 2432
32:17 by your great power and outstretched a. 2432
32:21 by a mighty hand and an outstretched a and 274
48:25 her a is broken," declares the LORD. 2432
Eze 4: 7 of Jerusalem and with bared a prophesy 2432
17: 9 not take a strong a or many people to pull it 2432
20:33 with a mighty hand and an outstretched a 2432
20:34 with a mighty hand and an outstretched a 2432
30:21 I have broken the a of Pharaoh king 2432
30:22 the good a as well as the broken one, NIH
Zec 11:17 the sword strike his a and his right eye! 2432
11:17 May his a be completely withered, 2432
Lk 1:51 He has performed mighty deeds with his a; 1098
Jn 12:38 the a of the Lord been revealed?" 1098
1Pe 4: 1 a yourselves also with the same attitude, 3959

ARMAGEDDON (1)

Rev 16:16 to the place that in Hebrew is called **A.** *762*

ARMED (48) [ARM]

Ex 13:18 up out of Egypt **a for battle.** 2821
Nu 31: 5 So twelve thousand *men* **a** *for* battle, 2741
32:21 and if all of you will go **a** over the Jordan 2741
32:27 But your servants, every *man* **a** *for* battle, 2741
32:29 every *man* **a** for battle, 2741
32:30 But if they do not cross over with you **a,** 2741
32:32 over before the LORD into Canaan **a,** 2741
Dt 3:18 all your able-bodied men, **a for battle,** 2741
Jos 1:14 but all your fighting men, **fully a,** 2821
4:12 **a,** in front of the Israelites, 2821
4:13 About forty thousand **a** *for* battle crossed 2741
6: 3 around the city once with all the **a** men. 4878
6: 7 with the **a guard** going ahead of the ark of 2741
6: 9 The **a guard** marched ahead of 2741
6:13 The **a** *men* went ahead of them and 2741
Jdg 18:11 the Danites, **a** *for* battle, set out 2520+3998
18:16 The six hundred Danites, **a** *for* battle, 2520+3998
18:17 the six hundred **a** men stood at the entrance 2520+3998
20: 2 four hundred thousand soldiers **a** 8990
20:25 all of them **a** *with* swords. 8990
20:35 Benjamites, all **a** *with* swords. 8990
1Sa 2: 4 but those who stumbled *are* **a** *with* strength. 273
2Sa 21:16 and who **was a** *with* a new [sword], 2520
22:40 *You* **a** me *with* strength for battle; 273
2Ki 3:25 but **men a with slings** surrounded it 7847
1Ch 12: 2 *they were* **a** *with* bows and were able 5976
12:23 of the men **a** for battle who came to David 2741
12:24 6,800 **a** *for* battle; 2741
12:37 *a* **with** every type of weapon—120,000. AIT
20: 1 Joab led out the **a forces.** 2657+7372
2Ch 14: 8 **a** *with* small shields and with bows. 5951
17:17 with 200,000 *men* **a** *with* bows and shields; 5976
17:18 Jehozabad, with 180,000 *men* **a** *for* battle. 2741
Est 8:11 to destroy, kill and annihilate any **a force** 2657
Ps 18:39 *You* **a** me *with* strength for battle; 273
65: 6 *having* **a yourself** with strength, 273
78: 9 men of Ephraim, though **a** *with* bows, 5976+8227
93: 1 the LORD is robed in majesty and *is* **a** 273
Pr 6:11 like a bandit and scarcity like an **a** man. 4482
24:34 like a bandit and scarcity like an **a** man. 4482
Isa 15: 4 Therefore the **a** *men* of Moab cry out, 2741
Jer 6:23 *They are* **a** *with* bow and spear; 2616
50:42 *They are* **a** *with* bows and spears; 2616
Eze 38: 4 your horses, your horsemen fully **a,** 4229
Da 11:31 "His **a forces** will rise up to desecrate 2432
Mt 26:47 With him was a large crowd **a** with swords *NIG*
Mk 14:43 With him was a crowd **a** with swords *NIG*
Lk 11:21 "When a strong man, **fully a,** *2774*

ARMENIA (KJV) See ARARAT

ARMIES (16) [ARM]

Ex 14:20 coming between the **a** *of* Egypt and Israel. 4722
Jdg 8:10 of the **a** *of* the eastern peoples; 4722
1Sa 17:26 that he should defy the **a** *of* the living God?" 5120
17:36 he has defied the **a** *of* the living God. 5120
17:45 the God of the **a** *of* Israel, 5120
1Ki 2: 5 to the two commanders of Israel's **a,** 7372
Ps 44: 9 you no longer go out with our **a.** 7372
60:10 and no longer go out with our **a?** 7372
68:12 "Kings and **a** flee in haste; 7372
108:11 and no longer go out with our **a?** 7372
Isa 34: 2 his wrath is upon all their **a.** 7372
Jer 35:11 to escape the Babylonian and Aramean **a.'** 2657
Lk 21:20 being surrounded by **a,** you will know *5136*
Heb 11:34 in battle and routed foreign **a.** *4213*
Rev 19:14 The **a** of heaven were following him, *5128*
19:19 and their **a** gathered together to make war *5128*

ARMLETS (1) [ARM]

Nu 31:50 **a,** bracelets, signet rings, 731

ARMONI (1)

2Sa 21: 8 But the king took **A** and Mephibosheth, 813

ARMOR (19) [ARM]

1Sa 14: 1 to the young man bearing his **a,** 3998
17: 5 on his head and wore a **coat of scale a** 7989+9234
17:38 a **coat of a** on him and a bronze helmet 9234
31: 9 and stripped off his **a,** 3998
31:10 They put his **a** in the temple of 3998
1Ki 20:11 *'One who* **puts on** *his* **a** should not boast 2520
22:34 of Israel between the sections of his **a.** 9234
1Ch 10: 9 and took his head and his **a,** 3998
10:10 They put his **a** *in* the temple of their gods 3998
2Ch 18:33 of Israel between the sections of his **a.** 9234
26:14 spears, helmets, **coats of a,** 9234
Ne 4:16 with spears, shields, bows and **a.** 9234
Isa 45: 1 and to strip kings of their **a,** to open doors 5516
Jer 46: 4 Polish your spears, put on your **a!** 6246
51: 3 nor let him put on his **a.** 6246
Lk 11:22 the **a** in which the man trusted and divides *4110*
Ro 13:12 the deeds of darkness and put on the **a** *3960*
Eph 6:11 Put on the **full a** of God so *4110*
6:13 Therefore put on the **full a** of God, *4110*

ARMOR-BEARER (18) [ARM]

Jdg 9:54 Hurriedly he called to his **a,** 3998+5951
1Sa 14: 6 Jonathan said to his young **a,** "Come, 3998+5951
14: 7 "Do all that you have in mind," his **a** said. 3998+5951
14:12 outpost shouted to Jonathan and his **a,** 3998+5951
14:12 Jonathan said to his **a,** "Climb up after me; 3998+5951
14:13 with his **a** right behind him. 3998+5951
14:13 his **a** followed and killed behind him. 3998+5951
14:14 and his **a** killed some twenty men in 3998+5951
14:17 it was Jonathan and his **a** who were 3998+5951
31: 4 Saul said to his **a,** 3998+5951
31: 4 But his **a** was terrified and would not do it; 3998+5951
31: 5 When the **a** saw that Saul was dead, 3998+5951
31: 6 and his **a** and all his men died together 3998+5951
2Sa 23:37 the **a** *of* Joab son of Zeruiah, 3998+5951
1Ch 10: 4 Saul said to his **a,** 3998+5951
10: 4 But his **a** was terrified and would not do it; 3998+5951
10: 5 When the **a** saw that Saul was dead, 3998+5951
11:39 the **a** *of* Joab son of Zeruiah, 3998+5951

ARMOR-BEARERS (2) [ARM]

1Sa 16:21 and David became one of his **a.** 3998+5951
2Sa 18:15 ten of Joab's **a** surrounded Absalom, 3998+5951

ARMORY (3) [ARM]

2Ki 20:13 his **a** and everything found 1074+3998
Ne 3:19 a point facing the ascent to the **a** as far as 5977
Isa 39: 2 the spices, the fine oil, his entire **a** 1074+3998

ARMRESTS (2) [ARM]

1Ki 10:19 On both sides of the seat were **a,** 3338
2Ch 9:18 On both sides of the seat were **a,** 3338

ARMS (49) [ARM]

Ge 16: 5 I put my servant in your **a,** 2668
24:30 and the bracelets on his sister's **a,** 3338
24:47 in her nose and the bracelets on her **a,** 3338
33: 4 *he* **threw** *his* **a around** his neck 5877+6584
45:14 Then *he* **threw** *his* **a around** 5877+6584+7418
46:29 *he* **threw** *his* **a around** his father and wept 5877+6584+7418
48:14 and crossing his **a,** he put his left hand 3338
49:24 his **strong a** stayed limber, 2432+3338
Nu 11:12 Why do you tell me to carry them in my **a,** 2668
Dt 33:27 and underneath are the everlasting **a.** 2432
Jdg 6:35 **calling** them **to a,** and also into Asher, 339+2410
10:17 When the Ammonites **were called to a** 7590
15:14 on his **a** became like charred flax, 2432
16:12 the ropes off his **a** as if they were threads. 2432
2Sa 12: 3 drank from his cup and even slept in his **a.** 2668
12: 8 and your master's wives into your **a.** 2668
22:33 It is God *who* **a** me *with* strength 273
22:35 my **a** can bend a bow of bronze. 2432
1Ki 17:19 He took him from her **a,** 2668
2Ki 3:21 *who could* **bear a** was called up 2514+2520
4:16 **hold** a son **in your a."** 2485
Ps 18:32 It is God who **a** me *with* strength 273
18:34 my **a** can bend a bow of bronze. 2432
129: 7 nor the one who gathers fill his **a.** 2950
Pr 31:17 her **a** are strong for her tasks. 2432
31:20 She opens her **a** to the poor 4090
SS 5:14 His **a** are rods of gold set with chrysolite. 3338
Isa 40:11 in his **a** and carries them close to his heart; 2432
49:22 they will bring your sons in their **a** 2950
Jer 38:12 worn-out clothes under your **a** to pad 723+3338
La 2:12 as their lives ebb away in their mothers' **a.** 2668
Eze 13:20 like birds and I will tear them from your **a;** 2432
16:11 on your **a** and a necklace around your neck, 3338
23:42 the rabble, and they put bracelets on the **a** 3338
30:22 I will break *both* his **a,** 2432
30:24 I will strengthen the **a** *of* the king 2432
30:24 but I will break the **a** *of* Pharaoh, 2432
30:25 I will strengthen the **a** *of* the king 2432
30:25 but the **a** *of* Pharaoh will fall limp. 2432
38: 8 many days *you will* **be called to a.** 7212
Da 2:32 its chest and **a** of silver, 10185
10: 6 his **a** and legs like the gleam 2432
Hos 11: 3 taking them by the **a;** 2432
Mk 9:36 **Taking** him **in his a,** *1878*
10:16 **took** the children **in his a,** *1878*
Lk 2:28 Simeon took him in his **a** and praised God, *44*
15:20 **threw his a around** him and kissed him. *2093+2158+3836+5549*
Ac 20:10 the young man and **put** *his* **a around** him. *5227*
Heb 12:12 strengthen your feeble **a** and weak knees. *5931*

ARMY (250) [ARM]

Ex 14: 4 for myself through Pharaoh and all his **a,** 2657
14: 6 and took his **a** with him. 6639
14:17 through Pharaoh and all his **a,** 2657
14:19 in front of Israel's **a,** 4722
14:24 the pillar of fire and cloud at the Egyptian **a** 4722
14:28 the entire **a** *of* Pharaoh that had followed 2657
15: 4 Pharaoh's chariots and his **a** he has hurled 2657
17:13 So Joshua overcame the Amalekite **a** with 6639
Nu 1: 3 or more who are able to serve in the **a.** 7372
1:20 to serve in the **a** were listed by name, 7372
1:22 in the **a** were counted and listed by name, 7372
1:24 to serve in the **a** were listed by name, 7372
1:26 to serve in the **a** were listed by name, 7372
1:28 to serve in the **a** were listed by name, 7372
1:30 to serve in the **a** were listed by name, 7372
1:32 to serve in the **a** were listed by name, 7372
1:34 to serve in the **a** were listed by name, 7372
1:36 to serve in the **a** were listed by name, 7372
1:38 to serve in the **a** were listed by name, 7372
1:40 to serve in the **a** were listed by name, 7372
1:42 to serve in the **a** were listed by name, 7372
1:45 in Israel's **a** were counted according 7372
20:20 against them with a large and powerful **a.** 6639
21:23 He mustered his entire **a** and marched out 6639
21:33 and his whole **a** marched out to meet them 6639
21:34 with his whole **a** and his land. 6639
21:35 together with his sons and his whole **a,** 6639
26: 2 or more who are able to serve in the **a** 7372
31:14 Moses was angry with the officers of the **a** 2657
31:48 officers who were over the units of the **a**— 7372
Dt 2:32 and all his **a** came out to meet us in battle 6639
2:33 together with his sons and his whole **a.** 6639
3: 1 with his whole **a** marched out to meet us 6639
3: 2 over to you with his whole **a** and his land. 6639
3: 3 of Bashan and all his **a.** 6639
11: 4 what he did to the Egyptian **a,** 2657
20: 1 and chariots and an **a** greater than yours, 6639
20: 2 and address the **a.** 6639
20: 5 The officers shall say to the **a:** 6639
20: 9 the officers have finished speaking to the **a,** 6639
Jos 5:14 of the **a** *of* the LORD I have now come." 7372
5:15 The commander of the LORD's **a** replied, 7372
8: 1 Take the whole **a** with you, 4878+6639
8: 3 the whole **a** moved out to attack Ai. 4878+6639
10: 7 up from Gilgal with his entire **a,** 4878+6639
10:21 The whole **a** then returned safely to Joshua 6639
10:24 the **a** commanders who had come with him, 408+4878
10:33 but Joshua defeated him and his **a**— 6639
11: 4 a huge **a,** as numerous as the sand on 6639
11: 7 So Joshua and his whole **a** came 4878+6639
Jdg 4: 2 The commander of his **a** was Sisera, 7372
4: 7 the commander of Jabin's **a,** 7372
4:15 and all his chariots and **a** by the sword, 4722
4:16 But Barak pursued the chariots and **a** as far 4722
7:22 The **a** fled to Beth Shittah toward Zererah 4722
8:11 and fell upon the unsuspecting **a.** 4722
8:12 routing their entire **a.** 4722
9:29 'Call out your whole **a!'** " 7372
20:10 to get provisions for the **a.** 6639
20:10 when **the a** arrives at Gibeah in Benjamin, 4392S
1Sa 4:17 and the **a** has suffered heavy losses. 6639
12: 9 the commander of the **a** *of* Hazor, 7372
13: 6 and that their **a** was hard pressed, 6639
14:15 Then panic struck the whole **a**— 6639
14:16 in Benjamin saw the **a** melting away 2162
14:25 The entire **a** entered the woods, 824
14:28 "Your father bound the **a** under 6639
14:38 all you who are leaders of the **a,** 6639
14:50 the commander of Saul's **a** was Abner son 7372
15: 9 the **a** spared Agag and the best of the sheep 6639
17:20 the **a** was going out to its battle positions, 2657
17:46 of the Philistine **a** to the birds of the air and 4722
17:55 he said to Abner, commander of the **a,** 7372
18: 5 that Saul gave him a high rank in the **a.** 408+4878
26: 5 the commander of the **a,** had lain down. 7372
26: 5 with the **a** encamped around him. 6639
26: 7 David and Abishai went to the **a** by night, 6639
26:14 He called out to the **a** and to Abner son 6639
28: 1 and your men will accompany me in the **a."** 4722
28: 5 Saul saw the Philistine **a,** he was afraid; 4722
28:19 over the **a** *of* Israel to the Philistines." 4722
29: 6 to have you serve with me in the **a.** 4722
31: 7 the Jordan saw that the Israelite **a** had fled 408
2Sa 1:12 **a** *of* the LORD and the house of Israel, 6639
2: 8 the commander of Saul's **a,** 7372
5:24 in front of you to strike the Philistine **a."** 4722
8: 9 that David had defeated the entire **a** 2657
8:16 Joab son of Zeruiah was over the **a;** 7372
10: 7 David sent Joab out with the entire **a** 7372
10:16 of Hadadezer's **a** leading them. 7372
10:18 down Shobach the commander of their **a,** 7372
11: 1 the king's men and the whole Israelite **a.** NIH
11:17 some of the men in David's **a** fell; 6639
12:29 So David mustered the entire **a** and went 6639
12:31 and his entire **a** returned to Jerusalem. 6639
17:25 Absalom had appointed Amasa over the **a** 7372
18: 6 The **a** marched into the field to fight Israel, 6639
18: 7 There the **a** *of* Israel was defeated 6639
19: 2 the whole **a** the victory that day was turned 6639
19:13 now on you are not the commander of my **a** 7372
20:23 Joab was over Israel's entire **a;** 7372
24: 2 the king said to Joab and the **a** commanders 2657
24: 4 overruled Joab and the **a** commanders; 2657
1Ki 1:19 and Joab the commander of the **a,** 7372
1:25 the commanders of the **a** and Abiathar 7372
2:32 Abner son of Ner, commander of Israel's **a,** 7372
2:32 commander of Judah's **a**— 7372
2:35 of Jehoiada over the **a** in Joab's position 7372
11:15 Joab the commander of the **a,** 7372
11:21 and that Joab the commander of the **a** was 7372
16:15 The **a** was encamped near Gibbethon, 6639
16:16 the commander of the **a,** 7372
20: 1 of Aram mustered his entire **a.** 2657
20:13 'Do you see this vast **a?** 2162
20:19 of the city with the **a** behind them 2657
20:25 also raise an **a** like the one you lost— 2657
20:28 I will deliver this vast **a** into your hands, 2162
22:36 a cry spread through the **a:** 4722

2Ki 3: 9 the **a** had no more water for themselves or 4722
4:13 to the king or the commander of the **a**?' " 7372
5: 1 Now Naaman was commander of the **a** *of* 7372
6:15 an **a** with horses and chariots 2657
6:24 of Aram mobilized his entire **a** 4722
7: 6 of chariots and horses and a great **a**, 2657
7:14 and the king sent them after the Aramean **a**. 4722
8:21 his **a**, however, fled back home. 6639
9: 5 he found the **a** officers sitting together. 2657
13: 7 of the **a** of Jehoahaz except fifty horsemen, 6639
18:17 and his field commander with a large **a**, 2657
25: 1 against Jerusalem with his whole **a**. 2657
25: 4 whole **a** fled at night through the gate 408+4878
25: 5 but the Babylonian **a** pursued the king 2657
25:10 The whole Babylonian **a**, 2657
25:23 When all the **a** officers and their men heard 2657
25:26 together with the **a** officers, 2657
1Ch 10: 7 in the valley saw that the **a** had fled and NIH
12:14 These Gadites were **a** commanders; 7372
12:21 and they were commanders in his **a**. 7372
12:22 until he had a great **a**, 4722
12:22 like the **a** *of* God. 4722
14:15 in front of you to strike the Philistine **a**." 4722
14:16 and they struck down the Philistine **a**, 4722
18: 9 the entire **a** *of* Hadadezer king of Zobah, 2657
18:15 Joab son of Zeruiah was over the **a**; 7372
19: 8 David sent Joab out with the entire **a** 7372
19:16 of Hadadezer's **a** leading them. 7372
19:18 the commander of their **a**. 7372
20: 3 and his entire **a** returned to Jerusalem. 6639
25: 1 together with the commanders of the **a**, 7372
26:26 and by the other **a** commanders. 7372
27: 1 that concerned the **a divisions** that were 4713
27: 3 of Perez and chief of all the **a** officers for 7372
27: 5 The third **a** commander, 7372
27:34 Joab was the commander of the royal **a**. 7372
2Ch 13: 8 You are indeed a vast **a** and have with you 2162
14: 8 an **a** of three hundred thousand men 2657
14: 9 with a vast **a** and three hundred chariots, 2657
14:11 we have come against this **vast a**. 2162
14:13 Asa and his **a** pursued them as far as Gerar. 6639
16: 7 on the LORD your God, the **a** *of* the king 2657
16: 8 and Libyans a mighty **a** with great numbers 2657
20: 2 "A vast **a** is coming against you 2162
20:12 For we have no power to face this vast **a** 2162
20:15 or discouraged because of this vast **a**. 2162
20:21 as they went out at the head of the **a**, 2741
20:24 the desert and looked toward the **vast a**, 2162
24:23 the **a** *of* Aram marched against Joash; 2657
24:24 Aramean **a** had come with only a few men, 2657
24:24 into their hands a much larger **a**, 2657
25:11 then marshaled his strength and led his **a** to 6639
25:12 The **a** *of* Judah also captured ten thousand 1201
26:11 Uzziah had a well-trained **a**, 2657
26:13 Under their command was an **a** of 307,500 2657+7372
26:14 bows and slingstones for the entire **a**. 7372
28: 9 to meet the **a** when it returned to Samaria. 7372
32: 7 the king of Assyria and the vast **a** with him, 2162
33:11 against them the **a** commanders of the king 7372
Ne 2: 9 also sent **a** officers and cavalry with me. 2657
4: 2 in the presence of his associates and the **a** 2657
Ps 27: 3 an **a** besiege me, my heart will not fear; 4722
33:16 No king is saved by the size of his **a**; 2657
136:15 swept Pharaoh and his **a** into the Red Sea; 2657
Pr 30:31 and a king with his **a** around him. 554
Isa 13: 4 The LORD Almighty is mustering an **a** 7372
36: 2 a large **a** from Lachish to King Hezekiah 2657
43:17 the **a** and reinforcements together, 2657
Jer 4:16 **besieging** *a* is coming from a distant land, AIT
6:22 an **a** is coming from the land of the north; 6639
32: 2 The **a** *of* the king of Babylon was 2657
34: 1 and all his **a** and all the kingdoms 2657
34: 7 the **a** *of* the king of Babylon was fighting 2657
34:21 to the **a** *of* the king of Babylon, 2657
37: 5 Pharaoh's **a** had marched out of Egypt, 2657
37: 7 to inquire of me, 'Pharaoh's **a**, 2657
37:10 to defeat the entire Babylonian **a** 2657
37:11 After the Babylonian **a** had withdrawn 2657
37:11 from Jerusalem because of Pharaoh's **a**, 2657
38: 3 over to the **a** *of* the king of Babylon, 2657
39: 1 with his whole **a** and laid siege to it. 2657
39: 5 But the Babylonian **a** pursued them 2657
40: 7 the **a** officers and their men who were still 2657
40:13 the **a** officers still in the open country came 2657
41:11 of Kareah and all the **a** officers who were 2657
41:13 of Kareah and the **a** officers who were 2657
41:16 of Kareah and all the **a** officers who were 2657
42: 1 Then all the **a** officers, 2657
42: 8 of Kareah and all the **a** officers who were 2657
43: 4 the **a** officers and all the people disobeyed 2657
43: 5 of Kareah and all the **a** officers led away all 2657
46: 2 the **a** *of* Pharaoh Neco king of Egypt, 2657
50:41 An **a** is coming from the north; 6639
51: 3 completely destroy her **a**. 7372
52: 4 against Jerusalem with his whole **a**. 2657
52: 7 and the whole **a** fled. 408+4878
52: 8 the Babylonian **a** pursued King Zedekiah 2657
52:14 The whole Babylonian **a** under 2657
La 1:15 an **a** against me to crush my young men. 4595
Eze 1:24 like the tumult of an **a**. 4722
17:15 to Egypt to get horses and a large **a**. 6639
17:17 with his mighty **a** and great horde will be 2657
26: 7 with horsemen and a great **a**. 2256+6639+7736
27:10 Lydia and Put served as soldiers in your **a**. 2657
29:18 of Babylon drove his **a** in a hard campaign 2657
29:18 Yet he and his **a** got no reward from 2657
29:19 and plunder the land as pay for his **a**. 2657
29:20 for his efforts because *he and his a* **did** it AIT
30:11 He and his **a**—the most ruthless 6639
32:22 "Assyria is there with her whole **a**; 7736
32:23 of the pit and her **a** lies around her grave. 7736
32:31 "Pharaoh—he and all his **a**— 2657
37:10 on their feet—a vast **a**. 2657
38: 4 and bring you out with your whole **a**— 2657
38:15 a great horde, a mighty **a**. 2657
Da 3:20 of the strongest soldiers in his **a** to tie 10264
11:10 for war and assemble a great **a**, 2162+2657
11:11 who will raise a large **a**, 2162
11:12 When the **a** is carried off, 2162
11:13 the king of the North will muster another **a**, 2162
11:13 with a huge **a** fully equipped. 2657
11:22 an overwhelming **a** will be swept away 2432
11:25 "With a large **a** he will stir up his strength 2657
11:25 with a large and very powerful **a**, 2657
11:26 his **a** will be swept away, 2657
Joel 2: 2 the mountains a large and mighty **a** comes, 6639
2: 5 like a mighty **a** drawn up for battle. 6639
2:11 The LORD thunders at the head of his **a**; 2657
2:20 "I will drive the **northern** *a* far from you, AIT
2:25 my great **a** that I sent among you. 2657
Mt 22: 7 He sent his **a** and destroyed those murderers *5128*
Rev 19:19 against the rider on the horse and his **a**. *5128*

ARNAN (1)

1Ch 3:21 of A, of Obadiah and of Shecaniah. 820

ARNON (24) [ARNON'S]

Nu 21:13 from there and camped alongside the A, 818
21:13 The A is the border of Moab, 818
21:14 "...Waheb in Suphah and the ravines, the A 818
21:24 over his land from the A to the Jabbok, 818
21:26 from him all his land as far as the A. 818
22:36 at the Moabite town on the A border, 818
Dt 2:24 "Set out now and cross the A Gorge. 818
2:36 From Aroer on the rim of the A Gorge, 818
3: 8 from the A Gorge as far as Mount Hermon. 818
3:12 the territory north of Aroer by the A Gorge, 818
3:16 the A Gorge (the middle of the gorge being 818
4:48 on the rim of the A Gorge to Mount Siyon 818
Jos 12: 1 from the A Gorge to Mount Hermon, 818
12: 2 from Aroer on the rim of the A Gorge— 818
13: 9 from Aroer on the rim of the A Gorge, 818
13:16 from Aroer on the rim of the A Gorge, 818
Jdg 11:13 they took away my land from the A to 818
11:18 and camped on the other side of the A. 818
11:18 for the A was its border. 818
11:22 capturing all of it from the A to the Jabbok 818
11:26 and all the towns along the A. 818
2Ki 10:33 from Aroer by the A Gorge through Gilead 818
Isa 16: 2 the women of Moab at the fords of the A. 818
Jer 48:20 Announce by the A that Moab is destroyed. 818

ARNON'S (1) [ARNON]

Nu 21:28 the citizens of A heights. 818

ARODI (2) [ARODITE]

Ge 46:16 Haggi, Shuni, Ezbon, Eri, A and Areli. 771
Nu 26:17 through A, the Arodite clan; 771

ARODITE (1) [ARODI]

Nu 26:17 the A clan; through Areli, the Arelite clan. 772

AROER (16) [AROERITE]

Nu 32:34 The Gadites built up Dibon, Ataroth, A, 6876
Dt 2:36 From A on the rim of the Arnon Gorge, 6876
3:12 and the Gadites the territory north of A by 6876
4:48 This land extended from A on the rim of 6876
Jos 12: 2 from A on the rim of the Arnon Gorge— 6876
13: 9 from A on the rim of the Arnon Gorge, 6876
13:16 from A on the rim of the Arnon Gorge, 6876
13:25 and half the Ammonite country as far as A, 6876
Jdg 11:26 A, the surrounding settlements and all 6876
11:33 He devastated twenty towns from A to 6876
1Sa 30:28 to those in A, Siphmoth, Eshtemoa 6876
2Sa 24: 5 crossing the Jordan, they camped near A, 6876
2Ki 10:33 from A by the Arnon Gorge through Gilead 6876
1Ch 5: 8 in the area from A to Nebo and Baal Meon. 6876
Isa 17: 2 The cities of A will be deserted and left 6876
Jer 48:19 you who live in A. 6876

AROERITE (1) [AROER]

1Ch 11:44 Shama and Jeiel the sons of Hotham the A, 6901

AROMA (41) [AROMATIC]

Ge 8:21 the pleasing **a** and said in his heart: 8194
Ex 29:18 the LORD, a pleasing **a**, an offering made 8194
29:25 with the burnt offering for a pleasing **a** to 8194
29:41 a pleasing **a**, an offering made to 8194
Lev 1: 9 an **a** pleasing to the LORD. 8194
1:13 an **a** pleasing to the LORD. 8194
1:17 an **a** pleasing to the LORD. 8194
2: 2 an **a** pleasing to the LORD. 8194
2: 9 an **a** pleasing to the LORD. 8194
2:12 to be offered on the altar as a pleasing **a**. 8194
3: 5 an **a** pleasing to the LORD. 8194
3:16 an offering made by fire, a pleasing **a**. 8194
4:31 on the altar as an **a** pleasing to the LORD. 8194
6:15 on the altar as an **a** pleasing to the LORD. 8194
6:21 in pieces as an **a** pleasing to the LORD. 8194
8:21 the altar as a burnt offering, a pleasing **a**, 8194
8:28 as an ordination offering, a pleasing **a**, 8194
17: 6 the fat as an **a** pleasing to the LORD. 8194
23:13 to the LORD by fire, a pleasing **a**— 8194
23:18 an **a** pleasing to the LORD. 8194
26:31 and I will take no delight in the pleasing **a** 8194
Nu 15: 3 as an **a** pleasing to the LORD— 8194
15: 7 Offer it as an **a** pleasing to the LORD. 8194
15:10 an **a** pleasing to the LORD. 8194
15:13 an offering made by fire as an **a** pleasing to 8194
15:14 an offering made by fire as an **a** pleasing to 8194
15:24 for a burnt offering as an **a** pleasing to 8194
18:17 an **a** pleasing to the LORD. 8194
28: 2 as an **a** pleasing to me.' 8194
28: 6 at Mount Sinai as a pleasing **a**, 8194
28: 8 an **a** pleasing to the LORD. 8194
28:13 This is for a burnt offering, a pleasing **a**, 8194
28:24 for seven days as an **a** pleasing to 8194
28:27 a year old as an **a** pleasing to the LORD. 8194
29: 2 As an **a** pleasing to the LORD, 8194
29: 6 by fire—a pleasing **a**. 8194
29: 8 Present as an **a** pleasing to the LORD 8194
29:13 an offering made by fire as an **a** pleasing to 8194
29:36 an offering made by fire as an **a** pleasing to 8194
Jer 48:11 and her **a** is unchanged. 8194
2Co 2:15 For we are to God the **a** of Christ *2380*

AROMATIC (1) [AROMA]

Ge 2:12 **a resin** and onyx are also there.) 978

AROSE (11) [RISE]

Ge 13: 7 And quarreling **a** between Abram's 2118
Jdg 5: 7 Deborah, **a**, arose a mother in Israel. 7756
5: 7 Deborah, arose, **a** a mother in Israel. 7756
1Sa 1:19 **Early** the next morning *they* **a** 8899
Est 8: 4 to Esther and she **a** and stood before him. 7756
SS 5: 5 I **a** to open for my lover, 7756
Jnh 1: 4 a violent storm **a** that the ship threatened 2118
Lk 22:24 Also a dispute **a** among them as to which *1181*
Ac 6: 9 **Opposition a**, however, *482*
19:23 About that time *there* **a** a great disturbance *1181+1254*
Gal 2: 4 [This matter **a**] because some false brothers *NIG*

AROUND (404) [ROUNDABOUT]

Ge 19:31 and there is no man **a** here to lie with us, 928
33: 4 *he* **threw** *his* **arms a** his neck and kissed him. 5877+6584
35: 5 of God fell upon the towns **all a** them so 6017
37: 7 while your sheaves **gathered a** mine 6015
37:15 a man found him **wandering a** in the fields 9494
41:42 in robes of fine linen and put a gold chain **a** 6584
45:14 Then *he* **threw** *his* **arms a** 5877+6584+7418
46:29 *he* **threw** *his* **arms a** his father and wept for 5877+6584+7418
49: 1 "Gather **a** so I can tell you what will happen 665
Ex 13:18 So God **led** the people **a** *by* the desert road 6015
14: 3 **wandering a** the land **in confusion,** 1003
16: 3 There we sat **a** pots of meat and ate all 6584
16:13 in the morning there was a layer of dew **a** 6017
18:13 and they stood **a** him from morning 6584
18:14 while all these people stand **a** you 6584
19:12 for the people **a** the mountain and tell them, 6017
19:23 **'Put limits a** the mountain and set it apart 1487
21:19 if the other gets up and **walks a** outside 2143
25:11 and make a gold molding **a** it. 6017
25:24 with pure gold and make a gold molding **a** 6017
25:25 Also make **a** it a rim a handbreadth wide 6017
27:17 All the posts **a** the courtyard are 6017
28:32 There shall be a woven edge like a collar **a** 6017
28:33 and scarlet yarn **a** the hem of the robe, 6017
28:34 the pomegranates are to alternate **a** the hem 6017
29:13 Then take all the fat **a** the inner parts, 4059
29:22 the fat tail, the fat **a** the inner parts, 4059
30: 3 and make a gold molding **a** it. 6017
32: 1 they gathered **a** Aaron and said, "Come, 6584
37: 2 and made a gold molding **a** it. 6017
37:11 with pure gold and made a gold molding **a** 6017
37:12 also made **a** it a rim a handbreadth wide 6017
37:26 and made a gold molding **a** it. 6017
38:16 All the curtains **a** the courtyard were 6017
39:23 and a band **a** this opening, 6017
39:24 and scarlet yarn and finely twisted linen **a** 6584
39:25 of pure gold and attached them **a** the hem 6017
39:26 and pomegranates alternated **a** the hem of 6017
40: 8 Set up the courtyard **a** it and put the curtain 6017
40:33 up the courtyard **a** the tabernacle and altar 6017
Lev 8: 7 **tied** the sash **a** him, 2520
8:13 **tied** sashes **a** them and put headbands 2520
8:16 Moses also took all the fat **a** the inner parts, 6584
8:25 the fat tail, all the fat **a** the inner parts, 6584
16: 4 **tie** the linen sash **a** 2520
25:31 without walls **a** them are to be considered 6017
25:44 to come from the nations **a** you; 6017
Nu 1:50 they are to take care of it and encamp **a** it. 6017
1:53 are to set up their tents **a** the tabernacle of 6017
2: 2 "The Israelites are to camp **a** the Tent 6017
11: 8 The people **went a** gathering it, 8763
11:24 of their elders and had them stand **a** 6017
11:31 It brought them down **all a** the camp to 6017
11:32 they spread them out **all a** the camp. 6017
16:34 At their cries, all the Israelites **a** them fled, 6017
21: 4 route to the Red Sea, to **go a** Edom. 6015
22: 4 "This horde is going to lick up everything **a** 6017

Nu 32:33 with its cities and the territory **a** them. 6017
35: 2 And give them pasturelands **a** the towns. 6017
35: 4 "The pasturelands **a** the towns 6017
Dt 1:40 **turn a** and set out toward the desert along 7155
2: 1 For a long time *we* **made** *our* **way a** 6015
2: 3 "You *have* **made** *your* **way a** 6015
2:37 the Jabbok nor that **a** the towns in the hills. NIH
6:14 the gods of the peoples **a** you; 6017
7:22 or the wild animals will multiply **a** you. 6584
12:10 rest from all your enemies **a** you 4946+6017
13: 7 gods of the peoples **a** you, 6017
17:14 a king over us like all the nations **a** us," 6017
22: 8 make a parapet **a** your roof so that you may 4200
25:19 from all the enemies **a** you in 4946+6017
Jos 6: 3 **March a** the city once with all 5938+6015
6: 4 **march a** the city seven times, 6015
6: 7 "Advance! **March a** the city, 6015
6:11 So *he had* the ark of the LORD **carried a** 6015
6:14 second day *they* **marched a** the city once 6015
6:15 they got up at daybreak and **marched a** 6015
6:16 The seventh time **a,** when the priests NIH
8:21 *they* **turned a** and attacked the men of Ai. 8740
10:38 with him **turned a** and attacked Debir. 8740
15: 3 past Hezron up to Addar and **curved a** 6015
15:12 These are the boundaries **a** the people 6017
19: 8 and all the villages **a** these towns as far 6017
19:14 There the boundary **went a** on the north 6015
21:12 and **villages** *a* the city they had given AIT
23: 1 from all their enemies **a** them, 4946+6017
Jdg 2:12 various gods of the peoples **a** them. 6017
2:14 He sold them to their enemies **all a,** 4946+6017
6:31 Joash replied to the hostile crowd **a** him, 6584
7:18 from **all a** the camp blow yours and shout, 6017
7:21 each man held his position **a** the camp, 6017
11: 3 where a group of adventurers gathered **a** 448
18:26 **turned a** and went back home. 7155
20:29 Then Israel set an ambush **a** Gibeah. 6017
1Sa 5:10 **brought** the ark of the god of Israel **a** 6015
9: 4 of Ephraim and through the **area** *a* AIT
17:39 over the tunic and tried **walking a,** 2143
22: 2 or in debt or discontented gathered **a** him, 448
22: 6 with all his officials standing **a** him. 6584
25:12 David's men **turned a** and went back. 2200
25:16 Night and day they were a wall **a** us all 6584
26: 5 with the army encamped **a** him. 6017
26: 7 Abner and the soldiers were lying **a** him. 6017
26:16 **Look a** you. Where are the king's spear 8011
31: 3 The fighting grew fierce **a** Saul, 448
2Sa 1: 7 When he turned **a** and saw me, 339
5: 9 He built up the **area a** it, 6017
5:23 but **circle a** behind them and attack them 6015
7: 1 from all his enemies **a** him, 4946+6017
11: 2 up from his bed and **walked a** on the roof 2143
22: 6 The cords of the grave **coiled a** me; 6015
22:12 He made darkness his canopy **a** him— 6017
24: 6 and on to Dan Jaan and **a** toward Sidon. 6017
1Ki 2: 5 with that blood stained the belt **a** his waist 928
3: 1 and the wall **a** Jerusalem. 6017
6: 5 and inner sanctuary he built a structure **a** 6017
6: 6 He made offset ledges **a** the outside of 6017
6:29 On the walls **all a** the temple, 4990
7:15 and twelve cubits **a,** 6015
7:20 pomegranates in rows **all a.** 6017
7:23 It took a line of thirty cubits *to* **measure a**
it. 6015+6017
7:31 **A** its opening there was engraving. 6584
7:36 with wreaths **all a.** 6017
8:14 the king **turned a** and blessed them. 6015
11:24 He gathered men **a** him and became 6584
16:18 the royal palace and set the palace on fire **a** 6584
18:26 And they danced **a** the altar they had made. 6584
18:32 a trench **a** it large enough to hold two seahs 6017
18:35 down **a** the altar and even filled the trench. 6017
19: 6 *He* **looked a,** and there by his head was 5564
19:19 Elijah went up to him and threw his cloak **a** 448
20:31 with sackcloth **a** our waists and ropes 928
20:31 around our waists and ropes **a** our heads. 928
20:32 Wearing sackcloth **a** their waists and ropes 928
20:32 around their waists and ropes **a** their heads, 928
21:27 He lay in sackcloth and **went a** meekly. 2143
22:19 with all the host of heaven standing **a** him 6584
22:34 **"Wheel a** and get me out of the fighting.
2200+3338
2Ki 1: 8 of hair and with a leather belt **a** his waist." 928
2:24 He turned **a,** looked at them and called 339
4: 3 Go **a** and ask all your neighbors 2021+2575+4946
6:17 of horses and chariots of fire **all a** Elisha. 6017
10:23 **"Look a** and see that no servants of 2924
11: 8 Station yourselves **a** the king, 6017
11:11 stationed themselves **a** the king— 6017
17:15 They imitated the nations **a** them although 6017
23: 5 of Judah and on *those* **a** Jerusalem— 4990
23:16 Then Josiah **looked a,** 7155
25: 1 the city and built siege works **all a** it. 6017
25:10 broke down the walls **a** Jerusalem. 6017
25:17 and pomegranates of bronze **all a.** 6017
1Ch 4:33 the villages **a** these towns as far as Baalath. 6017
6:56 and **villages** *a* the city were given AIT
9:27 They would spend the night **stationed a** 6017
10: 3 The fighting grew fierce **a** Saul, 6584
11: 8 He built up the city **a** it, 6017
14:14 but **circle a** them and attack them in front 6015
2Ch 4: 2 It took a line of thirty cubits *to* **measure a**
it. 6015+6017
6: 3 the king **turned a** and blessed them. 6015
13: 7 Some worthless scoundrels gathered **a** him 6584
13:13 Now Jeroboam *had* **sent** troops **a** to the rear, 6015
2Ch 14: 7 he said to Judah, "and **put** walls **a** them, 6015
14:14 They destroyed all the villages **a** Gerar, 6017
17: 9 *they* **went a** to all the towns of Judah 6015
18:33 **"Wheel a** and get me out of the fighting.
2200+3338
23: 7 The Levites are to station themselves **a** 6017
23:10 with his weapon in his hand, **a** the king— 6017
31:19 who lived on the **farm** lands *a* their towns AIT
34: 6 as far as Naphtali, and in the ruins **a** them, 6017
Ezr 3: 3 Despite their fear of the peoples **a** them, 824[S]
4: 4 the peoples **a** them set out to discourage 824[S]
9: 2 the holy race with the peoples **a** them. 824[S]
9: 4 at the words of the God of Israel gathered **a** 448
10: 1 and children—gathered **a** him. 448
10: 2 from the peoples **a** us. 824[S]
10:11 Separate yourselves from the peoples **a** you 824[S]
Ne 8:13 gathered **a** Ezra the scribe to give attention 448
10:30 to the peoples **a** us or take their daughters 824[S]
12:28 from the region **a** Jerusalem— 6017
12:29 for themselves **a** Jerusalem. 6017
12:44 the **fields** *a* the towns they were to bring AIT
Job 1:10 not put a hedge **a** him and his household
1237+4946+6017
8:17 it entwines its roots **a** a pile of rocks 6584
12:18 by kings and ties a loincloth **a** their waist. 928
19: 6 and drawn his net **a** me. 6584
19:12 a siege ramp against me and encamp **a** 6017
21: 8 They see their children established **a** them, 6640
22:10 That is why snares are **all a** you, 6017
29: 5 with me and my children were **a** me, 6017
37:12 At his direction they swirl **a** over the face 4991
Ps 3: 3 But you are a shield **a** me, O LORD; 1237
7: 7 *Let* the assembled peoples **gather a** you. 6015
18: 5 The cords of the grave **coiled a** me; 6015
18:11 his canopy **a** him— 6017
34: 7 the LORD encamps **a** those who fear him, 6017
44:13 the scorn and derision of *those* **a** us. 6017
48:12 Walk about Zion, **go a** her, 5938
50: 3 and **a** him a tempest rages. 6017
78:28 inside their camp, **all a** their tents. 6017
79: 3 like water **all a** Jerusalem, 6017
79: 4 of scorn and derision to *those* **a** us. 6017
109:19 like a belt **tied** forever **a** him. 2520
118:12 *They* **swarmed a** me like bees, 6015
128: 3 your sons will be like olive shoots **a** 6017
139:11 and the light become night **a** me," 1237
Pr 3: 3 bind them **a** your neck, 6584
6:21 fasten them **a** your neck. 6584
30:31 a he-goat, and a king with his army **a** him. 6640
Isa 11: 5 be his belt and faithfulness the **sash** *a* AIT
19:14 as a drunkard **staggers a** in his vomit. 9494
20: 2 he did so, **going a** stripped and barefoot. 2143
22:21 with your robe and **fasten** your sash *a* him AIT
28:20 the blanket too narrow *to* **wrap a** *you.* 4043
29: 3 I will encamp against you **all a;** 1885+2021+3869
32:11 **put sackcloth a** your waists. 2520
49:18 Lift up your eyes and look **a;** 6017
56:10 *they* **lie a** and dream, they love to sleep. 8886
Jer 5: 1 **look a** and consider, 8011
6: 3 they will pitch their tents **a** her, 6017
13: 1 and buy a linen belt and put it **a** your waist, 6584
13: 2 and put it **a** my waist. 6584
13: 4 the belt you bought and are **wearing a** 6584
13:11 For as a belt is bound **a** a man's waist, 448
17:26 the towns of Judah and the villages **a** 4946+6017
19:15 the villages **a** it every disaster I pronounced 3972
21:14 that will consume everything **a** you.' " 6017
26: 9 the people crowded **a** Jeremiah in the house 448
31:26 At this I awoke and **looked** *a.* AIT
32:44 in the villages **a** Jerusalem, 6017
33:13 in the villages **a** Jerusalem and in the towns 6017
34:16 *you have* **turned a** and profaned my name; 8740
40:15 and cause all the Jews who are gathered **a** 448
43:12 **wraps** his garment **a him,** 6486
43:12 so *will he* **wrap** Egypt **a himself** and depart 6486
46:14 for the sword devours *those* **a** you.' 6017
48:17 Mourn for her, all who live **a** her, 6017
48:39 an object of horror to all *those* **a** her." 6017
49: 5 I will bring terror on you from all *those* **a** 6017
50:14 "Take up your positions **a** Babylon, 6017
50:29 Encamp **all a** her; let no one escape. 6017
50:32 that will consume all who are **a** her." 6017
52: 4 the city and built siege works **all a** it. 6017
52:14 down all the walls **a** Jerusalem. 6017
52:22 and pomegranates of bronze all **a.** 6017
La 1:12 **Look a** and see. Is any suffering like my 5564
2: 3 a flaming fire that consumes **everything a** 6017
2: 8 down the **wall** *a* the Daughter of Zion. AIT
Eze 1:18 and all four rims were full of eyes **all a.** 6017
1:28 so was the radiance **a** him. 6017
2: 6 though briers and thorns are **all a** you 907
4: 2 against it and put battering rams **a** it. 6017
5: 2 and strike it with the sword **all a** the city. 6017
5: 5 with countries **all a** her. 6017
5: 6 the nations and countries **a** her. 6017
5: 7 the nations **a** you and have 6017
5: 7 to the standards of the nations **a** you. 6017
5:14 a ruin and a reproach among the nations **a** 6017
5:15 the nations **a** you when I inflict punishment 6017
6: 5 and I will scatter your bones **a** your altars. 6017
6:13 among their idols **a** their altars, 6017
11:12 to the standards of the nations **a** you." 6017
12:14 I will scatter to the winds all those **a** him— 6017
16:11 on your arms and a necklace **a** your neck, 6584
16:37 I will gather them against you from **all a** 6017
16:57 all *those* **a** you who despise you. 6017
23:15 with belts **a** their waists 928
Eze 23:42 "The noise of a carefree crowd was **a** her; 928
27:11 They hung their shields **a** your walls; 6017
31: 4 their streams flowed **all a** its base 6017
32:23 in the depths of the pit and her army lies **a** 6017
32:24 with all her hordes **a** her grave. 6017
32:25 with all her hordes **a** her grave. 6017
32:26 with all their hordes **a** their graves. 6017
36: 4 ridiculed by the rest of the nations **a** 4946+6017
36: 7 the nations **a** you will also suffer scorn 4946+6017
36:36 the nations **a** you that remain will know 6017
37:21 from **all a** and bring them back 6017
38: 4 *I will* **turn** you **a,** 8740
39: 2 *I will* **turn** you **a** and drag you along. 8740
39:17 from **all a** to the sacrifice I am preparing 6017
40:14 the faces of the projecting walls **all a** 6017+6017
40:16 by narrow parapet openings **all a,** 6017+6017
40:16 the openings **all a** faced inward. 6017+6017
40:17 had been constructed **all a** the court; 6017+6017
40:25 its portico had narrow openings **all a,** 6017+6017
40:29 and its portico had openings **all a.** 6017+6017
40:30 (The porticoes of the gateways **a** 6017+6017
40:33 and its portico had openings **all a.** 6017+6017
40:36 and it had openings **all a.** 6017+6017
40:43 were attached to the wall **all a.** 6017+6017
41: 5 and each side room **a** 6017+6017
41: 6 There were ledges **all a** the wall of 6017+6017
41: 7 The side rooms **all a** 6015
41: 8 the temple had a raised base **all a** it, 6017+6017
41:10 was twenty cubits wide **all a** 6017+6017
41:11 open area was five cubits wide **all a.** 6017+6017
41:12 building was five cubits thick **all a,** 6017+6017
41:16 and the narrow windows and galleries **a** 6017
41:17 on the walls at regular intervals **all a** 6017+6017
41:19 They were carved **all a** 6017+6017
42:15 east gate and measured the area **all a:** 6017+6017
42:20 It had a wall **a** it, 6017+6017
43:13 with a rim of one span **a** the edge. 6017
43:17 a cubit and a gutter of a cubit **all a.** 6017
43:20 of the upper ledge and **all a** the rim, 6017
44:18 on their heads and linen undergarments **a** 6584
45: 2 with 50 cubits **a** it for open land. 6017
46:21 and **led** me **a** to its four corners, 6296
46:23 **A** the inside of each of the four courts was 6017
46:23 with places for fire built **all a** under 6017
47: 2 the north gate and **led** me **a** the outside to 6015
48:35 "The distance **all a** will be 18,000 cubits. 6017
Da 3:25 I see four men **walking a** in the fire, 10207
3:27 governors and royal advisers **crowded a** 10359
5: 7 in purple and have a gold chain placed **a** 10542
5:16 and have a gold chain placed **a** your neck, 10542
5:29 a gold chain was placed **a** his neck, 10542
9:16 an object of scorn to all *those* **a** us. 6017
10: 5 with a belt of the finest gold **a** his waist. NIH
Jnh 2: 5 seaweed *was* **wrapped a** my head. 2502
Na 3: 8 situated on the Nile, with water **a** her? 6017
Hab 2:16 from the LORD's right hand *is* **coming a** 6015
Zec 2: 5 And I myself will be a wall of fire **a** it,' 6017
Mt 3: 4 and he had a leather belt **a** his waist. *4309*
8:18 When Jesus saw the crowd **a** him, *4309*
13: 2 Such large crowds gathered **a** him *4639*
18: 6 to have a large millstone hung **a** his neck *4309*
20: 6 and found still others standing **a.** *NIG*
21:33 *He* **put** a wall **a** it, *4363*
27:27 the whole company of soldiers **a** him. *2093*
Mk 1: 6 with a leather belt **a** his waist, *4309*
3: 5 He **looked a at** them in anger and, *4315*
3: 8 the regions across the Jordan and **a** Tyre *4309*
3:32 A crowd was sitting **a** him, *4309*
3:34 Then he looked at those seated in a circle **a** *4309*
4: 1 The crowd that gathered **a** him was so large *4639*
4:10 the Twelve and the others **a** him asked him *4309*
5:21 a large crowd gathered **a** him while he was *2093*
5:24 A large crowd followed and **pressed a** him. *5315*
5:30 He **turned a** in the crowd and asked, *2188*
5:32 But Jesus *kept* **looking a** *4315*
5:42 Immediately the girl stood up and walked **a** *NIG*
6: 6 Then Jesus **went a** teaching from village *4310*
6:30 The apostles gathered **a** Jesus and reported *4639*
7: 1 from Jerusalem gathered **a** Jesus and *4639*
8:24 they look like trees **walking a."** *4344*
8:27 and his disciples went on to the villages **a** *NIG*
9: 8 Suddenly, *when they* **looked a,** *4315*
9:14 a large crowd **a** them and the teachers of *4309*
9:20 *He* fell to the ground and **rolled a,** *3244*
9:42 into the sea with a large millstone **tied a** *4329*
10:23 Jesus **looked a** and said to his disciples, *4315*
11:11 *He* **looked a at** everything, *4315*
12: 1 *He* **put** a wall **a** it, *4363*
12:38 *to* **walk a** in flowing robes and be greeted *4344*
14:69 she said again *to* those **standing a,** *4225*
Lk 2: 9 and the glory of the Lord **shone a** them, *4334*
3: 3 He went into all the **country a** the Jordan, *4369*
5: 1 the people **crowding a** him and listening to *2130*
6:10 He **looked a at** them all, *4315*
10: 7 *Do* not **move a** from house to house. *3553*
13: 8 and I'll dig **a** it and fertilize it. *4309*
15: 1 and "sinners" were all **gathering a** *1581*
15:20 **threw his arms a** him and kissed him.
2093+2158+3836+5549
17: 2 the sea with a millstone **tied a** his neck than *4329*
20:46 like *to* **walk a** in flowing robes and love to *4344*
Jn 1:38 **Turning a,** Jesus saw them following *5138*
7: 1 After this, Jesus **went a** in Galilee, *4344*
8: 2 where all the people gathered **a** him, *4639*
10:24 The Jews **gathered a** him, saying, *3240*
11:44 and a cloth **a** his face. *4317*
13: 4 **wrapped** a towel **a** his **waist.** *1346*

Jn 13: 5 with the towel that was **wrapped a** *him.* 1346
18:18 and officials stood **a** a fire they had made NIG
20: 7 the burial cloth that had been **a** Jesus' head. 2093
20:14 *she* **turned a** and saw Jesus standing there, 1650+3836+3958+5138
21: 7 **wrapped** his outer garment **a** him 1346
Ac 5:16 Crowds gathered also from the towns **a** 4339
9: 3 suddenly a light from heaven **flashed a** 4313
9:39 All the widows **stood a** him, 4225
10:38 and how he **went a** doing good 1451
12: 8 **"Wrap** your cloak **a** *you* and follow me," 4314
14:20 But *after* the disciples *had* **gathered a** him, 3240
16:18 so troubled that he **turned a** and said to 2188
17:23 For *as I* **walked a** and looked carefully 1451
19:13 Some Jews who **went a** 4320
20:10 on the young man and **put** *his* **arms a** him. 5227
22: 6 a bright light from heaven **flashed a** me. 4313
25: 7 down from Jerusalem **stood a** him, 4325
26:13 **blazing a** me and my companions. 4334
Ro 15:19 from Jerusalem all the way **a** to Illyricum, 3241
2Co 4:10 We always **carry a** in our body the death 4367
Eph 6:14 with the belt of truth **buckled a** your **waist,** 4322
2Ti 4: 3 *they will* **gather a** them a great number 2197
Heb 11:30 people *had* **marched a** them for seven days. 3240
1Pe 5: 8 Your enemy the devil **prowls a** like 4344
1Jn 2:11 the darkness and **walks a** in the darkness; 4344
Rev 1:12 *I* **turned a** to see the voice 2188
1:13 down to his feet and with a golden sash **a** 4639
4: 6 In the center, **a** the throne, 3241
4: 8 and was covered with eyes **all a,** 3239
7:11 the angels were standing **a** the throne and 3241
7:11 around the throne and **a** the elders and NIG
15: 6 shining linen and wore golden sashes **a** 4309

AROUSE (5) [ROUSE]

SS 2: 7 *Do* not **a** or awaken love until it so desires. 6424
3: 5 *Do* not **a** or awaken love until it so desires. 6424
8: 4 *Do* not **a** or awaken love until it so desires. 6424
Ro 11:14 **a** my own people **to envy** 4143
1Co 10:22 **a** the Lord's **jealousy?** 4143

AROUSED (15) [ROUSE]

Ex 22:24 My anger *will be* **a,** 3013
Nu 11: 1 and when he heard them his anger *was* **a.** 3013
32:10 The LORD's anger *was* **a** that day 3013
Dt 9: 8 At Horeb *you* **a** the LORD's **wrath** so 7911
2Ch 21:16 The LORD **a** against Jehoram the hostility 6424
36:16 of the LORD *was* **a** against his people 6590
Job 17: 8 the innocent *are* **a** against the ungodly. 6424
32: 5 his anger *was* **a.** 3013
Ps 78:58 *they* **a** his **jealousy** with their idols. 7861
Jer 32:31 this city *has* so **a** my anger and wrath 2118+6584
51:39 But while they *are* **a,** 2801
Eze 38:18 my hot anger *will be* **a,** 6590
Hos 11: 8 all my compassion *is* **a** 4023
Ac 21:30 The whole city *was* **a,** 3075
Ro 7: 5 the sinful passions **a** by the law were NIG

AROUSES (1) [ROUSE]

Pr 6:34 for jealousy **a** a husband's fury, NIH

ARPAD (6)

2Ki 18:34 Where are the gods of Hamath and **A?** 822
19:13 is the king of Hamath, the king of **A,** 822
Isa 10: 9 Is not Hamath like **A,** 822
36:19 Where are the gods of Hamath and **A?** 822
37:13 is the king of Hamath, the king of **A,** 822
Jer 49:23 "Hamath and **A** are dismayed, 822

ARPHAD (KJV) See ARPAD

ARPHAXAD (10)

Ge 10:22 Elam, Asshur, **A,** Lud and Aram. 823
10:24 **A** was the father of Shelah, 823
11:10 he became the father of **A.** 823
11:11 And after he became the father of **A,** 823
11:12 When **A** had lived 35 years, 823
11:13 **A** lived 403 years and had other sons 823
1Ch 1:17 Elam, Asshur, **A,** Lud and Aram. 823
1:18 **A** was the father of Shelah, 823
1:24 Shem, **A,** Shelah, 823
Lk 3:36 the son *of* **A,** the son of Shem, 790

ARRANGE (4) [ARRANGED, ARRANGEMENT, ARRANGEMENTS]

Lev 1: 7 to put fire on the altar and **a** wood on 6885
1: 8 Aaron's sons the priests *shall* **a** the pieces, 6885
1:12 and the priest *shall* **a** them, 6885
6:12 to add firewood and **a** the burnt offering on 6885

ARRANGED (12) [ARRANGE]

Ge 15:10 and **a** the halves opposite each other; 5989
22: 9 an altar there and **a** the wood on it. 6885
Jdg 20:38 men of Israel *had* **a** with the ambush 2118+4595
2Sa 23: 5 **a** and secured in every part? 6885
1Ki 18:33 *He* **a** the wood, cut the bull into pieces 6885
2Ki 9:30 **a** her hair and looked out of a window. 3512
2Ch 35:10 The service **was a** and the priests stood 3922
Mt 26:48 Now the betrayer *had* **a** a signal with them: 1443
Mk 14:44 Now the betrayer *had* **a** a signal with them: 1443
Ac 28:23 They **a** to meet Paul on a certain day, 5435
1Co 12:18 But in fact God *has* **a** the parts in the body, 5502
Heb 9: 6 *When* everything *had been* **a** like this, 2941

ARRANGEMENT (2) [ARRANGE]

Eze 43:11 its **a,** its exits and entrances— 9414
Ac 20:13 *He had* **made** this **a** 1411

ARRANGEMENTS (1) [ARRANGE]

2Co 9: 5 and **finish the a for** the generous gift 4616

ARRAY (2) [ARRAYED]

Ge 2: 1 in all their **vast a.** 7372
Dt 4:19 all the heavenly **a—** 7372

ARRAYED (2) [ARRAY]

Ps 110: 3 **A in** holy majesty, 928
Isa 61:10 with garments of salvation and **a** me *in* 3598

ARREST (16) [ARRESTED, ARRESTING]

Jer 36:26 and Shelemiah son of Abdeel to **a** Baruch 4374
Mt 10:19 But when *they* **a** you, 4140
21:46 They looked for a way *to* **a** him, 3195
26: 4 and they plotted to **a** Jesus in some sly way 3195
26:48 "The one I kiss is the man; **a** him." 3195
26:55 and *you did* not **a** me. 3195
Mk 12:12 *to* **a** him because they knew he had spoken 3195
14: 1 for some sly way *to* **a** Jesus and kill him. 3195
14:44 **a** him and lead him away under guard." 3195
14:49 and *you did* not **a** me. 3195
Lk 20:19 looked for a way *to* **a** him immediately, 2093+2095+3836+5931
Jn 7:32 the Pharisees sent temple guards to **a** him. 4389
11:57 he should report it so that *they might* **a** him. 4389
18:36 my servants would fight to prevent *my* **a** by 4140
Ac 9:14 from the chief priests *to* **a** all who call 1313
2Co 11:32 the Damascenes guarded *in order to* **a** me. 4389

ARRESTED (14) [ARREST]

Jer 37:13 the son of Hananiah, **a** him and said, 9530
37:14 instead, *he* **a** Jeremiah and brought him to 9530
Mt 14: 3 Now Herod *had* **a** John and bound him 3195
26:50 seized Jesus and **a** him. 3195
26:57 Those who *had* **a** Jesus took him 3195
Mk 6:17 to have John **a,** 3195
13:11 Whenever you *are* **a** and brought to trial, 4140
14:46 The men seized Jesus and **a** him. 3195
Jn 18:12 and the Jewish officials **a** Jesus. 5197
Ac 1:16 as guide *for* those who **a** Jesus— 5197
5:18 *They* **a** the apostles and 2093+2095+3836+5931
12: 1 King Herod **a** some who 2095+3836+5931
21:33 up and **a** him and ordered him to be bound 2138
28:17 I was **a** in Jerusalem and handed over to 1300

ARRESTING (2) [ARREST]

Ac 12: 4 *After* **a** him, he put him in prison, 4389
22: 4 **a** both men and women and throwing them 1297

ARRIVAL (3) [ARRIVE]

Ge 43:25 They prepared their gifts for Joseph's **a** 995
Ezr 3: 8 of the second year after their **a** at the house 995
Jn 11:17 *On his* **a,** Jesus found 2262

ARRIVE (4) [ARRIVAL, ARRIVED, ARRIVES, ARRIVING]

Ex 1:19 and give birth before the midwives **a."** 448+995
Ne 2: 7 until *I* **a** in Judah? 995
Job 6:20 *they* **a** there, only to be disappointed. 995+6330
1Co 16: 3 when *I* **a,** I will give letters of introduction 4134

ARRIVED (89) [ARRIVE]

Ge 12: 5 for land of Canaan, and *they* **a** there. 995
19: 1 The two angels **a** at Sodom in the evening, 995
33:18 he **a** safely *at* the city of Shechem 995
37:14 When Joseph **a** at Shechem, 995
42: 6 So when Joseph's brothers **a,** 995
46:28 When *they* **a** in the region of Goshen, 995
Nu 10:21 to be set up before they **a.** 995
20: 1 the whole Israelite community **a** *at* 995
Dt 9: 7 the day you left Egypt until you **a** here, 995+6330
11: 5 in the desert until you **a** at this place, 995
Jos 8:11 and approached the city and **a** in front of it. 995
Jdg 3:27 When he **a** there, 995
7:13 Gideon **a** just as a man was telling 995
Ru 1:19 When they **a** *in* Bethlehem, 995
2: 4 then Boaz **a** from Bethlehem and greeted 995
1Sa 4:13 When *he* **a,** there was Eli sitting 995
10:10 When *they* **a** at Gibeah, 995
13:10 Samuel **a,** and Saul went out to greet him. 995
16: 4 When *he* **a** *at* Bethlehem, 995
16: 6 When they **a,** Samuel saw Eliab 995
25: 9 When David's men **a,** 995
25:12 When *they* **a,** they reported every word. 995
26: 4 and learned that Saul *had* definitely **a.** 995
30:26 When David **a** in Ziklag, 995
2Sa 1: 2 the third day a man **a** from Saul's camp, 995
2:32 and his men marched all night and **a** NIH
3:23 When Joab and all the soldiers with him **a,** 995
4: 5 and *they* **a** there in the heat of the day 995
11:22 when *he* **a** he told David everything Joab 995
15:32 When David **a** at the summit, 995
2Sa 15:37 So David's friend Hushai **a** *at* Jerusalem 995
16:14 with him **a** at their destination exhausted. 995
18:31 Then the Cushite **a** and said, 995
19:30 that my lord the king *has* **a** home safely." 995
1Ki 1:22 Nathan the prophet **a.** 995
1:42 Jonathan son of Abiathar the priest **a.** 995
8: 3 When all the elders of Israel *had* **a,** 995
12:21 When Rehoboam **a** *in* Jerusalem, 995
22:15 *he* **a,** the king asked him, "Micaiah, 448+995
2Ki 6:32 but before he **a,** Elisha said to the elders, 448+995
9: 5 When *he* **a,** he found the army officers 995
10: 7 When the letter **a,** these men took 448+995
10: 8 When the messenger **a,** he told Jehu, 995
2Ch 5: 4 When all the elders of Israel *had* **a,** 995
11: 1 When Rehoboam **a** *in* Jerusalem, 995
18:14 *he* **a,** the king asked him, "Micaiah, 448+995
22: 7 When Ahaziah **a,** he went out with Joram 995
Ezr 2:68 When they **a** at the house of the LORD 995
7: 8 Ezra **a** *in* Jerusalem in the fifth month of 995
7: 9 and *he* **a** in Jerusalem on the first day of 995
8:32 So *we* **a** in Jerusalem, 995
Est 6:14 the king's eunuchs **a** and hurried Haman 5595
Isa 30: 4 in Zoan and their envoys *have* **a** *in* Hanes, 5595
Eze 7:12 The time has come, the day *has* **a.** 5595
23:40 when *they* **a** you bathed yourself for them, 995
33:22 Now the evening before the man **a,** 995
47: 7 When I **a** there, I saw a great number 8740
Zec 6:10 who *have* **a** from Babylon. 995
Mt 8:28 *When* he **a** at the other side in the region of 2262
17:24 and his disciples **a** in Capernaum, 2262
25:10 to buy the oil, the bridegroom **a.** 2262
26:47 Judas, one of the Twelve, **a.** 2262
Mk 3:31 Then Jesus' mother and brothers **a.** 2262
11:27 *They* **a** again in Jerusalem, 1650+2262
14:17 Jesus **a** with the Twelve. 2262
Lk 8:51 *When he* **a** at the house of Jairus, 2262
Jn 4:45 When *he* **a** in Galilee, 2262
4:47 that Jesus *had* **a** in Galilee from Judea, 2457
12: 1 Jesus **a** at Bethany, where Lazarus lived, 2262
20: 6 **a** and went into the tomb. 2262
Ac 1:13 When *they* **a,** they went upstairs to 1656
5:21 *When* the high priest and his associates **a,** 4134
8:15 *When they* **a,** they prayed for them 2849
9:39 he **a** he was taken upstairs to the room. 4134
10:24 The following day *he* **a in** Caesarea. 1656
11:23 *When* he **a** and saw the evidence of 4134
13: 5 *When they* **a** at Salamis, 1181
18:19 *They* **a** at Ephesus, where Paul left 2918
19: 1 through the interior and **a** at Ephesus. 2982
20: 2 and finally **a** in Greece, 2262
20:15 from there and **a** off Kios. 2918
20:15 and on the following day **a** at Miletus. 2262
20:18 When *they* **a,** he said to them: 4134
21:17 *When* we **a** at Jerusalem, 1181
23:33 *When* the cavalry **a in** Caesarea, 1656
25:13 and Bernice **a** at Caesarea 2918
28:13 From there *we* set sail and **a** at Rhegium. 2918
1Co 16:17 Fortunatus and Achaicus **a,** 3836+4242
Gal 2:12 But when *they* **a,** he began to draw back 2262

ARRIVES (8) [ARRIVE]

Jdg 20:10 when the army **a** at Gibeah in Benjamin, 995
1Sa 16:11 we will not sit down until he **a."** 995+7024
1Ki 14: 5 When she **a,** she will pretend to 995
Hos 13:13 when the time **a,** he does not come NIH
Zep 2: 2 the appointed time **a** and that day sweeps 3528
Mt 12:44 *When it* **a,** it finds the house unoccupied, 2262
Lk 11:25 *When it* **a,** it finds the house swept clean 2262
Heb 13:23 *he* **a** soon, I will come with him to see you. 2262

ARRIVING (10) [ARRIVE]

Ru 1:22 **a** *in* Bethlehem as the barley harvest 995
1Ki 10: 2 **A** at Jerusalem with a very great caravan— 995
2Ch 9: 1 **A** with a very great caravan— NIH
28:12 confronted those *who were* **a** from the war. 995
Ac 5:22 But *on* **a** at the jail, 4134
14:27 *On* **a** there, they gathered 4134
17:10 *On* **a** there, they went to 4134
18:27 *On* **a,** he was a great help to those who 4134
25: 1 Three days after **a in** the province, 2094
27: 7 and had difficulty **a** off Cnidus. 1181

ARROGANCE (17) [ARROGANT]

Dt 1:43 and *in your* **a** you marched up into 2326
1Sa 2: 3 so proudly or let your mouth speak such **a,** 6981
15:23 and **a** like the evil of idolatry. 7210
Job 35:12 when men cry out because of the **a** *of* 1454
Ps 10: 2 In his **a** the wicked man hunts down 1452
17:10 and their mouths speak with **a.** 1455
73: 8 in their **a** they threaten oppression. 5294
Pr 8:13 I hate pride and **a,** 1454
Isa 2:17 The **a** *of* man will be brought low and 1471
9: 9 who say with pride and **a** *of* heart, 1542
13:11 I will put an end to the **a** *of* the haughty 1454
Jer 48:29 and **a** and the haughtiness of her heart. 1452
Eze 7:10 the rod has budded, **a** has blossomed! 2295
Hos 5: 5 Israel's **a** testifies against them; 1454
7:10 Israel's **a** testifies against him, 1454
Mk 7:22 deceit, lewdness, envy, slander, **a** and folly. 5661
2Co 12:20 factions, slander, gossip, **a** and disorder. 5883

ARROGANT (37) [ARROGANCE, ARROGANTLY]

2Ki 14:10 and now you *are* **a.** 4213+5951

2Ch 25:19 and now you *are* a and proud. 4213+5951
Ne 9:16 our forefathers, *became* a and stiff-necked, 2326
9:29 but they *became* a and disobeyed 2326
Ps 5:5 The a cannot stand in your presence; 2147
73:3 the a when I saw the prosperity of 2147
75:4 To the a I say, 'Boast no more,' 2147
86:14 The a are attacking me, O God; 2294
94:4 They pour out a words; 6981
119:21 You rebuke the a, who are cursed 2294
119:51 The a mock me without restraint, 2294
119:69 Though the a have smeared me with lies, 2294
119:78 the a be put to shame for wronging me 2294
119:85 a dig pitfalls for me, contrary to your law. 2294
119:122 let not the a oppress me. 2294
123:4 much contempt from the a. 1456
Pr 17:7 A lips are unsuited to a fool— 3856
21:24 The proud and a *man*—"Mocker" 3400
Isa 2:11 The eyes of the a man will be humbled and 1471
5:15 the eyes of the a humbled. 1469
33:19 You will see those a people no more, 3594
Jer 13:15 Hear and pay attention, *do* not *be* a, 1467
43:2 and all the a men said to Jeremiah, 2294
50:31 "See, I am against you, O a *one*," 2295
50:32 The a *one* will stumble and fall 2295
Eze 16:49 She and her daughters were a, 1454
Da 5:20 his heart *became* a and hardened with pride, 10659
Hab 2:5 he is a and never at rest. 3400
Zep 3:4 Her prophets *are* a; 7069
Mal 3:15 But now we call the a blessed. 2294
4:1 the a and every evildoer will be stubble, 2294
Ro 1:30 God-haters, insolent, a and boastful; *5662*
11:20 *Do* not *be* a, but be afraid. *5734+5858*
1Co 4:18 Some of you *have become* a, *5881*
4:19 not only how these a *people* are talking, *5881*
1Ti 6:17 not *to* be a nor to put their hope in wealth, *5735*
2Pe 2:10 Bold and a, these men are not afraid *881*

ARROGANTLY (4) [ARROGANT]

Ex 18:11 to *those* who *had* **treated** Israel a." 2326
Ne 9:10 knew how a the Egyptians **treated** them. 2326
Job 36:9 that they have sinned a. 1504
Ps 31:18 for with pride and contempt they speak a 6981

ARROW (18) [ARROWS]

1Sa 20:36 As the boy ran, he shot an a beyond him. 2943
20:37 to the place where Jonathan's a had fallen, 2943
20:37 "Isn't the a beyond you?" 2943
20:38 The boy picked up the a and returned 2943
2Ki 9:24 The a pierced his heart and he slumped 2943
13:17 "The LORD's a *of* victory, 2932
13:17 the a *of* victory over Aram!" 2932
19:32 not enter this city or shoot an a here. 2932
Job 20:24 a bronze-tipped a pierces him. 8008
34:6 his a inflicts an incurable wound.' 2932
Ps 91:5 nor the a that flies by day, 2932
Pr 7:23 till an a pierces his liver, 2932
25:18 Like a club or a sword or a sharp a is 2932
Isa 7:24 Men will go there with bow and a, 2932
37:33 not enter this city or shoot an a here. 2932
49:2 into a polished a and concealed me 2932
Jer 9:8 Their tongue is a deadly a; 2932
Zec 9:14 his a will flash like lightning. 2932

ARROWS (46) [ARROW]

Ex 19:13 shall surely be stoned or **shot with a;** 3721+3721
Nu 24:8 with their a they pierce them. 2932
Dt 32:23 upon them and spend my a against them. 2932
32:42 I will make my a drunk with blood, 2932
1Sa 20:20 I will shoot three a to the side of it, 2932
20:21 I will send a boy and say, 'Go, find the a.' 2932
20:21 'Look, the a are on this side of you; 2932
20:22 the a are beyond you,' then you must go, 2932
20:36 "Run and find the a I shoot." 2932
2Sa 11:20 Didn't you know *they would* **shoot** a from 3721
11:24 Then the archers **shot** a at your servants 3721
22:15 He shot a and scattered [the enemies], 2932
2Ki 13:15 Elisha said, "Get a bow and *some* a," 2932
13:18 Then he said, "Take the a," 2932
1Ch 12:2 to shoot a or to sling stones right-handed 2932
2Ch 26:15 and on the corner defenses to shoot a 2932
Job 6:4 The a *of* the Almighty are in me, 2932
41:28 A do not make him flee; 1201+8008
Ps 7:13 he makes ready his flaming a. 2932
11:2 they set their a against the strings to shoot 2932
18:14 He shot his a and scattered [the enemies], 2932
38:2 For your a have pierced me, 2932
45:5 Let your sharp a pierce the hearts of 2932
57:4 men whose teeth are spears and a, 2932
58:7 let their a be blunted. 2932
64:3 and aim their words like deadly a. 2932
64:7 But God will shoot them with a; 2932
76:3 There he broke the flashing a, 8008
77:17 your a flashed back and forth. 2932
120:4 He will punish you with a warrior's sharp a, 2932
127:4 Like a in the hands of 2932
144:6 shoot your a and rout them. 2932
Pr 26:18 a madman shooting firebrands or deadly a 2932
Isa 5:28 Their a are sharp, all their bows are strung; 2932
Jer 50:9 Their a will be like skilled warriors who do 2932
50:14 Spare no a, for she has sinned against 2932
51:11 "Sharpen the a, take up the shields! 2932
La 3:12 and made me the target for his a. 2932
3:13 He pierced my heart with a *from* his quiver. 1201[S]
Eze 5:16 at you with my deadly and destructive a 2932
21:21 He will cast lots with a, 2932
39:3 from your left hand and make your a drop 2932
39:9 the small and large shields, the bows and a, 2932
Hab 3:9 you called for many a. 4751
3:11 in the heavens at the glint of your flying a, 2932
Eph 6:16 the flaming a of the evil one. *1018*

ARSENAL (1)

Jer 50:25 The LORD has opened his a 238

ART (1) [ARTISANS, ARTISTIC, ARTS]

2Ch 2:7 experienced in the **a of engraving,** 7334+7338

ARTAXERXES (15)

Ezr 4:7 And in the days of A king of Persia, 831
4:7 the rest of his associates wrote a letter to A. 831
4:8 against Jerusalem to A the king as follows: 10078
4:11 To King A, From your servants, 10078
4:23 as the copy of the letter of King A was read 10078
6:14 Darius and A, kings of Persia. 10078
7:1 during the reign of A king of Persia, 831
7:7 to Jerusalem in the seventh year of King A. 831
7:11 of the letter King A had given to Ezra 831
7:12 A, king of kings, To Ezra the priest, 10078
7:21 King A, order all the treasurers 10078
8:1 from Babylon during the reign of King A: 831
Ne 2:1 of Nisan in the twentieth year of King A, 831
5:14 from the twentieth year of King A, 831
13:6 of A king of Babylon I had returned to 831

ARTEMAS (1)

Tit 3:12 As soon as I send A or Tychicus to you, *782*

ARTEMIS (5)

Ac 19:24 who made silver shrines *of* A, *783*
19:27 that the temple *of* the great goddess A will *783*
19:28 "Great is A of the Ephesians!" *783*
19:34 "Great is A of the Ephesians!" *783*
19:35 the temple *of* the great A and of her image, *783*

ARTICLE (14) [ARTICLES]

Lev 11:32 that a, whatever its use, will be unclean, 3998
13:49 or any leather a, is greenish or reddish, 3998
13:50 and isolate the **affected** a for seven days. 5596
13:51 destructive mildew; the a is unclean. 5596[S]
13:52 or any leather a that has the contamination 3998
13:52 the a must be burned up. NIH
13:53 or the leather a, 3998
13:54 he shall order that the **contaminated** a 5596
13:55 After the **affected** a has been washed, 5596
13:56 after **the** a has been washed, 2257[S]
13:57 or in the leather a, it is spreading, 3998
13:58 or any leather a that has been washed 3998
13:59 woven or knitted material, or any leather a, 3998
15:12 any wooden a is to be rinsed with water. 3998

ARTICLES (79) [ARTICLE]

Ge 24:53 and silver jewelry and **a of clothing** 955
Ex 3:22 for a *of* silver and gold and for clothing, 3998
11:2 to ask their neighbors for a *of* silver 3998
12:35 the Egyptians for a *of* silver and gold and 3998
27:19 All the other a *used* in the service of 3998
30:27 the table and all its a, 3998
31:8 the table and its a, 3998
35:13 with its poles and all its a and the bread of 3998
37:16 And they made from pure gold the a for 3998
39:36 with all its a and the bread of the Presence; 3998
Nu 3:31 the a *of* the sanctuary used in ministering, 3998
4:12 the a used for ministering in the sanctuary, 3998
4:15 the holy furnishings and all the holy a, 3998
4:16 including its holy furnishings and a." 3998
31:6 who took with him a *from* the sanctuary 3998
31:50 an offering to the LORD the gold a each 3998
31:51 all the crafted a. 3998
Jos 6:19 All the silver and gold and the a *of* bronze 3998
6:24 and gold and the a *of* bronze and iron into 3998
2Sa 8:10 with him a *of* silver and gold and bronze. 3998
8:11 King David dedicated **these** a to 4392[S]
17:28 brought bedding and bowls and a 3998
1Ki 10:21 the **household** a *in* the Palace of the Forest 3998
10:25 a *of* silver and gold, robes, 3998
15:15 of the LORD the silver and gold and the a 3998
2Ki 12:13 trumpets or any other a *of* gold or silver 3998
14:14 and silver and all the a found in the temple 3998
23:4 the a made for Baal and Asherah and all 3998
24:13 the gold a that Solomon king 3998
25:14 the bronze a used in the temple service. 3998
1Ch 9:28 Some of them were in charge of the a *used* 3998
9:29 of the furnishings and all the other a *of* 3998
18:8 the pillars and various bronze a. 3998
18:10 Hadoram brought all kinds of a *of* gold 3998
18:11 King David dedicated **these** a to 4392[S]
22:19 of the LORD and the sacred a *belonging* 3998
23:26 to carry the tabernacle or any of the a used 3998
28:13 as for all the a *to be used in* its service. 3998
28:14 the gold a *to be used in* various kinds 3998
28:14 and the weight of silver for all the silver a 3998
2Ch 4:16 shovels, meat forks and all related a. 3998
9:20 the **household** a *in* the Palace of the Forest 3998
9:24 a *of* silver and gold, and robes, 3998
15:18 of God the silver and gold and the a that he 3998
20:25 of equipment and clothing and also a 3998
21:3 of silver and gold and **a of value,** 4458
24:14 and with it were made a for 3998
24:14 a *for* the service and for 3998
25:24 and silver and all the a found in the temple 3998
29:18 the consecrated bread, with all its a. 3998
29:19 We have prepared and consecrated all the a 3998
36:7 to Babylon a *from* the temple of the LORD 3998
36:10 together with a *of* value from the temple of 3998
36:18 to Babylon all the a *from* the temple 3998
Ezr 1:6 All their neighbors assisted them with a 3998
1:7 King Cyrus brought out the a *belonging to* 3998
1:10 30 matching silver bowls 410 other a 3998
1:11 there were 5,400 a of gold and of silver. 3998
5:14 the temple of Babylon the gold and silver a 10398
5:15 'Take these a and go and deposit them in 10398
6:5 the gold and silver a *of* the house of God, 10398
7:19 to the God of Jerusalem *all* the a entrusted 10398
8:25 of silver and gold and the a that the king, 3998
8:26 silver a weighing 100 talents, 3998
8:27 darics, and two fine a *of* polished bronze, 3998
8:28 "You as well as these a are consecrated to 3998
8:30 and sacred a that had been weighed out to 3998
8:33 and gold and the sacred a into the hands 3998
Ne 10:39 the a *for* the sanctuary are kept and where 3998
13:5 and incense and temple a, 3998
Jer 27:16 now the a *from* the LORD's house will 3998
28:3 the a *of* the LORD's house 3998
28:6 by bringing the a *of* the LORD's house 3998
52:18 the bronze a used in the temple service. 3998
Eze 27:13 they exchanged slaves and a *of* bronze 3998
Da 1:2 with some of the a *from* the temple of God. 3998
11:8 their metal images and their valuable a 3998
2Ti 2:20 In a large house there are a not only of gold *5007*
Rev 18:12 and a of every kind made of ivory, *NIG*

ARTIFICER, ARTIFICERS (KJV) See CRAFTSMEN

ARTIFICIAL (1)

Ne 3:16 as the a pool and the House of the Heroes. 6913

ARTILLERY (KJV) See WEAPONS

ARTISANS (4) [ART]

2Ki 24:14 and all the craftsmen and a— 4994
24:16 and a thousand craftsmen and a. 4994
Jer 24:1 and the a *of* Judah were carried into exile 4994
29:2 the craftsmen and the a had gone into exile 4994

ARTISTIC (3) [ART]

Ex 31:4 to make **a designs** for work in gold, 4742
35:32 to make **a designs** for work in gold, 4742
35:33 to engage in all kinds of **a craftsmanship.** 4742

ARTS (7) [ART]

Ex 7:11 also did the same things by their **secret a:** 4268
7:22 the same things by their **secret a,** 4319
8:7 the same things by their **secret a;** 4319
8:18 to produce gnats by their **secret a,** 4319
Rev 9:21 their **magic a,** their sexual immorality *5760*
21:8 **those who practice magic a,** *5761*
22:15 those who **practice magic a,** *5761*

ARUBBOTH (1)

1Ki 4:10 in A (Socoh and all the land 749

ARUMAH (1)

Jdg 9:41 Abimelech stayed in A, 777

ARVAD (2) [ARVADITES]

Eze 27:8 Men of Sidon and A were your oarsmen; 770
27:11 Men of A and Helech manned your walls 770

ARVADITES (2) [ARVAD]

Ge 10:18 A, Zemarites and Hamathites. 773
1Ch 1:16 A, Zemarites and Hamathites. 773

ARZA (1)

1Ki 16:9 getting drunk in the home of A, 825

AS (4006) See Index of Articles Etc.

ASA (52) [ASA'S]

1Ki 15:8 And A his son succeeded him as king. 654
15:9 A became king of Judah, 654
15:11 A did what was right in the eyes of 654
15:13 A cut the pole down and burned it in 654
15:16 There was war between A and Baasha king 654
15:17 or entering the territory of A king of Judah. 654
15:18 A then took all the silver and gold 654
15:20 Ben-Hadad agreed with King A and sent 654
15:22 Then King A issued an order to all Judah— 654
15:22 With them King A built up Geba 654
15:24 Then A rested with his fathers 654
15:25 in the second year of A king of Judah, 654
15:28 of A king of Judah and succeeded him 654
15:32 There was war between A and Baasha king 654
15:33 In the third year of A king of Judah, 654
16:8 In the twenty-sixth year of A king of Judah, 654

1Ki 16:10 the twenty-seventh year of A king of Judah. 654
16:15 the twenty-seventh year of A king of Judah, 654
16:23 In the thirty-first year of A king of Judah, 654
16:29 In the thirty-eighth year of A king of Judah, 654
22:41 Jehoshaphat son of A became king of Judah 654
22:43 in the ways of his father A and did not stray 654
22:46 even after the reign of his father A. 654
1Ch 3:10 A his son, Jehoshaphat his son, 654
9:16 and Berekiah son of A, the son of Elkanah, 654
2Ch 14:1 A his son succeeded him as king, 654
14:2 A did what was good and right in the eyes 654
14:8 A had an army of three hundred thousand 654
14:10 A went out to meet him, 654
14:11 A called to the LORD his God and said, 654
14:12 down the Cushites before A and Judah. 654
14:13 and A and his army pursued them as far 654
15:2 He went out to meet A and said to him, 654
15:2 A and all Judah and Benjamin. 654
15:8 When A heard these words and 654
15:16 King A also deposed his grandmother Maacah from her position 654
15:16 A cut the pole down, 654
16:1 or entering the territory of A king of Judah. 654
16:2 A then took the silver and gold out of 654
16:4 Ben-Hadad agreed with King A and sent 654
16:6 Then King A brought all the men of Judah, 654
16:7 the seer came to A king of Judah and said 654
16:10 A was angry with the seer because of this; 654
16:10 the same time A brutally oppressed some of 654
16:12 of his reign A was afflicted with a disease 654
16:13 in the forty-first year of his reign A died 654
17:2 of Ephraim that his father A had captured. 654
20:32 in the ways of his father A and did not stray 654
21:12 of your father Jehoshaphat or of A king 654
Jer 41:9 the one King A had made as part 654
Mt 1:7 Abijah the father of A, *809*
1:8 A the father of Jehoshaphat, *809*

ASA'S (7) [ASA]
1Ki 15:14 A heart was fully committed to the LORD 654
15:23 As for all the other events of A reign, 654
2Ch 15:10 of the fifteenth year of A reign. 654
15:17 A heart was fully committed 654
15:19 until the thirty-fifth year of A reign. 654
16:1 the thirty-sixth year of A reign Baasha king 654
16:11 The events of A reign, 654

ASAHEL (18) [ASAHEL'S]
2Sa 2:18 Joab, Abishai and A. 6915
2:18 A was as fleet-footed as a wild gazelle. 6915
2:20 behind him and asked, "Is that you, A?" 6915
2:21 But A would not stop chasing him. 6915
2:22 Again Abner warned A, "Stop chasing me! 6915
2:23 But A refused to give up the pursuit; NIH
2:23 to the place where A had fallen and died. 6915
2:30 Besides A, nineteen of David's 6915
2:32 They took A and buried him 6915
3:27 there, to avenge the blood of his brother A, 6915
3:30 because he had killed their brother A in 6915
23:24 A the brother of Joab, 6915
1Ch 2:16 Zeruiah's three sons were Abishai, Joab and A. 6915
11:26 A the brother of Joab, 6915
27:7 was A the brother of Joab; 6915
2Ch 17:8 Shemaiah, Nethaniah, Zebadiah, A, 6915
31:13 Jehiel, Azaziah, Nahath, A, Jerimoth, 6915
Ezr 10:15 Only Jonathan son of A and Jahzeiah son 6915

ASAHEL'S (1) [ASAHEL]
2Sa 2:23 the butt of his spear into A stomach, 2084S

ASAHIAH (KJV) See ASAIAH

ASAIAH (8)
2Ki 22:12 the secretary and A the king's attendant: 6919
22:14 Shaphan and A went to speak to 6919
1Ch 4:36 Jaakobah, Jeshohaiah, A, Adiel, Jesimiel, 6919
6:30 Haggiah his son and A his son. 6919
9:5 A the firstborn and his sons. 6919
15:6 A the leader and 220 relatives; 6919
15:11 and Uriel, A, Joel, Shemaiah, 6919
2Ch 34:20 the secretary and A the king's attendant: 6919

ASAPH (45) [ASAPH'S]
2Ki 18:18 and Joah son of A the recorder went out 666
18:37 Shebna the secretary and Joah son of A 666
1Ch 6:39 and Heman's associate A, who served 666
6:39 A son of Berekiah, the son of Shimea, 666
9:15 the son of Zicri, the son of A; 666
15:17 from his brothers, A son of Berekiah; 666
15:19 A and Ethan were to sound 666
16:5 A was the chief, 666
16:5 A was to sound the cymbals, 666
16:7 to A and his associates this psalm of thanks 666
16:37 David left A and his associates before 666
25:1 set apart some of the sons of A, 666
25:2 From the sons of A: 666
25:2 of A were under the supervision of Asaph, 666
25:2 of Asaph were under the supervision of A, 666
25:6 A, Jeduthun and Heman were under 666
25:9 The first lot, which was for A, 666
26:1 one of the sons of A. 666
2Ch 5:12 All the Levites who were musicians—A, 666
20:14 a Levite and descendant of A, 666
29:13 from the descendants of A, 666
29:30 with the words of David and of A the seer. 666
35:15 The musicians, the descendants of A, 666
35:15 were in the places prescribed by David, A, 666
Ezr 2:41 The singers: the descendants of A 128 666
3:10 the Levites (the sons of A) with cymbals, 666
Ne 2:8 And may I have a letter to A, 666
7:44 The singers: the descendants of A 148 666
11:17 the son of Zabdi, the son of A, 666
12:35 the son of Zaccur, the son of A, 666
12:46 For long ago, in the days of David and A, 666
Ps 50:T A psalm of A. 666
73:T A psalm of A. 666
74:T A maskil of A. 666
75:T A psalm of A. 666
76:T A psalm of A. 666
77:T For Jeduthun. Of A. 666
78:T A maskil of A. 666
79:T A psalm of A. 666
80:T "The Lilies of the Covenant." Of A. 666
81:T According to gittith. Of A. 666
82:T A psalm of A. 666
83:T A song. A psalm of A. 666
Isa 36:3 Joah son of A the recorder went out to him. 666
36:22 and Joah son of A the recorder went 666

ASAPH'S (1) [ASAPH]
Ne 11:22 Uzzi was one of A descendants, 666

ASAREL (1)
1Ch 4:16 Ziph, Ziphah, Tiria and A. 832

ASARELAH (1)
1Ch 25:2 Zaccur, Joseph, Nethaniah and A. 833

ASCEND (7) [ASCENDED, ASCENDING, ASCENT, ASCENTS]
Dt 30:12 "Who *will* a into heaven to get it 6590
Ps 24:3 Who *may* a the hill of the LORD? 6590
Isa 14:13 *"I will* a *to* heaven; 6590
14:14 *I will* a above the tops of the clouds; 6590
Jn 6:62 the Son of Man a to where he was before! *326*
Ac 2:34 For David *did* not a to heaven, *326*
Ro 10:6 'Who *will* a into heaven?' " *326*

ASCENDED (8) [ASCEND]
Jdg 13:20 the angel of the LORD a in the flame. 6590
2Ki 19:23 "With my many chariots I *have* a 6590
Ps 47:5 God *has* a amid shouts of joy, 6590
68:18 *When you* a on high, 6590
Isa 37:24 'With my many chariots I *have* a 6590
Eph 4:8 This is why it says: *"When* he a on high, *326*
4:9 (What does *"he* a" mean except that he *326*
4:10 the very one who a higher than all *326*

ASCENDING (3) [ASCEND]
Ge 28:12 the angels of God *were* a and descending 6590
Eze 41:7 the temple was built **in a stages,** 2025+2025+4200+4200+5087+5087
Jn 1:51 and the angels of God a and descending on *326*

ASCENT (2) [ASCEND]
Ne 3:19 a point facing the a *to* the armory as far as 6590
12:37 up the steps of the City of David on the a to 5090

ASCENTS (15) [ASCEND]
Ps 120:T A song of a. 5092
121:T A song of a. 5092
122:T A song of a. Of David. 5092
123:T A song of a. 5092
124:T A song of a. Of David. 5092
125:T A song of a. 5092
126:T A song of a. 5092
127:T A song of a. Of Solomon. 5092
128:T A song of a. 5092
129:T A song of a. 5092
130:T A song of a. 5092
131:T A song of a. Of David. 5092
132:T A song of a. 5092
133:T A song of a. Of David. 5092
134:T A song of a. 5092

ASCRIBE (10)
1Ch 16:28 A to the LORD, O families of nations, 2035
16:28 a to the LORD glory and strength, 2035
16:29 a to the LORD the glory due his name. 2035
Job 36:3 *I will* a justice to my Maker. 5989
Ps 29:1 A to the LORD, O mighty ones, 2035
29:1 a to the LORD glory and strength. 2035
29:2 A to the LORD the glory due his name; 2035
96:7 A to the LORD, O families of nations, 2035
96:7 a to the LORD glory and strength. 2035
96:8 A to the LORD the glory due his name; 2035

ASENATH (3)
Ge 41:45 and gave him A daughter of Potiphera, 664
41:50 to Joseph by A daughter of Potiphera, 664
46:20 to Joseph by A daughter of Potiphera, 664

ASER (KJV) See ASHER

ASH (4) [ASHES]
Lev 4:12 and burn it in a wood fire on the a heap. 2016
1Sa 2:8 and lifts the needy from the **a heap;** 883
Ps 113:7 and lifts the needy from the **a heap;** 883
La 4:5 in purple now lie on **a heaps.** 883

ASHAMED (53) [SHAME]
2Sa 19:3 the city that day as men steal in who *are* a 4007
2Ki 2:17 they persisted until *he was* too a to refuse. 1017
8:11 with a fixed gaze until Hazael **felt a.** 1017
2Ch 30:15 The priests and the Levites *were* a 4007
Ezr 8:22 *I was* a to ask the king for soldiers 1017
9:6 *I am too* a and disgraced to lift up my face 1017
Ps 6:10 All my enemies *will be* a and dismayed; 1017
83:17 *May they* ever *be* a and dismayed; 1017
Isa 1:29 *"You will be* a because of the sacred oaks 1017
23:4 *Be* a, O Sidon, and you, 1017
24:23 The moon will be abashed, the sun a; 1017
29:22 "No longer *will* Jacob *be* a; 1017
33:9 Lebanon *is* a and withers; 2917
41:11 "All who rage against you *will* surely *be* a 1017
Jer 6:15 *Are they* a *of* their loathsome conduct? 1017
8:12 *Are they* a *of* their loathsome conduct? 1017
22:22 Then *you will be* a and disgraced because 1017
31:19 *I was* a and humiliated because I bore 1017
48:13 Then Moab *will be* a of Chemosh, 1017
48:13 of Israel *was* a when they trusted in Bethel. 1017
50:12 your mother *will be* greatly a; 1017
Eze 16:52 So then, *be* a and bear your disgrace, 1017
16:54 that you may bear your disgrace and *be* a 4007
16:61 and *be* a when you receive your sisters, 4007
16:63 and *be* a and never again open your mouth 1017
36:32 *Be* a and disgraced for your conduct, 1017
43:10 that *they may be* a of their sins. 4007
43:11 and if *they are* a of all they have done, 4007
Hos 10:6 Israel *will be* a of its wooden idols. 1017
Mic 3:7 *be* a and the diviners disgraced. 1017
7:16 Nations will see and *be* a, 1017
Zec 13:4 "On that day every prophet *will be* a 1017
Mk 8:38 If anyone *is* a **of** me and my words *2049*
8:38 of Man *will be* a **of** him when he comes *2049*
Lk 9:26 If anyone *is* a **of** me and my words, *2049*
9:26 of Man *will be* a **of** him when he comes *2049*
16:3 and *I'm* a to beg— *159*
Ro 1:16 *I am* not a **of** the gospel, *2049*
6:21 from the things *you are* now a **of?** *2049*
2Co 9:4 *would be* a **of** having been so confident. *2875*
10:8 *I will* not *be* a of it. *159*
Php 1:20 and hope that *I will* in no way *be* a, *159*
2Th 3:14 in order that *he may* **feel a.** *1956*
2Ti 1:8 So *do* not *be* a to testify about our Lord, *2049*
1:8 or a of me his prisoner. *NIG*
1:12 Yet *I am* not a, because I know whom I have believed, *2049*
1:16 and *was* not a **of** my chains. *2049*
2:15 a workman who **does not need to be a** *454*
Tit 2:8 *be* a because they have nothing bad to say *1956*
Heb 2:11 So Jesus *is* not a to call them brothers. *2049*
11:16 God *is* not a to be called their God, *2049*
1Pe 3:16 in Christ *may be* a of their slander. *2875*
4:16 if you suffer as a Christian, *do* not *be* a, *159*

ASHAN (4) [BOR ASHAN]
Jos 15:42 Libnah, Ether, A, 6941
19:7 Rimmon, Ether and A— 6941
1Ch 4:32 Ain, Rimmon, Token and A— 6941
6:59 A, Juttah and Beth Shemesh, together 6941

ASHBEA See BETH ASHBEA

ASHBEL (3) [ASHBELITE]
Ge 46:21 Bela, Beker, A, Gera, Naaman, Ehi, Rosh, 839
Nu 26:38 through A, the Ashbelite clan; 839
1Ch 8:1 A the second son, Aharah the third, 839

ASHBELITE (1) [ASHBEL]
Nu 26:38 through Ashbel, the A clan; 840

ASHCHENAZ (KJV) See ASHKENAZ

ASHDOD (21)
Jos 11:22 only in Gaza, Gath and A did any survive. 846
13:3 A, Ashkelon, Gath and Ekron— 847
15:46 all that were in the vicinity of A, 846
15:47 A, its surrounding settlements and villages; 846
1Sa 5:1 they took it from Ebenezer to A. 846
5:3 the **people of** A rose early the next day, 847
5:5 at A step on the threshold. 846
5:6 upon the **people of** A and its vicinity; 847
5:7 the men of A saw what was happening, 846
6:17 one each for A, Gaza, Ashkelon, 846
2Ch 26:6 down the walls of Gath, Jabneh and A. 846
26:6 He then rebuilt towns near A and elsewhere 846
Ne 4:7 the Ammonites and the **men of** A heard that 847
13:23 of Judah who had married women **from** A, 847
13:24 of their children spoke the **language of** A 848
Isa 20:1 came to A and attacked and captured it— 846
Jer 25:20 Gaza, Ekron, and the people left at A); 846
Am 1:8 of A and the one who holds the scepter 846

Am 3: 9 to the fortresses of A and to the fortresses 846
Zep 2: 4 At midday A will be emptied 846
Zec 9: 6 Foreigners will occupy A, 846

ASHDODITES, ASHDOTHITES (KJV)
See MEN OF ASHDOD

ASHDOTHPISGAH (KJV) See PISGAH

ASHER (45) [ASHER'S]
Ge 30:13 So she named him A. 888
35:26 of Leah's maidservant Zilpah: Gad and A. 888
46:17 The sons of A: Imnah, Ishvah, Ishvi, and 888
Ex 1: 4 Dan and Naphtali; Gad and A. 888
Nu 1:13 from A, Pagiel son of Ocran; 888
1:40 From the descendants of A: 888
1:41 number from the tribe of A was 41,500. 888
2:27 The tribe of A will camp next to them. 888
2:27 The leader of the people of A is Pagiel son 888
7:72 the leader of the people of A, 888
10:26 over the division of the tribe of A, 888+1201
13:13 from the tribe of A, Sethur son of Michael; 888
26:44 The descendants of A by their clans were: 888
26:46 (A had a daughter named Serah.) 888
26:47 These were the clans of A; 888+1201
34:27 the leader from the tribe of A; 888+1201
Dt 27:13 Reuben, Gad, A, Zebulun, 888
33:24 About A he said: "Most blessed of sons 888
33:24 "Most blessed of sons is A; 888
Jos 17: 7 The territory of Manasseh extended from A 888
17:10 and bordered A on the north and Issachar 888
17:11 Within Issachar and A, 888
19:24 The fifth lot came out for the tribe of A, 888+1201
19:31 the inheritance of the tribe of A, 888+1201
19:34 A on the west and the Jordan on the east. 888
21: 6 A, Naphtali and the half-tribe of Manasseh 888
21:30 from the tribe of A, Mishal, Abdon, 888
Jdg 1:31 Nor did A drive out those living in Acco 888
1:32 and because of this the **people of** A lived 896
5:17 A remained on the coast and stayed 888
6:35 and also into A, Zebulun and Naphtali, 888
7:23 A and all Manasseh were called out, 888
1Ki 4:16 Baana son of Hushai—in A and in Aloth; 888
1Ch 2: 2 Joseph, Benjamin, Naphtali, Gad and A. 888
6:62 from the tribes of Issachar, A and Naphtali, 888
6:74 from the tribe of A they received Mashal, 888
7:30 sons of A: Imnah, Ishvah, Ishvi and Beriah. 888
7:40 All these were descendants of A— 888
12:36 men of A, experienced soldiers prepared 888
2Ch 30:11 Nevertheless, some men of A, 888
Eze 48: 2 "A will have one portion; 888
48: 3 it will border the territory of A from east 888
48:34 the gate of A and the gate of Naphtali. 888
Lk 2:36 the daughter of Phanuel, of the tribe *of* A. *818*
Rev 7: 6 from the tribe *of* A 12,000, *818*

ASHER'S (1) [ASHER]
Ge 49:20 "A food will be rich; 888+4946

ASHERAH (39) [ASHERAHS]
Ex 34:13 and cut down their **A poles.** 895
Dt 7: 5 cut down their **A poles** and burn their idols 895
12: 3 and burn their **A poles** in the fire; 895
16:21 Do not set up any wooden **A pole** beside 895
Jdg 6:25 to Baal and cut down the **A pole** beside it. 895
6:26 the wood of the **A pole** that you cut down, 895
6:28 with the **A pole** beside it cut down and 895
6:30 down Baal's altar and cut down the **A pole** 895
1Ki 14:15 the LORD to anger by making **A poles.** 895
14:23 and **A poles** on every high hill and 895
15:13 because she had made a repulsive **A pole.** 895
16:33 Ahab also made an **A pole** and did more 895
18:19 of Baal and the four hundred prophets of **A,** 895
2Ki 13: 6 the **A pole** remained standing in Samaria. 895
17:10 They set up sacred stones and **A poles** 895
17:16 in the shape of calves, and an **A pole.** 895
18: 4 and cut down the **A poles.** 895
21: 3 to Baal and made an **A pole,** 895
21: 7 the carved **A pole** he had made and put it 895
23: 4 the articles made for Baal and A and all 895
23: 6 the **A pole** from the temple of the LORD 895
23: 7 and where women did weaving for **A.** 895
23:14 the sacred stones and cut down the **A poles** 895
23:15 and burned the **A pole** also. 895
2Ch 14: 3 and cut down the **A poles.** 895
15:16 because she had made a repulsive **A pole.** 895
17: 6 the high places and the **A poles** 895
19: 3 for you have rid the land of the **A poles** 895
24:18 and worshiped **A poles** and idols. 895
31: 1 and cut down the **A poles.** 895
33: 3 to the Baals and made **A poles.** 895
33:19 and set up **A poles** and idols 895
34: 3 **A poles,** carved idols and cast images. 895
34: 4 and smashed the **A poles,** 895
34: 7 he tore down the altars and the **A poles** 895
Isa 17: 8 have no regard for the **A poles** 895
27: 9 to pieces, no **A poles** or incense altars will 895
Jer 17: 2 and **A poles** beside the spreading trees and 895
Mic 5:14 from among you your **A poles** 895

ASHERAHS (1) [ASHERAH]
Jdg 3: 7 and served the Baals and the A. 895

ASHERITES (KJV) See ASHER

ASHES (35) [ASH]
Ge 18:27 though I am nothing but dust and **a,** 709
Ex 27: 3 its pots to **remove** the **a,** and its shovels, 2014
Lev 1:16 east side of the altar, where the **a** are. 2016
4:12 where the **a** are thrown, 2016
6:10 and shall remove the **a** of the burnt offering 2016
6:11 and carry the **a** outside the camp to a place 2016
Nu 4:13 *to* **remove** the **a** *from* the bronze altar 2014
19: 9 "A man who is clean shall gather up the **a** 709
19:10 The man who gathers up the **a** *of* 709
19:17 put some **a** *from* the burned purification 6760
2Sa 13:19 Tamar put **a** on her head and tore 709
1Ki 13: 3 The altar will be split apart and the **a** 2016
13: 5 the altar was split apart and its **a** poured out 2016
2Ki 23: 4 the Kidron Valley and took the **a** to Bethel. 6760
Est 4: 1 he tore his clothes, put on sackcloth and **a,** 709
4: 3 Many lay in sackcloth and **a.** 709
Job 2: 8 with it as he sat among the **a.** 709
13:12 Your maxims are proverbs of **a;** 709
30:19 and I am reduced to dust and **a.** 709
42: 6 and repent in dust and **a."** 709
Ps 102: 9 For I eat **a** as my food and mingle my drink 709
147:16 like wool and scatters the frost like **a.** 709
Isa 44:20 on **a,** a deluded heart misleads him; 709
58: 5 a reed and for lying on sackcloth and **a?** 709
61: 3 on them a crown of beauty instead of **a,** 709
Jer 6:26 put on sackcloth and roll in **a;** 709
31:40 where dead bodies and **a** are thrown, 2016
Eze 27:30 on their heads and roll in **a.** 709
28:18 and I reduced you to **a** on the ground in 709
Da 9: 3 in fasting, and in sackcloth and **a.** 709
Mal 4: 3 be **a** under the soles of your feet on the day 709
Mt 11:21 repented long ago, in sackcloth and **a.** *5075*
Lk 10:13 long ago, sitting in sackcloth and **a.** *5075*
Heb 9:13 The blood of goats and bulls and the **a** of *5075*
2Pe 2: 6 Sodom and Gomorrah *by* **burning** *them* **to a** *5491*

ASHHUR (2)
1Ch 2:24 of Hezron bore him A the father of Tekoa. 858
4: 5 A the father of Tekoa had two wives, 858

ASHIMA (1)
2Ki 17:30 and the men from Hamath made A; 860

ASHKELON (13)
Jos 13: 3 Ashdod, A, Gath and Ekron— 885
Jdg 1:18 A and Ekron—each city with its territory. 884
14:19 He went down to A, 884
1Sa 6:17 one each for Ashdod, Gaza, A, 884
2Sa 1:20 proclaim it not in the streets of A, 884
Jer 25:20 all the kings of the Philistines (those of A, 884
47: 5 A will be silenced. 884
47: 7 when he has ordered it to attack A and 884
Am 1: 8 and the one who holds the scepter in A. 884
Zep 2: 4 Gaza will be abandoned and A left in ruins. 884
2: 7 down in the houses of A. 884
Zec 9: 5 A will see it and fear; 884
9: 5 Gaza will lose her king and A will 884

ASHKENAZ (3)
Ge 10: 3 A, Riphath and Togarmah. 867
1Ch 1: 6 A, Riphath and Togarmah. 867
Jer 51:27 Ararat, Minni and A. 867

ASHNAH (2)
Jos 15:33 In the western foothills: Eshtaol, Zorah, A, 877
15:43 Iphtah, A, Nezib, 877

ASHORE (2) [SHORE]
Lk 8:27 When Jesus stepped **a,** he was met *1178+2093*
Jn 21:11 aboard and dragged the net **a.** *1178+1650+3836*

ASHPENAZ (1)
Da 1: 3 Then the king ordered A, 881

ASHRIEL (KJV) See ASRIEL

ASHTAROTH (6)
Dt 1: 4 king of Bashan, who reigned in A. 6958
Jos 9:10 and Og king of Bashan, who reigned in A. 6958
12: 4 who reigned in A and Edrei. 6958
13:12 in A and Edrei and had survived as one of 6958
13:31 and A and Edrei (the royal cities of Og 6958
1Ch 6:71 also A, together with their pasturelands; 6958

ASHTERATHITE (1)
1Ch 11:44 the A, Shama and Jeiel the sons of Hotham 6960

ASHTEROTH KARNAIM (1)
Ge 14: 5 and defeated the Rephaites in A, 6959

ASHTORETH (3) [ASHTORETHS]
1Ki 11: 5 He followed A the goddess of 6956
11:33 and worshiped A the goddess of 6956
2Ki 23:13 of Israel had built for A the vile goddess of 6956

ASHTORETHS (6) [ASHTORETH]
Jdg 2:13 and served Baal and the A. 6956
10: 6 They served the Baals and the A, 6956
1Sa 7: 3 the A and commit yourselves to the LORD 6956
7: 4 the Israelites put away their Baals and A, 6956
12:10 the LORD and served the Baals and the A. 6956
31:10 of the A and fastened his body to the wall 6956

ASHURBANIPAL (1)
Ezr 4:10 and honorable A deported and settled in 10055

ASHUR (KJV) See ASHHUR

ASHURITES (KJV) See ASHURI

ASHURI (1)
2Sa 2: 9 A and Jezreel, and also over Ephraim, 856

ASHVATH (1)
1Ch 7:33 The sons of Japhlet: Pasach, Bimhal and A. 6937

ASIA (19)
Ac 2: 9 Judea and Cappadocia, Pontus and A, *823*
6: 9 as well as the provinces of Cilicia and A. *823*
16: 6 the word in the **province of A.** *823*
19:10 in the **province of** A heard the word of *823*
19:22 while he stayed in the **province of A** *823*
19:26 *in* practically the whole **province of A.** *823*
19:27 throughout the **province of** A and *823*
20: 4 **from the province of A.** *824*
20:16 in the **province of A,** *823*
20:18 the first day I came into the **province of A.** *823*
21:27 the **province of** A saw Paul at the temple. *823*
24:19 from the **province of A,** *823*
27: 2 along the coast of the **province of A,** *823*
Ro 16: 5 to Christ *in* the **province of A.** *823*
1Co 16:19 *in* the **province of** A send you greetings. *823*
2Co 1: 8 in the **province of A.** *823*
2Ti 1:15 in the **province of** A has deserted me, *823*
1Pe 1: 1 Galatia, Cappadocia, A and Bithynia, *823*
Rev 1: 4 the seven churches in the **province of A:** *823*

ASIDE (72) [SIDE]
Ge 19: 2 "please **turn a** to your servant's house. 6073
Nu 18:11 *whatever* is **set a** *from* the gifts of all 9556
18:19 Whatever is **set a** *from* the holy offerings 9556
21:22 not **turn a** into any field or vineyard, 5742
23: 3 beside your offering while *I* **go a.** 2143
Dt 2:27 *we will* not **turn a** *to* the right or *to* 6073
4:41 Moses **set a** three cities east of the Jordan, 976
5:32 *do* not **turn a** *to* the right or to the left. 6073
9:16 *You had* **turned a** quickly from the way that 6073
14:22 **Be sure to set a a tenth** of all 6923+6923
17:11 *Do* not **turn a** from what they tell you, 6073
19: 2 then **set a** for yourselves three cities 976
19: 7 This is why I command you *to* **set a** 976
19: 9 then you are to set **a** three more cities. NIH
21:13 and **put a** the clothes she was wearing 6073
26:12 When you have finished **setting a a tenth** 5130+6923
26:13 *I have* not **turned a** from your commands 6296
28:14 *Do* not **turn a** from any of the commands 6073
Jos 16: 9 the towns and their villages that were **set a** 4426
23: 6 without **turning a** to the right or to the left. 6073
Jdg 14: 8 *he* **turned a** to look at the lion's carcass. 6073
1Sa 8: 3 *They* **turned a** after dishonest gain 5742
9:23 the one I told you to lay **a."** 6640
9:24 *it* **was set a** for you for this occasion, 9068
2Sa 2:21 **"Turn a** to the right or to the left; 5742
3:27 Joab **took** him **a** into the gateway, 5742
6:10 he **took** it **a** *to* the house of Obed-Edom 5742
18:30 The king said, **"Stand a** and wait here." 6015
18:30 So *he* **stepped a** and stood there. 6015
23: 6 evil men are all *to* **be cast a** like thorns, 5610
2Ki 22: 2 not **turning a** *to* the right or *to* the left. 6073
25:29 So Jehoiachin **put a** his prison clothes and 9101
1Ch 13:13 *he* **took** it **a** to the house of Obed-Edom 5742
2Ch 34: 2 not **turning a** *to* the right or *to* the left. 6073
35:12 *They* **set a** the burnt offerings to give them 6073
Ne 12:47 also **set a** the portion for the other Levites, 7727
12:47 and the Levites **set a** the portion for 7727
Job 6:18 Caravans **turn a** *from* their routes; 4369
23:11 I have kept to his way without **turning a.** 5742
29: 8 the young men saw me and **stepped a** and 2461
36:18 *do* not *let* a large bribe **turn** you **a.** 5742
Ps 14: 3 All *have* **turned a,** 6073
40: 4 to *those who* **turn a** *to* false gods. 8454
85: 3 *You* **set a** all your wrath and turned 665
102:10 for you have taken me up and **thrown** me **a.** 8959
Pr 5: 7 *do* not **turn a** from what I say. 6073
Jer 5:23 *they have* **turned a** and gone away. 6073
52:33 So Jehoiachin **put a** his prison clothes and 9101
Eze 26:16 from their thrones and **lay a** their robes 6073
31:11 according to its wickedness, *I* **cast it a,** 1763
48:20 **As a special gift** *you will* **set a** 8123
Mt 16:22 Peter **took** him **a** and began to rebuke him. *4689*
20:17 he took the twelve disciples **a** and said to them, *2625+2848*
Mk 7: 9 of **setting a** the commands of God in order *119*
7:33 After he took him **a,** away from the crowd, *2625+2848*
8:32 Peter **took** him **a** and began to rebuke him. *4689*

Mk 10:32 Again he took the Twelve a 4161
10:50 Throwing his cloak a, 610
Lk 18:31 Jesus took the Twelve a and told them, 4161
Jn 2: 9 Then he called the bridegroom a NIG
11:28 she went back and called her sister Mary a. 3277
Ac 7:27 the other pushed Moses a and said, 723
23:19 drew him a and asked, 2625+2848
Ro 13:12 So let us put a the deeds of darkness 700
1Co 16: 2 of you should set a a sum of money 5502
Gal 2:21 I do not set a the grace of God, 119
3:15 Just as no one can set a or add to 119
3:17 does not set a 218
2Ti 4: 4 from the truth and turn a to myths. 1762
Heb 7:18 The former regulation is set a 120
10: 9 He sets a the first to establish the second. 359
2Pe 1:14 because I know that I will soon put it a, 629+1639

ASIEL (1)

1Ch 4:35 the son of Seraiah, the son of A, 6918

ASK (184) [ASKED, ASKING, ASKS]

Ge 23: 9 A him to sell it to me for the full price as NIH
24:57 "Let's call the girl and a her about it." 8626
32:29 But he replied, "Why do you a my name?" 8626
34:11 and I will give you whatever you a. 606
34:12 and I'll pay whatever you a me. 606
50:17 I a you to forgive your brothers the sins 626
Ex 3:13 and they a me, 'What is his name?' 606
3:22 to a her neighbor and any woman living 8626
11: 2 and women alike are to a their neighbors 8626
12:26 And when your children a you, 606
Lev 25:20 You may a, "What will we eat in 606
Dt 4:32 A now about the former days, 8626
4:32 a from one end of the heavens to the other. NIH
10:12 the LORD your God a of you but to fear 8626
29:24 All the nations will a: 606
30:12 so that you have to a, 606
30:13 so that you have to a, 606
31:17 and on that day they will a, 606
32: 7 A your father and he will tell you, 8626
Jos 4: 6 In the future, when your children a you, 8626
4:21 when your descendants a their fathers, 8626
15:18 she urged him to a her father for a field. 907+8626
Jdg 1:14 she urged him to a her father for a field. 8626
9: 2 "A all the citizens of Shechem, 1819
13: 6 I didn't a him where he came from, 8626
13:18 He replied, "Why do you a my name? 8626
18:24 How can you a, 'What's the matter 606
Ru 3:11 I will do for you all you a. 606
1Sa 25: 8 A your own servants and they will tell you. 8626
2Sa 11:20 anger may flare up, and he may a you, 606
14:18 the answer to what I am going to a you." 8626
14:32 so I can send you to the king to a, 606
16:10 who can a, 'Why do you do this?' " 606
19:11 "A the elders of Judah, 1819
1Ki 2:17 he continued, "Please a King Solomon— 606
3: 5 "A for whatever you want me to give you." 8626
14: 5 "Jeroboam's wife is coming to a you 1821+2011
2Ki 1: 3 of the king of Samaria and a them, 1819
4: 3 and a all your neighbors for empty jars. 8626
4: 3 Don't a for just a few. NIH
4:26 Run to meet her and a her, 606
4:28 "Did I a you for a son, my lord?" 8626
8: 8 a him, 'Will I recover from this illness?' " 606
8: 9 of Aram has sent me to a, 606
9:17 "Send him to meet them and a, 606
14:10 Why a for trouble and cause 1741
2Ch 1: 7 "A for whatever you want me to give you." 8626
25:19 Why a for trouble and cause 1741
32:31 by the rulers of Babylon to a him about 2011
Ezr 7:21 may a of you— 10689
8:21 and a him for a safe journey for us 1335
8:22 I was ashamed to a the king for soldiers 8626
Est 5:14 and a the king in the morning 606
Job 8: 8 "A the former generations 8626
12: 7 "But a the animals, 8626
35: 3 Yet you a him, 'What profit is it to me, 606
37:20 Would any man a to be swallowed up? 606
Ps 2: 8 A of me, and I will make 8626
27: 4 One thing I a of the LORD, 8626
Pr 30: 7 "Two things I a of you, O LORD; 8626
Ecc 7:10 For it is not wise to a such questions. 8626
Isa 7:11 "A the LORD your God for a sign, 8626
7:12 But Ahaz said, "I will not a; 8626
21:12 If you would a, then ask; 1239
21:12 If you would ask, then a; 1239
41:28 no one to give answer when I a them. 8626
58: 2 They a me for just decisions 8626
65: 1 "I revealed myself to those who did not a 8626
Jer 2: 6 They did not a, 'Where is the LORD, 606
2: 8 priests did not a, 'Where is the LORD?' 606
5:19 And when the people a, 606
6:16 a for the ancient paths, 8626
6:16 a where the good way is, and walk in it, NIH
13:22 And if you a yourself, 606
15: 2 And if they a you, 'Where shall we go?' 606
15: 5 Who will stop to a how you are? 8626
16:10 and they a you, 'Why has the LORD decreed 606
22: 8 by this city and will a one another, 606
23:33 a you, 'What is the oracle of the LORD?' 8626
30: 6 A and see: Can a man bear children? 8626
38:14 "I am going to a you something," 8626
48:19 A the man fleeing and the woman escaping, 8626
48:19 a them, 'What has happened?' 606
50: 5 They will a the way to Zion 8626
Eze 12: 9 did not that rebellious house of Israel a you, 606
13:12 the wall collapses, will people not a you, 606
18:19 "Yet you a, 'Why does the son not share 606
21: 7 when they a you, 'Why are you groaning?' 606
37:18 "When your countrymen a you, 606
Hag 2: 2 of the people. A them, 606
2:11 'A the priests what the law says: 8626
Zec 7: 5 "A all the people of the land and 606
10: 1 A the LORD for rain in the springtime; 8626
Mal 1: 2 "But you a, 'How have you loved us?' 606
1: 6 "But you a, 'How have we shown contempt 606
1: 7 "But you a, 'How have we defiled you?' 606
2:14 You a, "Why?" 606
2:17 "How have we wearied him?" you a. 606
3: 7 "But you a, 'How are we to return?' 606
3: 8 "But you a, 'How do we rob you?' 606
3:13 you a, 'What have we said against you?' 606
Mt 6: 8 before you a him. 160
7: 7 "A and it will be given to you; 160
7:11 to those who a him! 160
9:38 A the Lord of the harvest, therefore, 1289
11: 3 to a him, "Are you the one who was 3306
18:19 on earth agree about anything you a for, 160
19:17 "Why do you a me about what is good?" 2263
21:22 you will receive whatever you a for 160
21:24 "I will also a you one question. 2263
21:25 "If we say, 'From heaven,' he will a, 3306
22:46 a him any more questions. 2089
27:20 and the elders persuaded the crowd to a for 160
Mk 5:31 his disciples answered, "and yet you can a, 3306
6:22 "A me for anything you want, 160
6:23 "Whatever you a I will give you, 160
6:24 "What shall I a for?" 160
8:12 "Why does this generation a for 2426
9:32 and were afraid to a him about it. 2089
10:35 "we want you to do for us whatever we a." 160
11:24 whatever you a for in prayer, 160
11:29 Jesus replied, "I will a you one question. 2089
11:31 "If we say, 'From heaven,' he will a, 3306
12:34 a him any more questions. 2089
Lk 6: 9 Then Jesus said to them, "I a you, 2089
7:19 he sent them to the Lord to a, 3306
7:20 "John the Baptist sent us to you to a, 3306
9:45 and they were afraid to a him about it. 2263
10: 2 A the Lord of the harvest, therefore, 1289
11: 9 A and it will be given to you; 160
11:13 the Holy Spirit to those who a him!" 160
14:32 the other is still a long way off and will a 2263
20: 3 He replied, "I will also a you a question. 2263
20: 5 he will a, 'Why didn't you believe him?' 3306
20:40 no one dared to a him any more questions. 2089
Jn 1:19 and Levites to a him who he was. 2263
4: 9 How can you a me for a drink?" 160
7:25 of the people of Jerusalem began to a, 3306
8:22 This made the Jews a, "Will he kill himself? 3306
9:21 we don't know. A him. 2263
9:23 "He is of age; a him." 2089
11:22 now God will give you whatever you a." 160
13:24 "A him which one he means." 4785
14:13 And I will do whatever you a in my name, 160
14:14 You may a me for anything in my name, 160
14:16 And I will a the Father, 2263
15: 7 words remain in you, a whatever you wish, 160
15:16 the Father will give you whatever you a 160
16:19 that they wanted to a him about this, 2263
16:23 day you will no longer a me anything. 2263
16:23 my Father will give you whatever you a 160
16:24 A and you will receive, 160
16:26 In that day you will a in my name. 160
16:26 I am not saying that I will a the Father 2263
16:30 even need to have anyone a you questions. 2263
18:21 A those who heard me. 2263
21:12 None of the disciples dared a him, 2004
Ac 9:11 of Judas on Straight Street and a for a man 2426
10:29 May I a why you sent for me?" 4785
23:20 "The Jews have agreed to a you 2263
Ro 10:18 But I a: Did they not hear? 3306
10:19 Again I a: Did Israel not understand? 3306
10:20 to those who did not a for me." 2089
11: 1 I a then: Did God reject his people? 3306
11:11 Again I a: Did they stumble 3306
16: 2 I a you to receive her in the Lord in NIG
1Co 14:35 they should a their own husbands at home; 2089
15:35 someone may a, "How are the dead raised? 3306
Eph 3:13 I a you, therefore, not to be discouraged 160
3:20 to do immeasurably more than all we a 160
Php 4: 3 Yes, and I a you, loyal yokefellow, 2263
1Th 4: 1 Now we a you and urge you in 2263
5:12 Now we a you, brothers, 2263
2Th 2: 1 and our being gathered to him, we a you, 2263
1Ti 5: 5 and day to pray and to a God for help. 4666
Phm 1:21 that you will do even more than I a. 3306
Jas 1: 5 lacks wisdom, he should a God, 160
4: 2 because you do not a God. 160
4: 3 When you a, you do not receive, 160
4: 3 because you a with wrong motives, 160
1Jn 3:22 and receive from him anything we a, 160
5:14 that if we a anything according to his will, 160
5:15 that he hears us—whatever we a— 160
2Jn 1: 5 I a that we love one another. 2263

ASKED (552) [ASK]

Ge 18: 9 "Where is your wife Sarah?" they a him. 606
20:10 And Abimelech a Abraham, 606
21:29 and Abimelech a Abraham, 606
24: 5 The servant a him, "What if the woman 606
24:23 Then he a, "Whose daughter are you? 606
24:39 "Then I a my master, 606
24:47 "I a her, 'Whose daughter are you?' 8626
24:58 So they called Rebekah and a her, 606
24:65 and a the servant, "Who is that man 606
26: 7 the men of that place a him about his wife, 8626
26:27 Isaac a them, "Why have you come to me, 606
27:20 Isaac a his son, "How did you find it 606
27:24 "Are you really my son Esau?" he a. 606
27:32 His father Isaac a him, "Who are you?" 606
27:36 now he's taken my blessing!" Then he a, 606
29: 4 Jacob a the shepherds, "My brothers, 606
29: 6 Then Jacob a them, "Is he well?" 606
30:31 "What shall I give you?" he a. 606
31:36 "What is my crime?" he a Laban. 6699
32:27 The man a him, "What is your name?" 606
33: 5 "Who are these with you?" he a. 606
33: 8 Esau a, "What do you mean 606
33:15 "But why do that?" Jacob a. 606
37:15 around in the fields and a him, 8626
38:16 to sleep with you?" she a. 606
38:17 until you send it?" she a. 606
38:21 He a the men who lived there, 8626
40: 7 So he a Pharaoh's officials who were 8626
41:38 So Pharaoh a them, "Can we find anyone 606
42: 7 "Where do you come from?" he a. 606
43: 6 Israel a, "Why did you bring this trouble 606
43: 7 'Is your father still living?' he a us. 606
43:27 He a them how they were, 4200+8626+8934
43:29 he a, "Is this your youngest brother, 606
44:19 My lord a his servants, 8626
47: 3 Pharaoh a the brothers, 606
47: 8 Pharaoh a him, "How old are you?" 606
48: 8 When Israel saw the sons of Joseph, he a, 606
Ex 1:18 the midwives and a them, 606
2: 7 Then his sister a Pharaoh's daughter, 606
2:13 He a the one in the wrong, 606
2:18 he a them, "Why have you returned 606
2:20 he a his daughters. 606
5:14 were beaten and were a, "Why didn't you 606
8:13 And the LORD did what Moses a. 1821
8:31 and the LORD did what Moses a: 1821
12:35 The Israelites did as Moses instructed and a 8626
12:36 gave them what they a for; 8626
33:17 "I will do the very thing you have a, 1819
Lev 10:16 Aaron's remaining sons, and a, 606
Nu 11:11 He a the LORD, "Why have you brought this 606
12: 2 LORD spoken only through Moses?" they a. 606
14:20 "I have forgiven them, as you a. 1821
22: 9 God came to Balaam and a, 606
22:32 The angel of the LORD a him, 606
23:17 Balak a him, "What did the LORD say?" 606
31:15 allowed all the women to live?" he a them. 606
Dt 18:16 For this is what you a of the LORD 8626
Jos 5:13 Joshua went up to him and a, 606
5:14 to the ground in reverence, and a him, 606
9: 8 But Joshua a, "Who are you and 606
15:18 When she got off her donkey, Caleb a her, 606
19:50 They gave him the town he a for— 8626
Jdg 1: 1 the Israelites a the LORD, 8626
1:14 When she got off her donkey, Caleb a her, 606
5:25 He a for water, and she gave him milk; 8626
6:15 "But Lord," Gideon a, 606
6:29 They a each other, "Who did this?" 606
8: 1 Now the Ephraimites a Gideon, 606
8:18 Then he a Zebah and Zalmunna, 606
8:26 The weight of the gold rings he a for came 8626
12: 5 the men of Gilead a him, 606
13:12 So Manoah a him, 606
15: 6 When the Philistines a, "Who did this?" 606
15:10 The men of Judah a, 606
17: 9 Micah a him, "Where are you from?" 606
18: 3 so they turned in there and a him, 606
18: 8 their brothers a them, 606
19:17 the old man a, "Where are you going? 606
20:28 They a, "Shall we go up again to battle 606
21: 5 Then the Israelites a, 606
21: 8 Then they a, "Which one of the tribes 606
Ru 2: 5 Boaz a the foreman of his harvesters, 606
2:19 Her mother-in-law a her, 606
3: 9 "Who are you?" he a. 606
3:16 Ruth came to her mother-in-law, Naomi a, 606
1Sa 1:17 of Israel grant you what you have a 8626
1:20 saying, "Because I a the LORD for him." 8626
1:27 LORD has granted me what I a of him. 8626
3:17 "What was it he said to you?" Eli a. 606
4: 3 the elders of Israel a, 606
4: 6 Hearing the uproar, the Philistines a, 606
4:14 Eli heard the outcry and a, 606
4:16 Eli a, "What happened, my son?" 606
5: 8 the rulers of the Philistines and a them, 606
6: 4 The Philistines a, "What guilt offering 606
6:20 and the men of Beth Shemesh a, 606
9:11 and they a them, "Is the seer here?" 606
9:18 approached Samuel in the gateway and a, 606
10:11 they a each other, "What is this 606
10:14 Now Saul's uncle a him and his servant, 606
11: 5 and he a, "What is wrong with the people? 606
11:12 "Who was it that a, 'Shall Saul reign 606
12:13 king you have chosen, the one you a for; 8626
12:17 in the eyes of the LORD when you a for 8626
13:11 "What have you done?" a Samuel. 606
14:37 So Saul a God, "Shall I go down 8626
16: 4 They a, "Do you come in peace?" 606
16:11 So he a Jesse, "Are these all the sons 606
17:26 David a the men standing near him, 606
17:28 he burned with anger at him and a, 606

1Sa 17:58 “Whose son are you, young man?” Saul **a** 606
19:22 And *he* **a**, “Where are Samuel and David?” 8626
20: 1 at Ramah and went to Jonathan and **a**, 606
20: 6 **earnestly a** my **permission** 8626+8626
20:10 David **a**, “Who will tell me 606
20:28 **earnestly a** me **for permission** 8626+8626
20:32 Jonathan **a** his father. 6699
21: 1 and **a**, “Why are you alone? 606
21: 8 David **a** Ahimelech, “Don't you have 606
23:12 Again David **a**, “Will the citizens 606
24:16 When David finished saying this, Saul **a**, 606
26: 6 David then **a** Ahimelech the Hittite 6699
27:10 When Achish **a**, “Where did you go 606
28:11 Then the woman **a**, “Whom shall I bring up 606
28:14 “What does he look like?” *he* **a**. 606
29: 3 The commanders of the Philistines **a**, 606
29: 8 “But what have I done?” **a** David. 606
30:13 David **a** him, “To whom do you belong, 606
30:15 David **a** him, “Can you lead me down 606
2Sa 1: 3 “Where have you come from?” David **a** him. 606
1: 4 “What happened?” David **a**. 606
1: 8 “*He* **a** me, ‘Who are you?’ 606
1:14 David **a** him, “Why were you not afraid 606
2: 1 of the towns of Judah?” he **a**. 606
2: 1 David **a**, “Where shall I go?” 606
2:20 Abner looked behind him and **a**, 606
9: 1 David **a**, “Is there anyone still left of 606
9: 3 The king **a**, “Is there no one still left of 606
9: 4 “Where is he?” the king **a**. 606
11: 7 David **a** him how Joab was, 8626
11:10 “Uriah did not go home,” he **a** him, 606
12:19 “Is the child dead?” he **a**. 606
12:21 His servants **a** him, 606
13: 4 *He* **a** Amnon, “Why do you, the king's son, 606
13:26 The king **a** him, “Why are you acting this 606
14: 5 The king **a** her, “What is troubling you?” 606
14:19 The king **a**, “Isn't the hand of Joab 606
16: 2 The king **a** Ziba, “Why have you brought 606
16: 3 The king then **a**, “Where is your master's 606
16:17 Absalom **a** Hushai, “Is this the love 606
17:20 at the house, *they* **a**, “Where are Ahimaaz 606
18:29 king **a**, “Is the young man Absalom safe?” 606
18:32 The king **a** the Cushite, “Is the young man 606
19:25 the king **a** him, “Why didn't you go with me 606
20:17 He went toward her, and she **a**, 606
21: 3 David **a** the Gibeonites, “What shall I do 606
21: 4 want me to do for you?” David **a**. 606
1Ki 1:11 Nathan **a** Bathsheba, Solomon's mother, 606
1:16 “What is it you want?” the king **a**. 606
1:41 the sound of the trumpet, Joab **a**, “What's 606
2:13 Solomon's mother. Bathsheba **a** him, 606
3:10 The Lord was pleased that Solomon *had* **a** 8626
3:11 “Since *you have* **a** *for* this and not 8626
3:11 nor *have* **a** *for* the death of your enemies 8626
3:12 I will do what you have **a**. 1821
3:13 I will give you what *you have* not **a** *for*— 8626
9:13 you have given me, my brother?” *he* **a**. 606
10:13 the queen of Sheba all she desired and **a** 8626
11:22 to your own country?” Pharaoh **a**. 606
12: 6 to answer these people?” he **a**. 606
12: 9 *He* **a** them, “What is your advice? 606
13:12 Their father **a** them, 1819
13:14 under an oak tree and **a**, 606
17:10 He called to her and **a**, 606
18: 9 “What have I done wrong,” **a** Obadiah, 606
20:14 “But who will do this?” **a** Ahab. 606
20:14 “And who will start the battle?” *he* **a**. 606
21: 5 His wife Jezebel came in and **a** him, 1819
22: 4 So *he* **a** Jehoshaphat, 606
22: 6 and **a** them, “Shall I go to war 606
22: 7 But Jehoshaphat **a**, “Is there not a prophet 606
22:15 When he arrived, the king **a** him, “Micaiah, 606
22:22 “ ‘By what means?’ the LORD **a**. 606
22:24 to speak to you?” *he* **a**. 606
2Ki 1: 5 messengers returned to the king, *he* **a** them, 606
1: 7 The king **a** them, “What kind of man 1819
2: 3 at Bethel came out to Elisha and **a**, 606
2: 5 at Jericho went up to Elisha and **a** him, 606
2:10 “*You have* **a** a difficult thing,” Elijah said, 8626
2:14 the God of Elijah?” *he* **a**. 606
3: 8 “By what route shall we attack?” *he* **a**. 606
3:11 But Jehoshaphat **a**, “Is there no prophet of 606
4:14 “What can be done for her?” Elisha **a**. 606
4:23 “Why go to him today?” *he* **a**. 606
4:43 before a hundred men?” his servant **a**. 606
5:21 “Is everything all right?” *he* **a**. 606
5:25 “Where have you been, Gehazi?” Elisha **a**. 606
6: 6 The man of God **a**, “Where did it fall?” 606
6:15 what shall we do?” the servant **a**. 606
6:18 as Elisha had **a**. 1821
6:21 *he* **a** Elisha, “Shall I kill them, my father? 606
6:28 Then he **a** her, “What's the matter?” 606
8: 6 The king **a** the woman *about* it, 8626
8:12 “Why is my lord weeping?” **a** Hazael. 606
8:14 When Ben-Hadad **a**, “What did Elisha say 606
9: 5 “For which of us?” **a** Jehu. 606
9:11 *one* of them **a** him, “Is everything all right? 606
9:22 When Joram saw Jehu *he* **a**, 606
9:31 As Jehu entered the gate, *she* **a**, 606
10:13 of Ahaziah king of Judah and **a**, 606
12: 7 the priest and the other priests and **a** them, 606
20: 8 Hezekiah *had* **a** Isaiah, 606
20:14 the prophet went to King Hezekiah and **a**, 606
20:15 The prophet **a**, “What did they see 606
23:17 The king **a**, “What is that tombstone I see?” 606
1Ch 13:12 David was afraid of God that day and **a**, 606
2Ch 1:11 and *you have* not **a** *for* wealth, 8626

2Ch 1:11 and since *you have* not **a** *for* a long life but 8626
9:12 of Sheba all she desired and **a** *for;* 8626
10: 6 to answer these people?” he **a**. 606
10: 9 *He* **a** them, “What is your advice? 606
18: 3 Ahab king of Israel **a** Jehoshaphat king 606
18: 5 and **a** them, “Shall we go to war 606
18: 6 But Jehoshaphat **a**, “Is there not a prophet 606
18:14 When he arrived, the king **a** him, “Micaiah, 606
18:20 “ ‘By what means?’ the LORD **a**. 606
18:23 he went from me to speak to you?” *he* **a**. 606
25: 9 Amaziah **a** the man of God, 606
31: 9 Hezekiah **a** the priests and Levites about 2011
Ezr 5: 3 and their associates went to them and **a**, 10042
5: 4 *They* also **a**, “What are the names of 10042
5: 9 We questioned the elders and **a** them, 10042
5:10 *We* also **a** them their names, 10689
7: 6 The king had granted him everything he **a**, 1336
Ne 2: 2 so the king **a** me, “Why does your face look 606
2: 6 **a** me, “How long will your journey take, 606
2:19 “What is this you are doing?” *they* **a**. 606
13: 6 Some time later *I* **a** his permission 8626
13:11 So I rebuked the officials and **a** them, 606
Est 1:15 what must be done to Queen Vashti?” he **a**. NIH
2:15 *she* **a for** nothing other than what Hegai, 1335
3: 3 at the king's gate **a** Mordecai, 606
5: 3 the king **a**, “What is it, Queen Esther? 606
5: 6 the king again **a** Esther, “Now what 606
6: 3 Mordecai received for this?” the king **a**. 606
6: 6 When Haman entered, the king **a** him, 606
7: 2 the king again **a**, “Queen Esther, 606
7: 5 King Xerxes **a** Queen Esther, “Who is he? 606
Job 42: 3 [You **a**,] ‘Who is this that obscures NIH
Ps 21: 4 *He* **a** you *for* life, and you gave it to him— 8626
105:40 *They* **a**, and he brought them quail 8626
106:15 So he gave them **what** they **a for**, 8629
137: 3 for there our captors **a** us *for* songs, 8626
Ecc 4: 8 “For whom am I toiling,” he **a**, NIH
Isa 1:12 who *has* **a** this of you, 1335
38:22 Hezekiah *had* **a**, “What will be the sign 606
39: 3 the prophet went to King Hezekiah and **a**, 606
39: 4 The prophet **a**, “What did they see 606
Jer 24: 3 Then the LORD **a** me, “What do you see, 606
36:17 Then *they* **a** Baruch, “Tell us, 8626
37:17 where he **a** him privately, 8626
Eze 24:19 Then the people **a** me, “Won't you tell us 606
37: 3 *He* **a** me, “Son of man, can these bones live? 606
47: 6 *He* **a** me, “Son of man, do you see this?” 606
Da 1: 8 **a** the chief official **for permission** 1335
2:10 *has ever* **a** such a thing of any magician 10689
2:15 *He* **a** the king's officer, 10558
2:16 Daniel went in to the king and **a for** time, 10114
2:23 you have made known to me what *we* **a** 10114
2:26 king **a** Daniel (also called Belteshazzar), 10558
2:27 to the king the mystery he *has* **a** *about,* 10689
3:24 to his feet in amazement and **a** his advisers, 10558
7:16 and **a** him the true meaning of all this. 10114
12: 8 So *I* **a**, “My lord, what will the outcome 606
Am 7: 8 LORD **a** me, “What do you see, Amos?” 606
8: 2 “What do you see, Amos?” *he* **a**. 606
Jnh 1: 8 So *they* **a** him, “Tell us, 606
1:10 This terrified them and *they* **a**, 606
1:11 So *they* **a** him, “What should we do to you 606
Zec 1: 9 *I* **a**, “What are these, my lord?” 606
1:19 *I* **a** the angel who was speaking to me, 606
1:21 *I* **a**, “What are these coming to do?” 606
2: 2 *I* **a**, “Where are you going?” 606
4: 2 *He* **a** me, “What do you see?” 606
4: 4 *I* **a** the angel who talked with me, 6699
4:11 Then *I* **a** the angel, “What are these two 6699
4:12 Again *I* **a** him, “What are these two 6699
5: 2 *He* **a** me, “What do you see?” 606
5: 6 *I* **a**, “What is it?” 606
5:10 *I* **a** the angel who was speaking to me. 606
6: 4 *I* **a** the angel who was speaking to me, 6699
Mt 2: 2 and **a**, “Where is the one who has been born king of the Jews? *3306*
2: 4 *he* **a** them where the Christ was to be born. *4785*
8:27 The men were amazed and **a**, *3306*
9:11 *they* **a** his disciples, *3306*
9:14 Then John's disciples came and **a** him, *3306*
9:28 the blind men came to him, and he **a** them, *3306*
12:10 to accuse Jesus, *they* **a** him, “Is it lawful *2089*
13:10 The disciples came to him and **a**, *3306*
13:28 “The servants **a** him, ‘Do you want *3306*
13:51 “Have you understood all these things?” Jesus **a**. *3306*
13:54 and these miraculous powers?” they **a**. *3306*
14: 7 with an oath to give her whatever *she* **a**. *160*
15: 1 to Jesus from Jerusalem and **a**, *3306*
15:12 Then the disciples came to him and **a**, *3306*
15:16 “Are you still so dull?” Jesus **a** them. *3306*
15:34 “How many loaves do you have?” Jesus **a**. *3306*
16: 8 Aware of their discussion, Jesus **a**, *3306*
16:13 *he* **a** his disciples, “Who do people say *2263*
16:15 “But what about you?” *he* **a**. *3306*
17:10 disciples **a** him, “Why then do the teachers *2089*
17:19 disciples came to Jesus in private and **a**, *3306*
17:24 the two-drachma tax came to Peter and **a**, *3306*
17:25 “What do you think, Simon?” he **a**. *NIG*
18: 1 that time the disciples came to Jesus and **a**, *3306*
18:21 Then Peter came to Jesus and **a**, “Lord, *3306*
19: 3 *They* **a**, “Is it lawful for a man *3306*
19: 7 then,” *they* **a**, “did Moses command that *3306*
19:16 Now a man came up to Jesus and **a**, *3306*
19:25 they were greatly astonished and **a**, *3306*
20: 6 *He* **a** them, ‘Why have you been standing *3306*
20:20 kneeling down, **a** a **favor** of him. *160*

Mt 20:21 “What is it you want?” he **a**. *3306*
20:32 What do you want me to do for you?” *he* **a**. *3306*
21:10 the whole city was stirred and **a**, *3306*
21:16 what these children are saying?” *they* **a** him. *3306*
21:20 “How did the fig tree wither so quickly?” *they* **a**. *3306*
21:23 “By what authority are you doing these things?” *they* **a**. *3306*
22:12 *he* **a**, ‘how did you get in here *3306*
22:20 and *he* **a** them, “Whose portrait is this? *3306*
22:41 While the Pharisees were gathered together, Jesus **a** them, *2089*
24: 2 “Do you see all these things?” he **a**. *3306*
26: 8 “Why this waste?” *they* **a**. *3306*
26:15 and **a**, “What are you willing to give me *3306*
26:17 the disciples came to Jesus and **a**, *3306*
26:40 watch with me for one hour?” *he* **a** Peter. *3306*
27:11 and the governor **a** him, *2089*
27:13 Then Pilate **a** him, “Don't you hear *3306*
27:17 the crowd had gathered, Pilate **a** them, *3306*
27:21 to release to you?” **a** the governor. *646*
27:22 with Jesus who is called Christ?” Pilate **a**. *3306*
27:23 What crime has he committed?” **a** Pilate. *5774*
27:58 Going to Pilate, he **a for** Jesus' body, *160*
Mk 1:27 so amazed that they **a** each other, *5184*
2:16 *they* **a** his disciples: “Why does he eat *3306*
2:18 Some people came and **a** Jesus, *3306*
3: 4 Then Jesus **a** them, “Which is lawful on *3306*
3:33 my mother and my brothers?” *he* **a**. *646*
4:10 and the others around him **a** him about *2263*
4:41 They were terrified and **a** each other, *3306*
5: 9 Then Jesus **a** him, “What is your name?” *2089*
5:30 *He* turned around in the crowd and **a**, *3306*
6: 2 “Where did this man get these things?” *they* **a**. *3306*
6:38 “How many loaves do you have?” he **a**. *3306*
7: 5 Pharisees and teachers of the law **a** Jesus, *2089*
7:17 his disciples **a** him **about** this parable. *2089*
7:18 “Are you so dull?” *he* **a**. *3306*
8: 5 “How many loaves do you have?” Jesus **a**. *2263*
8:11 *they* **a** him **for** a sign from heaven. *2426*
8:17 Aware of their discussion, Jesus **a** them: *3306*
8:23 Jesus **a**, “Do you see anything?” *2089*
8:27 On the way *he* **a** them, “Who do people say *2089*
8:29 “But what about you?” he **a**. *2089*
9:11 And *they* **a** him, “Why do the teachers *2089*
9:16 arguing with them about?” *he* **a**. *2089*
9:18 *I* **a** your disciples to drive out the spirit, *3306*
9:21 Jesus **a** the boy's father, “How long *2089*
9:28 his disciples **a** him privately, “Why *2089*
9:33 When he was in the house, *he* **a** them, *2089*
10:10 the disciples **a** Jesus about this. *2089*
10:17 *he* **a**, “what must I do to inherit eternal life? *2089*
10:36 “What do you want me to do for you?” he **a**. *3306*
10:51 do you want me to do for you?” Jesus **a** *646*
11: 5 some people standing there **a**, *3306*
11:28 “By what authority are you doing these things?” *they* **a**. *3306*
12:15 you trying to trap me?” *he* **a**. *3306*
12:16 They brought the coin, and *he* **a** them, *3306*
12:28 *he* **a** him, “Of all the commandments, *2089*
12:35 in the temple courts, *he* **a**, “How is it that *3306*
13: 3 James, John and Andrew **a** him privately, *2089*
14:12 Jesus' disciples **a** him, *3306*
14:60 up before them and **a** Jesus, *2089*
14:61 Again the high priest **a** him, *2089*
14:63 do we need any more witnesses?” *he* **a**. *3306*
15: 2 “Are you the king of the Jews?” **a** Pilate. *2089*
15: 4 So again Pilate **a** him, “Aren't you *2089*
15: 8 The crowd came up and **a** Pilate to do *160*
15: 9 to you the king of the Jews?” **a** Pilate, *646*
15:12 crime has he committed?” Pilate **a** them. *646*
15:14 What crime has he committed?” **a** Pilate. *3306*
15:43 to Pilate and **a for** Jesus' body. *160*
15:44 *he* **a** him if Jesus had already died. *2089*
16: 3 and *they* **a** each other, “Who will roll *3306*
Lk 1:18 Zechariah **a** the angel, “How can I be sure *3306*
1:34 “How will this be,” Mary **a** the angel, *3306*
1:63 *He* **a for** a writing tablet, *160*
2:49 “Why were you searching for me?” *he* **a**. *3306*
3:10 “What should we do then?” the crowd **a**. *2089*
3:12 “Teacher,” *they* **a**, “what should we do?” *3306*
3:14 Then some soldiers **a** him, *2089*
4:22 “Isn't this Joseph's son?” *they* **a**. *3306*
4:38 and *they* **a** Jesus to help her. *2263*
5: 3 and **a** him to put out a little from shore. *2263*
5:22 Jesus knew what they were thinking and **a**, *646*
6: 2 Some of the Pharisees **a**, *3306*
8: 9 His disciples **a** him what this parable meant. *2089*
8:25 “Where is you faith?” *he* **a** his disciples. *3306*
8:25 In fear and amazement *they* **a** one another, *3306*
8:30 Jesus **a** him, “What is your name?” *2089*
8:37 of the Gerasenes **a** Jesus to leave them, *2263*
8:45 “Who touched me?” Jesus **a**. *3306*
9:18 *he* **a** them, “Who do the crowds say I am?” *2089*
9:20 “But what about you?” *he* **a**. *3306*
9:54 *they* **a**, “Lord, do you want us to call fire *3306*
10:25 *he* **a**, “what must I do to inherit eternal life? *3306*
10:29 so *he* **a** Jesus, “And who is my neighbor?” *3306*
10:40 *She* came to him and **a**, “Lord, *3306*
12:41 Peter **a**, “Lord, are you telling this parable *3306*
12:48 entrusted with much, much more *will be* **a**. *160*
13:18 Jesus **a**, “What is the kingdom of God like? *3306*
13:20 Again *he* **a**, “What shall I compare *3306*
13:23 Someone **a** him, “Lord, are only a few *3306*
14: 3 Jesus **a** the Pharisees and experts in the law, *646*
14: 5 Then *he* **a** them, “If one of you has a son *3306*

Lk 15:26 the servants and **a** him what was going on. *4785*
16: 2 So *he* called him in and **a** him, *3306*
16: 5 *He* **a** the first, 'How much do you owe *3306*
16: 7 "Then *he* **a** the second, 'And how much *3306*
17:17 Jesus **a,** "Were not all ten cleansed? *646*
17:20 *having been* **a** by the Pharisees when *2089*
17:37 "Where, Lord?" *they* **a.** *646*
18:18 A certain ruler **a** him, "Good teacher, *2089*
18:26 Those who heard this **a,** "Who then can *3306*
18:36 *he* **a** what was happening. *4785*
18:40 When he came near, Jesus **a** him, *2089*
19:33 untying the colt, its owners **a** them, *3306*
20:17 Jesus looked directly at them and **a,** *3306*
21: 7 *they* **a,** "when will these things happen? *2089*
22: 9 want us to prepare for it?" they **a.** *3306*
22:31 Simon, Satan *has* **a** to sift you as wheat. *1977*
22:35 Then Jesus **a** them, "When I sent you *3306*
22:46 "Why are you sleeping?" *he* **a** them. *3306*
22:48 but Jesus **a** him, "Judas, are you betraying *3306*
22:68 and if *I* **a** you, you would not answer. *2263*
22:70 *They* all **a,** "Are you then the Son of God?" *3306*
23: 3 So Pilate **a** Jesus, "Are you the king *2263*
23: 6 Pilate **a** if the man was a Galilean. *2089*
23:25 the one *they* **a for,** *160*
23:52 Going to Pilate, he **a for** Jesus' body. *160*
24:17 *He* **a** them, "What are you discussing *3306*
24:18 One of them, named Cleopas, **a** him, *646*
24:19 "What things?" *he* **a.** "About Jesus *3306*
24:32 *They* **a** each other, "Were not our hearts *3306*
24:41 because of joy and amazement, *he* **a** them, *3306*
Jn 1:21 *They* **a** him, "Then who are you? *2263*
1:38 Jesus saw them following and **a,** *3306*
1:46 good come from there?" Nathanael **a.** *3306*
1:48 "How do you know me?" Nathanael **a.** *3306*
3: 4 when he is old?" Nicodemus **a.** *3306*
3: 9 "How can this be?" Nicodemus **a.** *646*
4:10 you would *have* **a** him *160*
4:27 But no one **a,** "What do you want?" *3306*
5: 6 *he* **a** him, "Do you want to get well?" *3306*
5:12 So *they* **a** him, "Who is this fellow *2263*
6: 6 *He* **a** this only to test him, *3306*
6:25 on the other side of the lake, *they* **a** him, *3306*
6:28 Then *they* **a** him, "What must we do *3306*
6:30 So *they* **a** him, "What miraculous sign *3306*
6:67 Jesus **a** the Twelve. *3306*
7:15 The Jews were amazed and **a,** *3306*
7:41 Still others **a,** "How can the Christ come *3306*
7:45 the chief priests and Pharisees, who **a** them, *3306*
7:50 and who was one of their own number, **a,** *3306*
8:10 Jesus straightened up and **a** her, "Woman, *3306*
8:19 Then *they* **a** him, "Where is your father?" *3306*
8:25 "Who are you?" *they* **a.** *3306*
9: 2 His disciples **a** him, "Rabbi, who sinned, *2263*
9: 8 those who had formerly seen him begging **a,** *3306*
9:17 "Where is this man?" *they* **a** him. *3306*
9:15 also **a** him how he had received his sight. *2263*
9:16 But others **a,** "How can a sinner do such *3306*
9:19 "Is this your son?" *they* **a.** *2263*
9:26 Then *they* **a** him, "What did he do to you? *3306*
9:36 "Who is he, sir?" the man **a.** *646*
9:40 with him heard him say this and **a,** *3306*
11:34 "Where have you laid him?" *he* **a.** *3306*
11:47 "What are we accomplishing?" *they* **a.** *3306*
11:56 in the temple area *they* **a** one another, *3306*
13:12 what I have done for you?" *he* **a** them. *3306*
13:25 Leaning back against Jesus, he **a** him, *3306*
13:36 Simon Peter **a** him, "Lord, where are you *3306*
13:37 Peter **a,** "Lord, why can't I follow you now? *3306*
16:24 Until now *you have* not **a for** anything *160*
18: 4 went out and **a** them, "Who is it you want?" *3306*
18: 7 Again *he* **a** them, "Who is it you want?" *2089*
18:17 the girl at the door **a** Peter. *3306*
18:25 he *was* **a,** "You are not one of his disciples, *3306*
18:29 So Pilate came out to them and **a,** *5774*
18:33 summoned Jesus and **a** him, *3306*
18:34 "Is that your own idea," Jesus **a,** *646*
18:38 "What is truth?" Pilate **a.** *3306*
19: 9 *he* **a** Jesus, but Jesus gave him no answer. *3306*
19:15 "Shall I crucify your king?" Pilate **a.** *3306*
19:31 *they* **a** Pilate to have the legs broken and *2263*
19:38 of Arimathea **a** Pilate for the body of Jesus. *2263*
20:13 They **a** her, "Woman, why are you crying?" *3306*
21:17 Peter was hurt because Jesus **a** him *3306*
21:21 When Peter saw him, *he* **a,** "Lord, *3306*
Ac 1: 6 So when they met together, *they* **a** him, *2263*
2: 7 Utterly amazed, *they* **a:** *3306*
2:12 Amazed and perplexed, *they* **a** one another, *3306*
3: 3 he **a** them **for** money. *2263*
3:14 and Righteous One and **a** that a murderer *160*
4: 9 to a cripple and are **a** how he was healed, *NIG*
4:16 we going to do with these men?" *they* **a.** *3306*
5: 8 Peter **a** her, "Tell me, is this the price *646*
7: 1 high priest **a** him, "Are these charges true?" *3306*
7:46 who enjoyed God's favor and **a** *160*
8:30 "Do you understand what you are reading?"
Philip **a.** *3306*
8:34 The eunuch **a** Philip, "Tell me, please, *646*
9: 2 and **a** him **for** letters to the synagogues *160*
9: 5 "Who are you, Lord?" Saul **a.** *3306*
9:21 and **a,** "Isn't he the man who raised havoc *3306*
10: 4 "What is it, Lord?" *he* **a.** *3306*
10:48 Then *they* **a** Peter to stay with them for *2263*
12:20 *they* **a for** peace, *160*
13:21 Then the *people* **a for** a king, *160*
13:28 *they* **a** Pilate to have him executed. *160*
16:30 He then brought them out and **a,** "Sirs, *5774*
17:18 Some of them **a,** "What is this babbler *3306*
18:20 *When* they **a** him to spend more time *2263*
19: 2 **a** them, "Did you receive the Holy Spirit *3306*
19: 3 So Paul **a,** "Then what baptism did you
receive?" *3306*
21:33 *he* **a** who he was and what he had done. *4785*
21:37 *he* **a** the commander, "May I say *3306*
22: 8 " 'Who are you, Lord?' I **a.** *646*
22:10 " 'What shall I do, Lord?' *I* **a.** *3306*
22:26 "What are you going to do?" *he* **a.** *3306*
22:27 The commander went to Paul and **a,** *3306*
23:18 for me and **a** me to bring this young man *2263*
23:19 drew him aside and **a,** "What is it *4785*
23:34 the letter and **a** what province he was from. *2089*
25:15 the Jews brought charges against him and **a** *160*
25:20 so *I* **a** if he would be willing to go *3306*
26:15 "Then I **a,** 'Who are you, Lord?' *3306*
28:20 For this reason *I have* **a** to see you and talk *4151*
Gal 2:10 **All they a was** that we should continue *3667*
1Jn 5:15 we know that we have what *we* **a** of him. *160+161*
Rev 7:13 Then one of the elders **a** me, *646*
10: 9 So I went to the angel and **a** him to give me *3306*
13: 4 and they also worshiped the beast and **a,** *3306*

ASKELON (KJV) See ASHKELON

ASKING (26) [ASK]

Ex 10:11 since that's what you *have been* **a for."** 1335
1Sa 8:10 the LORD to the people who *were* **a** him 8626
10: 2 He *is* **a,** "What shall I do about my son?" ' 606
12:19 to all our other sins the evil of **a** for a king. 8626
25:39 **a** her to become his wife. 1819
2Sa 15: 6 the Israelites who came to the king **a** NIH
1Ki 1: 6 with him by **a,** "Why do you behave as 606
Ps 4: 6 Many *are* **a,** "Who can show us any good?" 606
Da 6:11 and **a** God **for help.** 10274
Zec 7: 3 by **a** the priests of the house of 606
Mt 8: 5 a centurion came to him, **a for help.** *4151*
16: 1 by **a** him to show them a sign from heaven. *2089*
20:22 "You don't know what *you are* **a,"** *160*
Mk 10: 2 Some Pharisees came and tested him by **a,** *2089*
10:38 "You don't know what *you are* **a,"** *160*
Lk 1:66 **a,** "What then is this child going to be?" *3306*
2:46 listening to them and **a** them **questions.** *2089*
7: 3 **a** him to come and heal his servant. *2263*
11:16 Others tested him by **a for** a sign *2426*
Jn 7:11 the Jews were watching for him and **a,** *3306*
11:28 she said, "and *is* **a for** you." *5888*
16:18 *They kept* **a,** "What does he mean by *3306*
16:19 *"Are you* **a** one another what I meant *2426*
Ac 10:18 **a** if Simon who was known as Peter *4785*
Eph 1:17 I keep **a** that the God of our Lord Jesus *NIG*
Col 1: 9 and **a** God to fill you with the knowledge *160*

ASKS (33) [ASK]

Ge 32:17 "When my brother Esau meets you and **a,** 8626
46:33 When Pharaoh calls you in and **a,** 606
Ex 13:14 "In days to come, when your son **a** you, 8626
Dt 6:20 In the future, when your son **a** you, 8626
Jdg 4:20 "If someone comes by and **a** you, 8626
2Sa 11:21 If he **a** you this, then say to him, 'Also, NIH
14:15 perhaps he will do **what** his servant **a.** 1821
1Ki 8:43 and do whatever the foreigner **a** of you, 7924
2Ch 6:33 and do whatever the foreigner **a** of you, 7924
Est 5: 5 "so that we may do **what** Esther **a."** 1821
Jer 39:12 but do for him whatever *he* **a."** 1819
Da 2:10 "There is not a man on earth who can do
what the king **a!** 10418
2:11 What the king **a** is too difficult. 10689
Am 6:10 of the house and **a** anyone still hiding there, 606
Zec 13: 6 If *someone* **a** him, 'What are these wounds 606
Mt 5:42 Give *to* the one who **a** you, *160*
7: 8 For everyone who **a** receives; *160*
7: 9 "Which of you, if his son **a for** bread, *160*
7:10 Or if *he* **a for** a fish, will give him a snake? *160*
12:39 "A wicked and adulterous generation **a for** *2118*
Mk 11: 3 If anyone **a** you, 'Why are you doing this?' *3306*
14:14 of the house he enters, 'The Teacher **a:** *3306*
Lk 6:30 Give to everyone *who* **a** you, *160*
11:10 For everyone who **a** receives; *160*
11:11 *if* your son **a for** a fish, *160*
11:12 Or *if he* **a for** an egg, *160*
11:29 *It* **a for** a miraculous sign, *2426*
19:31 If anyone **a** you, 'Why are you untying it?' *2263*
22:11 to the owner of the house, 'The Teacher **a:** *3306*
Jn 4:10 of God and who it is that **a** you **for** a drink, *3306*
16: 5 yet none of you **a** me, 'Where are you *2263*
Jas 1: 6 But when *he* **a,** he must believe *160*
1Pe 3:15 to everyone who **a** you to give the reason *160*

ASLEEP (27) [SLEEP]

Ge 41: 5 *He* **fell a** again and had a second dream: 3822
Jdg 4:21 to him while he **lay fast a,** 8101
1Sa 26: 7 lying **a** inside the camp with his spear stuck 3825
1Ki 3:20 from my side while I your servant was **a.** 3825
19: 5 he lay down under the tree and **fell a.** 3822
Job 3:13 *I would be* **a** and at rest 3822
Mt 9:24 The girl is not dead but **a."** *2761*
25: 5 and they all became drowsy and **fell a.** *2761*
28:13 and stole him away *while* we *were* **a.'** *3121*
Mk 5:39 The child is not dead but **a."** *2761*
14:37 "Simon," he said to Peter, *"are you* **a**? *2761*
Lk 8:23 As they sailed, *he* **fell a.** *934*
8:52 "She is not dead but **a."** *2761*
22:45 he found them **a,** exhausted from sorrow. *3121*
Jn 11:11 "Our friend Lazarus *has* **fallen a;** *3121*
Ac 7:60 When he had said this, *he* **fell a.** *3121*
13:36 in his own generation, *he* **fell a;** *3121*
20: 9 *When he was* **sound a,** *608+2965+3836+5678*
1Co 11:30 and a number of you *have* **fallen a.** *3121*
15: 6 though some *have* **fallen a.** *3121*
15:18 also who *have* **fallen a** in Christ are lost. *3121*
15:20 the firstfruits *of* those who *have* **fallen a.** *3121*
1Th 4:13 to be ignorant about those who **fall a,** *3121*
4:14 with Jesus those who *have* **fallen a** *3121*
4:15 not precede those who *have* **fallen a.** *3121*
5: 6 then, *let us* not *be* like others, who are **a,** *2761*
5:10 whether we are awake or **a,** *2761*

ASNAH (1)

Ezr 2:50 **A,** Meunim, Nephussim, 663

ASNAPPER (KJV) See ASHURBANIPAL

ASP, ASPS (KJV) See COBRA, SERPENTS, VIPERS

ASPATHA (1)

Est 9: 7 They also killed Parshandatha, Dalphon, **A,** 672

ASRIEL (3) [ASRIELITE]

Nu 26:31 through **A,** the Asrielite clan; 835
Jos 17: 2 the clans of Abiezer, Helek, **A,** Shechem, 835
1Ch 7:14 **A** was his descendant 835

ASRIELITE (1) [ASRIEL]

Nu 26:31 through Asriel, the **A** clan; 834

ASS, ASS'S, ASSES (KJV) See DONKEY

ASSAIL (2) [ASSAILANT, ASSAILS]

Ps 17: 9 from the wicked who **a** me, 8720
55: 4 the terrors of death **a** me. 5877+6584

ASSAILANT (1) [ASSAIL]

Dt 25:11 to rescue her husband from his **a,** 5782

ASSAILS (1) [ASSAIL]

Job 16: 9 God **a** me and tears me in his anger 8475

ASSAR See TEL ASSAR

ASSASSINATE (2) [ASSASSINATED, ASSASSINATION, ASSASSINS]

Est 2:21 and conspired to **a** King Xerxes. 928+3338+8938
6: 2 had conspired to **a** King Xerxes. 928+3338+8938

ASSASSINATED (9) [ASSASSINATE]

2Ki 12:20 against him and **a** him *at* Beth Millo, 5782
15:10 **a** him and succeeded him as king. 4637
15:14 **a** him and succeeded him as king. 4637
15:25 *he* **a** Pekahiah, along with Argob and Arieh, 5782
15:30 He attacked and **a** him, 4637
21:23 against him and **a** the king in his palace. 4637
25:25 came with with ten men and **a** Gedaliah
2256+4637+5782
2Ch 33:24 against him and **a** him in his palace. 4637
Jer 41:16 of Nethaniah after *he had* **a** Gedaliah son 5782

ASSASSINATION (1) [ASSASSINATE]

Jer 41: 4 The day after Gedaliah's **a,** 4637

ASSASSINS (1) [ASSASSINATE]

2Ki 14: 6 he did not put the sons of the **a** to death, 5782

ASSAULT (2) [ASSAULTS]

Dt 21: 5 and to decide all cases of dispute and **a.** 5596
Ps 62: 3 How long *will you* **a** a man? 2109

ASSAULTED (KJV) See RUSHED TO

ASSAULTS (3) [ASSAULT]

Dt 17: 8 bloodshed, lawsuits or **a**— 4200+5596+5596
19:11 lies in wait for him, **a** and kills him, 6584+7756
Job 28: 9 Man's hand **a** the flinty rock 928+8938

ASSAY (KJV) See VENTURES

ASSEMBLE (33) [ASSEMBLED, ASSEMBLIES, ASSEMBLING, ASSEMBLY]

Ge 49: 2 **"A** and listen, sons of Jacob; 7695
Ex 3:16 "Go, **a** the elders of Israel and say to them, 665
Nu 8: 9 to the front of the Tent of Meeting and **a** 7735
10: 3 the whole community *is to* **a** before you at 3585
10: 4 *are to* **a** before you. 3585
Dt 4:10 **"A** the people before me to hear my words 7735
31:12 **A** the people—men, women and children 7735
31:28 **A** before me all the elders of your tribes 7735

Jdg 21: 5 from all the tribes of Israel *has* failed *to* a 928+2021+6590+7736
21: 5 a solemn oath that anyone who failed *to* a 6590
21: 8 of the tribes of Israel failed *to* a before 6590
1Sa 7: 5 "A all Israel at Mizpah and I will intercede 7695
2Sa 3:21 and a all Israel for my lord the king, 7695
1Ch 22: 2 So David gave orders to a the aliens living 4043
28: 1 **summoned** all the officials of Israel **to a** 7735
Ezr 10: 7 and Jerusalem for all the exiles to a 7695
Ne 7: 5 So my God put it into my heart *to* a 7695
Est 8:11 the right to a and protect themselves; 7735
Ps 47: 9 The nobles of the nations a as the people of 665
102:22 the kingdoms a to worship the LORD. 3481+7695
Isa 4: 5 of Mount Zion and over *those who* a there 5246
11:12 *he will* a the scattered people of Judah 7695
43: 9 nations gather together and the peoples a. 665
45:20 a, *you* fugitives from the nations. 3481+5602
60: 4 All a and come to you; 7695
Jer 49:14 "**A yourselves** to attack it! 7695
Eze 39:17 'A and come together from all around to 7695
Da 11:10 His sons will prepare for war and a 665
Joel 3:11 from every side, and a there. 7695
Am 3: 9 "**A** *yourselves* on the mountains 665
Mic 4: 6 I will gather the lame, *I will* a the exiles 7695
Zep 3: 8 I have decided to a the nations, 665
Ac 22:30 the chief priests and all the Sanhedrin *to* a. *5302*

ASSEMBLED (48) [ASSEMBLE]

Ex 35: 1 Moses a the whole Israelite community 7735
Dt 33: 5 when the leaders of the people a, 665
33:21 When the heads of the people a, 910
Jos 24: 1 Joshua a all the tribes of Israel at Shechem. 665
Jdg 9:47 Abimelech heard that they *had* a there, 7695
10:17 the Israelites a and camped at Mizpah. 665
16:23 of the Philistines a to offer a great sacrifice 665
20: 1 of Gilead came out as one man and a 7735
1Sa 7: 6 When *they had* a at Mizpah, 7695
7: 7 Philistines heard that Israel *had* a at Mizpah 7695
13: 5 The Philistines a to fight Israel, 665
14:20 Then Saul and all his men a and went to 2410
17: 1 for war and a *at* Socoh in Judah. 665
17: 2 the Israelites a and camped in the Valley 665
25: 1 and all Israel a and mourned for him; 7695
28: 4 The Philistines a and came and set up camp 7695
2Sa 2:30 from pursuing Abner and a all his men. 7695
1Ki 18:20 throughout all Israel and a the prophets 7695
20:15 Then *he* a the rest of the Israelites, 7,000 7212
1Ch 13: 5 So David a all the Israelites, 7735
15: 3 David a all Israel in Jerusalem to bring up 7735
2Ch 12: 5 the leaders of Judah who *had* a in Jerusalem 665
15: 9 Then *he* a all Judah and Benjamin and 7695
15:10 *They* a *at* Jerusalem in the third month of 7695
20:26 On the fourth day *they* a in the Valley 7735
29: 4 a them in the square on the east side 665
29:15 When *they had* a their brothers 665
30: 3 and the people *had* not a in Jerusalem. 665
30:13 of people a *in* Jerusalem to celebrate 665
30:25 Levites and all who *had* a from Israel, 995+7736
32: 4 A large force of men a, 7695
32: 6 over the people and a them before him in 7695
Ezr 3: 1 the people a as one man in Jerusalem. 665
8:15 *I* a them at the canal that flows 7695
Ne 5:16 All my men **were** a there for the work; 7695
8: 1 all the people a as one man in the square 665
Est 2:19 When the virgins **were** a a second time, 7695
9: 2 The Jews a in their cities in all 7735
9:16 also a to protect themselves and get relief 7735
9:18 *had* a on the thirteenth and fourteenth, 7735
Ps 7: 7 Let the a peoples gather around you. 6337
Da 3: 3 and all the other provincial officials a for 10359
Mt 26: 3 the people a in the palace of the high priest, *5251*
26:57 the teachers of the law and the elders *had* a. *5251*
Lk 1:10 all the a **worshipers** were praying outside. *3295+3836+4436*
24:33 the Eleven and those with them, a **together** *125*
Ac 28:17 *When* they *had* a, Paul said to them: *5302*
1Co 5: 4 *When* you *are* a in the name *5251*

ASSEMBLIES (5) [ASSEMBLE]

Lev 23: 2 which you are to proclaim as sacred a. 5246
23: 4 the sacred a you are to proclaim 5246
23:37 as sacred a for bringing offerings made to 5246
Isa 1:13 I cannot bear your evil a. 6809
Am 5:21 I cannot stand your a. 6809

ASSEMBLING (1) [ASSEMBLE]

1Sa 13:11 and that the Philistines *were* a at Micmash, 665

ASSEMBLY (160) [ASSEMBLE]

Ge 49: 6 let me not join their a, 7736
Ex 12:16 On the first day hold a sacred a, 5246
16: 3 into this desert to starve this entire a 7736
Lev 4:14 the a must bring a young bull as 7736
8: 3 and gather the entire a at the entrance to 6337
8: 4 the a gathered at the entrance to the Tent 6337
8: 5 Moses said to the a, 6337
9: 5 and the entire a came near and stood before 6337
19: 2 to the entire a *of* Israel and say to them: 6337
23: 3 a day of sacred a. 5246
23: 7 a sacred a and do no regular work. 5246
23: 8 And on the seventh day hold a sacred a 5246
23:21 a sacred a and do no regular work. 5246
23:24 a day of rest, a sacred a commemorated 5246
23:27 Hold a sacred a and deny yourselves, 5246
23:35 The first day is a sacred a; 5246
23:36 a sacred a and present an offering made to 5246
23:36 It is the **closing a;** do no regular work. 6809
24:14 and the entire a is to stone him. 6337
24:16 The entire a must stone him. 6337
Nu 10: 7 To gather the a, blow the trumpets, 7736
13:26 to the whole a and showed them the fruit of 6337
14: 2 and the whole a said to them, 6337
14: 5 of the whole Israelite a gathered there. 6337
14: 7 and said to the entire Israelite a, 6337
14:10 But the whole a talked about stoning them. 6337
15:33 to Moses and Aaron and the whole a, 6337
15:35 The whole a must stone him outside 6337
15:36 So the a took him outside the camp 6337
16: 3 you set yourselves above the LORD's a?" 7736
16:19 of the LORD appeared to the entire a. 6337
16:21 from this a so I can put an end to them 6337
16:22 with the entire a when only one man sins?" 6337
16:24 "Say to the a, 'Move away from the tents 6337
16:26 He warned the a, 'Move back from 6337
16:42 when the a gathered in opposition to Moses 6337
16:45 "Get away from this a so I can put an end 6337
16:46 hurry to the a to make atonement for them. 6337
16:47 and ran into the midst of the a. 7736
20: 6 the a to the entrance to the Tent of Meeting 7736
20: 8 your brother Aaron gather the a together. 6337
20:10 and Aaron gathered the a together in front 7736
25: 6 the eyes of Moses and the whole a *of* Israel 6337
25: 7 the priest, saw this, he left the a, 6337
27: 2 the leaders and the whole a, and said, 6337
27:19 before Eleazar the priest and the entire a 6337
27:22 before Eleazar the priest and the whole a. 6337
28:18 a sacred a and do no regular work. 5246
28:25 On the seventh day hold a sacred a 5246
28:26 hold a sacred a and do no regular work. 5246
29: 1 of the seventh month hold a sacred a 5246
29: 7 of this seventh month hold a sacred a. 5246
29:12 hold a sacred a and do no regular work. 5246
29:35 " 'On the eighth day hold an a 6809
31:12 the priest and the Israelite a at their camp 6337
35:12 not die before he stands trial before the a. 6337
35:24 the a must judge between him and 6337
35:25 The a must protect the one accused 6337
Dt 5:22 in a loud voice to your whole a there on 7736
9:10 on the day of the a. 7736
10: 4 out of the fire, on the day of the a. 7736
16: 8 and on the seventh day hold an a to 6809
18:16 at Horeb on the day of the a when you said, 7736
23: 1 or cutting may enter the a *of* the LORD. 7736
23: 2 nor any of his descendants may enter the a 7736
23: 3 or any of his descendants may enter the a 7736
23: 8 of children born to them may enter the a *of* 7736
31:30 in the hearing of the whole a *of* Israel: 7736
33: 4 the possession of the a *of* Jacob. 7737
Jos 8:35 that Joshua did not read to the whole a 7736
9:15 and the leaders of the a ratified it by oath. 6337
9:18 because the leaders of the a had sworn 6337
9:18 The whole a grumbled against the leaders, 6337
18: 1 The whole a *of* the Israelites gathered 6337
20: 6 that city until he has stood trial before the a 6337
20: 9 of blood prior to standing trial before the a. 6337
22:12 the whole a *of* Israel gathered at Shiloh 6337
22:16 "The whole a *of* the LORD says: 6337
Jdg 20: 2 the tribes of Israel took their places in the a 7736
21: 8 to the camp for the a. 7736
21:10 So the a sent twelve thousand fighting men 6337
21:13 Then the whole a sent an offer of peace to 6337
21:16 And the elders of the a said, 6337
1Ki 8: 5 and the entire a *of* Israel that had gathered 6337
8:14 the whole a *of* Israel was standing there, 7736
8:22 of the LORD in front of the whole a 7736
8:55 He stood and blessed the whole a *of* Israel 7736
8:65 a vast a, people from Lebo Hamath to 7736
12: 3 the whole a *of* Israel went to Rehoboam 7736
12:20 and called him to the a and made him king 6337
2Ki 10:20 Jehu said, "Call an a in honor of Baal." 6809
1Ch 13: 2 He then said to the whole a *of* Israel, 7736
13: 4 The whole a agreed to do this, 7736
28: 8 of the a *of* the LORD, and in the hearing 7736
29: 1 Then King David said to the whole a: 7736
29:10 the LORD in the presence of the whole a, 7736
29:20 Then David said to the whole a, 7736
2Ch 1: 3 and the whole a went to the high place 7736
1: 5 Solomon and the a inquired of him there. 7736
5: 6 and the entire a *of* Israel that had gathered 6337
6: 3 the whole a *of* Israel was standing there, 7736
6:12 the LORD in front of the whole a *of* Israel 7736
6:13 and then knelt down before the whole a 7736
7: 8 a vast a, people from Lebo Hamath to 7736
7: 9 On the eighth day they held an a, 6809
20: 5 the a *of* Judah and Jerusalem at the temple 7736
20:14 as he stood in the a. 7736
23: 3 the whole a made a covenant with the king 7736
24: 6 of the LORD and by the a of Israel for 7736
28:14 in the presence of the officials and all the a. 7736
29:23 before the king and the a, 7736
29:28 The whole a bowed in worship, 7736
29:31 a brought sacrifices and thank offerings, 7736
29:32 the a brought was seventy bulls, 7736
30: 2 The king and his officials and the whole a 7736
30: 4 both to the king and to the whole a. 7736
30:23 The whole a then agreed to celebrate 7736
30:24 and goats for the a, 7736
30:25 The entire a *of* Judah rejoiced, 7736
Ezr 10: 8 and would himself be expelled from the a 7736
10:12 The whole a responded with a loud voice: 7736
10:14 Let our officials act for the whole a. 7736
Ne 5:13 At this the whole a said, "Amen," 7736
8: 2 the priest brought the Law before the a, 7736
8:18 with the regulation, there was an a. 6809
13: 1 be admitted into the a *of* God, 7736
Job 30:28 I stand up in the a and cry for help. 7736
Ps 1: 5 nor sinners in the a *of* the righteous. 6337
22:25 the theme of my praise in the great a; 7736
26: 5 I abhor the a *of* evildoers and refuse to sit 7736
26:12 in the **great a** I will praise the LORD. 5220
35:18 I will give you thanks in the great a; 7736
40: 9 I proclaim righteousness in the great a; 7736
40:10 and your truth from the great a. 7736
68:26 praise the LORD in the a *of* Israel. 5227
82: 1 God presides in the great a; 6337
89: 5 in the a *of* the holy ones. 7736
107:32 Let them exalt him in the a *of* the people 7736
111: 1 in the council of the upright and in the a. 6337
149: 1 his praise in the a *of* the saints. 7736
Pr 5:14 utter ruin in the midst of the **whole a.**" 2256+6337+7736
24: 7 in the **a at the gate** he has nothing to say. 9133
26:26 his wickedness will be exposed in the a. 7736
Isa 14:13 I will sit enthroned on the mount of a, 4595
Jer 26:17 and said to the entire a *of* people, 7736
44:15 all the women who were present—a large a 7736
La 1:10 those you had forbidden to enter your a. 7736
Joel 1:14 Declare a holy fast; call a **sacred a.** 6809
2:15 declare a holy fast, call a **sacred a.** 6809
2:16 Gather the people, consecrate the a; 7736
Mic 2: 5 Therefore you will have no one in the a *of* 7736
Lk 23: 1 the whole a rose and led him off to Pilate. *4436*
Ac 5:21 the full a **of the elders** of Israel— *1172*
7:38 He was in the a in the desert, *1711*
15:12 The whole a became silent as they listened *4436*
19:32 The a was in confusion: *1711*
19:39 it must be settled in a legal a. *1711*
19:41 After he had said this, he dismissed the a. *1711*
23: 7 and the a was divided. *4436*
Heb 12:22 upon thousands of angels *in* **joyful a,** *4108*

ASSENT (KJV) See MAN

ASSERTED (1) [ASSERTING]

Lk 22:59 About an hour later another a, *1462*

ASSERTING (1) [ASSERTED]

Ac 24: 9 **a that** these things were true. *5763*

ASSESSMENTS (1)

2Ki 23:35 the people of the land according to their a. 6886

ASSHUR (7) [ASSHURITES]

Ge 2:14 it runs along the east side of A. 855
10:22 Elam, A, Arphaxad, Lud and Aram. 855
25:18 as you go toward A. 855
Nu 24:22 be destroyed when A takes you captive." 855
24:24 they will subdue A and Eber, 855
1Ch 1:17 Elam, A, Arphaxad, Lud and Aram. 855
Eze 27:23 A and Kilmad traded with you. 855

ASSHURITES (1) [ASSHUR]

Ge 25: 3 the descendants of Dedan were the A, 857

ASSIGN (12) [ASSIGNED, ASSIGNMENT, ASSIGNMENTS, ASSIGNS, REASSIGN]

Nu 4:19 and a to each man his work and what he is 8492
4:27 *You shall* a to them as their responsibility 7212
4:32 A to each man the specific things he is 7212
8:26 is how *you are to* a the responsibilities of 6913
34:13 "A this land by lot **as an inheritance.** 5706
34:17 a the land for you **as an inheritance:** 5706
34:18 from each tribe to **help** a the land. 5706
34:29 to a *the* **inheritance** *to* the Israelites in 5706
1Sa 8:12 Some he *will* a to be commanders 8492
Job 22:24 and a your nuggets to the dust, 8883
Mt 24:51 He will cut him to pieces and a him a place *5502*
Lk 12:46 He will cut him to pieces and a him a place *5502*

ASSIGNED (47) [ASSIGN]

Ge 40: 4 The captain of the guard a them *to* Joseph, 7212
Nu 2: 9 All the *men* a to the camp of Judah, 7212
2:16 All the *men* a to the camp of Reuben, 7212
2:24 All the *men* a to the camp of Ephraim, 7212
2:31 All the *men* a to the camp of Dan 7212
4:49 each *was* a his work and told what to carry. 7212
Jos 13: 8 the servant of the LORD, *had* a it to them. 5989
14: 2 Their inheritances *were* a by lot to NIH
19:51 and the heads of the tribal clans of Israel a 5706
21:10 (these towns were **a to** the descendants 4200
24: 4 *I* a the hill country of Seir to Esau, 5989
1Sa 15:20 "I went on the mission the LORD a me. 8938
27: 5 *be* a to me in one of the country towns, 5989
29: 4 that he may return to the place *you* a him. 7212
1Ki 7:14 to King Solomon and did all the **work** *a* AIT
14:27 and a these to the commanders of the guard 7212
2Ki 8: 6 he a an official to her case and said to him, 5989
1Ch 6:48 Their fellow Levites **were** a to all 5989
6:54 as their territory (they were **a to** 4200
9:22 gatekeepers *had been* **a to** their **positions** 3569
9:29 Others **were** a to take care of the furnishings 4948

1Ch 26:29 Kenaniah and his sons were a duties away 4200
2Ch 2:18 He a 70,000 of them to be carriers 6913
12:10 and a these to the commanders of the guard 7212
23: 6 to guard what the LORD has a to them. 5466
25: 5 the people of Judah together and a them 6641
30:22 For the seven days they ate their a portion 4595
31: 2 Hezekiah a the priests and Levites 6641
33: 8 the feet of the Israelites leave the land I a 6641
Ne 12:31 I also a two large choirs to give thanks. 6641
13:10 that the portions a to the Levites had AIT
13:30 and a them duties, each to his own task. 6641
Est 2: 9 He a to her seven maids selected from 5989
4: 5 one of the king's eunuchs a to attend her, 6641
Job 7: 3 and nights of misery have been a to me. 4948
Ps 16: 5 you have a me my portion and my cup; 4987
104: 8 to the place you a for them. 3569
Isa 53: 9 He was a a grave with the wicked, 5989
Eze 4: 5 I have a you the same number of days as 5989
4: 6 I have a you 40 days, a day for each year. 5989
Da 1: 5 The king a them a daily amount of food 4948
1:10 who has a your food and drink. 4948
Mk 13:34 each with his a task, NIG
Ac 22:10 be told all that you have been a to do.' 5435
1Co 3: 5 as the Lord has a to each his task. 1443
7:17 the place in life that the Lord a to him and 3532
2Co 10:13 to the field God has a to us, 3532

ASSIGNMENT (1) [ASSIGN]
1Ch 23:11 as one family with one a. 7213

ASSIGNMENTS (1) [ASSIGN]
2Ch 23:18 to whom David had made a in the temple, 2745

ASSIGNS (1) [ASSIGN]
Mic 2: 4 He a our fields to traitors.' " 2745

ASSIR (4)
Ex 6:24 The sons of Korah were A, 661
1Ch 6:22 Korah his son, A his son, 661
6:23 Ebiasaph his son, A his son, 661
6:37 the son of A, the son of Ebiasaph, 661

ASSIST (9) [ASSISTANCE, ASSISTANT, ASSISTANTS, ASSISTED]
Nu 1: 5 the names of the men who are to a you: 907+6641
3: 6 to Aaron the priest to a him. 9250
8:26 They may a their brothers 9250
18: 2 and a you when you and your sons minister 9250
2Ch 8:14 and the Levites to lead the praise and to a 9250
13:10 and the Levites a them. 4856
Ezr 8:20 and the officials had established to a 6275
Job 29:12 and the fatherless who had none to a him. 6468
Ro 15:24 a me on my journey 4636

ASSISTANCE (1) [ASSIST]
Ezr 8:36 then gave a to the people and to the house 5951

ASSISTANT (2) [ASSIST]
Dt 1:38 your a, Joshua son of Nun, will enter it. 4200+6641+7156
Ne 13:13 the son of Mattaniah, their a, 3338+6584

ASSISTANT (Anglicized) See also AIDE

ASSISTANTS (1) [ASSIST]
Ne 5:15 Their a also lorded it over the people. 5853

ASSISTED (3) [ASSIST]
2Ch 31:15 and Shecaniah a him faithfully in the towns 3338+6584
Ezr 1: 6 All their neighbors a them with articles 928+2616+3338
6:22 he a them in the work on the house 2616+3338

ASSOCIATE (10) [ASSOCIATED, ASSOCIATES]
Jos 23: 7 Do not a with these nations that remain 928+995
23:12 if you intermarry with them and a with 928+995
1Ch 6:39 and Heman's a Asaph, who served 278
Pr 22:24 do not a with one easily angered, 995
Jn 4: 9 (For Jews do not a with Samaritans.) 5178
Ac 10:28 that it is against our law for a Jew to a with 3140
Ro 12:16 but be willing to a with people 5270
1Co 5: 9 I have written you in my letter not to a with 5264
5:11 not a with anyone who calls himself 5264
2Th 3:14 Do not a with him, 5264

ASSOCIATED (4) [ASSOCIATE]
Ne 13: 4 He was closely a with Tobiah, 7940
Eze 37:16 to Judah and the Israelites a with him.' 2492
37:16 to Joseph and all the house of Israel a with 2492
37:19 and of the Israelite tribes a with him, 2492

ASSOCIATES (28) [ASSOCIATE]
1Ch 6:44 from their a, the Merarites, at his left hand: 278
16: 7 to Asaph and his a this psalm of thanks to 278
16:37 and his a before the ark of the covenant of 278
16:38 and his sixty-eight a to minister with them. 278
Ezr 3: 2 of Shealtiel and his a began to build 278
4: 7 Tabeel and the rest of his a wrote a letter 4056
4: 9 together with the rest of their a— 10360
4:17 of their a living in Samaria and elsewhere 10360
4:23 and Shimshai the secretary and their a, 10360
5: 3 and Shethar-Bozenai and their a went 10360
5: 6 and Shethar-Bozenai and their a, 10360
6:13 and their a carried it out with diligence. 10360
Ne 4: 2 and in the presence of his a and the army 278
10:10 and their a: Shebaniah, 278
11:12 and their a, who carried on work for 278
11:13 and his a, who were heads of families— 278
11:14 and his a, who were able men— 278
11:17 Bakbukiah, second among his a; 278
11:19 Akkub, Talmon and their a, 278
12: 7 the priests and their a in the days of Jeshua. 278
12: 8 who, together with his a, 278
12: 9 Bakbukiah and Unni, their a, 278
12:24 Jeshua son of Kadmiel, and their a, 278
12:36 and his a— Shemaiah, Azarel, 278
Job 34: 8 he a with wicked men. 2143
Zec 3: 8 O high priest Joshua and your a seated 8276
Ac 5:17 Then the high priest and all his a, 3836+5250
5:21 When the high priest and his a arrived, 3836+5250

ASSOS (2)
Ac 20:13 on ahead to the ship and sailed for A, 840
20:14 When he met us at A, 840

ASSUME (2) [ASSUMED]
Ne 10:32 a the responsibility for carrying out 6584+6641
10:35 "We also a responsibility for bringing to NIH

ASSUMED (2) [ASSUME]
1Sa 14:47 After Saul had a rule over Israel, 4334
Ac 21:29 with Paul and a that Paul had brought him 3787

ASSUR (KJV) See ASSYRIA

ASSURANCE (5) [ASSURE]
1Sa 17:18 and bring back some a from them. 6859
Est 9:30 words of goodwill and a— 622
Job 24:22 they have no a of life. 586
1Ti 3:13 and great a in their faith in Christ Jesus. 4244
Heb 10:22 near to God with a sincere heart in full a 4443

ASSURE (2) [ASSURANCE, ASSURED, ASSUREDLY, ASSURES, REASSURE, REASSURED]
Lk 4:25 I a you that there were many widows 237+2093+3306
Gal 1:20 I a you before God that what I am writing 2627

ASSURED (7) [ASSURE]
Dt 9: 3 But be a today that the LORD your God is 3359
Jos 2:14 "Our lives for your lives!" the men a her. 606
1Sa 10:16 "He a us that the donkeys had been found." 5583+5583
Job 36: 4 Be a that my words are not false; 597
Jer 26:15 Be a, however, that if you put me to death, 3359+3359
Ac 2:36 "Therefore let all Israel be a of this: 857+1182
Col 4:12 in all the will of God, mature and fully a. 4442

ASSUREDLY (1) [ASSURE]
Jer 32:41 in doing them good and will a plant them 622+928

ASSURES (1) [ASSURE]
Jer 5:24 who a us of the regular weeks of harvest,' 9068

ASSWAGE (KJV) See BRING RELIEF

ASSYRIA (122) [ASSYRIA'S, ASSYRIAN, ASSYRIANS]
Ge 10:11 From that land he went to A, 855
2Ki 15:19 Then Pul king of A invaded the land, 855
15:20 of silver to be given to the king of A. 855
15:20 So the king of A withdrew and stayed in 855
15:29 Tiglath-Pileser king of A came 855
15:29 and deported the people to A. 855
16: 7 to say to Tiglath-Pileser king of A, 855
16: 8 and sent it as a gift to the king of A. 855
16: 9 of A complied by attacking Damascus 855
16:10 to meet Tiglath-Pileser king of A. 855
16:18 in deference to the king of A. 855
17: 3 Shalmaneser king of A came up 855
17: 4 of A discovered that Hoshea was a traitor, 855
17: 4 he no longer paid tribute to the king of A, 855
17: 5 The king of A invaded the entire land, 855
17: 6 of A captured Samaria and deported 855
17: 6 and deported the Israelites to A. 855
17:23 from their homeland into exile in A, 855
17:24 of A brought people from Babylon, 855
17:26 It was reported to the king of A: 855
17:27 Then the king of A gave this order: 855
18: 7 against the king of A and did not serve him. 855
18: 9 Shalmaneser king of A marched 855
18:11 The king of A deported Israel to Assyria 855
18:11 The king of Assyria deported Israel to A 855
18:13 of A attacked all the fortified cities 855
18:14 of Judah sent this message to the king of A 855
18:14 The king of A exacted from Hezekiah king 855
18:16 and gave it to the king of A. 855
18:17 of A sent his supreme commander, 855
18:19 the great king, the king of A, says: 855
18:23 bargain with my master, the king of A: 855
18:28 the word of the great king, the king of A! 855
18:30 be given into the hand of the king of A.' 855
18:31 This is what the king of A says: 855
18:33 from the hand of the king of A? 855
19: 4 whom his master, the king of A, 855
19: 6 of the king of A have blasphemed me. 855
19: 8 that the king of A had left Lachish, 855
19:10 not be handed over to the king of A.' 855
19:11 of A have done to all the countries, 855
19:20 concerning Sennacherib king of A. 855
19:32 the LORD says concerning the king of A: 855
19:36 So Sennacherib king of A broke camp 855
20: 6 from the hand of the king of A. 855
23:29 the Euphrates River to help the king of A. 855
1Ch 5: 6 whom Tiglath-Pileser king of A took 855
5:26 up the spirit of Pul king of A (that is, 855
5:26 Tiglath-Pileser king of A), 855
2Ch 28:16 that time King Ahaz sent to the king of A 855
28:20 Tiglath-Pileser king of A came to him, 855
28:21 and presented them to the king of A, 855
30: 6 from the hand of the kings of A. 855
32: 1 of A came and invaded Judah. 855
32: 4 of A come and find plenty of water?" 855
32: 7 because of the king of A and the vast army 855
32: 9 of A and all his forces were laying siege 855
32:10 "This is what Sennacherib king of A says: 855
32:11 from the hand of the king of A,' 855
32:22 from the hand of Sennacherib king of A 855
33:11 the army commanders of the king of A, 855
Ezr 4: 2 since the time of Esarhaddon king of A, 855
6:22 by changing the attitude of the king of A, 855
Ne 9:32 from the days of the kings of A until today. 855
Ps 83: 8 Even A has joined them to lend strength to 855
Isa 7:17 he will bring the king of A." 855
7:18 of Egypt and for bees from the land of A. 855
7:20 hired from beyond the River—the king of A 855
8: 4 be carried off by the king of A." 855
8: 7 the king of A with all his pomp. 855
10:12 of A for the willful pride of his heart and 855
11:11 that is left of his people from A, 855
11:16 of his people that is left from A, 855
19:23 be a highway from Egypt to A. 855
19:23 to Egypt and the Egyptians to A. 855
19:24 along with Egypt and A, 855
19:25 be Egypt my people, A my handiwork, 855
20: 1 sent by Sargon king of A, 855
20: 4 of A will lead away stripped and barefoot 855
20: 6 and deliverance from the king of A! 855
27:13 in A and those who were exiled 824+855
30:31 The voice of the LORD will shatter A; 855
31: 8 "A will fall by a sword that is not of man; 855
36: 1 of A attacked all the fortified cities 855
36: 2 the king of A sent his field commander 855
36: 4 the great king, the king of A, says: 855
36: 8 bargain with my master, the king of A: 855
36:13 the great king, the king of A! 855
36:15 be given into the hand of the king of A.' 855
36:16 This is what the king of A says: 855
36:18 from the hand of the king of A? 855
37: 4 whom his master, the king of A, 855
37: 6 of the king of A have blasphemed me. 855
37: 8 that the king of A had left Lachish, 855
37:10 not be handed over to the king of A.' 855
37:11 of A have done to all the countries, 855
37:21 to me concerning Sennacherib king of A, 855
37:33 the LORD says concerning the king of A: 855
37:37 So Sennacherib king of A broke camp 855
38: 6 from the hand of the king of A. 855
52: 4 lately, A has oppressed them. 855
Jer 2:18 why go to A to drink water from the River? 855
2:36 by Egypt as you were by A. 855
50:17 The first to devour him was the king of A; 855
50:18 and his land as I punished the king of A. 855
La 5: 6 to Egypt and A to get enough bread. 855
Eze 31: 3 Consider A, once a cedar in Lebanon, 855
32:22 "A is there with her whole army; 855
Hos 5:13 then Ephraim turned to A, 855
7:11 now calling to Egypt, now turning to A. 855
8: 9 to A like a wild donkey wandering alone. 855
9: 3 to Egypt and eat unclean food in A. 855
10: 6 be carried to A as tribute for the great king. 855
11: 5 not A rule over them because they refuse 855
11:11 like doves from A. 824+855
12: 1 with A and sends olive oil to Egypt. 855
14: 3 A cannot save us; 855
Mic 5: 6 They will rule the land of A with 855
7:12 In that day people will come to you from A 855
Na 3:18 O king of A, your shepherds slumber; 855
Zep 2:13 against the north and destroy A, 855
Zec 10:10 from Egypt and gather them from A. 855

ASSYRIA'S (1) [ASSYRIA]
Zec 10:11 A pride will be brought down 855

ASSYRIAN (9) [ASSYRIA]
2Ki 19:17 the A kings have laid waste these nations 855
19:35 in the A camp. 855
2Ch 32:21 and officers in the camp of the A king. 855

Isa 10: 5 "Woe to the A, the rod of my anger, 855
14:25 I will crush the A in my land; 855
37:18 A kings have laid waste all these peoples 855
37:36 thousand men in the A camp. 855
Mic 5: 5 When the A invades our land and marches 855
5: 6 from the A when he invades our land 855

ASSYRIANS (11) [ASSYRIA]
2Ki 18:10 At the end of three years the A took it. NIH
Isa 10:24 do not be afraid of the A, 855
19:23 The A will go to Egypt and the Egyptians 855
19:23 The Egyptians and A will worship together. 855
23:13 A have made it a place for desert creatures; 855
Eze 16:28 You engaged in prostitution with the A too, 855+1201
23: 5 and she lusted after her lovers, the A— 855
23: 7 A and defiled herself with all the idols 855+1201
23: 9 the A, for whom she lusted. 855+1201
23:12 She too lusted after the A— 855+1201
23:23 and all the A with them, 855+1201

ASTAROTH (KJV) See ASHTAROTH

ASTIR (2) [STIR]
Ps 83: 2 See how your enemies *are* a, 2159
Isa 14: 9 The grave below *is* **all** a to meet you 8074

ASTONISHED (23) [ASTONISHMENT]
Job 21: 5 Look at me and *be* a; 9037
Mt 8:10 *he was* a and said to those following him, *2513*
12:23 All the people *were* a and said, *2014*
19:25 *they were* greatly a and asked, *1742*
22:33 *they were* a at his teaching. *1742*
Mk 5:42 At this *they were* completely a. *1749+2014*
10:32 and the disciples *were* a, *2501*
Lk 2:48 When his parents saw him, *they were* a. *1742*
5: 9 all his companions *were* a at the catch *2502+4321*
8:56 Her parents *were* a, *2014*
20:26 And a by his answer, they became silent. *2513*
Jn 7:21 "I did one miracle, and *you are* all a. *2513*
Ac 3:11 all the people were a and came running *1702*
4:13 *they were* a and they took note *2513*
8:13 a by the great signs and miracles he saw. *2014*
9:21 All those who heard him *were* a and asked, *2014*
10:45 with Peter *were* a that the gift of *2014*
12:16 the door and saw him, *they were* a. *2014*
Gal 1: 6 *I am* a that you are so quickly deserting *2513*
Rev 13: 3 The whole world *was* a and followed *2513*
17: 6 When I saw her, *I was* greatly a. *2512+2513*
17: 7 the angel said to me: "Why *are you* a? *2513*
17: 8 from the creation of the world *will be* a *2513*

ASTONISHING (1) [ASTONISHMENT]
Da 12: 6 be before these a **things** are fulfilled?" 7099

ASTONISHMENT (2) [ASTONISHED, ASTONISHING]
Ge 43:33 **looked** at each other **in** a. 9449
Lk 1:63 and to everyone's a he wrote, *2513*

ASTOUND (1) [ASTOUNDED, ASTOUNDING]
Isa 29:14 Therefore once more I *will* a these people 7098

ASTOUNDED (1) [ASTOUND]
Ps 48: 5 they saw [her] and *were* a; 9449

ASTOUNDING (2) [ASTOUND]
La 1: 9 Her fall was a; 7099
Da 8:24 He will cause a devastation 7098

ASTRAY (50) [STRAY]
Nu 5:12 a man's wife **goes** a and is unfaithful to him 8474
5:19 with you and *you have* not **gone** a 8474
5:20 But if you *have* **gone** a while married 8474
5:29 is the law of jealousy when a woman **goes** a 8474
Dt 13:13 **led** the people of their town a, 5615
17:17 or his heart *will be* **led** a. 6073
27:18 "Cursed is the man *who* **leads** the blind a on 8706
1Ki 11: 3 and his wives **led** him a. 4213+5742
2Ki 21: 9 Manasseh **led** them a, 9494
2Ch 21:11 and *had* **led** Judah a. 5615
33: 9 **led** Judah and the people of Jerusalem a, 9494
Job 19: 4 If it is true that *I have* **gone** a, 8706
Ps 58: 3 Even from birth the wicked **go** a; 2319
95:10 "They are a people whose hearts **go** a, 9494
119:67 Before I was afflicted I **went** a, 8704
Pr 5:23 **led** a by his own great folly. 8706
7:21 With persuasive words *she* **led** him a; 5742
10:17 whoever ignores correction **leads** others a. 9494
12:26 but the way of the wicked **leads** them a. 9494
14:22 *Do* not those who plot evil **go** a? 9494
20: 1 whoever *is* **led** a by them is not wise. 8706
Isa 3:12 O my people, your guides **lead** you a; 9494
9:16 and those who are guided **are led** a. 1182
19:13 of her peoples *have* **led** Egypt a. 9494
30:28 of the peoples a bit *that* **leads** them a. 9494
53: 6 We all, like sheep, *have* **gone** a, 9494
Jer 4: 1 of my sight and no longer **go** a, 5653
23:13 **led** my people Israel a. 9494
23:32 "They tell them and **lead** my people a 9494
50: 6 their shepherds *have* **led** them a 9494
Eze 13:10 " 'Because *they* **lead** my people a, saying, 3246
44:10 when Israel **went** a and who wandered 9494
44:15 of my sanctuary when the Israelites **went** a 9494
48:11 and *did* not **go** a as the Levites did when 9494
48:11 the Levites did when the Israelites **went** a. 9494
Hos 4:12 A spirit of prostitution **leads** them a; 9494
Am 2: 4 they *have been* **led** a *by* false gods, 9494
Mic 3: 5 "As for the prophets *who* **lead** my people a, 9494
Jn 16: 1 so that *you will* not **go** a. *4997*
Ac 19:26 and **led** a large numbers of people here *3496*
1Co 12: 2 or other you were influenced and **led** a *552*
2Co 11: 3 your minds *may* somehow *be* **led** a *5780*
Gal 2:13 even Barnabas *was* **led** a. *5270*
Heb 3:10 'Their hearts *are* always **going** a, *4414*
5: 2 those who are ignorant and *are* **going** a, *4414*
1Pe 2:25 For you were like sheep **going** a, *4414*
1Jn 2:26 about those who *are trying to* **lead** you a. *4414*
3: 7 *do* not *let* anyone **lead** you a. *4414*
Rev 12: 9 Satan, who **leads** the whole world a. *4414*
18:23 your magic spell all the nations *were* **led** a. *4414*

ASTROLOGER (1) [ASTROLOGERS]
Da 2:10 a thing of any magician or enchanter or a. 10373

ASTROLOGERS (9) [ASTROLOGER]
Isa 47:13 Let your a come forward, 2042+9028
Da 2: 2 and a to tell him what he had dreamed. 4169
2: 4 Then the a answered the king in Aramaic, 4169
2: 5 The king replied to the a, 10373
2:10 The a answered the king, 10373
3: 8 At this time some a came forward 10373
4: 7 a and diviners came, I told them the dream, 10373
5: 7 a and diviners to be brought and said 10373
5:11 enchanters, a and diviners. 10373

ASUPPIM (KJV) See SHUPPIM, STOREHOUSE

ASUNDER (2)
Ps 136:13 the Red Sea a His love endures forever. 1617
Isa 24:19 The earth is broken up, the earth **is split** a, 7297+7297

ASWAN (3)
Isa 49:12 some from the region of A." 6059
Eze 29:10 and a desolate waste from Migdol to A, 6059
30: 6 to A they will fall by the sword within her, 6059

ASYNCRITUS (1)
Ro 16:14 Greet A, Phlegon, Hermes, Patrobas, *850*

AT (2217) See Index of Articles Etc.

ATAD (2)
Ge 50:10 they reached the threshing floor of A, 354
50:11 the mourning at the threshing floor of A, 354

ATARAH (1)
1Ch 2:26 whose name was A; 6499

ATAROTH (4) [ATAROTH ADDAR]
Nu 32: 3 "A, Dibon, Jazer, Nimrah, 6500
32:34 The Gadites built up Dibon, A, Aroer, 6500
Jos 16: 2 over to the territory of the Arkites in A, 6500
16: 7 it went down from Janoah to A and Naarah, 6500

ATAROTH ADDAR (2) [ADDAR, ATAROTH]
Jos 16: 5 of their inheritance went from A in 6501
18:13 and went down to A on the hill south 6501

ATAROTHADAR (KJV) See ATAROTH ADDAR

ATE (107) [EAT]
Ge 3: 6 she took some and a it. 430
3: 6 who was with her, and *he* a it. 430
3:12 from the tree, and *I* a it." 430
3:13 "The serpent deceived me, and *I* a." 430
3:17 "Because you listened to your wife and a 430
18: 8 While *they* a, he stood near them under 430
19: 3 baking bread without yeast, and *they* a. 430
24:54 Then he and the men who were with him a 430
25:34 *He* a and drank, and then got up and left. 430
26:30 and *they* a and drank. 430
27:25 Jacob brought it to him and *he* a; 430
27:33 *I* a it just before you came 430
31:46 and *they* a there by the heap. 430
39: 6 with anything except the food he a. 430
41: 4 the cows that were ugly and gaunt a **up** 430
41:20 ugly cows a **up** the seven fat cows 430
41:21 But even after they a *them,* 448+995+7931
43:32 and the Egyptians who a with him 430
Ex 16: 3 There we sat around pots of meat and a all 430
16:35 The Israelites a manna forty years, 430
16:35 *they* a manna until they reached the border 430
24:11 they saw God, and *they* a and drank. 430
Nu 11: 5 We remember the fish *we* a in Egypt 430
25: 2 The people a and bowed down 430
Dt 9: 9 *I* a no bread and drank no water. 430
9:18 *I* a no bread and drank no water, 430
29: 6 *You* a no bread and drank no wine 430
32:38 the gods who a the fat of their sacrifices 430
Jos 5:11 *they* a some of the produce of the land: 430
5:12 the day after they a this food from the land; 430
5:12 that year *they* a of the produce of Canaan. 430
Jdg 14: 9 which he scooped out with his hands and a 430
14: 9 he gave them some, and *they* too a it. 430
19: 8 So the two of them a together. 430
Ru 2:14 *She* a all she wanted 430
1Sa 1:18 Then she went her way and a something, 430
14:32 on the ground and a them, 430
28:25 before Saul and his men, and *they* a. 430
30:12 *He* a and was revived, 430
2Sa 9:11 So Mephibosheth a at David's table 430
9:13 because he always a at the king's table, 430
11:13 *he* a and drank with him, 430
12:20 his request they served him food, and *he* a. 430
1Ki 4:20 *they* a, they drank and they were happy. 430
13:19 So the man of God returned with him and a 430
13:22 and a bread and drank water in the place 430
19: 6 *He* a and drank and then lay down again. 430
19: 8 So he got up and a and drank. 430
19:21 and gave it to the people, and *they* a. 430
2Ki 4:44 and *they* a and had some left over, 430
6:29 So we cooked my son and a him. 430
7: 8 *They* a and drank, and carried away silver, 430
9:34 Jehu went in and a and drank. 430
23: 9 *they* a unleavened bread 430
25:29 of his life a regularly at the king's table. 430
1Ch 29:22 *They* a and drank with great joy in 430
2Ch 30:18 yet *they* a the Passover, 430
30:22 the seven days *they* a their assigned portion 430
Ezr 6:21 who had returned from the exile a it, 430
10: 6 *he* a no food and drank no water, 430
Ne 5:14 nor my brothers a the food allotted to 430
5:17 and fifty Jews and officials a at my table, NIH
9:25 *They* a to the full and were well-nourished; 430
Job 42:11 before came and a with him in his house. 430
Ps 78:25 Men a the bread of angels; 430
78:29 *They* a till they had more than enough, 430
105:35 *they* a **up** every green thing in their land, 430
105:35 a **up** the produce of their soil. 430
106:28 to the Baal of Peor and a sacrifices offered 430
Isa 44:19 I roasted meat and *I* a. 430
Jer 15:16 When your words came, *I* a them; 430
52:33 of his life a regularly at the king's table. 430
La 4: 5 Those *who once* a delicacies are destitute in 430
Eze 3: 3 So *I* a it, and it tasted as sweet as honey 430
Da 1:15 of the young men who a the royal food. 430
4:33 from people and a grass like cattle. 10030
5:21 he lived with the wild donkeys and a grass 10301
10: 3 *I* a no choice food; 430
Mt 9:10 and "sinners" came and a **with** him *5263*
12: 4 and he and his companions a *2266*
13: 4 and the birds came and a it **up.** *2983*
14:20 *They* all a and were satisfied, *2266*
14:21 The number of those who a was *2266*
15:37 *They* all a and were satisfied. *2266*
15:38 of those who a was four thousand, *2266*
Mk 1: 6 and *he* a locusts and wild honey. *2266*
2:26 of God and a the consecrated bread, *2266*
4: 4 and the birds came and a it **up.** *2983*
6:42 *They* all a and were satisfied, *2266*
8: 8 The *people* a and were satisfied. *2266*
Lk 4: 2 *He* a nothing during those days, *2266*
6: 4 *he* a what is lawful only for priests to eat. *2266*
8: 5 and the birds of the air a it **up.** *2983*
9:17 *They* all a and were satisfied, *2266*
13:26 you will say, '*We* a and drank with you, *2266*
24:43 and *he* took it and a it in their presence. *2266*
Jn 6:26 because *you* a the loaves and had your fill. *2266*
6:31 Our forefathers a the manna in the desert; *2266*
6:49 Your forefathers a the manna in the desert, *2266*
6:58 Your forefathers a manna and died, *2266*
Ac 2:46 and a together with glad and sincere hearts, *5575*
10:41 by us who a and drank **with** him *5303*
11: 3 the house of uncircumcised men and a **with** *5303*
20:11 and broke bread and a. *1174*
27:36 and a some food *themselves.* *4689*
1Co 10: 3 *They* all a the same spiritual food *2266*
Rev 10:10 from the angel's hand and a it. *2983*

ATER (5)
Ezr 2:16 of A (through Hezekiah) 98 359
2:42 the descendants of Shallum, A, Talmon, 359
Ne 7:21 of A (through Hezekiah) 98 359
7:45 the descendants of Shallum, A, Talmon, 359
10:17 A, Hezekiah, Azzur, 359

ATHACH (1)
1Sa 30:30 to those in Hormah, Bor Ashan, A 6973

ATHAIAH (1)
Ne 11: 4 A son of Uzziah, the son of Zechariah, 6970

ATHALIAH (17)
2Ki 8:26 His mother's name was A, 6976
11: 1 When A the mother of Ahaziah saw 6975
11: 2 in a bedroom to hide him from A; 6976

2Ki 11: 3 of the LORD for six years while **A** ruled 6975
11:13 When **A** heard the noise made by 6975
11:14 **A** tore her robes and called out, "Treason! 6975
11:20 because **A** had been slain with the sword at 6976
1Ch 8:26 Shamsherai, Shehariah, **A,** 6975
2Ch 22: 2 His mother's name was **A,** 6976
22:10 When **A** the mother of Ahaziah saw 6976
22:11 the child from **A** so she could not kill him. 6976
22:12 of God for six years while **A** ruled the land. 6975
23:12 When **A** heard the noise of 6976
23:13 **A** tore her robes and shouted, "Treason! 6976
23:21 because **A** had been slain with the sword. 6976
24: 7 of that wicked woman **A** had broken into 6976
Ezr 8: 7 Jeshaiah son of **A,** and with him 70 men; 6975

ATHARIM (1)

Nu 21: 1 that Israel was coming along the road to **A,** 926

ATHENIANS (1) [ATHENS]

Ac 17:21 (All the **A** and the foreigners who lived there *122*

ATHENS (5) [ATHENIANS]

Ac 17:15 to **A** and then left with instructions for Silas *121*
17:16 While Paul was waiting for them in **A,** *121*
17:22 and said: "Men *of* **A!** *122*
18: 1 After this, Paul left **A** and went to Corinth. *121*
1Th 3: 1 to be left by ourselves in **A.** *121*

ATHLAI (1)

Ezr 10:28 Jehohanan, Hananiah, Zabbai and **A.** 6974

ATHLETE (1)

2Ti 2: 5 Similarly, if anyone **competes as an a,** *123*

ATONE (3) [ATONEMENT]

Ex 30:15 to the LORD to **a** for your lives. 4105
2Ch 29:24 the altar for a sin offering to **a** for all Israel, 4105
Da 9:24 to put an end to sin, to **a** *for* wickedness, 4105

ATONED (6) [ATONEMENT]

Dt 21: 8 And the bloodshed *will* **be a** for. 4105
1Sa 3:14 of Eli's house *will* never **be a for** 4105
Pr 16: 6 Through love and faithfulness sin **is a for;** 4105
Isa 6: 7 your guilt is taken away and your sin **a for."** 4105
22:14 this sin *will* not **be a for,"** 4105
27: 9 By this, then, *will* Jacob's guilt **be a for,** 4105

ATONEMENT (105) [ATONE, ATONED, ATONING]

Ex 25:17 "Make an **a cover** *of* pure gold— 4114
26:34 the **a cover** on the ark of the Testimony in 4114
29:33 to eat these offerings by which **a was made** 4105
29:36 a bull each day as a sin offering to make **a.** 4113
29:36 Purify the altar by **making a** for it, 4105
29:37 For seven days **make a** for the altar 4105
30: 6 the **a cover** that is over the Testimony— 4114
30:10 a year Aaron *shall* **make a** on its horns. 4105
30:10 This annual **a** *must be* **made** with the blood 4105
30:16 the **a** money from the Israelites and use it 4113
30:16 **making a** for your lives." 4105
31: 7 the ark of the Testimony with the **a cover** 4114
32:30 perhaps *I can* **make a** for your sin." 4105
35:12 the **a cover** and the curtain that shields it; 4114
37: 6 He made the **a cover** of pure gold— 4114
39:35 with its poles and the **a cover;** 4114
40:20 the poles to the ark and put the **a cover** 4114
Lev 1: 4 accepted on his behalf to **make a** for him. 4105
4:20 In this way the priest *will* **make a** for them, 4105
4:26 the priest *will* **make a** for the man's sin, 4105
4:31 In this way the priest *will* **make a** for him, 4105
4:35 In this way the priest *will* **make a** for him 4105
5: 6 the priest *shall* **make a** for him for his sin. 4105
5:10 in the prescribed way and **make a** for him 4105
5:13 In this way the priest *will* **make a** for him 4105
5:16 who *will* **make a** for him with the ram as 4105
5:18 In this way the priest *will* **make a** for him 4105
6: 7 In this way the priest *will* **make a** for him 4105
6:30 to **make a** in the Holy Place must 4105
7: 7 They belong to the priest who **makes a** 4105
8:15 So he consecrated it to **make a** for it. 4105
8:34 by the LORD to make **a** for you. 4105
9: 7 and **make a** for yourself and the people; 4105
9: 7 the offering that is for the people and **make a** for them, 4105
10:17 by **making a** for them before the LORD 4105
12: 7 before the LORD *to* **make a** for her, 4105
12: 8 In this way the priest *will* **make a** for her, 4105
14:18 the one to be cleansed and **make a** for him 4105
14:19 to sacrifice the sin offering and **make a** for 4105
14:20 and **make a** for him, and he will be clean. 4105
14:21 as a guilt offering to be waved to **make a** 4105
14:29 to **make a** for him before the LORD. 4105
14:31 the priest *will* **make a** before the LORD 4105
14:53 In this way *he will* **make a** for the house, 4105
15:15 In this way he *will* **make a** before 4105
15:30 In this way he *will* **make a** for her before 4105
16: 2 behind the curtain in front of the **a cover** 4114
16: 2 I appear in the cloud over the **a cover.** 4114
16: 6 the bull for his own sin offering *to* **make a** 4105
16:10 for **making a** by sending it into the desert as 4105
16:11 the bull for his own sin offering *to* **make a** 4105
Lev 16:13 the incense will conceal the **a cover** above 4114
16:14 on the front of the **a cover;** 4114
16:14 before the **a cover.** 4114
16:15 He shall sprinkle it on the **a cover** and 4114
16:16 In this way *he will* **make a** for 4105
16:17 from the time Aaron goes in to **make a** in 4105
16:17 *having* **made a** for himself, 4105
16:18 that is before the LORD and **make a** for it. 4105
16:20 "When Aaron has finished **making a** *for* 4105
16:24 *to* **make a** for himself and for the people. 4105
16:27 to **make a,** must be taken outside the camp; 4105
16:30 because on this day **a** *will be* **made** for you, 4105
16:32 as high priest *is to* **make a.** 4105
16:33 and **make a** *for* the Most Holy Place, 4105
16:34 **A** *is to be* **made** once a year for all the sins 4105
17:11 to you to **make a** for yourselves on the altar; 4105
17:11 it is the blood *that* **makes a** for one's life. 4105
19:22 of the guilt offering the priest *is to* **make a** 4105
23:27 of this seventh month is the Day of **A.** 4113
23:28 because it is the Day of **A,** 4113
23:28 when **a** *is* **made** for you before 4105
25: 9 on the Day of **A** sound the trumpet 4113
Nu 5: 8 the ram with which **a** *is* **made** for him. 4105+4113
6:11 and the other as a burnt offering *to* **make a** 4105
7:89 the **a cover** on the ark of the Testimony. 4114
8:12 to **make a** for the Levites. 4105
8:19 of the Israelites and to **make a** for them so 4105
8:21 before the LORD and **made a** for them 4105
15:25 The priest is *to* **make a** for 4105
15:28 The priest *is to* **make a** before the LORD 4105
15:28 and when **a** *has been* **made** for him, 4105
16:46 hurry to the assembly *to* **make a** for them. 4105
16:47 but Aaron offered the incense and **made a** 4105
25:13 of his God and **made a** for the Israelites." 4105
28:22 as a sin offering to **make a** for you. 4105
28:30 Include one male goat to **make a** for you. 4105
29: 5 as a sin offering to **make a** for you. 4105
29:11 in addition to the sin offering for **a** and 4113
31:50 to **make a** for ourselves before the LORD." 4105
35:33 and **a** cannot **be made** for the land 4105
Dt 21: 8 **Accept** *this* **a** for your people Israel, 4105
32:43 on his enemies and **make a** *for* his land 4105
1Ch 6:49 **making a** for Israel, 4105
28:11 its inner rooms and the place of **a.** 4114
Ne 10:33 for sin offerings to **make a** for Israel; 4105
Eze 16:63 I **make a** for you for all you have done, 4105
43:20 and so purify the altar and **make a** *for* it. 4105
43:26 For seven days *they are to* **make a** *for* 4105
45:15 and fellowship offerings to **make a** for 4105
45:17 and fellowship offerings to **make a** for 4105
45:20 so *you are to* **make a** *for* the temple. 4105
Ro 3:25 God presented him as a **sacrifice of a,** *2663*
Heb 2:17 and that *he might* **make a for** the sins of *2661*
9: 5 overshadowing the **a cover.** *2663*

ATONING (3) [ATONEMENT]

Ex 30:10 of the **a** sin offering for the generations 4113
1Jn 2: 2 He is the **a sacrifice** for our sins, *2662*
4:10 and sent his Son as an **a sacrifice** *2662*

ATROTH BETH JOAB (1)

1Ch 2:54 **A,** half the Manahathites, 6502

ATROTH SHOPHAN (1)

Nu 32:35 **A,** Jazer, Jogbehah, 6503

ATTACH (7) [ATTACHED, ATTACHING]

Ex 28:14 like a rope, and **a** the chains to the settings. 5989
28:26 and **a** them to the other two corners of 8492
28:27 Make two more gold rings and **a** them to 5989
28:37 Fasten a blue cord to it *to* **a** it to the turban; 2118
29: 6 on his head and **a** the sacred diadem to 5989
39:31 Then they fastened a blue cord to it to **a** it 5989
Eze 37: 6 *I will* **a** tendons to you 5989

ATTACHED (15) [ATTACH]

Ge 29:34 at last my husband *will become* **a** to me, 4277
32:32 the Israelites do not eat the tendon **a to** 6584
Ex 28: 7 It is to have two shoulder pieces **a** to two 2489
39: 4 *which were* **a** to two of its corners, 2489
39:19 They made two gold rings and **a** them to 8492
39:20 and **a** them to the bottom of 5989
39:25 of pure gold and **a** them around the hem 5989
40:20 **a** the poles to the ark and put 8492
1Ki 6:10 and *they were* **a to** the temple by beams 297
7:28 They had side panels **a to** uprights. 1068
7:32 the axles of the wheels were **a to** the stand. 928
7:35 The supports and panels were **a to** the top 6584
2Ch 3:16 a hundred pomegranates and **a** them to 5989
9:18 and a footstool of gold **was a** to it. 297
Eze 40:43 **were a** to the wall all around. 3922

ATTACHING (2) [ATTACH]

Ex 28:25 **a** them to the shoulder pieces of the ephod 5989
39:18 **a** them to the shoulder pieces of the ephod 5989

ATTACK (101) [ATTACKED, ATTACKER, ATTACKERS, ATTACKING, ATTACKS]

Ge 14:15 the night Abram divided his men to **a** them 6584
32:11 for I am afraid he will come and **a** me, 5782
34:30 and if they join forces against me and **a** me, 5782
43:18 to **a** us and overpower us and seize us 1670
Ge 49:19 but he *will* **a** them *at* their heels. 1574
Nu 13:31 "We can't **a** those people; 448+6590
20:18 if you try, we will march out and **a** you 7925
Dt 20:10 When you march up to **a** a city, 4309
Jos 8: 1 and go up and **a** Ai. 6590
8: 3 and the whole army moved out to **a** Ai. 6590
9:18 But the Israelites *did* not **a** them, 5782
10: 4 "Come up and help me **a** Gibeon," he said, 5782
10:19 Pursue your enemies, **a** them **from the rear** 2386
Jdg 7:10 If you are afraid to **a,** 3718
7:11 you will be encouraged *to* **a** the camp." 928+3718
9:43 he rose *to* **a** them. 5782
9:45 All that day Abimelech **pressed** *his* **a** 4309
10:18 *the* **a** against the Ammonites will be 4309
18: 9 They answered, "Come on, *let's* **a** them! 6584+6590
18:25 or some hot-tempered men *will* **a** you, 7003
20:34 of Israel's finest men **made** a frontal **a** 995
1Sa 7: 7 of the Philistines came up to **a** them. 448
14:14 In that first **a** Jonathan 4804
15: 3 Now go, **a** the Amalekites 5782
17:48 As the Philistine moved closer to **a** him, 7925
23: 2 saying, "Shall I go and **a** these Philistines?" 5782
23: 2 "Go, **a** the Philistines and save Keilah." 5782
24: 7 and did not allow them to **a** Saul. 448+7756
2Sa 5: 6 and his men marched to Jerusalem to **a** 448
5:19 "Shall I go and **a** the Philistines? 448
5:23 behind them and **a** them in front of 995+4200
11:25 Press the **a** against the city and destroy it.' 4878
17: 2 *I would* **a** him while he is weary 995+6584
17: 9 If *he should* **a** your troops first, 928+5877
17:12 *we will* **a** him wherever he may be found, 448+995
1Ki 20:12 and he ordered his men: "Prepare to **a."** NIH
20:12 So they prepared to **a** the city. 6584
20:22 the king of Aram *will* **a** you again." 6584+6590
22:12 **"A** Ramoth Gilead and be victorious," 6590
22:15 **"A** and be victorious," he answered, 6590
22:32 So they turned to **a** him, 4309
2Ki 3: 8 "By what route *shall we* **a?"** 6590
7: 6 the Hittite and Egyptian kings to **a** us!" 995+6584
12:17 Then he turned to **a** Jerusalem. 6584+6590
17: 3 of Assyria came up to **a** Hoshea, 6584
18:25 to **a** and destroy this place without word 6584
1Ch 11: 6 "Whoever leads the **a** *on* 5782
14:10 "Shall I go and **a** the Philistines? 6584
14:14 circle around them and **a** them in front 995+4200
2Ch 18: 2 and urged him to **a** Ramoth Gilead. 448+6590
18:11 **"A** Ramoth Gilead and be victorious," 6590
18:14 **"A** and be victorious," he answered, 6590
18:31 So they turned to **a** him, 4309
Ne 4:12 "Wherever you turn, they will **a** us." 6584
Est 8:11 that *might* **a** them and their women 7444
9: 2 to **a** those seeking their destruction, 928+3338+8938
Job 15:21 when all seems well, marauders **a** him. 995
15:24 like a king poised to **a,** 3960
19: 3 shamelessly *you* **a** me. 2686
30:21 with the might of your hand *you* **a** me. 8475
Ps 27: 2 when my enemies and my foes **a** me, 4200
56: 1 all day long they press *their* **a.** 4309
59: 4 yet they are ready *to* **a** me. 8132
109: 3 *they* **a** me without cause. 4309
109:28 *when they* **a** they will be put to shame, 7756
Isa 21: 2 the looter takes loot. Elam, **a!** 6590
29: 7 *that* **a** her and her fortress and besiege her, 7371
36:10 have I come to **a** and destroy this land 6584
54:15 *anyone does* **a** you, it will not be my doing; 1592+1592
Jer 5: 6 a lion from the forest *will* **a** them, 5782
6: 4 Arise, *let us* **a** at noon! 6590
6: 5 *let us* **a** at night 6590
6:23 like men in battle formation to **a** you, 6584
12: 9 that other birds of prey surround and **a?** 6584
18:18 *let's* **a** him with our tongues 5782
37: 8 the Babylonians will return and **a** this city; 4309
37:19 of Babylon *will* not **a** you or this land'? 995+6584
43:11 He will come and **a** Egypt, 5782
46:13 of Babylon to **a** Egypt: 5782
47: 7 when he has ordered it to **a** Ashkelon and 448
49: 4 'Who *will* **a** me?' 448+995
49:14 "Assemble yourselves *to* **a** it! 995+6584
49:28 **a** Kedar and destroy the people of the East. 448+6590
49:31 "Arise and **a** a nation at ease, 448+6590
50: 3 A nation from the north *will* **a** her 6584+6590
50:21 **"A** the land of Merathaim 6584+6590
50:42 like men in battle formation to **a** you, 6584
51:48 out of the north de-troyers *will* **a** her," 995+4200
Eze 38:11 *I will* **a** a peaceful 995
Da 8: 7 I saw him **a** the ram furiously, 5595
11: 7 *He will* **a** the forces of the king of 448+995
11:39 *He will* **a** the mightiest fortresses with 4200+6913
Hos 13: 8 *I will* **a** them and rip them open. 7008
Joel 3: 9 Let all the fighting men draw near and **a.** 6590
Zec 12: 9 destroy all the nations that **a** Jerusalem. 995+6584
14:13 and they *will* **a** each other. 3338+6584+6590
Ac 16:22 The crowd **joined in the a** against Paul *5308*
18:10 and no one *is going to* **a** and harm you, *2202*
18:12 the Jews **made a** united **a on** Paul *2987*
2Ti 4:18 The Lord will rescue me from every evil **a** *NIG*
Rev 11: 7 comes up from the Abyss *will* **a** them, *4472+4483*

ATTACKED (61) [ATTACK]

Ge 4: 8 Cain **a** his brother Abel and killed him. 448+7756
34:25 and **a** the unsuspecting city, 995+6584
49:19 "Gad *will be* **a** *by* a band of raiders, 1574

Ge 49:23 *With* **bitterness** archers **a** him; 5352
Ex 17: 8 The Amalekites came and **a** the Israelites 4309
Nu 14:45 and **a** them and beat them down all the way 5782
21: 1 *he* **a** the Israelites and captured some 4309
Jos 8:21 they turned around and **a** the men of Ai. 5782
10: 5 up positions against Gibeon and **a** it. 4309
10:29 on from Makkedah to Libnah and **a** it. 4309
10:31 he took up positions against it and **a** it. 4309
10:34 they took up positions against it and **a** it. 4309
10:36 up from Eglon to Hebron and **a** it. 4309
10:38 with him turned around and **a** Debir. 4309
11: 7 at the Waters of Merom and **a** them, 928+5877
19:47 so they went up and **a** Leshem, took it, 4309
Jdg 1: 4 When Judah **a,** the LORD gave 6590
1: 8 men of Judah **a** Jerusalem also and took it. 4309
1:17 with the Simeonites their brothers and **a** 5782
1:22 Now the house of Joseph **a** Bethel, 6590
3:13 Eglon came and **a** Israel, 5782
11:12 against us that *you have* **a** our country?" 4309
15: 8 *He* **a** them **viciously** and slaughtered many 3751+5782+6584+8797
18:27 *They* **a** them with the sword and burned 5782
1Sa 13: 3 Jonathan **a** the Philistine outpost at Geba, 5782
13: 4 "Saul *has* **a** the Philistine outpost, 5782
15: 7 Then Saul **a** the Amalekites all the way 5782
27: 9 Whenever David **a** an area, 5782
30: 1 *They had* **a** Ziklag and burned it, 5782
2Sa 12:29 and **a** and captured it. 4309
1Ki 2:32 of my father David *he* **a** two men 7003
9:16 of Egypt *had* **a** and captured Gezer. 6590
14:25 Shishak king of Egypt **a** Jerusalem. 6584+6590
20: 1 he went up and besieged Samaria and **a** it. 4309
2Ki 3:25 with slings surrounded it and **a** it as well. 5782
12:17 up and **a** Gath and captured it. 4309
14:11 so Jehoash king of Israel **a.** 6590
15:10 *He* **a** him in front of the people, 5782
15:14 *He* **a** Shallum son of Jabesh in Samaria, 5782
15:16 **a** Tiphsah and everyone in the city 5782
15:30 *He* **a** and assassinated him, 5782
18:13 king of Assyria **a** all the fortified cities of Judah 6584+6590
1Ch 4:41 *They* **a** the Hamites in their dwellings and 5782
20: 1 Joab **a** Rabbah and left it in ruins. 5782
2Ch 12: 2 Shishak king of Egypt **a** Jerusalem in 6584+6590
12: 9 When Shishak king of Egypt **a** Jerusalem, 6584+6590
13:14 that they were being **a** at both front 4878
14:15 *They* also **a** the camps of the herdsmen 5782
21:17 *They* **a** Judah, invaded it and carried off 928+6590
25:21 So Jehoash king of Israel **a.** 6590
28:17 The Edomites had again come and **a** Judah 5782
36: 6 Nebuchadnezzar king of Babylon **a** him 6584+6590
Est 8: 7 "Because Haman **a** the Jews, 928+3338+8938
Job 1:15 and the Sabeans **a** and carried them off. 5877
Ps 53: 5 God scattered the bones of *those who* **a** you; 2837
124: 2 not been on our side when men **a** us, 6584+7756
Isa 20: 1 came to Ashdod and **a** and captured it— 4309
36: 1 king of Assyria **a** all the fortified cities of Judah 6584+6590
Jer 47: 1 the Philistines before Pharaoh **a** Gaza: 5782
49:28 which Nebuchadnezzar king of Babylon **a:** 5782
Zec 14:16 nations that *have* **a** Jerusalem will go 995+6584

ATTACKER (1) [ATTACK]

Na 2: 1 An **a** advances against you, [Nineveh]. 7046

ATTACKERS (1) [ATTACK]

Ps 35:15 **a** gathered against me when I was unaware. 5784

ATTACKING (13) [ATTACK]

1Ki 22:20 into **a** Ramoth Gilead and going 6590
2Ki 16: 7 who *are* **a** me." 6584+7756
16: 9 of Assyria complied by **a** Damascus 448+6590
2Ch 18:19 of Israel into **a** Ramoth Gilead and going 6590
20:12 to face this vast army that *is* **a** us. 995+6584
35:21 It is not you I am **a** at this time, 6584
Ps 54: 3 Strangers *are* **a** me; 6584+7756
56: 2 many *are* **a** me in their pride. 4309
86:14 The arrogant are **a** me, O God; 6584+7756
Jer 21: 2 Nebuchadnezzar king of Babylon *is* **a** us. 4309
32:24 over to the Babylonians who *are* **a** it. 4309
32:29 The Babylonians who *are* **a** this city 4309
37:10 the entire Babylonian army that *is* **a** you 4309

ATTACKS (14) [ATTACK]

Ge 32: 8 "If Esau comes and **a** one group, 5782
Ex 21:15 *"Anyone who* **a** his father or his mother 5782
Dt 22:26 case is like that of someone *who* **a** 6584+7756
Jos 15:16 in marriage to the man who **a** 5782
Jdg 1:12 in marriage to the man who **a** 5782
2Sa 22:44 "You have delivered me from the **a** 8190
Job 30:12 On my right the tribe **a;** 7756
Ps 18:43 You have delivered me from the **a** *of* 8190
55:20 My companion **a** his friends; 928+3338+8938
Pr 21:22 A wise man **a** the city of the mighty 6590
Isa 54:15 whoever **a** you will surrender to you. 1592
Eze 38:18 When Gog **a** the land of Israel, 995+6584
Lk 11:22 someone stronger **a** and overpowers him, *2088*
Jn 10:12 Then the wolf **a** the flock and scatters it. *773*

ATTAI (4)

1Ch 2:35 and she bore him **A.** 6968
2:36 **A** was the father of Nathan, 6968
12:11 **A** the sixth, Eliel the seventh, 6968
2Ch 11:20 who bore him Abijah, **A,** 6968

ATTAIN (4) [ATTAINED, ATTAINING, ATTAINS]

Ps 139: 6 too lofty for *me to* **a.** 3523
Pr 2:19 None who go to her return or **a** the paths 5952
Gal 3: 3 *are you* now *trying to* **a** *your* **goal** *2200*
Php 3:11 to **a** to the resurrection from the dead. *2918*

ATTAINED (4) [ATTAIN]

Pr 16:31 *it* **is a** by a righteous life. 5162
Ro 9:31 law of righteousness, *has* not **a** it. *5777*
Php 3:16 up to what *we have already* **a.** *5777*
Heb 7:11 If perfection could have been **a** through *NIG*

ATTAINING (2) [ATTAIN]

Pr 1: 2 for **a** wisdom and discipline; 3359
Eph 4:13 **a** to the whole measure of the fullness *1650*

ATTAINS (1) [ATTAIN]

Pr 11:19 The truly righteous man **a** life, 4200

ATTALIA (2)

Ac 14:25 they went down to **A.** *877*
14:26 From **A** they sailed back to Antioch, *NIG*

ATTEMPT (1)

Ac 27:30 *In* **an a** to escape from the ship, *2426*

ATTEND (3) [ATTENDANCE, ATTENDANT, ATTENDANTS, ATTENDED, ATTENDING, ATTENDS]

Ge 39:11 One day he went into the house to **a to** 6913
1Ki 1: 2 a young virgin *to* **a** the king and take care 4200+6641+7156
Est 4: 5 one of the king's eunuchs assigned to **a** her, 4200+7156

ATTENDANCE (1) [ATTEND]

SS 8:13 in the gardens with friends *in* **a,** 7992

ATTENDANT (6) [ATTEND]

Ge 39: 4 in his eyes and *became* his **a.** 9250
1Ki 19:21 to follow Elijah and *became* his **a.** 9250
2Ki 22:12 the secretary and Asaiah the king's **a:** 6269
2Ch 34:20 the secretary and Asaiah the king's **a:** 6269
Lk 4:20 gave it back *to* the **a** and sat down. *5677*
Ac 13: 7 who was an **a of** the proconsul, *5250*

ATTENDANTS (26) [ATTEND]

Ge 45: 1 no longer control himself before all his **a,** 5893
Ex 2: 5 her **a** were walking along the river bank. 5855
Jdg 3:19 And all his **a** left him. 6584+6641
1Sa 8:14 and olive groves and give them to his **a.** 6269
8:15 and give it to his officials and **a.** 6269
16:15 Saul's **a** said to him, "See, 6269
16:17 So Saul said to his **a,** 6269
18:22 Then Saul ordered his **a:** 6269
18:22 and his **a** all like you; 6269
18:26 When the **a** told David these things, 6269
19: 1 Saul told his son Jonathan and all the **a** 6269
28: 7 Saul then said to his **a,** 6269
2Ki 5:15 and all his **a** went back to the man of God. 4722
24:12 Jehoiachin king of Judah, his mother, his **a,** 6269
Ezr 8:17 that they might bring **a** to us for the house 9250
Est 1:12 when the **a** delivered the king's command, 6247
2: 2 Then the king's **personal a** proposed, 5853+9250
6: 3 for him," his **a** answered. 5853+9250
6: 5 His **a** answered, "Haman is standing in 5853
Jer 25:19 his **a,** his officials and all his people, 6269
36:24 all his **a** who heard all these words showed no fear, 6269
36:31 I will punish him and his children and his **a** 6269
37: 2 Neither he nor his **a** nor the people of 6269
Mt 14: 2 he said *to* his **a,** "This is John the Baptist; *4090*
22:13 "Then the king told the **a,** *1356*
Ac 10: 7 and a devout soldier who *was one of* his **a.** *4674*

ATTENDED (6) [ATTEND]

Ge 40: 4 and *he* **a** them. 9250
Jdg 14:20 **a** him **at** his **wedding.** 8287
1Sa 25:42 **a by** her five maids, 2143+4200+8079
Da 7:10 Thousands upon thousands **a** him; 10727
Mt 4:11 devil left him, and angels came and **a** him. *1354*
Mk 1:13 and angels **a** him. *1354*

ATTENDING (6) [ATTEND]

1Sa 4:20 As she was dying, the *women* **a** her said, 5893
1Ki 1:15 where Abishag the Shunammite *was* **a** him. 9250
10: 5 the **a** servants in their robes, his cupbearers, 5096
2Ch 9: 4 the **a** servants in their robes, 5096
22: 8 relatives, *who had been* **a** Ahaziah, 9250
Est 7: 9 Harbona, one of the eunuchs **a** the king 4200+7156

ATTENDS (1) [ATTEND]

Jn 3:29 The friend who **a** the bridegroom waits *NIG*

ATTENTION (78) [ATTENTIVE, ATTENTIVELY]

Ge 39:23 The warden **paid** no **a** *to* anything 8011
Ex 4: 8 "If they do not believe you or **pay a** to 9048
5: 9 so that they keep working and **pay** no **a** 9120
15:26 if *you* **pay a** to his commands 263
16:20 some of them **paid** no **a** to Moses; 9048
23:21 **Pay a** to him and listen to what he says. 9068
Nu 5:15 a reminder offering *to* **draw a to** guilt. 2349
Dt 1:45 but he **paid** no **a** to your weeping 9048
7:12 If *you* **pay a** *to* these laws and are careful 9048
17: 4 **been brought** to your **a,** 2256+5583+9048
28:13 If *you* **pay a** to the commands of 9048
Jdg 11:28 **paid** no **a** to the message 9048
Ru 4: 4 **bring** the matter **to** your **a** 265+1655
1Sa 4:20 But she did not respond or pay *any* **a.** 4213
25:25 May my lord pay no **a** to 4213
1Ki 8:28 Yet **give a** to your servant's prayer 7155
18:29 no one answered, no one **paid a.** 7993
2Ch 6:19 Yet **give a** to your servant's prayer 7155
33:10 but *they* **paid** no **a.** 7992
Ne 8:13 gathered around Ezra the scribe to **give a** to 8505
9:30 Yet *they* **paid** no **a,** 263
9:34 *they did* not **pay a** to your commands or 7992
Est 9:25 But when the plot came to the king's **a** 4200+7156
Job 7:17 that you give him so much **a,** 4213
32:12 **gave** you *my* **full a.** 1067
33: 1 **pay a** *to* everything I say. 263
33:31 **"Pay a,** Job, and listen to me; 7992
35:13 the Almighty **pays** no **a** *to* it. 8800
Pr 4: 1 **pay a** and gain understanding. 7992
4:20 My son, **pay a** to what I say; 7992
5: 1 My son, **pay a** to my wisdom, 7992
7:24 my sons, listen to me; **pay a** to what I say. 7992
17: 4 a liar **pays a** to a malicious tongue. 263
22:17 **Pay a** and listen to the sayings of the wise; 265+5742
27:23 give **careful a** to your herds; 4213
Ecc 7:21 *Do* not pay **a** to every word people say, 4213
Isa 28:23 **pay a** and hear what I say. 7992
34: 1 Come near, you nations, and listen; **pay a,** 7992
42:20 but *have* **paid** no **a;** 9068
42:23 Which of you will listen to this or **pay close a** 2256+7992+9048
48:18 If only *you had* **paid a** to my commands, 7992
Jer 7:24 But they did not listen or **pay a;** 265+5742
7:26 But they did not listen to me or **pay a.** 265+5742
11: 8 But they did not listen or **pay a;** 265+5742
13:15 Hear and **pay a,** do not be arrogant, 263
17:23 Yet they did not listen or **pay a;** 265+5742
18:18 and **pay** no **a** to anything he says." 7992
25: 4 you have not listened or **paid any a.** 265+4200+5742+9048
34:14 did not listen to me or **pay a** to me. 265+5742
35:15 *you have* not **paid a** or listened to me. 265+5742
37: 2 nor the people of the land **paid** *any* **a** to 9048
44: 5 But they did not listen or **pay a;** 265+5742
Eze 40: 4 and pay **a** to everything I am going 4213
44: 5 and give **a** to everything I tell you 4213
44: 5 Give **a** to the entrance of the temple and all 4213
Da 3:12 who pay no **a** to you, O king. 10302
6:13 pays no **a** to you, O king, 10302
9:13 from our sins and **giving a** to your truth. 8505
11:18 Then he will turn his **a** to the coastlands 7156
Hos 5: 1 **Pay a,** *you* Israelites! 7992
Zec 1: 4 But they would not listen or **pay a** to me, 7992
7:11 "But they refused to **pay a;** 7992
Mal 2:13 and wail because *he* no longer **pays a** 7155
Mt 7: 3 and **pay** no **a to** the plank in your own eye? *2917*
22: 5 "But they **paid** no **a** and went off— *288*
22:16 **pay** no **a** to **who they are.** *476+1063+4725*
24: 1 up to him *to* **call** his **a to** its buildings. *2109*
Mk 12:14 **pay** no **a** to **who they are;** *476+1063+4725*
Lk 6:41 and **pay** no **a to** the plank in your own eye? *2917*
Ac 3: 5 So the man *gave* them *his* **a,** *2091*
6: 4 and *will* **give** *our* **a** to prayer and *4674*
8: 6 *they* all **paid close a** to what he said. *4668*
8:10 *gave* him *their* **a** and exclaimed, *4668*
Tit 1:14 and *will* **pay** no **a** to Jewish myths or to *4668*
Heb 2: 1 **pay** more careful **a,** therefore, **to** *4668*
Jas 2: 3 *If you* **show special a to** *2098*
2Pe 1:19 and you will do well to **pay a** to it, *4668*
3Jn 1:10 *I will* **call a to** what he is doing, *5703*

ATTENTIVE (7) [ATTENTION]

2Ch 6:40 may your eyes be open and your ears **a** to 7995
7:15 Now my eyes will be open and my ears **a** 7995
Ne 1: 6 let your ear be **a** and your eyes open to hear 7994
1:11 be **a** to the prayer of this your servant and 7994
Ps 34:15 the righteous and his ears are **a to** their cry; 448
130: 2 Let your ears be **a** to my cry for mercy. 7995
1Pe 3:12 on the righteous and his ears are **a** *NIG*

ATTENTIVELY (2) [ATTENTION]

Ne 8: 3 And all the people **listened a to** the Book of the Law. 265+448
Jer 8: 6 I have listened **a,** but they do not say 7992

ATTESTED (1)

1Sa 3:20 to Beersheba recognized that Samuel **was a** 586

ATTIRE (KJV) See DRESSED, WEDDING ORNAMENTS

ATTITUDE (8) [ATTITUDES]

Ge 31: 2 And Jacob noticed that Laban's **a** 7156
31: 5 "I see that your father's **a** toward me is 7156
1Ki 11:11 "Since this is your **a** and you have 6640
Ezr 6:22 by changing the **a** *of* the king of Assyria, 4213
Da 3:19 and his **a** toward them changed. 10049+10614
Eph 4:23 to be made new *in* the **a** of your minds; *4460*
Php 2: 5 Your **a** *should be* the same as that *5858*
1Pe 4: 1 arm yourselves also with the same **a,** *1936*

ATTITUDES (1) [ATTITUDE]

Heb 4:12 it judges the thoughts and **a** of the heart. *1936*

ATTRACT (1) [ATTRACTED, ATTRACTIVE]

Isa 53: 2 He had no beauty or majesty *to* **a** *us* 8011

ATTRACTED (2) [ATTRACT]

Dt 21:11 the captives a beautiful woman and *are* **a** 3137
Est 2:17 the king *was* **a** to Esther more than to any 170

ATTRACTIVE (3) [ATTRACT]

Jdg 15: 2 Isn't her younger sister more **a?** 3202
Zec 9:17 How **a** and beautiful they will be! 3206
Tit 2:10 **make** the teaching about God our Savior **a.** *3175*

AUDIENCE (5)

1Ki 10:24 The whole world sought **a** *with* Solomon 7156
2Ch 9:23 of the earth sought **a** *with* Solomon to hear 7156
Pr 29:26 Many **seek an a with** a ruler, 1335+7156
Ac 12:20 they now joined together and **sought an a** *4205*
25:23 the **a room** with the high ranking officers *211*

AUGMENT (KJV) See MORE

AUGUSTUS (1)

Lk 2: 1 In those days Caesar **A** issued a decree that *880*

AUL (KJV) See AWL

AUNT (2)

Lev 18:14 to have sexual relations; she is your **a.** 1860
20:20 " 'If a man sleeps with his **a,** 1860

AUSTERE (KJV) See HARD

AUTHOR (3)

Ac 3:15 You killed the **a** of life, *795*
Heb 2:10 should make the **a** of their salvation perfect *795*
12: 2 the **a** and perfecter of our faith, *795*

AUTHORITIES (13) [AUTHORITY]

Lk 12:11 before synagogues, rulers and **a,** do *2026*
Jn 7:26 the **a** really concluded that he is the Christ? *807*
Ac 16:19 into the marketplace to face the **a.** *807*
Ro 13: 1 must submit himself *to* the governing **a,** *2026*
13: 1 The **a** that exist have been established *NIG*
13: 5 it is necessary to submit to the **a,** *NIG*
13: 6 for the **a** are God's servants, *NIG*
Eph 3:10 *to* the rulers and **a** in the heavenly realms, *2026*
6:12 but against the rulers, against the **a,** *2026*
Col 1:16 whether thrones or powers or rulers or **a;** *2026*
2:15 And having disarmed the powers and **a,** *2026*
Tit 3: 1 the people to be subject *to* rulers and **a,** *2026*
1Pe 3:22 **a** and powers in submission to him. *2026*

AUTHORITY (88) [AUTHORITIES, AUTHORIZATION, AUTHORIZED]

Ge 41:35 up the grain under the **a** *of* Pharaoh, 3338
Nu 27:20 Give him some of your **a** so 2086
Dt 1:15 and appointed them to have **a** over you— 8031
Ezr 7:24 You are also to know that you have no **a** 10718
Ne 3: 7 the **a** *of* the governor of Trans-Euphrates. 4058
Est 9:29 with full **a** to confirm this second letter 9549
Isa 22:21 around him and hand your **a** over to him. 4939
Jer 5:31 the priests rule by their own **a,** 3338
Da 4:31 Your **royal a** has been taken from you. 10424
7: 6 and it was given **a to rule.** 10717
7:12 of their **a,** but were allowed to live for 10717
7:14 He was given **a,** glory 10717
Mt 7:29 because he taught as one who had **a,** *2026*
8: 9 For I myself am a man under **a,** *2026*
9: 6 Son of Man has **a** on earth to forgive sins *2026*
9: 8 who had given such **a** to men. *2026*
10: 1 and gave them **a** to drive out evil spirits *2026*
20:25 their high officials **exercise a over** them. *2980*
21:23 "By what **a** are you doing these things?" *2026*
21:23 "And who gave you this **a?"** *2026*
21:24 by what **a** I am doing these things. *2026*
21:27 by what **a** I am doing these things. *2026*
28:18 "All **a** in heaven and on earth *2026*
Mk 1:22 because he taught them as one who had **a,** *2026*
1:27 A new teaching—and with **a!** *2026*
2:10 Son of Man has **a** on earth to forgive sins *2026*
3:15 and to have **a** to drive out demons. *2026*
6: 7 by two and gave them **a over** evil spirits. *2026*
10:42 their high officials **exercise a over** them. *2980*
11:28 "By what **a** are you doing these things?" *2026*
11:28 "And who gave you **a** to do this?" *2026*
11:29 by what **a** I am doing these things. *2026*
11:33 by what **a** I am doing these things." *2026*
Lk 4: 6 "I will give you all their **a** and splendor, *2026*
4:32 because his message **had a.** *1639+1877+2026*
4:36 With **a** and power he gives orders *2026*
5:24 Son of Man has **a** on earth to forgive sins *2026*
7: 8 For I myself am a man under **a,** *2026*
9: 1 and **a** to drive out all demons and *2026*
10:19 I have given you **a** to trample on snakes *2026*
20: 2 by what **a** you are doing these things," *2026*
20: 2 "Who gave you this **a?"** *2026*
20: 8 by what **a** I am doing these things." *2026*
20:20 over *to* the power and **a** of the governor. *2026*
22:25 and those who **exercise a over** *2027*
Jn 2:18 to prove your **a** to do all this?" *NIG*
5:27 And he has given him **a** to judge *2026*
10:18 I have **a** to lay it down and authority *2026*
10:18 to lay it down and **a** to take it up again. *2026*
17: 2 For you granted him **a over** all people *2026*
Ac 1: 7 or dates the Father has set by his own **a.** *2026*
9:14 And he has come here **with a** from *2026+2400*
26:10 **On** the **a** of the chief priests I put many of the saints in prison, *2026+3284*
26:12 to Damascus with the **a** and commission of *2026*
Ro 7: 1 that the law *has* **a over** a man only as long *3259*
13: 1 for there is no **a** except *2026*
13: 2 he who rebels against the **a** is rebelling *2026*
13: 3 to be free from fear of the one in **a?** *2026*
1Co 11:10 the woman ought to have a sign of **a** *2026*
15:24 after he has destroyed all dominion, **a** *2026*
2Co 10: 8 even if I boast somewhat freely about the **a** *2026*
13:10 not have to be harsh in my use of **a—** *2026*
13:10 **the a** the Lord gave me for building you up, *4005S*
Eph 1:21 far above all rule and **a,** *2026*
Col 2:10 who is the head over every power and **a.** *2026*
1Th 4: 2 you know what instructions we gave you **by the a of** the Lord *1328*
1Ti 2: 2 for kings and all those in **a,** *5667*
2:12 a woman to teach or *to* **have a over** a man; *883*
Tit 2:15 Encourage and rebuke with all **a.** *2198*
Heb 13:17 Obey your leaders and submit to their **a.** *NIG*
1Pe 2:13 for the Lord's sake to every **a** instituted *3232*
2:13 whether to the king, as the **supreme a,** *5660*
2Pe 2:10 of the sinful nature and despise **a.** *3262*
Jude 1: 6 not keep their **positions of a** *794*
1: 8 reject **a** and slander celestial beings. *3262*
1:25 majesty, power and **a,** *2026*
Rev 2:26 I will give **a** over the nations— *2026*
2:27 just as I have received **a** from my Father. *NIG*
12:10 and the **a** of his Christ. *2026*
13: 2 and his throne and great **a.** *2026*
13: 4 the dragon because he had given **a** to *2026*
13: 5 and to exercise his **a** for forty-two months. *2026*
13: 7 And he was given **a** over every tribe, *2026*
13:12 He exercised all the **a** of the first beast *2026*
17:12 for one hour will receive **a** as kings along *2026*
17:13 and will give their power and **a** to *2026*
18: 1 He had great **a,** *2026*
20: 4 seated those who had been given **a** to judge. *NIG*

AUTHORIZATION (1) [AUTHORITY]

Ac 15:24 that some went out from us without our **a** *1403*

AUTHORIZED (3) [AUTHORITY]

Ezr 3: 7 as **a** *by* Cyrus king of Persia. 8397
5: 3 "Who **a** you to rebuild this temple 10302+10682
5: 9 "Who **a** you to rebuild this temple 10302+10682

AUTUMN (7)

Dt 11:14 both **a** and spring rains, 3453
Ps 84: 6 the **a rains** also cover it with pools. 4620
Jer 5:24 who gives **a** and spring rains in season, 3453
Joel 2:23 for he has given you the **a rains** 4620
2:23 both **a** and spring rains, as before. 4620
Jas 5: 7 how patient he is for the **a** and spring **rains.** *4611*
Jude 1:12 **a** trees, without fruit and uprooted— *5781*

AVA (KJV) See AVVA

AVAIL (2) [AVAILABLE]

Isa 16:12 *it is to* no **a.** 3523
Da 11:27 but *to* no **a,** 7503

AVAILABLE (1) [AVAIL]

1Ki 7:36 in every **a space,** with wreaths all around. 5113

AVEN (1) [BETH AVEN]

Am 1: 5 in the Valley of **A** and the one who holds 225

AVENGE (17) [VENGEANCE]

Lev 26:25 I will bring the sword upon you *to* **a** 5933+5934
Dt 32:35 It is mine to **a;** I will repay. 5934
32:43 for *he will* **a** the blood of his servants; 5933
1Sa 24:12 the LORD **a** *the* **wrongs** you have *done* 5933
2Sa 3:27 there, **to a** the blood of his brother Asahel, 928
2Ki 9: 7 and *I will* **a** the blood of my servants 5933
Est 8:13 that day to **a themselves** on their enemies. 5933
Ps 79:10 make known among the nations that *you* **a** 5935
Isa 1:24 from my foes and **a myself** on my enemies. 5933
Jer 5: 9 *"Should I* not **a** myself on such a nation 5933
5:29 *"Should I* not **a** myself on such a nation 5933
9: 9 *"Should I* not **a** myself on such a nation 5933
15:15 **A** me on my persecutors. 5933
51:36 I will defend your cause and **a** you; 5933+5935
Ro 12:19 "It is mine *to* **a;** *1689*
Heb 10:30 we know him who said, "It is mine to **a;** *1689*
Rev 6:10 of the earth and **a** our blood?" *1688*

AVENGED (11) [VENGEANCE]

Ge 4:24 If Cain **is a** seven times, 5933
Jos 10:13 till the nation **a** *itself on* its enemies, 5933
Jdg 9:24 *might be* **a** on their brother Abimelech and 8492
11:36 the LORD *has* **a** you of your enemies, 5935+6913
1Sa 14:24 before *I have* **a myself** on my enemies!" 5933
25:31 or of *having* **a** himself. 3828
2Sa 4: 8 This day the LORD *has* **a** my lord the king 5935+5989
Ps 58:10 The righteous will be glad when they are **a,** 5934
Eze 5:13 and *I will* **be a.** 5714
Ac 7:24 so *he* went to his defense and **a** him *1689+4472*
Rev 19: 2 *He has* **a** on her the blood of his servants." *1688*

AVENGER (14) [VENGEANCE]

Nu 35:12 They will be places of refuge from the **a,** 1457
35:19 **a** *of* blood shall put the murderer to death; 1457
35:21 The **a** *of* blood shall put the murderer 1457
35:24 between him and the **a** *of* blood according 1457
35:25 from the **a** *of* blood and send him back to 1457
35:27 the **a** *of* blood finds him outside the city, 1457
35:27 the **a** *of* blood may kill the accused 1457
Dt 19: 6 the **a** *of* blood might pursue him in a rage, 1457
19:12 and hand him over to the **a** *of* blood to die. 1457
Jos 20: 3 and find protection from the **a** *of* blood. 1457
20: 5 If the **a** *of* blood pursues him, 1457
20: 9 the **a** *of* blood prior to standing trial before 1457
2Sa 14:11 to prevent the **a** *of* blood from adding to 1457
Ps 8: 2 to silence the foe and the **a.** 5933

AVENGES (5) [VENGEANCE]

2Sa 22:48 He is the God who **a** me, 5935+5989
Ps 9:12 For *he who* **a** blood remembers; 2011
18:47 He is the God who **a** me, 5935+5989
94: 1 O LORD, the God who **a,** 5935
94: 1 the God who avenges, O God who **a,** 5935

AVENGING (3) [VENGEANCE]

1Sa 25:26 and from **a** yourself with your own hands, 3828
25:33 from bloodshed this day and from **a** myself 3828
Na 1: 2 The LORD is a jealous and **a** God; 5933

AVERSE (KJV) See RETURNING

AVERT (1)

Jer 11:15 *Can* consecrated meat **a** [your punishment]? 4946+6296+6584

AVIM (KJV) See AVVIM

AVIMS, AVITES (KJV) See AVVITES

AVITH (2)

Ge 36:35 His city was named **A.** 6400
1Ch 1:46 His city was named **A.** 6400

AVOID (18) [AVOIDS]

Ne 5: 9 to **a** the reproach of our Gentile enemies? 4946
Ps 38:11 My friends and companions **a** me because 6641
Pr 4:15 **A** it, do not travel on it; 7277
19: 7 how much more *do* his friends **a** him! 8178
20: 3 It is to a man's honor *to* **a** strife, 3782+4946
20:19 so **a** a man who talks too much. 4200+4202+6843
Ecc 7:18 The man who fears God *will* **a** all [extremes]. 3655
Eze 46:20 to **a** bringing them into the outer court 1194
Zep 1: 9 that day I will punish all who **a stepping** on 1925
Jn 18:28 to **a** ceremonial uncleanness the Jews did *3590*
Ac 15:29 You will do well *to* **a** these things. *1413*
20:16 to **a** spending time in the province of Asia, *3590*
2Co 8:20 *We want to* **a** any criticism of *5097*
Gal 6:12 to **a** being persecuted for the cross *3590*
1Th 4: 3 that you should **a** sexual immorality; *600*
5:22 **A** every kind of evil. *600*
2Ti 2:16 **A** godless chatter, *4325*
Tit 3: 9 But **a** foolish controversies and genealogies *4325*

AVOIDS (2) [AVOID]

Pr 16: 6 through the fear of the LORD *a man* **a** evil. 6073
16:17 The highway of the upright **a** evil; 6073

AVVA (1)

2Ki 17:24 from Babylon, Cuthah, **A,** Hamath 6379

AVVIM (1)

Jos 18:23 **A,** Parah, Ophrah, 6399

AVVITES (3)

Dt 2:23 the **A** who lived in villages as far as Gaza, 6398
Jos 13: 3 Gath and Ekron—that of the **A);** 6398
2Ki 17:31 the **A** made Nibhaz and Tartak, 6398

AWAIT (5) [WAIT]

Isa 24:17 Terror and pit and snare **a** you, 6584
Jer 48:43 Terror and pit and snare **a** you, 6584
Hos 9: 8 yet snares **a** him on all his paths, NIH
Gal 5: 5 by faith **eagerly a** through the Spirit the righteousness **for** *587*
Php 3:20 And *we* **eagerly a** a Savior from there, *587*

AWAITS (8) [WAIT]

Job 17: 1 my days are cut short, the grave **a** me. 4200
Ps 65: 1 Praise **a** you, O God, in Zion; 1875
Pr 15:10 Stern discipline **a** him who leaves the path; 4200
28:22 and is unaware that poverty **a** him. 995
Ecc 3:19 the same fate **a** them both: 4200
9: 1 no man knows whether love or hate **a** him. 4200+7156
Ob 1: 5 Oh, what a **disaster a** *you*— 1950
Hab 2: 3 For the revelation **a** an appointed time; 6388

AWAKE (28) [WAKE]

Job 14:12 the heavens are no more, men *will* not **a** 7810
Ps 7: 6 **A**, my God; decree justice. 6424
17:15 when **I a**, I will be satisfied 7810
35:23 **A**, and rise to my defense! 6424
44:23 **A**, O Lord! 6424
57: 8 **A**, my soul! 6424
57: 8 **A**, harp and lyre! 6424
102: 7 *I* **lie a**; I have become like a 9193
108: 2 **A**, harp and lyre! I will awaken the dawn. 6424
139:18 *When I* **a**, I am still with you. 7810
Pr 6:22 when *you* **a**, they will speak to you. 7810
20:13 **stay a** and you will have food to spare. 6524+7219
SS 4:16 **A**, north wind, and come, south wind! 6424
5: 2 I slept but my heart *was* **a**. 6424
Isa 51: 9 **A**, awake! Clothe yourself with strength, 6424
51: 9 **a!** Clothe yourself with strength, 6424
51: 9 **a**, as in days gone by, 6424
51:17 **A**, awake! Rise up, O Jerusalem, 6424
51:17 **a!** Rise up, O Jerusalem, 6424
52: 1 **A**, awake, O Zion, clothe yourself 6424
52: 1 **a**, O Zion, clothe yourself with strength. 6424
Jer 51:39 then sleep forever and not **a**," 7810
51:57 they will sleep forever and not **a**," 7810
Da 12: 2 in the dust of the earth *will* **a**: 7810
Zec 13: 7 "**A**, O sword, against my shepherd, 6424
Lk 9:32 but *when they became* **fully a**, *1340*
1Th 5:10 whether *we are* **a** or asleep, *1213*
Rev 16:15 Blessed is he who **stays a** *1213*

AWAKEN (6) [WAKE]

Ps 57: 8 *I will* **a** the dawn. 6424
80: 2 **A** your might; come and save us. 6424
108: 2 Awake, harp and lyre! *I will* **a** the dawn. 6424
SS 2: 7 Do not arouse or **a** love until it so desires. 6424
3: 5 Do not arouse or **a** love until it so desires. 6424
8: 4 Do not arouse or **a** love until it so desires. 6424

AWAKENED (2) [WAKE]

1Ki 18:27 Maybe he is sleeping and *must be* **a**." 3699
2Ki 4:31 "The boy *has* not **a**." 7810

AWAKENS (2) [WAKE]

Isa 29: 8 but *he* **a**, and his hunger remains; 7810
29: 8 but *he* **a** faint, with his thirst unquenched. 7810

AWAKES (1) [WAKE]

Ps 73:20 As a dream when *one* **a**, so when you arise, 7810

AWARD (1)

2Ti 4: 8 *will* **a** to me on that day— *625*

AWARE (21)

Ge 19:33 *He was* not **a** *of it* when she lay down or 3359
19:35 Again *he was* not **a** *of it* when she lay 3359
28:16 and I *was* not **a** *of it*." 3359
Ex 34:29 he *was* not **a** that his face was radiant 3359
Lev 4:14 *they* **become a** *of* the sin they committed, 3359
4:23 When he **is made a** *of* the sin he committed, 3359
4:28 When he **is made a** *of* the sin he committed, 3359
Nu 15:24 **without** the community **being a** 4946+6524
1Sa 14: 3 No one *was* **a** that Jonathan had left. 3359
1Ki 8:38 each one **a** *of* the afflictions 3359
2Ch 6:29 each one **a** *of* his afflictions and pains, 3359
Ne 4:15 When our enemies heard that we *were* **a** 3359
Mt 12:15 **A** of this, Jesus withdrew from that place. *1182*
16: 8 **A** of their discussion, Jesus asked, *1182*
24:50 and at an hour he is not **a of.** *1182*
26:10 **A** of this, Jesus said to them, *1182*
Mk 8:17 **A** of their discussion, Jesus asked them: *1182*
Lk 12:46 and at an hour *he is* not **a of.** *1182*
Jn 6:61 **A** that his disciples were grumbling *3857*
Ac 10:28 "You *are* **well a** that it is against our law *2179*
Gal 4:21 *are you* not **a** of what the law says? *201*

AWAY (798)

Ge 5:24 he was no more, because God **took** him **a.** 4374
6:21 be eaten and **store** it **a** as food for you and 665
14:11 then *they* **went a.** 2143
15:11 but Abram **drove** them **a.** 5959
16: 8 "I'm **running a** from my mistress Sarai," 1368
18:22 men turned **a** and went toward Sodom, 4946+9004
18:23 "*Will you* **sweep a** the righteous with 6200
18:24 *Will you* really **sweep** it **a** and not spare 6200
19:15 or *you will* **be swept a** when 6200
19:17 to the mountains or *you will* **be swept a!"** 6200
21:16 about a bowshot **a**, for she thought, 8178
25: 6 the sons of his concubines and **sent** them **a** 8938
26:16 Abimelech said to Isaac, "Move **a from** us; 4946+6640
26:17 So Isaac moved **a from** there and encamped 4946
26:27 you were hostile to me and sent me **a?"** 907+4946
26:29 but always treated you well and **sent** you **a** 8938
27:39 "Your dwelling will be **a from** 4946
27:39 **a from** the dew of heaven above. 4946
29: 3 the shepherds would roll the stone **a from** the well's mouth 4946+6584
29: 8 the stone has been rolled **a from** the mouth of the well. 4946+6584
29:10 and rolled the stone **a from** the mouth of the well 4946+6584
30:15 that you **took a** my husband? 4374
30:23 "God *has* **taken a** my disgrace." 665
31: 9 So God *has* **taken a** your father's livestock 5911
31:16 that God **took a** from our father belongs 5911
31:20 by not telling him he *was* **running a.** 1368
31:27 so *I could* **send** you **a** with joy and singing 8938
31:31 I thought you would take your daughters **a from** me by force. 4946+6640
31:42 surely *have* **sent** me **a** empty-handed. 8938
31:49 and me when *we are* **a** from each other. 6259
40:19 And the birds *will* **eat a** your flesh." 430
42:24 *He* **turned a** from them and began to weep, 6015
44:28 One of them **went a** from me, and I said, 3655
45:24 Then *he* **sent** his brothers **a**, 8938
47:13 Canaan **wasted a** because of the famine. 3532
Ex 2:17 along and **drove** them **a**, 1763
5: 4 why *are you* **taking** the people **a** 7277
8: 8 *to* **take** the frogs **a** from me and my people, 6073
10:17 **take** this deadly plague **a** 6073
14:25 "*Let's* **get a** from the Israelites! 5674
15:15 the people of Canaan *will* **melt a;** 4570
16:21 and when the sun grew hot, *it* **melted a.** 5022
18: 2 After Moses had **sent a** his wife Zipporah, 8933
21:14 take him **a from** my altar and put him 4946+6640
22:10 or **is taken a** while no one is looking, 8647
23:25 *I will* **take a** sickness from among you, 6073
32: 8 *to* **turn a** from what I commanded them 6073
33: 7 the camp **some distance a,** 4946+8178
Lev 10: 4 **a from** the front of the sanctuary." 907+4946
10:17 to you to **take a** the guilt of the community 5951
16:21 *He shall* **send** the goat **a** into the desert in 8938
26:16 and **drain a** your life. 1853
26:39 Those of you who are left *will* **waste a** in 5245
26:39 of their fathers' sins *they will* **waste a.** 5245
Nu 5: 2 *to* **send a** from the camp anyone who has 8938
5: 3 **Send a** male and female alike; 8938
5:21 *to* **waste a** and your abdomen to swell. 5877
5:22 and your thigh **wastes a."** 5877
5:27 and her thigh **waste a,** 5877
9:10 of a dead body or are **a** on a journey, 8158
12:12 with its flesh half **eaten a."** 430
14:43 *you have* **turned a** from the LORD, 8740
16:24 '**Move a** from the tents of Korah, 6590
16:26 or *you will* **be swept a** because 6200
16:27 So *they* **moved a** from the tents of Korah, 6590
16:37 and scatter the coals **some distance a**, for 2134
16:45 "**Get a** from this assembly so I can put 8250
20:21 Israel turned **a from** them. 4946+6584
21: 7 that the LORD *will* **take** the snakes **a** 6073
22:11 be able to fight them and **drive** them **a.'** " 1763
22:33 and **turned a** from me these three times. 5742
22:33 If *she had* not **turned a,** 5742
25: 4 that the LORD's fierce anger *may* **turn a** 8740
25:11 *has* **turned** my anger **a** from the Israelites; 8740
31:16 **turning** the Israelites **a** 5086
32:15 If *you* **turn a** from following him, 8740
36: 3 to us *will* **be taken a.** 1757
Dt 7: 4 for *they will* **turn** your sons **a** 6073
9:12 *They have* **turned a** quickly 6073
11:16 *to* **turn a** and worship other gods and bow 6073
12:21 to put his Name *is too* **far a** from you, 8178
12:32 do not add to it or **take a** from it. 1757
13:10 to **turn** you **a** from the LORD your God, 5615
14:24 to put his Name *is so* **far a**), 8178
15:13 do not send him **a** empty-handed. 4946+6640
23: 9 keep **a from** everything impure. 4946
23:14 and turn **a from** you. 339+4946
28:26 there will be no *one to* **frighten** them **a.** 3006
28:49 a nation against you from **far a,** 8158
29:18 among you today whose heart **turns a** from 7155
30:17 But if your heart **turns a** and you are 7155
30:17 and if *you* **are drawn a** to bow down 5615
Jos 2:21 So *she* **sent** them **a** and they departed. 8938
3:16 It piled up in a heap a great **distance a,** 8178
5: 9 "Today *I have* **rolled a** the reproach 1670
6:18 But **keep a** from the devoted things, 9068
8: 6 until *we have* **lured** them **a** from the city, 5998
8: 6 '*They are* **running a** from us 5674
8:16 and they pursued Joshua and **were lured a** 5998
22: 6 Then Joshua blessed them and **sent** them **a,** 8938
22:16 How could you **turn a** from the LORD 8740
22:18 *are* you now **turning a** from the LORD? 8740
22:23 If we have built our own altar to **turn a** 8740
22:29 and **turn a** from him today by building 8740
23:12 "But if *you* **turn a** and ally yourselves 8740+8740
24:14 **Throw a** the gods your forefathers worshiped beyond the River and in Egypt, 6073
24:23 "**throw a** the foreign gods that are 6073
Jos 24:28 Then Joshua **sent** the people **a,** 8938
Jdg 3:26 While they waited, Ehud **got a.** 4880
5:21 The river Kishon **swept** them **a,** 1759
6:18 Please *do* not **go a** until I come back 4631
11: 2 *they* **drove** Jephthah **a.** 1763
11:13 they **took a** my land from the Arnon to 4374
12: 9 **gave** his daughters **a in marriage** 8938
15:17 *he* **threw a** the jawbone; 8959
18:21 *they* **turned a** and left. 7155
18:24 and my priest, and **went a.** 2143
20:31 to meet them and **were drawn a** from 5998
20:32 "Let's retreat and **draw** them **a** from the city 5998
Ru 1:21 **I went a** full, but the LORD has brought me 2143
2: 8 in another field and don't **go a** from here. 6296
1Sa 2: 5 but she who has had many sons **pines a.** 581
5:11 "**Send** the ark of the god of Israel **a;** 8938
6: 3 *do* not **send** it **a** empty, 8938
6: 7 but **take** their calves **a** and pen them up. 8740
7: 4 Israelites **put a** their Baals and Ashtoreths, 6073
12:20 yet *do* not **turn a** from the LORD, 6073
12:21 *Do* not **turn a** after useless idols. 6073
12:25 both you and your king *will* **be swept a."** 6200
14:16 in Benjamin saw the army **melting a** 2143+2256+4570
15: 6 Then he said to the Kenites, "Go **a,** 6073
15: 6 the Kenites **moved a** from the Amalekites. 6073
15:11 because he has turned **a from** me 339+4946
17:30 then turned **a** to someone else and 725+4946
18:13 So he **sent** David **a** from him 6073
19:17 and **send** my enemy **a** so that he escaped?" 8938
19:17 "He said to me, '**Let** me **get a.** 8938
20:13 not let you know and send you **a** safely. 2143
20:22 because the LORD *has* **sent** you **a.** 8938
20:29 **let** *me* **get a** to see my brothers.' 4880
21: 6 by hot bread on the day it **was taken a.** 4374
23:26 hurrying to **get a** from Saul. 2143
24:19 *does he* **let** him **get a** unharmed? 928+2006+8938
25:10 Many servants *are* **breaking a** 7287
25:29 the lives of your enemies *he will* **hurl a** as 7843
26:13 and stood on top of the hill **some distance a;** 4946+8158
28:15 and God *has* **turned a** from me. 6073
28:16 now that the LORD *has* **turned a** from you 6073
30:17 and none of them **got a,** 4880
2Sa 3:15 and *had* her **taken a** 4374
3:21 David **sent** Abner **a,** and he went in peace. 8938
3:22 because David *had* **sent** him **a,** 8938
3:23 king *had* **sent** him **a** and that he had gone 8938
4: 6 Recab and his brother Baanah **slipped a.** 4880
7:15 my love *will* never *be* **taken a** from him, 6073
7:15 as *I* **took** it **a** from Saul, 6073
10: 4 and **sent** them **a.** 8938
12:13 "The LORD *has* **taken a** your sin. 6296
13:16 "**Sending** me **a** would be 8938
13:19 She put her hand on her head and **went a,** 2143
14:14 But God *does* not **take a** life; 5951
15:17 and they halted at a place **some distance a.** 5305
19:41 **steal** the king **a** and bring him 1704
22:23 *I have* not **turned a** from his decrees. 6073
24:10 I beg you, **take a** the guilt of your servant. 6296
1Ki 2:40 So Shimei **went a** and brought 2143
5: 9 and you *can* **take** them **a.** 5951
8:46 to his own land, **far a** or near; 8158
8:66 On the following day *he* **sent** the people **a.** 8938
9: 6 if you or your sons **turn a** from me 8740+8740
11: 9 because his heart *had* **turned a** from 5742
11:11 **most certainly tear** the kingdom **a** 7973+7973
12: 5 "**Go a** for three days and then come back 2143
12: 5 So the people **went a.** 2143
14: 8 *I* **tore** the kingdom **a** from the house 7973
15:22 and *they* **carried a** from Ramah the stones 5951
17:15 *She* **went a** and did as Elijah had told her. 2143
18:40 Don't **let** anyone **get a!"** 4880
20: 6 and **carry** it **a.'** " 4374
20:36 And after the man went **a,** 725+4946
2Ki 3: 3 *he did* not **turn a** from them. 6073
4:27 Gehazi came over to **push** her **a,** 2074
4:35 Elisha **turned a** and walked back and forth 8740
5:11 But Naaman **went a** angry and said, 2143
5:24 the servants and **put** them **a** in the house. 7212
5:24 *He* **sent** the men **a** and they left. 8938
6:23 *he* **sent** them **a,** 8938
7: 8 ate and drank, and carried **a** silver, 4946+9004
7:15 and equipment the Arameans *had* **thrown a** 8959
8: 1 "**Go a** with your family and stay for a 2143
8: 2 She and her family **went a** and stayed in 2143
9: 2 **get** him **a** from his companions 7756
10:21 not one **stayed a.** 995+4202
10:29 not **turn a** from the sins of Jeroboam son 6073
10:31 not **turn a** from the sins of Jeroboam, 6073
11: 2 took Joash son of Ahaziah and **stole** him **a** 1704
13: 2 and *he did* not **turn a** from them. 6073
13: 6 But *they did* not **turn a** from the sins of 6073
13:11 the LORD and *did* not **turn a** from any of 6073
14:24 the LORD and *did* not **turn a** from any of 6073
15: 9 not **turn a** from the sins of Jeroboam son 6073
15:18 not **turn a** from the sins of Jeroboam son 6073
15:24 not **turn a** from the sins of Jeroboam son 6073
15:28 not **turn a** from the sins of Jeroboam son 6073
16:17 King Ahaz **took a** the side panels 7915
16:18 *He* **took a** the Sabbath canopy 6015
17:21 *he* **tore** Israel **a** from the house of David, 7973
17:21 Jeroboam enticed Israel **a from** following 4946
17:22 of Jeroboam and *did* not **turn a** from them 6073
20:18 that will be born to you, *will be* **taken a,** 4374
23: 5 *He* **did a with** the pagan priests 8697

2Ki 23:26 not turn a from the heat of his fierce anger, 8740
24:13 and took a all the gold articles 7915
25:14 They also took a the pots, shovels, 4374
25:15 of the imperial guard took a the censers 4374
25:21 a from her land. 4946+6584
1Ch 12:19 after consultation, their rulers sent him a. 8938
12:40 their neighbors from as far a as Issachar, 6330
17:13 I will never take my love a from him, 6073
17:13 as I took it a from your predecessor. 6073
19: 4 and sent them a. 8938
21: 8 I beg you, take a the guilt of your servant. 6296
21:12 of being swept a before your enemies, 6200
26:29 and his sons were assigned duties a from 2667
2Ch 6:36 who takes them captive to a land far a 8158
7:19 "But if you turn a and forsake the decrees 8740
10: 5 So the people went a. 2143
16: 6 and they carried a from Ramah the stones 5951
18:31 God drew them a from him, 6077
20:10 so they turned a from them and did 6073
20:25 more than they could take a. 5362+5911
21:20 He passed a, to no one's regret, 2143
22:11 took Joash son of Ahaziah and stole him a 1704
25:27 that Amaziah turned a from following 6073
28:17 and attacked Judah and carried a prisoners, 8647
28:24 from the temple of God and took them a. 7915
29: 6 They turned their faces a from 6015
29:10 that his fierce anger will turn a from us. 8740
30: 8 that his fierce anger will turn a from you. 8740
30:14 the altars in Jerusalem and cleared a 6073
35:22 however, would not turn a from him, 6015+7156
35:23 and he told his officers, "Take me a; 6296
Ezr 1: 7 which Nebuchadnezzar had carried a 3655
3:13 And the sound was heard far a.
4200+4946+6330+8158
6: 6 stay a from there. 10663
10: 3 before our God to send a all these women 3655
10:14 of our God in this matter is turned a 8740
10:19 in pledge to put a their wives, 3655
Ne 6:11 But I said, "Should a man like me run a? 1368
8:12 Then all the people went a to eat and drink, 2143
12:43 in Jerusalem could be heard far a. 4946+8158
13:28 And I drove him a from me. 1368
Est 4:17 So Mordecai went a and carried out all 6296
6:14 and hurried Haman a to 995
Job 1:21 and the LORD has taken a; 4374
5:13 and the schemes of the wily are swept a. 4554
6:27 for the fatherless and barter a your friend. 4126
7:19 Will you never look a from me, 4946
8:19 Surely its life withers a, 5376
9:12 If he snatches a, who can stop him? 3166
9:25 they fly a without a glimpse of joy. 1368
10:20 Turn a from me so I can have 4946
11:14 if you put a the sin that is in your hand 8178
12:17 He leads counselors a stripped 2143
12:19 He leads priests a stripped 2143
12:20 the lips of trusted advisers and takes a 4374
13:28 "So man wastes a like something rotten, 1162
14: 2 He springs up like a flower and withers a; 4908
14: 6 So look a from him and let him alone, 4946+6584
14:19 as water wears a stones 8835
14:19 and torrents wash a the soil, 8851
14:20 and send him a. 8938
15:12 Why has your heart carried you a, 4374
15:30 of God's mouth will carry him a. 6073
16: 6 and if I refrain, it does not go a. 4946
18:13 It eats a parts of his skin; 430
19:14 My kinsmen have gone a; 2532
20: 8 Like a dream he flies a, 6414
21:18 like chaff swept a by a gale? 1704
22: 9 And you sent widows a empty-handed 8938
22:16 their foundations washed a by a flood. 3668
24: 3 They drive a the orphan's donkey and take 5627
24:19 heat and drought snatch a the melted snow, 1608
24:19 grave snatches a those who have sinned. NIH
24:22 But God drags a the mighty by his power; 5432
27: 8 when God takes a his life? 8923
27:20 a tempest snatches him a in the night. 1704
30:15 my dignity is driven a as by the wind, 8103
30:16 my life ebbs a; days of suffering grip me. 9161
32:22 my Maker would soon take me a. 5951
33:21 His flesh wastes a to nothing, 3983
34:20 the people are shaken and they pass a; 6296
36:20 to drag people a from their homes. 6590
39:22 he does not shy a from the sword. 8740
Ps 1: 4 They are like chaff that the wind blows a. 5622
6: 8 A from me, all you who do evil, 6073
18:22 I have not turned a from his decrees. 6073
22:14 it has melted a within me. 5022
25:18 and my distress and take a all my sins. 5951
26: 9 Do not take a my soul along with sinners, 665
27: 9 do not turn your servant a in anger; 5742
28: 3 Do not drag me a with the wicked, 5432
32: 3 my bones wasted a 1162
34: T who drove him a, and he left. 1763
35: 5 the angel of the LORD driving them a; 1890
36:11 nor the hand of the wicked drive me a. 5653
37: 2 like green plants they will soon die a. 5570
37:36 but he soon passed a and was no more; 6296
38:11 my neighbors stay far a. 4946+8158
39:13 Look a from me, 4946
51: 2 Wash a all my iniquity and cleanse me 3891
53: 3 Everyone has turned a, 6047
55: 6 I would fly a and be at rest— 6414
55: 7 I would flee far a and stay in the desert; 8178
58: 7 Let them vanish like water that flows a; 2143
58: 8 Like a slug melting a as it moves along, 9468
58: 9 the wicked will be swept a. 8548
Ps 65: 8 Those living far a fear your wonders; 7921
68: 2 As smoke is blown a by the wind, 5622
68: 2 may you blow them a; 5622
71: 9 Do not cast me a when I am old; 8959
73:19 completely swept a by terrors! 6200
80:18 Then we will not turn a from you; 6047
85: 4 and put a your displeasure toward us. 7296
90: 5 You sweep men a in the sleep of death; 2441
90: 9 All our days pass a under your wrath; 7155
90:10 for they quickly pass, and we fly a. 6414
102:11 I wither a like grass. 3312
102:24 So I said: "Do not take me a, O my God, 6590
104:22 The sun rises, and they steal a; 665
104:29 when you take a their breath, 665
106:43 on rebellion and they wasted a in their sin. 4812
107: 5 and their lives ebbed a. 6494
107:14 the deepest gloom and broke a their chains. 5998
107:26 in their peril their courage melted a. 4570
109:23 I fade a like an evening shadow; 2143
112:10 he will gnash his teeth and waste a; 5022
119:37 Turn my eyes a from worthless things; 6296
119:39 Take a the disgrace I dread, 6296
119:115 A from me, you evildoers, 6073
124: 5 the raging waters would have swept us a. 6296
139:19 A from me, you bloodthirsty men! 6073
148: 6 he gave a decree that will never pass a. 6296
Pr 1:19 it takes a the lives of those who get it. 4374
4:24 Put a perversity from your mouth; 6073
6:33 and his shame will never be wiped a; 4681
13:11 Dishonest money dwindles a, 5070
13:23 but injustice sweeps it a. 6200
14: 7 Stay a from a foolish man, 4946+5584
15: 1 A gentle answer turns a wrath, 8740
20:30 Blows and wounds cleanse a evil, 5347
21: 7 violence of the wicked will drag them a, 1760
24:11 Rescue those being led a to death; 4374
24:18 and disapprove and turn his wrath a 8740
25:20 Like one who takes a a garment on 6334
27:10 a neighbor nearby than a brother far a. 8158
29: 8 but wise men turn a anger. 8740
Ecc 3: 6 a time to keep and a time to throw a, 8959
SS 1: 4 Take me a with you—let us hurry! 5432
5: 7 they took a my cloak, 4946+6584
8: 7 rivers cannot wash it a. 8851
8:14 Come a, my lover, and be like a gazelle or 1368
Isa 1:25 I will thoroughly purge a your dross
1342+2021+3869+7671
2:20 In that day men will throw a to the rodents 8959
3:18 the Lord will snatch a their finery: 6073
4: 1 Take a our disgrace!" 665
4: 4 The Lord will wash a the filth of 8175
5: 5 I will take a its hedge, 6073
5:24 and their flowers blow a like dust; 6590
5:25 Yet for all this, his anger is not turned a, 8740
6: 7 your guilt is taken a 6073
6:12 until the LORD has sent everyone far a 8178
7:17 a time unlike any since Ephraim broke a 6073
9:12 Yet for all this, his anger is not turned a, 8740
9:17 Yet for all this, his anger is not turned a, 8740
9:21 Yet for all this, his anger is not turned a, 8740
10: 4 Yet for all this, his anger is not turned a, 8740
10:18 as when a sick man wastes a. 5022
12: 1 your anger has turned a 8740
14:31 Melt a, all you Philistines! 4570
15: 7 and stored up they carry a over the Ravine 5951
16:10 and gladness are taken a from the orchards; 665
17: 4 the fat of his body will waste a. 8135
17:13 when he rebukes them they flee far a, 4946+5305
18: 5 down and take a the spreading branches. 6073
19: 7 will blow a and be no more. 5622
19: 8 on the water will pine a. 581
20: 4 the king of Assyria will lead a stripped 5627
22: 3 while the enemy was still far a. 4946+8158
22: 4 Therefore I said, "Turn a from me; 9120
22: 8 the defenses of Judah are stripped a. 1655
22:17 take firm hold of you and hurl you a, 3214+3232
24:16 But I said, "I waste a, I waste away! 8140
24:16 But I said, "I waste away, I waste a! 8140
25: 8 The Sovereign LORD will wipe a 4681
28:17 hail will sweep a your refuge, the lie, 3589
28:19 As often as it comes it will carry you a; 4374
30:17 at the threat of five you will all flee a, 5674
30:22 you will throw them a like 2430
30:22 like a menstrual cloth and say to them, "A 3655
33: 9 The land mourns and wastes a, 581
33:13 You who are far a, hear what I have done; 8158
34:12 all her princes will vanish a. 700
35:10 and sorrow and sighing will flee a. 5674
39: 7 will be taken a, 4374
40:24 and a whirlwind sweeps them a like chaff. 5951
41:16 and a gale will blow them a. 7046
42:22 all of them trapped in pits or hidden a 2461
44:22 I have swept a your offenses like a cloud, 4681
46:13 it is not far a; 8178
47:11 and you will not know how to conjure it a. 8838
49:19 those who devoured you will be far a. 8178
50: 1 of divorce with which I sent her a? 8938
50: 1 because of your transgressions your mother
was sent a. 8938
51:11 and sorrow and sighing will flee a. 5674
52: 5 my people have been taken a for nothing, 4374
53: 8 oppression and judgment he was taken a. 4374
57: 1 devout men are taken a, 665
57: 1 that the righteous are taken a to be spared 665
57: 9 You sent your ambassadors far a; 4946+8158
57:13 a mere breath will blow them a. 4374
58: 7 to turn a from your own flesh and blood? 6623
Isa 58: 9 "If you do a with the yoke of oppression,
4946+6073+9348
59:11 for deliverance, but it is far a. 8178
64: 6 and like the wind our sins sweep us a. 5951
64: 7 and made us waste a because of our sins. 4570
65: 5 say, 'Keep a; don't come near 448+3870+7928
Jer 1:13 tilting a from the north," I answered. 4946+7156
3: 8 and sent her a because of all her adulteries. 8938
3:19 and not turn a from following me. 8740
4: 8 of the LORD has not turned a from us. 8740
4:25 every bird in the sky had flown a. 5610
5:23 they have turned aside and gone a. 2143
5:25 Your wrongdoings have kept these a; 5742
6: 8 or I will turn a from you 3697
6:29 The bellows blow fiercely to burn a 9462
7:29 Cut off your hair and throw it a; 8959
7:33 there will be no one to frighten them a. 3006
8: 4 When a man turns a, does he not return? 8740
8: 5 Why then have these people turned a? 8740
8: 5 Why does Jerusalem always turn a? 5412
8:13 " 'I will take a their harvest, 665
8:19 to the cry of my people from a land far a: 5305
9: 2 that I might leave my people and go a from
them; 907+4946
13:19 be carried into exile, carried completely a. 1655
15: 1 Send them a from my presence! 8938
15: 3 to kill and the dogs to drag a and the birds 6079
15:15 You are long-suffering—do not take me a; 4374
17: 3 and all your treasures I will give a 5989
17: 5 and whose heart turns a from the LORD. 6073
17:13 Those who turn a from you will be written 6073
17:16 I have not run a from being your shepherd; 4946
18:20 in their behalf to turn your wrath a 8740
20: 4 who will carry them a to Babylon 1655
20: 5 They will take it a as plunder 4374
22:19 dragged a and thrown outside the gates 6079
22:22 drive all your shepherds a, 8286
23: 2 and driven them a and have 5615
23:23 "and not a God far a? 4946+8158
24: 5 from Judah, whom I sent a from this place 8938
27:20 not take a when he carried Jehoiachin son 4374
29:20 all you exiles whom I have sent a 8938
32:40 so that they will never turn a from me. 6073
41:16 with him led a all the survivors 4374
43: 5 the army officers led a all the remnant 4374
43: 6 They also led a all the men, NIH
44:12 I will take a the remnant 4374
46:16 a from the sword of the oppressor.' 4946+7156
49: 5 "Every one of you will be driven a, 5615
49:20 The young of the flock will be dragged a; 6079
49:30 "Flee quickly a! 5653
50: 3 both men and animals will flee a. 2143
50:17 a scattered flock that lions have chased a. 5615
50:45 The young of the flock will be dragged a; 6079
52:18 They also took a the pots, shovels, 4374
52:19 of the imperial guard took a the basins, 4374
52:27 a from her land. 4946+6584
La 1: 8 she herself groans and turns a. 294
2: 8 together they wasted a. 581
2:12 as their lives ebb a in their mothers' arms. 9161
3: 2 He has driven me a and made me walk 5627
4: 9 they waste a for lack of food from the field. 2307
4:15 "Go a! You are unclean!" 6073
4:15 men cry to them. "A! 6073
4:15 men cry to them. "Away! A! 6073
Eze 3:14 The Spirit then lifted me up and took me a, 4374
4:17 at the sight of each other and will waste a 5245
5: 3 a few strands of hair and tuck them a in 7443
6: 9 which have turned a from me, 4946+6584
6:12 He that is far a will die of the plague, 8158
7:22 I will turn my face a from them, 4946
10: 5 of the cherubim could be heard as far a as 6330
11:15 'They are far a from the LORD; 8178
11:16 Although I sent them far a among 8178
16:42 and my jealous anger will turn a 6073
16:50 I did a with them as you have seen. 6073
17: 4 and carried it a to a land of merchants, 995
17:10 wither a in the plot where it grew?' " 3312
17:13 also carried a the leading men of the land, 4374
18:21 "But if a wicked man turns a from all 8740
18:27 But if a wicked man turns a from 8740
18:28 and turns a from them, he will surely live; 8740
18:30 Turn a from all your offenses; 8740
22: 5 near and those who are far a will mock you, 8158
23:10 took a her sons and daughters 4374
23:17 turned a from them in disgust. 3697
23:18 turned a from her in disgust, 3697
23:18 just as I had turned a from her sister. 5936
23:22 turned a from in disgust, 5936
23:25 They will take a your sons and daughters, 4374
23:28 turned a from in disgust. 5936
23:29 and take a everything you have worked for. 4374
23:40 for men who came from far a, 5305
24: 6 whose deposit will not go a! 4946
24:11 be melted and its deposit burned a. 9462
24:16 to take a from you the delight of your eyes. 4374
24:23 but will waste a because of your sins 5245
24:25 on the day I take a their stronghold, 4374
26: 4 I will scrape a her rubble and make her 6081
30: 4 her wealth will be carried a 4374
31:15 and all the trees of the field withered a. 6634
33: 6 that man will be taken a because of his sin, 4374
33:10 and we are wasting a because of them. 5245
33:14 but he then turns a from his sin 8740
33:19 a wicked man turns a from his wickedness 8740
34:21 you have driven them a, 448+2021+2025+2575
38:13 to take a livestock and goods and 4374

Eze 43: 9 Now *let them* **put a** from me 8178
Da 1:16 So the guard **took a** their choice food and 5951
2:35 The wind **swept** them a without leaving 10492
4:25 *be* **driven a** from people and will live with 10304
4:32 *be* **driven a** from people and will live with 10304
4:33 *He* **was driven a** from people and ate grass 10304
5:21 *He* **was driven a** from people and given 10304
7:14 that *will* not **pass a,** 10528
7:26 and his power *will be* **taken a** 10528
8:11 *it* **took a** the daily sacrifice from him, 8123
9: 5 we *have* **turned a** from your commands 6073
9:11 and **turned a,** refusing 6073
9:16 **turn a** your anger and your wrath 8740
11:22 an overwhelming army *will* **be swept a** 8851
11:26 his army *will be* **swept a,** 8851
Hos 2: 9 "Therefore *I will* **take a** my grain 4374
4: 3 and all who live in it **waste a;** 581
4:11 *which* **take a** the understanding 4374
4:19 A whirlwind *will* **sweep** them **a,** 928+4053+7674
5:14 I will tear them to pieces and **go a;** 2143
7:14 and new wine but **turn a** from me. 6073
8:10 to **waste a** under the oppression of 5071
9:11 Ephraim's glory *will* **fly a** like a bird— 6414
9:12 Woe to them when I **turn a** from them! 6073
10: 7 and its king *will* **float a** like a twig on 1950
13:11 and in my wrath *I* **took** him **a.** 4374
14: 4 for my anger *has* **turned a** from them. 8740
Joel 1: 7 and **thrown** it **a,** 8959
1:12 Surely the joy of mankind *is* **withered a.** 3312
3: 8 a nation **far a."** 8158
Am 2:15 the fleet-footed soldier *will* not **get a,** 4880
4: 2 surely come when you *will* **be taken a** 5951
4: 7 when the harvest was still three months **a.** NIH
5:23 **A** *with* the noise of your songs! 6073
6: 5 *You* **strum a** on your harps like David 7260
7:11 **a from** their native land.' " 4946+6584
7:17 **a from** their native land.' " 4946+6584
8: 4 you who trample the needy and **do a with** 8697
9: 1 Not one *will* **get a,** none will escape. 5674+5674
Jnh 1: 3 But Jonah **ran a** from the LORD 1368
1:10 (They knew he *was* **running a** from 1368
2: 7 "When my life *was* **ebbing a,** 6494
4: 3 Now, O LORD, take **a** my life, 4946
Mic 2: 9 *You* **take a** my blessing 4374
2:10 Get up, **go a!** 2143
4: 7 those **driven a** a strong nation. 2133
Na 1: 5 before him and the hills **melt a.** 4570
1:12 they will be cut off and **pass a.** 6296
1:13 from your neck and **tear** your shackles **a."** 5998
2: 7 that [the city] be exiled and **carried a.** 6590
2: 8 and its water *is* **draining a.** 5674
3:16 the land and then **fly a.** 6414
3:17 but when the sun appears *they* **fly a,** 5610
Zep 1: 2 *"I will* **sweep a** everything from the face of the earth," 665+6066
1: 3 *"I will* **sweep a** both men and animals; 6066
1: 3 *I will* **sweep a** the birds of the air and 6066
3:15 The LORD *has* **taken a** your punishment, 6073
Hag 1: 9 What you brought home, *I* **blew a.** 5870
Zec 3: 4 "See, *I have* **taken a** your sin, 6296
6:15 *Those who are* **far a** will come and help 8158
9: 4 But the Lord *will* **take a** her **possessions** 3769
9:10 *I will* **take a** the chariots from Ephraim 4162
10:11 down and Egypt's scepter *will* **pass a.** 6073
Mal 3: 7 of your forefathers *you have* **turned a** 6073
Mt 4:10 Jesus said to him, **"A from** me, Satan! *5632*
5:29 gouge it out and throw it **a.** *608*
5:30 cut it off and throw it **a.** *608*
5:42 and *do* not **turn a from** the one who wants *695*
6:26 they do not sow or reap or **store a** in barns, *5251*
7:23 **A from** me, you evildoers!' *713*
9:16 the patch *will* **pull a** from the garment, *149*
9:24 he said, **"Go a.** The girl is *432*
11: 6 the man who *does* not **fall a** on account *4997*
13:19 and **snatches a** what was sown in his heart. *773*
13:21 *he* quickly **falls a.** *4997*
13:25 among the wheat, and **went a.** *599*
13:46 he **went a** and sold everything he had *599*
13:48 but threw the bad **a.** *2032*
14:15 **Send** the crowds **a,** *668*
14:16 Jesus replied, "They do not need *to* **go a.** *599*
15:23 **"Send** her **a,** for she keeps crying out *668*
15:32 I do not want *to* **send** them **a** hungry, *668*
15:39 *After* Jesus *had* **sent** the crowd **a,** *668*
16: 4 Jesus then left them and **went a.** *599*
18: 8 cut it off and throw it **a.** *608*
18: 9 gouge it out and throw it **a.** *608*
18:12 and one of them **wanders a,** *4414*
19: 7 a certificate of divorce and **send** her **a?"** *668*
19:22 *he* **went a** sad, because he had great wealth. *599*
21: 3 and he will send them **right a."** *2317*
21:33 **went a on a journey.** *623*
21:43 of God *will be* **taken a** from you and given *149*
22:22 So *they* left him and **went a.** *599*
24: 1 and *was* **walking a** when his disciples came *4513*
24:10 that time many *will* **turn a** from the faith *4997*
24:34 this generation *will* certainly not **pass a** *4216*
24:35 Heaven and earth *will* **pass a,** *4216*
24:35 but my words *will* never **pass a.** *4216*
24:39 until the flood came and **took** them all **a.** *149*
24:48 'My master is **staying a long time,'** *5988*
25:46 they *will* **go a** to eternal punishment, *599*
26: 2 the Passover is two days **a—** *3552*
26:31 "This very night you *will* all **fall a** *4997*
26:33 "Even if all **fall a** on account of you, *4997*
26:42 He **went a** a second time and prayed, *599*
26:42 for this cup *to* **be taken a** unless I drink it, *4216*
Mt 26:44 So he left them and **went a** once more *599*
26:73 for your accent **gives** you **a."** *1316+4472*
27: 2 **led** him **a** and handed him over to Pilate, *552*
27: 5 Then he **went a** and hanged himself. *599*
27:31 Then *they* **led** him **a** to crucify him. *552*
27:60 of the entrance to the tomb and **went a.** *599*
28: 8 the women **hurried a from** the tomb, *599+5444*
28:13 and stole him **a** while we were asleep.' *NIG*
Mk 1:43 Jesus **sent** him **a** at once with *1675*
2:21 the new piece *will* **pull a** from the old, *149*
4:15 and **takes a** the word that was sown *149*
4:17 *they* quickly **fall a.** *4997*
5:20 So the *man* **went a** and began to tell in *599*
6:32 So *they* **went a** by themselves in a boat to *599*
6:36 **Send** the people **a** so they can go to *668*
7:33 **took** him aside, **a from** *655*
8: 9 And *having* **sent** them **a,** *668*
10: 4 a certificate of divorce and **send** her **a."** *668*
10:22 *He* **went a** sad, because he had great wealth. *599*
12: 1 and **went a on a journey.** *623*
12: 3 beat him and **sent** him **a** empty-handed. *690*
12:12 so *they* left him and **went a.** *599*
13:30 this generation *will* certainly not **pass a** *4216*
13:31 Heaven and earth *will* **pass a,** *4216*
13:31 but my words *will* never **pass a.** *4216*
13:34 It's like a man **going a:** *624*
14: 1 of Unleavened Bread were only two days **a,** *3552*
14:27 *"You will* all **fall a,"** Jesus told them, *4997*
14:29 Peter declared, "Even if all **fall a,** *4997*
14:39 Once more he **went a** and prayed *599*
14:44 arrest him and **lead** him **a** under guard." *552*
15: 1 **led** him **a** and handed him over to Pilate. *708*
15:16 The soldiers **led** Jesus **a** into the palace *552*
16: 3 "Who *will* **roll** the stone **a** from *653*
16: 4 which was very large, *had been* **rolled a.** *653*
Lk 1:25 and **taken a** my disgrace among *904*
1:53 but *has* **sent** the rich **a** empty. *1990*
5: 8 **"Go a** from me, Lord; I am a sinful man!" *2002*
7:23 the man who *does* not **fall a** on account *4997*
8:12 then the devil comes and **takes a** the word *149*
8:13 but in the time of testing *they* **fall a.** *923*
8:38 but Jesus **sent** him **a,** saying, *668*
8:39 So the man **went a** and told all over town *599*
9:12 **"Send** the crowd **a** so they can go to *668*
10:30 beat him and **went a,** leaving him half dead. *599*
10:42 and it *will* not *be* **taken a from** her." *904*
11:22 *he* **takes a** the armor in which *149*
11:52 *you have* **taken a** the key to knowledge. *149*
13:27 **A from** me, all you evildoers!' *923*
14: 4 he healed him and **sent** him **a.** *668*
16: 3 My master is **taking a** my job. *904*
16:23 he looked up and saw Abraham **far a,** *608+3427*
19:20 I have kept it **laid a** in a piece of cloth. *641*
19:24 **'Take** his mina **a** from him and give it to *149*
19:26 even what he has *will be* **taken a.** *149*
20: 9 to some farmers and **went a** for a long time. *623*
20:10 and **sent** him **a** empty-handed. *1990*
20:11 and **sent a** empty-handed. *1990*
21: 9 but the end will not come **right a."** *2311*
21:32 this generation *will* certainly not **pass a** *4216*
21:33 Heaven and earth *will* **pass a,** *4216*
21:33 but my words *will* never **pass a.** *4216*
22:54 *they* **led** him **a** and took him into the house *72*
23:18 **"A with** this man! *149*
23:26 As *they* **led** him **a,** *552*
23:48 *they* beat their breasts and **went a.** *5715*
24: 2 They found the stone **rolled a** from *653*
24:12 and he **went a,** *599*
Jn 1:29 who **takes a** the sin of the world! *149*
5:13 for Jesus *had* **slipped a** into the crowd *1728*
5:15 The man **went a** and told the Jews *599*
6:22 but that they *had* **gone a** alone. *599*
6:37 whoever comes to me I will never drive **a.** *2032*
7: 1 purposely **staying a from** Judea *1877+4024+4344*
8: 9 those who heard *began to* **go a** one at *2002*
8:21 "I *am* **going a,** and you will look for me, *5632*
8:59 **slipping a from** the temple grounds. *2002*
10: 5 *they will* **run a** from him because they do *5771*
10:12 he abandons the sheep and **runs a.** *5771*
10:13 The man runs **a** because he is a hired hand *NIG*
11:39 **"Take a** the stone," he said. *149*
11:41 So *they* **took a** the stone. *149*
11:48 and then the Romans will come and **take a** *149*
14:28 *'I am* **going a** and I am coming back *5632*
15: 6 like a branch that is thrown **a** and withers; *2032*
16: 7 It is for your good that I *am* **going a.** *599*
16: 7 Unless *I* **go a,** the Counselor will *599*
16:22 and no one *will* **take a** your joy. *149*
18:11 "Put your sword **a!** *1650+2557+3836*
19:15 But they shouted, **"Take** him **a!** *149*
19:15 **Take** him **a!** *149*
19:38 he came and **took** the body **a.** *149*
20:13 *"They have* **taken** my Lord **a,"** she said, *149*
20:15 she said, "Sir, if you *have* **carried** him **a,** *1002*
Ac 7:42 But God **turned a** and gave them over to *5138*
8:39 **suddenly took** Philip **a,** *773*
17:10 **sent** Paul and Silas **a** *1734*
20:30 in order to **draw a** disciples after them. *685*
21: 1 *After we had* **torn** *ourselves* **a** from them, *685*
21:21 among the Gentiles **to turn a from** Moses, *686*
21:36 that followed kept shouting, **"A with** him!" *149*
22:16 Get up, be baptized and **wash** your sins **a,** *666*
22:21 I will send you **far a** to the Gentiles.' " *3426*
23:10 the troops to go down and take him **a from** *1666*
27:32 that held the lifeboat and let it **fall a.** *1738*
27:42 to prevent any of them *from* **swimming a** *1713*
Ro 3:12 All *have* **turned a,** *1712*
Ro 6: 6 that the body of sin *might be* **done a with,** *2934*
11:26 **turn** godlessness **a from** *695*
11:27 with them when *I* **take a** their sins." *904*
16:17 *Keep* **a** from them. *1712*
1Co 7:31 this world in its present form *is* **passing a.** *4135*
13: 8 where there is knowledge, *it will* **pass a.** *2934*
2Co 3:11 And if what *was* **fading a** came with glory, *2934*
3:13 at it *while* the radiance *was* **fading a.** *2934*
3:14 because only in Christ *is it* **taken a.** *2934*
3:16 the veil *is* **taken a.** *4311*
4:16 Though outwardly we *are* **wasting a,** *1425*
5: 6 at home in the body *we are* **a** from the Lord. *1685*
5: 8 *to be* **a from** the body and at home with *1685*
5: 9 at home in the body or **a from** it. *1685*
10: 1 to face with you, but "bold" *when* **a!** *582*
12: 8 with the Lord to **take** it **a from** me. *923*
Gal 3:17 by God and thus **do a with** the promise. *2934*
5: 4 *you have* **fallen a from** grace. *1738*
Eph 2:13 in Christ Jesus you who once were **far a** have been brought near *3426*
2:17 and preached peace to you who were **far a** *3426*
Col 2:14 he **took** it **a,** nailing it to the cross. *149*
1Th 2:17 *when* we *were* **torn a from** you for *682*
2Th 3: 6 *to* **keep a** from every brother who is idle *5097*
1Ti 1: 6 Some *have* **wandered a from** these *1762*
5:15 in fact already **turned a** to follow Satan. *1762*
6:20 **Turn a from** godless chatter and *1762*
2Ti 2:18 who *have* **wandered a** from the truth. *846*
2:19 the Lord *must* **turn a from** wickedness." *923*
4: 4 **turn** their ears **a from** the truth *695*
Heb 2: 1 so that *we do* not **drift a.** *4184*
3:12 unbelieving heart that **turns a from** *923*
6: 6 *if they* **fall a,** to be brought back *4178*
8: 9 and I **turned a** from them, *288*
9:26 to **do a** with sin by the sacrifice of himself. *120*
9:28 so Christ was sacrificed once *to* **take a** *429*
10: 4 the blood of bulls and goats *to* **take a** sins. *904*
10:11 which can never **take a** sins. *4311*
10:35 So *do* not **throw a** your confidence; *610*
11: 5 because God *had* **taken** him **a.** *3572*
12:25 *if* we **turn a from** him who warns us *695*
13: 9 *Do* not *be* **carried a** by all kinds *4195*
Jas 1:10 because *he will* **pass a** like a wild flower. *4216*
1:11 the rich man *will* **fade a** even *3447*
1:14 *he is* **dragged a** and enticed. *1999*
1:24 and, after looking at himself, **goes a** *599*
1Pe 5: 4 the crown of glory that will **never fade a.** *277*
2Pe 3:17 not *be* **carried a** by the error of lawless men *5270*
1Jn 2:17 The world and its desires **pass a,** *4135*
3: 5 so that *he might* **take a** our sins. *149*
Rev 7:17 **wipe a** every tear **from** their eyes." *1981*
12:15 **sweep** her **a with the torrent.** *4472+4533*
16:20 Every island **fled a** and *5771*
17: 3 Then the angel **carried** me **a** in the Spirit *708*
21: 1 first heaven and the first earth *had* **passed a,** *599*
21: 4 for the old order of things *has* **passed a."** *599*
21:10 And he **carried** me **a** in the Spirit to *708*
22:19 if anyone **takes** words **a from** this book *904*
22:19 God *will* **take a from** him his share in *904*

AWE (16) [AWESOME, OVERAWED]

1Sa 12:18 all the people **stood in a** *of* the LORD 3707+4394
1Ki 3:28 **held** the king **in a,** 3707
Job 25: 2 "Dominion and **a** belong to God; 7065
Ps 119:120 *I* **stand in a** of your laws. 3707
Ecc 5: 7 Therefore **stand in a** *of* God. 3707
Isa 29:23 and *will* **stand in a** *of* the God of Israel. 6907
Jer 2:19 the LORD your God and have no **a** 7067
33: 9 and *they will be* **in a** and will tremble at 7064
Hab 3: 2 *I* **stand in a** *of* your deeds, O LORD. 3707
Mal 2: 5 and he revered me and **stood in a** 3169
Mt 9: 8 *they were* **filled with a;** *5828*
Lk 1:65 The neighbors were all filled with **a,** *5832*
5:26 They were filled *with* **a** and said, *5832*
7:16 They were all **filled with a** *3284+5832*
Ac 2:43 Everyone was filled with **a,** *5832*
Heb 12:28 with reverence and **a,** *1290*

AWESOME (34) [AWE]

Ge 28:17 "How **a** is this place! 3707
Ex 15:11 majestic in holiness, **a** *in* glory, 3707
34:10 among will see how **a** *is* the work that I, 3707
Dt 4:34 or by great and **a deeds,** 4616
7:21 who is among you, is a great and **a** God. 3707
10:17 the great God, mighty and **a,** 3707
10:21 **a wonders** you saw with your own eyes. 3707
28:58 do not revere this glorious and **a** name— 3707
34:12 the mighty power or performed the **a** deeds 4616
Jdg 13: 6 He looked like an angel of God, very **a.** 3707
2Sa 7:23 and **a wonders** by driving out nations 3707
1Ch 17:21 and **a wonders** by driving out nations from 3707
Ne 1: 5 God of heaven, the great and **a** God, 3707
4:14 Remember the Lord, who is great and **a,** 3707
9:32 O our God, the great, mighty and **a** God, 3707
Job 10:16 like a lion and again **display** *your* **a power** 7098
37:22 God comes in **a** majesty. 3707
Ps 45: 4 let your right hand display **a** *deeds.* 3707
47: 2 How **a** is the LORD Most High, 3707
65: 5 with **a deeds** of righteousness, 3707
66: 3 Say to God, "How **a** are your deeds! 3707
66: 5 *how* **a** his works in man's behalf! 3707
68:35 *You are* **a,** O God, in your sanctuary; 3707
89: 7 *he is* more **a** than all who surround him. 3707
99: 3 Let them praise your great and **a** name— 3707
106:22 miracles in the land of Ham and **a** *deeds* by 3707

Ps 111: 9 holy and a *is* his name. 3707
145: 6 They will tell of the power of your a works, 3707
Isa 64: 3 you did a *things* that we did not expect, 3707
Eze 1:18 Their rims were high and a, 3711
1:22 sparkling like ice, and a. 3707
Da 2:31 enormous, dazzling statue, a in appearance. 10167
9: 4 "O Lord, the great and a God, 3707
Zep 2:11 *be* a to them when he destroys all the gods 3707

AWFUL (5)

Jdg 20: 3 "Tell us how this a thing happened." 8288
20:12 about this a crime that was committed 8288
Ne 9:18 or when they committed a blasphemies. 1524
9:26 they committed a blasphemies. 1524
Jer 30: 7 How a that day will be! 1524+2098

AWHILE (3) [WHILE]

Ge 47: 4 "We have come to live here a, 1591
1Sa 9:27 "but you stay here a, 2021+3427+3869
1Co 16: 6 Perhaps *I will* stay with you a, *4169*

AWL (2)

Ex 21: 6 the doorpost and pierce his ear with an a. 5345
Dt 15:17 an a and push it through his ear lobe into 5345

AWNINGS (1)

Eze 27: 7 your a were of blue and purple from 4833

AWOKE (7) [WAKE]

Ge 9:24 When Noah a from his wine 3699
28:16 When Jacob a from his sleep, he thought, 3699
Jdg 16:14 *He* a from his sleep and pulled up the pin 3699
16:20 *He* a from his sleep and thought, 3699
1Ki 3:15 Then Solomon a—and he realized it had been a dream. 3699
Ps 78:65 Then the Lord a as from sleep, 3699
Jer 31:26 At this *I* a and looked around. 7810

AX (8) [AXES, AXHEAD]

Dt 19: 5 and as he swings his a to fell a tree, 1749
20:19 do not destroy its trees by putting an a 1749
Jdg 9:48 He took an a and cut off some branches, 7935
Ecc 10:10 If the a is dull and its edge unsharpened, 1366
Isa 10:15 the a raise itself above him who swings it, 1749
10:34 down the forest thickets with an a; 1366
Mt 3:10 The a is already at the root of the trees, *544*
Lk 3: 9 The a is already at the root of the trees, *544*

AXES (7) [AX]

1Sa 13:20 mattocks, a and sickles sharpened. 7935
13:21 of a shekel for sharpening forks and a and 7935
2Sa 12:31 with saws and with iron picks and a, 4477
1Ch 20: 3 with saws and with iron picks and a. 4490
Ps 74: 5 like men wielding a to cut through a thicket 7935
74: 6 the carved paneling with their a 4172
Jer 46:22 they will come against her with a, 7935

AXHEAD (1) [AX]

2Ki 6: 5 the iron a fell into the water. 1366

AXLES (3)

1Ki 7:30 with bronze a, and each had a basin resting 6248
7:32 a *of* the wheels were attached to the stand. 3338
7:33 the a, rims, spokes and hubs were all 3338

AXLETREES (KJV) See AXEL

AYYAH (1)

1Ch 7:28 and its villages all the way to A 6509

AZAL (KJV) See AZEL

AZALIAH (2)

2Ki 22: 3 Shaphan son of A, the son of Meshullam, 729
2Ch 34: 8 he sent Shaphan son of A and Maaseiah 729

AZANIAH (1)

Ne 10: 9 The Levites: Jeshua son of A, 271

AZARAEL, AZAREEL (KJV) See AZAREL

AZAREL (6)

1Ch 12: 6 A, Joezer and Jashobeam the Korahites; 6475
25:18 the eleventh to A, his sons and relatives, 12 6475
27:22 A son of Jeroham. 6475
Ezr 10:41 A, Shelemiah, Shemariah, 6475
Ne 11:13 Amashsai son of A, the son of Ahzai, 6475
12:36 Shemaiah, A, Milalai, Gilalai, Maai, 6475

AZARIAH (46) [AZARIAH'S, UZZIAH]

1Ki 4: 2 A son of Zadok— 6482
4: 5 A son of Nathan— 6482
2Ki 14:21 Then all the people of Judah took A, 6481
15: 1 A son of Amaziah king of Judah began 6481
15: 7 A rested with his fathers and was buried 6481
15: 8 In the thirty-eighth year of A king of Judah, 6482
15:17 In the thirty-ninth year of A king of Judah, 6481
15:23 In the fiftieth year of A king of Judah, 6481
15:27 In the fifty-second year of A king of Judah, 6481
1Ch 2: 8 The son of Ethan: A. 6481
2:38 Jehu the father of A, 6481
2:39 A the father of Helez, 6481
3:12 A his son, Jotham his son, 6481
6: 9 Ahimaaz the father of A, 6481
6: 9 A the father of Johanan, 6481
6:10 of A (it was he who served as priest in 6481
6:11 A the father of Amariah, 6481
6:13 Hilkiah the father of A, 6481
6:14 A the father of Seraiah, 6481
6:36 the son of A, the son of Zephaniah, 6481
9:11 A son of Hilkiah, the son of Meshullam, 6481
2Ch 15: 1 The Spirit of God came upon A son 6482
15: 8 the prophecy of A son of Oded the prophet, 6482
21: 2 the sons of Jehoshaphat, were A, Jehiel, 6481
23: 1 A son of Jeroham, 6482
23: 1 Ishmael son of Jehohanan, A son of Obed, 6482
26:17 A the priest with eighty other courageous priests 6482
26:20 When A the chief priest and all 6482
28:12 A son of Jehohanan, Berekiah son 6482
29:12 Mahath son of Amasai and Joel son of A; 6482
29:12 Kish son of Abdi and A son of Jehallelel; 6482
31:10 and A the chief priest, 6482
31:13 and A the official in charge of the temple 6482
Ezr 7: 1 Ezra son of Seraiah, the son of A, 6481
7: 3 the son of A, the son of Meraioth, 6481
Ne 3:23 and next to them, A son of Maaseiah, 6481
7: 7 A, Raamiah, Nahamani, Mordecai, Bilshan, 6481
8: 7 Shabbethai, Hodiah, Maaseiah, Kelita, A, 6481
10: 2 Seraiah, A, Jeremiah, 6481
12:33 along with A, Ezra, Meshullam, 6481
Jer 43: 2 A son of Hoshaiah and Johanan son 6481
Da 1: 6 Daniel, Hananiah, Mishael and A. 6481
1: 7 to Mishael, Meshach; and to A, 6481
1:11 Hananiah, Mishael and A, 6481
1:19 Hananiah, Mishael and A; 6481
2:17 to his friends Hananiah, Mishael and A. 10538

AZARIAH'S (2) [AZARIAH]

2Ki 15: 6 As for the other events of A reign, 6482
Ne 3:24 from A house to the angle and the corner, 6481

AZARIAHU (1)

2Ch 21: 2 Zechariah, A, Michael and Shephatiah. 6482

AZAZ (1)

1Ch 5: 8 and Bela son of A, 6452

AZAZIAH (3)

1Ch 15:21 Jeiel and A were to play the harps, 6453
27:20 Hoshea son of A; 6453
2Ch 31:13 Jehiel, A, Nahath, Asahel, Jerimoth, 6453

AZBUK (1)

Ne 3:16 Beyond him, Nehemiah son of A, 6443

AZEKAH (7)

Jos 10:10 down all the way to A and Makkedah. 6467
10:11 on the road down from Beth Horon to A, 6467
15:35 Jarmuth, Adullam, Socoh, A, 6467
1Sa 17: 1 between Socoh and A. 6467
2Ch 11: 9 Adoraim, Lachish, A, 6467
Ne 11:30 and in A and its settlements. 6467
Jer 34: 7 that were still holding out—Lachish and A. 6467

AZEL (7)

1Ch 8:37 Eleasah his son and A his son. 727
8:38 A had six sons, and these were their names: 727
8:38 All these were the sons of A. 727
9:43 Eleasah his son and A his son. 727
9:44 A had six sons, and these were their names: 727
9:44 These were the sons of A. 727
Zec 14: 5 for it will extend to A. 728

AZEM (KJV) See EZEM

AZGAD (4)

Ezr 2:12 of A 1,222 6444
8:12 of the descendants of A, Johanan son 6444
Ne 7:17 of A 2,322 6444
10:15 Bunni, A, Bebai, 6444

AZIEL (1)

1Ch 15:20 A, Shemiramoth, Jehiel, Unni, Eliab, 6456

AZIZA (1)

Ezr 10:27 Mattaniah, Jeremoth, Zabad and A. 6461

AZMAVETH (8) [BETH AZMAVETH]

2Sa 23:31 Abi-Albon the Arbathite, A the Barhumite, 6462
1Ch 8:36 of Alemeth, A and Zimri, and Zimri was 6462
9:42 of Alemeth, A and Zimri, and Zimri was 6462
11:33 A the Baharumite, Eliahba the Shaalbonite, 6462
12: 3 Jeziel and Pelet the sons of A; 6462
27:25 A son of Adiel was in charge of 6462
Ezr 2:24 of A 42 6463
Ne 12:29 and from the area of Geba and A, 6463

AZMON (2)

Nu 34: 4 to Hazar Addar and over to A, 6801
Jos 15: 4 then passed along to A and joined the Wadi 6801

AZNOTH TABOR (1) [TABOR]

Jos 19:34 through A and came out at Hukkok. 268

AZOR (2)

Mt 1:13 Eliakim the father of A, *110*
1:14 A the father of Zadok, *110*

AZOTUS (1)

Ac 8:40 however, appeared at A and traveled about, *111*

AZRIEL (3)

1Ch 5:24 Epher, Ishi, Eliel, A, Jeremiah, 6480
27:19 Jerimoth son of A; 6480
Jer 36:26 Seraiah son of A and Shelemiah son 6480

AZRIKAM (6)

1Ch 3:23 Elioenai, Hizkiah and A— three in all. 6483
8:38 A, Bokeru, Ishmael, Sheariah, 6483
9:14 Shemaiah son of Hasshub, the son of A, 6483
9:44 A, Bokeru, Ishmael, Sheariah, 6483
2Ch 28: 7 A the officer in charge of the palace, 6483
Ne 11:15 Shemaiah son of Hasshub, the son of A, 6483

AZUBAH (4)

1Ki 22:42 His mother's name was A daughter 6448
1Ch 2:18 of Hezron had children by his wife A (and 6448
2:19 When A died, Caleb married Ephrath, 6448
2Ch 20:31 His mother's name was A daughter 6448

AZUR (KJV) See AZZUR

AZZAH (KJV) See GAZA

AZZAN (1)

Nu 34:26 of A, the leader from the tribe of Issachar; 6464

AZZUR (3)

Ne 10:17 Ater, Hezekiah, A, 6473
Jer 28: 1 the prophet Hananiah son of A, 6473
Eze 11: 1 and I saw among them Jaazaniah son of A 6473

B

BAAL (63) [BAAL GAD, BAAL HAMON, BAAL HAZOR, BAAL HERMON, BAAL MEON, BAAL PEOR, BAAL PERAZIM, BAAL SHALISHAH, BAAL TAMAR, BAAL ZEPHON, BAAL'S, BAAL-BERITH, BAAL-HANAN, BAAL-ZEBUB, BAALS, BAMOTH BAAL]

Nu 25: 3 Israel joined in worshiping the B *of* Peor. 1251
25: 5 in worshiping the B *of* Peor." 1251
Dt 4: 3 among you everyone who followed the B 1251
Jdg 2:13 because they forsook him and served B and 1251
6:25 down your father's altar to B and cut down 1251
6:31 If B really is a god, 2085S
6:32 saying, "Let B contend with him," 1251
1Ki 16:31 and began to serve B and worship him. 1251
16:32 for B *in* the temple of Baal that he built 1251
16:32 in the temple of B that he built in Samaria. 1251
18:19 the four hundred and fifty prophets of B 1251
18:21 but if B is God, follow him." 1251
18:22 but B has four hundred and fifty prophets. 1251
18:25 Elijah said to the prophets of B, 1251
18:26 on the name of B from morning till noon. 1251
18:26 "O B, answer us!" 1251
18:40 "Seize the prophets of B. 1251
19:18 all whose knees have not bowed down to B 1251
22:53 He served and worshiped B and provoked 1251
2Ki 3: 2 He got rid of the sacred stone of B 1251
10:18 "Ahab served B a little; 1251
10:19 Now summon all the prophets of B, 1251
10:19 I am going to hold a great sacrifice for B. 1251
10:19 in order to destroy the ministers of B. 1251
10:20 Jehu said, "Call an assembly in honor of B." 1251
10:21 and all the ministers of B came; 1251
10:21 of B until it was full from one end to 1251
10:22 "Bring robes for all the ministers of B." 1251
10:23 of Recab went into the temple of B. 1251
10:23 Jehu said to the ministers of B, 1251
10:23 only ministers of B." 1251

2Ki 10:25 the inner shrine of the temple of **B**. 1251
10:26 the sacred stone out of the temple of **B** 1251
10:27 of **B** and tore down the temple of Baal, 1251
10:27 of Baal and tore down the temple of **B**, 1251
10:28 So Jehu destroyed **B worship** in Israel. 1251
11:18 to the temple of **B** and tore it down. 1251
11:18 and killed Mattan the priest of **B** in front of 1251
17:16 and they worshiped **B**. 1251
21: 3 he also erected altars to **B** and made 1251
23: 4 the articles made for **B** and Asherah and all 1251
23: 5 those who burned incense to **B**, 1251
1Ch 5: 5 Micah his son, Reaiah his son, **B** his son, 1252
8:30 followed by Zur, Kish, **B**, Ner, Nadab, 1252
9:36 followed by Zur, Kish, **B**, Ner, Nadab, 1252
2Ch 23:17 All the people went to the temple of **B** 1251
23:17 and killed Mattan the priest of **B** in front of 1251
Ps 106:28 to the **B** *of* Peor and ate sacrifices offered 1251
Jer 2: 8 The prophets prophesied by **B**, 1251
7: 9 to **B** and follow other gods you have 1251
11:13 to burn incense to that shameful god **B** are 1251
11:17 to anger by burning incense to **B**. 1251
12:16 they once taught my people to swear by **B**— 1251
19: 5 the high places of **B** to burn their sons in 1251
19: 5 in the fire as offerings to **B**— 1251
23:13 by **B** and led my people Israel astray. 1251
23:27 as their fathers forgot my name through **B worship**. 1251
32:29 by burning incense on the roofs to **B** and 1251
32:35 They built high places for **B** in the Valley 1251
Hos 2: 8 which they used for **B**. 1251
13: 1 But he became guilty of **B worship** and died. 1251
Zep 1: 4 from this place every remnant of **B**, 1251
Ro 11: 4 not bowed the knee *to* **B**." *955*

BAAL GAD (3) [BAAL, GAD]
Jos 11:17 to **B** in the Valley 1254
12: 7 from **B** in the Valley of Lebanon 1254
13: 5 the east, from **B** below Mount Hermon 1254

BAAL HAMON (1) [BAAL]
SS 8:11 Solomon had a vineyard in **B**; 1255

BAAL HAZOR (1) [BAAL, HAZOR]
2Sa 13:23 at **B** near the border of Ephraim, 1258

BAAL HERMON (2) [BAAL, HERMON, SENIR]
Jdg 3: 3 from Mount **B** to Lebo Hamath. 1259
1Ch 5:23 in the land from Bashan to **B**, 1259

BAAL MEON (3) [BETH BAAL MEON, BETH MEON]
Nu 32:38 and **B** (these names were changed) 1260
1Ch 5: 8 the area from Aroer to Nebo and **B**. 1260
Eze 25: 9 Beth Jeshimoth, **B** and Kiriathaim— 1260

BAAL PEOR (2) [BAAL, PEOR]
Dt 4: 3 the LORD did at **B**. 1261
Hos 9:10 But when they came to **B**, 1261

BAAL PERAZIM (4) [BAAL, PERAZIM]
2Sa 5:20 So David went to **B**, 1262
5:20 So that place was called **B**. 1262
1Ch 14:11 David and his men went up to **B**, 1262
14:11 So that place was called **B**. 1262

BAAL SHALISHAH (1) [BAAL]
2Ki 4:42 A man came from **B**, 1264

BAAL TAMAR (1) [BAAL, TAMAR]
Jdg 20:33 and took up positions at **B**, 1265

BAAL ZEPHON (3) [BAAL, ZEPHON]
Ex 14: 2 directly opposite **B**. 1263
14: 9 near Pi Hahiroth, opposite **B**. 1263
Nu 33: 7 to the east of **B**, 1263

BAAL'S (4) [BAAL]
Jdg 6:28 there was **B** altar, demolished, 1251
6:30 because he has broken down **B** altar and cut 1251
6:31 "Are you going to plead **B** cause? 1251
6:32 because he broke down **B** altar. 2257S

BAAL-BERITH (2) [BAAL]
Jdg 8:33 They set up **B** as their god 1253
9: 4 of silver from the temple of **B**, 1253

BAAL-HANAN (5) [BAAL]
Ge 36:38 **B** son of Acbor succeeded him as king. 1257
36:39 When **B** son of Acbor died, 1257
1Ch 1:49 **B** son of Acbor succeeded him as king. 1257
1:50 **B** died, Hadad succeeded him as king. 1257
27:28 **B** the Gederite was in charge of the olive 1257

BAAL-ZEBUB (4) [BAAL, BEELZEBUB]
2Ki 1: 2 "Go and consult **B**, the god of Ekron, 1256
1: 3 that you are going off to consult **B**, 1256
1: 6 that you are sending men to consult **B**, 1256
1:16 that you have sent messengers to consult **B**, 1256

BAALAH (6) [KIRIATH JEARIM]
Jos 15: 9 of Mount Ephron and went down toward **B** 1267
15:10 it curved westward from **B** to Mount Seir, 1267
15:11 along to Mount **B** and reached Jabneel. 1267
15:29 **B**, Iim, Ezem, 1267
2Sa 6: 2 He and all his men set out from **B** *of* Judah 1267
1Ch 13: 6 to **B** of Judah (Kiriath Jearim) to bring up 1267

BAALATH (4) [BAALATH BEER]
Jos 19:44 Eltekeh, Gibbethon, **B**, 1272
1Ki 9:18 **B**, and Tadmor in the desert, 1272
1Ch 4:33 the villages around these towns as far as **B**. 1272
2Ch 8: 6 as well as **B** and all his store cities, and all 1272

BAALATH BEER (1) [BAALATH]
Jos 19: 8 as far as **B** (Ramah in the Negev). 1273

BAALI (KJV) See MY MASTER

BAALIM (KJV) See BAALS

BAALIS (1)
Jer 40:14 "Don't you know that **B** king of 1271

BAALS (18) [BAAL]
Jdg 2:11 in the eyes of the LORD and served the **B**. 1251
3: 7 the LORD their God and served the **B** and 1251
8:33 prostituted themselves to the **B**. 1251
10: 6 They served the **B** and the Ashtoreths, 1251
10:10 forsaking our God and serving the **B**." 1251
1Sa 7: 4 Israelites put away their **B** and Ashtoreths, 1251
12:10 and served the **B** and the Ashtoreths. 1251
1Ki 18:18 and have followed the **B**. 1251
2Ch 17: 3 He did not consult the **B** 1251
24: 7 even its sacred objects for the **B**. 1251
28: 2 also made cast idols for worshiping the **B**. 1251
33: 3 to the **B** and made Asherah poles. 1251
34: 4 the altars of the **B** were torn down; 1251
Jer 2:23 I have not run after the **B'**? 1251
9:14 they have followed the **B**, 1251
Hos 2:13 for the days she burned incense to the **B**; 1251
2:17 the names of the **B** from her lips; 1251
11: 2 to the **B** and they burned incense to images. 1251

BAANA (3)
1Ki 4:12 **B** son of Ahilud— 1275
4:16 **B** son of Hushai—in Asher and in Aloth; 1275
Ne 3: 4 to him Zadok son of **B** also made repairs. 1275

BAANAH (9)
2Sa 4: 2 One was named **B** and the other Recab; 1276
4: 5 Now Recab and **B**, 1276
4: 6 Recab and his brother **B** slipped away. 1276
4: 9 David answered Recab and his brother **B**, 1276
23:29 Heled son of **B** the Netophathite, 1276
1Ch 11:30 Heled son of **B** the Netophathite, 1276
Ezr 2: 2 Bilshan, Mispar, Bigvai, Rehum and **B**): 1276
Ne 7: 7 Mispereth, Bigvai, Nehum and **B**): 1276
10:27 Malluch, Harim and **B**. 1276

BAARA (1)
1Ch 8: 8 after he had divorced his wives Hushim and **B**. 1281

BAASEIAH (1)
1Ch 6:40 the son of **B**, the son of Malkijah, 1283

BAASHA (25) [BAASHA'S]
1Ki 15:16 There was war between Asa and **B** king 1284
15:17 **B** king of Israel went up against Judah 1284
15:19 Now break your treaty with **B** king of Israel 1284
15:21 When **B** heard this, 1284
15:22 and timber **B** had been using there. 1284
15:27 **B** son of Ahijah of the house 1284
15:28 **B** killed Nadab in the third year 1284
15:32 There was war between Asa and **B** king 1284
15:33 **B** son of Ahijah became king of all Israel 1284
16: 1 to Jehu son of Hanani against **B**: 1284
16: 3 So I am about to consume **B** and his house, 1284
16: 4 Dogs will eat those belonging to **B** who die 1284
16: 6 **B** rested with his fathers and was buried 1284
16: 7 of Hanani to **B** and his house, because 1284
16: 8 Elah son of **B** became king of Israel, 1284
16:12 So Zimri destroyed the whole family of **B**, 1284
16:12 the word of the LORD spoken against **B** 1284
16:13 the sins **B** and his son Elah had committed 1284
21:22 of Jeroboam son of Nebat and that of **B** son 1284
2Ki 9: 9 and like the house of **B** son of Ahijah. 1284
2Ch 16: 1 the thirty-sixth year of Asa's reign **B** king 1284
16: 3 Now break your treaty with **B** king of Israel 1284
16: 5 When **B** heard this, 1284
16: 6 the stones and timber **B** had been using. 1284
Jer 41: 9 of his defense against **B** king of Israel. 1284

BAASHA'S (2) [BAASHA]
1Ki 16: 5 As for the other events of **B** reign, 1284
16:11 he killed off **B** whole family. 1284

BABBLER (1) [BABBLING]
Ac 17:18 "What is this **b** trying to say?" *5066*

BABBLING (1) [BABBLER]
Mt 6: 7 you pray, *do* not *keep on* **b** like pagans, *1006*

BABBLINGS (KJV) See CHATTER

BABE, BABES (KJV) See CHILDREN

BABEL (1) [BABYLON]
Ge 11: 9 That is why it was called **B**— 951

BABIES (5) [BABY]
Ge 25:22 The **b** jostled each other within her, 1201
Ex 2: 6 "This is one of the Hebrew **b**," she said. 3529
Lk 18:15 People were also bringing **b** to Jesus *1100*
Ac 7:19 to throw out their **newborn b** so *1100*
1Pe 2: 2 Like newborn **b**, crave pure spiritual milk, *1100*

BABOONS (2)
1Ki 10:22 silver and ivory, and apes and **b**. 9415
2Ch 9:21 silver and ivory, and apes and **b**. 9415

BABY (16) [BABIES, BABY'S]
Ex 2: 6 She opened it and saw the **b**. 3529
2: 7 the Hebrew women to nurse the **b** for you?" 3529
2: 9 "Take this **b** and nurse him for me, 3529
2: 9 So the woman took the **b** and nursed him. 3529
1Ki 3:17 ***I* had a b** while she was there with me. 3528
3:18 this woman also **had a b**. 3528
3:26 "Please, my lord, give her the living **b**! 3528
3:27 "Give the living **b** to the first woman. 3528
Isa 49:15 the **b at** her **breast** and have no compassion 6403
Lk 1:41 the **b** leaped in her womb, *1100*
1:44 the **b** in my womb leaped for joy. *1100*
1:57 for Elizabeth *to* **have** *her* **b**, *5503*
2: 6 the time came for the **b to be born**, *5503*
2:12 You will find a **b** wrapped in cloths *1100*
2:16 and the **b**, who was lying in the manger. *1100*
Jn 16:21 when her **b** is born she forgets the anguish *4086*

BABY'S (1) [BABY]
Ex 2: 8 And the girl went and got the **b** mother. 3529

BABYLON (281) [BABEL, BABYLON'S, BABYLONIA, BABYLONIAN, BABYLONIANS, BABYLONIANS']
Ge 10:10 The first centers of his kingdom were **B**, 951
2Ki 17:24 of Assyria brought people from **B**, 951
17:30 The men from **B** made Succoth Benoth, 951
20:12 of Baladan king of **B** sent Hezekiah letters 951
20:14 "They came from **B**." 951
20:17 will be carried off to **B**. 951
20:18 in the palace of the king of **B**." 951
24: 1 Nebuchadnezzar king of **B** invaded 951
24: 7 the king of **B** had taken all his territory, 951
24:10 of **B** advanced on Jerusalem and laid siege 951
24:12 of the reign of the king of **B**, 951
24:15 Nebuchadnezzar took Jehoiachin captive to **B**. 951
24:15 from Jerusalem to **B** the king's mother, 951
24:16 The king of **B** also deported to Babylon 951
24:16 The king of Babylon also deported to **B** 951
24:20 Zedekiah rebelled against the king of **B**. 951
25: 1 Nebuchadnezzar king of **B** marched 951
25: 6 He was taken to the king of **B** at Riblah, 951
25: 7 with bronze shackles and took him to **B**. 951
25: 8 of Nebuchadnezzar king of **B**, 951
25: 8 an official of the king of **B**, 951
25:11 over to the king of **B**. 951
25:13 and they carried the bronze to **B**. 951
25:20 and brought them to the king of **B** 951
25:22 of **B** appointed Gedaliah son of Ahikam, 951
25:23 that the king of **B** had appointed Gedaliah 951
25:24 down in the land and serve the king of **B**, 951
25:27 the year Evil-Merodach became king of **B**, 951
25:28 of the other kings who were with him in **B**. 951
1Ch 9: 1 of Judah were taken captive to **B** because 951
2Ch 32:31 of **B** to ask him about the miraculous sign 951
33:11 with bronze shackles and took him to **B**. 951
36: 6 Nebuchadnezzar king of **B** attacked him 951
36: 6 with bronze shackles to take him to **B**. 951
36: 7 to **B** articles from the temple of the LORD 951
36:10 for him and brought him to **B**, 951
36:18 to **B** all the articles from the temple of God, 951
36:20 He carried into exile to **B** the remnant, 951
Ezr 1:11 the exiles came up from **B** to Jerusalem. 951
2: 1 of **B** had taken captive 951
2: 1 to **B** (they returned to Jerusalem and Judah, 951
4: 9 Persia, Erech and **B**, the Elamites of Susa, 10094
5:12 king of **B**, who destroyed this temple 10093
5:12 and deported the people to **B**. 10093
5:13 in the first year of Cyrus king of **B**, 10093
5:14 the temple of **B** the gold and silver articles 10093

Ezr 5:14 and brought to the temple in **B**. 10093
5:17 a search be made in the royal archives of **B** 10093
6: 1 in the archives stored in the treasury at **B**. 10093
6: 5 the temple in Jerusalem and brought to **B**, 10093
7: 6 this Ezra came up from **B**. 951
7: 9 from **B** on the first day of the first month, 951
7:16 from the province of **B**, 10093
8: 1 with them who came up with me from **B** 951
Ne 7: 6 of **B** had taken captive (they returned 951
13: 6 of Artaxerxes king of **B** I had returned to 951
Est 2: 6 by Nebuchadnezzar king of **B**, 951
Ps 87: 4 "I will record Rahab and **B** 951
137: 1 By the rivers of **B** we sat and wept 951
137: 8 O Daughter of **B**, doomed to destruction, 951
Isa 13: 1 concerning **B** that Isaiah son of Amoz saw: 951
13:19 **B**, the jewel of kingdoms, 951
14: 4 up this taunt against the king of **B**: 951
14:22 from **B** her name and survivors, 951
21: 9 '**B** has fallen, has fallen! 951
39: 1 of Baladan king of **B** sent Hezekiah letters 951
39: 3 "They came to me from **B**." 951
39: 6 will be carried off to **B**. 951
39: 7 in the palace of the king of **B**." 951
43:14 "For your sake I will send to **B** and bring 951
47: 1 sit in the dust, Virgin Daughter of **B**; 951
48:14 The LORD's chosen ally will carry out his purpose against **B**; 951
48:20 Leave **B**, flee from the Babylonians! 951
Jer 20: 4 I will hand all Judah over to the king of **B**, 951
20: 4 who will carry them away to **B** or put them 951
20: 5 as plunder and carry it off to **B**. 951
20: 6 in your house will go into exile to **B**. 951
21: 2 of **B** is attacking us. 951
21: 4 which you are using to fight the king of **B** 951
21: 7 to Nebuchadnezzar king of **B** and 951
21:10 be given into the hands of the king of **B**, 951
22:25 to Nebuchadnezzar king of **B** and to 951
24: 1 to **B** by Nebuchadnezzar king of Babylon, 951
24: 1 to Babylon by Nebuchadnezzar king of **B**, 951
25: 1 the first year of Nebuchadnezzar king of **B**. 951
25: 9 and my servant Nebuchadnezzar king of **B**," 951
25:11 the king of **B** seventy years. 951
25:12 I will punish the king of **B** and his nation, 951
27: 6 to my servant Nebuchadnezzar king of **B**; 951
27: 8 not serve Nebuchadnezzar king of **B** 951
27: 9 'You will not serve the king of **B**.' 951
27:11 the yoke of the king of **B** and serve him, 951
27:12 under the yoke of the king of **B**; 951
27:13 that will not serve the king of **B**? 951
27:14 'You will not serve the king of **B**,' 951
27:16 be brought back from **B**.' 951
27:17 Serve the king of **B**, and you will live. 951
27:18 and in Jerusalem not be taken to **B**. 951
27:20 which Nebuchadnezzar king of **B** did 951
27:20 of Judah into exile from Jerusalem to **B**, 951
27:22 be taken to **B** and there they will remain 951
28: 2 'I will break the yoke of the king of **B**. 951
28: 3 that Nebuchadnezzar king of **B** removed 951
28: 3 from here and took to **B**. 951
28: 4 from Judah who went to **B**,' 951
28: 4 'for I will break the yoke of the king of **B**.' 951
28: 6 and all the exiles back to this place from **B**. 951
28:11 the yoke of Nebuchadnezzar king of **B** off 951
28:14 to make them serve Nebuchadnezzar king of **B**, 951
29: 1 into exile from Jerusalem to **B**. 951
29: 3 to King Nebuchadnezzar in **B**. 951
29: 4 into exile from Jerusalem to **B**: 951
29:10 "When seventy years are completed for **B**, 951
29:15 LORD has raised up prophets for us in **B**," 951
29:20 from Jerusalem to **B**. 951
29:21 over to Nebuchadnezzar king of **B**, 951
29:22 in **B** will use this curse: 951
29:22 whom the king of **B** burned in the fire.' 951
29:28 He has sent this message to us in **B**: 951
32: 2 of **B** was then besieging Jerusalem, 951
32: 3 to hand this city over to the king of **B**, 951
32: 4 be handed over to the king of **B**, 951
32: 5 He will take Zedekiah to **B**, 951
32:28 and to Nebuchadnezzar king of **B**, 951
32:36 be handed over to the king of **B**'; 951
34: 1 of **B** and all his army and all the kingdoms 951
34: 2 to hand this city over to the king of **B**, 951
34: 3 the king of **B** with your own eyes. 951
34: 3 And you will go to **B**. 951
34: 7 of **B** was fighting against Jerusalem and 951
34:21 to the army of the king of **B**, 951
35:11 of **B** invaded this land, 951
36:29 that the king of **B** would certainly come 951
37: 1 of Judah by Nebuchadnezzar king of **B**; 951
37:17 "you will be handed over to the king of **B**." 951
37:19 of **B** will not attack you or this land'? 951
38: 3 over to the army of the king of **B**, 951
38:17 the officers of the king of **B**, your life will 951
38:18 the king of **B**, this city will be handed over 951
38:22 to the officials of the king of **B**. 951
38:23 but will be captured by the king of **B**; 951
39: 1 Nebuchadnezzar king of **B** marched 951
39: 3 Then all the officials of the king of **B** came 951
39: 3 and all the other officials of the king of **B**. 951
39: 5 and took him to Nebuchadnezzar king of **B** 951
39: 6 at Riblah the king of **B** slaughtered the sons 951
39: 7 with bronze shackles to take him to **B**. 951
39: 9 of the imperial guard carried into exile to **B** 951
39:11 of **B** had given these orders about Jeremiah 951
39:13 and all the other officers of the king of **B** 951
40: 1 who were being carried into exile to **B**. 951
Jer 40: 4 Come with me to **B**, if you like, 951
40: 5 the king of **B** has appointed over the towns 951
40: 7 the king of **B** had appointed Gedaliah son 951
40: 7 not been carried into exile to **B**, 951
40: 9 down in the land and serve the king of **B**, 951
40:11 the king of **B** had left a remnant in Judah 951
41: 2 the one whom the king of **B** had appointed 951
41:18 the king of **B** had appointed as governor 951
42:11 Do not be afraid of the king of **B**, 951
43: 3 they may kill us or carry us into exile to **B**." 951
43:10 for my servant Nebuchadnezzar king of **B**, 951
44:30 over to Nebuchadnezzar king of **B**, 951
46: 2 of **B** in the fourth year of Jehoiakim son 951
46:13 the coming of Nebuchadnezzar king of **B** 951
46:26 to Nebuchadnezzar king of **B** 951
49:28 which Nebuchadnezzar king of **B** attacked: 951
49:30 "Nebuchadnezzar king of **B** has plotted 951
50: 1 through Jeremiah the prophet concerning **B** 951
50: 2 but say, '**B** will be captured; 951
50: 8 "Flee out of **B**; 951
50: 9 against **B** an alliance of great nations from 951
50:13 All who pass **B** will be horrified and scoff 951
50:14 "Take up your positions around **B**, 951
50:16 Cut off from **B** the sower, 951
50:17 the last to crush his bones was Nebuchadnezzar king of **B**." 951
50:18 "I will punish the king of **B** and his land 951
50:23 How desolate is **B** among the nations! 951
50:24 I set a trap for you, O **B**, 951
50:28 fugitives and refugees from **B** declaring 824+951
50:29 "Summon archers against **B**, 951
50:34 but unrest to those who live in **B**. 951
50:35 "against those who live in **B** and 951
50:42 to attack you, O Daughter of **B**. 951
50:43 king of **B** has heard reports about them, 951
50:44 I will chase **B** from its land in an instant. 4392S
50:45 against **B**, what he has purposed against 951
51: 1 up the spirit of a destroyer against **B** and 951
51: 2 I will send foreigners to **B** to winnow her 951
51: 4 They will fall down slain in **B**, 824+4169
51: 6 "Flee from **B**! 951
51: 7 **B** was a gold cup in the LORD's hand; 951
51: 8 **B** will suddenly fall and be broken. 951
51: 9 " 'We would have healed **B**, 951
51:11 because his purpose is to destroy **B**. 951
51:12 Lift up a banner against the walls of **B**! 951
51:12 his decree against the people of **B**. 951
51:24 "Before your eyes I will repay **B** 951
51:29 the LORD's purposes against **B** stand— 951
51:29 the land of **B** so that no one will live there. 951
51:31 of **B** that his entire city is captured, 951
51:33 "The Daughter of **B** is like a threshing floor 951
51:34 of **B** has devoured us, 951
51:35 the violence done to our flesh be upon **B**," 951
51:37 **B** will be a heap of ruins, 951
51:41 What a horror **B** will be among the nations! 951
51:42 The sea will rise over **B**; 951
51:44 I will punish Bel in **B** 951
51:44 And the wall of **B** will fall. 951
51:47 when I will punish the idols of **B**; 951
51:48 that is in them will shout for joy over **B**, 951
51:49 "**B** must fall because of Israel's slain, 951
51:49 in all the earth have fallen because of **B**. 951
51:53 Even if **B** reaches the sky 951
51:54 "The sound of a cry comes from **B**, 951
51:55 The LORD will destroy **B**; 951
51:56 A destroyer will come against **B**; 951
51:59 when he went to **B** with Zedekiah king 951
51:60 the disasters that would come upon **B**— 951
51:60 all that had been recorded concerning **B**. 951
51:61 He said to Seraiah, "When you get to **B**, 951
51:64 'So will **B** sink to rise no more because of 951
52: 3 Zedekiah rebelled against the king of **B**. 951
52: 4 Nebuchadnezzar king of **B** marched 951
52: 9 He was taken to the king of **B** at Riblah in 951
52:10 at Riblah the king of **B** slaughtered the sons 951
52:11 with bronze shackles and took him to **B**, 951
52:12 of Nebuchadnezzar king of **B**, 951
52:12 who served the king of **B**, 951
52:15 over to the king of **B**. 951
52:17 and they carried all the bronze to **B**. 951
52:26 and brought them to the king of **B** 951
52:31 the year Evil-Merodach became king of **B**, 951
52:32 of the other kings who were with him in **B**. 951
52:34 Day by day the king of **B** gave Jehoiachin 951
Eze 17:12 'The king of **B** went to Jerusalem 951
17:12 bringing them back with him to **B**. 951
17:16 he shall die in **B**, 951
17:20 I will bring him to **B** and execute judgment 951
19: 9 a cage and brought him to the king of **B**. 951
21:19 for the sword of the king of **B** to take, 951
21:21 king of **B** will stop at the fork in the road, 951
24: 2 because the king of **B** has laid siege 951
26: 7 against Tyre Nebuchadnezzar king of **B**, 951
29:18 Nebuchadnezzar king of **B** drove his army 951
29:19 to Nebuchadnezzar king of **B**, 951
30:10 by the hand of Nebuchadnezzar king of **B**. 951
30:24 the arms of the king of **B** and put my sword 951
30:25 I will strengthen the arms of the king of **B**, 951
30:25 of **B** and he brandishes it against Egypt. 951
32:11 " 'The sword of the king of **B** will come 951
Da 1: 1 of **B** came to Jerusalem and besieged it. 951
2:12 the execution of all the wise men of **B**. 10093
2:14 to put to death the wise men of **B**, 10093
2:18 with the rest of the wise men of **B**. 10093
2:24 to execute the wise men of **B**, 10093
2:24 "Do not execute the wise men of **B**. 10093
Da 2:48 the entire province of **B** and placed him 10093
2:49 over the province of **B**, 10093
3: 1 on the plain of Dura in the province of **B**. 10093
3:12 over the affairs of the province of **B**— 10093
3:30 and Abednego in the province of **B**. 10093
4: 6 So I commanded that all the wise men of **B** 10093
4:29 on the roof of the royal palace of **B**, 10093
4:30 "Is not this the great **B** I have built as 10093
5: 7 and said to these wise men of **B**, 10093
7: 1 In the first year of Belshazzar king of **B**, 10093
Mic 4:10 You will go to **B**; 951
Zec 2: 7 Escape, you who live in the Daughter of **B**!" 951
6:10 who have arrived from **B**. 951
Mt 1:11 at the time of the exile *to* **B**. *956*
1:12 After the exile *to* **B**: *956*
1:17 fourteen from David to the exile *to* **B**, *956*
Ac 7:43 into exile' beyond **B**. *956*
1Pe 5:13 She who is in **B**, chosen together with you, *956*
Rev 14: 8 Fallen is **B** the Great, *956*
16:19 God remembered **B** the Great and gave her *956*
17: 5 **B** THE GREAT THE MOTHER OF PROSTITUTES AND OF THE ABOMINATIONS OF THE EARTH. *956*
18: 2 Fallen is **B** the Great! *956*
18:10 Woe, O great city, O **B**, city of power! *956*
18:21 "With such violence the great city of **B** will *956*

BABYLON'S (3) [BABYLON]

Jer 50:46 of **B** capture the earth will tremble; 951
51:30 **B** warriors have stopped fighting; 951
51:58 "**B** thick wall will be leveled 951

BABYLONIA (10) [BABYLON]

Jos 7:21 in the plunder a beautiful robe from **B**, 9114
Isa 11:11 from Cush, from Elam, from **B**, 9114
Jer 50:10 So **B** will be plundered; 4169
51:24 in **B** for all the wrong they have done 4169
51:35 "May our blood be on those who live in **B**," 4169
Eze 11:24 to the exiles in **B** in the vision given by 4169
12:13 I will bring him to **B**, 951
16:29 to include **B**, a land of merchants, but even 4169
Da 1: 2 to the temple of his god in **B** and put in 824+9114
Zec 5:11 "To the country of **B** to build a house for it. 9114

BABYLONIAN (13) [BABYLON]

2Ki 24: 2 The LORD sent **B**, Aramean, 4169
25: 5 but the **B** army pursued the king 4169
25:10 The whole **B** army, 4169
25:24 "Do not be afraid of the **B** officials," 4169
Jer 35:11 we must go to Jerusalem to escape the **B** 4169
37:10 if you were to defeat the entire **B** army 4169
37:11 the **B** army had withdrawn from Jerusalem 4169
39: 5 But the **B** army pursued them 4169
41: 3 as well as the **B** soldiers who were there. 4169
52: 8 but the **B** army pursued King Zedekiah 4169
52:14 The whole **B** army under the commander of 4169
Eze 23:15 of them looked like **B** chariot officers, 951+1201
Da 9: 1 who was made ruler over the **B** kingdom— 4169

BABYLONIANS (53) [BABYLON]

2Ki 25: 4 though the **B** were surrounding the city. 4169
25:13 The **B** broke up the bronze pillars, 4169
25:25 also the men of Judah and the **B** who were 4169
25:26 fled to Egypt for fear of the **B**. 4169
2Ch 36:17 up against them the king of the **B**, 4169
Isa 23:13 Look at the land of the **B**, 4169
43:14 and bring down as fugitives all the **B**, 4169
47: 1 without a throne, Daughter of the **B**. 4169
47: 5 go into darkness, Daughter of the **B**; 4169
48:14 his arm will be against the **B**. 4169
48:20 Leave Babylon, flee from the **B**! 4169
Jer 21: 4 of Babylon and the **B** who are outside 4169
21: 9 to the **B** who are besieging you will live; 4169
22:25 of Babylon and to the **B**. 4169
24: 5 from this place to the land of the **B**. 4169
25:12 the land of the **B**, for their guilt," 4169
32: 4 of the **B** but will certainly be handed over 4169
32: 5 If you fight against the **B**, 4169
32:24 over to the **B** who are attacking it. 4169
32:25 the city will be handed over to the **B**, 4169
32:28 over to the **B** and to Nebuchadnezzar king 4169
32:29 The **B** who are attacking this city will come 4169
32:43 for it has been handed over to the **B**.' 4169
33: 5 in the fight with the **B**: 4169
37: 5 the **B** who were besieging Jerusalem heard 4169
37: 8 Then the **B** will return and attack this city; 4169
37: 9 thinking, 'The **B** will surely leave us.' 4169
37:13 "You are deserting to the **B**!" 4169
37:14 "I am not deserting to the **B**." 4169
38: 2 but whoever goes over to the **B** will live. 4169
38:18 over to the **B** and they will burn it down; 4169
38:19 of the Jews who have gone over to the **B**, 4169
38:19 for the **B** may hand me over to them NIH
38:23 and children will be brought out to the **B**. 4169
39: 8 The **B** set fire to the royal palace and 4169
40: 9 "Do not be afraid to serve the **B**," he said. 4169
40:10 to represent you before the **B** who come 4169
41:18 to escape the **B**. 4169
43: 3 against us to hand us over to the **B**, 4169
50: 1 concerning Babylon and the land of the **B**: 4169
50: 8 leave the land of the **B**, 4169
50:25 to do in the land of the **B**. 4169
50:35 "A sword against the **B**!" 4169
50:45 against the land of the **B**: 4169
51:54 of great destruction from the land of the **B**. 4169

Jer 52: 7 though the **B** were surrounding the city. 4169
52:17 The **B** broke up the bronze pillars, 4169
Eze 1: 3 by the Kebar River in the land of the **B.** 4169
23:17 the **B** came to her, to the bed of love, 951+1201
23:23 the **B** and all the Chaldeans, 951+1201
Da 1: 4 the language and literature of the **B.** 4169
5:30 That very night Belshazzar, king of the **B,** 10373
Hab 1: 6 I am raising up the **B,** 4169

BABYLONIANS' (1) [BABYLON]

Isa 13:19 the glory of the **B'** pride, 4169

BABYLONISH (KJV) See BABYLONIA

BACA (1)

Ps 84: 6 As they pass through the Valley of **B,** 1133

BACHRITES (KJV) See BEKER

BACK (619) [BACKBONE, BACKGROUND, BACKS, BACKSLIDING, BACKSLIDINGS, BACKWARD]

Ge 3:24 and a flaming sword **flashing b and forth** 2200
8: 7 and it kept flying **b** and forth until 8740
8: 9 the dove and **brought** it **b** to himself in 995
14: 7 Then *they* **turned b** and went to En Mishpat 8740
14:16 the goods and **brought b** his relative Lot 8740
15:16 fourth generation your descendants *will* **come b** here, 8740
16: 9 **"Go b** to your mistress and submit to her." 8740
19:10 and **pulled** Lot **b** into the house and shut 995
19:17 Don't look **b,** and don't stop anywhere in 339
19:26 But Lot's wife looked **b,** 339+4946
22: 5 We will worship and then *we will* **come b** 8740
24: 5 "What if the woman is unwilling to come **b** 339
24: 5 *Shall I then* **take** your son **b** to 8740+8740
24: 6 that *you do* not **take** my son **b** there," 8740
24: 8 If the woman is unwilling to come **b** 339
24: 8 Only *do* not **take** my son **b** there." 8740
24:20 ran **b** to the well to draw more water, 6388
24:39 if the woman will not come **b** *with* me?' 339
24:61 and mounted their camels and went **b** *with* 339
27: 5 to hunt game and **bring** it **b,** 995
27:45 I'll send word for you *to* **come b** from there. 4374
28:15 and *I will* **bring** you **b** to this land. 8740
29: 7 the sheep and **take** them **b** *to* pasture." 2143
30:25 so *I can* **go b** to my own homeland. 2143
31: 3 **"Go b** to the land of your fathers and 8740
31:13 at once and **go b** to your native land.' " 8740
32: 9 **'Go b** to your country and your relatives, 8740
33:16 **started** on his way **b** 8740
37:14 and **bring** word **b** *to* me." 8740
37:22 to rescue him from them and **take** him **b** 8740
37:30 *He* **went b** to his brothers and said, 8740
37:32 **took** the ornamented robe **b** 995+2256+8938
38:20 the Adullamite in order to **get** his pledge **b** 4374
38:22 So *he* **went b** to Judah and said, 8740
38:29 But when *he* **drew b** his hand, 8740
42:19 while the rest of you go and **take** grain **b** 995
42:24 but then **turned b** and spoke to them again. 8740
42:25 **put** each man's silver **b** 8740
42:34 Then *I will* **give** your brother **b** to you, 5989
42:37 of my sons to death if *I do* not **bring** him **b** 995
42:37 and I *will* **bring** him **b."** 8740
43: 2 **"Go b** and buy us a little more food." 8740
43: 9 not **bring** him **b** to you and set him here 995
43:12 the silver that *was* **put b** into the mouths 8740
43:13 Take your brother also and **go b** to the man 8740
43:14 and Benjamin **come b** with you. 8938
43:18 that *was* **put b** into our sacks the first time. 8740
43:21 So *we have* **brought** it **b** with us. 8740
44: 8 *We* even **brought b** to you from the land 8740
44:17 **go b** to your father in peace." 6590
44:24 When *we* **went b** to your servant my father, 6590
44:25 **'Go b** and buy a little more food.' 8740
44:30 when I **go b** to your servant my father and 995
44:32 I said, 'If *I do* not **bring** him **b** to you, 995
44:34 How *can I* **go b** to my father if the boy is 6590
45: 9 Now hurry **b** to my father and say to him, 6590
45:18 bring your father and your families **b** to me. 995
45:27 the carts Joseph had sent to **carry** him **b,** 5951
46: 4 and I *will* **surely bring** you **b** again. 6590+6590
48:21 but God will be with you and **take** you **b** to 8740
50:15 grudge against us and **pays** us **b** *for* all 8740+8740
Ex 4: 4 of the snake and *it* **turned** *b* **into** a staff AIT
4: 7 "Now **put** it **b** into your cloak," he said. 8740
4: 7 So Moses **put** his hand **b** into his cloak, 8740
4:18 Then Moses went **b** 8740
4:18 "Let me go **b** to my own people in Egypt 8740
4:19 "Go **b** *to* Egypt, 8740
4:20 on a donkey and **started b** to Egypt. 8740
5: 4 **Get b** to your work!" 2143
9: 2 and continue *to* **hold** them **b,** 2616
9:24 hail fell and lightning **flashed b and forth.** 928+4374+9348
10: 8 Then Moses and Aaron **were brought b** 8740
14: 2 "Tell the Israelites *to* **turn b** and encamp 8740
14:21 that night the LORD **drove** the sea **b** with 2143
14:26 the sea so that the waters *may* **flow b** over 8740
14:27 and at daybreak the sea **went b** to its place. 8740
14:28 The water **flowed b** and covered 8740
15:19 **brought** the waters of the sea **b** 8740
19: 7 So Moses **went b** and summoned the elders 995
Ex 19: 8 Moses **brought** their answer **b** 8740
22: 1 *he must* **pay b** five head of cattle for the ox 8966
22: 4 *he must* **pay b** double. 8966
22: 7 if he is caught, *must* **pay b** double. 8966
22: 9 judges declare guilty *must* **pay b** double 8966
22:29 not **hold b** offerings from your granaries 336
23: 4 **be sure to take** it **b** 8740+8740
24:14 "Wait here for us until *we* **come b** to you. 8740
32:15 on both sides, front and **b.** 2296[S]
32:27 **Go b** and forth through the camp 8740
32:31 So Moses **went b** to the LORD and said, 8740
33:23 and you will see my **b;** 294
34:31 leaders of the community **came b** to him, 8740
34:35 Then Moses *would* **put** the veil **b** 8740
Lev 19:13 **hold b** the wages of a hired man **overnight.** 1332+4328+6330
25:27 *he can* then **go b** to his own property. 8740
25:28 and *he can* then **go b** to his property. 8740
25:41 and *he will* **go b** to his own clan and to 8740
27:27 *he may* **buy** it **b** at its set value, 7009
Nu 10:30 *I am* **going b** to my own land 2143
12:14 after that *she can* **be brought b."** 665
12:15 not move on till she *was* **brought b.** 665
13:20 Do your best *to* **bring b** some of the fruit of 4374
13:26 *They* **came b** to Moses and Aaron and the whole Israelite community 995+2143+2256
14: 3 Wouldn't it be better for us *to* **go b** 8740
14: 4 "We should choose a leader and **go b** 8740
14:25 **turn b** tomorrow and set out toward 7155
16:26 **"Move b** from the tents 6073
17:10 **"Put b** Aaron's staff in front of 8740
22: 8 "and *I will* **bring** you **b** the answer 8740
22:13 **"Go b** to your own country, 2143
22:23 Balaam beat her to **get** her **b on** the road. 5742
22:34 Now if you are displeased, *I will* **go b."** 8740
23: 5 **"Go b** to Balak and give him this message." 8740
23: 6 So *he* **went b** to him and found him 8740
23:16 **"Go b** to Balak and give him this message." 8740
24:14 Now I *am* **going b** to my people, but come, 2143
33: 7 They left Etham, **turned b** to Pi Hahiroth, 8740
35:25 and **send** him **b** to the city of refuge 8740
35:32 a city of refuge and so *allow* him *to* **go b** 8740
Dt 1:22 ahead to spy out the land for us and **bring b** 8740
1:45 *You* **came b** and wept before the LORD, 8740
2: 1 Then *we* **turned b** and set out toward 7155
3:20 each of you *may* **go b** to 8740
10: 5 Then *I* **came b** down the mountain and put 7155
17:16 *"You are* not to **go b** that way again." 8740
19:12 **bring** him **b** from the city, 4374
22: 1 **be sure to take** it **b** 8740+8740
22: 2 Then **give** it **b** to him. 8740
24:19 *do* not **go b** to get it. 8740
28:68 The LORD *will* **send** you **b** in ships 8740
30: 4 and **bring** you **b.** 4374
Jos 1:15 *you may* **go b** and occupy your own land, 8740
2:23 Then the two men **started b.** 8740
8:15 **let themselves be driven b** 5595
8:20 men of Ai looked **b** and saw the smoke 339+7155
8:20 toward the desert *had* **turned b** 2200
8:26 not **draw b** the hand that held out his javelin 8740
11:10 At that time Joshua **turned b** 8740
14: 7 And *I* **brought** him **b** a report according 8740
19:29 The boundary then **turned b** *toward* Ramah 8740
20: 6 Then he *may* **go b** to his own home in 8740
Jdg 1: 7 God *has* **paid** me **b** *for* what I did to them." 8966
3:19 At the idols near Gilgal *he* himself **turned b** 8740
3:22 which came out his **b.** 7307
6:18 Please do not go away until I **come b** 995
7: 3 'Anyone who trembles with fear *may* **turn b** 8740
8:29 Jerub-Baal son of Joash **went b** home 2143
11: 9 "Suppose you **take** me **b** to fight 8740
11:13 Now **give** it **b** peaceably." 8740
11:14 Jephthah sent **b** messengers to 3578+6388
14: 8 when *he* **went b** to marry her, 8740
16:18 **"Come b** once more; 6590
16:31 *They* **brought** him **b** and buried him 6590
17: 3 *I will* **give** it **b** to you." 8740
18:26 turned around and **went b** home. 8740
19: 2 and went **b** to her father's house NIH
19:26 At daybreak the woman **went b** *to* 995
20:48 of Israel **went b** to Benjamin and put all 8740
Ru 1: 7 that *would* **take** them **b** to the land of Judah. 8740
1: 8 "Go **b,** each of you, to your mother's home. 8740
1:10 *"We will* **go b** with you to your people." 8740
1:15 "your sister-in-law *is* **going b** to her people 8740
1:15 **Go b** with her." 8740
1:16 "Don't urge me to leave you or to **turn b** 8740
1:21 but the LORD *has* **brought** me **b** empty. 8740
2: 4 *they* **called b.** 606
2: 6 the Moabitess who **came b** from Moab 8740
2:18 She carried it **b** *to* town, 995
3:15 Then *he* **went b** *to* town. 995
3:17 of barley, saying, 'Don't **go b** 995
4: 3 "Naomi, who *has* **come b** from Moab, 8740
1Sa 1:19 the LORD and then went **b** to their home 8740
3: 5 Eli said, "I did not call; **go b** and lie down." 8740
3: 6 **go b** and lie down." 8740
4: 4 they brought **b** the ark of the covenant 4946+9004
5: 3 They took Dagon and **put** him **b** 8740
5:11 *let* it **go b** to its own place, 8740
6: 2 how *we should* **send** it **b** to its place." 8938
6: 8 the gold objects *you are* **sending b** to him as 8740
7:17 But he always **went b** to Ramah, 9588
8:22 "Everyone **go b** to his town." 2143
9: 5 *let's* **go b,** or my father will stop thinking 8740
13: 2 of the men *he* **sent b** to their homes. 8938
15:20 and **brought b** Agag their king. 995
1Sa 15:25 forgive my sin and **come b** with me, 8740
15:26 *"I will* not **go b** with you. 8740
15:30 **come b** with me, 8740
15:31 So Samuel **went b** with Saul, 8740
17: 6 a bronze javelin was **slung on** his **b.** 1068+4190
17:15 but David went **b** and forth from Saul 8740
17:18 and **bring b** some assurance from them. 4374
19:15 Then Saul **sent** the men **b** to see David 8938
20:40 "Go, **carry** them **b** *to* town." 995
20:42 and Jonathan **went b** *to* the town. 995
23:23 and **come b** to me with definite information. 8740
24: 3 David and his men were **far b in** the cave. 928+3752
25:12 David's men turned around and **went b.** 8740
25:21 *He has* **paid** me **b** evil for good. 8740
26:21 **Come b,** David my son. 8740
29: 4 **"Send** the man **b,** 8740
29: 7 **Turn b** and go in peace; 8740
29:11 up early in the morning to go **b** to the land 8740
30:19 David **brought** everything **b.** 8740
2Sa 1:22 the bow of Jonathan did not turn **b,** 294
2:23 and the spear came out through his **b.** 339
3:16 Then Abner said to him, "Go **b** home!" 8740
3:16 So *he* **went b.** 8740
3:26 *they* **brought** him **b** from the well of Sirah. 8740
10: 5 and then **come b."** 8740
11: 4 Then *she* **went b** home. 8740
11:12 and tomorrow *I will* **send** you **b."** 8938
11:23 but *we* **drove** them **b** to the entrance to 2118+6584
12:23 Can I **bring** him **b** again? 8740
14:13 king *has* not **brought b** his banished son? 8740
14:21 Go, **bring b** the young man Absalom." 8740
14:23 and **brought** Absalom **b** *to* Jerusalem. 995
15: 8 'If the LORD **takes** me **b** to Jerusalem, 8740+8740
15:19 **Go b** and stay with King Absalom. 8740
15:20 **Go b,** and take your countrymen. 8740
15:25 **"Take** the ark of God **b** 8740
15:25 *he will* **bring** me **b** and let me see it 8740
15:27 **Go b** *to* the city in peace, 8740
15:29 **took** the ark of God **b** 8740
16: 3 the house of Israel *will* **give** me **b** my grandfather's kingdom.' " 8740
17: 3 **bring** all the people **b** 8740
19:10 about **bringing** the king **b?"** 8740
19:11 be the last to **bring** the king **b** to his palace, 8740
19:12 So why should you be the last to **bring b** 8740
19:43 the first to speak of **bringing b** our king?" 8740
20:22 And Joab **went b** to the king in Jerusalem. 8740
22:38 *I did* not **turn b** till they were destroyed. 8740
23:16 near the gate of Bethlehem and carried it **b** 995
24: 8 *they* **came b** *to* Jerusalem at the end 995
1Ki 2:26 **"Go b** to your fields in Anathoth. 2143
2:40 and **brought** the slaves **b** from Gath. 995
5: 2 Solomon **sent b** this message to Hiram: 8938
7: 8 **set farther b,** was similar in design. 337+2021+2958
8:33 *they* **turn b** to you and confess your name, 8740
8:34 of your people Israel and **bring** them **b** to 8740
8:48 and if *they* **turn b** to you with all their heart 8740
9:28 to Ophir and brought **b** 420 talents of gold, 4946+9004
10:19 and its **b** had a rounded top. 339+4946
11:22 to **go b** to your own country?" 2143
12: 5 "Go away for three days and then **come b** 8740
12:12 **"Come b** to me in three days." 8740
13: 4 so that he could not **pull** it **b.** 8740
13:16 "I cannot **turn b** and go with you, 8740
13:18 **'Bring** him **b** with you to your house so 8740
13:20 to the old prophet who *had* **brought** him **b.** 8740
13:22 *You* **came b** and ate bread and drank water 8740
13:23 the prophet who *had* **brought** him **b** 8740
13:26 When the prophet who *had* **brought** him **b** 8740
13:29 and **brought** it **b** to his own city to mourn 8740
14: 9 to anger and thrust me behind your **b.** 1567
14:12 "As for you, **go b** home. 2143
18:37 that you are turning their hearts **b** again." 345
18:43 Seven times Elijah said, **"Go b."** 8740
19: 7 of the LORD **came b** a second time 8740
19:15 "Go **b** the way you came, 8740
19:20 "Go **b,"** Elijah replied. 8740
19:21 So Elisha left him and **went b.** 8740
20: 9 and **took** the answer **b** *to* Ben-Hadad. 8740
22:26 **send** him **b** to Amon the ruler of the city 8740
2Ki 1: 5 he asked them, "Why *have you* **come b?"** 8740
1: 6 'Go **b** to the king who sent you 8740
2:13 that had fallen from Elijah and **went b** 8740
4:31 Gehazi **went b** to meet Elisha and told him, 8740
4:35 Elisha turned away and walked **b and forth** 285+285+2178+2178+2256
5: 7 Can I kill and **bring b to life?** 2649
5:15 Then Naaman and all his attendants **went b** 8740
6:13 *The* **report came b:** "He is in Dothan." 5583
6:22 that they may eat and drink and then go **b** 2143
8: 3 the seven years she **came b** from the land of 8740
8: 5 the woman whose son Elisha *had* **brought b to life** came 2649
8: 6 **"Give b** everything that belonged to her, 8740
8:21 his army, however, **fled b** home. 5674
9:18 but *he* isn't **coming b."** 8740
9:20 but *he* isn't **coming b** either. 8740
9:36 *They* **went b** and told Jehu, who said, 8740
14:20 *He was* **brought b** by horse and was buried 5951
16:12 the king **came b** from Damascus and saw 995
17:27 from Samaria go **b** to live there and teach 2025+9004[S]
20: 5 **"Go b** and tell Hezekiah, the leader 8740
20: 9 or *shall it* **go b** ten steps?" 8740

2Ki 20:10 "Rather, have it go b ten steps." 345+8740
20:11 made the shadow go b 8740
22:20 So they took her answer b to the king. 8740
23:20 Then he went b to Jerusalem. 8740
1Ch 11:18 near the gate of Bethlehem and carried it b 995
11:19 they risked their lives to bring it b, 995
13: 3 bring the ark of our God b 6015
19: 5 and then come b." 8740
19:15 So Joab went b to Jerusalem. 995
21: 2 Then report b to me so that I may know 995
21: 4 and went throughout Israel and then came b 995
21:27 and he put his sword b into its sheath. 8740
2Ch 6:24 when they turn b and confess your name, 8740
6:25 of your people Israel and bring them b to 8740
6:38 and if they turn b to you with all their heart 8740
8:18 and brought b four hundred and fifty talents 4946+9004
10: 5 "Come b to me in three days." 8740
10:12 "Come b to me in three days." 8740
11: 4 of the LORD and turned b from marching 8740
15:11 from the plunder they had brought b. 995
18:25 send him b to Amon the ruler of the city 8740
19: 4 and turned them b to the LORD, 8740
24:11 the chest and carry it b to its place. 8740
24:19 to the people to bring them b to him, 8740
25:13 Amaziah had sent b and had not allowed 8740
25:14 he brought b the gods of the people of Seir. 995
25:28 He was brought b by horse and was buried 5951
28: 8 which they carried b to Samaria. 995
28:11 Send b your fellow countrymen you have 8740
28:15 So they took them b 995
30: 9 by their captors and will come b 8740
33:13 so he brought him b to Jerusalem and 8740
34: 7 Then he went b to Jerusalem. 8740
34:28 So they took her answer b to the king. 8740
Ne 1: 3 "Those who survived the exile and are b in 9004
2: 6 and when will you get b?" 8740
2:15 I turned b and reentered through 8740
4: 2 bring the stones b to life 2649
4: 4 Turn their insults b on their own heads. 8740
5: 8 we have bought b our Jewish brothers who were sold 7864
5: 8 only for them to be sold b to us!" 4835
5:11 Give b to them immediately their fields, 8740
5:12 "We will give it b," they said. 8740
6: 7 Now this report will get b to the king; 9048
8:15 into the hill country and bring b branches 995
8:16 the people went out and brought b branches 995
9:26 in order to turn them b to you; 8740
13: 7 and came b to Jerusalem. 995
13: 9 and then I put b into them the equipment 8740
13:10 the service had gone b to their own fields. 1368
Est 2:11 Every day he walked b and forth near 2143
4: 9 Hathach went b and reported 995
4:13 he sent b this answer: 8740
9:25 should come b onto his own head, 8740
Job 1: 7 through the earth and going b and forth 2143
2: 2 through the earth and going b and forth 2143
12:15 If he holds b the waters, there is drought; 6806
20:10 his own hands must give b his wealth. 8740
20:18 What he toiled for he must give b uneaten; 8740
20:25 He pulls it out of his b, 1576
33:30 to turn b his soul from the pit, 8740
37: 4 his voice resounds, he holds nothing b. 6810
41:15 His b has rows of shields tightly sealed 1568
Ps 6:10 they will turn b in sudden disgrace. 8740
9: 3 My enemies turn b; 294
18:37 I did not turn b till they were destroyed. 8740
28: 4 for what their hands have done and bring b 8740
31:23 but the proud he pays b in full. 8966
35: 4 may those who plot my ruin be turned b 294
38: 7 My b is filled with searing pain; 4072
40:14 may all who desire my ruin be turned b 294
44: 5 Through you we push b our enemies; 5590
44:18 Our hearts had not turned b; 294
51:13 and sinners will turn b to you. 8740
56: 9 my enemies will turn b when I call for help. 294
70: 2 may all who desire my ruin be turned b 294
70: 3 turn b because of their shame. 8740
74:11 Why do you hold b your hand, 8740
77:17 your arrows flashed b and forth. 2143
78: 9 turned b on the day of battle; 2200
78:66 He beat b his enemies; 294
79:12 Pay b into the laps 8740
89:43 You have turned b the edge of his sword 8740
90: 3 You turn men b to dust, saying, 8740
94: 2 pay b to the proud what they deserve. 8740
114: 3 sea looked and fled, the Jordan turned b; 294
114: 5 that you fled, O Jordan, that you turned b, 294
118:13 I was pushed b and about to fall, 1890+1890
126: 1 the LORD brought b the captives to Zion, 8740
129: 3 Plowmen have plowed my b 1461
129: 5 May all who hate Zion be turned b 294
Pr 3:28 not say to your neighbor, "Come b later; 8740
10:13 rod is for the b of him who lacks judgment. 1568
14: 3 A fool's talk brings a rod to his b, 1452
17:13 If a man pays b evil for good, 8740
19:24 he will not even bring it b to his mouth! 8740
20:22 "I'll pay you b for this wrong!" 8966
24:11 hold b those staggering toward slaughter. 3104
24:29 I'll pay that man b for what he did." 8740
26:15 he is too lazy to bring it b to his mouth. 8740
26:27 it will roll b on him. 8740
Ecc 1: 5 and hurries b to where it rises. 8634
SS 6:13 Come b, come back, O Shulammite; 8740
6:13 Come back, come b, O Shulammite; 8740
6:13 come b, come back, that we may gaze 8740
SS 6:13 come b, that we may gaze on you! 8740
Isa 3:11 They will be paid b 6913
14:27 and who can turn it b? 8740
21: 9 And he gives b the answer: 6699
21:12 and come b yet again." 8740
28: 6 of strength to those who turn b the battle at 8740
31: 2 he does not take b his words. 6073
38: 8 I will make the shadow cast by the sun go b 345
38: 8 So the sunlight went b 8740
38:17 you have put all my sins behind your b. 1568
42:14 I have been quiet and held myself b. 706
42:17 will be turned b in utter shame. 294
42:22 with no one to say, "Send them b." 8740
43: 6 and to the south, 'Do not hold them b.' 3973
48: 9 the sake of my praise I hold it b from you, 2641
49: 5 the womb to be his servant to bring Jacob b 8740
49: 6 and bring b those of Israel I have kept. 8740
49:17 Your sons hasten b, NIH
50: 5 I have not drawn b. 294+6047
50: 6 I offered my b to those who beat me, 1568
51:23 And you made your b like the ground, 1568
54: 2 do not hold b; 3104
54: 6 The LORD will call you b as 7924
54: 7 with deep compassion I will bring you b. 7695
58: 1 "Shout it aloud, do not hold b. 3104
59:14 So justice is driven b, 294+6047
64:12 O LORD, will you hold yourself b? 706
65: 6 not keep silent but will pay b in full; 8966
65: 6 I will pay it b into their laps— 8966
Jer 4:28 I have decided and will not turn b." 8740
12:15 bring each of them b 8740
18:17 I will show them my b and not my face in 6902
22:27 You will never come b to the land you long 8740
23: 3 and will bring them b to their pasture, 8740
23:20 The anger of the LORD will not turn b 8740
24: 6 and I will bring them b to this land. 8740
27:16 from the LORD's house will be brought b 8740
27:22 'Then I will bring them b 6590
28: 3 Within two years I will bring b 8740
28: 4 also bring b to this place Jehoiachin son 8740
28: 6 bringing the articles of the LORD's house and all the exiles b 8740
29:10 to bring you b to this place. 8740
29:14 "and will bring you b from captivity. 8740
29:14 "and will bring you b to the place 8740
30: 3 bring my people Israel and Judah b 8740
30:24 not turn b until he fully accomplishes 8740
31: 9 they will pray as I bring them b. 3297
31:23 "When I bring them b from captivity, 8740
32:37 I will bring them b to this place 8740
33: 7 bring Judah and Israel b 8740
34:11 and took b the slaves they had freed 8740
34:16 each of you has taken b the male 8740
34:22 and I will bring them b to this city. 8740
37: 7 will go b to its own land, to Egypt. 8740
37:20 Do not send me b to the house of Jonathan 8740
38:26 not to send me b to Jonathan's house 8740
39:14 to take him b to his home. 3655
40: 5 "Go b to Gedaliah son of Ahikam, 8740
40:12 they all came b to the land of Judah, 8740
42: 4 the LORD says and will keep nothing b 4979
43: 5 remnant of Judah who had come b to live 8740
46: 5 They flee in haste without looking b, 7155
46:16 let us go b to our own people 8740
48:39 How Moab turns her b in shame! 6902
50: 2 keep nothing b, but say, 3948
50:19 But I will bring Israel b 8740
La 1:13 a net for my feet and turned me b. 294
3:64 Pay them b what they deserve, O LORD, 8740
Eze 1:13 Fire moved b and forth among 2143
1:14 The creatures sped b and forth like flashes 8740
9:11 the writing kit at his side brought b word, 8740
11:17 from the nations and bring you b from 665
11:17 and I will give you b the land 5989
17:12 bringing them b with him to Babylon. AIT
23:35 and thrust me behind your b, 1567
24:14 I will not hold b; 7277
29:14 I will bring them b from captivity 8740
31:15 I held b its streams, 4979
33:15 if he gives b what he took in pledge for 8740
34: 4 not brought b the strays or searched for 8740
34:16 I will search for the lost and bring b 8740
36:24 from all the countries and bring you b 995
37: 2 He led me b and forth among them, 6017+6017
37:12 I will bring you b to the land of Israel. 995
37:21 and bring them b into their own land. 995
39:25 I will now bring Jacob b from captivity 8740
39:27 When I have brought them b from 8740
40:49 and twelve cubits from front to b. 8145
44: 1 the man brought me b to the outer gate of 8740
47: 1 The man brought me b to the entrance of 8740
47: 6 Then he led me b to the bank of the river. 8740
Da 4:35 No one can hold b his hand or say to him: 10411
7: 6 And on its b it had four wings like those of 10128
11:18 and will turn his insolence b upon him. 8740
11:19 he will turn b toward the fortresses 8740
11:30 Then he will turn b and vent his fury 8740
Hos 2: 7 'I will go b to my husband as at first, 8740
2: 9 I will take b my wool and my linen, 5911
2:15 There I will give her b her vineyards, 5989
5:15 Then I will go b to my place 8740
Joel 3: 4 If you are paying me b, 1694
Am 1: 3 I will not turn b [my wrath]. 8740
1: 6 I will not turn b [my wrath]. 8740
1: 9 I will not turn b [my wrath]. 8740
1:11 I will not turn b [my wrath]. 8740
1:13 I will not turn b [my wrath]. 8740
Am 2: 1 I will not turn b [my wrath]. 8740
2: 4 I will not turn b [my wrath]. 8740
2: 6 I will not turn b [my wrath]. 8740
7:12 Go b to the land of Judah. 1368
9:14 I will bring b my exiled people Israel; 8740
Jnh 1:13 the men did their best to row b to land. 8740
Na 2: 4 rushing b and forth through the squares. 9212
2: 8 they cry, but no one turns b. 7155
Zep 1: 6 those who turn b from following 6047
3:15 he has turned b your enemy. 7155
Zec 5: 8 and he pushed her b into the basket 8959
8: 8 I will bring them b to live in Jerusalem; 995
10:10 I will bring them b from Egypt 8740
Mt 2:12 in a dream not to go b to Herod, 366
11: 4 "Go b and report to John what you hear NIG
18:26 he begged, 'and I will pay b everything.' 625
18:28 'Pay b what you owe me!' 625
18:29 and I will pay you b.' 625
18:34 until he should pay b all he owed. 625
21:18 as he was on his way b to the city, 2056
24:18 Let no one in the field go b to get his cloak. 3958
25:27 when I returned I would have received it b 3152
26:43 When he came b, 2262
26:52 "Put your sword b in its place," 695
28: 2 rolled b the stone and sat on it. 653
Mk 6:28 and brought b his head on a platter. NIG
8:13 got b into the boat and crossed to 4099
11: 3 and will send it b here shortly.'" 690
13:16 Let no one in the field go b to get his cloak. 1650+3836+3958
13:35 when the owner of the house will come b— 2262
14:40 When he came b, 2262
Lk 1:16 of the people of Israel will he bring b to 2188
2:45 they went b to Jerusalem to look for him. 5715
4:20 gave it b to the attendant and sat down. 625
6:30 do not demand it b. 555
6:35 expecting to get anything b. 594
7:15 and Jesus gave him b to his mother. NIG
7:22 "Go b and report to John NIG
7:42 of them had the money to pay him b, 625
9: 8 the prophets of long ago had come b to life. 482
9:19 of long ago has come b to life." 482
9:42 the boy and gave him b to his father. 625
9:61 but first let me go b and say good-by NIG
9:62 and looks b is fit for service in the kingdom 1650+3836+3958
14:12 they may invite you b and so you will 511
14:21 "The servant came b and reported this 4134
15:18 and go b to my father and say to him: 4513
15:27 the fattened calf because he has him b safe 655
17: 4 and seven times comes b to you and says, 2188
17:15 came b, praising God in a loud voice. 5715
17:31 in the field should go b for anything. 1650+3836+3958
19: 8 I will pay b four times the amount." 625
19:13 he said, 'until I come b.' 2262
19:23 so that when I came b, 2262
22:32 And when you have turned b, 2188
22:45 When he rose from prayer and went b to 2262
23:11 they sent him b to Pilate. 402
23:15 Neither has Herod, for he sent him b to us; 402
24: 9 When they came b from the tomb, 5715
Jn 1:22 an answer to take b to those who sent us. 1443
4: 3 he left Judea and went b once more 599
4:16 "Go, call your husband and come b." 1924
4:28 the woman went b to the town and said to 599
6:66 From this time many of his disciples turned b 599+1650+3836+3958
7:45 the temple guards went b to the chief priests 2262
10:40 Then Jesus went b across the Jordan to 4099
11: 7 "Let us go b to Judea." 4099
11: 8 and yet you are going b there?" 5632
11:28 she went b and called her sister Mary aside. 599
13:25 Leaning b against Jesus, he asked him, 404
14: 3 I will come b and take you to be with me 4099
14:28 'I am going away and I am coming b 2262
16:28 now I am leaving the world and going b to NIG
18: 6 drew b and fell to the ground. 1650+3836+3958
18:16 who was known to the high priest, came b, NIG
18:33 Pilate then went b inside the palace, 4099
18:40 They shouted b, "No, not him! 4099
19: 9 and he went b inside the palace. 4099
20:10 Then the disciples went b to their homes, 599
21:20 the one who had leaned b against Jesus at 404
Ac 1:11 will come b in the same way you have seen 2262
4:23 Peter and John went b to their own people 2262
5: 2 With his wife's full knowledge he kept b part of the money 3802
5:22 So they went b and reported, 418
7:16 Their bodies were brought b to Shechem 3572
7:34 Now come, I will send you b to Egypt.' 690
7:39 and in their hearts turned b to Egypt. 5138
10: 5 Now send men to Joppa to bring b 3569
10:16 and immediately the sheet was taken b 377
12:14 so overjoyed she ran b without opening it NIG
14:20 he got up and went b into the city. NIG
14:26 From Attalia they sailed b to Antioch, NIG
15:36 "Let us go b and visit the brothers in all 2188
18:21 "I will come b if it is God's will." 366
20: 3 he decided to go b through Macedonia. 5715
Ro 9:20 who are you, O man, to talk b to God? 503
1Co 15:34 Come b to your senses 1729
2Co 1:16 on my way to Macedonia and to come b 4099
Gal 2:12 he began to draw b and separate himself 5713
4: 9 that you are turning b to those weak 4099
Eph 4:14 tossed b and forth by the waves, 3115
Php 2:25 But I think it is necessary to send b NIG

1Th 5:15 that nobody **pays b** wrong for wrong, *625*
2Th 1: 6 *He will* **pay b** trouble *500*
2: 6 now you know what *is* **holding** him **b,** *2988*
2: 7 the one who now **holds** it **b** will continue *2988*
Tit 2: 9 to try to please them, not to **talk b** to them, *515*
Phm 1:12 **sending** him—who is my very heart—**b** *402*
1:15 a little while was that *you might* **have** him **b** *600*
1:19 I *will* **pay** it **b—** *702*
Heb 6: 6 *to be* **brought b** to repentance, *362*
10:38 *he* **shrinks b,** I will not be pleased with him." *5713*
10:39 not *of* those who **shrink b** and are destroyed, *5714*
11:19 *he did* **receive** Isaac **b** from death. *3152*
11:35 Women received **b** their dead, *NIG*
13:20 the blood of the eternal covenant **brought b** *343*
Jas 5:19 the truth and someone *should* **bring** him **b,** *2188*
2Pe 2:13 They will be paid **b** with harm for *NIG*
2:22 that is washed goes **b** to her wallowing in *NIG*
Rev 4: 6 in front and **in b.** *3957*
7: 1 **holding b** the four winds of the earth *3195*
12: 7 and the dragon and his angels fought **b.** *NIG*
18: 6 **Give b** to her as she has given; *625*
18: 6 **pay** her **b double** for what she has done. 1486+*1488*

BACKBITING, BACKBITINGS (KJV)
See SLY, SLANDER

BACKBONE (1) [BACK, BONE]
Lev 3: 9 the entire fat tail cut off close to the **b,** 6782

BACKGROUND (2) [BACK]
Est 2:10 not revealed her nationality and **family b,** 4580
2:20 But Esther had kept secret her **family b** 4580

BACKS (24) [BACK]
Ex 23:27 I will make all your enemies turn their **b** 6902
Jos 7:12 they turn their **b** and run 6902
23:13 whips on your **b** and thorns in your eyes, 7396
2Sa 22:41 You made my enemies turn their **b** in flight, 6902
2Ch 29: 6 and turned their **b** on him. 6902
Ne 9:26 they put your law behind their **b.** 1567
9:29 Stubbornly they turned their **b** on you, 4190
Ps 18:40 You made my enemies turn their **b** in flight, 6902
21:12 for you will make them turn their **b** 8900
66:11 into prison and laid burdens on our **b.** 5516
69:23 and their **b** be bent forever. 5516
Pr 19:29 and beatings for the **b** *of* fools. 1568
26: 3 and a rod for the **b** *of* fools! 1568
Isa 1: 4 the Holy One of Israel and turned their **b** 294
30: 6 the envoys carry their riches on donkeys' **b,** 4190
59:13 turning our **b** on our God, 339
Jer 2:27 They have turned their **b** to me and 6902
32:33 They turned their **b** to me and 6902
Eze 8:16 *With* their **b** toward the temple of 294
10:12 Their entire bodies, including their **b,** 1461
29: 7 you broke and their **b** were wrenched. 5516
Zec 7:11 stubbornly they turned their **b** and stopped 4190
Ro 11:10 and their **b** be bent forever." *3822*
2Pe 2:21 to have known it and then *to* **turn their b** *5715*

BACKSLIDERS, BACKSLIDING (KJV)
See also FAITHLESS, STUBBORN, UNFAITHFUL, WAYWARDNESS

BACKSLIDING (5) [BACK]
Jer 2:19 your **b** will rebuke you. 5412
3:22 I will cure you of **b."** 5412
14: 7 our **b** is great; we have sinned against you. 5412
15: 6 "You keep on **b.** 294
Eze 37:23 for I will save them from all their sinful **b,** 5412

BACKSLIDINGS (1) [BACK]
Jer 5: 6 for their rebellion is great and their **b** many. 5412

BACKWARD (5) [BACK]
Ge 9:23 in **b** and covered their father's nakedness. 345
49:17 the horse's heels so that its rider tumbles **b.** 294
1Sa 4:18 Eli fell **b** off his chair by the side of 345
Isa 28:13 so that they will go and fall **b,** 294
Jer 7:24 They went **b** and not forward. 294+4200

BACUTH See ALLON BACUTH

BAD (65) [BADLY]
Ge 18:21 down and see if what they have done is as **b** 3986
31:24 anything to Jacob, either good or **b."** 8273
31:29 to say anything to Jacob, either good or **b.'** 8273
37: 2 and he brought their father a **b** report 8273
Ex 7:21 and the river **smelled** so **b** that 944
Lev 27:10 or substitute a good one for a **b** *one,* 8273
27:10 or a **b** *one* for a good one; 8273
27:12 who will judge its quality as good or **b.** 8273
27:14 judge its quality as good or **b.** 8273
27:33 He must not pick out the good from the **b** 8273
Nu 13:19 Is it good or **b?** 8273
13:32 among the Israelites a **b report** *about* 1804
14:36 against him by spreading a **b report** 1804
14:37 the **b** report about the land were struck 8273
24:13 good or **b,** to go beyond the command of 8288
Dt 1:39 not yet know good from **b—** 8273
22:14 and slanders her and gives her a **b** name, 8273
22:19 an Israelite virgin a **b** name. 8273
2Sa 13:22 word to Amnon, either good or **b;** 8273
1Ki 14: 6 I have been sent to you with **b news.** 7997
22: 8 about me, but always **b.** 8273
22:18 about me, but only **b?"** 8273
2Ki 2:19 water is **b** and the land is unproductive." 8273
2Ch 18: 7 about me, but always **b.** 8288
18:17 about me, but only **b?"** 8273
Ne 6:13 and then they would give me a **b** name 8273
Ps 112: 7 He will have no fear of **b** news; 8273
Pr 25:10 and you will never lose your **b reputation.** 1804
25:19 Like a **b** tooth or a lame foot is reliance on 8317
Ecc 7:14 but when times are **b,** consider: 8288
8: 3 Do not stand up for a **b** cause, 8273
9: 2 the good and the **b,** 8273
10: 1 **give** perfume **a b smell,** 944+5580
Isa 5: 2 but it yielded only **b fruit.** 946
5: 4 why did it yield only **b?** 946
41:23 Do something, whether good or **b,** 8317
Jer 24: 2 so **b** they could not be eaten. 8278
24: 3 poor ones are so **b** they cannot be eaten." 8278
24: 8 which are so **b** they cannot be eaten,' 8278
29:17 like poor figs that are so **b** they cannot 8278
49:23 for they have heard **b** news. 8273
Zep 1:12 will do nothing, either good or **b.'** 8317
Mt 6:23 But if your eyes are **b,** *4505*
7:17 but a **b** tree bears bad fruit. *4911*
7:17 but a bad tree bears **b** fruit. *4505*
7:18 A good tree cannot bear **b** fruit, *4505*
7:18 and a **b** tree cannot bear good fruit. *4911*
12:33 or make a tree **b** and its fruit will be bad, *4911*
12:33 or make a tree bad and its fruit will be **b,** *4911*
13:48 but threw the **b** away. *4911*
22:10 both good and **b,** *4505*
Mk 9:39 the next moment **say** anything **b about** me, *2800*
Lk 6:43 "No good tree bears **b** fruit, *4911*
6:43 nor does a **b** tree bear good fruit. *4911*
11:34 But when they are **b,** *4505*
16:25 while Lazarus received **b** *things,* *2805*
Jn 11:39 "by this time *there is* **a b odor,** *3853*
Ac 17: 5 up some **b** characters from the marketplace, *4505*
28:21 from there has reported or said anything **b** *4505*
Ro 9:11 or had done anything good or **b—** *5765*
1Co 15:33 **"B** company corrupts good character." *2805*
2Co 5:10 whether good or **b.** *5765*
6: 8 **b report** and good report; *1556*
2Ti 3:13 and impostors will go **from b to worse,** 2093+*3836*+*5937*
Tit 2: 8 be ashamed because they have nothing **b** *5765*

BADGERS' (KJV) See SEA COWS

BADLY (4) [BAD]
Ge 50:17 wrongs they committed in treating you *so* **b.** 8288
1Sa 24:17 but I have treated you **b.** 8288
2Ch 35:23 I am **b** wounded." 4394
Mk 12:27 You are **b** mistaken!" *4498*

BAFFLED (2)
Da 5: 9 His nobles *were* **b.** 10698
Ac 9:22 and more powerful and **b** the Jews living *5177*

BAG (13) [BAGS, BAGGAGE]
Dt 25:13 not have two differing weights in your **b—** 3967
1Sa 17:40 put them in the pouch of his shepherd's **b** 3998
17:49 Reaching into his **b** and taking out a stone, 3998
Job 14:17 My offenses will be sealed up in a **b;** 7655
Pr 16:11 all the weights in the **b** are of his making. 3967
Mic 6:11 with a **b** *of* false weights? 3967
Mt 10:10 take no **b** for the journey, or extra tunic, *4385*
Mk 6: 8 no bread, no **b,** no money in your belts. *4385*
Lk 9: 3 no staff, no **b,** no bread, no money, *4385*
10: 4 Do not take a purse or **b** or sandals; *4385*
22:35 **b** or sandals, did you lack anything?" *4385*
22:36 take it, and also a **b;** *4385*
Jn 12: 6 **keeper of the money b,** 1186+*2400*

BAGGAGE (1) [BAG]
1Sa 10:22 "Yes, he has hidden himself among the **b."** 3998

BAGS (5) [BAG]
Ge 42:25 Joseph gave orders to fill their **b** with grain, 3998
43:11 in your **b** and take them down to the man as 3998
2Ki 5:23 tied up the two talents of silver in two **b,** 3038
12:10 the temple of the LORD and **put** it **into b.** 7443
Isa 46: 6 from their **b** and weigh out silver on 3967

BAHARUMITE (1)
1Ch 11:33 Azmaveth the **B,** Eliahba the Shaalbonite, 1049

BAHURIM (5)
2Sa 3:16 weeping behind her all the way to **B.** 1038
16: 5 As King David approached **B,** 1038
17:18 and went to the house of a man in **B.** 1038
19:16 Shimei son of Gera, the Benjamite from **B,** 1038
1Ki 2: 8 the Benjamite from **B,** 1038

BAJITH (KJV) See TEMPLE

BAKBAKKAR (1)
1Ch 9:15 **B,** Heresh, Galal and Mattaniah son 1320

BAKBUK (2)
Ezr 2:51 **B,** Hakupha, Harhur, 1317
Ne 7:53 **B,** Hakupha, Harhur, 1317

BAKBUKIAH (3)
Ne 11:17 **B,** second among his associates; 1319
12: 9 **B** and Unni, their associates, 1319
12:25 Mattaniah, **B,** Obadiah, Meshullam, 1319

BAKE (9) [BAKED, BAKER, BAKERS, BAKES, BAKING]
Ge 11: 3 let's make bricks and **b** them **thoroughly."** 4200+8596+8599
18: 6 and knead it and **b** some bread." 6913
Ex 16:23 So **b** what you want to bake 684
16:23 *to* **b** and boil what you want to boil. 684
Lev 24: 5 "Take fine flour and **b** twelve loaves 684
26:26 ten women *will be able to* **b** your bread 684
Eze 4:12 **b** it in the sight of the people, 6383
4:15 "I will let you **b** your bread 6913
46:20 the guilt offering and the sin offering and **b** 684

BAKED (14) [BAKE]
Ge 40:17 In the top basket were all kinds of **b goods** 685+4407+5126
Ex 12:39 *they* **b** cakes of unleavened bread. 684
Lev 2: 4 " 'If you bring a grain offering **b** *in* 4418
6:17 *It must* not **be b** *with* yeast; 684
7: 9 Every grain offering **b** in an oven or cooked 684
23:17 of an ephah of fine flour, **b** *with* yeast, as 684
1Sa 28:24 kneaded it and **b** bread without yeast. 684
2Sa 13: 8 made the bread in his sight and **b** it. 1418
1Ki 19: 6 a cake of bread **b over hot coals,** 8363
2Ki 4:42 of barley bread **b** *from* the first ripe grain, 4312
Isa 44:19 *I* even **b** bread over its coals, 684
Da 2:33 its feet partly of iron and partly of **b clay.** 10279
2:41 of **b clay** and partly of iron, so this will be 10279
2:43 you saw the iron mixed with **b clay,** 10279+10298

BAKEMEATS (KJV) See BAKED GOODS

BAKER (8) [BAKE]
Ge 40: 1 the cupbearer and the **b** of the king 685
40: 2 the chief cupbearer and the chief **b,** 685
40: 5 cupbearer and the **b** of the king of Egypt, 685
40:16 When the chief **b** saw that Joseph had given 685
40:20 the chief **b** in the presence of his officials: 685
40:22 but he hanged the chief **b,** 685
41:10 and the chief **b** in the house of the captain 685
Hos 7: 4 an oven whose fire the **b** need not stir from 685

BAKERS (2) [BAKE]
1Sa 8:13 to be perfumers and cooks and **b.** 685
Jer 37:21 from the street of the **b** each day until all 685

BAKES (1) [BAKE]
Isa 44:15 he kindles a fire and **b** bread. 684

BAKING (3) [BAKE]
Ge 19: 3 **b** bread without yeast, and they ate. 684
1Ch 9:31 was entrusted with the responsibility for **b** 5126
23:29 the **b** and the mixing, 4679

BALAAM (59) [BALAAM'S]
Nu 22: 5 sent messengers to summon **B** son of Beor, 1189
22: 7 When they came to **B,** 1189
22: 8 "Spend the night here," **B** said to them, 1189
22: 9 God came to **B** and asked, "Who are these 1189
22:10 **B** said to God, "Balak son of Zippor, 1189
22:12 But God said to **B,** "Do not go with them. 1189
22:13 The next morning **B** got up and said 1189
22:14 **"B** refused to come with us." 1189
22:16 They came to **B** and said: "This is what 1189
22:18 But **B** answered them, "Even if Balak gave 1189
22:20 That night God came to **B** and said, 1189
22:21 **B** got up in the morning, 1189
22:22 **B** was riding on his donkey, 2085S
22:23 **B** beat her to get her back on the road. 1189
22:27 she lay down under **B,** 1189
22:28 and she said to **B,** "What have I done to you 1189
22:29 **B** answered the donkey, "You made a fool 1189
22:30 The donkey said to **B,** "Am I not your own 1189
22:34 **B** said to the angel of the LORD, 1189
22:35 The angel of the LORD said to **B,** 1189
22:35 So **B** went with the princes of Balak. 1189
22:36 When Balak heard that **B** was coming, 1189
22:37 Balak said to **B,** "Did I not send you 1189
22:38 "Well, I have come to you now," **B** replied. 1189
22:39 Then **B** went with Balak to Kiriath Huzoth. 1189
22:40 to **B** and the princes who were with him. 1189
22:41 The next morning Balak took **B** up 1189
23: 1 **B** said, "Build me seven altars here, 1189
23: 2 Balak did as **B** said, 1189
23: 3 Then **B** said to Balak, "Stay here 1189

Nu 23: 4 God met with him, and **B** said, 1189
23: 7 Then **B** uttered his oracle: NIH
23:11 Balak said to **B**, "What have you done 1189
23:15 **B** said to Balak, "Stay here NIH
23:16 The LORD met with **B** and put a message 1189
23:25 Then Balak said to **B**, "Neither curse them 1189
23:26 **B** answered, "Did I not tell you 1189
23:27 Then Balak said to **B**, "Come, 1189
23:28 And Balak took **B** to the top of Peor, 1189
23:29 **B** said, "Build me seven altars here, 1189
23:30 Balak did as **B** had said, 1189
24: 1 when **B** saw that it pleased the LORD 1189
24: 2 When **B** looked out and saw Israel 1189
24: 3 "The oracle of **B** son of Beor, 1189
24:10 Then Balak's anger burned against **B**. 1189
24:12 **B** answered Balak, "Did I not tell 1189
24:15 "The oracle of **B** son of Beor, 1189
24:20 Then **B** saw Amalek and uttered his oracle: NIH
24:25 Then **B** got up and returned home 1189
31: 8 also killed **B** son of Beor with the sword. 1189
Dt 23: 4 and they hired **B** son of Beor from Pethor 1189
23: 5 the LORD your God would not listen to **B** 1189
Jos 13:22 the Israelites had put to the sword **B** son 1189
24: 9 for **B** son of Beor to put a curse on you. 1189
24:10 But I would not listen to **B**, 1189
Ne 13: 2 with food and water but had hired **B** to call 1189
Mic 6: 5 of Moab counseled and what **B** son 1189
2Pe 2:15 to follow the way *of* **B** son of Beor, *962*
Rev 2:14 hold to the teaching *of* **B**, *962*

BALAAM'S (5) [BALAAM]
Nu 22:25 crushing **B** foot against it. 1189
22:31 Then the LORD opened **B** eyes, 1189
23: 5 The LORD put a message in **B** mouth 1189
31:16 the ones who followed **B** advice and were 1189
Jude 1:11 they have rushed for profit into **B** error; *962*

BALAC (KJV) See BALAK

BALADAN (2)
2Ki 20:12 that time Merodach-Baladan son of **B** king 1156
Isa 39: 1 that time Merodach-Baladan son of **B** king 1156

BALAH (1)
Jos 19: 3 Hazar Shual, **B**, Ezem, 1163

BALAK (36) [BALAK'S]
Nu 22: 2 Now **B** son of Zippor saw all that Israel 1192
22: 4 So **B** son of Zippor, who was king of Moab 1192
22: 5 **B** said: "A people has come out of Egypt; NIH
22: 7 they told him what **B** had said. 1192
22:10 Balaam said to God, "**B** son of Zippor, 1192
22:14 the Moabite princes returned to **B** and said, 1192
22:15 Then **B** sent other princes, 1192
22:16 "This is what **B** son of Zippor says: 1192
22:18 if **B** gave me his palace filled with silver 1192
22:35 So Balaam went with the princes of **B**. 1192
22:36 When **B** heard that Balaam was coming, 1192
22:37 **B** said to Balaam, "Did I not send you 1192
22:39 Balaam went with **B** to Kiriath Huzoth. 1192
22:40 **B** sacrificed cattle and sheep, 1192
22:41 The next morning **B** took Balaam up 1192
23: 2 **B** did as Balaam said, 1192
23: 3 Then Balaam said to **B**, "Stay here 1192
23: 5 "Go back to **B** and give him this message." 1192
23: 7 "**B** brought me from Aram, 1192
23:11 **B** said to Balaam, "What have you done 1192
23:13 Then **B** said to him, "Come with me 1192
23:15 Balaam said to **B**, "Stay here 1192
23:16 "Go back to **B** and give him this message." 1192
23:17 **B** asked him, "What did the LORD say?" 1192
23:18 Then he uttered his oracle: "Arise, **B**, 1192
23:25 Then **B** said to Balaam, "Neither curse 1192
23:27 Then **B** said to Balaam, "Come, 1192
23:28 And **B** took Balaam to the top of Peor, 1192
23:30 **B** did as Balaam had said, 1192
24:12 Balaam answered **B**, "Did I not tell 1192
24:13 if **B** gave me his palace filled with silver 1192
24:25 and **B** went his own way. 1192
Jos 24: 9 When **B** son of Zippor, the king of Moab, 1192
Jdg 11:25 Are you better than **B** son of Zippor, 1192
Mic 6: 5 remember what **B** king of Moab counseled 1192
Rev 2:14 who taught **B** to entice the Israelites to sin *963*

BALAK'S (2) [BALAK]
Nu 22:13 up and said to **B** princes, 1192
24:10 Then **B** anger burned against Balaam. 1192

BALANCE (3) [BALANCES]
Lev 25:27 since he sold it and refund the **b** to the man 6369
Ps 62: 9 if weighed on a **b**, they are nothing; 4404
Isa 40:12 on the scales and the hills in a **b?** 4404

BALANCES (1) [BALANCE]
Pr 16:11 Honest scales and **b** are from the LORD; 7144

BALD (5) [BALDHEAD, BALDNESS]
Lev 13:40 "When a man has lost his hair and is **b**, 7944
13:41 the front of his scalp and has a **b forehead**, 1477
13:42 if he has a reddish-white sore on his **b head** 7949
Isa 3:17 the LORD *will* **make** their scalps **b**." 6867
Mic 1:16 **make** yourselves as **b** as the vulture, 7947+8143

BALDHEAD (2) [BALD]
2Ki 2:23 "Go on up, you **b!**" 7944
2:23 "Go on up, you **b!**" 7944

BALDNESS (1) [BALD]
Isa 3:24 instead of well-dressed hair, **b;** 7947

BALL (1)
Isa 22:18 like a **b** and throw you into a large country. 1885

BALM (7)
Ge 37:25 **b** and myrrh, and they were on their way 7661
43:11 a little **b** and a little honey, 7661
2Ch 28:15 food and drink, and **healing b.** 6057
Jer 8:22 Is there no **b** in Gilead? 7661
46:11 "Go up to Gilead and get **b**, 7661
51: 8 Get **b** for her pain; 7661
Eze 27:17 honey, oil and **b** for your wares. 7661

BALSAM (4)
2Sa 5:23 and attack them in front of the **b trees.** 1132
5:24 of marching in the tops of the **b trees,** 1132
1Ch 14:14 and attack them in front of the **b trees.** 1132
14:15 of marching in the tops of the **b trees,** 1132

BAMAH (1)
Eze 20:29 (It is called **B** to this day.) 1196

BAMOTH (2) [BAMOTH BAAL]
Nu 21:19 from Nahaliel to **B**, 1199
21:20 from **B** to the valley in Moab where the top 1199

BAMOTH BAAL (2) [BAAL, BAMOTH]
Nu 22:41 Balak took Balaam up to **B**, 1200
Jos 13:17 including Dibon, **B**, Beth Baal Meon, 1200

BAN (1)
1Ch 2: 7 on Israel *by* **violating the b** 5085

BAND (16) [BANDED, BANDS]
Ge 49:19 "Gad will be attacked by a **b of raiders**, 1522
Ex 39:23 and a **b** around this opening, 8557
2Sa 1:10 that was on his head and the **b** on his arm 731
23:13 while a **b** *of* Philistines was encamped in 2653
1Ki 7:35 the stand there was a **circular b** half 6017+6318
11:24 of a **b of rebels** when David destroyed 1522
2Ki 13:21 suddenly they saw a **b of raiders;** 1522
19:31 and out of Mount Zion a **b of survivors.** 7129
1Ch 11:15 while a **b** *of* Philistines was encamped in 4722
Ps 22:16 a **b** *of* evil men has encircled me, 6337
78:49 a **b** *of* destroying angels. 5449
86:14 a **b** *of* ruthless men seeks my life— 6337
94:21 *They* **b together** against the righteous 1518
Isa 31: 4 a **whole b** *of* shepherds is called together 4850
37:32 and out of Mount Zion a **b of survivors.** 7129
Ac 5:37 the days of the census and led a **b** of people *NIG*

BANDAGED (2)
Isa 1: 6 not cleansed or **b** or soothed with oil. 2502
Lk 10:34 He went to him and **b** his wounds, *2866*

BANDED (4) [BAND]
Nu 14:35 which *has* **b together** against me. 3585
16:11 and all your followers *have* **b together.** 3585
27: 3 who **b together** against the LORD, 3585
2Sa 23:11 When the Philistines **b together** at a place 665+2021+2653+4200

BANDIT (3) [BANDITS]
Pr 6:11 like a **b** and scarcity like an armed man. 2143
23:28 Like a **b** she lies in wait, 3167
24:34 like a **b** and scarcity like an armed man. 2143

BANDITS (3) [BANDIT]
Ezr 8:31 and he protected us from enemies and **b** 741
Hos 7: 1 **b** rob in the streets; 1522
2Co 11:26 in danger *from* **b**, in danger *3334*

BANDS (17) [BAND]
Ex 27:10 and with silver hooks and **b** on the posts. 3122
27:11 and with silver hooks and **b** on the posts. 3122
27:17 around the courtyard are to have silver **b** 3138
36:38 the tops of the posts and their **b** with gold 3122
38:10 and with silver hooks and **b** on the posts. 3122
38:11 with silver hooks and **b** on the posts. 3122
38:12 with silver hooks and **b** on the posts. 3122
38:17 The hooks and **b** on the posts were silver, 3122
38:17 all the posts of the courtyard had silver **b.** 3138
38:19 Their hooks and **b** were silver, 3122
38:28 and *to* **make** their **b.** 3138
2Sa 4: 2 Now Saul's son had two men who were leaders of **raiding b.** 1522
2Ki 5: 2 Now **b** from Aram had gone out 1522
6:23 So the **b** from Aram stopped raiding 1522
1Ch 12:18 and made them leaders of his **raiding b.** 1522
12:21 They helped David against **raiding b**, 1522
Hos 6: 9 so do **b** *of* priests; they murder 2490

BANGLES (1)
Isa 3:18 **b** and headbands and crescent necklaces, 6577

BANI (14)
1Ch 6:46 the son of **B**, the son of Shemer, 1220
9: 4 the son of Imri, the son of **B**, 1220
Ezr 2:10 of **B** 642 1220
8:10 of the descendants of **B**, Shelomith son NIH
10:29 From the descendants of **B:** 1220
10:34 From the descendants of **B:** 1220
Ne 3:17 by the Levites under Rehum son of **B.** 1220
8: 7 Jeshua, **B**, Sherebiah, Jamin, Akkub, 1220
9: 4 Jeshua, **B**, Kadmiel, Shebaniah, Bunni, 1220
9: 4 Bunni, Sherebiah, **B** and Kenani— 1220
9: 5 And the Levites—Jeshua, Kadmiel, **B**, 1220
10:13 Hodiah, **B** and Beninu. 1220
10:14 Parosh, Pahath-Moab, Elam, Zattu, **B**, 1220
11:22 in Jerusalem was Uzzi son of **B**, 1220

BANISH (11) [BANISHED, BANISHMENT]
2Ki 13:23 or **b** them from his presence. 8959
Ps 5:10 **B** them for their many sins, 5615
125: 5 to crooked ways the LORD *will* **b** with 2143
Ecc 11:10 **b** anxiety from your heart and cast off 6073
Jer 8: 3 Wherever *I* **b** them, 5615
24: 9 wherever *I* **b** them. 5615
25:10 *I will* **b** from them the sounds of joy 6
27:10 *I will* **b** you and you will perish. 5615
27:15 I *will* **b** you and you will perish, 5615
32:37 where *I* **b** them in my furious anger 5615
Zec 13: 2 *I will* **b** the names of the idols from 4162

BANISHED (16) [BANISH]
Ge 3:23 So the LORD God **b** him from the Garden 8938
Dt 30: 4 if you *have* **been b** to the most distant land 5615
2Sa 14:13 for the king has not brought back his **b** son? 5615
14:14 so that a **b** *person* may not remain estranged 5615
1Ch 12: 1 while *he* **was b** from the presence 6806
Job 18:18 into darkness and *is* **b** from the world. 5610
20: 8 **b** like a vision of the night. 5610
30: 5 *They* **were b** from their fellow men, 1763
Isa 24:11 all gaiety *is* **b** *from* the earth. 1655
Jer 16:15 of all the countries where *he had* **b** them.' 5615
23: 8 of all the countries where *he had* **b** them.' 5615
23:12 *be* **b** to darkness and there they will fall. 5615
29:14 and places where *I have* **b** you," 5615
Jnh 2: 4 I said, '*I have* **been b** from your sight; 1763
Zec 5: 3 every thief *will* **be b**, 5927
5: 3 everyone who swears falsely *will* **be b.** 5927

BANISHMENT (1) [BANISH]
Ezr 7:26 **b**, confiscation of property, 10744

BANK (13) [BANKERS, BANKS, EMBANKMENT]
Ge 41:17 "In my dream I was standing on the **b** *of* 8557
Ex 2: 3 in it and put it among the reeds along the **b** 8557
2: 5 along the river **b.** 3338
7:15 Wait on the **b** *of* the Nile to meet him, 8557
Jos 13:23 of the Reubenites was the **b** *of* the Jordan. 1473
2Ki 2:13 and went back and stood on the **b** *of* 8557
Eze 47: 6 Then he led me back to the **b** *of* the river. 8557
Da 10: 4 I was standing on the **b** *of* the great river, 3338
12: 5 one on this **b** *of* the river and one on 8557
12: 5 of the river and one on the opposite **b.** 8557
Mt 8:32 the whole herd rushed down the **steep b** into *3204*
Mk 5:13 the **steep b** into the lake and were drowned. *3204*
Lk 8:33 the **steep b** into the lake and was drowned. *3204*

BANKERS (1) [BANK]
Mt 25:27 on deposit *with* the **b**, *5545*

BANKS (3) [BANK]
1Ch 12:15 when it was overflowing all its **b**, 1536
Isa 8: 7 run over all its **b** 1536
Eze 47:12 Fruit trees of all kinds will grow on both **b** 8557

BANNER (15) [BANNERS]
Ex 17:15 an altar and called it The LORD is my **B.** 5812
Ps 60: 4 you have raised a **b** to be unfurled against 5812
SS 2: 4 and his **b** over me is love. 1840
Isa 5:26 He lifts up a **b** for the distant nations, 5812
11:10 that day the Root of Jesse will stand as a **b** 5812
11:12 He will raise a **b** for the nations and gather 5812
13: 2 Raise a **b** on a bare hilltop, shout to them; 5812
18: 3 when a **b** is raised on the mountains, 5812
30:17 like a **b** on a hill." 5812
49:22 I will lift up my **b** to the peoples; 5812
62:10 Raise a **b** for the nations. 5812
Jer 50: 2 lift up a **b** and proclaim it; 5812
51:12 Lift up a **b** against the walls of Babylon! 5812
51:27 "Lift up a **b** in the land! 5812
Eze 27: 7 and served as your **b;** 5812

BANNERS (3) [BANNER]
Nu 2: 2 each man under his standard with the **b** 253
Ps 20: 5 and *will* **lift up** *our* **b** in the name 1839

SS 6: 4 majestic as **troops with b.** 1839

BANQUET (31) [BANQUETS]

1Sa 25:36 he was in the house holding a **b** like that of 5492
Est 1: 3 of his reign he gave a **b** for all his nobles 5492
1: 5 the king gave a **b**, lasting seven days, 5492
1: 9 Queen Vashti also gave a **b** *for* the women 5492
2:18 And the king gave a great **b**, 5492
2:18 the king gave a great banquet, Esther's **b**, 5492
5: 4 come today to a **b** I have prepared for him." 5492
5: 5 to the **b** Esther had prepared. 5492
5: 8 to the **b** I will prepare for them. 5492
5:12 to accompany the king to the **b** she gave. 5492
6:14 to the **b** Esther had prepared. 5492
7: 8 from the palace garden to the **b** hall, 3516+5492
SS 2: 4 He has taken me to the **b hall,** 1074+3516
Isa 25: 6 a **b** *of* aged wine— 5492
Da 5: 1 a great **b** for a thousand of his nobles 10389
5:10 came into the **b** hall. 10447
Mt 22: 2 king who prepared a **wedding b** for his son. *1141*
22: 3 to those who had been invited to the **b** *1141*
22: 4 Come to the **wedding b.'** *1141*
22: 8 'The **wedding b** is ready, *1141*
22: 9 and invite to the **b** anyone you find.' *1141*
25:10 in with him to the **wedding b.** *1141*
Mk 6:21 On his birthday Herod gave a **b** *1270*
Lk 5:29 Levi held a great **b** for Jesus at his house, *1531*
12:36 for their master to return from a **wedding b,** *1141*
14:13 But when you give a **b**, invite the poor, *1531*
14:16 "A certain man was preparing a great **b** *1270*
14:17 At the time *of* the **b** he sent his servant *1270*
14:24 a taste *of* my **b.'** " *1270*
Jn 2: 8 and take it *to* the **master of the b."** *804*
2: 9 and the **master of the b** tasted the water *804*

BANQUETS (4) [BANQUET]

Isa 5:12 They have harps and lyres at their **b**, 5492
Mt 23: 6 of honor at **b** and the most important seats *1270*
Mk 12:39 and the places of honor at **b.** *1270*
Lk 20:46 and the places of honor at **b.** *1270*

BAPTISM (20) [BAPTIZE]

Mt 21:25 John's **b**—where did it come from? 967
Mk 1: 4 in the desert region and preaching a **b** 967
10:38 be baptized with the **b** I am baptized with?" 967
10:39 be baptized with the **b** I am baptized with, 967
11:30 John's **b**—was it from heaven, or from men? 967
Lk 3: 3 a **b** of repentance for the forgiveness 967
12:50 But I have a **b** *to* **undergo,** 966+967
20: 4 John's **b**—was it from heaven, 967
Ac 1:22 beginning from John's **b** to the time 967
10:37 in Galilee after the **b** that John preached— 967
13:24 John preached repentance and **b** to all 967
18:25 though he knew only the **b** of John. 967
19: 3 "Then what **b** *did you* **receive?"** 966
19: 3 "John's **b,"** they replied. 967
19: 4 "John's **b** was a baptism of repentance. 966
19: 4 "John's baptism was a **b** of repentance. 967
Ro 6: 4 with him through **b** into death in order that, 967
Eph 4: 5 one Lord, one faith, one **b**; 967
Col 2:12 in **b** and raised with him through your faith 967
1Pe 3:21 and this water symbolizes **b** that 967

BAPTISMS (1) [BAPTIZE]

Heb 6: 2 instruction *about* **b**, the laying on 968

BAPTIST (14) [BAPTIZE]

Mt 3: 1 In those days John the **B** came, 969
11:11 not risen anyone greater than John the **B**; 969
11:12 From the days *of* John the **B** until now, 969
14: 2 "This is John the **B**; 969
14: 8 on a platter the head *of* John the **B."** 969
16:14 They replied, "Some say John the **B**; 969
17:13 to them about John the **B.** 969
Mk 6:14 "John the **B** has been raised from the dead, 966
6:24 "The head *of* John the **B,"** she answered. 966
6:25 now the head *of* John the **B** on a platter." 969
8:28 They replied, "Some say John the **B**; 969
Lk 7:20 they said, "John the **B** sent us to you to ask, 969
7:33 For John the **B** came neither eating bread 969
9:19 They replied, "Some say John the **B**; 969

BAPTIZE (12) [BAPTISM, BAPTISMS, BAPTIST, BAPTIZED, BAPTIZING]

Mt 3:11 "I **b** you with water for repentance. 966
3:11 He *will* **b** you with the Holy Spirit and 966
Mk 1: 8 I **b** you with water, 966
1: 8 but he *will* **b** you with the Holy Spirit." 966
Lk 3:16 "I **b** you with water. 966
3:16 He *will* **b** you with the Holy Spirit and 966
Jn 1:25 then *do you* **b** if you are not the Christ, 966
1:26 "I **b** with water," John replied, 966
1:33 except that the one who sent me *to* **b** 966
1:33 down and remain is he who *will* **b** with 966
1Co 1:14 not **b** any of you except Crispus and Gaius, 966
1:17 For Christ did not send me *to* **b,** 966

BAPTIZED (50) [BAPTIZE]

Mt 3: 6 *they were* **b** by him in the Jordan River. 966
3:13 Galilee to the Jordan *to be* **b** by John. 966+3836
3:14 saying, "I need *to be* **b** by you, 966
3:16 As soon as Jesus *was* **b,** 966
Mk 1: 5 *they were* **b** by him in the Jordan River. 966
1: 9 from Nazareth in Galilee and *was* **b** by John 966
10:38 "Can you drink the cup I drink or *be* **b** with 966
10:38 be baptized with the baptism I *am* **b** with?" 966
10:39 *be* **b** with the baptism I am baptized with, 966
10:39 be baptized with the baptism I *am* **b** with, 966
16:16 Whoever believes and *is* **b** will be saved, 966
Lk 3: 7 John said to the crowds coming out *to be* **b** 966
3:12 Tax collectors also came *to be* **b.** 966
3:21 When all the people *were being* **b,** 966
3:21 Jesus *was* **b** too. 966
7:29 *because they had been* **b** by John. 966+967
7:30 *because they had not been* **b** by John.) 966
Jn 3:22 where he spent some time with them, and **b.** 966
3:23 and people were constantly coming *to be* **b.** 966
4: 2 although in fact it was not Jesus who **b,** 966
Ac 1: 5 For John **b** with water, 966
1: 5 but in a few days you *will be* **b** with 966
2:38 Peter replied, "Repent and *be* **b,** 966
2:41 Those who accepted his message *were* **b,** 966
8:12 *they were* **b,** both men and women. 966
8:13 Simon himself believed and was **b.** 966
8:16 *they had* simply *been* **b** into the name 966+5639
8:36 Why shouldn't I *be* **b?"** 966
8:38 down into the water and Philip **b** him. 966
9:18 *He* got up and *was* **b,** 966
10:47 from *being* **b** with water? 966
10:48 that they *be* **b** in the name of Jesus Christ. 966
11:16 'John **b** with water, 966
11:16 but you *will be* **b** with the Holy Spirit.' 966
16:15 and the members of her household *were* **b,** 966
16:33 immediately he and all his family *were* **b.** 966
18: 8 many of the Corinthians who heard him believed and *were* **b.** 966
19: 5 *they were* **b** into the name of the Lord Jesus. 966
22:16 Get up, *be* **b** and wash your sins away, 966
Ro 6: 3 Or don't you know that all of *us who were* **b** 966
6: 3 into Christ Jesus *were* **b** into his death? 966
1Co 1:13 *Were you* **b** into the name of Paul? 966
1:15 so no one can say that *you were* **b** 966
1:16 (Yes, *I* also **b** the household of Stephanas; 966
1:16 I don't remember if *I* **b** anyone else.) 966
10: 2 *They were* all **b** into Moses in the cloud and 966
12:13 we *were* all **b** by one Spirit into one body— 966
15:29 what will those do who *are* **b** for the dead? 966
15:29 why *are people* **b** for them? 966
Gal 3:27 for all of you who *were* **b** into Christ 966

BAPTIZING (9) [BAPTIZE]

Mt 3: 7 and Sadducees coming to where he *was* **b,** 967
28:19 **b** them in the name of the Father and of 966
Mk 1: 4 **b** in the desert region and preaching 966
Jn 1:28 where John was **b.** 966
1:31 but the reason I came **b** with water was 966
3:23 Now John also was **b** at Aenon near Salim, 966
3:26 he *is* **b,** and everyone is going to him." 966
4: 1 and **b** more disciples than John, 966
10:40 where John had been **b** in the early days. 966

BAR (3) [BARRED, BARS]

Jdg 16: 3 and tore them loose, **b** and all. 1378
Ne 7: 3 have them shut the doors and **b** them. 296
Isa 9: 4 the **b** *across* their shoulders, 4751

BAR-JESUS (1)

Ac 13: 6 and false prophet named **B,** *979*

BARABBAS (12)

Mt 27:16 a notorious prisoner, called **B.** *972*
27:17 **B,** or Jesus who is called Christ?" *972*
27:20 the elders persuaded the crowd to ask for **B** *972*
27:21 **"B,"** they answered. *972*
27:26 Then he released **B** to them. *972*
Mk 15: 7 A man called **B** was in prison with *972*
15:11 the crowd to have Pilate release **B** instead. *972*
15:15 Pilate released **B** to them. *972*
Lk 23:18 Release **B** to us!" *972*
23:19 (**B** had been thrown into prison for *4015*[S]
Jn 18:40 Give us **B!"** *972*
18:40 Now **B** had taken part in a rebellion. *972*

BARACHEL (KJV) See BARAKEL

BARACHIAS (KJV) See BARACHIAH

BARAH See BETH BARAH

BARAK (13) [BARAK'S]

Jdg 4: 6 for **B** son of Abinoam from Kedesh 1399
4: 8 **B** said to her, "If you go with me, I will go; 1399
4: 9 So Deborah went with **B** to Kedesh, 1399
4:12 that **B** son of Abinoam had gone up 1399
4:14 Then Deborah said to **B,** "Go! 1399
4:14 So **B** went down Mount Tabor, 1399
4:16 But **B** pursued the chariots and army as far 1399
4:22 **B** came by in pursuit of Sisera, 1399
5: 1 and **B** son of Abinoam sang this song: 1399
5:12 Arise, O **B!** 1399
5:15 yes, Issachar was with **B,** 1399
1Sa 12:11 Then the LORD sent Jerub-Baal, **B,** 1399
Heb 11:32 I do not have time to tell about Gideon, **B,** *973*

BARAK'S (1) [BARAK]

Jdg 4:15 At **B** advance, the LORD routed Sisera 1399

BARAKEL (2)

Job 32: 2 But Elihu son of **B** the Buzite, 1387
32: 6 So Elihu son of **B** the Buzite said: 1387

BARBARIAN (1)

Col 3:11 circumcised or uncircumcised, **b,** Scythian, *975*

BARBARIANS (KJV) See FOREIGNER, ISLANDER, NON-GREEKS

BARBAROUS (KJV) See ISLANDERS

BARBER'S (1)

Eze 5: 1 and use it as a **b** razor to shave your head 1647

BARBS (1)

Nu 33:55 those you allow to remain will become **b** 8493

BARE (28) [BARED, BAREFOOT, BARELY, BARREN]

Jdg 14: 6 that he tore the lion apart with his **b** hands 401+928+4399
2Sa 22:16 and the foundations of the earth **laid b** at 1655
2Ki 9:13 and spread them under him on the **b** steps. 1752
Job 28: 9 and **lays b** the roots of the mountains. 2200
Ps 18:15 and the foundations of the earth **laid b** 1655
29: 9 the oaks and **strips** the forests **b.** 3106
Isa 13: 2 a banner on a **b** hilltop, shout to them; 9142
23:13 **stripped** its fortresses **b** 6910
27:10 *they* **strip** its branches **b.** 3983
47: 2 Lift up your skirts, **b** *your* legs, 1655
52:10 The LORD *will* **lay b** his holy arm in 3106
Jer 2:25 until your feet are **b** and your throat is dry. 3504
49:10 But I *will* **strip** Esau **b;** 3106
Eze 13:14 so that its foundation *will* **be laid b.** 1655
16: 7 you who were naked and **b.** 6880
16:22 when you were naked and **b,** 6880
16:39 and leave you naked and **b.** 6880
23:29 They will leave you naked and **b,** 6880
24: 7 She poured it on the **b** rock; 7460
24: 8 I put her blood on the **b** rock, 7460
26: 4 and make her a **b** rock. 7460
26:14 I will make you a **b** rock, 7460
29:18 every head **was rubbed b** 7942
Hos 2: 3 and **make** her as **b** as on 3657
Mic 1: 6 into the valley and **lay b** her foundations. 1655
1Co 14:25 and the secrets of his heart will be **laid b.** *5745*
Heb 4:13 and **laid b** before the eyes of him *5548*
2Pe 3:10 earth and everything in it *will be* **laid b.** *2351*

BARED (2) [BARE]

Isa 20: 4 with buttocks **b**—to Egypt's shame. 3106
Eze 4: 7 of Jerusalem and with **b** arm prophesy 3106

BAREFOOT (5) [BARE, FOOT]

2Sa 15:30 his head was covered and he was **b.** 3504
Isa 20: 2 And he did so, going around stripped and **b.** 3504
20: 3 and **b** for three years, 3504
20: 4 of Assyria will lead away stripped and **b** 3504
Mic 1: 8 I will go about **b** and naked. 8768

BARELY (2) [BARE]

1Sa 3: 2 so weak that he could **b** see, 4202
Isa 26:16 *they could* **b whisper a prayer.** 4318+7440

BARGAIN (2)

2Ki 18:23 " 'Come now, **make a b** with my master, 6842
Isa 36: 8 " 'Come now, **make a b** with my master, 6842

BARHUMITE (1)

2Sa 23:31 Abi-Albon the Arbathite, Azmaveth the **B,** 1372

BARIAH (1)

1Ch 3:22 Hattush, Igal, **B,** Neariah and Shaphat— 1377

BARK (4)

Ge 30:37 on them *by* **peeling** *the* **b** and exposing AIT
Ex 11: 7 among the Israelites not a dog *will* **b** 3076+4383
Isa 56:10 they are all mute dogs, they cannot **b;** 5560
Joel 1: 7 *It has* **stripped off** their **b** 3106+3106

BARKOS (2)

Ezr 2:53 **B,** Sisera, Temah, 1401
Ne 7:55 **B,** Sisera, Temah, 1401

BARLEY (36)

Ex 9:31 (The flax and **b** were destroyed, 8555
9:31 **b** had headed and the flax was in bloom. 8555
Lev 27:16 fifty shekels of silver to a homer of **b** seed. 8555
Nu 5:15 a tenth of an ephah of **b** flour on her behalf. 8555
Dt 8: 8 a land with wheat and **b,** vines 8555
Jdg 7:13 "A round loaf of **b** bread came tumbling 8555
Ru 1:22 as the **b** harvest was beginning. 8555

Ru 2:17 Then she threshed the **b** she had gathered, 8555
2:23 the servant girls of Boaz to glean until the **b** 8555
3: 2 be winnowing **b** on the threshing floor. 8555
3:15 into it six measures of **b** and put it on her. 8555
3:17 "He gave me these six measures of **b**, 8555
2Sa 14:30 and he has **b** there. 8555
17:28 They also brought wheat and **b**, 8555
21: 9 just as the **b** harvest was beginning. 8555
1Ki 4:28 the proper place their quotas of **b** and straw 8555
2Ki 4:42 of **b** bread baked from the first ripe grain, 8555
7: 1 for a shekel and two seahs of **b** for a shekel 8555
7:16 and two seahs of **b** sold for a shekel, 8555
7:18 for a shekel and two seahs of **b** for a shekel 8555
1Ch 11:13 At a place where there was a field full of **b**, 8555
2Ch 2:10 twenty thousand cors of **b**, 8555
2:15 the wheat and **b** and the olive oil 8555
27: 5 of wheat and ten thousand cors of **b**. 8555
Job 31:40 instead of wheat and weeds instead of **b**." 8555
Isa 28:25 **b** in its plot, and spelt in its field? 8555
Jer 41: 8 We have wheat and **b**, oil and honey, 8555
Eze 4: 9 "Take wheat and **b**, beans and lentils, 8555
4:12 Eat the food as you would a **b** cake; 8555
13:19 for a few handfuls of **b** and scraps of bread. 8555
45:13 a sixth of an ephah from each homer of **b**. 8555
Hos 3: 2 and about a homer and a lethek of **b**. 8555
Joel 1:11 grieve for the wheat and the **b**, 8555
Jn 6: 9 "Here is a boy with five **small b** loaves *3209*
6:13 with the pieces of the five **b** loaves left over *3209*
Rev 6: 6 and three quarts *of* **b** for a day's wages, *3208*

BARN (5) [BARNS]

Hag 2:19 Is there yet any seed left in the **b**? 4476
Mt 3:12 gathering his wheat into the **b** and burning *630*
13:30 the wheat and bring it into my **b**.' " *630*
Lk 3:17 and to gather the wheat into his **b**, *630*
12:24 they have no storeroom or **b**; *630*

BARNABAS (34)

Ac 4:36 called **B** (which means Son of Encouragement), *982*
9:27 But **B** took him and brought him to *982*
11:22 and they sent **B** to Antioch. *982*
11:25 Then **B** went to Tarsus to look for Saul, *NIG*
11:26 So for a whole year **B and Saul** met with *899S*
11:30 sending their gift to the elders by **B** *982*
12:25 **B** and Saul had finished their mission, *982*
13: 1 **B**, Simeon called Niger, Lucius of Cyrene, *982*
13: 2 "Set apart for me **B** and Saul for the work *982*
13: 7 for **B** and Saul because he wanted to hear *982*
13:42 As **Paul and B** were leaving *899S*
13:43 to Judaism followed Paul and **B**, *982*
13:46 Then Paul and **B** answered them boldly: *982*
13:50 up persecution against Paul and **B**, *982*
14: 1 At Iconium **Paul and B** went as usual into *899S*
14: 3 and **B** spent considerable time there, *NIG*
14:12 **B** they called Zeus, *982*
14:14 when the apostles **B** and Paul heard of this, *982*
14:20 The next day he and **B** left for Derbe. *982*
14:23 Paul and **B** appointed elders for them *NIG*
15: 2 This brought Paul and **B** into sharp dispute *982*
15: 2 So Paul and **B** were appointed, *982*
15:12 as they listened to **B** and Paul telling about *982*
15:22 and send them to Antioch with Paul and **B**. *982*
15:25 to you with our dear friends **B** and Paul— *982*
15:35 But Paul and **B** remained in Antioch, *982*
15:36 Some time later Paul said to **B**, *982*
15:37 **B** wanted to take John, also called Mark, *982*
15:39 **B** took Mark and sailed for Cyprus, *982*
1Co 9: 6 Or is it only I and **B** who must work for *982*
Gal 2: 1 again to Jerusalem, this time with **B**. *982*
2: 9 gave me and **B** the right hand of fellowship *982*
2:13 by their hypocrisy even **B** was led astray. *982*
Col 4:10 as does Mark, the cousin *of* **B**. *982*

BARNEA See KADESH BARNEA

BARNS (5) [BARN]

Dt 28: 8 The LORD will send a blessing on your **b** 662
Ps 144:13 Our **b** will be filled with every kind 4646
Pr 3:10 then your **b** will be filled to overflowing, 662
Mt 6:26 they do not sow or reap or store away in **b**, *630*
Lk 12:18 down my **b** and build bigger ones, *630*

BARRACKS (6)

Ac 21:34 he ordered that Paul be taken into the **b**. *4213*
21:37 about to take Paul into the **b**, *4213*
22:24 to be taken into the **b**. *4213*
23:10 by force and bring him into the **b**. *4213*
23:16 he went into the **b** and told Paul. *4213*
23:32 while they returned to the **b**. *4213*

BARRED (4) [BAR]

Pr 18:19 disputes are like the **b gates** *of* a citadel. 1378
Isa 24:10 the entrance to every house **is b**. 6037
La 3: 9 *He has* **b** my way with blocks of stone; 1553
Jnh 2: 6 the earth beneath **b** me **in** forever. 1237+1378

BARREL, BARRELS (KJV) See JAR, JARS

BARREN (29) [BARE]

Ge 11:30 Now Sarai was **b**; she had no children. 6829
25:21 because she was **b**. 6829
29:31 he opened her womb, but Rachel was **b**. 6829
Ex 23:26 and none will miscarry or be **b** in your land. 6829
Nu 23: 3 Then he went off to a **b height**. 9155
Dt 32:10 in a **b** and howling waste. 9332
1Sa 2: 5 *She who was* **b** has borne seven children, 6829
Job 3: 7 May that night be **b**; 1678
15:34 For the company of the godless will be **b**, 1678
24:21 They prey on the **b** and childless woman, 6829
Ps 113: 9 the **b** *woman* in her home as a happy mother 6829
Pr 30:16 the **b** womb, land, which is never satisfied 6808
Isa 41:18 I will make rivers flow on **b heights**, 9155
49: 9 the roads and find pasture on every **b hill**. 9155
49:21 I was bereaved and **b**; 1678
54: 1 O **b** *woman*, you who never bore a child; 6829
Jer 2: 6 and led us through the **b wilderness**, 4497
3: 2 "Look up to the **b heights** and see. 9155
3:21 A cry is heard on the **b heights**, 9155
4:11 "A scorching wind from the **b heights** in 9155
7:29 take up a lament on the **b heights**, 9155
12:12 Over all the **b heights** in 9155
14: 6 on the **b heights** and pant like jackals; 9155
Joel 2:20 pushing it into a parched and **b** land, 9039
Lk 1: 7 because Elizabeth was **b**; *5096*
1:36 and she who was said to be **b** is *5096*
23:29 'Blessed are the **b women**, *5096*
Gal 4:27 For it is written: "Be glad, *O* **b woman**, *5096*
Heb 11:11 and Sarah herself was **b**— *5096*

BARRIER (2)

Jer 5:22 an everlasting **b** it cannot cross. 2976
Eph 2:14 the two one and has destroyed the **b**, *5850*

BARS (23) [BAR]

Lev 26:13 the **b** *of* your yoke and enabled you to walk 4574
Dt 3: 5 with high walls and with gates and **b**, 1378
1Sa 23: 7 by entering a town with gates and **b**." 1378
1Ki 4:13 with bronze **gate b**); 1378
2Ch 8: 5 with walls and with gates and **b**, 1378
14: 7 with towers, gates and **b**. 1378
Ne 3: 3 and put its doors and bolts and **b** in place. 1378
3: 6 and put its doors and bolts and **b** in place. 1378
3:13 and put its doors and bolts and **b** in place. 1378
3:14 and put its doors and bolts and **b** in place. 1378
3:15 over and putting its doors and bolts and **b** 1378
Job 38:10 for it and set its doors and **b** in place, 1378
Ps 68:30 Humbled, may it bring **b** *of* silver. 8349
107:16 down gates of bronze and cuts through **b** 1378
147:13 the **b** *of* your gates and blesses your people 1378
Isa 45: 2 down gates of bronze and cut through **b** 1378
Jer 49:31 "a nation that has neither gates nor **b**; 1378
51:30 the **b of** her **gates** are broken. 1378
La 2: 9 their **b** he has broken and destroyed. 1378
Eze 34:27 the **b** *of* their yoke and rescue them from 4574
38:11 without walls and without gates and **b**. 1378
Hos 11: 6 will destroy the **b of** their **gates** and put 964
Na 3:13 fire has consumed their **b**. 1378

BARSABBAS (2)

Ac 1:23 Joseph called **B** (also known as Justus) *984*
15:22 They chose Judas (called **B**) and Silas, *984*

BARTER (3)

Job 6:27 for the fatherless and **b away** your friend. 4126
41: 6 *Will* traders **b** for him? 4126
La 1:11 *they* **b** their treasures for food 5989

BARTHOLOMEW (4)

Mt 10: 3 Philip and **B**; Thomas *978*
Mk 3:18 Philip, **B**, Matthew, Thomas, *978*
Lk 6:14 his brother Andrew, James, John, Philip, **B**, *978*
Ac 1:13 Philip and Thomas, **B** and Matthew; *978*

BARTIMAEUS (1) [TIMAEUS]

Mk 10:46 **B** (that is, the Son of Timaeus), *985*

BARUCH (28)

Ne 3:20 Next to him, **B** son of Zabbai 1358
10: 6 Daniel, Ginnethon, **B**, 1358
11: 5 and Maaseiah son of **B**, 1358
Jer 32:12 and I gave this deed to **B** son of Neriah, 1358
32:13 In their presence I gave **B** these instructions: 1358
32:16 to **B** son of Neriah, I prayed to the LORD: 1358
36: 4 So Jeremiah called **B** son of Neriah, 1358
36: 4 **B** wrote them on the scroll. 1358
36: 5 Then Jeremiah told **B**, "I am restricted; 1358
36: 8 **B** son of Neriah did everything Jeremiah 1358
36:10 **B** read to all the people at 1358
36:13 Micaiah told them everything he had heard **B** read 1358
36:14 the son of Cushi, to say to **B**, 1358
36:14 So **B** son of Neriah went to them with 1358
36:15 So **B** read it to them. 1358
36:16 at each other in fear and said to **B**, 1358
36:17 Then they asked **B**, "Tell us, 1358
36:18 **B** replied, "he dictated all these words 1358
36:19 Then the officials said to **B**, 1358
36:26 and Shelemiah son of Abdeel to arrest **B** 1358
36:27 that **B** had written at Jeremiah's dictation, 1358
36:32 and gave it to the scribe **B** son of Neriah, 1358
Jer 36:32 **B** wrote on it all the words of the scroll NIH
43: 3 But **B** son of Neriah is inciting you 1358
43: 6 Jeremiah the prophet and **B** son of Neriah. 1358
45: 1 the prophet told **B** son of Neriah in 1358
45: 1 after **B** had written on a scroll 2257S
45: 2 the God of Israel, says to you, **B**: 1358

BARZILLAI (13)

2Sa 17:27 and **B** the Gileadite from Rogelim 1367
19:31 **B** the Gileadite also came down 1367
19:32 **B** was a very old man, eighty years of age. 1367
19:33 The king said to **B**, "Cross over with me 1367
19:34 But **B** answered the king, "How many more 1367
19:39 The king kissed **B** 1367
19:39 and **B** returned to his home. NIH
21: 8 whom she had borne to Adriel son of **B** 1367
1Ki 2: 7 to the sons of **B** of Gilead and let them be 1367
Ezr 2:61 and **B** (a man who had married a daughter 1367
2:61 (a man who had married a daughter of **B** 1367
Ne 7:63 the descendants of Hobaiah, Hakkoz and **B** 1367
7:63 (a man who had married a daughter of **B** 1367

BASE (21) [BASED, BASES, BASIC, BASING, BASIS]

Ex 25:31 and hammer it out, **b** and shaft; 3751
29:12 pour out the rest of it at the **b** *of* the altar. 3572
37:17 and hammered it out, **b** and shaft; 3751
38:27 one talent for each **b**. 149
Lev 4: 7 of the bull's blood he shall pour out at the **b** 3572
4:18 of the blood he shall pour out at the **b** *of* 3572
4:25 and pour out the rest of the blood at the **b** 3572
4:30 and pour out the rest of the blood at the **b** 3572
4:34 and pour out the rest of the blood at the **b** 3572
5: 9 of the blood must be drained out at the **b** *of* 3572
8:15 He poured out the rest of the blood at the **b** 3572
9: 9 the rest of the blood he poured out at the **b** 3572
Nu 8: 4 from its **b** to its blossoms. 3751
2Ki 16:17 that supported it and set it on a stone **b**. 5346
Job 30: 8 A **b** and nameless brood, 5572
SS 3:10 Its posts he made of silver, its **b** *of* gold. 8339
Isa 3: 5 the **b** against the honorable. 7829
Eze 31: 4 around its **b** and sent their channels to all 4760
41: 8 that the temple had a **raised** *b* all around it, AIT
41:11 and the **b** *adjoining* 5226
41:22 its corners, its **b** and its sides were of wood. 149

BASED (6) [BASE]

Lev 25:50 **b on the rate paid** to a hired man 3427+3869
Nu 26:53 to be allotted to them as an inheritance **b on** 928
Ro 2: 2 against those who do such things is **b on** *2848*
10: 2 but their zeal is not **b on** knowledge. *2848*
Gal 3:12 The law is not **b on** faith; *1666*
Col 2:22 because they are **b on** human commands *2848*

BASEMATH (7)

Ge 26:34 and also **B** daughter of Elon the Hittite. 1412
36: 3 also **B** daughter of Ishmael and sister 1412
36: 4 Adah bore Eliphaz to Esau, **B** bore Reuel, 1412
36:10 and Reuel, the son of Esau's wife **B**. 1412
36:13 These were grandsons of Esau's wife **B**. 1412
36:17 they were grandsons of Esau's wife **B**. 1412
1Ki 4:15 in Naphtali (he had married **B** daughter 1412

BASER (KJV) See BAD CHARACTERS

BASEST (KJV) See LOWLIEST

BASES (41) [BASE]

Ex 26:19 and make forty silver **b** to go under them— 149
26:19 two **b** for each frame, 149
26:21 and forty silver **b**—two under each frame. 149
26:25 be eight frames and sixteen silver **b**— 149
26:32 with gold and standing on four silver **b**. 149
26:37 And cast five bronze **b** for them. 149
27:10 with twenty posts and twenty bronze **b** and 149
27:11 with twenty posts and twenty bronze **b** and 149
27:12 with ten posts and ten **b**. 149
27:14 with three posts and three **b**, 149
27:15 with three posts and three **b**. 149
27:16 with four posts and four **b**. 149
27:17 and hooks, and bronze **b**. 149
27:18 and with bronze **b**. 149
35:11 clasps, frames, crossbars, posts and **b**; 149
35:17 of the courtyard with its posts and **b**, and 149
36:24 and made forty silver **b** to go under them— 149
36:24 two **b** for each frame, 149
36:26 and forty silver **b**—two under each frame. 149
36:30 there were eight frames and sixteen silver **b** 149
36:36 for them and cast their four silver **b**. 149
36:38 with gold and made their five **b** *of* bronze. 149
38:10 with twenty posts and twenty bronze **b**, 149
38:11 and had twenty posts and twenty bronze **b**, 149
38:12 with ten posts and ten **b**, 149
38:14 with three posts and three **b**, 149
38:15 with three posts and three **b**. 149
38:17 The **b** for the posts were bronze. 149
38:19 with four posts and four bronze **b**. 149
38:27 to cast the **b** *for* the sanctuary and for 149
38:27 100 **b** from the 100 talents, 149
38:30 They used it to make the **b** *for* the entrance 149
38:31 the **b** *for* the surrounding courtyard 149
39:33 its clasps, frames, crossbars, posts and **b**; 149

Ex 39:40 of the courtyard with its posts and **b,** and 149
40:18 he put the **b** in place, erected the frames, 149
Nu 3:36 its crossbars, posts, **b,** all its equipment, 149
3:37 of the surrounding courtyard with their **b,** 149
4:31 its crossbars, posts and **b,** 149
4:32 of the surrounding courtyard with their **b,** 149
SS 5:15 His legs are pillars of marble set on **b** 149

BASEWORK (1)

1Ki 7:31 its **b** it measured a cubit and a half. 4029+5126

BASHAN (60)

Nu 21:33 and went up along the road toward **B,** 1421
21:33 of **B** and his whole army marched out 1421
32:33 and the kingdom of Og king of **B—** 1421
Dt 1:4 and at Edrei had defeated Og king of **B,** 1421
3:1 and went up along the road toward **B,** 1421
3:1 of **B** with his whole army marched out 1421
3:3 also gave into our hands Og king of **B** 1421
3:4 of Argob, Og's kingdom in **B.** 1421
3:10 and all **B** as far as Salecah and Edrei, 1421
3:10 towns of Og's kingdom in **B.** 1421
3:11 (Only Og king of **B** was left of the remnant 1421
3:13 The rest of Gilead and also all of **B,** 1421
3:13 of Argob in **B** used to be known as a land 1421
3:14 so that to this day **B** is called Havvoth Jair.) 1421
4:43 and Golan in **B,** for the Manassites. 1421
4:47 of his land and the land of Og king of **B,** 1421
29:7 of Heshbon and Og king of **B** came out 1421
32:14 of **B** and the finest kernels of wheat. 1421
33:22 "Dan is a lion's cub, springing out of **B.**" 1421
Jos 9:10 Sihon king of Heshbon, and Og king of **B,** 1421
12:4 And the territory of Og king of **B,** 1421
12:5 of **B** to the border of the people of Geshur 1421
13:11 all of Mount Hermon and all **B** as far 1421
13:12 the whole kingdom of Og in **B,** 1421
13:30 from Mahanaim and including all of **B,** 1421
13:30 the entire realm of Og king of **B—** 1421
13:30 all the settlements of Jair in **B,** sixty towns, 1421
13:31 and Edrei (the royal cities of Og in **B**). 1421
17:1 who had received Gilead and **B** because 1421
17:5 of land besides Gilead and **B** east of 1421
20:8 and Golan in **B** in the tribe of Manasseh. 1421
21:6 and the half-tribe of Manasseh in **B.** 1421
21:27 of Manasseh, Golan in **B** (a city of refuge 1421
22:7 of Manasseh Moses had given land in **B,** 1421
1Ki 4:13 in **B** and its sixty large walled cities 1421
4:19 and the country of Og king of **B**). 1421
2Ki 10:33 by the Arnon Gorge through Gilead to **B.** 1421
1Ch 5:11 The Gadites lived next to them in **B,** 824+1421
5:12 then Janai and Shaphat, in **B.** 1421
5:16 in **B** and its outlying villages, 1421
5:23 in the land from **B** to Baal Hermon, 1421
6:62 of the tribe of Manasseh that is in **B.** 1421
6:71 of Manasseh they received Golan in **B** and 1421
Ne 9:22 and the country of Og king of **B.** 1421
Ps 22:12 strong bulls of **B** encircle me. 1421
68:15 mountains of **B** are majestic mountains; 1421
68:15 rugged are the mountains of **B.** 1421
68:22 The Lord says, "I will bring them from **B;** 1421
135:11 Og king of **B** and all the kings of Canaan— 1421
136:20 and Og king of **B—** 1421
Isa 2:13 tall and lofty, and all the oaks of **B,** 1421
33:9 and **B** and Carmel drop their leaves. 1421
Jer 22:20 let your voice be heard in **B,** 1421
50:19 and he will graze on Carmel and **B;** 1421
Eze 27:6 Of oaks from **B** they made your oars; 1421
39:18 all of them fattened animals from **B.** 1421
Am 4:1 you cows of **B** on Mount Samaria, 1421
Mic 7:14 in **B** and Gilead as in days long ago. 1421
Na 1:4 **B** and Carmel wither and the blossoms 1421
Zec 11:2 the stately trees are ruined! Wail, oaks of **B;** 1421

BASHAN-HAVOTH-JAIR (KJV) See HAVVOTH JAIR

BASHEMATH (KJV) See BASEMATH

BASIC (3) [BASE]

Gal 4:3 we were in slavery under the **b principles** *5122*
Col 2:8 the **b principles** of this world rather than *5122*
2:20 to the **b principles** of this world, why, as *5122*

BASIN (14) [BASINS, WASHBASIN]

Ex 12:22 the **b** and put some of the blood on the top 6195
30:18 "Make a bronze **b,** 3963
30:28 and the **b** with its stand. 3963
31:9 the **b** with its stand— 3963
35:16 the bronze **b** with its stand; 3963
38:8 the bronze **b** and its bronze stand from 3963
39:39 the **b** with its stand; 3963
40:7 place the **b** between the Tent of Meeting 3963
40:11 the **b** and its stand and consecrate them. 3963
40:30 the **b** between the Tent of Meeting and 3963
Lev 8:11 and all its utensils and the **b** with its stand, 3963
1Ki 7:30 and each had a **b** resting on four supports, 3963
7:38 one **b** to go on each of the ten stands. 3963
Jn 13:5 a **b** and began to wash his disciples' feet, *3781*

BASING (3) [BASE]

2Ki 18:19 **On** what *are you* **b** this confidence of yours 1053
2Ch 32:10 On what *are* you **b** your **confidence,** 1053
Isa 36:4 **On** what *are you* **b** this confidence of yours 1053

BASINS (9) [BASIN]

1Ki 7:38 He then made ten bronze **b,** 3963
7:40 the **b** and shovels and sprinkling bowls. 3963
7:43 the ten stands with their ten **b;** 3963
7:50 the pure gold **b,** 6195
2Ki 12:13 not spent for making silver **b,** 6195
16:17 the side panels and removed the **b** from 3963
2Ch 4:6 He then made ten **b** for washing 3963
4:14 the stands with their **b;** 3963
Jer 52:19 of the imperial guard took away the **b,** 6195

BASIS (15) [BASE]

Lev 25:15 to buy from your countryman **on the b of** 928
25:15 to you **on the b of** the number of years left 928
1Ki 20:34 **"On the b of** a treaty I will set you free." 928
Eze 16:61 but not **on the b of** my covenant with you. 4946
Da 6:5 "We will never find any **b for charges** 10544
Lk 23:4 "I find no **b for a charge** against this man." *165*
23:14 in your presence and have found no **b** *165*
Jn 8:6 in order to have a **b** for accusing him. *NIG*
18:38 "I find no **b for a charge** against him. *162*
19:4 to let you know that I find no **b for a charge** against him." *162*
19:6 I find no **b for a charge** against him." *162*
Phm 1:9 yet I appeal to you **on the b of** love. *1328*
Heb 7:11 the Levitical priesthood (for **on the b of** it *2093*
7:16 a priest not **on the b of** a regulation as *2848*
7:16 to his ancestry but **on the b of** the power of *2848*

BASKET (34) [BASKETFULS, BASKETS]

Ge 40:17 In the top **b** were all kinds of baked goods 6130
40:17 but the birds were eating them out of the **b** 6130
Ex 2:3 a papyrus **b** for him and coated it with tar 9310
2:5 She saw the **b** among the reeds 9310
29:3 Put them in a **b** and present them in it— 6130
29:23 From the **b** *of* bread made without yeast, 6130
29:32 of the ram and the bread that is in the **b.** 6130
Lev 8:2 and the **b** *containing* bread made 6130
8:26 from the **b** *of* bread made without yeast, 6130
8:31 and eat it there with the bread from the **b** 6130
Nu 6:15 and a **b** *of* bread made without yeast— 6130
6:17 to present the **b** *of* unleavened bread and is 6130
6:19 and a cake and a wafer from the **b,** 6130
Dt 23:24 but do not put any in your **b.** 3998
26:2 and put them in a **b.** 3244
26:4 The priest shall take the **b** from your hands 3244
26:10 Place **the b** before the LORD your God 2257[S]
28:5 Your **b** and your kneading trough will 3244
28:17 Your **b** and your kneading trough will 3244
Jdg 6:19 Putting the meat in a **b** and its broth in 6130
Ps 81:6 their hands were set free from the **b.** 1857
Isa 40:12 Who has held the dust of the earth in a **b,** 8955
Jer 24:2 One **b** had very good figs, 1857
24:2 the other **b** had very poor figs, 1857
Am 8:1 a **b** *of* ripe fruit. 3990
8:2 "A **b** *of* ripe fruit," I answered. 3990
Zec 5:6 He replied, "It is a **measuring b.**" 406
5:7 and there in the **b** sat a woman! 406
5:8 into the **b** and pushed the lead cover down 406
5:9 and they lifted up the **b** between heaven 406
5:10 "Where are they taking the **b?**" 406
5:11 the **b** will be set there in its place." NIH
Ac 9:25 and lowered him in a **b** through an opening *5083*
2Co 11:33 But I was lowered in a **b** from a window in *4914*

BASKETFULS (9) [BASKET]

Mt 14:20 and the disciples picked up twelve **b** *3186+4441*
15:37 the disciples picked up seven **b** *4441+5083*
16:9 and how many **b** you gathered? *3186*
16:10 and how many **b** you gathered? *5083*
Mk 6:43 up twelve **b** of broken pieces of bread *3186+4445*
8:8 Afterward the disciples picked up seven **b** *5083*
8:19 how many **b** of pieces did you pick up?" *3186+4441*
8:20 how many **b** of pieces did you pick up?" *4445+5083*
Lk 9:17 and the disciples picked up twelve **b** *3186*

BASKETS (6) [BASKET]

Ge 40:16 On my head were three **b** *of* bread. 6130
40:18 "The three **b** are three days. 6130
2Ki 10:7 They put their heads in **b** and sent them 1857
Jer 24:1 the LORD showed me two **b** 1857
Mt 13:48 down and collected the good fish in **b,** *35*
Jn 6:13 So they gathered them and filled twelve **b** *3186*

BASMATH (KJV) See BASEMATH

BASON, BASONS (KJV) See BASIN, BASINS, DISH, BOWLS

BASTARD, BASTARDS (KJV) See BORN OF A FORBIDDEN MARRIAGE, FOREIGNERS

BAT (2) [BATS]

Lev 11:19 any kind of heron, the hoopoe and the **b.** 6491
Dt 14:18 any kind of heron, the hoopoe and the **b.** 6491

BATCH (4)

Ro 11:16 then the whole **b** is holy; *5878*
1Co 5:6 through the whole **b of dough?** *5878*
5:7 that you may be a new **b** without yeast— *5878*
Gal 5:9 through the whole **b of dough."** *5878*

BATH (7) [BATHE]

Isa 5:10 A ten-acre vineyard will produce only a **b** 1427
Eze 45:10 an accurate ephah and an accurate **b.** 1427
45:11 ephah and the **b** are to be the same size, 1427
45:11 the **b** containing a tenth of a homer and 1427
45:14 measured by the **b,** 1427
45:14 a tenth of a **b** from each cor (which consists 1427
Jn 13:10 "A person who *has* **had a b** needs only *3374*

BATH RABBIM (1)

SS 7:4 of Heshbon by the gate of **B.** 1442

BATHE (26) [BATH, BATHED, BATHING, BATHS]

Ex 2:5 down to the Nile to **b,** 8175
Lev 14:8 shave off all his hair and **b** with water; 8175
14:9 He must wash his clothes and **b** himself 8175
15:5 and **b** with water, 8175
15:6 on must wash his clothes and **b** with water, 8175
15:7 a discharge must wash his clothes and **b** 8175
15:8 that person must wash his clothes and **b** 8175
15:10 up those things must wash his clothes and **b** 8175
15:11 with water must wash his clothes and **b** 8175
15:13 he must wash his clothes and **b** himself 8175
15:16 *he must* **b** his whole body with water, 8175
15:18 *both must* **b** with water, 8175
15:21 and **b** with water, 8175
15:22 on must wash his clothes and **b** with water, 8175
15:27 he must wash his clothes and **b** with water, 8175
16:4 so *he must* **b** himself with water 8175
16:24 *He shall* **b** himself with water in 8175
16:26 and **b** himself with water; 8175
16:28 and **b** himself with water; 8175
17:15 and **b** with water, and he will 8175
17:16 he does not wash his clothes and **b** himself, 8175
Nu 19:7 and **b** himself with water. 8175
19:8 also wash his clothes and **b** with water, 8175
19:19 and **b** with water, 8175
Dt 33:24 and *let him* **b** his feet in oil. 3188
Ps 58:10 *they* **b** their feet in the blood of the wicked. 8175

BATHED (5) [BATHE]

Lev 22:6 the sacred offerings unless *he has* **b** himself 8175
1Ki 22:38 a pool in Samaria (where the prostitutes **b**), 8175
Isa 34:6 The sword of the LORD *is* **b in** blood, 4848
Eze 16:9 " *'I* **b** you with water and washed 8175
23:40 and when they arrived *you* **b** *yourself* 8175

BATHING (2) [BATHE]

2Sa 11:2 From the roof he saw a woman **b.** 8175
Job 36:30 **b** the depths of the sea. 4059

BATHS (10) [BATHE]

1Ki 5:11 to twenty thousand **b** *of* pressed olive oil. 1427
7:26 It held two thousand **b.** 1427
7:38 each holding forty **b** 1427
2Ch 2:10 twenty thousand **b** of wine 1427
2:10 and twenty thousand **b** of olive oil." 1427
4:5 It held three thousand **b.** 1427
Ezr 7:22 a hundred **b** of wine, 10126
7:22 a hundred **b** of olive oil, 10126
Eze 45:14 from each cor (which consists of ten **b** 1427
45:14 for ten **b** are equivalent to a homer). 1427

BATHSHEBA (13)

2Sa 11:3 The man said, "Isn't this **B,** 1444
12:24 Then David comforted his wife **B,** 1444
1Ki 1:11 Then Nathan asked **B,** Solomon's mother, 1444
1:15 So **B** went to see the aged king in his room, 1444
1:16 **B** bowed low and knelt before the king. 1444
1:28 Then King David said, "Call in **B.**" 1444
1:31 Then **B** bowed low with her face to 1444
2:13 Adonijah, the son of Haggith, went to **B,** 1444
2:13 **B** asked him, "Do you come peacefully?" NIH
2:18 "Very well," **B** replied, 1444
2:19 When **B** went to King Solomon to speak 1444
1Ch 3:5 These four were by **B** daughter of Ammiel. 1444
Ps 51:T after David had committed adultery with **B.** 1444

BATS (1) [BAT]

Isa 2:20 throw away to the rodents and **b** their idols 6491

BATTERED (1) [BATTERING]

Isa 24:12 city is left in ruins, its gate *is* **b to pieces.** 4198+8625

BATTERING (7) [BATTERED]

2Sa 20:15 While *they were* **b** the wall to bring it down, 8845
Isa 22:5 a day of **b down** walls and of crying out to 7982
Eze 4:2 to it, set up camps against it and put **b rams** 4119
21:22 where he is to set up **b rams,** 4119
21:22 to set **b rams** against the gates, 4119
26:9 the blows of his **b rams** against your walls 7692
Ac 27:18 **took** such a violent **b from the storm** *5928*

BATTLE (210) [BATTLEMENTS, BATTLES]

Ge 14: 8 marched out and drew up their **b** lines 4878
Ex 13:18 went up out of Egypt **armed for b.** 2821
Nu 10: 9 When you go into **b** in your own land 4878
21:33 to meet them in **b** at Edrei. 4878
31: 4 Send into **b** a thousand men from each of 7372
31: 5 So twelve thousand men armed for **b,** 7372
31: 6 Moses sent them into **b,** 7372
31:14 who returned from the **b.** 4878+7372
31:21 into **b,** "This is the requirement of the law 4878
31:27 between the soldiers who took part in the **b** 7372
31:28 From the soldiers who fought in the **b,** 7372
31:36 of those who fought in the **b** was: 7372
32:20 before the LORD for **b,** 4878
32:27 But your servants, every man armed for **b,** 7372
32:29 every man armed for **b,** 4878
Dt 2:24 take possession of it and engage him in **b.** 4878
2:32 and all his army came out to meet us in **b** 4878
3: 1 to meet us in **b** at Edrei. 4878
3:18 But all your able-bodied men, **armed for b,** 2741
20: 2 When you are about to go into **b,** 4878
20: 3 "Hear, O Israel, today you are going into **b** 4878
20: 5 in **b** and someone else may dedicate it. 4878
20: 6 in **b** and someone else enjoy it. 4878
20: 7 in **b** and someone else marry her." 4878
20:12 to make peace and they engage you in **b,** 4878
Jos 4:13 About forty thousand armed for **b** crossed 7372
8:14 in the morning to meet Israel in **b** at 4878
11:19 who took them all in **b.** 4878
13:22 In addition to *those* **slain in b,** 2728
14:11 I'm just as vigorous to go out to **b** now 4878
Jdg 3: 2 not had previous **b** experience): 4392S
8:13 of Joash then returned from the **b** by 4878
18:11 the clan of the Danites, armed for **b,** set out 4878
18:16 The six hundred Danites, armed for **b,** 4878
20:20 the Benjamites and took up **b** positions 4878
20:23 up again to **b** against the Benjamites, 4878
20:28 up again to **b** with Benjamin our brother, 4878
20:39 then the men of Israel would turn in the **b.** 4878
20:39 "We are defeating them as in the first **b.**" 4878
20:42 but they could not escape the **b.** 4878
1Sa 4: 2 and as the **b** spread, 4878
4:12 a Benjamite ran from the **b line** and went 5120
4:16 "I have just come from the **b line;** 5120
7:10 near to engage Israel in **b.** 4878
13:22 on the day of the **b** not a soldier with Saul 4878
14:20 and went to the **b.** 4878
14:22 they joined the **b** in hot pursuit. 4878
14:23 and the **b** moved on beyond Beth Aven. 4878
17: 2 the Valley of Elah and drew up their **b** line 4878
17: 8 "Why do you come out and line up for **b?** 4878
17:20 the army was going out to its **b positions,** 5120
17:22 ran to the **b lines** and greeted his brothers. 5120
17:28 you came down only to watch the **b.**" 4878
17:47 for the **b** is the LORD's, 4878
17:48 David ran quickly toward the **b line** 5120
18:30 commanders continued to go out to **b,** NIH
23: 8 And Saul called up all his forces for **b,** 4878
26:10 or he will go into **b** and perish. 4878
29: 4 He must not go with us into **b,** 4878
29: 9 'He must not go up with us into **b.**' 4878
30:24 as that of him who went down to the **b.** 4878
2Sa 1: 4 He said, "The men fled from the **b.** 4878
1:25 "How the mighty have fallen in **b!** 4878
2:17 The **b** that day was very fierce, 4878
3:30 in the **b** at Gibeon.) 4878
8:10 and congratulate him on his victory *in* **b** 4309
10: 8 and drew up in **b formation** at the entrance 4878
10: 9 that there were **b lines** in front of him and 4878
10:17 The Arameans **formed** *their* **b lines** 6885
11:18 Joab sent David a full account of the **b.** 4878
11:19 the king this account of the **b,** 4878
17:11 with you yourself leading them into **b.** 7930
18: 6 The **b** took place in the forest of Ephraim. 4878
18: 8 The **b** spread out over 4878
19: 3 in who are ashamed when they flee from **b.** 4878
19:10 anointed to rule over us, has died in **b.** 4878
21:15 a **b** between the Philistines and Israel. 4878
21:17 "Never again will you go out with us to **b,** 4878
21:18 there was another **b** with the Philistines, 4878
21:19 In another **b** with the Philistines at Gob, 4878
21:20 In still another **b,** which took place at Gath, 4878
22:35 He trains my hands for **b;** 4878
22:40 You armed me with strength for **b;** 4878
23: 9 [at Pas Dammim] for **b.** 4878
1Ki 2: 5 in peacetime as if in **b,** 4878
20:14 "And who will start the **b?**" 4878
20:29 and on the seventh day the **b** was joined. 4878
20:39 "Your servant went into the thick of the **b,** 4878
22:30 "I will enter the **b** in disguise, 4878
22:30 of Israel disguised himself and went into **b.** 4878
22:35 All day long the **b** raged, 4878
2Ki 3:26 the king of Moab saw that the **b** had gone 4878
8:29 on him at Ramoth in his **b** with Hazael king 4309
9:15 on him in the **b** with Hazael king of Aram.) 4309
13:25 of Hazael the towns he had taken in **b** 4878
14: 7 in the Valley of Salt and captured Sela in **b,** 4878
23:29 King Josiah marched out to **meet** him **in b,** 7925
1Ch 5:18 and who were trained for **b.** 4878
5:20 because they cried out to him during the **b.** 4878
5:22 because the **b** was God's. 4878
7: 4 had 36,000 **men ready for b,** 1522+4878+7372
7:40 The number of men **ready for b,** 928+2021+4878+7372
11:13 when the Philistines gathered there for **b.** 4878
12: 1 among the warriors who helped him in **b;** 4878
1Ch 12: 8 They were brave warriors, **ready for b** 408+2021+4200+4878+7372
12:23 of the men armed for **b** who came to David 7372
12:24 6,800 armed for **b;** 7372
12:25 of Simeon, warriors ready for **b**—7,100; 7372
12:33 experienced soldiers prepared for **b** 4878
12:35 men of Dan, ready for **b**—28,600; 4878
12:36 experienced soldiers prepared for **b**— 4878
14:15 move out to **b,** 4878
18:10 and congratulate him on his victory *in* **b** 4309
19: 7 from their towns and moved out for **b.** 4878
19: 9 and drew up in **b formation** at the entrance 4878
19:10 that there were **b lines** in front of him and 4878
19:17 and **formed** *his* **b lines** opposite them. 6885
19:17 to meet the Arameans *in* **b,** 4878
20: 5 In another **b** with the Philistines, 4878
20: 6 In still another **b,** which took place at Gath, 4878
26:27 of the plunder taken in **b** they dedicated for 4878
2Ch 13: 3 Abijah went into **b** with a force 4878
13: 3 and Jeroboam drew up a **b** line against him 4878
13:12 with their trumpets will sound the **b cry** 9558
13:15 and the men of Judah **raised the b cry.** 8131
13:15 **sound of** their **b cry,** 8131
14:10 and they took up **b** positions in the Valley 4878
17:18 Jehozabad, with 180,000 men armed for **b.** 7372
18:29 "I will enter the **b** in disguise, 4878
18:29 of Israel disguised himself and went into **b.** 4878
18:34 All day long the **b** raged, 4878
20:15 For the **b** is not yours, but God's. 4878
20:17 You *will* not *have* to **fight** this **b.** 4309
22: 6 on him at Ramoth in his **b** with Hazael king 4309
25: 8 Even if you go and fight courageously in **b,** 4878
35:20 and Josiah marched out to **meet** him **in b.** 7925
35:22 but disguised himself to **engage** him **in b.** 4309
Job 5:20 and in **b** from the stroke of the sword. 4878
38:23 for days of war and **b?** 4878
39:25 He catches the scent of **b** from afar, 4878
39:25 the shout of commanders and the **b cry.** 9558
Ps 18:34 He trains my hands for **b;** 4878
18:39 You armed me with strength for **b;** 4878
24: 8 the LORD mighty in **b.** 4878
55:18 from the **b** waged against me, 7930
78: 9 turned back on the day of **b;** 7930
89:43 and have not supported him in **b.** 4878
110: 3 be willing on your day of **b.** 2657
140: 7 who shields my head in the day of **b**— 5977
144: 1 trains my hands for war, my fingers for **b.** 4878
Pr 21:31 The horse is made ready for the day of **b,** 4878
Ecc 9:11 or the **b** to the strong, nor does food come 4878
SS 3: 8 all experienced in **b,** 4878
Isa 3:25 your warriors in **b.** 4878
8: 9 **Prepare for b,** and be shattered! 273
8: 9 **Prepare for b,** and be shattered! 273
9: 5 in **b** and every garment rolled in blood will 8323
21:15 from the bent bow and from the heat of **b.** 4878
22: 2 nor did they die in **b.** 4878
27: 4 I would march against them in **b;** 4878
28: 6 of strength to those who turn back the **b** at 4878
30:32 as he fights them in **b** with the blows 4878
31: 4 to **do b** on Mount Zion and on its heights. 7371
31: 9 **b standard** their commanders will panic," 5812
42:13 with a shout *he will* **raise the b cry** 7658
Jer 4:19 I have heard the **b** cry. 4878
4:21 the **b standard** and hear the sound of 5812
6: 4 "Prepare for **b** against her! 4878
6:23 like men in **b** formation to attack you, 4878
8: 6 like a horse charging into **b.** 4878
18:21 their young men slain by the sword in **b.** 4878
20:16 a **b cry** at noon. 9558
46: 3 both large and small, and march out for **b!** 4878
48:14 'We are warriors, men valiant in **b**'? 4878
49: 2 "when I will sound the **b** cry 4878
49:14 Rise up for **b!**" 4878
50:22 The noise of **b** is in the land, 4878
50:42 like men in **b** formation to attack you, 4878
51:20 "You are my war club, my weapon for **b**— 4878
51:27 Prepare the nations for **b** against her; NIH
51:28 Prepare the nations for **b** against her— NIH
Eze 7:14 no one will go into **b,** 4878
13: 5 so that it will stand firm in the **b** on the day 4878
21:22 to sound the **b cry,** 9558
Da 11:10 **carry the b** as far as his fortress 1741+2256+8740
11:20 yet not in anger or in **b.** 4878
11:26 and many *will* **fall in b.** 2728+5877
11:40 the king of the South *will* **engage** him **in b,** 5590
Hos 1: 7 not by bow, sword or **b,** 4878
2:18 Bow and sword and **b** I will abolish from 4878
5: 8 **Raise the b cry** in Beth Aven; 8131
10:14 the **roar of b** will rise against your people, 8623
10:14 war cries on the day of **b,** 4878
Joel 2: 5 like a mighty army drawn up for **b.** 4878
Am 1:14 on the day of **b,** 4878
Ob 1: 1 "Rise, and let us go against her for **b**"— 4878
Mic 2: 8 like men returning from **b.** 4878
Zep 1:16 and **b cry** against the fortified cities and 9558
Zec 9:10 and the **b** bow will be broken. 4878
10: 3 and make them like a proud horse in **b.** 4878
10: 4 from him the tent peg, from him the **b** bow, 4878
10: 5 the muddy streets in **b.** 4878
14: 3 as he fights in the day of **b.** 7930
1Co 14: 8 who will get ready for **b?** *4483*
Heb 11:34 and who became powerful in **b** *4483*
Jas 4: 1 Don't they come from your desires that **b** *5129*
Rev 9: 7 like horses prepared for **b.** *4483*
9: 9 of many horses and chariots rushing into **b.** *4483*
16:14 for the **b** on the great day of God Almighty. *4483*
20: 8 to gather them for **b.** *4483*

BATTLEFIELD (2) [FIELD]

Jdg 20:21 cut down twenty-two thousand Israelites on the **b** that day. 824
1Sa 4: 2 about four thousand of them on the **b.** 5120+8441

BATTLEMENT (KJV) See PARAPET

BATTLEMENTS (1) [BATTLE]

Isa 54:12 I will make your **b** of rubies, 9087

BATTLES (4) [BATTLE]

1Sa 8:20 and to go out before us and fight our **b.**" 4878
18:17 only serve me bravely and fight the **b** *of* 4878
25:28 because he fights the LORD's **b.** 4878
2Ch 32: 8 to help us and to fight our **b.**" 4878

BAVAI (KJV) See BINNUI

BAY (4)

Jos 15: 2 Their southern boundary started from the **b** 4383
15: 5 the **b** *of* the sea at the mouth of the Jordan, 4383
18:19 and came out at the northern **b** *of* 4383
Ac 27:39 but they saw a **b** with a sandy beach, *3146*

BAZLUTH (2)

Ezr 2:52 **B,** Mehida, Harsha, 1296
Ne 7:54 **B,** Mehida, Harsha, 1296

BDELLIUM (KJV) See RESIN

BE (5161) [AM, ARE, AREN'T, BEEN, BEING, WAS, WASN'T, WERE, WEREN'T] See Index of Articles Etc.

BE ESHTARAH (1)

Jos 21:27 and **B,** together with their pasturelands— 1285

BEACH (3)

Ac 21: 5 and there on the **b** we knelt to pray. *129*
27:39 but they saw a bay with a **sandy b,** *129*
27:40 the foresail to the wind and made for the **b.** *129*

BEACON (KJV) See FLAGSTAFF

BEAK (1)

Ge 8:11 in its **b** was a freshly plucked olive leaf! 7023

BEALIAH (1)

1Ch 12: 5 **B,** Shemariah and Shephatiah 1270

BEALOTH (1)

Jos 15:24 Ziph, Telem, **B,** 1268

BEAM (1) [BEAMS]

Ezr 6:11 a **b** is to be pulled from his house and he is 10058

BEAMS (18) [BEAM]

1Ki 6: 9 roofing it with **b** and cedar planks. 1464
6:10 and they were attached to the temple by **b** 6770
6:36 and one course of **trimmed** cedar **b.** 4164
7: 2 columns supporting **trimmed** cedar **b.** 4164
7: 3 above the **b** that rested on the columns— 7521
7: 3 forty-five **b,** fifteen to a row. NIH
7:11 cut to size, and **cedar** *b.* AIT
7:12 and one course of **trimmed** cedar **b,** 4164
2Ch 3: 7 He overlaid the **ceiling b,** doorframes, 7771
34:11 and timber for joists and **b** *for* the buildings 7936
Ne 2: 8 to **make b** *for* the gates of the citadel by 7936
3: 3 They **laid** its **b** and put its doors and bolts 7936
3: 6 They **laid** its **b** and put its doors and bolts 7936
Ps 104: 3 and **lays** *the* **b** *of* his upper chambers 7936
SS 1:17 The **b** *of* our house are cedars; 7771
Jer 22: 7 up your fine **cedar** *b* and throw them into AIT
Hab 2:11 and the **b** of the woodwork will echo it. 4096
Zep 2:14 the **b of cedar** will be exposed. 781

BEANS (2)

2Sa 17:28 flour and roasted grain, **b** and lentils, 7038
Eze 4: 9 "Take wheat and barley, **b** and lentils, 7038

BEAR (125) [AFTERBIRTH, BEARABLE, BEARER, BEARING, BEARS, BIRTH, BIRTHDAY, BIRTHRIGHT, BORE, BORN, BORNE, CHILDBEARING, CHILDBIRTH, FIRSTBORN, HIGHBORN, LOWBORN, NATIVE-BORN, NEWBORN, REBIRTH, STILLBORN, UNBORN]

Ge 1:11 and trees on the land *that* **b** fruit with seed 6913
4:13 "My punishment is more than I *can* **b.** 5951
17:17 *Will* Sarah **b a child** at the age of ninety?" 3528
17:19 but your wife Sarah *will* **b** you a son, 3528
17:21 Isaac, whom Sarah *will* **b** to you 3528

Ge 30: 3 with her so that *she can* **b children** for me 3528
43: 9 *I will* **b the blame** before you all my life. 2627
44:32 *I will* **b the blame** before you, my father, 2627
Ex 16:29 **B in mind** that the LORD has given you 8011
28:12 Aaron *is to* **b** the names on his shoulders 5951
28:29 he *will* **b** the names of the sons of Israel 5951
28:30 Thus Aaron *will* always **b** the means 5951
28:38 and he *will* **b** the guilt involved in 5951
Lev 19:18 not seek revenge or **b a grudge against** one 5757
Nu 5:31 but the woman *will* **b** the consequences 5951
9:13 That man *will* **b** the consequences 5951
18: 1 your sons and your father's family *are to* **b** 5951
18: 1 *to* **b** the responsibility for offenses against 5951
18:22 or they *will* **b** the consequences 5951
18:23 the Tent of Meeting and **b** the responsibility 5951
Dt 1:12 But how *can I* **b** your problems 5951
21:15 both **b** him sons but the firstborn is the son 3528
Jdg 5:14 from Zebulun *those who* **b** a commander's 5432
10:16 **b** Israel's misery **no longer.** 7918
1Sa 17:34 a lion or a **b** came and carried off a sheep 1800
17:36 both the lion and the **b;** 1800
17:37 and the paw of the **b** will deliver me from 1800
2Sa 17: 8 and as fierce as a wild **b** robbed of her cubs. 1800
2Ki 3:21 old, *who could* **b arms** was called up 2514+2520
19:30 and **b** fruit above. 6913
Est 8: 6 *can I* **b** to see disaster fall on my people? 3523
8: 6 How *can I* **b** to see the destruction 3523
Job 9: 9 He is the Maker of the **B** and Orion, 6933
20:13 though *he* cannot **b** to let it go and keeps it 2798
21: 3 **B with** me while I speak, 5951
36: 2 "**B** with me a little longer 4192
38:32 in their seasons or lead out the **B** 6568
39: 2 Do you count the months till *they* **b?** 4848
Ps 38: 4 like a burden too heavy to **b.** NIH
89:50 I **b** in my heart the taunts of all the nations, 5951
92:14 *They will* still **b fruit** in old age, 5649
Pr 17:12 Better to meet a **b** robbed of her cubs than 1800
18:14 but a crushed spirit who *can* **b?** 5951
28:15 or a charging **b** is a wicked man ruling over 1800
30:21 under four it cannot **b up:** 5951
Isa 1:13 *I* **cannot b** your evil assemblies. 3523+4202
11: 1 from his roots a Branch *will* **b fruit.** 7238
11: 7 The cow will feed with the **b,** 1800
24: 6 its people *must* **b** *their* **guilt.** 870
37:31 and **b** fruit above. 6913
53:11 and he *will* **b** their iniquities. 6022
65:23 not toil in vain or **b children** doomed 3528
Jer 12: 2 they grow and **b** fruit. 6913
12:13 So **b** *the* **shame** of your harvest because of 1017
14: 9 we **b** your name; do not forsake us! 6584+7924
15:16 for I **b** your name, 6584+7924
17: 8 of drought and never fails *to* **b** fruit." 6913
30: 6 Ask and see: *Can* a man **b children?** 3528
La 3:10 Like a **b** lying in wait, like a lion in hiding, 1800
3:27 for a man *to* **b** the yoke while he is young. 5951
5: 7 and we **b** their punishment. 6022
Eze 4: 4 *You are to* **b** their sin for the number 5951
4: 5 So for 390 days *you will* **b** the sin of 5951
4: 6 and **b** the sin of the house of Judah. 5951
14:10 *They will* **b** their guilt— 5951
16:52 **B** your disgrace, for you have furnished 5951
16:52 So then, be ashamed and **b** your disgrace, 5951
16:54 so that *you may* **b** your disgrace and 5951
16:58 You *will* **b** the consequences 5951
17: 8 **b** fruit and become a splendid vine.' 5951
17:23 and **b** fruit and become a splendid cedar. 6913
23:35 behind your back, you *must* **b** 5951
23:49 for your lewdness and **b** the consequences 5951
32:24 *They* **b** their shame with those who go 5951
32:25 *they* **b** their shame with those who go down 5951
32:30 and **b** their shame with those who go down 5951
34:29 in the land or **b** the scorn of the nations. 5951
44:10 after their idols *must* **b** the consequences 5951
44:12 with uplifted hand that *they must* **b** 5951
44:13 *they must* **b** the shame 5951
47:12 Every month *they will* **b,** 1144
Da 7: 5 which looked like a **b.** 10155
9:19 your city and your people **b** your Name." 6584+7924
Hos 9:16 Even if *they* **b children,** 3528
10: 2 and now *they must* **b** *their* **guilt.** 870
13: 8 Like a **b** robbed of her cubs, 1800
13:16 people of Samaria *must* **b** *their* **guilt,** 870
Am 5:19 a man fled from a lion only to meet a **b,** 1800
7:10 The land cannot **b** all his words. 3920
9:12 and all the nations that **b** my name," 6584+7924
Mic 6:16 *you will* **b** the scorn of the nations." 5951
7: 9 *I will* **b** the LORD's wrath, 5951
Na 1:14 to **b** your name. NIH
Mt 7:18 A good tree cannot **b** bad fruit, *4472*
7:18 and a bad tree cannot **b** good fruit. *4472*
7:19 Every tree that *does* not **b** good fruit is cut *4472*
21:19 *"May* you never **b** fruit again!" *1181*
Mk 4: 7 so that *they did* not **b** grain. *1443*
Lk 1:13 Your wife Elizabeth *will* **b** you a son, *1164*
1:42 blessed is the **child** you will **b!** *2843+3120+3836*
6:43 nor *does* a bad tree **b** good fruit. *4472*
Jn 15: 2 *that does* **b** fruit he prunes so that it will be *5770*
15: 4 No branch can **b** fruit by itself; *5770*
15: 4 Neither can you **b** fruit unless you remain *NIG*
15: 5 he *will* **b** much fruit; *5770*
15: 8 that *you* **b** much fruit, *5770*
15:16 and appointed you to go and **b** fruit— *5770*
16:12 more than you can now **b.** *1002*
Ac 15:10 nor our fathers have been able *to* **b?** *1002*
15:17 and all the Gentiles who **b** my name, *2126*
Ro 7: 4 in order that *we might* **b fruit** to God. *2844*
13: 4 for *he does* not **b** the sword for nothing. *5841*
15: 1 *to* **b with** the failings of the weak and not *1002*
1Co 10:13 be tempted beyond what you can **b.** *NIG*
15:49 so *shall we* **b** the likeness of the man *5841*
Gal 6:17 for I **b** on my body the marks of Jesus. *1002*
Col 3:13 **B with** each other and forgive *462*
Heb 9:28 he will appear a second time, not to **b** sin, *NIG*
12:20 *they could* not **b** what was commanded: *5770*
13:22 to **b with** my word of exhortation, *462*
Jas 3:12 My brothers, can a fig tree **b** olives, *4472*
3:12 or a grapevine **b** figs? *NIG*
1Pe 4:16 but praise God that you **b** that name. *NIG*
2Pe 3:15 **B in mind** that our Lord's patience means salvation, *2451*
Rev 13: 2 but had feet like those of a **b** and a mouth *759*

BEARABLE (5) [BEAR]

Mt 10:15 it will be **more b** for Sodom and Gomorrah *445*
11:22 be **more b** for Tyre and Sidon on the day *445*
11:24 that it will be **more b** for Sodom on the day *445*
Lk 10:12 it will be **more b** on that day for Sodom *445*
10:14 But it will be **more b** for Tyre and Sidon at *445*

BEARD (12) [BEARDS]

Lev 14: 9 he must shave his head, his **b,** 2417
19:27 of your head or clip off the edges of your **b.** 2417
1Sa 21:13 the gate and letting saliva run down his **b.** 2417
2Sa 10: 4 shaved off half of each man's **b,** 2417
20: 9 by the **b** with his right hand to kiss him. 2417
Ezr 9: 3 from my head and **b** and sat down appalled. 2417
Ps 133: 2 running down on the **b,** 2417
133: 2 running down on Aaron's **b,** 2417
Isa 15: 2 Every head is shaved and every **b** cut off. 2417
50: 6 my cheeks to *those who* **pulled out** my **b;** 5307
Jer 48:37 Every head is shaved and every **b** cut off; 2417
Eze 5: 1 to shave your head and your **b.** 2417

BEARDS (5) [BEARD]

Lev 21: 5 the edges of their **b** or cut their bodies. 2417
2Sa 10: 5 "Stay at Jericho till your **b** have grown, 2417
1Ch 19: 5 "Stay at Jericho till your **b** have grown, 2417
Isa 7:20 and to take off your **b** also. 2417
Jer 41: 5 eighty men who had shaved off their **b,** 2417

BEARER (2) [BEAR]

1Sa 17: 7 His shield **b** went ahead of him. 5951
17:41 with his shield **b** in front of him, 5951

BEARING (18) [BEAR]

Ge 1:12 plants **b** seed according to their kinds 2445
1:12 and trees **b** fruit with seed in it according 6913
30: 1 that *she was* not **b** Jacob any **children,** 3528
Nu 13:23 they cut off a branch **b** a single cluster 2256
Jdg 8:18 "each one with the **b** *of* a prince." 9307
1Sa 14: 1 of Saul said to the young man **b** his armor, 5951
2Ch 12:11 the guards went with him, **b** the shields, 5951
Pr 30:29 four that move *with* **stately b:** 3512
Isa 1:14 I am weary of **b** them. 5951
60: 6 **b** gold and incense and proclaiming 5951
Jer 4:31 a groan as of *one* **b** *her* **first child—** 1144
Joel 2:22 The trees *are* **b** their fruit; 5951
Ro 2:15 their consciences also **b witness,** *5210*
Eph 4: 2 be patient, **b with** one another in love. *462*
Col 1: 6 All over the world this gospel is **b fruit** *2844*
1:10 **b fruit** in every good work, *2844*
Heb 13:13 **b** the disgrace he bore. *5770*
Rev 22: 2 **b** twelve crops of fruit, *4472*

BEARS (27) [BEAR]

Ge 49:21 a doe set free that **b** beautiful fawns. 5989
Ex 21: 4 a wife and *she* **b** him sons or daughters, 3528
Dt 25: 6 The first son *she* **b** shall carry on the name 3528
28:57 from her womb and the children *she* **b.** 3528
1Ki 8:43 this house I have built **b** your Name. 6584+7924
2Ki 2:24 Then two **b** came out of the woods 1800
2Ch 6:33 this house I have built **b** your Name. 6584+7924
20: 9 that **b** your Name and will cry out to you 928
Job 39: 1 Do you watch when the doe **b** her fawn? 2655
Ps 68:19 God our Savior, *who* daily **b** our **burdens.** 6673
Isa 59:11 We all growl like **b;** 1800
Jer 7:10 which **b** my Name, and say, 6584+7924
7:11 Has this house, which **b** my Name, 6584+7924
7:14 now do to the house that **b** my Name, 6584+7924
7:30 that **b** my Name and have defiled it. 6584+7924
25:29 on the city that **b** my Name, 6584+7924
32:34 house that **b** my Name and defiled it. 6584+7924
34:15 in the house that **b** my Name. 6584+7924
Da 9:18 the desolation of the city that **b** your Name. 6584+7924
Mt 7:17 Likewise every good tree **b** good fruit, *4472*
7:17 but a bad tree **b** bad fruit. *4472*
Lk 6:43 "No good tree **b** bad fruit, *1639+4472*
13: 9 If *it* **b** fruit next year, fine! *4472*
Jn 15: 2 cuts off every branch in me *that* **b** no fruit, *5770*
Gal 4:24 from Mount Sinai and **b children** who are *1164*
4:27 O barren woman, who **b** no **children;** *5503*
1Pe 2:19 For it is commendable if a *man* **b up under** *5722*

BEAST (58) [BEASTS]

2Ki 14: 9 Then a wild **b** in Lebanon came along 2651
2Ch 25:18 Then a wild **b** in Lebanon came along 2651
Ps 36: 6 O LORD, you preserve both man and **b.** 989
68:30 Rebuke the **b** *among* the reeds, 2651
73:22 I was a **brute b** before you. 989
Isa 35: 9 nor will *any* ferocious **b** get up on it; 2651
Jer 7:20 be poured out on this place, on man and **b,** 989
Da 7: 5 "And there before me was a second **b,** 10263
7: 6 and there before me was another **b,** NIH
7: 6 This **b** had four heads, 10263
7: 7 and there before me was a fourth **b—** 10263
7:11 until the **b** was slain and its body destroyed 10263
7:19 the fourth **b,** which was different from all 10263
7:19 the **b** that crushed and devoured its victims NIH
7:23 'The fourth **b** is a fourth kingdom 10263
Jnh 3: 7 Do not let any man or **b,** herd or flock, 989
3: 8 let man and **b** be covered with sackcloth. 989
Zec 8:10 that time there were no wages for man or **b.** 989
2Pe 2:16 for his wrongdoing by a **donkey—**a **b** *5689*
Rev 11: 7 the **b** that comes up from the Abyss *2563*
13: 1 And I saw a **b** coming out of the sea. *2563*
13: 2 The **b** I saw resembled a leopard, *2563*
13: 2 The dragon gave **the b** his power *899S*
13: 3 *of* **the b** seemed to have had a fatal wound, *899S*
13: 3 and followed the **b.** *2563*
13: 4 because he had given authority *to* the **b,** *2563*
13: 4 and they also worshiped the **b** and asked, *2563*
13: 4 "Who is like the **b?** *2563*
13: 5 **The b** was given a mouth *899S*
13: 8 of the earth will worship **the b—** *899S*
13:11 I saw another **b,** coming out of the earth. *2563*
13:12 He exercised all the authority *of* the first **b** *2563*
13:12 and its inhabitants worship the first **b,** *2563*
13:14 to do on behalf of the first **b,** *2563*
13:14 the **b** who was wounded by the sword and *2563*
13:15 to give breath to the image *of* the first **b,** *2563*
13:17 which is the name *of* the **b** or the number *2563*
13:18 let him calculate the number *of* the **b,** *2563*
14: 9 the **b** and his image and receives his mark *2563*
14:11 for those who worship the **b** and his image, *2563*
15: 2 those who had been victorious over the **b** *2563*
16: 2 the mark *of* the **b** and worshiped his image. *2563*
16:10 on the throne *of* the **b,** *2563*
16:13 the mouth *of* the **b** and out of the mouth of *2563*
17: 3 There I saw a woman sitting on a scarlet **b** *2563*
17: 7 of the woman and *of* the **b** she rides, *2563*
17: 8 The **b,** which you saw, once was, *2563*
17: 8 be astonished when they see the **b,** *2563*
17:11 The **b** who once was, and now is not, *2563*
17:12 authority as kings along with the **b.** *2563*
17:13 and authority *to* the **b.** *2563*
17:16 The **b** and the ten horns you saw will hate *2563*
17:17 by agreeing to give the **b** their power *2563*
19:19 Then I saw the **b** and the kings of the earth *2563*
19:20 But the **b** was captured, *2563*
19:20 the mark *of* the **b** and worshiped his image. *2563*
20: 4 They had not worshiped the **b** or his image *2563*
20:10 where the **b** and the false prophet had been thrown. *2563*

BEASTS (58) [BEAST]

Ge 1:30 the **b** *of* the earth and all the birds of the air 2651
2:19 the **b** *of* the field and all the birds of the air. 2651
2:20 the birds of the air and all the **b** *of* the field. 2651
9: 2 upon all the **b** *of* the earth and all the birds 2651
31:39 **animals torn by wild b;** 3274
Ex 22:31 **animal torn by** wild **b;** 3274
Lev 26: 6 I will remove savage **b** from the land, 2651
Dt 28:26 be food for all the birds of the air and the **b** 989
32:24 against them the fangs of **wild b,** 989
1Sa 17:44 the birds of the air and the **b** *of* the field!" 989
17:46 to the birds of the air and the **b** *of* the earth, 2651
Job 5:22 and need not fear the **b** *of* the earth. 2651
28: 8 **Proud b** do not set foot on it, 1201+8832
35:11 the **b** *of* the earth and makes us wiser than 989
Ps 8: 7 all flocks and herds, and the **b** *of* the field, 989
49:12 he is like the **b** that perish. 989
49:20 without understanding is like the **b** 989
57: 4 I lie among **ravenous b—** 4266
74:19 over the life of your dove to **wild b;** 2651
79: 2 the flesh of your saints to the **b** *of* the earth. 2651
104:11 They give water to all the **b** *of* the field; 2651
104:20 and all the **b** *of* the forest prowl. 2651
Pr 30:30 among **b,** who retreats before nothing; 989
Isa 46: 1 their idols are borne by **b of burden.** 989+2256+2651
56: 9 Come, all you **b** *of* the field, 2651
56: 9 come and devour, all you **b** of the forest! 2651
Jer 7:33 the birds of the air and the **b** *of* the earth, 989
12: 9 Go and gather all the wild **b;** 2651
15: 3 of the air and the **b** *of* the earth to devour 989
16: 4 the birds of the air and the **b** *of* the earth." 989
19: 7 to the birds of the air and the **b** *of* the earth. 989
34:20 the birds of the air and the **b** *of* the earth. 989
Eze 5:17 I will send famine and wild **b** against you, 2651
14:15 "Or if I send wild **b** through that country 2651
14:15 through it because of the **b,** 2651
14:21 sword and famine and wild **b** and plague— 2651
29: 5 to the **b** *of* the earth and the birds of the air. 2651
31: 6 all the **b** *of* the field gave birth 2651
31:13 the **b** *of* the field were among its branches. 2651
32: 4 the **b** *of* the earth gorge themselves on you. 2651
34:25 of wild **b** so that they may live in the desert 2651
38:20 the birds of the air, the **b** *of* the field, 2651
Da 2:38 the **b** *of* the field and the birds of the air. 10263
4:12 Under it the **b** *of* the field found shelter, 10263
4:21 giving shelter to the **b** *of* the field, 10263
7: 3 Four great **b,** each different from the others, 10263
7: 7 It was different from all the former **b,** 10263

Da 7:12 (The other b had been stripped 10263
7:17 'The four great b are four kingdoms 10263
Hos 2:18 a covenant for them with the b of the field 2651
4: 3 the b of the field and the birds of the air 2651
Mic 5: 8 like a lion among the b of the forest, 989
Zep 2:15 a lair for wild b! 2651
Ac 11: 6 wild b, reptiles, and birds of the air. 2563
1Co 15:32 If I fought wild b in Ephesus 2562
2Pe 2:12 They are like brute b, creatures of instinct, 2442
2:12 and like b they too will perish. NIG
Rev 6: 8 and by the wild b of the earth. 2563

BEAT (42) [BEATEN, BEATING, BEATINGS, BEATS]

Ex 9:25 it b down everything growing in the fields 5782
Nu 14:45 down and attacked them and b them down 4198
22:23 Balaam b her to get her back on the road. 5782
22:25 So he b her again. 5782
22:27 and he was angry and b her with his staff. 5782
22:28 to make you b me these three times?" 5782
Dt 1:44 and b you down from Seir all the way 5782
24:20 When you b the olives from your trees, 2468
2Sa 22:43 I b them as fine as the dust of the earth; 8835
Ne 13:25 I b some of the men 5782
Ps 18:42 I b them as fine as dust borne on the wind; 8835
78:66 He b back his enemies; 5782
Pr 23:35 They b me, but I don't feel it! 2150
SS 5: 7 They b me, they bruised me; 5782
Isa 2: 4 They will b their swords into plowshares 4198
10:24 the Assyrians, who b you with a rod and lift 5782
32:12 B your breasts for the pleasant fields, 6199
49:10 the desert heat or the sun b upon them. 5782
50: 6 I offered my back to those who b me, 5782
Jer 31:19 after I came to understand, I b my breast. 6215
Eze 21:12 Therefore b your breast. 6215
Joel 3:10 B your plowshares into swords 4198
Mic 4: 3 They will b their swords into plowshares 4198
Na 2: 7 Its slave girls moan like doves and b 9528
Mt 7:25 the winds blew and b against that house; 4700
7:27 the winds blew and b against that house, 4684
21:35 they b one, killed another, 1296
24:49 and he then begins to b his fellow servants 5597
Mk 12: 3 b him and sent him away empty-handed. 1296
12: 5 some of them they b, others they killed. 1296
14:65 And the guards took him and b him. 4825
Lk 10:30 b him and went away, 2202+4435
12:45 to b the menservants and maidservants and 5597
18:13 but b his breast and said, 'God, 5597
20:10 But the tenants b him 1296
20:11 that one also they b and treated shamefully 1296
23:48 they b their breasts and went away. 5597
Ac 16:37 "They b us publicly without a trial, 1296
18:17 the synagogue ruler and b him in front of 5597
22:19 to imprison and b those who believe 1296
1Co 9:27 I b my body and make it my slave so that 5724
Rev 7:16 The sun will not b upon them, 4406

BEATEN (18) [BEAT]

Ex 5:14 by Pharaoh's slave drivers were b 5782
5:16 Your servants are being b, 5782
Nu 22:32 "Why have you b your donkey these three times? 5782
Dt 25: 2 If the guilty man deserves to be b, 5782
Jdg 20:36 Then the Benjamites saw that they were b. 5597
1Ki 6:32 the cherubim and palm trees with b gold. 8096
Isa 1: 5 Why should you be b anymore? 5782
17: 6 as when an olive tree is b, 5939
24:13 as when an olive tree is b, 5939
28:18 you will be b down by it. 5330
28:27 caraway is b out with a rod, 2468
Jer 20: 2 he had Jeremiah the prophet b 5782
37:15 and had him b and imprisoned in the house 5782
Lk 12:47 will be b with many blows. 1296
12:48 will be b with few blows. 1296
Ac 16:22 to be stripped and b. 4810
2Co 6: 9 b, and yet not killed; 4084
11:25 Three times I was b with rods, 4810

BEATING (7) [BEAT]

Ex 2:11 He saw an Egyptian b a Hebrew, 5782
Pr 18: 6 and his mouth invites a b. 4547
Lk 22:63 The men who were guarding Jesus began mocking and b him. 1296
Ac 19:16 He gave them such a b 2710
21:32 they stopped b Paul. 5597
1Co 9:26 I do not fight like a man b the air. 1296
1Pe 2:20 how is it to your credit if you receive a b 3139

BEATINGS (3) [BEAT]

Pr 19:29 and b for the backs of fools. 4547
20:30 and b purge the inmost being. 4804
2Co 6: 5 in b, imprisonments and riots; 4435

BEATS (1) [BEAT]

Ex 21:20 a man b his male or female slave with a rod 5782

BEAUTIFUL (71) [BEAUTY]

Ge 6: 2 that the daughters of men were b, 3202
12:11 "I know what a b woman you are. 3637+5260
12:14 that she was a very b woman. 3637
24:16 The girl was very b, a virgin; 3202+5260
26: 7 because she is b." 3202+5260
29:17 but Rachel was lovely in form, and b. 3637+5260
49:21 a doe set free that bears b fawns. 9183
Nu 24: 5 "How b are your tents, 3201
Dt 21:11 captives a b woman and are attracted 3637+9307
Jos 7:21 in the plunder a b robe from Babylonia, 3202
1Sa 25: 3 She was an intelligent and b woman, 3637+9307
2Sa 11: 2 The woman was very b, 3202+5260
13: 1 the b sister of Absalom son of David. 3637
14:27 and she became a b woman. 3637+5260
1Ki 1: 3 for a b girl and found Abishag, 3637
1: 4 The girl was very b; 3637
Est 2: 2 "Let a search be made for b young virgins 3202+5260
2: 3 bring all these b girls into the harem 3202+5260
Job 38:31 "Can you bind the b Pleiades? 5051
42:15 in all the land were there found women as b 3637
Ps 48: 2 It is b in its loftiness, 3637
Pr 11:22 a b woman who shows no discretion. 3637
24: 4 with rare and b treasures. 5833
Ecc 3:11 He has made everything b in its time. 3637
SS 1: 8 If you do not know, most b of women, 3637
1:10 Your cheeks are b with earrings, 5533
1:15 How b you are, my darling! 3637
1:15 Oh, how b! 3637
2:10 my darling, my b one, and come with me. 3637
2:13 my b one, come with me." 3637
4: 1 How b you are, my darling! 3637
4: 1 Oh, how b! 3637
4: 7 All b you are, my darling; 3637
5: 9 most b of women? 3637
6: 1 has your lover gone, most b of women? 3637
6: 4 You are b, my darling, as Tirzah, 3637
7: 1 b your sandaled feet, O prince's daughter! 3636
7: 6 How b you are and how pleasing, O love, 3636
Isa 4: 2 that day the Branch of the LORD will be b 7382
28: 5 a b wreath for the remnant of his people. 7382
52: 7 How b on the mountains are the feet 5533
Jer 3:19 the most b inheritance of any nation.' 7382+7382
6: 2 so b and delicate. 5534
11:16 a thriving olive tree with fruit b in form. 3637
46:20 "Egypt is a b heifer, 3645
Eze 7:20 They were proud of their b jewelry 6344+7382
16: 7 and became the most b of jewels. 6344+6344
16:12 on your ears and a b crown on your head. 9514
16:13 You became very b and rose to be a queen. 3636
20: 6 the most b of all lands. 7382
20:15 most b of all lands— 7382
23:42 and her sister and b crowns on their heads. 9514
27:24 they traded with you b garments, 4815
31: 3 with b branches overshadowing the forest; 3637
31: 9 I made it b with abundant branches, 3637
33:32 a b voice and plays an instrument well, 3637
Da 4:12 Its leaves were b, its fruit abundant, 10736
4:21 with b leaves and abundant fruit, 10736
8: 9 and to the east and toward the B Land. 7382
11:16 He will establish himself in the B Land 7382
11:41 He will also invade the B Land. 7382
11:45 between the seas at the b holy mountain. 7382
Zec 9:17 How attractive and b they will be! 3642
Mt 23:27 which look b on the outside but on the 6053
26:10 She has done a b thing to me. 2819
Mk 14: 6 She has done a b thing to me. 2819
Lk 21: 5 how the temple was adorned with b stones 2819
Ac 3: 2 to the temple gate called B, 6053
3:10 to sit begging at the temple gate called B, 6053
Ro 10:15 "How b are the feet of those who bring 6053
1Pe 3: 5 in God used to make themselves b. 3175

BEAUTIFULLY (1) [BEAUTY]

Rev 21: 2 as a bride b dressed for her husband. 3175

BEAUTY (33) [BEAUTIFUL, BEAUTIFULLY]

Est 1:11 to display her b to the people and nobles, 3642
2: 3 and let b treatments be given to them. 9475
2: 9 with her b treatments and special food. 9475
2:12 of b treatments prescribed for the women, 5299
Ps 27: 4 upon the b of the LORD and to seek him 5840
37:20 The LORD's enemies will be like the b of 3701
45:11 The king is enthralled by your b; 3642
50: 2 From Zion, perfect in b, God shines forth. 3642
Pr 6:25 Do not lust in your heart after her b 3642
31:30 Charm is deceptive, and b is fleeting; 3642
Isa 3:24 instead of b, branding. 3642
28: 1 to the fading flower, his glorious b, 7382
28: 4 That fading flower, his glorious b, 7382
33:17 in his b and view a land that stretches afar. 3642
53: 2 He had no b or majesty to attract us to him, 9307
61: 3 to bestow on them a crown of b instead 6996
La 2:15 the city that was called the perfection of b, 3642
Eze 16:14 among the nations on account of your b, 3642
16:14 splendor I had given you made your b perfect, NIH
16:15 in your b and used your fame to become 3642
16:15 who passed by and your b became his. NIH
16:25 and degraded your b, 3642
27: 3 " 'You say, O Tyre, "I am perfect in b." 3642
27: 4 your builders brought your b to perfection. 3642
27:11 they brought your b to perfection. 3642
28: 7 they will draw their swords against your b 3642
28:12 full of wisdom and perfect in b. 3642
28:17 on account of your b, 3642
31: 7 It was majestic in b, 1542
31: 8 in the garden of God could match its b. 3642
Jas 1:11 its blossom falls and its b is destroyed. 2346
1Pe 3: 3 Your b should not come NIG
3: 4 the unfading b of a gentle and quiet spirit, NIG

BEBAI (6)

Ezr 2:11 of B 623 950
8:11 of the descendants of B, Zechariah son 950
8:11 Zechariah son of B, and with him 28 men; 950
10:28 From the descendants of B: 950
Ne 7:16 of B 628 950
10:15 Bunni, Azgad, B, 950

BECAME (329) [BECOME]

Ge 2: 7 and the man b a living being. 2118
4: 1 and she b pregnant and gave birth to Cain. AIT
4:17 she b pregnant and gave birth to Enoch. AIT
5: 6 he b the father of Enosh. AIT
5: 7 And after he b the father of Enosh, AIT
5: 9 he b the father of Kenan. AIT
5:10 And after he b the father of Kenan, AIT
5:12 he b the father of Mahalalel. AIT
5:13 And after he b the father of Mahalalel, AIT
5:15 he b the father of Jared. AIT
5:16 And after he b the father of Jared, AIT
5:18 he b the father of Enoch. AIT
5:19 And after he b the father of Enoch, AIT
5:21 he b the father of Methuselah. AIT
5:22 And after he b the father of Methuselah, AIT
5:25 he b the father of Lamech. AIT
5:26 And after he b the father of Lamech, AIT
5:32 he b the father of Shem, Ham and Japheth. AIT
8: 5 the tops of the mountains b visible. AIT
9:21 he b drunk and lay uncovered inside his tent. AIT
11:10 he b the father of Arphaxad. AIT
11:11 And after he b the father of Arphaxad, AIT
11:12 he b the father of Shelah. AIT
11:13 And after he b the father of Shelah, AIT
11:14 he b the father of Eber. AIT
11:15 And after he b the father of Eber, AIT
11:16 he b the father of Peleg. AIT
11:17 And after he b the father of Peleg, AIT
11:18 he b the father of Reu. AIT
11:19 And after he b the father of Reu, AIT
11:20 he b the father of Serug. AIT
11:21 And after he b the father of Serug, AIT
11:22 he b the father of Nahor. AIT
11:23 And after he b the father of Nahor, AIT
11:24 he b the father of Terah. AIT
11:25 And after he b the father of Terah, AIT
11:26 he b the father of Abram, AIT
11:27 Terah b the father of Abram, AIT
11:27 And Haran b the father of Lot. AIT
19:26 and she b a pillar of salt. 2118
19:36 So both of Lot's daughters b pregnant AIT
20:12 and she b my wife. 2118
21: 2 Sarah b pregnant and bore a son AIT
21:20 He lived in the desert and b an archer. 2118
22:23 Bethuel b the father of Rebekah. AIT
24:67 So she b his wife, and he loved her; 2118
25:19 Abraham b the father of Isaac, AIT
25:21 and his wife Rebekah b pregnant. AIT
25:27 and Esau b a skillful hunter, 2118
26:13 The man b rich, and his wealth AIT
26:13 to grow until he b very wealthy. AIT
29:32 Leah b pregnant and gave birth to a son. AIT
30: 1 she b jealous of her sister. AIT
30: 2 Jacob b angry with her and said, AIT
30: 5 and she b pregnant and bore him a son. AIT
30:17 she b pregnant and bore Jacob a fifth son. AIT
30:23 She b pregnant and gave birth to a son AIT
36:32 Bela son of Beor b king of Edom. AIT
38: 3 she b pregnant and gave birth to a son, AIT
38:18 and she b pregnant by him. AIT
39: 4 in his eyes and b his attendant. AIT
47:20 The land b Pharaoh's, 2118
Ex 1: 7 b exceedingly numerous, AIT
1:20 b even more numerous. AIT
2: 2 and she b pregnant and gave birth to a son. AIT
2:10 to Pharaoh's daughter and he b her son. 2118
4: 3 Moses threw it on the ground and it b 2118
7:10 and it b a snake. 2118
7:12 Each one threw down his staff and it b 2118
7:13 Yet Pharaoh's heart b hard and he would AIT
7:22 and Pharaoh's heart b hard; AIT
8:17 throughout the land of Egypt b gnats. 2118
15:25 and the water b sweet. AIT
Lev 18:24 to drive out before you b defiled. 3237
18:27 and the land b defiled. AIT
Nu 6:12 because he b defiled during his separation. AIT
11:10 The LORD b exceedingly angry, AIT
16: 1 and On son of Peleth—b insolent AIT
16:15 Then Moses b very angry and said to AIT
Dt 1:37 the LORD b angry with me also and said, AIT
26: 5 with a few people and lived there and b 2118
32:15 filled with food, he b heavy and sleek. AIT
Jos 7: 5 of the people melted and b like water. 2118
24:32 This b the inheritance of Joseph's 2118
Jdg 1:28 When Israel b strong, AIT
1:33 and Beth Anath b forced laborers for them. 2118
3:10 so that he b Israel's judge and went to war. AIT
8:27 and it b a snare to Gideon and his family. 2118
9: 4 who b his followers. AIT
10: 7 he b angry with them. AIT
15:14 The ropes on his arms b like charred flax, 2118
17:12 and the young man b his priest and lived 2118
Ru 4:13 So Boaz took Ruth and she b his wife. 2118
1Sa 10:12 So it b a saying: "Is Saul also among 2118
13: 1 Saul was [thirty] years old when he b king, AIT

1Sa 16:21 and David **b** one of his armor-bearers. 2118
18: 1 **b one** in spirit **with** 8003
18:29 Saul *b* still **more** afraid of him, AIT
18:30 and his name *b* **well known.** AIT
22: 2 and *he* **b** their leader. 2118
25:37 his heart failed him and he **b** like a stone. 2118
25:42 with David's messengers and **b** his wife. 2118
30:13 when *I b* **ill** three days ago. AIT
2Sa 2:10 of Saul was forty years old when he *b* **king** AIT
4: 1 he lost courage, and all Israel *b* **alarmed.** AIT
4: 4 he fell and **b crippled.** 7174
5: 4 David was thirty years old when he *b* **king,** AIT
5:10 And he **b more and more powerful,** 1524+2143+2143+2256
8: 2 So the Moabites **b** subject to David 2118
8: 6 and the Arameans **b** subject to him 2118
8:13 And David **b famous** after he returned 6913+9005
8:14 and all the Edomites **b** subject to David. 2118
10:19 with the Israelites and *b* **subject** *to* them. AIT
11:27 and *she* **b** his wife and bore him a son. 2118
12:15 borne to David, and *he b* **ill.** AIT
13: 2 Amnon *b* **frustrated** to the point of illness AIT
14:26 to time when it **b** too heavy for him— NIH
14:27 and she **b** a beautiful woman. 2118
21:15 and he *b* **exhausted.** AIT
23:18 and so he **b** as famous as the Three. 4200
23:19 *He* **b** their commander, 2118
1Ki 11: 9 The LORD *b* **angry** with Solomon AIT
11:24 around him and **b** the leader of a band 2118
12:30 And this thing **b** a sin; 2118
13: 6 and the king's hand was restored and **b** 2118
14: 1 that time Abijah son of Jeroboam *b* **ill,** AIT
14:21 He was forty-one years old when he *b* **king,** AIT
15: 1 Abijah *b* **king** of Judah, AIT
15: 9 Asa *b* **king** *of* Judah, AIT
15:23 In his old age, however, his feet *b* **diseased.** AIT
15:25 Nadab son of Jeroboam *b* **king** of Israel in AIT
15:33 Baasha son of Ahijah *b* **king** of all Israel AIT
16: 8 Elah son of Baasha *b* **king** of Israel, AIT
16:22 So Tibni died and Omri *b* **king.** AIT
16:23 Omri *b* **king** of Israel, AIT
16:29 Ahab son of Omri *b* **king** of Israel, AIT
17:17 the woman who owned the house *b* **ill.** AIT
19:21 to follow Elijah and *b* his **attendant.** AIT
22:41 Jehoshaphat son of Asa *b* **king** of Judah in AIT
22:42 years old when he *b* **king,** AIT
22:51 Ahaziah son of Ahab *b* **king** of Israel in Samaria AIT
2Ki 3: 1 Joram of Ahab *b* **king** of Israel in Samaria AIT
4:17 But the woman *b* **pregnant,** AIT
5:14 and his flesh was restored and *b* **clean** like AIT
8:17 years old when he *b* **king,** AIT
8:26 years old when he *b* **king,** AIT
12: 1 In the seventh year of Jehu, Joash *b* **king,** AIT
13: 1 Jehoahaz son of Jehu *b* **king** of Israel AIT
13:10 Jehoash son of Jehoahaz *b* **king** of Israel AIT
14: 2 years old when he *b* **king,** AIT
14:23 of Jehoash king of Israel *b* **king** in Samaria, AIT
15: 2 He was sixteen years old when he *b* **king,** AIT
15: 8 Zechariah son of Jeroboam *b* **king** of Israel AIT
15:13 of Jabesh *b* **king** in the thirty-ninth year AIT
15:17 Menahem son of Gadi *b* **king** of Israel, AIT
15:23 Pekahiah son of Menahem *b* **king** of Israel AIT
15:27 of Remaliah *b* **king** of Israel in Samaria, AIT
15:33 years old when he *b* **king,** AIT
16: 2 Ahaz was twenty years old when he *b* **king,** AIT
17: 1 Hoshea son of Elah *b* **king** of Israel AIT
17:15 and *themselves b* **worthless.** AIT
18: 2 years old when he *b* **king,** AIT
20: 1 In those days Hezekiah *b* **ill** and was at AIT
21: 1 years old when he *b* **king,** AIT
21:19 years old when he *b* **king,** AIT
22: 1 Josiah was eight years old when he *b* **king,** AIT
23:31 years old when he *b* **king,** AIT
23:36 years old when he *b* **king,** AIT
24: 1 and Jehoiakim **b** his vassal for three years. 2118
24: 8 years old when he *b* **king,** AIT
24:18 years old when he *b* **king,** AIT
25:27 the year Evil-Merodach *b* **king** *of* Babylon, AIT
1Ch 7:23 and *she b* **pregnant** and gave birth to a son. AIT
11: 9 David **b more and more powerful,** 1524+2143+2143+2256
11:20 and so he **b** as famous as the Three. NIH
11:21 above the Three and **b** their commander, 2118
14: 3 and *b the* **father** *of* more sons AIT
18: 2 they **b** subject to him and brought tribute. 2118
18: 6 and the Arameans **b** subject to him 2118
18:13 and all the Edomites **b** subject to David. 2118
19:19 they made peace with David and *b* **subject** AIT
2Ch 12:13 He was forty-one years old when he *b* **king,** AIT
13: 1 Abijah *b* **king** of Judah, AIT
17:12 Jehoshaphat **b** more and more powerful; 2118
20:31 He was thirty-five years old when he *b* **king** AIT
21: 5 years old when he *b* **king,** AIT
21:20 years old when he *b* **king,** AIT
22: 2 years old when he *b* **king,** AIT
22: 4 after his father's death they **b** his advisers, 2118
24: 1 Joash was seven years old when he *b* **king,** AIT
25: 1 years old when *he b* **king,** AIT
26: 3 years old when he *b* **king,** AIT
26:15 he was greatly helped until *he b* **powerful.** AIT
26:16 But after Uzziah **b powerful,** 2621
26:19 in his hand ready to burn incense, *b* **angry.** AIT
27: 1 years old when he *b* **king,** AIT
27: 8 years old when he *b* **king,** AIT
28: 1 Ahaz was twenty years old when he *b* **king,** AIT
28:22 King Ahaz *b* even **more** unfaithful AIT
2Ch 29: 1 years old when *he b* **king,** AIT
32:24 In those days Hezekiah *b* **ill** and was at AIT
33: 1 years old when he *b* **king,** AIT
33:21 years old when he *b* **king,** AIT
34: 1 Josiah was eight years old when he *b* **king,** AIT
35:25 These **b** a tradition in Israel and are written 5989
36: 2 years old when he *b* **king,** AIT
36: 5 years old when he *b* **king,** AIT
36: 9 years old when he *b* **king,** AIT
36:11 years old when he *b* **king,** AIT
36:13 *He b* **stiff-necked** and hardened his heart AIT
36:14 *b* **more and more unfaithful,** AIT
36:20 and *they* **b** servants to him and his sons 2118
Ne 4: 1 he *b* **angry** and was greatly incensed. AIT
9:16 *b* **arrogant** and stiff-necked, AIT
9:17 *They b* **stiff-necked** and AIT
9:29 but they *b* **arrogant** AIT
9:29 *b* **stiff-necked** and refused to listen. AIT
Est 1:12 the king *b* **furious** and burned with anger. AIT
2:21 *b* **angry** and conspired AIT
8:17 of other nationalities **b Jews** because fear of 3366
9: 4 he **b more and more powerful.** 1524+2143+2256
Job 26:13 By his breath the skies **b** fair; NIH
32: 2 *b* **very angry** with Job AIT
Ps 83:10 who perished at Endor and **b** like refuse on 2118
106:36 *which* **b** a snare to them. 2118
107:17 Some **b** fools through their rebellious ways NIH
114: 2 Judah **b** God's sanctuary, 2118
Ecc 2: 9 *I b* **greater** by far than anyone AIT
Isa 23: 3 and *she* **b** the marketplace of the nations. 2118
38: 1 In those days Hezekiah *b* **ill** and was at AIT
63: 8 and so *he* **b** their Savior. 2118
63:10 So *he* **turned and b** their enemy 2200
Jer 2: 5 and *b* **worthless** *themselves.* AIT
44:22 your land **b** an object of cursing and 2118
52: 1 years old when he *b* **king,** AIT
52:31 the year Evil-Merodach *b* **king** *of* Babylon, 4895
La 3:14 *I* **b** the laughingstock of all my people; 2118
4:10 *who* **b** their food 2118
Eze 16: 7 up and developed and **b** the most beautiful 995
16: 8 and *you* **b** mine. 2118
16:13 *You b* very **beautiful** and rose to be AIT
16:15 by and your beauty **b** his. 2118
16:47 in all your ways *you* soon *b* more **depraved** than they. AIT
17: 6 and it sprouted and **b** a low, 2118
17: 6 So *it* **b** a vine and produced branches 2118
19: 3 and *he* **b** a strong lion. 2118
23: 3 *They b* **prostitutes** in Egypt, AIT
23:10 *She* **b** a byword among women, 2118
23:19 Yet *she b* **more and more** promiscuous AIT
25:12 on the house of Judah and *b* **very guilty** AIT
28:17 Your heart *b* **proud** on account AIT
34: 5 and when they were scattered *they* **b** food 2118
35:15 of the house of Israel *b* **desolate,** AIT
36: 3 so that you **b** the possession of the rest of 2118
Da 2:35 to pieces at the same time and **b** like chaff 10201
2:35 that struck the statue **b** a huge mountain 10201
4:36 **b even greater** than before. 10323+10339+10650
5: 9 So King Belshazzar *b* even more **terrified** AIT
5:20 when his heart *b* **arrogant** and hardened AIT
8: 4 He did as he pleased and *b* **great.** AIT
8: 8 The goat *b* very **great,** AIT
Hos 9:10 to that shameful idol and **b** as vile as 2118
13: 1 But *he b* **guilty** of Baal worship and died. AIT
13: 6 when they were satisfied, they *b* **proud;** AIT
Jnh 4: 1 Jonah was greatly displeased and *b* **angry.** AIT
Mt 17: 2 and his clothes **b** as white as the light. *1181*
25: 5 and *they* all **b drowsy** and fell asleep. *3818*
28: 4 of him that *they* shook and **b** like dead men. *1181*
Mk 9: 3 His clothes **b** dazzling white, *1181*
10:41 *they* **b** indignant with James and John. *806*
Lk 1:24 After this his wife Elizabeth *b* **pregnant** *AIT*
1:80 And the child grew and *b* **strong** in spirit; *AIT*
2:40 And the child grew and **b strong;** *3194*
6:16 and Judas Iscariot, who **b** a traitor. *1181*
9:29 and his clothes **b** as bright as a flash *NIG*
9:32 but *when they b* **fully awake,** *AIT*
13:19 It grew and **b** a tree, *1181+1650*
14:21 the house *b* **angry** and ordered his servant, *AIT*
15:28 "The older brother *b* **angry** and refused *AIT*
18:23 When he heard this, *he* **b** very sad, *1181*
20:26 astonished by his answer, *they b* **silent.** *AIT*
23:12 That day Herod and Pilate **b** friends— *1181*
Jn 1:14 The Word **b** flesh and made his dwelling *1181*
4:41 of his words many more **b believers.** *4409*
Ac 3: 7 the man's feet and ankles *b* **strong.** *AIT*
6: 7 and a large number of priests *b* **obedient** to *AIT*
7: 8 And Abraham **b the father of** Isaac *1164*
7: 8 Later Isaac **b** the father of Jacob, *NIG*
7: 8 Jacob **b** the father of the twelve patriarchs. *NIG*
7:18 who knew nothing about Joseph, **b ruler** of Egypt. *482*
9:37 About that time *she* **b sick** and died, *AIT*
9:42 *This* **b** known all over Joppa, *1181*
10:10 *He* **b** hungry and wanted something to eat, *1181*
15:12 The whole assembly *b* **silent** *AIT*
16:18 Finally Paul *b* so **troubled** that he turned *AIT*
17:34 A few men **b followers of** Paul *3140*
18: 6 when the Jews opposed Paul and *b* **abusive,** *AIT*
19: 9 But some of them *b* **obstinate;** *AIT*
19:17 When this **b** known to the Jews *1181*
22: 2 *they* **b** very quiet. *4218*
23:10 The dispute **b** so violent that *1181*
Ro 1:21 but their thinking *b* **futile** *AIT*
1:22 they claimed to be wise, *they* **b fools** *AIT*
4:18 and so **b** the father of many nations, *1181*
1Co 4:15 for in Christ Jesus I **b** your **father** through *1164*
9:20 To the Jews *I* **b** like a Jew, *1181*
9:20 To those under the law I **b** like one under *NIG*
9:21 not having the law I **b** like one not having *NIG*
9:22 To the weak *I* **b** weak, to win the weak. *1181*
13:11 *I* **b** a man, I put childish ways behind me. *1181*
15:45 "The first man Adam **b** a living being"; *1181+1650*
2Co 7: 9 For *you b* **sorrowful** as God intended and *AIT*
8: 9 yet for your sakes *he b* **poor,** *AIT*
Gal 4:12 brothers, become like me, for I **b** like you. *NIG*
Eph 3: 7 *I* **b** a servant of this gospel by the gift *1181*
Php 2: 8 he humbled himself and **b** obedient *1181*
1Th 1: 6 You **b** imitators of us and of the Lord; *1181*
1: 7 And so you **b** a model to all the believers *1181*
2:14 **b** imitators of God's churches in Judea, *1181*
1Ti 2:14 it was the woman who was deceived and **b** a sinner. *1181*
Phm 1:10 who **b** *my* son while I was in chains. *1164*
Heb 1: 4 So *he* **b** as much superior to the angels as *1181*
5: 9 *he* **b** the source of eternal salvation *1181*
7:20 Others **b** priests without any oath, *1181+1639*
7:21 but he **b** a priest with an oath *NIG*
11: 7 and **b** heir of the righteousness that comes *1181*
11:34 and who **b** powerful in battle *1181*
Rev 16: 4 springs of water, and *they* **b** blood. *1181*
18:19 where all who had ships on the sea *b* **rich** *AIT*

BECAUSE (1672)

Ge 2: 3 **b** on it he rested from all the work 3954
3:10 and I was afraid **b** I was naked; so I hid." 3954
3:14 "**B** you have done this, 3954
3:17 "**B** you listened to your wife and ate from 3954
3:17 "Cursed is the ground **b of** you; 6288
3:20 **b** she would become the mother of all 3954
5:24 he was no more, **b** God took him away. 3954
6:13 the earth is filled with violence **b of** them. 4946+7156
7: 1 **b** I have found you righteous 3954
8: 9 the dove could find no place to set its feet **b** 3954
8:21 "Never again will I curse the ground **b of** 6288
10:25 **b** in his time the earth was divided; 3954
11: 9 **b** there the LORD confused the language 3954
12:10 down to Egypt to live there for a while **b** 3954
12:13 and my life will be spared **b of** you." 1673
12:17 his household **b of** Abram's wife Sarai 1821+6584
18:28 Will you destroy the whole city **b of** 928
19:13 **b** we are going to destroy this place. 3954
19:14 **b** the LORD is about to destroy the city!" 3954
19:22 **b** I cannot do anything until you reach it." 3954
20: 3 as dead **b of** the woman you have taken; 6584
20:11 and they will kill me **b of** my wife.' 1821+6584
20:18 in Abimelech's household **b of** 1821+6584
21:11 The matter distressed Abraham greatly **b** 6584
21:12 **b** it is through Isaac that your offspring will 3954
21:13 **b** he is your offspring." 3954
21:31 **b** the two men swore an oath there. 3954
22:12 **b** you have not withheld from me your son, 2256
22:16 that **b** you have done this and have 889+3610
22:18 **b** you have obeyed me." 889+6813
25:21 **b** she was barren. 3954
26: 5 **b** Abraham obeyed me 889+6813
26: 7 "She is my sister," **b** he was afraid to say, 3954
26: 7 **b** she is beautiful." 3954
26: 9 "**B** I thought I might lose my life 3954
26:12 **b** the LORD blessed him. 2256
26:20 **b** they disputed with him. 3954
27:41 Esau held a grudge against Jacob **b of** 6584
27:46 with living **b of** these Hittite women. 4946+7156
28:11 he stopped for the night **b** the sun had set. 3954
29: 2 with three flocks of sheep lying near it **b** 3954
29:15 "**Just b** you are a relative of mine, 3954
29:20 like only a few days to him **b of** his love 928
29:32 "It is **b** the LORD has seen my misery. 3954
29:33 "**B** the LORD heard that I am not loved, 3954
29:34 **b** I have borne him three sons." 3954
30: 6 **B of** this she named him Dan. 6584
30:20 **b** I have borne him six sons." 3954
30:27 that the LORD has blessed me **b of** you." 928+1673
31:30 Now you have gone off **b** you longed 3954
31:31 Jacob answered Laban, "I was afraid, **b** 3954
31:49 It was also called Mizpah, **b** he said, 889
32:28 **b** you have struggled with God and 3954
32:30 saying, "It is **b** I saw God face to face, 3954
32:31 and he was limping **b of** his hip. 6584
32:32 **b** the socket of Jacob's hip was touched 3954
33:11 **And b** Jacob insisted, Esau accepted it. 2256
34: 7 **b** Shechem had done a disgraceful thing 3954
34:13 **B** their sister Dinah had been defiled, 889
34:19 **b** he was delighted with Jacob's daughter. 3954
35: 7 **b** it was there that God revealed himself 3954
36: 7 not support them both **b of** their livestock. 4946+7156
37: 3 **b** he had been born to him in his old age; 3954
37: 8 And they hated him all the more **b of** 6584
39: 5 the household of the Egyptian **b of** Joseph. 1673
39: 9 **b** you are his wife. 889+928
39:23 **b** the LORD was with Joseph 889+928
41:31 **b** the famine that follows it will be 4946+7156
41:49 so much that he stopped keeping records **b** 3954
41:51 firstborn Manasseh and said, "It is **b** 3954
41:52 "It is **b** God has made me fruitful in 3954
41:57 **b** the famine was severe in all the world. 3954
42: 4 **b** he was afraid that harm might come 3954
42:21 "Surely we are being punished **b of** 6584
43: 5 we will not go down, **b** the man said to us, 3954

Ge 43:18 “We were brought here **b of** the silver 1821+6584
43:25 **b** they had heard that they were to eat there. 3954
43:32 **b** Egyptians could not eat with Hebrews, 3954
45: 3 **b** they were terrified at his presence. 3954
45: 5 **b** it was to save lives that God sent me 3954
45:11 **b** five years of famine are still to come. 3954
45:20 **b** the best of all Egypt will be yours.’ ” 3954
47: 4 **b** the famine is severe in Canaan 3954
47:13 the whole region **b** the famine was severe; 3954
47:13 Canaan wasted away **b of** the famine. 4946+7156
47:20 **b** the famine was too severe for them. 3954
47:22 **b** they received a regular allotment 3954
48:10 Israel’s eyes were failing **b of** old age, 4946
49:24 **b of** the hand of the Mighty One of Jacob, 4946
49:24 **b of** the Shepherd, the Rock of Israel, 4946+9004
49:25 **b of** your father’s God, 4946
49:25 who helps you, **b of** the Almighty, 907
Ex 1:21 And **b** the midwives feared God, 3954
2:23 for help **b of** their slavery went up to God. 4946
3: 6 **b** he was afraid to look at God. 3954
3: 7 I have heard them crying out **b of** 4946+7156
6: 1 **B of** my mighty hand he will let them go; 928
6: 1 **b of** my mighty hand he will drive them out of his country.” 928
6: 9 not listen to him **b of** their discouragement 4946
7:24 **b** they could not drink the water of 3954
9:11 before Moses **b of** the boils that were 4946+7156
9:19 **b** the hail will fall on every man and animal 2256
9:32 were not destroyed, **b** they ripen later.) 3954
10: 9 **b** we are to celebrate a festival to 3954
12:17 **b** it was on this very day 3954
12:39 without yeast **b** they had been driven out 3954
12:42 **B** the LORD kept vigil that night NIH
13: 3 **b** the LORD brought you out of it with 3954
13: 8 ‘I do this **b of** what the LORD did for me 6288
13:19 Moses took the bones of Joseph with him **b** 3954
14:11 “Was it **b** there were no graves in Egypt 4946
15:23 not drink its water **b** it was bitter. 3954
16: 7 **b** he has heard your grumbling against him. 928
16: 8 **b** he has heard your grumbling against him. 928
16:25 “**b** today is a Sabbath to the LORD. 3954
17: 7 and Meribah **b** the Israelites quarreled and 6584
17: 7 the Israelites quarreled and **b** they tested 6584
17:14 **b** I will completely blot out the memory 3954
18:15 “**B** the people come to me 3954
18:22 **b** they will share it with you. 2256
19:11 **b** on that day the LORD will come down 3954
19:18 **b** the LORD descended on it in fire. 4946+7156
19:23 **b** you yourself warned us, 3954
21: 8 **b** he has broken faith with her. 928
22:27 **b** his cloak is the only covering he has 3954
23: 9 **b** you were aliens in Egypt. 3954
23:29 **b** the land would become desolate and 7153
23:33 **b** the worship of their gods will certainly be 3954
29:33 **b** they are sacred. 3954
29:34 It must not be eaten, **b** it is sacred. 3954
31:14 “ ‘Observe the Sabbath, **b** it is holy to you. 3954
32: 7 “Go down, **b** your people, 3954
32:35 the people with a plague **b of** what they did 6584
33: 3 **b** you are a stiff-necked people 3954
33:17 **b** I am pleased with you and I know you 3954
34:29 he was not aware that his face was radiant **b** 928
36: 7 **b** what they already had was more than enough 2256
40:35 the Tent of Meeting **b** the cloud had settled 3954
Lev 5: 1 “ ‘If a person sins **b** he does not speak up 561
5:11 **b** it is a sin offering. 3954
10: 7 **b** the LORD’s anointing oil is on you.” 3954
10:13 **b** it is your share and your sons’ share of 3954
11:13 to detest and not eat **b** they are detestable: NIH
11:44 consecrate yourselves and be holy, **b** 3954
11:45 therefore be holy, **b** I am holy. 3954
13:11 **b** he is already unclean. 3954
13:44 The priest shall pronounce him unclean **b of** 928
13:52 **b** the mildew is destructive; 3954
14:48 **b** the mildew is gone. 3954
15:15 the LORD for the man **b of** his discharge. 4946
16: 2 on the ark, or else he will die, **b** I appear in 3954
16:16 the Most Holy Place **b of** the uncleanness 4946
16:30 **b** on this day atonement will be made 3954
17:14 **b** the life of every creature is its blood. 3954
17:14 **b** the life of every creature is its blood; 3954
18:13 **b** she is your mother’s close relative. 3954
18:24 **b** this is how the nations that I am going 3954
19: 2 ‘Be holy **b** I, the LORD your God, 3954
19: 8 Whoever eats it will be held responsible **b** 3954
19:20 **b** she had not been freed. 3954
20: 7 **b** I am the LORD your God. 3954
20:23 **B** they did all these things, 3954
20:26 You are to be holy to me **b** I, the LORD, 3954
21: 6 **B** they present the offerings made to 3954
21: 7 **b** priests are holy to their God. 3954
21: 8 **b** they offer up the food of your God. 3954
21: 8 **b** I the LORD am holy— 3954
21:12 **b** he has been dedicated by the anointing oil 3954
21:23 yet **b of** his defect, 3954
22:20 **b** it will not be accepted on your behalf. 3954
22:25 **b** they are deformed and have defects.’ ” 3954
23:28 **b** it is the Day of Atonement, 3954
24: 9 **b** it is a most holy part of their regular share 3954
25:16 **b** what he is really selling you is 3954
25:23 **b** the land is mine and you are but aliens 3954
25:33 in the Jubilee, **b** the houses in the towns of 3954
25:42 **B** the Israelites are my servants, 3954
26:16 **b** your enemies will eat it. 2256
26:20 **b** your soil will not yield its crops, 2256
26:39 in the lands of their enemies **b of** their sins; 928

Lev 26:39 **b of** their fathers’ sins they will waste away. 928
26:43 pay for their sins **b** they rejected my laws 928+2256+3610+3610
Nu 5: 2 or who is ceremonially unclean **b of** 4200
5:15 **b** it is a grain offering for jealousy, 3954
5:30 over a man **b** he suspects his wife. 2256
6: 7 **b** the symbol of his separation to God is 3954
6:11 to make atonement for him **b** he sinned 889+4946
6:12 **b** he became defiled during his separation. 3954
7: 9 **b** they were to carry on their shoulders 3954
9: 6 that day **b** they were ceremonially unclean NIH
9: 7 “We have become unclean **b of** 4200
9:10 or your descendants are unclean **b of** 4200
9:13 from his people **b** he did not present 3954
11: 3 **b** fire from the LORD had burned 3954
11:20 **b** you have rejected the LORD, 3610+3954
11:34 **b** there they buried 3954
12: 1 Aaron began to talk against Moses **b of** 128+6584
13:24 the Valley of Eshcol **b of** the cluster 128+6584
14: 9 **b** we will swallow them up. 3954
14:24 But **b** my servant Caleb has 6813
14:42 Do not go up, **b** the LORD is not with you. 3954
14:43 **B** you have turned away from the LORD, 3954+4027+6584
15:26 **b** all the people were involved in 3954
15:31 **B** he has despised the LORD’s word 3954
15:34 **b** it was not clear what should be done 3954
16:26 you will be swept away **b of** all their sins.” 928
16:49 in addition to those who had died **b of** Korah. 1821+6584
19:13 **B** the water of cleansing has 3954
19:20 **b** he has defiled the sanctuary of 3954
20:12 “**B** you did not trust in me enough 3610
20:24 **b** both of you rebelled 889+6584
21:24 **b** their border was fortified. 3954
22: 3 and Moab was terrified **b** there were 4946+7156
22: 3 Moab was filled with dread **b of** 4946+7156
22: 6 **b** they are too powerful for me. 3954
22:12 **b** they are blessed.” 3954
22:17 **b** I will reward you handsomely 3954
22:32 to oppose you **b** your path is a reckless one 3954
25:13 **b** he was zealous for the honor of his God 889+9393
25:18 **b** they treated you as enemies 3954
26:62 not counted along with the other Israelites **b** 3954
27: 4 from his clan **b** he had no son? 3954
30: 5 the LORD will release her **b** 3954
32:11 ‘**B** they have not followed me wholeheartedly, 3954
32:19 **b** our inheritance has come to us on 3954
34:14 **b** the families of the tribe of Reuben, 3954
Dt 1:36 **b** he followed the LORD wholeheartedly 889+3610
1:37 **B of** you the LORD became angry 928+1673
1:38 **b** he will lead Israel to inherit it. 3954
1:42 **b** I will not be with you. 3954
2:25 will tremble and be in anguish **b of** 4946+7156
3:26 But **b of** you the LORD was angry 5100
4:21 The LORD was angry with me **b of** you 1821+6584
4:37 **B** he loved your forefathers 3954+9393
5: 5 **b** you were afraid of the fire and did not go 3954
7: 7 on you and choose you **b** 4946
7: 8 But it was **b** the LORD loved you and kept 4946
9: 4 of this land **b of** my righteousness.” 928
9: 5 It is not **b of** your righteousness 928
9: 6 that it is not **b of** your righteousness that 928
9:12 **b** your people whom you brought out 3954
9:18 **b of** all the sin you had committed, 6584
9:25 and forty nights **b** 3954
9:28 ‘**B** the LORD was not able to take them 4946
9:28 and **b** he hated them, 4946
12: 7 **b** the LORD your God has blessed you. 889
12:23 **b** the blood is the life, 3954
12:25 **b** you will be doing what is right in the eyes 3954
12:28 **b** you will be doing what is good and right 3954
12:31 **b** in worshiping their gods, 3954
13: 5 **b** he preached rebellion against 3954
13:10 **b** he tried to turn you away from 3954
13:18 **b** you obey the LORD your God, 3954
14:24 and cannot carry your tithe (**b** the place 3954
15: 2 **b** the LORD’s time 3954
15:10 then **b of** this 1673
15:16 **b** he loves you and your family 3954
15:18 to set your servant free, **b** his service 3954
16: 1 **b** in the month of Abib he brought you out 3954
16: 3 **b** you left Egypt in haste— 3954
18:12 and **b of** these detestable practices 1673
19: 9 **b** you carefully follow all these laws I command you today— 3954
20: 1 **b** the LORD your God, 3954
20:19 **b** you can eat their fruit. 3954
21:23 **b** anyone who is hung on a tree is 3954
22:19 **b** this man has given an Israelite virgin 3954
22:24 the girl **b** she was in a town and did 1821+6584
22:24 man **b** he violated another man’s wife. 1821+6584
23: 5 **b** the LORD your God loves you. 3954
23: 7 **b** you lived as an alien in his country. 3954
23:10 If one of your men is unclean **b of** 4946
23:18 **b** the LORD your God detests them both. 3954
23:23 **b** you made your vow freely to NIH
24: 1 to him **b** he finds something indecent 3954
24: 6 **b** that would be taking a man’s livelihood 3954
24:15 **b** he is poor and is counting on it. 3954
28:20 to sudden ruin **b of** the evil you have done 4946+7156
28:38 **b** locusts will devour it. 3954
28:39 **b** worms will eat them. 3954
28:40 **b** the olives will drop off. 3954

Dt 28:41 **b** they will go into captivity. 3954
28:45 **b** you did not obey the LORD your God 3954
28:47 **B** you did not serve the LORD your God 889+9393
28:53 **B of** the suffering that your enemy 928
28:55 It will be all he has left **b of** 928
28:62 **b** you did not obey the LORD your God. 3954
28:67 **b of** the terror that will fill your hearts and 4946
29:25 “It is **b** this people abandoned the covenant 6584
31: 6 Do not be afraid or terrified **b of** them, 4946+7156
31:17 ‘Have not these disasters come upon us **b** 3954+6584
31:18 that day **b of** all their wickedness in turning 6584
31:21 **b** it will not be forgotten 3954
31:29 upon you **b** you will do evil in the sight of 3954
32:19 The LORD saw this and rejected them **b** 4946
32:51 This is **b** both of you broke faith with me in 6584
32:51 and **b** you did not uphold my holiness 6584
34: 9 of wisdom **b** Moses had laid his hands 3954
Jos 1: 6 **b** you will lead these people to inherit 3954
2: 3 and entered your house, **b** they have come 3954
2: 9 country are melting in fear **b of** you. 4946+7156
2:11 everyone’s courage failed **b of** you, 4946+7156
2:12 **b** I have shown kindness to you. 3954
2:24 all the people are melting in fear **b of** us.” 4946+7156
5: 7 They were still uncircumcised **b** they had 3954
6: 1 Now Jericho was tightly shut up **b of** 4946+7156
6:17 **b** she hid the spies we sent. 3954
6:25 **b** she hid the men Joshua had sent as spies 3954
7:12 and run **b** they have been made liable 3954
9: 9 from a very distant country **b of** the fame 4200
9:18 **b** the leaders of the assembly had sworn 3954
9:24 So we feared for our lives **b of** you, 4946+7156
10: 2 **b** Gibeon was an important city, 3954
10: 4 “**b** it has made peace with Joshua and 3954
10: 6 **b** all the Amorite kings from 3954
10:42 **b** the LORD, the God of Israel, 3954
11: 6 **b** by this time tomorrow I will hand all 3954
14: 9 **b** you have followed 3954
14:14 **b** he followed the LORD, 889+3610
17: 1 who had received Gilead and Bashan **b** 3954
17: 6 **b** the daughters of the tribe 3954
18: 7 **b** the priestly service of 3954
19: 9 from the share of Judah, **b** 3954
20: 5 **b** he killed his neighbor unintentionally and 3954
21:10 **b** the first lot fell to them): 3954
22:31 **b** you have not acted unfaithfully toward 889
23:10 **b** the LORD your God fights for you, 3954
24:18 **b** he is our God.” 3954
Jdg 1:19 **b** they had iron chariots. 3954
1:32 and **b of** this the people of Asher lived 3954
2:13 **b** they forsook him and served Baal and 2256
2:20 **B** this nation has violated the covenant 889+3610
3:12 and **b** they did this evil 3954+6584
4: 3 **B** he had nine hundred iron chariots 3954
4: 9 But **b of** the way you are going about this, 6584
4:17 **b** there were friendly relations 3954
5:23 **b** they did not come to help the LORD, 3954
6: 2 **B** the power of Midian was so oppressive, 4946+7156
6: 7 the Israelites cried to the LORD **b of** 128+6584
6:27 But **b** he was afraid of his family and 889+3869
6:30 **b** he has broken down Baal’s altar and cut 3954
6:32 **b** he broke down Baal’s altar. 3954
7: 9 **b** I am going to give it into your hands. 3954
8:20 **b** he was only a boy and was afraid. 3954
8:22 **b** you have saved us out of the hand 3954
9:18 king over the citizens of Shechem **b** 3954
9:21 **b** he was afraid of 4946+7156
10: 6 And **b** the Israelites forsook the LORD 2256
11: 2 “**b** you are the son of another woman.” 3954
11:35 **b** I have made a vow to the LORD 2256
11:37 **b** I will never marry.” 6584
11:38 the hills and wept **b** she would never marry. 6584
12: 4 The Gileadites struck them down **b** 3954
12: 6 **b** he could not pronounce 2256
13: 5 **b** you will conceive and give birth to a son 3954
13: 5 **b** the boy is to be a Nazirite, 3954
13: 7 **b** the boy will be a Nazirite of God 3954
14:17 **b** she continued to press him. 3954
15: 6 **b** his wife was given to his friend.” 3954
15:18 **B** he was very thirsty, 2256
16:17 “**b** I have been a Nazirite set apart to God 3954
18: 1 **b** they had not yet come into an inheritance 3954
18:28 to rescue them **b** they lived a long way 3954
20: 6 **b** they committed this lewd 3954
20:36 **b** they relied on the ambush they had set 3954
20:41 **b** they realized that disaster had come 3954
21:15 **b** the LORD had made a gap in the tribes 3954
21:22 **b** we did not get wives for them during 3954
Ru 1:13 **b** the LORD’s hand has gone out 3954
1:19 the whole town was stirred **b of** them, 6584
1:20 “Call me Mara, **b** the Almighty has made my life very bitter. 3954
2:22 **b** in someone else’s field you might 2256+4202
4: 6 “Then I cannot redeem it **b** 7153
1Sa 1: 5 But to Hannah he gave a double portion **b** 3954
1: 6 And **b** the LORD had closed her womb, 3954
1:20 saying, “**B** I asked the LORD for him.” 3954
3:13 that I would judge his family forever **b of** 928
4:13 **b** his heart feared for the ark of God. 3954
4:21 **b of** the capture of the ark of God and 448
5: 7 **b** his hand is heavy upon us and 3954
6: 4 **b** the same plague has struck both you 3954
6:19 to death **b** they had looked into the ark of 3954
6:19 The people mourned **b of** the heavy blow 3954
7: 7 they were afraid **b of** the Philistines. 4946+7156

1Sa 9: 9 b the prophet of today used to be called 3954
9:13 b he must bless the sacrifice; 3954
9:24 b it was set aside for you for this occasion, 3954
12: 7 b I am going to confront you with evidence 2256
12:21 nor can they rescue you, b they are useless. 3954
12:22 b the LORD was pleased 3954
13:14 and appointed him leader of his people, b 3954
13:19 b the Philistines had said, 3954
14:10 b that will be our sign that 2256
14:24 b Saul had bound the people under an oath, 2256
14:26 b they feared the oath. 3954
15:11 b he has turned away from me and has 3954
15:23 B you have rejected the word of 3610
17:36 like one of them, b he has defied the armies 3954
17:39 b he was not used to them. 3954
17:39 he said to Saul, "b I am not used to them." 3954
18: 3 with David b he loved him as himself. 928
18:12 b the LORD was with David 3954
18:14 b the LORD was with him. 2256
18:16 b he led them in their campaigns. 3954
20: 6 b an annual sacrifice is being made there 3954
20:17 b he loved him as he loved himself. 3954
20:18 b your seat will be empty. 3954
20:21 bring them here,' then come, b, 3954
20:22 b the LORD has sent you away. 3954
20:29 b our family is observing a sacrifice in 3954
20:34 the month he did not eat, b he was grieved 3954
21: 8 b the king's business was urgent." 3954
22:17 b they too have sided with David. 3954
24:10 b he is the LORD's anointed.' 3954
25:17 b disaster is hanging over our master 3954
25:28 b he fights the LORD's battles. 3954
26:12 b the LORD had put them into 3954
26:16 b you did not guard your master, 889
26:21 B you considered my life precious today, 889+9393
28:18 B you did not obey the LORD 889+3869
28:20 filled with fear b of Samuel's words. 4946
30: 6 David was greatly distressed b 3954
30: 6 each one was bitter in spirit b of his sons 6584
30:16 drinking and reveling b of the great amount 928
30:22 "B they did not go out with us, 889+3610
2Sa 1:10 b I knew that after he had fallen he could 3954
1:12 b they had fallen by the sword. 3954
2: 6 and I too will show you the same favor b 889
3: 8 Abner was very angry b of 6584
3:11 b he was afraid of him. 4946
3:22 b David had sent him away, 3954
3:30 and his brother Abishai murdered Abner b 6584
4: 3 b the people of Beeroth fled to Gittaim 2256
5:10 b the LORD God Almighty was with him. 2256
5:24 b that will mean the LORD has gone out 3954
6: 6 b the oxen stumbled. 3954
6: 7 against Uzzah b of his irreverent act; 6584
6: 8 Then David was angry b 6584
6:12 b of the ark of God." 6288
9:13 b he always ate at the king's table, 3954
12: 6 b he did such a thing and had no pity." 889+6813
12:10 b you despised me and took the wife 3954+6813
12:14 But b by doing this you have made 3954
12:24 and b the LORD loved him, 6288
13:22 he hated Amnon b 1821+6584
14:15 the king b the people have made me afraid. 3954
14:22 in your eyes, my lord the king, b 889
16: 3 "He is staying in Jerusalem, b he thinks, 3954
16: 8 You have come to ruin b you are a man 3954
16:10 If he is cursing b the LORD said to him, 3954
18:20 b the king's son is dead." 3954+4027+6584
19: 2 b on that day the troops heard it said, 3954
19: 9 he has fled the country b of Absalom; 4946+6584
19:42 "We did this b the king is closely related 3954
21: 1 it is b he put the Gibeonites to death." 889+6584
21: 7 b of the oath before the LORD 6584
22: 8 they trembled b he was angry. 3954
22:20 he rescued me b he delighted in me. 3954
24:16 the LORD was grieved b of the calamity 448
1Ki 2:26 b you carried the ark of 3954
2:32 b without the knowledge 889
3: 2 b a temple had not yet been built for 3954
3: 6 b he was faithful to you and righteous 889+3869
3:19 "During the night this woman's son died b 889
3:28 b they saw that he had wisdom from God 3954
5: 1 b he had always been on friendly terms 3954
5: 3 "You know that b of the wars waged 4946+7156
7:47 b there were so many; 4946
8:11 not perform their service b of the cloud, 4946+7156
8:18 'B it was in your heart to build a temple 889+3610
8:33 an enemy b they have sinned against you, 889
8:35 there is no rain b your people have sinned 3954
8:35 from their sin b you have afflicted them, 3954
8:41 but has come from a distant land b of 5100
8:64 b the bronze altar before the LORD 3954
9: 9 'B they have forsaken the LORD 889+6584
9:11 b Hiram had supplied him with all NIH
10: 9 B of the LORD's eternal love for Israel, 928
10:21 b silver was considered of little value NIH
11: 2 b they will surely turn your hearts 434
11: 9 The LORD became angry with Solomon b 3954
11:33 I will do this b they have forsaken me 889+3610
11:39 I will humble David's descendants b of 5100
14: 4 his sight was gone b of his age. 4946
14:10 B of this, I am going to bring disaster 4027+4200
14:13 b he is the only one in the house 3610
14:15 b they provoked the LORD to anger 889+3610
14:16 up b of the sins Jeroboam has committed 1673
15:13 b she had made a repulsive Asherah pole. 889
1Ki 15:30 b of the sins Jeroboam had committed 6584
15:30 and b he provoked the LORD, 928
16: 7 b of all the evil he had done in the eyes of 6584
16: 7 and also b he destroyed it. 889+6584
16:13 b of all the sins Baasha 448
16:19 b of the sins he had committed, 6584
17: 7 the brook dried up b there had been no rain 3954
20:22 b next spring the king 3954
20:28 B the Arameans think the LORD is a god 889+3610
20:36 "B you have not obeyed the LORD, 889+3610
21: 4 and angry b Naboth the Jezreelite had said, 6584
21: 6 "B I said to Naboth the Jezreelite, 3954
21:20 "b you have sold yourself to do evil in 3610
21:22 b you have provoked me to anger 448
21:29 B he has humbled himself, 3610+3954
22: 8 but I hate him b 3954
22:52 b he walked in the ways of his father 2256
2Ki 1: 3 'Is it b there is no God in Israel 4946
1: 6 Is it b there is no God in Israel 4946
1:16 Is it b there is no God in Israel for you 4946
1:16 B you have done this, 889+3610
1:17 B Ahaziah had no son, 3954
3:13 the king of Israel answered, "b it was 3954
5: 1 of his master and highly regarded, b 3954
6: 9 b the Arameans are going down there." 3954
8: 1 b the LORD has decreed a famine in 3954
8:12 "B I know the harm you will do to 3954
8:29 b he had been wounded. 3954
9:16 b Joram was resting there and Ahaziah king 3954
10:19 b I am going to hold a great sacrifice 3954
10:30 "B you have done well 889+3610
11:20 b Athaliah had been slain with the sword at 2256
12:15 b they acted with complete honesty. 3954
13:23 for them b of his covenant with Abraham, 5100
15:16 b they refused to open their gates. 3954
17: 7 All this took place b 3954
17:26 b the people do 889+3869
18:12 This happened b they had not obeyed 889+6584
18:36 b the king had commanded, 3954
19:28 B you rage against me 3610
20: 1 b you are going to die; 3954
20:12 b he had heard of Hezekiah's illness. 3954
21:15 b they have done evil in my eyes 889+3610
22: 7 b they are acting faithfully." 3954
22:13 LORD's anger that burns against us b 889+6584
22:17 B they have forsaken me 889+9393
22:19 B your heart was responsive 3610
22:19 and b you tore your robes and wept NIH
23:26 which burned against Judah b of all 6584
24: 3 to remove them from his presence b of 928
24: 7 from his own country again, b the king 3954
24:20 It was b of the LORD's anger 6584
1Ch 1:19 b in his time the earth was divided; 3954
4:14 It was called this b 3954
4:41 b there was pasture for their flocks. 3954
5: 9 b their livestock had increased in Gilead. 3954
5:20 b they cried out to him during the battle. 3954
5:20 b they trusted in him. 3954
5:22 b the battle was God's. 3954
6:54 b the first lot was for them): 3954
7:23 b there had been misfortune in his family. 3954
9: 1 to Babylon b of their unfaithfulness. 928
9:27 b they had to guard it; 3954
9:33 from other duties b they were responsible 3954
10:13 Saul died b he was unfaithful to 928
11: 9 b the LORD Almighty was with him. 2256
11:19 B they risked their lives to bring it back, 3954
12:19 and his men did not help the Philistines b, 3954
13: 4 b it seemed right to all the people. 3954
13: 9 b the oxen stumbled. 3954
13:10 down b he had put his hand on the ark. 889+6584
13:11 Then David was angry b 3954
14:15 b that will mean God has gone out 3954
15: 2 b the LORD chose them to carry the ark of 3954
15:13 It was b you, the Levites, 3954+4200+4537
15:22 that was his responsibility b he was skillful 3954
15:26 B God had helped 928
19: 2 b his father showed kindness to me." 3954
21: 6 b the king's command was repulsive 3954
21:15 and was grieved b of the calamity and said 6584
21:30 b he was afraid of the sword of the angel of 3954
22: 8 b you have shed much blood on the earth 3954
26: 6 who were leaders in their father's family b 3954
27:23 b the LORD had promised to make Israel 3954
28: 3 b you are a warrior and have shed blood.' 3954
29: 1 b this palatial structure is not for man but 3954
2Ch 1: 4 b he had pitched a tent for it in Jerusalem. 3954
2: 5 b our God is greater than all other gods. 3954
2: 9 b the temple I build must be large 3954
2:11 "B the LORD loves his people, 928
5:14 not perform their service b of the cloud, 4946+7156
6: 8 'B it was in your heart to build a temple 889+3610
6:24 an enemy b they have sinned against you 3954
6:26 up and there is no rain b 3954
6:26 from their sin b you have afflicted them, 3954
6:32 from a distant land b of your great name 5100
7: 2 the temple of the LORD b the glory of 3954
7: 7 b the bronze altar he had made could 3954
7:22 'B they have forsaken the LORD, 889+6584
8:11 b the places the ark of 3954
8:14 b this was what David the man 3954
9: 8 B of the love of your God for Israel 928
9:20 b silver was considered of little value NIH
11:14 to Judah and Jerusalem b Jeroboam 3954
12: 2 B they had been unfaithful to the LORD, 3954
12:12 B Rehoboam humbled himself, 928
2Ch 12:14 He did evil b he had not set his heart 3954
13:18 of Judah were victorious b they relied on 3954
14: 7 b we have sought the LORD our God; 3954
15: 6 b God was troubling them with every kind 3954
15:15 All Judah rejoiced about the oath b 3954
15:16 b she had made a repulsive Asherah pole. 889
16: 7 "B you relied on the king of Aram and not on the LORD your God, 4027+6584
16:10 Asa was angry with the seer b of this; 6584
17: 3 The LORD was with Jehoshaphat b 3954
18: 7 but I hate him b 3954
19: 2 B of this, the wrath of the LORD is 928
19: 6 b you are not judging for man but for 3954
20:15 'Do not be afraid or discouraged b of 4946+7156
20:37 "B you have made an alliance 3869
21: 3 but he had given the kingdom to Jehoram b 3954
21: 7 b of the covenant the LORD had made 5100
21:10 b Jehoram had forsaken the LORD, 3954
21:19 his bowels came out b of the disease, 6640
22: 6 down to Jezreel to see Joram son of Ahab b 3954
22:11 B Jehosheba, the daughter of King Jehoram 2256
23: 6 they may enter b they are consecrated, 3954
23:21 b Athaliah had been slain with the sword. 2256
24:16 b of the good he had done in Israel for God 3954
24:18 B of their guilt, 928
24:20 B you have forsaken the LORD, 3954
24:24 B Judah had forsaken the LORD, 3954
25:16 b you have done this and have not listened 3954
25:20 b they sought the gods of Edom. 3954
26: 8 b he had become very powerful. 3954
26:10 b he had much livestock in the foothills and 3954
26:20 b the LORD had afflicted him. 3954
27: 6 Jotham grew powerful b 3954
28: 6 b Judah had forsaken the LORD, 928
28: 9 He said to them, "B the LORD, 928
28:19 The LORD had humbled Judah b of 6288
29:24 b the king had ordered the burnt offering 3954
29:36 b it was done so quickly. 3954
30: 3 to celebrate it at the regular time b 3954
31:10 b the LORD has blessed his people, 3954
32: 7 discouraged b of the king of Assyria 4946+7156
34:21 b our fathers have not kept the word 889+6584
34:25 B they have forsaken me 889+9393
34:27 B your heart was responsive 3610
34:27 and b you humbled yourself before me NIH
35:14 b the priests, the descendants of Aaron, 3954
35:15 b their fellow Levites made 3954
36:15 b he had pity on his people and 3954
Ezr 3:11 b the foundation of the house of 6584
3:13 b the people made so much noise. 3954
4: 2 "Let us help you build b, like you, 3954
5:12 b our fathers angered the God of heaven, 10168+10427
6:13 Then, b of the decree King Darius had sent, 10168+10378+10619
6:22 b the LORD had filled them with joy 3954
7:28 B the hand of the LORD my God was 3869
8:18 B the gracious hand of our God was on us, 3869
8:22 b we had told the king, 3954
9: 4 the God of Israel gathered around me b of 6584
9: 6 to lift up my face to you, my God, b 3954
9: 7 B of our sins, 928
9:15 though b of it not one of us can stand 6584
10: 6 b he continued to mourn over 3954
10: 9 greatly distressed by the occasion and b of 4946
10:13 b we have sinned greatly in this thing. 3954
Ne 2: 8 And b the gracious hand of my God was 3869
2:16 b as yet I had said nothing to the Jews or 2256
5: 5 b our fields and our vineyards belong 2256
5: 8 b they could find nothing to say. 2256
5:18 b the demands were heavy on these people. 3954
6:10 b men are coming to kill you— 3954
6:12 that he had prophesied against me b Tobiah 2256
6:14 O my God, b of what they have done; 3869
6:16 and lost their self-confidence, b 2256
7: 2 b he was a man of integrity 3954
8: 5 the people could see him b he was standing 3954
8:12 b they now understood the words 3954
9: 8 You have kept your promise b 3954
9:19 "B of your great compassion you did 928
9:37 B of our sins, its abundant harvest goes 928
12:43 rejoicing b God had given them great joy. 3954
13: 2 b they had not met the Israelites with food 3954
13:13 b these men were considered trustworthy. 3954
13:26 Was it not b of marriages like these 6584
13:29 b they defiled the priestly office and 6584
Est 2: 7 up b she had neither father nor mother. 3954
2:10 b Mordecai had forbidden her to do so. 3954
4: 2 b no one clothed in sackcloth was allowed 3954
4:13 that b you are in the king's house you alone NIH
7: 4 b no such distress would justify disturbing 3954
8: 7 "B Haman attacked the Jews, 889+6584
8:17 of other nationalities became Jews b fear of 3954
9: 2 b the people of all 3954
9: 3 b fear of Mordecai had seized them. 3954
9:26 B of everything written in this letter 4027+6584
9:26 this letter and b of what they had seen 3970+6584
10: 3 b he worked for the good of his people NIH
Job 2:13 b they saw how great his suffering was. 3954
6:20 b they had been confident; 3954
11:18 You will be secure, b there is hope; 3954
15:25 b he shakes his fist at God 3954
20: 2 to answer b I am greatly disturbed. 6288
29:12 b I rescued the poor who cried for help, 3954
31:34 b I so feared the crowd and so dreaded 3954
32: 1 b he was righteous in his own eyes. 3954
32: 3 b they had found no way to refute Job, 889+6584

Job 32: 4 to Job **b** they were older than he. 3954
34:25 **B** he takes note of their deeds, 4027+4200
34:27 **b** they turned from following him 4027+6584
35:12 He does not answer when men cry out **b of** 4946+7156
37:19 we cannot draw up our case **b of** 4946+7156
42: 7 **b** you have not spoken of me what is right, 3954
Ps 3: 5 I wake again, **b** the LORD sustains me. 3954
5: 8 in your righteousness **b of** my enemies— 5100
6: 4 save me **b of** your unfailing love. 5100
6: 7 they fail **b of** all my foes. 928
7:17 I will give thanks to the LORD **b of** 3869
8: 2 and infants you have ordained praise **b of** 5100
12: 5 "**B of** the oppression of the weak and 4946
16: 8 **B** he is at my right hand, 3954
16:10 **b** you will not abandon me to the grave, 3954
18: 7 they trembled **b** he was angry. 3954
18:19 he rescued me **b** he delighted in me. 3954
25:21 **b** my hope is in you. 3954
27:11 in a straight path **b of** my oppressors. 5100
31:10 my strength fails **b of** my affliction, 928
31:11 **B of** all my enemies, 4946
37: 1 Do not fret **b of** evil men or be envious 928
37:40 **b** they take refuge in him. 3954
38: 3 **B of** your wrath there is no health 4946+7156
38: 3 my bones have no soundness **b of** my sin. 4946+7156
38: 5 My wounds fester and are loathsome **b of** 4946+7156
38:11 My friends and companions avoid me **b of** 4946+5584
44:16 **b of** the enemy, who is bent on revenge. 4946+7156
44:26 redeem us **b of** your unfailing love. 5100
48:11 of Judah are glad **b of** your judgments. 5100
63: 3 **B** your love is better than life, 3954
63: 7 **B** you are my help, 3954
68:29 **B of** your temple 4946
69: 6 in you not be disgraced **b of** me, O Lord, 928
69: 6 not be put to shame **b of** me, 928
69:18 redeem me **b of** my foes. 5100
70: 3 turn back **b of** their shame. 6584+6813
74:20 **b** haunts of violence fill the dark places of 3954
91:14 "**B** he loves me," says the LORD, 3954
97: 8 of Judah are glad **b of** your judgments, 5100
102: 5 **B of** my loud groaning I am reduced 4946
102:10 **b of** your great wrath, 4946+7156
105:38 **b** dread of Israel had fallen on them. 3954
106:32 and trouble came to Moses **b of** them; 6288
107:17 and suffered affliction **b of** their iniquities. 4946
107:34 **b of** the wickedness of those 4946
115: 1 **b of** your love and faithfulness. 6584
116: 2 **B** he turned his ear to me, 3954
119:47 I delight in your commands **b** I love them. 889
119:53 Indignation grips me **b of** the wicked, 4946
119:127 **B** I love your commands more than gold, 4027+6584
119:128 **b** I consider all your precepts right, 4027+6584
139:14 I praise you **b** I am fearfully 3954+6584
142: 7 the righteous will gather about me **b of** 3954
Pr 3:12 **b** the LORD disciplines those he loves, 3954
21:25 **b** his hands refuse to work. 3954
22:22 not exploit the poor **b** they are poor and do 3954
24:19 Do not fret **b of** evil men or be envious of 928
Ecc 2:17 **b** the work that is done under 3954
2:18 **b** I must leave them to the one who comes 8611
3:22 **b** that is his lot. 3954
4: 9 **b** they have a good return for their work: 889
5:20 **b** God keeps him occupied with gladness 3954
7: 3 **b** a sad face is good for the heart. 3954
8: 2 I say, **b** you took an oath before God. 1826+6584
8:13 Yet **b** the wicked do not fear God, 889
8:15 **b** nothing is better for a man under 889
10:20 **b** a bird of the air may carry your words, 3954
12: 3 when the grinders cease **b** they are few, 3954
SS 1: 6 Do not stare at me **b** I am dark, 8611
1: 6 **b** I am darkened by the sun. 8611
Isa 1:29 "You will be ashamed **b of** the sacred oaks 4946
1:29 you will be disgraced **b of** the gardens 4946
7: 4 Do not lose heart **b of** 4946
7: 4 **b of** the fierce anger of Rezin and Aram 928
7:22 **b of** the abundance of the milk they give, 4946
8: 6 "**B** this people has rejected 3610+3954
10:13 and by my wisdom, **b** I have understanding. 3954
10:27 the yoke will be broken **b** you have grown 4946+7156
13: 7 **B of this,** all hands will go limp, 4027+6584
17: 9 which they left **b of** the Israelites, 4946+7156
19:17 **b of** what the LORD Almighty is planning 4946+7156
19:20 When they cry out to the LORD **b of** 4946+7156
26: 3 whose mind is steadfast, **b** he trusts in you. 3954
30: 5 to shame **b of** a people useless to them, 6584
30:12 "**B** you have rejected this message, 3610
31: 9 Their stronghold will fall **b of** terror; 4946
36:21 **b** the king had commanded, 3954
37:21 **B** you have prayed to me 889
37:29 **B** you rage against me and 3610
37:29 and **b** your insolence has reached my ears, NIH
38: 1 **b** you are going to die; 3954
38:15 I will walk humbly all my years **b of** 6584
39: 1 **b** he had heard of his illness and recovery. 2256
40: 7 **b** the breath of the LORD blows on them. 3954
40:26 **B of** his great power and mighty strength, 4946
43: 4 and **b** I love you, NIH
43:20 **b** I provide water in the desert and streams 3954
49: 7 **b of** the LORD, who is faithful, 5100

Isa 50: 1 **B of** your sins you were sold; 928
50: 1 **b of** your transgressions your mother was sent away. 928
50: 7 **B** the Sovereign LORD helps me, 4027+6584
51:13 in constant terror every day **b of** the wrath of the oppressor, 4946+7156
52:15 and kings will shut their mouths **b of** him. 6584
53:12 **b** he poured out his life unto death, 889+9393
54: 1 **b** more are the children of 3954
55: 5 **b of** the LORD your God, 5100
57:11 not **b** I have long been silent that you do NIH
61: 1 **b** the LORD has anointed me 3610
64: 7 and made us waste away **b of** our sins. 928+3338
65: 7 "**B** they burned sacrifices on the mountains 889
66: 5 and exclude you **b of** my name, have said, 5100
66:18 I, **b** of their actions and their imaginations, NIH
Jer 1:16 on my people **b of** their wickedness 6584
2:35 But I will pass judgment on you **b** you say, 6584
3: 8 sent her away **b of** all her adulteries. 128+6584
3: 9 **B** Israel's immorality mattered so little 2256
3:21 **b** they have perverted their ways 3954
4: 4 like fire **b of** the evil you have done— 4946+7156
4:17 **b** she has rebelled against me,' " 3954
4:28 **b** I have spoken and will not relent, 3954+6584
5:14 "**B** the people have spoken these words, 3610
6:19 on this people, the fruit of their schemes, **b** 3954
6:30 **b** the LORD has rejected them." 3954
7:12 see what I did to it **b of** the wickedness 4946+7156
8:14 **b** we have sinned against him. 3954
9: 7 test them, for what else can I do **b of** 4946+7156
9:13 "It is **b** they have forsaken my law, 6584
9:19 We must leave our land **b** our houses are 3954
10: 5 they must be carried **b** they cannot walk. 3954
10:19 Woe to me **b of** my injury! 6584
11:14 **b** I will not listen when they call to me in 3954
11:17 **b** the house of Israel and the house 1673
11:18 **B** the LORD revealed their plot to me, 2256
11:23 **b** I will bring disaster on the men 3954
12: 4 **B** those who live in it are wicked, 4946
12:11 be laid waste **b** there is no one who cares. 3954
12:13 So bear the shame of your harvest **b of** 4946
13:17 I will weep in secret **b of** your pride; 4946+7156
13:17 **b** the LORD's flock will be taken captive. 3954
13:22 it is **b of** your many sins 928
13:25 "**b** you have forgotten me and trusted 889
14: 4 The ground is cracked **b** there is no rain in 3954
14: 5 in the field deserts her newborn fawn **b** 3954
14:16 Jerusalem **b of** the famine and sword. 4946+7156
15: 4 of the earth **b of** what Manasseh son 1673
15:13 **b of** all your sins throughout your country. 928
15:17 I sat alone **b** your hand was on me 4946+7156
16: 5 **b** I have withdrawn my blessing, 3954
16:11 'It is **b** your fathers forsook me,' 889+6584
16:18 **b** they have defiled my land with 6584
17: 3 **b of** sin throughout your country. 928
17:13 be written in the dust **b** they have forsaken 3954
19: 8 by will be appalled and will scoff **b of** 6584
19:15 **b** they were stiff-necked and would 3954
21: 2 the LORD for us **b** Nebuchadnezzar king 3954
21:12 like fire **b of** the evil you have done— 4946+7156
22: 9 '**B** they have forsaken the covenant of 889+6584
22:10 for him who is exiled, **b** 3954
22:22 and disgraced **b of** all your wickedness. 4946
23: 2 "**B** you have scattered my flock NIH
23: 9 **b of** the LORD and his holy words 4946+7156
23:10 **b of** the curse the land lies parched 3954+4946+7156
23:15 and drink poisoned water, **b** from 3954
23:36 'the oracle of the LORD' again, **b** 3954
25: 8 "**B** you have not listened to my words, 889+3610
25:16 and go mad **b of** the sword I will send 4946+7156
25:27 rise no more **b of** the sword I will send 4946+7156
25:37 be laid waste **b of** the fierce anger of 4946+7156
25:38 their land will become desolate **b of** 4946+7156
25:38 of the sword of the oppressor and **b of** 4946+7156
26: 3 the disaster I was planning **b of** 4946+7156
26:11 be sentenced to death **b** he has prophesied 3954
28:16 **b** you have preached rebellion against 3954
29: 7 Pray to the LORD for it, **b** if it prospers, 3954
29:22 **B of** them, all the exiles 4946
29:31 **B** Shemaiah has prophesied to you, 889+3610
29:32 **b** he has preached rebellion against me.' " 3954
30:14 **b** your guilt is so great and your sins 6584
30:15 **B of** your great guilt 6584
30:17 '**b** you are called an outcast, 3954
31: 9 **b** I am Israel's father, 3954
31:15 **b** her children are no more." 3954
31:18 **b** you are the LORD my God. 3954
31:19 I was ashamed and humiliated **b** I bore 3954
31:32 **b** they broke my covenant, 889
31:34 **b** they will all know me, 3954
31:37 of Israel **b of** all they have done," 6584
32: 7 **b** as nearest relative it is your right and duty 3954
32:24 **B of** the sword, famine and plague, 4946+7156
32:44 **b** I will restore their fortunes, 3954
33: 5 I will hide my face from this city **b of** 6584
35: 6 **b** our forefather Jonadab son 3954
35:14 **b** they obey their forefather's command. 3954
36:31 **b** they have not listened.' " 2256
37:11 from Jerusalem **b of** Pharaoh's army, 4946+7156
39:18 **b** you trust in me, declares the LORD.' " 3954
40: 3 All this happened **b** you people sinned NIH
41:18 They were afraid of them **b** Ishmael son 3954
44: 3 **b of** the evil they have done. 4946+7156
44:23 **B** you have burned incense 4946+7156
48: 8 **b** the LORD has spoken. 889
48:42 Moab will be destroyed as a nation **b** 3954

Jer 49:17 by will be appalled and will scoff **b of** 6584
49:20 he will completely destroy their pasture **b of** 6584
50:11 "**B** you rejoice and are glad, 3954
50:11 **b** you frolic like a heifer threshing grain 3954
50:13 **B of** the LORD's anger she will not 4946
50:13 be horrified and scoff **b of** all her wounds. 6584
50:16 **B of** the sword of the oppressor 4946+7156
50:24 and captured **b** you opposed the LORD. 3954
50:45 he will completely destroy their pasture **b of** 6584
51: 6 Do not be destroyed **b of** her sins. 928
51:11 **b** his purpose is to destroy Babylon. 3954
51:49 "Babylon must fall **b of** Israel's slain, NIH
51:49 as the slain in all the earth have fallen **b of** 4200
51:51 **b** foreigners have entered the holy places of 3954
51:64 rise no more **b of** the disaster I will bring 4946+7156
52: 3 It was **b of** the LORD's anger 6584
La 1: 5 The LORD has brought her grief **b of** 6584
1:16 My children are destitute **b** 3954
1:22 as you have dealt with me **b of** all my sins. 6584
2:11 on the ground **b** my people are destroyed, 6584
2:11 **b** children and infants faint in the streets of 928
3:22 **B of** the LORD's great love we are NIH
3:48 from my eyes **b** my people are destroyed. 6584
3:51 What I see brings grief to my soul **b of** all 4946
4: 4 **B of** thirst the infant's tongue sticks to 928
4:13 But it happened **b of** the sins 4946
5: 9 our lives **b of** the sword in the desert. 4946+7156
5:17 **B of** this our hearts are faint, 6584
5:17 **b of** these things our eyes grow dim 6584
Eze 1:20 **b** the spirit of the living creatures was in 3954
1:21 **b** the spirit of the living creatures was in 3954
3: 7 to you **b** they are not willing to listen to me, 3954
3:21 he will surely live **b** he took warning, 3954
4:17 of each other and will waste away **b of** 928
5: 9 **B of** all your detestable idols, 3610
5:11 **b** you have defiled my sanctuary 561+3610+4202
6:11 **b of** all the wicked and detestable practices 448
7:13 **B of** their sins, not one of them 928
7:16 each **b of** his sins. 928
7:23 **b** the land is full of bloodshed and 3954
10:17 the cherubim rose, they rose with them, **b** 3954
12:19 in it **b of** the violence of all who live there. 4946
13: 8 **B of** your false words and lying visions, 3610
13:10 " '**B** they lead my people astray, saying, 3610
13:10 "Peace," when there is no peace, and **b,** 928+3610
13:22 **B** you disheartened the righteous 3610
13:22 and **b** you encouraged the wicked not NIH
14:15 so that no one can pass through it **b of** 4946+7156
15: 8 I will make the land desolate **b** 3610
16:14 the nations on account of your beauty, **b** 3954
16:28 **b** you were insatiable; 4946
16:31 **b** you scorned payment. 4200
16:36 **B** you poured out your wealth 3610
16:36 and **b of** all your detestable idols, 6584
16:36 and **b** you gave them your children's blood, 3869
16:43 " '**B** you did not remember the days 889+3610
16:52 **B** your sins were more vile than theirs, 928
16:59 **b** you have despised my oath by breaking 889
16:63 and never again open your mouth **b of** 4946+7156
17:18 **B** he had given his hand in pledge and 2256
17:20 upon him there **b** he was unfaithful to me. 889
18:13 **B** he has done all these detestable things, NIH
18:18 **b** he practiced extortion, 3954
18:22 **B of** the righteous things he has done, 928
18:24 **B of** the unfaithfulness he is guilty of and 928
18:24 the unfaithfulness he is guilty of and **b of** 928
18:26 **b of** the sin he has committed he will die. 928
18:28 **B** he considers all 2256
19:10 and full of branches **b of** abundant water. 4946
20:16 **b** they rejected my laws and did 3610
20:24 **b** they had not obeyed my laws 3610
21: 4 **B** I am going to cut off the righteous 889+3610
21: 7 '**B of** the news that is coming. 448
21:24 '**B** you people have brought 3610
21:24 **b** you have done this, 3610
22: 4 you have become guilty **b of** 928
22:19 '**B** you have all become dross, 3610
23:30 **b** you lusted after the nations 928
23:45 **b** they are adulterous and blood is 3954
24: 2 **b** the king of Babylon has laid siege NIH
24:13 **B** I tried to cleanse you but you would not 3610
24:23 or weep but will waste away **b of** your sins 928
25: 3 **B** you said "Aha!" 3610
25: 6 **B** you have clapped your hands 3610
25: 8 '**B** Moab and Seir said, "Look, 3610
25:12 '**B** Edom took revenge on the house 3610
25:15 '**B** the Philistines acted in vengeance 3610
26: 2 **b** Tyre has said of Jerusalem, 'Aha! 889+3610
27:12 with you **b of** your great wealth of goods; 4946
27:16 " 'Aram did business with you **b of** 4946
27:18 **b of** your many products and great wealth 928
27:31 They will shave their heads **b of** you 448
28: 5 **b of** your wealth your heart has grown proud 928
28: 6 " '**B** you think you are wise, 3610
28:17 and you corrupted your wisdom **b of** 6584
29: 9 " '**B** you said, "The Nile is mine; 3610
29:20 for his efforts **b** he and his army did it 889
31: 5 spreading **b of** abundant waters. 4946
31:10 **B** it towered on high, 889+3610
31:10 and **b** it was proud of its height, NIH
31:15 **B of** it I clothed Lebanon with gloom, 6584
32:10 with horror **b of** you 6584
32:25 **B** their terror had spread in the land of 3954
32:26 by the sword **b** they spread their terror in 3954
33: 6 that man will be taken away **b of** his sin, 928
33:10 and we are wasting away **b of** them. 928

Eze 33:12 to live **b of** his former righteousness.' 928
33:29 the land a desolate waste **b of** all 6584
34: 5 So they were scattered **b** 4946
34: 8 **b** my flock lacks a shepherd and 4946
34: 8 and **b** my shepherds did not search NIH
34:21 **B** you shove with flank and shoulder, 3610
35: 5 " '**B** you harbored an ancient hostility 3610
35:10 " '**B** you have said, "These two nations 3610
35:15 **B** you rejoiced when the inheritance of 3869
36: 3 **B** they ravaged and hounded you 928+3610+3610
36: 6 in my jealous wrath **b** you have suffered 3610
36:13 **B** people say to you, 3610
36:18 on them **b** they had shed blood in the land 6584
36:18 and **b** they had defiled it with their idols. NIH
36:30 **disgrace** among the nations *b* AIT
39:10 **b** they will use the weapons for fuel. 3954
39:11 **b** Gog and all his hordes will 2256
39:23 **b** they were unfaithful to me. 889+6584
44: 2 It is to remain shut **b** the LORD, 3954
44:12 But **b** they served them in the presence 889+3610
47: 5 **b** the water had risen and was deep enough 3954
47: 9 **b** this water flows there and makes 3954
47:12 **b** the water from the sanctuary flows 3954
47:14 **B** I swore with uplifted hand to give it 889
48:14 **b** it is holy to the LORD. 3954
Da 1:10 king would then have my head **b of** *you.*" 2549
2: 8 are trying to gain time, **b** 10168+10353+10619
2:30 this mystery has been revealed to me, not **b** 10089
4:18 **b** the spirit of the holy gods is in you." 10168
4:37 **b** everything he does is right 10168
5:19 **B of** the high position he gave him, 10427
6: 4 **b** he was trustworthy and neither corrupt 10168+10353+10619
6:22 **b** I was found innocent in his sight. 10168+10353+10619
6:23 **b** he had trusted in his God. 10168
7:11 to watch **b of** the boastful words 10427
8:12 **B of** rebellion, the host [of the saints] and 928
8:19 **b** the vision concerns the appointed time of 3954
9: 7 where you have scattered us **b of** 928
9: 8 with shame **b** we have sinned against you. 889
9:11 **b** we have sinned against you. 3954
9:18 We do not make requests of you **b** 6584
9:18 but **b of** your great mercy. 6584
9:19 For your sake, O my God, do not delay, **b** 3954
10:13 **b** I was detained there with the king 2256
10:16 "I am overcome with anguish **b of** 928
11: 4 **b** his empire will be uprooted and given 3954
11:25 to stand **b of** the plots devised against him. 3954
11:27 **b** an end will still come at 3954
12: 9 **b** the words are closed up and sealed until 3954
Hos 1: 2 **b** the land is guilty of the vilest adultery 3954
1: 4 **b** I will soon punish the house of Jehu for 3954
2: 4 **b** they are the children of adultery. 3954
4: 1 **b** the LORD has a charge to bring 3954
4: 3 **B of** this the land mourns, 6584
4: 6 "**B** you have rejected knowledge, 3954
4: 6 **b** you have ignored the law of your God, 2256
4:10 but not increase, **b** they have deserted 3954
4:14 **b** the men themselves consort with harlots 3954
7:13 Woe to them, **b** they have strayed from me! 3954
7:13 **b** they have rebelled against me! 3954
7:16 Their leaders will fall by the sword **b of** 4946
8: 1 An eagle is over the house of the LORD **b** 3610
9: 7 **B** your sins are so many and your hostility 6584
9:15 "**B of** all their wickedness in Gilgal, NIH
9:15 **B of** their sinful deeds, 6584
9:17 My God will reject them **b** they have 3954
10: 3 "We have no king **b** we did not revere 3954
10: 5 **b** it is taken from them into exile. 3954
10:13 **B** you have depended on your own strength 3954
10:15 O Bethel, **b** your wickedness is great. 4946+7156
11: 5 not Assyria rule over them **b** they refuse 3954
13: 9 **b** you are against me, against your helper. 3954
13:16 **b** they have rebelled against their God. 3954
Joel 1: 5 wail **b of** the new wine, 6584
1:11 **b** the harvest of the field is destroyed. 3954
1:18 herds mill about **b** they have no pasture; 3954
3:19 **b of** violence done to the people of Judah, 4946
Am 1: 3 **B** she threshed Gilead 6584
1: 6 **B** she took captive whole communities 6584
1: 9 **B** she sold whole communities of captives 6584
1:11 **B** he pursued his brother with a sword, 6584
1:11 **b** his anger raged continually 2256
1:13 **B** he ripped open the pregnant women 6584
2: 1 **B** he burned, as if to lime, 6584
2: 4 **B** they have rejected the law of the LORD 6584
2: 4 **b** they have been led astray by false gods, 2256
4:12 Israel, and **b** I will do this to you, 3954+6813
7:13 **b** this is the king's sanctuary and the temple 3954
8:13 and strong young men will faint **b of** thirst. 928
Ob 1:10 **B of** the violence 4946
Jnh 1: 2 **b** its wickedness has come up before me." 3954
1:10 **b** he had already told them so.) 3954
Mic 1: 5 All this is **b of** Jacob's transgression, 928
1: 5 **b of** the sins of the house of Israel. 928
1: 8 **B of** this I will weep and wail; 6584
1:12 **b** disaster has come from the LORD, 3954
2: 1 At morning's light they carry it out **b** it is 3954
2:10 this is not your resting place, **b** it is defiled, 6288
3: 4 from them **b of** the evil they have done. 889+3869
3: 7 They will all cover their faces **b** 3954
3:12 Therefore **b of** you, 1673
6:13 to ruin you **b of** your sins. 6584
6:14 **b** what you save I will give to the sword. 2256
7: 9 **B** I have sinned against him, 3954
7:13 The earth will become desolate **b of** 6584

Na 3: 4 all **b of** the wanton lust of a harlot, 4946
Hab 2: 5 **B** he is as greedy as the grave and 889
2: 8 **B** you have plundered many nations, 3954
Zep 1:17 **b** they have sinned against the LORD. 3954
3:11 **b** I will remove from this city 3954
Hag 1: 9 "**B of** my house, which remains a ruin, 3610
1:10 Therefore, **b of** you the heavens have withheld their dew 6584
1:12 **b** the LORD their God had sent him. 889+3869
Zec 2: 4 without walls **b of** the great number of men 4946
2:13 **b** he has roused himself 3954
8: 4 each with cane in hand **b of** his age. 4946
8:10 about his business safely **b of** his enemy, 4946
8:23 **b** we have heard that God is with you.' " 3954
9:11 **b of** the blood of my covenant with you, 928
10: 5 **B** the LORD is with them, 3954
10: 6 I will restore them **b** I have compassion 3954
12: 5 **b** the LORD Almighty is their God.' 928
13: 3 **b** you have told lies in the LORD's name.' 3954
Mal 1:11 **b** my name will be great among 3954
2: 2 **b** you have not set your heart to honor me. 3954
2: 3 "**B of** you I will rebuke your descendants; 4200
2: 7 **b** he is the messenger of 3954
2: 9 **b** you have not followed my ways 889+3869+7023
2:13 and wail **b** he no longer pays attention 3954
2:14 **b** the LORD is acting as the witness 3954+6584
2:14 **b** you have broken faith with her, 889
2:15 **B** he was seeking godly offspring. NIH
3: 9 **b** you are robbing me. 2256
Mt 1:19 *B* Joseph her husband **was** AIT
1:20 **b** what is conceived in her is from 1142
1:21 **b** he will save his people from their sins." 1142
2:18 **b** they are no more." 4022
5:10 Blessed are those who are persecuted **b** 1915
5:11 of evil against you **b of** me. 1915
5:12 **b** great is your reward in heaven, 4022
6: 7 for they think they will be heard **b of** 1877
7:25 **b** it had its foundation on the rock. 1142
7:29 **b** he taught as one who had authority, 1142
9:36 **b** they were harassed and helpless, 4022
10:22 All men will hate you **b of** me, 1328
10:41 a prophet **b** he is a prophet will receive NIG
10:41 and anyone who receives a righteous man **b** NIG
10:42 of cold water to one of these little ones **b** NIG
11:20 **b** they did not repent. 4022
11:25 **b** you have hidden these things from 4022
13: 5 **b** the soil was shallow. 1328
13: 6 and they withered **b** they had no root. 1328
13:16 But blessed are your eyes **b** they see, 4022
13:16 and your ears **b** they hear. 4022
13:21 When trouble or persecution comes **b of** 1328
13:29 '**b** while you are pulling the weeds, 3607
13:58 And he did not do many miracles there **b of** their lack of faith. 1328
14: 3 and bound him and put him in prison **b of** 1328
14: 5 **b** they considered him a prophet. 4022
14: 9 but **b of** his oaths and his dinner guests, 1328
14:24 by the waves **b** the wind was against it. 1142
16: 7 "It is **b** we didn't bring any bread." 4022
17:20 He replied, "**B** you have so little faith. 1328
18: 7 the world **b of** the things that cause people 608
18:32 that debt of yours **b** you begged me to. 2075
19: 8 to divorce your wives **b** 4639
19:12 For some are eunuchs **b** they were born NIG
19:12 and others have renounced marriage **b of** 1328
19:22 he went away sad, **b** he had great wealth. 1142
20: 7 " '**B** no one has hired us,' they answered. 4022
20:15 Or are you envious **b** I am generous?' 4022
21:46 of the crowd **b** the people held that he was 2075
22:16 **b** you pay no attention to who they are. 1142
22:29 *b you do* not **know** the Scriptures AIT
24: 9 you will be hated by all nations **b of** me. 1328
24:12 **B of** the increase of wickedness, 1328
24:42 **b** you do not know 4022
24:44 **b** the Son of Man will come at an hour 4022
25:13 **b** you do not know the day or the hour. 4022
26:43 **b** their eyes were heavy. 1142
27:19 a great deal today in a dream **b of** him." 1328
Mk 1:22 **b** he taught them as one who had authority, 1142
1:34 the demons speak **b** they knew who he was. 4022
2: 4 Since they could not get him to Jesus **b of** 1328
3: 9 **B of** the crowd he told his disciples to have 1328
3:30 He said this **b** they were saying, 4022
4: 5 **b** the soil was shallow. 1328
4: 6 and they withered **b** they had no root. 1328
4:17 When trouble or persecution comes **b of** 1328
4:29 **b** the harvest has come." 4022
5:28 **b** she thought, "If I just touch his clothes, 1142
6:17 He did this **b of** Herodias, 1328
6:20 **b** Herod feared John and protected him, 1142
6:26 but **b of** his oaths and his dinner guests, 1328
6:31 **b** so many people were coming and going 1142
6:34 **b** they were like sheep without a shepherd. 4022
6:48 **b** the wind was against them. 1142
6:50 **b** they all saw him and were terrified. 1142
8: 3 **b** some of them have come 2779
8:16 "It is **b** we have no bread." 4022
9:31 **b** he was teaching his disciples. 1142
9:34 But they kept quiet **b** on 1142
9:38 **b** he was not one of us." 4022
9:41 a cup of water in my name **b** you belong 4022
10: 5 "It was **b** your hearts were hard 4639
10:22 He went away sad, **b** he had great wealth. 1142
11:13 **b** it was not the season for figs. 1142
11:18 **b** the whole crowd was amazed 1142
12:12 Then they looked for a way to arrest him **b** 1142
12:14 **b** you pay no attention to who they are; 1142

Mk 12:24 **b** you do not know the Scriptures or 1328+4047
13:13 All men will hate you **b of** me, 1328
13:19 **b** those will be days of distress unequaled 1142
13:35 "Therefore keep watch **b** you do not know 1142
14:40 **b** their eyes were heavy. 1142
16: 8 **b** they were afraid. 1142
Lk 1: 7 **b** Elizabeth was barren; 2776
1:14 and many will rejoice **b of** his birth, 2093
1:20 **b** you did not believe my words, 505+4005
1:68 **b** he has come and has redeemed 4022
1:78 **b of** the tender mercy of our God, 1328
2: 4 **b** he belonged to the house and line 1328
2: 7 **b** there was no room for them in the inn. 1484
3:19 when John rebuked Herod the tetrarch **b** of 4309
4:18 **b** he has anointed me to preach good news to the poor. 1641+4005
4:32 **b** his message had authority. 4022
4:41 **b** they knew he was the Christ. 4022
4:43 **b** that is why I was sent." 4022
5: 5 But **b** you say so, I will let down the nets." 2093
5:19 not find a way to do this **b of** the crowd, 1328
6:19 **b** power was coming from him 4022
6:22 **b** of the Son of Man. 1915
6:23 **b** great is your reward in heaven. 1142
6:35 **b** he is kind to the ungrateful and wicked. 4022
6:48 **b** it was well built. 1328+3836
7: 5 **b** he loves our nation 1142
7:29 *b they had been* **baptized** AIT
7:30 *b they had* not *been* **baptized** AIT
8: 6 the plants withered **b** they had no moisture. 1328
8:19 but they were not able to get near him **b of** 1328
8:30 **b** many demons had gone into him. 4022
8:37 **b** they were overcome with fear. 4022
8:42 **b** his only daughter, 4022
9: 7 **b** some were saying 1328
9:12 **b** we are in a remote place here." 4022
9:49 **b** he is not one of us." 4022
9:53 **b** he was heading for Jerusalem. 4022
10:21 **b** you have hidden these things from 4022
11: 6 **b** a friend of mine on a journey has come 2076
11: 8 give him the bread **b** he is his friend, 1328+3836
11: 8 yet **b of** the man's boldness he will get up 1328
11:18 say this **b** you claim that I drive out demons 4022
11:42 **b** you give God a tenth of your mint, 4022
11:43 **b** you love the most important seats in 4022
11:44 **b** you are like unmarked graves, 4022
11:46 **b** you load people down 4022
11:47 **b** you build tombs for the prophets, 4022
11:49 **B of** this, God in his wisdom said, 1328
11:52 **b** you have taken away the key 4022
12:40 **b** the Son of Man will come at an hour 4022
13: 2 other Galileans **b** they suffered this way? 4022
13:14 Indignant **b** Jesus had healed on the Sabbath, 4022
13:24 **b** many, I tell you, will try to enter 4022
15:27 the fattened calf **b** he has him back safe 4022
15:32 **b** this brother of yours was dead 4022
16: 2 **b** you cannot be manager any longer.' 1142
16: 8 commended the dishonest manager **b** 4022
16:24 **b** I am in agony in this fire.' 4022
17: 9 the servant **b** he did what he was told to do? 4022
17:21 **b** the kingdom of God is within you." 1142
18: 5 yet **b** this widow keeps bothering me, 1328
18:23 **b** he was a man of great wealth. 1142
19: 3 **b of** the crowd. 608
19: 9 **b** this man, too, is a son of Abraham. 2776
19:11 **b** he was near Jerusalem and 1328+3836
19:17 '**B** you have been trustworthy in 4022
19:21 I was afraid of you, **b** you are a hard man. 4022
19:44 **b** you did not recognize the time 505+4005
19:48 **b** all the people hung on his words. 1142
20: 6 **b** they are persuaded that John was 1142
20:19 **b** they knew he had spoken this parable 1142
21:17 All men will hate you **b of** me. 1328
21:28 **b** your redemption is drawing near." 1484
23: 8 **b** for a long time he had been wanting 1142
24:11 **b** their words seemed to them 2779
24:41 And while they still did not believe it **b of** 608
Jn 1:15 after me has surpassed me **b** he was 4022
1:30 after me has surpassed me **b** he was 4022
1:50 "You believe **b** I told you I saw you under 4022
3:18 not believe stands condemned already **b** 4022
3:19 but men loved darkness instead of light **b** 1142
3:23 **b** there was plenty of water, 4022
4:39 in him **b of** the woman's testimony, 1328
4:41 **b of** his words many more became believers 1328
4:42 "We no longer believe just **b of** 1328
5:16 **b** Jesus was doing these things on 1328+4047
5:19 **b** whatever the Father does the Son 1142
5:27 And he has given him authority to judge **b** 4022
5:39 You diligently study the Scriptures **b** 4022
6: 2 and a great crowd of people followed him **b** 4022
6:26 not **b** you saw miraculous signs but 4022
6:26 not because you saw miraculous signs but **b** 4022
6:41 the Jews began to grumble about him **b** 4022
6:57 as the living Father sent me and I live **b of** 1328
6:57 the one who feeds on me will live **b of** me. 1328
7: 1 from Judea **b** the Jews there were waiting 4022
7: 7 but it hates me **b** I testify 4022
7: 8 **b** for me the right time has not yet come." 4022
7:22 **b** Moses gave you circumcision 1328+4047
7:29 but I know him **b** I am from him 4022
7:30 **b** his time had not yet come. 4022
7:43 Thus the people were divided **b of** Jesus. 1328
8:16 my decisions are right, **b** I am not alone. 4022
8:20 **b** his time had not yet come. 4022
8:37 **b** you have no room for my word. 4022

Jn 8:43 **B** you are unable to hear what I say. *4022*
8:45 **b** I tell the truth, you do not believe me! *4022*
9:22 His parents said this **b** they were afraid of *4022*
10: 4 and his sheep follow him **b** *4022*
10: 5 they will run away from him **b** they do *4022*
10:13 The man runs away **b** he is a hired hand *4022*
10:26 you do not believe **b** you are not my sheep. *4022*
10:33 "but for blasphemy, **b** you, a mere man, *4022*
10:36 then do you accuse me of blasphemy **b** *4022*
12: 6 not say this **b** he cared about the poor but *4022*
12: 6 because he cared about the poor but **b** *4022*
12: 9 not only **b of** him but also to see Lazarus, *1328*
12:18 Many people, **b** they had heard *4022*
12:39 For this reason they could not believe, **b,** *4022*
12:41 Isaiah said this **b** he saw Jesus' glory *4022*
12:42 But **b of** the Pharisees they would *1328*
14:12 **b** I am going to the Father. *4022*
14:17 **b** it neither sees him nor knows him. *4022*
14:19 **B** I live, you also will live. *4022*
15: 3 You are already clean **b of** the word *1328*
15:15 **b** a servant does not know his master's *4022*
15:21 They will treat you this way **b of** my name, *1328*
16: 3 They will do such things **b** they have *4022*
16: 4 not tell you this at first **b** I was with you. *4022*
16: 6 **B** I have said these things, *4022*
16: 9 **b** men do not believe in me; *4022*
16:10 **b** I am going to the Father, *4022*
16:11 **b** the prince of this world *4022*
16:17 and '**B** I am going to the Father'?" *4022*
16:21 A woman giving birth to a child has pain **b** *4022*
16:21 the anguish **b of** her joy that a child is born *1328*
16:27 the Father himself loves you **b** *4022*
17:24 the glory you have given me **b** *4022*
18: 2 **b** Jesus had often met there *4022*
18:15 **B** this disciple was known to *1254*
19: 7 **b** he claimed to be the Son of God." *4022*
19:31 **B** the Jews did not want the bodies left on *2671*
19:38 but secretly **b** he feared the Jews. *1328*
19:42 **B** it was the Jewish day of Preparation and *1328*
20:29 Then Jesus told him, "**B** you have seen me, *4022*
21: 6 the net in **b of** the large number of fish. *608*
21:17 Peter was hurt **b** Jesus asked him *4022*
21:23 **B of** this, the rumor spread among *4036*
Ac 2: 6 **b** each one heard them speaking *4022*
2:24 **b** it was impossible for death *2776*
2:25 **B** he is at my right hand, *4022*
2:27 **b** you will not abandon me to the grave, *4022*
4: 2 They were greatly disturbed **b** *1328*
4: 3 and **b** it was evening, *1142*
4:21 **b** all the people were praising God *1328*
5:26 **b** they feared that the people would stone *1142*
5:41 rejoicing **b** they had been counted worthy *4022*
6: 1 against the Hebraic Jews **b** their widows *4022*
7: 9 "*B* the patriarchs *were* **jealous of** *AIT*
8:11 They followed him **b** he had amazed them *1328+3836*
8:16 **b** the Holy Spirit had not yet come *1142*
8:20 with you, **b** you thought you could buy *4022*
8:21 **b** your heart is not right before God. *1142*
10:38 **b** God was with him. *4022*
12:20 **b** they depended on the king's country *1328*
12:23 **b** Herod did not give praise to God, *505+4005*
13: 7 for Barnabas and Saul **b** he wanted to hear *NIG*
14:12 and Paul they called Hermes **b** he was *2076*
14:13 to the city gates **b** he and the crowd wanted *NIG*
15:38 *b he had* **deserted** them in Pamphylia *AIT*
16: 3 so he circumcised him **b of** the Jews *1328*
16:27 and was about to kill himself *b he* **thought** *AIT*
16:34 *b he had* **come to believe** *AIT*
17:18 They said this **b** Paul was preaching *4022*
17:25 *b he* himself **gives** all men life and breath *AIT*
18: 2 **b** Claudius had ordered all the Jews *1328*
18: 3 **b** he was a tentmaker as they were, *1328+3836*
18:10 **b** I have many people in this city." *1484*
18:18 he had his hair cut off at Cenchrea **b of** *1142*
19:40 in danger of being charged with rioting **b** *4309*
20: 3 *B* the Jews **made** a plot against him just *AIT*
20: 7 *b* he **intended** to leave the next day, *AIT*
20:13 He had made this arrangement *b* he was **going** there *AIT*
21:34 not get at the truth **b of** the uproar, *1328*
22:11 **b** the brilliance of the light had blinded me. *608*
22:18 **b** they will not accept your testimony *1484*
23: 6 on trial **b of** my hope in the resurrection of *4309*
23:18 to you *b he* **has** something to tell you." *AIT*
23:21 **b** more than forty of them are waiting *1142*
24:27 *b* Felix **wanted** to grant a favor to the Jews, *AIT*
25:25 *b* he **made** his **appeal to** the Emperor *AIT*
26: 3 and especially so **b** you **are** well acquainted *1639*
26: 6 And now it is **b of** my hope *2093*
26: 7 it is **b of** this hope that *4309*
26:26 **b** it was not done in a corner. *1142*
27: 4 Cyprus **b** the winds were against us. *1328+3836*
27: 9 sailing had already become dangerous **b** *1328+3836*
27:22 **b** not one of you will be lost; *1142*
28: 2 a fire and welcomed us all **b** it was raining *1328*
28:18 **b** I was not guilty *1328+3836*
28:20 It is **b** of the hope of Israel that I am bound *1915*
Ro 1: 8 **b** your faith is being reported all over *4022*
1:16 **b** it is the power of God for the salvation *1142*
1:19 **b** God has made it plain to them. *1142*
1:26 **B of** this, God gave them over *1328*
2: 1 **b** you who pass judgment do *1142*
2: 5 But **b of** your stubbornness *2848*
2:18 superior *b you are* **instructed** by the law; *AIT*
2:20 *b you* **have** in the law the embodiment *AIT*
Ro 2:24 among the Gentiles **b of** you." *1328*
3:25 **b** in his forbearance he had left *1328*
4:15 **b** law brings wrath. *1142*
5: 3 also rejoice in our sufferings, *b we* **know** *AIT*
5: 5 **b** God has poured out his love *4022*
5:12 in this way death came to all men, **b** *2093+4005*
6: 7 **b** anyone who has died has been freed *1142*
6:14 **b** you are not under law, but under grace. *1142*
6:15 Shall we sin **b** we are not under law but *4022*
6:19 I put this in human terms **b** you are weak *1328*
8: 2 **b** through Christ Jesus the law of the Spirit *1142*
8:10 Christ is in you, your body is dead **b of** sin, *1328*
8:10 yet your spirit is alive **b of** righteousness. *1328*
8:14 **b** those who are led by the Spirit *1142*
8:27 **b** the Spirit intercedes for the saints *4022*
9: 7 Nor **b** they are his descendants are they all Abraham's children. *4022*
9:32 **B** they pursued it not by faith but as *4022*
11:11 *b of* their **transgression,** *AIT*
11:20 But they were broken off *b of* **unbelief,** *AIT*
13: 5 not only **b of** possible punishment but also *1328*
13: 5 of possible punishment but also **b of** *1328*
13:11 **b** our salvation is nearer now than *1142*
14:15 If your brother is distressed **b of** *1328*
14:18 **b** anyone who serves Christ *1142*
14:23 **b** his eating is not from faith; *4022*
15:15 **b of** the grace God gave me *1328*
1Co 1: 4 **b of** his grace given you in Christ Jesus. *2093*
1: 6 **b** our testimony about Christ was confirmed in you. *2777*
1:30 It is **b of** him that you are in Christ Jesus, *1666*
2:14 **b** they are spiritually discerned. *4022*
3:13 **b** the Day will bring it to light. *1142*
7: 5 that Satan will not tempt you **b of** your lack *1328*
7:26 **B of** the present crisis, *1328*
9:10 **b** when the plowman plows and *4022*
10:17 **B** there is one loaf, we, who are many, *4022*
10:30 why am I denounced **b of** *5642*
11:10 For this reason, and **b of** the angels, *1328*
12:15 If the foot should say, "**B** I am not a hand, *4022*
12:16 if the ear should say, "**B** I am not an eye, *4022*
15: 9 **b** I persecuted the church of God. *1484*
15:58 *b you* **know** that your labor in the Lord is *AIT*
16: 9 **b** a great door for effective work *1142*
16:17 **b** they have supplied what was lacking *4022*
2Co 1: 7 *b we* **know** that just as you share *AIT*
1:15 *B I was* **confident of** this, *AIT*
1:24 **b** it is by faith you stand firm. *1142*
2:13 *b* I *did* not **find** my brother Titus *AIT*
3: 7 not look steadily at the face of Moses **b of** *1328*
3:14 **b** only in Christ is it taken away. *4022*
4:14 *b we* **know** that the one who raised *AIT*
5: 3 *b* when *we are* **clothed,** *AIT*
5: 4 **b** we do not wish to be unclothed *2093+4005*
5:14 *b we are* **convinced** that one died for all, *AIT*
7: 9 not **b** you were made sorry, *4022*
7: 9 but **b** your sorrow led you to repentance. *4022*
7:13 **b** his spirit has been refreshed by all of you. *4022*
8:22 *b of* his **great confidence** *AIT*
9:13 **B of** the service by which you have proved *1328*
9:14 their hearts will go out to you, **b of** *1328*
11:11 **B** I do not love you? *4022*
12: 6 **b** I would be speaking the truth. *1142*
12: 7 *b of* these **surpassingly great** *AIT*
12:14 **b** what I want is not your possessions *1142*
Gal 1:24 And they praised God **b of** me. *1877*
2: 4 [This matter arose] **b** some false brothers *1328*
2:11 **b** he was clearly in the wrong. *4022*
2:12 *b he was* **afraid of** those who belonged to *AIT*
2:16 **b** by observing the law no one will *4022*
3: 5 among you **b** you observe the law, *1666*
3: 5 or **b** you believe what you heard? *1666*
3:11 **b,** "The righteous will live by faith." *4022*
3:19 It was added **b of** transgressions until *5920*
4: 6 **B** you are sons, God sent the Spirit *4022*
4:13 it was **b of** an illness that I first preached *1328*
4:20 **b** I am perplexed about you! *4022*
4:25 **b** she is in slavery with her children. *1142*
4:27 **b** more are the children of the desolate *4022*
Eph 2: 4 But **b of** his great love for us, God, *1328*
3:13 be discouraged **b of** my sufferings for you, *1877*
4:18 the life of God **b of** the ignorance that is *1328*
5: 3 **b** these are improper for God's holy people. *2777*
5: 6 for **b of** such things God's wrath comes *1328*
5: 1 every opportunity, **b** the days are evil. *4022*
6: 8 *b* you **know** that the Lord will reward *AIT*
Php 1: 5 **b** of your partnership in the gospel from *2093*
1:14 *B of* my **chains,** *AIT*
1:18 And **b of** this I rejoice. *1877*
2:22 **b** as a son with his father he has served *NIG*
2:26 and is distressed **b** you heard he was ill. *1484*
2:30 **b** he almost died for the work of Christ, *4022*
4:11 I am not saying this **b** I am in need, *4022*
Col 1: 4 *b we have* **heard** of your faith in Christ Jesus *AIT*
1:21 in your minds **b of** your evil behavior. *1877*
2:22 **b** they are based on human commands *NIG*
3: 6 **B of** these, the wrath of God is coming. *1328*
4: 1 *b you* **know** that you also have a Master *AIT*
1Th 1: 5 **b** our gospel came to you not simply *4022*
2: 8 **b** you had become so dear to us. *1484*
2:13 And we also thank God continually **b,** *4022*
3: 7 about you **b of** your faith. *1328*
3: 9 in the presence of our God **b of** you? *1328*
5:13 the highest regard in love **b of** their work. *1328*
2Th 1: 3 **b** your faith is growing more and more, *4022*
1:10 **b** you believed our testimony to you. *4022*
2Th 2:10 They perish **b** they refused to love the truth *505+4005*
2:13 **b** from the beginning God chose you to *4022*
3: 9 not **b** we do not have the right to such help, *4022*
1Ti 1:13 I was shown mercy **b** I acted in ignorance *4022*
4: 5 **b** it is consecrated by the word of God *1142*
4:12 Don't let anyone look down on you **b** *NIG*
4:16 Persevere in them, **b** if you do, *1142*
5:12 **b** they have broken their first pledge. *4022*
5:23 and use a little wine **b of** your stomach *1328*
6: 2 not to show less respect for them **b** *4022*
6: 2 **b** those who benefit from their service *4022*
2Ti 1: 9 not **b of** anything we have done but *2848*
1: 9 because of anything we have done but **b of** *2848*
1:12 **b** I know whom I have believed, *1142*
1:16 **b** he often refreshed me and was *4022*
2:16 **b** those who indulge in it will become more *1142*
2:23 *b you* **know** they produce quarrels. *AIT*
3: 9 But they will not get very far **b,** *1142*
3:14 *b you* **know** those from whom you learned *AIT*
4:10 *b he* **loved** this world, *AIT*
4:11 **b** he is helpful to me in my ministry. *1142*
4:15 **b** he strongly opposed our message. *1142*
Tit 1:11 *b* they *are* **ruining** whole households *AIT*
2: 8 be ashamed *b they* **have** nothing bad to say *AIT*
3: 5 not **b of** righteous things we had done, *1666*
3: 5 but **b of** his mercy. *2848*
3: 9 **b** these are unprofitable and useless. *1142*
3:12 **b** I have decided to winter there. *1142*
Phm 1: 5 *b* I **hear** about your faith in the Lord Jesus *AIT*
1: 7 **b** you, brother, have refreshed the hearts of *1328*
1:22 a guest room for me, **b** I hope to be restored *1142*
Heb 2: 9 with glory and honor **b** he suffered death, *1328*
2:18 **B** he himself suffered when he was tempted *1142*
3:19 **b of** their unbelief. *1328*
4: 2 of no value to them, **b** those who heard did *NIG*
4: 6 **b of** their disobedience. *1328*
5: 7 he was heard **b of** his reverent submission. *608*
5:11 but it is hard to explain **b** you are slow *2075*
6: 6 *b* to their loss *they are* **crucifying** the Son of God **all over again** *AIT*
6:17 **B** God wanted to make *1877+4005*
7:10 **b** when Melchizedek met Abraham, *1142*
7:18 The former regulation is set aside **b** *1328+3836*
7:22 **B of** this oath, *2848*
7:24 but **b** Jesus lives forever, *1328+3836*
7:25 *b he* always **lives** to intercede for them. *AIT*
8: 9 **b** they did not remain faithful *4022*
8:11 'Know the Lord,' **b** they will all know me, *4022*
9:17 **b** a will is in force only *1142*
10: 4 **b** it is impossible for the blood of bulls *1142*
10:14 **b** by one sacrifice he has made perfect forever those who are being made holy. *1142*
10:34 *b you* **knew** that you yourselves had better *AIT*
11: 5 **b** God had taken him away. *1484*
11: 6 **b** anyone who comes to him must believe *1142*
11:11 was enabled to become a father **b** *2075*
11:23 **b** they saw he was no ordinary child, *1484*
11:26 **b** he was looking ahead to his reward. *1142*
11:27 persevered **b** he saw him who is invisible. *1142*
11:31 *b she* **welcomed** the spies, *AIT*
12: 6 **b** the Lord disciplines those he loves, *1142*
12:20 **b** they could not bear what was commanded *1142*
13: 5 **b** God has said, "Never will I leave you; *1142*
Jas 1: 3 *b you* **know** that the testing *AIT*
1: 6 **b** he who doubts is like a wave of the sea, *1142*
1:10 **b** he will pass away like a wild flower. *4022*
1:12 **b** when he has stood the test, *4022*
2:13 **b** judgment without mercy will be shown *1142*
3: 1 *b you* **know** that we who teach will *AIT*
4: 2 You do not have, **b** you do not ask God. *1328*
4: 3 **b** you ask with wrong motives, *1484*
5: 1 and wail **b of** the misery that is coming *2093*
5: 8 **b** the Lord's coming is near. *4022*
1Pe 1:16 for it is written: "Be holy, **b** I am holy." *4022*
2: 8 They stumble *b they* **disobey** the message— *AIT*
2:19 up under the pain of unjust suffering **b** *1328*
2:21 **b** Christ suffered for you, *4022*
3: 9 **b** to this you were called so *4022*
4: 1 **b** he who has suffered in his body is done *4022*
4: 8 **b** love covers over a multitude of sins. *4022*
4:14 If you are insulted **b of** the name of Christ, *1877*
5: 2 not *b* you **must,** but because you are willing, *AIT*
5: 2 because you must, but *b* you are **willing,** *AIT*
5: 5 **b,** "God opposes the proud but gives grace *4022*
5: 7 Cast all your anxiety on him **b** he cares *4022*
5: 9 *b you* **know** that your brothers throughout *AIT*
2Pe 1:14 *b I* **know** that I will soon put it aside, *AIT*
1Jn 2: 8 in him and you, **b** the darkness is passing *4022*
2:11 **b** the darkness has blinded him. *4022*
2:12 **b** your sins have been forgiven on account *4022*
2:13 **b** you have known him who is from *4022*
2:13 **b** you have overcome the evil one. *4022*
2:13 **b** you have known the Father. *4022*
2:14 **b** you have known him who is from *4022*
2:14 young men, **b** you are strong, *4022*
2:21 I do not write to you **b** you do not know *4022*
2:21 but **b** you do know it and *4022*
2:21 because you do know it and **b** no lie comes *4022*
3: 8 **b** the devil has been sinning from *4022*
3: 9 **b** God's seed remains in him; *4022*
3: 9 **b** he has been born of God. *4022*
3:12 **B** his own actions were evil *4022*
3:14 **b** we love our brothers. *4022*
3:22 **b** we obey his commands *4022*
4: 1 **b** many false prophets have gone out into *4022*
4: 4 **b** the one who is in you is greater than *4022*

1Jn 4: 8 does not know God, **b** God is love. *4022*
4: 13 **b** he has given us of his Spirit. *4022*
4: 17 **b** in this world we are like him. *4022*
4: 18 **b** fear has to do with punishment. *4022*
4: 19 We love **b** he first loved us. *4022*
5: 6 **b** the Spirit is the truth. *4022*
5: 9 but God's testimony is greater **b** it is *4022*
5: 10 **b** he has not believed *4022*
2Jn 1: 2 **b of** the truth, which lives in us and will be *1328*
Rev 1: 3 **b** the time is near. *1142*
1: 7 the peoples of the earth will mourn **b of** *2093*
1: 9 was on the island of Patmos **b of** the word *1328*
3: 16 So, **b** you are lukewarm— *4022*
5: 4 I wept and wept **b** no one was found *4022*
5: 9 to take the scroll and to open its seals, **b** *4022*
6: 9 the souls of those who had been slain **b of** *1328*
8: 13 **b** of the trumpet blasts about to be sounded *NIG*
11: 2 **b** it has been given to the Gentiles. *4022*
11: 10 by sending each other gifts, **b** *4022*
11: 17 **b** you have taken your great power *4022*
12: 12 **b** the devil has gone down to you! *4022*
12: 12 *b he* **knows** that his time is short." *AIT*
13: 4 the dragon **b** he had given authority to *4022*
13: 14 **B of** the signs he was given power to do *1328*
14: 7 **b** the hour of his judgment has come. *4022*
14: 15 **b** the time to reap has come, *4022*
14: 18 **b** its grapes are ripe." *4022*
15: 1 last, **b** with them God's wrath is completed. *4022*
16: 5 the Holy One, **b** you have so judged; *4022*
16: 11 of heaven **b of** their pains and their sores, *1666*
16: 21 **b** the plague was so terrible. *4022*
17: 8 **b** he once was, now is not, *4022*
17: 14 the Lamb will overcome them **b** he is Lord *4022*
18: 11 of the earth will weep and mourn over her **b** *4022*
20: 4 of those who had been beheaded **b of** *1328*
20: 4 of their testimony for Jesus and **b of** *1328*
21: 22 **b** the Lord God Almighty and *1142*
22: 10 **b** the time is near. *1142*

BECHER (KJV) See BEKER

BECHORATH (KJV) See BECORATH

BECKON (2)

Isa 13: 2 **b** *to* them to enter the gates of the nobles. 3338+5677
49: 22 "See, I *will* **b** to the Gentiles, 3338+5951

BECOME (398) [BECAME, BECOMES, BECOMING]

Ge 2: 24 and *they will* **b** one flesh. 2118
3: 20 she *would* **b** the mother of all the living. 2118
3: 22 "The man *has* now **b** like one of us, 2118
6: 5 man's wickedness on the earth had **b,** NIH
6: 12 **corrupt** the earth *had b,* AIT
9: 15 Never again *will* the waters **b** a flood 2118
13: 2 Abram *had b* very **wealthy** in livestock and AIT
18: 18 Abraham *will* **surely b** a great 2118+2118
24: 35 and *he has b* **wealthy.** AIT
24: 51 and *let her* **b** the wife of your master's son, 2118
26: 16 *you have b* too **powerful** for us." AIT
28: 3 and increase your numbers until *you* **b** 2118
29: 34 at last my husband *will b* **attached** to me, AIT
32: 10 but now *I have* **b** two groups. 2118
34: 15 that *you* **b** like us 2118
34: 16 We'll settle among you and **b** one people 2118
34: 23 and all their other animals **b** ours? NIH
38: 23 or *we will* **b** a laughingstock. 2118
44: 9 and the rest of us *will* **b** my lord's slaves." 2118
44: 10 to have it *will* **b** my slave; 2118
44: 17 to have the cup *will* **b** my slave. 2118
45: 11 to you *will b* **destitute.'** AIT
47: 19 and that the land *may* not *b* **desolate."** AIT
47: 26 of the priests that *did* not **b** Pharaoh's. 2118
48: 19 He too *will* **b** a people, 2118
48: 19 and he too *will b* **great.** AIT
48: 19 his descendants *will* **b** a group of nations." 2118
49: 13 "Zebulun will live by the seashore and **b** 4200
Ex 1: 9 Israelites have **b** much too numerous for us. NIH
1: 10 or *they will b even more* **numerous** and, AIT
2: 14 "What I did *must have* **b known."** 3359
2: 22 saying, *"I have* **b** an alien in a foreign land." 2118
4: 9 from the river *will* **b** blood on the ground." 2118
7: 9 and *it will* **b** a snake." 2118
8: 16 the land of Egypt the dust *will* **b** gnats." 2118
9: 9 *It will* **b** fine dust over the whole land 2118
9: 24 the land of Egypt since *it had* **b** a nation. 2118
15: 2 *he has* **b** my salvation. 2118
18: 3 *"I have* **b** an alien in a foreign land"; 2118
22: 24 your wives *will* **b** widows 2118
23: 29 because the land *would* **b** desolate and 2118
32: 7 up out of Egypt, *have b* **corrupt.** AIT
32: 25 and so **b** a laughingstock to their enemies. 4200
Lev 4: 14 *they* **b aware** *of* the sin they committed, 3359
5: 2 he *has b* **unclean** and is guilty. AIT
6: 18 Whatever touches them *will b* **holy.'"** AIT
6: 27 of the flesh *will b* **holy,** AIT
10: 6 *"Do* not *let* your hair *b* **unkempt,** AIT
13: 2 a rash or a bright spot on his skin that *may* **b** 2118
21: 10 *must* not *let* his hair *b* **unkempt** AIT
22: 8 and so *b* **unclean** through it. AIT
22: 9 not **b guilty** and die 2628+5951+6584
25: 45 and *they will* **b** your property. 2118
27: 10 both it and the substitute **b** holy. 2118
Lev 27: 15 and the house *will again* **b** his. 2118
27: 19 and the field *will again* **b** his. 7756
27: 21 it *will* **b** holy, like a field devoted to 2118
27: 21 *it will* **b** the property of the priests. 2118
27: 33 both the animal and its substitute **b** holy 2118
Nu 5: 19 not gone astray and **b** impure while married NIH
5: 27 and she *will* **b** accursed among her people. 2118
9: 7 "We have **b** unclean because of NIH
16: 38 before the LORD and *have b* **holy.** AIT
16: 40 or *he would* **b** like Korah and his followers. 2118
33: 55 those you allow to remain *will* **b** barbs 2118
Dt 4: 16 not *b* **corrupt** and make for yourselves AIT
4: 25 then *b* **corrupt** and make any kind of idol, AIT
8: 14 then your heart *will b* **proud** AIT
9: 12 of Egypt *have b* **corrupt.** AIT
15: 17 and *he will* **b** your servant for life. 2118
20: 7 *Has* anyone *b* **pledged** *to* a woman and AIT
20: 8 not *b* **disheartened** too." AIT
23: 17 or woman *is to* **b** a shrine prostitute. 2118
27: 9 now **b** the people of the LORD your God. 2118
28: 25 And *you will* **b** a thing of horror to all 2118
28: 37 *You will* **b** a thing of horror and an object 2118
31: 17 On that day I *will b* **angry** with them AIT
31: 29 *you are* **sure to b utterly corrupt** 8845+8845
Jos 14: 4 for the sons of Joseph *had* **b** two tribes— 2118
23: 13 *they will* **b** snares and traps for you, 2118
Jdg 16: 7 *I'll* **b** as weak as any other man." 2118
16: 11 *I'll* **b** as weak as any other man." 2118
16: 13 *I'll* **b** as weak as any other man." 2118
16: 17 and *I would* **b** as weak as any other man." 2118
17: 13 since this Levite *has* **b** my priest." 2118
Ru 1: 11 *who could* **b** your husbands? 2118
4: 7 and transfer of property to *b* **final,** AIT
4: 14 *May* he *b* **famous** throughout Israel! AIT
1Sa 8: 17 and *you* yourselves *will* **b** his slaves. 2118
13: 4 Israel *has b a* **stench** to the Philistines." AIT
15: 17 not **b** the head of the tribes of Israel? NIH
17: 9 *we will* **b** your subjects; 2118
17: 9 *you will* **b** our subjects and serve us." 2118
18: 18 that *I should* **b** the king's son-in-law?" 2118
18: 21 a second opportunity *to b* my **son-in-law."** AIT
18: 22 now *b* his **son-in-law.'"** AIT
18: 23 *b* the king's **son-in-law?** AIT
18: 26 *b* the king's **son-in-law.** AIT
18: 27 *b* the king's **son-in-law.** AIT
25: 39 asking her to **b** his **wife.** 851+4200+4374
25: 40 to you to take you to **b** his wife." NIH
27: 12 *"He has b* **so odious** to his people, AIT
28: 16 from you and **b** your enemy? 2118
2Sa 5: 2 and you *will* **b** their ruler.'" 2118
6: 22 **b** even more **undignified** 7837
7: 24 and you, O LORD, *have* **b** their God. 2118
10: 6 that *they had b a* **stench** in David's nostrils, AIT
16: 2 to refresh those who **b** exhausted in NIH
17: 29 "The people have **b** hungry and tired NIH
19: 22 This day *you have* **b** my adversaries! 2118
1Ki 1: 11 the son of Haggith, *has b* **king** AIT
1: 13 Why then *has* Adonijah *b* **king?'** AIT
1: 18 But now Adonijah *has b* **king,** and you, AIT
8: 46 and *you b* **angry** with them and give them AIT
9: 7 Israel *will* then **b** a byword and an object 2118
13: 33 *to* **b** a priest he consecrated for 2118
2Ki 8: 13 that you will **b** king of Aram," NIH
9: 29 Ahaziah *had b* **king** of Judah.) AIT
20: 18 and *they will* **b** eunuchs in the palace of 2118
22: 19 that they *would* **b** accursed and laid waste, 2118
25: 3 the famine in the city *had b so* **severe** AIT
1Ch 4: 27 so their entire clan *did* not *b* as **numerous** AIT
11: 2 and you *will* **b** their ruler.'" 2118
11: 6 the Jebusites *will* **b** commander-in-chief." 2118
17: 22 and you, O LORD, *have* **b** their God. 2118
19: 6 that *they had b a* **stench** in David's nostrils, AIT
2Ch 6: 36 and *you b* **angry** with them and give them AIT
12: 1 and he had **b strong,** 2621
12: 8 *They will,* however, **b** subject to him, 2118
13: 9 *may* **b** a priest of what are not gods. 2118
26: 8 because *he had b* very **powerful.** AIT
Ne 6: 6 *about to* **b** their king 2093
9: 21 not wear out nor *did* their feet *b* **swollen.** AIT
Est 1: 17 For the queen's conduct *will* **b known** to all 3655
Job 3: 9 *May* its morning stars *b* **dark;** AIT
7: 20 *Have I* **b** a burden to you? 2118
11: 12 But a witless man *can* no more **b wise** than 4220
11: 17 and darkness *will* **b** like morning. 2118
11: 20 their hope will **b** a dying gasp." NIH
12: 4 *"I have* **b** a laughingstock to my friends, 2118
16: 8 and *it has* **b** a witness; 2118
20: 14 it will **b** the venom of serpents within him. NIH
24: 22 though *they b* **established,** AIT
30: 9 *I have* **b** a byword among them. 2118
30: 29 *I have* **b** a brother of jackals, 2118
37: 10 and the broad waters **b** frozen. NIH
38: 30 *when* the waters **b hard** as stone, 2461
Ps 2: 7 today I *have b* your **Father.** AIT
14: 3 *they have* together *b* **corrupt;** AIT
31: 12 *I have* **b** like broken pottery. 2118
38: 14 *I have* **b** like a man who does not hear, 2118
53: 3 *they have* together *b* **corrupt;** AIT
63: 10 over to the sword and **b** food for jackals. 2118
69: 22 *May* the table set before them **b** a snare; 2118
69: 22 may it **b** retribution and a trap. NIH
71: 7 *I have* **b** like a portent to many, 2118
89: 41 *he has* **b** the scorn of his neighbors. 2118
94: 8 you fools, when *will you b* **wise?** AIT
94: 22 But the LORD *has* **b** my fortress, 2118
102: 7 *I have* **b** like a bird alone on a roof. 2118
118: 14 *he has* **b** my salvation. 2118
Ps 118: 21 *you have* **b** my salvation. 2118
118: 22 the builders rejected *has* **b** the capstone; 2118
139: 11 and the light **b** night around me," NIH
140: 8 or *they will b* **proud.** AIT
Pr 21: 17 He who loves pleasure will **b** poor; NIH
21: 18 The wicked **b** a ransom for the righteous, NIH
23: 21 for drunkards and gluttons *b* **poor,** AIT
29: 12 all his officials **b** wicked. NIH
30: 9 Or *I may* **b poor** and steal, 3769
SS 8: 10 Thus *I have* **b** in his eyes 2118
Isa 1: 9 *we would have* **b** like Sodom, 2118
1: 14 *They have* **b** a burden to me; 2118
1: 21 See how the faithful city *has* **b** a harlot! 2118
1: 22 Your silver *has* **b** dross, 2118
1: 31 The mighty man *will* **b** tinder 2118
5: 9 "Surely the great houses *will* **b** desolate, 2118
7: 25 *they will* **b** places where cattle are turned 2118
8: 21 *they will b* **enraged** and, looking upward, AIT
10: 17 The Light of Israel *will* **b** a fire, 2118
12: 2 *he has* **b** my salvation." 2118
14: 10 they will say to you, "You also *have b* **weak,** AIT
14: 10 *you have* **b like** us." 5439
17: 1 be a city but *will* **b** a heap of ruins. 2118
19: 7 along the Nile *will b* **parched,** AIT
19: 13 The officials of Zoan *have* **b fools,** 3282
21: 4 the twilight I longed for *has* **b** a horror 8492
28: 13 the word of the LORD to them *will* **b:** 2118
28: 22 or your chains *will b* **heavier;** AIT
29: 5 your many enemies *will* **b** like fine dust, 2118
30: 13 this sin *will* **b** for you like a high wall, 2118
32: 14 citadel and watchtower *will* **b** 2118
34: 9 her land *will* **b** blazing pitch! 2118
34: 13 *She will* **b** a haunt for jackals, 2118
35: 7 The burning sand *will* **b** a pool, 2118
39: 7 and *they will* **b** eunuchs in the palace of 2118
40: 4 the rough ground *shall* **b** level, 2118
42: 22 *They have* **b** plunder, with no one 2118
42: 24 Who handed Jacob over to **b** loot, NIH
51: 4 my justice *will* **b** a light to the nations. 8088
58: 10 and your night will **b** like the noonday. NIH
60: 22 The least of you *will* **b** a thousand, 2118
64: 6 All of us *have* **b** like one who is unclean, 2118
64: 10 Your sacred cities *have* **b** a desert; 2118
65: 10 Sharon *will* **b** a pasture for flocks, 2118
Jer 2: 14 Why then *has he* **b** plunder? 2118
5: 27 *they have b* **rich** and powerful AIT
7: 11 **b** a den of robbers to you? 2118
7: 33 the carcasses of this people *will* **b** food for 2118
7: 34 for the land *will* **b** desolate. 2118
12: 8 My inheritance *has* **b** to me like a lion in 2118
12: 9 Has not my inheritance **b** to me like NIH
16: 4 and their dead bodies *will* **b** food for 2118
22: 5 by myself that this palace *will* **b** a ruin.'" 2118
23: 12 "Therefore their path *will* **b** slippery; 2118
25: 11 whole country *will* **b** a desolate wasteland, 2118
25: 38 and their land *will* **b** desolate because of 2118
26: 18 Jerusalem *will* **b** a heap of rubble, 2118
27: 17 Why *should* this city **b** a ruin? 2118
34: 16 to **b** your slaves again. 2118
34: 20 Their dead bodies *will* **b** food for the birds 2118
44: 12 *They will* **b** an object of cursing 2118
47: 2 *they will* **b** an overflowing torrent. 2118
48: 6 **b** like a bush in the desert. 2118
48: 9 her towns *will* **b** desolate, 2118
48: 39 Moab *has* **b** an object of ridicule, 2118
49: 2 *it will* **b** a mound of ruins, 2118
49: 13 "that Bozrah *will* **b** a ruin and an object 2118
49: 17 "Edom *will* **b** an object of horror; 2118
49: 24 Damascus *has b* **feeble,** AIT
49: 32 Their camels *will* **b** plunder, 2118
49: 33 "Hazor *will* **b** a haunt of jackals, 2118
50: 36 *They will* **b fools.** 3282
50: 37 *They will* **b** women. 2118
51: 30 *they have* **b** like women. 2118
52: 6 the famine in the city *had b so* **severe** AIT
La 1: 1 among the provinces *has now* **b** a slave. 2118
1: 2 *they have* **b** her enemies. 2118
1: 5 Her foes *have* **b** her masters; 2118
1: 8 and so *has* **b** unclean. 2118
1: 17 for Jacob that his neighbors **b** his foes; NIH
1: 17 Jerusalem *has* **b** an unclean thing 2118
1: 21 the day you have announced so *they may* **b** 2118
4: 1 the fine gold *b* **dull!** AIT
4: 3 but my people have **b** heartless NIH
4: 8 *it has* **b** as dry as a stick. 2118
5: 3 *We have* **b** orphans and fatherless, 2118
Eze 7: 17 and every knee *will b as* **weak as** water. AIT
16: 15 and used your fame *to b a* **prostitute.** AIT
17: 8 bear fruit and **b** a splendid vine.' 2118
17: 23 and bear fruit and **b** a splendid cedar. 2118
20: 26 *I* **let** them **b defiled** through their gifts— 3237
21: 7 every spirit *will b* **faint** AIT
21: 7 and every knee *b as* **weak as** water.' AIT
22: 4 *you have b* **guilty** because of AIT
22: 4 the blood you have shed and *have b* **defiled** AIT
22: 18 the house of Israel *has* **b** dross to me; 2118
22: 19 'Because you *have* all **b** dross, 2118
25: 8 of Judah has **b** like all the other nations," NIH
26: 5 Out in the sea *she will* **b** a place 2118
26: 5 *She will* **b** plunder for the nations, 2118
26: 14 and *you will* **b** a place to spread fishnets. 2118
29: 9 Egypt *will* **b** a desolate wasteland. 2118
30: 21 in a splint so as to *b* **strong** *enough* to hold AIT
33: 28 the mountains of Israel *will b* **desolate** so AIT
34: 8 so has been plundered and *has* **b** food for all 2118
36: 2 The ancient heights *have* **b** our possession." 2118

Eze 36:11 and they will be fruitful and *b* **numerous.** AIT
36:35 "This land that was laid waste *has* **b** like 2118
37:17 into one stick so that *they will* **b** one 2118
37:19 and *they will* **b** one in my hand.' 2118
47:11 the swamps and marshes *will* not *b* **fresh;** AIT
47:14 this land *will* **b** your inheritance. 5877
Da 4:22 *You have b* **great** and strong; AIT
8:23 when rebels *have b* **completely** wicked, AIT
8:24 *He will b* **very strong,** AIT
11:5 "The king of the South *will b* **strong,** AIT
11:5 one of his commanders *will b even* **stronger** than he AIT
11:6 After some years, *they will b* **allies.** AIT
Hos 4:15 O Israel, *let* not Judah *b* **guilty.** AIT
7:5 of our king the princes *b* **inflamed** AIT
8:11 *these have* **b** altars for sinning. 2118
12:8 *I have* **b** wealthy. 5162
Am 7:17 " 'Your wife *will b a* **prostitute** in AIT
Jnh 1:12 he replied, "and it *will b* **calm.** AIT
Mic 3:12 Jerusalem *will* **b** a heap of rubble, 2118
7:13 The earth *will* **b** desolate because 2118
7:16 on their mouths and their ears *will b* **deaf.** AIT
Na 3:11 You too *will b* **drunk;** AIT
Hab 2:7 Then *you will* **b** their victim. 2118+4200
Zep 2:9 "surely Moab *will* **b** like Sodom, 2118
2:15 What a ruin *she has* **b**, a lair for wild beasts! 2118
Hag 2:12 oil or other food, *does it b* **consecrated?'** " AIT
2:13 *does it b* **defiled?"** AIT
Zec 2:11 in that day and *will* **b** my people. 2118
4:7 Before Zerubbabel you will **b** level ground. 4200
8:19 seventh and tenth months *will* **b** joyful 2118
9:7 to our God and **b** leaders in Judah, 2118
10:7 The Ephraimites *will* **b** like mighty men, 2118
14:10 south of Jerusalem, *will* **b** like the Arabah. 6015
Mt 4:3 tell these stones *to* **b** bread." *1181*
5:32 causes her *to* **b an adulteress,** *3658*
13:15 For this people's heart *has b* **calloused;** *AIT*
18:3 unless you change and **b** like little children, *1181*
19:5 and the two *will* **b** one flesh'? *1639+1650*
20:26 *to* **b** great among you must be your servant, *1181*
21:42 builders rejected *has* **b** the capstone; *1181+1650*
27:57 who *had* himself **b a disciple** of Jesus. *3411*
Mk 6:14 for Jesus' name *had* **b** well known. *1181*
10:8 and the two *will* **b** one flesh.' *1639+1650*
10:43 *to* **b** great among you must be your servant, *1181*
12:10 builders rejected *has* **b** the capstone; *1181+1650*
Lk 3:5 The crooked roads *shall* **b** straight, *1639*
4:3 tell this stone to **b** bread." *1181*
20:17 builders rejected *has* **b** the capstone'? *1181+1650*
Jn 1:12 he gave the right *to* **b** children of God— *1181*
3:30 He must **b greater;** I must become less. *889*
3:30 He must become greater; I must *b* **less.** *AIT*
4:14 the water I give him *will* **b** in him a spring *1181*
7:4 No one who wants *to* **b** a public figure acts *1639*
9:27 Do you want *to* **b** his disciples, too?" *1181*
9:39 and those who see *will* **b** blind." *1181*
12:36 so that *you may* **b** sons of light." *1181*
Ac 1:22 For one of these *must* **b** a witness with us *1181*
4:11 which *has* **b** the capstone.' *1181*
12:18 among the soldiers as to what *had* **b of** *1181*
13:33 today I *have* **b** your **Father.'** *1164*
26:29 to me today *may* **b** what I am, *1181*
27:9 and sailing *had* already **b** dangerous *1639*
28:27 For this people's heart *has b* **calloused;** *AIT*
Ro 1:29 *They have* **b filled** with every kind *AIT*
2:25 you *have* **b** as though you had *1181*
3:12 *they have* together **b worthless;** *946*
3:20 through the law we **b** conscious of sin. *NIG*
6:18 and *have* **b slaves** to righteousness. *1530*
6:22 from sin and *have* **b slaves** to God, *1530*
7:13 *Did* that which is good, then, **b** death to me? *1181*
7:13 sin *might* **b** utterly sinful. *1181*
9:29 *we* would *have* **b** like Sodom, *1181*
11:9 "*May* their table **b** a snare and a trap, *1181+1650*
11:31 so they too *have* now *b* **disobedient** in order *AIT*
15:8 For I tell you that Christ *has* **b** a servant of *1181*
15:16 the Gentiles *might* **b** an offering acceptable *1181*
1Co 1:30 who *has* **b** for us wisdom from God— *1181*
3:18 *he should* **b** a "fool" so he may *1181*
3:18 a "fool" so that *he may* **b** wise. *1181*
4:8 Already *you have b* **rich!** *AIT*
4:8 *You have b* **kings—**and that without us! *AIT*
4:8 that you really *had b* **kings** so that we might *AIT*
4:13 Up to this moment *we have* **b** the scum of *1181*
4:18 Some of you *have b* **arrogant,** *AIT*
6:16 it is said, "The two *will* **b** one flesh." *1639+1650*
7:18 *He should* not **b uncircumcised.** *2177*
7:23 *do* not **b** slaves of men. *1181*
8:9 that the exercise of your freedom *does* not **b** *1181*
9:22 *I have* **b** all things to all men so that *1181*
2Co 5:21 in him we *might* **b** the righteousness of God. *1181*
8:9 that you through his poverty *might* **b rich.** *4456*
Gal 4:12 I plead with you, brothers, **b** like me, *1181*
4:16 now **b** your enemy by telling you the truth? *1181*
5:26 *Let us* not **b** conceited, *1181*
6:9 *Let us* not **b weary** in doing good, *1591*
Eph 2:21 and rises to **b** a holy temple in the Lord. *NIG*
2:22 in him you too are being built together to **b** *NIG*
4:13 of the Son of God and **b** mature, *1650*
5:31 and the two *will* **b** one flesh." *1639+1650*
Php 1:13 it *has* **b** clear throughout *1181*
2:15 so that *you may* **b** blameless and pure, *1181*
Col 1:23 and of which I, Paul, *have* **b** a servant. *1181*
1:25 I *have* **b** its servant by the commission God *1181*
3:21 or *they will* **b discouraged.** *126*
1Th 1:8 your faith in God *has b* **known** everywhere. *AIT*
2:8 because *you had* **b** so dear to us. *1181*
2Th 2:2 not *to b* easily **unsettled** or alarmed *AIT*
1Ti 3:6 or *he may* **b conceited** and fall under *5605*
5:13 And not only do they **b** idlers, *NIG*
2Ti 2:16 because those who indulge in it will **b** more *NIG*
3:14 and *have b* **convinced** *of,* *AIT*
Tit 3:7 *we might* **b** heirs having the hope *1181*
Phm 1:11 now he has **b** useful both to you and to me. *NIG*
Heb 1:5 today I *have* **b** your **Father"?** *1164*
2:17 in order that *he might* **b** a merciful *1181*
5:5 today I *have* **b** your **Father."** *1164*
6:12 We do not want *you to* **b** lazy, *1181*
6:20 *He has* **b** a high priest forever, *1181*
7:5 of Levi who **b** priests to collect a tenth from *3284*
7:16 one who *has* **b** a priest not on the basis of *1181*
7:22 Jesus *has* **b** the guarantee of *1181*
11:11 was enabled to **b a father** *2856+3284+5065*
Jas 1:19 slow to speak and slow to **b** angry, *NIG*
2:4 and **b** judges with evil thoughts? *1181*
2:11 *you have* **b** a lawbreaker. *1181*
1Pe 2:7 builders rejected *has* **b** the capstone," *1181+1650*
4:18 what *will* **b** of the ungodly and the sinner?" *5743*
Rev 3:18 so *you can b* **rich;** *AIT*
8:11 from the waters that *had b* **bitter.** *AIT*
11:15 of the world *has* **b** the kingdom of our Lord *1181*
18:2 *She has* **b** a home for demons and a haunt *1181*

BECOMES (35) [BECOME]

Lev 6:4 when he thus sins and *b* **guilty,** AIT
11:35 of their carcasses falls on *b* **unclean;** AIT
12:2 'A woman *who b* **pregnant** and gives birth AIT
22:13 priest's daughter **b** a widow or is divorced, 2118
25:25 of your countrymen *b* **poor** and sells some AIT
25:35 of your countrymen *b* **poor** and is unable AIT
25:39 of your countrymen *b* **poor** among you AIT
25:47 or a temporary resident among you *b* **rich** AIT
25:47 and one of your countrymen *b* **poor** AIT
27:9 such an animal given to the LORD **b** holy. 2118
Nu 19:22 that an unclean person touches *b* **unclean,** AIT
19:22 and anyone who touches it *b* **unclean** AIT
Dt 24:1 If a man marries a woman *who* **b** displeasing to him 2118
24:2 if after she leaves his house *she* **b** the wife 2118
Job 14:11 the sea or a riverbed *b* **parched** and dry, AIT
18:6 The light in his tent *b* **dark;** AIT
30:18 In his great power [God] **b like** clothing 2924
38:38 when the dust *b* **hard** and the clods AIT
Ps 104:20 You bring darkness, *it* **b** night, 2118
Pr 30:22 a servant *who b* **king,** AIT
Isa 18:5 when the blossom is gone and the flower **b** 2118
32:15 and the desert **b** a fertile field, 2118
59:15 and whoever shuns evil **b** *a* **prey.** 8964
Jer 23:36 because every man's own word **b** his oracle 2118
Eze 14:15 and they leave it childless and *it* **b** desolate 2118
24:11 the coals till *it b* **hot** and its copper glows AIT
47:8 the water there *b* **fresh.** AIT
Hag 2:13 "Yes," the priests replied, *"it b* **defiled."** AIT
Mt 13:32 the largest of garden plants and **b** a tree, *1181*
23:15 and when *he* **b** one, *1181*
Mk 4:32 and **b** the largest of all garden plants, *1181*
9:18 gnashes his teeth and **b rigid.** *3830*
Gal 2:17 *it b* **evident** that we ourselves are sinners, *AIT*
Eph 5:13 everything exposed by the light *b* **visible,** *AIT*
Jas 4:4 be a friend of the world **b** an enemy of God. *2770*

BECOMING (8) [BECOME]

Lev 21:9 by *b a* **prostitute,** she disgraces her father; AIT
1Sa 3:2 whose eyes *were* **b** so weak 2725
1Ki 16:7 and **b** like the house of Jeroboam— 2118
Joel 2:22 for the open pastures *are b* **green.** AIT
2Co 12:7 To keep *me* from *b* **conceited** because *AIT*
Gal 3:13 the law *by* **b** a curse for us, for it is written: *1181*
Php 3:10 **b like** him in his death, *5214*
Heb 5:5 upon himself the glory *of* **b** a high priest. *1181*

BECORATH (1)

1Sa 9:1 the son of Zeror, the son of **B,** 1138

BED (76) [BEDDING, BEDRIDDEN, BEDROOM, BEDROOMS, BEDS, SICKBED]

Ge 19:4 Before *they had* **gone to b,** 8886
39:7 **"Come to b with** me!" 6640+8886
39:10 he refused to **go to b with** her 725+8886
39:12 **"Come to b with** me!" 6640+8886
48:2 and sat up on the **b.** 4753
49:4 for you went up onto your father's **b,** 5435
49:33 he drew his feet up into the **b,** 4753
Ex 8:3 and your bedroom and onto your **b,** 4753
21:18 and he does not die but is confined to **b,** 5435
Lev 15:4 " 'Any **b** the man with a discharge lies 5435
15:5 Anyone who touches his **b** must wash his clothes 5435
15:21 Whoever touches her **b** must wash his clothes 5435
15:23 the **b** or anything she was sitting on, 5435
15:24 any **b** he lies on will be unclean. 5435
15:26 Any **b** she lies on while her discharge 5435
15:26 as is her **b** during her monthly period, 5435
Dt 3:11 His **b** was *made of* iron 6911
22:30 *he must* not **dishonor** his father's **b.** 1655+4053
27:20 for *he* **dishonors** his father's **b."** 1655+4053
1Sa 19:13 Michal took an idol and laid it on the **b,** 4753
19:15 up to me in his **b** so that I may kill him." 4753
19:16 the men entered, there was the idol in the **b,** 4753
2Sa 4:7 while he was lying on the **b** in his bedroom. 4753
4:11 in his own house and on his own **b—** 5435
11:2 from his **b** and walked around on the roof 5435
13:5 "Go to **b** and pretend to be ill," 5435
13:11 "Come *to* **b with** me, my sister." 6640+8886
1Ki 1:47 And the king bowed in worship on his **b** 5435
17:19 and laid him on his **b.** 4753
21:4 He lay on his **b** sulking and refused to eat. 4753
2Ki 1:4 'You will not leave the **b** you are lying on. 4753
1:6 not leave the **b** you are lying on. 4753
1:16 you will never leave the **b** you are lying on. 4753
4:10 a small room on the roof and put in it a **b** 4753
4:21 and laid him on the **b** *of* the man of God, 4753
4:34 Then he got on the **b** and lay upon the boy, NIH
4:35 and forth in the room and then got on the **b** NIH
1Ch 5:1 when he defiled his father's **marriage b,** 3661
2Ch 24:25 and they killed him in his **b.** 4753
Job 7:13 When I think my **b** will comfort me 6911
17:13 if I spread out my **b** in darkness, 3661
33:19 Or a man may be chastened on a **b** of pain 5435
Ps 6:6 all night long I flood my **b** with weeping 4753
36:4 Even on his **b** he plots evil; 5435
41:3 on his sickbed and restore him from his **b** 5435
63:6 On my **b** I remember you; 3661
132:3 "I will not enter my house or go to my **b—** 3661+6911
139:8 if *I* **make** *my* **b** *in* the depths, you are there. 3667
Pr 7:16 I have covered my **b** with colored linens 6911
7:17 I have perfumed my **b** with myrrh, 5435
22:27 your very **b** will be snatched from 5435
26:14 so a sluggard turns on his **b.** 4753
31:22 She makes **coverings** for her **b;** 5267
SS 1:16 And our **b** is verdant. 6911
3:1 All night long on my **b** I looked for 5435
Isa 28:20 The **b** is too short to stretch out on, 5201
57:7 You have made your **b** on a high 5435
57:8 Forsaking me, you uncovered your **b,** 5435
Eze 22:10 **dishonor** their fathers' **b;** 1655+6872
23:17 Babylonians came to her, to the **b** *of* love, 5435
32:25 A **b** is made for her among the slain, 5435
Da 2:28 as you lay on your **b** are these: 10444
4:5 As I was lying in my **b,** 10444
4:10 the visions I saw while lying in my **b:** 10444
4:13 "In the visions I saw while lying in my **b,** 10444
7:1 through his mind as he was lying on his **b.** 10444
Mt 8:14 he saw Peter's mother-in-law lying in **b** *NIG*
Mk 1:30 Simon's mother-in-law *was* **in b** with *2879*
4:21 in a lamp to put it under a bowl or a **b?** *3109*
7:30 and found her child lying on the **b,** *3109*
Lk 8:16 and hides it in a jar or puts it under a **b.** *3109*
11:7 and my children are with me in **b.** *3130*
17:34 on that night two people will be in one **b;** *3109*
Ac 28:8 His father was **sick in b,** *2879*
Heb 13:4 and the **marriage b** kept pure, *3130*
Rev 2:22 So I will cast her on a **b of suffering,** *3109*

BEDAD (2)

Ge 36:35 When Husham died, Hadad son of **B,** 971
1Ch 1:46 When Husham died, Hadad son of **B,** 971

BEDAN (1)

1Ch 7:17 The son of Ulam: **B.** 979

BEDCHAMBER (KJV) See BEDROOM

BEDDING (1) [BED]

2Sa 17:28 brought **b** and bowls and articles of pottery. 5435

BEDEIAH (1)

Ezr 10:35 Benaiah, **B,** Keluhi, 973

BEDRIDDEN (1) [BED]

Ac 9:33 a paralytic *who had been* **b** for eight years. 2093+2879+3187

BEDROOM (8) [BED, ROOM]

Ex 8:3 up into your palace and your **b** 2540+5435
2Sa 4:7 while he was lying on the bed in his **b.** 2540+5435
13:10 "Bring the food here into my **b** so I may eat 2540
13:10 to her brother Amnon in his **b.** 2540
2Ki 6:12 the very words you speak in your **b."** 2540+5435
11:2 in a **b** to hide him from Athaliah; 2540+4753
2Ch 22:11 and put him and his nurse in a **b.** 2540+4753
Ecc 10:20 or curse the rich in your **b,** 2540+5435

BEDROOMS (1) [BED, ROOM]

Ps 105:30 which went up into the **b** *of* their rulers. 2540

BEDS (12) [BED]

Job 30:6 to live in the dry **stream b,** 5707
33:15 on men as they slumber in their **b,** 5435
Ps 4:4 when you are on your **b,** 5435
149:5 in this honor and sing for joy on their **b.** 5435
SS 5:13 like **b** *of* spice yielding perfume. 6870
6:2 to the **b** *of* spices, 6870
Isa 57:8 a pact with those whose **b** you love, 5435
Hos 7:14 from their hearts but wail upon their **b.** 5435
Am 3:12 on the edge of their **b** and in Damascus 4753
6:4 You lie on **b** *inlaid with* ivory and lounge 4753
Mic 2:1 to those who plot evil on their **b!** 5435

Ac 5:15 into the streets and laid them on **b** and mats *3108*

BEELIADA (1)

1Ch 14: 7 Elishama, **B** and Eliphelet. 1269

BEELZEBUB (7) [BAAL-ZEBUB]

Mt 10:25 If the head of the house *has been* called **B**, *1015*
12:24 "It is only by **B**, the prince of demons, *1015*
12:27 And if I drive out demons by **B**, *1015*
Mk 3:22 "He is possessed by **B**! *1015*
Lk 11:15 But some of them said, "By **B**, *1015*
11:18 that I drive out demons by **B**. *1015*
11:19 Now if I drive out demons by **B**, *1015*

BEEN (890) [BE] See Index of Articles Etc.

BEER (13) [BAALATH BEER, BEER LAHAI ROI, BEER ELIM]

Nu 21:16 From there they continued on to **B**, 932
Jdg 9:21 Then Jotham fled, escaping to **B**, 932
1Sa 1:15 I have not been drinking wine or **b**; 8911
Pr 20: 1 Wine is a mocker and **b** a brawler; 8911
31: 4 not for rulers to crave **b**, 8911
31: 6 Give **b** to those who are perishing, 8911
Isa 24: 9 the **b** is bitter to its drinkers. 8911
28: 7 also stagger from wine and reel from **b**: 8911
28: 7 from **b** and are befuddled with wine; 8911
28: 7 they reel from **b**, 8911
29: 9 but not from wine, stagger, but not from **b**. 8911
56:12 Let us drink our fill of **b**! 8911
Mic 2:11 for you plenty of wine and **b**,' 8911

BEER ELIM (1) [BEER, ELIM]

Isa 15: 8 their lamentation as far as **B**. 935

BEER LAHAI ROI (3) [BEER]

Ge 16:14 the well was called **B**; 936
24:62 Now Isaac had come from **B**, 936
25:11 who then lived near **B**. 936

BEERA (1)

1Ch 7:37 Hod, Shamma, Shilshah, Ithran and **B**. 938

BEERAH (2)

1Ch 5: 6 and **B** his son, 939
5: 6 **B** was a leader of the Reubenites. 2085S

BEERI (2)

Ge 26:34 he married Judith daughter of **B** the Hittite, 941
Hos 1: 1 of the LORD that came to Hosea son of **B** 941

BEEROTH (6) [BEEROTHITE]

Jos 9:17 Gibeon, Kephirah, **B** and Kiriath Jearim. 940
18:25 Gibeon, Ramah, **B**, 940
2Sa 4: 2 **B** is considered part of Benjamin, 940
4: 3 because the **people of B** fled to Gittaim 943
Ezr 2:25 of Kiriath Jearim, Kephirah and **B** 743 940
Ne 7:29 of Kiriath Jearim, Kephirah and **B** 743 940

BEEROTHITE (4) [BEEROTH]

2Sa 4: 2 they were sons of Rimmon the **B** from 943
4: 5 the sons of Rimmon the **B**, 943
4: 9 the sons of Rimmon the **B**, 943
23:37 the **B**, the armor-bearer of Joab son 943

BEERSHEBA (34)

Ge 21:14 and wandered in the desert of **B**. 937
21:31 So that place was called **B**, 937
21:32 After the treaty had been made at **B**, 937
21:33 Abraham planted a tamarisk tree in **B**, 937
22:19 and they set off together for **B**. 937
22:19 And Abraham stayed in **B**. 937
26:23 From there he went up to **B**. 937
26:33 the name of the town has been **B**. 937
28:10 Jacob left **B** and set out for Haran. 937
46: 1 and when he reached **B**, 937
46: 5 Then Jacob left **B**, 937
Jos 15:28 Hazar Shual, **B**, Biziothiah, 937
19: 2 It included: **B** (or Sheba), Moladah, 937
Jdg 20: 1 to **B** and from the land of Gilead came out 937
1Sa 3:20 to **B** recognized that Samuel was attested as 937
8: 2 and they served at **B**. 937
2Sa 3:10 over Israel and Judah from Dan to **B**." 937
17:11 Let all Israel, from Dan to **B**— 937
24: 2 from Dan to **B** and enroll the fighting men, 937
24: 7 they went on to **B** in the Negev of Judah. 937
24:15 of the people from Dan to **B** died. 937
1Ki 4:25 from Dan to **B**, lived in safety, 937
19: 3 When he came to **B** in Judah, 937
2Ki 12: 1 mother's name was Zibiah; she was from **B**. 937
23: 8 from Geba to **B**, 937
1Ch 4:28 They lived in **B**, Moladah, Hazar Shual, 937
21: 2 "Go and count the Israelites from **B** to Dan. 937
2Ch 19: 4 from **B** to the hill country of Ephraim 937
24: 1 she was from **B**. 937
30: 5 throughout Israel, from **B** to Dan, 937
Ne 11:27 in Hazar Shual, in **B** and its settlements, 937
11:30 So they were living all the way from **B** to 937
Am 5: 5 do not go to Gilgal, do not journey to **B**. 937
8:14 or, 'As surely as the god of **B** lives'— 937

BEES (4)

Dt 1:44 like a **swarm of b** and beat you down 1805
Jdg 14: 8 In it was a swarm of **b** and some honey, 1805
Ps 118:12 They swarmed around me like **b**, 1805
Isa 7:18 of Egypt and for **b** from the land of Assyria. 1805

BEESH-TERAH (KJV) See BE ESHTARAH

BEETLE (KJV) See CRICKET

BEEVES (KJV) See CATTLE

BEFALL (2) [BEFALLS]

Job 5:19 in seven no harm *will* **b** you. 5595
Ps 91:10 then no harm *will* **b** you, 448+628

BEFALLS (1) [BEFALL]

Pr 12:21 No harm **b** the righteous, 628+4200

BEFORE (1295) [BEFOREHAND]

Ge 10: 9 He was a mighty hunter **b** the LORD; 4200+7156
10: 9 a mighty hunter **b** the LORD." 4200+7156
13: 9 Is not the whole land **b** you? 4200+7156
13:10 This was **b** the LORD destroyed Sodom 4200+7156
17: 1 walk **b** me and be blameless. 4200+7156
18: 8 and set these **b** them. 4200+7156
18:22 Abraham remained standing **b** the LORD. 4200+7156
19: 4 **B** they had gone to bed, 3270
19:27 place where he had stood **b** the LORD. 907+7156
20:15 Abimelech said, "My land is **b** you; 4200+7156
20:16 This is to cover the offense against you **b** 4200
21:23 Now swear to me here **b** God that you will 928
23: 7 and bowed down **b** the people of the land, 4200
23:12 Abraham bowed down **b** the people 4200+7156
24: 7 he will send his angel **b** you so 4200+7156
24:15 **B** he had finished praying, 3270
24:33 Then food was set **b** him, but he said, 4200+7156
24:40 'The LORD, **b** whom I have walked, 4200+7156
24:45 "**B** I finished praying in my heart, 3270
24:52 down to the ground **b** the LORD. 4200
27: 4 I may give you my blessing **b** I die." 928+3270
27: 7 in the presence of the LORD **b** I die.' 4200+7156
27:10 so that he may give you his blessing **b** 4200+7156
27:33 I ate it **just b** you came 928+3270
29:26 to give the younger daughter in marriage **b** 4200+7156
30:30 The little you had **b** I came 4200+7156
31: 5 toward me is not what it was **b**, 8997+9453
33:14 slowly at the pace of the droves **b** me 4200+7156
36:31 in Edom **b** any Israelite king reigned: 4200+7156
37:10 and bow down to the ground **b** you?" 4200
37:18 and **b** he reached them, 928+3270
41:14 he came **b** Pharaoh. 448
41:21 they looked just as ugly as **b**. 928+2021+9378
41:43 and men shouted **b** him, "Make way!" 4200+7156
41:50 **B** the years of famine came, 928+3270
42:24 from them and bound **b** their eyes. 4200
43: 9 to you and set him here **b** you, 4200+7156
43: 9 I will bear the blame **b** you all my life. 4200
43:14 may God Almighty grant you mercy **b** 4200+7156
43:26 and they bowed down **b** him to the ground. 4200
43:33 The men had been seated **b** him 4200+7156
44:14 they threw themselves to the ground **b** him. 4200+7156
44:32 I will bear the blame **b** you, my father, 4200
45: 1 Joseph could no longer control himself **b** 4200
45:28 I will go and see him **b** I die." 928+3270
46:29 As soon as Joseph appeared **b** him, 448
47: 2 of his brothers and presented them **b** 4200+7156
47: 6 and the land of Egypt is **b** you; 4200+7156
47: 7 in and presented him **b** Pharaoh. 4200+7156
47:15 Why should we die **b** your eyes? 5584
47:19 Why should we perish **b** your eyes— 4200
48: 5 to you in Egypt **b** I came to you here will 6330
48:15 the God **b** whom my fathers Abraham 4200+7156
50:16 "Your father left these instructions **b** 4200+7156
50:18 and threw themselves down **b** him. 4200+7156
Ex 1:19 and give birth **b** the midwives arrive." 928+3270
4:21 see that you perform **b** Pharaoh all 4200+7156
4:30 also performed the signs **b** the people, 4200+6524
5: 8 make the same number of bricks as **b**; 8997+9453
5:14 of bricks yesterday or today, as **b**?" 8997+9453
7: 9 'Take your staff and throw it down **b** 4200+7156
9:10 from a furnace and stood **b** Pharaoh. 4200+7156
9:11 magicians could not stand **b** Moses 4200+7156
10: 3 to humble yourself **b** me? 4946+7156
10:14 Never **b** had there been such a plague 4200+7156
10:28 Make sure you do not appear **b** me again! 7156
10:29 "I will never appear **b** you again." 7156
11: 8 bowing down **b** me and saying, 'Go, 4200
11:10 Aaron performed all these wonders **b** 4200+7156
12:34 So the people took their dough **b** 3270
16: 9 'Come **b** the LORD, 4200+7156
16:33 Then place it **b** the LORD to be kept for 4200+7156
17: 6 I will stand there **b** you by the rock 4200+7156
18:19 You must be the people's representative **b** 4578
19: 7 people and set **b** them all the words 4200+7156
20: 3 "You shall have no other gods **b** me. 6584+7156
21: 1 are the laws you are to set **b** them: 4200+7156
21: 6 then his master must take him **b** the judges. 448
22: 8 of the house must appear **b** the judges 448
22: 9 parties are to bring their cases **b** the judges. 6330
22:11 an **oath** *b* the LORD that the neighbor did AIT
23:15 "No one is to appear **b** me empty-handed. 7156
23:17 to appear **b** the Sovereign LORD. 448+7156
23:24 not bow down **b** their gods or worship them 4200
23:30 Little by little I will drive them out **b** you, 7156
23:31 the land and you will drive them out **b** you. 7156
25:30 the Presence on this table to be **b** me 4200+7156
27:21 to keep the lamps burning **b** the LORD 4200+7156
28:12 names on his shoulders as a memorial **b** the LORD. 4200+7156
28:29 as a continuing memorial **b** the LORD. 4200+7156
28:30 Israelites over his heart **b** the LORD. 4200+7156
28:35 heard when he enters the Holy Place **b** 4200+7156
29:23 which is **b** the LORD, take a loaf, 4200+7156
29:24 his sons and wave them **b** the LORD 4200+7156
29:26 wave it **b** the LORD as a wave offering, 4200+7156
29:42 the entrance to the Tent of Meeting **b** 4200+7156
30: 6 Put the altar in front of the curtain that is **b** 6584
30: 6 **b** the atonement cover that is over 4200+7156
30: 8 so incense will burn regularly **b** the LORD 4200+7156
30:16 memorial for the Israelites **b** the LORD, 4200+7156
32: 1 "Come, make us gods who will go **b** us. 4200+7156
32:23 'Make us gods who will go **b** us. 4200+7156
32:34 and my angel will go **b** you. 4200+7156
33: 2 I will send an angel **b** you and drive 4200+7156
34:10 **B** all your people I will do wonders never 5584
34:10 all your people I will do wonders never **b** NIH
34:11 I will drive out **b** you the Amorites, 4946+7156
34:20 "No one is to appear **b** me empty-handed. 7156
34:23 a year all your men are to appear **b** 907+7156
34:24 I will drive out nations **b** you 4946+7156
34:24 up three times each year to appear **b** 907+7156
40:23 and set out the bread on it **b** the LORD, 4200+7156
40:25 and set up the lamps **b** the LORD, 4200+7156
Lev 1: 5 slaughter the young bull **b** the LORD, 4200+7156
1:11 to slaughter it at the north side of the altar **b** the LORD. 4200+7156
3: 1 he is to present **b** the LORD an animal 4200+7156
3: 7 he is to present it **b** the LORD. 4200+7156
3:12 he is to present it **b** the LORD. 4200+7156
4: 4 the entrance to the Tent of Meeting **b** 4200+7156
4: 4 on its head and slaughter it **b** the LORD. 4200+7156
4: 6 and sprinkle some of it seven times **b** 4200+7156
4: 7 is **b** the LORD in the Tent of Meeting. 4200+7156
4:14 a sin offering and present it **b** the Tent 4200+7156
4:15 to lay their hands on the bull's head **b** 4200+7156
4:15 bull shall be slaughtered **b** the LORD. 4200+7156
4:17 and sprinkle it **b** the LORD seven times 4200+7156
4:18 horns of the altar that is **b** the LORD in 4200+7156
4:24 the burnt offering is slaughtered **b** 4200+7156
6: 7 priest will make atonement for him **b** 4200+7156
6:14 Aaron's sons are to bring it **b** the LORD, 4200+7156
6:25 be slaughtered **b** the LORD in the place 4200+7156
7:30 breast **b** the LORD as a wave offering. 4200+7156
8:26 which was **b** the LORD, 4200+7156
8:27 his sons and waved them **b** the LORD 4200+7156
8:29 waved it **b** the LORD as a wave offering, 4200+7156
9: 2 and present them **b** the LORD. 4200+7156
9: 4 for a fellowship offering to sacrifice **b** 4200+7156
9: 5 entire assembly came near and stood **b** 4200+7156
9:21 breasts and the right thigh **b** the LORD 4200+7156
10: 1 and they offered unauthorized fire **b** 4200+7156
10: 2 and they died **b** the LORD. 4200+7156
10:15 waved **b** the LORD as a wave offering. 4200+7156
10:17 by making atonement for them **b** 4200+7156
10:19 and their burnt offering **b** the LORD, 4200+7156
12: 7 He shall offer them **b** the LORD 4200+7156
13: 7 he must appear **b** the priest again. 448
14:11 cleansed and his offerings **b** the LORD 4200+7156
14:12 he shall wave them **b** the LORD as 4200+7156
14:16 with his finger sprinkle some of it **b** 4200+7156
14:18 make atonement for him **b** the LORD. 4200+7156
14:23 the entrance to the Tent of Meeting, **b** 4200+7156
14:24 and wave them **b** the LORD as 4200+7156
14:27 from his palm seven times **b** the LORD. 4200+7156
14:29 make atonement for him **b** the LORD. 4200+7156
14:31 the priest will make atonement **b** 4200+7156
14:36 order the house to be emptied **b** he goes 928+3270
15:14 come **b** the LORD to the entrance to 4200+7156
15:15 In this way he will make atonement **b** 4200+7156
15:30 for her **b** the LORD for the uncleanness 4200+7156
16: 4 so he must bathe himself with water **b** 2256
16: 7 take the two goats and present them **b** 4200+7156
16:10 presented alive **b** the LORD to be used 4200+7156
16:12 the altar **b** the LORD and 4200+4946+7156
16:13 put the incense on the fire **b** the LORD, 4200+7156
16:14 of it with his finger seven times **b** 4200+7156
16:18 is **b** the LORD and make atonement 4200+7156
16:23 and take off the linen garments he put on **b** 928
16:30 Then, **b** the LORD, you will be clean 4200+7156
18:24 nations that I am going to drive out **b** 4946+7156
18:27 people who lived in the land **b** you, 4200+7156
18:28 it vomited out the nations that were **b** 4200+7156
18:30 the detestable customs that were practiced **b** 4200+7156
19:22 priest is to make atonement for him **b** 4200+7156
20:17 be cut off **b** the eyes of their people. 4200
20:23 nations I am going to drive out **b** you. 4946+7156
23:11 to wave the sheaf **b** the LORD so it will 4200+7156
23:20 to wave the two lambs **b** the LORD as 4200+7156

Lev 23:28 when atonement is made for you **b** 7156
23:40 and rejoice **b** the LORD your God 4200+7156
24: 3 Aaron is to tend the lamps **b** the LORD 4200+7156
24: 4 the pure gold lampstand **b** the LORD 4200+7156
24: 6 on the table of pure gold **b** the LORD. 4200+7156
24: 8 to be set out **b** the LORD regularly, 4200+7156
25:30 not redeemed **b** a full year has passed, 6330
26: 1 a carved stone in your land to bow down **b** 6584
26: 7 and they will fall by the sword **b** you. 4200+7156
26: 8 enemies will fall by the sword **b** you. 4200+7156
26:37 not be able to stand **b** your enemies. 4200+7156
Nu 3: 4 fell dead **b** the LORD when they made 4200+7156
3: 4 offering with unauthorized fire **b** him 4200+7156
5:16 and have her stand **b** the LORD. 4200+7156
5:18 After the priest has had the woman stand **b** the LORD 4200+7156
5:25 wave it **b** the LORD and bring it to 4200+7156
5:30 The priest is to have her stand **b** the LORD 4200+7156
6:16 to present them **b** the LORD and make 4200+7156
6:20 The priest shall then wave them **b** 4200+7156
7: 3 their gifts **b** the LORD six covered carts 4200+7156
7: 3 These they presented **b** the tabernacle. 4200+7156
7:10 for its dedication and presented them **b** 4200+7156
8:10 are to bring the Levites **b** the LORD, 4200+7156
8:11 Levites **b** the LORD as a wave offering 4200+7156
8:21 as a wave offering **b** the LORD 4200+7156
10: 3 the whole community is to assemble **b** you 448
10: 4 are to assemble **b** you. 448
10:10 and they will be a memorial for you **b** 4200+7156
10:21 The tabernacle was to be set up **b** 6330
10:33 The ark of the covenant of the LORD went **b** them 4200+7156
10:35 may your foes flee **b** you." 4946+7156
11:20 among you, and have wailed **b** him, 4200+7156
11:33 the meat was still between their teeth and **b** 3270
13:22 (Hebron had been built seven years **b** Zoan 4200+7156
13:30 Then Caleb silenced the people **b** Moses 448
14:14 that you go **b** them in a pillar of cloud 4200+7156
14:37 down and died of a plague **b** the LORD. 4200+7156
15:15 the alien shall be the same **b** the LORD: 4200+7156
15:28 to make atonement **b** the LORD for 4200+7156
16: 7 and incense in them **b** the LORD. 4200+7156
16: 9 to stand **b** the community and minister 4200+7156
16:16 "You and all your followers are to appear **b** the LORD 4200+7156
16:17 and present it **b** the LORD. 4200+7156
16:38 for they were presented **b** the LORD 4200+7156
16:40 Aaron should come to burn incense **b** 4200+7156
17: 7 Moses placed the staffs **b** the LORD in 4200+7156
18: 2 when you and your sons minister **b** the Tent 4200+7156
18:19 It is an everlasting covenant of salt **b** 4200+7156
20: 3 our brothers fell dead **b** the LORD! 4200+7156
20: 8 Speak to that rock **b** their eyes 4200
22:32 your path is a reckless one **b** me. 4200+5584
25: 2 The people ate and bowed down **b** 4200
25: 4 and expose them in broad daylight **b** 4200
25: 6 to his family a Midianite woman **right b** 4200
26:61 they made an offering **b** the LORD 4200+7156
27: 2 Tent of Meeting and stood **b** Moses, 4200+7156
27: 5 Moses brought their case **b** the LORD 4200+7156
27:14 to honor me as holy **b** their eyes." 4200
27:17 to go out and come in **b** them, 4200+7156
27:19 Have him stand **b** Eleazar the priest 4200+7156
27:21 He is to stand **b** Eleazar the priest, 4200+7156
27:21 by inquiring of the Urim **b** the LORD. 4200+7156
27:22 had him stand **b** Eleazar the priest 4200+7156
31:50 to make atonement for ourselves **b** 4200+7156
31:54 memorial for the Israelites **b** the LORD. 4200+7156
32: 4 land the LORD subdued **b** the people 4200+7156
32:20 if you will arm yourselves **b** the LORD 4200+7156
32:21 you will go armed over the Jordan **b** 4200+7156
32:21 until he has driven his enemies out **b** him— 4946+7156
32:22 when the land is subdued **b** the LORD, 4200+7156
32:22 this land will be your possession **b** 4200+7156
32:27 will cross over to fight **b** the LORD, 4200+7156
32:29 over the Jordan with you **b** the LORD, 4200+7156
32:29 then when the land is subdued **b** you, 4200+7156
32:32 over **b** the LORD into Canaan armed, 4200+7156
33:52 drive out all the inhabitants of the land **b** you, 4946+7156
35:12 a person accused of murder may not die **b** 6330
35:12 before he stands trial **b** the assembly. 4200+7156
35:32 and live on his own land **b** the death of 6330
36: 1 and spoke **b** Moses and the leaders, 4200+7156
Dt 1:30 The LORD your God, who is going **b** you, 4200+7156
1:30 did for you in Egypt, **b** your very eyes, 4200
1:45 You came back and wept **b** the LORD, 4200+7156
2:12 They destroyed the Horites from **b** them 7156
2:21 The LORD destroyed them from **b** 7156
2:22 when he destroyed the Horites from **b** them. 7156
4: 8 as this body of laws I am setting **b** 4200+7156
4:10 day you stood **b** the LORD your God 4200+7156
4:10 the people **b** me to hear my words so 4200
4:32 long **b** your time, from 4200+7156
4:34 for you in Egypt **b** your very eyes? 4200
4:38 to drive out **b** you nations greater 4946+7156
4:44 This is the law Moses set **b** the Israelites. 4200+7156
5: 7 "You shall have no other gods **b** me. 6584+7156
6:19 thrusting out all your enemies **b** you, 4946+7156
6:22 **B** our eyes the LORD sent miraculous signs 4200
6:25 if we are careful to obey all this law **b** 4200+7156

Dt 7: 1 and drives out **b** you many nations— 4946+7156
7:22 The LORD your God will drive out those nations **b** you, 4946+7156
8:20 Like the nations the LORD destroyed **b** 4946+7156
9: 3 he will subdue them **b** you. 4200+7156
9: 4 the LORD your God has driven them out **b** you, 4200+4946+7156
9: 4 the LORD is going to drive them out **b** 4946+7156
9: 5 the LORD your God will drive them out **b** you, 4946+7156
9:17 breaking them to pieces **b** your eyes. 4200
9:18 Then once again I fell prostrate **b** 4200+7156
9:25 I lay prostrate **b** 4200+7156
10: 4 on these tablets what he had written **b**, 8037
10: 8 to stand **b** the LORD to minister and 4200+7156
11:23 the LORD will drive out all these nations **b** you, 4200+4946+7156
11:26 I am setting **b** you today a blessing 4200+7156
11:32 the decrees and laws I am setting **b** 4200+7156
12:12 there rejoice **b** the LORD your God, 4200+7156
12:18 to rejoice **b** the LORD your God 4200+7156
12:29 The LORD your God will cut off **b** you 4946+7156
12:30 after they have been destroyed **b** you, 4946+7156
16:11 And rejoice **b** the LORD your God at 4200+7156
16:16 a year all your men must appear **b** 907+7156
16:16 No man should appear **b** 907+7156
17: 8 If cases come **b** your courts 928
18:12 the LORD your God will drive out those nations **b** you. 4946+7156
18:13 be blameless **b** the LORD your God. 6640
19:17 the presence of the LORD **b** the priests 4200+7156
20: 3 not be terrified or give way to panic **b** them. 4946+7156
22:17 Then her parents shall display the cloth **b** the elders 4200+7156
24:15 Pay him his wages each day **b** sunset, 4202
26: 5 shall declare **b** the LORD your God: 4200+7156
26:10 Place the basket **b** the LORD your God 4200+7156
26:10 your God and bow down **b** him. 4200+7156
28: 7 up against you will be defeated **b** you. 4200+7156
28:25 The LORD will cause you to be defeated **b** your enemies. 4200+7156
28:31 Your ox will be slaughtered **b** your eyes, 4200
30: 1 curses I have set **b** you come upon you 4200+7156
30:15 I set **b** you today life and prosperity, 4200+7156
30:19 witnesses against you that I have set **b** 4200+7156
31: 3 He will destroy these nations **b** you, 4200+4946+7156
31: 8 The LORD himself goes **b** you and 4200+7156
31:11 to appear **b** the LORD your God at 907+7156
31:11 you shall read this law **b** them 5584
31:21 even **b** I bring them into the land 928+3270
31:28 Assemble **b** me all the elders of your tribes 448
33: 1 of God pronounced on the Israelites **b** 4200+7156
33:10 He offers incense **b** you 678+928
33:27 He will drive out your enemy **b** you, 4946+7156
33:29 Your enemies will cower **b** you, 4200
Jos 2: 8 **B** the spies lay down for the night, 3270
3: 1 where they camped **b** crossing over. 3270
3: 4 you have never been this way **b**. 4946+8997+9453
3:10 that he will certainly drive out **b** you 4946+7156
4: 5 "Go over **b** the ark of the LORD your God 4200+7156
4: 7 the flow of the Jordan was cut off **b** the ark 4946+7156
4:13 **b** the LORD to the plains of Jericho 4200+7156
4:18 their place and ran at flood stage as **b**. 8997+9453
4:23 the LORD your God dried up the Jordan **b** you 4946+7156
4:23 the Red Sea when he dried it up **b** us 4946+7156
5: 1 the LORD had dried up the Jordan **b** 4946+7156
6: 8 the seven trumpets **b** 4200+7156
6:13 marching **b** the ark of the LORD 4200+7156
6:26 "Cursed **b** the LORD is the man 4200+7156
7: 6 fell facedown to the ground **b** the ark 4200+7156
7:23 all the Israelites and spread them out **b** 4200+7156
8: 5 as they did **b**, we will flee from them. 928+2021+8037
8: 6 from us as they did **b**.' 928+2021+8037
8:10 leaders of Israel marched **b** them to Ai 4200+7156
8:15 be driven back **b** them, 4200+7156
9:24 to wipe out all its inhabitants from **b** you. 7156
10:10 The LORD threw them into confusion **b** Israel, 4200+7156
10:11 As they fled **b** Israel on the road down 4946+7156
10:14 There has never been a day like it **b** or 4200+7156
13: 6 will drive them out **b** the Israelites. 4946+7156
18: 3 "How long will you wait **b** you begin NIH
20: 4 city gate and state his case **b** the elders 265+928
20: 6 in that city until he has stood trial **b** 4200+7156
20: 9 of blood prior to standing trial **b** 4200+7156
22:29 of the LORD our God that stands **b** 4200+7156
23: 5 He will push them out **b** you, 4200+4946+7156
23: 9 "The LORD has driven out **b** you great 4946+7156
23:13 LORD your God will no longer drive out these nations **b** you. 4200+4946+7156
24: 1 and they presented themselves **b** God. 4200+7156
24: 8 I destroyed them from **b** you. 7156
24:12 which drove them out **b** you— 4946+7156
24:17 and performed those great signs **b** our eyes. 4200
24:18 LORD drove out **b** us all the nations, 4946+7156
Jdg 2: 3 that I will not drive them out **b** you; 4946+7156
2:21 I will no longer drive out **b** them any 4946+7156
4:23 the Canaanite king, **b** the Israelites. 4200+7156
5: 5 The mountains quaked **b** the LORD, 4946+7156
5: 5 **b** the LORD, the God of Israel. 4946+7156
6: 9 from **b** you and gave you their land. 7156

Jdg 6:18 bring my offering and set it **b** you." 4200+7156
8:28 Midian was subdued **b** the Israelites 4200+7156
11:11 he repeated all his words **b** the LORD 4200+7156
11:23 the Amorites out **b** his people Israel, 4946+7156
14:18 **B** sunset on the seventh day the men of 928+3270
16:20 "I'll go out **as b** and shake myself free." 928+3869+7193+7193
20: 1 as one man and assembled **b** the LORD 448
20:23 up and wept **b** the LORD until evening, 4200+7156
20:26 and there they sat weeping **b** the LORD. 4200+7156
20:28 the son of Aaron, ministering **b** it.) 4200+7156
20:30 **as** they had **done b.** 928+3869+7193+7193
20:31 to inflict casualties on the Israelites **as b,** 928+3869+7193+7193
20:32 "We are defeating them as **b,"** 928+2021+8037
20:35 The LORD defeated Benjamin **b** Israel, 4200+7156
20:36 men of Israel had given way **b** Benjamin, 4200
20:42 fled **b** the Israelites in the direction 4200+7156
21: 2 where they sat **b** God until evening, 4200+7156
21: 5 has failed to assemble **b** the LORD?" 448
21: 5 that anyone who failed to assemble **b** 448
21: 8 of the tribes of Israel failed to assemble **b** 448
Ru 2:11 live with a people you did not know **b.** 8997+9453
3:14 got up **b** anyone could be recognized; 928+3270
1Sa 1:19 and worshiped **b** the LORD and 4200+7156
1:22 I will take him and present him **b** 907+7156
2:11 the boy ministered **b** the LORD under Eli 907
2:15 But even **b** the fat was burned, 928+3270
2:18 Samuel was ministering **b** the LORD— 907+7156
2:30 your father's house would minister **b** 4200+7156
2:35 minister **b** my anointed one always. 4200+7156
2:36 down **b** him for a piece of silver and a crust 4200
3: 1 The boy Samuel ministered **b** the LORD 907
4: 3 the LORD bring defeat upon us today **b** 4200+7156
4: 7 Nothing like this has happened **b.** 919+8997
4:17 "Israel fled **b** the Philistines, 4200+7156
5: 3 fallen on his face on the ground **b** the ark of the LORD! 4200+7156
5: 4 fallen on his face on the ground **b** the ark of the LORD! 4200+7156
7: 6 they drew water and poured it out **b** 4200+7156
7:10 such a panic that they were routed **b** 4200+7156
8:20 to go out **b** us and fight our battles." 4200+7156
8:21 he repeated it **b** the LORD. 265+928
9:13 you will find him **b** he goes up to 928+3270
9:15 Now the day **b** Saul came, 4200+7156
10: 5 flutes and harps being played **b** them, 4200+7156
10:19 So now present yourselves **b** the LORD 4200+7156
10:25 a scroll and deposited it **b** the LORD. 4200+7156
11:15 they sacrificed fellowship offerings **b** 4200+7156
12: 7 to confront you with evidence **b** the LORD 4200+7156
12:16 the LORD is about to do **b** your eyes! 4200
14:13 The Philistines fell **b** Jonathan, 4200+7156
14:24 "Cursed be any man who eats food **b** 6330
14:24 **b** I have avenged myself on my enemies!" NIH
15:30 But please honor me **b** the elders 5584
15:30 before the elders of my people and **b** Israel; 5584
15:33 And Samuel put Agag to death **b** 4200+7156
16: 6 the LORD's anointed stands here **b** 5584
16:10 Jesse had seven of his sons pass **b** Samuel, 4200+7156
17:30 and the men answered him as **b.** 8037
17:57 Abner took him and brought him **b** Saul, 4200+7156
18:26 **b** the allotted time **elapsed,** 4202+4848
19: 7 and David was with Saul as **b.** 919+8997
19: 8 with such force that they fled **b** him. 4946+7156
20: 8 into a **covenant** with you *b* the LORD. AIT
20:41 and **bowed** down *b* Jonathan three times, AIT
21: 6 had been removed from **b** the LORD! 4200+7156
21: 7 detained **b** the LORD; 4200+7156
23:18 of them made a covenant **b** the LORD. 4200+7156
25:23 bowed down **b** David with her face to the ground. 678+4200
26:19 may they be cursed **b** the LORD! 4200+7156
28:25 set it **b** Saul and his men, and they ate. 4200+7156
30:15 to me **b** God that you will not kill me 928
31: 1 the Israelites fled **b** them, 4946+7156
2Sa 2:26 How long **b** you order your men 4202
3:28 "I and my kingdom are forever innocent **b** the LORD 4946+6640
3:34 You fell as one falls **b** wicked men." 4200+7156
3:35 if I taste bread or anything else **b** 4200+7156
5: 3 with them at Hebron **b** the LORD, 4200+7156
5:20 against my enemies **b** me." 4200+7156
6: 5 with all their might **b** the LORD, 4200+7156
6:14 danced **b** the LORD with all his might, 4200+7156
6:16 and dancing **b** the LORD, 4200+7156
6:17 and fellowship offerings **b** the LORD. 4200+7156
6:21 David said to Michal, "It was **b** the LORD, 4200+7156
6:21 I will celebrate **b** the LORD. 4200+7156
7: 9 I have cut off all your enemies from **b** you. 7156
7:15 whom I removed from **b** you. 4200+7156
7:16 kingdom will endure forever **b** me; 4200+7156
7:18 David went in and sat **b** the LORD, 4200+7156
7:23 and their gods from **b** your people, 7156
7:26 house of your servant David will be established **b** you. 4200+7156
9: 2 They called him to appear **b** David, 448
10:13 and they fled **b** him. 4946+7156
10:14 they fled **b** Abishai and went inside 4946+7156
10:18 But they fled **b** Israel, 4946+7156
12:11 **B** your very eyes I will take your wives 4200
12:12 but I will do this thing in broad daylight **b** 5584
14:33 with his face to the ground **b** the king. 4200+7156

2Sa 15: 2 with a complaint to be placed **b** the king for 448
15: 5 to bow down **b** him, 4200
15:18 from Gath marched **b** the king. 6584+7156
18:21 The Cushite bowed down **b** Joab 4200
18:28 down **b** the king with his face to the ground 4200
19: 8 they all came **b** him. 4200+7156
19:18 he fell prostrate **b** the king 4200+7156
21: 6 to us to be killed and exposed **b** the LORD 4200
21: 7 of the **oath** *b* the LORD between David AIT
21: 9 exposed them on a hill **b** the LORD. 4200+7156
22:23 All his laws are **b** me; 4200+5584
22:24 I have been blameless **b** him 4200
23:16 instead, he poured it out **b** the LORD. 4200
24:11 **B** David got up the next morning, 2256
24:20 and bowed down **b** the king with his face to 4200
1Ki 1:16 Bathsheba bowed low and knelt **b** the king. 4200
1:23 So he went **b** the king and bowed 4200+7156
1:28 the king's presence and stood **b** him. 4200+7156
1:31 kneeling **b** the king, said, 4200
1:32 When they came **b** the king, 4200+7156
2: 4 and if they walk faithfully **b** me 4200+7156
2:26 the Sovereign LORD **b** my father David 4200+7156
2:45 David's throne will remain secure **b** 4200+7156
3:15 stood **b** the ark of the Lord's covenant 4200+7156
3:16 to the king and stood **b** him. 4200+7156
3:22 And so they argued **b** the king. 4200+7156
8: 5 gathered about him were **b** the ark, 4200+7156
8:22 Then Solomon stood **b** the altar of 4200+7156
8:25 'You shall never fail to have a man to sit **b** me on the throne 4200+4946+7156
8:25 to walk **b** me as you have done.' 4200+7156
8:31 and he comes and swears the oath **b** 4200+7156
8:54 he rose from **b** the altar of the LORD, 4200+7156
8:59 which I have prayed **b** the LORD, 4200+7156
8:62 all Israel with him offered sacrifices **b** 4200+7156
8:64 bronze altar **b** the LORD was too small 4200+7156
8:65 They celebrated it **b** the LORD our God 4200+7156
9: 3 prayer and plea you have made **b** me; 4200+7156
9: 4 if you walk **b** me in integrity of heart 4200+7156
9:25 burning incense **b** the LORD along 4200+7156
10: 8 who continually stand **b** you 4200+7156
11:36 a lamp **b** me in Jerusalem, 4200+7156
13: 6 and became as it was **b.** 928+2021+8037
14: 9 You have done more evil than all who lived **b** you. 4200+7156
14:24 the nations the LORD had driven out **b** 4946+7156
15: 3 the sins his father had done **b** him; 4200+7156
16:25 and sinned more than all those **b** him. 4200+7156
16:30 eyes of the LORD than any of those **b** 4200+7156
16:33 to anger than did all the kings of Israel **b** him. 4200+7156
18:21 Elijah went **b** the people and said, 448
18:44 'Hitch up your chariot and go down **b** 4202
19:11 and shattered the rocks **b** the LORD, 4200+7156
21:13 and brought charges against Naboth **b** 5584
21:26 like the Amorites the LORD drove out **b** Israel.) 4946+7156
21:29 how Ahab has humbled himself **b** me? 4200+4946+7156
22:10 all the prophets prophesying **b** them. 4200+7156
22:21 stood **b** the LORD and said, 4200+7156
2Ki 1:13 up and fell on his knees **b** Elijah. 4200+5584
2: 9 what can I do for you **b** I am taken 928+3270
2:15 to meet him and bowed to the ground **b** 4200
4:12 So he called her, and she stood **b** him. 4200+7156
4:43 "How can I set this **b** a hundred men?" 4200+7156
4:44 Then he set it **b** them, 4200+7156
5:15 He stood **b** him and said, 4200+7156
5:25 he went in and stood **b** his master Elisha. 448
6:22 and water **b** them so that they may eat 4200+7156
6:32 **b** he arrived, Elisha said to the elders, 928+3270
8: 9 He went in and stood **b** him, and said, 4200+7156
10: 9 He stood **b** all the people and said, 448
13: 5 in their own homes as they had **b.** 8997+9453
16: 3 the nations the LORD had driven out **b** 4946+7156
16:11 and finished it **b** King Ahaz returned. 6330
16:14 that stood **b** the LORD he brought from 4200+7156
17: 8 the nations the LORD had driven out **b** 4946+7156
17:11 the LORD had driven out **b** 4946+7156
18: 5 either **b** him or after him. 4200+7156
18:22 "You must worship **b** this altar 4200+7156
19:14 the LORD and spread it out **b** the LORD. 4200+7156
19:26 scorched **b** it grows up. 4200+7156
19:32 *He will* not **come b** it with shield or build 7709
20: 3 how I have walked **b** you faithfully 4200+7156
20: 4 **B** Isaiah had left the middle court, 4202
21: 2 the nations the LORD had driven out **b** 4946+7156
21: 9 LORD had destroyed **b** the Israelites. 4946+7156
22:19 and you humbled yourself **b** the LORD 4946+7156
23:25 Neither **b** nor after Josiah was there a king like him 4200+7156
25: 7 They killed the sons of Zedekiah **b** his eyes. 4200
1Ch 1:43 in Edom **b** any Israelite king reigned: 4200+7156
5:25 whom God had destroyed **b** them. 4946+7156
6:32 They ministered with music **b** 4200+7156
10: 1 the Israelites fled **b** them, 4946+7156
11: 3 he made a compact with them at Hebron **b** the LORD, 4200+7156
11:18 instead, he poured it out **b** the LORD. 4200
13: 8 with all their might **b** God, 4200+7156
13:10 So he died there **b** God. 4200+7156
15: 2 the LORD and to **minister** *b* him forever." AIT
15:24 priests were to blow trumpets **b** the ark 4200+7156
16: 1 and fellowship offerings **b** God. 4200+7156
16: 4 of the Levites to minister **b** the ark 4200+7156
16: 6 blow the trumpets regularly **b** the ark 4200+7156
16:27 Splendor and majesty are **b** him; 4200+7156
1Ch 16:29 Bring an offering and come **b** him; 4200+7156
16:30 Tremble **b** him, all the earth! 4200+4946+7156
16:33 will sing for joy **b** the LORD, 4200+4946+7156
16:37 his associates **b** the ark of the covenant 4200+7156
16:39 his fellow priests **b** the tabernacle of 4200+7156
17: 8 I have cut off all your enemies from **b** you. 7156
17:16 David went in and sat **b** the LORD, 4200+7156
17:21 by driving out nations from **b** your people, 7156
17:24 of your servant David will be established **b** you. 4200+7156
19:14 and they fled **b** him. 4946+7156
19:15 they too fled **b** his brother Abishai 4946+7156
19:18 But they fled **b** Israel, 4200+4946+7156
21:12 of being swept away **b** your enemies, 4946+7156
21:21 down **b** David with his face to the ground. 4200
21:30 David could not go **b** it to inquire of God, 4200+7156
22: 5 So David made extensive preparations **b** his death. 4200+7156
23:13 to offer sacrifices **b** the LORD, 4200+7156
23:13 to **minister** *b* him and AIT
23:31 were to serve **b** the LORD regularly 4200+7156
24: 2 Nadab and Abihu died **b** their father did, 4200+7156
29:20 they bowed low and fell prostrate **b** 4200
29:22 anointing him **b** the LORD to be ruler 4200
29:25 as no king over Israel ever had **b.** 4200+7156
2Ch 1: 6 the bronze altar **b** the LORD in the Tent 4200+7156
1:12 riches and honor, such as no king who was **b** you ever had 4200+7156
1:13 from **b** the Tent of Meeting. 4200+7156
2: 4 for burning fragrant incense **b** him, 4200+7156
2: 6 as a place to burn sacrifices **b** him? 4200+7156
5: 6 gathered about him were **b** the ark, 4200+7156
6:12 Then Solomon stood **b** the altar of 4200+7156
6:13 and then knelt down **b** the whole assembly 5584
6:16 'You shall never fail to have a man to sit **b** me on the throne 4200+4946+7156
6:16 in all they do to walk **b** me according 4200+7156
6:22 and he comes and swears the oath **b** 4200+7156
6:24 praying and making supplication **b** you 4200+7156
7: 4 people offered sacrifices **b** the LORD. 4200+7156
7:17 if you walk **b** me as David your father did, 4200+7156
9: 7 who continually stand **b** you 4200+7156
13:15 God routed Jeroboam and all Israel **b** 4200+7156
13:16 The Israelites fled **b** Judah, 4946+7156
14:12 The LORD struck down the Cushites **b** 4200+7156
14:13 they were crushed **b** the LORD 4200+7156
18: 9 all the prophets prophesying **b** them. 4200+7156
18:20 stood **b** the LORD and said, 4200+7156
19:10 In every case that comes **b** you 6584
19:11 Levites will serve as officials **b** you. 4200+7156
20: 7 not drive out the inhabitants of this land **b** your people 4200+4946+7156
20: 9 we will stand in your presence **b** 4200+7156
20:13 stood there **b** the LORD. 4200+7156
20:18 and Jerusalem fell down in worship **b** 4200+7156
24:20 He stood **b** the people and said, 4946+6584
25: 8 God will overthrow you **b** the enemy, 4200+7156
26:19 in their presence **b** the incense altar in 4946+6584
27: 6 because he walked steadfastly **b** 4200+7156
28: 3 the nations the LORD had driven out **b** 4946+7156
28:13 "or we will be **guilty** *b* the LORD. AIT
29:11 the LORD has chosen you to stand **b** him 4200+7156
29:11 to minister **b** him and to burn incense." 4200
29:23 sin offering were brought **b** the king 4200+7156
31:20 and faithful **b** the LORD his God. 4200+7156
32: 6 over the people and assembled them **b** him 448
32:12 'You must worship **b** one altar 4200+7156
33: 2 the nations the LORD had driven out **b** 4946+7156
33: 9 LORD had destroyed **b** the Israelites. 4946+7156
33:12 and humbled himself greatly **b** the God 4200+4946+7156
33:19 and set up Asherah poles and idols **b** 4200+7156
33:23 he did not humble himself **b** the LORD; 4200+4946+7156
34:27 you humbled yourself **b** God 4200+4946+7156
34:27 because you humbled yourself **b** me 4200+7156
36:12 not humble himself **b** Jeremiah the prophet, 4200+4946+7156
Ezr 7:28 to me **b** the king and his advisers 4200+7156
8:21 that we might humble ourselves **b** our God 4200+7156
8:29 the house of the LORD in Jerusalem **b** 4200+7156
9:15 Here we are **b** you in our guilt, 4200+7156
10: 1 down **b** the house of God, 4200+7156
10: 3 Now let us make a covenant **b** our God 4200
10: 6 Then Ezra withdrew from **b** the house 4200+7156
10: 9 all the people were sitting in the **square** *b* AIT
Ne 1: 4 and prayed **b** the God of heaven. 4200+7156
1: 6 hear the prayer your servant is praying **b** you day and night 4200+7156
2: 1 I had not been sad in his presence **b;** NIH
4:11 "**B** they know it or see us, 4202
8: 1 in the square **b** the Water Gate. 4200+7156
8: 2 Ezra the priest brought the Law **b** the assembly, 4200+7156
8: 3 the square **b** the Water Gate 4200+7156
9:11 You divided the sea **b** them, 4200+7156
9:24 You subdued **b** them the Canaanites, 4200+7156
13: 4 **B** this, Eliashib the priest had been put 4200+7156
13:19 the gates of Jerusalem **b** the Sabbath, 4200+7156
Est 1:11 to bring **b** him Queen Vashti, 4200+7156
1:17 to be brought **b** him, 4200+7156
2:12 **B** a girl's turn came to go in 928
Est 6: 9 through the city streets, proclaiming **b** him, 4200+7156
6:11 through the city streets, proclaiming **b** him, 4200+7156
6:13 **b** whom your downfall has started, 4200+7156
7: 6 Haman was terrified **b** the king and queen. 4200+4946+7156
8: 4 and she arose and stood **b** him. 4200+7156
Job 1: 6 the angels came to present themselves **b** 6584
2: 1 the angels came to present themselves **b** 6584
2: 1 also came with them to present himself **b** 6584
4:16 A form stood **b** my eyes, 4200+5584
5: 8 I would lay my cause **b** him. 448
7: 4 I lie down I think, '**How long** *b* I get up?' AIT
9: 2 But how can a mortal be righteous **b** God? 6640
10:18 I wish I had died **b** any eye saw me. 4202
10:21 **b** I go to the place of no return, 928+3270
13:16 no godless man would dare come **b** him! 4200+7156
14: 3 Will you bring him **b** you for judgment? 6640
15: 7 Were you brought forth **b** the hills? 4200+7156
15:32 **B** his time he will be paid in full, 928+4202
16:22 a few years will pass **b** I go on the journey 2256
21: 8 their offspring **b** their eyes. 4200
21:18 How often are they like straw **b** the wind, 4200+7156
21:33 and a countless throng goes **b** him. 4200+7156
22:16 They were carried off **b** their time, 4202
23: 4 I would state my case **b** him 4200+7156
23: 7 an upright man could present his case **b** 6640
23:15 That is why I am terrified **b** him; 4946+7156
25: 4 How then can a man be righteous **b** God? 6640
26: 6 Death is naked **b** God; 5584
30:22 You snatch me up and drive me **b** the wind; 448
32: 4 Now Elihu had waited **b** speaking to Job NIH
33: 6 I am just like you **b** God; 4200
34:23 that they should come **b** him for judgment. 448
34:28 They caused the cry of the poor to come **b** 6584
35:14 your case is **b** him and you must wait 4200+7156
41:22 dismay goes **b** him. 4200+7156
41:25 they retreat **b** his thrashing. 4946
42:10 and gave him twice as much as he had **b.** NIH
42:11 everyone who had known him **b** came 4200+7156
Ps 5: 3 in the morning I lay my requests **b** you 4200
5: 8 make straight your way **b** me. 4200+7156
9: 3 they stumble and perish **b** you. 4946+7156
16: 8 I have set the LORD always **b** me. 4200+5584
18: 6 my cry came **b** him, into his ears. 4200+7156
18:22 All his laws are **b** me; 4200+5584
18:23 I have been blameless **b** him 6640
18:44 foreigners cringe **b** me. 4200
22:25 **b** those who fear you will I fulfill my vows. 5584
22:27 the families of the nations will bow down **b** him, 4200+7156
22:29 all who go down to the dust will kneel **b** him— 4200+7156
23: 5 You prepare a table **b** me in the presence of my enemies. 4200+7156
26: 3 for your love is ever **b** me, 4200+5584+6524
34: T pretended to be insane **b** Abimelech, 4200+7156
35: 5 May they be like chaff **b** the wind, 4200+7156
36: 1 There is no fear of God **b** his eyes. 4200+5584
37: 7 Be still **b** the LORD and wait patiently 4200
38: 9 All my longings lie open **b** you, O Lord; 5584
39: 5 the span of my years is as nothing **b** you. 5584
39:13 that I may rejoice again **b** I depart 928+3270
44:10 You made us retreat **b** the enemy, 4974
44:15 My disgrace is **b** me all day long, 5584
50: 3 a fire devours **b** him, 4200+7156
50: 8 which are ever **b** me. 4200+5584
51: 3 and my sin is always **b** me. 5584
56:13 I may walk **b** God in the light of life. 4200+7156
58: 9 **B** your pots can feel [the heat of] 928+3270
59:10 God *will* **go b** me and will let me gloat 7709
66: 3 that your enemies cringe **b** you. 4200
68: 1 may his foes flee **b** him. 4946+7156
68: 2 as wax melts **b** the fire, 4946+7156
68: 2 may the wicked perish **b** God. 4946+7156
68: 3 But may the righteous be glad and rejoice **b** God; 4200+7156
68: 4 and rejoice **b** him. 4200+7156
68: 7 you went out **b** your people, O God, 4200+7156
68: 8 the heavens poured down rain, **b** God, 4946+7156
68: 8 **b** God, the God of Israel. 4946+7156
68:28 O God, as you have done **b.** NIH
69:19 all my enemies are **b** you. 5584
69:22 the table set **b** them become a snare; 4200+7156
72: 9 The desert tribes will bow **b** him 4200+7156
73:22 I was a brute beast **b** you. 6640
76: 7 Who can stand **b** you when you are angry? 4200+7156
78:30 **b** they turned from the food they craved, 4202
78:55 He drove out nations **b** them 4946+7156
79:10 **B** our eyes, make known among the nations 4200
79:11 May the groans of the prisoners come **b** you; 4200+7156
80: 2 **b** Ephraim, Benjamin 4200+7156
81:15 Those who hate the LORD would cringe **b** 4200
83:13 O my God, like chaff **b** the wind. 4200+7156
84: 7 till each appears **b** God in Zion. 448
85:13 Righteousness goes **b** him 4200+7156
86: 9 and worship **b** you, O Lord; 4200+7156
88: 1 day and night I cry out **b** you. 5584
88: 2 May my prayer come **b** you; 4200+7156
88:13 in the morning my prayer **comes b** you. 7709
89:14 love and faithfulness go **b** you. 7156
89:23 I will crush his foes **b** him and strike 4946+7156

Ps 89:36 and his throne endure **b** me like the sun; 5584
90: 2 **B** the mountains were born 928+3270
90: 8 You have set our iniquities **b** you, 4200+5584
95: 2 Let us come **b** him with thanksgiving 7156
95: 6 let us kneel **b** the LORD our Maker; 4200+7156
96: 6 Splendor and majesty are **b** him; 4200+7156
96: 9 tremble **b** him, all the earth. 4946+7156
96:13 they will sing **b** the LORD, 4200+7156
97: 3 Fire goes **b** him and consumes his foes 4200+7156
97: 5 The mountains melt like wax **b** the LORD, 4200+4946+7156
97: 5 **b** the Lord of all the earth. 4200+4946+7156
98: 6 shout for joy **b** the LORD, the King. 4200+7156
98: 9 let them sing **b** the LORD, 4200+7156
100: 2 come **b** him with joyful songs. 4200+7156
101: 3 I will set **b** my eyes no vile thing. 4200+5584
102: T and pours out his lament **b** the LORD 4200+7156
102:28 their descendants will be established **b** 4200+7156
105:17 and he sent a man **b** them— 4200+7156
106:23 stood in the breach **b** him 4200+7156
109:14 of his fathers be remembered **b** the LORD; 448
109:15 May their sins always remain **b** the LORD, 5584
116: 9 that I may walk **b** the LORD in the land of the living. 4200+7156
119:46 of your statutes **b** kings and will not be put 5584
119:67 **B** I was afflicted I went astray, 3270
119:147 I rise **b** dawn and cry for help; 928
119:169 May my cry come **b** you, O LORD; 4200+7156
119:170 May my supplication come **b** you; 4200+7156
129: 6 which withers **b** it can grow; 7712
138: 1 **b** the "gods" I will sing your praise. 5584
139: 4 **B** a word is 401+3954
139: 5 You hem me in—behind and **b;** 7710
139:16 in your book **b** one of them came to be. 4202
140:13 and the upright will live **b** you. 907+7156
141: 2 May my prayer be set **b** you like incense; 4200+7156
142: 2 I pour out my complaint **b** him; 4200+7156
142: 2 **b** him I tell my trouble. 4200+7156
143: 2 for no one living is righteous **b** you. 4200+7156
Pr 2:17 and ignored the **covenant** she *made b* God. AIT
4:25 fix your gaze directly **b** you. 5584
8:22 **b** his deeds of old; 7710
8:23 from the beginning, **b** the world **began.** 7710
8:25 **b** the mountains were settled in place, 928+3270
8:25 **b** the hills, I was given birth, 4200+7156
8:26 **b** he made the earth or its fields 4202+6330
15:11 and Destruction lie open **b** the LORD— 5584
15:33 and humility comes **b** honor. 4200+7156
16:18 Pride goes **b** destruction, 4200+7156
16:18 a haughty spirit **b** a fall. 4200+7156
17:14 drop the matter **b** a dispute breaks out. 4200+7156
18:12 **B** his downfall a man's heart is proud, 4200+7156
18:12 but humility comes **b** honor. 4200+7156
18:13 He who answers **b** listening— 928+3270
22:29 He will serve **b** kings; 4200+7156
22:29 he will not serve **b** obscure men. 4200+7156
23: 1 note well what is **b** you, 4200+7156
25: 7 to humiliate you **b** a nobleman. 4200+7156
27: 4 but who can stand **b** jealousy? 4200+7156
30: 7 do not refuse me **b** I die: 928+3270
30:30 who retreats **b** nothing; 4946+7156
Ecc 1:10 it was here **b** our **time.** 4200+4946+7156
1:16 over Jerusalem **b** me; 4200+7156
2: 7 flocks than anyone in Jerusalem **b** me. 4200+7156
2: 9 by far than anyone in Jerusalem **b** me. 4200+7156
3:15 and what will be has been **b;** 3893
4:16 to all the people who were **b** them. 4200+7156
5: 2 do not be hasty in your heart to utter anything **b** God. 4200+7156
6: 8 by knowing how to conduct himself **b** 5584
7:17 why die **b** your time? 928+4202
8: 2 I say, because you took an **oath** *b* God. AIT
8:12 who are reverent **b** God. 4200+4946+7156
10:11 If a snake bites **b** it is charmed, 928+4202
12: 1 **b** the days of trouble come and 889+4202+6330
12: 2 **b** the sun and the light and the moon and the stars grow dark, 889+4202+6330
12: 6 **b** the silver cord is severed, 889+4202+6330
12: 6 **b** the pitcher is shattered at the spring, NIH
SS 6:12 **B** I realized it, 4202
Isa 1: 7 by foreigners **right b** you, 4200+5584
1:12 When you come to **appear b** me, 7156+8011
1:23 the widow's case does not come **b** them. 448
7:16 But **b** the boy knows enough to reject 928+3270
8: 4 **B** the boy knows how to say 'My father' 928+3270
9: 3 they rejoice **b** you as people rejoice at 4200+7156
10:34 Lebanon will fall **b** the Mighty One. 928
13:16 Their infants will be dashed to pieces **b** 4200
17:13 driven **b** the wind like chaff 4200+7156
17:13 like tumbleweed **b** a gale. 4200+7156
17:14 **B** the morning, they are gone! 928+3270
18: 5 For, **b** the harvest, when the blossom is gone 4200+7156
19: 1 The idols of Egypt tremble **b** him, 4946+7156
23:18 Her profits will go to those who live **b** 4200+7156
24:23 and **b** its elders, gloriously. 5584
28: 4 will be like a fig ripe **b** harvest— 928+3270
31: 8 They will flee **b** the sword 4946+7156
36: 7 "You must worship **b** this altar"? 4200+7156
37:14 the LORD and spread it out **b** the LORD. 4200+7156
37:27 scorched **b** it grows up. 4200+7156
37:33 *He will* not **come b** it with shield or build 7709
38: 3 how I have walked **b** you faithfully 4200+7156
40:17 **B** him all the nations are as nothing; 5584
41: 1 "Be silent **b** me, you islands! 448
41: 2 over to him and subdues kings **b** him. 4200+7156
Isa 41: 3 by a path his feet have not traveled **b.** NIH
42: 9 **b** they spring into being 928+3270
42:16 I will turn the darkness into light **b** them 4200+7156
43:10 **B** me no god was formed, 4200+7156
44: 7 and lay out **b** me what has happened 4200
45: 1 to subdue nations **b** him 4200+7156
45: 1 to open doors **b** him so that gates 4200+7156
45: 2 I will go **b** you and will level 4200+7156
45:14 down **b** you and plead with you, saying, 448
45:23 **B** me every knee will bow; 4200
48: 5 **b** they happened I announced them to you 928+3270
48: 7 you have not heard of them **b** today. 4200+7156
48:19 be cut off nor destroyed from **b** me." 4200+7156
49: 1 **B** I was born the LORD called me; 4946
49:16 your walls are ever **b** me. 5584
49:23 They will bow down **b** you with their faces 4200
52:12 for the LORD will go **b** you, 4200+7156
53: 2 He grew up **b** him like a tender shoot, 4200+7156
53: 7 and as a sheep **b** her shearers is silent, 4200+7156
55:12 and hills will burst into song **b** you, 4200+7156
57:16 the spirit of man would grow faint **b** me— 4200+4946+7156
58: 8 then your righteousness will go **b** you, 4200+7156
60:14 of your oppressors will come bowing **b** 448
61:11 and praise spring up **b** all nations. 5584
63:12 who divided the waters **b** them, 4946+7156
64: 1 the mountains would tremble **b** you! 4946+7156
64: 2 and cause the nations to quake **b** you! 4946+7156
64: 3 and the mountains trembled **b** you. 4946+7156
65: 6 "See, it stands written **b** me: 4200+7156
65:24 **B** they call I will answer; 3270
66: 7 **"B** she goes into labor, she gives birth; 928+3270
66: 7 **b** the pains come upon her, 928+3270
66:22 the new earth that I make will endure **b** 4200+7156
66:23 all mankind will come and bow down **b** 4200+7156
Jer 1: 5 **"B** I formed you in the womb I knew you, 928+3270
1: 5 **b** you were born I set you apart; 928+3270
1:17 or I will terrify you **b** them. 4200+7156
2:22 the stain of your guilt is still **b** me," 4200+7156
4:26 all its towns lay in ruins **b** the LORD, 4946+7156
4:26 before the LORD, **b** his fierce anger. 4946+7156
6: 7 sickness and wounds are ever **b** me. 6584+7156
6:21 "I will put obstacles **b** this people. 448
7:10 come and stand **b** me in this house, 4200+7156
9:13 which I set **b** them; 4200+7156
12: 1 O LORD, when I bring a case **b** you. 448
12:11 parched and desolate **b** me; 6584
13:16 Give glory to the LORD your God **b** 928+3270
13:16 **b** your feet stumble on the darkening hills. 928+3270
15: 1 if Moses and Samuel were to stand **b** me, 4200+7156
15: 9 to the sword **b** their enemies," 4200+7156
16: 9 **B** your eyes and in your days I will bring 4200
17:16 What passes my lips is **open b** you. 5790+7156
18:17 I will scatter them **b** their enemies; 4200+7156
18:20 I stood **b** you and spoke in their behalf 4200+7156
18:23 Let them be overthrown **b** you; 4200+7156
19: 7 I will make them fall by the sword **b** 4200+7156
21: 8 I am setting **b** you the way of life and 4200+7156
26: 4 which I have set **b** you, 4200+7156
28: 5 the prophet Hananiah **b** the priests 4200+6524
28:11 and he said **b** all the people, 4200+6524
29:21 he will put them to death **b** your very eyes. 4200
30:20 their community will be established **b** me; 4200+7156
31:36 Israel ever cease to be a nation **b** me." 4200+7156
33: 7 will rebuild them as they were **b.** 928+2021+8037
33: 9 and honor **b** all nations on earth that hear 4200
33:11 the fortunes of the land as they were **b,'** 928+2021+8037
33:18 to have a man to stand **b** me continually 4200+4946+7156
33:21 the Levites who are priests **ministering** *b* AIT
33:22 the Levites *who* **minister** *b* me as countless AIT
34:15 made a covenant **b** me in the house 4200+7156
34:18 terms of the covenant they made **b** me, 4200+7156
35: 5 of wine and some cups **b** the men of 4200+7156
36: 7 Perhaps they will bring their petition **b** 4200+7156
36: 9 of fasting **b** the LORD was proclaimed 4200+7156
37:20 Let me bring my petition **b** you: 4200+7156
38:10 the prophet out of the cistern **b** he dies." 928+3270
39: 6 slaughtered the sons of Zedekiah **b** his eyes 4200
39:16 they will be fulfilled **b** your **eyes.** 4200+7156
40: 4 Look, the whole country lies **b** you; 4200+7156
40: 5 However, **b** Jeremiah turned to go, 4202+6388
40:10 at Mizpah to represent you **b** 4200+7156
41: 4 **b** anyone knew about it, 4202
44:10 decrees I set **b** you and your fathers. 4200+7156
47: 1 Philistines **b** Pharaoh attacked Gaza: 928+3270
49:37 I will shatter Elam **b** their foes, 4200+7156
49:37 **b** those who seek their lives; 4200+7156
50:24 and you were caught **b** you knew it; 4202
51: 5 though their land is full of guilt **b** 4946
51:24 **"B** your eyes I will repay Babylon 4200
52:10 the sons of Zedekiah **b** his eyes; 4200
La 1: 5 captive **b** the foe. 4200+7156
1: 6 in weakness they have fled **b** the pursuer. 4200+7156
1:22 "Let all their wickedness come **b** you; 4200+7156
3:35 deny a man his rights **b** the Most High, 5584+7156
Eze 2:10 which he unrolled **b** me. 4200+7156
3: 1 eat what *is* **b** *you,* eat this scroll; 5162
Eze 3:20 and I put a stumbling block **b** him, 4200+7156
5: 9 I will do to you what *I have* never **done** *b* AIT
8: 1 the elders of Judah were sitting **b** me, 4200+7156
8: 4 And there **b** me was the glory of the God NIH
14: 3 and put wicked stumbling blocks **b** 5790
14: 4 a wicked stumbling block **b** his face and 5790
14: 7 a wicked stumbling block **b** his face and 5790
16:18 offered my oil and incense **b** them. 4200+7156
16:19 offered as fragrant incense **b** them. 4200+7156
16:50 and did detestable things **b** me. 4200+7156
16:55 will return to *what* they were **b;** 7712
16:55 to *what* you were **b.** 7712
16:57 **b** your wickedness was uncovered. 928+3270
21: 6 Groan **b** them with broken heart 4200+6524
22:30 and stand **b** me in the gap on behalf of 4200+7156
23:41 with a table spread **b** it on which 4200+7156
28:17 I made a spectacle of you **b** kings. 4200+7156
30:24 and he will groan **b** him like 4200+7156
32:10 when I brandish my sword **b** them. 6584+7156
33:22 Now the evening **b** the man arrived, 4200+7156
33:22 and he opened my mouth **b** the man came 6330
33:31 and sit **b** you to listen to your words, 4200+7156
36:11 and will make you prosper more than **b.** 8035
36:23 when I show myself holy through you **b** 4200
37:20 Hold **b** their eyes the sticks 4200
38:16 when I show myself holy through you **b** 4200
40:46 near to the LORD to **minister** *b* him." AIT
41:22 "This is the table that is **b** the LORD." 4200+7156
42:14 They are to put on other clothes **b** they go 2256
43:11 Write these down **b** them so that 4200+6524
43:19 who come near to **minister** *b* me, AIT
43:24 You are to offer them **b** the LORD, 4200+7156
44:11 sacrifices for the people and stand **b** 4200+7156
44:15 are to come near to **minister** *b* me; AIT
44:15 are to stand **b** me to offer sacrifices 4200+7156
44:16 to **minister** *b* me and perform my service. AIT
45: 4 and who draw near to **minister** *b* AIT
46: 9 people of the land come **b** the LORD 4200+7156
Da 2: 2 they came in and stood **b** the king, 4200+7156
2:31 there **b** you stood a large statue— 10378+10619
2:46 Then King Nebuchadnezzar fell prostrate **b** NIH
3: 3 and they stood **b** it. 10378+10619
3:13 So these men were brought **b** the king, 10621
3:16 we do not need to **defend** ourselves *b* you AIT
4: 6 the wise men of Babylon be brought **b** me 10621
4:10 and there **b** me stood a tree in the middle of NIH
4:13 I looked, and there **b** me was a messenger, NIH
4:36 and became even greater than **b.** NIH
5:13 So Daniel was brought **b** the king, 10621
5:15 and enchanters were brought **b** me 10621
6:10 just as he had done **b.** 10180+10427+10622
6:22 Nor have I ever done any wrong **b** you, 10621
6:24 And **b** they reached the floor of the den, 10379
7: 2 "In my vision at night I looked, and there **b** NIH
7: 5 "And there **b** me was a second beast, NIH
7: 6 I looked, and there **b** me was another beast, NIH
7: 7 and there **b** me was a fourth beast— NIH
7: 8 there **b** me was another horn, a little one, NIH
7: 8 three of the first horns were uprooted **b** it. 10427+10621
7:10 coming out from **b** him. 10621
7:10 ten thousand times ten thousand stood **b** 10621
7:13 and there **b** me was one like a son of man, NIH
7:20 **b** which three of them fell— 10427+10621
8: 3 and there **b** me was a ram with two horns, NIH
8:15 there **b** me stood one who looked like 4200+5584
10: 5 and there **b** me was a man dressed in linen, NIH
10:12 and to humble yourself **b** your God, 4200+7156
10:16 I said to the one standing **b** me, 4200+5584
11:22 be swept away **b** him; 4200+4946+7156
11:29 be different from what it was **b.** 8037
12: 5 looked, and there **b** me stood two others, NIH
12: 6 be **b** these astonishing things are fulfilled?" NIH
Hos 2:10 now I will expose her lewdness **b** the eyes 4200
7: 2 they are always **b** me. 5584+7156
Joel 1: 9 *those who* **minister** *b* the LORD. AIT
1:13 wail, *you who* **minister** *b* the altar. AIT
1:13 *you who* **minister** *b* my God; AIT
1:16 not the food been cut off **b** our very eyes— 5584
2: 3 **B** them fire devours, 4200+7156
2: 3 **B** them the land is like the garden of Eden, 4200+7156
2:10 **B** them the earth shakes, the sky trembles, 4200+7156
2:17 Let the priests, *who* **minister** *b* the LORD, AIT
2:23 both autumn and spring rains, as **b.** 8037
2:31 the moon to blood **b** the coming 4200+7156
Am 1: 1 what he saw concerning Israel two years **b** the earthquake, 4200+7156
2: 9 "I destroyed the Amorite **b** them, 4946+7156
Jnh 1: 2 its wickedness has come up **b** me." 4200+7156
1:13 for the sea grew even wilder than **b.** NIH
Mic 1: 4 like wax **b** the fire, 4946+7156
2:13 One who breaks open the way will go up **b** them, 4200+7156
2:13 Their king will pass through **b** them, 4200+7156
6: 1 **plead** *your* **case** *b* the mountains; AIT
6: 6 With what *shall I* **come b** the LORD 7709
6: 6 before the LORD and bow down **b** 4200
6: 6 *Shall I* **come b** him with burnt offerings, 7709
Na 1: 5 The mountains quake **b** him and 4946
1: 6 the rocks are shattered **b** him. 4946
Hab 1: 3 Destruction and violence are **b** me; 4200+5584
2:20 let all the earth be silent **b** him." 4946+7156
3: 5 Plague went **b** him; 4200+7156
Zep 1: 7 Be silent **b** the Sovereign LORD, 4946+7156
2: 2 **b** the appointed time arrives and 928+3270

Zep 2: 2 **b** the fierce anger of the LORD comes 928+3270+4202
2: 2 **b** the day of the LORD's wrath comes 928+3270+4202
3:20 I restore your fortunes **b** your very eyes," 4200
Hag 2:15 how things were **b** one stone was laid 3270+4946
Zec 1: 8 there **b** me was a man riding a red horse! NIH
1:18 and there **b** me were four horns! NIH
2: 1 and there **b** me was a man with NIH
2:13 Be still **b** the LORD, all mankind, 4946+7156
3: 1 the high priest standing **b** the angel of 4200+7156
3: 3 filthy clothes as he stood **b** the angel. 4200+7156
3: 4 to those who were standing **b** him, 4200+7156
3: 8 and your associates seated **b** you, 4200+7156
4: 7 **B** Zerubbabel you will become level ground. 4200+7156
5: 1 and there **b** me was a flying scroll! NIH
5: 9 and there **b** me were two women, NIH
6: 1 and there **b** me were four chariots coming out from between two mountains— NIH
8:10 **B** that time there were no wages 4200+7156
10: 8 they will be as numerous as **b**. 8049[S]
12: 8 like the Angel of the LORD going **b** them. 4200+7156
Mal 2: 9 be despised and humiliated **b** all the people, 4200
3: 1 who will prepare the way **b** me. 4200+7156
3:14 like mourners **b** the LORD Almighty? 4946+7156
4: 5 I will send you the prophet Elijah **b** 4200+7156
Mt 1:18 but **b** they came together, 2445+4570
5:12 the prophets who were **b** you. 4574
5:16 In the same way, let your light shine **b** men, 1869
6: 1 to do your 'acts of righteousness' **b** men, 1869
6: 8 for your Father knows what you need **b** 4574
8: 2 with leprosy came and **knelt b** him and said, 4665
8:29 "Have you come here to torture us **b** 4574
9:18 a ruler came and **knelt b** him and said, 4686
10:18 On my account you will be brought **b** 2093
10:23 cities of Israel **b** the Son of Man comes. 323+2401
10:32 "Whoever acknowledges me **b** men, 1869
10:32 I will also acknowledge him **b** my Father 1869
10:33 But whoever disowns me **b** men, 1869
10:33 I will disown him **b** my Father in heaven. 1869
11:10 who will prepare your way **b** you.' 1869
15: 2 They don't wash their hands **b** they eat!" 4020
15:25 The woman came and **knelt b** him. 4686
16:28 not taste death **b** they see the Son 323+2401
17: 2 There he was transfigured **b** them. 1869
17: 3 Just then there appeared *b* **them** Moses AIT
17:14 a man approached Jesus and **knelt b** him. 1206
18:26 "The servant fell **on** *his* **knees b** him. 4686
24:38 For in the days **b** the flood, 4574
25:32 All the nations will be gathered **b** him, 1869
26:34 "this very night, **b** the rooster crows, 4570
26:70 But he denied it **b** them all. 1869
26:75 "**B** the rooster crows, 4570
27:11 Meanwhile Jesus stood **b** the governor, 1869
Mk 3:11 *they* **fell down b** him and cried out, 4700
6:41 Then he gave them to his disciples to **set b** 4192
8: 6 and gave them to his disciples to **set b** 4192
9: 1 not taste death **b** they see the kingdom 323+2401
9: 2 There he was transfigured **b** them. 1869
9: 4 there appeared *b* **them** Elijah and Moses, AIT
10:17 and **fell on** his **knees b** him. 1206
13: 9 of me you will stand **b** governors and kings 2093
14:30 **b** the rooster crows twice you yourself will disown me three times." 4570
14:60 high priest stood up **b them** and asked Jesus, 1650+3545
14:72 "**B** the rooster crows twice you will disown me three times." 4570
15:42 the **day b the Sabbath).** 4640
Lk 1: 8 on duty and he was serving as priest **b** God, 1882
1:17 And he will go on **b** the Lord, 1967
1:75 and righteousness **b** him all our days. 1967
1:76 on **b** the Lord to prepare the way for him, 1967
2:21 the name the angel had given him **b** 4574
2:26 by the Holy Spirit that he would not die **b** he had seen the Lord's Christ. 323+2445+4570
4:35 the demon threw the man down **b** them all 1650+3545+3836
5:18 to take him into the house to lay him **b** 1967
7:27 who will prepare your way **b** you.' 1869
9:16 Then he gave them to the disciples *to* **set b** 4192
9:27 not taste death **b** they see the kingdom 323+2401
10: 8 eat what *is* **set b** you. 4192
11: 6 and I have nothing *to* **set b** him.' 4192
11:38 that Jesus did not first wash **b** the meal, 4574
12: 8 whoever acknowledges me **b** men, 1869
12: 8 also acknowledge him **b** the angels of God. 1869
12: 9 But he who disowns me **b** men will 1967
12: 9 before men will be disowned **b** the angels 1967
12:11 "When you are brought **b** synagogues, 2093
18:14 went home **justified b God.** 1467
21:12 "But **b** all this, they will lay hands on you 4574
21:12 you will be brought **b** kings and governors, 2093
21:36 and that you may be able to stand **b** the Son 1869
22:15 to eat this Passover with you **b** I suffer. 4574
22:34 "I tell you, Peter, **b** the rooster crows today, 2401
22:61 "**B** the rooster crows today, 4570
22:66 met together, and Jesus was led **b** them. 1650
23:12 **b this** *they had* **been** 1639+4732
24:19 in word and deed **b** God and all the people. 1883
Jn 1:15 because he was **b** me.'" 4755
1:30 because he was **b** me.' 4755
1:48 while you were still under the fig tree **b** 4574
3:24 (This was **b** John was put in prison.) 4037
4:49 "Sir, come down **b** my child dies." 4570
5:45 do not think I will accuse you **b** the Father. 4639
6:62 the Son of Man ascend to where he was **b!** 4728
8: 3 They made her stand **b the group** 1877+3545
8:58 Jesus answered, "**b** Abraham was born, I am!" 4570
10: 8 All who ever came **b** me were thieves 4574
11:55 ceremonial cleansing **b** the Passover. 4574
12: 1 Six days **b** the Passover, 4574
12:35 **b** darkness overtakes you. 2671+3590
13: 1 It was just **b** the Passover Feast. 4574
13:19 "I am telling you now **b** it happens, 4574
13:38 I tell you the truth, **b** the rooster crows, 2401+4005
14:19 **B long,** the world will 2285+3625
14:29 I have told you now **b** it happens, 4570
17: 5 the glory I had with you **b** the world began. 4574
17:24 because you loved me **b** the creation of 4574
Ac 1: 9 he was taken up **b their very eyes,** 899+1063
2:20 the moon to blood **b** the coming of the great 4570
2:25 "'I saw the Lord always **b** me. 1967
3:13 and you disowned him **b** Pilate, 2848+4725
4: 7 They had Peter and John brought **b** them 1877+3545+3836
4:10 that this man stands **b** you healed. 1967
5: 4 Didn't it belong to you **b** it was sold? NIG
5:27 they made them appear **b** the Sanhedrin to 1877
6:12 They seized Stephen and brought him **b** 1650
7: 2 **b** he lived in Haran. 2445+4570
7:40 'Make us gods who *will* **go b** us. 4638
7:45 the land from the nations God drove out **b** them. 608+4725
8:21 because your heart is not right **b** God. 1882
8:32 and as a lamb **b** the shearer is silent, 1883
9:15 to carry my name **b** the Gentiles 1967
9:15 and their kings and **b** the people of Israel. NIG
10: 4 up as a memorial offering **b** God. 1869
10:30 Suddenly a man in shining clothes stood **b** 1967
12: 6 The night **b** Herod was to bring him to trial, 4021
13:24 **B** the coming of Jesus, 4574+4725
16:20 They **brought** them **b** the magistrates 4642
16:29 in and **fell** trembling **b** Paul and Silas. 4700
16:34 into his house and **set a meal b** them; 4192+5544
17: 6 and some other brothers **b** the city officials, 2093
18:18 **B** he sailed, he had his hair cut off NIG
19:30 Paul wanted to appear **b** the crowd, NIG
19:33 in order to make a defense *b* **the people.** AIT
22:30 he brought Paul and had him stand **b** them. 1650
23:15 the commander to bring him **b** you on 1650
23:15 We are ready to kill him **b** he gets here." 4574
23:20 to bring Paul **b** the Sanhedrin tomorrow on 1650
24: 1 against Paul *b* **the governor.** AIT
24: 2 Tertullus presented his case **b** Felix: NIG
24:16 to keep my conscience clear **b** God 4639
24:19 to be here **b** you and bring charges 2093
24:20 in me when I stood **b** the Sanhedrin— 2093
24:21 the dead that I am on trial **b** you today.'" 2093
25: 2 and Jewish leaders appeared *b* **him** AIT
25: 6 and ordered that Paul be brought **b** him. NIG
25: 9 up to Jerusalem and stand trial **b** me there 2093
25:10 "I am now standing **b** Caesar's court, 2093
25:16 not the Roman custom to hand over any man **b** he has faced his accusers 2445+4570
25:26 Therefore *I have* **brought** him **b** all of you, 4575
25:26 and especially **b** you, King Agrippa, 2093
26: 2 to stand **b** you today as I make my defense 2093
27:14 **B very long,** a wind of hurricane force, 3552+4024+4498
27:21 Paul stood up **b** them and said: 1877+3545
27:24 You must **stand trial b** Caesar; 4225
27:33 **Just b** dawn Paul urged them all to eat. 948+4005
Ro 3:18 "There is no fear of God **b** their eyes." 595
4: 2 but not **b** God. 4639
4:10 Was it after he was circumcised, or **b?** NIG
4:10 It was not after, but **b!** NIG
4:12 the faith our father Abraham had **b** he was **circumcised.** 213+1877
5:13 for **b** the law was given, 948
9:11 **Yet, b** the twins were born 3609
14:10 *we will* all **stand b** God's judgment seat. 4225
14:11 says the Lord, 'every knee will bow *b* **me;** AIT
16: 7 and they were in Christ **b** I was. 4574
1Co 1:29 so that no one may boast **b** him. 1967
2: 7 and that God destined for our glory **b** 4574
4: 5 judge nothing **b** the appointed time; 4574
6: 1 dare he take it **b** the ungodly 2093
6: 1 the ungodly for judgment instead of **b** 2093
10:27 eat whatever *is* **put b** you 4192
11:28 A man ought to examine himself **b** he eats NIG
2Co 2:17 in Christ we speak **b** God with sincerity, 2978
3: 4 as this is ours through Christ **b** God. 4639
5:10 For we must all appear **b** the judgment seat 1869
7: 3 *I have* **said b** that you have such a place 4625
7:12 that **b** God you could see for yourselves 1967
12:21 I come again my God will humble me **b** 4639
Gal 1:17 to see those who were apostles **b** I was, 4574
1:20 I assure you **b** God 1967
2: 2 I went in response to a revelation and **set b** 423
2:12 **B** certain men came from James, 4574
3: 1 **B** your very eyes Jesus Christ was clearly portrayed as crucified. 2848
3:11 Clearly no one is justified **b** God by 4123
3:23 **B** this faith came, we were held prisoners 4574
5:21 I warn you, as *I* **did b,** 4625[S]
Eph 1: 4 For he chose us in him **b** the creation of 4574
3:14 For this reason I kneel **b** the Father, 4639
Php 3:18 as I have often told you **b** and NIG
Col 1:17 He is **b** all things, 4574
1Th 1: 3 We continually remember **b** our God 1869
1Th 5:27 *I* **charge** you **b** the Lord 1941
1Ti 6:13 who while testifying **b** Pontius Pilate made 2093
2Ti 1: 9 This grace was given us in Christ Jesus **b** 4574
2:14 Warn them **b** God against quarreling 1967
4:21 Do your best to get here **b** winter. 4574
Tit 1: 2 promised **b** the beginning of time, 4574
Heb 4: 7 as *was* **said b:** "Today, if you hear 4625
4:13 and laid bare *b* **the eyes** of him AIT
6:20 who **went b** us, has entered on our behalf. 4596
11: 5 For **b** he was taken, 4574
12: 2 who for the joy **set b** him endured the cross, 4618
Jas 4:10 Humble yourselves **b** the Lord, 1967
1Pe 1:20 *He was* **chosen b** the creation of the world, 4589
2:20 this is commendable **b** God. 4123
1Jn 2:28 and unashamed **b** him at his coming. 608
3:21 we have confidence **b** God 4639
Jude 1:24 and to present you **b** his glorious presence 2979
1:25 through Jesus Christ our Lord, **b** all ages, 4574
Rev 1: 4 and from the seven spirits **b** his throne, 1967
3: 5 but will acknowledge his name **b** my Father 1967
3: 8 I have placed **b** you an open door 1967
4: 1 and **there b** me was a door standing open 2627
4: 2 and **there b** me was a throne in heaven 2627
4: 5 **B** the throne, seven lamps were blazing. 1967
4: 6 Also **b** the throne there was what looked 1967
4:10 down **b** him who sits on the throne, 1967
4:10 They lay their crowns **b** the throne and say: 1967
5: 8 and the twenty-four elders fell down **b** 1967
6: 2 I looked, and **there b** me was a white horse! 2627
6: 5 I looked, and **there b** me was a black horse! 2627
6: 8 I looked, and **there b** me was a pale horse! 2627
7: 9 After this I looked and **there b** me was 2627
7: 9 standing **b** the throne and in front of 1967
7:11 They fell down on their faces **b** the throne 1967
7:15 "they are **b** the throne of God 1967
8: 2 I saw the seven angels who stand **b** God, 1967
8: 3 on the golden altar **b** the throne. 1967
8: 4 went up **b** God from the angel's hand. 1967
9:13 the horns of the golden altar that is **b** God. 1967
11: 4 the two lampstands that stand **b** the Lord of 1967
11:16 who were seated on their thrones **b** God, 1967
12:10 who accuses them **b** our God day and night, 1967
14: 1 I looked, and **there b** me was the Lamb, 2627
14: 3 And they sang a new song **b** the throne and 1967
14: 3 the throne and **b** the four living creatures 1967
14:14 I looked, and **there b** me was a white cloud, 2627
15: 4 All nations will come and worship **b** you, 1967
19:11 I saw heaven standing open and **there b** 2627
20:12 great and small, standing **b** the throne, 1967

BEFOREHAND (7) [BEFORE]

Isa 41:26 or **b,** so we could say, 'He was right'? 4200+4946+7156
Mk 13:11 *do* not **worry b about** what to say. 4628
14: 8 on my body **b** to prepare for my burial. 4624
Lk 21:14 *to* **worry b** how you will defend yourselves. 4627
Ac 4:28 and will *had* **decided b** should happen. 4633
Ro 1: 2 the gospel *he* **promised b** through his prophets 4600
3:25 the sins **committed b** unpunished— 4588

BEFUDDLED (1)

Isa 28: 7 and prophets stagger from beer and *are* **b** 1182

BEG (19) [BEGGAR, BEGGARS, BEGGED, BEGGING]

Jdg 13: 8 "O Lord, **I b you,** let the man of God 5528
1Sa 15:25 Now **I b you,** forgive my sin 5528
2Sa 24:10 Now, O LORD, **I b you,** take away the guilt 5528
2Ki 8: 3 of the Philistines and went to the king to **b** 7590
8: 5 to life came *to* **b** the king for her house 7590
1Ch 21: 8 **I b you,** take away the guilt of your servant. 5528
Est 4: 8 into the king's presence to **b for mercy** 2858
7: 7 behind to **b** Queen Esther for his life. 1335
Job 19:16 though *I* **b** him with my own mouth. 2858
La 4: 4 the children **b** *for* bread, 8626
Am 7: 5 I cried out, "Sovereign LORD, **I b you,** 5528
Lk 8:28 *I* **b** you, don't torture me!" 1289
9:38 "Teacher, *I* **b** you to look at my son, 1289
16: 3 and I'm ashamed *to* **b—** 2050
16:27 "He answered, 'Then *I* **b** you, father, 2263
Jn 9: 8 the same man who *used to* sit and **b?"** 4644
Ac 3: 2 where he was put every day *to* **b** 160+1797+3836
26: 3 *I* **b** you to listen to me patiently. 1289
2Co 10: 2 *I* **b** you that when I come I may not have 1289

BEGAN (175) [BEGIN]

Ge 4:26 At that time *men* **b** to call on the name of the LORD. 2725
6: 1 When men **b** to increase in number on 2725
16: 4 she *b to* **despise** her mistress. AIT
21:16 And as she sat there nearby, *she* **b** to sob. 906+5951+7754
29:11 Jacob kissed Rachel and *b to* **weep** aloud. AIT
35:16 Rachel *b to* **give birth** AIT
41:54 and the seven years of famine **b,** 2725
41:55 *b to* **feel the famine,** AIT
42:24 He turned away from them and *b to* **weep,** AIT
Ex 16:20 but it was full of maggots and *b to* **smell.** AIT
33: 4 *they b to* **mourn** and no one put AIT
Nu 11: 4 *b to* **crave other food,** AIT
12: 1 and Aaron *b to* **talk** against Moses AIT
25: 1 the men **b** to indulge in sexual immorality 2725
Dt 1: 5 Moses **b** to expound this law, saying: 3283

Jos 16: 1 The allotment for Joseph **b** at the Jordan 3655
18:12 On the north side their boundary **b** at 2118
18:15 The southern side **b** at the outskirts 3655
Jdg 13:25 and the Spirit of the LORD **b** to stir him 2725
16:19 and so **b** to subdue him. 2725
16:22 But the hair on his head **b** to grow *again* 2725
20:31 *They* **b** to inflict casualties on the Israelites 2725
20:40 the column of smoke **b** to rise from the city, 2725
Ru 2: 3 and *b to* **glean** in the fields behind AIT
1Sa 13: 8 and Saul's men *b to* **scatter.** AIT
20:19 where you hid **when** this trouble **b,** 928+3427
23:25 Saul and his men **b** the search, 2143
1Ki 6: 1 *he b to* **build** the temple of the LORD. AIT
15:29 As soon as he *b to* **reign,** AIT
16:11 As soon as he *b to* **reign** and was seated on AIT
16:31 and **b** to serve Baal and worship him. 2143
18:27 At noon Elijah *b to* **taunt** them. AIT
2Ki 4:40 but as they *b to* **eat** it, they cried out, AIT
6: 4 They went to the Jordan and *b to* **cut down** AIT
8:11 Then the man of God *b to* **weep.** AIT
8:16 of Jehoshaphat *b his* **reign** as king of Judah. AIT
8:25 of Jehoram king of Judah *b to* **reign.** AIT
10:32 the LORD **b** to reduce the size of Israel. 2725
11:21 when he *b to* **reign.** AIT
14: 1 of Joash king of Judah *b to* **reign.** AIT
15: 1 of Amaziah king of Judah *b to* **reign.** AIT
15:32 of Uzziah king of Judah *b to* **reign.** AIT
15:37 the LORD **b** to send Rezin king of Aram 2725
16: 1 of Jotham king of Judah *b to* **reign.** AIT
18: 1 of Ahaz king of Judah *b to* **reign.** AIT
1Ch 27:24 Joab son of Zeruiah **b** to count the men 2725
2Ch 3: 1 Then Solomon **b** to build the temple of 2725
3: 2 *He* **b** building on the second day of 2725
20:22 As *they* **b** to sing and praise, 2725
22: 1 of Jehoram king of Judah *b to* **reign.** AIT
29:17 *They* **b** the consecration on the first day of 2725
29:27 As the offering **b,** singing to the LORD 2725
29:27 singing to the LORD **b** also, 2725
31: 7 *They* **b** doing this in the third month 2725
31:10 the people **b** to bring their contributions to 2725
34: 3 *he* **b** to seek the God of his father David. 2725
34: 3 In his twelfth year *he* **b** to purge Judah 2725
Ezr 3: 2 of Shealtiel and his associates **b** to build 7756
3: 6 the first day of the seventh month *they* **b** 2725
3: 8 from the captivity to Jerusalem) **b** the work, 2725
Ne 2:18 So they **b** this good work. 2616+3338
Job 2:12 *they b to* **weep** aloud, AIT
Pr 8:23 from the beginning, **before** the world **b.** 7710
Ecc 2:20 So my heart **b** to despair 6015
SS 5: 4 my heart *b to* **pound** for him. AIT
Jer 36: 2 the other nations from the time *I b* **speaking** AIT
Eze 9: 6 So *they* **b** with the elders who were in front 2725
9: 7 So they went out and *b* **killing** throughout AIT
23: 8 not give up the prostitution she **b** in Egypt, NIH
23:27 to the lewdness and prostitution you **b** NIH
Da 9:23 As soon as you **b** to pray, 9378
10:16 and I opened my mouth and *b to* **speak.** AIT
Hos 1: 2 *When* the LORD **b** to speak through Hosea, 9378
Hag 1:14 They came and **b** *to* work on the house of 6913
Mt 4:17 From that time on Jesus **b** to preach, *806*
5: 2 and *he b to* **teach** them, saying: *AIT*
8:15 and she got up and *b to* **wait on** him. *AIT*
11: 7 Jesus **b** to speak to the crowd about John: *806*
11:20 Then Jesus **b** to denounce the cities *806*
12: 1 and **b** to pick some heads of grain *806*
13:54 *he b* **teaching** the people in their synagogue, *AIT*
16:21 on Jesus **b** to explain to his disciples *806*
16:22 Peter took him aside and **b** to rebuke him. *806*
18:24 *As* he **b** the settlement, *806*
18:28 He grabbed him and *b to* **choke** him. *AIT*
20:11 *they b to* **grumble** against the landowner. *AIT*
26:22 *They* were very sad and **b** to say to him one *806*
26:37 and he **b** to be sorrowful and troubled. *806*
26:74 Then *he* **b** to call down curses on himself *806*
Mk 1:21 into the synagogue and *b to* **teach.** *AIT*
1:31 The fever left her and *she b to* **wait on** *AIT*
1:45 Instead *he* went out and **b** to talk freely, *806*
2:13 and *he b to* **teach** them. *AIT*
2:23 *they* **b** to pick some heads of grain. *806*
3: 6 Then the Pharisees went out and *b to* **plot** *AIT*
4: 1 Again Jesus **b** to teach by the lake. *806*
5:17 Then the *people* **b** to plead with Jesus *806*
5:20 So the man went away and **b** to tell in *806*
6: 2 *he* **b** to teach in the synagogue, *806*
6:34 So *he* **b** teaching them many things. *806*
7:35 and *he b* **to speak** plainly. *AIT*
8:11 The Pharisees came and **b** *806*
8:31 *He* then **b** to teach them that the Son *806*
8:32 Peter took him aside and **b** to rebuke him. *806*
10:47 *he* **b** to shout, "Jesus, Son of David, *806*
11:15 and **b** driving out those who were buying *806*
11:18 and *b* **looking for** a way to kill him, *AIT*
12: 1 *He* then **b** to speak to them in parables: *806*
14:33 *he* **b** to be deeply distressed and troubled. *806*
14:65 Then some **b** to spit at him; *806*
14:71 He **b** to call down curses on himself, *806*
15:18 And *they* **b** to call out to him, "Hail, *806*
Lk 1:64 and *he b to* **speak,** praising God. *AIT*
2:44 Then *they b* **looking for** him *AIT*
3:23 Jesus himself was about thirty years old
when he **b** his ministry. *806*
4:21 and *he* **b** by saying to them, *806*
4:31 and on the Sabbath **b** to teach the people. *1639*
4:39 *She* got up at once and *b to* **wait on** them. *AIT*
5: 6 of fish that their nets *b to* **break.** *AIT*
5: 7 both boats so full that they *b to* **sink.** *AIT*
5:21 and the teachers of the law **b** thinking *806*
Lk 6: 1 his disciples *b to* **pick** some heads of grain, *AIT*
6:11 But they were furious and *b to* **discuss** *AIT*
7:15 The dead man sat up and **b** to talk, *806*
7:24 Jesus **b** to speak to the crowd about John: *806*
7:38 *she* **b** to wet his feet with her tears. *806*
7:49 The other guests **b** to say *806*
11:53 the Pharisees and the teachers of the law **b** *806*
12: 1 Jesus **b** to speak first to his disciples, *806*
14:18 "But *they* all alike **b** to make excuses. *806*
14:30 'This fellow **b** to build and was not able *806*
15:14 and he **b** to be in need. *806*
15:24 So *they* **b** to celebrate. *806*
19: 7 All the people saw this and *b to* **mutter,** *AIT*
19:37 the whole crowd of disciples **b** joyfully *806*
19:45 and **b** driving out those who were selling. *806*
22:23 They **b** to question among themselves *806*
22:63 The men who were guarding Jesus *b*
mocking and beating him. *AIT*
23: 2 And *they* **b** to accuse him, saying, *806*
24:30 broke it and *b to* **give** it to them. *AIT*
Jn 6:14 *they b to* **say,** "Surely this is the Prophet *AIT*
6:41 At this the Jews *b to* **grumble** about him *AIT*
6:52 Then the Jews *b to* **argue sharply** *AIT*
7:25 of the people of Jerusalem *b to* **ask,** *AIT*
8: 9 those who heard *b to* **go away** one at *AIT*
13: 5 a basin and **b** to wash his disciples' feet, *806*
17: 5 the glory I had with you before the world **b.** *1639*
18:27 and at that moment a rooster *b to* **crow.** *AIT*
Ac 1: 1 about all that Jesus **b** to do and to teach *806*
2: 4 with the Holy Spirit and **b** to speak *806*
3: 8 He jumped to his feet and *b to* **walk.** *AIT*
4: 7 before them and *b to* **question** them: *AIT*
5:21 and *b to* **teach** the people. *AIT*
6: 9 These men **b** to argue with Stephen, *NIG*
7:58 of the city and *b to* **stone** him. *AIT*
8: 3 But Saul **b** *to* **destroy** the church. *3381*
8:35 Then Philip **b** with that very passage *806*
9:20 At once *he b to* **preach** in the synagogues *AIT*
10:34 Then Peter **b to speak:** *487+3306+3836+5125*
11: 4 Peter **b** and explained everything *806*
11:15 "As **I b** to speak, the Holy Spirit came on *806*
11:20 went to Antioch and *b to* **speak** to Greeks *AIT*
14:10 At that, the *man* jumped up and *b to* **walk.** *AIT*
16:13 *We* sat down and *b to* **speak** to *AIT*
17:18 and Stoic philosophers *b to* **dispute with** *AIT*
18:26 He **b** to speak boldly in the synagogue. *806*
19:28 they were furious and *b* **shouting:** *AIT*
26: 1 with his hand and *b his* **defense:** *AIT*
27:13 **gentle** south wind *b to* **blow,** *AIT*
27:18 the storm that the next day *they* **b** to throw *4472*
27:35 Then *he* broke it and **b** to eat. *806*
28:25 among themselves and *b to* **leave** *AIT*
1Co 2: 7 for our glory before time **b.** *NIG*
Gal 2:12 *b to* **draw back** and **separate** *AIT*
Php 1: 6 that he who **b** a good work in you *1887*

BEGAT, BEGET, BEGETTEST, BEGETTETH (KJV) See FATHER

BEGGAR (3) [BEG]

Lk 16:20 At his gate was laid a **b** named Lazarus, *4777*
16:22 when the **b** died and the angels carried him *4777*
Ac 3:11 While **the b** held on to Peter and John, *899S*

BEGGARS (1) [BEG]

Ps 109:10 May his children be wandering **b;** 8626

BEGGED (23) [BEG]

2Ki 1:13 "Man of God," *he* **b,** 2858
Est 8: 3 *She* **b** him to put an end to the evil plan 2858
Hos 12: 4 he wept and **b for** his **favor.** 2858
Mt 8:31 The demons **b** Jesus, "If you drive us out, *3306+4151*
14:36 and **b** him to let the sick just touch the edge *4151*
18:26 'Be patient with me,' *he* **b,** *3306*
18:29 to his knees and **b** him, *4151*
18:32 that debt of yours because *you* **b** me to. *4151*
Mk 1:40 A man with leprosy came to him and **b** him *4151*
5:10 And *he* **b** Jesus again and again not *4151*
5:12 The demons **b** Jesus, "Send us among *4151*
5:18 the man who had been demon-possessed **b** *4151*
6:56 *They* **b** him to let them touch even the edge *4151*
7:26 *She* **b** Jesus to drive the demon out *2263*
7:32 *they* **b** him to place his hand on the man. *4151*
8:22 a blind man and **b** Jesus to touch him. *4151*
Lk 5:12 with his face to the ground and **b** him, *1289*
8:31 And *they* **b** him *repeatedly* not *4151*
8:32 The demons **b** Jesus to let them go *4151*
8:38 the demons had gone out **b** to go with him, *1289*
9:40 *I* **b** your disciples to drive it out, *1289*
Jn 4:47 to him and **b** him to come and heal his son, *2263*
Heb 12:19 heard it **b** that no further word be spoken *4148*

BEGGING (8) [BEG]

Job 41: 3 Will he keep **b** you **for mercy?** 9384
Ps 37:25 or their children **b** bread. 1335
Mk 10:46 was sitting by the roadside **b.** *4644*
Lk 18:35 a blind man was sitting by the roadside **b.** *2050*
Jn 9: 8 those who had formerly seen him **b** asked, *4645*
Ac 3:10 to sit **b** at the temple gate called Beautiful, *1797+3836+4639*
16: 9 of a man of Macedonia standing and **b** him, *4151*
19:31 sent him a message **b** him not to venture *4151*

BEGIN (21) [BEGAN, BEGINNING, BEGINNINGS, BEGINS, BEGUN]

Dt 2:24 **B** to take possession of it and engage him 2725
2:25 This very day *I will* **b** to put the terror 2725
2:31 Now **b** to conquer and possess his land." 2725
16: 9 Count off seven weeks from the time you **b** 2725
28:30 but *you will* not *even b to* **enjoy** its fruit. AIT
Jos 3: 7 "Today *I will* **b** to exalt you in the eyes 2725
18: 3 before you **b** to take possession of the land 995
Jdg 13: 5 and he *will* **b** the deliverance of Israel 2725
1Sa 9:13 The people *will* not *b* **eating** AIT
1Ch 22:16 **b** the work, and the LORD be with you." 7756
22:19 **B** to build the sanctuary of the LORD God, 7756
Ps 81: 2 **B** the music, strike the tambourine, 5951
La 2:19 as the watches of the night **b;** 8031
Eze 9: 6 **B** at my sanctuary." 2725
39:14 the seven months *they will b their* **search.** AIT
Hos 8:10 *They will* **b** *to* waste away under 2725
Lk 3: 8 And *do* not **b** to say to yourselves, *806*
21:28 *When* these things **b** to take place, *806*
23:54 and the Sabbath *was* **about to b.** *2216*
Jn 7:14 up to the temple courts and *b to* **teach.** *AIT*
1Pe 4:17 for judgment *to* **b** with the family of God; *806*

BEGINNING (90) [BEGIN]

Ge 1: 1 In the **b** God created the heavens and 8040
44:12 **b** with the oldest and ending with 2725
Lev 23:39 " 'So **b with** the fifteenth day of 928
Dt 11:12 on it from the **b** *of* the year to its end. 8040
31:24 a book the words of this law **from b to** end, 6330
31:30 of this song **from b to** end in the hearing of 6330
Jdg 7:19 of the camp at the **b** *of* the middle watch, 8031
Ru 1:22 in Bethlehem as the barley harvest was **b.** 9378
1Sa 3:12 from **b** to end. 2725
2Sa 7:10 oppress them anymore, as they did at the **b** 8037
21: 9 just as the barley harvest was **b.** 9378
21:10 the **b** *of* the harvest till the rain poured 9378
1Ch 17: 9 as they did at the **b** 8037
29:29 events of King David's reign, from **b** to end, 8037
2Ch 9:29 events of Solomon's reign, from **b** to end, 8037
12:15 events of Rehoboam's reign, from **b** to end, 8037
16:11 The events of Asa's reign, from **b** to end, 8037
20:34 of Jehoshaphat's reign, from **b** to end, 8037
25:26 events of Amaziah's reign, from **b** to end, 8037
26:22 events of Uzziah's reign, from **b** to end, 8037
28:26 his reign and all his ways, from **b** to end, 8037
35:27 all the events, from **b** to end, 8037
Ezr 4: 6 At the **b** *of* the reign of Xerxes, 9378
Ps 102:25 the **b** you laid the foundations of the earth, 7156
111:10 The fear of the LORD is the **b** *of* wisdom; 8040
Pr 1: 7 fear of the LORD is the **b** *of* knowledge, 8040
8:23 from the **b,** before the world began. 8031
9:10 fear of the LORD is the **b** *of* wisdom, 9378
20:21 An inheritance quickly gained at the **b** will 8037
Ecc 3:11 what God has done from **b** to end. 8031
7: 8 The end of a matter is better than its **b,** 8040
10:13 At the **b** his words are folly; 9378
Isa 1:26 your counselors as at the **b.** 9378
40:21 Has it not been told you from the **b?** 8031
41: 4 calling forth the generations from the **b?** 8031
41:26 Who told of this from the **b,** 8031
46:10 I make known the end from the **b,** 8040
Jer 17:12 A glorious throne, exalted from the **b,** 8037
25:29 I am **b** to bring disaster on the city 2725
Eze 25: 9 **b** at its frontier towns— NIH
40: 1 at the **b** *of* the year, 8031
42:12 the **b** *of* the passageway that was parallel to 8031
48:30 **B** on the north side, which is 4,500 NIH
Da 12: 1 as has not happened from the **b** *of* nations 2118
Mic 1:13 You were the **b** *of* sin to the Daughter 8040
Mt 14:30 he was afraid and, **b** to sink, cried out, *806*
19: 4 "that at the **b** the Creator 'made them male *794*
19: 8 But it was not this way from the **b.** *794*
20: 8 **b** with the last ones hired and going on to *806*
24: 8 All these are the **b** of birth pains. *794*
24:21 from the **b** of the world until now— *794*
Mk 1: 1 The **b** of the gospel about Jesus Christ, *794*
10: 6 at the **b** of creation God 'made them male *794*
13: 8 These are the **b** of birth pains. *794*
13:19 be days of distress unequaled from the **b,** *794*
Lk 1: 3 I myself have carefully investigated
everything **from the b,** *540*
11:50 that has been shed since the **b** of the world, *2856*
24:27 And **b** with Moses and all the Prophets, *806*
24:47 in his name to all nations, **b** at Jerusalem. *806*
Jn 1: 1 In the **b** was the Word, *794*
1: 2 He was with God in the **b.** *794*
6:64 from the **b** which of them did not believe *794*
8:44 He was a murderer from the **b,** *794*
15:27 for you have been with me from the **b.** *794*
Ac 1:22 **b** from John's baptism to the time *806*
10:37 **b** in Galilee after the baptism *806*
11:15 on them as he had come on us at the **b.** *794*
26: 4 from the **b** of my life in my own country, *794*
2Co 3: 1 *Are we* **b** to commend ourselves again? *806*
8: 6 since *he had* **earlier made a b,** *4599*
Gal 3: 3 *After* **b** with the Spirit, *1887*
Col 1:18 he is the **b** and the firstborn from among *794*
2Th 2:13 from the **b** God chose you to be saved *794*
2Ti 1: 9 in Christ Jesus before the **b of time,** *173+5989*
Tit 1: 2 promised before the **b of time,** *173+5989*
Heb 1:10 He also says, "In the **b,** O Lord, *794*
7: 3 without **b** of days or end of life, *794*
2Pe 2:20 at the end than they were at the **b.** *4755*
3: 4 everything goes on as it has since the **b** *794*

1Jn 1:1 That which was from the **b**, 794
2:7 you have had since the **b**. 794
2:13 you have known him who is from the **b**. 794
2:14 you have known him who is from the **b**. 794
2:24 from the **b** remains in you. 794
3:8 the devil has been sinning from the **b**. 794
3:11 This is the message you heard from the **b**: 794
2Jn 1:5 but one we have had from the **b**. 794
1:6 As you have heard from the **b**, 794
Rev 21:6 the **B** and the End. 794
22:13 the First and the Last, the **B** and the End. 794

BEGINNINGS (1) [BEGIN]

Job 8:7 Your **b** will seem humble, 8040

BEGINS (7) [BEGIN]

Lev 23:5 The LORD's Passover **b** at twilight on NIH
23:6 the LORD's Feast of Unleavened Bread **b**; NIH
23:34 the LORD's Feast of Tabernacles **b**, NIH
Eze 45:25 which **b** in the seventh month on NIH
Mt 24:49 and *he* then **b** to beat his fellow servants and 806
Lk 12:45 and *he* then **b** to beat the menservants 806
1Pe 4:17 and if it **b** with us, 4754

BEGOTTEN (1)

Isa 45:10 'What *have you* **b**?' 3528

BEGRUDGE (1)

Dt 28:56 *will* **b** the husband she loves 6524+8317

BEGUILE, BEGUILED, BEGUILING (KJV) See DECEIVE, DISQUALIFY

BEGUN (9) [BEGIN]

Ge 11:6 the same language they *have* **b** to do this, 2725
Dt 2:31 *I have* **b** to deliver Sihon and his country 2725
3:24 you *have* **b** to show to your servant 2725
20:6 a vineyard and not *b to* **enjoy** it? AIT
Jdg 20:39 The Benjamites *had* **b** to inflict casualties 2725
Ezr 7:9 He *had* **b** his journey from Babylon on 3569
Est 9:23 to continue the celebration *they had* **b**, 2725
Mic 6:13 Therefore, I *have* **b** to destroy you, 2725
Rev 11:17 and *have b to* **reign.** AIT

BEHALF (46)

Ge 23:8 with Ephron son of Zohar **on** my **b** 4200
25:21 Isaac prayed to the LORD **on b of** 4200+5790
Lev 1:4 be accepted **on** his **b** to make atonement 4200
14:31 the LORD **on b of** the one to be cleansed." 6584
19:5 a way that it will be **accepted** *on* your *b*. AIT
22:19 in order that it may be **accepted** *on* your *b*. AIT
22:20 because it will not be accepted **on** your **b**. 4200
22:25 They will not be accepted **on** your **b**, 4200
22:29 a way that it will be **accepted** *on* your *b*. AIT
23:11 so it will be **accepted** *on* your *b;* AIT
24:8 **on b of** the Israelites, as a lasting covenant. 907+4946
Nu 3:38 of the sanctuary **on b of** the Israelites. 4200+5466
5:15 a tenth of an ephah of barley flour **on** her **b**. 6584
8:19 **work** at the Tent of Meeting *on b* AIT
1Sa 7:9 He cried out to the LORD **on** Israel's **b**, 1237
14:6 Perhaps the LORD will act **in** our **b**. 4200
2Sa 3:12 Then Abner sent messengers **on** his **b** to say 9393
14:8 and I will issue an order **in** your **b**." 6584
21:14 God answered prayer **in b of** the land. 4200
24:25 LORD answered prayer **in b of** the land, 4200
2Ki 4:13 Can we speak **on** your **b** to the king or 4200
Est 8:8 in the king's name **in b of** the Jews 6584
Job 6:22 Have I ever said, 'Give something **on** my **b**, 4200
8:6 even now he will rouse himself **on** your **b** 6584
13:7 Will you speak wickedly **on** God's **b**? 4200
16:21 **on b of** a man he pleads with God as 4200
36:2 that there is more to be said **in** God's **b**. 4200
Ps 45:4 In your majesty ride forth victoriously **in b of** truth, 1821+6584
66:5 how awesome his works **in** man's **b**! 6584
Isa 8:19 Why consult the dead **on b of** the living? 1237
58:10 if you spend yourselves **in b of** the hungry 4200
64:4 who acts **on b of** those who wait for him. 4200
65:8 so will I do **in b of** my servants; 5100
Jer 18:20 I stood before you and spoke **in** their **b** 3208+6584
Eze 22:30 and stand before me in the gap **on b of** 1237
Jn 8:14 "Even if I testify **on** my own **b**, 4309
16:26 that I will ask the Father **on** your **b**. 4309
Ro 15:8 a servant of the Jews **on b of** God's truth, 5642
2Co 1:11 Then many will give thanks **on** our **b** for 5642
5:20 We implore you **on** Christ's **b**: 5642
Php 1:29 to you **on b of** Christ not only to believe 5642
Col 1:7 a faithful minister of Christ **on** our **b**, 5642
Heb 6:20 who went before us, has entered **on** our **b**. 5642
Rev 13:12 the authority of the first beast **on** his **b**, 1967
13:14 the signs he was given power to do **on b of** 1967
19:20 the miraculous signs **on** his **b**. 1967

BEHAVE (2) [BEHAVED, BEHAVES, BEHAVIOR]

1Ki 1:6 "Why *do you* **b** as you do?" 6913
Ro 13:13 *Let us* **b** decently, as in the daytime, 4344

BEHAVED (5) [BEHAVE]

2Sa 15:6 Absalom **b** in this way toward all 6913
1Ki 21:26 *He* **b in the vilest manner** 4394+9493
Ps 74:5 *They* **b** like men wielding axes to cut 3359
Jer 2:23 See **how** you **b** in the valley; 2006
16:12 you *have* **b** more wickedly than your fathers. 6913

BEHAVES (1) [BEHAVE]

Pr 21:24 *he* **b** with overweening pride. 6913

BEHAVIOR (5) [BEHAVE]

Est 3:4 about it to see whether Mordecai's **b** would 1821
Pr 8:13 evil **b** and perverse speech. 2006
Col 1:21 in your minds because of your evil **b**. 2240
1Pe 3:1 over without words by the **b** of their wives, 419
3:16 against your good **b** in Christ may 419

BEHEADED (5)

Mt 14:10 and *had* John **b** in the prison. 642
Mk 6:16 he said, "John, the man I **b**, 642
6:27 The man went, **b** John in the prison, 642
Lk 9:9 But Herod said, "I **b** John. 642
Rev 20:4 the souls *of* those who *had been* **b** because 4284

BEHELD (1) [BEHOLD]

Ps 63:2 in the sanctuary and **b** your power 8011

BEHEMOTH (1)

Job 40:15 "Look at the **b**, which I made along with you 990

BEHIND (101)

Ge 18:10 which was **b** him. 339
19:6 to meet them and shut the door **b** him 339
32:18 and he is coming **b** us.' " 339
32:20 'Your servant Jacob is coming **b** us.' " 339
Ex 10:24 **leave** your flocks and herds **b**." 3657
10:26 not a hoof *is to be* **left b**. 8636
14:19 withdrew and went **b** them. 339+4946
14:19 moved from in front and stood **b** them, 339+4946
26:33 the ark of the Testimony **b** the curtain. 1074+4946
Lev 16:2 the Most Holy Place **b** the curtain 1074+4946
16:12 and take them **b** the curtain. 1074+4946
16:15 and take its blood **b** the curtain 1074+4946
Nu 3:23 to camp on the west, **b** the tabernacle. 339
Dt 25:18 and cut off all who were lagging **b**; 339
Jos 8:2 Set an ambush **b** the city." 339+4946
8:4 You are to set an ambush **b** the city. 339+4946
8:14 an ambush had been set against him **b** 339+4946
Jdg 3:23 of the upper room **b** him and locked them. 1237
5:28 **b** the lattice she cried out, 1237
Ru 2:2 to the fields and pick up the leftover grain **b** 339
2:3 to glean in the fields **b** the harvesters. 339
2:7 among the sheaves **b** the harvesters.' 339
1Sa 11:5 **b** his oxen, and he asked, 339
14:13 with his armor-bearer **right b** him. 339
14:13 his armor-bearer followed and killed **b** him. 339
21:9 it is wrapped in a cloth **b** the ephod. 339
24:8 When Saul looked **b** him, 339
30:9 where some **stayed b**, 6641
30:21 and who *were* **left b** at the Besor Ravine. 8740
2Sa 2:20 Abner looked **b** him and asked, 339
2:25 Then the men of Benjamin rallied **b** Abner. 339
3:16 weeping **b** her all the way to Bahurim. 339
3:31 King David himself walked **b** the bier. 339
5:23 around **b** them and attack them in front of 339
10:9 in front of him and **b** him; 294+4946
18:22 please let me run **b** the Cushite." 339
1Ki 14:9 to anger and thrust me **b** your back. 339
20:19 of the city with the army **b** them 339
2Ki 4:4 Then go inside and shut the door **b** you 1237
4:5 She left him and afterward shut the door **b** 1237
6:32 the sound of his master's footsteps **b** him?" 339
9:18 "Fall in **b** me." 339
9:19 Fall in **b** me." 339
9:25 and I were riding together in chariots **b** 339
11:6 and a third at the gate **b** the guard, 339
25:12 But the commander **left b** some of 8636
25:22 be over the people *he had* **left b** in Judah. 8636
1Ch 19:10 in front of him and **b** him; 294
28:9 and understands every **motive** *b* AIT
2Ch 13:13 front of Judah the ambush was **b** them. 339+4946
Ne 4:13 people **b** the lowest points of the wall 339+4946
4:16 The officers posted themselves **b** all 339
9:26 they put your law **b** their backs. 339
Est 7:7 **stayed b** to beg Queen Esther for his life. 6641
Job 21:21 about the family he **leaves b** 339
38:8 up the sea **b** doors when it burst forth from 928
39:10 Will he till the valleys **b** you? 339
41:32 **B** him he leaves a glistening wake; 339
Ps 50:17 and cast my words **b** you. 339
139:5 You hem me in—**b** and before; 294
SS 2:9 There he stands **b** our wall, 339
4:1 Your eyes **b** your veil are doves. 1237+4946
4:3 Your temples **b** your veil are like 1237+4946
6:7 Your temples **b** your veil are like 1237+4946
Isa 26:20 enter your rooms and shut the doors **b** you; 1237
30:21 your ears will hear a voice **b** you, 339+4946
38:17 you have put all my sins **b** your back. 339
45:14 they will trudge **b** you, 339
57:8 **B** your doors and your doorposts you have put your pagan symbols. 339
Jer 9:22 like cut grain **b** the reaper, 339+4946
39:10 the guard **left b** in the land of Judah some 8636
40:6 the people who *were* **left b** in the land. 8636
52:16 But Nebuzaradan **left b** the rest of 8636
Eze 3:12 and I heard **b** me a loud rumbling sound— 339
23:35 and thrust me **b** your back, 339
24:21 and daughters *you* **left b** will fall by 6440
39:28 not leaving any **b**. 9004
42:14 to go into the outer court until they leave **b** 9004
Joel 2:3 **b** them a flame blazes. 339
2:3 **b** them, a desert waste— 339
2:14 He may turn and have pity and leave **b** 339
Zec 1:8 **B** him were red, brown and white horses. 339
7:14 so desolate **b** them that no one could come 339
Mt 9:20 up **b** him and touched the edge of his cloak. 3957
16:23 Jesus turned and said to Peter, "Get **b** me, 3958
Mk 4:36 **Leaving** the crowd **b**, 918
5:27 she came up **b** him in the crowd 3957
8:33 "Get **b** me, Satan!" 3958
14:52 he fled naked, **leaving** his garment **b**. 2901
Lk 2:43 the boy Jesus **stayed b** in Jerusalem, 5702
7:38 and as she stood **b** him at his feet weeping, 3958
8:44 up **b** him and touched the edge of his cloak, 3957
23:26 the cross on him and made him carry it **b** 3957
Jn 20:6 Then Simon Peter, *who was* **b** him, 199
1Co 13:11 I became a man, *I* **put** childish ways **b** *me*. 2934
Php 3:13 Forgetting what is **b** and straining 3958
1Ti 5:24 the sins of others **trail b** them. 2051
Heb 6:19 It enters the inner sanctuary **b** the curtain, NIG
9:3 **B** the second curtain was a room called 3552
Rev 1:10 I heard **b** me a loud voice like a trumpet, 3958
6:8 and Hades *was* **following** close **b** him. 199

BEHOLD (6) [BEHELD]

Nu 24:17 *I* **b** him, but not near. 8800
Isa 65:17 "**B**, I will create new heavens and 2180
Rev 1:18 and **b** I am alive for ever and ever! 2627
16:15 "**B**, I come like a thief! 2627
22:7 "**B**, I am coming soon! 2627
22:12 "**B**, I am coming soon! 2627

BEHOVED (KJV) See HAD TO, HAVE TO

BEING (165) [BE, BEINGS]

Ge 2:7 and the man became a living **b**. 5883
38:25 *As* she **was** *b* **brought out**, AIT
40:5 who **were b held** in prison— AIT
40:15 *to deserve b* **put** in a dungeon." AIT
42:21 "Surely we are **b** punished because NIH
50:20 for good to accomplish what is now **b** done, NIH
Ex 5:16 Your servants *are* **b beaten**, 5782
6:6 I will free you from **b** slaves to them, NIH
23:1 a wicked man by **b** a malicious witness. 2118
Lev 24:17 " 'If anyone takes the life of a **human b**, 132
Nu 6:11 because he sinned by **b** in the presence of NIH
15:24 **without** the community **b aware** 4946+6524
19:19 The person **b** cleansed must wash his clothes NIH
24:11 the LORD has kept you from **b** rewarded." NIH
35:27 the accused without **b** guilty of murder. NIH
Dt 3:16 the Arnon Gorge (the middle of the gorge **b** NIH
22:21 in Israel by *b* **promiscuous** while still AIT
1Sa 2:13 and while the meat *was b* **boiled**, AIT
10:5 flutes and harps **b** played before them, NIH
20:6 because an annual sacrifice is **b** made there NIH
2Sa 13:13 not keep me from **b** married to you." NIH
17:17 they could not risk **b seen** entering the city. 8011
19:11 to his palace, since what is **b** said NIH
20:10 Without **b** stabbed again, Amasa died. NIH
1Ki 6:7 at the temple site while it **was b built**. AIT
1Ch 9:18 **b** stationed at the King's Gate on the east, NIH
21:12 of **b swept away** before your enemies, 6200
24:6 one family **b taken** from Eleazar and 296
28:7 as is **b** done at this time.' NIH
2Ch 13:14 that they were **b** attacked at both front NIH
15:6 One nation **was** *b* **crushed** by another AIT
Ezr 3:12 **the foundation** *of* this temple *b* **laid,** AIT
5:8 The work *is* **b carried on** with diligence 10522
Ne 4:7 ahead and that the gaps *were* **b closed**, 6258
8:8 people could understand what was **b** read. NIH
13:27 and *are* **b unfaithful** to our God AIT
Est 4:11 in the inner court without **b summoned** 7924
Job 4:7 Who, **b** innocent, has ever perished? NIH
10:19 If only *I had* never **come into b**, 2118+2118
33:20 so that his **very b** finds food repulsive 2652
Ps 11:3 When the foundations *are* **b destroyed**, 2238
35:10 My whole **b** will exclaim, 6795
103:1 all my **inmost b**, praise his holy name. 7931
119:126 your law *is* **b broken**. AIT
139:13 For you created my **inmost b**; 4000
Pr 3:26 and will keep your foot from **b** snared. NIH
6:27 into his lap without his clothes **b burned**? 8596
6:28 on hot coals without his feet **b scorched**? 3917
20:27 it searches out his **inmost b**. 1061+2540
20:30 and beatings purge the **inmost b**. 1061+2540
23:16 my **inmost b** will rejoice 4000
24:11 Rescue *those* **b led away** to death; 4374
Ecc 2:15 What then do I gain *by b* **wise?**" AIT
Isa 1:7 your fields *are b* **stripped** AIT
16:11 my **inmost b** for Kir Hareseth. 7931
42:9 before *they* **spring into b** I announce them 7541
50:4 wakens my ear to listen like one **b** taught. NIH
66:2 and so they **came into b**?" 2118
Jer 6:22 a great nation *is* **b stirred up** from the ends AIT
17:16 I have not run away from *b* your **shepherd**; AIT

Jer 40: 1 and Judah who *were* **b carried into exile** 1655
50:41 and many kings *are* **b stirred up** from 6424
Eze 3: 5 not **b sent** to a people of obscure speech 8938
10:13 I heard the wheels **b called** 7924
14:13 by *b* **unfaithful** and I stretch out my hand AIT
20: 9 from **b profaned** in the eyes of 2725
20:14 from **b profaned** in the eyes of the nations 2725
20:22 from **b profaned** in the eyes of the nations 2725
43:13 that cubit **b** a cubit and a handbreadth: NIH
Da 4:27 and your wickedness by *b* **kind** *to* AIT
6:18 and without any entertainment *b* **brought** AIT
Mt 20:13 'Friend, *I am* not *b* **unfair** *to* you. AIT
23:33 How will you escape **b** condemned to hell? NIG
Mk 1:10 he saw heaven *b* **torn open** and AIT
1:13 *b* **tempted** by Satan. AIT
Lk 3:21 When all the people *were b* **baptized,** AIT
7:12 a dead person *was b* **carried out—** AIT
8:23 so that the boat *was b* **swamped,** AIT
14: 1 he was *b* **carefully watched.** AIT
16:16 **the good news** of the kingdom of God *is b* **preached,** AIT
17:27 marrying and *b* **given in marriage** up to AIT
19: 3 but **b** a short man he could not, 1639
21:13 This will result in your **b** witnesses to them. NIG
21:20 "When you see Jerusalem *b* **surrounded** AIT
22:44 And **b** in anguish, 1181
Jn 13: 2 The evening meal *was* **b** served, 1181
Ac 2:47 the Lord added to their number daily those who *were b* **saved.** AIT
3: 2 a man crippled from birth *was b* **carried** to AIT
4: 9 *b* **called to account** AIT
6: 1 because their widows *were b* **overlooked** in AIT
7:24 of them *b* **mistreated** by an Egyptian, AIT
10:10 and *while* the meal *was b* **prepared,** AIT
10:11 like a large sheet *b* **let down** to earth AIT
10:47 from *b* **baptized** with water? AIT
11: 5 like a large sheet *b* **let down** from heaven AIT
17:28 in him *we* live and move and **have** *our* **b.'** 1639
17:29 the **divine b** is like gold or silver or stone— 2521
19:40 in danger of **b charged with** rioting because 1592
22:30 to find out exactly why Paul *was b* **accused** AIT
25: 4 "Paul *is b* **held** at Caesarea, AIT
27:20 we finally gave up all hope *of* **b saved.** AIT
27:27 fourteenth night we were *still b* **driven** AIT
Ro 1: 8 your faith *is b* **reported** all over the world. AIT
1:18 of God *is b* **revealed** from heaven AIT
1:20 *b* **understood** from what has been made, AIT
2: 9 for every **human b** who does evil: 476
3: 1 What advantage, then, is there in **b** a Jew, NIG
3: 8 *b* **slanderously reported** AIT
4:21 *b* **fully persuaded** that God had power AIT
7:22 For in my inner **b** I delight in God's law; 476
1Co 1:18 but *to* us who *are b* **saved** it is the power AIT
11:32 *we are b* **disciplined** so that we will not AIT
14: 7 will anyone know what tune *is b* **played** AIT
15:45 "The first man Adam became a living **b"**; 6034
2Co 2:15 of Christ among those who *are b* **saved** AIT
3:18 *are b* **transformed** into his likeness AIT
4:11 we who are alive *are* always *b* **given over** AIT
4:16 yet inwardly we *are b* **renewed** day by day. AIT
11: 9 I have kept myself from **b** a burden to you NIG
Gal 3:22 **b** given through faith in Jesus Christ, NIG
5:11 why *am I* still *b* **persecuted?** AIT
6:12 to avoid *b* **persecuted** for the cross AIT
Eph 2:22 And in him you too *are b* **built together** AIT
3:16 through his Spirit in your inner **b,** 476
3:17 *b* **rooted** and **established** AIT
4:22 which *is b* **corrupted** AIT
Php 1: 6 *b* **confident** *of* this, AIT
1:26 that through my **b** with you again your joy 4242
1:28 without *b* **frightened** in any way AIT
2: 1 from **b** united with Christ, NIG
2: 2 make my joy complete by **b like-minded,** 899+3836+5858
2: 2 **b** one in spirit and purpose. NIG
2: 6 **b** in very nature God, 5639
2: 7 *b* **made** in human likeness. AIT
2: 8 And *b* **found** in appearance as a man, AIT
2:17 *b* **poured out like a drink offering** AIT
4:12 I have learned the secret of **b** content in any NIG
Col 1:11 *b* **strengthened** with all power according AIT
3:10 which *is b* **renewed** in knowledge in AIT
4: 2 *b* **watchful** and thankful. AIT
2Th 2: 1 and our *b* **gathered** to him, AIT
1Ti 3: 1 **sets** his **heart on b** 3977
3:13 **get into the habit of b** 3443
2Ti 2: 9 to the point of *b* **chained** like a criminal. AIT
3:13 deceiving and *b* **deceived.** AIT
4: 6 *b* **poured out like a drink offering,** AIT
Tit 1: 6 and are not open to the charge of **b** wild NIG
3: 3 **b** hated and hating one another. NIG
Heb 1: 3 and the exact representation of his **b,** 5712
2:18 he is able to help those who *are b* **tempted.** AIT
5:13 Anyone who lives on milk, **b** still an infant, 1639
6: 8 and is in danger of **b cursed.** 2932
9: 9 that the gifts and sacrifices *b* **offered** were AIT
10: 2 would they not have stopped *b* **offered?** AIT
10:14 by one sacrifice he has made perfect forever those who *are b* **made holy.** AIT
11: 1 Now faith is *b* **sure** of what we hope for AIT
Jas 1:27 and to keep oneself **from b polluted** by 834
3: 7 reptiles and creatures of the sea *are b* **tamed** AIT
1Pe 2: 5 *are b* **built** into a spiritual house to be AIT
3:20 of Noah *while* the ark *was b* **built.** AIT
5: 3 but **b** examples to the flock. 1181
2Pe 1: 8 they will keep you from **b** ineffective NIG
3: 7 *b* **kept** for the day of judgment AIT
Rev 3: 1 you have a reputation of *b* **alive,** AIT
4:11 they were created and have *their* **b."** 1639

BEINGS (5) [BEING]
Ps 8: 5 a little lower than the **heavenly b** 466
89: 6 like the LORD among the **heavenly b?** 446+1201
2Pe 2:10 not afraid to slander **celestial b;** 1518
2:11 against **such b** in the presence of the Lord. 899
Jude 1: 8 reject authority and slander **celestial b.** 1518

BEKA (2) [BEKAS]
Ge 24:22 a gold nose ring weighing a **b** 1325
Ex 38:26 *one* **b** per person, 1325

BEKAS (3) [BEKA]
1Ki 10:16 six hundred **b** of gold went into each shield. NIH
2Ch 9:15 six hundred **b** of hammered gold went NIH
9:16 with three hundred **b** of gold in each shield. NIH

BEKER (5) [BEKERITE]
Ge 46:21 Bela, **B,** Ashbel, Gera, Naaman, Ehi, Rosh, 1146
Nu 26:35 through **B,** the Bekerite clan; 1146
1Ch 7: 6 Bela, **B** and Jediael. 1146
7: 8 The sons of **B:** 1146
7: 8 All these were the sons of **B.** 1146

BEKERITE (1) [BEKER]
Nu 26:35 through Beker, the **B** clan; 1151

BEL (3)
Isa 46: 1 **B** bows down, Nebo stoops low; 1155
Jer 50: 2 **B** will be put to shame, 1155
51:44 I will punish **B** in Babylon 1155

BELA (14) [BELAITE, ZOAR]
Ge 14: 2 and the king of **B** (that is, Zoar). 1186
14: 8 the king of Zeboiim and the king of **B** 1186
36:32 **B** son of Beor became king of Edom. 1185
36:33 When **B** died, Jobab son of Zerah 1185
46:21 The sons of Benjamin: **B,** Beker, Ashbel, 1185
Nu 26:38 through **B,** the Belaite clan; 1185
26:40 of **B** through Ard and Naaman were: 1185
1Ch 1:43 **B** son of Beor, 1185
1:44 When **B** died, Jobab son of Zerah 1185
5: 8 and **B** son of Azaz, 1185
7: 6 Three sons of Benjamin: **B,** 1185
7: 7 The sons of **B:** 1185
8: 1 Benjamin was the father of **B** his firstborn, 1185
8: 3 The sons of **B** were: Addar, Gera, Abihud, 1185

BELAH (KJV) See BELA

BELAITE (1) [BELA]
Nu 26:38 through Bela, the **B** clan; 1188

BELCH (KJV) See SPEW

BELIAL (1)
2Co 6:15 harmony is there between Christ and **B?** 1016

BELIEF (1) [BELIEVE]
2Th 2:13 of the Spirit and through **b** in the truth. 4411

BELIEFS (1) [BELIEVE]
Job 11: 4 'My **b** are flawless and I am pure 4375

BELIEVE (160) [BELIEF, BELIEFS, BELIEVED, BELIEVER, BELIEVERS, BELIEVES, BELIEVING]
Ge 45:26 Jacob was stunned; *he did* not **b** them. 586
Ex 4: 1 if *they do* not **b** me or listen to me and say, 586
4: 5 "is so that *they may* **b** that the LORD, 586
4: 8 "If *they do* not **b** you or pay attention to 586
4: 8 *they may* **b** the second. 586
4: 9 But if *they do* not **b** these two signs or listen 586
Nu 14:11 How long *will they* refuse *to* **b** in me, 586
1Ki 10: 7 But *I did* not **b** these things until I came 586
2Ch 9: 6 But *I did* not **b** what they said until I came 586
32:15 *Do* not **b** him, for no god of any nation 586
Job 9:16 *I do* not **b** he would give me a hearing. 586
Ps 78:22 not **b** in God or trust in his deliverance. 586
78:32 in spite of his wonders, *they did* not **b.** 586
106:24 *they did* not **b** his promise. 586
119:66 for *I* **b** in your commands. 586
Pr 26:25 his speech is charming, *do* not **b** him, 586
Isa 43:10 and **b** me and understand that I am he. 586
Jer 29:31 and *has* **led** you **to b** a lie, 1053
40:14 Gedaliah son of Ahikam *did* not **b** them. 586
La 4:12 The kings of the earth *did* not **b,** 586
Hab 1: 5 in your days that *you would* not **b,** 586
Mt 9:28 "*Do you* **b** that I am able to do this?" 4409
18: 6 of these little ones who **b** in me to sin, 4409
21:22 If *you* **b,** you will receive whatever you ask 4409
21:25 he will ask, 'Then why didn't *you* **b** him?' 4409
21:32 and *you did* not **b** him, 4409
21:32 you did not repent and **b** him. 4409
24:23 'There he is!' *do* not **b** it. 4409
24:26 'Here he is, in the inner rooms,' *do* not **b** it. 4409
27:42 and *we will* **b** in him. 4409
Mk 1:15 Repent and **b** the good news!" 1877+4409
5:36 "Don't be afraid; just **b."** 4409
9:24 "*I do* **b;** help me overcome my unbelief!" 4409
9:42 of these little ones who **b** in me to sin, 4409
11:24 **b** that you have received it, 4409
11:31 he will ask, 'Then why didn't *you* **b** him?' 4409
13:21 'Look, there he is!' *do* not **b** it. 4409
15:32 that we may see and **b."** 4409
16:11 *they did* **not b** it. 601
16:13 but *they did* not **b** them either. 4409
16:14 *to* **b** those who had seen him 4409
16:16 whoever *does* **not b** will be condemned. 601
16:17 these signs will accompany those who **b:** 4409
Lk 1:20 because *you did* not **b** my words, 4409
8:12 so that they may not **b** and be saved. 4409
8:13 They **b** for a while, 4409
8:50 just **b,** and she will be healed." 4409
20: 5 he will ask, 'Why didn't *you* **b** him?' 4409
22:67 "If I tell you, *you will* not **b** me, 4409
24:11 But *they did* **not b** the women, 601
24:25 *to* **b** all that the prophets have spoken! 4409
24:41 *while* they still *did* **not b** it because of joy 601
Jn 1: 7 so that through him all men *might* **b.** 4409
1:50 "*You* **b** because I told you I saw you under 4409
3:12 to you of earthly things and *you do* not **b;** 4409
3:12 *will you* **b** if I speak of heavenly things? 4409
3:18 not **b** stands condemned already 4409
4:21 Jesus declared, "**B** me, woman, 4409
4:42 "*We* no longer **b** just because 4409
4:48 Jesus told him, "*you will* never **b."** 4409
5:38 for you *do* not **b** the one he sent. 4409
5:44 How can you **b** if you accept praise 4409
5:46 If you believed Moses, *you* would **b** me, 4409
5:47 But since you *do* not **b** what he wrote, 4409
5:47 how *are you going to* **b** what I say?" 4409
6:29 *to* **b** in the one he has sent." 4409
6:30 that we may see it and **b** you? 4409
6:36 you have seen me and still *you do* not **b.** 4409
6:64 Yet there are some of you who *do* not **b."** 4409
6:64 from the beginning which of them *did* not **b** 4409
6:69 We **b** and know that you are the Holy One 4409
7: 5 For even his own brothers *did* not **b** in him. 4409
8:24 if *you do* not **b** that I am [the one I claim to 4409
8:45 because I tell the truth, *you do* not **b** me! 4409
8:46 I am telling the truth, why don't you **b** me? 4409
9:18 not **b** that he had been blind 4409
9:35 he said, "*Do* you **b** in the Son of Man?" 4409
9:36 "Tell me so that *I may* **b** in him." 4409
9:38 Then the man said, "Lord, *I* **b,"** 4409
10:25 "I did tell you, but *you do* not **b.** 4409
10:26 you *do* not **b** because you are not my sheep. 4409
10:37 not **b** me unless I do what my Father does. 4409
10:38 But if I do it, even though *you do* not **b** me, 4409
10:38 even though you do not believe me, **b** 4409
11:15 so that *you may* **b.** 4409
11:26 *Do you* **b** this?" 4409
11:27 "I **b** that you are the Christ, the Son of God, 4409
11:42 that *they may* **b** that you sent me." 4409
11:48 everyone *will* **b** in him, 4409
12:37 *they* still *would* not **b** in him. 4409
12:39 For this reason they could not **b,** because, 4409
12:44 *he does* not **b** in me only, 4409
13:19 it does happen *you will* **b** that I am He. 4409
14:10 Don't *you* **b** that I am in the Father, 4409
14:11 **B** me when I say that I am in the Father and 4409
14:11 or at least **b** on the evidence of 4409
14:29 so that when it does happen *you will* **b.** 4409
16: 9 in regard to sin, because *men do* not **b** in me; 4409
16:30 This makes *us* **b** that you came from God." 4409
16:31 "*You* **b** at last!" Jesus answered. 4409
17:20 I pray also for those who *will* **b** in me 4409
17:21 that the world *may* **b** that you have sent me. 4409
19:35 and he testifies so that you also *may* **b.** 4409
20:25 *I will* not **b** it." 4409
20:27 Stop doubting and **b."** 4412
20:31 that *you may* **b** that Jesus is the Christ, 4409
Ac 13:41 in your days that *you would* never **b,** 4409
14: 2 But the Jews who **refused to b** stirred up 578
15: 7 the message of the gospel and **b.** 4409
15:11 *We* **b** it is through the grace 4409
16:31 They replied, "**B** in the Lord Jesus, 4409
16:34 with joy *because he had* **come to b** in God 4409
19: 4 the people to **b** in the one coming after him, 4409
19: 9 *they* **refused to b** and publicly maligned 578
22:19 to another to imprison and beat those who **b** 4409
24:14 *I* **b** everything that agrees with the Law 4409
26:27 King Agrippa, *do you* **b** the prophets? 4409
28:24 but others *would* **not b.** 601
Ro 3:22 through faith in Jesus Christ to all who **b.** 4409
4:11 he is the father *of* all who **b** but have 4409
4:24 for us who **b** in him who raised Jesus 4409
6: 8 *we* **b** that we will also live with him. 4409
10: 9 and **b** in your heart that God raised him 4409
10:10 with your heart that *you* **b** and are justified, 4409
10:14 And how *can they* **b in** the one 4409
14:22 So whatever you **b** about these things 2400+4411
16:26 so that all nations might **b** and obey him— 4411
1Co 1:21 of what was preached to save those who **b.** 4409
3: 5 through whom *you came to* **b—** 4409
11:18 and to some extent *I* **b** it. 4409
2Co 4:13 With that same spirit of faith we also **b** and 4409
Gal 3: 5 or because you **b** what you heard? 4411
3: 7 those who **b** are children of Abraham. 1666+4411
3:22 might be given *to* those who **b.** 4409

Eph 1:19 his incomparably great power for us who **b**. *4409*
Php 1:29 on behalf of Christ not only *to* **b** on him, *4409*
1Th 2:13 which is at work in you who **b**. *4409*
4:14 *We* **b** that Jesus died and rose again and *4409*
4:14 that Jesus died and rose again and so we **b** *NIG*
2Th 2:11 a powerful delusion so that they *will* **b** *4409*
1Ti 1:16 an example for those who would **b** on him *4409*
4:3 *by* those who **b** and who know the truth. *4412*
4:10 and especially *of* those who **b**. *4412*
Tit 1:6 a man whose children **b** and are not open to *4412*
1:15 *to* those who are corrupted and do **not b**, *603*
Heb 10:39 but *of* those who **b** and are saved. *4411*
11:6 because anyone who comes to him must **b** *4409*
Jas 1:6 But when he asks, *he must* **b** and not doubt, *4411*
2:19 You **b** that there is one God. *4409*
2:19 Even the demons **b** that—and shudder. *4409*
1Pe 1:8 even though you do not see him now, you **b** *4409*
1:21 Through him you **b** in God, *4412*
2:7 Now to you who **b**, this stone is precious. *4409*
2:7 But *to* those who do **not b**, *601*
3:1 if any of them **do not b** the word, *578*
1Jn 3:23 to **b** in the name of his Son, Jesus Christ, *4409*
4:1 Dear friends, *do* not **b** every spirit, *4409*
5:10 not **b** God has made him out to be a liar, *4409*
5:13 to you who **b** in the name of the Son of God *4409*
Jude 1:5 but later destroyed those who *did* not **b**. *4409*

BELIEVED (66) [BELIEVE]

Ge 15:6 Abram **b** the LORD, and he credited to him as righteousness. 586
Ex 4:31 and they **b**. And when they heard 586
Job 29:24 When I smiled at them, *they* scarcely **b** it; 586
Ps 106:12 *they* **b** his promises and sang his praise. 586
116:10 *I* **b**; therefore I said, 586
Isa 53:1 Who *has* **b** our message and to whom has 586
Jnh 3:5 The Ninevites **b** God. 586
Mt 8:13 It will be done just as *you* **b** it would." *4409*
Lk 1:45 Blessed is she who *has* **b** that what *4409*
Jn 1:12 to those who **b** in his name, *4409*
2:22 Then *they* **b** the Scripture and the words *4409*
2:23 the miraculous signs he was doing and **b** *4409*
3:18 because *he has* not **b** in the name *4409*
4:39 of the Samaritans from that town **b** in him *4409*
4:53 So he and all his household **b**. *4409*
5:46 If *you* **b** Moses, you would believe me, *4409*
7:39 whom those who **b** in him were later *4409*
7:48 of the rulers or of the Pharisees **b** in him? *4409*
8:31 To the Jews who *had* **b** him, Jesus said, *4409*
10:42 And in that place many **b** in Jesus. *4409*
11:40 Jesus said, "Did I not tell you that if *you* **b**, *4409*
12:38 who *has* **b** our message and to whom has *4409*
12:42 even among the leaders **b** in him. *4409*
16:27 because you have loved me and *have* **b** *4409*
17:8 and *they* **b** that you sent me. *4409*
20:8 He saw and **b**. *4409*
20:29 "Because you have seen me, *you have* **b**; *4409*
20:29 who have not seen and yet *have* **b**." *4409*
Ac 4:4 But many who heard the message **b**, *4409*
5:14 and women **b** in the Lord and were added *4409*
8:12 But when *they* **b** Philip as he preached *4409*
8:13 Simon himself **b** and was baptized. *4409*
9:42 and many people **b** in the Lord. *4409*
11:17 *who* **b** in the Lord Jesus Christ, *4409*
11:21 and a great number of people **b** and turned *4409*
13:12 the proconsul saw what had happened, *he* **b**, *4409*
13:48 all who were appointed for eternal life **b**. *4409*
14:1 that a great number of Jews and Gentiles **b**. *4409*
17:12 Many of the Jews **b**, *4409*
17:34 A few men became followers of Paul and **b**. *4409*
18:8 and his entire household **b** in the Lord; *4409*
18:8 of the Corinthians who heard him **b** *4409*
18:27 a great help to those who by grace *had* **b**. *4409*
19:2 the Holy Spirit *when you* **b**?" *4409*
19:18 Many *of* those who **b** now came *4409*
21:20 how many thousands of Jews *have* **b**, *4409*
Ro 4:3 "Abraham **b** God, and it was credited *4409*
4:17 in the sight of God, in whom *he* **b**— *4409*
4:18 in hope **b** and so became the father *4409*
10:14 on the one *they have* not **b in**? *4409*
10:16 "Lord, who *has* **b** our message?" *4409*
13:11 now than when *we* first **b**. *4409*
1Co 15:2 Otherwise, *you have* **b** in vain. *4409*
15:11 and this is what *you* **b**. *4409*
2Co 4:13 It is written: "*I* **b**; therefore I have spoken." *4409*
Gal 3:6 Consider Abraham: "*He* **b** God, *4409*
Eph 1:13 *Having* **b**, you were marked in him with *4409*
1Th 2:10 and blameless we were among you who **b**. *4409*
2Th 1:10 be marveled at among all those who *have* **b**. *4409*
1:10 because you **b** our testimony to you. *4409*
2:12 that all will be condemned who *have* not **b** *4409*
1Ti 3:16 *was* **b on** in the world, *4409*
2Ti 1:12 because I know whom *I have* **b**, *4409*
Heb 4:3 Now we who *have* **b** enter that rest, *4409*
Jas 2:23 "Abraham **b** God, and it was credited *4409*
1Jn 5:10 not **b** the testimony God has given *4409*

BELIEVER (7) [BELIEVE]

1Ki 18:3 (Obadiah was a devout **b** *in* the LORD. 3707
Ac 16:1 whose mother was a Jewess and a **b**, *4412*
16:15 "If you consider me a **b** in the Lord," *1639+4412*
1Co 7:12 If any brother has a wife who is **not a b** *603*
7:13 a husband who is **not a b** and he is willing *603*
2Co 6:15 a **b** have in common with an unbeliever? *4412*
1Ti 5:16 If any woman who is a **b** has widows *4412*

BELIEVERS (21) [BELIEVE]

Jn 4:41 because of his words many more **became b**. *4409*
Ac 1:15 up among the **b** (a group numbering about *81*
2:44 All the **b** were together and had everything *4409*
4:32 All the **b** were one in heart and mind. *4409*
5:12 And all the **b** used to meet together *NIG*
9:41 the **b** and the widows and presented her *41*
10:45 The circumcised **b** who had come *4412*
11:2 the circumcised **b** criticized him *NIG*
15:2 along with some other **b**, *899+1666*[S]
15:5 *of* the **b** who belonged to the party of *4409*
15:23 your brothers, *To* the Gentile **b** in Antioch, *81*
21:25 As for the Gentile **b**, *4409*
1Co 6:5 to judge a dispute between **b**? *81*
14:22 are a sign, not *for* **b** but for unbelievers; *4409*
14:22 prophecy, however, is *for* **b**, *4409*
Gal 6:10 to those who belong to the family *of* **b**. *3836+4411*
1Th 1:7 And so you became a model *to* all the **b** *4409*
1Ti 4:12 but set an example *for* the **b** in speech, *4412*
6:2 those who benefit from their service are **b**, *4412*
Jas 2:1 as **b** in our glorious Lord Jesus Christ, *2400+3836+4411*
1Pe 2:17 Love the **brotherhood of b**, fear God, *82*

BELIEVES (24) [BELIEVE]

Pr 14:15 A simple man **b** anything, 586
Mk 9:23 "Everything is possible *for* him who **b**." *4409*
11:23 and does not doubt in his heart but **b** *4409*
16:16 Whoever **b** and is baptized will be saved, *4409*
Jn 3:15 that everyone who **b** *4409*
3:16 that whoever **b** in him shall not perish *4409*
3:18 Whoever **b** in him is not condemned, *4409*
3:36 Whoever **b** in the Son has eternal life, *4409*
5:24 and **b** him who sent me has eternal life *4409*
6:35 and he who **b** in me will never be thirsty. *4409*
6:40 the Son and **b** in him shall have eternal life, *4409*
6:47 he who **b** has everlasting life. *4409*
7:38 Whoever **b** in me, as the Scripture has said, *4409*
11:25 He who **b** in me will live, *4409*
11:26 whoever lives and **b** in me will never die. *4409*
12:44 Then Jesus cried out, "*When* a man **b** in me, *4409*
12:46 so that no one who **b** in me should stay *4409*
Ac 10:43 about him that everyone who **b** *4409*
13:39 Through him everyone who **b** is justified *4409*
Ro 1:16 for the salvation *of* everyone who **b**: *4409*
10:4 be righteousness for everyone who **b**. *4409*
1Jn 5:1 Everyone who **b** that Jesus is the Christ *4409*
5:5 Only he who **b** that Jesus is the Son of God. *4409*
5:10 Anyone who **b** in the Son *4409*

BELIEVING (7) [BELIEVE]

Jn 20:31 that *by* **b** you may have life in his name. *4409*
Ac 9:26 not **b** that he really was a disciple. *4409*
1Co 7:14 sanctified through her **b** husband. *NIG*
7:15 A **b man** or woman is not bound *81*
9:5 Don't we have the right to take a **b wife** *80+1222*
Gal 3:2 or by **b** what you heard? *4411*
1Ti 6:2 Those who have **b** masters are not *4412*

BELLOW (1) [BELLOWS]

Job 6:5 or an ox **b** when it has fodder? 1716

BELLOWS (1) [BELLOW]

Jer 6:29 The **b** blow fiercely to burn away the lead 5135

BELLS (6)

Ex 28:33 with gold **b** between them. 7194
28:34 The gold **b** and the pomegranates are 7194
28:35 of **the b** will be heard when he enters 2257[S]
39:25 And they made **b** *of* pure gold 7194
39:26 The **b** and pomegranates alternated around 7194
Zec 14:20 be inscribed on the **b** *of* the horses, 5197

BELLY (9)

Ge 3:14 on your **b** and you will eat dust all the days 1623
Lev 11:42 whether it moves on its **b** or walks 1623
Jdg 3:21 and plunged it into the king's **b**. 1061
2Sa 20:10 and Joab plunged it into his **b**, 2824
Job 15:2 with empty notions or fill his **b** with 1061
20:23 When he has filled his **b**, 1061
40:16 what power in the muscles of his **b**! 1061
Da 2:32 its **b** and thighs of bronze, 10435
Mt 12:40 and three nights in the **b** of a huge fish, *3120*

BELONG (81) [BELONGED, BELONGING, BELONGINGS, BELONGS]

Ge 32:17 '**To** whom do you **b**, 4200
32:18 'They **b to** your servant Jacob. 4200
40:8 "Do not interpretations **b to** God? 4200
45:11 and your household and all who **b to** 4200
Ex 13:12 the firstborn males of your livestock **b to** 4200
21:4 and her children *shall* **b to** her master, 2118+4200
29:27 of the ordination ram that **b to** Aaron 4200
29:29 "Aaron's sacred garments *will* **b to** 2118+4200
Lev 5:13 of the offering *will* **b to** the priest, 2118+4200
7:7 *They* **b to** the priest who makes atonement 2118+4200
25:30 in the walled city *shall* **b** permanently to 7756
25:55 for the Israelites **b to** me as servants. 4200
Nu 5:9 the Israelites bring to a priest *will* **b to** 2118+4200
5:10 what he gives to the priest *will* **b to** 2118+4200
6:20 they are holy and **b to** the priest, 4200
Dt 10:14 **To** the LORD your God **b** 4200
20:15 at a distance from you and do not **b to** 4946
29:29 The secret things **b to** the LORD our God, 4200
29:29 but the things revealed **b to** us and 4200
33:8 and Urim **b to** the man you favored. 4200
Jos 2:13 and all who **b to** them, 4200
6:22 and bring her out and all who **b to** her, 4200
1Sa 25:22 of all who **b to** him!" 4200
30:13 "**To** whom do you **b**, 4200
1Ki 8:41 not **b to** your people Israel but has come 4946
2Ch 6:32 not **b to** your people Israel but has come 4946
Ne 5:5 because our fields and our vineyards **b to** 4200
Job 12:13 "**To** God **b** wisdom and power; 6640
12:16 **To** him **b** strength and victory; 6640
25:2 "Dominion and awe **b to** God; 6640
Ps 47:9 for the kings of the earth **b to** God; 4200
95:4 and the mountain peaks **b to** him. 4200
104:18 The high mountains **b to** the wild goats; 4200
115:16 The highest heavens **b to** the LORD, 4200
Pr 16:1 **To** man **b** the plans of the heart, 4200
SS 7:10 I **b to** my lover, and his desire is for me. 4200
Isa 44:5 One will say, 'I **b to** the LORD'; 4200
Jer 5:10 for these people do not **b to** the LORD. 4200
Eze 13:9 not **b to** the council of my people or 928+2118
18:4 both alike **b to** me. 4200
44:29 in Israel devoted to the LORD *will* **b to** 2118+4200
44:30 and of all your special gifts *will* **b to** 2118+4200
45:5 cubits wide *will* **b** to the Levites, 2118
45:6 *it will* **b to** the whole house of Israel. 2118+4200
46:16 it *will* also **b to** his descendants; 2118+4200
48:21 and the city property will **b to** the prince. 4200
48:21 of the tribal portions will **b to** the prince, 4200
Zep 2:7 It *will* **b to** the remnant of the house 2118+4200
Zec 9:7 Those who are left will **b to** our God 4200
Mt 20:23 *b to* **those for whom** *AIT*
Mk 9:41 a cup of water in my name because *you* **b** *1639*
10:40 These places **b** to those *NIG*
13:14 where *it does* not **b**— *1256*
Jn 8:44 You **b to** your father, the devil, *1639+1666*
8:47 not hear is that *you do* not **b to** God." *1639+1666*
14:24 they *b to* the **Father** who sent me. *AIT*
15:19 As it is, *you do* not **b to** the world, *1639+1666*
Ac 5:4 Didn't *it* **b** to you before it was sold? *3531*
Ro 1:6 to *b to* **Jesus Christ.** *AIT*
7:4 that you *might* **b** to another, *1181*
8:9 he **does** not **b to** Christ. *1639*
14:8 whether we live or die, *we* **b to** the **Lord.** *1639+3261*
16:10 Greet those who **b to** the household *1666*
1Co 7:4 not **b to** her alone but also to her husband. *2027*
7:4 not **b to** him alone but also to his wife. *2027*
7:39 but he must **b to** the Lord. *1877*
9:19 **free and b to no man,** *1666+1801+4246*
12:15 I do not **b to** the body," *1666*
12:16 I do not **b to** the body," *1666*
15:23 then, when he comes, those who *b to* **him.** *AIT*
2Co 10:7 that we *b to* **Christ** just as much as he. *AIT*
Gal 3:29 If you *b to* **Christ,** *AIT*
5:24 Those who *b to* **Christ Jesus** have crucified *AIT*
6:10 to those who **b to** the **family** of believers. *3858*
Php 4:22 especially those who **b to** *1666*
1Th 5:5 We do not **b to** the night or to *1639*
5:8 But *since* we **b** to the day, *1639*
Jas 2:7 the noble name of him to whom you **b**? *2126*
1Jn 2:19 but *they did* not really **b to** us. *1639+1666*
3:19 then is how we know that *we* **b** to the truth, *1639*
Rev 19:1 and glory and power *b to* our **God,** *AIT*

BELONGED (51) [BELONG]

Ge 30:40 and dark-colored **animals** *that b to* Laban. AIT
31:1 from what **b to** our father." 4200
Nu 3:21 **To** Gershon **b** the clans of the Libnites 4200
3:27 **To** Kohath **b** the clans of the Amramites, 4200
3:33 **To** Merari **b** the clans of the Mahlites and 4200
27:1 **b** to the clans of Manasseh son of Joseph. 4200
Dt 11:6 tents and every living thing that **b to** 928+8079
30:5 He will bring you to the land that **b** 3769
Jos 6:23 and mother and brothers and all who **b to** 4200
6:25 with her family and all who **b to** her, 4200
14:14 So Hebron *has* **b to** Caleb son 2118+4200
17:6 Gilead **b to** the rest of the descendants 2118+4200
17:8 **b to** the Ephraimites.) 4200
17:10 On the south the land **b to** Ephraim, 4200
Jdg 6:11 under the oak in Ophrah that **b to** Joash 4200
Ru 4:3 of land that **b to** our brother Elimelech. 4200
1Sa 27:6 and it *has* **b to** the kings 2118+4200
2Sa 8:7 the gold shields that **b to** the officers 448+2118
8:8 **towns** *that b to* Hadadezer, AIT
9:7 the **land** *that b to* your grandfather Saul, AIT
9:9 that **b to** Saul and his family. 2118+4200
12:4 the **ewe lamb** *that b to* the poor man AIT
16:4 "All that **b to** Mephibosheth is now yours." 4200
1Ki 6:22 also overlaid with gold the altar that **b to** 4200
2Ki 8:6 "Give back everything that **b to** her, 4200
9:21 **plot of ground** *that had b* AIT
9:25 the **field** *that b to* Naboth the Jezreelite. AIT
11:10 that had **b to** King David and that were in 4200
12:16 *it* **b to** the priests. 2118+4200
14:28 which had **b to** Yaudi, 4200
1Ch 5:2 the rights of the firstborn **b to** Joseph)— 4200
18:8 **towns** *that b to* Hadadezer, AIT
2Ch 23:9 and small shields that had **b to** King David 4200
26:23 near them in a field for burial that **b to** 4200
Eze 23:41 the incense and **oil** *that b to* me. AIT
46:19 which **b to** the priests, 448

Lk 1: 5 who **b to** the priestly division of Abijah; *1666*
2: 4 because he **b to** the house and line *1639+1666*
5:30 the teachers of the law **who b to their sect** *899*
Jn 15:19 If *you* **b to** the world, *1639+1666*
Ac 9: 2 that if he found any there *who* **b to** the Way, *1639*
12: 1 that King Herod arrested some who **b to** *608*
15: 5 of the believers **who b to** the party of *608*
27: 1 *b to* the Imperial **Regiment.** *AIT*
28: 7 **was** an estate nearby **that b** *5639*
Gal 2:12 of those who **b to** the circumcision group. *1666*
Col 2:20 why, as though *you still* **b** to it, *2409*
Heb 7:13 *He* of whom these things are said **b to** *3576*
1Jn 2:19 For if *they had* **b to** us, *1639+1666*
2:19 that none of them **b to** us. *1639+1666*
3:12 who **b to** the evil one *1666*

BELONGING (37) [BELONG]

Ge 14:23 that I will accept nothing **b to** you, 4200
50: 8 *b to* his father's **household.** AIT
Ex 9: 4 no animal **b to** the Israelites will die.' " 4200
9: 6 but not one animal **b to** the Israelites died. 4946
Lev 7:20 of the fellowship offering **b to** the LORD, 4200
7:21 of the fellowship offering **b to** the LORD, 4200
25:34 But the **pastureland** *b to* their towns must AIT
Nu 1:50 over all its furnishings and everything **b to** 4200
16:26 Do not touch anything **b to** them, 4200
17: 5 The **staff** *b to* the man I choose AIT
31:42 The **half** *b to* the Israelites, AIT
Dt 2:19 not give you possession of any **land** *b to* AIT
Jos 17: 9 There were towns **b to** Ephraim lying 4200
Ru 2: 3 she found herself working in a field **b to** 4200
1Sa 6:18 of Philistine towns **b to** the five rulers— 4200
9: 3 donkeys **b to** Saul's father Kish were lost, 4200
25:34 not one male **b to** Nabal 4200
30:14 and the territory **b to** Judah and the Negev 4200
1Ki 14:11 Dogs will eat those **b to** Jeroboam who die 4200
14:13 He is the only one **b to** Jeroboam who will 4200
16: 4 Dogs will eat those **b to** Baasha who die in 4200
21: 1 a vineyard **b to** Naboth the Jezreelite. 2118+4200
21:24 "Dogs will eat those **b to** Ahab who die in 4200
1Ch 7: 5 The relatives who were fighting men **b to** 4200
9:18 These were the gatekeepers **b to** the camp 4200
22:19 of the LORD and the sacred **articles** *b* AIT
23: 7 **B to** the Gershonites: Ladan and Shimei. 4200
26:21 and who were heads of families **b to** Ladan 4200
28: 1 and livestock **b to** the king and his sons, 4200
2Ch 34:33 from all the territory **b to** the Israelites, 4200
Ezr 1: 7 King Cyrus brought out the **articles** *b to* AIT
Eze 37:16 **'B to** Judah and the Israelites associated 4200
37:16 **b to** Joseph and all the house 4200
48:22 The area **b to** the prince will lie between 4200
Lk 5: 3 the one **b to Simon,** *1639+4981*
1Pe 2: 9 a holy nation, a people **b** to God, *1650+4348*
Rev 13: 8 book of life *b to* **the Lamb** that was slain *AIT*

BELONGINGS (8) [BELONG]

Ge 45:20 Never mind about your **b**, 3998
Jdg 14:19 of their **b** and gave their clothes 2723
Jer 10:17 Gather up your **b** to leave the land, 4045
46:19 Pack your **b** *for* exile, 3998
Eze 12: 3 pack your **b** *for* exile and in the daytime, 3998
12: 4 bring out your **b** packed for exile. 3998
12: 5 dig through the wall and take your **b** out NIH
12: 7 I took my **b** out at dusk, NIH

BELONGS (58) [BELONG]

Ge 14:24 and the **share** *that b to* the men who went AIT
19:12 or anyone else in the city who **b to** you? 4200
23: 9 which **b to** him and is at the end 4200
31:16 that God took away from our father **b to** us 4200
31:37 what have you found that **b to** 4946
47:18 and our livestock **b to** you, 448
47:26 that a fifth of the produce **b to** Pharaoh. 4200
49:10 until he comes **to** whom it **b** and 4200
Ex 13: 2 of every womb among the Israelites **b to** 4200
20:17 or anything that **b to** your neighbor." 4200
34:19 first offspring of every womb **b to** me, 4200
40: 4 Bring in the table and set out **what b** *on* it. 6886
Lev 2: 3 the grain offering **b to** Aaron and his sons; 4200
2:10 the grain offering **b to** Aaron and his sons; 4200
7: 9 on a griddle **b to** the priest who offers it, 2118+4200
7:10 **b** equally to all the sons of Aaron. 2118
7:14 *it* **b to** the priest who sprinkles the blood 2118+4200
7:31 but the breast **b to** Aaron and his sons. 2118+4200
14:13 the guilt offering **b to** the priest; 4200
24: 9 *It* **b to** Aaron and his sons, 2118+4200
27:26 **firstborn** already **b to** the LORD 1144+4200
27:30 **b to** the LORD; it is holy to the LORD. 4200
Nu 5: 8 the restitution **b to** the LORD and must 4200
16: 5 the LORD will show who **b to** him 4200
16:30 with everything that **b to** them, 4200
18: 9 that part **b to** you and your sons. 4200
Dt 1:17 for judgment **b to** God. 4200
5:21 or anything that **b to** your neighbor." 4200
21:17 The right of the firstborn **b to** him. 4200
Jos 7:15 along with all that **b to** him. 4200
1Sa 15: 3 and totally destroy everything that **b to** 4200
1Ki 22: 3 "Don't you know that Ramoth Gilead **b to** 4200
1Ch 29:16 and all of it **b to** you. 4200
Job 41:11 Everything under heaven **b to** me. 4200
Ps 22:28 for dominion **b to** the LORD and he rules 4200
89:18 Indeed, our shield **b to** the LORD, 4200
111:10 *To* him *b* eternal **praise.** AIT
Jer 46:10 But that day **b to** the Lord, 4200
Eze 18: 4 For every living soul **b to** me, 4200
21:27 **to** whom it rightfully **b;** 4200
46:17 His inheritance **b to** his sons only; NIH
48:22 the center of the area that **b to** the prince. 4200
Mt 19:14 the kingdom of heaven **b to** such as these." *1639*
25:25 See, here is what **b to you.'** *2400+5050*
Mk 10:14 for the kingdom of God **b to** such as these. *1639*
Lk 6:30 and if anyone takes what **b to you,** *5050*
18:16 for the kingdom of God **b to** such as these. *1639*
Jn 3:29 The bride **b to** the bridegroom. *2400*
3:31 who is from the earth **b to** the earth, *1639+1666*
8:35 but a son **b to** it forever. *3531*
8:47 He who **b to** God hears what God says *1639+1666*
16:15 All that **b to** the Father is mine. *2400*
Ac 1:25 which Judas left to go where *he* **b."** *2625*
Ro 12: 5 and each member **b to** all the others. *NIG*
2Co 10: 7 If anyone is confident that he **b to Christ,** *1639+5986*
Col 3: 5 whatever **b** to your earthly nature: *NIG*
Rev 7:10 "Salvation *b to* our **God,** *AIT*
17:11 *He* **b to** the seven and is going *1639+1666*

BELOVED (4) [LOVE]

Dt 33:12 the **b** *of* the LORD rest secure in him, 3351
SS 5: 9 How is your **b** better than others, 1856
5: 9 How is your **b** better than others, 1856
Jer 11:15 "What is my **b** doing in my temple 3351

BELOW (42)

Ge 35: 8 was buried under the oak **b** Bethel. 4946+9393
49:25 blessings of the deep that lies **b,** 9393
Ex 20: 4 the earth beneath or in the waters **b.** 4946+9393
30: 4 Make two gold rings for the altar **b** 4946+9393
37:27 made two gold rings **b** the molding— 4946+9393
Dt 3:17 **b** the slopes of Pisgah. 9393
4:18 the ground or any fish in the waters **b.** 4946+9393
4:39 in heaven above and on the earth **b.** 4946+9393
4:49 **b** the slopes of Pisgah. 9393
5: 8 the earth beneath or in the waters **b.** 4946+9393
32:22 one that burns to the realm of death **b.** 9397
33:13 above and with the deep waters that lie **b;** 9393
Jos 2:11 in heaven above and on the earth **b.** 4946+9393
11: 3 and to the Hivites **b** Hermon in the region 9393
11:17 in the Valley of Lebanon **b** Mount Hermon. 9393
12: 3 and then southward **b** the slopes of Pisgah. 9393
13: 5 the east, from Baal Gad **b** Mount Hermon 9393
Jdg 7: 8 the camp of Midian lay **b** him in the valley. 4946+9393
1Sa 7:11 along the way to a point **b** Beth Car. 4946+9393
1Ki 4:12 Beth Shan next to Zarethan **b** Jezreel, 4946+9393
7:24 **B** the rim, gourds encircled it— 4946+9393
7:29 and **b** the lions and bulls were wreaths 4946+9393
8:23 like you in heaven above or on earth **b** 4946+9393
2Ki 19:30 of the house of Judah will take root **b** 4200+4752
2Ch 4: 3 **B** the rim, figures of bulls encircled it— 9393
Job 18:16 up **b** and his branches wither above. 4946+9393
28: 5 is transformed **b** as by fire; 9393
Isa 14: 9 The grave **b** is all astir to meet you 4946+9393
24:21 and the kings on the earth **b.** 141+2021+6584
37:31 of the house of Judah will take root **b** 4200+4752
Jer 31:37 the earth **b** be searched out 4200+4752
Eze 26:20 I will make you dwell in the earth **b,** 9397
31:14 for the earth **b,** among mortal men, 9397
31:16 were consoled in the earth **b.** 9397
31:18 down with the trees of Eden to the earth **b;** 9397
32:18 of Egypt and consign to the earth **b** both her 9397
32:24 down uncircumcised to the earth **b.** 9397
Am 2: 9 I destroyed his fruit above and his roots **b.** 4946+9393
Jnh 1: 5 But Jonah had gone **b deck,** 2021+3752+6208
Mk 14:66 While Peter was **b** in the courtyard, *3004*
Jn 8:23 But he continued, "You are from **b;** *3004*
Ac 2:19 the heaven above and signs on the earth **b,** *3004*

BELSHAZZAR (6) [BELSHAZZAR'S]

Da 5: 1 King **B** gave a great banquet for a thousand 10109
5: 2 While **B** was drinking his wine, 10109
5: 9 So King **B** became even more terrified 10109
5:22 "But you his son, O **B,** 10109
5:30 That very night **B,** king of the Babylonians, 10105
7: 1 In the first year of **B** king of Babylon, 10105

BELSHAZZAR'S (2) [BELSHAZZAR]

Da 5:29 Then at **B** command, 10109
8: 1 In the third year of King **B** reign, I, Daniel, 1157

BELT (25) [BELTS]

Ex 12:11 **cloak tucked into** your **b,** 2520+5516
1Sa 18: 4 and even his sword, his bow and his **b.** 2512
2Sa 18:11 of silver and a **warrior's b."** 2514
20: 8 over it at his waist was a **b** with a dagger 2512
1Ki 2: 5 that blood stained the **b** around his waist 2514
18:46 **tucking** his **cloak into** *his* **b,** 5516+9113
2Ki 1: 8 with a garment of hair and with a leather **b** 258
4:29 **"Tuck** your **cloak into** your **b,** 2520+5516
9: 1 **"Tuck** *your* **cloak into** your **b,** 2520+5516
Ps 109:19 like a **b** tied forever around him. 4652
Isa 5:27 not a **b** is loosened at the waist, 258
11: 5 Righteousness will be his **b** and 258+5516
Jer 13: 1 a linen **b** and put it around your waist, 258
13: 2 So I bought a **b,** as the LORD directed, 258
13: 4 "Take the **b** you bought and are wearing 258
13: 6 "Go now to Perath and get the **b** I told you 258
13: 7 to Perath and dug up the **b** and took it from 258
13:10 will be like this **b**—completely useless! 258
13:11 For as a **b** is bound around a man's waist, 258
Da 10: 5 with a **b** of the finest gold around his waist. 2520
Mt 3: 4 and he had a leather **b** around his waist. *2438*
Mk 1: 6 with a leather **b** around his waist, *2438*
Ac 21:11 Coming over to us, he took Paul's **b,** *2438*
21:11 the owner of this **b** and will hand him over *2438*
Eph 6:14 the **b** of truth buckled around your waist, *4019*

BELTESHAZZAR (10)

Da 1: 7 to Daniel, the name **B;** 1171
2:26 The king asked Daniel (also called **B**), 10108
4: 8 (He is called **B,** after the name of my god, 10108
4: 9 I said, **"B,** chief of the magicians, 10108
4:18 Now, **B,** tell me what it means, 10108
4:19 (also called **B**) was greatly perplexed for 10108
4:19 So the king said, **"B,** 10108
4:19 **B** answered, "My lord, 10108
5:12 This man Daniel, whom the king called **B,** 10108
10: 1 to Daniel (who was called **B**). 1171

BELTS (3) [BELT]

Eze 23:15 with **b** around their waists 258+2513
Mt 10: 9 or silver or copper in your **b;** *2438*
Mk 6: 8 no bread, no bag, no money in your **b.** *2438*

BEMOAN, BEMOANED, BEMOANING (KJV) See MOURN, SHOW SYMPATHY

BEN HINNOM (10)

Jos 15: 8 Valley of **B** along the southern slope of 1208
18:16 of the hill facing the Valley of **B,** 1208
2Ki 23:10 which was in the Valley of **B,** 1208
2Ch 28: 3 of **B** and sacrificed his sons in 1208
33: 6 in the fire in the Valley of **B,** 1208
Jer 7:31 the Valley of **B** to burn their sons 1208
7:32 or the Valley of **B,** 1208
19: 2 and go out to the Valley of **B,** 1208
19: 6 or the Valley of **B,** 1208
32:35 for Baal in the Valley of **B** 1208

BEN-ABINADAB (1) [ABINADAB]

1Ki 4:11 **B**—in Naphoth Dor (he was married to 1203

BEN-AMMI (1)

Ge 19:38 and she named him **B;** 1214

BEN-DEKER (1)

1Ki 4: 9 **B**—in Makaz, Shaalbim, 1206

BEN-GEBER (1) [GEBER]

1Ki 4:13 **B**—in Ramoth Gilead 1205

BEN-HADAD (28) [BEN-HADAD'S, HADAD]

1Ki 15:18 and sent them to **B** son of Tabrimmon, 1207
15:20 **B** agreed with King Asa and sent 1207
20: 1 **B** king of Aram mustered his entire army. 1207
20: 2 saying, "This is what **B** says: 1207
20: 5 "This is what **B** says: 1207
20: 9 They left and took the answer back to **B.** 2084S
20:10 Then **B** sent another message to Ahab: 1207
20:12 **B** heard this message while he and NIH
20:16 at noon while **B** and the 32 kings allied 1207
20:17 Now **B** had dispatched scouts, 1207
20:20 But **B** king of Aram escaped on horseback 1207
20:26 The next spring **B** mustered the Arameans 1207
20:30 And **B** fled to the city and hid in 1207
20:32 "Your servant **B** says: 1207
20:33 "Yes, your brother **B!"** 1207
20:33 When **B** came out, 1207
20:34 from your father," **B** offered. NIH
2Ki 6:24 **B** king of Aram mobilized his entire army 1207
8: 7 and **B** king of Aram was ill. 1207
8: 9 "Your son **B** king of Aram has sent me 1207
8:14 **B** asked, "What did Elisha say to you?" NIH
13: 3 of Hazael king of Aram and **B** his son. 1207
13:24 and **B** his son succeeded him as king. 1207
13:25 of Jehoahaz recaptured from **B** son 1207
2Ch 16: 2 and of his own palace and sent it to **B** king 1207
16: 4 **B** agreed with King Asa and sent 1207
Jer 49:27 it will consume the fortresses of **B."** 1207
Am 1: 4 that will consume the fortresses of **B.** 1207

BEN-HADAD'S (1) [BEN-HADAD]

1Ki 20: 9 So he replied to **B** messengers, 1207

BEN-HAIL (1)

2Ch 17: 7 of his reign he sent his officials **B,** 1211

BEN-HANAN (1) [HANAN]

1Ch 4:20 Amnon, Rinnah, **B** and Tilon. 1212

BEN-HESED (1)

1Ki 4:10 **B**—in Arubboth (Socoh 1213

BEN-HUR (1) [HUR]

1Ki 4: 8 These are their names: **B**— 1210

BEN-ONI (1)
Ge 35:18 she named her son **B**. 1204

BEN-ZOHETH (1)
1Ch 4:20 The descendants of Ishi: Zoheth and **B**. 1209

BENAIAH (45)
2Sa 8:18 **B** son of Jehoiada was over the Kerethites 1226
20:23 **B** son of Jehoiada was over the Kerethites 1225
23:20 **B** son of Jehoiada was a valiant fighter 1226
23:21 **B** went against him with a club. NIH
23:22 the exploits of **B** son of Jehoiada; 1226
23:30 **B** the Pirathonite, Hiddai from the ravines 1226
1Ki 1: 8 But Zadok the priest, **B** son of Jehoiada, 1226
1:10 not invite Nathan the prophet or **B** or 1226
1:26 and **B** son of Jehoiada, 1226
1:32 Nathan the prophet and **B** son of Jehoiada." 1226
1:36 **B** son of Jehoiada answered the king, 1226
1:38 Nathan the prophet, **B** son of Jehoiada, 1226
1:44 Nathan the prophet, **B** son of Jehoiada, 1226
2:25 So King Solomon gave orders to **B** son 1226
2:29 Then Solomon ordered **B** son of Jehoiada, 1226
2:30 So **B** entered the tent of the LORD 1226
2:30 **B** reported to the king, 1226
2:31 the king commanded **B**, "Do as he says. 2257S
2:34 So **B** son of Jehoiada went up and struck 1226
2:35 The king put **B** son of Jehoiada over 1226
2:46 king gave the order to **B** son of Jehoiada, 1226
4: 4 **B** son of Jehoiada— 1226
1Ch 4:36 Jeshohaiah, Asaiah, Adiel, Jesimiel, **B**, 1225
11:22 **B** son of Jehoiada was a valiant fighter 1225
11:23 **B** went against him with a club. NIH
11:24 the exploits of **B** son of Jehoiada; 1226
11:31 of Ribai from Gibeah in Benjamin, **B** 1225
15:18 Eliab, **B**, Maaseiah, Mattithiah, Eliphelehu, 1226
15:20 and **B** were to play the lyres according 1226
15:24 **B** and Eliezer the priests were 1226
16: 5 Mattithiah, Eliab, **B**, Obed-Edom and Jeiel. 1226
16: 6 and **B** and Jahaziel the priests were to blow 1226
18:17 **B** son of Jehoiada was over the Kerethites 1226
27: 5 was **B** son of Jehoiada the priest. 1226
27: 6 This was the **B** who was a mighty man 1226
27:14 was **B** the Pirathonite, an Ephraimite. 1225
27:34 by Jehoiada son of **B** and by Abiathar. 1226
2Ch 20:14 the son of **B**, the son of Jeiel, 1225
31:13 and **B** were supervisors under Conaniah 1226
Ezr 10:25 Mijamin, Eleazar, Malkijah and **B**. 1225
10:30 Adna, Kelal, **B**, Maaseiah, Mattaniah, 1225
10:35 **B**, Bedeiah, Keluhi, 1225
10:43 Zabad, Zebina, Jaddai, Joel and **B**. 1225
Eze 11: 1 of Azzur and Pelatiah son of **B**, 1226
11:13 Pelatiah son of **B** died. 1225

BENCHES (2)
Mt 21:12 the tables of the money changers and the **b** *2756*
Mk 11:15 the tables of the money changers and the **b** *2756*

BEND (9) [BENDING, BENT]
Ge 49:15 *he will* **b** his shoulder to the burden 5742
2Sa 22:35 my arms *can* **b** a bow of bronze. 5737
Ps 7:12 *he will* **b** and string his bow. 2005
11: 2 For look, the wicked **b** their bows; 2005
18:34 my arms *can* **b** a bow of bronze. 5737
37:14 The wicked draw the sword and **b** the bow 2005
Isa 65:12 and you *will* all **b down** for the slaughter; 4156
Zec 9:13 *I will* **b** Judah as I bend my bow and fill it 2005
9:13 I will bend Judah as I **b** my bow and fill it NIH

BENDING (1) [BEND]
Lk 24:12 **B over,** he saw the strips of linen lying *4160*

BENE BERAK (1)
Jos 19:45 Jehud, **B**, Gath Rimmon, 1222

BENE JAAKAN (2) [JAAKANITES]
Nu 33:31 and camped at **B**. 1223
33:32 They left **B** and camped 1223

BENEATH (22) [UNDERNEATH]
Ex 20: 4 on the earth **b** or in the waters below. 4946+9393
Lev 26:19 like iron and the **ground** *b* you like bronze. AIT
Dt 5: 8 on the earth **b** or in the waters below. 4946+9393
28:23 the ground **b** you iron. 9393
2Sa 22:37 You broaden the path **b** me, 9393
22:39 they fell **b** my feet. 9393
1Ki 8: 6 and put it **b** the wings of the cherubim. 9393
2Ch 5: 7 and put it **b** the wings of the cherubim. 9393
Job 26: 5 those **b** the waters and all that live in them. 4946+9393
37: 3 He unleashes his lightning **b** 9393
Ps 18:36 You broaden the path **b** me, 9393
18:38 they fell **b** my feet. 9393
45: 5 let the nations fall **b** your feet. 9393
Isa 14:11 maggots are spread out **b** you 9393
44:23 shout aloud, O earth **b**. 9397
51: 6 look at the earth **b**; 4946+9393
Eze 10: 2 "Go in among the wheels **b** the cherubim. 9393
10:20 These were the living creatures I had seen **b** 9393
24: 5 Pile wood **b** it for the bones; 9393
Joel 1:17 The seeds are shriveled **b** the clods. 9393
Jnh 2: 6 the earth **b** barred me in forever. NIH
Mic 1: 4 The mountains melt **b** him and 9393

BENEFACTORS (1)
Lk 22:25 over them call themselves **B**. *2309*

BENEFICIAL (2) [BENEFIT]
1Co 6:12 but not everything *is* **b**. *5237*
10:23 but not everything **is b**. *5237*

BENEFIT (16) [BENEFICIAL, BENEFITED, BENEFITS]
Job 22: 2 "*Can* a man **be of b** to God? 6122
22: 2 *Can* even a wise man **b** him? 6122
Ecc 5:11 And what **b** are they to the owner except 4179
Isa 38:17 it was for my **b** that I suffered such anguish. 8934
57:12 and *they will* not **b** you. 3603
Jer 23:32 **b** these people **in the least**," 3603+3603
Jn 11:42 but I said this **for the b of** *1328*
12:30 Jesus said, "This voice was **for** your **b**, *1328*
Ro 6:21 What **b** did you reap at that time from *2843*
6:22 the **b** you reap leads to holiness, *2843*
1Co 4: 6 to myself and Apollos **for** your **b**, *1328*
2Co 1:15 I planned to visit you first so that *you might* **b** twice. *2400+5921*
4:15 All this is **for** your **b**, *1328*
Eph 4:29 that *it may* **b** those who listen. *1443+5921*
1Ti 6: 2 because those who **b** *514*
Phm 1:20 *I may have* some **b** from you in the Lord; *3949*

BENEFITED (1) [BENEFIT]
1Sa 19: 4 and what he has done has **b** you greatly. 3202

BENEFITS (5) [BENEFIT]
Dt 18: 8 He is to share equally in their **b**, 2750
Ps 103: 2 O my soul, and forget not all his **b**— 1691
Pr 11:17 A kind man **b** himself, 1694
Ecc 7:11 is a good thing and **b** those who see the sun. 3463
Jn 4:38 and you *have* **reaped the b of** their labor." *1656*

BENINU (1)
Ne 10:13 Hodiah, Bani and **B**. 1231

BENJAMIN (136) [BENJAMIN'S, BENJAMITE, BENJAMITES]
Ge 35:18 But his father named him **B**. 1228
35:24 The sons of Rachel: Joseph and **B**. 1228
42: 4 But Jacob did not send **B**, Joseph's brother, 1228
42:36 and now you want to take **B**. 1228
43:14 and **B** come back with you. 1228
43:15 the amount of silver, and **B** also. 1228
43:16 When Joseph saw **B** with them, 1228
43:29 As he looked about and saw his brother **B**, 1228
45:12 and so can my brother **B**, 1228
45:14 around his brother **B** and wept, 1228
45:14 and **B** embraced him, weeping. 1228
45:22 to **B** he gave three hundred shekels of silver 1228
46:19 sons of Jacob's wife Rachel: Joseph and **B**. 1228
46:21 The sons of **B**: 1228
49:27 "**B** is a ravenous wolf; 1228
Ex 1: 3 Issachar, Zebulun and **B**; 1228
Nu 1:11 from **B**, Abidan son of Gideoni; 1228
1:36 From the descendants of **B**: 1228
1:37 number from the tribe of **B** was 35,400. 1228
2:22 The tribe of **B** will be next. 1228
2:22 The leader of the people of **B** is Abidan son 1228
7:60 the leader of the people of **B**, 1228
10:24 over the division of the tribe of **B**. 1201+1228
13: 9 from the tribe of **B**, Palti son of Raphu; 1228
26:38 The descendants of **B** by their clans were: 1228
26:41 These were the clans of **B**; 1201+1228
34:21 Elidad son of Kislon, from the tribe of **B**; 1228
Dt 27:12 Levi, Judah, Issachar, Joseph and **B**. 1228
33:12 About **B** he said: 1228
Jos 18:11 The lot came up for the tribe of **B**, 1201+1228
18:20 the inheritance of the clans of **B** 1201+1228
18:21 The tribe of **B**, clan by clan, 1201+1228
18:28 the inheritance of **B** for its clans. 1201+1228
21: 4 from the tribes of Judah, Simeon and **B**. 1228
21:17 from the tribe of **B** they gave them Gibeon, 1228
Jdg 5:14 **B** was with the people who followed you. 1228
10: 9 **B** and the house of Ephraim; 1228
19:14 and the sun set as they neared Gibeah in **B**. 1228
20: 4 "I and my concubine came to Gibeah in **B** 1228
20:10 when the army arrives at Gibeah in **B**, 1228
20:12 throughout the tribe of **B**, 1228
20:17 Israel, apart from **B**, mustered four hundred thousand swordsmen, 1228
20:24 drew near to **B** the second day. 1201+1228
20:28 up again to battle with **B** our brother, 1201+1228
20:35 The LORD defeated **B** before Israel, 1228
20:36 the men of Israel had given way before **B**, 1228
20:41 and the men of **B** were terrified, 1228
20:48 to **B** and put all the towns to the sword 1201+1228
21:15 The people grieved for **B**, 1228
21:16 "With the women of **B** destroyed, 1228
21:21 the girls of Shiloh and go to the land of **B**. 1228
1Sa 9: 1 the son of Aphiah of **B**. 408+1201+3549
9: 4 Then he passed through the territory of **B**, 3549
9:16 a man from the land of **B**. 1228
9:21 the least of all the clans of the tribe of **B**? 1228
10: 2 at Zelzah on the border of **B**. 1228
10:20 the tribe of **B** was chosen. 1228
10:21 Then he brought forward the tribe of **B**, 1228
13: 2 with Jonathan at Gibeah in **B**. 1228
13:15 and went up to Gibeah in **B**, 1228
13:16 with them were staying in Gibeah in **B**, 1228
14:16 at Gibeah in **B** saw the army melting away 1228
22: 7 Saul said to them, "Listen, **men of B**! 1229
2Sa 2: 9 and also over Ephraim, **B** and all Israel. 1228
2:15 twelve men for **B** and Ish-Bosheth son 1228
2:25 Then the men of **B** rallied behind Abner. 1228
3:19 that Israel and the whole house of **B** wanted 1228
4: 2 the Beerothite from the tribe of **B**— 1228
4: 2 Beeroth is considered part of **B**, 1228
21:14 Saul's father Kish, at Zela in **B**, 824+1228
23:29 Ithai son of Ribai from Gibeah in **B**, 1201+1228
1Ki 4:18 Shimei son of Ela—in **B**; 1228
12:21 whole house of Judah and the tribe of **B**— 1228
12:23 to the whole house of Judah and **B**, 1228
15:22 With them King Asa built up Geba in **B**, 1228
1Ch 2: 2 Dan, Joseph, **B**, Naphtali, Gad and Asher. 1228
6:60 the tribe of **B** they were given Gibeon, 1228
6:65 Simeon and **B** they allotted 1201+1228
7: 6 Three sons of **B**: Bela, Beker and Jediael. 1228
7:10 The sons of Bilhan: Jeush, **B**, Ehud, 1228
8: 1 **B** was the father of Bela his firstborn, 1228
8:40 All these were the descendants of **B**. 1228
9: 3 Those from Judah, from **B**, 1201+1228
9: 9 The **people from B**, 278+2157
11:31 Ithai son of Ribai from Gibeah in **B**, 1201+1228
12: 2 of Saul from the **tribe of B**): 1228
12:29 men of **B**, Saul's kinsmen— 1228
21: 6 not include Levi and **B** in the numbering, 1228
27:21 Iddo son of Zechariah; over **B**: 1228
2Ch 11: 1 he mustered the house of Judah and **B**— 1228
11: 3 and to all the Israelites in Judah and **B**, 1228
11:10 These were fortified cities in Judah and **B**. 1228
11:12 So Judah and **B** were his. 1228
11:23 throughout the districts of Judah and **B**, 1228
14: 8 two hundred and eighty thousand from **B**, 1228
15: 2 "Listen to me, Asa and all Judah and **B**. 1228
15: 8 and **B** and from the towns he had captured 1228
15: 9 Then he assembled all Judah and **B** and 1228
17:17 From **B**: Eliada, a valiant soldier, 1228
25: 5 of hundreds for all Judah and **B**. 1228
31: 1 and the altars throughout Judah and **B** and 1228
34: 9 and from all the people of Judah and **B** and 1228
34:32 in Jerusalem and **B** pledge themselves to it; 1228
Ezr 1: 5 Then the family heads of Judah and **B**, 1228
4: 1 and **B** heard that the exiles were building 1228
10: 9 of Judah and **B** had gathered in Jerusalem. 1228
10:32 **B**, Malluch and Shemariah. 1228
Ne 3:23 **B** and Hasshub made repairs in front 1228
11: 4 from both Judah and **B** lived in Jerusalem): 1228
11: 7 From the descendants of **B**: 1228
11:36 of the Levites of Judah settled in **B**. 1228
12:34 Judah, **B**, Shemaiah, Jeremiah, 1228
Est 2: 5 citadel of Susa a Jew of the **tribe of B**, 408+3549
Ps 68:27 There is the little **tribe of B**, leading them, 1228
80: 2 before Ephraim, **B** and Manasseh. 1228
Jer 1: 1 the priests at Anathoth in the territory of **B**. 1228
6: 1 "Flee for safety, people of **B**! 1228
17:26 the territory of **B** and the western foothills, 1228
20: 2 in the stocks at the Upper Gate of **B** at 1228
32: 8 at Anathoth in the territory of **B**. 1228
32:44 sealed and witnessed in the territory of **B**, 1228
33:13 in the territory of **B**, 1228
37:12 to go to the territory of **B** to get his share of 1228
37:13 But when he reached the **B** Gate, 1228
38: 7 While the king was sitting in the **B** Gate, 1228
Eze 48:22 the border of Judah and the border of **B**. 1228
48:23 **B** will have one portion; 1228
48:24 it will border the territory of **B** from east 1228
48:32 the gate of **B** and the gate of Dan. 1228
Hos 5: 8 lead on, O **B**. 1228
Ob 1:19 and **B** will possess Gilead. 1228
Zec 14:10 the **B** Gate to the site of the First Gate, 1228
Ac 13:21 of the tribe *of* **B**, who ruled forty years. *1021*
Ro 11: 1 from the tribe *of* **B**. *1021*
Php 3: 5 of the people of Israel, of the tribe *of* **B**, *1021*
Rev 7: 8 from the tribe *of* **B** 12,000. *1021*

BENJAMIN'S (2) [BENJAMIN]
Ge 43:34 **B** portion was five times as much 1228
44:12 And the cup was found in **B** sack. 1228

BENJAMITE (14) [BENJAMIN]
Jdg 3:15 a left-handed man, the son of Gera the **B**. 1229
20:46 day twenty-five thousand **B** swordsmen fell, 1228
21: 1 in marriage to a **B**." 1228
21:17 The **B** survivors must have heirs," 1228
21:18 be anyone who gives a wife to a **B**.' 1228
1Sa 4:12 That same day a **B** ran from the battle line 408+1228
9: 1 There was a **B**, a man of standing, 1228+4946
9:21 Saul answered, "But am I not a **B**, 1229
2Sa 16:11 How much more, then, this **B**! 1229
19:16 Shimei son of Gera, the **B** from Bahurim, 1229
20: 1 Sheba son of Bicri, a **B**, 408+3549
1Ki 2: 8 Shimei son of Gera, the **B** from Bahurim, 1229
1Ch 27:12 was Abiezer the Anathothite, a **B**, 1229
Ps 7: T to the LORD concerning Cush, a **B**. 1229

BENJAMITES (33) [BENJAMIN]
Jdg 1:21 The **B**, however, failed to dislodge 1201+1228
1:21 the Jebusites live there with the **B**. 1201+1228
19:16 in Gibeah (the men of the place were **B**), 1229

Jdg 20: 3 (The **B** heard that the Israelites had gone up 1201+1228
20:13 **B** would not listen to their fellow Israelites. 1201+1228
20:15 **B** mobilized twenty-six thousand swordsmen 1201+1228
20:18 shall go first to fight against the **B?"** 1201+1228
20:20 to fight the **B** and took up battle positions 1228
20:21 The **B** came out of Gibeah and cut 1201+1228
20:23 up again to battle against the **B,** 1201+1228
20:25 **B** came out from Gibeah to oppose them, 1228
20:30 went up against the **B** on the third day 1201+1228
20:31 The **B** came out to meet them 1201+1228
20:32 While the **B** were saying, 1201+1228
20:34 The fighting was so heavy that **the B** did 2156^S
20:35 **B,** all armed with swords. 1228
20:36 Then the **B** saw that they were beaten. 1201+1228
20:39 The **B** had begun to inflict casualties on 1228
20:40 the **B** turned and saw the smoke of 1228
20:43 They surrounded the **B,** 1228
20:44 Eighteen thousand **B** fell, 1228
20:45 after **the B** as far as Gidom and struck 2257^S
21: 6 Israelites grieved for their brothers, the **B.** 1228
21:13 peace to the **B** at the rock of Rimmon. 1201+1228
21:14 the **B** returned at that time and were given 1228
21:20 So they instructed the **B,** saying, 1201+1228
21:23 So that is what the **B** did. 1201+1228
2Sa 2:31 three hundred and sixty **B** who were with Abner. 408+1228+4946
3:19 Abner also spoke to the **B** in person. 1228
19:17 With him were a thousand **B,** 1228+4946
1Ch 9: 7 Of the **B:** Sallu son of Meshullam, 1201+1228
12:16 Other **B** and some men from Judah 1201+1228
Ne 11:31 The descendants of the **B** from Geba lived 1228

BENO (2)

1Ch 24:26 The son of Jaaziah: **B.** 1217
24:27 **B,** Shoham, Zaccur and Ibri. 1217

BENOTH See SUCCOTH BENOTH

BENT (21) [BEND]

Ex 10:10 Clearly you are **b on** evil. 5584+7156
1Sa 24: 9 'David *is* **b on** harming you'? 1335
1Ki 18:42 **b down** to the ground and put his face 1566
Ps 44:16 because of the enemy, *who is* **b on revenge.** 5933
69:23 and their backs *be* **b** forever. 5048
106:43 but they were **b on** rebellion 928+6783
Pr 16:30 he who purses his lips *is* **b on** evil. 3983
17:11 An evil man *is* **b** only **on** rebellion; 1335
Isa 21:15 from the **b** bow and from the heat of battle. 2005
51:13 who *is* **b on** destruction? 3922
Eze 22: 9 In you are slanderous men **b on** 5100
Da 11:27 The two kings, with their hearts **b on** evil, 4200
Hos 11: 4 from their neck and **b down** to feed them. 5742
Hab 1: 9 they all come **b on** violence. 4200
Lk 4:39 So he **b** over her and rebuked the fever, *2392*
13:11 She was **b over** and could not straighten up *5174*
Jn 8: 6 But Jesus **b** down and started to write on *3252*
20: 5 He **b over** and looked in at the strips *4160*
20:11 *she* **b over to look** into the tomb *4160*
Ro 11:10 and their backs *be* **b** forever." *5159*
Rev 6: 2 he rode out as a conqueror **b on** conquest. *2671*

BEON (1)

Nu 32: 3 Heshbon, Elealeh, Sebam, Nebo and **B—** 1274

BEOR (11)

Ge 36:32 Bela son of **B** became king of Edom. 1242
Nu 22: 5 to summon Balaam son of **B,** 1242
24: 3 "The oracle of Balaam son of **B,** 1242
24:15 "The oracle of Balaam son of **B,** 1242
31: 8 also killed Balaam son of **B** with the sword. 1242
Dt 23: 4 of **B** from Pethor in Aram Naharaim 1242
Jos 13:22 to the sword Balaam son of **B,** 1242
24: 9 for Balaam son of **B** to put a curse on you. 1242
1Ch 1:43 Bela son of **B,** 1242
Mic 6: 5 and what Balaam son of **B** answered. 1242
2Pe 2:15 to follow the way of Balaam son *of* **B,** *1027*

BERA (1)

Ge 14: 2 went to war against **B** king of Sodom, 1396

BERACAH (3)

1Ch 12: 3 **B,** Jehu the Anathothite, 1389
2Ch 20:26 in the Valley of **B,** 1390
20:26 This is why it is called the Valley of **B** 1390

BERACHIAH, BERECHIAH (KJV) See BEREKIAH

BERAIAH (1)

1Ch 8:21 **B** and Shimrath were the sons of Shimei. 1349

BERAK See BENE BERAK

BEREA (4) [BEREANS]

Ac 17:10 the brothers sent Paul and Silas away to **B.** *1023*
17:13 the word of God at **B,** *1023*
17:14 but Silas and Timothy stayed **at B.** *1695^S*
20: 4 by Sopater son of Pyrrhus **from B,** *1024*

BEREANS (1) [BEREA]

Ac 17:11 Now **the B** were of more noble character *4047^S*

BEREAVE (1) [BEREAVED, BEREAVEMENT, BEREAVES]

Hos 9:12 *I will* **b** them of every one. 8897

BEREAVED (3) [BEREAVE]

Ge 43:14 As for me, if *I am* **b,** I am bereaved." 8897
43:14 As for me, if I am bereaved, *I am* **b."** 8897
Isa 49:21 I was **b** and barren; 8892

BEREAVEMENT (2) [BEREAVE]

Isa 49:20 during your **b** will yet say in your hearing, 8898
Jer 15: 7 *I will* **bring b** and destruction 8897

BEREAVES (1) [BEREAVE]

La 1:20 Outside, the sword **b;** 8897

BERED (2)

Ge 16:14 it is still there, between Kadesh and **B.** 1354
1Ch 7:20 Shuthelah, **B** his son, Tahath his son, 1355

BEREKIAH (12)

1Ch 3:20 Ohel, **B,** Hasadiah and Jushab-Hesed. 1392
6:39 Asaph son of **B,** the son of Shimea, 1393
9:16 and **B** son of Asa, the son of Elkanah, 1392
15:17 from his brothers, Asaph son of **B;** 1393
15:23 **B** and Elkanah were to be doorkeepers for 1392
2Ch 28:12 **B** son of Meshillemoth, 1393
Ne 3: 4 Next to him Meshullam son of **B,** 1392
3:30 Meshullam son of **B** made repairs opposite his living quarters. 1392
6:18 the daughter of Meshullam son of **B.** 1392
Zec 1: 1 to the prophet Zechariah son of **B,** the son 1392
1: 7 to the prophet Zechariah son of **B,** 1393
Mt 23:35 to the blood of Zechariah son *of* **B,** *974*

BERI (1) [BERITES]

1Ch 7:36 Suah, Harnepher, Shual, **B,** Imrah, 1373

BERIAH (11) [BERIITE]

Ge 46:17 Imnah, Ishvah, Ishvi and **B.** 1380
46:17 The sons of **B:** Heber and Malkiel. 1380
Nu 26:44 through **B,** the Beriite clan; 1380
26:45 and through the descendants of **B:** 1380
1Ch 7:23 He named him **B,** 1380
7:30 sons of Asher: Imnah, Ishvah, Ishvi and **B.** 1380
7:31 The sons of **B:** 1380
8:13 and **B** and Shema, 1380
8:16 Ishpah and Joha were the sons of **B.** 1380
23:10 sons of Shimei: Jahath, Ziza, Jeush and **B.** 1380
23:11 but Jeush and **B** did not have many sons; 1380

BERIITE (1) [BERIAH]

Nu 26:44 through Beriah, the **B** clan; 1381

BERITES (1) [BERI]

2Sa 20:14 and through the entire region of the **B,** 1379

BERITH (KJV) See EL-BERITH

BERNICE (3)

Ac 25:13 and **B** arrived at Caesarea *1022*
25:23 and **B** came with great pomp and entered *1022*
26:30 the governor and **B** and those sitting *1022*

BERODACHBALADAN (KJV) See MERODACH-BALADAN

BEROTHAH (1)

Eze 47:16 **B** and Sibraim (which lies on the border 1363

BEROTHAI (1) [BEROTHITE]

2Sa 8: 8 From Tebah and **B,** 1408

BEROTHITE (1) [BEROTHAI]

1Ch 11:39 the **B,** the armor-bearer of Joab son 1409

BERRIES (KJV) See OLIVES

BERYL (4)

Ex 28:17 a topaz and a **b;** 1403
39:10 a topaz and a **b;** 1403
Eze 28:13 onyx and jasper, sapphire, turquoise and **b.** 1404
Rev 21:20 the seventh chrysolite, the eighth **b,** *1039*

BESAI (2)

Ezr 2:49 Uzza, Paseah, **B,** 1234
Ne 7:52 **B,** Meunim, Nephussim, 1234

BESEECH, BESEECHING, BESOUGHT (KJV) See APPEAL, ASKING, BEG, BEGGED, PLEAD, PLEASE, URGE

BESET (2)

Ps 41: 8 "A vile disease *has* **b** him; 3668
55: 5 Fear and trembling *have* **b** me; 928+995

BESIDE (88) [BESIDES, SIDE]

Ge 16: 7 it was the spring that is **b** the road to Shur. 928
23: 3 Abraham rose from **b** his dead wife 6584+7156
24:13 See, I am standing **b** this spring, 6584
24:43 See, I am standing **b** this spring; 6584
38:21 "Where is the shrine prostitute who was **b** 6584
39:15 he left his cloak **b** me and ran out of 725
39:16 She kept his cloak **b** her 725
39:18 he left his cloak **b** me and ran out of 725
41: 3 the Nile and stood **b** those on the riverbank. 725
48: 7 So I buried her there **b** the road to Ephrath" 928
Lev 6:10 on the altar and place them **b** the altar. 725
10:12 and eat it prepared without yeast **b** the altar, 725
Nu 23: 3 "Stay here **b** your offering while I go aside. 6584
23: 6 and found him standing **b** his offering, 6584
23:15 "Stay here **b** your offering while I meet 6584
23:17 and found him standing **b** his offering, 6584
24: 6 like gardens **b** a river, 6584
24: 6 like cedars **b** the waters. 6584
Dt 12:27 of your sacrifices must be poured **b** the altar 6584
16:21 Do not set up any wooden Asherah pole **b** 725
22: 6 If you come across a bird's nest **b** the road, 928
31:26 "Take this Book of the Law and place it **b** the ark of the covenant 4946+7396
Jdg 6:25 to Baal and cut down the Asherah pole **b** it. 6584
6:28 with the Asherah pole **b** it cut down and 6584
6:30 and cut down the Asherah pole **b** it." 6584
9: 6 and Beth Millo gathered **b** the great tree at 6640
1Sa 1:26 the woman who stood here **b** you praying 6640
5: 2 into Dagon's temple and set it **b** Dagon. 725
6: 8 and in a chest **b** it put 4946+7396
6:14 and there it stopped **b** a large rock. 9004
26: 3 Saul made his camp **b** the road on the hill 6584
2Sa 6: 7 down and he died there **b** the ark of God. 6640
12:17 of his household stood **b** him to get him up 6584
18: 4 So the king stood **b** the gate while all 448+3338
20:11 One of Joab's men stood **b** Amasa and said, 6584
1Ki 1: 2 She can lie **b** him so that our lord 928+2668
2:29 the tent of the LORD and was **b** the altar. 725
10:19 with a lion standing **b** each of them. 725
13:24 both the donkey and the lion standing **b** it. 725
13:25 with the lion standing **b** the body, 725
13:28 with the donkey and the lion standing **b** it. 725
13:31 lay my bones **b** his bones. 725
2Ki 11:14 The officers and the trumpeters were **b** 448
12: 9 He placed it **b** the altar, 725
2Ch 9:18 with a lion standing **b** each of them. 725
23:13 The officers and the trumpeters were **b** 6584
Ne 2: 6 Then the king, with the queen sitting **b** him, 725
3:17 **B** him, Hashabiah, ruler of half the district 3338+6584
3:23 made repairs **b** his house. 725
8: 4 **B** him on his right stood Mattithiah, 725
Job 18: 6 the lamp **b** him goes out. 6584
Ps 23: 2 he leads me **b** quiet waters, 6584
110: 7 He will drink from a brook **b** the way; 928
Pr 8: 3 **b** the gates leading into the city, at 3338+4200
SS 1: 7 Why should I be like a veiled woman **b** 6584
Isa 49: 9 "They will feed **b** the roads and find pasture 6584
49:10 on them will guide them and lead them **b** 6584
Jer 17: 2 and Asherah poles **b** the spreading trees and 6584
31: 9 I will lead them **b** streams of water on 448
36:21 the king and all the officials standing **b** him. 4946+6584
Eze 1:15 I saw a wheel on the ground **b** each creature 725
1:19 the wheels **b** them moved; 725
3:13 and the sound of the wheels **b** them, 4200+6645
9: 2 They came in and stood **b** the bronze altar. 725
10: 6 the man went in and stood **b** a wheel. 725
10: 9 and I saw **b** the cherubim four wheels, 725
10: 9 one **b** each of the cherubim; 725
10:16 the wheels **b** them moved; 725
11:22 the cherubim, with the wheels **b** them, 4200+6645
32:13 from **b** abundant waters no longer to 6584
39:15 he will set up a marker **b** it until 725
43: 6 While the man was standing **b** me, 725
43: 8 to my threshold and their doorposts **b** 725
Da 8: 2 in the vision I was **b** the Ulai Canal. 6584
8: 3 standing **b** the canal, 4200+7156
8: 6 the two-horned ram I had seen standing **b** the canal 4200+7156
Am 2: 8 down **b** every altar on garments taken 725
Zec 4:12 "What are these two olive branches **b** 928+3338
Mt 4:18 As Jesus was walking **b** the Sea of Galilee, *4123*
Mk 1:16 As Jesus **walked b** the Sea of Galilee, *4135*
2:13 Once again Jesus went out **b** the lake. *4123*
Lk 9:47 took a little child and had him stand **b** him. *4123*
24: 4 that gleamed like lightning **stood b** them. *2392*
Ac 1:10 in white **stood b** them. *4225*
5:10 carried her out and buried her **b** *4639*
22:13 He **stood b** me and said, 'Brother Saul, *2392*
27:23 and whom I serve **stood b** me *4225*
Rev 15: 2 standing **b** the sea, *2093*

BESIDES (42) [BESIDE]

Ge 20:12 **B,** she really is my sister, 1685+2256
26: 1 **b** the earlier famine of Abraham's time— 963+4200+4946
31:50 or if you take any wives **b** my daughters, 6584
38:22 **B,** the men who lived there said, 1685+2256
46:15 **b** his daughter Dinah. 2256
50: 8 **b** all the members of Joseph's household 2256
Ex 12:37 **b** women and children. 963+4200+4946
Nu 28:15 **B** the regular burnt offering 6584
Dt 4:35 **b** him there is no other. 963+4200+4946
32:39 There is no god **b** me. 6643
Jos 17: 5 of land **b** Gilead and Bashan east of 963+4200
1Sa 2: 2 there is no one **b** you; 1194
2Sa 2:30 **B** Asahel, nineteen of David's 2256
17: 8 **B,** your father is an experienced fighter; 2256
19:43 and **b,** we have a greater claim 1685
22:32 For who is God **b** the LORD? 1187+4946
1Ki 10:13 **b** what he had given her out 963+4200+4946
11: 1 Solomon, however, loved many foreign women **b** Pharaoh's daughter— 2256
2Ki 21:16 **b** the sin that he had caused Judah to commit, 963+4200+4946
1Ch 3: 9 **b** his sons by his concubines. 963+4200+4946
29: 3 **B,** in my devotion to the temple 6388
2Ch 17:19 **b** those he stationed in the fortified cities 963+4200+4946
Ezr 2:65 **b** their 7,337 menservants 963+4200+4946
10:13 **B,** this matter cannot be taken care of in 2256
Ne 7:67 **b** their 7,337 menservants 963+4200+4946
Ps 18:31 For who is God **b** the LORD? 1187+4946
73:25 And earth has nothing I desire **b** you. 6640
120: 3 What will he do to you, and what **more b,** 3578
Isa 26:13 other lords **b** you have ruled over us, 2314
44: 8 Is there any God **b** me? 1187+4946
45: 6 men may know there is none **b** me. 1187
47: 8 'I am, and there is none **b** me.' 6388
47:10 'I am, and there is none **b** me.' 6388
56: 8 to them **b** those already gathered." 4200
64: 4 no eye has seen any God **b** you, 2314
Zep 2:15 "I am, and there is none **b** me." 6388
Mt 14:21 **b** women and children. *6006*
15:38 **b** women and children. *6006*
Lk 16:26 And **b** all this, *1877*
Ac 21:28 And **b,** he has brought Greeks into *2285*
2Co 11:28 **B everything else,** I face daily the pressure of my concern for all *3836+4211+6006*
1Ti 5:13 **B,** they get into the habit of being idle *275*

BESIEGE (10) [SIEGE]

Dt 20:19 that you *should* **b** them? 928+995+2021+5189
28:52 *They will* **b** all the cities throughout 7674
1Sa 23: 8 down to Keilah to **b** David and his men. 7443
2Sa 12:28 and **b** the city and capture it. 2837+6584
2Ch 6:28 when enemies **b** them in any of their cities, 7443
Ps 27: 3 an army **b** me, my heart will not fear; 2837+6584
Isa 29: 2 Yet *I will* **b** Ariel; 7439
29: 7 that attack her and her fortress and **b** her, 7439
Eze 4: 3 It will be under siege, and *you shall* **b** it. 7443
Lk 11:53 and *to* **b** him **with questions,** *694+4309+4498*

BESIEGED (11) [SIEGE]

Jdg 9:50 Abimelech went to Thebez and **b** it 928+2837
1Sa 11: 1 up and **b** Jabesh Gilead. 2837+6584
2Sa 11: 1 the Ammonites and **b** Rabbah. 7443
20:15 All the troops with Joab came and **b** Sheba 7443
1Ki 20: 1 he went up and **b** Samaria and attacked it. 7443
2Ki 16: 5 up to fight against Jerusalem and **b** Ahaz, 7443
1Ch 20: 1 and went to Rabbah and **b** it, 7443
Ps 31:21 to me when I was in a **b** city. 5189
La 3: 5 *He has* **b** me and surrounded me 1215+6584
Da 1: 1 of Babylon came to Jerusalem and **b** it. 7443
Zec 12: 2 Judah will be **b** as well as Jerusalem. 5189

BESIEGES (1) [SIEGE]

1Ki 8:37 an enemy **b** them in any of their cities, 7443

BESIEGING (7) [SIEGE]

1Ki 15:27 while Nadab and all Israel *were* **b** it. 7443
2Ki 24:11 up to the city while his officers *were* **b** it. 7443
Jer 4:16 'A **b** *army* is coming from a distant land, 7443
21: 4 who are outside the wall **b** you. 7443
21: 9 to the Babylonians who *are* **b** you will live; 7443
32: 2 the king of Babylon *was* then **b** Jerusalem, 7443
37: 5 Babylonians who *were* **b** Jerusalem heard 7443

BESODEIAH (1)

Ne 3: 6 of Paseah and Meshullam son of **B.** 1233

BESOM (KJV) See BROOM

BESOR (2)

1Sa 30: 9 with him came to the **B** Ravine, 1410
30:21 and who were left behind at the **B** Ravine. 1410

BEST (69) [GOOD]

Ge 16: 6 "Do with her whatever you think **b.**" 3202
27:15 the **b** clothes of Esau her older son, 2776
43:11 of the **b products** *of* the land in your bags 2380
45:18 I will give you the **b** *of* the land of Egypt 3206
45:20 because the **b** *of* all Egypt will be yours.'" 3206
45:23 ten donkeys loaded with the **b things** 3206
47: 6 and your brothers in the **b** *part of* the land. 4774
47:11 and gave them property in the **b** *part of* 4774
Ex 14: 7 He took six hundred of the **b** chariots, 1047
15: 4 The **b** *of* Pharaoh's officers are drowned in 4436
22: 5 from the **b** *of* his own field or vineyard. 4774
23:19 "Bring the **b** *of* the firstfruits of your soil to 8040
34:26 "Bring the **b** *of* the firstfruits of your soil to 8040
Nu 13:20 **Do** *your* **b** to bring back some of the fruit of 2616
18:29 the LORD's portion the **b** and holiest part 2693
18:30 'When you present the **b** part, 2693
18:32 By presenting the **b** part of it you will not 2693
Dt 33:14 the **b** the sun brings forth and the finest 4458
33:16 with the **b** gifts *of* the earth and its fullness 4458
33:21 He chose the **b** land for himself; 8040
Jos 8: 3 his **b fighting men** and sent them out 1475+2657
10: 7 including all the **b fighting men.** 1475+2657
Jdg 10:15 Do with us whatever you think **b.** 3202
Ru 3: 3 and put on your **b clothes.** 8529
1Sa 1:23 "Do what seems **b** to you," 3202
8:14 the **b** of your fields and vineyards 3202
8:16 and maidservants and the **b** of your cattle 3202
14:36 "Do whatever seems **b** to you," 3202
14:40 "Do what seems **b** to you," the men replied. 3202
15: 9 the **b** *of* the sheep and cattle, the fat calves 4774
15:15 the **b** *of* the sheep and cattle to sacrifice to 4774
15:21 the **b** *of* what was devoted to God, 8040
27: 1 The **b** *thing* I can do is to escape to the land 3202
2Sa 10: 9 of the **b** *troops in* Israel and deployed them 1047
18: 4 "I will do whatever seems **b** to you." 3512
23:20 He struck down two of Moab's **b men.** 738
1Ki 20: 3 and the **b** of your wives 3202
2Ki 10: 3 choose the **b** and most worthy 3202
10: 5 you do whatever you think **b.**" 3202
1Ch 11:22 He struck down two of Moab's **b men.** 738
19:10 so he selected some of the **b** *troops* in Israel 1047
Ezr 7:18 then do whatever **seems b** with the rest of 10320
Est 2: 9 and her maids into the **b** *place in* 3202
3: 8 **in** the king's **b interest** 8750
8: 8 the Jews as seems **b** to you, and seal it with 3202
Pr 5: 9 lest you give your **b strength** to others 2086
SS 7: 9 and your mouth like the **b** wine. 3202
Isa 1:19 you will eat the **b** *from* the land; 3206
25: 6 the **b** *of* meats and the finest of wines. 9043
48:17 who teaches you *what is* **b** for you, 3603
Jer 18: 4 shaping it as seemed **b** to him. 3837
Eze 24: 4 Fill it with the **b** *of* these bones; 4436
31:16 the choicest and **b** *of* Lebanon, 3202
44:30 The **b** *of* all the firstfruits and 8040
48:14 This is the **b** *of* the land and must not pass 8040
Da 11:15 even their **b** troops will not have 4436
Jnh 1:13 the men *did their b to* **row** back to land. AIT
Mic 7: 4 The **b** *of* them is like a brier, 3202
Zec 11:12 I told them, "If you think it **b,** 3202
Lk 15:22 Bring the **b** robe and put it on him. *4755*
Jn 2:10 but you have saved the **b** till now." *2819*
2Co 8:10 And here is my advice about what is **b** *5237*
Php 1:10 you may be able to discern **what is b** *1422+3836*
1Th 3: 1 *we* **thought it b** to be left by ourselves *2305*
2Ti 2:15 **Do** *your* **b** to present yourself to God *5079*
4: 9 **Do** *your* **b** to come to me quickly, *5079*
4:21 **Do** *your* **b** to get here before winter. *5079*
Tit 3:12 **do** *your* **b** to come to me at Nicopolis, *5079*
Heb 12:10 for a little while as they thought **b;** *NIG*

BESTOW (6) [BESTOWED, BESTOWER, BESTOWING, BESTOWS]

Ps 3: 3 you **b** glory on me and lift up my head. NIH
31:19 which *you* **b** in the sight of men 7188
Isa 45: 4 **b** *on* you **a title of honor,** 4033
61: 3 to **b** on them a crown of beauty instead 5989
62: 2 that the mouth of the LORD *will* **b.** 5918
Jer 23: 2 on them, I *will* **b punishment** on you *for* 7212

BESTOWED (4) [BESTOW]

1Ch 29:25 and **b** on him royal splendor such 5989
Ps 21: 5 *you have* **b** on him splendor and majesty. 8751
89:19 *"I have* **b** strength on a warrior; 8751
Jer 23: 2 and *have* not **b care on** them, 7212

BESTOWER (1) [BESTOW]

Isa 23: 8 against Tyre, the **b of crowns,** 6497

BESTOWING (1) [BESTOW]

Pr 8:21 **b** wealth on those who love me 5706

BESTOWS (3) [BESTOW]

Job 5:10 He **b** rain on the earth; 5989
Ps 84:11 the LORD **b** favor and honor; 5989
133: 3 For there the LORD **b** his blessing, 7422

BETEN (1)

Jos 19:25 Their territory included: Helkath, Hali, **B,** 1062

BETH (1)

1Sa 31:12 through the night to **B** Shan. NIH

BETH ANATH (3) [ANATH]

Jos 19:38 Horem, **B** and Beth Shemesh. 1117
Jdg 1:33 in Beth Shemesh or **B;** 1117
1:33 and **B** became forced laborers 1117

BETH ANOTH (1)

Jos 15:59 **B** and Eltekon— 1116

BETH ARABAH (4) [ARABAH]

Jos 15: 6 of **B** to the Stone of Bohan son 1098
15:61 In the desert: **B,** Middin, Secacah, 1098
18:18 of **B** and on down into the Arabah. 1098
18:22 **B,** Zemaraim, Bethel, 1098

BETH ARBEL (1)

Hos 10:14 as Shalman devastated **B** on the day 1079

BETH ASHBEA (1)

1Ch 4:21 the clans of the linen workers at **B,** 1080

BETH AVEN (7) [AVEN]

Jos 7: 2 which is near **B** to the east of Bethel, 1077
18:12 coming out at the desert of **B.** 1077
1Sa 13: 5 camped at Micmash, east of **B.** 1077
14:23 and the battle moved on beyond **B.** 1077
Hos 4:15 do not go up to **B.** 1077
5: 8 Raise the battle cry in **B;** 1077
10: 5 for the calf-idol of **B.** 1077

BETH AZMAVETH (1) [AZMAVETH]

Ne 7:28 of **B** 42 1115

BETH BAAL MEON (1) [BAAL MEON]

Jos 13:17 Bamoth Baal, **B,** 1081

BETH BARAH (2)

Jdg 7:24 ahead of them as far as **B.**" 1083
7:24 the waters of the Jordan as far as **B.** 1083

BETH BIRI (1)

1Ch 4:31 Hazar Susim, **B** and Shaaraim. 1082

BETH CAR (1)

1Sa 7:11 along the way to a point below **B.** 1105

BETH DAGON (2) [DAGON]

Jos 15:41 **B,** Naamah and Makkedah— 1087
19:27 It then turned east toward **B,** 1087

BETH DIBLATHAIM (1) [ALMON DIBLATHAIM]

Jer 48:22 to Dibon, Nebo and **B,** 1086

BETH EDEN (1) [EDEN]

Am 1: 5 the one who holds the scepter in **B.** 1114

BETH EKED (2)

2Ki 10:12 At **B** *of* the Shepherds, 1118
10:14 by the well of **B**— 1118

BETH EMEK (1)

Jos 19:27 and went north to **B** and Neiel, 1097

BETH EZEL (1) [EZEL]

Mic 1:11 **B** is in mourning; 1089

BETH GADER (1)

1Ch 2:51 and Hareph the father of **B.** 1084

BETH GAMUL (1) [GAMUL]

Jer 48:23 to Kiriathaim, **B** and Beth Meon, 1085

BETH GILGAL (1) [GILGAL]

Ne 12:29 from **B,** and from the area of Geba 1090

BETH HAGGAN (1)

2Ki 9:27 he fled up the road to **B.** 1091

BETH HAKKEREM (2)

Ne 3:14 ruler of the district of **B.** 1094
Jer 6: 1 Raise the signal over **B!** 1094

BETH HARAM (1)

Jos 13:27 **B,** Beth Nimrah, 1099

BETH HARAN (1) [HARAN]

Nu 32:36 and **B** as fortified cities, 1100

BETH HOGLAH (3) [HOGLAH]

Jos 15: 6 went up to **B** and continued north 1102
18:19 to the northern slope of **B** 1102
18:21 Jericho, **B,** Emek Keziz, 1102

BETH HORON (14) [HORONITE]

Jos 10:10 the road going up to **B** and cut them 1103
10:11 on the road down from **B** to Azekah, 1103

Jos 16: 3 as far as the region of Lower **B** and 1103
16: 5 in the east to Upper **B** 1103
18:13 on the hill south of Lower **B.** 1103
18:14 From the hill facing **B** on the south 1103
21:22 Kibzaim and **B,** together 1103
1Sa 13:18 another toward **B,** 1103
1Ki 9:17 He built up Lower **B,** 1103
1Ch 6:68 Jokmeam, **B,** 1103
7:24 who built Lower and Upper **B** 1103
2Ch 8: 5 He rebuilt Upper **B** 1103
8: 5 and Lower **B** as fortified cities, 1103
25:13 from Samaria to **B.** 1103

BETH JESHIMOTH (4)
Nu 33:49 along the Jordan from **B** 1093
Jos 12: 3 to **B,** and then southward below 1093
13:20 the slopes of Pisgah, and **B** 1093
Eze 25: 9 **B,** Baal Meon and Kiriathaim— 1093

BETH LEBAOTH (1) [LEBAOTH]
Jos 19: 6 **B** and Sharuhen— 1106

BETH MARCABOTH (2)
Jos 19: 5 Ziklag, **B,** Hazar Susah, 1096
1Ch 4:31 **B,** Hazar Susim, Beth Biri 1112

BETH MEON (1) [BAAL MEON]
Jer 48:23 to Kiriathaim, Beth Gamul and **B,** 1110

BETH MILLO (4)
Jdg 9: 6 and **B** gathered beside the great tree 1109
9:20 citizens of Shechem and **B,** 1109
9:20 citizens of Shechem and **B,** 1109
2Ki 12:20 and assassinated him at **B,** 1109

BETH NIMRAH (2) [NIMRAH]
Nu 32:36 **B** and Beth Haran 1113
Jos 13:27 Beth Haram, **B,** 1113

BETH OPHRAH (1) [OPHRAH]
Mic 1:10 In **B** roll in the dust. 1108

BETH PAZZEZ (1)
Jos 19:21 En Gannim, En Haddah and **B.** 1122

BETH PELET (2) [PELET]
Jos 15:27 Hazar Gaddah, Heshmon, **B,** 1120
Ne 11:26 in Jeshua, in Moladah, in **B,** 1120

BETH PEOR (4) [PEOR]
Dt 3:29 So we stayed in the valley near **B.** 1121
4:46 in the valley near **B** east of the Jordan, 1121
34: 6 in the valley opposite **B,** 1121
Jos 13:20 **B,** the slopes of Pisgah, 1121

BETH RAPHA (1) [RAPHA]
1Ch 4:12 Eshton was the father of **B,** 1125

BETH REHOB (2) [REHOB]
Jdg 18:28 The city was in a valley near **B.** 1124
2Sa 10: 6 from **B** and Zobah, 1124

BETH SHAN (9)
Jos 17:11 Manasseh also had **B,** 1126
17:16 in **B** and its settlements and those in 1126
Jdg 1:27 the people of **B** or Taanach or Dor 1126
1Sa 31:10 fastened his body to the wall of **B.** 1126
31:12 the wall of **B** and went to Jabesh, 1126
2Sa 21:12 from the public square at **B,** 1126
1Ki 4:12 of **B** next to Zarethan below Jezreel, 1126
4:12 to Zarethan below Jezreel, from **B** 1126
1Ch 7:29 the borders of Manasseh were **B,** 1126

BETH SHEMESH (22)
Jos 15:10 continued down to **B** and crossed 1127
19:22 Shahazumah and **B,** 1127
19:38 Horem, Beth Anath and **B.** 1127
21:16 Juttah and **B,** 1127
Jdg 1:33 in **B** or Beth Anath; 1127
1:33 of the land, and those living in **B** 1127
1Sa 6: 9 up to its own territory, toward **B,** 1127
6:12 cows went straight up toward **B,** 1127
6:12 as far as the border of **B.** 1127
6:13 of **B** were harvesting their wheat 1127
6:14 to the field of Joshua **of B,** 1128
6:15 of **B** offered burnt offerings 1127
6:18 in the field of Joshua **of B.** 1128
6:19 down some of the men of **B,** 1127
6:20 and the men of **B** asked, 1127
1Ki 4: 9 Shaalbim, **B** and Elon Bethhanan; 1127
2Ki 14:11 of Judah faced each other at **B** 1127
14:13 the son of Ahaziah, at **B.** 1127
1Ch 6:59 Juttah and **B,** 1127
2Ch 25:21 of Judah faced each other at **B** 1127
25:23 the son of Ahaziah, at **B.** 1127
28:18 They captured and occupied **B,** 1127

BETH SHITTAH (1)
Jdg 7:22 The army fled to **B** toward Zererah 1101

BETH TAPPUAH (1) [TAPPUAH]
Jos 15:53 Janim, **B,** Aphekah, 1130

BETH TOGARMAH (2) [TOGARMAH]
Eze 27:14 of **B** exchanged work horses, 1129
38: 6 and **B** from the far north 1129

BETH ZUR (4) [ZUR]
Jos 15:58 Halhul, **B,** Gedor, 1123
1Ch 2:45 and Maon was the father of **B.** 1123
2Ch 11: 7 **B,** Soco, Adullam, 1123
Ne 3:16 ruler of a half-district of **B,** 1123

BETH-HACCEREM (KJV) See BETH HAKKEREM

BETH-HOGLA (KJV) See BETH HOGLAH

BETH-LEHEM-JUDAH (KJV) See BETHLEHEM, JUDAH

BETH-MEON (KJV) See BETH BAAL MEON, BAAL MEON

BETH-PALET (KJV) See BETH PELET

BETH-SHEAN (KJV) See BETH SHAN

BETH-SHEMITE (KJV) See BETH SHEMESH

BETHABARA (KJV) See BETHANY

BETHANY (12)
Mt 21:17 he left them and went out of the city to **B,** *1029*
26: 6 in **B** in the home of a man known as Simon *1029*
Mk 11: 1 to Bethphage and **B** at the Mount of Olives, *1029*
11:11 he went out to **B** with the Twelve. *1029*
11:12 The next day as they were leaving **B,** *1029*
14: 3 While he was in **B,** reclining at the table *1029*
Lk 19:29 As he approached Bethphage and **B** at *1029*
24:50 he had led them out to the vicinity of **B,** *1029*
Jn 1:28 This all happened at **B** on the other side of *1029*
11: 1 He was from **B,** the village of Mary *1029*
11:18 **B** was less than two miles from Jerusalem, *1029*
12: 1 Jesus arrived at **B,** where Lazarus lived, *1029*

BETHARAM (KJV) See BETH HARAM

BETHBIREI (KJV) See BETH BIRI

BETHEL (71) [EL BETHEL, LUZ]
Ge 12: 8 the hills east of **B** and pitched his tent, 1078
12: 8 with **B** on the west and Ai on the east. 1078
13: 3 from place to place until he came to **B,** 1078
13: 3 to the place between **B** and Ai 1078
28:19 He called that place **B,** 1078
31:13 I am the God of **B,** 1078
35: 1 "Go up to **B** and settle there, 1078
35: 3 Then come, let us go up to **B,** 1078
35: 6 Luz (that is, **B**) in the land of Canaan. 1078
35: 8 and was buried under the oak below **B.** 1078
35:15 where God had talked with him **B.** 1078
35:16 Then they moved on from **B.** 1078
Jos 7: 2 which is near Beth Aven to the east of **B,** 1078
8: 9 between **B** and Ai, to the west of Ai— 1078
8:12 and set them in ambush between **B** and Ai, 1078
8:17 a man remained in Ai or **B** who did not go 1078
12: 9 the king of Ai (near **B**) one 1078
12:16 king of Makkedah one the king of **B** one 1078
16: 1 the desert into the hill country of **B.** 1078
16: 2 It went on from **B** (that is, Luz), 1078
18:13 slope of Luz (that is, **B**) and went down 1078
18:22 Beth Arabah, Zemaraim, **B,** 1078
Jdg 1:22 Now the house of Joseph attacked **B,** 1078
1:23 to spy out **B** (formerly called Luz), 1078
4: 5 between Ramah and **B** in the hill country 1078
20:18 The Israelites went up to **B** and inquired 1078
20:26 the Israelites, all the people, went up to **B,** 1078
20:31 the one leading to **B** and the other 1078
21: 2 The people went to **B,** 1078
21:19 to the north of **B,** 1078
21:19 of the road that goes from **B** to Shechem, 1078
1Sa 7:16 on a circuit from **B** to Gilgal to Mizpah, 1078
10: 3 up to God at **B** will meet you there. 1078
13: 2 at Micmash and in the hill country of **B,** 1078
30:27 He sent it to those who were in **B,** 1078
1Ki 12:29 One he set up in **B,** and the other in Dan. 1078
12:32 This he did in **B,** 1078
12:32 And at **B** he also installed priests at 1078
12:33 on the altar he had built at **B.** 1078
13: 1 a man of God came from Judah to **B,** 1078
1Ki 13: 4 of God cried out against the altar at **B,** 1078
13:10 not return by the way he had come to **B.** 1078
13:11 there was a certain old prophet living in **B,** 1078
13:32 the altar in **B** and against all the shrines on 1078
16:34 In Ahab's time, Hiel **of B** rebuilt Jericho. 1088
2Ki 2: 2 the LORD has sent me to **B."** 1078
2: 2 So they went down to **B.** 1078
2: 3 The company of the prophets at **B** came out 1078
2:23 From there Elisha went up to **B.** 1078
10:29 the worship of the golden calves at **B** 1078
17:28 in **B** and taught them how to worship 1078
23: 4 the Kidron Valley and took the ashes to **B.** 1078
23:15 Even the altar at **B,** 1078
23:17 the altar of **B** the very things you have done 1078
23:19 Just as he had done at **B,** 1078
1Ch 7:28 Their lands and settlements included **B** 1078
2Ch 13:19 and took from him the towns of **B,** 1078
Ezr 2:28 of **B** and Ai 223 1078
Ne 7:32 of **B** and Ai 123 1078
11:31 Aija, **B** and its settlements, 1078
Jer 48:13 when they trusted in **B.** 1078
Hos 10:15 Thus will it happen to you, O **B,** 1078
12: 4 at **B** and talked with him there— 1078
Am 3:14 I will destroy the altars of **B;** 1078
4: 4 "Go to **B** and sin; 1078
5: 5 do not seek **B,** 1078
5: 5 and **B** will be reduced to nothing." 1078
5: 6 and **B** will have no one to quench it. 1078
7:10 of **B** sent a message to Jeroboam king 1078
7:13 Don't prophesy anymore at **B,** 1078
Zec 7: 2 of **B** had sent Sharezer and Regem-Melech, 1078

BETHELITE (KJV) See BETHEL

BETHESDA (1)
Jn 5: 2 which in Aramaic is called **B** *1031*

BETHHANAN See ELON BETHHANAN

BETHLEHEM (51) [BETHLEHEMITE, EPHRATH]
Ge 35:19 on the way to Ephrath (that is, **B**). 1107
48: 7 beside the road to Ephrath" (that is, **B**). 1107
Jos 19:15 Nahalal, Shimron, Idalah and **B.** 1107
Jdg 12: 8 After him, Ibzan of **B** led Israel. 1107
12:10 Then Ibzan died, and was buried in **B.** 1107
17: 7 A young Levite from **B** *in* Judah, 1107
17: 9 "I'm a Levite from **B** *in* Judah," he said, 1107
19: 1 of Ephraim took a concubine from **B** 1107
19: 2 and went back to her father's house in **B,** 1107
19:18 "We are on our way from **B** *in* Judah to 1107
19:18 to **B** *in* Judah and now I am going to 1107
Ru 1: 1 and a man from **B** *in* Judah, 1107
1: 2 They were Ephrathites from **B,** Judah. 1107
1:19 two women went on until they came to **B.** 1107
1:19 When they arrived in **B,** 1107
1:22 in **B** as the barley harvest was beginning. 1107
2: 4 Just then Boaz arrived from **B** and greeted 1107
4:11 in Ephrathah and be famous in **B.** 1107
1Sa 16: 1 I am sending you to Jesse **of B.** 1095
16: 4 When he arrived at **B,** 1107
16:18 a son of Jesse **of B** who knows how to play 1095
17:12 who was from **B** *in* Judah. 1107
17:15 from Saul to tend his father's sheep at **B.** 1107
17:58 "I am the son of your servant Jesse **of B."** 1095
20: 6 to hurry to **B,** 1107
20:28 for permission to go to **B.** 1107
2Sa 2:32 and buried him in his father's tomb at **B.** 1107
23:14 and the Philistine garrison was at **B.** 1107
23:15 of water from the well near the gate of **B!"** 1107
23:16 drew water from the well near the gate of **B** 1107
23:24 Elhanan son of Dodo from **B,** 1107
1Ch 2:51 Salma the father of **B,** 1107
2:54 **B,** the Netophathites, Atroth Beth Joab, 1107
4: 4 the firstborn of Ephrathah and father of **B.** 1107
11:16 and the Philistine garrison was at **B.** 1107
11:17 of water from the well near the gate of **B!"** 1107
11:18 drew water from the well near the gate of **B** 1107
11:26 Elhanan son of Dodo from **B,** 1107
2Ch 11: 6 **B,** Etam, Tekoa, 1107
Ezr 2:21 the men of **B** 123 1107
Ne 7:26 the men of **B** and Netophah 188 1107
Jer 41:17 at Geruth Kimham near **B** on their way 1107
Mic 5: 2 "But you, **B** Ephrathah, 1107
Mt 2: 1 After Jesus was born in **B** in Judea, *1033*
2: 5 "In **B** in Judea," they replied, *1033*
2: 6 **B,** in the land of Judah, *1033*
2: 8 He sent them to **B** and said, *1033*
2:16 and he gave orders to kill all the boys in **B** *1033*
Lk 2: 4 to **B** the town of David, *1033*
2:15 to **B** and see this thing that has happened, *1033*
Jn 7:42 from David's family and from **B,** *1033*

BETHLEHEMITE (1) [BETHLEHEM]
2Sa 21:19 of Jaare-Oregim **the B** killed Goliath 1095

BETHPHAGE (3)
Mt 21: 1 and came to **B** on the Mount of Olives, *1036*
Mk 11: 1 to **B** and Bethany at the Mount of Olives, *1036*
Lk 19:29 As he approached **B** and Bethany at *1036*

BETHPHELET (KJV) See BETH PELET

BETHSAIDA (7)

Mt 11:21 Woe to you, **B!** *1034*
Mk 6:45 into the boat and go on ahead of him to **B,** *1034*
8:22 They came to **B,** *1034*
Lk 9:10 by themselves to a town called **B,** *1034*
10:13 Woe to you, **B!** *1034*
Jn 1:44 was from the town of **B.** *1034*
12:21 who was from **B** in Galilee, with a request. *1034*

BETHUEL (10)

Ge 22:22 Kesed, Hazo, Pildash, Jidlaph and **B."** 1432
22:23 **B** became the father of Rebekah. 1432
24:15 She was the daughter of **B** son of Milcah, 1432
24:24 "I am the daughter of **B,** 1432
24:47 'The daughter of **B** son of Nahor, 1432
24:50 Laban and **B** answered, 1432
25:20 when he married Rebekah daughter of **B** 1432
28: 2 to the house of your mother's father **B.** 1432
28: 5 to Laban son of **B** the Aramean, 1432
1Ch 4:30 **B,** Hormah, Ziklag, 1433

BETHUL (1)

Jos 19: 4 Eltolad, **B,** Hormah, 1434

BETIMES (KJV) See AGAIN, EARLY, CAREFUL, FORAGING, LOOK

BETONIM (1)

Jos 13:26 and **B,** and from Mahanaim to the territory 1064

BETRAY (24) [BETRAYED, BETRAYER, BETRAYING, BETRAYS]

1Ch 12:17 if you have come to **b** me to my enemies 8228
Ps 89:33 nor *will I ever* **b** my faithfulness. 9213
Pr 16:10 and his mouth *should* not **b** justice. 5085
25: 9 *do* not **b** another man's confidence, 1655
Isa 16: 3 Hide the fugitives, *do* not **b** the refugees. 1655
24:16 The treacherous **b!** 953
24:16 *With* treachery the treacherous **b!"** 953
Mt 10:21 "Brother *will* **b** brother to death, *4140*
24:10 the faith and *will* **b** and hate each other, *4140*
26:21 one of you *will* **b** me." *4140*
26:23 into the bowl with me *will* **b** me. *4140*
26:25 Then Judas, the one who *would* **b** him, *4140*
Mk 13:12 "Brother *will* **b** brother to death, *4140*
14:10 went to the chief priests to **b** Jesus to them. *4140*
14:18 one of you *will* **b** me— *4140*
Lk 22: 4 with them how *he might* **b** Jesus. *4140*
22:21 *of* him who *is going to* **b** me is with mine *4140*
Jn 6:64 and who *would* **b** him. *1639+3836+4140*
6:71 one of the Twelve, was later *to* **b** him.) *4140*
12: 4 Judas Iscariot, who was later *to* **b** him, *4140*
13: 2 son of Simon, to **b** Jesus. *4140*
13:11 For he knew who *was going to* **b** him, *4140*
13:21 one of you *is going to* **b** me." *4140*
21:20 "Lord, who is *going to* **b** you?") *4140*

BETRAYED (22) [BETRAY]

2Sa 19:26 But Ziba my servant **b** me. 8228
Ps 73:15 *I would have* **b** your children. 953
Isa 33: 1 O traitor, you who *have* not *been* **b!** 953
33: 1 when you stop betraying, you *will be* **b.** 953
Jer 12: 6 even they *have* **b** you; 953
La 1: 2 All her friends *have* **b** her; 953
1:19 "I called to my allies but they **b** me. 8228
Mt 10: 4 the Zealot and Judas Iscariot, who **b** him. *4140*
17:22 of Man is going to *be* **b** into the hands *4140*
20:18 *be* **b** to the chief priests and the teachers of *4140*
26:45 Son of Man *is* **b** into the hands of sinners. *4140*
27: 3 When Judas, who *had* **b** him, *4140*
27: 4 he said, *"for I have* **b** innocent blood." *4140*
Mk 3:19 and Judas Iscariot, who **b** him. *4140*
9:31 of Man *is going to be* **b** into the hands *4140*
10:33 *be* **b** to the chief priests and teachers of *4140*
14:41 Son of Man *is* **b** into the hands of sinners. *4140*
Lk 9:44 of Man is going to *be* **b** into the hands *4140*
21:16 *You will be* **b** even by parents, brothers, *4140*
Jn 18: 2 Now Judas, who **b** him, knew the place, *4140*
Ac 7:52 now you *have* **b** and murdered him— *1181+4595*
1Co 11:23 The Lord Jesus, on the night *he was* **b,** *4140*

BETRAYER (4) [BETRAY]

Mt 26:46 Rise, let us go! Here comes my **b!"** *4140*
26:48 Now the **b** had arranged a signal with them: *4140*
Mk 14:42 Rise! Let us go! Here comes my **b!"** *4140*
14:44 Now the **b** had arranged a signal with them: *4140*

BETRAYING (2) [BETRAY]

Isa 33: 1 when you stop **b,** you will be betrayed. 953
Lk 22:48 *are you* **b** the Son of Man with a kiss?" *4140*

BETRAYS (7) [BETRAY]

Pr 11:13 A gossip **b** a confidence, 1655
20:19 A gossip **b** a confidence; 1655
Isa 21: 2 The traitor **b,** the looter takes loot. 953
Hab 2: 5 wine **b** him; he is arrogant and never at rest. 953
Mt 26:24 woe to that man who **b** the Son of Man! *4140*
Mk 14:21 woe to that man who **b** the Son of Man! *4140*
Lk 22:22 but woe to that man who **b** *him."* *4140*

BETROTH (3) [BETROTHED]

Hos 2:19 *I will* **b** you to me forever; 829
2:19 *I will* **b** you in righteousness and justice, 829
2:20 *I will* **b** you in faithfulness, 829

BETROTHED (2) [BETROTH]

Dt 22:27 and though the **b** girl screamed, 829
2Sa 3:14 whom *I* **b** to myself for the price of 829

BETTER (133) [GOOD]

Ge 29:19 "It's **b** that I give her to you than 3202
Ex 14:12 It would have been **b** for us to serve 3202
Nu 11:18 We were **b off** in Egypt!" 3202
14: 3 Wouldn't it be **b** for us to go back 3202
Dt 17:20 and not **consider** himself **b** than his brothers 4222+8123
Jdg 8: 2 the gleanings of Ephraim's grapes **b** than 3202
9: 2 'Which is **b** for you: 3202
11:25 Are you **b** than Balak son of Zippor, 3201+3201
18:19 Isn't it **b** that you serve a tribe and clan 3202
Ru 4:15 and who is **b** to you than seven sons, 3202
1Sa 14:30 **How much b** it would have been if 677+3954
15:22 To obey is **b** than sacrifice, 3202
15:22 and to heed is **b than** the fat of rams. 4946
15:28 to one **b** than you. 3202
16:16 and you *will* **feel b."** 3201
16:23 he *would* **feel b,** 3201
29: 4 **b** could he regain his master's favor **than** 4202
2Sa 14:32 It would be **b** for me if I were still there!" ' 3202
17:14 "The advice of Hushai the Arkite is **b** than 3202
18: 3 be **b** now for you to give us support from 3202
1Ki 2:32 were **b** *men* and more upright than he. 3202
19: 4 I am no **b** than my ancestors." 3202
21: 2 In exchange I will give you a **b** vineyard or, 3202+4946
2Ki 5:12 **b** than any of the waters of Israel? 3202
2Ch 21:13 men *who were* **b** than you. 3202
Est 1:19 to someone else who is **b** than she. 3202
Ps 37:16 **B** the little that the righteous have than 3202
63: 3 Because your love is **b** than life, 3202
84:10 **B** is one day in your courts than 3202
118: 8 It is **b** to take refuge in the LORD than 3202
118: 9 It is **b** to take refuge in the LORD than 3202
Pr 3:14 and yields **b** returns **than** gold. 4946
8:19 My fruit is **b** than fine gold; 3202
12: 9 **B** to be a nobody and yet have a servant 3202
15:16 **B** a little with the fear of the LORD than 3202
15:17 **B** a meal of vegetables where there is love 3202
16: 8 **B** a little with righteousness 3202
16:16 How much **b** to get wisdom than gold, 3202
16:19 **B** to be lowly in spirit and among 3202
16:32 **B** a patient man than a warrior, 3202
17: 1 **B** a dry crust with peace and quiet than 3202
17:12 **B** to meet a bear robbed of her cubs **than** 440
19: 1 **B** a poor man whose walk is blameless than 3202
19:22 **b** to be poor than a liar. 3202
21: 9 **B** to live on a corner of the roof than share 3202
21:19 **B** to live in a desert than with 3202
22: 1 to be esteemed is **b** than silver or gold. 3202
25: 7 it is **b** for him to say to you, 3202
25:24 **B** to live on a corner of the roof than share 3202
27: 5 **B** is open rebuke than hidden love. 3202
27:10 **b** a neighbor nearby than 3202
28: 6 **B** a poor man whose walk is blameless than 3202
Ecc 2:13 I saw that wisdom is **b** than folly, 3862
2:13 just as light is **b** than darkness. 3862
2:24 A man can do nothing **b** than to eat 3202
3:12 I know that there is nothing **b** for men than 3202
3:22 that there is nothing **b** for a man than 3202
4: 3 But **b** than both is he who has not yet been, 3202
4: 6 **B** one handful with tranquillity 3202
4: 9 Two are **b** than one, 3202
4:13 **B** a poor but wise youth than an old 3202
5: 5 It is **b** not to vow than to make a vow and 3202
6: 3 I say that a stillborn child is **b off** than he. 3202
6: 9 **B** what the eye sees than the roving of 3202
7: 1 A good name is **b** than fine perfume, 3202
7: 1 and the day of death **b than** the day of birth. 4946
7: 2 It is **b** to go to a house of mourning than 3202
7: 3 Sorrow is **b** than laughter, 3202
7: 5 It is **b** to heed a wise man's rebuke than 3202
7: 8 The end of a matter is **b** than its beginning, 3202
7: 8 and patience is **b** than pride. 3202
7:10 "Why were the old days **b** than these?" 3202
8:12 that it will go **b** with God-fearing men, 3202
8:15 because nothing is **b** for a man under 3202
9: 4 even a live dog is **b off** than a dead lion! 3202
9:16 So I said, "Wisdom is **b** than strength." 3202
9:18 Wisdom is **b** than weapons of war, 3202
SS 5: 9 How is your beloved **b than** others, 4946
5: 9 How is your beloved **b than** others, 4946
Isa 56: 5 and a name **b** than sons and daughters; 3202
56:12 tomorrow will be like today, or even far **b."** 1524
La 4: 9 by the sword are **b off** than those who die 3202
Eze 15: 2 of a vine **b than** that of a branch on any of 4946
Da 1:15 and **b** nourished **than** any of 4946
1:20 he found them ten times **b than** all 6584
Hos 2: 7 for then I was **b off** than now.' 3202
Am 6: 2 Are *they* **b off** than your two kingdoms? 3202
Jnh 4: 3 for it is **b** for me to die than to live." 3202
4: 8 "It would be **b** for me to die than to live." 3202
Na 3: 8 *Are you* **b** than Thebes, 3512
Mt 5:29 *It is* **b** for you to lose one part *5237*
5:30 *It is* **b** for you to lose one part *5237*
18: 6 *be* **b** for him to have a large millstone hung *5237*
Mt 18: 8 It is **b** for you to enter life maimed *2819*
18: 9 It is **b** for you to enter life *2819*
19:10 *it is* **b** not to marry." *5237*
26:24 be **b** for him if he had not been born." *2819*
Mk 5:26 yet instead of **getting b** she grew worse. *6067*
9:42 be **b** for him to be thrown into the sea with *2819*
9:43 It is **b** for you to enter life maimed than *2819*
9:45 It is **b** for you to enter life crippled than *2819*
9:47 It is **b** for you to enter the kingdom of God *2819*
14:21 be **b** for him if he had not been born." *2819*
Lk 5:39 for he says, 'The old is **b.'** " *5982*
10:42 Mary has chosen what is **b,** *19*
14:10 'Friend, move up to a **b** place.' *NIG*
17: 2 *be* **b** for him to be thrown into the sea with *3387*
Jn 4:52 as to the time when his son got **b,** *3153*
11:12 "Lord, if he sleeps, *he will* **get b."** *5392*
11:50 that *it is* **b** for you that one man die for *5237*
Ro 3: 9 *Are we* any **b?** Not at all! *4604*
14:21 It is **b** not to eat meat or drink wine or *2819*
1Co 7: 9 it is **b** to marry than to burn with passion. *3202*
7:38 but he who does not marry her does even **b.** *3202*
8: 8 and no **b** if we do. *4355*
Eph 1:17 so that you may **know** him **b.** *2106*
Php 1:23 be with Christ, which is **b** by far; *3202+3437*
2: 3 in humility consider others **b than** yourselves. *5660*
1Ti 6: 2 Instead, they are to serve them even **b,** *NIG*
Phm 1:16 but **b than** a slave, as a dear brother. *5642*
Heb 6: 9 we are confident of **b** *things* in your case— *3202*
7:19 and a **b** hope is introduced, *3202*
7:22 the guarantee *of* a **b** covenant. *3202*
8: 6 and it is founded on **b** promises. *3202*
9:23 *with* **b** sacrifices than these. *3202*
10:34 you knew that you yourselves had **b** and lasting possessions. *3202*
11: 4 a **b** sacrifice than Cain did. *4498*
11:16 they were longing for a **b** country— *3202*
11:35 so that they might gain a **b** resurrection. *3202*
11:40 God had planned something **b** for us so *3202*
12:24 that speaks a **b** word than the blood *3202*
1Pe 3:17 It is **b,** if it is God's will, to suffer for doing good *3202*
2Pe 2:21 It would have been **b** for them not to have known the way of righteousness, *3202*

BETWEEN (223)

Ge 1: 6 expanse **b** the waters to separate water 928+9348
3:15 I will put enmity **b** you and the woman, 1068
3:15 and **b** your offspring and hers; 1068
9:12 of the covenant I am making **b** me and you 1068
9:13 the sign of the covenant **b** me and the earth. 1068
9:15 I will remember my covenant **b** me and you 1068
9:16 and remember the everlasting covenant **b** 1068
9:17 of the covenant I have established **b** me 1068
10:12 which is **b** Nineveh and Calah; 1068
13: 3 to the place **b** Bethel and Ai 1068
13: 7 And quarreling arose **b** Abram's herdsmen 1068
13: 8 not have any quarreling **b** you and me, 1068
13: 8 or **b** your herdsmen and mine, 1068
15:17 with a blazing torch appeared and passed **b** 1068
16: 5 May the LORD judge **b** you and me." 1068
16:14 it is still there, **b** Kadesh and Bered. 1068
17: 2 I will confirm my covenant **b** me and you 1068
17: 7 as an everlasting covenant **b** me and you 1068
17:11 and it will be the sign of the covenant **b** me 1068
20: 1 the region of the Negev and lived **b** Kadesh 1068
23:15 but what is that **b** me and you? 1068
26:28 'There ought to be a sworn agreement **b** us 1068
26:28 sworn agreement **b** us and you. 1068
30:36 Then he put a three-day journey **b** himself 1068
31:37 and let them judge **b** the two of us. 1068
31:44 and let it serve as a witness **b** us." 1068
31:48 a witness **b** you and me today." 1068
31:49 "May the LORD keep watch **b** you and me 1068
31:50 remember that God is a witness **b** you 1068
31:51 and here is this pillar I have set up **b** you 1068
31:53 the God of their father, judge **b** us." 1068
32:16 and keep some space **b** the herds." 1068
49:10 nor the ruler's staff from **b** his feet, 1068
49:14 a rawboned donkey lying down **b** 1068
Ex 8:23 a distinction **b** my people and your people. 1068
9: 4 But the LORD will make a distinction **b** 1068
11: 7 the LORD makes a distinction **b** Egypt 1068
14: 2 **b** Migdol and the sea. 1068
14:20 coming **b** the armies of Egypt and Israel. 1068
16: 1 which is **b** Elim and Sinai, 1068
18:16 and I decide **b** the parties and inform them 1068
22:11 the issue **b** them will be settled by 1068
25:22 above the cover **b** the two cherubim 1068+4946
28:33 with gold bells **b** them. 928+9348
30:18 Place it **b** the Tent of Meeting and the altar, 1068
31:13 be a sign **b** me and you for the generations 1068
31:17 be a sign **b** me and the Israelites forever, 1068
39:25 around the hem **b** the pomegranates. 928+9348
40: 7 place the basin **b** the Tent of Meeting and 1068
40:30 He placed the basin **b** the Tent of Meeting 1068
Lev 10:10 You must distinguish **b** the holy and 1068
10:10 **b** the unclean and the clean, 1068
11:47 You must distinguish **b** the unclean and 1068
11:47 **b** living creatures that may be eaten 1068
20:25 " 'You must therefore make a distinction **b** 1068
20:25 between clean and unclean animals and **b** 1068
24:10 and a fight broke out in the camp **b** him and NIH
Lev 26:46 on Mount Sinai **b** himself and the Israelites 1068
27: 3 set the value of a male **b** the ages of twenty 2256+4946+6330

Lev 27: 5 **b** the ages of five and twenty, 2256+4946+6330
27: 6 If it is a person **b** one month and five years, 2256+4946+6330
Nu 7:89 he heard the voice speaking to him from **b** 1068
11:33 But while the meat was still **b** their teeth 1068
13:23 Two of them carried it on a pole **b** them, 928
16:48 He stood **b** the living and the dead, 1068
21:13 **b** Moab and the Amorites. 1068
22:24 of the LORD stood in a **narrow path** *b* AIT
30:16 **relationships b** a man and his wife, 1068
30:16 and **b** a father and his your daughter 1068
31:27 the spoils **b** the soldiers who took part in 1068
35:24 the assembly must judge **b** him and 1068
Dt 1: 1 opposite Suph, **b** Paran and Tophel, Laban, 1068
1:16 Hear the disputes **b** your brothers 1068
1:16 whether the case is **b** brother Israelites or 1068
1:16 between brother Israelites or **b** one of them 1068
5: 5 (At that time I stood **b** the LORD and you 1068
33:12 the LORD loves rests **b** his shoulders." 1068
Jos 3: 4 a distance of about a thousand yards **b** you 1068
8: 9 in wait **b** Bethel and Ai, to the west of Ai— 1068
8:11 with the valley **b** them and the city. 1068
8:12 and set them in ambush **b** Bethel and Ai, 1068
18:11 Their allotted territory lay **b** the tribes 1068
22:25 the Jordan a boundary **b** us and you— 1068
22:27 a witness **b** us and you and the generations 1068
22:28 but as a witness **b** us and you.' 1068
22:34 A Witness **B** Us that the LORD is God. 1068
23: 4 **b** the Jordan and the Great Sea in the west. 4946
24: 7 he put darkness **b** you and the Egyptians; 1068
Jdg 4: 5 She held court under the Palm of Deborah **b** 1068
4:17 because there were friendly relations **b** 1068
9:23 an evil spirit **b** Abimelech and the citizens 1068
11:27 decide the dispute this day **b** the Israelites 1068
13:25 **b** Zorah and Eshtaol. 1068
16:31 They brought him back and buried him **b** 1068
1Sa 4: 4 *who is* **enthroned** *b* the cherubim. AIT
7:12 Then Samuel took a stone and set it up **b** 1068
7:14 there was peace **b** Israel and the Amorites. 1068
14:42 "Cast the lot **b** me and Jonathan my son." 1068
17: 1 **b** Socoh and Azekah. 1068
17: 3 with the valley **b** them. 1068
20: 3 there is only a step **b** me and death." 1068
20:23 LORD is witness **b** you and me forever." 1068
20:42 'The LORD is witness **b** you and me, 1068
20:42 and **b** your descendants 1068
24:12 May the LORD judge **b** you and me. 1068
24:15 May the LORD be our judge and decide **b** 1068
26:13 there was a wide space **b** them. 1068
2Sa 3: 1 The war **b** the house of Saul and the house 1068
3: 6 the war **b** the house of Saul and the house 1068
6: 2 *who is* **enthroned** *b* the cherubim AIT
18:24 While David was sitting **b** the inner 1068
19:35 Can I tell the difference **b** what is good 1068
21: 7 because of the oath before the LORD **b** 1068
21:15 a battle **b** the Philistines and Israel, 4200
1Ki 3: 9 to govern your people and to distinguish **b** 1068
5:12 There were peaceful relations **b** Hiram 1068
7:29 On the panels **b** the uprights were lions, 1068
7:46 in clay molds in the plain of the Jordan **b** 1068
8:32 **Judge** *b* your servants, AIT
14:30 There was continual warfare **b** Rehoboam 1068
15: 6 There was war **b** Rehoboam and Jeroboam 1068
15: 7 There was war **b** Abijah and Jeroboam. 1068
15:16 There was war **b** Asa and Baasha king 1068
15:19 "Let there be a treaty **b** me and you," 1068
15:19 "as there was **b** my father and your father. 1068
15:32 There was war **b** Asa and Baasha king 1068
18:21 "How long will you waver **b** two opinions? 6584
18:42 bent down to the ground and put his face **b** 1068
22: 1 For three years there was no war **b** Aram 1068
22:34 and hit the king of Israel **b** the sections 1068
2Ki 9:24 Then Jehu drew his bow and shot Joram **b** 1068
11:15 "Bring her out **b** the ranks and put to 4200
11:17 then made a covenant **b** the LORD and 1068
11:17 He also made a covenant **b** the king and 1068
16:14 from **b** the new altar and the temple of 1068
19:15 God of Israel, **enthroned** *b* the cherubim, AIT
25: 4 at night through the gate **b** the two walls 1068
1Ch 13: 6 *who is* **enthroned** *b* the cherubim— AIT
21:16 and saw the angel of the LORD standing **b** 1068
2Ch 4:17 in clay molds in the plain of the Jordan **b** 1068
6:23 **Judge** *b* your servants, AIT
12: 8 **learn the difference b** serving me and 3359
12:15 There was continual **warfare** *b* Rehoboam AIT
13: 2 There was war **b** Abijah and Jeroboam. 1068
16: 3 "Let there be a treaty **b** me and you," 1068
16: 3 "as there was **b** my father and your father. 1068
18:33 and hit the king of Israel **b** the sections 1068
23:14 **"Bring** her **out** *b* the ranks and put to AIT
35:21 "What **quarrel** is there **b** you and me, 4200
Ne 3:32 and **b** the room above the corner and 1068
Job 4:20 **B** dawn and dusk they are broken to pieces; 4946
9:33 only there were someone to arbitrate **b** us, 1068
26:10 the face of the waters for a **boundary** *b* light and darkness. AIT
41:16 so close to the next that no air can pass **b.** 1068
Ps 80: 1 you *who* **sit enthroned** *b* the cherubim, AIT
99: 1 *he* **sits enthroned** *b* the cherubim, AIT
104:10 it flows **b** the mountains. 1068
SS 1:13 a sachet of myrrh resting **b** my breasts. 1068
Isa 2: 4 He will judge **b** the nations 1068
5: 3 judge **b** me and my vineyard. 1068
22:11 a reservoir **b** the two walls for the water of 1068
37:16 God of Israel, **enthroned** *b* the cherubim, AIT
Jer 34:18 the calf they cut in two and then walked **b** 1068
34:19 and all the people of the land who walked **b** 1068
Jer 39: 4 through the gate **b** the two walls, 1068
52: 7 at night through the gate **b** the two walls 1068
Eze 4: 3 place it as an iron wall **b** you and the city 1068
8: 3 The Spirit lifted me up **b** earth and heaven 1068
8:16 **b** the portico and the altar, 1068
18: 8 from doing wrong and judges fairly **b** man 1068
20:12 Also I gave them my Sabbaths as a sign **b** 1068
20:20 that they may be a sign **b** us. 1068
22:26 not distinguish **b** the holy and the common; 1068
22:26 that there is no **difference b** the unclean and 1068
34:17 I will judge **b** one sheep and another, 1068
34:17 and **b** rams and goats. 4200
34:20 See, I myself will judge **b** the fat sheep and 1068
34:22 I will judge **b** one sheep and another. 1068
40: 7 and the projecting walls **b** 1068
41: 9 The open area **b** the side rooms of 1075
43: 8 with only a wall **b** me and them, 1068
44:23 to teach my people **the difference b** the holy and the common 1068
44:23 to distinguish **b** the unclean and the clean. 1068
47:16 on the border **b** Damascus and Hamath), 1068
47:18 the east side the boundary will run **b** 1068+4946
47:18 Jordan **b** Gilead and the land of Israel, 1068+4946
48:22 the prince will lie **b** the border of Judah and 1068
Da 7: 5 and it had three ribs in its mouth **b** its teeth. 10099
8: 5 suddenly a goat with a prominent horn **b** 1068
8:21 the large horn **b** his eyes is the first king. 1068
11:45 He will pitch his royal tents **b** the seas at 1068
Hos 2: 2 from her face and the unfaithfulness from **b** 1068
Joel 2:17 weep **b** the temple porch and the altar. 1068
Mic 4: 3 He will judge **b** many peoples 1068
Zec 5: 9 and they lifted up the basket **b** heaven 1068
6: 1 from **b** two mountains— 1068
6:13 And there will be harmony **b** the two.' 1068
9: 7 the forbidden food from **b** their teeth. 1068
11:14 the brotherhood **b** Judah and Israel. 1068
Mal 2:14 the LORD is acting as the witness **b** you 1068
3:18 And you will again see the **distinction b** 1068
3:18 **b** those who serve God 1068
Mt 18:15 just **b** the two of you. *3568*
19:10 "If this is the situation **b** a husband *3552*
23:35 whom you murdered **b** the temple and *3568*
Lk 11:51 who was killed **b** the altar and *3568*
12:14 who appointed me a judge or an arbiter **b** *2093*
15:12 So he **divided** his property **b** them. *1349*
16:26 **b** us and you a great chasm has been fixed, *3568*
17:11 Jesus traveled along the border **b** Samaria *3545*
Jn 3:25 An argument developed **b** some *3552*
Ac 12: 6 Peter was sleeping **b** two soldiers, *3568*
15: 9 He made no distinction **b** us and them, *3568*
23: 7 *b* **the Pharisees** and the Sadducees, *AIT*
Ro 10:12 there is no difference **b** Jew and Gentile— *5445*
14:22 about these things keep **b** yourself and God. *NIG*
1Co 6: 5 to judge a dispute **b** believers? *324+3545*
12:10 to another **distinguishing b** spirits, *1360*
2Co 6:15 What harmony is there **b** Christ and Belial? *NIG*
6:16 What agreement is there **b** the temple *3552*
Php 1:23 I am torn **b** the two: *1666*
1Ti 2: 5 For there is one God and one **mediator b** *3542*
6: 5 **constant friction b** men of corrupt mind, *1384*

BEULAH (1)

Isa 62: 4 called Hephzibah, and your land **B;** 1241

BEWAIL, BEWAILED (KJV) See GRIEVED, MOURN, MOURNED, WEEP

BEWARE (7)

2Ki 6: 9 **"B** of passing that place, 9068
Job 36:21 **B** *of* turning to evil, 440+9068
Isa 22:17 **"B,** the LORD is about to take firm hold 2180
Jer 7:32 So **b,** the days are coming, 2180
9: 4 **"B** of your friends; 9068
19: 6 So **b,** the days are coming, 2180
Lk 20:46 **"B** of the teachers of the law. *4668*

BEWILDERED (3) [BEWILDERMENT]

Est 3:15 but the city of Susa *was* **b.** 1003
Isa 21: 3 *I* **am b** by what I see. 987
Mk 16: 8 and **b,** the women went out and fled from *1749*

BEWILDERMENT (1) [BEWILDERED]

Ac 2: 6 a crowd came together in **b,** *5177*

BEWITCHED (1) [WITCHCRAFT]

Gal 3: 1 Who *has* **b** you? *1001*

BEWRAY (KJV) See BETRAY

BEYOND (65)

Ge 35:21 and pitched his tent **b** Migdal Eder. 2134+4946
41:49 because it was **b** measure. 401
Lev 15:25 a discharge that continues **b** her period, 6584
Nu 22:18 not do anything great or small to **go b** 6296
24:13 *to* **go b** the command of the LORD— 6296
Dt 3:25 and see the good land **b** the Jordan— 928+6298
30:11 not too difficult for you or **b** your **reach.** 8158
30:13 Nor is it **b** the sea, so that you have to ask, 4946+6298
Jos 24: 2 lived **b** the River and worshiped other gods. 928+6298
Jos 24: 3 from the **land b** the River and led him 6298
24:14 the gods your forefathers worshiped **b** 928+6298
24:15 the gods your forefathers served **b** 928+6298
Jdg 1:36 from Scorpion Pass to Sela and **b.** 2025+5087
5:17 Gilead stayed **b** the Jordan. 928+6298
13:18 It is **b understanding."** 7100
1Sa 14:23 and the battle **moved on b** Beth Aven. 6296
20:22 the arrows are **b** you,' then you must go, 2134+2256+4946
20:36 As the boy ran, he shot an arrow **b** him. 6296
20:37 "Isn't the arrow **b** you?" 2134+2256+4946
2Sa 10:16 Hadadezer had Arameans brought from **b** 6298
16: 1 When David had gone a short distance **b** 4946
1Ki 14:15 to their forefathers and scatter them **b** 4946+6298
1Ch 19:16 and had Arameans brought from **b** 6298
22:16 and iron—craftsmen **b** number. 401
Ne 3:16 **B** him, Nehemiah son of Azbuk, 339
3:23 **B** them, Benjamin 339
Job 28:18 the price of wisdom is **b** rubies. 4946
36:26 How great is God—**b** our understanding! 4202
37: 5 he does great things **b** our understanding. 4202
37:23 The Almighty is **b** our reach and exalted 4202
Ps 104:25 teeming with creatures **b** number— 401
Ecc 7:23 but this was **b** me. 8158
SS 6: 8 and virgins **b** number; 401
Isa 7:20 the Lord will use a razor hired from **b** 6298
52:14 his appearance was so disfigured **b** that 4946
52:14 and his form marred **b** human likeness— 4946
64: 9 Do not be angry **b measure,** O LORD; 4394+6330
64:12 and punish us **b measure?** 4394+6330
Jer 17: 9 above all things and **b cure.** 631
30:12 your injury **b healing.** 2703
La 5:22 and are angry with us **b measure.** 4394+6330
Eze 41:16 everything **b** and including 5584
Da 8:27 it was **b** understanding. 401
Joel 2:11 his forces are **b number,** 4394+8041
Am 5:27 I will send you into exile **b** Damascus," 2134+4200+4946
Mic 2:10 it is ruined, **b all remedy.** 5344
Zep 3:10 From **b** the rivers of Cush my worshipers, 6298
Mal 1: 5 **even b** the borders of Israel!' 4946+6584
Mt 5:37 anything **b** this comes from the evil one. *4356*
Lk 22:41 He withdrew about a stone's throw **b** them, *608*
Ac 7:43 Therefore I will send you into exile' **b** *2084*
15:28 and to us not to burden you with anything **b** *4440*
26:22 I am saying nothing **b** what the prophets *1760*
Ro 11:11 Did they stumble so as to fall **b** recovery? *NIG*
11:33 and his paths **b tracing out!** *453*
1Co 1:16 **b that,** I don't remember *3370*
4: 6 "Do not go **b** what is written." *5642*
10:13 not let you be tempted **b** what you can bear. *5642*
2Co 1: 8 far **b** our ability to endure, *5642*
8: 3 and even **b** their ability, *4123*
10:13 however, will not boast **b** proper **limits,** *296+1650+3836*
10:15 Neither do we go **b** our **limits** by boasting of work done by others. *296+1650+3836*
10:16 the gospel in the regions **b** you. *5654*
Gal 1:14 I was advancing in Judaism **b** many Jews *5642*
1Ti 3:16 **B all question,** the mystery *3935*

BEZAI (3)

Ezr 2:17 of **B** 323 1291
Ne 7:23 of **B** 324 1291
10:18 Hodiah, Hashum, **B,** 1291

BEZALEL (9)

Ex 31: 2 I have chosen **B** son of Uri, the son of Hur, 1295
35:30 "See, the LORD has chosen **B** son of Uri, 1295
36: 1 So **B,** Oholiab and every skilled person 1295
36: 2 Then Moses summoned **B** and Oholiab 1295
37: 1 **B** made the ark of acacia wood— 1295
38:22 (**B** son of Uri, the son of Hur, 1295
1Ch 2:20 and Uri the father of **B.** 1295
2Ch 1: 5 But the bronze altar that **B** son of Uri, 1295
Ezr 10:30 Kelal, Benaiah, Maaseiah, Mattaniah, **B,** 1295

BEZEK (2) [ADONI-BEZEK]

Jdg 1: 4 down ten thousand men at **B.** 1028
1Sa 11: 8 When Saul mustered them at **B,** 1028

BEZER (5)

Dt 4:43 **B** in the desert plateau, for the Reubenites; 1311
Jos 20: 8 of the Jordan of Jericho they designated **B** 1311
21:36 from the tribe of Reuben, **B,** Jahaz, 1311
1Ch 6:78 the Jordan east of Jericho they received **B** 1311
7:37 **B,** Hod, Shamma, Shilshah, Ithran 1310

BICRI (8)

2Sa 20: 1 a troublemaker named Sheba son of **B,** 1152
20: 2 to follow Sheba son of **B.** 1152
20: 6 Sheba son of **B** will do us more harm than Absalom did. 1152
20: 7 from Jerusalem to pursue Sheba son of **B.** 1152
20:10 and his brother Abishai pursued Sheba son of **B.** 1152
20:13 on with Joab to pursue Sheba son of **B.** 1152
20:21 A man named Sheba son of **B,** 1152
20:22 and they cut off the head of Sheba son of **B** 1152

BID, BIDDEN, BIDDETH (KJV) See SAID, SAY, SAYS

BIDDING (2)
Ps 103:20 you mighty ones who do his **b**, 1821
148: 8 stormy winds that do his **b**, 1821

BIDKAR (1)
2Ki 9:25 Jehu said to **B**, his chariot officer, 982

BIER (2)
2Sa 3:31 King David himself walked behind the **b**. 4753
2Ch 16:14 They laid him on a **b** covered with spices 5435

BIG (14) [BIGGER]
Ex 29:20 and on the **b toes** *of* their right feet. 991
Lev 8:23 and on the **b toe** *of* his right foot. 991
8:24 of their right hands and on the **b toes** 991
14:14 and on the **b toe** *of* his right foot. 991
14:17 and on the **b toe** *of* his right foot, 991
14:25 and on the **b toe** *of* his right foot. 991
14:28 and on the **b toe** *of* his right foot. 991
Jdg 1: 6 and cut off his thumbs and **b toes.** 8079
1: 7 and **b toes** cut off have picked up scraps 8079
9:38 "Where is your **b talk** now, you who said, 7023
2Sa 18:17 into a **b** pit in the forest and piled up 1524
Mt 27:60 He rolled a **b** stone in front of the entrance *3489*
Mk 4:32 with such **b** branches that the birds of *3489*
Ac 22:28 "I had to pay a **b** price for my citizenship." *4498*

BIGGER (2) [BIG]
Lk 7:43 the one who had the **b** debt canceled." *4498*
12:18 I will tear down my barns and build **b** *ones,* *3505*

BIGTHA (1)
Est 1:10 Mehuman, Biztha, Harbona, **B**, Abagtha, 960

BIGTHANA (2)
Est 2:21 at the king's gate, **B** and Teresh, two of 961
6: 2 that Mordecai had exposed **B** and Teresh, 962

BIGVAI (6)
Ezr 2: 2 Bilshan, Mispar, **B**, Rehum and Baanah): 958
2:14 of **B** 2,056 958
8:14 of the descendants of **B**, 958
Ne 7: 7 Mispereth, **B**, Nehum and Baanah): 958
7:19 of **B** 2,067 958
10:16 Adonijah, **B**, Adin, 958

BILDAD (5)
Job 2:11 **B** the Shuhite and Zophar the Naamathite, 1161
8: 1 Then **B** the Shuhite replied: 1161
18: 1 Then **B** the Shuhite replied: 1161
25: 1 Then **B** the Shuhite replied: 1161
42: 9 **B** the Shuhite and Zophar 1161

BILEAM (1)
1Ch 6:70 the Israelites gave Aner and **B**, 1190

BILGAH (2) [BILGAH'S]
1Ch 24:14 the fifteenth to **B**, the sixteenth to Immer, 1159
Ne 12: 5 Mijamin, Moadiah, **B**, 1159

BILGAH'S (1) [BILGAH]
Ne 12:18 of **B**, Shammua; of Shemaiah's, 1159

BILGAI (1)
Ne 10: 8 **B** and Shemaiah. These were the priests. 1160

BILHAH (10)
Ge 29:29 Laban gave his servant girl **B** to his 1167
30: 3 Then she said, "Here is **B**, my maidservant. 1167
30: 4 So she gave him her servant **B** as a wife. 1167
30: 7 Rachel's servant **B** conceived again 1167
35:22 in and slept with his father's concubine **B**, 1167
35:25 The sons of Rachel's maidservant **B:** 1167
37: 2 the sons of **B** and the sons of Zilpah, 1167
46:25 These were the sons born to Jacob by **B**, 1167
1Ch 4:29 **B**, Ezem, Tolad, 1168
7:13 the descendants of **B**. 1167

BILHAN (4)
Ge 36:27 The sons of Ezer: **B**, Zaavan and Akan. 1169
1Ch 1:42 The sons of Ezer: **B**, Zaavan and Akan. 1169
7:10 The son of Jediael: **B**. 1169
7:10 The sons of **B:** Jeush, Benjamin, Ehud, 1169

BILL (2)
Lk 16: 6 "The manager told him, 'Take your **b**, *1207*
16: 7 'Take your **b** and make it eight hundred.' *1207*

BILLOWED (1) [BILLOWS]
Ex 19:18 The smoke **b up** *from* it like smoke from 6590

BILLOWS (2) [BILLOWED]
Joel 2:30 blood and fire and **b** *of* smoke. 9406
Ac 2:19 blood and fire and **b** of smoke. *874*

BILSHAN (2)
Ezr 2: 2 Nehemiah, Seraiah, Reelaiah, Mordecai, **B**, 1193
Ne 7: 7 **B**, Mispereth, Bigvai, Nehum and Baanah): 1193

BIMHAL (1)
1Ch 7:33 Pasach, **B** and Ashvath. 1197

BIND (19) [BINDING, BINDINGS, BINDS, BOUND]
Dt 6: 8 and **b** them on your foreheads 2118+3213+4200
11:18 and **b** them on your foreheads 2118+3213+4200
Ne 10:29 **b themselves with** a curse and an oath 928+995
Job 38:31 *"Can you* **b** the beautiful Pleiades? 8003
Ps 119:61 Though the wicked **b** me *with* ropes, 6386
149: 8 to **b** their kings with fetters, 673
Pr 3: 3 **b** them around your neck, 8003
6:21 **B** them upon your heart forever; 8003
7: 3 **B** them on your fingers; 8003
Isa 8:16 **B up** the testimony and seal up the law 7674
56: 6 And foreigners who **b themselves** to 4277
61: 1 He has sent me to **b up** the brokenhearted, 2502
Jer 50: 5 They will come and **b themselves** to 4277
Eze 34:16 *I will* **b up** the injured and strengthen 2502
Hos 6: 1 he has injured us but *he will* **b up** 2502
Mt 16:19 whatever *you* **b** on earth will be bound *1313*
18:18 whatever *you* **b** on earth will be bound *1313*
Mk 5: 3 and no one could **b** him any more, *1313*
Ac 21:11 of Jerusalem *will* **b** the owner of this belt *1313*

BIND, BINDS, BOUND (Anglicized) See also OBLIGATE, OBLIGATED, OBLIGATES

BINDING (7) [BIND]
Ge 37: 7 We *were* **b** sheaves of grain out in the field 520
Nu 30: 9 by a widow or divorced woman *will be* **b** 7756
30:14 or the pledges **b on** her. 6584
Jos 2:17 "This oath you made us swear will **not** be **b** 5929
Jdg 16:21 **B** him with bronze shackles, 673
Ne 9:38 we are making a **b agreement,** 591
Heb 2: 2 For if the message spoken by angels was **b**, *1010*

BINDINGS (1) [BIND]
Jdg 15:14 and the **b** dropped from his hands. 657

BINDS (5) [BIND]
Job 5:18 For he wounds, but *he* also **b up;** 2502
30:18 *he* **b** me like the neck of my garment. 273
Ps 147: 3 the brokenhearted and **b up** their wounds. 2502
Isa 30:26 the LORD **b up** the bruises of his people 2502
Col 3:14 love, which **b** them all **together** in perfect unity. *1639+5278*

BINEA (2)
1Ch 8:37 Moza was the father of **B;** 1232
9:43 Moza was the father of **B;** 1232

BINNUI (8)
Ezr 8:33 of Jeshua and Noadiah son of **B**. 1218
10:30 Mattaniah, Bezalel, **B** and Manasseh. 1218
10:38 From the descendants of **B:** Shimei, 1218
Ne 3:18 by their countrymen under **B** son 1218
3:24 **B** son of Henadad repaired another section, 1218
7:15 of **B** 648 1218
10: 9 **B** of the sons of Henadad, Kadmiel, 1218
12: 8 The Levites were Jeshua, **B**, Kadmiel, 1218

BIRD (38) [BIRD'S, BIRDS]
Ge 1:21 and every winged **b** according to its kind. 6416
6:20 Two of every kind of **b**, 6416
7: 3 and also seven of every kind of **b**, 6416
7:14 according to its kind and every **b** according 6416
Lev 7:26 not eat the blood of any **b** or animal. 6416
14: 6 He is then to take the live **b** and dip it, 7606
14: 6 of the **b** that was killed over the fresh water. 7606
14: 7 he is to release the live **b** in the open fields. 7606
14:51 the hyssop, the scarlet yarn and the live **b**, 7606
14:51 the blood of the dead **b** and the fresh water, 7606
14:52 the fresh water, the live **b**, the cedar wood, 7606
14:53 the live **b** in the open fields outside 7606
17:13 among you who hunts any animal or **b** 6416
20:25 Do not defile yourselves by any animal or **b** 6416
Dt 4:17 any animal on earth or any **b** that flies 4053+7606
14:11 You may eat any clean **b**. 7606
Job 28: 7 No **b of prey** knows that hidden path, 6514
41: 5 like a **b** or put him on a leash for your girls? 7606
Ps 11: 1 "Flee like a **b** to your mountain. 7606
50:11 I know every **b** *in* the mountains, 6416
102: 7 I have become like a **b** alone on a roof. 7606
124: 7 like a **b** out of the fowler's snare; 7606
Pr 6: 5 like a **b** from the snare of the fowler. 7606
7:23 like a **b** darting into a snare, 7606
27: 8 Like a **b** that strays from its nest is 7606
Ecc 10:20 a **b** *of* the air may carry your words, 6416
10:20 a **b on the wing** may report what you say. 1251+4053
Isa 46:11 From the east I summon a **b of prey;** 6514
Jer 4:25 every **b** *in* the sky had flown away. 6416
12: 9 like a speckled **b of prey** that other birds 6514
La 3:52 without cause hunted me like a **b**. 7606
Eze 39:17 to every kind of **b** and all the wild animals: 7606
Eze 44:31 priests must not eat anything, **b** or animal, 6416
Da 4:33 an eagle and his nails like the claws of a **b**. 10616
7: 6 four wings like those of a **b**. 10533
Hos 9:11 Ephraim's glory will fly away like a **b**— 6416
Am 3: 5 Does a **b** fall into a trap on the ground 7606
Rev 18: 2 a haunt *for* every unclean and detestable **b**. *3997*

BIRD'S (2) [BIRD]
Lev 14:52 He shall purify the house with the **b** blood, 7606
Dt 22: 6 If you come across a **b** nest beside the road, 7606

BIRDS (97) [BIRD]
Ge 1:20 and let **b** fly above the earth across 6416
1:22 and let the **b** increase on the earth." 6416
1:26 over the fish of the sea and the **b** *of* the air, 6416
1:28 over the fish of the sea and the **b** *of* the air, 6416
1:30 the beasts of the earth and all the **b** *of* the air 6416
2:19 the beasts of the field and all the **b** *of* the air 6416
2:20 the **b** *of* the air and all the beasts of 6416
6: 7 and **b** *of* the air— 6416
7: 8 of **b** and of all creatures that move along 6416
7:21 **b**, livestock, wild animals, 6416
7:23 the ground and the **b** *of* the air were wiped 6416
8:17 the **b**, the animals, and all the creatures 6416
8:19 that move along the ground and all the **b**— 6416
8:20 of all the clean animals and clean **b**, 6416
9: 2 the beasts of the earth and all the **b** *of* the air 6416
9:10 the **b**, the livestock and all 6416
15:10 the **b**, however, he did not cut in half. 7606
15:11 **b of prey** came down on the carcasses, 6514
40:17 but the **b** were eating them out of the basket 6416
40:19 And the **b** will eat away your flesh." 6416
Lev 1:14 to the LORD is a burnt offering of **b**, 6416
11:13 " 'These are the **b** you are to detest and 6416
11:46 concerning animals, **b**, every living thing 6416
14: 4 that two live clean **b** and some cedar wood, 7606
14: 5 Then the priest shall order that one of the **b** 7606
14:49 To purify the house he is to take two **b** 7606
14:50 He shall kill one of the **b** over fresh water 7606
20:25 and between unclean and clean **b**. 6416
Dt 28:26 Your carcasses will be food for all the **b** *of* 6416
1Sa 17:44 the **b** *of* the air and the beasts of the field!" 6416
17:46 the carcasses of the Philistine army to the **b** 6416
2Sa 21:10 not let the **b** *of* the air touch them by day or 6416
1Ki 4:33 He also taught about animals and **b**, 6416
14:11 the **b** *of* the air will feed on those who die 6416
16: 4 the **b** *of* the air will feed on those who die 6416
21:24 the **b** *of* the air will feed on those who die 6416
Job 12: 7 and they will teach you, or the **b** *of* the air, 6416
28:21 concealed even from the **b** *of* the air. 6416
35:11 the earth and makes us wiser than the **b** *of* 6416
Ps 8: 8 the **b** *of* the air, 7606
78:27 flying **b** like sand on the seashore. 6416
79: 2 of your servants as food to the **b** *of* the air, 6416
104:12 The **b** *of* the air nest by the waters; 6416
104:17 There the **b** make their nests; 7606
148:10 small creatures and flying **b**, 7606
Pr 1:17 to spread a net in full view of all the **b**! 1251+4053
Ecc 9:12 or **b** are taken in a snare, 7606
12: 4 when men rise up at the sound of **b**, 7606
Isa 16: 2 Like fluttering **b** pushed from the nest, 6416
18: 6 be left to the mountain **b of prey** and to 6514
18: 6 the **b** will feed on them all summer, 6514
31: 5 Like **b** hovering overhead, 7606
Jer 5:26 in wait like **men who snare b** and 3687
5:27 Like cages full of **b**, 6416
7:33 of this people will become food for the **b** *of* 6416
9:10 The **b** *of* the air have fled and 6416
12: 4 the animals and **b** have perished. 6416
12: 9 that other **b of prey** surround and attack? 6514
15: 3 to kill and the dogs to drag away and the **b** 6416
16: 4 the **b** *of* the air and the beasts of the earth." 6416
19: 7 as food to the **b** *of* the air and the beasts of 6416
34:20 the **b** *of* the air and the beasts of the earth. 6416
Eze 13:20 like **b** and I will tear them from your arms; 7256
13:20 the people that you ensnare like **b**. 7256
17:23 **B** of every kind will nest in it; 4053+7606
29: 5 the beasts of the earth and the **b** *of* the air. 6416
31: 6 All the **b** *of* the air nested in its boughs, 6416
31:13 the **b** *of* the air settled on the fallen tree, 6416
32: 4 I will let all the **b** *of* the air settle on you 6416
38:20 The fish of the sea, the **b** *of* the air, 6416
39: 4 as food to all kinds of **carrion b** and to 6514+7606
Da 2:38 the beasts of the field and the **b** *of* the air. 10533
4:12 and the **b** *of* the air lived in its branches; 10616
4:14 Let the animals flee from under it and the **b** 10616
4:21 in its branches for the **b** *of* the air— 10616
Hos 2:18 the **b** *of* the air and the creatures that move 6416
4: 3 the field and the **b** *of* the air and the fish of 6416
7:12 I will pull them down like **b** *of* the air. 6416
11:11 They will come trembling like **b** 7606
Zep 1: 3 the **b** of the air and the fish of the sea. 6416
Mt 6:26 Look at the **b** of the air; *4374*
8:20 "Foxes have holes and **b** of the air *4374*
13: 4 and the **b** came and ate it up. *4374*
13:32 so that the **b** of the air come and perch *4374*
Mk 4: 4 and the **b** came and ate it up. *4374*
4:32 that the **b** of the air can perch in its shade." *4374*
Lk 8: 5 and the **b** of the air ate it up. *4374*
9:58 "Foxes have holes and **b** of the air *4374*
12:24 how much more valuable you are than **b**! *4374*
13:19 the **b** of the air perched in its branches." *4374*
Ac 10:12 as well as reptiles of the earth and **b** of *4374*
11: 6 wild beasts, reptiles, and **b** of the air. *4374*
Ro 1:23 to look like mortal man and **b** and animals *4374*

1Co 15:39 b another and fish another. *4764*
Jas 3: 7 All kinds *of* animals, b, *4374*
Rev 19:17 who cried in a loud voice *to* all the b flying *3997*
19:21 all the b gorged themselves on their flesh. *3997*

BIRI See BETH BIRI

BIRSHA (1)
Ge 14: 2 B king of Gomorrah, 1407

BIRTH (143) [BEAR]
Ge 3:16 with pain *you will* give b *to* children. 3528
4: 1 she became pregnant and gave b *to* Cain. 3528
4: 2 Later *she* gave b *to* his brother Abel. 3528
4:17 she became pregnant and gave b *to* Enoch. 3528
4:20 Adah gave b *to* Jabal; 3528
4:25 *she* gave b *to* a son and named him Seth, 3528
11:28 in the land of his b. 4580
25:13 listed in the order of their b: 9352
25:24 When the time came for her to give b, 3528
25:26 when Rebekah gave b *to* them. 3528
29:32 Leah became pregnant and gave b *to* 3528
29:33 and when *she* gave b *to* a son she said, 3528
29:34 and when *she* gave b *to* a son she said, 3528
29:35 and when *she* gave b *to* a son she said, 3528
30:21 Some time later *she* gave b *to* a daughter 3528
30:23 She became pregnant and gave b *to* a son 3528
30:25 After Rachel gave b *to* Joseph, 3528
31: 8 all the flocks gave b *to* speckled young; 3528
35:16 *to* give b and had great difficulty. 3528
38: 3 she became pregnant and gave b *to* a son, 3528
38: 4 and gave b *to* a son and named him Onan. 3528
38: 5 *She* gave b *to* still another son 3528
38: 5 It was at Kezib that she gave b *to* him. 3528
38:27 When the time came for her *to* give b, 3528
38:28 As she *was* giving b, 3528
50:23 of Manasseh *were* placed at b 3528
Ex 1:19 and give b before the midwives arrive." 3528
2: 2 she became pregnant and gave b *to* a son. 3528
2:22 Zipporah gave b *to* a son, 3528
21:22 and she gives b prematurely 3529+3655
28:10 in the order of their b— 9352
Lev 12: 2 and gives b *to* a son will 3528
12: 5 If *she* gives b *to* a daughter, 3528
12: 7 the regulations for the *woman who* gives b 3528
Nu 11:12 *Did* I give them b? 3528
Dt 32:18 you forgot the God *who* gave you b. 2655
Jdg 13: 5 you will conceive and give b *to* a son. 3528
13: 5 set apart to God from b, 1061
13: 7 'You will conceive and give b *to* a son. 3528
13: 7 of God from b until the day of his death.' " 1061
13:24 The woman gave b *to* a boy 3528
16:17 a Nazirite set apart to God since b. 562+1061
Ru 1:12 if I had a husband tonight and then gave b 3528
4:13 and *she* gave b *to* a son. 3528
4:15 *has* given him b." 3528
1Sa 1:20 of time Hannah conceived and gave b *to* 3528
2:21 she conceived and gave b *to* three sons 3528
4:19 she went into labor and gave b, 3528
4:20 *you have* given b *to* a son." 3528
2Sa 12:24 *She* gave b *to* a son, 3528
1Ki 11: 3 He had seven hundred wives of royal b 8576
2Ki 4:17 about that same time *she* gave b *to* a son, 3528
19: 3 to the point of b and there is no strength 5402
1Ch 2:49 *She* also gave b *to* Shaaph the father 3528
4: 9 saying, "*I* gave b *to* him in pain." 3528
4:17 One of Mered's wives gave b *to* Miriam, 2225
4:18 (His Judean wife gave b *to* Jered the father 3528
7:14 *She* gave b *to* Makir the father of Gilead. 3528
7:16 Makir's wife Maacah gave b *to* a son 3528
7:18 His sister Hammoleketh gave b *to* Ishhod, 3528
7:23 she became pregnant and gave b *to* a son. 3528
Job 3: 1 and cursed the day of his b. NIH
3: 3 "May the day of *my* b perish, 3528
3:11 "Why did I not perish at b, 8167
15:35 They conceive trouble and give b *to* evil; 3528
31:18 and from my b I guided the widow— 562+1061
38:29 Who gives b *to* the frost from the heavens 3528
39: 1 when the mountain goats give b? 3528
39: 2 Do you know the time they give b? 3528
Ps 7:14 with evil and conceives trouble gives b 3528
22:10 From b I was cast upon you; 8167
51: 5 Surely *I was* sinful at b, 2655
58: 3 Even from b the wicked go astray; 8167
71: 6 From b I have relied on you; 1061
Pr 8:24 When there were no oceans, *I* was given b, 2655
8:25 before the hills, *I* was given b, 2655
23:25 may *she who* gave you b rejoice! 3528
Ecc 7: 1 the day of death better than the day of b. 3528
10:17 of noble b and whose princes eat at 1201
SS 8: 5 there she who was in labor gave you b. 3528
Isa 7:14 be with child and *will* give b *to* a son, 3528
8: 3 and she conceived and gave b *to* a son. 3528
23: 4 "I have neither been in labor nor given b; 3528
26:17 to give b writhes and cries out in her pain, 3528
26:18 we writhed in pain, but *we* gave b *to* wind. 3528
26:18 *we have* not given b *to* people of the world. 5877
26:19 the earth *will* give b *to* her dead. 5877
33:11 You conceive chaff, *you* give b *to* straw; 3528
37: 3 to the point of b and there is no strength 5402
45:10 'What *have you* brought to b?' 2655
46: 3 and have carried since your b. 8167
48: 8 you were called a rebel from b. 1061
49: 1 from my b he has made mention 562+5055
51: 2 your father, and to Sarah, *who* gave you b. 2655
Isa 59: 4 they conceive trouble and give b *to* evil. 3528
66: 7 "Before she goes into labor, *she* gives b; 3528
66: 8 in labor than *she* gives b *to* her children. 3528
66: 9 Do I bring to the moment of b 8689
Jer 2:14 Is Israel a servant, a slave by b? 1074+3535
2:27 and to stone, 'You gave me b.' 3528
15:10 Alas, my mother, that *you* gave me b, 3528
22:26 and the mother who gave you b 3528
50:12 *she who* gave you b will be disgraced. 3528
Eze 16: 3 and b were in the land of the Canaanites; 4580
23: 4 They were mine and gave b *to* sons 3528
31: 6 of the field gave b under its branches; 3528
Hos 1: 6 Gomer conceived again and gave b *to* 3528
5: 7 *they* give b *to* illegitimate children. 3528
9:11 no b, no pregnancy, no conception. 4256
Mic 5: 3 the time when she who is in labor gives b 3528
Mt 1:18 how the b of Jesus Christ came about: *1161*
1:21 *She will* give b to a son, *5503*
1:23 be with child and *will* give b to a son, *5503*
1:25 with her until *she* gave b to a son. *5503*
24: 8 All these are the beginning *of* b pains. *6047*
Mk 13: 8 These are the beginning *of* b pains. *6047*
Lk 1:14 and many will rejoice because of his b, *1161*
1:15 filled with the Holy Spirit even from b *3120+3613*
1:31 You will be with child and give b to a son, *5503*
1:57 *she* gave b to a son. *1164*
2: 7 and *she* gave b to her firstborn, *5503*
11:27 "Blessed is the mother who gave you b *1002*
19:12 *of* noble b went to a distant country *2302*
Jn 3: 6 Flesh gives b to flesh, *1164*
3: 6 but the Spirit gives b to spirit. *1164*
9: 1 he saw a man blind from b. *1162*
9:34 "You *were* steeped in sin at b; *1164*
16:21 A woman giving b to a child has pain *5503*
Ac 3: 2 a man crippled from b was being carried to the temple gate *3120+3613*
7: 8 and circumcised him eight days after his b. *NIG*
14: 8 from b and had never walked. *3120+3613*
1Co 1:26 not many were of noble b. *2302*
Gal 1:15 who set me apart from b and called me *3120+3613*
2:15 *by* b and not 'Gentile sinners' *5882*
Eph 2:11 that formerly you who are Gentiles by b *4922*
Jas 1:15 desire has conceived, *it* gives b to sin; *5503*
1:15 when *it is* full-grown, gives b to death. *652*
1:18 *He* chose *to* give us b through the word *652*
1Pe 1: 3 In his great mercy he *has* given us new b *335*
Rev 12: 2 in pain *as she was about to* give b. *5503+6048*
12: 4 of the woman who was about to give b, *5503*
12: 5 *She* gave b to a son, a male child, *5503*
12:13 he pursued the woman who *had* given b to *5503*

BIRTHDAY (3) [BEAR]
Ge 40:20 Now the third day was Pharaoh's b, 3427+3528
Mt 14: 6 On Herod's b the daughter *1160*
Mk 6:21 *On* his b Herod gave a banquet *1160*

BIRTHRIGHT (6) [BEAR]
Ge 25:31 Jacob replied, "First sell me your b." 1148
25:32 "What good is the b to me?" 1148
25:33 selling his b to Jacob. 1148
25:34 So Esau despised his b. 1148
27:36 He took my b, 1148
1Ch 5: 1 in accordance with his b, 1148

BIRZAITH (1)
1Ch 7:31 who was the father of B. 1365

BISHLAM (1)
Ezr 4: 7 in the days of Artaxerxes king of Persia, B, 1420

BISHOPRICK (KJV) See LEADERSHIP

BIT (5) [BITES, BIT]
Nu 21: 6 *they* b the people and many Israelites died. 5966
2Ki 19:28 I will put my hook in your nose and my b 5496
Ps 32: 9 be controlled by b and bridle or they will 5496
Isa 30:28 of the peoples a b that leads them astray. 8270
37:29 I will put my hook in your nose and my b 5496

BITE (4) [BIT, BITES, BITING, BITTEN]
Jer 8:17 and *they will* b you," declares the LORD. 5966
Am 5:19 on the wall only to have a snake b him. 5966
9: 3 the serpent *to* b them. 5966
Jn 6: 7 for each one to have a b!" *NIG*

BITES (3) [BITE]
Ge 49:17 that b the horse's heels so 5966
Pr 23:32 the end *it* b like a snake and poisons like 5966
Ecc 10:11 If a snake b before it is charmed, 5966

BITHIAH (1)
1Ch 4:18 the children of Pharaoh's daughter B, 1437

BITHRON (1)
2Sa 2:29 continued through the whole B and came 1443

BITHYNIA (2)
Ac 16: 7 they tried to enter B, *1049*
1Pe 1: 1 Galatia, Cappadocia, Asia and B, *1049*

BITING (1) [BITE]
Gal 5:15 *on* b and devouring each other, *1231*

BITS (2) [BIT]
Am 6:11 into pieces and the small house into b. 1323
Jas 3: 3 When we put b into the mouths of horses *5903*

BITTEN (3) [BITE]
Nu 21: 8 anyone who is b can look at it and live." 5966
21: 9 when anyone *was* b *by* a snake and looked 5966
Ecc 10: 8 whoever breaks through a wall *may be* b *by* 5966

BITTER (44) [BITTERLY, BITTERNESS, EMBITTER, EMBITTERED]
Ge 27:34 with a loud and b cry and said to his father, 5253
Ex 1:14 *They* made their lives b with hard labor 5352
12: 8 along with b herbs, 5353
15:23 not drink its water because it was b. 5253
Nu 5:18 while he himself holds the b water 5253
5:19 may this b water that brings a curse 5253
5:23 and then wash them off into the b water. 5253
5:24 He shall have the woman drink the b water 5253
5:24 and cause b suffering. 5253
5:27 it will go into her and cause b suffering; 5253
9:11 with unleavened bread and b herbs. 5353
Dt 29:18 among you that produces such b poison. 4360
Ru 1:13 It is more b for me than for you, 5253
1:20 the Almighty made my life very b. 5352
1Sa 14:52 of Saul there was b war with the Philistines, 2617
30: 6 each one *was* b *in* spirit because of his sons 5352
1Ki 2: 8 down b curses on me the day I went 5344
2Ki 4:27 She *is* in b distress, 5352
Job 3:20 and life to the b *of* soul, 5253
13:26 For you write down b things against me 5353
23: 2 "Even today my complaint is b; 5308
Ps 71:20 many and b, you will restore my life again; 8273
107:12 So he subjected them to b labor; 6662
Pr 5: 4 but in the end she is b as gall, 5253
27: 7 to the hungry even *what* is b tastes sweet. 5253
Ecc 7:26 I find more b than death the woman who is 5253
Isa 5:20 who put b for sweet and sweet for bitter. 5253
5:20 who put bitter for sweet and sweet for b. 5253
24: 9 the beer *is* b to its drinkers. 5352
Jer 2:19 then and realize how evil and b it is for you 5253
4:18 How b it is! 5253
6:26 mourn with b wailing as for an only son, 9476
9:15 "See, I will make this people eat b food 4360
23:15 "I will make them eat b food 4360
La 1: 4 her maidens grieve, and she is in b anguish. 5253
3:15 He has filled me with b herbs and sated me 5353
Eze 21: 6 before them with broken heart and b grief. 5320
27:31 with anguish of soul and with b mourning 5253
Am 8:10 an only son and the end of it like a b day. 5253
Zep 1:14 The cry on the day of the LORD will be b, 5253
Heb 12:15 and that no b root grows up to cause trouble *4394*
Jas 3:14 if you harbor b envy and selfish ambition *4395*
Rev 8:11 A third of the waters turned b, *952*
8:11 from the waters that *had become* b. *4393*

BITTERLY (21) [BITTER]
Ge 50:10 they lamented loudly and b; 3878+4394
Nu 14:39 to all the Israelites, they mourned b. 4394
Jdg 5:23 'Curse its people b, 826+826
21: 2 raising their voices and weeping b. 1524
2Sa 13:36 too, and all his servants wept very b. 1524
2Ki 14:26 how b everyone in Israel, whether slave 5253
20: 3 And Hezekiah wept b. 1524
Ezr 10: 1 They too wept b. 1134+1135+2221
Est 4: 1 wailing loudly and b. 5253
Isa 22: 4 *let me* weep b. 5352
33: 7 the envoys of peace weep b. 5253
38: 3 And Hezekiah wept b. 1524
Jer 13:17 my eyes *will* weep b, 1963+1963
22:10 rather, weep b for him who is exiled, 1134+1134
48: 5 weeping b as they go; 1140+1140
La 1: 2 B *she* weeps at night, 1134+1134
Eze 27:30 They will raise their voice and cry b 5253
Hos 12:14 But Ephraim has b provoked him to anger; 9476
Zec 12:10 and grieve b for him as one grieves for 5352
Mt 26:75 And he went outside and wept b. *4396*
Lk 22:62 And he went outside and wept b. *4396*

BITTERN (KJV) See OWL

BITTERNESS (19) [BITTER]
Ge 49:23 *With* b archers attacked him; 5352
Dt 32:32 and their clusters with b. 5353
1Sa 1:10 In b *of* soul Hannah wept much and prayed 5253
15:32 thinking, "Surely the b *of* death is past." 5253
2Sa 2:26 Don't you realize that this will end in b? 5253
Job 7:11 I will complain in the b *of* my soul. 5253
10: 1 to my complaint and speak out in the b 5253
21:25 Another man dies in b of soul, 5253
27: 2 *who has* made me taste b of soul, 5352
Pr 14:10 Each heart knows its own b, 5289
17:25 to his father and b to the one who bore him. 4933
La 3: 5 and surrounded me with b and hardship. 8032
La 3:19 the b and the gall. 8032
Eze 3:14 I went *in* b and in the anger of my spirit, 5253
Am 5: 7 into b and cast righteousness to the ground 4360
6:12 and the fruit of righteousness into b— 4360
Ac 8:23 For I see that you are full of b *4394+5958*

Ro 3:14 "Their mouths are full of cursing and **b**." *4394*
Eph 4:31 Get rid of all **b**, rage and anger, *4394*

BITUMEN (Anglicized) See TAR

BIZIOTHIAH (1)
Jos 15:28 Hazar Shual, Beersheba, **B**, 1026

BIZJOTHJAH (KJV) See BIZIOTHIAH

BIZTHA (1)
Est 1:10 Mehuman, **B**, Harbona, Bigtha, Abagtha, 1030

BLACK (16) [BLACKENED, BLACKER, BLACKEST, BLACKNESS]
Ex 10:15 They covered all the ground until it *was* **b**. 3124
Lev 11:13 the eagle, the vulture, the **b vulture**, 6465
11:14 the red kite, any kind of **b kite**, 370
13:31 and there is no **b** hair in it, 8839
13:37 and **b** hair has grown in it, 8839
Dt 4:11 with **b** clouds and deep darkness. 3125
14:12 the eagle, the vulture, the **b vulture**, 6465
14:13 the red kite, the **b kite**, any kind of falcon, 370
1Ki 18:45 Meanwhile, the sky *grew* **b** *with* clouds, 7722
Job 30:30 My skin **grows b** and peels; 8837
SS 5:11 his hair is wavy and **b** as a raven. 8839
Zec 6:2 first chariot had red horses, the second **b**, 8839
6:6 The one with the **b** horses is going toward 8839
Mt 5:36 you cannot make even one hair white or **b**. *3506*
Rev 6:5 and there before me was a **b** horse! *3506*
6:12 The sun turned **b** like sackcloth made *3506*

BLACKENED (1) [BLACK]
Job 30:28 I go about **b**, but not by the sun; 7722

BLACKER (1) [BLACK]
La 4:8 But now they *are* **b** than soot; 3124

BLACKEST (3) [BLACK]
Job 28:3 for ore in the **b** darkness. 7516
2Pe 2:17 **B** darkness is reserved for them. *2432*
Jude 1:13 whom **b** darkness has been reserved forever. *2432*

BLACKNESS (4) [BLACK]
Job 3:5 may **b** overwhelm its light. 4025
Joel 2:2 a day of clouds and **b**. 6906
Am 5:8 who turns **b** into dawn and darkens day 7516
Zep 1:15 a day of clouds and **b**, 6906

BLACKSMITH (3)
1Sa 13:19 Not a **b** could be found in the whole land 3093
Isa 44:12 The **b** takes a tool and works with it 1366+3093
54:16 it is I who created the **b** who fans the coals 3093

BLADE (2)
Jdg 3:22 Even the handle sank in after the **b**, 4258
Eze 21:16 then to the left, wherever your **b** is turned. 7156

BLAINS (KJV) See FESTERING

BLAME (8) [BLAMELESS, BLAMELESSLY]
Ge 43:9 *I will* **bear the b** before you all my life. 2627
44:10 the rest of you will be **free from b**." 5929
44:32 *I will* **bear the b** before you, my father, 2627
1Sa 25:24 "My lord, let the **b** be on me alone. 6411
2Sa 14:9 the **b** rest on me and on my father's family, 6411
Ro 9:19 "Then why *does* God still **b** us? *3522*
1Ti 5:7 **no** one may be **open to b**. *455*
6:14 to keep this command without spot or **b** *455*

BLAMELESS (55) [BLAME]
Ge 6:9 **b** among the people of his time, 9459
17:1 walk before me and be **b**. 9459
Dt 18:13 be **b** before the LORD your God. 9459
2Sa 22:24 I have been **b** before him 9459
22:26 to the **b** you show yourself blameless, 1475+9459
22:26 to the blameless *you* **show yourself b**, 9462
Job 1:1 This man was **b** and upright; 9447
1:8 he is **b** and upright, 9447
2:3 he is **b** and upright, 9447
4:6 and your **b** ways your hope? 9448
8:20 not reject a **b** *man* or strengthen the hands 9447
9:20 if I were **b**, it would pronounce me guilty. 9447
9:21 I am **b**, I have no concern for myself; 9447
9:22 'He destroys both the **b** and the wicked.' 9447
12:4 though righteous and **b**! 9459
22:3 What would he gain if your ways *were* **b**? 9462
31:6 and he will know that I am **b**— 9450
Ps 15:2 He whose walk is **b** 9459
18:23 I have been **b** before him 9459
18:25 to the **b** you show yourself blameless, 1505+9459
18:25 to the blameless *you* **show yourself b**, 9462
19:13 Then *will I be* **b**, 9462
26:1 O LORD, for I have led a **b** life; 9448
26:11 But I lead a **b** life; 9448
37:18 The days of the **b** are known to the LORD, 9459
37:37 Consider the **b**, observe the upright; 9447
84:11 from those whose walk is **b**. 9459
Ps 101:2 I will be careful to lead a **b** life— 9459
101:2 I will walk in my house with **b** heart. 9448
101:6 he whose walk is **b** will minister to me. 9459
119:1 Blessed are *they* whose ways are **b**, 9459
119:80 May my heart be **b** toward your decrees, 9459
Pr 2:7 he is a shield to those whose walk is **b**, 9448
2:21 and the **b** will remain in it; 9459
11:5 of the **b** makes a straight way for them, 9459
11:20 but he delights in *those whose* ways are **b**. 9459
19:1 Better a poor man whose walk is **b** than 9448
20:7 The righteous man leads a **b** life; 9448
28:6 Better a poor man whose walk is **b** than 9448
28:10 but the **b** will receive a good inheritance. 9459
28:18 He whose walk is **b** is kept safe, 9459
Eze 28:15 You were **b** in your ways from 9459
1Co 1:8 be **b** on the day of our Lord Jesus Christ. *441*
Eph 1:4 the creation of the world to be holy and **b** *320*
5:27 or any other blemish, but holy and **b**. *320*
Php 1:10 be pure and **b** until the day of Christ, *718*
2:15 so that you may become **b** and pure, *289*
1Th 2:10 and **b** we were among you who believed. *290*
3:13 that you will be **b** and holy in the presence *289*
5:23 soul and body be kept **b** at the coming *290*
Tit 1:6 An elder must be **b**, *441*
1:7 he must be **b—**not overbearing, *441*
Heb 7:26 one who is holy, **b**, pure, *179*
2Pe 3:14 **b** and at peace with him. *318*
Rev 14:5 in their mouths; they are **b**. *320*

BLAMELESSLY (1) [BLAME]
Lk 1:6 observing all the Lord's commandments and regulations **b**. *289*

BLANKET (1) [BLANKETS]
Isa 28:20 the **b** too narrow to wrap around you. 5012

BLANKETS (2) [BLANKET]
Jdg 5:10 sitting on your **saddle b**, 4496
Eze 27:20 " 'Dedan traded in saddle **b** with you. 955+2927

BLASPHEME (5) [BLASPHEMED, BLASPHEMER, BLASPHEMES, BLASPHEMIES, BLASPHEMING, BLASPHEMOUS, BLASPHEMY]
Ex 22:28 not **b** God or curse the ruler of your people. 7837
Ac 26:11 and I tried to force them *to* **b**. *1059*
1Ti 1:20 over to Satan to be taught not *to* **b**. *1059*
2Pe 2:12 But these men **b** in matters they do *1059*
Rev 13:6 He opened his mouth to **b** God, *1060*

BLASPHEMED (9) [BLASPHEME]
Lev 24:11 The son of the Israelite woman **b** the Name 5919
2Ki 19:6 of the king of Assyria *have* **b** me. 1552
19:22 Who is it you have insulted and **b**? 1552
Isa 37:6 of the king of Assyria *have* **b** me. 1552
37:23 Who is it you have insulted and **b**? 1552
52:5 "And all day long my name **is** constantly **b**. 5540
Eze 20:27 also your fathers **b** me by forsaking me: 1552
Ac 19:37 nor **b** our goddess. *1059*
Ro 2:24 "God's name *is* **b** among the Gentiles *1059*

BLASPHEMER (3) [BLASPHEME]
Lev 24:14 "Take the **b** outside the camp. 7837
24:23 the **b** outside the camp and stoned him. 7837
1Ti 1:13 though I was once a **b** and a persecutor and *1061*

BLASPHEMES (5) [BLASPHEME]
Lev 24:16 *anyone who* **b** the name of the LORD must 5919
24:16 when he **b** the Name, 5919
Nu 15:30 whether native-born or alien, **b** the LORD, 1552
Mk 3:29 But whoever **b** against the Holy Spirit *1059*
Lk 12:10 but anyone who **b** against the Holy Spirit *1059*

BLASPHEMIES (4) [BLASPHEME]
Ne 9:18 or when they committed awful **b**. 5542
9:26 they committed awful **b**. 5542
Mk 3:28 and **b** of men will be forgiven them. *1059+1060*
Rev 13:5 a mouth to utter proud words and **b** and *1060*

BLASPHEMING (2) [BLASPHEME]
Mt 9:3 "This fellow *is* **b**!" *1059*
Mk 2:7 "Why does this fellow talk like that? *He's* **b**! *1059*

BLASPHEMOUS (2) [BLASPHEME]
Rev 13:1 and on each head a **b** name. *1060*
17:3 with **b** names and had seven heads *1060*

BLASPHEMY (9) [BLASPHEME]
Mt 12:31 every sin and **b** will be forgiven men, *1060*
12:31 **b against** the Spirit will not be forgiven. *1060*
26:65 *"He has* **spoken b**! *1059*
26:65 Look, now you have heard the **b**. *1060*
Mk 14:64 "You have heard the **b**. *1060*
Lk 5:21 "Who is this fellow who speaks **b**? *1060*
Jn 10:33 replied the Jews, "but for **b**, because you, *1060*
10:36 then do you accuse me of **b** because I said, *1059*
Ac 6:11 "We have heard Stephen speak words *of* **b** *1061*

BLAST (19) [BLASTS]
Ex 15:8 the **b** *of* your nostrils the waters piled up. 8120
19:13 ram's horn **sounds a long b** may they go 5432
19:16 and a very loud trumpet **b**. 7754
Nu 10:5 When a **trumpet b** is sounded, 9558
10:6 At the sounding of a second **b**, 9558
10:6 The **b** will be the signal for setting out. 9558
10:9 **sound a b** on the trumpets. 8131
Jos 6:5 When you hear them sound a long **b** 7754+8795
6:16 **sounded** the trumpet **b**, 9546
2Sa 22:16 at the **b** *of* breath from his nostrils. 5972
Job 4:9 at the **b** *of* his anger they perish. 8120
39:25 **At the b** *of* the trumpet he snorts, 'Aha! 928+1896
Ps 18:15 at the **b** *of* breath from your nostrils. 5972
98:6 and the **b** *of* the ram's horn— 7754
147:17 Who can withstand his **icy b**? 7938
Isa 27:8 with his fierce **b** he drives her out, 8120
Eze 22:20 into a furnace to melt it with a fiery **b**, 5870
Am 2:2 amid war cries and the **b** *of* the trumpet. 7754
Heb 12:19 *to* a trumpet **b** or to such *2491*

BLASTS (2) [BLAST]
Lev 23:24 a sacred assembly commemorated with **trumpet b**. 9558
Rev 8:13 of the trumpet **b** about to be sounded by *5889*

BLASTUS (1)
Ac 12:20 Having secured the support *of* **B**, *1058*

BLAZE (2) [BLAZED, BLAZES, BLAZING]
Nu 21:28 a **b** from the city of Sihon. 4259
Jer 48:45 a **b** from the midst of Sihon; 4259

BLAZED (7) [BLAZE]
Dt 4:11 the foot of the mountain while it **b** with fire 1277
Jdg 13:20 As the flame **b up** from the altar 6590
2Sa 22:9 burning coals **b** out of it. 1277
22:13 of his presence bolts of lightning **b forth**. 1277
Ps 18:8 burning coals **b** out of it. 1277
106:18 Fire **b** among their followers; 1277
Jnh 4:8 sun **b** on Jonah's head so that he grew faint. 5782

BLAZES (2) [BLAZE]
Hos 7:6 in the morning it **b** like a flaming fire. 1277
Joel 2:3 behind them a flame **b**. 4265

BLAZING (22) [BLAZE]
Ge 15:17 with a **b** torch appeared and passed between 836
SS 8:6 It burns like **b** fire, like a mighty flame. 8404
Isa 10:16 a fire will be kindled like a **b** flame. 3679
34:9 her land will become **b** pitch! 1277
62:1 her salvation like a **b** torch. 1277
Eze 20:47 The **b** flame will not be quenched, 4259
Da 3:6 be thrown into a **b** furnace." 10328+10471
3:11 be thrown into a **b** furnace. 10328+10471
3:15 be thrown immediately into a **b** furnace. 10328+10471
3:17 If we are thrown into the **b** furnace, 10328+10471
3:20 and throw them into the **b** furnace. 10328+10471
3:21 were bound and thrown into the **b** furnace. 10328+10471
3:23 firmly tied, fell into the **b** furnace. 10328+10471
3:26 the opening of the **b** furnace and shouted, 10328+10471
7:11 and thrown into the **b** fire. 10329
Ac 26:13 **b around** me and my companions. *4334*
2Th 1:7 in **b** fire with his powerful angels. *5825*
Rev 1:14 and his eyes were like **b** fire. *5825*
2:18 the Son of God, whose eyes are like **b** fire *5825*
4:5 Before the throne, seven lamps were **b**. *2794*
8:10 and a great star, **b** like a torch, *2794*
19:12 His eyes are like **b** fire, *5825*

BLEACH (1)
Mk 9:3 in the world could **b** them. *3326*

BLEAT (1) [BLEATING]
Isa 34:14 and wild goats *will* **b** to each other; 7924

BLEATING (1) [BLEAT]
1Sa 15:14 "What then is this **b** *of* sheep in my ears? 7754

BLEEDING (8) [BLOOD]
Lev 12:4 to be purified from her **b**. 1947
12:5 to be purified from her **b**. 1947
Mt 9:20 then a woman *who had been* **subject to b** *137*
Mk 5:25 woman was there who had been **subject to b** for twelve years. *135+1877+4868*
5:29 Immediately her **b** stopped *135+3836+4380*
Lk 8:43 woman was there who had been **subject to b** for twelve years, *135+1877+4868*
8:44 immediately her **b** stopped. *135+3836+4868*
Ac 19:16 that they ran out of the house naked and **b**. *5547*

BLEMISH (6) [BLEMISHED, BLEMISHES]
Lev 22:21 be without defect or **b** to be acceptable. 4583
Nu 19:2 to bring you a red heifer without defect or **b** 4583
2Sa 14:25 the sole of his foot there was no **b** in him. 4583
Eph 5:27 stain or wrinkle or any other **b**, *3836+5525*[S]

Col 1:22 **without b** and free from accusation— 320
1Pe 1:19 a lamb **without b** or defect. 320

BLEMISHED (1) [BLEMISH]

Mal 1:14 but then sacrifices a **b** animal to the Lord. 8845

BLEMISHES (2) [BLEMISH]

2Pe 2:13 They are blots and **b,** 3700
Jude 1:12 These men are **b** at your love feasts, 5069

BLEND (2) [BLENDED]

Ex 30:25 a fragrant **b,** the work of a perfumer. 8381
30:35 and make a **fragrant b** of incense, 8381

BLENDED (2) [BLEND]

2Ch 16:14 with spices and various **b** perfumes, 8379
SS 7:2 a rounded goblet that never lacks **b wine.** 4641

BLESS (95) [BLESSED, BLESSEDNESS, BLESSES, BLESSING, BLESSINGS]

Ge 12:2 into a great nation and I will **b** you; 1385
12:3 I will **b** those who bless you, 1385
12:3 I will bless those who **b** you, 1385
17:16 I will **b** her and will surely give you a son 1385
17:16 I will **b** her so that she will be the mother 1385
17:20 I will surely **b** him; 1385
22:17 I will **surely b** you 1385+1385
26:3 and I will be with you and will **b** you. 1385
26:24 I will **b** you and will increase the number 1385
27:29 be cursed and those who **b** you be blessed." 1385
27:34 "**B** me—me too, my father!" 1385
27:38 **B** me too, my father!" 1385
28:3 May God Almighty **b** you 1385
32:26 "I will not let you go unless you **b** me." 1385
48:9 "Bring them to me so I may **b** them." 1385
48:16 may he **b** these boys. 1385
Ex 12:32 And also **b** me." 1385
20:24 I will come to you and **b** you. 1385
Nu 6:23 'This is how you are to **b** the Israelites. 1385
6:24 " ' "The LORD **b** you and keep you; 1385
6:27 and I will **b** them." 1385
22:6 For I know that those you **b** are blessed, 1385
23:11 you have **done nothing but b** them!" 1385+1385
23:20 I have received a command to **b;** 1385
23:25 at all nor **b** them **at all!"** 1385+1385
24:1 that it pleased the LORD to **b** Israel, 1385
24:9 "May those who **b** you be blessed 1385
Dt 1:11 increase you a thousand times and **b** you 1385
7:13 and **b** you and increase your numbers. 1385
7:13 He will **b** the fruit of your womb, 1385
14:29 and so that the LORD your God may **b** you 1385
15:4 he will **richly b** you, 1385+1385
15:6 For the LORD your God will **b** you 1385
15:10 of this the LORD your God will **b** you 1385
15:18 And the LORD your God will **b** you 1385
16:15 For the LORD your God will **b** you 1385
23:20 so that the LORD your God may **b** you 1385
24:19 that the LORD your God may **b** you in all 1385
26:15 and **b** your people Israel and 1385
27:12 on Mount Gerizim to **b** the people: 1385
28:8 The LORD your God will **b** you in 1385
28:12 on your land in season and to **b** all the work 1385
30:16 and the LORD your God will **b** you in 1385
33:11 **B** all his skills, O LORD, 1385
33:13 "May the LORD **b** his land with 1385
Jos 8:33 when he gave instructions to **b** the people 1385
Jdg 17:2 Then his mother said, "The LORD **b** you, 1385
Ru 2:4 "The LORD **b** you!" 1385
2:20 "The LORD **b** him!" 1385
3:10 "The LORD **b** you, my daughter," 1385
1Sa 2:20 Eli would **b** Elkanah and his wife, saying, 1385
9:13 because he must **b** the sacrifice; 1385
15:13 Saul said, "The LORD **b** you! 1385
23:21 "The LORD **b** you for your concern 1385
2Sa 2:5 "The LORD **b** you 1385
6:20 David returned home to **b** his household, 1385
7:29 be pleased to **b** the house of your servant, 1385
21:3 so that you will **b** the LORD's inheritance?" 1385
1Ch 4:10 you would **b** me and enlarge my territory! 1385+1385
16:43 and David returned home to **b** his family. 1385
17:27 Now you have been pleased to **b** the house 1385
2Ch 30:27 The priests and the Levites stood to **b** 1385
Job 31:20 and his heart did not **b** me for warming him 1385
Ps 5:12 For surely, O LORD, you **b** the righteous; 1385
28:9 Save your people and **b** your inheritance; 1385
41:2 he will **b** him in the land and 887
62:4 With their mouths they **b,** 1385
65:10 you soften it with showers and **b** its crops. 1385
67:1 and **b** us and make his face shine upon us, 1385
67:6 and God, our God, will **b** us. 1385
67:7 God will **b** us, 1385
72:15 for him and **b** him all day long. 1385
109:28 They may curse, but you will **b;** 1385
115:12 The LORD remembers us and will **b** us: 1385
115:12 He will **b** the house of Israel, 1385
115:12 he will **b** the house of Aaron, 1385
115:13 he will **b** those who fear the LORD— 1385
118:26 From the house of the LORD we **b** you. 1385
128:5 the LORD **b** you from Zion all the days 1385
129:8 we **b** you in the name of the LORD." 1385
132:15 I will **b** her with **abundant** provisions; 1385+1385
134:3 **b** you from Zion. 1385
Pr 30:11 and do not **b** their mothers; 1385
Isa 19:25 The LORD Almighty will **b** them, saying, 1385
Jer 31:23 'The LORD **b** you, O righteous dwelling, 1385
Eze 34:26 I will **b** them and the places 1388+5989
Hag 2:19 " 'From this day on I will **b** you.' " 1385
Zec 4:7 the capstone to shouts of 'God **b** it! 2834
4:7 God **b** it!' " 2834
Lk 6:28 **b** those who curse you, 2328
Ac 3:26 to you to **b** you by turning each of you 2328
Ro 12:14 **B** those who persecute you; 2328
12:14 **b** and do not curse. 2328
1Co 4:12 When we are cursed, we **b;** 2328
Heb 6:14 "I will surely **b** you 2328+2328

BLESSED (234) [BLESS]

Ge 1:22 God **b** them and said, 1385
1:28 God **b** them and said to them, 1385
2:3 God **b** the seventh day and made it holy, 1385
5:2 and female and **b** them. 1385
9:1 Then God **b** Noah and his sons, 1385
9:26 He also said, "**B** be the LORD, 1385
12:3 and all peoples on earth will **be b** 1385
14:19 and he **b** Abram, 1385
14:19 saying, "**B** be Abram by God Most High, 1385
14:20 And **b** be God Most High, 1385
18:18 all nations on earth will **be b** through him. 1385
22:18 on earth will **be b,** 1385
24:1 and the LORD had **b** him in every way. 1385
24:31 "Come, you who are **b** by the LORD," 1385
24:35 The LORD has **b** my master abundantly, 1385
24:60 And they **b** Rebekah and said to her, 1385
25:11 God **b** his son Isaac, 1385
26:4 on earth will **be b,** 1385
26:12 because the LORD **b** him. 1385
26:29 And now you are **b** by the LORD." 1385
27:23 so he **b** him. 1385
27:27 he **b** him and said, "Ah, 1385
27:27 the smell of a field that the LORD has **b.** 1385
27:29 be cursed and those who bless you **be b."** 1385
27:33 I ate it just before you came and I **b** him— 1385
27:33 and indeed he will **be b!"** 1385
28:1 for Jacob and **b** him and commanded him: 1385
28:6 Now Esau learned that Isaac had **b** Jacob 1385
28:6 that when he **b** him he commanded him, 1385
28:14 All peoples on earth will **be b** through you 1385
30:27 that the LORD has **b** me because of you." 1385
30:30 LORD has **b** you wherever I have been. 1385
31:55 and his daughters and **b** them. 1385
32:29 Then he **b** him there. 1385
35:9 God appeared to him again and **b** him. 1385
39:5 the LORD **b** the household of the Egyptian 1385
47:7 After Jacob **b** Pharaoh, 1385
47:10 Then Jacob **b** Pharaoh and went out 1385
48:3 and there he **b** me 1385
48:15 Then he **b** Joseph and said, 1385
48:20 He **b** them that day and said, 1385
49:28 to them when he **b** them, 1385
Ex 20:11 Therefore the LORD **b** the Sabbath day 1385
32:29 and he has **b** you this day." 1388+5989
39:43 So Moses **b** them. 1385
Lev 9:22 toward the people and **b** them. 1385
9:23 When they came out, they **b** the people; 1385
Nu 22:6 For I know that those you bless are **b,** 1385
22:12 because they are **b."** 1385
23:20 he has **b,** and I cannot change it. 1385
24:9 "May those who bless you **be b** 1385
24:10 but you have **b** them these three times. 1385+1385
Dt 2:7 The LORD your God has **b** you in all 1385
7:14 You will be **b** more than any other people; 1385
12:7 because the LORD your God has **b** you. 1385
14:24 and you have been **b** by 1385
15:14 to him as the LORD your God has **b** you. 1385
16:17 the way the LORD your God has **b** you. 1388+5989
28:3 You will **be b** in the city and blessed in 1385
28:3 be blessed in the city and **b** in the country. 1385
28:4 The fruit of your womb will **be b,** 1385
28:5 and your kneading trough will **be b.** 1385
28:6 You will **be b** when you come in 1385
28:6 when you come in and **b** when you go out. 1385
33:20 "**B** is he who enlarges Gad's domain! 1385
33:24 "Most **b** of sons is Asher; 1385
33:29 **B** are you, O Israel! 897
Jos 14:13 Then Joshua **b** Caleb son of Jephunneh 1385
17:14 and the LORD has **b** us abundantly." 1385
22:6 Then Joshua **b** them and sent them away, 1385
22:7 When Joshua sent them home, he **b** them, 1385
24:10 **b** you **again and again,** 1385+1385
Jdg 5:24 "Most **b** of women be Jael, 1385
5:24 most **b** of tent-dwelling women. 1385
13:24 He grew and the LORD **b** him, 1385
Ru 2:19 **B** be the man who took notice of you!" 1385
1Sa 25:33 May you be **b** for your good judgment and 1385
26:25 Then Saul said to David, "May you **be b,** 1385
2Sa 6:11 the LORD **b** him and his entire household. 1385
6:12 "The LORD has **b** the household 1385
6:18 he **b** the people in the name of the LORD 1385
7:29 of your servant will **be b** forever." 1385
14:22 and he **b** the king. 1385
1Ki 2:45 But King Solomon will **be b,** 1385
8:14 the king turned around and **b** them. 1385
8:55 and **b** the whole assembly of Israel in 1385
8:66 They **b** the king and then went home, 1385
1Ch 13:14 and the LORD **b** his household 1385
16:2 he **b** the people in the name of the LORD. 1385
17:27 for you, O LORD, have **b** it, 1385
17:27 have blessed it, and it will **be b** forever." 1385
1Ch 26:5 (For God had **b** Obed-Edom.) 1385
2Ch 6:3 the king turned around and **b** them. 1385
31:8 the LORD and **b** his people Israel. 1385
31:10 because the LORD has **b** his people, 1385
Ne 9:5 "**B** be your glorious name, 1385
Job 1:10 You have **b** the work of his hands, 1385
5:17 "**B** is the man whom God corrects; 897
29:4 God's intimate friendship **b** my house, 6584
29:13 The man who was dying **b** me; 995+1388
42:12 The LORD **b** the latter part 1385
Ps 1:1 **B** is the man who does not walk in 897
2:12 **B** are all who take refuge in him. 897
32:1 **B** is he whose transgressions are forgiven, 897
32:2 **B** is the man whose sin the LORD does 897
33:12 **B** is the nation whose God is the LORD, 897
34:8 **b** is the man who takes refuge in him. 897
37:26 their children will be **b.** 1388
40:4 **B** is the man who makes 897
41:1 **B** is he who has regard for the weak; 897
45:2 since God has **b** you forever. 1385
49:18 Though while he lived he **counted** himself **b—** 1385
65:4 **B** are those you choose and bring near 897
72:17 All nations will **be b** through him, 1385
72:17 and they will **call** him **b.** 887
84:4 **B** are those who dwell in your house; 897
84:5 **B** are those whose strength is in you, 897
84:12 **b** is the man who trusts in you. 897
89:15 **B** are those who have learned 897
94:12 **B** is the man you discipline, O LORD, 897
106:3 **B** are they who maintain justice, 897
107:38 he **b** them, and their numbers greatly increased, 1385
112:1 **B** is the man who fears the LORD, 897
112:2 the generation of the upright will **be b.** 1385
115:15 May you **be b** by the LORD, 1385
118:26 **B** is he who comes in the name of 1385
119:1 **B** are they whose ways are blameless, 897
119:2 **B** are they who keep his statutes 897
127:5 **B** is the man whose quiver is full of them. 897
128:1 **B** are all who fear the LORD, 897
128:4 Thus **is** the man **b** who fears the LORD. 1385
144:15 **B** are the people of whom this is true; 897
144:15 **b** are the people whose God is the LORD. 897
146:5 **B** is he whose help is the God of Jacob, 897
Pr 3:13 **B** is the man who finds wisdom, 897
3:18 those who lay hold of her will **be b.** 887
5:18 May your fountain be **b,** 1385
8:32 **b** are those who keep my ways. 897
8:34 **B** is the man who listens to me, 897
14:21 but **b** is he who is kind to the needy. 897
16:20 and **b** is he who trusts in the LORD. 897
20:7 **b** are his children after him. 897
20:21 at the beginning will not **be b** at the end. 1385
22:9 A generous man will himself **be b,** 1385
28:14 **B** is the man who always fears the LORD, 897
28:20 A faithful man will be richly **b,** 1388
29:18 but **b** is he who keeps the law. 890
31:28 Her children arise and **call** her **b;** 887
Ecc 10:17 **B** are you, O land whose king is 897
SS 6:9 The maidens saw her and **called** her **b;** 887
Isa 19:25 saying, "**B** be Egypt my people, 1385
30:18 **B** are all who wait for him! 897
32:20 how **b** you will be, 897
51:2 and I **b** him and made him many. 1385
56:2 **B** is the man who does this, 897
61:9 that they are a people the LORD has **b."** 1385
65:23 for they will be a people **b** by the LORD, 1385
Jer 4:2 then the nations will **be b** by him and 1385
17:7 **b** is the man who trusts in the LORD, 1385
20:14 May the day my mother bore me not be **b!** 1385
Da 12:12 **B** is the one who waits for and reaches 897
Mal 3:12 "Then all the nations will **call** you **b,** 887
3:15 But now we **call** the arrogant **b.** 887
Mt 5:3 "**B** are the poor in spirit, 3421
5:4 **B** are those who mourn, 3421
5:5 **B** are the meek, 3421
5:6 **B** are those who hunger and thirst 3421
5:7 **B** are the merciful, 3421
5:8 **B** are the pure in heart, 3421
5:9 **B** are the peacemakers, 3421
5:10 **B** are those who are persecuted because 3421
5:11 "**B** are you when people insult you, 3421
11:6 **B** is the man who does not fall away 3421
13:16 But **b** are your eyes because they see, 3421
16:17 Jesus replied, "**B** are you, 3421
21:9 "**B** is he who comes in the name of the Lord 2328
23:39 '**B** is he who comes in the name of the Lord 2328
25:34 'Come, you who are **b** by my Father; 2328
Mk 10:16 put his hands on them and **b** them. 2986
11:9 "**B** is he who comes in the name of the Lord 2328
11:10 "**B** is the coming kingdom 2328
14:61 the Son of the **B** One?" 2329
Lk 1:42 "**B** are you among women, 2328
1:42 and **b** is the child you will bear! 2328
1:45 **B** is she who has believed that what 3421
1:48 now on all generations will **call** me **b,** 3420
2:34 Then Simeon **b** them and said to Mary, 2328
6:20 "**B** are you who are poor, 3421
6:21 **B** are you who hunger now, 3421
6:21 **B** are you who weep now, 3421
Lk 6:22 **B** are you when men hate you, 3421
7:23 **B** is the man who does not fall away 3421
10:23 "**B** are the eyes that see what you see. 3421
11:27 "**B** is the mother who gave you birth 3421
11:28 "**B** rather are those who hear the word 3421
13:35 '**B** is he who comes in the name of 2328

Lk 14:14 and you will be **b**. *3421*
14:15 "**B** is the man who will eat at the feast in *3421*
19:38 "**B** is the king who comes in the name of *2328*
23:29 '**B** are the barren women, *3421*
24:50 he lifted up his hands and **b** them. *2328*
Jn 12:13 "**B** is he who comes in the name of the Lord *2328*
12:13 "**B** is the King of Israel!" *NIG*
13:17 you will be **b** if you do them. *3421*
20:29 **b** are those who have not seen and yet have believed." *3421*
Ac 3:25 all peoples on earth *will be* **b**.' *1922*
20:35 'It is more **b** to give than to receive.'" *3421*
Ro 4: 7 "**B** are they whose transgressions are forgiven, *3421*
4: 8 **B** is the man whose sin the Lord will never count against him." *3421*
14:22 **B** is the man who does not condemn himself *3421*
Gal 3: 8 "All nations *will be* **b through** you." *1922*
3: 9 So those who have faith *are* **b** along *2328*
Eph 1: 3 who *has* **b** us in the heavenly realms *2328*
1Ti 1:11 to the glorious gospel *of* the **b** God, *3421*
6:15 God, the **b** and only Ruler, *3421*
Tit 2:13 while we wait for the **b** hope— *3421*
Heb 7: 1 from the defeat of the kings and **b** him, *2328*
7: 6 a tenth from Abraham and **b** him who had *2328*
7: 7 And without doubt the lesser person *is* **b** *2328*
11:20 By faith Isaac **b** Jacob and Esau in regard *2328*
11:21 **b** each of Joseph's sons, *2328*
Jas 1:12 **B** is the man who perseveres under trial, *3421*
1:25 he will be **b** in what he does. *3421*
5:11 *we* **consider b** those who have persevered. *3420*
1Pe 3:14 suffer for what is right, you are **b**. *3421*
4:14 insulted because of the name of Christ, you are **b**, *3421*
Rev 1: 3 **B** is the one who reads the words *3421*
1: 3 and **b** are those who hear it and take *NIG*
14:13 **B** are the dead who die in the Lord *3421*
16:15 **B** is he who stays awake and keeps *3421*
19: 9 '**B** are those who are invited to the wedding *3421*
20: 6 **B** and holy are those who have part in the first resurrection. *3421*
22: 7 **B** is he who keeps the words of the prophecy *3421*
22:14 "**B** are those who wash their robes, *3421*

BLESSEDNESS (2) [BLESS]

Ro 4: 6 the same thing when he speaks of the **b** of *3422*
4: 9 Is this **b** only for the circumcised, *3422*

BLESSES (8) [BLESS]

Ge 49:25 *who* **b** you *with* blessings of the heavens 1385
Ps 10: 3 *he* **b** the greedy and reviles the LORD. 1385
29:11 the LORD **b** his people with peace. 1385
37:22 *those* the LORD **b** will inherit the land, 1385
147:13 of your gates and **b** your people within you. 1385
Pr 3:33 but *he* **b** the home of the righteous. 1385
27:14 If a *man* loudly **b** his neighbor early in 1385
Ro 10:12 of all and richly **b** all who call on him, *NIG*

BLESSING (65) [BLESS]

Ge 12: 2 and you will be a **b**. 1388
17:18 "If only Ishmael might live **under** your **b**!" 4200+7156
27: 4 so that I *may* **give** you my **b** before I die." 1385
27: 7 so that *I may* **give** you *my* **b** in the presence 1385
27:10 that *he may* **give** you *his* **b** before he dies." 1385
27:12 down a curse on myself rather than a **b**." 1388
27:19 so that you *may* **give** me your **b**." 1385
27:25 so that I *may* **give** you my **b**." 1385
27:30 After Isaac finished **b** him 1385
27:31 so that you *may* **give** me your **b**." 1385
27:35 and took your **b**." 1388
27:36 and now he's taken my **b**!" 1388
27:36 "Haven't you reserved any **b** for me?" 1388
27:38 "Do you have only one **b**, my father? 1388
27:41 because of the **b** his father had given him. 1388
28: 4 and your descendants the **b** *given* 1388
39: 5 The **b** *of* the LORD was on everything 1388
48:20 "In your name *will* Israel **pronounce** *this* **b**: 1385
49:28 **giving** each the **b** appropriate to him. 1385+1388
Ex 23:25 and *his* **b** *will be on* your food and water. 1385
Lev 25:21 I will send you such a **b** in the sixth year 1388
Dt 11:26 I am setting before you today a **b** and 1388
11:27 the **b** if you obey the commands of 1388
12:15 to the **b** the LORD your God gives you. 1388
23: 5 to Balaam but turned the curse into a **b** 1388
28: 8 The LORD will send a **b** on your barns 1388
29:19 *he* **invokes a b on himself** 1385
33: 1 This is the **b** that Moses the man 1388
33:23 the favor of the LORD and is full of his **b**; 1388
2Sa 7:29 with your **b** the house of your servant will 1388
13:25 he still refused to go, but **gave** him *his* **b**. 1385
19:39 and **gave** him *his* **b**, 1385
Ne 9: 5 may it be exalted above all **b** and praise. 1388
13: 2 however, turned the curse into a **b**.) 1388
Ps 3: 8 May your **b** be on your people. 1388
24: 5 He will receive **b** from the LORD 1388
109:17 he found no pleasure in **b**— 1388
129: 8 "The **b** *of* the LORD be upon you; 1388
133: 3 For there the LORD bestows his **b**, 1388
Pr 10: 7 The memory of the righteous will be a **b**, 1388
10:22 The **b** *of* the LORD brings wealth, 1388
11:11 the **b** *of* the upright a city is exalted, 1388
11:26 but **b** crowns him who is willing to sell. 1388
24:25 and rich **b** will come upon them. 1388
Isa 19:24 a **b** on the earth. 1388
Isa 44: 3 and my **b** on your descendants. 1388
65:16 Whoever **invokes a b** in the land will do so 1385
Jer 16: 5 because I have withdrawn my **b**, 8934
Eze 34:26 there will be showers of **b**. 1388
44:30 of your ground meal so that a **b** may rest 1388
Joel 2:14 and have pity and leave behind a **b**— 1388
Mic 2: 9 You take away my **b** from their children 2077
Zec 8:13 so will I save you, and you will be a **b**. 1388
Mal 3:10 and pour out so much **b** that you will 1388
Lk 24:51 While he *was* **b** them, *2328*
Jn 1:16 of his grace we have all received one **b** *5921*
Ac 15:33 by the brothers with **the b of peace** to return *1645*
Ro 15:29 I will come in the full measure *of* the **b** *2330*
Gal 3:14 that the **b** given to Abraham might come to *2330*
Eph 1: 3 the heavenly realms with every spiritual **b** *2330*
Heb 6: 7 for whom it is farmed receives the **b** *2330*
12:17 when he wanted to inherit this **b**, *2330*
12:17 though he sought **the b** with tears. *899S*
1Pe 3: 9 but with **b**, because to this you were called *2328*
3: 9 so that you may inherit a **b**. *2330*

BLESSINGS (24) [BLESS]

Ge 49:25 who blesses you with **b** *of* the heavens 1388
49:25 **b** *of* the deep that lies below, 1388
49:25 **b** *of* the breast and womb. 1388
49:26 Your father's **b** are greater than 1388
49:26 the **b** *of* the ancient mountains, 1388
Dt 10: 8 to minister and to **pronounce b** in his name, 1385
11:29 to proclaim on Mount Gerizim the **b**, 1388
16:10 **b** the LORD your God *has* **given** 1385
21: 5 to minister and to **pronounce b** in the name 1385
28: 2 All these **b** will come upon you 1388
30: 1 When all these **b** and curses I have set 1388
30:19 that I have set before you life and death, **b** 1388
Jos 8:34 the **b** and the curses— 1388
1Ch 23:13 to minister before him and to **pronounce b** 1385
Ps 21: 3 with rich **b** and placed a crown of pure gold 1388
21: 6 Surely you have granted him eternal **b** 1388
128: 2 **b** and prosperity will be yours. 897
Pr 10: 6 **B** crown the head of the righteous, 1388
Hos 3: 5 to the LORD and to his **b** in the last days. 3206
Mal 2: 2 and I will curse your **b**. 1388
Ac 13:34 **holy** and sure **b promised** *4008*
Ro 15:27 Gentiles have shared in the Jews' spiritual **b**, *NIG*
15:27 to share with them their material **b**. *NIG*
1Co 9:23 that I may share in its **b**. *NIG*

BLEW (13) [BLOW]

Ex 15:10 But *you* **b** with your breath, 5973
Jos 6: 9 ahead of the priests *who* **b** the trumpets, 9546
Jdg 3:27 *he* **b** a trumpet in the hill country 9546
6:34 and *he* **b** a trumpet, 9546
7:19 *They* **b** their trumpets and broke the jars 9546
7:20 The three companies **b** the trumpets 9546
2Sa 2:28 So Joab **b** the trumpet, 9546
2Ki 9:13 Then *they* **b** the trumpet and shouted, 9546
2Ch 7: 6 the priests **b** *their* **trumpets**, 2955
13:14 The priests **b** their trumpets 2955
Hag 1: 9 What you brought home, *I* **b away**. 5870
Mt 7:25 the winds **b** and beat against that house; *4463*
7:27 and the winds **b** and beat against that house, *4463*

BLIGHT (5) [BLIGHTED]

Dt 28:22 with **b** and mildew, 8730
1Ki 8:37 or **b** or mildew, locusts or grasshoppers, 8730
2Ch 6:28 or **b** or mildew, locusts or grasshoppers, 8730
Am 4: 9 I struck them with **b** and mildew. 8730
Hag 2:17 I struck all the work of your hands with **b**, 8730

BLIGHTED (2) [BLIGHT]

Ps 102: 4 My heart **is b** and withered like grass; 5782
Hos 9:16 Ephraim *is* **b**, their root is withered, 5782

BLIND (82) [BLINDED, BLINDFOLDS, BLINDNESS, BLINDS]

Ex 4:11 Who gives him sight or makes him **b**? 6426
Lev 19:14 or put a stumbling block in front of the **b**, 6426
21:18 no man who is **b** or lame, 6426
22:22 Do not offer to the LORD the **b**, 6428
Dt 15:21 If an animal has a defect, is lame or **b**, 6426
27:18 "Cursed is the man who leads the **b** astray 6426
28:29 about like a **b** *man* in the dark. 6426
1Sa 2:33 be spared only to **b** your eyes with tears and 3983
2Sa 5: 6 even the **b** and the lame can ward you off." 6426
5: 8 and **b**' who are David's enemies." 6426
5: 8 '**b** and lame' will not enter the palace." 6426
Job 29:15 I was eyes to the **b** and feet to the lame. 6426
Ps 146: 8 the LORD gives sight to the **b**, 6426
Isa 29: 9 **b yourselves** and be sightless; 9129
29:18 and darkness the eyes of the **b** will see. 6426
35: 5 the eyes of the **b** be opened and the ears of 6426
42: 7 to open eyes that are **b**, 6426
42:16 the **b** by ways they have not known, 6426
42:18 "Hear, you deaf; look, you **b**, and see! 6426
42:19 Who is **b** but my servant, 6426
42:19 Who is **b** like the one committed to me, 6426
42:19 **b** like the servant of the LORD? 6426
43: 8 Lead out those who have eyes but are **b**, 6426
44: 9 Those who would speak up for them *are* **b**; 1153+8011
56:10 Israel's watchmen are **b**, 6426
59:10 Like the **b** we grope along the wall, 6426
Jer 31: 8 Among them will be the **b** and the lame, 6426
La 4:14 through the streets like *men who* are **b**. 6426
Zep 1:17 on the people and they will walk like **b** *men*, 6426
Zec 12: 4 but *I will* **b** all the horses of the nations. 928+2021+5782+6427
Mal 1: 8 When you bring **b** *animals* for sacrifice, 6426
Mt 9:27 two **b** *men* followed him, calling out, *5603*
9:28 the **b** *men* came to him, and he asked them, *5603*
11: 5 The **b** receive sight, *5603*
12:22 a demon-possessed man who was **b** *5603*
15:14 Leave them; they are **b** guides. *5603*
15:14 If a **b** *man* leads a blind man, *5603*
15:14 If a blind man leads a **b** *man*, *5603*
15:30 bringing the lame, the **b**, the crippled, *5603*
15:31 the lame walking and the **b** seeing. *5603*
20:30 Two **b** *men* were sitting by the roadside, *5603*
21:14 The **b** and the lame came to him at *5603*
23:16 "Woe to you, **b** guides! *5603*
23:17 *You* **b** fools! *5603*
23:19 *You* **b** *men*! *5603*
23:24 *You* **b** guides! *5603*
23:26 **B** Pharisee! First clean the inside of the cup *5603*
Mk 8:22 a **b** *man* and begged Jesus to touch him. *5603*
8:23 the **b** *man* by the hand and led him outside *5603*
10:46 were leaving the city, a **b** *man*, *5603*
10:49 So they called to the **b** *man*, "Cheer up! *5603*
10:51 The **b** *man* said, "Rabbi, I want to see." *5603*
Lk 4:18 and recovery of sight *for* the **b**, *5603*
6:39 "Can a **b** *man* lead a blind man? *5603*
6:39 "Can a blind man lead a **b** *man*? *5603*
7:21 and gave sight *to* many who were **b**. *5603*
7:22 The **b** receive sight, the lame walk, *5603*
14:13 the crippled, the lame, the **b**, *5603*
14:21 the crippled, the **b** and the lame.' *5603*
18:35 a **b** *man* was sitting by the roadside begging. *5603*
Jn 5: 3 the **b**, the lame, the paralyzed. *5603*
9: 1 he saw a man **b** from birth. *5603*
9: 2 that he was born **b**?" *5603*
9:13 to the Pharisees the man who had been **b**. *5603*
9:17 Finally they turned again *to* the **b** *man*, *5603*
9:18 not believe that he had been **b** *5603*
9:19 "Is this the one you say was born **b**? *5603*
9:20 "and we know he was born **b**. *5603*
9:24 the man who had been **b**. *5603*
9:25 I was **b** but now I see!" *5603*
9:32 of opening the eyes *of* a man born **b**. *5603*
9:39 so that the **b** will see *1063+3590*
9:39 and those who see will become **b**." *5603*
9:40 Are we **b** too?" *5603*
9:41 Jesus said, "If you were **b**, *5603*
10:21 Can a demon open the eyes *of* the **b**?" *5603*
11:37 the **b** *man* have kept this man from dying?" *5603*
Ac 9: 9 For three days he was **b**, *1063+3590*
13:11 You are going to be **b**, *5603*
Ro 2:19 that you are a guide *for* the **b**, *5603*
2Pe 1: 9 he is nearsighted and **b**, *5603*
Rev 3:17 pitiful, poor, **b** and naked. *5603*

BLINDED (5) [BLIND]

Zec 11:17 his right eye **totally b**!" 3908+3908
Jn 12:40 "*He has* **b** their eyes *5604*
Ac 22:11 because the brilliance of the light *had* **b** *me*. *1838+4024*
2Co 4: 4 The god of this age *has* **b** the minds of unbelievers, *5604*
1Jn 2:11 because the darkness *has* **b** him. *5604*

BLINDFOLDED (2)

Mk 14:65 they **b** him, struck him with their fists, *3836+4328+4725*
Lk 22:64 They **b** him and demanded, "Prophesy! *4328*

BLINDFOLDS (1) [BLIND]

Job 9:24 *he* **b** its judges. 4059+7156

BLINDNESS (4) [BLIND]

Ge 19:11 with **b** so that they could not find the door. 6177
Dt 28:28 **b** and confusion of mind. 6427
2Ki 6:18 "Strike these people with **b**." 6177
6:18 he struck them with **b**, as Elisha had asked. 6177

BLINDS (2) [BLIND]

Ex 23: 8 for a bribe **b** those who see and twists 6422
Dt 16:19 for a bribe **b** the eyes of the wise and twists 6422

BLOCK (13) [BLOCKED, BLOCKING, BLOCKS]

Lev 19:14 or put a **stumbling b** in front of the blind, 4842
Isa 44:19 Shall I bow down to a **b** *of* wood?" 1005
Eze 3:20 and I put a **stumbling b** before him, 4842
14: 4 in his heart and puts a wicked **stumbling b** 4842
14: 7 in his heart and puts a wicked **stumbling b** 4842
39:11 It *will* **b the way** *of* travelers, 2888
Hos 2: 6 Therefore I *will* **b** her path 8455
Mt 16:23 You are a **stumbling b** to me; *4998*
Ro 11: 9 a **stumbling b** and a retribution for them. *4998*
14:13 up your mind not to put any **stumbling b** *4682*
1Co 1:23 a **stumbling b** to Jews and foolishness *4998*
1Co 8: 9 not become a **stumbling b** to the weak. *4682*
2Co 6: 3 We put no **stumbling b** in anyone's path, *4683*

BLOCKED (5) [BLOCK]

Lev 15: 3 from his body or *is* **b**, 3159

2Ch 32: 4 and they b all the springs and the stream 6258
32:30 It was Hezekiah who b the upper outlet of 6258
Job 19: 8 He has b my way so I cannot pass; 1553
Pr 15:19 The way of the sluggard is b with thorns, 5379

BLOCKING (1) [BLOCK]

2Ch 32: 3 and military staff about b off the water 6258

BLOCKS (5) [BLOCK]

1Ki 5:17 from the quarry large b of quality stone 74
6: 7 only b dressed at the quarry were used, 74
7: 9 were made of b of high-grade stone cut AIT
La 3: 9 He has barred my way with b of stone; 1607
Eze 14: 3 in their hearts and put wicked stumbling b 4842

BLOOD (405) [AKELDAMA, BLEEDING, BLOOD-STAINED, BLOODSHED, BLOODSHOT, BLOODSTAINS, BLOODTHIRSTY, LIFEBLOOD]

Ge 4:10 Your brother's b cries out to me from 1947
4:11 to receive your brother's b from your hand. 1947
9: 6 "Whoever sheds the b of man, 1947
9: 6 by man shall his b be shed; 1947
29:14 "You are my own flesh and b." 6795
37:22 "Don't shed any b. 1947
37:26 if we kill our brother and cover up his b? 1947
37:27 all, he is our brother, our own flesh and b." 1414
37:31 a goat and dipped the robe in the b. 1947
42:22 Now we must give an accounting for his b." 1947
49:11 his robes in the b of grapes. 1947
Ex 4: 9 the river will become b on the ground." 1947
4:25 "Surely you are a bridegroom of b to me," 1947
4:26 (At that time she said "bridegroom of b," 1947
7:17 and it will be changed into b. 1947
7:19 and they will turn to b. 1947
7:19 B will be everywhere in Egypt, 1947
7:20 and all the water was changed into b. 1947
7:21 B was everywhere in Egypt. 1947
12: 7 to take some of the b and put it on the sides 1947
12:13 The b will be a sign for you on the houses 1947
12:13 and when I see the b, I will pass over you. 1947
12:22 the b in the basin and put some of the blood 1947
12:22 the blood in the basin and put some of the b 1947
12:23 the b on the top and sides of the doorframe 1947
23:18 not offer the b of a sacrifice to me along 1947
24: 6 Moses took half of the b and put it 1947
24: 8 Moses then took the b, 1947
24: 8 "This is the b of the covenant that 1947
29:12 of the bull's b and put it on the horns of 1947
29:16 Slaughter it and take the b and sprinkle it 1947
29:20 take some of its b and put it on the lobes of 1947
29:20 sprinkle b against the altar on all sides. 1947
29:21 And take some of the b on the altar 1947
30:10 with the b of the atoning sin offering for 1947
34:25 not offer the b of a sacrifice to me along 1947
Lev 1: 5 the priests shall bring the b and sprinkle it 1947
1:11 the priests shall sprinkle its b against 1947
1:15 its b shall be drained out on the side of 1947
3: 2 the priests shall sprinkle the b against 1947
3: 8 Then Aaron's sons shall sprinkle its b 1947
3:13 Then Aaron's sons shall sprinkle its b 1947
3:17 You must not eat any fat or any b.' " 1947
4: 5 of the bull's b and carry it into the Tent 1947
4: 6 the b and sprinkle some of it seven times 1947
4: 7 The priest shall then put some of the b on 1947
4: 7 the bull's b he shall pour out at the base of 1947
4:16 to take some of the bull's b into the Tent 1947
4:17 He shall dip his finger into the b 1947
4:18 the b on the horns of the altar that is before 1947
4:18 of the b he shall pour out at the base of 1947
4:25 Then the priest shall take some of the b of 1947
4:25 and pour out the rest of the b at the base of 1947
4:30 the b with his finger and put it on the horns 1947
4:30 and pour out the rest of the b at the base of 1947
4:34 Then the priest shall take some of the b of 1947
4:34 and pour out the rest of the b at the base of 1947
5: 9 to sprinkle some of the b of the sin offering 1947
5: 9 of the b must be drained out at the base of 1947
6:27 if any of the b is spattered on a garment, 1947
6:30 But any sin offering whose b is brought 1947
7: 2 and its b is to be sprinkled against the altar 1947
7:14 it belongs to the priest who sprinkles the b 1947
7:26 not eat the b of any bird or animal. 1947
7:27 If anyone eats b, 1947
7:33 of Aaron who offers the b and the fat of 1947
8:15 the bull and took some of the b, 1947
8:15 He poured out the rest of the b at the base 1947
8:19 the ram and sprinkled the b against the altar 1947
8:23 and took some of its b and put it on the lobe 1947
8:24 of the b on the lobes of their right ears, 1947
8:24 he sprinkled b against the altar on all sides. 1947
8:30 of the anointing oil and some of the b from 1947
9: 9 His sons brought the b to him, 1947
9: 9 the b and put it on the horns of the altar; 1947
9: 9 the rest of the b he poured out at the base of 1947
9:12 His sons handed him the b, 1947
9:18 His sons handed him the b, 1947
10:18 its b was not taken into the Holy Place, 1947
12: 7 be ceremonially clean from her flow of b. 1947
14: 6 into the b of the bird that was killed over 1947
14:14 to take some of the b of the guilt offering 1947
14:17 on top of the b of the guilt offering. 1947
14:25 and take some of its b and put it on the lobe 1947
14:28 to put on the same places he put the b of 1947
Lev 14:51 the b of the dead bird and the fresh water, 1947
14:52 He shall purify the house with the bird's b, 1947
15:19 a woman has her regular flow of b, 1947
15:25 " 'When a woman has a discharge of b 1947
16:14 the bull's b and with his finger sprinkle it 1947
16:15 the sin offering for the people and take its b 1947
16:15 and do with it as he did with the bull's b: 1947
16:18 He shall take some of the bull's b and some 1947
16:18 of the bull's blood and some of the goat's b 1947
16:19 of the b on it with his finger seven times 1947
16:27 whose b was brought into 1947
17: 4 he has shed b and must be cut off 1947
17: 6 the b against the altar of the LORD at 1947
17:10 among them who eats any b— 1947
17:10 that person who eats b and will cut him off 1947
17:11 For the life of a creature is in the b, 1947
17:11 the b that makes atonement for one's life. 1947
17:12 "None of you may eat b, 1947
17:12 nor may an alien living among you eat b." 1947
17:13 be eaten must drain out the b and cover it 1947
17:14 because the life of every creature is its b. 1947
17:14 "You must not eat the b of any creature, 1947
17:14 because the life of every creature is its b; 1947
19:26 " 'Do not eat any meat with the b still in it. 1947
20: 9 and his b will be on his own head. 1947
20:11 their b will be on their own heads. 1947
20:12 their b will be on their own heads. 1947
20:13 their b will be on their own heads. 1947
20:16 their b will be on their own heads. 1947
20:27 their b will be on their own heads.' " 1947
25:49 An uncle or a cousin or any b relative 1414+8638
Nu 18:17 Sprinkle their b on the altar 1947
19: 4 to take some of its b on his finger 1947
19: 5 its hide, flesh, b and offal. 1947
23:24 till he devours his prey and drinks the b 1947
35:19 The avenger of b shall put the murderer 1947
35:21 The avenger of b shall put the murderer 1947
35:24 of b according to these regulations. 1947
35:25 of b and send him back to the city of refuge 1947
35:27 the avenger of b finds him outside the city, 1947
35:27 the avenger of b may kill the accused 1947
35:33 for the land on which b has been shed, 1947
35:33 except by the b of the one who shed it. 1947
Dt 12:16 But you must not eat the b; 1947
12:23 But be sure you do not eat the b, 1947
12:23 because the b is the life, 1947
12:24 You must not eat the b; 5647S
12:27 both the meat and the b. 1947
12:27 The b of your sacrifices must be poured 1947
15:23 But you must not eat the b; 1947
19: 6 avenger of b might pursue him in a rage, 1947
19:10 Do this so that innocent b will not be shed 1947
19:12 hand him over to the avenger of b to die. 1947
19:13 guilt of shedding innocent b, 1947
21: 7 "Our hands did not shed this b, 1947
21: 8 not hold your people guilty of the b of 1947
21: 9 guilt of shedding innocent b, 1947
32:14 You drank the foaming b of the grape. 1947
32:42 I will make my arrows drunk with b, 1947
32:42 the b of the slain and the captives, 1947
32:43 for he will avenge the b of his servants; 1947
Jos 2:19 his b will be on his own head; 1947
2:19 his b will be on our head if a hand is laid 1947
20: 3 and find protection from the avenger of b. 1947
20: 5 If the avenger of b pursues him, 1947
20: 9 and not be killed by the avenger of b prior 1947
Jdg 9: 2 Remember, I am your flesh and b." 6795
9:24 the shedding of their b, 1947
1Sa 14:32 together with the b. 1947
14:33 the LORD by eating meat that has b in it." 1947
14:34 the LORD by eating meat with b still 1947
26:20 Now do not let my b fall to the ground far 1947
2Sa 1:16 "Your b be on your own head. 1947
1:22 From the b of the slain, 1947
3:27 to avenge the b of his brother Asahel, 1947
3:28 the LORD concerning the b of Abner son 1947
3:29 May his b fall upon the head of Joab and NIH
4:11 now demand his b from your hand and rid 1947
5: 1 "We are your own flesh and b. 6795
14:11 to prevent the avenger of b from adding to 1947
16: 7 get out, you man of b, you scoundrel! 1947
16: 8 the b you shed in the household of Saul, 1947
16: 8 to ruin because you are a man of b!" 1947
19:12 You are my brothers, my own flesh and b. 6795
19:13 'Are you not my own flesh and b? 6795
20:12 Amasa lay wallowing in his b in the middle 1947
23:17 "Is it not the b of men who went at the risk 1947
1Ki 2: 5 shedding their b in peacetime as if 1947
2: 5 with that b stained the belt around his waist 1947
2: 9 Bring his gray head down to the grave in b." 1947
2:31 guilt of the innocent b 1947
2:32 for the b he shed, 1947
2:33 May the guilt of their b rest on the head 1947
2:37 your b will be on your own head." 1947
8:19 but your son, who is your own flesh and b— 2743+3655+4946
18:28 as was their custom, until their b flowed. 1947
21:19 the place where dogs licked up Naboth's b, 1947
21:19 dogs will lick up your b—yes, yours!' " 1947
22:35 The b from his wound ran onto the floor of 1947
22:38 and the dogs licked up his b, 1947
2Ki 3:22 the water looked red—like b. 1947
3:23 "That's b!" they said. "Those kings 1947
9: 7 and I will avenge the b of my servants 1947
9: 7 of my servants the prophets and the b of all 1947
9:26 the b of Naboth and the blood of his sons, 1947
2Ki 9:26 the blood of Naboth and the b of his sons, 1947
9:33 of her b spattered the wall and the horses 1947
16:13 the b of his fellowship offerings on 1947
16:15 on the altar all the b of the burnt offerings 1947
20:18 your own flesh and b, 3655+3870+4946
21:16 so much innocent b that he filled Jerusalem 1947
24: 4 including the shedding of innocent b. 1947
24: 4 with innocent b, and the LORD was 1947
25:25 the son of Elishama, who was of royal b, 2446
1Ch 11: 1 "We are your own flesh and b. 6795
11:19 the b of these men who went at the risk 1947
22: 8 'You have shed much b 1947
22: 8 because you have shed much b on the earth 1947
28: 3 because you are a warrior and have shed b.' 1947
2Ch 6: 9 but your son, who is your own flesh and b— 2743+3655+4946
29:22 and the priests took the b and sprinkled it 1947
29:22 the rams and sprinkled their b on the altar; 1947
29:22 the lambs and sprinkled their b on the altar. 1947
29:24 the goats and presented their b on the altar 1947
30:16 The priests sprinkled the b handed to them 1947
35:11 the priests sprinkled the b handed to them, NIH
Ne 5: 5 of the same flesh and b as our countrymen 1414
Job 16:18 "O earth, do not cover my b; 1947
39:30 His young ones feast on b, 1947
Ps 9:12 For he who avenges b remembers; 1947
16: 4 not pour out their libations of b or take 1947
50:13 the flesh of bulls or drink the b of goats? 1947
58:10 they bathe their feet in the b of the wicked. 1947
68:23 that you may plunge your feet in the b 1947
72:14 for precious is their b in his sight. 1947
78:44 He turned their rivers to b; 1947
79: 3 They have poured out b like water all 1947
79:10 the nations that you avenge the outpoured b 1947
105:29 He turned their waters into b, 1947
106:38 They shed innocent b, 1947
106:38 the b of their sons and daughters, 1947
106:38 and the land was desecrated by their b. 1947
Pr 1:11 let's lie in wait for someone's b, 1947
1:16 they are swift to shed b. 1947
1:18 These men lie in wait for their own b; 1947
6:17 a lying tongue, hands that shed innocent b, 1947
12: 6 The words of the wicked lie in wait for b, 1947
30:33 and as twisting the nose produces b, 1947
Isa 1:11 in the b of bulls and lambs and goats. 1947
1:15 Your hands are full of b; 1947
9: 5 in battle and every garment rolled in b will 1947
15: 9 Dimon's waters are full of b, 1947
26:21 The earth will disclose the b shed upon her; 1947
34: 3 the mountains will be soaked with their b. 1947
34: 6 The sword of the LORD is bathed in b, 1947
34: 6 the b of lambs and goats, 1947
34: 7 Their land will be drenched with b, 1947
39: 7 your own flesh and b 3655+3870+4946
49:26 they will be drunk on their own b, 1947
58: 7 to turn away from your own flesh and b? 1414
59: 3 For your hands are stained with b, 1947
59: 7 they are swift to shed innocent b. 1947
63: 3 their b spattered my garments, 5906
63: 6 and poured their b on the ground." 5906
66: 3 like one who presents pig's b, 1947
Jer 7: 6 or the widow and do not shed innocent b 1947
19: 4 and they have filled this place with the b of 1947
22: 3 and do not shed innocent b in this place. 1947
22:17 on shedding innocent b and on oppression 1947
26:15 the guilt of innocent b on yourselves and 1947
41: 1 who was of royal b and had been one of 2446
46:10 till it has quenched its thirst with b. 1947
51:35 "May our b be on those who live 1947
La 4:13 who shed within her the b of the righteous. 1947
4:14 They are so defiled with b that no one dares 1947
Eze 3:18 and I will hold you accountable for his b. 1947
3:20 and I will hold you accountable for his b. 1947
11:15 your brothers who are your b relatives 408+1460
16: 6 by and saw you kicking about in your b, 1947
16: 6 and as you lay there in your b I said to you, 1947
16: 9 the b from you and put ointments on you. 1947
16:22 kicking about in your b. 1947
16:36 because you gave them your children's b, 1947
16:38 and who shed b; 1947
16:38 upon you the b vengeance of my wrath 1947
18:10 who sheds b or does any 1947
18:13 he will surely be put to death and his b will 1947
21:32 your b will be shed in your land, 1947
22: 3 on herself doom by shedding b in her midst 1947
22: 4 because of the b you have shed 1947
22: 6 in you uses his power to shed b. 1947
22: 9 In you are slanderous men bent on shedding b; 1947
22:12 In you men accept bribes to shed b; 1947
22:13 and at the b you have shed in your midst. 1947
22:27 they shed b and kill people 1947
23:37 for they have committed adultery and b is 1947
23:45 and shed b, because they are adulterous 1947
23:45 they are adulterous and b is on their hands. 1947
24: 7 " 'For the b she shed is in her midst: 1947
24: 8 up wrath and take revenge I put her b on 1947
28:23 upon her and make b flow in her streets. 1947
32: 6 the land with your flowing b all the way to 1947
33: 4 his b will be on his own head. 1947
33: 5 his b will be on his own head. 1947
33: 6 the watchman accountable for his b.' 1947
33: 8 and I will hold you accountable for his b. 1947
33:25 with the b still in it and look to your idols 1947
33:25 in it and look to your idols and shed b, 1947
36:18 because they had shed b in the land and 1947
39:17 There you will eat flesh and drink b. 1947

Eze 39:18 the flesh of mighty men and drink the **b** *of* 1947
39:19 till you are glutted and drink **b** 1947
43:18 and sprinkling **b** upon the altar 1947
43:20 You are to take some of its **b** and put it on 1947
44:7 fat and **b**, and you broke my covenant. 1947
44:15 before me to offer sacrifices of fat and **b**, 1947
45:19 to take some of the **b** *of* the sin offering 1947
Hos 6:8 stained with footprints of **b**. 1947
Joel 2:30 **b** and fire and billows of smoke. 1947
2:31 be turned to darkness and the moon to **b** 1947
3:19 in whose land they shed innocent **b**. 1947
Mic 7:2 All men lie in wait to shed **b**; 1947
Na 3:1 Woe to the city of **b**, full of lies, 1947
Hab 2:8 For you have shed man's **b**; 1947
2:17 For you have shed man's **b**; 1947
Zep 1:17 Their **b** will be poured out like dust 1947
Zec 9:7 I will take the **b** from their mouths, 1947
9:11 because of the **b** *of* my covenant with you, 1947
Mt 23:30 in shedding the **b** of the prophets.' *135*
23:35 the righteous **b** that has been shed on earth, *135*
23:35 from the **b** of righteous Abel to the blood *135*
23:35 of righteous Abel to the **b** of Zechariah son *135*
26:28 This is my **b** of the covenant, *135*
27:4 he said, "for I have betrayed innocent **b**." *135*
27:6 since it is **b money**." *135+5507*
27:8 the Field *of* **B** to this day. *135*
27:24 "I am innocent of this man's **b**," he said. *135*
27:25 "Let his **b** be on us and on our children!" *135*
Mk 14:24 "This is my **b** of the covenant, *135*
Lk 11:50 the **b** of all the prophets that has been shed *135*
11:51 the **b** of Abel to the blood of Zechariah, *135*
11:51 the blood of Abel to the **b** of Zechariah, *135*
13:1 the Galileans whose **b** Pilate had mixed *135*
22:20 "This cup is the new covenant in my **b**, *135*
22:44 and his sweat was like drops of **b** falling to *135*
Jn 6:53 the flesh of the Son of Man and drink his **b**, *135*
6:54 and drinks my **b** has eternal life, *135*
6:55 my flesh is real food and my **b** is real drink. *135*
6:56 and drinks my **b** remains in me, *135*
19:34 bringing a sudden flow of **b** and water. *135*
Ac 1:19 Akeldama, that is, Field *of* **B**.) *135*
2:19 **b** and fire and billows of smoke. *135*
2:20 be turned to darkness and the moon to **b** *135*
5:28 to make us guilty of this man's **b**." *135*
15:20 the meat of strangled animals and from **b**. *135*
15:29 *from* **b**, from the meat of strangled animals *135*
18:6 "Your **b** be on your own heads! *135*
20:26 to you today that I am innocent of the **b** *135*
20:28 which he bought with his own **b**. *135*
21:25 from **b**, from the meat of strangled animals *135*
22:20 the **b** of your martyr Stephen was shed, *135*
Ro 3:15 "Their feet are swift *to* shed **b**; *135*
3:25 through faith in his **b**. *135*
5:9 Since we have now been justified by his **b**, *135*
1Co 10:16 a participation *in* the **b** of Christ? *135*
11:25 "This cup is the new covenant in my **b**; *135*
11:27 be guilty of sinning against the body and **b** *135*
15:50 that flesh and **b** cannot inherit the kingdom *135*
Eph 1:7 In him we have redemption through his **b**, *135*
2:13 near through the **b** of Christ. *135*
6:12 For our struggle is not against flesh and **b**, *135*
Col 1:20 by making peace through his **b**, *135*
Heb 2:14 Since the children have flesh and **b**, *135*
9:7 and never without **b**, *135*
9:12 He did not enter by means of the **b** of goats *135*
9:12 for all by his own **b**, *135*
9:13 The **b** of goats and bulls and the ashes of *135*
9:14 How much more, then, will the **b** of Christ, *135*
9:18 not put into effect without **b**. *135*
9:19 he took the **b** of calves, together with water, *135*
9:20 He said, "This is the **b** of the covenant, *135*
9:21 he sprinkled *with* the **b** both the tabernacle *135*
9:22 that nearly everything be cleansed with **b**, *135*
9:22 the **shedding of b** there is no forgiveness. *136*
9:25 the Most Holy Place every year with **b** *135*
10:4 the **b** of bulls and goats to take away sins. *135*
10:19 the Most Holy Place by the **b** of Jesus, *135*
10:29 who has treated as an unholy thing the **b** of *135*
11:28 the Passover and the sprinkling *of* **b**, *135*
12:4 yet resisted to the point of **shedding** your **b**. *135*
12:24 and *to* the sprinkled **b** that speaks *135*
12:24 that speaks a better word than the **b** *NIG*
13:11 The high priest carries the **b** of animals into *135*
13:12 to make the people holy through his own **b**. *135*
13:20 the **b** of the eternal covenant brought back *135*
1Pe 1:2 to Jesus Christ and sprinkling *by* his **b**: *135*
1:19 but *with* the precious **b** of Christ, *135*
1Jn 1:7 and the **b** of Jesus, his Son, *135*
5:6 This is the one who came by water and **b**— *135*
5:6 but by water and **b**. *135*
5:8 the water and the **b**; *135*
Rev 1:5 and has freed us from our sins by his **b**, *135*
5:9 with your **b** you purchased men for God *135*
6:10 of the earth and avenge our **b**?" *135*
6:12 the whole moon turned **b red**, *135+6055*
7:14 and made them white in the **b** of the Lamb. *135*
8:7 and there came hail and fire mixed with **b**, *135*
8:8 A third of the sea turned into **b**, *135*
11:6 the waters into **b** and to strike the earth *135*
12:11 They overcame him by the **b** of the Lamb *135*
14:20 and **b** flowed out of the press, *135*
16:3 and it turned into **b** like that of a dead man, *135*
16:4 and they became **b**. *135*
16:6 for they have shed the **b** of your saints *135*
16:6 and you have given them **b** to drink *135*
17:6 I saw that the woman was drunk with the **b** *135*
17:6 the **b** of those who bore testimony to Jesus. *135*
Rev 18:24 In her was found the **b** of prophets and of *135*
19:2 on her the **b** of his servants." *135*
19:13 He is dressed in a robe dipped *in* **b**, *135*

BLOOD-STAINED (1) [BLOOD]

2Sa 21:1 "It is on account of Saul and his **b** house; 1947

BLOODGUILT (2) [GUILT]

Ps 51:14 Save me from **b**, O God, 1947
Joel 3:21 Their **b**, which I have not pardoned, 1947

BLOODSHED (30) [BLOOD]

Ex 22:2 the defender is not **guilty of b**; 1947
22:3 he is **guilty of b**. 1947
Lev 17:4 that man shall be considered **guilty of b**; 1947
Nu 35:33 **B** pollutes the land, 1947
Dt 17:8 whether **b**, lawsuits or assaults 1947+1947+4200
19:10 and so that you will not be **guilty of b**. 1947
21:8 And the **b** will be atoned for. 1947
22:8 so that you may not bring the **guilt of b** 1947
1Sa 25:26 **b** and from avenging yourself 928+995+1947
25:31 burden of needless **b** or of having avenged himself. 1947+9161
25:33 keeping me from **b** this day and from avenging myself 928+995+1947
2Ch 19:10 **b** or other concerns of the law, 1947+1947+4200
Isa 5:7 And he looked for justice, but saw **b**; 5384
Jer 48:10 on him who keeps his sword from **b**! 1947
Eze 5:17 Plague and **b** will sweep through you, 1947
7:23 the land is full of **b** and the city is full 1947+5477
9:9 the land is full of **b** and the city is full 1947
14:19 and pour out my wrath upon it through **b**, 1947
22:2 Will you judge this city of **b**? 1947
24:6 " 'Woe to the city of **b**, 1947
24:9 " 'Woe to the city of **b**! 1947
35:6 over to **b** and it will pursue you. 1947
35:6 Since you did not hate **b**, 1947
35:6 **b** will pursue you. 1947
38:22 upon him with plague and **b**; 1947
Hos 4:2 and **b** follows bloodshed. 1947
4:2 and bloodshed follows **b**. 1947
12:14 the **guilt of** his **b** and will repay him 1947
Mic 3:10 who build Zion with **b**, 1947
Hab 2:12 "Woe to him who builds a city with **b** 1947

BLOODSHOT (1) [BLOOD]

Pr 23:29 Who has **b** eyes? 2680

BLOODSTAINS (1) [BLOOD]

Isa 4:4 he will cleanse the **b** from Jerusalem by 1947

BLOODTHIRSTY (6) [BLOOD]

Ps 5:6 **b** and deceitful men the LORD abhors. 1947
26:9 my life with **b** men, 1947
55:23 **b** and deceitful men will 1947
59:2 from evildoers and save me from **b** men. 1947
139:19 Away from me, you **b** men! 1947
Pr 29:10 **B** men hate a man of integrity and seek 1947

BLOOM (5)

Ex 9:31 the barley had headed and the flax was **in b**. 1499
SS 2:15 our vineyards that are **in b**. 6163
6:11 or the pomegranates *were* **in b**. 5914
7:12 and if the pomegranates *are* **in b**— 5914
Isa 35:2 *it will* **burst into b**; 7255+7255

BLOSSOM (8) [BLOSSOMED, BLOSSOMING, BLOSSOMS]

1Ki 7:26 like the rim of a cup, like a lily **b**. 7258
2Ch 4:5 like the rim of a cup, like a lily **b**. 7258
Isa 18:5 when the **b** is gone and the flower becomes 7258
27:6 Israel will bud and **b** and fill all the world 7255
35:1 the wilderness will rejoice and **b**. 7255
Hos 14:5 *he will* **b** like a lily. 7255
14:7 *He will* **b** like a vine, 7255
Jas 1:11 its **b** falls and its beauty is destroyed. *470*

BLOSSOMED (3) [BLOSSOM]

Ge 40:10 As soon as it budded, it **b**, 5890+6590
Nu 17:8 **b** and produced almonds. 7437+7488
Eze 7:10 the rod has budded, arrogance *has* **b**! 7255

BLOSSOMING (1) [BLOSSOM]

SS 2:13 the **b** vines spread their fragrance. 6163

BLOSSOMS (12) [BLOSSOM]

Ex 25:31 buds and **b** shall be of one piece with it. 7258
25:33 like almond flowers with buds and **b** are to 7258
25:34 like almond flowers with buds and **b**. 7258
37:17 buds and **b** were of one piece with it. 7258
37:19 like almond flowers with buds and **b** were 7258
37:20 like almond flowers with buds and **b**. 7258
Nu 8:4 from its base to its **b**. 7258
Job 15:33 like an olive tree shedding its **b**. 5900
Ecc 12:5 when the almond tree **b** and 5914
SS 1:14 My lover is to me a cluster of **henna b** from 4110
7:12 if their **b** have opened, 6163
Na 1:4 Bashan and Carmel wither and the **b** 7258

BLOT (14) [BLOTS, BLOTTED]

Ex 17:14 because *I will* **completely b out** 4681+4681
32:32 **b** me **out** of the book you have written." 4681
32:33 against me *I will* **b out** of my book. 4681
Dt 9:14 and **b out** their name from under heaven. 4681
25:19 *you shall* **b out** the memory of Amalek 4681
29:20 and the LORD *will* **b out** his name from 4681
32:26 and **b out** their memory from mankind, 8697
2Ki 14:27 not said he *would* **b out** the name of Israel 4681
Ne 4:5 not cover up their guilt or **b out** their sins 4681
13:14 not **b out** what I have so faithfully done for 4681
Ps 51:1 to your great compassion **b out** my transgressions. 4681
51:9 from my sins and **b out** all my iniquity. 4681
Jer 18:23 not forgive their crimes or **b out** their sins 4681
Rev 3:5 never **b out** his name **from** the book of life, *1981*

BLOTS (2) [BLOT]

Isa 43:25 am he *who* **b out** your transgressions, 4681
2Pe 2:13 They are **b** and blemishes, *5070*

BLOTTED (5) [BLOT]

Dt 25:6 that his name *will* not **be b out** from Israel. 4681
Ps 9:5 *you have* **b out** their name for ever 4681
69:28 *May they* **be b out** of the book of life and 4681
109:13 their names **b out** from the next generation. 4681
109:14 *may* the sin of his mother never **be b out**. 4681

BLOW (31) [BLEW, BLOWING, BLOWN, BLOWS, WINDBLOWN]

Ex 10:13 **made** an east wind **b** 5627
21:19 the *one who* **struck the b** will not 5782
Nu 10:7 To gather the assembly, **b** *the* **trumpets**, 9546
10:8 the priests, *are to* **b** the trumpets. 9546
Jdg 7:18 I and all who are with me **b** our trumpets, 9546
7:18 then from all around the camp **b** yours 9546
7:20 the trumpets *they were to* **b**, 9546
16:28 with **one** *b* get revenge on the Philistines AIT
1Sa 6:19 of the heavy **b** the LORD had dealt them, 4804
1Ki 1:34 **B** the trumpet and shout, 9546
1Ch 15:24 and Eliezer the priests *were to* **b** trumpets 2955
16:6 to **b** the trumpets regularly before the ark of NIH
2Ch 21:14 with a heavy **b**. 4487
Ps 39:10 I am overcome by the **b** *of* your hand. 9327
68:2 *may you* **b** them **away**; 5622
SS 4:16 **B** *on* my garden, 7031
Isa 5:24 and their flowers **b away** like dust; 6590
19:7 *will* **b away** and be no more. 5622
41:16 and a gale *will* **b** them **away**. 7046
57:13 a mere breath *will* **b** them **away**. 4374
Jer 6:29 The bellows **b fiercely** to burn away 5723
14:17 a grievous wound, a crushing **b**. 4804
51:27 **B** the trumpet among the nations! 9546
Eze 7:9 that it is I the LORD *who* **strikes the b**. 5782
7:14 Though *they* **b** the trumpet 9546
22:21 and *I will* **b** on you with my fiery wrath, 5870
24:16 with *one* **b** I am about to take away 4487
33:6 not **b** the trumpet to warn the people and 9546
Joel 2:1 **B** the trumpet in Zion; 9546
2:15 **B** the trumpet in Zion, declare a holy fast, 9546
Ac 27:13 **gentle** south wind *began to* **b**, *5710*

BLOWING (9) [BLOW]

Jos 6:4 with the priests **b** the trumpets. 9546
6:8 the LORD went forward, **b** their trumpets, 9546
6:13 the ark of the LORD and **b** the trumpets. 9546
2Ki 11:14 of the land *were* rejoicing and **b** trumpets. 9546
2Ch 23:13 of the land *were* rejoicing and **b** trumpets, 9546
Hos 13:15 **b** in from the desert; 6590
Jn 6:18 A strong wind *was* **b** and *4463*
Ac 2:2 the **b** of a violent wind came from heaven *5770*
Rev 7:1 **prevent** any wind **from b** *3590+4463*

BLOWN (6) [BLOW]

1Sa 13:3 Then Saul **had** the trumpet **b** throughout 9546
Ps 68:2 As smoke **is b away** by the wind, 5622
Isa 29:5 the ruthless hordes like **b** chaff. 6296
Eph 4:14 and **b here and there** by every wind *4367*
Jas 1:6 **b** and tossed **by the wind**. *448*
Jude 1:12 **b along** by the wind; *4195*

BLOWS (18) [BLOW]

Job 20:23 against him and rain down his **b** upon him. 4303
Ps 1:4 They are like chaff that the wind **b away**. 5622
103:16 the wind **b** over it and it is gone, 6296
Pr 6:33 **B** and disgrace are his lot, 5596
20:30 **B** and wounds cleanse away evil, 2467
Ecc 1:6 wind **b** to the south and turns to the north; 2143
Isa 14:6 down peoples with unceasing **b**, 4804
27:8 as on a day the east wind **b**. NIH
30:32 as he fights them in battle with the **b** 9485
40:7 the breath of the LORD **b** on them. 5959
40:24 than *he* **b** on them and they wither, 5973
Jer 4:11 in the desert **b** toward my people, but not NIH
Eze 26:9 He will direct the **b** *of* his battering rams 4693
33:3 against the land and **b** the trumpet to warn 9546
Lk 12:47 *be* **beaten with** many **b**. *1296*
12:48 *be* **beaten with** few **b**. *1296*
12:55 And when the south **wind b**, you say, *4463*
Jn 3:8 The wind **b** wherever it pleases. *4463*

BLUE (50)

Ex 25: 4 **b,** purple and scarlet yarn and fine linen; 9418
26: 1 of finely twisted linen and **b,** 9418
26: 4 Make loops of **b material** along the edge 9418
26:31 "Make a curtain of **b,** 9418
26:36 the entrance to the tent make a curtain of **b,** 9418
27:16 provide a curtain twenty cubits long, of **b,** 9418
28: 5 Have them use gold, and **b,** 9418
28: 6 "Make the ephod of gold, and of **b,** 9418
28: 8 and with **b,** purple and scarlet yarn, 9418
28:15 of gold, and of **b,** purple and scarlet yarn, 9418
28:28 to the rings of the ephod with **b** cord, 9418
28:31 the robe of the ephod entirely of **b cloth,** 9418
28:33 Make pomegranates of **b,** 9418
28:37 a **b** cord to it to attach it to the turban; 9418
35: 6 **b,** purple and scarlet yarn and fine linen; 9418
35:23 Everyone who had **b,** 9418
35:25 **b,** purple or scarlet yarn or fine linen. 9418
35:35 designers, embroiderers in **b,** 9418
36: 8 of finely twisted linen and **b,** 9418
36:11 Then they made loops of **b material** along 9418
36:35 They made the curtain of **b,** 9418
36:37 to the tent they made a curtain of **b,** purple 9418
38:18 for the entrance to the courtyard was of **b,** 9418
38:23 and an embroiderer in **b,** 9418
39: 1 From the **b,** purple 9418
39: 2 They made the ephod of gold, and of **b,** 9418
39: 3 and cut strands to be worked into the **b,** 9418
39: 5 and with **b,** purple and scarlet yarn, 9418
39: 8 of gold, and of **b,** purple and scarlet yarn, 9418
39:21 with **b** cord, connecting it to the waistband 9418
39:22 the robe of the ephod entirely of **b cloth—** 9418
39:24 They made pomegranates of **b,** 9418
39:29 The sash was of finely twisted linen and **b,** 9418
39:31 Then they fastened a **b** cord to it to attach it 9418
Nu 4: 6 a cloth of solid **b** over that and put the poles 9418
4: 7 of the Presence they are to spread a **b** cloth 9418
4: 9 to take a **b** cloth and cover the lampstand 9418
4:11 the gold altar they are to spread a **b** cloth 9418
4:12 wrap them in a **b** cloth, 9418
15:38 with a **b** cord on each tassel. 9418
2Ch 2: 7 and in purple, crimson and **b yarn,** 9418
2:14 and with purple and **b** and crimson **yarn** 9418
3:14 **b,** purple and crimson **yarn** 9418
Est 1: 6 garden had hangings of white and **b** linen, 9418
8:15 royal garments of **b** and white, 9418
Jer 10: 9 then dressed in **b** and purple— 9418
Eze 23: 6 in **b,** governors and commanders, all 9418
27: 7 of **b** and purple from the coasts of Elishah. 9418
27:24 with you beautiful garments, **b** fabric, 9418
Rev 9:17 Their breastplates were fiery red, **dark b,** *5610*

BLUNTED (1)

Ps 58: 7 *let* their arrows **be b.** 4908

BLURTS (1)

Pr 12:23 but the heart of fools **b out** folly. 7924

BLUSH (3)

Jer 3: 3 you refuse *to* **b with shame.** 4007
6:15 they do not even know how *to* **b.** 4007
8:12 they do not even know how *to* **b.** 4007

BLUSTERING (1)

Job 8: 2 Your words are a **b** wind. 3888

BOANERGES (1)

Mk 3:17 the name **B,** which means Sons *1065*

BOARD (5) [ABOARD, BOARDED, BOARDS]

Eze 27: 9 Veteran craftsmen of Gebal were **on b** 928
27:27 and everyone else **on b** will sink into 928+9348
Ac 21: 2 **went on b** and set sail. *2094*
27: 6 for Italy and **put us on b.** *899+1650+1837*
27:37 Altogether there were 276 of us **on b.** *1877+3836+4450*

BOARDED (1) [BOARD]

Ac 27: 2 *We* **b** a ship from Adramyttium about to sail *2094*

BOARDS (4) [BOARD]

Ex 27: 8 Make the altar hollow, out of **b.** 4283
38: 7 They made it hollow, out of **b.** 4283
1Ki 6:15 He lined its interior walls with cedar **b,** 7521
6:16 with cedar **b** from floor to ceiling to form 7521

BOARS (1)

Ps 80:13 **B** from the forest ravage it and 2614

BOAST (56) [BOASTED, BOASTERS, BOASTFUL, BOASTFULLY, BOASTING, BOASTS]

Jdg 7: 2 In order that Israel *may* not **b** against me 6995
1Ki 20:11 'One who puts on his armor *should* not **b** 2146
Ps 34: 2 My soul *will* **b** in the LORD; 2146
44: 8 In God *we* **make** *our* **b** all day long, 2146
49: 6 in their wealth and **b** of their great riches? 2146
52: 1 Why *do you* **b** of evil, you mighty man? 2146
52: 1 Why do you **b** all day long, NIH
75: 4 **'B** no more,' and to the wicked, 2147
97: 7 those *who* **b** in idols— 2146
Pr 27: 1 *Do* not **b** about tomorrow, 2146
Isa 10:15 or the saw **b** against him who uses it? 1540
28:15 *You* **b,** "We have entered into a covenant 606
61: 6 and in their riches *you will* **b.** 607
Jer 9:23 *"Let* not the wise man **b** of his wisdom or 2146
9:23 or the strong man **b** of his strength or 2146
9:23 of his strength or the rich man **b** 2146
9:24 but let him who boasts **b** about this: 2146
49: 4 Why *do you* **b** of your valleys, 2146
49: 4 **b** of your valleys so fruitful? NIH
51:41 the **b** *of* the whole earth seized! 9335
Am 4: 5 **b** *about* them, you Israelites, 9048
Ob 1:12 nor **b so much** in the day of their trouble. 1540+3870+7023
Ro 4: 2 he had **something to b about—** *3017*
11:18 *do* not **b over** those branches. *2878*
1Co 1:29 so that no one *may* **b** before him. *3016*
1:31 *"Let* him who boasts **b** in the Lord." *3016*
4: 7 why *do you* **b** as though you did not? *3016*
9:15 I would rather die than have anyone deprive me of this **b.** *3017*
9:16 Yet when I preach the gospel, I cannot **b,** *3017*
13: 4 It does not envy, it *does* not **b,** *4371*
2Co 1:12 Now this is our **b:** *3018*
1:14 to understand fully that you can **b** of us *NIG*
1:14 just as *we will* **b** of you in the day of *1639+3017*
10: 8 if *I* **b** somewhat freely about the authority *3016*
10:13 however, *will* not **b** beyond proper limits, *3016*
10:16 not *want to* **b about** work already done *3016*
10:17 But, "Let him who boasts **b** in the Lord." *3016*
11:12 with us in the things *they* **b about.** *3016*
11:18 I too *will* **b.** *3016*
11:21 What anyone else dares to **b** about— *NIG*
11:21 I also dare to **b** about. *NIG*
11:30 If I must **b,** I will boast of the things *3016*
11:30 *I will* **b of** the things that show my weakness *3016*
12: 5 *I will* **b** about a man like that, *3016*
12: 5 but *I will* not **b** about myself, *3016*
12: 6 Even if I should choose *to* **b,** *3016*
12: 9 Therefore *I will* **b** all the more gladly *3016*
Gal 6:13 to be circumcised that *they may* **b** *3016*
6:14 May I never **b** except in the cross *3016*
Eph 2: 9 not by works, so that no one *can* **b.** *3016*
Php 2:16 that I may **b** on the day of Christ that I did *3017*
2Th 1: 4 among God's churches we **b** about your *1595*
Heb 3: 6 to our courage and the hope of which we **b.** *3017*
Jas 3:14 *do* not **b** about it or deny the truth. *2878*
4:16 As it is, you **b** and brag. *3016*
Jude 1:16 they **b** about themselves and flatter others *3281+5665*

BOASTED (7) [BOAST]

Ex 15: 9 "The enemy **b,** 'I will pursue, 606
Est 5:11 Haman **b** to them *about* his vast wealth, 6218
Isa 20: 5 in Cush and **b** *in* Egypt will be afraid 9514
Jer 13:20 the sheep of which you **b?** 9514
Eze 35:13 You **b** against me and spoke against me 928+1540+7023
Ac 8: 9 *He* **b** that he was someone great, *3306*
2Co 7:14 *I had* **b** to him about you, *3016*

BOASTERS (1) [BOAST]

Jer 48:45 the skulls of the **noisy b.** 1201+8623

BOASTFUL (5) [BOAST]

Ps 12: 3 and every **b** tongue 1524+1819
Da 7:11 of the **b** words the horn was speaking. 10647
Ro 1:30 God-haters, insolent, arrogant and **b;** *225*
2Ti 3: 2 lovers of money, **b,** proud, abusive, *225*
2Pe 2:18 For they mouth empty, **b** words and, *5665*

BOASTFULLY (2) [BOAST]

Da 7: 8 the eyes of a man and a mouth that spoke **b.** 10647
7:20 and that had eyes and a mouth that spoke **b.** 10647

BOASTING (17) [BOAST]

Ps 94: 4 all the evildoers *are* **full of b.** 607
Ro 3:27 Where, then, is **b?** *3018*
1Co 3:21 So then, no more **b** about men! *3016*
5: 6 Your **b** is not good. *3017*
2Co 7:14 so our **b about** you to Titus has proved to *3018*
9: 2 and *I have been* **b about** it to *3016*
9: 3 that our **b** about you in this matter should *3017*
10:13 but will confine our **b** to *NIG*
10:14 We are not going too far in our **b,** *NIG*
10:15 Neither do we go beyond our limits *by* **b of** *3016*
11:10 in the regions of Achaia will stop this **b** *3018*
11:16 so that I *may do* a little **b.** *3016*
11:17 In this self-confident **b** I am not talking as *3018*
11:18 many *are* **b** in the way the world does, *3016*
12: 1 I must *go on* **b.** *3016*
Jas 4:16 All such **b** is evil. *3018*
1Jn 2:16 the lust of his eyes and the **b** of what he has *224*

BOASTS (12) [BOAST]

1Sa 2: 1 My mouth **b** over my enemies, 8143
Ps 10: 3 He **b** of the cravings of his heart; 2146
Pr 20:14 then off he goes and **b** *about* his purchase. 2146
25:14 without rain is a man *who* **b** of gifts he does 2146
Isa 16: 6 but her **b** are empty. 966
Jer 9:24 but *let* him *who* **b** boast about this: 2146
48:30 "and her **b** accomplish nothing. 966
Hos 12: 8 Ephraim **b,** "I am very rich; 606
1Co 1:31 "Let him who **b** boast in the Lord." *3016*
2Co 10:17 But, *"Let* him who **b** boast in the Lord." *3016*
Jas 3: 5 but *it* **makes** great **b.** *902*
Rev 18: 7 In her heart *she* **b,** 'I sit as queen; *3306*

BOAT (43) [BOATS, LIFEBOAT]

Mt 4:21 They were in a **b** with their father Zebedee, *4450*
4:22 the **b** and their father and followed him. *4450*
8:23 into the **b** and his disciples followed him. *4450*
8:24 so that the waves swept over the **b.** *4450*
9: 1 Jesus stepped into a **b,** *4450*
13: 2 around him that he got into a **b** and sat in it, *4450*
14:13 by **b** privately to a solitary place. *4450*
14:22 the disciples get into the **b** and go on ahead *4450*
14:24 the **b** was already a considerable distance *4450*
14:29 Then Peter got down out of the **b,** *4450*
14:32 And when they climbed into the **b,** *4450*
14:33 those who were in the **b** worshiped him, *4450*
15:39 the **b** and went to the vicinity of Magadan. *4450*
Mk 1:19 of Zebedee and his brother John in a **b,** *4450*
1:20 the **b** with the hired men and followed him. *4450*
3: 9 to have a **small b** ready for him, *4449*
4: 1 around him was so large that he got into a **b** *4450*
4:36 just as he was, in the **b.** *4450*
4:37 and the waves broke over the **b,** *4450*
5: 2 When Jesus got out of the **b,** *4450*
5:18 As Jesus was getting into the **b,** *4450*
5:21 When Jesus had again crossed over by **b** to *4450*
6:32 So they went away by themselves in a **b** to *4450*
6:45 the **b** and go on ahead of him to Bethsaida, *4450*
6:47 the **b** was in the middle of the lake, *4450*
6:51 Then he climbed into the **b** with them, *4450*
6:54 As soon as they got out of the **b,** *4450*
8:10 he got into the **b** with his disciples and went *4450*
8:13 into the **b** and crossed to the other side. *4450*
8:14 for one loaf they had with them in the **b.** *4450*
Lk 5: 3 down and taught the people from the **b.** *4450*
5: 7 in the other **b** to come and help them, *4450*
8:22 So they got into a **b** and set out. *4450*
8:23 so that the **b** was being swamped, *NIG*
8:37 So he got into the **b** and left. *4450*
Jn 6:17 where they got into a **b** and set off across *4450*
6:19 they saw Jesus approaching the **b,** *4450*
6:21 they were willing to take him into the **b,** *4450*
6:21 and immediately the **b** reached the shore *4450*
6:22 that only one **b** had been there, *4449*
21: 3 So they went out and got into the **b,** *4450*
21: 6 "Throw your net on the right side *of* the **b** *4450*
21: 8 The other disciples followed *in* the **b,** *4449*

BOATS (9) [BOAT]

Job 9:26 They skim past like **b** *of* papyrus, 641
Isa 18: 2 which sends envoys by sea in papyrus **b** 3998
Mk 4:36 There were also other **b** with him. *4450*
Lk 5: 2 he saw at the water's edge two **b,** *4450*
5: 3 He got into one *of* the **b,** *4450*
5: 7 and filled both **b** so full that they began *4450*
5:11 So they pulled their **b** up on shore, *4450*
Jn 6:23 Then some **b** from Tiberias landed near *4449*
6:24 into the **b** and went to Capernaum in search *4449*

BOAZ (29)

Ru 2: 1 a man of standing, whose name was **B.** 1244
2: 3 in a field belonging to **B,** 1244
2: 4 then **B** arrived from Bethlehem and greeted 1244
2: 5 **B** asked the foreman of his harvesters, 1244
2: 8 **B** said to Ruth, "My daughter, listen to me. 1244
2:11 **B** replied, "I've been told all 1244
2:14 At mealtime **B** said to her, 1244
2:15 **B** gave orders to his men, 1244
2:19 of the man I worked with today is **B,"** 1244
2:23 to the servant girls of **B** to glean until 1244
3: 2 Is not **B,** with whose 1244
3: 7 When **B** had finished eating and drinking 1244
3:16 she told her everything **B** had done for her 408+2021[S]
4: 1 Meanwhile **B** went up to the town gate 1244
4: 1 **B** said, "Come over here, my friend, 1244
4: 2 **B** took ten of the elders of the town NIH
4: 5 Then **B** said, "On the day you buy the land 1244
4: 8 So the kinsman-redeemer said to **B,** 1244
4: 9 Then **B** announced to the elders and all 1244
4:13 So **B** took Ruth and she became his wife. 1244
4:21 Salmon the father of **B,** 1244
4:21 **B** the father of Obed, 1244
1Ki 7:21 and the one to the north **B.** 1245
1Ch 2:11 Salmon the father of **B,** 1244
2:12 **B** the father of Obed and Obed the father 1244
2Ch 3:17 and the one to the north **B.** 1245
Mt 1: 5 Salmon the father of **B,** *1067*
1: 5 **B** the father of Obed, *1067*
Lk 3:32 the son *of* **B,** the son of Salmon, *1078*

BOCHERU (KJV) See BOKERU

BOCHIM (KJV) See BOKIM

BODIES (70) [BODY]

Ge 34:27 of Jacob came upon the **dead b** and looted 2728
47:18 for our lord except our **b** and our land. 1581

Ex 30:32 on men's **b** and do not make any oil with 1414
Lev 19:28 " 'Do not cut your **b** for the dead 1414
21:5 the edges of their beards or cut their **b.** 1414
26:30 and pile your **dead b** on the lifeless forms 7007
Nu 8:7 then have them shave their whole **b** 1414
14:29 In this desert your **b** will fall— 7007
14:32 But you—your **b** will fall in this desert. 7007
14:33 until the last of your **b** lies in the desert. 7007
1Sa 31:12 They took down the **b** *of* Saul and his sons 1581
2Sa 4:12 and hung the **b** by the pool in Hebron. NIH
21:10 down from the heavens on **the b,** 2157[S]
2Ki 10:25 The guards and officers threw the **b** out and NIH
19:35 there were all the dead **b!** 7007
1Ch 10:12 all their valiant men went and took the **b** 1590
2Ch 20:24 they saw only **dead b** lying on the ground; 7007
Ne 9:37 over our **b** and our cattle as they please. 1581
Ps 44:25 our **b** cling to the ground. 1061
73:4 their **b** are healthy and strong. 214
79:2 the **dead b** *of* your servants as food to 5577
Isa 5:25 and the **dead b** are like refuse in the streets. 5577
26:19 But your dead will live; their **b** will rise. 5577
34:3 their **dead b** will send up a stench; 7007
37:36 there were all the dead **b!** 7007
66:24 upon the **dead b** *of* those who rebelled 7007
Jer 9:22 " 'The **dead b** *of* men will lie like refuse on 5577
16:4 and their **dead b** will become food for 5577
31:40 where **dead b** and ashes are thrown, 7007
33:5 'They will be filled with the **dead b** *of* 7007
34:20 Their **dead b** will become food for the birds 5577
41:9 Now the cistern where he threw all the **b** *of* 7007
La 4:7 their **b** more ruddy than rubies, 6795
Eze 6:5 I will lay the **dead b** *of* the Israelites in front 7007
10:12 Their entire **b,** including their backs, 1414
11:7 The **b** you have thrown there are the meat 2728
Da 3:27 the fire had not harmed their **b,** nor was 10151
Am 6:10 And if a relative who is to burn the **b** comes 6795
8:3 Many, many **b**—flung everywhere! 7007
Na 2:10 Hearts melt, knees give way, **b** tremble, 5516
3:3 piles of dead, **b** without number, 1581
Hab 2:15 so that he can gaze on their **naked b.** 5067
Mt 24:29 and the heavenly **b** will be shaken.' *NIG*
27:52 The tombs broke open and the **b** *5393*
Mk 13:25 and the heavenly **b** will be shaken.' *1539*
Lk 21:26 the **heavenly b** will be shaken. *1539+3836+4041*
Jn 19:31 the **b** left on the crosses during the Sabbath, *5393*
19:31 the legs broken and the **b** taken down. *NIG*
Ac 7:16 Their **b** were brought back to Shechem *NIG*
7:42 over to the worship *of* the heavenly **b.** *5131*
Ro 1:24 the degrading of their **b** with one another. *5393*
7:5 by the law were at work in our **b,** *3517*
8:11 the dead will also give life *to* your mortal **b** *5393*
8:23 the redemption *of* our **b.** *5393*
12:1 to offer your **b** as living sacrifices, *5393*
1Co 6:15 that your **b** are members of Christ himself? *5393*
10:5 their **b** were scattered over the desert. *NIG*
15:40 There are also heavenly **b** *5393*
15:40 and there are earthly **b;** *5393*
15:40 the splendor of the heavenly **b** is one kind, *NIG*
15:40 and the splendor of the earthly **b** is another. *NIG*
Eph 5:28 to love their wives as their own **b.** *5393*
Php 3:21 will transform our lowly **b** so that they will *5393*
Heb 3:17 whose **b** fell in the desert? *3265*
10:22 and having our **b** washed with pure water. *5393*
13:11 but the **b** are burned outside the camp. *5393*
Jude 1:8 these dreamers pollute their own **b,** *4922*
Rev 11:8 Their **b** will lie in the street of *4773*
11:9 language and nation will gaze on their **b** *4773*
18:13 and **b** and souls of men. *5393*

BODILY (4) [BODY]

Lev 15:2 'When any man has a **b** discharge, 1414+4946
22:4 an infectious skin disease or a **b discharge,** 2307
Lk 3:22 on him *in* **b** form like a dove. *5394*
Col 2:9 the fullness of the Deity lives **in b form,** *5395*

BODY (253) [BODIES, BODILY, EMBODIMENT]

Ge 15:4 but a son coming from your own **b** will 5055
25:25 and his **whole** *b* was like a hairy garment; AIT
35:11 and kings will come from your **b.** 2743
Ex 22:27 the only covering he has for his **b.** 6425
28:42 as a covering for the **b,** 1414+6872
Lev 6:10 with linen undergarments next to his **b,** 1414
13:13 and if the disease has covered his whole **b,** 1414
15:3 Whether it continues flowing from his **b** 1414
15:16 he must bathe his whole **b** with water, 1414
16:4 with linen undergarments next to his **b;** 1414
21:11 not enter a place where there is a dead **b.** 5883
Nu 5:2 because of a **dead b.** 5883
5:22 that brings a curse enter your **b** so 5055
6:6 to the LORD he must not go near a dead **b.** 5883
6:11 by being in the presence of the **dead b.** 5883
9:6 on account of a dead **b.** 132
9:7 because of a dead **b,** 132
9:10 of a **dead b** or are away on a journey, 5883
19:11 the dead **b** of anyone will be unclean 5883
19:13 Whoever touches the dead **b** *of* anyone 5883
25:8 the Israelite and into the woman's **b.** 7687
Dt 4:8 and laws as this **b** *of* laws I am setting 3972
21:2 and measure the distance from the **b** to 2728
21:3 of the town nearest the **b** shall take a heifer 2728
21:6 the **b** shall wash their hands over 2728
21:22 to death and **his b** is hung on a tree, 2257[S]
21:23 not leave his **b** on the tree overnight. 5577
Jos 8:29 Joshua ordered them to take his **b** from 5577
1Sa 5:4 only **his b** remained. 1837[S]
31:10 and fastened his **b** to the wall of Beth Shan. 1581
2Sa 7:12 who will come from your own **b,** 5055
1Ki 13:22 Therefore your **b** will not be buried in 5577
13:24 and his **b** was thrown down on the road, 5577
13:25 by saw the **b** thrown down there, 5577
13:25 with the lion standing beside the **b,** 5577
13:28 and found the **b** thrown down on the road, 5577
13:28 The lion had neither eaten the **b** nor mauled 5577
13:29 prophet picked up the **b** *of* the man of God, 5577
13:30 Then he laid the **b** in his own tomb, 5577
2Ki 4:34 the boy's **b** grew warm. 1414
6:30 underneath, he had sackcloth on his **b.** 1414
9:37 Jezebel's **b** will be like refuse on 5577
13:21 they threw the **man's b** into Elisha's tomb. 408
13:21 When the **b** touched Elisha's bones, NIH
23:30 Josiah's servants brought *his* **b** in a chariot 4637
Ezr 8:20 a **b** *that* David and the officials 8611[S]
Job 4:15 and the hair on my **b** stood on end. 1414
7:5 My **b** is clothed with worms and scabs, 1414
7:15 rather than this **b** *of* mine. 6795
14:22 of his own **b** and mourns only for himself." 1414
21:6 trembling seizes my **b.** 1414
21:24 his **b** well nourished, 6489
30:30 my **b** burns with fever. 6795
Ps 16:9 my **b** also will rest secure, 1414
31:9 my soul and my **b** with grief. 1061
38:3 of your wrath there is no health in my **b;** 1414
38:7 there is no health in my **b.** 1414
63:1 my soul thirsts for you, my **b** longs for you, 1414
109:18 it entered into his **b** like water, 7931
109:24 my **b** is thin and gaunt. 1414
139:16 your eyes saw my **unformed b.** 1677
Pr 3:8 to your **b** and nourishment to your bones. 9219
4:22 and health to a man's whole **b.** 1414
5:11 when your flesh and **b** are spent. 8638
14:30 A heart at peace gives life to the **b,** 1414
Ecc 11:5 how the **b** is formed in a mother's womb, 6795
11:10 and cast off the troubles of your **b,** 1414
12:12 and much study wearies the **b.** 1414
SS 5:14 His **b** is like polished ivory decorated 5055
Isa 17:4 the fat of his **b** will waste away. 1414
20:2 the sackcloth from your **b** and the sandals 5516
21:3 At this my **b** is racked with pain, 5516
Jer 13:22 and your **b** mistreated. 6811
26:23 down with a sword and his **b** thrown into 5577
36:30 his **b** will be thrown out and exposed to 5577
Eze 1:11 and two wings covering its **b.** 1581
1:23 and each had two wings covering its **b.** 1581
16:25 **offering** your **b** with increasing promiscuity 906+7316+8079
Da 4:33 His **b** was drenched with the dew of heaven 10151
5:21 his **b** was drenched with the dew of heaven, 10151
7:11 until the beast was slain and its **b** destroyed 10151
10:6 His **b** was like chrysolite, 1581
Mic 6:7 the fruit of my **b** for the sin of my soul? 1061
Hag 2:13 with a **dead b** touches one of these things, 5883
Zec 13:6 'What are these wounds on your **b?'** 3338
Mt 5:29 for you to lose one **part of** your **b** than *3517*
5:29 for your whole **b** to be thrown into hell. *5393*
5:30 for you to lose one **part of** your **b** than *3517*
5:30 of your body than for your whole **b** to go *5393*
6:22 "The eye is the lamp *of* the **b.** *5393*
6:22 your whole **b** will be full of light. *5393*
6:23 your whole **b** will be full of darkness. *5393*
6:25 or about your **b,** what you will wear. *5393*
6:25 and the **b** more important than clothes? *5393*
10:28 Do not be afraid of those who kill the **b** *5393*
10:28 of the One who can destroy both soul and **b** *5393*
14:12 John's disciples came and took his **b** *4773*
15:17 into the stomach and then out of the **b?** *NIG*
26:12 When she poured this perfume on my **b,** *5393*
26:26 "Take and eat; this is my **b."** *5393*
26:41 The spirit is willing, but the **b** is weak." *4922*
27:58 Going to Pilate, he asked for Jesus' **b,** *5393*
27:59 Joseph took the **b,** *5393*
27:64 his disciples may come and steal **the b** *899[S]*
Mk 5:29 and she felt *in* her **b** that she was freed *5393*
6:29 John's disciples came and took his **b** *4773*
7:19 and then out of his **b."** *NIG*
14:8 She poured perfume on my **b** beforehand *5393*
14:22 "Take it; this is my **b."** *5393*
14:38 The spirit is willing, but the **b** is weak." *4922*
15:43 to Pilate and asked for Jesus' **b.** *5393*
15:45 he gave the **b** to Joseph. *4773*
15:46 took down **the b,** wrapped it in the linen, *899[S]*
16:1 so that they might go to anoint **Jesus' b.** *899[S]*
Lk 11:34 Your eye is the lamp *of* your **b.** *5393*
11:34 your whole **b** also is full of light. *5393*
11:34 they are bad, your **b** also is full of darkness. *5393*
11:36 Therefore, if your whole **b** is full of light, *5393*
12:4 do not be afraid of those who kill the **b** and *5393*
12:5 Fear him who, after the killing of the **b,** *NIG*
12:22 or about your **b,** what you will wear. *5393*
12:23 and the **b** more than clothes. *5393*
17:37 He replied, "Where there is a **dead b,** *5393*
22:19 saying, "This is my **b** given for you; *5393*
23:52 Going to Pilate, he asked for Jesus' **b.** *5393*
23:55 and saw the tomb and how his **b** was laid *5393*
24:3 they did not find the **b** of the Lord Jesus. *5393*
24:23 but didn't find his **b.** *5393*
Jn 2:21 But the temple he had spoken of was his **b.** *5393*
13:10 his whole **b** is clean. *NIG*
19:38 Joseph of Arimathea asked Pilate for the **b** *5393*
19:38 he came and took the **b** away. *5393*
19:40 Taking Jesus' **b,** the two *5393*
20:12 seated where Jesus' **b** had been, *5393*
Ac 1:18 there he fell headlong, his **b** burst open *NIG*
2:26 my **b** also will live in hope, *4922*
2:31 nor did his **b** see decay. *4922*
5:6 wrapped up his **b,** *NIG*
9:37 and her **b** was washed and placed in *NIG*
13:36 with his fathers and *his* **b decayed.** *1426+3972*
Ro 4:19 the fact that his **b** was as good as dead— *5393*
6:6 that the **b** of sin might be done away with, *5393*
6:12 not let sin reign in your mortal **b** so *5393*
6:13 Do not offer the **parts of** your **b** to sin, *3517*
6:13 the **parts of** your **b** to him as instruments *3517*
6:19 the **parts of** your **b** in slavery to impurity *3517*
7:4 also died to the law through the **b** of Christ, *5393*
7:23 at work in the **members of** my **b,** *3517*
7:24 Who will rescue me from this **b** of death? *5393*
8:10 your **b** is dead because of sin, *5393*
8:13 to death the misdeeds *of* the **b,** *5393*
12:4 of us has one **b** with many members, *5393*
12:5 so in Christ we who are many form one **b,** *5393*
1Co 6:13 The **b** is not meant for sexual immorality, *5393*
6:13 but for the Lord, and the Lord *for* the **b.** *5393*
6:16 with a prostitute is one with her in **b?** *5393*
6:18 a man commits are outside his **b,** *5393*
6:18 who sins sexually sin against his own **b.** *5393*
6:19 know that your **b** is a temple of the Holy
Spirit, who is in you, *5393*
6:20 Therefore honor God with your **b.** *5393*
7:4 The wife's **b** does not belong to her alone *5393*
7:4 the husband's **b** does not belong *5393*
7:34 be devoted to the Lord *in* both **b** and spirit. *5393*
9:27 I beat my **b** and make it my slave so that *5393*
10:16 that we break a participation *in* the **b** *5393*
10:17 are one **b,** for we all partake of the one loaf. *5393*
11:24 he broke it and said, "This is my **b,** *5393*
11:27 be guilty of sinning against the **b** and blood *5393*
11:29 the **b** of the Lord eats and drinks judgment *5393*
12:12 The **b** is a unit, though it is made up of
many parts; *5393*
12:12 all its parts are many, they form one **b.** *5393*
12:13 by one Spirit into one **b—** *5393*
12:14 Now the **b** is not made up of one part but *5393*
12:15 I do not belong to the **b,"** *5393*
12:15 not for that reason cease to be part of the **b.** *5393*
12:16 I do not belong to the **b,"** *5393*
12:16 not for that reason cease to be part of the **b.** *5393*
12:17 If the whole **b** were an eye, *5393*
12:17 If the whole **b** were an ear, *NIG*
12:18 in fact God has arranged the parts in the **b,** *5393*
12:19 where would the **b** be? *5393*
12:20 As it is, there are many parts, but one **b.** *5393*
12:22 those parts *of* the **b** that seem to *5393*
12:24 of the **b** and has given greater honor to *5393*
12:25 so that there should be no division in the **b,** *5393*
12:27 Now you are the **b** of Christ, *5393*
13:3 the poor and surrender my **b** to the flames, *5393*
15:35 With what kind of **b** will they come?" *5393*
15:37 you do not plant the **b** that will be, *5393*
15:38 But God gives it a **b** as he has determined, *5393*
15:38 and to each kind of seed he gives its own **b.** *5393*
15:42 The **b** that is sown is perishable, *NIG*
15:44 it is sown a natural **b,** *5393*
15:44 it is raised a spiritual **b.** *5393*
15:44 If there is a natural **b,** *5393*
15:44 there is also a spiritual **b.** *NIG*
2Co 4:10 We always carry around in our **b** the death *5393*
4:10 life of Jesus may also be revealed in our **b.** *5393*
4:11 his life may be revealed in our mortal **b.** *4922*
5:6 as we are at home in the **b** we are away *5393*
5:8 and would prefer to be away from the **b** and *5393*
5:9 whether we are at home in the **b** or away *NIG*
5:10 for the things done while in the **b,** *5393*
7:1 from everything that contaminates **b** *4922*
7:5 this **b** of ours had no rest, *4922*
12:2 in the **b** or out of the body I do not know— *5393*
12:2 in the body or out of the **b** I do not know— *5393*
12:3 whether in the **b** or apart from the body I do *5393*
12:3 whether in the body or apart from the **b** I do *5393*
Gal 2:20 The life I live in the **b,** *4922*
6:17 for I bear on my **b** the marks of Jesus. *5393*
Eph 1:23 which is his **b,** the fullness of him *5393*
2:11 (that done in the **b** by the hands of men)— *4922*
2:16 and in this one **b** to reconcile both of them *5393*
3:6 **members together of one b,** *5362*
4:4 There is one **b** and one Spirit— *5393*
4:12 so that the **b** of Christ may be built up *5393*
4:16 From him the whole **b,** *5393*
4:25 for we are all members *of* **one b.** *253*
5:23 his **b,** of which he is the Savior. *5393*
5:29 After all, no one ever hated his own **b,** *4922*
5:30 for we are members *of* his **b.** *5393*
Php 1:20 as always Christ will be exalted in my **b,** *5393*
1:22 If I am to go on living in the **b,** *4922*
1:24 for you that I remain in the **b.** *4922*
3:21 so that they will be like his glorious **b.** *5393*
Col 1:18 And he is the head *of* the **b,** the church; *5393*
1:22 by Christ's physical **b** through death *5393*
1:24 for the sake of his **b,** which is the church. *5393*
2:5 For though I am absent from you in **b,** *4922*
2:19 from whom the whole **b,** *5393*
2:23 and their harsh treatment *of* the **b,** *5393*
3:15 members of one **b** you were called to peace. *5393*
1Th 4:4 of you should learn to control his own **b** in *5007*
5:23 soul and **b** be kept blameless at the coming *5393*
1Ti 3:16 He appeared in a **b,** *4922*
4:14 the **b of elders** laid their hands on you. *4564*
Heb 7:10 Levi was still in the **b** of his ancestor. *4019*
10:5 but a **b** you prepared for me; *5393*

Heb 10:10 the sacrifice *of* the **b** of Jesus Christ once *5393*
10:20 for us through the curtain, that is, his **b**, *4922*
Jas 2:26 As the **b** without the spirit is dead, *5393*
3: 2 able to keep his whole **b** in check. *5393*
3: 5 the tongue is a small **part of the b**, *3517*
3: 6 a world of evil among the **parts of the b**. *3517*
1Pe 2:24 in his **b** on the tree, so that we might die *5393*
3:18 He was put to death *in* the **b** but made alive *4922*
3:21 the **b** but the pledge of a good conscience *4922*
4: 1 Therefore, since Christ suffered *in* his **b**, *4922*
4: 1 who has suffered *in* his **b** is done with sin. *4922*
4: 6 according to men *in regard to* the **b**, *4922*
2Pe 1:13 as long as I live in the tent of this **b**, *NIG*
Jude 1: 9 with the devil about the **b** of Moses, *5393*

BODYGUARD (4) [GUARD]

1Sa 22:14 captain of your **b** and highly respected 5463
28: 2 I will make you my **b** for life." 4200+8031+9068
2Sa 23:23 And David put him in charge of his **b**. 5463
1Ch 11:25 And David put him in charge of his **b**. 5463

BOHAN (2)

Jos 15: 6 of Beth Arabah to the Stone of **B** son 992
18:17 ran down to the Stone of **B** son of Reuben. 992

BOIL (10) [BOILED, BOILING, BOILS]

Ex 16:23 to bake and **b** what you want to boil. 1418
16:23 to bake and boil what *you want to* **b**. 1418
Lev 13:18 "When someone has a **b** on his skin 8825
13:19 and in the place where the **b** was, 8825
13:20 that has broken out where the **b** was. 8825
13:23 it is only a scar from the **b**, 8825
2Ki 20: 7 They did so and applied it to the **b**, 8825
Isa 38:21 a poultice of figs and apply it to the **b**, 8825
64: 2 fire sets twigs ablaze and **causes** water **to b**, 1240
Eze 24: 5 **bring** it **to a b** and cook the bones 8409+8410

BOILED (4) [BOIL]

Nu 6:19 in his hands a **b** shoulder of the ram, 1419
1Sa 2:13 a sacrifice and while the meat *was being* **b**, 1418
2:15 he won't accept **b** meat from you, 1418
2Ch 35:13 and **b** the holy offerings in pots, 1418

BOILING (3) [BOIL]

Job 41:20 from his nostrils as from a **b** pot over a fire 5870
41:31 He makes the depths churn like a **b** caldron NIH
Jer 1:13 "I see a **b** pot, tilting away from the north," 5870

BOILS (5) [BOIL]

Ex 9: 9 and festering **b** will break out on men 8825
9:10 festering **b** broke out on men and animals. 8825
9:11 before Moses because of the **b** that were 8825
Dt 28:27 The LORD will afflict you with the **b** 8825
28:35 with painful **b** that cannot be cured, 8825

BOKERU (2)

1Ch 8:38 Azrikam, **B**, Ishmael, Sheariah, 1150
9:44 Azrikam, **B**, Ishmael, Sheariah, 1150

BOKIM (2)

Jdg 2: 1 of the LORD went up from Gilgal to **B** 1141
2: 5 and they called that place **B**. 1141

BOLD (10) [BOLDLY, BOLDNESS, EMBOLDENED]

Ge 18:27 "Now *that I have been so* **b** *as* to speak to 3283
18:31 "Now *that I have been so* **b** *as* to speak to 3283
Ps 138: 3 *you* **made** me **b** and stouthearted. 8104
Pr 21:29 A wicked man **puts up a b front**, 928+6451+7156
28: 1 but the righteous *are* as **b** as a lion. 1053
2Co 3:12 since we have such a hope, *we are* very **b**. *4244+5968*
10: 1 to face with you, but **"b"** when away! *2509*
10: 2 that when I come *I may* not have *to be* as **b** *2509*
Phm 1: 8 although in Christ I could **be b** and order you to do what you ought *2400+4244+4498*
2Pe 2:10 **B** and arrogant, these men are not afraid *5532*

BOLDLY (12) [BOLD]

Ex 14: 8 who were marching out **b**. 928+3338+8123
Nu 33: 3 They marched out **b** in full view of all the Egyptians, 928+3338+8123
Mk 15:43 went **b** to Pilate and asked for Jesus' body. *5528*
Ac 4:31 and spoke the word of God **b**. *3552+4244*
9:28 **speaking b** in the name of the Lord. *4245*
13:46 Then Paul and Barnabas answered them **b**: *4245*
14: 3 **speaking b** for the Lord, *4245*
18:26 He began *to* **speak b** in the synagogue. *4245*
19: 8 and **spoke b** there for three months, *4245*
28:31 **B** and without hindrance he preached *4244*
Ro 10:20 And Isaiah **b** says, "I was found *703*
15:15 I have written you **quite b** on some points, *5529*

BOLDNESS (2) [BOLD]

Lk 11: 8 of the man's **b** he will get up and give him *357*
Ac 4:29 to speak your word with great **b**. *4244*

BOLSTER (KJV) See HEAD

BOLT (1) [BOLTED, BOLTS]

2Sa 13:17 "Get this woman out of here and **b** the door 5835

BOLTED (1) [BOLT]

2Sa 13:18 So his servant put her out and **b** the door 5835

BOLTS (12) [BOLT]

Dt 33:25 **b of** your **gates** will be iron and bronze, 4981
2Sa 22:13 of his presence **b** *of* lightning blazed forth. 1624
22:15 **b of lightning** and routed them. 1398
Ne 3: 3 They laid its beams and put its doors and **b** 4980
3: 6 They laid its beams and put its doors and **b** 4980
3:13 and put its doors and **b** and bars in place. 4980
3:14 and put its doors and **b** and bars in place. 4980
3:15 roofing it over and putting its doors and **b** 4980
Job 38:35 Do you send the **lightning b** on their way? 1398
Ps 18:12 with hailstones and **b** *of* lightning. 1624
18:14 great **b of lightning** and routed them. 1398
78:48 their livestock to **b of lightning.** 8404

BOND (3) [BONDAGE, BONDS]

Eze 20:37 I will bring you into the **b** *of* the covenant. 5037
Ac 17: 9 Then they made Jason and the others **post b** *2653*
Eph 4: 3 to keep the unity of the Spirit through the **b** *5278*

BONDAGE (9) [BOND]

Ge 47:19 we with our land will be **in b** to Pharaoh. 6269
47:25 we will be **in b** to Pharaoh." 6269
Ex 6: 9 of their discouragement and cruel **b**. 6275
Ezr 9: 8 to our eyes and a little relief in our **b**. 6285
9: 9 our God has not deserted us in our **b**. 6285
Isa 14: 3 suffering and turmoil and cruel **b**, 6268+6275
Jer 34: 9 **hold** a fellow Jew **in b**. 6268
34:10 and no longer **hold** them **in b**. 6268
Ro 8:21 be liberated from its **b** to decay and brought *1525*

BONDMAID, BONDMAIDS (KJV) See SLAVE GIRL, SLAVES

BONDMAN, BONDMEN (KJV) See SLAVE, SERVANT

BONDS (4) [BOND]

Jer 2:20 and tore off your **b**; 4593
5: 5 the yoke and torn off the **b**. 4593
30: 8 and will tear off their **b**; 4593
Hos 10:10 be gathered against them *to* **put** them **in b** 673

BONDSERVANT (KJV) See SLAVE

BONDWOMAN, BONDWOMEN (KJV) See SLAVE

BONE (7) [BACKBONE, BONES]

Ge 2:23 now **b** of my bones and flesh of my flesh; 6795
Nu 19:16 anyone who touches a human **b** or a grave, 6795
19:18 anyone who touches a human **b** or a grave 6795
Pr 25:15 and a gentle tongue can break a **b**. 1752
Eze 37: 7 and the bones came together, **b** to bone. 6795
37: 7 and the bones came together, bone to **b**. 6795
39:15 the land and one of them sees a human **b**, 6795

BONES (90) [BONE]

Ge 2:23 now bone of my **b** and flesh of my flesh; 6795
50:25 and then you must carry my **b** up 6795
Ex 12:46 Do not break any of the **b**. 6795
13:19 Moses took the **b** *of* Joseph with him 6795
13:19 and then you must carry my **b** up with you 6795
Nu 9:12 of it till morning or break any of its **b**. 6795
24: 8 and break their **b** in pieces; 6795
Jos 24:32 And Joseph's **b**, which 6795
1Sa 31:13 Then they took their **b** and buried them 6795
2Sa 21:12 and took the **b** of Saul and his son Jonathan 6795
21:13 the **b** *of* Saul and his son Jonathan 6795
21:13 and the **b** *of* those who had been killed 6795
21:14 the **b** *of* Saul and his son Jonathan in 6795
1Ki 13: 2 and human **b** will be burned on you.' " 6795
13:31 lay my **b** beside his bones. 6795
13:31 lay my bones beside his **b**. 6795
2Ki 13:21 When the body touched Elisha's **b**, 6795
23:14 and covered the sites with human **b**. 6795
23:16 the **b** removed from them and burned on 6795
23:18 "Don't let anyone disturb his **b**." 6795
23:18 So they spared his **b** and those of 6795
23:20 on the altars and burned human **b** on them. 6795
1Ch 10:12 Then they buried their **b** under 6795
2Ch 34: 5 the **b** *of* the priests on their altars, 6795
Job 2: 5 and strike his flesh and **b**, 6795
4:14 and made all my **b** shake. 6795
10:11 and knit me together with **b** and sinews? 6795
19:20 I am nothing but skin and **b**; 6795
20:11 that fills his **b** will lie with him in the dust. 6795
21:24 his **b** rich with marrow. 6795
30:17 Night pierces my **b**; 6795
33:19 a bed of pain with constant distress in his **b**, 6795
33:21 and his **b**, once hidden, now stick out. 6795
Job 40:18 His **b** are tubes of bronze, 6795
Ps 6: 2 O LORD, heal me, for my **b** are in agony. 6795
22:14 and all my **b** are out of joint. 6795
22:17 I can count all my **b**; 6795
31:10 and my **b** grow weak. 6795
32: 3 my **b** wasted away 6795
34:20 he protects all his **b**, 6795
38: 3 my **b** have no soundness because of my sin. 6795
42:10 My **b** suffer mortal agony 6795
51: 8 let the **b** you have crushed rejoice. 6795
53: 5 the **b** *of* those who attacked you; 6795
102: 3 my **b** burn like glowing embers. 6795
102: 5 I am reduced to skin and **b**. 6795
109:18 into his **b** like oil. 6795
141: 7 so our **b** have been scattered at the mouth 6795
Pr 3: 8 to your body and nourishment to your **b**. 6795
12: 4 but a disgraceful wife is like decay in his **b**. 6795
14:30 but envy rots the **b**. 6795
15:30 and good news gives health to the **b**. 6795
16:24 sweet to the soul and healing to the **b**. 6795
17:22 but a crushed spirit dries up the **b**. 1752
Isa 38:13 but like a lion he broke all my **b**; 6795
Jer 8: 1 the **b** *of* the kings and officials of Judah, 6795
8: 1 the **b** *of* the priests and prophets, 6795
8: 1 and the **b** *of* the people of Jerusalem will 6795
20: 9 a fire shut up in my **b**. 6795
23: 9 heart is broken within me; all my **b** tremble. 6795
50:17 *to* **crush** his **b** was Nebuchadnezzar king 6793
La 1:13 sent it down into my **b**. 6795
3: 4 and has broken my **b**. 6795
4: 8 Their skin has shriveled on their **b**; 6795
Eze 6: 5 and I will scatter your **b** around your altars. 6795
24: 4 Fill it with the best of these **b**; 6795
24: 5 Pile wood beneath it for the **b**; 6795
24: 5 bring it to a boil and cook the **b** in it. 6795
24:10 and let the **b** be charred. 6795
32:27 for their sins rested on their **b**, 6795
37: 1 the middle of a valley; it was full of **b**. 6795
37: 2 a great many **b** on the floor of the valley, NIH
37: 2 **b** that were very dry. NIH
37: 3 "Son of man, can these **b** live?" 6795
37: 4 "Prophesy to these **b** and say to them, 6795
37: 4 'Dry **b**, hear the word of the LORD! 6795
37: 5 the Sovereign LORD says to these **b**: 6795
37: 7 a rattling sound, and the **b** came together, 6795
37:11 these **b** are the whole house of Israel. 6795
37:11 'Our **b** are dried up and our hope is gone; 6795
Da 6:24 and crushed all their **b**. 10150
Am 2: 1 as if to lime, the **b** *of* Edom's king, 6795
3:12 the lion's mouth only two **leg b** or a piece 4157
Mic 3: 2 from my people and the flesh from their **b**; 6795
3: 3 strip off their skin and break their **b** 6795
Hab 3:16 decay crept into my **b**, 6795
Mt 23:27 but on the inside are full *of* dead men's **b** *4014*
Lk 24:39 a ghost does not have flesh and **b**, *4014*
Jn 19:36 "Not one of his **b** will be broken," *4014*
Heb 11:22 and gave instructions about his **b**. *4014*

BONNETS (KJV) See HEADBANDS, HEADDRESSES, TURBANS

BOOK (130) [BOOKS]

Ex 24: 7 Then he took the **B** *of* the Covenant 6219
32:32 then blot me out of the **b** you have written." 6219
32:33 against me I will blot out of my **b**. 6219
Nu 21:14 the **B** *of* the Wars of the LORD says: 6219
Dt 28:58 which are written in this **b**, 6219
28:61 and disaster not recorded in this **B** *of* 6219
29:20 All the curses written in this **b** will fall 6219
29:21 the curses of the covenant written in this **B** 6219
29:27 on it all the curses written in this **b**. 6219
30:10 and decrees that are written in this **B** *of* 6219
31:24 in a **b** the words of this law from beginning 6219
31:26 "Take this **B** *of* the Law and place it beside 6219
Jos 1: 8 Do not let this **B** *of* the Law depart 6219
8:31 according to what is written in the **B** *of* 6219
8:34 just as it is written in the **B** *of* the Law. 6219
10:13 as it is written in the **B** *of* Jashar. 6219
23: 6 to obey all that is written in the **B** *of* 6219
24:26 And Joshua recorded these things in the **B** 6219
2Sa 1:18 of the bow (it is written in the **B** *of* Jashar): 6219
1Ki 11:41 are they not written in the **b** *of* the annals 6219
14:19 in the **b** *of* the annals of the kings of Israel. 6219
14:29 in the **b** *of* the annals of the kings of Judah? 6219
15: 7 in the **b** *of* the annals of the kings of Judah? 6219
15:23 in the **b** *of* the annals of the kings of Judah? 6219
15:31 in the **b** *of* the annals of the kings of Israel? 6219
16: 5 in the **b** *of* the annals of the kings of Israel? 6219
16:14 in the **b** *of* the annals of the kings of Israel? 6219
16:20 in the **b** *of* the annals of the kings of Israel? 6219
16:27 in the **b** *of* the annals of the kings of Israel? 6219
22:39 in the **b** *of* the annals of the kings of Israel? 6219
22:45 in the **b** *of* the annals of the kings of Judah? 6219
2Ki 1:18 in the **b** *of* the annals of the kings of Israel? 6219
8:23 in the **b** *of* the annals of the kings of Judah? 6219
10:34 in the **b** *of* the annals of the kings of Israel? 6219
12:19 in the **b** *of* the annals of the kings of Judah? 6219
13: 8 in the **b** *of* the annals of the kings of Israel? 6219
13:12 in the **b** *of* the annals of the kings of Israel? 6219
14: 6 in accordance with what is written in the **B** 6219
14:15 in the **b** *of* the annals of the kings of Israel? 6219
14:18 in the **b** *of* the annals of the kings of Judah? 6219
14:28 in the **b** *of* the annals of the kings of Israel? 6219
15: 6 in the **b** *of* the annals of the kings of Judah? 6219
15:11 in the **b** *of* the annals of the kings of Israel. 6219

2Ki 15:15 in the **b** *of* the annals of the kings of Israel. 6219
15:21 in the **b** *of* the annals of the kings of Israel? 6219
15:26 in the **b** *of* the annals of the kings of Israel. 6219
15:31 in the **b** *of* the annals of the kings of Israel? 6219
15:36 in the **b** *of* the annals of the kings of Judah? 6219
16:19 in the **b** *of* the annals of the kings of Judah? 6219
20:20 in the **b** *of* the annals of the kings of Judah? 6219
21:17 in the **b** *of* the annals of the kings of Judah? 6219
21:25 in the **b** *of* the annals of the kings of Judah? 6219
22: 8 "I have found the **B** *of* the Law in 6219
22:10 "Hilkiah the priest has given me a **b."** 6219
22:11 When the king heard the words of the **B** *of* 6219
22:13 for all Judah about what is written in this **b** 6219
22:13 not obeyed the words of this **b;** 6219
22:16 according to everything written in the **b** 6219
23: 2 in their hearing all the words of the **B** *of* 6219
23: 3 the words of the covenant written in this **b.** 6219
23:21 as it is written in this **B** *of* the Covenant." 6219
23:24 the requirements of the law written in the **b** 6219
23:28 the **b** *of* the annals of the kings of Judah? 6219
24: 5 the **b** *of* the annals of the kings of Judah? 6219
1Ch 9: 1 in the genealogies recorded in the **b** *of* 6219
27:24 and the number was not entered in the **b** *of* 6219
2Ch 16:11 are written in the **b** *of* the kings of Judah 6219
17: 9 with them the **B** *of* the Law of the LORD; 6219
20:34 which are recorded in the **b** *of* the kings 6219
24:27 in the annotations on the **b** *of* the kings. 6219
25: 4 in the **B** *of* Moses, 6219
25:26 not written in the **b** *of* the kings of Judah 6219
27: 7 are written in the **b** *of* the kings of Israel 6219
28:26 are written in the **b** *of* the kings of Judah 6219
32:32 the prophet Isaiah son of Amoz in the **b** *of* 6219
34:14 Hilkiah the priest found the **B** *of* the Law 6219
34:15 "I have found the **B** *of* the Law in 6219
34:16 the **b** to the king and reported to him: 6219
34:18 "Hilkiah the priest has given me a **b."** 6219
34:21 and Judah about what is written in this **b** 6219
34:21 with all that is written in this **b."** 6219
34:24 the **b** that has been read in the presence of 6219
34:30 in their hearing all the words of the **B** *of* 6219
34:31 the words of the covenant written in this **b.** 6219
35:12 as is written in the **B** *of* Moses. 6219
35:27 are written in the **b** *of* the kings of Israel 6219
36: 8 are written in the **b** *of* the kings of Israel 6219
Ezr 6:18 to what is written in the **B** *of* Moses. 10515
Ne 8: 1 They told Ezra the scribe to bring out the **B** 6219
8: 3 the people listened attentively to the **B** *of* 6219
8: 5 Ezra opened the **b.** 6219
8: 8 They read from the **B** of the Law of God, 6219
8:18 Ezra read from the **B** *of* the Law of God. 6219
9: 3 the **B** *of* the Law of the LORD their God 6219
12:23 of Eliashib were recorded in the **b** *of* 6219
13: 1 On that day the **B** *of* Moses was read aloud 6219
Est 2:23 All this was recorded in the **b** *of* the annals 6219
6: 1 so he ordered the **b** *of* the chronicles, 6219
10: 2 in the **b** *of* the annals of the kings of Media 6219
Ps 69:28 May they be blotted out of the **b** *of* life and 6219
139:16 in your **b** before one of them came to be. 6219
Jer 25:13 all that are written in this **b** and prophesied 6219
30: 2 in a **b** all the words I have spoken to you. 6219
Da 10:21 written in the **B** *of* Truth. 4181
12: 1 everyone whose name is found written in the **b—** 6219
Na 1: 1 **b** *of* the vision of Nahum the Elkoshite. 6219
Mk 12:26 have you not read in the **b** of Moses, *1047*
Lk 3: 4 As is written in the **b** of the words of Isaiah *1047*
20:42 David himself declares in the **B** of Psalms: *1047*
Jn 20:30 which are not recorded in this **b.** *1046*
Ac 1: 1 In my former **b,** Theophilus, *3364*
1:20 said Peter, "it is written in the **b** of Psalms, *1047*
7:42 This agrees with what is written in the **b** of *1047*
8:28 in his chariot reading the **b** of Isaiah *NIG*
Gal 3:10 to do everything written in the **B** of *1046*
Php 4: 3 whose names are in the **b** of life. *1047*
Rev 3: 5 I will never blot out his name from the **b** *1047*
13: 8 not been written in the **b** of life belonging *1046*
17: 8 not been written in the **b** of life from *1046*
20:12 Another **b** was opened, *1046*
20:12 which is the **b** of life. *NIG*
20:15 not found written in the **b** of life, *1047*
21:27 in the Lamb's **b** of life. *1046*
22: 7 the words of the prophecy *in* this **b."** *1046*
22: 9 and of all who keep the words *of* this **b.** *1046*
22:10 up the words of the prophecy *of* this **b,** *1046*
22:18 the words of the prophecy *of* this **b:** *1046*
22:18 to him the plagues described in this **b.** *1046*
22:19 if anyone takes words away from this **b** *1046*
22:19 which are described in this **b.** *1046*

BOOKS (5) [BOOK]

Ecc 12:12 Of making many **b** there is no end, 6219
Da 7:10 court was seated, and the **b** were opened. 10515
Jn 21:25 not have room for the **b** that would *1046*
Rev 20:12 before the throne, and **b** were opened. *1046*
20:12 to what they had done as recorded in the **b.** *1046*

BOOSTING (1)

Am 8: 5 the measure, **b** the price and cheating 1540

BOOT (1)

Isa 9: 5 Every warrior's **b** used in battle 6007

BOOTH (3) [BOOTHS]

Mt 9: 9 at the **tax collector's b.** *5468*
Mk 2:14 at the **tax collector's b.** *5468*
Lk 5:27 by the name of Levi sitting at his **tax b.** *5468*

BOOTHS (7) [BOOTH]

Lev 23:42 Live in **b** for seven days: 6109
23:42 All native-born Israelites are to live in **b** 6109
23:43 in **b** when I brought them out of Egypt. 6109
Ne 8:14 in **b** during the feast of the seventh month 6109
8:15 palms and shade trees, to make **b"—** 6109
8:16 and built themselves **b** on their own roofs, 6109
8:17 from exile built **b** and lived in them. 6109

BOOTY (2)

2Ch 14:14 since there was much **b** there. 1023
Jer 49:32 and their large herds will be **b.** 8965

BOOZ (KJV) See BOAZ

BOR ASHAN (1) [ASHAN]

1Sa 30:30 to those in Hormah, **B,** Athach 1016

BORDER (59) [BORDERED, BORDERING, BORDERS]

Ge 25:18 near the **b** *of* Egypt, 7156
49:13 his **b** will extend toward Sidon. 3752
Ex 16:35 they ate manna until they reached the **b** 7895
Nu 20:23 At Mount Hor, near the **b** *of* Edom, 1473
21:13 The Arnon is the **b** *of* Moab, 1473
21:15 that lead to the site of Ar and lie along the **b** 1473
21:24 because their **b** was fortified. 1473
22:36 at the Moabite town on the Arnon **b,** 1473
33:37 on the **b** *of* Edom. 7895
33:44 on the **b** *of* Moab. 1473
34: 3 of the Desert of Zin along the **b** *of* Edom. 3338
Dt 3:14 the whole region of Argob as far as the **b** *of* 1473
3:16 (the middle of the gorge being the **b)** 1473
3:16 which is the **b** *of* the Ammonites. 1473
3:17 Its western **b** was the Jordan in the Arabah, 1473
Jos 4:19 and camped at Gilgal on the eastern **b** 7895
12: 2 which is the **b** *of* the Ammonites. 1473
12: 5 the **b** *of* the people of Geshur and Maacah, 1473
12: 5 and half of Gilead to the **b** *of* Sihon king 1473
13:10 out to the **b** *of* the Ammonites. 1473
16: 8 the **b** went west to the Kanah Ravine 1473
22:11 the **b** *of* Canaan at Geliloth near the Jordan 4578
Jdg 7:22 as the **b** *of* Abel Meholah near Tabbath. 8557
11:18 for the Arnon was its **b.** 1473
1Sa 6:12 the Philistines followed them as far as the **b** 1473
10: 2 at Zelzah on the **b** *of* Benjamin. 1473
2Sa 13:23 at Baal Hazor near the **b** of Ephraim, NIH
1Ki 4:21 as far as the **b** *of* Egypt. 1473
2Ki 3:21 up and stationed on the **b.** 1473
2Ch 9:26 as far as the **b** *of* Egypt. 1473
26: 8 his fame spread as far as the **b** *of* Egypt, 995
Ps 78:54 Thus he brought them to the **b** 1473
Isa 15: 8 Their outcry echoes along the **b** *of* Moab; 1473
19:19 and a monument to the LORD at its **b.** 1473
Eze 29:10 as far as the **b** *of* Cush. 1473
45: 7 the western to the eastern **b** parallel to one 1473
47:16 Berothah and Sibraim (which lies on the **b** 1473
47:16 which is on the **b** *of* Hauran. 1473
47:17 along the northern **b** *of* Damascus, 1473
47:17 with the **b** *of* Hamath to the north. 1473
48: 1 and the northern **b** *of* Damascus next 1473
48: 1 of its **b** *from* the east side to the west side. 6991
48: 2 it will **b** the territory of Dan from east 6584
48: 3 it will **b** the territory of Asher from east 6584
48: 4 it will **b** the territory of Naphtali from east 6584
48: 5 it will **b** the territory of Manasseh from east 6584
48: 6 it will **b** the territory of Ephraim from east 6584
48: 7 it will **b** the territory of Reuben from east 6584
48:21 cubits of the sacred portion to the eastern **b,** 1473
48:21 cubits to the western **b.** 1473
48:22 the **b** *of* Judah and the border of Benjamin. 1473
48:22 the border of Judah and the **b** *of* Benjamin. 1473
48:24 it will **b** the territory of Benjamin from east 6584
48:25 it will **b** the territory of Simeon from east 6584
48:26 it will **b** the territory of Issachar from east 6584
48:27 it will **b** the territory of Zebulun from east 6584
Ob 1: 7 All your allies will force you to the **b;** 1473
Lk 17:11 Jesus traveled along the **b** between Samaria *NIG*
Ac 16: 7 When they came to the **b** of Mysia, *NIG*

BORDERED (1) [BORDER]

Jos 17:10 of Manasseh reached the sea and **b** Asher 7003

BORDERING (4) [BORDER]

Eze 45: 7 " 'The prince will have the land **b each side** 2256+2296+2296+4946+4946[S]
48: 8 **"B** the territory of Judah from east 6584
48:12 **b** the territory of the Levites. 448
48:18 **b** *on* the sacred portion and running 4200+6645

BORDERLAND (1) [LAND]

1Sa 13:18 and the third toward the **b** overlooking 1473

BORDERS (14) [BORDER]

Ge 10:19 and the **b** *of* Canaan reached from Sidon 1473
23:17 and all the trees within the **b** of the field— 1473
Ex 13: 7 be seen anywhere within your **b.** 1473
23:31 "I will establish your **b** from the Red Sea to 1473
1Ch 7:29 Along the **b** *of* Manasseh were Beth Shan, 3338
Ps 147:14 He grants peace to your **b** and satisfies you 1473
Isa 26:15 you have extended all the **b** *of* the land. 7898
60:18 nor ruin or destruction within your **b,** 1473
Eze 11:10 and I will execute judgment on you at the **b** 1473
11:11 I will execute judgment on you at the **b** 1473
Am 1:13 of Gilead in order to extend his **b,** 1473
Mic 5: 6 and marches into our **b.** 1473
Zec 9: 2 *which* **b** on it, and upon Tyre and Sidon, 1487
Mal 1: 5 even beyond **the b** *of* Israel!' 1473

BORE (62) [BEAR]

Ge 16:15 So Hagar **b** Abram a son, 3528
16:16 when Hagar **b** him Ishmael. 3528
21: 2 and **b** a son to Abraham in his old age, 3528
21: 3 the name Isaac to the son Sarah **b** him. 3528
22:23 Milcah **b** these eight sons 3528
24:24 the son that Milcah **b** to Nahor." 3528
24:47 whom Milcah **b** to him.' 3528
25: 2 *She* **b** him Zimran, Jokshan, Medan, 3528
25:12 Hagar the Egyptian, **b** to Abraham. 3528
30: 5 and she became pregnant and **b** him a son. 3528
30: 7 and **b** Jacob a second son. 3528
30:10 Leah's servant Zilpah **b** Jacob a son. 3528
30:12 Leah's servant Zilpah **b** Jacob a second son. 3528
30:17 and she became pregnant and **b** Jacob 3528
30:19 Leah conceived again and **b** Jacob 3528
30:39 And they **b young** that were streaked 3528
31: 8 then all the flocks **b** streaked young. 3528
31:39 I **b the loss** myself. 2627
36: 4 Adah **b** Eliphaz to Esau, 3528
36: 4 to Esau, Basemath **b** Reuel, 3528
36: 5 and Oholibamah **b** Jeush, 3528
36:12 Timna, *who* **b** him Amalek. 3528
36:14 Zibeon, whom *she* **b** to Esau: 3528
44:27 'You know that my wife **b** me two sons. 3528
46:15 the sons Leah **b** to Jacob in Paddan Aram, 3528
Ex 6:20 *who* **b** him Aaron and Moses. 3528
6:23 and *she* **b** him Nadab and Abihu, 3528
6:25 and *she* **b** him Phinehas. 3528
Nu 26:59 To Amram *she* **b** Aaron, 3528
Jdg 8:31 who lived in Shechem, also **b** him a son, 3528
11: 2 Gilead's wife also **b** him sons, 3528
Ru 4:12 whom Tamar **b** to Judah." 3528
1Sa 20:30 and to the shame of the **mother** *who b* you? AIT
2Sa 11:27 and she became his wife and **b** him a son. 3528
1Ki 11:20 of Tahpenes **b** him a son named Genubath, 3528
14:28 the guards **b** the shields, 5951
1Ch 2: 4 **b** him Perez and Zerah. 3528
2:19 Caleb married Ephrath, *who* **b** him Hur. 3528
2:21 and *she* **b** him Segub. 3528
2:24 the wife of Hezron **b** him Ashhur the father 3528
2:29 *who* **b** him Ahban and Molid. 3528
2:35 and *she* **b** him Attai. 3528
4: 6 Naarah **b** him Ahuzzam, Hepher, 3528
2Ch 11:19 *She* **b** him sons: 3528
11:20 *who* **b** him Abijah, Attai, 3528
Pr 17:25 and bitterness to the *one who* **b** him. 3528
SS 6: 9 the favorite of the *one who* **b** her. 3528
Isa 49:21 'Who **b** me these? 3528
51:18 the sons *she* **b** there was none to guide her; 3528
53:12 For he **b** the sin of many, 5951
54: 1 O barren woman, *you who* never **b a child;** 3528
Jer 20:14 the day my mother **b** me not be blessed! 3528
31:19 I was ashamed and humiliated because *I* **b** 5951
Eze 16:20 and daughters whom *you* **b** to me 3528
23:37 whom *they* **b** to me, as food for them. 3528
Hos 1: 3 and she conceived and **b** him a son. 3528
Lk 23:29 the wombs that never **b** and the breasts *1164*
Ro 7: 5 so that *we* **b fruit** for death. *2844*
9:22 **b** with great patience the objects *5770*
Heb 13:13 bearing the disgrace he **b.** *NIG*
1Pe 2:24 He himself **b** our sins in his body on *429*
Rev 17: 6 the blood *of* those who **b testimony** *3459*

BORED (1) [BEAR]

2Ki 12: 9 Jehoiada the priest took a chest and **b** a hole 5918

BORN (144) [BEAR]

Ge 4:18 To Enoch **was b** Irad, 3528
5: 4 After Seth *was* **b,** 3528
5:30 After Noah *was* **b,** 3528
6: 1 and daughters **were b** to them, 3528
10:21 *Sons* **were** also **b** to Shem, 3528
10:25 Two sons **were b** to Eber: 3528
14:14 the 318 trained men **b** *in* his household 3535
17:12 including **those b** *in* your household 3535
17:13 Whether **b** *in* your household or bought 3535
17:17 a **son be b** to a man a hundred years old? 3528
17:23 and all **those b** *in* his household or bought 3535
17:27 including **those b** *in* his household 3535
21: 5 when his son Isaac **was b** to him. 3528
35:26 who **were b** to him in Paddan Aram. 3528
36: 5 who **were b** to him in Canaan. 3528
37: 3 he had been **b** to him *in* his old age; 1201
41:50 two sons **were b** to Joseph 3528
44:20 a young **son** *b* to him *in* his old age. AIT
46:18 These were the children **b** to Jacob 3528
46:20 Manasseh and Ephraim **were b** to Joseph 3528
46:22 These were the sons of Rachel who **were b** 3528
46:25 These were the sons **b** to Jacob by Bilhah, 3528
46:27 the two sons who *had* **been b** to Joseph 3528
48: 5 your two sons **b** to you in Egypt 3528
48: 6 Any children **b** *to* you after them will 3528
Ex 1:22 "Every boy that is **b** you must throw into 3533

Ex 12:48 then he may take part like *one* **b** *in* 275
23:12 **slave b** in your **household,** 563+1201
Lev 18: 9 **b in the same home** 1074+4580
18:11 **b** *to* your father; she is your sister. 4580
22:11 or if a slave is **b** *in* his household, 3535
22:27 a lamb or a goat **is b,** 3528
25:45 among you and members of their clans **b** 3528
Nu 26:59 who *was* **b** to the Levites in Egypt. 3528
Dt 23: 2 **one b of a forbidden marriage** 4927
23: 8 The third generation of children **b** 3528
Jos 5: 5 but all the people **b** in the desert during 3533
Jdg 13: 8 how to bring up the boy who *is to* **be b."** 3528
18:29 who **was b** to Israel— 3528
2Sa 3: 2 Sons **were b** to David in Hebron: 3528
3: 5 These **were b** to David in Hebron. 3528
5:13 and more sons and daughters **were b** to him. 3528
5:14 the names of the **children b** to him there: 3533
12:14 the son **b** to you will die." 3533
14:27 and a daughter **were b** to Absalom. 3528
1Ki 1: 6 He was also very handsome and *was* **b** next 3528
3:18 The third day after my **child was b,** 3528
13: 2 'A son named Josiah *will* **be b** to the house 3528
2Ki 20:18 that *will be* **b** *to you,* will be taken away, 3528
1Ch 1:19 Two sons **were b** to Eber: 3528
1:32 The sons **b** *to* Keturah, 3528
2: 3 These three **were b** to him by 3528
2: 9 The sons **b** to Hezron were: 3528
3: 1 These were the sons of David **b** to him 3528
3: 4 These six **were b** to David in Hebron, 3528
3: 5 and these were *the children* **b** to him there: 3528
8: 8 Sons *were* **b** *to* Shaharaim in Moab 3528
14: 4 the names of the **children b** to him there: 3528
Job 3: 3 and the night it was said, 'A boy **is b!'** 2225
5: 7 Yet man **is b** to trouble as surely 3528
8: 9 for we were **b** only yesterday NIH
11:12 a wild donkey's colt *can* **be b** a man. 3528
14: 1 "Man **b** *of* woman is of few days and full 3528
15: 7 *"Are you* the first man ever **b?** 3528
15:14 that he could be pure, or *one* **b** *of* woman, 3528
25: 4 How can *one* **b** *of* woman be pure? 3528
38:21 Surely you know, for *you* **were** already **b!** 3528
Ps 78: 6 even the children *yet to* **be b,** 3528
87: 4 and will say, 'This one **was b** in Zion.'" 3528
87: 5 "This one and that one **were b** in her, 3528
87: 6 "This one **was b** in Zion." 3528
90: 2 the mountains **were b** or you brought forth 3528
127: 4 of a warrior are **sons** *b in* one's youth. AIT
Pr 17:17 and a brother **is b** for adversity. 3528
Ecc 2: 7 and had other slaves *who* were **b** 1201
3: 2 a time to *be* **b** and a time to die, 3528
4:14 or *he may have* **been b** in poverty 3528
Isa 9: 6 For to us a child **is b,** to us a son is given, 3528
39: 7 your own flesh and blood who *will be* **b** 3528
49: 1 Before I was **b** the LORD called me; 1061
49:20 The **children** *b during* your bereavement AIT
66: 8 *Can a* country **be b** in a day or a nation 2655
Jer 1: 5 before *you were* **b** I set you apart; 3655+4946+8167
16: 3 about the sons and daughters **b** in this land 3533
20:14 Cursed be the day *I was* **b!** 3528
20:15 saying, "A child **is b** to you—a son!" 3528
22:26 where neither *of you* **was b,** 3528
Eze 16: 4 the day you **were b** your cord was not cut, 3528
16: 5 on the day you **were b** you were despised. 3528
Hos 2: 3 as bare as on the day she **was b;** 3528
Zec 13: 3 his father and mother, to whom he *was* **b,** 3528
Mt 1:16 the husband of Mary, of whom *was* **b** Jesus, *1164*
2: 1 *After* Jesus *was* **b** in Bethlehem in Judea, *1164*
2: 2 is the one who *has been* **b** king of the Jews? *5503*
2: 4 where the Christ *was to be* **b.** *1164*
11:11 Among *those* **b** of women there has *1168*
19:12 For some are eunuchs because *they were* **b** *1164*
26:24 be better for him if he *had* not **been b."** *1164*
Mk 7:26 **b** in Syrian Phoenicia. *1169*
14:21 be better for him if he *had* not **been b."** *1164*
Lk 1:35 the holy one *to be* **b** will be called the Son *1164*
2: 6 the time came for the **baby to be b,** *5503*
2:11 town of David a Savior *has been* **b to** you; *5503*
7:28 I tell you, among *those* **b** *1168*
Jn 1:13 children **b** not of natural descent, *1164*
1:13 but **b of** God. *NIG*
3: 3 the kingdom of God unless he *is* **b** again." *1164*
3: 4 "How can a man *be* **b** when he is old?" *1164*
3: 4 into his mother's womb *to be* **b!"** *1164*
3: 5 the kingdom of God unless he *is* **b** of water *1164*
3: 7 'You must *be* **b** again.' *1164*
3: 8 So it is with everyone **b** of the Spirit." *1164*
8:58 Jesus answered, "before Abraham **was b,** *1181*
9: 2 that *he was* **b** blind?" *1164*
9:19 "Is this the one you say *was* **b** blind? *1164*
9:20 "and we know *he was* **b** blind. *1164*
9:32 of opening the eyes *of a man* **b** blind. *1164*
16:21 when her baby *is* **b** she forgets the anguish *1164*
16:21 of her joy that a child *is* **b** into the world. *1164*
18:37 In fact, for this reason *I was* **b,** *1164*
Ac 7:20 "At that time Moses *was* **b,** *1164*
22: 3 **b** in Tarsus of Cilicia, *1164*
22:28 "But I *was* **b** a citizen," Paul replied. *1164*
Ro 9:11 the twins *were* **b** or had done anything good *1164*
1Co 11:12 so also man is **b** of woman. *NIG*
15: 8 as to one **abnormally b.** *1765*
Gal 4: 4 God sent his Son, **b** of a woman, *1181*
4: 4 born of a woman, **b** under law, *1181*
4:23 the slave woman *was* **b** in the ordinary way; *1164*
4:23 by the free woman was **b** as the result of *NIG*
4:29 the son **b** in the ordinary way persecuted *1164*
4:29 in the ordinary way persecuted the son **b** by *NIG*
Heb 11:23 for three months *after he was* **b,** *1164*
1Pe 1:23 *For you have been* **b again,** *335*
2Pe 2:12 **b** only to be caught and destroyed, *1164*
1Jn 2:29 everyone who does what is right *has been* **b** *1164*
3: 9 No one who *is* **b** of God will continue *1164*
3: 9 because *he has been* **b** of God. *1164*
4: 7 Everyone who loves *has been* **b** of God *1164*
5: 1 that Jesus is the Christ *is* **b** of God, *1164*
5: 4 everyone **b** of God overcomes the world. *1164*
5:18 that anyone **b** of God does not continue *1164*
5:18 the one who *was* **b** of God keeps him safe, *1164*
Rev 12: 4 the moment *it was* **b.** *5503*

BORNE (21) [BEAR]

Ge 16: 1 Sarai, Abram's wife, *had* **b** him no **children.** 3528
16:15 the name Ishmael to the son she *had* **b.** 3528
21: 7 Yet *I have* **b** him a son in his old age." 3528
21: 9 the son whom Hagar the Egyptian *had* **b** 3528
22:20 she *has* **b** sons to your brother Nahor: 3528
24:36 My master's wife Sarah *has* **b** him a son 3528
29:34 because *I have* **b** him three sons." 3528
30:20 because *I have* **b** him six sons." 3528
31:43 or about the children they *have* **b?** 3528
34: 1 Dinah, the daughter Leah *had* **b** to Jacob, 3528
1Sa 2: 5 She who was barren *has* **b** seven **children,** 3528
2Sa 12:15 the child that Uriah's wife *had* **b** to David, 3528
21: 8 whom *she had* **b** to Saul, 3528
21: 8 whom *she had* **b** to Adriel son of Barzillai 3528
1Ki 3:21 I saw that it wasn't the son *I had* **b."** 3528
Ps 18:42 I beat them as fine as dust **b on** the wind; 6584+7156
Isa 46: 1 their idols are **b by** beasts of burden. 4200
49:15 on the child she has **b?** 1061
Hag 2:19 and the olive tree *have* not **b fruit.** 5951
Mt 20:12 to us who *have* **b** the burden of the work *1002*
1Co 15:49 just as *we have* **b** the likeness of the earthly man, *5841*

BORROW (5) [BORROWED, BORROWER, BORROWS]

Dt 15: 6 to many nations but *will* **b** from none. 6292
28:12 You will lend to many nations but *will* **b** 4278
Ne 5: 4 *to* **b** money to pay the king's tax 4278
Ps 37:21 The wicked **b** and do not repay, 4278
Mt 5:42 not turn away from the one who wants *to* **b** *1247*

BORROWED (2) [BORROW]

2Ki 6: 5 "Oh, my lord," he cried out, "it **was b!"** 8626
Jer 15:10 I have neither lent nor **b,** 928+5957

BORROWER (3) [BORROW]

Ex 22:15 the **b** will not have to pay NIH
Pr 22: 7 and the **b** is servant to the lender. 4278
Isa 24: 2 for seller as for buyer, for **b** as for lender, 4278

BORROWS (1) [BORROW]

Ex 22:14 "If a man **b** an animal from his neighbor 8626

BOSCATH (KJV) See BOZKATH

BOSOM (3) [BOSOMS]

Pr 5:20 Why embrace the **b** *of* another man's wife? 2668
Eze 23: 8 caressed her virgin **b** 1843
23:21 when in Egypt your **b** was caressed 1843

BOSOMS (1) [BOSOM]

Eze 23: 3 and their virgin **b** caressed. 1843

BOSOR (KJV) See BEOR

BOTH (289)

Ge 2:25 The man and his wife were **b** naked, 9109
3: 7 Then the eyes of **b** *of* them were opened, 9109
6:13 I am surely going to destroy **b** them **and** 907
11:29 Abram and Nahor **b** married. 2157[S]
11:29 the father of **b** Milcah **and** Iscah. 2256
17:26 Abraham and his son Ishmael **were** *b* **circumcised** on that same day. AIT
19: 4 **b** young and old—surrounded the house. 2256
19:36 So **b** *of* Lot's daughters became pregnant 9109
23:17 **b** the field **and** the cave in it, 2256
27:45 Why should I lose **b** *of* you in one day?" 9109
36: 7 not support **them** *b* because AIT
39: 5 **b** in the house **and** in the field. 2256
40: 8 *"We b* **had dreams,"** they answered, AIT
42:37 "You may put **b** *of* my sons to death if I do 9109
47:13 **b** Egypt and Canaan wasted away because 2256
48:13 And Joseph took **b** *of* them, 9109
Ex 4:15 I will help **b of you** speak 2084+2256+3870
9:25 **b** men **and** animals; 2256
12:12 **b** men **and** animals— 2256
12:22 on the top and on **b sides** *of* the doorframe. 9109
12:38 **b** flocks **and** herds. 2256
13:15 **b** man **and** animal. 2256
21:35 to sell the live one and divide **b** the money 2256
22: 9 **b** *parties* are to bring their cases before 9109
25:11 Overlay it with pure gold, **b** inside **and** out, 2256
26:13 cubit longer **on b sides;** 2256+2296+2296+4946[S]
26:24 **b** shall be like that. 9109
Ex 29:13 and **b** kidneys with the fat on them, 9109
29:22 **b** kidneys with the fat on them, 9109
31:10 **b** the sacred garments for Aaron the priest 2256
32:15 They were inscribed on **b** sides, 9109
35:19 **b** the sacred garments for Aaron the priest **and** the garments 2256
35:34 And he has given **b** him **and** Oholiab son 2256
36:29 **b** were made alike. 9109
37: 2 **b** inside **and** out, 2256
39:41 **b** the sacred garments for Aaron the priest **and** the garments 2256
Lev 3: 4 **b** kidneys with the fat on them near 9109
3:10 **b** kidneys with the fat on them near 9109
3:15 **b** kidneys with the fat on them near 9109
4: 9 **b** kidneys with the fat on them near 9109
7: 4 **b** kidneys with the fat on them near 9109
7: 7 **b** the sin offering **and** the guilt offering: 3869
8:16 and **b** kidneys and their fat, 9109
8:25 **b** kidneys and their fat and the right thigh. 9109
9: 2 *b* **without defect,** and present them before AIT
9: 3 *b* a year **old** and without defect— AIT
14:11 **b** the one to be cleansed **and** 2256
15:18 **b** *must* **bathe** with water, AIT
16:21 to lay **b** hands on the head of the live goat 9109
18:17 with **b** a woman **and** her daughter. 2256
20: 5 and will cut off from their people **b** him **and** 2256
20:10 **b** the adulterer **and** the adulteress must 2256
20:11 **B** the man and the woman must be put 9109
20:12 **b** *of* them must be put to death. 9109
20:13 **b** *of* them have done what is detestable. 9109
20:14 a man marries **b** a woman **and** her mother, 2256
20:14 **B** he **and** they must be burned in the fire, 2256
20:16 kill **b** the woman **and** the animal. 2256
20:18 **B** *of* them must be cut off 9109
20:19 *b of* **you** would be held responsible. AIT
27:10 **b** it and the substitute become holy. 2256
27:33 **b** the animal and its substitute become holy 2256
Nu 6:19 **b** made without yeast. NIH
7:13 **b** according to the sanctuary shekel, NIH
7:19 **b** according to the sanctuary shekel, NIH
7:25 **b** according to the sanctuary shekel, NIH
7:31 **b** according to the sanctuary shekel, NIH
7:37 **b** according to the sanctuary shekel, NIH
7:43 **b** according to the sanctuary shekel, NIH
7:49 **b** according to the sanctuary shekel, NIH
7:55 **b** according to the sanctuary shekel, NIH
7:61 **b** according to the sanctuary shekel, NIH
7:67 **b** according to the sanctuary shekel, NIH
7:73 **b** according to the sanctuary shekel, NIH
7:79 **b** according to the sanctuary shekel, NIH
10: 3 When **b** are sounded, 2177[S]
12: 5 When **b** *of* them stepped forward, 9109
15:16 and regulations will apply **b** to you **and** to 2256
18: 3 or **b** they and you will die. 1685
18:15 **b** man **and** animal, 2256
18:19 the LORD for **b** you **and** your offspring." 2256
19:10 **b** for the Israelites **and** 2256
20:24 because *b of you* **rebelled** AIT
22:24 walls **on b sides.** 2256+2296+2296+4946+4946[S]
25: 8 He drove the spear through **b** *of* them— 9109
27:14 *b of you* **disobeyed** my command AIT
Dt 1:17 **b** small *and* great **alike.** 3869
11: 3 **b** to Pharaoh king of Egypt **and** 2256
11:14 **b** autumn **and** spring rains, 2256
12:15 **B** the ceremonially unclean **and** 2256
12:22 **B** the ceremonially unclean and 3481
12:27 **b** the meat **and** the blood. 2256
13:15 **b** its people and its livestock. 2256
15:22 **B** the ceremonially unclean and 3481
21:15 **b** bear him sons but 170+2021+2021+2256+8533[S]
22:22 **b** the man who slept with her and 9109
22:24 you shall take **b** *of* them to the gate of 9109
23:18 the LORD your God detests them **b.** 9109
28:66 filled with dread **b** night **and** day, 2256
32:51 *b of you* **broke faith** AIT
Jos 8:22 with Israelites **on b sides.** 2256+2296+2296+4946+4946[S]
8:33 were standing **on b sides** of the ark 2256+2296+2296+4946+4946[S]
17:16 **b** those in Beth Shan and its settlements NIH
Jdg 9: 9 by which **b** gods **and** men are honored, 2256
9:13 which cheers **b** gods **and** men, 2256
19:19 We have **b** straw and fodder 1685
Ru 1: 5 **b** Mahlon and Kilion also died, 9109
1Sa 2:34 they will **b** die on the same day. 9109
5: 9 **b** young and old, 4946
6: 4 the same plague has struck **b** you **and** 2256
12:14 and if **b** you and the king who reigns 1685
12:25 **b** you and your king will be swept away." 1685
14:11 So **b** *of* them showed themselves to 9109
17:36 Your servant has killed **b** the lion and 1685
25:43 and they **b** were his wives. 9109
28:19 The LORD will hand over **b** Israel and you 1685
30: 2 **b** young and old. 4946
2Sa 4: 4 of Saul had a son who was lame in *b* **feet.** AIT
6:19 **b** men and women. 4946
9: 3 he is crippled in *b* **feet."** AIT
9:13 and he was crippled in **b** feet. 9109
14:16 of the man who is trying to cut off **b** me 3480
16:23 how **b** David and Absalom regarded all 1685
1Ki 2:32 with the sword. **B** of them— NIH
3:13 **b** riches and honor— 1685
6:29 in **b** the inner **and** outer rooms, 2256
6:30 of **b** the inner **and** outer rooms 2256
7:20 On the capitals of **b** pillars, 9109
10:19 **On b sides** of the seat were armrests, 2256+2296+2296+4946+4946[S]

1Ki 13:24 **with b** the donkey **and** the lion standing 2256
21:10 that he has cursed **b** God **and** the king. 2256
21:13 "Naboth has cursed **b** God **and** the king." 2256
2Ki 14:28 for Israel **b** Damascus **and** Hamath, 2256
21: 5 In **b** courts of the temple of the LORD, 9109
1Ch 24: 5 the descendants of **b** Eleazar **and** Ithamar. 2256
2Ch 9:18 **On b sides** of the seat were armrests, 2256+2296+2296+4946+4946S
13:14 that they were being attacked at **b** front **and** 2256
30: 4 **b** to the king **and** 2256
33: 5 In **b** courts of the temple of the LORD, 9109
36:18 **b** large **and** small, 2256
Ezr 3: 3 **b** the morning **and** evening sacrifices. 2256
Ne 11: 4 while other people from **b** Judah **and** 2256
Job 9:22 'He destroys **b** the blameless **and** 2256
9:33 to lay his hand upon us **b**, 9109
12:16 **b** deceived **and** deceiver are his. 2256
21:26 and worms cover **them** *b*. AIT
31:15 the same one form **us** *b* within our mothers? AIT
Ps 36: 6 O LORD, you preserve **b** man **and** beast. 2256
36: 7 **B** high **and** low among men find refuge in 2256
49: 2 **b** low and high, rich and poor alike: 1685
74:17 you made **b** summer **and** winter. 2256
76: 6 **b** horse and chariot lie still. 2256
104:25 living things **b** large **and** small. 6640
113: 2 **b** now **and** forevermore. 2256
115:14 **b** you **and** your children. 2256
115:18 **b** now **and** forevermore. 2256
121: 8 over your coming and going **b** now **and** 2256
125: 2 the LORD surrounds his people **b** now **and** 2256
131: 3 put your hope in the LORD **b** now **and** 2256
Pr 17:15 the LORD detests them **b**. 9109
20:10 the LORD detests them **b**. 9109
20:12 the LORD has made them **b**. 9109
22:16 **b** come to poverty. 421
27: 3 but provocation by a fool is heavier than **b**. 9109
29:13 The LORD gives sight to the eyes of **b**. 9109
Ecc 2:14 that the same fate overtakes them **b**. 3972
2:16 in days to come **b** will be forgotten. 3972
3:17 to judgment **b** the righteous **and** the wicked, 2256
3:19 the same fate awaits **them** *b*: AIT
4: 3 better than **b** is he who has not yet been, 9109
5: 8 and over **them** *b* are others higher still. AIT
7:15 of mine I have seen **b** of these: 3972
11: 6 or whether **b** will do equally well. 9109
SS 7:13 **b** new **and** old, 1685
Isa 1:28 But rebels and sinners will **b** be broken, 3481
1:31 **b** will burn together, 9109
3: 1 from Jerusalem and Judah **b** supply **and** 2256
8:14 but for **b** houses of Israel he will be a stone 9109
9:14 from Israel **b** head **and** tail, 2256
9:14 **b** palm branch **and** reed in a single day; 2256
31: 3 **b** will perish together. 3972
47: 9 **B** *of* these will overtake you in a moment, 9109
65: 7 **b** your sins and the sins of your fathers," 3481
Jer 3:25 **b** we **and** our fathers; 2256
6:11 **b** husband and wife will be caught in it, 1685
11:10 **B** the house of Israel **and** 2256
14:18 **B** prophet and priest have gone to 1685
16: 6 "**B** high and low will die in this land. 2256
21: 6 **b** men and animals— 2256
22:26 and there *you b will* **die.** AIT
23:11 "**B** prophet and priest are godless; 1685
27:15 **b** you **and** the prophets who prophesy 2256
32:14 Take these documents, **b** the sealed **and** 2256
32:20 **b** in Israel and among all mankind, 2256
34: 9 **b** male **and** female; 2256
36:29 and destroy this land and cut off **b** men **and** 2256
44:20 **b** men **and** women, 2256
46: 3 **b** large **and** small, and march out for battle! 2256
46:12 **b** will fall down together." 9109
50: 3 **b** men and animals will flee away. 4946
La 2: 6 in his fierce anger he has spurned **b** king **and** priest. 2256
3:38 that **b** calamities **and** good things come? 2256
Eze 2:10 **On b sides** of it were written words of lament 294+2256+7156
7:13 as long as *b of* **them** live, AIT
15: 4 on the fire as fuel and the fire burns **b** ends 9109
16:61 **b** those who are older than you **and** 448
18: 4 **b** *alike* belong to me. 2179
20:47 **b** green **and** dry. 2256
21: 3 from you **b** the righteous **and** the wicked. 2256
21:19 **b** starting from the same country. 9109
23:13 **b** *of* them went the same way. 9109
30:22 I will break *b* his **arms,** AIT
32:18 to the earth below **b** her **and** the daughters 2256
41:23 **B** the outer sanctuary **and** 2256
42: 3 **B** in the section twenty cubits from the inner court **and** 2256
43:23 and a ram from the flock, **b** without defect. NIH
43:25 and a ram from the flock, *b* **without defect.** AIT
45:11 to be the standard measure for **b**. 2257S
47:12 Fruit trees of all kinds will grow **on b** banks 2256+2296+2296+4946+4946
48:21 "What remains **on b sides** of the area formed by 2256+2296+2296+4946+4946S
48:21 **B** these areas running the length of NIH
Da 9: 7 of Jerusalem and all Israel, **b** near **and** far, 2256
11:22 **b** it and a prince of the covenant will 2256
Hos 4: 9 I will punish *b of* **them** for their ways AIT
Joel 2:23 **b** autumn **and** spring rains, as before. 2256
2:29 Even on my servants, **b** men **and** women, 2256
Mic 7: 3 *B* **hands** are skilled in doing evil; AIT
Zep 1: 3 "I will sweep away **b** men **and** animals; 2256
Zec 5: 4 **b** its timbers and its stones.' " 2256
13: 2 "I will remove **b** the prophets and the spirit 1685

Mt 6:24 You cannot serve **b** God and Money. *NIG*
9:17 and **b** are preserved." *317*
10:28 be afraid of the One who can destroy **b** soul *2779*
12:22 so that he could **b** talk and see. *NIG*
13:30 Let **b** grow together until the harvest. *317*
15:14 **b** will fall into a pit." *317*
22:10 **b** good and bad, *5445*
25: 9 'there may not be enough for **b** us and you. *NIG*
Mk 2:22 **and b** the wine and the wineskins will *2779*
Lk 1: 6 **B** of them were upright in the sight of God, *317*
1: 7 and they were **b** well along in years. *317*
5: 7 and filled **b** boats so full that they began *317*
6:39 Will they not **b** fall into a pit? *317*
7:42 so he canceled the debts of **b**. *317*
14: 9 the host who invited **b of you** will come *899+2779+5148*
16:13 You cannot serve **b** God and Money." *NIG*
22:66 **b** the chief priests and teachers of the law, *5445*
23:32 Two other men, **b** criminals, *NIG*
Jn 2:15 **b** sheep and cattle; *5445*
11:48 and take away **b** our place and our nation." *2779*
15:24 yet they have hated **b** me and my Father. *2779*
20: 4 **B** were running, but the other disciple outran Peter *1545+3836S*
Ac 2:11 (**b** Jews and converts to Judaism); *5445*
2:18 Even on my servants, **b** men and women, *NIG*
2:36 whom you crucified, **b** Lord and Christ." *2779*
8:10 **b** high and low, *608*
8:12 they were baptized, **b** men and women. *5445*
8:38 Then **b** Philip and the eunuch went down *317*
20:21 to **b** Jews and Greeks that they must turn *5445*
22: 4 arresting **b** men and women *5445*
24:15 be a resurrection of **b** the righteous and *5445*
27:12 facing **b** southwest and northwest. *NIG*
Ro 1:14 I am obligated **b** to Greeks and non-Greeks, *5445*
1:14 **b** to the wise and the foolish. *5445*
14: 9 that he might be the Lord of **b** the dead and *2779*
1Co 1:24 **b** Jews and Greeks, *5445*
6:13 but God will destroy them **b**. *2779+4047*
7:34 be devoted to the Lord in **b** body and spirit. *2779*
10:21 you cannot have a part in **b** the Lord's table *NIG*
10:28 **b** for the sake of the man who told you and *NIG*
2Co 1:21 Now it is God who makes **b** us *NIG*
Eph 2:16 and in this one body to reconcile **b** of them *317*
2:18 through him we **b** have access to the Father *317*
6: 9 that he who is **b** their Master and yours is *2779*
1Ti 4: 8 holding promise for **b** the present life and *NIG*
4:16 you will save **b** yourself and your hearers. *2779*
Tit 1:15 In fact, **b** their minds and consciences *2779*
Phm 1:11 he has become useful **b** to you and to me. *2779*
1:16 **b** as a man and as a brother in the Lord. *2779*
Heb 2:11 **B** the one who makes men holy *5445*
8: 3 Every high priest is appointed to offer **b** *5445*
9:21 he sprinkled with the blood **b** the tabernacle *2779*
Jas 3:11 Can **b** fresh water and salt water flow from *NIG*
2Pe 3: 1 I have written **b of them** as reminders *1877+4005*
3:18 To him be glory **b** now and forever! *2779*
2Jn 1: 9 the teaching has **b** the Father and the Son. *2779*
Rev 5: 1 on the throne a scroll with writing **on b sides** *2277+2779+3957*
11:18 **b** small and great— *NIG*
19: 5 you who fear him, **b** small and great!" *NIG*

BOTHER (4) [BOTHERING]

2Sa 14:10 and *he will* not **b** you again." 5595
Mk 5:35 "Why **b** the teacher any more?" *5035*
Lk 8:49 "Don't **b** the teacher any more." *5035*
11: 7 the one inside answers, 'Don't **b** me. *3160+4218*

BOTHERING (3) [BOTHER]

Mt 26:10 "Why *are you* **b** this woman? *3160+4218*
Mk 14: 6 "Why *are you* **b** her? *3160+4218*
Lk 18: 5 yet because this widow *keeps* **b** me, *3160+4218*

BOTTLED-UP (1)

Job 32:19 inside I am like **b** wine, 4202+7337

BOTTLES (1)

Isa 3:20 the perfume **b** and charms, 1074

BOTTOM (9)

Ex 26:24 be double from the **b** all the way to the top, 4752
28:27 the **b** *of* the shoulder pieces 4200+4752+4946
36:29 from the **b** all the way to the top and fitted 4752
39:20 the **b** *of* the shoulder pieces 4200+4752+4946
Dt 28:13 never at the **b**. 4752
Am 9: 3 Though they hide from me at the **b** *of* 7977
Mt 27:51 of the temple was torn in two from top to **b**. *3004*
Mk 15:38 of the temple was torn in two from top to **b**. *3004*
Jn 19:23 woven in one piece from top **to b**. *1328+3910*

BOTTOMLESS (KJV) See ABYSS

BOUGHS (10)

Ps 80:11 It sent out its **b** to the Sea, 7908
118:27 With **b** in hand, join the festal procession 6291
Isa 10:33 will lop off the **b** with great power. 6998
17: 6 four or five on the fruitful **b**," 6187
Eze 17: 6 and put out **leafy b**. 6997
31: 5 its **b** increased and its branches grew long, 6250
31: 6 All the birds of the air nested in its **b**, 6190
31: 7 with its spreading **b**, 1936
31: 8 nor could the pine trees equal its **b**, 6190
31:12 Its **b** fell on the mountains and in all 1936

BOUGHT (47) [BUY]

Ge 17:12 including those born in your household or **b** 5239
17:13 in your household or **b** *with* your money, 5239
17:23 and all those born in his household or **b** 5239
17:27 those born in his household or **b** 4084+5239
25:10 the field Abraham *had* **b** from the Hittites. 7864
33:19 *he* **b** from the sons of Hamor, 7864
39: 1 the captain of the guard, **b** him from 7864
47:20 Joseph **b** all the land in Egypt for Pharaoh. 7864
47:23 that *I have* **b** you and your land today 7864
49:30 which Abraham **b** as a burial place 7864
49:32 and the cave in it were **b** from the Hittites." 5238
50:13 which Abraham *had* **b** as a burial place 7864
Ex 12:44 Any slave you have **b** may eat of it 4084+5239
15:16 O LORD, until the people *you* **b** pass by. 7864
Lev 27:22 to the LORD a field he has **b**, 5239
27:24 to the person from whom *he* **b** it, 7864
Jos 24:32 at Shechem in the tract of land that Jacob **b** 7864
Ru 4: 9 that *I have* **b** from Naomi all the property 7864
2Sa 12: 3 poor man had nothing except one little ewe lamb *he had* **b**. 7864
24:24 So David **b** the threshing floor and the oxen 7864
1Ki 16:24 *He* **b** the hill of Samaria from Shemer 7864
Ne 5: 8 we *have* **b back** our Jewish brothers who were sold 7864
Job 28:15 It cannot **be b** *with* the finest gold, 5989
28:16 *It* cannot **be b** with the gold of Ophir, 6137
28:19 *it* cannot **be b** with pure gold. 6137
Ecc 2: 7 *I* **b** male and female slaves 7864
Isa 43:24 *You have* not **b** any fragrant calamus for me, 928+2021+4084+7864
Jer 13: 2 So *I* **b** a belt, as the LORD directed, 7864
13: 4 "Take the belt *you* **b** and are wearing 7864
32: 9 so *I* **b** the field at Anathoth 7864
32:15 and vineyards *will* again **be b** in this land.' 7864
32:43 Once more fields *will* **be b** in this land 7864
32:44 Fields *will be* **b** for silver, 7864
Eze 27:19 and Greeks from Uzal **b** your merchandise; NIH
Hos 3: 2 So *I* **b** her for fifteen shekels of silver and 4126
Mt 13:44 in his joy went and sold all he had and **b** *60*
13:46 and sold everything he had and **b** it. *60*
Mk 15:46 So Joseph **b** some linen cloth, *60*
16: 1 and Salome **b** spices so that they might go *60*
Lk 14:18 The first said, '*I have* just **b** a field, *60*
14:19 '*I have* just **b** five yoke of oxen, *60*
Ac 1:18 got for his wickedness; Judas **b** a field; *3227*
7:16 that Abraham *had* **b** from the sons of Hamor *6050*
20:28 which *he* **b** with his own blood. *4347*
1Co 6:20 *you were* **b** at a price. *60*
7:23 *You were* **b** at a price; do not become slaves *60*
2Pe 2: 1 denying the sovereign Lord *who* **b** them— *60*

BOULDER (1)

Rev 18:21 a **b** the size of a large millstone and threw it *3345*

BOUND (58) [BIND]

Ge 22: 9 *He* **b** his son Isaac and laid him on the altar, 6818
42:24 He had Simeon taken from them and **b** 673
44:30 whose life *is* **closely b up** with the boy's 8003
Jdg 15:13 So *they* **b** him with two new ropes 673
1Sa 14:24 **b** the people **under an oath,** 457
14:27 **b** the people **with the oath,** 8678
14:28 **b** the army **under a strict oath,** 8678+8678
25:29 be **b securely** in the bundle of the living by 7674
2Sa 3:34 Your hands **were** not **b**, 673
2Ki 25: 7 **b** him with bronze shackles and took him 673
2Ch 33:11 **b** him with bronze shackles and took him 673
36: 6 and **b** him with bronze shackles to take him 673
Job 16: 8 *You have* **b** me— 7855
36: 8 But if *men* **are b** in chains, 673
Pr 22:15 Folly **is b up** in the heart of a child, 8003
Isa 16:14 **servant b by contract** would count 8502
21:16 **servant b by contract** would count 8502
24:22 be herded together like **prisoners** *b* in AIT
56: 3 Let no foreigner who *has* **b himself** to 4277
Jer 13:11 For as a belt *is* **b** around a man's waist, 1815
13:11 so *I* **b** the whole house of Israel and 1815
39: 7 and **b** him with bronze shackles to take him 673
40: 1 He had found Jeremiah **b** in chains 673
52:11 **b** him with bronze shackles and took him 673
La 1:14 "My sins *have* **been b** *into* a yoke; 8567
Eze 3:25 you *will be* **b** so that you cannot go out 673
30:21 not **been b up** for healing or put in a splint 2502
34: 4 or healed the sick or **b up** the injured. 2502
Da 3:21 **were b** and thrown into the blazing furnace. 10366
4:15 **b** with iron and bronze, 10054
4:23 **b** with iron and bronze, 10054
Jnh 1: 3 where he found a ship **b** *for* that port. 995
Mt 14: 3 and **b** him and put him in prison because *1313*
16:19 whatever you bind on earth will be **b** *1313*
18:18 whatever you bind on earth will be **b** *1313*
23:16 *he is* **b by his oath.'** *4053*
23:18 *he is* **b by his oath.'** *4053*
27: 2 They **b** him, led him away and handed him *1313*
Mk 6:17 and *he* had him **b** and put in prison. *1313*
15: 1 They **b** Jesus, led him away *1313*
Lk 13:16 whom Satan *has kept* **b** *1313*
13:16 on the Sabbath day from what **b** her?" *1301*
17: 1 cause people to sin are **b to come,** *450+2262+3590*
Jn 18:12 arrested Jesus. *They* **b** him *1313*
18:24 Then Annas sent him, *still* **b**, *1313*
Ac 12: 6 **b** with two chains, and sentries stood guard *1313*

Ac 21:13 I am ready not only *to be* **b**, *1313*
21:33 and arrested him and ordered him *to be* **b** *1313*
23:12 **b** themselves **with an oath** *354*
28:20 because of the hope of Israel that *I am* **b** *4329*
Ro 7: 2 a married woman *is* **b** to her husband *1313*
7: 6 But now, by dying to what once **b** *us*, *2988*
11:32 For God *has* **b** all men **over** to disobedience *5168*
1Co 7:15 or woman *is* not **b** in such circumstances; *1530*
7:39 A woman *is* **b** to her husband as long *1313*
Jude 1: 6 **b** with everlasting chains for judgment on *NIG*
Rev 9:14 "Release the four angels who *are* **b** at *1313*
20: 2 or Satan, and **b** him for a thousand years. *1313*

BOUNDARIES (11) [BOUNDARY]

Nu 34: 2 to you as an inheritance will have these **b:** 1473
34:12 with its **b** on every side.' " 1473
Dt 32: 8 he set up **b** *for* the peoples according to 1473
Jos 15:12 These are the **b** around the people of Judah 1473
18:20 the **b** that marked out the inheritance of 1473
2Ki 14:25 He was the one who restored the **b** *of* Israel 1473
Ps 74:17 It was you who set all the **b** *of* the earth; 1473
Pr 15:25 but he keeps the widow's **b** intact. 1473
Isa 10:13 I removed the **b** *of* nations, 1473
Eze 47:13 "These are the **b** by which you are to divide 1473
Mic 7:11 the day for extending your **b.** 2976

BOUNDARY (59) [BOUNDARIES, BOUNDLESS, BOUNDS]

Nu 34: 3 your southern **b** will start from the end of 1473
34: 6 " 'Your western **b** will be the coast of 1473
34: 6 This will be your **b** *on* the west. 1473
34: 7 " 'For your northern **b,** 1473
34: 8 Then the **b** will go to Zedad, 1473
34: 9 This will be your **b** *on* the north. 1473
34:10 " 'For your eastern **b,** run a line 1473
34:11 The **b** will go down from Shepham 1473
34:12 Then the **b** will go down along the Jordan 1473
Dt 19:14 Do not move your neighbor's **b stone** set up 1473
27:17 man who moves his neighbor's **b stone."** 1473
Jos 13:23 The **b** *of* the Reubenites was the bank of 1473
15: 2 Their southern **b** started from the bay at 1473
15: 4 This is their southern **b.** 1473
15: 5 The eastern **b** is the Salt Sea as far as 1473
15: 5 The northern **b** started from the bay of 1473
15: 7 The **b** then went up to Debir from 1473
15: 9 the hilltop the **b** headed toward the spring 1473
15:11 The **b** ended at the sea. 1473
15:12 The western **b** is the coastline of 1473
15:21 the tribe of Judah in the Negev toward the **b** 1473
16: 5 The **b** *of* their inheritance went 1473
17: 7 The **b** ran southward from there to include 1473
17: 8 but Tappuah itself, on the **b** *of* Manasseh, 1473
17: 9 the **b** continued south to the Kanah Ravine. 1473
17: 9 the **b** *of* Manasseh was the northern side of 1473
18:12 the north side their **b** began at the Jordan, 1473
18:14 the **b** turned south along the western side 1473
18:15 the **b** came out at the spring of the waters 1473
18:16 The **b** went down to the foot of 1473
18:19 This was the southern **b.** 1473
18:20 Jordan **formed the b** on the eastern side. 1487
19:10 The **b** *of* their inheritance went as far 1473
19:14 There the **b** went around on the north 1473
19:22 The **b** touched Tabor, 1473
19:26 the **b** touched Carmel and Shihor Libnath. NIH
19:29 The **b** then turned back toward Ramah 1473
19:33 Their **b** went from Heleph and the large tree 1473
19:34 The **b** ran west through Aznoth Tabor 1473
22:25 the Jordan a **b** between us and you— 1473
Jdg 1:36 The **b** *of* the Amorites was 1473
Job 24: 2 Men move **b stones;** 1474
26:10 the horizon on the face of the waters for a **b** 9417
Ps 16: 6 The **b lines** have fallen for me 2475
104: 9 You set a **b** they cannot cross; 1473
Pr 8:29 the sea its **b** so the waters would 2976
22:28 Do not move an ancient **b stone** set up 1473
23:10 Do not move an ancient **b stone** or encroach 1473
Jer 5:22 I made the sand a **b** for the sea, 1473
Eze 47:15 "This is to be the **b** *of* the land: 1473
47:17 The **b** will extend from the sea 1473
47:17 This will be the north **b.** 6991
47:18 the east side the **b** will run between Hauran 1473
47:18 This will be the east **b.** 6991
47:19 This will be the south **b.** 6991
47:20 be the **b** to a point opposite Lebo Hamath. 1473
47:20 This will be the west **b.** 6991
48:28 "The southern **b** *of* Gad will run south 1473
Hos 5:10 like those who move **b stones.** 1473

BOUNDING (1)

SS 2: 8 leaping across the mountains, **b** over the hills. 7890

BOUNDLESS (2) [BOUNDARY]

Ps 119:96 but your commands are **b.** 4394+8146
Na 3: 9 Cush and Egypt were her **b** strength; 401+7897

BOUNDS (2) [BOUNDARY]

Hos 4: 2 *they* **break all b,** 7287
2Co 7: 4 in all our troubles my joy **knows no b.** *5668*

BOUNTY (7)

Ge 49:26 than the **b** *of* the age-old hills. 9294
Dt 28:12 the heavens, the storehouse of his **b,** 3202
1Ki 10:13 what he had given her out of his royal **b.** 3338
Ps 65:11 You crown the year with your **b,** 3208
68:10 Your people settled in it, and from your **b,** 3208
Jer 31:12 they will rejoice in the **b** *of* the LORD— 3206
31:14 and my people will be filled with my **b,"** 3206

BOW (105) [BOWED, BOWING, BOWMEN, BOWS, BOWSHOT]

Ge 27: 3 your quiver and **b—** 8008
27:29 May nations serve you and peoples **b down** 2556
27:29 *may* the sons of your mother **b down** to you. 2556
37:10 your brothers actually come and **b down** 2556
48:22 the Amorites with my sword and my **b."** 8008
49: 8 your father's sons *will* **b down** to you. 2556
49:24 But his **b** remained steady, 8008
Ex 20: 5 not **b down** to them or worship them; 2556
23:24 *Do* not **b down** before their gods 2556
Lev 26: 1 a carved stone in your land to **b down** 2556
Dt 5: 9 not **b down** to them or worship them; 2556
8:19 and worship and **b down** to them, 2556
11:16 worship other gods and **b down** to them. 2556
26:10 before the LORD your God and **b down** 2556
30:17 *to* **b down** to other gods and worship them, 2556
33: 3 At your feet they all **b down,** 9413
Jos 23: 7 You must not serve them or **b down** 2556
23:16 and serve other gods and **b down** to them, 2556
24:12 not do it with your own sword and **b.** 8008
1Sa 2:36 and **b down** before him for a piece of silver 2556
18: 4 and even his sword, his **b** and his belt. 8008
2Sa 1:18 this lament of the **b** (it is written in the Book of Jashar): 8008
1:22 the **b** *of* Jonathan did not turn back, 8008
15: 5 to **b down** before him, 2556
16: 4 *"I* **humbly b,"** Ziba said. 2556
22:35 my arms can bend a **b** *of* bronze. 8008
22:40 *you* **made** my adversaries **b** at my feet. 4156
1Ki 22:34 But someone drew his **b** at random and hit 8008
2Ki 5:18 of Rimmon to **b down** and he is leaning 2556
5:18 on my arm and *I* **b** there also— 2556
5:18 when I **b down** *in* the temple of Rimmon, 2556
6:22 with your own sword or **b?** 8008
9:24 Then Jehu drew his **b** and shot Joram 8008
13:15 Elisha said, "Get a **b** and some arrows," 8008
13:16 "Take the **b** in your hands," 8008
17:35 "Do not worship any other gods or **b down** 2556
17:36 To him *you shall* **b down** and 2556
1Ch 5:18 who could use a **b,** 8008
8:40 brave warriors who could handle the **b.** 8008
2Ch 18:33 But someone drew his **b** at random and hit 8008
Job 29:20 the **b** ever new in my hand.' 8008
30:11 God has unstrung my **b** and afflicted me, 3857
Ps 5: 7 in reverence *will I* **b down** 2556
7:12 he will bend and string his **b.** 8008
18:34 my arms can bend a **b** *of* bronze. 8008
18:39 *you* **made** my adversaries **b** at my feet. 4156
21:12 when you aim at them with **drawn b.** 4798
22:27 the families of the nations *will* **b down** 2556
37:14 The wicked draw the sword and bend the **b** 8008
44: 6 I do not trust in my **b,** 8008
46: 9 he breaks the **b** and shatters the spear, 8008
58: 7 *when they* **draw the b,** 2005
60: 4 a banner to be unfurled against the **b.** 8000
72: 9 The desert tribes *will* **b** before him 4156
72:11 All kings *will* **b down** to him 2556
78:57 as unreliable as a faulty **b.** 8008
81: 9 *you shall* not **b down** to an alien god. 2556
95: 6 Come, *let us* **b down** in worship, 4156
138: 2 *I will* **b down** toward your holy temple 2556
Pr 14:19 Evil men *will* **b down** in the presence of 8820
Isa 2: 8 *they* **b down** to the work of their hands, 2556
7:24 Men will go there with **b** and arrow, 8008
21:15 from the bent **b** and from the heat of battle. 8008
22: 3 without using the **b.** 8008
41: 2 to windblown chaff with his **b.** 8008
44:19 *Shall I* **b down** to a block of wood?" 6032
45:14 *They will* **b down** before you and plead 2556
45:23 Before me every knee *will* **b;** 4156
46: 2 They stoop and **b down** together; 4156
46: 6 and *they* **b down** and worship it. 6032
49: 7 princes will see and **b down,** 2556
49:23 *They will* **b down** before you 2556
60:14 all who despise you *will* **b down** 2556
66:23 all mankind will come and **b down** 2556
Jer 6:23 They are armed with **b** and spear; 8008
9: 3 "They make ready their tongue like a **b,** 8008
27: 8 of Babylon or **b** its neck under his yoke, 5989
27:11 if any nation *will* **b** its neck under the yoke 995
27:12 **"B** your neck under the yoke of the king 995
46: 9 men of Lydia who draw the **b.** 8008
49:35 "See, I will break the **b** *of* Elam, 8008
50:14 all you who draw the **b.** 8008
50:29 all those who draw the **b.** 8008
51: 3 Let not the archer string his **b,** 8008
La 2: 4 Like an enemy he has strung his **b;** 8008
3:12 He drew his **b** and made me the target 8008
Eze 39: 3 Then I will strike your **b** 8008
Hos 1: 5 that day I will break Israel's **b** in the Valley 8008
1: 7 not by **b,** sword or battle, 8008
2:18 **B** and sword and battle I will abolish from 8008
7:16 they are like a faulty **b.** 8008
Mic 5:13 *you will* no longer **b down** to the work 2556
6: 6 before the LORD and **b down** before 4104
Hab 3: 9 You uncovered your **b,** 8008
Zep 1: 5 **b down** on the roofs **to worship** 2556
1: 5 those *who* **b down** and swear by the LORD 2556
Zec 9:10 and the battle **b** will be broken. 8008
Zec 9:13 I will bend Judah as I bend my **b** and fill it 8008
10: 4 from him the battle **b,** 8008
Mt 4: 9 "if you will **b down** and worship me." *4406*
Ac 27:30 to lower some anchors from the **b.** *4749*
27:41 The **b** stuck fast and would not move, *4749*
Ro 14:11 'every knee *will* **b** before me; *2828*
Php 2:10 at the name of Jesus every knee **should b,** *2828*
Rev 6: 2 Its rider held a **b,** *5534*

BOWED (68) [BOW]

Ge 18: 2 to meet them and **b low** to the ground. 2556
19: 1 and **b down** *with* his face to the ground. 2556
23: 7 and **b down** before the people of the land, 2556
23:12 Again Abraham **b down** before the people 2556
24:26 the man **b down** and worshiped the LORD, 7702
24:48 and *I* **b down** and worshiped the LORD. 7702
24:52 *he* **b down** to the ground before the LORD. 2556
33: 3 and **b down** to the ground seven times 2556
33: 6 and their children approached and **b down.** 2556
33: 7 Leah and her children came and **b down.** 2556
33: 7 and *they* too **b down.** 2556
37: 7 around mine and **b down** to it." 2556
42: 6 *they* **b down** to him *with* their faces to 2556
43:26 and *they* **b down** before him to the ground. 2556
43:28 And *they* **b low** to pay him honor. 7702
48:12 and **b down** *with* his face to the ground. 2556
Ex 4:31 *they* **b down** and worshiped. 7702
12:27 Then the people **b down** and worshiped. 7702
18: 7 to meet his father-in-law and **b down** 2556
32: 8 *They have* **b down** to it and sacrificed to it 2556
34: 8 Moses **b** to the ground at once 7702
Nu 22:31 So *he* **b low** and fell facedown. 7702
25: 2 and **b down** before these gods. 2556
Dt 29:26 and worshiped other gods and **b down** 2556
Ru 2:10 *she* **b** down with her face to the ground. 2556
1Sa 20:41 up from the south side [of the stone] and **b** 2556
24: 8 David **b down** and prostrated himself 7702
25:23 she quickly got off her donkey and **b** down 2556
25:41 *She* **b down** with her face to the ground 2556
28:14 and *he* **b down** and prostrated himself 7702
2Sa 9: 6 *he* **b down** to pay him honor. 5877+6584+7156
9: 8 Mephibosheth **b down** and said, 2556
14:33 and he came in and **b down** with his face to 2556
18:21 Cushite **b down** before Joab and ran off. 2556
18:28 *He* **b down** before the king with his face to 2556
24:20 and **b down** before the king with his face to 2556
1Ki 1:16 Bathsheba **b low** and knelt before the king. 7702
1:23 the king and **b** with his face to the ground. 2556
1:31 Then Bathsheba **b low** with her face to 7702
1:47 And the king **b in worship** on his bed 2556
1:53 And Adonijah came and **b down** 2556
2:19 **b down** to her and sat down on his throne. 2556
18: 7 **b down to the ground,** 5877+6584+7156
19:18 all whose knees *have* not **b down** to Baal 4156
2Ki 2:15 And they went to meet him and **b** to 2556
4:37 fell at his feet and **b** to the ground. 2556
17:16 *They* **b down** to all the starry hosts, 2556
21: 3 *He* **b down** to all the starry hosts 2556
21:21 and **b down** to them. 2556
1Ch 21:21 threshing floor and **b down** before David 2556
29:20 *they* **b low** and fell prostrate before 7702
2Ch 20:18 Jehoshaphat **b** with his face to the ground, 7702
25:14 **b down** to them and burned sacrifices 2556
29:28 The whole assembly **b in worship,** 2556
29:30 and **b** *their* **heads** and worshiped. 7702
33: 3 *He* **b down** to all the starry hosts 2556
Ne 8: 6 Then *they* **b down** and worshiped 7702
Ps 35:14 *I* **b** *my* **head** in grief as though weeping 8820
38: 6 *I am* **b down** and brought very low; 6390
57: 6 I *was* **b down in distress.** 4104
145:14 and lifts up all who **are b down.** 4104
146: 8 the LORD lifts up *those who* **are b down,** 4104
La 2:10 of Jerusalem *have* **b** their heads to 3718
Da 10:15 *I* **b** with my face toward the ground 5989
Mt 2:11 and they **b down** and worshiped him. *4406*
Lk 24: 5 the *women* **b down** with their faces to *3111*
Jn 19:30 he **b** his head and gave up his spirit. *3111*
Ro 11: 4 for myself seven thousand who *have* not **b** *2828*

BOWELS (4)

2Ch 21:15 be very ill with a lingering disease of the **b,** 5055
21:15 the disease causes your **b** to come out.' " 5055
21:18 with an incurable disease of the **b.** 5055
21:19 his **b** came out because of the disease, 5055

BOWING (7) [BOW]

Ge 37: 9 and moon and eleven stars *were* **b down** 2556
Ex 11: 8 **b down** before me and saying, 'Go, 2556
Dt 4:19 into **b down** to them and worshiping things 2556
17: 3 **b down** to them or to the sun or the moon or 2556
Isa 58: 5 Is it only for **b** one's head like a reed and 4104
60:14 of your oppressors will come **b** before you; 8820
Eze 8:16 they *were* **b down** to the sun in the east. 2556

BOWL (31) [BOWL-SHAPED, BOWLFUL, BOWLS]

Nu 7:13 one silver **sprinkling b** weighing seventy shekels, 4670
7:19 one silver **sprinkling b** weighing seventy shekels, 4670
7:25 one silver **sprinkling b** weighing seventy shekels, 4670
7:31 one silver **sprinkling b** weighing seventy shekels, 4670

Nu 7:37 one silver **sprinkling b** weighing seventy shekels, 4670
7:43 one silver **sprinkling b** weighing seventy shekels, 4670
7:49 one silver **sprinkling b** weighing seventy shekels, 4670
7:55 one silver **sprinkling b** weighing seventy shekels, 4670
7:61 one silver **sprinkling b** weighing seventy shekels, 4670
7:67 one silver **sprinkling b** weighing seventy shekels, 4670
7:73 one silver **sprinkling b** weighing seventy shekels, 4670
7:79 one silver **sprinkling b** weighing seventy shekels, 4670
7:85 and each **sprinkling b** seventy shekels. 4670
Jdg 5:25 in a **b** *fit* for nobles 6210
2Ki 2:20 "Bring me a new **b**," he said, 7504
Ecc 12:6 or the golden **b** is broken; 1657
Zec 4:2 a solid gold lampstand with a **b** at the top 1657
4:3 the right of the **b** and the other on its left." 1657
9:15 will be full like a **b used for sprinkling** 4670
Mt 5:15 a lamp and put it under a **b**. *3654*
26:23 into the **b** with me will betray me. *5581*
Mk 4:21 "Do you bring in a lamp to put it under a **b** *3654*
14:20 "one who dips bread into the **b** with me. *5581*
Lk 11:33 where it will be hidden, or under a **b**. *3654*
Rev 16:2 The first angel went and poured out his **b** *5786*
16:3 The second angel poured out his **b** on *5786*
16:4 The third angel poured out his **b** on *5786*
16:8 The fourth angel poured out his **b** on *5786*
16:10 The fifth angel poured out his **b** on *5786*
16:12 The sixth angel poured out his **b** on *5786*
16:17 The seventh angel poured out his **b** into *5786*

BOWL-SHAPED (7) [BOWL]

1Ki 7:20 above the **b part** next to the network, 1061
7:41 the two **b** capitals on top of the pillars; 1657
7:41 of network decorating the two **b** capitals 1657
7:42 the **b** capitals on top of the pillars); 1657
2Ch 4:12 the two **b** capitals on top of the pillars; 1657
4:12 of network decorating the two **b** capitals 1657
4:13 the **b** capitals on top of the pillars); 1657

BOWLFUL (3) [BOWL]

Jdg 6:38 wrung out the dew—a **b** of water. 4850+6210
Ps 80:5 you have made them drink tears *by* the **b**. 8955
Am 6:6 by the **b** and use the finest lotions, 4670

BOWLS (35) [BOWL]

Ex 24:6 of the blood and put it in **b**, 110
25:29 as its pitchers and **b** for the pouring out 4984
27:3 **sprinkling b**, meat forks and firepans. 4670
37:16 its plates and dishes and **b** and its pitchers 4984
38:3 its pots, shovels, **sprinkling b**, 4670
Nu 4:7 and **b**, and the jars for drink offerings; 4984
4:14 meat forks, shovels and **sprinkling b**. 4670
7:84 twelve silver **sprinkling b** 4670
2Sa 17:28 brought bedding and **b** and articles 6195
1Ki 7:40 the basins and shovels and **sprinkling b**. 4670
7:45 shovels and **sprinkling b**. 4670
7:50 **sprinkling b**, dishes and censers; 4670
2Ki 12:13 wick trimmers, **sprinkling b**, 4670
25:15 the censers and **sprinkling b**— 4670
1Ch 28:17 **sprinkling b** and pitchers; 4670
2Ch 4:8 He also made a hundred gold **sprinkling b**. 4670
4:11 the pots and shovels and **sprinkling b**. 4670
4:22 **sprinkling b**, dishes and censers; 4670
Ezr 1:10 gold **b** 30 matching silver bowls 410 4094
1:10 gold bowls 30 matching silver **b** 410 4094
8:27 20 **b** *of* gold valued at 1,000 4094
Ne 7:70 50 **b** and 530 garments for priests. 4670
Pr 23:30 who go to sample **b of mixed wine.** 4932
Isa 22:24 from the **b** to all the jars. 110
65:11 a table for Fortune and fill **b of mixed wine** 4932
Jer 35:5 Then I set **b** full of wine and some cups 1483
52:18 shovels, wick trimmers, **sprinkling b**, 4670
52:19 censers, **sprinkling b**, pots, lampstands, 4670
52:19 **b used for drink offerings**— 4984
Zec 14:20 be like the **sacred b** in front of the altar. 4670
Rev 5:8 a harp and they were holding golden **b** full *5786*
15:7 the seven angels seven golden **b** filled with *5786*
16:1 the seven **b** of God's wrath on the earth." *5786*
17:1 the seven angels who had the seven **b** came *5786*
21:9 the seven angels who had the seven **b** full *5786*

BOWMEN (1) [BOW]

Isa 21:17 The survivors of the **b**, 5031+8008

BOWS (19) [BOW]

1Sa 2:4 "The **b** *of* the warriors are broken, 8008
1Ch 12:2 with **b** and were able to shoot arrows or 8008
2Ch 14:8 armed with small shields and **with b**. 2005+8008
17:17 men armed with **b** and shields; 8008
26:14 **b** and slingstones for the entire army. 8008
Ne 4:13 with their swords, spears and **b**. 8008
4:16 with spears, shields, **b** and armor. 8008
Ps 11:2 For look, the wicked bend their **b**; 8008
37:15 and their **b** will be broken. 8008
66:4 All the earth **b down** to you; 2556
78:9 The men of Ephraim, though armed with **b**, 8008
Isa 5:28 all their **b** are strung; 8008
13:18 Their **b** will strike down the young men; 8008
44:15 he makes an idol and **b down** to it. 6032
44:17 *he* **b down** to it and worships. 6032
46:1 Bel **b down**, Nebo stoops low; 4156
Jer 50:42 They are armed with **b** and spears; 8008
51:56 and their **b** will be broken. 8008
Eze 39:9 the **b** and arrows, the war clubs and spears. 8008

BOWSHOT (1) [BOW]

Ge 21:16 about a **b** away, for she thought, 3217+8008

BOX (KJV) See CHEST, HORN, FLASK

BOY (79) [BOY'S, BOYHOOD, BOYS]

Ge 21:12 "Do not be so distressed about the **b** 5853
21:14 and then sent her off with the **b**. 3529
21:15 she put the **b** under one of the bushes. 3529
21:16 for she thought, "I cannot watch the **b** die." 3529
21:17 God heard the **b** crying, 5853
21:17 God has heard the **b** crying as he lies there. 5853
21:18 Lift the **b** up and take him by the hand, 5853
21:19 the skin with water and gave the **b** a drink. 5853
21:20 God was with the **b** as he grew up. 5853
22:5 the donkey while I and the **b** go over there. 5853
22:12 "Do not lay a hand on the **b**," he said. 5853
37:30 "The **b** isn't there! 3529
42:22 "Didn't I tell you not to sin against the **b**? 3529
43:8 the **b** along with me and we will go at once, 5853
44:22 'The **b** cannot leave his father; 5853
44:30 if the **b** is not with us when I go back 5853
44:31 sees that the **b** isn't there, 5853
44:33 as my lord's slave in place of the **b**, 5853
44:33 and let the **b** return with his brothers. 5853
44:34 How can I go back to my father if the **b** is 5853
Ex 1:16 if it is a **b**, kill him; 1201
1:22 "Every **b** that is born you must throw into 1201
Lev 12:3 the eighth day **the b** is to be circumcised. 2257[S]
12:7 the woman who gives birth to a **b** or a girl. 2351
Jdg 8:20 because he was only a **b** and was afraid. 5853
13:5 because the **b** is to be a Nazirite, 5853
13:7 the **b** will be a Nazirite of God from birth 5853
13:8 to teach us how to bring up the **b** who is to 5853
13:24 to a **b** and named him Samson. 1201
1Sa 1:22 "After the **b** is weaned, 5853
1:24 she took the **b** with her, young as he was, 5853
1:25 they brought the **b** to Eli, 5853
2:11 but the **b** ministered before the LORD 5853
2:18 a **b** wearing a linen ephod. 5853
2:21 the **b** Samuel grew up in the presence of 5853
2:26 the **b** Samuel continued to grow in stature 5853
3:1 The **b** Samuel ministered before 5853
3:8 that the LORD was calling the **b**. 5853
4:21 She named the **b** Ichabod, saying, 5853
17:33 you are only a **b**, and he has been a fighting 5853
17:42 over and saw that he was only a **b**, 5853
20:21 Then I will send a **b** and say, 'Go, 5853
20:22 But if I say to the **b**, 'Look, 6624
20:35 He had a small **b** with him, 5853
20:36 and he said to the **b**, 5853
20:36 As the **b** ran, he shot an arrow beyond him. 5853
20:37 When the **b** came to the place 5853
20:38 The **b** picked up the arrow and returned 5853
20:39 (The **b** knew nothing of all this; 5853
20:40 Then Jonathan gave his weapons to the **b** 5853
20:41 After the **b** had gone, 5853
30:19 young or old, **b** or girl, 1201
1Ki 11:17 But Hadad, still only a **b**, 5853+7783
14:3 He will tell you what will happen to the **b**." 5853
14:12 you set foot in your city, the **b** will die. 3529
14:17 over the threshold of the house, the **b** died. 5853
17:21 the **b** three times and cried to the LORD, 3529
2Ki 4:20 the **b** sat on her lap until noon, NIH
4:31 "The **b** has not awakened." 5853
4:32 there was the **b** lying dead on his couch. 5853
4:34 Then he got on the bed and lay upon the **b**, 3529
4:35 The **b** sneezed seven times and opened his 5853
5:14 and became clean like that of a young **b**. 5853
Job 3:3 and the night it was said, 'A **b** is born!' 1505
Pr 4:3 When I was a **b** in my father's house, 1201
Isa 7:16 But before the **b** knows enough to reject 5853
8:4 Before the **b** knows how to say 'My father' 5853
Mt 17:17 Bring **the b** here to me." *899[S]*
17:18 and it came out of the **b**, *4090*
Mk 9:19 Bring **the b** to me." *899[S]*
9:20 it immediately threw **the b** into *899[S]*
9:26 The **b** looked so much like a corpse *NIG*
10:20 "all these I have kept since I was a **b**." *3744*
Lk 2:43 the **b** Jesus stayed behind in Jerusalem, *4090*
9:42 Even while the **b** was coming, *899[S]*
9:42 the **b** and gave him back to his father. *4090*
18:21 "All these I have kept since I was a **b**," *3744*
Jn 4:51 with the news that his **b** was living. *4090*
6:9 "Here is a **b** with five small barley loaves *4081*

BOY'S (10) [BOY]

Ge 44:30 is closely bound up with **the b** life, 2257[S]
44:32 Your servant guaranteed the **b** safety 5853
Jdg 13:12 to be the rule for the **b** life and work?" 5853
1Ki 17:21 let this **b** life return to him!" 3529
17:22 and the **b** life returned to him, and he lived. 3529
2Ki 4:29 Lay my staff on the **b** face." 5853
4:31 on ahead and laid the staff on the **b** face, 5853
4:34 the **b** body grew warm. 3529
Mk 9:21 Jesus asked the **b** father, "How long *899[S]*
9:24 Immediately the **b** father exclaimed, *4086*

BOYHOOD (1) [BOY]

Ge 46:34 have tended livestock from our **b** on, 5830

BOYS (14) [BOY]

Ge 25:24 there were **twin** *b* in her womb. AIT
25:27 The **b** grew up, 5853
38:27 there were **twin** *b* in her womb. AIT
48:16 may he bless these **b**. 5853
Ex 1:17 they let the **b** live. 3529
1:18 Why have you let the **b** live?" 3529
Nu 31:17 Now kill all the **b**. 2351+3251
2Ki 4:1 to take my two **b** as his slaves." 3529
Job 19:18 Even the **little b** scorn me; 6396
Isa 3:4 I will make **b** their officials; 5853
La 5:13 **b** stagger under loads of wood. 5853
Joel 3:3 for my people and traded **b** for prostitutes; 3529
Zec 8:5 be filled with **b** and girls playing there." 3529
Mt 2:16 and he gave orders to kill all the **b** *4090*

BOZEZ (1)

1Sa 14:4 one was called **B**, and the other Seneh. 1010

BOZKATH (2)

Jos 15:39 Lachish, **B**, Eglon, 1304
2Ki 22:1 she was from **B**. 1304

BOZRAH (8)

Ge 36:33 Jobab son of Zerah from **B** succeeded him 1313
1Ch 1:44 Jobab son of Zerah from **B** succeeded him 1313
Isa 34:6 For the LORD has a sacrifice in **B** and 1313
63:1 Who is this coming from Edom, from **B**, 1313
Jer 48:24 to Kerioth and **B**— 1313
49:13 "that **B** will become a ruin and an object 1313
49:22 spreading its wings over **B**. 1313
Am 1:12 that will consume the fortresses of **B**." 1313

BRACE (3) [BRACING]

Job 38:3 **B** yourself like a man; 273+2743
40:7 "**B** yourself like a man; 273+2743
Na 2:1 **b yourselves**, marshal all your strength! 2616+5516

BRACELETS (7)

Ge 24:22 and two gold **b** weighing ten shekels. 3338+6584+7543
24:30 and the **b** on his sister's arms, 7543
24:47 the ring in her nose and the **b** on her arms, 7543
Nu 31:50 armlets, **b**, signet rings, 7543
Isa 3:19 the earrings and **b** and veils, 9217
Eze 16:11 I put **b** on your arms and a necklace 7543
23:42 from the rabble, and they put **b** on the arms 7543

BRACING (1) [BRACE]

Jdg 16:29 **B** *himself* against them, 6164

BRAG (4)

Am 4:5 and **b** *about* your freewill offerings— 7924
Ro 2:17 on the law and **b about** your relationship *3016*
2:23 You who **b** about the law, *3016*
Jas 4:16 As it is, you boast and **b**. *224+1877+3836*

BRAIDED (5) [BRAIDS]

Ex 28:14 and two **b** chains of pure gold, 4456
28:22 the breastpiece make **b** chains of pure gold, 1491
39:15 For the breastpiece they made **b** chains 1491
1Ti 2:9 not with **b hair** or gold or pearls *4427*
1Pe 3:3 as **b** hair and the wearing of gold jewelry *1862*

BRAIDS (3) [BRAIDED]

Jdg 16:13 "If you weave the seven **b** *of* my head into 4710
16:13 Delilah took the seven **b** *of* his head, 4710
16:19 a man to shave off the seven **b** *of* his hair, 4710

BRAMBLE (KJV) See THORNBUSH

BRAMBLES (1)

Isa 34:13 nettles and **b** her strongholds. 2560

BRANCH (26) [BRANCHES]

Ge 49:11 his colt to the **choicest b**; 8605
Ex 25:33 with buds and blossoms are to be on one **b**, 7866
25:33 three on the next **b**, 7866
37:19 with buds and blossoms were on one **b**, 7866
37:19 three on the next **b** and the same 7866
Nu 4:2 a census of the Kohathite **b of** the Levites 4946+9348
13:23 they cut off a **b** bearing a single cluster 2367
Isa 4:2 the **B** *of* the LORD will be beautiful 7542
9:14 both **palm b** and reed in a single day; 4093
11:1 from his roots a **B** will bear fruit. 5916
14:19 of your tomb like a rejected **b**; 5916
19:15 head or tail, **palm b** or reed. 4093
Jer 1:11 "I see the **b** *of* an almond tree," I replied. 5234
23:5 I will raise up to David a righteous **B**, 7542
33:15 that time I will make a righteous **B** sprout 7542
Eze 8:17 Look at them putting the **b** to their nose! 2367
15:2 that of a **b** on any of the trees in the forest? 2367
19:14 No strong **b** is left on it fit for 4751

Zec 3: 8 I am going to bring my servant, the **B.** 7542
6:12 'Here is the man whose name is the **B,** 7542
6:12 and *he will* **b out** from his place and build 7541
Mal 4: 1 "Not a root or a **b** will be left to them. 6733
Jn 15: 2 He cuts off every **b** in me that bears no fruit, *3097*
15: 2 while every **b** that does bear fruit he prunes *NIG*
15: 4 No **b** can bear fruit by itself; *3097*
15: 6 like a **b** that is thrown away and withers; *3097*

BRANCHES (80) [BRANCH]

Ge 30:37 however, took fresh-cut **b** *from* poplar, 5234
30:37 the white inner wood of the **b.** 5234
30:38 the peeled **b** in all the watering troughs, 5234
30:39 they mated in front of the **b.** 5234
30:41 the **b** in the troughs in front of the animals 5234
30:41 the animals so they would mate near the **b,** 5234
40:10 and on the vine were three **b.** 8585
40:12 "The three **b** are three days. 8585
49:22 whose **b** climb over a wall. 1426
Ex 25:32 Six **b** are to extend from the sides of 7866
25:33 for all six **b** extending from the lampstand. 7866
25:35 be under the first pair of **b** extending from 7866
25:35 six **b** in all. 7866
25:36 The buds and **b** shall all be of one piece 7866
37:18 Six **b** extended from the sides of 7866
37:19 for all six **b** extending from the lampstand. 7866
37:21 under the first pair of **b** extending from 7866
37:21 under the third pair—six **b** in all. 7866
37:22 The buds and the **b** were all of one piece 7866
Lev 23:40 and palm fronds, leafy **b** and poplars, 6733
Dt 24:20 not **go over the b a second time.** 339+6994
Jdg 9:48 He took an ax and cut off *some* **b,** 6770+8457
9:49 all the men cut **b** and followed Abimelech. 8456
2Sa 18: 9 mule went under the **thick b** *of* a large oak, 8449
Ne 8:15 the hill country and bring back **b** *from* olive 6591
8:16 So the people went out and brought back **b** NIH
Job 15:32 and his **b** will not flourish. 4093
18:16 up below and his **b** wither above. 7908
29:19 and the dew will lie all night on my **b.** 7908
Ps 80:10 the mighty cedars with its **b.** 6733
104:12 they sing among the **b.** 6751
Isa 17: 6 or three olives on the topmost **b,** 580
18: 5 cut down and take away the **spreading b.** 5746
27:10 they strip its **b** bare. 6187
Jer 5:10 Strip off her **b,** 5746
6: 9 pass your hand over the **b** again, 6151
11:16 and its **b** will be broken. 1936
48:32 Your **b** spread as far as the sea; 5746
Eze 17: 6 Its **b** turned toward him, 1936
17: 6 and produced **b** and put out leafy boughs. 964
17: 7 where it was planted and stretched out its **b** 1936
17: 8 so that it would produce **b,** 6733
17:23 it will produce **b** and bear fruit and become 6733
17:23 they will find shelter in the shade of its **b.** 1936
19:10 and **full of b** because of abundant water. 6734
19:11 Its **b** were strong, fit for a ruler's scepter. 4751
19:11 for its height and for its many **b.** 1936
19:12 its strong **b** withered 4751
19:14 of its **main b** and consumed its fruit. 964+4751
21:19 a signpost where the road **b off** *to* the city. 8031
31: 3 with beautiful **b** overshadowing the forest; 6733
31: 5 its boughs increased and its **b** grew long, 6997
31: 6 of the field gave birth under its **b;** 6997
31: 8 nor could the plane trees compare with its **b** 6997
31: 9 I made it beautiful with abundant **b,** 1936
31:12 its **b** lay broken in all the ravines of 6997
31:13 the beasts of the field were among its **b.** 6997
36: 8 will produce **b** and fruit 6733
Da 4:12 and the birds of the air lived in its **b;** 10561
4:14 'Cut down the tree and trim off its **b;** 10561
4:14 from under it and the birds from its **b.** 10561
4:21 and having nesting places in its **b** for 10561
Joel 1: 7 leaving their **b** white. 8585
Zec 4:12 "What are these two olive **b** beside 8672
Mt 13:32 the birds of the air come and perch in its **b."** *3080*
21: 8 while others cut **b** from the trees *3080*
Mk 4:32 with such big **b** that the birds of *3080*
11: 8 others spread **b** they had cut in the fields. *5115*
Lk 13:19 and the birds of the air perched in its **b."** *3080*
Jn 12:13 They took palm **b** and went out *961*
15: 5 "I am the vine; you are the **b.** *3097*
15: 6 such **b** are picked up, *NIG*
Ro 11:16 if the root is holy, so are the **b.** *3080*
11:17 If some *of* the **b** have been broken off, *3080*
11:18 do not boast over those **b.** *3080*
11:19 "**B** were broken off so that I could *3080*
11:21 For if God did not spare the natural **b,** *3080*
11:24 the natural **b,** be grafted *NIG*
Heb 9:19 scarlet wool and **b of hyssop,** *5727*
Rev 7: 9 and were holding **palm b** in their hands. *5836*

BRAND (KJV) See BURNING STICK

BRANDING (1)

Isa 3:24 instead of beauty, **b.** 3953

BRANDISH (3) [BRANDISHED, BRANDISHES, BRANDISHING]

Ps 35: 3 **B** spear and javelin 8197
Isa 10:15 or a club **b** him who is not wood! 8123
Eze 32:10 of you when I **b** my sword before them. 6758

BRANDISHED (1) [BRANDISH]

Na 2: 3 the spears of pine *are* **b.** 8302

BRANDISHES (1) [BRANDISH]

Eze 30:25 the hand of the king of Babylon and *he* **b** it 5742

BRANDISHING (1) [BRANDISH]

Eze 38: 4 all of them **b** their swords. 9530

BRASEN, BRASS (KJV) See BRONZE

BRAVE (15) [BRAVELY, BRAVEST]

1Sa 14:52 whenever Saul saw a mighty or **b** man, 1201+2657
16:18 He is a **b man** and a warrior. 1475+2657
2Sa 2: 7 Now then, be strong and **b,** 1201+2657
13:28 Be strong and **b."** 1201+2657
17:10 a fighter and that those with him are **b.** 1201+2657
1Ch 5:24 They were **b** warriors, famous men, 2657
7:40 **b warriors** and outstanding leaders. 1475+2657
8:40 were **b warriors** who could handle 1475+2657
12: 8 They were **b warriors,** 1475+2657
12:21 for all of them were **b warriors,** 1475+2657
12:28 a **b** young **warrior,** with 22 officers 1475+2657
12:30 **b warriors,** famous in their own clans 1475+2657
28: 1 the mighty men and all the **b warriors.** 1475+2657
2Ch 14: 8 All these were **b fighting men.** 1475+2657
Isa 33: 7 Look, their **b men** cry aloud in the streets; 737

BRAVELY (3) [BRAVE]

1Sa 18:17 serve me **b** and fight the battles 1201+2657+4200
2Sa 10:12 and *let us* **fight b** for our people and 2616
1Ch 19:13 and *let us* **fight b** for our people and 2616

BRAVERY (KJV) See FINERY

BRAVEST (2) [BRAVE]

2Sa 17:10 Then even the **b soldier,** 1201+2657
Am 2:16 **b** warriors will flee naked on that day," 579+4213

BRAWLER (1) [BRAWLERS, BRAWLING]

Pr 20: 1 Wine is a mocker and beer a **b;** 2159

BRAWLERS (1) [BRAWLER]

Isa 5:14 and masses with all their **b** and revelers. 8623

BRAWLING (1) [BRAWLER]

Eph 4:31 rage and anger, **b** and slander, *3199*

BRAY (1) [BRAYED]

Job 6: 5 *Does* a wild donkey **b** when it has grass, 5640

BRAYED (1) [BRAY]

Job 30: 7 *They* **b** among the bushes and huddled in 5640

BRAZEN (3)

Pr 7:13 and kissed him and *with* a **b** face she said: 6451
Jer 3: 3 Yet you have the **b look** *of* a prostitute; 5195
Eze 16:30 acting like a **b** prostitute! 8951

BRAZIER (Anglicized) See FIRE POT

BREACH (2) [BREAK]

Job 30:14 They advance as through a gaping **b;** 7288
Ps 106:23 stood in the **b** before him to keep his wrath 7288

BREACHES (1) [BREAK]

Isa 22: 9 of David had many **b in** its **defenses;** 1323

BREACHING (2) [BREAK]

Ps 144:14 There will be no **b of walls,** 7288
Pr 17:14 Starting a quarrel is like **b** a dam; 7080

BREAD (271)

Ge 14:18 of Salem brought out **b** and wine. 4312
18: 6 of fine flour and knead it and bake *some* **b."** 6314
19: 3 baking **b without yeast,** and they ate. 5174
25:34 Then Jacob gave Esau *some* **b** 4312
27:17 the tasty food and the **b** she had made. 4312
40:16 On my head were three baskets of **b.** 3035
45:23 and **b** and other provisions for his journey. 4312
Ex 12: 8 and **b made without yeast.** 5174
12:15 to eat **b made without yeast.** 5174
12:17 **Feast of Unleavened B,** 5174
12:18 to eat **b made without yeast,** 5174
12:20 you must eat **unleavened b."** 5174
12:39 they baked cakes of **unleavened b.** 5174
13: 6 For seven days eat **b made without yeast** 5174
13: 7 Eat **unleavened b** during those seven days; 5174
16: 4 "I will rain down **b** from heaven for you. 4312
16: 8 to eat in the evening and all the **b** you want 4312
16:12 in the morning you will be filled with **b.** 4312
16:15 "It is the **b** the LORD has given you to eat. 4312
16:29 that is why on the sixth day he gives you **b** 4312
16:31 The people of Israel called **the b** manna. 2257[S]
16:32 to come, so they can see the **b** I gave you 4312
Ex 18:12 of Israel to eat **b** with Moses' father-in-law 4312
23:15 "Celebrate the Feast of **Unleavened B;** 5174
23:15 for seven days eat **b made without yeast,** 5174
25:30 Put the **b** *of* the Presence on this table to be 4312
29: 2 make **b,** and cakes mixed with oil, 4312
29:23 From the basket of **b made without yeast,** 5174
29:32 to eat the meat of the ram and the **b** that is 4312
29:34 of the ordination ram or any **b** is left over 4312
34:18 "Celebrate the Feast of **Unleavened B.** 5174
34:18 For seven days eat **b made without yeast,** 5174
34:28 without eating **b** or drinking water. 4312
35:13 with its poles and all its articles and the **b** 4312
39:36 the table with all its articles and the **b** *of* 4312
40:23 and set out the **b** on it before the LORD, 4312
Lev 7:12 offer cakes of **b made without yeast** 5174
7:13 to present an offering with cakes of **b** made 4312
8: 2 the basket containing **b made without yeast,** 5174
8:26 from the basket of **b made without yeast,** 5174
8:26 he took a cake of **b,** and one made with oil, 5174
8:31 of Meeting and eat it there with the **b** from 4312
8:32 Then burn up the rest of the meat and the **b.** 4312
23: 6 of **Unleavened B** begins; 5174
23: 6 seven days you must eat **b made without yeast.** 5174
23:14 You must not eat any **b,** 4312
23:18 Present with this **b** seven male lambs, 4312
23:20 together with the **b** *of* the firstfruits. 4312
24: 5 and bake twelve **loaves of b,** 2705
24: 7 as a memorial portion to represent the **b** and 4312
24: 8 **This b** is to be set out before 5647[S]
26:26 When I cut off your supply of **b,** 4312
26:26 ten women will be able to bake your **b** 4312
26:26 and they will dole out the **b** by weight. 4312
Nu 4: 7 the **b** that is continually there is to remain 4312
6:15 and a basket of **b made without yeast—** 5174
6:17 He is to present the basket of **unleavened b** 5174
9:11 with **unleavened b** and bitter herbs. 5174
21: 5 There is no **b!** 4312
28:17 for seven days eat **b made without yeast.** 5174
Dt 8: 3 on **b** alone but on every word that comes 4312
8: 9 a land where **b** will not be scarce 4312
9: 9 I ate no **b** and drank no water. 4312
9:18 I ate no **b** and drank no water, 4312
16: 3 Do not eat it with **b made with yeast,** 2809
16: 3 but for seven days eat **unleavened b,** 5174
16: 3 the **b** *of* affliction, because you left Egypt 4312
16: 8 For six days eat **unleavened b** and on 5174
16:16 at the Feast of **Unleavened B,** 5174
23: 4 to meet you with **b** and water on your way 4312
29: 6 You ate no **b** and drank no wine 4312
Jos 5:11 **unleavened b** and roasted grain. 5174
9: 5 All the **b** *of* their food supply was dry 4312
9:12 This **b** *of* ours was warm 4312
Jdg 6:19 an ephah of flour he made **b without yeast.** 5174
6:20 "Take the meat and the **unleavened b,** 5174
6:21 the meat and the **unleavened b.** 5174
6:21 consuming the meat and the **b.** 5174
7:13 "A round loaf of barley **b** came tumbling 4312
8: 5 "Give my troops *some* **b;** 3971+4312
8: 6 Why should we give **b** to your troops?" 4312
8:15 Why should we give **b** 4312
19:19 and fodder for our donkeys and **b** and wine 4312
Ru 2:14 Have some **b** and dip it in the wine vinegar 4312
1Sa 2:36 a piece of silver and a crust of **b** and plead, 4312
10: 3 another three loaves of **b,** 4312
10: 4 and offer you two loaves of **b,** 4312
16:20 So Jesse took a donkey loaded with **b,** 4312
17:17 of roasted grain and these ten **loaves of b** 4312
21: 3 Give me five **loaves of b,** 4312
21: 4 "I don't have any ordinary **b** on hand; 4312
21: 4 there is *some* consecrated **b** here— 4312
21: 6 So the priest gave him the consecrated **b,** NIH
21: 6 since there was no **b** there except the bread 4312
21: 6 since there was no bread there except the **b** 4312
21: 6 before the LORD and replaced by hot **b** on 4312
22:13 giving him **b** and a sword and inquiring 4312
25:11 Why should I take my **b** and water, 4312
25:18 She took two hundred **loaves of b,** 4312
28:24 kneaded it and baked **b without yeast.** 5174
2Sa 3:35 with me, be it ever so severely, if I taste **b** 4312
6:19 Then he gave a loaf of **b,** 4312
13: 6 and **make** some **special b** in my sight, 4221+4223
13: 8 **made** *the* **b** in his sight and baked it. 4221
13: 9 she took the pan and served him the **b,** NIH
13:10 And Tamar took the **b** she had prepared 4223
16: 1 and loaded with two hundred **loaves of b,** 4312
16: 2 the **b** and fruit are for the men to eat, 4312
1Ki 7:48 the golden table on which was the **b** *of* 4312
13: 8 nor would I eat **b** or drink water here. 4312
13: 9 'You must not eat **b** or drink water or return 4312
13:16 nor can I eat **b** or drink water with you 4312
13:17 not eat **b** or drink water there or return by 4312
13:18 with you to your house so that he may eat **b** 4312
13:22 You came back and ate **b** and drank water 4312
14: 3 Take ten **loaves of b** with you, 4312
17: 6 The ravens brought him **b** and meat in 4312
17: 6 the morning and **b** and meat in the evening, 4312
17:11 "And bring me, please, a piece of **b."** 4312
17:12 she replied, "I don't have any **b—** 5056
17:13 But first make a small **cake of b** for me 6314
19: 6 and there by his head was a **cake of b** baked 6314
22:27 but **b** and water until I return safely.' " 4312
2Ki 4:42 of God twenty **loaves of** barley **b** baked 4312
18:32 a land of **b** and vineyards, 4312
23: 9 they ate **unleavened b** with their fellow 5174
1Ch 9:31 the responsibility for baking the **offering b.** 2503

1Ch 9:32 for every Sabbath the **b** set out on the table. 4312
16: 3 Then he gave a loaf of **b,** 4312
23:29 They were in charge of the **b** set out on 4312
28:16 of gold for each table for **consecrated b;** 5121
2Ch 2: 4 for setting out the **consecrated b** regularly, 5121
4:19 on which was the **b** *of* the Presence; 4312
8:13 the Feast of **Unleavened B,** 5174
13:11 the **b** on the ceremonially clean table 4312
18:26 but **b** and water until I return safely.' " 4312
29:18 **setting out the consecrated b,** 5121
30:13 to celebrate the Feast of **Unleavened B** in 5174
30:21 the Feast of **Unleavened B** for seven days 5174
35:17 the Feast of **Unleavened B** for seven days. 5174
Ezr 6:22 with joy the Feast of **Unleavened B,** 5174
Ne 9:15 In their hunger you gave them **b** 4312
10:33 for the **b** set out on the table; 4312
Job 23:12 of his mouth more than my **daily b.** 2976
31:17 if I have kept my **b** to myself, not sharing it 7326
Ps 14: 4 those who devour my people as men eat **b** 4312
37:25 or their children begging **b.** 4312
41: 9 whom I trusted, he who shared my **b,** 4312
53: 4 those who devour my people as men eat **b** 4312
78:25 Men ate the **b** *of* angels; 4312
80: 5 You have fed them with the **b** *of* tears; 4312
104:15 and **b** that sustains his heart. 4312
105:40 and satisfied them with the **b** *of* heaven. 4312
Pr 4:17 They eat the **b** *of* wickedness and drink 4312
6:26 for the prostitute reduces you to a loaf of **b,** 4312
28:21 yet a man will do wrong for a piece of **b.** 4312
30: 8 but give me only my **daily b.** 2976+4312
31:27 of her household and does not eat the **b** 4312
Ecc 11: 1 Cast your **b** upon the waters, 4312
Isa 28:28 Grain must be ground to make **b;** 4312
30:20 the Lord gives you the **b** *of* adversity and 4312
33:16 His **b** will be supplied, 4312
36:17 a land of **b** and vineyards. 4312
44:15 he kindles a fire and bakes **b.** 4312
44:19 I even baked **b** over its coals, 4312
51:14 nor will they lack **b.** 4312
55: 2 Why spend money on *what* is not **b,** 4312
55:10 so that it yields seed for the sower and **b** for 4312
Jer 7:18 and make **cakes of b** for the Queen 3924
37:21 given **b** from the street of the bakers 3971+4312
37:21 of the bakers each day until all the **b** in 4312
38: 9 when there is no longer any **b** in the city." 4312
42:14 or hear the trumpet or be hungry for **b,**' 4312
La 1:11 All her people groan as they search for **b;** 4312
2:12 "Where is **b** and wine?" 1841
4: 4 the children beg for **b,** 4312
5: 6 to Egypt and Assyria to get enough **b.** 4312
5: 9 We get our **b** at the risk of our lives because 4312
Eze 4: 9 in a storage jar and use them to make **b** 4312
4:15 "I will let you bake your **b** over cow manure 4312
13:19 a few handfuls of barley and scraps of **b.** 4312
45:21 which you shall eat **b made without yeast.** 5174
Hos 9: 4 Such sacrifices will be to them like the **b** 4312
Am 4: 5 Burn **leavened b** as a thank offering 2809
4: 6 in every city and lack of **b** in every town, 4312
7:12 Earn your **b** there and do your prophesying 4312
Ob 1: 7 those who eat your **b** will set a trap for you, 4312
Hag 2:12 and that fold touches some **b** or stew, 4312
Mt 4: 3 tell these stones to become **b."** 788
4: 4 'Man does not live on **b** alone, 788
6:11 Give us today our daily **b.** 788
7: 9 "Which of you, if his son asks for **b,** 788
12: 4 and his companions ate the consecrated **b—** 788
14:17 "We have here only five **loaves of b** 788
15:26 not right to take the children's **b** and toss it 788
15:33 "Where could we get enough **b** 788
16: 5 the disciples forgot to take **b.** 788
16: 7 "It is because we didn't bring any **b."** 788
16: 8 among yourselves about having no **b?** 788
16:11 that I was not talking to you about **b?** 788
16:12 to guard against the yeast used *in* **b,** 788
26:17 **Feast of Unleavened B,** *109*
26:26 While they were eating, Jesus took **b,** 788
Mk 2:26 the house of God and ate the consecrated **b,** 788
6: 8 no **b,** no bag, no money in your belts. 788
6:37 that much on **b** and give it to them to eat?" 788
6:43 up twelve basketfuls of broken pieces of **b** *NIG*
7:27 not right to take the children's **b** and toss it 788
8: 4 this remote place can anyone get enough **b** 788
8:14 The disciples had forgotten to bring **b,** 788
8:16 "It is because we have no **b."** 788
8:17 "Why are you talking about having no **b?** 788
14: 1 **Feast of Unleavened B** *109*
14:12 **Feast of Unleavened B,** *109*
14:20 "one who dips **b** into the bowl with me. *NIG*
14:22 While they were eating, Jesus took **b,** 788
Lk 4: 3 tell this stone to become **b."** 788
4: 4 'Man does not live on **b** alone.' " 788
6: 4 and taking the consecrated **b,** 788
7:33 For John the Baptist came neither eating **b** 788
9: 3 no staff, no bag, no **b,** no money, 788
9:13 "We have only five **loaves of b** 788
11: 3 Give us each day our daily **b.** 788
11: 5 'Friend, lend me three **loaves of b,** 788
11: 8 and give him the **b** because he is his friend, *NIG*
22: 1 Now the Feast *of* **Unleavened B,** *109*
22: 7 Then came the day *of* **Unleavened B** *109*
22:19 And he took **b,** gave thanks and broke it, 788
24:30 he took **b,** gave thanks, 788
24:35 by them when he broke the **b.** 788
Jn 6: 5 shall we buy **b** for these people to eat?" 788
6: 7 not buy enough **b** for each one to have 788
6:23 the place where the people had eaten the **b** 788
6:31 'He gave them **b** from heaven to eat.' " 788
Jn 6:32 it is not Moses who has given you the **b** 788
6:32 but it is my Father who gives you the true **b** 788
6:33 For the **b** of God is he who comes down 788
6:34 they said, "from now on give us this **b."** 788
6:35 Then Jesus declared, "I am the **b** of life. 788
6:41 "I am the **b** that came down from heaven." 788
6:48 I am the **b** of life. 788
6:50 here is the **b** that comes down from heaven, 788
6:51 the living **b** that came down from heaven. 788
6:51 If anyone eats of this **b,** he will live forever. 788
6:51 This **b** is my flesh, which I give 788
6:58 This is the **b** that came down from heaven. 788
6:58 he who feeds on this **b** will live forever." 788
13:18 'He who shares my **b** has lifted up his heel 788
13:26 the one to whom I will give this **piece of b** *6040*
13:26 Then, dipping the **piece of b,** *6040*
13:27 As soon as Judas took the **b,** *6040*
13:30 As soon as Judas had taken the **b,** *6040*
21: 9 with fish on it, and some **b.** 788
21:13 Jesus came, took the **b** and gave it to them, 788
Ac 2:42 to the breaking *of* **b** and to prayer. 788
2:46 They broke **b** in their homes 788
12: 3 **Feast of Unleavened B.** *109*
20: 6 **Feast of Unleavened B,** *109+2465*
20: 7 of the week we came together to break **b.** 788
20:11 he went upstairs again and broke **b** and ate. 788
27:35 he took some **b** and gave thanks to God 788
1Co 5: 8 but with **b without yeast,** *109*
5: 8 the **b** of sincerity and truth. *NIG*
10:16 not the **b** that we break a participation in 788
11:23 on the night he was betrayed, took **b,** 788
11:26 whenever you eat this **b** and drink this cup, 788
11:27 whoever eats the **b** or drinks the cup of 788
11:28 to examine himself before he eats of the **b** 788
2Co 9:10 to the sower and **b** for food will also supply 788
2Th 3:12 to settle down and earn the **b** they eat. 788
Heb 9: 2 the table and the **consecrated b;** *788+4606*

BREADTH (5)

Ge 13:17 walk through the length and **b** of the land, 8145
1Ki 4:29 and a **b** *of* understanding as measureless as 8145
Isa 8: 8 Its outspread wings will cover the **b** 8145
40:12 the **b of** his **hand** marked off the heavens? 2455
Rev 20: 9 the **b** of the earth and surrounded the camp *4424*

BREAK (96) [BREACH, BREACHES, BREACHING, BREAKERS, BREAKING, BREAKS, BROKE, BROKEN, BROKENNESS, LAWBREAKER, LAWBREAKERS]

Ge 19: 9 and moved forward to **b down** the door. 8689
Ex 9: 9 and festering boils will **b out** on men 7255
12:46 *Do* not **b** any of the bones. 8689
13:13 but if you do not redeem it, **b** its **neck.** 6904
19:22 or the LORD *will* **b out** against them." 7287
19:24 or *he will* **b out** against them." 7287
23:24 **b** their sacred stones **to pieces.** 8689+8689
34:13 **B down** their altars, 5997
34:20 but if you do not redeem it, **b** its **neck.** 6904
Lev 11:33 and *you must* **b** the pot. 8689
26:19 *I will* **b down** your stubborn pride 8689
Nu 9:12 not leave any of it till morning or **b** any 8689
24: 8 **b** their bones **in pieces;** 1751
30: 2 *he must* not **b** his word 2725
Dt 1: 7 **B camp** and advance into the hill country of 7155
7: 5 **B down** their altars, 5997
12: 3 **B down** their altars, 5997
21: 4 in the valley *they are to* **b** the heifer's **neck.** 6904
31:16 and **b** the covenant I made with them. 7296
Jos 22:16 'How *could you* **b faith** with the God 5085+5086
Jdg 2: 1 '*I will* never **b** my covenant with you, 7296
2: 2 but *you shall* **b down** their altars.' 5997
5:12 Wake up, wake up, **b out** *in* song! 1819
11:35 a vow to the LORD that I cannot **b."** 8740
2Sa 5:20 He said, "As waters **b out,** 7288
1Ki 15:19 Now **b** your treaty with Baasha king 7296
2Ki 3:26 to **b through** to the king of Edom, 1324
1Ch 14:11 He said, "As waters **b out,** 7288
2Ch 16: 3 Now **b** your treaty with Baasha king 7296
Ezr 9:14 Shall we again **b** your commands 7296
Ne 4: 3 *he would* **b down** their wall of stones!" 7287
Job 24:16 In the dark, *men* **b into** houses, 3168
30:13 *They* **b up** my road; 5995
Ps 2: 3 "*Let us* **b** their chains," they say, 5998
3: 7 **b** the teeth of the wicked. 8689
10:15 **B** the arm of the wicked and evil man; 8689
27: 3 though war **b out** against me, 7756
46: 5 God will help her at **b of day.** 1332+7155
58: 6 **B** the teeth in their mouths, O God; 2238
Pr 25:15 and a gentle tongue *can* **b** a bone. 8689
Isa 5: 5 I *will* **b down** its wall, 7287
11:15 *He will* **b** it **up** into seven streams so 5782
14: 7 *they* **b** *into* singing. 7200
30:14 It will **b in pieces** like pottery, 8691
42: 3 A bruised reed *he will* not **b,** 8689
45: 2 *I will* **b down** gates of bronze and cut 8689
58: 6 to set the oppressed free and **b** every yoke? 5998
58: 8 Then your light *will* **b forth** like the dawn, 1324
Jer 4: 3 **"B up** your unplowed ground and do 5774
4: 4 or my wrath *will* **b out** and burn like fire 3655
14:21 with us and *do* not **b** it. 7296
15:12 *"Can a man* **b** iron— 8318
19:10 "Then **b** the jar while those who go 8689
21:12 or my wrath *will* **b out** and burn like fire 3655
Jer 28: 2 '*I will* **b** the yoke of the king of Babylon. 8689
28: 4 'for *I will* **b** the yoke of the king 8689
28:11 'In the same way *will I* **b** the yoke 8689
30: 8 '*I will* **b** the yoke off their necks 8689
33:20 'If *you can* **b** my covenant with the day 7296
49:35 "See, I *will* **b** the bow of Elam, 8689
50:26 **B open** her granaries; 7337
Eze 17:15 *Will he* **b** the treaty and yet escape? 7296
17:22 *I will* **b off** a tender sprig 7786
26:12 *they will* **b down** your walls 2238
27:26 But the east wind *will* **b** you **to pieces** in 8689
30:18 Dark will be the day at Tahpanhes when I **b** 8689
30:22 *I will* **b** both his arms, 8689
30:24 but *I will* **b** the arms of Pharaoh, 8689
34:27 when I **b** the bars of their yoke 8689
Da 2:40 so it will crush and **b** all the others. 10671
Hos 1: 5 In that day *I will* **b** Israel's bow in 8689
4: 2 *they* **b all bounds,** 7287
7: 1 They practice deceit, thieves **b into** houses, 995
10:11 and Jacob *must* **b up the ground.** 8440
10:12 and **b up** your unplowed ground; 5774
Am 1: 5 *I will* **b down** the gate of Damascus; 8689
Jnh 1: 4 that the ship threatened to **b up.** 8689
Mic 2:13 *they will* **b** through the gate and go out. 7287
3: 3 **b** their bones **in pieces;** 7200
4:13 and *you will* **b to pieces** many nations." 1990
Na 1:13 Now *I will* **b** their yoke from your neck 8689
Mal 2:15 *do* not **b faith** with the wife of your youth. 953
2:16 and *do* not **b faith.** 953
Mt 5:33 '*Do* not **b** *your* **oath,** *2155*
6:19 and where thieves **b in** and steal. *1482*
6:20 and where thieves *do* not **b in** and steal. *1482*
12:20 A bruised reed *he will* not **b,** *2862*
15: 2 "Why *do* your disciples **b** the tradition of *4124*
15: 3 "And why *do* you **b** the command of God *4124*
Lk 5: 6 of fish that their nets *began to* **b.** *1396*
Jn 19:33 *they did* not **b** his legs. *2862*
Ac 20: 7 of the week we came together *to* **b** bread. *3089*
Ro 2:25 but if *you* **b** the law, *1639+4127*
1Co 10:16 not the bread that *we* **b** a participation in *3089*
Gal 4:27 **b forth** and cry aloud, *4838*
Rev 5: 2 "Who is worthy *to* **b** the seals and open *3395*

BREAKERS (3) [BREAK]

Ps 42: 7 all your waves and **b** have swept over me. 1644
93: 4 mightier than the **b** *of* the sea— 5403
Jnh 2: 3 all your waves and **b** swept over me. 5403

BREAKFAST (1)

Jn 21:12 Jesus said to them, "Come and *have* **b."** *753*

BREAKING (23) [BREAK]

Ex 22: 2 "If a thief is caught **b in** and is struck so 4747
32:19 **b** them **to pieces** at the foot of 8689
Lev 13:42 it is an infectious disease **b out** on his head 7255
26:25 upon you to avenge the **b** of the covenant. NIH
26:44 **b** my covenant with them. 7296
Dt 9:17 **b** them **to pieces** before your eyes. 8689
31:20 rejecting me and **b** my covenant. 7296
Jos 9:20 on us for **b** the oath we swore to them." NIH
1Sa 25:10 Many servants *are* **b away** 7287
Isa 28:24 *Does he keep on* **b up** and harrowing 7337
58:13 "If you keep your feet from **b** the Sabbath NIH
Jer 2:34 though you did not catch them **b in.** 4747
Eze 16:59 because you have despised my oath by **b** 7296
17:18 He despised the oath by **b** the covenant. 7296
Joel 2: 8 through defenses without **b ranks.** 1298
Zec 11:14 **b** the brotherhood between Judah 7296
Mal 2:10 of our fathers *by* **b faith** with one another? 953
Jn 5:18 not only *was he* **b** the Sabbath, *3395*
Ac 2:42 to the **b** of bread and to prayer. *3082*
21:13 "Why are you weeping and **b** my heart? *5316*
Ro 2:23 do you dishonor God by **b** the law? *4126*
5:14 even over those who did not sin by **b a command,** *4126*
Jas 2:10 at just one point is guilty of **b** all of it. *NIG*

BREAKS (23) [BREAK]

Ex 1:10 if war **b out,** will join our enemies, 7925
22: 6 a fire **b out** and spreads into thornbushes so 3655
Lev 13:12 the disease **b out all over** his skin 7255+7255
Jdg 6:31 when *someone* **b down** his altar." 5997
Ps 29: 5 The voice of the LORD **b** the cedars; 8689
29: 5 the LORD **b in pieces** the cedars 8689
46: 9 *he* **b** the bow and shatters the spear, 8689
76:12 *He* **b** the spirit of rulers; 1306
107:16 for *he* **b down** gates of bronze and cuts 8689
141: 7 "As one plows and **b up** the earth, 1324
Pr 17:14 so drop the matter before a dispute **b out.** 1679
Ecc 10: 8 *whoever* **b through** a wall may be bitten by 7287
SS 2:17 Until the day **b** and the shadows flee, turn, 7031
4: 6 Until the day **b** and the shadows flee, 7031
Isa 66: 3 like *one who* **b** a dog's **neck;** 6904
Jer 23:29 **b** a rock **in pieces?** 7207
Eze 13: 5 to the **b** in the wall to repair it for the house 7288
Da 2:40 for iron **b** and smashes everything— 10182
2:40 and as iron **b** things **to pieces,** 10671
Am 4: 3 through **b in the wall,** 7288
Mic 2:13 One *who* **b open** the way will go up 7287
Mt 5:19 Anyone who **b** one of the least *3395*
1Jn 3: 4 Everyone who sins **b** the **law;** *490+4472*

BREAST (22) [BREASTPIECE, BREASTPLATE, BREASTPLATES, BREASTS]

Ge 49:25 blessings of the **b** and womb. 8716
Ex 29:26 the **b** of the ram for Aaron's ordination, 2601
29:27 the **b** that was waved and the thigh 2601
Lev 7:30 he is to bring the fat, together with the **b**, 2601
7:30 the **b** before the LORD as a wave offering. 2601
7:31 but the **b** belongs to Aaron and his sons. 2601
7:34 I have taken the **b** that is waved and 2601
8:29 He also took the **b**— 2601
10:14 the **b** that was waved and the thigh 2601
10:15 the **b** that was waved must be brought with 2601
Nu 6:20 and belong to the priest, together with the **b** 2601
18:18 just as the **b** *of* the wave offering and 2601
1Ki 3:20 by her **b** and put her dead son by my breast. 2668
3:20 by her breast and put her dead son by my **b**. 2668
Job 24:9 The fatherless child is snatched from the **b**; 8718
Ps 22:9 in you even at my mother's **b**. 8716
Isa 28:9 to those just taken from the **b**? 8716
49:15 the **baby at** her **b** and have no compassion 6403
Jer 31:19 after I came to understand, I beat my **b**. 3751
Eze 21:12 Therefore beat your **b**. 3751
Joel 2:16 gather the children, those nursing at the **b**. 8716
Lk 18:13 but beat his **b** and said, 'God, *5111*

BREASTPIECE (23) [BREAST]

Ex 25:7 to be mounted on the ephod and **b**. 3136
28:4 a **b**, an ephod, a robe, a woven tunic, 3136
28:15 "Fashion a **b** *for* making decisions— 3136
28:22 the **b** make braided chains of pure gold, 3136
28:23 and fasten them to two corners of the **b**. 3136
28:24 to the rings at the corners of the **b**, 3136
28:26 the **b** on the inside edge next to the ephod. 3136
28:28 the **b** are to be tied to the rings of the ephod 3136
28:28 the **b** will not swing out from the ephod. 3136
28:29 of Israel over his heart on the **b** *of* decision 3136
28:30 put the Urim and the Thummim in the **b**, 3136
29:5 the ephod itself and the **b**. 3136
35:9 to be mounted on the ephod and **b**. 3136
35:27 to be mounted on the ephod and **b**. 3136
39:8 They fashioned the **b**— 3136
39:15 For the **b** they made braided chains 3136
39:16 the rings to two of the corners of the **b**. 3136
39:17 to the rings at the corners of the **b**, 3136
39:19 the **b** on the inside edge next to the ephod. 3136
39:21 the rings of the **b** to the rings of the ephod 3136
39:21 so that the **b** would not swing out from 3136
Lev 8:8 He placed the **b** on him and put the Urim 3136
8:8 and put the Urim and Thummim in the **b**. 3136

BREASTPLATE (3) [BREAST]

Isa 59:17 He put on righteousness as his **b**, 9234
Eph 6:14 with the **b** of righteousness in place, *2606*
1Th 5:8 putting on faith and love as a **b**, *2606*

BREASTPLATES (3) [BREAST]

Rev 9:9 They had **b** like breastplates of iron, *2606*
9:9 They had breastplates like **b** of iron, *2606*
9:17 **Their b were** fiery red, dark blue, *2400+2606*

BREASTS (25) [BREAST]

Lev 9:20 these they laid on the **b**, 2601
9:21 the **b** and the right thigh before the LORD 2601
Job 3:12 to receive me and **b** that I might be nursed? 8716
Pr 5:19 may her **b** satisfy you always, 1843
SS 1:13 a sachet of myrrh resting between my **b**. 8716
4:5 Your two **b** are like two fawns, 8716
7:3 Your **b** are like two fawns, 8716
7:7 and your **b** like clusters of fruit. 8716
7:8 May your **b** be like the clusters of the vine, 8716
8:1 who was nursed at my mother's **b**! 8716
8:8 and her **b** are not yet grown. 8716
8:10 I am a wall, and my **b** are like towers. 8716
Isa 32:12 Beat your **b** for the pleasant fields, 8716
60:16 of nations and be nursed at royal **b**. 8718
66:11 and be satisfied at her comforting **b**; 8718
La 4:3 jackals offer their **b** to nurse their young, 8716
Eze 16:7 Your **b** were formed and your hair grew, 8716
23:3 In that land their **b** were fondled 8716
23:21 and your young **b** fondled. 8716
23:34 you will dash it to pieces and tear your **b**. 8716
Hos 2:2 and the unfaithfulness from between her **b**. 8716
9:14 Give them wombs that miscarry and **b** 8716
Na 2:7 like doves and beat upon their **b**. 4222
Lk 23:29 the wombs that never bore and the **b** *3466*
23:48 they beat their **b** and went away. *5111*

BREATH (60) [BREATHE, BREATHED, BREATHES, BREATHING, GOD-BREATHED]

Ge 1:30 everything that has the **b** *of* life in it— 5883
2:7 and breathed into his nostrils the **b** *of* life, 5972
6:17 every creature that has the **b** *of* life in it. 8120
7:15 Pairs of all creatures that have the **b** *of* life 8120
7:22 that had the **b** *of* life in its nostrils died. 5972+8120
Ex 15:10 But you blew with your **b**, 8120
2Sa 22:16 at the blast of **b** *from* his nostrils. 8120
Job 4:9 At the **b** *of* God they are destroyed; 5972
7:7 Remember, O God, that my life is but a **b**; 8120
9:18 He would not let me regain my **b** 8120
12:10 of every creature and the **b** *of* all mankind. 8120
15:30 the **b** *of* God's mouth will carry him away. 8120
19:17 My **b** is offensive to my wife; 8120
26:13 By his **b** the skies became fair; 8120
27:3 the **b** *of* God in my nostrils, 8120
32:8 the **b** *of* the Almighty, 5972
33:4 the **b** *of* the Almighty gives me life. 5972
34:14 and he withdrew his spirit and **b**, 5972
37:10 The **b** *of* God produces ice, 5972
41:21 His **b** sets coals ablaze, 5883
Ps 18:15 at the blast of **b** *from* your nostrils. 8120
33:6 their starry host by the **b** *of* his mouth. 8120
39:5 Each man's life is but a **b**. 2039
39:11 each man is but a **b**. 2039
62:9 Lowborn men are but a **b**, the highborn are 2039
62:9 together they are only a **b**. 2039
104:29 when you take away their **b**, 8120
135:17 nor is there **b** in their mouths. 8120
144:4 Man is like a **b**; 2039
150:6 Let everything that has **b** praise 5972
Ecc 3:19 All have the same **b**; 8120
SS 7:8 the fragrance of your **b** like apples, 678
Isa 2:22 who has but a **b** in his nostrils. 5972
11:4 the **b** *of* his lips he will slay the wicked. 8120
25:4 the **b** *of* the ruthless is like a storm driving 8120
30:28 His **b** is like a rushing torrent, 8120
30:33 the **b** *of* the LORD, 5972
33:11 your **b** is a fire that consumes you. 8120
40:7 the **b** *of* the LORD blows on them. 8120
42:5 who gives **b** to its people, 5972
57:13 a **mere b** will blow them away. 2039
57:16 the **b** of man that I have created. 5972
59:19 that the **b** *of* the LORD drives along. 8120
Jer 4:31 cry of the Daughter of Zion **gasping for b**, 3640
10:14 they have no **b** in them. 8120
38:16 who has given us **b**, 5883
51:17 they have no **b** in them. 8120
La 4:20 The LORD's anointed, our very **life b**, 678+8120
Eze 37:5 I will make **b** enter you, 8120
37:6 I will put **b** in you, 8120
37:8 but there was no **b** in them. 8120
37:9 Then he said to me, "Prophesy to the **b**; 8120
37:9 Come from the four winds, O **b**, 8120
37:10 and **b** entered them; 8120
Hab 2:19 there is no **b** in it. 8120
Ac 17:25 because he himself gives all men life and **b** *4466*
2Co 1:17 so that in the same **b** I say, *NIG*
2Th 2:8 the Lord Jesus will overthrow *with* the **b** *4460*
Rev 11:11 after the three and a half days a **b** of life *4460*
13:15 He was given power to give **b** to the image *4460*

BREATHE (4) [BREATH]

Jer 15:9 of seven will grow faint and **b** her **last.** 5870+5883
Eze 21:31 and **b out** my fiery anger against you; 7032
37:9 and **b** into these slain, that they may live.' " 7032
Da 10:17 My strength is gone and I **can hardly b.**" 4202+5972+8636

BREATHED (13) [BREATH]

Ge 2:7 the ground and **b** into his nostrils the breath 5870
25:8 Then Abraham **b his last** and died at 1588
25:17 *He* **b his last** and died, 1588
35:18 As she **b her last**— 3655+5883
35:29 Then he **b his last** and died 1588
49:33 **b his last** and was gathered to his people. 1588
Jos 10:40 He totally destroyed all who **b**, 5972
11:11 not sparing anything that **b**, 5972
11:14 not sparing anyone that **b**. 5972
1Ki 15:29 He did not leave Jeroboam anyone that **b**, 5972
Mk 15:37 With a loud cry, Jesus **b his last.** *1743*
Lk 23:46 When he had said this, *he* **b his last.** *1743*
Jn 20:22 And with that *he* **b on** them and said, *1874*

BREATHES (2) [BREATH]

Dt 20:16 do not leave alive anything that **b**. 5972
Job 14:10 he **b his last** and is no more. 1588

BREATHING (3) [BREATH]

1Ki 17:17 and finally stopped **b**. 5972
Ps 27:12 up against me, **b out** violence. 3641
Ac 9:1 Saul *was* still **b out** murderous threats *1863*

BRED (1) [BREED]

Est 8:10 who rode fast horses **especially b** for the king. 1201+2021+8247

BREECHES (KJV) See UNDERGARMENT

BREED (1) [BRED, BREEDING, BREEDS]

Job 21:10 Their bulls never fail *to* **b**; 6296

BREEDING (1) [BREED]

Ge 31:10 "In **b** season I once had a dream 2021+3501+7366

BREEDS (1) [BREED]

Pr 13:10 Pride only **b** quarrels, 5989

BREEZE (1) [BREEZES]

Ps 78:39 a passing **b** that does not return. 8120

BREEZES (1) [BREEZE]

Ps 147:18 he stirs up his **b**, and the waters flow. 8120

BRETHREN (KJV) See BROTHERS

BRIBE (16) [BRIBERY, BRIBES, BRIBING]

Ex 23:8 "Do not accept a **b**, 8816
23:8 for a **b** blinds those who see and twists 8816
Dt 16:19 Do not accept a **b**, 8816
16:19 a **b** blinds the eyes of the wise and twists 8816
27:25 "Cursed is the man who accepts a **b** to kill 8816
1Sa 12:3 From whose hand have I accepted a **b** 4111
Job 36:18 do not let a large **b** turn you aside. 4111
Ps 15:5 without usury and does not accept a **b** 8816
Pr 6:35 he will refuse the **b**, however great it is. 8816
17:8 A **b** is a charm to the one who gives it; 8816
17:23 a **b** in secret to pervert the course of justice. 8816
21:14 a **b** concealed in the cloak pacifies 8816
Ecc 7:7 and a **b** corrupts the heart. 5510
Isa 5:23 who acquit the guilty for a **b**, 8816
Mic 3:11 Her leaders judge for a **b**, 8816
Ac 24:26 that Paul would offer him a **b**, *5975*

BRIBERY (1) [BRIBE]

2Ch 19:7 there is no injustice or partiality or **b.**" 5228+8816

BRIBES (11) [BRIBE]

Dt 10:17 who shows no partiality and accepts no **b**. 8816
1Sa 8:3 and accepted **b** and perverted justice. 8816
Job 15:34 the tents of **those who love b**. 8816
Ps 26:10 whose right hands are full of **b**. 8816
Pr 15:27 but he who hates **b** will live. 5510
29:4 but one who is greedy for **b** tears it down. 9556
Isa 1:23 they all love **b** and chase after gifts. 8816
33:15 and keeps his hand from accepting **b**, 8816
Eze 22:12 In you men accept **b** to shed blood; 8816
Am 5:12 the righteous and take **b** and you deprive 4111
Mic 7:3 ruler demands gifts, the judge accepts **b**, 8936

BRIBING (1) [BRIBE]

Eze 16:33 **b** them to come to you from everywhere 8815

BRICK (4) [BRICKMAKING, BRICKS, BRICKWORK]

Ge 11:3 They used **b** instead of stone, 4246
Ex 1:14 in **b** and mortar and with all kinds of work 4246
Isa 65:3 and burning incense on **altars of b**; 4246
Jer 43:9 and bury them in clay in the **b pavement** at 4861

BRICKKILN (KJV) See BRICK PAVEMENT, BRICKWORK, BRICKMAKING

BRICKMAKING (1) [BRICK]

2Sa 12:31 and he made them work at **b**. 4861

BRICKS (8) [BRICK]

Ge 11:3 *let's* **make b** and bake them thoroughly." 4236+4246
Ex 5:7 the people with straw for **making b**; 4236+4246
5:8 to make the same number of **b** as before; 4246
5:14 of **b** yesterday or today, 4236
5:16 yet we are told, 'Make **b**!' 4246
5:18 yet you must produce your full quota of **b.**" 4246
5:19 to reduce the number of **b** *required of* you 4246
Isa 9:10 "The **b** have fallen down, 4246

BRICKWORK (1) [BRICK]

Na 3:14 tread the mortar, repair the **b**! 4861

BRIDAL (1) [BRIDE]

Ge 29:27 Finish this daughter's **b week**; 8651

BRIDE (25) [BRIDAL]

Ge 34:12 the **price for the b** and the gift I am to bring 4558
1Sa 18:25 king wants no other **price for** *the* **b** than 4558
Ps 45:9 at your right hand is the **royal b** in gold 8712
SS 4:8 Come with me from Lebanon, my **b**, 3987
4:9 You have stolen my heart, my sister, my **b**; 3987
4:10 delightful is your love, my sister, my **b**! 3987
4:11 as the honeycomb, my **b**; 3987
4:12 a garden locked up, my sister, my **b**; 3987
5:1 into my garden, my sister, my **b**; 3987
Isa 49:18 you will put them on, like a **b**. 3987
61:10 and as a **b** adorns herself with her jewels. 3987
62:5 as a bridegroom rejoices over his **b**, 3987
Jer 2:2 a **b** you loved me and followed me through 3994
2:32 a **b** her wedding ornaments? 3987
7:34 of **b** and bridegroom in the towns of Judah 3987
16:9 of joy and gladness and to the voices of **b** 3987
25:10 the voices of **b** and bridegroom, 3987
33:11 the voices of **b** and bridegroom, 3987
Joel 2:16 and the **b** her chamber. 3987
Jn 3:29 The **b** belongs to the bridegroom. *3811*
Rev 18:23 The voice of bridegroom and **b** will never *3811*
19:7 and his **b** has made herself ready. *1222*
21:2 as a **b** beautifully dressed for her husband. *3811*
21:9 "Come, I will show you the **b**, *3811*
22:17 The Spirit and the **b** say, "Come!" *3811*

BRIDE-PRICE (2)

Ex 22:16 *he* **must pay** the **b**, and she shall be his wife. 4555+4555
22:17 he must still pay the **b** *for* virgins. 4558

BRIDECHAMBER (KJV) See BRIDEGROOM

BRIDEGROOM (24) [BRIDEGROOM'S, BRIDEGROOMS]

Ex 4:25 "Surely you are a **b** *of* blood to me," 3163
4:26 (At that time she said "**b** *of* blood," 3163
Ps 19:5 like a **b** coming forth from his pavilion, 3163
Isa 61:10 as a **b** adorns his head like a priest, 3163
62:5 as a **b** rejoices over his bride, 3163
Jer 7:34 and **b** in the towns of Judah and the streets 3163
16:9 to the voices of bride and **b** in this place. 3163
25:10 the voices of bride and **b**, 3163
33:11 the voices of bride and **b**, 3163
Joel 2:16 Let the **b** leave his room and 3163
Mt 9:15 *of* the **b** mourn while he is with them? *3813*
9:15 when the **b** will be taken from them; *3812*
25:1 and went out to meet the **b**. *3812*
25:5 The **b** was a long time in coming, *3812*
25:6 At midnight the cry rang out: 'Here's the **b**! *3812*
25:10 on their way to buy the oil, the **b** arrived. *3812*
Mk 2:19 *of* the **b** fast while he is with them? *3813*
2:20 the time will come when the **b** will be taken *3812*
Lk 5:34 "Can you make the guests *of* the **b** fast *3813*
5:35 the time will come when the **b** will be taken *3812*
Jn 2:9 Then he called the **b** aside *3812*
3:29 The bride belongs to the **b**. *3812*
3:29 The friend who attends the **b** waits *3812*
Rev 18:23 The voice *of* **b** and bride will never *3812*

BRIDEGROOM'S (1) [BRIDEGROOM]

Jn 3:29 and is full of joy when he hears the **b** voice. *3812*

BRIDEGROOMS (1) [BRIDEGROOM]

Jdg 14:10 as was customary for **b**. 1033

BRIDLE (2) [BRIDLES]

Job 41:13 Who would approach him with a **b**? 4101+8270
Ps 32:9 by bit and **b** or they will not come to you. 6344+8270

BRIDLES (1) [BRIDLE]

Rev 14:20 rising as high as the horses' **b** for a distance *5903*

BRIEF (3) [BRIEFLY]

Ezr 9:8 "But now, for a **b** moment, 5071
Job 20:5 that the mirth of the wicked is **b**, 4946+7940
Isa 54:7 "For a **b** moment I abandoned you, 7785

BRIEFLY (3) [BRIEF]

Ac 24:4 that you be kind enough to hear us **b**. *5339*
Eph 3:3 as I have already written **b**. *1877+3900*
1Pe 5:12 I have written to you **b**, *1328+3900*

BRIER (1) [BRIERS]

Mic 7:4 The best of them is like a **b**, 2537

BRIERS (16) [BRIER]

Jdg 8:7 with desert thorns and **b**." 1402
8:16 by punishing them with desert thorns and **b**. 1402
Job 31:40 then let **b** come up instead of wheat 2560
Isa 5:6 and **b** and thorns will grow there. 9031
7:23 there will be only **b** and thorns. 9031
7:24 the land will be covered with **b** and thorns. 9031
7:25 you will no longer go there for fear of the **b** 9031
9:18 it consumes **b** and thorns, 9031
10:17 and consume his thorns and his **b**. 9031
27:4 If only there were **b** and thorns confronting 9031
32:13 a land overgrown with thorns and **b**— 9031
55:13 and instead of **b** the myrtle will grow. 6252
Eze 2:6 though **b** and thorns are all around you 6235
28:24 people of Israel have malicious neighbors who are painful **b** 6141
Hos 9:6 of silver will be taken over by **b**, 7853
Lk 6:44 or grapes from **b**. *1003*

BRIGANDINE (KJV) See ARMOR

BRIGHT (12) [BRIGHTENED, BRIGHTENS, BRIGHTER, BRIGHTLY, BRIGHTNESS]

Lev 13:2 a swelling or a rash or a **b spot** on his skin 994
14:56 and for a swelling, a rash or a **b spot**, 994
Job 25:5 the moon *is* not **b** and the stars are not pure 183
37:21 **b** as it is in the skies after 986
SS 6:10 fair as the moon, **b** as the sun, 1338
Eze 1:13 it was **b**, and lightning flashed out of it. 5586
8:2 and from there up his appearance was as **b** 2303
Mt 17:5 a **b** cloud enveloped them, *5893*
Lk 9:29 and his clothes became as **b** as a flash *3328*
Ac 22:6 a **b** light from heaven flashed around me. *2653*
Rev 19:8 Fine linen, **b** and clean, *3287*
22:16 and the **b** Morning Star." *3287*

BRIGHTENED (2) [BRIGHT]

1Sa 14:27 and his eyes **b**. 239
14:29 See how my eyes **b** when I tasted a little 239

BRIGHTENS (2) [BRIGHT]

Pr 16:15 When a king's face **b**, it means life; 240
Ecc 8:1 Wisdom **b** a man's face 239

BRIGHTER (5) [BRIGHT]

Job 11:17 Life *will be* **b** than noonday, 7756
Pr 4:18 **shining ever b** till the full light of day. 239+2143+2256
Isa 30:26 and the sunlight will be **seven** *times* *b*, AIT
La 4:7 Their princes *were* **b** than snow 2348
Ac 26:13 I saw a light from heaven, **b than** the sun, *3288+5642*

BRIGHTLY (1) [BRIGHT]

Pr 13:9 The light of the righteous **shines b**, 8523

BRIGHTNESS (8) [BRIGHT]

2Sa 22:13 Out of the **b** *of* his presence bolts 5586
23:4 the **b** after rain that brings the grass from 5586
Ps 18:12 of the **b** *of* his presence clouds advanced, 5586
Isa 59:9 for **b**, but we walk in deep shadows. 5588
60:3 and kings to the **b** *of* your dawn. 5586
60:19 nor will the **b** *of* the moon shine on you, 5586
Da 12:3 Those who are wise will shine like the **b** *of* the heavens, 2303
Am 5:20 pitch-dark, without a **ray of b**? 5586

BRILLIANCE (3) [BRILLIANT]

Ac 22:11 because the **b** of the light had blinded me. *1518*
Rev 1:16 like the sun shining in all its **b**. *1539*
21:11 its **b** was like that of a very precious jewel, *5891*

BRILLIANT (3) [BRILLIANCE]

Ecc 9:11 or wealth to the **b** or favor to the learned; 1067
Eze 1:4 and surrounded by **b light**. 5586
1:27 and **b light** surrounded him. 5586

BRIM (2)

Pr 3:10 and your vats *will* **b over** *with* new wine. 7287
Jn 2:7 so they filled them to **the b**. *539*

BRIMSTONE (KJV) See SULPHUR

BRING (728) [BRINGING, BRINGS, BROUGHT]

Ge 6:17 I *am going to* **b** floodwaters on the earth 995
6:19 *to* **b** into the ark two of all living creatures, 995
8:17 **B out** every kind of living creature that is 3655
9:14 Whenever I **b clouds** over the earth 6725+6727
15:9 So the LORD said to him, "**B** me a heifer, 4374
18:19 so that the LORD *will* **b about** 995
19:5 **B** them **out** to us so that we can have sex 3655
19:8 *Let me* **b** them **out** to you, 3655
27:4 the kind of tasty food I like and **b** it to me 995
27:5 to hunt game and **b** it **back**, 995
27:7 '**B** me some game 995
27:9 the flock and **b** me two choice young goats, 4374
27:12 be tricking him and *would* **b down** a curse 995
27:25 "My son, **b** me some of your game to eat, 5602
28:15 and *I will* **b** you **back** to this land. 8740
31:39 not **b** you animals torn by wild beasts; 995
34:12 the price for the bride and the gift **I** *am to b* AIT
37:14 and **b** word **back** *to* me." 8740
38:24 "**B** her **out** and have her burned to death!" 3655
42:20 *you must* **b** your youngest brother to me, 995
42:34 But **b** your youngest brother to me 995
42:37 of my sons to death if *I do* not **b** him **back** 995
42:37 and I *will* **b** him **back**." 8740
42:38 **b** my gray head **down** to the grave 3718
43:6 "Why *did you* **b** *this* **trouble** on me 8317
43:7 '**B** your brother **down** here'?" 3718
43:9 not **b** him **back** to you and set him here 995
44:21 '**B** him **down** to me so I can see him 3718
44:29 **b** my gray head **down** to the grave 3718
44:31 **b** the gray head of our father **down** 3718
44:32 I said, 'If *I do* not **b** him **back** to you, 995
45:13 And **b** my father **down** here quickly." 3718
45:18 **b** your father and your families back to me. 4374
46:4 and I *will* **surely b** you **back** again. 6590+6590
47:16 "Then **b** your livestock," said Joseph. 2035
48:9 "**B** them to me so I may bless them." 4374
Ex 3:8 the hand of the Egyptians and to **b** them **up** 6590
3:10 **b** my people the Israelites **out** 3655
3:11 and **b** the Israelites **out** of Egypt?" 3655
3:17 *to* **b** you **up** out of your misery in Egypt 6590
6:6 and *I will* **b** you **out** from under the yoke 3655
6:8 And *I will* **b** you to the land I swore 995
6:13 to **b** the Israelites **out** of Egypt. 3655
6:26 "**B** the Israelites **out** of Egypt 3655
7:4 of judgment *I will* **b out** my divisions, 3655
7:5 against Egypt and **b** the Israelites **out** of it." 3655
9:3 of the LORD *will* **b** a terrible plague 2118
9:19 **b** your livestock and everything you have in the field **to a place of shelter**, 6395
9:20 of the LORD **hurried to b** their slaves 5674
10:4 I *will* **b** locusts into your country 995
11:1 "*I will* **b** one more plague on Pharaoh and 995
12:12 and *I will* **b** judgment on all the gods 6913
12:42 that night to **b** them **out** of Egypt, 3655
14:13 the LORD *will* **b** you today. 6913
15:17 *You will* **b** them *in* and plant them on 995
15:26 not **b** on you any of the diseases I brought 8492
16:5 to prepare what *they* **b in**, 995
17:3 "Why *did you* **b** us **up** out of Egypt 6590
18:19 before God and **b** their disputes to him. 995
18:22 but *have them* **b** every difficult case to you; 995
19:24 "Go down and *b* Aaron **up** with you. AIT
22:9 both parties *are to* **b** their cases before 995
22:13 *he shall* **b in** the remains as evidence 995
23:19 "**B** the best of the firstfruits of your soil *to* 995
23:20 to guard you along the way and to **b** you to 995
23:23 My angel will go ahead of you and **b** you 995
25:2 "Tell the Israelites *to* **b** me an offering. 4374
27:20 "Command the Israelites *to* **b** you clear oil 4374
29:4 Then **b** Aaron and his sons to the entrance 7928
29:8 **B** his sons and dress them in tunics 7928
29:10 "**B** the bull to the front of the Tent 7928
32:2 and **b** them to me." 995
32:12 **relent and do not b** disaster on your people 5714
32:14 Then the LORD relented and did not **b** 6913
34:26 "**B** the best of the firstfruits of your soil to 995
35:5 *to* **b** to the LORD an offering of gold, 995
36:3 *to* **b** freewill offerings morning 995
40:4 **B in** the table and set out what belongs 995
40:4 **b in** the lampstand and set up its lamps. 995
40:12 "**B** Aaron and his sons to the entrance to 7928
40:14 **B** his sons and dress them in tunics. 7928
Lev 1:2 to the LORD, **b** as your offering an animal 7928
1:5 the priests *shall* **b** the blood and sprinkle it 7928
1:13 and the priest *is to* **b** all of it and burn it 7928
1:15 The priest *shall* **b** it to the altar, 7928
2:4 " 'If *you* **b** a grain offering baked in 7928
2:8 **B** the grain offering made of these things to 995
2:11 " 'Every grain offering *you* **b** to 7928
2:12 *You may* **b** them to the LORD as 7928
2:14 " 'If *you* **b** a grain offering of firstfruits to 7928
3:3 *to* **b** a sacrifice made to the LORD by fire: 7928
3:9 *to* **b** a sacrifice made to the LORD by fire: 7928
4:3 *he must* **b** to the LORD a young bull 7928
4:14 the assembly *must* **b** a young bull as 7928
4:23 *he must* **b** as his offering a male goat 995
4:28 *he must* **b** as his offering for 995
4:32 *he is to* **b** a female without defect. 995
5:6 *he must* **b** to the LORD a female lamb 995
5:7 *he is to* **b** two doves or two young pigeons 995
5:8 *He is to* **b** them to the priest, 995
5:11 *he is to* **b** as an offering for his sin a tenth 995
5:12 *He is to* **b** it to the priest, 995
5:15 *he is to* **b** to the LORD as a penalty a ram 995
5:18 *to* **b** to the priest as a guilt offering a ram 995
6:6 And as a penalty *he must* **b** to the priest, 995
6:14 Aaron's sons *are to* **b** it before the LORD, 7928
6:20 the offering Aaron and his sons *are to* **b** to 7928
6:21 **b** it well-mixed and present 995
7:14 *He is to* **b** one of each kind as an offering, 7928
7:29 *to* **b** part of it as his sacrifice to 995
7:30 *to* **b** the offering made to the LORD 995
7:30 *he is to* **b** the fat, together with the breast, 995
7:38 the Israelites to **b** their offerings to 7928
8:2 "**B** Aaron and his sons, 4374
12:6 *to* **b** to the priest at the entrance to the Tent 995
12:8 *to* **b** two doves or two young pigeons, 4374
14:10 the eighth day *he must* **b** two male lambs 4374
14:23 "On the eighth day *he must* **b** them 995
15:3 This is how his discharge *will* **b about** 928+2118
15:29 and **b** them to the priest at the entrance to 995
16:9 Aaron *shall* **b** the goat whose lot falls to 7928
16:11 "Aaron *shall* **b** the bull 7928
16:20 *he shall* **b forward** the live goat. 7928
17:5 so the Israelites *will* **b** to the LORD 995
17:5 *They must* **b** them to the priest, that is, 995
17:9 and *does* not **b** it to the entrance to the Tent 995
19:21 *must* **b** a ram to the entrance to the Tent 995
22:16 to eat the sacred offerings and so **b upon** 5951
22:20 *Do* not **b** anything with a defect, 7928
23:10 to give you and you reap its harvest, **b** to 995
23:14 until the very day you **b** this offering 995
23:17 **b** two loaves made of two-tenths of 995
24:2 "Command the Israelites *to* **b** you clear oil 4374
26:16 *I will* **b** upon you sudden terror, 7212
26:25 And *I will* **b** the sword upon you 995
Nu 3:6 "**B** the tribe of Levi and present them 7928
5:9 All the sacred contributions the Israelites **b** 7928
5:16 " 'The priest *shall* **b** her and have her stand 7928
5:25 before the LORD and **b** it to the altar. 7928
6:10 on the eighth day *he must* **b** two doves 995
6:12 for the period of his separation and *must* **b** 995
7:11 "Each day one leader *is to* **b** his offering 7928
8:9 **B** the Levites to the front of the Tent 7928
8:10 *You are to* **b** the Levites before the LORD, 7928
11:16 "**B** me seventy of Israel's elders 665
13:20 Do your best *to* **b back** some of the fruit of 4374
14:16 'The LORD was not able to **b** these people 995
14:24 *I will* **b** him into the land he went to, 995
14:31 *I will* **b** them **in** to enjoy 995
15:9 **b** with the bull a grain offering 7928
15:10 **b** half a hin of wine as a drink offering. 7928
15:27 *he must* **b** a year-old female goat for 7928
18:2 **B** your fellow Levites 7928
18:9 the gifts *they* **b** me as most holy offerings, 8740
18:13 that *they* **b** to the LORD will be yours. 995
19:2 Tell the Israelites *to* **b** you a red heifer 4374
20:4 Why *did you* **b** the LORD's community 995

Nu 20: 5 Why *did you* **b** us **up** out of Egypt 6590
20: 8 *You will* **b** water **out** of the rock for 3655
20:10 *must we* **b** you water **out** of this rock?" 3655
20:12 *you will* not **b** this community into 995
22: 8 "and *I will* **b** you **back** the answer 8740
27:17 one who will lead them out and **b** them **in,** 995
Dt 1:17 **B** me any case too hard for you, 7928
1:22 ahead to spy out the land for us and **b back** 8740
4:38 to **b** you **into** their land to give it to you 995
6:23 But he brought us out from there to **b** us **in** 995
7:26 *Do* not **b** a detestable thing into your house 995
12: 6 there **b** your burnt offerings and sacrifices, 995
12:11 *to* **b** everything I command you: 995
14:28 **b** all the tithes of that year's produce 3655
16:17 Each of you must **b** a gift in proportion to NIH
19:12 **b** him **back** from the city, 4374
21:12 **B** her into your home 995
21:19 of him and **b** him to the elders at the gate 3655
22: 8 so that *you may* not **b** the guilt of bloodshed 8492
22:15 the girl's father and mother *shall* **b** proof
that she was a virgin 2256+3655+4374
23:18 not **b** the earnings of a female prostitute or 995
24: 4 *Do* not **b sin** *upon* the land 2627
24: 5 stay at home and **b happiness** *to* the wife 8523
24:11 the loan **b** the pledge **out** to you. 3655
26:10 now *I* **b** the firstfruits of the soil that you, 995
28:49 The LORD *will* **b** a nation against you 5951
28:60 *He will* **b** upon you all the diseases 8740
28:61 The LORD *will* also **b** on you every kind 6623
29:19 This *will* **b disaster** *on* the watered land 6200
30: 4 and **b** you **back.** 4374
30: 5 He *will* **b** you to the land that belonged 995
31:21 even before *I* **b** them into 995
31:23 "Be strong and courageous, for you *will* **b** 995
32:39 I put to death and *I* **b to life,** 2649
33: 7 **b** him to his people. 995
Jos 2: 3 **"B out** the men who came to you 3655
6:18 **b about** *your own* **destruction** 3049
6:18 to destruction and **b trouble** *on* it. 6579
6:22 and **b** her **out** and all who belong to her, 3655
7: 7 why *did you ever* **b** this people **across** 6296+6296
7:25 LORD *will* **b trouble** *on* you today." 6579
10:22 **b** those five kings **out** 3655
18: 6 **b** them here to me and I will cast lots 995
23:15 so the LORD *will* **b** on you all 995
24:20 he will turn and **b disaster** on you and make 8317
Jdg 6:13 *'Did* not the LORD **b** us **up** out of Egypt?' 6590
6:18 and **b** my offering and set it before you." 3655
6:30 **"B out** your son. 3655
13: 8 to teach us how *to* **b up** the boy who is to 6913
16:25 **"B out** Samson to entertain us." 7924
19:22 **"B out** the man who came to your house 3655
19:24 *I will* **b** them **out** to you now, 3655
Ru 3:15 "**B** me the shawl you are wearing 2035
4: 4 **b** the matter **to** your **attention** 265+1655
1Sa 4: 3 the LORD **b defeat upon** us today before 5597
4: 3 *Let us* **b** the ark of the LORD's covenant 4374
9:23 **"B** the piece of meat I gave you, 5989
11: 2 of you and so **b** disgrace on all Israel." 8492
11:12 **B** these men to us and we will put them 5989
13: 9 **"B** me the burnt offering and 5602
14:18 Saul said to Ahijah, **"B** the ark of God." 5602
14:34 'Each of you **b** me your cattle and sheep, 5602
15:32 "**B** me Agag king of the Amalekites." 5602
16:17 "Find someone who plays well and **b** him 995
17:18 and **b back** some assurance from them. 4374
19:15 **"B** him **up** to me in his bed so 6590
20:21 **b** them here,' then come, because, 4374
20:31 Now send and **b** him to me, 4374
21:14 Why **b** him to me? 995
21:15 that *you have to* **b** this fellow here to carry 995
23: 9 to Abiathar the priest, **"B** the ephod." 5602
28: 8 he said, "and **b up** for me the one I name." 6590
28: 9 a trap for my life to **b about** my **death?"** 4637
28:11 "Whom *shall I* **b up** for you?" 6590
28:11 **"B up** Samuel," he said. 6590
30: 7 the son of Ahimelech, **"B** me the ephod." 5602
2Sa 3:12 I will help you **b** all Israel **over** to you." 6015
3:13 unless you **b** Michal daughter of Saul 995
6: 2 of Judah to **b up** from there the ark of God, 6590
9:10 to farm the land for him and **b in** the crops, 995
12:11 *to* **b** calamity upon you. 7756
12:23 Can I **b** him **back** again? 8740
13:10 **"B** the food here **into** 995
14:10 **b** him to me, 995
14:17 word of my lord the king **b** me rest, 2118+4200
14:21 Go, **b back** the young man Absalom." 8740
15:14 to overtake us and **b** ruin upon us and put 5616
15:25 *he will* **b** me **back** and let me see it 8740
17: 3 **b** all the people **back** 8740
17:13 then all Israel *will* **b** ropes to that city, 5951
17:14 of Ahithophel in order to **b** disaster 995
18:22 *that will* **b** you **a reward."** 5162
19:11 be the last to **b** the king **back** to his palace, 8740
19:12 So why should you be the last to **b back** 8740
19:15 the king and **b** him **across** the Jordan. 6296
19:41 **b** him and his household **across** 6296
20:15 they were battering the wall to **b** it **down,** 5877
22:28 on the haughty *to* **b** them **low.** 9164
23: 5 *Will he* not **b to fruition** my salvation 7541
1Ki 2: 9 **B** his gray head **down** 3718
3:24 Then the king said, **"B** me a sword." 4374
8: 1 to **b up** the ark of the LORD's covenant 6590
8:34 of your people Israel and **b** them **back** to 8740
13:18 **'B** him **back** with you to your house so 8740
14:10 *to* **b** disaster on the house of Jeroboam. 995
17:10 *"Would you* **b** me a little water in a jar 4374
1Ki 17:11 "And **b** me, please, a piece of bread." 4374
17:13 for me from what you have and **b** it to me, 3655
18:19 And **b** the four hundred and fifty prophets 7695
21:21 'I *am going to* **b** disaster on you. 995
21:29 *I will* not **b** this disaster in his day, 995
21:29 but *I will* **b** it on his house in the days 995
22: 9 **"B** Micaiah son of Imlah **at once."** 4554
2Ki 2:20 **"B** me a new bowl," he said, 4374
3:15 But now **b** me a harpist." 4374
4: 6 she said to her son, **"B** me another one." 5602
5: 7 Can I kill and **b back to life?** 2649
10:22 **"B** robes for all the ministers of Baal." 3655
11:15 **"B** her **out** between the ranks and put to 3655
21:12 *to* **b** such disaster on Jerusalem and Judah 995
22:16 *to* **b** disaster on this place and its people, 995
22:20 the disaster I *am going to* **b** on this place.' " 995
1Ch 11:19 Because they risked their lives *to* **b** it **back,** 995
13: 3 **b** the ark of our God **back** 6015
13: 5 to **b** the ark of God from Kiriath Jearim. 995
13: 6 of Judah (Kiriath Jearim) to **b up** from there 6590
13:12 "How *can I ever* **b** the ark of God to me?" 995
15: 3 in Jerusalem to **b up** the ark of the LORD 6590
15:12 to consecrate yourselves and **b up** the ark of 6590
15:13 *did* not **b** it up the first time that NIH
15:14 in order to **b up** the ark of the LORD, 6590
15:25 of units of a thousand went to **b up** the ark 6590
16:29 **B** an offering and come before him; 5951
21: 3 Why *should he* **b** guilt on Israel?" 2118+4200
22:19 so that you *may* **b** the ark of the covenant of 995
2Ch 5: 2 to **b up** the ark of the LORD's covenant 6590
6:25 of your people Israel and **b** them **back** to 8740
18: 8 **"B** Micaiah son of Imlah **at once."** 4554
23:14 **"B** her **out** *between* the ranks and put to 3655
24: 6 to **b in** from Judah and Jerusalem 995
24: 9 in Judah and Jerusalem that they *should* **b** 995
24:19 to the people to **b** them **back** to him, 8740
28:13 *"You must* not **b** those prisoners here," 995
29:31 Come and **b** sacrifices and thank offerings 995
31:10 the people began to **b** their contributions *to* 995
34:24 *to* **b** disaster on this place and its people— 995
34:28 the disaster I *am going to* **b** on this place 995
Ezr 3: 7 so that they *would* **b** cedar logs by sea 995
7:27 into the king's heart to **b honor** *to* the house 6995
8:17 so that they *might* **b** attendants to us for 995
Ne 1: 9 I will gather them from there and **b** them to 995
4: 2 **b** the stones **back to life** 2649
8: 1 They told Ezra the scribe to **b out** the Book 995
8:15 into the hill country and **b back** branches 995
10:31 the neighboring peoples **b** merchandise 995
10:34 when each of our families is to **b** to 995
10:36 we *will* **b** the firstborn of our sons and 995
10:37 *we will* **b** to the storerooms of the house 995
10:37 we will **b** a tithe of our crops to the Levites, NIH
10:38 **b** a tenth of the tithes **up** 6590
10:39 *are to* **b** their contributions of grain, 995
11: 1 the rest of the people cast lots to **b** one out 995
12:44 the fields around the towns they were to **b** 4043
Est 1:11 to **b** before him Queen Vashti, 995
2: 3 *to* **b** all these beautiful girls into the harem 7695
5: 5 **"B** Haman **at once,"** the king said, 4554
6: 5 **"B** *him* **in,"** the king ordered. 995
6: 8 *have them* **b** a royal robe the king has worn 995
Job 8:10 *Will they* not **b forth** words 3655
10:17 *You* **b new** witnesses against me 2542
10:18 "Why then *did you* **b** me **out** of the womb? 3655
12:12 Does not long life **b** understanding? NIH
13:19 *Can* anyone **b charges** against me? 8189
14: 3 *Will you* **b** him before you for judgment? 995
14: 4 Who *can* **b** what is pure from the impure? 5989
16: 5 comfort from my lips *would* **b** you **relief.** 3104
19:29 for wrath will **b** punishment by the sword, NIH
30:23 I know *you will* **b** me **down** *to* death, 8740
38:32 *Can you* **b forth** the constellations 3655
39: 3 They crouch down and **b forth** their young; 7114
39:12 Can you trust him *to* **b in** your grain 8740
40:11 look at every proud man and **b** him **low,** 9164
40:20 The hills **b** him their produce, 5951
Ps 7: 9 **b to an end** the violence of the wicked 1698
17:13 O LORD, confront them, **b** them **down;** 4156
18:27 but **b low** those whose eyes are haughty. 9164
28: 4 for what their hands have done and **b back** 8740
37:14 the bow to **b down** the poor and needy, 5877
43: 3 *let them* **b** me to your holy mountain, 995
44: 3 nor *did* their arm **b** them **victory;** 3828
44: 6 my sword *does* not **b** me **victory;** 3828
51:16 or *I would* **b** it; 5989
52: 5 **b** you **down** to everlasting **ruin:** 5997
55: 3 for *they* **b down** suffering upon me 4572
55:23 *will* **b down** the wicked into the pit 3718
56: 7 in your anger, O God, **b down** the nations. 3718
59:11 and **b** them **down.** 3718
60: 9 Who *will* **b** me to the fortified city? 3297
64: 8 against them and **b** them to **ruin;** 4173
65: 4 Blessed are those you choose and **b near** 7928
68:22 Lord says, *"I will* **b** them from Bashan; 8740
68:22 *I will* **b** them from the depths of the sea, 8740
68:29 at Jerusalem kings *will* **b** you gifts. 3297
68:30 Humbled, may it **b** bars of silver. NIH
71:20 of the earth you will again **b** me **up.** 6590
72: 3 mountains *will* **b** prosperity to the people, 5951
72:10 and of distant shores *will* **b** tribute to him; 8740
74:12 *you* **b** salvation upon the earth. 7188
76:11 the neighboring lands **b** gifts to the One to 3297
86: 4 **B joy** *to* your servant, for to you, O Lord, 8523
86: 9 *they will* **b glory** to your name. 3877
96: 8 **b** an offering and come into his courts. 5951
104:20 *You* **b** darkness, it becomes night, 8883
Ps 108:10 Who *will* **b** me *to* the fortified city? 3297
143: 2 *Do* not **b** your servant into judgment, 907+995
143: 8 *Let* the morning **b** me **word** 9048
143:11 in your righteousness, **b** me **out** of trouble. 3655
Pr 3: 2 and **b** you prosperity. 3578
3: 8 *This will* **b** health to your body 2118
10: 4 but diligent hands **b wealth.** 6947
10:16 The wages of the righteous **b** them life, 4200
13: 5 but the wicked **b shame** and disgrace. 944
18: 6 A fool's lips **b** him strife, 995
19:24 *he will* not even **b** it **back** to his mouth! 8740
22: 4 of the LORD **b** wealth and honor and life. 6813
24:22 who knows what calamities they can **b?** NIH
25: 8 *do* not **b** hastily to court, 3655
26:15 he is too lazy to **b** it **back** to his mouth. 8740
27: 1 you do not know what a day *may* **b forth.** 3528
27: 9 Perfume and incense **b joy** *to* the heart, 8523
27:11 Be wise, my son, and **b joy** *to* my heart; 8523
29:17 *he will* **b** delight to your soul. 5989
29:21 *he will* **b** grief in the end. 2118
31:31 and *let* her works **b** her **praise** at 2146
Ecc 3:17 "God *will* **b to judgment** both 9149
3:22 For who *can* **b** him to see what will happen 995
10:10 but skill *will* **b** success. 4178
11: 9 that for all these things God *will* **b** you 995
12:14 For God *will* **b** every deed into judgment, 995
SS 1: 4 *Let* the king **b** me **into** his chambers. 995
8: 2 and **b** you to my mother's house— 995
8:11 *to* **b** for its fruit a thousand shekels 995
Isa 3:17 the Lord *will* **b sores on** the heads of 8558
7:17 The LORD *will* **b** on you and 995
7:17 he will **b** the king of Assyria." NIH
8: 7 *to* **b** against them the mighty floodwaters 6590
14: 2 Nations will take them and **b** them 995
15: 9 but *I will* **b** still more upon Dimon— 8883
17:11 *you* **b** them **to bud,** 7255
19: 3 **b** their plans **to nothing;** 1182
19:17 Judah *will* **b** terror *to* the Egyptians; 2118+4200
21: 2 *I will* **b to an end** all 8697
21:14 **b** water for the thirsty; 910
21:14 **b** food for the fugitives. 7709
23: 9 to **b low** the pride of all glory and 2725
25:11 God *will* **b down** their pride despite 9164
25:12 *He will* **b down** your high fortified walls 8820
25:12 *he will* **b** them **down** to the ground, 5595
28:19 of this message *will* **b** sheer terror. 2118
30: 3 Egypt's shade will **b** you disgrace. NIH
30: 5 who **b** neither help nor advantage, NIH
31: 2 Yet he too is wise and *can* **b** disaster; 995
40: 9 You *who* **b good tidings** *to* Zion, 1413
40: 9 You *who* **b good tidings** *to* Jerusalem, 1413
41:22 **"B in** [your idols] to tell us what is going 5602
42: 1 on him and *he will* **b** justice to the nations. 3655
42: 3 In faithfulness *he will* **b forth** justice; 3655
43: 5 *I will* **b** your children from the east 995
43: 6 **B** my sons from afar and my daughters 995
43: 9 *Let them* **b** *in* their witnesses 5989
43:14 and **b down** as fugitives all the Babylonians 3718
45: 7 I **b** prosperity and create disaster; 6913
46:11 What I have said, that *will I* **b about;** 995
48:15 *I will* **b** him, 995
49: 5 the womb to be his servant to **b** Jacob **back** 8740
49: 6 and **b back** those of Israel I have kept. 8740
49: 6 that you *may* **b** my salvation to the ends of 2118
49:22 *they will* **b** your sons in their arms 995
50: 8 Who then *will* **b charges** against me? 8189
51: 5 and my arm *will* **b justice** *to* the nations. 9149
52: 7 the feet of *those who* **b good news,** 1413
52: 7 *who* **b** good **tidings,** who proclaim
salvation, 1413
54: 7 with deep compassion *I will* **b** you **back.** 7695
56: 7 these *I will* **b** to my holy mountain 995
60:11 men *may* **b** you the wealth of the nations— 995
60:17 Instead of bronze *I will* **b** you gold, 995
60:17 Instead of wood *I will* **b** you bronze, 995
65: 9 *I will* **b forth** descendants from Jacob, 3655
66: 4 and *will* **b** upon them what they dread. 995
66: 9 **b to the moment of birth** 8689
66: 9 up the womb when I **b to delivery?"** 3528
66:15 *he will* **b down** his anger with fury, 8740
66:20 And *they will* **b** all your brothers, 995
66:20 "They will **b** them, NIH
66:20 as the Israelites **b** their grain offerings, 995
Jer 2: 9 "Therefore *I* **b charges** against you again," 8189
2: 9 "And *I will* **b charges** 8189
2:29 "Why *do you* **b charges** against me? 8189
3:14 and **b** you *to* Zion. 995
7:34 *I will* **b an end** *to* the sounds of joy 8697
10:18 *I will* **b distress** on them so that they may 7674
11:11 'I *will* **b** on them 995
11:23 because *I will* **b** disaster on the men 995
12: 1 O LORD, when *I* **b a case** before you. 8189
12: 9 **b** them to devour. 910
12:15 **b** each of them **back** 8740
14:22 the worthless idols of the nations **b rain?** 1772
15: 7 *I will* **b bereavement** and destruction 8897
15: 8 At midday *I will* **b** a destroyer against 995
15: 8 suddenly *I will* **b down** on them anguish 5877
16: 9 in your days I *will* **b an end** *to* the sounds 8697
17:18 **B** on them the day of disaster; 995
17:21 on the Sabbath day or **b** it through the gates 995
17:22 *Do* not **b** a load **out** of your houses 3655
17:24 and **b** no load through the gates of this city 995
18:22 when *you* suddenly **b** invaders 995
19: 3 *to* **b** a disaster on this place that will make 995
19:15 I *am going to* **b** on this city and the villages 995
23: 3 and *will* **b** them **back** to their pasture, 8740

Jer 23:12 *I will* **b** disaster on them in 995
23:40 *I will* **b** upon you everlasting disgrace— 5989
24: 6 and *I will* **b** them **back** to this land. 8740
25: 9 "and *I will* **b** them against this land 995
25:13 *I will* **b** upon that land all 995
25:29 I am beginning to **b disaster** on the city 8317
25:31 for the LORD will **b** charges against NIH
25:31 he *will* **b judgment** on all mankind and put 9149
26: 3 not **b** on them the disaster I was planning 6913
26:13 Then the LORD *will* **relent and not b** 5714
26:15 you *will* **b** the guilt of innocent blood 5989
26:19 **relent, so that** he *did* **not b** 5714
26:19 *to* **b** a terrible disaster on ourselves!" 6913
27:22 'Then *I will* **b** them **back** and restore them 6590
28: 3 Within two years I *will* **b back** 8740
28: 4 also **b back** to this place Jehoiachin son 8740
29:10 to **b** you **back** to this place. 8740
29:14 "and *will* **b** you **back** *from* captivity. 8740
29:14 "and *will* **b** you **back** to the place 8740
30: 3 **b** my people Israel and Judah **back** 8740
30:19 *I will* **b** them **honor,** 3877
30:21 *I will* **b** him **near** and he will come close 7928
31: 8 I *will* **b** them from the land of the north 995
31: 9 they will pray *as I* **b** them **back.** 3297
31:23 "When I **b** them **back** *from* captivity, 8740
31:28 and to overthrow, destroy and **b disaster,** 8317
32:18 but **b** *the* **punishment** *for* the fathers' sins 8966
32:37 *I will* **b** them **back** to this place 8740
33: 6 I *will* **b** health and healing to it; 6590
33: 7 **b** Judah and Israel **back** 8740
33: 9 Then this city *will* **b** me renown, joy, 2118+4200
33:11 the voices of *those who* **b** thank offerings *to* 995
34:22 and *I will* **b** them **back** to this city. 8740
35:17 *to* **b** on Judah and on everyone living 995
36: 7 Perhaps they *will* **b** their petition before 5877
36:14 **"B** the scroll from which you have read to 4374
36:31 *I will* **b** on them and those living 995
37:20 *Let* me **b** my petition before you: 5877
42:17 or escape the disaster I *will* **b** on them.' 995
44: 7 Why **b** such great disaster on yourselves 6913
44:11 I am determined to **b** disaster on you and NIH
45: 5 For I *will* **b** disaster on all people, 995
46:25 "I *am about to* **b punishment** on Amon god 7212
48:44 for *I will* **b** upon Moab the year 995
49: 5 I *will* **b** terror on you from all those 995
49: 8 for *I will* **b** disaster on Esau at 995
49:16 from there *I will* **b** you **down,"** 3718
49:32 in distant places and *will* **b** disaster 995
49:36 *I will* **b** against Elam the four winds from 995
49:37 *I will* **b** disaster upon them, 995
50: 9 For I will stir up and **b** against Babylon 6590
50:19 But *I will* **b** Israel **back** to his own pasture 8740
50:34 so that *he may* **b rest** *to* their land, 8089
51:40 "*I will* **b** them **down** like lambs to 3718
51:64 because of the disaster I *will* **b** upon her. 995
La 1:21 *May you* **b** the day you have announced 995
3:33 For *he does* not willingly **b affliction** 6700
Eze 5:16 *I will* **b more and more** famine upon you 3578
5:17 and *I will* **b** the sword against you. 995
6: 3 I *am about to* **b** a sword against you, 995
6:10 I did not threaten in vain to **b** this calamity 6913
7:24 *I will* **b** the most wicked of the nations 995
9: 1 **"B** the guards of the city **here,** 7928
9:10 but *I will* **b down** on their own heads 5989
11: 8 the sword is what *I will* **b** against you, 995
11:17 from the nations and **b** you **back** from 665
11:21 *I will* **b down** on their own heads 5989
12: 4 **b out** your belongings packed for exile. 3655
12:13 *I will* **b** him to Babylonia, 995
14:17 if *I* **b** a sword against that country and say, 995
16:38 *I will* **b** *upon* you the blood vengeance 5989
16:40 *They will* **b** a mob against you, 6590
16:43 I *will* surely **b down** 5989
17:19 *I will* **b down** on his head my oath 5989
17:20 *I will* **b** him to Babylon 995
17:24 the LORD **b down** the tall tree and make 9164
20: 6 to them that *I would* **b** them **out** of Egypt 3655
20:15 not **b** them into the land I had given them— 995
20:34 *I will* **b** you from the nations 3655
20:35 *I will* **b** you into the desert of the nations 995
20:37 and *I will* **b** you into the bond of 995
20:38 Although *I will* **b** them **out** of the land 3655
20:41 as fragrant incense when **I b** you **out** from 3655
20:42 when I **b** you into the land of Israel, 995
23:22 in disgust, and *I will* **b** them against you 995
23:32 *it will* **b** scorn and derision, 2118+4200
23:46 **B** a mob against them and give them over 6590
24: 5 **b** it **to a boil** and cook the bones 8409+8410
26: 3 and *I will* **b** many nations against you, 6590
26: 7 *to* **b** against Tyre Nebuchadnezzar king 995
26:19 like cities no longer inhabited, and when I **b** 6590
26:20 then *I will* **b** you **down** with those who go 3718
26:21 *I will* **b** you *to* a horrible end 5989
28: 7 I *am going to* **b** foreigners against you, 995
28: 8 *They will* **b** you **down** to the pit, 3718
29: 8 I *will* **b** a sword against you 995
29:14 *I will* **b** them **back** *from* captivity 8740
32: 8 *I will* **b** darkness over your land, 5989
32: 9 the hearts of many peoples when I **b about** 995
33: 2 'When *I* **b** the sword against a land, 995
34:13 *I will* **b** them **out** from the nations 3655
34:13 and *I will* **b** them into their own land. 995
34:16 I will search for the lost and **b back** 8740
36:24 from all the countries and **b** you **back** 995
36:29 and make it plentiful and *will* not **b** famine 5989
37:12 to open your graves and **b** you **up** 6590
37:12 *I will* **b** you **back** to the land of Israel. 995
Eze 37:13 when I open your graves and **b** you **up** 6590
37:21 and **b** them **back** into their own land. 995
38: 4 and **b** you **out** with your whole army— 3655
38:16 O Gog, *I will* **b** you against my land, 995
38:17 for years that I *would* **b** you against them. 995
39: 2 *I will* **b** you from the far north 6590
39:25 *I will* now **b** Jacob **back** *from* captivity 8740
Da 1: 3 to **b in** some of the Israelites from 995
1:18 of the time set by the king to **b** them **in,** 995
2:44 **b** them **to an end,** 10508
5: 2 to **b in** the gold and silver goblets 10085
9:14 not hesitate *to* **b** the disaster upon us, for 995
9:24 to **b in** everlasting righteousness, 995
Hos 4: 1 because the LORD has a charge to **b** NIH
4: 4 "But *let* no man **b a charge,** 8189
4: 4 for your people are like *those who* **b charges** against a priest. 8189
4:19 and their sacrifices *will* **b** *them* **shame.** 1017
9:13 But Ephraim *will* **b out** their children to 3655
12: 2 The LORD has a charge to **b** NIH
12:13 The LORD used a prophet *to* **b** Israel **up** 6590
Joel 2:16 **b together** the elders, gather the children, 7695
3: 2 I will gather all nations and **b** them **down** to 3718
3:11 **B down** your warriors, O LORD! 5737
Am 4: 1 **"B** us some drinks!" 995
4: 4 **B** your sacrifices every morning, 995
5:22 Even though *you* **b** me burnt offerings 6590
5:22 Though you **b** choice fellowship offerings, NIH
5:25 *"Did you* **b** me sacrifices 5602
6: 3 You put off the evil day and **b near** a reign 5602
9: 1 **B** them **down** on the heads of all the people; 1298
9: 2 from there *I will* **b** them **down.** 3718
9: 7 *"Did I* not **b** Israel **up** from Egypt, 6590
9:14 *I will* **b back** my exiled people Israel; 8740
Ob 1: 3 'Who *can* **b** me **down** to the ground?' 3718
1: 4 from there *I will* **b** you **down,"** 3718
Jnh 3:10 he had compassion and *did* not **b** upon them 6913
Mic 1:15 *I will* **b** a conqueror against you who live 995
2:12 *I will* **surely b together** the remnant 7695+7695
2:12 *I will* **b** them together like sheep in a pen, 8492
7: 9 *He will* **b** me **out** into the light; 3655
Na 1: 9 against the LORD he *will* **b** to an end; 6913
Zep 1:17 *I will* **b distress** on the people 7674
3:10 my scattered people, *will* **b** me offerings. 3297
3:20 at that time *I will* **b** you **home.** 995
Hag 1: 8 the mountains and **b down** timber and build 995
Zec 3: 8 I *am going to* **b** my servant, the Branch. 995
4: 7 Then *he will* **b out** the capstone to shouts 3655
8: 8 *I will* **b** them **back** to live in Jerusalem; 995
8:14 as I had determined to **b disaster** upon you 8317
10:10 *I will* **b** them **back** from Egypt 8740
10:10 *I will* **b** them to Gilead and Lebanon, 995
13: 9 This third *I will* **b** into the fire; 995
14:18 The LORD *will* **b** on them 2118
Mal 1: 8 When *you* **b** blind animals for sacrifice, 5602
1:13 "When *you* **b** injured, 995
3: 3 LORD will have *men who will* **b** offerings 5602
3:10 **B** the whole tithe into the storehouse, 995
Mt 10:34 not suppose that I have come *to* **b** peace to *965*
10:34 I did not come *to* **b** peace, but a sword. *965*
13:30 the wheat and **b** it into my barn.' " *NIG*
14:18 **"B** them here to me," he said. *5770*
16: 7 "It is because *we* didn't **b** any bread." *3284*
17:17 **B** the boy here to me." *5770*
21: 2 Untie them and **b** them to me. *72*
21:41 **b** those wretches to a wretched **end,"** *660*
Mk 4:21 *"Do* you **b** in a lamp to put it under a bowl *2262*
6:27 with orders *to* **b** John's head. *5770*
8:14 The disciples had forgotten *to* **b** bread, *3284*
9:19 **B** the boy to me." *5770*
11: 2 Untie it and **b** it here. *5770*
12:15 **"B** me a denarius and let me look at it." *5770*
Lk 1:16 of the people of Israel *will he* **b back to** *2188*
2:10 *I* **b** you **good news** of great joy that will be *2294*
9:31 which he was about to **b to fulfillment** *4444*
9:41 **B** your son here." *4642*
12:49 "I have come *to* **b** fire on the earth, *965*
12:51 Do you think I came *to* **b** peace on earth? *1443*
14:21 the streets and alleys of the town and **b in** *1652*
15:22 **B** the best robe and put it on him. *1766*
15:23 **B** the fattened calf and kill it. *5770*
18: 7 And *will* not God **b about** justice *4472*
19:27 **b** them here and kill them in front of me.' " *72*
19:30 Untie it and **b** it here. *72*
19:42 on this day what would **b** you peace— *NIG*
Jn 7:45 "Why didn't *you* **b** him in?" *72*
10:16 I must **b** them also. *72*
11:52 to **b** them **together** and make them one. *5251*
14:13 so that the Son *may* **b glory to** the Father. *1519*
16:14 He *will* **b glory to** me by taking *1519*
21:10 **"B** some of the fish you have just caught." *5770*
Ac 7:42 " *'Did you* **b** me sacrifices *4712*
10: 5 Now send men to Joppa *to* **b back** *3569*
11:14 He *will* **b** you **a message** through *3281+4839*
12: 4 *to* **b** him **out** for public trial after *343*
12: 6 The night before Herod was *to* **b** him *4575*
13:47 the Gentiles, *that* you *may* **b** salvation *1639+1650*
17: 5 of Paul and Silas *in order to* **b** them **out** to *4575*
19:39 If there is anything further *you* **want to b up,** *2118*
22: 5 *to* **b** these people as prisoners to Jerusalem *72*
23:10 by force and **b** him into the barracks. *72*
23:15 the commander to **b** him before you on *2864*
23:18 for me and asked me *to* **b** this young man *72*
23:20 to **b** Paul before the Sanhedrin tomorrow on *2864*
24:17 I came to Jerusalem *to* **b** my people gifts *4472*
24:19 to be here before you and **b charges** *2989*
Ac 27:10 to be disastrous and **b** great loss to ship *NIG*
28:19 not that I had any **charge to b against** *2989*
Ro 5:21 through righteousness **to b** eternal life *1650*
7:10 commandment that was **intended to b** life actually brought death. *1650*
8:33 Who *will* **b any charge** *1592*
10: 6 (that is, *to* **b** Christ **down)** *2864*
10: 7 (that is, *to* **b** Christ **up** from the dead). *343*
10:15 the feet *of* those who **b** good **news!"** *2294*
11:12 much greater riches will their fullness **b!** *NIG*
13: 2 and those who do so *will* **b** judgment *3284*
13: 4 **agent** of wrath **to b punishment** *1690*
15: 7 in order to **b** praise to God. *NIG*
1Co 3:13 because the Day *will* **b** it **to light.** *1317*
4: 5 He *will* **b to light** what is hidden *5894*
8: 8 But food *does* not **b** us **near** to God; *4225*
14: 6 unless *I* **b** you some revelation *3281*
2Co 8: 6 to **b** also **to completion** this act of grace *2200*
Eph 1:10 **b** all things in heaven and on earth **together under one head,** *368*
6: 4 **b** them **up** in the training and instruction of *1763*
Php 3:21 **b** everything **under** his **control,** *5718*
1Th 4:14 and so we believe that God *will* **b** *72*
1Ti 5:12 Thus *they* **b** judgment on themselves, *2400*
6:15 which God *will* **b about** in his own time— *1259*
2Ti 4:11 Get Mark and **b** him with you, *72*
4:13 **b** the cloak that I left with Carpus at Troas, *5770*
4:18 and *will* **b** me **safely** *5392*
Heb 9:28 but to **b** salvation to those who are waiting *1650*
12:17 *He could* **b about** no change of mind, *2351*
Jas 1:20 for man's anger *does* not **b about** *2237*
5:19 the truth and someone *should* **b** him **back,** *2188*
1Pe 3:18 to **b** you to God. *4642*
2Pe 2: 2 **b** the way of truth **into disrepute.** *1059*
2:11 *do* not **b** slanderous accusations *5770*
3:12 That day will **b about** the destruction of *1328*
2Jn 1:10 to you and *does* not **b** this teaching, *5770*
Jude 1: 9 **b** a slanderous accusation **against** *2214*
1:21 the mercy of our Lord Jesus Christ to **b** you *NIG*
Rev 15: 4 O Lord, and **b glory to** your name? *1519*
17:16 They *will* **b** her to ruin *4472*
21:24 the kings of the earth *will* **b** their splendor *5770*

BRING UP, BRINGING UP (Anglicized)

See REAR, REARING

BRINGING (67) [BRING]

Ge 19: 9 *They* **kept b pressure** on Lot 4394+7210
Ex 6:27 about **b** the Israelites **out** of Egypt. 3655
14:11 What have you done to us by **b** us **out** 3655
36: 5 "The people *are* **b** more than enough 995
36: 6 so the people were restrained from **b** more, 995
Lev 4: 3 **b** guilt on the people, 4200
17: 4 instead of **b** it to the entrance to the Tent 995
18: 3 where I *am* **b** you. 995
20:22 that the land where I *am* **b** you to live may 995
23:37 as sacred assemblies for **b** offerings made 7928
Nu 14: 3 Why *is* the LORD **b** us to this land only 995
Dt 8: 7 For the LORD your God *is* **b** you into 995
1Sa 28:15 "Why have you disturbed me by **b** me **up?"** 6590
2Sa 4:10 and thought he was **b good news,** 1413
18:26 The king said, "He *must be* **b good news,** 1413
19:10 about **b** the king **back?"** 8740
19:43 not the first to speak of **b back** our king?" 8740
1Ki 1:42 like you *must be* **b** good **news."** 1413
8:32 condemning the guilty and **b down** 5989
2Ki 4:42 **b** the man of God twenty loaves 995
1Ch 12:40 and Naphtali **came b** food on donkeys, 995
2Ch 6:23 repaying the guilty by **b down** 5989
34:14 While they *were* **b out** the money 3655
Ne 10:35 for **b** to the house of the LORD each year 995
13:15 on the Sabbath and **b in** grain and loading it 995
13:15 And *they were* **b** all this **into** Jerusalem on 995
13:16 from Tyre who lived in Jerusalem *were* **b in** 995
Est 2:20 as she had done when he was **b** her **up.** 594
Ps 104:14 **b forth** food from the earth: 3655
Pr 31:14 **b** her food from afar. 995
SS 8:10 in his eyes like *one* **b** contentment. 3655
Isa 1:13 Stop **b** meaningless offerings! 995
46:13 **b** my righteousness **near,** 7928
60: 9 **b** your sons from afar, 995
Jer 4: 6 For I *am* **b** disaster from the north, 995
5:15 "I *am* **b** a distant nation against you— 995
6:19 I am **b** disaster on this people, 995
17:26 **b** burnt offerings and sacrifices, 995
28: 6 **b** the articles of the LORD's house and all the exiles **back** 8740
41: 5 **b** grain offerings and incense with them to 995
43:11 **b** death to those destined for death, NIH
Eze 17:12 **b** them *back* with him to Babylon. 995
20: 9 to the Israelites by **b** them **out** of Egypt. 3655
22:31 with my fiery anger, **b down** 5989
27:10 and helmets on your walls, **b** you splendor. 5989
46:20 to avoid **b** them into the outer court 3655
Da 9:12 against us and against our rulers by **b** 995
Mt 15:30 Great crowds came to him, **b** the lame, *1571+2400+3552*
26:62 **testimony** that these men *are* **b against** *2909*
27:13 **testimony** *they are* **b against** *2909*
Mk 2: 3 Some men came, **b** to him a paralytic, *5770*
10:13 *People were* **b** little children to Jesus *4712*
14:60 What *is* this **testimony** *that* these men *are* **b against** you?" *2909*
Lk 18:15 *People were* also **b** babies to Jesus *4712*
Jn 18:29 "What charges *are you* **b** *5770*

Jn 19: 4 *I am* **b** him out to you to let you know 72
19:34 **b** a sudden flow of blood and water. 2002
Ac 5:16 **b** their sick and those tormented 5770
7:11 **b** great suffering, and our fathers could NIG
14:15 We are **b** you **good news,** 2294
17:20 **b** some strange ideas **to** 1662
24: 8 **charges** we *are* **b against** 2989
25: 7 **b** many serious charges **against** 2965
Ro 3: 5 That God is unjust in **b** his wrath on us? 2214
1Ti 5:10 such as **b up children,** showing hospitality, 5452
Heb 2:10 In **b** many sons to glory, 72
2Pe 2: 1 **b** swift destruction **on** themselves. 2042

BRINGS (85) [BRING]

Ex 13: 5 When the LORD **b** you into the land of 995
13:11 "After the LORD **b** you into the land of 995
Lev 1: 2 any of you **b** an offering to the LORD, 7928
2: 1 " 'When someone **b** a grain offering to 7928
4:32 " 'If *he* **b** a lamb as his sin offering, 995
7:29 'Anyone *who* **b** a fellowship offering to 7928
22:21 When anyone **b** from the herd or flock 7928
Nu 5:18 the bitter water that **b a curse.** 826
5:19 may this bitter water that **b a curse** 826
5:22 that **b a curse** enter your body so 826
5:24 the bitter water that **b a curse,** 826
5:27 to drink the water that **b a curse,** it will go 826
15: 4 then the *one who* **b** his offering shall present 7928
15:13 in this way when *he* **b** an offering made 7928
16:30 the LORD **b about** something totally new, 1343
Dt 6:10 When the LORD your God **b** you into 995
7: 1 When the LORD your God **b** you into 995
33:14 with the best the sun **b forth** and the finest 9311
1Sa 2: 6 "The LORD **b death** and makes alive; 4637
2: 6 *he* **b down** *to* the grave and raises up. 3718
2Sa 23: 4 like the brightness after rain that **b** the grass NIH
Job 9:23 When a scourge **b** sudden **death,** 4637
12:22 of darkness and **b** deep shadows into 3655
22: 4 that he rebukes you and **b** charges 995
28:11 of the rivers and **b** hidden things *to* light. 3655
34:11 *he* **b upon** him what his conduct deserves. 5162
37:13 *He* **b** the clouds to punish men, 5162
Ps 75: 7 *He* **b** one **down,** he exalts another. 9164
76:10 your wrath against men **b** you **praise,** 3344
94:20 *one that* **b on** misery by its decrees? 3670
135: 7 he sends lightning with the rain and **b out** 3655
Pr 10: 1 A wise son **b joy** *to* his father, 8523
10:16 income of the wicked **b** them punishment. 4200
10:22 The blessing of the LORD **b wealth,** 6947
10:31 mouth of the righteous **b forth** wisdom, 5649
11:17 but a cruel man **b trouble** *on* himself. 6579
11:29 *He who* **b trouble** on his family 6579
12:18 but the tongue of the wise **b** healing. NIH
13:17 but a trustworthy envoy **b** healing. NIH
14: 3 A fool's talk **b** a rod to his back, 928
14:23 All hard work **b** a profit, 2118
15: 4 The tongue that **b** healing is a tree of life, NIH
15: 6 the income of the wicked **b** them **trouble.** 6579
15:20 A wise son **b joy** *to* his father, 8523
15:27 A greedy man **b trouble** *to* his family, 6579
15:30 A cheerful look **b joy** *to* the heart, 8523
16:22 but folly **b** punishment to fools. NIH
17:21 To have a fool for a son **b** grief; 4200
17:25 A foolish son **b** grief to his father NIH
19: 4 Wealth **b** many friends, 3578
19:15 Laziness **b on** deep sleep, 5877
19:26 a son *who* **b shame** and disgrace. 1017
21:12 **b** the wicked **to ruin.** 2021+4200+6156+8273
21:15 it **b** joy to the righteous but terror NIH
25:23 As a north wind **b** rain, 2655
25:23 so a sly tongue **b** angry looks. NIH
29: 3 man who loves wisdom **b joy** *to* his father, 8523
29:23 A man's pride **b** him **low,** 9164
31:12 *She* **b** him good, not harm, 1694
Isa 40:23 He **b** princes to naught and reduces 5989
40:26 He *who* **b out** the starry host one by one, 3655
Jer 10:13 He sends lightning with the rain and **b out** 3655
13:16 before *he* **b** *the* **darkness,** 3124
51:16 He sends lightning with the rain and **b out** 3655
La 3:32 Though *he* **b grief,** 3324
3:51 What I see **b grief** to my soul because of all 6618
Eze 22: 3 *that* **b** *on* herself doom by shedding blood 995
46: 4 The burnt offering the prince **b** to 7928
Am 5: 9 on the stronghold and **b** the fortified city 995
Na 1:15 the feet of *one who* **b good news,** 1413
Mal 2:12 *he* **b** offerings to the LORD Almighty. 5602
Mt 12:35 The good man **b** good things out of *1675*
12:35 and the evil man **b** evil things out of *1675*
13:52 like the owner of a house who **b out** *1675*
Lk 6:45 The good man **b** good things out of *4734*
6:45 and the evil man **b** evil things out of *4734*
Jn 2:10 "Everyone **b out** the choice wine first and *5502*
Ro 3: 5 **b out** God's righteousness **more clearly,** *5319*
4:15 because law **b** wrath. *2981*
5:18 *that* **b life** for all men. *2437*
2Co 3: 9 the ministry that **b** righteousness! *NIG*
7:10 Godly sorrow **b** repentance that leads *2237*
7:10 but worldly sorrow **b** death. *2981*
Tit 2:11 that **b** salvation has appeared to all men. *NIG*
Heb 1: 6 God **b** his firstborn **into** the world, *1650+1652*

BRINK (1)

Pr 5:14 I have come to the **b** of utter ruin in 5071

BRITTLE (1)

Da 2:42 be partly strong and partly **b.** 10752

BROAD (11) [BROADEN]

Nu 25: 4 kill them and expose them in **b daylight** 9087
2Sa 12:11 he will lie with your wives **in b daylight.** 2021+2021+2296+4200+6524+9087
12:12 but I will do this thing **in b daylight** 2021+5584+9087
Ne 3: 8 as far as the **B** Wall. 8146
12:38 past the Tower of the Ovens to the **B** Wall, 8146
Job 37:10 and the **b** waters become frozen. 8145
Isa 30:23 your cattle will graze in **b** meadows. 8143
33:21 be like a place of **b** rivers and streams. 3338+8146
Am 8: 9 at noon and darken the earth in **b daylight.** 240+3427
Mt 7:13 and **b** is the road that leads to destruction, *2353*
2Pe 2:13 of pleasure is to carouse in **b daylight.** *2465*

BROADEN (2) [BROAD]

2Sa 22:37 *You* **b** the path beneath me, 8143
Ps 18:36 *You* **b** the path beneath me, 8143

BROIDED (KJV) See BRAIDED HAIR

BROILED (1)

Lk 24:42 They gave him a piece *of* **b** fish, *3966*

BROKE (81) [BREAK]

Ex 9:10 festering boils **b out** on men and animals. 7255
34: 1 that were on the first tablets, which *you* **b.** 8689
Lev 24:10 and a **fight b out** in the camp between him 5897
26:13 *I* **b** the bars of your yoke and enabled you 8689
Dt 10: 2 that were on the first tablets, which *you* **b.** 8689
32:51 *of you* **b faith** with me in the presence of 5085
Jos 3:14 when the people **b camp** to cross the Jordan, 185+4946+5825
Jdg 6:32 because *he* **b down** Baal's altar. 5997
7:19 They blew their trumpets and **b** the jars 5879
1Sa 11:11 during the last watch of the night *they* **b** 995
19: 8 Once more war **b out,** 2118
23:28 Then Saul **b off** his pursuit of David 4946+8740
2Sa 23:16 So the three mighty men **b** through 1324
2Ki 8:21 but he rose up and **b through** by night; 5782
14:13 Then Jehoash went to Jerusalem and **b down** the wall 7287
18: 4 *He* **b into pieces** the bronze snake 4198
19:36 So Sennacherib king of Assyria **b camp** 5825
23: 8 *He* **b down** the shrines at the gates— 5997
25:10 **b down** the walls around Jerusalem. 5997
25:13 The Babylonians **b up** the bronze pillars, 8689
1Ch 11:18 So the Three **b** through the Philistine lines, 1324
15:13 that the LORD our God **b out in anger** 7287
20: 4 war **b out** with the Philistines, at Gezer. 6641
2Ch 15:16 **b** it **up** and burned it in the Kidron Valley. 1990
21: 9 but he rose up and **b through** by night. 5782
25:23 and **b down** the wall of Jerusalem from 7287
26: 6 against the Philistines and **b down** the walls 7287
26:19 leprosy **b out** on his forehead. 2436
34: 4 These *he* **b to pieces** and scattered over 1990
36:19 They set fire to God's temple and **b down** 5997
Job 22: 9 and **b** the strength of the fatherless. 1917
29:17 *I* **b** the fangs of the wicked and snatched 8689
Ps 74:13 *you* **b** the heads of the monster in 8689
76: 3 There *he* **b** the flashing arrows, 8689
78:21 his fire **b out** against Jacob, 5956
102:23 In the course of my life *he* **b** my strength; 6700
106:29 and a plague **b out** among them. 7287
107:14 the deepest gloom and **b away** their chains. 5998
Isa 7:17 a time unlike any since Ephraim **b away** 6073
37:37 So Sennacherib king of Assyria **b camp** 5825
38:13 but like a lion *he* **b** all my bones; 8689
Jer 2:20 "Long ago *you* **b off** your yoke 8689
28:10 the neck of the prophet Jeremiah and **b** it, 8689
31:32 because they **b** my covenant, 7296
39: 8 and the houses of the people and **b down** 5997
52:14 of the imperial guard **b down** all the walls 5997
52:17 The Babylonians **b up** the bronze pillars, 8689
Eze 17: 4 *he* **b off** its topmost shoot 7786
17:16 and whose treaty *he* **b.** 7296
17:19 that he despised and my covenant that *he* **b.** 7296
19: 7 *He* **b down** their strongholds 1548
29: 7 *you* **b** and their backs were wrenched. 8689
44: 7 fat and blood, and *you* **b** my covenant. 7296
Da 2:45 **b** the iron, the bronze, the clay, the silver and the gold **to pieces.** 10182
Zec 11:10 Then I took my staff called Favor and **b** it, 1548
11:14 Then *I* **b** my second staff called Union, 1548
Mt 14:19 he gave thanks and **b** the loaves. *3089*
15:36 *he* **b** them and gave them to the disciples, *3089*
26:26 Jesus took bread, gave thanks and **b** it, *3089*
27:52 The tombs **b open** and the bodies *487*
Mk 4:37 and the waves **b** over the boat, *2095*
5: 4 the chains apart and **b** the irons on his feet. *5341*
6:41 he gave thanks and **b** the loaves. *2880*
8: 6 *he* **b** them and gave them to his disciples *3089*
8:19 *I* **b** the five loaves for the five thousand, *3089*
8:20 I **b** the seven loaves for the four thousand, *NIG*
14: 3 She **b** the jar and poured the perfume *5341*
14:22 Jesus took bread, gave thanks and **b** it, *3089*
14:72 And he **b down** and wept. *2095*
Lk 9:16 he gave thanks and **b** them. *2880*
22:19 And *he* took bread, gave thanks and **b** it, *3089*
24:30 **b** it and began to give it to them. *3089*
24:35 by them when he **b** the bread. *3082*
Jn 19:32 The soldiers therefore came and **b** the legs *2862*
Ac 2:46 They **b** bread in their homes *3089*
8: 1 a great persecution **b out** against the church *1181*
20:11 *he* went upstairs again and **b** bread and ate. *3089*
23: 7 a dispute **b out** between the Pharisees and *1181*
27:35 Then he **b** it and began to eat. *3089*
1Co 11:24 *he* **b** it and said, "This is my body, *3089*
Rev 16: 2 and ugly and painful sores **b out** on *1181*

BROKEN (130) [BREAK]

Ge 17:14 he *has* **b** my covenant." 7296
38:29 "So this is how *you have* **b out!"** 7287+7288
Ex 21: 8 because he *has* **b faith** with her. 953
Lev 6:21 and present the grain offering **b** *in* pieces 9519
6:28 the meat is cooked in *must* **be b;** 8689
11:35 an oven or cooking pot *must* **be b up.** 5997
13:20 an infectious skin disease *that has* **b out** 7255
13:25 it is an infectious disease *that has* **b out** in 7255
13:39 a harmless rash *that has* **b out** on the skin; 7255
15:12 that the man touches *must* **be b,** 8689
Nu 15:31 the LORD's word and **b** his commands, 7296
Dt 21: 6 the heifer whose **neck was b** in the valley, 6904
Jdg 6:30 because *he has* **b down** Baal's altar and cut 5997
1Sa 2: 4 "The bows of the warriors are **b,** 3146
4:18 His neck **was b** and he died, 8689
5: 4 and hands *had* **been b off** and were lying on 4162
14:33 *"You have* **b faith,"** he said. 953
2Sa 5:20 the LORD *has* **b out** *against* my enemies 7287
6: 8 because the LORD's wrath *had* **b out** 7287
1Ki 19:10 **b down** your altars, 2238
19:14 **b down** your altars, 2238
2Ki 25: 4 Then the city wall **was b through,** 1324
1Ch 13:11 because the LORD's wrath *had* **b out** 7287
14:11 God *has* **b out** *against* my enemies 7287
2Ch 24: 7 of that wicked woman Athaliah *had* **b into** 7287
32: 5 the **b** *sections* of the wall 7287
Ne 1: 3 The wall of Jerusalem *is* **b down,** 7287
2:13 which *had been* **b down,** and its gates, 7287
Job 2: 8 a **piece of b pottery** and scraped himself 3084
4:10 yet the teeth of the great lions are **b.** 5996
4:20 and dusk *they* **are b to pieces;** 4198
7: 5 my skin *is* **b** and festering. 8090
17: 1 My spirit **is b,** my days are cut short, 2472
24:20 but **are b** like a tree. 8689
30:24 a hand on a **b man** when he cries for help 6505
31:22 *let* it **be b off** at the joint. 8689
31:39 without payment or **b** the spirit 5870
38:15 and their upraised arm **is b.** 8689
Ps 31:12 I have become like **b** pottery. 6
34:20 not one of them *will* **be b.** 8689
37:15 and their bows *will* **be b.** 8689
37:17 for the power of the wicked *will* **be b,** 8689
51:17 The sacrifices of God are a **b** spirit; 8689
51:17 a **b** and contrite heart, O God, 8689
69:20 Scorn *has* **b** my heart 8689
80:12 Why *have you* **b down** its walls so 7287
89:40 *You have* **b through** all his walls 7287
119:126 your law *is being* **b.** 7296
124: 7 the snare *has* **been b,** and we have escaped. 8689
Pr 25:28 Like a city whose walls **are b down** is 7287
Ecc 4:12 A cord of three strands is not quickly **b.** 5998
12: 6 or the golden bowl *is* **b;** 8368
12: 6 or the wheel **b** at the well, 8368
Isa 1:28 But rebels and sinners will both be **b,** 8691
5:27 not a sandal thong *is* **b.** 5998
8:15 they will fall and **be b,** 8689
10:27 the yoke *will* **be b** because you have grown 2472
14: 5 The LORD *has* **b** the rod of the wicked, 8689
14:29 that the rod that struck you *is* **b;** 8689
24: 5 the statutes and **b** the everlasting covenant. 7296
24:19 The earth **is b up,** the earth is split asunder, 8318+8318
27:11 *they* **are b off** and women come 8689
33: 8 The treaty *is* **b,** its witnesses are despised, 7296
33:20 nor any of its ropes **b.** 5998
58:12 you will be called Repairer of **B** Walls, 7288
59: 5 and *when* one is **b,** an adder is hatched. 2318
Jer 2:13 **b** cisterns that cannot hold water. 8689
5: 5 with one accord they too *had* **b off** the yoke 8689
11:10 of Israel and the house of Judah *have* **b** 7296
11:16 and its branches *will be* **b.** 8318
22:28 Is this man Jehoiachin a despised, **b** pot, 7046
23: 9 My heart *is* **b** within me; 8689
28:12 Shortly after the prophet Hananiah *had* **b** 8689
28:13 *You have* **b** a wooden yoke, 8689
33:21 *can* **be b** and David will no longer have 7296
39: 2 the city wall **was b through.** 1324
48: 4 Moab *will* **be b;** 8689
48:17 say, 'How **b** *is* the mighty scepter, 8689
48:17 how **b** the glorious staff!' NIH
48:25 her arm **is b,"** declares the LORD. 8689
48:38 for *I have* **b** Moab like a jar 8689
50:23 How **b** and shattered is the hammer of 1548
51: 8 Babylon will suddenly fall and **be b.** 8689
51:30 the bars of her gates **are b.** 8689
51:56 and their bows *will be* **b.** 3169
52: 7 Then the city wall **was b through,** 1324
La 2: 9 their bars *he has* **b** and destroyed. 8689
3: 4 and my flesh grow old and *has* **b** my bones. 8689
3:16 *He has* **b** my teeth with gravel; 1756
Eze 6: 6 your incense altars **b down,** 1548
21: 6 before them with **b** heart and bitter grief. 8695
26: 2 The gate to the nations **is b,** 8689
26:10 a city whose walls *have* **been b through.** 1324
30:21 *I have* **b** the arm of Pharaoh king of Egypt. 8689
30:22 the good arm as well as the **b** *one,* 8689
31:12 its branches *lay* **b** in all the ravines of 8689
32:28 *will* **be b** and will lie among 8689

Da 2:35 the gold *were* **b to pieces** at the same time 10182
8:8 of his power his large horn **was b off,** 8689
8:22 *that* **was b off** represent four kingdoms 8689
11:4 his empire *will* **be b up** and parceled out 8689
12:7 of the holy people *has been* finally **b,** 5879
Hos 6:7 Like Adam, they *have* **b** the covenant— 6296
8:1 the people *have* **b** my covenant and rebelled 6296
8:6 It will be **b in pieces,** that calf of Samaria. 8646
Joel 1:17 the granaries *have* **been b down,** 2238
Am 9:11 I will repair its **b places,** restore its ruins, 7288
Mic 1:7 All her idols *will* **be b to pieces;** 4198
Zec 9:10 and the battle bow *will* **be b.** 4162
Mal 2:11 Judah *has* **b faith.** 953
2:14 because you *have* **b faith** with her, 953
Mt 14:20 up twelve basketfuls *of* **b pieces** *3083*
15:37 up seven basketfuls *of* **b pieces** *3083*
21:44 on this stone *will* **be b to pieces,** *5314*
24:43 and would not have let his house *be* **b into.** *1482*
Mk 6:43 up twelve basketfuls of **b pieces** of bread *3083*
8:8 up seven basketfuls *of* **b pieces** *3083*
Lk 8:29 *he had* **b** his chains and had been driven by *1396*
9:17 up twelve basketfuls *of* **b pieces** *3083*
12:39 he would not have let his house *be* **b into.** *1482*
20:18 on that stone *will* **be b to pieces,** *5314*
Jn 7:23 so that the law of Moses *may* not *be* **b,** *3395*
10:35 and the Scripture cannot *be* **b—** *3395*
19:31 they asked Pilate to *have* the legs **b** and *2862*
19:36 "Not one of his bones *will* **be b,"** *5341*
Ac 27:41 the stern *was* **b to pieces** by the pounding of *3395*
Ro 11:17 If some of the branches *have been* **b off,** *1709*
11:19 "Branches *were* **b off** so that I could *1709*
11:20 But *they were* **b off** because of unbelief, *1709*
1Ti 5:12 because *they have* **b** *their* first pledge. *119*

BROKENHEARTED (4) [HEART]

Ps 34:18 the **b** and saves those who are crushed 4213+8689
109:16 the poor and the needy and the **b.** 3874+4222
147:3 He heals the **b** and binds up their wounds. 4213+8689
Isa 61:1 He has sent me to bind up the **b,** 4213+8689

BROKENNESS (1) [BREAK]

Isa 65:14 from anguish of heart and wail in **b** 8691

BRONZE (159) [BRONZE-TIPPED]

Ge 4:22 who forged all kinds of tools out of **b** 5733
Ex 25:3 gold, silver and **b;** 5733
26:11 Then make fifty **b** clasps and put them in 5733
26:37 And cast five **b** bases for them. 5733
27:2 and overlay the altar with **b.** 5733
27:3 Make all its utensils of **b—** 5733
27:4 Make a grating for it, a **b** network, 5733
27:4 a **b** ring at each of the four corners of 5733
27:6 for the altar and overlay them with **b.** 5733
27:10 with twenty posts and twenty **b** bases and 5733
27:11 with twenty posts and twenty **b** bases and 5733
27:17 and hooks, and **b** bases. 5733
27:18 and with **b** bases. 5733
27:19 those for the courtyard, are to be of **b.** 5733
30:18 "Make a **b** basin, with its bronze stand, 5733
30:18 with its **b** stand, for washing. 5733
31:4 for work in gold, silver and **b,** 5733
35:5 an offering of gold, silver and **b;** 5733
35:16 of burnt offering with its **b** grating, its poles 5733
35:16 the **b** basin with its stand; NIH
35:24 or **b** brought it as an offering to the LORD, 5733
35:32 for work in gold, silver and **b,** 5733
36:18 They made fifty **b** clasps to fasten 5733
36:38 with gold and made their five bases of **b.** 5733
38:2 and they overlaid the altar with **b.** 5733
38:3 They made all its utensils of **b—** 5733
38:4 a **b** network, to be under its ledge, 5733
38:5 They cast **b** rings to hold the poles for NIH
38:5 for the four corners of the **b** grating. 5733
38:6 of acacia wood and overlaid them with **b.** 5733
38:8 They made the **b** basin and its bronze stand 5733
38:8 They made the bronze basin and its **b** stand 5733
38:10 with twenty posts and twenty **b** bases, 5733
38:11 and had twenty posts and twenty **b** bases, 5733
38:17 The bases for the posts were **b.** 5733
38:19 with four posts and four **b** bases. 5733
38:20 and of the surrounding courtyard were **b.** 5733
38:29 The **b** *from* the wave offering was 70 talents 5733
38:30 the **b** altar with its bronze grating 5733
38:30 with its **b** grating and all its utensils, 5733
39:39 the **b** altar with its bronze grating, its poles 5733
39:39 the bronze altar with its **b** grating, its poles 5733
Lev 6:28 but if it is cooked in a **b** pot, 5733
26:19 like iron and the ground beneath you like **b.** 5703
Nu 4:13 the **b** altar and spread a purple cloth over it. NIH
16:39 the priest collected the **b** censers brought 5733
21:9 So Moses made a **b** snake and put it up on 5733
21:9 by a snake and looked at the **b** snake, 5733
31:22 Gold, silver, **b,** iron, tin, lead 5733
Dt 28:23 The sky over your head will be **b,** 5733
33:25 The bolts of your gates will be iron and **b,** 5733
Jos 6:19 All the silver and gold and the articles of **b** 5733
6:24 the articles of **b** and iron into the treasury of 5733
22:8 with silver, gold, **b** and iron, 5733
Jdg 16:21 Binding him with **b** *shackles,* 5733
1Sa 17:5 He had a **b** helmet on his head and wore 5733
17:5 of **b** weighing five thousand shekels; 5733
17:6 on his legs he wore **b** greaves, 5733
17:6 and a **b** javelin was slung on his back. 5733
17:38 a coat of armor on him and a **b** helmet 5733
2Sa 8:8 King David took a great quantity of **b.** 5733
8:10 with him articles of silver and gold and **b.** 5733
21:16 **b** spearhead weighed three hundred shekels 5733
22:35 my arms can bend a bow of **b.** 5703
1Ki 4:13 with **b** gate bars); 5733
7:14 a man of Tyre and a craftsman in **b.** 5733
7:14 and experienced in all kinds of **b** work. 5733
7:15 He cast two **b** pillars, 5733
7:16 He also made two capitals of cast **b** to set 5733
7:27 He also made ten movable stands of **b;** 5733
7:30 Each stand had four **b** wheels 5733
7:30 with **b** axles, and each had a basin resting 5733
7:38 He then made ten **b** basins, 5733
7:45 of the LORD were of burnished **b.** 5733
7:47 the weight of the **b** was not determined. 5733
8:64 the **b** altar before the LORD was too small 5733
14:27 So King Rehoboam made **b** shields 5733
2Ki 16:14 The **b** altar that stood before 5733
16:15 I will use the **b** altar for seeking guidance." 5733
16:17 from the **b** bulls that supported it and set it 5733
18:4 into pieces the **b** snake Moses had made, 5733
25:7 with **b shackles** and took him to Babylon. 5733
25:13 The Babylonians broke up the **b** pillars, 5733
25:13 the movable stands and the **b** Sea that were 5733
25:13 of the LORD and they carried the **b** 5733
25:14 the **b** articles used in the temple service. 5733
25:16 The **b** *from* the two pillars, 5733
25:17 The **b** capital on top of one pillar was four 5733
25:17 and pomegranates of **b** all around. 5733
1Ch 15:19 and Ethan were to sound the **b** cymbals; 5733
18:8 David took a great quantity of **b,** 5733
18:8 which Solomon used to make the **b** Sea, 5733
18:8 the pillars and various **b** articles. 5733
18:10 of articles of gold and silver and **b.** 5733
22:3 and more **b** than could be weighed. 5733
22:14 of **b** and iron too great to be weighed, 5733
22:16 **b** and iron—craftsmen beyond number. 5733
29:2 silver for the silver, **b** for the bronze, 5733
29:2 silver for the silver, bronze for the **b,** 5733
29:7 of **b** and a hundred thousand talents of iron. 5733
2Ch 1:5 But the **b** altar that Bezalel son of Uri, 5733
1:6 to the **b** altar before the LORD in the Tent 5733
2:7 **b** and iron, and in purple, 5733
2:14 **b** and iron, stone and wood, 5733
4:1 He made a **b** altar twenty cubits long, 5733
4:9 and overlaid the doors with **b.** 5733
4:16 of the LORD were of polished **b.** 5733
4:18 that the weight of the **b** was not determined. 5733
6:13 Now he had made a **b** platform, 5733
7:7 the **b** altar he had made could not hold 5733
12:10 So King Rehoboam made **b** shields 5733
24:12 workers in iron and **b** to repair the temple. 5733
33:11 with **b shackles** and took him to Babylon. 5733
36:6 and bound him with **b shackles** to take him 5733
Ezr 8:27 darics, and two fine articles of polished **b,** 5733
Job 6:12 Is my flesh **b?** 5702
37:18 hard as a mirror of **cast b?** 4607
40:18 His bones are tubes of **b,** 5703
41:27 like straw and **b** like rotten wood. 5703
Ps 18:34 my arms can bend a bow of **b.** 5703
107:16 for he breaks down gates of **b** and cuts 5733
Isa 45:2 down gates of **b** and cut through bars 5703
48:4 your forehead was **b.** 5703
60:17 Instead of **b** I will bring you gold, 5733
60:17 Instead of wood I will bring you **b,** 5733
Jer 1:18 a **b** wall to stand against the whole land— 5733
6:28 They are **b** and iron; they all act corruptly. 5733
15:12 from the north—or **b?** 5733
15:20 a fortified wall of **b;** 5733
39:7 and bound him with **b shackles** to take him 5733
52:11 with **b shackles** and took him to Babylon, 5733
52:17 The Babylonians broke up the **b** pillars, 5733
52:17 the movable stands and the **b** Sea that were 5733
52:17 of the LORD and they carried all the **b** 5733
52:18 the **b** articles used in the temple service. 5733
52:20 The **b** *from* the two pillars, 5733
52:20 the Sea and the twelve **b** bulls under it, 5733
52:22 The **b** capital on top of 5733
52:22 and pomegranates of **b** all around. 5733
Eze 1:7 of a calf and gleamed like burnished **b.** 5733
9:2 They came in and stood beside the **b** altar. 5733
27:13 they exchanged slaves and articles of **b** 5733
40:3 a man whose appearance was like **b;** 5733
Da 2:32 its belly and thighs of **b,** 10473
2:35 Then the iron, the clay, the **b,** 10473
2:39 Next, a third kingdom, one of **b,** 10473
2:45 a rock that broke the iron, the **b,** the clay, 10473
4:15 bound with iron and **b,** 10473
4:23 but leave the stump, bound with iron and **b,** 10473
5:4 of **b,** iron, wood and stone. 10473
5:23 of **b,** iron, wood and stone, 10473
7:19 with its iron teeth and **b** claws— 10473
10:6 and legs like the gleam of burnished **b,** 5733
Mic 4:13 I will give you hoofs of **b** 5703
Zec 6:1 between two mountains—mountains of **b!** 5733
Rev 1:15 His feet were like **b** glowing in a furnace, *5909*
2:18 and whose feet are like **burnished b.** *5909*
9:20 silver, **b,** stone and wood— *5905*
18:12 costly wood, **b,** iron and marble; *5910*

BRONZE-TIPPED (1) [BRONZE]

Job 20:24 a **b** arrow pierces him. 5703

BROOCHES (1)

Ex 35:22 **b,** earrings, rings and ornaments, 2626

BROOD (9)

Nu 32:14 "And here you are, a **b** *of* sinners, 9551
Job 30:8 A base and nameless **b,** 1201
Isa 1:4 a people loaded with guilt, a **b** *of* evildoers, 2446
57:4 Are you not a **b** *of* rebels, 3529
Mt 3:7 *"You* **b** of vipers! Who warned you to flee *1165*
12:34 *You* **b** of vipers, how can you who are evil *1165*
23:33 *You* **b** of vipers! How will you escape *1165*
Lk 3:7 *"You* **b** of vipers! Who warned you to flee *1165*
2Pe 2:14 experts in greed—an accursed **b!** *5451*

BROOK (7)

2Sa 17:20 "They crossed over the **b."** 4782+4784
1Ki 17:4 You will drink from the **b,** 5707
17:6 and he drank from the **b.** 5707
17:7 Some time later the **b** dried up 5707
Ps 110:7 He will drink from a **b** beside the way; 5707
Pr 18:4 but the fountain of wisdom is a bubbling **b.** 5707
Jer 15:18 Will you be to me like a deceptive **b,** NIH

BROOKS (KJV) See BROOK, RAVINES, RIVERS, WADI

BROOM (4)

1Ki 19:4 He came to a **b tree,** 8413
Job 30:4 and their food was the root of the **b tree.** 8413
Ps 120:4 with burning coals of the **b tree.** 8413
Isa 14:23 I will sweep her with the **b** *of* destruction," 4748

BROTH (3)

Jdg 6:19 Putting the meat in a basket and its **b** in 5348
6:20 place them on this rock, and pour out the **b.** 5348
Isa 65:4 and whose pots hold **b** *of* unclean meat; 5348

BROTHER (327) [BROTHER-IN-LAW, BROTHER'S, BROTHERHOOD, BROTHERLY, BROTHERS]

Ge 4:2 Later she gave birth to his **b** Abel. 278
4:8 Now Cain said to his **b** Abel, 278
4:8 Cain attacked his **b** Abel and killed him. 278
4:9 "Where is your **b** Abel?" 278
10:21 whose older **b** was Japheth; 278
10:25 his **b** was named Joktan. 278
14:13 a **b** *of* Eshcol and Aner, 278
20:5 and didn't she also say, 'He is my **b'?** 278
20:13 say of me, "He is my **b."** '" 278
20:16 "I am giving your **b** a thousand shekels 278
22:20 she has borne sons to your **b** Nahor: 278
22:21 Buz his **b,** Kemuel (the father of Aram), 278
22:23 to Abraham's **b** Nahor. 278
24:15 who was the wife of Abraham's **b** Nahor. 278
24:29 Now Rebekah had a **b** named Laban, 278
24:48 to get the granddaughter of my master's **b** 278
24:53 he also gave costly gifts to her **b** and 278
24:55 But her **b** and her mother replied, 278
25:26 After this, his **b** came out, 278
27:6 I overheard your father say to your **b** Esau, 278
27:11 "But my **b** Esau is a hairy man, 278
27:23 like those of his **b** Esau; 278
27:30 his **b** Esau came in from hunting. 278
27:35 "Your **b** came deceitfully 278
27:40 by the sword and you will serve your **b.** 278
27:41 then I will kill my **b** Jacob." 278
27:42 "Your **b** Esau is consoling himself with 278
27:43 Flee at once to my **b** Laban in Haran. 278
27:45 When your **b** is no longer angry with you 278
28:2 the daughters of Laban, your mother's **b.** 278
28:5 the Aramean, the **b** *of* Rebekah, 278
29:10 his mother's **b,** and Laban's sheep, 278
32:3 of him to his **b** Esau in the land of Seir, 278
32:6 they said, "We went to your **b** Esau, 278
32:11 I pray, from the hand of my **b** Esau, 278
32:13 with him he selected a gift for his **b** Esau: 278
32:17 "When my **b** Esau meets you and asks, 278
33:3 as he approached his **b.** 278
33:9 Esau said, "I already have plenty, my **b.** 278
35:1 when you were fleeing from your **b** Esau." 278
35:7 to him when he was fleeing from his **b.** 278
36:6 to a land some distance from his **b** Jacob. 278
37:26 if we kill our **b** and cover up his blood? 278
37:27 all, he is our **b,** our own flesh and blood." 278
38:8 to produce offspring for your **b."** 278
38:9 to keep from producing offspring for his **b.** 278
38:29 his **b** came out, and she said, 278
38:30 Then his **b,** who had the scarlet thread 278
42:4 Jacob did not send Benjamin, Joseph's **b,** 278
42:15 unless your youngest **b** comes here. 278
42:16 Send one of your number to get your **b;** 278
42:20 But you must bring your youngest **b** to me, 278
42:21 punished because of our **b.** 278
42:34 But bring your youngest **b** to me 278
42:34 Then I will give your **b** back to you, 278
42:38 his **b** is dead and he is the only one left. 278
43:3 not see my face again unless your **b** is 278
43:4 If you will send our **b** along with us, 278
43:5 not see my face again unless your **b** is 278
43:6 by telling the man you had another **b?"** 278
43:7 'Do you have another **b?'** 278
43:7 'Bring your **b** down here'?" 278
43:13 Take your **b** also and go back to the man 278
43:14 the man so that he will let your other **b** 278
43:29 he looked about and saw his **b** Benjamin, 278

Ge 43:29 he asked, "Is this your youngest **b**, 278
43:30 Deeply moved at the sight of his **b**, 278
44:19 'Do you have a father or a **b**?' 278
44:20 His **b** is dead, 278
44:23 your youngest **b** comes down with you, 278
44:26 if our youngest **b** is with us will we go. 278
44:26 the man's face unless our youngest **b** is 278
45: 4 he said, "I am your **b** Joseph, 278
45:12 and so can my **b** Benjamin, 278
45:14 around his **b** Benjamin and wept, 278
48:19 his younger **b** will be greater than he, 278
Ex 4:14 "What about your **b**, Aaron the Levite? 278
7: 1 and your **b** Aaron will be your prophet. 278
7: 2 and your **b** Aaron is to tell Pharaoh to let 278
28: 1 "Have Aaron your **b** brought to you from 278
28: 2 Make sacred garments for your **b** Aaron, 278
28: 4 for your **b** Aaron and his sons, 278
28:41 on your **b** Aaron and his sons, 278
32:27 each killing his **b** and friend 278
Lev 16: 2 "Tell your **b** Aaron not to come whenever 278
18:14 " 'Do not dishonor your father's **b** 278
18:16 that would dishonor your **b**. 278
19:17 " 'Do not hate your **b** in your heart. 278
20:21 he has dishonored his **b**. 278
21: 2 his son or daughter, his **b**, 278
Nu 6: 7 his own father or mother or **b** or sister dies, 278
20: 8 and you and your **b** Aaron gather 278
20:14 "This is what your **b** Israel says: 278
27:13 as your **b** Aaron was, 278
36: 2 to give the inheritance of our **b** Zelophehad 278
Dt 1:16 whether the case is between **b Israelites** or 278
3:18 must cross over ahead of your **b** Israelites. 278
13: 6 If your **very own b**, 278+562+1201+3870
15: 2 from his fellow Israelite or **b**, 278
15: 3 you must cancel any debt your **b** owes you. 278
15: 7 or tightfisted toward your poor **b**. 278
15: 9 toward your needy **b** and give him nothing. 278
17:15 one who is not a **b** Israelite. 278
19:18 giving false testimony against his **b**, 278
19:19 then do to him as he intended to do to his **b**. 278
22: 2 If the **b** does not live near you or if you do 278
23: 7 Do not abhor an Edomite, for he is your **b**. 278
23:19 Do not charge your **b** interest, 278
23:20 but not a **b Israelite**, 278
24: 7 of his **b** Israelites and treats him as a slave 278
24:14 a **b Israelite** or an alien living in one 278
25: 3 your **b** will be degraded in your eyes. 278
25: 5 Her **husband's b** shall take her and marry her 3303
25: 6 of the dead **b** so that his name will not 278
25: 7 "My **husband's b** refuses to carry 3303
28:54 on his own **b** or the wife he loves 278
32:50 just as your **b** Aaron died on Mount Hor 278
Jos 15:17 Othniel son of Kenaz, Caleb's **b**, took it; 278
Jdg 1:13 Othniel son of Kenaz, Caleb's younger **b**, 278
3: 9 Othniel son of Kenaz, Caleb's younger **b**, 278
9: 3 for they said, "He is our **b**." 278
9:18 of Shechem because he is your **b**)— 278
9:21 because he was afraid of his **b** Abimelech. 278
9:24 might be avenged on their **b** Abimelech and 278
20:28 up again to battle with Benjamin our **b**, 278
Ru 4: 3 of land that belonged to our **b** Elimelech. 278
1Sa 14: 3 He was a son of Ichabod's **b** Ahitub son 278
17:28 When Eliab, David's oldest **b**, 278
20:29 in the town and my **b** has ordered me to 278
26: 6 Joab's **b**, "Who will go down into the camp 278
2Sa 1:26 I grieve for you, Jonathan my **b**; 278
2:22 How could I look your **b** Joab in the face?" 278
3:27 there, to avenge the blood of his **b** Asahel, 278
3:30 (Joab and his **b** Abishai murdered Abner 278
3:30 because he had killed their **b** Asahel in 278
4: 6 Recab and his **b** Baanah slipped away. 278
4: 9 David answered Recab and his **b** Baanah, 278
10:10 of Abishai his **b** and deployed them against 278
13: 3 Jonadab son of Shimeah, David's **b**. 278
13: 4 my **b** Absalom's sister." 278
13: 7 of your **b** Amnon and prepare some food 278
13: 8 Tamar went to the house of her **b** Amnon, 278
13:10 to her **b** Amnon in his bedroom. 278
13:12 "Don't, my **b**!" she said to him. 278
13:20 Her **b** Absalom said to her, 278
13:20 "Has that Amnon, your **b**, been with you? 278
13:20 Be quiet now, my sister; he is your **b**. 278
13:20 And Tamar lived in her **b** Absalom's house, 278
13:26 please let my **b** Amnon come with us." 278
13:32 But Jonadab son of Shimeah, David's **b**, 278
14: 7 'Hand over the one who struck his **b** down, 278
14: 7 for the life of his **b** whom he killed; 278
18: 2 of Joab, a third under Joab's **b** Abishai son 278
20: 9 Joab said to Amasa, "How are you, my **b**?" 278
20:10 and his **b** Abishai pursued Sheba son 278
21:21 Jonathan son of Shimeah, David's **b**, 278
23:18 the **b** *of* Joab son of Zeruiah was chief of 278
23:24 Asahel the **b** *of* Joab, 278
1Ki 1:10 or the special guard or his **b** Solomon. 278
2: 7 by me when I fled from your **b** Absalom. 278
2:15 and the kingdom has gone to my **b**; 278
2:21 be given in marriage to your **b** Adonijah." 278
2:22 after all, he is my older **b**— 278
9:13 towns are these you have given me, my **b**?" 278
13:30 over him and said, "Oh, my **b**!" 278
20:32 "Is he still alive? He is my **b**." 278
20:33 "Yes, your **b** Ben-Hadad!" 278
1Ch 1:19 his **b** was named Joktan. 278
2:32 The sons of Jada, Shammai's **b**: 278
2:42 The sons of Caleb the **b** *of* Jerahmeel: 278
4:11 Shuhah's **b**, was the father of Mehir, 278
1Ch 7:16 His **b** was named Sheresh, 278
7:35 The sons of his **b** Helem: 278
8:39 The sons of his **b** Eshek: 278
11:20 the **b** *of* Joab was chief of the Three. 278
11:26 Asahel the **b** *of* Joab, 278
11:38 Joel the **b** *of* Nathan, Mibhar son of Hagri, 278
11:45 Jediael son of Shimri, his **b** Joha the Tizite, 278
19:11 under the command of Abishai his **b**, 278
19:15 they too fled before his **b** Abishai and went 278
20: 5 Elhanan son of Jair killed Lahmi the **b** 278
20: 7 Jonathan son of Shimea, David's **b**, 278
24:25 The **b** *of* Micah: 278
24:31 the oldest **b** were treated the same as those 278
26:22 Zetham and his **b** Joel. 278
27: 7 was Asahel the **b** *of* Joab; 278
27:18 Elihu, a **b** *of* David; 278
2Ch 31:12 and his **b** Shimei was next in rank. 278
31:13 under Conaniah and Shimei his **b**, 278
36: 4 a **b** *of* Jehoahaz, 278
36: 4 But Neco took Eliakim's **b** Jehoahaz 278
Ezr 7:18 You and your **b Jews** may 10017
Ne 7: 2 I put in charge of Jerusalem my **b** Hanani, 278
Job 30:29 I have become a **b** of jackals, 278
Ps 35:14 as though for my friend or **b**. 278
50:20 You speak continually against your **b** 278
Pr 17:17 and a **b** is born for adversity. 278
18: 9 in his work is **b** to one who destroys. 278
18:19 An offended **b** is more unyielding than 278
18:24 a friend who sticks closer than a **b**. 278
27:10 better a neighbor nearby than a **b** far away. 278
Ecc 4: 8 he had neither son nor **b**. 278
SS 8: 1 If only you were to me like a **b**, 278
Isa 9:19 no one will spare his **b**. 278
19: 2 **b** will fight against brother, 408
19: 2 brother will fight against **b**, 278
41: 6 each helps the other and says to his **b**, 278
Jer 9: 4 For every **b** is a deceiver, 278
22:18 for him: 'Alas, my **b**! 278
31:34 or a man his **b**, saying, 'Know the LORD,' 278
Eze 18:18 robbed his **b** and did what was wrong 278
38:21 Every man's sword will be against his **b**. 278
44:25 son or daughter, **b** or unmarried sister, 278
Am 1:11 Because he pursued his **b** with a sword, 278
Ob 1:10 of the violence against your **b** Jacob, 278
1:12 You should not look down on your **b** in 278
Mic 7: 2 each hunts his **b** with a net. 278
Hag 2:22 each by the sword of his **b**. 278
Mal 1: 2 "Was not Esau Jacob's **b**?" 278
Mt 4:18 Simon called Peter and his **b** Andrew. 81
4:21 James son of Zebedee and his **b** John. 81
5:22 that anyone who is angry *with* his **b** will 81
5:22 Again, anyone who says *to* his **b**, 'Raca,' 81
5:23 that your **b** has something against you, 81
5:24 First go and be reconciled *to* your **b**; 81
7: 4 How can you say *to* your **b**, 81
10: 2 (who is called Peter) and his **b** Andrew; 81
10: 2 James son of Zebedee, and his **b** John; 81
10:21 "**B** will betray brother to death, 81
10:21 "Brother will betray **b** to death, 81
12:50 in heaven is my **b** and sister and mother." 81
14: 3 Herodias, his **b** Philip's wife, 81
17: 1 James and John the **b** of James, 81
18:15 "If your **b** sins against you, 81
18:15 you have won your **b** over. 81
18:21 how many times shall I forgive my **b** 81
18:35 unless you forgive your **b** from your heart." 81
22:24 his **b** must marry the widow 81
22:25 he left his wife *to* his **b**. 81
22:26 to the second and third **b**, NIG
Mk 1:16 he saw Simon and his **b** Andrew casting 81
1:19 of Zebedee and his **b** John in a boat, 81
3:17 of Zebedee and his **b** John (to them he gave 81
3:35 Whoever does God's will is my **b** and sister 81
5:37 James and John the **b** of James. 81
6: 3 Isn't this Mary's son and the **b** of James, 81
6:17 his **b** Philip's wife, whom he had married. 81
12:19 "Moses wrote for us that if a man's **b** dies 81
12:19 the widow and have children *for* his **b**. 81
13:12 "**B** will betray brother to death, 81
13:12 "Brother will betray **b** to death, 81
Lk 3: 1 of Galilee, his **b** Philip tetrarch of Iturea 81
6:14 his **b** Andrew, James, John, Philip, 81
6:42 How can you say *to* your **b**, 'Brother, 81
6:42 How can you say to your brother, '**B**, 81
12:13 tell my **b** to divide the inheritance 81
15:27 'Your **b** has come,' he replied, 81
15:28 "The older **b** became angry and refused NIG
15:32 this **b** of yours was dead and is alive again; 81
17: 3 "If your **b** sins, rebuke him, 81
20:28 "Moses wrote for us that if a man's **b** dies 81
20:28 the widow and have children *for* his **b**. 81
Jn 1:40 Andrew, Simon Peter's **b**, 81
1:41 to find his **b** Simon and tell him, 81
6: 8 Andrew, Simon Peter's **b**, spoke up, 81
11: 2 This Mary, whose **b** Lazarus now lay sick, 81
11:19 to comfort them in the loss of their **b**. 81
11:21 my **b** would not have died. 81
11:23 Jesus said to her, "Your **b** will rise again." 81
11:32 my **b** would not have died." 81
Ac 9:17 Placing his hands on Saul, he said, "**B** Saul, 81
12: 2 He had James, the **b** of John, 81
21:20 Then they said to Paul: "You see, **b**, 81
22:13 He stood beside me and said, '**B** Saul, 81
Ro 14:10 You, then, why do you judge your **b**? 81
14:10 Or why do you look down on your **b**? 81
14:15 If your **b** is distressed because 81
14:15 Do not by your eating destroy **your b** 1697S
Ro 14:21 or to do anything else that will cause your **b** 81
16:23 and our **b** Quartus send you their greetings. 81
1Co 1: 1 and our **b** Sosthenes, 81
5:11 a **b** but is sexually immoral or greedy, 81
6: 6 one **b** goes to law against another— 81
7:12 If any **b** has a wife who is not a believer 81
8:11 So this weak **b**, for whom Christ died, 81
8:13 if what I eat causes my **b** to fall into sin, 81
16:12 Now about our **b** Apollos: 81
2Co 1: 1 and Timothy our **b**, To the church of God 81
2:13 because I did not find my **b** Titus there. 81
8:18 along with him the **b** who is praised by all 81
8:22 with them our **b** who has often proved to us 81
12:18 I urged Titus to go to you and I sent our **b** 81
Gal 1:19 only James, the Lord's **b**. 81
Eph 6:21 the dear **b** and faithful servant in the Lord, 81
Php 2:25 my **b**, fellow worker and fellow soldier, 81
Col 1: 1 and Timothy our **b**, 81
4: 7 He is a dear **b**, a faithful minister 81
4: 9 our faithful and dear **b**, who is one of you. 81
1Th 3: 2 who is our **b** and God's fellow worker 81
4: 6 in this matter no one should wrong his **b** 81
2Th 3: 6 from every **b** who is idle and does not live 81
3:15 as an enemy, but warn him as a **b**. 81
Phm 1: 1 and Timothy our **b**, 81
1: 7 **b**, have refreshed the hearts of the saints. 81
1:16 but better than a slave, as a dear **b**. 81
1:16 both as a man and as a **b** in the Lord. NIG
1:20 **b**, that I may have some benefit from you 81
Heb 8:11 or a man his **b**, saying, 'Know the Lord,' 81
13:23 that our **b** Timothy has been released. 81
Jas 1: 9 The **b** in humble circumstances ought 81
2:15 Suppose a **b** or sister is without clothes 81
4:11 against his **b** or judges him speaks against 81
1Pe 5:12 whom I regard as a faithful **b**, 81
2Pe 3:15 just as our dear **b** Paul also wrote you with 81
1Jn 2: 9 to be in the light but hates his **b** is still in 81
2:10 Whoever loves his **b** lives in the light, 81
2:11 But whoever hates his **b** is in the darkness 81
3:10 nor is anyone who does not love his **b**. 81
3:12 to the evil one and murdered his **b**. 81
3:15 Anyone who hates his **b** is a murderer, 81
3:17 and sees his **b** in need but has no pity 81
4:20 anyone says, "I love God," yet hates his **b**, 81
4:20 For anyone who does not love his **b**, 81
4:21 Whoever loves God must also love his **b**. 81
5:16 If anyone sees his **b** commit a sin that does 81
Jude 1: 1 a servant of Jesus Christ and a **b** of James, 81
Rev 1: 9 your **b** and companion in the suffering 81

BROTHER'S (28) [BROTHER]

Ge 4: 9 "Am I my **b** keeper?" 278
4:10 Your **b** blood cries out to me from 278
4:11 to receive your **b** blood from your hand. 278
4:21 His **b** name was Jubal; 278
27:44 for a while until your **b** fury subsides. 278
38: 8 with your **b** wife and fulfill your duty to her 278
38: 9 so whenever he lay with his **b** wife, 278
Lev 18:16 not have sexual relations with your **b** wife; 278
20:21 " 'If a man marries his **b** wife, 278
Dt 22: 1 If you see your **b** ox or sheep straying, 278
22: 3 Do the same if you find **your b** donkey 2257S
22: 4 If you see your **b** donkey or his ox fallen on 278
25: 7 if a man does not want to marry his **b wife**, 3304
25: 7 to carry on his **b** name in Israel. 278
25: 9 his **b widow** shall go up to him in 3304
25: 9 not build up his **b** family line." 278
Job 1:13 and drinking wine at the oldest **b** house, 278
1:18 and drinking wine at the oldest **b** house, 278
Pr 27:10 to your **b** house when disaster strikes you— 278
Hos 12: 3 In the womb he grasped his **b** heel; 278
Mt 7: 3 at the speck of sawdust in your **b** eye 81
7: 5 to remove the speck from your **b** eye. 81
Mk 6:18 not lawful for you to have your **b** wife." 81
Lk 3:19 the tetrarch because of Herodias, his **b** wife, 81
6:41 at the speck of sawdust in your **b** eye 81
6:42 to remove the speck from your **b** eye. 81
Ro 14:13 or obstacle in your **b** way. 81
1Jn 3:12 and his **b** were righteous. 81

BROTHER-IN-LAW (4) [BROTHER]

Ge 38: 8 **fulfill** *your* **duty** *to* her **as a b** 3302
Dt 25: 5 **fulfill the duty of a b** to her. 3302
25: 7 not **fulfill the duty of a b** to me." 3302
Jdg 4:11 the descendants of Hobab, Moses' **b**, 3162

BROTHERHOOD (3) [BROTHER]

Am 1: 9 disregarding a treaty of **b**, 278
Zec 11:14 breaking the **b** between Judah and Israel. 288
1Pe 2:17 Love the **b of believers**, fear God, 82

BROTHERLY (4) [BROTHER]

Ro 12:10 Be devoted to one another *in* **b love**. 5789
1Th 4: 9 Now about **b love** we do not need to write 5789
2Pe 1: 7 **b kindness**; and to brotherly kindness, love. 5789
1: 7 and to **b kindness**, love. 5789

BROTHERS (429) [BROTHER]

Ge 9:22 and told his two **b** outside. 278
9:25 The lowest of slaves will he be to his **b**." 278
13: 8 your herdsmen and mine, for we are **b**. 278
16:12 he will live in hostility toward all his **b**." 278
25:18 they lived in hostility toward all their **b**. 278
27:29 Be lord over your **b**, and may the sons 278

Ge 29: 4 Jacob asked the shepherds, "My **b**, 278
34:11 Shechem said to Dinah's father and **b**, 278
34:25 Simeon and Levi, Dinah's **b**, 278
37: 2 was tending the flocks with his **b**, 278
37: 4 When his **b** saw that their father loved him 278
37: 5 and when he told it to his **b**, 278
37: 8 His **b** said to him, 278
37: 9 and he told it to his **b**. 278
37:10 When he told his father as well as his **b**, 278
37:10 and your **b** actually come and bow down to 278
37:11 His **b** were jealous of him, 278
37:12 Now his **b** had gone 278
37:13 your **b** are grazing the flocks near Shechem. 278
37:14 and see if all is well with your **b** and with 278
37:16 He replied, "I'm looking for my **b**. 278
37:17 So Joseph went after his **b** and found them 278
37:23 So when Joseph came to his **b**, 278
37:26 Judah said to his **b**, 278
37:27 His **b** agreed. 278
37:28 his **b** pulled Joseph up out of the cistern NIH
37:30 He went back to his **b** and said, 278
38: 1 Judah left his **b** and went down to stay with 278
38:11 he thought, "He may die too, just like his **b**. 278
42: 3 *of* Joseph's **b** went down to buy grain 278
42: 6 So when Joseph's **b** arrived, 278
42: 7 As soon as Joseph saw his **b**, 278
42: 8 Although Joseph recognized his **b**, 278
42:13 they replied, "Your servants were twelve **b**, 278
42:19 let one of your **b** stay here in prison, 278
42:28 he said to his **b**. 278
42:32 We were twelve **b**, sons of one father. 278
42:33 Leave one of your **b** here with me, 278
43:32 **the b** by themselves, 2157S
44:14 in the house when Judah and his **b** came in, 278
44:33 and let the boy return with his **b**. 278
45: 1 when he made himself known to his **b**. 278
45: 3 Joseph said to his **b**, "I am Joseph! 278
45: 3 But his **b** were not able to answer him, 278
45: 4 Joseph said to his **b**, "Come close to me." 278
45:15 And he kissed all his **b** and wept over them. 278
45:15 Afterward his **b** talked with him. 278
45:16 that Joseph's **b** had come, 278
45:17 Pharaoh said to Joseph, "Tell your **b**, 278
45:24 Then he sent his **b** away, 278
46:31 to his **b** and to his father's household, 278
46:31 'My **b** and my father's household, 278
47: 1 "My father and **b**, with their flocks 278
47: 2 of his **b** and presented them before Pharaoh. 278
47: 3 Pharaoh asked the **b**, "What is your 278
47: 5 "Your father and your **b** have come to you, 278
47: 6 settle your father and your **b** in the best part 278
47:11 and his **b** in Egypt and gave them property 278
47:12 Joseph also provided his father and his **b** 278
48: 6 be reckoned under the names of their **b**. 278
48:22 And to you, as one who is over your **b**, 278
49: 5 "Simeon and Levi are **b**— 278
49: 8 "Judah, your **b** will praise you; 278
49:26 on the brow of the prince among his **b**. 278
50: 8 of Joseph's household and his **b** 278
50:14 with his **b** and all the others who had gone 278
50:15 Joseph's **b** saw that their father was dead, 278
50:17 I ask you to forgive your **b** the sins and 278
50:18 His **b** then came and threw themselves 278
50:24 Joseph said to his **b**, "I am about to die. 278
Ex 1: 6 and all his **b** and all that generation died, 278
32:29 for you were against your own sons and **b**, 278
Lev 21:10 the one among his **b** who has had 278
Nu 8:26 They may assist their **b** in performing 278
20: 3 "If only we had died when our **b** fell dead 278
27: 9 give his inheritance to his **b**. 278
27:10 If he has no **b**, give his inheritance 278
27:10 give his inheritance to his father's **b**. 278
27:11 If his father had no **b**, 278
Dt 1:16 Hear the disputes between your **b** 278
1:28 Our **b** have made us lose heart. 278
2: 4 about to pass through the territory of your **b** 278
2: 8 So we went on past our **b** the descendants 278
3:20 the LORD gives rest to your **b** as he has 278
10: 9 or inheritance among their **b**; 278
15: 7 If there is a poor man among your **b** in any 278
15:11 be openhanded toward your **b** and toward 278
17:15 He must be from among your own **b**. 278
17:20 and not consider himself better than his **b** 278
18: 2 shall have no inheritance among their **b**; 278
18:15 a prophet like me from among your own **b**. 278
18:18 a prophet like you from among their **b**; 278
20: 8 Let him go home so that his **b** will 278
25: 5 If **b** are living together and one of them dies 278
33: 9 He did not recognize his **b** 278
33:16 on the brow of the prince among his **b**. 278
33:24 let him be favored by his **b**, 278
Jos 1:14 must cross over ahead of your **b**. 278
1:14 You are to help **your b** 4392S
2:13 my father and mother, my **b** and sisters, 278
2:18 your **b** and all your family into your house. 278
6:23 and mother and **b** and all who belonged 278
14: 8 but my **b** who went up with me made 278
17: 4 to give us an inheritance among our **b**." 278
17: 4 along with the **b** *of* their father, 278
22: 3 not deserted your **b** but have carried out 278
22: 4 the LORD your God has given your **b** rest 278
22: 7 on the west side of the Jordan with their **b**.) 278
22: 8 and divide with your **b** the plunder 278
Jdg 1: 3 of Judah said to the Simeonites their **b**, 278
1:17 of Judah went with the Simeonites their **b** 278
8:19 Gideon replied, "Those were my **b**, 278
9: 1 to his mother's **b** in Shechem and said 278

Jdg 9: 3 the **b** repeated all this to the citizens 278+562
9: 5 and on one stone murdered his seventy **b**, 278
9:24 who had helped him murder his **b**. 278
9:26 of Ebed moved with his **b** into Shechem, 278
9:31 of Ebed and his **b** have come to Shechem 278
9:41 and Zebul drove Gaal and his **b** out 278
9:56 to his father by murdering his seventy **b**. 278
11: 3 So Jephthah fled from his **b** and settled in 278
16:31 Then his **b** and his father's whole family went down to get him. 278
18: 8 their **b** asked them, "How did you find 278
18:14 the land of Laish said to their **b**, 278
20:23 to battle against the Benjamites, our **b**?" 278
21: 6 Now the Israelites grieved for their **b**, 278
21:22 When their fathers or **b** complain to us, 278
1Sa 16:13 and anointed him in the presence of his **b**, 278
17:17 of bread for your **b** and hurry to their camp. 278
17:18 See how your **b** are and bring back 278
17:22 ran to the battle lines and greeted his **b**. 278
20:29 let me get away to see my **b**.' 278
22: 1 of Adullam. When his **b** 278
30:23 David replied, "No, my **b**, 278
2Sa 2:26 to stop pursuing their **b**?" 278
2:27 the pursuit of their **b** until morning." 278
19:12 You are my **b**, my own flesh and blood. 278
19:41 "Why did our **b**, the men of Judah, 278
1Ki 1: 9 He invited all his **b**, the king's sons, 278
12:24 Do not go up to fight against your **b**, 278
1Ch 4: 9 Jabez was more honorable than his **b**. 278
4:27 but his **b** did not have many children; 278
5: 2 and though Judah was the strongest of his **b** 278
9:17 Akkub, Talmon, Ahiman and their **b**, 278
9:25 Their **b** in their villages had to come 278
9:32 Some of their Kohathite **b** were in charge 278
13: 2 of our **b** throughout the territories of Israel, 278
15:16 the leaders of the Levites to appoint their **b** 278
15:17 from his **b**, Asaph son of Berekiah; 278
15:17 and from their **b** the Merarites, 278
15:18 and with them their **b** next in rank: 278
23:32 under their **b** the descendants of Aaron, 278
24:31 just as their **b** the descendants of Aaron did, 278
28: 2 "Listen to me, my **b** and my people. 278
2Ch 11: 4 Do not go up to fight against your **b**. 278
11:22 to be the chief prince among his **b**, 278
19:10 his wrath will come on you and your **b**. 278
21: 2 Jehoram's **b**, the sons of Jehoshaphat, 278
21: 4 he put all his **b** to the sword along 278
21:13 You have also murdered your own **b**, 278
29:15 When they had assembled their **b** 278
30: 7 Do not be like your fathers and **b**, 278
30: 9 then your **b** and your children will 278
35: 9 his **b**, and Hashabiah, Jeiel and Jozabad, 278
Ezr 3: 8 and the rest of their **b** (the priests and 278
3: 9 Jeshua and his sons and **b** and Kadmiel 278
3: 9 the sons of Henadad and their sons and **b**— 278
6:20 for their **b** the priests and for themselves. 278
8:18 and Sherebiah's sons and **b**, 18 men; 278
8:19 and his **b** and nephews, 20 men. 278
8:24 Hashabiah and ten of their **b**, 278
10:18 of Jeshua son of Jozadak, and his **b**: 278
Ne 1: 2 Hanani, one of my **b**, came from Judah 278
4:14 and fight for your **b**, 278
4:23 nor my **b** nor my men nor the guards 278
5: 1 a great outcry against their Jewish **b**. 278
5: 8 we have bought back our Jewish **b** who were sold 278
5: 8 Now you are selling your **b**, 278
5:10 I and my **b** and my men are also lending 278
5:14 neither I nor my **b** ate the food allotted to 278
10:29 all these now join their **b** the nobles, 278
13:13 for distributing the supplies to their **b**. 278
Job 6:15 But my **b** are as undependable 278
19:13 "He has alienated my **b** from me; 278
19:17 I am loathsome to my own **b**. 1061+1201
22: 6 You demanded security from your **b** 278
42:11 All his **b** and sisters 278
42:15 an inheritance along with their **b**. 278
Ps 22:22 I will declare your name to my **b**; 278
69: 8 I am a stranger to my **b**, 278
122: 8 For the sake of my **b** and friends, I will say, 278
133: 1 and pleasant it is when **b** live together 278
Pr 6:19 a man who stirs up dissension among **b**. 278
17: 2 will share the inheritance as one of the **b**. 278
Isa 3: 6 A man will seize *one of* his **b** 278
66: 5 "Your **b** who hate you, 278
66:20 And they will bring all your **b**, 278
Jer 7:15 just as I did all your **b**, 278
9: 4 do not trust your **b**. 278
12: 6 Your **b**, your own family— 278
35: 3 and his **b** and all his sons— 278
Eze 11:15 "Son of man, your **b**— 278
11:15 your **b** who are your blood relatives and 278
Hos 2: 1 "Say of your **b**, 'My people,' 278
13:15 even though he thrives among his **b**. 278
Mic 5: 3 the rest of his **b** return to join the Israelites. 278
Mt 1: 2 Jacob the father of Judah and his **b**, 81
1:11 the father of Jeconiah and his **b** at the time 81
4:18 he saw two **b**, James son of Zebedee 81
4:21 Going on from there, he saw two other **b**, 81
5:47 And if you greet only your **b**, 81
12:46 his mother and **b** stood outside, 81
12:47 "Your mother and **b** are standing outside, 81
12:48 "Who is my mother, and who are my **b**?" 81
12:49 he said, "Here are my mother and my **b**. 81
13:55 and aren't his **b** James, Joseph, 81
19:29 And everyone who has left houses or **b** 81
20:24 they were indignant with the two **b**. 81

Mt 22:25 Now there were seven **b** among us. 81
23: 8 you have only one Master and you are all **b**. 81
25:40 for one of the least *of* these **b** of mine, 81
28:10 Go and tell my **b** to go to Galilee; 81
Mk 3:31 Then Jesus' mother and **b** arrived. 81
3:32 "Your mother and **b** are outside looking 81
3:33 "Who are my mother and my **b**?" he asked. 81
3:34 "Here are my mother and my **b**! 81
10:29 "no one who has left home or **b** or sisters 81
10:30 **b**, sisters, mothers, children and fields— 81
12:20 Now there were seven **b**. 81
Lk 8:19 Now Jesus' mother and **b** came to see him, 81
8:20 "Your mother and **b** are standing outside, 81
8:21 and **b** are those who hear God's word 81
14:12 your **b** or relatives, or your rich neighbors; 81
14:26 his wife and children, his **b** and sisters— 81
16:28 for I have five **b**. 81
18:29 or **b** or parents or children for the sake of 81
20:29 Now there were seven **b**. 81
21:16 You will be betrayed even by parents, **b**, 81
22:32 you have turned back, strengthen your **b**." 81
Jn 2:12 down to Capernaum with his mother and **b** 81
7: 3 Jesus' **b** said to him, "You ought to leave 81
7: 5 For even his own **b** did not believe in him. 81
7:10 However, after his **b** had left for the Feast, 81
20:17 Go instead to my **b** and tell them, 81
21:23 the **b** that this disciple would not die. 81
Ac 1:14 Mary the mother of Jesus, and with his **b**. 81
1:16 "**B**, the Scripture had to be fulfilled which 81+467
2:29 "**B**, I can tell you confidently that 81
2:37 "**B**, what shall we do?" 81+467
3:17 **b**, I know that you acted in ignorance, 81
6: 3 **B**, choose seven men from 81
7: 2 "**B** and fathers, listen to me! 81+467
7:13 Joseph told his **b** who he was, 81
7:26 by saying, 'Men, you are **b**; 81
9:30 When the **b** learned of this, 81
10:23 and some *of* the **b** from Joppa went along. 81
11: 1 and the **b** throughout Judea heard that 81
11:12 These six **b** also went with me, 81
11:29 to provide help *for* the **b** living in Judea. 81
12:17 "Tell James and the **b** about this," he said, 81
13:15 to them, saying, "**B**, if you have a message 81+467
13:26 "**B**, children of Abraham, 81+467
13:38 "Therefore, my **b**, I want you to know that 81+467
14: 2 and poisoned their minds against the **b**. 81
15: 1 to Antioch and were teaching the **b**: 81
15: 3 This news made all the **b** very glad. 81
15: 7 "**B**, you know that some time ago God made a choice among you 81+467
15:13 When they finished, James spoke up: "**B**, 81+467
15:22 two men who were leaders among the **b**. 81
15:23 The apostles and elders, your **b**, 81
15:32 to encourage and strengthen the **b**. 81
15:33 by the **b** with the blessing of peace to return 81
15:36 the **b** in all the towns where we preached 81
15:40 commended by the **b** to the grace of 81
16: 2 The **b** at Lystra and Iconium spoke well 81
16:40 they met with the **b** and encouraged them. 81
17: 6 they dragged Jason and some other **b** before 81
17:10 the **b** sent Paul and Silas away to Berea. 81
17:14 The **b** immediately sent Paul to the coast, 81
18:18 Then he left the **b** and sailed for Syria, 81
18:27 the **b** encouraged him and wrote to 81
21: 7 the **b** and stayed with them for a day. 81
21:17 the **b** received us warmly. 81
22: 1 "**B** and fathers, listen now to my defense." 81+467
22: 5 I even obtained letters from them to their **b** 81
23: 1 and said, "My **b**, I have fulfilled my duty 81+467
23: 5 "**B**, I did not realize that he was 81
23: 6 called out in the Sanhedrin, "My **b**, 81+467
28:14 There we found some **b** who invited us 81
28:15 The **b** there had heard that we were coming, 81
28:17 "My **b**, although I have done nothing 81+467
28:21 and none *of* the **b** who have come 81
Ro 1:13 I do not want you to be unaware, **b**, 81
7: 1 Do you not know, **b**— 81
7: 4 So, my **b**, you also died to the law through 81
8:12 Therefore, **b**, we have an obligation— 81
8:29 be the firstborn among many **b**. 81
9: 3 from Christ for the sake of my **b**, 81
10: 1 **B**, my heart's desire and prayer to God for 81
11:25 **b**, so that you may not be conceited: 81
12: 1 Therefore, I urge you, **b**, 81
15:14 I myself am convinced, my **b**, 81
15:30 **b**, by our Lord Jesus Christ and by the love 81
16:14 Patrobas, Hermas and the **b** with them. 81
16:17 I urge you, **b**, to watch out 81
1Co 1:10 I appeal to you, **b**, in the name of our Lord 81
1:11 My **b**, some from Chloe's 81
1:26 **B**, think of what you were 81
2: 1 When I came to you, **b**, 81
3: 1 **B**, I could not address you as spiritual but 81
4: 6 **b**, I have applied these things to myself 81
6: 8 and you do this to your **b**. 81
7:24 **B**, each man, as responsible to God, 81
7:29 What I mean, **b**, is that the time is short. 81
8:12 When you sin against your **b** in this way 81
9: 5 as do the other apostles and the Lord's **b** 81
10: 1 of the fact, **b**, that our forefathers were all 81
11:33 my **b**, when you come together to eat, 81
12: 1 Now about spiritual gifts, **b**, 81
14: 6 **b**, if I come to you and speak in tongues, 81
14:20 **B**, stop thinking like children. 81
14:26 What then shall we say, **b**? 81
14:39 Therefore, my **b**, be eager to prophesy, 81
15: 1 Now, **b**, I want to remind you of 81

1Co 15: 6 *to* more than five hundred of the **b** at *81*
15:31 I die every day—I mean that, **b**— *81*
15:50 I declare to you, **b**, that flesh and blood
cannot inherit *81*
15:58 Therefore, my dear **b**, stand firm. *81*
16:11 I am expecting him along with the **b**. *81*
16:12 to go to you with the **b**. *81*
16:15 of the saints. I urge you, **b**, *81*
16:20 All the **b** here send you greetings. *81*
2Co 1: 8 We do not want you to be uninformed, **b**, *81*
8: 1 And now, **b**, we want you to know about *81*
8:23 as for our **b**, they are representatives *81*
9: 3 the **b** in order that our boasting about you *81*
9: 5 the **b** to visit you in advance and finish *81*
11: 9 for the **b** who came from Macedonia *81*
11:26 and in danger from **false b**. *6012*
13:11 Finally, **b**, good-by. *81*
Gal 1: 2 the **b** with me, To the churches in Galatia: *81*
1:11 I want you to know, **b**, that the gospel *81*
2: 4 some **false b** had infiltrated our ranks *6012*
3:15 **B**, let me take an example *81*
4:12 I plead with you, **b**, become like me, *81*
4:28 you, **b**, like Isaac, are children of promise. *81*
4:31 **b**, we are not children of the slave woman, *81*
5:11 **B**, if I am still preaching circumcision, *81*
5:13 You, my **b**, were called to be free. *81*
6: 1 **B**, if someone is caught in a sin, *81*
6:18 The grace of our Lord Jesus Christ be with
your spirit, **b**. *81*
Eph 6:23 Peace *to* the **b**, and love with faith *81*
Php 1:12 Now I want you to know, **b**, *81*
1:14 *of* the **b** in the Lord have been encouraged *81*
3: 1 Finally, my **b**, rejoice in the Lord! *81*
3:13 **B**, I do not consider myself yet *81*
3:17 in following my example, **b**, and take note *81*
4: 1 my **b**, you whom I love and long for, *81*
4: 8 Finally, **b**, whatever is true, *81*
4:21 The **b** who are with me send greetings. *81*
Col 1: 2 the holy and faithful **b** in Christ at Colosse: *81*
4:15 Give my greetings to the **b** at Laodicea, *81*
1Th 1: 4 For we know, **b** loved by God, *81*
2: 1 **b**, that our visit to you was not a failure. *81*
2: 9 you remember, **b**, our toil and hardship; *81*
2:14 **b**, became imitators of God's churches *81*
2:17 But, **b**, when we were torn away from you *81*
3: 7 Therefore, **b**, in all our distress *81*
4: 1 **b**, we instructed you how to live in order *81*
4:10 the **b** throughout Macedonia. *81*
4:10 we urge you, **b**, to do so more and more. *81*
4:13 **B**, we do not want you to be ignorant *81*
5: 1 **b**, about times and dates we do not need *81*
5: 4 But you, **b**, are not in darkness so *81*
5:12 Now we ask you, **b**, to respect those *81*
5:14 And we urge you, **b**, warn those *81*
5:25 **B**, pray for us. *81*
5:26 Greet all the **b** with a holy kiss. *81*
5:27 the Lord to have this letter read *to* all the **b**. *81*
2Th 1: 3 We ought always to thank God for you, **b**, *81*
2: 1 to him, we ask you, **b**, *81*
2:13 **b** loved by the Lord, *81*
2:15 So then, **b**, stand firm and hold to *81*
3: 1 **b**, pray for us that the message of *81*
3: 6 the Lord Jesus Christ, we command you, **b**, *81*
3:13 for you, **b**, never tire of doing what is right. *81*
1Ti 4: 6 If you point these things out *to* the **b**, *81*
5: 1 Treat younger men as **b**, *81*
6: 2 for them because they are **b**. *81*
2Ti 4:21 Linus, Claudia and all the **b**. *81*
Heb 2:11 So Jesus is not ashamed to call them **b**. *81*
2:12 "I will declare your name *to* my **b**; *81*
2:17 For this reason he had to be made like his **b** *81*
3: 1 holy **b**, who share in the heavenly calling, *81*
3:12 See to it, **b**, that none of you has a sinful, *81*
7: 5 that is, their **b**— *81*
7: 5 their **b** are descended from Abraham. *NIG*
10:19 Therefore, **b**, since we have confidence *81*
13: 1 Keep on **loving each other as b**. *5789*
13:22 **B**, I urge you to bear with my word *81*
Jas 1: 2 Consider it pure joy, my **b**, *81*
1:16 Don't be deceived, my dear **b**. *81*
1:19 My dear **b**, take note of this: *81*
2: 1 My **b**, as believers in our *81*
2: 5 my dear **b**: Has God not chosen *81*
2:14 What good is it, my **b**, if a man claims *81*
3: 1 to be teachers, my **b**, because you know *81*
3:10 My **b**, this should not be. *81*
3:12 My **b**, can a fig tree bear olives, *81*
4:11 **B**, do not slander one another. *81*
5: 7 Be patient, then, **b**, until the Lord's coming. *81*
5: 9 Don't grumble against each other, **b**, *81*
5:10 **B**, as an example of patience in the face *81*
5:12 Above all, my **b**, do not swear— *81*
5:19 My **b**, if one of you should wander from *81*
1Pe 1:22 so that you have sincere **love for** your **b**, *5789*
3: 8 be sympathetic, **love as b**, *5790*
5: 9 because you know that your **b** throughout *82*
2Pe 1:10 Therefore, my **b**, be all the more eager *81*
1Jn 3:13 Do not be surprised, my **b**, *81*
3:14 because we love our **b**. *81*
3:16 we ought to lay down our lives for our **b**. *81*
3Jn 1: 3 It gave me great joy to have some **b** come *81*
1: 5 in what you are doing for the **b**, *81*
1:10 he refuses to welcome the **b**. *81*
Rev 6:11 of their fellow servants and **b** who were to *81*
12:10 For the accuser *of* our **b**, *81*
19:10 and with your **b** who hold to the testimony *81*
22: 9 with you and with your **b** the prophets and *81*

BROUGHT (763) [BRING]

Ge 2:19 *He* **b** them to the man 995
2:22 and *he* **b** her to the man. 995
4: 1 the help of the LORD *I have* **b forth** 7865
4: 3 the course of time Cain **b** some of the fruits 995
4: 4 But Abel **b** fat portions from some of 995
8: 9 the dove and **b** it **back** to himself in the ark. 995
14:16 the goods and **b back** his relative Lot 8740
14:18 of Salem **b out** bread and wine. 3655
15: 7 who **b** you **out** of Ur of the Chaldeans 3655
15:10 Abram **b** all these to him, 4374
18: 4 *Let* a little water **be b**, 4374
18: 8 *He* then **b** some curds and milk and the calf 4374
19:17 As soon as they *had* **b** them out, 3655
19:29 and *he* **b** Lot out of the catastrophe 8938
20: 9 that *you have* **b** such great guilt upon me 995
20:14 Then Abimelech **b** sheep and cattle 4374
21: 6 Sarah said, "God *has* **b** me laughter, 6913
21:27 So Abraham **b** sheep and cattle 4374
24: 7 who **b** me out of my father's household 4374
24:32 Straw and fodder *were* **b** for the camels, 5989
24:53 the servant **b out** gold and silver jewelry 3655
24:67 Isaac **b** her into the tent 995
26:10 and *you would have* **b** guilt upon us." 995
27:14 and got them and **b** them to his mother, 995
27:25 Jacob **b** it to him and he ate; 5602
27:25 and *he* **b** some wine and he drank. 995
27:31 He too prepared some tasty food and **b** it 995
27:33 then, that hunted game and **b** it to me? 995
29:13 and kissed him and **b** him to his home, 995
29:22 So Laban **b together** all the people of 665
30:14 which *he* **b** to his mother Leah. 995
33:11 Please accept the present that **was b** to you, 995
34:30 *"You have* **b trouble** *on* me by making me 6579
37: 2 he **b** their father a bad report about them. 995
38:25 *As* she **was** *being* **b out**, 3655
39:14 "this Hebrew *has been* **b** to us 995
39:17 "That Hebrew slave *you* **b** us came to me 995
41:14 and he *was* **quickly b** from the dungeon. 8132
43: 2 when they had eaten all the grain *they had* **b** 995
43:18 "We **were b** here because of the silver 995
43:21 So *we have* **b** it **back** with us. 8740
43:22 also **b** additional silver with us to buy food. 3718
43:23 Then *he* **b** Simeon **out** to them. 3655
43:26 him the gifts they had **b** into the house, 928+3338
44: 8 even **b back** to you from the land of Canaan 8740
46:32 and *they have* **b** *along* their flocks and herds 995
47: 7 **b** his father Jacob **in** 995
47:14 and he **b** it to Pharaoh's palace. 995
47:17 So *they* **b** their livestock to Joseph, 995
47:17 And *he* **b** them through that year with food 5633
48:10 So Joseph **b** his sons **close** to him, 5602
48:13 and **b** them **close** to him. 5602
Ex 3:12 When you *have* **b** the people **out** of Egypt, 3655
4:29 Moses and Aaron **b together** all the elders 665
5:22 why *have you* **b trouble** upon this people? 8317
5:23 *he has* **b trouble** upon this people, 8317
6: 7 who **b** you **out** from under the yoke of 3655
8:12 to the LORD about the frogs *he had* **b** 8492
9:19 every man and animal that *has* not **been b** 665
10: 8 Moses and Aaron **were b back** to Pharaoh. 8740
10:13 By morning the wind *had* **b** the locusts; 5951
12:17 on this very day that *I* **b** your divisions **out** 3655
12:39 With the dough *they had* **b** from Egypt, 3655
12:51 the LORD **b** the Israelites **out** of Egypt 3655
13: 3 LORD **b** you **out** of it with a mighty hand. 3655
13: 9 For the LORD **b** you **out** of Egypt 3655
13:14 'With a mighty hand the LORD **b** us **out** 3655
13:16 on your forehead that the LORD **b** us **out** 3655
14:11 in Egypt *that you* **b** us to the desert to die? 4374
14:20 Throughout the night the cloud **b** darkness 2118
15:19 **b** the waters of the sea **back** 8740
15:26 not bring on you any of the diseases *I* **b** on 8492
16: 3 but *you have* **b** us **out** into this desert 3655
16: 6 that it was the LORD *who* **b** you **out** 3655
16:32 in the desert when I **b** you **out** of Egypt.' " 3655
18: 1 how the LORD *had* **b** Israel **out** of Egypt. 3655
18:12 **b** a burnt offering and other sacrifices 4374
18:16 a dispute, *it is* **b** to me, 995
18:26 The difficult cases *they* **b** to Moses, 995
19: 4 on eagles' wings and **b** you to myself. 995
19: 8 Moses **b** their answer **back** to the LORD. 8740
20: 2 who **b** you **out** of Egypt, 3655
28: 1 **"Have** Aaron your brother **b** to you from 7928
29:46 who **b** them **out** of Egypt so 3655
32: 1 As for this fellow Moses who **b** us **up** out 6590
32: 3 and **b** them to Aaron. 995
32: 4 O Israel, who **b** you **up** out of Egypt." 6590
32: 7 whom *you* **b up** out of Egypt, 6590
32: 8 O Israel, who **b** you **up** out of Egypt.' 6590
32:11 whom *you* **b out** of Egypt 3655
32:12 'It was with evil intent *that he* **b** them **out**, 3655
32:23 As for this fellow Moses who **b** us **up** out 6590
33: 1 you and the people *you* **b up** out of Egypt, 6590
35:21 and whose heart moved him came and **b** 995
35:22 came and **b** gold jewelry of all kinds: 995
35:23 or hides of sea cows **b** them. 995
35:24 or bronze **b** it as an offering to the LORD, 995
35:24 for any part of the work **b** it. 995
35:25 with her hands and **b** what she had spun— 995
35:27 The leaders **b** onyx stones and other gems 995
35:28 They also **b** spices and olive oil for the light NIH
35:29 and women who were willing **b** to 995
36: 3 the offerings the Israelites *had* **b** to carry out 995
39:33 Then *they* **b** the tabernacle to Moses: 995
40:21 Then *he* **b** the ark into the tabernacle 995
Lev 6:30 But any sin offering whose blood **is b** into 995
8: 6 **b** Aaron and his sons **forward** 7928
8:13 **b** Aaron's sons **forward**, 7928
8:24 **b** Aaron's sons **forward** 7928
9: 9 His sons **b** the blood to him, 7928
9:15 then **b** the offering that was for the people. 7928
9:16 *He* **b** the burnt offering and offered it in 7928
9:17 *He* also **b** the grain offering, 7928
10:15 the breast that was waved *must be* **b** with 995
11:45 I am the LORD who **b** you **up** out of Egypt 6590
13: 2 *he must* **be b** to Aaron the priest or to one 995
13: 9 *he must* **be b** to the priest. 995
14: 2 when *he is* **b** to the priest: 995
14: 4 and hyssop **be b** for the one to be cleansed. 4374
16:27 whose blood **was b** into 995
19:36 who **b** you **out** of Egypt. 3655
22:33 who **b** you **out** of Egypt to be your God. 3655
23:15 the day you **b** the sheaf of 995
23:43 in booths when I **b** them **out** of Egypt. 3655
24:11 so *they* **b** him to Moses. 995
25:38 who **b** you **out** of Egypt to give you 3655
25:42 whom *I* **b out** of Egypt, 3655
25:55 whom *I* **b out** of Egypt. 3655
26:13 who **b** you **out** of Egypt so 3655
26:45 with their ancestors whom *I* **b out** 3655
Nu 6:13 *be* **b** to the entrance to the Tent of Meeting. 995
7: 3 *They* **b** as their gifts before 995
7:10 the leaders **b** their offerings 7928
7:12 The *one who* **b** his offering on 7928
7:18 the leader of Issachar, **b** his **offering.** 7928
7:19 offering *he* **b** was one silver plate weighing 7928
7:24 of the people of Zebulun, **b** his offering. NIH
7:30 of the people of Reuben, **b** his offering. NIH
7:36 of the people of Simeon, **b** his offering. NIH
7:42 of the people of Gad, **b** his offering. NIH
7:48 of the people of Ephraim, **b** his offering. NIH
7:54 of the people of Manasseh, **b** his offering. NIH
7:60 of the people of Benjamin, **b** his offering. NIH
7:66 of the people of Dan, **b** his offering. NIH
7:72 of the people of Asher, **b** his offering. NIH
7:78 of the people of Naphtali, **b** his offering. NIH
11:11 "Why *have you* **b** *this* **trouble** 8317
11:24 *He* **b together** seventy of their elders 665
11:31 *It* **b** them **down** all around the camp to 5759
12:14 after that *she can* **be b back."** 665
12:15 people did not move on till she *was* **b back.** 665
14:13 By your power *you* **b** these people **up** from 6590
15:25 for it was not intentional and they *have* **b** to 995
15:33 Those who found him gathering wood **b**
him to Moses 7928
15:41 who **b** you **out** of Egypt to be your God. 3655
16: 9 of the Israelite community and **b** you **near** 7928
16:10 **b** you and all your fellow Levites **near** 7928
16:13 Isn't it enough that *you have* **b** us **up** out of 6590
16:14 *you* haven't **b** us into a land flowing 995
16:39 the priest collected the bronze censers **b** 7928
17: 9 Then Moses **b out** all the staffs from 3655
20:16 and sent an angel and **b** us **out** of Egypt. 3655
21: 5 "Why *have you* **b** us **up** out of Egypt to die 6590
23: 7 "Balak **b** me from Aram, 5663
23:11 *I* **b** you to curse my enemies, 4374
23:22 God **b** them **out** of Egypt; 3655
24: 8 "God **b** them **out** of Egypt; 3655
25: 6 Then an Israelite man **b** to his family 7928
27: 5 So Moses **b** their case before the LORD 7928
31:12 and **b** the captives, spoils and plunder 995
31:50 So *we have* **b** as an offering to the LORD 7928
31:54 and commanders of hundreds and **b** it into 995
32:17 ahead of the Israelites until *we have* **b** them 995
33: 4 the LORD *had* **b** judgment on their gods. 6913
Dt 1:25 *they* **b** it **down** to us and reported, 3718
1:27 so *he* **b** us **out** of Egypt to deliver us into 3655
4:20 and **b** you **out** of the iron-smelting furnace, 3655
4:37 *he* **b** you **out** of Egypt by his Presence 3655
5: 6 who **b** you **out** of Egypt, 3655
5:15 and that the LORD your God **b** you **out** 3655
6:12 who **b** you **out** of Egypt, 3655
6:21 in Egypt, but the LORD **b** us **out** of Egypt 3655
6:23 But *he* **b** us **out** from there to bring us in 3655
7: 8 to your forefathers that he **b** you **out** with 3655
7:19 the LORD your God **b** you **out.** 3655
8:14 who **b** you **out** of Egypt, 3655
8:15 He **b** you water **out** of hard rock. 3655
9: 4 "The LORD *has* **b** me here 995
9:12 because your people whom *you* **b out** 3655
9:26 by your great power and **b out** of Egypt 3655
9:28 the country from which *you* **b** us will say, 3655
9:28 *he* **b** them **out** to put them to death in 3655
9:29 that *you* **b out** by your great power 3655
11: 4 and how the LORD **b** lasting **ruin** *on* them. 6
11:29 When the LORD your God *has* **b** you into 995
13: 5 who **b** you **out** of Egypt and redeemed you 3655
13:10 who **b** you **out** of Egypt, 3655
16: 1 in the month of Abib he **b** you **out** of Egypt 3655
17: 4 **been b** to your **attention,** 2256+5583+9048
20: 1 who **b** you **up** out of Egypt, 6590
22:21 *be* **b** to the door of her father's house 3655
26: 8 So the LORD **b** us **out** of Egypt with 3655
26: 9 *He* **b** us to this place and gave us this land, 995
29:25 with them when he **b** them **out** of Egypt. 3655
29:27 *he* **b** on it all the curses written in this book. 995
31:20 When *I have* **b** them into the land flowing 995
Jos 2:18 unless *you have* **b** your father and mother, 665
6:23 the spying went in and **b out** Rahab, 3655
6:23 *They* **b out** her entire family and put them 3655
7:23 **b** them to Joshua and all the Israelites 995
7:25 "Why *have you* **b** *this* **trouble** *on* us? 6579

Jos 8:23 the king of Ai alive and **b** him to Joshua. 7928
10:23 **b** the five kings **out** 3655
10:24 When they *had* **b** these kings to Joshua, 3655
14: 7 And *I* **b** him **back** a report according 8740
18: 1 **was b under** their **control,** 3899
24: 5 and *I* **b** you **out.** 3655
24: 6 When *I* **b** your fathers **out** of Egypt, 3655
24: 7 *he* **b** the sea over them and covered them. 995
24: 8 " '*I* **b** you to the land of 995
24:17 **b** us and our fathers **up** 6590
24:32 which the Israelites *had* **b up** from Egypt, 6590
Jdg 1: 7 *They* **b** him to Jerusalem, and he died there. 995
2: 1 "*I* **b** you **up** out of Egypt and led you into 6590
2:12 whom *had* **b** them **out** of Egypt. 3655
5:25 for nobles *she* **b** him curdled milk. 7928
6: 8 I **b** you **up** out of Egypt, 6590
6:19 *he* **b** them **out** and offered them to him 3655
7:25 the Midianites and **b** the heads of Oreb 995
12: 9 **b in** thirty young women **as wives** 995
16: 8 of the Philistines **b** her seven fresh thongs 6590
16:31 *They* **b** him **back** and buried him 6590
18: 3 in there and asked him, "Who **b** you here? 995
Ru 1:21 but the LORD *has* **b** me **back** empty. 8740
1:21 the Almighty *has* **b misfortune** upon me." 8317
2:18 also **b out** and gave her what she had left 3655
1Sa 1:24 **b** him *to* the house of the LORD at Shiloh. 995
1:25 *they* **b** the boy to Eli, 995
2:14 for himself whatever the fork **b up.** 6590
4: 4 and *they* **b** back the ark of the covenant of 5951
4:17 The *man who* **b the news** replied, 1413
5: 6 *he* **b devastation** *upon* them 9037
5:10 **b** the ark of the god of Israel **around** 6015
6: 9 the LORD *has* **b** this great disaster on us. 6913
8: 8 from the day *I* **b** them **up** out of Egypt 6590
9:22 Then Samuel **b** Saul and his servant into 995
10:18 'I **b** Israel **up** out of Egypt, 6590
10:20 **b** all the tribes of Israel **near,** 7928
10:21 Then *he* **b forward** the tribe of Benjamin, 7928
10:23 They ran and **b** him out, 4374
10:27 They despised him and **b** him no gifts. 995
12: 6 and Aaron and **b** your forefathers **up** out 6590
12: 8 **b** your forefathers **out** 3655
14:34 So everyone **b** his ox that night 5602
14:45 *he* who *has* **b about** this great deliverance 6913
15:15 "The soldiers **b** them from the Amalekites; 995
15:20 the Amalekites and **b back** Agag their king. 995
16:12 So he sent and **had** him **b in.** 995
17:30 then turned away to someone else and **b up** 606
17:54 the Philistine's head and **b** it *to* Jerusalem, 995
17:57 Abner took him and **b** him before Saul, 995
18:27 He **b** their foreskins and presented 995
19: 7 He **b** him to Saul, 995
20: 8 for *you have* **b** him into a covenant 995
21: 8 *I* haven't **b** my sword 4374
23: 6 of Ahimelech *had* **b** the ephod **down** 3718
25:27 which your servant *has* **b** to my master, 995
25:31 when the LORD *has* **b** my master **success,** 3512
25:35 from her hand what *she had* **b** him and said, 995
25:39 **b** Nabal's wrongdoing **down** 8740
27:11 not leave a man or woman alive to *be* **b** 995
30: 7 Abiathar **b** it to him, 5602
30:11 an Egyptian in a field and **b** him to David. 4374
30:19 David **b** everything **back.** 8740
2Sa 1: 5 to the young man who **b** him *the* **report,** 5583
1:10 the band on his arm and *have* **b** them here 995
1:13 to the young man who **b** him *the* **report,** 5583
2: 8 of Saul and **b** him **over** *to* Mahanaim. 6296
3:22 from a raid and **b** with them a great deal 995
3:26 and *they* **b** him **back** from the well of Sirah. 8740
4: 8 *They* **b** the head of Ish-Bosheth to David 995
6: 1 David again **b together** out 665
6: 3 the ark of God on a new cart and **b** it from 5951
6:12 and **b up** the ark of God from the house 6590
6:15 while he and the entire house of Israel **b up** 6590
6:17 *They* **b** the ark of the LORD and set it 995
7: 6 in a house from the day I **b** the Israelites **up** 6590
7:18 that *you have* **b** me this far? 995
8: 2 to David and **b** tribute. 5951
8: 6 to him and **b** tribute. 5951
8: 7 to the officers of Hadadezer and **b** them 995
8:10 Joram **b with** him articles of silver and gold 928+2118+3338
9: 5 So King David **had** him **b** from Lo Debar, 2256+4374+8938
10:16 Hadadezer **had** Arameans **b** from beyond 3655
11:27 David **had** her **b** to his house, 665
12:31 and **b out** the people who were there, 3655
13:10 the bread she had prepared and **b** it 995
14: 2 **had** a wise woman **b** 4374
14:13 the king *has* not **b back** his banished son? 8740
14:23 and **b** Absalom **back** *to* Jerusalem. 995
16: 2 "Why have you **b** these?" 4200
17:28 **b** bedding and bowls and articles of pottery. NIH
17:28 *They* also **b** wheat and barley, 5602
21:13 David **b** the bones of Saul 6590
22:20 *He* **b** me **out** into a spacious place; 3655
23:10 The LORD **b about** a great victory 6913
23:12 and the LORD **b about** a great victory. 6913
1Ki 1: 3 a Shunammite, and **b** her to the king. 995
1:53 and *they* **b** him **down** from the altar. 3718
2:19 *He* **had** a throne **b** for the king's mother, 8492
2:40 So Shimei went away and **b** the slaves **back** 995
3: 1 *He* **b** her to the City of David 995
3:24 So *they* **b** a sword for the king. 995
4:21 *These* countries **b** tribute 5602
4:28 *They* also **b** to the proper place their quotas 995
7:13 King Solomon sent to Tyre and **b** Huram, 4374
1Ki 7:51 of the LORD was finished, he **b in** 995
8: 4 and *they* **b up** the ark of the LORD and 6590
8: 6 then **b** the ark of the LORD's covenant 995
8:16 **b** my people Israel **out** 3655
8:21 with our fathers when he **b** them **out** 3655
8:51 whom *you* **b out** of Egypt, 3655
8:53 **b** our fathers **out** of Egypt." 3655
9: 9 who **b** their fathers **out** of Egypt, 3655
9: 9 the LORD **b** all this disaster on them.' " 995
9:28 They sailed to Ophir and **b** back 420 talents 4374
10:10 so many spices **b in** as those the queen 995
10:11 (Hiram's ships **b** gold from Ophir; 5951
10:11 and from there *they* **b** great cargoes 995
10:25 everyone who came **b** a gift— 995
11:20 whom Tahpenes **b up** in the royal palace. 1694
12:28 O Israel, who **b** you **up** out of Egypt." 6590
13:20 to the old prophet who *had* **b** him **back.** 8740
13:23 the prophet who *had* **b** him **back** saddled his donkey 8740
13:26 When the prophet who *had* **b** him **back** 8740
13:29 and **b** it **back** to his own city to mourn 8740
15:15 *He* **b into** the temple of the LORD 995
17: 6 The ravens **b** him bread and meat in 995
17:20 *have you* **b tragedy** also 8317
18:40 and Elijah *had* them **b down** to 3718
21:13 and sat opposite him and **b charges against** 6386
22: 6 the king of Israel **b together** the prophets— 7695
22:37 So the king died and *was* **b** *to* Samaria, 995
2Ki 2:20 So *they* **b** it to him. 4374
4: 5 They **b** the jars to her and she kept pouring. 5602
5:20 by not accepting from him what *he* **b.** 995
8: 5 the woman whose son Elisha *had* **b back to life** came 2649
10: 8 "*They have* **b** the heads of the princes." 995
10:18 **b** all the people **together** 7695
10:22 So *he* **b out** robes for them. 3655
10:26 **b** the sacred stone **out** 3655
11: 4 the Carites and the guards and **had** them **b** 995
11:12 Jehoiada **b out** the king's son and put 3655
11:19 and *together they* **b** the king **down** from 3718
12: 4 that **is b** as sacred offerings *to* the temple of 995
12: 4 and the money **b** voluntarily *to* the temple. 995
12: 9 into the chest all the money that **was b** *to* 995
12:10 the money that *had* **been b** *into* the temple 5162
12:13 The money **b into** the temple was not spent 995
12:16 and sin offerings **was** not **b into** the temple 995
14:20 *He was* **b back** by horse and was buried 5951
16:14 before the LORD *he* **b** from the front of 7928
17: 7 who *had* **b** them **up** out of Egypt from under 6590
17:24 of Assyria **b** people from Babylon, 995
17:33 of the nations from which they *had been* **b.** 1655
17:36 who **b** you **up** out of Egypt 6590
19:25 now *I have* **b** it **to pass,** 995
20:20 the tunnel by which *he* **b** water into the city, 995
22: 4 the money that *has* **been b into** the temple 995
23: 8 Josiah **b** all the priests from the towns 995
23:30 Josiah's servants **b** his body in a chariot 995
25:20 the commander took them all and **b** them to 2143
1Ch 2: 7 who **b trouble** *on* Israel by violating 6579
9:28 they counted them *when* they *were* **b** in and 995
10:12 the bodies of Saul and his sons and **b** them 995
11:14 the LORD **b about** a great **victory.** 3828+9591
15:28 So all Israel **b up** the ark of the covenant of 6590
16: 1 *They* **b** the ark of God and set it inside 995
17: 5 in a house from the day *I* **b** Israel **up** out 6590
17:16 that *you have* **b** me this far? 995
18: 2 they became subject to him and **b** tribute. 5951
18: 6 to him and **b** tribute. 5951
18: 7 by the officers of Hadadezer and **b** them 995
18:10 Hadoram **b** all kinds of articles of gold NIH
19:16 **had** Arameans **b** from beyond the River, 3655
20: 3 and **b out** the people who were there, 3655
22: 4 and Tyrians **had b** large numbers of them 995
2Ch 1: 4 Now David *had* **b up** the ark of God 6590
5: 1 temple of the LORD was finished, he **b in** 995
5: 5 and *they* **b up** the ark and the Tent 6590
5: 7 then **b** the ark of the LORD's covenant 995
6: 5 the day *I* **b** my people **out** of Egypt, 3655
7:22 who **b** them **out** of Egypt, 3655
7:22 that is why *he* **b** all this disaster on them.' " 995
8:11 **b** Pharaoh's daughter **up** 6590
8:18 and **b** back four hundred and fifty talents 4374
9:10 of Hiram and the men of Solomon **b** gold 995
9:10 also **b** algumwood and precious stones. 995
9:12 he gave her more than *she had* **b** to him. 995
9:14 the revenues **b in** *by* merchants and traders. 995
9:14 the governors of the land **b** gold and silver 995
9:24 everyone who came **b** a gift— 995
15:11 and goats from the plunder *they had* **b back.** 995
15:18 *He* **b into** the temple of God the silver 995
16: 6 Then King Asa **b** all the men of Judah, 4374
17: 5 and all Judah **b** gifts to Jehoshaphat, 5989
17:11 Some Philistines **b** Jehoshaphat gifts 995
17:11 and the Arabs **b** him flocks: 995
18: 5 the king of Israel **b together** the prophets— 7695
22: 7 God **b about** Ahaziah's downfall. 2118+4946
22: 9 He *was* **b** to Jehu and put to death. 995
23:11 Jehoiada and his sons **b out** the king's son 3655
23:20 the people of the land and **b** the king **down** 3718
24:10 the people **b** their contributions gladly, 995
24:11 Whenever the chest *was* **b in** by the Levites 995
24:14 *they* **b** the rest of the money to the king 995
25:14 *he* **b back** the gods of the people of Seir. 995
25:23 Then Jehoash **b** him *to* Jerusalem 995
25:28 He *was* **b back** by horse and was buried 5951
26: 8 The Ammonites **b** tribute to Uzziah, 5989
27: 5 The Ammonites **b** him the same amount 8740
2Ch 28: 5 as prisoners and **b** them *to* Damascus. 995
29: 4 *He* **b in** the priests and the Levites, 995
29:16 *They* **b out** to the courtyard of 3655
29:21 *They* **b** seven bulls, seven rams, 995
29:23 The goats for the sin offering *were* **b** before 5602
29:31 assembly **b** sacrifices and thank offerings, 995
29:31 all whose hearts were willing **b** burnt offerings. NIH
29:32 the assembly **b** was seventy bulls, 995
29:36 the people rejoiced at what God *had* **b about** 3922
30:15 and burnt offerings *to* the temple of 995
31: 5 *They* **b** a great amount, 995
31: 6 also **b** a tithe of their herds and flocks and 995
31:12 Then *they* faithfully **b in** the contributions, 995
32:23 Many **b** offerings to Jerusalem for 995
33:11 So the LORD **b** against them 995
33:13 so *he* **b** him **back** *to* Jerusalem and 8740
34: 9 gave him the money that *had* **been b into** 995
35:24 in the other chariot he had and **b** him 2143
36:10 for him and **b** him to Babylon, 995
36:17 *He* **b up** against them the king of 6590
Ezr 1: 7 King Cyrus **b out** the articles belonging to 3655
1: 8 of Persia **had** them **b** by Mithredath 3655
1:11 Sheshbazzar **b** all these **along** when 6590
3: 5 **b as freewill offerings** to the LORD 5605+5607
4: 2 king of Assyria, who **b** us here." 6590
5:14 the temple in Jerusalem and **b** to the temple 10308
6: 5 the temple in Jerusalem and **b** to Babylon, 10308
8:18 *they* **b** us Sherebiah, a capable man, 995
8:20 They also **b** 220 of the temple servants— NIH
Ne 2: 1 when wine was **b** for him, NIH
8: 2 the seventh month Ezra the priest **b** the Law 995
8:16 So the people went out and **b back** branches 995
9: 7 who chose Abram and **b** him **out** of Ur of 3655
9:15 and in their thirst *you* **b** them water from 3655
9:18 who **b** you **up** out of Egypt,' 6590
9:23 and *you* **b** them into the land 995
12:27 where they lived and *were* **b** to Jerusalem 995
12:28 The singers also **were b together** from 665
13:12 All Judah **b** the tithes of grain, 995
13:18 that our God **b** all this calamity upon us and 995
13:19 the gates so that no load *could be* **b in** on 995
Est 1:17 Queen Vashti to *be* **b** before him, 995
2: 7 Hadassah, whom he *had* **b up** 587
2: 8 many girls **were b** to the citadel of Susa 7695
6: 1 to *be* **b in** and read to him. 995
Job 4:12 "A word **was secretly b** to me, 1704
14:21 if *they are* **b low,** he does not see it. 7592
15: 7 **Were** *you* **b forth** before the hills? 2655
22:29 *men are* **b low** and you say, 'Lift them up!' 9164
24:24 *they* **are b low** and gathered up 4812
42:11 the trouble the LORD *had* **b** upon him, 995
Ps 18:19 *He* **b** me **out** into a spacious place; 3655
20: 8 They *are* **b** *to their* **knees** and fall, 4156
22: 9 Yet you **b** me out of the womb; 1631
30: 3 O LORD, *you* **b** me **up** from the grave; 6590
37:33 be condemned when **b to trial.** 9149
38: 6 I am bowed down and **b** very **low;** 8820
44:25 We *are b* **down** to the dust; AIT
45:14 her virgin companions follow her and **are b** 995
46: 8 the desolations *he has* **b** on the earth. 8492
66:11 *You* **b** us into prison and laid burdens 995
66:12 but *you* **b** us to a place of abundance. 3655
71: 6 you **b** me **forth** from my mother's womb. 1602
74: 3 **destruction** the enemy *has* **b** 8317
78:16 *he* **b** streams **out** of a rocky crag 3655
78:52 But *he* **b** his people **out** like a flock; 5825
78:54 Thus *he* **b** them to the border 995
78:71 from tending the sheep *he* **b** him to be 995
80: 8 *You* **b** a vine **out** of Egypt; 5825
81:10 who **b** you **up** out of Egypt. 6590
90: 2 the mountains were born or *you* **b forth** 2655
94:19 your consolation **b joy** *to* my soul. 9130
105:37 *He* **b out** Israel, laden with silver and gold, 3655
105:40 and *he* **b** them quail and satisfied them with 995
105:43 *He* **b out** his people with rejoicing, 3655
107:14 *He* **b** them **out** of darkness and 3655
107:28 and *he* **b** them **out** of their distress. 3655
107:36 **b** the hungry **to live,** 3782
126: 1 the LORD **b back** the captives *to* Zion, 8740
136:11 and **b** Israel **out** from 3655
136:14 and **b** Israel through the midst of it, 6296
Pr 7:26 Many are the victims *she has* **b down;** 5877
8:22 LORD **b** me **forth** as the first of his works, 7865
11: 5 but the wicked *are* **b down** 5877
14:32 calamity comes, the wicked **are b down,** 1890
21:27 how much more so *when* **b** with evil intent! 995
24:16 but the wicked **are b down** by calamity. 4173
SS 3: 4 and would not let him go till *I had* **b** him 995
Isa 1: 2 "I reared children and **b** them **up,** 8123
2: 9 So man *will* **be b low** 8820
2:11 be humbled and the pride of men **b low;** 8820
2:17 The arrogance of man *will be* **b low** and 8820
3: 9 *They have* **b** disaster upon themselves. 1694
5:15 man *will* **be b low** and mankind humbled, 8820
10:33 the tall ones *will be* **b low.** 9164
14:11 All your pomp *has* **been b down** *to* 3718
14:15 But *you* **are b down** to the grave, 3718
18: 7 At that time gifts *will* **be b** to 3297
18: 7 the gifts will be **b** to Mount Zion, NIH
23: 4 I have neither reared sons nor **b up** 8123
26:14 You punished them and **b** them **to ruin;** 9012
26:18 *We have* not **b** salvation *to* the earth; 6913
29: 4 **B low,** you will speak from the ground; 9164
29:10 The LORD *has* **b** over you a deep sleep: 5818
37:26 now *I have* **b** it **to pass,** 995

Isa 43:23 not b me sheep for burnt offerings, 995
44:11 *they will be* b down to terror and infamy. 7064
45:10 to his mother, 'What *have you* b to birth?' 2655
49:21 Who b these up? 1540
53: 5 punishment *that* b us peace was upon him, AIT
60: 5 the wealth on the seas *will* be b to you, 2200
63:11 where is he *who* b them through the sea, 6590
66: 8 in a day or a nation be b forth in a moment? 3528
Jer 2: 6 who b us up out of Egypt and led us 6590
2: 7 *I* b you into a fertile land to eat its fruit 995
2:17 not b this on yourselves by forsaking 6913
4:18 "Your own conduct and actions *have* b this 6913
6:15 *they will* be b down when I punish them," 4173
7:22 b your forefathers out 3655
8:12 *they will* be b down 4173
10: 9 Hammered silver is b from Tarshish 995
11: 4 when I b them out of Egypt, 3655
11: 7 the time I b your forefathers up from Egypt 6590
11: 8 So *I* b on them all the curses of 995
16:14 who b the Israelites up out of Egypt,' 6590
16:15 who b the Israelites up out of the land of 6590
20: 8 So the word of the LORD *has* b me insult 2118
20:15 b my father the news, 1413
23: 7 who b the Israelites up out of Egypt,' 6590
23: 8 b the descendants of Israel up 6590
25: 7 and you have b harm to yourselves." NIH
26:23 *They* b Uriah out of Egypt and took him 3655
27:16 from the LORD's house *will* be b back 8740
32:21 b your people Israel out 3655
32:23 b all this disaster upon 7925
32:42 As *I have* b all this great calamity 995
34:13 with your forefathers when *I* b them out 3655
35: 4 *I* b them into the house of the LORD, 995
36:21 and Jehudi b it from the room of Elishama 4374
37:14 instead, he arrested Jeremiah and b him to 995
37:17 for him and *had* him b to the palace, 4374
38:14 for Jeremiah the prophet and *had* him b to 4374
38:22 of Judah *will* be b out to the officials of 3655
38:23 and children *will be* b out to 3655
40: 3 And now the LORD *has* b it about; 995
41:16 and court officials *he had* b from Gibeon. 8740
44: 2 the great disaster *I* b on Jerusalem and 995
50:25 and b out the weapons of his wrath, 3655
52:26 the commander took them all and b them to 2143
La 1: 5 The LORD *has* b her grief because 3324
1:12 that the LORD b on me in the day 3324
2: 2 b her kingdom and its princes down 5595
Eze 8: 7 Then *he* b me to the entrance to the court. 995
8:14 Then *he* b me to the entrance to 995
8:16 then b me into the inner court of the house 995
9:11 with the writing kit at his side b back word, 8740
11: 1 the Spirit lifted me up and b me to the gate 995
11:24 up and b me to the exiles in Babylonia in 995
12: 7 the day *I* b out my things packed for exile. 3655
13:22 when I *had* b them no grief, 3872
14:22 sons and daughters who *will* be b out of it. 3655
14:22 be consoled regarding the disaster *I have* b 995
14:22 every disaster *I have* b upon it. 995
17:14 so that the kingdom would be *b* low, AIT
19: 3 *She* b up one of her cubs, 6590
19: 9 a cage and b him to the king of Babylon. 995
20:10 of Egypt and b them into the desert. 995
20:14 in whose sight *I had* b them out. 3655
20:22 in whose sight *I had* b them out. 3655
20:28 When *I* b them into the land I had sworn 995
21:24 you people *have* b to mind your guilt 2349
21:26 be exalted and the exalted *will be* b low. 9164
22: 4 b your days to a close, 7928
23:30 *have* b this upon you, 6913
23:42 Sabeans were b from the desert along 995
27: 4 b your beauty to perfection. 4005
27:11 b your beauty to perfection. 4005
30:11 *will* be b in to destroy the land. 995
31:15 the day it *was* b down to the grave 3718
31:16 at the sound of its fall when I b it down to 3718
31:18 *will* be b down with the trees of Eden to 3718
34: 4 *You have* not b back the strays or searched 8740
37: 1 and *he* b me out by the Spirit of the LORD 3655
38: 8 They *had* been b out from the nations, 3655
39:27 When I *have* b them back from the nations 8740
40: 4 for that is why *you have* been b here. 995
40:17 Then *he* b me into the outer court. 995
40:28 Then *he* b me into the inner court through 995
40:32 *he* b me to the inner court on the east side, 995
40:35 *he* b me to the north gate and measured it. 995
40:48 *He* b me to the portico of the temple 995
41: 1 Then the man b me to the outer sanctuary 995
42: 1 into the outer court and b me to 995
43: 1 Then the man b me to the gate facing east, 2143
43: 5 Then the Spirit lifted me up and b me into 995
44: 1 Then the man b me back to the outer gate 8740
44: 4 the man b me by way of the north gate to 995
44: 7 you b foreigners uncircumcised in heart 995
46:19 Then the man b me through the entrance at 995
46:21 *He* then b me to the outer court and led me 3655
47: 1 The man b me back to the entrance of 8740
47: 2 *He* then b me out through the north gate 3655
Da 3:13 So these men were b before the king, 10085
4: 6 the wise men of Babylon *be* b before me 10549
5: 3 So *they* b in the gold goblets 10085
5: 7 astrologers and diviners to *be* b and said 10549
5:13 So Daniel was b before the king, 10549
5:13 the exiles my father the king b from Judah? 10085
5:15 The wise men and enchanters were b 10549
5:23 You had the goblets from his temple b 10085
5:26 days of your reign and b it to an end. 10719
6:16 and *they* b Daniel and threw him into 10085
Da 6:17 A stone was b and placed over the mouth of 10085
6:18 without any entertainment *being* b to him. 10549
6:24 the men who had falsely accused Daniel *were* b in 10085
8:11 and the place of his sanctuary was b low. 8959
9:15 who b your people out of Egypt with 3655
Hos 10: 1 *he* b forth fruit for himself. 8751
12: 9 [who b you] out of Egypt; NIH
13: 4 [who b you] out of Egypt. NIH
Am 2:10 "I b you up out of Egypt, 6590
3: 1 the whole family *I* b up out of Egypt: 6590
Jnh 2: 6 But *you* b my life up from the pit, 6590
Mic 4: 6 the exiles and those *I have* b to grief. 8317
6: 4 *I* b you up out of Egypt and redeemed you 6590
Hag 1: 9 What *you* b home, I blew away. 995
Zec 10:11 Assyria's pride *will* be b down 3718
Mal 1:11 and pure offerings *will* be b to my name, 5602
Mt 4:24 and people b to him all who were ill *4712*
8:16 many who were demon-possessed *were* b to *4712*
9: 2 *Some men* b to him a paralytic, *4712*
9:32 and could not talk *was* b to Jesus. *4712*
10:18 *be* b before governors and kings *72*
12:22 Then *they* b him a demon-possessed man *4712*
14:11 His head *was* b in on a platter and given to *5770*
14:35 *People* b all their sick to him *4712*
17:16 *I* b him to your disciples, *4712*
18:24 man who owed him ten thousand talents *was* b to him. *4712*
19:13 Then little children *were* b to Jesus for him *4712*
19:13 the disciples rebuked those who b them. *NIG*
21: 7 *They* b the donkey and the colt, *72*
22:19 They b him a denarius, *4712*
25:20 the five talents b the other five. *4712*
Mk 1:32 That evening after sunset the *people* b *5770*
4:22 to be b out into the open. *2262*
6:28 and b back his head on a platter. *5770*
7:32 There *some people* b to him *5770*
8:22 and *some people* b a blind man *5770*
9:17 "Teacher, *I* b you my son, *5770*
9:20 So *they* b him. *5770*
11: 7 When *they* b the colt to Jesus *5770*
12:16 They b the coin, and he asked them, *5770*
13:11 Whenever you are arrested and b to trial, *72*
15:22 *They* b Jesus to the place called Golgotha *5770*
Lk 1:52 *He has* b down rulers from their thrones *2747*
2:27 When the parents b in the child Jesus to do *1652*
4:16 where he had been b up, *5555*
4:40 When the sun was setting, the people b *72*
7:37 *she* b an alabaster jar of perfume, *3152*
8:17 not be known or b out into the open. *2262*
12:11 "When you *are* b before synagogues, *1662*
18:40 Jesus stopped and ordered the man *to be* b *72*
19:35 *They* b it to Jesus, *72*
21:12 *you will be* b before kings and governors, *552*
23:14 "*You* b me this man as one who was inciting the people to rebellion. *4712*
Jn 1:42 And *he* b him to Jesus. *72*
4:33 "Could someone *have* b him food?" *5770*
8: 3 The teachers of the law and the Pharisees b *72*
9:13 *They* b to the Pharisees *72*
10: 4 When *he has* b out all his own, *1675*
17: 4 I *have* b you glory on earth by completing *1519*
17:23 May they be b to complete unity to let *NIG*
18:13 and b him first to Annas, *72*
18:16 to the girl on duty there and b Peter in. *1652*
19:13 *he* b Jesus out and sat down on *72*
19:39 Nicodemus b a mixture of myrrh and aloes, *5770*
Ac 4: 7 *They had* Peter and John b before them *2705*
4:34 b the money from the sales *5770*
4:37 a field he owned and b the money and put it *5770*
5: 2 but b the rest and put it at the apostles' feet. *5770*
5:15 people b the sick into the streets *1766*
5:19 the doors of the jail and b them out. *1974*
5:26 the captain went with his officers and b *72*
5:27 *Having* b the apostles, *72*
6:12 They seized Stephen and b him before *72*
7:16 Their bodies *were* b back to Shechem *3572*
7:21 Pharaoh's daughter took him and b him up *427*
7:41 *They* b sacrifices to it and held *343*
7:45 under Joshua b it with them when they took *1652*
9:27 But Barnabas took him and b him to *72*
11:24 great number of people *were* b to the Lord. *4707*
11:26 *he* b him to Antioch. *72*
12:17 and described how the Lord *had* b him out *1974*
13: 1 Manaen (who had been b up with Herod *5343*
13:23 "From this man's descendants God *has* b *72*
14:13 b bulls and wreaths to the city gates *5770*
15: 2 This b Paul and Barnabas into sharp dispute *1181*
16:20 They b them before the magistrates *4642*
16:30 *He* then b them out and asked, "Sirs, *4575*
16:34 The jailer b them into his house and set *343*
17:15 The men who escorted Paul b him *72*
17:19 Then *they* took him and b him to a meeting *72*
18:12 a united attack on Paul and b him *72*
19:19 b their scrolls together *5237*
19:24 b in no little business for the craftsmen. *4218*
19:37 *You have* b these men here, *72*
21:16 from Caesarea accompanied us and b us to *72*
21:28 *he has* b Greeks into the temple area *1652*
21:29 that Paul *had* b him into the temple area.) *1652*
22: 3 but b up in this city. *427*
22:30 he b Paul and had him stand before them. *2864*
23:28 so *I* b him to their Sanhedrin. *2864*
23:31 with them during the night and b him as far *72*
24: 1 and they b their charges against Paul before *1872*
24: 2 under you, and your foresight *has* b about *1181*
25: 6 and ordered that Paul *be* b before him. *72*
Ac 25:11 the charges b against me by these Jews are *2989*
25:15 elders of the Jews b charges against him *1872*
25:17 and ordered the man *to be* b in. *72*
25:23 At the command of Festus, Paul *was* b in. *72*
25:26 Therefore *I have* b him before all of you, *4575*
Ro 5:16 followed one sin and b condemnation, *1650*
5:16 but the gift followed many trespasses and b justification. *1650*
6:13 b from death to life; *2409*
7:10 to bring life actually b death. *1650*
8:21 to decay and b into the glorious freedom of *NIG*
2Co 3: 7 Now if the ministry that b death, *NIG*
Eph 2:13 in Christ Jesus you who once were far away *have been* b near *1181*
Col 1:13 and b us into the kingdom of the Son *3496*
1Th 3: 6 to us from you and *has* b good news about *2294*
1Ti 4: 6 b up in the truths of the faith and of *1957*
5:19 an accusation against an elder unless it is b *NIG*
6: 7 For *we* b nothing into the world, *1662*
2Ti 1:10 b life and immortality to light *5894*
Tit 1: 3 b his word to light *5746*
Heb 6: 6 *to be* b back to repentance, *362*
13:20 the blood of the eternal covenant b back *343*
Jas 5:11 have seen what the Lord finally b about. *NIG*
2Pe 2: 5 *when he* b the flood on its ungodly people, *2042*
Rev 18:17 In one hour such great wealth *has been* b to ruin!' *2246*
18:19 In one hour *she has been* b to ruin! *2246*
21:26 and honor of the nations *will be* b into it. *5770*

BROUGHT (Anglicized) See also TOOK

BROUGHT UP (Anglicized) See REARED

BROW (5)

Ge 3:19 the sweat of your b you will eat your food 678
49:26 on the b *of* the prince among his brothers. 7721
Dt 33:16 on the b *of* the prince among his brothers. 7721
Job 16:15 over my skin and buried my b in the dust. 7967
Lk 4:29 and took him to the b of the hill on which *4059*

BROWN (1)

Zec 1: 8 Behind him were red, b and white horses. 8601

BROWSE (2) [BROWSES]

SS 4: 5 like twin fawns of a gazelle that b among 8286
6: 2 to b in the gardens and to gather lilies. 8286

BROWSES (2) [BROWSE]

SS 2:16 he b among the lilies. 8286
6: 3 he b among the lilies. 8286

BRUISE (2) [BRUISED, BRUISES]

Ex 21:25 wound for wound, b for bruise. 2467
21:25 wound for wound, bruise for b. 2467

BRUISED (5) [BRUISE]

Lev 22:24 the LORD an animal whose testicles *are* b, 5080
Ps 105:18 *They* b his feet with shackles, 6700
SS 5: 7 They beat me, *they* b me; 7205
Isa 42: 3 A b reed he will not break, 8368
Mt 12:20 A b reed he will not break, *5341*

BRUISES (2) [BRUISE]

Pr 23:29 Who has needless b? 7206
Isa 30:26 the LORD binds up the b *of* his people 8691

BRUISES (Anglicized) See also WELTS

BRUIT (KJV) See REPORT, NEWS

BRUSH (1) [BRUSHWOOD, UNDERBRUSH]

Job 30: 4 In the b they gathered salt herbs, 8489

BRUSHING (1)

Eze 3:13 the living creatures b against each other and 5976

BRUSHWOOD (1) [BRUSH, WOOD]

Ac 28: 3 Paul gathered a pile *of* b and, *5866*

BRUTAL (2) [BRUTE]

Eze 21:31 I will hand you over to b men, 1279
2Ti 3: 3 slanderous, without self-control, b, *466*

BRUTALLY (3) [BRUTE]

2Ch 16:10 At the same time Asa b oppressed some of 8368
Eze 34: 4 You have ruled them harshly and b. 928+7266
1Co 4:11 *we are* b treated, we are homeless. *3139*

BRUTE (2) [BRUTAL, BRUTALLY, BRUTES]

Ps 73:22 I was a b beast before you. 989
2Pe 2:12 They are like b beasts, creatures of instinct, *263*

BRUTES (1) [BRUTE]
Tit 1:12 "Cretans are always liars, evil **b**, *2563*

BUBASTIS (1)
Eze 30:17 of Heliopolis and **B** will fall by the sword, 7083

BUBBLING (2)
Pr 18: 4 but the fountain of wisdom is a **b** brook. 5580
Isa 35: 7 the thirsty ground **b springs.** 4432+4784

BUCKET (1) [BUCKETS]
Isa 40:15 Surely the nations are like a drop in a **b**; 1932

BUCKETS (2) [BUCKET]
Ex 7:19 *even* in the **wooden** *b* and stone jars." AIT
Nu 24: 7 Water will flow from their **b**; 1932

BUCKLED (1) [BUCKLER]
Eph 6:14 with the belt of truth **b around** your **waist,** *4322*

BUCKLER (1) [BUCKLED]
Ps 35: 2 Take up shield and **b**; 7558

BUCKLERS (KJV) See SHIELDS

BUD (11) [BUDDED, BUDS]
Ex 25:35 One **b** shall be under the first pair 4117
25:35 a second **b** under the second pair, 4117
25:35 and a third **b** under the third pair— 4117
37:21 One **b** was under the first pair 4117
37:21 a second **b** under the second pair, 4117
37:21 and a third **b** under the third pair— 4117
Job 14: 9 of water *it will* **b** and put forth shoots like 7255
Isa 17:11 *you* **bring** them **to b**, 7255
27: 6 Israel *will* **b** and blossom and fill all 7437
55:10 without watering the earth and **making** it **b** 3528
Hab 3:17 not **b** and there are no grapes on the vines, 7255

BUDDED (6) [BUD]
Ge 40:10 As soon as it **b**, it blossomed, 7255
Nu 17: 8 had not only sprouted but *had* **b**, 3655+7258
SS 6:11 if the vines *had* **b** or the pomegranates were 7255
7:12 to the vineyards to see if the vines *have* **b**, 7255
Eze 7:10 Doom has burst forth, the rod *has* **b**, 7437
Heb 9: 4 Aaron's staff that *had* **b**, *1056*

BUDS (8) [BUD]
Ex 25:31 its flowerlike cups, **b** and blossoms shall be 4117
25:33 with **b** and blossoms are to be 4117
25:34 like almond flowers with **b** and blossoms. 4117
25:36 The **b** and branches shall all be of one piece 4117
37:17 **b** and blossoms were of one piece with it. 4117
37:19 with **b** and blossoms were on one branch, 4117
37:20 like almond flowers with **b** and blossoms. 4117
37:22 The **b** and the branches were all 4117

BUFFET (KJV) See BEAT, STRUCK, TORMENT

BUFFETED (1)
Mt 14:24 **b** by the waves because the wind was *989*

BUILD (152) [BUILDER, BUILDERS, BUILDING, BUILDINGS, BUILDS, BUILT, REBUILD, REBUILDING, REBUILT, WELL-BUILT]
Ge 6:15 This is how *you are to* **b** it: 6913
11: 4 "Come, *let us* **b** ourselves a city, 1215
16: 2 perhaps *I can* **b a family** through her." 1215
30: 3 and that through her I too *can* **b a family."** 1215
35: 1 and **b** an altar there to God, 6913
35: 3 where *I will* **b** an altar to God, 6913
Ex 20:25 *do* not **b** it *with* dressed stones, 1215
27: 1 **"B** an altar of acacia wood, 6913
Nu 23: 1 Balaam said, **"B** me seven altars here, 1215
23:29 Balaam said, **"B** me seven altars here, 1215
32:16 *to* **b** pens here for our livestock and cities 1215
32:24 **B** cities for your women and children, 1215
Dt 6:10 flourishing cities *you did* not **b**, 1215
8:12 when *you* **b** fine houses and settle down, 1215
16:21 the altar *you* **b** to the LORD your God, 6913
19: 3 **B** roads to them and divide into three parts 3922
20:20 *to* **b** siege works until the city at war 1215
22: 8 When *you* **b** a new house, 1215
25: 9 not **b up** his brother's family line." 1215
27: 5 **B** there an altar to the LORD your God, 1215
27: 6 **B** the altar of the LORD your God 1215
28:30 *You will* **b** a house, 1215
Jos 22:16 from the LORD and **b** yourselves an altar 1215
22:26 'Let us get ready and **b** an altar— 1215
24:13 not toil and cities *you did* not **b**; 1215
Jdg 6:26 Then **b** a proper kind of altar to 1215
2Sa 7: 5 the one *to* **b** me a house to dwell in? 1215
7:13 the one *who will* **b** a house for my Name, 1215
7:27 saying, '*I will* **b** a house for you.' 1215
24:18 "Go up and **b** an altar to the LORD on 7756
24:21 "so I *can* **b** an altar to the LORD, 1215
1Ki 2:36 **"B** yourself a house in Jerusalem 1215
5: 3 he could not **b** a temple for the Name of 1215
5: 5 to **b** a temple for the Name of 1215
5: 5 the throne in your place *will* **b** the temple 1215
6: 1 *he began to* **b** the temple of the LORD. 1215
8:17 to **b** a temple for the Name of the LORD, 1215
8:18 'Because it was in your heart to **b** a temple 1215
8:19 you *are* not *the one to* **b** the temple, 1215
8:19 he *is the one who will* **b** the temple 1215
9:15 to **b** the LORD's temple, 1215
9:19 whatever he desired to **b** in Jerusalem, 1215
11:38 *I will* **b** you a dynasty as enduring as 1215
2Ki 6: 2 and *let us* **b** a place there for us to live." 6913
19:32 He will not come before it with shield or **b** 9161
1Ch 14: 1 stonemasons and carpenters to **b** a palace 1215
17: 4 not the one *to* **b** me a house to dwell in. 1215
17:10 " 'I declare to you that the LORD *will* **b** 1215
17:12 He *is the one who will* **b** a house for me, 1215
17:25 to your servant that you *will* **b** a house 1215
21:18 to go up and **b** an altar to the LORD on 7756
21:22 of your threshing floor so *I can* **b** an altar 1215
22: 6 for his son Solomon and charged him to **b** 1215
22: 7 "My son, I had it in my heart to **b** a house 1215
22: 8 *You are* not *to* **b** a house for my Name, 1215
22:10 *the one who will* **b** a house for my Name. 1215
22:11 and may you have success and **b** the house 1215
22:19 *to* **b** the sanctuary of the LORD God, 1215
28: 2 to **b** a house as a place of rest for the ark of 1215
28: 2 and I made plans to **b** it. 1215
28: 3 *'You are* not *to* **b** a house for my Name, 1215
28: 6 the one *who will* **b** my house 1215
28:10 the LORD has chosen you to **b** a temple as 1215
29:19 to do everything to **b** the palatial structure 1215
2Ch 2: 1 to **b** a temple for the Name of the LORD 1215
2: 3 when you sent him cedar to **b** a palace 1215
2: 4 *about to* **b** a temple for the Name of 1215
2: 5 "The temple I *am going to* **b** will be great, 1215
2: 6 But who is able to **b** a temple for him, 1215
2: 6 Who then am I *to* **b** a temple for him, 1215
2: 9 temple I **b** must be large and magnificent. 1215
2:12 who *will* **b** a temple for the LORD and 1215
3: 1 to **b** the temple of the LORD in Jerusalem 1215
6: 7 to **b** a temple for the Name of the LORD, 1215
6: 8 'Because it was in your heart to **b** a temple 1215
6: 9 you are not *the one to* **b** the temple, 1215
6: 9 he is *the one who will* **b** the temple 1215
6:38 whatever he desired to **b** in Jerusalem, 1215
14: 7 *"Let us* **b up** these towns," 1215
36:23 to **b** a temple for him at Jerusalem in Judah. 1215
Ezr 1: 2 to **b** a temple for him at Jerusalem in Judah. 1215
1: 3 up to Jerusalem in Judah and **b** the temple 1215
1: 5 to go up and **b** the house of the LORD 1215
3: 2 of Shealtiel and his associates began *to* **b** 1215
4: 2 *"Let us* help you **b** because, like you, 1215
4: 3 We alone *will* **b** it for the LORD, 1215
6:14 So the elders of the Jews *continued to* **b** 10111
Job 19:12 *they* **b** a siege ramp against me and encamp 6148
20:19 he has seized houses *he did* not **b**. 1215
30:12 *they* **b** their siege ramps against me. 6148
39:27 **b** his nest **on high?** 8123
Ps 28: 5 down and never **b** them **up** *again.* 1215
51:18 **b up** the walls of Jerusalem. 1215
Pr 24:27 after that, **b** your house. 1215
Ecc 3: 3 a time to tear down and a time to **b**, 1215
SS 8: 9 *we will* **b** towers of silver on her. 1215
Isa 37:33 with shield or **b** a siege ramp against it. 9161
54:11 I *will* **b** you with stones of turquoise, 8069
57:14 **"B up,** build up, prepare the road! 6148
57:14 "Build up, **b up,** prepare the road! 6148
62:10 **B up,** build up the highway! 6148
62:10 Build up, **b up** the highway! 6148
65:21 *They will* **b** houses and dwell in them; 1215
65:22 No longer *will they* **b** houses 1215
66: 1 Where is the house *you will* **b** for me? 1215
Jer 1:10 to **b** and to plant." 1215
6: 6 "Cut down the trees and **b** siege ramps 9161
22:14 '*I will* **b** myself a great palace 1215
24: 6 *I will* **b** them **up** and not tear them down; 1215
29: 5 **"B** houses and settle down; 1215
29:28 Therefore **b** houses and settle down; 1215
31: 4 *I will* **b** you **up** again and you will 1215
31:28 I will watch over them to **b** and to plant," 1215
35: 7 Also *you must* never **b** houses, 1215
42:10 *I will* **b** you **up** and not tear you down; 1215
49:16 **b** your nest as **high** 1467
Eze 4: 2 **b** a ramp up to it, 9161
11: 3 'Will it not soon be time *to* **b** houses? 1215
21:22 to **b** a ramp and to erect siege works. 9161
22:30 a man among them *who would* **b up** the wall 1553
26: 8 he will set up siege works against you, **b** 9161
28:26 and *will* **b** houses and plant vineyards; 1215
Da 11:15 the North will come and **b up** siege ramps 9161
Am 9:11 restore its ruins, and **b** it as it used to be, 1215
Mic 3:10 *who* **b** Zion with bloodshed, 1215
Hab 1:10 *they* **b** earthen ramps and capture them. 7392
Zep 1:13 *They will* **b** houses but not live in them; 1215
Hag 1: 8 the mountains and bring down timber and **b** 1215
Zec 5:11 the country of Babylonia to **b** a house for it. 1215
6:12 and he will branch out from his place and **b** 1215
6:13 It is he *who will* **b** the temple of 1215
6:15 and *help to* **b** the temple of the LORD, 1215
Mal 1: 4 "They *may* **b**, but I will demolish. 1215
Mt 16:18 and on this rock *I will* **b** my church, *3868*
23:29 *You* **b** tombs for the prophets and decorate *3868*
27:40 to destroy the temple and **b** it in three days, *3868*
Mk 14:58 and in three days *will* **b** another, *3868*
15:29 to destroy the temple and **b** it in three days, *3868*
Lk 11:47 because *you* **b** tombs for the prophets, *3868*
11:48 and you **b** their tombs. *3868*
12:18 down my barns and **b** bigger ones, *3868*
14:28 "Suppose one of you wants *to* **b** a tower. *3868*
14:30 'This fellow began *to* **b** and was not able *3868*
19:43 when your enemies *will* **b** an embankment *4212*
Jn 2:20 *to* **b** this temple, *3868*
Ac 7:49 What kind of house *will you* **b** for me? *3868*
20:32 which can **b** you **up** and give you *3868*
Ro 15: 2 to **b** him **up.** *3869*
1Co 14:12 try to excel in gifts that **b up** the church. *3869*
1Th 5:11 encourage one another and **b** each other **up,** *3868*
Heb 8: 5 when he was about to **b** the tabernacle: *2200*
Jude 1:20 **b** yourselves **up** in your most holy faith *2224*

BUILDER (4) [BUILD]
1Co 3:10 I laid a foundation as an expert **b**, *802*
Heb 3: 3 as the **b of** a house has greater honor than *2941*
3: 4 but God is the **b of** everything. *2941*
11:10 whose architect and **b** is God. *1321*

BUILDERS (14) [BUILD]
2Ki 12:11 the carpenters and **b**, 1215
22: 6 the **b** and the masons, 1215
2Ch 34:11 also gave money to the carpenters and **b** 1215
Ezr 3:10 the **b** laid the foundation of the temple of 1215
Ne 4: 5 in the face of the **b.** 1215
4:18 and each of the **b** wore his sword at his side 1215
Ps 118:22 the **b** rejected has become the capstone; 1215
127: 1 its **b** labor in vain. 1215
Eze 27: 4 your **b** brought your beauty to perfection. 1215
Mt 21:42 the **b** rejected has become the capstone; *3868*
Mk 12:10 the **b** rejected has become the capstone; *3868*
Lk 20:17 the **b** rejected has become the capstone'? *3868*
Ac 4:11 He is " 'the stone you **b** rejected, *3871*
1Pe 2: 7 the **b** rejected has become the capstone," *3868*

BUILDING (50) [BUILD]
Ge 4:17 Cain was then **b** a city, 1215
11: 5 the city and the tower that the men *were* **b**. 1215
11: 8 and they stopped **b** the city. 1215
Jos 22:19 or against us by **b** an altar for yourselves, 1215
22:29 and turn away from him today by **b** an altar 1215
1Ki 3: 1 of David until he finished **b** his palace and 1215
5:18 and prepared the timber and stone for the **b** 1215
6: 5 a structure around the **b**, 1074
6: 7 In **b** the temple, 1215
6:12 "As for this temple you *are* **b**, 1215
6:38 *He had spent* seven years **b** it. 1215
9: 1 When Solomon had finished **b** the temple 1215
15:21 he stopped **b** Ramah and withdrew 1215
2Ki 25: 9 Every important **b** he burned down. 1074
1Ch 22: 2 to prepare dressed stone for **b** the house 1215
29:16 that we have provided for **b** you a temple 1215
2Ch 3: 2 He began **b** on the second day of 1215
3: 3 The foundation Solomon laid for **b** 1215
3: 4 the width of the **b** and twenty cubits high. 1074
16: 5 he stopped **b** Ramah 1215
32: 5 the broken sections of the wall and **b** towers 6590
Ezr 3: 8 and older to supervise the **b** *of* the house of 4856
4: 1 the exiles *were* **b** a temple for the LORD, 1215
4: 3 "You have no part with us in **b** a temple 1215
4: 4 of Judah and make them afraid to *go on* **b**. 1215
5: 4 the names of the men constructing this **b?"** 10112
5: 8 The people *are* **b** it *with* large stones 10111
6:14 They finished **b** the temple according to 10111
Ne 3: 1 **b** as far as the Tower of the Hundred, NIH
4: 3 who was at his side, said, "What they *are* **b** 1215
4:17 who *were* **b** the wall. 1215
6: 6 and therefore you *are* **b** the wall. 1215
Jer 52:13 Every important **b** he burned down. 1074
Eze 41:12 The **b** facing the temple courtyard on 1230
41:12 The wall of the **b** was five cubits thick all 1230
41:13 and the temple courtyard and the **b** 1224
41:15 Then he measured the length of the **b** facing 1230
42: 2 The **b** whose door faced north was NIH
42: 5 on the lower and middle floors of the **b.** 1230
Mic 7:11 The day for **b** your walls will come, 1215
Lk 6:48 He is like a man **b** a house, *3868*
17:28 buying and selling, planting and **b.** *3868*
Ro 15:20 not *be* **b** on someone else's foundation. *3868*
1Co 3: 9 you are God's field, God's **b.** *3869*
3:10 and someone else *is* **b on** it. *2224*
2Co 5: 1 we have a **b** from God, *3869*
10: 8 the authority the Lord gave us for **b** you **up** *3869*
13:10 authority the Lord gave me for **b** you **up,** *3869*
Eph 2:21 the whole **b** is joined together and rises *3869*
4:29 for **b** others **up** according to their needs, *3869*

BUILDINGS (12) [BUILD]
1Ki 9:10 during which Solomon built these two **b—** 1074
1Ch 15: 1 After David had constructed **b** for himself 1074
28:11 its **b**, its storerooms, its upper parts, 1074
29: 4 for the overlaying of the walls of the **b**, 1074
2Ch 32:28 also made **b to store** the harvest of grain, 5016
34:11 for joists and beams for the **b** that the kings 1074
Isa 22:10 the **b** *in* Jerusalem and tore down houses 1074
Jer 22:23 who are nestled in cedar **b**, NIH
Eze 40: 2 on whose south side were *some* **b** 4445
Mt 24: 1 up to him to call his attention to its **b.** *3869*
Mk 13: 1 What magnificent **b!"** *3869*
13: 2 "Do you see all these great **b?"** *3869*

BUILDS (13) [BUILD]

Job 27:18 The house *he* **b** is like a moth's cocoon, 1215
Ps 127: 1 Unless the LORD **b** the house, 1215
147: 2 The LORD **b up** Jerusalem; 1215
Pr 14: 1 The wise woman **b** her house, 1215
17:19 *he who* **b** a **high** gate invites destruction. 1467
Jer 22:13 to *him who* **b** his palace by unrighteousness, 1215
Am 9: 6 he *who* **b** his lofty palace in the heavens 1215
Hab 2: 9 "Woe to *him who* **b** his realm by unjust gain 1298
2:12 "Woe to *him who* **b** a city with bloodshed 1215
1Co 3:10 But each one should be careful how *he* **b**. *2224*
3:12 If any man **b on** this foundation using gold, *2224*
8: 1 Knowledge puffs up, but love **b up**. *3868*
Eph 4:16 grows and **b** itself **up** in love, *3869*

BUILT (200) [BUILD]

Ge 8:20 Then Noah **b** an altar to the LORD and, 1215
10:11 where *he* **b** Nineveh, Rehoboth Ir, 1215
12: 7 So *he* **b** an altar there to the LORD, 1215
12: 8 There *he* **b** an altar to the LORD and called 1215
13: 4 and where *he had* first **b** an altar. 6913
13:18 where *he* **b** an altar to the LORD. 1215
22: 9 Abraham **b** an altar there and arranged 1215
26:25 Isaac **b** an altar there and called on 1215
33:17 where *he* **b** a place for himself 1215
35: 7 There *he* **b** an altar, 1215
Ex 1:11 and *they* **b** Pithom and Rameses 1215
17:15 Moses **b** an altar and called it 1215
24: 4 up early the next morning and **b** an altar at 1215
32: 5 *he* **b** an altar in front of the calf 1215
38: 1 *They* **b** the altar of burnt offering 6913
Nu 13:22 (Hebron *had* **been b** seven years before Zoan 1215
23:14 and there *he* **b** seven altars and offered 1215
32:34 The Gadites **b up** Dibon, Ataroth, Aroer, 1215
32:36 and **b** pens for their flocks. NIH
Dt 20: 5 *"Has* anyone **b** a new house and 1215
Jos 8:30 Then Joshua **b** on Mount Ebal an altar to 1215
8:31 He **b** it according to what is written in NIH
11:13 Yet Israel did not burn any of the cities **b** 6641
19:50 And *he* **b up** the town and settled there. 1215
22:10 of Manasseh **b** an imposing altar there by 1215
22:11 the Israelites heard that *they had* **b** the altar 1215
22:23 If we *have* **b** our own altar to turn away 1215
22:28 of the LORD's altar, which our fathers **b**, 6913
Jdg 1:26 where *he* **b** a city and called it Luz, 1215
6:24 So Gideon **b** an altar to the LORD there 1215
6:28 on the **newly b** altar! 1215
21: 4 Early the next day the people **b** an altar 1215
Ru 4:11 who together **b up** the house of Israel. 1215
1Sa 7:17 And *he* **b** an altar there to the LORD. 1215
14:35 Then Saul **b** an altar to the LORD; 1215
2Sa 5: 9 He **b up** the area around it, 1215
5:11 and *they* **b** a palace for David. 1215
7: 7 "Why *have you* not **b** me a house 1215
20:15 *They* **b** a siege ramp up to the city, 9161
24:25 David **b** an altar to the LORD there 1215
1Ki 3: 2 not yet **been b** for the Name of the LORD. 1215
6: 2 The temple that King Solomon **b** for 1215
6: 5 and inner sanctuary *he* **b** a structure around 1215
6: 7 at the temple site while it **was** *being* **b**. 1215
6: 9 So *he* **b** the temple and completed it, 1215
6:10 *he* **b** the side rooms all along the temple. 1215
6:14 So Solomon **b** the temple and completed it, 1215
6:36 And *he* **b** the inner courtyard 1215
7: 2 *He* **b** the Palace of the Forest of Lebanon 1215
7: 7 *He* **b** the throne hall, the Hall of Justice, 6913
8:13 *I have* **indeed b** a magnificent temple 1215+1215
8:16 to *have* a temple **b** for my Name to be there, 1215
8:20 and *I have* **b** the temple for the Name of 1215
8:27 How much less this temple *I have* **b!** 1215
8:43 that this house *I have* **b** bears your Name. 1215
8:44 and the temple *I have* **b** for your Name, 1215
8:48 and the temple *I have* **b** for your Name; 1215
9: 3 this temple, which *you have* **b**, 1215
9:10 during which Solomon **b** these two buildings— 1215
9:17 He **b** up Lower Beth Horon, NIH
9:24 of David to the palace Solomon *had* **b** 1215
9:25 fellowship offerings on the altar *he had* **b** 1215
9:26 King Solomon also **b** ships at Ezion Geber, 6913
10: 4 of Solomon and the palace *he had* **b**, 1215
11: 7 Solomon **b** a high place for Chemosh 1215
11:27 Solomon *had* **b** the supporting terraces 1215
11:38 the one *I* **b** for David and will give Israel 1215
12:25 From there he went out and **b up** Peniel. 1215
12:31 Jeroboam **b** shrines on high places 6913
12:33 he offered sacrifices on the altar *he had* **b** 6913
15:22 With them King Asa **b up** Geba 1215
15:23 all he did and the cities *he* **b**, 1215
16:24 from Shemer for two talents of silver and **b** 1215
16:32 in the temple of Baal that *he* **b** in Samaria. 1215
18:32 *With* the stones *he* **b** an altar in the name of 1215
22:39 the palace *he* **b** and inlaid with ivory, 1215
22:48 Now Jehoshaphat **b** a fleet of trading ships 6913
2Ki 16:11 So Uriah the priest **b** an altar in accordance 1215
16:18 that *had been* **b** at the temple and removed 1215
17: 9 fortified city *they* **b** themselves high places 1215
21: 4 *He* **b** altars in the temple of the LORD, 1215
21: 5 *he* **b** altars to all the starry hosts. 1215
23:12 the altars Manasseh *had* **b** in the two courts 6913
23:13 the ones Solomon king of Israel *had* **b** 1215
23:19 the high places that the kings of Israel *had* **b** 6913
25: 1 the city and **b** siege works all around it. 1215
1Ch 6:10 in the temple Solomon **b** in Jerusalem), 1215
6:32 until Solomon **b** the temple of the LORD 1215
7:24 *who* **b** Lower and Upper Beth Horon as well 1215
8:12 Eber, Misham, Shemed (who **b** Ono 1215
11: 8 *He* **b up** the city around it, 1215
17: 6 "Why *have you* not **b** me a house 1215
21:26 David **b** an altar to the LORD there 1215
22: 5 the house to *be* **b** for the LORD should be 1215
22:19 into the temple that *will* **be b** for the Name 1215
2Ch 3: 8 *He* **b** the Most Holy Place, 6913
6: 2 I *have* **b** a magnificent temple for you, 1215
6: 5 to *have* a temple **b** for my Name to be there, 1215
6:10 and *I have* **b** the temple for the Name of 1215
6:18 How much less this temple *I have* **b!** 1215
6:33 that this house *I have* **b** bears your Name. 1215
6:34 and the temple *I have* **b** for your Name, 1215
6:38 toward the temple *I have* **b** for your Name; 1215
8: 1 during which Solomon **b** the temple of 1215
8: 4 *He* also **b up** Tadmor in the desert and all 1215
8: 4 in the desert and all the store cities *he had* **b** 1215
8:11 the City of David to the palace *he had* **b** 1215
8:12 the altar of the LORD that *he had* **b** in front 1215
9: 3 as well as the palace *he had* **b**, 1215
11: 5 in Jerusalem and **b up** towns for defense 1215
14: 6 *He* **b up** the fortified cities of Judah, 1215
14: 7 So *they* **b** and prospered. 1215
16: 6 With them *he* **b up** Geba and Mizpah. 1215
17:12 *he* **b** forts and store cities in Judah 1215
20: 8 and *have* **b** in it a sanctuary for your Name, 1215
20:36 After these *were* **b** at Ezion Geber, 6913
21:11 also **b** high places on the hills of Judah 6913
26: 9 Uzziah **b** towers in Jerusalem at 1215
26:10 *He* also **b** towers in the desert 1215
27: 4 *He* **b** towns in the Judean hills and forts 1215
28:25 in Judah *he* **b** high places to burn sacrifices 6913
32: 5 He **b** another wall outside that one NIH
32:29 *He* **b** villages and acquired great numbers 6913
33: 4 *He* **b** altars in the temple of the LORD, 1215
33: 5 *he* **b** altars to all the starry hosts. 1215
33:15 as all the altars *he had* **b** on the temple hill 1215
33:19 and the sites where *he* **b** high places and set 1215
35: 3 that Solomon son of David king of Israel **b**. 1215
Ezr 3: 3 *they* **b** the altar on its foundation 3922
4:13 the king should know that if this city **is b** 10111
4:16 if this city **is b** and its walls are restored, 10111
5:11 the temple that was **b** many years ago, 10111
5:11 that a great king of Israel **b** and finished. 10111
Ne 3: 2 The men of Jericho **b** the adjoining section, 1215
3: 2 and Zaccur son of Imri **b** next to them. 1215
8: 4 a high wooden platform **b** for the occasion. 6913
8:16 and **b** themselves booths 6913
8:17 from exile **b** booths and lived in them. 6913
12:29 for the singers *had* **b** villages for themselves 1215
Est 5:14 *"Have* a gallows **b**, seventy-five feet high, 6913
5:14 and *he had* the gallows **b**. 6913
Job 3:14 who **b** for themselves places now lying 1215
Ps 78:69 *He* **b** his sanctuary like the heights, 1215
122: 3 Jerusalem **is b** like a city 1215
Pr 9: 1 Wisdom *has* **b** her house; 1215
24: 3 By wisdom a house **is b**, 1215
Ecc 2: 4 *I* **b** houses for myself 1215
9:14 surrounded it and **b** huge siegeworks 1215
SS 4: 4 like the tower of David, **b** with elegance; 1215
Isa 5: 2 *He* **b** a watchtower in it and cut out 1215
22:11 *You* **b** a reservoir between the two walls for 6913
44:26 of the towns of Judah, *'They shall* **be b**,' 1215
Jer 7:31 *They have* **b** the high places of Topheth in 1215
18: 9 that a nation or kingdom *is to be* **b up** 1215
18:15 in bypaths and on roads not **b up**. 6148
19: 5 *They have* **b** the high places of Baal 1215
32:24 "See how the siege ramps *are* **b up** to take 995
32:31 From the day it *was* **b** until now, 1215
32:35 *They* **b** high places for Baal in the Valley 1215
35: 9 or **b** houses to live in or had vineyards, 1215
45: 4 I will overthrow what *I have* **b** 1215
52: 4 the city and **b** siege works all around it. 1215
Eze 13:10 and because, when a flimsy wall *is* **b**, 1215
16:24 *you* **b** a mound for yourself and made 1215
16:25 of every street *you* **b** your lofty shrines 1215
16:31 When you **b** your mounds at the head 1215
17:17 when ramps *are* **b** and siege works erected 9161
41: 7 The structure surrounding the temple was **b** NIH
43:18 upon the altar when it **is b:** 6913
46:23 with places for fire **b** all around under 6913
Da 4:30 "Is not this the great Babylon I *have* **b** as 10111
Hos 8:11 Ephraim **b many** altars for sin offerings, 8049
8:14 Israel has forgotten his Maker and **b** palaces; 1215
10: 1 As his fruit increased, *he* **b more** altars; 8049
Am 5:11 though *you have* **b** stone mansions, 1215
7: 7 by a wall that had been **b** true to plumb, NIH
Hag 1: 2 yet come for the LORD's house to **be b.'** " 1215
Zec 8: 9 be strong so that the temple *may* **be b.** 1215
9: 3 Tyre *has* **b** herself a stronghold; 1215
Mt 7:24 a wise man who **b** his house on the rock. *3868*
7:26 like a foolish man who **b** his house on sand. *3868*
21:33 dug a winepress in it and **b** a watchtower. *3868*
Mk 12: 1 a pit for the winepress and **b** a watchtower. *3868*
Lk 4:29 of the hill on which the town *was* **b**, *3868*
6:48 because it *was* well **b**. *3868*
6:49 into practice is like a man *who* **b** a house on *3868*
7: 5 and *has* **b** our synagogue." *3868*
Ac 7:47 it was Solomon who **b** the house for him. *3868*
17:24 and does not live in temples **b by hands.** *5935*
28: 2 They **b** a fire and welcomed us all *721*
1Co 3:14 If what *he has* **b** survives, *2224*
2Co 5: 1 an eternal house in heaven, **not b by human hands.** *942*
Eph 2:20 **b on** the foundation of the apostles *2224*
2:22 And in him you too *are being* **b together** *5325*
4:12 so that the body of Christ may be **b up** *3869*
Col 2: 7 rooted and **b up** in him, *2224*
Heb 3: 4 For every house *is* **b** by someone, *2941*
11: 7 in holy fear **b** an ark to save his family. *2941*
1Pe 2: 5 *are being* **b** into a spiritual house to be *3868*
3:20 the days of Noah *while* the ark *was being* **b**. *2941*

BUKKI (5)

Nu 34:22 **B** son of Jogli, the leader from the tribe 1321
1Ch 6: 5 Abishua the father of **B**, 1321
6: 5 **B** the father of Uzzi, 1321
6:51 **B** his son, Uzzi his son, Zerahiah his son, 1321
Ezr 7: 4 the son of Uzzi, the son of **B**, 1321

BUKKIAH (2)

1Ch 25: 4 As for Heman, from his sons: **B**, 1322
25:13 the sixth to **B**, his sons and relatives, 1322

BUL (1)

1Ki 6:38 In the eleventh year in the month of **B**, 1004

BULGES (1) [BULGING]

Job 15:27 with fat and his waist **b with flesh**, 6913+7089

BULGING (1) [BULGES]

Isa 30:13 cracked and **b**, that collapses suddenly, 1240

BULL (98) [BULL'S, BULLS]

Ex 21:28 "If a **b** gores a man or a woman to death, 8802
21:28 the **b** must be stoned to death, 8802
21:28 of the **b** will not be held responsible. 8802
21:29 the **b** has had the habit of goring and 8802
21:29 the **b** must be stoned and the owner 8802
21:31 This law also applies if the **b** gores a son NIH
21:32 If the **b** gores a male or female slave, 8802
21:32 and the **b** must be stoned. 8802
21:35 "If a man's **b** injures the bull of another 8802
21:35 "If a man's bull injures the **b** *of* another 8802
21:36 if it was known that the **b** had the habit 8802
29: 1 young **b** and two rams without defect. 1330+7228
29: 3 along with the **b** and the two rams. 7228
29:10 the **b** to the front of the Tent of Meeting, 7228
29:36 Sacrifice a **b** each day as a sin offering 7228
Lev 1: 5 to slaughter the young **b** before the LORD, 1330
4: 3 to the LORD a young **b** without defect 1330+7228
4: 4 the **b** at the entrance to the Tent of Meeting 7228
4: 8 He shall remove all the fat from the **b** *of* 7228
4:11 But the hide of the **b** and all its flesh, 7228
4:12 all the rest of the **b**— 7228
4:14 young **b** as a sin offering and present 1330+7228
4:15 and the **b** shall be slaughtered before 7228
4:20 with this **b** just as he did with the bull for 7228
4:20 with this bull just as he did with the **b** *for* 7228
4:21 Then he shall take the **b** outside the camp 7228
4:21 and burn it as he burned the first **b**. 7228
8: 2 the anointing oil, the **b** *for* the sin offering, 7228
8:14 He then presented the **b** *for* the sin offering, 7228
8:15 Moses slaughtered the **b** and took some of NIH
8:17 But the **b** with its hide and its flesh 7228
9: 2 "Take a **b** calf for your sin offering 1201+1330
16: 3 young **b** for a sin offering and a ram 1330+7228
16: 6 to offer the **b** for his own sin offering 7228
16:11 the **b** for his own sin offering 7228
16:11 to slaughter the **b** for his own sin offering. 7228
16:27 The **b** and the goat for the sin offerings, 7228
23:18 one young **b** and two rams. 1330+7228
Nu 7:15 one young **b**, one ram and one male 1330+7228
7:21 one young **b**, one ram and one male 1330+7228
7:27 one young **b**, one ram and one male 1330+7228
7:33 one young **b**, one ram and one male 1330+7228
7:39 one young **b**, one ram and one male 1330+7228
7:45 one young **b**, one ram and one male 1330+7228
7:51 one young **b**, one ram and one male 1330+7228
7:57 one young **b**, one ram and one male 1330+7228
7:63 one young **b**, one ram and one male 1330+7228
7:69 one young **b**, one ram and one male 1330+7228
7:75 one young **b**, one ram and one male 1330+7228
7:81 one young **b**, one ram and one male 1330+7228
8: 8 a young **b** with its grain offering 1330+7228
8: 8 a second young **b** for a sin offering. 1330+7228
15: 8 a young **b** as a burnt offering or sacrifice, 1330
15: 9 with the **b** a grain offering of three-tenths of 1330
15:11 Each **b** or ram, each lamb or young goat, 8802
15:24 whole community is to offer a young **b** 1330+7228
23: 2 of them offered a **b** and a ram on each altar. 7228
23: 4 on each altar I have offered a **b** and a ram." 7228
23:14 and offered a **b** and a ram on each altar. 7228
23:30 and offered a **b** and a ram on each altar. 7228
28:12 With each **b** there is to be a grain offering 7228
28:14 With each **b** there is to be a drink offering 7228
28:20 With each **b** prepare a grain offering 7228
28:28 With each **b** there is to be a grain offering 7228
29: 2 a burnt offering of one young **b**, 1330+7228
29: 3 With the **b** prepare a grain offering 7228
29: 8 a burnt offering of one young **b**, 1330+7228
29: 9 With the **b** prepare a grain offering 7228
29:36 a burnt offering of one **b**, 7228
29:37 With the **b**, the ram and the lambs, 7228
Dt 18: 3 the people who sacrifice a **b** or a sheep: 8802
33:17 In majesty he is like a firstborn **b**; 8802
Jdg 6:25 "Take the second **b** from your father's herd, 7228

Jdg 6:26 offer the second **b** as a burnt offering." 7228
6:28 down and the second **b** sacrificed on 7228
1Sa 1:24 along with a three-year-old **b**, 7228
1:25 When they had slaughtered the **b**, 7228
2Sa 6:13 he sacrificed a **b** and a fattened calf. 8802
1Ki 18:23 I will prepare the other **b** and put it on 7228
18:26 they took the **b** given them and prepared it. 7228
18:33 the **b** into pieces and laid it on the wood. 7228
2Ch 13: 9 a young **b** and seven rams may become 1330
Ps 50: 9 I have no need of a **b** from your stall or 7228
69:31 more than a **b** with its horns and hoofs. 7228
106:20 for an image of a **b**, 8802
Isa 34: 7 the **b calves** and the great bulls. 7228
66: 3 a **b** is like one who kills a man, 8802
Eze 43:19 are to give a young **b** as a sin offering 1330+7228
43:21 to take the **b** *for* the sin offering and burn it 7228
43:22 to be purified as it was purified with the **b**. 7228
43:23 a young **b** and a ram from the flock, 1330+7228
43:25 also to provide a young **b** and a ram 1330+7228
45:18 take a young **b** without defect and purify the sanctuary. 1330+7228
45:22 the prince is to provide a **b** as a sin offering 7228
45:24 as a grain offering an ephah for each **b** and 7228
46: 6 New Moon he is to offer a young **b**, 1330+7228
46: 7 as a grain offering one ephah with the **b**, 7228
46:11 grain offering is to be an ephah with a **b**, 7228

BULL'S (9) [BULL]

Ex 29:12 of the **b** blood and put it on the horns of 7228
29:14 the **b** flesh and its hide and its offal outside 7228
Lev 4: 5 of the **b** blood and carry it into the Tent 7228
4: 7 the **b** blood he shall pour out at the base of 7228
4:15 to lay their hands on the **b** head before 7228
4:16 to take some of the **b** blood into the Tent 7228
16:14 the **b** blood and with his finger sprinkle it 7228
16:15 and do with it as he did with the **b** blood: 7228
16:18 He shall take some of the **b** blood and some 7228

BULLOCK (KJV) See BULL

BULLS (64) [BULL]

Ge 32:15 forty cows and ten **b**, 7228
Ex 24: 5 and sacrificed **young b** 7228
Nu 7:87 the burnt offering came to twelve **young b**, 7228
8:12 on the heads of the **b**, 7228
23: 1 and prepare seven **b** and seven rams 7228
23:29 and prepare seven **b** and seven rams 7228
28:11 a burnt offering of two young **b**, 1330+7228
28:19 a burnt offering of two young **b**, 1330+7228
28:27 Present a burnt offering of two young **b**, 1330+7228
29:13 a burnt offering of thirteen young **b**, 1330+7228
29:14 of the thirteen **b** prepare a grain offering 7228
29:17 second day prepare twelve young **b**, 1330+7228
29:18 With the **b**, rams and lambs, 7228
29:20 " 'On the third day prepare eleven **b**, 7228
29:21 With the **b**, rams and lambs, 7228
29:23 " 'On the fourth day prepare ten **b**, 7228
29:24 With the **b**, rams and lambs, 7228
29:26 " 'On the fifth day prepare nine **b**, 7228
29:27 With the **b**, rams and lambs, 7228
29:29 " 'On the sixth day prepare eight **b**, 7228
29:30 With the **b**, rams and lambs, 7228
29:32 " 'On the seventh day prepare seven **b**, 7228
29:33 With the **b**, rams and lambs, 7228
1Ki 7:25 The Sea stood on twelve **b**, 1330
7:29 the uprights were lions, **b** and cherubim— 1330
7:29 and **b** were wreaths of hammered work. 1330
7:44 the Sea and the twelve **b** under it; 1330
18:23 Get two **b** for us. 7228
18:25 "Choose one of the **b** and prepare it first, 7228
2Ki 16:17 the Sea from the bronze **b** that supported it 1330
1Ch 15:26 seven **b** and seven rams were sacrificed. 7228
29:21 a thousand **b**, a thousand rams and 7228
2Ch 4: 3 Below the rim, figures of **b** encircled it— 1330
4: 3 The **b** were cast in two rows in one piece 1330
4: 4 The Sea stood on twelve **b**, 1330
4:15 the Sea and the twelve **b** under it; 1330
29:21 They brought seven **b**, seven rams, 7228
29:22 So they slaughtered the **b**, 1330
29:32 the assembly brought was seventy **b**, 1330
29:33 to six hundred **b** and three thousand sheep 1330
30:24 a thousand **b** and seven thousand sheep 7228
30:24 with a thousand **b** and ten thousand sheep 7228
Ezr 6: 9 Whatever is needed—young **b**, rams, 10756
6:17 of God they offered a hundred **b**, 10756
7:17 With this money be sure to buy **b**, 10756
8:35 twelve **b** for all Israel, ninety-six rams, 7228
Job 21:10 Their **b** never fail to breed; 8802
42: 8 So now take seven **b** and seven rams and go 7228
Ps 22:12 Many **b** surround me; 7228
22:12 strong **b** of Bashan encircle me. NIH
50:13 the flesh of **b** or drink the blood of goats? 52
51:19 then **b** will be offered on your altar. 7228
66:15 I will offer **b** and goats. 1330
68:30 herd of **b** among the calves of the nations. 52
Isa 1:11 in the blood of **b** and lambs and goats. 7228
34: 7 the bull calves and the great **b**. NIH
Jer 50:27 Kill all her **young b**; 7228
52:20 the Sea and the twelve bronze **b** under it, 1330
Eze 39:18 as if they were rams and lambs, goats and **b** 7228
45:23 of the Feast he is to provide seven **b** 7228
Hos 12:11 Do they sacrifice **b** in Gilgal? 8802
Ac 14:13 brought **b** and wreaths to the city gates *5436*
Heb 9:13 The blood of goats and **b** and the ashes of *5436*
Heb 10: 4 the blood *of* **b** and goats to take away sins. *5436*

BULRUSH, BULRUSHES (KJV) See PAPYRUS

BULWARKS (KJV) See SEIGEWORKS, CORNER DEFENSES

BUNAH (1)

1Ch 2:25 Ram his firstborn, **B**, Oren, 1007

BUNCH (1)

Ex 12:22 Take a **b** *of* hyssop, 99

BUNDLE (1) [BUNDLES]

1Sa 25:29 be bound securely in the **b** *of* the living by 7655

BUNDLES (2) [BUNDLE]

Ru 2:16 from the **b** and leave them for her to pick 7395
Mt 13:30 First collect the weeds and tie them in **b** to *1299*

BUNNI (3)

Ne 9: 4 Jeshua, Bani, Kadmiel, Shebaniah, **B**, 1221
10:15 **B**, Azgad, Bebai, 1221
11:15 the son of Hashabiah, the son of **B**; 1221

BURDEN (37) [BURDENED, BURDENS, BURDENSOME]

Ge 49:15 to the **b** and submit to forced labor. 6022
Nu 11:11 that you put the **b** *of* all these people 5362
11:14 the **b** is too heavy for me. NIH
11:17 the **b** *of* the people so that you will 5362
Dt 1: 9 **too heavy a b** for me **to carry** 3523+4202+5951
1Sa 25:31 not have on his conscience the **staggering b** of needless bloodshed 2256+4842+7050
2Sa 13:25 *we would* only *be a* **b** to you." 3877
15:33 "If you go with me, you will be a **b** to me. 5362
19:35 Why should your servant be an added **b** 5362
Ne 5:15 **placed a heavy b** on the people 3877
Job 7:20 Have I become a **b** to you? 5362
Ps 38: 4 like a **b** too heavy to bear. 5362
81: 6 "I removed the **b** from their shoulders; 6023
Pr 27: 3 Stone is heavy and sand a **b**, 5748
Ecc 1:13 What a heavy **b** God has laid on men! 6701+6721
3:10 I have seen the **b** God has laid on men. 6701+6721
Isa 1:14 They have become a **b** to me; 3268
10:27 In that day their **b** will be lifted 6024
14:25 and his **b** removed from their shoulders." 6024
46: 1 idols are borne by **beasts of b.** 989+2256+2651
46: 1 a **b** for the weary. 5362
46: 2 unable to rescue the **b**, 5362
Zep 3:18 they are a **b** and a reproach to you. 5368
Mal 1:13 And you say, 'What a **b!**' 9430
Mt 11:30 For my yoke is easy and my **b** is light." *5845*
20:12 to us who have borne the **b** of the work and *983*
Ac 15:28 to us not **to b** you with anything beyond *983+2202*
2Co 11: 9 *I was* not **a b to** anyone, *2915*
11: 9 I have kept myself from being a **b** to you *4*
12:13 except that I *was* never a **b** to you? *2915*
12:14 and *I will* not *be* a **b** to you, *2915*
12:16 I *have* not *been* a **b to** you. *2851*
1Th 2: 6 of Christ we could have been a **b** to you, *983*
2: 9 not to **be a b to** anyone while we preached *2096*
2Th 3: 8 so that *we would* not **be a b to** any of you. *2096*
Heb 13:17 so that their work will be a joy, not a **b**, for *5100*
Rev 2:24 not impose any other **b** on you): *983*

BURDENED (7) [BURDEN]

Isa 43:23 *I have* not **b** you with grain offerings 6268
43:24 But *you have* **b** me with your sins 6268
Mic 6: 3 How *have I* **b** you? 4206
Mt 11:28 "Come to me, all you who are weary and **b**, *5844*
2Co 5: 4 we groan and are **b**, *976*
Gal 5: 1 not *let yourselves be* **b** again by a yoke *1923*
1Ti 5:16 and not *let* the church *be* **b** with them, *976*

BURDENS (8) [BURDEN]

Nu 4:24 as they work and carry **b**: 5362
Dt 1:12 and your **b** and your disputes all by myself? 5362
Ps 66:11 You brought us into prison and laid **b** 4601
68:19 to God our Savior, *who* daily **bears** our **b**. 6673
73: 5 They are free from the **b** *common to* man; 6662
Isa 9: 4 you have shattered the yoke that **b** them, 6024
Lk 11:46 down with **b** they can hardly carry, *5845*
Gal 6: 2 Carry each other's **b**, *983*

BURDENSOME (2) [BURDEN]

Isa 46: 1 The images that are carried about *are* **b**, 6673
1Jn 5: 3 And his commands are not **b**, *987*

BURIAL (18) [BURY]

Ge 23: 4 for a **b site** here so I can bury my dead." 7700
23: 9 to sell it to me for the full price as a **b** site 7700
23:20 to Abraham by the Hittites as a **b** site. 7700
49:30 as a **b** place from Ephron the Hittite, 7700
50:13 which Abraham had bought as a **b** place 7700
2Ch 26:23 near them in a field for **b** that belonged to 7690
Ecc 6: 3 and does not receive **proper b**, 7690
Isa 14:20 you will not join them in **b**, 7690
Jer 22:19 *He will* **have** *the* **b** *of* a donkey— 7690+7699
26:23 into the **b place** *of* the common people.) 7700
Eze 39:11 that day I will give Gog a **b** place in Israel, 7700
Mt 26:12 she did it to **prepare** me **for b.** *1946*
27: 7 to buy the potter's field as a **b place** *5438*
Mk 14: 8 to prepare for my **b**. *1947*
Jn 12: 7 for the day *of* my **b**. *1947*
19:40 in accordance with Jewish **b** customs. *1946*
20: 7 as well as the **b cloth** that had been *5051*
Rev 11: 9 gaze on their bodies and refuse them **b.** *1650+3645+5502*

BURIED (112) [BURY]

Ge 15:15 will go to your fathers in peace and **be b** at 7699
23:19 Afterward Abraham **b** his wife Sarah in 7699
25: 9 His sons Isaac and Ishmael **b** him in 7699
25:10 There Abraham **was b** with his wife Sarah. 7699
35: 4 Jacob **b** them under the oak at Shechem. 3243
35: 8 died and **was b** under the oak below Bethel. 7699
35:19 and **was b** on the way to Ephrath (that is, 7699
35:29 And his sons Esau and Jacob **b** him. 7699
47:30 of Egypt and bury me where they are **b.**" 7690
48: 7 So *I* **b** her there beside the road 7699
49:31 There Abraham and his wife Sarah *were* **b**, 7699
49:31 there Isaac and his wife Rebekah *were* **b**, 7699
49:31 and there *I* **b** Leah. 7699
50:13 of Canaan and **b** him in the cave in the field 7699
Nu 11:34 because there *they* **b** 7699
20: 1 There Miriam died and **was b.** 7699
Dt 10: 6 There Aaron died and **was b**, 7699
34: 6 *He* **b** him in Moab, 7699
Jos 24:30 *they* **b** him in the land of his inheritance, 7699
24:32 *were* **b** at Shechem in the tract of land 7699
24:33 And Eleazar son of Aaron died and *was* **b** 7699
Jdg 2: 9 *they* **b** him in the land of his inheritance, 7699
8:32 of Joash died at a good old age and **was b** in 7699
10: 2 then he died, and **was b** in Shamir. 7699
10: 5 When Jair died, *he* **was b** in Kamon. 7699
12: 7 and **was b** in a town in Gilead. 7699
12:10 Then Ibzan died, and **was b** in Bethlehem. 7699
12:12 and **was b** in Aijalon in the land of Zebulun. 7699
12:15 and **was b** at Pirathon in Ephraim, 7699
16:31 and **b** him between Zorah and Eshtaol in 7699
Ru 1:17 and there *I will* **be b.** 7699
1Sa 25: 1 and *they* **b** him at his home in Ramah. 7699
28: 3 and **b** him in his own town of Ramah. 7699
31:13 and **b** them under a tamarisk tree at Jabesh, 7699
2Sa 2: 4 the men of Jabesh Gilead who *had* **b** Saul, 7699
2:32 and **b** him in his father's tomb 7699
3:32 *They* **b** Abner in Hebron, 7699
4:12 of Ish-Bosheth and **b** it in Abner's tomb 7699
17:23 So he died and **was b** in his father's tomb. 7699
21:14 *They* **b** the bones of Saul 7699
1Ki 2:10 with his fathers and **was b** in the City 7699
2:34 and *he* **was b** on his own land in the desert. 7699
11:43 Then he rested with his fathers and **was b** in 7699
13:22 not *be* **b** in the tomb of your fathers.' " 995
13:31 in the grave where the man of God **is b**; 7699
14:13 to Jeroboam *who will be* **b**, 448+995+7700
14:18 *They* **b** him, and all Israel mourned for him, 7699
14:31 and **was b** with them in the City of David. 7699
15: 8 with his fathers and *was* **b** in the City 7699
15:24 Then Asa rested with his fathers and **was b** 7699
16: 6 Baasha rested with his fathers and **was b** 7699
16:28 Omri rested with his fathers and **was b** 7699
22:37 and *they* **b** him there. 7699
22:50 with his fathers and **was b** with them in 7699
2Ki 8:24 and **was b** with them in the City of David. 7699
9:28 and **b** him with his fathers in his tomb in 7699
10:35 with his fathers and *was* **b** in Samaria. 7699
12:21 and *was* **b** with his fathers in the City 7699
13: 9 Jehoahaz rested with his fathers and **was b** 7699
13:13 Jehoash **was b** in Samaria with the kings 7699
13:20 Elisha died and *was* **b.** 7699
14:16 with his fathers and **was b** in Samaria with 7699
14:20 He was brought back by horse and **was b** 7699
15: 7 and *was* **b** near them in the City of David. 7699
15:38 and **was b** with them in the City of David, 7699
16:20 and **was b** with them in the City of David. 7699
21:18 Manasseh rested with his fathers and **was b** 7699
21:26 He *was* **b** in his grave in the garden 7699
22:20 and *you will* **be b** in peace. 448+665+7700
23:30 to Jerusalem and **b** him in his own tomb. 7699
1Ch 10:12 Then *they* **b** their bones under the great tree 7699
2Ch 9:31 Then he rested with his fathers and *was* **b** in 7699
12:16 Rehoboam rested with his fathers and **was b** 7699
14: 1 with his fathers and *was* **b** in the City 7699
16:14 *They* **b** him in the tomb that he had cut out 7699
21: 1 and **was b** with them in the City of David. 7699
21:20 and *was* **b** in the City of David, 7699
22: 9 *They* **b** him, for they said, 7699
24:16 He *was* **b** with the kings in the City 7699
24:25 So he died and *was* **b** in the City of David, 7699
25:28 He was brought back by horse and *was* **b** 7699
26:23 Uzziah rested with his fathers and *was* **b** 7699
27: 9 Jotham rested with his fathers and *was* **b** in 7699
28:27 Ahaz rested with his fathers and *was* **b** in 7699
32:33 with his fathers and *was* **b** on the hill where 7699
33:20 Manasseh rested with his fathers and *was* **b** 7699
34:28 and *you will* **be b** in peace. 448+665+7700
35:24 *He* **was b** in the tombs of his fathers, 7699
Ne 2: 3 the city where my fathers are **b** lies in ruins, 7700
2: 5 the city in Judah where my fathers are **b** so 7700
Job 16:15 over my skin and **b** my brow in the dust. 6619
Ps 106:17 *it* **b** the company of Abiram. 4059

Ecc 8:10 Then too, I saw the wicked **b—** 7699
Jer 8: 2 They will not be gathered up or **b,** 7699
16: 4 They will not be mourned or **b** but will be 7699
16: 6 *They will* not **be b** or mourned, 7699
20: 6 There you will die and **be b,** 7699
25:33 not be mourned or gathered up or **b,** 7699
43:10 over these stones *I have* **b** here; 3243
Eze 39:11 Gog and all his hordes *will be* **b** there. 7699
39:15 beside it until the gravediggers *have* **b** it in 7699
Mt 14:12 and took his body and **b** it. *2507*
Lk 16:22 The rich man also died and *was* **b.** *2507*
Ac 2:29 that the patriarch David died and *was* **b,** *2507*
5: 6 and carried him out and **b** him. *2507*
5: 9 of the men who **b** your husband are at *2507*
5:10 and **b** her beside her husband. *2507*
8: 2 Godly men **b** Stephen and mourned deeply *5172*
13:36 *he was* **b** with his fathers *4707*
Ro 6: 4 therefore **b** with him through baptism *5313*
1Co 15: 4 that *he was* **b,** that he was raised *2507*
Col 2:12 *having been* **b with** him in baptism *5313*

BURIES (2) [BURY]

Pr 19:24 The sluggard **b** his hand in the dish; 3243
26:15 The sluggard **b** his hand in the dish; 3243

BURN (136) [BURNED, BURNED-OUT, BURNING, BURNS, BURNT]

Ex 3: 2 though the bush was on fire it *did* not **b up.** 430
3: 3 why the bush *does* not **b up.**" 1277
12:10 if some is left till morning, *you must* **b** it. 836+928+2021+8596
21:25 **b** for burn, wound for wound, bruise 3918
21:25 burn for **b,** wound for wound, bruise 3918
29:13 and **b** them on the altar. 7787
29:14 But **b** the bull's flesh and its hide 836+928+2021+8596
29:18 Then **b** the entire ram on the altar. 7787
29:25 from their hands and **b** them on the altar 7787
29:34 over till morning, **b** it **up.** 836+928+2021+8596
30: 7 "Aaron *must* **b** fragrant incense on 7787
30: 8 *He must* **b** incense again when he lights 7787
30: 8 at twilight so incense will **b** regularly NIH
32:10 Now leave me alone so that my anger *may* **b** 3013
32:11 "why *should* your anger **b** 3013
Lev 1: 9 and the priest *is to* **b** all of it on the altar. 7787
1:13 and the priest is to bring all of it and **b** it on 7787
1:15 wring off the head and **b** it on the altar; 7787
1:17 then the priest *shall* **b** it on the wood that is 7787
2: 2 **b** this as a memorial portion on the altar, 7787
2: 9 from the grain offering and **b** it on the altar 7787
2:11 for *you are* not *to* **b** any yeast or honey in 7787
2:16 The priest *shall* **b** the memorial portion of 7787
3: 5 Then Aaron's sons *are to* **b** it on the altar 7787
3:11 The priest *shall* **b** them on the altar 7787
3:16 The priest *shall* **b** them on the altar 7787
4:10 Then the priest *shall* **b** them on the altar 7787
4:12 and **b** it in a wood fire on the ash heap. 8596
4:19 He shall remove all the fat from it and **b** it 7787
4:21 the camp and **b** it as he burned the first bull. 8596
4:26 *He shall* **b** all the fat on the altar 7787
4:31 and the priest *shall* **b** it on the altar as 7787
4:35 and the priest *shall* **b** it on the altar on top 7787
5:12 as a memorial portion and **b** it on the altar 7787
6:12 the burnt offering on the fire and **b** the fat 7787
6:15 and **b** the memorial portion on the altar as 7787
7: 5 The priest *shall* **b** them on the altar as 7787
7:31 The priest *shall* **b** the fat on the altar, 7787
8:32 **b up** the rest of the meat and the bread. 836+928+2021+8596
13:24 "When someone has a **b** on his skin 836+4805
13:24 in the raw flesh of the **b,** 4805
13:25 that has broken out in the **b.** 4805
13:28 it is a swelling from the **b,** 4805
13:28 it is only a scar from the **b.** 4805
13:52 *He must* **b up** the clothing, 8596
13:55 **B** it with fire, 8596
16:25 also **b** the fat of the sin offering on the altar. 7787
17: 6 at the entrance to the Tent of Meeting and **b** 7787
Nu 5:26 as a memorial offering and **b** it on the altar; 7787
16:40 of Aaron should come to **b** incense before 7787
18:17 the altar and **b** their fat as an offering made 7787
Dt 6:15 is a jealous God and his anger *will* **b** 3013
7: 4 and the LORD's anger *will* **b** against you 3013
7: 5 down their Asherah poles and **b** their idols 8596
7:25 The images of their gods *you are to* **b** in 8596
11:17 the LORD's anger *will* **b** against you, 3013
12: 3 and **b** their Asherah poles in the fire; 8596
12:31 **b** their sons and daughters in the fire **as sacrifices** 8596
13:16 and completely **b** the town 836+928+2021+8596
29:20 his wrath and zeal *will* **b** against that man. 6939
Jos 11: 6 and **b** their chariots." 836+928+2021+8596
11:13 Yet Israel *did* not **b** any of the cities built 8596
23:16 the LORD's anger *will* **b** against you, 3013
Jdg 12: 1 *to* **b down** your house over your head." 836+928+2021+8596
14:15 **b** you and your father's household **to death.** 836+928+2021+8596
1Sa 2:28 to go up to my altar, to **b** incense, 7787
1Ki 14:10 *I will* **b up** the house of Jeroboam 1277
22:43 to offer sacrifices and **b incense** there. 7787
2Ki 12: 3 to offer sacrifices and **b incense** there. 7787
14: 4 to offer sacrifices and **b incense** there. 7787
15: 4 to offer sacrifices and **b incense** there. 7787
15:35 to offer sacrifices and **b incense** there. 7787

2Ki 22:17 my anger *will* **b** against this place and will 3675
23: 5 *to* **b incense** on the high places of the towns 7787
1Ch 14:12 and David gave orders *to* **b** *them* in the fire. 8596
2Ch 2: 6 as a place to **b sacrifices** before him? 7787
4:20 to **b** in front of the inner sanctuary 1277
26:16 the temple of the LORD to **b incense** on 7787
26:18 Uzziah, to **b incense** to the LORD. 7787
26:18 who have been consecrated to **b incense.** 7787
26:19 a censer in his hand *ready* to **b incense,** 7787
28:25 in Judah he built high places to **b sacrifices** 7787
29: 7 not **b** incense or present any burnt offerings 7787
29:11 to minister before him and *to* **b incense."** 7787
32:12 before one altar and **b sacrifices** on it'? 7787
Ne 10:34 a contribution of wood to **b** on the altar of 1277
Ps 79: 5 How long *will* your jealousy **b** like fire? 1277
89:46 How long *will* your wrath **b** like fire? 1277
102: 3 my bones **b** like glowing embers. 3081
Isa 1:31 both *will* **b** together, 1277
10:17 in a single day *it will* **b** 1277
47:14 the fire *will* **b** them **up.** 8596
57: 5 You **b with lust** among the oaks and 2801
Jer 4: 4 or my wrath will break out and **b** like fire 1277
4: 4 **b** with no one to quench it. NIH
6:29 The bellows blow fiercely *to* **b away** 9462
7: 9 **b incense** to Baal 7787
7:20 and *it will* **b** and not be quenched. 1277
7:31 in the Valley of Ben Hinnom *to* **b** their sons 8596
11:12 to the gods to whom they **b incense,** 7787
11:13 and the altars you have set up to **b incense** 7787
15:14 for my anger will kindle a fire *that will* **b** 3678
17: 4 and *it will* **b** forever." 3678
18:15 *they* **b incense** to worthless idols, 7787
19: 5 the high places of Baal to **b** their sons in 8596
21:12 or my wrath will break out and **b** like fire 1277
21:12 **b** with no one to quench it. NIH
32:29 *they will* **b** it **down,** 8596
33:18 *to* **b** grain offerings and 7787
34: 2 and *he will* **b** it **down.** 836+928+2021+8596
34:22 take it and **b** it **down.** 836+928+2021+8596
36:25 and Gemariah urged the king not *to* **b** 8596
37: 8 they will capture it and **b** it **down.'** 836+928+2021+8596
37:10 they would come out and **b** this city **down."** 836+928+2021+8596
38:18 the Babylonians and *they will* **b** it **down;** 836+928+2021+8596
43:12 *he will* **b** their temples 8596
43:13 and *will* **b down** the temples of the gods 836+928+2021+8596
44:17 We *will* **b incense** to the Queen of Heaven 7787
44:25 to **b incense** and pour out drink offerings to 7787
48:35 the high places and **b incense** to their gods," 7787
Eze 5: 2 **b** a third of the hair with fire inside the city. 1277
5: 4 and throw them into the fire and **b** them **up.** 836+928+2021+8596
16:41 *They will* **b down** your houses 836+928+2021+8596
23:47 and daughters and **b down** their houses. 836+928+2021+8596
39: 9 use the weapons for fuel and **b** them **up—** 5956
43:21 to take the bull for the sin offering and **b** it 8596
Hos 4:13 on the mountaintops and **b offerings** on 7787
Am 4: 5 **B** leavened bread as a thank offering 7787
6:10 *to* **b** the bodies comes to carry them out of 6251
Na 2:13 *"I will* **b up** your chariots in smoke, 1277
Mal 4: 1 the day is coming; *it will* **b** like a furnace 1277
Lk 1: 9 into the temple of the Lord and **b incense.** *2594*
3:17 but *he will* **b up** the chaff *2876*
1Co 7: 9 it is better to marry than *to* **b with passion.** *4792*
2Co 11:29 and I *do* not **inwardly b?** *4792*
Rev 17:16 they will eat her flesh and **b** her with fire. *2876*

BURNED (150) [BURN]

Ge 38:24 "Bring her out and *have her* **b to death!"** 8596
39:19 he **b** *with* anger. 3013
Ex 4:14 Then the LORD's anger **b** against Moses 3013
32:19 his anger **b** and he threw the tablets out 3013
32:20 And he took the calf they had made and **b** it 8596
40:27 and **b** fragrant incense on it, 7787
Lev 4:21 the bull outside the camp and burn it as *he* **b** 8596
4:26 He shall burn all the fat on the altar as he **b** NIH
6:22 and *is to* **be b** completely. 7787
6:23 of a priest shall be **b** completely; NIH
6:30 *it must* **be b.** 836+928+2021+8596
7:17 over till the third day *must* **be b up.** 836+928+2021+8596
7:19 must not be eaten; *it must* **be b up.** 836+928+2021+8596
8:16 and **b** it on the altar. 7787
8:17 and its flesh and its offal *he* **b up** outside 836+928+2021+8596
8:20 He cut the ram into pieces and **b** the head, 7787
8:21 with water and **b** the whole ram on the altar 7787
8:28 from their hands and **b** them on the altar 7787
9:10 On the altar *he* **b** the fat, 7787
9:11 and the hide *he* **b up** outside the camp. 836+928+2021+8596
9:13 and *he* **b** them on the altar. 7787
9:14 and **b** them on top of the burnt offering on 7787
9:17 took a handful of it and **b** it on the altar 7787
9:20 and then Aaron **b** the fat on the altar. 7787
10:16 and found that *it had* **been b up,** 8596
13:52 the article *must* **be b up.** 836+928+2021+8596
13:57 and whatever has the mildew *must be* **b** 8596
16:27 their hides, flesh and offal *are to be* **b up.** 836+928+2021+8596

Lev 19: 6 over until the third day *must* **be b up.** 836+928+2021+8596
20:14 Both he and they *must be* **b** in the fire, 8596
21: 9 *she must* **be b** in the fire. 8596
Nu 11: 1 Then fire from the LORD **b** among them 1277
11: 3 fire from the LORD *had* **b** among them. 1277
11:33 of the LORD **b** against the people, 3013
12: 9 The anger of the LORD **b** against them, 3013
16:39 by those *who had* **been b up,** 8596
19: 5 While he watches, the heifer *is to be* **b—** 8596
19:17 from the **b** purification offering into a jar 8599
24:10 Then Balak's anger **b** against Balaam. 3013
25: 3 And the LORD's anger **b** against them. 3013
31:10 *They* **b** all the towns where 836+928+2021+8596
32:13 The LORD's anger **b** against Israel 3013
Dt 9:21 the calf you had made, and **b** it in the fire. 8596
29:27 the LORD's anger **b** against this land, 3013
Jos 6:24 *they* **b** the whole city and everything in it, 836+928+2021+8596
7: 1 So the LORD's anger **b** against Israel. 3013
7:25 after they had stoned the rest, *they* **b** them. 836+928+2021+8596
8:28 So Joshua **b** Ai and made it 8596
11: 9 and **b** their chariots. 836+928+2021+8596
11:11 and *he* **b up** Hazor itself. 836+928+2021+8596
11:13 except Hazor, which Joshua **b.** 8596
Jdg 3: 8 The anger of the LORD **b** against Israel so 3013
15: 5 *He* **b up** the shocks and standing grain, 1277
15: 6 **b** her and her father **to death.** 836+928+2021+8596
18:27 with the sword and **b down** their city. 836+928+2021+8596
1Sa 2:15 But even before the fat *was* **b,** 7787
2:16 said to him, *"Let* the fat *be* **b up** first, 7787+7787
11: 6 and he **b** with anger. 3013+4394
17:28 he **b** *with* anger at him and asked, 3013
30: 1 attacked Ziklag and **b** it, 836+928+2021+8596
30:14 And *we* **b** Ziklag." 836+928+2021+8596
31:12 where *they* **b** them. 8596
2Sa 6: 7 The LORD's anger **b** against Uzzah 3013
12: 5 David **b** *with* anger against the man 3013+4394
23: 7 *they* **are b up** where they lie." 836+928+2021+8596+8596
24: 1 the anger of the LORD **b** against Israel, 3013
1Ki 3: 3 that he offered sacrifices and **b incense** on 7787
11: 8 *who* **b incense** and offered sacrifices 7787
13: 2 and human bones *will be* **b** on you.' " 8596
15:13 down and **b** it in the Kidron Valley. 8596
18:38 Then the fire of the LORD fell and **b up** 430
19:21 **b** the plowing equipment **to cook** 1418
2Ki 10:26 of the temple of Baal and **b** it. 8596
13: 3 So the LORD's anger **b** against Israel, 3013
16: 4 He offered sacrifices and **b incense** at 7787
17:11 At every high place *they* **b incense,** 7787
17:31 **b** their children in the fire **as sacrifices** 8596
22:17 and **b incense** to other gods 7787
23: 4 *He* **b** them outside Jerusalem in the fields of 8596
23: 5 those *who* **b incense** to Baal, 7787
23: 6 and **b** it there. 8596
23: 8 where the priests *had* **b incense.** 7787
23:11 then **b** the chariots dedicated to the sun. 836+928+2021+8596
23:15 *He* **b** the high place and ground it 8596
23:15 and **b** the Asherah pole also. 8596
23:16 he had the bones removed from them and **b** 8596
23:20 on the altars and **b** human bones on them. 8596
23:26 which **b** against Judah because of all 3013
25: 9 Every important building *he* **b down.** 836+928+2021+8596
1Ch 13:10 The LORD's anger **b** against Uzzah, 3013
2Ch 15:16 broke it up and **b** it in the Kidron Valley. 8596
25:14 down to them and **b sacrifices** to them. 7787
25:15 of the LORD **b** against Amaziah, 3013
28: 3 He **b sacrifices** in the Valley 7787
28: 4 He offered sacrifices and **b incense** at 7787
34: 5 *He* **b** the bones of the priests on their altars, 8596
34:25 and **b incense** to other gods 7787
36:19 *they* **b** all the palaces 836+928+2021+8596
Ne 1: 3 and its gates *have* **been b** with fire." 3675
2:17 and its gates *have* **been b** with fire. 3675
4: 2 **b** as they are?" 8596
Est 1:12 the king became furious and **b** *with* anger. 1277
Job 1:16 the sky and **b up** the sheep and the servants, 1277
Ps 39: 3 and as I meditated, the fire **b;** 1277
74: 7 *They* **b** your sanctuary to the ground; 836+928+2021+8938
74: 8 *They* **b** every place where God 8596
80:16 Your vine is cut down, *it* **is b** with fire; 8596
Pr 6:27 into his lap without his clothes **being b?** 8596
Isa 1: 7 your cities **b** *with* fire; 8596
24: 6 Therefore earth's inhabitants *are* **b up,** 3081
33:12 The peoples will be **b** *as if to* lime; 5386
43: 2 *you will* not **be b;** 3917
64:11 has been **b** *with* fire, 8599
65: 7 "Because *they* **b sacrifices** on 7787
Jer 2:15 his towns **are b** and deserted. 3675
19: 4 *they have* **b sacrifices** in it to gods 7787
19:13 where *they* **b incense** on the roofs to all 7787
29:22 whom the king of Babylon **b** in the fire.' 7828
36:23 until the entire scroll *was* **b** in the fire. 9462
36:27 the king **b** the scroll containing the words 8596
36:28 which Jehoiakim king of Judah **b up.** 8596
36:29 You **b** that scroll and said, 8596
36:32 scroll that Jehoiakim king of Judah *had* **b** 8596
38:17 be spared and this city *will* not **be b down;** 836+928+2021+8596
38:23 and this city *will be* **b down."** 836+2021+8596

Jer 44:19 "When we **b incense** to the Queen 7787
44:21 and think about the incense **b** in the towns 7787
44:23 Because *you have* **b incense** 7787
52:13 Every important building *he* **b down.** 836+928+2021+8596
La 2: 3 *He has* **b** in Jacob like a flaming fire 1277
Eze 15: 5 into something useful *when* the fire *has* **b** it 430
24:11 be melted and its deposit **b away.** 9462
Da 11:33 the sword or be **b** or captured or plundered. 4259
Hos 2:13 I will punish her for the days *she* **b incense** 7787
11: 2 to the Baals and *they* **b incense** to images. 7787
Joel 1:19 the open pastures and flames *have* **b up** all 4265
Am 2: 1 Because he **b**, as if to lime, 8596
Mic 1: 7 all her temple gifts *will* **be b** with fire; 8596
Mt 13:30 the weeds and tie them in bundles to *be* **b;** *2876*
13:40 the weeds are pulled up and **b** in the fire, *2876*
22: 7 and **b** their city. *1856*
Jn 5:35 John was a lamp that **b** and gave light, *2794*
15: 6 thrown into the fire and **b.** *2794*
Ac 19:19 and **b** them publicly. *2876*
1Co 3:15 If it *is* **b up,** he will suffer loss; *2876*
Heb 6: 8 In the end it will be **b.** *3011*
13:11 but the bodies *are* **b** outside the camp. *2876*
Rev 8: 7 A third of the earth *was* **b up,** *2876*
8: 7 a third of the trees *were* **b up,** *2876*
8: 7 and all the green grass *was* **b up.** *2876*

BURNED-OUT (1) [BURN]

Jer 51:25 and make you a **b** mountain. 8599

BURNING (77) [BURN]

Ge 19:24 the LORD rained down **b** sulfur on Sodom 836
Ex 15: 7 You unleashed your **b anger;** 3019
27:20 the light so that the lamps *may be* kept **b.** 6590
27:21 and his sons are to keep the lamps **b** before NIH
30: 1 an altar of acacia wood for **b** incense. 5230
Lev 1: 8 on the **b** wood that is on the altar. 836+2021+6584
1:12 on the **b** wood that is on the altar. 836+2021+6584
3: 5 the burnt offering that is on the **b** wood, 836+2021+6584
6: 9 and the fire *must* **be kept b** on the altar. 3678
6:12 The fire on the altar *must* **be kept b;** 3678
6:13 The fire *must* **be kept b** on 3678
16:12 a censer full of **b** coals from the altar before 836
24: 2 so that the lamps *may be* **kept b** continually. 6590
Nu 19: 6 and throw them onto the **b** heifer. 8599
Dt 29:23 The whole land will be a **b waste** *of* salt 8599
29:24 Why this fierce, **b** anger?" 3034
33:16 the favor of him who dwelt in the **b** bush. NIH
Jdg 14:19 **B** *with* anger, he went up 3013
2Sa 14: 7 the only **b coal** I have left, 1625
22: 9 **b coals** blazed out of it. 1624
1Ki 9:25 **b incense** before the LORD along 7787
2Ki 18: 4 the Israelites had been **b incense** to it. 7787
2Ch 2: 4 to dedicate it to him for **b** fragrant incense 7787
Job 18: 5 the flame of his fire stops **b.** 5585
18:15 **b sulfur** is scattered over his dwelling. 1730
20:23 God will vent his **b** anger against him 3019
Ps 11: 6 On the wicked he will rain fiery coals and **b sulfur;** 1730
18: 8 **b coals** blazed out of it. 1624
18:28 You, O LORD, **keep** my lamp **b;** 239
118:12 but they died out as quickly as **b** thorns; 836
120: 4 with **b coals** *of* the broom tree. 1624
140:10 Let **b coals** fall upon them; 1624
Pr 25:22 you will heap **b coals** on his head, 1624
Isa 9: 5 in blood will be destined for **b,** 8599
13:13 in the day of his **b** anger. 3019
30:27 with **b** anger and dense clouds of smoke; 1277
30:33 like a stream of **b sulfur,** sets it ablaze. 1730
33:14 Who of us can dwell with everlasting **b?"** 4611
34: 9 her dust into **b sulfur;** 1730
35: 7 The **b sand** will become a pool, 9220
42:25 So he poured out on them his **b** anger, 2779
44:15 It is man's fuel for **b;** 1277
65: 3 offering sacrifices in gardens and **b incense** 7787
65: 5 a fire *that keeps* **b** all day. 3678
Jer 1:16 *in* **b incense** to other gods and 7787
11:17 and provoked me to anger by **b incense** 7787
32:29 to anger by **b incense** on the roofs to Baal 7787
36:22 with a fire **b** in the firepot in front of him. 1277
44: 3 by **b incense** and by worshiping other gods 7787
44: 5 from their wickedness or stop **b incense** 7787
44: 8 **b incense** to other gods in Egypt, 7787
44:15 that their wives *were* **b incense** 7787
44:18 since we stopped **b incense** to the Queen 7787
Eze 1:13 the living creatures was like **b** coals of fire 1277
10: 2 Fill your hands with **b** coals from among 836
36: 5 In my **b** zeal I have spoken against the rest 836
38:22 of rain, hailstones and **b** sulfur on him and 836
Hos 7: 4 **b** like an oven whose fire the baker need 1277
13: 5 in the land of **b heat.** 9429
Am 4:11 You were like a **b stick** snatched from 202
Zec 3: 2 Is not this man a **b stick** snatched from 202
8: 2 I am **b** *with* jealousy for her." 2779
Mt 3:12 and **b up** the chaff with unquenchable fire." *2876*
Lk 1:10 when the time *for* the **b of incense** came, *2592*
12:35 for service and *keep* your lamps **b,** *2794*
24:32 not our hearts **b** within us while he talked *2794*
Jn 21: 9 they saw a **fire of b coals** there with fish *471*
Ac 7:30 *of* a **b** bush in the desert near Mount Sinai. *4786*
Ro 12:20 you will heap **b** coals on his head." *4786*
Heb 12:18 that can be touched and that *is* **b** with fire; *2794*
2Pe 2: 6 Sodom and Gomorrah by **b** *them* **to ashes,** *5491*
Rev 14:10 be tormented with **b** sulfur in the presence *4786*
18: 9 the smoke *of* her **b,** *4796*
18:18 When they see the smoke *of* her **b,** *4796*
19:20 into the fiery lake *of* **b** sulfur. *2794*
20:10 was thrown into the lake *of* **b** sulfur, *4786*
21: 8 be in the fiery lake of **b** sulfur. *2794*

BURNISHED (4)

1Ki 7:45 the temple of the LORD were of **b** bronze. 5307
Eze 1: 7 of a calf and gleamed like **b** bronze. 7838
Da 10: 6 and legs like the gleam of **b** bronze, 7838
Rev 2:18 and whose feet are like **b bronze.** *5909*

BURNS (20) [BURN]

Ex 22: 6 that *it* **b** shocks of grain or standing grain 430
Lev 16:28 The *man who* **b** them must wash his clothes 8596
Nu 19: 8 The *man who* **b** it must also wash his clothes 8596
Dt 32:22 *one that* **b** to the realm of death below. 3678
1Ki 14:10 up the house of Jeroboam as *one* **b** dung, 1277
2Ki 22:13 that **b** against us because our fathers have 3675
Job 19:11 His anger **b** against me; 3013
30:30 my body **b** with fever. 3081
31:12 It is a fire *that* **b** to Destruction; 430
Ps 46: 9 *he* **b** the shields with fire. 8596
SS 8: 6 It **b** like blazing fire, like a mighty flame. 8404
Isa 5:25 the LORD's anger **b** against his people; 3013
9:18 Surely wickedness **b** like a fire; 1277
44:16 Half of the wood *he* **b** in the fire; 8596
66: 3 and *whoever* **b memorial** incense, 2349
Jer 48:45 *it* **b** the foreheads of Moab, 430
Eze 15: 4 on the fire as fuel and the fire **b** both ends 430
Hos 8: 5 My anger **b** against them. 3013
Hab 1:16 to his net and **b incense** to his dragnet, 7787
Zec 10: 3 "My anger **b** against the shepherds, 3013

BURNT (275) [BURN]

Ge 8:20 he sacrificed **b offerings** on it. 6592
22: 2 Sacrifice him there as a **b offering** on one 6592
22: 3 he had cut enough wood for the **b offering,** 6592
22: 6 Abraham took the wood for the **b offering** 6592
22: 7 "but where is the lamb for the **b offering?"** 6592
22: 8 the lamb for the **b offering,** 6592
22:13 and sacrificed it as a **b offering** instead 6592
Ex 10:25 to have sacrifices and **b offerings** to present 6592
18:12 brought a **b offering** and other sacrifices 6592
20:24 for me and sacrifice on it your **b offerings** 6592
24: 5 and they offered **b offerings** 6592
29:18 It is a **b offering** to the LORD, 6592
29:25 with the **b offering** for a pleasing aroma to 6592
29:42 the generations to come this **b offering** is 6592
30: 9 or any **b offering** or grain offering, 6592
30:28 the altar of **b offering** and all its utensils, 6592
31: 9 of **b offering** and all its utensils, the basin 6592
32: 6 and sacrificed **b offerings** 6592
35:16 of **b offering** with its bronze grating, 6592
38: 1 the altar of **b offering** *of* acacia wood, 6592
40: 6 "Place the altar of **b offering** in front of 6592
40:10 the altar of **b offering** and all its utensils; 6592
40:29 the altar of **b offering** near the entrance to 6592
40:29 on it **b offerings** and grain offerings, 6592
Lev 1: 3 the offering is a **b offering** from the herd, 6592
1: 4 on the head of the **b offering,** 6592
1: 6 to skin the **b offering** and cut it into pieces. 6592
1: 9 It is a **b offering,** an offering made by fire, 6592
1:10 the offering is a **b offering** from the flock, 6592
1:13 It is a **b offering,** an offering made by fire, 6592
1:14 the offering to the LORD is a **b offering** 6592
1:17 It is a **b offering,** an offering made by fire, 6592
3: 5 the **b offering** that is on the burning wood, 6592
4: 7 of the altar of **b offering** at the entrance to 6592
4:10 on the altar of **b offering.** 6592
4:18 of the altar of **b offering** at the entrance to 6592
4:24 where the **b offering** is slaughtered before 6592
4:25 the altar of **b offering** and pour out the rest 6592
4:29 at the place of the **b offering.** 6592
4:30 the altar of **b offering** and pour out the rest 6592
4:33 where the **b offering** is slaughtered. 6592
4:34 the altar of **b offering** and pour out the rest 6592
5: 7 and the other for a **b offering.** 6592
5:10 then offer the other as a **b offering** in 6592
6: 9 the regulations for the **b offering:** 6592
6: 9 The **b offering** is to remain on 6592
6:10 of the **b offering** that the fire has consumed 6592
6:12 to add firewood and arrange the **b offering** 6592
6:25 in the place the **b offering** is slaughtered; 6592
7: 2 where the **b offering** is slaughtered, 6592
7: 8 a **b offering** *for* anyone may keep its hide 6592
7:37 then, are the regulations for the **b offering,** 6592
8:18 then presented the ram for the **b** *offering,* 6592
8:21 the whole ram on the altar as a **b offering,** 6592
8:28 of the **b offering** as an ordination offering, 6592
9: 2 and a ram for your **b offering,** 6592
9: 3 for a **b offering,** 6592
9: 7 and your **b offering** and make atonement 6592
9:12 Then he slaughtered the **b offering.** 6592
9:13 They handed him the **b offering** piece 6592
9:14 and burned them on top of the **b offering** 6592
9:16 He brought the **b offering** and offered it in 6592
9:17 in addition to the morning's **b offering.** 6592
9:22 the **b offering** and the fellowship offering, 6592
9:24 the LORD and consumed the **b offering** 6592
10:19 and their **b offering** before the LORD, 6592
12: 6 of Meeting a year-old lamb for a **b offering** 6592
12: 8 one for a **b offering** and the other for 6592
14:13 and the **b offering** are slaughtered. 6592
Lev 14:19 the priest shall slaughter the **b offering** 6592
14:22 and the other for a **b offering.** 6592
14:31 a sin offering and the other as a **b offering,** 6592
15:15 and the other for a **b offering.** 6592
15:30 and the other for a **b offering.** 6592
16: 3 a sin offering and a ram for a **b offering.** 6592
16: 5 a sin offering and a ram for a **b offering.** 6592
16:24 and sacrifice the **b offering** *for* himself and 6592
16:24 for himself and the **b offering** *for* 6592
17: 8 among them who offers a **b offering** 6592
22:18 a gift for a **b offering** to the LORD, 6592
23:12 as a **b offering** to the LORD a lamb 6592
23:18 They will be a **b offering** to the LORD, 6592
23:37 the **b offerings** and grain offerings, 6592
Nu 6:11 as a **b offering** to make atonement for him 6592
6:14 without defect for a **b offering,** 6592
6:16 the sin offering and the **b offering.** 6592
7:15 one male lamb a year old, for a **b offering;** 6592
7:21 one male lamb a year old, for a **b offering;** 6592
7:27 one male lamb a year old, for a **b offering;** 6592
7:33 one male lamb a year old, for a **b offering;** 6592
7:39 one male lamb a year old, for a **b offering;** 6592
7:45 one male lamb a year old, for a **b offering;** 6592
7:51 one male lamb a year old, for a **b offering;** 6592
7:57 one male lamb a year old, for a **b offering;** 6592
7:63 one male lamb a year old, for a **b offering;** 6592
7:69 one male lamb a year old, for a **b offering;** 6592
7:75 one male lamb a year old, for a **b offering;** 6592
7:81 one male lamb a year old, for a **b offering;** 6592
7:87 the **b offering** came to twelve young bulls, 6592
8:12 the LORD and the other for a **b offering,** 6592
10:10 to sound the trumpets over your **b offerings** 6592
15: 3 whether **b offerings** or sacrifices, 6592
15: 5 With each lamb for the **b offering** or 6592
15: 8 a young bull as a **b offering** or sacrifice, 6592
15:24 for a **b offering** as an aroma pleasing to 6592
28: 3 as a regular **b offering** each day. 6592
28: 6 This is the regular **b offering** instituted 6592
28:10 This is the **b offering** *for* every Sabbath, 6592
28:10 in addition to the regular **b offering** 6592
28:11 present to the LORD a **b offering** 6592
28:13 This is for a **b offering,** a pleasing aroma, 6592
28:14 This is the monthly **b offering** to be made 6592
28:15 Besides the regular **b offering** 6592
28:19 a **b offering** of two young bulls, 6592
28:23 to the regular morning **b offering.** 6592
28:24 in addition to the regular **b offering** 6592
28:27 Present a **b offering** of two young bulls, 6592
28:31 in addition to the regular **b offering** 6592
29: 2 prepare a **b offering** of one young bull, 6592
29: 6 to the monthly and daily **b offerings** 6592
29: 8 the LORD a **b offering** of one young bull, 6592
29:11 for atonement and the regular **b offering** 6592
29:13 a **b offering** of thirteen young bulls, 6592
29:16 in addition to the regular **b offering** 6592
29:19 in addition to the regular **b offering** 6592
29:22 in addition to the regular **b offering** 6592
29:25 in addition to the regular **b offering** 6592
29:28 in addition to the regular **b offering** 6592
29:31 in addition to the regular **b offering** 6592
29:34 in addition to the regular **b offering** 6592
29:36 a **b offering** of one bull, 6592
29:38 in addition to the regular **b offering** 6592
29:39 your **b offerings,** grain offerings, 6592
Dt 12: 6 there bring your **b offerings** and sacrifices, 6592
12:11 your **b offerings** and sacrifices, 6592
12:13 not to sacrifice your **b offerings** anywhere you please. 6592
12:27 Present your **b offerings** on the altar of 6592
13:16 and all its plunder as a **whole b offering** to 4003
27: 6 with fieldstones and offer **b offerings** on it 6592
33:10 and **whole b offerings** on your altar. 4003
Jos 8:31 to the LORD **b offerings** 6592
22:23 and to offer **b offerings** and grain offerings, 6592
22:26 but not for **b offerings** or sacrifices.' 6592
22:27 at his sanctuary with our **b offerings,** 6592
22:28 not for **b offerings** and sacrifices, 6592
22:29 by building an altar for **b offerings,** 6592
Jdg 6:26 offer the second bull as a **b offering."** 6592
11:31 and I will sacrifice it as a **b offering."** 6592
13:16 But if you prepare a **b offering,** 6592
13:23 he would not have accepted a **b offering** 6592
20:26 until evening and presented **b offerings** 6592
21: 4 an altar and presented **b offerings** 6592
1Sa 6:14 and sacrificed the cows as a **b offering** to 6592
6:15 of Beth Shemesh offered **b offerings** 6592
7: 9 and offered it up as a whole **b offering** to 6592
7:10 Samuel was sacrificing the **b offering,** 6592
10: 8 down to you to sacrifice **b offerings** 6592
13: 9 "Bring me the **b offering** and 6592
13: 9 And Saul offered up the **b offering.** 6592
13:12 So I felt compelled to offer the **b offering."** 6592
15:22 "Does the LORD delight in **b offerings** 6592
2Sa 6:17 and David sacrificed **b offerings** 6592
6:18 the **b offerings** and fellowship offerings, 6592
24:22 Here are oxen for the **b offering,** 6592
24:24 to the LORD my God **b offerings** 6592
24:25 the LORD there and sacrificed **b offerings** 6592
1Ki 3: 4 a thousand **b offerings** on that altar. 6592
3:15 and sacrificed **b offerings** 6592
8:64 and there he offered **b offerings,** 6592
8:64 to hold the **b offerings,** 6592
9:25 a year Solomon sacrificed **b offerings** 6592
10: 5 and the **b offerings** he made at the temple 6592
2Ki 5:17 your servant will never again make **b offerings** and sacrifices to any other god 6592
10:24 in to make sacrifices and **b offerings.** 6592

2Ki 10:25 the **b offering,** he ordered the guards 6592
16:13 up his **b offering** and grain offering, 6592
16:15 offer the morning **b offering** and 6592
16:15 the king's **b offering** 6592
16:15 the **b offering** *of* all the people of the land, 6592
16:15 on the altar all the blood of the **b offerings** 6592
1Ch 6:49 on the altar of **b offering** and on the altar 6592
16: 1 and they presented **b offerings** 6592
16: 2 the **b offerings** and fellowship offerings, 6592
16:40 to present **b offerings** to the LORD on 6592
16:40 on the altar of **b offering** regularly, 6592
21:23 I will give the oxen for the **b offerings,** 6592
21:24 a **b offering** that costs me nothing." 6592
21:26 the LORD there and sacrificed **b offerings** 6592
21:26 from heaven on the altar of **b offering.** 6592
21:29 and the altar of **b offering** were at that time 6592
22: 1 and also the altar of **b offering** for Israel." 6592
23:31 and whenever **b offerings** were presented 6592
29:21 to the LORD and presented **b offerings** 6592
2Ch 1: 6 and offered a thousand **b offerings** on it. 6592
2: 4 and for making **b offerings** every morning 6592
4: 6 to be used for the **b offerings** were rinsed, 6592
7: 1 from heaven and consumed the **b offering** 6592
7: 7 and there he offered **b offerings** and the fat 6592
7: 7 not hold the **b offerings,** 6592
8:12 Solomon sacrificed **b offerings** to 6592
9: 4 in their robes and the **b offerings** he made 6592
13:11 and evening they present **b offerings** 6592
23:18 the **b offerings** *of* the LORD as written in 6592
24:14 for the service and for the **b offerings,** 6592
24:14 **b offerings** were presented continually in 6592
29: 7 not burn incense or present any **b offerings** 6592
29:18 the altar of **b offering** with all its utensils, 6592
29:24 the king had ordered the **b offering** and 6592
29:27 the order to sacrifice the **b offering** on 6592
29:28 of the **b offering** was completed. 6592
29:31 all whose hearts were willing brought **b offerings.** 6592
29:32 The number of **b offerings** 6592
29:32 all of them for **b offerings** to the LORD. 6592
29:34 were too few to skin all the **b offerings;** 6592
29:35 There were **b offerings** in abundance, 6592
29:35 that accompanied the **b offerings.** 6592
30:15 and brought **b offerings** to the temple of 6592
31: 2 to offer **b offerings** 6592
31: 3 the morning and evening **b offerings** and 6592
31: 3 and for the **b offerings** on the Sabbaths, 6592
35:12 They set aside the **b offerings** to give them 6592
35:14 were sacrificing the **b offerings** and 6592
35:16 the Passover and the offering of **b offerings** 6592
Ezr 3: 2 of the God of Israel to sacrifice **b offerings** 6592
3: 3 on its foundation and sacrificed **b offerings** 6592
3: 4 of **b offerings** prescribed for each day. 6592
3: 5 they presented the regular **b offerings,** 6592
3: 6 to offer **b offerings** to the LORD, 6592
6: 9 male lambs for **b offerings** to the God 10545
8:35 from captivity sacrificed **b offerings** to 6592
8:35 All this was a **b offering** to the LORD. 6592
Ne 10:33 the regular grain offerings and **b offerings;** 6592
Job 1: 5 a **b offering** for each of them, 6592
42: 8 and sacrifice a **b offering** for yourselves. 6592
Ps 20: 3 and accept your **b offerings.** 6592
40: 6 **b offerings** and sin offerings you did 6592
50: 8 for your sacrifices or your **b offerings,** 6592
51:16 you do not take pleasure in **b offerings.** 6592
51:19 whole **b offerings** to delight you; 6592
66:13 I will come to your temple with **b offerings** 6592
Isa 1:11 "I have more than enough of **b offerings,** 6592
40:16 nor its animals enough for **b offerings.** 6592
43:23 not brought me sheep for **b offerings,** 6592
56: 7 Their **b offerings** and sacrifices will 6592
Jer 6:20 Your **b offerings** are not acceptable; 6592
7:21 Go ahead, add your **b offerings** 6592
7:22 about **b offerings** and sacrifices, 6592
14:12 though they offer **b offerings** 6592
17:26 bringing **b offerings** and sacrifices, 6592
33:18 before me continually to offer **b offerings,** 6592
Eze 40:38 where the **b offerings** were washed. 6592
40:39 on which the **b offerings,** 6592
40:42 of dressed stone for the **b offerings,** 6592
40:42 the utensils for slaughtering the **b offerings** 6592
43:18 the regulations for sacrificing **b offerings** 6592
43:24 on them and sacrifice them as a **b offering** 6592
43:27 the priests are to present your **b offerings** 6592
44:11 the **b offerings** and sacrifices for the people 6592
45:15 **b offerings** and fellowship offerings 6592
45:17 to provide the **b offerings,** grain offerings 6592
45:17 **b offerings** and fellowship offerings 6592
45:23 without defect as a **b offering** to 6592
45:25 **b offerings,** grain offerings and oil. 6592
46: 2 The priests are to sacrifice his **b offering** 6592
46: 4 The **b offering** the prince brings to 6592
46:12 a **b offering** or fellowship offerings— 6592
46:12 He shall offer his **b offering** 6592
46:13 without defect for a **b offering** to 6592
46:15 by morning for a regular **b offering.** 6592
Hos 6: 6 of God rather than **b offerings.** 6592
Am 5:22 Even though you bring me **b offerings** 6592
Mic 6: 6 Shall I come before him with **b offerings,** 6592
Mk 12:33 love your neighbor as yourself is more important than all **b offerings** *3906*
Heb 10: 6 with **b offerings** and sin offerings you were *3906*
10: 8 **b offerings** and sin offerings you did not *3906*

BURNT-OUT (Anglicized) See BURNED-OUT

BURST (21) [BURSTS]

Ge 7:11 the springs of the great deep **b forth,** 1324
27:34 *he* **b out** *with* a loud and bitter cry and said 7590
Job 26: 8 yet the clouds *do* not **b** under their weight. 1324
32:19 like new wineskins **ready to b.** 1324
38: 8 the sea behind doors when it **b** forth from 1631
Ps 60: 1 O God, and **b forth** *upon* us; 7287
98: 4 **b** *into* jubilant song with music; 7200
Isa 35: 2 *it will* **b into bloom;** 7255+7255
44:23 **B** *into* song, *you* mountains, 7200
49:13 **b** *into* song, O mountains! 7200
52: 9 **B** *into* songs of joy together, 7200
54: 1 **b** *into* song, shout for joy, 7200
55:12 the mountains and hills *will* **b** *into* song 7200
Jer 23:19 storm of the LORD *will* **b out** in wrath, 3655
30:23 storm of the LORD *will* **b out** *in* wrath, 3655
Eze 7:10 Doom *has* **b forth,** the rod has budded, 3655
13:11 and violent winds *will* **b forth.** 1324
Mt 9:17 If they do, the skins *will* **b,** *4838*
Mk 2:22 If he does, the wine *will* **b** the skins, *4838*
Lk 5:37 If he does, the new wine *will* **b** the skins, *4838*
Ac 1:18 there he fell headlong, his body **b** open *3279*

BURSTS (1) [BURST]

Job 16:14 **Again and again** *he* **b** upon me 7287+7288+7288

BURY (38) [BURIAL, BURIED, BURIES, BURYING]

Ge 23: 4 for a burial site here so *I can* **b** my dead." 7699
23: 6 **B** your dead in the choicest of our tombs. 7699
23: 8 "If you are willing to *let* me **b** my dead, 7699
23:11 **B** your dead." 7699
23:13 from me so *I can* **b** my dead there." 7699
23:15 **B** your dead." 7699
47:29 *Do* not **b** me in Egypt, 7699
47:30 of Egypt and **b** me where they are buried." 7699
49:29 **B** me with my fathers in the cave in 7699
50: 5 **b** me in the tomb I dug for myself in 7699
50: 5 Now let me go up and **b** my father; 7699
50: 6 Pharaoh said, "Go up and **b** your father, 7699
50: 7 So Joseph went up to **b** his father. 7699
50:14 with him to **b** his father. 7699
Dt 21:23 **Be sure to b** him that same day, 7699+7699
1Ki 2:31 Strike him down and **b** him, 7699
11:15 who had gone up to **b** the dead, 7699
13:29 to his own city to mourn for him and **b** him. 7699
13:31 **b** me in the grave where the man 7699
14:13 All Israel will mourn for him and **b** him. 7699
2Ki 9:10 and no *one will* **b** her.' " 7699
9:34 "and **b** her, for she was a king's daughter." 7699
9:35 But when they went out to **b** her, 7699
Job 27:15 The plague *will* **b** those who survive him, 7699
40:13 **B** them all in the dust together; *3243*
Ps 79: 3 and there is no *one to* **b** the dead. 7699
Jer 7:32 for *they will* **b** the dead in Topheth 7699
14:16 be no *one to* **b** them or their wives, 7699
19:11 *They will* **b** the dead in Topheth 7699
43: 9 take some large stones with you and **b** them 3243
La 3:29 *Let him* **b** his face in the dust— 5989
Eze 39:13 All the people of the land *will* **b** them, 7699
39:14 *others will* **b** those that remain on 7699
Hos 9: 6 and Memphis *will* **b** them. 7699
Mt 8:21 "Lord, first let me go and **b** my father." *2507*
8:22 and let the dead **b** their own dead." *2507*
Lk 9:59 "Lord, first let me go and **b** my father." *2507*
9:60 "Let the dead **b** their own dead, *2507*

BURYING (7) [BURY]

Ge 23: 6 his tomb for **b** your dead." 7699
50:14 After **b** his father, Joseph returned to Egypt, 7699
Nu 33: 4 who *were* **b** all their firstborn, whom 7699
2Sa 2: 5 to Saul your master *by* **b** him. 7699
1Ki 13:31 After **b** him, he said to his sons, 7699
2Ki 13:21 Once *while* some Israelites *were* **b** a man, 7699
Eze 39:12 of Israel *will be* **b** them in order to cleanse 7699

BUSH (11) [BUSHES]

Ex 3: 2 to him in flames of fire from within a **b.** 6174
3: 2 though the **b** was on fire it did not burn up 6174
3: 3 why the **b** does not burn up." 6174
3: 4 God called to him from within the **b,** 6174
Dt 33:16 of him who dwelt in the burning **b.** 6174
Jer 17: 6 He will be like a **b** in the wastelands; 6899
48: 6 become like a **b** in the desert. 6899
Mk 12:26 the book of Moses, in the account *of* the **b,** *1003*
Lk 20:37 But in the account *of* the **b,** *1003*
Ac 7:30 a burning **b** in the desert near Mount Sinai. *1003*
7:35 the angel who appeared to him in the **b.** *1003*

BUSHELS (1)

Lk 16: 7 'A **thousand b** of wheat,' he replied. *1669+3174*

BUSHES (2) [BUSH]

Ge 21:15 she put the boy under one of the **b.** 8489
Job 30: 7 They brayed among the **b** and huddled in 8489

BUSHY (KJV) See WAVY

BUSINESS (17)

1Sa 21: 8 because the king's **b** was urgent." 1821
Est 3: 9 for the men who carry out this **b."** 4856
Ecc 4: 8 This too is meaningless—a miserable **b!** 6721
Eze 27:12 " 'Tarshish **did b with** you because 6086
27:16 " 'Aram **did b with** you because 6086
27:18 **did b with** you in wine from Helbon 6086
27:21 *they* **did b with** you in lambs, 6086
Da 8:27 Then I got up and went about the king's **b.** 4856
Zec 8:10 No one *could* **go about** *his* **b** safely 995+2256+3655
Mt 22: 5 one to his field, another to his **b.** *1865*
Jn 15:15 a servant does not know his master's **b.** *4472+5515*
Ac 19:24 brought in no little **b** for the craftsmen. *2238*
19:25 a good income from this **b.** *2238*
1Co 5:12 **What b is it of mine** to judge *1609+5515*
1Th 4:11 *to* **mind** your own **b** and to work *4556*
Jas 1:11 even while he **goes about his b.** *4512*
4:13 **carry on b** and make money." *1864*

BUSTLES (1)

Ps 39: 6 *He* **b about,** but only in vain; 2159

BUSY (6)

1Ki 18:27 Perhaps he is deep in thought, or **b,** 8485
20:40 While your servant was **b** here and there, 6913
Isa 32: 6 fool speaks folly, his mind *is* **b** *with* evil: 6913
Hag 1: 9 while each of you *is* **b** with his own house. 8132
2Th 3:11 *They are* not **b;** they are busybodies. *2237*
Tit 2: 5 to be **b at home,** to be kind, *3877*

BUSYBODY (KJV) See MEDDLER

BUSYBODIES (2)

2Th 3:11 They are not busy; *they are* **b.** *4318*
1Ti 5:13 but also gossips and **b,** *4319*

BUT (3983) See Index of Articles Etc.

BUTCHERED (4)

1Sa 14:32 they **b** them on the ground and ate them, 8821
28:24 which *she* **b** at once. 2284
Jer 12: 3 Drag them off like sheep to be **b!** 3186
Mt 22: 4 My oxen and fattened cattle *have been* **b,** *2604*

BUTLER (KJV) See CUPBEARER

BUTT (1) [BUTTING]

2Sa 2:23 the **b** *of* his spear into Asahel's stomach, 339

BUTTER (2)

Ps 55:21 His speech is smooth as **b,** 4717
Pr 30:33 For as churning the milk produces **b,** 2772

BUTTING (1) [BUTT]

Eze 34:21 **b** all the weak sheep with your horns 5590

BUTTOCKS (3)

2Sa 10: 4 in the middle at the **b,** 9268
1Ch 19: 4 in the middle at the **b,** 5156
Isa 20: 4 with **b** bared—to Egypt's shame. 9268

BUY (54) [BOUGHT, BUYER, BUYERS, BUYING, BUYS]

Ge 41:57 the countries came to Egypt to **b grain** 8690
42: 2 Go down there and **b** some for us, 8690
42: 3 of Joseph's brothers went down to **b** grain 8690
42: 5 among those who went to **b grain,** 8690
42: 7 they replied, "to **b** food." 8690
42:10 "Your servants have come to **b** food. 8690
43: 2 "Go back and **b** us a little more food." 8690
43: 4 we will go down and **b** food for you. 8690
43:20 down here the first time to **b** food. 8690
43:22 with us to **b** food. 8690
44:25 'Go back and **b** a little more food.' 8690
47:19 **B** us and our land in exchange for food, 7864
47:22 *he did* not **b** the land of the priests, 7864
Ex 21: 2 "If *you* **b** a Hebrew servant, 7864
Lev 25:14 of your countrymen or **b** any from him, 7864
25:15 *to* **b** from your countryman on the basis of 7864
25:44 from them *you may* **b** slaves. 7864
25:45 *You may* also **b** some of 7864
27:27 *he may* **b back** at its set value, 7009
Dt 14:26 *Use* the silver *to* **b** whatever you like: 5989
28:68 but no *one will* **b** you. 7864
Ru 4: 4 to your attention and suggest that *you* **b** it 7864
4: 5 "On the day you **b** the land from Naomi 7864
4: 8 to Boaz, **"B** it yourself." 7864
2Sa 24:21 "To **b** your threshing floor," 7864
Ezr 7:17 With this money be sure *to* **b** bulls, 10632
Ne 10:31 *we will* not **b** from them on the Sabbath or 4374
Pr 23:23 **B** the truth and do not sell it; 7864
Isa 55: 1 you who have no money, come, **b** and eat! 8690
55: 1 **b** wine and milk without money and 8690
Jer 13: 1 "Go and **b** a linen belt and put it 7864
19: 1 "Go and **b** a clay jar from a potter. 7864
32: 7 **'B** my field at Anathoth, 7864
32: 7 and duty to **b** it.' 7864
32: 8 **'B** my field at Anathoth in the territory 7864
32: 8 **b** it for yourself.' 7864
32:25 **'B** the field with silver and have 7864
La 5: 4 We must **b** the water we drink; 928+4084

Mt 14:15 the villages and **b** themselves some food." *60*
25: 9 go to those who sell oil and **b** some *60*
25:10 while they were on their way *to* **b** the oil, *60*
27: 7 to use the money to **b** the potter's field as *60*
27:10 and *they* used them to **b** the potter's field, *1443*
Mk 6:36 and villages and **b** themselves something *60*
Lk 9:13 unless we go and **b** food for all this crowd." *60*
22:36 sell your cloak and **b** one. *60*
Jn 4: 8 into the town to **b** food.) *60*
6: 5 *shall we* **b** bread for these people to eat?" *60*
6: 7 not **b** enough bread for each one to have *NIG*
13:29 *to* **b** what was needed for the Feast, *60*
Ac 8:20 because you thought *you could* **b** the gift *3227*
1Co 7:30 those who **b** something, *60*
Rev 3:18 I counsel you *to* **b** from me gold refined in *60*
13:17 so that no one could **b** or sell unless he had *60*

BUYER (6) [BUY]

Lev 25:28 in the possession of the **b** until the Year 7864
25:30 to the **b** and his descendants. 7864
25:50 He and his **b** are to count the time from 7864
Pr 20:14 it's no good!" says the **b**; 7864
Isa 24: 2 for mistress as for maid, for seller as for **b**, 7864
Eze 7:12 Let not the **b** rejoice nor the seller grieve, 7864

BUYERS (1) [BUY]

Zec 11: 5 Their **b** slaughter them and go unpunished. 7864

BUYING (5) [BUY]

Ge 47:14 in payment for the grain they *were* **b**, 8690
Am 8: 6 **b** the poor with silver and the needy for 7864
Mt 21:12 and drove out all who *were* **b** *4797*
Mk 11:15 and began driving out those who *were* **b** *4797*
Lk 17:28 **b** and selling, planting and building. *60*

BUYS (3) [BUY]

Lev 22:11 But if a priest **b** a slave *with* money, 7864+7871
Pr 31:16 She considers a field and **b** it; 4374
Rev 18:11 because no one **b** their cargoes any more— *60*

BUZ (3) [BUZITE]

Ge 22:21 **B** his brother, Kemuel (the father of Aram), 998
1Ch 5:14 the son of Jahdo, the son of **B**. 998
Jer 25:23 Tema, **B** and all who are in distant places; 998

BUZI (1)

Eze 1: 3 Ezekiel the priest, the son of **B**, 1001

BUZITE (2) [BUZ]

Job 32: 2 But Elihu son of Barakel the **B**, 1000
32: 6 So Elihu son of Barakel the **B** said: 1000

BY (2431) See Index of Articles Etc.

BYPATHS (1) [PATH]

Jer 18:15 They made them walk in **b** and on roads 5986

BYWORD (9) [WORD]

1Ki 9: 7 then become a **b** and an object of ridicule 5442
2Ch 7:20 I will make it a **b** and an object of ridicule 5442
Job 17: 6 "God has made me a **b** to everyone, 5439
30: 9 I have become a **b** among them. 4863
Ps 44:14 You have made us a **b** among the nations; 5442
Jer 24: 9 a reproach and a **b**, 5442
Eze 14: 8 and make him an example and a **b**. 5442
23:10 She became a **b** among women, 9005
Joel 2:17 a **b** among the nations. 5442

C

CAB (1)

2Ki 6:25 quarter of a **c** *of* seed pods for five shekels. 7685

CABBON (1)

Jos 15:40 **C**, Lahmas, Kitlish, 3887

CABINS (KJV) See VAULTED CELL

CABUL (2)

Jos 19:27 passing **C** on the left. 3886
1Ki 9:13 And he called them the Land of **C**, 3886

CAESAR (20) [CAESAR'S]

Mt 22:17 Is it right to pay taxes *to* **C** or not?" *2790*
22:21 "Give *to* **C** what is Caesar's, *2790*
Mk 12:14 Is it right to pay taxes *to* **C** or not? *2790*
12:17 "Give *to* **C** what is Caesar's and *2790*
Lk 2: 1 In those days **C** Augustus issued a decree *2790*
3: 1 fifteenth year of the reign *of* Tiberius **C**— *2790*
Lk 20:22 Is it right for us to pay taxes *to* **C** or not?" *2790*
20:25 "Then give *to* **C** what is Caesar's, *2790*
23: 2 of taxes *to* **C** and claims to be Christ, *2790*
Jn 19:12 you are no friend *of* **C**. *2790*
19:12 to be a king opposes **C**." *2790*
19:15 "We have no king but **C**," *2790*
Ac 25: 8 Jews or against the temple or against **C**." *2790*
25:11 I appeal to **C**!" *2790*
25:12 "You have appealed *to* **C**. *2790*
25:12 To **C** you will go!" *2790*
25:21 until I could send him to **C**." *2790*
26:32 if he had not appealed to **C**." *2790*
27:24 You must stand trial before **C**; *2790*
28:19 I was compelled to appeal to **C**— *2790*

CAESAR'S (9) [CAESAR]

Mt 22:21 "**C**," they replied. *2790*
22:21 "Give to Caesar what is **C**, *2790*
Mk 12:16 "**C**," they replied. *2790*
12:17 "Give to Caesar what *is* **C** and *2790*
Lk 20:25 "**C**," they replied. *2790*
20:25 "Then give to Caesar what *is* **C**, *2790*
Ac 17: 7 They are all defying **C** decrees, *2790*
25:10 "I am now standing before **C** court, *2790*
Php 4:22 especially those who belong to **C** household *2790*

CAESAREA (19)

Mt 16:13 to the region *of* **C** Philippi, *2791*
Mk 8:27 on to the villages around **C** Philippi. *2791*
Ac 8:40 in all the towns until he reached **C**. *2791*
9:30 they took him down to **C** and sent him off *2791*
10: 1 At **C** there was a man named Cornelius, *2791*
10:24 The following day he arrived in **C**. *2791*
11:11 to me from **C** stopped at the house *2791*
12:19 from Judea to **C** and stayed there a while. *2791*
18:22 When he landed at **C**, *2791*
21: 8 we reached **C** and stayed at the house *2791*
21:16 from **C** accompanied us and brought us to *2791*
23:23 and two hundred spearmen to go to **C** *2791*
23:33 When the cavalry arrived in **C**, *2791*
24: 1 the high priest Ananias went down to **C** *NIG*
25: 1 Festus went up from **C** to Jerusalem, *2791*
25: 4 Festus answered, "Paul is being held at **C**, *2791*
25: 6 he went down to **C**, *2791*
25:13 at **C** to pay their respects to Festus. *2791*
25:24 about him in Jerusalem and here in **C**, *NIG*

CAGE (1) [CAGES]

Eze 19: 9 With hooks they pulled him into a **c** 6050

CAGES (1) [CAGE]

Jer 5:27 Like **c** full of birds, 3990

CAIAPHAS (9)

Mt 26: 3 high priest, whose name was **C**, *2780*
26:57 to **C**, the high priest, where the teachers of *2780*
Lk 3: 2 during the high priesthood of Annas and **C**, *2780*
Jn 11:49 Then one of them, named **C**, *2780*
18:13 who was the father-in-law *of* **C**, *2780*
18:14 **C** was the one who had advised the Jews *2780*
18:24 still bound, to **C** the high priest. *2780*
18:28 the Jews led Jesus from **C** to the palace of *2780*
Ac 4: 6 and so were **C**, John, Alexander *2780*

CAIN (20)

Ge 4: 1 she became pregnant and gave birth to **C**. 7803
4: 2 Abel kept flocks, and **C** worked the soil. 7803
4: 3 In the course of time **C** brought some of 7803
4: 5 but on **C** and his offering he did not look 7803
4: 5 So **C** was very angry, 7803
4: 6 LORD said to **C**, "Why are you angry? 7803
4: 8 Now **C** said to his brother Abel, 7803
4: 8 **C** attacked his brother Abel and killed him. 7803
4: 9 Then the LORD said to **C**, 7803
4:13 **C** said to the LORD, 7803
4:15 if anyone kills **C**, 7803
4:15 Then the LORD put a mark on **C** so 7803
4:16 So **C** went out from the LORD's presence 7803
4:17 **C** lay with his wife, 7803
4:17 **C** was then building a city, NIH
4:24 If **C** is avenged seven times, 7803
4:25 since **C** killed him." 7803
Heb 11: 4 a better sacrifice than **C** did. *2782*
1Jn 3:12 Do not be like **C**, *2782*
Jude 1:11 They have taken the way *of* **C**; *2782*

CAINAN (1)

Lk 3:36 the son *of* **C**, *2783*

CAKE (13) [CAKES]

Ex 29:23 and a **c** *made with* oil, and a wafer. 2705+4312
Lev 8:26 he took a **c** *of* bread, 2705
Nu 6:19 and a **c** and a wafer from the basket, 2705
15:20 a **c** from the first of your ground meal 2705
1Sa 30:12 a **c of pressed figs** and two cakes of raisins. 1811
2Sa 6:19 a **c of dates** and a cake of raisins 882
6:19 of dates and a **c of raisins** to each person in 862
1Ki 17:13 But first make a small **c of bread** for me 6314
19: 6 by his head was a **c of bread** baked 6314
1Ch 16: 3 a **c of dates** and a cake of raisins 882
16: 3 and a **c of raisins** to each Israelite man 862
Eze 4:12 Eat the food as you would a barley **c**; 6314
Hos 7: 8 Ephraim is a **flat c** not turned over. 6314

CAKES (19) [CAKE]

Ex 12:39 they baked **c** *of* unleavened bread. 6314
29: 2 make bread, and **c** mixed with oil, 2705
Lev 2: 4 **c** *made* without yeast and mixed with oil, 2705
7:12 with this thank offering he is to offer **c** 2705
7:12 and **c** *of* fine flour well-kneaded and mixed 2705
7:13 to present an offering with **c** *of* bread made 2705
Nu 6:15 **c** *made of* fine flour mixed with oil, 2705
11: 8 They cooked it in a pot or made it into **c**. 6314
1Sa 25:18 a hundred **c of raisins** 7540
25:18 and two hundred **c of pressed figs**, 1811
30:12 a cake of pressed figs and two **c of raisins**. 7540
2Sa 16: 1 a hundred **c of raisins**, 7540
16: 1 a hundred **c of figs** and a skin of wine. 7811
1Ki 14: 3 *some* **c** and a jar of honey, and go to him. 5926
1Ch 12:40 **fig c**, raisin cakes, wine, oil, 1811
12:40 **raisin c**, wine, oil, cattle and sheep, 7540
Jer 7:18 and make **c of bread** for the Queen 3924
44:19 that we were making **c** like her image 3924
Hos 3: 1 to other gods and love the **sacred** raisin **c**." 862

CALAH (2)

Ge 10:11 where he built Nineveh, Rehoboth Ir, **C** 3996
10:12 which is between Nineveh and **C**; 3996

CALAMITIES (8) [CALAMITY]

Dt 29:22 the **c** that have fallen on the land and 4804
32:23 "I will heap **c** upon them 8288
1Sa 10:19 who saves you out of all your **c** 8288
2Sa 19: 7 This will be worse for you than all the **c** 8288
Job 5:19 From six **c** he will rescue you; 7650
Pr 24:22 and who knows what **c** they can bring? 7085
Isa 51:19 These double **c** have come upon you— NIH
La 3:38 the mouth of the Most High that both **c** 8288

CALAMITY (29) [CALAMITIES]

2Sa 12:11 to bring **c** upon you. 8288
24:16 the LORD was grieved because of the **c** 8288
1Ch 21:15 and was grieved because of the **c** and said 8288
2Ch 20: 9 'If **c** comes upon us, 8288
Ne 13:18 that our God brought all this **c** upon us and 8288
Job 18:12 **C** is hungry for him; 224
21:17 How often does **c** come upon them, 369
21:30 the evil man is spared from the day of **c**, 369
Ps 107:39 and they were humbled by oppression, **c** 8288
Pr 1:26 I will mock when **c** overtakes you— 7065
1:27 when **c** overtakes you like a storm, 7065
14:32 When **c** comes, the wicked are brought 8288
21:23 and his tongue keeps himself from **c**. 7650
24:16 but the wicked are brought down by **c**. 8288
Isa 47:11 A **c** will fall upon you 2096
Jer 14:16 I will pour out on them the **c** they *deserve*. 8288
32:42 As I have brought all this great **c** 8288
48:16 her **c** will come quickly. 8288
Eze 6:10 not threaten in vain to bring this **c** on them. 8288
7:26 **C** upon calamity will come, 2096
7:26 Calamity upon **c** will come, 2096
35: 5 over to the sword at the time of their **c**, 369
Joel 2:13 and he relents from sending **c**. 8288
Ob 1:13 nor look down on them in their **c** in the day 8288
Jnh 1: 7 to find out who is responsible for this **c**." 8288
4: 2 a God who relents from sending **c**. 8288
Mic 2: 3 for it will be a time of **c**. 8288
Hab 3:16 Yet I will wait patiently for the day of **c** 7650
Zec 1:15 but they added to the **c**.' 8288

CALAMUS (4)

SS 4:14 **c** and cinnamon, with every kind 7866
Isa 43:24 You have not bought *any* **fragrant c** 7866
Jer 6:20 from Sheba or sweet **c** from a distant land? 7866
Eze 27:19 cassia and **c** for your wares. 7866

CALCOL (2)

1Ki 4:31 wiser than Heman, **C** and Darda, 4004
1Ch 2: 6 Zimri, Ethan, Heman, **C** and Darda— 4004

CALCULATE (1) [CALCULATED]

Rev 13:18 *let him* **c** the number of the beast, *6028*

CALCULATED (1) [CALCULATE]

Ac 19:19 When *they* **c** the value of the scrolls, *5248*

CALDRON (2) [CALDRONS]

1Sa 2:14 into the pan or kettle or **c** or pot, 7831
Job 41:31 He makes the depths churn like a boiling **c** 6105

CALDRONS (1) [CALDRON]

2Ch 35:13 **c** and pans and served them quickly to all 1857

CALEB (33) [CALEB EPHRATHAH, CALEB'S, CALEBITE]

Nu 13: 6 **C** son of Jephunneh; 3979
13:30 Then **C** silenced the people before Moses 3979
14: 6 of Nun and **C** son of Jephunneh, 3979
14:24 because my servant **C** has a different spirit 3979
14:30 except **C** son of Jephunneh and Joshua son 3979
14:38 of Nun and **C** son of Jephunneh survived. 3979

Nu 26:65 and not one of them was left except **C** son 3979
32:12 not one except **C** son of Jephunneh 3979
34:19 These are their names: **C** son of Jephunneh, 3979
Dt 1:36 except **C** son of Jephunneh. 3979
Jos 14:6 and **C** son of Jephunneh the Kenizzite said 3979
14:13 Then Joshua blessed **C** son of Jephunneh 3979
14:14 to **C** son of Jephunneh the Kenizzite ever 3979
15:13 to **C** son of Jephunneh a portion in Judah— 3979
15:14 From Hebron **C** drove out 3979
15:16 And **C** said, "I will give my daughter Acsah in marriage 3979
15:17 so **C** gave his daughter Acsah to him NIH
15:18 When she got off her donkey, **C** asked her, 3979
15:19 So **C** gave her the upper and lower springs. NIH
21:12 to **C** son of Jephunneh as his possession. 3979
Jdg 1:12 And **C** said, "I will give my daughter Acsah in marriage 3979
1:13 so **C** gave his daughter Acsah to him NIH
1:14 When she got off her donkey, **C** asked her, 3979
1:15 **C** gave her the upper and lower springs. 3979
1:20 Hebron was given to **C**, 3979
1Sa 30:14 to Judah and the Negev of **C**. 3979
1Ch 2:9 Jerahmeel, Ram and **C**. 3992
2:18 **C** son of Hezron had children 3979
2:19 When Azubah died, **C** married Ephrath, 3979
2:42 The sons of **C** the brother of Jerahmeel: 3979
2:50 These were the descendants of **C**. 3979
4:15 The sons of **C** son of Jephunneh: 3979
6:56 the city were given to **C** son of Jephunneh. 3979

CALEB EPHRATHAH (1) [CALEB, EPHRATHAH]

1Ch 2:24 After Hezron died in **C**, 3980

CALEB'S (6) [CALEB]

Jos 15:17 Othniel son of Kenaz, **C** brother, took it; 3979
Jdg 1:13 Othniel son of Kenaz, **C** younger brother, 3979
3:9 Othniel son of Kenaz, **C** younger brother, 3979
1Ch 2:46 **C** concubine Ephah was the mother 3979
2:48 **C** concubine Maacah was the mother 3979
2:49 **C** daughter was Acsah. 3979

CALEBITE (1) [CALEB]

1Sa 25:3 a **C**, was surly and mean in his dealings. 3982

CALF (33) [CALF-IDOL, CALF-IDOLS, CALVE, CALVED, CALVES]

Ge 18:7 tender **c** and gave it to a servant, 1201+1330
18:8 milk and the **c** that had been prepared, 1201+1330
Ex 32:4 into an idol cast in the **shape of a c**, 6319
32:5 an altar in front of **the c** and announced, 2257[S]
32:8 an idol cast in the **shape of a c**. 6319
32:19 the camp and saw the **c** and the dancing, 6319
32:20 the **c** they had made and burned it in 6319
32:24 and out came this **c**!" 6319
32:35 with the **c** Aaron had made. 6319
Lev 9:2 "Take a bull **c** for your sin offering and 6319
9:3 a sin offering, a **c** and a lamb— 6319
9:8 and slaughtered the **c** as a sin offering 6319
22:27 a **c**, a lamb or a goat is born, it is to remain 8802
Dt 9:16 an idol cast in the **shape of a c**. 6319
9:21 the **c** you had made, 6319
1Sa 28:24 The woman had a fattened **c** at the house, 6319
2Sa 6:13 he sacrificed a bull and a **fattened c**. 5309
2Ch 11:15 and for the goat and **c** idols he had made. 6319
Ne 9:18 for themselves an image of a **c** and said, 6319
Ps 29:6 He makes Lebanon skip like a **c**, 6319
106:19 a **c** and worshiped an idol cast from metal. 6319
Pr 15:17 where there is love than a fattened **c** 8802
Isa 11:6 the **c** and the lion and the yearling together; 6319
Jer 31:18 'You disciplined me like an unruly **c**, 6319
34:18 like the **c** they cut in two and then walked 6319
34:19 between the pieces of the **c**, 6319
Eze 1:7 of a **c** and gleamed like burnished bronze. 6319
Hos 8:6 They are from Israel! This **c**— NIH
8:6 that **c** *of* Samaria. 6319
Lk 15:23 Bring the fattened **c** and kill it. *3675*
15:27 the fattened **c** because he has him back safe *3675*
15:30 you kill the fattened **c** for him!' *3675*
Ac 7:41 **made** an idol **in the form of a c**. *3674*

CALF-IDOL (2) [CALF, IDOL]

Hos 8:5 Throw out your **c**, O Samaria! 6319
10:5 in Samaria fear for the **c** *of* Beth Aven. 6319

CALF-IDOLS (1) [CALF, IDOL]

Hos 13:2 "They offer human sacrifice and kiss the **c**." 6319

CALL (192) [CALLED, CALLING, CALLS, SO-CALLED]

Ge 4:26 At that time men began to **c** on the name of 7924
17:15 *you are* no longer *to* **c** her Sarai; 7924+9005
17:19 and *you will* **c** him Isaac. 7924+9005
24:57 *"Let's* **c** the girl and ask her about it." 7924
30:13 The women *will* **c** me **happy.**" 887
Dt 3:9 the Amorites **c** it Senir.) 7924
4:26 **c** heaven and earth **as witnesses** 6386
18:19 *I* myself *will* **c** him **to account.** 2011+4946+6640
30:19 **c** heaven and earth **as witnesses** 6386
31:14 **C** Joshua and present yourselves at 7924
31:28 **c** heaven and earth **to testify** 6386
Jos 22:23 *may* the LORD himself **c** us **to account.** 1335
Jdg 8:1 Why didn't *you* **c** us when you went 7924
9:29 '**C out** your whole army!' " 3655
Ru 1:20 "Don't **c** me Naomi," she told them. 7924
1:20 "**C** me Mara, because the Almighty has made my life very bitter. 7924
1:21 Why **c** me Naomi? 7924
1Sa 3:5 But Eli said, *"I did* not **c**; 7924
3:6 "My son," Eli said, *"I did* not **c**; 7924
12:17 *I will* **c** upon the LORD to send thunder 7924
20:16 **c** David's enemies **to account."** 1335+3338+4946
23:28 That is why *they* **c** this place Sela Hammahlekoth. 7924
2Sa 15:2 Absalom *would* **c out** to him, 7924
22:4 *I* **c** *to* the LORD, 7924
1Ki 1:28 Then King David said, "**C in** Bathsheba." 7924
1:32 King David said, "**C in** Zadok the priest, 7924
18:24 Then *you* **c** on the name of your god, 7924
18:24 and I *will* **c** on the name of the LORD. 7924
18:25 **C** on the name of your god, 7924
2Ki 4:12 to his servant Gehazi, "**C** 7924
4:15 Then Elisha said, "**C** her." 7924
4:36 and said, "**C** the Shunammite." 7924
5:11 and **c** on the name of the LORD his God, 7924
10:20 "**C** an assembly **in honor of** 4200+7727
1Ch 16:8 **c** on his name; 7924
2Ch 24:22 the LORD see this and **c** you **to account."** 2011
Ne 13:2 but had hired Balaam to **c a curse down** 7837
Job 5:1 "**C** if you will, but who will answer you? 7924
14:15 *You will* **c** and I will answer you; 7924
19:7 though *I* **c for help,** there is no justice. 8775
27:10 *Will he* **c upon** God at all times? 7924
Ps 4:1 Answer me when I **c** to you, 7924
4:3 the LORD will hear when I **c** to him. 7924
10:13 *"He* won't **c** me **to account"?** 2011
10:15 **c** him **to account** *for* his wickedness 2011
14:4 as men eat bread and *who do* not **c on** 7924
17:6 I **c on** you, O God, for you will answer me; 7924
18:3 *I* **c** *to* the LORD, 7924
20:9 Answer us when we **c**! 7924
27:7 Hear my voice *when I* **c**, O LORD; 7924
28:1 To you *I* **c**, O LORD my Rock; 7924
28:2 **c** to you **for help,** 8775
50:15 and **c upon** me in the day of trouble; 7924
53:4 as men eat bread and *who do* not **c on** God? 7924
55:16 But I **c** to God, and the LORD saves me. 7924
56:9 when *I* **c for help.** 7924
61:2 From the ends of the earth *I* **c** to you, 7924
61:2 I **c** as my heart grows faint; NIH
65:8 **c forth songs of joy.** 8264
72:17 and *they will* **c** him **blessed.** 887
79:6 the kingdoms that *do* not **c** on your name; 7924
80:18 revive us, and *we will* **c** on your name. 7924
86:3 O Lord, for *I* **c** to you all day long. 7924
86:5 abounding in love to all *who* **c** *to* you. 7924
86:7 In the day of my trouble *I will* **c** to you, 7924
88:9 *I* **c** *to* you, O LORD, every day; 7924
89:26 He *will* **c out** *to* me, 'You are my Father, 7924
91:15 *He will* **c upon** me, and I will answer him; 7924
102:2 when *I* **c**, answer me quickly. 7924
105:1 Give thanks to the LORD, **c** on his name; 7924
116:2 *I will* **c** *on* him as long as I live. 7924
116:13 up the cup of salvation and **c** on the name 7924
116:17 a thank offering to you and **c** on the name 7924
119:145 *I* **c** with all my heart; 7924
119:146 *I* **c out** *to* you; 7924
120:1 *I* **c** on the LORD in my distress, 7924
141:1 O LORD, *I* **c** *to* you; 7924
141:1 Hear my voice when I **c** to you. 7924
145:18 The LORD is near to all *who* **c** *on* him, 7924
145:18 to all who **c** *on* him in truth. 7924
147:9 and for the young ravens when *they* **c**. 7924
Pr 1:28 *they will* **c** *to* me but I will not answer; 7924
2:3 and if *you* **c out** for insight and cry aloud 7924
7:4 and **c** understanding your kinsman; 7924
8:1 *Does* not wisdom **c out?** 7924
8:4 *I* **c out;** I raise my voice to all mankind. 7924
31:28 Her children arise and **c** her **blessed;** 887
Ecc 3:15 **c** the past **to account.** 1335
Isa 5:20 Woe to those *who* **c** evil good and good evil, 606
7:14 and *will* **c** him Immanuel. 7924+9005
8:2 **c in** Uriah the priest and Zechariah son of Jeberekiah **as reliable witnesses** 6332+6386
8:12 *"Do* not **c** conspiracy everything 606
8:12 that these people **c** conspiracy; 606
12:4 "Give thanks to the LORD, **c** on his name; 7924
30:7 Therefore *I* **c** her Rahab the Do-Nothing. 7924
44:5 another *will* **c** *himself* by the name 7924
48:2 *you who* **c yourselves** citizens of 7924
54:6 The LORD *will* **c** you **back** as if you were 7924
55:6 **c** *on* him while he is near. 7924
58:5 Is that what *you* **c** a fast, 7924
58:9 *you will* **c**, and the LORD will answer; 7924
58:13 if *you* **c** the Sabbath a delight and 7924
60:14 down at your feet and *will* **c** you the City 7924
60:18 but *you will* **c** your walls Salvation 7924
62:4 No longer *will they* **c** you Deserted, 606
62:6 You who **c** on the LORD, 2349
65:1 To a nation *that did* not **c** on my name, 7924
65:24 Before *they* **c** I will answer; 7924
Jer 3:17 At that time *they will* **c** Jerusalem 7924
3:19 I thought *you would* **c** me 'Father' and 7924
7:27 when *you* **c** to them, they will not answer. 7924
7:32 when people *will* no longer **c** *it* Topheth 606
9:17 **C** for the wailing women to come; 7924
10:25 on the peoples who *do* not **c** on your name. 7924
11:14 because I will not listen when they **c** to me 7924
Jer 19:6 *people will* no longer **c** this place Topheth 7924
29:12 Then *you will* **c upon** me and come 7924
33:3 '**C** to me and I will answer you 7924
La 3:8 Even when *I* **c out** or cry for help, 2410
3:21 this I **c to mind** and therefore I have hope: 448+4213+8740
Eze 9:1 Then I heard *him* **c out** *in* a loud voice, 7924
36:29 *I will* **c** for the grain and make it plentiful 7924
39:17 **C out** to every kind of bird and all 606
Da 5:12 **C** *for* Daniel, and he will tell you what 10637
Hos 1:4 LORD said to Hosea, "**C** him Jezreel, 7924+9005
1:6 to Hosea, "**C** her Lo-Ruhamah, 7924+9005
1:9 the LORD said, "**C** him Lo-Ammi, 7924+9005
2:16 *"you will* **c** me 'my husband'; 7924
2:16 *you will* no longer **c** me 'my master.' 7924
11:7 Even *if they* **c** to the Most High, 7924
Joel 1:14 Declare a holy fast; **c** a sacred assembly. 7924
1:19 To you, O LORD, *I* **c**, 7924
2:15 declare a holy fast, **c** a sacred assembly. 7924
Jnh 1:6 Get up and **c** on your god! 7924
3:8 *Let everyone* **c** urgently on God. 7924
Hab 1:2 How long, O LORD, *must I* **c for help,** 8775
Zep 3:9 of them *may* **c** on the name of the LORD 7924
Zec 13:9 They *will* **c** on my name 7924
Mal 3:12 "Then all the nations *will* **c** you **blessed,** 887
3:15 **c** the arrogant **blessed.** 887
Mt 1:23 and *they will* **c** him Immanuel" *2813+3836+3950*
9:13 For I have not come *to* **c** the righteous, *2813*
20:8 '**C** the workers and pay them their wages, *2813*
23:7 and to have men **c** them 'Rabbi.' *2813*
23:9 And *do* not **c** anyone on earth 'father,' *2813*
24:1 to him *to* **c** his **attention to** its buildings. *2109*
24:31 with a loud **trumpet c,** *4894*
26:53 Do you think I cannot **c on** my Father, *4151*
26:74 Then he began *to* **c down curses** on himself *2874*
Mk 2:17 I have not come *to* **c** the righteous, *2813*
3:31 they sent someone in *to* **c** him. *2813*
10:18 "Why *do you* **c** me good?" *3306*
10:49 Jesus stopped and said, "**C** him." *5888*
14:71 He began *to* **c down curses** on himself, *354*
15:12 with the one *you* **c** the king of the Jews?" *3306*
15:18 And they began *to* **c out to** him, "Hail, *832*
Lk 1:48 now on all generations *will* **c** me **blessed,** *3420*
5:32 I have not come *to* **c** the righteous, *2813*
6:46 "Why *do you* **c** me, 'Lord, Lord,' *2813*
9:54 do you want *us to* **c** fire down *3306*
18:19 "Why *do you* **c** me good?" *3306*
22:25 over them **c** *themselves* Benefactors. *2813*
Jn 4:16 "Go, **c** your husband and come back." *5888*
9:11 "The man they **c** Jesus made some mud *3306*
13:13 "You **c** me 'Teacher' and 'Lord,' *5888*
15:15 *I* no longer **c** you servants, *3306*
Ac 2:39 for all whom the Lord our God *will* **c**." *4673*
9:14 from the chief priests to arrest all who **c on** *2126*
9:21 in Jerusalem among those who **c on** *2126*
10:15 *"Do* not **c** anything **impure** *3123*
10:28 that I *should* not **c** any man impure *3306*
11:9 *'Do* not **c** anything **impure** *3123*
24:14 which *they* **c** a sect. *3306*
Ro 1:5 and apostleship to **c** people from among all *NIG*
2:17 Now you, if *you* **c** *yourself* a Jew; *2226*
9:25 *"I will* **c** them 'my people' who are *2813*
9:25 and I will **c** her 'my loved one' who is *NIG*
10:12 of all and richly blesses all who **c on** him, *2126*
10:14 *can they* **c on** the one they have *2126*
11:29 for God's gifts and his **c** are irrevocable. *3104*
1Co 1:2 with all those everywhere who **c on** *2126*
14:8 if the trumpet does not sound a clear **c**, *5889*
2Co 1:23 I **c** God as my witness that it was in order *2126*
Eph 2:11 by those who **c** *themselves* *3306*
1Th 4:7 For God *did* not **c** us to be impure, *2813*
4:16 of the archangel and with the **trumpet c** *4894*
2Ti 2:22 along with those who **c on** the Lord out of *2126*
Heb 2:11 Jesus is not ashamed *to* **c** them brothers. *2813*
Jas 5:14 *He should* **c** the elders of the church to pray *4673*
1Pe 1:17 Since *you* **c on** a Father who judges each *2126*
3Jn 1:10 *I will* **c attention to** what he is doing, *5703*
Rev 8:13 an eagle that was flying in midair **c out** in *3306*

CALL (Anglicized) See also GET

CALLED (502) [CALL]

Ge 1:5 God **c** the light "day," 7924
1:5 and the darkness *he* **c** "night." 7924
1:8 God **c** the expanse "sky." 7924
1:10 God **c** the dry ground "land," 7924
1:10 and the gathered waters *he* **c** "seas." 7924
2:19 whatever the man **c** each living creature, 7924
2:23 she *shall* **be c** 'woman,' 7924
3:9 But the LORD God **c** to the man, 7924
5:2 they were created, *he* **c** them "man." 7924+9005
11:9 That is why it *was* **c** Babel— 7924+9005
12:8 an altar to the LORD and **c** on the name of 7924
13:4 There Abram **c** on the name of the LORD. 7924
14:14 *he* **c out** the 318 trained men born 8197
16:14 That is why the well *was* **c** Beer Lahai Roi; 7924
17:5 No longer *will* you **be c** Abram; 7924+9005
19:5 *They* **c** to Lot, 7924
19:22 (That is why the town *was* **c** Zoar.) 7924+9005
20:9 Then Abimelech **c** Abraham **in** and said, 7924
21:17 the angel of God **c** to Hagar from heaven 7924
21:31 So that place *was* **c** Beersheba, 7924
21:33 and there *he* **c** upon the name of 7924
22:11 But the angel of the LORD **c out** to him 7924
22:14 So Abraham **c** that place 7924+9005

Ge 22:15 of the LORD c to Abraham from heaven 7924
24:58 So *they* c Rebekah and asked her, 7924
25:30 (That is why he *was* also c Edom.) 7924+9005
26:25 Isaac built an altar there and c on the name 7924
26:33 *He* c it Shibah, 7924
27: 1 *he* c *for* Esau his older son and said to him, 7924
28: 1 So Isaac c for Jacob and blessed him 7924
28:19 *He* c that place Bethel, 7924+9005
28:19 though the city used to *be* c Luz. 9005
31:47 Laban c it Jegar Sahadutha, 7924
31:47 and Jacob c it Galeed. 7924
31:48 That is why it *was* c Galeed. 7924+9005
31:49 It was also c Mizpah, because he said, NIH
32:30 So Jacob c the place Peniel, saying, 7924+9005
33:17 That is why the place *is* c Succoth. 7924+9005
33:20 up an altar and c it El Elohe Israel. 7924
35: 7 and *he* c the place El Bethel, 7924
35:10 but you *will* no longer **be** c Jacob; 7924+9005
35:15 Jacob c the place where God had talked 7924+9005
39:14 *she* c her household servants. 7924
47:29 *he* c for his son Joseph and said to him, 7924
48:16 *May* they **be** c by my name and the names 7924
49: 1 Then Jacob c for his sons and said: 7924
50:11 near the Jordan *is* c Abel Mizraim. 7924+9005
Ex 3: 4 God c to him from within the bush, 7924
15:23 (That is why the place *is* c Marah.) 7924+9005
16:31 people of Israel c the bread manna. 7924+9005
17: 7 *he* c the place Massah and Meribah 7924+9005
17:15 altar and c it The LORD is my Banner. 7924+9005
19: 3 and the LORD c to him from the mountain 7924
19:20 of Mount Sinai and c Moses to the top of 7924
24:16 on the seventh day the LORD c to Moses 7924
34:31 But Moses c to them; 7924
Lev 1: 1 The LORD c to Moses and spoke to him 7924
Nu 1:18 c the whole community **together** 7735
11: 3 So that place *was* c Taberah, 7924+9005
13:24 That place *was* c the Valley of Eshcol 7924
32:41 and c them Havvoth Jair. 7924
32:42 and c it Nobah after himself. 7924
Dt 2:11 but the Moabites c them Emites. 7924
2:20 but the Ammonites c them Zamzummites. 7924
3: 9 (Hermon *is* c Sirion by the Sidonians; 7924
3:14 that to this day Bashan is c Havvoth Jair.) NIH
28:10 on earth will see that you *are* c *by* the name 7924
Jos 3:16 a town c Adam in the vicinity of Zarethan, NIH
4: 4 So Joshua c **together** 7924
5: 9 So the place *has been* c Gilgal to this day. 7924+9005
6: 6 So Joshua son of Nun c the priests and said 7924
7:26 Therefore that place *has been* c the Valley of Achor 7924+9005
8:16 All the men of Ai **were** c to pursue them, 2410
14:15 (Hebron used to be c Kiriath Arba 9005
15:15 in Debir (formerly c Kiriath Sepher). 9005
Jdg 1:10 in Hebron (formerly c Kiriath Arba) 9005
1:11 in Debir (formerly c Kiriath Sepher). 9005
1:17 Therefore it *was* c Hormah. 7924+9005
1:23 to spy out Bethel (formerly c Luz), 9005
1:26 where he built a city and c it Luz, 7924+9005
2: 5 and *they* c that place Bokim. 7924+9005
6:24 an altar to the LORD there and c it 7924
6:32 So that day *they* c Gideon "Jerub-Baal," 7924
7:15 to the camp of Israel and c **out,** 606
7:23 Asher and all Manasseh **were** c **out,** 7590
7:24 So all the men of Ephraim **were** c **out** 7590
9:54 Hurriedly *he* c to his armor-bearer, 7924
10: 4 which to this day *are* c Havvoth Jair. 7924
10:17 the Ammonites **were** c **to arms** and camped 7590
12: 1 The men of Ephraim c **out** their forces, 7590
12: 2 and *although I* c, 2410
12: 4 Jephthah then c **together** the men of Gilead 7695
15:17 and the place *was* c Ramath Lehi. 7924
15:19 So the spring *was* c En Hakkore, 7924+9005
16: 9 With men hidden in the room, *she* c to him, 606
16:12 with men hidden in the room, *she* c to him, 606
16:14 Again *she* c to him, "Samson, 606
16:19 *she* c a man to shave off the seven braids 7924
16:20 Then *she* c, "Samson, 606
16:25 So *they* c Samson out of the prison, 7924
18:12 of Kiriath Jearim *is* c Mahaneh Dan 7924
18:22 near Micah **were** c **together** and overtook 2410
18:23 c **out** your men **to fight?"** 2410
18:29 though the city used to be c Laish. 9005
Ru 2: 4 "The LORD bless you!" *they* c **back.** 606
1Sa 1: 2 one was c Hannah and the other Peninnah. 9005
3: 4 Then the LORD c Samuel. 7924
3: 5 "Here I am; *you* c me." 7924
3: 6 Again the LORD c, "Samuel!" 7924
3: 6 "Here I am; *you* c me." 7924
3: 8 The LORD c Samuel a third time, 7924
3: 8 "Here I am; *you* c me." 7924
3:16 but Eli c him and said, 7924
5: 8 So *they* c **together** all the rulers 665+2256+8938
5:11 So *they* c **together** all the rulers 665+2256+8938
6: 2 the Philistines c for the priests and 7924
9: 9 the prophet of today used to **be** c a seer.) 7924
9:26 about daybreak and Samuel c to Saul on 7924
12:18 Then Samuel c upon the LORD, 7924
14: 4 one was c Bozez, and the other Seneh. 9005
16: 8 Then Jesse c Abinadab and had him pass 7924
19: 7 So Jonathan c David and told him 7924
20:37 Jonathan c **out** after him, 7924
23: 8 And Saul c **up** all his forces for battle, 9048
24: 8 Then David went out of the cave and c **out** 7924
26:14 He c **out** to the army and to Abner son 7924
28:15 So *I have* c on you to tell me what to do." 7924
29: 6 So Achish c David and said to him, 7924
2Sa 1: 7 *he* c **out** to me, and I said, 'What can I do?' 7924
1:15 Then David c one of his men and said, 7924
2:16 in Gibeon *was* c Helkath Hazzurim. 7924
2:26 Abner c **out** to Joab, 7924
5: 9 up residence in the fortress and c it the City 7924
5:20 So that place *was* c Baal Perazim. 7924+9005
6: 2 which **is** c *by* the Name, 7924
6: 8 and to this day that place *is* c Perez Uzzah. 7924
9: 2 *They* c him to appear before David, 7924
13:17 *He* c his personal servant and said, 7924
18:18 it **is** c Absalom's Monument to this day. 7924
18:25 The watchman c **out** to the king 7924
18:26 and he c down to the gatekeeper, "Look, 7924
18:28 Ahimaaz c **out** to the king, "All is well!" 7924
20:16 a wise woman c from the city, 7924
22: 7 In my distress *I* c *to* the LORD; 7924
22: 7 *I* c **out** to my God. 7924
1Ki 2: 8 who c **down** bitter **curses** *on* me 7837+7839
9:13 And *he* c them the Land of Cabul, 7924
12:20 they sent and c him to the assembly 7924
17:10 *He* c to her and asked, 7924
17:11 As she was going to get it, *he* c, 7924
18:26 Then *they* c on the name of Baal 7924
20:39 the prophet c **out** to him, 7590
22: 9 So the king of Israel c one of his officials 7924
2Ki 2:24 looked at them and c **down a curse** *on* them 7837
3:10 c us three kings **together** 7924
3:13 c us three kings **together** 7924
3:21 who could bear arms **was** c **up** and stationed 7590
4:12 So *he* c her, and she stood before him. 7924
4:15 So *he* c her, and she stood in the doorway. 7924
4:22 *She* c her husband and said, 7924
7:10 and c **out** to the city gatekeepers 7924
9:17 *he* c **out,** "I see some troops coming." 606
9:32 He looked up at the window and c **out,** 606
11:14 Then Athaliah tore her robes and c **out,** 7924
18: 4 (It *was* c Nehushtan.) 7924
18:18 *They* c for the king; 7924
18:28 the commander stood and c **out** in Hebrew: 928+1524+7754+7924
20:11 Then the prophet Isaiah c upon the LORD, 7924
23: 1 the king c **together** all the elders of Judah 665+2256+8938
1Ch 4:14 It was c this because its people NIH
9:23 the house c the Tent. NIH
11: 7 and so it *was* c the City of David. 7924
13: 6 the ark that **is** c *by* the Name. 7924
13:11 and to this day that place *is* c Perez Uzzah. 7924
14:11 So that place *was* c Baal Perazim. 7924+9005
15: 4 He c **together** the descendants of Aaron 665
21:26 *He* c on the LORD, 7924
22: 6 Then *he* c for his son Solomon 7924
2Ch 7:14 who **are** c *by* my name, 7924
14:11 Asa c to the LORD his God and said, 7924
18: 8 So the king of Israel c one of his officials 7924
20:26 is why it *is* c the Valley of Beracah 7924+9005
24: 5 *He* c **together** the priests and Levites 7695
25: 5 c the people of Judah **together** 7695
32:18 Then *they* c **out** in Hebrew to the people 928+1524+7754+7924
34:29 the king c **together** all the elders of Judah 665+2256+8938
Ezr 2:61 of Barzillai the Gileadite and **was** c by 7924
Ne 5: 7 So *I* c **together** a large meeting to deal 5989
7:63 of Barzillai the Gileadite and **was** c by 7924
9: 4 *who* c with loud voices to 2410
13:11 Then *I* c them **together** and stationed them 7695
13:25 I rebuked them and c **curses down** *on* them. 7837
Est 4:11 But thirty days have passed since I **was** c 7924
9:26 (Therefore these days *were* c Purim, 7924
Job 12: 4 though *I* c upon God and he answered— 7924
31:14 What will I answer when c **to account?** 7212
Ps 18: 6 In my distress *I* c *to* the LORD; 7924
30: 2 c to you **for help** 8775
30: 8 To you, O LORD, *I* c; 7924
31:22 c to you **for help.** 8775
34: 6 This poor man c, and 7924
81: 7 In your distress *you* c and I rescued you, 7924
99: 6 among *those who* c *on* his name; 7924
99: 6 *they* c on the LORD 7924
105:16 *He* c **down** famine on the land 7924
116: 4 Then *I* c on the name of the LORD: 7924
138: 3 When *I* c, you answered me; 7924
Pr 1:24 But since you rejected me *when I* c 7924
16:21 The wise in heart **are** c discerning, 7924
SS 5: 6 *I* c him but he did not answer. 7924
6: 9 The maidens saw her and c her **blessed;** 887
Isa 1:26 Afterward you *will* **be** c the City 7924
4: 1 only *let* us **be** c *by* your name. 7924
4: 3 who remain in Jerusalem, *will* **be** c holy, 606
9: 6 And he *will* **be** c Wonderful Counselor 7924+9005
19:18 of them *will* **be** c the City of Destruction. 606
22:12 c you on that day to weep and to wail, 7924
31: 4 of shepherds **is** c **together** against him, he is 7924
32: 5 No longer *will* the fool **be** c noble nor 7924
34:12 Her nobles will have nothing there *to be* c 7924
35: 8 it *will* **be** c the Way of Holiness. 7924
36:13 the commander stood and c **out** in Hebrew, 928+1524+7754+7924
41: 9 from its farthest corners *I* c you. 7924
42: 6 the LORD, *have* c you in righteousness; 7924
43: 7 everyone who **is** c by my name, 7924
43:22 "Yet *you have* not c *upon* me, O Jacob, 7924
47: 1 No more *will* you *be* c tender or delicate. 7924
47: 5 no more *will* you *be* c queen of kingdoms. 7924
48: 1 you who **are** c by the name of Israel 7924
48: 8 you **were** c a rebel from birth. 7924
Isa 48:12 O Jacob, Israel, *whom I have* c: 7924
48:15 I, even I, have spoken; yes, *I have* c him. 7924
49: 1 Before I was born the LORD c me; 7924
50: 2 *I* c, why was there no one to answer? 7924
51: 2 When *I* c him he was but one, 7924
54: 5 *he* **is** c the God of all the earth. 7924
56: 7 for my house *will* **be** c a house of prayer 7924
58:12 you *will be* c Repairer of Broken Walls, 7924
61: 3 They *will* **be** c oaks of righteousness, 7924
61: 6 And you *will* **be** c priests of the LORD, 7924
62: 2 you *will* **be** c *by* a new name that 7924
62: 4 But you *will* **be** c Hephzibah, 7924
62:12 They *will be* c the Holy People, 7924
62:12 and you *will* **be** c Sought After, 7924
63:19 they *have* not **been** c *by* your name. 7924
65:12 for *I* c but you did not answer, 7924
66: 4 For *when I* c, no one answered, 7924
Jer 3: 4 *Have you* not just c to me: 7924
6:30 They *are* c rejected silver, 7924
7:13 *I* c you, but you did not answer. 7924
11:16 The LORD c you a thriving olive tree 7924+9005
23: 6 This is the name by which he *will be* c: 7924
30:17 'because you *are* c an outcast, 7924
33:16 This is the name by which it *will be* c: 7924
35:17 *I* c to them, but they did not answer.' " 7924
36: 4 So Jeremiah c Baruch son of Neriah, 7924
42: 8 So *he* c **together** Johanan son of Kareah 7924
La 1:19 "*I* c to my allies but they betrayed me. 7924
2:15 the city that *was* c the perfection of beauty, 606
3:55 *I* c *on* your name, O LORD, 7924
3:57 You came near when *I* c you, 7924
Eze 9: 3 Then the LORD c to the man clothed 7924
10:13 the wheels **being** c "the whirling wheels." 7924
20:29 (It **is** c Bamah to this day.) 7924+9005
38: 8 After many days *you will* **be** c **to arms.** 7212
39:11 So *it will* be c the Valley of Hamon Gog. 7924
39:16 (Also a town c Hamonah will be there.) 9005
Da 2:26 king asked Daniel (also c Belteshazzar), 10721
4: 8 (He is c Belteshazzar, 10721
4:14 *He* c in a loud voice: 10637
4:19 (also c Belteshazzar) was greatly perplexed 10721
5: 7 The king c **out** for the enchanters, 10637
5:12 whom the king c Belteshazzar, 10682+10721
6:20 he c to Daniel in an anguished voice, 10237
10: 1 to Daniel (who **was** c Belteshazzar). 7924+9005
Hos 1:10 they *will* **be** c 'sons of the living God.' 606
2:23 to the one I c 'Not my loved one.' NIH
2:23 I will say to those c 'Not my people,' NIH
11: 1 I loved him, and out of Egypt *I* c my son. 7924
11: 2 But the more *I* c Israel, 7924
Jnh 2: 2 He said: "In my distress *I* c to the LORD, 7924
2: 2 From the depths of the grave *I* c **for help,** 8775
Hab 3: 9 *you* c *for* many arrows. 606
Hag 1:11 *I* c *for* a drought on the fields and 7924
Zec 6: 8 Then *he* c to me, "Look, 2410
7:13 " 'When *I* c, they did not listen; 7924
7:13 so *when they* c, I would not listen,' 7924
8: 3 Jerusalem *will* **be** c the City of Truth, 7924
8: 3 of the LORD Almighty will be c NIH
11: 7 Then I took two staffs and c one Favor and 7924
11:10 Then I took my staff c Favor and broke it, NIH
11:14 Then I broke my second staff c Union, NIH
Mal 1: 4 They *will be* c the Wicked Land, 7924
2: 5 this c for reverence and he revered me NIH
Mt 1:16 of whom was born Jesus, who *is* c Christ. *3306*
2: 4 *When* he *had* c **together** all *5251*
2: 7 Then Herod c the Magi secretly *2813*
2:15 "Out of Egypt *I* c my son." *2813*
2:23 he went and lived in a town c Nazareth. *3306*
2:23 *"He will be* c a Nazarene." *2813*
4:18 Simon c Peter and his brother Andrew. *3306*
4:21 preparing their nets. Jesus c them, *2813*
5: 9 for they *will be* c sons of God. *2813*
5:19 the same *will be* c least in the kingdom *2813*
5:19 *be* c great in the kingdom of heaven. *2813*
10: 1 c his twelve disciples **to** him *4673*
10: 2 first, Simon (who *is* c Peter) *3306*
10:25 head of the house has been c Beelzebub, *2126*
15:10 Jesus c the crowd *to him* and said, *4673*
15:32 Jesus c his disciples **to** him and said, *4673*
18: 2 He c a little child and had him stand *4673*
18:32 "Then the master c the servant **in.** *4673*
20:25 Jesus c them **together** and said, *4673*
20:32 Jesus stopped and c them. *5888*
21:13 " 'My house *will be* c a house of prayer,' *2813*
23: 8 "But you *are* not *to be* c 'Rabbi,' *2813*
23:10 Nor *are you to be* c 'teacher,' *2813*
25:14 who c his servants *2813*
26:14 the one c Judas Iscariot— *3306*
26:36 with his disciples to a place c Gethsemane, *3306*
27: 8 That is why it *has been* c the Field *2813*
27:16 a notorious prisoner, c Barabbas. *3306*
27:17 Barabbas, or Jesus who *is* c Christ?" *3306*
27:22 then, with Jesus who *is* c Christ?" *3306*
27:33 to a place c Golgotha (which means *3306*
Mk 1:20 Without delay *he* c them, *2813*
3:13 Jesus went up on a mountainside and c **to** *4673*
3:23 So Jesus c them and spoke to them *4673*
7:14 Again Jesus c the crowd **to** *him* and said, *4673*
8: 1 Jesus c his disciples **to** *him* and said, *4673*
8:34 Then he c the crowd **to** him along *4673*
9:35 Sitting down, Jesus c the Twelve and said, *5888*
10:42 Jesus c them **together** and said, *4673*
10:49 So *they* c **to** the blind man, "Cheer up! *5888*
11:17 " 'My house *will be* c a house of prayer *2813*
14:32 went to a place c Gethsemane, *3836+3950+4005*
15: 7 A man c Barabbas was in prison with *3306*

Mk 15:16 and **c together** the whole company *5157*
15:22 to the place **c** Golgotha (which means *NIG*
Lk 1:32 He will be great and *will be* **c** the Son of *2813*
1:35 the holy one to be born *will be* **c** the Son *2813*
1:60 *He is to be* **c** John." *2813*
1:76 *will be* **c** a prophet of the Most High; *2813*
2:25 was a man in Jerusalem **c** Simeon, *3950+4005*
6:13 *he* **c** his disciples **to** *him* and chose twelve *4715*
6:15 Simon who *was* **c** the Zealot, *2813*
7:11 Jesus went to a town **c** Nain, *2813*
8: 2 Mary (**c** Magdalene) from whom seven demons had come out; *2813*
8: 8 When he said this, *he* **c out,** *5888*
9: 1 **c** the Twelve **together,** *5157*
9:10 by themselves to a town **c** Bethsaida, *2813*
9:38 A man in the crowd **c out,** "Teacher, *1066*
10:39 She had a sister **c** Mary, *2813*
11:27 a woman in the crowd **c out,** *2048+5889*
13:12 *he* **c** her **forward** and said to her, "Woman, *4715*
15:19 I am no longer worthy *to be* **c** your son; *2813*
15:21 I am no longer worthy *to be* **c** your son.' *2813*
15:26 So he **c** one of the servants *4673*
16: 2 So he **c** him **in** and asked him, *5888*
16: 5 *he* **c in** each one of his master's debtors. *4673*
16:24 So he **c to** him, 'Father Abraham, *5888*
17:13 **c out in a loud voice,** *149+5889*
18:16 But Jesus **c** the children **to** *him* and said, *4673*
18:38 *He* **c out,** "Jesus, Son of David, *1066*
19:13 So he **c** ten of his servants *2813*
19:29 and Bethany at the hill **c** the Mount *2813*
21:37 the night on the hill **c** the Mount of Olives, *2813*
22: 1 Feast of Unleavened Bread, **c** the Passover, *3306*
22: 3 Then Satan entered Judas, **c** Iscariot, *2813*
22:47 and the man who *was* **c** Judas, *3306*
23:13 Pilate **c together** the chief priests, *5157*
23:33 When they came to the place **c** the Skull, *2813*
23:46 Jesus **c out** with a loud voice, "Father, *5888*
24:13 of them were going to a village **c** Emmaus, *3950*
Jn 1:42 You *will be* **c** Cephas" (which, *2813*
1:48 under the fig tree before Philip **c** you." *5888*
2: 9 Then he **c** the bridegroom aside *5888*
4: 5 So he came to a town in Samaria **c** Sychar, *3306*
4:25 that Messiah" (**c** Christ) "is coming. *3306*
5: 2 which in Aramaic *is* **c** Bethesda *2141*
10:35 If *he* **c** them 'gods,' *3306*
11:16 Then Thomas (**c** Didymus) said to the rest *3306*
11:28 she went back and **c** her sister Mary aside. *5888*
11:43 Jesus **c** in a loud voice, "Lazarus, *3198*
11:47 the Pharisees **c** a **meeting** of the Sanhedrin. *5251*
11:54 to a village **c** Ephraim, *3306*
12:17 with him when *he* **c** Lazarus from the tomb *5888*
15:15 Instead, *I have* **c** you friends, *3306*
19:17 in Aramaic *is* **c** Golgotha). *3306*
20:24 Now Thomas (**c** Didymus), *3306*
21: 2 Thomas (**c** Didymus), *3306*
21: 5 He **c out** to them, "Friends, *3306*
Ac 1:12 to Jerusalem from the hill **c** the Mount *2813*
1:19 so they **c** that field *2813*
1:23 Joseph **c** Barsabbas (also known as Justus) *2813*
3: 2 to the temple gate **c** Beautiful, *3306*
3:10 at the temple gate **c** Beautiful, *NIG*
3:11 in the place **c** Solomon's Colonnade. *2813*
4: 9 If we *are being* **c to account** today for *373*
4:18 Then *they* **c** them in again *2813*
4:36 the apostles **c** Barnabas (which means Son *2126*
5:21 *they* **c together** the Sanhedrin— *5157*
5:40 *They* **c** the apostles **in** *4673*
6: 9 of the Freedmen (as *it was* **c**)— *3306*
9:10 The Lord **c** to him in a vision, "Ananias!" *3306*
9:41 Then he **c** the believers and the widows *5888*
10: 5 a man named Simon who *is* **c** Peter. *2126*
10: 7 Cornelius **c** two of his servants and *5888*
10:18 *They* **c out,** asking *5888*
10:24 and *had* **c together** his relatives *5157*
10:32 Send to Joppa for Simon who *is* **c** Peter. *2126*
11:13 'Send to Joppa for Simon who *is* **c** Peter. *2126*
11:26 The disciples *were* **c** Christians first *5976*
12:12 of Mary the mother of John, also **c** Mark, *2126*
12:25 taking with them John, also **c** Mark. *2126*
13: 1 Barnabas, Simeon **c** Niger, *2813*
13: 2 for the work to which *I have* **c** them." *4673*
13: 9 Then Saul, who was also **c** Paul, *NIG*
14:10 and **c out,** "Stand up *3306+3489+5889*
14:12 Barnabas *they* **c** Zeus, *2813*
14:12 and Paul they **c** Hermes because he was *NIG*
15:22 They chose Judas (**c** Barsabbas) and Silas, *2813*
15:37 Barnabas wanted to take John, also **c** Mark, *2813*
16:10 concluding that God *had* **c** us to preach *4673*
16:29 The jailer **c for** lights, *160*
17: 7 that there is another king, one **c** Jesus." *NIG*
19:25 He **c** them **together,** along with *5255*
23: 6 **c out** in the Sanhedrin, "My brothers, *3189*
23:17 Then Paul **c** one of the centurions and said, *4673*
23:23 Then he **c** two of his centurions *4673*
24: 2 *When* Paul *was* **c** in, *2813*
27: 8 and came to a place **c** Fair Havens, *2813*
27:14 of hurricane force, **c** the "northeaster," *2813*
27:16 to the lee of a small island **c** Cauda, *2813*
28: 1 we found out that the island *was* **c** Malta. *2813*
28:17 Three days later he **c together** the leaders *5157*
Ro 1: 1 **c** to be an apostle and set apart for *3105*
1: 6 also are among those who are **c** to belong *3105*
1: 7 in Rome who are loved by God and **c** to *3105*
7: 3 *she is* **c** an adulteress. *5976*
8:28 who have been **c** according to his purpose. *3105*
8:30 And those he predestined, *he* also **c;** *2813*
8:30 those *he* **c,** he also justified; *2813*
Ro 9:24 even us, whom *he* also **c,** *2813*
9:26 *they will be* **c** 'sons of the living God.' " *2813*
1Co 1: 1 **c** to be an apostle of Christ Jesus by *3105*
1: 2 to those sanctified in Christ Jesus and **c** to *3105*
1: 9 who *has* **c** *you* into fellowship *2813*
1:24 but to those whom God *has* **c,** *3105*
1:26 think of what you were when you were **c.** *3104*
7:15 God *has* **c** us to live in peace. *2813*
7:17 to him and to which God *has* **c** him. *2813*
7:18 a man already circumcised when *he was* **c?** *2813*
7:18 Was a man uncircumcised when *he was* **c?** *2813*
7:20 which he was in when God **c** him. *2813*
7:21 Were you a slave when *you were* **c?** *2813*
7:22 For he who was a slave *when he was* **c** by *2813*
7:22 a free man *when he was* **c** is Christ's slave. *2813*
7:24 should remain in the situation God **c** *him* to. *2813*
15: 9 and do not even deserve *to be* **c** an apostle, *2813*
Gal 1: 6 so quickly deserting the one who **c** you by *2813*
1:15 who set me apart from birth and **c** me *2813*
5:13 You, my brothers, *were* **c** to be free. *2813*
Eph 1:18 the hope to which he has **c** you, *3104*
2:11 by birth and **c** "uncircumcised" *3306*
4: 4 just as *you were* **c** to one hope *2813*
4: 4 to one hope when you were **c**— *3104*
Php 3:14 for which God has **c** me heavenward *3104*
Col 3:15 members of one body *you were* **c** to peace. *2813*
4:11 Jesus, who *is* **c** Justus, *3306*
2Th 2: 4 that is **c** God or is worshiped, *3306*
2:14 *He* **c** you to this through our gospel, *2813*
1Ti 6:12 of the eternal life to which *you were* **c** *2813*
6:20 *of* what *is* **falsely c** knowledge, *6024*
2Ti 1: 9 who has saved us and **c** us to a holy life— *2813*
Heb 3:13 as long as *it is* **c** Today, *2813*
5: 4 *he* must *be* **c** by God, just as Aaron was. *2813*
9: 2 this *was* **c** the Holy Place. *3306*
9: 3 Behind the second curtain was a room **c** the Most Holy Place, *3306*
9:15 that those who are **c** may receive *2813*
11: 8 By faith Abraham, *when* **c** to go *2813*
11:16 God is not ashamed *to be* **c** their God, *2126*
Jas 2:23 and *he was* **c** God's friend. *2813*
1Pe 1:15 But just as he who **c** you is holy, *2813*
2: 9 *of* him who **c** you out of darkness *2813*
2:21 To this *you were* **c,** *2813*
3: 6 and **c** him her master. *2813*
3: 9 to this *you were* **c** so that you may inherit *2813*
5:10 who **c** you to his eternal glory in Christ, *2813*
2Pe 1: 3 through our knowledge *of* him who **c** us *2813*
1Jn 3: 1 that *we should be* **c** children of God! *2813*
Jude 1: 1 To those who *have been* **c,** *3105*
Rev 6:10 *They* **c out** in a loud voice, "How long, *3189*
6:16 *They* **c** to the mountains and the rocks, *3306*
7: 2 *He* **c out** in a loud voice to the four angels *3189*
11: 8 which *is* figuratively **c** Sodom and Egypt, *2813*
12: 9 that ancient serpent **c** the devil, or Satan, *2813*
14:15 of the temple and **c** in a loud voice *3189*
14:18 came from the altar and **c** in a loud voice *5888*
16:16 the place that in Hebrew is **c** Armageddon. *2813*
17:14 and with him will be his **c,** *3105*
19:11 whose rider *is* **c** Faithful and True. *2813*

CALLING (43) [CALL]

Ex 33: 7 **c** it the "tent of meeting." 7924
Nu 10: 2 **c** the community **together** 5246
Jdg 6:35 **c** them **to arms,** and also into Asher, 339+2410
12: 1 to fight the Ammonites without **c** us to go 7924
1Sa 3: 8 Eli realized that the LORD *was* **c** the boy. 7924
3:10 **c** as at the other times, "Samuel! 7924
1Ki 16:24 **c** it Samaria, after Shemer, 7924+9005
2Ki 9:23 **c out** to Ahaziah, "Treachery, Ahaziah!" 606
14: 7 **c** it Joktheel, the name it has to this day. 7924
2Ch 30: 5 **c** the people to come to Jerusalem NIH
Est 5:10 **C together** his friends and Zeresh, his wife, 995+2256+8938
Ps 69: 3 I am worn out **c for help;** 7924
Pr 9:15 **c out** to those who pass by, 7924
Isa 6: 3 And *they were* **c** to one another: 7924
40: 3 A voice of *one* **c:** "In the desert prepare 7924
41: 2 **c** him in righteousness to his service? 7924
41: 4 **c forth** the generations from 7924
Jer 25:29 for I *am* **c down** a sword upon all who live 7924
Da 8:16 And I heard a man's voice from the Ulai **c,** 7924
Hos 7:11 now **c** *to* Egypt, now turning to Assyria. 7924
Am 7: 4 The Sovereign LORD *was* **c** for judgment 7924
Mic 6: 9 The LORD *is* **c** to the city— 7754+7924
Mt 3: 3 "A voice *of one* **c** in the desert, *1066*
9:27 **c out,** "Have mercy on us, Son of David!" *3189*
11:16 in the marketplaces and **c out** to others: *4715*
27:47 they said, "He's **c** Elijah." *5888*
Mk 1: 3 "a voice *of one* **c** in the desert, *1066*
6: 7 **C** the Twelve **to** *him,* *4673*
10:49 On your feet! *He's* **c** you." *5888*
12:43 **C** his disciples **to** him, Jesus said, *4673*
15:35 they said, "Listen, *he's* **c** Elijah." *5888*
Lk 3: 4 "A voice *of one* **c** in the desert, *1066*
7:18 **C** two of them, *4673*
7:32 in the marketplace and **c out** to each other: *4715*
Jn 1:23 "I am the voice *of one* **c** in the desert, *1066*
5:18 but *he was* even **c** God his own Father, *3306*
Ac 22:16 and wash your sins away, **c on** his name.' *2126*
Eph 4: 1 live a life worthy *of* the **c** *you have* **received.** *2813+3104*
2Th 1:11 our God may count you worthy *of* his **c,** *3104*
Heb 3: 1 holy brothers, who share in the heavenly **c,** *3104*
4: 7 God again set a certain day, **c** it Today, *NIG*
8:13 By **c** this covenant "new," *3306*
2Pe 1:10 be all the more eager to make your **c** *3104*

CALLOUS (3) [CALLOUSED]

Ps 17:10 They close up their **c hearts,** 2693
73: 7 From their **c hearts** comes iniquity; 2693
119:70 Their hearts are **c** and unfeeling, 2021+2693+3869

CALLOUSED (3) [CALLOUS]

Isa 6:10 **Make** the heart of this people **c;** 9042
Mt 13:15 For this people's heart *has become* **c;** *4266*
Ac 28:27 For this people's heart *has become* **c;** *4266*

CALLS (40) [CALL]

Ge 46:33 When Pharaoh **c** you **in** and asks, 7924
1Sa 3: 9 "Go and lie down, and if *he* **c** you, say, 7924
26:14 "Who are you *who* **c** to the king?" 7924
Ps 42: 7 Deep **c** to deep in the roar 7924
147: 4 the number of the stars and **c** them each 7924
Pr 1:20 Wisdom **c aloud** in the street, 8264
9: 3 and *she* **c** from the highest point of the city. 7924
Isa 21:11 *Someone* **c** to me from Seir, "Watchman, 7924
40:26 and **c** them each by name. 7924
41:25 one from the rising sun *who* **c** on my name. 7924
59: 4 No *one* **c** for justice; 7924
64: 7 No *one* **c** on your name or strives 7924
Hos 7: 7 and none of them **c** on me. 7924
Joel 2:32 everyone who **c** on the name of the LORD 7924
2:32 among the survivors whom the LORD **c.** 7924
Am 5: 8 who **c** for the waters of the sea 7924
9: 6 who **c** for the waters of the sea 7924
Zep 2:14 Their **c** will echo through the windows, 7754
Mt 22:43 speaking by the Spirit, **c** him 'Lord'? *2813*
22:45 If then David **c** him 'Lord,' *2813*
Mk 12:37 David himself **c** him 'Lord.' *3306*
Lk 15: 6 **c** his friends and neighbors **together** *5157*
15: 9 **c** her friends and neighbors **together** *5157*
20:37 for *he* **c** the Lord 'the God of Abraham, *3306*
20:44 David **c** him 'Lord.' *2813*
Jn 10: 3 *He* **c** his own sheep by name *5888*
Ac 2:21 And everyone who **c on** the name of *2126*
Ro 4:17 to the dead and **c** things that are not as *2813*
9:12 not by works but by him who **c**— *2813*
10:13 "Everyone who **c on** the name of the Lord *2126*
1Co 5:11 not associate with anyone who **c** *himself* *3951*
Gal 4: 6 the Spirit who **c out,** "Abba, Father." *3189*
5: 8 not come from the one who **c** you. *2813*
1Th 2:12 who **c** you into his kingdom and glory. *2813*
5:24 one who **c** you is faithful and he will do it. *2813*
Rev 2:20 who **c** herself a prophetess. *3306*
13:10 This **c for** patient endurance *1639*
13:18 This **c for** wisdom. *1639*
14:12 This **c for** patient endurance on the part of *1639*
17: 9 "This **c for** a mind with wisdom. *6045*

CALM (9) [CALMED, CALMNESS, CALMS]

Ps 107:30 They were glad when *it grew* **c,** 9284
Isa 7: 4 'Be careful, *keep* **c** and don't be afraid. 9200
Eze 16:42 *I will be* **c** and no longer angry. 9200
Jnh 1:11 to you *to make* the sea **c down** for us?" 9284
1:12 he replied, "and it *will become* **c.** 9284
1:15 and the raging sea *grew* **c.** 6641
Mt 8:26 and it was completely **c.** *1132*
Mk 4:39 wind died down and it was completely **c.** *1132*
Lk 8:24 the storm subsided, and all was **c.** *1132*

CALMED (1) [CALM]

Ne 8:11 The Levites **c** all the people, saying, 3120

CALMNESS (1) [CALM]

Ecc 10: 4 **c** can lay great errors to rest. 5341

CALMS (1) [CALM]

Pr 15:18 but a patient man **c** a quarrel. 9200

CALNEH (2)

Ge 10:10 Erech, Akkad and **C,** in Shinar. 4011
Am 6: 2 Go to **C** and look at it; 4011

CALNO (1)

Isa 10: 9 'Has not **C** fared like Carchemish? 4012

CALVARY (KJV) See SKULL

CALVE (1) [CALF]

Job 21:10 their cows **c** and do not miscarry. 7117

CALVED (1) [CALF]

1Sa 6: 7 *that have* **c** and have never been yoked. 6402

CALVES (25) [CALF]

Dt 7:13 the **c** *of* your herds and the lambs 8715
28: 4 the **c** *of* your herds and the lambs 8715
28:18 and the **c** *of* your herds and the lambs 8715
28:51 nor any **c** *of* your herds or lambs 8715
1Sa 6: 7 but take their **c** away and pen them up. 1201
6:10 to the cart and penned up their **c.** 1201
14:32 taking sheep, cattle and **c,** 1201+1330
15: 9 the **fat** *c* and lambs— AIT
1Ki 1: 9 and **fattened c** at the Stone of Zoheleth 5309

1Ki 1:19 **fattened c,** and sheep, 5309
1:25 **fattened c,** and sheep. 5309
12:28 the king made two golden **c.** 6319
12:32 sacrificing to the **c** he had made. 6319
2Ki 10:29 the worship of the golden **c** at Bethel 6319
17:16 two idols cast in the **shape of c,** 6319
2Ch 13:8 a vast army and have with you the golden **c** 6319
Ps 68:30 herd of bulls among the **c** *of* the nations. 6319
Isa 27:10 there the **c** graze, there they lie down; 6319
34:7 the **bull c** and the great bulls. 7228
Jer 46:21 in her ranks are like fattened **c.** 6319
Am 6:4 You dine on choice lambs and fattened **c.** 6319
Mic 6:6 with **c** a year old? 6319
Mal 4:2 and leap like **c** released *from* the stall. 6319
Heb 9:12 by means of the blood of goats and **c;** *3675*
9:19 he took the blood *of* **c,** *3675*

CAME (1193) [COME]

Ge 2:6 but streams **c up** from the earth 6590
7:6 when the floodwaters **c** on the earth. 2118
7:9 **c** to Noah and entered the ark, 995
7:10 And after the seven days the floodwaters **c** 2118
7:15 in them **c** to Noah and entered the ark. 995
8:4 of the seventh month the ark **c to rest** on 5663
8:18 So Noah **c out,** together with his sons 3655
8:19 **c out** of the ark, one kind after another. 3655
9:10 all *those that* **c out** *of* the ark with you— 3655
9:18 of Noah who **c out** of the ark were Shem, 3655
9:19 from them **c** the people who were scattered NIH
10:14 Casluhites (from whom the Philistines **c**) 3655
11:5 But the LORD **c down** to see the city and 3718
11:31 when *they* **c** to Haran, they settled there. 995
12:14 When Abram **c** to Egypt, 995
13:3 from place to place until he **c** to Bethel, NIH
14:13 *One* who had escaped **c** and reported this 995
14:17 of Sodom **c out** to meet him in the Valley 3655
15:1 the word of the LORD **c** to Abram in 2118
15:4 Then the word of the LORD **c** to him: NIH
15:11 Then birds of prey **c down** on the carcasses, 3718
15:12 a thick and dreadful darkness **c** over him. 5877
19:5 "Where are the men who **c** to you tonight? 995
19:9 they said, "This fellow **c** here as an alien, 995
20:3 But God **c** to Abimelech in 995
24:5 to the country *you* **c** from?" 3655
24:15 Rebekah **c out** with her jar 3655
24:16 filled her jar and **c up** again. 6590
24:42 "When *I* **c** to the spring today, I said, 995
24:45 Rebekah **c out,** with her jar 3655
25:24 When the time **c** for her to give birth, 4848
25:26 After this, his brother **c out,** 3655
25:29 Esau **c in** from the open country, famished. 995
26:32 That day Isaac's servants **c** and told him 995
27:30 his brother Esau **c in** from hunting. 995
27:33 before *you* **c** and I blessed him— 995
27:35 "Your brother **c** deceitfully 995
29:1 Then Jacob continued on his journey and **c** 2143
29:9 Rachel **c** with her father's sheep, 995
29:23 But when evening **c,** 2118
29:25 When morning **c,** there was Leah! 2118
30:16 Jacob **c in** from the fields that evening, 995
30:30 before I **c** has increased greatly, NIH
30:38 be directly in front of the flocks *when they* **c** 995
30:38 the flocks were in heat and **c** to drink, 995
30:43 and *c to* **own** large flocks, AIT
31:24 Then God **c** to Laban the Aramean in 995
31:33 After *he* **c out** of Leah's tent, 3655
33:7 Leah and her children **c** and bowed down. 5602
33:7 Last of all **c** Joseph and Rachel, 5602
33:18 After Jacob **c** from Paddan Aram, 995
34:5 so he kept quiet about it until they **c home.** 995
34:27 of Jacob **c** upon the dead bodies and looted 995
35:6 Jacob and all the people with him **c** to Luz 995
35:27 Jacob **c home** to his father Isaac in Mamre, 995
37:23 So when Joseph **c** to his brothers, 995
37:28 So when the Midianite merchants **c by,** 6296
37:35 and daughters **c** to comfort him, 7756
38:27 When the time **c** for her to give birth, 2118
38:28 "This one **c out** first." 3655
38:29 his brother **c out,** and she said, 3655
38:30 **c out** and he was given the name Zerah. 3655
39:14 *He* **c** in here to sleep with me, 995
39:16 beside her until his master **c** home. 995
39:17 "That Hebrew slave you brought us **c** to me 995
40:6 When Joseph **c** to them the next morning, 995
41:2 out of the river *there* **c up** seven cows, 6590
41:3 **c up** out of the Nile and stood beside those 6590
41:14 *he* **c** before Pharaoh. 995
41:18 out of the river *there* **c up** seven cows, 6590
41:19 After them, seven other cows **c up—** 6590
41:20 ugly cows ate up the seven fat cows that **c** NIH
41:27 that **c up** afterward are seven years, and 6590
41:50 Before the years of famine **c,** 995
41:53 of abundance in Egypt **c to an end,** 3983
41:57 the countries **c** to Egypt to buy grain 995
42:29 When *they* **c** to their father Jacob in 995
43:20 *"we* **c down** here the first time to buy food. 3718+3718
43:26 When Joseph **c** home, 995
43:31 After he had washed his face, *he* **c out** and, 3655
44:14 the house when Judah and his brothers **c** in, 995
45:25 up out of Egypt and **c** to their father Jacob 995
47:15 all Egypt **c** to Joseph and said, 995
47:18 *they* **c** to him the following year and said, 995
48:5 to you in Egypt before I **c** to you here will 995
50:17 When their **message c** to him, Joseph wept. 1819
50:18 His brothers then **c** and threw themselves 2143

Ex 1:8 **c to power** in Egypt. 7756
1:12 so the Egyptians *c to* **dread** the Israelites AIT
2:16 and *they* **c** to draw water and fill 995
2:17 Some shepherds **c along** 995
2:17 but Moses got up and **c to** their **rescue** 3828
3:1 to the far side of the desert and **c** to Horeb, 995
8:6 and the frogs **c up** and covered the land. 6590
8:17 gnats **c** upon men and animals. 2118
13:3 the day *you* **c out** of Egypt, 3655
13:8 the LORD did for me when I **c out** 3655
15:23 When *they* **c** to Marah, 995
15:27 Then *they* **c** to Elim, 995
16:1 from Elim and **c** to the Desert of Sin, 995
16:13 That evening quail **c** and covered the camp, 6590
16:22 of the community **c** and reported this 995
16:35 until they **c** to a land that was settled; 995
17:8 The Amalekites **c** and attacked 995
18:5 **c** to him in the desert, 995
18:12 and Aaron **c** with all the elders of Israel 995
19:1 *they* **c** *to* the Desert of Sinai. 995
23:15 for in that month *you* **c out** of Egypt. 3655
32:24 and **out c** this calf!" 3655
34:5 Then the LORD **c down** in the cloud 3718
34:18 for in that month *you* **c out** of Egypt. 3655
34:29 When Moses **c down** from Mount Sinai 3718
34:31 the leaders of the community **c back** to him, 8740
34:32 Afterward all the Israelites **c near** him, 5602
34:34 he removed the veil until he **c out.** 3655
34:34 And when *he* **c out** and told 3655
35:21 and whose heart moved him **c** and brought 995
35:22 **c** and brought gold jewelry of all kinds: 995
Lev 9:5 the entire assembly **c near** and stood before 7928
9:8 So Aaron **c** to the altar and slaughtered 7928
9:23 When *they* **c out,** they blessed the people; 3655
9:24 Fire **c out** from the presence of the LORD 3655
10:2 So fire **c out** from the presence of 3655
10:5 So *they* **c** and carried them, 7928
18:30 before you **c** and do not defile yourselves NIH
Nu 1:1 of the second year after the Israelites **c out** 3655
4:35 from thirty to fifty years of age who **c** 995
4:39 from thirty to fifty years of age who **c** 995
4:43 from thirty to fifty years of age who **c** 995
4:47 from thirty to fifty years of age who **c** to do 995
7:87 the burnt offering **c** to twelve young bulls, NIH
7:88 for the sacrifice of the fellowship offering **c** NIH
8:22 the Levites **c** to do their work at the Tent 995
9:1 the second year after they **c out** of Egypt. 3655
9:6 *they* **c** to Moses and Aaron that same day 7928
10:12 from place to place until the cloud **c to rest** 8905
10:36 Whenever it **c to rest,** he said, "Return, 5663
11:9 the manna also **c down.** 3718
11:25 the LORD **c down** in the cloud and spoke 3718
12:4 So the three of them **c out.** 3655
12:5 the LORD **c down** in a pillar of cloud; 3718
13:22 up through the Negev and **c** to Hebron, 995
13:26 *They* **c back** to Moses and Aaron 995+2143+2256
14:45 that hill country **c down** and attacked them 3718
16:3 *They* **c as a group** to oppose Moses 7735
16:35 And fire **c out** from the LORD 3655
20:20 Then Edom **c out** against them with a large 3655
20:22 from Kadesh and **c** *to* Mount Hor. 995
20:28 and Eleazar **c down** from the mountain, 3718
21:7 The people **c** to Moses and said, 995
22:7 When *they* **c** to Balaam, 995
22:9 God **c** to Balaam and asked, 995
22:16 *They* **c** to Balaam and said: 995
22:20 That night God **c** to Balaam and said, 995
24:2 the Spirit of God **c** upon him 2118
25:18 when the plague **c** as a result of Peor." NIH
26:4 These were the Israelites who **c out** 3655
30:12 or pledges that **c from** her lips will stand. 4604
32:2 So they **c** to Moses and Eleazar the priest 995
32:11 the men twenty years old or more who **c up** 6590
32:16 Then *they* **c up** to him and said, 5602
33:1 of the Israelites when *they* **c out** of Egypt 3655
33:38 of the fortieth year after the Israelites **c out** 3655
36:1 **c** and spoke before Moses and the leaders, 7928
Dt 1:22 Then all of you **c** to me and said, 7928
1:24 **c** to the Valley of Eshcol and explored it. 995
1:44 in those hills **c out** against you; 3655
1:45 *You* **c back** and wept before the LORD, 8740
2:32 and all his army **c out** to meet us in battle 3655
4:11 *You* **c near** and stood at the foot of 7928
4:45 when they **c out** of Egypt 3655
4:46 by Moses and the Israelites as they **c out** 3655
5:23 of your tribes and your elders **c** to me. 7928
10:5 Then *I* **c back** down the mountain and put AIT
23:4 and water on your way when you **c out** 3655
24:9 to Miriam along the way after you **c out** 3655
25:17 along the way when you **c out** of Egypt. 3655
29:7 of Heshbon and Og king of Bashan **c out** 3655
31:14 and Joshua **c** and presented themselves at 2143
32:44 Moses **c** with Joshua son of Nun 995
33:2 "The LORD **c** from Sinai and dawned 995
33:2 *He* **c** with myriads of holy ones from 910
Jos 2:3 "Bring out the men who **c** to you 995
2:4 She said, "Yes, the men **c** to me, 995
2:10 of the Red Sea for you when you **c out** 3655
2:23 forded the river and **c** to Joshua son of Nun 995
4:11 priests **c to the other side** 6296
4:18 the priests **c up** out of the river carrying 6590
5:4 All those who **c out** of Egypt— 3655
5:5 that **c out** had been circumcised, 3655
6:1 No one went out and no *one* **c in.** 995
7:17 The clans of Judah **c forward,** 7928
8:22 The men of the ambush also **c out** of the city 3655

Jos 9:2 *they* **c together** to make war against Joshua 3481+7695
9:17 the Israelites set out and on the third day **c** 995
10:24 So *they* **c forward** and placed their feet 7928
11:4 They **c out** with all their troops and 3655
11:7 So Joshua and his whole army **c** 995
15:7 to the waters of En Shemesh and **c** out 2118
15:9 **c out** at the towns of Mount Ephron 3655
15:18 One day when she **c** to Othniel, 995
16:7 touched Jericho and **c out** at the Jordan. 3655
18:11 The lot **c up** for the tribe of Benjamin, 6590
18:14 the western side and **c** out at Kiriath Baal 2118
18:15 and the boundary **c out** at the spring of 3655
18:19 and **c** out at the northern bay of 2118
19:1 The second lot **c out** for the tribe 3655
19:10 The third lot **c up** for Zebulun, 6590
19:13 *it* **c out** at Rimmon and turned 3655
19:17 fourth lot **c out** for Issachar, clan by clan. 3655
19:24 The fifth lot **c out** for the tribe of Asher, 3655
19:29 turned toward Hosah and **c** out at the sea in 2118
19:32 sixth lot **c out** for Naphtali, clan by clan: 3655
19:34 through Aznoth Tabor and **c out** 3655
19:40 The seventh lot **c out** for the tribe of Dan, 3655
21:4 The first lot **c out** for the Kohathites, 3655
22:10 When *they* **c** to Geliloth near the Jordan in 995
24:6 *you* **c** to the sea, and the Egyptians pursued 995
24:11 you crossed the Jordan and **c** to Jericho. 995
Jdg 1:14 One day when she **c** *to* Othniel, 995
3:10 The Spirit of the LORD **c** upon him, 2118
3:13 Eglon **c** and attacked Israel, 2143
3:22 blade, *which* **c out** his back. 3655
3:24 the servants **c** and found the doors of 995
3:31 After Ehud **c** Shamgar son of Anath, 2118
4:5 and the Israelites **c** to her 6590
4:22 Barak **c by in pursuit** *of* Sisera, 8103
5:8 war **c** to the city gates, NIH
5:13 the men who were left **c down** to the nobles; 3718
5:13 of the LORD **c** to me with the mighty. 3718
5:14 Some **c** from Ephraim, NIH
5:14 From Makir captains **c down,** 3718
5:19 "Kings **c,** they fought; 995
6:5 They **c up** with their livestock 6590
6:11 the LORD **c** and sat down under the oak 995
6:34 the Spirit of the LORD **c upon** Gideon, 4252
7:13 "A round loaf of barley bread **c tumbling** 2200
8:4 **c** to the Jordan and crossed it. 995
8:15 Gideon **c** and said to the men of Succoth, 995
8:26 for **c** to seventeen hundred shekels, 2118
9:35 as Abimelech and his soldiers **c out** 7756
9:57 The curse of Jotham son of Jerub-Baal **c** 995
11:13 "When Israel **c up** out of Egypt, 6590
11:16 But when they **c up** out of Egypt, 6590
11:29 the Spirit of the LORD **c** upon Jephthah. 2118
13:6 "A man of God **c** to me. 995
13:6 I didn't ask him where he **c** from, NIH
13:9 and the angel of God **c** again to the woman 995
13:11 When *he* **c** to the man, he said, 995
14:5 suddenly a young lion **c** roaring **toward** 7925
14:6 Spirit of the LORD **c** upon him **in power** 7502
14:19 Spirit of the LORD **c** upon him **in power.** 7502
15:14 the Philistines **c toward** him shouting. 7925
15:14 Spirit of the LORD **c** upon him **in power.** 7502
15:19 and water **c out** of it. 3655
16:30 and **down c** the temple on the rulers and all 5877
17:8 On his way *he* **c** to Micah's house in 995
18:2 of Ephraim and **c** to the house of Micah, NIH
18:7 So the five men left and **c** to Laish, 995
18:13 on to the hill country of Ephraim and **c** 995
19:16 **c in** from his work in the fields. 995
19:22 "Bring out the man who **c** to your house 995
19:30 the day the Israelites **c up** out of Egypt. 6590
20:1 of Gilead **c out** as one man and assembled 3655
20:4 and my concubine **c** to Gibeah in Benjamin 995
20:5 the night the men of Gibeah **c** after me 7756
20:14 From their towns they **c together** at Gibeah 665
20:21 The Benjamites **c out** of Gibeah and cut 3655
20:25 when the Benjamites **c out** from Gibeah 3655
20:31 The Benjamites **c out** to meet them 3655
20:42 of Israel who **c** out of the towns cut them NIH
20:48 All the towns they **c across** they set on fire. 5162
Ru 1:19 So the two women went on until they **c** 995
2:6 the Moabitess who **c back** from Moab 8740
2:11 and your homeland and **c** to live with 2143
3:14 "Don't let it be known that a woman **c** *to* 995
3:16 When Ruth **c** to her mother-in-law, 995
4:1 the kinsman-redeemer he had mentioned **c along,** 6296
1Sa 1:4 the day **c** for Elkanah to sacrifice, 2118
2:14 how they treated all the Israelites who **c** 995
2:27 Now a man of God **c** to Eli and said to him, 995
3:10 The LORD **c** and stood there, 995
4:1 And Samuel's word **c** to all Israel. 2118
4:5 of the LORD's covenant **c** into the camp, 995
6:14 The cart **c** to the field of Joshua 995
7:1 So the men of Kiriath Jearim **c** and took up 995
7:7 of the Philistines **c up** to attack them. 6590
8:4 of Israel gathered together and **c** to Samuel 995
9:15 Now the day before Saul **c,** 995
9:25 After *they* **c down** from the high place to 3718
10:10 Spirit of God **c** upon him **in power,** 7502
11:4 When the messengers **c** *to* Gibeah of Saul 995
11:6 Spirit of God **c** upon him **in power,** 7502
15:2 when they waylaid them as they **c up** 6590
15:6 the Israelites when they **c up** out of Egypt." 6590
15:10 Then the word of the LORD **c** to Samuel: 2118
15:32 Agag **c** to him confidently, thinking, 2143
16:13 Spirit of the LORD **c** upon David **in power.** 7502

1Sa 16:21 David **c** to Saul and entered his service. 995
16:23 Whenever the spirit from God **c** upon Saul, 2118
17: 4 **c out** of the Philistine camp. 3655
17:16 the Philistine **c forward** every morning 5602
17:28 *you* **c down** only to watch the battle." 3718
17:34 a lion or a bear **c** and carried off a sheep 995
18: 6 the women **c out** from all the towns 3655
18:10 an evil spirit from God **c forcefully** 7502
18:19 So when the time **c** for Merab, 2118
19: 9 an evil spirit from the LORD **c** upon Saul 2118
19:19 **Word c** to Saul: "David is in Naioth 5583
19:20 the Spirit of God **c** upon Saul's men 2118
19:23 But the Spirit of God **c** even upon him, 2118
19:23 and he walked along prophesying until he **c** 995
20:24 and when the New Moon festival **c,** 2118
20:37 When the boy **c** to the place 995
22:11 and they all **c** to the king. 995
23:27 a messenger **c** to Saul, 995
24: 3 *He* **c** to the sheep pens along the way; 995
25:20 As she **c riding** her donkey into 8206
26:15 Someone **c** to destroy your lord the king. 995
28: 4 The Philistines assembled and **c** and set 995
28:21 When the woman **c** to Saul and saw 995
29: 6 From the day you **c** to me until now, 995
29: 8 against your servant from the day *I* **c** 2118
30: 3 When David and his men **c** to Ziklag, 995
30: 9 David and the six hundred men with him **c** 995
30:21 Then David **c** to the two hundred men 995
30:21 *They* **c out** to meet David and the people 3655
30:23 and handed over to us the forces that **c** 995
31: 7 And the Philistines **c** and occupied them. 995
31: 8 when the Philistines **c** to strip the dead, 995
2Sa 1: 2 When he **c** to David, 995
2: 4 Then the men of Judah **c** to Hebron 995
2:23 and the spear **c out** through his back. 3655
2:23 And every man stopped when he **c** to 995
2:24 they **c** to the hill of Ammah, 995
2:28 and all the men **c to a halt;** 6641
2:29 continued through the whole Bithron and **c** 995
3:20 **c** to David at Hebron, 995
3:24 Look, Abner **c** to you. 995
3:25 *he* **c** to deceive you 995
3:35 Then they all **c** and urged David 995
4: 4 when the news about Saul and Jonathan **c** 995
5: 1 All the tribes of Israel **c** to David at Hebron 995
5:22 the Philistines **c up** and spread out in 6590
6: 6 *they* **c** to the threshing floor of Nacon, 995
6:20 Michal daughter of Saul **c out** to meet him 3655
7: 4 the word of the LORD **c** to Nathan, 2118
8: 5 of Damascus **c** to help Hadadezer king 995
9: 6 the son of Saul, **c** to David, 995
10: 2 When David's men **c** *to* the land of 995
10: 8 The Ammonites **c out** and drew up 3655
10:14 the Ammonites and **c** to Jerusalem. 995
11: 4 *She* **c** to him, and he slept with her. 995
11: 7 When Uriah **c** to him, 995
11:17 When the men of the city **c out** and fought 3655
11:23 "The men overpowered us and **c out** 3655
12: 1 When *he* **c** to him, he said, 995
12: 4 "Now a traveler **c** to the rich man, 995
13: 6 When the king **c** to see him, 995
13:30 the report **c** to David: 995
13:36 the king's sons **c in,** wailing loudly. 995
14:33 and *he* **c** in and bowed down with his face 995
15: 2 Whenever anyone **c** with a complaint to 2118
15: 6 in this way toward all the Israelites who **c** 995
15:13 A messenger **c** and told David, 995
15:20 You **c** only yesterday. 995
16: 5 from the same clan as Saul's family **c out** 3655
16: 5 and he cursed *as he* **c out.** 3655+3655
16:15 and all the men of Israel **c** *to* Jerusalem, 995
17: 6 When Hushai **c** to him, Absalom said, 995
17:20 When Absalom's men **c** to the woman at 995
17:27 When David **c** to Mahanaim, 995
18:25 And the man **c** closer and closer. 2143
19: 8 they all **c** before him. 995
19:25 When *he* **c** *from* Jerusalem to meet the king, 995
19:31 the Gileadite also **c down** from Rogelim 3718
20: 8 Amasa **c** to meet them. 995
20:12 that all the troops **c to a halt** there. 6641
20:12 that everyone who **c** up to Amasa stopped, 995
20:15 the troops with Joab **c** and besieged Sheba 995
21:17 of Zeruiah **c** to David's **rescue;** 6468
22: 7 my cry **c** to his ears. NIH
22: 9 consuming fire **c** from his mouth, NIH
22:10 He parted the heavens and **c down;** 3718
23:13 of the thirty chief men **c** down to David at 995
24: 8 *they* **c back** *to* Jerusalem at the end 995
1Ki 1:28 So *she* **c** into the king's presence and stood 995
1:32 When *they* **c** before the king, 995
1:53 And Adonijah **c** and bowed down 995
2: 8 When he **c down** to meet me at the Jordan, 3718
3:16 Now two prostitutes **c** to the king and stood 995
4:27 for King Solomon and all who **c** to 7929
4:34 *Men* of all nations **c** to listen 995
6:11 The word of the LORD **c** to Solomon: 2118
7:14 *He* **c** to King Solomon and did all 995
8: 2 of Israel **c together** to King Solomon at 7735
8: 9 the Israelites after they **c out** of Egypt. 3655
10: 1 *she* **c** to test him with hard questions. 995
10: 2 *she* **c** to Solomon and talked with him 995
10: 7 But I did not believe these things until *I* **c** 995
10:25 everyone who **c** brought a gift— NIH
12:22 of God **c** to Shemaiah the man of God: 2118
13: 1 By the word of the LORD a man of God **c** 995
13: 9 or return by the way *you* **c.'** " 2143
13:11 whose sons **c** and told him all that the man 995
1Ki 13:14 the man of God *who* **c** from Judah?" 995
13:17 or return by the way *you* **c.'** " 2143
13:20 the word of the LORD **c** to 2118
13:22 *You* **c back** and ate bread and drank water 8740
16: 1 Then the word of the LORD **c** to Jehu son 2118
16: 7 the LORD **c** through the prophet Jehu son 2118
16:10 Zimri **c in,** struck him down and killed him 995
17: 2 Then the word of the LORD **c** to Elijah: 2118
17: 8 Then the word of the LORD **c** to him: 2118
17:10 When *he* **c** to the town gate, 995
18: 1 the word of the LORD **c** to Elijah: 2118
18:30 They **c** to him, 5602
18:45 a heavy rain **c on** and Ahab rode off 2118
18:46 The power of the LORD **c** upon Elijah 2118
19: 3 When *he* **c** *to* Beersheba in Judah, 995
19: 4 *He* **c** *to* a broom tree, 995
19: 7 of the LORD **c back** a second time 8740
19: 9 And the word of the LORD **c** to him: 606
19:12 After the earthquake **c** a fire, NIH
19:12 And after the fire **c** a gentle whisper. NIH
19:15 "Go back the way you **c,** NIH
20: 5 The messengers **c again** and said, 8740
20:13 Meanwhile a prophet **c** to Ahab king 5602
20:22 the prophet **c** to the king of Israel and said, 5602
20:28 of God **c up** and told the king of Israel, 5602
20:33 When Ben-Hadad **c out,** 3655
20:39 someone **c** to me **with** a captive and said, 995
21: 5 His wife Jezebel **c** in and asked him, 995
21:13 Then two scoundrels **c** 995
21:17 Then the word of the LORD **c** to Elijah 2118
21:28 Then the word of the LORD **c** to Elijah 2118
22:21 Finally, a spirit **c forward,** 3655
2Ki 1: 6 "A man **c** to meet us," they replied. 6590
1: 7 of man was it who **c** to meet you 6590
2: 3 of the prophets at Bethel **c out** to Elisha 3655
2:23 some youths **c out** of the town and jeered 3655
2:24 Then two bears **c out** of the woods 3655
3:15 the hand of the LORD **c** upon Elisha 2118
3:24 when the Moabites **c** to the camp of Israel, 995
4: 8 So whenever he **c by,** 6296
4:11 One day when Elisha **c,** 995
4:25 and **c** to the man of God at Mount Carmel. 995
4:27 Gehazi **c over** to push her away, 5602
4:36 When *she* **c,** he said, "Take your son." 995
4:37 *She* **c in,** fell at his feet and bowed to 995
4:42 A man **c** from Baal Shalishah, 995
5:24 When Gehazi **c** to the hill, 995
6:13 *The* **report c back:** "He is in Dothan." 5583
6:18 As the enemy **c down** toward him, 3718
6:33 the messenger **c down** to him. 3718
7:17 of God had foretold when the king **c down** 3718
8: 3 the seven years she **c back** from the land of 8740
8: 5 to life **c** to beg the king for her house NIH
9:19 When *he* **c** to them he said, 995
10:15 *he* **c upon** Jehonadab son of Recah 5162
10:17 When Jehu **c** *to* Samaria, 995
10:21 and all the ministers of Baal **c;** 995
11: 9 and **c** to Jehoiada the priest. 995
12:10 the royal secretary and the high priest **c,** 6590
13:21 the man **c to life** and stood up on his feet. 2649
14: 9 Then a wild beast in Lebanon **c along** 6296
15:29 Tiglath-Pileser king of Assyria **c** 995
16:12 the king **c back** from Damascus and saw 995
17: 3 Shalmaneser king of Assyria **c up** 6590
17:28 from Samaria **c** to live in Bethel 995
18:17 *They* **c** up to Jerusalem and stopped at 995
19: 5 King Hezekiah's officials **c** to Isaiah, 995
19:28 I will make you return by the way *you* **c.'** 995
19:33 By the way that *he* **c** he will return; 995
20: 4 the word of the LORD **c** to him: 2118
20:14 *"They* **c** from Babylon." 995
21:15 the day their forefathers **c out** of Egypt 3655
23:17 of God who **c** from Judah and pronounced 995
24:11 and Nebuchadnezzar *himself* **c up** to 995
25: 8 of the king of Babylon, **c** *to* Jerusalem. 995
25:23 *they* **c** to Gedaliah at Mizpah— 995
25:25 **c** with ten men and assassinated Gedaliah 995
1Ch 1:12 Casluhites (from whom the Philistines **c**) 3655
2:55 the Kenites who **c** from Hammath, 995
4:41 The men whose names were listed **c** in 995
5: 2 the strongest of his brothers and a ruler **c** NIH
6:31 of the LORD after the ark **c to rest** there. 4955
7:22 and his relatives **c** to comfort him. 995
10: 7 And the Philistines **c** and occupied them. 995
10: 8 when the Philistines **c** to strip the dead, 995
11: 1 All Israel **c together** to David at Hebron 7695
11:15 the thirty chiefs **c down** to David to the rock 3718
12: 1 These were the *men who* **c** to David 995
12:16 and *some men* from Judah also **c** to David 995
12:18 Then the Spirit **c upon** Amasai, 4252
12:22 Day after day *men* **c** to help David, 995
12:23 of the men armed for battle *who* **c** to David 995
12:38 *They* **c** to Hebron fully determined 995
12:40 and Naphtali **c bringing** food on donkeys, 995
13: 9 *they* **c** to the threshing floor of Kidon, 995
17: 3 That night the word of God **c** to Nathan, 2118
18: 5 of Damascus **c** to help Hadadezer king 995
19: 2 When David's men **c** to Hanun in the land 995
19: 5 *someone* **c** and told David about the men, 2143
19: 7 *who* **c** and camped near Medeba, 995
19: 9 The Ammonites **c out** and drew up 3655
21: 4 and went throughout Israel and then **c back** 995
22: 8 But this word of the LORD **c** to me: 2118
27:24 Wrath **c** on Israel on account 2118
2Ch 5: 3 of Israel **c together** to the king at the time 7735
5:10 the Israelites after they **c out** of Egypt. 3655
7: 1 fire **c down** from heaven and consumed 3718
2Ch 9: 1 *she* **c** to Jerusalem to test him 995
9: 1 *she* **c** to Solomon and talked with him 995
9: 6 until *I* **c** and saw with my own eyes. 995
9:24 everyone who **c** brought a gift— NIH
11: 2 But this word of the LORD **c** to Shemaiah 2118
11:14 and **c** to Judah and Jerusalem 2143
12: 3 and Cushites that **c** with him from Egypt, 995
12: 4 the fortified cities of Judah and **c** as far 995
12: 5 Then the prophet Shemaiah **c** to Rehoboam 995
12: 7 this word of the LORD **c** to Shemaiah: 2118
14: 9 and **c** as far as Mareshah. 995
15: 1 The Spirit of God **c** upon Azariah son 2118
16: 7 At that time Hanani the seer **c** to Asa king 995
18:20 Finally, a spirit **c forward,** 3655
20: 1 with some of the Meunites **c** to make war 995
20: 2 *Some men* **c** and told Jehoshaphat, 995
20: 4 The people of Judah **c together** to seek help 7695
20: 4 indeed, *they* **c** from every town in Judah 995
20:10 not allow Israel to invade when they **c** 995
20:14 of the LORD **c** upon Jahaziel son 2118
20:24 When the men of Judah **c** to the place 995
20:29 The fear of God **c** upon all the kingdoms of 2118
21:19 his bowels **c out** because of the disease, 3655
22: 1 who **c** with the Arabs into the camp, 995
23: 2 When *they* **c** to Jerusalem, 995
24:17 the officials of Judah **c** and paid homage to 995
24:18 God's anger **c** upon Judah and Jerusalem. 2118
24:20 of God **c upon** Zechariah son of Jehoiada 4252
25: 7 But a man of God **c** to him and said, 995
25:18 Then a wild beast in Lebanon **c along** 6296
28:20 Tiglath-Pileser king of Assyria **c** to him, 995
30:18 Although most of the many people who **c** NIH
31: 8 When Hezekiah and his officials **c** and saw 995
32: 1 of Assyria **c** and invaded Judah. 995
36:20 until the kingdom of Persia **c to power.** 4887
Ezr 1:11 the exiles **c up** from Babylon to Jerusalem. 6590
2: 1 the province who **c up** from the captivity of 6590
2:59 The following **c up** from the towns 6590
3: 1 When the seventh month **c** and 5595
4: 2 *they* **c** to Zerubbabel and to the heads of 5602
4:12 that the Jews who **c up** to us 10513
4:24 of God in Jerusalem **c to a standstill** 10098
5:16 So this Sheshbazzar **c** and laid 10085
7: 6 this Ezra **c up** from Babylon. 6590
7: 7 also **c up** to Jerusalem in the seventh year 6590
8: 1 with them who **c up** with me from Babylon 6590
9: 1 the leaders **c** to me and said, 5602
Ne 1: 2 **c** from Judah with some other men, 995
4:12 near them **c** and told us ten times over, 995
4:21 the first light of dawn till the stars **c out.** 3655
5:17 as well as those *who* **c** to us from 995
6: 1 When **word c** to Sanballat, Tobiah, 9048
7: 6 the province who **c up** from the captivity of 6590
7:61 The following **c up** from the towns 6590
7:73 When the seventh month **c** and 5595
9:13 *"You* **c down** on Mount Sinai; 3718
13: 7 and **c back** to Jerusalem. 995
13:21 From that time on *they* no longer **c** on 995
Est 2:12 a girl's turn **c** to go in to King Xerxes, 5595
2:15 When the turn **c** *for* Esther 5595
4: 3 to which the edict and order of the king **c,** 5595
4: 4 When Esther's maids and eunuchs **c** 995
8: 1 And Mordecai **c** into the presence of 995
9:15 in Susa **c together** on the fourteenth day of 7735
9:25 But when the plot **c** *to* the king's attention, 995
Job 1: 6 One day the angels **c** to present themselves 995
1: 6 and Satan also **c** with them. 995
1:14 a messenger **c** to Job and said, 995
1:16 another messenger **c** and said, 995
1:17 another messenger **c** and said, 995
1:18 yet another messenger **c** and said, 995
1:21 "Naked *I* **c** from my mother's womb, 3655
2: 1 the angels **c** to present themselves before 995
2: 1 also **c** with them to present himself 995
3:11 and die *as I* **c** from the womb? 3655
30:26 Yet when I hoped for good, evil **c;** 995
30:26 when I looked for light, then **c** darkness. 995
31:29 or gloated over the trouble *that* **c** *to* him— 5162
42:11 and everyone who had known him before **c** 995
Ps 18: 6 my cry **c** before him, into his ears. 995
18: 8 consuming fire **c** from his mouth, NIH
18: 9 He parted the heavens and **c down;** 3718
33: 9 For he spoke, and *it* **c to be;** 2118
51: T When the prophet Nathan **c** to him 995
105:19 till what he foretold **c to pass,** 995
105:31 He spoke, and *there* **c** swarms of flies, 995
105:34 He spoke, and the locusts **c,** 995
106:32 and **trouble c** to Moses because of them; 8317
106:33 and **rash words c** from Moses' lips. 1051
114: 1 When Israel **c out** of Egypt, 3655
116: 3 the anguish of the grave **c upon** me; 5162
132: 6 *we* **c upon** it in the fields of Jaar: 5162
139:16 in your book before one of them **c** to be. NIH
Pr 7:10 **out c** a woman **to meet** 7925
7:15 So *I* **c out** to meet you; 3655
Ecc 2:14 but I **c** *to* **realize** that AIT
4:16 But those who **c** later were not pleased NIH
9:14 And a powerful king **c** against it, 995
12: 7 the dust returns to the ground *it* **c** *from,* 2118
Isa 11:16 as there was for Israel when they **c up** 6590
14:28 This oracle **c** in the year King Ahaz died: 2118
20: 1 **c** to Ashdod and attacked and captured it— 995
23: 3 the great waters **c** the grain of the Shihor; NIH
26:16 LORD, *they* **c** *to* you in their distress; 7212
37: 5 King Hezekiah's officials **c** to Isaiah, 995
37:29 I will make you return by the way *you* **c.** 995
37:34 By the way that *he* **c** he will return; 995

Isa 38: 4 Then the word of the LORD **c** to Isaiah: 2118
39: 3 *"They* **c** to me from Babylon." 995
48: 3 then suddenly I acted, and *they* **c to pass.** 995
50: 2 *When* I **c,** why was there no one? 995
64: 3 *you* **c down,** and the mountains trembled 3718
66: 2 and so they **c into being?"** 2118
Jer 1: 2 the LORD **c** to him in the thirteenth year 2118
1: 4 The word of the LORD **c** to me, saying, 2118
1:11 The word of the LORD **c** to me: 2118
1:13 The word of the LORD **c** to me again: 2118
2: 1 The word of the LORD **c** to me: 2118
2: 7 But *you* **c** and defiled my land 995
7: 1 This is the word that **c** to Jeremiah from 2118
11: 1 This is the word that **c** to Jeremiah from 2118
13: 3 word of the LORD **c** to me a second time: 2118
13: 8 Then the word of the LORD **c** to me: 2118
15:16 *When* your words **c,** I ate them; 5162
16: 1 Then the word of the LORD **c** to me: 2118
18: 1 This is the word that **c** to Jeremiah from 2118
18: 5 Then the word of the LORD **c** to me: 2118
21: 1 The word **c** to Jeremiah from the LORD 2118
24: 4 Then the word of the LORD **c** to me: 2118
25: 1 The word **c** to Jeremiah concerning all 2118
26: 1 this word **c** from the LORD: 2118
27: 1 this word **c** to Jeremiah from the LORD: 2118
28:12 the word of the LORD **c** to Jeremiah: 2118
29:30 the word of the LORD **c** to Jeremiah: 2118
30: 1 This is the word that **c** to Jeremiah from 2118
31:19 after I *c to* **understand,** I beat my breast. AIT
32: 1 This is the word that **c** to Jeremiah from 2118
32: 6 "The word of the LORD **c** to me: 2118
32: 8 my cousin Hanamel **c** to me in 995
32:23 *They* **c in** and took possession of it, 995
32:26 the word of the LORD **c** to Jeremiah: 2118
33: 1 of the LORD **c** to him a second time: 2118
33:19 The word of the LORD **c** to Jeremiah: 2118
33:23 The word of the LORD **c** to Jeremiah: 2118
34: 1 this word **c** to Jeremiah from the LORD: 2118
34: 8 The word **c** to Jeremiah from the LORD 2118
34:12 the word of the LORD **c** to Jeremiah: 2118
35: 1 that **c** to Jeremiah from the LORD during 2118
35:12 word of the LORD **c** to Jeremiah, saying: 2118
36: 1 this word **c** to Jeremiah from the LORD: 2118
36:27 the word of the LORD **c** to Jeremiah: 2118
37: 6 Then the word of the LORD **c** to Jeremiah 2118
39: 3 of the king of Babylon **c** and took seats in 995
39:15 the word of the LORD **c** to him: 2118
40: 1 The word **c** to Jeremiah from the LORD 2118
40: 8 *they* **c** to Gedaliah at Mizpah— 995
40:12 they all **c back** to the land of Judah, 8740
40:13 the army officers still in the open country **c** 995
41: 1 **c** with ten men to Gedaliah son of Ahikam 995
41: 5 torn their clothes and cut themselves **c** 995
42: 7 Ten days later the word of the LORD **c** 2118
43: 8 In Tahpanhes the word of the LORD **c** 2118
44: 1 This word **c** to Jeremiah concerning all 2118
44:28 the whole remnant of Judah who **c** to live 995
46: 1 the word of the LORD that **c** to Jeremiah 2118
47: 1 the word of the LORD that **c** to Jeremiah 2118
49: 9 If grape pickers **c** to you, 995
49: 9 If thieves **c** during the night, NIH
49:34 the word of the LORD that **c** to Jeremiah 2118
52:12 the king of Babylon, **c** to Jerusalem. 995
La 3:57 *You* **c near** when I called you, and you said, 7928
Eze 1: 3 the word of the LORD **c** to Ezekiel 2118+2118
1:25 Then *there* **c** a voice from above 2118
2: 2 the Spirit **c** into me and raised me 995
3:15 *I* **c** to the exiles who lived at Tel Abib 995
3:16 of seven days the word of the LORD **c** 2118
3:24 Spirit **c** into me and raised me to my feet. 995
6: 1 The word of the LORD **c** to me: 2118
7: 1 The word of the LORD **c** to me: 2118
8: 1 of the Sovereign LORD **c** upon me there. 5877
9: 2 *They* **c in** and stood beside the bronze altar. 995
11: 5 Then the Spirit of the LORD **c** upon me, 5877
11:14 The word of the LORD **c** to me: 2118
12: 1 The word of the LORD **c** to me: 2118
12: 8 In the morning the word of the LORD **c** 2118
12:17 The word of the LORD **c** to me: 2118
12:21 The word of the LORD **c** to me: 2118
12:26 The word of the LORD **c** to me: 2118
13: 1 The word of the LORD **c** to me: 2118
14: 1 Some of the elders of Israel **c** to me and sat 995
14: 2 Then the word of the LORD **c** to me: 2118
14:12 The word of the LORD **c** to me: 2118
15: 1 The word of the LORD **c** to me: 2118
16: 1 The word of the LORD **c** to me: 2118
17: 1 The word of the LORD **c** to me: 2118
17: 3 and full plumage of varied colors **c** 995
17:11 Then the word of the LORD **c** to me: 2118
18: 1 The word of the LORD **c** to me: 2118
19: 8 Then the nations **c** against him, 5989
20: 1 some of the elders of Israel **c** to inquire of 995
20: 2 Then the word of the LORD **c** to me: 2118
20:45 The word of the LORD **c** to me: 2118
21: 1 The word of the LORD **c** to me: 2118
21: 8 The word of the LORD **c** to me: 2118
21:18 The word of the LORD **c** to me: 2118
22: 1 The word of the LORD **c** to me: 2118
22:17 Then the word of the LORD **c** to me: 2118
22:23 Again the word of the LORD **c** to me: 2118
23: 1 The word of the LORD **c** to me: 2118
23:17 Then the Babylonians **c** to her, 995
23:40 "They even sent messengers for men *who* **c** 995
24: 1 the word of the LORD **c** to me: 2118
24:15 The word of the LORD **c** to me: 2118
24:20 "The word of the LORD **c** to me: 2118
Eze 25: 1 The word of the LORD **c** to me: 2118
26: 1 the word of the LORD **c** to me: 2118
27: 1 The word of the LORD **c** to me: 2118
27: 9 the sea and their sailors **c** alongside to trade 2118
28: 1 The word of the LORD **c** to me: 2118
28:11 The word of the LORD **c** to me: 2118
28:20 The word of the LORD **c** to me: 2118
29: 1 the word of the LORD **c** to me: 2118
29:17 the word of the LORD **c** to me: 2118
30: 1 The word of the LORD **c** to me: 2118
30:20 the word of the LORD **c** to me: 2118
31: 1 the word of the LORD **c** to me: 2118
31:12 of the earth **c out** from under its shade 3718
32: 1 the word of the LORD **c** to me: 2118
32:17 the word of the LORD **c** to me: 2118
33: 1 The word of the LORD **c** to me: 2118
33:21 a man who had escaped from Jerusalem **c** 995
33:22 and he opened my mouth before the man **c** 995
33:23 Then the word of the LORD **c** to me: 2118
34: 1 The word of the LORD **c** to me: 2118
35: 1 The word of the LORD **c** to me: 2118
36:16 Again the word of the LORD **c** to me: 2118
37: 7 a rattling sound, and the bones **c together,** 7928
37:10 *they* **c to life** and stood up on their feet— 2649
37:15 The word of the LORD **c** to me: 2118
38: 1 The word of the LORD **c** to me: 2118
43: 3 the vision I had seen when he **c** to destroy 995
Da 1: 1 of Babylon **c** *to* Jerusalem and besieged it. 995
2: 2 When *they* **c in** and stood before the king, 995
3: 8 At this time some astrologers **c forward** 10638
3:26 Meshach and Abednego **c out** of the fire, 10485
4: 7 enchanters, astrologers and diviners **c,** 10549
4: 8 Daniel **c into** my presence and I told him 10549
4:31 on his lips *when* a voice **c** from heaven, 10484
5: 8 Then all the king's wise men **c in,** 10549
5:10 **c** into the banquet hall. 10549
6:20 When he **c near** the den, 10638
7: 3 **c up** out of the sea. 10513
7: 8 a little one, *which* **c up** among them; 10513
7:20 that **c up,** before which three of them fell— 10513
7:22 of Days **c** and pronounced judgment 10085
7:22 time **c** when they possessed the kingdom. 10413
8: 5 a prominent horn between his eyes **c** from 995
8: 6 *He* **c** toward the two-horned ram I had seen 995
8: 9 Out of one of them **c** another horn, 3655
8:17 *he* **c** near the place where I was standing, 995
9:21 **c** to me in swift flight about the time of 5595
10: 1 The understanding of the message **c** to him NIH
10:13 one of the chief princes, **c** to help me, 995
Hos 1: 1 of the LORD that **c** to Hosea son of Beeri 2118
2:15 as in the day she **c up** out of Egypt. 6590
9:10 But when they **c** *to* Baal Peor, 995
Joel 1: 1 of the LORD that **c** to Joel son of Pethuel. 2118
Ob 1: 5 thieves **c** to you, if robbers in the night— 995
1: 5 If grape pickers **c** to you, 995
Jnh 1: 1 of the LORD **c** to Jonah son of Amittai: 2118
3: 1 Then the word of the LORD **c** to Jonah 2118
Mic 1: 1 the LORD that **c** to Micah of Moresheth 2118
7:15 "As in the days when you **c out** of Egypt, 3655
Hab 3: 3 God **c** from Teman, 995
3:13 *You* **c out** to deliver your people, 3655
Zep 1: 1 that **c** to Zephaniah son of Cushi, the son 2118
Hag 1: 1 the LORD **c** through the prophet Haggai 2118
1: 3 the LORD **c** through the prophet Haggai: 2118
1:14 *They* **c** and began to work on the house of 995
2: 1 the LORD **c** through the prophet Haggai: 2118
2: 5 with you when you **c out** of Egypt. 3655
2:10 of the LORD **c** to the prophet Haggai: 2118
2:16 anyone **c** to a heap of twenty measures, 995
2:20 the LORD **c** to Haggai a second time on 2118
Zec 1: 1 the LORD **c** to the prophet Zechariah son 2118
1: 7 the LORD **c** to the prophet Zechariah son 2118
2: 3 and another angel **c** to meet him 3655
4: 8 Then the word of the LORD **c** to me: 2118
5: 5 to me **c forward** and said to me, 3655
6: 9 The word of the LORD **c** to me: 2118
7: 1 the word of the LORD **c** to Zechariah on 2118
7: 4 the word of the LORD Almighty **c** to me: 2118
7: 8 word of the LORD **c** again to Zechariah: 2118
8: 1 the word of the LORD Almighty **c** to me. 2118
8:18 the word of the LORD Almighty **c** to me. 2118
Mt 1:18 how the birth of Jesus Christ **c about:** *1639*
1:18 but before they **c together,** *5302*
2: 1 Magi from the east **c** to Jerusalem *4134*
3: 1 In those days John the Baptist **c,** *4134*
3:13 Then Jesus **c** from Galilee to the Jordan to *4134*
4: 3 The tempter **c to** him and said, *4665*
4:11 and angels **c** and attended him. *4665*
5: 1 His disciples **c to** him, *4665*
7:25 The rain **c down,** the streams rose, *2849*
7:27 The rain **c down,** the streams rose, *2849*
8: 1 *When* he **c down** from the mountainside, *2849*
8: 2 A man with leprosy **c** and knelt before him *4665*
8: 5 a centurion **c to** him, asking for help. *4665*
8:14 *When* Jesus **c** into Peter's house, *2262*
8:16 *When* evening **c,** many who were
demon-possessed were brought to him, *1181*
8:19 a teacher of the law **c to** him and said, *4665*
8:24 a furious storm **c up** on the lake, *1181*
8:32 So they **c out** and went into the pigs, *2002*
9: 1 crossed over and **c** to his own town. *2262*
9:10 many tax collectors and "sinners" **c** and ate *2262*
9:14 Then John's disciples **c** and asked him, *4665*
9:18 a ruler **c** and knelt before him and said, *2262*
9:20 for twelve years **c up** behind him *4665*
9:28 the blind men **c to** him, and he asked them, *4665*
11:18 For John **c** neither eating nor drinking, *2262*
Mt 11:19 The Son of Man **c** eating and drinking, *2262*
12:42 for *she* **c** from the ends of the earth to listen *2262*
13: 4 and the birds **c** and ate it up. *2262*
13: 6 But *when* the sun **c up,** *422*
13:10 The disciples **c to** him and asked, *4665*
13:25 his enemy **c** and sowed weeds among *2262*
13:27 "The owner's servants **c to** him and said, *4665*
13:36 His disciples **c to** him and said, *4665*
14:12 John's disciples **c** and took his body *4665*
14:15 the disciples **c to** him and said, *4665*
14:23 *When* evening **c,** he was there alone, *1181*
14:29 walked on the water and **c** toward Jesus. *2262*
15: 1 of the law **c to** Jesus from Jerusalem *4665*
15:12 Then the disciples **c to** him and asked, *4665*
15:22 A Canaanite woman from that vicinity **c** *2002*
15:23 So his disciples **c to** him and urged him, *4665*
15:25 The woman **c** and knelt before him. *2262*
15:30 Great crowds **c to** him, bringing the lame, *4665*
16: 1 and Sadducees **c to** Jesus and tested him *4665*
16:13 *When* Jesus **c** to the region *2262*
17: 7 But Jesus **c** and touched them. *4665*
17:14 *When they* **c** to the crowd, *2262*
17:18 and it **c out** of the boy, *2002*
17:19 disciples **c to** Jesus in private and asked, *4665*
17:22 *When* they **c together** in Galilee, *5370*
17:24 the two-drachma tax **c to** Peter and asked, *4665*
17:25 *When* Peter **c** into the house, *2262*
18: 1 At that time the disciples **c to** Jesus *4665*
18:21 Then Peter **c to** Jesus and asked, "Lord, *4665*
19: 3 Some Pharisees **c to** him to test him. *4665*
19:16 Now a man **c up to** Jesus and asked, *4665*
20: 8 *"When* evening **c,** the owner of *1181*
20: 9 the eleventh hour **c** and each received *2262*
20:10 So *when* those **c** who were hired first, *2262*
20:20 of Zebedee's sons **c to** Jesus with her sons *4665*
21: 1 As they approached Jerusalem and **c** *2262*
21:14 and the lame **c to** him at the temple, *4665*
21:23 and the elders of the people **c to** him. *4665*
21:32 For John **c** to you to show you the way *2262*
22:11 "But *when* the king **c in** to see the guests, *1656*
22:23 **c to** him with a question. *4665*
24: 1 when his disciples **c up to** him *4665*
24: 3 the disciples **c to** him privately. *4665*
24:39 about what would happen until the flood **c** *2262*
25:11 "Later the others also **c.** *2262*
25:22 "The man with the two talents also **c.** *4665*
25:24 the man who had received the one talent **c.** *4665*
25:36 I was in prison and *you* **c** to visit me.' *2262*
26: 7 a woman **c to** him with an alabaster jar *4665*
26:17 the disciples **c to** Jesus and asked, *4665*
26:20 *When* evening **c,** Jesus was reclining at *1181*
26:43 *When he* **c back,** *2262*
26:50 Jesus replied, "Friend, *do* what *you* **c for."** *4205*
26:60 *though* many false witnesses **c forward.** *4665*
26:60 Finally two **c forward** *4665*
26:69 and a servant girl **c to** him. *4665*
27: 1 of the people **c** to the decision to put Jesus *1181*
27:33 *They* **c** to a place called Golgotha *2262*
27:45 the ninth hour darkness **c** over all the land. *1181*
27:53 *They* **c out of** the tombs, *2002*
27:57 *there* **c** a rich man from Arimathea, *2262*
28: 2 angel of the Lord **c down** from heaven and, *2849*
28: 9 They **c to** him, *4665*
28:13 'His disciples **c** during the night *2262*
28:18 Then Jesus **c to** them and said, *4665*
Mk 1: 4 And so John **c,** baptizing in the desert *1181*
1: 9 that time Jesus **c** from Nazareth in Galilee *2262*
1:11 And a voice **c** from heaven: *1181*
1:21 and when the Sabbath **c,** *NIG*
1:26 the man violently and **c out** of him with *2002*
1:40 with leprosy **c** to him and begged him *2262*
1:45 the *people* still **c** to him from everywhere. *2262*
2: 3 Some *men* **c,** bringing to him a paralytic, *2262*
2:13 A large crowd **c** to him, *2262*
2:18 *Some people* **c** and asked Jesus, *2262*
3: 8 many people **c** to him from Judea, *2262*
3:13 and *they* **c** to him. *599*
3:22 of the law who **c down** from Jerusalem said, *2849*
4: 4 and the birds **c** and ate it up. *2262*
4: 6 But when the sun **c up,** *422*
4: 8 It **c up,** grew and produced a crop, *326*
4:35 That day *when* evening **c,** *1181*
4:37 A furious squall **c up,** *1181*
5: 2 an evil spirit **c** from the tombs to meet him. *NIG*
5:13 the evil spirits **c out** and went into the pigs. *2002*
5:15 When *they* **c** to Jesus, *2262*
5:22 the synagogue rulers, named Jairus, **c** there. *2262*
5:27 *she* **c** up behind him in the crowd *2262*
5:33 **c** and fell at his feet and, *2262*
5:35 *some men* **c** from the house of Jairus, *2262*
5:38 When *they* **c** to the home of *2262*
6: 2 *When* the Sabbath **c,** *1181*
6:21 Finally the opportune time **c.** *1181*
6:22 the daughter of Herodias **c in** and danced, *1656*
6:29 John's disciples **c** and took his body *2262*
6:35 so his disciples **c to** him. *4665*
6:47 *When* evening **c,** the boat was in the middle *1181*
7:25 by an evil spirit **c** and fell at his feet. *2262*
8:11 The Pharisees **c** and began *2002*
8:22 *They* **c** to Bethsaida, *2262*
9: 7 and a voice **c** from the cloud: *1181*
9:14 *When they* **c** to the other disciples, *2262*
9:26 convulsed him violently and **c out.** *2002*
9:33 *They* **c** to Capernaum. *2262*
10: 1 Again crowds of people **c** to him, *5233*
10: 2 Some Pharisees **c** and tested him by asking, *4665*
10:35 the sons of Zebedee, **c to** him. *4702*

Mk 10:46 Then *they* c to Jericho. *2262*
10:50 he jumped to his feet and c to Jesus. *2262*
11: 1 As they approached Jerusalem and c *NIG*
11:19 When evening **c,** they went out of the city. *1181*
11:27 the teachers of the law and the elders c *2262*
12:14 They c to him and said, "Teacher, *2262*
12:18 c to him with a question. *2262*
12:28 of the law c and heard them debating. *4665*
12:42 But a poor widow c and put *2262*
14: 3 a woman c with an alabaster jar *2262*
14:17 *When* evening **c,** Jesus arrived with *1181*
14:40 *When he* c **back,** he again found them *2262*
14:53 elders and teachers of the law **c together.** *5302*
14:66 of the servant girls of the high priest c by. *2262*
15: 8 The crowd **c up** and asked Pilate to do *326*
15:33 At the sixth hour darkness c over *1181*
Lk 1:10 when the time for the burning of incense **c,** *NIG*
1:22 *When he* **c out,** he could not speak to them. *2002*
1:59 On the eighth day *they* c to circumcise *2262*
2: 6 the time c for the baby to be born, *4398*
3: 2 the word of God c to John son of Zechariah *1181*
3:12 Tax collectors also c to be baptized. *2262*
3:22 And a voice c from heaven: *1181*
4:22 at the gracious words that **c from** his lips. *1744*
4:35 the man down before them all and **c out** *2002*
4:41 Moreover, demons **c out** of many people, *2002*
4:42 for him and when *they* c to where he was, *2262*
5: 7 and *they* c and filled both boats so full *2262*
5:12 a man c along who was covered *NIG*
5:15 so that crowds of people c to hear him and *5302*
5:18 Some men c carrying a paralytic on a mat *NIG*
6:13 When morning **c,** he called his disciples *1181*
6:48 *When* a flood **c,** the torrent struck *1181*
7: 4 *When* they c to Jesus, *4134*
7:20 *When* the men c to Jesus, they said, *4134*
7:33 For John the Baptist c neither eating bread *2262*
7:34 The Son of Man c eating and drinking, *2262*
7:44 *I* **c into** your house. *1656*
8: 6 Some fell on rock, and *when it* **c up,** *5886*
8: 8 *It* **c up** and yielded a crop, *5886*
8:19 Jesus' mother and brothers c to see him, *4134*
8:23 A squall **c down** on the lake, *2849*
8:33 *When* the demons **c out** of the man, *2002*
8:35 When *they* c to Jesus, *2262*
8:41 c and fell at Jesus' feet, *2262*
8:44 She **c up** behind him and touched the edge *4665*
8:47 c trembling and fell at his feet. *2262*
8:49 someone c from the house of Jairus, *2262*
9:12 Late in the afternoon the Twelve **c to** him *4665*
9:35 A voice c from the cloud, saying, *1181*
9:37 *when* they **c down** from the mountain, *2982*
10:32 *when he* c to the place and saw him, *1181*
10:33 as he traveled, c where the man was; *2262*
10:38 he **c to** a village where *1656*
10:40 She c to him and asked, "Lord, *2392*
11:31 for *she* c from the ends of the earth to listen *2262*
12:51 Do you think *I* c to bring peace on earth? *4134*
13:31 At that time some Pharisees **c to** Jesus *4665*
14:21 "The servant **c back** and reported this *4134*
15:17 *"When he* c to his senses, he said, *2262*
15:25 When he c near the house, *2262*
16:21 Even the dogs c and licked his sores. *2262*
16:22 **"The time c when** the beggar died *1181+1254*
17:15 **c back,** praising God in a loud voice. *5715*
17:27 Then the flood c and destroyed them all. *2262*
18:40 *When* he **c near,** Jesus asked him, *1581*
19: 6 So *he* **c down** at once *2849*
19:10 For the Son of Man c to seek and *2262*
19:16 "The first one c and said, 'Sir, *4134*
19:18 "The second c and said, 'Sir, *2262*
19:20 "Then another servant c and said, 'Sir, *2262*
19:23 so that *when* I **c back,** *2262*
19:37 *When* he **c near** the place where *1581*
20: 1 together with the elders, **c up** to him. *2392*
20:27 **c to** Jesus with a question. *4665*
21:38 **c early in the morning** *3983*
22: 7 Then c the day of Unleavened Bread *2262*
22:14 When the hour **c,** *1181*
22:47 While he was still speaking a crowd **c** up, *NIG*
23:33 When *they* c to the place called the Skull, *2262*
23:36 The soldiers also **c up** and mocked him. *4665*
23:44 and darkness c over the whole land until *1181*
23:51 He c from the Judean town of Arimathea *NIG*
24: 9 *When they* **c back** from the tomb, *5715*
24:15 Jesus himself **c up** and walked along *1581*
24:23 *They* c and told us that they had seen *2262*
Jn 1: 6 *There* c a man who was sent from God; *1181*
1: 7 He c as a witness to testify concerning *2262*
1: 8 he c only as a witness to the light. *NIG*
1:11 *He* c to that which was his own, *2262*
1:14 who c from the Father, *NIG*
1:17 grace and truth c through Jesus Christ. *1181*
1:31 but the reason I c baptizing with water was *2262*
3: 2 He c to Jesus at night and said, "Rabbi, *2262*
3:13 into heaven except the one who c *2849*
3:26 *They* c to John and said to him, "Rabbi, *2262*
4: 5 So *he* c to a town in Samaria called Sychar, *2262*
4: 7 When a Samaritan woman c to draw water, *2262*
4:30 *They* **c out** of the town and made their way *2002*
4:40 So when the Samaritans c to him, *2262*
6:16 When evening **c,** his disciples went down *1181*
6:41 "I am the bread that **c down** from heaven." *2849*
6:42 can he now say, *'I* **c down** from heaven'?" *2849*
6:51 the living bread that **c down** from heaven. *2849*
6:58 This is the bread that **c down** from heaven. *2849*
8:14 where *I* c from and where I am going. *2262*
8:42 for I **c from** God and now am here. *2002*

Jn 9: 7 man went and washed, and c home seeing. *2262*
10: 8 All who ever c before me were thieves *2262*
10:22 c the Feast of Dedication at Jerusalem. *1181*
10:35 to whom the word of God **c—** *1181*
10:41 and many people c to him. *2262*
11:38 once more deeply moved, c to the tomb. *2262*
11:44 The dead man **c out,** *2002*
12: 9 that Jesus was there and **c,** *2262*
12:21 They **c to** Philip, *4665*
12:27 it was for this very reason *I* c to this hour. *2262*
12:28 Then a voice c from heaven, *2262*
13: 6 *He* c to Simon Peter, who said to him, *2262*
16:27 and have believed that I c from God. *2002*
16:28 *I* c from the Father and entered the world; *2002*
16:30 This makes us believe that *you* **c** *2002*
17: 8 They knew with certainty that *I* c *2002*
18: 3 So Judas c to the grove, *2262*
18:16 who was known to the high priest, c back, *2002*
18:29 So Pilate **c out** to them and asked, *2002*
18:37 and for this *I* c into the world, *2262*
19: 4 Once more Pilate **c out** and said to *2002*
19: 5 When Jesus **c out** wearing the crown *2002*
19:32 The soldiers therefore c and broke the legs *2262*
19:33 But *when they* c to Jesus and found *2262*
19:38 *he* c and took the body away. *2262*
20: 2 So *she* c running to Simon Peter and *2262*
20:19 Jesus c and stood among them and said, *2262*
20:24 was not with the disciples when Jesus **c.** *2262*
20:26 Jesus c and stood among them and said, *2262*
21:13 Jesus **c,** took the bread and gave it to them, *2262*
Ac 2: 1 When the day of Pentecost **c,** *5230*
2: 2 of a violent wind c from heaven and filled *1181*
2: 3 of fire that separated and **c to rest** on each *2767*
2: 6 a crowd **c together** in bewilderment, *5302*
3:11 the people were astonished and **c running** *5340*
4: 1 and the Sadducees **c up** to Peter and John *2392*
5: 6 Then the young men **c forward,** *482*
5: 7 About three hours later his wife **c in,** *1656*
5:10 Then the young men **c in** and, *1656*
5:25 Then someone c and said, "Look! *4134*
5:36 and *it* all c to nothing. *1181*
7:26 The next day Moses **c upon** *3972*
8: 7 With shrieks, evil spirits **c out of** many, *2002*
8:36 *they* c to some water and the eunuch said, *2262*
8:39 When *they* **c up** out of the water, *326*
9:26 *When he* c to Jerusalem, *4134*
10: 3 *who* c to him and said, "Cornelius!" *1656*
10:29 *I* c without raising any objection. *2262*
10:44 Holy Spirit **c on** all who heard the message. *2158*
11: 5 and *it* c down to where I was. *2262*
11:15 the Holy Spirit **c on** them as he had come *2158*
11:27 During this time some prophets **c down** *2982*
12:10 and c to the iron gate leading to the city. *2262*
12:11 Then Peter c to himself and said, *1181*
12:13 and a servant girl named Rhoda c to answer *4665*
13: 6 the whole island until they c to Paphos. *NIG*
13:11 Immediately mist and darkness c over him, *4406*
14:19 Then some Jews c from Antioch *2088*
14:24 *they* c into Pamphylia, *2262*
15: 1 Some men **c down** from Judea to Antioch *2982*
15: 4 *When they* c to Jerusalem, *4134*
16: 1 *He* c to Derbe and then to Lystra, *2918*
16: 7 *When they* c to the border of Mysia, *2262*
16:26 and everybody's chains **c loose.** *479*
16:39 *They* c to appease them and escorted them *2262*
16:40 *After* Paul and Silas **c out** of the prison, *2002*
17: 1 *they* c to Thessalonica, *2262*
18: 5 and Timothy c from Macedonia, *2982*
18:24 a native of Alexandria, **c to** Ephesus. *2918*
19: 6 the Holy Spirit c on them, *2262*
19:18 Many of those who believed now c *2262*
19:19 the total c to fifty thousand drachmas. *NIG*
20: 7 On the first day of the week we **c together** *5251*
20:18 the first day *I* c into the province of Asia. *2094*
21:10 prophet named Agabus **c down** from Judea. *2982*
21:30 the people c running from all directions. *1181*
21:33 The commander **c up** and arrested him *1581*
22: 6 "About noon *as* I c near Damascus, *4513*
22:12 "A man named Ananias c to see me. *2262*
23:27 but I c with my troops and rescued him, *2392*
24:17 *I* c to Jerusalem to bring my people gifts *4134*
24:24 Several days later Felix c *4134*
25:17 *When* they c here **with** me, *5302*
25:23 and Bernice c with great pomp and entered *2262*
27: 8 along the coast with difficulty and c to *2262*
27:39 When daylight **c,** they did not recognize *1181*
28: 9 of the sick on the island c and were cured. *4665*
28:13 The next day the south wind **c up,** *2104*
28:14 And so *we* c to Rome. *2262*
28:23 and c in even larger numbers to the place *2262*
28:30 and welcomed all who c to see him. *1660*
Ro 3:24 by his grace through the redemption that c *NIG*
5:12 and in this way death c to all men, *1451*
5:15 the gift that c by the grace of the one man, *NIG*
7: 9 but *when* the commandment **c,** *2262*
1Co 2: 1 When I c to you, brothers, *2262*
2: 3 I c to you in weakness and fear, *1181*
3: 5 through whom *you* c *to* **believe—** *AIT*
8: 6 from whom all things c and *NIG*
8: 6 through whom all things c and *NIG*
11:12 For as woman c from man, *NIG*
15:21 For since death c through a man, *NIG*
2Co 2: 3 so that *when I* c I should not be distressed *2262*
3: 7 c with glory, so that the Israelites could *1181*
3:11 And if what was fading away c with glory, *NIG*
7: 5 For *when* we c into Macedonia, *2262*
11: 9 for the brothers *who* c from Macedonia *2262*

Gal 2:11 When Peter c to Antioch, *2262*
2:12 Before certain men c from James, *2262*
3:23 Before this faith **c,** we were held prisoner *2262*
Eph 2:17 He c and preached peace *2262*
1Th 1: 5 our gospel c to you not simply with words, *1181*
1Ti 1:15 Christ Jesus c into the world *2262*
2Ti 4:16 no one **c to** my **support,** *4134*
Heb 7:28 but the oath, which c after the law, *NIG*
9:11 *When* Christ c as high priest of *4134*
10: 5 *when* Christ **c into** the world, he said: *1656*
11:12 **c descendants** as numerous as the stars in *1164*
2Pe 1:17 the voice c to him from the Majestic Glory, *5770*
1:18 that c from heaven when we were with him *5770*
1:20 that no prophecy of Scripture **c about** by *1181*
1Jn 5: 6 This is the one who c by water and blood— *2262*
Rev 1:16 **out** of his mouth c a sharp double-edged sword. *1744*
2: 8 who died and **c to life** again. *2409*
4: 5 **From** the throne c flashes of lightning, *1744*
5: 7 *He* c and took the scroll from the right hand *2262*
6: 4 Then another horse **c out,** a fiery red one. *2002*
8: 3 c and stood at the altar. *2262*
8: 5 and *there* c peals of thunder, rumblings, *1181*
8: 7 and *there* c hail and fire mixed with blood, *1181*
9: 3 **out** of the smoke locusts **c** *2002*
9:17 **out** of their mouths c fire, smoke and sulfur. *1744*
9:18 and sulfur that **c out** of their mouths. *1744*
11:19 And *there* c flashes of lightning, *1181*
14:15 Then another angel **c out** of the temple *2002*
14:17 Another angel **c out** of the temple *2002*
14:18 c from the altar and called in a loud voice *NIG*
15: 6 **Out** of the temple c the seven angels *2002*
16:13 they c out of the mouth of the dragon, *NIG*
16:17 **out** of the temple c a loud voice *2002*
16:18 Then *there* c flashes of lightning, *1181*
17: 1 the seven bowls c and said to me, *2262*
19: 5 Then a voice c **from** the throne, saying: *2002*
19:21 with the sword that **c out** of the mouth of *2002*
20: 4 *They* **c to life** and reigned with Christ *2409*
20: 9 But fire **c down** from heaven *2849*
21: 9 of the seven last plagues c and said to me, *2262*

CAMEL (7) [CAMEL'S, CAMEL-LOADS, CAMELS, CAMELS', SHE-CAMEL]

Ge 24:64 She got down from her c 1695
Lev 11: 4 The **c,** though it chews the cud, 1695
Dt 14: 7 not eat the **c,** the rabbit or the coney. 1695
Mt 19:24 it is easier for a c to go through the eye of *2823*
23:24 You strain out a gnat but swallow a **c.** *2823*
Mk 10:25 It is easier for a c to go through the eye of *2823*
Lk 18:25 it is easier for a c to go through the eye of *2823*

CAMEL'S (3) [CAMEL]

Ge 31:34 inside her c saddle and was sitting on them. 1695
Mt 3: 4 John's clothes were made of c hair, *2823*
Mk 1: 6 John wore clothing made *of* c hair, *2823*

CAMEL-LOADS (1) [LOAD]

2Ki 8: 9 taking with him as a gift forty c of all 1695+5362

CAMELS (48) [CAMEL]

Ge 12:16 menservants and maidservants, and **c.** 1695
24:10 servant took ten of his master's c and left, 1695
24:11 the c kneel down near the well outside 1695
24:14 'Drink, and I'll water your c too'— 1695
24:19 she said, "I'll draw water for your c too, 1695
24:20 and drew enough for all his **c.** 1695
24:22 When the c had finished drinking, 1695
24:30 to the man and found him standing by the c 1695
24:31 the house and a place for the **c."** 1695
24:32 and the c were unloaded. 1695
24:32 Straw and fodder were brought for the **c,** 1695
24:35 and c and donkeys. 1695
24:44 "Drink, and I'll draw water for your c too," 1695
24:46 'Drink, and I'll water your c too.' 1695
24:46 So I drank, and she watered the c also. 1695
24:61 and mounted their c and went back with 1695
24:63 and as he looked up, he saw c approaching. 1695
30:43 and c and donkeys. 1695
31:17 Jacob put his children and his wives on **c,** 1695
32: 7 and the flocks and herds and c as well. 1695
32:15 thirty female c with their young, 1695
37:25 Their c were loaded with spices, 1695
Ex 9: 3 on your horses and donkeys and c and 1695
Jdg 6: 5 to count the men and their **c;** 1695
7:12 Their c could no more be counted than 1695
1Sa 15: 3 cattle and sheep, c and donkeys.' " 1695
27: 9 but took sheep and cattle, donkeys and **c,** 1695
30:17 who rode off on c and fled. 1695
1Ki 10: 2 with c carrying spices, 1695
1Ch 5:21 of the Hagrites—fifty thousand **c,** 1695
12:40 Naphtali came bringing food on donkeys, **c,** 1695
27:30 Obil the Ishmaelite was in charge of the **c.** 1695
2Ch 9: 1 with c carrying spices, 1695
14:15 of sheep and goats and **c.** 1695
Ezr 2:67 435 c and 6,720 donkeys. 1695
Ne 7:69 435 c and 6,720 donkeys. 1695
Job 1: 3 three thousand **c,** five hundred yoke 1695
1:17 down on your c and carried them off. 1695
42:12 six thousand c, a thousand yoke of oxen 1695
Isa 21: 7 riders on donkeys or riders on **c,** 1695
30: 6 their treasures on the humps of **c,** 1695
60: 6 Herds of c will cover your land, 1695
60: 6 **young c** *of* Midian and Ephah. 1145

Isa 66:20 and on mules and c," says the LORD. 4140
Jer 49:29 be carried off with all their goods and c. 1695
49:32 Their c will become plunder, 1695
Eze 25: 5 I will turn Rabbah into a pasture for c 1695
Zec 14:15 the c and donkeys, 1695

CAMELS' (2) [CAMEL]

Jdg 8:21 and took the ornaments off their c' necks. 1695
8:26 or the chains that were on their c' necks. 1695

CAMON (KJV) See KAMON

CAMP (180) [CAMPED, CAMPFIRES, CAMPING, CAMPS, ENCAMP, ENCAMPED, ENCAMPS]

Ge 32: 2 he said, "This is the c *of* God!" 4722
32:21 but he himself spent the night in the c. 4722
Ex 16:13 That evening quail came and covered the c, 4722
16:13 a layer of dew around the c. 4722
19:16 Everyone in the c trembled. 4722
19:17 the people out of the c to meet with God, 4722
29:14 and its hide and its offal outside the c. 4722
32:17 "There is the sound of war in the c." 4722
32:19 When Moses approached the c and saw 4722
32:26 he stood at the entrance to the c and said, 4722
32:27 through the c from one end to the other, 4722
33: 7 the c some distance away, 4722
33: 7 to the tent of meeting outside the c. 4722
33:11 Then Moses would return to the c, 4722
36: 6 and they sent this word throughout the c: 4722
Lev 4:12 the c to a place ceremonially clean, 4722
4:21 the c and burn it as he burned the first bull. 4722
6:11 and carry the ashes outside the c to a place 4722
8:17 and its offal he burned up outside the c, 4722
9:11 and the hide he burned up outside the c. 4722
10: 4 carry your cousins outside the c, 4722
10: 5 still in their tunics, outside the c, 4722
13:46 he must live outside the c. 4722
14: 3 to go outside the c and examine him. 4722
14: 8 After this he may come into the c, 4722
16:26 afterward he may come into the c. 4722
16:27 must be taken outside the c; 4722
16:28 afterward he may come into the c. 4722
17: 3 a lamb or a goat in the c or outside of it 4722
24:10 and a fight broke out in the c between him 4722
24:14 "Take the blasphemer outside the c. 4722
24:23 and they took the blasphemer outside the c 4722
Nu 1:52 in his own c under his own standard. 4722
2: 2 "The Israelites *are to* c around the Tent 2837
2: 3 the divisions of the c *of* Judah are 4722
2: 5 The tribe of Issachar *will* c next to them. 2837
2: 9 All the men assigned to the c *of* Judah, 4722
2:10 On the south will be the divisions of the c 4722
2:12 The tribe of Simeon *will* c next to them. 2837
2:16 All the men assigned to the c *of* Reuben, 4722
2:17 Then the Tent of Meeting and the c *of* 4722
2:18 of the c *of* Ephraim under their standard. 4722
2:24 All the men assigned to the c *of* Ephraim, 4722
2:25 On the north will be the divisions of the c 4722
2:27 The tribe of Asher *will* c next to them. 2837
2:31 to the c *of* Dan number 157,600. 4722
3:23 Gershonite clans *were to* c on the west, 2837
3:29 *to* c on the south side of the tabernacle. 2837
3:35 *to* c on the north side of the tabernacle. 2837
3:38 Moses and Aaron and his sons *were to* c to 2837
4: 5 When the c is to move, 4722
4:15 and when the c is ready to move, 4722
5: 2 to send away from the c anyone who has 4722
5: 3 the c so they will not defile their camp, 4722
5: 3 the camp so they will not defile their c, 4722
5: 4 they sent them outside the c. 4722
9:18 *they* **remained in** c. 2837
9:22 the Israelites *would* **remain in** c and 2837
10:14 The divisions of the c *of* Judah went first, 4722
10:18 divisions of the c *of* Reuben went next, 4722
10:22 divisions of the c *of* Ephraim went next, 4722
10:25 the divisions of the c *of* Dan set out, 4722
10:31 You know where we *should* c in the desert, 2837
10:34 by day when they set out from the c. 4722
11: 1 of the outskirts of the c. 4722
11: 9 When the dew settled on the c at night, 4722
11:26 had remained in the c. 4722
11:26 and they prophesied in the c. 4722
11:27 and Medad are prophesying in the c." 4722
11:30 and the elders of Israel returned to the c. 4722
11:31 the c to about three feet above the ground, 4722
11:32 Then they spread them out all around the c. 4722
12:14 Confine her outside the c for seven days; 4722
12:15 So Miriam was confined outside the c 4722
14:44 the LORD's covenant moved from the c. 4722
15:35 assembly must stone him outside the c." 4722
15:36 So the assembly took him outside the c 4722
19: 3 to be taken outside the c and slaughtered 4722
19: 7 He may then come into the c, 4722
19: 9 in a ceremonially clean place outside the c. 4722
31:12 and the Israelite assembly at their c on 4722
31:13 to meet them outside the c. 4722
31:19 must stay outside the c seven days. 4722
31:24 Then you may come into the c." 4722
Dt 1: 7 **Break** c and advance into the hill country of 7155
1:33 to search out places for you to c and 2837
2:14 of fighting men had perished from the c, 4722
2:15 until he had completely eliminated them from the c. 4722
23:10 he is to go outside the c and stay there. 4722
23:11 and at sunset he may return to the c. 4722
23:12 the c where you can go to relieve yourself. 4722
23:14 about in your c to protect you and 4722
23:14 Your c must be holy, 4722
Jos 1:11 "Go through the c and tell the people, 4722
3: 2 the officers went throughout the c, 4722
3:14 when the people **broke** c to cross the Jordan, 185+4946+5825
4: 8 they carried them over with them to their c, 4869
5: 8 they remained where they were in c 4722
6:11 Then the people returned to c and spent 4722
6:14 around the city once and returned to the c. 4722
6:18 the c *of* Israel liable to destruction 4722
6:23 and put them in a place outside the c 4722
8:11 *They* **set up** c north of Ai, 2837
8:13 all those in the c to the north of the city and 4722
9: 6 the c at Gilgal and said to him and the men 4722
10: 6 then sent word to Joshua in the c at Gilgal: 4722
10:15 with all Israel to the c at Gilgal. 4722
10:21 then returned safely to Joshua in the c 4722
10:43 with all Israel to the c at Gilgal. 4722
11: 5 and **made** c together at the Waters 2837
18: 9 and returned to Joshua in the c at Shiloh. 4722
Jdg 7: 1 The c *of* Midian was north of them in 4722
7: 8 c *of* Midian lay below him in the valley. 4722
7: 9 "Get up, go down against the c, 4722
7:10 go down to the c with your servant Purah 4722
7:11 you will be encouraged to attack the c." 4722
7:11 down to the outposts of the c. 4722
7:13 into the Midianite c. 4722
7:14 and the whole c into his hands." 4722
7:15 to the c *of* Israel and called out, 4722
7:15 The LORD has given the Midianite c 4722
7:17 When I get to the edge of the c, 4722
7:18 from all around the c blow yours and shout, 4722
7:19 the c at the beginning of the middle watch, 4722
7:21 each man held his position around the c, 4722
7:22 throughout the c to turn on each other 4722
18:12 On their way *they* **set up** c 2837
20:19 the Israelites got up and **pitched** c 2837
21: 8 from Jabesh Gilead had come to the c for 4722
21:12 and they took them to the c *at* Shiloh 4722
1Sa 4: 3 When the soldiers returned to c, 4722
4: 5 of the LORD's covenant came into the c, 4722
4: 6 in the Hebrew c?" 4722
4: 6 the ark of the LORD had come into the c, 4722
4: 7 "A god has come into the c," they said. 4722
11:11 of the night they broke into the c of 4722
13:17 from the Philistine c in three detachments. 4722
14:15 those in the c and field, 4722
14:19 the Philistine c increased more and more. 4722
14:21 and had gone up with them to their c went 4722
17: 1 *They* **pitched** c at Ephes Dammim, 2837
17: 4 came out of the Philistine c. 4722
17:17 for your brothers and hurry to their c. 4722
17:20 He reached the c as the army was going out 5046
17:53 they plundered their c. 4722
26: 3 Saul **made** *his* c beside the road on the hill 2837
26: 5 Saul was lying inside the c, 5046
26: 6 "Who will go down into the c with me 4722
26: 7 the c with his spear stuck in the ground 5046
28: 4 and came and **set up** c at Shunem, 2837
28: 4 the Israelites and **set up** c at Gilboa. 2837
2Sa 1: 2 the third day a man arrived from Saul's c, 4722
1: 3 "I have escaped from the Israelite c." 4722
1Ki 16:16 the c heard that Zimri had plotted against 2837
16:16 king over Israel that very day there in the c. 4722
2Ki 3:24 when the Moabites came to the c *of* Israel, 4722
6: 8 "I will **set up** my c in such and such 9381
7: 4 So let's go over to the c *of* the Arameans 4722
7: 5 At dusk they got up and went to the c *of* 4722
7: 5 When they reached the edge of the c, 4722
7: 7 the c as it was and ran for their lives. 4722
7: 8 of the c and entered one of the tents. 4722
7:10 the Aramean c and not a man was there— 4722
7:12 so they have left the c to hide in 4722
7:16 the people went out and plundered the c *of* 4722
19:35 men in the Assyrian c. 4722
19:36 So Sennacherib king of Assyria **broke** c 5825
1Ch 9:18 the gatekeepers belonging to the c *of* 4722
2Ch 22: 1 who came with the Arabs into the c, 4722
32:21 and officers in the c *of* the Assyrian king. 4722
Ps 78:28 He made them come down inside their c, 4722
106:16 In the c they grew envious of Moses and 4722
Isa 10:29 and say, "We will c **overnight** at Geba." 4869
21:13 *who* c in the thickets of Arabia, 4328
37:36 in the Assyrian c. 4722
37:37 So Sennacherib king of Assyria **broke** c 5825
Mic 4:10 for now you must leave the city *to* c in 8905
Heb 13:11 but the bodies are burned outside the c. *4213*
13:13 Let us, then, go to him outside the c, *4213*
Rev 20: 9 and surrounded the c of God's people, *4213*

CAMPAIGN (3) [CAMPAIGNS]

Jos 10:42 and their lands Joshua conquered in one c, 7193
Eze 29:18 of Babylon drove his army in a hard c 6275
29:18 from the c he led against Tyre. 6275

CAMPAIGNS (4) [CAMPAIGN]

1Sa 18:13 **led** the troops **in** their c. 995+2256+3655+4200+7156
18:16 **led** them **in** their c. 995+2256+3655+4200+7156
2Sa 5: 2 **led** Israel **on** their **military** c. 995+2256+3655
1Ch 11: 2 **led** Israel **on** their **military** c. 995+2256+3655

CAMP (Anglicized) See also ENCAMP

CAMPED (79) [CAMP]

Ge 31:25 and Laban and his relatives c there too. 9546
33:18 of Shechem in Canaan and c within sight 2837
Ex 13:20 After leaving Succoth *they* c at Etham on 2837
14: 9 the Israelites and overtook them *as they* c 2837
15:27 and *they* c there near the water. 2837
17: 1 *They* c at Rephidim, 2837
18: 5 where he *was* c near the mountain of God. 2837
19: 2 and Israel c there in the desert in front of 2837
Nu 21:10 The Israelites moved on and c at Oboth. 2837
21:11 Then they set out from Oboth and c 2837
21:12 From there they moved on and c in 2837
21:13 They set out from there and c alongside 2837
22: 1 and c along the Jordan across from Jericho. 2837
33: 5 The Israelites left Rameses and c 2837
33: 6 They left Succoth and c at Etham, 2837
33: 7 and c near Migdol. 2837
33: 8 *they* c at Marah. 2837
33: 9 and *they* c there. 2837
33:10 They left Elim and c by the Red Sea. 2837
33:11 They left the Red Sea and c in the Desert 2837
33:12 the Desert of Sin and c at Dophkah. 2837
33:13 They left Dophkah and c at Alush. 2837
33:14 They left Alush and c at Rephidim, 2837
33:15 They left Rephidim and c in the Desert 2837
33:16 of Sinai and c at Kibroth Hattaavah. 2837
33:17 They left Kibroth Hattaavah and c 2837
33:18 They left Hazeroth and c at Rithmah. 2837
33:19 They left Rithmah and c at Rimmon Perez. 2837
33:20 They left Rimmon Perez and c at Libnah. 2837
33:21 They left Libnah and c at Rissah. 2837
33:22 They left Rissah and c at Kehelathah. 2837
33:23 They left Kehelathah and c 2837
33:24 They left Mount Shepher and c at Haradah. 2837
33:25 They left Haradah and c at Makheloth. 2837
33:26 They left Makheloth and c at Tahath. 2837
33:27 They left Tahath and c at Terah. 2837
33:28 They left Terah and c at Mithcah. 2837
33:29 They left Mithcah and c at Hashmonah. 2837
33:30 They left Hashmonah and c at Moseroth. 2837
33:31 They left Moseroth and c at Bene Jaakan. 2837
33:32 They left Bene Jaakan and c 2837
33:33 They left Hor Haggidgad and c 2837
33:34 They left Jotbathah and c at Abronah. 2837
33:35 They left Abronah and c at Ezion Geber. 2837
33:36 They left Ezion Geber and c at Kadesh, 2837
33:37 They left Kadesh and c at Mount Hor, 2837
33:41 They left Mount Hor and c at Zalmonah. 2837
33:42 They left Zalmonah and c at Punon. 2837
33:43 They left Punon and c at Oboth. 2837
33:44 They left Oboth and c at Iye Abarim, 2837
33:45 They left Iyim and c at Dibon Gad. 2837
33:46 and c at Almon Diblathaim. 2837
33:47 They left Almon Diblathaim and c in 2837
33:48 and c on the plains of Moab by the Jordan 2837
33:49 the plains of Moab *they* c along the Jordan 2837
Jos 3: 1 where *they* c before crossing over. 4328
4:19 the people went up from the Jordan and c 2837
5:10 *while* c at Gilgal on the plains of Jericho, 2837
Jdg 6: 4 *They* c on the land and ruined the crops all 2837
6:33 the Jordan and c in the Valley of Jezreel. 2837
7: 1 and all his men c at the spring of Harod. 2837
10:17 the Ammonites were called to arms and c 2837
10:17 the Israelites assembled and c at Mizpah. 2837
11:18 and c on the other side of the Arnon. 2837
15: 9 The Philistines went up and c in Judah, 2837
1Sa 4: 1 The Israelites c at Ebenezer, 2837
13: 5 They went up and c at Micmash, 2837
13:16 while the Philistines c at Micmash. 2837
17: 2 the Israelites assembled and c in the Valley 2837
26: 5 and went to the place where Saul *had* c. 2837
29: 1 and Israel c by the spring in Jezreel. 2837
2Sa 11:11 and my lord's men *are* c in the open fields. 2837
17:26 The Israelites and Absalom c *in* the land 2837
24: 5 crossing the Jordan, *they* c near Aroer, 2837
1Ki 20:27 The Israelites c opposite them 2837
20:29 For seven days they c opposite each other, 2837
1Ch 19: 7 who came and c near Medeba, 2837
Ezr 8:15 and *we* c there three days. 2837
Jer 52: 4 *They* c outside the city 2837

CAMPFIRES (2) [CAMP, FIRE]

Jdg 5:16 the c to hear the whistling for the flocks? 5478
Ps 68:13 Even while you sleep among the c, 9190

CAMPHIRE (KJV) See HENNA

CAMPING (1) [CAMP]

Nu 10: 5 the tribes c on the east are to set out. 2837

CAMPS (13) [CAMP]

Ge 25:16 according to their settlements and c. 3227
Nu 2:17 in the middle of the c. 4722
2:32 All those in the c, by their divisions, 4722
10: 2 and for having the c set out. 4722
10: 6 the c on the south are to set out. 4722
31:10 as well as all their c. 3227
Dt 29:11 in your c who chop your wood 4722
2Ch 14:15 They also attacked the c *of* the herdsmen 185
Ps 68:12 in the c men divide the plunder. 1074+5661
Eze 4: 2 set up c against it and put battering rams 4722

Eze 25: 4 They will set up their c and pitch their tents 3227
Am 4:10 with the stench of your c, 4722
Zec 14:15 and all the animals in those c. 4722

CAN (718) [CAN'T, CANNOT]

Ge 4:13 "My punishment is more than I c bear. AIT
8:17 so they c multiply on the earth and AIT
15: 2 what c you give me AIT
15: 5 if indeed you c count them." 3523
15: 8 how c I know that I will gain possession AIT
16: 2 perhaps I c build a family through her." AIT
18: 5 so you c be refreshed and then go AIT
18:30 What if only thirty c be found there?" AIT
18:31 what if only twenty c be found there?" AIT
18:32 What if only ten c be found there?" AIT
19: 2 You c wash your feet and spend the night AIT
19: 5 to us so that we c have sex with them." AIT
19: 8 and you c do what you like with them. AIT
19:34 with him so we c preserve our family line AIT
20:13 'This is how you c show your love to me: AIT
23: 4 for a burial site here so I c bury my dead." AIT
23:13 from me so I c bury my dead there." AIT
24: 7 so that you c get a wife for my son AIT
24:40 so that you c get a wife for my son AIT
24:50 we c say nothing to you one way or 3523
27: 9 I c prepare some tasty food for your father, AIT
27:21 "Come near so I c touch you, my son, AIT
27:37 So what c I possibly do for you, AIT
30: 3 with her so that she c bear children for me AIT
30: 3 that through her I too c build a family." AIT
30:15 "he c sleep with you tonight in return AIT
30:25 so I c go back to my own homeland. AIT
31:43 Yet what c I do today AIT
34:10 You c settle among us; AIT
34:21 We c marry their daughters AIT
34:21 and they c marry ours. AIT
37:16 C you tell me where they are AIT
37:30 Where c I turn now?" AIT
41:15 "I had a dream, and no one c interpret it. AIT
41:15 when you hear a dream you c interpret it." AIT
41:38 "C we find anyone like this man, AIT
42:34 and you c trade in the land.' " AIT
43: 9 c hold me personally responsible AIT
44: 1 with as much food as they c carry, 3523
44:15 c find things out by divination?" AIT
44:16 "What c we say to my lord?" AIT
44:16 "What c we say? AIT
44:16 c we prove our innocence? AIT
44:21 down to me so I c see him for myself.' AIT
44:34 How c I go back to my father if the boy is AIT
45:12 "You c see for yourselves, AIT
45:12 and so c my brother Benjamin, NIH
45:18 the land of Egypt and you c enjoy the fat AIT
47:23 here is seed for you so you c plant AIT
49: 1 around so I c tell you what will happen AIT
Ex 4:14 I know he c speak well. AIT
4:17 so you c perform miraculous signs with it." AIT
5:11 get your own straw wherever you c find it, AIT
10:21 darkness that c be felt." AIT
14:16 the water so that the Israelites c go through AIT
16:32 to come, so they c see the bread I gave you AIT
18:22 the simple cases they c decide themselves. AIT
24:14 anyone involved in a dispute c go to them." AIT
28: 7 so it c be fastened. AIT
29:29 so that they c be anointed and ordained AIT
32:30 perhaps I c make atonement for your sin." AIT
Lev 13:12 so far as the priest c see, NIH
14:22 which he c afford, AIT
14:30 which the person c afford, AIT
25:27 he c then go back to his own property. AIT
25:28 and he c then go back to his property. AIT
25:31 They c be redeemed, AIT
25:35 so he c continue to live among you. AIT
25:46 You c will them to your children AIT
25:46 and c make them slaves for life, AIT
27: 8 to what the man making the vow c afford. AIT
27:20 it c never be redeemed. AIT
Nu 5: 8 to whom restitution c be made for AIT
6:21 in addition to whatever else he c afford. AIT
10:31 and you c be our eyes. AIT
11:13 Where c I get meat for all these people? AIT
12:14 after that she c be brought back." AIT
13:30 for we c certainly do it." 3523+3523
16:21 from this assembly so I c put an end AIT
16:45 from this assembly so I c put an end AIT
20: 8 so they and their livestock c drink." AIT
21: 8 anyone who is bitten c look at it and live." AIT
22:38 "But c I say just anything? 3523+3523
23: 8 c I curse those whom God has not cursed? AIT
23: 8 How c I denounce those whom AIT
23:10 Who c count the dust of Jacob or number AIT
23:13 to another place where you c see them; AIT
24:23 "Ah, who c live when God does this? AIT
31:23 and anything else that c withstand fire must AIT
35:15 anyone who has killed another accidentally c flee there. AIT
Dt 1:12 But how c I bear your problems AIT
1:28 Where c we go? AIT
3:24 in heaven or on earth who c do the deeds AIT
5:24 a man c live even if God speaks with him. AIT
7:17 How c we drive them out?" 3523
8: 9 the rocks are iron and you c dig copper out AIT
9: 2 "Who c stand up against the Anakites?" AIT
18:21 "How c we know when a message has AIT
20:19 because you c eat their fruit. AIT
22:20 of the girl's virginity c be found, AIT
Dt 22:29 He c never divorce her as long as he lives. 3523
23:12 a place outside the camp where you c go AIT
31:12 so they c listen and learn to fear AIT
31:28 that I c speak these words in their hearing AIT
32:39 and no one c deliver out of my hand. AIT
33:14 and the finest the moon c yield; NIH
Jos 7: 8 O Lord, what c I say, AIT
9: 7 How then c we make a treaty with you?" AIT
15:18 Caleb asked her, "What c I do for you?" NIH
17:18 you c drive them out." AIT
Jdg 1:14 Caleb asked her, "What c I do for you?" NIH
6:15 Gideon asked, "how c I save Israel? AIT
6:31 he c defend himself when someone breaks AIT
7:14 "This c be nothing other than the sword NIH
11: 6 so we c fight the Ammonites." AIT
14:12 c give me the answer AIT
16: 5 "See if you c lure him into showing you AIT
16: 5 how we c overpower him so we may tie him up AIT
16: 6 and how you c be tied up and subdued." AIT
16:10 Come now, tell me how you c be tied." AIT
16:13 Tell me how you c be tied." AIT
16:15 Then she said to him, "How c you say, AIT
16:26 where I c feel the pillars that support AIT
18:24 How c you ask, AIT
19: 5 then you c go." AIT
19: 9 Early tomorrow morning you c get up AIT
19:22 to your house so we c have sex with him." AIT
19:24 and you c use them and do AIT
20:10 it c give them what they deserve AIT
21: 7 c we provide wives for those who are left, AIT
Ru 1:19 "C this be Naomi?" NIH
1Sa 2:36 c have food to eat." '" AIT
6:20 "Who c stand in the presence of 3523
9: 7 "If we go, what c we give the man? AIT
10:27 "How c this fellow save us?" AIT
11: 3 so we c send messengers throughout Israel; AIT
11:10 and you c do to us whatever seems good AIT
12:21 c do you no good, AIT
12:21 nor c they rescue you, AIT
14: 6 Nothing c hinder the LORD from saving, NIH
16: 2 But Samuel said, "How c I go? AIT
16:16 to search for someone who c play the harp. 3359
18: 8 What more c he get but the kingdom?" NIH
20: 7 you c be sure that he is determined AIT
21: 3 or whatever you c find." AIT
25: 8 and your son David whatever you c find AIT
25:17 Now think it over and see what you c do, AIT
25:17 a wicked man that no one c talk to him." AIT
26: 9 Who c lay a hand on AIT
27: 1 The best thing I c do is to escape to NIH
28: 2 for yourself what your servant c do." AIT
30:15 "C you lead me down AIT
2Sa 1: 7 and I said, 'What c I do?' 2180
5: 6 the blind and the lame c ward you off." AIT
6: 9 c the ark of the LORD ever come AIT
7:10 so that they c have a home of their own AIT
7:20 "What more c David say to you? AIT
9: 1 of Saul to whom I c show kindness AIT
9: 3 of Saul to whom I c show God's kindness?" AIT
12:18 How c we tell him the child is dead? AIT
12:23 C I bring him back again? 3523
14:19 no one c turn to the right or to the left NIH
14:32 'Come here so I c send you to the king AIT
15:34 c help me by frustrating AIT
16:10 who c ask, 'Why do you do this?' " AIT
17: 5 so we c hear what he has to say." AIT
17:13 until not even a piece of it c be found." AIT
19:26 so I c go with the king.' AIT
19:35 C I tell the difference AIT
19:35 C your servant taste what he eats AIT
19:35 C I still hear the voices of men AIT
20:16 Tell Joab to come here so I c speak AIT
22:30 With your help I c advance against AIT
22:30 with my God I c scale a wall. AIT
22:35 my arms c bend a bow of bronze. AIT
24:21 "so I c build an altar to the LORD, AIT
1Ki 1: 2 She c lie beside him so that our lord AIT
1:12 how you c save your own life and the life AIT
2:37 you c be sure you will die; AIT
2:42 you c be sure you will die'? AIT
5: 9 and you c take them away. AIT
13:16 nor c I eat bread or drink water with you AIT
18: 5 Maybe we c find some grass to keep AIT
20:25 so we c fight Israel on the plains. AIT
22: 7 of the LORD here whom we c inquire of?" AIT
22: 8 through whom we c inquire of the LORD, AIT
22:14 I c tell him only what AIT
2Ki 2: 9 what c I do for you before I am taken AIT
2:19 this town is well situated, as you c see, AIT
4: 2 Elisha replied to her, "How c I help you? AIT
4: 7 You and your sons c live on what is left." AIT
4:10 he c stay there whenever he comes to us." AIT
4:13 Now what c be done for you? AIT
4:13 C we speak on your behalf to the king or AIT
4:14 "What c be done for her?" AIT
4:22 c go to the man of God quickly AIT
4:43 "How c I set this before a hundred men?" AIT
5: 7 C I kill and bring back to life? AIT
5:17 as much earth as a pair of mules c carry, NIH
6: 2 where each of us c get a pole; AIT
6:13 "so I c send men and capture him." AIT
6:20 open the eyes of these men so they c see." AIT
6:27 c I get help for you? AIT
8: 1 and stay for a while wherever you c, 1591S
9:22 "How c there be peace," Jehu replied, NIH
10: 4 not resist him, how c we?" 6641S
2Ki 18:23 if you c put riders on them! 3523
18:24 How c you repulse one officer of the least AIT
18:35 How then c the LORD deliver Jerusalem AIT
1Ch 13:12 c I ever bring the ark of God to me?" AIT
17: 9 so that they c have a home of their own AIT
17:18 "What more c David say to you NIH
21:22 of your threshing floor so I c build AIT
2Ch 2:14 and c execute any design given to him. AIT
2:16 c then take them up AIT
18: 6 of the LORD here whom we c inquire of?" AIT
18: 7 through whom we c inquire of the LORD, AIT
18:13 I c tell him only what my God says." AIT
20: 6 and no one c withstand you. AIT
25: 9 "The LORD c give you much more than that." AIT
29: 8 as you c see with your own eyes. AIT
32:14 then c your god deliver you from my hand? 3523
Ezr 9:10 now, O our God, what c we say after this? AIT
9:15 though because of it not one of us c stand AIT
Ne 2: 2 This c be nothing but sadness of heart." NIH
2: 5 so that I c rebuild it." AIT
4: 2 C they bring the stones back to life AIT
4:22 so they c serve us as guards by night AIT
Est 8: 6 c I bear to see disaster fall on my people? AIT
8: 6 How c I bear to see the destruction AIT
8: 8 and sealed with his ring c be revoked." AIT
Job 4: 2 But who c keep from speaking? 3523
4:17 'C a mortal be more righteous AIT
4:17 C a man be more pure AIT
6:30 C my mouth not discern AIT
8:11 C papyrus grow tall AIT
8:11 C reeds thrive without water? AIT
9: 2 c a mortal be righteous AIT
9:12 If he snatches away, who c stop him? AIT
9:12 Who c say to him, 'What are you doing?' AIT
9:14 "How then c I dispute with him? AIT
9:14 How c I find words to argue with him? AIT
10: 7 that no one c rescue me from your hand? AIT
10:20 c have a moment's joy AIT
11: 7 "C you fathom the mysteries of God? AIT
11: 7 C you probe the limits of the Almighty? AIT
11: 8 what c you do? AIT
11: 8 what c you know? AIT
11:10 who c oppose him? AIT
11:12 c no more become wise AIT
11:12 a wild donkey's colt c be born a man. AIT
13:19 C anyone bring charges AIT
14: 4 Who c bring what is pure from the impure? AIT
17:15 Who c see any hope for me? AIT
18: 2 Be sensible, and then we c talk. AIT
21:22 "C anyone teach knowledge to God, AIT
21:34 c you console me with your nonsense? AIT
22: 2 "C a man be of benefit AIT
22: 2 C even a wise man benefit AIT
22:17 What c the Almighty do to us?' AIT
23:13 he stands alone, and who c oppose him? AIT
24:25 who c prove me false AIT
25: 3 C his forces be numbered? AIT
25: 4 c a man be righteous AIT
25: 4 c one born of woman be pure? AIT
26:14 Who then c understand the thunder AIT
28:12 "But where c wisdom be found? AIT
28:15 c its price be weighed AIT
28:17 Neither gold nor crystal c compare with it, AIT
28:17 nor c it be had for jewels of gold. NIH
33: 5 Answer me then, if you c; 3523
34:17 C he who hates justice govern? AIT
34:22 no deep shadow, where evildoers c hide. AIT
34:26 where everyone c see them, AIT
34:29 if he remains silent, who c condemn him? AIT
34:29 If he hides his face, who c see him? AIT
36:29 Who c understand how he spreads out AIT
37:18 c you join him in spreading out AIT
37:21 Now no one c look at the sun, AIT
38:20 C you take them to their places? AIT
38:31 "C you bind the beautiful Pleiades? AIT
38:31 C you loose the cords of Orion? AIT
38:32 C you bring forth the constellations AIT
38:33 C you set up [God's] dominion over AIT
38:34 "C you raise your voice to the clouds AIT
38:37 Who c tip over the water jars of AIT
39:10 C you hold him to the furrow with AIT
39:12 C you trust him to bring in your grain AIT
40: 4 how c I reply to you? AIT
40: 9 and c your voice thunder like his? AIT
40:14 to you that your own right hand c save you. AIT
40:19 his Maker c approach him with his sword. AIT
40:24 C anyone capture him by the eyes, AIT
41: 1 "C you pull in the leviathan with AIT
41: 2 C you put a cord through his nose AIT
41: 5 C you make a pet AIT
41: 7 C you fill his hide with harpoons AIT
41:13 Who c strip off his outer coat? AIT
41:16 to the next that no air c pass between. AIT
42: 2 "I know that you c do all things; 3523
42: 2 no plan of yours c be thwarted. AIT
Ps 2:12 for his wrath c flare up in a moment. AIT
4: 6 "Who c show us any good?" AIT
5: 9 Not a word from their mouth c be trusted; AIT
11: 1 How then c you say to me: AIT
11: 3 what c the righteous do?" AIT
18:29 With your help I c advance against AIT
18:29 with my God I c scale a wall. AIT
18:34 my arms c bend a bow of bronze. AIT
19:12 Who c discern his errors? AIT
22:17 I c count all my bones; AIT
38:14 whose mouth c offer no reply. NIH

Ps 40: 5 for us no one c recount to you; AIT
42: 2 When c I go and meet with God? AIT
49: 7 No man c redeem the life of another or give AIT
49:10 For all c see that wise men die; AIT
56: 4 What c mortal man do to me? AIT
56:11 What c man do to me? AIT
58: 9 Before your pots c feel [the heat of] the thorns— AIT
59: 7 and they say, "Who c hear us?" AIT
71: 3 to which I c always go; AIT
73:11 They say, "How c God know? AIT
75: 6 the west or from the desert c exalt a man. AIT
76: 5 not one of the warriors c lift his hands. AIT
76: 7 Who c stand before you AIT
78:19 "C God spread a table in the desert? 3523
78:20 But c he also give us food? 3523
78:20 C he supply meat for his people?" AIT
86: 8 no deeds c compare with yours. NIH
89: 6 For who in the skies above c compare with AIT
89:48 What man c live and not see death, AIT
94:20 C a corrupt throne be allied with AIT
104: 5 it c never be moved. AIT
106: 2 Who c proclaim the mighty acts of AIT
115: 7 c they utter a sound AIT
116:12 How c I repay the LORD AIT
118: 6 What c man do to me? AIT
119: 9 c a young man keep his way pure? AIT
119:165 and nothing c make them stumble. NIH
129: 6 which withers before it c grow; AIT
137: 4 How c we sing the songs of the LORD AIT
139: 7 Where c I go from your Spirit? AIT
139: 7 Where c I flee from your presence? AIT
145: 3 his greatness no one c fathom. NIH
147:17 Who c withstand his icy blast? AIT
Pr 3:15 nothing you desire c compare with her. AIT
6:27 C a man scoop fire into his lap AIT
6:28 C a man walk on hot coals AIT
8:11 and nothing you desire c compare with her. AIT
14:10 and no one else c share its joy. AIT
18:14 but a crushed spirit who c bear? AIT
20: 6 but a faithful man who c find? AIT
20: 9 Who c say, "I have kept my heart pure; AIT
20:24 then c anyone understand his own way? AIT
21:30 no plan that c succeed against the LORD. NIH
22:21 so that you c give sound answers AIT
23:35 will I wake up so I c find another drink?" AIT
24:22 who knows what calamities they c bring? NIH
25:15 Through patience a ruler c be persuaded, AIT
25:15 and a gentle tongue c break a bone. AIT
27: 4 but who c stand before jealousy? AIT
27: 6 Wounds from a friend c be trusted, AIT
27:11 then I c answer anyone who treats me AIT
29: 6 but a righteous one c sing and be glad. AIT
30:28 a lizard c be caught with the hand, AIT
31:10 A wife of noble character who c find? AIT
31:25 she c laugh at the days to come. AIT
Ecc 1: 8 more than one c say. 3523
1:10 Is there anything of which one c say, AIT
2:12 c the king's successor do AIT
2:24 A man c do nothing better than to eat NIH
2:25 who c eat or find enjoyment? AIT
3:14 nothing c be added to it and nothing taken AIT
3:22 For who c bring him AIT
4:10 his friend c help him up. AIT
4:11 But how c one keep warm alone? AIT
4:12 two c defend themselves. AIT
5:15 from his labor that he c carry in his hand. AIT
6:10 no man c contend 3523
6:12 Who c tell him what will happen under AIT
7:13 Who c straighten what he has made crooked? 3523
7:24 who c discover it? AIT
8: 4 a king's word is supreme, who c say to him, AIT
8: 7 who c tell him what is to come? AIT
8:17 No one c comprehend what goes on under 3523
10: 4 c lay great errors to rest. AIT
10:14 who c tell him what will happen AIT
Isa 11:15 into seven streams so that men c cross over AIT
14:27 and who c thwart him? AIT
14:27 and who c turn it back? AIT
19:11 How c you say to Pharaoh, AIT
19:15 There is nothing Egypt c do— AIT
20: 6 How then c we escape?' " AIT
22:22 what he opens no one c shut, AIT
22:22 and what he shuts no one c open. AIT
29:11 give the scroll to someone who c read, 3359+6219
29:16 C the pot say of the potter, AIT
31: 2 Yet he too is wise and c bring disaster; AIT
33:14 of us c dwell with the consuming fire? AIT
33:14 of us c dwell with everlasting burning?" AIT
36: 8 if you c put riders on them! 3523
36: 9 then c you repulse one officer of the least AIT
36:20 c the LORD deliver AIT
38:15 But what c I say? AIT
40:28 and his understanding no one c fathom. NIH
43:13 No one c deliver out of my hand. AIT
43:13 When I act, who c reverse it?" AIT
44:10 which c profit him nothing? AIT
47:15 That is all they c do for you— AIT
47:15 there is not one that c save you. AIT
48:11 c I let myself be defamed? AIT
49:15 "C a mother forget the baby at her breast AIT
49:24 C plunder be taken from warriors, AIT
51:19 who c comfort you?— AIT
51:19 who c console you? AIT
53: 8 And who c speak of his descendants? AIT
64: 5 How then c we be saved? AIT
Isa 66: 8 C a country be born in a day AIT
Jer 2:23 "How c you say, 'I am not defiled; AIT
2:24 in her heat who c restrain her? AIT
2:28 if they c save you when you are in trouble! AIT
2:33 of women c learn from your ways. AIT
3: 5 but you do all the evil you c." 3523
5: 1 If you c find but one person AIT
6: 8 so no one c live in it." AIT
6:10 To whom c I speak and give warning? AIT
8: 8 " 'How c you say, "We are wise, AIT
9: 7 and test them, for what else c I do because AIT
9:11 of Judah so no one c live there." AIT
9:12 by the LORD and c explain it? AIT
9:12 like a desert that no one c cross? AIT
10: 5 they c do no harm AIT
10: 5 c they do any good." AIT
11:15 C consecrated meat avert AIT
12: 5 how c you compete with horses? AIT
13:23 C the Ethiopian change AIT
13:23 Neither c you do good who are accustomed 3523
15: 6 I c no longer show compassion. 4206
15:12 "C a man break iron— AIT
17: 9 Who c understand it? AIT
18: 6 c I not do with you as this potter does?" 3523
21:13 you who say, "Who c come against us? AIT
21:13 Who c enter our refuge?" AIT
23:24 C anyone hide in secret places so AIT
25: 5 and you c stay in the land the LORD gave AIT
30: 6 C a man bear children? AIT
31:37 "Only if the heavens above c be measured AIT
33:20 'If you c break my covenant with the day AIT
33:21 c be broken and David will no longer have AIT
34:22 of Judah so no one c live there." AIT
38: 5 "The king c do nothing to oppose you." 3523
47: 7 But how c it rest when AIT
48:14 "How c you say, 'We are warriors, AIT
49:11 Your widows too c trust in me." AIT
49:19 Who is like me and who c challenge me? AIT
49:19 And what shepherd c stand against me?" AIT
50:44 Who is like me and who c challenge me? AIT
50:44 And what shepherd c stand against me?" AIT
51: 8 perhaps she c be healed. AIT
La 2:13 What c I say for you? AIT
2:13 With what c I compare you, AIT
2:13 To what c I liken you, AIT
2:13 Who c heal you? AIT
3:37 Who c speak and have it happen if AIT
3:44 a cloud so that no prayer c get through. AIT
4:15 "They c stay here no longer." AIT
5: 4 our wood c be had only at a price. AIT
Eze 14:15 so that no one c pass through it because of AIT
15: 5 how much less c it be made AIT
31: 2 " 'Who c be compared with you AIT
31:18 the trees of Eden c be compared with you AIT
33:10 How then c we live?" ' AIT
34:10 the shepherds c no longer feed themselves. AIT
37: 3 "Son of man, c these bones live?" AIT
Da 2: 9 I will know that you c interpret it for me." AIT
2:10 on earth who c do what the king asks! 10321
2:11 No one c reveal it to the king except AIT
2:25 among the exiles from Judah who c tell AIT
2:27 magician or diviner c explain to the king 10321
3:29 for no other god c save in this way." 10321
4:18 the wise men in my kingdom c interpret it 10321
4:18 But you c, because the spirit of 10346
4:35 No one c hold back his hand or say to him: AIT
5:16 If you c read this writing 10321
6:15 or edict that the king issues c be changed." AIT
10:17 How c I, your servant, talk with you, 3523
10:17 My strength is gone and I c hardly breathe." 4202+5972+8636
Hos 4:16 then c the LORD pasture them like lambs AIT
6: 4 "What c I do with you, Ephraim? AIT
6: 4 What c I do with you, Judah? AIT
11: 8 c I give you up, AIT
11: 8 c I hand you over, AIT
11: 8 How c I treat you like Admah? AIT
11: 8 How c I make you like Zeboiim? AIT
Joel 2:11 Who c endure it? AIT
Am 3: 8 who c but prophesy? AIT
7: 2 How c Jacob survive? AIT
7: 5 How c Jacob survive? AIT
Ob 1: 3 'Who c bring me down to the ground?' AIT
Jnh 1: 6 "How c you sleep? AIT
Mic 5: 8 and no one c rescue. AIT
Na 1: 6 Who c withstand his indignation? AIT
1: 6 Who c endure his fierce anger? AIT
3: 7 Where c I find anyone to comfort you?" AIT
3:19 Nothing c heal your wound; NIH
Hab 2:15 so that he c gaze on their naked bodies. AIT
2:19 C it give guidance? AIT
Mal 3: 2 But who c endure the day of his coming? AIT
3: 2 Who c stand when he appears? AIT
Mt 3: 9 And do not think you c say to yourselves, NIG
3: 9 of these stones God c raise up children 1538
5:13 c it be made salty AIT
6:24 "No one c serve two masters. 1538
6:27 by worrying c add a single hour to his life? 1538
7: 4 How c you say to your brother, 4802
8: 2 if you are willing, you c make me clean." 1538
9:15 "How c the guests of 1538
10:28 the One who c destroy both soul and body 1538
11:16 "To what c I compare this generation? NIG
12:26 c his kingdom stand? AIT
12:29 how c anyone enter a strong man's house 1538
12:29 Then he c rob his house. AIT
12:34 c you who are evil say anything good? 1538
Mt 14:15 c go to the villages and buy AIT
16:26 Or what c a man give in exchange AIT
17:20 you c say to this mountain, NIG
19:11 "Not everyone c accept this word, NIG
19:12 one who c accept this should accept it." 1538
19:25 "Who then c be saved?" 1538
20:22 "C you drink the cup I am going to drink?" 1538
20:22 "We c," they answered. 1538
21:21 not only c you do what was done to AIT
21:21 but also you c say to this mountain, 'Go, AIT
22:45 how c he be his son?" 4802
Mk 1:38 so I c preach there also. AIT
1:40 "If you are willing, you c make me clean." 1538
2: 7 Who c forgive sins but God alone?" 1538
2:19 "How c the guests of the bridegroom fast 1538
3:23 "How c Satan drive out Satan? 1538
3:27 no one c enter a strong man's house 1538
3:27 Then he c rob his house. NIG
4:32 the birds of the air c perch in its shade." 1538
5:31 his disciples answered, "and yet you c ask, NIG
6:36 c go to the surrounding countryside and villages and buy themselves something to eat." AIT
7:15 a man c make him 'unclean' by going 1538
7:18 from the outside c make him 'unclean'? 1538
8: 4 this remote place c anyone get enough bread 1538
8:37 Or what c a man give in exchange NIG
9:22 But if you c do anything, 1538
9:23 " 'If you c'?" 1538
9:29 "This kind c come out only by prayer." 1538
9:39 "No one who does a miracle in my name c 1538
9:50 c you make it salty AIT
10:26 "Who then c be saved?" 1538
10:38 "C you drink the cup I drink or be baptized 1538
10:39 "We c," they answered. 1538
12:37 How then c he be his son?" 4470
14: 7 and you c help them any time you want. 1538
Lk 1:18 "How c I be sure of this? AIT
3: 8 of these stones God c raise up children 1538
4: 6 and I c give it to anyone I want to. AIT
5:12 if you are willing, you c make me clean." 1538
5:21 Who c forgive sins but God alone?" 1538
5:34 "C you make the guests of 1538
6:39 "C a blind man lead a blind man? 1538
6:42 How c you say to your brother, 'Brother, 1538
7:31 c I compare the people of this generation? AIT
8:16 so that those who come in c see the light. AIT
9:12 so they c go to the surrounding villages AIT
11:18 c his kingdom stand? AIT
11:46 down with burdens they c hardly carry, AIT
12: 4 the body and after that c do no more. 2400S
12:25 by worrying c add a single hour to his life? 1538
12:36 and knocks they c immediately open AIT
13:33 surely no prophet c die outside Jerusalem! 1896
14:34 c it be made salty AIT
16:10 "Whoever c be trusted with very little can 4412
16:10 with very little c also be trusted with much, 4412
16:13 "No servant c serve two masters. 1538
16:26 nor c anyone cross over from there to us.' NIG
17: 6 you c say to this mulberry tree, AIT
18:26 "Who then c be saved?" 1538
20:36 and they c no longer die; 1538
20:44 How then c he be his son?" AIT
21:30 c see for yourselves and know AIT
23:15 as you c see, 2627
Jn 1:46 C anything good come from there?" 1538
2:18 c you show us to prove AIT
3: 3 no one c see the kingdom of God 1538
3: 4 "How c a man be born when he is old?" 1538
3: 5 no one c enter the kingdom of God 1538
3: 9 "How c this be?" Nicodemus asked. 1538
3:27 "A man c receive only what is given him 1538
3:28 You yourselves c testify that I said, AIT
4: 9 How c you ask me for a drink?" NIG
4:11 Where c you get this living water? AIT
4:19 "I c see that you are a prophet. 2555
5:19 the Son c do nothing by himself; 1538
5:19 he c do only what he sees his Father doing, NIG
5:30 By myself I c do nothing; 1538
5:44 How c you believe if you accept praise 1538
6:42 How c he now say, 4802
6:44 "No one c come to me unless 1538
6:52 "How c this man give us his flesh to eat?" 1538
6:60 Who c accept it?" 1538
6:65 "This is why I told you that no one c come 1538
7:23 a child c be circumcised on the Sabbath so AIT
7:41 "How c the Christ come from Galilee? AIT
8:33 How c you say that we shall be set free?" AIT
8:46 C any of you prove me guilty AIT
9: 4 Night is coming, when no one c work. 1538
9:16 c a sinner do such miraculous signs?" 1538
9:19 How is it that now he c see?" AIT
9:21 But how he c see now, AIT
9:41 you claim you c see, your guilt remains. AIT
10:21 C a demon open the eyes of the blind?" 1538
10:28 no one c snatch them out of my hand. AIT
10:29 no one c snatch them out 1538
12:34 so how c you say, AIT
12:40 so they c neither see with their eyes, AIT
14: 5 so how c we know the way?" 1538
14: 9 How c you say, 'Show us the Father'? AIT
15: 4 No branch c bear fruit by itself; 1538
15: 4 Neither c you bear fruit unless you remain NIG
15: 5 apart from me you c do nothing. 1538
16:10 where you c see me no longer; AIT
16:12 more than you c now bear. 1538
16:30 Now we c see that you know all things and 3857

Ac 2:29 I **c** tell you confidently that 2003
3:16 as **you c** all **see.** 595+5148
8:31 "How **c** *I*," he said, *1538*
8:33 Who *c* **speak of** his descendants? *AIT*
10:47 "**C** anyone keep these people *1538*
16:36 Now *you c* **leave.** *AIT*
19:38 *They c* **press charges.** *AIT*
20:32 which **c** build you up and give you *1538*
21:24 *c have* their heads **shaved.** *AIT*
22:5 high priest and all the Council *c* **testify.** *AIT*
24:11 You **c** easily verify *1538*
26:5 for a long time and **c** testify, *NIG*
26:26 and I **c** speak freely to him. *NIG*
26:28 that in such a short time *you c* **persuade** me *AIT*
27:10 *I c* **see** that our voyage is going to *AIT*
Ro 6:2 how *c we* **live** in it any longer? *AIT*
8:7 not submit to God's law, nor **c** it do so. *1538*
8:31 If God is for us, who **c** be against us? *NIG*
10:2 For *I c* **testify** about them *AIT*
10:14 *c they* **call on** the one they have *AIT*
10:14 And how *c they* **believe in** the one *AIT*
10:14 how *c they* **hear** without someone preaching *AIT*
10:15 how *c they* **preach** unless they are sent? *AIT*
1Co 1:15 so no one *c* **say** that you were baptized *AIT*
3:11 For no one **c** lay any foundation other than *1538*
7:21 if *you* **c** gain your freedom, do so. *1538*
7:32 how *he c* **please** the Lord. *AIT*
7:33 how *he c* **please** his wife— *AIT*
7:34 how *she c* **please** her husband. *AIT*
10:13 be tempted beyond what *you* **c** bear. *1538*
10:13 also provide a way out so that you **c** stand *1538*
12:3 "Jesus be cursed," and no one **c** say, *1538*
13:2 of prophecy and **c** fathom all mysteries *NIG*
13:2 and if I have a faith that **c** move mountains, *NIG*
14:16 how **c** one who finds himself *NIG*
14:31 For *you* **c** all prophesy in turn so *1538*
15:12 **how c** some of you say *4802*
16:6 so that you **c** help me on my journey, *NIG*
2Co 1:4 that we **c** comfort those in any trouble with *1538*
1:14 that you **c** boast of us just as we will boast *NIG*
5:12 so that *you* **c** answer those who take pride *2400*
6:14 Or what fellowship **c** light have *NIG*
7:16 I am glad I **c** have complete confidence *NIG*
8:24 so that the churches **c see it.** *4725*[S]
9:11 that you **c** be generous on every occasion, *NIG*
10:16 that we **c** preach the gospel in the regions *NIG*
Gal 3:15 Just as no one *c* **set aside** or add to *AIT*
4:15 I **c** testify that, if you could have done so, *NIG*
6:4 Then *he c* take **pride** in himself, *AIT*
Eph 1:21 **title** *that c be* **given,** *AIT*
2:9 not by works, so that no one *c* **boast.** *AIT*
5:5 For of this *you c* **be sure:** *AIT*
6:11 so that you **c** take your stand against *1538*
6:16 with which *you* **c** extinguish all *1538*
Php 1:8 God **c** testify how I long for all of you with *NIG*
1:17 that they **c** stir up trouble for me while I am *NIG*
4:13 *I* **c do** everything *2710*
1Th 3:9 How **c** *we* thank God enough for you *1538*
1Ti 3:5 how *c he* **take care of** God's church?) *AIT*
5:16 church *c* **help** those widows who are really *AIT*
6:7 and *we* **c** take nothing out of it. *1538*
6:16 whom no one has seen or **c** see. *1538*
Tit 1:9 so that *he* **c** encourage others *1543+1639*
2:4 Then *they c* **train** the younger women *AIT*
2:10 but to show that they **c** be fully trusted, *NIG*
3:13 Do **everything you c** to help Zenas *5081*
Heb 10:1 For this reason *it* **c** never, *1538*
10:11 which **c** never take away sins. *1538*
12:18 not come to a mountain that **c** be touched *NIG*
12:27 the removing of what *c be* **shaken—** *AIT*
13:6 What *c* man **do** to me?" *AIT*
Jas 1:21 which **c** save you. *1538*
2:14 **C** such faith save him? *1538*
3:3 we **c** turn the whole animal. *NIG*
3:8 but no man **c** tame the tongue. *1538*
3:11 *C* both fresh water and salt water **flow** *AIT*
3:12 My brothers, **c** a fig tree bear olives, *1538*
3:12 Neither **c** a salt spring produce fresh water. *NIG*
1Pe 1:4 into an inheritance that **c never perish,** spoil or fade— *915*
4:7 and self-controlled so that you **c** pray. *NIG*
1Jn 3:17 **how c** the love of God be in him? *4802*
4:2 how *you c* **recognize** the Spirit of God: *AIT*
Rev 3:7 What he opens no one **c** shut, *NIG*
3:7 and what he shuts no one **c** open. *NIG*
3:8 before you an open door that no one **c** shut. *1538*
3:18 so *you c become* **rich;** *AIT*
3:18 so *you c* **cover** your shameful nakedness; *AIT*
3:18 and salve to put on your eyes, so *you c* **see.** *AIT*
6:17 and who **c** stand?" *1538*
13:4 Who **c** make war against him?" *1538*

CAN'T (16) [CAN, CANNOT, NOT]

Ge 19:19 But I **c** flee to the mountains; 3523+4202
29:8 *"We* **c**," they replied, "until all 3523+4202
34:14 They said to them, *"We* **c** do such a thing; 3523+4202
34:14 we **c** give our sister to a man who is NIH
Nu 13:31 *"We* **c** attack those people; 3523+4202
Jdg 9:54 so that they **c** say, 'A woman killed him.' " 7153
14:13 If *you* **c** tell me the answer, 3523+4202
21:18 We **c** give them our daughters as wives, 3523+4202
1Sa 17:29 "**C** I even speak?" 4202
29:8 Why **c** I go and fight against the enemies 4202
Isa 29:11 he will answer, *"I* **c**; it is sealed." 3523+4202
Mt 27:42 they said, "but *he* **c** save himself! *1538+4024*
Mk 15:31 they said, "but *he* **c** save himself! *1538+4024*
Lk 11:7 *I* **c** get up and give you anything.' *1538+4024*
14:20 'I just got married, so *I* **c** come.' *1538+4024*
Jn 13:37 "Lord, why **c** I follow you now? *1538+4024*

CANA (4)

Jn 2:1 On the third day a wedding took place at **C** *2830*
2:11 Jesus performed at **C** in Galilee. *2830*
4:46 Once more he visited **C** in Galilee, *2830*
21:2 Nathanael from **C** in Galilee, *2830*

CANAAN (84) [CANAANITE, CANAANITES]

Ge 9:18 (Ham was the father of **C**.) 4046
9:22 Ham, the father of **C**, 4046
9:25 he said, "Cursed be **C**! 4046
9:26 May **C** be the slave of Shem. 4046
9:27 and may **C** be his slave." 4046
10:6 Cush, Mizraim, Put and **C**. 4046
10:15 **C** was the father of Sidon his firstborn, 4046
10:19 and the borders of **C** reached from Sidon 4050
11:31 from Ur of the Chaldeans to go to **C**. 824+4046
12:5 and they set out for the land of **C**, 4046
13:12 Abram lived in the land of **C**, 4046
16:3 Abram had been living in **C** ten years, 824+4046
17:8 The whole land of **C**, 4046
23:2 Hebron) in the land of **C**, 4046
23:19 at Hebron) in the land of **C**. 4046
31:18 to go to his father Isaac in the land of **C**. 4046
33:18 of Shechem in **C** and camped 824+4046
35:6 Bethel) in the land of **C**. 4046
36:2 Esau took his wives from the women of **C**: 4046
36:5 who were born to him in **C**. 824+4046
36:6 and all the goods he had acquired in **C**, 824+4046
37:1 where his father had stayed, the land of **C**. 4046
42:5 for the famine was in the land of **C** also. 4046
42:7 "From the land of **C**," they replied, 4046
42:13 who lives in the land of **C**. 4046
42:29 to their father Jacob in the land of **C**, 4046
42:32 youngest is now with our father in **C**.' 824+4046
44:8 of **C** the silver we found inside the mouths 4046
45:17 and return to the land of **C**, 4046
45:25 to their father Jacob in the land of **C**. 4046
46:6 the possessions they had acquired in **C**, 824+4046
46:12 and Onan had died in the land of **C**). 4046
46:31 who were living in the land of **C**, 4046
47:1 have come from the land of **C** and are now 4046
47:4 because the famine is severe in **C** 824+4046
47:13 **C** wasted away because of the famine. 824+4046
47:14 to be found in Egypt and **C** in payment 824+4046
47:15 of the people of Egypt and **C** was gone, 824+4046
48:3 to me at Luz in the land of **C**, 4046
48:7 to my sorrow Rachel died in the land of **C** 4046
49:30 Machpelah, near Mamre in **C**, 824+4046
50:5 the tomb I dug for myself in the land of **C**." 4046
50:13 of **C** and buried him in the cave in the field 4046
Ex 6:4 with them to give them the land of **C**, 4046
15:15 the people of **C** will melt away; 4046
16:35 until they reached the border of **C**. 824+4046
Lev 14:34 "When you enter the land of **C**, 4046
18:3 not do as they do in the land of **C**, 4046
25:38 of Egypt to give you the land of **C** and to 4046
Nu 13:2 "Send some men to explore the land of **C**, 4046
13:17 When Moses sent them to explore **C**, 824+4046
26:19 but they died in **C**. 824+4046
32:30 possession with you in **C**." 824+4046
32:32 over before the LORD into **C** armed, 824+4046
33:40 who lived in the Negev of **C**, 824+4046
33:51 'When you cross the Jordan into **C**, 824+4046
34:2 'When you enter **C**, the land that will 824+4046
34:29 to the Israelites in the land of **C**. 4046
35:10 'When you cross the Jordan into **C**, 824+4046
35:14 on this side of the Jordan and three in **C** 824+4046
Dt 32:49 across from Jericho, and view **C**, 4046
Jos 5:12 that year they ate of the produce of **C**. 824+4046
14:1 as an inheritance in the land of **C**, 4046
21:2 at Shiloh in **C** and said to them, 824+4046
22:9 the Israelites at Shiloh in **C** to return 824+4046
22:10 to Geliloth near the Jordan in the land of **C**, 4046
22:11 the altar on the border of **C** at Geliloth 824+4046
22:32 and the leaders returned to **C** 824+4046
24:3 the River and led him throughout **C** 824+4046
Jdg 3:1 not experienced any of the wars in **C** 4046
4:2 a king of **C**, who reigned in Hazor. 4046
5:19 of **C** fought at Taanach by the waters 4046
21:12 took them to the camp at Shiloh in **C**. 824+4046
1Ch 1:8 sons of Ham: Cush, Mizraim, Put and **C**. 4046
1:13 **C** was the father of Sidon his firstborn, 4046
16:18 of **C** as the portion you will inherit." 4046
Ps 105:11 of **C** as the portion you will inherit." 4046
106:38 whom they sacrificed to the idols of **C**, 4046
135:11 Og king of Bashan and all the kings of **C**— 4046
Isa 19:18 the language of **C** and swear allegiance to 4046
Ob 1:20 of Israelite exiles who are **in C** will possess 4050
Zep 2:5 word of the LORD is against you, O **C**, 4046
Ac 7:11 "Then a famine struck all Egypt and **C**, *5913*
13:19 in **C** and gave their land to his people *1178+5913*

CANAANITE (19) [CANAAN]

Ge 10:18 Later the **C** clans scattered 4050
28:1 "Do not marry a **C** woman. 4046
28:6 "Do not marry a **C** woman," 4046
28:8 the **C** women were to his father Isaac; 4046
38:2 the daughter of a **C** man named Shua. 4050
46:10 Zohar and Shaul the son of a **C** *woman.* 4050
Ex 6:15 Zohar and Shaul the son of a **C** *woman.* 4050
Nu 21:1 When the **C** king of Arad, 4050
33:40 The **C** king of Arad, 4050
Jos 5:1 and all the **C** kings along the coast heard 4050
13:3 all of it counted as **C** (the territory of 4050
Jdg 1:32 of Asher lived among the **C** inhabitants of 4050
1:33 among the **C** inhabitants of the land, 4050
4:23 the **C** king, before the Israelites. 4046
4:24 the **C** king, until they destroyed him. 4046
1Ki 9:16 He killed its **C** inhabitants and then gave it 4050
1Ch 2:3 to him by a **C** *woman,* 4050
Zec 14:21 And on that day there will no longer be a **C** 4050
Mt 15:22 A **C** woman from that vicinity came *5914*

CANAANITES (57) [CANAAN]

Ge 12:6 At that time the **C** were in the land. 4050
13:7 The **C** and Perizzites were also living in 4050
15:21 Amorites, **C**, Girgashites and Jebusites." 4050
24:3 for my son from the daughters of the **C**, 4050
24:37 for my son from the daughters of the **C**, 4050
34:30 on me by making me a stench to the **C** 4050
50:11 the **C** who lived there saw the mourning at 4050
Ex 3:8 the home of the **C**, Hittites, Amorites, 4050
3:17 in Egypt into the land of the **C**, 4050
13:5 of the **C**, Hittites, Amorites, Hivites 4050
13:11 into the land of the **C** and gives it to you, 4050
23:23 Perizzites, **C**, Hivites and Jebusites, 4050
23:28 **C** and Hittites out of your way. 4050
33:2 an angel before you and drive out the **C**, 4050
34:11 I will drive out before you the Amorites, **C**, 4050
Nu 13:29 **C** live near the sea and along the Jordan." 4050
14:25 Amalekites and **C** are living in the valleys, 4050
14:43 the Amalekites and **C** will face you there. 4050
14:45 and **C** who lived in that hill country came 4050
21:3 to Israel's plea and gave the **C** over 4050
Dt 1:7 to the land of the **C** and to Lebanon, 4050
7:1 the Hittites, Girgashites, Amorites, **C**, 4050
11:30 the territory of those **C** living in the Arabah 4050
20:17 the Hittites, Amorites, **C**, Perizzites, 4050
Jos 3:10 drive out before you the **C**, 4050
7:9 The **C** and the other people of 4050
9:1 **C**, Perizzites, Hivites and Jebusites)— 4050
11:3 to the **C** in the east and west; 4050
12:8 the lands of the Hittites, Amorites, **C**, 4050
13:4 all the land of the **C**, 4050
16:10 not dislodge the **C** living in Gezer; 4050
16:10 the **C** live among the people of Ephraim 4050
17:12 **C** were determined to live in that region. 4050
17:13 they subjected the **C** to forced labor but did 4050
17:16 and all the **C** who live in 4050
17:18 though the **C** have iron chariots and 4050
24:11 as did also the Amorites, Perizzites, **C**, 4050
Jdg 1:1 to go up and fight for us against the **C**?" 4050
1:3 to fight against the **C**. 4050
1:4 the LORD gave the **C** and Perizzites 4050
1:5 putting to rout the **C** and Perizzites. 4050
1:9 against the **C** living in the hill country, 4050
1:10 They advanced against the **C** living 4050
1:17 and attacked the **C** living in Zephath, 4050
1:27 the **C** were determined to live in that land. 4050
1:28 they pressed the **C** into forced labor 4050
1:29 Nor did Ephraim drive out the **C** living 4050
1:29 the **C** continued to live there among them. 4050
1:30 Neither did Zebulun drive out the **C** living 4050
3:3 all the **C**, the Sidonians, 4050
3:5 The Israelites lived among the **C**, Hittites, 4050
2Sa 24:7 and all the towns of the Hivites and **C**. 4050
Ezr 9:1 like those of the **C**, Hittites, Perizzites, 4050
Ne 9:8 to his descendants the land of the **C**, 4050
9:24 You subdued before them the **C**, 4050
9:24 you handed **the C** over to them, 4392[S]
Eze 16:3 and birth were in the land of the **C**; 4050

CANAL (6) [CANALS]

Ezr 8:15 I assembled them at the **c** that flows 5643
8:21 There, by the Ahava **C**, I proclaimed a fast, 5643
8:31 from the Ahava **C** to go to Jerusalem. 5643
Da 8:2 in the vision I was beside the Ulai **C**. 67
8:3 standing beside the **c**, 67
8:6 the **c** and charged at him in great rage. 67

CANALS (3) [CANAL]

Ex 7:19 over the streams and **c**, 3284
8:5 with your staff over the streams and **c** 3284
Isa 19:6 The **c** will stink; 5643

CANCEL (4) [CANCELED, CANCELING]

Dt 15:1 of every seven years *you must* **c debts.** 6913+9024
15:2 Every creditor *shall* **c** 9023
15:3 you *must* **c** *any* **debt** your brother owes you. 9023
Ne 10:31 the land and will **c** all debts. NIH

CANCELED (5) [CANCEL]

Mt 18:27 **c** the debt and let him go. *918*
18:32 *'I* **c** all that debt of yours *918*
Lk 7:42 so *he* **c** the debts of both. *5919*
7:43 the one who *had* the bigger debt **c**." *5919*
Col 2:14 *having* **c** the written code, *1981*

CANCELING (3) [CANCEL]

Dt 15:2 the LORD's **time for c debts** has been proclaimed. 9024
15:9 "The seventh year, the year for **c debts,** 9024

Dt 31:10 in the year for **c** debts, 9024

CANDACE (1)

Ac 8:27 in charge of all the treasury *of* **C**, *2833*

CANDLE (KJV) See LAMP

CANDLESTICK, CANDLESTICK (KJV) See LAMPSTAND, LAMPSTANDS

CANE (2)

Ex 30:23 250 shekels of fragrant **c**, 7866
Zec 8: 4 each with **c** in hand because of his age. 5475

CANKER (KJV) See GANGRENE

CANKERWORM (KJV) See LOCUST, GRASSHOPPER

CANNEH (1)

Eze 27:23 **C** and Eden and merchants of Sheba, 4034

CANNOT (249) [CAN]

Ge 19:22 *I* **c** do anything until you reach it." 3523+4202
21:16 for she thought, "I **c** watch the boy die." 440
31:35 that *I* **c** stand up in your presence; 3523+4202
32:12 which **c** be counted.' " 4202
41:16 "I **c** do it," Joseph replied to Pharaoh, 1187
44:22 'The boy **c** leave his father; 3523+4202
44:26 But we said, '*We* **c** go down. 3523+4202
44:26 *We* **c** see the man's face 3523+4202
47:18 "We **c** hide from our lord the fact that 4202
Ex 10: 5 They will cover the face of the ground so that it **c** be seen. 3523+4202
18:18 *you* **c** handle it alone. 3523+4202
19:23 "The people **c** come up Mount Sinai, 3523+4202
33:20 But," he said, "*you* **c** see my face, 3523+4202
Lev 5: 7 " 'If he **c** afford a lamb, 4202
5:11 he **c** afford two doves 4202
12: 8 If she **c** afford a lamb, 4202
14:21 "If, however, he is poor and **c** afford these, 401
14:32 an infectious skin disease and who **c** afford 4202
27:33 and its substitute become holy and **c** 4202
Nu 11:14 I **c** carry all these people by myself; 3523+4202
23:20 he has blessed, and I **c** change it. 4202
31:23 And whatever **c** withstand fire must be put 4202
35:33 and atonement **c** be made for the land 4202
Dt 4:28 which **c** see or hear or eat or smell. 4202
14:24 and **c** carry your tithe 3523+4202
28:27 from which *you* **c** be cured. 3523+4202
28:35 legs with painful boils that **c** be cured, 3523+4202
Jos 7:12 Israelites **c** stand against their enemies; 3523+4202
7:13 *You* **c** stand against your enemies 3523+4202
9:19 and *we* **c** touch them now. 3523+4202
Jdg 11:35 a vow to the LORD that *I* **c** break." 3523+4202
Ru 4: 6 "Then *I* **c** redeem it 3523+4202
4: 6 *I* **c** do it." 3523+4202
1Sa 17:39 "*I* **c** go in these," he said to Saul, 3523+4202
2Sa 5: 6 They thought, "David **c** get in here." 4202
14:14 which **c** be recovered, so we must die. 4202
1Ki 8:27 even the highest heaven, **c** contain you. 4202
13:16 "*I* **c** turn back and go with you, 3523+4202
20: 9 but this demand *I* **c** meet.' " 3523+4202
2Ki 18:29 *He* **c** deliver you from my hand. 3523+4202
1Ch 16:30 it **c** be moved. 1153
2Ch 2: 6 even the highest heavens, **c** contain him? 4202
6:18 even the highest heavens, **c** contain you. 4202
Ezr 10:13 so we **c** stand outside. 401+3946
10:13 this matter **c** be taken care of in a day 4202
Ne 4:10 there is so much rubble that we **c** rebuild the wall." 3523+4202
6: 3 on a great project and **c** go down. 3523+4202
Est 1:19 which **c** be repealed, 4202
6:13 *you* **c stand** against him— 3523+4202
Job 5: 9 He performs wonders that **c** be fathomed, 401
5: 9 miracles that **c** be counted. 401
9:10 He performs wonders that **c** be fathomed, 401
9:10 miracles that **c** be counted. 401
9:11 When he passes me, I **c** see him; 4202
9:11 when he goes by, I **c** perceive him. 4202
9:35 but as it now stands with me, I **c**. 4202
10:15 Even if I am innocent, I **c** lift my head, 4202
12:14 What he tears down **c** be rebuilt; 4202
12:14 the man he imprisons **c** be released. 4202
14: 5 and have set limits he **c** exceed. 4202
19: 8 He has blocked my way so I **c** pass; 4202
20:13 though he **c** bear to let it go and keeps it 4202
20:20 he **c** save himself by his treasure. 4202
22:11 why it is so dark you **c** see, 4202
28:13 it **c** be found in the land of the living. 4202
28:15 It **c** be bought with the finest gold, 4202
28:16 It **c** be bought with the gold of Ophir, 4202
28:19 The topaz of Cush **c** compare with it; 4202
28:19 it **c** be bought with pure gold. 4202
34:32 Teach me what I **c** see; 1187
37:19 we **c** draw up our case because 4202
39:13 but they **c** compare with the pinions 561
39:24 he **c** stand still when the trumpet sounds. 4202
41:17 they cling together and **c** be parted. 4202
Ps 5: 4 with you the wicked **c** dwell. 4202
5: 5 The arrogant **c** stand in your presence; 4202
21:11 and devise wicked schemes, they **c** succeed; 1153
22:29 those who **c** keep themselves alive. 4202
33:17 despite all its great strength it **c** save. 4202
38:13 I am like a deaf man, who **c** hear, 4202
38:13 like a mute, who **c** open his mouth; 4202
40:12 sins have overtaken me, and *I* **c** see. 3523+4202
69:23 May their eyes be darkened **so** they **c** see, 4946
88: 8 I am confined and **c** escape; 4202
93: 1 it **c** be moved. 1153
96:10 it **c** be moved; 1153
104: 9 You set a boundary they **c** cross; 1153
115: 5 They have mouths, but **c** speak, eyes, 4202
115: 5 but cannot speak, eyes, but they **c** see; 4202
115: 6 but **c** hear, noses, but they cannot smell; 4202
115: 6 but cannot hear, noses, but they **c** smell; 4202
115: 7 but **c** feel, feet, but they cannot walk; 4202
115: 7 but cannot feel, feet, but they **c** walk; 4202
125: 1 which **c** be shaken but endures forever. 4202
129: 7 with it the reaper **c** fill his hands, 4202
135:16 They have mouths, but **c** speak, eyes, 4202
135:16 but cannot speak, eyes, but they **c** see; 4202
135:17 but **c** hear, nor is there breath 4202
146: 3 in mortal men, who **c** save. 401
Pr 4:16 For they **c** sleep till they do evil; 4202
12: 3 man **c** be established through wickedness, 4202
12: 3 but the righteous **c** be uprooted. 1153
29:19 A servant **c** be corrected by mere words; 4202
30:21 under four *it* **c** bear up: 3523+4202
31: 8 up for **those who c speak** *for themselves,* 522
Ecc 1:15 What is twisted **c** be straightened; 3523+4202
1:15 what is lacking **c** be counted. 3523+4202
3:11 yet they **c** fathom what God has done 4202
6: 3 if he **c** enjoy his prosperity and does 4202
7:14 a man **c** discover anything about his future. 4202
8:17 man **c** discover its meaning. 4202
8:17 *he* **c** really comprehend it. 3523+4202
11: 5 so you **c** understand the work of God, 4202
SS 8: 7 Many waters **c** quench love; 3523+4202
8: 7 rivers **c** wash it away. 4202
Isa 1:13 *I* **c bear** your evil assemblies. 3523+4202
28:15 it **c** touch us, 4202
29:12 you give the scroll to someone *who* **c read,** 3359+4202+6219
36:14 *He* **c** deliver you! 3523+4202
38:18 For the grave **c** praise you, 4202
38:18 death **c** sing your praise; NIH
38:18 to the pit **c** hope for your faithfulness. 4202
44:18 their eyes are plastered over *so* they **c** see, 4946
44:18 their minds closed *so* they **c** understand. 4946
44:20 he **c** save himself, or say, 4202
45:20 who pray to gods that **c** save. 4202
46: 7 From that spot it **c** move. 4202
46: 7 it **c** save him from his troubles. 4202
47:11 that *you* **c** ward off with a ransom; 3523+4202
47:11 a catastrophe you **c** foresee will suddenly come 4202
47:14 They **c** even save themselves from 4202
48: 7 **So** you **c** say, 'Yes, I knew of them.' 7153
56:10 they are all mute dogs, *they* **c** bark; 3523+4202
57:20 the wicked are like the tossing sea, *which* **c** rest, 3523+4202
58: 4 You **c** fast as you do today 4202
59: 6 they **c** cover themselves 4202
59:14 in the streets, honesty **c** enter. 3523+4202
Jer 2:13 broken cisterns that **c** hold water. 4202
4:19 My heart pounds within me, I **c** keep silent. 4202
5:22 an everlasting barrier it **c** cross. 4202
5:22 The waves may roll, but *they* **c** prevail; 4202
5:22 they may roar, but they **c** cross it. 4202
6:10 Their ears are closed so *they* **c** hear. 3523+4202
6:11 and *I* **c** hold it in. 4206
8:17 vipers that **c** be charmed, 401
10: 5 their idols **c** speak; 4202
10: 5 they must be carried because they **c** walk. 4202
10:10 the nations **c** endure his wrath. 4202
11:11 on them a disaster *they* **c** escape. 3523+4202
14:19 Why have you afflicted us so that we **c** 401
19:11 as this potter's jar is smashed and **c** 3523+4202
20: 9 I am weary of holding it in; indeed, *I* **c**. 3523+4202
23:24 in secret places so that I **c** see him?" 4202
24: 3 the poor ones are so bad they **c** be eaten." 4202
24: 8 which are so bad they **c** be eaten,' 4202
29:17 like poor figs that are so bad they **c** 4202
36: 5 *I* **c** go to the LORD's temple. 3523+4202
46: 6 "The swift **c** flee nor the strong escape. 440
46:15 **c** stand, for the LORD will push them down. 4202
46:23 they **c** be counted. 401
49:10 so that *he* **c** conceal himself. 3523+4202
51: 9 but she **c** be healed; 4202
La 1:14 over to those *I* **c** withstand. 3523+4202
3: 7 He has walled me in so I **c** escape; 4202
Eze 3: 6 whose words you **c** understand. 4202
3:25 so that you **c** go out among the people. 4202
4: 8 with ropes so that you **c** turn from one side 4202
12: 6 Cover your face so that you **c** see the land, 4202
12:12 He will cover his face so that he **c** see 4202
Da 5:23 which **c** see or hear or understand. 10379
6: 8 the decree and put it in writing so that it **c** 10379
6: 8 and Persians, which **c** be repealed." 10379
6:12 and Persians, which **c** be repealed." 10379
Hos 1:10 which **c** be measured or counted. 4202
2: 6 I will wall her in so that she **c** find her way. 4202
14: 3 Assyria **c** save us; 4202
Am 5:21 I **c** stand your assemblies. 4202
7:10 The land **c** bear all his words. 3523+4202
Jnh 4:11 twenty thousand people who **c** tell their right hand from their left, 4202
Mic 2: 3 from which you **c** save yourselves. 4202
Hab 1:13 *you* **c** tolerate wrong. 3523+4202
2:18 he makes idols **that c speak.** 522
Mt 5:14 A city on a hill **c** be hidden. *1538+4024*
5:36 *you* **c** make even one hair white or black. *1538+4024*
6:24 *You* **c** serve both God and Money. *1538+4024*
7:18 A good tree **c** bear bad fruit, *1538+4024*
7:18 and a bad tree **c** bear good fruit. *NIG*
10:28 of those who kill the body but **c** kill *1538+3590*
16: 3 you **c** interpret the signs of the times. *1538+4024*
26:53 Do you think *I* **c** call on my Father, *1538+4024*
Mk 2:19 *They* **c**, so long as they have him *1538+4024*
3:24 that kingdom **c** stand. *1538+4024*
3:25 that house **c** stand. *1538+4024*
3:26 *he* **c** stand; his end has come. *1538+4024*
Lk 12:26 Since *you* **c do** this very little thing, *1538+4028*
14:14 Although *they* **c** repay you, *2400+4024*
14:26 *he* **c** be my disciple. *1538+4024*
14:27 not carry his cross and follow me **c** *1538+4024*
14:33 up everything he has **c** be my disciple. *1538+4024*
16: 2 because *you* **c** be manager any longer.' *1538+4024*
16:13 *You* **c** serve both God and Money." *1538+4024*
16:26 who want to go from here to you **c**, *1538+3590*
Jn 3: 4 "Surely *he* **c** enter a second time *1538+3590*
3: 8 but you **c** tell where it comes from or *4024*
7: 7 The world **c** hate you, *1538+4024*
7:34 and where I am, you **c** come." *1538+4024*
7:35 to go that we **c** find him? *4024*
7:36 and 'Where I am, you **c** come'?" *1538+4024*
8:21 Where I go, you **c** come." *1538+4024*
8:22 'Where I go, you **c** come'?" *1538+4024*
10:35 and the Scripture **c** be broken— *1538+4024*
13:33 Where I am going, you **c** come. *1538+4024*
13:36 "Where I am going, *you* **c** follow now, *1538+4024*
14:17 The world **c** accept him, *1538+4024*
Ac 4:16 and *we* **c** deny it. *1538+4024*
4:20 For we **c** help speaking *1538+4024*
15: 1 to the custom taught by Moses, *you* **c** *1538+4024*
24:13 **And** *they* **c** prove to you *1538+4028*
27:31 you **c** be saved." *1538+4024*
Ro 6: 9 he **c** die **again;** *4033*
7:18 but I **c** carry it out. *4024*
8: 8 by the sinful nature **c** please God. *1538+4024*
8:26 for us with groans *that* **words c express.** *227*
11:10 May their eyes be darkened so they **c** see, *3590*
1Co 2:14 and *he* **c** understand them, *1538+4024*
7: 9 But if they **c** control themselves, *4024*
9:16 when I preach the gospel, I **c** boast, *1639+4024*
10:21 *You* **c** drink the cup of the Lord and the cup of demons *1538+4024*
10:21 *you* **c** have a part in both the Lord's table of demons. *1538+4024*
12:21 The eye **c** say to the hand, *1538+4024*
12:21 And the head **c** say to the feet, *NIG*
15:50 flesh and blood **c** inherit the kingdom *1538+4024*
2Co 1:13 not write you anything you **c** read *NIG*
4: 4 so that they **c** see the light of the gospel of *3590*
13: 8 For *we* **c do** anything against the truth, *1538+4024*
Gal 6: 7 Do not be deceived: God **c** be mocked. *4024*
1Ti 5:25 even those that are not **c** be hidden. *1538+4024*
2Ti 2:13 for *he* **c** disown himself. *1538+4024*
Tit 2: 8 soundness of speech *that* **c be condemned,** *183*
Heb 9: 5 But we **c** discuss these things in detail *1639+4024*
12:27 so that what **c** be shaken may remain. *3590*
12:28 a kingdom that **c be shaken,** *810*
Jas 1:13 For God **c** be **tempted** by evil, *585*
4: 2 but *you* **c** have what you want. *1538+4024*
1Jn 3: 9 *he* **c** go on sinning, *1538+4024*
4:20 **c** love God, whom he has not seen. *1538+4024*
5:18 and the evil one **c** harm him. *4024*
Rev 2: 2 I know that *you* **c** tolerate wicked men, *1538+4024*
9:20 idols that **c** see or hear or walk. *1538+4046*

CANOPY (6)

2Sa 22:12 He made darkness his **c** around him— 6109
2Ki 16:18 the Sabbath **c** that had been built at 4590
Ps 18:11 his **c** around him— 6109
Isa 4: 5 over all the glory will be a **c.** 2903
40:22 He stretches out the heavens like a **c**, 1988
Jer 43:10 he will spread his **royal c** above them. 9188

CAPABLE (6)

Ex 18:21 But select **c** men from all the people— 2657
18:25 He chose **c** men from all Israel 2657
1Ch 26: 6 because they were **very c men.** 1475+2657
26: 8 and their relatives were **c** men with 2657
26:31 and **c men** among 1475+2657
Ezr 8:18 they brought us Sherebiah, a **c** man, 8507

CAPERNAUM (16)

Mt 4:13 Leaving Nazareth, he went and lived in **C**, *3019*
8: 5 When Jesus had entered **C**, *3019*
11:23 you, **C**, will you be lifted up to the skies? *3019*
17:24 After Jesus and his disciples arrived in **C**, *3019*
Mk 1:21 They went to **C**, *3019*
2: 1 when Jesus again entered **C**, *3019*
9:33 They came to **C**. *3019*
Lk 4:23 that you did in **C**.' " *3019*
4:31 Then he went down to **C**, *3019*
7: 1 in the hearing of the people, he entered **C**. *3019*
10:15 you, **C**, will you be lifted up to the skies? *3019*
Jn 2:12 down to **C** with his mother and brothers *3019*
4:46 And there was a certain royal official whose son lay sick at **C**. *3019*

Jn 6:17 into a boat and set off across the lake for C. 3019
6:24 the boats and went to C in search of Jesus. 3019
6:59 while teaching in the synagogue in C. 3019

CAPES (1)

Isa 3:22 the fine robes and the c and cloaks, 5074

CAPHTOR (3) [CAPHTORITES]

Dt 2:23 from C destroyed them and settled 4116
Jer 47:4 the remnant from the coasts of C. 4116
Am 9:7 the Philistines from C and the Arameans 4116

CAPHTORITES (3) [CAPHTOR]

Ge 10:14 (from whom the Philistines came) and C. 4118
Dt 2:23 the C coming out from Caphtor 4118
1Ch 1:12 (from whom the Philistines came) and C. 4118

CAPITAL (7) [CAPITALS]

Dt 21:22 If a man guilty of a c offense is put to death 4638+5477
1Ki 7:16 each c was five cubits high. 4196
7:17 seven for each c. 4196
7:18 He did the same for each c. 4196
2Ki 25:17 The bronze c on top of one pillar was four 4196
2Ch 3:15 each with a c on top measuring five cubits. 7633
Jer 52:22 The bronze c on top of 4196

CAPITALS (12) [CAPITAL]

1Ki 7:16 He also made two c of cast bronze to set on 4196
7:17 of interwoven chains festooned the c on top 4196
7:18 to decorate the c on top of the pillars. 4196
7:19 The c on top of the pillars in 4196
7:20 On the c of both pillars, 4196
7:22 The c on top were in the shape of lilies. NIH
7:41 the two bowl-shaped c on top of the pillars; 4196
7:41 the two bowl-shaped c on top of the pillars; 4196
7:42 the bowl-shaped c on top of the pillars); 4196
2Ch 4:12 the two bowl-shaped c on top of the pillars; 4196
4:12 the two bowl-shaped c on top of the pillars; 4196
4:13 the bowl-shaped c on top of the pillars); 4196

CAPPADOCIA (2)

Ac 2:9 residents of Mesopotamia, Judea and C, 2838
1Pe 1:1 scattered throughout Pontus, Galatia, C, 2838

CAPSTONE (7) [STONE]

Ps 118:22 The stone the builders rejected has become the c; 7157+8031
Zec 4:7 Then he will bring out the c to shouts 74+8036
Mt 21:42 " 'The stone the builders rejected has become the c; 1224+3051
Mk 12:10 " 'The stone the builders rejected has become the c; 1224+3051
Lk 20:17 " 'The stone the builders rejected has become the c'? 1224+3051
Ac 4:11 " 'the stone you builders rejected, which has become the c.' 1224+3051
1Pe 2:7 " 'The stone the builders rejected has become the c," 1224+3051

CAPTAIN (22) [CAPTAINS]

Ge 37:36 the c of the guard. 8569
39:1 the c of the guard, 8569
40:3 in custody in the house of the c of 8569
40:4 The c of the guard assigned them 8569
41:10 and the chief baker in the house of the c of 8569
41:12 a servant of the c of the guard. 8569
1Sa 22:14 c of your bodyguard and highly respected 6233
2Ki 1:9 a c with his company of fifty men. 2822+8569
1:9 The c went up to Elijah, NIH
1:10 Elijah answered the c, 2822+8569
1:10 and consumed the c and his men. 2257[S]
1:11 this the king sent to Elijah another c 2822+8569
1:11 The c said to him, "Man of God, NIH
1:13 king sent a third c with his fifty men. 2822+8569
1:13 third c went up and fell on his knees 2822+8569
Isa 3:3 the c of fifty and man of rank, 8569
Jer 37:13 the c of the guard, 1251
Jnh 1:6 The c went to him and said, 2021+2480+8042
Ac 4:1 The priests and the c of the temple guard 5130
5:24 the c of the temple guard and 5130
5:26 the c went with his officers and brought 5130
Rev 18:17 "Every sea c, and all who travel by ship, 3237

CAPTAINS (4) [CAPTAIN]

Jdg 5:14 From Makir c came down, 2980
1Ki 9:22 his government officials, his officers, his c, 8957
2Ki 1:14 and consumed the first two c 2822+8569
2Ch 8:9 commanders of his c, 8957

CAPTIVATE (1) [CAPTURE]

Pr 6:25 after her beauty or let her c you 4374

CAPTIVATED (2) [CAPTURE]

Pr 5:19 may you ever be c by her love. 8706
5:20 Why be c, my son, by an adulteress? 8706

CAPTIVE (43) [CAPTURE]

Ge 14:14 that his relative had been taken c, 8647
Nu 24:22 be destroyed when Asshur takes you c." 8647
Dt 1:39 little ones that you said would be taken c, 1020
Jdg 5:12 Take c your captives, O son of Abinoam.' 8647
1Sa 30:2 and had taken c the women 8647
30:3 and sons and daughters taken c. 8647
1Ki 8:46 who takes them c to his own land, 8647+8647
8:47 the land where they are held c, and repent 8647
8:48 of their enemies who took them c, and pray 8647
20:39 and someone came to me with a c and said, 408
2Ki 5:2 from Aram had gone out and had taken c 8647
17:27 "Have one of the priests you took c 1655
24:15 Nebuchadnezzar took Jehoiachin c 1655
1Ch 3:17 The descendants of Jehoiachin the c: 660
5:21 also took one hundred thousand people c, NIH
9:1 of Judah were taken c to Babylon because 1655
2Ch 6:36 who takes them c to a land far away or near; 8647+8647
6:37 the land where they are held c, and repent 8647
28:8 The Israelites took c 8647
Ezr 2:1 king of Babylon had taken c 1655
Ne 7:6 king of Babylon had taken c 1655
Est 2:6 among those taken c with Jehoiachin king 1655
Ps 69:33 and does not despise his c people. 659
106:46 to be pitied by all who held them c. 8647
SS 7:5 the king is held c by its tresses. 673
Isa 52:2 O c Daughter of Zion. 8665
Jer 13:17 the LORD's flock will be taken c. 8647
22:12 in the place where they have led him c; 1655
41:10 Ishmael son of Nethaniah took them c 8647
41:14 All the people Ishmael had taken c 8647
43:12 and take their gods c. 8647
48:7 you too will be taken c, 4334
La 1:5 c before the foe. NIH
Eze 6:9 the nations where they have been carried c, 8647
21:23 of their guilt and take them c. 9530
21:24 you have done this, you will be taken c. 928+2021+4090+9530
Am 1:6 Because she took c whole communities 1655
Na 3:10 Yet she was taken c and went into exile. 1583
Hab 2:5 to himself all the nations and takes c all 7695
Ac 8:23 that you are full of bitterness and c to sin." 5278
2Co 10:5 and we take c every thought 170
Col 2:8 See to it that no one takes you c through hollow and deceptive 1639+5194
2Ti 2:26 who has taken them c to do his will. 2436

CAPTIVES (25) [CAPTURE]

Ge 31:26 and you've carried off my daughters like c 8647
Nu 21:29 and his daughters as c to Sihon king of 8669
31:12 and brought the c, 8660
31:19 third and seventh days you must purify yourselves and your c. 8660
Dt 21:10 into your hands and you take c, 8647+8660
21:11 the c a beautiful woman and are attracted 8664
32:42 the blood of the slain and the c, 8664
Jdg 5:12 Take captive your c, O son of Abinoam.' 8660
Job 3:18 C also enjoy their ease; 659
Ps 68:18 you led c in your train; 8660
126:1 the LORD brought back the c to Zion, 8860
Isa 10:4 but to cringe among the c or fall among 660
14:2 They will make c of their captors and rule 8647
14:17 and would not let his c go home?" 659
20:4 the Egyptian c and Cushite exiles, young 8660
42:7 to free c from prison and to release from 660
49:9 to say to the c, 673
49:24 or c rescued from the fierce? 8660
49:25 "Yes, c will be taken from warriors, 8660
61:1 to proclaim freedom for the c and release 8647
Jer 40:1 in chains among all the c from Jerusalem 1661
41:10 Ishmael made c of all the rest of 8647
Eze 12:11 They will go into exile as c. 8660
Am 1:9 she sold whole communities of c to Edom, 1661
Eph 4:8 he led c in his train 168+169

CAPTIVITY (32) [CAPTURE]

Dt 28:41 because they will go into c. 8660
Jdg 18:30 for the tribe of Dan until the time of the c 1655
2Ki 25:21 So Judah went into c, away from her land. 1655
2Ch 6:37 and plead with you in the land of their c 8660
6:38 of their c where they were taken, and pray 8660
29:9 and daughters and our wives are in c. 8660
Ezr 2:1 of the province who came up from the c of 8660
3:8 from the c to Jerusalem) began the work, 8660
8:35 from c sacrificed burnt offerings to the God 8660
9:7 to the sword and c, 8660
Ne 4:4 Give them over as plunder in a land of c. 8664
7:6 of the province who came up from the c of 8660
Ps 78:61 He sent [the ark of] his might into c, 8660
144:14 no going into c, 3448
Isa 46:2 they themselves go off into c. 8660
Jer 15:2 those for c, to captivity.' 8660
15:2 those for captivity, to c.' 8660
29:14 "and will bring you back from c. 8654
30:3 and Judah back from c and restore them to 8654
31:23 "When I bring them back from c, 8654
33:7 I will bring Judah and Israel back from c 8654
43:11 c to those destined for captivity, 8660
43:11 captivity to those destined for c, 8660
48:46 into exile and your daughters into c. 8664
52:27 So Judah went into c, away from her land. 1655
La 2:14 not expose your sin to ward off your c. 8654
Eze 29:14 from c and return them to Upper Egypt, 8654
30:17 and the cities themselves will go into c. 8660
30:18 and her villages will go into c. 8660
39:25 from c and will have compassion on all 8654
Rev 13:10 If anyone is to go into c, 168
13:10 into c he will go. 168

CAPTORS (4) [CAPTURE]

2Ch 30:9 by their c and will come back to this land, 8647
Ps 137:3 for there our c asked us for songs, 8647
Isa 14:2 They will make captives of their c and rule 8647
Jer 50:33 All their c hold them fast, 8647

CAPTURE (19) [CAPTIVATE, CAPTIVATED, CAPTIVE, CAPTIVES, CAPTIVITY, CAPTORS, CAPTURED, CAPTURES, CAPTURING, RECAPTURE, RECAPTURED]

Dt 20:19 fighting against it to c it, 9530
1Sa 4:21 of the c of the ark of God and the deaths 4374
19:14 When Saul sent the men to c David, 4374
19:20 so he sent men to c him. 4374
23:26 in on David and his men to c them, 9530
2Sa 12:28 of the troops and besiege the city and c it. 4334
2Ki 6:13 "so I can send men and c him." 4374
2Ch 32:18 and make them afraid in order to c the city. 4334
Job 40:24 Can anyone c him by the eyes, 4374
Jer 18:22 to c me and have hidden snares for my feet. 4334
32:3 and he will c it. 4334
32:28 of Babylon, who will c it. 4334
37:8 they will c it and burn it down.' 4334
38:3 of the king of Babylon, who will c it.' " 4334
50:46 of Babylon's c the earth will tremble; 9530
Da 11:15 up siege ramps and will c a fortified city. 4334
Hab 1:10 they build earthen ramps and c them. 4334
Mt 26:55 with swords and clubs to c me? 5197
Mk 14:48 with swords and clubs to c me? 5197

CAPTURED (75) [CAPTURE]

Nu 21:1 he attacked the Israelites and c some 8647+8660
21:25 Israel c all the cities of the Amorites 4374
21:32 the Israelites c its surrounding settlements 4334
31:9 The Israelites c the Midianite women 8647
31:26 the people and animals that were c. 8660
32:39 c it and drove out the Amorites 4334
32:41 of Manasseh, c their settlements 4334
32:42 And Nobah c Kenath 4334
Dt 2:35 from the towns we had c we carried off 4334
21:13 the clothes she was wearing when c. 8660
Jos 8:19 the city and c it and quickly set it on fire. 4334
10:35 They c it that same day and put it to 4334
11:10 and c Hazor and put its king to the sword. 4334
11:17 He c all their kings and struck them down, 4334
Jdg 7:25 They also c two of the Midianite leaders, 4334
8:12 fled, but he pursued them and c them, 4334
9:45 city until he had c it and killed its people. 4334
9:50 to Thebez and besieged it and c it. 4334
12:5 The Gileadites c the fords of 4334
1Sa 4:11 The ark of God was c, and Eli's two sons, 4374
4:17 are dead, and the ark of God has been c." 4374
4:19 the ark of God had been c and that her father-in-law 4374
4:22 for the ark of God has been c." 4374
5:1 After the Philistines had c the ark of God, 4374
7:14 to Gath that the Philistines had c 4374
30:5 David's two wives had been c— 8647
2Sa 5:7 Nevertheless, David c the fortress of Zion, 4334
8:4 David c a thousand of his chariots, 4334
12:26 of the Ammonites and c the royal citadel. 4334
12:29 and attacked and c it. 4334
1Ki 9:16 of Egypt had attacked and c Gezer. 4334
2Ki 6:22 "Would you kill men you have c 8647
12:17 up and attacked Gath and c it. 4334
14:7 in the Valley of Salt and c Sela in battle, 9530
14:13 Jehoash king of Israel c Amaziah king 9530
17:6 the king of Assyria c Samaria and deported 4334
18:10 So Samaria was c in Hezekiah's sixth year, 4334
18:13 the fortified cities of Judah and c them. 9530
25:6 and he was c. 9530
1Ch 2:23 (But Geshur and Aram c Havvoth Jair, 4374
11:5 Nevertheless, David c the fortress of Zion, 4334
18:4 David c a thousand of his chariots, 4334
2Ch 8:3 then went to Hamath Zobah and c it. 2616
12:4 he c the fortified cities of Judah and came 4334
15:8 and Benjamin and from the towns he had c 4334
17:2 of Ephraim that his father Asa had c. 4334
22:9 and his men c him while he was hiding 4334
25:12 of Judah also c ten thousand men alive, 8647
25:23 Jehoash king of Israel c Amaziah king 9530
28:18 They c and occupied Beth Shemesh, 4334
Ne 9:25 They c fortified cities and fertile land; 4334
Isa 8:15 they will be snared and c." 4334
13:15 Whoever is c will be thrust through; 5162
20:1 came to Ashdod and attacked and c it— 4334
22:3 they have been c without using the bow. 673
28:13 be injured and snared and c. 4334
36:1 the fortified cities of Judah and c them. 9530
Jer 10:18 on them so that they may be c." 5162
34:3 but will surely be c and handed over 9530+9530
38:23 from their hands but will be c by the king 9530
38:28 of the guard until the day Jerusalem was c. 4334
39:5 They c him and took him 4374
48:1 Kiriathaim will be disgraced and c; 4334
48:41 Kerioth will be c and 4334
50:2 but say, 'Babylon will be c; 4334
50:9 and from the north she will be c. 4334
50:24 you were found and c because you opposed 9530

Jer 51:31 the king of Babylon that his entire city **is c,** 4334
51:41 "How Sheshach *will* **be c,** 4334
51:56 her warriors *will* **be c,** 4334
52: 9 and he *was* **c.** 9530
Da 11:33 the sword or be burned or **c** or plundered. 8660
Am 4:10 along with your **c** horses. 8660
Zec 14: 2 the city *will* **be c,** the houses ransacked, 4334
Rev 19:20 But the beast *was* **c,** *4389*

CAPTURES (2) [CAPTURE]

Jos 15:16 the man who attacks and **c** Kiriath Sepher." 4334
Jdg 1:12 the man who attacks and **c** Kiriath Sepher." 4334

CAPTURING (2) [CAPTURE]

Jdg 11:22 **c** all of it from the Arnon to the Jabbok and 3769
2Ki 16: 9 by attacking Damascus and **c** it. 9530

CAR See BETH CAR

CARAVAN (3) [CARAVANS]

Ge 37:25 a **c** *of* Ishmaelites coming from Gilead. 785
1Ki 10: 2 Arriving at Jerusalem with a very great **c**— 2657
2Ch 9: 1 Arriving with a very great **c**— 2657

CARAVANS (3) [CARAVAN]

Job 6:18 **C** turn aside from their routes; 785
6:19 The **c** *of* Tema look for water, 785
Isa 21:13 You **c** *of* Dedanites, 785

CARAWAY (3)

Isa 28:25 does he not sow **c** and scatter cummin? 7902
28:27 **C** is not threshed with a sledge, 7902
28:27 **c** is beaten out with a rod, 7902

CARBUNCLE, CARBUNCLES (KJV) See BERYL, JEWELS

CARCAS (1)

Est 1:10 Harbona, Bigtha, Abagtha, Zethar and **C**— 4139

CARCASE, CARCASES (KJV) See CARCASSES, BODIES, CORPSES

CARCASS (9) [CARCASSES]

Lev 11:26 whoever touches [the **c** of] any of them will NIH
11:37 a **c** falls on any seeds that are to be planted, 5577
11:38 on the seed and a **c** falls on it, 5577
11:39 anyone who touches the **c** will be unclean 5577
11:40 of the **c** must wash his clothes, 5577
11:40 up the **c** must wash his clothes, 5577
Jdg 14: 8 he turned aside to look at the lion's **c.** 5147
14: 9 the honey from the lion's **c.** 1581
Mt 24:28 Wherever there is a **c,** *4773*

CARCASSES (15) [CARCASS]

Ge 15:11 Then birds of prey came down on the **c,** 7007
Lev 5: 2 whether the **c** *of* unclean wild animals or 5577
11: 8 not eat their meat or touch their **c;** 5577
11:11 and you must detest their **c.** 5577
11:24 whoever touches their **c** will be unclean 5577
11:25 up one of their **c** must wash his clothes, 5577
11:27 whoever touches their **c** will be unclean 5577
11:28 up their **c** must wash his clothes, 5577
11:35 of their **c** falls on becomes unclean; 5577
11:36 of these **c** is unclean. 5577
Dt 14: 8 not to eat their meat or touch their **c.** 5577
28:26 Your **c** will be food for all the birds of 5577
1Sa 17:46 the **c** *of* the Philistine army to the birds of 7007
Jer 7:33 Then the **c** *of* this people will become food 5577
19: 7 and I will give their **c** as food to the birds 5577

CARCHEMISH (3)

2Ch 35:20 Neco king of Egypt went up to fight at **C** 4138
Isa 10: 9 'Has not Calno fared like **C**? 4138
Jer 46: 2 of Egypt, which was defeated at **C** on 4138

CARE (91) [CARED, CAREFREE, CAREFUL, CAREFULLY, CARELESS, CARELESSLY, CARES, CARING]

Ge 2:15 the Garden of Eden to work it and **take c of** 9068
30:29 how your livestock has fared **under** my **c.** 907
30:35 and he placed them in the **c** *of* his sons. 3338
32:16 He put them in the **c** *of* his servants, 3338
33:13 and that I must **c for** the ewes and cows 6584
39: 4 he entrusted to his **c** everything he owned. 3338
39: 6 So he left in Joseph's **c** everything he had; 3338
39: 8 everything he owns he has entrusted to my **c** 3338
39:23 to anything under Joseph's **c,** 3338
42:37 Entrust him to my **c,** 3338
Ex 12: 6 **Take c of** them until the fourteenth day 2118+4200+5466
Lev 6: 2 to him or left in his **c** or stolen, 3338
16:21 into the desert in the **c** *of* a man appointed 3338
Nu 1:50 *to* **take c of** it and encamp around it. 9250
1:53 be responsible for the **c** *of* the tabernacle of 5466
3: 8 *They are to* **take c of** all the furnishings of 9068
3:25 the Gershonites were **responsible for** the **c** 5466
Nu 3:28 The Kohathites were responsible for the **c** 9068
3:31 They were **responsible for** the **c** *of* the ark, 5466
3:32 over *those who were* responsible for the **c** 9068
3:36 The Merarites were appointed to **take c of** 5466
3:38 for the **c** *of* the sanctuary on behalf of 9068
4: 4 the **c** of the most holy things. NIH
18: 4 to join you and be responsible for the **c** *of* 5466
18: 5 to be responsible for the **c** *of* the sanctuary 5466
31:30 for the **c** *of* the LORD's tabernacle." 5466
31:47 for the **c** *of* the LORD's tabernacle. 5466
Dt 7:11 Therefore, **take c** to follow the commands, 9068
2Sa 15:16 but he left ten concubines to **take c of** 9068
16:21 to **take c of** the palace. 9068
18: 3 *they* won't **c about** us. 448+4213+8492
18: 3 if half of us die, *they* won't **c;** 448+4213+8492
19:24 *He had* not **taken c of** his feet 6913
20: 3 the ten concubines he had left to **take c of** 9068
1Ki 1: 2 to attend the king and **take c of** him. 2118+6125
1: 4 *she* **took c of** the king and waited on him, 2118+6125
2Ki 9:34 **"Take c of** that cursed woman," he said, 7212
1Ch 9:29 to **take c of** the furnishings and all 6584
9:30 the priests **took c of mixing** the spices. 5351+8379
26:28 the other dedicated things were in the **c** 3338
27:32 of Hacmoni **took c of** the king's sons. 6640
2Ch 25:24 the temple of God that had been **in the c of** 6640
32:22 *He* **took c of** them on every side. 5633
Ezr 10:13 this matter cannot be taken **c** of in a day NIH
Est 2: 3 Let them be placed under the **c** *of* Hegai, 3338
2: 8 to the citadel of Susa and put under the **c** 3338
2:14 to another part of the harem to the **c** 3338
Job 3: 4 *may* God above not **c about** it; 2011
21:21 For what does he **c** about 2914
Ps 8: 4 the son of man that *you* **c for** him? 7212
65: 9 *You* **c for** the land and water it; 7212
88: 5 who are cut off from your **c.** 3338
95: 7 the flock **under** his **c.** 3338
144: 3 O LORD, what is man that *you* **c for** him, 3359
Pr 29: 7 The righteous **c about** justice for the poor, 3359
SS 1: 6 and made me **take c of** the vineyards; 5757
Isa 13:17 who *do* not **c for** silver and have no delight 3108
34:15 and **c for** *her* **young** under the shadow 1842
Jer 6:20 **What do I c about** 2296+3276+4200+4200+4537
15:15 remember me and **c for** me. 7212
23: 2 and *have* not **bestowed c on** them, 7212
30:14 *they* **c** nothing **for** you. 2011
Eze 34: 2 the shepherds of Israel who *only* **take c of** 8286
34: 2 *Should* not shepherds **take c of** the flock? 8286
34: 3 but *you do* not **take c of** the flock. 8286
Hos 14: 8 I will answer him and **c for** him. 8800
Am 7:14 and I also **took c of** sycamore-fig trees. 1179
Mic 2: 8 from those who pass by **without a c,** 1055
Zep 2: 7 The LORD their God *will* **c for** them; 7212
Zec 10: 3 the LORD Almighty *will* **c for** his flock, 7212
11:16 a shepherd over the land *who will* not **c for** 7212
Mt 27:55 from Galilee to **c for** his needs. *1354*
Mk 4:38 "Teacher, don't you **c** if we drown?" *3508*
5:26 She had suffered a great deal under the **c** *NIG*
Lk 10:34 took him to an inn and **took c of** him. *2150*
10:40 don't you **c** that my sister has left me to do *3508*
13: 7 **took c of the vineyard,** *307*
18: 4 though I don't fear God or **c about** men, *1956*
Jn 21:16 Jesus said, **"Take c of** my sheep." *4477*
Ac 9:34 **take c of** *your* **mat."** *4932+5143*
13:40 **Take c** that what *1063*
24:23 **take c of** his **needs.** *5676*
1Co 4: 3 **I c very little** if I am judged by you *1639+1650+1788*
Php 2:25 whom you sent to **take c of** my needs. *3313*
1Ti 3: 5 how *can he* **take c of** God's church?) *2150*
6:20 **what has been entrusted** to *your* **c.** *4146*
Heb 2: 6 the son of man that *you* **c for** him? *2170*
1Pe 1:10 **searched intently and with the greatest c,** *1699+2001+2779*
5: 2 that is under your **c,** serving as overseers— *NIG*
Rev 12: 6 where she *might be* **taken c of** for 1,260 *5555*
12:14 where she *would be* **taken c of** for a time, *5555*

CAREAH (KJV) See KAREAH

CARED (11) [CARE]

Dt 32:10 He shielded him and **c for** him; 1067
Ru 4:16 laid him in her lap and **c** for him. 587
La 2:20 the children they have **c for?** 3259
2:22 those *I* **c for** and reared, 3254
Eze 34: 8 not search for my flock but **c for** 8286
Hos 12:13 by a prophet *he* **c for** *him.* 9068
13: 5 **I c for** you in the desert, 3359
Mk 15:41 and **c for** his **needs.** *1354*
Lk 18: 2 nor **c about** men. *1956*
Jn 12: 6 not say this because he **c** about the poor but *3508*
Ac 7:20 For three months he *was* **c for** *427*

CAREFREE (3) [CARE]

Ps 73:12 always **c,** they increase in wealth. 8929
Eze 23:42 "The noise of a **c** crowd was around her; 8929
Zep 2:15 This is the **c** city that lived in safety. 6611

CAREFUL (78) [CARE]

Ge 31:24 **"Be c** not to say anything to Jacob, 9068
31:29 **'Be c** not to say anything to Jacob, 9068
Ex 19:12 *'Be* **c** *that* you do not go up the mountain 9068
23:13 *"Be* **c to do** everything I have said to you. 9068
34:12 *Be* **c** not to make a treaty 9068
Ex 34:15 "Be **c** not to make a treaty NIH
Lev 18: 4 You must obey my laws and *be* **c** 9068
25:18 " 'Follow my decrees and *be* **c** 9068
26: 3 " 'If you follow my decrees and *are* **c** 9068
Dt 2: 4 They will be afraid of you, but *be* very **c.** 9068
4: 9 Only *be* **c,** and watch yourselves closely so 9068
4:23 *Be* **c** not to forget the covenant of 9068
5:32 So *be* **c** to do what 9068
6: 3 and *be* **c** to obey so that it may go well 9068
6:12 *be* **c** that you do not forget the LORD, 9068
6:25 And if *we are* **c** to obey all this law before 9068
7:12 If you pay attention to these laws and *are* **c** 9068
8: 1 *Be* **c** to follow every command I am giving you today, 9068
8:11 *Be* **c** that you do not forget 9068
11:16 *Be* **c,** or you will be enticed to turn away 9068
12: 1 *be* **c** to follow in the land that the LORD, 9068
12:13 *Be* **c** not to sacrifice 9068
12:19 *Be* **c** not to neglect the Levites as long 9068
12:28 *Be* **c** to obey all these regulations I am giving you, 9068
12:30 *be* **c** not to be ensnared by inquiring 9068
15: 5 the LORD your God and *are* **c** 9068
15: 9 *Be* **c** not to harbor this wicked thought: 9068
17:10 *Be* **c** to do everything they direct you 9068
24: 8 leprous diseases *be* very **c** to do exactly as the priests, 9068+9068
Jos 1: 7 *Be* **c** to obey all the law 9068
1: 8 *you may be* **c** to do everything written in it. 9068
22: 5 But *be* very **c** to keep the commandment 9068
23: 6 *be* **c** to obey all that is written in the Book 9068
23:11 So *be* very **c** to love the LORD your God. 9068
1Ki 8:25 if only your sons *are* **c** in all they do 9068
2Ki 10:31 Yet Jehu *was* not **c** to keep the law of 9068
17:37 *You must* always *be* **c** to keep the decrees 9068
21: 8 *be* **c** to do everything I commanded them 9068
1Ch 22:13 Then you will have success if *you are* **c** 9068
28: 8 *Be* **c** to follow all the commands of 9068
2Ch 6:16 if only your sons *are* **c** in all they do 9068
33: 8 *be* **c** to do everything I commanded them 9068
Ezr 4:22 Be **c** not to neglect this matter. 10224
Job 36:18 *Be* **c** that no one entices you by riches; 2778
Ps 101: 2 *I will be* **c** to lead a blameless life— 8505
Pr 13:24 he who loves him *is* **c** to discipline him. 8838
27:23 give **c attention** to your herds; 4213
Isa 7: 4 Say to him, *'Be* **c,** 9068
Jer 17:21 *Be* **c** not to carry a load on the Sabbath day 9068
17:24 But if *you are* **c to obey** me, 9048+9048
22: 4 if *you are* **c to carry out** these commands, 6913+6913
Eze 11:20 Then they will follow my decrees and *be* **c** 9068
18:19 and *has been* **c** to keep all my decrees, 9068
20:19 follow my decrees and *be* **c** 9068
20:21 *they were* not **c** to keep my laws— 9068
36:27 to follow my decrees and *be* **c** 9068
37:24 They will follow my laws and *be* **c** 9068
Mic 7: 5 with her who lies in your embrace *be* **c** 9068
Hag 1: 5 **"Give c thought** to your ways. 4222+8492
1: 7 **"Give c thought** to your ways. 4222+8492
2:15 " 'Now **give c thought** to this 4222+8492
2:18 **give c thought** to the day when 4222+8492
2:18 **Give c thought:** 4222+8492
Mt 2: 8 "Go and make a **c** search for the child. *209*
6: 1 *"Be* **c** not to do your 'acts of righteousness' *4668*
16: 6 *"Be* **c,"** Jesus said to them. *3972*
Mk 8:15 *"Be* **c,"** Jesus warned them. *3972*
Lk 17:20 not come with your **c observation,** *4191*
21:34 *"Be* **c,** or your hearts will be weighed down *4668*
Ro 12:17 *Be* **c** to do what is right in the eyes *4629*
1Co 3:10 But each one *should be* **c** how he builds. *1063*
8: 9 *Be* **c,** however, that the exercise *1063*
10:12 *be* **c that** you don't fall! *1063*
Eph 5:15 Be **very c,** then, how you live— *209*
2Ti 4: 2 with great patience and **c instruction.** *1439*
Tit 3: 8 in God *may be* **c** to devote themselves *5863*
Heb 2: 1 We must pay **more c** attention, therefore, *4359*
4: 1 *let us* **be c** that none of you be found *5828*

CAREFULLY (41) [CARE]

Ge 27: 8 my son, **listen c** and do what I tell you: 928+7754+9048
Ex 15:26 "If *you* **listen c** to the voice of 9048+9048
23:22 If *you* **listen c** to what he says and do 9048+9048
Dt 4: 6 Observe them **c,** for this will show your wisdom 9068
4:15 **watch** yourselves very **c,** 9068
11:22 If you **c observe** all these commands I am giving you 9068+9068
16:12 and follow **c** these decrees. 9068
17:19 and follow **c** all the words of this law 9068
19: 9 *you* **c** follow all these laws I command you today— 9068
24: 8 You must follow **c** what I have commanded 9068
26:16 **c** observe them with all your heart and 9068
28: 1 **c** follow all his commands I give you today, 9068
28:13 that I give you this day and **c** follow them, 9068
28:15 and do not **c** follow all his commands 9068
28:58 not **c** follow all the words of this law, 9068
29: 9 **C** follow the terms of this covenant, 9068
31:12 and follow **c** all the words of this law. 9068
32:46 to obey **c** all the words of this law. 9068
Jos 8: 4 with these orders: **"Listen c.** 8011
Jdg 6:29 When *they* **c investigated,** 1335+2011+2256
2Ch 19: 6 He told them, **"Consider c** what you do, 8011
19: 7 Judge **c,** for with the LORD our God there is no injustice 9068

Ezr 8:29 Guard them **c** until you weigh them out in 9068
Ne 10:29 of God and to obey **c** all the commands, 9068
Job 13:17 **Listen c** *to* my words; 9048+9048
21: 2 **"Listen c** *to* my words; 9048+9048
Eze 3:10 **listen c** and take to heart all 265+928+9048
44: 5 "Son of man, **look c,** 928+6524+8011
Da 10:11 **consider c** the words I am about to speak 1067
Mk 4:24 **"Consider c** what you hear," he continued. *1063*
Lk 1: 3 I myself have **c** investigated everything *209*
4:10 concerning you *to* **guard** you **c;** *1428+3836*
8:18 Therefore **consider c** how you listen. *1063*
9:44 **"Listen c** *to* what I am about to tell you: *1650+3836+4044+5148+5148+5502*
14: 1 he was *being* **c watched.** *4190*
15: 8 the house and search **c** until she finds it? *2151*
Ac 2:14 **listen c** *to* what I say. *1969*
5:35 "Men of Israel, **consider c** what you intend *4668*
16:23 the jailer was commanded to guard them **c.** *857*
17:23 and **looked c at** your objects of worship, I *355*
1Co 14:29 and the others *should* **weigh c** what is said. *1359*

CARELESS (1) [CARE]

Mt 12:36 for every **c** word they have spoken. *734*

CARELESSLY (1) [CARE]

Lev 5: 4 in any matter one *might* **c** swear about— 1051

CARES (12) [CARE]

Dt 11:12 It is a land the LORD your God **c for;** 2011
Job 39:16 she **c** not that her labor was in vain, 7065
Ps 55:22 Cast your **c** on the LORD 3365
142: 4 I have no refuge; no *one* **c for** my life. 2011
Pr 12:10 A righteous man **c for** the needs 3359
Ecc 5: 3 As a dream comes when there are many **c,** 6721
Jer 12:11 be laid waste because there is no one *who* **c.** 4213+6584+8492
30:17 Zion for whom no *one* **c.'** 2011
Na 1: 7 *He* **c for** those who trust in him, 3359
Jn 10:13 a hired hand and **c** nothing for the sheep. *3508*
Eph 5:29 but *he* feeds and **c for** it, *2499*
1Pe 5: 7 Cast all your anxiety on him because he **c** *3508*

CARESSED (3) [CARESSING]

Eze 23: 3 and their virgin bosoms **c.** 6914
23: 8 **c** her virgin bosom 6914
23:21 when in Egypt your bosom *was* **c** 6914

CARESSING (1) [CARESSED]

Ge 26: 8 and saw Isaac **c** his wife Rebekah. 7464

CARGO (5) [CARGOES]

Eze 27:25 You are filled with **heavy c** in the heart of AIT
Jnh 1: 5 And they threw the **c** into the sea to lighten 641+889+928+2021+3998
Ac 21: 3 where our ship was to unload its **c.** *1203*
27:10 and bring great loss to ship and **c,** *5845*
27:18 **throw the c overboard.** *1678*

CARGOES (4) [CARGO]

1Ki 10:11 and from there they brought **great c** AIT
Rev 18:11 because no one buys their **c** any more— *1203*
18:12 **c** of gold, silver, precious stones *1203*
18:13 **c** of cinnamon and spice, of incense, myrrh *NIG*

CARING (2) [CARE]

1Th 2: 7 like a mother **c for** her little children. *2499*
1Ti 5: 4 **put** *their* **religion into practice by c for** *2355*

CARITES (2)

2Ki 11: 4 the **C** and the guards and had them brought 4133
11:19 the **C,** the guards and all the people of 4133

CARMEL (27) [CARMELITE]

Jos 12:22 the king of Jokneam in **C** one 4151
15:55 Maon, **C,** Ziph, Juttah, 4150
19:26 On the west the boundary touched **C** 4151
1Sa 15:12 but he was told, "Saul has gone to **C.** 4150
25: 2 who had property there at **C,** 4150
25: 2 which he was shearing in **C.** 4150
25: 5 to Nabal at **C** and greet him in my name. 4150
25: 7 and the whole time they were at **C** nothing 4150
25:40 His servants went to **C** and said to Abigail, 4150
27: 3 Ahinoam of Jezreel and Abigail of **C,** 4153
30: 5 the widow of Nabal **of C.** 4153
2Sa 2: 2 the widow of Nabal **of C.** 4153
3: 3 of Abigail the widow of Nabal **of C;** 4153
1Ki 18:19 over Israel to meet me on Mount **C.** 4151
18:20 and assembled the prophets on Mount **C.** 4151
18:42 but Elijah climbed to the top of **C,** 4151
2Ki 2:25 on to Mount **C** and from there returned 4151
4:25 and came to the man of God at Mount **C.** 4151
1Ch 3: 1 second, Daniel the son of Abigail **of C;** 4153
SS 7: 5 Your head crowns you like Mount **C.** 4151
Isa 33: 9 and Bashan and **C** drop their leaves. 4151
35: 2 the splendor of **C** and Sharon; 4151
Jer 46:18 like **C** by the sea. 4151
50:19 to his own pasture and he will graze on **C** 4151
Am 1: 2 and the top of **C** withers." 4151
9: 3 on the top of **C,** 4151
Na 1: 4 Bashan and **C** wither and the blossoms 4151

CARMELITE (2) [CARMEL]

2Sa 23:35 Hezro the **C,** Paarai the Arbite, 4153
1Ch 11:37 Hezro the **C,** Naarai son of Ezbai, 4153

CARMI (8) [CARMITE]

Ge 46: 9 Hanoch, Pallu, Hezron and **C.** 4145
Ex 6:14 and Pallu, Hezron and **C.** 4145
Nu 26: 6 through **C,** the Carmite clan. 4145
Jos 7: 1 Achan son of **C,** the son of Zimri, 4145
7:18 and Achan son of **C,** the son of Zimri, 4145
1Ch 2: 7 The son of **C:** 4145
4: 1 Perez, Hezron, **C,** Hur and Shobal. 4145
5: 3 Hanoch, Pallu, Hezron and **C.** 4145

CARMITE (1) [CARMI]

Nu 26: 6 through Carmi, the **C** clan. 4146

CARNAL (KJV) See UNSPIRITUAL, SINFUL NATURE, SINFUL, MATERIAL, WORLDLY, MERE MEN

CARNALLY (KJV) See SINFUL MAN, INTERCOURSE

CARNELIAN (2)

Rev 4: 3 the appearance of jasper and **c.** *4917*
21:20 the sixth **c,** the seventh chrysolite, *4917*

CAROUSE (1) [CAROUSING]

2Pe 2:13 of pleasure is to **c** in broad daylight. *5588*

CAROUSING (1) [CAROUSE]

1Pe 4: 3 orgies, **c** and detestable idolatry. *4542*

CARPENTER (2) [CARPENTER'S, CARPENTERS]

Isa 44:13 The **c** measures with a line and makes 3093+6770
Mk 6: 3 Isn't this the **c?** *5454*

CARPENTER'S (1) [CARPENTER]

Mt 13:55 "Isn't this the **c** son? *5454*

CARPENTERS (8) [CARPENTER]

2Sa 5:11 with cedar logs and **c** and stonemasons 3093+6770
2Ki 12:11 the **c** and builders, 3093+6770
22: 6 the **c,** the builders and 3093
1Ch 14: 1 stonemasons and **c** to build a palace 3093+6770
22:15 stonecutters, masons and **c,** 6770
2Ch 24:12 and **c** to restore the LORD's temple, 3093
34:11 They also gave money to the **c** and builders 3093
Ezr 3: 7 they gave money to the masons and **c,** 3093

CARPUS (1)

2Ti 4:13 bring the cloak that I left with **C** at Troas, *2842*

CARRIAGE (2) [CARRIAGES]

SS 3: 7 It is Solomon's **c,** 4753
3: 9 King Solomon made for himself the **c;** 712

CARRIAGES (1) [CARRIAGE]

Rev 18:13 horses and **c;** and bodies and souls of men. *4832*

CARRIED (156) [CARRY]

Ge 14:12 *They* also **c** off Abram's nephew Lot 4374
22: 6 and *he* himself **c** the fire and the knife. 928+3338+4374
31:26 and *you've* **c off** my daughters 5627
34:29 *They* **c off** all their wealth 8647
40:15 For *I* **was forcibly c off** from the land 1704+1704
50:13 They **c** him to the land of Canaan 5951
Ex 10:19 up the locusts and **c** them into the Red Sea. 9546
12:34 and **c** it on their shoulders NIH
19: 4 and how *I* **c** you on eagles' wings 5951
27: 7 be on two sides of the altar when it *is* **c.** 5951
34: 4 and *he* **c** the two stone tablets in his hands. 4374
Lev 10: 5 So they came and **c** them, 5951
Nu 10:17 and the Gershonites and Merarites, *who* **c** it, 5951
13:23 Two of them **c** it on a pole between them, 5951
Dt 1:31 how the LORD your God **c** you, 5951
2:35 from the towns we had captured *we* **c off** 1024
3: 7 and the plunder from their cities *we* **c off** 1024
31: 9 who **c** the ark of the covenant of 5951
31:25 the Levites *who* **c** the ark of the covenant of 5951
33:21 *he* **c out** the LORD's righteous will, 6913
Jos 3:15 the priests *who* **c** the ark reached the Jordan 5951
3:17 The priests *who* **c** the ark of the covenant of 5951
4: 8 *they* **c** them **over** with them to their camp, 6296
4: 9 at the spot where the priests *who* **c** the ark of 5951
4:10 the priests *who* **c** the ark remained standing 5951
6:11 So *he had* the ark of the LORD **c around** 6015
8:33 facing *those who* **c** it— 5951
11:14 The Israelites **c off** for themselves all 1024
22: 3 not deserted your brothers but *have* **c out** 9068
Jdg 3:18 he sent on their way the men *who had* **c** it. 5951
5:19 but *they* **c off** no silver, no plunder. 4374
16: 3 He lifted them to his shoulders and **c** them 6590
Jdg 21:23 each man caught one and **c** her **off** to 5951
Ru 2:18 *She* **c** it back to town, 5951
1Sa 5: 2 Then they **c** the ark *into* Dagon's temple 4374
15:11 and *has* not **c out** my instructions." 7756
15:13 *I have* **c out** the LORD's instructions." 7756
17:34 a lion or a bear came and **c off** a sheep 5951
23: 5 the Philistines and **c off** their livestock. 5627
30: 2 but **c** them **off** as they went on their way. 5627
2Sa 5:21 and David and his men **c** them **off.** 5951
23:16 near the gate of Bethlehem and **c** it back 5951
1Ki 2:26 because *you* **c** the ark of the Sovereign 5951
8: 4 The priests and Levites **c** them **up,** 6590
14:26 *He* **c off** the treasures of the temple of 4374
15:22 and *they* **c away** from Ramah the stones 5951
16:20 and the rebellion *he* **c out,** 8003
17:19 **c** him to the upper room 6590
17:23 up the child and **c** him **down** from the room 3718
2Ki 4:20 the servant had lifted him up and **c** him 995
5:23 and *they* **c** them ahead of Gehazi. 5951
7: 8 They ate and drank, and **c** away silver, 5951
18:12 to the commands nor **c** them **out.** 6913
20:17 *will* **be c off** to Babylon. 5951
23:34 he took Jehoahaz and **c** him **off** *to* Egypt, 995
24:14 *He* **c into exile** all Jerusalem: 1655+1655
25:11 the commander of the guard **c into exile** 1655
25:13 at the temple of the LORD and *they* **c** 5951
1Ch 11:18 near the gate of Bethlehem and **c** it back 5951
15:15 the Levites **c** the ark of God with the poles 5951
18: 7 the gold shields **c by** the officers 2118+6584
23:32 the Levites **c out** their responsibilities for 9068
2Ch 5: 5 The priests, who were Levites, **c** them **up;** 6590
8:16 All Solomon's work **was c out,** 3922
12: 9 *he* **c off** the treasures of the temple of 4374
14:13 of Judah **c off** a large amount of plunder. 5951
14:15 of the herdsmen and **c off** droves of sheep 8647
16: 6 and *they* **c away** from Ramah the stones 5951
21:17 invaded it and **c off** all the goods found in 8647
24:12 to the *men who* **c out** the work required for 6913
25:13 and **c off** great quantities of plunder. 1024
28: 8 which *they* **c back** to Samaria. 995
28:17 and attacked Judah and **c away** prisoners, 8647
29:16 The Levites took it and **c** it **out** to 3655
35: 3 It is not to be **c about** on your shoulders. 5362
35:16 the LORD **was c out** for the celebration of 3922
36: 4 and **c** him **off** to Egypt. 995
36:18 *He* **c** *to* Babylon all the articles from 995
36:20 *He* **c into exile** to Babylon the remnant, 1655
Ezr 1: 7 which Nebuchadnezzar *had* **c away** 3655
5: 8 The work *is* **being c on** with diligence 10522
6:12 *Let it* **be c out** with diligence. 10522
6:13 and their associates **c** it **out** with diligence. 10522
Ne 3:17 **c out repairs** for his district. 2616
4:17 Those *who* **c** materials did their work 5951+6673
11:12 *who* **c on** work for the temple— 6913
Est 2: 6 who *had* **been c into exile** from Jerusalem 1655
4:17 So Mordecai went away and **c out** all 6913
9: 1 by the king was to **be c out.** 6913
Job 1:15 and the Sabeans attacked and **c** them **off.** 4374
1:17 down on your camels and **c** them **off.** 4374
10:19 or *had* **been c** straight from the womb to 3297
15:12 Why *has* your heart **c** you **away,** 4374
21:32 He **is c** to the grave, 3297
22:16 They **were c off** before their time, 7855
Ecc 8:11 **is** not quickly **c out,** 6913
Isa 8: 4 and the plunder of Samaria *will* **be c off** 5951
39: 6 *will* **be c off** to Babylon. 5951
41: 4 Who has done this and **c** *it* **through,** 6913
46: 1 **images that are c about** 5953
46: 3 and *have* **c** since your birth. 5951
53: 4 up our infirmities and **c** our sorrows, 6022
60: 4 and your daughters **are c** on the arm. 587
63: 9 he lifted them up and **c** them all the days 5951
66:12 you will nurse and **be c** on her arm 5951
Jer 10: 5 *they* **must be c** because they cannot walk. 5951+5951
13:19 All Judah *will* **be c into exile,** 1655
13:19 be carried into exile, **c** completely **away.** 1655
24: 1 and the artisans of Judah *were* **c into exile** 1655
27:20 **c** Jehoiachin son of Jehoiakim king of Judah **into exile** 1655
29: 1 people Nebuchadnezzar *had* **c into exile** 1655
29: 4 to all those *I* **c into exile** from Jerusalem 1655
29: 7 the city to which *I have* **c** you **into exile.** 1655
29:14 the place from which *I* **c** you **into exile."** 1655
35:16 of Jonadab son of Recab *have* **c out** 7756
39: 9 the imperial guard **c into exile** *to* Babylon 1655
40: 1 and Judah who *were* **being c into exile** 1655
40: 7 the land and who *had* not **been c into exile** 1655
49:29 *be* **c off** with all their goods and camels. 5951
52:15 of the guard **c into exile** some of 1655
52:17 at the temple of the LORD and *they* **c** all 5951
52:28 the people Nebuchadnezzar **c into exile:** 1655
Eze 6: 9 where *they have* **been c captive,** 8647
16:16 **c on** *your* **prostitution.** 2388
17: 4 he broke off its topmost shoot and **c** it **away** 995
17:12 and **c off** her king and her nobles, 4374
17:13 *He* also **c away** the leading men of the land, 4374
23:14 **c** her prostitution **still further.** 3578
23:18 **c on** her prostitution **openly** 1655
30: 4 *be* **c away** and her foundations torn down. 4374
44:15 and who **faithfully c out** the duties 9068
Da 1: 2 These *he* **c off** *to* the temple of his god 995
11:12 When the army **is c off,** 5951
Hos 10: 6 It *will* **be c** to Assyria as tribute for 3297
Joel 3: 5 and my gold and **c off** my finest treasures 995
Ob 1:11 while strangers **c off** his wealth 8647
Na 2: 7 that [the city] be exiled and **c away.** 6590

Mal 2: 3 and you *will be* **c off** with it. 5951
Mt 8:17 up our infirmities and c our diseases." *1002*
14:11 *who* c it to her mother. *5770*
Mk 2: 3 paralytic, c by four of them. *149*
6:55 throughout that whole region and c the sick *4367*
Lk 7:12 a dead person *was being* **c out—** *1714*
16:22 when the beggar died and the angels c him *708*
Jn 20:15 she said, "Sir, if you *have* **c** him **away,** *1002*
Ac 3: 2 Now a man crippled from birth *was being* c *1002*
5: 6 and c him **out** and buried him. *1766*
5:10 **c** her **out** and buried her *1766*
13:29 When *they had* **c out** all that was written *5464*
21:35 of the mob was so great he had to be c by *1002*
23:30 When I was informed of a plot to be c out *NIG*
Heb 13: 9 *be* **c away** by all kinds of strange teachings. *4195*
2Pe 1:21 but men spoke from God *as they were* c *5770*
3:17 so that you may not *be* **c away** by the error *5270*
Rev 17: 3 angel c me **away** in the Spirit into a desert. *708*
21:10 And *he* c me **away** in the Spirit to *708*

CARRIERS (7) [CARRY]

Jos 9:21 but let them be woodcutters and water c for 8612
9:23 as woodcutters and water c for the house 8612
9:27 the Gibeonites woodcutters and water c for 8612
1Ki 5:15 Solomon had seventy thousand c 5951+6025
2Ch 2: 2 as c and eighty thousand as stonecutters in 6025
2:18 of them to be c and 80,000 6025
Eze 27:25 of Tarshish *serve as* c *for* your wares. 8801

CARRIES (9) [CARRY]

Nu 11:12 as a nurse c an infant, 5951
Dt 1:31 as a father c his son, 5951
32:11 to catch them and c them on its pinions. 5951
Job 23:14 *He* **c out** his decree against me, 8966
27:21 The east wind c him **off,** and he is gone; 5951
Isa 40:11 in his arms and c them close to his heart; 5951
44:26 *who* c out the words of his servants 7756
Hag 2:12 If a person c consecrated meat in the fold 5951
Heb 13:11 The high priest c the blood of animals into *1662*

CARRION (1)

Eze 39: 4 as food to all kinds of c **birds** and to 6514+7606

CARRY (132) [CARRIED, CARRIERS, CARRIES, CARRYING]

Ge 44: 1 with as much food as they can **c,** 5951
45:27 the carts Joseph had sent to c him **back,** 5951
47:30 c me out of Egypt and bury me 5951
50:25 and then *you must* c my bones **up** 6590
Ex 13:19 then *you must* c my bones **up** with you 6590
25:14 the rings on the sides of the chest to c it. 5951
25:28 overlay them with gold and c the table 5951
30: 4 to hold the poles used to c it. 5951
36: 1 how to **c out** all the work of constructing 6913
36: 3 the Israelites had brought to **c out** the work 6913
37: 5 into the rings on the sides of the ark to c it. 5951
37:27 to hold the poles used to c it. 5951
Lev 4: 5 of the bull's blood and c it into the Tent 995
6:11 and c the ashes outside the camp to a place 3655
10: 4 c your cousins outside the camp, 5951
16:22 The goat *will* c on itself all their sins to 5951
26:14 to me and **c out** all these commands, 6913
26:15 and fail *to* **c out** all my commands and 6913
Nu 1:50 *to* c the tabernacle and all its furnishings; 5951
4:15 The Kohathites are to c those things 5362
4:19 **what** he is **to c.** 5362
4:24 as they work and c burdens: NIH
4:25 *They are to* c the curtains of the tabernacle, 5951
4:27 as their responsibility all they are to **c.** 5362
4:31 to c the frames of the tabernacle, 5362
4:32 to each man the specific things he is to **c.** 5362
4:49 and told **what to c.** 5362
7: 9 because *they were to* c on their shoulders 5951
11:12 Why do you tell me *to* c them in my arms, 5951
11:14 I cannot c all these people by myself; 5951
11:17 *They will* help you c the burden of 5951
11:17 so that you *will* not *have to* c it alone. 5951
31: 3 to **c out** the LORD's vengeance on them. 5989
Dt 1: 9 **too heavy a burden** for me **to c** 3523+4202+5951
10: 8 to c the ark of the covenant of the LORD, 5951
14:24 and cannot c your tithe (because the place 5951
25: 6 The first son she bears *shall* **c on** the name of the dead brother 6584+7756
25: 7 "My husband's brother refuses to **c on** 7756
29:11 and c your water. 8612
Jos 3: 8 the priests *who* c the ark of the covenant: 5951
3:13 as the priests *who* c the ark of the LORD— 5951
4: 3 where the priests stood and *to* c them **over** 6296
6: 4 *Have* seven priests c trumpets 5951
6: 6 and *have* seven priests c trumpets in front 5951
8: 2 except that *you may* **c off** their plunder 1024
8:27 But Israel *did* **c off** for themselves 1024
1Sa 3:12 At that time *I will* **c out** 7756
20:40 "Go, c them **back** *to* town." 995
21:15 to bring this fellow here to **c on** like this 8713
28:18 the LORD or **c out** his fierce wrath 6913
2Sa 18:18 "I have no son to **c on the memory** 2349
24:12 of them *for me to* **c out** against you.' " 6913
1Ki 1:30 surely **c out** today what I swore to you by 6913
3: 7 and do not know how *to* **c out** *my* **duties.** 995+2256+3655
6:12 **c out** my regulations 6913
18:12 of the LORD *may* c you when I leave you. 5951
20: 6 and c it **away.' "** 4374
2Ki 4:19 "C him to his mother." 5951
5:17 as much earth as a pair of mules can **c,** 5362
1Ch 15: 2 "No one but the Levites *may* c the ark 5951
15: 2 because the LORD chose them to c the ark 5951
21:10 of them *for me to* **c out** against you.' " 6913
23:26 the Levites no *longer need* to c 5951
2Ch 20:25 and his men went to **c off** their plunder, 1024
24:11 the chest and c it back to its place. 5951
30:12 to give them unity of mind to **c out** what 6913
Est 3: 9 for the *men who* **c out** this business." 6913
9:13 to **c out** this day's edict tomorrow also, 6913
Job 12: 6 *those* who c their god in their hands. 995
15:30 of God's mouth *will* **c** *him* **away.** 6073
20:28 A flood *will* **c off** his house, 1655
24:10 *they* c the sheaves, but still go hungry. 5951
Ps 28: 9 be their shepherd and c them forever. 5951
37: 7 when they **c out** their wicked schemes. 6913
149: 9 to **c out** the sentence written against them. 6913
Ecc 5:15 from his labor that *he can* c in his hand. 2143
10:20 because a bird of the air *may* c your words, 2143
Isa 5:29 as they seize their prey and **c** it **off** 7117
10:23 *will* **c out** the destruction decreed upon 6913
13: 3 to c out my wrath— NIH
15: 7 and stored up *they* **c away** over the Ravine 5951
28:19 As often as it comes *it will* c you **away;** 4374
30: 1 "to those *who* **c out** plans that are not mine, 6913
30: 6 envoys c their riches on donkeys' backs, 5951
33:23 and even the lame *will* **c off** plunder. 1024
45:20 Ignorant are those *who* **c about** idols 5951
46: 4 I have made you and I *will* c you; 5951
46: 7 They lift it to their shoulders and c it; 6022
48:14 LORD's chosen ally *will* **c out** his purpose 6913
49:22 and c your daughters on their shoulders. 5951
52:11 you *who* c the vessels of the LORD. 5951
57:13 c all of them **off,** 5951
Jer 17:21 *to* c a load on the Sabbath day or bring it 5951
20: 4 *who will* c them **away** to Babylon 1655
20: 5 as plunder and **c** it **off** to Babylon. 995
22: 4 *you are* **careful** to **c out** these commands, 6913+6913
43: 3 so they may kill us or c us **into exile** 1655
44:25 you said, '*We will* **certainly c out** 6913+6913
46: 9 men of Cush and Put *who* c shields, 9530
51:12 The LORD *will* **c out** *his* **purpose,** 2372
Eze 12: 6 as they are watching and c them **out** 3655
25:17 *I will* **c out** great vengeance on them 6913
29:19 and *he will* **c off** its wealth. 5951
38:13 to **c off** silver and gold, 5951
Da 11: 8 and gold and c them **off** *to* Egypt. 928+995+2021+8660
11:10 and **c the battle** as far as his 1741+2256+8740
Hos 5:14 *I will* c them **off,** 5951
11: 9 *I will* not **c out** my fierce anger, 6913
Am 6:10 to burn the bodies comes *to* c them out of 5951
Mic 2: 1 At morning's light *they* **c** it **out** 6913
Mt 3:11 whose sandals I am not fit *to* **c.** *1002*
12:29 and **c off** his possessions *773*
27:32 and they forced him to c the cross. *149*
Mk 3:27 and **c off** his possessions *1395*
11:16 not allow anyone *to* c merchandise *1422*
15:21 and they forced *him to* c the cross. *149*
Lk 11:46 down with burdens *they can* **hardly c,** *1546*
14:27 And anyone who *does* not c his cross *1002*
23:26 and put the cross on him and made him c it *5770*
Jn 5:10 the law forbids you *to* c your mat." *149*
8:44 and you want *to* **c out** your father's desire. *4472*
Ac 5: 9 and *they will* c you **out** also." *1766*
9:15 to c my name before the Gentiles *1002*
Ro 7:18 but *I* cannot **c** it **out.** *2981*
9:28 the Lord *will* **c out** his sentence on earth *4472*
2Co 4:10 We always **c around** in our body the death *4367*
8:19 by the churches to accompany us as we c *NIG*
Gal 6: 2 C each other's burdens, *1002*
6: 5 for each one *should* c his own load. *1002*
Php 1: 6 **c it on to completion** *2200*
Heb 9: 6 into the outer room *to* **c on** their ministry. *2200*
Jas 4:13 **c on business** and make money." *1864*

CARRYING (50) [CARRY]

Ex 25:27 to the rim to hold the poles *used in* c 5951
37:14 the rim to hold the poles used in c the table. 5951
37:15 for c the table were made of acacia wood 5951
38: 7 be on the sides of the altar for c it. 5951
Nu 4:10 of sea cows and put it on a c **frame.** 4573
4:12 of sea cows and put them on a c **frame.** 4573
4:15 the Kohathites are to come to *do the* **c.** 5951
4:27 whether c or doing other work, 5362
4:47 to do the work of serving and c the Tent 5362
10:21 the Kohathites set out, c the holy things. 5951
Dt 27:26 the words of this law by c them **out."** 6913
Jos 3: 3 and the priests, who are Levites, c it, 5951
3:14 the priests c the ark of the covenant went 5951
4:16 the priests c the ark of the Testimony 5951
4:18 up out of the river c the ark of the covenant 5951
6: 8 the seven priests c the seven trumpets 5951
6:13 The seven priests c the seven trumpets 5951
1Sa 10: 3 One *will be* c three young goats, 5951
2Sa 6:13 When *those who were* c the ark of 5951
15:24 with him *were* c the ark of the covenant 5951
1Ki 8: 7 and overshadowed the ark and its c **poles.** 964
10: 2 with camels c spices, large quantities 5951
10:22 Once every three years it returned, c gold, 5951
1Ch 12:24 c shield and spear— 5951
12:34 men c shields and spears; 928
15:26 the Levites *who were* c the ark of 5951
15:27 as were all the Levites who *were* c the ark, 5951
1Ch 28: 7 if he is unswerving in **c out** my commands 6913
2Ch 5: 8 the ark and covered the ark and its **c poles.** 964
7:11 and *had* **succeeded in c out** all he had 7503
9: 1 with camels c spices, large quantities 5951
9:21 Once every three years it returned, c gold, 5951
Ne 6: 3 "I *am* **c on** a great project 6913
10:32 **assume the responsibility for c out** 6584+6641
Ps 126: 6 He who goes out weeping, c seed to sow, 5951
126: 6 c sheaves with him. 5951
Jer 17:27 the Sabbath day holy by not c any load 5951
Eze 12: 7 c them on my shoulders 5951
44: 8 Instead of **c out** *your* duty in regard 9068
Mal 3:14 by **c out** his requirements and going about 9068
Mk 14:13 and a man c a jar of water will meet you. *1002*
Lk 5:18 Some men came c a paralytic on a mat *5770*
7:14 and those c it stood still. *1002*
22:10 a man c a jar of water will meet you. *1002*
Jn 18: 3 They were c torches, lanterns and weapons. *NIG*
19:17 C his own cross, *1002*
Ac 23:31 So the soldiers, **c out** their orders, *2848*
27:43 and kept them from c out their plan. *NIG*
1Co 16:10 for *he is* **c on** the work of the Lord, *2237*
1Jn 5: 2 by loving God and **c out** his commands. *4472*

CARSHENA (1)

Est 1:14 **C,** Shethar, Admatha, Tarshish, Meres, 4161

CART (14) [CARTS, CARTWHEEL]

Nu 7: 3 from each leader and a c from every two. 6322
1Sa 6: 7 "Now then, get a new c ready, 6322
6: 7 Hitch the cows to the **c,** 6322
6: 8 the ark of the LORD and put it on the **c,** 6322
6:10 and hitched them to the c and penned 6322
6:11 They placed the ark of the LORD on the c 6322
6:14 The c came to the field of Joshua 6322
6:14 The people chopped up the wood of the c 6322
2Sa 6: 3 on a new c and brought it from the house 6322
6: 3 were guiding the new c 6322
1Ch 13: 7 of God from Abinadab's house on a new **c,** 6322
Isa 5:18 and wickedness as with c ropes, 6322
28:28 the wheels of his **threshing** c over it, 6322
Am 2:13 I will crush you as a c crushes when loaded 6322

CARTS (9) [CART]

Ge 45:19 Take *some* c from Egypt for your children 6322
45:21 Joseph gave them **c,** 6322
45:27 the c Joseph had sent to carry him back, 6322
46: 5 and their children and their wives in the c 6322
Nu 7: 3 before the LORD six covered c 6322
7: 6 the c and oxen and gave them to 6322
7: 7 He gave two c and four oxen to 6322
7: 8 and he gave four c and eight oxen to 6322
Ps 65:11 and your c overflow with abundance. 5047

CARTWHEEL (1) [CART]

Isa 28:27 nor is a c rolled over cummin; 236+6322

CARVED (26) [CARVES, CARVINGS]

Lev 26: 1 not place a c stone in your land to bow 5381
Nu 33:52 Destroy all their c **images** 5381
Jdg 17: 3 to the LORD for my son to make a **c image** 7181
18:14 a **c image** and a cast idol? 7181
18:17 the land went inside and took the **c image,** 7181
18:18 into Micah's house and took the **c image,** 7181
18:20 the **c image** and went along with the people. 7181
1Ki 6:18 c *with* gourds and open flowers. 5237
6:29 and outer rooms, *he* c cherubim, 5237+7844
6:32 two olive wood doors *he* c cherubim, 5237+7844
6:35 *He* c cherubim, palm trees and open flowers 7844
2Ki 21: 7 the c Asherah pole he had made and put it 7181
2Ch 3: 7 and *he* c cherubim on the walls. 7338
33: 7 He took the c image he had made and put it 7181
34: 3 Asherah poles, **c idols** and cast images. 7178
Ps 74: 6 They smashed all the c **paneling** 7334
144:12 and our daughters will be like pillars c 2634
Eze 41:18 were c cherubim and palm trees. 6913
41:19 *They* **were** c all around the whole temple. 6913
41:20 cherubim and palm trees **were** c on the wall 6913
41:25 of the outer sanctuary **were** c cherubim 6913
41:25 and palm trees like *those* c on the walls, 6913
41:26 with palm trees c on each side. NIH
Mic 5:13 I will destroy your **c images** 7178
Na 1:14 I will destroy the **c images** and cast idols 7181
Hab 2:18 since a man *has* c it? 7180

CARVES (1) [CARVED]

Dt 27:15 "Cursed is the man who c an image or casts 6913

CARVINGS (1) [CARVED]

1Ki 6:35 with gold hammered evenly over the **c.** 2977

CASE (58) [CASES]

Ex 18:22 have them bring every difficult c to you; 1821
Lev 5: 4 of it, in any c when he learns of it he will 465[S]
5:13 **as in the c** of the grain offering.' " 3869
Nu 27: 5 Moses brought their c before the LORD 5477
Dt 1:16 whether the c is between brother Israelites NIH
1:17 Bring me any c too hard for you, 1821
6:24 **as is the c** today. 3869
22:26 This c is like that of someone who attacks 1821
25: 1 to court and the judges will decide **the c,** 4392[S]
Jos 20: 4 and state his c before the elders of that city. 1821

2Sa 15: 4 or **c** could come to me and I would see 5477
20:21 That is not the **c**. 1821
1Ki 15: 5 except in the **c** *of* Uriah the Hittite. 1821
2Ki 8: 6 Then he assigned an official to her **c** NIH
2Ch 19:10 In every **c** that comes before you 8190
Job 13: 3 the Almighty and *to* **argue** my **c** with God. 3519
13: 8 *Will you* **argue the c** for God? 8189
13:18 Now that I have prepared my **c**, 5477
23: 4 I would state my **c** before him 5477
23: 7 There an upright man *could* **present** his **c** 3519
29:16 I took up the **c** of the stranger. 8190
35:14 that your **c** is before him and you must wait 1907
37:19 *we* cannot **draw up** our **c** because 6885
Pr 18:17 The first to present his **c** seems right, 8190
22:23 for the LORD will take up their **c** 8190
23:11 he will take up their **c** against you. 8190
25: 9 If you argue your **c** with a neighbor, 8190
Isa 1:17 **plead** the **c** *of* the widow. 8189
1:23 the widow's **c** does not come before them. 8190
41:21 "Present your **c**," says the LORD. 8190
43:26 state the *c for* your **innocence**. AIT
59: 4 no *one* **pleads** *his* **c** with integrity. 9149
Jer 5:28 not plead the **c** *of* the fatherless to win it, 1907
12: 1 O LORD, when *I* **bring a c** before you. 8189
La 3:58 O Lord, you took up my **c**; 8190
Mic 6: 1 **plead** *your* **c** *before* the mountains; 8189
6: 2 For the LORD has a **c** against his people; 8190
7: 9 until he pleads my **c** 8190
Lk 13:33 **In any c**, I must keep going today *4440*
Ac 5:38 Therefore, in the present **c** I advise you: *NIG*
19:40 **In that c** we would not be able to account *4005+4309*
23:15 of wanting more accurate information about his **c**. *NIG*
23:30 to present to you their **c** against him. *NIG*
23:35 *"I will* **hear** your **c** *1358*
24: 2 Tertullus **presented** his **c** before Felix: *2989*
24:22 he said, "I will decide your **c**." *2848+3836*
25:14 Festus discussed Paul's **c** with the king. *2848+3836*
25:17 I did not delay the **c**, *NIG*
1Co 5:10 **In that c** you would have to leave *726+2075*
14: 7 **Even in the c of** lifeless things *3940*
2Co 10:14 as would be the **c** if we had not come *NIG*
Gal 3:15 so it is in this **c**. *NIG*
5:11 **In that c** the offense of *726*
2Ti 3: 9 as in the **c** of those men, *NIG*
Heb 6: 9 we are confident of better things **in** your **c**— *4309*
7: 8 **In the one c**, the tenth is collected *3525+6045*
7: 8 **but in the other c**, by him *1254+1695*
9:16 **In the c of** a will, *3963*

CASEMENT (KJV) See LATTICE

CASES (9) [CASE]

Ex 18:22 the simple **c** they can decide themselves. 1821
18:26 The difficult **c** they brought to Moses, 1821
22: 9 In all **c** *of* illegal possession of an ox, 1821
22: 9 both parties are to bring their **c** before 1821
Dt 17: 8 If **c** come before your courts 1821+8191
21: 5 and to decide all **c of dispute** and assault. 8190
24: 8 In **c** of leprous diseases be very careful NIH
Ezr 10:16 down to investigate the **c**, 1821
1Co 6: 2 are you not competent *to* **judge** trivial **c**? *3215*

CASIPHIA (2)

Ezr 8:17 I sent them Iddo, the leader in **C**. 4085
8:17 the temple servants in **C**, 4085

CASLUHITES (2)

Ge 10:14 **C** (from whom the Philistines came) 4078
1Ch 1:12 **C** (from whom the Philistines came) 4078

CASSIA (3)

Ex 30:24 500 shekels of **c**— 7703
Ps 45: 8 with myrrh and aloes and **c**; 7904
Eze 27:19 **c** and calamus for your wares. 7703

CAST (90) [CASTING, CASTS, OUTCAST]

Ex 25:12 **C** four gold rings for it and fasten them 3668
26:37 And **c** five bronze bases for them. 3668
32: 4 and made it into an **idol c** in the shape of 5011
32: 8 and have made themselves an **idol c** in 5011
34:17 "Do not make **c** idols. 5011
36:36 for them and **c** their four silver bases. 3668
37: 3 *He* **c** four gold rings for it 3668
37:13 *They* **c** four gold rings for the table 3668
38: 5 *They* **c** bronze rings to hold the poles for 3668
38:27 The 100 talents of silver were used to **c** 3668
Lev 16: 8 He *is to* **c** lots for the two goats— 5989
19: 4 not turn to idols or make gods of **c metal** 5011
Nu 33:52 and their **c** idols, 5011
Dt 9:12 and have made a **c idol** for themselves." 5011
9:16 you had made for yourselves an **idol c** in 5011
Jos 18: 6 and *I will* **c** lots for you in the presence 3721
18: 8 and *I will* **c** lots for you here at Shiloh in 8959
18:10 Joshua then **c** lots for them in Shiloh in 8959
Jdg 17: 3 to make a carved image and a **c idol**. 5011
18:14 a carved image and a **c idol**? 5011
18:17 the other household gods and the **c idol** 5011
18:18 the other household gods and the **c idol**, 5011
1Sa 14:42 "**C** the lot between me 5877
2Sa 23: 6 evil men are all *to* **be c aside** like thorns, 5610
1Ki 7:15 *He* **c** two bronze pillars, 7445
7:16 also made two capitals of **c** bronze to set on 4607
7:23 He made the Sea of **c metal**, 4607
7:24 The gourds **were c** in two rows in one piece 3668
7:30 **c** *with* wreaths on each side. 3668
7:33 rims, spokes and hubs were all of **c metal**. 4607
7:37 **c in** the same **molds** 4607
7:46 The king *had* them **c** in clay molds in 3668
2Ki 17:16 and made for themselves two **idols c** in 5011
1Ch 24:31 They also **c** lots, 5877
25: 8 **c** lots for their duties. 5877
26:13 Lots *were* **c** for each gate, 5877
26:14 Then lots *were* **c** *for* his son Zechariah, 5877
2Ch 4: 2 He made the Sea of **c metal**, 4607
4: 3 The bulls **were c** in two rows in one piece 3668
4:17 The king *had* them **c** in clay molds in 3668
28: 2 of the kings of Israel and also made **c idols** 5011
34: 3 Asherah poles, carved idols and **c images**. 5011
Ne 9:18 even when *they* **c** for themselves an image 6913
10:34 *have* **c** lots to determine when each 5877
11: 1 the rest of the people **c** lots to bring one out 5877
Est 3: 7 the month of Nisan, *they* **c** the pur (that is, 5877
9:24 against the Jews to destroy them and *had* **c** 5877
Job 6:27 *You would* even **c** lots for the fatherless 5877
37:18 hard as a mirror of **c bronze**? 4607
Ps 22:10 From birth *I was* **c** upon you; 8959
22:18 among them and **c** lots for my clothing. 5877
50:17 You hate my instruction and **c** my words 8959
51:11 *Do* not **c** me from your presence 8959
55:22 **C** your cares on the LORD 8959
71: 9 *Do* not **c** me **away** when I am old; 8959
73:18 *you* **c** them **down** to ruin. 5877
89:44 an end to his splendor and **c** his throne to 4489
106:19 and worshiped an **idol c from metal**. 5011
Pr 16:33 The lot is **c** into the lap, 3214
23: 5 **C** but a glance at riches, and they are gone, 6414
29:18 the people **c off restraint**; 7277
Ecc 11: 1 **C** your bread upon the waters, 8938
11:10 banish anxiety from your heart and **c off** 6296
Isa 14:12 *You have* **been c down** to the earth, 1548
14:19 But you **are c** out of your tomb like 8959
19: 8 all *who* **c** hooks into the Nile; 8959
38: 8 the shadow **c** by the sun go back NIH
57:20 whose waves **c up** mire and mud. 1764
Jer 22:28 **c** into a land they do not know? 8959
23:39 and **c** you **out** of my presence along with 5759
La 3:31 For *men are* not **c off** *by* the Lord forever. 2396
Eze 21:21 *He will* **c lots** with arrows, 7837
31:11 according to its wickedness, *I* **c** it **aside**, 1763
32: 3 a great throng of people *I will* **c** my net 7298
Joel 3: 3 *They* **c** lots for my people and traded boys 3341
Am 4: 3 and *you will be* **c out** toward Harmon," 8959
5: 7 into bitterness and **c** righteousness to 5663
Ob 1:11 and foreigners entered his gates and **c** lots 3341
Jnh 1: 7 *let us* **c** lots to find out who is responsible 5877
1: 7 *They* **c** lots and the lot fell on Jonah. 5877
Mic 5:12 and you will no longer **c spells**, 6726
Na 1:14 the carved images and **c idols** that are in 5011
3:10 Lots *were* **c** for her nobles, 3341
Mal 3:11 in your fields *will* not **c** *their* **fruit**," 8897
Mk 15:24 they **c** lots to see what each would get. *965*
Jn 19:24 among them and **c** lots for my clothing." *965*
Ac 1:26 *they* **c** lots, and the lot fell to Matthias; *1443*
26:10 *I* **c** *my* vote **against** them. *2965*
1Pe 5: 7 **C** all your anxiety **on** on him because he cares for you. *2166*
Rev 2:22 So *I will* **c** her on a bed of suffering, *965*

CASTAWAY (KJV) See DISQUALIFIED

CASTING (7) [CAST]

Pr 18:18 **C** the lot settles disputes NIH
Eze 24: 6 Empty it piece by piece without **c** lots 5877
26: 3 like the sea **c up** its waves. 6590
Mt 4:18 *They were* **c** a net into the lake, *965*
27:35 they divided up his clothes *by* **c** lots. *965*
Mk 1:16 and his brother Andrew **c a net** into *311*
Lk 23:34 And *they* divided up his clothes by **c** lots. *965*

CASTLE, CASTLES (KJV) See FORT, FORTRESS

CASTOR (1)

Ac 28:11 **twin gods C and Pollux.** *1483*

CASTS (7) [CAST]

Dt 18:11 or **c spells**, or who is a medium 2489+2490
27:15 the man who carves an image or **c** NIH
Ps 15: 3 and **c** no slur on his fellowman, 5951
147: 6 the humble but **c** the wicked to the ground. 9164
Isa 26: 5 he levels it to the ground and **c** it **down** to 5595
40:19 As for an idol, a craftsman **c** it, 5818
44:10 Who shapes a god and **c** an idol, 5818

CASUALTIES (7)

Jdg 20:31 They began to inflict **c** on the Israelites as 2728
20:39 The Benjamites had begun to inflict **c** on 2728
2Sa 18: 7 and the **c** that day were great— 4487
1Ki 20:29 **inflicted** a hundred thousand **c** 5782
2Ch 13:17 so that there were five hundred thousand **c** 2728
28: 5 who inflicted heavy **c** on him. 4804
Na 3: 3 Many **c**, piles of dead, 2728

CATASTROPHE (2)

Ge 19:29 of the **c** that overthrew the cities 2202
Isa 47:11 a **c** you cannot foresee will suddenly come 8739

CATCH (19) [CATCHES, CAUGHT]

Ge 44: 4 and when *you* **c up** *with* them, say to them, 5952
Dt 32:11 *to* **c** them and carries them on its pinions. 4374
Jos 2: 5 *You may* **c up** *with* them." 5952
Job 23: 9 *I* **c** no **glimpse** of him. 8011
Ps 10: 9 he lies in wait to **c** the helpless; 2642
SS 2:15 **C** for us the foxes, 296
Jer 2:34 though *you did* not **c** them breaking in. 5162
5:26 and like those who set traps *to* **c** men. 4334
16:16 "and *they will* **c** them. 1899
Hos 2: 7 after her lovers but not **c** them; 5952
7:12 *I will* **c** them. 3579
Am 3: 5 when there is nothing *to* **c**? 4334+4334
Mt 17:27 Take the first fish you **c**; *NIG*
Mk 12:13 and Herodians to Jesus to **c** him *65*
Lk 5: 4 and let down the nets for a **c**." *62*
5: 9 at the **c** of fish they had taken, *62*
5:10 from now on *you will* **c** men." *1639+2436*
11:54 *to* **c** him in something he might say. *2561*
20:20 *to* **c** Jesus in something he said so *2138*

CATCHES (5) [CATCH]

Job 5:13 *He* **c** the wise in their craftiness, 4334
39:25 *He* **c the scent** *of* battle from afar, 8193
Ps 10: 9 *he* **c** the helpless and drags them off 2642
Hab 1:15 *he* **c** them in his net, 1760
1Co 3:19 "He **c** the wise in their craftiness"; *1533*

CATERPILLER, CATERPILLERS (KJV) See GRASSHOPPER, GRASSHOPPERS

CATTLE (85)

Ge 12:16 and Abram acquired sheep and **c**, 1330
20:14 Then Abimelech brought sheep and **c** 1330
21:27 and **c** and gave them to Abimelech, 1330
24:35 He has given him sheep and **c**, 1330
32: 5 I have **c** and donkeys, sheep and goats, 8802
47:17 sheep and goats, their **c** and donkeys. 1330+5238
Ex 9: 3 and donkeys and camels and on your **c** 1330
11: 5 and all the firstborn of the **c** as well. 989
20:24 your sheep and goats and your **c**. 1330
22: 1 he must pay back five *head of* **c** for the ox 1330
22:30 Do the same with your **c** and your sheep. 8802
Lev 7:23 'Do not eat any of the fat of **c**, 8802
22:19 a male without defect from the **c**, 1330
26:22 destroy your **c** and make you so few 989
Nu 22:40 Balak sacrificed **c** and sheep, 1330
31:28 whether persons, **c**, donkeys, 1330
31:30 **c**, donkeys, sheep, goats or other animals. 1330
31:33 72,000 **c**, 1330
31:38 36,000 **c**, of which the tribute for 1330
31:44 36,000 **c**, 1330
35: 3 to live in and pasturelands for their **c**, 989
Dt 11:15 I will provide grass in the fields for your **c**, 989
14:26 Use the silver to buy whatever you like: **c**, 1330
Jos 6:21 men and women, young and old, **c**, 8802
7:24 his sons and daughters, his **c**, 8802
Jdg 6: 4 neither sheep nor **c** nor donkeys. 8802
1Sa 8:16 the best of your **c** and donkeys he will take 1330
14:32 taking sheep, **c** and calves, 1330
14:34 'Each of you bring me your **c** and sheep, 8802
15: 3 **c** and sheep, camels and donkeys.'" 8802
15: 9 the sheep and **c**, the fat calves and lambs— 1330
15:14 What is this lowing of **c** that I hear?" 1330
15:15 and **c** to sacrifice to the LORD your God, 1330
15:21 The soldiers took sheep and **c** from 1330
22:19 its children and infants, and its **c**, 8802
27: 9 but took sheep and **c**, donkeys and camels, 1330
2Sa 12: 2 a very large number of sheep and **c**, 1330
12: 4 of his own sheep or **c** to prepare a meal for 1330
1Ki 1: 9 **c** and fattened calves at the Stone 1330
1:19 He has sacrificed great numbers of **c**, 8802
1:25 down and sacrificed great numbers of **c**, 8802
4:23 ten *head of* stall-fed **c**, 1330
4:23 of pasture-fed **c** and a hundred sheep 1330
8: 5 so many sheep and **c** that they could not 1330
8:63 twenty-two thousand **c** and a hundred 1330
2Ki 3:17 your **c** and your other animals will drink. 5238
1Ch 12:40 oil, **c** and sheep, for there was joy in Israel. 1330
2Ch 5: 6 so many sheep and **c** that they could not 1330
7: 5 of twenty-two thousand *head of* **c** and 1330
15:11 *of* **c** and seven thousand sheep and goats 1330
18: 2 and **c** for him and the people with him 1330
32:28 made stalls for various **kinds of c**, 989+989+2256
35: 7 and also three thousand **c**— 1330
35: 8 and three hundred **c**. 1330
35: 9 and five hundred *head of* **c** for the Levites. 1330
35:12 They did the same with the **c**. 1330
Ne 9:37 over our bodies and our **c** as they please. 989
10:36 the firstborn of our sons and of our **c**, 989
Job 18: 3 as **c** and considered stupid in your sight? 989
36:33 even the **c** make known its approach. 5238
Ps 50:10 and the **c** on a thousand hills. 989
78:48 He gave over their **c** to the hail, 1248
104:14 He makes grass grow for the **c**, 989
147: 9 He provides food for the **c** and for 989
148:10 wild animals and all **c**, 989
Isa 7:25 where **c** are turned loose and 8802
22:13 slaughtering of **c** and killing of sheep, 1330

Isa 30:23 In that day your c will graze 5238
32:20 and letting your c and donkeys range free. 8802
63:14 like c that go down to the plain, 989
Jer 9:10 and the lowing of c is not heard. 5238
Eze 32:13 I will destroy all her c from 989
32:13 of man or muddied by the hoofs of c. 989
Da 4:25 you will eat grass like c and be drenched 10756
4:32 you will eat grass like c. 10756
4:33 from people and ate grass like c. 10756
5:21 with the wild donkeys and ate grass like c; 10756
Joel 1:18 How the c moan! 989
Jnh 4:11 and many c as well. 989
Hab 3:17 in the pen and no c in the stalls, 1330
Hag 1:11 on men and c, 989
Mt 22:4 and **fattened** c have been butchered, *4990*
Jn 2:14 the temple courts he found men selling c, *1091*
2:15 both sheep and c; *1091*
Rev 18:13 and wheat; c and sheep; *3229*

CAUDA (1)

Ac 27:16 to the lee of a small island called C, *3007*

CAUGHT (57) [CATCH]

Ge 22:13 and there in a thicket he saw a ram c 296
27:27 When Isaac **c the smell** *of* his clothes, 8193+8194
31:23 he pursued Jacob for seven days and **c up** 1815
39:12 *She* c him by his cloak and said, 9530
44:6 When *he* **c up** *with* them, 5952
Ex 10:19 *which* **c up** the locusts and carried them into 5951
21:16 or still has him *when he* **is c** must be put 5162
22:2 "If a thief **is c** breaking in and is struck so 5162
22:7 the thief, if *he* **is c**, must pay back double. 5162
Nu 5:13 *she has* not **been c in the act),** 9530
11:22 if all the fish in the sea **were c** for them?" 665
Dt 24:7 If a man **is c** kidnapping one 5162
Jos 7:15 *He* who **is c** with the devoted things shall 4334
8:22 so that *they were* c in the middle, 2118
Jdg 1:6 but they chased him and c him, 296
8:14 *He* c a young man of Succoth 4334
15:4 So he went out and c three hundred foxes 4334
21:23 each man c one and carried her off to 1608
1Sa 9:17 When Samuel **c sight of** Saul, 8011
15:27 Saul **c hold** of the hem of his robe, 2616
2Sa 18:9 Absalom's head *got* c in the tree. 2616
Job 4:12 my ears c a whisper of it. 4374
Ps 9:15 their feet **are** c in the net they have hidden. 4334
10:2 *who* **are** c in the schemes he devises. 9530
59:12 *let them* **be** c in their pride. 4334
Pr 6:31 Yet if *he* **is c**, he must pay sevenfold, 5162
30:28 a lizard *can be* c with the hand, 9530
Ecc 9:12 As fish **are** c in a cruel net, 296
Isa 13:15 all who **are** c will fall by the sword. 6200
22:3 All you *who* **were** c were taken prisoner together, 5162
24:18 whoever climbs out of the pit *will* **be** c in 4334
51:20 like **antelope** *c in* a net. AIT
Jer 2:26 "As a thief is disgraced when *he* **is c,** 5162
6:11 both husband and wife *will* **be** c in it, 4334
41:12 *They* **c up** *with* him near the great pool 5162
48:27 **Was** *she* c among thieves, 5162
48:44 whoever climbs out of the pit *will* **be** c in 4334
50:24 and *you* **were** c before you knew it; 4334
La 4:20 our very life breath, **was** c in their traps. 4334
Eze 12:13 and *he will* **be** c in my snare; 9530
17:20 and *he will* **be** c in my snare. 9530
Am 3:4 in his den when *he has* c nothing? 4334
Mt 13:47 down into the lake and c all kinds of fish. *5251*
14:31 Immediately Jesus reached out his hand and c him. *2138*
Lk 5:5 and haven't c anything. *3284*
5:6 *they* c such a large number of fish *5168*
Jn 8:3 and the Pharisees brought in a woman c *2898*
8:4 this woman *was* **c in the act** of adultery. *900+2093+2898*
21:3 but that night *they* c nothing. *4389*
21:10 "Bring some of the fish *you have* just **c.**" *4389*
Ac 27:15 The ship *was* c by the storm and could *5275*
2Co 12:2 a man in Christ *who* fourteen years ago *was* **c up** to the third heaven. *773*
12:4 *was* **c up** to paradise. *773*
12:16 *I* c you by trickery! *3284*
Gal 6:1 Brothers, if someone *is* c in a sin, *4624*
1Th 4:17 *be* **c up** together with them in the clouds *773*
2Pe 2:12 born only to *be* c and destroyed, *274*

CAUL, CAULS (KJV) See COVERING

CAULK (1)

Eze 27:9 on board as shipwrights *to* c your seams. 2616

CAUSE (87) [CAUSED, CAUSES, CAUSING]

Ex 20:24 c my name **to be honored,** 2349
23:33 or *they will* c you **to sin** against me, 2627
33:19 c all my goodness **to pass** 6296
Nu 5:21 *"may* the LORD c your people to curse 5989
5:24 and c bitter suffering. 4200
5:27 it will go into her and c bitter suffering; 4200
16:5 The man he chooses *he will* **c to come near** 7928
32:15 **c of their destruction."** 8845
Dt 3:28 across and *will* c them **to inherit** the land 5706
10:18 He defends the c *of* the fatherless and 5477
28:25 The LORD *will* c you to be defeated 5989
33:7 With his own hands *he* **defends** his **c.** 8189
Jos 22:25 your descendants *might* c ours **to stop** fearing the LORD. 8697
Jdg 6:31 *"Are you going to* **plead** Baal's c? 8189
1Sa 24:15 May he consider my c and uphold it; 8190
25:39 who has upheld my c against Nabal 8190
1Ki 8:45 and uphold their **c.** 5477
8:49 and uphold their c. 5477
8:50 c their conquerors to show them mercy; 5989
8:59 that he may uphold the c *of* his servant and 5477
8:59 of his servant and the c *of* his people Israel 5477
2Ki 2:21 Never again *will* it c death or make 2118+4946
14:10 *c* your own **downfall** AIT
2Ch 6:35 and uphold their **c.** 5477
6:39 and uphold their **c.** 5477
20:27 **given** them **c to rejoice** 8523
25:19 *c* your own **downfall** AIT
Job 5:8 I would lay my c before him. 1826
Ps 7:4 or **without** c have robbed my foe— 8200
9:4 For you have upheld my right and my **c;** 1907
35:7 Since they hid their net for me **without c** 2855
35:7 for me without cause and **without** c dug 2855
35:19 over me who are my enemies **without c;** 9214
37:6 the **justice of** your c like the noonday sun. 5477
43:1 and plead my c against an ungodly nation; 8190
69:4 many are my enemies **without c,** 9214
74:22 Rise up, O God, and defend your **c;** 8190
82:3 **Defend** the c *of* the weak and fatherless; 9149
109:3 they attack me **without c.** 2855
119:78 to shame for wronging me **without c;** 9214
119:86 help me, for men persecute me **without c.** 9214
119:154 Defend my c and redeem me; 8190
119:161 Rulers persecute me **without c,** 2855
140:12 the poor and upholds the c *of* the needy. 5477
146:7 the c of the oppressed and gives food to 5477
Pr 24:28 not testify against your neighbor **without c,** 2855
Ecc 8:3 Do not stand up for a bad **c,** 1821
Isa 1:17 **Defend the** c *of* the fatherless, 9149
1:23 *They do* not **defend the** c *of* the fatherless; 9149
16:5 in judging seeks justice and speeds the c NIH
30:30 The LORD *will* c men **to hear** his majestic voice 9048
34:8 a year of retribution, to **uphold** Zion's **c.** 8189
40:27 my c is disregarded by my God"? 5477
47:12 perhaps *you will* c **terror.** 6907
53:10 to crush him and c him **to suffer,** 2703
58:14 and *I will* c you **to ride** on the heights of 8206
64:2 *c* the nations *to* **quake** AIT
Jer 11:20 for to you I have committed my **c.** 8190
20:12 for to you I have committed my **c.** 8190
22:16 He defended the c *of* the poor and needy, 1907
30:13 There is no one to plead your **c,** 1907
40:15 *c* all the Jews who are gathered around you *to* **be scattered** AIT
50:34 He will vigorously defend their c so 8190
51:36 "See, I will defend your c and avenge you; 8190
La 3:52 Those who were my enemies **without c** hunted me 2855
3:59 Uphold my **c!** 5477
Eze 14:23 that I have done nothing in it **without c,** 2855
32:10 c many peoples **to be appalled** 9037
32:12 c your hordes **to fall** 5877
33:12 of the wicked man *will* not *c him to* **fall** AIT
36:12 c people, my people Israel, **to walk** 2143
36:15 c your nation **to fall,** 4173
Da 8:24 c astounding **devastation** 8845
8:25 He will c deceit to prosper, 928+3338
Mt 18:7 **things that** c people **to sin!** *4998*
Lk 2:34 "This child is destined to c the falling *1650*
17:1 that **c people to sin** are bound to come, *4998*
17:2 c one of these little ones **to sin.** *4997*
Ro 14:21 c your brother *to* **fall.** *4684*
16:17 for those who c divisions and put obstacles *4472*
1Co 8:13 so that *I will* not c him **to fall.** *4997*
10:32 **not** c anyone **to stumble,** *718*
2Co 4:15 and more people may c thanksgiving *NIG*
Gal 6:17 Finally, *let* no one c me trouble, *4218*
Php 4:3 at my side **in the** c *of* the gospel, *1877*
Heb 12:15 that no bitter root grows up to **c trouble** *1943*
Rev 13:15 and c all who refused to worship the image *4472*

CAUSED (48) [CAUSE]

Ge 2:21 c the man **to fall** into a deep sleep; 5877
5:29 painful toil of our hands **c by** the ground 4946
Jdg 7:22 c the men throughout the camp **to turn** 8492
1Ki 11:25 adding to the trouble c *by* Hadad. 6913
14:16 and *has* c Israel **to commit.**" 2627
15:26 in his sin, which *he had* c Israel **to commit.** 2627
15:30 and *had* c Israel **to commit,** 2627
15:34 in his sin, which *he had* c Israel **to commit.** 2627
16:2 c my people Israel **to sin** 2627
16:13 and *had* c Israel **to commit,** 2627
16:19 and *had* c Israel **to commit.** 2627
16:26 in his sin, which *he had* c Israel **to commit,** 2627
21:22 to anger and *have* c Israel **to sin.'** 2627
22:52 who c Israel **to sin.** 2627
2Ki 3:3 which *he had* c Israel **to commit;** 2627
7:6 c the Arameans **to hear** 9048
10:29 which *he had* c Israel **to commit—** 2627
10:31 which *he had* c Israel **to commit.** 2627
13:2 which *he had* c Israel **to commit,** 2627
13:6 which *he had* c Israel **to commit;** 2627
13:11 which *he had* c Israel **to commit;** 2627
14:24 which *he had* c Israel **to commit.** 2627
15:9 which *he had* c Israel **to commit.** 2627
15:18 which *he had* c Israel **to commit.** 2627
15:24 which *he had* c Israel **to commit.** 2627
15:28 which *he had* c Israel **to commit.** 2627
17:21 the LORD and c them **to commit** 2627
21:16 the sin that *he had* c Judah **to commit,** 2627
23:15 who *had* c Israel **to sin—** 2627
2Ch 21:11 c the people of Jerusalem **to prostitute themselves** 2388
Ezr 6:12 c his Name **to dwell** 10709
Job 34:28 c the cry of the poor **to come** 995
Ps 106:46 *He* c them to be pitied 5989
111:4 *He has* c his wonders to be remembered; 6913
140:9 **trouble** their lips have *c.* AIT
Isa 21:2 to an end all the groaning she **c.** NIH
Jer 50:6 and c them **to roam** on the mountains. 8740
Eze 32:30 the slain in disgrace despite the terror **c by** 4946
Da 1:9 Now God *had* c the official to show favor 5989
Am 3:6 *has* not the LORD c it? 6913
Mal 2:8 by your teaching *have* c many **to stumble;** 4173
2:9 "So I *have* c you to be despised 5989
Ac 10:40 from the dead on the third day and c him to *1443*
17:6 "These men who *have* c **trouble** all over *415*
2Co 2:5 If anyone *has* **c grief,** *3382*
7:8 Even if *I* c you **sorrow** by my letter, *3382*
Jas 4:5 the spirit he c to live in us envies intensely? *NIG*
2Pe 1:4 and escape the corruption in the world **c by** *1877*

CAUSED (Anglicized) See also RAISED

CAUSES (31) [CAUSE]

Nu 5:21 and denounce you when he c your thigh 5989
2Ch 21:15 the disease c your bowels to come out.'" 4946
Ps 7:16 The **trouble** he *c* recoils on himself; AIT
Pr 10:10 He who winks maliciously c grief, 5989
Isa 8:14 a stone that c men **to stumble** and a rock 5598
61:11 up and a garden c seeds **to grow,** 7541
64:2 fire sets twigs ablaze and c water **to boil,** 1240
Da 8:13 the rebellion *that* **c desolation,** 9037
9:27 up an abomination *that* **c desolation,** 9037
11:31 up the abomination *that* **c desolation.** 9037
12:11 the abomination *that* **c desolation** is set 9037
Mt 5:29 If your right eye c you *to* **sin,** *4997*
5:30 And if your right hand c you **to sin,** *4997*
5:32 c her to become an adulteress, *4472*
5:45 *He* c his sun **to rise** *422*
13:41 of his kingdom everything that **c sin** *4998*
18:6 c one of these little ones who believe in me **to sin,** *4997*
18:8 If your hand or your foot c you **to sin,** *4997*
18:9 And if your eye c you **to sin,** *4997*
24:15 that *c* **desolation,'** spoken of through *AIT*
Mk 9:42 c one of these little ones who believe in me **to sin,** *4997*
9:43 If your hand c you **to sin,** cut it off. *4997*
9:45 And if your foot c you **to sin,** cut it off. *4997*
9:47 And if your eye c you **to sin,** pluck it out. *4997*
13:14 that *c* **desolation'** standing where it does *AIT*
Ro 9:33 I lay in Zion a stone that **c men to stumble** *4682*
14:20 a man to eat anything that c someone else *1328*
1Co 8:13 c my brother *to* **fall into sin,** *4997*
Col 2:19 grows as God c it to grow. *NIG*
Jas 4:1 **What** c fights and quarrels among you? *4470*
1Pe 2:8 "A stone that **c men to stumble** and a rock *4682*

CAUSEWAY (KJV) See ROAD

CAUSING (4) [CAUSE]

Dt 8:3 c you **to hunger** and then feeding you 8279
1Ki 17:20 c her son **to die?"** 4637
Ps 105:29 c their fish **to die.** 4637
Rev 13:13 even c fire to come down from heaven *4472*

CAUTIONED (1) [CAUTIOUS]

Ac 23:22 the young man and c him, *4133*

CAUTIOUS (1) [CAUTIONED]

Pr 12:26 A righteous man *is* c in friendship, 9365

CAVALRY (7)

Ne 2:9 The king had also sent army officers and c 7305
Da 11:40 with chariots and c and a great fleet 7305
Joel 2:4 they gallop along like **c.** 7305
Na 3:3 Charging **c,** flashing swords 7305
Hab 1:8 Their c gallops headlong; 7305
Ac 23:32 The next day they let the c go on with him, *2689*
23:33 When **the c** arrived in Caesarea, *4015S*

CAVE (35) [CAVERNS, CAVES]

Ge 19:30 He and his two daughters lived in a **c.** 5117
23:9 so he will sell me the c *of* Machpelah, 5117
23:11 and I give you the c that is in it. 5117
23:17 both the field and the c in it, 5117
23:19 in the c *in* the field of Machpelah 5117
23:20 and the c in it were deeded to Abraham by 5117
25:9 in the c *of* Machpelah near Mamre, 5117
49:29 in the c in the field of Ephron the Hittite, 5117
49:30 the c in the field of Machpelah, 5117
49:32 The field and the c in it were bought from 5117
50:13 the land of Canaan and buried him in the c 5117
Jos 10:16 the five kings had fled and hidden in the c 5117
10:17 in the c at Makkedah, 5117
10:18 "Roll large rocks up to the mouth of the c, 5117
10:22 the c and bring those five kings out to me." 5117

Jos 10:23 So they brought the five kings out of the c— 5117
10:27 from the trees and threw them into the c 5117
10:27 the mouth of the c they placed large rocks, 5117
Jdg 15: 8 Then he went down and stayed in a c *in* 6186
15:11 down to the c *in* the rock of Etam and said 6186
1Sa 22: 1 David left Gath and escaped to the c 5117
24: 3 a c was there, 5117
24: 3 David and his men were far back in the c. 5117
24: 7 And Saul left the c and went his way. 5117
24: 8 of the c and called out to Saul, 5117
24:10 into my hands in the c. 5117
2Sa 17: 9 he is hidden in a c or some other place. 7074
23:13 down to David at the c *of* Adullam, 5117
1Ki 19: 9 There he went into a c and spent the night. 5117
19:13 and stood at the mouth of the c. 5117
1Ch 11:15 to David to the rock at the c *of* Adullam, 5117
Ps 57: T When he had fled from Saul into the c. 5117
142: T When he was in the c. 5117
Jer 48:28 that makes its nest at the mouth of a c. 7074
Jn 11:38 a c with a stone laid across the entrance. *5068*

CAVERNS (1) [CAVE]

Isa 2:21 They will flee to c *in* the rocks and to 5942

CAVES (10) [CAVE]

Jdg 6: 2 in mountain clefts, c and strongholds. 5117
1Sa 13: 6 they hid in c and thickets, among the rocks, 5117
1Ki 18: 4 and hidden them in two c, 5117
18:13 of the LORD's prophets in two c, 5117
Isa 2:19 Men will flee to c *in* the rocks and to holes 5117
Jer 49: 8 Turn and flee, hide in deep c, NIH
49:30 Stay in deep c, you who live in Hazor," NIH
Eze 33:27 and those in strongholds and c will die of 5117
Heb 11:38 and in c and holes in the ground. *5068*
Rev 6:15 and every slave and every free man hid in c *5068*

CEASE (17) [CEASED, CEASING]

Ge 8:22 day and night *will* never c." 8697
Jos 9:23 You *will* never c to serve as woodcutters 4162
2Ki 18: 6 to the LORD and *did* not c to follow him; 6073
Ne 9:19 the pillar of cloud *did* not c to guide them 6073
Est 9:28 And these days of Purim *should* never c to 6296
Job 3:17 There the wicked c *from* turmoil, 2532
6:17 but that c **to flow** in the dry season, 7551
Ps 46: 9 *He* **makes** wars c to the ends of the earth; 8697
Ecc 12: 3 when the grinders c because they are few, 1060
Isa 16: 4 and destruction *will* c; 3983
Jer 18:14 from distant sources *ever* c to flow? 5980
31:36 "*will* the descendants of Israel ever c to be 8697
47: 6 Return to your scabbard; c and be still.' 8089
Eze 5:13 "Then my anger *will* c and my wrath 3983
1Co 12:15 *it would* not for that reason c **to be** part of the body. 1639+4024
12:16 *it would* not for that reason c **to be** part of the body. 1639+4024
13: 8 where there are prophecies, *they will* c, *2934*

CEASED (3) [CEASE]

Jdg 5: 7 Village life in Israel c, ceased until I, 2532
5: 7 Village life in Israel ceased, c until I, 2532
Ps 36: 3 *he has* c to be wise and to do good. 2532

CEASING (2) [CEASE]

Ps 35:15 They slandered me without c. 1957
Jer 14:17 with tears **night** and day without c; 1949

CEDAR (57) [CEDARS]

Lev 14: 4 that two live clean birds and some c wood, 780
14: 6 together with the c wood, 780
14:49 to take two birds and some c wood, 780
14:51 Then he is to take the c wood, the hyssop, 780
14:52 the c wood, the hyssop and the scarlet yarn. 780
Nu 19: 6 The priest is to take some c wood, 780
2Sa 5:11 along with c logs and carpenters 780
7: 2 "Here I am, living in a palace of c, 780
7: 7 not built me a house of c?" ' 780
1Ki 4:33 from the c of Lebanon to the hyssop 780
5: 8 and will do all you want in providing the c 780
5:10 with all the c and pine logs he wanted, 780
6: 9 roofing it with beams and c planks. 780
6:10 to the temple by beams of c. 780
6:15 He lined its interior walls with c boards, 780
6:16 with c boards from floor to ceiling to form 780
6:18 The inside of the temple was c, 780
6:18 Everything was c; no stone was to be seen. 780
6:20 and he also overlaid the altar of c. 780
6:36 and one course of trimmed c beams. 780
7: 2 c columns supporting trimmed cedar beams. 780
7: 2 cedar columns supporting trimmed c beams. 780
7: 3 with c above the beams that rested on 780
7: 7 he covered it with c from floor to ceiling. 780
7:11 cut to size, and c *beams*. 780
7:12 and one course of trimmed c beams, 780
9:11 with all the c and pine and gold he wanted. 780
10:27 and c as plentiful as sycamore-fig trees in 780
2Ki 14: 9 "A thistle in Lebanon sent a message to a c 780
1Ch 14: 1 along with c logs, 780
17: 1 "Here I am, living in a palace of c, 780
17: 6 not built me a house of c?" ' 780
22: 4 He also provided more c logs than could 780
2Ch 1:15 and c as plentiful as sycamore-fig trees in 780
2: 3 "Send me c logs as you did NIH
2: 3 for my father David when you sent him c 780
2Ch 2: 8 "Send me also c, pine and algum logs 780
9:27 and c as plentiful as sycamore-fig trees in 780
25:18 "A thistle in Lebanon sent a message to a c 780
Ezr 3: 7 so that they would bring c logs by sea 780
Job 40:17 His tail sways like a c; 780
Ps 92:12 they will grow like a c of Lebanon; 780
SS 8: 9 we will enclose her with panels of c. 780
Isa 41:19 I will put in the desert the c and the acacia, 780
Jer 22: 7 up your fine c *beams* and throw them into 780
22:14 panels it with c and decorates it in red. 780
22:15 a king to have more and more c? 780
22:23 who are nestled in c buildings, 780
Eze 17: 3 Taking hold of the top of a c, 780
17:22 from the very top of a c and plant it; 780
17:23 and bear fruit and become a splendid c. 780
27: 5 they took a c from Lebanon to make a mast 780
31: 3 Consider Assyria, once a c in Lebanon, 780
Hos 14: 5 Like a **c of Lebanon** he will send 4248
14: 6 his fragrance like a **c of Lebanon.** 4248
Zep 2:14 the **beams of** c will be exposed. 781
Zec 11: 2 Wail, O pine tree, for the c has fallen; 780

CEDARS (19) [CEDAR]

Nu 24: 6 like c beside the waters. 780
Jdg 9:15 of the thornbush and consume the c 780
1Ki 5: 6 "So give orders that c of Lebanon be cut 780
2Ki 19:23 I have cut down its tallest c, 780
Ps 29: 5 The voice of the LORD breaks the c; 780
29: 5 the LORD breaks in pieces the c 780
80:10 the mighty c with its branches. 780
104:16 the c *of* Lebanon that he planted. 780
148: 9 fruit trees and all c, 780
SS 1:17 The beams of our house are c; 780
5:15 choice as its c. 780
Isa 2:13 for all the c *of* Lebanon, 780
9:10 but we will replace them with c." 780
14: 8 the c *of* Lebanon exult over you and say, 780
37:24 I have cut down its tallest c, 780
44:14 He cut down c, 780
Eze 31: 8 c in the garden of God could not rival it, 780
Am 2: 9 he was tall as the c and strong as the oaks. 780
Zec 11: 1 O Lebanon, so that fire may devour your c! 780

CEDRON (KJV) See KIDRON

CEILING (4)

1Ki 6:15 from the floor of the temple to the c, 6212
6:16 with cedar boards from floor to c to form 7815
7: 7 he covered it with cedar from floor to c. 6212
2Ch 3: 7 He overlaid the c **beams,** doorframes, 7771

CELEBRATE (53) [CELEBRATED, CELEBRATING, CELEBRATION, CELEBRATIONS]

Ex 10: 9 because we are to c a festival to NIH
12:14 for the generations to come *you shall* c it 2510
12:17 "C the Feast of Unleavened Bread, 9068
12:17 C this day as a lasting ordinance for 9068
12:47 The whole community of Israel *must* c it. 6913
12:48 "An alien living among you *who wants to* c 6913
23:14 a year *you are to* c **a festival** to me. 2510
23:15 "C the Feast of Unleavened Bread; 9068
23:16 "C the Feast of Harvest with the firstfruits NIH
23:16 "C the Feast of Ingathering at the end of NIH
34:18 "C the Feast of Unleavened Bread. 9068
34:22 "C the Feast of Weeks with the firstfruits 6913
Lev 23:39 c the festival to the LORD for seven days; 2510
23:41 C this as a festival to the LORD 2510
23:41 c it in the seventh month. 2510
Nu 9: 2 "*Have* the Israelites c the Passover at 6913
9: 3 C it at the appointed time, 6913
9: 4 Moses told the Israelites to c the Passover, 6913
9: 6 But some of them could not c the Passover 6913
9:10 *they may still* c the LORD's Passover. 6913
9:11 *They are to* c it on the fourteenth day of 6913
9:12 *When they* c the Passover, 6913
9:13 and not on a journey fails to c the Passover, 6913
9:14 *to* c the LORD's Passover must do so 6913
29:12 C a festival to the LORD for seven days. 2510
Dt 16: 1 the month of Abib and c the Passover of 6913
16:10 Then c the Feast of Weeks to 6913
16:13 C the Feast of Tabernacles for seven days 6913
16:15 For seven days **c the Feast** to 2510
Jdg 16:23 to Dagon their god and to c, 8525
2Sa 6:21 *I will* c before the LORD. 8471
2Ki 23:21 "C the Passover to the LORD your God, 6913
2Ch 30: 1 in Jerusalem and c the Passover to 6913
30: 2 in Jerusalem decided to c the Passover in 6913
30: 3 not been able to c it at the regular time 6913
30: 5 to come to Jerusalem and c the Passover to 6913
30:13 of people assembled in Jerusalem to c 6913
30:23 The whole assembly then agreed to c 6913
Ne 8:12 to send portions of food and to c 6913
12:27 and were brought to Jerusalem to c joyfully 6913
Est 9:21 to have them c annually the fourteenth 6913
Ps 145: 7 *They will* c your abundant goodness 2352+5580
Isa 30:29 as on the night you c a **holy** festival; 7727
Na 1:15 C your festivals, O Judah, 2510
Zec 14:16 and to c the Feast of Tabernacles. 2510
14:18 the nations that do not go up to c the Feast 2510
14:19 the nations that do not go up to c the Feast 2510
Mt 26:18 *to* c the Passover with my disciples *4472*
Lk 15:23 *Let's* have a feast and c. *2370*
Lk 15:24 So they began *to* c. *2370*
15:29 even a young goat so *I could* c *2370*
15:32 But we had *to* c and be glad, *2370*
Rev 11:10 the earth will gloat over them and *will* c *2370*

CELEBRATED (18) [CELEBRATE]

Jos 5:10 the Israelites c the Passover. 6913
1Ki 8:65 They c it before the LORD our God NIH
2Ki 23:23 this Passover **was** c to the LORD 6913
2Ch 7: 9 for *they had* c the dedication of the altar 6913
30: 5 not *been* c in large numbers according 6913
30:21 in Jerusalem c the Feast 6913
30:23 so for another seven days *they* c joyfully. 6913
35: 1 Josiah c the Passover to the LORD 6913
35:17 The Israelites who were present c 6913
35:18 of the kings of Israel *had ever* c such 6913
35:19 This Passover **was** c in the eighteenth year 6913
Ezr 3: 4 *they* c the Feast of Tabernacles with 6913
6:16 c the dedication of the house of God 10522
6:19 the exiles c the Passover. 6913
6:22 For seven days *they* c with joy the Feast 6913
Ne 8:17 the Israelites *had* not c it like this. 6913
8:18 *They* c the feast for seven days, 6913
Est 9:28 of Purim should never cease to be c by NIH

CELEBRATING (5) [CELEBRATE]

Ex 31:16 c it for the generations to come as 6913
2Sa 6: 5 David and the whole house of Israel *were* c 8471
1Ch 13: 8 the Israelites *were* c with all their might 8471
15:29 when she saw King David dancing and c, 8471
Est 8:17 with feasting and c. 3202+3427

CELEBRATION (7) [CELEBRATE]

1Sa 11:15 Saul and all the Israelites **held a** great c. 8523
2Ch 35:16 of the LORD was carried out for the c *of* 6913
Est 8:15 And the city of Susa **held a** joyous c. 7412
9:22 into joy and their mourning into a day of c. 3202
9:23 to continue **the** c they had begun, 889[S]
Ac 7:41 They brought sacrifices to it and **held a** c *2370*
Col 2:16 a **New Moon** c or a Sabbath day. *3741*

CELEBRATIONS (1) [CELEBRATE]

Hos 2:11 I will stop all her c: 5375

CELESTIAL (2)

2Pe 2:10 not afraid to slander c **beings;** *1518*
Jude 1: 8 reject authority and slander c **beings.** *1518*

CELL (3)

Jer 37:16 Jeremiah was put into a **vaulted** c in 2844
Ac 12: 7 and a light shone in the c. *3862*
16:24 in the inner c and fastened their feet in *5871*

CELLARS (KJV) See VATS, SUPPLIES

CENCHREA (2)

Ac 18:18 he had his hair cut off at C because of *3020*
Ro 16: 1 a servant of the church in C. *3020*

CENSER (8) [CENSERS]

Lev 16:12 He is to take a c full of burning coals from 4746
Nu 16:17 Each man is to take his c and put incense 4746
16:18 So each man took his c, 4746
16:46 "Take your c and put incense in it, 4746
2Ch 26:19 a c in his hand ready to burn incense, 5233
Eze 8:11 Each had a c in his hand, 5233
Rev 8: 3 Another angel, who had a golden c, *3338*
8: 5 Then the angel took the c, *3338*

CENSERS (13) [CENSER]

Lev 10: 1 and Abihu took their c, put fire in them 4746
Nu 16: 6 your followers are to do this: Take c 4746
16:17 250 c in all— 4746
16:17 You and Aaron are to present your c also." 4746
16:37 to take the c out of the smoldering remains 4746
16:37 for the c are holy— NIH
16:38 the c *of* the men who sinned at the cost 4746
16:38 Hammer the c into sheets to overlay 4392[S]
16:39 the priest collected the bronze c brought 4746
1Ki 7:50 sprinkling bowls, dishes and c; 4746
2Ki 25:15 of the imperial guard took away the c 4746
2Ch 4:22 sprinkling bowls, dishes and c; 4746
Jer 52:19 c, sprinkling bowls, pots, lampstands, 4746

CENSUS (17)

Ex 30:12 "When *you* **take a** c *of* the Israelites 906+5951+8031
38:25 **were counted in the** c 7212
Nu 1: 2 "**Take a** c *of* the whole Israelite 5951+8031
1:49 **include** them **in the** c 906+5951+8031
4: 2 "**Take a** c *of* the Kohathite branch of the Levites 906+5951+8031
4:22 "**Take a** c also *of* the Gershonites 5951+8031
14:29 in the c and who has grumbled against me. 5031
26: 2 "**Take a** c *of* the whole Israelite 906+5951+8031
26: 4 a c of the men twenty years old or more, NIH
2Sa 24: 1 "Go and **take a** c *of* Israel and Judah." 4948
2Ki 12: 4 the money collected in the c, 408+6296
1Ch 21: 1 against Israel and incited David to **take a** c 4948
2Ch 2:17 Solomon **took a** c *of* all the aliens 6218

2Ch 2:17 c his father David *had* **taken;** 6218+6222
Lk 2: 1 c *should* **be taken of** *616*
2: 2 (This was the first c that took place *615*
Ac 5:37 *of* the c and led a band of people in revolt. *615*

CENTER (20) [CENTERS, CENTRAL, CENTRALLY]

Ex 26:28 The c crossbar is to extend from end to end 9399
28:32 with an opening for the head in its **c.** 9348
36:33 the c crossbar so that it extended from end 9399
39:23 with an opening in the c *of* the robe like 9348
Nu 35: 5 with the town in the **c.** 9348
Jdg 9:37 "Look, people are coming down from the c 3179
1Ki 7:25 and their hindquarters were toward the **c.** 1074
2Ch 4: 4 and their hindquarters were toward the **c.** 1074
6:13 and had placed it in the c *of* 9348
Eze 1: 4 The c *of* the fire looked like 9348
5: 5 which I have set in the c *of* the nations, 9348
38:12 living at the c *of* the land." 3179
48: 8 the sanctuary will be in the c *of* it. 9348
48:10 In the c *of* it will be the sanctuary of 9348
48:15 The city will be in the c *of* it 9348
48:21 with the temple sanctuary will be in the c 9348
48:22 the c *of* the area that belongs to the prince. 9348
Rev 4: 6 In the **c,** around the throne, *3545*
5: 6 standing in the c of the throne, *3545*
7:17 at the c of the throne will be their shepherd; *3545*

CENTERS (1) [CENTER]

Ge 10:10 The **first** *c of* his kingdom were Babylon, AIT

CENTRAL (1) [CENTER]

Jdg 16:29 the two c pillars on which the temple stood. 9348

CENTRALLY (1) [CENTER]

Dt 19: 2 for yourselves three cities **c located in** 928+9348

CENTURION (21) [CENTURION'S, CENTURIONS]

Mt 8: 5 a c came to him, asking for help. *1672*
8: 8 The c replied, "Lord, I do not deserve *1672*
8:13 Then Jesus said *to* the **c,** "Go! *1672*
27:54 When the c and those with him *1672*
Mk 15:39 And when the **c,** who stood there *3035*
15:44 Summoning the **c,** he asked him *3035*
15:45 When he learned from the c that it was so, *3035*
Lk 7: 3 The c heard of Jesus and sent some elders *NIG*
7: 6 the house when the c sent friends to say *1672*
23:47 The **c,** seeing what had happened, *1672*
Ac 10: 1 Cornelius, a c in what was known as *1672*
10:22 "We have come from Cornelius the **c.** *1672*
22:25 Paul said to the c standing there, *1672*
22:26 When the c heard this, *1672*
23:18 The c said, "Paul, the prisoner, *NIG*
24:23 He ordered the c to keep Paul under guard *1672*
27: 1 over *to* a c named Julius, *1672*
27: 6 the c found an Alexandrian ship sailing *1672*
27:11 But the **c,** instead of listening *1672*
27:31 Then Paul said *to* the c and the soldiers, *1672*
27:43 But the c wanted to spare Paul's life *1672*

CENTURION'S (1) [CENTURION]

Lk 7: 2 There a c servant, whom his master valued *1672*

CENTURIONS (2) [CENTURION]

Ac 23:17 Then Paul called one *of* the c and said, *1672*
23:23 he called two *of* his c and ordered them, *1672*

CEPHAS (4) [PETER]

Jn 1:42 You will be called **C"** (which, when translated, is Peter). *3064*
1Co 1:12 another, "I follow **C";** *3064*
3:22 whether Paul or Apollos or C or the world *3064*
9: 5 and the Lord's brothers and **C?** *3064*

CEREMONIAL (9) [CEREMONY]

Lev 14: 2 of his **c cleansing,** when he is brought to 3200
15:13 for his **c cleansing;** 3200
Mk 7: 3 unless they give their hands a c washing, *4778*
Jn 2: 6 the kind used by the Jews for **c washing,** *2752*
3:25 a certain Jew over the matter of **c washing.** *2752*
11:55 for their **c cleansing** before the Passover. *49*
18:28 and to avoid **c uncleanness** the Jews did *3620*
Heb 9:10 of food and drink and various **c washings—** *968*
13: 9 strengthened by grace, not by c foods, *NIG*

CEREMONIALLY (40) [CEREMONY]

Lev 4:12 the camp to a place **c clean,** 3196
5: 2 if a person touches anything **c unclean—** 3238
6:11 the camp to a place that is **c clean.** 3196
7:19 that touches anything **c unclean** must not 3238
7:19 anyone **c clean** may eat it. 3196
10:14 Eat them in a **c clean** place; 3196
11: 4 it is **c unclean** for you. 3238
12: 2 to a son *will be* **c unclean** for seven days, 3237
12: 7 then *she will be* **c clean** from her flow 3197
13: 3 **pronounce** him **c unclean.** 3237
14: 8 then *he will be* **c clean.** 3197
15:28 and after that *she will be* **c clean.** 3197
15:33 with a *woman who is* **c unclean.** 3238
Lev 17:15 and *he will be* **c unclean** till evening; 3237
21: 1 **make himself c unclean** 3237
22: 3 if any of your descendants is **c unclean** 3240
27:11 If what he vowed is a **c unclean** animal— 3238
Nu 5: 2 who is **c unclean** because of a dead body. 3238
6: 7 **make himself c unclean** 3237
8: 6 the other Israelites and **make** them **c clean.** 3197
9: 6 on that day because they were **c unclean** 3238
9:13 But if a man who is **c clean** and not on 3196
18:11 in your household who is **c clean** may eat it. 3196
18:13 in your household who is **c clean** may eat it. 3196
19: 7 but he *will be* **c unclean** till evening. 3237
19: 9 and put them in a **c clean** place outside 3196
19:18 Then a man who is **c clean** is 3196
Dt 12:15 the **c unclean** and the clean may eat it. 3238
12:22 Both the **c unclean** and the clean may eat. 3238
14: 7 they are **c unclean** for you. 3238
15:22 the **c unclean** and the clean may eat it, 3238
1Sa 20:26 to David to make him **c unclean—** 1194+3196
2Ch 13:11 on the **c clean** table and light the lamps on 3196
30:17 for all *those who* were not **c clean** 3196
Ezr 6:20 and were all **c clean.** 3196
Ne 12:30 **purified themselves c,** 3197
Isa 66:20 of the LORD in **c clean** vessels. 3196
Eze 22:10 when they are **c unclean.** 3238
Ac 24:18 *I was* **c clean** when they found me in *49*
Heb 9:13 on those who *are* **c unclean** sanctify them *3124*

CEREMONIES (1) [CEREMONY]

Heb 9:21 the tabernacle and everything used *in* its **c.** *3311*

CEREMONY (4) [CEREMONIAL, CEREMONIALLY, CEREMONIES]

Ge 50:11 a solemn **c of mourning."** 65
Ex 12:25 as he promised, observe this **c.** 6275
12:26 'What does this c mean to you?' 6275
13: 5 you are to observe this c in this month: 6275

CERTAIN (37) [CERTAINTY, CERTAINLY]

Ge 15:13 **"Know for c** that your descendants 3359+3359
28:11 When he reached a c place, 2021
Nu 16: 1 the son of Levi, and c Reubenites— NIH
Jos 8:14 at a **c place** overlooking the Arabah. 4595
Jdg 13: 2 A c man of Zorah, named Manoah, 285
1Sa 1: 1 There was a c man from Ramathaim, 285
21: 2 "The king charged me with a *c* **matter** AIT
21: 2 I have told them to meet me at a c place 532+7141
25: 2 A c man in Maon, NIH
2Sa 12: 1 he said, "There were two men in a c town, 285
1Ki 13:11 there was a c old prophet living in Bethel, 285
2Ki 19: 7 in him that when he hears a c report, NIH
2Ch 17: 8 With them were c Levites— 2021
Ne 7:73 along with c *of* the people and the rest of 4946
Est 3: 8 a c people dispersed and scattered among 285
Isa 37: 7 in him so that when he hears a c report, NIH
Da 2: 8 "I *am* c that you are trying to gain time, 10313+10327+10427
Hos 5: 9 the tribes of Israel I proclaim *what is* **c.** 586
Mt 26:18 "Go into the city to a c *man* and tell him, *1265*
Mk 15:21 A c *man* from Cyrene, Simon, *5516*
Lk 7:41 "Two men owed money to **a c** moneylender. *5516*
11: 1 One day Jesus was praying in **a c** place. *5516*
12:16 "The ground **of a c** rich man produced *5516*
14:16 **"A c** man was preparing a great banquet *5516*
18: 2 **"In a c** town there was a judge *5516*
18:18 **A c** ruler asked him, "Good teacher, *5516*
Jn 3:25 of John's disciples and a c Jew over *NIG*
4:46 *a* c royal official whose son lay sick *5516*
Ac 7:16 the sons of Hamor at Shechem for a c sum *NIG*
28:23 They arranged to meet Paul on a c day, *NIG*
Gal 2:12 Before c *men* came from James, *5516*
1Ti 1: 3 so that you may command c *men* not *5516*
4: 3 and order them to abstain from c foods, *NIG*
Heb 4: 7 Therefore God again set **a c** day, *5516*
11: 1 of what we hope for and c of what we do *1793*
2Pe 1:19 the word of the prophets made *more* **c,** *1010*
Jude 1: 4 c men whose condemnation was written *5516*

CERTAINLY (49) [CERTAIN]

Ex 22: 3 "A thief **must c make restitution,** 8966+8966
22:23 *I will* **c hear** their cry. 9048+9048
23:33 because the worship of their gods will c be 3954
Nu 13:30 for *we* **can c do** it." 3523+3523
22:33 I would c have killed you by now, 3954
27: 7 *You* **must c give** them property as 5989+5989
Dt 4:26 not live there long but *will* **c be destroyed.** 9012+9012
13: 9 **must c put** him **to death.** 2222+2222
13:15 *you* **must c put** to the sword all who live in that town. 5782+5782
23:21 the LORD your God *will* **c demand** it 2011+2011
30:18 that *you will* **c be destroyed.** 6+6
31:18 And I *will* **c hide** my face on that day 6259+6259
Jos 3:10 that *he will* **c drive out** before you 3769+3769
Jdg 11:10 we will c do as you say." 561+4202
21: 5 **c be put to death.** 4637+4637
1Sa 25:28 the LORD *will* **c make** a lasting dynasty 6913+6913
30: 8 *"You will* **c overtake** them and 5952+5952
1Ki 11:11 **most c tear** the kingdom **away** 7973+7973
13:32 towns of Samaria *will* **c come true."** 2118+2118
2Ki 1: 4 *You will* **c die!' "** 4637+4637
1: 6 *You will* **c die!" '** 4637+4637
1:16 *You will* **c die!"** 4637+4637
8:10 *'You will* **c recover';** 2649+2649
2Ki 8:14 He told me that *you would* **c recover.** 2649+2649
Jer 32: 4 the Babylonians but *will* **c be handed over** 928+3338+5989+5989
36:29 that the king of Babylon *would* **c come** 995+995
38: 3 'This city *will* **c be handed over** *to* the army 928+3338+5989+5989
42: 4 "I will c pray to the LORD your God 2180
44:17 *We will* **c do** everything we said we would: 6913+6913
44:25 *'We will* **c carry out** the vows we made 6913+6913
Da 3:24 They replied, **"C,** O king." 10002+10327
Am 7:17 And Israel *will* **c go into exile,** 1655+1655
Hab 2: 3 *it will* **c come** and will not delay. 995+995
Mal 3:15 C the evildoers prosper, 1685
Mt 5:20 you will **c not** enter the kingdom *3590+4024*
10:42 he will **c not** lose his reward." *3590+4024*
24:34 this generation will **c not** pass away *3590+4024*
Mk 9:41 because you belong to Christ will **c not** lose his reward. *3590+4024*
13:30 this generation will **c not** pass away *3590+4024*
Lk 21:32 this generation will **c not** pass away *3590+4024*
22:59 **"C** this fellow was with him, *237+2093*
Ac 21:22 They will c hear that you have come, *4122*
Ro 3: 6 **C not!** If that were so, *1181+3590*
6: 5 we will c also be united with him *247*
7: 7 Is the law sin? **C not!** *1181+3590*
1Co 11:22 Shall I praise you for this? C not! *NIG*
Gal 3:21 then righteousness would c have come by *3953*
1Th 2:18 c I, Paul, did, again and again— *3525*
4:15 will **c not** precede those who have fallen asleep. *3590+4024*

CERTAINTY (2) [CERTAIN]

Lk 1: 4 the c of the things you have been taught. *854*
Jn 17: 8 They knew **with c** that I came from you, *242*

CERTIFICATE (7) [CERTIFIED]

Dt 24: 1 and he writes her a c *of* divorce, 6219
24: 3 and writes her a c *of* divorce, 6219
Isa 50: 1 "Where is your mother's c *of* divorce 6219
Jer 3: 8 I gave faithless Israel her c *of* divorce 6219
Mt 5:31 must give her a **c of divorce.'** *687*
19: 7 that a man give his wife a c of divorce *1046*
Mk 10: 4 to write a c of divorce and send her away." *1046*

CERTIFIED (1) [CERTIFICATE]

Jn 3:33 The man who has accepted it *has* c that God is truthful. *3456+3836+5381*

CHAFF (18)

Job 13:25 Will you chase after dry **c?** 7990
21:18 like c swept away by a gale? 5161
41:28 slingstones are like c to him. 7990
Ps 1: 4 They are like c that the wind blows away. 5161
35: 5 May they be like c before the wind, 5161
83:13 O my God, like c before the wind. 7990
Isa 17:13 driven before the wind like c *on* the hills, 5161
29: 5 the ruthless hordes like blown c. 5161
33:11 You conceive **c,** you give birth to straw; 3143
40:24 and a whirlwind sweeps them away like **c.** 7990
41: 2 to windblown c with his bow. 7990
41:15 and reduce the hills to **c.** 5161
Jer 13:24 "I will scatter you like c driven by 7990
Da 2:35 like c on a threshing floor in the summer. 10534
Hos 13: 3 like c swirling from a threshing floor, 5161
Zep 2: 2 and that day sweeps on like **c,** 5161
Mt 3:12 into the barn and burning up the c *949*
Lk 3:17 up the c with unquenchable fire." *949*

CHAIN (9) [CHAINED, CHAINS]

Ge 41:42 in robes of fine linen and put a gold c 8054
2Ch 3: 5 with palm tree and c designs. 9249
Pr 1: 9 be a garland to grace your head and a c 6736
Da 5: 7 and have a gold c placed around his neck, 10212
5:16 and have a gold c placed around your neck, 10212
5:29 a gold c was placed around his neck, 10212
Mk 5: 3 not even *with* a **c.** *268*
Ac 28:20 of Israel that I am bound with this **c."** *268*
Rev 20: 1 and holding in his hand a great **c.** *268*

CHAINED (5) [CHAIN]

Mk 5: 4 For he had often *been* **c hand** and foot, *268+1313*
Lk 8:29 and though *he was* **c hand** and foot *268+1297*
2Ti 2: 9 even to the point of *being* c like a criminal. *1301*
2: 9 But God's word *is* not **c.** *1313*
Heb 11:36 while still others were c and put in prison. *1301*

CHAINS (50) [CHAIN]

Ex 28:14 and two braided c *of* pure gold, 9249
28:14 and attach the c to the settings. 6310+9249
28:22 "For the breastpiece make braided c 9249
28:24 the two gold c to the rings at the corners of 6310
28:25 the other ends of the c to the two settings, 6310
39:15 For the breastpiece they made braided c 9249
39:17 They fastened the two gold c to the rings at 6310
39:18 the other ends of the c to the two settings, 6310
Jdg 8:26 or the c that were on their camels' necks. 6736
1Ki 6:21 and he extended gold c across the front of 8411
7:17 of **interwoven** c festooned the capitals 5126+9249
2Ki 23:33 Pharaoh Neco **put** him **in** c at Riblah in 673
2Ch 3:16 He made interwoven c and put them on top 9249

2Ch 3:16 and attached them to the c. 9249
Job 36: 8 But if men are bound in c, 2414
Ps 2: 3 "Let us break their c," they say, 4593
107:10 prisoners suffering in iron c, 1366
107:14 the deepest gloom and broke away their c. 4593
116:16 you have freed me from my c. 4591
Ecc 7:26 a trap and whose hands are c. 657
Isa 3:20 the headdresses and ankle c and sashes, 7578
28:22 or your c will become heavier; 4591
40:19 with gold and fashions silver c for it. 8416
45:14 coming over to you in c. 2414
52: 2 Free yourself from the c on your neck, 4591
58: 6 the c of injustice and untie the cords of 3078
Jer 40: 1 in c among all the captives from Jerusalem 272
40: 4 But today I am freeing you from the c 272
La 3: 7 he has weighed me down with c. 5733
Eze 7:23 "Prepare c, because the land is full 8408
Na 3:10 all her great men were put in c. 928+2414+8415
Mk 5: 4 the c apart and broke the irons on his feet. 268
Lk 8:29 he had broken his c and had been driven by 1301
Ac 12: 6 bound with two c, 268
12: 7 he said, and the c fell off Peter's wrists. 268
16:26 and everybody's c came loose. 1301
21:33 and ordered him to be bound with two c. 268
22:29 put Paul, a Roman citizen, in c. 1313
26:29 except for these c." 1301
Eph 6:20 for which I am an ambassador in c. 268
Php 1: 7 for whether I am in c or defending 1301
1:13 to everyone else that I am in c for Christ. 1301
1:14 Because of my c, 1301
1:17 up trouble for me while I am in c. 1301
Col 4: 3 for which I am in c. 1313
4:18 Remember my c. 1301
2Ti 1:16 and was not ashamed of my c. 268
Phm 1:10 who became my son while I was in c. 1301
1:13 in helping me while I am in c for 1301
Jude 1: 6 bound with everlasting c for judgment 1301

CHAIR (4)
1Sa 1: 9 the priest was sitting on a c by the doorpost 4058
4:13 there was Eli sitting on his c by the side of 4058
4:18 Eli fell backward off his c by the side of 4058
2Ki 4:10 a c and a lamp for him. 4058

CHALCEDONY (1)
Rev 21:19 the second sapphire, the third c, 5907

CHALCOL (KJV) See CALCOL

CHALDAEANS (KJV) See BABYLON, BABYLONIA

CHALDEA (2) [CHALDEAN, CHALDEANS]
Eze 23:15 Babylonian chariot officers, natives of C. 4169
23:16 and sent messengers to them in C. 4169

CHALDEAN (1) [CHALDEA]
Ezr 5:12 over to Nebuchadnezzar the C, 10373

CHALDEANS (9) [CHALDEA]
Ge 11:28 Haran died in Ur of the C, 4169
11:31 and together they set out from Ur of the C 4169
15: 7 who brought you out of Ur of the C 4169
Ne 9: 7 of Ur of the C and named him Abraham. 4169
Job 1:17 "The C formed three raiding parties 4169
Eze 12:13 the land of the C, but he will not see it, 4169
23:14 figures of C portrayed in red, 4169
23:23 the Babylonians and all the C, 4169
Ac 7: 4 "So he left the land of the C and settled 5900

CHALDEES (KJV) See CHALDEAN

CHALK (1)
Isa 27: 9 the altar stones to be like c stones crushed 1732

CHALLENGE (5) [CHALLENGED]
2Ki 14: 8 with the c: "Come, meet me face to face." 606
2Ch 25:17 he sent this c to Jehoash son of Jehoahaz, 606
Jer 49:19 Who is like me and who can c me? 3585
50:44 Who is like me and who can c me? 3585
Mal 3:15 and even those who c God escape.' " 1043

CHALLENGED (2) [CHALLENGE]
Jn 8:13 The Pharisees c him, "Here you are, 3306
18:26 the man whose ear Peter had cut off, c him, 3306

CHAMBER (3) [CHAMBERS]
Job 37: 9 The tempest comes out from its c, 2540
Ps 45:13 All glorious is the princess within [her c]; NIH
Joel 2:16 and the bride her c. 2903

CHAMBERLAIN (KJV) See EUNUCH, OFFICERS

CHAMBERS (5) [CHAMBER]
Ezr 8:29 until you weigh them out in the c of 4384
Ps 104: 3 the beams of his upper c on their waters. 6608
Ps 104:13 He waters the mountains from his upper c; 6608
Pr 7:27 leading down to the c of death. 2540
SS 1: 4 Let the king bring me into his c. 2540

CHAMELEON (1)
Lev 11:30 the wall lizard, the skink and the c. 9491

CHAMOIS (KJV) See MOUNTAIN SHEEP

CHAMPAIGN (KJV) See ARABAH

CHAMPION (3) [CHAMPIONS]
1Sa 17: 4 A c named Goliath, who was from Gath, 408+1227+2021
17:23 Goliath, the Philistine c from Gath, 408+1227+2021
Ps 19: 5 like a c rejoicing to run his course. 1475

CHAMPIONS (1) [CHAMPION]
Isa 5:22 at drinking wine and c at mixing drinks, 408+2657

CHANAAN (KJV) See CANAAN

CHANCE (5)
Jos 8:20 but they had no c to escape in any direction, 928+2118+3338
1Sa 6: 9 and that it happened to us by c." 5247
19: 2 "My father Saul is looking for a c 1335
Ecc 9:11 but time and c happen to them all. 7004
Mk 6:31 and going that they did not even have a c 2320

CHANCELLOR (KJV) See COMMANDING OFFICER

CHANGE (33) [CHANGED, CHANGERS, CHANGES, CHANGING]
Ge 35: 2 and purify yourselves and c your clothes. 2736
Ex 13:17 they might c their minds and return 5714
Lev 13:16 Should the raw flesh c and turn white, 8740
Nu 23:19 nor a son of man, that he should c his mind. 5714
23:20 he has blessed, and I cannot c it. 8740
1Sa 15:29 of Israel does not lie or c his mind; 5714
15:29 he is not a man, that he should c his mind." 5714
2Sa 14:20 Your servant Joab did this to c 6015
1Ki 8:47 and if they have a c of heart in the land 8740
13:33 after this, Jeroboam did not c his evil ways, 8740
2Ch 6:37 and if they have a c of heart in the land 8740
Ezr 6:12 or people who lifts a hand to c this decree 10731
Job 9:27 I will c my expression, and smile,' 6440
14:20 you c his countenance and send him away. 9101
Ps 55:19 men who never c their ways 2722
102:26 Like clothing you will c them 2736
110: 4 LORD has sworn and will not c his mind: 5714
Jer 7: 5 If you really c your ways 3512+3512
13:16 but he will turn it to thick darkness and c it 8883
13:23 Can the Ethiopian c his skin or 2200
Da 2: 9 hoping the situation will c. 10731
7:25 and try to c the set times and the laws. 10731
Mal 3: 6 "I the LORD do not c. 9101
Mt 18: 3 you c and become like little children, 5138
Ac 6:14 of Nazareth will destroy this place and c 248
Gal 4:20 be with you now and c my tone, 248
Heb 7:12 For when there is a c of the priesthood, 3572
7:12 there must also be a c of the law. 3557
7:21 Lord has sworn and will not c his mind: 3564
12:17 He could bring about no c of mind, 3567
Jas 1:17 who does not c like shifting shadows. 1913+4164
4: 9 C your laughter to mourning and your joy 3573
Jude 1: 4 who c the grace of our God into a license 3572

CHANGED (32) [CHANGE]
Ge 31:41 and you c my wages ten times. 2736
41:14 When he had shaved and c his clothes, 2736
Ex 7:15 and take in your hand the staff that was c 2200
7:17 and it will be c into blood. 2200
7:20 and all the water was c into blood. 2200
10:19 And the LORD c the wind to 2200
14: 5 and his officials c their minds about them 2200
Lev 13:55 and if the mildew has not c its appearance, 2200
Nu 32:38 and Baal Meon (these names were c) 6015
Jdg 7:19 just after they had c the guard. 7756+7756
1Sa 10: 6 and you will be c into a different person. 2200
10: 9 God c Saul's heart, 337+2200
2Sa 12:20 put on lotions and c his clothes, 2736
1Ki 2:15 But things c, and the kingdom has gone 6015
2Ki 23:34 of his father Josiah and c Eliakim's name 6015
24: 1 But then he c his mind and rebelled 8740
24:17 in his place and c his name to Zedekiah. 6015
2Ch 36: 4 and Jerusalem and c Eliakim's name 6015
Jer 2:11 Has a nation ever c its gods? 3558
15: 7 for they have not c their ways. 8740
34:11 But afterward they c their minds 8740
Da 3:19 and his attitude toward them c. 10731
4:16 Let his mind be c from that of a man 10731
6:15 or edict that the king issues can be c." 10731
6:17 so that Daniel's situation might not be c. 10731
Hos 11: 8 My heart is c within me; 2200
Mt 21:29 but later he c his mind and went. 3564
Lk 9:29 the appearance of his face c, 1181+2283
Ac 28: 6 they c their minds and said he was a god. 3554
1Co 15:51 We will not all sleep, but we will all be c— 248
15:52 raise imperishable, and we will be c. 248
Heb 1:12 like a garment they will be c. 248

CHANGERS (3) [CHANGE]
Mt 21:12 He overturned the tables of the money c and 3142
Mk 11:15 He overturned the tables of the money c and 3142
Jn 2:15 of the money c and overturned their tables. 3142

CHANGES (3) [CHANGE]
Ezr 6:11 I decree that if anyone c this edict, 10731
Ecc 8: 1 a man's face and c its hard appearance. 9101
Da 2:21 He c times and seasons; 10731

CHANGING (3) [CHANGE]
Ge 31: 7 by c my wages ten times. 2736
Ezr 6:22 the LORD had filled them with joy by c 6015
Jer 2:36 about so much, c your ways? 9101

CHANNEL (1) [CHANNELED, CHANNELS]
Job 38:25 Who cuts a c for the torrents of rain, 9498

CHANNELED (1) [CHANNEL]
2Ch 32:30 the upper outlet of the Gihon spring and c 3837

CHANNELS (4) [CHANNEL]
Job 6:17 and in the heat vanish from their c. 5226
Isa 8: 7 It will overflow all its c, 692
Eze 31: 4 and sent their c to all the trees of the field. 9498
Zec 4: 2 with seven c to the lights. 4609

CHANT (3)
Eze 32:16 "This is the lament they will c for her. 7801
32:16 The daughters of the nations will c it; 7801
32:16 for Egypt and all her hordes they will c it, 7801

CHAOS (1)
Isa 34:11 the measuring line of c and the plumb line 9332

CHAPEL (KJV) See SANCTUARY

CHAPITER, CHAPITERS (KJV) See CAPITALS, TOPS

CHARACTER (7) [CHARACTERS]
Ru 3:11 that you are a woman of noble c. 2657
Pr 12: 4 A wife of noble c is her husband's crown, 2657
31:10 A wife of noble c who can find? 2657
Ac 17:11 the Bereans were of more noble c than 2302
Ro 5: 4 perseverance, c; and character, hope. 1509
5: 4 perseverance, character; and c, hope. 1509
1Co 15:33 "Bad company corrupts good c." 2456

CHARACTERS (1) [CHARACTER]
Ac 17: 5 up some bad c from the marketplace, 467

CHARASHIM (KJV) See GE HARASHIM

CHARCHEMISH (KJV) See CARCHEMISH

CHARCOAL (1)
Pr 26:21 As c to embers and as wood to fire, 7073

CHARGE (162) [CHARGED, CHARGES, CHARGING]
Ge 24: 2 the one in c of all that he had, 5440
39: 4 Potiphar put him in c of his household, 7212
39: 5 the time he put him in c of his household 7212
39: 6 with Joseph in c, NIH
39: 8 "With me in c," he told her, NIH
39:22 warden put Joseph in c of all those held 928+3338
41:33 and wise man and put him in c of the land 6584
41:40 You shall be in c of my palace, 6584
41:41 "I hereby put you in c of the whole land 6584
41:43 Thus he put him in c of the whole land 6584
47: 6 put them in c of my own livestock." 8569
Ex 5: 6 to the slave drivers and foremen in c of 928
22:25 c him no interest. 8492
23: 7 Have nothing to do with a false c and do 1821
Lev 5: 1 not speak up when he hears a public c 460
Nu 1:50 the Levites to be in c of the tabernacle of 6584
4:16 is to have c of the oil for the light, 7213
4:16 He is to be in c of the entire tabernacle 7213
7: 2 who were the tribal leaders in c 6584+6641
18: 8 "I myself have put you in c of 5466
Dt 22:20 the c is true and no proof of 1821
23:19 c your brother interest, 5967+5968
23:20 c a foreigner interest, 5967
2Sa 20:24 Adoniram was in c of forced labor; 6584
23:23 And David put him in c of his bodyguard. 448
1Ki 2: 1 he gave a c to Solomon his son. 7422
4: 5 in c of the district officers; 6584
4: 6 in c of the palace; 6584
4: 6 in c of forced labor. 6584
5:14 Adoniram was in c of the forced labor. 6584
9:23 They were also the chief officials in c of 6584

1Ki 11:28 he put him in c of the whole labor force of 7212
12:18 who was in c of forced labor, 6584
16: 9 the man in c of the palace at Tirzah. 6584
18: 3 who was in c of his palace. 6584
2Ki 7:17 put the officer on whose arm he leaned in c 7212
11:15 who were in c of the troops: 7212
15: 5 Jotham the king's son had c of the palace 6584
25:19 he took the officer in c of the fighting men 7224
25:19 in c of conscripting the people of the land NIH
1Ch 6:31 the men David put in c of the music 3338+6584+6641
9:11 the official in c of the house of God; 5592
9:20 of Eleazar was in c of the gatekeepers, 5592
9:23 They and their descendants were in c of 6584
9:27 and they had c of the key 6584
9:28 Some of them were in c of the articles used 6584
9:32 of their Kohathite brothers were in c of 6584
11:25 And David put him in c of his bodyguard. 6584
15:22 the head Levite was in c of the singing; 6254
15:27 who was in c of the singing of the choirs. 8569
23:28 to be in c of the courtyards, the side rooms, 6584
23:29 They were in c of the bread set out on 4200
26:20 Their fellow Levites were in c of 6584
26:22 They were in c of the treasuries of 6584
26:24 was the officer in c of the treasuries. 6584
26:26 Shelomith and his relatives were in c of all 6584
26:32 and King David put them in c of 7212
27: 2 In c of the first division, 6584
27: 4 In c of the division for 6584
27: 6 His son Ammizabad was in c NIH
27:25 of Adiel was in c of the royal storehouses. 6584
27:25 of Uzziah was in c of the storehouses in 6584
27:26 Ezri son of Kelub was in c of 6584
27:27 the Ramathite was in c of the vineyards. 6584
27:27 the Shiphmite was in c of the produce of 6584
27:28 Baal-Hanan the Gederite was in c of 6584
27:28 Joash was in c of the supplies of olive oil. 6584
27:29 the Sharonite was in c of the herds grazing 6584
27:29 Shaphat son of Adlai was in c of the herds 6584
27:30 Obil the Ishmaelite was in c of the camels. 6584
27:30 the Meronothite was in c of the donkeys. 6584
27:31 Jaziz the Hagrite was in c of the flocks. 6584
27:31 All these were the officials in c 8569
28: 1 of hundreds, and the officials in c of all 8569
28: 8 now I c you in the sight of all Israel and of NIH
29: 6 and the officials in c of 8569
2Ch 10:18 who was in c of forced labor, 6584
23:14 who were in c of the troops, 7212
24:13 The men in c of the work were diligent, 6913
26:21 Jotham his son had c of the palace 6584
28: 7 Azrikam the officer in c of the palace, 5592
31:12 a Levite, was in c of these things, 5592
31:13 the official in c of the temple of God. 5592
31:14 was in c of the freewill offerings given 6584
34:13 had c of the laborers and supervised all 6584
Ne 7: 2 I put in c of Jerusalem my brother Hanani, 7422
11:16 who had c of the outside work of the house 6584
11:21 and Ziha and Gishpa were in c of them. 6584
12: 8 was in c of the songs of thanksgiving. 6584
12:44 that time men were appointed to be in c of 6584
13: 4 Eliashib the priest had been put in c of 928
13:13 put Shelemiah the priest, Zadok the scribe, and a Levite named Pedaiah in c of the storerooms 238+732+6584
Est 2: 3 who is in c of the women; 9068
2: 8 who had c of the harem. 9068
2:14 the king's eunuch who was in c of 9068
2:15 king's eunuch who was in c of the harem, 9068
Job 34:13 Who put him in c of the whole world? 8492
Ps 69:27 C them with crime upon crime; 5989
SS 2: 7 I c you by the gazelles and by the does of 8678
3: 5 I c you by the gazelles and by the does of 8678
5: 8 O daughters of Jerusalem, I c you— 8678
5: 9 that you c us so? 8678
8: 4 Daughters of Jerusalem, I c you: 8678
Isa 3: 6 take c of this heap of ruins!" 3338+9393
22:15 to Shebna, who is in c of the palace: 6584
33:18 Where is the officer in c of the towers?" 6221
Jer 15:13 without c, because of all your sins 4697
29:26 in place of Jehoiada to be in c of the house 7224
40: 7 the land and had put him in c of the men, 7212
46: 9 C, O horses! 6590
52:25 he took the officer in c of the fighting men, 7224
52:25 in c of conscripting the people of the land NIH
Eze 40:45 the priests who have c of the temple, 5466+9068
40:46 the priests who have c of the altar. 5466+9068
44: 8 you put others in c of my sanctuary. 9068
44:11 having c of the gates of the temple 7213
44:14 Yet I will put them in c of the duties of 9068
Da 2:48 placed him in c of all its wise men. 10505+10647
Hos 4: 1 because the LORD has a c to bring 8190
4: 4 "But let no man bring a c, 8189
12: 2 The LORD has a c to bring against Judah; 8190
Joel 2: 7 They c like warriors; 8132
Mic 6: 2 he is lodging a c against Israel. 3519
Zec 3: 6 of the LORD gave this c to Joshua: 6386
3: 7 and have c of my courts, 9068
Mt 24:45 the master has put in c of the servants 2770
24:47 he will put him in c of all his possessions. 2770
25:21 I will put you in c of many things. 2770
25:23 I will put you in c of many things. 2770
26:63 "I c you under oath by the living God: 2019
27:14 Jesus made no reply, not even to a single c 4839
27:37 the written c against him: 162
Mk 3:21 they went to take c of him, for they said, 3195
13:34 and puts his servants in c, 2026
15:26 The written notice of the c 162
Lk 12:42 whom the master puts in c of his servants 2770
12:44 he will put him in c of all his possessions. 2770
19:17 take c of ten cities.' 2026
19:19 'You take c of five cities.' 1181+2062
23: 4 "I find no basis for a c against this man." 165
Jn 13:29 Since Judas had c of the money, 2400
18:38 "I find no basis for a c against him. 162
19: 4 to let you know that I find no basis for a c 162
19: 6 I find no basis for a c against him." 162
19:16 So the soldiers took c of Jesus. 4161
Ac 8:27 an important official in c of all the treasury 1639+2093
23:29 but there was no c against him 1598
25:18 they did not c him with any of 162+5770
28:19 not that I had any c to bring against 2989
Ro 3: 9 We have already made the c that Jews 4577
8:33 Who will bring any c 1592
1Co 9:18 the gospel I may offer it free of c, 78
2Co 11: 7 the gospel of God to you free of c? 1562
Gal 3:24 So the law was put in c to lead us to Christ 4080
1Th 5:27 I c you before the Lord 1941
1Ti 5:21 I c you, in the sight of God 1371
6:13 the good confession, I c you 4133
2Ti 4: 1 I give you this c: 1371
Tit 1: 6 and are not open to the c of being wild 2990
Phm 1:18 owes you anything, c it to me. 1823
Rev 14:18 Still another angel, who had c of the fire, 2026
16: 5 I heard the angel in c of the waters say: NIG

CHARGED (10) [CHARGE]

Dt 1:16 And I c your judges at that time: 7422
Jos 6:20 so every man c straight in, 6590
Jdg 20:33 and the Israelite ambush c out of its place 1631
1Sa 21: 2 "The king c me with a certain matter 7422
1Ch 22: 6 and c him to build a house for the LORD, 7422
Eze 18:20 of the wicked will be c against him. 6584
Da 8: 4 I watched the ram as he c toward the west 5590
8: 6 beside the canal and c at him in great rage. 8132
Ac 18:13 they c, "is persuading the people 3306
19:40 in danger of being c with rioting because 1592

CHARGER (KJV) See PLATE, PLATTER

CHARGES (34) [CHARGE]

1Ki 21:13 and sat opposite him and brought c against 6386
Ne 5: 6 When I heard their outcry and these c, 1821
Job 4:18 if he c his angels with error, 8492
10: 2 but tell me what c you have against me. 8189
13:19 Can anyone bring c against me? 8189
22: 4 that he rebukes you and brings c 5477
23: 6 No, he would not press c against me. 8492
24:12 But God c no one with wrongdoing. 8492
39:21 and c into the fray. 3655
Isa 50: 8 Who then will bring c against me? 8189
Jer 2: 9 "Therefore I bring c against you again," 8189
2: 9 "And I will bring c against your 8189
2:29 "Why do you bring c against me? 8189
25:31 the LORD will bring c against the nations; 8190
Da 6: 4 and the satraps tried to find grounds for c 10544
6: 5 "We will never find any basis for c 10544
Hos 4: 4 for your people are like those who bring c 8189
Lk 23:14 and have found no basis for your c 2989
Jn 18:29 "What c are you bringing 2990
Ac 7: 1 high priest asked him, "Are these c true?" NIG
19:38 They can press c. 1592
24: 1 and they brought their c against Paul before 1872
24: 8 c we are bringing against 2989
24:13 c they are now making against 2989
24:19 to be here before you and bring c 2989
25: 2 appeared before him and presented the c 1872
25: 5 with me and press c against the man there, 2989
25: 7 bringing many serious c against him, 166
25: 9 and stand trial before me there on these c?" NIG
25:11 the c brought against me by these Jews are 2989
25:15 the Jews brought c against him and asked 1872
25:16 to defend himself against their c. 1598
25:20 and stand trial there on these c. NIG
25:27 without specifying the c against him." 162

CHARGING (6) [CHARGE]

Ne 5:11 and also the usury you are c them— 5957
Job 1:22 Job did not sin by c God with wrongdoing. 5989
15:26 defiantly c against him with a thick, 8132
Pr 28:15 or a c bear is a wicked man ruling over 9212
Jer 8: 6 Each pursues his own course like a horse c 8851
Na 3: 3 C cavalry, flashing swords 6590

CHARIOT (65) [CHARIOTEERS, CHARIOTS]

Ge 41:43 in a c as his second-in-command, 5324
46:29 Joseph had his c made ready and went 5324
Ex 14: 6 So he had his c made ready 8207
Jdg 4:15 Sisera abandoned his c and fled on foot. 5324
5:28 'Why is his c so long in coming? 8207
2Sa 8: 4 but a hundred of the c horses. 8207
15: 1 a c and horses and with fifty men to run 5324
1Ki 4:26 Solomon had four thousand stalls for c horses, 5323
4:28 of barley and straw for the c horses and 8224
7:33 The wheels were made like c wheels; 5324
10:26 the c cities and also with him in Jerusalem. 8207
10:29 a c from Egypt for six hundred shekels 5324
12:18 to get into his c and escape to Jerusalem. 5324
18:44 'Hitch up your c and go down before NIH
20:25 horse for horse and c for chariot— 8207
20:25 horse for horse and chariot for c— 8207
20:33 Ahab had him come up into his c. 5324
22:31 the king of Aram had ordered his thirty-two c commanders, 8207
22:32 When the c commanders saw Jehoshaphat, 8207
22:33 the c commanders saw that he was not 8207
22:34 The king told his c driver, 8208
22:35 and the king was propped up in his c facing 5324
22:35 from his wound ran onto the floor of the c, 8207
22:38 They washed the c at a pool in Samaria 8207
2Ki 2:11 a c of fire and horses of fire appeared 8207
5:21 he got down from the c to meet him. 5324
5:26 the man got down from his c to meet you? 5324
8:21 and his c commanders, but he rose up 8207
9:16 Then he got into his c and rode to Jezreel, 8206
9:21 "Hitch up my c," Joram ordered. 8207
9:21 each in his own c, to meet Jehu. 8207
9:24 and he slumped down in his c. 8207
9:25 Jehu said to Bidkar, his c officer, 8957
9:27 in his c on the way up to Gur near Ibleam, 5324
9:28 His servants took him by c to Jerusalem 8206
10:15 he did, and Jehu helped him up into the c. 5324
10:16 Then he had him ride along in his c. 8207
23:30 Josiah's servants brought his body in a c 8206
1Ch 18: 4 but a hundred of the c horses. 8207
28:18 He also gave him the plan for the c, that is, 5324
2Ch 1:14 the c cities and also with him in Jerusalem. 8207
1:17 a c from Egypt for six hundred shekels 5324
9:25 the c cities and also with him in Jerusalem. 8207
10:18 to get into his c and escape to Jerusalem. 5324
18:30 of Aram had ordered his c commanders, 8207
18:31 When the c commanders saw Jehoshaphat, 8207
18:32 when the c commanders saw that he was 8207
18:33 The king told the c driver, 8208
18:34 of Israel propped himself up in his c facing 5324
21: 9 and his c commanders, 8207
35:24 So they took him out of his c, 5324
35:24 in the other c he had and brought him 8207
Ps 76: 6 O God of Jacob, both horse and c lie still. 8207
104: 3 the clouds his c and rides on the wings of 8213
Isa 5:28 their c wheels like a whirlwind. 1649
21: 9 here comes a man in a c with a team 8207
Jer 51:21 with you I shatter c and driver, 8207
Eze 23:15 of them looked like Babylonian c officers, 8957
23:23 c officers and men of high rank, 8957
Mic 1:13 harness the team to the c. 5324
Zec 6: 2 The first c had red horses, 5324
Ac 8:28 in his c reading the book of Isaiah 761
8:29 "Go to that c and stay near it." 761
8:30 to the c and heard the man reading Isaiah NIG
8:38 And he gave orders to stop the c. 761

CHARIOTEERS (11) [CHARIOT]

1Sa 13: 5 six thousand c, and soldiers as numerous as 7305
2Sa 8: 4 of his chariots, seven thousand c 7305
10:18 and David killed seven hundred of their c 7305
1Ki 9:22 and the commanders of his chariots and c. 7305
1Ch 18: 4 of his chariots, seven thousand c 7305
19: 6 of silver to hire chariots and c 7305
19: 7 They hired thirty-two thousand chariots and c, 8207
19:18 and David killed seven thousand of their c 8207
2Ch 8: 9 and commanders of his chariots and c. 7305
Isa 22: 6 with her c and horses; 132+8207
Jer 46: 9 Drive furiously, O c! 8207

CHARIOTS (102) [CHARIOT]

Ge 50: 9 C and horsemen also went up with him. 8207
Ex 14: 7 He took six hundred of the best c, 8207
14: 7 along with all the other c of Egypt, 8207
14: 9 all Pharaoh's horses and c, 8207
14:17 through his c and his horsemen. 8207
14:18 his c and his horsemen." 8207
14:23 and c and horsemen followed them into 8207
14:25 He made the wheels of their c come off so 5324
14:26 the Egyptians and their c and horsemen." 8207
14:28 The water flowed back and covered the c 8207
15: 4 Pharaoh's c and his army he has hurled 5324
15:19 c and horsemen went into the sea, 8207
Dt 11: 4 to its horses and c, 8207
20: 1 against your enemies and see horses and c 8207
Jos 11: 4 and a large number of horses and c— 8207
11: 6 to hamstring their horses and burn their c." 5324
11: 9 and burned their c. 5324
17:16 in the plain have iron c, 8207
17:18 though the Canaanites have iron c and 8207
24: 6 with c and horsemen as far as the Red Sea. 8207
Jdg 1:19 because they had iron c. 8207
4: 3 Because he had nine hundred iron c 8207
4: 7 Jabin's army, with his c and his troops 8207
4:13 Sisera gathered together his nine hundred iron c 8207
4:15 the LORD routed Sisera and all his c 8207
4:16 But Barak pursued the c and army as far 8207
5:28 Why is the clatter of his c delayed?' 5324
1Sa 8:11 and make them serve with his c and horses, 5324
8:11 and they will run in front of his c. 5324
8:12 of war and equipment for his c. 8207
13: 5 with three thousand c, 8207
2Sa 1: 6 with the c and riders almost upon him. 8207
8: 4 David captured a thousand of his c, 8207
1Ki 1: 5 So he got c and horses ready, 8207
9:19 and the towns for his c and for his horses— 8207

1Ki 9:22 the commanders of his **c** and charioteers. 8207
10:26 Solomon accumulated **c** and horses; 8207
10:26 he had fourteen hundred **c** 8207
16: 9 who had command of half his **c,** 8207
20: 1 by thirty-two kings with their horses and **c,** 8207
20:21 the horses and **c** and inflicted heavy losses 8207
2Ki 2:12 The **c** and horsemen of Israel!" 8207
5: 9 So Naaman went with his horses and **c** 8207
6:14 and **c** and a strong force there. 8207
6:15 an army with horses and **c** had surrounded 8207
6:17 of horses and **c** *of* fire all around Elisha. 8207
7: 6 the sound of **c** and horses and a great army, 8207
7:14 So they selected two **c** *with* their horses, 8207
8:21 So Jehoram went to Zair with all his **c.** 8207
9:25 how you and I *were* **riding** together **in c** 8206
10: 2 with you and you have **c** and horses, 8207
13: 7 ten **c** and ten thousand foot soldiers, 8207
13:14 "The **c** and horsemen of Israel!" 8207
18:24 though you are depending on Egypt for **c** 8207
19:23 "With my many **c** I have ascended 8207
23:11 then burned the **c** *dedicated to* the sun. 5324
1Ch 18: 4 David captured a thousand of his **c,** 8207
19: 6 a thousand talents of silver to hire **c** 8207
19: 7 They hired thirty-two thousand **c and charioteers,** 8207
2Ch 1:14 Solomon accumulated **c** and horses; 8207
1:14 he had fourteen hundred **c** 8207
8: 6 all the cities for his **c** and for his horses— 8207
8: 9 and commanders of his **c** and charioteers. 8207
9:25 for horses and **c,** 5324
12: 3 With twelve hundred **c** 8207
14: 9 with a vast army and three hundred **c,** 5324
16: 8 with great numbers of **c** and horsemen? 8207
21: 9 with his officers and all his **c.** 8207
Ps 20: 7 Some trust in **c** and some in horses, 8207
68:17 The **c** *of* God are tens of thousands 8207
SS 1: 9 to a mare harnessed to one of the **c** 8207
6:12 my desire set me among the royal **c** 5324
Isa 2: 7 there is no end to their **c.** 5324
21: 7 When he sees **c** *with* teams of horses, 8207
22: 7 Your choicest valleys are full of **c,** 8207
22:18 and there your splendid **c** will remain— 5324
31: 1 who trust in the multitude of their **c** and in 8207
36: 9 though you are depending on Egypt for **c** 8207
37:24 'With my many **c** I have ascended 8207
43:17 who drew out the **c** and horses, the army 8207
66:15 and his **c** are like a whirlwind; 5324
66:20 on horses, in **c** and wagons, 8207
Jer 4:13 his **c** come like a whirlwind, 5324
17:25 and their officials will come riding in **c** and 8207
22: 4 riding in **c** and on horses, 8207
47: 3 of enemy **c** and the rumble of their wheels. 8207
50:37 A sword against her horses and **c** and all 8207
Eze 23:24 **c** and wagons and with a throng of people; 8207
26: 7 king of kings, with horses and **c,** 8207
26:10 wagons and **c** when he enters your gates 8207
Da 11:40 the North will storm out against him with **c** 8207
Joel 2: 5 that of **c** they leap over the mountaintops, 5324
Mic 5:10 from among you and demolish your **c.** 5324
Na 2: 3 The metal on the **c** flashes on 8207
2: 4 The **c** storm through the streets, 8207
2:13 "I will burn up your **c** in smoke, 8207
3: 2 galloping horses and jolting **c!** 5324
Hab 3: 8 with your horses and your victorious **c?** 5324
Hag 2:22 I will overthrow **c** and their drivers; 5324
Zec 6: 1 before me were four **c** coming out from 5324
9:10 I will take away the **c** from Ephraim and 8207
Rev 9: 9 *of* many horses and **c** rushing into battle. *761*

CHARITY (KJV) See LOVE

CHARM (2) [CHARMED, CHARMER, CHARMING, CHARMS]
Pr 17: 8 A bribe is a **c** to the one who gives it; 74+2834
31:30 **C** is deceptive, and beauty is fleeting; 2834

CHARMED (2) [CHARM]
Ecc 10:11 If a snake bites before it is **c,** 4318
Jer 8:17 vipers that cannot be **c,** 4318

CHARMER (2) [CHARM]
Ps 58: 5 that will not heed the tune of the **c,** 4317
Ecc 10:11 there is no profit for the **c.** 1251+4383

CHARMING (2) [CHARM]
Pr 26:25 Though his speech *is* **c,** 2858
SS 1:16 Oh, how **c!** 5833

CHARMS (3) [CHARM]
Isa 3:20 the perfume bottles and **c,** 4318
Eze 13:18 Woe to the women who sew **magic c** 4086
13:20 I am against your **magic c** 4086

CHARRAN (KJV) See HARAN

CHARRED (3) [CHARS]
Jdg 15:14 The ropes on his arms became like **c** flax, 836+928+1277+2021
Eze 15: 5 when the fire has burned it and *it* **is c?** 3081
24:10 and *let* the bones **be c.** 3081

CHARS (1) [CHARRED]
Eze 15: 4 the fire burns both ends and **c** the middle, 3081

CHASE (8) [CHASED, CHASES, CHASING]
Lev 26: 8 Five of you *will* **c** a hundred, 8103
26: 8 and a hundred of you *will* **c** ten thousand, 8103
Dt 32:30 How *could* one man **c** a thousand, 8103
Job 13:25 *Will you* **c after** dry chaff? 8103
Isa 1:23 they all love bribes and **c after** gifts. 8103
Jer 49:19 *I will* **c** Edom from its land in an instant. 8132
50:44 *I will* **c** Babylon from its land in 8132
Hos 2: 7 *She will* **c after** her lovers but 8103

CHASED (10) [CHASE]
Dt 1:44 *they* **c** you like a swarm of bees 8103
Jos 7: 5 *They* **c** the Israelites from the city gate 8103
8:24 and in the desert where *they had* **c** them, 8103
Jdg 1: 6 but *they* **c** him and caught him, 8103
9:40 Abimelech **c** him, and many fell wounded 8103
20:43 **c** them and easily overran them in 8103
2Sa 2:19 He **c** Abner, turning neither to the right nor 8103
2Ki 9:27 Jehu **c** him, shouting, "Kill him too!" 8103
Jer 50:17 a scattered flock that lions *have* **c away.** 5615
La 4:19 *they* **c** us over the mountains and lay 1944

CHASES (2) [CHASE]
Pr 12:11 but *he who* **c** fantasies lacks judgment. 8103
28:19 but the *one who* **c** fantasies will have his fill 8103

CHASING (12) [CHASE]
1Sa 17:53 Israelites returned from **c** the Philistines 339+1944
2Sa 2:21 But Asahel would not stop **c** him. 339
2:22 Again Abner warned Asahel, "Stop **c** me! 339
Ecc 1:14 meaningless, a **c after** the wind. 8296
1:17 too, is a **c after** the wind. 8301
2:11 meaningless, a **c after** the wind; 8296
2:17 All of it is meaningless, a **c after** the wind. 8296
2:26 meaningless, a **c after** the wind. 8296
4: 4 meaningless, a **c after** the wind. 8296
4: 6 with toil and **c after** the wind. 8296
4:16 meaningless, a **c after** the wind. 8301
6: 9 meaningless, a **c after** the wind. 8296

CHASM (1)
Lk 16:26 between us and you a great **c** has been fixed, *5926*

CHASTE (KJV) See PURE

CHASTENED (2)
Job 33:19 Or a man *may* **be c** on a bed of pain 3519
Ps 118:18 The LORD *has* **c** me **severely,** 3579+3579

CHASTISE (KJV) See PUNISH, SCOURGE, CATCH, TRAINED

CHATTER (2) [CHATTERING]
1Ti 6:20 from godless **c** and the opposing ideas *3032*
2Ti 2:16 Avoid godless **c,** *3032*

CHATTERING (2) [CHATTER]
Pr 10: 8 but a **c** fool comes to ruin. 8557
10:10 and a **c** fool comes to ruin. 8557

CHEAPER (1)
Jn 2:10 the choice wine first and then the **c** wine *1781*

CHEAT (2) [CHEATED, CHEATING, CHEATS]
Mal 1:14 the **c** who has an acceptable male 5792
1Co 6: 8 Instead, *you* yourselves **c** and do wrong, *691*

CHEATED (5) [CHEAT]
Ge 31: 7 yet your father *has* **c** me 9438
1Sa 12: 3 Whom *have I* **c?** 6943
12: 4 *"You have* not **c** or oppressed us," 6943
Lk 19: 8 and if *I have* **c** anybody **out of** anything, *5193*
1Co 6: 7 Why not rather *be* **c?** *691*

CHEATING (1) [CHEAT]
Am 8: 5 the measure, boosting the price and **c** 6430

CHEATS (1) [CHEAT]
Lev 6: 2 or if *he* **c** him, 6943

CHEBAR (KJV) See KEBAR

CHECK (2) [CHECKED]
Ge 30:33 whenever *you* **c** on the wages 995+4200+7156
Jas 3: 2 **keep** his whole body **in c.** *5902*

CHECKED (3) [CHECK]
2Ki 6:10 king of Israel **c on** the place indicated 448+8938
Ezr 8:15 *I* **c** among the people and the priests, 1067
Ps 106:30 and the plague **was c.** 6806

CHECKER WORK (KJV) See INTERWOVEN CHAINS

CHEDORLAOMER (KJV) See KEDORLAOMER

CHEEK (5) [CHEEKS]
Job 16:10 they strike my **c** in scorn and unite together 4305
La 3:30 Let him offer his **c** 4305
Mic 5: 1 They will strike Israel's ruler on the **c** with 4305
Mt 5:39 If someone strikes you on the right **c,** *4965*
Lk 6:29 If someone strikes you on one **c,** *4965*

CHEEKS (4) [CHEEK]
SS 1:10 Your **c** are beautiful with earrings, 4305
5:13 His **c** are like beds of spice 4305
Isa 50: 6 my **c** to those who pulled out my beard; 4305
La 1: 2 tears are upon her **c.** 4305

CHEER (2) [CHEERED, CHEERFUL, CHEERFULLY, CHEERING, CHEERS]
1Ki 21: 7 Get up and eat! **C up.** 3512+4213
Mk 10:49 So they called to the blind man, **"C up!** *2510*

CHEERED (1) [CHEER]
Php 2:19 that I also *may be* **c** when I receive news *2379*

CHEERFUL (5) [CHEER]
Pr 15:13 A happy heart **makes** the face **c,** 3512
15:15 but the **c** heart has a continual feast. 3202
15:30 A **c** look brings joy to the heart, 4401
17:22 A **c** heart is good medicine, 8524
2Co 9: 7 for God loves a **c** giver. *2659*

CHEERFULLY (1) [CHEER]
Ro 12: 8 if it is showing mercy, let him do it **c.** *1877+2660*

CHEERING (3) [CHEER]
1Ki 1:45 From there they have gone up **c,** 8524
2Ch 23:12 the noise of the people running and **c** 2146
Ecc 2: 3 I tried **c** myself with wine, 5432

CHEERS (2) [CHEER]
Jdg 9:13 my wine, which **c** both gods and men, 8523
Pr 12:25 but a kind word **c** him **up.** 8523

CHEESE (2) [CHEESES]
2Sa 17:29 and **c** *from* cows' milk for David 9147
Job 10:10 like milk and curdle me like **c,** 1482

CHEESES (1) [CHEESE]
1Sa 17:18 Take along these ten **c** to the commander 2692+3043

CHELAL (KJV) See KELAL

CHELLUH (KJV) See KELUHI

CHELUB (KJV) See KELUB

CHELUBAI (KJV) See CALEB

CHEMARIMS (KJV) See PAGAN

CHEMOSH (8)
Nu 21:29 You are destroyed, O people of **C!** 4019
Jdg 11:24 not take what your god **C** gives you? 4019
1Ki 11: 7 a high place for **C** the detestable god 4019
11:33 **C** the god of the Moabites, 4019
2Ki 23:13 for **C** the vile god of Moab, 4019
Jer 48: 7 and **C** will go into exile, 4019
48:13 Then Moab will be ashamed of **C,** 4019
48:46 The people of **C** are destroyed; 4019

CHENAANAH (KJV) See KENAANAH

CHENANI (KJV) See KENANI

CHENANIAH (KJV) See KENANIAH

CHEPHAR-HAAMMONAI (KJV) See KEPHAR AMMONI

CHEPHIRAH (KJV) See KEPHIRAH

CHERAN (KJV) See KERAN

CHERETHIMS, CHERETHITES (KJV) See KERETHITES

CHERISH (2) [CHERISHED, CHERISHES]
Ps 17:14 You still the hunger of those you **c**; 7621
83: 3 they plot against *those* you **c**. 7621

CHERISHED (2) [CHERISH]
Ps 66:18 If *I had* **c** sin in my heart, 8011
Hos 9:16 I will slay their **c** offspring." 4718

CHERISHES (1) [CHERISH]
Pr 19: 8 *he who* **c** understanding prospers. 9068

CHERITH (KJV) See KERITH

CHERUB (16) [CHERUBIM]
Ex 25:19 Make one **c** on one end and 4131
25:19 on one end and the second **c** on the other; 4131
37: 8 He made one **c** on one end and 4131
37: 8 on one end and the second **c** on the other; 4131
1Ki 6:24 of the first **c** was five cubits long, and 4131
6:25 The second **c** also measured ten cubits, 4131
6:26 The height of each **c** was ten cubits. 4131
6:27 The wing of one **c** touched one wall, 4131
2Ch 3:11 One wing of the first **c** was five cubits long NIH
3:11 touched the wing of the other **c**. 4131
3:12 of the second **c** was five cubits long 4131
3:12 touched the wing of the first **c**. 4131
Eze 10:14 One face was that of a **c**, 4131
28:14 You were anointed as a guardian **c**, 4131
28:16 O guardian **c**, from among the fiery stones. 4131
41:18 Each **c** had two faces: 4131

CHERUBIM (73) [CHERUB]
Ge 3:24 the east side of the Garden of Eden **c** and 4131
Ex 25:18 And make two **c** out of hammered gold at 4131
25:19 make the **c** of one piece with the cover, 4131
25:20 The **c** are to have their wings spread upward 4131
25:20 The **c** are to face each other, 4131
25:22 above the cover between the two **c** that are 4131
26: 1 with **c** worked into them by 4131
26:31 with **c** worked into it by 4131
36: 8 with **c** worked into them by 4131
36:35 with **c** worked into it by 4131
37: 7 Then he made two **c** out of hammered gold 4131
37: 9 The **c** had their wings spread upward, 4131
37: 9 The **c** faced each other, 4131
Nu 7:89 the two **c** above the atonement cover on 4131
1Sa 4: 4 who is enthroned between the **c**. 4131
2Sa 6: 2 who is enthroned between the **c** that are on 4131
22:11 He mounted the **c** and flew; 4131
1Ki 6:23 In the inner sanctuary he made a pair of **c** 4131
6:25 the two **c** were identical in size and shape. 4131
6:27 He placed the **c** inside the innermost room 4131
6:28 He overlaid the **c** with gold. 4131
6:29 he carved **c**, palm trees and open flowers. 4131
6:32 on the two olive wood doors he carved **c**, 4131
6:32 the **c** and palm trees with beaten gold. 4131
6:35 He carved **c**, palm trees and open flowers 4131
7:29 bulls and **c**—and on the uprights as well. 4131
7:36 He engraved **c**, lions and palm trees on 4131
8: 6 and put it beneath the wings of the **c**. 4131
8: 7 The **c** spread their wings over the place of 4131
2Ki 19:15 God of Israel, enthroned between the **c**, 4131
1Ch 13: 6 who is enthroned between the **c**— 4131
28:18 the **c** of gold that spread their wings 4131
2Ch 3: 7 and he carved **c** on the walls. 4131
3:10 a pair of sculptured **c** and overlaid them 4131
3:11 of the **c** was twenty cubits. 4131
3:13 wings of these **c** extended twenty cubits. 4131
3:14 with **c** worked into it. 4131
5: 7 and put it beneath the wings of the **c**. 4131
5: 8 The **c** spread their wings over the place of 4131
Ps 18:10 He mounted the **c** and flew; 4131
80: 1 you who sit enthroned between the **c**, 4131
99: 1 he sits enthroned between the **c**, 4131
Isa 37:16 God of Israel, enthroned between the **c**, 4131
Eze 9: 3 of Israel went up from above the **c**, 4131
10: 1 that was over the heads of the **c**. 4131
10: 2 "Go in among the wheels beneath the **c**. 4131
10: 2 from among the **c** and scatter them over 4131
10: 3 Now the **c** were standing on the south side 4131
10: 4 above the **c** and moved to the threshold of 4131
10: 5 The sound of the wings of the **c** could 4131
10: 6 from among the **c**," 4131
10: 7 Then one of the **c** reached out his hand to 4131
10: 8 of the **c** could be seen what looked like 4131
10: 9 and I saw beside the **c** four wheels, 4131
10: 9 one beside each of the **c**; 4131
10:11 of the four directions **the c** faced; 2157S
10:11 the wheels did not turn about as **the c** went. 4392S
10:11 The **c** went in whatever direction NIH
10:14 Each of the **c** had four faces: NIH
10:15 Then the **c** rose upward. 4131
10:16 When the **c** moved, the wheels 4131
10:16 when the **c** spread their wings to rise from 4131
10:17 When **the c** stood still, they also stood still; 4392S
10:17 and when **the c** rose, they rose with them, 4392S
10:18 of the temple and stopped above the **c**. 4131
10:19 the **c** spread their wings and rose from 4131
10:20 and I realized that they were **c**. 4131
11:22 Then the **c**, with the wheels beside them, 4131
41:18 were carved **c** and palm trees. 4131
41:18 Palm trees alternated with **c**. 4131
41:20 **c** and palm trees were carved on the wall of 4131
Eze 41:25 of the outer sanctuary were carved **c** 4131
Heb 9: 5 Above the ark were the **c** of the Glory, *5938*

CHESALON (KJV) See KESALON

CHESED (KJV) See KESED

CHESIL (KJV) See KESIL

CHESNUT (KJV) See PLANE

CHEST (17) [CHESTS]
Ex 25:10 "Have them make a **c** *of* acacia wood— 778
25:14 the poles into the rings on the sides of the **c** 778
Dt 10: 1 Also make a wooden **c**. 778
10: 2 Then you are to put them in the **c**." 778
1Sa 6: 8 and in a **c** beside it put 761
6:11 along with it the **c** containing the gold rats 761
6:15 with the **c** containing the gold objects, 761
2Ki 12: 9 Jehoiada the priest took a **c** and bored 778
12: 9 into **the c** all the money that was brought 9004S
12:10 a large amount of money in the **c**, 778
2Ch 24: 8 a **c** was made and placed outside, 778
24:10 dropping them into the **c** until it was full. 778
24:11 the **c** was brought in by the Levites to 778
24:11 the **c** and carry it back to its place. 778
Job 41:24 His **c** is hard as rock, 4213
Da 2:32 its **c** and arms of silver, 10249
Rev 1:13 and with a golden sash around his **c**. *3466*

CHESTS (1) [CHEST]
Rev 15: 6 and wore golden sashes around their **c**. *5111*

CHESULLOTH (KJV) See KESULLOTH

CHEW (6) [CHEWED, CHEWS]
Lev 11: 4 " 'There are some *that* only **c** the cud 6590
11: 7 *does* not **c** the cud; it is unclean for you. 1760
11:26 *that does* not **c** the cud is unclean for you; 6590
Dt 14: 7 of *those that* **c** the cud or that have 6590
14: 7 Although they **c** the cud, 6590
14: 8 it does not **c** the cud. NIH

CHEWED (1) [CHEW]
Jnh 4: 7 *which* **c** the vine so that it withered. 5782

CHEWS (5) [CHEW]
Lev 11: 3 a split hoof completely divided and *that* **c** 6590
11: 4 The camel, though it **c** the cud, 6590
11: 5 The coney, though it **c** the cud, 6590
11: 6 The rabbit, though it **c** the cud, 6590
Dt 14: 6 a split hoof divided in two and that **c** 6590

CHEZIB (KJV) See KEZIB

CHICKENS (KJV) See CHICKS

CHICKS (2)
Mt 23:37 as a hen gathers her **c** under her wings, *3800*
Lk 13:34 as a hen gathers her **c** under her wings, *3799*

CHIDE (KJV) See QUARREL; CRITICIZED, ACCUSE

CHIDON (KJV) See KIDON

CHIEF (145) [CHIEFS]
Ge 24: 2 He said to the **c** servant *in* his household, 2418
40: 2 the **c** cupbearer and the chief baker, 8569
40: 2 the chief cupbearer and the **c** baker, 8569
40: 9 So the **c** cupbearer told Joseph his dream. 8569
40:16 the **c** baker saw that Joseph had given 8569
40:20 He lifted up the heads of the **c** cupbearer 8569
40:20 the **c** baker in the presence of his officials: 8569
40:21 He restored the **c** cupbearer to his position, 8569
40:22 but he hanged the **c** baker, 8569
40:23 The **c** cupbearer, however, 8569
41: 9 Then the **c** cupbearer said to Pharaoh, 8569
41:10 and the **c** baker in the house of the captain 8569
Nu 3:32 The **c leader** *of* the Levites 5954+5954
25:15 a tribal **c** of a Midianite family. 8031
Dt 29:10 your leaders and **c men**, 8657
Jos 22:14 With him they sent ten of the **c** *men*, 5954
2Sa 23: 8 a Tahkemonite, was **c** *of* the Three; 8031
23:13 of the thirty **c** *men* came down to David at 8031
23:18 the brother of Joab son of Zeruiah was **c** *of* 8031
1Ki 4: 2 And these were his **c officials:** 8569
4: 4 of Jehoiada—**commander in c**; 2021+6584+7372
9:23 They were also the **c** officials in charge 8569
2Ki 10:11 as well as all his **c** *men*, 1524
15:25 One of his **c officers,** 8957
18:17 his **c** officer and his field commander with 8042
25:18 as prisoners Seraiah the **c** priest, 8031
25:19 the secretary who was **c officer** in charge 2021+7372+8569
1Ch 5: 7 Jeiel the **c**, Zechariah, 8031
1Ch 5:12 Joel was the **c**, Shapham the second, 8031
9:17 and their brothers, Shallum their **c** 8031
11:11 a Hacmonite, was **c** *of* the officers; 8031
11:20 the brother of Joab was **c** *of* the Three. 8031
11:42 who was **c** of the Reubenites, 8031
12: 3 Ahiezer their **c** and Joash the sons 8031
12: 9 Ezer was the **c**, 8031
12:18 Spirit came upon Amasai, **c** *of* the Thirty, 8031
16: 5 Asaph was the **c**, 8031
18:17 and David's sons were **c officials** at 8037
26:12 through their **c** men, 8031
26:31 Jeriah was their **c** according to 8031
27: 3 He was a descendant of Perez and **c** of all 8031
27: 5 He was **c** and there were 24,000 8031
2Ch 8:10 also King Solomon's **c** officials— 8569
11:22 to be the **c** prince among his brothers, 8031
19:11 the **c** priest will be over you in any matter 8031
24: 6 the king summoned Jehoiada the **c** priest 8031
24:11 and the officer of the **c** priest would come 8031
26:20 the **c** priest and all the other priests looked 8031
31:10 and Azariah the **c** priest, 8031
Ezr 7: 5 the son of Aaron the **c** priest— 8031
Ne 11: 9 Joel son of Zicri was their **c officer,** 7224
11:14 Their **c officer** was Zabdiel son 7224
11:22 The **c officer** *of* the Levites 7224
Job 29: 9 the **c men** refrained from speaking 8569
29:25 I chose the way for them and sat as their **c**; 8031
Isa 2: 2 be established as **c** *among* the mountains; 8031
33:18 "Where is that **c officer?** 6221
Jer 20: 1 the **c** officer in the temple of the LORD, 5592
39: 3 Nebo-Sarsekim a **c** officer, 8042
39:13 Nebushazban a **c** officer, 8042
52:24 as prisoners Seraiah the **c** priest, 8031
52:25 the secretary who was **c officer** in charge 2021+7372+8569
Eze 38: 2 the **c** prince of Meshech and Tubal; 8031
38: 3 O Gog, **c** prince of Meshech and Tubal. 8031
39: 1 O Gog, **c** prince of Meshech and Tubal. 8031
Da 1: 3 **c** *of* his court officials, 8041
1: 7 The **c** official gave them new names: 8569
1: 8 and he asked the **c** official for permission 8569
1:11 the **c** official had appointed over Daniel, 8569
1:18 the **c** official presented them 8569
4: 9 I said, "Belteshazzar, **c** *of* the magicians, 10647
5:11 appointed him **c** *of* the magicians, 10647
10:13 Then Michael, one of the **c** princes, 8037
Mic 4: 1 be established as **c** *among* the mountains; 8031
Mt 2: 4 the people's **c priests** and teachers of *797*
16:21 **c priests** and teachers of the law, *797*
20:18 *to* the **c priests** and the teachers of the law. *797*
21:15 the **c priests** and the teachers of the law saw *797*
21:23 the **c priests** and the elders of *797*
21:45 When the **c priests** and the Pharisees *797*
26: 3 Then the **c priests** and the elders of *797*
26:14 went to the **c priests** *797*
26:47 the **c priests** and the elders of the people. *797*
26:59 The **c priests** and the whole Sanhedrin *797*
27: 1 all the **c priests** and the elders of *797*
27: 3 the thirty silver coins *to* the **c priests** and *797*
27: 6 The **c priests** picked up the coins and said, *797*
27:12 When he was accused by the **c priests** and *797*
27:20 But the **c priests** and the elders persuaded *797*
27:41 In the same way the **c priests,** *797*
27:62 **c priests** and the Pharisees went to Pilate. *797*
28:11 the **c priests** everything that had happened. *797*
28:12 When the **c** priests had met with the elders *NIG*
Mk 8:31 **c priests** and teachers of the law, *797*
10:33 be betrayed *to* the **c priests** and teachers of *797*
11:18 The **c priests** and the teachers of *797*
11:27 the temple courts, the **c priests,** the teachers *797*
14: 1 and the **c priests** and the teachers of *797*
14:10 to the **c priests** to betray Jesus to them. *797*
14:43 sent from the **c priests,** the teachers *797*
14:53 and all the **c priests,** elders and teachers *797*
14:55 The **c priests** and the whole Sanhedrin *797*
15: 1 Very early in the morning, the **c priests,** *797*
15: 3 The **c priests** accused him of many things. *797*
15:10 the **c priests** had handed Jesus over to him. *797*
15:11 But the **c priests** stirred up the crowd *797*
15:31 the same way the **c priests** and the teachers *797*
Lk 9:22 **c priests** and teachers of the law, *797*
19: 2 a **c tax collector** and was wealthy. *803*
19:47 But the **c priests,** the teachers of the law *797*
20: 1 the **c priests** and the teachers of the law, *797*
20:19 the law and the **c priests** looked for a way *797*
22: 2 and the **c priests** and the teachers of *797*
22: 4 And Judas went *to* the **c priests** and *797*
22:52 Then Jesus said to the **c priests,** *797*
22:66 both the **c priests** and teachers of the law, *797*
23: 4 Then Pilate announced to the **c priests** and *797*
23:10 The **c priests** and the teachers of *797*
23:13 Pilate called together the **c priests,** *797*
23:20 The **c priests** and our rulers handed him *797*
Jn 7:32 Then the **c priests** and the Pharisees *797*
7:45 the temple guards went back to the **c priests** *797*
11:47 Then the **c priests** and the Pharisees called *797*
11:57 the **c priests** and Pharisees had given orders *797*
12:10 **c priests** made plans to kill Lazarus as well, *797*
18: 3 and some officials from the **c priests** *797*
18:35 and your **c priests** who handed you over *797*
19: 6 as the **c priests** and their officials saw him, *797*
19:15 the **c priests** answered. *797*
19:21 The **c priests** of the Jews protested *797*
Ac 4:23 the **c priests** and elders had said to them. *797*
5:24 and the **c priests** were puzzled, *797*
9:14 from the **c priests** to arrest all who call *797*
9:21 to take them as prisoners to the **c priests?**" *797*

Ac 14:12 because he was the c speaker. *2451*
19:14 Seven sons of Sceva, a Jewish c **priest,** *797*
22:30 he released him and ordered the c **priests** *797*
23:14 They went to the c **priests** and elders *797*
25: 2 the c **priests** and Jewish leaders appeared *797*
25:15 the c **priests** and elders of the Jews *797*
26:10 On the authority of the c **priests** I put many *797*
26:12 and commission *of* the c **priests.** *797*
28: 7 the c **official** of the island. *4755*
Eph 2:20 himself as the c **cornerstone.** *214+1639*
1Pe 5: 4 And when the C **Shepherd** appears, *799*

CHIEFS (25) [CHIEF]

Ge 36:15 These were the c *among* Esau's descendants: 477
36:15 C Teman, Omar, Zepho, Kenaz, 477
36:16 These were the c *descended from* Eliphaz 477
36:17 C Nahath, Zerah, Shammah and Mizzah. 477
36:17 These were the c *descended from* Reuel 477
36:18 C Jeush, Jalam and Korah. 477
36:18 These were the c *descended* 477
36:19 Edom), and these were their c. 477
36:21 These sons of Seir in Edom were Horite c. 477
36:29 These were the Horite c: 477
36:30 These were the Horite c, 477
36:40 These were the c *descended from* Esau, 477
36:43 These were the c *of* Edom, 477
Ex 15:15 The c *of* Edom will be terrified, 477
Jos 13:21 and the Midianite c, Evi, Rekem, Zur, Hur 5954
1Ki 8: 1 the tribes and the c of the Israelite families, 5954
1Ch 1:51 The c *of* Edom were: 477
1:54 These were the c *of* Edom. 477
7: 3 All five of them were c. 8031
8:28 c as listed in their genealogy, 8031
9:34 c as listed in their genealogy, 8031
11:10 These were the c *of* David's mighty men— 8031
11:15 the thirty c came down to David to the rock 8031
12:32 200 c, with all their relatives 8031
2Ch 5: 2 the tribes and the c of the Israelite families, 5954

CHILD (121) [CHILD'S, CHILDHOOD, CHILDISH, CHILDLESS, CHILDREN, CHILDREN'S, GRANDCHILDREN]

Ge 4:25 "God has granted me another c in place 2446
16:11 "You are now **with** c and you will have 2226
17:17 *Will* Sarah **bear a** c at the age of ninety?" 3528
18:13 *'Will I* really **have a** c, 3528
21: 8 The c grew and was weaned, 3529
Ex 2: 2 When she saw that he was a **fine** *c,* AIT
2: 3 the c in it and put it among the reeds along 3529
2:10 When the c grew older, 3529
Jdg 11:34 She was an **only** c. 3495
Ru 4:16 Then Naomi took the c, 3529
1Sa 1:27 I prayed for this c, 5853
2Sa 12:15 the c that Uriah's wife had borne to David, 3529
12:16 David pleaded with God for the c. 5853
12:18 On the seventh day the c died. 3529
12:18 to tell him that the c was dead, 3529
12:18 "While the c was still living, 3529
12:18 How can we tell him the c is dead? 3529
12:19 and he realized the c was dead. 3529
12:19 "Is the c dead?" 3529
12:21 While the c was alive, you fasted and wept, 3529
12:21 but now that the c is dead, 3529
12:22 He answered, "While the c was still alive, 3529
12:22 be gracious to me and let the c live.' 3529
1Ki 3: 7 But I am only a little c and do not know 5853
3:18 The third day after my c **was born,** 3528
3:25 the living c in two and give half to one 3529
3:26 the c and carried him down from the room 3529
2Ki 4:18 The c grew, and one day he went out 3529
4:26 Is your c all right?' " 3529
2Ch 22:11 she hid **the** c from Athaliah so she could 2084[S]
Job 3:16 in the ground like a **stillborn** c, 5878
24: 9 **fatherless** c is snatched from the breast; 3846
Ps 58: 8 like a **stillborn** c, 851+5878
131: 2 like a **weaned** *c* with its mother, AIT
131: 2 like a **weaned** *c* is my soul within me. AIT
Pr 4: 3 still tender, and an **only** c of my mother, 3495
20:11 Even a c is known by his actions, 5853
22: 6 Train a c in the way he should go, 5853
22:15 Folly is bound up in the heart of a c, 5853
23:13 Do not withhold discipline from a c; 5853
29:15 but a c left to himself disgraces his mother. 5853
Ecc 6: 3 that a **stillborn** c is better off than he. 5878
Isa 7:14 The virgin will be **with** c and will give birth to a son, 2226
9: 6 For to us a c is born, to us a son is given, 3529
10:19 be so few that a c could write them down. 5853
11: 6 and a little c will lead them. 5853
11: 8 **young** c put his hand into the viper's nest. 1694
26:17 As a *woman* **with** c and about 2225
26:18 *We were* **with** c, we writhed in pain, 2225
49:15 on the c she has borne? 1201
54: 1 O barren woman, *you who* never **bore a** c; 3528
66:13 As a mother comforts her c, 408
Jer 1: 6 I am only a c." 5853
1: 7 "Do not say, 'I am only a c.' 5853
4:31 a groan as of *one* **bearing** *her* **first** c— 1144
20:15 saying, "A c is born to you—a son!" 1201
31:20 the c *in whom* I delight? 3529
Hos 11: 1 "When Israel was a c, I loved him, 5853
13:13 but he is a c without wisdom; 1201
Zec 12:10 for him as one mourns for an **only** c, 3495
Mt 1:18 she was found *to be* **with** c through the Holy Spirit. *1143+1877+2400*
1:23 "The virgin *will be* **with** c and will give birth to a son, *1143+1877+2400*
2: 8 "Go and make a careful search for the c. *4086*
2: 9 over the place where the c was. *4086*
2:11 they saw the c with his mother Mary, *4086*
2:13 the c and his mother and escape to Egypt. *4086*
2:13 for Herod is going to search for the c *4086*
2:14 took the c and his mother during the night *4086*
2:20 take the c and his mother and go to the land *4086*
2:21 the c and his mother and went to the land *4086*
10:21 and a father his c; *5451*
18: 2 He called a **little** c and had him stand *4086*
18: 4 like this c is the greatest in the kingdom *4086*
18: 5 "And whoever welcomes a **little** c *4086*
Mk 5:39 The c is not dead but asleep." *4086*
5:40 and went in where the c was. *4086*
7:30 She went home and found her c lying on *4086*
9:36 He took a **little** c and had him stand *4086*
10:15 of God like a **little** c will never enter it." *4086*
12:21 but he also died, leaving no c. *5065*
13:12 and a father his c. *5451*
Lk 1:31 *You will be* **with** c and give birth to a son, *1143+1877+5197*
1:36 to have a c in her old age, *5626*
1:42 blessed is the c you will **bear!** *2843+3120+3836*
1:59 to circumcise the c, *4086*
1:62 like to name **the** c. *899[S]*
1:66 asking, "What then is this c going to be?" *4086*
1:76 my c, will be called a prophet of *4086*
1:80 the c grew and became strong in spirit; *4086*
2: 5 be married to him and was **expecting a** c. *1607*
2:17 what had been told them about this c, *4086*
2:27 the c Jesus to do for him what the custom *4086*
2:34 "This c is destined to cause the falling *NIG*
2:38 about **the** c to all who were looking forward *899[S]*
2:40 And the c grew and became strong; *4086*
8:54 he took her by the hand and said, "My c, *4090*
9:38 for he is my **only** *c.* *3666*
9:47 a **little** c and had him stand beside him. *4086*
9:48 "Whoever welcomes this **little** c *4086*
18:17 of God like a **little** c will never enter it." *4086*
Jn 4:49 "Sir, come down before my c dies." *4086*
7:22 you circumcise a c on the Sabbath. *476*
7:23 if a c can be circumcised on the Sabbath so *476*
16:21 A woman **giving birth to a** c has pain *5503*
16:21 of her joy that a c is born into the world. *476*
Ac 7: 5 though at that time Abraham had no c. *5451*
7:20 and he was no ordinary c. *NIG*
13:10 a c of the devil and an enemy of everything *5626*
26: 4 the way I have lived ever since I was a c, *3744*
1Co 13:11 When I was a c, I talked like a child, *3758*
13:11 When I was a child, I talked like a c, *3758*
13:11 I thought like a c, I reasoned like a child. *3758*
13:11 I thought like a child, I reasoned like a c. *3758*
Gal 4: 1 that as long as the heir is a c, *3758*
Heb 11:23 because they saw he was no ordinary c, *4086*
1Jn 3:10 not do what is right is not a c of God, *NIG*
5: 1 the father loves his c as well. *1164*
Rev 12: 4 so that he might devour her c *5451*
12: 5 She gave birth to a son, a male c, *NIG*
12: 5 And her c was snatched up to God and *5451*
12:13 who had given birth to the male c. *NIG*

CHILD'S (6) [CHILD]

2Ki 4:30 But the c mother said, 5853
Job 33:25 then his flesh is renewed like a c; 5854
Mt 2:20 to take the c life are dead." *4086*
Mk 5:40 he took the c father and mother and *4086*
Lk 2:33 The c father and mother marveled *899[S]*
8:51 and the c father and mother. *4090*

CHILDBEARING (3) [BEAR]

Ge 3:16 "I will greatly increase your pains in c; 2228
18:11 Sarah was past the **age of** c. 784+851+2021+3869
1Ti 2:15 But women will be saved through c— *5450*

CHILDBIRTH (6) [BEAR]

Ge 35:17 And as she was having great difficulty in c, 3528
Ex 1:16 **help** the Hebrew women **in** c 3528
Isa 42:14 like a *woman* **in** c, I cry out, I gasp and pant. 3528
Hos 13:13 Pains as of a *woman* **in** c come to him, 3528
Ro 8:22 groaning as **in the pains of** c *5349*
Gal 4:19 for whom I am again **in the pains of** c *6048*

CHILDHOOD (4) [CHILD]

Ge 8:21 every inclination of his heart is evil from c. 5830
Isa 47:12 which you have labored at since c. 5830
47:15 with and trafficked with since c. 5830
Mk 9:21 "From c," he answered. *4085*

CHILDISH (1) [CHILD]

1Co 13:11 I became a man, I put c *ways* behind me. *3758+3836*

CHILDLESS (16) [CHILD]

Ge 15: 2 what can you give me since I remain c and 6884
Lev 20:20 they will die c. 6884
20:21 They will be c. 6884
Dt 7:14 none of your men or *women* will be c, 6829
32:25 In the street the sword *will* **make** them c; 8897
Jdg 13: 2 wife who was sterile and **remained** c. 3528+4202
13: 3 "You are sterile and c, 3528+4202
1Sa 15:33 "As your sword *has* **made** women c, 8897
15:33 so *will* your mother *be* c among women." 8897
Job 24:21 They prey on the barren and c *woman,* 3528+4202
Jer 18:21 Let their wives be made c and widows; 8891
22:30 "Record this man as if c, 6884
Eze 5:17 and *they will* **leave** you c. 8897
14:15 through that country and *they* **leave** it c 8897
36:14 or **make** your nation c, 8897
Lk 20:29 The first one married a woman and died c. *866*

CHILDREN (435) [CHILD]

Ge 3:16 with pain you will give birth to c. 1201
6: 4 to the daughters of men and **had** c by them. 3528
11:30 Now Sarai was barren; she had no c. 2263
15: 3 Abram said, "You have given me no c; 2446
16: 1 Sarai, Abram's wife, *had* **borne** him no c. 3528
16: 2 "The LORD has kept me from **having** c. 3528
18:19 that he will direct his c and his household 1201
20:17 so *they could* **have** c again, 3528
21: 7 to Abraham that Sarah would nurse c? 1201
21:23 with me or my c or my descendants. 5769
29:35 Then she stopped **having** c. 3528
30: 1 that *she was* not **bearing** Jacob any c, 3528
30: 1 she said to Jacob, "Give me c, or I'll die!" 1201
30: 2 who has kept you from *having* c?" 1061+7262
30: 3 Sleep with her so that *she can* **bear** c for me 3528
30: 9 Leah saw that she had stopped **having** c, 3528
30:26 Give me my wives and c, 3529
31:16 from our father belongs to us and our c. 1201
31:17 Jacob put his c and his wives on camels, 1201
31:43 the c are my children, 1201
31:43 the children are my c, 1201
31:43 or about the c they have borne? 1201
32:11 and also the mothers with their c. 1201
33: 1 so he divided the c among Leah, 3529
33: 2 the maidservants and their c in front, 3529
33: 2 Leah and her c next, 3529
33: 5 Esau looked up and saw the women and c. 3529
33: 5 c God has graciously given your servant." 3529
33: 6 and their c approached and bowed down. 3529
33: 7 Leah and her c came and bowed down. 3529
33:13 that the c are tender and that I must care for 3529
33:14 of the droves before me and that of the c, 3529
34:29 and all their women and c, 3251
36:25 The c *of* Anah: 1201
42:36 **deprived** me of my c. 8897
43: 8 we and you and our c may live and not die. 3251
45:10 you, your c and grandchildren, 1201
45:19 Take some carts from Egypt for your c 3251
46: 5 and their c and their wives in the carts 3251
46:18 These were the c born to Jacob *by* Zilpah, 1201
47:12 according to the number of their c. 3251
47:24 and your households and your c." 3251
48: 6 Any c born to you after them will be yours; 4580
48:11 God has allowed me to see your c too." 2446
50: 8 Only their c and their flocks 3251
50:21 I will provide for you and your c." 3251
50:23 saw the third generation of Ephraim's c. 1201
50:23 Also the c *of* Makir son of Manasseh 1201
Ex 10: 2 that you may tell your c and grandchildren 1201
10:10 I let you go, along with your **women and** c! 3251
10:24 Even your **women and** c may go with you; 3251
12:26 And when your c ask you, 1201
12:37 besides **women and** c. 3251
17: 3 to make us and our c and livestock die 1201
20: 5 punishing the c for the sin of the fathers to 1201
21: 4 and her c shall belong to her master, 3529
21: 5 'I love my master and my wife and c 1201
22:24 and your c fatherless. 1201
34: 7 he punishes the c and their children for 1201
34: 7 he punishes the children and their c for 1201
Lev 10:14 they have been given to you and your c 1201
10:15 be the regular share for you and your c, 1201
18:21 not give any of your c to be sacrificed 2446
20: 2 of his c to Molech must be put to death. 2446
20: 3 for by giving his c to Molech, 2446
20: 4 when that man gives one of his c to Molech 2446
22:13 yet has no c, 2446
25:41 Then he and his c are to be released, 1201
25:46 to your c as inherited property 1201
25:54 he and his c are to be released in the Year 1201
26:22 **rob** you **of** your c, 8897
Nu 5:28 and *will* **be able to have** c. 2445+2446
14: 3 Our wives and c will be taken as plunder. 3251
14:18 he punishes the c for the sin of the fathers 1201
14:31 As for your c that you said would be taken 3251
14:33 Your c will be shepherds here 1201
16:27 c and little ones at the entrances 1201
31: 9 the Midianite women and c and took all 3251
32:16 and cities for our **women and** c. 3251
32:17 Meanwhile our **women and** c will live 3251
32:24 Build cities for your **women and** c, 3251
32:26 Our c and wives, 3251
Dt 1:39 your c who do not yet know good 1201
2:34 men, women and c. 3251
3: 6 men, women and c. 3251
3:19 However, your wives, your c 3251
4: 9 Teach them to your c and to their children 1201
4: 9 Teach them to your children and to their c 1201
4:10 in the land and may teach them to their c." 1201
4:25 After you have had c and grandchildren 1201
4:40 so that it may go well with you and your c 1201
5: 9 punishing the c for the sin of the fathers to 1201
5:29 with them and their c forever! 1201
6: 2 your c and their children 1201
6: 2 and their c after them may fear 1201
6: 7 Impress them on your c. 1201

Dt	11: 2	that your c were not the ones who saw	1201
	11: 5	not your c who saw what he did for you in	NIH
	11:19	Teach them to your c,	1201
	11:21	the days of your c may be many in the land	1201
	12:25	so that it may go well with you and your c	1201
	12:28	with you and your c after you,	1201
	14: 1	You are the c of the LORD your God.	1201
	20:14	As for the women, the c,	3251
	23: 8	of c born to them may enter the assembly	1201
	24:16	Fathers shall not be put to death for their c,	1201
	24:16	nor c put to death for their fathers;	1201
	28:54	or the wife he loves or his surviving c,	1201
	28:55	to one of them any of the flesh of his c	1201
	28:57	from her womb and the c she bears.	1201
	29:11	together with your c and your wives,	3251
	29:22	Your c who follow you in later generations	1201
	29:29	to us and to our c forever,	1201
	30: 2	and your c return to the LORD your God	1201
	30:19	so that you and your c may live	2446
	31:12	Assemble the people—men, women and c,	3251
	31:13	Their c, who do not know this law,	1201
	32: 5	to their shame they are no longer his c,	1201
	32:20	a perverse generation, c who are unfaithful.	1201
	32:46	so that you may command your c	1201
	33: 9	or acknowledge his own c,	1201
Jos	1:14	your c and your livestock may stay in	3251
	4: 6	In the future, when your c ask you,	1201
	8:35	including the women and c,	3251
	14: 9	and that of your c forever,	1201
Jdg	18:21	Putting their **little** c,	3251
	21:10	including the women and c.	3251
1Sa	1: 2	Peninnah had c, but Hannah had none.	3529
	2: 5	She who was barren *has* **borne** seven c,	3528
	2:20	the LORD give you c by this woman	2446
	15: 3	put to death men and women, c and infants,	6407
	22:19	with its men and women, its c and infants,	6407
	30:22	each man may take his wife and c and go."	1201
2Sa	5:14	the names of the c **born** to him there:	3533
	6:23	And Michal daughter of Saul had no c to	3529
	12: 3	and it grew up with him and his c.	1201
1Ki	11:20	with Pharaoh's own c.	1201
	20: 3	the best of your wives and c are mine.' "	1201
	20: 5	your wives and your c.	1201
	20: 7	When he sent for my wives and my c,	1201
2Ki	8:12	dash their **little** c to the ground,	6407
	10: 1	**guardians of** Ahab's c.	587
	14: 6	be put to death for their c, nor children put	1201
	14: 6	nor c put to death for their fathers;	1201
	17:31	the Sepharvites burned their c in the fire	1201
	17:41	To this day their c and grandchildren	1201
	19: 3	and disgrace, as when c come to the point	1201
1Ch	2:18	of Hezron **had** c by his wife Azubah (and	3528
	2:30	Seled died without c.	1201
	2:32	Jether died without c.	1201
	3: 5	and these were *the c* **born** to him there:	AIT
	4:18	the c *of* Pharaoh's daughter Bithiah,	1201
	4:27	but his brothers did not have many c;	1201
	6: 3	The c *of* Amram:	1201
	7: 4	for they had many wives and c.	1201
	14: 4	the names of the c **born** to him there:	3528
2Ch	20:13	with their wives and c and little ones,	1201
	25: 4	be put to death for their c, nor children put	1201
	25: 4	nor c put to death for their fathers;	1201
	30: 9	and your c will be shown compassion	1201
Ezr	8:21	for a safe journey for us and our c,	3251
	9:12	to your c as an everlasting inheritance.'	1201
	10: 1	men, women and c—gathered around him.	3529
	10: 3	to send away all these women and their c,	3528
	10:44	and some of them had c by these wives.	1201
Ne	12:43	The women and c also rejoiced.	3529
	13:24	of their c spoke the language of Ashdod or	1201
Est	3:13	young and old, women and **little** c—	3251
	8:11	and their women and c;	3251
Job	1: 5	"Perhaps my c have sinned and cursed God	1201
	5: 4	His c are far from safety,	1201
	5:25	You will know that your c will be many,	2446
	8: 4	When your c sinned against him,	1201
	17: 5	the eyes of his c will fail.	1201
	20:10	His c must make amends to the poor;	1201
	21: 8	They see their c established around them,	2446
	21:11	They send forth their c as a flock;	6396
	24: 5	the wasteland provides food for their c.	5853
	27:14	many his c, their fate is the sword;	1201
	29: 5	with me and my c were around me,	5853
	42:16	he saw his c and their children to	1201
	42:16	and their c to the fourth generation.	1201
Ps	8: 2	of c and infants you have ordained praise	6407
	17:14	and they store up wealth for their c.	6407
	34:11	Come, my c, listen to me;	1201
	37:25	or their c begging bread.	2446
	37:26	their c will be blessed.	2446
	69:36	the c *of* his servants will inherit it,	2446
	72: 4	the people and save the c *of* the needy;	1201
	73:15	I would have betrayed your c.	1201+1887
	78: 4	We will not hide them from their c;	1201
	78: 5	to teach their c,	1201
	78: 6	even the c yet to be born,	1201
	78: 6	and they in turn would tell their c.	1201
	90:16	your splendor to their c.	1201
	102:28	The c *of* your servants will live	1201
	103:13	As a father has compassion on his c,	1201
	103:17	his righteousness with their children's c—	1201
	109: 9	May his c be fatherless and his wife	1201
	109:10	May his c be wandering beggars;	1201
	109:12	to him or take pity on his **fatherless** c.	3846
	112: 2	His c will be mighty in the land;	2446
	113: 9	in her home as a happy mother of c.	1201
Ps	115:14	both you and your c.	1201
	127: 3	c a reward from him.	1061+2021+7262
	128: 6	and may you live to see your children's c.	1201
	148:12	young men and maidens, old men and c.	5853
Pr	13:22	an inheritance for his children's c,	1201
	14:26	and for his c it will be a refuge.	1201
	17: 6	Children's c are a crown to the aged,	1201
	17: 6	and parents are the pride of their c.	1201
	20: 7	blessed are his c after him.	1201
	31:28	Her c arise and call her blessed;	1201
Ecc	6: 3	A man *may* **have** a hundred c	3528
Isa	1: 2	"I reared c and brought them up,	1201
	1: 4	a brood of evildoers, c given to corruption!	1201
	3: 4	**mere** c will govern them.	9500
	8:18	and the c the LORD has given me.	3529
	13:18	nor will they look with compassion on c.	1201
	28: 9	To *c* **weaned** from their milk,	AIT
	29:23	When they see among them their c,	3529
	30: 1	"Woe to the obstinate c,"	1201
	30: 9	These are rebellious people, deceitful c,	1201
	30: 9	c unwilling to listen to	1201
	37: 3	and disgrace, as when c come to the point	1201
	38:19	fathers tell their c about your faithfulness.	1201
	43: 5	I will bring your c from the east	2446
	45:11	do you question me about my c,	1201
	47: 8	be a widow or suffer the **loss of** c.'	8890
	47: 9	**loss of** c and widowhood.	8890
	48:19	your c like its numberless grains;	5055+7368
	49:20	The c *born during* your bereavement will	1201
	49:25	and your c I will save.	1201
	54: 1	the c *of* the desolate woman than	1201
	57: 5	you sacrifice your c in the ravines and	3529
	59:21	or from the mouths of your c,	2446
	65:23	They will not toil in vain or **bear** c doomed	3528
	66: 8	in labor than she gives birth to her c.	1201
Jer	2: 9	against your children's c.	1201
	4:22	They are senseless c;	1201
	5: 7	Your c have forsaken me and sworn	1201
	6:11	"Pour it out on the c in the street and on	6408
	7:18	The c gather wood,	1201
	9:21	the c from the streets and the young men	6408
	17: 2	Even their c remember their altars	1201
	18:21	So give their c over to famine;	1201
	22:28	Why will he and his c be hurled out,	2446
	30: 6	Ask and see: *Can* a man **bear** c?	3528
	30:20	Their c will be as in days of old,	1201
	31:15	Rachel weeping for her c and refusing to	1201
	31:15	because her c are no more."	1201
	31:17	"Your c will return to their own land.	1201
	32:18	for the fathers' sins into the laps of their c	1201
	32:39	for their own good and the good of their c	1201
	36:31	and his c and his attendants	2446
	38:23	"All your wives and c will be brought out	1201
	40: 7	and c who were the poorest in the land	3251
	41:16	c and court officials he had brought	3251
	43: 6	led away all the men, women and c and	3251
	44: 7	the men and women, the c and infants,	6407
	47: 3	Fathers will not turn to help their c;	1201
	49:10	His c, relatives and neighbors will perish,	2446
La	1: 5	Her c have gone into exile,	6408
	1:16	My c are destitute because	1201
	2:11	c and infants faint in the streets of the city.	6407
	2:19	to him for the lives of your c,	6408
	2:20	the c they have cared for?	6407
	3:33	or grief to the c *of* men.	1201
	4: 4	c beg for bread, but no one gives it to them.	6408
	4:10	With their own hands compassionate women have cooked their own c,	3529
Eze	5:10	in your midst fathers will eat their c,	1201
	5:10	and c will eat their fathers.	1201
	9: 6	young men and maidens, women and c,	3251
	16:21	You slaughtered my c and sacrificed them	1201
	16:45	who despised her husband and her c;	1201
	16:45	who despised their husbands and their c.	1201
	20:18	I said to their c in the desert,	1201
	20:21	" 'But the c rebelled against me:	1201
	23:37	they even sacrificed their c,	1201
	23:39	On the very day they sacrificed their c	1201
	36:12	**deprive** them **of** their c.	8897
	36:13	**deprive** your nation **of** *its* c,"	8897
	37:25	They and their c	1201
	37:25	their children's c will live there forever,	1201
	47:22	among you and who have c.	1201
Da	6:24	along with their wives and c.	10120
Hos	1: 2	an adulterous wife and c *of* unfaithfulness,	3529
	2: 4	I will not show my love to her c,	1201
	2: 4	because they are the c *of* adultery.	1201
	4: 6	I also will ignore your c.	1201
	5: 7	they give birth to illegitimate c.	1201
	9:12	Even if they rear c,	1201
	9:13	But Ephraim will bring out their c to	1201
	9:16	Even if *they* **bear** c,	3528
	10:14	to the ground with their c.	1201
	11:10	his c will come trembling from the west.	1201
Joel	1: 3	Tell it to your c,	1201
	1: 3	and let your c tell it to their children,	1201
	1: 3	and let your children tell it to their c,	1201
	1: 3	and their c to the next generation.	1201
	2:16	bring together the elders, gather the c,	6408
Mic	1:16	in mourning for the c *in whom* you delight;	1201
	2: 9	from their c forever.	6408
Zec	10: 7	Their c will see it and be joyful;	1201
	10: 9	They and their c will survive,	1201
Mal	4: 6	of the fathers to their c, and the hearts of	1201
	4: 6	and the hearts of the c to their fathers;	1201
Mt	2:18	Rachel weeping for her c and refusing to	*5451*
	3: 9	that out of these stones God can raise up c	*5451*
Mt	7:11	know how to give good gifts *to* your c,	*5451*
	10:21	c will rebel against their parents	*5451*
	11:16	They are like c sitting in the marketplaces	*4086*
	11:25	and revealed them *to* **little** c.	*3758*
	14:21	besides women and c.	*4086*
	15:38	besides women and c.	*4086*
	18: 3	you change and become like **little** c,	*4086*
	18:25	and his wife and his c and all that he had	*5451*
	19:13	Then **little** c were brought to Jesus	*4086*
	19:14	Jesus said, "Let the **little** c come to me,	*4086*
	19:29	or sisters or father or mother or c or fields	*5451*
	21:15	and the c shouting in the temple area,	*4090*
	21:16	"Do you hear what these c are saying?"	*NIG*
	21:16	" 'From the lips *of* c and infants	*3758*
	22:24	that if a man dies without having c,	*5451*
	22:24	the widow and **have** c for him.	*482+5065*
	22:25	and since he had no c,	*5065*
	23:37	to gather your c together,	*5451*
	27:25	"Let his blood be on us and on our c!"	*5451*
Mk	7:27	"First let the c eat all they want,"	*5451*
	9:37	"Whoever welcomes one *of* these **little** c	*4086*
	10:13	People were bringing **little** c to Jesus	*4086*
	10:14	"Let the **little** c come to me,	*4086*
	10:16	And he took **the** c in his arms,	*899S*
	10:24	But Jesus said again, "C,	*5451*
	10:29	or mother or father or c or fields for me and	*5451*
	10:30	brothers, sisters, mothers, c and fields—	*5451*
	12:19	and leaves a wife but no c,	*5451*
	12:19	must marry the widow and **have** c	*1985+5065*
	12:20	and died without leaving any c.	*5065*
	12:22	In fact, none of the seven left any c.	*5065*
	13:12	C will rebel against their parents	*5451*
Lk	1: 7	But they had no c,	*5451*
	1:17	of the fathers to their c and the disobedient	*5451*
	3: 8	that out of these stones God can raise up c	*5451*
	7:32	They are like c sitting in the marketplace	*4086*
	7:35	But wisdom is proved right by all her c."	*5451*
	10:21	and revealed them *to* **little** c.	*3758*
	11: 7	and my c are with me in bed.	*4086*
	11:13	know how to give good gifts *to* your c,	*5451*
	13:34	to gather your c together,	*5451*
	14:26	his wife and c, his brothers and sisters—	*5451*
	18:16	But Jesus called **the** c to him and said,	*899S*
	18:16	"Let the **little** c come to me,	*4086*
	18:29	or parents or c for the sake of the kingdom	*5451*
	19:44	you and the c within your walls.	*5451*
	20:28	and leaves a wife but **no** c,	*866*
	20:28	must marry the widow and **have** c	*1985+5065*
	20:31	the same way the seven died, leaving no c.	*5451*
	20:36	They are God's c,	*5626*
	20:36	since they are c of the resurrection.	*5626*
	23:28	weep for yourselves and for your c.	*5451*
Jn	1:12	he gave the right to become c of God—	*5451*
	1:13	c born not of natural descent,	*4005S*
	8:39	"If you were Abraham's c," said Jesus,	*5451*
	8:41	"We *are* not **illegitimate** c,"	*1164+1666+4518*
	11:52	for that nation but also for the scattered c	*5451*
	13:33	"My c, I will be with you only	*5448*
Ac	2:39	and your c and for all who are far off—	*5451*
	13:26	"Brothers, c of Abraham,	*1169+5626*
	13:33	their c, by raising up Jesus.	*5451*
	21: 5	and their wives and c accompanied us out	*5451*
	21:21	not to circumcise their c or live according	*5451*
Ro	8:16	with our spirit that we are God's c.	*5451*
	8:17	Now if we are c, then we are heirs—	*5451*
	8:21	into the glorious freedom *of* the c of God.	*5451*
	9: 7	Nor because they are his descendants are they all Abraham's c.	*5451*
	9: 8	not the natural c who are God's children,	*5451*
	9: 8	not the natural children who are God's c,	*5451*
	9: 8	the c of the promise who are regarded	*5451*
	9:10	Rebekah's c had one and the same father,	*NIG*
1Co	4:14	but to warn you, as my dear c.	*5451*
	7:14	Otherwise your c would be unclean,	*5451*
	14:20	Brothers, stop thinking *like* c.	*4086*
2Co	6:13	As a fair exchange—I speak as *to* my c—	*5451*
	12:14	c should not have to save up	*5451*
	12:14	but parents *for* their c.	*5451*
Gal	3: 7	that those who believe are c of Abraham.	*5626*
	4: 3	So also, when we were c,	*3758*
	4:19	My **dear** c, for whom I am again in	*5451*
	4:24	from Mount Sinai and **bears** c who are to	*1164*
	4:25	because she is in slavery with her c.	*5451*
	4:27	O barren woman, who **bears** no c;	*5503*
	4:27	the c of the desolate woman than	*5451*
	4:28	you, brothers, like Isaac, are c of promise.	*5451*
	4:31	brothers, we are not c of the slave woman,	*5451*
Eph	5: 1	Be imitators of God, therefore, as dearly loved c	*5451*
	5: 8	Live as c of light	*5451*
	6: 1	C, obey your parents in the Lord,	*5451*
	6: 4	Fathers, do not exasperate your c;	*5451*
Php	2:15	c of God without fault in a crooked	*5451*
Col	3:20	C, obey your parents in everything,	*5451*
	3:21	Fathers, do not embitter your c,	*5451*
1Th	2: 7	like a mother caring for her little c.	*5451*
	2:11	of you as a father deals with his own c,	*5451*
1Ti	3: 4	that his c obey him with proper respect.	*5451*
	3:12	of but one wife and must manage his c	*5451*
	5: 4	But if a widow has c or grandchildren,	*5451*
	5:10	such as **bringing up** c, showing hospitality,	*5452*
	5:14	to marry, *to* **have** c, to manage their homes	*5449*
Tit	1: 6	a man whose c believe and are not open to	*5451*
	2: 4	to love their husbands and c,	*5817*
Heb	2:13	"Here am I, and the c God has given me."	*4086*
	2:14	Since the c have flesh and blood,	*4086*
	12: 8	you are **illegitimate** c and not true sons.	*3785*

1Pe 1:14 As obedient c, do not conform to the evil 5451
1Jn 2: 1 My dear c, I write this to you so 5448
2:12 I write to you, dear c, 5448
2:13 I write to you, dear c, 4086
2:18 Dear c, this is the last hour; 4086
2:28 And now, dear c, continue in him, 5448
3: 1 that we should be called c of God! 5451
3: 2 Dear friends, now we are c of God, 5451
3: 7 Dear c, do not let anyone lead you astray. 5448
3:10 This is how we know who the c of God are 5451
3:10 of God are and who the c of the devil are: 5451
3:18 Dear c, let us not love with words 5448
4: 4 You, dear c, are from God 5448
5: 2 how we know that we love the c of God: 5451
5:19 We know that we are c of God, NIG
5:21 Dear c, keep yourselves from idols. 5448
2Jn 1: 1 The elder, To the chosen lady and her c, 5451
1: 4 to find some of your c walking in the truth, 5451
1:13 c of your chosen sister send their greetings. 5451
3Jn 1: 4 to hear that my c are walking in the truth. 5451
Rev 2:23 I will strike her c dead. 5451

CHILDREN'S (13) [CHILD]
Ps 103:17 his righteousness with their c children— 1201
128: 6 may you live to see your c children. 1201+4200
Pr 13:22 an inheritance for his c children, 1201
17: 6 C children are a crown to the aged, 1201
Isa 54:13 and great will be your c peace. 1201
Jer 2: 9 I will bring charges against your c children. 1201
31:29 and the c teeth are set on edge.' 1201
Eze 16:36 and because you gave them your c blood, 1201
18: 2 and the c teeth are set on edge'? 1201
37:25 and their c children will live there forever, 1201
Mt 15:26 not right to take the c bread and toss it 5451
Mk 7:27 not right to take the c bread and toss it 5451
7:28 the dogs under the table eat the c crumbs." 4086

CHILEAB (KJV) See KILEAB

CHILION (KJV) See KILION

CHILMAD (KJV) See KILMAD

CHIMHAM (KJV) See KIMHAM

CHIMNEY (KJV) See WINDOW

CHIN (2)
Lev 13:29 a sore on the head or on the c, 2417
13:30 an infectious disease of the head or c. 2417

CHINNERETH, CHINNEROTH (KJV) See KINNERETH

CHIOS (KJV) See KIOS

CHIRP (1)
Isa 10:14 or opened its mouth to c.' " 7627

CHISEL (4) [CHISELED, CHISELING, CHISELS]
Ex 34: 1 "C out two stone tablets like the first ones, 7180
Dt 10: 1 "C out two stone tablets like the first ones 7180
1Ki 6: 7 c or any other iron tool was heard at 1749
Jer 10: 3 and a craftsman shapes it with his c. 5108

CHISELED (2) [CHISEL]
Ex 34: 4 So Moses c out two stone tablets like 7180
Dt 10: 3 of acacia wood and c out two stone tablets 7180

CHISELING (1) [CHISEL]
Isa 22:16 on the height and c your resting place in 2980

CHISELS (1) [CHISEL]
Isa 44:13 with c and marks it with compasses. 5244

CHISLEU (KJV) See KISLEV

CHISLON (KJV) See KISLON

CHISLOTH-TABOR (KJV) See KISLOTH TABOR

CHITTIM (KJV) See KITTIM

CHIUN (KJV) See PEDESTAL

CHLOE'S (1)
1Co 1:11 some from C household have informed me 5951

CHOICE (34) [CHOOSE]
Ge 18: 7 Then he ran to the herd and selected a c, 3202
27: 9 the flock and bring me two c young goats, 3202
Lev 23:40 On the first day you are to take c fruit from 2077
Dt 12:11 and all the c possessions you have vowed to 4436
32:14 with c rams of Bashan and 1201
1Sa 2:29 on the c parts of every offering made 8040
1Ki 4:23 gazelles, roebucks and c fowl. 80
1Ch 7:40 heads of families, c men, 1405
21:11 "This is what the LORD says: 'Take your c: 7691
Ne 5:18 Each day one ox, six c sheep 1405
8:10 "Go and enjoy c food and sweet drinks, 5460
Job 36:16 of your table laden with c food. 2016
Pr 8:10 knowledge rather than c gold, 1047
8:19 what I yield surpasses c silver. 1047
10:20 The tongue of the righteous is c silver, 1047
18: 8 The words of a gossip are like c morsels; 4269
21:20 In the house of the wise are stores of c food 2773
26:22 The words of a gossip are like c morsels; 4269
SS 4:13 an orchard of pomegranates with c fruits, 4458
4:16 into his garden and taste its c fruits. 4458
5:15 c as its cedars. 1047
Isa 1:22 your c wine is diluted with water. 6011
Jer 2:21 like a c vine of sound and reliable stock. 8603
Eze 20:40 and your c gifts, 8040
24: 4 all the c pieces—the leg and the shoulder. 3202
34: 3 with the wool and slaughter the c animals, 1374
Da 1:16 So the guard took away their c food and 7329
10: 3 I ate no c food; 2776
Am 5:22 Though you bring c fellowship offerings, 5309
6: 4 You dine on c lambs and fattened calves. 4119+4946+7366
Zec 11:16 but will eat the meat of the c sheep, 1374
Jn 2:10 the c wine first and then the cheaper wine 2819
Ac 15: 7 you know that some time ago God made a c 1721
Ro 8:20 not by its own c, but by the will of the one 1776

CHOICEST (12) [CHOOSE]
Ge 23: 6 Bury your dead in the c of our tombs. 4436
49:11 his colt to the c branch; 8605
Dt 33:15 with the c gifts of the ancient mountains 8031
2Ki 19:23 the c of its pines. 4435
Job 22:25 the c silver for you. 9361
33:20 and his soul loathes the c meal. 9294
Isa 5: 2 of stones and planted it with the c vines. 8603
16: 8 down the c vines, 8602
22: 7 Your c valleys are full of chariots, 4436
37:24 the c of its pines. 4436
Eze 31:16 the c and best of Lebanon, 4436
Hab 1:16 in luxury and enjoys the c food. 1374

CHOIR (1) [CHOIRS]
Ne 12:38 The second c proceeded in 9343

CHOIRS (4) [CHOIR]
1Ch 15:27 who was in charge of the singing of the c. 8876
Ne 12:31 I also assigned two large c to give thanks. 9343
12:40 The two c that gave thanks 9343
12:42 The c sang under the direction of Jezrahiah. 8876

CHOKE (3) [CHOKED]
Mt 13:22 and the deceitfulness of wealth c it, 5231
18:28 He grabbed him and began to c him. 4464
Mk 4:19 the desires for other things come in and c 5231

CHOKED (4) [CHOKE]
Mt 13: 7 which grew up and c the plants. 4464
Mk 4: 7 which grew up and c the plants, 5231
Lk 8: 7 which grew up with it and c the plants. 678
8:14 on their way they are c by life's worries, 5231

CHOLER (KJV) See FURIOUSLY, RAGE

CHOOSE (66) [CHOICE, CHOICEST, CHOOSES, CHOOSING, CHOSE, CHOSEN]
Ex 12: 5 The animals you c must be year-old males 4200
17: 9 "C some of our men and go out to fight 1047
34:16 c some of their daughters as wives 4374
Nu 14: 4 "We should c a leader and go back 5989
17: 5 to the man I c will sprout, 1047
Dt 1:13 C some wise, understanding 2035
7: 7 not set his affection on you and c you 1047
12: 5 the place the LORD your God will c 1047
12:11 the LORD your God will c as a dwelling 1047
12:14 the LORD will c in one of your tribes, 1047
12:18 at the place the LORD your God will c— 1047
12:26 and go to the place the LORD will c. 1047
14:23 the LORD your God at the place he will c 1047
14:24 the LORD will c to put his Name is 1047
14:25 to the place the LORD your God will c. 1047
15:20 at the place he will c. 1047
16: 2 the place the LORD will c as a dwelling 1047
16: 6 except in the place he will c as a dwelling 1047
16: 7 at the place the LORD your God will c. 1047
16:11 at the place he will c as a dwelling 1047
16:15 at the place the LORD will c. 1047
16:16 at the place he will c: 1047
17: 8 to the place the LORD your God will c. 1047
17:10 at the place the LORD will c. 1047
18: 6 to the place the LORD will c, 1047
26: 2 the LORD your God will c as a dwelling 1047
30:19 Now c life, so that you and your children 1047
31:11 at the place he will c, 1047
Jos 3:12 then, c twelve men from the tribes of Israel, 4374
Jos 4: 2 "C twelve men from among the people, 4374
9:27 at the place the LORD would c. 1047
24:15 if serving the LORD seems undesirable to you, then c for yourselves this day whom 1047
1Sa 17: 8 C a man and have him come down to me. 1405
2Sa 17: 1 "I would c twelve thousand men 1047
24:12 C one of them for me to carry out 1047
1Ki 18:23 Let them c one for themselves, 1047
18:25 "C one of the bulls and prepare it first, 1047
2Ki 10: 3 c the best and most worthy 8011
18:32 C life and not death! 2649
1Ch 21:10 C one of them for me to carry out 1047
Ps 65: 4 Blessed are those you c and bring near 1047
75: 2 You say, "I c the appointed time; 4374
78:67 he did not c the tribe of Ephraim; 1047
Pr 1:29 Since they hated knowledge and did not c 1047
3:31 Do not envy a violent man or c any 1047
8:10 C my instruction instead of silver, 4374
16:16 to c understanding rather than silver! 1047+7864
Isa 7:15 to reject the wrong and c the right. 1047
7:16 to reject the wrong and c the right, 1047
14: 1 once again he will c Israel 1047
56: 4 who c what pleases me and hold fast 1047
66: 4 so I also will c harsh treatment for them 1047
Jer 3:14 I will c you—one from a town 4374
33:26 and will not c one of his sons to rule over 4374
Eze 33: 2 the people of the land c one of their men 4374
Hos 8: 4 they c princes without my approval. 8606
Zec 1:17 and the LORD will again comfort Zion and c Jerusalem.' " 1047
2:12 the holy land and will again c Jerusalem. 1047
Jn 15:16 You did not c me, but I chose you 1721
Ac 1:21 to c one of the men who have been with us NIG
6: 3 c seven men from among you 2170
15:22 to c some of their own men and send them 1721
15:25 to c some men and send them to you 1721
2Co 12: 6 Even if I should c to boast, 2527
Php 1:22 Yet what shall I c? 145
1Pe 4: 3 in the past doing what pagans c to do— 1088

CHOOSES (13) [CHOOSE]
Lev 16: 2 not to come whenever he c into NIH
Nu 16: 5 The man he c he will cause to come 1047
16: 7 the LORD c will be the one who is holy. 1047
Dt 12:21 If the place where the LORD your God c 1047
17:15 over you the king the LORD your God c. 1047
23:16 and in whatever town he c. 1047
2Sa 15:15 to do whatever our lord the king c." 1047
Ps 68:16 at the mountain where God c to reign, 2773
Isa 41:24 he who c you is detestable. 1047
Mt 11:27 and those to whom the Son c to reveal him. 1089
Lk 10:22 the Son and those to whom the Son c 1089
Jn 7:17 If anyone c to do God's will, 2527
Jas 4: 4 Anyone who c to be a friend of the world 1089

CHOOSING (2) [CHOOSE]
1Ki 12:33 a month of his own c, 968
Ro 9:22 What if God, c to show his wrath 2527

CHOP (3) [CHOPPED]
Dt 29:11 in your camps who c your wood 2634
Jer 46:23 They will c down her forest," 4162
Mic 3: 3 who c them up like meat for the pan, 7298

CHOPPED (1) [CHOP]
1Sa 6:14 The people c up the wood of the cart 1324

CHORASHAN (KJV) See BOR ASHAN

CHORAZIN (KJV) See KORAZIN

CHOSE (45) [CHOOSE]
Ge 6: 2 and they married any of them they c. 1047
13:11 So Lot c for himself the whole plain of 1047
47: 2 He c five of his brothers and presented them 4374
Ex 18:25 He c capable men from all Israel 1047
Dt 4:37 and c their descendants after them, 1047
10:15 and he c you, their descendants, 1047
33:21 He c the best land for himself; 8011
Jos 8: 3 He c thirty thousand of his best fighting 1047
Jdg 5: 8 When they c new gods, 1047
1Sa 2:28 I c your father out of all the tribes of Israel 1047
13: 2 Saul c three thousand men from Israel; 1047
17:40 c five smooth stones from the stream, 1047
2Sa 6:21 who c me rather than your father or anyone 1047
1Ki 11:34 the sake of David my servant, whom I c 1047
11:36 the city where I c to put my Name. 1047
2Ki 23:27 and I will reject Jerusalem, the city I c, 1047
1Ch 15: 2 because the LORD c them to carry the ark 1047
28: 4 c me from my whole family to be king 1047
28: 4 He c Judah as leader, 1047
28: 4 from the house of Judah he c my family, NIH
2Ch 24: 3 Jehoiada c two wives for him, 5951
Ne 9: 7 who c Abram and brought him out of Ur of 1047
Job 29:25 I c the way for them and sat as their chief; 1047
Ps 33:12 the people he c for his inheritance. 1047
47: 4 He c our inheritance for us, 1047
78:68 but he c the tribe of Judah, 1047
78:70 He c David his servant and took him from 1047
Isa 65:12 in my sight and c what displeases me." 1047
66: 4 in my sight and c what displeases me." 1047
Jer 33:24 the two kingdoms he c'? 1047

Eze 20: 5 On the day I **c** Israel, 1047
Lk 6:13 he called his disciples to him and **c** twelve *1721*
Jn 5:35 and you **c** for a time to enjoy his light. *2527*
15:16 but I **c** you and appointed you to go *1721*
Ac 6: 5 *They* **c** Stephen, a man full of faith and of *1721*
13:17 God of the people of Israel **c** our fathers; *1721*
15:22 They **c** Judas (called Barsabbas) and Silas, *NIG*
15:40 but Paul **c** Silas and left, *2141*
1Co 1:27 But God **c** the foolish things of the world *1721*
1:27 God **c** the weak things of the world *1721*
1:28 He **c** the lowly things of this world and *1721*
Eph 1: 4 For *he* **c** us in him before the creation of *1721*
2Th 2:13 from the beginning God **c** you to be saved *145*
Heb 11:25 *He* **c** to be mistreated along with the people *145*
Jas 1:18 He **c** to give us birth through the word *1089*

CHOSEN (125) [CHOOSE]

Ge 18:19 For *I have* **c** him, 3359
24:14 the one *you have* **c** for your servant Isaac. 3519
24:44 the LORD *has* **c** for my master's son.' 3519
Ex 31: 2 *I have* **c** Bezalel son of Uri, 928+7924+9005
35:30 "See, the LORD *has* **c** Bezalel 928+7924+9005
Lev 16:10 But the goat **c** *by* lot as the scapegoat shall 6590
Dt 7: 6 The LORD your God *has* **c** you out of all 1047
14: 2 the LORD *has* **c** you to be his treasured 1047
18: 5 for the LORD your God *has* **c** them 1047
21: 5 for the LORD your God *has* **c** them 1047
Jos 24:22 against yourselves that you *have* **c** to serve 1047
Jdg 10:14 Go and cry out to the gods *you have* **c**. 1047
20:15 to seven hundred **c** men from those living 1047
20:16 seven hundred **c** men who were left-handed, 1047
1Sa 8:18 for relief from the king *you have* **c**, 1047
10:20 the tribe of Benjamin **was c.** 4334
10:21 clan by clan, and Matri's clan **was c.** 4334
10:21 Finally Saul son of Kish **was c.** 4334
10:24 "Do you see the man the LORD *has* **c**? 1047
12:13 Now here is the king *you have* **c**, 1047
16: 1 *I have* **c** one of his sons to be king." 8011
16: 8 "The LORD *has* not **c** this one either." 1047
16: 9 "Nor *has* the LORD **c** this one." 1047
16:10 "The LORD *has* not **c** these." 1047
24: 2 So Saul took three thousand **c** men 1047
26: 2 with his three thousand **c** men of Israel, 1047
2Sa 6: 1 brought together out of Israel **c** *men*, 1047
16:18 the one **c** by the LORD, by these people, 1047
21: 6 at Gibeah of Saul—the LORD's **c** *one*." 1040
1Ki 3: 8 among the people *you have* **c**, 1047
8:16 not **c** a city in any tribe of Israel to have 1047
8:16 *I have* **c** David to rule my people Israel.' 1047
8:44 the LORD toward the city *you have* **c** and 1047
8:48 toward the city *you have* **c** and 1047
11:13 Jerusalem, which *I have* **c**." 1047
11:32 which *I have* **c** out of all the tribes 1047
14:21 the LORD *had* **c** out of all the tribes 1047
2Ki 21: 7 which *I have* **c** out of all the tribes 1047
1Ch 9:22 those **c** to be gatekeepers at 1405
16:13 O sons of Jacob, his **c** *ones*. 1040
16:41 the rest of those **c** and designated by name 1405
28: 5 *he has* **c** my son Solomon to sit on 1047
28: 6 for *I have* **c** him to be my son, 1047
28:10 for the LORD *has* **c** you to build a temple 1047
29: 1 the one whom God *has* **c**, 1047
2Ch 6: 5 not **c** a city in any tribe of Israel to have 1047
6: 5 nor *have I* **c** anyone to be the leader 1047
6: 6 But now *I have* **c** Jerusalem for my Name 1047
6: 6 *I have* **c** David to rule my people Israel.' 1047
6:34 to you toward this city *you have* **c** and 1047
6:38 toward the city *you have* **c** and toward 1047
7:12 and *have* **c** this place for myself as a temple 1047
7:16 *I have* **c** and consecrated this temple so 1047
12:13 the LORD *had* **c** out of all the tribes 1047
29:11 the LORD *has* **c** you to stand before him 1047
33: 7 which *I have* **c** out of all the tribes 1047
Ne 1: 9 and bring them to the place *I have* **c** as 1047
Ps 25:12 He will instruct him in the way **c** for him. 1047
89: 3 "I have made a covenant with my **c** *one*, 1040
105: 6 O sons of Jacob, his **c** *ones*. 1040
105:26 and Aaron, whom *he had* **c**. 1047
105:43 his **c** *ones* with shouts of joy; 1040
106: 5 I may enjoy the prosperity of your **c** *ones*, 1040
106:23 had not Moses, his **c** *one*, 1040
119:30 *I have* **c** the way of truth; 1047
119:173 for *I have* **c** your precepts. 1047
132:13 For the LORD *has* **c** Zion, 1047
135: 4 For the LORD *has* **c** Jacob to be his own, 1047
Isa 1:29 because of the gardens that *you have* **c**. 1047
41: 8 my servant, Jacob, whom *I have* **c**, 1047
41: 9 *I have* **c** you and have not rejected you. 1047
42: 1 my **c** *one* in whom I delight; 1040
43:10 "and my servant whom *I have* **c**, 1047
43:20 to give drink to my people, my **c**, 1040
44: 1 my servant, Israel, whom *I have* **c**. 1047
44: 2 my servant, Jeshurun, whom *I have* **c**. 1047
45: 4 sake of Jacob my servant, of Israel my **c**, 1040
48:14 LORD's **c ally** will carry out his purpose 170
49: 7 the Holy One of Israel, *who has* **c** you." 1047
58: 5 Is this the kind of fast *I have* **c**, 1047
58: 6 "Is not this the kind of fasting *I have* **c**: 1047
65: 9 my **c** *people* will inherit them, 1040
65:15 You will leave your name to my **c** *ones* as 1040
65:22 my **c** *ones* will long enjoy the works 1040
66: 3 They *have* **c** their own ways, 1047
Jer 49:19 Who *is the* **c** *one* I will appoint for this? 1047
50:44 Who *is the* **c** *one* I will appoint for this? 1047
Am 3: 2 "You only *have I* **c** of all the families of 3359
Hag 2:23 for *I have* **c** you,' 1047
Zec 3: 2 The LORD, who *has* **c** Jerusalem, 1047
Mt 12:18 "Here is my servant whom *I have* **c**, *147*
22:14 "For many are invited, but few are **c**." *1723*
27:15 at the Feast to release a prisoner **c** by *2527*
Mk 13:20 for the sake of the elect, whom *he has* **c**, *1721*
Lk 1: 9 *he was* **c by lot,** *3275*
9:35 saying, "This is my Son, whom *I have* **c**; *1721*
10:42 Mary *has* **c** what is better, *1721*
18: 7 not God bring about justice *for* his **c** *ones*, *1723*
23:35 if he is the Christ of God, the **C** *One*." *1723*
Jn 6:70 Jesus replied, "*Have* I not **c** you, the Twelve? *1721*
13:18 I know those *I have* **c**. *1721*
15:19 but I *have* **c** you out of the world. *1721*
Ac 1: 2 the Holy Spirit to the apostles *he had* **c**. *1721*
1:24 Show us which of these two *you have* **c** *1721*
9:15 This man is my **c** instrument *1724*
10:41 but *by* witnesses whom God *had* **already c** *4742*
22:14 of our fathers *has* **c** you to know his will *4741*
Ro 8:33 against those whom God has **c**? *1723*
11: 5 at the present time there is a remnant **c** *1724*
16:13 Greet Rufus, **c** in the Lord, and his mother, *1723*
2Co 8:19 *he was* **c** by the churches to accompany us *5936*
Eph 1:11 In him *we were* also **c**, *3103*
Col 1:27 To them God *has* **c** to make known among *2527*
3:12 Therefore, as God's **c** *people*, *1723*
1Th 1: 4 brothers loved by God, that he has **c** you, *1724*
Jas 2: 5 not God **c** those who are poor in the eyes of *1721*
1Pe 1: 2 have been **c** according to the foreknowledge *NIG*
1:20 *He was* **c before** the creation of the world, *4589*
2: 4 rejected by men but **c** by God and precious *1723*
2: 6 a **c** and precious cornerstone, *1723*
2: 9 But you are a **c** people, a royal priesthood, *1723*
5:13 She who is in Babylon, **c together with** you, *5293*
2Jn 1: 1 The elder, *To* the **c** lady and her children, *1723*
1:13 *of* your **c** sister send their greetings. *1723*
Rev 17:14 **c** and faithful followers." *1723*

CHOZEBA (KJV) See COZEBA

CHRIST (530) [CHRIST'S, CHRISTIAN, CHRISTIANS, CHRISTS, MESSIAH]

Mt 1: 1 the genealogy *of* Jesus **C** the son of David, *5986*
1:16 of whom was born Jesus, who is called **C**. *5986*
1:17 and fourteen from the exile to the **C**. *5986*
1:18 how the birth *of* Jesus **C** came about: *5986*
2: 4 he asked them where the **C** was to be born. *5986*
11: 2 in prison what **C** was doing, *5986*
16:16 Simon Peter answered, "You are the **C**, *5986*
16:20 not to tell anyone that he was the **C**. *5986*
22:42 "What do you think about the **C**? *5986*
23:10 for you have one Teacher, the **C**. *5986*
24: 5 'I am the **C**,' and will deceive many. *5986*
24:23 'Look, here is the **C**!' *5986*
26:63 Tell us if you are the **C**, the Son of God." *5986*
26:68 and said, "Prophesy to us, **C**. *5986*
27:17 Barabbas, or Jesus who is called **C**?" *5986*
27:22 then, with Jesus who is called **C**?" *5986*
Mk 1: 1 beginning of the gospel *about* Jesus **C**, *5986*
8:29 Peter answered, "You are the **C**." *5986*
9:41 because you belong *to* **C** will certainly *5986*
12:35 that the teachers of the law say that the **C** is *5986*
13:21 'Look, here is the **C**!' *5986*
14:61 "Are you the **C**, the Son of the Blessed One *5986*
15:32 Let this **C**, this King of Israel, *5986*
Lk 2:11 he is **C** the Lord. *5986*
2:26 not die before he had seen the Lord's **C**. *5986*
3:15 if John might possibly be the **C**. *5986*
4:41 because they knew he was the **C**. *5986*
9:20 Peter answered, "The **C** of God." *5986*
20:41 "How is it that they say the **C** is the Son *5986*
22:67 "If you are the **C**," they said, "tell us." *5986*
23: 2 of taxes to Caesar and claims to be **C**, *5986*
23:35 let him save himself if he is the **C** of God, *5986*
23:39 "Aren't you the **C**? *5986*
24:26 Did not the **C** have to suffer these things *5986*
24:46 The **C** will suffer and rise from the dead on *5986*
Jn 1:17 grace and truth came through Jesus **C**. *5986*
1:20 but confessed freely, "I am not the **C**." *5986*
1:25 then do you baptize if you are not the **C**, *5986*
1:41 the Messiah" (that is, the **C**). *5986*
3:28 'I am not the **C** but am sent ahead of him.' *5986*
4:25 that Messiah" (called **C**) "is coming. *5986*
4:29 Could this be the **C**?" *5986*
7:26 that he is the **C**? *5986*
7:27 when the **C** comes, *5986*
7:31 They said, "When the **C** comes, *5986*
7:41 Others said, "He is the **C**." *5986*
7:41 "How can the **C** come from Galilee? *5986*
7:42 not the Scripture say that the **C** will come *5986*
9:22 the **C** would be put out of the synagogue. *5986*
10:24 If you are the **C**, tell us plainly." *5986*
11:27 she told him, "I believe that you are the **C**, *5986*
12:34 the Law that the **C** will remain forever, *5986*
17: 3 and Jesus **C**, whom you have sent. *5986*
20:31 that you may believe that Jesus is the **C**, *5986*
Ac 2:31 he spoke of the resurrection *of* the **C**, *5986*
2:36 whom you crucified, both Lord and **C**." *5986*
2:38 of Jesus **C** for the forgiveness of your sins. *5986*
3: 6 In the name *of* Jesus **C** of Nazareth, walk." *5986*
3:18 saying that his **C** would suffer. *5986*
3:20 the **C**, who has been appointed for you— *5986*
4:10 It is by the name of Jesus **C** of Nazareth, *5986*
5:42 the good news that Jesus is the **C**. *5986*
Ac 8: 5 in Samaria and proclaimed the **C** there. *5986*
8:12 of God and the name *of* Jesus **C**, *5986*
9:22 in Damascus by proving that Jesus is the **C**. *5986*
9:34 Peter said to him, "Jesus **C** heals you. *5986*
10:36 the good news of peace through Jesus **C**, *5986*
10:48 be baptized in the name *of* Jesus **C**. *5986*
11:17 who believed in the Lord Jesus **C**, *5986*
15:26 for the name *of* our Lord Jesus **C**. *5986*
16:18 "In the name *of* Jesus **C** I command you *5986*
17: 3 the **C** had to suffer and rise from the dead. *5986*
17: 3 I am proclaiming to you is the **C**," *5986*
18: 5 testifying to the Jews that Jesus was the **C**. *5986*
18:28 from the Scriptures that Jesus was the **C**. *5986*
24:24 to him as he spoke about faith in **C** Jesus. *5986*
26:23 that the **C** would suffer and, *5986*
28:31 of God and taught about the Lord Jesus **C**. *5986*
Ro 1: 1 Paul, a servant *of* **C** Jesus, *5986*
1: 4 Jesus **C** our Lord. *5986*
1: 6 to *belong to* Jesus **C**. *5986*
1: 7 and from the Lord Jesus **C**. *5986*
1: 8 I thank my God through Jesus **C** for all *5986*
2:16 when God will judge men's secrets through Jesus **C**, *5986*
3:22 through faith *in* Jesus **C** to all who believe. *5986*
3:24 the redemption that came by **C** Jesus. *5986*
5: 1 with God through our Lord Jesus **C**, *5986*
5: 6 **C** died for the ungodly. *5986*
5: 8 While we were still sinners, **C** died for us. *5986*
5:11 in God through our Lord Jesus **C**, *5986*
5:15 Jesus **C**, overflow to the many! *5986*
5:17 in life through the one man, Jesus **C**. *5986*
5:21 through Jesus **C** our Lord. *5986*
6: 3 into **C** Jesus were baptized into his death? *5986*
6: 4 just as **C** was raised from the dead through *5986*
6: 8 Now if we died with **C**, *5986*
6: 9 For we know that since **C** was raised from *5986*
6:11 to sin but alive to God in **C** Jesus. *5986*
6:23 of God is eternal life in **C** Jesus our Lord. *5986*
7: 4 also died to the law through the body *of* **C**, *5986*
7:25 through Jesus **C** our Lord! *5986*
8: 1 for those who are in **C** Jesus, *5986*
8: 2 through **C** Jesus the law of the Spirit *5986*
8: 9 if anyone does not have the Spirit *of* **C**, *5986*
8: 9 he does not belong to **C**. *899S*
8:10 But if **C** is in you, *5986*
8:11 he who raised **C** from the dead will *5986*
8:17 heirs of God and co-heirs with **C**, *5986*
8:34 **C** Jesus, who died— *5986*
8:35 Who shall separate us from the love *of* **C**? *5986*
8:39 the love of God that is in **C** Jesus our Lord. *5986*
9: 1 I speak the truth in **C**—I am not lying, *5986*
9: 3 cut off from **C** for the sake of my brothers, *5986*
9: 5 the human ancestry of **C**, *5986*
10: 4 **C** is the end of the law so that there may *5986*
10: 6 (that is, to bring **C** down) *5986*
10: 7 (that is, to bring **C** up from the dead). *5986*
10:17 message is heard through the word *of* **C**. *5986*
12: 5 so in **C** we who are many form one body, *5986*
13:14 clothe yourselves with the Lord Jesus **C**, *5986*
14: 9 **C** died and returned to life so that he might *5986*
14:15 your brother for whom **C** died. *5986*
14:18 because anyone who serves **C** *5986*
15: 3 For even **C** did not please himself but, *5986*
15: 5 among yourselves as you follow **C** Jesus, *5986*
15: 6 the God and Father *of* our Lord Jesus **C**. *5986*
15: 7 then, just as **C** accepted you, *5986*
15: 8 For I tell you that **C** has become a servant *5986*
15:16 to be a minister *of* **C** Jesus to the Gentiles *5986*
15:17 I glory in **C** Jesus in my service to God. *5986*
15:18 not venture to speak of anything except what **C** has accomplished *5986*
15:19 I have fully proclaimed the gospel *of* **C**. *5986*
15:20 the gospel where **C** was not known, *5986*
15:29 in the full measure of the blessing *of* **C**. *5986*
15:30 by our Lord Jesus **C** and by the love of *5986*
16: 3 my fellow workers in **C** Jesus. *5986*
16: 5 the first convert to **C** in the province *5986*
16: 7 and they were in **C** before I was. *5986*
16: 9 Greet Urbanus, our fellow worker in **C**, *5986*
16:10 Greet Apelles, tested and approved in **C**. *5986*
16:16 All the churches *of* **C** send greetings. *5986*
16:18 such people are not serving our Lord **C**, *5986*
16:25 and the proclamation *of* Jesus **C**, *5986*
16:27 be glory forever through Jesus **C**! *5986*
1Co 1: 1 an apostle *of* **C** Jesus by the will of God, *5986*
1: 2 to those sanctified in **C** Jesus and called to *5986*
1: 2 on the name *of* our Lord Jesus **C**— *5986*
1: 3 from God our Father and the Lord Jesus **C**. *5986*
1: 4 because of his grace given you in **C** Jesus. *5986*
1: 6 *about* **C** was confirmed in you. *5986*
1: 7 as you eagerly wait for our Lord Jesus **C** to *5986*
1: 8 on the day *of* our Lord Jesus **C**. *5986*
1: 9 with his Son Jesus **C** our Lord, *5986*
1:10 brothers, in the name *of* our Lord Jesus **C**, *5986*
1:12 still another, "I follow **C**." *5986*
1:13 Is **C** divided? Was Paul crucified for you? *5986*
1:17 For **C** did not send me to baptize, *5986*
1:17 lest the cross *of* **C** be emptied of its power. *5986*
1:23 but we preach **C** crucified: *5986*
1:24 **C** the power of God and the wisdom *5986*
1:30 It is because of him that you are in **C** Jesus, *5986*
2: 2 with you except Jesus **C** and him crucified. *5986*
2:16 But we have the mind *of* **C**. *5986*
3: 1 as worldly—mere infants in **C**. *5986*
3:11 one already laid, which is Jesus **C**. *5986*
3:23 and you are *of* **C**, and Christ is of God. *5986*
3:23 and you are of Christ, and **C** is of God. *5986*

1Co 4: 1 men ought to regard us as servants *of* C 5986
4:10 We are fools for C, 5986
4:10 but you are so wise in C! 5986
4:15 in C, you do not have many fathers, for 5986
4:15 for in C Jesus I became your father through 5986
4:17 of my way of life in C Jesus, 5986
5: 7 C, our Passover lamb, has been sacrificed. 5986
6:11 in the name *of* the Lord Jesus C and by 5986
6:15 that your bodies are members *of* C himself? 5986
6:15 then take the members *of* C and unite them 5986
8: 6 and there is but one Lord, Jesus C, 5986
8:11 So this weak brother, for whom C died, 5986
8:12 wound their weak conscience, you sin
against C. 5986
9:12 rather than the gospel *of* C. 5986
10: 4 and that rock was C. 5986
10:16 a participation in the blood *of* C? 5986
10:16 a participation in the body *of* C? 5986
11: 1 as I follow the example *of* C. 5986
11: 3 to realize that the head of every man is C, 5986
11: 3 and the head *of* C is God. 5986
12:12 So it is with C. 5986
12:27 Now you are the body *of* C, 5986
15: 3 that C died for our sins according to 5986
15:12 if it is preached that C has been raised from 5986
15:13 then not even C has been raised. 5986
15:14 And if C has not been raised, 5986
15:15 about God that he raised C from the dead. 5986
15:16 then C has not been raised either. 5986
15:17 if C has not been raised, your faith is futile; 5986
15:18 also who have fallen asleep in C are lost. 5986
15:19 If only for this life we have hope in C, 5986
15:20 C has indeed been raised from the dead, 5986
15:22 so in C all will be made alive. 5986
15:23 But each in his own turn: C, the firstfruits; 5986
15:27 who put everything under C. 899[S]
15:31 as I glory over you in C Jesus our Lord. 5986
15:57 the victory through our Lord Jesus C. 5986
16:24 My love to all of you in C Jesus. Amen. 5986
2Co 1: 1 an apostle *of* C Jesus by the will of God, 5986
1: 2 from God our Father and the Lord Jesus C. 5986
1: 3 to the God and Father *of* our Lord Jesus C, 5986
1: 5 For just as the sufferings *of* C flow over 5986
1: 5 so also through C our comfort overflows. 5986
1:19 For the Son of God, Jesus C, 5986
1:20 they are "Yes" in C. 899[S]
1:21 both us and you stand firm in C. 5986
2:10 I have forgiven in the sight *of* C 5986
2:12 *of* C and found that the Lord had opened 5986
2:14 in C and through us spreads everywhere 5986
2:15 *of* C among those who are being saved 5986
2:17 in C we speak before God with sincerity, 5986
3: 3 You show that you are a letter *from* C, 5986
3: 4 Such confidence as this is ours through C 5986
3:14 because only in C is it taken away. 5986
4: 4 the light of the gospel of the glory *of* C, 5986
4: 5 but Jesus C as Lord, 5986
4: 6 of the glory of God in the face *of* C. 5986
5:10 before the judgment seat *of* C, 5986
5:16 Though we once regarded C in this way, 5986
5:17 if anyone is in C, he is a new creation; 5986
5:18 who reconciled us to himself through C 5986
5:19 the world to himself in C, 5986
6:15 What harmony is there between C 5986
8: 9 you know the grace *of* our Lord Jesus C, 5986
8:23 of the churches and an honor *to* C. 5986
9:13 confession of the gospel *of* C, 5986
10: 1 By the meekness and gentleness *of* C, 5986
10: 5 to make it obedient *to* C. 5986
10: 7 is confident that he **belongs to C**, 1639+5986
10: 7 that we *belong to* C just as much as he. 5986
10:14 as far as you with the gospel *of* C. 5986
11: 2 I promised you to one husband, *to* C, 5986
11: 3 from your sincere and pure devotion to C. 5986
11:10 As surely as the truth *of* C is in me, 5986
11:13 masquerading as apostles *of* C. 5986
11:23 Are they servants *of* C? 5986
12: 2 in C who fourteen years ago was caught up 5986
12:19 in the sight of God as those in C; 5986
13: 3 that C is speaking through me. 5986
13: 5 Do you not realize that C Jesus is in you— 5986
13:14 May the grace *of* the Lord Jesus C, 5986
Gal 1: 1 but by Jesus C and God the Father, 5986
1: 3 from God our Father and the Lord Jesus C, 5986
1: 6 the one who called you by the grace *of* C 5986
1: 7 and are trying to pervert the gospel *of* C. 5986
1:10 I would not be a servant *of* C. 5986
1:12 I received it by revelation *from* Jesus C. 5986
1:22 to the churches of Judea that are in C. 5986
2: 4 to spy on the freedom we have in C Jesus 5986
2:16 but by faith *in* Jesus C. 5986
2:16 in C Jesus that we may be justified by faith 5986
2:16 by faith *in* C and not by observing the law, 5986
2:17 "If, while we seek to be justified in C, 5986
2:17 does that mean that C promotes sin? 5986
2:20 I have been crucified with C 5986
2:20 but C lives in me. 5986
2:21 gained through the law, C died for nothing! 5986
3: 1 Before your very eyes Jesus C was clearly
portrayed as crucified. 5986
3:13 C redeemed us from the curse of the law 5986
3:14 to the Gentiles through C Jesus, 5986
3:16 meaning one person, who is C. 5986
3:22 being given through faith *in* Jesus C, 5986
3:24 to lead us to C that we might be justified 5986
3:26 of God through faith in C Jesus, 5986
3:27 into C have clothed yourselves with Christ. 5986
Gal 3:27 into Christ have clothed yourselves with C. 5986
3:28 for you are all one in C Jesus. 5986
3:29 If you *belong to* C, then you are Abraham's 5986
4:14 as if I were C Jesus himself. 5986
4:19 in the pains of childbirth until C is formed 5986
5: 1 It is for freedom that C has set us free. 5986
5: 2 C will be of no value to you at all. 5986
5: 4 by law have been alienated from C; 5986
5: 6 For in C Jesus neither circumcision 5986
5:24 *to* C Jesus have crucified the sinful nature 5986
6: 2 in this way you will fulfill the law *of* C. 5986
6:12 for the cross *of* C. 5986
6:14 in the cross *of* our Lord Jesus C, 5986
6:18 *of* our Lord Jesus C be with your spirit, 5986
Eph 1: 1 an apostle *of* C Jesus by the will of God, 5986
1: 1 the faithful in C Jesus: 5986
1: 2 from God our Father and the Lord Jesus C. 5986
1: 3 to the God and Father *of* our Lord Jesus C, 5986
1: 3 with every spiritual blessing in C. 5986
1: 5 as his sons through Jesus C, in accordance 5986
1: 9 which he purposed in C, 899[S]
1:10 on earth together under one head, even C. 5986
1:12 who were the first to hope in C, 5986
1:13 also were included in C when you heard 4005[S]
1:17 that the God *of* our Lord Jesus C, 5986
1:20 which he exerted in C when he raised him 5986
2: 5 with C even when we were dead 5986
2: 6 And God raised us up with C and seated us NIG
2: 6 with him in the heavenly realms in C Jesus, 5986
2: 7 expressed in his kindness to us in C Jesus. 5986
2:10 created in C Jesus to do good works, 5986
2:12 that at that time you were separate from C, 5986
2:13 in C Jesus you who once were far away
have been brought near 5986
2:13 near through the blood *of* C. 5986
2:20 C Jesus himself as the chief cornerstone. 5986
3: 1 *of* C Jesus for the sake of you Gentiles— 5986
3: 4 into the mystery *of* C, 5986
3: 6 sharers together in the promise in C Jesus. 5986
3: 8 the Gentiles the unsearchable riches *of* C, 5986
3:11 accomplished in C Jesus our Lord. 5986
3:17 C may dwell in your hearts through faith. 5986
3:18 and high and deep is the love *of* C, 5986
3:21 and in C Jesus throughout all generations, 5986
4: 7 grace has been given as C apportioned it. 5986
4:12 so that the body *of* C may be built up 5986
4:13 to the whole measure of the fullness *of* C. 5986
4:15 up into him who is the Head, that is, C. 5986
4:20 did not come to know C that way. 5986
4:32 just as in C God forgave you. 5986
5: 2 as C loved us and gave himself up for us as 5986
5: 5 has any inheritance in the kingdom *of* C 5986
5:14 and C will shine on you." 5986
5:20 in the name *of* our Lord Jesus C. 5986
5:21 to one another out of reverence *for* C. 5986
5:23 the husband is the head of the wife as C is 5986
5:24 Now as the church submits *to* C, 5986
5:25 just as C loved the church and gave himself 5986
5:29 just as C does the church— 5986
5:32 but I am talking about C and the church. 5986
6: 5 just as you would obey C. 5986
6: 6 but like slaves *of* C, doing the will of God 5986
6:23 from God the Father and the Lord Jesus C. 5986
6:24 Grace to all who love our Lord Jesus C 5986
Php 1: 1 Paul and Timothy, servants *of* C Jesus, 5986
1: 1 To all the saints in C Jesus at Philippi, 5986
1: 2 from God our Father and the Lord Jesus C. 5986
1: 6 on to completion until the day *of* C Jesus. 5986
1: 8 for all of you with the affection *of* C Jesus. 5986
1:10 be pure and blameless until the day *of* C, 5986
1:11 that comes through Jesus C— 5986
1:13 to everyone else that I am in chains for C. 5986
1:15 that some preach C out of envy and rivalry, 5986
1:17 former preach C out of selfish ambition, 5986
1:18 from false motives or true, C is preached. 5986
1:19 and the help given by the Spirit *of* Jesus C, 5986
1:20 as always C will be exalted in my body, 5986
1:21 For to me, to live is C and to die is gain. 5986
1:23 I desire to depart and be with C, 5986
1:26 in C Jesus will overflow on account of me. 5986
1:27 in a manner worthy of the gospel *of* C. 5986
1:29 on behalf of C not only to believe on him, 5986
2: 1 from being united with C, 5986
2: 5 be the same as that of C Jesus: 5986
2:11 every tongue confess that Jesus C is Lord, 5986
2:16 *of* C that I did not run or labor for nothing. 5986
2:21 not those of Jesus C. 5986
2:30 because he almost died for the work *of* C, 5986
3: 3 who glory in C Jesus, 5986
3: 7 now consider loss for the sake of C. 5986
3: 8 of knowing C Jesus my Lord, 5986
3: 8 that I may gain C 5986
3: 9 but that which is through faith *in* C— 5986
3:10 I want to know C and the power 899[S]
3:12 of that for which C Jesus took hold of me. 5986
3:14 God has called me heavenward in C Jesus. 5986
3:18 many live as enemies of the cross *of* C. 5986
3:20 the Lord Jesus C, 5986
4: 7 and your minds in C Jesus. 5986
4:19 according to his glorious riches in C Jesus. 5986
4:21 Greet all the saints in C Jesus. 5986
4:23 *of* the Lord Jesus C be with your spirit. 5986
Col 1: 1 an apostle *of* C Jesus by the will of God, 5986
1: 2 To the holy and faithful brothers in C 5986
1: 3 the Father *of* our Lord Jesus C, 5986
1: 4 in C Jesus and of the love you have for all 5986
1: 7 a faithful minister *of* C on our behalf, 5986
Col 1:27 which is C in you, the hope of glory. 5986
1:28 that we may present everyone perfect in C. 5986
2: 2 the mystery of God, namely, C, 5986
2: 5 and how firm your faith in C is. 5986
2: 6 then, just as you received C Jesus as Lord, 5986
2: 8 of this world rather than on C. 5986
2: 9 For in C all the fullness of the Deity lives 899[S]
2:10 and you have been given fullness in C, 899[S]
2:11 but with the circumcision done *by* C, 5986
2:13 God made you alive with C. 899[S]
2:17 the reality, however, is found in C. 5986
2:20 with C to the basic principles of this world, 5986
3: 1 Since, then, you have been raised with C, 5986
3: 1 where C is seated at the right hand of God. 5986
3: 3 and your life is now hidden with C in God. 5986
3: 4 When C, who is your life, appears, 5986
3:11 slave or free, but C is all, and is in all. 5986
3:15 Let the peace *of* C rule in your hearts, 5986
3:16 Let the word *of* C dwell in you richly 5986
3:24 It is the Lord C you are serving. 5986
4: 3 so that we may proclaim the mystery *of* C, 5986
4:12 who is one of you and a servant *of* C Jesus, 5986
1Th 1: 1 in God the Father and the Lord Jesus C: 5986
1: 3 by hope *in* our Lord Jesus C. 5986
2: 6 *of* C we could have been a burden to you, 5986
2:14 which are in C Jesus: 5986
3: 2 in spreading the gospel *of* C, 5986
4:16 and the dead in C will rise first. 5986
5: 9 through our Lord Jesus C. 5986
5:18 for this is God's will for you in C Jesus. 5986
5:23 at the coming *of* our Lord Jesus C. 5986
5:28 grace *of* our Lord Jesus C be with you. 5986
2Th 1: 1 in God our Father and the Lord Jesus C: 5986
1: 2 from God the Father and the Lord Jesus C. 5986
1:12 the grace of our God and the Lord Jesus C. 5986
2: 1 the coming *of* our Lord Jesus C 5986
2:14 in the glory *of* our Lord Jesus C. 5986
2:16 May our Lord Jesus C himself 5986
3: 6 In the name *of* the Lord Jesus C, 5986
3:12 and urge in the Lord Jesus C to settle down 5986
3:18 grace *of* our Lord Jesus C be with you all. 5986
1Ti 1: 1 an apostle *of* C Jesus by the command 5986
1: 1 and *of* C Jesus our hope, 5986
1: 2 from God the Father and C Jesus our Lord. 5986
1:12 I thank C Jesus our Lord, 5986
1:14 with the faith and love that are in C Jesus. 5986
1:15 C Jesus came into the world to save sinners 5986
1:16 C Jesus might display his unlimited
patience as an example 5986
2: 5 between God and men, the man C Jesus, 5986
3:13 in their faith in C Jesus. 5986
4: 6 you will be a good minister *of* C Jesus, 5986
5:11 when their sensual desires overcome their
dedication to C, 5986
5:21 of God and C Jesus and the elect angels, 5986
6: 3 *of* our Lord Jesus C and to godly teaching, 5986
6:13 and *of* C Jesus, who while testifying 5986
6:14 until the appearing *of* our Lord Jesus C, 5986
2Ti 1: 1 an apostle *of* C Jesus by the will of God, 5986
1: 1 to the promise of life that is in C Jesus, 5986
1: 2 from God the Father and C Jesus our Lord. 5986
1: 9 This grace was given us in C Jesus before 5986
1:10 the appearing *of* our Savior, C Jesus, 5986
1:13 with faith and love in C Jesus. 5986
2: 1 be strong in the grace that is in C Jesus. 5986
2: 3 with us like a good soldier *of* C Jesus. 5986
2: 8 Remember Jesus C, raised from the dead, 5986
2:10 the salvation that is in C Jesus, 5986
3:12 a godly life in C Jesus will be persecuted, 5986
3:15 for salvation through faith in C Jesus. 5986
4: 1 In the presence of God and *of* C Jesus, 5986
Tit 1: 1 a servant of God and an apostle *of* Jesus C 5986
1: 4 the Father and C Jesus our Savior. 5986
2:13 *of* our great God and Savior, Jesus C, 5986
3: 6 through Jesus C our Savior, 5986
Phm 1: 1 Paul, a prisoner *of* C Jesus, 5986
1: 3 from God our Father and the Lord Jesus C. 5986
1: 6 of every good thing we have in C. 5986
1: 8 in C I could be bold and order you 5986
1: 9 and now also a prisoner *of* C Jesus— 5986
1:20 refresh my heart in C. 5986
1:23 Epaphras, my fellow prisoner in C Jesus, 5986
1:25 *of* the Lord Jesus C be with your spirit. 5986
Heb 3: 6 But C is faithful as a son over God's house. 5986
3:14 to share in C if we hold firmly till the end 5986
5: 5 So C also did not take upon himself 5986
6: 1 the elementary teachings *about* C and go 5986
9:11 When C came as high priest of 5986
9:14 much more, then, will the blood *of* C, 5986
9:15 For this reason C is the mediator of NIG
9:24 For C did not enter a man-made sanctuary 5986
9:26 C would have had to suffer many times 899[S]
9:28 so C was sacrificed once to take away 5986
10: 5 when C came into the world, he said: NIG
10:10 the sacrifice of the body *of* Jesus C once 5986
11:26 He regarded disgrace *for the sake of* C as 5986
13: 8 Jesus C is the same yesterday and today 5986
13:21 through Jesus C, to whom be glory for ever 5986
Jas 1: 1 a servant of God and *of* the Lord Jesus C, 5986
2: 1 as believers *in* our glorious Lord Jesus C, 5986
1Pe 1: 1 Peter, an apostle *of* Jesus C, 5986
1: 2 for obedience *to* Jesus C and sprinkling 5986
1: 3 to the God and Father *of* our Lord Jesus C! 5986
1: 3 the resurrection *of* Jesus C from the dead, 5986
1: 7 glory and honor when Jesus C is revealed. 5986
1:11 and circumstances to which the Spirit *of* C 5986
1:11 when he predicted the sufferings of C and 5986

1Pe 1:13 to be given you when Jesus C is revealed. 5986
1:19 but with the precious blood of C, 5986
2: 5 acceptable to God through Jesus C. 5986
2:21 because C suffered for you, 5986
3:15 But in your hearts set apart C as Lord. 5986
3:16 in C may be ashamed of their slander. 5986
3:18 For C died for sins once for all, 5986
3:21 It saves you by the resurrection of Jesus C, 5986
4: 1 Therefore, since C suffered in his body, 5986
4:11 be praised through Jesus C. 5986
4:13 that you participate in the sufferings of C, 5986
4:14 you are insulted because of the name of C, 5986
5:10 who called you to his eternal glory in C, 5986
5:14 Peace to all of you who are in C. 5986
2Pe 1: 1 a servant and apostle of Jesus C, 5986
1: 1 and Savior Jesus C have received a faith 5986
1: 8 in your knowledge of our Lord Jesus C. 5986
1:11 of our Lord and Savior Jesus C. 5986
1:14 as our Lord Jesus C has made clear to me. 5986
1:16 and coming of our Lord Jesus C, 5986
2:20 and Savior Jesus C and are again entangled 5986
3:18 of our Lord and Savior Jesus C. 5986
1Jn 1: 3 with the Father and with his Son, Jesus C. 5986
2: 1 Jesus C, the Righteous One. 5986
2:22 It is the man who denies that Jesus is the C. 5986
3:16 Jesus C laid down his life for us. 1697S
3:23 to believe in the name of his Son, Jesus C, 5986
4: 2 that acknowledges that Jesus C has come in 5986
5: 1 that Jesus is the C is born of God, 5986
5: 6 by water and blood—Jesus C. 5986
5:20 even in his Son Jesus C. 5986
2Jn 1: 3 from God the Father and from Jesus C, 5986
1: 7 not acknowledge Jesus C as coming in 5986
1: 9 in the teaching of C does not have God; 5986
Jude 1: 1 servant of Jesus C and a brother of James, 5986
1: 1 by God the Father and kept by Jesus C: 5986
1: 4 and deny Jesus C our only Sovereign 5986
1:17 the apostles of our Lord Jesus C foretold. 5986
1:21 the mercy of our Lord Jesus C to bring you 5986
1:25 through Jesus C our Lord, before all ages, 5986
Rev 1: 1 The revelation of Jesus C, 5986
1: 2 word of God and the testimony of Jesus C. 5986
1: 5 and from Jesus C, 5986
11:15 the kingdom of our Lord and of his C, 5986
12:10 and the authority of his C. 5986
20: 4 to life and reigned with C a thousand years. 5986
20: 6 be priests of God and of C and will reign 5986

CHRIST'S (11) [CHRIST]

1Co 7:22 a free man when he was called is C slave. 5986
9:21 from God's law but am under C law), 5986
2Co 5:14 For C love compels us, 5986
5:20 We are therefore C ambassadors, 5642+5986
5:20 We implore you on C behalf: 5986
12: 9 so that C power may rest on me. 5986
12:10 That is why, for C sake, 5986
Col 1:22 by C physical body through death 899S
1:24 in regard to C afflictions, 5986
2Th 3: 5 into God's love and C perseverance. 5986
1Pe 5: 1 of C sufferings and one who also will share 5986

CHRISTIAN (2) [CHRIST]

Ac 26:28 you can persuade me to be a C?" 5985
1Pe 4:16 However, if you suffer as a C, 5985

CHRISTIANS (1) [CHRIST]

Ac 11:26 The disciples were called C first at Antioch. 5985

CHRISTS (2) [CHRIST]

Mt 24:24 For false C and false prophets will appear 6023
Mk 13:22 For false C and false prophets will appear 6023

CHRONIC (1)

Lev 13:11 it is a c skin disease and the priest shall 3823

CHRONICLES (1)

Est 6: 1 so he ordered the book of the c, 2355

CHRYSOLITE (8)

Ex 28:20 in the fourth row a c, 9577
39:13 in the fourth row a c, 9577
SS 5:14 His arms are rods of gold set with c. 9577
Eze 1:16 They sparkled like c, 9577
10: 9 the wheels sparkled like c. 74+9577
28:13 ruby, topaz and emerald, c, 9577
Da 10: 6 His body was like c, his face like lightning, 9577
Rev 21:20 the sixth carnelian, the seventh c, 5994

CHRYSOPRASE (1)

Rev 21:20 the tenth c, the eleventh jacinth, 5995

CHUB (KJV) See LIBYA

CHUN (KJV) See CUN

CHURCH (79) [CHURCHES]

Mt 16:18 and on this rock I will build my c, 1711
18:17 refuses to listen to them, tell it to the c; 1711
18:17 and if he refuses to listen even to the c, 1711
Ac 5:11 fear seized the whole c and all who heard 1711
8: 1 a great persecution broke out against the c 1711
8: 3 But Saul began to destroy the c. 1711
9:31 Then the c throughout Judea, 1711
11:22 News of this reached the ears of the c 1711
11:26 the c and taught great numbers of people. 1711
12: 1 that King Herod arrested some who belonged to the c, intending 1711
12: 5 the c was earnestly praying to God for him. 1711
13: 1 In the c at Antioch there were prophets 1711
14:23 elders for them in each c and, 1711
14:27 gathered the c together and reported all 1711
15: 3 The c sent them on their way, 1711
15: 4 by the c and the apostles and elders, 1711
15:22 the apostles and elders, with the whole c, 1711
15:30 the c together and delivered the letter. 4436
18:22 he went up and greeted the c and then went 1711
20:17 Paul sent to Ephesus for the elders of the c. 1711
20:28 Be shepherds of the c of God, 1711
Ro 16: 1 a servant of the c in Cenchrea. 1711
16: 5 Greet also the c that meets at their house. 1711
16:23 and the whole c here enjoy, 1711
1Co 1: 2 the c of God in Corinth, to those sanctified 1711
4:17 with what I teach everywhere in every c. 1711
5:12 of mine to judge those outside the c? NIG
6: 4 even men of little account in the c! 1711
10:32 whether Jews, Greeks or the c of God— 1711
11:18 I hear that when you come together as a c, 1711
11:22 Or do you despise the c of God 1711
12:28 And in the c God has appointed first 1711
14: 4 but he who prophesies edifies the c. 1711
14: 5 so that the c may be edified. 1711
14:12 try to excel in gifts that build up the c. 1711
14:19 But in the c I would rather speak five intelligible words 1711
14:23 So if the whole c comes together 1711
14:26 be done for the strengthening of the c. NIG
14:28 in the c and speak to himself and God. 1711
14:35 for a woman to speak in the c. 1711
15: 9 because I persecuted the c of God. 1711
16:19 and so does the c that meets at their house. 1711
2Co 1: 1 To the c of God in Corinth, 1711
Gal 1:13 how intensely I persecuted the c of God 1711
Eph 1:22 to be head over everything for the c, 1711
3:10 His intent was that now, through the c, 1711
3:21 to him be glory in the c and in Christ Jesus 1711
5:23 of the wife as Christ is the head of the c, 1711
5:24 Now as the c submits to Christ, 1711
5:25 just as Christ loved the c and gave himself 1711
5:27 and to present her to himself as a radiant c, 1711
5:29 just as Christ does the c— 1711
5:32 but I am talking about Christ and the c. 1711
Php 3: 6 as for zeal, persecuting the c; 1711
4:15 not one c shared with me in the matter 1711
Col 1:18 And he is the head of the body, the c; 1711
1:24 for the sake of his body, which is the c. 1711
4:15 and to Nympha and the c in her house. 1711
4:16 also read in the c of the Laodiceans and 1711
1Th 1: 1 To the c of the Thessalonians in God 1711
2Th 1: 1 To the c of the Thessalonians 1711
1Ti 3: 5 how can he take care of God's c?) 1711
3:15 which is the c of the living God, 1711
5:16 and not let the c be burdened with them, 1711
5:16 the c can help those widows who are really NIG
5:17 of the c well are worthy of double honor, NIG
Phm 1: 2 and to the c that meets in your home: 1711
Heb 12:23 to the c of the firstborn, 1711
Jas 5:14 He should call the elders of the c to pray 1711
3Jn 1: 6 They have told the c about your love. 1711
1: 9 I wrote to the c, but Diotrephes, 1711
1:10 to do so and puts them out of the c. 1711
Rev 2: 1 "To the angel of the c in Ephesus write: 1711
2: 8 "To the angel of the c in Smyrna write: 1711
2:12 "To the angel of the c in Pergamum write: 1711
2:18 "To the angel of the c in Thyatira write: 1711
3: 1 "To the angel of the c in Sardis write: 1711
3: 7 "To the angel of the c in Philadelphia write: 1711
3:14 "To the angel of the c in Laodicea write: 1711

CHURCHES (35) [CHURCH]

Ac 15:41 and Cilicia, strengthening the c. 1711
16: 5 So the c were strengthened in the faith 1711
Ro 16: 4 the c of the Gentiles are grateful to them. 1711
16:16 All the c of Christ send greetings. 1711
1Co 7:17 This is the rule I lay down in all the c. 1711
11:16 nor do the c of God. 1711
14:34 women should remain silent in the c. 1711
16: 1 Do what I told the Galatian c to do. 1711
16:19 The c in the province of Asia 1711
2Co 8: 1 that God has given the Macedonian c. 1711
8:18 by all the c for his service to the gospel. 1711
8:19 he was chosen by the c to accompany us 1711
8:23 they are representatives of the c and 1711
8:24 so that the c can see it. 1711
11: 8 I robbed other c by receiving support 1711
11:28 the pressure of my concern for all the c. 1711
12:13 How were you inferior to the other c, 1711
Gal 1: 2 To the c in Galatia: 1711
1:22 to the c of Judea that are in Christ. 1711
1Th 2:14 became imitators of God's c in Judea, 1711
2:14 the same things those c suffered from NIG
2Th 1: 4 among God's c we boast 1711
Rev 1: 4 To the seven c in the province of Asia: 1711
1:11 and send it to the seven c: 1711
1:20 seven stars are the angels of the seven c, 1711
1:20 and the seven lampstands are the seven c. 1711
2: 7 let him hear what the Spirit says to the c. 1711
2:11 let him hear what the Spirit says to the c. 1711
2:17 let him hear what the Spirit says to the c. 1711
2:23 Then all the c will know 1711
2:29 let him hear what the Spirit says to the c. 1711
3: 6 let him hear what the Spirit says to the c. 1711
3:13 let him hear what the Spirit says to the c. 1711
3:22 let him hear what the Spirit says to the c." 1711
22:16 to give you this testimony for the c. 1711

CHURN (1) [CHURNED, CHURNING, CHURNS]

Job 41:31 He makes the depths c like a boiling caldron 8409

CHURNED (1) [CHURN]

Job 26:12 By his power he c up the sea; 8088

CHURNING (5) [CHURN]

Job 30:27 The c inside me never stops; 8409
Pr 30:33 For as c the milk produces butter, 4790
Eze 32: 2 the seas thrashing about in your streams, c 1931
Da 7: 2 the four winds of heaven c up the great sea. 10137
Hab 3:15 c the great waters. 2816

CHURNS (1) [CHURN]

Isa 51:15 who c up the sea so that its waves roar— 8088

CHUSHAN-RISHATHAIM (KJV) See CUSHAN-RISHATHAIM

CHUZA (Anglicized, KJV) See CUZA

CIELED (KJV) See COVERED, PANELED, PANELS

CILICIA (8)

Ac 6: 9 as well as the provinces of C and Asia. 3070
15:23 Syria and C: Greetings. 3070
15:41 He went through Syria and C, 3070
21:39 "I am a Jew, from Tarsus in C, 3070
22: 3 born in Tarsus of C, 3070
23:34 Learning that he was from C, 3070
27: 5 across the open sea off the coast of C 3070
Gal 1:21 Later I went to Syria and C. 3070

CINNAMON (4)

Ex 30:23 250 shekels) of fragrant c, 7872
Pr 7:17 with myrrh, aloes and c. 7872
SS 4:14 and c, with every kind of incense tree, 7872
Rev 18:13 cargoes of c and spice, of incense, myrrh 3077

CINNEROTH (KJV) See KINNEROTH

CIRCLE (4) [CIRCLED, CIRCLING, CIRCUIT, CIRCULAR, CIRCUMFERENCE, ENCIRCLE, ENCIRCLED, ENCIRCLING]

2Sa 5:23 but c around behind them and attack them 6015
1Ch 14:14 but c around them and attack them in front 6015
Isa 40:22 He sits enthroned above the c of the earth, 2553
Mk 3:34 at those seated in a c around him and said, 3241

CIRCLED (1) [CIRCLE]

Jos 6:15 that on that day they c the city seven times. 6015

CIRCLING (1) [CIRCLE]

Jos 6:11 around the city, c it once. 5938

CIRCUIT (2) [CIRCLE]

1Sa 7:16 on a c from Bethel to Gilgal to Mizpah, 6015
Ps 19: 6 of the heavens and makes its c to the other; 9543

CIRCULAR (4) [CIRCLE]

1Ki 7:23 He made the Sea of cast metal, c in shape, 6017+6318
7:31 that had a c frame one cubit deep. 4196
7:35 top of the stand there was a c band 6017+6318
2Ch 4: 2 He made the Sea of cast metal, c in shape, 6017+6318

CIRCULATED (1)

Mt 28:15 And this story has been widely c among 1424

CIRCUMCISE (9) [CIRCUMCISED, CIRCUMCISING, CIRCUMCISION]

Dt 10:16 C your hearts, therefore, 4576+6889
30: 6 The LORD your God will c your hearts 4576
Jos 5: 2 and c the Israelites again." 4909
Jer 4: 4 C yourselves to the LORD, 4576
4: 4 c your hearts, you men of Judah 6073+6889
Lk 1:59 On the eighth day they came to c the child, 4362
2:21 when it was time to c him, 4362
Jn 7:22 you c a child on the Sabbath. 4362
Ac 21:21 telling them not to c their children or live 4362

CIRCUMCISED (51) [CIRCUMCISE]
Ge 17:10 Every male among you shall be c. 4576
17:12 among you who is eight days old must be c, 4576
17:13 they must be c. 4576+4576
17:14 who has not been c in the flesh, 4576+6889
17:23 every male in his household, and c them, as God told him. 1414+4576+6889
17:24 Abraham was ninety-nine years old when he was c, 1414+4576+6889
17:26 Abraham and his son Ishmael were both c 4576
17:27 was c with him. 4576
21: 4 Abraham c him, as God commanded him. 4576
34:14 to a man who is not c. 2257+4200+6889
34:17 But if you will not agree to be c, 4576
34:22 on the condition that our males be c, 4576
34:24 and every male in the city was c. 4576
Ex 12:44 of it after you have c him, 4576
12:48 the males in his household c; 4576
Lev 12: 3 On the eighth day the boy is to be c. 1414+4576+6889
Jos 5: 3 and c the Israelites at Gibeath Haaraloth. 4576
5: 5 All the people that came out had been c, 4576
5: 7 and these were the ones Joshua c. 4576
5: 7 because they had not been c on the way. 4576
5: 8 And after the whole nation had been c, 4576
Jer 9:25 "when I will punish all who are c only in 4576
Jn 7:23 Now if a child can be c on the Sabbath 3284+4364
Ac 7: 8 the father of Isaac and c him eight days 4362
10:45 The c believers who had come 1666+4364
11: 2 the c believers criticized him 1666+4364
15: 1 "Unless you are c, according to the custom 4362
15: 5 "The Gentiles must be c and required 4362
16: 3 so he c him because of the Jews 3284+4362
Ro 2:25 as though you had not been c. 213
2:26 If those who are not c keep 213
2:26 not be regarded as though they were c? 4364
2:27 The one who is not c physically and 213
3:30 who will justify the c by faith and 4364
4: 9 Is this blessedness only for the c, 4364
4:10 Was it after he was c, or before? 1639+1877+4364
4:11 of all who believe but have not been c, 213
4:12 father of the c who not only are circumcised 4364
4:12 of the circumcised who not only are c 1666+4364
4:12 father Abraham had before he was c. 213+1877
1Co 7:18 Was a man already c when he was called? 4362
7:18 He should not be c. 4362
Gal 2: 3 who was with me, was compelled to be c, 4362
5: 2 tell you that if you let yourselves be c, 4362
5: 3 to every man who lets himself be c 4362
6:12 trying to compel you to be c. 4362
6:13 Not even those who are c obey the law, 4362
6:13 be c that they may boast about your flesh. 4362
Php 3: 5 c on the eighth day, of the people of Israel, 4364
Col 2:11 In him you were also c, 4362
3:11 c or uncircumcised, barbarian, Scythian, 4364

CIRCUMCISING (1) [CIRCUMCISE]
Ge 34:15 you become like us by c all your males. 4576

CIRCUMCISION (21) [CIRCUMCISE]
Ge 17:11 You are to undergo c, 906+1414+4576+6889
Ex 4:26 "bridegroom of blood," referring to c.) 4581
Jn 7:22 because Moses gave you c 4364
Ac 7: 8 Then he gave Abraham the covenant of c. 4364
Ro 2:25 C has value if you observe the law, 4364
2:27 though you have the written code and c, 4364
2:28 nor is c merely outward and physical. 4364
2:29 and c is circumcision of the heart, 4364
2:29 and circumcision is c of the heart, NIG
3: 1 or what value is there in c? 4364
4:11 And he received the sign of c, 4364
1Co 7:19 C is nothing and uncircumcision is nothing. 4364
Gal 2:12 of those who belonged to the c group. 4364
5: 6 For in Christ Jesus neither c 4364
5:11 Brothers, if I am still preaching c, 4364
6:15 Neither c nor uncircumcision means anything; 4364
Eph 2:11 "the c" (that done in the body by the hands 4364
Php 3: 3 For it is we who are the c, 4364
Col 2:11 with a c done by the hands of men but with 4364
2:11 by the hands of men but with the c done 4364
Tit 1:10 especially those of the c group. 4364

CIRCUMFERENCE (1) [CIRCLE]
Jer 52:21 and twelve cubits in c; 2562+6015

CIRCUMSPECT (KJV) See CAREFUL

CIRCUMSTANCES (8)
1Ch 29:30 and the c that surrounded him and Israel 6961
Ro 4:10 Under what c was it credited? 4802
1Co 7:15 or woman is not bound in such c; AIT
Php 4:11 I have learned to be content whatever the c. NIG
Col 4: 8 that you may know about our c and 3836
1Th 5:18 give thanks in all c, AIT
Jas 1: 9 The brother in humble c ought to take pride 5424
1Pe 1:11 to find out the time and c to which the Spirit AIT

CIS (KJV) See KISH

CISTERN (20) [CISTERNS]
Ge 37:22 Throw him into this c here in the desert, 1014
37:24 they took him and threw him into the c. 1014
37:24 the c was empty; there was no water in it. 1014
37:28 his brothers pulled Joseph up out of the c 1014
37:29 to the c and saw that Joseph was not there, 1014
Lev 11:36 or a c for collecting water remains clean, 1014
1Sa 19:22 for Ramah and went to the great c at Secu. 1014
2Ki 18:31 and drink water from his own c, 1014
Pr 5:15 Drink water from your own c, 1014
Isa 30:14 from a hearth or scooping water out of a c." 1465
36:16 and drink water from his own c, 1014
Jer 38: 6 and put him into the c of Malkijah, 1014
38: 6 lowered Jeremiah by ropes into the c; 1014
38: 7 heard that they had put Jeremiah into the c. 1014
38: 9 They have thrown him into a c, 1014
38:10 and lift Jeremiah the prophet out of the c 1014
38:11 down with ropes to Jeremiah in the c. 1014
38:13 with the ropes and lifted him out of the c. 1014
41: 7 and threw them into a c. 1014
41: 9 Now the c where he threw all the bodies of 1014

CISTERNS (6) [CISTERN]
Ge 37:20 and throw him into one of these c and say 1014
1Sa 13: 6 among the rocks, and in pits and c. 1014
2Ch 26:10 in the desert and dug many c, 1014
Jer 2:13 and have dug their own c, 1014
2:13 broken c that cannot hold water. 1014
14: 3 they go to the c but find no water. 1463

CITADEL (20) [CITADELS]
2Sa 12:26 of the Ammonites and captured the royal c. 6551
1Ki 16:18 the c of the royal palace and set the palace 810
2Ki 15:25 in the c of the royal palace at Samaria. 810
Ezr 6: 2 the c of Ecbatana in the province of Media, 10101
Ne 1: 1 while I was in the c of Susa, 1072
2: 8 of the c by the temple and for the city wall 1072
7: 2 with Hananiah the commander of the c, 1072
Est 1: 2 from his royal throne in the c of Susa, 1072
1: 5 who were in the c of Susa. 1072
2: 3 into the harem at the c of Susa. 1072
2: 5 Now there was in the c of Susa a Jew of 1072
2: 8 many girls were brought to the c of Susa 1072
3:15 and the edict was issued in the c of Susa. 1072
8:14 the edict was also issued in the c of Susa. 1072
9: 6 In the c of Susa, 1072
9:11 of those slain in the c of Susa was reported 1072
9:12 and the ten sons of Haman in the c of Susa. 1072
Pr 18:19 disputes are like the barred gates of a c. 810
Isa 32:14 c and watchtower will become 6755
Da 8: 2 In my vision I saw myself in the c of Susa 1072

CITADELS (4) [CITADEL]
Ps 48: 3 God is in her c; 810
48:13 view her c, that you may tell of them to 810
122: 7 and security within your c." 810
Isa 34:13 Thorns will overrun her c, 810

CITIES (150) [CITY]
Ge 13:12 while Lot lived among the c of the plain 6551
19:25 Thus he overthrew those c and 6551
19:25 including all those living in the c— 6551
19:29 So when God destroyed the c of the plain, 6551
19:29 that overthrew the c where Lot had lived. 6551
22:17 of the c of their enemies, 9133
41:35 to be kept in the c for food. 6551
41:48 in Egypt and stored it in the c. 6551
Ex 1:11 and Rameses as store c for Pharaoh. 6551
Lev 26:25 When you withdraw into your c, 6551
26:31 I will turn your c into ruins 6551
26:33 and your c will lie in ruins. 6551
Nu 13:28 and the c are fortified and very large. 6551
21: 2 we will totally destroy their c." 6551
21:25 the c of the Amorites and occupied them, 6551
32:16 to build pens here for our livestock and c 6551
32:17 and children will live in fortified c, 6551
32:24 Build c for your women and children, 6551
32:26 and herds will remain here in the c 6551
32:33 the whole land with its c and the territory 6551
32:36 Beth Nimrah and Beth Haran as fortified c, 6551
32:38 They gave names to the c they rebuilt. 6551
35: 6 of the towns you give the Levites will be c 6551
35:11 select some towns to be your c of refuge, 6551
35:13 These six towns you give will be your c 6551
35:14 of the Jordan and three in Canaan as c 6551
Dt 1:28 the c are large, with walls up to the sky. 6551
3: 4 At that time we took all his c. 6551
3: 4 not one of the sixty c that we did not take 6551
3: 5 All these c were fortified with high walls 6551
3: 7 and the plunder from their c we carried off 6551
4:41 Moses set aside three c east of the Jordan, 6551
4:42 into one of these c and save his life. 6551
4:43 The c were these: NIH
6:10 flourishing c you did not build, 6551
9: 1 with large c that have walls up to the sky. 6551
19: 2 for yourselves three c centrally located in 6551
19: 5 That man may flee to one of these c 6551
19: 7 to set aside for yourselves three c. 6551
19: 9 then you are to set aside three more c. 6551
19:11 and then flees to one of these c, 6551
20:15 the c that are at a distance from you and do 6551
20:16 in the c of the nations 6551
28:52 to all the c throughout your land until 9133
28:52 They will besiege all the c throughout 9133
28:55 on you during the siege of all your c. 9133
28:57 inflict on you in your c. 9133
Jos 9:17 and on the third day came to their c: 6551
10: 2 like one of the royal c; 6551
10:19 the rear and don't let them reach their c, 6551
10:20 few who were left reached their fortified c. 6551
11:12 Joshua took all these royal c 6551
11:13 Yet Israel did not burn any of the c built 6551
11:14 the plunder and livestock of these c, 6551
13:31 and Ashtaroth and Edrei (the royal c of Og 6551
14:12 and their c were large and fortified, 6551
18:21 clan by clan, had the following c: 6551
19:35 The fortified c were Ziddim, Zer, 6551
20: 2 the Israelites to designate the c of refuge, 6551
20: 4 "When he flees to one of these c, 6551
20: 9 to these designated c and not be killed by 6551
24:13 on which you did not toil and c you did 6551
2Sa 10:12 for our people and the c of our God. 6551
20: 6 he will find fortified c and escape from us." 6551
1Ki 4:13 in Bashan and its sixty large walled c 6551
8:37 enemy besieges them in any of their c, 824+9133
9:19 as well as all his store c and the towns 6551
10:26 which he kept in the chariot c and also 6551
15:23 all he did and the c he built, 6551
20:34 the c my father took from your father," 6551
22:39 and the c he fortified, 6551
2Ki 18:13 the fortified c of Judah and captured them. 6551
19:25 that you have turned fortified c into piles 6551
1Ch 19:13 for our people and the c of our God. 6551
2Ch 1:14 which he kept in the chariot c and also 6551
6:28 besiege them in any of their c, 824+9133
8: 4 in the desert and all the store c he had built 6551
8: 5 and Lower Beth Horon as fortified c, 6551
8: 6 as well as Baalath and all his store c, 6551
8: 6 the c for his chariots and for his horses— 6551
9:25 which he kept in the chariot c and also 6551
11:10 These were fortified c in Judah 6551
11:12 He put shields and spears in all the c, 2256+6551+6551
11:23 and to all the fortified c. 6551
12: 4 the fortified c of Judah and came as far 6551
14: 6 He built up the fortified c of Judah, 6551
16: 4 Abel Maim and all the store c of Naphtali. 6551
17: 2 the fortified c of Judah and put garrisons 6551
17:12 he built forts and store c in Judah 6551
17:19 besides those he stationed in the fortified c 6551
19: 5 in each of the fortified c of Judah. 6551
19:10 fellow countrymen who live in the c— 6551
21: 3 as well as fortified c in Judah, 6551
32: 1 He laid siege to the fortified c, 6551
33:14 in all the fortified c in Judah. 6551
Ne 9:25 They captured fortified c and fertile land; 6551
Est 9: 2 The Jews assembled in their c in all 6551
Ps 9: 6 you have uprooted their c; 6551
69:35 for God will save Zion and rebuild the c 6551
Isa 1: 7 your c burned with fire; 6551
6:11 the c lie ruined and without inhabitant, 6551
14:17 who overthrew its c and would 6551
14:21 the land and cover the earth with their c. 6551
17: 2 The c of Aroer will be deserted and left 6551
17: 9 In that day their strong c, 6551
19:18 In that day five c in Egypt will speak 6551
25: 3 c of ruthless nations will revere you. 7953
36: 1 the fortified c of Judah and captured them. 6551
37:26 that you have turned fortified c into piles 6551
54: 3 and settle in their desolate c. 6551
61: 4 the ruined c that have been devastated 6551
64:10 Your sacred c have become a desert; 6551
Jer 4: 5 Let us flee to the fortified c!' 6551
4:16 raising a war cry against the c of Judah. 6551
5:17 the sword they will destroy the fortified c 6551
8:14 to the fortified c and perish there! 6551
13:19 The c in the Negev will be shut up, 6551
14: 2 "Judah mourns, her c languish; 9133
34: 7 against Jerusalem and the other c of Judah 6551
34: 7 These were the only fortified c left 6551
46: 8 I will destroy c and their people.' 6551
48:18 up against you and ruin your fortified c. 4448
Eze 26:19 like c no longer inhabited, 6551
29:12 and her c will lie desolate forty years 6551
29:12 and her cities will lie desolate forty years among ruined c. 6551
30: 7 and their c will lie among ruined cities. 6551
30: 7 and their cities will lie among ruined c. 6551
30:17 and the c themselves will go into captivity. NIH
36:35 the c that were lying in ruins, 6551
36:38 the ruined c be filled with flocks of people. 6551
Hos 8:14 But I will send fire upon their c 6551
11: 6 Swords will flash in their c, 6551
Am 9:14 they will rebuild the ruined c and live 6551
Mic 5:11 I will destroy the c of your land and tear 6551
5:14 and demolish your c. 6551
7:12 to you from Assyria and the c of Egypt, 6551
Hab 1:10 They laugh at all fortified c; 4448
2: 8 you have destroyed lands and c 7953
2:17 you have destroyed lands and c 7953
Zep 1:16 and battle cry against the fortified c and 6551
3: 6 Their c are destroyed; 6551
Zec 8:20 the inhabitants of many c will yet come, 6551
Mt 10:23 you will not finish going through the c 4484
11:20 Then Jesus began to denounce the c in which most of his miracles 4484
Lk 19:17 take charge of ten c.' 4484
19:19 'You take charge of five c.' 4484
Ac 14: 6 the Lycaonian c of Lystra and Derbe and to 4484
26:11 I even went to foreign c to persecute them. 4484
2Pe 2: 6 if he condemned the c of Sodom and Gomorrah 4484
Rev 16:19 and the c of the nations collapsed. 4484

CITIZEN (8) [CITIZENS, CITIZENSHIP]

Lk 15:15 and hired himself out to a **c** of that country, *4489*
Ac 21:39 a **c** of no ordinary city. *4489*
22:25 for you to flog a **Roman c** who hasn't *476+4871*
22:26 "This man is a **Roman c.**" *4871*
22:27 "Tell me, are you a **Roman c?**" *4871*
22:28 "But I was born a **c,**" Paul replied. *NIG*
22:29 put Paul, a **Roman c,** in chains. *4871*
23:27 for I had learned that he is a **Roman c.** *4871*

CITIZENS (24) [CITIZEN]

Nu 21:28 the **c** *of* Arnon's heights. 1251
Jos 8:33 All Israel, aliens and **c** alike, 275
24:11 The **c** of Jericho fought against you, 1251
Jdg 9:2 the **c** *of* Shechem, 'Which is better for you: 1251
9:3 When the brothers repeated all this to the **c** 1251
9:6 the **c** *of* Shechem and Beth Millo gathered 1251
9:7 "Listen to me, **c** *of* Shechem, 1251
9:18 king over the **c** *of* Shechem 1251
9:20 **c** *of* Shechem and Beth Millo, 1251
9:20 **c** *of* Shechem and Beth Millo, 1251
9:23 between Abimelech and the **c** *of* Shechem, 1251
9:24 on their brother Abimelech and on the **c** 1251
9:25 to him these **c** *of* Shechem set men on 1251
9:26 and its **c** put their confidence in him. 1251
9:39 the **c** *of* Shechem and fought Abimelech. 1251
9:46 the **c** *in* the tower of Shechem went into 1251
1Sa 23:11 Will the **c** *of* Keilah surrender me to him? 1251
23:12 the **c** *of* Keilah surrender me and my men 1251
2Sa 21:12 of Saul and his son Jonathan from the **c** 1251
Isa 48:2 you who call yourselves **c of** the holy city 4946^{S}
Eze 26:17 you and your **c**; 3782
Ac 16:37 even though we are **Roman c,** *476+4871*
16:38 that Paul and Silas were **Roman c,** *4871*
Eph 2:19 but **fellow c with** God's people *5232*

CITIZENSHIP (3) [CITIZEN]

Ac 22:28 "I had to pay a big price for my **c.**" *4486*
Eph 2:12 excluded *from* **c** in Israel and foreigners to *4486*
Php 3:20 But our **c** is in heaven. *4487*

CITRON (1)

Rev 18:12 every sort of **c** wood, *2591*

CITY (718) [CITIES, CITY'S]

Ge 4:17 Cain was then building a **c,** 6551
10:12 that is the great **c.** 6551
11:4 "Come, let us build ourselves a **c,** 6551
11:5 But the LORD came down to see the **c** 6551
11:8 and they stopped building the **c.** 6551
18:24 if there are fifty righteous people in the **c?** 6551
18:26 "If I find fifty righteous people in the **c** 6551
18:28 Will you destroy the whole **c** because 6551
19:1 and Lot was sitting in the gateway of **the c.** 6042^{S}
19:4 from every part of the **c** *of* Sodom— 6551
19:12 or anyone else in the **c** who belongs 6551
19:14 the LORD is about to destroy the **c!**" 6551
19:15 be swept away when the **c** is punished." 6551
19:16 and led them safely out of the **c,** 6551
23:10 to the gate of his **c.** 6551
23:18 to the gate of the **c.** 6551
28:19 though the **c** used to be called Luz. 6551
33:18 at the **c** *of* Shechem in Canaan and camped 6551
33:18 and camped within sight of the **c.** 6551
34:20 to the gate of their **c** to speak 6551
34:24 the men who went out of the **c** gate agreed 6551
34:24 and every male in the **c** was circumcised. 6551
34:25 and attacked the unsuspecting **c,** 6551
34:27 the **c** where their sister had been defiled. 6551
34:28 of theirs in the **c** and out in the fields. 6551
36:32 His **c** was named Dinhabah. 6551
36:35 His **c** was named Avith. 6551
36:39 His **c** was named Pau. 6551
41:48 In each **c** he put the food grown in 6551
44:4 from the **c** when Joseph said to his steward, 6551
44:13 and returned to the **c.** 6551
Ex 9:29 "When I have gone out of the **c,** 6551
9:33 Moses left Pharaoh and went out of the **c.** 6551
Lev 25:29 " 'If a man sells a house in a walled **c,** 6551
25:30 in the walled **c** shall belong permanently to 6551
Nu 21:26 the **c** *of* Sihon king of the Amorites, 6551
21:27 let Sihon's **c** be restored. 6551
21:28 a blaze from the **c** *of* Sihon. 7953
24:19 of Jacob and destroy the survivors of the **c.**" 6551
35:25 and send him back to the **c** *of* refuge 6551
35:26 of the **c** *of* refuge to which he has fled 6551
35:27 avenger of blood finds him outside the **c,** 6551
35:28 The accused must stay in his **c** *of* refuge 6551
35:32 a **c** *of* refuge and so allow him to go back 6551
Dt 3:6 of Heshbon, destroying every **c—** 6551
17:5 to your **c gate** and stone that person 9133
19:12 bring him back from **the c,** 9004^{S}
20:10 When you march up to attack a **c,** 6551
20:12 lay siege to **that c.** 2023^{S}
20:14 the livestock and everything else in the **c,** 6551
20:19 When you lay siege to a **c** for a long time, 6551
20:20 to build siege works until the **c** at war 6551
28:3 You will be blessed in the **c** and blessed in 6551
28:16 You will be cursed in the **c** and cursed in 6551
34:3 the C *of* Palms, as far as Zoar. 6551
Jos 2:5 when it was time to close the **c gate,** 9133
2:15 house she lived in was part of the **c** wall. 7815
6:3 around the **c** once with all the armed men. 6551
6:4 march around the **c** seven times, 6551
Jos 6:5 of the **c** will collapse and the people will go 6551
6:7 March around the **c,** 6551
6:11 the ark of the LORD carried around the **c,** 6551
6:14 the **c** once and returned to the camp. 6551
6:15 and marched around the **c** seven times in 6551
6:15 on that day they circled the **c** seven times. 6551
6:16 For the LORD has given you the **c!** 6551
6:17 The **c** and all that is in it are to be devoted 6551
6:20 and they took the **c.** 6551
6:21 the **c** to the LORD and destroyed with 6551
6:24 the whole **c** and everything in it, 6551
6:26 the man who undertakes to rebuild this **c,** 6551
7:5 from the **c gate** as far as the stone quarries 9133
8:1 his people, his **c** and his land. 6551
8:2 Set an ambush behind the **c.**" 6551
8:4 You are to set an ambush behind the **c.** 6551
8:5 with me will advance on the **c,** 6551
8:6 until we have lured them away from the **c,** 6551
8:7 to rise up from ambush and take the **c.** 6551
8:8 When you have taken the **c,** set it on fire. 6551
8:11 with him marched up and approached the **c** 6551
8:11 with the valley between them and the **c.** 6504^{S}
8:12 to the west of the **c.** 6551
8:13 all those in the camp to the north of the **c** 6551
8:14 and all the men of the **c** hurried out early in 6551
8:14 against him behind the **c.** 6551
8:16 and were lured away from the **c.** 6551
8:17 They left the **c** open and went in pursuit 6551
8:18 for into your hand I will deliver **the c.**" 5626^{S}
8:19 the **c** and captured it and quickly set it 6551
8:20 and saw the smoke of the **c** rising against 6551
8:21 the **c** and that smoke was going up from 6551
8:21 and that smoke was going up from the **c,** 6551
8:22 of the ambush also came out of the **c** 6551
8:27 the livestock and plunder of this **c,** 6551
8:29 down at the entrance of the **c** gate. 6551
10:2 because Gibeon was an important **c,** 6551
10:28 He put **the c** and its king to the sword 2023^{S}
10:30 The LORD also gave **that c** and its king 2023^{S}
10:30 **The c** and everyone in it Joshua put to 2023^{S}
10:32 **The c** and everyone in it he put to 2023^{S}
10:37 They took **the c** and put it to the sword, 2023^{S}
10:39 They took **the c,** its king and its villages, 2023^{S}
11:19 not one **c** made a treaty of peace with 6551
15:8 the southern slope of the Jebusite **c** (that is, NIH
15:62 the C *of* Salt and En Gedi— 6551
18:16 the southern slope of the **Jebusite** *c* and so AIT
18:28 Haeleph, the **Jebusite** *c* (that is, Jerusalem), AIT
19:29 toward Ramah and went to the fortified **c** 6551
20:4 the entrance of the **c** gate and state his case 6551
20:4 before the elders of that **c.** 6551
20:4 into their **c** and give him a place to live 6551
20:6 to stay in that **c** until he has stood trial 6551
21:12 around the **c** they had given to Caleb son 6551
21:13 (a **c** *of* refuge for one accused of murder), 6551
21:21 (a **c** *of* refuge for one accused of murder) 6551
21:27 (a **c** *of* refuge for one accused of murder) 6551
21:32 (a **c** *of* refuge for one accused of murder), 6551
21:38 (a **c** *of* refuge for one accused of murder), 6551
Jdg 1:8 They put the **c** to the sword and set it 6551
1:16 from the C *of* Palms with the men of Judah 6551
1:17 and they totally destroyed the **c.** 6551
1:18 each **c** with its territory. NIH
1:24 a man coming out of the **c** and they said 6551
1:24 how to get into the **c** and we will see 6551
1:25 and they put the **c** to the sword but spared 6551
1:26 where he built a **c** and called it Luz, 6551
3:13 they took possession of the C *of* Palms. 6551
5:8 war came to the **c gates,** 9133
5:11 of the LORD went down to the **c gates.** 9133
9:30 of the **c** heard what Gaal son of Ebed said, 6551
9:31 and are stirring up the **c** against you. 6551
9:33 advance against the **c.** 6551
9:35 the entrance to the **c** gate just as Abimelech 6551
9:43 he saw the people coming out of the **c,** 6551
9:44 to a position at the entrance to the **c** gate. 6551
9:45 against the **c** until he had captured it 6551
9:45 he destroyed the **c** and scattered salt over it. 6551
9:51 Inside the **c,** however, was a strong tower, 6551
9:51 all the people of the **c**—fled. 6551
16:2 in wait for him all night at the **c** gate. 6551
16:3 up and took hold of the doors of the **c** gate, 6551
18:27 with the sword and burned down their **c.** 6551
18:28 **The c** was in a valley near Beth Rehob. 2085^{S}
18:28 The Danites rebuilt the **c** and settled there. 6551
18:29 though the **c** used to be called Laish. 6551
19:11 at this **c** *of* the Jebusites and spend 6551
19:12 We won't go into an alien **c,** 6551
19:15 They went and sat in the **c** square, 6551
19:17 and saw the traveler in the **c** square, 6551
19:22 of the wicked men of the **c** surrounded 6551
20:11 and united as one man against the **c.** 6551
20:31 and were drawn away from the **c.** 6551
20:32 and draw them away from the **c** to 6551
20:37 and put the whole **c** to the sword. 6551
20:38 up a great cloud of smoke from the **c,** 6551
20:40 column of smoke began to rise from the **c,** 6551
20:40 and saw the smoke of the whole **c** going up 6551
1Sa 5:9 the LORD's hand was against that **c,** 6551
5:9 He afflicted the people of the **c,** 6551
5:11 For death had filled the **c** with panic; 6551
5:12 and the outcry of the **c** went up to heaven. 6551
15:5 to the **c** *of* Amalek and set an ambush in 6551
27:5 Why should your servant live in the royal **c** 6551
2Sa 5:7 fortress of Zion, the C *of* David. 6551
5:9 in the fortress and called it the C *of* David. 6551
6:10 of the LORD to be with him in the C 6551
2Sa 6:12 the house of Obed-Edom to the C *of* David 6551
6:16 the LORD was entering the C *of* David, 6551
10:3 the **c** and spy it out and overthrow it?" 6551
10:8 at the entrance to their **c gate,** 9133
10:14 before Abishai and went inside the **c.** 6551
11:16 So while Joab had the **c** under siege, 6551
11:17 of the **c** came out and fought against Joab, 6551
11:20 'Why did you get so close to the **c** to fight? 6551
11:23 to the entrance to the **c gate.** 9133
11:25 the attack against the **c** and destroy it.' 6551
12:28 the troops and besiege the **c** and capture it. 6551
12:28 Otherwise I will take the **c,** 6551
12:30 a great quantity of plunder from the **c** 6551
15:2 the side of the road leading to the **c gate.** 9133
15:14 and bring ruin upon us and put the **c** to 6551
15:24 the people had finished leaving the **c.** 6551
15:25 "Take the ark of God back into the **c.** 6551
15:27 Go back to the **c** in peace, 6551
15:34 if you return to the **c** and say to Absalom, 6551
15:37 as Absalom was entering the **c.** 6551
17:13 If he withdraws into a **c,** 6551
17:13 then all Israel will bring ropes to that **c,** 6551
17:17 not risk being seen entering the **c.** 6551
18:3 now for you to give us support from the **c.**" 6551
19:3 The men stole into the **c** that day 6551
20:15 They built a siege ramp up to the **c,** 6551
20:16 a wise woman called from the **c,** 6551
20:19 to destroy a **c** that is a mother in Israel. 6551
20:21 and I'll withdraw from the **c.**" 6551
20:22 and his men dispersed from the **c,** 6551
1Ki 1:41 the meaning of all the noise in the **c?**" 7953
1:45 and the **c** resounds with it. 7953
2:10 with his fathers and was buried in the C 6551
3:1 He brought her to the C *of* David 6551
8:1 from Zion, the C *of* David. 6551
8:16 not chosen a **c** in any tribe of Israel to have 6551
8:44 the LORD toward the **c** you have chosen 6551
8:48 toward the **c** you have chosen and 6551
9:24 up from the C *of* David to 6551
11:27 and had filled in the gap in the wall of the **c** 6551
11:32 for the sake of my servant David and the **c** 6551
11:36 the **c** where I chose to put my Name. 6551
11:43 and was buried in the **c** *of* David his father. 6551
13:25 and they went and reported it in the **c** 6551
13:29 and brought it back to his own **c** to mourn 6551
14:11 to Jeroboam who die in the **c,** 6551
14:12 When you set foot in your **c,** 6551
14:21 the **c** the LORD had chosen out of all 6551
14:31 and was buried with them in the C 6551
15:8 with his fathers and was buried in the C 6551
15:24 with them in the **c** *of* his father David. 6551
16:4 to Baasha who die in the **c,** 6551
16:18 When Zimri saw that the **c** was taken, 6551
16:24 for two talents of silver and built a **c** on 6551
20:2 He sent messengers into the **c** to Ahab king 6551
20:12 So they prepared to attack the **c.** 6551
20:19 of the **c** with the army behind them 6551
20:30 The rest of them escaped to the **c** of Aphek, 6551
20:30 And Ben-Hadad fled to the **c** and hid in 6551
21:8 and nobles who lived in Naboth's **c** 6551
21:11 and nobles who lived in Naboth's **c** did 6551
21:13 So they took him outside the **c** 6551
21:24 to Ahab who die in the **c,** 6551
22:26 to Amon the ruler of the **c** and to Joash 6551
22:50 with them in the **c** *of* David his father. 6551
2Ki 2:19 The men of the **c** said to Elisha, "Look, 6551
3:19 You will overthrow every fortified **c** 6551
3:27 offered him as a sacrifice on the **c wall.** 2570
6:14 They went by night and surrounded the **c.** 6551
6:15 and chariots had surrounded the **c.** 6551
6:19 "This is not the road and this is not the **c.** 6551
6:20 After they entered **the c,** Elisha said, 9076^{S}
6:25 There was a great famine in **the c;** 9076^{S}
7:3 with leprosy at the entrance of the **c gate.** 9133
7:4 If we say, 'We'll go into the **c'**— 6551
7:10 the **c** gatekeepers and told them, "We went 6551
7:12 and get into the **c.**' " 6551
7:13 of the horses that are left in **the c.** 2023^{S}
8:24 and was buried with them in the C 6551
9:15 of the **c** to go and tell the news in Jezreel." 6551
9:28 with his fathers in his tomb in the C 6551
10:2 a fortified **c** and weapons, 6551
10:5 So the palace administrator, the **c** governor, 6551
10:6 were with the leading men of the **c,** 6551
10:8 the entrance of the **c gate** until morning." 9133
11:20 And the **c** was quiet, 6551
12:21 and was buried with his fathers in the C 6551
14:20 in the C *of* David. 6551
15:7 and was buried near them in the C 6551
15:16 attacked Tiphsah and everyone in **the c** 2023^{S}
15:38 and was buried with them in the C 6551
15:38 the **c** of his father. NIH
16:20 and was buried with them in the C 6551
17:9 fortified **c** they built themselves high places 6551
18:8 From watchtower to fortified **c,** 6551
18:30 this **c** will not be given into the hand of 6551
19:13 the king of the **c** *of* Sepharvaim, 6551
19:32 not enter this **c** or shoot an arrow here. 6551
19:33 he will not enter this **c,** 6551
19:34 I will defend this **c** and save it, 6551
20:6 And I will deliver you and this **c** from 6551
20:6 I will defend this **c** for my sake and for 6551
20:20 by which he brought water into the **c,** 6551
23:8 to the Gate of Joshua, the **c** governor, 6551
23:8 which is on the left of the **c** gate. 6551
23:17 The men of the **c** said, 6551
23:27 and I will reject Jerusalem, the **c** I chose, 6551

2Ki 24:11 to the c while his officers were besieging it. 6551
25: 1 He encamped outside the c 2023S
25: 2 The c was kept under siege until 6551
25: 3 the famine in the c had become so severe 6551
25: 4 Then the c wall was broken through, 6551
25: 4 the Babylonians were surrounding the c. 6551
25:11 the people who remained in the c, 6551
25:19 Of those still in the c, 6551
25:19 of his men who were found in the c. 6551
1Ch 1:43 whose c was named Dinhabah. 6551
1:46 His c was named Avith. 6551
1:50 His c was named Pau, 6551
6:56 around the c were given to Caleb son 6551
6:57 of Aaron were given Hebron (a c 6551
6:67 of Ephraim they were given Shechem (a c 6551
11: 5 fortress of Zion, the C *of* David. 6551
11: 7 and so it was called the C *of* David. 6551
11: 8 He built up the c around it, 6551
11: 8 while Joab restored the rest of the c. 6551
13:13 the ark to be with him in the C *of* David. 6551
15: 1 for himself in the C *of* David, 6551
15:29 the LORD was entering the C *of* David, 6551
19: 9 at the entrance to their c, 6551
19:15 and went inside the c. 6551
20: 2 a great quantity of plunder from the c 6551
2Ch 5: 2 from Zion, the C *of* David. 6551
6: 5 not chosen a c in any tribe of Israel to have 6551
6:34 to you toward this c you have chosen and 6551
6:38 toward the c you have chosen and toward 6551
8:11 the C *of* David to the palace he had built 6551
9:31 and was buried in the c *of* David his father. 6551
12:13 the c the LORD had chosen out of all 6551
12:16 with his fathers and was buried in the C 6551
14: 1 with his fathers and was buried in the C 6551
15: 6 by another and *one* c by another, 6551
16:14 that he had cut out for himself in the C 6551
18:25 to Amon the ruler of the c and to Joash 6551
21: 1 and was buried with them in the C 6551
21:20 and was buried in the C *of* David, 6551
23:21 And the c was quiet, 6551
24:16 He was buried with the kings in the C 6551
24:25 he died and was buried in the C *of* David, 6551
25:28 and was buried with his fathers in the C 6551
27: 9 with his fathers and was buried in the C 6551
28:15 the C *of* Palms, and returned to Samaria. 6551
28:27 with his fathers and was buried in the c 6551
29:20 the c officials together and went up to 6551
32: 3 the water from the springs outside the c, 6551
32: 5 the supporting terraces of the C *of* David. 6551
32: 6 before him in the square at the c gate 6551
32:18 in order to capture the c. 6551
32:30 down to the west side of the C *of* David. 6551
33:14 Afterward he rebuilt the outer wall of the C 6551
33:15 and he threw them out of the c. 6551
34: 8 of Azaliah and Maaseiah the ruler of the c, 6551
Ezr 4:10 in the c of Samaria and elsewhere 10640
4:12 that rebellious and wicked c. 10640
4:13 the king should know that if this c is built 10640
4:15 In these records you will find that this c is 10640
4:15 that this city is a rebellious c, 10640
4:15 That is why this c was destroyed. 10640
4:16 if this c is built and its walls are restored, 10640
4:19 that this c has a long history of revolt 10640
4:21 this c will not be rebuilt until I so order. 10640
Ne 2: 3 when the c where my fathers are buried lies 6551
2: 5 the c in Judah where my fathers are buried 6551
2: 8 the citadel by the temple and for the c wall 6551
3:15 the steps going down from the C *of* David. 6551
7: 4 Now the c was large and spacious, 6551
11: 1 the holy c, while the remaining nine were 6551
11: 9 over the Second District of the c. 6551
11:18 The Levites in the holy c totaled 284. 6551
12:37 the steps of the C *of* David on the ascent to 6551
13:18 upon us and upon this c? 6551
Est 3:15 but the c *of* Susa was bewildered. 6551
4: 1 and went out into the c, 6551
4: 6 to Mordecai in the open square of the c 6551
6: 9 on the horse through the c streets, 6551
6:11 led him on horseback through the c streets, 6551
8:11 the Jews in every c the right to assemble 6551
8:15 the c *of* Susa held a joyous celebration. 6551
8:17 In every province and in every c, 6551
9:28 every province and in every c. 2256+6551+6551
Job 24:12 The groans of the dying rise from the c, 6551
29: 7 the c and took my seat in the public square, 7984
Ps 31:21 to me when I was in a besieged c. 6551
46: 4 a river whose streams make glad the c 6551
48: 1 in the c *of* our God, his holy mountain. 6551
48: 2 the c *of* the Great King. 7953
48: 8 the c *of* the LORD Almighty, in the city 6551
48: 8 in the c *of* our God: 6551
55: 9 for I see violence and strife in the c. 6551
55:11 Destructive forces are at work in the c; 2023S
59: 6 snarling like dogs, and prowl about the c. 6551
59:14 snarling like dogs, and prowl about the c. 6551
60: 9 Who will bring me to the fortified c? 6551
87: 3 Glorious things are said of you, O c *of* God: 6551
101: 8 I will cut off every evildoer from the c *of* 6551
107: 4 to a c where they could settle. 6551
107: 7 He led them by a straight way to a c 6551
107:36 they founded a c *where* they could settle. 6551
108:10 Who will bring me to the fortified c? 6551
122: 3 like a c that is closely compacted together. 6551
127: 1 Unless the LORD watches over the c, 6551
Pr 1:21 of the c she makes her speech: 6551
8: 3 into the c, at the entrances, she cries aloud: 7984
9: 3 she calls from the highest point of the c. 7984
Pr 9:14 on a seat at the highest point of the c, 7984
10:15 The wealth of the rich is their fortified c, 7953
11:10 When the righteous prosper, the c rejoices; 7953
11:11 the blessing of the upright a c is exalted, 7984
16:32 a man who controls his temper than one who takes a c. 6551
18:11 The wealth of the rich is their fortified c; 7953
18:19 a fortified c, and disputes are like 7953
21:22 A wise man attacks the c *of* the mighty 6551
25:28 Like a c whose walls are broken down is 6551
29: 8 Mockers stir up a c, 7953
31:23 Her husband is respected at the c gate, 9133
31:31 her works bring her praise at the c gate. 9133
Ecc 7:19 Wisdom makes one wise man more powerful than ten rulers in a c. 6551
8:10 the holy place and receive praise in the c 6551
9:14 a small c with only a few people in it. 6551
9:15 there lived in that c a man poor but wise, 2023S
9:15 and he saved the c by his wisdom. 6551
SS 3: 2 I will get up now and go about the c, 6551
3: 3 as they made their rounds in the c. 6551
5: 7 as they made their rounds in the c. 6551
Isa 1: 8 like a c under siege. 6551
1:21 See how the faithful c has become a harlot! 7953
1:26 Afterward you will be called the C 6551
1:26 the City of Righteousness, the Faithful C." 7953
14:31 Howl, O c! 6551
17: 1 be a c but will become a heap of ruins. 6551
17: 3 The fortified c will disappear NIH
19: 2 c against city, kingdom against kingdom. 6551
19: 2 city against c, kingdom against kingdom. 6551
19:18 One of them will be called the C 6551
22: 2 O c *of* tumult and revelry? 7953
22: 7 and horsemen are posted at the c gates; 9133
22: 9 that the C *of* David had many breaches 6551
23: 7 Is this your c of revelry, the old, old city, NIH
23: 7 Is this your city of revelry, the old, old c, 2023S
23:16 walk through the c, O prostitute forgotten; 6551
24:10 The ruined c lies desolate; 7953
24:12 The c is left in ruins, 6551
25: 2 You have made the c a heap of rubble, 6551
25: 2 the foreigners' stronghold a c no more; 6551
26: 1 We have a strong c; 6551
26: 5 he lays the lofty c low; 7953
27:10 The fortified c stands desolate, 6551
28: 1 to that c, the pride of those laid low NIH
29: 1 Ariel, Ariel, the c *where* David settled! 7953
32:13 for all houses of merriment and for this c 7953
32:14 the noisy c deserted; 6551
32:19 the forest and the c is leveled completely, 6551
33:20 Look upon Zion, the c *of* our festivals; 7953
36:15 this c will not be given into the hand of 6551
37:13 the king of the c *of* Sepharvaim, 6551
37:33 not enter this c or shoot an arrow here. 6551
37:34 he will not enter this c," 6551
37:35 "I will defend this c and save it, 6551
38: 6 And I will deliver you and this c from 6551
38: 6 I will defend this c. 6551
45:13 He will rebuild my c 6551
48: 2 the holy c and rely on the God of Israel— 6551
52: 1 O Jerusalem, the holy c. 6551
54:11 "O afflicted c, lashed by storms and NIH
60:14 down at your feet and will call you the C 6551
62:12 the C No Longer Deserted. 6551
66: 6 Hear that uproar from the c, 6551
Jer 1:18 Today I have made you a fortified c, 6551
5: 1 I will forgive this c, 2023S
6: 6 This c must be punished; 6551
8:16 the c and all who live there." 6551
14:18 if I go into the c, 6551
15: 7 with a winnowing fork at the c gates *of* 9133
17:24 through the gates of this c on the Sabbath, 6551
17:25 the gates of this c with their officials. 6551
17:25 and this c will be inhabited forever. 6551
19: 8 I will devastate this c and make it an object 6551
19:11 I will smash this nation and this c just 6551
19:12 I will make this c like Topheth. 6551
19:15 to bring on this c and the villages 6551
20: 5 to their enemies all the wealth of this c— 6551
21: 4 And I will gather them inside this c. 6551
21: 6 I will strike down those who live in this c— 6551
21: 7 the people in this c who survive the plague, 6551
21: 9 Whoever stays in this c will die by 6551
21:10 I have determined to do this c harm and 6551
22: 8 from many nations will pass by this c 6551
22: 8 a thing to this great c?' 6551
23:39 with the c I gave to you and your fathers. 6551
25:29 I am beginning to bring disaster on the c 6551
26: 6 like Shiloh and this c an object of cursing 6551
26: 9 and this c will be desolate and deserted?" 6551
26:11 because he has prophesied against this c. 6551
26:12 to prophesy against this house and this c all 6551
26:15 and on this c and on those who live in it, 6551
26:20 against this c and this land as Jeremiah did. 6551
27:17 Why should this c become a ruin? 6551
27:19 the other furnishings that are left in this c, 6551
29: 7 the c to which I have carried you into exile. 6551
29:16 in this c, your countrymen who did not go 6551
30:18 the c will be rebuilt on her ruins, 6551
31:38 "when this c will be rebuilt for me from 6551
31:40 The c will never again be uprooted NIH
32: 3 to hand this c over to the king of Babylon, 6551
32:24 the siege ramps are built up to take the c. 6551
32:24 the c will be handed over to 6551
32:25 And though the c will be handed over to 6551
32:28 to hand this c over to the Babylonians and 6551
32:29 The Babylonians who are attacking this c 6551
Jer 32:31 this c has so aroused my anger and wrath 6551
32:36 "You are saying about this c, 6551
33: 4 the houses in this c and the royal palaces 6551
33: 5 from this c because of all its wickedness. 6551
33: 9 Then this c will bring me renown, joy, NIH
34: 2 to hand this c over to the king of Babylon, 6551
34:22 and I will bring them back to this c. 6551
37: 8 Babylonians will return and attack this c; 6551
37:10 and burn this c down." 6551
37:12 Jeremiah started to leave the c to go to 3731S
37:21 until all the bread in the c was gone. 6551
38: 2 'Whoever stays in this c will die by 6551
38: 3 'This c will certainly be handed over to 6551
38: 4 the soldiers who are left in this c, 6551
38: 9 when there is no longer any bread in the c." 6551
38:17 your life will be spared and this c will not 6551
38:18 this c will be handed over to 6551
38:23 and this c will be burned down." 6551
39: 2 the c wall was broken through. 6551
39: 4 the c at night by way of the king's garden, 6551
39: 9 the people who remained in the c, 6551
39:16 about to fulfill my words against this c 6551
41: 7 When they went into the c, 6551
49:25 the c *of* renown not been abandoned, 6551
51:31 of Babylon that his entire c is captured, 6551
52: 4 They camped outside the c 2023S
52: 5 The c was kept under siege until 6551
52: 6 the famine in the c had become so severe 6551
52: 7 Then the c wall was broken through, 6551
52: 7 They left the c at night through the gate 6551
52: 7 the Babylonians were surrounding the c. 6551
52:15 and those who remained in the c, 6551
52:25 Of those still in the c, 6551
52:25 of his men who were found in the c. 6551
La 1: 1 deserted lies the c, once so full of people! 6551
1:19 My priests and my elders perished in the c 6551
2:11 and infants faint in the streets of the c. 7953
2:12 like wounded men in the streets of the c, 6551
2:15 "Is this the c that was called the perfection 6551
3:51 because of all the women of my c. 6551
5:14 The elders are gone from the c gate; 9133
Eze 4: 1 in front of you and draw the c of Jerusalem 6551
4: 3 between you and the c and turn your face 6551
5: 2 a third of the hair with fire inside the c. 6551
5: 2 with the sword all around the c. 2023S
7:15 by the sword, and those in the c will 6551
7:23 of bloodshed and the c is full of violence. 6551
9: 1 "Bring the guards of the c here, 6551
9: 4 "Go throughout the c *of* Jerusalem and put 6551
9: 5 "Follow him through the c and kill, 6551
9: 7 and began killing throughout the c. 6551
9: 9 of bloodshed and the c is full of injustice. 6551
10: 2 the cherubim and scatter them over the c." 6551
11: 2 and giving wicked advice in this c. 6551
11: 3 This c is a cooking pot, 2085S
11: 6 in this c and filled its streets with the dead. 6551
11: 7 the meat and this c is the pot, 2085S
11: 9 I will drive you out of the c and hand you 2023S
11:11 This c will not be a pot for you, 2085S
11:23 the c and stopped above the mountain east 6551
17: 4 where he planted it in a c *of* traders. 6551
21:19 where the road branches off to the c. 6551
22: 2 Will you judge this c *of* bloodshed? 6551
22: 3 O c that brings on herself doom 6551
22: 5 O infamous c, full of turmoil. NIH
22:20 and my wrath and put you inside the c NIH
24: 6 " 'Woe to the c *of* bloodshed, 6551
24: 9 " 'Woe to the c *of* bloodshed! 6551
26:10 a c whose walls have been broken through. 6551
26:17 " 'How you are destroyed, O c *of* renown, 6551
26:19 When I make you a desolate c, 6551
33:21 "The c has fallen!" 6551
40: 1 the fourteenth year after the fall of the c— 6551
40: 2 that looked like a c. 6551
43: 3 when he came to destroy the c and like 6551
45: 6 to give the c as its property an area 5,000 6551
45: 7 the sacred district and the property of the c. 6551
48:15 will be for the common use of the c, 6551
48:15 The c will be in the center of it 6551
48:17 The pastureland for the c will be 250 cubits 6551
48:18 for the workers of the c. 6551
48:19 from the c who farm it will come from all 6551
48:20 along with the property of the c. 6551
48:21 the c property will belong to the prince. 6551
48:22 the property of the c will lie in the center of 6551
48:30 "These will be the exits of the c: 6551
48:31 of the c will be named after the tribes 6551
48:35 the name of the c from that time on will be: 6551
Da 9:16 Jerusalem, your c, your holy hill. 6551
9:18 of the c that bears your Name. 6551
9:19 your c and your people bear your Name." 6551
9:24 and your holy c to finish transgression, 6551
9:26 the ruler who will come will destroy the c 6551
11:15 and will capture a fortified c. 6551
Hos 6: 8 Gilead is a c *of* wicked men, 7953
Joel 2: 9 They rush upon the c; 6551
Am 3: 6 When a trumpet sounds in a c, 6551
3: 6 When disaster comes to a c, 6551
4: 6 in every c and lack of bread in every town, 6551
5: 3 "The c that marches out a thousand strong 6551
5: 9 the stronghold and brings the fortified c 4448
6: 8 I will deliver up the c and everything in it." 6551
7:17 a prostitute in the c, 6551
Jnh 1: 2 "Go to the great c of Nineveh and preach 6551
3: 2 to the great c *of* Nineveh and proclaim to it 6551
3: 3 Now Nineveh was a very important c— 6551
3: 4 On the first day, Jonah started into the c. 6551

Jnh 4: 5 and sat down at a place east of the c. 6551
4: 5 to see what would happen to the c. 6551
4: 11 not be concerned about that great c?" 6551
Mic 4: 10 for now you must leave the c to camp in 7953
5: 1 Marshal your troops, O c *of* troops, 1426
6: 9 The LORD is calling to the c— 6551
Na 2: 5 They dash to the **c wall;** 2570
2: 7 that [the c] be exiled and carried away. NIH
3: 1 Woe to the c *of* blood, full of lies, 6551
Hab 2: 12 a c with bloodshed and establishes a town 6551
Zep 2: 15 This is the carefree c that lived in safety. 6551
3: 1 Woe to the c *of* oppressors, 6551
3: 7 I said to the c, 'Surely you will fear me NIH
3: 11 from **this** c those who rejoice in their pride. 3871S
Zec 2: 4 'Jerusalem will be a c **without walls** 7252
8: 3 Jerusalem will be called the C *of* Truth, 6551
8: 5 The c streets will be filled with boys 6551
8: 21 the inhabitants of one c will go to another NIH
14: 2 the c will be captured, 6551
14: 2 Half of the c will go into exile, 6551
14: 2 of the people will not be taken from the c. 6551
Mt 4: 5 Then the devil took him to the holy c *4484*
5: 14 A c on a hill cannot be hidden. *4484*
5: 35 for it is the c of the Great King. *4484*
12: 25 and every c or household divided *4484*
21: 10 the whole c was stirred and asked, *4484*
21: 17 And he left them and went out of the c *4484*
21: 18 as he was on his way back to the c, *4484*
22: 7 and burned their c. *4484*
26: 18 into the c to a certain man and tell him, *4484*
27: 53 the holy c and appeared to many people. *4484*
28: 11 of the guards went into the c and reported *4484*
Mk 10: 46 were leaving the c, a blind man, *NIG*
11: 19 they went out *of* the c. *4484*
14: 13 telling them, "Go into the c, *4484*
14: 16 went into the c and found things just *4484*
Lk 19: 41 As he approached Jerusalem and saw the c, *4484*
21: 21 let those in the c get out, *899S*
21: 21 and let those in the country not enter **the c.** *899S*
22: 10 He replied, "As you enter the c, *4484*
23: 19 into prison for an insurrection in the c, *4484*
24: 49 in the c until you have been clothed *4484*
Jn 19: 20 where Jesus was crucified was near the c, *4484*
Ac 1: 12 a Sabbath day's walk from the c. *NIG*
4: 27 and the people of Israel in this c to conspire *4484*
7: 58 dragged him out *of* the c and began *4484*
8: 5 down to a c in Samaria and proclaimed *4484*
8: 8 So there was great joy in that c. *4484*
8: 9 the c and amazed all the people of Samaria. *4484*
9: 6 "Now get up and go into the c, *4484*
9: 24 on the **c gates** in order to kill him. *4783*
10: 9 on their journey and approaching the c, *4484*
11: 5 "I was in the c of Joppa praying, *4484*
12: 10 and came to the iron gate leading to the c. *4484*
13: 44 the whole c gathered to hear the word of *4484*
13: 50 and the leading men *of* the c. *4484*
14: 4 The people *of* the c were divided; *4484*
14: 13 whose temple was just outside the c, *4484*
14: 13 and wreaths to the c gates because he and *NIG*
14: 19 and dragged him outside the c, *4484*
14: 20 he got up and went back into the c. *4484*
14: 21 that c and won a large number of disciples. *4484*
15: 21 For Moses has been preached in every c *4484*
16: 12 the leading c of that district of Macedonia. *4484*
16: 13 On the Sabbath we went outside the **c gate** *4783*
16: 14 in purple cloth *from* the c of Thyatira, *4484*
16: 20 and are throwing our c into an uproar *4484*
16: 39 requesting them to leave the c. *4484*
17: 5 formed a mob and started a riot *in* the c. *4484*
17: 6 before the **c officials,** shouting: *4485*
17: 8 the crowd and the **c officials** were thrown *4485*
17: 16 to see that the c was full of idols. *4484*
18: 10 because I have many people in this c." *4484*
19: 29 Soon the whole c was in an uproar. *4484*
19: 35 The c clerk quieted the crowd and said: *NIG*
19: 35 the world know that the c of Ephesus is *4484*
20: 23 that in every c the Holy Spirit warns me *4484*
21: 5 and children accompanied us out of the c, *4484*
21: 29 in the c with Paul and assumed *4484*
21: 30 The whole c was aroused, *4484*
21: 31 that the whole **c of Jerusalem** was in *2647*
21: 39 a citizen *of* no ordinary c. *4484*
22: 3 but brought up in this c. *4484*
24: 12 the synagogues or anywhere else in the c. *4484*
25: 23 and the leading men *of* the c. *4484*
2Co 11: 26 in danger in the c, in danger in the country, *4484*
11: 32 the governor under King Aretas had the c *4484*
Gal 4: 25 *to* the present **c of Jerusalem,** *2647*
Heb 11: 10 For he was looking forward to the c *4484*
11: 16 for he has prepared a c for them. *4484*
12: 22 the c of the living God. *4484*
13: 12 so Jesus also suffered outside the **c gate** *4783*
13: 14 For here we do not have an enduring c, *4484*
13: 14 but we are looking for the c that is to come. *NIG*
Jas 4: 13 or tomorrow we will go to this or that c, *4484*
Rev 2: 13 who was put to death in your c— *NIG*
3: 12 the name of my God and the name *of* the c *4484*
11: 2 They will trample on the holy c *4484*
11: 8 in the street *of* the great c, *4484*
11: 13 and a tenth *of* the c collapsed. *4484*
14: 20 in the winepress outside the c, *4484*
16: 19 The great c split into three parts, *4484*
17: 18 the great c that rules over the kings of *4484*
18: 10 Woe, O great c, O Babylon, city of power! *4484*
18: 10 Woe, O great city, O Babylon, c of power! *4484*
18: 16 Woe, O great c, dressed in fine linen, *4484*
18: 18 'Was there ever a c like this great city?' *NIG*
Rev 18: 18 'Was there ever a city like this great c?' *4484*
18: 19 O great c, where all who had ships on *4484*
18: 21 the great c of Babylon will be thrown *4484*
20: 9 camp of God's people, the c he loves. *4484*
21: 2 I saw the Holy C, the new Jerusalem, *4484*
21: 10 and showed me the Holy C, Jerusalem, *4484*
21: 14 The wall *of* the c had twelve foundations, *4484*
21: 15 a measuring rod of gold to measure the c, *4484*
21: 16 The c was laid out like a square, *4484*
21: 16 the c with the rod and found it to be 12,000 *4484*
21: 18 and the c of pure gold, as pure as glass. *4484*
21: 19 the c walls were decorated with every kind *4484*
21: 21 The great street *of* the c was of pure gold, *4484*
21: 22 I did not see a temple in **the c,** *899S*
21: 23 The c does not need the sun or the moon *4484*
22: 2 the middle of the great street *of* **the c.** *899S*
22: 3 of God and of the Lamb will be in **the c,** *899S*
22: 14 and may go through the gates into the c. *4484*
22: 19 in the tree of life and in the holy c, *4484*

CITY'S (1) [CITY]

Ro 16: 23 who is the c director of public works, *4484*

CIVILIAN (1)

2Ti 2: 4 a soldier gets involved in **c affairs**— *1050+4548*

CLAD (2)

Na 2: 3 the warriors *are* c **in scarlet.** 9443
Zep 1: 8 and the king's sons and all those c 4252

CLAIM (23) [CLAIMED, CLAIMING, CLAIMS, RECLAIM, RECLAIMED]

2Sa 19: 43 **have a** greater c **on** David than you have. 928
Ne 2: 20 you have no share in Jerusalem or any c 7407
Job 3: 5 and deep shadow c it once more; 1457
41: 11 Who **has a** c **against** me that I must pay? 7709
Ps 73: 9 Their mouths **lay** c to heaven, 9286
Pr 25: 6 and *do* not c a place among great men; 6641
Jer 23: 38 Although *you* c, 'This is the oracle of 606
23: 38 though I told you that *you must* not c, 606
Lk 11: 18 because *you* c that I drive out demons *3306*
Jn 4: 20 but you Jews c that the place *3306*
8: 24 if you do not believe that I am [the one I c *NIG*
8: 28 then you will know that I am [the one I c to *NIG*
8: 54 My Father, whom you c as your God, *3306*
9: 41 that *you* c you can see, your guilt remains. *3306*
10: 33 because you, a mere man, c to be God. *4472+4932*
Ro 3: 8 as saying and as some c that we say— *5774*
2Co 3: 5 in ourselves *to* c anything for ourselves, *3357*
Tit 1: 16 *They* c to know God, *3933*
1Jn 1: 6 If *we* c to have fellowship with him *3306*
1: 8 If *we* c to be without sin, *3306*
1: 10 If *we* c we have not sinned, *3306*
Rev 2: 2 that you have tested those who c to *3306*
3: 9 who c to be Jews though they are not, *3306*

CLAIMED (9) [CLAIM]

2Sa 18: 8 forest c more lives that day than the sword. 430
1Ki 18: 10 a nation or kingdom c you were not there, 606
Mk 6: 15 And still others c, "He is a prophet, *3306*
Jn 9: 9 Some c that he was. *3306*
19: 7 because *he* **c to be** the Son of God." *1571+4472*
19: 21 but that this man c to be king of the Jews." *3306*
Ac 4: 32 No one c that any of his possessions *3306*
25: 19 about a dead man named Jesus who Paul c was alive. *5763*
Ro 1: 22 *Although they* c to be wise, *5763*

CLAIMING (5) [CLAIM]

Mt 24: 5 For many will come in my name, c, *3306*
Mk 13: 6 Many will come in my name, c, 'I am he,' *3306*
Lk 21: 8 For many will come in my name, c, *3306*
Jn 8: 25 "Just what *I have been* c all along," *3281*
Ac 5: 36 c to be somebody, *3306*

CLAIMS (9) [CLAIM]

2Sa 15: 3 "Look, your c are valid and proper, 1821
Pr 20: 6 Many a man c to have unfailing love, 7924
Ecc 8: 17 Even if a wise man c he knows, 606
Jer 23: 34 If a prophet or a priest or anyone else c, 606
Lk 23: 2 of taxes to Caesar and c to be Christ, *3306*
Jn 19: 12 Anyone who **c to be a** king *1571+4472*
Jas 2: 14 if a man c to have faith but has no deeds? *3306*
1Jn 2: 6 Whoever c to live in him must walk *3306*
2: 9 Anyone who c to be in the light *3306*

CLAMOR (2)

Ps 74: 23 Do not ignore the c *of* your adversaries, 7754
Isa 31: 4 by their shouts or disturbed by their c— 2162

CLAN (170) [CLANS]

Ge 24: 38 go to my father's family and to my own c, 5476
24: 40 a wife for my son from my own c and 5476
24: 41 Then, when you go to my c, 5476
Ex 6: 25 the heads of the Levite families, c by clan. NIH
6: 25 the heads of the Levite families, clan by c. 5476
Lev 25: 10 and each to his own c. 5476
25: 41 and he will go back to his own c and to 5476
25: 47 among you or to a member of the alien's c, 5476
25: 49 in his c may redeem him. 5476
Nu 2: 34 each with his c and family. 5476
Nu 26: 5 through Hanoch, the Hanochite c; 5476
26: 5 through Pallu, the Palluite c; 5476
26: 6 through Hezron, the Hezronite c; 5476
26: 6 through Carmi, the Carmite c. 5476
26: 12 through Nemuel, the Nemuelite c; 5476
26: 12 through Jamin, the Jaminite c; 5476
26: 12 through Jakin, the Jakinite c; 5476
26: 13 through Zerah, the Zerahite c; 5476
26: 13 through Shaul, the Shaulite c. 5476
26: 15 through Zephon, the Zephonite c; 5476
26: 15 through Haggi, the Haggite c; 5476
26: 15 through Shuni, the Shunite c; 5476
26: 16 through Ozni, the Oznite c; 5476
26: 16 through Eri, the Erite c; 5476
26: 17 through Arodi, the Arodite c; 5476
26: 17 through Areli, the Arelite c. 5476
26: 20 through Shelah, the Shelanite c; 5476
26: 20 through Perez, the Perezite c; 5476
26: 20 through Zerah, the Zerahite c. 5476
26: 21 through Hezron, the Hezronite c; 5476
26: 21 through Hamul, the Hamulite c. 5476
26: 23 through Tola, the Tolaite c; 5476
26: 23 through Puah, the Puite c; 5476
26: 24 through Jashub, the Jashubite c; 5476
26: 24 through Shimron, the Shimronite c. 5476
26: 26 through Sered, the Seredite c; 5476
26: 26 through Elon, the Elonite c; 5476
26: 26 through Jahleel, the Jahleelite c. 5476
26: 29 through Makir, the Makirite c (Makir was 5476
26: 29 through Gilead, the Gileadite c. 5476
26: 30 through Iezer, the Iezerite c; 5476
26: 30 through Helek, the Helekite c; 5476
26: 31 through Asriel, the Asrielite c; 5476
26: 31 through Shechem, the Shechemite c; 5476
26: 32 through Shemida, the Shemidaite c; 5476
26: 32 through Hepher, the Hepherite c. 5476
26: 35 through Shuthelah, the Shuthelahite c; 5476
26: 35 through Beker, the Bekerite c; 5476
26: 35 through Tahan, the Tahanite c. 5476
26: 36 through Eran, the Eranite c. 5476
26: 38 through Bela, the Belaite c; 5476
26: 38 through Ashbel, the Ashbelite c; 5476
26: 38 through Ahiram, the Ahiramite c; 5476
26: 39 through Shupham, the Shuphamite c; 5476
26: 39 through Hupham, the Huphamite c. 5476
26: 40 through Ard, the Ardite c; 5476
26: 40 through Naaman, the Naamite c. 5476
26: 42 through Shuham, the Shuhamite c. 5476
26: 44 through Imnah, the Imnite c; 5476
26: 44 through Ishvi, the Ishvite c; 5476
26: 44 through Beriah, the Beriite c; 5476
26: 45 through Heber, the Heberite c; 5476
26: 45 through Malkiel, the Malkielite c. 5476
26: 48 through Jahzeel, the Jahzeelite c; 5476
26: 48 through Guni, the Gunite c; 5476
26: 49 through Jezer, the Jezerite c; 5476
26: 49 through Shillem, the Shillemite c. 5476
26: 57 through Gershon, the Gershonite c; 5476
26: 57 through Kohath, the Kohathite c; 5476
26: 57 through Merari, the Merarite c. 5476
26: 58 These also were Levite clans: the Libnite c, 5476
26: 58 the Libnite clan, the Hebronite c, 5476
26: 58 the Hebronite clan, the Mahlite c, 5476
26: 58 the Mushite c, the Korahite clan. 5476
26: 58 the Mushite clan, the Korahite c. 5476
27: 4 from his c because he had no son? 5476
27: 11 to the nearest relative in his c, 5476
36: 1 The family heads of the c *of* Gilead son 5476
36: 6 as long as they marry within the tribal c 5476
36: 8 in her father's tribal c, 5476
36: 12 in their father's c and tribe. 5476
Dt 29: 18 or woman, c or tribe 5476
Jos 7: 14 that the LORD takes shall come forward c NIH
7: 14 that the LORD takes shall come forward clan by c; 5476
7: 14 the c that the LORD takes shall come forward family by family; 5476
7: 17 the c *of* the Zerahites come forward 5476
13: 15 to the tribe of Reuben, c by clan: NIH
13: 15 to the tribe of Reuben, clan by c: 5476
13: 23 the inheritance of the Reubenites, c NIH
13: 23 of the Reubenites, clan by c. 5476
13: 24 to the tribe of Gad, c by clan: NIH
13: 24 to the tribe of Gad, clan by c: 5476
13: 28 the inheritance of the Gadites, c by clan. NIH
13: 28 the inheritance of the Gadites, clan by c. 5476
13: 29 of the descendants of Manasseh, c by clan: NIH
13: 29 of the descendants of Manasseh, clan by c: 5476
13: 31 for half of the sons of Makir, c by clan. NIH
13: 31 for half of the sons of Makir, clan by c. 5476
15: 1 for the tribe of Judah, c by clan, extended NIH
15: 1 for the tribe of Judah, clan by c, extended 5476
15: 20 the inheritance of the tribe of Judah, c NIH
15: 20 of the tribe of Judah, clan by c: 5476
16: 5 the territory of Ephraim, c by clan: NIH
16: 5 the territory of Ephraim, clan by c: 5476
16: 8 of the tribe of the Ephraimites, c by clan. NIH
16: 8 of the tribe of the Ephraimites, clan by c. 5476
18: 11 up for the tribe of Benjamin, c by clan. NIH
18: 11 up for the tribe of Benjamin, clan by c. 5476
18: 21 The tribe of Benjamin, c by clan, NIH
18: 21 The tribe of Benjamin, clan by c, 5476
19: 1 for the tribe of Simeon, c by clan. NIH
19: 1 for the tribe of Simeon, clan by c. 5476
19: 8 of the tribe of the Simeonites, c by clan. NIH
19: 8 of the tribe of the Simeonites, clan by c. 5476
19: 10 The third lot came up for Zebulun, c NIH

Jos 19:10 up for Zebulun, clan by **c**: 5476
19:16 the inheritance of Zebulun, **c** by clan. NIH
19:16 the inheritance of Zebulun, clan by **c.** 5476
19:17 fourth lot came out for Issachar, **c** by clan. NIH
19:17 fourth lot came out for Issachar, clan by **c.** 5476
19:23 the inheritance of the tribe of Issachar, **c** NIH
19:23 of the tribe of Issachar, clan by **c.** 5476
19:24 for the tribe of Asher, **c** by clan. NIH
19:24 for the tribe of Asher, clan by **c.** 5476
19:31 the inheritance of the tribe of Asher, **c** NIH
19:31 of the tribe of Asher, clan by **c.** 5476
19:32 sixth lot came out for Naphtali, **c** by clan: NIH
19:32 sixth lot came out for Naphtali, clan by **c**: 5476
19:39 the inheritance of the tribe of Naphtali, **c** NIH
19:39 of the tribe of Naphtali, clan by **c.** 5476
19:40 for the tribe of Dan, **c** by clan. NIH
19:40 for the tribe of Dan, clan by **c.** 5476
19:48 the inheritance of the tribe of Dan, **c** NIH
19:48 of the tribe of Dan, clan by **c.** 5476
21: 4 The first lot came out for the Kohathites, **c** NIH
21: 4 for the Kohathites, clan by **c.** 5476
21: 7 The descendants of Merari, **c** by clan, NIH
21: 7 The descendants of Merari, clan by **c,** 5476
Jdg 4:17 of Hazor and the **c** *of* Heber the Kenite. 1074
6:15 My **c** is the weakest in Manasseh, 548
9: 1 to them and to all his mother's **c,** 3+1074+5476
12: 9 in marriage to those **outside** his *c.* AIT
12: 9 as wives from **outside** his *c.* AIT
13: 2 named Manoah, from the **c** *of* the Danites, 5476
17: 7 who had been living within the **c** *of* Judah, 5476
18:11 six hundred men from the **c** *of* the Danites, 5476
18:19 Isn't it better that you serve a tribe and **c** 5476
Ru 2: 1 from the **c** *of* Elimelech, 5476
2: 3 who was from the **c** *of* Elimelech. 5476
1Sa 9:21 and is not my **c** the least of all the clans of 5476
10:21 **c** by clan, and Matri's clan was chosen. NIH
10:21 clan by **c,** and Matri's clan was chosen. 5476
10:21 clan by clan, and Matri's **c** was chosen. 5476
18:18 and what is my family or my father's **c** 5476
20: 6 for his whole **c.'** 5476
2Sa 14: 7 Now the whole **c** has risen up 5476
16: 5 from the *same* **c** *as* Saul's family came out 5476
1Ch 4:27 so their entire **c** did not become 5476
6:54 of Aaron who were from the Kohathite **c,** 5476
6:62 descendants of Gershon, **c by clan,** 4200+5476
6:62 descendants of Gershon, **clan by c,** 4200+5476
6:63 The descendants of Merari, **c by clan,** 4200+5476
6:63 The descendants of Merari, **clan by c,** 4200+5476
6:71 From the **c** *of* the half-tribe 5476
Jer 3:14 one from a town and two from a **c**— 5476
Zec 12:12 The land will mourn, **each c** by itself, 5476+5476
12:12 **c** *of* the house of David and their wives, 5476
12:12 the **c** *of* the house of Nathan and their wives, 5476
12:13 the **c** *of* the house of Levi and their wives, 5476
12:13 the **c** *of* Shimei and their wives, 5476

CLANGING (1)

1Co 13: 1 I am only a resounding gong or a **c** cymbal. *226*

CLANS (137) [CLAN]

Ge 10: 5 by their **c** within their nations, 5476
10:18 Later the Canaanite **c** scattered 5476
10:20 the sons of Ham by their **c** and languages, 5476
10:31 the sons of Shem by their **c** and languages, 5476
10:32 These are the **c** *of* Noah's sons, 5476
36:40 by name, according to their **c** and regions: 5476
Ex 6:14 These were the **c** *of* Reuben. 5476
6:15 These were the **c** *of* Simeon. 5476
6:17 The sons of Gershon, by **c,** 5476
6:19 the **c** *of* Levi according to their records. 5476
6:24 These were the Korahite **c.** 5476
Lev 25:45 among you and members of their **c** born 5476
Nu 1: 2 of the whole Israelite community by their **c** 5476
1:16 They were the heads of the **c** *of* Israel. 548
1:18 by their **c** and families, 5476
1:20 by one, according to the records of their **c** 5476
1:22 by one, according to the records of their **c** 5476
1:24 by name, according to the records of their **c** 5476
1:26 by name, according to the records of their **c** 5476
1:28 by name, according to the records of their **c** 5476
1:30 by name, according to the records of their **c** 5476
1:32 by name, according to the records of their **c** 5476
1:34 by name, according to the records of their **c** 5476
1:36 by name, according to the records of their **c** 5476
1:38 by name, according to the records of their **c** 5476
1:40 by name, according to the records of their **c** 5476
1:42 by name, according to the records of their **c** 5476
3:15 "Count the Levites by their families and **c.** 5476
3:18 These were the names of the Gershonite **c**: 5476
3:19 The Kohathite **c**: Amram, 5476
3:20 The Merarite **c**: Mahli and Mushi. 5476
3:20 These were the Levite **c,** 5476
3:21 To Gershon belonged the **c** *of* the Libnites 5476
3:21 these were the Gershonite **c.** 5476
3:23 Gershonite **c** were to camp on the west, 5476
3:27 To Kohath belonged the **c** *of* 5476
3:27 these were the Kohathite **c.** 5476
3:29 The Kohathite **c** were to camp on 5476
3:30 of the Kohathite **c** was Elizaphan son 5476
3:33 To Merari belonged the **c** *of* the Mahlites 5476
3:33 these were the Merarite **c.** 5476
3:35 of the Merarite **c** was Zuriel son of Abihail; 5476
3:39 by Moses and Aaron according to their **c,** 5476
4: 2 of the Levites by their **c** and families. 5476
4:18 the Kohathite tribal **c** are not cut off from 5476
4:22 of the Gershonites by their families and **c.** 5476
4:24 "This is the service of the Gershonite **c** 5476
4:28 of the Gershonite **c** at the Tent of Meeting. 5476
4:29 the Merarites by their **c** and families. 5476
4:33 the service of the Merarite **c** as they work 5476
4:34 the Kohathites by their **c** and families. 5476
4:36 counted by **c,** were 2,750. 5476
4:37 of all those in the Kohathite **c** who served 5476
4:38 The Gershonites were counted by their **c** 5476
4:40 counted by their **c** and families, 5476
4:41 in the Gershonite **c** who served at the Tent 5476
4:42 The Merarites were counted by their **c** 5476
4:44 counted by their **c,** were 3,200. 5476
4:45 the total of those in the Merarite **c.** 5476
4:46 of Israel counted all the Levites by their **c** 5476
10: 4 the heads of the **c** *of* Israel— 548
26: 7 These were the **c** *of* Reuben; 5476
26:12 descendants of Simeon by their **c** were: 5476
26:14 These were the **c** *of* Simeon; 5476
26:15 The descendants of Gad by their **c** were: 5476
26:18 These were the **c** *of* Gad; 5476
26:20 The descendants of Judah by their **c** were: 5476
26:22 These were the **c** *of* Judah; 5476
26:23 descendants of Issachar by their **c** were: 5476
26:25 These were the **c** *of* Issachar; 5476
26:26 descendants of Zebulun by their **c** were: 5476
26:27 These were the **c** *of* Zebulun; 5476
26:28 of Joseph by their **c** through Manasseh 5476
26:34 These were the **c** *of* Manasseh; 5476
26:35 the descendants of Ephraim by their **c**: 5476
26:37 These were the **c** *of* Ephraim; 5476
26:37 the descendants of Joseph by their **c.** 5476
26:38 descendants of Benjamin by their **c** were: 5476
26:41 These were the **c** *of* Benjamin; 5476
26:42 the descendants of Dan by their **c**: 5476
26:42 These were the **c** *of* Dan: 5476
26:43 All of them were Shuhamite **c**; 5476
26:44 The descendants of Asher by their **c** were: 5476
26:47 These were the **c** *of* Asher; 5476
26:48 descendants of Naphtali by their **c** were: 5476
26:50 These were the **c** *of* Naphtali; 5476
26:57 the Levites who were counted by their **c**: 5476
26:58 These also were Levite **c**: 5476
27: 1 to the **c** *of* Manasseh son of Joseph. 5476
31: 5 were supplied from the **c** *of* Israel. 548
33:54 according to your **c.** 5476
36: 1 from the **c** *of* the descendants of Joseph, 5476
36:12 the **c** *of* the descendants of Manasseh son 5476
Jos 7:17 The **c** *of* Judah came forward, 5476
14: 1 the heads of the tribal **c** of Israel allotted 3
15:12 around the people of Judah by their **c.** 5476
17: 2 the **c** *of* Abiezer, Helek, Asriel, Shechem, 1201
17: 2 of Manasseh son of Joseph by their **c.** 5476
18:20 that marked out the inheritance of the **c** 5476
18:28 the inheritance of Benjamin for its **c.** 5476
19:51 the heads of the tribal **c** of Israel assigned 3
21: 5 from the **c** *of* the tribes of Ephraim, 5476
21: 6 from the **c** *of* the tribes of Issachar, 5476
21:10 of Aaron who were from the Kohathite **c** of 5476
21:20 The rest of the Kohathite **c** *of* 5476
21:26 to the rest of the Kohathite **c.** 5476
21:27 The Levite **c** of the Gershonites 5476
21:33 the towns of the Gershonite **c** were thirteen, 5476
21:34 The Merarite **c** (the rest of 5476
21:40 All the towns allotted to the Merarite **c,** 5476
22:14 of a family division among the Israelite **c.** 548
22:21 of Manasseh replied to the heads of the **c** 548
22:30 the heads of the **c** *of* the Israelites— 548
Jdg 18: 2 These men represented all their **c.** 5476
21:24 and went home to their tribes and **c,** 5476
1Sa 9:21 and is not my clan the least of all the **c** *of* 5476
10:19 before the LORD by your tribes and **c."** 548
23:23 I will track him down among all the **c** 548
1Ch 2:53 and the **c** *of* Kiriath Jearim: 5476
2:55 and the **c** *of* scribes who lived at Jabez: 5476
4: 2 These were the **c** *of* the Zorathites. 5476
4: 8 and of the **c** *of* Aharhel son of Harum. 5476
4:21 Laadah the father of Mareshah and the **c** *of* 5476
4:38 above by name were leaders of their **c.** 5476
5: 7 Their relatives by **c,** listed according 5476
6:19 the **c** *of* the Levites listed according 5476
6:60 among the Kohathite **c,** 5476
6:61 from the **c** *of* half the tribe of Manasseh. 5476
6:66 Some of the Kohathite **c** were given 5476
6:70 to the rest of the Kohathite **c.** 5476
7: 5 to all the **c** *of* Issachar, 5476
12:30 brave warriors, famous in their own **c**— 3+1074
Job 31:34 the contempt of the **c** that I kept silent 5476
Jer 2: 4 all you **c** *of* the house of Israel. 5476
31: 1 "I will be the God of all the **c** *of* Israel, 5476
Mic 5: 2 you are small among the **c** *of* Judah, 548
Zec 12:14 and all the rest of the **c** and their wives. 5476

CLAP (6) [CLAPPED, CLAPS]

Job 21: 5 **c** your hand over your mouth. 8492
Ps 47: 1 **C** your hands, all you nations; 9546
98: 8 *Let* the rivers **c** their hands, 4673
Pr 30:32 **c** your hand over your mouth! NIH
Isa 55:12 all the trees of the field *will* **c** their hands. 4673
La 2:15 All who pass your way **c** their hands 6215

CLAPPED (2) [CLAP]

2Ki 11:12 and the people **c** their hands and shouted, 5782
Eze 25: 6 Because you *have* **c** your hands 4673

CLAPS (3) [CLAP]

Job 27:23 **c** its hands **in derision** 8562
34:37 **scornfully** *he* **c** *his* **hands** 6215
Na 3:19 the news about you **c** his hands at your fall, 9546

CLASH (1)

Ps 150: 5 praise him with the **c** *of* cymbals, 9049

CLASP (1) [CLASPED, CLASPS]

Isa 2: 6 the Philistines and **c hands** with pagans. 8562

CLASPED (1) [CLASP]

Mt 28: 9 **c** his feet and worshiped him. *3195*

CLASPS (7) [CLASP]

Ex 26: 6 Then make fifty gold **c** and use them 7971
26:11 Then make fifty bronze **c** and put them in 7971
26:33 the curtain from the **c** and place the ark of 7971
35:11 **c,** frames, crossbars, posts and bases; 7971
36:13 Then they made fifty gold **c** and used them 7971
36:18 They made fifty bronze **c** to fasten 7971
39:33 the tent and all its furnishings, its **c,** 7971

CLASSIFY (1)

2Co 10:12 We do not dare *to* **c** or compare ourselves *1605*

CLATTER (2)

Jdg 5:28 Why is the **c** *of* his chariots delayed?' 7193
Na 3: 2 The crack of whips, the **c** *of* wheels, 7754+8323

CLAUDA (KJV) See CAUDA

CLAUDIA (1)

2Ti 4:21 Linus, **C** and all the brothers. *3086*

CLAUDIUS (3)

Ac 11:28 (This happened during the reign of **C.**) *3087*
18: 2 **C** had ordered all the Jews to leave Rome. *3087*
23:26 **C** Lysias, To His Excellency, *3087*

CLAVE (KJV) See CUT, SPLIT, DIVIDED, DRAWN, CLUNG

CLAWS (2)

Da 4:33 of an eagle and his nails like the **c** of a bird. NIH
7:19 with its iron teeth and bronze **c**— 10303

CLAY (40)

Lev 6:28 The **c** pot the meat is cooked in must 3084
11:33 If one of them falls into a **c** pot, 3084
14: 5 be killed over fresh water in a **c** pot. 3084
14:42 to replace these and take new **c** and plaster 6760
14:50 of the birds over fresh water in a **c** pot. 3084
15:12 " 'A **c** pot that the man touches must 3084
Nu 5:17 in a **c** jar and put some dust from 3084
1Ki 7:46 The king had them cast in **c** molds in 141
2Ch 4:17 The king had them cast in **c** molds in 141
Job 4:19 much more those who live in houses of **c,** 2817
10: 9 Remember that you molded me like **c.** 2817
13:12 your defenses are defenses of **c.** 2817
27:16 like dust and clothes like piles of **c,** 2817
33: 6 I too have been taken from **c.** 2817
38:14 The earth takes shape like **c** *under* a seal; 2817
Ps 12: 6 like silver refined in a furnace of **c,** 824
Isa 29:16 if the potter were thought to be like the **c**! 2817
41:25 as if he were a potter treading the **c.** 3226
45: 9 Does the **c** say to the potter, 2817
64: 8 We are the **c,** you are the potter; 2817
Jer 18: 4 from the **c** was marred in his hands; 2817
18: 6 "Like **c** in the hand of the potter, 2817
19: 1 "Go and buy a **c** jar from a potter. 3084
32:14 and put them in a **c** jar so they will last 3084
43: 9 and bury them in **c** in the brick pavement at 4879
La 4: 2 are now considered as pots of **c,** 3084
Eze 4: 1 "Now, son of man, take a **c tablet,** 4246
Da 2:33 its feet partly of iron and partly of **baked c.** 10279
2:34 on its feet of iron and **c** and smashed them. 10279
2:35 Then the iron, the **c,** the bronze, 10279
2:41 of **baked c** and partly of iron, so this will be 10279
2:41 even as you saw iron mixed with **c.** 10279+10298
2:42 As the toes were partly iron and partly **c,** 10279
2:43 saw the iron mixed with **baked c,** 10279+10298
2:43 any more than iron mixes with **c.** 10279
2:45 the **c,** the silver and the gold to pieces. 10279
Na 3:14 Work the **c,** tread the mortar, 3226
Ro 9:21 of the same **lump of c** some pottery *5878*
2Co 4: 7 But we have this treasure in jars of **c** *4017*
2Ti 2:20 but also of wood and **c**; *4017*

CLEAN (120) [CLEANNESS, CLEANSE, CLEANSED, CLEANSES, CLEANSING]

Ge 7: 2 with you seven of every kind of **c** animal, 3196
7: 8 Pairs of **c** and unclean animals, 3196
8:20 of all the **c** animals and clean birds, 3196
8:20 of all the clean animals and **c** birds, 3196
20: 5 with a clear conscience and **c** hands." 5931
Lev 4:12 the camp to a place **ceremonially c,** 3196

Lev 6:11 the camp to a place that is **ceremonially c.** 3196
7:19 anyone **ceremonially c** may eat it. 3196
10:10 between the unclean and the **c,** 3196
10:14 Eat them in a **ceremonially c** place; 3196
11:32 and then *it will be* **c.** 3197
11:36 or a cistern for collecting water remains **c,** 3196
11:37 that are to be planted, they remain **c.** 3196
11:47 between the unclean and the **c,** 3196
12: 7 *be* **ceremonially c** from her flow of blood. 3197
12: 8 and *she will be* **c.'** " 3197
13: 6 the priest *shall* **pronounce** him **c;** 3197
13: 6 and *he will be* **c.** 3197
13: 7 to the priest to be **pronounced c,** 3200
13:13 **pronounce** that person **c.** 3197
13:13 Since it has all turned white, he is **c.** 3196
13:17 **pronounce** the infected person **c;** 3197
13:17 then he will be **c.** 3196
13:23 and the priest *shall* **pronounce** him **c.** 3197
13:28 and the priest *shall* **pronounce** him **c;** 3197
13:34 the priest *shall* **pronounce** him **c.** 3197
13:34 and *he will be* **c.** 3197
13:35 in the skin after he is **pronounced c,** 3200
13:37 He is **c,** and the priest shall pronounce him clean. 3196
13:37 and the priest *shall* **pronounce** him **c.** 3197
13:39 that person is **c.** 3196
13:40 a man has lost his hair and is bald, he is **c.** 3196
13:41 and has a bald forehead, he is **c.** 3196
13:58 must be washed again, and *it will be* **c."** 3197
13:59 for **pronouncing** them **c** or unclean. 3197
14: 4 that two live **c** birds and some cedar wood, 3196
14: 7 and **pronounce** him **c.** 3197
14: 8 then *he will be* **ceremonially c.** 3197
14: 9 and *he will be* **c.** 3197
14:11 The priest who **pronounces** him **c** shall 3197
14:20 and *he will be* **c.** 3197
14:48 **pronounce** the house **c,** 3197
14:53 and *it will be* **c."** 3197
14:57 to determine when something is **c** 3196
15: 8 the discharge spits on someone who is **c,** 3196
15:13 and *he will be* **c.** 3197
15:28 and after that *she will be* **ceremonially c.** 3197
16:30 *you will be* **c** from all your sins. 3197
17:15 then *he will be* **c.** 3197
20:25 therefore make a distinction between **c** 3196
20:25 and between unclean and **c** birds. 3196
22: 7 When the sun goes down, *he will be* **c,** 3197
Nu 8: 6 **make** them **ceremonially c.** 3197
9:13 if a man who is **ceremonially c** and not on 3196
18:11 in your household who is **ceremonially c** may eat it. 3196
18:13 in your household who is **ceremonially c** may eat it. 3196
19: 9 "A man who is **c** shall gather up the ashes 3196
19: 9 a **ceremonially c** place outside the camp. 3196
19:12 then *he will be* **c.** 3197
19:12 *he will* not *be* **c.** 3197
19:18 Then a man who is **ceremonially c** is 3196
19:19 The *man* who is **c** is to sprinkle 3196
19:19 and that evening *he will be* **c.** 3197
31:23 and then *it will be* **c.** 3197
31:24 and *you will be* **c.** 3197
Dt 12:15 ceremonially unclean and the **c** may eat it. 3196
12:22 ceremonially unclean and the **c** may eat. 3196
14:11 You may eat any **c** bird. 3196
14:20 any winged creature that is **c** you may eat. 3196
15:22 ceremonially unclean and the **c** may eat it, 3196
2Ki 5:14 and his flesh was restored and *became* **c** 3197
2Ch 13:11 the bread on the **ceremonially c** table 3196
30:17 for all *those who* were not **ceremonially c** 3196
30:19 even if he is not **c** according to the rules of 3200
Ezr 6:20 and were all **ceremonially c.** 3196
Job 17: 9 and those with **c** hands will grow stronger. 3198
33: 9 I am **c** and free from guilt. 2899
37:21 the skies after the wind has swept them **c.** 3197
Ps 24: 4 *He who* has **c** hands and a pure heart, 5929
51: 7 Cleanse me with hyssop, and *I will be* **c;** 3197
Pr 20: 9 *I am* **c** and without sin"? 3197
Ecc 9: 2 the **c** and the unclean, 3196
Isa 1:16 wash and **make yourselves c.** 2342
66:20 of the LORD in **ceremonially c** vessels. 3196
Eze 16: 4 with water to **make** you **c,** 5470
22:26 between the unclean and the **c;** 3196
24:13 *you will* not *be* **c** again until my wrath 3197
36:25 I will sprinkle **c** water on you, 3196
36:25 and *you will be* **c;** 3197
44:23 between the unclean and the **c.** 3196
Am 7: 2 When *they had* **stripped** the land **c,** 430
Zec 3: 5 Then I said, "Put a **c** turban on his head." 3196
3: 5 a **c** turban on his head and clothed him, 3196
Mt 8: 2 if you are willing, you can **make** me **c."** *2751*
8: 3 "I am willing," he said. *"Be* **c!"** *2751*
12:44 **swept c** and put in order. *4924*
23:25 *You* **c** the outside of the cup and dish, *2751*
23:26 First **c** the inside of the cup and dish, *2751*
23:26 and then the outside also will be **c.** *2754*
27:59 wrapped it in a **c** linen cloth, *2754*
Mk 1:40 "If you are willing, you can **make** me **c."** *2751*
1:41 "I am willing," he said. *"Be* **c!"** *2751*
7:19 Jesus declared all foods **"c.")** *2751*
Lk 5:12 if you are willing, you can **make** me **c."** *2751*
5:13 "I am willing," he said. *"Be* **c!"** *2751*
11:25 it finds the house **swept c** and put in order. *4924*
11:39 you Pharisees **c** the outside of the cup *2751*
11:41 and everything will be **c** for you. *2754*
Jn 13:10 his whole body is **c.** *2754*
13:10 you are **c,** though not every one of you." *2754*
13:11 that was why he said not every one was **c.** *2754*
15: 3 You are already **c** because of the word *2754*
Ac 10:15 that God *has* **made c."** *2751*
11: 9 that God *has* **made c.'** *2751*
24:18 *I was* **ceremonially c** when they found me *49*
Ro 14:20 All food is **c,** but it is wrong for a man to *2754*
Heb 9:13 so that they are outwardly **c.** *2755*
Rev 15: 6 They were dressed in **c,** *2754*
19: 8 Fine linen, bright and **c,** *2754*
19:14 and dressed in fine linen, white and **c.** *2754*

CLEANNESS (5) [CLEAN]

2Sa 22:21 to the **c** *of* my hands he has rewarded me. 1341
22:25 according to my **c** in his sight. 1341
Job 22:30 be delivered through the **c** *of* your hands." 1341
Ps 18:20 to the **c** *of* my hands he has rewarded me. 1341
18:24 according to the **c** *of* my hands in his sight. 1341

CLEANSE (20) [CLEAN]

Lev 16:19 on it with his finger seven times *to* **c** it and 3197
16:30 be made for you, to **c** you. 3197
Ps 51: 2 Wash away all my iniquity and **c** me 3197
51: 7 **C** me with hyssop, and I will be clean; 2627
Pr 20:30 Blows and wounds **c away** evil, 5347
Isa 4: 4 *he will* **c** the bloodstains from Jerusalem 1866
Jer 4:11 but not to winnow or **c;** 1405
33: 8 *I will* **c** them from all 3197
Eze 24:13 Because *I tried to* **c** you but you would 3197
36:25 *I will* **c** you from all your impurities and 3197
36:33 On the day I **c** you from all your sins, 3197
37:23 and *I will* **c** them. 3197
39:12 of Israel will be burying them in order to **c** 3197
39:14 " 'Men will be regularly employed to **c** 3197
39:16 And so *they will* **c** the land.' 3197
43:26 to make atonement for the altar and **c** it; 3197
Zec 13: 1 to **c** them from sin and impurity. NIH
Mt 10: 8 raise the dead, **c** those who have leprosy, *2751*
Heb 9:14 **c** our consciences from acts that lead *2751*
10:22 *having* our hearts **sprinkled to c** us from *4822*

CLEANSED (30) [CLEAN]

Lev 14: 4 and hyssop be brought for the *one to* **be c.** 3197
14: 7 the *one to* **be c** of the infectious disease 3197
14: 8 "The *person to* **be c** must wash his clothes, 3197
14:11 *to* **be c** and his offerings before the LORD 3197
14:14 the lobe of the right ear of the *one to* **be c,** 3197
14:17 the lobe of the right ear of the *one to* **be c,** 3197
14:18 *to* **be c** and make atonement for him before 3197
14:19 for the *one to* **be c** from his uncleanness. 3197
14:25 the lobe of the right ear of the *one to* **be c,** 3197
14:28 the lobe of the right ear of the *one to* **be c,** 3197
14:29 on the head of the *one to* **be c,** 3197
14:31 the LORD on behalf of the *one to* **be c."** 3197
15:13 " 'When a man *is* **c** from his discharge, 3197
15:28 " 'When *she is* **c** from her discharge, 3197
22: 4 not eat the sacred offerings until *he is* **c.** 3197
Nu 19:19 The person being **c** must wash his clothes NIH
Jos 22:17 Up to this very day *we have* not **c** ourselves 3197
2Ki 5:10 be restored and *you will be* **c."** 3197
5:12 Couldn't I wash in them and *be* **c?"** 3197
5:13 then, when he tells you, 'Wash and *be* **c'!"** 3197
Pr 30:12 in their own eyes and yet **are** not **c** 8175
Isa 1: 6 not **c** or bandaged or soothed with oil. 2318
Eze 24:13 to cleanse you but *you would* not *be* **c** 3197
44:26 After he is **c,** he must wait seven days. 3200
Lk 4:27 yet not one of them *was* **c—** *2751*
17:14 And as they went, *they were* **c.** *2751*
17:17 Jesus asked, *"Were* not all ten **c?** *2751*
Heb 9:22 the law requires that nearly everything *be* **c** *2751*
10: 2 For the worshipers *would have been* **c** once *2751*
2Pe 1: 9 that he has been **c** from his past sins. *2752*

CLEANSES (1) [CLEAN]

2Ti 2:21 If a man **c** himself from the latter, *1705*

CLEANSING (16) [CLEAN]

Lev 14: 2 of his **ceremonial c,** when he is brought to 3200
14:23 the eighth day he must bring them for his **c** 3200
14:32 the regular offerings for his **c.** 3200
15:13 seven days for his **ceremonial c;** 3200
Nu 6: 9 he must shave his head on the day of his **c—** 3200
8: 7 Sprinkle the water of **c** on them; 2633
19: 9 for use in the water of **c;** 5614
19:13 water of **c** has not been sprinkled on him, 5614
19:20 water of **c** has not been sprinkled on him, 5614
19:21 the water of **c** must also wash his clothes, 5614
19:21 and anyone who touches the water of **c** will 5614
31:23 it must also be purified with the water of **c.** 5614
Mk 1:44 that Moses commanded for your **c,** *2752*
Lk 5:14 that Moses commanded for your **c,** *2752*
Jn 11:55 for their **ceremonial c** before the Passover. *49*
Eph 5:26 **c** her by the washing with water through *2751*

CLEAR (41) [CLEARED, CLEARLY]

Ge 20: 5 with a **c** conscience and clean hands." 9448
20: 6 I know you did this with a **c** conscience, 9448
Ex 24:10 made of sapphire, **c** as the sky itself. 3198
27:20 "Command the Israelites to bring you **c** oil 2341
Lev 24: 2 "Command the Israelites to bring you **c** oil 2341
24:12 of the LORD *should be* **made c** to them. 7300
Nu 15:34 *it was* not **c** what should be done to him. 7300
Jos 17:15 and **c land** for yourselves there in the land 1345
17:18 **C** it, and its farthest limits will be yours; 1345
2Sa 19: 6 *You have* **made** *it* **c** today that 5583
1Ki 2:31 so **c** me and my father's house *of* the guilt 6073
Ne 8: 8 **making** it **c** and giving the meaning so that 7300
Isa 32: 4 the stammering tongue will be fluent and **c.** 7456
Eze 34:18 Is it not enough for you to drink **c** water? 5488
Mt 3:12 and *he will* **c** his threshing floor, *1351*
Lk 3:17 in his hand *to* **c** his threshing floor and *1350*
Jn 8:43 Why *is* my language **not c** to you? *1182+4024*
Ac 18: 6 I am **c** of my responsibility. *2754*
24:16 So I strive always to keep my conscience **c** *718*
1Co 4: 4 My **conscience is c,** *4029+5323*
14: 8 if the trumpet does **not** sound a **c** call, *83*
15:27 it is **c** that this does *1316*
2Co 7:11 what **eagerness** to **c** yourselves, *665*
11: 6 *We have* **made** this perfectly **c** to you *5746*
Php 1:13 it has become **c** throughout *5745*
3:15 that too God *will* **make c** to you. *636*
1Th 3:11 and Father himself and our Lord Jesus **c** *2985*
1Ti 3: 9 of the faith with a **c** conscience. *2754*
2Ti 1: 3 as my forefathers did, with a **c** conscience, *2754*
3: 9 their folly will be **c** to everyone. *1684*
Heb 6:17 **make** the unchanging nature of his purpose very **c** to the heirs *2109*
7:14 For *it is* **c** that our Lord descended *4593*
7:15 And what we have said is even more **c** *2867*
9: 9 *to* **c** the conscience of the worshiper. *5457*
13:18 a **c** conscience and desire to live honorably *2819*
1Pe 3:16 keeping a **c** conscience, *19*
4: 7 Therefore *be* **c minded** and self-controlled *5404*
2Pe 1:14 as our Lord Jesus Christ *has* **made c** to me. *1317*
Rev 4: 6 like a sea of glass, **c** as crystal. *NIG*
21:11 like a jasper, **c as crystal.** *3222*
22: 1 river of the water of life, as **c** as crystal, *3287*

CLEARED (7) [CLEAR]

Nu 5:28 she *will* **be c of guilt** and will be able 5927
1Sa 14:41 and the men *were* **c.** 3655
2Ch 30:14 in Jerusalem and **c away** the incense altars 6073
Job 33:32 speak up, for I want you *to be* **c.** 7405
35: 2 You say, 'I will be **c** by God.' 7406
Ps 80: 9 *You* **c** *the* **ground** for it, 7155
Isa 5: 2 up and **c** it **of stones** and planted it with 6232

CLEARLY (20) [CLEAR]

Ge 26:28 *We* **saw c** that the LORD was with you; 8011+8011
Ex 10:10 **C** you are bent on evil. 3954+8011
Nu 12: 8 face to face, **c** and not in riddles; 5260
24: 3 the oracle of one whose eye **sees c,** 9280
24:15 the oracle of one whose eye **sees c,** 9280
Dt 27: 8 And you shall write very **c** all the words 930
Jos 9:24 "Your servants **were c told** how 5583+5583
1Sa 2:27 not **c reveal myself** to your father's house 1655+1655
Jer 23:20 In days to come *you will* **understand** it **c.** 1067+1069
Mt 7: 5 then *you will* **see c** to remove the speck *1332*
Mk 8:25 and he saw everything **c.** *5495*
Lk 6:42 then *you will* **see c** to remove the speck *1332*
Jn 16:29 "Now you are speaking **c** and *1877+4244*
Ro 1:20 *have been* **c seen,** *2775*
3: 5 **brings out** God's righteousness **more c,** *5319*
Gal 2:11 because he was **c in the wrong.** *2861*
3: 1 Before your very eyes Jesus Christ was **c** portrayed as crucified. *NIG*
3:11 **C** no one is justified before God by *1316*
Col 4: 4 Pray that *I may* **proclaim** it **c,** as I should. *5746*
1Ti 4: 1 The Spirit **c** says that *4843*

CLEAVE, CLEAVED, CLEAVETH (KJV) ALLY, CLING, CLUNG, DIVIDED, HELD FAST, HOLD FAST, REMAIN TRUE, STICK, STUCK, UNITED

CLEFT (1) [CLEFTS]

Ex 33:22 in a **c** *in* the rock and cover you 5942

CLEFTS (4) [CLEFT]

Jdg 6: 2 for themselves in **mountain c,** 2215
SS 2:14 My dove in the **c** *of* the rock, 2511
Jer 49:16 you who live in the **c** *of* the rocks, 2511
Ob 1: 3 the **c** *of* the rocks and make your home on 2511

CLEMENCY (KJV) See KIND

CLEMENT (1)

Php 4: 3 with **C** and the rest of my fellow workers, *3098*

CLEOPAS (1)

Lk 24:18 One of them, named **C,** asked him, *3093*

CLEOPHAS (KJV) See CLOPAS

CLERESTORY (1)

1Ki 6: 4 He made narrow **c** windows in the temple. 9209

CLERK (1)

Ac 19:35 The city **c** quieted the crowd and said: *1208*

CLEVER (2) [CLEVERLY, CLEVERNESS]
Isa 3: 3 skilled craftsman and **c** enchanter. 1067
5:21 in their own eyes and **c** in their own sight. 1067

CLEVERLY (2) [CLEVER]
Hos 13: 2 from their silver, **c fashioned** images, 9312
2Pe 1:16 We did not follow **c invented** stories *5054*

CLEVERNESS (1) [CLEVER]
Isa 25:11 down their pride despite the **c** 747

CLIFF (5) [CLIFFS]
1Sa 14: 4 to reach the Philistine outpost was a **c;** 6152+9094
14: 5 One **c** stood to the north toward Micmash, 9094
2Ch 25:12 took them to the top of a **c** and threw them 6152
Job 39:28 He dwells on a **c** and stays there at night; 6152
Lk 4:29 **throw** him **down the c.** *2889*

CLIFFS (3) [CLIFF]
Ps 141: 6 be thrown down from the **c,** 6152
Jer 51:25 roll you off the **c,** 6152
Eze 38:20 the **c** will crumble and every wall will fall 4533

CLIFT (KJV) See CLEFT

CLIMAX (3)
Eze 21:25 of punishment has reached its **c,** 7891
21:29 of punishment has reached its **c.** 7891
35: 5 the time their punishment reached its **c,** 7891

CLIMB (7) [CLIMBED, CLIMBING, CLIMBS]
Ge 49:22 whose branches **c** over a wall. 7575
1Sa 14:10 if they say, 'Come up to us,' *we will* **c up,** 6590
14:12 **"C up** after me; 6590
SS 7: 8 I said, *"I will* **c** the palm tree; 6590
Jer 4:29 *some* **c up** among the rocks. 6590
Joel 2: 9 *They* **c** into the houses; 6590
Am 9: 2 Though *they* **c up** *to* the heavens, 6590

CLIMBED (17) [CLIMB]
Dt 32:50 the mountain that you *have* **c** you will die 6590
34: 1 Then Moses **c** Mount Nebo from the plains 6590
Jos 15: 8 From there it **c** to the top of the hill west of 6590
Jdg 9: 7 *he* **c up** on the top of Mount Gerizim 2143
9:51 They locked themselves in and **c up** on 6590
1Sa 14:13 Jonathan **c up,** using his hands and feet, 6590
2Sa 17:18 and *they* **c down** *into* it. 3718
17:21 the two **c** out of the well and went 6590
1Ki 18:42 but Elijah **c** to the top of Carmel, 6590
Ne 4: 3 if even a fox **c up** on it, 6590
Isa 57: 8 *you* **c** *into* it and opened it wide; 6590
Jer 9:21 Death *has* **c in** through our windows 6590
Eze 40: 6 *He* **c** its steps and measured the threshold of 6590
Mt 14:32 they **c** into the boat, the wind died down. *326*
Mk 6:51 Then *he* **c** into the boat with them, *326*
Lk 19: 4 ahead and **c** a sycamore-fig tree to see him, *326*
Jn 21:11 Simon Peter **c aboard** and dragged *326*

CLIMBING (1) [CLIMB]
2Ch 20:16 They *will be* **c up** by the Pass of Ziz, 6590

CLIMBS (3) [CLIMB]
Isa 24:18 whoever **c** out of the pit will be caught in 6590
Jer 48:44 whoever **c** out of the pit will be caught in 6590
Jn 10: 1 but **c in** by some other way, *326*

CLING (10) [CLINGING, CLINGS, CLUNG]
Dt 28:60 and *they will* **c** to you. 1815
2Ki 5:27 Naaman's leprosy *will* **c** to you and 1815
Job 41:17 *they* **c together** and cannot be parted. 4334
Ps 31: 6 I hate those *who* **c** *to* worthless idols; 9068
44:25 our bodies **c** to the ground. 1815
101: 3 *they will* not **c** to me. 1815
119:31 I hold fast to your statutes, O LORD; 1815
137: 6 *May* my tongue **c** to the roof of my mouth 1815
Jer 8: 5 *They* **c** to deceit; they refuse to return. 2616
Jnh 2: 8 *"Those who* **c** *to* worthless idols forfeit 9068
Ro 12: 9 Hate what is evil; **c** to what is good. *3140*

CLINGING (1) [CLING]
1Ki 1:51 of King Solomon and *is* **c** to the horns of 296

CLINGS (2) [CLING]
Job 8:15 *he* **c** to it, but it does not hold. 2616
Ps 63: 8 My soul **c** to you; 1815

CLIP (1)
Lev 19:27 at the sides of your head or **c off** the edges 8845

CLOAK (51) [CLOAKS]
Ge 39:12 She caught him by his **c** and said, 955
39:12 But he left his **c** in her hand and ran out of 955
39:13 When she saw that he had left his **c** 955
39:15 he left his **c** beside me and ran out of 955
39:16 She kept his **c** beside her 955
39:18 he left his **c** beside me and ran out of 955
Ex 4: 6 LORD said, "Put your hand inside your **c.**" 2668
4: 6 So Moses put his hand into his **c,** 2668
Ex 4: 7 "Now put it back into your **c,**" he said. 2668
4: 7 So Moses put his hand back into his **c,** 2668
12:11 **c tucked into** your **belt,** 2520+5516
22:26 If you take your neighbor's **c** as a pledge, 8515
22:27 because his **c** is the only covering he has 8529
Dt 22: 3 if you find your brother's donkey or his **c** 8529
22:12 on the four corners of the **c** you wear. 4064
24:13 Return his **c** to him by sunset so 8515
24:17 or take the **c** *of* the widow as a pledge. 955
1Ki 11:29 wearing a new **c.** 8515
11:30 of the new **c** he was wearing and tore it 8515
18:46 **tucking** his **c into** *his* **belt,** 5516+9113
19:13 he pulled his **c** over his face and went out 168
19:19 up to him and threw his **c** around him. 168
2Ki 2: 8 Elijah took his **c,** 168
2:13 up the **c** that had fallen from Elijah 168
2:14 Then he took the **c** that had fallen from him 168
4:29 **"Tuck** your **c into** your **belt,** 2520+5516
4:39 of its gourds and filled the **fold of** his **c.** 955
9: 1 **"Tuck** *your* **c into** your **belt,** 2520+5516
Ezr 9: 3 When I heard this, I tore my tunic and **c,** 5077
9: 5 with my tunic and **c** torn, 5077
Ps 109:19 May it be like a **c** wrapped about him, 955
109:29 and wrapped in shame as in a **c.** 5077
Pr 21:14 in the **c** pacifies great wrath. 2668
30: 4 Who has wrapped up the waters in his **c?** 8529
SS 5: 7 they took away my **c,** 8100
Isa 3: 6 and say, "You have a **c,** you be our leader; 8529
59:17 and wrapped himself in zeal as in a **c.** 5077
Mt 5:40 let him have your **c** as well. *2668*
9:20 behind him and touched the edge *of* his **c.** *2668*
9:21 She said to herself, "If I only touch his **c,** *2668*
14:36 to let the sick just touch the edge *of* his **c,** *2668*
24:18 Let no one in the field go back to get his **c.** *2668*
Mk 5:27 behind him in the crowd and touched his **c,** *2668*
6:56 to let them touch even the edge *of* his **c,** *2668*
10:50 Throwing his **c** aside, *2668*
13:16 Let no one in the field go back to get his **c.** *2668*
Lk 6:29 If someone takes your **c,** *2668*
8:44 behind him and touched the edge *of* his **c,** *2668*
22:36 sell your **c** and buy one. *2668*
Ac 12: 8 "Wrap your **c** around you and follow me," *2668*
2Ti 4:13 bring the **c** that I left with Carpus at Troas, *5742*

CLOAKS (9) [CLOAK]
2Ki 9:13 and took their **c** and spread them under him 955
Isa 3:22 the fine robes and the capes and **c,** 4762
Mt 21: 7 placed their **c** on them, *2668*
21: 8 A very large crowd spread their **c** on *2668*
Mk 11: 7 the colt to Jesus and threw their **c** over it, *2668*
11: 8 Many people spread their **c** on the road, *2668*
Lk 19:35 threw their **c** on the colt and put Jesus on it. *2668*
19:36 people spread their **c** on the road. *2668*
Ac 22:23 and throwing off their **c** and flinging dust *2668*

CLODS (2)
Job 38:38 and the **c of earth** stick together? 8073
Joel 1:17 The seeds are shriveled beneath the **c.** 4493

CLOPAS (1)
Jn 19:25 Mary the wife *of* **C,** and Mary Magdalene. *3116*

CLOSE (65) [CLOSED, CLOSELY, CLOSER, CLOSES, CLOSEST, CLOSING, ENCLOSE, ENCLOSED]
Ge 27:22 Jacob **went c** to his father Isaac, 5602
45: 4 Joseph said to his brothers, **"Come c** to me." 5602
46: 4 And Joseph's own hand *will* **c** your eyes." 8883
48:10 So Joseph **brought** his sons **c** to him, 5602
48:13 and **brought** them **c** to him. 5602
Ex 25:27 to be **c to** the rim to hold the poles 4200+6645
28:27 **c to** the seam just above the waistband 4200+6645
37:14 The rings were put **c to** the rim to hold 4200+6645
39:20 **c to** the seam just above the waistband 4200+6645
Lev 3: 9 entire fat tail cut off **c to** the backbone, 4200+6645
14:38 of the house and **c** it **up** for seven days. 6037
18: 6 'No one is to approach any **c relative** 1414+8638
18:12 she is your father's **c relative.** 8638
18:13 because she is your mother's **c relative.** 8638
18:17 they are her **c relatives.** 8638
20: 4 If the people of the community **c** their eyes 6623+6623
20:19 for that would dishonor a **c relative;** 8638
21: 2 except for a **c relative,** 7940+8638
Nu 5: 8 But if that person has no **c relative** 1457
22:25 *she* **pressed c** to the wall, 4315
Jos 2: 5 when it was time to **c** the city gate, 6037
Jdg 16: 9 of string snaps when it **comes c** *to* a flame. 8193
Ru 2:20 She added, "That man is our **c relative;** 7940
2:23 So Ruth **stayed c** to the servant girls 1815
2Sa 11:20 'Why *did you* **get so c** to the city to fight? 5602
11:21 Why *did you* **get so c** to the wall?' 5602
12:11 and give them to **one who is c** *to* you, 8276
1Ki 21: 1 **c to** the palace of Ahab king of Samaria. 725
21: 2 since it is **c to** my palace. 725+7940
2Ki 10:11 his **c friends** and his priests, 3359
11: 8 Stay **c to** the king wherever he goes." 907
2Ch 23: 7 Stay **c to** the king wherever he goes." 907
Ne 6:10 and *let us* **c** the temple doors, 6037
Job 13:27 *you* **keep c watch on** all my paths 9068
33:11 *he* **keeps c watch on** all my paths.' 9068
41:16 each *is so* **c** to the next 5602
Ps 17:10 *They* **c up** their callous hearts, 6037
34:18 The LORD is **c** to the brokenhearted 7940
41: 9 Even my **c friend,** whom I trusted, 408+8934
55:13 my companion, my **c friend,** 3359
69:15 up or the pit **c** its mouth over me. 358
88:15 and **c to death;** 1588
148:14 of Israel, the people **c to** his **heart.** 7940
Pr 16:28 and a gossip separates **c friends.** 476
17: 9 the matter separates **c friends.** 476
Isa 6:10 make their ears dull and **c** their eyes. 9129
40:11 the lambs in his arms and carries them **c to** 928
42:23 listen to this or **pay c attention** 2256+7992+9048
56: 1 and do what is right, for my salvation is **c** 7940
66: 9 *"Do I* **c up** the womb when I bring 6806
Jer 30:21 I will bring him near and *he will* **come c** 5602
30:21 to *be* **c** to me?' 5602
La 3:56 *"Do* not **c** your ears to my cry for relief." 6623
Eze 22: 4 **brought** your days **to a c,** 7928
Da 12: 4 **c up** and seal the words of the scroll until 6258
Joel 2: 1 It is **c at hand—** 7940
Zec 13: 7 against the man who is **c** *to* me!" 6660
Mt 6: 6 **c** the door and pray to your Father, *3091*
Lk 20:20 **Keeping a c watch** on him, they sent spies, *4190*
21:34 day *will* **c** on you unexpectedly like a trap. *2392*
Jn 4:47 *who was* **c** to death. *3516*
Ac 8: 6 *they* all **paid c attention** to what he said. *4668*
9:24 Day and night *they* **kept c watch on** *4190*
10:24 called together his relatives and **c** friends. *338*
Rev 6: 8 and Hades was following **c** behind him. *3552*

CLOSE-KNIT (1) [KNIT]
Job 40:17 the sinews of his thighs *are* **c.** 8571

CLOSED (18) [CLOSE]
Ge 2:21 he took one of the man's ribs and **c up** 6037
8: 2 the floodgates of the heavens *had* **been c,** 6126
20:18 for the LORD *had* **c up** every womb 6806+6806
Lev 14:46 the house while it *is* **c up** will be unclean 6037
Nu 16:33 the earth **c** over them, 4059
Jdg 3:22 and the fat **c in** over it. 6037
1Sa 1: 5 and the LORD *had* **c** her womb. 6037
1: 6 And because the LORD *had* **c** her womb, 6037
Ne 4: 7 ahead and that the gaps *were* **being c,** 6258
Job 17: 4 *You have* **c** their minds to understanding; 7621
Ecc 12: 4 the doors to the street **are c** and the sound 6037
Isa 32: 3 eyes of those who see *will* no *longer be* **c,** 9129
44:18 their minds **c** so they cannot understand. NIH
Jer 6:10 Their ears are **c** so they cannot hear. 6888
La 3:54 the waters **c** over my head, 7429
Da 12: 9 the words *are* **c up** and sealed until the time 6258
Mt 13:15 and *they have* **c** their eyes. *2826*
Ac 28:27 and *they have* **c** their eyes. *2826*

CLOSELY (18) [CLOSE]
Ge 24:21 the man **watched** her **c** to learn whether or 8617
43: 7 man **questioned** us **c** about ourselves 8626+8626
44:30 whose life *is* **c bound up** with 8003
Dt 4: 9 and watch yourselves **c** so that you do 4394
2Sa 19:42 "We did this because the king is **c related** 7940
1Ki 3:21 *I* **looked** at him **c** in the morning light, 1067
Ne 13: 4 He was **c associated** with Tobiah, 7940
Job 23:11 My feet *have* **c followed** his steps; 296
Ps 122: 3 like a city that **is c compacted** together. 2489
Pr 4:20 **listen c** to my words. 265+5742
Jer 2:10 send to Kedar and observe **c;** 4394
Eze 44: 5 **listen c** and give attention 265+928+9048
Mk 3: 2 so *they* **watched** him **c** to see *4190*
14:67 *she* **looked c at** him. *1838*
Lk 6: 7 so *they* **watched** him **c** to see *4190*
22:56 She **looked c at** him and said, *867*
Ac 7:31 As he went over *to* **look more c,** *2917*
1Ti 4:16 **Watch** your life and doctrine **c.** *2091*

CLOSER (6) [CLOSE]
Ex 3: 5 *"Do* not **come** *any* **c,"** God said. 7928
1Sa 17:41 kept coming **c** to David. 7929
17:48 As the Philistine moved **c** to attack him, 7928
2Sa 18:25 the man came **c and closer.** 2143+2256+7929
18:25 the man came **closer and c.** 2143+2256+7929
Pr 18:24 but there is a friend *who* **sticks c** than 1816

CLOSES (2) [CLOSE]
Pr 28:27 but *he who* **c** his eyes 6623
Lk 13:25 Once the owner of the house gets up and **c** *643*

CLOSEST (4) [CLOSE]
Dt 13: 6 or your **c friend** secretly entices you, 889+3869+3870+5883+8276
Est 1:14 and were **c** to the king— 7940
Ps 88: 8 You have taken from me my **c friends** 3359
88:18 the darkness *is* my **c friend.** 3359

CLOSET (KJV) See CHAMBER, ROOM

CLOSING (4) [CLOSE]
Lev 23:36 It is the **c assembly;** do no regular work. 6809
1Sa 23:26 As Saul and his forces *were* **c in** on David 6496
Ps 77: 4 **kept** my eyes **from c;** 296+9073
Eze 21:14 **c in** on them **from every side.** 2539

CLOTH (27) [CLOTHS]

Ex 28:31 the robe of the ephod entirely of **blue c**, 9418
39:22 the robe of the ephod entirely of **blue c**— 9418
Lev 11:32 whether it is made of wood, c, 955
Nu 4: 6 a c *of* solid blue over that and put the poles 955
4: 7 of the Presence they are to spread a blue c 955
4: 8 Over these they are to spread a scarlet c, 955
4: 9 to take a blue c and cover the lampstand 955
4:11 to spread a blue c and cover that with hides 955
4:12 wrap them in a blue c, 955
4:13 from the bronze altar and spread a purple c 955
Dt 22:17 Then her parents shall display the c before 8529
1Sa 21: 9 it is wrapped in a c behind the ephod. 8529
2Ki 8:15 But the next day he took a **thick c**, 4802
Isa 19:10 The **workers in c** will be dejected, 9271
30:22 like a **menstrual c** and say to them, 1865
Eze 16:13 and costly fabric and **embroidered c**. 8391
Mt 9:16 a patch *of* unshrunk c on an old garment, *4820*
27:59 wrapped it in a clean **linen c**, *4984*
Mk 2:21 a patch *of* unshrunk c on an old garment. *4820*
15:46 So Joseph bought some **linen c**, *4984*
Lk 19:20 I have kept it laid away in a **piece of c**. *5051*
23:53 *in* **linen c** and placed it in a tomb cut in *4984*
Jn 11:44 and a c around his face. *5051*
20: 7 as well as the **burial c** that had been *5051*
20: 7 The c was folded up by itself, *NIG*
Ac 16:14 a **dealer in purple c** from the city *4527*
Rev 18:12 fine linen, purple, silk and scarlet c; *NIG*

CLOTHE (21) [CLOTHED, CLOTHES, CLOTHING]

Job 10:11 c me *with* skin and flesh 4252
39:19 the horse his strength or c his neck *with* 4252
40:10 and c *yourself in* honor and majesty. 4252
Ps 45: 3 c yourself with splendor and majesty. NIH
73: 6 *they* c themselves *with* violence. 6493+8884
132:16 *I will* c her priests *with* salvation, 4252
132:18 *I will* c his enemies *with* shame, 4252
Isa 22:21 *I will* c him *with* your robe 4252
50: 3 *I* c the sky *with* darkness 4252
51: 9 C *yourself with* strength, 4252
52: 1 awake, O Zion, c *yourself with* strength. 4252
58: 7 when you see the naked, *to* c him, 4059
Eze 34: 3 c *yourselves with* the wool and slaughter 4252
Mt 6:30 *will he* not much more c you, *NIG*
25:38 or needing clothes and c you? *4314*
25:43 I needed clothes and *you did* not c me, *4314*
Lk 12:28 how much more will he c you, *NIG*
Ro 13:14 c *yourselves* **with** the Lord Jesus Christ, *1907*
1Co 15:53 For the perishable must c *itself* **with** *1907*
Col 3:12 c *yourselves* **with** compassion, kindness, *1907*
1Pe 5: 5 c *yourselves* **with** humility *1599*

CLOTHED (47) [CLOTHE]

Ge 3:21 of skin for Adam and his wife and c them. 4252
Lev 8: 7 c him *with* the robe and put the ephod 4252
2Sa 1:24 who c you *in* scarlet and finery, 4252
1Ch 15:27 Now David **was** c in a robe of fine linen, 4124
21:16 Then David and the elders, c in sackcloth, 4059
2Ch 6:41 O LORD God, *be* c *with* salvation, 4252
28:15 the plunder *they* c all who were naked. 4252
Est 4: 2 because no *one* c in sackcloth was allowed 4230
Job 7: 5 My body *is* c *with* worms and scabs, 4252
8:22 Your enemies *will be* c *in* shame, 4252
Ps 30:11 you removed my sackcloth and c me 273
35:26 *may* all who exalt themselves over me *be* c 4252
65:12 the hills *are* c *with* gladness. 2520
104: 1 *you are* c *with* splendor and majesty. 4252
109:29 *be* c *with* disgrace and wrapped in shame 4252
132: 9 *May* your priests *be* c *with* righteousness; 4252
Pr 31:21 for all of them are c *in* scarlet. 4229
31:22 she is c in fine linen and purple. 4230
31:25 She is c *with* strength and dignity; 4230
Ecc 9: 8 Always be c *in* white, 955
Isa 61:10 For *he has* c me *with* garments of salvation 4252
Eze 7:18 They will put on sackcloth and *be* c 4059
7:27 the prince *will be* c *with* despair, 4252
9: 2 With them was a man c *in* linen who had 4229
9: 3 the man c *in* linen who had the writing kit 4229
10: 2 The LORD said to the man c *in* linen, 4229
16:10 *I* c you *with* an embroidered dress 4252
23: 6 c *in* blue, governors and commanders, all 4229
26:16 C *with* terror, they will sit on the ground, 4252
31:15 c Lebanon **with gloom,** 7722
Da 5: 7 and tells me what it means *will be* c 10383
5:16 *you will be* c *in* purple and have 10383
5:29 Daniel *was* c *in* purple, 10383
12: 6 One of them said to the man c *in* linen, 4229
12: 7 The man c *in* linen, 4229
Zec 3: 5 a clean turban on his head and c him, 955+4252
6:13 and he *will be* c **with** majesty and will sit 5951
Mt 25:36 I needed clothes and *you* c me, *4314*
Lk 24:49 the city until *you have been* c **with** power *1907*
Jn 19: 2 *They* c him **in** a purple robe *4314*
1Co 15:54 When the perishable *has been* c **with** *1907*
2Co 5: 2 *to be* c with our heavenly dwelling, *2086*
5: 3 *because when we are* c, *1907*
5: 4 but *to be* c with our heavenly dwelling, *2086*
Gal 3:27 into Christ *have* c *yourselves* **with** Christ. *1907*
Rev 11: 3 and they will prophesy for 1,260 days, **c in** *4314*
12: 1 a woman c with the sun, *4314*

CLOTHES (169) [CLOTHE]

Ge 27:15 the best c *of* Esau her older son, 955
27:27 When Isaac caught the smell of his c, 955
28:20 and will give me food to eat and c to wear 955
35: 2 and purify yourselves and change your c. 8529
37:29 saw that Joseph was not there, he tore his c. 955
37:34 Then Jacob tore his c, put on sackcloth 8529
38:14 she took off her widow's c, 955
38:19 and put on her widow's c again. 955
41:14 When he had shaved and changed his c, 8529
44:13 At this, they tore their c. 8529
45:22 of silver and five sets of c. 8529
Ex 19:10 Have them wash their c 8529
19:14 and they washed their c. 8529
28:41 After *you* **put** these **c on** 4252
Lev 6:10 The priest shall then put on his linen c, 4496
6:11 he is to take off these c and put on others, 955
10: 6 and do not tear your c, 955
11:25 up one of their carcasses must wash his c, 955
11:28 up their carcasses must wash his c, 955
11:40 of the carcass must wash his c, 955
11:40 up the carcass must wash his c, 955
13: 6 The man must wash his c, 955
13:34 He must wash his c, and he will be clean. 955
13:45 an infectious disease must wear torn c, 955
14: 8 to be cleansed must wash his c, 955
14: 9 He must wash his c and bathe himself 955
14:47 or eats in the house must wash his c. 955
15: 5 who touches his bed must wash his c 955
15: 6 on must wash his c and bathe with water, 955
15: 7 a discharge must wash his c and bathe 955
15: 8 that person must wash his c and bathe 955
15:10 up those things must wash his c and bathe 955
15:11 with water must wash his c and bathe 955
15:13 he must wash his c and bathe himself 955
15:21 Whoever touches her bed must wash his c 955
15:22 on must wash his c and bathe with water, 955
15:27 he must wash his c and bathe with water, 955
16:26 the goat as a scapegoat must wash his c 955
16:28 The man who burns them must wash his c 955
17:15 by wild animals must wash his c and bathe 955
17:16 if he does not wash his c and bathe himself, NIH
21:10 let his hair become unkempt or tear his c. 955
Nu 8: 7 shave their whole bodies and wash their c, 955
8:21 purified themselves and washed their c. 955
14: 6 the land, tore their c 955
19: 7 the priest must wash his c 955
19: 8 The man who burns it must also wash his c 955
19:10 of the heifer must also wash his c, 955
19:19 The person being cleansed must wash his c 955
19:21 of cleansing must also wash his c, 955
31:24 the seventh day wash your c and you will 955
Dt 8: 4 Your c did not wear out and your feet did 8529
21:13 the c she was wearing when captured. 8529
22:11 *Do* not **wear** c of wool and linen 4252
29: 5 your c did not wear out, 8515
Jos 7: 6 Then Joshua tore his c and fell facedown to 8529
9: 5 on their feet and wore old c. 8515
9:13 And our c and sandals are worn out by 8515
Jdg 11:35 When he saw her, he tore his c and cried, 955
14:12 and thirty sets of c. 955
14:13 and thirty sets of c." 955
14:19 of their belongings and gave their c 2722
17:10 your c and your food." 955+6886
Ru 3: 3 and put on your **best c**. 8529
1Sa 4:12 his c torn and dust on his head. 4496
27: 9 donkeys and camels, and c. 955
28: 8 Saul disguised himself, putting on other c, 955
2Sa 1: 2 with his c torn and with dust on his head. 955
1:11 the men with him took hold of their c 955
3:31 "Tear your c and put on sackcloth and walk 955
12:20 put on lotions and changed his c, 8529
13:31 tore his c and lay down on the ground; 955
13:31 all his servants stood by with their c torn. 955
14: 2 Dress in mourning c, 955
19:24 or washed his c from the day the king left 955
1Ki 21:27 he tore his c, put on sackcloth and fasted. 955
2Ki 2:12 of his own c and tore them apart. 955
5:26 or to accept c, olive groves, vineyards, 955
7: 8 gold and c, and went off and hid them. 955
18:37 with their c torn, 955
19: 1 he tore his c and put on sackcloth and went 955
25:29 So Jehoiachin put aside his prison c and for 955
2Ch 28:15 *They* **provided** them **with** c and sandals, 4252
Ne 4:23 nor the guards with me took off our c; 955
9:21 they lacked nothing, their c did 8515
Est 4: 1 he tore his c, put on sackcloth and ashes, 955
4: 4 She sent c for him to put on instead 955
Job 9:31 so that even my c would detest me. 8515
24: 7 Lacking c, they spend the night naked; 4230
24:10 Lacking c, they go about naked; 4230
27:16 up silver like dust and c like piles of clay, 4860
37:17 in your c when the land lies hushed under 955
Pr 6:27 into his lap without his c being burned? 955
23:21 and drowsiness c them *in* rags. 4252
Isa 4: 1 and provide our own c; 8529
23:18 for abundant food and fine c. 4833
32:11 **Strip off** *your* c, 2256+6910+7320
36:22 with their c torn, 955
37: 1 he tore his c and put on sackcloth and went 955
Jer 2:34 On your c men find the lifeblood of 4053
36:24 nor did they tear their c. 955
38:11 and worn-out c from there and let them 4874
38:12 and worn-out c under your arms to pad 4874
41: 5 torn their c and cut themselves came 955
52:33 So Jehoiachin put aside his prison c and for 955
Eze 16:13 your c were of fine linen and costly fabric 4860
16:18 And you took your embroidered c to put 955
16:39 of your c and take your fine jewelry 955
23:26 of your c and take your fine jewelry. 955
42:14 They are to put on other c before they go 955
44:17 they are to wear linen c; 955
44:19 to take off the c they have been ministering 955
44:19 and put on other c, 955
Da 3:21 trousers, turbans and other c, 10382
Zep 1: 8 and all those clad in foreign c. 4860
Hag 1: 6 *You* **put on** c, but are not warm. 4252
Zec 3: 3 in filthy c as he stood before the angel. 955
3: 4 "Take off his filthy c." 955
Mt 3: 4 John's c were made of camel's hair, *1903*
6:25 and the body more important than c? *1903*
6:28 "And why do you worry about c? *1903*
6:30 If that is how God c the grass of the field, *314*
11: 8 A man dressed in **fine** c? *3434*
11: 8 those who wear **fine** c are *3434*
17: 2 and his c became as white as the light. *2668*
22:11 not wearing wedding c. *1903*
22:12 in here without wedding c?' *1903*
25:36 I **needed** c and you clothed me, *1218*
25:38 or **needing** c and clothe you? *1218*
25:43 I **needed** c and you did not clothe me, *1218*
25:44 a stranger or **needing** c or sick or in prison, *1218*
26:65 Then the high priest tore his c and said, *2668*
27:31 they took off the robe and put his own c *2668*
27:35 they divided up his c by casting lots. *2668*
28: 3 and his c were white as snow. *1903*
Mk 5:28 "If I just touch his c, I will be healed." *2668*
5:30 "Who touched my c?" *2668*
9: 3 His c became dazzling white, *2668*
14:63 The high priest tore his c. *5945*
15:20 the purple robe and put his own c on him. *2668*
15:24 Dividing up his c, they cast lots *2668*
Lk 7:25 A man dressed in fine c? *2668*
7:25 those who wear expensive c and indulge *2669*
8:27 For a long time this man had not worn c *2668*
9:29 and his c became as bright as a flash *2669*
10:30 **stripped** him **of** his c, *1694*
12:23 and the body more than c. *1903*
12:28 If that is how God c the grass of the field, *313*
23:34 And they divided up his c by casting lots. *2668*
24: 4 in c that gleamed like lightning stood *2264*
Jn 11:44 "Take off the grave c and let him go." *NIG*
13:12 he put on his c and returned to his place. *2668*
19:23 they took his c, dividing them into four *2668*
Ac 7:58 the witnesses laid their c at the feet of *2668*
10:30 a man in shining c stood before me *2264*
12: 8 **"Put on** your c and sandals." *2439*
14:14 they tore their c and rushed out into *2668*
18: 6 he shook out his c in protest and said *2668*
22:20 the c of those who were killing him.' *2668*
1Ti 2: 9 or gold or pearls or expensive c, *2669*
Jas 2: 2 a gold ring and fine c, *2264*
2: 2 and a poor man in shabby c also comes in. *2264*
2: 3 to the man wearing fine c and say, *2264*
2:15 Suppose a brother or sister is **without** c *1218*
5: 2 and moths have eaten your c. *2668*
1Pe 3: 3 and the wearing of gold jewelry and fine c. *2668*
Rev 3: 4 in Sardis who have not soiled their c. *2668*
3:18 and white c to wear, *2668*
16:15 and keeps his c with him, *2668*

CLOTHING (52) [CLOTHE]

Ge 24:53 and silver jewelry and **articles of** c 955
45:22 To each of them he gave new c, 8529
Ex 3:22 for articles of silver and gold and for c, 8529
12:34 in kneading troughs wrapped in c. 8529
12:35 for articles of silver and gold and for c. 8529
21:10 c and marital rights. 4064
Lev 13:47 "If any c is contaminated with mildew— 955
13:47 any woolen or linen c, 955
13:49 and if the contamination in the c, 955
13:51 and if the mildew has spread in the c, 955
13:52 He must burn up the c, 955
13:53 the mildew has not spread in the c, 955
13:56 to tear the contaminated part out of the c, 955
13:57 But if it reappears in the c, 955
13:58 The c, or the woven or knitted material, 955
13:59 by mildew in woolen or linen c, 955
14:55 for mildew in c or in a house, 955
15:17 Any c or leather that has semen on it must 955
19:19 not wear c woven of two kinds of material. 955
Dt 10:18 and loves the alien, giving him food and c. 8529
22: 5 A woman must not wear men's c, 3998
22: 5 nor a man wear women's c, 8529
Jos 22: 8 bronze and iron, and a great quantity of c— 8515
Jdg 3:16 to his right thigh under his c. 4496
2Ki 5: 5 of gold and ten sets of c. 955
5:22 a talent of silver and two sets of c.' " 955
5:23 with two sets of c. 955
7:15 the whole road strewn with the c 955
2Ch 20:25 a great amount of equipment and c and 955
Job 22: 6 you stripped men of their c, 955
29:14 **put on** righteousness **as** *my* c; 4252
30:18 In his great power [God] becomes like c 4230
31:19 I have seen anyone perishing for lack of c, 4230
Ps 22:18 among them and cast lots for my c. 4230
102:26 Like c you will change them and they will 4230
Pr 27:26 the lambs will provide you with c, 4230
Isa 3: 7 I have no food or c in my house; 8529
3:24 instead of **fine** c, sackcloth; 7345
59: 6 Their cobwebs are useless for c; 955
63: 3 and I stained all my c. 4860
Eze 18: 7 to the hungry and provides c for the naked. 955
18:16 to the hungry and provides c for the naked. 955
Da 7: 9 His c was as white as snow; 10382

Zec 14:14 great quantities of gold and silver and **c.** 955
Mt 7:15 They come to you in sheep's **c,** *1903*
Mk 1:6 John **wore c** made of camel's hair, *1639+1907*
Jn 13:4 took off his **outer c,** *2668*
19:24 among them and cast lots for my **c."** *2669*
Ac 9:39 the robes and other **c** that Dorcas had made *2668*
20:33 not coveted anyone's silver or gold or **c.** *2669*
1Ti 6:8 But if we have food and **c,** *5004*
Jude 1:23 even the **c** stained by corrupted flesh. *5945*

CLOTHS (3) [CLOTH]

Eze 16:4 with salt or **wrapped in c.** 3156+3156
Lk 2:7 *She* **wrapped** him **in c** and placed him in *5058*
2:12 a baby **wrapped in c** and lying in a manger." *5058*

CLOUD (97) [CLOUDBURST, CLOUDLESS, CLOUDS, THUNDERCLOUD]

Ex 13:21 a pillar of **c** to guide them on their way and 6727
13:22 Neither the pillar of **c** by day nor the pillar 6727
14:19 The pillar of **c** also moved from in front 6727
14:20 the **c** brought darkness to the one side 6727
14:24 the pillar of fire and **c** at the Egyptian army 6727
16:10 the glory of the LORD appearing in the **c.** 6727
19:9 "I am going to come to you in a dense **c,** 6727
19:16 with a thick **c** over the mountain, 6727
24:15 went up on the mountain, the **c** covered it, 6727
24:16 For six days the **c** covered the mountain, 6727
24:16 to Moses from within the **c.** 6727
24:18 Then Moses entered the **c** as he went on up 6727
33:9 the pillar of **c** would come down and stay 6727
33:10 the people saw the pillar of **c** standing at 6727
34:5 down in the **c** and stood there with him 6727
40:34 Then the **c** covered the Tent of Meeting, 6727
40:35 of Meeting because the **c** had settled 6727
40:36 the **c** lifted from above the tabernacle, 6727
40:37 if the **c** did not lift, they did not set out— 6727
40:38 So the **c** *of* the LORD was over 6727
40:38 and fire was in **the c** by night, 2257[S]
Lev 16:2 I appear in the **c** over the atonement cover. 6727
Nu 9:15 was set up, the **c** covered it. 6727
9:15 the **c** above the tabernacle looked like fire. NIH
9:16 **c** covered it, and at night it looked like fire. 6727
9:17 Whenever the **c** lifted from above the Tent, 6727
9:17 wherever the **c** settled, 6727
9:18 As long as the **c** stayed over the tabernacle, 6727
9:19 When the **c** remained over the tabernacle 6727
9:20 the **c** was over the tabernacle only 6727
9:21 Sometimes the **c** stayed only from evening 6727
9:21 whenever the **c** lifted, they set out. 6727
9:22 Whether the **c** stayed over the tabernacle 6727
10:11 the **c** lifted from above the tabernacle of 6727
10:12 from place to place until the **c** came to rest 6727
10:34 The **c** *of* the LORD was over them by day 6727
11:25 the LORD came down in the **c** and spoke 6727
12:5 the LORD came down in a pillar of **c;** 6727
12:10 When the **c** lifted from above the Tent, 6727
14:14 that your **c** stays over them, 6727
14:14 and that you go before them in a pillar of **c** 6727
16:42 suddenly the **c** covered it and the glory of 6727
Dt 1:33 in fire by night and in a **c** by day, 6727
5:22 the **c** and the deep darkness; 6727
31:15 at the Tent in a pillar of **c,** 6727
31:15 the **c** stood over the entrance to the Tent. 6727
Jdg 20:38 that they should send up a great **c** *of* smoke 5368
1Ki 8:10 the **c** filled the temple of the LORD. 6727
8:11 not perform their service because of the **c,** 6727
8:12 that he would dwell in a **dark c;** 6906
18:44 "A **c** as small as a man's hand is rising 6265
2Ch 5:13 temple of the LORD was filled with a **c,** 6727
5:14 not perform their service because of the **c,** 6727
6:1 that he would dwell in a **dark c;** 6906
Ne 9:12 By day you led them with a pillar of **c,** 6727
9:19 the pillar of **c** did not cease to guide them 6727
Job 3:5 may a **c** settle over it; 6729
7:9 As a **c** vanishes and is gone, 6727
30:15 my safety vanishes like a **c.** 6265
Ps 78:14 He guided them with the **c** by day and 6727
99:7 He spoke to them from the pillar of **c;** 6727
105:39 He spread out a **c** as a covering, 6727
Pr 16:15 his favor is like a rain **c** in spring. 6265
Isa 4:5 and over those who assemble there a **c** 6727
14:31 A **c of smoke** comes from the north, 6940
18:4 like a **c** *of* dew in the heat of harvest." 6265
19:1 on a swift **c** and is coming to Egypt. 6265
25:5 as heat is reduced by the shadow of a **c,** 6265
44:22 I have swept away your offenses like a **c,** 6265
La 2:1 **covered** the Daughter of Zion **with the c** 6380
3:44 with a **c** so that no prayer can get through. 6727
Eze 1:4 an immense **c** with flashing lightning 6727
8:11 and a fragrant **c** *of* incense was rising. 6727
10:3 and a **c** filled the inner court. 6727
10:4 The **c** filled the temple, 6727
32:7 I will cover the sun with a **c,** 6727
38:9 you will be like a **c** covering the land. 6727
38:16 against my people Israel like a **c** that covers 6727
Mt 17:5 a bright **c** enveloped them, *3749*
17:5 and a voice from the **c** said, *3749*
Mk 9:7 Then a **c** appeared and enveloped them, *3749*
9:7 and a voice came from the **c:** *3749*
Lk 9:34 a **c** appeared and enveloped them, *3749*
9:34 and they were afraid as they entered the **c.** *3749*
9:35 A voice came from the **c,** saying, *3749*
12:54 "When you see a **c** rising in the west, *3749*
21:27 the Son of Man coming in a **c** with power *3749*
Ac 1:9 and a **c** hid him from their sight. *3749*
1Co 10:1 that our forefathers were all under the **c** and *3749*
10:2 They were all baptized into Moses in the **c** *3749*
Heb 12:1 since we are surrounded by such a great **c** *3751*
Rev 10:1 He was robed in a **c,** *3749*
11:12 And they went up to heaven in a **c,** *3749*
14:14 and there before me was a white **c,** *3749*
14:14 on the **c** was one "like a son of man" with *3749*
14:15 to him who was sitting on the **c,** *3749*
14:16 on the **c** swung his sickle over the earth, *3749*

CLOUDBURST (1) [CLOUD]

Isa 30:30 with **c,** thunderstorm and hail. 5881

CLOUDLESS (1) [CLOUD]

2Sa 23:4 of morning at sunrise on a **c** morning, 4202+6265

CLOUDS (67) [CLOUD]

Ge 9:13 I have set my rainbow in the **c,** 6727
9:14 Whenever I **bring c** over the earth and 6725+6727
9:14 the earth and the rainbow appears in the **c,** 6727
9:16 Whenever the rainbow appears in the **c,** 6727
Dt 4:11 with black **c** and deep darkness. 6727
33:26 on the heavens to help you and on the **c** 8836
Jdg 5:4 the **c** poured down water. 6265
2Sa 22:10 **dark c** were under his feet. 6906
22:12 the dark rain **c of the sky.** 6265+8836
1Ki 18:45 Meanwhile, the sky grew black with **c,** 6265
Job 20:6 to the heavens and his head touches the **c,** 6265
22:14 **Thick c** veil him, 6265
26:8 He wraps up the waters in his **c,** 6265
26:8 yet the **c** do not burst under their weight. 6727
26:9 spreading his **c** over it. 6727
35:5 gaze at the **c** so high above you. 8836
36:28 the **c** pour down their moisture 8836
36:29 how he spreads out the **c,** 6265
37:11 He loads the **c** with moisture; 6265
37:13 He brings **the c** to punish men, 2084[S]
37:15 Do you know how God controls the **c** 6727
37:16 Do you know how the **c** hang poised, 6265
38:9 the **c** its garment and wrapped it 6727
38:34 to the **c** and cover yourself with a flood 6265
38:37 Who has the wisdom to count the **c?** 8836
Ps 18:9 **dark c** were under his feet. 6906
18:11 the dark rain **c of the sky.** 6265+8836
18:12 the brightness of his presence **c** advanced, 6265
68:4 extol him who rides on the **c—** 6265
77:17 The **c** poured down water, 6265
97:2 **C** and thick darkness surround him; 6727
104:3 the **c** his chariot and rides on the wings of 6265
135:7 He makes **c** rise from the ends of the earth; 5955
147:8 He covers the sky with **c;** 6265
148:8 and hail, snow and **c,** stormy winds 7798
Pr 3:20 and the **c** let drop the dew. 8836
8:28 when he established the **c** above 8836
25:14 Like **c** and wind without rain is 5955
Ecc 11:3 If **c** are full of water, 6265
11:4 whoever looks at the **c** will not reap. 6265
12:2 and the **c** return after the rain; 6265
Isa 5:6 I will command the **c** not to rain on it." 6265
5:30 even the light will be darkened by the **c.** 6882
14:14 I will ascend above the tops of the **c;** 6265
30:27 with burning anger and dense **c of smoke;** 5366
45:8 let the **c** shower it down. 8836
60:8 "Who are these that fly along like **c,** 6265
Jer 4:13 He advances like the **c,** 6727
10:13 he makes **c** rise from the ends of the earth. 5955
51:9 it rises as high as the **c.'** 8836
51:16 he makes **c** rise from the ends of the earth. 5955
Eze 1:28 Like the appearance of a rainbow in the **c** 6727
30:3 a day of **c,** a time of doom for the nations. 6727
30:18 She will be covered with **c,** 6727
34:12 where they were scattered on a day of **c** 6727
Da 7:13 coming with the **c** *of* heaven. 10560
Joel 2:2 a day of **c** and blackness. 6727
Na 1:3 and **c** are the dust of his feet. 6727
Zep 1:15 a day of **c** and blackness, 6727
Zec 10:1 it is the LORD who makes the **storm c.** 2613
Mt 24:30 the Son of Man coming on the **c** of the sky, *3749*
26:64 of the Mighty One and coming on the **c** *3749*
Mk 13:26 of Man coming in **c** with great power *3749*
14:62 of the Mighty One and coming on the **c** *3749*
1Th 4:17 be caught up together with them in the **c** *3749*
Jude 1:12 They are **c** without rain, *3749*
Rev 1:7 Look, he is coming with the **c,** *3749*

CLOVEN (KJV) See DIVIDED, SEPARATED

CLUB (8) [CLUBS]

2Sa 23:21 Benaiah went against him with a **c.** 8657
1Ch 11:23 Benaiah went against him with a **c.** 8657
Job 41:29 A **c** seems to him but a piece of straw; 9371
Pr 25:18 Like a **c** or a sword or a sharp arrow is 5138
Isa 10:5 in whose hand is the **c** of my wrath! 4751
10:15 or a **c** brandish him who is not wood! 4751
10:24 who beat you with a rod and lift up a **c** 4751
Jer 51:20 "You are my **war c,** 5151

CLUBS (6) [CLUB]

Eze 39:9 bows and arrows, the **war c** and spears 3338+5234
Mt 26:47 a large crowd armed with swords and **c,** *3833*
26:55 that you have come out with swords and **c** *3833*
Mk 14:43 a crowd armed with swords and **c,** *3833*
14:48 "that you have come out with swords and **c** *3833*
Lk 22:52 that you have come with swords and **c?** *3833*

CLUNG (3) [CLING]

Ru 1:14 but Ruth **c** to her. 1815
2Ki 3:3 *he* **c** to the sins of Jeroboam son of Nebat, 1815
La 1:9 Her filthiness **c to** her skirts; 928

CLUSTER (5) [CLUSTERS]

Nu 13:23 they cut off a branch bearing a single **c** 864
13:24 the **c of grapes** the Israelites cut off there. 864
SS 1:14 a **c** *of* henna blossoms from the vineyards 864
Isa 65:8 when juice is still found in a **c of grapes** 864
Mic 7:1 there is no **c of grapes** to eat, 864

CLUSTERS (5) [CLUSTER]

Ge 40:10 it blossomed, and its **c** ripened into grapes. 864
Dt 32:32 and their **c** *with* bitterness. 864
SS 7:7 and your breasts like **c of fruit.** 864
7:8 May your breasts be like the **c** *of* the vine, 864
Rev 14:18 the **c of grapes** from the earth's vine, *1084*

CLUTCHES (5)

Job 5:15 he saves them from the **c** *of* the powerful. 3338
6:23 ransom me from the **c** *of* the ruthless'? 3338
16:11 over to evil men and thrown me into the **c** 3338
Hab 2:9 to escape the **c** *of* ruin! 4090
Ac 12:11 from Herod's **c** and from everything *5931*

CNIDUS (1)

Ac 27:7 and had difficulty arriving off **C.** *3118*

CO-HEIRS (1) [INHERIT]

Ro 8:17 heirs of God and **c with** Christ, *5169*

COAL (2) [COALS]

2Sa 14:7 the only **burning c** I have left, 1625
Isa 6:6 of the seraphs flew to me with a **live c** 8365

COALS (21) [COAL]

Lev 16:12 He is to take a censer full of burning **c** from 1624
Nu 16:37 and scatter the **c** some distance away, for 836
2Sa 22:9 **burning c** blazed out of it. 1624
1Ki 19:6 a cake of bread **baked over hot c,** 8363
Job 41:21 His breath sets **c** ablaze, 1624
Ps 11:6 On the wicked he will rain fiery **c** 7073
18:8 **burning c** blazed out of it. 1624
120:4 with **burning c** *of* the broom tree. 1624
140:10 Let **burning c** fall upon them; 1624
Pr 6:28 on **hot c** without his feet being scorched? 1624
25:22 you will heap **burning c** on his head, 1624
Isa 30:14 a fragment will be found for taking **c** from 836
44:12 a tool and works with it in the **c;** 7073
44:19 I even baked bread over its **c,** 1624
47:14 Here are no **c** to warm anyone; 1625
54:16 the blacksmith who fans the **c** into flame 7073
Eze 1:13 of the living creatures was like burning **c** 1624
10:2 Fill your hands with burning **c** from among 1624
24:11 the empty pot on the **c** till it becomes hot 1624
Jn 21:9 they saw a **fire of burning c** there with fish *471*
Ro 12:20 you will heap burning **c** on his head." *472*

COARSE (1)

Eph 5:4 foolish talk or **c joking,** *2365*

COAST (15) [COASTLANDS, COASTLINE, COASTS]

Nu 34:6 " 'Your western boundary will be the **c** of 1473
Dt 1:7 in the Negev and along the **c,** 2572+3542
Jos 5:1 the Canaanite kings along the **c** heard how 3542
9:1 the western foothills, and along the entire **c** 2572
Jdg 5:17 Asher remained on the **c** and stayed 2572+3542
2Ch 8:17 to Ezion Geber and Elath on the **c** 3542+8557
Isa 20:6 the people who live on this **c** will say, 362
Jer 47:7 to attack Ashkelon and the **c?"** 2572+3542
Eze 25:16 destroy those remaining along the **c.** 2572+3542
26:16 Then all the princes of the **c** will step down 3542
Lk 6:17 and from the **c** of Tyre and Sidon, *4163*
Ac 17:14 to the **c,** but Silas and Timothy stayed *2498*
27:2 to sail for ports along the **c** of the province *NIG*
27:5 across the open sea off the **c** of Cilicia *NIG*
27:8 along the **c** with difficulty and came to *NIG*

COASTLANDS (9) [COAST]

Jer 25:22 the kings of the **c** across the sea; 362
31:10 proclaim it in distant **c:** 362
Eze 26:15 not the **c** tremble at the sound of your fall, 362
26:18 Now the **c** tremble on the day of your fall; 362
27:15 and many **c** were your customers; 362
27:35 All who live in the **c** are appalled at you; 362
39:6 and on those who live in safety in the **c,** 362
Da 11:18 Then he will turn his attention to the **c** 362
11:30 Ships of the **western c** will oppose him, 4183

COASTLINE (2) [COAST]

Jos 15:12 The western boundary is the **c** of 1473
15:47 as far as the Wadi of Egypt and the **c** of 1473

COASTS (5) [COAST]
Jer 2:10 Cross over to the c *of* Kittim and look, 362
47: 4 the remnant from the c *of* Caphtor. 362
Eze 27: 3 merchant of peoples on many c, 362
27: 6 from the c *of* Cyprus they made your deck, 362
27: 7 of blue and purple from the c *of* Elishah. 362

COAT (6) [COATED, COATING, COATS]
Ge 6:14 make rooms in it and c it with pitch inside 4106
Dt 27: 2 set up some large stones and c them 8486
27: 4 and c them with plaster. 8486
1Sa 17: 5 his head and wore a **c of scale armor** 7989+9234
17:38 a **c of armor** on him and a bronze helmet 9234
Job 41:13 Who can strip off his outer c? 4230

COAT OF MANY COLOURS (KJV) See RICHLY ORNAMENTED ROBE

COATED (1) [COAT]
Ex 2: 3 a papyrus basket for him and c it with tar 2814

COATING (1) [COAT]
Pr 26:23 Like a c *of* glaze 7596

COATS (1) [COAT]
2Ch 26:14 spears, helmets, **c of armor,** 9234

COAX (1)
Jdg 14:15 "C your husband *into* explaining 7331

COBRA (3) [COBRAS]
Ps 58: 4 like that of a c that has stopped its ears, 7352
91:13 You will tread upon the lion and the c; 7352
Isa 11: 8 The infant will play near the hole of the c, 7352

COBRAS (1) [COBRA]
Dt 32:33 the deadly poison of c. 7352

COBWEBS (1) [WEB]
Isa 59: 6 Their c are useless for clothing; 7770

COCK (Anglicized, KJV) See ROOSTER

COCKATRICE (KJV) See VIPER

COCKCROWING (KJV) See ROOSTER, CROWING

COCKLE (KJV) See WEED

COCOON (1)
Job 27:18 The house he builds is like a **moth's c,** 6931

CODE (4)
Ro 2:27 you have the written c and circumcision, *NIG*
2:29 by the Spirit, not by the written c. *NIG*
7: 6 and not in the old way *of* the **written c.** *1207*
Col 2:14 the **written c,** with its regulations, that was *5934*

COFFER (KJV) See CHEST

COFFIN (2)
Ge 50:26 he was placed in a c in Egypt. 778
Lk 7:14 Then he went up and touched the c, *5049*

COGNITIONS (KJV) See THOUGHTS

COHORTS (1)
Job 9:13 even the c *of* Rahab cowered at his feet. 6468

COILED (2) [COILING]
2Sa 22: 6 The cords of the grave **c around** me; 6015
Ps 18: 5 The cords of the grave **c around** me; 6015

COILING (1) [COILED]
Isa 27: 1 Leviathan the c serpent; 6825

COIN (4) [COINS]
Mt 17:27 and you will find a **four-drachma c.** *5088*
22:19 Show me the c used for paying the tax." *3790*
Mk 12:16 They brought the c, and he asked them, *NIG*
Lk 15: 9 I have found my lost c.' *1534*

COINS (9) [COIN]
Mt 26:15 counted out for him thirty **silver c.** *736*
27: 3 the thirty **silver** c to the chief priests and *736*
27: 6 The chief priests picked up the c and said, *736*
27: 9 "They took the thirty **silver c,** *736*
Mk 12:42 and put in two very **small copper c,** *3321*
Lk 10:35 The next day he took out two **silver c** *1324*
15: 8 a woman has ten **silver** c and loses one. *1534*
Lk 21: 2 in two very **small copper c.** *3321*
Jn 2:15 he scattered the c of the money changers *3047*

COL-HOZEH (2)
Ne 3:15 by Shallun son of C, 3997
11: 5 the son of C, the son of Hazaiah, 3997

COLD (15)
Ge 8:22 seedtime and harvest, c and heat, 7923
31:40 in the daytime and the c at night, 7943
Job 24: 7 to cover themselves in the c. 7938
37: 9 the c from the driving winds. 7938
Pr 25:20 a garment on a c day, 7938
25:25 Like c water to a weary soul is good news 7922
Na 3:17 that settle in the walls on a c day— 7938
Zec 14: 6 no c or frost. 7938
Mt 10:42 And if anyone gives even a cup *of* c water *6037*
24:12 the love of most *will* **grow c,** *6038*
Jn 18:18 It was c, and the servants *6036*
Ac 28: 2 because it was raining and c. *6036*
2Co 11:27 I have been c and naked. *6036*
Rev 3:15 that you are neither c nor hot. *6037*
3:16 neither hot nor c— *6037*

COLLAPSE (5) [COLLAPSED, COLLAPSES]
Jos 6: 5 the city *will* c and the people will go up, 5877
Ps 10:10 His victims are crushed, *they* c; 8820
Eze 26:18 in the sea are terrified at your c.' 3655
Mt 15:32 or *they may* c on the way." *1725*
Mk 8: 3 *they will* c on the way, *1725*

COLLAPSED (8) [COLLAPSE]
Jos 6:20 the people gave a loud shout, the wall c; 5877
Jdg 7:13 that the tent overturned and c." 5877
1Ki 20:30 where the wall c on twenty-seven thousand 5877
Job 1:19 *It* c on them and they are dead, 5877
Hab 3: 6 and the age-old hills c. 8820
Lk 6:49 *it* c and its destruction was complete." *5229*
Rev 11:13 and a tenth of the city c. *4406*
16:19 and the cities of the nations c. *4406*

COLLAPSES (3) [COLLAPSE]
Isa 30:13 cracked and bulging, that c suddenly, 995+8691
Eze 13:12 When the wall c, will people not ask you, 5877
Na 2: 6 and the palace c. 4570

COLLAR (3)
Ex 28:32 a woven edge like a c around this 7023+9389
39:23 of the robe like the opening of a c, 9389
Ps 133: 2 down upon the c *of* his robes. 7023

COLLECT (13) [COLLECTED, COLLECTING, COLLECTION, COLLECTIONS, COLLECTOR, COLLECTOR'S, COLLECTORS, COLLECTS]
Ge 41:35 *They should* c all the food 7695
Nu 3:47 c five shekels for each one, 4374
2Ki 12: 4 "C all the money that is brought NIH
12: 8 not c any more money from the people and 4374
2Ch 20:25 that it took three days *to* c it. 1024
24: 5 of Judah and c the money due annually 7695
Ne 10:37 the Levites who c *the* **tithes** in all the towns 6923
Mt 13:30 First c the weeds and tie them in bundles to *5198*
17:25 the kings of the earth c duty and taxes— *3284*
21:34 to the tenants *to* c his fruit. *3284*
Mk 12: 2 the tenants to c from them some of the fruit *3284*
Lk 3:13 "Don't c any more than you are required *4556*
Heb 7: 5 *to* **c a tenth from** the people— *620+2400*

COLLECTED (15) [COLLECT]
Ge 41:48 Joseph c all the food produced 7695
47:14 Joseph c all the money that was to be found 4377
Nu 3:49 So Moses c the redemption money 4374
3:50 of the Israelites *he* c silver weighing 1,365 4374
16:39 the priest c the bronze censers brought 4374
2Ki 12: 4 the **money** *c in* the census, AIT
22: 4 the doorkeepers *have* c from the people. 665
2Ch 24:11 and c a great amount of money. 665
34: 9 the Levites who were the doorkeepers *had* c 665
Ecc 12:11 their **c sayings** like firmly embedded nails— 670+1251
Zec 14:14 of all the surrounding nations *will* **be c**— 665
Mt 13:48 Then *they* sat down and c the good fish *5198*
Lk 19:23 *I* could *have* c it with interest?' *4556*
Heb 7: 6 yet *he* **c a tenth** from Abraham *1282*
7: 8 the tenth is c by men who die; *3284*

COLLECTING (1) [COLLECT]
Lev 11:36 or a cistern for c water remains clean, 5224

COLLECTION (2) [COLLECT]
Isa 57:13 let your c [of idols] save you! 7689
1Co 16: 1 Now about the c for God's people: *3356*

COLLECTIONS (1) [COLLECT]
1Co 16: 2 when I come no c will have to be made. *3356*

COLLECTOR (8) [COLLECT]
Da 11:20 a **tax c** to maintain the royal splendor. 5601
Mt 10: 3 Thomas and Matthew the **tax c;** *5467*
18:17 treat him as you would a pagan or a **tax c.** *5467*
Lk 5:27 and saw a **tax c** by the name of Levi sitting *5467*
18:10 one a Pharisee and the other a **tax c.** *5467*
18:11 or even like this **tax c.** *5467*
18:13 "But the **tax c** stood at a distance. *5467*
19: 2 he was a **chief tax c** and was wealthy. *803*

COLLECTOR'S (2) [COLLECT]
Mt 9: 9 at the **tax c booth.** *5468*
Mk 2:14 of Alphaeus sitting at the **tax c booth.** *5468*

COLLECTORS (16) [COLLECT]
Mt 5:46 Are not even the **tax c** doing that? *5467*
9:10 many **tax c** and "sinners" came and ate *5467*
9:11 "Why does your teacher eat with **tax c** *5467*
11:19 a friend *of* **tax c** and "sinners." ' *5467*
17:24 **c of** the two-drachma **tax** *3284*
21:31 the **tax c** and the prostitutes are entering *5467*
21:32 but the **tax c** and the prostitutes did. *5467*
Mk 2:15 many **tax c** and "sinners" were eating *5467*
2:16 and **tax c,** they asked his disciples: *5467*
2:16 "Why does he eat with **tax c** *5467*
Lk 3:12 **Tax c** also came to be baptized. *5467*
5:29 *of* **tax c** and others were eating with them. *5467*
5:30 "Why do you eat and drink with **tax c** *5467*
7:29 (All the people, even the **tax c,** *5467*
7:34 a friend *of* **tax c** and "sinners." ' *5467*
15: 1 the **tax c** and "sinners" were all gathering *5467*

COLLECTS (1) [COLLECT]
Heb 7: 9 who c the tenth, *3284*

COLLEGE (KJV) See SECOND DISTRICT

COLONNADE (4) [COLUMN]
1Ki 7: 6 a c fifty cubits long and thirty wide. 395+6647
Jn 10:23 in the temple area walking in Solomon's C. *5119*
Ac 3:11 to them in the place called Solomon's C. *5119*
5:12 to meet together in Solomon's C. *5119*

COLONNADES (1) [COLUMN]
Jn 5: 2 and which is surrounded by five **covered c.** *5119*

COLONY (1)
Ac 16:12 a **Roman c** and the leading city of *3149*

COLORED (1) [COLORFUL, COLORS, DARK-COLORED, MULTICOLORED]
Pr 7:16 I have covered my bed with c linens 2635

COLORFUL (2) [COLORED]
Jdg 5:30 **c garments** as plunder for Sisera, 7389
5:30 **c garments** embroidered, 7389

COLORS (2) [COLORED]
1Ch 29: 2 turquoise, stones of **various c,** 8391
Eze 17: 3 and full plumage *of* **varied** c came 8391

COLOSSE (1)
Col 1: 2 and faithful brothers in Christ at C: *3145*

COLT (15)
Ge 49:11 his c to the choicest branch; 912+1201
Job 11:12 a wild donkey's c can be born a man. 6555
Zec 9: 9 gentle and riding on a donkey, on a c, 6555
Mt 21: 2 with her c by her. *4798*
21: 5 gentle and riding on a donkey, on a c, *4798*
21: 7 They brought the donkey and the c, *4798*
Mk 11: 2 you will find a c tied there, *4798*
11: 4 They went and found a c outside in *4798*
11: 5 "What are you doing, untying that c?" *4798*
11: 7 the c to Jesus and threw their cloaks *4798*
Lk 19:30 you will find a c tied there, *4798*
19:33 As they were untying the c, *4798*
19:33 "Why are you untying the c?" *4798*
19:35 threw their cloaks on the c and put Jesus *4798*
Jn 12:15 seated on a donkey's c." *4798*

COLUMN (3) [COLONNADE, COLONNADES, COLUMNS]
Jdg 20:40 the c *of* smoke began to rise from the city, 6647
SS 3: 6 up from the desert like a c *of* smoke, 9406
Isa 9:18 so that it rolls upward in a c *of* smoke. 1455

COLUMNS (5) [COLUMN]
1Ki 7: 2 of cedar c supporting trimmed cedar beams. 6647
7: 3 above the beams that rested on the c— 6647
Jer 36:23 Whenever Jehudi had read three or four c 1946
Joel 2:20 with its **front** c going into the eastern sea 7156
Zep 2:14 and the screech owl will roost on her c. 4117

COMB (2) [COMBED]
Ps 19:10 than honey from the c. 7430

Pr 24:13 **honey from the c** is sweet to your taste. 5885

COMBED (1) [COMB]

Isa 19: 9 Those who work with **c** flax will despair, 8591

COMBINE (1) [COMBINED]

Heb 4: 2 those who heard *did* not **c** it **with** faith. *5166*

COMBINED (1) [COMBINE]

1Co 12:24 But God *has* **c** the members of the body *5166*

COME (1463) [CAME, COMES, COMING]

Ge 6:20 that moves along the ground *will* **c** to you 995
8:16 **"C out** of the ark, 3655
9:12 a covenant for all generations **to c:** 6409
11: 3 They said to each other, **"C,** 2035
11: 4 **"C,** let us build ourselves a city, 2035
11: 7 **C,** let us go down 2035
15:14 and afterward *they will* **c out** 3655
15:16 fourth generation your descendants *will* **c back** here, 8740
16: 8 servant of Sarai, where *have you* **c** from, 995
17: 6 and kings *will* **c** from you. 3655
17: 7 after you for the **generations to c,** 1887
17: 9 after you for the **generations to c.** 1887
17:12 For the **generations to c** every male 1887
17:16 kings of peoples *will* **c** from her." 2118
18: 5 now that *you have* **c** to your servant." 6296
19: 8 for *they have* **c** under the protection 995
22: 5 We will worship and then *we will* **c back** 8740
23:10 hearing of all the Hittites *who had* **c** *to* 995
23:18 the Hittites *who had* **c** *to* the gate of the city. 995
24: 5 "What if the woman is unwilling to **c** back 2143
24: 8 the woman is unwilling to **c** back with you, 2143
24:31 **"C,** you who are blessed by the LORD," 995
24:39 if the woman *will* not **c** back with me?' 2143
24:42 to the journey on which I *have* **c.** 2143
24:62 Now Isaac *had* **c** from Beer Lahai Roi, 995
25:25 The first *to* **c out** was red, 3655
26:26 Abimelech *had* **c** to him from Gerar, 2143
26:27 Isaac asked them, "Why *have you* **c** to me, 995
27:21 **"C near** so I can touch you, my son, 5602
27:26 Then his father Isaac said to him, **"C here,** 5602
27:45 I'll send word for you *to* **c back** from there. 4374
31: 4 to **c** out to the fields where his flocks were. NIH
31:44 **C** now, let's make a covenant, you and I, 2143
32:11 for I am afraid he *will* **c** and attack me, 995
33:14 until *I* **c** to my lord in Seir." 995
34: 7 Now Jacob's sons *had* **c in** from the fields 995
35: 3 Then **c,** let us go up to Bethel, 7756
35:11 a community of nations *will* **c** from you, 2118
35:11 and kings *will* **c** from your body. 3655
37:10 and your brothers **actually c** and bow 995+995
37:13 **C,** I am going to send you to them." 2143
37:20 **"C** now, let's kill him and throw him 2143
37:27 **C,** let's sell him to the Ishmaelites and 2143
38:16 **"C** now, let me sleep with you." 2035
39: 7 **"C to bed with** me!" 6640+8886
39:12 **"C to bed with** me!" 6640+8886
41:36 the seven years of famine that *will* **c** 2118
42: 4 he was afraid that harm *might* **c** to him. 7925
42: 7 "Where *do you* **c** from?" 995
42: 9 *You have* **c** to see 995
42:10 "Your servants *have* **c** to buy food. 995
42:12 *"You have* **c** to see 995
42:21 that's why this distress *has* **c** upon us." 995
43:14 and Benjamin **c back** with you. 8938
44:34 not let me see the misery that *would* **c upon** 5162
45: 4 **"C close** to me." 5602
45: 9 **C down** to me; don't delay. 3718
45:11 five years of famine are **still** *to c.* AIT
45:16 that Joseph's brothers *had* **c,** 995
45:19 and get your father and **c.** 995
46:31 *have* **c** to me. 995
47: 1 *have* **c** from the land of Canaan and are 995
47: 4 *"We have* **c** to live here awhile, 995
47: 5 "Your father and your brothers *have* **c** 995
48: 2 "Your son Joseph *has* **c** to you," 995
49: 1 to you in days **to c.** 344
50:24 **surely c to your aid** 7212+7212
50:25 **surely c to your aid,** 7212+7212
Ex 1:10 **C,** we must deal shrewdly with them 2035
3: 5 *"Do* not **c** *any* **closer,"** God said. 7928
3: 8 So *I have* **c down** to rescue them from 3718
8: 3 *They will* **c** up into your palace 995
8: 5 and **make** frogs **c up** on the land of Egypt.' 6590
8: 7 also **made** frogs **c up** on the land of Egypt. 6590
11: 8 All these officials of yours *will* **c** to me, 3718
12:14 the **generations to c** you shall celebrate it 1887
12:17 for the **generations to c.** 1887
12:42 the LORD for the **generations to c.** 1887
13:14 *"In* **days to c,** when your son asks you, 4737
13:19 **surely c to your aid,** 7212+7212
14:25 **made** the wheels of their chariots **c off** 6073
16: 1 of the second month after they *had* **c out** 3655
16: 9 **'C** before the LORD, 7928
16:32 and keep it for the **generations to c,** 1887
16:33 to be kept for the **generations to c."** 1887
17: 6 and water *will* **c out** of it for the people 3655
18:15 the people **c** to me to seek God's will. 995
18:18 You and these people who **c** NIH
19: 9 "I *am going to* **c** to you in a dense cloud, 995
19:11 the LORD *will* **c down** on Mount Sinai in 3718
19:23 "The people cannot **c up** Mount Sinai, 6590
Ex 19:24 not force their way through to **c up** to 6590
20:20 God *has* **c** to test you, 995
20:24 *I will* **c** to you and bless you. 995
23: 4 "If *you* **c across** your enemy's ox 7003
24: 1 he said to Moses, **"C up** to the LORD, 6590
24: 2 the others *must* not **c near.** 5602
24: 2 And the people *may* not **c up** with him." 6590
24:12 **"C up** to me on the mountain and stay here, 6590
24:14 "Wait here for us until *we* **c back** to you. 8740
27:21 the Israelites for the **generations to c.** 1887
29:42 the **generations to c** this burnt offering is 1887
30: 8 before the LORD for the **generations to c.** 1887
30:10 for the **generations to c.** 1887
30:12 Then no plague *will* **c** on them 2118
30:21 for the **generations to c."** 1887
30:31 for the **generations to c.** 1887
31:13 and you for the **generations to c,** 1887
31:16 the **generations to c** as a lasting covenant. 1887
32: 1 they gathered around Aaron and said, **"C,** 7756
32:26 "Whoever is for the LORD, **c** to me." NIH
33: 9 the pillar of cloud *would* **c down** and stay at 3718
34: 2 and then **c up** on Mount Sinai. 6590
34: 3 *to* **c** with you or be seen anywhere on 6590
34:30 and they were afraid *to* **c near** him. 5602
35:10 among you *are to* **c** and make everything 995
36: 2 and who was willing to **c** and do the work. 7928
40:15 that will continue for all **generations to c."** 1887
Lev 3:17 the **generations to c,** wherever you live: 1887
6:18 the LORD by fire for the **generations to c.** 1887
7:36 for the **generations to c.** 1887
9: 7 **"C** to the altar and sacrifice 7928
10: 4 and said to them, **"C here;** 7928
10: 9 for the **generations to c.** 1887
14: 8 After this *he may* **c** into the camp, 995
15:14 and **c** before the LORD to the entrance to 995
16: 2 not *to* **c** whenever he chooses into 995
16:18 "Then *he shall* **c out** to the altar that is 3655
16:24 Then *he shall* **c out** and sacrifice 3655
16:26 afterward *he may* **c** into the camp. 995
16:28 afterward *he may* **c** into the camp. 995
17: 7 for them and for the **generations to c.'** 1887
21:17 'For the **generations to c** none 1887
21:17 a defect *may* **c near** to offer the food 7928
21:18 No man who has any defect *may* **c near:** 7928
21:21 the priest who has any defect *is to* **c near** 5602
21:21 not **c near** to offer the food of his God. 5602
22: 3 "Say to them: 'For the **generations to c,** 1887
23:14 for the **generations to c,** 1887
23:21 for the **generations to c,** 1887
23:31 for the **generations to c,** 1887
23:41 for the **generations to c;** 1887
24: 3 for the **generations to c.** 1887
25:25 his nearest relative *is to* **c** 995
25:44 and female slaves *are to* **c** from the nations 2118
Nu 4: 3 of age *who* **c** to serve in the work in the Tent 995
4:15 the Kohathites *are to* **c** to do the carrying. 995
4:19 when they **c near** the most holy things, 5602
4:23 from thirty to fifty years of age who **c** 995
4:30 from thirty to fifty years of age who **c** 995
5:14 if feelings of jealousy **c** over her husband 6296
5:30 or when feelings of jealousy **c** over a man 6296
8:15 they *are to* **c** to do their work at the Tent 995
8:24 Men twenty-five years old or more *shall* **c** 995
10: 8 for you and the **generations to c.** 1887
10:29 **C** with us and we will treat you well, 2143
10:32 If *you* **c** with us, 2143
11:16 **Have** them **c** to the Tent of Meeting, 4374
11:17 *I will* **c down** and speak with you there, 3718
11:23 or not what I say *will* **c true** *for* you." 7936
12: 4 **"C out** to the Tent of Meeting, 3655
13:33 (the descendants of Anak **c** from NIH
15:14 For the **generations to c,** 1887
15:15 for the **generations to c.** 1887
15:21 Throughout the **generations to c** you are 1887
15:23 through the **generations to c—** 1887
15:38 'Throughout the **generations to c** you are 1887
16: 5 **have** that person **c near** 7928
16: 5 The man he chooses *he will* **cause to c near** 7928
16:12 But they said, *"We will* not **c!** 6590
16:14 No, *we will* not **c!"** 6590
16:27 and Abiram *had* **c out** and were standing 3655
16:40 of Aaron *should* **c** to burn incense before 7928
16:46 Wrath *has* **c out** from the LORD; 3655
18: 4 and no *one* else *may* **c near** where you are. 7928
18:23 for the **generations to c.** 1887
19: 7 *He may* then **c** into the camp, 995
20:14 about all the hardships that *have* **c upon** us. 5162
21:27 **"C** *to* Heshbon and let it be rebuilt; 995
22: 5 Balak said: "A people *has* **c out** of Egypt; 3655
22: 6 Now **c** and put a curse on these people, 2143
22:11 that *has* **c out** of Egypt covers the face of 3655
22:11 Now **c** and put a curse on them for me. 2143
22:14 "Balaam refused *to* **c** with us." 2143
22:17 **C** and put a curse on these people for me." 2143
22:20 "Since these men *have* **c** to summon you, 995
22:32 I *have* **c** here to oppose you 3655
22:37 Why didn't *you* **c** to me? 2143
22:38 "Well, *I have* **c** to you now," 995
23: 3 the LORD *will* **c** to meet with me. 7936
23: 7 **'C,'** he said, 'curse Jacob for me; 2143
23: 7 'Come,' he said, 'curse Jacob for me; **c,** 2143
23:13 **"C** with me to another place 2143
23:27 Then Balak said to Balaam, **"C,** 2143
24:14 Now I am going back to my people, but **c,** 2143
24:14 to your people in days **to c."** 344
24:17 A star *will* **c** out of Jacob; 2005
24:19 A ruler will **c** out of Jacob and destroy NIH
Nu 24:20 but he will **c to** ruin at last." 6330
24:24 Ships will **c** from the shores of Kittim; NIH
24:24 but they too will **c to** ruin." 6330
27:17 to go out and **c in** before them, 995
27:21 and at his command *they will* **c in."** 995
31:24 Then *you may* **c** into the camp." 995
32:19 because our inheritance *has* **c** to us on 995
35:29 for you throughout the **generations to c,** 1887
Dt 1:22 to take and the towns *we will* **c** to." 995
2:19 When *you* **c** to the Ammonites, 7928
10: 1 like the first ones and **c up** to me on 6590
11:10 from which *you have* **c,** 3655
14:29 the widows who live in your towns *may* **c** 995
17: 8 If cases **c** before your courts NIH
18:22 the LORD does not take place or **c true,** 995
20: 2 the priest *shall* **c forward** and address 5602
22: 6 you **c across** a bird's nest beside the road, 4200+7156+7925
23: 4 For *they did* not **c** to **meet** you with bread 7709
26: 3 that *I have* **c** to the land the LORD swore 995
28: 2 All these blessings *will* **c** upon you 995
28: 6 be blessed when you **c in** and blessed 995
28: 7 *They will* **c** at you from one direction 3655
28:15 all these curses *will* **c** upon you 995
28:19 when you **c in** and cursed when you go out. 995
28:20 and **c** to sudden **ruin** because of 6
28:24 *it will* **c down** from the skies 3718
28:25 *You will* **c** at them from one direction 3655
28:45 All these curses *will* **c** upon you. 995
29:22 in later generations and foreigners who **c** 995
30: 1 before you **c** upon you and you take them 995
31:17 and difficulties *will* **c upon** them, 5162
31:17 *'Have* not these disasters **c upon** us 5162
31:21 and difficulties **c upon** them, 5162
31:29 In days **to c,** disaster will fall upon you 344
Jos 2: 2 the Israelites *have* **c** here tonight to spy out 995
2: 3 *they have* **c** to spy out the whole land." 995
2: 4 but I did not know where they had **c** from. NIH
3: 9 **"C** here and listen to the words of 5602
4:16 the Testimony *to* **c up** out of the Jordan." 6590
4:17 **"C up** out of the Jordan." 6590
5:14 of the army of the LORD I *have* now **c."** 995
7:14 that the LORD takes *shall* **c forward** clan 7928
7:14 the LORD takes *shall* **c forward** family 7928
7:14 that the LORD takes *shall* **c forward** man 7928
7:16 next morning Joshua **had** Israel **c forward** 7928
7:17 **had** the clan of the Zerahites **c forward** 7928
7:18 **had** his family **c forward** 7928
8: 5 and when the men **c out** against us, 3655
9: 6 *"We have* **c** from a distant country; 995
9: 8 "Who are you and where *do you* **c** from?" 995
9: 9 "Your servants *have* **c** from 995
9:12 at home on the day we left to **c** to you. 2143
10: 4 **"C up** and help me attack Gibeon," he said, 6590
10: 6 **C up** to us quickly and save us! 6590
10:24 said to the army commanders who *had* **c** 2143
10:24 **"C here** and put your feet on the necks 7928
10:33 of Gezer *had* **c up** to help Lachish, 6590
22:19 **c over** to the LORD's land, 6296
22:20 *did* not wrath **c** upon the whole community 2118
23:15 of the LORD your God *has* **c true,** 995
Jdg 1: 3 **"C up** with us into the territory allotted 6590
1:34 not allowing them to **c down** into the plain. 3718
4:18 **"C,** my lord, come right in. 6073
4:18 "Come, my lord, **c** right in. 6073
4:22 **"C,"** she said, "I will show you 2143
5:23 because *they did* not **c** to help the LORD, 995
6:18 Please do not go away until I **c back** 995
7:24 **"C down** against the Midianites and seize 3718
8:21 Zebah and Zalmunna said, **"C,** 7756
9:10 **'C** and be our king.' 2143
9:12 trees said to the vine, **'C** and be our king.' 2143
9:14 **'C** and be our king.' 2143
9:15 **c** and take refuge in my shade; 995
9:15 if not, then *let* fire **c out** of the thornbush 3655
9:20 *let* fire **c out** from Abimelech 3655
9:20 and *let* fire **c out** from you, 3655
9:31 of Ebed and his brothers *have* **c** to Shechem 995
9:32 and your men *should* **c** and lie in wait in 7756
9:33 When Gaal and his men **c out** against you, 3655
11: 6 **"C,"** they said, "be our commander, 2143
11: 7 Why *do you* **c** to me now, 995
11: 8 **c** with us to fight the Ammonites, 2143
11:34 *who should* **c out** to meet him 3655
12: 3 why *have you* **c up** today to fight me?" 6590
13: 8 *let* the man of God you sent to us **c** again 995
15:10 "Why *have you* **c** to fight us?" 6590
15:10 *"We have* **c** to take Samson prisoner," 6590
15:12 *"We've* **c** to tie you up and hand you over to 3718
16:10 **C now,** tell me how you can be tied." 5528+6964
16:18 **"C back** once more; 6590
18: 1 **c into** an inheritance among the tribes 928+5877
18: 9 They answered, **"C on,** let's attack them! 7756
18:19 **C** with us, and be our father and priest. 2143
19:11 the servant said to his master, **"C,** 2143
19:13 **"C,** let's try to reach Gibeah or Ramah 2143
19:17 Where *did you* **c** from?" 995
20:41 they realized that disaster *had* **c** upon them. 5595
21: 8 from Jabesh Gilead *had* **c** to the camp for 995
21:21 When the girls of Shiloh **c out** to join in 3655
Ru 1: 6 the LORD *had* **c to the aid of** his people 7212
1:11 Why *would you* **c** with me? 2143
2:12 under whose wings *you have* **c** 995
2:14 At mealtime Boaz said to her, **"C** 5602
4: 1 **"C over** here, my friend, and sit down." 6073
4: 3 "Naomi, who *has* **c back** from Moab, 8740
1Sa 2:13 the servant of the priest *would* **c** with 995

1Sa 2:15 the servant of the priest *would* **c** and say to 995
2:36 in your family line *will* **c** and bow down 995
4: 6 the ark of the LORD *had* **c** into the camp, 995
4: 7 "A god *has* **c** into the camp," they said. 995
4:16 "I *have just* **c** from the battle line; 995
6:21 **C down** and take it up to your place." 3718
9: 5 to the servant who was with him, **"C,** 2143
9: 9 he would say, **"C,** let us go to the seer," 2143
9:10 **"C,** let's go." 2143
9:12 Hurry now; *he has* just **c** to our town today, 995
10: 6 **c** upon you **in power,** 7502
10: 8 I *will* surely **c down** to you 3718
10: 8 until I **c** to you and tell you what you are 995
10:22 *"Has* the man **c** here yet?" 995
11: 9 They told the messengers who *had* **c,** 995
11:14 Then Samuel said to the people, **"C,** 2143
13: 8 but Samuel *did* not **c** *to* Gilgal, 995
13:11 and that you *did* not **c** at the set time, 995
13:12 the Philistines *will* **c down** against me 3718
14: 1 **"C,** let's go over to the Philistine outpost 2143
14: 6 to his young armor-bearer, **"C,** let's go 2143
14: 8 Jonathan said, **"C, then;** 2180
14: 9 'Wait there until we **c** to you,' 5595
14:10 But if they say, '**C up** to us,' 6590
14:12 **"C up** to us and we'll teach you a lesson." 6590
14:38 Saul therefore said, **"C** here, 5602
15:25 forgive my sin and **c back** with me, 8740
15:30 **c back** with me, so that I may worship 8740
16: 2 *'I have* **c** to sacrifice to the LORD.' 995
16: 4 They asked, *"Do* you **c** in peace?" 995
16: 5 *I have* **c** to sacrifice to the LORD. 995
16: 5 Consecrate yourselves and **c** to the sacrifice 995
16:23 Then **relief** *would* **c** to Saul; 8118
17: 8 "Why *do you* **c out** and line up for battle? 3655
17: 8 Choose a man and *have him* **c down** to me. 3718
17:28 "Why *have you* **c down** here? 3718
17:43 "Am I a dog, that you **c** at me with sticks?" 995
17:44 **"C** here," he said, "and I'll give your flesh 2143
17:45 "You **c** against me with sword and spear 995
17:45 but I **c** against you in the name of 995
20:11 **"C,"** Jonathan said, "let's go out into 2143
20:21 bring them here,' then **c,** because, 995
20:27 "Why hasn't the son of Jesse **c** to the meal, 995
20:29 That is why *he has* not **c** to 995
21:15 *Must* this man **c** into my house?" 995
22: 3 *"Would you let* my father and mother **c** 3655
22: 9 "I saw the son of Jesse **c** to Ahimelech son 995
23:10 that Saul plans to **c** to Keilah and destroy 995
23:11 *Will* Saul **c down,** 3718
23:15 that Saul *had* **c out** to take his life. 3655
23:20 **c down** whenever it pleases you to do so, 3718
23:23 and **c back** to me with definite information. 8740
23:27 to Saul, saying, **"C** quickly! 2143
24:13 'From evildoers **c** evil deeds,' 3655
24:14 the king of Israel **c out?** 3655
25: 8 since *we* **c** at a festive time. 995
25:34 if *you had* not **c** quickly to meet me, 995
26:10 either his time *will* **c** and he will die, 995
26:20 The king of Israel *has* **c out** to look for 3655
26:21 **C back,** David my son. 8740
26:22 of your young men **c over** and get it. 6296
29:10 with your master's servants who *have* **c** 995
30:13 and where do you **c** from?" NIH
31: 4 or these uncircumcised fellows *will* **c** 995
2Sa 1: 3 "Where *have you* **c** from?" 995
3:13 *Do* not **c into** my **presence** 906+7156+8011
3:13 of Saul when you **c** to see me." 995
3:23 that Abner son of Ner *had* **c** to the king and 995
5: 3 of Israel *had* **c** to King David at Hebron, 995
5:18 Now the Philistines *had* **c** and spread out in 995
6: 9 *can* the ark of the LORD *ever* **c** to me?" 995
7:12 who *will* **c** from your own body, 3655
10: 5 and then **c back."** 8740
10:11 then *you are to* **c** to my rescue; 2118
10:11 then *I will* **c** to rescue you. 2143
11:10 "Haven't you *just* **c** from a distance? 995
12: 4 to prepare a meal for the traveler who *had* **c** 995
12: 4 and prepared it for the one who *had* **c** 995
13: 5 *to* **c** and give me something to eat. 995
13: 6 "I would like my sister Tamar *to* **c** 995
13:11 **"C** to bed with me, my sister." 995
13:23 he invited all the king's sons to **c** there. NIH
13:24 "Your servant has had shearers **c.** 2180
13:26 please *let* my brother Amnon **c** with us." 2143
14:15 "And now *I have* **c** to say this to my lord 995
14:29 but Joab refused to **c** to him. 995
14:29 he sent a second time, but he refused to **c.** 995
14:32 '**C** here so I can send you to the king 995
14:32 "Why *have I* **c** from Geshur? 995
15: 4 or case *could* **c** to me and I would see 995
15:12 David's counselor, to **c** from Giloh, NIH
15:14 with him in Jerusalem, **"C!** 7756
15:19 "Why *should* you **c** along with us? 2143
16: 8 You have **c** to ruin because you are a man NIH
18:22 again said to Joab, **"C what may,** 2118+4537
18:23 He said, **"C what may,** I want to run." 2118+4537
19: 7 for you than all the calamities that *have* **c** 995
19:15 of Judah *had* **c** to Gilgal to go out and meet 995
19:20 but today *I have* **c** here as the first of 995
19:20 of the whole house of Joseph to **c down** 3718
20: 4 "Summon the men of Judah to **c** to me NIH
20:16 Tell Joab *to* **c** here so I can speak to him." 7928
22:45 and foreigners **c cringing** to me; 3950
22:46 *they* **c trembling** from their strongholds. 3004
24:11 of the LORD *had* **c** to Gad the prophet, 2118
24:13 *"Shall there* **c** upon you three years 995
24:21 "Why *has* my lord the king **c** 995

1Ki 1:14 I *will* **c in** and confirm what you have said 995
1:35 and he *is to* **c** and sit on my throne 995
1:42 Adonijah said, **"C in.** 995
1:47 the royal officials *have* **c** 995
2:13 *"Do* you **c** peacefully?" 995
2:15 for *it has* **c** to him from the LORD. 2118
2:30 "The king says, '**C out!'** " 3655
6: 1 after the Israelites *had* **c out** of Egypt, 3655
8:26 let your word that you promised your servant David my father **c true.** 586
8:37 whatever disaster or disease *may* **c,** 2118
8:41 not belong to your people Israel but *has* **c** 995
9:24 After Pharaoh's daughter *had* **c up** from 6590
12: 5 "Go away for three days and then **c back** 8740
12:12 **"C back** to me in three days." 8740
13: 7 **"C** home with me and have something 995
13:10 not return by the way *he had* **c** to Bethel. 995
13:15 **"C** home with me and eat." 2143
13:21 of God who *had* **c** from Judah, "This is what 995
13:32 of Samaria *will* **certainly c true."** 2118+2118
14: 6 he said, **"C in,** wife of Jeroboam. 995
17:18 *Did you* **c** to remind me of my sin 995
18:30 Elijah said to all the people, **"C here** to me." 5602
18:31 to whom the word of the LORD *had* **c,** 2118
19:20 he said, "and then *I will* **c** with you." 2143
20:18 He said, "If *they have* **c out** for peace, 3655
20:18 if *they have* **c out** for war, 3655
20:33 Ahab **had** him **c up** into his chariot. 6590
2Ki 1: 5 he asked them, "Why *have you* **c back?"** 8740
1: 9 "Man of God, the king says, '**C down!'** " 3718
1:10 *may* fire **c down** from heaven 3718
1:11 '**C down** at once!' " 3718
1:12 *"may* fire **c down** from heaven 3718
3:21 the Moabites had heard that the kings *had* **c** 6590
5: 8 *Have* the man **c** to me and he will know 995
5:11 that *he would* **surely c out** to me and 3655+3655
5:22 the company of the prophets *have* just **c** 995
6: 3 *"Won't you* please **c** with your servants?" 2143
7:12 thinking, *'They will* surely **c out,** 3655
8: 7 "The man of God *has* **c** all the way 995
9:11 Why *did* this madman **c** to you?" 995
9:17 'Do you **c in peace?'** " 8934
9:18 'Do you **c in peace?'** " 8934
9:19 'Do you **c in peace?'** " 8934
9:22 "Have you **c in peace,** Jehu?" 8934
9:31 she asked, "Have you **c in peace,** Zimri, 8934
10: 6 the heads of your master's sons and **c** to me 995
10:13 and *we have* **c down** to greet the families of 3718
10:16 **"C** with me and see my zeal for 2143
10:19 Anyone who **fails to c** will no longer live." 7212
14: 8 **"C,** meet me face to face." 2143
16: 7 **C up** and save me out of the hand of 6590
18:23 " '**C now,** make a bargain with my master, 5528+6964
18:25 *have I* **c** to attack and destroy this place 6590
18:31 Make peace with me and **c out** to me. 3655
18:32 until I **c** and take you to a land 995
19: 3 as when children **c** to the point of birth 995
19:27 where you stay and *when* you **c** and go and 995
19:31 For out of Jerusalem *will* **c** a remnant, 3655
19:32 *He will* not **c before** it with shield or build 7709
20:14 and where *did they* **c** from?" 995
20:17 surely **c** when everything in your palace, 995
23:18 of the prophet who *had* **c** from Samaria. 995
1Ch 9:25 in their villages *had* to **c** from time to time 995
10: 4 or these uncircumcised fellows *will* **c** 995
11: 3 of Israel *had* **c** to King David at Hebron, 995
12:17 "If *you have* **c** to me in peace, to help me, 995
12:17 if you have **c** to betray me to my enemies NIH
12:31 by name to **c** and make David king— 995
13: 2 *to* **c and join** us. 7695
14: 9 the Philistines *had* **c** and raided the Valley 995
16:29 Bring an offering and **c** before him; 995
19: 3 Haven't his men **c** to you to explore 995
19: 5 and then **c back."** 8740
19: 9 the kings who *had* **c** were by themselves in 995
23:25 and *has* **c to dwell** in Jerusalem forever, 8905
29:12 Wealth and honor **c** from you; NIH
2Ch 6:17 you promised your servant David **c true.** 586
6:28 whatever disaster or disease *may* **c,** 2118
6:32 not belong to your people Israel but *has* **c** 995
6:41 O LORD God, and **c** to your resting place, NIH
10: 5 **"C back** to me in three days." 8740
10:12 **"C back** to me in three days." 8740
14:11 and in your name *we have* **c** 995
15: 9 for large numbers *had* **c over** to him 5877
19:10 otherwise his wrath *will* **c** on you 2118
21:15 the disease causes your bowels *to* **c out.'** " 3655
24:11 and the officer of the chief priest *would* **c** 995
24:24 Aramean army *had* **c** with only a few men, 995
25:10 So Amaziah dismissed the troops who *had* **c** 995
25:17 **"C,** meet me face to face." 2143
28:17 The Edomites *had* again **c** 995
29:31 **C** and bring sacrifices and thank offerings 5602
30: 1 inviting them to **c** to the temple of 995
30: 5 the people to **c** to Jerusalem and celebrate 995
30: 8 **C** to the sanctuary, 995
30: 9 by their captors and *will* **c back** 8740
30:25 including the aliens who *had* **c** from Israel 995
32: 2 When Hezekiah saw that Sennacherib *had* **c** 995
32: 4 of Assyria **c** and find plenty of water?" 995
32:26 the LORD's wrath *did* not **c** upon them 995
Ezr 10:14 a foreign woman **c** at a set time, 995
Ne 2:10 that someone *had* **c** to promote the welfare 995
2:17 **C,** let us rebuild the wall of Jerusalem, 2143
4: 8 to **c** and fight against Jerusalem and stir 995

Ne 6: 2 **"C,** let us meet together in one of 2143
6: 7 so **c,** let us confer together." 2143
9:32 the hardship that *has* **c upon** us, 5162
Est 1:12 Queen Vashti refused to **c.** 995
1:17 but *she would* not **c.'** 995
4:14 that *you have* **c** to royal position for such 5595
5: 4 **c** today to a banquet I have prepared 995
5: 8 *let* the king and Haman **c** tomorrow to 995
6:13 *you will* **surely c to ruin!"** 5877+5877
9:25 the Jews *should* **c back** onto his own head, 8740
Job 1: 7 "Where *have you* **c** from?" 995
2: 2 "Where *have you* **c** from?" 995
2:11 about all the troubles that *had* **c** upon him, 995
3:21 to those who long for death that does not **c,** NIH
3:25 What I feared *has* **c** *upon* me; 910
5:26 *You will* **c** to the grave in full vigor, 995
7: 6 and *they* **c to an end** without hope. 3983
7:10 *He will* never **c** to his house again; 8740
9: 4 and **c** *out* **unscathed?** AIT
10:17 your forces **c** against me wave upon wave. NIH
10:19 If only *I had* never **c into being,** 2118+2118
13:13 then *let* **c** to me what may. 6296
13:16 no godless man *would* dare **c** before him! 995
14:14 for my renewal *to* **c.** 995
17:10 "But **c on,** all of you, try again! 995
20:22 the full force of misery *will* **c** *upon* him. 995
20:25 Terrors *will* **c** over him; 2143
21:17 How often *does* calamity **c** upon them, 995
21:21 when his allotted months **c to an end?** 2951
22:21 in this way prosperity *will* **c** *to* you. 995
23:10 *I will* **c forth** as gold. 3655
28: 6 sapphires **c** from its rocks, NIH
28:20 "Where then *does* wisdom **c** from? 995
30:14 amid the ruins *they* **c rolling in.** 1670
31:40 then *let* briers **c up** instead of wheat 3655
33: 3 My words **c** from an upright heart; NIH
34:23 they *should* **c** before him for judgment. 2143
34:28 **caused** the cry of the poor **to c** 995
38:11 'This far *you may* **c** and no farther; 995
Ps 5: 7 *will* **c into** your house; 995
14: 7 that salvation for Israel would **c** out NIH
17: 2 *May* my vindication **c** from you; 3655
18:45 *they* **c trembling** from their strongholds. 3004
22:19 O my Strength, **c quickly** to help me. 2590
24: 7 that the King of glory *may* **c in.** 995
24: 9 that the King of glory *may* **c in.** 995
31: 2 **c** quickly **to** my **rescue;** 5911
32: 9 by bit and bridle or they *will* not **c** to you. 7928
34:11 **C,** my children, listen to me; 2143
35: 2 **arise and c** to my aid. 7756
35:11 Ruthless witnesses **c forward;** 7756
36:11 *May* the foot of the proud not **c** *against* me, 995
38: 2 and your hand *has* **c down** upon me. 5737
38:22 **C quickly** to help me, O Lord my Savior. 2590
40: 7 Then I said, "Here I am, *I have* **c**— 995
40:13 O LORD, **c quickly** to help me. 2590
45:12 The Daughter of Tyre will **c** with a gift, NIH
46: 8 **C** and see the works of the LORD, 2143
49: 5 Why should I fear when evil days **c,** NIH
53: 6 salvation for Israel would **c** out of Zion! NIH
65: 2 to you all men *will* **c.** 995
66: 5 **C** and see what God has done, 2143
66: 6 *c, let us* **rejoice** in him. AIT
66:13 *I will* **c** *to* your temple 995
66:16 **C** and listen, all you who fear God; 2143
68:17 Lord [has **c**] from Sinai into his sanctuary. NIH
68:24 Your procession *has* **c into view,** O God, 8011
68:31 Envoys *will* **c** from Egypt; 910
69: 1 for the waters *have* **c** up to my neck. 995
69: 2 *I have* **c** into the deep waters; 995
69:18 **C near** and rescue me; 7928
70: 1 O LORD, **c quickly** to help me. 2590
70: 5 **c quickly** to me, O God. 2590
71:12 **c quickly,** O my God, to help me. 2590
71:16 *I will* **c** and proclaim your mighty acts, 995
71:18 your might to all *who are to* **c.** 995
78:28 *He* **made** them **c down** inside their camp, 5877
79: 8 *may* your mercy **c** quickly **to meet** us, 7709
79:11 the groans of the prisoners **c** before you; 995
80: 2 Awaken your might; **c** and save us. 2143
83: 4 **"C,"** they say, "let us destroy them as 2143
86: 9 All the nations you have made *will* **c** 995
88: 2 *May* my prayer **c** before you; 995
91: 7 but *it will* not **c near** you. 5602
91:10 no disaster *will* **c near** your tent. 7928
95: 1 **C,** let us sing for joy to the LORD; 2143
95: 2 *Let us* **c** before him with thanksgiving 7709
95: 6 **C,** let us bow down in worship, 995
96: 8 bring an offering and **c** into his courts. 995
100: 2 **c** before him with joyful songs. 995
101: 2 when *will you* **c** to me? 995
102: 1 *let* my cry for help **c** to you. 995
102:13 the appointed time *has* **c.** 995
106: 4 **c** to my **aid** when you save them, 7212
106:31 for endless **generations to c.** 1887+1887+2256
109:17 *may it* **c** *on* him; 995
112: 5 Good will **c** to him who is generous NIH
112:10 longings of the wicked *will* **c to nothing.** 6
119:13 With my lips I recount all the **laws** *that c* AIT
119:41 *May* your unfailing love **c** *to* me, 995
119:77 *Let* your compassion **c** *to* me 995
119:143 Trouble and distress *have* **c upon** me, 5162
119:169 *May* my cry **c** before you, O LORD; 7928
119:170 *May* my supplication **c** before you; 995
121: 1 where *does* my help **c** from? 995
132: 8 O LORD, and **c** to your resting place, NIH
141: 1 O LORD, I call to you; **c quickly** to me. 2590

Ps 143: 1 and righteousness **c to** my **relief.** 6699
144: 5 Part your heavens, O LORD, and **c down;** 3718
146: 4 on that very day their plans **c to nothing.** 6
Pr 1:11 If they say, "**C** along with us; 2143
2: 6 and from his mouth **c** knowledge NIH
3:28 Do not say to your neighbor, "**C** back later; 2143
5:14 *I have* **c** to the brink of utter ruin in 2118
6:11 and poverty *will* **c** *on* you like a bandit 995
7:18 **C,** let's drink deep of love till morning; 2143
9: 4 *"Let all* who are simple **c in** here!" 6073
9: 5 "**C,** eat my food and drink 2143
9:16 *"Let all* who are simple **c in** here!" 6073
10:28 but the hopes of the wicked **c to nothing.** 6
13: 3 but he who speaks rashly will **c** to ruin. NIH
18:24 A man of many companions *may* **c to ruin,** 8318
22:16 both **c** to poverty. NIH
24:25 and rich blessing *will* **c** upon them. 995
24:31 thorns *had* **c up** everywhere, 6590
24:34 and poverty *will* **c** *on* you like a bandit 995
25: 7 "**C up** here," than for him to humiliate you 6590
26: 2 an undeserved curse *does* not **c to rest.** 995
30: 4 Who has gone up to heaven and **c down?** 3718
31:25 she can laugh at the days **to c.** 340
Ecc 1: 4 Generations **c** and generations go, 2143
1: 7 To the place the streams **c** from, 2143
1:11 and even those who are **yet to c** will not 340
2: 1 I thought in my heart, "**C** now, 2143
2:16 in days *to* **c** both will be forgotten. 995
3:20 all **c** from dust, and to dust all return. 2118
4:14 The youth *may have* **c** from prison to 3655
8: 5 Whoever obeys his command *will* **c to** 3359
8: 7 who can tell him what *is to* **c?** 2118
8:10 *those who used to* **c** and go from 995
9:11 or the battle to the strong, nor does food **c** NIH
9:12 no man knows when his hour will **c:** NIH
11: 2 for you do not know what disaster *may* **c** 2118
11: 8 Everything *to* **c** is meaningless. 995
12: 1 of trouble **c** and the years approach 995
SS 2:10 my beautiful one, and **c** with me. 2143
2:12 the season of singing *has* **c,** 5595
2:13 Arise, **c,** my darling; 2143
2:13 my beautiful one, **c** with me." 2143
3:11 **C out,** you daughters of Zion, 3655
4: 8 **C** with me from Lebanon, my bride, NIH
4: 8 my bride, **c** with me from Lebanon. 995
4:16 Awake, north wind, and **c,** south wind! 995
4:16 *Let* my lover **c** into his garden 995
5: 1 *I have* **c** into my garden, my sister, 995
6:13 **C back,** come back, O Shulammite; 8740
6:13 Come back, **c back,** O Shulammite; 8740
6:13 **c back,** come back, that we may gaze 8740
6:13 **c back,** that we may gaze on you! 8740
7:11 **C,** my lover, let us go to the countryside, 2143
8:14 **C away,** my lover, and be like a gazelle or 1368
Isa 1:12 When *you* **c** to appear before me, 995
1:18 "**C** now, let us reason together," 2143
1:23 the widow's case *does* not **c** before them. 995
2: 3 Many peoples *will* **c** and say, "Come, 2143
2: 3 Many peoples will come and say, "**C,** 2143
2: 5 **C,** O house of Jacob, 2143
5:19 *let* the plan of the Holy One of Israel **c,** 995
5:26 Here *they* **c,** swiftly and speedily! 995
7:19 They *will* all **c** and settle in 995
11: 1 A shoot *will* **c up** from the stump of Jesse; 3655
13: 5 *They* **c** from faraway lands, 995
13: 6 *it will* **c** like destruction from 995
14: 4 How the oppressor *has* **c to an end!** 8697
16: 4 The oppressor *will* **c to an end,** 699
21:12 and **c** back yet again." 910
21:16 all the pomp of Kedar *will* **c to an end.** 3983
23: 1 the land of Cyprus **word** *has* **c** to them.. 1655
26: 9 When your judgments **c** upon the earth, NIH
27: 5 Or else *let them* **c** *to* me for refuge; 2616
27: 6 *In days to* **c** Jacob will take root, 995
27:11 and women **c** and make fires with them. 995
27:13 and those who were exiled in Egypt *will* **c** 995
29: 4 Your voice *will* **c** ghostlike from 2118
29: 6 the LORD Almighty *will* **c** with thunder 7212
29:13 "These people **c near** to me 5602
30: 8 days **to c** it may be an everlasting witness. 340
31: 4 so the LORD Almighty *will* **c down** 3718
32:10 and the harvest of fruit *will* not **c.** 995
34: 1 **C near,** you nations, and listen; 7928
35: 4 your God will **c,** he will come NIH
35: 4 *he will* **c** *with* vengeance; 995
35: 4 with divine retribution he *will* **c** 995
36: 8 " '**C now,** make a bargain with my master, 5528+6964
36:10 *have I* **c** to attack and destroy this land 6590
36:16 Make peace with me and **c out** to me. 3655
36:17 until I **c** and take you to a land 995
37: 3 as when children **c** to the point of birth 995
37:28 "But I know where you stay and *when* you **c** 995
37:32 For out of Jerusalem *will* **c** a remnant, 3655
37:33 *He will* not **c before** it with shield or build 7709
38:14 I am troubled; O Lord, **c to** my **aid!"** 6842
39: 3 and where *did they* **c** from?" 995
39: 6 surely **c** when everything in your palace, 995
41: 1 *Let them* **c forward** and speak; 5602
41: 5 They approach and **c forward;** 910
41:22 Or declare to us the *things to* **c,** 995
42:23 to this or pay close attention in **time to c?** 294
44: 7 and *what is yet to* **c—** 910
44: 7 yes, let him foretell what *will* **c.** 995
44:11 *Let* them all **c together** 7695
45:11 Concerning **things to c,** 910
45:14 *they will* **c over** to you and will be yours; 6296
Isa 45:20 "Gather together and **c;** 995
45:24 All who have raged against him *will* **c** 995
46:10 from ancient times, what *is* **still to c.** 4202+6913
47: 9 *They will* **c** upon you in full measure, 995
47:11 Disaster *will* **c** upon you, 995
47:11 a catastrophe you cannot foresee *will* suddenly **c** upon you. 995
47:13 *Let* your astrologers **c forward,** 6641
48: 1 by the name of Israel and **c** from the line 3655
48:14 "**C together,** all of you, and listen: 7695
48:16 "**C near** me and listen to this: 7928
49: 9 '**C out,**' and to those in darkness, 3655
49:12 See, they *will* **c** from afar— 995
49:18 all your sons gather and **c** to you. 995
49:21 where have they **c** from?' " NIH
51:19 These double calamities *have* **c upon** you— 7925
52:11 **C out** from it and be pure, 3655
54:14 *it will* not **c near** you. 7928
55: 1 "**C,** all you who are thirsty, 2098
55: 1 all you who are thirsty, **c** to the waters; 2143
55: 1 you who have no money, **c,** buy and eat! 2143
55: 1 **C,** buy wine and milk without money and 2143
55: 3 Give ear and **c** to me; 2143
55:10 the rain and the snow **c down** from heaven, 3718
56: 9 **C,** all *you* beasts of the field, 910
56: 9 **c** and devour, all you beasts of the forest! NIH
56:12 "**C,**" each one cries, "let me get wine! 910
57: 3 "But you—**c** here, *you* sons of a sorceress, 7928
58: 2 and seem eager for God to **c near** them. 7932
59:19 For *he will* **c** like a pent-up flood that 995
59:20 "The Redeemer *will* **c** to Zion, 995
60: 1 "Arise, shine, for your light *has* **c,** 995
60: 3 Nations *will* **c** to your light, 2143
60: 4 All assemble and **c** to you; 995
60: 4 your sons **c** from afar, 995
60: 5 to you the riches of the nations *will* **c.** 995
60: 6 And all from Sheba *will* **c,** 995
60:13 "The glory of Lebanon *will* **c** to you, 995
60:14 The sons of your oppressors *will* **c** bowing 2143
61:11 **makes** the sprout **c up** 3655
63: 4 and the year of my redemption *has* **c.** 995
64: 1 you would rend the heavens and **c down,** 3718
64: 2 **c** down to make your name known NIH
64: 5 You **c to the help of** 7003
65: 5 don't **c near** me, 5602
65:17 nor *will they* **c** to mind. 6590
66: 7 before the pains **c** upon her, 995
66:18 *to* **c** and gather all nations and tongues, 995
66:18 and *they will* **c** and see my glory. 995
66:23 all mankind *will* **c** and bow down 995
Jer 1:15 "Their kings *will* **c** and set 995
1:15 they will **c** against all her surrounding walls NIH
2:27 they say, '**C** and save us!' 7756
2:28 *Let them* **c** if they can save you 7756
2:31 *we will* **c** to you no more'? 995
3:18 and together *they will* **c** from 995
3:22 "Yes, we *will* **c** *to* you, 910
4: 7 A lion *has* **c** out of his lair; 6590
4:13 his chariots **c** like a whirlwind, NIH
5:12 No harm *will* **c** to us; 995
6: 3 with their flocks *will* **c** against her; 995
6:23 they **c** like men in battle formation NIH
6:26 for suddenly the destroyer *will* **c** upon us. 995
7: 2 the LORD, all you people of Judah who **c** 995
7:10 then **c** and stand before me in this house, 995
8:15 We hoped for peace but no good has **c,** NIH
8:16 *They have* **c** to devour the land 995
9:17 Call for the wailing women *to* **c;** 995
9:18 *Let them* **c quickly** and wail over us 4554
13:18 "**C down** from your thrones, 9164
14:19 We hoped for peace but no good has **c,** NIH
16:19 to you the nations *will* **c** from the ends of 995
17:20 in Jerusalem who **c** through these gates. 995
17:25 on David's throne *will* **c** through the gates 995
17:25 and their officials will **c** riding in chariots NIH
17:26 *People will* **c** from the towns of Judah 995
17:27 as you **c** through the gates of Jerusalem on 995
18:18 "**C,** let's make plans against Jeremiah; 2143
18:18 So **c,** let's attack him with our tongues 2143
20:18 Why *did I ever* **c out** of the womb 3655
21:13 you who say, "Who *can* **c** against us? 5737
22: 2 and your people who **c** through these gates. 995
22: 4 on David's throne *will* **c** through the gates 995
22:23 you will groan when pangs **c** upon you, 995
22:27 *You will* never **c back** to the land you long 8740
23:17 'No harm *will* **c** to you.' 995
23:20 In days **to c** you will understand it clearly. 344
25: 3 the LORD *has* **c** to me and I have spoken 2118
25:34 For your time to be slaughtered *has* **c;** 4848
26: 2 of the towns of Judah who **c** to worship in 995
27: 3 and Sidon through the envoys who *have* **c** 995
27:22 and there they will remain until the day I **c** 7212
29:10 for Babylon, *I will* **c** *to* you 7212
29:12 Then you will call upon me and **c** and pray 2143
30:19 From them *will* **c** songs of thanksgiving 3655
30:21 I will bring him near and *he will* **c close** 5602
30:24 In days **to c** you will understand this. 344
31: 2 I *will* **c** to give rest to Israel." 2143
31: 6 '**C,** let us go up to Zion, 7756
31: 9 *They will* **c** with weeping; 995
31:12 *They will* **c** and shout for joy on 995
32: 7 of Shallum your uncle *is going to* **c** to you 995
32:29 The Babylonians who are attacking this city *will* **c in** 995
33:20 the night, so that day and night no *longer* **c** 2118
35: 2 to the Recabite family and invite them *to* **c** 995
35:11 of Babylon invaded this land, we said, '**C,** 995
Jer 36: 6 of Judah who **c in** from their towns. 995
36: 9 the people in Jerusalem and those *who had* **c** 995
36:14 to the people and **c.**" 2143
36:17 "Tell us, how *did you* **c** *to* **write** all this? AIT
36:29 the king of Babylon *would* **certainly c** 995+995
37: 4 Now Jeremiah *was free to* **c** and go among 995
37:10 *they would* **c out** and burn this city down." 7756
38:25 and *they* "**c** to you and say, 995
38:27 All the officials *did* **c** to Jeremiah 995
40: 4 **C** with me to Babylon, if you like, 995
40: 4 but if you do not want to, then don't **c.** 995
40:10 before the Babylonians who **c** to us, 995
41: 6 he said, "**C** to Gedaliah son of Ahikam." 995
43: 5 remnant of Judah who *had* **c back** to live 8740
43:11 *He will* **c** and attack Egypt, 995
44: 8 where you *have* **c** to live? 995
44:23 this disaster *has* **c upon** you, 7925
46:18 *"one will* **c** who is like Tabor among 995
46:22 *they will* **c** against her with axes, 995
47: 4 the day *has* **c** to destroy all the Philistines 995
48: 2 '**C,** let us put an end to that nation.' 2143
48: 8 The destroyer *will* **c** against every town, 995
48:16 her calamity *will* **c quickly.** 4394+4554
48:18 "**C down** from your glory and sit on 3718
48:18 for he who destroys Moab *will* **c up** 6590
48:21 Judgment *has* **c** to the plateau— 995
48:47 the fortunes of Moab in days **to c,"** 344
49:39 the fortunes of Elam in days **to c,"** 344
50: 5 *They will* **c** and bind themselves to 995
50:26 **C** against her from afar. 995
50:27 For their day *has* **c,** 995
50:31 the LORD Almighty, "for your day *has* **c,** 995
50:42 they **c** like men in battle formation NIH
51:10 " 'The LORD has vindicated us; **c,** 995
51:13 your end *has* **c,** 995
51:33 the time to harvest her *will* soon **c."** 995
51:45 "**C out** of her, my people! 3655
51:47 the time *will* surely **c** when I will punish 995
51:56 A destroyer *will* **c** against Babylon; 995
51:60 the disasters that *would* **c** upon Babylon— 995
La 1:14 *They have* **c** upon my neck and 6590
1:22 *"Let* all their wickedness **c** before you; 995
3:38 that both calamities and good things **c?** 3655
4:18 our days were numbered, for our end *had* **c.** 995
Eze 5: 2 When the days of your siege **c to an end,** 4848
7: 2 end *has* **c** upon the four corners of the land. 995
7: 6 The end *has* **c!** 995
7: 6 The end *has* **c!** 995
7: 6 It has roused itself against you. *It has* **c!** 995
7: 7 Doom *has* **c** upon you— 995
7: 7 The time *has* **c,** the day is near; 995
7:10 "The day is here! *It has* **c!** 995
7:12 The time *has* **c,** the day has arrived 995
7:26 Calamity upon calamity *will* **c,** 995
13:11 Rain *will* **c** in torrents, 2118
14:22 They *will* **c** to you, 3655
15: 7 Although *they have* **c out** of the fire, 3655
16:33 bribing them to **c** to you from everywhere 995
20: 3 *Have* you **c** to inquire of me? 995
21:13 " '**Testing** *will* surely *c.* AIT
21:20 to **c** against Rabbah of the Ammonites 995
21:22 Into his right hand *will* **c** the lot 2118
21:25 wicked prince of Israel, whose day *has* **c,** 995
21:29 are to be slain, whose day *has* **c,** 995
22: 4 and the end of your years *has* **c.** 995
23:24 *They will* **c** against you with weapons, 995
24:14 The time *has* **c** for me to act. 995
24:26 on that day a fugitive *will* **c** to tell you 995
27:36 *you have* **c** *to* a horrible end and will 2118
28:18 **made** a fire **c out,** and it consumed you, 3655
28:19 *you have* **c** *to* a horrible end and will 2118
30: 4 A sword *will* **c** against Egypt, 995
30: 4 and anguish *will* **c** upon Cush. 2118
30: 9 for it is sure **to c.** 995
30:18 there her proud strength *will* **c to an end.** 8697
32:11 of the king of Babylon *will* **c** *against* you. 995
32:21 *'They have* **c down** and they lie with 3718
33:28 and her proud strength *will* **c to an end,** 8697
33:30 '**C** and hear the message that has come 995
33:30 the message that *has* **c** from the LORD.' 3655
33:31 My people **c** to you, as they usually do, 995
35: 7 and cut off from it *all who* **c** and go. 6296
36: 8 for *they will* soon **c home.** 995
37: 5 and *you will* **c to life.** 2649
37: 6 I will attach tendons to you and **make** flesh **c** upon you 6590
37: 6 and *you will* **c to life.** 2649
37: 9 **C** from the four winds, O breath, 995
38:10 that day thoughts *will* **c** into your mind 6590
38:13 *"Have* you **c** to plunder? 995
38:15 *You will* **c** from your place in 995
38:16 In days **to c,** O Gog, 344
39:17 'Assemble and **c** together from all around 995
43:19 who **c near** to minister before me, 7940
44:13 *to* **c near** to serve me as priests or come 5602
44:13 as priests or **c near** any of my holy things 5602
44:15 *are to* **c near** to minister before me; 7928
44:16 *to* **c near** my table to minister before me 7928
46: 8 and *he is to* **c out** the same way. 3655
46: 9 the people of the land **c** before the LORD 995
48:19 from the city who farm it will **c** from all NIH
Da 2:28 in days **to c.** 10022
2:29 O king, your mind turned to things **to c,** 10021+10180+10201
3: 2 and all the other provincial officials to **c** to 10085
3:26 servants of the Most High God, **c out!** 10485
3:26 of the Most High God, come out! **C** here!" 10085

Da 7:24 The ten horns are ten kings *who will* **c** 10624
9:13 all this disaster *has* **c** upon us, 995
9:22 *I have* now **c** to give you insight 3655
9:23 which I *have* **c** to tell you, 995
9:26 the ruler who *will* **c** will destroy the city 995
9:26 The end will **c** like a flood: NIH
10:12 and I *have* **c** in response to them. 995
10:14 Now *I have* **c** to explain 995
10:14 for the vision concerns a time **yet to c."** 6388
10:20 "Do you know why *I have* **c** to you? 995
10:20 the prince of Greece *will* **c;** 995
11:15 the North *will* **c** and build up siege ramps 995
11:17 to **c** with the might of his entire kingdom 995
11:27 an end will still **c** at the appointed time. NIH
11:35 for it will still **c** at the appointed time. NIH
11:45 Yet *he will* **c** to his end, 995
Hos 1:11 and *will* **c up** out of the land, 6590
3:5 *They will* **c trembling** to the LORD and 7064
4:14 without understanding *will* **c to ruin!** 4231
6:1 **"C,** let us return to the LORD. 2143
6:3 *he will* **c** to us like the winter rains, 995
9:4 not **c into** the temple of the LORD. 995
11:9 *I will* not **c** in wrath. 995
11:10 his children *will* **c trembling** from 3006
11:11 *They will* **c trembling** like birds 3006
13:7 So *I will* **c** upon them like a lion, 2118
13:13 Pains as of a woman in childbirth **c** to him, 995
13:13 *he does* not **c** to the opening of the womb. 6641
13:15 An east wind from the LORD *will* **c,** 995
Joel 1:13 **C,** spend the night in sackcloth, 995
1:15 *it will* **c** like destruction from 995
2:2 nor ever will be in ages **to c.** 1887+1887+2256
3:11 **C** quickly, all you nations from every side, 995
3:13 **C,** trample the grapes, 995
Am 4:2 "The time *will* surely **c** when you will 995
6:1 to whom the people of Israel **c!** 995
Jnh 1:2 its wickedness *has* **c up** before me." 6590
1:7 Then the sailors said to each other, **"C,** 2143
1:8 Where *do you* **c** from? 995
1:12 that it is my fault that this great storm has **c** NIH
Mic 1:9 her wound is incurable; *it has* **c** to Judah. 995
1:11 Those who live in Zaanan *will* not **c out.** 3655
1:12 because disaster *has* **c** from the LORD, 3718
1:15 the glory of Israel *will* **c** to Adullam. 995
3:6 Therefore night will **c** over you, NIH
3:11 No disaster *will* **c** upon us." 995
4:2 Many nations *will* **c** and say, "Come, 2143
4:2 Many nations will come and say, **"C,** 2143
4:8 kingship *will* **c** to the Daughter 995
5:2 of you *will* **c** for me one who will be ruler 3655
6:6 With what *shall I* **c before** the LORD 7709
6:6 *Shall I* **c before** him with burnt offerings, 7709
7:4 The day of your watchmen *has* **c,** 995
7:11 The day for building your walls will **c,** NIH
7:12 that day *people will* **c** to you from Assyria 995
7:17 *They will* **c trembling** out of their dens; 8074
Na 1:9 trouble *will* **c** a second time. 7756
1:11 *has one* **c forth** who plots evil against 3655
Hab 1:8 their horsemen **c** from afar. 995
1:9 they all **c** bent on violence. 995
2:3 *it will* **certainly c** and will not delay. 995+995
2:19 to him who says to wood, **'C to life!'** 7810
3:16 of calamity to **c** on the nation invading us. 6590
Zep 3:7 nor all *my* **punishments c** upon her. 7212
Hag 1:2 *yet* **c** for the LORD's house to be built.' " 995
2:7 and the desired of all nations *will* **c,** 995
Zec 1:21 but the craftsmen *have* **c** to terrify them 995
2:6 **"C!** Come! Flee from the 2098
2:6 **C!** Flee from the land of the 2098
2:7 **"C,** O Zion! 2098
3:8 men **symbolic of things to c:** 4603
6:15 Those who are far away *will* **c** and help 995
7:14 behind them that no *one could* **c** or go. 8740
8:20 the inhabitants of many cities *will* yet **c,** 995
8:22 and powerful nations *will* **c** to Jerusalem 995
10:4 From Judah *will* **c** the cornerstone, 3655
14:5 Then the LORD my God *will* **c,** 995
14:21 and all who **c** to sacrifice will take some of 995
Mal 3:1 the Lord you are seeking *will* **c** 995
3:1 *will* **c,"** says the LORD Almighty. 995
3:5 "So *I will* **c near** to you for judgment. 7928
4:6 or else *I will* **c** and strike the land with 995
Mt 2:2 in the east and *have* **c** to worship him." *2262*
2:6 **out of** you *will* **c** a ruler *2002*
3:11 me *will* **c** one who is more powerful than I, *2262*
3:14 and *do* you **c** to me?" *2262*
4:19 **"C,** follow me," Jesus said, *1307*
5:17 not think that *I have* **c** to abolish the Law *2262*
5:17 not **c** to abolish them but to fulfill them. *2262*
5:24 then **c** and offer your gift. *2262*
6:10 your kingdom **c,** your will be done on earth *2262*
7:15 They **c** to you in sheep's clothing, *2262*
8:8 not deserve to have *you* **c** under my roof. *1656*
8:9 and that one, **'C,'** and he comes. *2262*
8:11 I say to you that many *will* **c** from the east *2457*
8:29 *"Have you* **c** here to torture us before *2262*
9:13 For *I have* not **c** to call the righteous, *2262*
9:15 The time *will* **c** when the bridegroom will *2262*
9:18 But **c** and put your hand on her, *2262*
10:34 not suppose that *I have* **c** to bring peace to *2262*
10:34 *I did* not **c** to bring peace, but a sword. *2262*
10:35 *I have* **c** to turn " 'a man against his father, *2262*
11:3 "Are you the one who *was* to **c,** *2262*
11:14 he is the Elijah who *was* **to c.** *2262+3516*
11:28 **"C** to me, all *you* who are weary *1307*
12:28 then the kingdom of God *has* **c** upon you. *5777*
12:32 either in this age or in the age **to c.** *3516*

Mt 13:27 Where then did the weeds **c** from?' *2400*
13:32 birds of the air **c** and perch in its branches." *2262*
13:49 The angels *will* **c** and separate the wicked *2002*
14:28 "tell me *to* **c** to you on the water." *2262*
14:29 **"C,"** he said. *2262*
15:18 the things that **c out** of the mouth come *1744*
15:18 that come out of the mouth **c from** *2002*
15:19 **out of** the heart **c** *2002*
16:24 "If anyone would **c** after me, *2262*
16:27 of Man is going to **c** in his Father's glory *2262*
17:10 of the law say that Elijah must **c** first?" *2262*
17:12 But I tell you, Elijah *has* already **c,** *2262*
18:7 Such things must **c,** *2262*
18:7 but woe to the man through whom they **c!** *2262*
18:20 two or three **c together** in my name, *1639+5251*
19:14 Jesus said, "Let the little children **c** to me, *2262*
19:21 Then **c,** follow me." *1306*
20:28 as the Son of Man *did* not **c** to be served, *2262*
21:25 John's baptism—where did it **c** from? *NIG*
21:38 **C,** let's kill him and take his inheritance.' *1307*
22:3 to the banquet to tell them to **c,** *NIG*
22:3 but they refused *to* **c.** *2262*
22:4 **C** to the wedding banquet.' *1307*
22:8 but those I invited did not deserve to **c.** *NIG*
23:35 so upon you *will* **c** all the righteous blood *2262*
23:36 all this *will* **c** upon this generation. *2457*
24:5 For many *will* **c** in my name, claiming, *2262*
24:6 but the end is **still to c.** *4037*
24:14 and then the end *will* **c.** *2457*
24:32 as its twigs get tender and its leaves **c out,** *1770*
24:42 not know on what day your Lord *will* **c.** *2262*
24:44 because the Son of Man *will* **c** at an hour *2262*
24:50 The master of that servant *will* **c** on a day *2457*
25:6 **C out** to meet him!' *2002*
25:21 **C** and share your master's happiness!' *1656*
25:23 **C** and share your master's happiness!' *1656*
25:34 the King will say to those on his right, **'C,** *1307*
26:55 that *you have* **c out** with swords and clubs *2002*
27:40 **C down** from the cross, *2849*
27:42 *Let him* **c down** now from the cross, *2849*
27:64 his disciples *may* **c** and steal the body *2262*
28:6 **C** and see the place where he lay. *1307*
Mk 1:7 "After me *will* **c** one more powerful than I, *2262*
1:15 "The time *has* **c,"** he said. *4444*
1:17 **"C,** follow me," Jesus said, *1307*
1:24 *Have you* **c** to destroy us? *2262*
1:25 **"C out** of him!" *2002*
1:38 That is why *I have* **c."** *2002*
2:1 the people heard that *he had* **c** home. *1639*
2:17 *I have* not **c** to call the righteous, *2262*
2:20 the time *will* **c** when the bridegroom will *2262*
3:26 his end has **c.** *NIG*
4:19 the desires for other things **c in** and choke *1656*
4:29 because the harvest *has* **c."** *4225*
5:8 Jesus had said to him, **"C out** of this man, *2002*
5:23 Please **c** and put your hands on her so *2262*
6:31 **"C** with me by yourselves to a quiet place *1307*
7:1 the law *who had* **c** from Jerusalem gathered *2262*
7:4 When *they* **c** from the marketplace they do *2262*
7:21 **out** of men's hearts, **c** evil thoughts, *1744*
7:23 All these evils **c** from inside and make *1744*
8:3 some of them *have* **c** a long distance." *2457*
8:34 "If anyone would **c** after me, *199*
9:1 before they see the kingdom of God **c** *2262*
9:11 of the law say that Elijah must **c** first?" *2262*
9:12 Elijah *does* **c** first, and restores all things. *2262*
9:13 But I tell you, Elijah *has* **c,** *2262*
9:25 **c out** of him and never enter him again." *2002*
9:29 "This kind can **c out** only by prayer." *2002*
10:14 "Let the little children **c** to me, *2262*
10:21 Then **c,** follow me." *1306*
10:30 persecutions) and in the age *to* **c,** *2262*
10:45 even the Son of Man *did* not **c** to be served, *2262*
12:7 **C,** let's kill him, and the inheritance will *1307*
12:9 *He will* **c** and kill those tenants and give *2262*
13:6 Many *will* **c** in my name, claiming, *2262*
13:7 but the end is **still to c.** *4037*
13:28 as its twigs get tender and its leaves **c out,** *1770*
13:33 You do not know when that time *will* **c.** *1639*
13:35 when the owner of the house *will* **c back—** *2262*
14:41 The hour *has* **c.** *2262*
14:48 "that *you have* **c out** with swords and clubs *2002*
15:30 **c down** from the cross and save yourself!" *2849*
15:32 **c down** now from the cross, *2849*
15:41 Many other women who *had* **c up with** him *5262*
Lk 1:20 which *will* **c true** at their proper time." *4444*
1:35 "The Holy Spirit *will* **c upon** you, *2088*
1:43 the mother of my Lord *should* **c** to me? *2262*
1:68 *he has* **c** and has redeemed his people. *2170*
1:78 the rising sun *will* **c to** us from heaven *2170*
3:16 But one more powerful than I *will* **c,** *2262*
4:34 *Have you* **c** to destroy us? *2262*
4:35 **"C out** of him!" *2002*
4:36 to evil spirits and *they* **c out!"** *2002*
5:7 in the other boat to **c** and help them, *2262*
5:17 who had **c** from every village of Galilee *2262*
5:32 *I have* not **c** to call the righteous, *2262*
5:35 the time *will* **c** when the bridegroom will *2262*
6:18 who *had* **c** to hear him and to be healed *2262*
7:3 asking him to **c** and heal his servant. *2262*
7:6 not deserve to *have you* **c** under my roof. *1656*
7:7 even consider myself worthy *to* **c** to you. *2262*
7:8 and that one, **'C,'** and he comes. *2262*
7:16 "God *has* **c to help** his people." *2170*
7:19 "Are you the one who *was to* **c,** *2262*
7:20 'Are you the one who *was to* **c,** *2262*
8:2 from whom seven demons *had* **c out;** *2002*

Lk 8:16 so that those who **c in** can see the light. *1660*
8:29 the evil spirit *to* **c out** of the man. *2002*
8:41 pleading with him *to* **c to** his house *1656*
9:8 the prophets of long ago *had* **c back to life.** *482*
9:19 of long ago *has* **c back to life."** *482*
9:23 "If anyone would **c** after me, *2262*
11:2 hallowed be your name, your kingdom **c.** *2262*
11:6 a friend of mine on a journey *has* **c** to me, *4134*
11:20 then the kingdom of God *has* **c** to you. *5777*
11:33 so that those who **c in** may see the light. *1660*
12:37 at the table and will **c** and wait on them. *4216*
12:40 because the Son of Man *will* **c** at an hour *2262*
12:46 The master of that servant *will* **c** on a day *2457*
12:49 *"I have* **c** to bring fire on the earth, *2262*
13:14 So **c** and be healed on those days, *2262*
13:25 'I don't know you or where *you* **c** from.' *1639*
13:27 'I don't know you or where *you* **c** from. *1639*
13:29 *People will* **c** from east and west *2457*
14:9 the host who invited both of you will **c** *2262*
14:17 **'C,** for everything is now ready.' *2262*
14:20 'I just got married, so I can't **c.'** *2262*
14:23 and country lanes and make them **c in,** *1656*
15:27 'Your brother **has c,'** he replied, *2457*
16:28 so that they *will* not also **c** to this place *2262*
17:1 "Things that cause people to sin are **bound** *to* **c,** *450+2262+3590*
17:1 woe to that person through whom *they* **c.** *2262*
17:7 **'C along** now and sit down to eat'? *4216*
17:20 when the kingdom of God *would* **c,** *2262*
17:20 not **c** with your careful observation, *2262*
18:16 "Let the little children **c** to me, *2262*
18:22 Then **c,** follow me." *1306*
18:30 in the age *to* **c,** eternal life." *2262*
19:5 "Zacchaeus, **c down** immediately. *2849*
19:9 "Today salvation *has* **c** to this house, *1181*
19:13 he said, 'until *I* **c back.'** *2262*
19:43 The days *will* **c** upon you *2457*
20:16 *He will* **c** and kill those tenants and give *2262*
21:6 the time *will* **c** when not one stone will *2262*
21:8 For many *will* **c** in my name, claiming, *2262*
21:9 but the end will not **c** right away." *NIG*
21:35 For *it will* **c upon** all those who live on *2082*
22:52 and the elders, who *had* **c** for him, *4134*
22:52 that *you have* **c** with swords and clubs? *2002*
23:5 in Galilee and has **c** all the way here." *NIG*
23:29 For the time *will* **c** when you will say, *2262*
23:42 when *you* **c** into your kingdom." *2262*
23:55 The women who had **c with** Jesus *5302*
Jn 1:32 the Spirit **c down** from heaven as a dove *2849*
1:33 on whom you see the Spirit **c down** *2849*
1:39 **"C,"** he replied, "and you will see." *2262*
1:46 Can anything good **c** from there?" *1639*
1:46 **"C** and see," said Philip. *2262*
2:4 "My time *has* not yet **c."** *2457*
2:9 He did not realize where *it had* **c** from, *1639*
3:2 we know *you are* a teacher who *has* **c** *2262*
3:19 Light *has* **c** into the world, *2262*
3:20 and *will* not **c** into the light for fear *2262*
4:16 "Go, call your husband and **c** back." *2262*
4:23 Yet a time is coming and *has* now **c** when *1639*
4:29 **"C,** see a man who told me everything I ever did. *1307*
4:47 and begged him *to* **c** and heal his son, *2849*
4:49 "Sir, **c down** before my child dies." *2849*
4:54 *having* **c** from Judea to Galilee. *2262*
5:25 now **c** when the dead will hear the voice of *1639*
5:29 and **c out**—those who have done good will rise to live, *1744*
5:40 yet you refuse *to* **c** to me to have life. *2262*
5:43 I *have* **c** in my Father's name, *2262*
6:14 "Surely this is the Prophet who *is to* **c** into *2262*
6:15 that they intended *to* **c** and make him king *2262*
6:37 All that the Father gives me *will* **c** to me, *2457*
6:38 For *I have* **c down** from heaven not *2849*
6:44 "No one can **c** to me unless *2262*
6:65 "This is why I told you that no one can **c** *2262*
7:6 "The right time for me *has* not yet **c;** *4205*
7:8 because for me the right time *has* not yet **c."** *4444*
7:22 (though actually *it did* not **c** from Moses, *1639*
7:30 because his time *had* not yet **c.** *2262*
7:34 and where I am, you cannot **c."** *2262*
7:36 and 'Where I am, you cannot **c'?"** *2262*
7:37 *let him* **c** to me and drink. *2262*
7:41 "How *can* the Christ **c** from Galilee? *2262*
7:42 not the Scripture say that the Christ *will* **c** *2262*
7:52 that a prophet *does* not **c** out of Galilee." *1586*
8:14 But you have no idea where *I* **c** from or *2262*
8:20 because his time *had* not yet **c.** *2262*
8:21 Where I go, you cannot **c."** *2262*
8:22 'Where I go, you cannot **c'?"** *2262*
8:42 *I have* not **c** on my own; but he sent me. *2262*
9:39 "For judgment I *have* **c** into this world, *2262*
10:9 *He will* **c in** and go out, and find pasture. *1656*
10:10 I *have* **c** that they may have life, *2262*
11:19 and many Jews *had* **c** to Martha and Mary *2262*
11:27 who *was to* **c** into the world." *2262*
11:33 and the Jews who *had* **c along with** her *5302*
11:34 **"C** and see, Lord," they replied. *2262*
11:43 in a loud voice, "Lazarus, **c** out!" *1306*
11:45 many of the Jews who *had* **c** to visit Mary, *2262*
11:48 and then the Romans *will* **c** and take away *2262*
12:12 that *had* **c** for the Feast heard that Jesus was *2262*
12:23 "The hour *has* **c** for the Son of Man to *2262*
12:46 I *have* **c** into the world as a light, *2262*
12:47 For *I did* not **c** to judge the world, *2262*
13:1 the time *had* **c** for him to leave this world *2262*
13:3 that *he had* **c** from God and was returning *2002*

Jn 13:33 Where I am going, you cannot **c.** *2262*
14: 3 *I will* **c** back and take you to be with me *2262*
14:18 *I will* **c** to you. *2262*
14:23 and *we will* **c** to him and make our home *2262*
14:31 **"C now;** let us leave. *1586*
15:22 If *I had* not **c** and spoken to them, *2262*
16: 7 the Counselor *will* not **c** to you; *2262*
16:13 and he will tell you what *is* yet *to* **c.** *2262*
16:21 to a child has pain because her time *has* **c;** *2262*
16:32 "But a time is coming, and *has* **c,** *2262*
17: 1 "Father, the time *has* **c.** *2262*
17:10 And **glory** *has* **c to** *me* through them. *1519*
18:20 where all the Jews **c together.** *5302*
19: 9 "Where *do* you **c** from?" *1639*
21:12 Jesus said to them, **"C** and have breakfast." *1307*
Ac 1:11 *will* **c back** in the same way *2262*
3:19 times of refreshing *may* **c** from the Lord, *2262*
5:24 wondering what would **c of** this. *1181*
7: 7 'and afterward *they will* **c out of** *2002*
7:34 I have heard their groaning and *have* **c**
down to set them free. *2849*
7:34 Now **c,** I will send you back to Egypt.' *1306*
8:16 Holy Spirit *had* not yet **c upon** any of them;
1639+2158
8:31 he invited Philip *to* **c up** and sit with him. *326*
9:12 he has seen a man named Ananias **c** *1656*
9:14 And he has **c** here with authority from *NIG*
9:21 And *hasn't he* **c** here to take them *2262*
9:38 to him and urged him, "Please **c** at once!" *1451*
10: 4 the poor *have* **c up** as a memorial offering *326*
10:21 Why *have you* **c?"** *4205*
10:22 "We have **c** from Cornelius the centurion. *NIG*
10:22 A holy angel told him *to have* you **c** *3569*
10:33 and it was good of you *to* **c.** *4134*
10:45 The circumcised believers who *had* **c with** *5302*
11:15 on them as he had **c** on us at the beginning. *NIG*
14:11 "The gods *have* **c down** to us *2849*
16: 9 **"C over** to Macedonia and help us." *1329*
16:15 she said, **"c** and stay **at** my house." *1656*
16:18 of Jesus Christ I command you *to* **c out** *2002*
16:34 *because he had* **c to believe** in God— *4409*
16:37 Let them **c** themselves and escort us out." *2262*
17: 6 over the world *have* now **c** here, *4205*
18: 2 *who had* recently **c** from Italy *2262*
18:21 *"I will* **c back** if it is God's will." *366*
19:13 **command** you **to c out."** *3991*
20:29 savage wolves *will* **c in among** you *1656*
21:22 They will certainly hear that *you have* **c,** *2262*
24:25 self-control and the judgment **to c,** *3516*
25: 5 of your leaders **c with** me and press charges *5160*
25: 7 the Jews *who had* **c down** *2849*
28:21 and none of the brothers *who have* **c from** *4134*
Ro 1:10 the way may be opened for me *to* **c** to you. *2262*
1:13 that I planned many times *to* **c** to you *2262*
5:14 who was a pattern *of* the one **to c.** *3516*
11:11 salvation has **c** to the Gentiles *NIG*
11:25 the full number of the Gentiles *has* **c in.** *1656*
11:26 "The deliverer *will* **c** from Zion; *2457*
13:11 The hour has **c** for you to wake up *NIG*
14:23 everything that does not **c** from faith is sin. *NIG*
15:29 I know that *when I* **c** to you, *2262*
15:29 *I will* **c** in the full measure of the blessing *2262*
15:32 that by God's will I may **c** to you with joy *2262*
1Co 2: 1 not **c** with eloquence or superior wisdom *2262*
2:14 not accept the things that *c from* **the Spirit** *AIT*
4:19 But *I will* **c** to you very soon, *2262*
4:21 *Shall I* **c** to you with a whip, *2262*
7: 5 Then **c together** again so that Satan will
899+1639+2093+3836
10:11 on whom the fulfillment of the ages *has* **c.** *2918*
11: 8 For man *did* not **c** from woman, *1639*
11:18 I hear that *when* you **c together** as a church, *5302*
11:20 *When* you **c together,** *5302*
11:31 *we* would not **c under judgment.** *3212*
11:33 my brothers, *when you* **c together** to eat, *5302*
11:34 when *I* **c** I will give further directions. *2262*
14: 6 if *I* **c** to you and speak in tongues, *2262*
14:23 not understand or some unbelievers **c in,** *1656*
14:26 When you **c together,** *5302*
15:24 Then the end will **c,** *NIG*
15:34 **C back to** *your* **senses** *1729*
15:35 With what kind of body *will they* **c?"** *2262*
15:36 What you sow *does* not **c to life** *2443*
15:46 The spiritual did not **c** first, but the natural, *NIG*
15:54 then the saying that is written *will* **c true:** *1181*
16: 2 *I* **c** no collections will have to be made. *2262*
16: 5 *I will* **c** to you— *2262*
16:22 **C, O Lord!** *3448*
2Co 1:14 *you will* **c to understand** fully *2105*
1:16 on my way to Macedonia and *to* **c** back *2262*
1:22 guaranteeing what is to **c.** *NIG*
5: 5 guaranteeing what is to **c.** *NIG*
5:17 the old has gone, the new *has* **c!** *1181*
6:17 **c out** from them and be separate, *2002*
9: 4 For if any Macedonians **c** with me *2262*
10: 2 that *when I* **c** I may not have to be as bold *4205*
10:14 as would be the case if *we had* not **c** to you, *2391*
12:20 *when I* **c** I may not find you as I want you *2262*
12:21 that *when* I **c** again my God will humble me *2262*
13:10 that *when I* **c** I may not have to be harsh *4205*
Gal 3:14 that the blessing given to Abraham *might* **c** *1181*
3:19 to whom the promise referred *had* **c.** *2262*
3:21 then righteousness would certainly *have* **c** *1639*
3:25 Now that faith *has* **c,** *2262*
4: 4 But when the time *had* fully **c,** *2262*
5: 8 That kind of persuasion does not **c** from *NIG*
Eph 1:21 in the present age but also in the one **to c.** *3516*
Eph 4:20 however, *did* not *c to* **know** Christ that way. *AIT*
4:29 *Do* not *let* any unwholesome talk **c out** *1744*
Php 1:27 whether I **c** and see you or only hear *2262*
2:24 in the Lord that I myself *will* **c** soon. *2262*
Col 1: 6 that *has* **c** to you. *4205*
2:17 a shadow *of* the things that *were to* **c;** *3516*
1Th 2:16 The wrath of God *has* **c** upon them at last. *5777*
2:18 For we wanted *to* **c** to you— *2262*
3: 6 But Timothy *has* just now **c** to us from you *2262*
3:11 and our Lord Jesus clear the way for us to **c** *NIG*
4:16 the Lord himself *will* **c down** from heaven, *2849*
5: 2 of the Lord *will* **c** like a thief in the night. *2262*
5: 3 destruction *will* **c on** them suddenly, *2392*
2Th 2: 2 report or letter supposed to have **c** from us, *NIG*
2: 2 that the day of the Lord *has already* **c.** *1931*
2: 3 not **c]** until the rebellion occurs and *NIG*
1Ti 2: 4 who wants all men to be saved and *to* **c** to *2262*
3:14 Although I hope *to* **c** to you soon, *2262*
4: 2 Such teachings **c** through hypocritical liars, *NIG*
4: 8 for both the present life and the life **to c.** *3516*
4:13 Until *I* **c,** devote yourself to *2262*
2Ti 2:26 that *they will* **c** *to their* **senses** and escape *392*
4: 3 For the time *will* **c** when men will not put *1639*
4: 6 and the time *has* **c** for my departure. *2392*
4: 9 Do your best *to* **c** to me quickly, *2262*
4:13 *When* you **c,** bring the cloak that I left *2262*
Tit 3:12 do your best *to* **c** to me at Nicopolis, *2262*
Heb 2: 5 that he has subjected the world **to c,** *3516*
3:14 *We have* **c** to share in Christ *1181*
7:11 for another priest *to* **c—** *482*
7:25 to save completely those who **c to** God *4665*
10: 7 *I* **have c** to do your will, O God.' " *2457*
10: 9 "Here I am, *I* **have c** to do your will." *2457*
10:37 "He who is coming *will* **c** and will *2457*
12:18 not **c to** a mountain that can be touched *4665*
12:22 But *you have* **c to** Mount Zion, *4665*
12:22 You have **c** to thousands upon thousands *NIG*
12:23 You have **c** to God, the judge of all men, *NIG*
13:14 but we are looking for the city that *is* **to c.** *3516*
13:23 I will **c** with him to see you. *NIG*
Jas 3:10 **Out** of the same mouth **c** *2002*
3:15 not **c down** from heaven but is earthly, *2982*
4: 1 Don't they **c** from your desires that battle *NIG*
4: 8 **C near** to God and he will come near *1581*
4: 8 near to God and *he will* **c near** to you. *1581*
1Pe 1: 7 These have **c** so that your faith— *NIG*
1:10 who spoke of the grace that was to **c** *NIG*
2: 4 *As you* **c** to him, the living Stone— *4665*
3: 3 not **c** from outward adornment, *1639*
2Pe 3: 3 that in the last days scoffers *will* **c,** *2262*
3: 9 but everyone *to* **c** to repentance. *6003*
3:10 But the day of the Lord *will* **c** like a thief. *2457*
1Jn 2: 3 We know that *we have c to* **know** him *AIT*
2:18 even now many antichrists *have* **c.** *1181*
4: 2 that acknowledges that Jesus Christ *has* **c** in *2262*
5: 6 He did not **c** by water only, *NIG*
5:20 We know also that the Son of God **has c** *2457*
3Jn 1: 3 to have some brothers **c** and tell *2262*
1:10 So if *I* **c,** I will call attention *2262*
Rev 1: 4 and who was, and who *is to* **c,** *2262*
1: 8 "who is, and who was, and who *is to* **c,** *2262*
2: 5 *I will* **c** to you *2262*
2:16 *I will* soon **c** to you and will fight *2262*
2:25 Only hold on to what you have until *I* **c.** *2457*
3: 3 you do not wake up, *I will* **c** like a thief, *2457*
3: 3 not know at what time *I will* **c** to you. *2457*
3: 9 I will make them **c** and fall down *2457*
3:10 that is going to **c** upon the whole world *2262*
3:20 *I will* **c in** and eat with him, *1656*
4: 1 to me like a trumpet said, **"C up** here, *326*
4: 8 who was, and is, and *is to* **c."** *2262*
6: 1 in a voice like thunder, **"C!"** *2262*
6: 3 I heard the second living creature say, **"C!"** *2262*
6: 5 I heard the third living creature say, **"C!"** *2262*
6: 7 of the fourth living creature say, **"C!"** *2262*
6:17 For the great day of their wrath *has* **c,** *2262*
7:13 who are they, and where *did they* **c** from?" *2262*
7:14 "These are they who *have* **c** out of *2262*
9:12 two other woes are yet *to* **c.** *2262*
11:12 from heaven saying to them, **"C up** here." *326*
11:18 and your wrath *has* **c.** *2262*
11:18 The time has **c** for judging the dead, *NIG*
12:10 "Now *have* **c** the salvation and the power *1181*
13:13 *to* **c down** from heaven to earth in full view *2849*
14: 7 because the hour of his judgment *has* **c.** *2262*
14:15 because the time to reap *has* **c,** *2262*
15: 4 All nations *will* **c** and worship before you, *2457*
16:15 "Behold, *I* **c** like a thief! *2262*
17: 1 to me, **"C,** I will show you the punishment *1306*
17: 8 and will **c up** out of the Abyss and go *326*
17: 8 now is not, and yet *will* **c.** *4205*
17:10 one is, the other *has* not yet **c;** *2262*
17:10 *he does* **c,** he must remain for a little while. *2262*
18: 4 **"C out** of her, my people, *2002*
18:10 In one hour your doom *has* **c!'** *2262*
19: 7 For the wedding of the Lamb *has* **c,** *2262*
19:17 **"C,** gather together for the great supper *1307*
20: 5 (The rest of the dead *did* not **c to life** until *2409*
21: 9 **"C,** I will show you the bride, *1306*
22:17 The Spirit and the bride say, **"C!"** *2262*
22:17 And let him who hears say, **"C!"** *2262*
22:17 Whoever is thirsty, *let him* **c;** *2262*
22:20 **C,** Lord Jesus. *2262*

COMES (290) [COME]

Ge 24:43 if a maiden **c out** to draw water and I say 3655
Ge 29: 6 here **c** his daughter Rachel with the sheep." 995
32: 8 "If Esau **c** and attacks one group, 995
37:19 "Here **c** that dreamer!" 995
37:20 Then we'll see what **c of** his dreams." 2118
42:15 unless your youngest brother **c** here. 995
42:38 If harm **c** *to* him on the journey 7925
44:23 your youngest brother **c down** with you, 3718
44:29 from me too and harm **c** *to* him, 7936
47:24 But when the **crop c in,** 9311
49:10 until *he* **c** to whom it belongs and 995
Ex 21: 3 If *he* **c** alone, he is to go free alone; 995
21: 3 but if he has a wife when he **c,** NIH
28:35 before the LORD and when he **c out,** 3655
29:30 and **c** to the Tent of Meeting to minister in 995
32:34 when the time **c** for me to punish, NIH
Lev 14:36 "But if the priest **c** to examine it and 995+995
16:17 in the Most Holy Place until he **c out,** 3655
22: 3 and yet **c near** the sacred offerings that 7928
25:22 until the harvest of the ninth year **c in.** 995
Nu 6: 4 not eat anything that **c** from the grapevine, 6913
11:20 until *it* **c out** of your nostrils 3655
17:13 who **even c near** the tabernacle 7929+7929
18: 7 Anyone else who **c near** the sanctuary must 7929
36: 4 the Year of Jubilee for the Israelites **c,** 2118
Dt 2: 8 which **c** up from Elath and Ezion Geber, NIH
8: 3 but on every **word that c from** the mouth of 4604
18: 6 and **c** in all earnestness to the place 995
22: 2 with you and keep it until he **c looking for** 2011
25:11 of one of them **c** to rescue her husband 7928
31:11 when all Israel **c** to appear before 995
32:32 Their vine **c** from the vine of Sodom and NIH
Jdg 4:20 "If someone **c by** and asks you, 995
11:31 whatever **c out** of the door of my house 3655
11:39 From this **c** the Israelite custom 2118
13:14 not eat anything that **c** from the grapevine, 3655
13:17 when your word **c true?"** 995
16: 9 of string snaps when it **c close** *to* a flame. 8193
1Sa 8:18 When that day **c,** NIH
9: 6 and everything he says **c true.** 995+995
9:13 The people will not begin eating until he **c,** 995
11: 3 if no one **c** to rescue us, NIH
14:24 be any man who eats food before evening **c,** NIH
16:16 when the evil spirit from God **c** upon you, 2118
17:25 *He* **c out** to defy Israel. 6590
2Sa 13: 5 "When your father **c** to see you, say to him, 995
15:28 until word **c** from you to inform me." 995
18:27 *"He* **c** with good news." 995
1Ki 8:31 to take an oath and *he* **c** and swears the oath 995
8:37 "When famine or plague **c** to the land, 2118
8:42 when *he* **c** and prays toward this temple, 995
2Ki 4: 9 that this man *who* often **c** our way is 6296
4:10 he can stay there whenever he **c** to us." 995
6:32 Look, when the messenger **c,** 995
1Ch 16:33 for *he* **c** to judge the earth. 995
29:14 Everything **c** from you, NIH
29:14 and we have given you only what **c** NIH
29:16 it **c** from your hand, NIH
2Ch 6:22 to take an oath and *he* **c** and swears the oath 995
6:28 "When famine or plague **c** to the land, 2118
6:32 when *he* **c** and prays toward this temple, 995
13: 9 Whoever **c** to consecrate himself with 995
19:10 In every case that **c** before you 995
20: 9 'If calamity **c** upon us, 995
Job 3:24 For sighing **c** *to* me instead of food; 995
4: 5 trouble **c** to you, and you are discouraged; 995
5:14 Darkness **c** *upon* them in the daytime; 7008
5:21 and need not fear when destruction **c.** 995
11:10 "If *he* **c along** and confines you in prison 2736
27: 9 Does God listen to his cry when distress **c** 995
28: 5 The earth, from which food **c,** 3655
33:27 Then *he* **c** to men and says, 'I sinned, 8801
37: 2 to the rumbling *that* **c** from his mouth. 3655
37: 4 **c** the sound of *his* **roar;** 8613
37: 9 The tempest **c** out from its chamber, 995
37:22 Out of the north *he* **c** in golden splendor; 910
37:22 God **c** in awesome majesty. NIH
38:29 From whose womb **c** the ice? 3655
Ps 3: 8 From the LORD **c** deliverance. NIH
7:16 his violence **c down** on his own head. 3718
22:25 From you **c** the theme of my praise in NIH
30: 5 but rejoicing **c** in the morning. NIH
37:39 The salvation of the righteous **c** from NIH
41: 6 Whenever *one* **c** to see me, 995
50: 3 Our God **c** and will not be silent; 995
62: 1 my salvation **c** from him. NIH
62: 5 my hope **c** from him. NIH
68:20 the Sovereign LORD **c** escape from death. NIH
73: 7 From their callous hearts **c** iniquity; 3655
88:13 in the morning my prayer **c before** you. 7709
96:13 for *he* **c,** he comes to judge the earth. 995
96:13 for he comes, *he* **c** to judge the earth. 995
98: 9 for *he* **c** to judge the earth. 995
118:26 Blessed is he *who* **c** in the name of 995
121: 2 My help **c** from the LORD, NIH
Pr 10: 8 but a chattering fool **c to ruin.** 4231
10:10 and a chattering fool **c to ruin.** 4231
11: 2 *When* pride **c,** then comes disgrace, 995
11: 2 When pride comes, then **c** disgrace, 995
11: 2 but with humility **c** wisdom. NIH
11: 7 from his power **c to nothing.** 6
11: 8 and *it* **c** *on* the wicked instead. 995
11:24 another withholds unduly, but **c** to poverty. NIH
11:27 but evil **c** *to* him who searches for it. 995
13:18 He who ignores discipline **c** to poverty NIH
14: 4 the strength of an ox **c** an abundant harvest. NIH
14: 6 but knowledge **c easily** to the discerning. 7837
14:32 When calamity **c,** the wicked are brought NIH

Pr 15:33 and humility c before honor. NIH
16: 1 from the LORD c the reply of the tongue. NIH
18: 3 When wickedness c, so does contempt, 995
18: 3 and with shame c disgrace. NIH
18:12 but humility c before honor. NIH
18:17 till another c *forward* and questions him. 995
21:16 from the path of understanding **c to rest** in 5663
25: 4 and **out** c material for the silversmith; 3655
Ecc 1:18 For with much wisdom c much sorrow; NIH
2:18 because I must leave them to the one who c 2118
5: 3 As a dream c when there are many cares, 995
5:15 Naked a *man* c from his mother's womb, 3655
5:15 and as *he* c, so he departs. 995
5:16 This too is a grievous evil: As a *man* c, 995
6: 4 *It* c without meaning, 995
SS 2: 8 Here *he* c, leaping across the mountains, 995
Isa 10: 3 when disaster c from afar? 995
14: 8 no woodsman c to cut us down." 6590
14:31 A cloud of smoke c from the north, 995
21: 1 *an invader* c from the desert, 995
21: 9 here c a man in a chariot with a team 995
23: 5 When word c to Egypt, NIH
28:19 As often as it c it will carry you away; 6296
28:29 All this also c from the LORD Almighty, 3655
30:23 the food *that* c *from* the land will be rich 9311
30:27 See, the Name of the LORD c from afar, 995
34: 1 the world, and all **that c out** *of* it! 7368
40:10 See, the Sovereign LORD c with power, 995
41:25 up one from the north, and *he* c— 910
42: 5 the earth and **all that** c **out** *of* it, 7368
62:11 the Daughter of Zion, 'See, your Savior **c**! 995
Jer 4:12 a wind too strong for that c from me. 995
10:15 when their judgment c, they will perish. NIH
17: 6 he will not see prosperity when *it* **c**. 995
17: 8 It does not fear when heat **c**; 995
27: 7 until the time for his land **c**; 995
28: 9 by the LORD only if his prediction **c true."** 995
51:18 when their judgment c, they will perish. NIH
51:46 one rumor c this year, another the next, 995
51:54 "The sound of a cry c from Babylon, NIH
La 1: 4 for no *one* c *to* her appointed feasts. 995
Eze 7:25 *When* terror c, they will seek peace, 995
12:22 by and every vision **c to nothing'?** 6
21:27 until he c to whom it rightfully belongs; 995
33: 4 but does not take warning and the sword **c** 995
33: 6 and the sword c and takes the life of one 995
33:33 "When all this **c true—** 995
Da 9:25 the ruler, c, there will be seven 'sevens,' NIH
Hos 10:12 for it is time to seek the LORD, until *he* c 995
14: 8 your fruitfulness c from me." 5162
Joel 2: 2 the mountains a large and mighty army **c**, NIH
Am 3: 6 When disaster c to a city, 2118
6:10 the bodies c to carry them out of the house NIH
Jnh 2: 9 Salvation c from the LORD." NIH
Mic 1: 3 *he* **c down** and treads the high places of 3718
2:11 If a liar and deceiver c and says, 2143
Zep 2: 2 the fierce anger of the LORD c upon you, 995
2: 2 the day of the LORD's wrath c upon you. 995
Zec 9: 9 See, your king c to you, 995
14: 7 When evening **c**, there will be light. 2118
Mal 4: 5 and dreadful day of the LORD **c**. 995
Mt 4: 4 but on every word that c from the mouth *1744*
5:37 anything beyond this c from the evil one. *1639*
8: 9 and that one, 'Come,' and *he* **c**. *2262*
10:23 the cities of Israel before the Son of Man **c**. *2262*
12:43 "When an evil spirit **c out** of a man, *2002*
13:19 the evil one c and snatches away *2262*
13:21 *When* trouble or persecution c because of *1181*
15:11 but what **c out** of his mouth, *1744*
16: 2 He replied, "*When* evening **c**, you say, *1181*
17:11 Elijah c and will restore all things. *2262*
21: 5 'See, your king c to you, *2262*
21: 9 Blessed is he who c in the name of the Lord! *2262*
21:40 when the owner of the vineyard **c**, *2262*
23:39 Blessed is he who c in the name of the Lord. *2262*
24:27 as lightning that c from the east is visible *2002*
25:31 "When the Son of Man c in his glory, *2262*
26:46 Rise, let us go! Here c my betrayer!" *1581*
27:49 Let's see if Elijah c to save him." *2262*
Mk 4:15 Satan c and takes away the word *2262*
4:17 When trouble or persecution c because of *1181*
7:15 **c out** of a man that makes him 'unclean.' *1744*
7:20 **c out** of a man is what makes him 'unclean.' *1744*
8:38 of him when *he* c in his Father's glory with *2262*
11: 9 Blessed is he who c in the name of the Lord! *2262*
13:36 If *he* c suddenly, *2262*
14:42 Rise! Let us go! Here c my betrayer!" *1581*
15:36 Let's see if Elijah c to take him down," *2262*
Lk 6:47 I will show you what he is like who c to me *2262*
7: 8 and that one, 'Come,' and *he* **c**. *2262*
8:12 then the devil c and takes away the word *2262*
9:26 of Man will be ashamed of him when *he* c *2262*
11:24 "When an evil spirit **c out** of a man, *2002*
12:33 no thief **c near** and no moth destroys. *1581*
12:36 so that *when he* c *2262*
12:37 master finds them watching *when he* **c**. *2262*
12:38 even if *he* c in the second or third watch of *2262*
13:35 Blessed is he who c in the name of the Lord. *2262*
14:10 so that when your host **c**, *2262*
14:26 "If anyone c to me and does *2262*
15:30 with prostitutes **c home**, *2262*
17: 4 and seven times **c back** to you and says, *2188*
17: 7 to the servant when he **c in** from the field, *1656*
18: 8 However, *when* the Son of Man **c**, *2262*
19:38 Blessed is the king who c in the name of *2262*
22:18 of the vine until the kingdom of God **c**." *2262*
Jn 1:15 'He who c after me has surpassed me *2262*
Jn 1:27 He is the one who c after me, *2262*
1:30 'A man who c after me has surpassed me *2262*
3: 8 but you cannot tell where *it* c from or *2262*
3:21 whoever lives by the truth c into the light, *2262*
3:31 "The one who c from above is above all; *2262*
3:31 The one who c from heaven is above all. *2262*
4:25 *he* **c**, he will explain everything to us." *2262*
5:43 but if someone else c in his own name, *2262*
5:44 the praise that c from the only God? *NIG*
6:33 For the bread of God is he who **c down** *2849*
6:35 He who c to me will never go hungry, *2262*
6:37 whoever c to me I will never drive away. *2262*
6:45 to the Father and learns from him c to me. *2262*
6:50 here is the bread that **c down** from heaven, *2849*
7:16 It c from him who sent me. *NIG*
7:17 he will find out whether my teaching c *1639*
7:27 when the Christ **c**, *2262*
7:31 They said, "When the Christ **c**, *2262*
9:29 we don't even know where *he* c from." *1639*
9:30 You don't know where *he* c from, *1639*
10:10 thief c only to steal and kill and destroy; *2262*
12:13 "Blessed is he who c in the name of *2262*
14: 6 No one c to the Father except through me. *2262*
15:26 "When the Counselor **c**, *2262*
16: 4 so that when the time c you will remember *2262*
16: 8 *When* he c, he will convict the world *2262*
16:13 But when he, the Spirit of truth, **c**, *2262*
17: 7 that everything you have given me c *1639*
Ac 1: 8 *when* the Holy Spirit **c on** you; *2088*
3:16 It is Jesus' name and the faith that c *NIG*
3:21 He must remain in heaven until the time c *NIG*
24:22 "When Lysias the commander **c**," he said, *2849*
Ro 1: 5 the Gentiles to the obedience that c *NIG*
3:22 from God c through faith in Jesus Christ *NIG*
4:13 through the righteousness that c by faith. *NIG*
4:16 Therefore, the promise c by faith, *NIG*
10: 3 the righteousness that c from God *NIG*
10:17 faith c from hearing the message, *NIG*
1Co 4: 5 wait till the Lord **c**. *2262*
11:12 But everything c from God. *NIG*
11:26 you proclaim the Lord's death until *he* **c**. *2262*
13:10 but when perfection **c**, *2262*
14:23 whole church **c together** *899+2093+3836+5302*
14:24 or someone who does not understand **c in** *1656*
14:30 And if a **revelation c** *636*
15:21 the resurrection of the dead c also through *NIG*
15:23 then, when he **c**, those who belong to him. *4242*
16:10 If Timothy **c**, see to it that he has nothing *2262*
2Co 3: 5 but our competence c from God. *NIG*
3:18 which c from the Lord, who is the Spirit. *NIG*
11: 4 For if someone c to you and preaches *2262*
Eph 5: 6 for because of such things God's wrath c *2262*
6:13 so that when the day of evil **c**, *NIG*
6:15 with the readiness that c from the gospel *NIG*
Php 1:11 filled with the fruit of righteousness that c *NIG*
3: 9 a righteousness of my own that c from *NIG*
3: 9 the righteousness that c from God and is *NIG*
Col 4:10 if *he* c to you, welcome him.) *2262*
1Th 2:19 the presence of our Lord Jesus when he **c**? *4242*
3:13 and Father when our Lord Jesus c *4242*
2Th 1:10 on the day *he* c to be glorified *2262*
1Ti 1: 5 which c from a pure heart and *NIG*
Heb 11: 6 because anyone who c to him must believe *4665*
11: 7 and became heir of the righteousness that c *NIG*
Jas 2: 2 a man **c into** your meeting wearing *1656*
2: 2 and a poor man in shabby clothes also **c in**. *1656*
3:13 by deeds done in the humility that c *NIG*
3:17 But the wisdom that c from heaven is first *NIG*
1Jn 2:16 c not from the Father but from the world. *1639*
2:21 and because no lie c from the truth. *1639*
4: 7 for love c from God. *1639*
2Jn 1:10 If anyone c to you and does *2262*
Rev 11: 5 fire **c from** their mouths *1744*
11: 7 that **c up** from the Abyss will attack them, *326*
19:15 **Out** of his mouth c a sharp sword *1744*

COMFORT (47) [COMFORTED, COMFORTER, COMFORTERS, COMFORTING, COMFORTS]

Ge 5:29 "He *will* c us in the labor and painful toil 5714
37:35 All his sons and daughters came to c him, 5714
Ru 2:13 "*You have* **given** me c 5714
1Ch 7:22 and his relatives came to c him. 5714
Job 2:11 to go and sympathize with him and c him. 5714
7:13 When I think my bed *will* c me 5714
16: 5 c *from* my lips would bring you relief. 5764
36:16 the c *of* your table laden with choice food. 5739
Ps 23: 4 your rod and your staff, they c me. 5714
71:21 and c me once again. 5714
119:50 My c in my suffering is this: 5717
119:52 O LORD, and *I* **find** c in them. 5714
119:76 May your unfailing love be my **c**, 5714
119:82 I say, "When *will you* c me?" 5714
Isa 40: 1 **C**, comfort my people, says your God. 5714
40: 1 Comfort, c my people, says your God. 5714
51: 3 The LORD *will* surely c Zion 5714
51:19 who *can* c you?— 5653
57:18 I will guide him and restore c to him, 5719
61: 2 to c all who mourn, 5714
66:13 mother comforts her child, so *will* I c you; 5714
Jer 16: 7 to c those who mourn for the dead— 5714
31:13 *I will* **give** them c and joy instead 5714
La 1: 2 Among all her lovers there is none *to* c her. 5714
1: 9 there was none *to* c her. 5714
1:16 No one is near *to* c me, 5714
La 1:17 but there is no *one to* c her. 5714
1:21 but there is no *one to* c me. 5714
2:13 To what can I liken you, that *I may* c you, 5714
Eze 16:54 of all you have done in **giving** them **c**. 5714
Na 3: 7 Where can I find *anyone to* c you?" 5714
Zec 1:17 and the LORD *will* again c Zion 5714
10: 2 *they* **give** c in vain. 5714
Lk 6:24 for you have already received your **c**. *4155*
Jn 11:19 to Martha and Mary to c them in the loss *4170*
1Co 14: 3 encouragement and **c**. *4171*
2Co 1: 3 Father of compassion and the God *of* all **c**, *4155*
1: 4 so that we can c those in any trouble with *4151*
1: 4 with the c we ourselves have received *4155*
1: 5 so also through Christ our c overflows. *4155*
1: 6 it is for your c and salvation; *4155*
1: 6 if we are comforted, it is for your **c**, *4155*
1: 7 so also you share *in* our **c**. *4155*
2: 7 instead, you *ought to* forgive and c him, *4151*
7: 7 but also by the c you had given him. *4155*
Php 2: 1 if any c from his love, *4172*
Col 4:11 and they have proved a c to me. *4219*

COMFORTED (17) [COMFORT]

Ge 24:67 and Isaac **was** c after his mother's death. 5714
37:35 but he refused to **be c**. 5714
2Sa 12:24 Then David c his wife Bathsheba, 5714
Job 42:11 *They* c and consoled him over all 5653
Ps 77: 2 and my soul refused *to* **be c**. 5714
86:17 O LORD, have helped me and c me. 5714
Isa 12: 1 and *you have* c me. 5714
52: 9 for the LORD *has* c his people, 5714
54:11 lashed by storms and not **c**, 5714
66:13 and *you will* **be** c over Jerusalem." 5714
Jer 31:15 for her children and refusing to **be c**, 5714
Mt 2:18 for her children and refusing *to be* **c**, *4151*
5: 4 for they *will be* **c**. *4151*
Lk 16:25 but now *he is* c here and you are in agony. *4151*
Ac 20:12 and *were* greatly **c**. *4151*
2Co 1: 6 if *we are* **c**, it is for your comfort, *4151*
7: 6 c us by the coming of Titus, *4151*

COMFORTER (3) [COMFORT]

Ecc 4: 1 and they have no **c**; 5714
4: 1 and they have no **c**. 5714
Jer 8:18 O my C in sorrow, 4443

COMFORTER (KJV) See COUNSELOR

COMFORTERS (2) [COMFORT]

Job 16: 2 miserable c are you all! 5714
Ps 69:20 but there was none, for c, but I found none. 5714

COMFORTING (4) [COMFORT]

Isa 66:11 and be satisfied at her c breasts; 9488
Zec 1:13 So the LORD spoke kind and c words to 5714
Jn 11:31 with Mary in the house, c her, noticed *4170*
1Th 2:12 c and urging you to live lives worthy *4170*

COMFORTS (6) [COMFORT]

Job 29:25 I was like *one who* c mourners. 5714
Isa 49:13 For the LORD c his people 5714
51:12 "I, even I, am he *who* c you. 5714
66:13 a mother c her child, so will I comfort you; 5714
2Co 1: 4 who c us in all our troubles, *4151*
7: 6 But God, who c the downcast, *4151*

COMING (245) [COME]

Ge 7:17 For forty days the flood *kept* c on 2118
15: 4 "This man will not be your heir, but a son **c** 3655
19:15 With the c *of* dawn, the angels urged Lot, 6590
24:13 the daughters of the townspeople *are* **c out** 3655
24:65 that man in the field c to meet us?" 2143
32: 6 and now *he is* c to meet you, 2143
32:18 and he is c behind us.' " NIH
32:20 'Your servant Jacob is c behind us.' " NIH
33: 1 c with his four hundred men; 995
37:25 a caravan of Ishmaelites c from Gilead. 995
41:29 Seven years of great abundance *are* c 995
41:35 of these good years that *are* c and store up 995
Ex 14:20 c between the armies of Egypt and Israel. 995
18: 6 *am* c to you with your wife 995
32: 1 that Moses was so long in **c down** from 3718
Nu 12:12 a stillborn infant c from its mother's womb 3655
21: 1 that Israel *was* c *along* the road to Atharim, 995
22:16 Do not let anything keep you from c to me, 2143
22:36 When Balak heard that Balaam *was* **c**, 995
33:40 heard that the Israelites *were* **c**. 995
Dt 2:23 the Caphtorites **c out** 3655
Jos 18:12 c out at the desert of Beth Aven. 2118
Jdg 1:24 a man **c out** of the city and they said 3655
5:28 'Why is his chariot so long in **c**? 995
9:36 people *are* **c down** from the tops of 3718
9:37 "Look, people *are* **c down** from the center 3718
9:37 the center of the land, and a company *is* **c** 995
9:43 When he saw the people **c out** of the city, 3655
Ru 4:11 the LORD make the woman who *is* **c** 995
1Sa 2:31 The time *is* c when I will cut short 995
9:11 they met some girls **c out** to draw water, 3655
9:14 c toward them on his way up to 3655
10: 5 of prophets **c down** from the high place 3718
17:25 "Do you see how this man *keeps* **c out**? 6590
17:41 **kept** c closer to David. 2143+2143

1Sa 25:11 give it to men c from who knows where?" NIH
28:13 "I see a spirit c up out of the ground." 6590
28:14 "An old man wearing a robe is c up," 6590
2Sa 13:34 c down the side of the hill. 2143
19:41 of Israel were c to the king and saying 995
24:20 the king and his men c toward him, 6296
1Ki 14:5 "Jeroboam's wife is c to ask you 995
2Ki 4:1 now his creditor is c to take my two boys 995
9:17 he called out, "I see some troops c." NIH
9:18 but he isn't c back." 8740
9:20 but he isn't c back either. 8740
2Ch 7:3 the fire c down and the glory of the LORD 3718
20:2 "A vast army is c against you from Edom, 995
20:11 See how they are repaying us by c 995
Ne 6:10 because men are c to kill you— 995
6:10 by night they are c to kill you." 995
6:17 and replies from Tobiah kept c to them. 995
Job 36:33 His thunder announces the c storm; 2257S
Ps 19:5 a bridegroom c forth from his pavilion, 3655
37:13 for he knows their day is c. 995
121:8 the LORD will watch over your c 995
Ecc 10:14 No one knows what is c— 2118
SS 3:6 Who is this c up from the desert like 6590
4:2 c up from the washing. 6590
6:6 Your teeth are like a flock of sheep c up 6590
8:5 Who is this c up from the desert leaning 6590
Isa 13:9 See, the day of the LORD is c— 995
14:9 to meet you at your c; 995
19:1 the LORD rides on a swift cloud and is c 995
21:12 The watchman replies, "Morning is c, 910
26:21 the LORD is c out of his dwelling 3655
30:30 and will make them see his arm c down 5738
45:14 c over to you in chains. 6296
47:13 let them save you from what is c 995
63:1 Who is this c from Edom, from Bozrah, 995
66:15 See, the LORD is c with fire, 995
Jer 4:16 'A besieging army is c from a distant land, 995
6:22 an army is c from the land of the north; 995
7:32 So beware, the days are c, 995
9:25 "The days are c," declares the LORD, 995
10:22 The report is c— 995
13:20 up your eyes and see those who are c from 995
16:14 "However, the days are c," 995
19:6 So beware, the days are c, 995
23:5 "The days are c," declares the LORD, 995
23:7 "So then, the days are c," 995
30:3 The days are c,' declares the LORD, 995
31:27 "The days are c," declares the LORD, 995
31:31 "The time is c," declares the LORD, 995
31:38 "The days are c," declares the LORD, 995
33:14 " 'The days are c,' declares the LORD, 995
46:13 the c of Nebuchadnezzar king of Babylon 995
46:20 a gadfly is c against her from the north. 995
46:21 for the day of disaster is c upon them, 995
48:12 But days are c," declares the LORD, 995
49:2 But the days are c," declares the LORD, 995
49:19 "Like a lion c up from Jordan's thickets to 6590
50:41 An army is c from the north; 995
50:44 Like a lion c up from Jordan's thickets to 6590
51:52 "But days are c," declares the LORD, 995
Eze 1:4 and I saw a windstorm c out of the north— 995
7:5 An unheard-of disaster is c. 995
9:2 And I saw six men c from the direction of 995
21:7 'Because of the news that is c. 995
21:7 It is c! It will surely take place, 995
33:3 and he sees the sword c against the land 995
33:6 the sword c and does not blow the trumpet 995
39:8 It is c! It will surely take place, 995
43:2 and I saw the glory of the God of Israel c 995
47:1 and I saw water c out from under 3655
47:1 The water was c down from under 3718
Da 4:13 a holy one, c down from heaven. 10474
4:23 a holy one, c down from heaven and saying, 10474
7:10 c out from before him. 10485
7:13 c with the clouds of heaven. 10085
11:23 After c to an agreement with him, 2489
Hos 9:7 The days of punishment are c, 995
Joel 2:1 for the day of the LORD is c. 995
2:31 the moon to blood before the c of the great 995
Am 7:1 and just as the second crop was c up. 6590
8:11 "The days are c," declares 995
9:13 "The days are c," declares the LORD, 995
Mic 1:3 The LORD is c from his dwelling place; 3655
Hab 2:16 from the LORD's right hand is c around 6015
Zep 1:14 near and c quickly. 4394+4554
Zec 1:21 I asked, "What are these c to do?" 995
2:10 For I am c, and I will live among you," 995
6:1 before me were four chariots c out from 3655
14:1 of the LORD is c when your plunder will 995
Mal 3:2 But who can endure the day of his c? 995
4:1 the day is c; it will burn like a furnace. 995
4:1 that day that is c will set them on fire," 995
Mt 2:11 On c to the house, 2262
3:7 of the Pharisees and Sadducees c to 2262
3:7 Who warned you to flee from the c wrath? 3516
8:28 two demon-possessed men c from 2002
13:54 C to his hometown, 2262
16:28 the Son of Man c in his kingdom." 2262
17:9 As they were c down the mountain, 2849
24:3 and what will be the sign of your c and of 4242
24:27 so will be the c of the Son of Man. 4242
24:30 the Son of Man c on the clouds of the sky, 2262
24:37 so it will be at the c of the Son of Man. 4242
24:39 is how it will be at the c of the Son of Man. 4242
24:43 at what time of night the thief was c, 2262
25:5 The bridegroom was a long time in c, 5988
26:64 the right hand of the Mighty One and c on 2262

Mk 1:10 As Jesus was c up out of the water, 326
6:31 because so many people were c and going 2262
9:9 As they were c down the mountain, 2849
11:10 the c kingdom of our father David!" 2262
13:26 that time men will see the Son of Man c 2262
14:62 the right hand of the Mighty One and c on 2262
Lk 2:38 C up to them at that very moment, 2392
3:7 to the crowds c out to be baptized by him, 1744
3:7 Who warned you to flee from the c wrath? 3516
6:19 because power was c from him 2002
8:4 and people were c to Jesus from town 2164
9:42 Even while the boy was c, 4665
12:39 at what hour the thief was c, 2262
12:45 'My master is taking a long time in c,' 2262
13:7 'For three years now I've been c to look 2262
14:31 with ten thousand men to oppose the one c 2262
17:22 "The time is c when you will long 2262
18:3 that town who kept c to him with the plea, 2262
18:5 that she won't eventually wear me out with her c!' " 2262
19:4 since Jesus was c that way. 1451+3516
19:44 not recognize the time of God's c to you." 2175
21:26 apprehensive of what is c on the world, 2088
21:27 At that time they will see the Son of Man c 2262
Jn 1:9 that gives light to every man was c into 2262
1:29 The next day John saw Jesus c toward him 2262
3:23 and people were constantly c to 4134
4:15 and have to keep c here to draw water." 1451
4:21 a time is c when you will worship 2262
4:23 Yet a time is c and has now come when 2262
4:25 "I know that Messiah" (called Christ) "is c. 2262
5:25 a time is c and has now come when 2262
5:28 for a time is c when all who are 2262
6:5 up and saw a great crowd c toward him, 2262
9:4 Night is c, when no one can work. 2262
10:12 So when he sees the wolf c, 2262
11:20 When Martha heard that Jesus was c, 2262
11:56 Isn't he c to the Feast at all?" 2262
12:15 see, your king is c, 2262
14:28 'I am going away and I am c back to you.' 2262
14:30 for the prince of this world is c. 2262
16:2 a time is c when anyone who kills you 2262
16:25 a time is c when I will no longer use 2262
16:32 "But a time is c, and has come, 2262
17:11 and I am c to you. 2262
17:13 "I am c to you now, 2262
Ac 2:20 the moon to blood before the c of the great 2262
7:52 They even killed those who predicted the c 1803
9:17 to you on the road as you were c here— 2262
13:24 Before the c of Jesus, 1658
13:25 No, but he is c after me, 2262
19:4 the people to believe in the one c after him, 2262
21:11 C over to us, he took Paul's belt, 2262
28:15 brothers there had heard that we were c, NIG
Ro 15:22 hindered from c to you. 2262+3836
1Co 2:6 who are c to nothing. 2934
4:18 as if I were not c to you. 2262
2Co 7:6 comforted us by the c of Titus, 4242
7:7 and not only by his c but also by 4242
8:17 but he is c to you with much enthusiasm 2002
Eph 2:7 in order that in the c ages he might show 2088
Php 2:17 the sacrifice and service c from your faith, AIT
Col 3:6 Because of these, the wrath of God is c. 2262
4:9 He is c with Onesimus, NIG
1Th 1:10 Jesus, who rescues us from the c wrath. 2262
4:15 who are left till the c of the Lord, 4242
5:23 soul and body be kept blameless at the c 4242
2Th 2:1 Concerning the c of our Lord Jesus Christ 4242
2:8 and destroy by the splendor of his c. 4242
2:9 The c of the lawless one will be 4242
1Ti 6:19 as a firm foundation for the c age, 3516
Heb 6:5 of God and the powers of the c age, 3516
8:8 "The time is c, declares the Lord, 2262
10:1 a shadow of the good things that are c— 3516
10:37 "He who is c will come and will not delay. 2262
Jas 1:17 c down from the Father of 2849
5:1 because of the misery that is c upon you. 2088
5:7 then, brothers, until the Lord's c. 4242
5:8 because the Lord's c is near. 4242
1Pe 1:5 by God's power until the c of the salvation NIG
2Pe 1:16 the power and c of our Lord Jesus Christ, 4242
3:4 "Where is this 'c' he promised? 4242
3:12 to the day of God and speed its c. 4242
1Jn 2:18 as you have heard that the antichrist is c, 2262
2:28 and unashamed before him at his c. 4242
4:3 which you have heard is c and even 2262
2Jn 1:7 who do not acknowledge Jesus Christ as c 2262
Jude 1:14 "See, the Lord is c with thousands 2262
Rev 1:7 Look, he is c with the clouds, 2262
3:11 I am c soon. 2262
3:12 which is c down out of heaven 2849
7:2 I saw another angel c up from the east, 326
9:13 a voice c from the horns of the golden altar NIG
10:1 Then I saw another mighty angel c down 2849
11:14 the third woe is c soon. 2262
13:1 And I saw a beast c out of the sea. 326
13:11 I saw another beast, c out of the earth. 326
18:1 After this I saw another angel c down 2849
20:1 And I saw an angel c down out of heaven, 2849
21:2 c down out of heaven from God, 2849
21:10 Jerusalem, c down out of heaven from God. 2849
22:7 "Behold, I am c soon! 2262
22:12 "Behold, I am c soon! 2262
22:20 "Yes, I am c soon." 2262

COMMAND (195) [COMMANDED, COMMANDER, COMMANDER-IN-CHIEF, COMMANDER'S, COMMANDERS, COMMANDING, COMMANDMENT, COMMANDMENTS, COMMANDS, SECOND-IN-COMMAND]

Ex 7:2 You are to say everything I c you, 7422
27:20 "C the Israelites to bring you clear oil 7422
34:11 Obey what I c you today. 7422
38:21 which were recorded at Moses' c by 7023
Lev 6:9 "Give Aaron and his sons this c: 7422
10:1 before the LORD, contrary to his c. 7422
24:2 "C the Israelites to bring you clear oil 7422
Nu 3:39 at the LORD's c by Moses and Aaron 7023
4:37 to the LORD's c through Moses. 7023
4:41 according to the LORD's c. 7023
4:45 to the LORD's c through Moses. 7023
4:49 At the LORD's c through Moses, 7023
5:2 "C the Israelites to send away from 7422
9:18 At the LORD's c the Israelites set out, 7023
9:18 and at his c they encamped. 7023
9:20 at the LORD's c they would encamp, 7023
9:20 and then at his c they would set out. 7023
9:23 At the LORD's c they encamped, 7023
9:23 and at the LORD's c they set out. 7023
9:23 in accordance with his c through Moses. 7023
10:13 at the LORD's c through Moses. 7023
10:14 Nahshon son of Amminadab was in c. 6584+7372
10:18 Elizur son of Shedeur was in c. 6584+7372
10:22 Elishama son of Ammihud was in c. 6584+7372
10:25 Ahiezer son of Ammishaddai was in c. 6584+7372
13:3 So at the LORD's c Moses sent them out 7023
14:41 "Why are you disobeying the LORD's c? 7023
20:24 because both of you rebelled against my c 7023
22:18 to go beyond the c of the LORD my God. 7023
23:20 I have received a c to bless; NIH
24:13 to go beyond the c of the LORD— 7023
27:14 of you disobeyed my c to honor me as holy 7023
27:21 At his c he and the entire community of 7023
27:21 and at his c they will come in." 7023
28:2 "Give this c to the Israelites and say 7422
31:49 the soldiers under our c, 3338
33:2 the LORD's c Moses recorded the stages 7023
33:38 At the LORD's c Aaron the priest went 7023
34:2 "C the Israelites and say to them: 7422
35:2 "C the Israelites to give the Levites towns 7422
36:5 at the LORD's c Moses gave this order to 7023
Dt 1:26 against the c of the LORD your God. 7023
1:43 You rebelled against the LORD's c and 7023
2:37 with the c of the LORD our God, 7422
4:2 to what I c you and do not subtract from it, 7422
8:1 to follow every c I am giving you today, 5184
9:23 against the c of the LORD your God. 7023
11:28 that I c you today by following other gods, 7422
12:11 there you are to bring everything I c you: 7422
12:14 and there observe everything I c you. 7422
12:32 See that you do all I c you; 7422
15:11 Therefore I c you to be openhanded 7422
15:15 That is why I give you this c today. 1821
17:3 contrary to my c has worshiped other gods, 7422
18:18 and he will tell them everything I c him. 7422
19:7 This is why I c you to set aside 7422
19:9 carefully follow all these laws I c you today 7422
24:18 That is why I c you to do this. 7422
24:22 That is why I c you to do this. 7422
27:4 as I c you today, 7422
30:2 according to everything I c you today, 7422
30:16 I c you today to love the LORD your God, 7422
31:23 The LORD gave this c to Joshua son 7422
31:25 he gave this c to the Levites who carried 7422
32:46 so that you may c your children 7422
Jos 1:13 "Remember the c that Moses the servant of 1821
1:18 whatever you may c them, 7422
4:16 "C the priests carrying the ark of 7422
15:13 In accordance with the LORD's c to him, 7023
17:4 according to the LORD's c. 7023
22:9 with the c of the LORD through Moses. 7023
Jdg 9:29 If only this people were under my c! 3338
1Sa 13:13 the c the LORD your God gave you; 5184
13:14 because you have not kept the LORD's c." 7422
15:24 the LORD's c and your instructions. 7023
16:16 Let our lord c his servants here to search 606
18:13 and gave him c over a thousand men, 8569
2Sa 10:10 the men under the c of Abishai his brother 3338
18:2 a third under the c of Joab, 3338
20:7 the mighty warriors went out under the c of 339
1Ki 2:43 to the LORD and obey the c I gave you?" 5184
5:17 At the king's c they removed from 7422
9:4 and do all I c and observe my decrees 7422
11:10 Solomon did not keep the LORD's c. 7422
11:38 If you do whatever I c you and walk 7422
13:21 of the LORD and have not kept the c 5184
16:9 who had c of half his chariots, 8569
18:36 and have done all these things at your c. 1821
2Ki 24:3 to Judah according to the LORD's c, 7023
1Ch 11:6 and so he received the c. 8031
12:9 Obadiah the second in c, Eliab the third, 9108
12:32 with all their relatives under their c; 7023
19:11 the men under the c of Abishai his brother, 3338
21:6 because the king's c was repulsive to him. 1821
21:7 This c was also evil in the sight of God; 1821
22:12 and understanding when he puts you in c 7422
28:21 and all the people will obey your every c." 1821
2Ch 7:13 or c locusts to devour the land or send 7422
7:17 and do all I c, 7422
24:8 At the king's c, 606

2Ch 26:13 Under their c was an army of 307,500 3338
30: 6 At the king's c, couriers went 5184
35:22 not listen to what Neco had said at God's c 7023
Ezr 6:14 according to the c *of* the God of Israel and 10302
Est 1: 8 By the king's c each guest was allowed 2017
1:12 when the attendants delivered the king's c, 1821
1:15 "She has not obeyed the c *of* King Xerxes 4411
3: 3 "Why do you disobey the king's c?" 5184
3:15 Spurred on by the king's c, 1821
8:14 raced out, spurred on by the king's c. 1821
Job 39:27 the eagle soar at your c and build his nest 7023
Ps 71: 3 **give** *the* c to save me, 7422
78:23 Yet *he* **gave** *a* c *to* the skies above 7422
91:11 For *he will* c his angels concerning you 7422
147:15 He sends his c to the earth; 614
Pr 8:29 so the waters would not overstep his c, 7023
13:13 but he who respects a c is rewarded. 5184
Ecc 8: 2 Obey the king's c, I say, 7023
8: 5 Whoever obeys his c will come to no harm, 5184
Isa 5: 6 *I will* c the clouds not to rain on it." 7422
Jer 1: 7 and say whatever *I* c you. 7422
1:17 Stand up and say to them whatever I c you. 7422
7:23 but *I* **gave** them this c: 7422
7:23 Walk in all the ways *I* c you, 7422
7:31 something *I did* not c, 7422
11: 4 'Obey me and do everything *I* c you, 7422
19: 5 something *I did* not c or mention, 7422
26: 2 Tell them everything *I* c you; 7422
35: 6 of Recab **gave** us *this* c: 7422
35:14 not to drink wine and this c has been kept. 1821
35:14 because they obey their forefather's c. 5184
35:16 the c their forefather gave them, 5184
35:18 the c *of* your forefather Jonadab 5184
43: 4 the LORD's c to stay in the land of Judah. 7754
La 1:18 yet I rebelled against his c. 7023
Eze 21:22 to **give** *the* c to slaughter, 7023+7337
38: 7 and **take** c of them. 2118+4200+5464
Da 3:22 The king's c was so urgent and the furnace 10418
3:28 They trusted in him and defied the king's c 10418
4:26 *The* c to leave the stump of the tree 10042
5:29 Then *at* Belshazzar's c, 10042
6:24 *At* the king's c, 10042
Joel 2:11 and mighty are those who obey his c. 1821
Am 6:11 For the LORD *has* **given the** c, 7422
9: 3 there *I will* c the serpent to bite them. 7422
9: 4 there *I will* c the sword to slay them. 7422
9: 9 "For I *will* **give** *the* c, 7422
Na 1:14 The LORD *has* **given a** c concerning you, 7422
Mt 4: 6 " '*He will* c his angels concerning you, *1948*
15: 3 the c of God for the sake of your tradition? *1953*
19: 7 "*did* Moses c that a man give his wife *1948*
Mk 9:25 he said, "I c you, *2199*
10: 3 "What *did* Moses c you?" he replied. *1948*
Lk 4:10 " '*He will* c his angels concerning you *1948*
Jn 10:18 This c I received from my Father." *1953*
12:50 I know that his c leads to eternal life. *1953*
13:34 "A new c I give you: Love one another. *1953*
14:15 "If you love me, you will obey what I c. *1953*
15:12 My c is this: Love each other as I have *1953*
15:14 You are my friends if you do what I c. *1948*
15:17 This *is my* c: Love each other. *1948*
Ac 1: 4 *he* **gave** them this c: *4133*
16:18 "In the name of Jesus Christ *I* c you *4133*
19:13 c you **to come out."** *3991*
25:23 *At the* c of Festus, Paul was brought in. *3027*
Ro 5:14 over those who did not sin by **breaking a** c, *4126*
16:26 through the prophetic writings by the c of *2198*
1Co 7: 6 I say this as a concession, not as a c. *2198*
7:10 To the married *I* **give this** c (not I, *4133*
7:25 I have no c from the Lord, *2198*
14:37 to you is the Lord's c. *1953*
Gal 5:14 The entire law is summed up in a single c: *3364*
1Th 4:16 with a **loud** c, *3026*
2Th 3: 4 and will continue to do the things *we* c. *4133*
3: 6 the Lord Jesus Christ, *we* c you, brothers, *4133*
3:12 Such people *we* c and urge in *4133*
1Ti 1: 1 of Christ Jesus by the c of God our Savior *2198*
1: 3 in Ephesus so that *you may* c certain men *4133*
1: 5 The goal *of* this c is love, *4132*
4:11 C and teach these things. *4133*
6:14 to keep this c without spot or blame until *1953*
6:17 C those who are rich in this present world *4133*
6:18 C them to do good, *NIG*
Tit 1: 3 the preaching entrusted to me by the c *2198*
Heb 11: 3 that the universe was formed *at* God's c, *4839*
2Pe 2:21 on the sacred c that was passed on to them. *1953*
3: 2 past by the holy prophets and the c given *1953*
1Jn 2: 7 not writing you a new c but an old one, *1953*
2: 7 This old c is the message you have heard. *1953*
2: 8 Yet I am writing you a new c; *1953*
3:23 And this is his c: to believe in the name *1953*
4:21 And he has given us this c: *1953*
2Jn 1: 5 a new c but one we have had from *1953*
1: 6 his c is that you walk in love. *1953*
Rev 3:10 you have kept my c to endure patiently, *3364*

COMMANDED (271) [COMMAND]

Ge 2:16 And the LORD God c the man, 7422
3:11 from the tree that *I* c you not to eat from?" 7422
3:17 the tree *about* which *I* c you, 'You must 7422
6:22 Noah did everything just as God c him. 7422
7: 5 And Noah did all that the LORD c him. 7422
7: 9 as God *had* c Noah. 7422
7:16 as God *had* c Noah. 7422
21: 4 Abraham circumcised him, as God c him. 7422
28: 1 for Jacob and blessed him and c him: 7422
Ge 28: 6 and that when he blessed him *he* c him, 7422
45:21 Joseph gave them carts, as Pharaoh had c, 7023
50:12 So Jacob's sons did as *he had* c them: 7422
Ex 4:28 about all the miraculous signs *he had* c him 7422
6:13 and *he* c them to bring the Israelites out 7422
7: 6 and Aaron did just as the LORD c them. 7422
7:10 to Pharaoh and did just as the LORD c. 7422
7:20 and Aaron did just as the LORD *had* c. 7422
12:28 the LORD c Moses and Aaron. 7422
12:50 the LORD *had* c Moses and Aaron. 7422
16:16 This is what the LORD *has* c: 7422
16:23 "This is what the LORD c: 1819
16:24 So they saved it until morning, as Moses c, 7422
16:32 "This is what the LORD *has* c: 7422
16:34 As the LORD c Moses, 7422
17: 1 from place to place as the LORD c. 7023
19: 7 the words the LORD *had* c him to speak. 7422
23:15 without yeast, as *I* c you. 7422
29:35 and his sons everything *I have* c you, 7422
31: 6 to make everything *I have* c you: 7422
31:11 They are to make them just as *I* c you." 7422
32: 8 to turn away from what *I* c them 7422
32:28 The Levites did as Moses c, 1821
34: 4 as the LORD *had* c him; 7422
34:18 eat bread made without yeast, as *I* c you. 7422
34:34 and told the Israelites what *he had* **been** c, 7422
35: 1 "These are the things the LORD *has* c you 7422
35: 4 "This is what the LORD *has* c: 7422
35:10 and make everything the LORD *has* c: 7422
35:29 the LORD through Moses *had* c them 7422
36: 1 to do the work just as the LORD *has* c." 7422
36: 5 the work the LORD c to be done." 7422
38:22 made everything the LORD c Moses; 7422
39: 1 as the LORD c Moses. 7422
39: 5 as the LORD c Moses. 7422
39: 7 as the LORD c Moses. 7422
39:21 as the LORD c Moses. 7422
39:26 as the LORD c Moses. 7422
39:29 as the LORD c Moses. 7422
39:31 as the LORD c Moses. 7422
39:32 as the LORD c Moses. 7422
39:42 as the LORD *had* c Moses. 7422
39:43 as the LORD *had* c. 7422
40:16 as the LORD c him. 7422
40:19 as the LORD c him. 7422
40:21 as the LORD c him. 7422
40:23 as the LORD c him. 7422
40:25 as the LORD c him. 7422
40:27 as the LORD c him. 7422
40:29 as the LORD c him. 7422
40:32 as the LORD c Moses. 7422
Lev 7:36 the LORD c that the Israelites give this 7422
7:38 on Mount Sinai on the day he c 7422
8: 4 Moses did as the LORD c him, 7422
8: 5 "This is what the LORD *has* c to be done." 7422
8: 9 on the front of it, as the LORD c Moses. 7422
8:13 as the LORD c Moses. 7422
8:17 as the LORD c Moses. 7422
8:21 as the LORD c Moses. 7422
8:29 as the LORD c Moses. 7422
8:31 the basket of ordination offerings, as *I* c, 7422
8:34 What has been done today *was* c by 7422
8:35 for that is what *I have* **been** c." 7422
8:36 and his sons did everything the LORD c 7422
9: 5 the things Moses c to the front of the Tent 7422
9: 6 "This is what the LORD *has* c you to do, 7422
9: 7 as the LORD *has* c." 7422
9:10 as the LORD c Moses; 7422
9:21 the LORD as a wave offering, as Moses c. 7422
10:13 for so *I have* **been** c. 7422
10:15 as the LORD *has* c." 7422
10:18 the goat in the sanctuary area, as *I* c." 7422
16:34 And it was done, as the LORD c Moses. 7422
17: 2 'This is what the LORD *has* c: 7422
24:23 The Israelites did as the LORD c Moses. 7422
Nu 1:19 as the LORD c Moses. 7422
1:54 as the LORD c Moses. 7422
2:33 as the LORD c Moses. 7422
2:34 the LORD c Moses; 7422
3:16 as *he* **was** c by the word of the LORD. 7422
3:42 as the LORD c him. 7422
3:51 as he *was* c by the word of the LORD. 7422
4:49 as the LORD c Moses. 7422
8: 3 just as the LORD c Moses. 7422
8:20 the Levites just as the LORD c Moses. 7422
8:22 the Levites just as the LORD c Moses. 7422
9: 5 as the LORD c Moses. 7422
15:36 as the LORD c Moses. 7422
17:11 Moses did just as the LORD c him. 7422
19: 2 of the law that the LORD *has* c: 7422
20: 9 just as *he* c him. 7422
20:27 Moses did as the LORD c: 7422
26: 4 as the LORD c Moses." 7422
27:11 as the LORD c Moses.' " 7422
27:22 Moses did as the LORD c him. 7422
29:40 the Israelites all that the LORD c him. 7422
31: 7 as the LORD c Moses, 7422
31:31 the priest did as the LORD c Moses. 7422
31:41 as the LORD c Moses. 7422
31:47 as the LORD c him, 7422
34:13 Moses c the Israelites: 7422
34:29 These are the men the LORD c to assign 7422
36: 2 the LORD c my lord to give the land as 7422
36:10 as the LORD c Moses. 7422
Dt 1: 3 that the LORD *had* c him concerning them. 7422
1:19 Then, as the LORD our God c us, 7422
1:41 as the LORD our God c us." 7422
Dt 3:18 *I* c you at that time: 7422
3:21 At that time *I* c Joshua: 7422
4: 5 and laws as the LORD my God c me, 7422
4:13 which *he* c you to follow and 7422
5:12 as the LORD your God *has* c you. 7422
5:15 the LORD your God *has* c you to observe 7422
5:16 as the LORD your God *has* c you, 7422
5:32 to do what the LORD your God *has* c you; 7422
5:33 that the LORD your God *has* c you, 7422
6:20 and laws the LORD our God *has* c you?" 7422
6:24 The LORD c us to obey all these decrees 7422
6:25 as *he has* c us, 7422
9:12 from what *I* c them and have made 7422
9:16 from the way that the LORD *had* c you. 7422
10: 5 as the LORD c me, 7422
12:21 as *I have* c you, 7422
13: 5 from the way the LORD your God c you 7422
18:20 in my name anything *I have* not c him 7422
20:17 as the LORD your God *has* c you. 7422
24: 8 You must follow carefully what *I have* c them. 7422
26:13 according to all you c. 5184+7422
26:14 I have done everything *you* c me. 7422
27: 1 Moses and the elders of Israel c the people: 7422
27:11 On the same day Moses c the people: 7422
29: 1 the covenant the LORD c Moses to make 7422
31: 5 must do to them all that *I have* c you. 5184+7422
31:10 Then Moses c them: 7422
31:29 and to turn from the way *I have* c you. 7422
34: 9 and did what the LORD *had* c Moses. 7422
Jos 1: 9 *Have I* not c you? 7422
1:16 "Whatever *you have* c us we will do, 7422
4: 8 So the Israelites did as Joshua c them. 7422
4:10 the LORD *had* c Joshua was done by 7422
4:17 So Joshua c the priests, 7422
6:10 But Joshua *had* c the people, 7422
6:16 Joshua c the people, "Shout! 606
7:11 which *I* c them to keep. 7422
8: 8 Do what the LORD has c. 1821
8:31 as Moses the servant of the LORD *had* c 7422
8:33 the servant of the LORD *had* formerly c 7422
8:35 that Moses *had* c that Joshua did not read to 7422
9:24 LORD your God *had* c his servant Moses 7422
10:40 just as the LORD, the God of Israel, *had* c. 7422
11:12 as Moses the servant of the LORD *had* c. 7422
11:15 As the LORD c his servant Moses, 7422
11:15 so Moses c Joshua, and Joshua did it; 7422
11:15 of all that the LORD c Moses. 7422
11:20 as the LORD *had* c Moses. 7422
14: 2 as the LORD *had* c through Moses. 7422
14: 5 just as the LORD *had* c Moses. 7422
17: 4 "The LORD c Moses to give us 7422
19:50 as the LORD had c. 7023
21: 2 "The LORD c through Moses 7422
21: 3 So, as the LORD had c, 7023
21: 8 as the LORD *had* c through Moses. 7422
22: 2 that Moses the servant of the LORD c, 7422
22: 2 and you have obeyed me in everything *I* c. 7422
23:16 which *he* c you, 7422
Jdg 13:14 She must do everything *I have* c her." 7422
2Sa 5:25 So David did as the LORD c him, 7422
7: 7 to any of their rulers whom *I* c 7422
18: 5 The king c Joab, Abishai and Ittai, 7422
18:12 In our hearing the king c you and Abishai 7422
21:14 and did everything the king c. 7422
24:19 as the LORD *had* c through Gad. 7422
1Ki 2:31 Then the king c Benaiah, "Do as he says. 606
11:11 which *I* c you, 7422
13: 9 For I *was* c by the word of the LORD: 7422
17: 9 *I have* c a widow in that place 7422
18:40 Elijah c them, "Seize the prophets of Baal. 606
2Ki 7:14 *He* c the drivers, 606
11: 5 *He* c them, saying, "This is what you are 7422
14: 6 of the Law of Moses where the LORD c: 7422
17:13 the entire Law that *I* c your fathers to obey 7422
17:35 a covenant with the Israelites, *he* c them: 7422
18:12 all that Moses the servant of the LORD c. 7422
18:36 because the king had c, 5184
21: 8 to do everything *I* c them and will keep 7422
1Ch 6:49 that Moses the servant of God *had* c. 7422
14:16 So David did as God c him, 7422
15:15 as Moses *had* c in accordance with the word 7422
16:15 the word *he* c, for a thousand generations, 7422
17: 6 to any of their leaders whom *I* c 7422
24:19 as the LORD, the God of Israel, *had* c him. 7422
2Ch 8:13 to the daily requirement for offerings c 5184
8:18 Hiram sent him ships c by his own officers, 3338
14: 4 *He* c Judah to seek the LORD, 606
25: 4 in the Book of Moses, where the LORD c: 7422
29:21 The king c the priests, 606
29:25 this was c by the LORD 5184
33: 8 to do everything *I* c them concerning all 7422
35: 6 doing what the LORD c through Moses." 1821
Ezr 4: 3 as King Cyrus, the king of Persia, c us." 7422
Ne 8: 1 which the LORD *had* c *for* Israel. 7422
8:14 which the LORD *had* c through Moses, 7422
13:22 Then *I* c the Levites to purify themselves 606
Est 1:10 *he* c the seven eunuchs who served him— 606
1:17 'King Xerxes c Queen Vashti to be brought 606
3: 2 for the king *had* c this concerning him. 7422
6:10 "Go at once," the king c Haman. 606
9: 1 the edict c *by* the king was to 1821
9:14 So the king c that this be done. 606
Ps 33: 9 he c, and it stood firm. 7422
78: 5 which *he* c our forefathers 7422
105: 8 the word *he* c, for a thousand generations, 7422
106:34 the peoples as the LORD *had* c them, 606

Ps 148: 5 for he c and they were created. 7422
Isa 13: 3 I *have* c my holy ones; 7422
36:21 because the king had c, 5184
Jer 11: 4 the terms *I* c your forefathers 7422
11: 8 of the covenant *I had* c them to follow but 7422
17:22 as *I* c your forefathers. 7422
26: 8 the people everything the LORD *had* c him 7422
32:23 they did not do what *you* c them to do. 7422
32:35 though *I* never c, 7422
35: 8 Jonadab son of Recab c us. 7422
35:10 have fully obeyed everything our forefather Jonadab c us. 7422
36:26 Instead, the king c Jerahmeel, 7422
38:10 Then the king c Ebed-Melech the Cushite, 7422
47: 7 how can it rest when the LORD *has* c it, 7422
50:21 "Do everything *I have* c you. 7422
Eze 9:11 saying, "I have done as *you* c." 7422
10: 6 When the LORD c the man in linen, 7422
12: 7 So I did as *I* **was** c. 7422
24:18 The next morning I did as *I had* **been** c. 7422
37: 7 So I prophesied as *I* **was** c. 7422
37:10 So I prophesied as *he* c me, 7422
Da 3: 4 "This is what you *are* c to do, O peoples, 10042
3:20 and c some of the strongest soldiers 10042
4: 6 So I c that all the wise men of Babylon 10302+10682
Am 2:12 the Nazirites drink wine and c the prophets 7422
Jnh 2:10 And the LORD c the fish, 606
Zec 1: 6 which *I* c my servants the prophets, 7422
Mt 1:24 he did what the angel of the Lord *had* c him *4705*
8: 4 to the priest and offer the gift Moses c, *4705*
27:10 buy the potter's field, as the Lord c me." *5332*
28:20 to obey everything *I have* c you. *1948*
Mk 1:44 and offer the sacrifices that Moses c *4705*
7:36 Jesus c them not to tell anyone. *1403*
Lk 5:14 and offer the sacrifices that Moses c *4705*
8:29 For Jesus *had* c the evil spirit to come out of *4133*
Jn 8: 5 the Law Moses c us to stone such women. *1948*
12:49 Father who sent me c me what to say *1443+1953*
14:31 that I do exactly what my Father *has* c me. *1948*
18:11 Jesus c Peter, "Put your sword away! *3306*
Ac 4:18 Then they called them in again and c them *4133*
10:33 to everything the Lord *has* c you to tell us." *4705*
10:42 *He* c us to preach to the people and *4133*
13:47 For this is what the Lord *has* c us: *1948*
16:23 and the jailer *was* c to guard them carefully. *4133*
1Co 9:14 the Lord *has* c that those who preach *1411*
Heb 9:20 which God *has* c you **to keep."** *1948*
12:20 because they could not bear what *was* c: *1403*
1Jn 3:23 and to love one another as *he* c us. *1443+1953*
2Jn 1: 4 just as the Father c us. *1953+3284*

COMMANDER (105) [COMMAND]

Ge 21:22 At that time Abimelech and Phicol the c 8569
21:32 the c *of* his forces returned to the land of 8569
26:26 and Phicol the c *of* his forces. 8569
Jos 5:14 "but as c *of* the army of the LORD I have 8569
5:15 The c *of* the LORD's army replied, 8569
Jdg 4: 2 The c *of* his army was Sisera, 8569
4: 7 I will lure Sisera, the c *of* Jabin's army, 8569
11: 6 "Come," they said, "be our c, 7903
11:11 the people made him head and c over them. 7903
1Sa 12: 9 the c *of* the army of Hazor, 8569
14:50 the c *of* Saul's army was Abner son of Ner, 8569
17:18 Take along these ten cheeses to the c 8569
17:55 he said to Abner, c *of* the army, "Abner, 8569
26: 5 the c *of* the army, had lain down. 8569
2Sa 2: 8 Abner son of Ner, the c *of* Saul's army, 8569
10:16 the c *of* Hadadezer's army leading them. 8569
10:18 He also struck down Shobach the c 8569
19:13 from now on you are not the c *of* my army 8569
23:19 He became their c, 8569
1Ki 1:19 the priest and Joab the c *of* the army, 8569
2:32 Abner son of Ner, c *of* Israel's army, 8569
2:32 of Jether, c *of* Judah's army— 8569
4: 4 Benaiah son of Jehoiada—**c in chief;** 2021+6584+7372
11:15 Joab the c *of* the army, 8569
11:21 that Joab the c *of* the army was also dead. 8569
16:16 they proclaimed Omri, the c *of* the army, 8569
2Ki 4:13 on your behalf to the king or the c *of* 8569
5: 1 Now Naaman was c *of* the army of 8569
9: 5 "I have a message for you, c," he said. 8569
9: 5 "For you, c," he replied. 8569
18:17 The king of Assyria sent his **supreme** c, 9580
18:17 his chief officer and his **field** c with 8072
18:19 The **field** c said to them, "Tell Hezekiah: 8072
18:26 and Shebna and Joah said to the **field** c, 8072
18:27 the c replied, "Was it only to your master 8072
18:28 Then the c stood and called out in Hebrew: 8072
18:37 and told him what the **field** c had said. 8072
19: 4 the words of the **field** c, 8072
19: 8 When the **field** c heard that the king 8072
25: 8 Nebuzaradan c *of* the imperial guard, 8042
25:10 under the c *of* the imperial guard, 8042
25:11 Nebuzaradan the c *of* the guard carried 8042
25:12 But the c left behind some of 8042
25:15 The c *of* the imperial guard took away 8042
25:18 The c *of* the guard took 8042
25:20 the c took them all and brought them to 8042
1Ch 11:21 above the Three and became their c, 8569
19:16 the c *of* Hadadezer's army leading them. 8569
19:18 also killed Shophach the c *of* their army. 8569
27: 5 The third army c, for the third month, 8569
27: 8 was the c Shamhuth the Izrahite. 8569
27:34 Joab was the c of the royal army. 8569
2Ch 17:14 Adnah the c, with 300,000 fighting men; 8569
17:15 next, Jehohanan the c, with 280,000; 8569
Ne 7: 2 along with Hananiah the c *of* the citadel, 8569
Pr 6: 7 It has no c, no overseer or ruler, 7903
Isa 20: 1 In the year that the **supreme** c, 9580
36: 2 Then the king of Assyria sent his **field** c 8072
36: 2 When the c stopped at the aqueduct of NIH
36: 4 The **field** c said to them, "Tell Hezekiah, 8072
36:11 Shebna and Joah said to the **field** c, 8072
36:12 the c replied, "Was it only to your master 8072
36:13 Then the c stood and called out in Hebrew, 8072
36:22 and told him what the **field** c had said. 8072
37: 4 the words of the **field** c, 8072
37: 8 When the **field** c heard that the king 8072
55: 4 a leader and c *of* the peoples. 7422
Jer 39: 9 Nebuzaradan c *of* the imperial guard carried into exile 8042
39:10 the c *of* the guard left behind in the land 8042
39:11 about Jeremiah through Nebuzaradan c *of* 8042
39:13 So Nebuzaradan the c *of* the guard, 8042
40: 1 from the LORD after Nebuzaradan c *of* 8042
40: 2 When the c *of* the guard found Jeremiah, 8042
40: 5 the c gave him provisions and a present 8042
41:10 over whom Nebuzaradan c *of* 8042
43: 6 the king's daughters whom Nebuzaradan c 8042
51:27 Appoint a c against her; 3261
52:12 Nebuzaradan c *of* the imperial guard, 8042
52:14 The whole Babylonian army under the c *of* 8042
52:15 the c *of* the guard carried into exile some 8042
52:19 The c *of* the imperial guard took away 8042
52:24 The c *of* the guard took 8042
52:26 the c took them all and brought them to 8042
52:30 into exile by Nebuzaradan the c *of* 8042
Da 2:14 When Arioch, the c *of* the king's guard, 10647
11:18 but a c will put an end to his insolence 7903
Jn 18:12 Then the detachment of soldiers with its c *5941*
Ac 21:31 news reached the c of the Roman troops *5941*
21:32 When the rioters saw the c and his soldiers, *5941*
21:33 The c came up and arrested him *5941*
21:34 and since **the** c could not get at the truth *899S*
21:37 he asked the c, *5941*
22:24 the c ordered Paul to be taken into *5941*
22:26 he went to the c and reported it. *5941*
22:27 The c went to Paul and asked, "Tell me, *5941*
22:28 Then the c said, *5941*
22:29 The c himself was alarmed *5941*
22:30 since the c wanted to find out *NIG*
23:10 so violent that the c was afraid Paul would *5941*
23:15 the c to bring him before you on the pretext *5941*
23:17 "Take this young man to the c; *5941*
23:18 So he took him to the c. *5941*
23:19 The c took the young man by the hand, *5941*
23:22 The c dismissed the young man *5941*
24:22 "When Lysias the c comes," he said, *5941*

COMMANDER'S (2) [COMMAND]

Jdg 5:14 from Zebulun those who bear a c staff. 6221
Ac 21:40 Having received **the** c permission, *899S*

COMMANDER-IN-CHIEF (1) [COMMAND]

1Ch 11: 6 "Whoever leads the attack on the Jebusites will become c." 2256+8031+8569

COMMANDERS (88) [COMMAND]

Nu 31:14 the c *of* thousands and commanders 8569
31:14 the commanders of thousands and c 8569
31:48 the c *of* thousands and commanders 8569
31:48 the commanders of thousands and c 8569
31:52 from the c *of* thousands and commanders 8569
31:52 of thousands and c *of* hundreds that Moses 8569
31:54 from the c *of* thousands and commanders 8569
31:54 from the commanders of thousands and c NIH
Dt 1:15 as c *of* thousands, *of* hundreds, 8569
20: 9 they shall appoint c over it. 7372+8569
Jos 10:24 to the army c who had come with him, 7903
1Sa 8:12 Some he will assign to be c *of* thousands 8569
8:12 to be commanders of thousands and c 8569
18:30 The Philistine c continued to go out 8569
22: 7 of you c *of* thousands and commanders 8569
22: 7 of you commanders of thousands and c 8569
29: 3 The c *of* the Philistines asked, 8569
29: 4 Philistine c were angry with him and said, 8569
29: 9 nevertheless, the Philistine c have said, 8569
2Sa 18: 1 over them c *of* thousands and commanders 8569
18: 1 over them commanders of thousands and c 8569
18: 5 concerning Absalom to each of the c. 8569
19: 6 the c and their men mean nothing to you. 8569
24: 2 king said to Joab and the army c with him, 8569
24: 4 however, overruled Joab and the army c; 8569
1Ki 1:25 the c *of* the army and Abiathar the priest. 8569
2: 5 what he did to the two c *of* Israel's armies, 8569
9:22 and the c *of* his chariots and charioteers. 8569
14:27 to replace them and assigned these to the c 8569
15:20 with King Asa and sent the c *of* his forces 8569
20:14 of the provincial c will do it.' " 8569
20:15 the young officers of the provincial c, 8569
20:17 of the provincial c went out first. 8569
20:19 of the provincial c marched out of the city 8569
22:31 the king of Aram had ordered his thirty-two chariot c, 8569
22:32 When the chariot c saw Jehoshaphat, 8569
22:33 the chariot c saw that he was not the king 8569
2Ki 8:21 and his chariot c, but he rose up and broke 8569
11: 4 In the seventh year Jehoiada sent for the c 8569
11: 9 The c *of* units of a hundred did just 8569
2Ki 11:10 Then he gave the c the spears and shields 8569
11:15 Jehoiada the priest ordered the c *of* units of 8569
11:19 He took with him the c *of* hundreds, 8569
1Ch 12:14 These Gadites were army c; 8031
12:21 and they were c in his army. 8569
13: 1 the c *of* thousands and commanders 8569
13: 1 the commanders of thousands and c NIH
15:25 So David and the elders of Israel and the c 8569
21: 2 David said to Joab and the c *of* the troops, 8569
25: 1 David, together with the c *of* the army, 8569
26:26 of families who were the c *of* thousands 8569
26:26 the commanders of thousands and c NIH
26:26 and by the other army c. 8569
27: 1 heads of families, c *of* thousands 8569
27: 1 commanders of thousands and c NIH
28: 1 over the tribes, the c *of* the divisions in 8569
28: 1 the service of the king, the c *of* thousands 8569
28: 1 the commanders of thousands and c 8569
29: 6 the c *of* thousands and commanders 8569
29: 6 the commanders of thousands and c NIH
2Ch 1: 2 to the c *of* thousands and commanders 8569
1: 2 and c of hundreds, to the judges and to all NIH
8: 9 they were his fighting men, c 8569
8: 9 and c *of* his chariots and charioteers. 8569
11:11 He strengthened their defenses and put c 5592
12:10 to replace them and assigned these to the c 8569
16: 4 with King Asa and sent the c *of* his forces 8569
17:14 From Judah, c *of* units of 1,000: 8569
18:30 the king of Aram had ordered his chariot c, 8569
18:31 When the chariot c saw Jehoshaphat, 8569
18:32 for when the chariot c saw that he was not 8569
21: 9 surrounded him and his chariot c, 8569
23: 1 He made a covenant with the c *of* units of 8569
23: 9 the c *of* units of a hundred the spears and 8569
23:14 Jehoiada the priest sent out the c *of* units 8569
23:20 He took with him the c *of* hundreds, 8569
25: 5 to c *of* thousands and commanders 8569
25: 5 to commanders of thousands and c 8569
33:11 against them the army c of the king 8569
33:14 He stationed military c in all 8569
Job 39:25 the shout of c and the battle cry. 8569
Isa 10: 8 'Are not my c all kings?' he says. 8569
31: 9 of the battle standard their c will panic," 8569
Eze 23: 6 and c, all of them handsome young men, 6036
23:12 governors and c, warriors in full dress, 6036
23:23 all of them governors and c, 6036
Da 11: 5 of his c will become even stronger than he 8569
Mk 6:21 *for* his high officials and **military** c and *5941*

COMMANDING (7) [COMMAND]

Dt 30:11 Now what I *am* c you today is 7422
Ezr 4: 8 Rehum the c **officer** and Shimshai 10116+10302
4: 9 Rehum the c **officer** and Shimshai 10116+10302
4:17 To Rehum the c **officer**, 10116+10302
Ac 23: 3 yet *you* yourself violate the law by c that I *3027*
2Co 8: 8 *I am* not c you, *2198+2848+3306*
2Ti 2: 4 he wants to please his c **officer.** *5133*

COMMANDMENT (15) [COMMAND]

Jos 22: 5 the c and the law that Moses the servant of 5184
Mt 22:36 which is the greatest c in the Law?" *1953*
22:38 This is the first and greatest c. *1953*
Mk 12:31 There is no c greater than these." *1953*
Lk 23:56 on the Sabbath in obedience to the c. *1953*
Ro 7: 8 seizing the opportunity afforded by the c, *1953*
7: 9 the c came, sin sprang to life and I died. *1953*
7:10 I found that the very c that was intended *1953*
7:11 seizing the opportunity afforded by the c, *1953*
7:11 and through **the** c put me to death. *899S*
7:12 So then, the law is holy, and the c is holy, *1953*
7:13 the c sin might become utterly sinful. *1953*
13: 9 and whatever other c there may be, *1953*
Eph 6: 2 which is the first c with a promise— *1953*
Heb 9:19 When Moses had proclaimed every c of *1953*

COMMANDMENTS (20) [COMMAND]

Ex 20: 6 of those who love me and keep my c. 5184
34:28 of the covenant—the Ten C. 1821
Dt 4:13 the Ten C, which he commanded you 1821
5:10 of those who love me and keep my c. 5184
5:22 These are the c the LORD proclaimed in 1821
6: 6 These c that I give you today are to be 1821
9:10 the c the LORD proclaimed to you on 1821
10: 4 the Ten C he had proclaimed to you on 1821
Ecc 12:13 Fear God and keep his c, 5184
Mt 5:19 the least *of* these c and teaches others to do *1953*
19:17 If you want to enter life, obey the c." *1953*
22:40 and the Prophets hang on these two c." *1953*
Mk 10:19 You know the c: *1953*
12:28 he asked him, "Of all the c, *1953*
Lk 1: 6 the Lord's c and regulations blamelessly. *1953*
18:20 You know the c: *1953*
Ro 13: 9 The c, "Do not commit adultery," *NIG*
Eph 2:15 by abolishing in his flesh the law *with* its c *1953*
Rev 12:17 those who obey God's c and hold to *1953*
14:12 on the part of the saints who obey God's c *1953*

COMMANDS (183) [COMMAND]

Ge 26: 5 my c, my decrees and my laws." 5184
Ex 8:27 as *he* c us." 606
15:26 to his c and keep all his decrees, 5184
16:28 "How long will you refuse to keep my c 5184
18:23 If you do this and God so c, 7422
24:12 and c I have written for their instruction." 5184

Ex 25:22 I will meet with you and give you all *my* **c** 7422
34:32 **gave** them all *the* **c** 7422
Lev 4: 2 in any of the LORD's **c**— 5184
4:13 in any of the LORD's **c**, 5184
4:22 and does what is forbidden in any of the **c** 5184
4:27 in any of the LORD's **c**, 5184
5:17 in any of the LORD's **c**, 5184
22:31 "Keep my **c** and follow them. 5184
26: 3 and are careful to obey my **c**, 5184
26:14 not listen to me and carry out all these **c**, 5184
26:15 and fail to carry out all my **c** and 5184
27:34 These are the **c** the LORD gave Moses 5184
Nu 9: 8 "Wait until I find out what the LORD **c** 7422
15:22 of these **c** the LORD gave Moses— 5184
15:23 any of the LORD's **c** to you through him, 7422
15:31 and broken his **c**, that person must surely 5184
15:39 and so you will remember all the **c** *of* 5184
15:40 Then you will remember to obey all my **c** 5184
30: 1 "This is what the LORD **c**: 7422
32:25 "We your servants will do as our lord **c**. 7422
36: 6 the LORD **c** for Zelophehad's daughters: 7422
36:13 the **c** and regulations the LORD gave 5184
Dt 4: 2 but keep the **c** *of* the LORD your God 5184
4:40 Keep his decrees and **c**, 5184
5:29 to fear me and keep all my **c** always, 5184
5:31 with me so that I may give you all the **c**, 5184
6: 1 These are the **c**, decrees and laws 5184
6: 2 as you live by keeping all his decrees and **c** 5184
6:17 to keep the **c** *of* the LORD your God and 5184
7: 9 of those who love him and keep his **c**. 5184
7:11 Therefore, take care to follow the **c**, 5184
8: 2 whether or not you would keep his **c**. 5184
8: 6 Observe the **c** *of* the LORD your God, 5184
8:11 failing to observe his **c**, 5184
10:13 and to observe the LORD's **c** and decrees 5184
11: 1 his decrees, his laws and his **c** always. 5184
11: 8 therefore all the **c** I am giving you today, 5184
11:13 the **c** I am giving you today— 5184
11:22 If you carefully observe all these **c** I am giving you 5184
11:27 if you obey the **c** *of* the LORD your God 5184
11:28 the **c** *of* the LORD your God and turn 5184
13: 4 Keep his **c** and obey him; 5184
13:18 keeping all his **c** that I am giving you today 5184
15: 5 to follow all these **c** I am giving you today. 5184
26:13 from your **c** nor have I forgotten any 5184
26:16 The LORD your God **c** you this day 7422
26:17 that you will keep his decrees, **c** and laws, 5184
26:18 and that you are to keep all his **c**. 5184
27: 1 "Keep all these **c** that I give you today. 5184
27:10 the LORD your God and follow his **c** 5184
28: 1 carefully follow all his **c** I give you today, 5184
28: 9 if you keep the **c** *of* the LORD your God 5184
28:13 to the **c** *of* the LORD your God 5184
28:14 from any of the **c** I give you today, 1821
28:15 and do not carefully follow all his **c** 5184
28:45 and observe the **c** and decrees he gave you. 5184
30: 8 and follow all his **c** I am giving you today. 5184
30:10 and keep his **c** and decrees that are written 5184
30:16 to walk in his ways, and to keep his **c**, 5184
Jos 22: 5 to walk in all his ways, to obey his **c**, 5184
Jdg 2:17 the way of obedience to the LORD's **c**. 5184
3: 4 see whether they would obey the LORD's **c**, 5184
4: 6 "The LORD, the God of Israel, **c** you: 7422
1Sa 12:14 not rebel against his **c**, and if both you and 7023
12:15 and if you rebel against his **c**, 7023
2Sa 9:11 the king **c** his servant to do." 7422
1Ki 2: 3 and keep his decrees and **c**, 5184
3:14 in my ways and obey my statutes and **c** 5184
6:12 carry out my regulations and keep all my **c** 5184
8:58 to walk in all his ways and to keep the **c**, 5184
8:61 to live by his decrees and obey his **c**, 5184
9: 6 the **c** and decrees I have given you 5184
11:34 whom I chose and who observed my **c** 5184
11:38 in my eyes by keeping my statutes and **c**, 5184
14: 8 who kept my **c** and followed me 5184
15: 5 not failed to keep any of the LORD's **c** all 7422
18:18 You have abandoned the LORD's **c** 5184
20:24 the kings from their **c** and replace them 5226
2Ki 17:13 Observe my **c** and decrees, 5184
17:16 the **c** *of* the LORD their God and made 5184
17:19 not keep the **c** *of* the LORD their God. 5184
17:34 and **c** that the LORD gave the descendants 5184
17:37 the laws and **c** he wrote for you. 5184
18: 6 he kept the **c** the LORD had given Moses. 5184
18:12 They neither listened to the **c** NIH
23: 3 to follow the LORD and keep his **c**, 5184
1Ch 28: 7 if he is unswerving in carrying out my **c** 5184
28: 8 to follow all the **c** *of* the LORD your God, 5184
29:19 the wholehearted devotion to keep your **c**, 5184
2Ch 7:19 the decrees and **c** I have given you 5184
8:15 not deviate from the king's **c** to the priests 5184
14: 4 and to obey his laws and **c**. 5184
17: 4 and followed his **c** rather than the practices 5184
19:10 **c**, decrees or ordinances— 5184
24:20 'Why do you disobey the LORD's **c**? 5184
31:21 and in obedience to the law and the **c**, 5184
34:31 to follow the LORD and keep his **c**, 5184
Ezr 7:11 concerning the **c** and decrees of the LORD 5184
9:10 For we have disregarded the **c** 5184
9:14 Shall we again break your **c** and intermarry 5184
10: 3 and of those who fear the **c** *of* our God. 5184
Ne 1: 5 with those who love him and obey his **c**, 5184
1: 7 We have not obeyed the **c**, 5184
1: 9 but if you return to me and obey my **c**, 5184
9:13 and decrees and **c** that are good. 5184
9:14 and gave them **c**, 5184
Ne 9:16 and did not obey your **c**. 5184
9:29 and disobeyed your **c**. 5184
9:34 to your **c** or the warnings you gave them. 5184
10:29 of God and to obey carefully all the **c**, 5184
10:32 the **c** to give a third of a shekel each year 5184
12:45 to the **c** *of* David and his son Solomon. 5184
Job 23:12 I have not departed from the **c** *of* his lips; 5184
36:10 to correction and **c** them to repent 606
36:32 with lightning and **c** it to strike its mark. 7422
37:12 the whole earth to do whatever *he* **c** them. 7422
Ps 19: 8 The **c** *of* the LORD are radiant, 5184
78: 7 not forget his deeds but would keep his **c**. 5184
89:31 and fail to keep my **c**, 5184
112: 1 who finds great delight in his **c**. 5184
119: 6 be put to shame when I consider all your **c**. 5184
119:10 do not let me stray from your **c**. 5184
119:19 do not hide your **c** from me. 5184
119:21 who are cursed and who stray from your **c**. 5184
119:32 I run in the path of your **c**, 5184
119:35 Direct me in the path of your **c**, 5184
119:47 for I delight in your **c** because I love them. 5184
119:48 I lift up my hands to your **c**, which I love, 5184
119:60 I will hasten and not delay to obey your **c**. 5184
119:66 for I believe in your **c**. 5184
119:73 give me understanding to learn your **c**. 5184
119:86 All your **c** are trustworthy; 5184
119:96 but your **c** are boundless. 5184
119:98 Your **c** make me wiser than my enemies, 5184
119:115 that I may keep the **c** *of* my God! 5184
119:127 Because I love your **c** more than gold, 5184
119:131 longing for your **c**. 5184
119:143 but your **c** are my delight. 5184
119:151 O LORD, and all your **c** are true. 5184
119:166 O LORD, and I follow your **c**. 5184
119:172 for all your **c** are righteous. 5184
119:176 for I have not forgotten your **c**. 5184
Pr 2: 1 if you accept my words and store up my **c** 5184
3: 1 but keep my **c** in your heart, 5184
4: 4 keep my **c** and you will live. 5184
6:20 keep your father's **c** and do 5184
6:23 For these **c** are a lamp, 5184
7: 1 keep my words and store up my **c** 5184
7: 2 Keep my **c** and you will live; 5184
10: 8 The wise in heart accept **c**, 5184
Isa 48:18 If only you had paid attention to my **c**, 5184
58: 2 and has not forsaken the **c** *of* its God. 5477
Jer 7:22 not *just* **give** them **c** about burnt offerings 7422
22: 4 For if you are careful to carry out these **c**, 1821
22: 5 But if you do not obey these **c**, 1821
Da 9: 4 with all who love him and obey his **c**, 5184
9: 5 we have turned away from your **c** and laws. 5184
Zep 2: 3 you who do what he **c**. 5477
Mt 5:19 and teaches these **c** will be called great in NIG
Mk 7: 8 of the **c** of God and are holding on to 1953
7: 9 "You have a fine way of setting aside the **c** 1953
Lk 8:25 *He* **c** even the winds and the water, 2199
Jn 14:21 Whoever has my **c** and obeys them, 1953
15:10 If you obey my **c**, you will remain in my love, 1953
15:10 as I have obeyed my Father's **c** and remain 1953
Ac 17:30 now *he* **c** all people everywhere to repent. 4133
1Co 7:19 Keeping God's **c** is what counts. 1953
Col 2:22 they are based on human **c** and teachings. 1945
Tit 1:14 or *to* the **c** of those who reject the truth. 1953
1Jn 2: 3 to know him if we obey his **c**. 1953
2: 4 but does not do what he **c** is a liar, 1953
3:22 we obey his **c** and do what pleases him. 1953
3:24 Those who obey his **c** live in him, 1953
5: 2 by loving God and carrying out his **c**. 1953
5: 3 This is love for God: to obey his **c**. 1953
5: 3 And his **c** are not burdensome, 1953
2Jn 1: 6 that we walk in obedience to his **c**. 1953

COMMEMORATE (4) [COMMEMORATED]

Ex 12:14 "This is a day you are to **c**; 2355
13: 3 Then Moses said to the people, "**C** this day, 2349
Jdg 11:40 to **c** the daughter of Jephthah the Gileadite. 9480
2Ch 35:25 and women singers **c** Josiah in the laments. 606

COMMEMORATED (1) [COMMEMORATE]

Lev 23:24 a sacred assembly **c** *with* trumpet blasts. 2355

COMMEND (10) [COMMENDABLE, COMMENDED, COMMENDS]

Ps 145: 4 One generation *will* **c** your works 8655
Ecc 8:15 So I **c** the enjoyment of life, 8655
Ro 13: 3 do what is right and he *will* **c** *you.* 2047+2400
16: 1 *I* **c** to you our sister Phoebe, 5319
2Co 3: 1 Are we beginning *to* **c** ourselves again? 5319
4: 2 the truth plainly *we* **c** ourselves 5319
5:12 not *trying to* **c** ourselves to you again, 5319
6: 4 of God *we* **c** ourselves in every way: 5319
10:12 with some who **c** themselves. 5319
1Pe 2:14 and to **c** those who do right. 2047

COMMENDABLE (2) [COMMEND]

1Pe 2:19 For it is **c** if a man bears up under the pain 5921
2:20 this is **c** before God. 5921

COMMENDED (9) [COMMEND]

Ne 11: 2 The people **c** all the men who volunteered 1385
Job 29:11 and those who saw me **c** me, 6386
Lk 16: 8 "The master **c** the dishonest manager 2046
Ac 15:40 **c** by the brothers to the grace of the Lord. 4140
2Co 12:11 I ought *to have been* **c** by you, 5319
Heb 11: 2 This is what the ancients *were* **c** for. 3455
11: 4 By faith *he was* **c** as a righteous man, 3455
11: 5 *he was* **c** as one who pleased God. 3455
11:39 These *were* all **c** for their faith, 3455

COMMENDS (3) [COMMEND]

Pr 15: 2 The tongue of the wise **c** knowledge, 3512
2Co 10:18 not the one who **c** himself who is approved, 5319
10:18 but the one whom the Lord **c**. 5319

COMMISSION (5) [COMMISSIONED, COMMISSIONERS]

Nu 27:19 and the entire assembly and **c** him 7422
Dt 3:28 But **c** Joshua, and encourage 7422
31:14 where *I will* **c** him." 7422
Ac 26:12 with the authority and **c** of the chief priests. 2207
Col 1:25 by the **c** God gave me to present to you 3873

COMMISSIONED (1) [COMMISSION]

Nu 27:23 Then he laid his hands on him and **c** him, 7422

COMMISSIONERS (2) [COMMISSION]

Ge 41:34 Let Pharaoh appoint **c** over the land to take 7224
Est 2: 3 Let the king appoint **c** in every province 7224

COMMIT (56) [COMMITS, COMMITTED, COMMITTING]

Ex 20:14 *"You shall* not **c adultery.** 5537
Dt 5:18 *"You shall* not **c adultery.** 5537
1Sa 7: 3 the Ashtoreths and **c** yourselves to the LORD 3922
1Ki 14:16 and *has* **caused** Israel **to c."** 2627
15:26 his sin, which *he had* **caused** Israel **to c.** 2627
15:30 and *had* **caused** Israel **to c,** 2627
15:34 his sin, which *he had* **caused** Israel **to c.** 2627
16:13 and *had* **caused** Israel **to c,** 2627
16:19 and *had* **caused** Israel **to c,** 2627
16:26 his sin, which *he had* **caused** Israel **to c,** 2627
16:31 not only considered it trivial *to* **c** the sins of Jeroboam 928+2143
2Ki 3: 3 which *he had* **caused** Israel **to c;** 2627
10:29 which *he had* **caused** Israel **to c**— 2627
10:31 which *he had* **caused** Israel **to c.** 2627
13: 2 which *he had* **caused** Israel **to c,** 2627
13: 6 which *he had* **caused** Israel **to c;** 2627
13:11 which *he had* **caused** Israel **to c;** 2627
14:24 which *he had* **caused** Israel **to c.** 2627
15: 9 which *he had* **caused** Israel **to c.** 2627
15:18 which *he had* **caused** Israel **to c.** 2627
15:24 which *he had* **caused** Israel **to c.** 2627
15:28 which *he had* **caused** Israel **to c.** 2627
17:21 the LORD and **caused** them **to c** 2627
21:16 the sin that *he had* **caused** Judah **to c,** 2627
Ezr 9:14 the **peoples** *who* **c** such detestable practices? AIT
Ne 6:13 to intimidate me so that *I would* **c a sin** 2627
Ps 31: 5 Into your hands *I* **c** my spirit; 7212
37: 5 **C** your way to the LORD; 1670
Pr 16: 3 **C** to the LORD whatever you do, 1670
Jer 7: 9 **c adultery** and perjury, 5537
23:14 They **c adultery** and live a lie. 5537
Eze 16:38 to the punishment of *women who* **c adultery** 5537
16:51 Samaria *did* not **c** half the sins you did. 2627
18: 7 *He does* not **c robbery** but gives his food to the hungry 1608+1611
18:16 *He does* not **c robbery** but gives his food to the hungry 1608+1611
22: 9 at the mountain shrines and **c** lewd acts. 6913
22:29 practice extortion and **c robbery;** 1608+1610
23:45 to the punishment of *women who* **c adultery** 5537
Hos 4:14 when *they* **c adultery,** because 5537
4:15 "Though you **c adultery,** O Israel, 2388
Mt 5:27 *'Do* not **c adultery.'** 3658
19:18 " 'Do not murder, *do* not **c adultery,** 3658
Mk 10:19 'Do not murder, *do* not **c adultery,** 3658
Lk 18:20 *'Do* not **c adultery,** do not murder, 3658
23:46 "Father, into your hands *I* **c** my spirit." 4192
Ac 20:32 "Now *I* **c** you to God and to the word 4192
Ro 2:22 that people *should* not **c adultery,** 3658
2:22 *do you* **c adultery?** 3658
13: 9 The commandments, *"Do* not **c adultery,"** 3658
1Co 10: 8 not **c sexual immorality,** 4519
Jas 2:11 For he who said, *"Do* not **c adultery,"** 3658
2:11 not **c adultery** but do commit murder, 3658
2:11 not commit adultery but *do* **c murder,** 5839
1Pe 4:19 to God's will *should* **c** themselves 4192
1Jn 5:16 If anyone sees his brother **c a sin** that does not lead to death, 279+281
Rev 2:22 and I will make those who **c adultery** 3658

COMMITS (20) [COMMIT]

Lev 5:15 "When a person **c a violation** 5085+5086
6: 3 if he **c** any such **sin** that people may do— 2627
20:10 " 'If a man **c adultery** 5537
Ps 10:14 The victim **c** *himself* to you; 6440
36: 4 *he* **c himself** to a sinful course and does 3656
Pr 6:32 But *a man who* **c adultery** lacks judgment; 5537
29:22 and a hot-tempered one **c** many sins. NIH
Ecc 8:12 Although a wicked man **c** a hundred crimes 6913
Eze 18:12 *He* **c robbery.** 1608+1611
18:14 a son who sees all the sins his father **c**, and 6913
18:24 man turns from his righteousness and **c** sin 6913

Eze 18:26 turns from his righteousness and **c** sin, 6913
22:11 In you one man **c** a detestable offense 6913
Mt 5:32 the divorced woman **c adultery.** *3656*
19: 9 and marries another woman **c adultery."** *3656*
Mk 10:11 and marries another woman **c adultery** *3656*
10:12 and marries another man, *she* **c adultery."** *3656*
Lk 16:18 and marries another woman **c adultery,** *3658*
16:18 a divorced woman **c adultery.** *3658*
1Co 6:18 All other sins a man **c** are outside his body, *4472*

COMMITTED (89) [COMMIT]

Ge 31:36 "What **sin** *have* I *c* that you hunt me down? AIT
50:17 and the wrongs *they* **c** *in treating* you 1694
Ex 32:30 "You *have* **c** a great **sin.** 2627+2631
32:31 a great **sin** these people *have* **c**! 2627+2631
Lev 4: 3 as a sin offering for the sin *he has* **c.** 2627
4:14 When they become aware of the sin *they* **c,** 2627
4:23 When he is made aware of the sin *he* **c,** 2627
4:28 When he is made aware of the sin *he* **c,** 2627
4:28 as his offering for the sin *he* **c** a female goat 2627
4:35 for him for the sin *he has* **c,** 2627
5: 6 as a penalty for the sin *he has* **c,** 2627
5:10 for him for the sin *he has* **c,** 2627
5:13 for him for any of these sins *he has* **c,** 2627
5:18 **wrong** *he has* **c unintentionally,** 8704+8705
19:22 before the LORD for the sin *he has* **c,** 2627
Nu 5: 7 and must confess the sin *he has* **c.** 6913
12:11 against us the sin *we have* so foolishly **c.** 2627
Dt 9:18 because of all the sin *you had* **c,** 2627
19:15 any crime or offense *he may have* **c.** 2627+2628
22:26 she has **c** no sin deserving death. NIH
Jdg 20: 6 because *they* **c** this lewd 6913
20:12 "What about this awful crime that **was c** 2118
1Sa 14:38 let us find out what sin *has been* **c** today. 2118
1Ki 8:50 the offenses *they have* **c** against you, 7321
8:61 be **fully c** to the LORD our God, 8969
14:16 up because of the sins Jeroboam *has* **c** 2627
14:22 By the sins *they* **c** they stirred 2627
15: 3 *He* **c** all the sins his father had done 928+2143
15:14 Asa's heart was **fully c** to 8969
15:30 because of the sins Jeroboam *had* **c** 2627
16:13 and his son Elah *had* **c** and had caused Israel 2627
16:19 because of the sins *he had* **c,** 2627
16:19 ways of Jeroboam and in the sin *he had* **c** 6913
2Ki 21:11 of Judah *has* **c** these detestable sins. 6913
21:17 and all he did, including the sin *he* **c,** 2627
1Ch 16: 7 That day David first **c** to Asaph 5989
2Ch 15:17 Asa's heart was **fully c** [to 8969
16: 9 to strengthen those whose hearts are **fully c** 8969
34:16 that *has* **been c** to them. 5989
Ne 1: 6 *have* **c** against you. 2627
9:18 or when *they* **c** awful blasphemies. 6913
9:26 *they* **c** awful blasphemies. 6913
Job 13:23 How many wrongs and sins have I **c?** 4200
Ps 51: T David *had* **c adultery with** Bathsheba. 448+995
Isa 42:19 Who is blind like the *one* **c** to me, 8966
Jer 2:13 "My people *have* **c** two sins: 6913
3: 6 and *has* **c adultery** there. 2388
3: 8 she also went out and **c adultery.** 2388
3: 9 and **c adultery** with stone and wood. 5537
5: 7 yet *they* **c adultery** and thronged to 5537
11:20 for to you *I have* **c** my cause. 1655
16:10 What sin *have we* **c** against 2627
20:12 for to you *I have* **c** my cause. 1655
29:23 *they have* **c adultery** 5537
33: 8 from all the sin *they have* **c** against me 2627
37:18 "What **crime** *have I* **c** against you 2627
41:11 the crimes Ishmael son of Nethaniah *had* **c,** 6913
44: 9 the wickedness **c** by your fathers and by 6913
44: 9 the wickedness **c** by you and your wives in NIH
Eze 18:21 the sins *he has* **c** and keeps all my decrees 6913
18:22 of the offenses *he has* **c** will be remembered 6913
18:24 of and because of the sins *he has* **c,** 2627
18:26 because of the sin *he has* **c** he will die. 6913
18:27 from the wickedness *he has* **c** 6913
18:28 the offenses *he has* **c** and turns away 6913
18:31 of all the offenses *you have* **c,** 7321
23:37 for *they have* **c adultery** and blood is 5537
23:37 *They* **c adultery** with their idols; 5537
33:16 of the sins *he has* **c** will be remembered 2627
Mal 2:11 A detestable thing *has* **been c** in Israel and 6913
Mt 5:28 who looks at a woman lustfully *has* already
c adultery with her in his heart. *3658*
11:27 "All things *have been* **c** to me *4140*
27:23 What crime *has he* **c?"** *4472*
Mk 15: 7 with the insurrectionists who *had* **c** murder *4472*
15:14 What crime *has he* **c?"** *4472*
Lk 10:22 "All things *have been* **c** to me *4140*
23:22 What crime *has* this man **c?** *4472*
Ac 14:23 with prayer and fasting, **c** them to the Lord, *4192*
14:26 where they had been **c** to the grace of God *4140*
Ro 1:27 Men **c** indecent acts with other men, *2981*
3:25 the sins **c beforehand** unpunished— *4588*
1Co 9:17 I am simply discharging the trust **c** to *me.* *4409*
2Co 5:19 *he has* **c** to us the message of reconciliation. *5502*
Heb 9: 7 **sins** the people had **c in ignorance.** *52*
9:15 as a ransom to set them free from the sins **c** *NIG*
1Pe 2:22 "He **c** no sin, and no deceit was found *4472*
Rev 17: 2 the earth **c adultery** and the inhabitants of *4519*
18: 3 The kings of the earth **c adultery** with her, *4519*
18: 9 the kings of the earth who **c adultery** *4519*

COMMITTING (2) [COMMIT]

Hos 6: 9 on the road to Shechem, **c** shameful crimes. 6913
Rev 2:14 and by **c sexual immorality.** *4519*

COMMON (26)

Ge 11: 1 world had one language and a **c** speech. 285
Lev 10:10 between the holy and the **c,** 2687
2Sa 16:10 king said, "What do you and I **have in c,** 4200
19:22 "What do you and I **have in c,** 4200
1Ki 10:27 silver **as c** in Jerusalem **as** stones, 3869
2Ki 23: 6 dust over the graves of the **c people.** 1201+6639
2Ch 1:15 gold **as c** in Jerusalem **as** stones, 3869
9:27 silver **as c** in Jerusalem **as** stones, 3869
Ne 7: 5 the **c people** for registration by families. 6639
Ps 73: 5 They are free from the **burdens** *c to* man; AIT
Pr 1:14 and we will share a **c** purse"— 285
22: 2 Rich and poor **have** *this* **in c:** 7008
29:13 poor man and the oppressor **have** *this* **in c:** 7008
Ecc 9: 2 All share a **c** destiny— 285
Jer 26:23 into the burial place of the **c people.)** 1201+6639
Eze 22:26 not distinguish between the holy and the **c;** 2687
42:20 to separate the holy from the **c.** 2687
44:23 between the holy and the **c** and show them 2687
48:15 cubits long, will be for the **c use** of the city, 2687
Ac 2:44 and had everything **in c.** *3123*
Ro 9:21 for noble purposes and some for **c** use? *871*
1Co 10:13 No temptation has seized you except what
is **c to man.** *474*
12: 7 of the Spirit is given for the **c** good. *NIG*
2Co 6:14 and wickedness have **in c?** *3580*
6:15 a believer have **in c** with an unbeliever? *3535*
Tit 1: 4 my true son in our **c** faith: *3123*

COMMONWEALTH (KJV) See CITIZENSHIP

COMMOTION (8)

Job 39: 7 He laughs at the **c** *in* the town; 2162
Isa 22: 2 O town full of **c,** 9583
Jer 3:23 Surely the [idolatrous] **c** on the hills 2162
10:22 a great **c** from the land of the north! 8323
Mk 5:38 Jesus saw a **c,** *2573*
5:39 "Why all this **c** and wailing? *2572*
Ac 12:18 there was no small **c** among the soldiers as *5431*
19:40 not be able to account for this **c,** *5371*

COMMUNION (KJV) See PARTICIPATION, FELLOWSHIP

COMMUNITIES (2) [COMMUNITY]

Am 1: 6 Because she took captive whole **c** 1661
1: 9 she sold whole **c of captives** to Edom, 1661

COMMUNITY (86) [COMMUNITIES, COMMUNITY'S]

Ge 28: 3 until you become a **c** *of* peoples. 7736
35:11 and a **c** *of* nations will come from you, 7736
48: 4 I will make you a **c** *of* peoples, 7736
Ex 12: 3 the whole **c** *of* Israel that on the tenth day 6337
12: 6 of the **c** *of* Israel must slaughter them 6337
12:19 with yeast in it must be cut off from the **c** 6337
12:47 The whole **c** *of* Israel must celebrate it. 6337
16: 1 The whole Israelite **c** set out from Elim 6337
16: 2 the whole **c** grumbled against Moses 6337
16: 9 "Say to the entire Israelite **c,** 6337
16:10 to the whole Israelite **c,** 6337
16:22 the leaders of the **c** came and reported this 6337
17: 1 The whole Israelite **c** set out from 6337
34:31 the leaders of the **c** came back to him, 6337
35: 1 Moses assembled the whole Israelite **c** 6337
35: 4 Moses said to the whole Israelite **c,** 6337
35:20 Then the whole Israelite **c** withdrew 6337
38:25 from those of the **c** who were counted in 6337
Lev 4:13 the whole Israelite **c** sins unintentionally 6337
4:13 even though the **c** is unaware of the matter, 7736
4:15 The elders of the **c** are to lay their hands on 6337
4:21 This is the sin offering for the **c.** 7736
4:27 " 'If a member of the **c** sins unintentionally
824+2021+6639
10: 6 the LORD will be angry with the whole **c.** 6337
10:17 the **c** by making atonement for them before 6337
16: 5 the Israelite **c** he is to take two male goats 6337
16:17 his household and the whole **c** *of* Israel. 7736
16:33 for the priests and all the people of the **c.** 7736
20: 2 The people of the **c** are to stone him. 824
20: 4 If the people of the **c** close their eyes when 824
Nu 1: 2 "Take a census of the whole Israelite **c** 6337
1:16 These were the men appointed from the **c,** 6337
1:18 and they called the whole **c** together on 6337
1:53 so that wrath will not fall on the Israelite **c.** 6337
3: 7 and for the whole **c** at the Tent of Meeting 6337
4:34 the **c** counted the Kohathites by their clans 6337
8: 9 and assemble the whole Israelite **c.** 6337
8:20 Aaron and the whole Israelite **c** did with 6337
10: 2 and use them for calling the **c** together and 6337
10: 3 the whole **c** is to assemble before you at 6337
13:26 and the whole Israelite **c** at Kadesh in 6337
14: 1 of the **c** raised their voices and wept aloud. 6337
14:27 "How long will this wicked **c** grumble 6337
14:35 to this whole wicked **c,** 6337
14:36 and made the whole **c** grumble against him 6337
15:15 The **c** is to have the same rules for you and 7736
15:24 without the **c** being aware of it, 6337
15:24 then the whole **c** is to offer a young bull for 6337
15:25 for the whole Israelite **c,** 6337
15:26 The whole Israelite **c** and the aliens living 6337
Nu 16: 2 well-known **c** leaders who had been
appointed members of the council. 6337
16: 3 The whole **c** is holy, every one of them, 6337
16: 9 the Israelite **c** and brought you near himself 6337
16: 9 to stand before the **c** and minister to them? 6337
16:33 they perished and were gone from the **c.** 7736
16:41 the whole Israelite **c** grumbled 6337
19: 9 They shall be kept by the Israelite **c** for use 6337
19:20 he must be cut off from the **c,** 7736
20: 1 the first month the whole Israelite **c** arrived 6337
20: 2 Now there was no water for the **c,** 6337
20: 4 Why did you bring the LORD's **c** 7736
20: 8 the **c** so they and their livestock can drink." 6337
20:11 and the **c** and their livestock drank. 6337
20:12 not bring this **c** into the land I give them." 7736
20:22 The whole Israelite **c** set out from Kadesh 6337
20:27 up Mount Hor in the sight of the whole **c.** 6337
20:29 the whole **c** learned that Aaron had died, 6337
26: 2 "Take a census of the whole Israelite **c** 6337
26: 9 the **c** officials who rebelled against Moses 6337
27:14 the **c** rebelled at the waters in the Desert 6337
27:16 appoint a man over this **c** 6337
27:20 so the whole Israelite **c** will obey him. 6337
27:21 and the entire **c** of the Israelites will go out, 6337
31:13 the **c** went to meet them outside the camp. 6337
31:26 the priest and the family heads of the **c** are 6337
31:27 in the battle and the rest of the **c.** 6337
32: 2 the priest and to the leaders of the **c,** 6337
Jos 9:21 and water carriers for the entire **c."** 6337
9:27 and water carriers for the **c** and for the altar 6337
22:17 a plague fell on the **c** *of* the LORD! 6337
22:18 be angry with the whole **c** *of* Israel. 6337
22:20 did not wrath come upon the whole **c** 6337
22:30 Phinehas the priest and the leaders of the **c** 6337
2Ch 31:18 the sons and daughters of the whole **c** listed 7736
Jer 30:20 and their **c** will be established before me; 6337
Ac 25:24 The whole **Jewish c** has petitioned me *2681+4436*

COMMUNITY'S (1) [COMMUNITY]

Nu 31:43 the **c** half—was 337,500 sheep, 6337

COMPACT (3) [COMPACTED]

2Sa 3:21 so that they may make a **c** with you, 1382
5: 3 the king made a **c** with them at Hebron 1382
1Ch 11: 3 he made a **c** with them at Hebron before 1382

COMPACTED (1) [COMPACT]

Ps 122: 3 like a city that **is closely c** together. 2489

COMPANIES (8) [COMPANY]

Jdg 7:16 the three hundred men into three **c,** 8031
7:20 The three **c** blew the trumpets and smashed 8031
9:34 near Shechem in four **c.** 8031
9:43 into three **c** and set an ambush in the fields. 8031
9:44 the **c** with him rushed forward to a position 8031
9:44 Then two **c** rushed upon those in the fields 8031
2Ki 11: 5 You who are in the three **c** that are going NIH
11: 7 and you who are in the other two **c** 3338

COMPANION (8) [COMPANIONS]

1Ki 20:35 of the sons of the prophets said to his **c,** 8276
Job 30:29 a **c** of owls. 8276
Ps 55:13 But it is you, a man like myself, my **c,** 476
55:20 **My c** attacks his friends; 2257S
Pr 13:20 but a **c** *of* fools suffers harm. 8287
28: 7 but a **c** *of* gluttons disgraces his father. 8287
29: 3 but a **c** *of* prostitutes squanders his wealth. 8287
Rev 1: 9 and **c** in the suffering and kingdom *5171*

COMPANIONS (27) [COMPANION]

Jdg 14:11 When he appeared, he was given thirty **c.** 5335
2Ki 9: 2 from his **c** and take him into an inner room. 278
Ps 38:11 and **c** avoid me because of my wounds; 8276
45: 7 above your **c** by anointing you with the oil 2492
45:14 her virgin **c** follow her and are brought 8292
88:18 You have taken my **c** and loved ones 8276
Pr 18:24 A man of *many* **c** may come to ruin, 8276
Isa 1:23 Your rulers are rebels, **c** *of* thieves; 2492
Mt 12: 3 when he and his **c** were hungry? *3552+3836*
12: 4 he and his **c** ate the consecrated bread *3552+3836*
26:51 one *of* Jesus' **c** reached for his sword, *3552+3836*
Mk 1:36 Simon and his **c** went to look for him, *3552+3836*
2:25 and his **c** were hungry and in need? *3552+3836*
2:26 he also gave some *to* his **c."** *1639+3836+5250*
Lk 5: 9 all his **c** were astonished at the catch *3836+5250*
6: 3 when he and his **c** were hungry? *1639+3552+3836*
6: 4 And he also gave some *to* his **c."** *3552*
9:32 Peter and his **c** were very sleepy, *3836+5250*
24:24 some *of* **our c** went to the tomb *1609+3836+5250*
Ac 13:13 and his **c** sailed to Perga in Pamphylia, *3836+4309*
16: 6 and his **c** traveled throughout the region *NIG*
19:29 Paul's **traveling c** from Macedonia, *5292*
20:34 and the needs of my **c.** *1639+3552+3836*
22: 9 My **c** saw the light, *1639+3836+5250*
22:11 My **c** led me by the hand into Damascus, *5289*
26:13 blazing around me and my **c.** *4513+5250*
Heb 1: 9 above your **c** by anointing you with the oil *3581*

COMPANY (36) [COMPANIES]

Ge 13: 9 *Let's* **part c.** 7233
13:11 The two men **parted c:** 7233
50: 9 It was a very large **c.** 4722

Jdg 9:37 the center of the land, and a **c** is coming 8031
2Ki 1: 9 to Elijah a captain with his *c of* **fifty** *men.* AIT
2: 3 The **c** *of* the prophets at Bethel came out 1201
2: 5 The **c** *of* the prophets at Jericho went up 1201
2: 7 of the **c** *of* the prophets went and stood at 1201
2:15 The **c** *of* the prophets from Jericho, 1201
4: 1 a man from the **c** *of* the prophets cried out 1201
4:38 **c** *of* the prophets was meeting with him, 1201
5:22 the **c** *of* the prophets have just come to me 1201
6: 1 The **c** *of* the prophets said to Elisha, 1201
9: 1 from the **c** *of* the prophets and said to him, 1201
Ezr 2: 2 **in c with** Zerubbabel, 6640
2:64 The whole **c** numbered 42,360, 7736
Ne 7: 7 **in c with** Zerubbabel, 6640
7:66 The whole **c** numbered 42,360, 7736
8:17 The whole **c** that had returned 7736
Job 15:34 For the **c** *of* the godless will be barren, 6337
34: 8 *He* **keeps c** with evildoers; 782+2495+4200
Ps 14: 5 for God is present in the **c** *of* the righteous. 1887
68:11 great was the **c** of those who proclaimed it: 7372
106:17 it buried the **c** *of* Abiram. 6337
Pr 21:16 of understanding comes to rest in the **c** *of* 7736
24: 1 do not desire their **c;** 907+2118
Jer 15:17 I never sat in the **c** *of* revelers, 6051
Eze 27:34 your wares and all your **c** have gone down 7736
Ob 1:20 This **c** of Israelite exiles who are 2657
Mt 27:27 and gathered the whole **c of soldiers** *5061*
Mk 15:16 the whole **c of soldiers.** *5061*
Lk 2:13 a **great c** of the heavenly host appeared *4436*
2:44 Thinking he was in their **c,** *5322*
Ac 15:39 They had a sharp disagreement that they **parted c.** *253+608+714*
Ro 15:24 after *I have* **enjoyed** your **c** for a while. *1855*
1Co 15:33 "Bad **c** corrupts good character." *3918*

COMPARE (20) [COMPARED, COMPARING, COMPARISON]

Job 28:17 Neither gold nor crystal *can* **c** *with* it, 6885
28:19 The topaz of Cush cannot **c with** it; 6885
39:13 but they cannot **c** with the pinions NIH
Ps 86: 8 no deeds can **c with** yours. 3869
89: 6 in the skies above *can* **c** with the LORD? 6885
Pr 3:15 nothing you desire *can* **c** with her. 8750
8:11 and nothing you desire *can* **c** with her. 8750
Isa 40:18 To whom, then, *will you* **c** God? 1948
40:18 What image *will you* **c** him to? 6885
40:25 "To whom *will you* **c** me? 1948
46: 5 "To whom *will you* **c** me 1948
La 2:13 With what *can I* **c** you, 1948
Eze 31: 8 the plane trees **c with** its branches— 2118+3869
Da 1:13 Then **c** our appearance with that of 8011
Mt 11:16 "To what can *I* **c** this generation? *3929*
Lk 7:31 then, *can I* **c** the people of this generation? *3929*
13:18 What *shall I* **c** it to? *3929*
13:20 "What *shall I* **c** the kingdom of God to? *3929*
2Co 10:12 We do not dare to classify or **c** ourselves *5173*
10:12 and **c** themselves with themselves, *5173*

COMPARED (6) [COMPARE]

Jdg 8: 2 "What have I accomplished **c to** you? 3869
8: 3 What was I able to do **c to** you?" 3869
Isa 46: 5 that *we may be* **c**? 1948
Eze 31: 2 " 'Who *can be* **c** with *you* in majesty? 1948
31:18 *be* **c** with *you* in splendor and majesty? 1948
Php 3: 8 a loss **c to** the surpassing greatness *1328*

COMPARING (3) [COMPARE]

Ro 8:18 not worth **c with** the glory that will *4639*
2Co 8: 8 of your love by **c** it with the earnestness *NIG*
Gal 6: 4 without **c** himself to somebody else, *NIG*

COMPARISON (1) [COMPARE]

2Co 3:10 now in **c with** the surpassing glory. *3538*

COMPASS (KJV) See AROUND

COMPASSES (1)

Isa 44:13 with chisels and marks it with **c.** 4684

COMPASSION (77) [COMPASSIONATE, COMPASSIONS]

Ex 33:19 and *I will* **have c** on whom I will have 8163
33:19 compassion on whom *I will* **have c.** 8163
Dt 13:17 he will show you mercy, **have c** *on* you, 8163
28:54 among you *will* **have no c** 6524+8317
30: 3 and **have c** on you and gather you again 8163
32:36 and **have c** on his servants 5714
Jdg 2:18 the LORD **had c** *on* them as they groaned 5714
1Ki 3:26 with **c** for her son and said to the king, 8171
2Ki 13:23 the LORD was gracious to them and **had c** 8163
2Ch 30: 9 and your children will be shown **c** 8171
Ne 9:19 of your great **c** you did not abandon them 8171
9:27 in your great **c** you gave them deliverers, 8171
9:28 and in your **c** you delivered them time 8171
Ps 51: 1 to your great **c** blot out my transgressions. 8171
77: 9 Has he in anger withheld his **c**?" 8171
90:13 **Have c** on your servants. 5714
102:13 You will arise and **have c** *on* Zion, 8163
103: 4 the pit and crowns you with love and **c,** 8171
103:13 As a father **has c** on his children, 8163
103:13 so the LORD **has c** on those who fear him; 8163
116: 5 our God *is* **full of c.** 8163
119:77 Let your **c** come to me that I may live, 8171
119:156 Your **c** is great, O LORD; 8171
135:14 and **have c** on his servants. 5714
145: 9 he has **c** on all he has made. 8171
Isa 13:18 nor *will* they **look with c** on children. 2571+6524
14: 1 The LORD *will* **have c** *on* Jacob; 8163
27:11 so their Maker *has* no **c** *on* them, 8163
30:18 he rises to **show** you **c.** 8163
49:10 *He who* **has c** *on* them will guide them 8163
49:13 and *will have* **c** *on* his afflicted ones. 8163
49:15 and **have** no **c** *on* the child she has borne? 8163
51: 3 surely comfort Zion and *will* **look with c** 5714
54: 7 but with deep **c** I will bring you back. 8171
54: 8 with everlasting kindness *I will* **have c** 8163
54:10 says the LORD, *who* **has c** *on* you. 8163
60:10 in favor *I will* **show** you **c.** 8163
63: 7 according to his **c** and many kindnesses. 8171
63:15 Your tenderness and **c** are withheld 8171
Jer 12:15 I will again **have c** and will bring each 8163
13:14 or **c** to keep me from destroying them.' " 8163
15: 6 I can no longer **show c.** 5714
21: 7 he will show them no mercy or pity or **c.'** 8163
30:18 the fortunes of Jacob's tents and **have c** 8163
31:20 *I* **have great c** *for* him," 8163+8163
33:26 For I will restore their fortunes and **have c** 8163
42:12 I will show you **c** so 8171
42:12 that *he will* **have c** *on* you and restore you 8163
La 3:32 Though he brings grief, *he will* **show c,** 8163
Eze 9: 5 without showing pity or **c.** 2798
16: 5 on you with pity or **had c** *enough* to do any 2798
39:25 and *will* **have c** *on* all the people of Israel, 8163
Hos 2:19 in righteousness and justice, in love and **c.** 8171
11: 8 all my **c** is aroused. 5719
13:14 "I will have no **c,** 5716
14: 3 for in you the fatherless **find c."** 8163
Am 1:11 with a sword, stifling *all* **c,** 8171
Jnh 3: 9 and *with* **c** turn from his fierce anger so 5714
3:10 he *had* **c** and did not bring upon them 5714
Mic 7:19 You will again **have c** *on* us; 8163
Zec 7: 9 show mercy and **c** to one another. 8171
10: 6 I will restore them because *I* **have c** 8163
Mal 3:17 as **in c** a man **spares** his son 2798
Mt 9:36 When he saw the crowds, *he* **had c** on them, *5072*
14:14 *he* **had c** on them and healed their sick. *5072*
15:32 "*I* **have c** for these people; *5072*
20:34 Jesus **had c** on them and touched their eyes. *5072*
Mk 1:41 **Filled with c,** Jesus reached out his hand *5072*
6:34 *he* **had c** on them, *5072*
8: 2 "*I* **have c** for these people; *5072*
Lk 15:20 and *was* **filled with c for** him; *5072*
Ro 9:15 *I will have* **c** on whom I have compassion." *3882*
9:15 I will have compassion on whom *I have* **c."** *3882*
2Co 1: 3 the Father *of* **c** and the God of all comfort, *3880*
Php 2: 1 if any tenderness and **c,** *3880*
Col 3:12 clothe yourselves with **c,** kindness, *3880*
Jas 5:11 The Lord is **full of c** and mercy. *4499*

COMPASSIONATE (14) [COMPASSION]

Ex 22:27 I will hear, for I am **c.** 2843
34: 6 the **c** and gracious God, slow to anger, 8157
2Ch 30: 9 for the LORD your God is gracious and **c.** 8157
Ne 9:17 you are a forgiving God, gracious and **c,** 8157
Ps 86:15 But you, O Lord, are a **c** and gracious God, 8157
103: 8 The LORD is **c** and gracious, 8157
111: 4 the LORD is gracious and **c.** 8157
112: 4 for the gracious and **c** and righteous man. 8157
145: 8 The LORD is gracious and **c,** 8157
La 4:10 With their own hands **c** women have cooked their own children, 8172
Joel 2:13 for he is gracious and **c,** 8157
Jnh 4: 2 I knew that you are a gracious and **c** God, 8157
Eph 4:32 Be kind and **c** to one another, *2359*
1Pe 3: 8 love as brothers, *be* **c** and humble. *2359*

COMPASSIONS (1) [COMPASSION]

La 3:22 for his **c** never fail. 8171

COMPEL (1) [COMPELLED, COMPELS, COMPULSION]

Gal 6:12 *to* **c** you to be circumcised. *337*

COMPELLED (6) [COMPEL]

1Sa 13:12 So *I* **felt c** to offer the burnt offering." 706
Ezr 4:23 the Jews in Jerusalem and **c** them by force 10264
Ac 20:22 "And now, **c** by the Spirit, *1313*
28:19 *I was* **c** to appeal to Caesar— *337*
1Co 9:16 I cannot boast, for I am **c** to preach. *340+2130*
Gal 2: 3 who was with me, *was* **c** to be circumcised, *337*

COMPELS (3) [COMPEL]

Ex 3:19 not let you go unless a mighty hand **c** him. 928
Job 32:18 and the spirit within me **c** me; 7439
2Co 5:14 For Christ's love **c** us, *5309*

COMPENSATE (2) [COMPENSATION]

Ex 21:26 he must let the servant go free **to c for** 9393
21:27 he must let the servant go free **to c for** 9393

COMPENSATION (1) [COMPENSATE]

Pr 6:35 He will not accept any **c;** 4111

COMPETE (1) [COMPETES]

Jer 12: 5 how *can you* **c** with horses? 3013

COMPETENCE (1) [COMPETENT]

2Co 3: 5 but our **c** comes from God. *2654*

COMPETENT (4) [COMPETENCE]

Ro 15:14 in knowledge and **c** to instruct one another. *1538*
1Co 6: 2 are you **not c** to judge trivial cases? *396*
2Co 3: 5 that we are **c** in ourselves to claim anything *2653*
3: 6 He *has* **made** us **c** as ministers of *2655*

COMPETES (3) [COMPETE]

1Co 9:25 Everyone who **c in the games** goes *76*
2Ti 2: 5 Similarly, if anyone **c as an athlete,** *123*
2: 5 the victor's crown unless *he* **c** according to *123*

COMPLACENCY (2) [COMPLACENT]

Pr 1:32 and the **c** *of* fools will destroy them; 8932
Eze 30: 9 in ships to frighten Cush out of her **c.** 1055

COMPLACENT (4) [COMPLACENCY]

Isa 32: 9 You women *who* are *so* **c,** 8633
32:11 Tremble, you **c** *women;* 8633
Am 6: 1 Woe to *you who* are **c** in Zion, 8633
Zep 1:12 with lamps and punish those who *are* **c,** 7884

COMPLAIN (7) [COMPLAINED, COMPLAINING, COMPLAINT, COMPLAINTS]

Jdg 21:22 When their fathers or brothers **c** to us, 8189
Job 7:11 *I will* **c** in the bitterness of my soul. 8488
33:13 Why *do you* **c** to him that he answers none 8189
Isa 29:24 *those who* **c** will accept instruction." 8087
40:27 Why do you say, O Jacob, and **c,** O Israel, 1819
56: 3 And *let* not any eunuch **c,** 606
La 3:39 Why *should* any living man **c** 645

COMPLAINED (4) [COMPLAIN]

Ge 21:25 Then Abraham **c** *to* Abimelech about 3519
Nu 11: 1 Now the people **c** *about* their hardships in 645
Lk 5:30 of the law who belonged to their sect **c** *1197*
Ac 6: 1 Grecian Jews among them **c** against *1181+1198*

COMPLAINING (1) [COMPLAIN]

Php 2:14 Do everything without **c** or arguing, *1198*

COMPLAINT (11) [COMPLAIN]

2Sa 15: 2 with a **c** to be placed before the king 8190
15: 4 a **c** or case could come to me 8190
Job 7:13 and my couch will ease my **c,** 8490
9:27 If I say, 'I will forget my **c,** 8490
10: 1 to my **c** and speak out in the bitterness 8490
21: 4 "Is my **c** directed to man? 8490
23: 2 "Even today my **c** is bitter; 8490
Ps 64: 1 Hear me, O God, as I voice my **c;** 8490
142: 2 I pour out my **c** before him; 8490
Hab 2: 1 and what answer I am to give to this **c.** 9350
Ac 18:14 "If you Jews *were* **making a c about** *1639S*

COMPLAINTS (2) [COMPLAIN]

Nu 14:27 the **c** *of* these grumbling Israelites. 9442
Pr 23:29 Who has **c?** Who has needless bruises? 8490

COMPLETE (29) [COMPLETED, COMPLETELY, COMPLETING, COMPLETION]

Ex 5:13 **"C** the work required of you for each day, 3983
Dt 16:15 and your joy will be **c.** 421
1Ki 7: 1 *to* **c** the construction of his palace. 3983
2Ki 12:15 because they acted with **c honesty.** 575
Est 2:12 she *had to* **c** twelve months 2118+4946+7891
Zec 4: 9 his hands *will* also **c** it. 1298
Lk 6:49 it collapsed and its destruction was **c."** *3489*
14:28 to see if he has enough money to **c** it? *568*
Jn 3:29 That joy is mine, and *it is now* **c.** *4444*
15:11 be in you and that your joy *may be* **c.** *4444*
16:24 and your joy will be **c.** *4444*
17:23 be brought to **c** unity to let the world know *5457*
Ac 3:16 through him that has given this **c healing** *3907*
20:24 if only I may finish the race and **c** the task *NIG*
Ro 15:14 **c** in knowledge and competent *4246+4444*
2Co 7:16 I am glad I can have **c** confidence in you. *1877+4246*
8: 7 *in* **c** earnestness and in your love for us— *4246*
10: 6 once your obedience *is* **c.** *4444*
Php 2: 2 then **make** my joy **c** by being like-minded, *4444*
Col 2: 2 the full riches *of* **c** understanding, *4443*
4:17 to it that *you* **c** the work you have received *4444*
Jas 1: 4 so that you may be mature and **c,** *3908*
2:22 and his faith *was* **made c** by what he did. *5457*
1Jn 1: 4 We write this to **make** our joy **c.** *1639+4444*
2: 5 God's love *is* truly **made c** in him. *5457*
4:12 God lives in us and his love is **made c** in us. *5457*
4:17 love *is* **made c** among us so *5457*
2Jn 1:12 so that our joy may be **c.** *4444*
Rev 3: 2 for I have not found your deeds **c** in the sight of my God. *4444*

COMPLETED (26) [COMPLETE]
Ge 2: 1 and the earth **were c** in all their vast array. 3983
29:21 My time *is* c, and I want to lie with her." 4848
Ex 39:32 the Tent of Meeting, *was* c. 3983
Lev 8:33 until the days of your ordination *are* c, 4848
Jos 3:17 by until the whole nation *had* c the crossing 9462
1Ki 6: 9 So he built the temple and c it, 3983
6:14 So Solomon built the temple and c it. 3983
7:22 And so the work on the pillars *was* c. 9462
2Ch 29:28 the sacrifice of the burnt offering *was* c. 3983
36:21 until the seventy years *were* c in fulfillment 4848
Ezr 6:15 The temple *was* c on the third day of 10707
Ne 6: 9 and *it will* not **be c."** 6913
6:15 the wall *was* c on the twenty-fifth of Elul, 8966
Isa 40: 2 to her that her hard service *has been* c, 4848
Jer 29:10 "When seventy years *are* c for Babylon, 4848
Da 11:36 be successful until the time of wrath *is* c, 3983
12: 7 all these things *will be* **c."** 3983
Lk 1:23 When his time of service *was* c, *4398*
2:22 according to the Law of Moses *had been* c, *4398*
12:50 and how distressed I am until *it is* c! *5464*
Jn 19:28 Later, knowing that all *was* now c, *5464*
Ac 14:26 of God for the work *they had* now c. *4444*
Ro 15:28 So *after I have* c this task *2200*
Rev 6:11 to be killed as they had been *was* c. *4444*
15: 1 last, because with them God's wrath *is* c. *5464*
15: 8 seven plagues of the seven angels *were* c. *5464*

COMPLETELY (91) [COMPLETE]
Ge 8:14 of the second month the earth *was* **c dry.** 3312
20:16 you are c vindicated." 3972
Ex 11: 1 and when he does, he will drive you out **c.** 3986
17:14 because *I will* c **blot out** the memory 4681+4681
21:19 **see that** *he* **is c healed.** 8324+8324
Lev 1:17 not **severing** it c, 976
5: 8 not **severing** it c, 976
6:22 and is to be burned c. 4003
6:23 of a priest shall be burned c. 4003
11: 3 a split hoof **c divided** and that chews 9117+9118
11: 7 the pig, though it has a split hoof **c divided,** 9117+9118
11:26 a split hoof not **c divided** or that does 9117+9118
26:44 or abhor them so as to **destroy** them **c,** 3983
Nu 21: 3 *They* **c destroyed** them and their towns; 3049
Dt 2:15 against them until he had **c** eliminated them 9462
2:34 and **c destroyed** them— 3049
3: 6 *We* **c destroyed** them, as we had done 3049
12: 2 **Destroy c** all the places on 6+6
13:15 **Destroy** it **c,** both its people 3049
13:16 the middle of the public square and **c** burn NIH
14: 7 or that have a split hoof **c divided** you may 9117
20:17 **C destroy** them—the Hittites, 3049+3049
Jos 2:10 whom *you* **c destroyed.** 3049
3:16 of the Arabah (the Salt Sea) was c cut off. 9462
10:20 Joshua and the Israelites destroyed them **c—** 3983
11:14 to the sword until they **c destroyed** them, 9012
17:13 but *did* not **drive** them **out c.** 3769+3769
Jdg 1:28 but never **drove** them **out c.** 3769+3769
1Sa 15: 9 These they were unwilling *to* **destroy c,** 3049
15:18 'Go and **c destroy** those wicked people, 3049
15:20 *I* **c destroyed** the Amalekites 3049
2Sa 22:39 *I* **crushed** them **c,** 430+2256+4730
1Ki 11: 6 **did** not follow the LORD **c,** 4848
2Ki 13:17 "You will **c** destroy the Arameans 3983+6330
13:19 and **c destroyed** it. 3983+6330
19:11 to all the countries, **destroying** them **c.** 3049
1Ch 4:41 and **c destroyed** them, 3049
Job 19:13 my acquaintances are c estranged from me. 421
21:23 c secure and at ease, 3972
Ps 73:19 c swept away by terrors! 9462
74: 8 "We will crush them **c!"** 3480
78:59 he rejected Israel **c.** 4394
88:17 they have c engulfed me. 3480
139: 4 a word is on my tongue you know it **c,** 3972
Isa 10:18 and fertile fields it will **c** destroy, 1414+2256+4946+5883+6330
24: 3 The earth *will* **be c laid waste** 1327+1327
32:19 the forest and the city *is* **leveled c,** 928+2021+9164+9168
37:11 to all the countries, **destroying** them **c.** 3049
Jer 3: 1 *Would* not the land *be* **c defiled?** 2866+2866
4:10 how **c** *you have* **deceived** this people 5958+5958
4:27 though *I will* not **destroy** it **c.** 3986+6913
5:10 but *do* not **destroy** them **c.** 3986+6913
5:18 *"I will* not **destroy** you **c.** 3986+6913
10:25 they have devoured him **c** 3983
12:17 *I will* **c uproot** and destroy it," 6004+6004
13: 7 now it was ruined and **c** useless. 2021+3972+4200
13:10 like this belt—**c** useless! 2021+3972+4200
13:19 be carried into exile, carried **c** away. 8934
14:19 *Have you* **rejected** Judah **c?** 4415+4415
25: 9 *I will* **c destroy** them and make them 3049
30:11 'Though *I* **c destroy** all the nations 3986+6913
30:11 *I will* not **c destroy** you. 3986+6913
46:28 "Though *I* **c destroy** all the nations 3986+6913
46:28 *I will* not **c destroy** you. 3986+6913
49:20 *he will* **c destroy** their pasture because 9037
50:13 not be inhabited but will be **c** desolate. 3972
50:21 Pursue, kill and **c destroy** them," 3049
50:26 **C destroy** her and leave her no remnant. 3049
50:45 *he will* **c destroy** their pasture because 9037
51: 3 **c destroy** her army. 3049
Eze 10:12 **c** full of eyes, as were their four wheels. 6017
11:13 *Will* you **c destroy** the remnant of Israel?" 3986+6913
17:10 not **wither c** when the east wind strikes it— 3312+3312
40: 5 a wall **c surrounding** the temple area. 6017+6017
Da 7:26 his power will be taken away and **c destroyed** forever. 10005+10221+10722
8:23 when rebels *have become* **c** wicked, 9462
Hos 10:15 the king of Israel *will* **be c destroyed.** 1950+1950
Na 1:15 they will be **c** destroyed. 3972
Zec 11:17 *May* his arm *be* **c withered,** 3312+3312
Mt 8:26 and it was **c** calm. *3489*
12:13 So he stretched it out and it was **c restored,** *635*
Mk 3: 5 and his hand *was* **c restored.** *635*
4:39 the wind died down and it was **c** calm. *3489*
5:42 At this they were **c** astonished. *3489*
6:51 They were **c** amazed, *1666+3336+4356*
Lk 6:10 He did so, and his hand *was* **c restored.** *635*
11:36 and no part of it dark, it will be **c** lighted, *3910*
Ac 3:23 not listen to him *will be* **c cut off from** *2017*
1Co 6: 7 lawsuits among you means you have been **c** defeated already. *3914*
Eph 4: 2 Be **c** humble and gentle; *4246*
Heb 7:25 save **c** those who come to God *1650+3836+4117*

COMPLETING (2) [COMPLETE]
Jn 17: 4 on earth *by* **c** the work you gave me to do. *5457*
Ac 13:25 As John *was* **c** his work, he said: *4444*

COMPLETION (4) [COMPLETE]
2Ch 8:16 of the LORD was laid until its **c.** 3983
2Co 8: 6 to **bring** also to **c** this act of grace *2200*
8:11 to do it may be matched by your **c** of it, *2200*
Php 1: 6 who began a good work in you *will* **carry it on to c** *2200*

COMPLIED (1) [COMPLY]
2Ki 16: 9 of Assyria **c** *by* attacking Damascus 9048

COMPLIMENTS (1)
Pr 23: 8 and will have wasted your **c.** 1821+5833

COMPLY (1) [COMPLIED]
Est 3: 4 to him but *he* refused *to* **c.** 9048

COMPOSED (1) [COMPOSE]
2Ch 35:25 Jeremiah **c laments** for Josiah, 7801

COMPREHEND (3) [COMPREHENDED]
Job 28:13 Man *does* not **c** its worth; 3359
Ecc 8:17 No one can **c** what goes on under the sun. 5162
8:17 he cannot *really* **c** it. 5162

COMPREHENDED (1) [COMPREHEND]
Job 38:18 *Have you* **c** the vast expanses of the earth? 1067

COMPULSION (2) [COMPEL]
1Co 7:37 who is under no **c** but has control *340*
2Co 9: 7 not reluctantly or under **c,** *340*

COMPUTE (1)
Lev 25:52 *he is to* **c** that and pay 3108

CONANIAH (3)
2Ch 31:12 **C,** a Levite, was in charge of these things, 4042
31:13 and Benaiah were supervisors under **C** 4042
35: 9 Also **C** along with Shemaiah and Nethanel, 4042

CONCEAL (8) [CONCEALED, CONCEALS]
Lev 16:13 of the incense *will* **c** the atonement cover 4059
Job 14:13 and **c** me till your anger has passed! 6259
27:11 the ways of the Almighty *I will* not **c.** 3948
40:22 The lotuses **c** him in their shadow; 6114
Ps 40:10 *I do* not **c** your love and your truth from 3948
Pr 25: 2 It is the glory of God *to* **c** a matter; 6259
Isa 26:21 *she will* **c** her slain no longer. 4059
Jer 49:10 so that he cannot **c himself.** 2464

CONCEALED (13) [CONCEAL]
Jdg 9:34 and **took up c positions** near Shechem 741
Job 10:13 "But this is what *you* **c** in your heart, 7621
24:15 and he keeps his face **c.** 6260
28:21 **c** even from the birds of the air. 6259
31:33 if *I have* **c** my sin as men do, 4059
Pr 21:14 a bribe **c in** the cloak pacifies great wrath. 928
26:26 His malice *may be* **c** by deception, 4059
Isa 49: 2 he made me into a polished arrow and **c** me 6259
Jer 16:17 nor is their sin **c** from my eyes. 7621
Mt 10:26 There is nothing **c** that will not be disclosed, *2821*
Mk 4:22 and whatever is **c** is meant to *649*
Lk 8:17 and nothing **c** that will not be known *649*
12: 2 There is nothing **c** that will not be disclosed, *5158*

CONCEALS (2) [CONCEAL]
Pr 10:18 *He who* **c** his hatred has lying lips, 4059
28:13 *He who* **c** his sins does not prosper, 4059

CONCEDE (1) [CONCESSION]
Dt 32:31 as even our enemies **c.** 7130

CONCEIT (3) [CONCEITED, CONCEITS]
Isa 16: 6 her overweening pride and **c,** 1452
Jer 48:29 her overweening pride and **c,** 1470
Php 2: 3 of selfish ambition or **vain c,** *3029*

CONCEITED (8) [CONCEIT]
1Sa 17:28 I know how **c** you are and 2295
Ro 11:25 brothers, so that you may not be **c:** *5861*
12:16 Do not be **c.** *4123+4932+5861*
2Co 12: 7 To keep *me* from *becoming* **c** because *5643*
Gal 5:26 Let us not become **c,** *3030*
1Ti 3: 6 or *he may* **become c** and fall under *5605*
6: 4 *he is* **c** and understands nothing. *5605*
2Ti 3: 4 **c,** lovers of pleasure rather than lovers *5605*

CONCEITS (1) [CONCEIT]
Ps 73: 7 the **evil c** *of* their minds know no limits. 5381

CONCEIVE (8) [CONCEIVED, CONCEIVES, CONCEPTION]
Nu 11:12 *Did* I **c** all these people? 2225
Jdg 13: 3 but *you are going to* **c** and have a son. 2225
13: 5 because you *will* **c** and give birth to a son. 2225
13: 7 'You *will* **c** and give birth to a son. 2225
Ru 4:13 and the LORD enabled her to **c,** 2231
Job 15:35 They **c** trouble and give birth to evil; 2225
Isa 33:11 *You* **c** chaff, you give birth to straw; 2225
59: 4 they **c** trouble and give birth to evil. 2225

CONCEIVED (23) [CONCEIVE]
Ge 16: 4 He slept with Hagar, and *she* **c.** 2225
29:33 *She* **c** again, and when she gave birth to 2225
29:34 Again *she* **c,** and when she gave birth to 2225
29:35 *She* **c** again, and when she gave birth to 2225
30: 7 Rachel's servant Bilhah **c** again 2225
30:19 Leah **c** again and bore Jacob a sixth son. 2225
38: 4 *She* **c** again and gave birth to a son 2225
1Sa 1:20 the course of time Hannah **c** and gave birth 2225
2:21 *she* **c** and gave birth to three sons 2225
2Sa 11: 5 The woman **c** and sent word to David, 2225
Ps 51: 5 sinful from the time my mother **c** me. 3501
SS 3: 4 to the room of the *one who* **c** me. 2225
8: 5 there your mother **c** you, 2473
Isa 8: 3 and *she* **c** and gave birth to a son. 2225
46: 3 you whom I have upheld since you were **c,** 1061
59:13 uttering lies our hearts *have* **c.** 2225
Hos 1: 3 and *she* **c** and bore him a son. 2225
1: 6 Gomer **c** again and gave birth to 2225
2: 5 and *has* **c** them in disgrace. 2225
Mt 1:20 what *is* **c** in her is from the Holy Spirit. *1164*
Lk 2:21 before he *had been* **c.** *1877+3120+3836+5197*
1Co 2: 9 no mind *has* **c** what God has prepared *326*
Jas 1:15 *after* desire *has* **c,** it gives birth to sin; *5197*

CONCEIVES (1) [CONCEIVE]
Ps 7:14 and **c** trouble gives birth to disillusionment. 2225

CONCEPTION (1) [CONCEIVE]
Hos 9:11 no birth, no pregnancy, no **c.** 2231

CONCERN (18) [CONCERNED, CONCERNING, CONCERNS]
Ge 39: 6 with Joseph in charge, *he did* not **c** *himself* 3359
39: 8 not **c** *himself with* anything in the house; 3359
1Sa 23:21 "The LORD bless you for *your* **c** for me. 2798
2Ki 13:23 and had compassion and **showed c for** them 448+7155
Job 9:21 I am blameless, *I* **have** no **c for** myself; 3359
19: 4 my error remains my **c** alone. 907
Ps 131: 1 *I do* not **c** *myself* with great matters 2143
Pr 29: 7 but the wicked **have** no *such* **c.** 1067+1981
Eze 36:21 *I* **had c** for my holy name, 2798
Ac 15:14 how God at first **showed** *his* **c** by taking *2170*
18:17 But Gallio **showed** no **c** whatever. *3508*
1Co 7:32 I would like you to be **free from c.** *291*
12:25 its parts *should* **have** equal **c** for each other. *3534*
2Co 7: 7 your deep sorrow, your **ardent c** for me, *2419*
7:11 what **c,** what readiness to see justice done. *2419*
8:16 the heart of Titus the same **c** I have for you. *5082*
11:28 the pressure of my **c** for all the churches. *3533*
Php 4:10 at last you have renewed your **c** for me. *5858*

CONCERNED (21) [CONCERN]
Ge 21:11 because it **c** his son. 128
Ex 2:25 on the Israelites and *was* **c about** them. 3359
3: 7 and *I am* **c about** their suffering. 3359
4:31 that the LORD *was* **c about** them 7212
1Sa 22: 8 None of you *is* **c** about me or tells me 2703
2Sa 13:33 the king *should* not *be* **c about** the report 448+4213+8492
1Ch 27: 1 in all *that* **c** the army divisions that were 1821
Ps 142: 4 no *one is* **c** for me. 5795
Eze 36: 9 I am **c for** you and will look on you 448
Da 10: 1 Its message was true and it **c** a great war. NIH
Jnh 4:10 "You *have been* **c** about this vine, 2571
4:11 *Should* I not *be* **c** about that great city?" 2571
Ro 11:28 As far as the gospel **is c,** *2848*
11:28 but as far as election **is c,** *2848*
1Co 7:32 An unmarried man *is* **c about** *3534*
7:33 But a married man *is* **c about** the affairs *3534*

1Co 7:34 An unmarried woman or virgin *is* c about 3534
7:34 a married woman *is* c about the affairs 3534
9: 9 Is it about oxen that God *is* c? 3508
Php 4:10 Indeed, *you have been* c, 5858
2Ti 3: 8 who, as far as the faith is c, are rejected. 4309

CONCERNING (111) [CONCERN]

Ge 24: 9 and swore an oath to him c this matter. 6584
47:26 So Joseph established it as a law c land 6584
Lev 11:46 " 'These are the regulations *c* animals, AIT
13:59 These are the regulations *c* contamination AIT
Nu 9: 8 the LORD commands c you." 4200
18:24 That is why I said c them: 4200
30:16 the regulations the LORD gave Moses c NIH
Dt 1: 3 the LORD had commanded him c them. 448
19: 4 the rule *c* the man who kills another AIT
33:21 and his judgments c Israel." 6640
1Sa 25:30 my master every good thing he promised c 6584
2Sa 1:17 up this lament c Saul and his son Jonathan, 6584
3:28 the LORD c the blood of Abner son 4946
7:25 keep forever the promise you have made c 6584
10: 2 to express his sympathy to Hanun c 448
13:39 for he was consoled c Amnon's death. 6584
18: 5 the king giving orders c Absalom 1821+6584
1Ki 21:23 "And also c Jezebel the LORD says: 4200
2Ki 19:20 I have heard your prayer c Sennacherib 448
19:32 "Therefore this is what the LORD says c 448
22:13 in accordance with all that is written there c 6584
22:18 says c the words you heard: NIH
1Ch 17:23 the promise you have made c your servant 6584
19: 2 to express his sympathy to Hanun c 6584
2Ch 9:29 the visions of Iddo the seer c Jeroboam son 6584
19:11 be over you in any matter *c* the LORD, AIT
19:11 will be over you in any matter *c* the king, AIT
23: 3 as the LORD promised c the descendants 6584
33: 8 to do everything I commanded them c all 4200
34:26 says c the words you heard: NIH
Ezr 6: 3 king issued a decree *c* the temple of God AIT
7:11 in matters *c* the commands and decrees of AIT
Est 3: 2 for the king had commanded this c him. 4200
9:29 to confirm this second letter *c* Purim. AIT
Ps 7: T which he sang to the LORD c Cush, 1821+6584
36: 1 oracle is within my heart *c* AIT
91:11 For he will command his angels c you 4200
Isa 1: 1 The vision c Judah and Jerusalem 6584
2: 1 This is what Isaiah son of Amoz saw c 6584
13: 1 An oracle *c* Babylon that Isaiah son AIT
15: 1 An oracle *c* Moab: AIT
16:13 the word the LORD has already spoken c 448
17: 1 An oracle *c* Damascus: AIT
19: 1 An oracle *c* Egypt: AIT
21: 1 An oracle *c* the Desert by the Sea: AIT
21:11 An oracle *c* Dumah: AIT
21:13 An oracle c Arabia: 928
22: 1 An oracle *c* the Valley of Vision: AIT
23: 1 oracle *c* Tyre: Wail, O ships of Tarshish! AIT
23:11 an order c Phoenicia that her fortresses 448
30: 6 An oracle *c* the animals of the Negev: AIT
32: 6 and spreads error c the LORD; 448
37:21 to me c Sennacherib king of Assyria, 448
37:33 "Therefore this is what the LORD says c 448
45:11 C things to come, NIH
Jer 9:10 and take up a lament c the desert pastures. 6584
14: 1 of the LORD to Jeremiah c the drought: 1821+6584
23: 9 C the prophets: My heart is broken within 4200
23:15 the LORD Almighty says c the prophets: 6584
25: 1 The word came to Jeremiah c all the people 6584
30: 4 These are the words the LORD spoke c 448
34: 4 This is what the LORD says c you: 6584
36: 2 on it all the words I have spoken to you c 6584
44: 1 This word came to Jeremiah c all 448
46: 1 to Jeremiah the prophet c the nations: 6584
46: 2 C Egypt: This is the message against the 4200
47: 1 to Jeremiah the prophet c the Philistines 448
48: 1 C Moab: This is what the LORD Almighty, 4200
49: 1 C the Ammonites: This is what the LORD says: 4200
49: 7 C Edom: This is what the LORD Almighty says: 4200
49:23 C Damascus: "Hamath and Arpad are 4200
49:28 C Kedar and the kingdoms of Hazor, 4200
49:34 that came to Jeremiah the prophet c Elam, 448
50: 1 through Jeremiah the prophet c Babylon 448
51:60 all that had been recorded c Babylon. 448
Eze 7:13 for the vision c the whole crowd will not 448
19: 1 "Take up a lament c the princes of Israel 448
21:29 Despite false visions c you 4200
26:17 Then they will take up a lament c you 6584
27: 2 "Son of man, take up a lament c Tyre. 6584
27:32 they will take up a lament c you: 6584
28:12 take up a lament c the king of Tyre and say 6584
32: 2 a lament c Pharaoh king of Egypt and say 6584
36: 6 Therefore prophesy c the land of Israel 6584
44: 5 and give attention to everything I tell you c 4200
Da 2:18 from the God of heaven c this mystery, 10542
8:13 the vision c the daily sacrifice, NIH
Joel 3: 2 against them c my inheritance, 6584
Am 1: 1 what he saw c Israel two years before 6584
5: 1 this lament I take up c you: 6584
Mic 1: 1 the vision he saw c Samaria and Jerusalem. 6584
Na 1: 1 An oracle c Nineveh. AIT
1:14 The LORD has given a command c you, 6584
Zec 12: 1 An Oracle This is the word of the LORD c 6584
Mal 3:16 in his presence c those who feared 4200
Mt 4: 6 " 'He will command his angels c you, 4309
Lk 2:17 they spread the word *c* what *had been* told AIT
4:10 " 'He will command his angels c you 4309
24:27 in all the Scriptures c himself. 4309
Jn 1: 7 He came as a witness to testify c that light, 4309
1:15 John testifies c him. 4309
5:37 Father who sent me has himself testified c 4309
Ac 1:16 the mouth of David c Judas, who served 4309
13:22 He testified *c* him: AIT
24:21 'It is c the resurrection of the dead 4309
28:21 not received any letters from Judea c you, 4309
Ro 9:27 Isaiah cries out c Israel: 5642
10:21 But c Israel he says, 4639
2Th 2: 1 C the coming of our Lord Jesus Christ 5642
1Pe 1:10 C this salvation, the prophets, 4309
1Jn 1: 1 this we proclaim c the Word of life. 4309

CONCERNS (6) [CONCERN]

2Ch 19:10 whether bloodshed or other c of the law, NIH
Eze 12:10 This oracle *c* the prince in Jerusalem and AIT
Da 8:17 "understand that the vision c the time of 4200
8:19 the vision c the appointed time of the end. 4200
8:26 for it c the distant future." 4200
10:14 for the vision c a time yet to come." 4200

CONCESSION (1) [CONCEDE]

1Co 7: 6 I say this as a c, not as a command. 5152

CONCISION (KJV) See MUTILATORS OF THE FLESH

CONCLUDE (1) [CONCLUDED, CONCLUDES, CONCLUDING, CONCLUSION]

Ro 3: 9 What shall we c then? 4036

CONCLUDED (2) [CONCLUDE]

Ecc 9: 1 on all this and c that the righteous and 1013
Jn 7:26 the authorities really c that he is the Christ? 1182

CONCLUDES (1) [CONCLUDE]

Ps 72:20 *This* c the prayers of David son of Jesse. 3983

CONCLUDING (1) [CONCLUDE]

Ac 16:10 c that God had called us to preach 5204

CONCLUSION (1) [CONCLUDE]

Ecc 12:13 here is the c *of* the matter: Fear God 6067

CONCORD (KJV) See HARMONY

CONCOURSE (KJV) See COMMOTION, NOISY

CONCUBINE (21) [CONCUBINES]

Ge 22:24 His c, whose name was Reumah, 7108
35:22 in and slept with his father's c Bilhah, 7108
36:12 also had a c named Timna, 7108
Jdg 8:31 His c, who lived in Shechem, 7108
19: 1 in the hill country of Ephraim took a c 7108
19: 9 when the man, with his c and his servant, 7108
19:10 with his two saddled donkeys and his c. 7108
19:24 here is my virgin daughter, and his c. 7108
19:25 So the man took his c and sent her outside 7108
19:27 there lay his c, 7108
19:29 he took a knife and cut up his c, 7108
20: 4 "I and my c came to Gibeah in Benjamin 7108
20: 5 They raped my c, and she died. 7108
20: 6 I took my c, 7108
2Sa 3: 7 a c named Rizpah daughter of Aiah. 7108
3: 7 "Why did you sleep with my father's c?" 7108
21:11 When David was told what Aiah's daughter Rizpah, Saul's c, 7108
1Ch 1:32 The sons born to Keturah, Abraham's c: 7108
2:46 Caleb's c Ephah was the mother of Haran, 7108
2:48 Caleb's c Maacah was the mother 7108
7:14 through his Aramean c. 7108

CONCUBINES (17) [CONCUBINE]

Ge 25: 6 to the sons of his c and sent them away 7108
2Sa 5:13 David took more c and wives in Jerusalem, 7108
15:16 but he left ten c to take care of the palace. 7108
16:21 "Lie with your father's c whom he left 7108
16:22 with his father's c in the sight of all Israel. 7108
19: 5 and the lives of your wives and c. 7108
20: 3 he took the ten c he had left to take care of 7108
1Ki 11: 3 of royal birth and three hundred c, 7108
1Ch 3: 9 besides his sons by his c. 7108
2Ch 11:21 of his other wives and c. 7108
11:21 In all, he had eighteen wives and sixty c, 7108
Est 2:14 king's eunuch who was in charge of the c. 7108
SS 6: 8 Sixty queens there may be, and eighty c, 7108
6: 9 the queens and c praised her. 7108
Da 5: 2 his wives and his c might drink from them. 10390
5: 3 his wives and his c drank from them. 10390
5:23 and your c drank wine from them. 10390

CONCUPISCENCE (KJV) See COVETOUS DESIRE, EVIL DESIRE, LUST

CONDEMN (26) [CONDEMNATION, CONDEMNED, CONDEMNING, CONDEMNS, SELF-CONDEMNED]

Job 9:20 if I were innocent, my mouth *would* c me; 8399
10: 2 I will say to God: *Do* not c me, 8399
34:17 *Will you* c the just and mighty One? 8399
34:29 But if he remains silent, who *can* c him? 8399
40: 8 *Would you* c me to justify yourself? 8399
Ps 94:21 the righteous and c the innocent *to* death. 8399
109: 7 and *may* his prayers c him. 2118+2631+4200
109:31 to save his life from *those who* c him. 9149
Isa 50: 9 Who is he *that will* c me? 8399
Mt 12:41 the judgment with this generation and c it; 2891
12:42 the judgment with this generation and c it; 2891
20:18 *They will* c him to death 2891
Mk 10:33 *They will* c him to death 2891
Lk 6:37 *Do* not c, and you will not be condemned. 2868
11:31 with the men of this generation and c them; 2891
11:32 the judgment with this generation and c it; 2891
Jn 3:17 not send his Son into the world to c 3212
7:51 *"Does* our law c anyone without first 3212
8:11 "Then neither *do* I c you," Jesus declared. 2891
12:48 that very word which I spoke *will* c him at 3212
Ro 2:27 and yet obeys the law *will* c you who, 3212
14: 3 not eat everything *must* not c the man 3212
14:22 Blessed is the man who *does* not c himself 3212
2Co 7: 3 I do not say this to c you; 2892
1Jn 3:20 whenever our hearts c us. 2861
3:21 Dear friends, if our hearts *do* not c us, 2861

CONDEMNATION (8) [CONDEMN]

Jer 42:18 of c and reproach; 7839
44:12 of c and reproach. 7839
Ro 3: 8 Their c is deserved. 3210
5:16 judgment followed one sin and brought c, 2890
5:18 the result of one trespass was c for all men, 2890
8: 1 now no c for those who are in Christ Jesus, 2890
2Pe 2: 3 Their c has long been hanging over them, 3210
Jude 1: 4 For certain men whose c was written 3210

CONDEMNED (35) [CONDEMN]

Dt 13:17 None of those c things shall be found 3051
Job 32: 3 and yet *had* c him. 8399
Ps 34:21 the foes of the righteous *will be* c. 870
34:22 no one *will be* c who takes refuge in him. 870
37:33 or let them be c when brought to trial. 8399
79:11 of your arm preserve *those* c to die. 1201
102:20 the prisoners and release *those* c to death." 1201
Mt 12: 7 *you* would not *have* c the innocent. 2868
12:37 and by your words *you will be* c." 2868
23:33 How will you escape being c to hell? 3213
27: 3 saw that Jesus *was* c, 2891
Mk 14:64 They all c him as worthy of death. 2891
16:16 but whoever does not believe *will be* c. 2891
Lk 6:37 Do not condemn, and *you will* not *be* c. 2868
Jn 3:18 Whoever believes in him *is* not c, 3212
3:18 not believe *stands* c already 3212
5:24 and *will* not *be* c; 1650+2262+3213
5:29 those who have done evil will rise to be c. 3213
8:10 *Has* no one c you?" 2891
16:11 the prince of this world *now stands* c. 3212
Ac 25:15 against him and asked that he be c. 2869
Ro 3: 7 why *am* I still c as a sinner?" 3212
8: 3 And so *he* c sin in sinful man, 2891
14:23 But the man who has doubts *is* c if he eats, 2891
1Co 4: 9 like *men* c to die in the arena. 2119
11:32 so that *we will* not *be* c with the world. 2891
Gal 1: 8 let him be eternally c! 353
1: 9 let him be eternally c! 353
2Th 2:12 so that all *will be* c who have not believed 3212
Tit 2: 8 and soundness of speech *that* cannot be c, 183
Heb 11: 7 By his faith *he* c the world and became heir 2891
Jas 5: 6 *You have* c and murdered innocent men, 2868
5:12 your "No," no, or *you will* be c. 3213+4406+5679
2Pe 2: 6 if *he* c the cities of Sodom and Gomorrah 2891
Rev 19: 2 *He has* c the great prostitute who corrupted 3212

CONDEMNING (5) [CONDEMN]

Dt 25: 1 acquitting the innocent and c the guilty. 8399
1Ki 8:32 c the guilty and bringing down 8399
Pr 17:15 Acquitting the guilty and c the innocent— 8399
Ac 13:27 yet *in* c him they fulfilled the words of 3212
Ro 2: 1 *you are* c yourself, 2891

CONDEMNS (4) [CONDEMN]

Job 15: 6 Your own mouth c you, not mine; 8399
Pr 12: 2 but the LORD c a crafty man. 8399
Ro 8:34 Who is he that c? 2891
2Co 3: 9 If the ministry that c men is glorious, 2892

CONDESCEND (KJV) See WILLING TO ASSOCIATE

CONDITION (7) [CONDITIONS]

Ge 34:15 to you on one c only: 2296S
34:22 to live with us as one people only on the c 2296S
1Sa 11: 2 with you only on the c that I gouge out 928+2296
Pr 27:23 Be sure you know the c *of* your flocks, 7156
Mt 12:45 final *c* of that man is worse than the first. AIT
Lk 11:26 And the final *c* of that man is worse than AIT
Jn 5: 6 that he had been in this c for a long time, NIG

CONDITIONS (1) [CONDITION]
Jer 32:11 the sealed copy containing the terms and c, 2976

CONDUCT (31) [CONDUCTED, CONDUCTS, SAFE-CONDUCT]
Est 1:17 For the queen's c will become known to all 1821
1:18 about the queen's c will respond to all 1821
Job 21:31 Who denounces his c to his face? 2006
34:11 he brings upon him what his c deserves. 784
Pr 10:23 A fool finds pleasure in evil c, 6913
20:11 by whether his c is pure and right. 7189
21: 8 but the c *of* the innocent is upright. 7189
Ecc 6: 8 how to c *himself* before others? 2143
Jer 4:18 "Your own c and actions have brought this 2006
6:15 Are they ashamed of *their* loathsome c? 6913
8:12 Are they ashamed of *their* loathsome c? 6913
17:10 to reward a man according to his c, 2006
32:19 you reward everyone according to his c and 2006
Eze 7: 3 I will judge you according to your c 2006
7: 4 for your c and the detestable practices 2006
7: 8 I will judge you according to your c 2006
7: 9 I will repay you in accordance with your c 2006
7:27 I will deal with them according to their c, 2006
14:22 and when you see their c and their actions, 2006
14:23 You will be consoled when you see their c 2006
16:27 who were shocked by your lewd c. 2006
20:43 There you will remember your c and all 2006
24:14 You will be judged according to your c 2006
36:17 they defiled it by their c and their actions. 2006
36:17 Their c was like a woman's monthly 2006
36:19 according to their c and their actions. 2006
36:32 Be ashamed and disgraced for your c, 2006
Da 6: 4 for charges against Daniel in his c NIH
Ac 13:18 he endured their c for about forty years in *NIG*
Php 1:27 c **yourselves in a manner** worthy *4488*
1Ti 3:15 *to* c *themselves* in God's household, *418*

CONDUCTED (1) [CONDUCT]
2Co 1:12 that *we have* c **ourselves** in the world, *418*

CONDUCTS (1) [CONDUCT]
Ps 112: 5 *who* c his affairs with justice. 3920

CONDUIT (KJV) See AQUEDUCT, TUNNEL

CONEY (2) [CONEYS]
Lev 11: 5 The c, though it chews the cud, 9176
Dt 14: 7 the rabbit or the c. 9176

CONEYS (2) [CONEY]
Ps 104:18 the crags are a refuge for the c. 9176
Pr 30:26 c are creatures of little power, 9176

CONFECTION (KJV) See PERFUMER

CONFECTIONARIES (KJV) See PERFUMERS

CONFECTIONS (1)
Eze 27:17 they exchanged wheat from Minnith and c, 7154

CONFEDERACY (KJV) See CONSPIRACY, ALLIES

CONFER (2) [CONFERRED, CONFERRING]
Ne 6: 7 so come, *let us* c together." 3619
Lk 22:29 And I c on you a kingdom, *1416*

CONFERRED (6) [CONFER]
2Sa 3:17 Abner c with the elders of Israel and said, 1821
1Ki 1: 7 Adonijah c with Joab son of Zeruiah 1821+2118
1Ch 13: 1 David c with each of his officers, 3619
Lk 22:29 just as my Father c one on me, *1416*
Ac 4:15 from the Sanhedrin and then c together. *5202*
25:12 *After* Festus *had* c **with** his council, *5196*

CONFERRING (1) [CONFER]
2Ki 6: 8 After c with his officers, he said, 3619

CONFESS (21) [CONFESSED, CONFESSES, CONFESSING, CONFESSION]
Lev 5: 5 *he must* c in what way he has sinned 3344
16:21 on the head of the live goat and c over it all 3344
26:40 " 'But if *they will* c their sins and the sins 3344
Nu 5: 7 and *must* c the sin he has committed. 3344
1Ki 8:33 they turn back to you and c your name, 3344
8:35 toward this place and c your name and turn 3344
2Ch 6:24 and when they turn back and c your name, 3344
6:26 toward this place and c your name and turn 3344
Ne 1: 6 *I* c the sins we Israelites, 3344
Ps 32: 5 *"I will* c my transgressions to 3344
38:18 *I* c my iniquity; I am troubled by my sin. 5583
Jn 1:20 *He did* not fail *to* c, but confessed freely, *3933*
12:42 because of the Pharisees *they would* not c their faith *3933*
Ro 10: 9 That if *you* c with your mouth, *3933*
10:10 with your mouth that *you* c and are saved. *3933*
14:11 every tongue *will* c to God.' " *2018*
Php 2:11 every tongue c that Jesus Christ is Lord, *2018*
Heb 3: 1 the apostle and high priest whom we c. *3934*
13:15 the fruit of lips that c his name. *3933*
Jas 5:16 Therefore c your sins to each other *2018*
1Jn 1: 9 If *we* c our sins, he is faithful and just *3933*

CONFESSED (5) [CONFESS]
1Sa 7: 6 On that day they fasted and there *they* c, 606
Ne 9: 2 They stood in their places and c their sins 3344
Da 9: 4 I prayed to the LORD my God and c: 3344
Jn 1:20 He did not fail to confess, but c freely, *3933*
Ac 19:18 now came and **openly** c their evil deeds. *334+2018*

CONFESSES (2) [CONFESS]
Pr 28:13 *whoever* c and renounces them finds mercy. 3344
2Ti 2:19 and, "Everyone who c the name of *3951*

CONFESSING (4) [CONFESS]
Ezr 10: 1 While Ezra was praying and c, 3344
Da 9:20 c my sin and the sin of my people Israel 3344
Mt 3: 6 C their sins, they were baptized by him in *2018*
Mk 1: 5 C their sins, they were baptized by him in *2018*

CONFESSION (5) [CONFESS]
Ezr 10:11 Now make c to the LORD, 9343
Ne 9: 3 and *spent* another quarter *in* c and 3344
2Co 9:13 for the obedience that *accompanies* your c *3934*
1Ti 6:12 *when you* **made** *your* good c in the presence of many witnesses. *3933+3934*
6:13 before Pontius Pilate **made** the good c, *3934*

CONFIDE (1) [CONFIDES, CONFIDING]
Jdg 16:15 'I love you,' when you won't c **in** me? 907+4213

CONFIDENCE (36) [CONFIDENT, CONFIDENTLY, SELF-CONFIDENCE, SELF-CONFIDENT]
Jdg 9:26 and its citizens **put** *their* c in him. 1053
2Ki 18:19 On what are you basing this c of yours? 1059
2Ch 32: 8 the people **gained** c from what Hezekiah 6164
32:10 On what *are* you **basing** your c, 1053
Job 4: 6 Should not your piety be your c 4074
Ps 71: 5 O Sovereign LORD, my c since my youth. 4440
Pr 3:26 be your c and will keep your foot 4073
3:32 but takes the upright into his c. 6051
11:13 A gossip betrays a c, 6051
20:19 A gossip betrays a c; 6051
25: 9 do not betray another man's c, 6051
31:11 Her husband **has full** c in her 1053+4213
Isa 32:17 be quietness and c forever. 1055
36: 4 On what are you basing this c of yours? 1059
Jer 17: 7 whose c is in him. 4440
49:31 which lives in c," declares the LORD, 1055
Eze 29:16 Egypt will no longer be a **source of** c for 4440
Mic 7: 5 **put** no c in a friend; 1053
2Co 2: 3 *I had* c in all of you, *4275*
3: 4 Such c as this is ours through Christ *4301*
7: 4 I have great c in you; *4244*
7:16 I am glad *I* can *have* complete c in you. *2509*
8:22 more so *because of* his great c in you. *4301*
Eph 3:12 with freedom and c. *4301*
Php 3: 3 and who **put** no c in the flesh— *4275*
3: 4 though I myself have reasons for such c. *4301*
3: 4 to **put** c in the flesh, I have more: *4275*
2Th 3: 4 *We have* c in the Lord that you are doing *4275*
Heb 3:14 if we hold firmly till the end the c we had *5712*
4:16 then approach the throne of grace with c, *4244*
10:19 we have c to enter the Most Holy Place *4244*
10:35 So do not throw away your c; *4244*
13: 6 So we say **with** c, "The Lord is my helper; *2509*
1Jn 3:21 we have c before God *4244*
4:17 that we will have c on the day of judgment, *4244*
5:14 This is the c we have in approaching God: *4244*

CONFIDENT (15) [CONFIDENCE]
Job 6:20 because *they had been* c; 1053
Ps 27: 3 even then *will* I *be* c. 1053
27:13 *I am* still c of this: I will see the goodness 586
Lk 18: 9 To some who *were* c of their own *4275*
2Co 1:15 *Because I was* c **of** this, *4301*
5: 6 Therefore *we are* always c and know that *2509*
5: 8 *We are* c, I say, and would prefer to be *2509*
9: 4 would be ashamed of having been so c. *1877+5712*
10: 7 If anyone *is* c that he belongs to Christ, *4275*
Gal 5:10 *I am* c in the Lord that you will take no *4275*
Php 1: 6 *being* c *of* this, that he who began a good *4275*
2:24 And *I am* c in the Lord *4275*
Phm 1:21 C of your obedience, I write to you, *4275*
Heb 6: 9 *we are* c **of** better things in your case— *4275*
1Jn 2:28 so that when he appears *we may be* c *2400+4244*

CONFIDENTLY (3) [CONFIDENCE]
1Sa 15:32 Agag came to him c, thinking, 5051
Ac 2:29 I can tell you c that the patriarch *3552+4244*
1Ti 1: 7 about or what *they* so c **affirm.** *1331*

CONFIDES (1) [CONFIDE]
Ps 25:14 The LORD c in those who fear him; 6051

CONFIDING (1) [CONFIDE]
1Sa 20: 2 great or small, without c **in** me. 265+906+1655

CONFINE (2) [CONFINED, CONFINEMENT, CONFINES]
Nu 12:14 C *her* outside the camp for seven days; 6037
2Co 10:13 but will c our boasting to the field God has *NIG*

CONFINED (9) [CONFINE]
Ge 39:20 the place where the king's prisoners **were** c. 673
40: 3 in the same prison where Joseph **was** c. 673
Ex 21:18 or with his fist and he does not die but *is* c 5877
Nu 12:15 So Miriam *was* c outside the camp 6037
Jdg 1:34 Amorites c the Danites to the hill country, 4315
Ps 88: 8 I **am** c and cannot escape; 3973
Jer 32: 2 the prophet was c in the courtyard of 3973
33: 1 While Jeremiah **was** still c in the courtyard 6806
39:15 While Jeremiah had been c in the courtyard 6806

CONFINEMENT (1) [CONFINE]
2Sa 20: 3 They were **kept in** c till the day 7674

CONFINES (1) [CONFINE]
Job 11:10 and c you **in prison** and convenes a court, 6037

CONFIRM (9) [CONFIRMED, CONFIRMING, CONFIRMS]
Ge 17: 2 *I will* c my covenant between me 5989
26: 3 and *will* c the oath I swore 7756
Nu 30:13 Her husband *may* c 7756
Dt 29:13 to c you this day as his people, 7756
1Ki 1:14 I will come in and c what you have said." 4848
Est 9:29 to c this second letter concerning Purim. 7756
Da 9:27 *He will* c a covenant with many 1504
Ac 15:27 and Silas *to* c by word *550*
Ro 15: 8 to c the promises made to the patriarchs *1011*

CONFIRMED (13) [CONFIRM]
Dt 4:31 which *he* c to them **by oath.** 8678
1Sa 11:15 the people went to Gilgal and c Saul **as king** 4887
1Ch 16:17 *He* c it to Jacob as a decree, 6641
2Ch 1: 9 *let* your promise to my father David **be** c, 586
Est 9:32 Esther's decree c these regulations 7756
Job 28:27 *he* c it and tested it. 3922
Ps 105:10 *He* c it to Jacob as a decree, 6641
119:106 I have taken an oath and c it, 7756
Mk 16:20 the Lord worked with them and c his word *1011*
Ac 14: 3 who c the message of his grace *3455*
1Co 1: 6 our testimony about Christ *was* c in you. *1011*
Heb 2: 3 *was* c to us by those who heard him. *1011*
6:17 *he* c it with an oath. *3541*

CONFIRMING (2) [CONFIRM]
2Ki 23: 3 thus c the words of the covenant written 7756
Php 1: 7 in chains or defending and c the gospel, *1012*

CONFIRMS (5) [CONFIRM]
Nu 30:14 then *he* c all her vows or 7756
30:14 *He* c them by saying nothing to her 7756
Dt 8:18 and so c his covenant, 7756
Ro 9: 1 my conscience c it in the Holy Spirit— *5210*
Heb 6:16 and the oath c what is said and *1012+1650*

CONFISCATION (2)
Ezr 7:26 c *of* property, or imprisonment. 10562
Heb 10:34 in prison and joyfully accepted the c *771*

CONFLICT (2) [CONFLICTS]
Hab 1: 3 there is strife, and c abounds. 4506
Gal 5:17 They *are* **in** c with each other, *512*

CONFLICTS (1) [CONFLICT]
2Co 7: 5 c on the outside, fears within. *3480*

CONFORM (2) [CONFORMED, CONFORMITY, CONFORMS]
Ro 12: 2 c *any longer* **to the pattern of** this world, *5372*
1Pe 1:14 *do* not c to the evil desires you had *5372*

CONFORMED (3) [CONFORM]
Eze 5: 7 not even c **to** the standards of the nations 3869+6913
11:12 or kept my laws but *have* c **to** the standards of the nations 3869+6913
Ro 8:29 predestined to be c to the likeness of his Son *5215*

CONFORMITY (1) [CONFORM]
Eph 1:11 of him who works out everything **in** c **with** *2848*

CONFORMS (1) [CONFORM]
1Ti 1:11 c **to** the glorious gospel of the blessed God *2848*

CONFOUND (1)
Ps 55: 9 O Lord, c their speech, 7103

CONFRONT (13) [CONFRONTED, CONFRONTING, CONFRONTS]
Ex 8:20 "Get up early in the morning and c Pharaoh 3656
9:13 c Pharaoh and say to him, 3656
Jdg 14: 4 who was seeking an occasion to c 4946
1Sa 12: 7 because I am going to c you with evidence 9149
Job 9:32 that we might c each other in court. 995
30:27 days of suffering c me. 7709
33: 5 prepare yourself and c me. 3656
Ps 17:13 Rise up, O LORD, c them, 7709
Isa 50: 8 Let him c me! 5602
Eze 16: 2 c Jerusalem with her detestable practices 3359
20: 4 Then c them with the detestable practices 3359
22: 2 Then c her with all her detestable practices 3359
23:36 Then c them with their detestable practices, 5583

CONFRONTED (6) [CONFRONT]
2Sa 22: 6 the snares of death c me. 7709
22:19 They c me in the day of my disaster, 7709
2Ch 26:18 They c him and said, 6584+6641
28:12 c those who were arriving from the war. 6584+7756
Ps 18: 5 the snares of death c me. 7709
18:18 They c me in the day of my disaster, 7709

CONFRONTING (2) [CONFRONT]
Isa 27: 4 If only there were briers and thorns c me! NIH
30:11 stop c us with the Holy One of Israel!" 4946+7156

CONFRONTS (1) [CONFRONT]
Job 31:14 what will I do when God c me? 7756

CONFUSE (2) [CONFUSED, CONFUSING, CONFUSION]
Ge 11: 7 down and c their language so they will 1176
Ps 55: 9 C the wicked, O Lord, 1182

CONFUSED (1) [CONFUSE]
Ge 11: 9 because there the LORD c the language of 1176

CONFUSING (1) [CONFUSE]
Pr 23:33 and your mind imagine c things. 9337

CONFUSION (19) [CONFUSE]
Ex 14: 3 wandering around the land in c, 1003
14:24 at the Egyptian army and threw it into c. 2169
23:27 throw into c every nation you encounter. 2169
Dt 7:23 throwing them into great c 2169+4539
28:20 The LORD will send on you curses, c 4539
28:28 blindness and c of mind. 9451
Jos 10:10 The LORD threw them into c 2169
1Sa 14:20 They found the Philistines in total c, 4539
2Sa 18:29 "I saw great c just as Joab was about 2162
Ps 35:26 over my distress be put to shame and c; 2917
40:14 to take my life be put to shame and c; 2917
70: 2 be put to shame and c; 2917
71:24 to harm me have been put to shame and c. 2917
Isa 41:29 their images are but wind and c. 9332
Jer 51:34 he has thrown us into c, 2169
Mic 7: 4 Now is the time of their c. 4428
Ac 19:32 The assembly was in c: 5177
Gal 1: 7 some people are throwing you into c 5429
5:10 The one who is throwing you into c will pay the penalty, 5429

CONGEALED (1)
Ex 15: 8 the deep waters c in the heart of the sea. 7884

CONGRATULATE (3)
2Sa 8:10 to King David to greet him and c him 1385
1Ki 1:47 to c our lord King David, 1385
1Ch 18:10 to King David to greet him and c him 1385

CONGREGATION (4) [CONGREGATIONS]
Ps 22:22 in the c I will praise you. 7736
68:26 Praise God in the great c; 5220
Ac 13:43 When the c was dismissed, 5252
Heb 2:12 of the c I will sing your praises." 1711

CONGREGATIONS (1) [CONGREGATION]
1Co 14:33 As in all the c of the saints, 1711

CONIES (Anglicized, KJV) See CONEYS

CONJURE (1)
Isa 47:11 and you will not know how to c it away. 8838

CONNECTED (4) [CONNECTING, CONNECTION]
Lev 3: 3 the fat that covers the inner parts or is c to 6584
3: 9 the fat that covers the inner parts or is c to 6584
3:14 the fat that covers the inner parts or is c to 6584
4: 8 the fat that covers the inner parts or is c to 6584

CONNECTING (2) [CONNECTED]
Ex 28:28 c it to the waistband, 2118
39:21 c it to the waistband so that 2118

CONNECTION (4) [CONNECTED]
Nu 18: 7 and your sons may serve as priests in c with 4200
1Ch 6:49 of incense in c with all that was done in 4200
Ac 11:19 those who had been scattered by the persecution in c with Stephen 2093
Col 2:19 He has lost c with the Head, 3195+4024

CONONIAH (KJV) See CONIAH

CONQUER (3) [CONQUERED, CONQUEROR, CONQUERORS, CONQUERS, CONQUEST]
Dt 2:31 Now begin to c and possess his land." 3769
2Ch 32: 1 thinking to c them for himself. 1324
Rev 13: 7 against the saints and to c them. 3771

CONQUERED (11) [CONQUER]
Ge 14: 7 and they c the whole territory of 5782
Nu 24:18 Edom will be c; 3771
24:18 Seir, his enemy, will be c, 3771
Jos 10:42 and their lands Joshua c in one campaign, 4334
12: 6 and the Israelites c them. 5782
12: 7 the land that Joshua and the Israelites c on 5782
23: 4 the nations I c— 4162
1Ki 15:20 He c Ijon, Dan, Abel Beth Maacah 5782
2Ch 16: 4 They c Ijon, Dan, Abel Maim and all 5782
27: 5 the king of the Ammonites and c them. 2616+6584
Heb 11:33 who through faith c kingdoms, 2865

CONQUEROR (2) [CONQUER]
Mic 1:15 a c against you who live in Mareshah. 3769
Rev 6: 2 and he rode out as a c bent on conquest. 3771

CONQUERORS (3) [CONQUER]
1Ki 8:47 and plead with you in the land of their c 8647
8:50 and cause their c to show them mercy; 8647
Ro 8:37 in all these things we are more than c 5664

CONQUERS (1) [CONQUER]
2Sa 5: 8 "Anyone who c the Jebusites will have 5782

CONQUEST (2) [CONQUER]
Am 6:13 you who rejoice in the c of Lo Debar NIH
Rev 6: 2 and he rode out as a conqueror bent on c. 3771

CONSCIENCE (29) [CONSCIENCE', CONSCIENCE-STRICKEN, CONSCIENCES, CONSCIENTIOUS]
Ge 20: 5 with a clear c and clean hands." 4222
20: 6 "Yes, I know you did this with a clear c, 4222
1Sa 25:31 not have on his c the staggering burden 4213
Job 27: 6 my c will not reproach me as long as I live. 4222
Ac 23: 1 to God in all good c to this day." 5287
24:16 to keep my c clear before God and man. 5287
Ro 9: 1 my c confirms it in the Holy Spirit— 5287
13: 5 but also because of c. 5287
1Co 4: 4 My c is clear, 4029+5323
8: 7 and since their c is weak, it is defiled. 5287
8:10 if anyone with a weak c sees you who have this knowledge eating 5287
8:12 in this way and wound their weak c, 5287
10:25 without raising questions of c, 5287
10:27 before you without raising questions of c. 5287
10:29 the other man's c, I mean, not yours. 5287
10:29 be judged by another's c? 5287
2Co 1:12 c testifies that we have conducted ourselves in the world, 5287
4: 2 to every man's c in the sight of God. 5287
5:11 and I hope it is also plain to your c. 5287
1Ti 1: 5 from a pure heart and a good c and 5287
1:19 holding on to faith and a good c. 5287
3: 9 of the deep truths of the faith with a clear c. 5287
2Ti 1: 3 as my forefathers did, with a clear c, 5287
Heb 9: 9 not able to clear the c of the worshiper. 5287
10:22 to cleanse us from a guilty c and 4505+5287
13:18 a clear c and desire to live honorably 5287
1Pe 3:16 keeping a clear c, 5287
3:21 from the body but the pledge of a good c 5287

CONSCIENCE' [CONSCIENCE]
1Co 10:28 of the man who told you and for c sake— 5287

CONSCIENCE-STRICKEN (2) [CONSCIENCE]
1Sa 24: 5 David was c for having cut off a corner 4213+5782
2Sa 24:10 David was c after he had counted 4213+5782

CONSCIENCES (4) [CONSCIENCE]
Ro 2:15 their c also bearing witness, 5287
1Ti 4: 2 whose c have been seared as with 5287
Tit 1:15 both their minds and c are corrupted. 5287
Heb 9:14 cleanse our c from acts that lead to death, 5287

CONSCIENTIOUS (1) [CONSCIENCE]
2Ch 29:34 for the Levites had been more c 3838+4222

CONSCIOUS (2)
Ro 3:20 rather, through the law we become c of sin. 2106
1Pe 2:19 the pain of unjust suffering because he is c 5287

CONSCRIPTED (5) [CONSCRIPTING]
1Ki 5:13 King Solomon c laborers from all Israel— 6590
9:15 the forced labor King Solomon c to build 6590
9:21 these Solomon c for his slave labor force, 6590
2Ch 2: 2 He c seventy thousand men as carriers 6218
8: 8 these Solomon c for his slave labor force, 6590

CONSCRIPTING (2) [CONSCRIPTED]
2Ki 25:19 in charge of c the people of the land 7371
Jer 52:25 in charge of c the people of the land 7371

CONSECRATE (43) [CONSECRATED, CONSECRATING, CONSECRATION, RECONSECRATED]
Ex 13: 2 "C to me every firstborn male. 7727
19:10 the people and c them today and tomorrow. 7727
19:22 the LORD, must c themselves, or 7727
28:38 in the sacred gifts the Israelites c, 7727
28:41 C them so they may serve me as priests. 7727
29: 1 "This is what you are to do to c them, 7727
29:27 "C those parts of the ordination ram 7727
29:36 and anoint it to c it. 7727
29:37 for the altar and c it. 7727
29:44 "So I will c the Tent of Meeting and 7727
29:44 and the altar and will c Aaron and his sons 7727
30:29 You shall c them so they will 7727
30:30 "Anoint Aaron and his sons and c them 7727
40: 9 c it and all its furnishings, 7727
40:10 c the altar, and it will be most holy. 7727
40:11 Anoint the basin and its stand and c them. 7727
40:13 anoint him and c him so he may serve me 7727
Lev 8:11 and the basin with its stand, to c them. 7727
8:12 and anointed him to c him. 7727
11:44 c yourselves and be holy, 7727
16:19 and to c it from the uncleanness of 7727
20: 7 " 'C yourselves and be holy, 7727
22: 2 the sacred offerings the Israelites c to me, 7727
22: 3 the sacred offerings that the Israelites c to 7727
25:10 C the fiftieth year and proclaim liberty 7727
Nu 6:11 That same day he is to c his head. 7727
11:18 'C yourselves in preparation 7727
Jos 3: 5 Joshua told the people, "C yourselves, 7727
7:13 "Go, c the people. 7727
7:13 'C yourselves in preparation 7727
Jdg 17: 3 "I solemnly c my silver to the LORD 7727+7727
1Sa 16: 5 C yourselves and come to the sacrifice 7727
1Ch 15:12 to c yourselves and bring up the ark of 7727
23:13 to c the most holy things, 7727
29: 5 who is willing to c himself today to the LORD? 2257+3338+4848
2Ch 13: 9 Whoever comes to c himself with 3338+4848
29: 5 C yourselves now and consecrate 7727
29: 5 now and c the temple of the LORD, 7727
30:17 not c [their lambs] to the LORD. 7727
35: 6 c yourselves and prepare [the lambs] 7727
Isa 66:17 "Those who c and purify themselves to go 7727
Eze 44:19 so that they do not c the people by means 7727
Joel 2:16 Gather the people, c the assembly; 7727

CONSECRATED (57) [CONSECRATE]
Ex 19:14 he c them, and they washed their clothes. 7727
29:21 and his sons and their garments will be c. 7727
29:43 and the place will be c by my glory. 7727
Lev 8:10 and so c them. 7727
8:15 So he c it to make atonement for it. 7727
8:30 So he c Aaron and his garments 7727
Nu 6: 8 of his separation he is c to the LORD. 7705
7: 1 and c it and all its furnishings. 7727
7: 1 and c the altar and all its utensils. 7727
15:40 to obey all my commands and will be c 7705
Dt 12:26 But take your c things 7731
1Sa 7: 1 on the hill and c Eleazar his son to guard 7727
16: 5 Then he c Jesse and his sons 7727
21: 4 however, there is some c bread here— 7731
21: 6 So the priest gave him the c bread, 7731
1Ki 8:64 On that same day the king c the middle part 7727
9: 3 I have c this temple, which you have built, 7727
9: 7 and will reject this temple I have c 7727
13:33 a priest he c for the high places. 906+3338+4848
1Ch 15:14 and Levites c themselves in order to bring 7727
28:16 of gold for each table for c bread; 5121
2Ch 2: 4 for setting out the c bread regularly, 5121
5:11 priests who were there had c themselves, 7727
7: 7 Solomon c the middle part of the courtyard 7727
7:16 and c this temple so that my Name may 7727
7:20 and will reject this temple I have c 7727
23: 6 they may enter because they are c, 7731
26:18 who have been c to burn incense. 7727
29:15 and c themselves, they went in to purify 7727
29:17 For eight more days they c the temple of 7727
29:18 setting out the c bread, 5121
29:19 We have prepared and c all the articles 7727
29:33 The animals c as sacrifices amounted 7731
29:34 and until other priests had been c, 7727
30: 3 not enough priests had c themselves 7727

2Ch 30: 8 the sanctuary, which *he has* **c** forever. 7727
30:15 the Levites were ashamed and **c themselves** 7727
30:17 many in the crowd *had* not **c themselves,** 7727
30:24 A great number of priests **c themselves.** 7727
31:14 to the LORD and also the **c gifts.** 7731+7731
35: 3 and who had been **c** to the LORD: 7705
36:14 which *he had* **c** in Jerusalem. 7727
Ezr 8:28 "You as well as these articles are **c** to 7731
Ps 50: 5 "Gather to me my **c** *ones,* 2883
106:16 who was **c** *to* the LORD. 7705
Jer 11:15 Can **c** meat avert [your punishment]? 7731
Eze 48:11 This will be for the **c** priests, the Zadokites, 7727
Hos 9:10 *they* **c themselves** to that shameful idol 5692
Zep 1: 7 *he has* **c** those he has invited. 7727
Hag 2:12 If a person carries **c** meat in the fold 7731
2:12 oil or other food, *does it become* **c?' "** 7727
Mt 12: 4 he and his companions ate the **c** bread— *4606*
Mk 2:26 the house of God and ate the **c** bread, *4606*
Lk 2:23 "Every firstborn male is *to be* **c** to *41+2813*
6: 4 and taking the **c** bread, *4606*
1Ti 4: 5 *it is* **c** by the word of God and prayer. *39*
Heb 9: 2 the table and the **c bread;** *788+4606*

CONSECRATING (3) [CONSECRATE]

2Ch 29:34 in **c themselves** than the priests had been. 7727
31:18 For they *were* faithful in **c themselves.** 7727+7731
Eze 46:20 into the outer court and **c** the people." 7727

CONSECRATION (3) [CONSECRATE]

Ex 28: 3 for his **c**, so he may serve me as priest. 7727
29:33 for their ordination and **c.** 7727
2Ch 29:17 the **c** on the first day of the first month, 7727

CONSENT (8) [CONSENTED]

Ge 34:15 *We will* **give** *our* **c** to you 252
34:22 But the men will **c** to live with us 252
34:23 So *let us* **give** *our* **c** to them, 252
Job 39: 9 *"Will* the wild ox **c** to serve you? 14
Hos 8: 4 They set up kings without my **c;** 4946
Ac 23:21 waiting for your **c** to their request." *2039*
1Co 7: 5 not deprive each other except by **mutual c** *5247*
Phm 1:14 not want to do anything without your **c,** *1191*

CONSENTED (3) [CONSENT]

Mt 3:15 Then John **c.** *918*
Lk 22: 6 *He* **c**, and watched for an opportunity *2018*
23:51 who had not **c** to their decision and action. *5163*

CONSEQUENCES (8) [CONSEQUENTLY]

Nu 5:31 but the woman will bear the **c** of her **sin.' "** 6411
9:13 That man will bear the **c of** his **sin.** 2628
18:22 or they will bear the **c of** their **sin** 2628
Eze 16:58 You will bear the **c** of your **lewdness** 2365
23:35 the **c of** your **lewdness** and prostitution." 2365
23:49 and bear the **c of** your **sins** *of* idolatry. 2628
44:10 after their idols must bear the **c of** their **sin.** 6411
44:12 that they must bear the **c of** their **sin,** 6411

CONSEQUENTLY (4) [CONSEQUENCES]

Ro 5:18 **C**, just as the result of one trespass *726+4036*
10:17 **C**, faith comes from hearing the message, *726*
13: 2 **C**, he who rebels against the authority *6063*
Eph 2:19 **C**, you are no longer foreigners *726+4036*

CONSIDER (92) [CONSIDERABLE, CONSIDERATE, CONSIDERED, CONSIDERS, RECONSIDER]

Ex 30:32 It is sacred, and you *are to* **c** *it* sacred. 2118+4200
30:37 **c** *it* holy to the LORD. 2118+4200
Lev 19:23 three years you *are to* **c** it forbidden; 2118+4200
21: 8 **C** *them* holy, because I 2118+4200
Nu 23: 9 and *do* not **c themselves** one of the nations. 3108
Dt 15:18 Do not **c** it a hardship to set your servant free, 928+6524
17:20 not **c** himself **better** than his brothers 4222+8123
32: 7 **c** the generations long past. 1067
Jdg 5:10 and you who walk along the road, **c** 8488
19:30 Think about it! **C** it! 6418
1Sa 12:24 **c** what great things he has done for you. 7011
16: 7 *"Do* not **c** his appearance or his height, 5564
24:15 *May he* **c** my cause and uphold it; 8011
1Ki 2: 9 But now, *do* not **c** him **innocent.** 5927
1Ch 28:10 **C** now, for the LORD has chosen you 8011
2Ch 19: 6 He told them, **"C carefully** what you do, 8011
Job 4: 7 **"C** now: Who, being innocent, 2349
13:24 and **c** me your enemy? 3108
23: 5 and **c** what he would say. 1067
37:14 stop and **c** God's wonders. 1067
Ps 5: 1 O LORD, **c** my sighing. 1067
8: 3 When *I* **c** your heavens, 8011
10:14 *you* **c** it to take it in hand. 5564
37:37 **C** the blameless, observe the upright; 9068
45:10 Listen, O daughter, **c** and give ear: 8011
48:13 **c well** her ramparts, 4213+8883
50:22 **"C** this, *you* who forget God, 1067
77:12 and **c** all your mighty deeds. 8488
107:43 and **c** the great love of the LORD. 1067
119: 6 to shame when I **c** all your commands. 5564
119:15 on your precepts and **c** your ways. 5564
119:128 **c** all your precepts **right,** 3837
137: 6 if *I do* not **c** Jerusalem my highest joy. 6590
143: 5 and **c** what your hands have done. 8488
Pr 6: 6 **c** its ways and be wise! 8011
20:25 and only later to **c** his vows. 1329
Ecc 2:12 Then I turned my thoughts to **c** wisdom, 8011
7:13 **C** what God has done: 8011
7:14 but when times are bad, **c:** 8011
Isa 41:20 *may* **c** and understand, 8492
41:22 so that we *may* **c** them 4213+8492
47: 7 But *you did* not **c** these things 4213+6584+8492
Jer 2:19 **C** then and realize how evil and bitter it is 3359
2:23 **c** what you have done. 3359
2:31 **c** the word of the LORD: 8011
5: 1 look around and **c,** 3359
9:17 This is what the LORD Almighty says: **"C** now! 1067
La 1: 9 *she did* not **c** her future. 2349
1:11 "Look, O LORD, and **c,** 5564
2:20 "Look, O LORD, and **c:** 5564
Eze 31: 3 **C** Assyria, once a cedar in Lebanon, 2180
43:10 *Let them* **c** the plan, 4499
47:22 You *are to* **c** them as native-born Israelites; 2118+4200
Da 8:25 and he will **c** himself superior. 928+4222
9:23 **c** the message and understand the vision: 1067
10:11 **c carefully** the words I am about 1067
Hag 2:15 **c** how things were before one stone was laid NIH
Mk 4:24 **"C carefully** what you hear," *1063*
Lk 7: 7 That is why *I did* not even **c** myself **worthy** *546*
8:18 Therefore **c carefully** how you listen. *1063*
12:24 **C** the ravens: They do not sow or reap, *2917*
12:27 **"C** how the lilies grow. *2917*
14:31 not first sit down and **c** whether he is able *1086*
Ac 4:29 **c** their threats and enable your servants *2078*
5:35 of Israel, **c carefully** what you intend *4668*
13:46 not **c** yourselves worthy of eternal life, *3212*
15: 6 and elders met *to* **c** this question. *3972+4309*
16:15 "If *you* **c** me a believer in the Lord," *3212*
20:24 However, *I* **c** my life worth nothing to me, *4472*
26: 2 *I* **c** myself fortunate to stand *2451*
26: 8 Why *should* any of you **c** it incredible *3212*
Ro 8:18 *I* **c** that our present sufferings are *3357*
11:18 If you do, **c** this: *NIG*
11:22 **C** therefore the kindness and sternness *3972*
14:16 Do not allow what you **c** good to be spoken *NIG*
1Co 10:18 **C** the people of Israel: *1063*
2Co 10: 7 *he should* **c** again that we belong *3357*
Gal 3: 6 **C** Abraham: "He believed God, *NIG*
Php 2: 3 in humility **c** others better than yourselves. *2451*
2: 6 *did* not **c** equality with God something to *2451*
3: 7 But whatever was to my profit *I now* **c** loss *2451*
3: 8 *I* **c** everything a loss compared to *2451*
3: 8 *I* **c** them rubbish, *2451*
3:13 not **c** myself yet to have taken hold of it. *3357*
1Ti 6: 1 of slavery *should* **c** their masters worthy *2451*
Phm 1:17 So if *you* **c** me a partner, *2400*
Heb 10:24 And *let us* **c** how we may spur one another on toward love *2917*
12: 3 **C** him who endured such opposition *382*
13: 7 **C** the outcome of their way of life *355*
Jas 1: 2 **C** it pure joy, my brothers, *2451*
3: 5 **C** what a great forest is set on fire by *2627*
5:11 *we* **c blessed** those who have persevered. *3420*

CONSIDERABLE (2) [CONSIDER]

Mt 14:24 boat was already a **c** distance from land, *4498*
Ac 14: 3 So Paul and Barnabas spent **c** time there, *2653*

CONSIDERATE (4) [CONSIDER]

Tit 3: 2 to be peaceable and **c,** *2117*
Jas 3:17 then peace-loving, **c**, submissive, *2117*
1Pe 2:18 not only *to* those who are good and **c,** *2117*
3: 7 be **c** as you live with your wives, *1194+2848*

CONSIDERED (31) [CONSIDER]

Ge 30:33 *will* **be c stolen."** 1704
Lev 17: 4 that man *shall* **be c** guilty of bloodshed; 3108
25:31 around them *are to* **be c** as open country. 3108
Dt 2:11 they too **were c** Rephaites, 3108
2:20 (That too **was c** a land of the Rephaites, 3108
1Sa 26:21 Because you **c** my life precious today, 928+6524
2Sa 4: 2 Beeroth **is c** part of Benjamin, 3108
1Ki 10:21 because silver **was c** of little value 3108
16:31 not only **c** *it* **trivial** to commit the sins 7837
2Ch 9:20 because silver **was c** of little value 3108
Ne 13:13 because *these men* **were c** trustworthy. 3108
Job 1: 8 *"Have you* **c** my servant Job? 4213+8492
2: 3 *"Have you* **c** my servant Job? 4213+8492
18: 3 Why are we regarded as cattle and **c stupid** 3241
34: 6 Although I am right, *I am* **c a liar;** 3941
Ps 44:22 *we* **are c** as sheep to be slaughtered. 3108
119:59 *I have* **c** my ways 3108
Isa 53: 4 yet we **c** him stricken by God, 3108
65:20 to reach a hundred *will* **be c accursed.** 7837
La 4: 2 **are** now **c** as pots of clay, 3108
Hos 9: 7 the prophet is **c** a fool, NIH
Mt 1:20 But *after* he *had* **c** this, *1926*
14: 5 because *they* **c** him a prophet. *2400+6055*
Lk 20:35 But those who *are* **c worthy of** taking part *2921*
22:24 among them as to which of them *was* **c** to *1506*
Ro 8:36 *we are* **c** as sheep to be slaughtered." *3357*
2Co 11:12 an opportunity to *be* **c** equal with us in *2351*
1Ti 1:12 that *he* **c** me faithful, *2451*
Heb 11:11 because *he* **c** him faithful who had made *2451*
Jas 2:21 *Was* not our ancestor Abraham **c righteous** *1467*
2:25 the prostitute **c righteous** for what she did *1467*

CONSIDERS (7) [CONSIDER]

Job 33:10 *he* **c** me his enemy. 3108
Ps 33:15 who **c** everything they do. 1067
Pr 31:16 *She* **c** a field and buys it; 2372
Eze 18:28 Because *he* **c** all the offenses 8011
Ro 14: 5 One man **c** one day more sacred than another; *3212*
14: 5 another man **c** every day alike. *3212*
Jas 1:26 If anyone **c himself** religious and yet *1506+1639*

CONSIGN (2) [CONSIGNING]

Isa 43:28 and *I will* **c** Jacob to destruction 5989
Eze 32:18 of Egypt and **c** to the earth below both her 3718

CONSIGNING (2) [CONSIGN]

2Sa 12:31 **c** them **to labor** with saws and 8492
1Ch 20: 3 **c** them **to labor** with saws and 8492

CONSIST (3) [CONSISTED, CONSISTING, CONSISTS]

Lev 2: 4 it is to **c** of fine flour: NIH
Eze 45:12 The shekel *is to* **c of** twenty gerahs. 2118
Lk 12:15 not **c** in the abundance of his possessions." *1639*

CONSISTED (2) [CONSIST]

Jos 17: 5 Manasseh's share **c of** ten tracts 5877
1Ch 27: 1 Each division **c** of 24,000 men. NIH

CONSISTING (1) [CONSIST]

Eze 46:14 **c** of a sixth of an ephah with a third of NIH

CONSISTS (2) [CONSIST]

Eze 45:14 is a tenth of a bath from each cor (which **c** NIH
Eph 5: 9 (for the fruit of the light **c** in all goodness, *NIG*

CONSOLATION (4) [CONSOLE]

Job 6:10 Then I would still have this **c—** 5717
21: 2 let this be the **c** you give me. 9487
Ps 94:19 your **c** brought joy to my soul. 9488
Lk 2:25 He was waiting for the **c** of Israel, *4155*

CONSOLATIONS (1) [CONSOLE]

Job 15:11 Are God's **c** not enough for you, 9487

CONSOLE (4) [CONSOLATION, CONSOLATIONS, CONSOLED, CONSOLING]

Job 21:34 how *can you* **c** me *with* your nonsense? 5714
Isa 22: 4 to **c** me over the destruction of my people." 5714
51:19 who *can* **c** you? 5714
Jer 16: 7 will anyone give them a drink to **c** them. 9488

CONSOLED (6) [CONSOLE]

2Sa 13:39 for *he* **was c** concerning Amnon's death. 5714
Job 42:11 They comforted and **c** him over all 5714
Eze 14:22 *you will* **be c** regarding 5714
14:23 You *will be* **c** when you see their conduct 5714
31:16 **were c** in the earth below. 5714
32:31 and *he will* **be c** for all his hordes 5714

CONSOLING (1) [CONSOLE]

Ge 27:42 "Your brother Esau *is* **c himself** with 5714

CONSORT (2)

Ps 26: 4 nor *do I* **c** with hypocrites; 995
Hos 4:14 because the men themselves **c** with harlots 7233

CONSPICUOUS (1)

Eze 19:11 **c** for its height and for its many branches. 8011

CONSPIRACY (9) [CONSPIRE]

2Sa 15:12 And so the **c** gained strength, 8004
2Ki 15:15 and the **c** he **led,** 8003+8004
Ps 64: 2 Hide me from the **c** *of* the wicked, 6051
Isa 8:12 "Do not call **c** everything 8004
8:12 that these people call **c;** 8004
Jer 11: 9 "There is a **c** among the people of Judah 8004
Eze 22:25 There is a **c** *of* her princes within her like 8004
Am 7:10 "Amos *is* **raising a c** against you in 8003
Ac 23:12 the Jews formed a **c** and bound themselves *5371*

CONSPIRATORS (1) [CONSPIRE]

2Sa 15:31 among the **c** with Absalom." 8003

CONSPIRE (9) [CONSPIRACY, CONSPIRATORS, CONSPIRED]

Ps 2: 1 the nations **c** and the peoples plot in vain? 8093
31:13 they **c** against me and plot to take my life. 3570
56: 6 *They* **c**, they lurk, they watch my steps, 1592
59: 3 Fierce men **c** against me for no offense 1592
71:10 those who wait to kill me **c** together. 3619
83: 3 With cunning they **c** against your people; 6051
105:25 to **c** against his servants. 5792
Mic 7: 3 *they all* **c** *together.* 6309
Ac 4:27 and the people of Israel in this city to **c** *NIG*

CONSPIRED (19) [CONSPIRE]

1Sa 22: 8 Is that why you *have* all **c** against me? 8003
22:13 "Why *have you* **c** against me, 8003
1Ki 2:28 who *had* **c** with Adonijah though not 5742
2Ki 9:14 the son of Nimshi, **c** against Joram. 8003
10: 9 It was I *who* **c** against my master 8003
12:20 His officials **c** *against* him 8003+8004
14:19 *They* **c** against him in Jerusalem, 8003+8004
15:10 Shallum son of Jabesh **c** against Zechariah. 8003
15:25 Pekah son of Remaliah, **c** against him. 8003
15:30 **c** against Pekah son of Remaliah. 8003+8004
21:23 Amon's officials **c** against him 8003
2Ch 24:25 His officials **c** against him for murdering 8003
24:26 Those *who* **c** against him were Zabad, 8003
25:27 *they* **c** against him in Jerusalem and 8003+8004
33:24 Amon's officials **c** against him 8003
Est 2:21 and **c** to assassinate King Xerxes. 1335
6: 2 who *had* **c** to assassinate King Xerxes. 1335
Da 2: 9 *You have* **c** to tell me misleading 10231
Ac 9:23 the Jews **c** to kill him, *5205*

CONSTANT (10) [CONSTANTLY]

Nu 17: 5 I will rid myself of this **c grumbling** 4296+9442
Dt 28:66 You will live in **c** suspense, 4946+5584
Job 33:19 a bed of pain with **c** distress in his bones, 419
Pr 19:13 quarrelsome wife is like a **c dripping.** 1942+3265
27:15 quarrelsome wife is like a **c dripping** 1942+3265
Isa 51:13 that you live in **c** terror every day because 9458
Eze 30:16 Memphis will be in **c** distress. 3429
Ac 27:33 "you have been in **c** suspense *NIG*
1Ti 6: 5 **c friction between** men of corrupt mind, *1384*
Heb 5:14 who by **c** use have trained themselves *NIG*

CONSTANTLY (9) [CONSTANT]

Ps 106: 3 who **c** do what is right. 928+3972+6961
119:109 Though I **c** take my life in my hands, 9458
Isa 52: 5 all day long my name is **c** blasphemed. 9458
Jn 3:23 and *people were* **c** *coming* to be baptized. *AIT*
Ac 1:14 They all **joined** together **c** in prayer, *4674*
Ro 1: 9 is my witness how **c** I remember you *90*
2Co 11:26 I have been **c** on the move. *4490*
2Th 1:11 With this in mind, we **c** pray for you, *4121*
2Ti 1: 3 and day I **c** remember you in my prayers. *89*

CONSTELLATIONS (4)

2Ki 23: 5 to the **c** and to all the starry hosts. 4655
Job 9: 9 the Pleiades and the **c** *of* the south. 2540
38:32 Can you bring forth the **c** in their seasons 4666
Isa 13:10 and their **c** will not show their light. 4068

CONSTRAIN (KJV) See COMPEL

CONSTRUCT (1) [CONSTRUCTED, CONSTRUCTING, CONSTRUCTION, CONSTRUCTIVE]

2Ch 20:36 with him to **c** a fleet of trading ships. 6913

CONSTRUCTED (3) [CONSTRUCT]

1Ki 9:24 *he* **c** the supporting terraces. 1215
1Ch 15: 1 After David *had* **c** buildings for himself in 6913
Eze 40:17 and a pavement *that had* **been c** all around 6913

CONSTRUCTING (3) [CONSTRUCT]

Ex 36: 1 of **c** the sanctuary are to do the work just as 6275
36: 3 to carry out the work of **c** the sanctuary. 6275
Ezr 5: 4 the names of the men **c** this building?" 10111

CONSTRUCTION (4) [CONSTRUCT]

1Ki 7: 1 however, to complete the **c** *of* his palace. 1215
2Ki 16:10 with detailed plans for its **c.** 5126
Ezr 5:16 to the present *it has been* **under c** but is not 10111
6: 8 of the Jews in the **c** *of* this house of God: 10111

CONSTRUCTIVE (1) [CONSTRUCT]

1Co 10:23 is permissible"—but not everything *is* **c.** *3868*

CONSULT (19) [CONSULTATION, CONSULTED, CONSULTING, CONSULTS]

1Sa 28: 8 "**C** a spirit for me," he said, 7876
28:16 Samuel said, "Why *do you* **c** me, 8626
2Ki 1: 2 Go and **c** Baal-Zebub, the god of Ekron 928+2011
1: 3 that you are going off to **c** Baal-Zebub, 928+2011
1: 6 you are sending men to **c** Baal-Zebub, 928+2011
1:16 is no God in Israel for you to **c** 928+1821+2011
1:16 to **c** Baal-Zebub, the god of Ekron? 928+2011
8: 8 **C** the LORD through him; 2011
2Ch 17: 3 *He did* not **c** the Baals 2011
25:15 "Why *do you* **c** this people's gods, 2011
Est 1:13 the king to **c** experts in matters of law 4200+7156
Pr 15:12 *he will* not **c** the wise. 448+2143
Isa 8:19 When men tell you *to* **c** mediums 2011
8:19 Why **c** the dead on behalf of the living? 448
19: 3 *they will* **c** the idols and the spirits of 2011
40:14 Whom *did* the LORD **c** to enlighten him, 3619
Eze 21:21 *he will* **c** his idols, 8626
Hos 4:12 *They* **c** a wooden idol and are answered by 8626
Gal 1:16 *I did* not **c** any man, *4651*

CONSULTATION (1) [CONSULT]

1Ch 12:19 after **c**, their rulers sent him away. 6783

CONSULTED (10) [CONSULT]

1Ki 12: 6 Then King Rehoboam **c** the elders 3619
12: 8 and **c** the young men who had grown up 3619
2Ki 21: 6 and **c** mediums and spiritists. 6913
1Ch 10:13 of the LORD and even **c** a medium 8626
2Ch 10: 6 Then King Rehoboam **c** the elders 3619
10: 8 and **c** the young men who had grown up 3619
25:17 Amaziah king of Judah **c** *his* **advisers,** 3619
32: 3 *he* **c** with his officials and military staff 3619
33: 6 and **c** mediums and spiritists. 6913
Jer 8: 2 and which they have followed and **c** 2011

CONSULTING (2) [CONSULT]

2Ch 20:21 After **c** the people, 3619
Isa 30: 2 who go down to Egypt without **c** me; 7023+8626

CONSULTS (2) [CONSULT]

Dt 18:11 or who is a medium or spiritist or *who* **c** 2011
Eze 14:10 be as guilty as the *one who* **c** him. 2011

CONSUME (39) [CONSUMED, CONSUMES, CONSUMING]

Dt 5:25 This great fire *will* **c** us, 430
Jdg 9:15 of the thornbush and **c** the cedars 430
9:20 from Abimelech and **c** you, 430
9:20 and Beth Millo, and **c** Abimelech!" 430
1Ki 16: 3 So I *am about to* **c** Baasha and his house, 1277
21:21 *I will* **c** your descendants and cut off 1277
2Ki 1:10 and **c** you and your fifty men!" 430
1:12 and **c** you and your fifty men!" 430
Job 5: 5 The hungry **c** his harvest, 430
15:34 and fire *will* **c** the tents 430
20:26 A fire unfanned *will* **c** him 430
Ps 21: 9 and his fire *will* **c** them. 430
39:11 *you* **c** their wealth like a moth— 4998
59:13 **c** them in wrath, 3983
59:13 **c** them till they are no more. 3983
Ecc 5:11 As goods increase, so do *those who* **c** them. 430
Isa 10:17 in a single day it will burn and **c** his thorns 430
26:11 the fire reserved for your enemies **c** them. 430
Jer 17:27 of Jerusalem that *will* **c** her fortresses.' " 430
21:14 *that will* **c** everything around you.' " 430
49:27 *it will* **c** the fortresses of Ben-Hadad." 430
50:32 a fire in her towns *that will* **c** all who are 430
Eze 15: 7 the fire *will yet* **c** them. 430
20:47 and *it will* **c** all your trees, 430
21:28 polished to **c** and to flash like lightning! 430
22:31 on them and **c** them with my fiery anger, 3983
Hos 8:14 *that will* **c** their fortresses." 430
Am 1: 4 *that will* **c** the fortresses of Ben-Hadad. 430
1: 7 of Gaza *that will* **c** her fortresses. 430
1:10 of Tyre *that will* **c** her fortresses." 430
1:12 I will send fire upon Teman *that will* **c** 430
1:14 *that will* **c** her fortresses amid war cries 430
2: 2 I will send fire upon Moab *that will* **c** 430
2: 5 *that will* **c** the fortresses of Jerusalem." 430
Ob 1:18 and they will set it on fire and **c** it. 430
Na 3:15 like grasshoppers, **c** you. 430
Zec 12: 6 *They will* **c** right and left all 430
Jn 2:17 "Zeal for your house *will* **c** me." *2983*
Heb 10:27 of judgment and of raging fire *that* will **c** *2266*

CONSUMED (33) [CONSUME]

Ge 31:40 The heat **c** me in the daytime and the cold 430
Ex 15: 7 *it* **c** them like stubble. 430
Lev 6:10 of the burnt offering that the fire *has* **c** on 430
9:24 and **c** the burnt offering and the fat portions 430
10: 2 the presence of the LORD and **c** them, 430
Nu 11: 1 among them and **c** some of the outskirts of 430
11:33 and before *it could* **be c,** 4162
16:35 And fire came out from the LORD and **c** 430
21:28 *It* **c** Ar of Moab, 430
2Ki 1:10 from heaven and **c** the captain and his men. 430
1:12 the fire of God fell from heaven and **c** him 430
1:14 from heaven and **c** the first two captains 430
2Ch 7: 1 down from heaven and **c** the burnt offering 430
Ps 31:10 My life *is* **c** by anguish and my years 3983
78:63 Fire **c** their young men, 430
90: 7 *We are* **c** by your anger and terrified 3983
106:18 a flame **c** the wicked. 4265
119:20 My soul *is* **c** with longing for your laws 1756
Ecc 10:12 but a fool *is* **c** *by* his own lips. 1180
Isa 42:25 *it* **c** them, but they did not take it to heart. 1277
Jer 3:24 From our youth shameful gods *have* **c** 430
La 3:22 of the LORD's great love *we are* not **c,** 9462
4:11 a fire in Zion that **c** her foundations. 430
Eze 19:12 and fire **c** them. 430
19:14 of its main branches and **c** its fruit. 430
23:25 and those of you who are left *will* **be c** 430
28:18 and it **c** you, 430
Na 1:10 *they will* **be c** like dry stubble. 430
3:13 fire *has* **c** their bars. 430
Zep 1:18 of his jealousy the whole world *will* **be c,** 430
3: 8 The whole world *will* **be c** by the fire 430
Zec 9: 4 and she *will* **be c** by fire. 430
Rev 18: 8 *She will be* **c** by fire, *2876*

CONSUMES (8) [CONSUME]

Ps 69: 9 for zeal for your house **c** me, 430
83:14 As fire **c** the forest or a flame sets 1277
97: 3 before him and **c** his foes on every side. 4265
Isa 9:18 *it* **c** briers and thorns, 430
24: 6 Therefore a curse **c** the earth; 430
33:11 your breath is a fire *that* **c** you. 430
Jer 5:14 a fire and these people the wood *it* **c.** 430
La 2: 3 a flaming fire *that* **c** everything around it. 430

CONSUMING (11) [CONSUME]

Ex 24:17 glory of the LORD looked like a **c** fire on 430
Dt 4:24 LORD your God is a **c** fire, a jealous God. 430
32:24 **c** pestilence and deadly plague; 4310
Jdg 6:21 **c** the meat and the bread. 430
2Sa 22: 9 **c** fire came from his mouth, 430
Ps 18: 8 **c** fire came from his mouth, 430
Isa 30:27 and his tongue *is* a **c** fire. 430
30:30 down with raging anger and **c** fire, 430
33:14 "Who of us can dwell with the **c** fire? 430
Joel 2: 5 like a crackling fire **c** stubble, 430
Heb 12:29 for our "God is a **c** fire." *2914*

CONSUMMATION (KJV) See END

CONSUMPTION (KJV) See DISEASE, DESTRUCTION

CONTACT (1)

Hag 2:13 "If a *person* **defiled** *by* **c** *with* a dead body AIT

CONTAIN (5) [CONTAINED, CONTAINER, CONTAINING, CONTAINS]

1Ki 8:27 even the highest heaven, cannot **c** you. 3920
2Ch 2: 6 even the highest heavens, cannot **c** him? 3920
6:18 even the highest heavens, cannot **c** you. 3920
Ecc 8: 8 No man has power over the wind to **c** it; 3973
2Pe 3:16 His letters **c** some things that are hard *NIG*

CONTAINED (2) [CONTAIN]

Ac 10:12 It **c** all kinds of four-footed animals, *1877+5639*
Heb 9: 4 This ark **c** the gold jar of manna, *1877+2400*

CONTAINER (1) [CONTAIN]

Nu 19:15 and every open **c** without a lid fastened 3998

CONTAINING (9) [CONTAIN]

Ex 13: 3 Eat nothing **c yeast.** 2809
23:18 to me along with **anything c yeast.** 2809
34:25 to me along with **anything c yeast,** 2809
Lev 8: 2 and the **basket** *c* bread made without yeast, AIT
1Sa 6:11 the chest **c** the gold rats and the models of NIH
6:15 together with the chest **c** the gold objects, 928
Jer 32:11 the sealed copy **c** the terms and conditions, NIH
36:27 After the king burned the scroll **c** the words NIH
Eze 45:11 the bath **c** a tenth of a homer and the ephah 5951

CONTAINS (2) [CONTAIN]

Job 28: 6 and its dust **c** nuggets of gold. 4200
Pr 15: 6 The house of the righteous **c** great treasure, NIH

CONTAMINATED (4) [CONTAMINATES, CONTAMINATION]

Lev 13:47 "If any clothing is **c** *with* mildew— 5596
13:54 he shall order that the **c article** 5596
13:56 he is to tear **the c part** out of the clothing, 2257[S]
14:40 he is to order that the **c** stones be torn out 5596

CONTAMINATES (1) [CONTAMINATED]

2Co 7: 1 from everything **that c** body and spirit, *3663*

CONTAMINATION (3) [CONTAMINATED]

Lev 13:49 and if the **c** in the clothing, 5596
13:52 or any leather article that has the **c** in it, 5596
13:59 the regulations concerning **c** *by* mildew 5596

CONTEMN (KJV) See REVILE, DESPISES

CONTEMPLATING (1) [CONTEMPLATE]

Isa 33:15 and shuts his eyes against **c** evil— 8011

CONTEMPT (31) [CONTEMPTIBLE, CONTEMPTUOUS, CONTEMPTUOUSLY]

Lev 22: 9 and die for **treating** them **with c.** 2725
Nu 14:11 "How long *will* these people **treat** me **with c?** 5540
14:23 No one *who has* **treated** me **with c** will ever see it. 5540
16:30 these men *have* **treated** the LORD **with c."** 5540
Dt 17:12 The man who shows **c** for the judge or for 2295
1Sa 2:17 **treating** the LORD's offering **with c.** 5540
25:39 against Nabal for treating me with **c.** 3075
2Sa 12:14 *you have* **made** the enemies of the LORD **show utter c,** 5540+5540
19:43 So why *do you* **treat** us **with c?** 7837
Job 12: 5 at ease have **c** for misfortune as the fate 997
12:21 He pours **c** on nobles and disarms 997
31:34 the crowd and so dreaded the **c** *of* the clans 997

Ps 31:11 I am the utter c of my neighbors; 3075
31:18 for with pride and c they speak arrogantly 997
107:40 he who pours c on nobles 997
119:22 Remove from me scorn and c, 997
123: 3 for we have endured much c. 997
123: 4 much c from the arrogant. 997
Pr 14:31 He who oppresses the poor **shows** c 3070
17: 5 the poor **shows** c *for* their Maker; 3070
18: 3 When wickedness comes, so does c, 997
27:11 I can answer *anyone who* **treats** me **with** c. 3070
Eze 22: 7 **treated** father and mother **with** c; 7837
Da 12: 2 others to shame and everlasting c. 1994
Hos 12:14 and will repay him for his c. 3075
Na 3: 6 *I will* **treat** you **with** c and make you 5571
Mal 1: 6 O priests, *who* **show** c *for* my name. 1022
1: 6 'How *have we* **shown** c *for* your name?' 1022
Ro 2: 4 Or *do you* **show** c **for** the riches *2969*
Gal 4:14 *you did* not **treat** me **with** c or scorn. *2024*
1Th 5:20 *do* not **treat** prophecies **with** c. *2024*

CONTEMPTIBLE (5) [CONTEMPT]
1Sa 3:13 his sons **made** themselves c, 7837
Eze 35:12 the c **things** you have said against 5542
Da 11:21 by a c *person* who has not been given 1022
Mal 1: 7 "By saying that the LORD's table *is* c. 1022
1:12 'It is defiled,' and of its food, 'It *is* c.' 1022

CONTEMPTUOUS (2) [CONTEMPT]
Dt 17:13 and *will* not *be* c again. 2326
Pr 19:16 but *he who is* c *of* his ways will die. 1022

CONTEMPTUOUSLY (1) [CONTEMPT]
Mal 1:13 and *you* **sniff** *at* it c," 5870

CONTEND (11) [CONTENDED, CONTENDING, CONTENDS, CONTENTION, CONTENTIOUS]
Ge 6: 3 "My Spirit *will* not c with man forever, 1906
Jdg 6:32 saying, "*Let* Baal c with him," 8189
Ps 35: 1 C, O LORD, with those who contend 8189
35: 1 O LORD, with *those who* c *with* me; 3742
35:23 C *for* me, my God and Lord. 8190
127: 5 to shame when *they* c with their enemies in 1819
Ecc 6:10 no man can c with one who is stronger 1906
Isa 27: 8 By warfare and exile *you* c *with* her— 8189
49:25 I *will* c with those who contend with you, 8189
49:25 I will contend with *those who* c *with* you, 3742
Jude 1: 3 I felt I had to write and urge you *to* c for *2043*

CONTENDED (2) [CONTEND]
Dt 33: 8 *you* c *with* him at the waters of Meribah, 8189
Php 4: 3 help these women who *have* c **at** my **side** in the cause of the gospel, *5254*

CONTENDING (1) [CONTEND]
Php 1:27 c **as** one man for the faith of the gospel *5254*

CONTENDS (2) [CONTEND]
Job 40: 2 "*Will* the *one who* c with 8189
Jer 15:10 with whom the whole land strives and c! 4506

CONTENT (9) [CONTENTED, CONTENTMENT, CONTENTS]
Jos 7: 7 If only *we had been* c to stay on 3283
Pr 13:25 The righteous eat to their hearts' c, 8427
19:23 Then one rests c, untouched by trouble. 8428
Ecc 4: 8 yet his eyes *were* not c *with* his wealth. 8425
Lk 3:14 *be* c with your pay." *758*
Php 4:11 to be c whatever the circumstances. *895*
4:12 I have learned the secret of being c in any *NIG*
1Ti 6: 8 *we will be* c with that. *758*
Heb 13: 5 of money and *be* c with what you have, *758*

CONTENTED (1) [CONTENT]
Da 4: 4 at home in my palace, c and prosperous. 10710

CONTENTION (1) [CONTEND]
Ps 80: 6 You have made us a **source of** c 4506

CONTENTIOUS (1) [CONTEND]
1Co 11:16 If anyone wants to be c about this, *5809*

CONTENTMENT (3) [CONTENT]
Job 36:11 in prosperity and their years in c. 5833
SS 8:10 in his eyes like one bringing c. 8934
1Ti 6: 6 But godliness with c is great gain. *894*

CONTENTS (1) [CONTENT]
Lev 1:16 to remove the crop with its c and throw it 5901

CONTEST (1)
Heb 10:32 when you stood your ground in a great c in *124*

CONTINUAL (4) [CONTINUE]
1Ki 14:30 There was c warfare between Rehoboam and Jeroboam. 2021+3427+3972
2Ch 12:15 There was c warfare between Rehoboam and Jeroboam. 2021+3427+3972
Pr 15:15 but the cheerful heart has a c feast. 9458
Eph 4:19 with a c lust for more. *NIG*

CONTINUALLY (26) [CONTINUE]
Ex 28:38 be on Aaron's forehead c so that they will 9458
Lev 24: 2 so that the lamps may be kept burning c. 9458
24: 3 the LORD from evening till morning, c. 9458
24: 4 before the LORD must be tended c. 9458
Nu 4: 7 the bread that is c there is to remain on it. 9458
Dt 11:12 the eyes of the LORD your God are c on it 9458
1Ki 10: 8 who c stand before you 9458
2Ch 9: 7 who c stand before you 9458
24:14 burnt offerings were presented c in 9458
Ps 26: 3 and *I* **walk** c in your truth. 2143
50:20 You speak c against your brother 3782
74:23 the uproar of your enemies, which rises c. 9458
Isa 27: 3 I water it c. 4200+8092
28:24 does he plow c? 2021+3427+3972
65: 3 a people who c provoke me 9458
Jer 33:18 ever fail to have a man to stand before me c to offer burnt offerings, 2021+3427+3972
Eze 8:17 with violence and c provoke me to anger? 8740
Da 6:16 "May your God, whom you serve c, rescue you!" 10002+10089+10753
6:20 has your God, whom you serve c, been able to rescue you 10002+10089+10753
Am 1:11 because his anger raged c 4200+6329
Ob 1:16 so all the nations will drink c; 9458
Lk 24:53 stayed c at the temple, praising God. *1328+4246*
1Th 1: 3 We c remember before our God *90*
2:13 And we also thank God c because, *90*
5:17 pray c; *90*
Heb 13:15 c offer to God a sacrifice of praise— *1328+4246*

CONTINUE (65) [CONTINUAL, CONTINUALLY, CONTINUED, CONTINUES, CONTINUING, CONTINUOUSLY]
Ex 9: 2 to let them go and c to hold them back, 6388
33:13 so I may know you and *c to* **find** favor AIT
40:15 a priesthood that will c for all generations 6409
Lev 25:22 from the old crop and *will c to* **eat** *from* it AIT
25:35 so *he can c to* **live** among you. AIT
25:36 so that your countryman *may c to* **live** AIT
26: 5 Your threshing *will* c **until** grape harvest 5952
26: 5 the grape harvest *will* c **until** planting, 5952
26:23 not accept my correction but c *to* 2143
26:27 of this you still do not listen to me but c *to* 2143
Nu 34: 4 c **on** to Zin and go south of Kadesh Barnea. 6296
34: 9 c to Ziphron and end at Hazar Enan. 3655
34:11 to Riblah on the east side of Ain and c 4682
Dt 22:19 *She shall c to* **be** his wife; AIT
Jos 13:13 so they *c to* **live** among the Israelites AIT
Jdg 19:27 the house and stepped out to c on his way, 2143
Ru 2:13 "*May I c to* **find** favor in your eyes, AIT
2Sa 7:29 that *it may* c forever in your sight; 2118
1Ki 8:23 with your servants who c wholeheartedly 2143
2Ki 17:41 and grandchildren *c to* **do** AIT
1Ch 17:27 that *it may* c forever in your sight; 2118
2Ch 6:14 with your servants who c wholeheartedly 2143
Est 9:23 to c the celebration they had begun, 6913
Ps 36:10 C your love to those who know you, 5432
72:17 *may* it c as long as the sun. 5672
89:36 that his line *will* c forever 2118
Isa 47: 7 You said, '*I will* c forever— 2118
Jer 3: 5 *Will* your wrath c forever?' 9068
18:12 *We will* c with our own plans; 2143
23:26 How long *will this* c in the hearts 3780
Eze 20:31 *c to* **defile yourselves** AIT
21:13 which the sword despises, *does* not c? 2118
Da 4:27 It may be that then your prosperity will c." 10073
9:26 War will c until the end, NIH
12:10 but the wicked *will c to be* **wicked.** AIT
Hos 4:18 c *their* **prostitution;** 2388+2388
Mal 2: 4 so that my covenant with Levi *may* c," 2118
Jn 17:26 *c to* **make** you **known** *AIT*
Ac 13:43 with them and urged them *to* c **in** the grace *4693*
Ro 1:32 *they* not only *c to* **do** these very things but *AIT*
11:22 provided that *you* c **in** his kindness. *2152*
2Co 1:10 On him we have set our hope that he will c *2285*
11: 9 and *will c to* **do so.** *AIT*
Gal 2:10 that *we should c to* **remember** the poor, *AIT*
3:10 not c to do everything written in the Book *1844*
Php 1:18 Yes, and *I will c to* **rejoice,** *AIT*
1:25 and *I will* c **with** all of you *4169*
2:12 *c to* **work out** your salvation with fear *AIT*
Col 1:23 if *you* c **in** your faith, *2152*
2: 6 *c to* **live** in him, *AIT*
2Th 2: 7 the one who now holds it back will c to do *NIG*
3: 4 and *will c to* **do** the things we command. *AIT*
1Ti 2:15 if *they* c in faith, *3531*
2Ti 3:14 c in what you have learned *3531*
Heb 6:10 and *c to* **help** them. *AIT*
1Pe 4:19 to their faithful Creator and c to do good. *NIG*
1Jn 2:28 And now, dear children, c in him, *3531*
3: 9 No one who is born of God *will c to* **sin,** *AIT*
5:18 that anyone born of God *does* not *c to* **sin;** *AIT*
2Jn 1: 9 Anyone who runs ahead and *does* not c in *3531*
3Jn 1: 3 to the truth and how you *c to* **walk** in *AIT*
Rev 22:11 Let him who does wrong c to do wrong; *2285*
22:11 let him who is vile c to be vile; *2285*
22:11 let him who does right c to do right; *2285*
22:11 and let him who is holy c to be holy." *2285*

CONTINUED (77) [CONTINUE]
Ge 8: 5 The waters c to recede until 2118+2143
12: 9 Abram set out and c toward the Negev. 2143
26:13 and his wealth c to grow 2143
29: 1 Then Jacob c **on** his **journey** and 5951+8079
30:36 Jacob *c to* **tend** the rest of Laban's flocks. AIT
42: 2 *He* c, "I have heard that there is grain 606
Ex 36: 3 the people c to bring freewill offerings 6388
Nu 9:16 That is how it c to be; 9458
21:16 From there they c on to Beer, NIH
Jos 9:21 They c, "Let them live, 606
15: 3 c **on** to Zin and went over to the south 6296
15: 6 to Beth Hoglah and c north of Beth Arabah 6296
15: 7 It c **along** to the waters of En Shemesh 6296
15:10 c **down** *to* Beth Shemesh and crossed 3718
16: 6 and c to the sea. 3655
17: 9 the boundary c south *to* the Kanah Ravine. 3718
18:16 *It* c **down** the Hinnom Valley along 3718
18:17 went to En Shemesh, c to Geliloth, 3655
18:18 *It* c to the northern slope of Beth Arabah 6296
19:13 Then *it* c eastward to Gath Hepher 6296
Jdg 1:29 Canaanites *c to* **live** there among them. AIT
14:17 because *she c to* **press** him. AIT
18:31 *They c to* **use** the idols Micah had made, AIT
1Sa 2:26 And the boy Samuel c **to grow** in stature 2143
3:21 The LORD c to appear at Shiloh, 3578
7:15 Samuel *c as* **judge** *over* Israel all the days AIT
18:30 The Philistine commanders *c to* **go out** AIT
30:10 and four hundred men *c the* **pursuit.** AIT
2Sa 2:27 the men *would have* c the pursuit 6590
2:29 c *through* the whole Bithron and came 2143
15:30 But David *c* **up** the Mount of Olives, AIT
16:13 So David and his men c along the road 2143
20:18 *She* c, "Long ago they used to say, 606
1Ki 2:17 So *he* c, "Please ask King Solomon— 606
3: 6 *You have* c this great kindness to him 9068
5:11 Solomon *c to* **do** this for Hiram year AIT
18:29 *c their* **frantic prophesying** AIT
22:19 Micaiah c, "Therefore hear the word of 606
22:43 and the people c to offer sacrifices 6388
2Ki 12: 3 the people c to offer sacrifices 6388
13: 6 *they* c in them. 2143
13:11 *he* c in them. 2143
14: 4 the people c to offer sacrifices 6388
15: 4 the people c to offer sacrifices 6388
15:35 the people c to offer sacrifices 6388
2Ch 12:13 in Jerusalem and *c as* **king.** AIT
18:18 Micaiah c, "Therefore hear the word of 606
27: 2 people, however, c their corrupt practices. 6388
29:28 All this c until the sacrifice of the burnt NIH
33:17 however, c to sacrifice at the high places, 6388
Ezr 6:14 of the Jews *c to* **build** and prosper under AIT
10: 6 because *he c to* **mourn** over AIT
Ne 4:21 So we c the work with half 6913
5: 9 So *I* c, "What you are doing is not right. 606
12:37 At the Fountain Gate *they* c directly **up** 6590
Est 2:20 she *c to* **follow** Mordecai's instructions AIT
Job 27: 1 And Job c his discourse: 3578
29: 1 Job c his discourse: 3578
36: 1 Elihu c: 3578
Ps 78:17 But *they* c to sin against him, 3578+6388
Isa 64: 5 But when we c to sin against them, 6409
Jer 32:20 and wonders in Egypt and have c them NIH
Da 7:11 "Then *I* c to watch because of 10201
10:12 Then *he* c, "Do not be afraid, Daniel. 606
Mk 4:24 "Consider carefully what you hear," *he* c. *3306*
Lk 4:24 "I tell you the truth," *he* c, *3306*
15:11 Jesus c: "There was a man who had two sons. *3306*
Jn 8:23 But *he* c, "You are from below; *3306*
12:17 *c to* **spread the word.** *AIT*
Ac 2:46 Every day *they* c to meet together in *4674*
4:33 the apostles *c* **to testify to** the resurrection *AIT*
12:24 the word of God *c to* **increase** and spread. *AIT*
14: 7 where *they* c to preach the good news. *1639*
15:38 in Pamphylia and *had* not c **with** them in *5302*
21: 5 our time was up, *we* left and c **on** *our* **way.** *4513*
21: 7 We c our voyage from Tyre and landed *1382*
27:20 for many days and the storm c **raging,** *2130+3900+4024*

CONTINUES (10) [CONTINUE]
Lev 15: 3 Whether it *c* **flowing** *from* his body AIT
15:25 or has a discharge that c beyond her period, NIH
15:26 **while** her discharge c will be unclean, 3427+3972
Ps 100: 5 his faithfulness c through all generations. NIH
119:90 Your faithfulness c through all generations; NIH
2Co 10:15 Our hope is that, *as* your faith *c to* **grow,** *AIT*
1Ti 5: 5 and c night and day to pray and to ask God *4693*
Jas 1:25 and c to do this, not forgetting *4169*
1Jn 3: 6 No one who *c to* **sin** has either seen him *AIT*
2Jn 1: 9 whoever c in the teaching has both *3531*

CONTINUING (5) [CONTINUE]
Ex 28:29 the breastpiece of decision as a c memorial 9458
Nu 15:23 from the day the LORD gave them and c 2134
Ro 13: 8 except the c debt to love one another, *NIG*
Heb 7:23 since death prevented them from c *4169*
2Pe 2: 9 *while c* their **punishment.** *AIT*

CONTINUOUSLY (1) [CONTINUE]
Lev 6:13 fire must be kept burning on the altar c; 9458

CONTRACT (2)
Isa 16:14 as a **servant bound by** c would count them, 8502
21:16 as a **servant bound by** c would count it, 8502

CONTRADICT (1)
Lk 21:15 be able to resist or c. *515*

CONTRARIWISE (KJV) See INSTEAD, CONTRARY, BUT

CONTRARY (23)
Lev 10: 1 before the LORD, **c** *to* his command. 4202
Dt 17: 3 **c to** my command has worshiped other gods 4202
Jos 22:27 **On the c,** it is to be a witness between us 3954
2Ch 30:18 **c to** what was written. 928+3869+4202
Ps 119:85 arrogant dig pitfalls for me, **c to** your law. 3869+4202
Ac 18:13 the people to worship God in ways **c to** *4123*
Ro 9: 7 **On the c,** "It is through Isaac *247*
11:24 and **c to** nature were grafted into *4123*
12:20 **On the c:** "If your enemy is hungry, *247*
16:17 that are **c to** the teaching you have learned. *4123*
1Co 9:12 **On the c,** we put up *247*
12:22 **On the c,** those parts of the body that seem to be weaker *247+3437+4498*
2Co 2:17 **On the c,** in Christ we speak before God *247*
4: 2 **On the c,** by setting forth *247*
10: 4 **On the c,** they have divine power *247*
Gal 2: 7 **On the c,** they saw that I had been entrusted with the task *247+1883*
3:12 The law is not based on faith; **on the c,** *247*
5:17 sinful nature desires what is **c to** the Spirit, *2848*
5:17 and the Spirit what is **c to** the sinful nature. *2848*
1Th 2: 4 **On the c,** we speak as men approved *247*
2Th 3: 8 **On the c,** we worked night and day, *247*
1Ti 1:10 whatever else *is* c to the sound doctrine *512*
2Ti 1:17 **On the c,** when he was in Rome, *247*

CONTRIBUTE (1) [CONTRIBUTED, CONTRIBUTING, CONTRIBUTION, CONTRIBUTIONS]
2Ki 15:20 Every wealthy man had to **c** fifty shekels 6584

CONTRIBUTED (4) [CONTRIBUTE]
2Ch 31: 3 The king **c** from his own possessions for 4987
35: 8 also **c** voluntarily to the people and 8123
Ne 7:70 of the heads of the families **c** to the work. 5989
12:47 all Israel **c** the daily portions for the singers 5989

CONTRIBUTING (1) [CONTRIBUTE]
Ro 12: 8 if it is **c** to the needs of others, *3556*

CONTRIBUTION (5) [CONTRIBUTE]
Ex 29:28 It is the **c** the Israelites are to make to 9556
Lev 7:14 a **c** to the LORD; 9556
7:32 to the priest as a **c.** 9556
Ne 10:34 at set times each year a **c** *of* wood to burn 7934
Ro 15:26 to make a **c** for the poor among the saints *3126*

CONTRIBUTIONS (10) [CONTRIBUTE]
Lev 22:12 she may not eat any of the sacred **c.** 9556
Nu 5: 9 All the sacred **c** the Israelites bring to 9556
2Ch 24:10 and all the people brought their **c** gladly, NIH
31:10 "Since the people began to bring their **c** to 9556
31:12 Then they faithfully brought in the **c,** 9556
31:14 distributing the **c** *made to* the LORD and 9556
Ne 10:39 are to bring their **c** *of* grain, 9556
12:44 to be in charge of the storerooms for the **c,** 9556
13: 5 as well as the **c** *for* the priests. 9556
13:31 I also made provision for **c** *of* wood 7934

CONTRITE (4)
Ps 51:17 a broken and **c** heart, O God, 1920
Isa 57:15 also with *him who* is **c** and lowly in spirit, 1918
57:15 the lowly and to revive the heart of the **c.** 1917
66: 2 he who is humble and **c** *in* spirit, 5783

CONTROL (23) [CONTROLLED, CONTROLLING, CONTROLS, SELF-CONTROL, SELF-CONTROLLED]
Ge 45: 1 Then Joseph could no longer **c himself** 706
Ex 32:25 that Aaron *had let* them **get out of c** and 7277
Jos 18: 1 The country **was brought under** their **c,** 3899
2Sa 8: 1 and he took Metheg Ammah from the **c** *of* 3338
8: 3 to restore his **c** along the Euphrates River. 3338
1Ki 11:24 where they settled and **took c.** 4887
1Ch 18: 1 and its surrounding villages from the **c** *of* 3338
18: 3 when he went to establish his **c** along 3338
2Ch 17: 5 the kingdom under his **c;** 3338
25: 3 After the kingdom was firmly **in** his **c,** 6584
Pr 29:11 but a wise man keeps himself **under c.** 294+928
Ecc 2:19 Yet *he will* **have c** over all the work 8948
Jer 28:14 even give him **c** over the wild animals.' " NIH
Da 11:43 *He will* **gain c** of the treasures of gold 5440
Ro 6:20 you were free from the **c** of righteousness. *NIG*
1Co 7: 9 But if *they* cannot **c themselves,** *1603*
7:37 who is under no compulsion but has **c** *2026*
14:32 The spirits of prophets *are* **subject to the c** *5718*
Php 3:21 **bring** everything **under** his **c,** *5718*
1Th 4: 4 of you should learn *to* **c** his own body in *3227*
2Ti 3: 6 and **gain c over** weak-willed women, *170*
1Jn 5:19 whole world *is* **under the c** of the evil one. *3023*
Rev 16: 9 who had **c** over these plagues, *2026*

CONTROLLED (7) [CONTROL]
Jdg 10: 4 They **c** thirty towns in Gilead, 4200
1Ch 2:22 who **c** twenty-three towns in Gilead. 2118+4200
Ps 32: 9 but *must be* **c** by bit and bridle or they will 1178
Ro 7: 5 For when we were **c** by the sinful nature, *NIG*
8: 6 the mind **c** by the Spirit is life and peace; *NIG*
8: 8 Those **c** by the sinful nature cannot please God. *1639*
8: 9 *are* **c** not by the sinful nature but by *1639*

CONTROLLING (1) [CONTROL]
Ge 43:31 **c himself,** said, "Serve the food." 706

CONTROLS (2) [CONTROL]
Job 37:15 Do you know how God **c** the clouds 8492
Pr 16:32 a *man who* **c** his temper than one who takes 5440

CONTROVERSIES (4)
Ac 26: 3 with all the Jewish customs and **c.** *2427*
1Ti 1: 4 These promote **c** rather than God's work— *1700*
6: 4 in **c** and quarrels about words that result *2428*
Tit 3: 9 But avoid foolish **c** and genealogies *2428*

CONVENED (2) [CONVENES]
Ac 25: 6 and the next day he **c the court** and ordered *1037+2093+2767+3836*
25:17 but **c** the court the next day and ordered *2767*

CONVENES (1) [CONVENED]
Job 11:10 and confines you in prison and **c a court,** 7735

CONVENIENT (1)
Ac 24:25 *When I* **find** it **c,** I will send for you." *2789+3561*

CONVERSATION (4)
1Sa 19: 7 and told him the whole **c.** 1821
Jer 38:24 "Do not let anyone know about this **c,** 1821
38:27 for no one had heard his **c** with the king. 1821
Col 4: 6 Let your **c** be always full of grace, *3364*

CONVERT (4) [CONVERTED, CONVERTS]
Mt 23:15 over land and sea to win a single **c,** *4670*
Ac 6: 5 and Nicolas from Antioch, a **c to Judaism.** *4670*
Ro 16: 5 the **first c** to Christ in the province *569*
1Ti 3: 6 He must not be a **recent c,** *3745*

CONVERTED (1) [CONVERT]
Ac 15: 3 they told how the Gentiles **had been c.** *2189+3836*

CONVERTS (3) [CONVERT]
Ac 2:11 (both Jews and **c to Judaism);** *4670*
13:43 and devout **c to Judaism** followed Paul *4670*
1Co 16:15 the household of Stephanas were the first **c** *NIG*

CONVEY (KJV) See FLOAT, SAFE-CONDUCT

CONVICT (5) [CONVICTED, CONVICTION, CONVICTIONS]
Dt 19:15 *to* **c** a man accused of any crime 7756
2Sa 14:13 does he not **c** himself, 872
Pr 24:25 it will go well with those *who* **c** the guilty, 3519
Jn 16: 8 **c** the world of **guilt** *1794*
Jude 1:15 and *to* **c** all the ungodly of all *1794*

CONVICTED (1) [CONVICT]
Jas 2: 9 and *are* **c** by the law as lawbreakers. *1794*

CONVICTION (1) [CONVICT]
1Th 1: 5 with the Holy Spirit and with deep **c.** *4443*

CONVICTIONS (1) [CONVICT]
Jos 14: 7 a report according to my **c,** 4222+6640

CONVINCE (1) [CONVINCED, CONVINCING]
Ac 28:23 the kingdom of God and *tried to* **c** them *4275*

CONVINCED (16) [CONVINCE]
Ge 45:28 And Israel said, "I'm **c!** 8041
Lk 16:31 *they will not be* **c** even if someone rises *4275*
Ac 19:26 and hear how this fellow Paul *has* **c** *4275*
26: 9 "I too *was* **c** that I ought to do all *1506*
26:26 *I am* **c** that none of this has escaped his *4275*
28:24 Some *were* **c** by what he said, *4275*
Ro 2:19 if *you are* **c that** you are a guide for *4275*
8:38 For *I am* **c** that neither death nor life, *4275*
14: 5 Each one *should be* **fully c** *4442*
14:14 *I am* **fully c** that no food is unclean *2779+3857+4275*
15:14 I myself *am* **c,** my brothers, *4275*
1Co 14:24 **c** by all **that** *he* **is a sinner** *1794*
2Co 5:14 *because we are* **c** that one died for all, *3212*
Php 1:25 **C** of this, I know that I will remain, *4275*
2Ti 1:12 and *am* **c** that he is able to guard *4275*
3:14 you have learned and *have become* **c** *of,* *4413*

CONVINCING (1) [CONVINCE]
Ac 1: 3 and gave many **c proofs** that he was alive. *5447*

CONVOCATIONS (1)
Isa 1:13 New Moons, Sabbaths and **c—** 5246+7924

CONVULSED (2) [CONVULSION]
Ps 77:16 the very depths *were* **c.** 8074
Mk 9:26 **c** him violently and came out. *5057*

CONVULSION (2) [CONVULSED, CONVULSIONS]
Mk 9:20 it immediately **threw** the boy **into a c.** *5360*
Lk 9:42 the demon threw him to the ground **in a c.** *5360*

CONVULSIONS (1) [CONVULSION]
Lk 9:39 *it* **throws** him **into c** so that he foams at *5057*

COOING (1)
SS 2:12 the **c** *of* doves is heard in our land. 7754

COOK (14) [COOKED, COOKING, COOKS]
Ex 23:19 *"Do* not **c** a young goat in its mother's milk. 1418
29:31 the ram for the ordination and **c** the meat in 1418
34:26 not **c** a young goat in its mother's milk." 1418
Lev 8:31 **"C** the meat at the entrance to the Tent 1418
Dt 14:21 *Do* not **c** a young goat in its mother's milk. 1418
1Sa 9:23 Samuel said to the **c,** 3184
9:24 the **c** took up the leg with what was on it 3184
1Ki 19:21 **burned** the plowing equipment **to c** 1418
2Ki 4:38 "Put on the large pot and **c** some stew 1418
Eze 24: 5 bring it to a boil and **c** the bones in it. 1418
24:10 **C** the meat **well,** mixing in the spices; 9462
46:20 "This is the place where the priests *will* **c** 1418
46:24 at the temple *will* **c** the sacrifices of 1418
Zec 14:21 to sacrifice will take some of the pots and **c** 1418

COOKED (8) [COOK]
Ex 12: 9 Do not eat the meat raw or **c** in water, 1418+1419
Lev 2: 7 If your grain offering is **c** in a pan, NIH
6:28 The clay pot the meat *is* **c** in must 1418
6:28 but if *it is* **c** in a bronze pot, 1418
7: 9 Every grain offering baked in an oven or **c** 6913
Nu 11: 8 *They* **c** it in a pot or made it into cakes. 1418
2Ki 6:29 So *we* **c** my son and ate him. 1418
La 4:10 *With* their own hands compassionate women *have* **c** their own children, 1418

COOKING (5) [COOK]
Ge 25:29 Once when Jacob *was* **c** some stew, 2326
Lev 11:35 an oven or **c pot** must be broken up. 3968
Eze 11: 3 This city is a **c pot,** and we are the meat.' 6105
24: 3 " 'Put on the **c pot;** 6105
Zec 14:20 and the **c pots** in the LORD's house will 6105

COOKS (1) [COOK]
1Sa 8:13 to be perfumers and **c** and bakers. 3185

COOL (3) [COOLNESS]
Ge 3: 8 as he was walking in the garden in the **c** *of* 8120
Jer 18:14 Do its **c** waters from distant sources 7922
Lk 16:24 of his finger in water and **c** my tongue, *2976*

COOLNESS (1) [COOL]
Pr 25:13 Like the **c** *of* snow at harvest time is 7557

COOS (KJV) See COS

COPIED (3) [COPY]
Jos 8:32 Joshua **c** on stones the law of Moses, 4180+5467
Pr 25: 1 **c** *by* the men of Hezekiah king of Judah: 6980
Eze 16:47 and **c** their detestable practices, 6913

COPIES (2) [COPY]
Jer 32:14 both the sealed and **unsealed** *c* of the deed AIT
Heb 9:23 the **c** of the heavenly things to be purified *5682*

COPPER (8)
Dt 8: 9 the rocks are iron and you can dig **c** out of 5733
Job 28: 2 and **c** is smelted from ore. 5703
Eze 22:18 all of them are the **c,** tin, 5733
22:20 As men gather silver, **c,** iron, 5733
24:11 the coals till it becomes hot and its **c** glows 5733
Mt 10: 9 along any gold or silver or **c** in your belts; *5910*
Mk 12:42 and put in two very **small c coins,** *3321*
Lk 21: 2 in two very **small c coins.** *3321*

COPPERSMITH (KJV) See METALWORKER

COPULATION (KJV) See EMISSION

COPY (14) [COPIED, COPIES]
Dt 17:18 he is to write for himself on a scroll a **c** 5467
2Ki 11:12 he presented him with a **c of** the **covenant** 6343
2Ch 23:11 with a **c of** the **covenant** 6343
Ezr 4:11 (This is a **c** *of* the letter they sent him.) 10598
4:23 As soon as the **c** *of* the letter 10598
5:6 This is a **c** *of* the letter that Tattenai, 10598
7:11 a **c** *of* the letter King Artaxerxes had given 7306
Est 3:14 A **c** *of* the text of the edict was to be issued 7358
4:8 also gave him a **c** *of* the text of the edict 7358
8:13 A **c** *of* the text of the edict was to be issued 7358
Jer 32:11 the **sealed** *c* containing the terms AIT
32:11 as well as the **unsealed** *c*— AIT
Heb 8:5 that is a **c** and shadow of what is in heaven. *5682*
9:24 a man-made sanctuary that was only a **c** of *531*

COR (1) [CORS]
Eze 45:14 from each **c** (which consists of ten baths 4123

CORAL (2)
Job 28:18 **C** and jasper are not worthy of mention; 8029
Eze 27:16 **c** and rubies for your merchandise. 8029

CORBAN (1)
Mk 7:11 from me is **C'** (that is, a gift devoted to God), *3167*

CORD (15) [CORDS]
Ge 38:18 "Your seal and its **c**, 7348
38:25 "See if you recognize whose seal and **c** 7348
Ex 28:28 to the rings of the ephod with blue **c**, 7348
28:37 a blue **c** to it to attach it to the turban; 7348
39:21 with blue **c**, connecting it to the waistband 7348
39:31 Then they fastened a blue **c** to it to attach it 7348
Nu 15:38 with a blue **c** on each tassel. 7348
Jos 2:18 have tied this scarlet **c** in the window 2562+9535
2:21 And she tied the scarlet **c** in the window. 9535
2Sa 8:2 and measured them off with a **length of c.** 2475
Job 41:2 a **c** through his nose or pierce his jaw with 109
Ecc 4:12 A **c** of three strands is not quickly broken. 2562
12:6 before the silver **c** is severed, 2475
Eze 16:4 the day you were born your **c** was not cut, 9219
40:3 a linen **c** and a measuring rod in his hand. 7348

CORDIAL (1) [CORDIALLY]
Ezr 5:7 To King Darius: **C greetings.** 10002+10002+10353+10720

CORDIALLY (2) [CORDIAL]
Ps 28:3 who speak **c** with their neighbors 8934
Jer 9:8 With his mouth each speaks **c** 8934

CORDS (17) [CORD]
2Sa 22:6 The **c** *of* the grave coiled around me; 2475
Est 1:6 with **c** *of* white linen and purple material 2475
Job 4:21 Are not the **c of** their **tent** pulled up, 3857
36:8 held fast by **c** *of* affliction, 2475
38:31 Can you loose the **c** *of* Orion? 5436
Ps 18:4 The **c** *of* death entangled me; 2475
18:5 The **c** *of* the grave coiled around me; 2475
116:3 The **c** *of* death entangled me, 2475
129:4 he has cut me free from the **c** *of* 6310
140:5 the **c** of their net and have set traps for me 2475
Pr 5:22 the **c** *of* his sin hold him fast. 2475
Isa 5:18 Woe to those who draw sin along with **c** 2475
54:2 lengthen your **c**, strengthen your stakes. 4798
58:6 the chains of injustice and untie the **c** *of* 99
Eze 27:24 and multicolored rugs with **c** twisted 2475
Hos 11:4 I led them with **c** *of* human kindness, 2475
Jn 2:15 So he made a whip out of **c**, *5389*

CORIANDER (2)
Ex 16:31 like **c** seed and tasted like wafers made 1512
Nu 11:7 The manna was like **c** seed and looked 1512

CORINTH (7) [CORINTHIANS]
Ac 18:1 After this, Paul left Athens and went to **C.** *3172*
18:18 Paul stayed on in **C** for some time. *NIG*
19:1 While Apollos was at **C**, *3172*
1Co 1:2 the church of God in **C**, to those sanctified *3172*
2Co 1:1 To the church of God in **C**, *3172*
1:23 to spare you that I did not return to **C.** *3172*
2Ti 4:20 Erastus stayed in **C**, *3172*

CORINTHIANS (2) [CORINTH]
Ac 18:8 and many *of* the **C** who heard him believed *3171*
2Co 6:11 We have spoken freely to you, **C**, *3171*

CORMORANT (2)
Lev 11:17 the little owl, the **c**, the great owl, 8960
Dt 14:17 the desert owl, the osprey, the **c**, 8960

CORN [EARS OF] (Anglicized, KJV) See GRAIN [HEADS OF], KERNEL

CORNELIUS (10)
Ac 10:1 At Caesarea there was a man named **C**, *3173*
10:3 who came to him and said, **"C!"** *3173*
10:4 **C** stared at him in fear. *1254+3836*[S]
10:7 **C** called two of his servants and *NIG*
10:17 by **C** found out where Simon's house was *3173*
10:22 "We have come from **C** the centurion. *3173*
10:24 **C** was expecting them *3173*
10:25 **C** met him and fell at his feet in reverence. *3173*
10:30 **C** answered: "Four days ago I was in my *3173*
10:31 and said, **'C**, God has heard your prayer *3173*

CORNER (26) [CORNERS, CORNERSTONE, CORNERSTONES]
Ru 3:9 "Spread the **c of** your **garment** over me, 4053
1Sa 24:4 up unnoticed and cut off a **c** *of* Saul's robe. 4053
24:5 for having cut off a **c** *of* his robe. 4053
24:11 the **c** *of* your robe but did not kill you. 4053
1Ki 7:34 one on each **c**, projecting from the stand. 7157
7:39 at the southeast **c** of the temple. 4578
2Ki 14:13 from the Ephraim Gate to the **C** Gate— 7157
2Ch 4:10 at the southeast **c.** 4578
25:23 from the Ephraim Gate to the **C** Gate— 7157
26:9 in Jerusalem at the **C** Gate, 7157
26:15 for use on the towers and on the **c defenses** 7157
28:24 up altars at every **street c** in Jerusalem. 7157
Ne 3:24 to the angle and the **c**, 7157
3:31 and as far as the room above the **c;** 7157
3:32 the room above the **c** and the Sheep Gate 7157
Pr 7:8 He was going down the street near her **c**, 7157
7:12 now in the squares, at every **c** she lurks.) 7157
21:9 to live on a **c** *of* the roof than share a house 7157
25:24 to live on a **c** *of* the roof than share a house 7157
Jer 31:38 from the Tower of Hananel to the **C** Gate. 7157
31:40 the Kidron Valley on the east as far as the **c** 7157
Eze 16:8 I spread the **c of** my **garment** over you 4053
46:21 and I saw **in each c** another court. 928+928+5243+5243
Zep 1:16 the fortified cities and against the **c** towers. 7157
Zec 14:10 Tower of Hananel to the **C** Gate, 7157
Ac 26:26 because it was not done in a **c.** *1224*

CORNERS (36) [CORNER]
Ex 25:26 for the table and fasten them to the four **c**, 6991
26:23 make two frames for the **c** at the far end. 7910
26:24 At these two **c** they must be double from 5243
27:2 Make a horn at each of the four **c**, 7157
27:4 a bronze ring at each of the four **c** *of* 7896
28:7 to two of its **c**, 7896
28:23 for it and fasten them to two **c** *of* 7896
28:24 the two gold chains to the rings at the **c** *of* 7896
28:26 to the other two **c** *of* the breastpiece on the 7896
36:28 for the **c** *of* the tabernacle at the far end. 7910
36:29 At these two **c** the frames were double 5243
37:13 the table and fastened them to the four **c**, 6991
38:2 They made a horn at each of the four **c**, 7157
38:5 for the four **c** of the bronze grating. 7921
39:4 which were attached to two of its **c**, 7896
39:16 the rings to two of the **c** *of* the breastpiece. 7896
39:17 the two gold chains to the rings at the **c** *of* 7896
39:19 to the other two **c** *of* the breastpiece on the 7896
Nu 15:38 to make tassels on the **c** *of* your garments, 4053
Dt 22:12 on the four **c** *of* the cloak you wear. 4053
Job 1:19 in from the desert and struck the four **c** *of* 7157
Isa 41:9 from its **farthest c** I called you. 721
Eze 7:2 end has come upon the four **c** *of* the land. 4053
41:22 its **c**, its base and its sides were of wood. 5243
43:20 the four **c** *of* the upper ledge and all around 7157
45:19 on the four **c** *of* the upper ledge of the altar 7157
46:21 and led me around to its four **c**, 5243
46:22 In the four **c** *of* the outer court 5243
46:22 the courts in the four **c** was the same size. 7910
Zec 9:15 be full like a bowl used for sprinkling the **c** 2312
Mt 6:5 in the synagogues and on the street **c** to *1224*
22:9 Go to the street **c** and invite to *1447*
Ac 10:11 down to earth *by* its four **c.** *794*
11:5 down from heaven *by* its four **c**, *794*
Rev 7:1 at the four **c** of the earth, *1224*
20:8 the nations in the four **c** of the earth— *1224*

CORNERSTONE (6) [CORNER, STONE]
Job 38:6 or who laid its **c**— 74+7157
Isa 28:16 a precious **c** *for* a sure foundation; 7157
Jer 51:26 No rock will be taken from you for a **c**, 7157
Zec 10:4 From Judah will come the **c**, 7157
Eph 2:20 with Christ Jesus himself as the **chief c.** *214+1639*
1Pe 2:6 a chosen and precious **c**, *214*

CORNERSTONES (1) [CORNER, STONE]
Isa 19:13 the **c** *of* her peoples have led Egypt astray. 7157

CORNET, CORNETS (KJV) See RAM'S HORNS, HORN

CORNFIELD, CORNFIELDS (Anglicized) See GRAINFIELD, GRAINFIELDS

CORNFLOOR (KJV) See THRESHING FLOOR

CORPSE (3) [CORPSES]
Lev 22:4 by a **c** or by anyone who has an emission 5883
Isa 14:19 Like a **c** trampled underfoot, 7007
Mk 9:26 The boy looked so much like a **c** *3738*

CORPSES (1) [CORPSE]
Na 3:3 people stumbling over the **c**— 1581

CORRECT (4) [CORRECTED, CORRECTING, CORRECTION, CORRECTIONS, CORRECTLY, CORRECTS]
Job 6:26 Do you mean to **c** what I say, 3519
40:2 with the Almighty **c** him? 3574
Jer 10:24 **C** me, LORD, but only with justice— 3579
2Ti 4:2 **c**, rebuke and encourage— *1794*

CORRECTED (1) [CORRECT]
Pr 29:19 A servant cannot **be c** by mere words; 3579

CORRECTING (1) [CORRECT]
2Ti 3:16 rebuking, **c** and training in righteousness, *2061*

CORRECTION (16) [CORRECT]
Lev 26:23 not **accept** my **c** but continue to be hostile 3579
Job 36:10 to **c** and commands them to repent 4592
Pr 5:12 How my heart spurned **c!** 9350
10:17 but whoever ignores **c** leads others astray. 9350
12:1 but he who hates **c** is stupid. 9350
13:18 but whoever heeds **c** is honored. 9350
15:5 but whoever heeds **c** shows prudence. 9350
15:10 he who hates **c** will die. 9350
15:12 A mocker resents **c;** 3519
15:32 but whoever heeds **c** gains understanding. 9350
29:15 The rod of **c** imparts wisdom, 9350
Jer 2:30 they did not respond to **c.** 4592
5:3 you crushed them, but they refused **c.** 4592
7:28 the LORD its God or responded to **c.** 4592
Zep 3:2 She obeys no one, she accepts no **c.** 4592
3:7 'Surely you will fear me and accept **c!'** 4592

CORRECTIONS (1) [CORRECT]
Pr 6:23 and the **c** *of* discipline are the way to life, 9350

CORRECTLY (5) [CORRECT]
Jdg 12:6 he could not pronounce the word **c**, 4026
Jer 1:12 The LORD said to me, *"You have* seen **c**, 3512
Lk 7:43 "You have judged **c**," Jesus said. *3987*
10:28 "You have answered **c**," Jesus replied. *3987*
2Ti 2:15 who does not need to be ashamed and *who* **c handles** the word *3982*

CORRECTS (2) [CORRECT]
Job 5:17 "Blessed is the man whom God **c;** 3519
Pr 9:7 *"Whoever* **c** a mocker invites insult; 3579

CORRESPONDING (3) [CORRESPONDS]
1Ch 23:6 David divided the Levites into groups **c to** 4200
2Ch 3:8 length **c to** the width of the temple— 6584+7156
Eze 42:12 to the **c** wall extending eastward, 2054

CORRESPONDS (1) [CORRESPONDING]
Gal 4:25 and **c** to the present city of Jerusalem, *5368*

CORRODED (1) [CORROSION]
Jas 5:3 Your gold and silver *are* **c.** *2995*

CORROSION (1) [CORRODED]
Jas 5:3 Their **c** will testify against you *2675*

CORRUPT (26) [CORRUPTED, CORRUPTION, CORRUPTLY, CORRUPTS]
Ge 6:11 the earth *was* **c** in God's sight and was full 8845
6:12 God saw *how* **c** the earth *had become,* 8845
Ex 32:7 up out of Egypt, *have become* **c.** 8845
Dt 4:16 not *become* **c** and make for yourselves 8845
4:25 then *become* **c** and make any kind of idol, 8845
9:12 of Egypt *have become* **c.** 8845
31:29 *you are* **sure to become utterly c** 8845+8845
Jdg 2:19 even more **c** than those of their fathers, 8845
2Ch 27:2 however, continued *their* **c practices.** 8845
Job 15:16 who is vile and **c**, 480
Ps 14:1 *They are* **c**, their deeds are vile; 8845
14:3 *they have* together *become* **c;** 480
53:1 *They are* **c**, and their ways are vile; 8845
53:3 *they have* together *become* **c;** 480
94:20 Can a **c** throne be allied with you— 2095
Pr 4:24 keep **c talk** far from your lips. 4299
6:12 who goes about with a **c** mouth, 6838
19:28 A **c** witness mocks at justice, 1175
Jer 2:21 did you turn against me into a **c**, wild vine? 6074
Eze 20:44 to your evil ways and your **c** practices, 8845
Da 6:4 because he was trustworthy and neither **c** 10705

Da 11:32 With flattery *he will* **c** those who have violated the covenant, 2866
Hos 5: 3 turned to prostitution; Israel *is* **c.** 3237
Ac 2:40 "Save yourselves from this *c* generation." *5021*
1Ti 6: 5 constant friction between men *of* **c** mind, *1425*
2Pe 2:10 of those who follow the **c** desire of *3622*

CORRUPTED (8) [CORRUPT]

Ge 6:12 for all the people on earth *had* **c** their ways. 8845
Eze 28:17 and *you* **c** your wisdom because 8845
2Co 7: 2 *we have* **c** no one, *5780*
Eph 4:22 which *is being* **c** by its deceitful desires; *5780*
Tit 1:15 but *to* those who *are* **c** and do not believe, *3620*
1:15 both their minds and consciences *are* **c.** *3620*
Jude 1:23 hating even the clothing stained by **c flesh.** *4922*
Rev 19: 2 the great prostitute who **c** the earth *5780*

CORRUPTION (9) [CORRUPT]

2Ki 23:13 of Jerusalem on the south of the Hill of **C**— 5422
Ezr 9:11 a land polluted by the **c** *of* its peoples. 5614
Job 17:14 if I say to **c,** 'You are my father,' 8846
Ps 55:23 down the wicked into the pit of **c;** 8846
Isa 1: 4 a brood of evildoers, children **given to c!** 8845
Da 6: 4 They could find no **c** in him, 10705
Hos 9: 9 They have sunk deep into **c,** 8845
2Pe 1: 4 the **c** in the world caused by evil desires. *5785*
2:20 the **c** of the world by knowing our Lord *3621*

CORRUPTLY (3) [CORRUPT]

Dt 32: 5 *They have* **acted c** toward him; 8845
Jer 6:28 They are bronze and iron; they all **act c.** 8845
Zep 3: 7 But they were still eager *to* **act c** 8845

CORRUPTS (3) [CORRUPT]

Ecc 7: 7 and a bribe **c** the heart. 6
1Co 15:33 "Bad company **c** good character." *5780*
Jas 3: 6 *It* **c** the whole person, *5071*

CORS (8) [COR]

1Ki 4:22 Solomon's daily provisions were thirty **c** 4123
4:22 of fine flour and sixty **c** *of* meal, 4123
5:11 Solomon gave Hiram twenty thousand **c** 4123
2Ch 2:10 twenty thousand **c** of ground wheat, 4123
2:10 twenty thousand **c** of barley, 4123
27: 5 ten thousand **c** of wheat 4123
27: 5 of wheat and ten thousand **c** of barley. NIH
Ezr 7:22 a hundred **c** of wheat, 10367

COS (1)

Ac 21: 1 we put out to sea and sailed straight to **C.** *3271*

COSAM (1)

Lk 3:28 the son *of* **C,** the son of Elmadam, *3272*

COSMETIC (1) [COSMETICS]

2Sa 14: 2 and don't use any **c lotions.** 9043

COSMETICS (1) [COSMETIC]

Est 2:12 of myrrh and six with perfumes and **c.** 9475

COST (14) [COSTLY, COSTS]

Nu 11: 5 the fish we ate in Egypt **at no c**— 2855
16:38 the men who sinned **at the c of** their lives. 928
Jos 6:26 **"At the c of** his firstborn son will he lay 928
6:26 **at the c of** his youngest will he set 928
2Sa 24:24 burnt offerings that **c** me **nothing."** 2855
1Ki 16:34 He laid its foundations **at the c of** 928
16:34 and he set up its gates **at the c of** 928
1Ch 12:19 "It will **c** us our heads if he deserts 928
Pr 4: 7 it **c** all you have, get understanding. 928
7:23 little knowing it will **c** him his life. 928
23: 7 of man who is always thinking about the **c.** 5883
Isa 55: 1 and milk without money and without **c.** 4697
Lk 14:28 Will he not first sit down and estimate the **c** *1252*
Rev 21: 6 to drink **without c** from the spring of *1562*

COSTLY (8) [COST]

Ge 24:53 he also gave **c gifts** to her brother and 4458
Est 1: 6 marble, mother-of-pearl and other **c stones.** 6090
Ps 49: 8 a life **is c,** no payment is ever enough— 3700
Eze 16:10 and covered you with **c garments.** 5429
16:13 and **c fabric** and embroidered cloth. 5429
Da 11:38 with precious stones and **c gifts.** 2776
1Co 3:12 silver, **c** stones, wood, hay or straw, *5508*
Rev 18:12 **c** wood, bronze, iron and marble; *5508*

COSTS (3) [COST]

1Ch 21:24 a burnt offering that **c** me **nothing."** 2855
Ezr 6: 4 The **c** are to be paid by the royal treasury. 10486
Pr 6:31 though *it* **c** *him* all the wealth of his house. 5989

COTES (KJV) See PEN

COUCH (7) [COUCHES]

Ge 49: 4 onto my **c** and defiled it. 3661
1Sa 28:23 He got up from the ground and sat on the **c.** 4753
2Ki 4:32 there was the boy lying dead on his **c.** 4753
Est 7: 8 on the **c** where Esther was reclining. 4753
Job 7:13 and my **c** will ease my complaint, 5435
Ps 6: 6 with weeping and drench my **c** with tears. 6911
Eze 23:41 You sat on an elegant **c,** 4753

COUCHES (3) [COUCH]

Est 1: 6 There were **c** *of* gold and silver on 4753
Am 3:12 of their beds and in Damascus on their **c."** 6911
6: 4 with ivory and lounge on your **c.** 6911

COULD (285) [COULDN'T]

Ge 8: 9 But the dove *c* **find** no place to set its feet AIT
13: 6 But the land *c* not **support** them AIT
13:16 so that if anyone *c* count the dust, 3523
13:16 then your offspring *c* **be counted.** AIT
19:11 with blindness so that *they* **c not** find 4206
20:17 so *they c* **have children** again, AIT
27: 1 so weak that *he c* no longer **see,** AIT
31:27 so *I c* **send** you **away** with joy and singing AIT
31:35 but *c* not **find** the household gods. AIT
32:25 the man saw that *he c* not **overpower** him, AIT
36: 7 where they were staying **c** not support them 3523
37: 4 they hated him and **c** not speak a kind word 3523
39: 9 then *c I* **do** such a wicked thing and sin AIT
41: 8 but no *one c* **interpret** them for him. AIT
41:21 no *one c* **tell** that they had done so; AIT
41:24 but none *c* **explain** it to me." AIT
42:23 not realize that Joseph *c* **understand** them, AIT
43:10 *c have* gone and **returned** AIT
43:32 because Egyptians **c** not eat with Hebrews, 3523
45: 1 Then Joseph **c** no longer control himself 3523
48:10 and *he* **c** hardly see. 3523
Ex 2: 3 But when *she* **c** hide him no longer, 3523
7:21 that the Egyptians **c** not drink its water. 3523
7:24 *they* **c** not drink the water of the river. 3523
8:18 by their secret arts, *they* **c** not. 3523
9:11 The magicians **c** not stand before Moses 3523
9:15 For by now *I c have* **stretched out** my hand AIT
10:23 No one *c* **see** anyone else or leave his place AIT
13:21 so that they *c* **travel** by day or night. AIT
15:23 *they* **c** not drink its water 3523
39: 4 so *it c* **be fastened.** AIT
40:35 Moses **c** not enter the Tent of Meeting 3523
Lev 11:34 that *c* **be eaten** but has water on it AIT
11:34 any liquid that *c* **be drunk** from it is unclean. AIT
Nu 9: 6 of them **c** not celebrate the Passover on 3523
11:33 and before *it c* **be consumed,** AIT
22:18 *I* **c** not do anything great or small to go 3523
24:13 *I* **c** not do anything of my own accord, 3523
35:17 anyone has a stone in his hand that *c* **kill,** AIT
35:18 a wooden object in his hand that *c* **kill,** AIT
35:23 drops a stone on him that *c* **kill** him, AIT
Dt 4:42 anyone who had killed a person *c* **flee** AIT
4:42 *He c* **flee** into one of these cities AIT
32:30 How *c* one man **chase** a thousand, AIT
Jos 15:63 Judah **c** not dislodge the Jebusites, 3523
20: 9 among them who killed someone accidentally *c* **flee** AIT
22:16 'How *c you* **break faith** with the God AIT
22:16 How **c** you turn away from the LORD NIH
Jdg 7:12 Their camels **c** no more be counted than NIH
10:16 *c* **bear** Israel's misery **no longer.** AIT
12: 6 he **c** not *pronounce* the word correctly, 3922
14:14 For three days *they* **c** not give the answer. 3523
20:16 each of whom *c* **sling** a stone at a hair and AIT
20:42 but they *c* not **escape** the battle. AIT
Ru 1:11 *who c* **become** your husbands? AIT
3:14 but got up before anyone *c be* **recognized;** AIT
1Sa 3: 2 so weak that *he* **c** barely see, 3523
4:15 and whose eyes were set so that *he* **c** 3523
6: 6 *c* **go on** *their* **way?** AIT
13:19 a blacksmith *c* **be found** in the whole land AIT
29: 4 *c* he **regain** his master's **favor** AIT
2Sa 1:10 that after he had fallen *he c* not **survive.** AIT
2:22 *c I* **look** your brother Joab **in the face?"** AIT
11:11 *How c* I **go** to my house to eat and drink AIT
13:13 *c I* **get rid of** my disgrace? AIT
15: 4 or case *c* **come** to me and I would see AIT
17:17 *they* **c** not **risk** being seen entering the city. 3523
22:39 and *they* **c** not **rise;** AIT
24: 9 able-bodied men *who c* **handle** a sword, AIT
1Ki 1: 1 he *c* not *keep* **warm** even AIT
5: 3 *he* **c** not build a temple for the Name of 3523
8: 5 that *they c* not **be recorded** or counted. AIT
8: 8 their ends *c* **be seen** from the Holy Place AIT
8:11 And the priests **c** not perform their service 3523
9:21 whom the Israelites **c** not exterminate— 3523
13: 4 so that *he* **c** not pull it back. 3523
14: 4 Now Ahijah **c** not see; 3523
18:10 he made them swear *they c* not **find** you. AIT
2Ki 3:21 *who c* **bear arms** was called up AIT
4:40 And *they* **c** not eat it. 3523
7: 2 of the heavens, *c* this **happen?"** AIT
7:19 of the heavens, *c* this **happen?"** AIT
8:13 *c* your servant, a mere dog, **accomplish** AIT
10: 4 "If two kings *c* not **resist** him, AIT
16: 5 but *they* **c** not overpower him. 3523
23:10 *c use* it *to* **sacrifice** AIT
25:16 was more than **c** be weighed. NIH
1Ch 5: 1 *c* not **be listed in the genealogical record** AIT
5:18 able-bodied men *who c* **handle** shield AIT
5:18 *who c* **use** a bow, AIT
8:40 of Ulam were brave warriors *who c* **handle** AIT
21: 5 men *who c* **handle** a sword, AIT
21:30 David **c** not go before it to inquire of God, 3523
1Ch 22: 3 and more bronze than **c** be weighed. NIH
22: 4 He also provided more cedar logs than **c** NIH
2Ch 5: 6 that *they c* not **be recorded** or counted. AIT
5: 9 *c* **be seen** *from* in front of AIT
5:14 and the priests **c** not perform their service 3523
7: 2 The priests **c** not enter the temple of 3523
7: 7 the bronze altar he had made **c** not hold 3523
14:13 a great number of Cushites fell that they **c** NIH
20:25 more than *they c* **take away.** AIT
22:11 from Athaliah so *she c* not **kill** him. AIT
25:15 which *c* not **save** their own people AIT
30:17 and *c* not **consecrate** [their lambs] to AIT
31: 4 so *they c* **devote** *themselves* to the Law of AIT
Ezr 2:59 but *they* **c** not show 3523
2:62 but they *c* not **find** *them* and AIT
3:13 No one *c* **distinguish** the sound of the shouts AIT
5: 5 a report *c* **go** to Darius and his written reply AIT
5:10 so that *we c* **write down** the names AIT
Ne 5: 8 because *they c* **find** nothing to say. AIT
7:61 but *they* **c** not show 3523
7:64 but they *c* not **find** *them* and AIT
8: 3 women and others *who c* **understand.** AIT
8: 5 All the people **c** see him NIH
8: 8 people *c* **understand** what was being read. AIT
9:36 so they *c* **eat** its fruit and AIT
12:43 **sound** of rejoicing in Jerusalem *c* **be heard** AIT
13:19 the gates so that no load *c* **be brought in** on AIT
Est 6: 1 That night the king **c not** sleep; 5610
9: 2 No one *c* **stand** against them, AIT
Job 2:12 *they c* hardly **recognize** him; AIT
4:16 It stopped, but *I c* not **tell** what it was. AIT
6: 2 "If only my anguish *c* **be weighed** AIT
9: 3 *he c* not **answer** him one time out of AIT
9:15 *I c* not **answer** him; AIT
9:15 *c* only **plead** with my Judge **for mercy.** AIT
13: 9 *C you* **deceive** him AIT
15:14 "What is man, that *he c be* **pure,** AIT
15:14 that *he c be* **righteous?** AIT
16: 4 I also *c* **speak** like you, AIT
16: 4 *I c* **make fine speeches** against you AIT
23: 3 if only *I c* **go** to his dwelling! AIT
23: 7 There an upright man *c* **present** his **case** AIT
31:23 fear of his splendor *I* **c** not **do** such things. 3523
Ps 18:38 I crushed them so that *they* **c** not rise; 3523
37:36 though I looked for him, *he c* not **be found.** AIT
55:12 *I c* **endure** it; AIT
55:12 *I c* **hide** from him. AIT
78:25 **all** the food they **c eat.** 8427
78:44 *they c* not **drink** *from* their streams. AIT
78:64 and their widows *c* not **weep.** AIT
107: 4 to a city where they **c** settle. NIH
107: 7 a straight way to a city where they **c** settle. NIH
107:36 and they founded a city where they **c** settle. NIH
130: 3 O Lord, who *c* **stand?** AIT
Isa 5: 4 What more *c have been* **done** AIT
7: 1 but *they* **c** not overpower it. 3523
10:19 be so few that a child *c* **write** them **down.** AIT
26:16 *c* **barely whisper a prayer.** AIT
41:26 so *we c* **know,** or beforehand, AIT
41:26 or beforehand, so *we c* **say,** 'He was right'? AIT
48: 5 so that *you c* not **say,** 'My idols did them; AIT
Jer 24: 2 so bad *they c* not **be eaten.** AIT
44:22 the LORD **c** no longer endure your wicked actions 3523
47: 4 and to cut off all survivors *who c* **help** Tyre AIT
52:20 was more than **c** be weighed. NIH
La 4:12 and foes *c* **enter** the gates of Jerusalem. AIT
4:17 for a nation *that c* not **save** us. AIT
4:18 so we *c* not **walk** in our streets. AIT
Eze 10: 5 of the cherubim *c* **be heard** as far away as AIT
10: 8 of the cherubim *c* **be seen** what looked like AIT
14:14 were in it, they *c* **save** only themselves AIT
14:16 *they c* not **save** their own sons AIT
14:18 *they c* not **save** their own sons AIT
14:20 *they c* **save** neither son nor daughter. AIT
20:25 not good and laws *they c* not **live** by; AIT
31: 8 cedars in the garden of God *c* not **rival** it, AIT
31: 8 *c* the pine trees **equal** AIT
31: 8 *c* the plane trees **compare with** AIT
31: 8 in the garden of God *c* **match** its beauty. AIT
47: 5 but now it was a river that *I* **c** not cross, 3523
47: 5 a river that no *one c* **cross.** AIT
Da 1:17 And Daniel *c* **understand** visions AIT
2: 1 mind was troubled and he **c not** sleep. 2118+6584
4: 7 but *they c* not **interpret** it for me. AIT
5: 8 but *they* **c** not read the writing or tell 10346
5:15 but *they* **c** not explain it. 10346
6: 4 *They c* **find** no corruption in him, AIT
6:18 And he **c not** sleep. 10463
8: 4 No animal *c* **stand** against him, AIT
8: 4 and none *c* **rescue** from his power. AIT
8: 7 and none *c* **rescue** the ram from his power. AIT
Hos 10: 3 even if we had a king, what *c he* **do** for us?" AIT
Jnh 1:13 But *they* **c** not, 3523
2: 8 forfeit the grace that **c** be theirs. NIH
Zec 1:21 so that no one *c* **raise** his head, AIT
7:14 so desolate behind them that no *one c* **come** AIT
8:10 *c* **go about** *his* **business** AIT
Mt 8:28 They were so violent that no one **c** pass *2710*
9:32 and **c not talk** was brought to Jesus. *3273*
12:22 *c* both **talk** and **see.** *AIT*
12:23 **"C** this be the Son of David?" *NIG*
15:33 "Where **c** we get enough bread *NIG*
17:16 but *they* **c** not heal him." *1538*
18:30 the man thrown into prison until *he c* **pay** *AIT*
22:10 and gathered all the people they **c** find, *NIG*

Mt 22:46 No one c say a word in reply, 1538
26: 9 "This perfume c have been sold at 1538
26:40 "C you men not keep watch with me 2710
26:59 c put him to death. AIT
Mk 1:45 Jesus c no longer enter a town openly 1538
2: 4 Since they c not get him to Jesus because 1538
4:33 as much as they c understand. 1538
5: 3 and no one c bind him any more, 1538
6: 5 He c not do any miracles there, 1538
7:24 yet he c not keep his presence secret. 1538
7:32 a man who was deaf and c hardly talk, 3652
9: 3 in the world c bleach them. 1538
9:18 but they c not." 2710
14: 5 It c have been sold for more than 1538
14: 8 She did what she c. 2400
14:37 C you not keep watch for one hour? 2710
14:55 against Jesus so that they c put him NIG
Lk 1:22 When he came out, he c not speak to them. 1538
5:19 When they c not find a way to do this NIG
6:48 torrent struck that house but c not shake it, 2710
8:43 but no one c heal her. 2710
8:47 woman, seeing that she c not go unnoticed, AIT
9:40 but they c not." 1538
13:11 She was bent over and c not straighten up 1538
15:29 even a young goat so I c celebrate AIT
19: 3 but being a short man he c not, 1538
19:23 I c have collected it with interest?' 323
19:48 Yet they c not find any way to do it, AIT
24:45 so they c understand the Scriptures. AIT
Jn 3: 2 For no one c perform the miraculous 1538
4:29 C this be the Christ?" NIG
4:33 "C someone have brought him food?" NIG
9:11 So I went and washed, and then I c see." AIT
9:33 he c do nothing." 1538
11:37 "C not he who opened the eyes of 1538
12:39 For this reason they c not believe, because, 1538
Ac 4:14 But since they c see AIT
4:14 there was nothing they c say. NIG
4:21 They c not decide how to punish them, NIG
5: 9 c you agree to test the Spirit of the Lord? AIT
6:10 but they c not stand up against his wisdom 2710
7:11 and our fathers c not find food. AIT
8:20 with you, because you thought you c buy AIT
9: 8 when he opened his eyes he c see nothing. AIT
9:18 and he c see again. AIT
10:22 so that he c hear what you have to say." AIT
11:17 who was I to think that I c oppose God?" 1543
13:39 from everything you c not be justified 1538
21:34 since the commander c not get at the truth 1538
25: 7 which they c not prove. 2710
25:21 I ordered him held until I c send him AIT
26:32 "This man c have been set free if he had 1538
27:15 by the storm and c not head into the wind; 1538
27:39 to run the ship aground if they c. 1538
27:43 He ordered those who c swim 1538
Ro 3: 6 how c God judge the world? AIT
9: 3 For I c wish that I myself were cursed AIT
11: 8 a spirit of stupor, eyes so that they c not see AIT
11: 8 not see and ears so that they c not hear, AIT
11:19 so that I c be grafted in." AIT
1Co 3: 1 I c not address you as spiritual but 1538
2Co 3: 7 the Israelites c not look steadily at the face 1538
7:12 that before God you c see for yourselves NIG
Gal 2:21 righteousness c be gained through the law, NIG
3:21 if a law had been given that c impart life, 1538
4:15 I can testify that, if you c have done so, 1543
4:20 how I wish I c be with you now NIG
Php 2:30 to make up for the help you c not give me. 5729
1Th 2: 6 of Christ we c have been a burden to you, 1538
3: 1 So when we c stand it no longer, AIT
3: 5 For this reason, when I c stand it no longer, AIT
Phm 1: 8 in Christ I c be bold and order you NIG
1:13 c take your place in helping AIT
Heb 5: 7 to the one who c save him from death, 1538
7:11 If perfection c have been attained through AIT
10: 2 If it c, would they have stopped 2075
11: 5 he c not be found, AIT
11:19 Abraham reasoned that God c raise 1543
12:17 He c bring about no change of mind, AIT
12:20 they c not bear what was commanded: AIT
Rev 5: 3 on earth or under the earth c open the scroll 1538
7: 9 a great multitude that no one c count, 1538
13:15 so that it c speak and cause all who refused AIT
13:17 so that no one c buy or sell unless he had 1538
14: 3 No one c learn the song except the 144,000 1538
15: 8 and no one c enter the temple until 1538
16:20 and the mountains c not be found. AIT

COULDN'T (3) [COULD, NOT]

2Ki 5:12 C I wash in them and be cleansed?" 4202
Mt 17:19 "Why c we drive it out?" 1538+4024
Mk 9:28 "Why c we drive it out?" 1538+4024

COUNCIL (16) [COUNCILS]

Ge 49: 6 Let me not enter their c, 6051
Nu 16: 2 who had been appointed members of the c. 4595
Job 15: 8 Do you listen in on God's c? 6051
Ps 89: 7 In the c of the holy ones 6051
107:32 of the people and praise him in the c of 4632
111: 1 in the c of the upright and in the assembly. 6051
Jer 23:18 of them has stood in the c of the LORD 6051
23:22 But if they had stood in my c, 6051
Eze 13: 9 They will not belong to the c of my people 6051
Mk 15:43 a prominent member of the C, 1085
Lk 22:66 At daybreak the c of the elders 4564
23:50 Joseph, a member of the C, a good and upright man, 1085
Jn 3: 1 a member of the Jewish ruling c. NIG
Ac 17:33 At that, Paul left the C. 899S
22: 5 the high priest and all the C can testify. 4564
25:12 After Festus had conferred with his c, 5206

COUNCILS (2) [COUNCIL]

Mt 10:17 they will hand you over to the local c 5284
Mk 13: 9 the local c and flogged in the synagogues. 5284

COUNSEL (33) [COUNSELED, COUNSELOR, COUNSELORS, COUNSELS]

2Sa 15:31 turn Ahithophel's c into foolishness." 6783
1Ki 22: 5 "First seek the c of the LORD." 1821
2Ch 18: 4 "First seek the c of the LORD." 1821
22: 5 He also followed their c when he went 6783
25:16 and have not listened to my c." 6783
Ezr 10: 3 in accordance with the c of my lord and 6783
Job 12:13 c and understanding are his. 6783
21:16 so I stand aloof from the c of the wicked. 6783
22:18 so I stand aloof from the c of the wicked. 6783
29:21 waiting in silence for my c. 6783
38: 2 "Who is this that darkens my c with words 6783
42: 3 that obscures my c without knowledge?' 6783
Ps 1: 1 not walk in the c of the wicked or stand in 6783
32: 8 I will c you and watch over you. 3619
73:24 You guide me with your c, 6783
106:13 and did not wait for his c. 6783
107:11 the words of God and despised the c of 6783
Pr 8:14 C and sound judgment are mine; 6783
15:22 Plans fail for lack of c, 6051
22:20 sayings of c and knowledge, 4600
27: 9 of one's friend springs from his earnest c. 6783
Isa 11: 2 the Spirit of c and of power, 6783
16: 3 "Give us c, render a decision. 6783
28:29 wonderful in c and magnificent in wisdom. 6783
41:28 one among them to give c, 3446
45:21 let them take c together. 3619
47:13 c you have received has only worn you out! 6783
Jer 18:18 nor will c from the wise, 6783
38:15 Even if I did give you c, 3619
49: 7 Has c perished from the prudent? 6783
Eze 7:26 as will the c of the elders. 6783
1Ti 5:14 So I c younger widows to marry, 1089
Rev 3:18 I c you to buy from me gold refined in 5205

COUNSELED (1) [COUNSEL]

Mic 6: 5 remember what Balak king of M 3619

COUNSELOR (13) [COUNSEL]

2Sa 15:12 Ahithophel the Gilonite, David's c, 3446
1Ch 26:14 a wise c, and the lot for the North Gate fell 3446
27:32 Jonathan, David's uncle, was a c, 3446
27:33 Ahithophel was the king's c. 3446
Isa 3: 3 the captain of fifty and man of rank, the c, 3446
9: 6 And he will be called Wonderful C, 3446
40:13 or instructed him as his c? 408+6783
Mic 4: 9 Has your c perished, 3446
Jn 14:16 he will give you another C to be with you 4156
14:26 But the C, the Holy Spirit, 4156
15:26 "When the C comes, whom I will send 4156
16: 7 the C will not come to you; 4156
Ro 11:34 Or who has been his c?" 5207

COUNSELORS (6) [COUNSEL]

Ezr 4: 5 They hired c to work against them 3446
Job 3:14 with kings and c of the earth, 3446
12:17 He leads c away stripped and makes fools 3446
Ps 119:24 they are my c. 408+6783
Isa 1:26 your c as at the beginning. 3446
19:11 wise c of Pharaoh give senseless advice. 3446

COUNSELS (2) [COUNSEL]

Ps 16: 7 I will praise the LORD, who c me; 3619
Na 1:11 against the LORD and c wickedness. 3619

COUNT (45) [COUNTED, COUNTING, COUNTLESS, COUNTS]

Ge 13:16 so that if anyone could c the dust, 4948
15: 5 "Look up at the heavens and c the stars— 6218
15: 5 if indeed you can c them." 6218
16:10 that they will be too numerous to c." 6218
Ex 30:12 a census of the Israelites to c them, 7212
Lev 15:13 he is to c off seven days 6218
15:28 she must c off seven days, 6218
23:15 c off seven full weeks. 6218
23:16 C off fifty days up to the day after 6218
25: 8 " 'C off seven sabbaths of years— 6218
25:50 to c the time from the year he sold himself 3108
Nu 1:49 not c the tribe of Levi or include them in 7212
3:15 "C the Levites by their families and clans. 7212
3:15 C every male a month old or more." 7212
3:40 "C all the firstborn Israelite males who are 7212
4: 3 C all the men from thirty to fifty years NIH
4:23 C all the men from thirty to fifty years 7212
4:29 "C the Merarites by their clans 7212
4:30 C all the men from thirty to fifty years 7212
6:12 The previous days do not c, 5877
23:10 Who can c the dust of Jacob or number 4948
31:26 heads of the community are to c all the people 906+5951+8031
Dt 16: 9 C off seven weeks from 6218
Jdg 6: 5 It was impossible to c the men 5031
1Ki 3: 8 too numerous to c or number. 6218
1Ch 21: 2 and c the Israelites from Beersheba to Dan. 6218
27:24 Joab son of Zeruiah began to c the men 4948
Job 14:16 Surely then you will c my steps but 6218
19:15 and my maidservants c me a stranger; 3108
31: 4 not see my ways and c my every step? 6218
38:37 Who has the wisdom to c the clouds? 6218
39: 2 Do you c the months till they bear? 6218
Ps 22:17 I can c all my bones; 6218
32: 2 the man whose sin the LORD does not c 3108
48:12 go around her, c her towers, 6218
139:18 Were I to c them, 6218
139:22 I c them my enemies. 2118+4200
Isa 16:14 a servant bound by contract would c them, NIH
21:16 as a servant bound by contract would c it, NIH
46: 5 or c me equal? 8750
Ro 4: 8 the man whose sin the Lord will never c 3357
6:11 c yourselves dead to sin but alive to God 3357
2Th 1:11 our God may c you worthy of his calling, 546
Rev 7: 9 a great multitude that no one could c, 749
11: 1 and c the worshipers there. NIG

COUNTED (67) [COUNT]

Ge 13:16 then your offspring could be c. 4948
32:12 which cannot be c.' " 6218
Ex 30:12 a ransom for his life at the time he is c. 7212
30:13 to those already c is to give a half shekel, 7212
38:25 the community who were c in the census 7212
38:26 who had crossed over to those c, 7212
Nu 1:19 And so he c them in the Desert of Sinai: 7212
1:22 in the army were c and listed by name, 7212
1:44 were the men c by Moses and Aaron 7212+7212
1:45 to serve in Israel's army were c according 7212
1:47 however, were not c along with the others. 7212
2:32 c according to their families. 7212
2:33 were not c along with the other Israelites, 7212
3:16 So Moses c them, 7212
3:22 a month old or more who were c was 7,500. 7212
3:34 a month old or more who were c was 6,200. 7212
3:39 of Levites c at the LORD's command 7212
3:42 Moses c all the firstborn of the Israelites, 7212
4:34 Aaron and the leaders of the community c 7212
4:36 c by clans, were 2,750. 7212
4:37 Moses and Aaron c them according to 7212
4:38 The Gershonites were c by their clans 7212
4:40 c by their clans and families, were 2,630. 7212
4:41 Moses and Aaron c them according to 7212
4:42 The Merarites were c by their clans 7212
4:44 c by their clans, were 3,200. 7212
4:45 Moses and Aaron c them according to 7212
4:46 and the leaders of Israel c all the Levites 7212
4:49 Thus they were c, 7212
7: 2 in charge of those who were c, 7212
14:29 of you twenty years old or more who was c 7212
26:57 the Levites who were c by their clans: 7212
26:62 They were not c along with 7212
26:63 These are the ones c by Moses and Eleazar 7212
26:63 when they c the Israelites on the plains 7212
26:64 of them was among those c by Moses 7212
26:64 by Moses and Aaron the priest when they c 7212
31:49 Your servants have c the soldiers 906+5951+8031
Jos 13: 3 all of it c as Canaanite (the territory of 3108
Jdg 7:12 Their camels could no more be c than 5031
21: 9 For when they c the people, 7212
1Sa 13:15 and Saul c the men who were with him. 7212
2Sa 2:15 So they stood up and were c off 928+5031+6296
24:10 David was conscience-stricken after he had c the fighting men, 6218
1Ki 8: 5 that they could not be recorded or c. 4948
2Ki 12:10 c the money that had been brought into 4948
1Ch 9:28 they c them when they were brought in and 5031
21:17 the fighting men to be c? 4948
22: 4 be c, for the Sidonians 5031
23: 3 The Levites thirty years old or more were c, 6218
23:11 so they were c as one family NIH
23:14 of Moses the man of God were c as part of 7924
23:24 under their names and c individually, 5031
23:27 the Levites were c 5031
2Ch 5: 6 that they could not be recorded or c. 4948
Ezr 1: 8 who c them out to Sheshbazzar the prince 6218
Job 5: 9 miracles that cannot be c. 5031
9:10 miracles that cannot be c. 5031
Ps 49:18 Though while he lived he c himself blessed— 1385
88: 4 I am c among those who go down to 3108
Ecc 1:15 what is lacking cannot be c. 4948
Isa 22:10 You c the buildings in Jerusalem and tore 6218
Jer 46:23 they cannot be c. 5031
Hos 1:10 which cannot be measured or c. 6218
Mt 26:15 So they c out for him thirty silver coins. 2705
Ac 5:41 rejoicing because they had been c worthy 2921
2Th 1: 5 and as a result you will be c worthy of 2921

COUNTENANCE (1)

Job 14:20 you change his c and send him away. 7156

COUNTERFEIT (2)

2Th 2: 9 in all kinds of c miracles, 6022
1Jn 2:27 and as that anointing is real, not c— 6022

COUNTING (4) [COUNT]

Ge 46:26 **not c** his sons' wives— 963+4200+4946
Dt 24:15 because he is poor and *is* **c on** it. 448+906+5883+5951
Jdg 8:26 **not c** the ornaments, 963+4200+4946
2Co 5:19 not **c** men's sins against them. *3357*

COUNTLESS (4) [COUNT]

Nu 10:36 O LORD, to the **c** thousands of Israel." 8047
Job 21:33 and a **c** throng goes before him. 401+5031
Jer 33:22 **make** the descendants of David my servant and the Levites who minister before me as **c** 889+4202+6218+8049
Heb 11:12 as numerous as the stars in the sky and as **c** *410*

COUNTRIES (43) [COUNTRY]

Ge 41:57 And all the **c** came to Egypt to buy grain 824
Dt 29:16 in Egypt and how we passed through the **c** 1580
1Ki 4:21 These **c** brought tribute NIH
2Ki 18:35 of these **c** has been able to save his land 824
19:11 the kings of Assyria have done to all the **c**, 824
2Ch 9:28 from Egypt and from all other **c**. 824
20:29 the kingdoms of the **c** when they heard 824
Isa 10:14 so I gathered all the **c**; 824
36:20 of these **c** has been able to save his land 824
37:11 the kings of Assyria have done to all the **c**, 824
Jer 16:15 of the land of the north and out of all the **c** 824
23: 3 the remnant of my flock out of all the **c** 824
23: 8 of the land of the north and out of all the **c** 824
27: 6 Now I will hand all your **c** over 824
28: 8 against many **c** and great kingdoms. 824
40:11 and all the other **c** heard that the king 824
40:12 the **c** where they had been scattered. 5226
51:28 and all the **c** they rule. 824
Eze 5: 5 with **c** all around her. 824
5: 6 and decrees more than the nations and **c** 824
11:16 and scattered them among the **c**, 824
11:16 for them in the **c** where they have gone.' 824
11:17 from the **c** where you have been scattered, 824
12:15 the nations and scatter them through the **c**. 824
20:23 the nations and scatter them through the **c**, 824
20:34 from the nations and gather you from the **c** 824
20:41 from the nations and gather you from the **c** 824
22: 4 the nations and a laughingstock to all the **c**. 824
22:15 the nations and scatter you through the **c**; 824
25: 7 the nations and exterminate you from the **c**. 824
29:12 the nations and scatter them through the **c**. 824
30:23 the nations and scatter them through the **c**. 824
30:26 the nations and scatter them through the **c**. 824
34:13 the nations and gather them from the **c**, 824
35:10 "These two nations and **c** will be ours 824
36:19 and they were scattered through the **c**; 824
36:24 from all the **c** and bring you back 824
39:27 and have gathered them from the **c** 824
Da 9: 7 and all Israel, both near and far, in all the **c** 824
11:40 He will invade *many* **c** and sweep 824
11:41 **Many** *c* will fall, but Edom, AIT
11:42 He will extend his power over *many* **c**; 824
Zec 8: 7 "I will save my people from the **c** *of* 824

COUNTRY (245) [COUNTRIES, COUNTRYSIDE, COUNTRYMAN, COUNTRYMAN]

Ge 10:30 in the eastern **hill c**. 2215
12: 1 to Abram, "Leave your **c**, your people 824
14: 6 and the Horites in the **hill c** *of* Seir, 2215
15:13 be strangers in a **c** not their own, 824
21:23 Show to me and the **c** where you are living 824
24: 4 but will go to my **c** and my own relatives 824
24: 5 to the **c** you came from?" 824
25:27 a man of the **open c**, 8441
25:29 Esau came in from the **open c**, famished. 8441
27: 3 the **open c** to hunt some wild game for me. 8441
27: 5 When Esau left for the **open c** to hunt game 8441
31:21 he headed for the **hill c** *of* Gilead. 2215
31:23 and caught up with him in the **hill c** 2215
31:25 Jacob had pitched his tent in the **hill c** 2215
31:54 He offered a sacrifice there in the **hill c** 2215
32: 3 the **c** *of* Edom. 8441
32: 9 'Go back to your **c** and your relatives, 824
36: 8 Edom) settled in the **hill c** *of* Seir. 2215
36: 9 the father of the Edomites in the **hill c** 2215
36:35 who defeated Midian in the **c** *of* Moab, 8441
41:36 be held in reserve for the **c**, 824
41:36 the **c** may not be ruined by the famine." 824
41:56 the famine had spread over the whole **c**, 824
Ex 1:10 fight against us and leave the **c**." 824
6: 1 Because of my mighty hand he will drive them out of his **c**." 824
6:11 of Egypt to let the Israelites go out of his **c**." 824
7: 2 to let the Israelites go out of his **c**. 824
8: 2 I will plague your whole **c** with frogs. 1473
10: 4 I will bring locusts into your **c** tomorrow. 1473
10:14 in every area of the **c** in great numbers. 5213
11:10 not let the Israelites go out of his **c**. 824
12:33 the people to hurry and leave the **c**. 824
13:17 on the road through the Philistine **c**, 824
18:27 and Jethro returned to his own **c**. 824
Lev 25:24 the **c** *that* you hold as a possession, 824
25:31 to be considered as open **c**. 824
25:45 and members of their clans born in your **c**, 824
26: 6 and the sword will not pass through your **c**. 824
26:34 that it lies desolate and you are in the **c** 824
Nu 13:17 through the Negev and on into the **hill c**. 2215
13:29 Jebusites and Amorites live in the **hill c**; 2215
14:40 up toward the high **hill c**. 2215
14:44 up toward the high **hill c**, 2215
14:45 that **hill c** came down and attacked them 2215
20:17 Please let us pass through your **c**. 824
21:22 "Let us pass through your **c**. 824
22: 6 to defeat them and drive them out of the **c**. 824
22:13 "Go back to your own **c**, 824
Dt 1: 7 Break camp and advance into the **hill c** 2215
1:19 from Horeb and went toward the **hill c** *of* 2215
1:20 "You have reached the **hill c** *of* 2215
1:24 They left and went up into the **hill c**, 2215
1:41 thinking it easy to go up into the **hill c**. 2215
1:43 up into the **hill c**. 2215
2: 1 around the **hill c** *of* Seir. 2215
2: 3 around this **hill c** long enough; 2215
2: 5 I have given Esau the **hill c** *of* Seir 2215
2:24 king of Heshbon, and his **c**. 824
2:27 "Let us pass through your **c**. 824
2:31 I have begun to deliver Sihon and his **c** 824
3:12 including half the **hill c** *of* Gilead, 2215
3:25 that fine **hill c** and Lebanon." 2215
9:28 the **c** from which you brought us will say, 824
11: 3 of Egypt and to his whole **c**; 824
22:25 the **c** a man happens to meet a girl pledged 8441
22:27 for the man found the girl out in the **c**, 8441
23: 7 because you lived as an alien in his **c**. 824
28: 3 be blessed in the city and blessed in the **c**. 8441
28:16 be cursed in the city and cursed in the **c**. 8441
28:24 the rain of your **c** into dust and powder; 824
28:40 You will have olive trees throughout your **c** 1473
Jos 1: 4 all the Hittite **c**— 824
2: 9 in this **c** are melting in fear because of you. 824
7: 9 and the other people of the **c** will hear 824
9: 1 those in the **hill c**, 2215
9: 6 "We have come from a distant **c**; 824
9: 9 from a very distant **c** because of the fame 824
9:11 and all those living in our **c** said to us, 824
10: 6 the **hill c** have joined forces against us." 2215
10:40 including the **hill c**, the Negev, 2215
11: 3 Perizzites and Jebusites in the **hill c**; 2215
11:16 So Joshua took this entire land: the **hill c**, 2215
11:21 the Anakites from the **hill c**: 2215
11:21 from all the **hill c** *of* Judah, 2215
11:21 and from all the **hill c** *of* Israel. 2215
12: 8 the **hill c**, the western foothills, 2215
13:21 who lived in that **c**. 824
13:25 of Gilead and half the Ammonite **c** as far 824
14:12 Now give me this **hill c** that 2215
15:48 In the **hill c**: Shamir, Jattir, Socoh, 2215
16: 1 the desert into the **hill c** *of* Bethel. 2215
17:15 "and if the **hill c** *of* Ephraim is too small 2215
17:16 "The **hill c** is not enough for us, 2215
17:18 but the forested **hill c** as well. 2215
18: 1 The **c** was brought under their control, 824
18:12 and headed west into the **hill c**, 2215
19:50 Timnath Serah in the **hill c** *of* Ephraim. 2215
20: 7 in Galilee in the **hill c** *of* Naphtali, 2215
20: 7 Shechem in the **hill c** *of* Ephraim, 2215
20: 7 Hebron) in the **hill c** *of* Judah. 2215
21:11 in the **hill c** *of* Judah. 2215
21:21 In the **hill c** *of* Ephraim they were given 2215
22:33 to devastate the **c** where the Reubenites and 824
24: 4 I assigned the **hill c** *of* Seir to Esau, 2215
24:30 at Timnath Serah in the **hill c** 2215
24:33 to his son Phinehas in the **hill c** 2215
Jdg 1: 9 against the Canaanites living in the **hill c**, 2215
1:19 They took possession of the **hill c**, 2215
1:34 the Danites to the **hill c**, 2215
2: 9 at Timnath Heres in the **hill c** 2215
3:27 a trumpet in the **hill c** *of* Ephraim, 2215
4: 5 between Ramah and Bethel in the **hill c** 2215
6: 3 and other eastern peoples invaded **the c**. 2257[S]
7:24 throughout the **hill c** *of* Ephraim, 2215
10: 1 in the **hill c** *of* Ephraim. 2215
11:12 against us that you have attacked our **c?"** 824
11:17 'Give us permission to go through your **c**,' 824
11:18 along the eastern side of the **c** *of* Moab, 824
11:19 through your **c** to our own place.' 824
11:21 of the Amorites who lived in that **c**, 824
12:15 in the **hill c** *of* the Amalekites. 2215
17: 1 Now a man named Micah from the **hill c** 2215
17: 8 to Micah's house in the **hill c** 2215
18: 2 The men entered the **hill c** *of* Ephraim 2215
18:13 on to the **hill c** *of* Ephraim and came 2215
19: 1 in the **hill c** *of* Ephraim took a concubine 2215
19:16 That evening an old man from the **hill c** 2215
19:18 to a remote area in the **hill c** *of* Ephraim 2215
Ru 1: 1 went to live for a while in the **c** *of* Moab. 8441
1Sa 1: 1 a Zuphite from the **hill c** *of* Ephraim, 2215
6: 5 and of the rats that are destroying the **c**, 824
6:18 the fortified towns with their **c** villages. 7253
9: 4 the **hill c** *of* Ephraim and through 2215
13: 2 at Micmash and in the **hill c** *of* Bethel, 2215
14:22 the Israelites who had hidden in the **hill c** 2215
14:29 "My father has made trouble for the **c**. 824
27: 5 be assigned to me in one of the **c** towns, 8441
2Sa 10: 8 by themselves in the **open c**. 8441
19: 9 now he has fled the **c** because of Absalom; 824
20:21 from the **hill c** *of* Ephraim, 2215
1Ki 4: 8 in the **hill c** *of* Ephraim; 2215
4:19 (the **c** *of* Sihon king of the Amorites and 824
4:19 of Sihon king of the Amorites and the **c** NIH
10: 6 in my own **c** about your achievements 824
10:13 and returned with her retinue to her own **c**. 824
11:21 "Let me go, that I may return to my own **c**." 824
1Ki 11:22 that you want to go back to your own **c?"** 824
11:29 The two of them were alone out in the **c**, 8441
12:25 in the **hill c** *of* Ephraim and lived there. 2215
14:11 the air will feed on those who die in the **c**. 8441
16: 4 the air will feed on those who die in the **c**." 8441
21:24 the air will feed on those who die in the **c**." 8441
2Ki 5:22 to me from the **hill c** *of* Ephraim. 2215
8: 6 from her land from the day she left the **c** 824
13:20 to enter the **c** every spring. 824
17:26 not know what the god of that **c** requires. 824
18:25 to march against this **c** and destroy it.' " 824
19: 7 he will return to his own **c**, 824
24: 7 not march out from his own **c** again, 824
1Ch 1:46 who defeated Midian in the **c** *of* Moab, 8441
4:42 invaded the **hill c** *of* Seir. 2215
6:67 In the **hill c** *of* Ephraim they were given 2215
19: 3 and spy out the **c** and overthrow it?" 824
19: 9 by themselves in the **open c**. 8441
2Ch 9: 5 in my own **c** about your achievements 824
9:12 and returned with her retinue to her own **c**. 824
13: 4 in the **hill c** *of* Ephraim, and said, 2215
14: 1 in his days the **c** was at peace for ten years. 824
19: 4 from Beersheba to the **hill c** *of* Ephraim 2215
Ne 8:15 into the **hill c** and bring back branches 2215
9:22 over the **c** *of* Sihon king of Heshbon and 824
9:22 of Sihon king of Heshbon and the **c** 824
Ps 78:54 to the **hill c** his right hand had taken. 2215
105:31 and gnats throughout their **c**. 1473
105:33 and shattered the trees of their **c**. 1473
Pr 28: 2 When a **c** is rebellious, it has many rulers, 824
29: 4 By justice a king gives a **c** stability, 824
Isa 1: 7 Your **c** is desolate, your cities burned 824
13: 5 to destroy the whole **c**. 824
22:18 like a ball and throw you into a large **c**. 824
36:10 to march against this **c** and destroy it.' " 824
37: 7 he will return to his own **c**, 824
63:13 Like a horse in **open c**, 4497
66: 8 Can a **c** be born in a day or a nation 824
Jer 12: 5 If you stumble in safe **c**, 824
12:15 to his own inheritance and his own **c**. 824
14:18 If I go into the **c**, 8441
15:13 because of all your sins throughout your **c**. 1473
17: 3 because of sin throughout your **c**. 1473
17:26 from the **hill c** and the Negev, 2215
22:26 into another **c**, where neither 824
25:11 This whole **c** will become a desolate 824
32:44 of Judah and in the towns of the **hill c**, 2215
33:13 In the towns of the **hill c**, 2215
40: 4 Look, the whole **c** lies before you; 824
40: 7 in the **open c** heard that the king 8441
40:13 in the **open c** came to Gedaliah at Mizpah 8441
Eze 7:15 those in the **c** will die by the sword, 8441
14:13 if a **c** sins against me by being unfaithful 824
14:15 through that **c** and they leave it childless 824
14:17 if I bring a sword against that **c** and say, 824
21:19 both starting from the same **c**. 824
33:27 by the sword, those out in the **c** I will give 8441
Da 11: 9 of the South but will retreat to his own **c**. 141
11:19 the fortresses of his own **c** but will stumble 824
11:28 of the North will return to his own **c** 824
11:28 against it and then return to his own **c**. 824
Hos 12:12 Jacob fled to the **c** *of* Aram; 8441
Am 7:17 and you yourself will die in a pagan **c**. 141
Jnh 1: 8 What is your **c?** 824
Zec 5:11 the **c** *of* Babylonia to build a house for it. 824
6: 6 toward the north **c**, 824
6: 8 the north **c** have given my Spirit rest in 824
Mt 2:12 they returned to their **c** by another route. *6001*
14:35 they sent word to all the **surrounding c**. *4369*
Mk 15:21 was passing by on his way in from the **c**, *69*
16:12 of them while they were walking in the **c**. *69*
Lk 1:39 and hurried to a town in the **hill c** *3978*
1:65 the **hill c** of Judea people were talking *3978*
3: 3 He went into all the **c around** the Jordan, *4369*
7:17 throughout Judea and the **surrounding c**. *4369*
14:23 the roads and **c lanes** and make them come *5850*
15: 4 the ninety-nine in the **open c** and go after *2245*
15:13 a distant **c** and there squandered his wealth *6001*
15:14 there was a severe famine in that whole **c**, *6001*
15:15 and hired himself out to a citizen *of* that **c**, *6001*
19:12 a distant **c** to have himself appointed king *6001*
21:21 and let those in the **c** not enter the city. *6001*
23:26 who was on his way in from the **c**, *69*
Jn 4:44 that a prophet has no honor in his own **c**.) *4258*
11:55 many went up from the **c** to Jerusalem *6001*
Ac 7: 3 'Leave your **c** and your people,' God said, *1178*
7: 6 'Your descendants will be strangers in a **c** *1178*
7: 7 'and afterward they will come out of that **c** *NIG*
9:32 As Peter **traveled about the c**, *1328+1451+4246*
10:39 of everything he did in the **c** of the Jews *6001*
12:20 because they depended on the king's **c** *NIG*
13:17 with mighty power he led them out of **that c**, *899[S]*
14: 6 and Derbe and to the **surrounding c**, *4369*
26: 4 from the beginning of my life in my own **c**, *1620*
2Co 11:26 in danger in the city, in danger in the **c**, *2244*
Heb 11: 9 like a stranger in a foreign **c**; *NIG*
11:14 that they are looking for a **c of their own**. *4258*
11:15 of the **c** they had left, *NIG*
11:16 Instead, they were longing for a better **c**— *NIG*

COUNTRYMAN (3) [COUNTRY, MAN]

Lev 25:15 You are to buy from your **c** on the basis of 6660
25:25 to come and redeem what his **c** has sold. 278
25:36 your **c** may continue to live among you. 278

COUNTRYMEN (27) [COUNTRY, MAN]

Lev 25:14 to one of your **c** or buy any from him, 6660
25:25 of your **c** becomes poor and sells some 278
25:35 of your **c** becomes poor and is unable 278
25:39 of your **c** becomes poor among you 278
25:47 of your **c** becomes poor and sells himself to 278
Nu 32: 6 "Shall your **c** go to war while you sit here? 278
2Sa 15:20 Go back, and take your **c**, 278
2Ch 19:10 before you from your **fellow c** who live 278
28:11 Send back your **fellow c** you have taken 278
28:15 So they took them back to their **fellow c** 278
35: 5 of the families of your **fellow c**, 278
35: 6 [the lambs] for your **fellow c**, 278
Ne 3:18 by their **c** under Binnui son of Henadad, 278
5: 5 and blood as our **c** and though our sons are 278
5: 7 "You are exacting usury from your own **c**!" 278
Jer 22:13 making his **c** work for nothing, 8276
29:16 your **c** who did not go with you 278
34:15 Each of you proclaimed freedom to his **c**. 8276
34:17 not proclaimed freedom for your fellow **c**. 8276
Eze 3:11 to your **c** in exile and speak to them. 1201+6639
33: 2 speak to your **c** and say to them: 1201+6639
33:12 "Therefore, son of man, say to your **c**, 1201+6639
33:17 "Yet your **c** say, 1201+6639
33:30 your **c** are talking together about you 1201+6639
37:18 "When your **c** ask you, 1201+6639
2Co 11:26 in danger from my own **c**, *1169*
1Th 2:14 You suffered from your own **c** *5241*

COUNTRYSIDE (15) [COUNTRY]

1Sa 30:16 and there they were, scattered over the **c**, 824
2Sa 15:23 The whole **c** wept aloud as all 824
18: 8 The battle spread out over the whole **c**, 824
1Ki 20:27 while the Arameans covered the **c**. 824
2Ki 7:12 so they have left the camp to hide in the **c**, 8441
Job 5:10 he sends water upon the **c**. 2575
SS 7:11 Come, my lover, let us go to the **c**, 8441
Mk 1: 5 The whole Judean **c** and all the people *6001*
5:14 and reported this in the town and **c**, *69*
6:36 so they can go to the surrounding **c** *69*
6:56 into villages, towns or **c**— *69*
Lk 4:14 about him spread through the whole **c**. *4369*
8:34 and reported this in the town and **c**, *69*
9:12 to the surrounding villages and **c** *69*
Jn 3:22 disciples went out into the Judean **c**, *1178*

COUNTS (6) [COUNT]

Job 19:11 *he* **c** me among his enemies. 3108
Jer 33:13 under the hand of the *one who* **c** them,' 4948
Jn 6:63 Spirit gives life; the flesh **c for** nothing. *6067*
1Co 7:19 Keeping God's commands is what **c**. *NIG*
Gal 5: 6 that **c** is faith expressing itself *NIG*
6:15 what **c** is a new creation. *NIG*

COURAGE (21) [COURAGEOUS, COURAGEOUSLY]

Jos 2:11 our hearts melted and everyone's **c** failed 8120
5: 1 and they no longer had the **c** to face 8120
2Sa 4: 1 he **lost c**, and all Israel became alarmed. 3338+8332
7:27 So your servant has found **c** 4213
1Ch 17:25 So your servant *has* **found c** to pray to you. 5162
2Ch 15: 8 of Oded the prophet, *he* **took c**. 2616
19:11 Act *with* **c**, and may the LORD be 2616
Ezr 7:28 I **took c** and gathered leading men 2616
10: 4 We will support you, so **take c** and do it." 2616
Ps 107:26 in their peril their **c** melted away. 5883
Eze 22:14 Will your **c** endure or your hands be strong 4213
Da 11:25 up his strength and **c** against the king of 4222
Mt 14:27 Jesus immediately said to them: **"Take c!** *2510*
Mk 6:50 to them and said, **"Take c!** *2510*
Ac 4:13 When they saw the **c** of Peter and John *4244*
23:11 the Lord stood near Paul and said, **"Take c!** *2510*
27:22 But now I urge you *to* **keep up** your **c**, *2313*
27:25 So **keep up** *your* **c**, men, *2313*
1Co 16:13 *be* **men of c**; be strong. *437*
Php 1:20 but will have sufficient **c** so that now *4244*
Heb 3: 6 on to our **c** and the hope of which we boast. *4244*

COURAGEOUS (12) [COURAGE]

Dt 31: 6 Be strong and **c**. 599
31: 7 "Be strong and **c**, 599
31:23 "Be strong and **c**, 599
Jos 1: 6 "Be strong and **c**, 599
1: 7 Be strong and very **c**. 599
1: 9 Be strong and **c**. 599
1:18 Only be strong and **c**!" 599
10:25 Be strong and **c**. 599
1Ch 22:13 Be strong and **c**. 599
28:20 "Be strong and **c**, and do the work. 599
2Ch 26:17 Azariah the priest with eighty other **c** priests of the LORD 1201+2657
32: 7 "Be strong and **c**. 599

COURAGEOUSLY (2) [COURAGE]

2Ch 25: 8 Even if you go and fight **c** in battle, 2616
Php 1:14 the word of God more **c** and fearlessly. *5528*

COURIER (1) [COURIERS]

Jer 51:31 *One* **c** follows another 8132

COURIERS (6) [COURIER]

2Ch 30: 6 **c** went throughout Israel and Judah 8132
30:10 The **c** went from town to town in Ephraim 8132
Est 3:13 by **c** to all the king's provinces with 8132
3:15 the **c** went out, 8132
8:10 and sent them by mounted **c**, 8132
8:14 The **c**, riding the royal horses, raced out, 8132

COURSE (33) [COURSES]

Ge 4: 3 In the **c** *of* time Cain brought some of 7891
Dt 2:37 the land along the **c** *of* the Jabbok nor that 5707
1Sa 1:20 So in the **c** *of* time Hannah conceived 9543
22:15 **Of c not!** 2721
2Sa 2: 1 **In the c of time,** 339+4027
8: 1 **In the c of time,** 339+4027
10: 1 **In the c of time,** 339+4027
13: 1 **In the c of time,** 339+4027
15: 1 **In the c of time,** 339+4027+4946
21:18 **In the c of time,** 339+4027
1Ki 6:36 of three courses of dressed stone and one **c** 3215
7:12 of three courses of dressed stone and one **c** 3215
1Ch 18: 1 **In the c of time,** 339+4027
19: 1 **In the c of time,** 339+4027
20: 4 **In the c of time,** 339+4027
2Ch 21:19 **In the c of time,** 3427+3427+4200+4946
Job 1: 5 When a period of feasting *had* **run** *its* **c**, 5938
Ps 19: 5 like a champion rejoicing to run his **c**. 784
36: 4 he commits himself to a sinful **c** and does 2006
102:23 In the **c of** my **life** he broke my strength; 2006
Pr 2: 8 for he guards the **c** *of* the just and protects 784
15:21 a man of understanding keeps a straight **c**. 2143
16: 9 In his heart a man plans his **c**, 2006
17:23 a bribe in secret to pervert the **c** *of* justice. 784
Ecc 1: 6 ever returning on its **c**. 6017
Jer 8: 6 Each pursues his own **c** like 5297
23:10 an evil **c** and use their power unjustly. 5297
Joel 2: 7 not swerving from their **c**. 784
Ac 27: 7 **allow us to hold** our **c**, *4661*
Ro 10:18 **Of c** they did: *3529*
2Co 12:18 in the same spirit and **follow the same c**? *2717*
13: 5 unless, of **c**, you fail the test? *NIG*
Jas 3: 6 sets the whole **c** of his life on fire, *5580*

COURSES (4) [COURSE]

Jdg 5:20 from their **c** they fought against Sisera. 5019
1Ki 6:36 And he built the inner courtyard of three **c** 3215
7:12 of three **c** of dressed stone and one course 3215
Ezr 6: 4 with three **c** of large stones and one 10462

COURTEOUS (KJV) See HUMBLE

COURT (90) [COURTS, COURTYARD, COURTYARDS]

Ge 50: 4 Joseph said to Pharaoh's **c**, 1074
50: 7 of his **c** and all the dignitaries of Egypt— 1074
Ex 21:22 and the **c** allows. 7130
Dt 25: 1 to take it to **c** and the judges will decide 5477
Jdg 4: 5 She **held c** under the Palm of Deborah 3782
1Ki 3:15 Then he gave a feast for all his **c**. 6269
2Ki 20: 4 Before Isaiah had left the middle **c**, 2958
23:11 They were in the **c** near the room of 7247
1Ch 26:18 As for the **c** to the west, 7232
26:18 at the road and two at the **c** itself. 7232
2Ch 4: 9 and the large **c** and the doors for the court, 6478
4: 9 and the large court and the doors for the **c**, 6478
6:13 in the center of the **outer c**. 6478
Ne 3:25 the upper palace near the **c** *of* the guard. 2958
Est 4:11 in the inner **c** without being summoned 2958
5: 1 on her royal robes and stood in the inner **c** 2958
5: 2 he saw Queen Esther standing in the **c**, 2958
6: 4 The king said, "Who is in the **c**?" 2958
6: 4 Now Haman had just entered the outer **c** *of* 2958
6: 5 "Haman is standing in the **c**." 2958
Job 5: 4 crushed in **c** without a defender. 9133
9:32 that we might confront each other in **c**. 5477
11:10 in prison and **convenes a c**, 7735
11:19 and many *will* **c** your **favor**. 2704+7156
31:21 knowing that I had influence in **c**, 9133
Pr 22:22 and do not crush the needy in **c**, 9133
25: 8 do not bring hastily to **c**, 8190
29: 9 If a wise man **goes to c** with a fool, 9149
Isa 3:13 The LORD takes his place **in c**; 8189
29:21 in **c** and with false testimony deprive 9133
Jer 19:14 and stood in the **c** *of* the LORD's temple 2958
29: 2 the **c officials** and the leaders of Judah 6247
34:19 and Jerusalem, the **c officials**, the priests 6247
41:16 children and **c officials** he had brought 6247
Eze 8: 3 to the north gate of the inner **c**, NIH
8: 7 he brought me to the entrance to the **c**. 2958
8:16 into the inner **c** *of* the house of the LORD, 2958
10: 3 and a cloud filled the inner **c**. 2958
10: 4 the **c** was full of the radiance of the glory 2958
10: 5 be heard as far away as the outer **c**, 2958
40:17 Then he brought me into the outer **c**. 2958
40:17 that had been constructed all around the **c**; 2958
40:19 to the outside of the inner **c**; 2958
40:20 leading into the outer **c**. 2958
40:23 a gate to the inner **c** facing the north gate, 2958
40:27 The inner **c** also had a gate facing south, 2958
40:28 into the inner **c** through the south gate, 2958
40:30 the inner **c** were twenty-five cubits wide NIH
40:31 Its portico faced the outer **c**; 2958
40:32 Then he brought me to the inner **c** *on* 2958
Eze 40:34 Its portico faced the outer **c**; 2958
40:37 Its portico faced the outer **c**; 2958
40:44 Outside the inner gate, within the inner **c**, 2958
40:47 Then he measured the **c**: 2958
41:15 and the portico facing the **c**, 2958
42: 1 the man led me northward into the outer **c** 2958
42: 3 from the inner **c** and in the section opposite 2958
42: 3 the pavement of the outer **c**, 2958
42: 7 to the rooms and the outer **c**; 2958
42: 8 to the outer **c** was fifty cubits long, 2958
42: 9 as one enters them from the outer **c**. 2958
42:10 along the length of the wall of the outer **c**, 2958
42:14 not to go into the outer **c** until they leave 2958
43: 5 up and brought me into the inner **c**, 2958
44:17 " 'When they enter the gates of the inner **c**, 2958
44:17 while ministering at the gates of the inner **c** 2958
44:19 When they go out into the outer **c** where 2958
44:21 to drink wine when he enters the inner **c**. 2958
44:27 into the inner **c** of the sanctuary to minister 2958
45:19 the altar and on the gateposts of the inner **c**. 2958
46: 1 of the inner **c** facing east is to be shut on 2958
46:20 the outer **c** and consecrating the people." 2958
46:21 then brought me to the outer **c** and led me 2958
46:21 and I saw in each corner another **c**. 2958
46:22 of the outer **c** were enclosed courts, 2958
Da 1: 3 chief of his **c officials**, 6247
2:49 Daniel himself remained at the royal **c**. 10776
7:10 **c** was seated, and the books were opened. 10170
7:26 " 'But the **c** will sit, 10170
Am 5:10 in **c** and despise him who tells the truth. 9133
Mt 5:25 **adversary who is taking** you **to c**. *508*
Ac 18:12 on Paul and brought him into **c**. *1037*
18:16 So he had them ejected from the **c**. *1037*
18:17 and beat him in front of the **c**. *1037*
25: 6 the next day he **convened the c** and ordered *1037+2093+2767+3836*
25:10 "I am now standing before Caesar's **c**, *1037*
25:17 but convened the **c** the next day *1037+2093*
1Co 4: 3 if I am judged by you or by any human **c**; *2465*
Jas 2: 6 not the ones who are dragging you into **c**? *3215*
Rev 11: 2 But exclude the outer **c**; *885*

COURTS (51) [COURT]

Dt 17: 8 before your **c** that are too difficult for you 9133
2Ki 21: 5 In both **c** *of* the temple of the LORD, 2958
23:12 the altars Manasseh had built in the two **c** 2958
1Ch 28: 6 the one who will build my house and my **c**, 2958
28:12 that the Spirit had put in his mind for the **c** 2958
2Ch 33: 5 In both **c** *of* the temple of the LORD, 2958
Ne 8:16 the **c** *of* the house of God and in the square 2958
13: 7 in providing Tobiah a room in the **c** *of* 2958
Ps 65: 4 and bring near to live in your **c**! 2958
84: 2 even faints, for the **c** *of* the LORD; 2958
84:10 in your **c** than a thousand elsewhere; 2958
92:13 they will flourish in the **c** *of* our God. 2958
96: 8 bring an offering and come into his **c**. 2958
100: 4 Enter his gates with thanksgiving and his **c** 2958
116:19 in the **c** *of* the house of the LORD— 2958
135: 2 in the **c** *of* the house of our God. 2958
Isa 1:12 this trampling of my **c**? 2958
62: 9 the grapes will drink it in the **c** 2958
Eze 9: 7 the temple and fill the **c** with the slain. 2958
42: 6 had no pillars, as the **c** had; 2958
46:22 of the outer court were enclosed **c**, 2958
46:22 *the* **c** in the four corners was the same size. 4392[S]
46:23 Around the inside of *each of the* four **c** was 4392[S]
Am 5:12 and you deprive the poor of justice in the **c**. 9133
5:15 maintain justice in the **c**. 9133
Zec 3: 7 and have charge of my **c**, 2958
8:16 and sound judgment in your **c**; 9133
Mt 21:23 Jesus entered the **temple c**, and, *2639*
26:55 Every day I sat in the **temple c** teaching, *2639*
Mk 11:16 to carry merchandise through the **temple c**. *2639*
11:27 while Jesus was walking in the **temple c**, *2639*
12:35 While Jesus was teaching in the **temple c**, *2639*
14:49 teaching in the **temple c**, *2639*
Lk 2:27 he went into the **temple c**. *2639*
2:46 they found him in the **temple c**, *2639*
20: 1 in the **temple c** and preaching the gospel, *2639*
22:53 Every day I was with you in the **temple c**, *2639*
Jn 2:14 the **temple c** he found men selling cattle, *2639*
7:14 the Feast did Jesus go up to the **temple c** *2639*
7:28 Then Jesus, still teaching in the **temple c**, *2639*
8: 2 he appeared again in the **temple c**, *2639*
Ac 2:46 to meet together in the **temple c**. *2639*
3: 2 to beg from those going into the **temple c**. *2639*
3: 8 Then he went with them into the **temple c**, *2639*
5:20 "Go, stand in the **temple c**," he said, *2639*
5:21 At daybreak they entered the **temple c**, *2639*
5:25 in jail are standing in the **temple c** teaching *2639*
5:42 in the **temple c** and from house to house, *2639*
19:38 the **c are open** and there are proconsuls. *61+72*
24:18 in the **temple c** doing this. *2639*
26:21 in the **temple c** and tried to kill me. *2639*

COURTYARD (73) [COURT]

Ex 27: 9 "Make a **c** *for* the tabernacle. 2958
27:12 of the **c** shall be fifty cubits wide 2958
27:13 the **c** shall also be fifty cubits wide. 2958
27:16 "For the entrance to the **c**, 2958
27:17 the **c** are to have silver bands and hooks, 2958
27:18 The **c** shall be a hundred cubits long 2958
27:19 the tent pegs for it and those for the **c**, 2958
35:17 of the **c** with its posts and bases, and 2958
35:17 and the curtain for the entrance to the **c**; 2958

Ex 35:18 for the tabernacle and for the **c**, 2958
38: 9 Next they made the **c**. 2958
38:15 on the other side of the entrance to the **c**, 2958
38:16 around the **c** were of finely twisted linen. 2958
38:17 so all the posts of the **c** had silver bands. 2958
38:18 to the **c** was of blue, purple and scarlet yarn 2958
38:18 like the curtains of the **c**, five cubits high, 2958
38:20 and of the surrounding **c** were bronze. 2958
38:31 the surrounding **c** and those for its entrance 2958
38:31 and those for the surrounding **c**. 2958
39:40 of the **c** with its posts and bases, and 2958
39:40 and the curtain for the entrance to the **c**; 2958
39:40 the ropes and tent pegs for **the c**; 2023S
40: 8 Set up the **c** around it and put the curtain at 2958
40: 8 and put the curtain at the entrance to the **c**. 2958
40:33 up the **c** around the tabernacle and altar 2958
40:33 up the curtain at the entrance to the **c**. 2958
Lev 6:16 to eat it in the **c** *of* the Tent of Meeting. 2958
6:26 in the **c** *of* the Tent of Meeting. 2958
Nu 3:26 of the **c**, the curtain at the entrance to 2958
3:26 the **c** surrounding the tabernacle and altar, 2958
3:37 as well as the posts of the surrounding **c** 2958
4:26 the **c** surrounding the tabernacle and altar, 2958
4:32 as well as the posts of the surrounding **c** 2958
2Sa 17:18 He had a well in his **c**, 2958
1Ki 6:36 the inner **c** of three courses of dressed stone 2958
7: 9 to the great **c** and from foundation to eaves, 2958
7:12 The great **c** was surrounded by a wall 2958
7:12 the inner **c** *of* the temple of the LORD 2958
8:64 the **c** in front of the temple of the LORD, 2958
2Ch 4: 9 He made the **c** *of* the priests, 2958
7: 7 the **c** in front of the temple of the LORD, 2958
20: 5 of the LORD in the front of the new **c** 2958
24:21 the king they stoned him to death in the **c** 2958
29:16 They brought out to the **c** *of* 2958
Est 2:11 near the **c** *of* the harem to find out 2958
Jer 26: 2 in the **c** *of* the LORD's house and speak 2958
32: 2 in the **c** *of* the guard in the royal palace 2958
32: 8 my cousin Hanamel came to me in the **c** *of* 2958
32:12 of all the Jews sitting in the **c** *of* the guard. 2958
33: 1 While Jeremiah was still confined in the **c** 2958
36:10 the upper **c** at the entrance of the New Gate 2958
36:20 to the king in the **c** and reported everything 2958
37:21 in the **c** *of* the guard and given bread from 2958
37:21 Jeremiah remained in the **c** *of* the guard. 2958
38: 6 which was in the **c** *of* the guard. 2958
38:13 Jeremiah remained in the **c** *of* the guard. 2958
38:28 And Jeremiah remained in the **c** *of* 2958
39:14 sent and had Jeremiah taken out of the **c** *of* 2958
39:15 While Jeremiah had been confined in the **c** 2958
Eze 40:14 up to the portico facing the **c**. 2958
41:12 The building facing the temple **c** on 1619
41:13 a hundred cubits long, and the temple **c** and 1619
41:14 The width of the temple **c** on the east, 1619
41:15 of the building facing the **c** at the rear of 1619
42: 1 the temple **c** and opposite the outer wall on 1619
42:10 the temple **c** and opposite the outer wall, 1619
42:13 and south rooms facing the temple **c** are 1619
Mt 26:58 right up to the **c** of the high priest. *885*
26:69 Now Peter was sitting out in the **c**, *885*
Mk 14:54 right into the **c** of the high priest. *885*
14:66 While Peter was below in the **c**, *885*
Lk 22:55 a fire in the middle *of* the **c** and had sat *885*
Jn 18:15 he went with Jesus into the high priest's **c**, *885*

COURTYARDS (4) [COURT]

Ex 8:13 in the **c** and in the fields. 2958
1Ch 23:28 to be in charge of the **c**, the side rooms, 2958
2Ch 23: 5 to be in the **c** *of* the temple of the LORD. 2958
Ne 8:16 in their **c**, in the courts of the house of God 2958

COUSIN (6) [COUSINS]

Lev 25:49 An uncle or a **c** or any blood relative 1201+1856
Est 2: 7 Mordecai had a **c** named Hadassah, 1426+1856
Jer 32: 8 my **c** Hanamel came to me in the courtyard 1201+1856
32: 9 field at Anathoth from my **c** Hanamel 1201+1856
32:12 in the presence of my **c** Hanamel and of 1856
Col 4:10 as does Mark, the **c** of Barnabas. *463*

COUSINS (3) [COUSIN]

Lev 10: 4 carry your **c** outside the camp, 278
Nu 36:11 **c on their father's side.** 1201+1856
1Ch 23:22 Their **c**, the sons of Kish, married them. 278

COVENANT (297) [COVENANTED, COVENANTS]

Ge 6:18 But I will establish my **c** with you, 1382
9: 9 "I now establish my **c** with you and 1382
9:11 I establish my **c** with you: 1382
9:12 of the **c** I am making between me and you 1382
9:12 a **c** for all generations to come: NIH
9:13 the sign of the **c** between me and the earth. 1382
9:15 I will remember my **c** between me and you 1382
9:16 I will see it and remember the everlasting **c** 1382
9:17 "This is the sign of the **c** I have established 1382
15:18 the LORD made a **c** with Abram and said, 1382
17: 2 I will confirm my **c** between me and you 1382
17: 4 this is my **c** with you: 1382
17: 7 I will establish my **c** as an everlasting 1382
17: 7 as an everlasting **c** between me and you 1382
17: 9 "As for you, you must keep my **c**, 1382
17:10 This is my **c** with you 1382
17:10 **the c** you are to keep: 889S
17:11 and it will be the sign of the **c** between me 1382
17:13 My **c** in your flesh is to be an everlasting 1382
17:13 in your flesh is to be an everlasting **c**. 1382
17:14 he has broken my **c**." 1382
17:19 I will establish my **c** with him as 1382
17:19 as an everlasting **c** for his descendants 1382
17:21 But my **c** I will establish with Isaac, 1382
31:44 Come now, let's make a **c**, you and I, 1382
Ex 2:24 and he remembered his **c** with Abraham, 1382
6: 4 I also established my **c** with them 1382
6: 5 and I have remembered my **c**. 1382
19: 5 Now if you obey me fully and keep my **c**, 1382
23:32 not make a **c** with them or with their gods. 1382
24: 7 the Book of the C and read it to the people. 1382
24: 8 of the **c** that the LORD has made with you 1382
31:16 for the generations to come as a lasting **c**. 1382
34:10 LORD said: "I am making a **c** with you. 1382
34:27 with these words I have made a **c** with you 1382
34:28 he wrote on the tablets the words of the **c**— 1382
Lev 2:13 not leave the salt of the **c** *of* your God out 1382
24: 8 on behalf of the Israelites, as a lasting **c**. 1382
26: 9 and I will keep my **c** with you. 1382
26:15 and so violate my **c**, 1382
26:25 upon you to avenge the breaking of the **c**. 1382
26:42 I will remember my **c** *with* Jacob 1382
26:42 and my **c** *with* Isaac and my covenant 1382
26:42 and my covenant with Isaac and my **c** 1382
26:44 breaking my **c** with them. 1382
26:45 But for their sake I will remember the **c** 1382
Nu 10:33 of the **c** *of* the LORD went before them 1382
14:44 nor the ark of the LORD's **c** moved from 1382
18:19 an everlasting **c** *of* salt before the LORD 1382
25:12 Therefore tell him I am making my **c** 1382
25:13 He and his descendants will have a **c** *of* 1382
Dt 4:13 He declared to you his **c**, 1382
4:23 the **c** *of* the LORD your God that he made 1382
4:31 not abandon or destroy you or forget the **c** 1382
5: 2 The LORD our God made a **c** with us 1382
5: 3 that the LORD made this **c**, 1382
7: 9 the faithful God, keeping his **c** *of* love to 1382
7:12 then the LORD your God will keep his **c** 1382
8:18 and so confirms his **c**, 1382
9: 9 the **c** that the LORD had made with you, 1382
9:11 the tablets of the **c**. 1382
9:15 the two tablets of the **c** were in my hands. 1382
10: 8 the tribe of Levi to carry the ark of the **c** *of* 1382
17: 2 the LORD your God in violation of his **c**, 1382
29: 1 of the **c** the LORD commanded Moses 1382
29: 1 in addition to the **c** he had made with them 1382
29: 9 Carefully follow the terms of this **c**, 1382
29:12 to enter into a **c** *with* the LORD your God, 1382
29:12 a **c** the LORD is making with you this day 889S
29:14 I am making this **c**, with its oath, 1382
29:21 according to all the curses of the **c** written 1382
29:25 "It is because this people abandoned the **c** 1382
29:25 of their fathers, **the c** he made with them 889S
31: 9 who carried the ark of the **c** *of* the LORD, 1382
31:16 and break the **c** I made with them. 1382
31:20 rejecting me and breaking my **c**. 1382
31:25 the Levites who carried the ark of the **c** *of* 1382
31:26 the Law and place it beside the ark of the **c** 1382
33: 9 over your word and guarded your **c**. 1382
Jos 3: 3 the ark of the **c** *of* the LORD your God, 1382
3: 6 "Take up the ark of the **c** and pass on ahead 1382
3: 8 Tell the priests who carry the ark of the **c**: 1382
3:11 of the **c** *of* the Lord of all the earth will go 1382
3:14 the priests carrying the ark of the **c** went 1382
3:17 The priests who carried the ark of the **c** *of* 1382
4: 7 before the ark of the **c** *of* the LORD. 1382
4: 9 the ark of the **c** had stood. 1382
4:18 up out of the river carrying the ark of the **c** 1382
6: 6 "Take up the ark of the **c** *of* the LORD 1382
6: 8 the ark of the LORD's **c** followed them. 1382
7:11 Israel has sinned; they have violated my **c**, 1382
7:15 He has violated the **c** *of* the LORD 1382
8:33 on both sides of the ark of the **c** *of* 1382
23:16 you violate the **c** *of* the LORD your God, 1382
24:25 that day Joshua made a **c** for the people, 1382
Jdg 2: 1 I said, 'I will never break my **c** with you, 1382
2: 2 and you shall not make a **c** with the people 1382
2:20 the **c** that I laid down for their forefathers 1382
20:27 the ark of the **c** *of* God was there, 1382
1Sa 4: 3 the ark of the LORD's **c** from Shiloh, 1382
4: 4 and they brought back the ark of the **c** *of* 1382
4: 4 were there with the ark of the **c** *of* God. 1382
4: 5 When the ark of the LORD's **c** came into 1382
18: 3 a **c** with David because he loved him 1382
20: 8 for you have brought him into a **c** with you 1382
20:16 Jonathan **made a c** with the house of David, 4162
22: 8 No one tells me when my son **makes a c** 4162
23:18 of them made a **c** before the LORD. 1382
2Sa 15:24 with him were carrying the ark of the **c** 1382
23: 5 Has he not made with me an everlasting **c**, 1382
1Ki 3:15 the Lord's **c** and sacrificed burnt offerings 1382
6:19 to set the ark of the **c** *of* the LORD there. 1382
8: 1 up the ark of the LORD's **c** from Zion, 1382
8: 6 the ark of the LORD's **c** to its place in 1382
8: 9 the LORD **made a c** with the Israelites 4162
8:21 the **c** *of* the LORD that he made 1382
8:23 you who keep your **c** of love 1382
11:11 not kept my **c** and my decrees, 1382
19:10 The Israelites have rejected your **c**, 1382
19:14 The Israelites have rejected your **c**, 1382
2Ki 11: 4 a **c** with them and put them under oath at 1382
11:12 a **copy of** the **c** and proclaimed him king. 6343
11:17 then made a **c** between the LORD and 1382
11:17 He also made a **c** between the king and NIH
2Ki 13:23 for them because of his **c** with Abraham, 1382
17:15 the **c** he had made with their fathers and 1382
17:35 the LORD made a **c** with the Israelites, 1382
17:38 Do not forget the **c** I have made with you, 1382
18:12 but had violated his **c**— 1382
23: 2 the words of the Book of the **C**, 1382
23: 3 the pillar and renewed the **c** in the presence 1382
23: 3 thus confirming the words of the **c** written 1382
23: 3 all the people pledged themselves to the **c**. 1382
23:21 as it is written in this Book of the **C**." 1382
1Ch 15:25 a thousand went to bring up the ark of the **c** 1382
15:26 the ark of the **c** *of* the LORD, 1382
15:28 the ark of the **c** *of* the LORD with shouts, 1382
15:29 the ark of the **c** *of* the LORD was entering 1382
16: 6 before the ark of the **c** *of* God. 1382
16:15 He remembers his **c** forever, 1382
16:16 **the c** he made with Abraham, 889S
16:17 to Israel as an everlasting **c**: 1382
16:37 and his associates before the ark of the **c** *of* 1382
17: 1 ark of the **c** *of* the LORD is under a tent." 1382
22:19 so that you may bring the ark of the **c** *of* 1382
28: 2 of rest for the ark of the **c** *of* the LORD, 1382
28:18 and shelter the ark of the **c** *of* the LORD. 1382
2Ch 5: 2 up the ark of the LORD's **c** from Zion, 1382
5: 7 the ark of the LORD's **c** to its place in 1382
5:10 the LORD **made a c** with the Israelites 4162
6:11 the **c** *of* the LORD that he made with 1382
6:14 you who keep your **c** of love 1382
13: 5 to David and his descendants forever by a **c** 1382
15:12 They entered into a **c** to seek the LORD, 1382
21: 7 of the **c** the LORD had made with David, 1382
23: 1 He made a **c** with the commanders of units 1382
23: 3 the whole assembly made a **c** with the king 1382
23:11 a **copy of** the **c** and proclaimed him king. 6343
23:16 then made a **c** that he and the people and 1382
29:10 Now I intend to make a **c** with the LORD, 1382
34:30 the words of the Book of the **C**, 1382
34:31 the **c** in the presence of the LORD— 1382
34:31 the words of the **c** written in this book. 1382
34:32 in accordance with the **c** *of* God, 1382
Ezr 10: 3 Now let us make a **c** before our God 1382
Ne 1: 5 and awesome God, who keeps his **c** of love 1382
9: 8 a **c** with him to give to his descendants 1382
9:32 who keeps his **c** of love, 1382
13:29 the **c** *of* the priesthood and of the Levites. 1382
Job 5:23 For you will have a **c** with the stones of 1382
31: 1 a **c** with my eyes not to look lustfully at 1382
Ps 25:10 for those who keep the demands of his **c**. 1382
25:14 he makes his **c** known to them. 1382
44:17 not forgotten you or been false to your **c**. 1382
50: 5 who made a **c** *with* me by sacrifice." 1382
50:16 to recite my laws or take my **c** 1382
55:20 he violates his **c**. 1382
60: T To [the tune of] "The Lily of the **C**." 6343
74:20 Have regard for your **c**, 1382
78:10 they did not keep God's **c** and refused 1382
78:37 they were not faithful to his **c**. 1382
80: T To [the tune of] "The Lilies of the **C**." 6343
89: 3 "I have made a **c** with my chosen one, 1382
89:28 and my **c** with him will never fail. 1382
89:34 I will not violate my **c** 1382
89:39 You have renounced the **c** 1382
103:18 with those who keep his **c** and remember 1382
105: 8 He remembers his **c** forever, 1382
105: 9 **the c** he made with Abraham, 889S
105:10 to Israel as an everlasting **c**: 1382
106:45 for their sake he remembered his **c** and out 1382
111: 5 he remembers his **c** forever. 1382
111: 9 he ordained his **c** forever— 1382
132:12 if your sons keep my **c** and 1382
Pr 2:17 and ignored the **c** she *made before* God. 1382
Isa 24: 5 the statutes and broken the everlasting **c**. 1382
28:15 "We have entered into a **c** with death, 1382
28:18 Your **c** with death will be annulled; 1382
42: 6 I will keep you and will make you to be a **c** 1382
49: 8 I will keep you and will make you to be a **c** 1382
54:10 be shaken nor my **c** *of* peace be removed," 1382
55: 3 I will make an everlasting **c** with you, 1382
56: 4 and hold fast to my **c**— 1382
56: 6 and who hold fast to my **c**— 1382
59:21 "As for me, this is my **c** with them," 1382
61: 8 and make an everlasting **c** with them. 1382
Jer 3:16 'The ark of the **c** *of* the LORD.' 1382
11: 2 "Listen to the terms of this **c** and tell them 1382
11: 3 not obey the terms of this **c**— 1382
11: 6 to the terms of this **c** and follow them. 1382
11: 8 the **c** I had commanded them to follow but 1382
11:10 the **c** I made with their forefathers. 1382
14:21 Remember your **c** with us and do 1382
22: 9 'Because they have forsaken the **c** *of* 1382
31:31 "when I will make a new **c** with the house 1382
31:32 be like the **c** I made with their forefathers 1382
31:32 because they broke my **c**, 1382
31:33 the **c** I will make with the house of Israel 1382
32:40 I will make an everlasting **c** with them: 1382
33:20 'If you can break my **c** *with* the day 1382
33:20 with the day and my **c** *with* the night, 1382
33:21 then my **c** with David my servant— 1382
33:21 and my **c** with the Levites NIH
33:25 not established my **c** with day and night 1382
34: 8 after King Zedekiah had made a **c** with all 1382
34:10 and people who entered into this **c** agreed 1382
34:13 I made a **c** with your forefathers 1382
34:15 You even made a **c** before me in the house 1382
34:18 The men who have violated my **c** and have 1382
34:18 not fulfilled the terms of the **c** they made 1382
50: 5 the LORD in an everlasting **c** that will not 1382

Eze 16: 8 and entered into a c with you, 1382
16:59 by breaking the c. 1382
16:60 Yet I will remember the c I made with you 1382
16:60 I will establish an everlasting c with you. 1382
16:61 but not on the basis of my c *with* you. 1382
16:62 So I will establish my c with you, 1382
17:18 He despised the oath by breaking the c. 1382
17:19 that he despised and my c that he broke. 1382
20:37 and I will bring you into the bond of the c. 1382
30: 5 Libya and the people of the c land will fall 1382
34:25 a c *of* peace with them and rid the land 1382
37:26 I will make a c *of* peace with them; 1382
37:26 it will be an everlasting c. 1382
44: 7 fat and blood, and you broke my c. 1382
Da 9: 4 and awesome God, who keeps his c of love 1382
9:27 He will confirm a c with many 1382
11:22 it and a prince of the c will be destroyed. 1382
11:28 but his heart will be set against the holy c. 1382
11:30 and vent his fury against the holy c. 1382
11:30 to those who forsake the holy c. 1382
11:32 With flattery he will corrupt those who have violated the c, 1382
Hos 2:18 a c for them with the beasts of the field and 1382
6: 7 Like Adam, they have broken the c— 1382
8: 1 the people have broken my c and rebelled 1382
Zec 9:11 because of the blood of my c *with* you, 1382
11:10 the c I had made with all the nations. 1382
Mal 2: 4 so that my c with Levi may continue," 1382
2: 5 "My c was with him, 1382
2: 5 a c of life and peace, NIH
2: 8 you have violated the c *with* Levi," 1382
2:10 Why do we profane the c *of* our fathers 1382
2:14 the wife of your **marriage** c. 1382
3: 1 the messenger of the c, whom you desire, 1382
Mt 26:28 This is my blood *of* the c, *1347*
Mk 14:24 "This is my blood *of* the c, *1347*
Lk 1:72 to our fathers and to remember his holy c, *1347*
22:20 saying, "This cup is the new c in my blood, *1347*
Ac 3:25 *of* the c God **made** with your fathers. *1347+1416*
7: 8 he gave Abraham the c of circumcision. *1347*
Ro 11:27 And this is my c with them *1347*
1Co 11:25 saying, "This cup is the new c in my blood; *1347*
2Co 3: 6 as ministers *of* a new c— *1347*
3:14 when the old c is read. *1347*
Gal 3:15 as no one can set aside or add to a human c *1347*
3:17 not set aside the c previously established *1347*
4:24 One c is from Mount Sinai *NIG*
Heb 7:22 the guarantee of a better c. *1347*
8: 6 as the c of which he is mediator is superior *1347*
8: 7 had been nothing wrong with that first c, *NIG*
8: 8 a new c with the house of Israel and with *1347*
8: 9 be like the c I made with their forefathers *1347*
8: 9 they did not remain faithful to my c, *1347*
8:10 c *I will* **make** with the house of Israel *1347+1416*
8:13 By calling this c "new," *NIG*
9: 1 Now the first c had regulations for worship *NIG*
9: 4 and the gold-covered ark *of* the c. *1347*
9: 4 and the stone tablets *of* the c. *1347*
9:15 the mediator *of* a new c, *1347*
9:15 from the sins committed under the first c. *1347*
9:18 This is why even the first c was not put *NIG*
9:20 He said, "This is the blood *of* the c, *1347*
10:16 the c *I will* **make** with them after that time, *1347+1416*
10:29 the blood *of* the c that sanctified him, *1347*
12:24 to Jesus the mediator *of* a new c, *1347*
13:20 the blood *of* the eternal c brought back *1347*
Rev 11:19 within his temple was seen the ark of his c. *1347*

COVENANTED (2) [COVENANT]

2Ch 7:18 as *I* c with David your father when I said, 4162
Hag 2: 5 'This is what *I* c with you 4162

COVENANTS (3) [COVENANT]

Ro 9: 4 theirs the divine glory, the c, *1347*
Gal 4:24 for the women represent two c. *1347*
Eph 2:12 and foreigners *to* the c of the promise, *1347*

COVER (98) [COVER-UP, COVERED, COVERING, COVERINGS, COVERS, GOLD-COVERED]

Ge 20:16 This is to c **the offense** against you 4064+6524
37:26 if we kill our brother and c **up** his blood? 4059
Ex 10: 5 *They will* c the face of the ground so 4059
21:33 and fails *to* c it and an ox or a donkey falls 4059
25:17 "Make an **atonement** c *of* pure gold— 4114
25:18 of hammered gold at the ends of the c. 4114
25:19 make the cherubim of one piece with the c, 4114
25:20 overshadowing the c with them. 4114
25:20 looking toward the c. 4114
25:21 the c on top of the ark and put in the ark 4114
25:22 the c between the two cherubim that are 4114
26:13 over the sides of the tabernacle so as to c it. 4059
26:34 Put the **atonement** c on the ark of 4114
30: 6 before the **atonement** c that is over 4114
31: 7 the Testimony with the **atonement** c on it, 4114
33:22 a cleft in the rock and c you *with* my hand 8503
35:12 the ark with its poles and the **atonement** c 4114
37: 6 He made the **atonement** c of pure gold— 4114
37: 7 of hammered gold at the ends of the c. 4114
37: 8 of one piece with the c. 4114
37: 9 overshadowing the c with them. 4114
37: 9 looking toward the c. 4114
39:35 with its poles and the **atonement** c; 4114
Ex 40:20 the poles to the ark and put the **atonement** c 4114
Lev 13:45 c the lower part of his face and cry out, 6486
16: 2 the curtain in front of the **atonement** c on 4114
16: 2 I appear in the cloud over the **atonement** c. 4114
16:13 of the incense will conceal the **atonement** c 4114
16:14 on the front of the **atonement** c; 4114
16:14 before the **atonement** c. 4114
16:15 He shall sprinkle it on the **atonement** c and 4114
17:13 be eaten must drain out the blood and c it 4059
Nu 4: 5 down the shielding curtain and c the ark of 4059
4: 6 *they are to* c this *with* hides of sea cows, 4062+5989
4: 8 c that with hides of sea cows 4059+4832
4: 9 to take a blue cloth and c the lampstand 4059
4:11 a blue cloth and c that with hides 4059+4832
4:12 c that with hides of sea cows 4059+4832
7:89 the two cherubim above the **atonement** c on 4114
22: 5 *they* c the face of the land 4059
Dt 23:13 dig a hole and c **up** your excrement. 2256+4059+8740
Jdg 9:31 **Under** c he sent messengers to Abimelech, 928+9564
1Ki 18: 6 So they divided the land they *were* to c, 6296
Ne 4: 5 *Do* not c **up** their guilt or blot out their sins 4059
Job 14:17 *you will* c over my sin. 3260
16:18 "O earth, *do* not c my blood; 4059
21:26 and worms c them both. 4059
24: 7 they have nothing to c themselves in 4064
37: 8 The animals take c; 743
38:34 to the clouds and c yourself *with* a flood 4059
Ps 10: 9 He lies in wait like a lion in c; 6108
17:12 like a great lion crouching in c. 5041
32: 5 to you and *did* not c **up** my iniquity. 4059
83:16 C their faces *with* shame so 4848
84: 6 the autumn rains also c it *with* pools. 6486
91: 4 *He will* c you with his feathers, 6114
104: 9 never again *will they* c the earth. 4059
Isa 8: 8 Its outspread wings will c the breadth 4850
10:31 the people of Gebim **take** c. 6395
11: 9 of the LORD as the waters c the sea. 4059
14:11 and worms c you. 4833
14:21 rise to inherit the land and c the earth 4848+7156
54: 9 waters of Noah *would* never again c 6296+6584
59: 6 *they* cannot c **themselves** 4059
60: 6 Herds of camels *will* c your land, 4059
Jer 3:25 and *let* our disgrace c us. 4059
14: 3 and despairing, *they* c their heads. 2902
14: 4 the farmers are dismayed and c their heads. 2902
46: 8 She says, 'I will rise and c the earth; 4059
51:42 its roaring waves *will* c *her*. 4059
Eze 12: 6 C your face so that you cannot see the land, 4059
12:12 *He will* c his face so that he cannot see 4059
13:10 they c it *with* whitewash, 3212
13:11 therefore tell *those who* c it *with* whitewash 3212
24: 7 where the dust *would* c it. 4059
24:17 *do* not c the lower part of your face or eat 6486
24:22 *You will* not c the lower part of your face 6486
26:10 be so many that *they will* c you *with* dust. 4059
26:19 over you and its vast waters c you, 4059
32: 7 *I will* c the heavens 4059
32: 7 *I will* c the sun with a cloud, 4059
37: 6 and make flesh come upon you and c you 7965
Hos 2: 9 intended to c her nakedness. 4059
10: 8 and thistles will grow up and c their altars. 6584
10: 8 they will say to the mountains, "C us!" 4059
Mic 3: 7 They *will* all c their faces 6486
Hab 2:14 as the waters c the sea. 4059
2:16 and disgrace will c your glory. 6584
Zec 5: 7 Then the c *of* lead was raised, 3971
5: 8 and pushed the lead c down over its mouth. 74
Lk 23:30 and to the hills, "C us!"' *2821*
1Co 11: 6 If a woman *does* not c her head, *2877*
11: 6 *she should* c her head. *2877*
11: 7 A man ought not *to* c his head, *2877*
1Th 2: 5 nor *did we* **put on a mask to** c **up** greed *4733*
Heb 9: 5 overshadowing the **atonement** c. *2663*
Jas 5:20 from death and c **over** a multitude of sins. *2821*
Rev 3:18 so *you can* c your shameful nakedness; *3590+5746*

COVER-UP (1) [COVER]

1Pe 2:16 but *do* not *use* your freedom as a c for evil; *2127+2400*

COVERED (101) [COVER]

Ge 7:19 under the entire heavens **were** c. 4059
7:20 The waters rose and c the mountains to 4059
9:23 in backward and c their father's nakedness. 4059
24:65 So she took her veil and c **herself.** 4059
27:16 *She* also c his hands and the smooth part 4252
38:14 c *herself* with a veil to disguise herself, 4059
38:15 for *she had* c her face. 4059
Ex 8: 6 and the frogs came up and c the land. 4059
10:15 *They* c all the ground until it was black. 4059
10:22 total darkness c all Egypt for three days. 928+2118
14:28 The water flowed back and c the chariots 4059
15: 5 The deep waters *have* c them; 4059
15:10 and the sea c them. 4059
16:13 That evening quail came and c the camp, 4059
19:18 Mount Sinai *was* c **with smoke,** 6939
24:15 the cloud c it, 4059
24:16 For six days the cloud c the mountain, 4059
40:34 Then the cloud c the Tent of Meeting, 4059
Lev 13:13 and if the disease *has* c his whole body, 4059
Nu 7: 3 as their gifts before the LORD six c carts 7369
9:15 was set up, the cloud c it. 4059
Nu 9:16 cloud c it, and at night it looked like fire. 4059
16:42 suddenly the cloud c it and the glory of 4059
Jos 24: 7 he brought the sea over them and c them. 4059
Jdg 4:19 gave him a drink, and c him **up.** 4059
6:39 the fleece dry and the ground c **with** dew." 6584
6:40 all the ground was c **with** dew. 6584
2Sa 15:30 his head **was** c and he was barefoot. 2902
15:30 All the people with him c their heads too 2902
19: 4 The king c his face and cried aloud, 4286
1Ki 6:15 and c the floor of the temple with planks 7596
6:21 Solomon c the inside of the temple 7596
6:30 *He* also c the floors of both the inner 7596
7: 7 and *he* c it with cedar from floor to ceiling. 6211
20:27 while the Arameans c the countryside. 4848
2Ki 3:25 a stone on every good field until it *was* c. 4848
18:16 which he *had* c the doors and doorposts 7596
23:14 down the Asherah poles and c the sites 4848
2Ch 3: 5 He paneled the main hall with pine and c it 2902
5: 8 the ark and c the ark and its carrying poles. 4059
16:14 They laid him on a bier c *with* spices 4848
Est 6:12 with his head c *in* grief, 2902
7: 8 *they* c Haman's face. 2902
Job 15:27 "Though his face *is* c with fat 4059
29: 9 and c their mouths *with* their hands; 4200+8492
Ps 32: 1 are forgiven, *whose* sins **are** c. 4059
34: 5 their faces *are* never c **with shame.** 2917
44:15 and my face *is* c *with* shame 4059
44:19 and made us a haunt for jackals and c us 4059
65:13 The meadows *are* c *with* flocks and 4252
71:13 to harm me *be* c *with* scorn and disgrace. 6486
80:10 The mountains **were** c *with* its shade, 4059
85: 2 of your people and c all their sins. 4059
89:45 c him **with a mantle** 6486
104: 6 *You* c it *with* the deep as with a garment; 4059
106:11 The waters c their adversaries; 4059
140: 9 *be* c *with* the trouble their lips have caused. 4059
Pr 7:16 *I have* c my bed *with* colored linens 5267+8048
24:31 the ground **was** c *with* weeds, 4059
Isa 6: 2 With two wings *they* c their faces, 4059
6: 2 with two *they* c their feet, 4059
7:24 for the land will be c **with** briers and thorns. 3972
14:19 you are c *with* the slain, 4229
28: 8 the tables *are* c *with* vomit and there is not 4848
29:10 *he has* c your heads (the seers). 4059
30:22 with silver and your images c *with* gold; 682
34: 6 *it* **is** c with fat— 2014
51:16 in your mouth and c you with the shadow 4059
Jer 48:37 and every waist is c **with** sackcloth. 6584
La 2: 1 c the Daughter of Zion **with the cloud** 6380
3:43 *"You have* c yourself with anger 6114
3:44 *You have* c yourself with a cloud so 6114
Eze 7:18 be c *with* shame and their heads will 448
13:12 "Where is the whitewash *you* c it *with?"* 3212
13:14 down the wall *you have* c *with* whitewash 3212
13:15 and against those *who* c it *with* whitewash. 3212
16: 8 over you and c your nakedness. 4059
16:10 I dressed you in fine linen and c you 4059
24: 8 so that it *would* not **be** c. 4059
30:18 She *will be* c *with* clouds, 4059
31:15 down to the grave *I* c the deep springs 4059
37: 8 on them and skin c them, 7965
41:16 including the threshold was c **with** wood. 6017+6017+8470
41:16 and the windows **were** c. 4059
Da 9: 7 but this day we are c **with** shame— 4200+7156
9: 8 our princes and our fathers are c **with** shame 4200+7156
Ob 1:10 you *will be* c *with* shame; 4059
Jnh 3: 6 c *himself* with sackcloth and sat down in 4059
3: 8 But *let* man and beast **be** c with sackcloth. 4059
Mic 7:10 Then my enemy will see it and *will* **be** c 4059
Hab 2:19 It *is* c *with* gold and silver; 9530
3: 3 His glory c the heavens 4059
Lk 5:12 a man came along who was c with leprosy. *4441*
16:20 a beggar named Lazarus, c **with sores** *1815*
Jn 5: 2 by five c **colonnades.** *5119*
Ac 7:57 At this *they* c their ears and, *5309*
Ro 4: 7 are forgiven, whose sins *are* c. *2128*
1Co 11: 4 with his head c dishonors his head. *2400+2848*
Rev 4: 6 and *they* were c **with** eyes, *1154*
4: 8 and *was* c **with** eyes all around, *1154*
17: 3 that *was* c **with** blasphemous names *1154*

COVERING (38) [COVER]

Ge 8:13 the c *from* the ark and saw that the surface 4832
Ex 22:27 his cloak is the only c he has for his body. 4064
26:14 for the tent a c *of* ram skins dyed red, 4832
26:14 and over that a c *of* hides of sea cows. 4832
28:42 "Make linen undergarments as a c *for* 4059
29:13 the c of the liver, 3866
29:22 the c *of* the liver, 3866
35:11 and its c, clasps, frames, crossbars, posts 4832
36:19 for the tent a c *of* ram skins dyed red, 4832
36:19 and over that a c *of* hides of sea cows. 4832
39:34 the c *of* ram skins dyed red, the covering 4832
39:34 the c *of* hides of sea cows and 4832
40:19 the tabernacle and put the c over the tent, 4832
Lev 3: 4 and the c of the liver, 3866
3:10 and the c of the liver, 3866
3:15 and the c of the liver, 3866
4: 9 and the c of the liver, 3866
7: 4 and the c of the liver, 3866
8:16 the c *of* the liver, 3866
8:25 the c *of* the liver, 3866
9:10 and the c of the liver from the sin offering, 3866
9:19 the kidneys and the c *of* the liver— 3866

Nu 4:10 in a c of hides of sea cows and put it on 4832
4:14 a c of hides of sea cows and put its poles 4062
4:15 "After Aaron and his sons have finished c 4059
4:25 its c and the outer covering of hides 4832
4:25 and the outer c of hides of sea cows, 4832
Jdg 4:18 and she put a c over him. 8526
1Sa 19:13 c it with a garment 4059
2Sa 17:19 a c and spread it out over the opening of 5009
Ps 18:11 He made darkness his c, 6260
105:39 He spread out a cloud as a c, 5009
Isa 50:3 with darkness and make sackcloth its c." 4064
Eze 1:11 and two wings c its body. 4059
1:23 and each had two wings c its body. 4059
38:9 you will be like a cloud c the land. 4059
Mal 2:16 a man's c himself with violence as well as 4059
1Co 11:15 For long hair is given to her as a c. 4316

COVERINGS (3) [COVER]

Ge 3:7 and made c for themselves. 2514
Nu 3:25 for the care of the tabernacle and tent, its c, 4832
Pr 31:22 She makes c for her bed; 5267

COVERS (23) [COVER]

Ex 22:15 the money paid for the hire c the loss. 928+995
Lev 3:3 the fat that c the inner parts or is connected 4059
3:9 the fat that c the inner parts or is connected 4059
3:14 the fat that c the inner parts or is connected 4059
4:8 the fat that c the inner parts or is connected 4059
7:3 the fat tail and the fat that c the inner parts, 4059
13:12 it c all the skin of the infected person 4059
Nu 22:11 that has come out of Egypt c the face of 4059
1Ki 1:1 not keep warm even when they put c 955
Job 22:11 and why a flood of water c you. 4059
23:17 by the thick darkness that c my face. 4059
26:9 He c the face of the full moon, 297
Ps 10:11 he c his face and never sees." 6259
69:7 and shame c my face. 4059
147:8 He c the sky with clouds; 4059
Pr 10:12 but love c over all wrongs. 4059
17:9 He who c over an offense promotes love, 4059
Isa 25:7 the sheet that c all nations; 5819
60:2 darkness c the earth and thick darkness is 4059
Jer 51:51 and shame c our faces, 4059
Eze 38:16 against my people Israel like a cloud that c 4059
2Co 3:15 a veil c their hearts. 2093+3023
1Pe 4:8 because love c over a multitude of sins. 2821

COVES (1)

Jdg 5:17 on the coast and stayed in his c. 5153

COVET (9) [COVETED, COVETING, COVETOUS]

Ex 20:17 "You shall not c your neighbor's house. 2773
20:17 You shall not c your neighbor's wife, 2773
34:24 and no one will c your land when you go 2773
Dt 5:21 "You shall not c your neighbor's wife. 2773
7:25 Do not c the silver and gold on them, 2773
Mic 2:2 They c fields and seize them, and houses, 2773
Ro 7:7 if the law had not said, "Do not c." 2121
13:9 Do not murder," "Do not steal," "Do not c," 2121
Jas 4:2 You kill and c, 2420

COVETED (2) [COVET]

Jos 7:21 I c them and took them. 2773
Ac 20:33 not c anyone's silver or gold or clothing. 2121

COVETING (1) [COVET]

Ro 7:7 not have known what c really was if 2123

COVETOUS (1) [COVET]

Ro 7:8 produced in me every kind of c desire. 2123

COW (4) [COWS, COWS']

Lev 22:28 not slaughter a c or a sheep and its young 8802
Isa 7:21 a man will keep alive a young c 1330+6320
11:7 The c will feed with the bear, 7239
Eze 4:15 bake your bread over c manure instead 1330

COWARDLY (1) [COWER]

Rev 21:8 But the c, the unbelieving, the vile, 1264

COWER (1) [COWARDLY, COWERED, COWERING]

Dt 33:29 Your enemies will c before you, 3950

COWERED (1) [COWER]

Job 9:13 even the cohorts of Rahab c at his feet. 8820

COWERING (1) [COWER]

Isa 51:14 The c prisoners will soon be set free; 7579

COWS (33) [COW]

Ge 32:15 forty c and ten bulls, 7239
33:13 the ewes and c that are nursing their young. 1330
41:2 out of the river there came up seven c, 7239
41:3 After them, seven other c, ugly and gaunt, 7239
41:4 And the c that were ugly and gaunt ate up 7239
41:4 and gaunt ate up the seven sleek, fat c. 7239
41:18 out of the river there came up seven c, 7239
41:19 After them, seven other c came up— 7239
41:19 I had never seen such ugly c in all the land 2179S
41:20 ugly c ate up the seven fat cows that came 7239
41:20 ugly cows ate up the seven fat c that came 7239
41:26 The seven good c are seven years, 7239
41:27 The seven lean, ugly c that came 7239
Ex 25:5 ram skins dyed red and hides of sea c; 9391
26:14 and over that a covering of hides of sea c. 9391
35:7 ram skins dyed red and hides of sea c; 9391
35:23 or hides of sea c brought them. 9391
36:19 and over that a covering of hides of sea c. 9391
39:34 of hides of sea c and the shielding curtain; 9391
Nu 4:6 they are to cover this with hides of sea c, 9391
4:8 that with hides of sea c and put its poles 9391
4:10 in a covering of hides of sea c and put it on 9391
4:11 that with hides of sea c and put its poles 9391
4:12 cover that with hides of sea c and put them 9391
4:14 of hides of sea c and put its poles in place. 9391
4:25 and the outer covering of hides of sea c, 9391
1Sa 6:7 with two c that have calved 7239
6:7 Hitch the c to the cart, 7239
6:10 They took two such c and hitched them to 7239
6:12 c went straight up toward Beth Shemesh, 7239
6:14 up the wood of the cart and sacrificed the c 7239
Job 21:10 their c calve and do not miscarry. 7239
Am 4:1 you c of Bashan on Mount Samaria, 7239

COWS' (1) [COW]

2Sa 17:29 from c' milk for David and his people 1330

COZ (KJV) See KOZ

COZBI (2)

Nu 25:15 to death was C daughter of Zur, 3944
25:18 in the affair of Peor and their sister C, 3944

COZEBA (1)

1Ch 4:22 the men of C, and Joash and Saraph, 3943

CRACK (1) [CRACKED]

Na 3:2 The c of whips, the clatter of wheels, 7754

CRACKED (5) [CRACK]

Jos 9:4 with worn-out sacks and old wineskins, c 1324
9:13 but see how c they are. 1324
Jdg 9:53 on his head and c his skull. 8368
Isa 30:13 c and bulging, that collapses suddenly, 5877+7288
Jer 14:4 The ground is c because there is no rain in 3169

CRACKLING (2)

Ecc 7:6 Like the c of thorns under the pot, 7754
Joel 2:5 like a c fire consuming stubble, 7754

CRACKNELS (KJV) See CAKES

CRAFT (1) [CRAFTED, CRAFTINESS, CRAFTS, CRAFTSMAN, CRAFTSMAN'S, CRAFTSMANSHIP, CRAFTSMEN, CRAFTY]

1Ch 28:21 in any c will help you in all the work. 6275

CRAFTED (1) [CRAFT]

Nu 31:51 all the c articles. 5126

CRAFTINESS (3) [CRAFT]

Job 5:13 He catches the wise in their c, 6891
1Co 3:19 "He catches the wise in their c"; 4111
Eph 4:14 and c of men in their deceitful scheming. 4111

CRAFTS (2) [CRAFT]

Ex 31:3 ability and knowledge in all kinds of c— 4856
35:31 ability and knowledge in all kinds of c— 4856

CRAFTSMAN (18) [CRAFT]

Ex 26:1 into them by a skilled c. 3110
26:31 into it by a skilled c. 3110
28:6 the work of a skilled c. 3110
28:15 the work of a skilled c. 3110
36:8 into them by a skilled c. 3110
36:35 into it by a skilled c. 3110
38:23 a c and designer, 3093
39:3 the work of a skilled c. 3110
39:8 the work of a skilled c. 3110
1Ki 7:14 a man of Tyre and a c in bronze. 3086
Pr 8:30 Then I was the c at his side. 570
Isa 3:3 skilled c and clever enchanter. 3093
40:19 As for an idol, a c casts it, 3093
40:20 He looks for a skilled c to set up an idol 3093
41:7 The c encourages the goldsmith, 3093
Jer 10:3 and a c shapes it with his chisel. 3093
10:9 What the c and goldsmith have made is 3093
Hos 8:6 This calf—a c has made it; it is not God. 3093

CRAFTSMAN'S (2) [CRAFT]

Dt 27:15 the work of the c hands— 3093
SS 7:1 the work of a c hands. 588

CRAFTSMANSHIP (2) [CRAFT]

Ex 31:5 and to engage in all kinds of c. 4856
35:33 and to engage in all kinds of artistic c. 4742

CRAFTSMEN (23) [CRAFT]

Ex 31:6 Also I have given skill to all the c 2682+4213
35:35 with skill to do all kinds of work as c, 3093
35:35 all of them master c and designers. 4856+6913
36:4 the skilled c who were doing all the work 2682
1Ki 5:18 The c of Solomon and Hiram and the men 1215
2Ki 24:14 and all the c and artisans— 3093
24:16 and a thousand c and artisans. 3093
1Ch 4:14 It was called this because its people were c. 3093
22:16 and iron—c beyond number. NIH
29:5 and for all the work to be done by the c. 3093
2Ch 2:7 in Judah and Jerusalem with my skilled c, 2682
2:14 He will work with your c and with those 2682
Ne 11:35 in Lod and Ono, and in the Valley of the C. 3093
Isa 44:11 c are nothing but men. 3093
Jer 24:1 the c and the artisans of Judah were carried 3093
29:2 the c and the artisans had gone into exile 3093
52:15 the rest of the c and those who had gone 570
Eze 27:9 Veteran c of Gebal were on board 2682
Hos 13:2 all of them the work of c. 3093
Zec 1:20 Then the LORD showed me four c. 3093
1:21 but the c have come to terrify them 465S
Ac 19:24 brought in no little business for the c. 5493
19:38 and his fellow c have a grievance 5493

CRAFTY (8) [CRAFT]

Ge 3:1 Now the serpent was more c than any of 6874
1Sa 23:22 They tell me he is very c. 6891+6891
Job 5:12 He thwarts the plans of the c, 6874
15:5 you adopt the tongue of the c. 6874
Pr 7:10 dressed like a prostitute and with c intent. 5915
12:2 but the LORD condemns a c man. 4659
14:17 and a c man is hated. 4659
2Co 12:16 Yet, c fellow that I am, 4112

CRAG (3) [CRAGS]

Dt 32:13 and with oil from the flinty c, 7446
Job 39:28 a rocky c is his stronghold. 9094
Ps 78:16 of a rocky c and made water flow down 6152

CRAGS (6) [CRAG]

1Sa 24:2 and his men near the C of the Wild Goats. 7446
Ps 104:18 the c are a refuge for the coneys. 6152
Pr 30:26 yet they make their home in the c; 6152
Isa 2:21 and to the overhanging c from dread of 6152
57:5 in the ravines and under the overhanging c. 6152
Am 6:12 Do horses run on the rocky c? 6152

CRANE (KJV) See SWIFT

CRASH (2)

Zep 1:10 and a loud c from the hills. 8691
Mt 7:27 that house, and it fell with a great c." 899+1639+3489+3836+4774

CRAVE (7) [CRAVED, CRAVES, CRAVING, CRAVINGS]

Nu 11:4 with them began to c other food, 203+9294
Dt 12:20 and you c meat and say, 203
Pr 23:3 Do not c his delicacies, 203
23:6 do not c his delicacies; 203
31:4 kings to drink wine, not for rulers to c beer, 197
Mic 7:1 none of the early figs that I c. 203
1Pe 2:2 Like newborn babies, c pure spiritual milk, 2160

CRAVED (4) [CRAVE]

Nu 11:34 the people who had c other food. 203
Ps 78:18 to the test by demanding the food they c. 5883
78:29 for he had given them what they c. 9294
78:30 before they turned from the food they c, 9294

CRAVES (3) [CRAVE]

Pr 13:4 The sluggard c and gets nothing, 203
21:10 The wicked man c evil; 203
21:26 All day long he c for more, 203+9294

CRAVING (6) [CRAVE]

Job 20:20 "Surely he will have no respite from his c; 1061
Ps 106:14 they gave in to their c; 203+9294
Pr 10:3 but he thwarts the c of the wicked. 2094
13:2 but the unfaithful have a c for violence. 5883
21:25 The sluggard's c will be the death of him, 9294
Jer 2:24 sniffing the wind in her c— 205+5883

CRAVINGS (3) [CRAVE]

Ps 10:3 He boasts of the c of his heart; 9294
Eph 2:3 gratifying the c of our sinful nature 2123
1Jn 2:16 the c of sinful man, 2123

CRAWL (2) [CRAWLING]

Ge 3:14 You will c on your belly 2143
Mic 7:17 like creatures that c on the ground. 2323

CRAWLING (3) [CRAWL]

Lev 22: 5 or if he touches any c thing 9238
1Sa 14:11 "The Hebrews *are* c out of the holes 3655
Eze 8:10 of c things and detestable animals and all 8254

CREAM (2)

Job 20:17 the rivers flowing with honey and c. 2772
29: 6 when my path was drenched with c and 2772

CREATE (11) [CREATED, CREATES, CREATING, CREATION, CREATOR]

Ps 51:10 C in me a pure heart, O God, 1343
Isa 4: 5 the LORD *will* c over all of Mount Zion 1343
45: 7 I form the light and c darkness, 1343
45: 7 I bring prosperity and c disaster; 1343
45:18 *he did* not c it to be empty, 1343
65:17 I *will* c new heavens and a new earth. 1343
65:18 and rejoice forever in what I *will* c, 1343
65:18 for I *will* c Jerusalem to be a delight 1343
Jer 31:22 The LORD *will* c a new thing on earth— 1343
Mal 2:10 *Did* not one God c us? 1343
Eph 2:15 to c in himself one new man out of the two, *3231*

CREATED (47) [CREATE]

Ge 1: 1 In the beginning God c the heavens and 1343
1:21 So God c the great creatures of the sea 1343
1:27 So God c man in his own image, 1343
1:27 in the image of God *he* c him; 1343
1:27 male and female *he* c them. 1343
2: 4 the heavens and the earth when they were c. 1343
5: 1 When God c man, 1343
5: 2 *He* c them male and female 1343
5: 2 when they were c, he called them "man." 1343
6: 7 "I will wipe mankind, whom *I have* c, 1343
Dt 4:32 from the day God c man on the earth; 1343
Ps 89:12 You c the north and the south; 1343
89:47 For what futility *you have* c all men! 1343
102:18 a people not yet c may praise the LORD: 1343
104:30 When you send your Spirit, *they* are c, 1343
139:13 For you c my inmost being; 7865
148: 5 for he commanded and *they* were c. 1343
Isa 40:26 Who c all these? 1343
41:20 that the Holy One of Israel *has* c it. 1343
42: 5 *he who* c the heavens 1343
43: 1 *he who* c you, O Jacob, he who formed you, 1343
43: 7 whom *I* c for my glory, 1343
45: 8 I, the LORD, *have* c it. 1343
45:12 It is I who made the earth and c mankind 1343
45:18 *he who* c the heavens, he is God, 1343
48: 7 *They* are c now, and not long ago; 1343
54:16 it is I *who* c the blacksmith who fans 1343
54:16 And it is I *who have* c the destroyer 1343
57:16 the breath of man that I *have* c. 6913
Eze 21:30 In the place where *you* were c, 1343
28:13 on the day you were c they were prepared. 1343
28:15 in your ways from the day you were c 1343
Mk 13:19 when God c the world, until now— *3231*
Ro 1:25 and served c things rather than *3232*
1Co 11: 9 neither *was* man c for woman, *3231*
Eph 2:10 c in Christ Jesus to do good works, *3231*
3: 9 in God, who c all things. *3231*
4:24 c to be like God in true righteousness *3231*
Col 1:16 For by him all things *were* c: *3231*
1:16 all things *were* c by him and for him. *3231*
1Ti 4: 3 which God c to be received *3231*
4: 4 For everything God c is good, *3233*
Heb 12:27 that is, c things— *4472*
Jas 1:18 be a kind of firstfruits *of* all he c. *3233*
Rev 4:11 for you c all things, *3231*
4:11 and by your will *they were* c *3231*
10: 6 who c the heavens and all that is in them, *3231*

CREATES (1) [CREATE]

Am 4:13 He who forms the mountains, c the wind, 1343

CREATING (2) [CREATE]

Ge 2: 3 from all the work *of* c that he had done. 1343
Isa 57:19 c praise on the lips of the mourners 1343

CREATION (25) [CREATE]

Hab 2:18 For he who makes it trusts in his own c; 3671
Mt 13:35 I will utter things hidden since the c of *2856*
25:34 the kingdom prepared for you since the c *2856*
Mk 10: 6 the beginning *of* c God 'made them male *3232*
16:15 and preach the good news *to* all c. *3232*
Jn 17:24 because you loved me before the c of *2856*
Ro 1:20 c of the world God's invisible qualities— *3232*
8:19 The c waits in eager expectation for *3232*
8:20 For the c was subjected to frustration, *3232*
8:21 that the c itself will be liberated *3232*
8:22 that the whole c has been groaning as in *3232*
8:39 nor anything else in all c, *3232*
2Co 5:17 if anyone is in Christ, he is a new c; *3232*
Gal 6:15 what counts is a new c. *3232*
Eph 1: 4 the c of the world to be holy and blameless *2856*
Col 1:15 the firstborn *over* all c. *3232*
Heb 4: 3 yet his work has been finished since the c *2856*
4:13 Nothing in all c is hidden *3232*
9:11 that is to say, not *a part of* this c. *3232*
9:26 to suffer many times since the c of *2856*
1Pe 1:20 He was chosen before the c of the world, *2856*
2Pe 3: 4 on as it has since the beginning *of* c." *3232*
Rev 3:14 the ruler *of* God's c. *3232*
13: 8 Lamb that was slain from the c of the world. *2856*
17: 8 the book of life from the c of the world will *2856*

CREATOR (11) [CREATE]

Ge 14:19 God Most High, C *of* heaven and earth. 7865
14:22 God Most High, C *of* heaven and earth, 7865
Dt 32: 6 Is he not your Father, your C, 7865
Ecc 12: 1 Remember your C in the days 1343
Isa 27:11 and their C shows them no favor. 3670
40:28 the C *of* the ends of the earth. 1343
43:15 your Holy One, Israel's C, your King." 1343
Mt 19: 4 at the beginning the C 'made them male *3231*
Ro 1:25 and served created things rather than the C *3231*
Col 3:10 in knowledge in the image *of* its C. *3231*
1Pe 4:19 *to* their faithful C and continue to do good. *3234*

CREATURE (37) [CREATURES]

Ge 1:28 the air and over every living c that moves 2651
2:19 and whatever the man called each living c, 5883
6:17 every c that has the breath of life in it. NIH
6:20 of animal and of every kind of c that moves 8254
7: 4 of the earth every living c I have made." 3685
7:14 every c that moves along the ground 8254
8:17 Bring out every kind of living c that is 1414
9: 2 upon every c that moves along the ground, 889S
9:10 with every living c that was with you— 5883
9:10 every living c *on* earth. 2651
9:12 and every living c with you, a covenant 5883
Lev 11:41 " 'Every c that moves about on 9238
11:42 You are not to eat any c that moves about 9238
11:44 Do not make yourselves unclean by any c 9238
11:46 the water and every c that moves about on 5883
17:11 For the life of a c is in the blood, 1414
17:14 because the life of every c is its blood. 1414
17:14 "You must not eat the blood of any c, 1414
17:14 because the life of every c is its blood; 1414
Dt 4:18 or like any c that moves along the ground 8253
14:20 But any winged c that is clean you may eat. 6416
Job 12:10 of every c and the breath of all mankind. 2644
14:15 c your hands have made. 5126
41:33 a c without fear. 6913
Ps 136:25 and who gives food to every c. 1414
145:21 Let every c praise his holy name for ever 1414
Isa 47: 8 "Now then, listen, you wanton *c,* AIT
Eze 1:11 one touching the wing of another c on 408S
1:15 I saw a wheel on the ground beside each c 2651
38:20 every c that moves along the ground, 8254
Da 4:12 from it every c was fed. 10125
Col 1:23 and that has been proclaimed to every c *3232*
Rev 4: 7 The first living c was like a lion, *2442*
5:13 Then I heard every c in heaven and *3233*
6: 3 I heard the second living c say, "Come!" *2442*
6: 5 I heard the third living c say, "Come!" *2442*
6: 7 the voice *of* the fourth living c say, *2442*

CREATURES (82) [CREATURE]

Ge 1:20 "Let the water teem with living c, 5883
1:21 the great c of the sea and every living 9490
1:24 "Let the land produce living c according 5883
1:24 livestock, c that move along the ground, 8254
1:25 the c that move *along* the ground according 8254
1:26 over all the c that move along the ground." 8254
1:30 the birds of the air and all the c that move 8253
6: 7 c that move along the ground, 8254
6:19 to bring into the ark two of all living c, 1414
7: 8 and of all c that move along the ground, 889S
7:15 Pairs of all c that have the breath of life 1414
7:21 all the c that swarm over the earth, 9238
7:23 men and animals and the c that move along 8254
8:17 and all the c that move along the ground— 8254
8:19 the animals and all the c that move along 8254
8:21 And never again will I destroy all living c, 2645
9:15 and you and all living c of every kind. 5883
9:16 and all living c of every kind on the earth." 5883
Lev 5: 2 c that move along the ground— 9238
11: 9 " 'Of all the c living in the water of the seas 889S
11:10 But all c in the seas or streams that do NIH
11:10 among all the other living c in the water— 5883
11:21 some winged c that walk on all fours 9238
11:23 But all other winged c 9238
11:43 Do not defile yourselves by any of these c. 9238
11:47 between living c that may be eaten 2651
Dt 14: 9 Of all the c living in the water, 889S
Ps 50:11 and the c *of* the field are mine. 2328
74:14 and gave him as food to the c of the desert. 7470
80:13 Boars from the forest ravage it and the c *of* 2328
104:24 the earth is full of your c. 7871
104:25 teeming with c beyond number— 8254
148: 7 you great sea c and all ocean depths, 9490
148:10 small c and flying birds, 8254
Pr 30:25 Ants are c of little strength, yet they store 6639
30:26 coneys are c of little power, 6639
Isa 13:21 But desert c will lie there, 7470
23:13 a place for desert c; 7470
34:14 Desert c will meet with hyenas, 7470
34:14 there the night c will also repose and find 4327
Jer 50:39 "So desert c and hyenas will live there, 7470
Eze 1: 5 like four living c. 2651
1:13 the living c was like burning coals of fire 2651
1:13 Fire moved back and forth among the c; 2651
1:14 The c sped back and forth like flashes 2651
1:15 As I looked at the living c, 2651
1:17 of the four directions the c faced; NIH
1:17 the wheels did not turn about as the c went. 5527S
Eze 1:19 When the living c moved, 2651
1:19 when the living c rose from the ground, 2651
1:20 spirit of the living c was in the wheels. 2651
1:21 When the c moved, they also moved; 4392S
1:21 when the c stood still, they also stood still; 4392S
1:21 and when the c rose from the ground, 4392S
1:21 spirit of the living c was in the wheels. 2651
1:22 the heads of the living c was what looked 2651
1:24 When the c moved, 4392S
3:13 the living c brushing against each other 2651
10:15 These were the living c I had seen by 2651
10:17 the spirit of the living c was in them. 2651
10:20 the living c I had seen beneath the God 2651
47: 9 Swarms of living c will live wherever 5883
Hos 2:18 and the birds of the air and the c that move 8254
Mic 7:17 like *c that* crawl *on* the ground. AIT
Hab 1:14 like sea c that have no ruler. 8254
Zep 2:14 c *of* every kind. 2651
Jas 3: 7 reptiles and c of the sea are being tamed *1879*
2Pe 2:12 They are like brute beasts, c of instinct, *5879*
Rev 4: 6 around the throne, were four living c, *2442*
4: 8 Each of the four living c had six wings *2442*
4: 9 Whenever the living c give glory, *2442*
5: 6 *by* the four living c and the elders. *2442*
5: 8 the four living c and the twenty-four elders *2442*
5:11 They encircled the throne and the living c *2442*
5:14 The four living c said, "Amen," *2442*
6: 1 Then I heard one of the four living c say *2442*
6: 6 like a voice among the four living c, *2442*
7:11 around the elders and the four living c. *2442*
8: 9 a third *of* the living c in the sea died, *3233*
14: 3 before the four living c and the elders. *2442*
15: 7 Then one of the four living c gave to *2442*
19: 4 and the four living c fell down *2442*

CREDIT (6) [ACCREDITED, CREDITED, CREDITOR, CREDITORS, CREDITS]

Est 2:22 giving c to Mordecai. 928+9005
Lk 6:32 what c is that to you? *5921*
6:33 what c is that to you? *5921*
6:34 what c is that to you? *5921*
Ro 4:24 to whom God will c righteousness— *3357*
1Pe 2:20 how is it to your c if you receive a beating *3094*

CREDITED (16) [CREDIT]

Ge 15: 6 and *he* c it to him *as* righteousness. 3108
Lev 7:18 *It will* not be c to the one who offered it, 3108
1Sa 18: 8 *"They have* c David *with* tens of thousands, 5989
Ps 106:31 *This* was c to him as righteousness 3108
Eze 18:20 of the righteous man will be c to him, 6584
Ro 4: 3 and *it was* c to him as righteousness." *3357*
4: 4 his wages *are* not c to him as a gift, *3357*
4: 5 his faith *is* c as righteousness. *3357*
4: 9 that Abraham's faith *was* c to him *3357*
4:10 Under what circumstances *was it* c? *3357*
4:11 that righteousness *might be* c to them. *3357*
4:22 This is why *"it was* c to him *3357*
4:23 The words *"it was* c to him" were written *3357*
Gal 3: 6 and *it was* c to him as righteousness." *3357*
Php 4:17 but I am looking for what may be c *4429*
Jas 2:23 and *it was* c to him as righteousness," *3357*

CREDITOR (4) [CREDIT]

Dt 15: 2 Every c shall cancel the loan he has made 1251+2257+3338+5408
2Ki 4: 1 now his c is coming to take my two boys 5957
Ps 109:11 May a c seize all he has; 5957
Isa 24: 2 for debtor as for c. 5957

CREDITORS (1) [CREDIT]

Isa 50: 1 Or to which of my c did I sell you? 5957

CREDITS (1) [CREDIT]

Ro 4: 6 to whom God c righteousness apart *3357*

CREPT (2)

1Sa 24: 4 Then David c up unnoticed and cut off 7756
Hab 3:16 decay c into my bones, 995

CRESCENS (1)

2Ti 4:10 C has gone to Galatia, *3206*

CRESCENT (1)

Isa 3:18 bangles and headbands and c necklaces, 8448

CREST (2)

Est 6: 8 one with a royal c placed on its head. 4195
SS 4: 8 Descend from the c *of* Amana, 8031

CRETANS (2) [CRETE]

Ac 2:11 to Judaism); C and Arabs— *3205*
Tit 1:12 "C are always liars, evil brutes, *3205*

CRETE (5) [CRETANS]

Ac 27: 7 we sailed to the lee of C, *3207*
27:12 This was a harbor *in* C, *3207*
27:13 and sailed along the shore of C. *3207*
27:21 not to sail from C; *3207*
Tit 1: 5 The reason I left you in C was *3207*

CRETES, CRETIANS (KJV) See CRETANS

CREVICE (1) [CREVICES]
Jer 13: 4 now to Perath and hide it there in a c in 5932

CREVICES (2) [CREVICE]
Isa 7:19 the steep ravines and in the c in the rocks, 5932
Jer 16:16 on every mountain and hill and from the c 5932

CRIB (KJV) See MANGER

CRICKET (1)
Lev 11:22 katydid, c or grasshopper. 3005

CRIED (94) [CRY]
Ge 41:55 the people c to Pharaoh for food. 7590
45: 1 and he c out, "Have everyone leave 7924
Ex 2:23 in their slavery and c out, 2410
8:12 Moses c out to the LORD about 7590
14:10 They were terrified and c out to 7590
15:25 Then Moses c out to the LORD, 7590
17: 4 Then Moses c out to the LORD, 7590
Nu 11: 2 When the people c out to Moses, 7590
12:13 So Moses c out to the LORD, "O God, 7590
16:22 Moses and Aaron fell facedown and c out, 606
20:16 but when we c out to the LORD, 7590
Dt 26: 7 Then we c out to the LORD, 7590
Jos 24: 7 c to the LORD for help, 7590
Jdg 3: 9 But when they c out to the LORD, 2410
3:15 Again the Israelites c out to the LORD, 2410
4: 3 c to the LORD for help. 7590
5:28 behind the lattice she c out, 3291
6: 6 c out to the LORD for help. 2410
6: 7 the Israelites c to the LORD because 2410
10:10 Then the Israelites c out to the LORD, 2410
10:12 c to me for help, 7590
11:35 When he saw her, he tore his clothes and c, 606
14:17 She c the whole seven days of the feast. 1134
15:18 he was very thirsty, he c out to the LORD, 7924
21: 3 "O LORD, the God of Israel," they c, 606
1Sa 5:10 the people of Ekron c out, 2410
7: 9 He c out to the LORD on Israel's behalf, 2410
12: 8 c to the LORD for help, 2410
12:10 They c out to the LORD and said, 2410
15:11 and he c out to the LORD all that night. 2410
28:12 she c out at the top of her voice and said 2410
2Sa 19: 4 The king covered his face and c aloud, 2410
22:42 They c for help, but there was no one 8775
1Ki 13: 2 He c out against the altar by the word of 7924
13: 4 of God c out against the altar at Bethel, 7924
13:21 He c out to the man of God who had come 7924
17:20 Then he c out to the LORD, 7924
17:21 on the boy three times and c to the LORD, 7924
18:39 they fell prostrate and c, "The LORD— 606
22:32 but when Jehoshaphat c out, 2410
2Ki 2:12 Elisha saw this and c out, "My father! 7590
4: 1 from the company of the prophets c out 7590
4:40 but as they began to eat it, they c out, 7590
6: 5 "Oh, my lord," he c out, 7590
6:26 a woman c to him, "Help me, 7590
13:14 "My father! My father!" he c. 606
1Ch 4:10 Jabez c out to the God of Israel, "Oh, 7924
5:20 they c out to him during the battle. 2410
2Ch 13:14 Then they c out to the LORD. 7590
18:31 but Jehoshaphat c out, 2410
32:20 and the prophet Isaiah son of Amoz c out 2410
Ne 9:27 they were oppressed they c out to you. 7590
9:28 And when they c out to you again, 2410
Job 29:12 because I rescued the poor who c for help, 8775
Ps 18: 6 c to my God for help. 8775
18:41 They c for help, but there was no one 8775
22: 5 They c to you and were saved; 2410
30: 8 to the Lord I c for mercy: 2858
31:17 O LORD, for I have c out to you; 7924
66:17 I c out to him with my mouth; 7924
77: 1 c out to God for help; 7590+7754
77: 1 I c out to God to hear me. 7754
107: 6 they c out to the LORD in their trouble, 7590
107:13 Then they c to the LORD in their trouble, 2410
107:19 Then they c to the LORD in their trouble, 2410
107:28 they c out to the LORD in their trouble, 7590
118: 5 In my anguish I c to the LORD, 7924
137: 7 "Tear it down," they c, 606
Isa 6: 5 "Woe to me!" I c. 606
38:14 I c like a swift or thrush, 7627
Eze 11:13 I fell facedown and c out in a loud voice, 2410
Am 7: 2 I c out, "Sovereign LORD, forgive! 606
7: 5 Then I c out, "Sovereign LORD, 606
Jnh 1: 5 All the sailors were afraid and each c out 2410
1:14 Then they c to the LORD, "O LORD, 7924
Mt 14:26 "It's a ghost," they said, and c out in fear. 3189
14:30 to sink, c out, "Lord, save me!" 3189+3306
27:46 the ninth hour Jesus c out in a loud voice, 331
27:50 when Jesus had c out again in a loud voice, 3189
Mk 1:23 by an evil spirit c out, 371
3:11 they fell down before him and c out, 3189
6:49 they thought he was a ghost. They c out, 371
15:34 the ninth hour Jesus c out in a loud voice, 1066
Lk 4:33 He c out at the top of his voice, 371
8:28 he c out and fell at his feet, 371
23:18 With one voice they c out, 371
Jn 7:28 still teaching in the temple courts, c out, 3189
Jn 12:44 Then Jesus c out, 3189
20:16 toward him and c out in Aramaic, 3306
Ac 7:60 Then he fell on his knees and c out, "Lord, 3189+3489+5889
Rev 7:10 And they c out in a loud voice: 3189
12: 2 She was pregnant and c out in pain 3189
19: 4 And they c: "Amen, Hallelujah!" 3306
19:17 who c in a loud voice to all the birds flying 3189

CRIES (26) [CRY]
Ge 4:10 Your brother's blood c out to me from 7590
Ex 22:27 When he c out to me, I will hear, 7590
Nu 16:34 At their c, all the Israelites 7754
Job 30:24 on a broken man when he c for help 8780
31:38 "if my land c out against me 2410
Ps 47: 1 shout to God with c of joy. 7754
Pr 1:21 at the head of the noisy streets she c out, in 7924
8: 3 at the entrances, she c aloud: 8264
Isa 5: 7 for righteousness, but heard c of distress. 7591
15: 5 My heart c out over Moab; 2410
26:17 to give birth writhes and c out in her pain, 2410
46: 7 Though one c out to it, it does not answer; 7590
56:12 "Come," each one c, "let me get wine! NIH
Jer 30: 5 " 'C of fear are heard—terror, not peace. 7754
46:12 your c will fill the earth. 7424
48: 3 Listen to the c from Horonaim, 7591
48: 3 c of great havoc and destruction. NIH
48: 5 on the road down to Horonaim anguished c 7591
Hos 8: 2 Israel c out to me, 'O our God, 2410
Am 1:14 that will consume her fortresses amid war c 9558
2: 2 in great tumult amid war c and the blast of 9558
5:16 and c of anguish in every public square. 606
Jn 1:15 He c out, saying, "This was he 3189
Ro 9:27 Isaiah c out concerning Israel: 3189
Heb 5: 7 and petitions with loud c and tears to 3199
Jas 5: 4 The c of the harvesters have reached 1068

CRIME (19) [CRIMES, CRIMINAL, CRIMINALS]
Ge 31:36 "What is my c?" 7322
Dt 19:15 to convict a man accused of any c 6411
19:16 the stand to accuse a man of a c, 6240
25: 2 with the number of lashes his c deserves, 8402
Jdg 9:24 the c against Jerub-Baal's seventy sons, 2805
20:12 about this awful c that was committed 8288
1Sa 20: 1 What is my c? 6411
Ezr 6:11 And for this c his house is to be made a pile AIT
Ps 69:27 Charge them with c upon crime; 6411
69:27 Charge them with crime upon c; 6411
Ecc 8:11 When a sentence for a c is not quickly carried out, 5126+8288
Jer 37:18 "What c have I committed against you 2627
Hab 2:12 and establishes a town by c! 6406
Mt 27:23 What c has he committed?" 2805
Mk 15:14 What c has he committed?" 2805
Lk 23:22 What c has this man committed? 2805
Ac 18:14 about some misdemeanor or serious c, 4815
24:20 these who are here should state what c they found in me 93
28:18 not guilty of any c deserving death. 162

CRIMES (7) [CRIME]
Ecc 8:12 a hundred c and still lives a long time, 8273
Jer 18:23 Do not forgive their c or blot out their sins 6411
41:11 with him heard about all the c Ishmael son 8288
Hos 6: 9 committing shameful c. 2365
7: 1 the sins of Ephraim are exposed and the c 8288
Ac 25:18 with any of the c I had expected. 4505
Rev 18: 5 and God has remembered her c. 93

CRIMINAL (4) [CRIME]
Lk 23:40 But the other c rebuked him. NIG
Jn 18:30 "If he were not a c," they replied, 2805+4472
2Ti 2: 9 even to the point of being chained like a c. 2806
1Pe 4:15 a murderer or thief or any other kind of c, 2804

CRIMINALS (4) [CRIME]
1Ki 1:21 I and my son Solomon will be treated as c." 2629
Lk 23:32 Two other men, both c, 2806
23:33 there they crucified him, along with the c— 2806
23:39 One of the c who hung there hurled insults 2806

CRIMSON (5)
2Ch 2: 7 and in purple, c and blue yarn, 4147
2:14 and with purple and blue and c yarn 4147
3:14 purple and c yarn and fine linen, 4147
Isa 1:18 they are red as c, they shall be like wool. 9355
63: 1 from Bozrah, with his garments stained c? 2808

CRINGE (4) [CRINGING]
Ps 18:44 foreigners c before me. 3950
66: 3 So great is your power that your enemies c 3950
81:15 Those who hate the LORD would c 3950
Isa 10: 4 but to c among the captives or fall among 4156

CRINGING (1) [CRINGE]
2Sa 22:45 and foreigners come c to me; 3950

CRIPPLE (1) [CRIPPLED, CRIPPLES]
Ac 4: 9 to a c and are asked how he was healed, 476+822

CRIPPLED (15) [CRIPPLE]
Lev 21:19 no man with a c foot or hand, 8691
2Sa 4: 4 he fell and became c. 7174
9: 3 he is c in both feet." 5783
9:13 and he was c in both feet. 7177
Mal 1: 8 When you sacrifice c or diseased animals, 7177
1:13 c or diseased animals and offer them 7177
Mt 15:30 the blind, the c, the mute and many others, 3245
15:31 the c made well, 3245
18: 8 or c than to have two hands or two feet and 6000
Mk 9:45 for you to enter life c than to have two feet 6000
Lk 13:11 a woman was there who had been c by 819+2400
14:13 you give a banquet, invite the poor, the c, 401
14:21 the c, the blind and the lame.' 401
Ac 3: 2 Now a man c from birth was being carried 6000
14: 8 In Lystra there sat a man c in his feet, 105

CRIPPLES (1) [CRIPPLE]
Ac 8: 7 and many paralytics and c were healed. 6000

CRISIS (1)
1Co 7:26 Because of the present c, 340

CRISPUS (2)
Ac 18: 8 C, the synagogue ruler, 3214
1Co 1:14 not baptize any of you except C and Gaius, 3214

CRITICAL (1) [CRITICISM]
1Sa 13: 6 of Israel saw that their situation was c and 7639

CRITICALLY (1) [CRITICISM]
1Sa 31: 3 they wounded him c. 4394

CRITICISM (1) [CRITICAL, CRITICALLY, CRITICIZED]
2Co 8:20 We want to avoid any c of 3699

CRITICIZED (2) [CRITICISM]
Jdg 8: 1 And they c him sharply. 8189
Ac 11: 2 the circumcised believers c him 1359

CROCUS (1)
Isa 35: 1 and blossom. Like the c, 2483

CROOKED (13)
Dt 32: 5 but a warped and c generation. 7350
2Sa 22:27 but to the c you show yourself shrewd. 6836
Ps 18:26 but to the c you show yourself shrewd. 6836
125: 5 to c ways the LORD will banish with 6824
Pr 2:15 whose paths are c and who are devious 6836
5: 6 her paths are c, but she knows it not. 5675
8: 8 none of them is c or perverse. 7349
10: 9 but he who takes c paths will be found out. 6835
Ecc 7:13 Who can straighten what he has made c? 6430
Isa 59: 8 They have turned them into c roads; 6835
La 3: 9 he has made my paths c. 6390
Lk 3: 5 The c roads shall become straight, 5021
Php 2:15 children of God without fault in a c 5021

CROP (17) [CROPS]
Ge 47:24 But when the c comes in, 9311
Lev 1:16 He is to remove the c with its contents 5263
25:22 the old c and will continue to eat from it 9311
Isa 5: 2 Then he looked for a c of good grapes, 6913
Am 7: 1 and just as the second c was coming up. 4381
Hab 3:17 olive c fails and the fields produce no food, 5126
Mt 13: 8 where it produced a c— 2843
13:23 He produces a c, yielding a hundred, 2844
21:41 who will give him his share of the c 2843
Mk 4: 8 It came up, grew and produced a c, 2843
4:20 hear the word, accept it, and produce a c— 2844
Lk 8: 8 It came up and yielded a c, 2843
8:15 retain it, and by persevering produce a c. 2844
12:16 of a certain rich man produced a good c. 2369
Jn 4:36 even now he harvests the c for eternal life, 2843
Heb 6: 7 on it and that produces a c useful to those 1083
Jas 5: 7 to yield its valuable c and how patient he is 2843

CROPS (43) [CROP]
Ge 4:12 it will no longer yield its c for you. 3946
26:12 Isaac planted c in that land and 2445
Ex 23:10 to sow your fields and harvest the c, 9311
23:16 with the firstfruits of the c you sow 5126
23:16 when you gather in your c from the field. 5126
Lev 23:39 after you have gathered the c of the land, 9311
25: 3 and gather their c. 9311
25:15 the number of years left for harvesting c. 9311
25:16 the number of c. 9311
25:20 if we do not plant or harvest our c?" 9311
26: 4 and the ground will yield its c and the trees 3292
26:20 because your soil will not yield its c, 3292
Dt 7:13 the c of your land— 7262
22: 9 not only the c you plant but also the fruit of 4852
28: 4 and the c of your land and the young 7262
28:11 the young of your livestock and the c 7262
28:18 and the c of your land, 7262
28:42 over all your trees and the c of your land. 7262
28:51 the c of your land until you are destroyed. 7262
30: 9 of your livestock and the c of your land. 7262

Jdg 6: 3 Whenever the Israelites planted *their* c, 2445
6: 4 the c all the way to Gaza and did not spare 3292
2Sa 9: 10 to farm the land for him and bring in the c, NIH
Ne 10: 35 the LORD each year the firstfruits of our c 141
10: 37 we will bring a tithe of our c to the Levites, 141
Job 31: 8 and may my c be uprooted. 7368
Ps 65: 10 you soften it with showers and bless its c. 7542
78: 46 He gave their c to the grasshopper, 3292
Pr 3: 9 with the firstfruits of all your c; 9311
10: 5 *He who* gathers c in summer is a wise son, 112
28: 3 like a driving rain that leaves no c. 4312
Jer 35: 9 to live in or had vineyards, fields or c. 2446
Eze 34: 27 and the ground will yield its c; 3292
34: 29 land renowned for its c, 4760
36: 30 the fruit of the trees and the c *of* the field, 9482
Hag 1: 10 and the earth its c. 3292
Zec 8: 12 the ground will produce its c, 3292
Mal 3: 11 I will prevent pests from devouring your c, 141+2021+7262
Lk 12: 17 I have no place to store my c.' *2843*
Ac 14: 17 by giving you rain from heaven and c *2845*
2Ti 2: 6 be the first to receive a share *of* the c. *2843*
Jas 5: 18 and the earth produced its c. *2843*
Rev 22: 2 bearing twelve c of fruit, *NIG*

CROSS (85) [ACROSS, CROSSED, CROSSES, CROSSING, CROSSINGS]

Ex 30: 14 All who c over, 6296
Nu 32: 5 *Do* not make us c the Jordan." 6296
32: 27 *will* c over to fight before the LORD, 6296
32: 29 c over the Jordan with you before 6296
32: 30 But if *they do* not c over with you armed, 6296
32: 32 We *will* c over before the LORD 6296
33: 51 'When you c the Jordan into Canaan, 6296
34: 4 c south of Scorpion Pass, 6015
35: 10 'When you c the Jordan into Canaan, 6296
Dt 2: 13 "Now get up and c the Zered Valley." 6296
2: 24 "Set out now and c the Arnon Gorge. 6296
2: 29 until *we* c the Jordan into the land 6296
3: 18 *must* c over ahead of your brother 6296
3: 27 since *you are* not *going to* c this Jordan. 6296
4: 21 and he solemnly swore that I *would* not c 6296
4: 22 I *will* not c the Jordan; 6296
4: 22 *about to* c over and take possession of 6296
9: 1 You *are* now *about to* c the Jordan to go 6296
11: 31 You *are about to* c the Jordan to enter 6296
12: 10 But *you will* c the Jordan and settle in 6296
30: 13 "Who *will* c the sea to get it 6296
31: 2 '*You shall* not c the Jordan.' 6296
31: 3 The LORD your God himself *will* c over 6296
31: 3 Joshua also *will* c over ahead of you, 6296
34: 4 but *you will* not c over into it." 6296
Jos 1: 2 *to* c the Jordan River into the land I am 6296
1: 11 from now you *will* c the Jordan here to go 6296
1: 14 *must* c over ahead of your brothers. 6296
3: 14 the people broke camp to c the Jordan, 6296
Jdg 3: 28 they allowed no one to c over. 6296
12: 5 "*Let me* c over," 6296
1Sa 14: 4 to c to reach the Philistine outpost was 6296
14: 8 we *will* c over toward the men 6296
30: 10 *to* c the ravine. 6296
2Sa 17: 16 c over without fail, 6296+6296
17: 21 "Set out and c the river at once; 6296
19: 31 down from Rogelim *to* c the Jordan with 6296
19: 33 "C over with me and stay with me 6296
19: 36 Your servant *will* c over the Jordan with 6296
19: 37 *Let him* c over with my lord the king. 6296
19: 38 "Kimham *shall* c over with me, 6296
1Ki 2: 37 The day you leave and c the Kidron Valley, 6296
Ps 104: 9 You set a boundary *they* cannot c; 6296
Isa 11: 15 into seven streams so that *men can* c over 2005
23: 6 C over to Tarshish; 6296
23: 12 "Up, c over *to* Cyprus; 6296
51: 10 the sea so that the redeemed *might* c over? 6296
Jer 2: 10 C over *to* the coasts of Kittim and look, 6296
5: 22 an everlasting barrier *it* cannot c. 6296
5: 22 they may roar, but *they* cannot c it. 6296
9: 12 like a desert that no *one can* c? 6296
41: 10 and set out to c over to the Ammonites. 6296
Eze 33: 28 so that no *one will* c them. 6296
47: 5 but now it was a river that I could not c, 6296
47: 5 a river that no *one could* c. 6296
Mt 8: 18 he gave orders *to* c to the other side of *599*
10: 38 not take his c and follow me is not worthy *5089*
16: 24 he must deny himself and take up his c *5089*
27: 32 and they forced him to carry the c. *5089*
27: 40 Come down from the c, *5089*
27: 42 Let him come down now from the c, *5089*
Mk 8: 34 he must deny himself and take up his c *5089*
15: 21 and they forced him to carry the c. *5089*
15: 30 come down from the c and save yourself!" *5089*
15: 32 come down now from the c, *5089*
Lk 9: 23 and take up his c daily and follow me. *5089*
14: 27 And anyone who does not carry his c *5089*
16: 26 nor can anyone c over from there to us.' *1385*
23: 26 and put the c on him and made him carry it *5089*
Jn 19: 17 Carrying his own c, *5089*
19: 19 a notice prepared and fastened to the c. *5089*
19: 25 Near the c of Jesus stood his mother, *5089*
Ac 2: 23 nailing him to the c. *4699*
1Co 1: 17 lest the c of Christ be emptied of its power. *5089*
1: 18 For the message *of* the c is foolishness *5089*
Gal 5: 11 the offense *of* the c has been abolished. *5089*
6: 12 to avoid being persecuted *for* the c *5089*
6: 14 May I never boast except in the c *5089*
Eph 2: 16 both of them to God through the c, *5089*
Php 2: 8 obedient to death—even death on a c! *5089*
3: 18 many live as enemies *of* the c of Christ. *5089*
Col 1: 20 peace through his blood, shed on the c. *5089*
2: 14 he took it away, nailing it *to* the c. *5089*
2: 15 triumphing over them by the c. *899S*
Heb 12: 2 for the joy set before him endured the c, *5089*

CROSS-EXAMINED (1) [EXAMINE]

Ac 12: 19 *he* c the guards and ordered that they *373*

CROSSBAR (2) [CROSSBARS]

Ex 26: 28 The center c is to extend from end to end at 1378
36: 33 They made the center c so that it extended 1378

CROSSBARS (12) [CROSSBAR]

Ex 26: 26 "Also make c *of* acacia wood: 1378
26: 29 and make gold rings to hold the c. 1378
26: 29 Also overlay the c with gold. 1378
35: 11 clasps, frames, c, posts and bases; 1378
36: 31 They also made c *of* acacia wood: 1378
36: 34 and made gold rings to hold the c. 1378
36: 34 They also overlaid the c with gold. 1378
39: 33 its clasps, frames, c, posts and bases; 1378
40: 18 inserted the c and set up the posts. 1378
Nu 3: 36 its c, posts, bases, all its equipment, 1378
4: 31 to carry the frames of the tabernacle, its c, 1378
Jer 27: 2 "Make a yoke out of straps and c and put it 4574

CROSSED (58) [CROSS]

Ge 32: 10 I had only my staff *when I* c this Jordan, 6296
32: 22 and his eleven sons and c the ford of 6296
Ex 38: 26 from everyone who *had* c over 6296
Dt 2: 13 So *we* c the valley. 6296
2: 14 the time we left Kadesh Barnea until *we* c 6296
27: 2 When *you have* c the Jordan into the land 6296
27: 3 the words of this law when you *have* c over 6296
27: 4 And when you *have* c the Jordan, 6296
27: 12 When you *have* c the Jordan, 6296
Jos 3: 16 So the people c over opposite Jericho. 6296
4: 7 When it c the Jordan, 6296
4: 11 and as soon as all of them *had* c, 6296
4: 12 Gad and the half-tribe of Manasseh c over, 6296
4: 13 for battle c over before the LORD to 6296
4: 22 'Israel c the Jordan on dry ground.' 6296
4: 23 the Jordan before you until you *had* c over. 6296
4: 23 up before us until we *had* c over. 6296
5: 1 before the Israelites until we *had* c over, 6296
15: 3 c south of Scorpion Pass, 3655
15: 10 down to Beth Shemesh and c *to* Timnah. 6296
16: 2 c over to the territory of the Arkites 6296
18: 13 From there it c to the south slope of Luz 6296
24: 11 *you* c the Jordan and came to Jericho. 6296
Jdg 6: 33 and c over the Jordan and camped in 6296
8: 4 came to the Jordan and c it. 6296
10: 9 The Ammonites also c the Jordan to fight 6296
11: 29 *He* c Gilead and Manasseh, 6296
12: 1 c over to Zaphon and said to Jephthah, 6296
12: 3 I took my life in my hands and c over 6296
1Sa 13: 7 even c the Jordan *to* the land of Gad 6296
26: 13 Then David c over *to* the other side 6296
2Sa 2: 29 *They* c the Jordan, 6296
10: 17 c the Jordan and went to Helam. 6296
15: 23 The king also c the Kidron Valley, 6296
17: 20 "*They* c over the brook." 6296
17: 22 and all the people with him set out and c 6296
17: 22 no one was left who *had* not c the Jordan. 6296
17: 24 and Absalom c the Jordan with all the men 6296
19: 18 *They* c *at* the ford to take 6296
19: 18 When Shimei son of Gera c the Jordan, 6296
19: 39 So all the people c the Jordan, 6296
19: 39 and then the king c over. 6296
19: 40 When the king c over to Gilgal, 6296
19: 40 Kimham c with him. 6296
2Ki 2: 8 and the two of them c over on dry ground. 6296
2: 9 When they *had* c, Elijah said to Elisha, 6296
2: 14 and he c over. 6296
1Ch 12: 15 It was they who c the Jordan in 6296
19: 17 he gathered all Israel and c the Jordan; 6296
Mt 9: 1 c over and came to his own town. *1385*
14: 34 *When they had* c over, *1385*
Mk 5: 21 *When* Jesus *had* again c over by boat to *1385*
6: 53 *When they had* c over, *1385*
8: 13 into the boat and c to the other side. *599*
Jn 5: 24 *he has* c over from death to life. *3553*
6: 1 Jesus c to the far shore of the Sea *599*
18: 1 with his disciples and c the Kidron Valley. *4305*
Ac 20: 15 The day after that *we* c over to Samos, *4125*

CROSSES (2) [CROSS]

Ex 30: 13 Each *one* who c over 6296
Jn 19: 31 the bodies left on the c during the Sabbath, *5089*

CROSSING (16) [CROSS]

Ge 31: 21 So he fled with all he had, and c the River, 6296
48: 14 though he was the younger, and c his arms, 8506
Dt 4: 14 that you *are* c the Jordan to possess. 6296
4: 26 from the land that you *are* c the Jordan 6296
6: 1 that you *are* c the Jordan to possess, 6296
11: 8 in and take over the land that you *are* c 6296
11: 11 But the land you *are* c the Jordan 6296
30: 18 You will not live long in the land you *are* c 6296
31: 13 as you live in the land you *are* c the Jordan 6296
32: 47 the land you *are* c the Jordan to possess." 6296
Jos 3: 1 where they camped before c over. 6296
3: 17 until the whole nation had completed the c 6296
4: 1 the whole nation had finished c the Jordan, 6296
2Sa 24: 5 After c the Jordan, 6296
Da 8: 5 c the whole earth without touching 6584+7156
Ac 21: 2 We found a ship c over to Phoenicia, *1385*

CROSSINGS (1) [CROSS]

Jer 51: 32 the river c seized, the marches set on fire, 5045

CROSSROADS (2) [ROAD]

Jer 6: 16 "Stand at the c and look; 2006
Ob 1: 14 not wait at the c to cut down their fugitives, 7294

CROUCH (3) [CROUCHES, CROUCHING]

Nu 24: 9 Like a lion *they* c and lie down, 4156
Job 38: 40 when *they* c in their dens or lie in wait in 8820
39: 3 *They* c down and bring forth their young; 4156

CROUCHES (1) [CROUCH]

Ge 49: 9 Like a lion *he* c and lies down, 4156

CROUCHING (2) [CROUCH]

Ge 4: 7 sin *is* c at your door; 8069
Ps 17: 12 like a great lion c in cover. 3782

CROW (1) [CROWED, CROWS]

Jn 18: 27 and at that moment a rooster *began to* c. *5888*

CROWD (136) [CROWDED, CROWDING, CROWDS]

Ex 23: 2 "Do not follow the c in doing wrong. 8041
23: 2 do not pervert justice by siding with the c, 8041
Jdg 6: 31 Joash replied to the hostile c around him, 889+3972+6641
2Sa 6: 19 to each person in the whole c *of* Israelites, 2162
2Ch 30: 13 A very large c of people assembled 7736
30: 17 in the c had not consecrated themselves, 7736
Ezr 10: 1 a large c of Israelites— 7736
Job 31: 34 so feared the c and so dreaded the contempt 2162
Ps 64: 2 from that noisy c *of* evildoers. 8095
Jer 9: 2 a c *of* unfaithful people. 6809
Eze 7: 11 none of that c—no wealth, nothing of value. 2162
7: 12 for wrath is upon the whole c. 2162
7: 13 the vision concerning the whole c will not 2162
7: 14 for my wrath is upon the whole c. 2162
23: 42 "The noise of a carefree c was around her; 2162
Mt 8: 18 When Jesus saw the c around him, *4063*
9: 8 When the c saw this, *4063*
9: 23 and saw the flute players and the noisy c, *4063*
9: 25 After the c had been put outside, *4063*
9: 33 The c was amazed and said, *4063*
11: 7 Jesus began to speak *to* the c about John: *4063*
12: 46 While Jesus was still talking *to* the c, *4063*
13: 34 Jesus spoke all these things *to* the c *4063*
13: 36 Then he left the c and went into the house. *4063*
14: 14 When Jesus landed and saw a large c, *4063*
14: 22 while he dismissed the c. *4063*
15: 10 Jesus called the c to him and said, *4063*
15: 33 in this remote place to feed such a c?" *4063*
15: 35 He told the c to sit down on the ground. *4063*
15: 39 After Jesus had sent the c away, *4063*
17: 14 When they came to the c, *4063*
20: 29 a large c followed him. *4063*
20: 31 The c rebuked them and told them to *4063*
21: 8 A very large c spread their cloaks on *4063*
21: 46 the c because the people held that he was *4063*
26: 47 With him was a large c armed with swords *4063*
26: 55 At that time Jesus said *to* the c, *4063*
27: 15 to release a prisoner chosen *by* the c. *4063*
27: 17 So when the c had gathered, *899S*
27: 20 and the elders persuaded the c to ask *4063*
27: 24 and washed his hands in front of the c. *4063*
Mk 2: 4 not get him to Jesus because of the c, *4063*
2: 13 A large c came to him, *4063*
3: 7 and a large c from Galilee followed. *4436*
3: 9 Because of the c he told his disciples *4063*
3: 20 and again a c gathered, *4063*
3: 32 A c was sitting around him, *4063*
4: 1 The c that gathered around him was *4063*
4: 36 Leaving the c behind, they took him along, *4063*
5: 21 a large c gathered around him while he was *4063*
5: 24 A large c followed and pressed *4063*
5: 27 behind him in the c and touched his cloak, *4063*
5: 30 He turned around in the c and asked, *4063*
6: 34 When Jesus landed and saw a large c, *4063*
6: 45 while he dismissed the c. *4063*
7: 14 Again Jesus called the c to him and said, *4063*
7: 17 After he had left the c and entered *4063*
7: 33 After he took him aside, away from the c, *4063*
8: 1 During those days another large c gathered. *4063*
8: 6 He told the c to sit down on the ground. *4063*
8: 34 the c to him along with his disciples *4063*
9: 14 a large c around them and the teachers of *4063*
9: 17 A man in the c answered, "Teacher, *4063*
9: 25 When Jesus saw that a c was running to *4063*
10: 46 together with a large c, *4063*
11: 18 the whole c was amazed at his teaching. *4063*
12: 12 But they were afraid of the c; *4063*
12: 37 The large c listened to him with delight. *4063*
12: 41 and watched the c putting their money into *4063*
14: 43 With him was a c armed with swords *4063*

Mk 15: 8 The c came up and asked Pilate to do *4063*
15:11 But the chief priests stirred up the c *4063*
15:15 Wanting to satisfy the c, *4063*
Lk 3:10 "What should we do then?" the c asked. *4063*
4:30 But he walked right through the c and went *NIG*
5:19 not find a way to do this because of the c, *4063*
5:19 through the tiles into the middle of the c, *NIG*
5:29 and a large c of tax collectors *4063*
6:17 A large c of his disciples was there and *4063*
7: 9 and turning *to* the c following him, *4063*
7:11 and his disciples and a large c went along *4063*
7:12 And a large c from the town was with her. *4063*
7:24 Jesus began to speak to the c about John: *4063*
8: 4 While a large c was gathering *4063*
8:19 not able to get near him because of the c. *4063*
8:40 when Jesus returned, a c welcomed him, *4063*
9:12 "Send the c away so they can go to *4063*
9:13 unless we go and buy food for all this c." *3295*
9:37 a large c met him. *4063*
9:38 A man in the c called out, "Teacher, *4063*
11:14 and the c was amazed. *4063*
11:27 a woman in the c called out, *4063*
12: 1 when a c of many thousands had gathered, *4063*
12:13 Someone in the c said to him, "Teacher, *4063*
12:54 He said *to* the c: *4063*
18:36 When he heard the c going by, *4063*
19: 3 because of the c. *4063*
19:37 the whole c of disciples began joyfully *4436*
19:39 of the Pharisees in the c said to Jesus, *4063*
22: 6 over to them when no c was present. *4063*
22:47 While he was still speaking a c came up, *4063*
23: 4 to the chief priests and the c, *4063*
Jn 5:13 for Jesus had slipped away into the c *4063*
6: 2 and a great **c of people** followed him *4063*
6: 5 up and saw a great c coming toward him, *4063*
6:22 the c that had stayed on the opposite shore *4063*
6:24 Once the c realized that neither Jesus *4063*
7:20 "You are demon-possessed," the c answered *4063*
7:31 Still, many in the c put their faith in him. *4063*
7:32 the c whispering such things about him. *4063*
12: 9 Meanwhile a large c of Jews found out *4063*
12:12 The next day the great c that had come for *4063*
12:17 Now the c that was with him *4063*
12:29 The c that was there and heard it *4063*
12:34 The c spoke up, "We have heard *4063*
Ac 2: 6 a c came together in bewilderment, *4436*
2:14 raised his voice and addressed **the c:** *899S*
14:11 When the c saw what Paul had done, *4063*
14:13 the city gates because he and the c wanted *4063*
14:14 and rushed out into the c, shouting: *4063*
14:18 they had difficulty keeping the c *4063*
14:19 and Iconium and won the c over. *4063*
16:22 The c joined in the attack against Paul *4063*
17: 5 in order to bring them out to the c. *1322*
17: 8 the c and the city officials were thrown *4063*
19:30 Paul wanted to appear before the c, *1322*
19:33 some of the c shouted instructions to him. *4063*
19:35 The city clerk quieted the c and said: *4063*
21:27 They stirred up the whole c and seized him, *4063*
21:32 and soldiers and ran down to **the c.** *899S*
21:34 the c shouted one thing and some another, *4063*
21:36 c that followed kept shouting, *3295+3836+4436*
21:40 on the steps and motioned *to* the c. *3295*
22:22 The c listened to Paul until he said this. *NIG*
24:12 up a c in the synagogues or anywhere else *4063*
24:18 There was no c with me, *4063*

CROWDED (4) [CROWD]

Jdg 16:27 the temple *was* c *with* men and women; 4848
2Ki 10:21 *They* c **into** the temple of Baal 995
Jer 26: 9 the people c around Jeremiah in the house 7735
Da 3:27 governors and royal advisers **c around** 10359

CROWDING (4) [CROWD]

Mk 3: 9 to keep the *people* from c him. *2567*
5:31 "You see the people **c against** you," *5315*
Lk 5: 1 with the people **c around** him and listening *2130*
8:45 c and pressing **against** *5309*

CROWDS (27) [CROWD]

Mt 4:25 Large c from Galilee, the Decapolis, *4063*
5: 1 Now when he saw the c, *4063*
7:28 the c were amazed at his teaching, *4063*
8: 1 large c followed him. *4063*
9:36 When he saw the c, *4063*
13: 2 Such large c gathered around him *4063*
14:13 the c followed him on foot from the towns. *4063*
14:15 Send the c away, *4063*
15:30 Great c came to him, bringing the lame, *4063*
19: 2 Large c followed him, *4063*
21: 9 The c that went ahead of him and those *4063*
21:11 The c answered, "This is Jesus, *4063*
22:33 *When* the c heard this, *4063*
23: 1 Jesus said *to* the c and to his disciples: *4063*
Mk 10: 1 Again c of people came to him, *4063*
Lk 3: 7 *to* the c coming out to be baptized by him, *4063*
5:15 so that **c of people** came to hear him and *4063*
8:42 the c almost crushed him. *4063*
9:11 but the c learned about it and followed him. *4063*
9:18 he asked them, "Who do the c say I am?" *4063*
11:29 As the c increased, Jesus said, *4063*
14:25 Large c were traveling with Jesus, *4063*
Jn 7:12 the c there was widespread whispering *4063*
Ac 5:16 C gathered also from the towns *4436*
8: 6 When the c heard Philip and saw *4063*

Ac 13:45 When the Jews saw the c, *4063*
17:13 agitating the c and stirring them up. *4063*

CROWED (3) [CROW]

Mt 26:74 Immediately a rooster c. *5888*
Mk 14:72 Immediately the rooster c the second time. *5888*
Lk 22:60 Just as he was speaking, the rooster c. *5888*

CROWN (53) [CROWNED, CROWNS]

Jdg 9: 6 the pillar in Shechem *to* c Abimelech king. 4887
2Sa 1:10 And I took the c that was on his head and 5694
12:30 He took the c from the head of their king— 6498
2Ki 11:12 the king's son and put the c on him; 5694
1Ch 20: 2 the c from the head of their king— 6498
2Ch 23:11 the king's son and put the c on him; 5694
Est 1:11 wearing her royal c, 4195
2:17 So he set a royal c on her head 4195
8:15 a large c *of* gold and a purple robe 6498
Job 19: 9 and removed the c *from* my head. 6498
31:36 I would put it on like a c. 6498
Ps 21: 3 and placed a c *of* pure gold on his head. 6498
65:11 *You* c the year with your bounty, 6497
89:39 with your servant and have defiled his c in 5694
132:18 but the c on his head will be resplendent." 5694
Pr 4: 9 and present you with a c *of* splendor." 6498
10: 6 Blessings c the head of the righteous, 4200
12: 4 wife of noble character is her husband's c, 6498
14:24 The wealth of the wise is their c, 6498
16:31 Gray hair is a c *of* splendor; 6498
17: 6 Children's children are a c *to* the aged, 6498
27:24 and a c is not secure for all generations. 5694
SS 3:11 and look at King Solomon wearing the c, 6498
3:11 the c with which his mother crowned him NIH
Isa 28: 5 the LORD Almighty will be a glorious c, 7619
35:10 everlasting joy will c their heads. 6584
51:11 everlasting joy will c their heads. 6584
61: 3 to bestow on them a **c of beauty** instead 6996
62: 3 be a c *of* splendor in the LORD's hand, 6498
Jer 2:16 the **c of** your **head.** 7721
La 5:16 The c has fallen *from* our head. 6498
Eze 16:12 earrings on your ears and a beautiful c 6498
21:26 Take off the turban, remove the c. 6498
Zec 6:11 Take the silver and gold and make a c, 6498
6:14 The c will be given to Heldai, Tobijah, 6498
9:16 in his land like jewels in a c. 5694
Mt 27:29 then twisted together a c of thorns and set it *5109*
Mk 15:17 then twisted together a c of thorns and set it *5109*
Jn 19: 2 The soldiers twisted together a c of thorns *5109*
19: 5 When Jesus came out wearing the c *5109*
1Co 9:25 They do it to get a c that will not last; *5109*
9:25 but we do it to get a c that will last forever. *NIG*
Php 4: 1 my joy and c, *5109*
1Th 2:19 the c in which we will glory in the presence *5109*
2Ti 2: 5 *he does not* **receive the victor's c** *5110*
4: 8 the c of righteousness, which the Lord, *5109*
Jas 1:12 the c of life that God has promised *5109*
1Pe 5: 4 the c of glory that will never fade away. *5109*
Rev 2:10 and I will give you the c of life. *5109*
3:11 so that no one will take your c. *5109*
6: 2 Its rider held a bow, and he was given a c, *5109*
12: 1 under her feet and a c of twelve stars *5109*
14:14 a son of man" with a c of gold on his head *5109*

CROWNED (5) [CROWN]

Ps 8: 5 the heavenly beings and c him *with* glory 6497
Pr 14:18 but the prudent *are* c *with* knowledge. 4194
SS 3:11 the crown with which his mother c him on 6497
Heb 2: 7 *you* c him with glory and honor *5110*
2: 9 now c with glory and honor *5110*

CROWNS (14) [CROWN]

Ps 68:21 the hairy c *of* those who go on in their sins. 7721
103: 4 and c you *with* love and compassion, 6497
149: 4 *he* c the humble with salvation. 6995
Pr 11:26 blessing c him who is willing to sell. 4200+8031
SS 7: 5 Your head c you like Mount Carmel. 6584
Isa 23: 8 the **bestower of c,** 6497
Jer 13:18 your glorious c will fall from your heads." 6498
Eze 23:42 of the woman and her sister and beautiful c 6498
Rev 4: 4 in white and had c of gold on their heads. *5109*
4:10 They lay their c before the throne and say: *5109*
9: 7 On their heads they wore something like c *5109*
12: 3 with seven heads and ten horns and seven c *1343*
13: 1 with ten c on his horns, *1343*
19:12 and on his head are many c. *1343*

CROWS (8) [CROW]

Mt 26:34 "this very night, before the rooster c, you will disown me three times." *5888*
26:75 "Before the rooster c, you will disown me three times." *5888*
Mk 13:35 or at midnight, or **when the rooster c,** *231*
14:30 before the rooster c twice you yourself will disown me three times." *5888*
14:72 "Before the rooster c twice you will disown me three times." *5888*
Lk 22:34 Peter, before the rooster c today, *5888*
22:61 "Before the rooster c today, *5888*
Jn 13:38 I tell you the truth, before the rooster c, *5888*

CRUCIBLE (2)

Pr 17: 3 The c for silver and the furnace for gold, 5214
27:21 The c for silver and the furnace for gold, 5214

CRUCIFIED (36) [CRUCIFY]

Mt 20:19 to *be* mocked and flogged and c. *5090*
26: 2 Son of Man will be handed over to *be* c." *5090*
27:26 and handed him over to *be* c. *5090*
27:35 *When they had* c him, *5090*
27:38 Two robbers *were* c with him, *5090*
27:44 the same way the robbers who *were* **c with** *5365*
28: 5 that you are looking for Jesus, who *was* c. *5090*
Mk 15:15 and handed him over to *be* c. *5090*
15:24 And *they* c him. *5090*
15:25 It was the third hour when *they* c him. *5090*
15:27 *They* c two robbers with him, *5090*
15:32 Those **c with** him also heaped insults *5365*
16: 6 for Jesus the Nazarene, who *was* c. *5090*
Lk 23:23 they insistently demanded that he *be* c, *5090*
23:33 there *they* c him, along with *5090*
24: 7 *be* c and on the third day be raised again.' " *5090*
24:20 sentenced to death, and *they* c him; *5090*
Jn 19:16 over to them to *be* c. *5090*
19:18 Here *they* c him, and *5090*
19:20 place where Jesus *was* c was near the city, *5090*
19:23 When the soldiers c Jesus, *5090*
19:32 of the first man who *had been* **c with** Jesus, *5365*
19:41 At the place where Jesus *was* c, *5090*
Ac 2:36 God has made this Jesus, whom you c, *5090*
4:10 of Jesus Christ of Nazareth, whom you c *5090*
Ro 6: 6 For we know that our old self *was* **c with** *5365*
1Co 1:13 *Was* Paul c for you? *5090*
1:23 but we preach Christ c: *5090*
2: 2 with you except Jesus Christ and him c. *5090*
2: 8 *they* would not *have* c the Lord of glory. *5090*
2Co 13: 4 For to be sure, *he was* c in weakness, *5090*
Gal 2:20 *I have been* **c with** Christ *5365*
3: 1 Before your very eyes Jesus Christ was clearly portrayed as c. *5090*
5:24 Those who belong to Christ Jesus *have* c *5090*
6:14 through which the world *has been* c to me, *5090*
Rev 11: 8 where also their Lord *was* c. *5090*

CRUCIFY (15) [CRUCIFIED, CRUCIFYING]

Mt 23:34 Some of them *you will* kill and c; *5090*
27:22 They all answered, "C *him!*" *5090*
27:23 But they shouted all the louder, "C *him!*" *5090*
27:31 Then they led him away to c him. *5090*
Mk 15:13 "C him!" they shouted. *5090*
15:14 But they shouted all the louder, "C him!" *5090*
15:20 Then they led him out to c him. *5090*
Lk 23:21 But they kept shouting, "C him! *5090*
23:21 "Crucify him! C him!" *5090*
Jn 19: 6 their officials saw him, they shouted, "C! *5090*
19: 6 they shouted, "Crucify! C!" *5090*
19: 6 "You take him and c him. *5090*
19:10 either to free you or *to* c you?" *5090*
19:15 Take him away! C him!" *5090*
19:15 "*Shall I* c your king?" *5090*

CRUCIFYING (1) [CRUCIFY]

Heb 6: 6 c the Son of God **all over again** *416*

CRUEL (16) [CRUELLY, CRUELTY]

Ge 49: 7 so fierce, and their fury, so c! 7996
Ex 6: 9 of their discouragement and c bondage. 7997
Dt 28:33 but c oppression all your days. 8368
Ps 71: 4 from the grasp of evil and c *men.* 2807
Pr 5: 9 to others and your years to *one who* is c, 426
11:17 but a c *man* brings trouble on himself. 426
12:10 but the kindest acts of the wicked are c. 426
27: 4 Anger is c and fury overwhelming, 427
Ecc 9:12 As fish are caught in a c net, 8273
Isa 13: 9 a c day, with wrath and fierce anger— 426
14: 3 from suffering and turmoil and c bondage, 7997
19: 4 over to the power of a c master, 7997
Jer 6:23 they are c and show no mercy. 426
15:21 and redeem you from the grasp of the c." 6883
30:14 and punished you as would the c, 426
50:42 they are c and without mercy. 426

CRUELLY (1) [CRUEL]

Jdg 4: 3 and had c oppressed the Israelites 928+2622

CRUELTY (1) [CRUEL]

Na 3:19 for who has not felt your endless c? 8288

CRUMBLE (2) [CRUMBLED, CRUMBLES, CRUMBLING]

Lev 2: 6 C it and pour oil on it; it is a grain offering. 7326+7359
Eze 38:20 the cliffs *will* c and every wall will fall to 5877

CRUMBLED (1) [CRUMBLE]

Hab 3: 6 The ancient mountains c and 7207

CRUMBLES (1) [CRUMBLE]

Job 14:18 "But as a mountain erodes and c and as 5570

CRUMBLING (1) [CRUMBLE]

Job 15:28 houses c to rubble. 6963

CRUMBS (2)

Mt 15:27 the c that fall from their masters' table." *6033*

Mk 7:28 under the table eat the children's c." *6033*

CRUSE (KJV) See JUG, JAR

CRUSH (27) [CRUSHED, CRUSHES, CRUSHING]

Ge 3:15 he *will* c your head, and you will strike 8789
Nu 24:17 *He will* c the foreheads of Moab, 4730
Job 6:9 that God would be willing *to* c me, 1917
9:17 He *would* c me with a storm 8789
19:2 "How long will you torment me and c me 1917
24:11 *They* c **olives** among the terraces; 7414
39:15 unmindful that a foot *may* c them, 2318
40:12 c the wicked where they stand. 2070
Ps 68:21 God *will* c the heads of his enemies, 4730
72:4 *he will* c the oppressor. 1917
74:8 *"We will* c them completely!" 3561
89:23 *I will* c his foes before him and strike 4198
94:5 *They* c your people, O LORD; 1917
110:5 *he will* c kings on the day of his wrath. 4730
Pr 22:22 and *do* not c the needy in court, 1917
Isa 14:25 I *will* c the Assyrian in my land; 8689
41:15 You will thresh the mountains and c them, 1990
53:10 the LORD's will *to* c him and cause him 1917
Jer 50:17 *to* c his **bones** was Nebuchadnezzar king 6793
La 1:15 an army against me to c my young men. 8689
3:34 To c underfoot all prisoners in the land, 1917
Da 2:40 so *it will* c and break all the others. 10182
2:44 *It will* c all those kingdoms 10182
Am 2:13 I *will* c you as a cart crushes when loaded 6421
4:1 and c the needy and say to your husbands, 8368
Mic 6:15 you will c grapes but not drink the wine. NIH
Ro 16:20 The God of peace *will* soon c Satan *5341*

CRUSHED (45) [CRUSH]

Lev 2:14 offer c heads of new grain roasted in 1762
2:16 the memorial portion of the c **grain** and 1762
22:24 an animal whose testicles are bruised, c, 4198
Nu 11:8 ground it in a handmill or c it in a mortar. 1870
Dt 9:21 Then *I* c it and ground it to powder as fine 4198
Jdg 5:26 She struck Sisera, *she* c his head, 4735
10:8 who that year shattered and c them. 8368
2Sa 22:38 "I pursued my enemies and c them; 9012
22:39 *I* c them **completely**, 430+2256+4730
2Ch 14:13 *they* **were** c before the LORD 8689
15:6 One nation **was** *being* c by another 4198
34:7 the altars and the Asherah poles and c 4198
Job 4:19 who *are* c more readily than a moth! 1917
5:4 c in court without a defender. 1917
16:12 he seized me by the neck and c me. 7207
34:25 in the night and *they are* c. 1917
Ps 10:10 His victims *are* c, they collapse; 1920
18:38 *I* c them so that they could not rise; 4730
34:18 and saves *those who* are c *in* spirit. 1918
38:8 I am feeble and utterly c; 1920
44:2 *you* c the peoples 8317
44:19 But *you* c us and made us a haunt 1920
51:8 let the bones *you have* c rejoice. 1920
74:14 It was you *who* c the heads of Leviathan 8368
89:10 You c Rahab like one of the slain; 1917
Pr 17:22 but a c spirit dries up the bones. 5779
18:14 but a c spirit who can bear? 5779
Isa 21:10 O my people, c *on* the threshing floor, 4536
23:12 O Virgin Daughter of Sidon, *now* c! 6943
27:9 to be like chalk stones c **to pieces**, 5879
53:5 *he* **was** c for our iniquities; 1917
Jer 5:3 *you* c them, but they refused correction. 3983
8:21 Since my people are c, I am crushed; 8691
8:21 Since my people are crushed, *I am* c; 8689
22:20 for all your allies **are** c. 8689
Eze 30:8 I set fire to Egypt and all her helpers **are** c. 8689
Da 6:24 and c all their bones. 10182
7:7 *it* c and devoured its victims 10182
7:19 the beast *that* c and devoured its victims 10182
Hab 3:13 *You* c the leader of the land of wickedness, 4730
Mal 1:4 Edom may say, *"Though we have* **been** c, 8406
Mt 21:44 but *he* on whom it falls *will be* c." *3347*
Lk 8:42 the crowds *almost* c him. *5231*
20:18 but he on whom it falls *will be* c." *3347*
2Co 4:8 on every side, but not c; *5102*

CRUSHES (4) [CRUSH]

Ps 143:3 *he* c me to the ground; 1917
Pr 15:4 but a deceitful tongue c the spirit. 8691
15:13 but heartache c the spirit. 5779
Am 2:13 I will crush you as a cart c when loaded 6421

CRUSHING (6) [CRUSH]

Nu 22:25 close to the wall, c Balaam's foot against it. 4315
Dt 23:1 by c or cutting may enter the assembly of 1918
Ps 110:6 the dead and c the rulers of the whole earth. 4730
Isa 3:15 by c my people and grinding the faces of 1917
Jer 14:17 suffered a grievous wound, a c blow. 2703+4394
Da 7:23 trampling it down and c it. 10182

CRUST (2) [ENCRUSTED]

1Sa 2:36 before him for a piece of silver and a c 3971
Pr 17:1 Better a dry c with peace and quiet than 7326

CRUTCH (1)

2Sa 3:29 or leprosy or who leans on a c or who falls 7134

CRY (168) [CRIED, CRIES, CRYING]

Ge 27:34 a loud and bitter c and said to his father, 7591
Ex 2:23 and their c **for help** because 8784
3:9 now the c *of* the Israelites has reached me, 7591
22:23 If you do and *they* c **out** to me, 7590+7590
22:23 I will certainly hear their c. 7591
Lev 13:45 cover the lower part of his face and c **out,** 7924
Nu 20:16 he heard our c and sent an angel 7754
Dt 24:15 Otherwise *he may* c to the LORD 7924
33:7 "Hear, O LORD, the c *of* Judah; 7754
Jos 6:10 *"Do* not **give a war** c, 8131
Jdg 10:14 Go and c **out** to the gods you have chosen. 2410
1Sa 4:13 the whole town **sent up a** c. 2410
8:18 *you will* c **out** for relief from 2410
9:16 for their c has reached me." 7591
17:20 shouting the **war** c. 4878
2Sa 22:7 my c came to his ears. 8784
1Ki 8:28 Hear the c and the prayer 8262
8:52 to them whenever they c **out** to you. 7924
17:22 The LORD heard Elijah's c, 7754
22:36 a c spread through the army: 8262
1Ch 16:35 C **out,** "Save us, O God our Savior; 606
2Ch 6:19 Hear the c and the prayer 8262
13:12 the **battle** c against you. 9558
13:15 and the men of Judah **raised the battle** c. 8131
13:15 **sound of** their **battle** c, 8131
20:9 and *will* c **out** to you in our distress, 2410
Ne 9:9 you heard their c at the Red Sea. 2411
Job 16:18 may my c never be laid to rest! 2411
19:7 "Though *I* c, 'I've been wronged!' 7590
24:12 the souls of the wounded c **out for help.** 8775
27:9 to his c when distress comes upon him? 7591
30:20 *"I* c **out** to you, O God, 8775
30:28 I stand up in the assembly and c **for help.** 8775
34:28 They caused the c *of* the poor to come 7591
34:28 so that he heard the c *of* the needy. 7591
35:9 *"Men* c **out** under a load of oppression; 2410
35:12 when *men* c **out** because of the arrogance 7590
36:13 he fetters them, *they do* not c **for help.** 8775
38:41 for the raven when its young c **out** to God 8775
39:25 shout of commanders and the **battle** c. 9558
Ps 3:4 To the LORD *I* c aloud, 7924
5:2 Listen to my c **for help,** 7754+8776
6:9 The LORD has heard my c **for mercy;** 9382
9:12 he does not ignore the c *of* the afflicted. 7591
10:17 and you listen to their c, NIH
17:1 listen to my c. 8262
18:6 my c came before him, into his ears. 8784
22:2 O my God, *I* c **out** by day, 7924
22:24 from him but has listened to his c **for help.** 8775
28:2 Hear my c **for mercy** as I call to you 7754+9384
28:6 for he has heard my c **for mercy.** 7754+9384
29:9 And in his temple all c, "Glory!" 606
31:22 Yet you heard my c **for mercy** 7754+9384
34:15 and his ears are attentive to their c; 8784
34:17 The righteous c **out,** and 7590
39:12 O LORD, listen to my c **for help;** 8784
40:1 he turned to me and heard my c. 8784
55:17 morning and noon *I* c **out** in distress, 2159
57:2 *I* c **out** to God Most High, to God, 7924
61:1 Hear my c, O God; listen to my prayer. 8262
72:12 For he will deliver the needy *who* c **out,** 8775
84:2 and my flesh c **out** for the living God. 8264
86:6 listen to my c **for mercy.** 7754+9384
88:1 day and night *I* c **out** before you. 7590
88:2 turn your ear to my c. 8262
88:13 c to you **for help,** 8775
102:1 let my c **for help** come to you. 8784
106:44 of their distress when he heard their c; 8262
116:1 he heard my c **for mercy.** 9384
119:147 I rise before dawn and c **for help;** 8775
119:169 May my c come before you, O LORD; 8262
130:1 Out of the depths *I* c *to* you, O LORD; 7924
130:2 be attentive to my c **for mercy.** 7754+9384
140:6 Hear, O LORD, my c **for mercy.** 7754+9384
142:1 *I* c aloud to the LORD; 2410
142:5 *I* c to you, O LORD; 2410
142:6 Listen to my c, for I am in desperate need; 8262
143:1 hear my prayer, listen to my c **for mercy;** 9384
144:14 no c **of distress** in our streets. 7424
145:19 he hears their c and saves them. 8784
Pr 2:3 and c **aloud** for understanding, 5989+7754
21:13 If a man shuts his ears to the c *of* the poor, 2411
21:13 he too *will* c **out** and not be answered. 7924
30:15 "The leech has two daughters. 'Give! Give!' they c. NIH
Isa 3:7 But in that day *he will* c **out,** 606+4200+5951
8:9 **Raise the war** c, *you* nations, 8131
10:30 C **out,** O Daughter of Gallim! 7412+7754
15:4 Heshbon and Elealeh c **out,** 2410
15:4 Therefore the armed men of Moab c **out,** 8131
19:20 When *they* c **out** to the LORD because 7590
24:11 In the streets they c **out** for wine; 7424
30:19 How gracious he will be when you c **for help!** 2410+7754
33:7 their brave men c **aloud** in the streets; 7590
40:6 A voice says, "C **out.**" 7924
40:6 And I said, "What *shall I* c?" 7924
42:2 He will not shout or c **out,** 9048
42:13 with a shout *he will* **raise the battle** c 7658
42:14 now, like a woman in childbirth, *I* c **out,** 7184
57:13 When you c **out for help,** 2410
58:9 *you will* c **for help,** and he will say: 8775
65:14 but you *will* c **out** from anguish of heart 7590
Jer 3:21 A c is heard on the barren heights, 7754
4:5 C aloud and say: 'Gather together! 7924
4:16 raising a **war** c against the cities of Judah. 7754
4:19 I have heard the battle c. 9558
4:31 I hear a c as of a woman in labor, 7754
4:31 the c *of* the Daughter of Zion gasping 7754
8:19 the c *of* my people from a land far away: 8784
11:11 Although *they* c **out** to me, 2410
11:12 of Jerusalem will go and c **out** to the gods 2410
12:6 they *have* **raised a** loud c against you. 7924
14:2 and a c goes up *from* Jerusalem. 7424
14:12 they fast, I will not listen to their c; 8262
18:22 Let a c be heard from their houses 2411
20:8 *I* c **out** proclaiming violence 2410
20:16 a **battle** c at noon. 9558
22:20 "Go up to Lebanon and c **out,** 7590
22:20 c **out** from Abarim, 7590
25:36 Hear the c *of* the shepherds, 7591
30:15 Why *do you* c **out** over your wound, 2410
31:6 be a day *when* watchmen c **out** on the hills 7924
47:2 The people *will* c **out;** 2410
47:6 " 'Ah, sword of the LORD,' [you c,] NIH
48:4 her little ones *will* c **out.** 2411+9048
48:20 Wail and c **out!** 2410
48:31 for all Moab *I* c **out,** 2410
48:34 "The sound of their c rises from Heshbon 2411
49:2 "when I will sound the battle c 9558
49:3 C **out,** O inhabitants of Rabbah! 7590
49:21 their c will resound to the Red Sea. 7591+7754
50:46 its c will resound among the nations. 2411
51:54 "The sound of a c comes from Babylon, 2411
La 2:18 The hearts of the people c **out** to the Lord. 7590
2:19 Arise, c **out** in the night, 8264
3:8 Even when I call out or c **for help,** 8775
3:56 "Do not close your ears to my c for relief." 8784
4:15 *men* c to them. 7924
Eze 6:11 and stamp your feet and c **out** "Alas!" 606
21:12 C **out** and wail, son of man, 2410
21:22 to sound the **battle** c, 9558
27:28 when your seamen c **out.** 2411+7754
27:30 They will raise their voice and c bitterly 2410
Hos 5:8 **Raise the battle** c in Beth Aven; 8131
7:14 not c **out** to me from their hearts but wail 2410
Joel 1:14 and c **out** to the LORD. 2410
Jnh 2:2 and you listened to my c. 7754
Mic 3:4 Then *they will* c **out** to the LORD, 2410
4:9 Why *do you* now c **aloud—** 8131+8275
Na 2:8 they c, but no one turns back. NIH
Hab 1:2 Or c **out** to you, "Violence!" 2410
2:11 The stones of the wall *will* c **out,** 2410
Zep 1:10 "a c will go up from the Fish Gate, 7591+7754
1:14 c *on* the day of the LORD will be bitter, 7754
1:16 and **battle** c against the fortified cities 9558
Mt 12:19 He will not quarrel or c **out;** *3198*
25:6 "At midnight the c rang out: *3199*
Mk 5:5 in the hills he would c **out** and cut himself *3189*
15:37 With a loud c, Jesus breathed his last. *5889*
15:39 heard his c and saw how he died, he said, *3189*
Lk 7:13 to her and he said, "Don't c." *3081*
7:32 we sang a dirge, and *you did* not c.' *3081*
18:7 who c **out** to him day and night? *1066*
19:40 "if they keep quiet, the stones *will* c **out.**" *3189*
Ro 8:15 And by him *we* c, "Abba, Father." *3189*
Gal 4:27 break forth and c **aloud,** *1066*
Rev 18:10 they will stand far off and c: " 'Woe! *3306*
18:16 and c **out:** " 'Woe! Woe, *3306*
18:19 and with weeping and mourning c **out:** *3189*

CRYING (20) [CRY]

Ge 21:17 God heard the boy c, 7754
21:17 God has heard the boy c as he lies there. 7754
Ex 2:6 He *was* c, and she felt sorry for him. 1134
3:7 I have heard them c **out** because 7591
5:8 They are lazy; that is why they *are* c **out,** 7590
14:15 "Why *are you* c **out** to me? 7590
Jdg 7:21 all the Midianites ran, c **out** as they fled. 8131
1Sa 7:8 "Do not stop c **out** to the LORD our God 2410
Isa 22:5 a day of battering down walls and of c **out** 8779
65:19 and of c will be heard in it no more. 2411
Eze 9:8 c **out,** "Ah, Sovereign LORD! 2410
Mt 15:22 c **out,** "Lord, Son of David, *3189+3306*
15:23 for *she keeps* c **out** after us." *3189*
Mk 5:38 with people c and wailing loudly. *3081*
Jn 20:11 but Mary stood outside the tomb c. *3081*
20:13 They asked her, "Woman, why *are you* c?" *3081*
20:15 "Woman," he said, "why *are you* c? *3081*
Ac 9:39 c and showing him the robes *3081*
Jas 5:4 workmen who mowed your fields *are* c **out** *3189*
Rev 21:4 be no more death or mourning or c or pain, *3199*

CRYSTAL (4)

Job 28:17 Neither gold nor c can compare with it, 2343
Rev 4:6 like a sea of glass, clear as c. *3223*
21:11 like a jasper, **clear as** c. *3222*
22:1 the river of the water of life, as clear as c, *3223*

CUB (2) [CUBS]

Ge 49:9 You are a lion's c, O Judah; 1594
Dt 33:22 About Dan he said: "Dan is a lion's c, 1594

CUBIT (37) [CUBITS]

Ex 25:10 a c and a half wide, 564
25:10 and a c and a half high. 564
25:17 a half cubits long and a c and a half wide. 564
25:23 a c wide and a cubit and a half high. 564
25:23 a cubit wide and a c and a half high. 564

Ex 26:13 The tent curtains will be a **c** longer on 564
26:16 Each frame is to be ten cubits long and a **c** 564
30: 2 It is to be square, a **c** long and a cubit wide, 564
30: 2 It is to be square, a cubit long and a **c** wide, 564
36:21 Each frame was ten cubits long and a **c** and 564
37: 1 a **c** and a half wide, 564
37: 1 and a **c** and a half high. 564
37: 6 a half cubits long and a **c** and a half wide. 564
37:10 two cubits long, a **c** wide, 564
37:10 a cubit wide, and a **c** and a half high. 564
37:25 It was square, a **c** long and a cubit wide, 564
37:25 It was square, a cubit long and a **c** wide, 564
1Ki 7:24 gourds encircled it—ten to a **c**. 564
7:31 that had a circular frame one **c** deep. 564
7:31 and with its basework it measured a **c** and 564
7:32 The diameter of each wheel was a **c** and 564
7:35 a circular band half a **c** deep. 564
2Ch 3: 3 and twenty cubits wide (using the **c** of 564
4: 3 figures of bulls encircled it—ten to a **c**. 564
Eze 40: 5 each of which was a **c** and a handbreadth. 564
40:12 of each alcove was a wall one **c** high, 564
40:42 each a **c** and a half long, 564
40:42 a **c** and a half wide and a cubit high. 564
40:42 a cubit and a half wide and a **c** high. 564
43:13 that **c** being a cubit and a handbreadth: 564
43:13 that cubit being a **c** and a handbreadth: 564
43:13 Its gutter is a **c** deep and a cubit wide, 564
43:13 Its gutter is a cubit deep and a **c** wide, 564
43:14 and a **c** wide, 564
43:14 and a **c** wide. 564
43:17 a **c** and a gutter of a cubit all around. 564
43:17 a cubit and a gutter of a **c** all around. 564

CUBITS (220) [CUBIT]

Ex 25:10 *two* and a half **c** long, 564
25:17 a half **c** long and a cubit and a half wide. 564
25:23 *two* **c** long, a cubit wide and a cubit and 564
26: 2 twenty-eight **c** long and four cubits wide. 564
26: 2 twenty-eight cubits long and four **c** wide. 564
26: 8 thirty **c** long and four cubits wide. 564
26: 8 thirty cubits long and four **c** wide. 564
26:16 to be ten **c** long and a cubit and a half wide, 564
27: 1 an altar of acacia wood, three **c** high; 564
27: 1 five **c** long and five cubits wide. 564
27: 1 five cubits long and five **c** wide. 564
27: 9 be a hundred **c** long and is to have curtains 564
27:11 be a hundred **c** long and is to have curtains, NIH
27:12 of the courtyard shall be fifty **c** wide 564
27:13 the courtyard shall also be fifty **c** wide. 564
27:14 Curtains fifteen **c** long are to be on one side 564
27:15 and curtains fifteen **c** long are to be on NIH
27:16 provide a curtain twenty **c** long, of blue, 564
27:18 be a hundred **c** long and fifty cubits wide, 564
27:18 be a hundred cubits long and fifty **c** wide, NIH
27:18 of finely twisted linen five **c** high, 564
30: 2 and *two* **c** high— 564
36: 9 twenty-eight **c** long and four cubits wide. 564
36: 9 twenty-eight cubits long and four **c** wide. 564
36:15 thirty **c** long and four cubits wide. 564
36:15 thirty cubits long and four **c** wide. 564
36:21 Each frame was ten **c** long and a cubit and 564
37: 1 *two* and a half **c** long, 564
37: 6 a half **c** long and a cubit and a half wide. 564
37:10 *two* **c** long, a cubit wide, 564
37:25 and *two* **c** high— 564
38: 1 of acacia wood, three **c** high; 564
38: 1 five **c** long and five cubits wide. 564
38: 1 five cubits long and five **c** wide. 564
38: 9 The south side was a hundred **c** long 564
38:11 also a hundred **c** long and had twenty posts 564
38:12 The west end was fifty **c** wide 564
38:13 toward the sunrise, was also fifty **c** wide. 564
38:14 Curtains fifteen **c** long were on one side of 564
38:15 and curtains fifteen **c** long were on 564
38:18 It was twenty **c** long and, 564
38:18 the curtains of the courtyard, five **c** high, 564
1Ki 6: 2 for the LORD was sixty **c** long, 564
6: 3 that is twenty **c**, 564
6: 3 and projected ten **c** from the front of 564
6: 6 The lowest floor was five **c** wide, 564
6: 6 the middle floor six **c** and 564
6:10 The height of each was five **c**, 564
6:16 He partitioned off twenty **c** at the rear of 564
6:17 in front of this room was forty **c** long. 564
6:20 The inner sanctuary was twenty **c** long, 564
6:23 each ten **c** high. 564
6:24 of the first cherub was five **c** long, and 564
6:24 and the other wing five **c**— 564
6:24 ten **c** from wing tip to wing tip. 564
6:25 The second cherub also measured ten **c**, 564
6:26 The height of each cherub was ten **c**. 564
7: 2 of the Forest of Lebanon a hundred **c** long, 564
7: 6 a colonnade fifty **c** long and thirty wide. 564
7:10 some measuring ten **c** and some eight. 564
7:15 each eighteen **c** high and twelve cubits 564
7:15 each eighteen cubits high and twelve **c** 564
7:16 each capital was five **c** high. 564
7:19 in the shape of lilies, four **c** high. 564
7:23 measuring ten **c** from rim to rim 564
7:23 from rim to rim and five **c** high. 564
7:23 a line of thirty **c** to measure around it. 564
7:27 each was four **c** long, 564
7:38 and measuring four **c** across, 564
2Ch 3: 3 the temple of God was sixty **c** long 564
3: 3 and twenty **c** wide (using the cubit of 564
3: 4 at the front of the temple was twenty **c** long 564

2Ch 3: 4 of the building and twenty **c** high. NIH
3: 8 twenty **c** long and twenty cubits wide. 564
3: 8 twenty cubits long and twenty **c** wide. 564
3:11 of the cherubim was twenty **c**. 564
3:11 of the first cherub was five **c** long 564
3:11 while its other wing, also five **c** long, 564
3:12 of the second cherub was five **c** long 564
3:12 and its other wing, also five **c** long, 564
3:13 of these cherubim extended twenty **c**. 564
3:15 which [together] were thirty-five **c** long, 564
3:15 each with a capital on top measuring five **c**. 564
4: 1 He made a bronze altar twenty **c** long, 564
4: 1 twenty **c** wide and ten cubits high. 564
4: 1 twenty cubits wide and ten **c** high. 564
4: 2 measuring ten **c** from rim to rim 564
4: 2 from rim to rim and five **c** high. 564
4: 2 a line of thirty **c** to measure around it. 564
6:13 he had made a bronze platform, five **c** long, 564
6:13 five **c** wide and three cubits high, 564
6:13 five cubits wide and three **c** high, 564
Jer 52:21 Each of the pillars was eighteen **c** high 564
52:21 and twelve **c** in circumference; 564
52:22 on top of the one pillar was five **c** high 564
Eze 40: 5 in the man's hand was six **long c**, 564
40: 7 between the alcoves were five **c** thick. 564
40: 9 it was eight **c** deep 564
40: 9 and its jambs were two **c** thick. 564
40:11 it was ten **c** and its length 564
40:11 and its length was thirteen **c**. 564
40:12 and the alcoves were six **c** square. 564
40:13 the distance was twenty-five **c** 564
40:14 of the gateway—sixty **c**. 564
40:15 to the far end of its portico was fifty **c**. 564
40:19 it was a hundred **c** on the east side as well 564
40:21 It was fifty **c** long 564
40:21 and twenty-five **c** wide. 564
40:23 it was a hundred **c**. 564
40:25 It was fifty **c** long 564
40:25 and twenty-five **c** wide. 564
40:27 it was a hundred **c**. 564
40:29 It was fifty **c** long 564
40:29 and twenty-five **c** wide. 564
40:30 the inner court were twenty-five **c** wide 564
40:30 and five **c** deep.) 564
40:33 It was fifty **c** long 564
40:33 and twenty-five **c** wide. 564
40:36 It was fifty **c** long 564
40:36 and twenty-five **c** wide. 564
40:47 hundred **c** long and a hundred cubits wide. 564
40:47 hundred cubits long and a hundred **c** wide. 564
40:48 they were five **c** wide on either side. 564
40:48 The width of the entrance was fourteen **c** 564
40:48 and its projecting walls were three **c** wide 564
40:49 The portico was twenty **c** wide, 564
40:49 and twelve **c** from front to back. 564
41: 1 width of the jambs was six **c** on each side. 564
41: 2 The entrance was ten **c** wide, 564
41: 2 on each side of it were five **c** wide. 564
41: 2 it was forty **c** long and twenty cubits wide. 564
41: 2 it was forty cubits long and twenty **c** wide. 564
41: 3 each was two **c** wide. 564
41: 3 The entrance was six **c** wide, 564
41: 3 on each side of it were seven **c** wide. 564
41: 4 it was twenty **c**, 564
41: 4 and its width was twenty **c** across the end 564
41: 5 it was six **c** thick, 564
41: 5 around the temple was four **c** wide. 564
41: 8 It was the length of the rod, six long **c**. 564
41: 9 of the side rooms was five **c** thick. 564
41:10 the [priests'] rooms was twenty **c** wide all 564
41:11 the open area was five **c** wide all around. 564
41:12 on the west side was seventy **c** wide. 564
41:12 The wall of the building was five **c** thick all 564
41:12 and its length was ninety **c**. 564
41:13 it was a hundred **c** long, 564
41:13 with its walls were also a hundred **c** long. 564
41:14 was a hundred **c**. 564
41:15 it was a hundred **c**. 564
41:22 There was a wooden altar three **c** high 564
41:22 and two **c** square; 564
42: 2 a hundred **c** long and fifty cubits wide. 564
42: 2 a hundred cubits long and fifty **c** wide. 564
42: 3 in the section twenty **c** from the inner court NIH
42: 4 an inner passageway ten **c** wide and 564
42: 4 and a hundred **c** long. 564
42: 7 it extended in front of the rooms for fifty **c**. 564
42: 8 to the outer court was fifty **c** long, 564
42: 8 the sanctuary was a hundred **c** long. 564
42:16 it was five hundred **c**. 564
42:17 it was five hundred **c** by the measuring rod. 564
42:18 it was five hundred **c** by the measuring rod. 564
42:19 it was five hundred **c** by the measuring rod. 564
42:20 five hundred **c** long NIH
42:20 and five hundred **c** wide, NIH
43:13 the altar in **long c**, that cubit being a cubit 564
43:14 up to the lower ledge it is two **c** high and 564
43:14 up to the larger ledge it is four **c** high and 564
43:15 The altar hearth is four **c** high, 564
43:16 twelve **c** long and twelve cubits wide. NIH
43:16 twelve cubits long and twelve **c** wide. NIH
43:17 fourteen **c** long and fourteen cubits wide, NIH
43:17 fourteen cubits long and fourteen **c** wide, NIH
45: 1 25,000 **c** long and 20,000 cubits wide; NIH
45: 1 25,000 cubits long and 20,000 **c** wide; NIH
45: 2 a section 500 **c** square is to be for NIH
45: 2 with 50 **c** around it for open land. 564
45: 3 **c** long and 10,000 cubits wide. NIH

Eze 45: 3 cubits long and 10,000 **c** wide. NIH
45: 5 An area 25,000 **c** long and 10,000 NIH
45: 5 **c** wide will belong to the Levites, NIH
45: 6 **c** wide and 25,000 cubits long, NIH
45: 6 **c** long, adjoining the sacred portion; NIH
46:22 forty **c** long and thirty cubits wide; NIH
46:22 forty cubits long and thirty **c** wide; NIH
47: 3 a thousand **c** and then led me through water 564
47: 4 He measured off another thousand **c** NIH
48: 8 It will be 25,000 **c** wide, NIH
48: 9 **c** long and 10,000 cubits wide. NIH
48: 9 cubits long and 10,000 **c** wide. NIH
48:10 It will be 25,000 **c** long on the north side, NIH
48:10 10,000 **c** wide on the west side, 10,000 NIH
48:10 10,000 **c** wide on the east side and 25,000 NIH
48:10 **c** long on the south side. NIH
48:13 **c** long and 10,000 cubits wide. NIH
48:13 cubits long and 10,000 **c** wide. NIH
48:13 **c** and its width 10,000 cubits. NIH
48:13 cubits and its width 10,000 **c**. NIH
48:15 5,000 **c** wide and 25,000 cubits long, NIH
48:15 5,000 cubits wide and 25,000 **c** long, NIH
48:16 the north side 4,500 **c**, the south side 4,500 NIH
48:16 the south side 4,500 **c**, the east side 4,500 NIH
48:16 **c**, and the west side 4,500 cubits. NIH
48:16 cubits, and the west side 4,500 **c**. NIH
48:17 The pastureland for the city will be 250 **c** NIH
48:17 250 **c** on the south, 250 cubits on the east, NIH
48:17 250 cubits on the south, 250 **c** on the east, NIH
48:17 and 250 **c** on the west. NIH
48:18 **c** on the east side and 10,000 NIH
48:18 **c** on the west side. NIH
48:20 25,000 **c** on each side. NIH
48:21 **c** of the sacred portion to NIH
48:21 **c** to the western border. NIH
48:30 which is 4,500 **c** long, NIH
48:32 "On the east side, which is 4,500 **c** long, NIH
48:33 which measures 4,500 **c**, NIH
48:34 "On the west side, which is 4,500 **c** long, NIH
48:35 "The distance all around will be 18,000 **c**. NIH
Rev 21:17 its wall and it was 144 **c** thick, *4388*

CUBS (11) [CUB]

2Sa 17: 8 and as fierce as a wild bear **robbed of** her **c**. 8891
Job 4:11 and the **c** *of* the lioness are scattered. 1201
38:32 or lead out the Bear with its **c**? 1201
Pr 17:12 Better to meet a bear robbed of her **c** than 408
Jer 51:38 they growl like lion **c**. 1596
Eze 19: 2 among the young lions and reared her **c**. 1594
19: 3 She brought up one of her **c**, 1594
19: 5 she took another of her **c** and made him 1594
Hos 13: 8 Like a bear **robbed of** *her* **c**, 8891
Na 2:11 the lion and lioness went, and the **c**, 793+1594
2:12 The lion killed enough for his **c** 1596

CUCKOW (KJV) See GULL

CUCUMBERS (1)

Nu 11: 5 also the **c**, melons, leeks, onions and garlic. 7991

CUD (11)

Lev 11: 3 and that chews the **c**. 1742
11: 4 " 'There are some that only chew the **c** 1742
11: 4 The camel, though it chews the **c**, 1742
11: 5 The coney, though it chews the **c**, 1742
11: 6 The rabbit, though it chews the **c**, 1742
11: 7 does not chew the **c**; it is unclean for you. 1742
11:26 that does not chew the **c** is unclean for you; 1742
Dt 14: 6 in two and that chews the **c**. 1742
14: 7 of those that chew the **c** or that have 1742
14: 7 Although they chew the **c**, 1742
14: 8 it does not chew the **c**. 1742

CULTIVATE (2) [CULTIVATED]

Dt 28:39 and **c** them but you will not drink the wine 6268
Ps 104:14 and plants for man to **c**— 6275

CULTIVATED (5) [CULTIVATE]

Isa 5: 6 neither pruned nor **c**, 6371
7:25 As for all the hills *once* **c** by the hoe, 6371
Jer 13:21 over you those you **c** as your special allies? 4340
Eze 36:34 The desolate land *will* **be c** instead 6268
Ro 11:24 to nature were grafted into a **c olive tree**, *2814*

CUMBERED (KJV) See DISTRACTED

CUMI (KJV) See KOUM

CUMMIN (4)

Isa 28:25 does he not sow caraway and scatter **c**? 4021
28:27 nor is a cartwheel rolled over **c**; 4021
28:27 and **c** with a stick. 4021
Mt 23:23 mint, dill and **c**. *3248*

CUN (1)

1Ch 18: 8 From Tebah and C, 3923

CUNNING (4)

Ps 64: 6 Surely the mind and heart of man are **c**. 6678
83: 3 *With* **c** *they* conspire against your people; 6891

2Co 11: 3 as Eve was deceived by the serpent's c, *4111*
Eph 4:14 by every wind of teaching and by the c *3235*

CUP (65) [CUPS]

Ge 40:11 Pharaoh's c was in my hand, 3926
40:11 squeezed them into Pharaoh's c and put 3926
40:11 into Pharaoh's cup and put the c 3926
40:13 and you will put Pharaoh's c in his hand, 3926
40:21 so that he once again put the c 3926
44: 2 Then put my c, the silver one, 1483
44: 5 Isn't this **the** c my master drinks from and 889S
44:12 And the c was found in Benjamin's sack. 1483
44:16 and the one who was found to have the c." 1483
44:17 to have the c will become my slave. 1483
2Sa 12: 3 drank from his c and even slept in his arms. 3926
1Ki 7:26 and its rim was like the rim of a c, 3926
2Ch 4: 5 and its rim was like the rim of a c, 3926
Ps 16: 5 you have assigned me my portion and my c; 3926
23: 5 with oil; my c overflows. 3926
75: 8 a c full of foaming wine mixed with spices; 3926
116:13 up the c *of* salvation and call on the name 3926
Pr 23:31 when it sparkles in the c, 3926
Isa 51:17 the hand of the LORD the c *of* his wrath, 3926
51:22 of your hand the c that made you stagger; 3926
51:22 from that c, the goblet of my wrath, NIH
Jer 25:15 from my hand this c *filled with* the wine 3926
25:17 the c from the LORD's hand and made all 3926
25:28 if they refuse to take the c from your hand 3926
49:12 not deserve to drink the c must drink it, 3926
51: 7 a gold c in the LORD's hand; 3926
La 4:21 But to you also the c will be passed; 3926
Eze 23:31 so I will put her c into your hand. 3926
23:32 "You will drink your sister's c, 3926
23:32 a c large and deep; NIH
23:33 the c *of* ruin and desolation, 3926
23:33 the c *of* your sister Samaria. 3926
Hab 2:16 c *from* the LORD's right hand is coming around to you, 3926
Zec 12: 2 to make Jerusalem a c *that sends* all 6195
Mt 10:42 And if anyone gives even a c of cold water *4539*
20:22 "Can you drink the c I am going to drink?" *4539*
20:23 "You will indeed drink from my c, *4539*
23:25 You clean the outside *of* the c and dish, *4539*
23:26 First clean the inside *of* the c and dish, *4539*
26:27 Then he took the c, gave thanks *4539*
26:39 may this c be taken from me. *4539*
26:42 for this c to be taken away unless I drink it, *NIG*
Mk 9:41 anyone who **gives** you a c of water *4539+4540*
10:38 "Can you drink the c I drink or be baptized *4539*
10:39 the c I drink and be baptized with *4539*
14:23 Then he took the c, gave thanks *4539*
14:36 Take this c from me. *4539*
Lk 11:39 you Pharisees clean the outside *of* the c *4539*
22:17 After taking the c, he gave thanks and said, *4539*
22:20 after the supper he took the c, saying, *4539*
22:20 "This c is the new covenant in my blood, *4539*
22:42 if you are willing, take this c from me; *4539*
Jn 18:11 not drink the c the Father has given me?" *4539*
1Co 10:16 Is not the c of thanksgiving *4539*
10:21 You cannot drink the c of the Lord and *4539*
10:21 of the Lord and the c of demons too; *4539*
11:25 In the same way, after supper he took the c, *4539*
11:25 "This c is the new covenant in my blood; *4539*
11:26 whenever you eat this bread and drink this c *4539*
11:27 whoever eats the bread or drinks the c of *4539*
11:28 of the bread and drinks of the c. *4539*
Rev 14:10 into the c of his wrath. *4539*
16:19 and gave her the c filled with the wine of *4539*
17: 4 She held a golden c in her hand, *4539*
18: 6 Mix her a double portion from her own c. *4539*

CUPBEARER (10) [CUPBEARERS]

Ge 40: 1 the c and the baker *of* the king 5482
40: 2 the chief c and the chief baker, 5482
40: 5 the c and the baker of the king of Egypt, 5482
40: 9 So the chief c told Joseph his dream. 5482
40:13 just as you used to do when you were his c. 5482
40:20 the heads of the chief c and the chief baker 5482
40:21 He restored the chief c to his position, 5482
40:23 The chief c, however, did not remember 5482
41: 9 Then the chief c said to Pharaoh, 5482
Ne 1:11 I was c to the king. 5482

CUPBEARERS (2) [CUPBEARER]

1Ki 10: 5 the attending servants in their robes, his c, 5482
2Ch 9: 4 the c in their robes and 5482

CUPS (8) [CUP]

Ex 25:31 its flowerlike c, buds and blossoms shall be 1483
25:33 Three c shaped like almond flowers 1483
25:34 the lampstand there are to be four c shaped 1483
37:17 its flowerlike c, buds and blossoms were 1483
37:19 Three c shaped like almond flowers 1483
37:20 And on the lampstand were four c shaped 1483
Jer 35: 5 Then I set bowls full of wine and *some* c 3926
Mk 7: 4 such as the washing *of* c, *4539*

CURDLE (1) [CURDS]

Job 10:10 not pour me out like milk and c me 7884

CURDLED (1) [CURDS]

Jdg 5:25 for nobles she brought him c **milk.** 2772

CURDS (7) [CURDLE, CURDLED]

Ge 18: 8 then brought *some* c and milk and the calf 2772
Dt 32:14 with c and milk from herd and flock and 2772
2Sa 17:29 and c, sheep, and cheese from cows' milk 2772
Isa 7:15 He will eat c and honey 2772
7:22 he will have c to eat. 2772
7:22 All who remain in the land will eat c 2772
Eze 34: 3 You eat the c, 2693

CURE (8) [CURED]

2Ki 5: 3 *He would* c him of his leprosy." 665
5: 6 so that *you may* c him of his leprosy." 665
5:11 over the spot and c me *of* my leprosy. 665
Jer 3:22 *I will* c you *of* backsliding." 8324
17: 9 above all things and **beyond** c. 631
30:15 your pain that has **no** c? 631
Hos 5:13 But he is not able to c you, 8324
Lk 9: 1 to drive out all demons and *to* c diseases, *2543*

CURED (14) [CURE]

Dt 28:27 from which you cannot **be** c. 8324
28:35 and legs with painful boils that cannot **be** c, 8324
2Ki 5: 7 to me to *be* c of his leprosy? 665
Mt 8: 3 Immediately *he was* c of his leprosy. *2751*
11: 5 those who have leprosy *are* c, *2751*
Mk 1:42 the leprosy left him and *he was* c. *2751*
Lk 6:18 Those troubled by evil spirits *were* c, *2543*
7:21 very time Jesus c many who had diseases, *2543*
7:22 those who have leprosy *are* c, *2751*
8: 2 also some women who *had been* c *1639+2543*
8:36 how the demon-possessed man *had been* c. *5392*
Jn 5: 9 At once the man was c; *5618*
Ac 19:12 and their illnesses *were* c and *557*
28: 9 of the sick on the island came and *were* c. *2543*

CURRENT (1) [CURRENTS]

Ge 23:16 **according to the weight** c among the merchants. 6296

CURRENTS (1) [CURRENT]

Jnh 2: 3 and the c swirled about me; 5643

CURRY (1)

Pr 19: 6 Many c **favor with** a ruler, 2704+7156

CURSE (87) [ACCURSED, CURSED, CURSES, CURSING]

Ge 4:11 Now you *are* **under a** c and driven from 826
8:21 "Never again *will I* c the ground because 7837
12: 3 and whoever curses you *I will* c; 826
27:12 down a c on myself rather than a blessing." 7839
27:13 "My son, let the c fall on me. 7839
27:29 May *those who* c you be cursed 826
Ex 22:28 "Do not blaspheme God or c the ruler 826
Lev 19:14 not c the deaf or put a stumbling block 7837
24:11 the Name with a c; 7837
Nu 5:18 the bitter water that **brings a** c. 826
5:19 may this bitter water that **brings a** c 826
5:21 to put the woman under this c of the oath— 460
5:21 "may the LORD cause your people to c 460
5:22 that **brings a** c enter your body so 826
5:24 the bitter water that **brings a** c, 826
5:27 to drink the water that **brings a** c, it will go 826
22: 6 Now come and **put a** c **on** these people, 826
22: 6 and those *you* c are cursed." 826
22:11 Now come and **put a** c **on** them for me. 7686
22:12 *You must* not **put a** c **on** those people, 826
22:17 Come and **put a** c **on** these people for me." 7686
23: 7 'Come,' he said, 'c Jacob for me; 826
23: 8 *can I* c those whom God has not cursed? 7686
23:11 I brought you to c my enemies, 7686
23:13 And from there, c them for me." 7686
23:25 "Neither c them **at all** nor bless them 7686+7686
23:27 *to let you* c them for me from there." 7686
24: 9 be blessed and *those who* c you be cursed!" 826
24:10 "I summoned you to c my enemies, 7686
Dt 11:26 before you today a blessing and a c— 7839
11:28 the c if you disobey the commands of 7839
21:23 on a tree is *under* God's c. 7839
23: 4 in Aram Naharaim to **pronounce a** c **on** 7837
23: 5 to Balaam but turned the c into a blessing 7839
Jos 9:23 You *are* now **under a** c: 826
24: 9 for Balaam son of Beor to **put a** c **on** you. 7837
Jdg 5:23 'C Meroz,' said the angel of the LORD. 826
5:23 'C its people **bitterly,** 826+826
9:57 The c *of* Jotham son of Jerub-Baal came 7839
17: 2 and about which I heard you **utter a** c— 457
2Sa 16: 9 "Why *should* this dead dog c my lord 7837
16:10 'C David,' who can ask, 7837
16:11 *let* him c, for the LORD has told him to. 7837
2Ki 2:24 and **called down a** c *on* them in the name 7837
Ne 10:29 and bind themselves with a c and an oath 460
13: 2 but had hired Balaam to **call a** c **down** 7837
13: 2 however, turned the c into a blessing.) 7839
Job 1:11 and *he will* surely c you to your face." 1385
2: 5 and *he will* surely c you to your face." 1385
2: 9 C God and die!" 1385
3: 8 May *those who* c days curse that day, 826
3: 8 *May* those who curse days c that day, 7686
31:30 to sin by invoking a c against his life— 460
Ps 62: 4 but in their hearts *they* c. 7837
102: 8 rail against me **use** my **name as a** c. 928+8678
109:17 He loved to pronounce a c— 7839
109:28 They *may* c, but you will bless; 7837
Pr 3:33 LORD's c is on the house of the wicked, 4423
11:26 People c the man who hoards grain, 7686
24:24 peoples *will* c him 7686
26: 2 an undeserved c does not come to rest. 7839
27:14 it will be taken as a c. 7839
30:10 or *he will* c you, and you will pay for it. 7837
30:11 "There are those *who* c their fathers and do 7837
Ecc 10:20 or c the rich in your bedroom, 7837
Isa 8:21 *will* c their king and their God. 7837
24: 6 Therefore a c consumes the earth; 460
65:15 to my chosen ones as a c; 8652
Jer 23:10 the c the land lies parched and the pastures 460
29:22 in Babylon will use this c: 7839
48:10 "A c *on* him who is lax in doing 826
48:10 A c *on* him who keeps his sword 826
La 3:65 and may your c be on them! 9297
Zec 5: 3 the c that is going out over the whole land; 460
Mal 2: 2 "I will send a c upon you, 4423
2: 2 and *I will* c your blessings. 826
3: 9 You *are* under a c— 826+4423
4: 6 and strike the land with a c." 3051
Lk 6:28 bless those who c you, *2933*
Jn 7:49 there is a c on them." *2063*
Ro 12:14 bless and *do* not c. *2933*
1Co 16:22 does not love the Lord—a c be on *him*. *353*
Gal 3:10 the law are under a c, for it is written: *2932*
3:13 the c of the law by becoming a curse for us, *2932*
3:13 the curse of the law by becoming a c for us, *2932*
Jas 3: 9 and with it *we* c men, *2933*
Rev 22: 3 No longer will there be any c. *2873*

CURSED (64) [CURSE]

Ge 3:14 "C *are* you above all the livestock and all 826
3:17 "C *is* the ground because of you; 826
5:29 by the ground the LORD *has* c." 826
9:25 he said, "C *be* Canaan! 826
27:29 *May* those who curse you **be** c 826
49: 7 C *be* their anger, so fierce, and their fury, 826
Lev 20: 9 *He has* c his father or his mother, 7837
Nu 22: 6 and those you curse *are* c." 826
23: 8 can I curse those whom God *has* not c? 7686
24: 9 be blessed and those who curse you **be** c!" 826
Dt 27:15 "C is the man who carves an image or casts 826
27:16 "C *is* the man who dishonors his father 826
27:17 "C *is* the man who moves his neighbor's boundary stone." 826
27:18 "C *is* the man who leads the blind astray 826
27:19 "C *is* the man who withholds justice from 826
27:20 "C *is* the man who sleeps with his father's wife, 826
27:21 "C *is* the man who has sexual relations 826
27:22 "C *is* the man who sleeps with his sister, 826
27:23 "C *is* the man who sleeps with his mother-in-law." 826
27:24 "C *is* the man who kills his neighbor 826
27:25 "C *is* the man who accepts a bribe to kill 826
27:26 "C *is* the man who does not uphold 826
28:16 You *will* **be** c in the city and cursed in 826
28:16 be cursed in the city and c in the country. 826
28:17 and your kneading trough *will* **be** c. 826
28:18 The fruit of your womb *will* **be** c, 826
28:19 You *will* **be** c when you come in 826
28:19 when you come in and c when you go out. 826
Jos 6:26 "C before the LORD is the man who 826
Jdg 9:27 and drinking, *they* c Abimelech. 7837
21:18 'C *be* anyone who gives a wife to 826
1Sa 14:24 "C *be* any man who eats food 826
14:28 'C *be* any man who eats food today!' 826
17:43 And the Philistine c David by his gods. 7837
26:19 *may* they **be** c before the LORD! 826
2Sa 16: 5 and *he* c as he came out. 7837
16: 7 As he c, Shimei said, "Get out, get out, 7837
19:21 *He* c the LORD's anointed." 7837
1Ki 21:10 that he *has* c both God and the king. 1385
21:13 "Naboth *has* c both God and the king." 1385
2Ki 9:34 "Take care of that c *woman*," he said, 826
Job 1: 5 and c God in their hearts." 1385
3: 1 Job opened his mouth and c the day 7837
5: 3 but suddenly his house *was* c. 7686
24:18 their portion of the land **is** c, 7837
Ps 119:21 *who are* c and who stray 826
Ecc 7:22 that many times *you* yourself *have* c others. 7837
Jer 11: 3 'C *is* the man who does not obey 826
17: 5 "C *is* the one who trusts in man, 826
20:14 C *be* the day I was born! 826
20:15 C *be* the man who brought my father 826
Mal 1:14 "C *is* the cheat who has 826
2: 2 Yes, *I have already* c them, 826
Mt 25:41 'Depart from me, you who *are* c, *2933*
Mk 11:21 The fig tree *you* c has withered!" *2933*
Ro 9: 3 that I myself were c and cut off from Christ *353*
1Co 4:12 *When we are* c, we bless; *3366*
12: 3 "Jesus be c," and no one can say, *353*
Gal 3:10 "C is everyone who does not continue *2129*
3:13 "C is everyone who is hung on a tree." *2129*
Heb 6: 8 and is in danger of **being** c. *2932*
Rev 16: 9 by the intense heat and *they* c the name *1059*
16:11 and c the God of heaven because *1059*
16:21 And they c God on account of the plague *1059*

CURSES (32) [CURSE]

Ge 12: 3 and *whoever* c you I will curse; 7837
Ex 21:17 "*Anyone who* c his father or mother must 7837

Lev 20: 9 “ ‘If anyone **c** his father or mother, 7837
24:15 Say to the Israelites: ‘If anyone **c** his God, 7837
Nu 5:23 “ ‘The priest is to write these **c** on a scroll 460
Dt 11:29 and on Mount Ebal the **c.** 7839
27:13 on Mount Ebal to **pronounce c:** 7839
28:15 all these **c** will come upon you 7839
28:20 The LORD will send on you **c,** 4423
28:45 All these **c** will come upon you. 7839
29:20 All the **c** written in this book will fall 460
29:21 the **c** *of* the covenant written in this Book 460
29:27 so that he brought on it all the **c** written 7839
30: 1 and **c** I have set before you come upon you 7839
30: 7 The LORD your God will put all these **c** 460
30:19 before you life and death, blessings and **c.** 7839
Jos 8:34 the blessings and the **c**— 7839
1Ki 2: 8 who **called down** bitter **c** *on* me 7837+7839
2Ch 34:24 the **c** written in the book that has been read 460
Ne 13:25 I rebuked them and **called c down** 7837
Ps 10: 7 His mouth is full of **c** and lies and threats; 460
37:22 but *those* he **c** will be cut off. 7837
59:12 For the **c** and lies they utter, 460
Pr 20:20 If a *man* **c** his father or mother, 7837
28:27 to them receives many **c.** 4423
Jer 11: 8 I brought on them all the **c** *of* the covenant 1821
15:10 yet everyone **c** me. 7837
Da 9:11 the **c** and sworn judgments written in 460
Mt 15: 4 and ‘Anyone who **c** his father or mother *2800*
26:74 Then he began *to* **call down c** on himself *2874*
Mk 7:10 ‘Anyone who **c** his father or mother must *2800*
14:71 He began *to* **call down c** on himself, *354*

CURSING (18) [CURSE]

2Sa 16:10 If *he is* **c** because the LORD said to him, 7837
16:12 with good for the **c** I am receiving today.” 7839
16:13 **c** as he went and throwing stones at him 7837
Ps 109:18 He wore **c** as his garment; 7839
Ecc 7:21 or you may hear your servant **c** you— 7837
Jer 24: 9 an object of ridicule and **c,** 7839
25:18 and an object of horror and scorn and **c,** 7839
26: 6 an **object of c** among all the nations of 7839
29:18 of the earth and an **object of c** and horror, 460
42:18 You will be an **object of c** and horror, 460
44: 8 an **object of c** and reproach among all 7839
44:12 They will become an **object of c** 460
44:22 your land became an **object of c** and 7839
49:13 of reproach and of **c;** 7839
Hos 4: 2 There is only **c,** lying and murder, 457
Zec 8:13 As you have been an **object of c** among 7839
Ro 3:14 “Their mouths are full *of* **c** and bitterness.” *725*
Jas 3:10 Out of the same mouth come praise and **c.** *2932*

CURTAIN (62) [CURTAINS]

Ex 26: 4 of blue material along the edge of the end **c** 3749
26: 4 do the same with the end **c** in the other set. 3749
26: 5 on one **c** and fifty loops on the end curtain 3749
26: 5 and fifty loops on the end **c** of the other set, 3749
26: 9 the sixth **c** double at the front of the tent. 3749
26:10 the end **c** in one set and also along the edge 3749
26:10 along the edge of the end **c** *in* the other set. 3749
26:12 the half **c** that is left over is to hang down 3749
26:31 “Make a **c** *of* blue, 7267
26:33 the **c** from the clasps and place the ark of 7267
26:33 the ark of the Testimony behind the **c.** 7267
26:33 The **c** will separate the Holy Place from 7267
26:35 the table outside the **c** on the north side of 7267
26:36 the entrance to the tent make a **c** of blue, 5009
26:37 Make gold hooks for this **c** and five posts 5009
27:16 provide a **c** twenty cubits long, of blue, 5009
27:21 the **c** that is in front of the Testimony, 7267
30: 6 Put the altar in front of the **c** that is before 7267
35:12 and the atonement cover and the **c** 7267
35:15 the **c** *for* the doorway at the entrance to 5009
35:17 and the **c** *for* the entrance to the courtyard; 5009
36:11 of blue material along the edge of the end **c** 3749
36:11 and the same was done with the end **c** in 3749
36:12 on one **c** and fifty loops on the end curtain 3749
36:12 and fifty loops on the end **c** of the other set, 3749
36:17 the end **c** in one set and also along the edge 3749
36:17 along the edge of the end **c** in the other set. 3749
36:35 They made the **c** of blue, 7267
36:37 For the entrance to the tent they made a **c** 5009
38:18 The **c** *for* the entrance to the courtyard was 5009
38:27 the bases for the sanctuary and for the **c**— 7267
39:34 of hides of sea cows and the shielding **c;** 7267
39:38 and the **c** *for* the entrance to the tent; 5009
39:40 and the **c** for the entrance to the courtyard; 5009
40: 3 in it and shield the ark with the **c.** 7267
40: 5 the Testimony and put the **c** *at* the entrance 5009
40: 8 Set up the courtyard around it and put the **c** 5009
40:21 into the tabernacle and hung the shielding **c** 7267
40:22 of the tabernacle outside the **c** 7267
40:26 in the Tent of Meeting in front of the **c** 7267
40:28 up the **c** *at* the entrance to the tabernacle. 5009
40:33 and altar and put up the **c** *at* the entrance to 5009
Lev 4: 6 in front of the **c** *of* the sanctuary. 7267
4:17 the LORD seven times in front of the **c.** 7267
16: 2 the Most Holy Place behind the **c** in front 7267
16:12 and take them behind the **c.** 7267
16:15 the people and take its blood behind the **c** 7267
21:23 not go near the **c** or approach the altar, 7267
24: 3 Outside the **c** *of* the Testimony in the Tent 7267
Nu 3:25 the **c** *at* the entrance to the Tent 5009
3:26 the **c** *at* the entrance to the courtyard 5009
3:31 the **c,** and everything related to their use. 5009
4: 5 in and take down the shielding **c** and cover 7267
4:26 the **c** *for* the entrance, 5009
18: 7 at the altar and inside the **c.** 7267
2Ch 3:14 He made the **c** *of* blue, 7267
Mt 27:51 that moment the **c** of the temple was torn *2925*
Mk 15:38 The **c** of the temple was torn in two *2925*
Lk 23:45 And the **c** of the temple was torn in two. *2925*
Heb 6:19 It enters the inner sanctuary behind the **c,** *2925*
9: 3 Behind the second **c** was a room called *2925*
10:20 living way opened for us through the **c,** *2925*

CURTAINS (36) [CURTAIN]

Ex 26: 1 with ten **c** *of* finely twisted linen and blue, 3749
26: 2 All the **c** are to be the same size— 3749
26: 3 Join five of the **c** together, 3749
26: 6 and use them to fasten the **c** together so 3749
26: 7 “Make **c** *of* goat hair for the tent over 3749
26: 8 All eleven **c** are to be the same size— 3749
26: 9 the **c** together into one set and the other six 3749
26:12 As for the additional length of the tent **c,** 3749
26:13 The tent **c** will be a cubit longer on 3749
27: 9 be a hundred cubits long and is to have **c** 7846
27:11 be a hundred cubits long and is to have **c,** 7846
27:12 be fifty cubits wide and have **c,** 7846
27:14 **C** fifteen cubits long are to be on one side 7846
27:15 and **c** fifteen cubits long are to be on 7846
27:18 and fifty cubits wide, with **c** NIH
35:17 the **c** *of* the courtyard with its posts 7846
36: 8 with ten **c** *of* finely twisted linen and blue, 3749
36: 9 All the **c** were the same size— 3749
36:10 They joined five of the **c** together and did 3749
36:13 to fasten the *two sets of* **c** together so that 3749
36:14 They made **c** *of* goat hair for the tent over 3749
36:15 All eleven **c** were the same size— 3749
36:16 They joined five of the **c** into one set and 3749
38: 9 and had **c** *of* finely twisted linen, 7846
38:12 and had **c,** with ten posts and ten bases, 7846
38:14 **C** fifteen cubits long were on one side of 7846
38:15 and **c** fifteen cubits long were on 7846
38:16 All the **c** around the courtyard were 7846
38:18 like the **c** *of* the courtyard, five cubits high, 7846
39:40 the **c** *of* the courtyard with its posts 7846
Nu 3:26 the **c** *of* the courtyard, the curtain at 7846
4:25 They are to carry the **c** *of* the tabernacle, 3749
4:25 the **c** *for* the entrance to the Tent 5009
4:26 the **c** *of* the courtyard surrounding 7846
SS 1: 5 like the **tent c** *of* Solomon. 3749
Isa 54: 2 stretch your tent **c** wide, do not hold back; 3749

CURVED (4)

Jos 15: 3 past Hezron up to Addar and **c around** 6015
15:10 it **c** westward from Baalah to Mount Seir, 6015
16: 6 the north it **c** eastward to Taanath Shiloh, 6015
18:17 *It* then **c** north, went to En Shemesh, 9305

CUSH (27) [CUSHITE, CUSHITES]

Ge 2:13 it winds through the entire land of **C.** 3932
10: 6 **C,** Mizraim, Put and Canaan. 3932
10: 7 The sons of **C:** 3932
10: 8 **C** was the father of Nimrod, 3932
1Ch 1: 8 sons of Ham: **C,** Mizraim, Put and Canaan. 3932
1: 9 The sons of **C:** 3932
1:10 **C** was the father of Nimrod, 3932
Est 1: 1 from India to **C:** 3932
8: 9 from India to **C.** 3932
Job 28:19 The topaz of **C** cannot compare with it; 3932
Ps 7: T to the LORD concerning **C,** 3933
68:31 **C** will submit herself to God. 3932
87: 4 Philistia too, and Tyre, along with **C**— 3932
Isa 11:11 from Upper Egypt, from **C,** from Elam, 3932
18: 1 of whirring wings along the rivers of **C,** 3932
20: 3 as a sign and portent against Egypt and **C,** 3932
20: 5 in **C** and boasted in Egypt will be afraid 3932
43: 3 **C** and Seba in your stead. 3932
45:14 of Egypt and the merchandise of **C,** 3932
Jer 46: 9 men of **C** and Put who carry shields, 3932
Eze 29:10 as far as the border of **C.** 3932
30: 4 and anguish will come upon **C.** 3932
30: 5 **C** and Put, Lydia and all Arabia, 3932
30: 9 to frighten **C** out of her complacency. 3932
38: 5 Persia, **C** and Put will be with them, 3932
Na 3: 9 **C** and Egypt were her boundless strength; 3932
Zep 3:10 beyond the rivers of **C** my worshipers, 3932

CUSHAN (1)

Hab 3: 7 I saw the tents of **C** in distress, 3936

CUSHAN-RISHATHAIM (2)

Jdg 3: 8 that he sold them into the hands of **C** king 3937
3:10 The LORD gave **C** king of Aram into 3937

CUSHI (2)

Jer 36:14 the son of Shelemiah, the son of **C,** 3935
Zep 1: 1 that came to Zephaniah son of **C,** the son 3935

CUSHION (1)

Mk 4:38 Jesus was in the stern, sleeping on a **c.** *4676*

CUSHITE (17) [CUSH]

Nu 12: 1 against Moses because of his **C** wife, 3934
12: 1 for he had married a **C.** 3934
2Sa 18:21 Then Joab said to a **C,** “Go, 3934
18:21 The **C** bowed down before Joab 3934
18:22 please let me run behind the **C.**” 3934
18:23 by way of the plain and outran the **C.** 3934
18:31 Then the **C** arrived and said, 3934
18:32 The king asked the **C,** 3934
18:32 The **C** replied, “May the enemies 3934
2Ki 19: 9 Tirhakah, the **C** king [of Egypt], 3932
2Ch 14: 9 Zerah the **C** marched out against them with 3934
Isa 20: 4 the Egyptian captives and **C** exiles, young 3932
37: 9 Tirhakah, the **C** king [of Egypt], 3932
Jer 38: 7 But Ebed-Melech, a **C,** 3934
38:10 the king commanded Ebed-Melech the **C,** 3934
38:12 Ebed-Melech the **C** said to Jeremiah, 3934
39:16 the **C,** ‘This is what the LORD Almighty, 3934

CUSHITES (8) [CUSH]

2Ch 12: 3 and **C** that came with him from Egypt, 3934
14:12 The LORD struck down the **C** before Asa 3934
14:12 before Asa and Judah. The **C** fled, 3934
14:13 a great number of **C** fell that they could 3934
16: 8 Were not the **C** and Libyans a mighty army 3934
21:16 and of the Arabs who lived near the **C.** 3934
Am 9: 7 the same to me as the **C?**” 1201+3934
Zep 2:12 “You too, O **C,** will be slain by my sword.” 3934

CUSTODY (7)

Ge 40: 3 in **c** *in* the house of the captain of 5464
40: 4 After they had been in **c** for some time, 5464
40: 7 in **c** with him *in* his master’s house, 5464
42:17 And he put them all in **c** for three days. 5464
Lev 24:12 in **c** until the will of the LORD should 5464
Nu 15:34 and they kept him in **c,** 5464
1Ch 29: 8 the temple of the LORD in the **c** *of* Jehiel 3338

CUSTOM (19) [ACCUSTOMED, CUSTOMARY, CUSTOMS]

Ge 19:31 as is the **c** all over the earth. 2006
29:26 not our **c** here to give the younger daughter in marriage before the older on. 4027+6913
Jdg 8:24 **(It was the c of** the Ishamaelites 3954
11:39 From this comes the Israelite **c** 2976
1Ki 18:28 as was their **c,** until their blood flowed. 5477
2Ki 11:14 standing by the pillar, as the **c** was. 5477
Est 9:27 upon themselves to **establish the c** 7756
Job 1: 5 This *was* Job’s regular **c.** 6913
Mt 27:15 Now *it was* the governor’s **c** at the Feast *1665*
Mk 10: 1 and as *was* his **c,** he taught them. *1665*
15: 6 Now it was the **c** at the Feast to release *NIG*
Lk 1: 9 according to the **c** of the priesthood, *1621*
2:27 the child Jesus to do for him what the **c** of *1616*
2:42 went up to the Feast, according to the **c.** *1621*
4:16 went into the synagogue, as was his **c.** *1665*
Jn 18:39 But it is your **c** for me to release *5311*
Ac 15: 1 *according to* the **c** taught by Moses, *1621*
17: 2 As his **c** was, Paul went into the synagogue, *1665*
25:16 not the Roman **c** to hand over any man *1621*

CUSTOMARY (6) [CUSTOM]

Jdg 14:10 as *was* **c** *for* bridegrooms. 6913
1Sa 20:25 He sat in his **c** place by the wall, 928+3869+7193+7193
Est 1:13 Since it was **c** *for* the king 1821+4027
Eze 24:17 the lower part of your face or eat the **c** food NIH
24:22 the lower part of your face or eat the **c** food NIH
Mk 14:12 it was **c** to sacrifice the Passover lamb, *NIG*

CUSTOMERS (2)

Eze 27:15 and many coastlands were your **c;** 3338+6088
27:21 all the princes of Kedar were your **c;** 3338+6086

CUSTOMS (13) [CUSTOM]

Lev 18:30 and do not follow any of the detestable **c** 2978
20:23 the **c** *of* the nations I am going to drive out 2978
2Ki 17:33 in accordance with the **c** *of* the nations 5477
Est 3: 8 of your kingdom whose **c** are different 2017
Ps 106:35 with the nations and adopted their **c.** 5126
Jer 10: 3 For the **c** *of* the peoples are worthless; 2978
Jn 19:40 in accordance with Jewish burial **c.** *1621*
Ac 6:14 and change the **c** Moses handed down *1621*
16:21 by advocating **c** unlawful for us Romans *1621*
21:21 or live *according to* our **c.** *1621*
26: 3 with all the Jewish **c** and controversies. *1621*
28:17 against our people or against the **c** *1621*
Gal 2:14 you force Gentiles *to* **follow Jewish c?** *2678*

CUT (288) [CUTS, CUTTER, CUTTING, FRESH-CUT]

Ge 9:11 Never again *will* all life **be c off** by the waters of a flood; 4162
15:10 **c** them in two and arranged 1439
15:10 the birds, however, *he did* not **c in half.** 1439
17:14 *will* **be c off** from his people; 4162
22: 3 When *he had* **c** enough wood for the burnt offering, 1324
Ex 4:25 **c off** her son’s foreskin 4162
12:15 the seventh *must* **be c off** from Israel. 4162
12:19 in it *must* **be c off** from the community 4162
29:17 **C** the ram into pieces and wash 5983
30:33 a priest *must* **be c off** from his people.’ ” 4162
30:38 like it to enjoy its fragrance *must* **be c off** 4162
31: 5 to **c** and set stones, 3098
31:14 on that day *must* **be c off** from his people. 4162
34:13 and **c down** their Asherah poles. 4162

Ex 35:33 to **c** and set stones, 3098
39: 3 and **c** strands to be worked into the blue, 7915
Lev 1: 6 He is to skin the burnt offering and **c** it 5983
1:12 *He is to* **c** it into pieces, 5983
3: 9 entire fat tail **c off** close to the backbone, 6073
7:20 that person *must* **be c off** from his people. 4162
7:21 to the LORD, that person *must* **be c off** 4162
7:25 the LORD *must* **be c off** from his people. 4162
7:27 that person *must* **be c off** 4162
8:20 *He* **c** the ram into pieces and burned 5983
17: 4 he has shed blood and *must* **be c off** 4162
17: 9 that man *must* **be c off** from his people. 4162
17:10 and *will* **c** him **off** from his people. 4162
17:14 anyone who eats it *must* **be c off."** 4162
18:29 such persons *must* **be c off** 4162
19: 8 that person *must* **be c off** from his people. 4162
19:27 *'Do* not **c** the **hair** at the sides of your head 5938
19:28 " *'Do* not **c** your bodies for the dead 5989+8582
20: 3 and *I will* **c** him **off** from his people; 4162
20: 5 and *will* **c off** from their people both him 4162
20: 6 and *I will* **c** him **off** from his people. 4162
20:17 *They must* **be c off** before the eyes 4162
20:18 of them *must* **be c off** from their people. 4162
21: 5 edges of their beards or **c** their bodies. 8581+8583
22: 3 to the LORD, that person *must* **be c off** 4162
22:24 to the LORD an animal whose testicles are
bruised, crushed, torn or **c.** 4162
23:29 not deny himself on that day *must* **be c off** 4162
26:26 When I **c off** your supply of bread, 8689
26:30 **c down** your incense altars 4162
Nu 4:18 the Kohathite tribal clans *are* not **c off** 4162
9:13 that person *must* **be c off** from his people 4162
13:23 *they* **c off** a branch bearing a single cluster 4162
13:24 of grapes the Israelites **c off** there. 4162
15:30 that person *must* **be c off** from his people. 4162
15:31 **must surely be c off;** 4162+4162
19:13 That person *must* **be c off** from Israel. 4162
19:20 he *must* **be c off** from the community, 4162
Dt 7: 5 **c down** their Asherah poles 1548
12: 3 **c down** the idols of their gods 1548
12:29 The LORD your God *will* **c off** 4162
14: 1 *Do* not **c yourselves** or shave the front 1517
19: 5 into the forest with his neighbor to **c** wood, 2634
20:19 *Do* not **c** them **down.** 4162
20:20 *you may* **c down** trees that you know are 4162
25:12 *you shall* **c off** her hand. 7915
25:18 and **c off** all who were lagging behind; 2386
Jos 3:13 its waters flowing downstream *will* **be c off** 4162
3:16 (the Salt Sea) **was** completely **c off.** 4162
4: 7 that the flow of the Jordan **was c off** before 4162
4: 7 the waters of the Jordan **were c off.** 4162
8:22 Israel **c** them **down,** 5782
10:10 to Beth Horon and **c** them **down** all the way 5782
Jdg 1: 6 and **c off** his thumbs and big toes. 7915
1: 7 and big toes **c off** have picked up scraps 7915
6:25 down your father's altar to Baal and **c down** 4162
6:26 of the Asherah pole that *you* **c down,** 4162
6:28 with the Asherah pole beside it **c down** and 4162
6:30 and **c down** the Asherah pole beside it." 4162
9:48 He took an ax and **c off** some branches, 4162
9:49 So all the men **c** branches 4162
19:29 he took a knife and **c up** his concubine, 5983
20: 6 **c** her **into pieces** and sent one piece 5983
20:21 and **c down** twenty-two thousand Israelites 8845
20:25 from Gibeah to oppose them, *they* **c down** 8845
20:42 of the towns **c** them **down** there. 8845
20:45 the Israelites **c down** five thousand men 6618
21: 6 "Today one tribe *is* **c off** from Israel," 1548
1Sa 2:31 when *I will* **c short** your strength and 1548
2:33 not **c off** from my altar will be spared only 4162
11: 7 He took a pair of oxen, **c** them **into pieces,** 5983
17:46 I'll strike you down and **c off** your head. 6073
17:51 *he* **c off** his head with the sword. 4162
20:15 and *do* not ever **c off** your kindness 4162
20:15 even when the LORD *has* **c off** every one 4162
24: 4 Then David crept up unnoticed and **c off** 4162
24: 5 for *having* **c off** a corner of his robe. 4162
24:11 I **c off** the corner of your robe but did 4162
24:21 that *you will* not **c off** my descendants 4162
28: 9 *He has* **c off** the mediums and spiritists 4162
31: 9 *They* **c off** his head 4162
2Sa 4: 7 *they* **c off** his head, 6073
4:12 *They* **c off** their hands and feet and hung 7915
7: 9 and *I have* **c off** all your enemies from 4162
10: 4 **c off** their garments in the middle at 4162
14:16 the hand of the man *who is trying to* **c off** 9012
14:26 Whenever he **c** *the* **hair** *of* his head— 1662
14:26 he used to **c** *his* **hair** from time to time 1662
16: 9 Let me go over and **c off** his head." 6073
20:22 and *they* **c off** the head of Sheba son 4162
1Ki 3:25 **"C** the living child in two and give half 1615
3:26 **C** him **in two!"** 1615
5: 6 that cedars of Lebanon *be* **c** for me. 4162
5:18 the men of Gebal **c** and prepared the timber 7180
7: 9 were made of blocks of high-grade stone **c** 1607
7:11 Above were high-grade stones, **c** to size, 1607
9: 7 then *I will* **c off** Israel from 4162
14:10 *I will* **c off** from Jeroboam every last male 4162
14:14 over Israel who *will* **c off** the family 4162
15:13 Asa **c** the pole **down** and burned it in 4162
18:23 and *let them* **c** it **into pieces** and put it on 5983
18:33 **c** the bull **into pieces** 5983
21:21 I will consume your descendants and **c off** 4162
2Ki 3:19 *You will* **c down** every good tree, 5877
3:25 They stopped up all the springs and **c down** 5877
4:39 *he* **c** them **up** into the pot of stew, 7114
6: 4 to the Jordan and *began to* **c down** trees. 1615
2Ki 6: 6 Elisha **c** a stick and threw it there, 7892
6:32 to **c off** my head? 6073
9: 8 *I will* **c off** from Ahab every last male 4162
10:25 So *they* **c** them **down** with the sword. 5782
18: 4 smashed the sacred stones and **c down** 4162
19: 7 and there *I will* **have** him **c down** with 5877
19:23 *I have* **c down** its tallest cedars, 4162
19:37 and Sharezer **c** him **down** with the sword, 5782
23:14 and **c down** the Asherah poles and covered 4162
1Ch 17: 8 and *I have* **c off** all your enemies from 4162
19: 4 **c off** their garments in the middle at 4162
2Ch 2:10 the woodsmen *who* **c** the timber, 4162
2:16 and we *will* **c** all the logs from Lebanon 4162
14: 3 smashed the sacred stones and **c down** 1548
15:16 Asa **c** the pole **down,** 4162
16:14 in the tomb that *he had* **c out** for himself in 4125
31: 1 smashed the sacred stones and **c down** 1548
32:21 of his sons **c** him **down** with the sword. 5877
34: 4 *he* **c to pieces** the incense altars that were 1548
34: 7 the idols to powder and **c to pieces** all 1548
Job 6: 9 to let loose his hand and **c** me **off!** 1298
14: 7 If *it* **is c down,** it will sprout again, 4162
17: 1 My spirit is broken, my days **are c short,** 2403
24:24 *they* **are c off** like heads of grain. 4909
26:12 by his wisdom *he* **c** Rahab **to pieces.** 4730
27: 8 the godless when *he is* **c off,** 1298
Ps 12: 3 *May* the LORD **c off** all flattering lips 4162
31:22 *"I* **am c off** from your sight!" 1746
34:16 to **c off** the memory of them from 4162
37: 9 For evil men *will* **be c off,** 4162
37:22 but those he curses *will* **be c off.** 4162
37:28 the offspring of the wicked *will* **be c off;** 4162
37:34 when the wicked **are c off,** you will see it. 4162
37:38 the future of the wicked *will* **be c off.** 4162
74: 5 They behaved like men wielding axes to **c** NIH
75:10 *I will* **c off** the horns of all the wicked, 1548
80:16 Your vine **is c down,** it is burned with fire; 4065
88: 5 who **are c off** from your care. 1615
89:45 *You have* **c short** the days of his youth; 7918
101: 8 I *will* **c off** every evildoer from the city 4162
102:23 *he* **c short** my days. 7918
109:13 May his descendants be **c off,** 4162
109:15 that *he may* **c off** the memory of them from 4162
118:10 in the name of the LORD *I* **c** them **off.** 4577
118:11 in the name of the LORD *I* **c** them **off.** 4577
118:12 in the name of the LORD *I* **c** them **off.** 4577
129: 4 *he has* **c** me **free** *from* the cords of 7915
Pr 2:22 the wicked *will* **be c off** from the land, 4162
10:27 but the years of the wicked *are* **c short.** 7918
10:31 but a perverse tongue *will* **be c out.** 4162
23:18 and your hope *will* not **be c off.** 4162
24:14 and your hope *will* not **be c off.** 4162
Isa 5: 2 a watchtower in it and **c out** a winepress 2933
6:13 when they are **c down,** 8961
9:14 So the LORD *will* **c off** from Israel 4162
10:34 *He will* **c down** the forest thickets with 5937
11:13 and Judah's enemies *will* **be c off;** 4162
14: 8 no *woodsman comes to* **c** us **down."** 4162
14:22 *"I will* **c off** from Babylon her name 4162
15: 2 and every beard **c off.** 1757
18: 5 *he will* **c off** the shoots 4162
18: 5 and **c down** and take away 9372
22:16 and who gave you permission *to* **c out** 2933
22:25 and the load hanging on it *will* **be c down."** 4162
29:20 all who have an eye for evil *will* **be c down** 4162
33:12 like **c** thornbushes they will be set ablaze." 4065
37: 7 and there *I will* **have** him **c down** with 5877
37:24 *I have* **c down** its tallest cedars, 4162
37:38 and Sharezer **c** him **down** with the sword, 5782
38:12 and he *has* **c** me **off** from the loom; 1298
44:14 He **c down** cedars, 4162
45: 2 down gates of bronze and **c through** bars 1548
48: 9 so as not *to* **c** you **off.** 4162
48:19 their name *would* never **be c off** 4162
51: 1 to the rock from which you **were c** and to 2933
51: 9 Was it not you who **c** Rahab **to pieces,** 2933
53: 8 For *he* **was c off** from the land of the living; 1615
56: 5 an everlasting name that *will* not **be c off.** 4162
Jer 6: 6 **"C down** the trees and build siege ramps 4162
7:29 **C off** your hair and throw it away; 1605
9:21 *it has* **c off** the children from the streets 4162
9:22 like **c grain** behind the reaper, 6658
10: 3 *they* **c** a tree out of the forest, 4162
11:19 *let us* **c** him **off** from the land of the living 4162
16: 6 and no *one will* **c himself** 1517
22: 7 and *they will* **c up** your fine cedar beams 4162
34:18 like the calf *they* **c** in two and then walked 4162
36:23 the king **c** them **off** with a scribe's knife 7973
36:29 and **c off** both men and animals from it?" 8697
41: 5 torn their clothes and **c themselves** came 1517
46:22 like *men who* **c down** trees. 2634
47: 4 to **c off** all survivors who could help Tyre 4162
47: 5 how long *will you* **c yourselves?** 1517
48:25 Moab's horn **is c off;** 1548
48:37 and every beard **c off;** 1757
50:16 **C off** from Babylon the sower, 4162
51:13 the time for you to be **c off.** 1299
La 2: 3 In fierce anger *he has* **c off** every horn 1548
3:54 and I thought *I was about to* **be c off.** 1615
Eze 4:16 of man, I *will* **c off** the supply of food 8689
5:16 upon you and **c off** your supply of food. 8689
14: 8 *I will* **c** him **off** from my people. 4162
14:13 *to* **c off** its food supply and send famine 8689
16: 4 the day you were born your cord *was* not **c,** 4162
21: 3 from its scabbard and **c off** from you both 4162
21: 4 Because *I am going to* **c off** the righteous 4162
23:25 *They will* **c off** your noses and your ears, 6073
Eze 23:47 The mob will stone them and **c** them **down** 1345
25: 7 *I will* **c** you **off** from the nations 4162
25:16 against the Philistines, and *I will* **c off** 4162
30:15 and **c off** the hordes of Thebes. 4162
31:12 of foreign nations **c** it **down** and left it. 4162
35: 7 and **c off** from it all who come and go. 4162
37:11 our hope is gone; we **are c off.'** 1615
39:10 to gather wood from the fields or **c** it from 2634
Da 2: 5 and interpret it, I *will have you* **c into** 10522
2:34 you were watching, a rock **was c out,** 10140
2:45 the meaning of the vision of the rock **c out** 10140
3:29 Meshach and Abednego **be c into** pieces 10522
4:14 **'C down** the tree and trim off its branches; 10134
4:23 **'C down** the tree and destroy it, 10134
9:26 the Anointed One *will* **be c off** 4162
Hos 6: 5 Therefore *I* **c** you **in pieces** 2933
Joel 1: 9 and drink offerings *are* **c off** from 4162
1:16 the food **been c off** before our very eyes— 4162
Am 3:14 the horns of the altar *will* **be c off** and fall 1548
Ob 1: 9 in Esau's mountains *will* **be c down** in 4162
1:14 at the crossroads to **c down** their fugitives, 4162
Na 1:12 *they will* **be c off** and pass away. 1605
3:15 the sword *will* **c** you **down** and, 4162
Zep 1: 3 of rubble when *I* **c off** man from the face 4162
1: 4 *I will* **c off** from this place every remnant of 4162
3: 6 *"I have* **c off** nations; 4162
3: 7 Then her dwelling *would* not **be c off,** 4162
Zec 9: 6 *I will* **c off** the pride of the Philistines. 4162
11: 2 the dense forest *has been* **c down!** 3718
Mal 2:12 *may* the LORD **c** him **off** from the tents 4162
Mt 3:10 not produce good fruit *will be* **c down** *1716*
5:30 **c** it **off** and throw it away. *1716*
7:19 not bear good fruit *is* **c down** and thrown *1716*
18: 8 **c** it **off** and throw it away. *1716*
21: 8 while others **c** branches from the trees *3164*
24:22 If those days *had* not *been* **c short,** *3143*
24:51 *He will* **c** him **to pieces** and assign him *1497*
27:60 in his own new tomb that *he had* **c out** of *3300*
Mk 5: 5 in the hills he would cry out and **c** himself *2888*
9:43 If your hand causes you to sin, **c** it **off.** *644*
9:45 And if your foot causes you to sin, **c** it **off.** *644*
11: 8 while others spread branches *they had* **c** in *3164*
13:20 If the Lord *had* not **c short** those days, *3143*
15:46 and placed it in a tomb **c** out of rock. *1639+3300*
Lk 3: 9 not produce good fruit *will be* **c down** *1716*
12:46 *He will* **c** him **to pieces** and assign him *1497*
13: 7 **C** it **down!** *1716*
13: 9 If not, then **c** it **down.'"** *1716*
23:53 and placed it in a tomb **c in the rock,** *3292*
Jn 18:26 of the man whose ear Peter *had* **c off,** *644*
Ac 2:37 *they were* **c to** the heart and said to Peter *2920*
3:23 **completely c off from** among his people.' *2017*
18:18 *he had* his hair **c off** at Cenchrea because of *3025*
27:32 So the soldiers **c** the ropes that held *644*
Ro 9: 3 that I myself were cursed and **c off from** *608*
11:22 Otherwise, you also *will be* **c off.** *1716*
11:24 if you *were* **c out** of an olive tree *1716*
1Co 11: 6 *she should have* her hair **c off;** *3025*
11: 6 a woman *to have her* **hair c** or shaved off, *3025*
2Co 11:12 **c** the ground **from under** those *1716*
Gal 5: 7 Who **c in on** you and kept you *1601*

CUTHAH (2)

2Ki 17:24 **C,** Avva, Hamath and Sepharvaim 3940
17:30 the men from **C** made Nergal, 3939

CUTS (4) [CUT]

Job 28: 4 Far from where people dwell *he* **c** a shaft, 7287
38:25 Who **c** a channel for the torrents of rain, 7103
Ps 107:16 down gates of bronze and **c through** bars 1548
Jn 15: 2 *He* **c off** every branch in me *149*

CUTTER (1) [CUT]

Ex 28:11 the two stones the way a gem **c** engraves 3093

CUTTING (11) [CUT]

Dt 23: 1 **c** may enter the assembly of the LORD. 4162+9163
2Ki 6: 5 As one of them was **c down** a tree, 5877
2Ch 2: 8 that your men are skilled in **c** timber there. 4162
Ps 78:31 **c down** the young men of Israel. 4156
Pr 26: 6 Like **c off** one's feet 7894
Jer 44: 7 on yourselves by **c off** from Judah the men 4162
Mt 26:51 servant of the high priest, **c off** his ear. *904*
Mk 14:47 servant of the high priest, **c off** his ear. *904*
Lk 22:50 servant of the high priest, **c off** his right ear. *904*
Jn 18:10 the high priest's servant, **c off** his right ear. *644*
Ac 27:40 **C loose** the anchors, *4311*

CUZA (1)

Lk 8: 3 Joanna the wife *of* **C,** the manager of
Herod's household; *5966*

CYCLE (1)

Isa 29: 1 **c** of festivals **go on.** 5938

CYMBAL (1) [CYMBALS]

1Co 13: 1 a resounding gong or a clanging **c.** *3247*

CYMBALS (16) [CYMBAL]

2Sa 6: 5 lyres, tambourines, sistrums and **c.** 7529
1Ch 13: 8 lyres, tambourines, **c** and trumpets. 5199
15:16 musical instruments: lyres, harps and **c.** 5199

1Ch 15:19 and Ethan were to sound the bronze **c**; 5199
15:28 of rams' horns and trumpets, and of **c**, and 5199
16: 5 Asaph was to sound the **c**, 5199
16:42 of the trumpets and **c** and for the playing of 5199
25: 1 accompanied by harps, lyres and **c**. 5199
25: 6 with **c**, lyres and harps, 5199
2Ch 5:12 dressed in fine linen and playing **c**, 5199
5:13 **c** and other instruments, 5199
29:25 in the temple of the LORD with **c**, harps 5199
Ezr 3:10 and the Levites (the sons of Asaph) with **c**, 5199
Ne 12:27 of thanksgiving and with the music of **c**, 5199
Ps 150: 5 praise him with the clash of **c**, 7529
150: 5 praise him with resounding **c**. 7529

CYPRESS (5)

Ge 6:14 So make yourself an ark of **c** wood; 1729
Isa 41:19 the fir and the **c** together, 9309
44:14 or perhaps took a **c** or oak. 9560
60:13 the pine, the fir and the **c** together, 9309
Eze 27: 6 of **c wood** from the coasts 9309

CYPRUS (11)

Isa 23: 1 From the land of **C** word has come to them. 4183
23:12 "Up, cross over to **C**; 4183
Eze 27: 6 from the coasts of **C** they made your deck, 4183
Ac 4:36 Joseph, a Levite **from C**, *3250*
11:19 as far as Phoenicia, **C** and Antioch, telling *3251*
11:20 however, men **from C** and Cyrene, *3250*
13: 4 to Seleucia and sailed from there to **C**. *3251*
15:39 Barnabas took Mark and sailed for **C**, *3251*
21: 3 After sighting **C** and passing to the south *3251*
21:16 He was a man **from C** and one of *3250*
27: 4 of **C** because the winds were against us. *3251*

CYRENE (7)

Mt 27:32 they met a man **from C**, named Simon, *3254*
Mk 15:21 A certain man **from C**, Simon, *3254*
Lk 23:26 they seized Simon **from C**, *3254*
Ac 2:10 Egypt and the parts of Libya near **C**; *3255*
6: 9 Jews **of C** and Alexandria as well as *3254*
11:20 however, men from Cyprus and **C**, *3254*
13: 1 Simeon called Niger, Lucius **of C**, *3254*

CYRENIAN, CYRENIANS (KJV) See CYRENE

CYRENIUS (KJV) See QUIRINIUS

CYRUS (23)

2Ch 36:22 In the first year of **C** king of Persia, 3931
36:22 of **C** king of Persia to make a proclamation 3931
36:23 "This is what **C** king of Persia says: 3931
Ezr 1: 1 In the first year of **C** king of Persia, 3931
1: 1 of **C** king of Persia to make a proclamation 3931
1: 2 "This is what **C** king of Persia says: 3931
1: 7 King **C** brought out the articles belonging 3931
1: 8 **C** king of Persia had them brought 3931
3: 7 as authorized by **C** king of Persia. 3931
4: 3 as King **C**, the king of Persia, 3931
4: 5 during the entire reign of **C** king of Persia 3931
5:13 in the first year of **C** king of Babylon, 10350
5:13 King **C** issued a decree 10350
5:14 "Then King **C** gave them to 10350
5:17 to see if King **C** did in fact issue a decree 10350
6: 3 In the first year of King **C**, the king issued 10350
6:14 of the God of Israel and the decrees of **C**, 10350
Isa 44:28 who says of **C**, 'He is my shepherd 3931
45: 1 to **C**, whose right hand I take hold of 3931
45:13 I will raise up **C** in my righteousness: 2084S
Da 1:21 until the first year of King **C**. 3931
6:28 of Darius and the reign of **C** the Persian. 10350
10: 1 In the third year of **C** king of Persia, 3931

D

DABAREH (KJV) See DABERATH

DABBESHETH (1)

Jos 19:11 Going west it ran to Maralah, touched **D**, 1833

DABERATH (3)

Jos 19:12 of Kisloth Tabor and went on to **D** and up 1829
21:28 from the tribe of Issachar, Kishion, **D**, 1829
1Ch 6:72 of Issachar they received Kedesh, **D**, 1829

DAGGER (3)

2Sa 2:16 and thrust his **d** into his opponent's side, 2995
20: 8 at his waist was a belt with a **d** in its sheath. 2995
20:10 Amasa was not on his guard against the **d** 2995

DAGON (8) [BETH DAGON, DAGON'S]

Jdg 16:23 to offer a great sacrifice to **D** their god and 1837
1Sa 5: 2 into Dagon's temple and set it beside **D**. 1837
5: 3 the next day, there was **D**, fallen on his face 1837
5: 3 They took **D** and put him back in his place. 1837
5: 4 when they rose, there was **D**, fallen 1837
5: 5 to this day neither the priests of **D** 1837
5: 7 upon us and upon **D** our god." 1837
1Ch 10:10 and hung up his head in the temple of **D**. 1837

DAGON'S (2) [DAGON]

1Sa 5: 2 Then they carried the ark into **D** temple 1837
5: 5 nor any others who enter **D** temple 1837

DAILY (30) [DAY]

Nu 29: 6 to the monthly and **d** burnt offerings 9458
1Ki 4:22 Solomon's **d** provisions were 285+3427+4200
2Ch 8:13 the **d** requirement for offerings commanded by Moses 928+3427+3427
31:16 to perform the **d** duties 928+2257+3427+3427
Ezr 6: 9 must be given them **d** without fail, 10089+10317+10317
Ne 11:23 which regulated their **d** activity. 928+3427+3427
12:47 all Israel contributed the **d** portions for the singers and gatekeepers. 928+1821+3427+3427
Job 23:12 of his mouth more than my **d bread.** 2976
Ps 68:19 who **d** bears our burdens. 3427+3427
Pr 8:34 watching **d** at my doors, 3427+3427
30: 8 but give me only my **d bread.** 2976+4312
Eze 43:25 to provide a male goat **d** for a sin offering; 2021+3427+4200
Da 1: 5 The king assigned them a **d** amount of food and wine 928+3427+3427
8:11 it took away the **d sacrifice** from him, 9458
8:12 and the **d sacrifice** were given over to it. 9458
8:13 the vision concerning the **d sacrifice,** 9458
11:31 and will abolish the **d sacrifice.** 9458
12:11 the time that the **d sacrifice** is abolished 9458
Mt 6:11 Give us today our **d** bread. *2157*
Lk 9:23 and take up his cross **d** and follow me. *2465+2848*
11: 3 Give us each day our **d** bread. *2157*
Ac 2:47 the Lord added to their number **d** those who were being saved. *2465+2848*
6: 1 overlooked in the **d** distribution of food. *2766*
16: 5 in the faith and grew **d** in numbers. *2465+2848*
19: 9 had discussions **d** in the lecture hall *2465+2848*
2Co 11:28 I face **d** the pressure of my concern *2465+2848*
1Th 4:12 so that *your* **d life** may win the respect *4344*
Tit 3:14 that they may provide for **d necessities** *338+5970*
Heb 3:13 But encourage one another **d**, *1667+2465+2848*
Jas 2:15 or sister is without clothes and **d** food. *2390*

DAINTY (KJV) See CHOICEST, DELICACIES, RICHES

DALAIAH (KJV) See DELAIAH

DALE (KJV) See VALLEY

DALMANUTHA (1)

Mk 8:10 and went to the region *of* **D**. *1236*

DALMATIA (1)

2Ti 4:10 and Titus to **D**. *1237*

DALPHON (1)

Est 9: 7 They also killed Parshandatha, **D**, Aspatha, 1943

DAM (1)

Pr 17:14 Starting a quarrel is like breaching a **d**; 4784

DAMAGE (4) [DAMAGED]

2Ki 12: 5 be used to repair whatever **d** is found *in* 981
12: 7 "Why aren't you repairing the **d** *done to* 981
Ac 27:21 you would have spared yourselves this **d** *5615*
Rev 6: 6 and *do* not **d** the oil and the wine!" *92*

DAMAGED (1) [DAMAGE]

Lev 21:20 or running sores or **d** testicles. 5293

DAMARIS (1)

Ac 17:34 also a woman named **D**, *1240*

DAMASCENES (1) [DAMASCUS]

2Co 11:32 *of* **the D** guarded in order to arrest me. *1241*

DAMASCUS (59) [DAMASCENES]

Ge 14:15 pursuing them as far as Hobah, north of **D**. 1966
15: 2 who will inherit my estate is Eliezer *of* **D**?" 1966
2Sa 8: 5 of **D** came to help Hadadezer king 1966
8: 6 in the Aramean kingdom of **D**, 1966
1Ki 11:24 the rebels went to **D**, 1966
15:18 the king of Aram, who was ruling in **D**. 1966
19:15 and go to the Desert of **D**. 1966
20:34 up your own market areas in **D**, 1966
2Ki 5:12 Are not Abana and Pharpar, the rivers of **D**, 1966
8: 7 Elisha went to **D**, 1966
8: 9 of all the finest wares of **D**. 1966
14:28 how he recovered for Israel both **D** 1966
16: 9 of Assyria complied by attacking **D** 1966
16:10 to **D** to meet Tiglath-Pileser king 1877
16:10 in **D** and sent to Uriah the priest a sketch of 1966
16:11 the plans that King Ahaz had sent from **D** 1966
16:12 king came back from **D** and saw the altar, 1966
1Ch 18: 5 of **D** came to help Hadadezer king 2008
18: 6 in the Aramean kingdom of **D**, 2008
2Ch 16: 2 who was ruling in **D**. 2008
24:23 They sent all the plunder to their king in **D**. 2008
28: 5 as prisoners and brought them to **D**. 2008
28:23 He offered sacrifices to the gods of **D**, 2008
SS 7: 4 the tower of Lebanon looking toward **D**. 1966
Isa 7: 8 for the head of Aram is **D**, 1966
7: 8 and the head of **D** is only Rezin. 1966
8: 4 of **D** and the plunder of Samaria will 1966
10: 9 and Samaria like **D**? 1966
17: 1 An oracle concerning **D**: 1966
17: 1 **D** will no longer be a city but will become 1966
17: 3 and royal power from **D**; 1966
Jer 49:23 Concerning **D**: "Hamath 1966
49:24 **D** has become feeble, she has turned to flee 1966
49:27 "I will set fire to the walls of **D**; 1966
Eze 27:18 " '**D**, because of your many products 1966
47:16 on the border between **D** and Hamath), 1966
47:17 along the northern border of **D**, 1966
47:18 between Hauran and **D**, 1966
48: 1 and the northern border of **D** next 1966
Am 1: 3 "For three sins of **D**, even for four, 1966
1: 5 I will break down the gate of **D**; 1966
3:12 of their beds and in **D** on their couches." 1966
5:27 I will send you into exile beyond **D**," 1966
Zec 9: 1 the land of Hadrach and will rest upon **D**— 1966
Ac 9: 2 for letters to the synagogues in **D**, *1242*
9: 3 As he neared **D** on his journey, *1242*
9: 8 So they led him by the hand into **D**. *1242*
9:10 In **D** there was a disciple named Ananias. *1242*
9:19 with the disciples in **D**. *1242*
9:22 the Jews living in **D** by proving that Jesus is *1242*
9:27 in **D** he had preached fearlessly in the name *1242*
22: 5 from them to their brothers in **D**, *1242*
22: 6 "About noon *as* I came near **D**, *1242*
22:10 " 'Get up,' the Lord said, 'and go into **D**. *1242*
22:11 My companions led me by the hand into **D**, *1242*
26:12 "On one of these journeys I was going to **D** *1242*
26:20 First to those in **D**, *1242*
2Co 11:32 In **D** the governor under King Aretas had *1242*
Gal 1:17 into Arabia and later returned to **D**. *1242*

DAMMIM See EPHES DAMMIM, PAS DAMMIM

DAMNATION (KJV) See CONDEMNED, CONDEMNATION, DESTRUCTION, JUDGMENT, PUNISHED SEVERELY, SIN

DAMPNESS (1)

SS 5: 2 my hair with the **d** *of* the night." 8268

DAMSEL (KJV) See CHILD, LITTLE GIRL, SERVANT GIRL, SLAVE GIRL, VIRGIN, YOUNG WOMAN

DAN (59) [DAN JAAN, DANITE, DANITES, LAISH, LESHEM, MAHANEH DAN]

Ge 14:14 and went in pursuit as far as **D**. 1969
30: 6 Because of this she named him **D**. 1968
35:25 of Rachel's maidservant Bilhah: **D** and Naphtali. 1968
46:23 The son of **D**: Hushim. 1968
49:16 "**D** will provide justice for his people 1968
49:17 **D** will be a serpent by the roadside, 1968
Ex 1: 4 **D** and Naphtali; Gad and Asher. 1968
31: 6 of the tribe of **D**, to help him. 1968
35:34 of the tribe of **D**, the ability to teach others. 1968
38:23 of the tribe of **D**— 1968
Nu 1:12 from **D**, Ahiezer son of Ammishaddai; 1968
1:38 From the descendants of **D**: 1968
1:39 number from the tribe of **D** was 62,700. 1968
2:25 be the divisions of the camp of **D**, 1968
2:25 of **D** is Ahiezer son of Ammishaddai. 1968
2:31 to the camp of **D** number 157,600. 1968
7:66 the leader of the people of **D**, 1968
10:25 the divisions of the camp of **D** set out, 1201+1968
13:12 the tribe of **D**, Ammiel son of Gemalli; 1968
26:42 the descendants of **D** by their clans: 1968
26:42 These were the clans of **D**: 1968
34:22 the leader from the tribe of **D**; 1201+1968
Dt 27:13 Gad, Asher, Zebulun, **D** and Naphtali. 1968
33:22 About **D** he said: 1968
33:22 About Dan he said: "**D** is a lion's cub, 1968
34: 1 from Gilead to **D**, 1968
Jos 19:40 seventh lot came out for the tribe of **D**, 1201+1968
19:47 They settled in Leshem and named it **D** 1969
19:48 the inheritance of the tribe of **D**, 1201+1968
21: 5 **D** and half of Manasseh. 1968
21:23 from the tribe of **D** they received Eltekeh, 1968
Jdg 5:17 And **D**, why did he linger by the ships? 1968
18:29 They named it **D** after their forefather Dan, 1969
18:29 They named it Dan after their forefather **D**, 1968

Jdg 18:30 the tribe of **D** until the time of the captivity 1974
20: 1 the Israelites from **D** to Beersheba and from 1969
1Sa 3:20 from **D** to Beersheba recognized 1969
2Sa 3:10 and Judah from **D** to Beersheba." 1969
17:11 Let all Israel, from **D** to Beersheba— 1969
24: 2 "Go throughout the tribes of Israel from **D** 1969
24:15 and seventy thousand of the people from **D** 1969
1Ki 4:25 from **D** to Beersheba, lived in safety, 1969
12:29 One he set up in Bethel, and the other in **D.** 1969
12:30 the people went even as far as **D** to worship 1969
15:20 He conquered Ijon, **D,** 1969
2Ki 10:29 of the golden calves at Bethel and **D.** 1969
1Ch 2: 2 **D,** Joseph, Benjamin, Naphtali, Gad 1968
12:35 **men of D,** ready for battle—28,600; 1974
21: 2 the Israelites from Beersheba to **D.** 1969
27:22 over **D:** Azarel son of Jeroham. 1968
2Ch 2:14 from **D** and whose father was from Tyre. 1968
16: 4 They conquered Ijon, **D,** 1969
30: 5 from Beersheba to **D,** 1969
Jer 4:15 A voice is announcing from **D,** 1969
8:16 of the enemy's horses is heard from **D;** 1969
Eze 48: 1 **D** will have one portion; 1968
48: 2 it will border the territory of **D** from east 1968
48:32 the gate of Benjamin and the gate of **D.** 1968
Am 8:14 or say, 'As surely as your god lives, O **D,'** 1969

DAN JAAN (1) [DAN]

2Sa 24: 6 and on to **D** and around toward Sidon. 1970

DANCE (7) [DANCED, DANCES, DANCING]

Job 21:11 their little ones **d about.** 8376
Ecc 3: 4 a time to mourn and a time *to* **d,** 8376
SS 6:13 the Shulammite as on the **d** *of* Mahanaim? 4703
Jer 31: 4 up your tambourines and go out to **d** *with* 4688
31:13 Then maidens will **d** and be glad, 4688
Mt 11:17 and *you did* not **d;** *4004*
Lk 7:32 and *you did* not **d;** *4004*

DANCED (5) [DANCE]

1Sa 18: 7 As they **d,** they sang: 8471
2Sa 6:14 **d** before the LORD with all his might, 4159
1Ki 18:26 And *they* **d** around the altar they had made. 7174
Mt 14: 6 of Herodias **d** for them and pleased Herod *4004*
Mk 6:22 the daughter of Herodias came in and **d,** *4004*

DANCES (2) [DANCE]

1Sa 21:11 Isn't he the one they sing about in their **d:** 4703
29: 5 the David they sang about in their **d:** 4703

DANCING (13) [DANCE]

Ex 15:20 with tambourines and **d,** 4703
32:19 the camp and saw the calf and the **d,** 4703
Jdg 11:34 **d** to the sound of tambourines! 4703
21:21 the girls of Shiloh come out to join in the **d,** 4703
21:23 While the *girls were* **d,** 2565
1Sa 18: 6 to meet King Saul with singing and **d,** 4703
2Sa 6:16 when she saw King David leaping and **d** 4159
1Ch 15:29 she saw King David **d** and celebrating, 8376
Ps 30:11 You turned my wailing into **d;** 4688
149: 3 Let them praise his name with **d** 4688
150: 4 praise him with tambourine and **d,** 4688
La 5:15 our **d** has turned to mourning. 4688
Lk 15:25 he heard music and **d.** *5962*

DANDLED (1)

Isa 66:12 be carried on her arm and **d** on her knees. 9130

DANGER (17) [DANGEROUS, DANGERS, ENDANGER, ENDANGERED, ENDANGERS]

1Sa 20:21 you are safe; there is no **d.** 1821
Pr 22: 3 A prudent man sees **d** and takes refuge, 8288
27:12 The prudent see **d** and take refuge, 8288
Mt 5:22 will be **in d** of the fire of hell. *1944*
Lk 8:23 and *they were in* great **d.** *3073*
Ac 19:27 *There is* **d** not only **that** *3073*
19:40 *we are in* **d** of being charged with rioting *3073*
Ro 8:35 or persecution or famine or nakedness or **d** *3074*
2Co 11:26 I have been *in* **d** from rivers, *3074*
11:26 *in* **d** from bandits, in danger *3074*
11:26 *in* **d** from my own countrymen, *3074*
11:26 *in* **d** from Gentiles; *3074*
11:26 *in* **d** in the city, in danger in the country, *3074*
11:26 in danger in the city, *in* **d** in the country, *3074*
11:26 in danger in the country, *in* **d** at sea; *3074*
11:26 and *in* **d** from false brothers. *3074*
Heb 6: 8 and thistles is worthless and is **in d of** *1584*

DANGEROUS (1) [DANGER]

Ac 27: 9 and sailing had already become **d** because *2195*

DANGERS (1) [DANGER]

Ecc 12: 5 when men are afraid of heights and of **d** in 3152

DANGLES (1)

Job 28: 4 far from men *he* **d** and sways. 1938

DANIEL (76) [DANIEL'S]

1Ch 3: 1 the second, **D** the son of Abigail of Carmel; 1975
Ezr 8: 2 of the descendants of Ithamar, **D;** 1975
Ne 10: 6 **D,** Ginnethon, Baruch, 1975
Eze 14:14 Noah, **D** and Job— 1975
14:20 even if Noah, **D** and Job were in it, 1975
28: 3 Are you wiser than **D?** 1975
Da 1: 6 **D,** Hananiah, Mishael and Azariah. 1975
1: 7 to **D,** the name Belteshazzar; 1975
1: 8 But **D** resolved not to defile himself with 1975
1: 9 to show favor and sympathy to **D,** 1975
1:10 but the official told **D,** 1975
1:11 **D** then said to the guard whom 1975
1:11 the chief official had appointed over **D,** 1975
1:17 And **D** could understand visions 1975
1:19 and he found none equal to **D,** Hananiah, 1975
1:21 And **D** remained there until the first year 1975
2:13 for **D** and his friends to put them to death. 10181
2:14 **D** spoke to him with wisdom and tact. 10181
2:15 Arioch then explained the matter to **D.** 10181
2:16 **D** went in to the king and asked for time, 10181
2:17 Then **D** returned to his house and explained 10181
2:19 the night the mystery was revealed to **D** in 10181
2:19 Then **D** praised the God of heaven 10181
2:24 Then **D** went to Arioch, 10181
2:25 Arioch took **D** to the king at once and said, 10181
2:26 king asked **D** (also called Belteshazzar), 10181
2:27 **D** replied, "No wise man, enchanter, 10181
2:46 before **D** and paid him honor and ordered 10181
2:47 The king said to **D,** 10181
2:48 Then the king placed **D** in a high position 10181
2:49 **D** himself remained at the royal court. 10181
4: 8 **D** came into my presence and I told him 10181
4:19 Then **D** (also called Belteshazzar) was greatly perplexed 10181
5:12 This man **D,** whom the king called Belteshazzar, 10181
5:12 Call for **D,** and he will tell you what 10181
5:13 So **D** was brought before the king, 10181
5:13 and the king said to him, "Are you **D,** 10181
5:17 Then **D** answered the king, 10181
5:29 **D** was clothed in purple, 10181
6: 2 one of whom was **D.** 10181
6: 3 Now **D** so distinguished himself among 10181
6: 4 to find grounds for charges against **D** 10181
6: 5 against this man **D** unless it has something 10181
6:10 Now when **D** learned that 10181
6:11 and found **D** praying and asking God 10181
6:13 Then they said to the king, **"D,** 10181
6:14 to rescue **D** and made every effort 10181
6:16 and they brought **D** and threw him into 10181
6:16 The king said to **D,** "May your God, 10181
6:20 he called to **D** in an anguished voice, 10181
6:20 **"D,** servant of the living God, 10181
6:21 **D** answered, "O king, live forever! 10181
6:23 and gave orders to lift **D** out of the den. 10181
6:23 And when **D** was lifted from the den, 10181
6:24 the men who had falsely accused **D** were 10181
6:26 and reverence the God of **D.** 10181
6:27 He has rescued **D** from the power of 10181
6:28 So **D** prospered during the reign of Darius 10181
7: 1 **D** had a dream, 10181
7: 2 **D** said: "In my vision at night 10181
7:15 "I, **D,** was troubled in spirit, 10181
7:28 I, **D,** was deeply troubled by my thoughts, 10181
8: 1 I, **D,** had a vision, 1975
8:15 **D,** was watching the vision and trying 1975
8:27 **D,** was exhausted and lay ill 1975
9: 2 I, **D,** understood from the Scriptures, 1975
9:22 He instructed me and said to me, **"D,** 1975
10: 1 to **D** (who was called Belteshazzar). 1975
10: 2 At that time I, **D,** mourned for three weeks. 1975
10: 7 I, **D,** was the only one who saw the vision; 1975
10:11 He said, **"D,** you who are highly esteemed, 1975
10:12 Then he continued, "Do not be afraid, **D.** 1975
12: 4 **D,** close up and seal the words of the scroll 1975
12: 5 Then I, **D,** looked, and there 1975
12: 9 He replied, "Go your way, **D,** 1975
Mt 24:15 spoken of through the prophet **D—** *1248*

DANIEL'S (2) [DANIEL]

Da 2:49 at **D** request the king appointed Shadrach, 10181
6:17 so that **D** situation might not be changed. 10089+10181

DANITE (1) [DAN]

Lev 24:11 the daughter of Dibri the **D.)** 1968+4200+4751

DANITES (14) [DAN]

Jos 19:47 the **D** had difficulty taking possession 1201+1968
Jdg 1:34 The Amorites confined the **D** to 1201+1968
13: 2 named Manoah, from the clan of the **D,** 1974
18: 1 in those days the tribe of the **D** was seeking 1974
18: 2 So the **D** sent five warriors from Zorah 1201+1968
18:11 six hundred men from the clan of the **D,** 1974
18:16 The six hundred **D,** armed for battle, 1201+1968
18:22 and overtook the **D.** 1201+1968
18:23 the **D** turned and said to Micah, 1201+1968
18:25 The **D** answered, "Don't argue with us, 1201+1968
18:26 So the **D** went their way, and Micah, 1201+1968
18:28 The **D** rebuilt the city and settled there. NIH
18:30 the **D** set up for themselves the idols, 1201+1968
Eze 27:19 " '**D** and Greeks from Uzal 1968

DANNAH (1)

Jos 15:49 **D,** Kiriath Sannah (that is, Debir), 1972

DAPPLED (2)

Zec 6: 3 and the fourth **d—**all of them powerful. 1353
6: 6 the one with the **d** horses toward the south." 1353

DARDA (2)

1Ki 4:31 wiser than Heman, Calcol and **D,** 1997
1Ch 2: 6 Zimri, Ethan, Heman, Calcol and **D—** 1997

DARE (12) [DARED, DARES, DARING]

2Sa 3:11 Ish-Bosheth *did* not **d** to say another word 3523
Job 13:16 no godless man *would* **d come** before him! AIT
Pr 29:24 he is put under oath and *d* not **testify.** AIT
Jn 2:16 **How d you** turn my Father's house into *3590*
9:34 how **d** you lecture us!" *NIG*
Ac 7:32 Moses trembled with fear and *did* not **d** *5528*
23: 4 "You **d** to insult God's high priest?" *NIG*
Ro 5: 7 good man someone *might* possibly **d** to die. *5528*
1Co 6: 1 **d** *he* take it before the ungodly *5528*
2Co 10:12 not **d** to classify or compare ourselves *5528*
11:21 I also **d** to boast about. *5528*
Jude 1: 9 *did* not **d** to bring a slanderous accusation *5528*

DARED (7) [DARE]

Est 7: 5 man who *has* **d** to do such a thing?" 4213+4848
Mt 22:46 no one **d** to ask him any more questions. *5528*
Mk 12:34 no one **d** ask him any more questions. *5528*
Lk 20:40 no *one* **d** to ask him any more questions. *5528*
Jn 21:12 None of the disciples **d** ask him, *5528*
Ac 5:13 No one else **d** join them, *5528*
1Th 2: 2 of our God *we* **d** to tell you his gospel *4245*

DARES (5) [DARE]

Ge 49: 9 who *d to* **rouse** him? AIT
Nu 24: 9 who *d to* **rouse** them? AIT
Job 41:14 Who *d* **open** the doors of his mouth, AIT
La 4:14 that no *one* **d** to touch their garments. 3523
2Co 11:21 What anyone else **d** to boast about— *5528*

DARICS (2)

1Ch 29: 7 and ten thousand **d** of gold, 163
Ezr 8:27 **d,** and two fine articles of polished bronze, 163

DARING (1) [DARE]

Job 32: 6 **not d** to tell you what I know. 3707

DARIUS (25)

Ezr 4: 5 and down to the reign of **D** king of Persia. 2003
4:24 until the second year of the reign of **D** king 10184
5: 5 a report could go to **D** and his written reply 10184
5: 6 sent to King **D.** 10184
5: 7 To King **D:** Cordial greetings. 10184
6: 1 King **D** then issued an order, 10184
6:12 I **D** have decreed it. 10184
6:13 because of the decree King **D** had sent, 10184
6:14 **D** and Artaxerxes, kings of Persia. 10184
6:15 in the sixth year of the reign of King **D.** 10184
Ne 12:22 were recorded in the reign of **D** the Persian. 2003
Da 5:31 and **D** the Mede took over the kingdom, 10184
6: 1 It pleased **D** to appoint 120 satraps to rule 10184
6: 6 "O King **D,** live forever! 10184
6: 9 So King **D** put the decree in writing. 10184
6:25 Then King **D** wrote to all the peoples, 10184
6:28 during the reign of **D** and the reign of Cyrus 10184
9: 1 In the first year of **D** son of Xerxes (a Mede 2003
11: 1 And in the first year of **D** the Mede, 2003
Hag 1: 1 In the second year of King **D,** 2003
1:15 in the second year of King **D.** 2003
2:10 in the second year of **D,** 2003
Zec 1: 1 the eighth month of the second year of **D,** 2003
1: 7 in the second year of **D,** 2003
7: 1 In the fourth year of King **D,** 2003

DARK (39) [DARK-COLORED, DARKEN, DARKENED, DARKENING, DARKENS, DARKER, DARKEST, DARKNESS, PITCH-DARK]

Dt 28:29 about like a blind man in the **d.** 696
2Sa 22:10 **d clouds** were under his feet. 6906
22:12 the **d** rain clouds of the sky. 3128
1Ki 8:12 that he would dwell in a **d cloud;** 6906
2Ch 6: 1 that he would dwell in a **d cloud;** 6906
Job 3: 9 *May* its morning stars *become* **d;** 3124
18: 6 The light in his tent *becomes* **d;** 3124
22:11 why it is so **d** you cannot see, 3125
24:16 In the **d,** men break into houses, 3125
34:22 There is no **d place,** no deep shadow, 3125
Ps 18: 9 **d clouds** were under his feet. 6906
18:11 the **d** rain clouds of the sky. 3128
35: 6 may their path be **d** and slippery, 3125
74:20 because haunts of violence fill the **d places** 4743
105:28 He sent darkness and **made** the land **d—** 3124
139:12 even the darkness *will* not *be* **d** to you; 3124
Pr 2:13 the straight paths to walk in **d** ways, 3125
7: 9 as the **d** of night set in. 413+696
31:15 She gets up while it is still **d;** 4326
Ecc 12: 2 the light and the moon and the stars *grow* **d,** 3124
SS 1: 5 **D** am I, yet lovely, 8839
1: 5 **d** like the tents of Kedar, NIH
1: 6 Do not stare at me because I am **d,** 8842
Isa 50:10 Let him who walks in the **d,** 3128

Jer 4:28 and the heavens above *grow* **d,** 7722
Eze 30:18 **D** *will be* the day at Tahpanhes 3124
Mic 3: 6 and the day *will* **go d** for them. 7722
Mt 10:27 What I tell you in the **d,** *5028*
Mk 1:35 **while it was still d,** Jesus got up, *1939*
Lk 11:36 and no part of it **d,** *5027*
12: 3 What you have said in the **d** will be heard *5028*
Jn 6:17 By now it was **d,** *5028*
12:35 The man who walks in the **d** does not know *5028*
20: 1 while it was still **d,** *5028*
Ro 2:19 a light for those who are in the **d,** *5030*
Eph 6:12 against the powers of this **d** world and *5030*
2Pe 1:19 as to a light shining in a **d** place, *903*
Rev 8:12 so that a third of them **turned d.** *5029*
9:17 Their breastplates were fiery red, **d blue,** *5610*

DARK-COLORED (4) [DARK, COLORED]

Ge 30:32 every **d** lamb and every spotted 2569
30:33 or any lamb that is not **d,** 2569
30:35 that had white on them) and all the **d** lambs, 2569
30:40 the streaked and **d** animals that belonged 2569

DARKEN (3) [DARK]

Eze 32: 7 I will cover the heavens and **d** their stars; 7722
32: 8 the shining lights in the heavens *I will* **d** 7722
Am 8: 9 "I will make the sun go down at noon and **d** 3124

DARKENED (13) [DARK]

Job 6:16 *when* **d** by thawing ice and swollen 7722
Ps 69:23 *May* their eyes *be* **d** so they cannot see, 3124
SS 1: 6 because I *am* **d** *by* the sun. 8812
Isa 5:30 even the light *will be* **d** by the clouds. 3124
13:10 The rising sun *will be* **d** and the moon will 3124
Joel 2:10 the sky trembles, the sun and moon *are* **d,** 7722
3:15 The sun and moon *will be* **d,** 7722
Mt 24:29 *be* **d,** and the moon will not give its light; *5029*
Mk 13:24 " 'the sun *will be* **d,** *5029*
Ro 1:21 and their foolish hearts *were* **d.** *5029*
11:10 *May* their eyes *be* **d** so they cannot see, *5029*
Eph 4:18 They are **d** in their understanding *5031*
Rev 9: 2 The sun and sky *were* **d** by the smoke from *5029*

DARKENING (1) [DARK]

Jer 13:16 before your feet stumble on the **d** hills. 5974

DARKENS (2) [DARK]

Job 38: 2 "Who is this *that* **d** my counsel with words 3124
Am 5: 8 into dawn and **d** day *into* night, who calls 3124

DARKER (1) [DARK]

Ge 49:12 His eyes will be **d** than wine, 2679

DARKEST (1) [DARK]

Ps 88: 6 in the **d** depths. 4743

DARKNESS (158) [DARK]

Ge 1: 2 **d** was over the surface of the deep, 3125
1: 4 and he separated the light from the **d.** 3125
1: 5 and the **d** he called "night." 3125
1:18 and to separate light from **d.** 3125
15:12 and a thick and dreadful **d** came over him. 3128
15:17 When the sun had set and **d** had fallen, 6602
Ex 10:21 the sky so that **d** will spread over Egypt— 3125
10:21 **d** that can be felt." 3125
10:22 **total d** covered all Egypt for three days. 696+3125
14:20 Throughout the night the cloud brought **d** to 3125
20:21 while Moses approached the **thick d** 6906
Dt 4:11 with black clouds and **deep d.** 6906
5:22 the cloud and the **deep d;** 6906
5:23 When you heard the voice out of the **d,** 3125
Jos 24: 7 he put **d** between you and the Egyptians; 4419
1Sa 2: 9 but the wicked will be silenced in **d.** 3125
2Sa 22:12 He made **d** his canopy around him— 3125
22:29 the LORD turns my **d** into light. 3125
Job 3: 4 That day—may it turn to **d;** 3125
3: 5 May **d** and deep shadow claim it once more; 3125
3: 6 That night—may **thick d** seize it; 694
5:14 **D** comes upon them in the daytime; 3125
10:22 where even the light is like **d."** 694
11:17 and **d** will become like morning. 9507
12:22 of **d** and brings deep shadows into the light. 3125
12:25 They grope in **d** with no light; 3125
15:22 He despairs of escaping the **d;** 3125
15:23 he knows the day of **d** is at hand. 3125
15:30 He will not escape the **d;** 3125
17:12 in the face of **d** they say, 'Light is near.' 3125
17:13 if I spread out my bed in **d,** 3125
18:18 into **d** and is banished from the world. 3125
19: 8 he has shrouded my paths in **d.** 3125
20:26 total **d** lies in wait for his treasures. 3125
22:13 Does he judge through such **d?** 6906
23:17 Yet I am not silenced by the **d,** 3125
23:17 by the **thick d** that covers my face. 694
24:17 For all of them, **deep d** is their morning; 7516
24:17 they make friends with the terrors of **d.** 7516
26:10 for a boundary between light and **d.** 3125
28: 3 Man puts an end to the **d;** 3125
28: 3 for ore in the blackest **d.** 694
29: 3 and by his light I walked through **d!** 3125
30:26 when I looked for light, then came **d.** 694
37:19 up our case because of our **d.** 3125
38: 9 and wrapped it in **thick d,** 6906
Job 38:19 And where does **d** reside? 3125
Ps 18:11 He made **d** his covering, 3125
18:28 my God turns my **d** into light. 3125
44:19 for jackals and covered us over with **deep d.** 7516
82: 5 They walk about in **d;** 3128
88:12 Are your wonders known in the *place of* **d,** 3125
88:18 the **d** is my closest friend. 4743
91: 6 nor the pestilence that stalks in the **d,** 694
97: 2 Clouds and **thick d** surround him; 6906
104:20 You bring **d,** it becomes night, 3125
105:28 He sent **d** and made the land dark— 3125
107:10 Some sat in **d** and the deepest gloom, 3125
107:14 He brought them out of **d** and 3125
112: 4 Even in **d** light dawns for the upright, 3125
139:11 "Surely the **d** will hide me and 3125
139:12 even the **d** will not be dark to you; 3125
139:12 for **d** is as light to you. 3128
143: 3 in **d** like those long dead. 4743
Pr 4:19 But the way of the wicked is like **deep d;** 696
20:20 his lamp will be snuffed out in **pitch d.** 854+3125
Ecc 2:13 just as light is better than **d.** 3125
2:14 while the fool walks in the **d;** 3125
5:17 All his days he eats in **d,** 3125
6: 4 It comes without meaning, it departs in **d,** 3125
6: 4 and in **d** its name is shrouded. 3125
11: 8 But let him remember the days of **d,** 3125
Isa 5:20 who put **d** for light and light for darkness, 3125
5:20 who put darkness for light and light for **d,** 3125
5:30 he will see **d** and distress; 3125
8:22 toward the earth and see only distress and **d** 3128
8:22 and they will be thrust into **utter d.** 696
9: 2 people walking in **d** have seen a great light; 3125
29:15 who do their work in **d** and think, 4743
29:18 and **d** the eyes of the blind will see. 3125
42: 7 from the dungeon those who sit in **d.** 3125
42:16 I will turn the **d** into light before them 4743
45: 3 I will give you the treasures of **d,** 3125
45: 7 I form the light and create **d,** 3125
45:19 from somewhere in a land of **d;** 3125
47: 5 "Sit in silence, go into **d,** 3125
49: 9 'Come out,' and to those in **d,** 'Be free!' 3125
50: 3 with **d** and make sackcloth its covering." 7725
58:10 then your light will rise in the **d,** 3125
59: 9 We look for light, but all is **d;** 3125
60: 2 **d** covers the earth and thick darkness is 3125
60: 2 and **thick d** is over the peoples, 6906
61: 1 for the captives and **release from d** for 7223
Jer 2: 6 a land of drought and **d,** 7516
2:31 a desert to Israel or a land of **great d?** 4420
13:16 before *he* **brings** *the* **d,** 3124
13:16 but he will turn it to **thick d** and change it 7516
23:12 be banished to **d** and there they will fall. 696
La 3: 2 and made me walk in **d** rather than light; 3125
3: 6 He has made me dwell in **d** 4743
Eze 8:12 of the house of Israel are doing in the **d,** 3125
32: 8 I will bring **d** over your land, 3125
34:12 on a day of clouds and **d.** 6906
Da 2:22 he knows what lies in **d,** 10286
Joel 2: 2 a day of **d** and gloom, 3125
2:31 be turned to **d** and the moon to blood before 3125
Am 4:13 he who turns dawn to **d,** 6547
5:18 That day will be **d,** not light. 3125
5:20 Will not the day of the LORD be **d,** 3125
Mic 3: 6 without visions, and **d,** without divination. 3127
7: 8 I sit in **d,** the LORD will be my light. 3125
Na 1: 8 he will pursue his foes into **d.** 3125
Zep 1:15 a day of **d** and gloom, 3125
Mt 4:16 people living in **d** have seen a great light; *5030*
6:23 your whole body will be **full of d.** *5027*
6:23 If then the light within you is **d,** *5030*
6:23 how great is that **d!** *5030*
8:12 into the **d,** where there will be weeping *5030*
22:13 and throw him outside, into the **d,** *5030*
25:30 that worthless servant outside, into the **d,** *5030*
27:45 the sixth hour until the ninth hour **d** came *5030*
Mk 15:33 the sixth hour **d** came over the whole land *5030*
Lk 1:79 on those living in **d** and in the shadow *5030*
11:34 they are bad, your body also is **full of d.** *5027*
11:35 then, that the light within you is not **d.** *5030*
22:53 But this is your hour—when **d** reigns." *5030*
23:44 and **d** came over the whole land until *5030*
Jn 1: 5 The light shines in the **d,** *5028*
1: 5 but the **d** has not understood it. *5028*
3:19 the world, but men loved **d** instead of light *5030*
8:12 Whoever follows me will never walk in **d,** *5028*
12:35 before **d** overtakes you. *5028*
12:46 no one who believes in me should stay in **d.** *5028*
Ac 2:20 be turned to **d** and the moon to blood before *5030*
13:11 Immediately mist and **d** came over him, *5030*
26:18 to open their eyes and turn them from **d** *5030*
Ro 13:12 So let us put aside the deeds *of* **d** and put *5030*
1Co 4: 5 to light what is hidden in **d** and will expose *5030*
2Co 4: 6 God, who said, "Let light shine out of **d,"** *5030*
6:14 Or what fellowship can light have with **d?** *5030*
Eph 5: 8 For you were once **d,** *5030*
5:11 to do with the fruitless deeds *of* **d,** *5030*
Col 1:13 from the dominion *of* **d** and brought us into *5030*
1Th 5: 4 not in **d** so that this day should surprise you *5030*
5: 5 We do not belong to the night or to the **d.** *5030*
Heb 12:18 *to* **d,** gloom and storm; *1190*
1Pe 2: 9 the praises of him who called you out of **d** *5030*
2Pe 2:17 Blackest **d** is reserved for them. *5030*
1Jn 1: 5 in him there is no **d** at all. *5028*
1: 6 with him yet walk in the **d,** *5030*
2: 8 in him and you, because the **d** is passing *5028*
2: 9 but hates his brother is still in the **d.** *5028*
2:11 in the **d** and walks around in the darkness; *5028*
1Jn 2:11 in the darkness and walks around in the **d;** *5028*
2:11 because the **d** has blinded him. *5028*
Jude 1: 6 these he has kept in **d,** *2432*
1:13 whom blackest **d** has been reserved forever. *5030*
Rev 16:10 and his kingdom was plunged into **d.** *5031*

DARKON (2)

Ezr 2:56 Jaala, **D,** Giddel, 2010
Ne 7:58 Jaala, **D,** Giddel, 2010

DARLING (9)

SS 1: 9 I liken you, my **d,** to a mare harnessed 8299
1:15 How beautiful you are, my **d!** 8299
2: 2 among thorns is my **d** among the maidens. 8299
2:10 my **d,** my beautiful one, and come with me. 8299
2:13 my **d;** my beautiful one, come with me." 8299
4: 1 How beautiful you are, my **d!** 8299
4: 7 All beautiful you are, my **d;** 8299
5: 2 "Open to me, my sister, my **d,** my dove, 8299
6: 4 You are beautiful, my **d,** as Tirzah, 8299

DART (3) [DARTING]

Job 41:21 and flames **d** from his mouth. 3655
41:26 nor does the spear or the **d** or the javelin. 5025
Na 2: 4 *they* **d about** like lightning. 8132

DARTING (4) [DART]

Pr 7:23 like a bird **d** into a snare, 4554
26: 2 Like a fluttering sparrow or a **d** swallow, 6414
Isa 14:29 its fruit will be a **d,** venomous serpent. 6414
30: 6 of adders and **d** snakes, 6414

DARTS (KJV) See ARROWS, CLUB, JAVELINS, WEAPONS

DASH (7) [DASHED, DASHES]

Jdg 20:37 in ambush **made a** sudden **d** into Gibeah, 7320
2Ki 8:12 **d** their little children **to the ground,** 8187
Ps 2: 9 *you will* **d** them **to pieces** like pottery." 5879
Eze 23:34 *you will* **d** it *to* pieces 1751
Na 2: 5 *They* **d** to the city wall; 4554
Lk 19:44 **d** you **to the ground,** *1610*
Rev 2:27 *he will* **d** them **to pieces** like pottery'— *5341*

DASHED (7) [DASH]

2Ch 25:12 down so that all **were d to pieces.** 1324
Ps 119:116 **let** my hopes **be d.** 1017
Isa 13:16 Their infants *will* **be d to pieces** 8187
Hos 10:14 mothers **were d to the ground** 8187
13:16 little ones *will* **be d to the ground,** 8187
Na 3:10 Her infants **were d to pieces** at the head 8187
Ac 27:29 that *we would be* **d** against the rocks, *1738*

DASHES (1) [DASH]

Ps 137: 9 he who seizes your infants and **d** them 5879

DATE (3) [DATES]

Eze 24: 2 record this **d,** this very date, 3427
24: 2 record this date, this very **d,** 3427
Ac 21:26 to the temple to give notice of the **d** when *NIG*

DATES (4) [DATE]

2Sa 6:19 a **cake of d** and a cake of raisins 882
1Ch 16: 3 a **cake of d** and a cake of raisins 882
Ac 1: 7 or **d** the Father has set by his own authority. *2789*
1Th 5: 1 about times and **d** we do not need to write *2789*

DATHAN (10)

Nu 16: 1 **D** and Abiram, sons of Eliab, 2018
16:12 Then Moses summoned **D** and Abiram, 2018
16:24 from the tents of Korah, **D** and Abiram.' " 2018
16:25 Moses got up and went to **D** and Abiram, 2018
16:27 from the tents of Korah, **D** and Abiram. 2018
16:27 **D** and Abiram had come out 2018
26: 9 of Eliab were Nemuel, **D** and Abiram. 2018
26: 9 The same **D** and Abiram were 2018
Dt 11: 6 and what he did to **D** and Abiram, 2018
Ps 106:17 The earth opened up and swallowed **D;** 2018

DAUB (KJV) See COVER

DAUGHTER (281) [DAUGHTER'S, DAUGHTER-IN-LAW, DAUGHTERS, DAUGHTERS-IN-LAW, GRANDDAUGHTER, GRANDDAUGHTERS]

Ge 11:29 she was the **d** *of* Haran, 1426
19:31 One day the **older** *d* said to the younger, AIT
19:33 and the **older** *d* went in and lay with him. AIT
19:34 The next day the **older** *d* said to AIT
19:35 and the **younger** *d* went and lay with him. AIT
19:37 The **older** *d* had a son, AIT
19:38 The **younger** *d* also had a son, AIT
20:12 **d** *of* my father though not *of* my mother; 1426
24:15 She *was the* **d** of Bethuel son of Milcah, 3528
24:23 Then he asked, "Whose **d** are you? 1426
24:24 She answered him, "I am the **d** *of* Bethuel, 1426

Ge 24:47 “I asked her, ‘Whose **d** are you?’ 1426
24:47 “She said, ‘The **d** *of* Bethuel son of Nahor, 1426
25:20 when he married Rebekah **d** *of* Bethuel 1426
26:34 he married Judith **d** *of* Beeri the Hittite, 1426
26:34 and also Basemath **d** *of* Elon the Hittite. 1426
28: 9 the sister of Nebaioth and **d** *of* Ishmael son 1426
29: 6 here comes his **d** Rachel with the sheep.” 1426
29:10 When Jacob saw Rachel **d** *of* Laban, 1426
29:18 in return for your younger **d** Rachel.” 1426
29:23 he took his **d** Leah and gave her to Jacob, 1426
29:24 to his **d** as her maidservant. 1426
29:26 not our custom here to give the **younger** *d* AIT
29:28 Laban gave him his **d** Rachel to be his wife. 1426
29:29 to his **d** Rachel as her maidservant. 1426
30:21 Some time later she gave birth to a **d** 1426
34: 1 Now Dinah, the **d** Leah had borne to Jacob, 1426
34: 3 His heart was drawn to Dinah **d** *of* Jacob, 1426
34: 5 that his **d** Dinah had been defiled, 1426
34: 7 in Israel by lying with Jacob's **d—** 1426
34: 8 My son Shechem has his heart set on your **d** 1426
34:19 because he was delighted with Jacob's **d.** 1426
36: 2 Adah **d** *of* Elon the Hittite, 1426
36: 2 the Hittite, and Oholibamah **d** *of* Anah 1426
36: 3 also Basemath **d** *of* Ishmael and sister 1426
36:14 The sons of Esau's wife Oholibamah **d** 1426
36:18 from Esau's wife Oholibamah **d** *of* Anah. 1426
36:25 Dishon and Oholibamah **d** *of* Anah. 1426
36:39 and his wife's name was Mehetabel **d** 1426
36:39 the **d** *of* Me-Zahab. 1426
38: 2 the **d** *of* a Canaanite man named Shua. 1426
38:12 long time Judah's wife, the **d** *of* Shua, died. 1426
41:45 and gave him Asenath **d** *of* Potiphera, 1426
41:50 two sons were born to Joseph by Asenath **d** 1426
46:15 besides his **d** Dinah. 1426
46:18 whom Laban had given to his **d** Leah— 1426
46:20 to Joseph by Asenath **d** *of* Potiphera, 1426
46:25 whom Laban had given to his **d** Rachel— 1426
Ex 2: 5 Pharaoh's **d** went down to the Nile to bathe, 1426
2: 7 Then his sister asked Pharaoh's **d,** 1426
2: 9 Pharaoh's **d** said to her, 1426
2:10 to Pharaoh's **d** and he became her son. 1426
2:21 who gave his **d** Zipporah to Moses 1426
6:23 **d** *of* Amminadab and sister of Nahshon, 1426
20:10 neither you, nor your son or **d,** 1426
21: 7 “If a man sells his **d** as a servant, 1426
21: 9 he must grant her the rights of a **d.** 1426
21:31 also applies if the bull gores a son or **d.** 1426
Lev 12: 5 If she gives birth to a **d,** 5922
12: 6 of her purification for a son or **d** are over, 1426
18: 9 your father's **d** or your mother's daughter, 1426
18: 9 your father's daughter or your mother's **d,** 1426
18:10 not have sexual relations with your son's **d** 1426
18:10 or your daughter's **d;** 1426
18:11 “ ‘Do not have sexual relations with the **d** 1426
18:17 with both a woman and her **d.** 1426
18:17 with either her son's **d** 1426
18:17 or her daughter's **d;** 1426
19:29 “ ‘Do not degrade your **d** by making her 1426
20:17 the **d** *of* either his father or his mother, 1426
21: 2 such as his mother or father, his son or **d,** 1426
21: 9 a priest's **d** defiles herself by becoming 1426
22:12 If a priest's **d** marries anyone other than 1426
22:13 priest's **d** becomes a widow or is divorced, 1426
24:11 the **d** *of* Dibri the Danite.) 1426
Nu 25:15 to death was Cozbi **d** *of* Zur, 1426
25:18 the **d** *of* a Midianite leader, 1426
26:46 (Asher had a **d** named Serah.) 1426
27: 8 turn his inheritance over to his **d.** 1426
27: 9 If he has no **d,** give his inheritance 1426
30:16 between a father and his young **d** still living 1426
36: 8 Every **d** who inherits land 1426
Dt 5:14 neither you, nor your son or **d,** 1426
13: 6 If your very own brother, or your son or **d,** 1426
18:10 among you who sacrifices his son or **d** in 1426
22:16 “I gave my **d** in marriage to this man, 1426
22:17 ‘I did not find your **d** to be a virgin.’ 1426
27:22 the **d** *of* his father or the daughter 1426
27:22 of his father or the **d** *of* his mother.” 1426
28:56 the husband she loves and her own son or **d** 1426
Jos 15:16 “I will give my **d** Acsah in marriage to 1426
15:17 Caleb gave his **d** Acsah to him in marriage. 1426
Jdg 1:12 “I will give my **d** Acsah in marriage to 1426
1:13 Caleb gave his **d** Acsah to him in marriage. 1426
11:34 to meet him but his **d,** 1426
11:34 Except for her he had neither son nor **d.** 1426
11:35 and cried, “Oh! My **d!** 1426
11:40 for four days to commemorate the **d** 1426
19:24 Look, here is my virgin **d,** 1426
21: 1 “Not one of us will give his **d** in marriage 1426
Ru 2: 2 Naomi said to her, “Go ahead, my **d.”** 1426
2: 8 So Boaz said to Ruth, “My **d,** listen to me. 1426
2:22 “It will be good for you, my **d,** 1426
3: 1 “My **d,** should I not try to find a home 1426
3:10 “The LORD bless you, my **d,”** he replied. 1426
3:11 And now, my **d,** don't be afraid. 1426
3:16 Naomi asked, “How did it go, my **d?”** 1426
3:18 Then Naomi said, “Wait, my **d,** 1426
1Sa 14:49 The name of his older **d** was Merab, 1426
14:50 His wife's name was Ahinoam **d** 1426
17:25 He will also give him his **d** in marriage 1426
18:17 “Here is my older **d** Merab. 1426
18:19 when the time came for Merab, Saul's **d,** 1426
18:20 Saul's **d** Michal was in love with David, 1426
18:27 Saul gave him his **d** Michal in marriage. 1426
18:28 and that his **d** Michal loved David, 1426
25:44 But Saul had given his **d** Michal, 1426
2Sa 3: 3 of Maacah **d** *of* Talmai king of Geshur; 1426
3: 7 a concubine named Rizpah **d** *of* Aiah. 1426
3:13 into my presence unless you bring Michal **d** 1426
6:16 Michal **d** *of* Saul watched from a window. 1426
6:20 Michal **d** *of* Saul came out to meet him 1426
6:23 And Michal **d** *of* Saul had no children to 1426
11: 3 the **d** *of* Eliam and the wife of Uriah 1426
12: 3 It was like a **d** to him. 1426
14:27 Three sons and a **d** were born to Absalom. 1426
17:25 the **d** *of* Nahash and sister of Zeruiah 1426
21: 8 the two sons of Aiah's **d** Rizpah, 1426
21: 8 with the five sons of Saul's **d** Merab, 1426
21:10 Rizpah **d** *of* Aiah took sackcloth 1426
21:11 David was told what Aiah's **d** Rizpah, 1426
1Ki 3: 1 of Egypt and married his **d.** 1426
4:11 to Taphath **d** *of* Solomon); 1426
4:15 in Naphtali (he had married Basemath **d** 1426
7: 8 a palace like this hall for Pharaoh's **d,** 1426
9:16 and then gave it as a wedding gift to his **d,** 1426
9:24 After Pharaoh's **d** had come up from 1426
11: 1 Solomon, however, loved many foreign
women besides Pharaoh's **d—** 1426
15: 2 His mother's name was Maacah **d** 1426
15:10 His grandmother's name was Maacah **d** 1426
16:31 also married Jezebel **d** *of* Ethbaal king of 1426
22:42 His mother's name was Azubah **d** 1426
2Ki 8:18 for he married a **d** *of* Ahab. 1426
9:34 “and bury her, for she was a king's **d.”** 1426
11: 2 **d** *of* King Jehoram and sister of Ahaziah, 1426
14: 9 ‘Give your **d** to my son in marriage.’ 1426
15:33 His mother's name was Jerusha **d** 1426
18: 2 His mother's name was Abijah **d** 1426
19:21 ‘The Virgin **D** *of* Zion despises you 1426
19:21 **D** *of* Jerusalem tosses her head as you flee. 1426
21:19 His mother's name was Meshullemeth **d** 1426
22: 1 His mother's name was Jedidah **d** 1426
23:10 to sacrifice his son or **d** in the fire 1426
23:31 His mother's name was Hamutal **d** 1426
23:36 His mother's name was Zebidah **d** 1426
24: 8 His mother's name was Nehushta **d** 1426
24:18 His mother's name was Hamutal **d** 1426
1Ch 1:50 and his wife's name was Mehetabel **d** 1426
1:50 the **d** *of* Me-Zahab. 1426
2: 3 the **d** *of* Shua. 1426
2:21 Hezron lay with the **d** *of* Makir the father 1426
2:35 Sheshan gave his **d** in marriage 1426
2:49 Caleb's **d** was Acsah. 1426
3: 2 of Maacah **d** *of* Talmai king of Geshur; 1426
3: 5 These four were by Bathsheba **d** 1426
4:18 the children of Pharaoh's **d** Bithiah, 1426
7:24 His **d** was Sheerah, 1426
15:29 Michal **d** *of* Saul watched from a window. 1426
2Ch 8:11 Solomon brought Pharaoh's **d** up from 1426
11:18 who was the **d** *of* David's son Jerimoth and 1426
11:18 the **d** *of* Jesse's son Eliab. 1426
11:20 Then he married Maacah **d** *of* Absalom, 1426
11:21 Rehoboam loved Maacah **d** 1426
13: 2 a **d** *of* Uriel of Gibeah. 1426
20:31 His mother's name was Azubah **d** 1426
21: 6 for he married a **d** *of* Ahab. 1426
22:11 But Jehosheba, the **d** *of* King Jehoram, 1426
22:11 the **d** *of* King Jehoram and wife of 1426
25:18 ‘Give your **d** to my son in marriage.’ 1426
27: 1 His mother's name was Jerusha **d** 1426
29: 1 His mother's name was Abijah **d** 1426
Ezr 2:61 and Barzillai (a man who had married a **d** 1426
Ne 6:18 and his son Jehohanan had married the **d** 1426
7:63 and Barzillai (a man who had married a **d** 1426
Est 2: 7 and Mordecai had taken her as his own **d** 1426
2:15 the **d** *of* his uncle Abihail) to go to 1426
9:29 So Queen Esther, **d** *of* Abihail, 1426
Job 42:14 The first **d** he named Jemimah, NIH
Ps 9:14 the gates of the **D** *of* Zion and there rejoice 1426
45:10 Listen, O **d,** consider and give ear: 1426
45:12 The **D** *of* Tyre will come with a gift, 1426
137: 8 O **D** *of* Babylon, doomed to destruction, 1426
SS 6: 9 is unique, the only **d** of her mother, 2085[S]
7: 1 beautiful your sandaled feet, O prince's **d!** 1426
Isa 1: 8 The **D** *of* Zion is left like a shelter in 1426
10:30 Cry out, O **D** *of* Gallim! 1426
10:32 at the mount of the **D** *of* Zion, 1426
16: 1 to the mount of the **D** *of* Zion. 1426
23:10 O **D** *of* Tarshish, 1426
23:12 O Virgin **D** *of* Sidon, now crushed! 1426
37:22 Virgin **D** *of* Zion despises and mocks you. 1426
37:22 **D** *of* Jerusalem tosses her head as you flee. 1426
47: 1 sit in the dust, Virgin **D** *of* Babylon; 1426
47: 1 **D** *of* the Babylonians. 1426
47: 5 go into darkness, **D** *of* the Babylonians; 1426
52: 2 O captive **D** *of* Zion. 1426
62:11 “Say to the **D** *of* Zion, ‘See, 1426
Jer 4:31 the cry of the **D** *of* Zion gasping for breath, 1426
6: 2 I will destroy the **D** *of* Zion, 1426
6:23 in battle formation to attack you, O **D** 1426
14:17 for my virgin **d—** 1426
31:22 How long will you wander, O unfaithful **d?** 1426
46:11 O Virgin **D** *of* Egypt. 1426
46:24 The **D** *of* Egypt will be put to shame, 1426
48:18 O inhabitants of the **D** *of* Dibon, 1426
49: 4 O unfaithful **d,** you trust in your riches 1426
50:42 in battle formation to attack you, O **D** 1426
51:33 “The **D** *of* Babylon is like a threshing floor 1426
52: 1 His mother's name was Hamutal **d** 1426
La 1: 6 All the splendor has departed from the **D** 1426
1:15 the Lord has trampled the Virgin **D** 1426
2: 1 the **D** *of* Zion with the cloud of his anger! 1426
2: 2 down the strongholds of the **D** *of* Judah. 1426
2: 4 like fire on the tent of the **D** *of* Zion. 1426
2: 5 and lamentation for the **D** *of* Judah. 1426
2: 8 to tear down the wall around the **D** *of* Zion. 1426
2:10 the **D** *of* Zion sit on the ground in silence; 1426
2:13 O **D** *of* Jerusalem? 1426
2:13 O Virgin **D** *of* Zion? 1426
2:15 they scoff and shake their heads at the **D** 1426
2:18 O wall of the **D** *of* Zion, 1426
4:21 Rejoice and be glad, O **D** *of* Edom, 1426
4:22 O **D** *of* Zion, your punishment will end; 1426
4:22 But, O **D** *of* Edom, 1426
Eze 14:20 they could save neither son nor **d.** 1426
16:44 “Like mother, like **d.”** 1426
16:45 You are a true **d** *of* your mother, 1426
22:11 his own father's **d.** 1426
44:25 son or **d,** brother or unmarried sister, 1426
Da 11: 6 The **d** *of* the king of the South will go to 1426
11:17 a **d** in marriage in order to overthrow 1426
Hos 1: 3 So he married Gomer **d** *of* Diblaim, 1426
1: 6 and gave birth to a **d.** 1426
Mic 1:13 You were the beginning of sin to the **D** 1426
4: 8 O stronghold of the **D** *of* Zion, 1426
4: 8 kingship will come to the **D** *of* Jerusalem.” 1426
4:10 Writhe in agony, O **D** *of* Zion, 1426
4:13 “Rise and thresh, O **D** *of* Zion, 1426
7: 6 a **d** rises up against her mother, 1426
Zep 3:14 Sing, O **D** *of* Zion; shout aloud, O Israel! 1426
3:14 O **D** *of* Jerusalem! 1426
Zec 2: 7 you who live in the **D** *of* Babylon!” 1426
2:10 “Shout and be glad, O **D** *of* Zion. 1426
9: 9 Rejoice greatly, O **D** *of* Zion! 1426
9: 9 Shout, **D** *of* Jerusalem! 1426
Mal 2:11 by marrying the **d** *of* a foreign god. 1426
Mt 9:18 “My **d** has just died. *2588*
9:22 “Take heart, **d,”** he said, *2588*
10:35 a **d** against her mother, *2588*
10:37 or **d** more than me is not worthy of me; *2588*
14: 6 the **d** of Herodias danced for them *2588*
15:22 My **d** is suffering terribly *2588*
15:28 And her **d** was healed from that very hour. *2588*
21: 5 “Say *to* the **D** of Zion, *2588*
Mk 5:23 “My **little d** is dying. *2589*
5:34 He said to her, **“D,** *2588*
5:35 “Your **d** is dead,” they said. *2588*
6:22 the **d** of Herodias came in and danced, *2588*
7:25 a woman whose **little d** was possessed *2589*
7:26 to drive the demon out *of* her **d.** *2588*
7:29 the demon has left your **d.”** *2588*
Lk 2:36 the **d** of Phanuel, of the tribe of Asher. *2588*
8:42 because his only **d,** *2588*
8:48 Then he said to her, **“D,** *2588*
8:49 “Your **d** is dead,” he said. *2588*
12:53 against **d** and daughter against mother, *2588*
12:53 against daughter and **d** against mother, *2588*
13:16 should not this woman, a **d** of Abraham, *2588*
Jn 12:15 *O* **D** of Zion; *2588*
Ac 7:21 Pharaoh's **d** took him and brought him up *2588*
Heb 11:24 to be known as the son *of* Pharaoh's **d.** *2588*

DAUGHTER'S (5) [DAUGHTER]

Ge 29:27 Finish **this** *d* bridal week; AIT
Lev 18:10 or your **d** daughter; 1426
18:17 either her son's daughter or her **d** daughter; 1426
Dt 22:17 But here is the proof of my **d** virginity.” 1426
2Sa 14:27 **The d** name was Tamar, 2023[S]

DAUGHTER-IN-LAW (17) [DAUGHTER]

Ge 11:31 and his **d** Sarai, the wife of his son Abram, 3987
38:11 Judah then said to his **d** Tamar, 3987
38:16 Not realizing that she was his **d,** 3987
38:24 “Your **d** Tamar is guilty of prostitution, 3987
Lev 18:15 “ ‘Do not have sexual relations with your **d.** 3987
20:12 “ ‘If a man sleeps with his **d,** 3987
Ru 1:22 the Moabitess, her **d,** arriving in Bethlehem 3987
2:20 Naomi said to her **d.** 3987
2:22 Naomi said to Ruth her **d,** 3987
4:15 For your **d,** who loves you 3987
1Sa 4:19 His **d,** the wife of Phinehas, 3987
1Ch 2: 4 Judah's **d,** bore him Perez and Zerah. 3987
Eze 22:11 another shamefully defiles his **d,** 3987
Mic 7: 6 a **d** against her mother-in-law— 3987
Mt 10:35 a **d** against her mother-in-law— *3811*
Lk 12:53 mother-in-law against **d** *3811*
12:53 and **d** against mother-in-law.” *3811*

DAUGHTERS (214) [DAUGHTER]

Ge 5: 4 and had other sons and **d.** 1426
5: 7 and had other sons and **d.** 1426
5:10 and had other sons and **d.** 1426
5:13 and had other sons and **d.** 1426
5:16 and had other sons and **d.** 1426
5:19 and had other sons and **d.** 1426
5:22 and had other sons and **d.** 1426
5:26 and had other sons and **d.** 1426
5:30 and had other sons and **d.** 1426
6: 1 in number on the earth and **d** were born 1426
6: 2 saw that the **d** *of* men were beautiful, 1426
6: 4 when the sons of God went to the **d** *of* men 1426
11:11 and had other sons and **d.** 1426
11:13 and had other sons and **d.** 1426
11:15 and had other sons and **d.** 1426
11:17 and had other sons and **d.** 1426
11:19 and had other sons and **d.** 1426
11:21 and had other sons and **d.** 1426
11:23 and had other sons and **d.** 1426
11:25 and had other sons and **d.** 1426

Ge 19: 8 I have two **d** who have never slept with 1426
19:12 sons-in-law, sons or **d,** 1426
19:14 who were pledged to marry his **d.** 1426
19:15 and your two **d** who are here, 1426
19:16 and of his two **d** and led them safely out of 1426
19:30 Lot and his two **d** left Zoar and settled in 1426
19:30 He and his two **d** lived in a cave. 1426
19:36 of Lot's **d** became pregnant by their father. 1426
24: 3 for my son from the **d** *of* the Canaanites, 1426
24:13 the **d** *of* the townspeople are coming out 1426
24:37 for my son from the **d** *of* the Canaanites, 1426
28: 2 from among the **d** *of* Laban, 1426
29:16 Now Laban had two **d;** 1426
31:26 and you've carried off my **d** like captives 1426
31:28 and my **d** good-by. 1426
31:31 I thought you would take your **d** away 1426
31:41 for you fourteen years for your two **d** 1426
31:43 "The women are my **d,** 1426
31:43 Yet what can I do today about these **d** 1426
31:50 If you mistreat my **d** or 1426
31:50 or if you take any wives besides my **d,** 1426
31:55 and his **d** and blessed them. 1426
34: 9 give us your **d** and take our daughters 1426
34: 9 give us your daughters and take our **d** 1426
34:16 Then we will give you our **d** 1426
34:16 and take your **d** for ourselves. 1426
34:21 We can marry their **d** 1426
36: 6 Esau took his wives and sons and **d** and all 1426
37:35 All his sons and **d** came to comfort him, 1426
46: 7 to Egypt his sons and grandsons and his **d** 1426
46:15 These sons and **d** *of* his were thirty-three 1426
Ex 2:16 Now a priest of Midian had seven **d,** 1426
2:20 he asked his **d.** 1426
3:22 which you will put on your sons and **d.** 1426
6:25 Eleazar son of Aaron married one of the **d** 1426
10: 9 with our sons and **d,** 1426
21: 4 a wife and she bears him sons or **d,** 1426
32: 2 your sons and your **d** are wearing, 1426
34:16 when you choose some of their **d** as wives 1426
34:16 and those **d** prostitute themselves 1426
Lev 10:14 and your sons and your **d** may eat the breast 1426
26:29 of your sons and the flesh of your **d.** 1426
Nu 18:11 and your sons and **d** as your regular share. 1426
18:19 and your sons and **d** as your regular share. 1426
21:29 and his **d** as captives to Sihon king of 1426
26:33 he had only **d,** whose names were Mahlah, 1426
27: 1 The **d** *of* Zelophehad son of Hepher, 1426
27: 1 The names of the **d** were Mahlah, Noah, 1426
27: 7 "What Zelophehad's **d** are saying is right. 1426
36: 2 of our brother Zelophehad to his **d.** 1426
36: 6 the LORD commands for Zelophehad's **d:** 1426
36:10 So Zelophehad's **d** did as the LORD 1426
36:11 Zelophehad's **d**—Mahlah, 1426
Dt 7: 3 Do not give your **d** to their sons 1426
7: 3 to their sons or take their **d** for your sons, 1426
12:12 you, your sons and **d,** 1426
12:18 you, your sons and **d,** 1426
12:31 They even burn their sons and **d** in the fire 1426
16:11 you, your sons and **d,** 1426
16:14 you, your sons and **d,** 1426
28:32 and **d** will be given to another nation, 1426
28:41 You will have sons and **d** but you will 1426
28:53 and **d** the LORD your God has given you. 1426
32:19 because he was angered by his sons and **d.** 1426
Jos 7:24 the gold wedge, his sons and **d,** his cattle, 1426
17: 3 had no sons but only **d,** 1426
17: 6 the **d** *of* the tribe of Manasseh received 1426
Jdg 3: 6 They took their **d** in marriage 1426
3: 6 and gave their own **d** to their sons, 1426
12: 9 He had thirty sons and thirty **d.** 1426
12: 9 He gave his **d** away in marriage NIH
21: 7 not to give them any of our **d in marriage?** 1426
21:18 We can't give them our **d** as wives, 1426
21:22 since you did not give your **d** to them.' " NIH
Ru 1:11 But Naomi said, "Return home, my **d.** 1426
1:12 Return home, my **d;** I am too old to have 1426
1:13 No, my **d.** 1426
1Sa 1: 4 and to all her sons and **d.** 1426
2:21 and gave birth to three sons and two **d.** 1426
8:13 He will take your **d** to be perfumers 1426
30: 3 and sons and **d** taken captive. 1426
30: 6 in spirit because of his sons and **d.** 1426
2Sa 1:20 lest the **d** *of* the Philistines be glad, 1426
1:20 lest the **d** *of* the uncircumcised rejoice. 1426
1:24 "O **d** *of* Israel, weep for Saul, 1426
5:13 and more sons and **d** were born to him. 1426
13:18 of garment the virgin **d** *of* the king wore. 1426
19: 5 the lives of your sons and **d** and the lives 1426
2Ki 17:17 They sacrificed their sons and **d** in the fire. 1426
1Ch 2:34 Sheshan had no sons—only **d.** 1426
4:27 Shimei had sixteen sons and six **d,** 1426
7:15 who had only **d.** 1426
14: 3 and became the father of more sons and **d.** 1426
23:22 he had only **d.** 1426
25: 5 God gave Heman fourteen sons and three **d.** 1426
2Ch 11:21 twenty-eight sons and sixty **d.** 1426
13:21 and had twenty-two sons and sixteen **d.** 1426
24: 3 and he had sons and **d.** 1426
28: 8 from their kinsmen two hundred thousand wives, sons and **d.** 1426
29: 9 and why our sons and **d** and our wives are 1426
31:18 and **d** of the whole community listed 1426
Ezr 9: 2 They have taken some of their **d** as wives 1426
9:12 do not give your **d** in marriage to their sons 1426
9:12 to their sons or take their **d** for your sons. 1426
Ne 3:12 the next section with the help of his **d.** 1426
4:14 your sons and your **d,** 1426
Ne 5: 2 "We and our sons and **d** are numerous; 1426
5: 5 yet we have to subject our sons and **d** 1426
5: 5 Some of our **d** have already been enslaved, 1426
10:28 and all their sons and **d** who are able 1426
10:30 not to give our **d** in marriage to the peoples 1426
10:30 to the peoples around us or take their **d** 1426
13:25 not to give your **d** in marriage to their sons, 1426
13:25 to take their **d** in marriage for your sons or 1426
Job 1: 2 He had seven sons and three **d,** 1426
1:13 and **d** were feasting and drinking wine at 1426
1:18 and **d** were feasting and drinking wine at 1426
42:13 And he also had seven sons and three **d.** 1426
42:15 as beautiful as Job's **d,** 1426
Ps 45: 9 **D** *of* kings are among your honored 1426
106:37 They sacrificed their sons and their **d** 1426
106:38 the blood of their sons and **d,** 1426
144:12 and our **d** will be like pillars carved 1426
Pr 30:15 "The leech has two **d.** 'Give! Give!' 1426
SS 1: 5 Dark am I, yet lovely, O **d** *of* Jerusalem, 1426
2: 7 **D** *of* Jerusalem, I charge you by 1426
3: 5 **D** *of* Jerusalem, I charge you by 1426
3:10 its interior lovingly inlaid by the **d** 1426
3:11 Come out, you **d** *of* Zion, 1426
5: 8 O **d** *of* Jerusalem, I charge you— 1426
5:16 this my friend, O **d** *of* Jerusalem. 1426
8: 4 **D** *of* Jerusalem, I charge you: 1426
Isa 23: 4 I have neither reared sons nor brought up **d.** 1435
32: 9 you **d** who feel secure, 1426
32:11 shudder, you **d** who feel secure! NIH
43: 6 Bring my sons from afar and my **d** from 1426
49:22 and carry your **d** on their shoulders. 1426
56: 5 and a name better than sons and **d;** 1426
60: 4 and your **d** are carried on the arm. 1426
Jer 3:24 their flocks and herds, their sons and **d.** 1426
5:17 devour your sons and **d;** 1426
7:31 of Ben Hinnom to burn their sons and **d** in 1426
9:20 Teach your **d** how to wail; 1426
11:22 their sons and **d** by famine. 1426
14:16 their sons or their **d.** 1426
16: 2 not marry and have sons or **d** in this place." 1426
16: 3 the LORD says about the sons and **d** born 1426
19: 9 the flesh of their sons and **d,** 1426
29: 6 Marry and have sons and **d;** 1426
29: 6 for your sons and give your **d** in marriage, 1426
29: 6 so that they too may have sons and **d.** 1426
32:35 of Ben Hinnom to sacrifice their sons and **d** 1426
35: 8 nor our sons and **d** have ever drunk wine 1426
41:10 the king's **d** along with all 1426
43: 6 king's **d** whom Nebuzaradan commander 1426
48:46 your sons are taken into exile and your **d** 1426
Eze 13:17 the **d** *of* your people who prophesy out 1426
14:16 they could not save their own sons or **d.** 1426
14:18 they could not save their own sons or **d.** 1426
14:22 sons and **d** who will be brought out of it. 1426
16:20 and **d** whom you bore to me 1426
16:27 the **d** *of* the Philistines, 1426
16:46 who lived to the north of you with her **d;** 1426
16:46 who lived to the south of you with her **d,** 1426
16:48 and her **d** never did what you 1426
16:48 and your **d** have done. 1426
16:49 She and her **d** were arrogant, 1426
16:53 the fortunes of Sodom and her **d** and 1426
16:53 and of Samaria and her **d,** 1426
16:55 with her **d** and Samaria with her daughters, 1426
16:55 with her daughters and Samaria with her **d,** 1426
16:55 and you and your **d** will return 1426
16:57 by the **d** *of* Edom and all her neighbors and 1426
16:57 of Edom and all her neighbors and the **d** *of* 1426
16:61 I will give them to you as **d,** 1426
23: 2 **d** *of* the same mother. 1426
23: 4 and gave birth to sons and **d.** 1426
23:10 took away her sons and **d** and killed her 1426
23:25 They will take away your sons and **d,** 1426
23:47 they will kill their sons and **d** and burn 1426
24:21 and **d** you left behind will fall by the sword. 1426
24:25 and their sons and **d** as well— 1426
32:16 The **d** *of* the nations will chant it; 1426
32:18 both her and the **d** *of* mighty nations, 1426
Hos 4:13 Therefore your **d** turn to prostitution 1426
4:14 "I will not punish your **d** when they turn 1426
Joel 2:28 Your sons and **d** will prophesy, 1426
3: 8 I will sell your sons and **d** to the people 1426
Am 7:17 and your sons and **d** will fall by the sword. 1426
Lk 23:28 "**D** of Jerusalem, do not weep for me; *2588*
Ac 2:17 Your sons and **d** will prophesy, *2588*
21: 9 He had four unmarried **d** who prophesied. *2588*
2Co 6:18 and you will be my sons and **d,** *2588*
1Pe 3: 6 You are her **d** if you do what is right and do *5451*

DAUGHTERS-IN-LAW (5) [DAUGHTER]

Ru 1: 6 Naomi and her **d** prepared to return home 3987
1: 7 With her two **d** she left the place 3987
1: 8 Then Naomi said to her two **d,** "Go back, 3987
Hos 4:13 to prostitution and your **d** to adultery. 3987
4:14 nor your **d** when they commit adultery, 3987

DAVID (1004) [DAVID'S]

Ru 4:17 He was the father of Jesse, the father of **D.** 1858
4:22 and Jesse the father of **D.** 1858
1Sa 16:13 on the Spirit of the LORD came upon **D** 1858
16:19 "Send me your son **D,** 1858
16:20 a young goat and sent them with his son **D** 1858
16:21 **D** came to Saul and entered his service. 1858
16:21 and **D** became one of his armor-bearers. NIH
16:22 saying, "Allow **D** to remain in my service, 1858
1Sa 16:23 **D** would take his harp and play. 1858
17:12 Now **D** was the son of an Ephrathite 1858
17:14 **D** was the youngest. 1858
17:15 but **D** went back and forth from Saul 1858
17:17 Now Jesse said to his son **D,** 1858
17:20 Early in the morning **D** left the flock with 1858
17:22 **D** left his things with the keeper 1858
17:23 and **D** heard it. 1858
17:26 **D** asked the men standing near him, 1858
17:29 "Now what have I done?" said **D.** 1858
17:31 What **D** said was overheard and reported 1858
17:32 **D** said to Saul, "Let no one lose heart 1858
17:34 But **D** said to Saul, "Your servant 1858
17:37 Saul said to **D,** "Go, 1858
17:38 Then Saul dressed **D** in his own tunic. 1858
17:39 **D** fastened on his sword over the tunic 1858
17:41 kept coming closer to **D.** 1858
17:42 He looked **D** over and saw that he was only 1858
17:43 He said to **D,** "Am I a dog, 1858
17:43 And the Philistine cursed **D** by his gods. 1858
17:45 **D** said to the Philistine, 1858
17:48 **D** ran quickly toward the battle line 1858
17:50 So **D** triumphed over the Philistine with 1858
17:51 **D** ran and stood over him. 1858
17:54 **D** took the Philistine's head and brought it 1858
17:55 As Saul watched **D** going out to meet 1858
17:57 as **D** returned from killing the Philistine, 1858
17:57 with **D** still holding the Philistine's head. 2257[S]
17:58 **D** said, "I am the son of your servant Jesse 1858
18: 1 After **D** had finished talking with Saul, 2257[S]
18: 1 Jonathan became one in spirit with **D,** 1858
18: 2 From that day Saul kept **D** with him and 2084[S]
18: 3 with **D** because he loved him as himself. 1858
18: 4 the robe he was wearing and gave it to **D,** 1858
18: 5 **D** did it so successfully that Saul gave him 1858
18: 6 after **D** had killed the Philistine, 1858
18: 7 and **D** his tens of thousands." 1858
18: 8 "They have credited **D** with tens 1858
18: 9 that time on Saul kept a jealous eye on **D.** 1858
18:10 while **D** was playing the harp, 1858
18:11 saying to himself, "I'll pin **D** to the wall." 1858
18:11 But **D** eluded him twice. 1858
18:12 Saul was afraid of **D,** 1858
18:12 the LORD was with **D** but had left Saul. 2257[S]
18:13 So he sent **D** away from him 2084[S]
18:13 and **D** led the troops in their campaigns. NIH
18:16 But all Israel and Judah loved **D,** 1858
18:17 Saul said to **D,** "Here is my older daughter 1858
18:18 But **D** said to Saul, "Who am I, 1858
18:19 Saul's daughter, to be given to **D,** 1858
18:20 Saul's daughter Michal was in love with **D,** 1858
18:21 So Saul said to **D,** "Now you have 1858
18:22 "Speak to **D** privately and say, 'Look, 1858
18:23 They repeated these words to **D.** 1858
18:23 But **D** said, "Do you think it is 1858
18:24 Saul's servants told him what **D** had said, 1858
18:25 "Say to **D,** 'The king wants no other price 1858
18:25 Saul's plan was to have **D** fall by the hands 1858
18:26 When the attendants told **D** these things, 1858
18:27 **D** and his men went out 1858
18:28 that the LORD was with **D** and 1858
18:28 and that his daughter Michal loved **D,** 2084[S]
18:30 **D** met with more success than the rest 1858
19: 1 and all the attendants to kill **D.** 1858
19: 1 But Jonathan was very fond of **D** 1858
19: 4 of **D** to Saul his father and said to him, "Let 1858
19: 4 not the king do wrong to his servant **D;** 1858
19: 5 to an innocent man like **D** by killing him 1858
19: 6 LORD lives, **D** will not be put to death." NIH
19: 7 So Jonathan called **D** and told him 1858
19: 7 and **D** was with Saul as before. 1858
19: 8 and **D** went out and fought the Philistines. 1858
19: 9 While **D** was playing the harp, 1858
19:10 but **D** eluded him as Saul drove the spear 1858
19:10 That night **D** made good his escape. 1858
19:12 So Michal let **D** down through a window, 1858
19:14 When Saul sent the men to capture **D,** 1858
19:15 Then Saul sent the men back to see **D** 1858
19:18 When **D** had fled and made his escape, 1858
19:19 "**D** is in Naioth at Ramah"; 1858
19:22 And he asked, "Where are Samuel and **D?**" 1858
20: 1 Then **D** fled from Naioth at Ramah 1858
20: 3 But **D** took an oath and said, 1858
20: 4 Jonathan said to **D,** "Whatever you want me 1858
20: 5 So **D** said, "Look, tomorrow is 1858
20: 6 '**D** earnestly asked my permission to hurry 1858
20:10 **D** asked, "Who will tell me 1858
20:12 Then Jonathan said to **D:** 1858
20:16 a covenant with the house of **D,** 1858
20:17 And Jonathan had **D** reaffirm his oath out 1858
20:18 Then Jonathan said to **D:** 2257[S]
20:24 So **D** hid in the field, 1858
20:26 to **D** to make him ceremonially unclean— 2085[S]
20:28 "**D** earnestly asked me for permission to go 1858
20:33 that his father intended to kill **D.** 1858
20:34 at his father's shameful treatment of **D.** 1858
20:35 to the field for his meeting with **D.** 1858
20:39 only Jonathan and **D** knew.) 1858
20:41 **D** got up from the south side [of the stone] 1858
20:41 but **D** wept the most. 1858
20:42 Jonathan said to **D,** "Go in peace, 1858
20:42 **D** left, and Jonathan went back to the town. NIH
21: 1 **D** went to Nob, to Ahimelech the priest. 1858
21: 2 **D** answered Ahimelech the priest, 1858
21: 4 But the priest answered **D,** 1858
21: 5 **D** replied, "Indeed women have been kept 1858
21: 8 **D** asked Ahimelech, "Don't you have 1858

1Sa 21: 9 **D** said, "There is none like it; 1858
21:10 That day **D** fled from Saul and went 1858
21:11 "Isn't this **D**, the king of the land? 1858
21:11 and **D** his tens of thousands'?" 1858
21:12 **D** took these words to heart 1858
22: 1 **D** left Gath and escaped to the cave 1858
22: 3 From there **D** went to Mizpah in Moab 1858
22: 4 and they stayed with him as long as **D** was 1858
22: 5 But the prophet Gad said to **D**, 1858
22: 5 So **D** left and went to the forest of Hereth. 1858
22: 6 that **D** and his men had been discovered. 1858
22:14 "Who of all your servants is as loyal as **D**, 1858
22:17 because they too have sided with **D**. 1858
22:20 escaped and fled to join **D**. 1858
22:21 He told **D** that Saul had killed the priests of 1858
22:22 Then **D** said to Abiathar: 1858
23: 1 When **D** was told, "Look, 1858
23: 4 Once again **D** inquired of the LORD, 1858
23: 5 So **D** and his men went to Keilah, 1858
23: 6 the ephod down with him when he fled to **D** 1858
23: 7 Saul was told that **D** had gone to Keilah, 1858
23: 7 for **D** has imprisoned himself by entering NIH
23: 8 down to Keilah to besiege **D** and his men. 1858
23: 9 When **D** learned that Saul was plotting 1858
23:10 **D** said, "O LORD, God of Israel, 1858
23:12 Again **D** asked, "Will the citizens 1858
23:13 So **D** and his men, 1858
23:13 When Saul was told that **D** had escaped 1858
23:14 **D** stayed in the desert strongholds and in 1858
23:14 but God did not give **D** into his hands. 2257[S]
23:15 **D** was at Horesh in the Desert of Ziph, 1858
23:16 to **D** at Horesh and helped him find strength 1858
23:18 but **D** remained at Horesh. 1858
23:19 not **D** hiding among us in the strongholds 1858
23:22 Find out where **D** usually goes 2257[S]
23:24 **D** and his men were in the Desert of Maon, 1858
23:25 and when **D** was told about it, 1858
23:25 into the Desert of Maon in pursuit of **D**. 1858
23:26 and **D** and his men were on the other side, 1858
23:26 As Saul and his forces were closing in on **D** 1858
23:28 of **D** and went to meet the Philistines. 1858
23:29 And **D** went up from there and lived in 1858
24: 1 "**D** is in the Desert of En Gedi." 1858
24: 2 to look for **D** and his men near the Crags of 1858
24: 3 **D** and his men were far back in the cave. 1858
24: 4 Then **D** crept up unnoticed and cut off 1858
24: 5 **D** was conscience-stricken 1858
24: 7 With these words **D** rebuked his men 1858
24: 8 Then **D** went out of the cave and called out 1858
24: 8 **D** bowed down and prostrated himself 1858
24: 9 '**D** is bent on harming you'? 1858
24:16 When **D** finished saying this, Saul asked, 1858
24:16 Saul asked, "Is that your voice, **D** my son?" 1858
24:22 So **D** gave his oath to Saul. 1858
24:22 but **D** and his men went up to 1858
25: 1 **D** moved down into the Desert of Maon. 1858
25: 4 While **D** was in the desert, 1858
25: 8 and your son **D** whatever you can find 1858
25:10 "Who is this **D**? 1858
25:13 **D** said to his men, "Put on your swords!" 1858
25:13 and **D** put on his. 1858
25:13 About four hundred men went up with **D**, 1858
25:14 "**D** sent messengers from the desert 1858
25:20 there were **D** and his men descending 1858
25:21 **D** had just said, "It's been useless— 1858
25:22 May God deal with **D**, 1858
25:23 When Abigail saw **D**, 1858
25:23 down before **D** with her face to the ground. 1858
25:32 **D** said to Abigail, "Praise be to the LORD, 1858
25:35 Then **D** accepted from her 1858
25:39 When **D** heard that Nabal was dead, 1858
25:39 Then **D** sent word to Abigail, 1858
25:40 "**D** has sent us to you to take you 1858
25:43 **D** had also married Ahinoam of Jezreel, 1858
26: 1 "Is not **D** hiding on the hill of Hakilah, 1858
26: 2 to search there for **D**. 1858
26: 3 but **D** stayed in the desert. 1858
26: 5 Then **D** set out and went to the place 1858
26: 6 **D** then asked Ahimelech the Hittite 1858
26: 7 **D** and Abishai went to the army by night, 1858
26: 8 Abishai said to **D**, 1858
26: 9 But **D** said to Abishai, "Don't destroy him! 1858
26:12 So **D** took the spear and water jug 1858
26:13 Then **D** crossed over to the other side 1858
26:15 **D** said, "You're a man, aren't you? 1858
26:17 "Is that your voice, **D** my son?" 1858
26:17 **D** replied, "Yes it is, my lord the king." 1858
26:21 Come back, **D** my son. 1858
26:22 "Here is the king's spear," **D** answered. 1858
26:25 Then Saul said to **D**, "May you be blessed, 1858
26:25 "May you be blessed, my son **D**; 1858
26:25 So **D** went on his way, 1858
27: 1 But **D** thought to himself, 1858
27: 2 So **D** and the six hundred men with him left 1858
27: 3 **D** and his men settled in Gath with Achish. 1858
27: 3 and **D** had his two wives: 1858
27: 4 Saul was told that **D** had fled to Gath, 1858
27: 5 Then **D** said to Achish, 1858
27: 7 **D** lived in Philistine territory a year 1858
27: 8 Now **D** and his men went up and raided 1858
27: 9 Whenever **D** attacked an area, 1858
27:10 **D** would say, "Against the Negev of Judah" 1858
27:11 'This is what **D** did.' " 1858
27:12 Achish trusted **D** and said to himself, 1858
28: 1 Achish said to **D**, 1858
28: 2 **D** said, "Then you will see 1858
28:17 of your neighbors—to **D**. 1858

1Sa 29: 2 **D** and his men were marching at the rear 1858
29: 3 Achish replied, "Is this not **D**, 1858
29: 5 the **D** they sang about in their dances: 1858
29: 5 and **D** his tens of thousands'?" 1858
29: 6 So Achish called **D** and said to him, 1858
29: 8 "But what have I done?" asked **D**. 1858
29:11 So **D** and his men got up early in 1858
30: 1 **D** and his men reached Ziklag on 1858
30: 3 When **D** and his men came to Ziklag, 1858
30: 4 So **D** and his men wept aloud 1858
30: 6 **D** was greatly distressed because 1858
30: 6 But **D** found strength in 1858
30: 7 Then **D** said to Abiathar the priest, 1858
30: 8 and **D** inquired of the LORD, 1858
30: 9 **D** and the six hundred men with him came 1858
30:10 But **D** and four hundred men continued 1858
30:11 in a field and brought him to **D**. 1858
30:13 **D** asked him, "To whom do you belong, 1858
30:15 **D** asked him, "Can you lead me down 1858
30:16 He led **D** down, and there they were, 2084[S]
30:17 **D** fought them from dusk until the evening 1858
30:18 **D** recovered everything 1858
30:19 **D** brought everything back. 1858
30:21 Then **D** came to the two hundred men 1858
30:21 They came out to meet **D** and the people 1858
30:21 As **D** and his men approached, 1858
30:23 **D** replied, "No, my brothers, 1858
30:25 **D** made this a statute and ordinance NIH
30:26 When **D** arrived in Ziklag, 1858
30:31 and to those in all the other places where **D** 1858
2Sa 1: 1 **D** returned from defeating the Amalekites 1858
1: 2 When he came to **D**, 1858
1: 3 "Where have you come from?" **D** asked 1858
1: 4 "What happened?" **D** asked. 1858
1: 5 Then **D** said to the young man 1858
1:11 Then **D** and all the men with him took hold 1858
1:13 **D** said to the young man who brought him 1858
1:14 **D** asked him, "Why were you not afraid 1858
1:15 Then **D** called one of his men and said, 1858
1:16 For **D** had said to him, 1858
1:17 **D** took up this lament concerning Saul 1858
2: 1 **D** inquired of the LORD. 1858
2: 1 **D** asked, "Where shall I go?" 1858
2: 2 So **D** went up there with his two wives, 1858
2: 3 **D** also took the men who were with him, 1858
2: 4 to Hebron and there they anointed **D** king 1858
2: 4 When **D** was told that it was the men 1858
2:10 The house of Judah, however, followed **D**. 1858
2:11 The length of time **D** was king in Hebron 1858
2:15 of Saul, and twelve for **D**. 1858
3: 1 the house of Saul and the house of **D** lasted 1858
3: 1 **D** grew stronger and stronger, 1858
3: 2 Sons were born to **D** in Hebron: 1858
3: 5 These were born to **D** in Hebron. 1858
3: 6 the house of Saul and the house of **D**, 1858
3: 8 I haven't handed you over to **D**. 1858
3: 9 for **D** what the LORD promised him 1858
3:12 on his behalf to say to **D**, 1858
3:13 "Good," said **D**. NIH
3:14 Then **D** sent messengers to Ish-Bosheth son 1858
3:17 to make **D** your king. 1858
3:18 For the LORD promised **D**, 1858
3:18 'By my servant **D** I will rescue my people Israel 1858
3:19 to Hebron to tell **D** everything that Israel 1858
3:20 came to **D** at Hebron, 1858
3:20 **D** prepared a feast for him and his men. 1858
3:21 Then Abner said to **D**, 1858
3:21 **D** sent Abner away, and he went in peace. 1858
3:22 But Abner was no longer with **D** in Hebron, 1858
3:22 because **D** had sent him away, NIH
3:26 Joab then left **D** and sent messengers 1858
3:26 But **D** did not know it. 1858
3:28 Later, when **D** heard about this, he said, 1858
3:31 **D** said to Joab and all the people with him, 1858
3:31 King **D** himself walked behind the bier. 1858
3:35 Then they all came and urged **D** 1858
3:35 but **D** took an oath, saying, 1858
4: 8 They brought the head of Ish-Bosheth to **D** 1858
4: 9 **D** answered Recab and his brother Baanah, 1858
4:12 So **D** gave an order to his men, 1858
5: 1 All the tribes of Israel came to **D** at Hebron 1858
5: 3 of Israel had come to King **D** at Hebron, 1858
5: 3 and they anointed **D** king over Israel 1858
5: 4 **D** was thirty years old 1858
5: 6 The Jebusites said to **D**, 1858
5: 6 They thought, "**D** cannot get in here." 1858
5: 7 **D** captured the fortress of Zion, 1858
5: 7 the fortress of Zion, the City of **D**. 1858
5: 8 On that day, **D** said, 1858
5: 9 **D** then took up residence in the fortress 1858
5: 9 in the fortress and called it the City of **D**. 1858
5:11 Hiram king of Tyre sent messengers to **D**, 1858
5:11 and they built a palace for **D**. 1858
5:12 And **D** knew that the LORD 1858
5:13 **D** took more concubines and wives 1858
5:17 that **D** had been anointed king over Israel, 1858
5:17 but **D** heard about it and went down to 1858
5:19 so **D** inquired of the LORD, 1858
5:20 So **D** went to Baal Perazim, 1858
5:21 and **D** and his men carried them off. 1858
5:23 so **D** inquired of the LORD, 1858
5:25 So **D** did as the LORD commanded him, 1858
6: 1 **D** again brought together out 1858
6: 5 **D** and the whole house of Israel 1858
6: 8 Then **D** was angry because 1858
6: 9 **D** was afraid of the LORD that day 1858

2Sa 6:10 the LORD to be with him in the City of **D**. 1858
6:12 Now King **D** was told, 1858
6:12 So **D** went down and brought up the ark 1858
6:12 the house of Obed-Edom to the City of **D** 1858
6:14 **D**, wearing a linen ephod, 1858
6:16 of the LORD was entering the City of **D**, 1858
6:16 when she saw King **D** leaping and dancing 1858
6:17 inside the tent that **D** had pitched for it, 1858
6:17 and **D** sacrificed burnt offerings 1858
6:20 **D** returned home to bless his household, 1858
6:21 **D** said to Michal, "It was before 1858
7: 5 "Go and tell my servant **D**, 'This is what 1858
7: 8 "Now then, tell my servant **D**, 1858
7:17 to **D** all the words of this entire revelation. 1858
7:18 King **D** went in and sat before the LORD, 1858
7:20 "What more can **D** say to you? 1858
7:26 And the house of your servant **D** will 1858
8: 1 **D** defeated the Philistines 1858
8: 2 **D** also defeated the Moabites. NIH
8: 2 So the Moabites became subject to **D** 1858
8: 3 **D** fought Hadadezer son of Rehob, 1858
8: 4 **D** captured a thousand of his chariots, 1858
8: 5 **D** struck down twenty-two thousand 1858
8: 6 The LORD gave **D** victory wherever he went. 1858
8: 7 **D** took the gold shields that belonged to 1858
8: 8 King **D** took a great quantity of bronze. 1858
8: 9 of Hamath heard that **D** had defeated 1858
8:10 he sent his son Joram to King **D** 1858
8:11 King **D** dedicated these articles to 1858
8:13 And **D** became famous after he returned 1858
8:14 and all the Edomites became subject to **D**. 1858
8:14 The LORD gave **D** victory wherever he went. 1858
8:15 **D** reigned over all Israel, 1858
9: 1 **D** asked, "Is there anyone still left of 1858
9: 2 They called him to appear before **D**, 1858
9: 5 So King **D** had him brought from Lo Debar, 1858
9: 6 the son of Saul, came to **D**, 1858
9: 6 **D** said, "Mephibosheth!" 1858
9: 7 "Don't be afraid," **D** said to him, 1858
10: 2 **D** thought, "I will show kindness 1858
10: 2 So **D** sent a delegation 1858
10: 3 "Do you think **D** is honoring your father 1858
10: 3 Hasn't **D** sent them to you to explore 1858
10: 5 When **D** was told about this, 1858
10: 7 **D** sent Joab out with the entire army 1858
10:17 When **D** was told of this, 1858
10:17 to meet **D** and fought against him. 1858
10:18 and **D** killed seven hundred 1858
11: 1 **D** sent Joab out with the king's men and 1858
11: 1 But **D** remained in Jerusalem 1858
11: 2 One evening **D** got up from his bed 1858
11: 3 and **D** sent someone to find out about her. 1858
11: 4 Then **D** sent messengers to get her. 1858
11: 5 The woman conceived and sent word to **D**, 1858
11: 6 So **D** sent this word to Joab: 1858
11: 6 And Joab sent him to **D**. 1858
11: 7 **D** asked him how Joab was, 1858
11: 8 Then **D** said to Uriah, 1858
11:10 When **D** was told, 1858
11:11 Uriah said to **D**, "The ark and Israel and 1858
11:12 Then **D** said to him, 1858
11:13 and **D** made him drunk. NIH
11:14 In the morning **D** wrote a letter to Joab 1858
11:18 Joab sent **D** a full account of the battle. 1858
11:22 he told **D** everything Joab had sent him 1858
11:23 The messenger said to **D**, 1858
11:25 **D** told the messenger, "Say this to Joab: 1858
11:27 **D** had her brought to his house, 1858
11:27 thing **D** had done displeased the LORD. 1858
12: 1 The LORD sent Nathan to **D**. 1858
12: 5 **D** burned with anger against the man 1858
12: 7 Then Nathan said to **D**, "You are the man! 1858
12:13 Then **D** said to Nathan, 1858
12:15 the child that Uriah's wife had borne to **D**, 1858
12:16 **D** pleaded with God for the child. 1858
12:18 we spoke to **D** but he would not listen to us. 2257[S]
12:19 **D** noticed that his servants were whispering 1858
12:20 Then **D** got up from the ground. 1858
12:24 Then **D** comforted his wife Bathsheba, 1858
12:27 Joab then sent messengers to **D**, saying, 1858
12:29 So **D** mustered the entire army and went 1858
12:31 Then **D** and his entire army returned 1858
13: 1 Amnon son of **D** fell in love with Tamar, 1858
13: 1 the beautiful sister of Absalom son of **D**. 1858
13: 7 **D** sent word to Tamar at the palace: 1858
13:21 When King **D** heard all this, he was furious. 1858
13:30 the report came to **D**: 1858
13:37 But King **D** mourned for his son every day. NIH
15:13 A messenger came and told **D**, 1858
15:14 Then **D** said to all his officials who were 1858
15:22 **D** said to Ittai, "Go ahead, march on." 1858
15:30 But **D** continued up the Mount of Olives, 1858
15:31 Now **D** had been told, 1858
15:31 So **D** prayed, "O LORD, 1858
15:32 When **D** arrived at the summit, 1858
15:33 **D** said to him, "If you go with me, 1858
16: 1 When **D** had gone a short distance beyond 1858
16: 5 As King **D** approached Bahurim, 1858
16: 6 He pelted **D** and all the king's officials 1858
16:10 'Curse **D**,' who can ask, 1858
16:11 **D** then said to Abishai and all his officials, 1858
16:13 So **D** and his men continued along the road 1858
16:23 how both **D** and Absalom regarded all 1858
17: 1 and set out tonight in pursuit of **D**. 1858
17:16 a message immediately and tell **D**, 'Do 1858
17:17 and they were to go and tell King **D**, 1858
17:21 of the well and went to inform King **D**. 1858

2Sa 17:22 So **D** and all the people with him set out 1858
17:24 **D** went to Mahanaim, 1858
17:27 When **D** came to Mahanaim, 1858
17:29 from cows' milk for **D** and his people 1858
18: 1 **D** mustered the men who were with him 1858
18: 2 **D** sent the troops out— 1858
18:24 While **D** was sitting between the inner 1858
19:11 King **D** sent this message to Zadok 1858
19:16 with the men of Judah to meet King **D**. 1858
19:22 **D** replied, "What do you and I have 1858
19:43 a greater claim on **D** than you have. 1858
20: 1 "We have no share in **D**, 1858
20: 2 of Israel deserted **D** to follow Sheba son 1858
20: 3 **D** returned to his palace in Jerusalem, 1858
20: 6 **D** said to Abishai, 1858
20:11 and whoever is for **D**, let him follow Joab!" 1858
20:21 up his hand against the king, against **D**. 1858
21: 1 During the reign of **D**, 1858
21: 1 so **D** sought the face of the LORD. 1858
21: 3 **D** asked the Gibeonites, 1858
21: 4 to do for you?" **D** asked. NIH
21: 7 of the oath before the LORD between **D** 1858
21:11 **D** was told what Aiah's daughter Rizpah, 1858
21:13 **D** brought the bones of Saul NIH
21:15 **D** went down with his men to fight against 1858
21:16 said he would kill **D**. 1858
21:22 and they fell at the hands of **D** and his men. 1858
22: 1 **D** sang to the LORD the words 1858
22:51 to **D** and his descendants forever." 1858
23: 1 These are the last words of **D**: 1858
23: 1 "The oracle of **D** son of Jesse, 1858
23: 9 he was with **D** when they taunted 1858
23:13 of the thirty chief men came down to **D** at 1858
23:14 At that time **D** was in the stronghold, 1858
23:15 **D** longed for water and said, "Oh, 1858
23:16 of Bethlehem and carried it back to **D**. 1858
23:17 And **D** would not drink it. NIH
23:23 And **D** put him in charge of his bodyguard. 1858
24: 1 and he incited **D** against them, saying, 1858
24:10 **D** was conscience-stricken 1858
24:11 Before **D** got up the next morning, 1858
24:12 and tell **D**, 'This is what the LORD says: 1858
24:13 So Gad went to **D** and said to him, 1858
24:14 **D** said to Gad, "I am in deep distress. 1858
24:17 When **D** saw the angel who was striking 1858
24:18 On that day Gad went to **D** and said to him, 1858
24:19 So **D** went up, as the LORD had commanded 1858
24:21 "To buy your threshing floor," **D** answered, 1858
24:22 Araunah said to **D**, "Let my lord the king 1858
24:24 So **D** bought the threshing floor and 1858
24:25 **D** built an altar to the LORD there 1858
1Ki 1: 1 King **D** was old and well advanced in years, 1858
1:13 Go in to King **D** and say to him, 1858
1:28 Then King **D** said, "Call in Bathsheba." 1858
1:31 said, "May my lord King **D** live forever!" 1858
1:32 King **D** said, "Call in Zadok the priest, 1858
1:37 the throne of my lord King **D**!" 1858
1:43 "Our lord King **D** has made Solomon king. 1858
1:47 to congratulate our lord King **D**, 1858
2: 1 When the time drew near for **D** to die, 1858
2:10 Then **D** rested with his fathers 1858
2:10 and was buried in the City of **D**. 1858
2:12 Solomon sat on the throne of his father **D**, 1858
2:24 the throne of my father **D** and has founded 1858
2:26 the Sovereign LORD before my father **D** 1858
2:32 of my father **D** he attacked two men 1858
2:33 But on **D** and his descendants, 1858
2:44 the wrong you did to my father **D**. 1858
3: 1 of **D** until he finished building his palace 1858
3: 3 according to the statutes of his father **D**, 1858
3: 6 my father **D**, because he was faithful to you 1858
3: 7 king in place of my father **D**. 1858
3:14 and commands as **D** your father did, 1858
5: 1 to succeed his father **D**, NIH
5: 1 on friendly terms with **D**. 1858
5: 3 of the wars waged against my father **D** 1858
5: 5 as the LORD told my father **D**, 1858
5: 7 for he has given **D** a wise son to rule 1858
6:12 the promise I gave to **D** your father. 1858
7:51 in the things his father **D** had dedicated— 1858
8: 1 from Zion, the City of **D**. 1858
8:15 with his own mouth to my father **D**. 1858
8:16 I have chosen **D** to rule my people Israel.' 1858
8:17 "My father **D** had it in his heart to build 1858
8:18 But the LORD said to my father **D**, 1858
8:20 I have succeeded **D** my father and now I sit 1858
8:24 to your servant **D** my father; 1858
8:25 keep for your servant **D** my father 1858
8:26 let your word that you promised your servant **D** my father come true. 1858
8:66 for his servant **D** and his people Israel. 1858
9: 4 as **D** your father did, and do all 1858
9: 5 as I promised **D** your father when I said, 1858
9:24 of **D** to the palace Solomon had built 1858
11: 4 as the heart of **D** his father had been. 1858
11: 6 as **D** his father had done. 1858
11:12 Nevertheless, for the sake of **D** your father, 1858
11:13 the sake of **D** my servant and for the sake 1858
11:15 Earlier when **D** was fighting with Edom, 1858
11:21 that **D** rested with his fathers and that Joab 1858
11:24 when **D** destroyed the forces [of Zobah]; 1858
11:27 in the wall of the city of **D** his father. 1858
11:32 of my servant **D** and the city of Jerusalem, 1858
11:33 nor kept my statutes and laws as **D**, 1858
11:34 of his life for the sake of **D** my servant, 1858
11:36 that **D** my servant may always have a lamp 1858
11:38 as **D** my servant did, I will be with you. 1858
1Ki 11:38 as the one I built for **D** and will give Israel 1858
11:43 and was buried in the city of **D** his father. 1858
12:16 "What share do we have in **D**, 1858
12:16 Look after your own house, O **D**!" 1858
12:19 in rebellion against the house of **D** 1858
12:20 of Judah remained loyal to the house of **D**. 1858
12:26 now likely revert to the house of **D**. 1858
13: 2 be born to the house of **D**. 1858
14: 8 from the house of **D** and gave it to you, 1858
14: 8 but you have not been like my servant **D**, 1858
14:31 and was buried with them in the City of **D**. 1858
15: 3 as the heart of **D** his forefather had been. 1858
15: 5 For **D** had done what was right in the eyes 1858
15: 8 and was buried in the City of **D**. 1858
15:11 as his father **D** had done. 1858
15:24 with them in the city of his father **D**. 1858
22:50 with them in the city of **D** his father. 1858
2Ki 8:19 Nevertheless, for the sake of his servant **D**, 1858
8:19 He had promised to maintain a lamp for **D** 2257[S]
8:24 and was buried with them in the City of **D**. 1858
9:28 in his tomb in the City of **D**. 1858
11:10 that had belonged to King **D** and that were 1858
12:21 with his fathers in the City of **D**. 1858
14: 3 but not as his father **D** had done. 1858
14:20 in the City of **D**. 1858
15: 7 and was buried near them in the City of **D**. 1858
15:38 and was buried with them in the City of **D**, 1858
16: 2 Unlike **D** his father, he did not do what 1858
16:20 and was buried with them in the City of **D**. 1858
17:21 he tore Israel away from the house of **D**, 1858
18: 3 just as his father **D** had done. 1858
19:34 my sake and for the sake of **D** my servant." 1858
20: 5 the God of your father **D**, says: 1858
20: 6 and for the sake of my servant **D**.' " 1858
21: 7 of which the LORD had said to **D** and 1858
22: 2 and walked in all the ways of his father **D**, 1858
1Ch 2:15 the sixth Ozem and the seventh **D**. 1858
3: 1 These were the sons of **D** born to him 1858
3: 4 These six were born to **D** in Hebron, 2257[S]
3: 4 **D** reigned in Jerusalem thirty-three years, NIH
3: 9 All these were the sons of **D**, 1858
4:31 These were their towns until the reign of **D**. 1858
6:31 the men **D** put in charge of the music in 1858
7: 2 During the reign of **D**, 1858
9:22 to their positions of trust by **D** and Samuel 1858
10:14 and turned the kingdom over to **D** son 1858
11: 1 All Israel came together to **D** at Hebron 1858
11: 3 of Israel had come to King **D** at Hebron, 1858
11: 3 and they anointed **D** king over Israel, 1858
11: 4 **D** and all the Israelites marched 1858
11: 5 said to **D**, "You will not get in here." 1858
11: 5 **D** captured the fortress of Zion, 1858
11: 5 the fortress of Zion, the City of **D**. 1858
11: 6 **D** had said, "Whoever leads the attack on 1858
11: 7 **D** then took up residence in the fortress, 1858
11: 7 and so it was called the City of **D**. 1858
11: 9 And **D** became more and more powerful, 1858
11:13 He was with **D** at Pas Dammim when 1858
11:15 the thirty chiefs came down to **D** to the rock 1858
11:16 At that time **D** was in the stronghold, 1858
11:17 **D** longed for water and said, "Oh, 1858
11:18 of Bethlehem and carried it back to **D**. 1858
11:19 **D** would not drink it. NIH
11:25 And **D** put him in charge of his bodyguard. 1858
12: 1 to **D** at Ziklag, while he was banished from 1858
12: 8 to **D** at his stronghold in the desert. 1858
12:16 and some men from Judah also came to **D** 1858
12:17 **D** went out to meet them and said to them, 1858
12:18 "We are yours, O **D**! 1858
12:18 So **D** received them and made them leaders 1858
12:19 of Manasseh defected to **D** when he went 1858
12:20 When **D** went to Ziklag, 2257[S]
12:21 They helped **D** against raiding bands, 1858
12:22 Day after day men came to help **D**, 1858
12:23 to **D** at Hebron to turn Saul's kingdom over 1858
12:31 by name to come and make **D** king— 1858
12:33 to help **D** with undivided loyalty— NIH
12:38 to Hebron fully determined to make **D** king 1858
12:38 also of one mind to make **D** king. 1858
12:39 The men spent three days there with **D**, 1858
13: 1 **D** conferred with each of his officers, 1858
13: 5 So **D** assembled all the Israelites, 1858
13: 6 **D** and all the Israelites with him went 1858
13: 8 **D** and all the Israelites were celebrating 1858
13:11 Then **D** was angry because 1858
13:12 **D** was afraid of God that day and asked, 1858
13:13 the ark to be with him in the City of **D**. 1858
14: 1 Hiram king of Tyre sent messengers to **D**, 1858
14: 2 And **D** knew that the LORD had 1858
14: 3 In Jerusalem **D** took more wives 1858
14: 8 that **D** had been anointed king 1858
14: 8 **D** heard about it and went out to meet them. 1858
14:10 so **D** inquired of God: 1858
14:11 So **D** and his men went up to Baal Perazim, 1858
14:12 and **D** gave orders to burn them in the fire. 1858
14:14 so **D** inquired of God again, 1858
14:16 So **D** did as God commanded him, 1858
15: 1 After **D** had constructed buildings NIH
15: 1 for himself in the City of **D**, 1858
15: 2 Then **D** said, "No one but the Levites 1858
15: 3 **D** assembled all Israel in Jerusalem to bring 1858
15:11 Then **D** summoned Zadok and Abiathar 1858
15:16 **D** told the leaders of the Levites 1858
15:25 So **D** and the elders of Israel and 1858
15:27 Now **D** was clothed in a robe of fine linen, 1858
15:27 **D** also wore a linen ephod. 1858
15:29 of the LORD was entering the City of **D**, 1858
1Ch 15:29 she saw King **D** dancing and celebrating, 1858
16: 1 and set it inside the tent that **D** had pitched 1858
16: 2 After **D** had finished sacrificing 1858
16: 7 That day **D** first committed to Asaph 1858
16:37 **D** left Asaph and his associates before NIH
16:39 **D** left Zadok the priest NIH
16:43 and **D** returned home to bless his family. 1858
17: 1 After **D** was settled in his palace, 1858
17: 2 Nathan replied to **D**, 1858
17: 4 "Go and tell my servant **D**, 'This is what 1858
17: 7 "Now then, tell my servant **D**, 1858
17:15 to **D** all the words of this entire revelation. 1858
17:16 King **D** went in and sat before the LORD, 1858
17:18 "What more can **D** say to you 1858
17:24 And the house of your servant **D** will 1858
18: 1 **D** defeated the Philistines 1858
18: 2 **D** also defeated the Moabites, 1858
18: 3 **D** fought Hadadezer king of Zobah, 1858
18: 4 **D** captured a thousand of his chariots, 1858
18: 5 **D** struck down twenty-two thousand 1858
18: 6 The LORD gave **D** victory everywhere he went. 1858
18: 7 **D** took the gold shields carried by 1858
18: 8 **D** took a great quantity of bronze, 1858
18: 9 of Hamath heard that **D** had defeated 1858
18:10 he sent his son Hadoram to King **D** 1858
18:11 King **D** dedicated these articles to 1858
18:13 and all the Edomites became subject to **D**. 1858
18:13 The LORD gave **D** victory everywhere he went. 1858
18:14 **D** reigned over all Israel, 1858
19: 2 **D** thought, "I will show kindness 1858
19: 2 So **D** sent a delegation 1858
19: 3 "Do you think **D** is honoring your father 1858
19: 5 someone came and told **D** about the men, 1858
19: 8 **D** sent Joab out with the entire army 1858
19:17 When **D** was told of this, 1858
19:17 **D** formed his lines to meet the Arameans 1858
19:18 and **D** killed seven thousand 1858
19:19 with **D** and became subject to him. 1858
20: 1 but **D** remained in Jerusalem. 1858
20: 2 **D** took the crown from the head 1858
20: 3 **D** did this to all the Ammonite towns. 1858
20: 3 Then **D** and his entire army returned 1858
20: 8 and they fell at the hands of **D** and his men. 1858
21: 1 against Israel and incited **D** to take a census 1858
21: 2 So **D** said to Joab and the commanders of 1858
21: 5 the number of the fighting men to **D**: 1858
21: 8 Then **D** said to God, 1858
21:10 and tell **D**, 'This is what the LORD says: 1858
21:11 So Gad went to **D** and said to him, 1858
21:13 **D** said to Gad, "I am in deep distress. 1858
21:16 **D** looked up and saw the angel of 1858
21:16 Then **D** and the elders, clothed in sackcloth, 1858
21:17 **D** said to God, 1858
21:18 the LORD ordered Gad to tell **D** to go up 1858
21:19 So **D** went up in obedience to the word 1858
21:21 Then **D** approached, and 1858
21:21 down before **D** with his face to the ground. 1858
21:22 **D** said to him, 1858
21:23 Araunah said to **D**, "Take it! 1858
21:24 But King **D** replied to Araunah, "No, 1858
21:25 So **D** paid Araunah six hundred shekels 1858
21:26 **D** built an altar to the LORD there 1858
21:28 when **D** saw that 1858
21:30 **D** could not go before it to inquire of God, 1858
22: 1 Then **D** said, "The house of 1858
22: 2 So **D** gave orders to assemble 1858
22: 4 brought large numbers of them to **D**. 1858
22: 5 **D** said, "My son Solomon is young 1858
22: 5 So **D** made extensive preparations 1858
22: 7 **D** said to Solomon: 1858
22:17 Then **D** ordered all the leaders of Israel 1858
23: 1 When **D** was old and full of years, 1858
23: 4 **D** said, "Of these, twenty-four thousand are NIH
23: 6 **D** divided the Levites 1858
23:25 For **D** had said, "Since the LORD, 1858
23:27 According to the last instructions of **D**, 1858
24: 3 **D** separated them into divisions 1858
24:31 in the presence of King **D** and of Zadok, 1858
25: 1 **D**, together with the commanders of 1858
26:26 for the things dedicated by King **D**, 1858
26:32 and King **D** put them in charge of 1858
27:18 Elihu, a brother of **D**; 1858
27:23 **D** did not take the number of 1858
27:24 in the book of the annals of King **D**. 1858
28: 1 **D** summoned all the officials of Israel 1858
28: 2 King **D** rose to his feet and said: 1858
28:11 Then **D** gave his son Solomon the plans for 1858
28:19 **D** said, "I have in writing from the hand of NIH
28:20 **D** also said to Solomon his son, 1858
29: 1 Then King **D** said to the whole assembly: 1858
29: 9 **D** the king also rejoiced greatly. 1858
29:10 **D** praised the LORD in the presence of 1858
29:20 Then **D** said to the whole assembly, 1858
29:22 Then they acknowledged Solomon son of **D** 1858
29:23 the LORD as king in place of his father **D**. 1858
29:26 **D** son of Jesse was king over all Israel. 1858
2Ch 1: 1 of **D** established himself firmly 1858
1: 4 Now **D** had brought up the ark of God 1858
1: 8 to **D** my father and have made me king 1858
1: 9 let your promise to my father **D** 1858
2: 3 for my father **D** when you sent him cedar 1858
2: 7 whom my father **D** provided. 1858
2:12 He has given King **D** a wise son, 1858
2:14 and with those of my lord, **D** your father. 1858
2:17 after the census his father **D** had taken; 1858

2Ch 3: 1 the LORD had appeared to his father **D.** 1858
3: 1 the place provided by **D.** 1858
5: 1 in the things his father **D** had dedicated— 1858
5: 2 from Zion, the City of **D.** 1858
6: 4 with his mouth to my father **D.** 1858
6: 6 I have chosen **D** to rule my people Israel.' 1858
6: 7 "My father **D** had it in his heart to build 1858
6: 8 But the LORD said to my father **D,** 1858
6:10 I have succeeded **D** my father and now I sit 1858
6:15 to your servant **D** my father; 1858
6:16 keep for your servant **D** my father 1858
6:17 you promised your servant **D** come true. 1858
6:42 the great love promised to **D** your servant." 1858
7: 6 which King **D** had made for praising 1858
7:10 the good things the LORD had done for **D** 1858
7:17 if you walk before me as **D** your father did, 1858
7:18 as I covenanted with **D** your father 1858
8:11 the City of **D** to the palace he had built 1858
8:11 not live in the palace of **D** king of Israel, 1858
8:14 with the ordinance of his father **D,** 1858
8:14 because this was what **D** the man 1858
9:31 and was buried in the city of **D** his father. 1858
10:16 "What share do we have in **D,** 1858
10:16 Look after your own house, O **D!"** 1858
10:19 in rebellion against the house of **D** 1858
11:17 walking in the ways of **D** and Solomon 1858
12:16 and was buried in the City of **D.** 1858
13: 5 of Israel to **D** and his descendants forever 1858
13: 6 an official of Solomon son of **D,** 1858
14: 1 and was buried in the City of **D.** 1858
16:14 for himself in the City of **D.** 1858
17: 3 in the ways his father **D** had followed. 1858
21: 1 and was buried with them in the City of **D.** 1858
21: 7 the covenant the LORD had made with **D,** 1858
21: 7 not willing to destroy the house of **D.** 1858
21:12 the God of your father **D,** says: 1858
21:20 and was buried in the City of **D,** 1858
23: 3 concerning the descendants of **D.** 1858
23: 9 that had belonged to King **D** and that were 1858
23:18 to whom **D** had made assignments in 1858
23:18 and singing, as **D** had ordered. 1858
24:16 with the kings in the City of **D,** 1858
24:25 So he died and was buried in the City of **D,** 1858
27: 9 and was buried in the City of **D.** 1858
28: 1 Unlike **D** his father, he did not do what 1858
29: 2 just as his father **D** had done. 1858
29:25 harps and lyres in the way prescribed by **D** 1858
29:27 by trumpets and the instruments of **D** king 1858
29:30 with the words of **D** and of Asaph the seer. 1858
30:26 of **D** king of Israel there had been nothing 1858
32: 5 the supporting terraces of the City of **D.** 1858
32:30 down to the west side of the City of **D.** 1858
33: 7 of which God had said to **D** and 1858
33:14 of the City of **D,** west of the Gihon spring 1858
34: 2 and walked in the ways of his father **D,** 1858
34: 3 he began to seek the God of his father **D.** 1858
35: 3 that Solomon son of **D** king of Israel built. 1858
35: 4 to the directions written by **D** king of Israel 1858
35:15 were in the places prescribed by **D,** Asaph, 1858
Ezr 3:10 as prescribed by **D** king of Israel. 1858
8: 2 of the descendants of **D,** 1858
8:20 that **D** and the officials had established 1858
Ne 3:15 as the steps going down from the City of **D.** 1858
3:16 up to a point opposite the tombs of **D,** 1858
12:24 as prescribed by **D** the man of God. 1858
12:36 with musical instruments [prescribed by] **D** 1858
12:37 up the steps of the City of **D** on the ascent 1858
12:37 the wall and passed above the house of **D** to 1858
12:45 the commands of **D** and his son Solomon. 1858
12:46 For long ago, in the days of **D** and Asaph, 1858
Ps 3: T A psalm of **D.** 1858
4: T A psalm of **D.** 1858
5: T A psalm of **D.** 1858
6: T A psalm of **D.** 1858
7: T A shiggaion of **D,** 1858
8: T A psalm of **D.** 1858
9: T A psalm of **D.** 1858
11: T For the director of music. Of **D.** 1858
12: T A psalm of **D.** 1858
13: T For the director of music. A psalm of **D.** 1858
14: T For the director of music. Of **D.** 1858
15: T A psalm of **D.** 1858
16: T A miktam of **D.** 1858
17: T A prayer of **D.** 1858
18: T Of **D** the servant of the LORD. 1858
18:50 to **D** and his descendants forever. 1858
19: T For the director of music. A psalm of **D.** 1858
20: T For the director of music. A psalm of **D.** 1858
21: T For the director of music. A psalm of **D.** 1858
22: T A psalm of **D.** 1858
23: T A psalm of **D.** 1858
24: T Of **D.** A psalm. 1858
25: T Of **D.** 1858
26: T Of **D.** 1858
27: T Of **D.** 1858
28: T Of **D.** 1858
29: T A psalm of **D.** 1858
30: T of the temple. Of **D.** 1858
31: T For the director of music. A psalm of **D.** 1858
32: T Of **D.** A maskil. 1858
34: T Of **D.** When he pretended to be 1858
35: T Of **D.** 1858
36: T Of **D** the servant of the LORD. 1858
37: T Of **D.** 1858
38: T A psalm of **D.** A petition. 1858
39: T A psalm of **D.** 1858
40: T For the director of music. Of **D.** A psalm. 1858
Ps 41: T For the director of music. A psalm of **D.** 1858
51: T A psalm of **D.** 1858
51: T to him after **D** had committed adultery NIH
52: T A maskil of **D.** 1858
52: T "**D** has gone to the house of Ahimelech." 1858
53: T A maskil of **D.** 1858
54: T A maskil of **D.** 1858
54: T "Is not **D** hiding among us?" 1858
55: T A maskil of **D.** 1858
56: T on Distant Oaks." Of **D.** 1858
57: T "Do Not Destroy." Of **D.** 1858
58: T "Do Not Destroy." Of **D.** 1858
59: T "Do Not Destroy." Of **D.** 1858
60: T A miktam of **D.** 1858
61: T With stringed instruments. Of **D.** 1858
62: T A psalm of **D.** 1858
63: T A psalm of **D.** 1858
64: T For the director of music. A psalm of **D.** 1858
65: T A psalm of **D.** 1858
68: T For the director of music. Of **D.** 1858
69: T To [the tune of] "Lilies." Of **D.** 1858
70: T For the director of music. Of **D.** A petition. 1858
72:20 This concludes the prayers of **D** son 1858
78:70 He chose **D** his servant and took him from 1858
78:72 **D** shepherded them with integrity of heart; NIH
86: T A prayer of **D.** 1858
89: 3 I have sworn to **D** my servant, 1858
89:20 I have found **D** my servant; 1858
89:35 and I will not lie to **D**— 1858
89:49 in your faithfulness you swore to **D?** 1858
101: T Of **D.** A psalm. 1858
103: T Of **D.** 1858
108: T A song. A psalm of **D.** 1858
109: T For the director of music. Of **D.** A psalm. 1858
110: T Of **D.** A psalm. 1858
122: T A song of ascents. Of **D.** 1858
122: 5 the thrones of the house of **D.** 1858
124: T A song of ascents. Of **D.** 1858
131: T A song of ascents. Of **D.** 1858
132: 1 remember **D** and all 1858
132:10 For the sake of **D** your servant, 1858
132:11 The LORD swore an oath to **D,** 1858
132:17 "Here I will make a horn grow for **D** 1858
133: T A song of ascents. Of **D.** 1858
138: T Of **D.** 1858
139: T For the director of music. Of **D.** A psalm. 1858
140: T For the director of music. A psalm of **D.** 1858
141: T A psalm of **D.** 1858
142: T A maskil of **D.** 1858
143: T A psalm of **D.** 1858
144: T Of **D.** 1858
144:10 who delivers his servant **D** from 1858
145: T A psalm of praise. Of **D.** 1858
Pr 1: 1 The proverbs of Solomon son of **D,** 1858
Ecc 1: 1 The words of the Teacher, son of **D,** 1858
SS 4: 4 Your neck is like the tower of **D,** 1858
Isa 7: 2 Now the house of **D** was told, 1858
7:13 Isaiah said, "Hear now, you house of **D!** 1858
16: 5 one from the house of **D**— 1858
22: 9 of **D** had many breaches in its defenses; 1858
22:22 on his shoulder the key to the house of **D;** 1858
29: 1 Ariel, Ariel, the city where **D** settled! 1858
37:35 my sake and for the sake of **D** my servant!" 1858
38: 5 the God of your father **D,** says: 1858
55: 3 my faithful love promised to **D.** 1858
Jer 21:12 O house of **D,** this is what the LORD says: 1858
22:30 the throne of **D** or rule anymore in Judah." 1858
23: 5 I will raise up to **D** a righteous Branch, 1858
30: 9 the LORD their God and **D** their king, 1858
33:17 '**D** will never fail to have a man to sit on 1858
33:21 then my covenant with **D** my servant— 1858
33:21 can be broken and **D** will no longer have 2257[S]
33:22 the descendants of **D** my servant and 1858
33:26 the descendants of Jacob and **D** my servant 1858
36:30 to sit on the throne of **D;** 1858
Eze 34:23 my servant **D,** and he will tend them; 1858
34:24 my servant **D** will be prince among them. 1858
37:24 " 'My servant **D** will be king over them, 1858
37:25 **D** my servant will be their prince forever. 1858
Hos 3: 5 the LORD their God and **D** their king. 1858
Am 6: 5 You strum away on your harps like **D** 1858
Zec 12: 7 of **D** and of Jerusalem's inhabitants may 1858
12: 8 that the feeblest among them will be like **D,** 1858
12: 8 and the house of **D** will be like God, 1858
12:10 "And I will pour out on the house of **D** and 1858
12:12 the clan of the house of **D** and their wives, 1858
13: 1 a fountain will be opened to the house of **D** 1858
Mt 1: 1 the genealogy of Jesus Christ the son *of* **D,** *1253*
1: 6 and Jesse the father of King **D.** *1253*
1: 6 **D** was the father of Solomon, *1253*
1:17 in all from Abraham to **D,** *1253*
1:17 fourteen from **D** to the exile to Babylon, *1253*
1:20 "Joseph son *of* **D,** *1253*
9:27 calling out, "Have mercy on us, Son *of* **D!"** *1253*
12: 3 "Haven't you read what **D** did when he *1253*
12:23 "Could this be the Son *of* **D?"** *1253*
15:22 "Lord, Son *of* **D,** have mercy on me! *1253*
20:30 "Lord, Son *of* **D,** have mercy on us!" *1253*
20:31 "Lord, Son *of* **D,** have mercy on us!" *1253*
21: 9 "Hosanna to the Son *of* **D!"** *1253*
21:15 "Hosanna to the Son *of* **D,"** *1253*
22:42 "The son *of* **D,"** they replied. *1253*
22:43 He said to them, "How is it then that **D,** *1253*
22:45 **D** calls him 'Lord,' how can he be his son?" *1253*
Mk 2:25 "Have you never read what **D** did when he *1253*
10:47 "Jesus, Son *of* **D,** have mercy on me!" *1253*
10:48 but he shouted all the more, "Son *of* **D,** *1253*
Mk 11:10 the coming kingdom *of* our father **D!"** *1253*
12:35 the law say that the Christ is the son *of* **D?** *1253*
12:36 **D** himself, speaking by the Holy Spirit, *1253*
12:37 **D** himself calls him 'Lord.' *1253*
Lk 1:27 a descendant *of* **D.** *1253*
1:32 the throne of his father **D,** *1253*
1:69 for us in the house *of* his servant **D** *1253*
2: 4 to Bethlehem the town *of* **D,** *1253*
2: 4 to the house and line *of* **D.** *1253*
2:11 in the town *of* **D** a Savior has been born *1253*
3:31 the son of Nathan, the son *of* **D,** *1253*
6: 3 "Have you never read what **D** did when he *1253*
18:38 He called out, "Jesus, Son *of* **D,** *1253*
18:39 but he shouted all the more, "Son *of* **D,** *1253*
20:41 that they say the Christ is the Son *of* **D?** *1253*
20:42 **D** himself declares in the Book of Psalms: *1253*
20:44 **D** calls him 'Lord.' *1253*
Jn 7:42 the town where **D** lived?" *1253*
Ac 1:16 through the mouth *of* **D** concerning Judas, *1253*
2:25 **D** said about him: *1253*
2:29 that the patriarch **D** died and was buried, *1253*
2:34 For **D** did not ascend to heaven, *1253*
4:25 the mouth of your servant, our father **D:** *1253*
7:45 It remained in the land until the time *of* **D,** *1253*
13:22 After removing Saul, he made **D** their king. *1253*
13:22 'I have found **D** son of Jesse a man *1253*
13:34 the holy and sure blessings promised to **D.'** *1253*
13:36 "For when **D** had served God's purpose *1253*
Ro 1: 3 to his human nature was a descendant of **D,** *1253*
4: 6 **D** says the same thing when he speaks of *1253*
11: 9 **D** says: "May their table become a snare *1253*
2Ti 2: 8 raised from the dead, descended from **D.** *1253*
Heb 4: 7 when a long time later he spoke through **D,** *1253*
11:32 Jephthah, **D,** Samuel and the prophets, *1253*
Rev 3: 7 who holds the key *of* **D.** *1253*
5: 5 the Root *of* **D,** has triumphed. *1253*
22:16 I am the Root and the Offspring *of* **D,** *1253*

DAVID'S (85) [DAVID]

1Sa 17:28 When Eliab, **D** oldest brother, 2257[S]
19:11 Saul sent men to **D** house to watch it and 1858
19:11 But Michal, **D** wife, warned him, 1858
20:15 of **D** enemies from the face of the earth." 1858
20:16 the LORD call **D** enemies to account." 1858
20:25 but **D** place was empty. 1858
20:27 **D** place was empty again. 1858
23: 3 But **D** men said to him, 1858
25: 9 When **D** men arrived, 1858
25: 9 they gave Nabal this message in **D** name. 1858
25:10 Nabal answered **D** servants, 1858
25:12 **D** men turned around and went back. 1858
25:42 with **D** messengers and became his wife. 1858
25:44 **D** wife, to Paltiel son of Laish, 1858
26:17 Saul recognized **D** voice and said, 1858
30: 5 **D** two wives had been captured— 1858
30:20 saying, "This is **D** plunder." 1858
30:22 and troublemakers among **D** followers said, 1858
2Sa 2:13 Joab son of Zeruiah and **D** men went out 1858
2:17 the men of Israel were defeated by **D** men. 1858
2:30 nineteen of **D** men were found missing. 1858
2:31 But **D** men had killed three hundred 1858
3: 5 Ithream the son of **D** wife Eglah. 1858
3:10 of Saul and establish **D** throne over Israel 1858
3:22 then **D** men and Joab returned from a raid 1858
5: 8 and blind' who are **D** enemies." 1858
8:18 and **D** sons were royal advisers. 1858
9:11 So Mephibosheth ate at **D** table like one of 2257[S]
10: 2 **D** men came to the land of the Ammonites, 1858
10: 4 So Hanun seized **D** men, 1858
10: 6 that they had become a stench in **D** nostrils, 1858
11:13 At **D** invitation, he ate and drank with him, 1858
11:17 some of the men in **D** army fell; 1858
12:18 **D** servants were afraid to tell him that 1858
12:30 and it was placed on **D** head. 1858
13: 3 of Shimeah, **D** brother. 1858
13:32 But Jonadab son of Shimeah, **D** brother, 1858
15:12 **D** counselor, to come from Giloh, 1858
15:37 So **D** friend Hushai arrived at Jerusalem 1858
16: 6 the special guard were on **D** right and left. 2257[S]
16:16 Then Hushai the Arkite, **D** friend, 1858
18: 7 the army of Israel was defeated by **D** men, 1858
18: 9 Now Absalom happened to meet **D** men. 1858
20:26 and Ira the Jairite was **D** priest. 1858+4200
21:17 Abishai son of Zeruiah came to **D** rescue; 2257[S]
21:17 Then **D** men swore to him, saying, 1858
21:21 Jonathan son of Shimeah, **D** brother, 1858
23: 8 are the names of **D** mighty men: 1858+4200
24:11 to Gad the prophet, **D** seer: 1858
1Ki 1: 8 **D** special guard did not join Adonijah. 1858+4200
1:11 without our lord **D** knowing it? 1858
1:38 on King **D** mule and escorted him to Gihon. 1858
2:45 and **D** throne will remain secure before 1858
11:39 I will humble **D** descendants because 1858
15: 4 for **D** sake the LORD his God gave him 1858
1Ch 11:10 were the chiefs of **D** mighty men— 1858+4200
11:11 this is the list of **D** mighty men: 1858+4200
14:17 So **D** fame spread throughout every land, 1858
18:17 and **D** sons were chief officials at 1858
19: 2 When **D** men came to Hanun in the land of 1858
19: 4 So Hanun seized **D** men, shaved them, 1858
19: 6 that they had become a stench in **D** nostrils, 1858
20: 2 and it was placed on **D** head. 1858
20: 7 Jonathan son of Shimea, **D** brother, 1858
21: 9 The LORD said to Gad, **D** seer, 1858
26:31 of **D** reign a search was made in 1858
27:31 officials in charge of King **D** property. 1858+4200

1Ch 27:32 Jonathan, **D** uncle, was a counselor, 1858
29:24 as well as all of King **D** sons, 1858
29:29 As for the events of King **D** reign, 1858
2Ch 11:18 who was the daughter of **D** son Jerimoth 1858
13: 8 which is in the hands of **D** descendants. 1858
29:26 the Levites stood ready with **D** instruments, 1858
32:33 where the tombs of **D** descendants are. 1858
Ps 59: T When Saul had sent men to watch **D** house 2021S
Isa 9: 7 on **D** throne and over his kingdom, 1858
Jer 13:13 the kings who sit on **D** throne, 1858+4200
17:25 then kings who sit on **D** throne will come 1858
22: 2 O king of Judah, you who sit on **D** throne— 1858
22: 4 kings who sit on **D** throne will come 1858+4200
29:16 about the king who sits on **D** throne and all 1858
33:15 a righteous Branch sprout from **D line;** 1858
Am 9:11 "In that day I will restore **D** fallen tent. 1858
Jn 7:42 that the Christ will come from **D** family and *1253*
Ac 15:16 this I will return and rebuild **D** fallen tent. *1253*

DAWN (33) [DAWNED, DAWNS]

Ge 19:15 With the coming of **d**, the angels urged Lot, 8840
Jdg 16: 2 saying, "At **d** we'll kill him." 240+1332+2021
19:25 and at **d** they let her go. 8840
1Sa 14:36 by night and plunder them till **d**, 240+1332+2021
Ne 4:21 **first light of d** till the stars came out. 6590+8840
Job 3: 9 in vain and not see the first rays of **d**, 8840
4:20 Between **d** and dusk they are broken 1332
7: 4 The night drags on, and I toss till **d**. 5974
38:12 or shown the **d** its place, 8840
41:18 his eyes are like the rays of **d**. 8840
Ps 37: 6 like the **d**, the justice of your cause like 240
57: 8 I will awaken the **d**. 8840
108: 2 Awake, harp and lyre! I will awaken the **d**. 8840
110: 3 the womb of the **d** you will receive the dew 5423
119:147 I rise before **d** and cry for help; 5974
139: 9 If I rise on the wings of the **d**, 8840
Pr 4:18 of the righteous is like the first gleam of **d**, 5586
SS 6:10 Who is this that appears like the **d**, 8840
Isa 8:20 they have no **light of d**. 8840
14:12 O morning star, son of the **d**! 8840
38:13 I waited patiently till **d**, 1332
58: 8 Then your light will break forth like the **d**, 8840
60: 3 and kings to the brightness of your **d**. 2437
62: 1 till her righteousness shines out like the **d**, 5586
Da 6:19 At the first light of **d**, 10740
Joel 2: 2 Like **d** spreading across the mountains 8840
Am 4:13 he who turns **d** to darkness, 8840
5: 8 into **d** and darkens day into night, who calls 1332
Jnh 4: 7 at **d** the next day God provided a worm, 8840
Mt 28: 1 *at* **d** on the first day of the week, *2216*
Mk 13:35 or when the rooster crows, or **at d**. *4745*
Jn 8: 2 *At* **d** he appeared again in the temple *3986*
Ac 27:33 Just before **d** Paul urged them all to eat. *1181+2465+3516*

DAWNED (5) [DAWN]

Ge 44: 3 *As* morning **d**, the men were sent 239
Dt 33: 2 from Sinai and **d** over them from Seir; 2436
Isa 9: 2 of the shadow of death a light *has* **d**. 5585
Mt 4:16 of the shadow of death a light *has* **d**." *422*
Ac 12:12 *When* this *had* **d on** him, *5328*

DAWNS (4) [DAWN]

Ps 65: 8 morning **d** and evening fades you call forth songs of 4604
112: 4 Even in darkness light **d** for the upright, 2436
Hos 10:15 When that **day d**, 8840
2Pe 1:19 until the day **d** and the morning star rises *1419*

DAY (1419) [DAILY, DAY'S, DAYBREAK, DAYLIGHT, DAYS, DAYTIME, EVERYDAY, MIDDAY, SEVEN-DAY, THREE-DAY]

Ge 1: 5 God called the light **"d,"** 3427
1: 5 and there was morning—the first **d**. 3427
1: 8 and there was morning—the second **d**. 3427
1:13 and there was morning—the third **d**. 3427
1:14 of the sky to separate the **d** from the night, 3427
1:16 the greater light to govern the **d** and 3427
1:18 to govern the **d** and the night, 3427
1:19 and there was morning—the fourth **d**. 3427
1:23 and there was morning—the fifth **d**. 3427
1:31 and there was morning—the sixth **d**. 3427
2: 2 By the seventh **d** God had finished 3427
2: 2 the seventh **d** he rested from all his work. 3427
2: 3 the seventh **d** and made it holy, 3427
3: 8 in the garden in the cool of the **d**, 3427
7:11 on the seventeenth **d** of the second month— 3427
7:11 on that **d** all the springs of 3427
7:13 On that very **d** Noah and his sons, Shem, 3427
8: 4 on the seventeenth **d** of the seventh month 3427
8: 5 on the first **d** of the tenth month the tops of NIH
8:13 By the first **d** of the first month NIH
8:14 the twenty-seventh **d** of the second month 3427
8:22 **d** and night will never cease." 3427
15:18 On that **d** the LORD made a covenant 3427
17:23 that very **d** Abraham took his son Ishmael 3427
17:26 both circumcised on that same **d**. 3427
18: 1 the entrance to his tent in the heat of the **d**. 3427
19:31 **One d** the older daughter said to 2256
19:34 The **next d** the older daughter said to 4740
21: 8 on the **d** Isaac was weaned Abraham held 3427
22: 4 On the third **d** Abraham looked up and saw 3427
22:14 And to this **d** it is said, 3427
Ge 26:32 That **d** Isaac's servants came and told him 3427
26:33 and to this **d** the name of the town 3427
27: 2 now an old man and don't know the **d** 3427
27:45 Why should I lose both of you *in* one **d**?" 3427
30:35 That same **d** he removed all the male goats 3427
31:22 On the third **d** Laban was told 3427
31:39 from me for whatever was stolen by **d** 3427
32:32 Therefore to this **d** the Israelites do not eat 3427
33:13 If they are driven hard just one **d**, 3427
33:16 that **d** Esau started on his way back to Seir. 3427
35: 3 who answered me in the **d** *of* my distress 3427
35:20 to this **d** that pillar marks Rachel's tomb. 3427
39:10 though she spoke to Joseph **d** *after* day, 3427
39:10 though she spoke to Joseph day after **d**, 3427
39:11 One **d** he went into the house to attend 3427
40:20 Now the third **d** was Pharaoh's birthday, 3427
42:18 On the third **d**, Joseph said to them, 3427
48:15 the God who has been my shepherd all my life to this **d**, 3427
48:20 He blessed them that **d** and said, 3427
Ex 2:11 One **d**, after Moses had grown up, 3427
2:13 The next **d** he went out 3427
5: 6 That same **d** Pharaoh gave this order to 3427
5:13 the work required of you **for each d**, 928+1821+3427+3427
5:19 of bricks required of you **for each d."** 928+1821+3427+3427
8:22 " 'But on that **d** I will deal differently with 3427
9: 6 And the **next d** the LORD did it: 4740
9:18 from the **d** it was founded till now. 3427
10: 6 the **d** they settled in this land till now.' " 3427
10:13 an east wind blow across the land all that **d** 3427
10:28 The **d** you see my face you will die." 3427
12: 3 on the tenth **d** of this month each man is NIH
12: 6 of them until the fourteenth **d** of the month, 3427
12:14 "This is a **d** you are to commemorate; 3427
12:15 On the first **d** remove the yeast 3427
12:15 from the first **d** through the seventh must 3427
12:16 On the first **d** hold a sacred assembly, 3427
12:16 and another one on the seventh **d**. 3427
12:17 because it was on this very **d** 3427
12:17 Celebrate this **d** as a lasting ordinance for 3427
12:18 from the evening of the fourteenth **d** until 3427
12:18 until the evening of the twenty-first **d**. 3427
12:41 At the end of the 430 years, to the very **d**, 3427
12:51 And on that very **d** the LORD brought 3427
13: 3 "Commemorate this **d**, 3427
13: 3 **the d** you came out of Egypt, 889S
13: 6 the seventh **d** hold a festival to the LORD. 3427
13: 8 On that **d** tell your son, 3427
13:21 **By d** the LORD went ahead of them in 3429
13:21 so that they could travel **by d** or night. 3429
13:22 the pillar of cloud **by d** nor the pillar of fire 3429
14:30 That **d** the LORD saved Israel from 3427
16: 1 on the fifteenth **d** of the second month 3427
16: 4 to go out each **d** and gather enough for NIH
16: 4 and gather enough for **that d**. 3427+3427
16: 5 On the sixth **d** they are 3427
16:22 the sixth **d**, they gathered twice as much— 3427
16:23 'Tomorrow is to be a **d of rest**, 8702
16:26 but on the seventh **d**, the Sabbath, 3427
16:27 of the people went out on the seventh **d** 3427
16:29 the sixth **d** he gives you bread for two days. 3427
16:29 to stay where he is on the seventh **d**; 3427
16:30 So the people rested on the seventh **d**. 3427
18:13 The **next d** Moses took his seat to serve 4740
19: 1 on the very **d—**they came to the Desert of 3427
19:11 and be ready by the third **d**, 3427
19:11 because on that **d** the LORD will come 3427
19:15 "Prepare yourselves for the third **d**. 3427
19:16 the third **d** there was thunder and lightning, 3427
20: 8 the Sabbath **d** by keeping it holy. 3427
20:10 but the seventh **d** is a Sabbath to 3427
20:11 but he rested on the seventh **d**. 3427
20:11 the LORD blessed the Sabbath **d** 3427
21:21 to be punished if the slave gets up after a **d** 3427
22:30 but give them to me on the eighth **d**. 3427
23:12 but on the seventh **d** do not work, 3427
24:16 the seventh **d** the LORD called to Moses 3427
29:36 Sacrifice a bull each **d** as a sin offering 3427
29:38 to offer on the altar regularly each **d**: 3427
31:14 on **that d** must be cut off from his people. 2023S
31:15 but the seventh **d** is a Sabbath of rest, 3427
31:15 on the Sabbath **d** must be put to death. 3427
31:17 on the seventh **d** he abstained from work 3427
32: 6 So the **next d** the people rose early 4740
32:28 and that **d** about three thousand of 3427
32:29 and he has blessed you this **d."** 3427
32:30 The **next d** Moses said to the people, 4740
34:21 but on the seventh **d** you shall rest; 3427
35: 2 but the seventh **d** shall be your holy day, 3427
35: 2 but the seventh day shall be your holy **d**, NIH
35: 3 in any of your dwellings on the Sabbath **d."** 3427
40: 2 on the first **d** *of* the first month. 3427
40:17 So the tabernacle was set up on the first **d** NIH
40:37 until the **d** it lifted. 3427
40:38 of the LORD was over the tabernacle **by d**, 3429
Lev 6: 5 on the **d** he presents his guilt offering. 3427
6:20 to the LORD on the **d** he is anointed: 3427
7:15 be eaten on the **d** it is offered; 3427
7:16 sacrifice shall be eaten on the **d** he offers it, 3427
7:16 over may be eaten on the **next d**. 4740
7:17 of the sacrifice left over till the third **d** must 3427
7:18 on the third **d**, 3427
7:35 and his sons on the **d** they were presented 3427
7:36 On the **d** they were anointed, 3427
7:38 on Mount Sinai on the **d** he commanded 3427
Lev 8:35 at the entrance to the Tent of Meeting **d** 3429
9: 1 On the eighth **d** Moses summoned Aaron 3427
12: 3 the eighth **d** the boy is to be circumcised. 3427
13: 5 the seventh **d** the priest is to examine him, 3427
13: 6 On the seventh **d** the priest is 3427
13:27 the seventh **d** the priest is to examine him, 3427
13:32 On the seventh **d** the priest is to examine 3427
13:34 On the seventh **d** the priest is to examine 3427
13:51 On the seventh **d** he is to examine it, 3427
14: 9 the seventh **d** he must shave off all his hair; 3427
14:10 the eighth **d** he must bring two male lambs 3427
14:23 "On the eighth **d** he must bring them 3427
14:39 On the seventh **d** the priest shall return 3427
15:14 On the eighth **d** he must take two doves 3427
15:29 On the eighth **d** she must take two doves 3427
16:29 On the tenth **d** of the seventh month NIH
16:30 on this **d** atonement will be made for you, 3427
19: 6 on the **d** you sacrifice it or on the next day; 3427
19: 6 on the day you sacrifice it or on the **next d**; 4740
19: 6 over until the third **d** must be burned up. 3427
19: 7 If any of it is eaten on the third **d**, 3427
22:27 From the eighth **d** on, 3427
22:28 or a sheep and its young on the same **d**. 3427
22:30 It must be eaten that same **d**; 3427
23: 3 but the seventh **d** is a Sabbath of rest, 3427
23: 3 a **d** of sacred assembly. NIH
23: 5 on the fourteenth **d** of the first month. NIH
23: 6 On the fifteenth **d** of that month 3427
23: 7 On the first **d** hold a sacred assembly 3427
23: 8 on the seventh **d** hold a sacred assembly 3427
23:11 to wave it on the **d after** the Sabbath. 4740
23:12 On the **d** you wave the sheaf, 3427
23:14 until the very **d** you bring this offering 3427
23:15 " 'From the **d after** the Sabbath, 4740
23:15 the **d** you brought the sheaf of 3427
23:16 up to the **d after** the seventh Sabbath, 4740
23:21 On that same **d** you are to proclaim 3427
23:24 'On the first **d** of the seventh month you are NIH
23:24 to have a **d of rest**, 8702
23:27 "The tenth **d** of this seventh month is NIH
23:27 this seventh month is the **D** of Atonement. 3427
23:28 Do no work on that **d**, 3427
23:28 because it is the **D** *of* Atonement, 3427
23:29 not deny himself on that **d** must be cut off 3427
23:30 among his people anyone who does any work on that **d**. 3427
23:32 the evening of the ninth **d** of the month NIH
23:34 'On the fifteenth **d** of the seventh month 3427
23:35 The first **d** is a sacred assembly; 3427
23:36 and on the eighth **d** hold a sacred assembly 3427
23:37 and drink offerings required for **each d**. 928+3427+3427
23:39 with the fifteenth **d** of the seventh month, 3427
23:39 the first **d** is a day of rest, 3427
23:39 the first day is a **d of rest**, 8702
23:39 and the eighth **d** also is a day of rest. 3427
23:39 and the eighth day also is a **d of rest.** 8702
23:40 the first **d** you are to take choice fruit from 3427
25: 9 on the tenth **d** of the seventh month; NIH
25: 9 on the **D** *of* Atonement sound the trumpet 3427
27:23 on that **d** as something holy to the LORD. 3427
Nu 1: 1 of Sinai on the first **d** of the second month NIH
1:18 the whole community together on the first **d** NIH
6: 9 he must shave his head on the **d** 3427
6: 9 of his cleansing—the seventh **d**. 3427
6:10 on the eighth **d** he must bring two doves 3427
6:11 That same **d** he is to consecrate his head. 3427
7:11 **"Each d** one leader is to bring his offering 2021+2021+3427+3427+4200+4200
7:12 the first **d** was Nahshon son of Amminadab 3427
7:18 On the second **d** Nethanel son of Zuar, 3427
7:24 On the third **d**, Eliab son of Helon, 3427
7:30 On the fourth **d** Elizur son of Shedeur, 3427
7:36 the fifth **d** Shelumiel son of Zurishaddai, 3427
7:42 On the sixth **d** Eliasaph son of Deuel, 3427
7:48 the seventh **d** Elishama son of Ammihud, 3427
7:54 On the eighth **d** Gamaliel son of Pedahzur, 3427
7:60 On the ninth **d** Abidan son of Gideoni, 3427
7:66 the tenth **d** Ahiezer son of Ammishaddai, 3427
7:72 On the eleventh **d** Pagiel son of Ocran, 3427
7:78 On the twelfth **d** Ahira son of Enan, 3427
9: 3 on the fourteenth **d** of this month, 3427
9: 5 of Sinai at twilight on the fourteenth **d** of 3427
9: 6 not celebrate the Passover on that **d** 3427
9: 6 they came to Moses and Aaron that same **d** 3427
9:11 They are to celebrate it on the fourteenth **d** 3427
9:15 On the **d** the tabernacle, 3427
9:21 Whether **by d** or by night, 3429
10:11 On the twentieth **d** of the second month of NIH
10:34 over them **by d** when they set out from 3429
11:19 You will not eat it *for* just one **d**, 3427
11:32 All that **d** and night and all the next day 3427
11:32 All that day and night and all the next **d** 3427
14:14 in a pillar of cloud **by d** and a pillar of fire 3429
15:23 the **d** the LORD gave them and continuing 3427
15:32 on the Sabbath **d**. 3427
16:41 The **next d** the whole Israelite community grumbled against Moses 4740
17: 8 The **next d** Moses entered the Tent of 4740
19:12 on the third **d** and on the seventh day; 3427
19:12 on the third day and on the seventh **d**; 3427
19:19 and on the seventh **d** he is to purify him. 3427
22:30 which you have always ridden, to this **d**? 3427
28: 3 as a regular burnt offering each **d**. 3427
28: 9 " 'On the Sabbath **d**, make an offering 3427
28:16 " 'On the fourteenth **d** of the first month 3427
28:17 On the fifteenth **d** of this month there is to 3427

Nu 28:18 On the first **d** hold a sacred assembly 3427
28:24 for the offering made by fire every **d** 3427
28:25 On the seventh **d** hold a sacred assembly 3427
28:26 " 'On the **d** *of* firstfruits, 3427
29: 1 " 'On the first **d** of the seventh month hold NIH
29: 1 It is a **d** for you to sound the trumpets. 3427
29: 7 the tenth **d** of this seventh month hold NIH
29:12 " 'On the fifteenth **d** of the seventh month, 3427
29:17 the second **d** prepare twelve young bulls, 3427
29:20 " 'On the third **d** prepare eleven bulls, 3427
29:23 " 'On the fourth **d** prepare ten bulls, 3427
29:26 " 'On the fifth **d** prepare nine bulls, 3427
29:29 " 'On the sixth **d** prepare eight bulls, 3427
29:32 " 'On the seventh **d** prepare seven bulls, 3427
29:35 " 'On the eighth **d** hold an assembly 3427
30:14 to her about it from **d** to day, 3427
30:14 to her about it from day to **d,** 3427
31:24 On the seventh **d** wash your clothes 3427
32:10 The LORD's anger was aroused that **d** 3427
33: 3 on the fifteenth **d** of the first month, 3427
33: 3 the **d after** the Passover. 4740
33:38 on the first **d** of the fifth month of NIH
Dt 1: 3 on the first **d** of the eleventh month, NIH
1:33 in fire by night and in a cloud **by d,** 3429
2:22 and have lived in their place to this **d.** 3427
2:25 This very **d** I will begin to put the terror 3427
3:14 to this **d** Bashan is called Havvoth Jair.) 3427
4:10 Remember the **d** you stood before 3427
4:15 the **d** the LORD spoke to you at Horeb out 3427
4:26 and earth as witnesses against you this **d** 3427
4:32 from the **d** God created man on the earth; 3427
4:39 Acknowledge and take to heart this **d** that 3427
5:12 "Observe the Sabbath **d** by keeping it holy, 3427
5:14 but the seventh **d** is a Sabbath to 3427
5:15 to observe the Sabbath **d.** 3427
8:11 and his decrees that I am giving you this **d.** 3427
9: 7 the **d** you left Egypt until you arrived here, 3427
9:10 on the **d** *of* the assembly. 3427
10: 4 out of the fire, on the **d** *of* the assembly. 3427
16: 4 on the evening of the first **d** remain 3427
16: 8 and on the seventh **d** hold an assembly to 3427
18:16 the LORD your God at Horeb on the **d** *of* 3427
21:23 Be sure to bury him that same **d,** 3427
24:15 Pay him his wages each **d** before sunset, 3427
26:16 LORD your God commands you this **d** 3427
26:17 You have declared this **d** that 3427
26:18 And the LORD has declared this **d** 3427
27:11 the same **d** Moses commanded the people: 3427
28:13 the LORD your God that I give you this **d** 3427
28:29 **d after day** you will be oppressed 2021+3427+3972
28:29 **day after d** you will be oppressed 2021+3427+3972
28:32 for them **d after day,** 2021+3427+3972
28:32 for them **day after d,** 2021+3427+3972
28:66 filled with dread both night and **d,** 3429
29: 4 But to this **d** the LORD has not given you 3427
29:12 with you this **d** and sealing with an oath, 3427
29:13 to confirm you this **d** as his people, 3427
30:18 to you this **d** that you will certainly 3427
30:19 This **d** I call heaven and earth as witnesses 3427
31:14 "Now the **d** *of* your death is near. 3427
31:17 On that **d** I will become angry with them 3427
31:17 and on that **d** they will ask, 3427
31:18 And I will certainly hide my face on that **d** 3427
31:22 So Moses wrote down this song that **d** 3427
32:35 their **d** *of* disaster is near 3427
32:46 solemnly declared to you this **d,** 3427
32:48 On that same **d** the LORD told Moses, 3427
33:12 for he shields him all **d** *long,* 3427
34: 6 to this **d** no one knows where his grave is. 3427
Jos 1: 8 meditate on it **d** and night, 3429
4: 9 And they are there to this **d.** 3427
4:14 That **d** the LORD exalted Joshua in 3427
4:19 On the tenth **d** of the first month NIH
5: 9 the place has been called Gilgal to this **d.** 3427
5:10 On the evening of the fourteenth **d** of 3427
5:11 The **d after** the Passover, that very day, 4740
5:11 The day after the Passover, that very **d,** 3427
5:12 the **d after** they ate this food from the land; 4740
6: 4 On the seventh **d,** march around the city 3427
6:10 do not say a word until the **d** I tell you 3427
6:14 So on the second **d** they marched around 3427
6:15 On the seventh **d,** they got up 3427
6:15 on that **d** they circled the city seven times. 3427
6:25 and she lives among the Israelites to this **d.** 3427
7:26 which remains to this **d.** 3427
8:25 and women fell that **d—** 3427
8:28 a desolate place to this **d.** 3427
8:29 which remains to this **d.** 3427
9:12 when we packed it at home on the **d** we left 3427
9:17 and on the third **d** came to their cities: 3427
9:27 That **d** he made the Gibeonites woodcutters 3427
9:27 And that is what they are to this **d.** 3427
10:12 the **d** the LORD gave the Amorites over 3427
10:13 and delayed going down about a full **d.** 3427
10:14 There has never been a **d** like it before or 3427
10:14 a **d** when the LORD listened to a man. NIH
10:27 which are there to this **d.** 3427
10:28 That **d** Joshua took Makkedah. 3427
10:32 and Joshua took it on the second **d.** 3427
10:35 They captured it that same **d** and put it to 3427
13:13 to live among the Israelites to this **d.** 3427
14: 9 So on that **d** Moses swore to me, 3427
14:11 as strong today as the **d** Moses sent me out; 3427
14:12 that the LORD promised me that **d.** 3427
15:18 **One d** when she came to Othniel, 2118+2256

Jos 15:63 to this **d** the Jebusites live there with 3427
16:10 to this **d** the Canaanites live among 3427
22: 3 For a long time now—to this very **d—** 3427
22:17 Up to this very **d** we have 3427
22:22 do not spare us this **d.** 3427
22:24 that **some d** your descendants might say 4737
23: 9 to this **d** no one has been able 3427
24:15 for yourselves this **d** whom you will serve, 3427
24:25 On that **d** Joshua made a covenant for 3427
Jdg 1:14 **One d** when she came to Othniel, 2118+2256
1:21 to this **d** the Jebusites live there with 3427
1:26 which is its name to this **d.** 3427
3:30 That **d** Moab was made subject to Israel, 3427
4:14 This is the **d** the LORD has given Sisera 3427
4:23 On that **d** God subdued Jabin, 3427
5: 1 On that **d** Deborah and Barak son 3427
6:24 To this **d** it stands in Ophrah of 3427
6:32 So that **d** they called Gideon "Jerub-Baal," 3427
6:38 Gideon rose early the **next d;** 4740
9: 8 One **d** the trees went out to anoint a king NIH
9:42 The **next d** the people of Shechem went out 4740
9:45 that **d** Abimelech pressed his attack against 3427
10: 4 which to this **d** are called Havvoth Jair. 3427
11:27 the dispute this **d** between the Israelites and 3427
13: 7 be a Nazirite of God from birth until the **d** 3427
13:10 The man who appeared to me the other **d!"** 3427
14:15 On the fourth **d,** they said 3427
14:17 So on the seventh **d** he finally told her, 3427
14:18 Before sunset on the seventh **d** the men of 3427
16: 1 **One d** Samson went to Gaza, 2256
16:16 With such nagging she prodded him **d after day** 2021+3427+3972
16:16 With such nagging she prodded him **day after d** 2021+3427+3972
18:12 is called Mahaneh Dan to this **d.** 3427
19: 5 On the fourth **d** they got up early 3427
19: 8 On the morning of the fifth **d,** 3427
19: 9 Spend the night here; the **d** is nearly over. 3427
19:11 near Jebus and the **d** was almost gone, 3427
19:30 the **d** the Israelites came up out of Egypt. 3427
20:21 on the battlefield that **d.** 3427
20:22 where they had stationed themselves the first **d.** 3427
20:24 near to Benjamin the second **d.** 3427
20:26 They fasted that **d** until evening 3427
20:30 up against the Benjamites on the third **d** 3427
20:35 on that **d** the Israelites struck down 25,100 3427
20:46 On that **d** twenty-five thousand Benjamite swordsmen fell, 3427
21: 4 Early the **next d** the people built an altar 4740
Ru 3: 1 **One d** Naomi her mother-in-law said to her, 2256
4: 5 "On the **d** you buy the land from Naomi 3427
4:14 to the LORD, who this **d** has not left you 3427
1Sa 1: 4 the **d** came for Elkanah to sacrifice, 3427
2:34 they will both die on the same **d.** 3427
4:12 That same **d** a Benjamite ran from 3427
4:16 I fled from it this very **d."** 3427
5: 3 the people of Ashdod rose early the **next d,** 4740
5: 5 That is why to this **d** neither the priests 3427
6:15 On that **d** the people 3427
6:16 and then returned that same **d** to Ekron. 3427
6:18 is a witness to this **d** in the field of Joshua 3427
7: 6 that **d** they fasted and there they confessed, 3427
7:10 But that **d** the LORD thundered 3427
8: 8 from the **d** I brought them up out of Egypt 3427
8: 8 up out of Egypt until this **d,** 3427
8:18 When that **d** comes, 3427
8:18 the LORD will not answer you in that **d."** 3427
9:15 Now the **d** before Saul came, 3427
9:24 And Saul dined with Samuel that **d.** 3427
10: 9 and all these signs were fulfilled that **d.** 3427
11:11 The **next d** Saul separated his men 4740
11:11 until the heat of the **d.** 3427
11:13 for this **d** the LORD has rescued Israel." 3427
12: 2 from my youth until this **d.** 3427
12: 5 and also his anointed is witness this **d,** 3427
12:18 and that same **d** the LORD sent thunder 3427
13:22 the **d** *of* the battle not a soldier with Saul 3427
14: 1 One **d** Jonathan son of Saul said to 3427
14:23 So the LORD rescued Israel that **d,** 3427
14:24 the men of Israel were in distress that **d,** 3427
14:31 That **d,** after the Israelites had struck down 3427
14:37 But God did not answer him that **d.** 3427
15:35 Until the **d** Samuel died, 3427
16:13 that **d** on the Spirit of the LORD came 3427
17:10 "This **d** I defy the ranks of Israel! 3427
17:46 This **d** the LORD will hand you over 3427
18: 2 that **d** Saul kept David with him and did 3427
18:10 The **next d** an evil spirit 4740
19:24 He lay that way all that **d** and night. 3427
20: 5 until the evening of the **d after tomorrow.** 8958
20:12 by this time the **d after** tomorrow! 8958
20:19 The **d after tomorrow,** 8992
20:26 Saul said nothing that **d,** for he thought, 3427
20:27 But the **next d,** 4740
20:27 the next day, the second **d** of the month, NIH
20:34 that second **d** *of* the month he did not eat, 3427
21: 6 by hot bread on the **d** it was taken away. 3427
21: 7 one of Saul's servants was there that **d,** 3427
21:10 That **d** David fled from Saul and went 3427
22:15 Was that **d** the first time I inquired of God 3427
22:18 That **d** he killed eighty-five men who wore 3427
22:22 "That **d,** when Doeg the Edomite was there, 3427
23:14 **D after day** Saul searched for him, 2021+3427+3972
23:14 **Day after d** Saul searched for him, 2021+3427+3972

1Sa 24: 4 the **d** the LORD spoke of when he said 3427
24:10 This **d** you have seen with your own eyes 3427
25:16 Night and **d** they were a wall around us all 3429
25:33 for keeping me from bloodshed this **d** and 3427
27: 6 So on that **d** Achish gave him Ziklag, 3427
28:20 for he had eaten nothing all that **d** 3427
29: 3 and from the **d** he left Saul until now, 3427
29: 6 From the **d** you came to me until now, 3427
29: 8 against your servant from the **d** I came 3427
30: 1 and his men reached Ziklag on the third **d.** 3427
30:17 from dusk until the evening of the **next d,** 4740
30:25 and ordinance for Israel from that **d** to this. 3427
31: 6 and all his men died together that same **d.** 3427
31: 8 The **next d,** when the Philistines came 4740
2Sa 1: 2 the third **d** a man arrived from Saul's camp, 3427
2:17 The battle that **d** was very fierce, 3427
3: 8 This very **d** I am loyal to the house 3427
3:35 to eat something while it was still **d;** 3427
3:37 that **d** all the people and all Israel knew that 3427
3:38 and a great man has fallen in Israel this **d?** 3427
4: 3 and have lived there as aliens to this **d.** 3427
4: 5 the **d** while he was taking his noonday rest. 3427
4: 8 This **d** the LORD has avenged my lord 3427
5: 8 On that **d,** David said, 3427
6: 8 to this **d** that place is called Perez Uzzah. 3427
6: 9 David was afraid of the LORD that **d** 3427
6:23 of Saul had no children to the **d** 3427
7: 6 a house from the **d** I brought the Israelites 3427
7: 6 the Israelites up out of Egypt to this **d.** 3427
11:12 David said to him, "Stay here one more **d,** 3427
11:12 So Uriah remained in Jerusalem that **d** and 3427
12:18 On the seventh **d** the child died. 3427
13:32 since the **d** Amnon raped his sister Tamar. 3427
13:37 King David mourned for his son every **d.** 3427
18: 7 and the casualties that **d** were great— 3427
18: 8 the forest claimed more lives that **d** than 3427
18:18 it is called Absalom's Monument to this **d.** 3427
19: 2 that **d** was turned into mourning, 3427
19: 2 because on that **d** the troops heard it said, 3427
19: 3 that **d** as men steal in who are ashamed 3427
19:19 on the **d** my lord the king left Jerusalem. 3427
19:22 This **d** you have become my adversaries! 3427
19:24 or washed his clothes from the **d** 3427
19:24 the king left until the **d** he returned safely. 3427
20: 3 They were kept in confinement till the **d** 3427
21:10 the air touch them **by d** or the wild animals 3429
22:19 They confronted me in the **d** 3427
23:10 about a great victory that **d.** 3427
23:20 He also went down into a pit on a snowy **d** 3427
24:18 that **d** Gad went to David and said to him, 3427
1Ki 2: 8 down bitter curses on me the **d** I went 3427
2:37 The **d** you leave and cross 3427
2:42 'On the **d** you leave to go anywhere else, 3427
3: 6 a son to sit on his throne this very **d.** 3427
3:18 The third **d** after my child was born, 3427
8:16 **d** I brought my people Israel out of Egypt, 3427
8:28 in your presence this **d.** 3427
8:29 be open toward this temple night and **d,** 3427
8:59 be near to the LORD our God **d** and night, 3429
8:64 On that same **d** the king consecrated 3427
8:66 the following **d** he sent the people away. 3427
9:13 a name they have to this **d.** 3427
9:21 as it is to this **d.** 3427
10:12 or seen since that **d.)** 3427
12:19 against the house of David to this **d.** 3427
12:32 He instituted a festival on the fifteenth **d** of 3427
12:33 On the fifteenth **d** of the eighth month, 3427
13: 3 That same **d** the man of God gave a sign: 3427
13:11 that the man of God had done there that **d.** 3427
14:14 This is the **d!** 3427
16:16 over Israel that very **d** there in the camp. 3427
17:14 the **d** the LORD gives rain on the land.' " 3427
17:15 So there was food **every d** for Elijah and for 3427
20:29 and on the seventh **d** the battle was joined. 3427
20:29 on the Aramean foot soldiers in one **d.** 3427
21: 9 "Proclaim a **d of fasting** and seat Naboth 7427
21:29 I will not bring this disaster in his **d,** 3427
22:25 "You will find out on the **d** you go to hide 3427
22:35 **All d long** the battle raged, 928+2021+2021+2085+3427
2Ki 2:22 water has remained wholesome to this **d,** 3427
4: 8 One **d** Elisha went to Shunem. 3427
4:11 One **d** when Elisha came, 3427
4:18 and one **d** he went out to his father, 3427
6:29 The next **d** I said to her, 3427
7: 9 a **d** *of* good news and we are keeping it 3427
8: 6 from the **d** she left the country until now." 3427
8:15 But the **next d** he took a thick cloth, 4740
8:22 To this **d** Edom has been in rebellion 3427
10:27 people have used it for a latrine to this **d.** 3427
13:23 To **this d** he has been unwilling 6964
14: 7 calling it Joktheel, the name it has to this **d.** 3427
15: 5 the king with leprosy until the **d** he died, 3427
16: 6 into Elath and have lived there to this **d.** 3427
17:34 To this **d** they persist 3427
17:41 To this **d** their children 3427
19: 3 This **d** is a day of distress and rebuke 3427
19: 3 a **d** *of* distress and rebuke and disgrace, 3427
19:37 **One d,** while he was worshiping in 2118+2256
20: 5 On the third **d** from now you will go up to 3427
20: 8 to the temple of the LORD on the third **d** 3427
20:17 that your fathers have stored up until this **d,** 3427
21:15 the **d** their forefathers came out of Egypt 3427
21:15 of Egypt until this **d."** 3427
25: 1 on the tenth **d** of the tenth month, NIH
25: 3 the ninth **d** of the [fourth] month the famine NIH
25: 8 On the seventh **d** of the fifth month, NIH

2Ki 25:27 the twenty-seventh **d** of the twelfth month. NIH
25:30 **D by day** the king gave Jehoiachin a regular allowance 928+1821+2257+3427+3427
25:30 **Day by d** the king gave Jehoiachin a regular allowance 928+1821+2257+3427+3427
1Ch 4:41 as is evident to this **d.** 3427
4:43 and they have lived there to this **d.** 3427
5:26 where they are to this **d.** 3427
9:33 for the work **d** and night. 3429
10: 8 The **next d,** when the Philistines came 4740
11:22 He also went down into a pit on a snowy **d** 3427
12:22 **D** after day men came to help David, 3427
12:22 Day after **d** men came to help David, 3427
13:11 to this **d** that place is called Perez Uzzah. 3427
13:12 David was afraid of God that **d** and asked, 3427
16: 7 That **d** David first committed to Asaph 3427
16:23 proclaim his salvation **d** after day. 3427
16:23 proclaim his salvation day after **d.** 3427
17: 5 from the **d** I brought Israel up out of Egypt 3427
17: 5 up out of Egypt to this **d.** 3427
26:17 There were six Levites a **d** on the east, 3427
26:17 four a **d** on the north, NIH
26:17 four a **d** on the south and two at a time at 3427
29:21 The next **d** they made sacrifices to 3427
29:22 in the presence of the LORD that **d.** 3427
2Ch 3: 2 on the second **d** of the second month in NIH
6: 5 the **d** I brought my people out of Egypt, 3427
6:20 be open toward this temple **d** and night, 3429
7: 9 On the eighth **d** they held an assembly, 3427
7:10 On the twenty-third **d** of 3427
8: 8 as it is to this **d.** 3427
8:16 from the **d** the foundation of the temple of 3427
9:20 of little value in Solomon's **d.** 3427
10:19 against the house of David to this **d.** 3427
18:24 "You will find out on the **d** you go to hide 3427
18:34 **All d long** the battle raged, 928+2021+2021+2085+3427
20:26 the fourth **d** they assembled in the Valley 3427
20:26 the Valley of Beracah to this **d.** 3427
21:10 To this **d** Edom has been in rebellion 3427
26:21 until the **d** he died. 3427
28: 6 In one **d** Pekah son of Remaliah killed 3427
29:17 They began the consecration on the first **d** NIH
29:17 by the eighth **d** of the month they reached 3427
29:17 on the sixteenth **d** of the first month. 3427
30:15 on the fourteenth **d** of the second month. NIH
30:21 priests sang to the LORD **every d,** 928+3427+3427
35: 1 on the fourteenth **d** of the first month. NIH
35:25 and to this **d** all the men 3427
Ezr 3: 4 offerings prescribed for **each d.** 928+3427+3427
3: 6 the first **d** of the seventh month they began 3427
5:16 From **that d** to the present it has been 10008[S]
6:15 The temple was completed on the third **d** of 10317
6:19 On the fourteenth **d** of the first month, NIH
7: 9 on the first **d** of the first month, NIH
7: 9 and he arrived in Jerusalem on the first **d** of NIH
8:31 the twelfth **d** of the first month we set out NIH
8:33 On the fourth **d,** in the house of our God, 3427
9:15 We are left this **d** as a remnant. 3427
10: 9 And on the twentieth **d** of the ninth month, NIH
10:13 this matter cannot be taken care of in a **d** 3427
10:16 the first **d** of the tenth month they sat down 3427
10:17 and by the first **d** of the first month 3427
Ne 1: 6 before you **d** and night for your servants, 3429
4: 2 Will they finish in a **d?** 3427
4: 9 to our God and posted a guard **d** and night 3429
4:16 From that **d** on, half of my men did 3427
4:22 as guards by night and workmen *by* **d."** 3427
5:18 Each **d** one ox, 3427
6:10 **One d** I went to the house of Shemaiah son 2256
8: 2 So on the first **d** of the seventh month Ezra 3427
8: 9 "This **d** is sacred to the LORD your God. 3427
8:10 This **d** is sacred to our Lord. 3427
8:11 saying, "Be still, for this is a sacred **d.** 3427
8:13 On the second **d** of the month, 3427
8:17 the days of Joshua son of Nun until that **d,** 3427
8:18 **D** after day, from the first day to the last, 3427
8:18 Day after **d,** from the first day to the last, 3427
8:18 Day after day, from the first **d** to the last, 3427
8:18 and on the eighth **d,** 3427
9: 1 On the twenty-fourth **d** of the same month, 3427
9: 3 the LORD their God *for* a quarter of the **d,** 3427
9:10 which remains to this **d.** 3427
9:12 **By d** you led them with a pillar of cloud, 3429
9:19 **By d** the pillar of cloud did not cease 928+3429
10:31 from them on the Sabbath or on any holy **d.** 3427
12:43 And on that **d** they offered great sacrifices, 3427
13: 1 that **d** the Book of Moses was read aloud in 3427
13:15 against selling food on that **d.** 3427
13:17 desecrating the Sabbath **d?** 3427
13:19 be brought in on the Sabbath **d.** 3427
13:22 in order to keep the Sabbath **d** holy. 3427
Est 1:10 On the seventh **d,** when King Xerxes was 3427
1:18 This very **d** the Persian and Median women 3427
2:11 **Every d** he walked back and forth near 2256+3427+3427+3972
3: 4 **D** after day they spoke to him 3427
3: 4 after **d** they spoke to him but he refused 3427
3: 7 in the presence of Haman to **select a d** 3427+3427+4200+4946
3:12 Then on the thirteenth **d** of the first month 3427
3:13 on a single **d,** the thirteenth day 3427
3:13 the thirteenth **d** of the twelfth month, NIH
3:14 so they would be ready for that **d.** 3427
4:16 not eat or drink for three days, night or **d.** 3427
5: 1 On the third **d** Esther put on her royal robes 3427
5: 9 Haman went out that **d** happy and 3427
Est 7: 2 they were drinking wine on that second **d,** 3427
8: 1 That same **d** King Xerxes gave Queen Esther 3427
8: 9 on the twenty-third **d** of the third month, NIH
8:12 The **d** appointed for the Jews to do this 3427
8:12 of King Xerxes was the thirteenth **d** of NIH
8:13 so that the Jews would be ready on that **d** 3427
9: 1 On the thirteenth **d** of the twelfth month, 3427
9: 1 On this **d** the enemies of the Jews 3427
9:11 to the king that same **d.** 3427
9:15 in Susa came together on the fourteenth **d** 3427
9:17 on the thirteenth **d** of the month of Adar, 3427
9:17 the fourteenth they rested and made it a **d** 3427
9:18 on the fifteenth they rested and made it a **d** 3427
9:19 the fourteenth of the month of Adar as a **d** 3427
9:19 a **d** for giving presents to each other. 3427
9:22 and their mourning into a **d** *of* celebration. 3427
Job 1: 6 One **d** the angels came 3427
1:13 One **d** when Job's sons 3427
2: 1 On another **d** the angels came 3427
3: 1 Job opened his mouth and cursed the **d** 3427
3: 3 "May the **d** *of* my birth perish, 3427
3: 4 That **d—**may it turn to darkness; 3427
3: 8 May those who curse days curse **that d,** 2084[S]
3:16 an infant who never saw the **light of d?** 240
15:23 he knows the **d** *of* darkness is at hand. 3427
17:12 These men turn night into **d;** 3427
20:28 rushing waters on the **d** *of* God's wrath. 3427
21:30 evil man is spared from the **d** *of* calamity, 3427
21:30 that he is delivered from the **d** *of* wrath? 3427
24:16 but **by d** they shut themselves in; 3429
Ps 1: 2 and on his law he meditates **d** and night. 3429
7:11 a God who expresses his wrath every **d.** 3427
13: 2 with my thoughts and **every d** have sorrow 3429
18:18 They confronted me in the **d** 3427
19: 2 **D** after day they pour forth speech; 3427
19: 2 Day after **d** they pour forth speech; 3427
22: 2 O my God, I cry out **by d,** 3429
25: 5 and my hope is in you all **d** *long.* 3427
27: 5 For in the **d** *of* trouble he will keep me safe 3427
32: 3 through my groaning all **d** *long.* 3427
32: 4 **d** and night your hand was heavy upon me; 3429
35:28 and of your praises all **d** *long.* 3427
37:13 for he knows their **d** is coming. 3427
38: 6 all **d** *long* I go about mourning. 3427
38:12 all **d** *long* they plot deception. 3427
42: 3 My tears have been my food **d** and night, 3429
42: 3 while men say to me all **d** *long,* 3427
42: 8 **By d** the LORD directs his love, 3429
42:10 saying to me all **d** *long,* 3427
44: 8 In God we make our boast all **d** *long,* 3427
44:15 My disgrace is before me all **d** *long,* 3427
44:22 Yet for your sake we face death all **d** *long;* 3427
46: 5 God will help her at **break of d.** 1332+7155
50:15 and call upon me in the **d** *of* trouble; 3427
52: 1 Why do you boast all **d** *long,* 3427
55:10 **D** and night they prowl about on its walls; 3429
56: 1 all **d** *long* they press their attack. 3427
56: 2 My slanderers pursue me all **d** *long;* 3427
56: 5 All **d** *long* they twist my words; 3427
61: 8 to your name and fulfill my vows **d** 3427
61: 8 and fulfill my vows day after **d.** 3427
71: 8 declaring your splendor all **d** *long.* 3427
71:15 of your salvation all **d** *long,* 3427
71:17 to **this d** I declare your marvelous deeds. 2178[S]
71:24 of your righteous acts all **d** *long,* 3427
72:15 for him and bless him all **d** *long.* 3427
73:14 All **d** *long* I have been plagued; 3427
74:16 The **d** is yours, and yours also the night; 3427
74:22 remember how fools mock you all **d** *long.* 3427
78: 9 turned back on the **d** *of* battle; 3427
78:14 He guided them with the cloud **by d** and 3429
78:42 the **d** he redeemed them from the oppressor, 3427
78:43 **the d** he displayed his miraculous signs 889[S]
81: 3 on the **d** *of* our Feast; 3427
84:10 Better is *one* **d** in your courts than 3427
86: 3 O Lord, for I call to you all **d** *long.* 3427
86: 7 In the **d** *of* my trouble I will call to you, 3427
88: 1 **d** and night I cry out before you. 3427
88: 9 I call to you, O LORD, every **d;** 3427
88:17 All **d** *long* they surround me like a flood; 3427
89:16 They rejoice in your name all **d** *long;* 3427
90: 4 a thousand years in your sight are like a **d** that has just gone by, 919+3427
91: 5 nor the arrow that flies **by d,** 3429
92: T A psalm. A song. For the Sabbath **d.** 3427
95: 8 as you did that **d** *at* Massah in the desert, 3427
96: 2 proclaim his salvation **d** after day. 3427
96: 2 proclaim his salvation day after **d.** 3427
102: 8 All **d** *long* my enemies taunt me; 3427
110: 3 Your troops will be willing on your **d** 3427
110: 5 he will crush kings on the **d** *of* his wrath. 3427
118:24 This is the **d** the LORD has made; 3427
119:91 Your laws endure to this **d,** 3427
119:97 I meditate on it all **d** *long.* 3427
119:164 a **d** I praise you for your righteous laws. 3427
121: 6 the sun will not harm you **by d,** 3429
136: 8 the sun to govern the **d,** 3427
137: 7 the Edomites did on the **d** Jerusalem fell. 3427
139:12 the night will shine like the **d,** 3427
140: 2 in their hearts and stir up war every **d.** 3427
140: 7 who shields my head in the **d** *of* battle— 3427
145: 2 Every **d** I will praise you 3427
146: 4 on that very **d** their plans come to nothing. 3427
Pr 4:18 shining ever brighter till the full light of **d.** 3427
7: 9 as the **d** was fading, 3427
8:30 I was filled with delight **d** *after* day, 3427
Pr 8:30 I was filled with delight day after **d,** 3427
11: 4 Wealth is worthless in the **d** *of* wrath, 3427
16: 4 even the wicked for a **d** *of* disaster. 3427
21:26 All **d** *long* he craves for more, 3427
21:31 The horse is made ready for the **d** *of* battle, 3427
25:20 a garment on a cold **d,** 3427
27: 1 you do not know what a **d** may bring forth. 3427
27:15 like a constant dripping on a rainy **d;** 3427
Ecc 7: 1 the **d** *of* death better than the day of birth. 3427
7: 1 the day of death better than the **d** *of* birth. 3427
8: 8 no one has power over the **d** *of* his death. 3427
8:16 his eyes not seeing sleep **d** or night— 3427
SS 2:17 Until the **d** breaks and the shadows flee, 3427
3:11 on the **d** *of* his wedding, 3427
3:11 the **d** his heart rejoiced. 3427
4: 6 Until the **d** breaks and the shadows flee, 3427
8: 8 for our sister for the **d** she is spoken for? 3427
Isa 2:11 the LORD alone will be exalted in that **d.** 3427
2:12 The LORD Almighty has a **d** in store 3427
2:17 the LORD alone will be exalted in that **d,** 3427
2:20 that **d** men will throw away to the rodents 3427
3: 7 in that **d** he will cry out, "I have no remedy. 3427
3:18 In that **d** the Lord will snatch away their finery: 3427
4: 1 In that **d** seven women will take hold 3427
4: 2 In that **d** the Branch of the LORD will 3427
4: 5 of smoke **by d** and a glow of flaming fire 3429
4: 6 a shelter and shade from the heat of the **d,** 3429
5:30 that **d** they will roar over it like the roaring 3427
7:18 that **d** the LORD will whistle for flies from 3427
7:20 that **d** the Lord will use a razor hired from 3427
7:21 that **d,** a man will keep alive a young cow 3427
7:23 In that **d,** in every place where there were 3427
9: 4 For as in the **d** *of* Midian's defeat, 3427
9:14 both palm branch and reed *in* a single **d;** 3427
10: 3 What will you do on the **d** *of* reckoning, 3427
10:17 in a single **d** it will burn 3427
10:20 In that **d** the remnant of Israel, 3427
10:27 In that **d** their burden will be lifted 3427
10:32 This **d** they will halt at Nob; 3427
11:10 In that **d** the Root of Jesse will stand as 3427
11:11 In that **d** the Lord will reach out his hand 3427
12: 1 In that **d** you will say: 3427
12: 4 In that **d** you will say: 3427
13: 6 Wail, for the **d** *of* the LORD is near; 3427
13: 9 See, the **d** *of* the LORD is coming— 3427
13: 9 a cruel **d,** with wrath and fierce anger— NIH
13:13 in the **d** *of* his burning anger. 3427
14: 3 On the **d** the LORD gives you relief 3427
17: 4 "In that **d** the glory of Jacob will fade; 3427
17: 7 In that **d** men will look to their Maker 3427
17: 9 In that **d** their strong cities, 3427
17:11 though on the **d** you set them out, 3427
17:11 yet the harvest will be as nothing in the **d** 3427
19:16 In that **d** the Egyptians will be like women. 3427
19:18 In that **d** five cities in Egypt will speak 3427
19:19 that **d** there will be an altar to the LORD in 3427
19:21 that **d** they will acknowledge the LORD. 3427
19:23 that **d** there will be a highway from Egypt 3427
19:24 In that **d** Israel will be the third, 3427
20: 6 In that **d** the people who live 3427
21: 8 the lookout shouted, **"D after day,** 3429+9458
21: 8 the lookout shouted, **"Day after d,** 3429+9458
22: 5 has a **d** *of* tumult and trampling and terror 3427
22: 5 a **d** of battering down walls and NIH
22: 8 And you looked in that **d** to the weapons in 3427
22:12 called you on that **d** to weep and to wail, 3427
22:14 **"Till** your dying *d* this sin will not AIT
22:20 "In that **d** I will summon my servant, 3427
22:25 "In that **d,"** declares the LORD Almighty, 3427
24:21 In that **d** the LORD will punish the powers 3427
25: 9 In that **d** they will say, 3427
26: 1 In that **d** this song will be sung in the land 3427
27: 1 In that **d,** the LORD will punish 3427
27: 2 In that **d—**"Sing about a fruitful vineyard: 3427
27: 3 I guard it **d** and night so 3427
27: 8 as on a **d** the east wind blows. 3427
27:12 In that **d** the LORD will thresh from 3427
27:13 And in that **d** a great trumpet will sound. 3427
28: 5 In that **d** the LORD Almighty will be 3427
28:19 morning after morning, by **d** and by night, 3427
29:18 In that **d** the deaf will hear the words of 3427
30:23 In that **d** your cattle will graze 3427
30:25 In the **d** *of* great slaughter, 3427
31: 7 that **d** every one of you will reject the idols 3427
34: 8 For the LORD has a **d** *of* vengeance, 3427
34:10 It will not be quenched night and **d;** 3429
37: 3 This **d** is a day of distress and rebuke 3427
37: 3 a **d** *of* distress and rebuke and disgrace, 3427
37:38 **One d,** while he was worshiping in 2118+2256
38:12 **d** and night you made an end of me. 3427
38:13 **d** and night you made an end of me. 3427
39: 6 that your fathers have stored up until this **d,** 3427
47: 9 on a single **d:** 3427
49: 8 and in the **d** *of* salvation I will help you; 3427
51:13 that you live in constant terror every **d** 3427
52: 5 all **d** *long* my name is constantly blasphemed. 3427
52: 6 therefore in that **d** they will know 3427
58: 2 For **d** *after* day they seek me out; 3427
58: 2 For day after **d** they seek me out; 3427
58: 3 "Yet on the **d** *of* your fasting, 3427
58: 5 only a **d** *for* a man to humble himself? 3427
58: 5 a **d** acceptable to the LORD? 3427
58:13 from doing as you please on my holy **d,** 3427
58:13 and the LORD's holy **d** honorable, NIH
60:11 they will never be shut, **d** or night, 3429

Isa 60:19 The sun will no more be your light **by d,** 3429
61: 2 the LORD's favor and the **d** *of* vengeance 3427
62: 6 they will never be silent **d** or night. 3427
63: 4 For the **d** *of* vengeance was in my heart, 3427
65: 2 All **d** *long* I have held out my hands to 3427
65: 5 a fire that keeps burning all **d.** 3427
66: 8 be born in a **d** or a nation be brought forth 3427
Jer 3:25 from our youth till this **d** we have 3427
4: 9 "In that **d,"** declares the LORD, 3427
7:25 until now, **d after day,** again 3427
7:25 until now, **day after d,** again 3427
9: 1 I would weep **d** and night for the slain 3429
12: 3 Set them apart for the **d** *of* slaughter! 3427
14:17 with tears night and **d** without ceasing; 3429
15: 9 Her sun will set while it is still **d;** 3429
16:13 there you will serve other gods **d** and night, 3429
17:16 you know I have not desired the **d** 3427
17:17 you are my refuge in the **d** *of* disaster. 3427
17:18 Bring on them the **d** *of* disaster; 3427
17:21 a load on the Sabbath **d** or bring it through 3427
17:22 but keep the Sabbath **d** holy, 3427
17:24 the Sabbath **d** holy by not doing any work 3427
17:27 the Sabbath **d** holy by not carrying any load 3427
17:27 the gates of Jerusalem on the Sabbath **d,** 3427
18:17 and not my face in the **d** *of* their disaster." 3427
20: 3 The **next d,** when Pashhur released him 4740
20: 7 I am ridiculed all **d** *long;* 3427
20: 8 and reproach all **d** *long.* 3427
20:14 Cursed be the **d** I was born! 3427
20:14 the **d** my mother bore me not be blessed! 3427
25: 3 of Amon king of Judah until this very **d—** 3427
27:22 until the **d** I come for them,' 3427
30: 7 How awful that **d** will be! 3427
30: 8 " 'In that **d,'** declares the LORD 3427
31: 6 be a **d** when watchmen cry out on the hills 3427
31:35 he who appoints the sun to shine **by d,** 3429
32:20 in Egypt and have continued them to this **d,** 3427
32:31 From the **d** it was built until now, 3427
33:20 with the **d** and my covenant with the night, 3427
33:20 and my covenant with the night, so that **d** 3429
33:25 not established my covenant with **d** 3429
35:14 To this **d** they do not drink wine, 3427
36: 6 of the LORD on a **d** *of* fasting and read to 3427
36:30 be thrown out and exposed to the heat by **d** 3427
37:21 given bread from the street of the bakers **each d** until 2021+3427+4200
38:28 until the **d** Jerusalem was captured. 3427
39: 2 And on the ninth **d** of the fourth month NIH
39:17 But I will rescue you on that **d,** 3427
41: 4 The **d** after Gedaliah's assassination, 3427
44:10 To this **d** they have not humbled 3427
46:10 But that **d** belongs to the Lord, 3427
46:10 **d** *of* vengeance, for vengeance on his foes. 3427
46:21 for the **d** *of* disaster is coming upon them, 3427
47: 4 the **d** has come to destroy all the Philistines 3427
48:41 that **d** the hearts of Moab's warriors will be 3427
49:22 that **d** the hearts of Edom's warriors will be 3427
49:26 all her soldiers will be silenced in that **d,"** 3427
50:27 For their **d** has come, 3427
50:30 all her soldiers will be silenced in that **d,"** 3427
50:31 "for your **d** has come, 3427
51: 2 they will oppose her on every side in the **d** 3427
52: 4 on the tenth **d** of the tenth month, NIH
52: 6 the ninth **d** of the fourth month the famine NIH
52:11 where he put him in prison till the **d** 3427
52:12 On the tenth **d** of the fifth month, NIH
52:31 on the twenty-fifth **d** of the twelfth month. NIH
52:34 **D by day** the king 928+1821+3427+3427
52:34 **Day by d** the king 928+1821+3427+3427
52:34 till the **d** *of* his death. 3427
La 1:12 that the LORD brought on me in the **d** 3427
1:13 He made me desolate, faint all the **d** *long.* 3427
1:21 May you bring the **d** you have announced 3427
2: 1 not remembered his footstool in the **d** 3427
2: 7 in the house of the LORD as on the **d** *of* 3427
2:16 This is the **d** we have waited for; 3427
2:18 let your tears flow like a river **d** and night; 3429
2:21 You have slain them in the **d** *of* your anger; 3427
2:22 "As you summon to a feast **d,** 3427
2:22 In the **d** *of* the LORD's anger 3427
3: 3 against me again and again, all **d** *long.* 3427
3:14 they mock me in song all **d** *long.* 3427
3:62 and mutter against me all **d** *long.* 3427
Eze 1: 1 in the fourth month on the fifth **d,** NIH
1:28 of a rainbow in the clouds on a rainy **d,** 3427
2: 3 in revolt against me to this very **d.** 3427
4: 6 a **d** for each year. 3427
4:10 of food to eat each **d** and eat it at set times. 3427
7: 7 The time has come, the **d** is near; 3427
7:10 "The **d** is here! 3427
7:12 The time has come, the **d** has arrived. 3427
7:19 not be able to save them in the **d** *of* 3427
8: 1 in the sixth month on the fifth **d,** NIH
12: 7 **During the d** I brought out my things packed 3429
13: 5 that it will stand firm in the battle on the **d** 3427
16: 4 the **d** you were born your cord was not cut, 3427
16: 5 on the **d** you were born you were despised. 3427
16:56 even mention your sister Sodom in the **d** 3427
20: 1 in the fifth month on the tenth **d,** NIH
20: 5 On the **d** I chose Israel, 3427
20: 6 On that **d** I swore to them 3427
20:29 (It is called Bamah to this **d.**) 3427
20:31 with all your idols to this **d.** 3427
21:25 whose **d** has come, 3427
21:29 whose **d** has come, 3427
22:14 or your hands be strong in the **d** I deal 3427
Eze 22:24 that has had no rain or showers in the **d** 3427
23:39 On the very **d** they sacrificed their children 3427
24: 1 in the tenth month on the tenth **d,** NIH
24: 2 to Jerusalem this very **d.** 3427
24:25 on the **d** I take away their stronghold, 3427
24:26 on that **d** a fugitive will come to tell you 3427
26: 1 on the first **d** of the month, NIH
26:18 coastlands tremble *on* the **d** *of* your fall; 3427
27:27 of the sea on the **d** *of* your shipwreck. 3427
28:13 the **d** you were created they were prepared. 3427
28:15 in your ways from the **d** you were created 3427
29: 1 in the tenth month on the twelfth **d,** NIH
29:17 in the first month on the first **d,** NIH
29:21 that **d** I will make a horn grow for the house 3427
30: 2 " 'Wail and say, "Alas for that **d!"** 3427
30: 3 **d** is near, the day of the LORD is near— 3427
30: 3 day is near, the **d** of the LORD is near— 3427
30: 3 **d** *of* clouds, a time of doom for the nations. 3427
30: 9 that **d** messengers will go out from me 3427
30: 9 Anguish will take hold of them on the **d** 3427
30:18 the **d** at Tahpanhes when I break the yoke 3427
30:20 in the first month on the seventh **d,** NIH
31: 1 in the third month on the first **d,** NIH
31:15 On the **d** it was brought down to 3427
32: 1 in the twelfth month on the first **d,** NIH
32:10 On the **d** *of* your downfall each 3427
32:17 on the fifteenth **d** of the month, NIH
33:21 in the tenth month on the fifth **d,** NIH
34:12 the places where they were scattered on a **d** 3427
36:33 On the **d** I cleanse you from all your sins, 3427
38:10 that **d** thoughts will come into your mind 3427
38:14 In that **d,** when my people Israel are living 3427
38:18 This is what will happen in that **d:** 3427
39: 8 This is the **d** I have spoken of. 3427
39:11 " 'On that **d** I will give Gog a burial place 3427
39:13 and the **d** I am glorified will be 3427
39:13 be a memorable **d** for them, NIH
39:22 that **d** forward the house of Israel will know 3427
40: 1 on that very **d** the hand of the LORD was 3427
43:22 the second **d** you are to offer a male goat 3427
43:27 from the eighth **d** on, 3427
44:27 On the **d** he goes into the inner court of 3427
45:18 the first month on the first **d** you are to take NIH
45:20 You are to do the same on the seventh **d** of NIH
45:21 the first month on the fourteenth **d** you are 3427
45:22 On that **d** the prince is to provide a bull as 3427
45:23 Every **d** *during* the seven days of 3427
45:25 in the seventh month on the fifteenth **d,** 3427
46: 1 the six working days, but on the Sabbath **d** 3427
46: 1 the **d** *of* the New Moon it is to be opened. 3427
46: 4 the Sabbath **d** is to be six male lambs and 3427
46: 6 On the **d** *of* the New Moon he is to offer 3427
46:12 as he does on the Sabbath **d.** 3427
46:13 **" 'Every d** you are to provide 2021+3427+4200
Da 6:10 Three times a **d** he got down on his knees 10317
6:13 He still prays three times a **d."** 10317
9: 7 but this **d** we are covered with shame— 3427
9:15 for yourself a name that endures to this **d,** 3427
10: 4 On the twenty-fourth **d** of the first month, 3427
10:12 Since the first **d** that you set your mind 3427
Hos 1: 5 In that **d** I will break Israel's bow in 3427
1:11 for great will be the **d** *of* Jezreel. 3427
2: 3 as bare as on the **d** she was born; 3427
2:15 as in the **d** she came up out of Egypt. 3427
2:16 "In that **d,"** declares the LORD, 3427
2:18 that **d** I will make a covenant for them with 3427
2:21 "In that **d** I will respond," 3427
4: 5 You stumble **d** and night, 3427
5: 9 be laid waste on the **d** *of* reckoning. 3427
6: 2 on the third **d** he will restore us, 3427
7: 5 On the **d** *of* the festival of our king 3427
9: 5 on the **d** *of* your appointed feasts, 3427
10:14 as Shalman devastated Beth Arbel on the **d** 3427
10:15 When that **d dawns,** 8840
12: 1 the east wind all **d** and multiplies lies 3427
Joel 1:15 Alas for that **d!** 3427
1:15 For the **d** *of* the LORD is near; 3427
2: 1 for the **d** *of* the LORD is coming. 3427
2: 2 a **d** *of* darkness and gloom, 3427
2: 2 a **d** *of* clouds and blackness. 3427
2:11 The **d** *of* the LORD is great; it is dreadful. 3427
2:31 of the great and dreadful **d** *of* the LORD. 3427
3:14 the **d** *of* the LORD is near in the valley 3427
3:18 that **d** the mountains will drip new wine, 3427
Am 1:14 on the **d** *of* battle, 3427
1:14 amid violent winds on a stormy **d.** 3427
2:16 bravest warriors will flee naked on that **d,"** 3427
3:14 "On the **d** I punish Israel for her sins, 3427
5: 8 and darkens **d** into night, who calls for 3427
5:18 to you who long for the **d** *of* the LORD! 3427
5:18 Why do you long for the **d** *of* the LORD? 3427
5:18 That **d** will be darkness, not light. NIH
5:20 Will not the **d** *of* the LORD be darkness, 3427
6: 3 the evil **d** and bring near a reign of terror. 3427
8: 3 "In that **d,"** declares the Sovereign LORD, 3427
8: 9 "In that **d,"** declares the Sovereign LORD, 3427
8:10 an only son and the end of it like a bitter **d.** 3427
8:13 "In that **d** "the lovely young women 3427
9:11 "In that **d** I will restore David's fallen tent. 3427
Ob 1: 8 "In that **d,"** declares the LORD, 3427
1:11 On the **d** you stood aloof 3427
1:12 on your brother in the **d** *of* his misfortune, 3427
1:12 of Judah in the **d** *of* their destruction, 3427
1:12 nor boast so much in the **d** *of* their trouble. 3427
1:13 through the gates of my people in the **d** 3427
1:13 in their calamity in the **d** *of* their disaster, 3427
1:13 nor seize their wealth in the **d** 3427
Ob 1:14 nor hand over their survivors in the **d** 3427
1:15 "The **d** *of* the LORD is near 3427
Jnh 3: 4 On the first **d,** Jonah started into the city. 3427
4: 7 at dawn the **next d** God provided a worm, 4740
Mic 2: 4 In that **d** men will ridicule you; 3427
3: 6 and the **d** will go dark for them. 3427
4: 6 "In that **d,"** declares the LORD, 3427
4: 7 in Mount Zion from **that d** and forever. 6964
5:10 "In that **d,"** declares the LORD, 3427
7: 4 The **d** *of* your watchmen has come, 3427
7: 4 the **d** God visits you. NIH
7:11 The **d** for building your walls will come, 3427
7:11 the **d** for extending your boundaries. 3427
7:12 In that **d** people will come to you 3427
Na 2: 3 on the **d** they are made ready; 3427
3:17 locusts that settle in the walls on a cold **d—** 3427
Hab 3: 2 Renew them in our **d,** 9102
3:16 Yet I will wait patiently for the **d** 3427
Zep 1: 7 for the **d** *of* the LORD is near. 3427
1: 8 On the **d** *of* the LORD's sacrifice 3427
1: 9 that **d** I will punish all who avoid stepping 3427
1:10 "On that **d,"** declares the LORD, 3427
1:14 "The great **d** *of* the LORD is near— 3427
1:14 cry on the **d** *of* the LORD will be bitter, 3427
1:15 That **d** will be a day of wrath, 3427
1:15 That day will be a **d** *of* wrath, 3427
1:15 a **d** *of* distress and anguish, 3427
1:15 a **d** *of* trouble and ruin, 3427
1:15 a **d** *of* darkness and gloom, 3427
1:15 a **d** *of* clouds and blackness, 3427
1:16 a **d** *of* trumpet and battle cry against 3427
1:18 on the **d** *of* the LORD's wrath. 3427
2: 2 and that **d** sweeps on like chaff, 3427
2: 2 before the **d** *of* the LORD's wrath comes 3427
2: 3 perhaps you will be sheltered on the **d** *of* 3427
3: 5 and every **new d** he does not fail, 240
3: 8 "for the **d** I will stand up to testify. 3427
3:11 that **d** you will not be put to shame for all 3427
3:16 On that **d** they will say to Jerusalem, 3427
Hag 1: 1 on the first **d** of the sixth month, 3427
1:15 on the twenty-fourth **d** of the sixth month in 3427
2: 1 On the twenty-first **d** of the seventh month, NIH
2:10 On the twenty-fourth **d** of the ninth month, NIH
2:15 to this from this **d** on— 3427
2:18 'From this **d** on, 3427
2:18 from this twenty-fourth **d** of 3427
2:18 give careful thought to the **d** when 3427
2:19 " 'From this **d** on I will bless you.' " 3427
2:20 a second time on the twenty-fourth **d** of NIH
2:23 " 'On that **d,'** declares the LORD 3427
Zec 1: 7 the twenty-fourth **d** of the eleventh month, 3427
2:11 in that **d** and will become my people. 3427
3: 9 the sin of this land in a single **d.** 3427
3:10 that **d** each of you will invite his neighbor 3427
4:10 "Who despises the **d** *of* small things? 3427
6:10 Go the same **d** to the house of Josiah son 3427
7: 1 on the fourth **d** of the ninth month, NIH
9:16 on that **d** as the flock of his people. 3427
11:11 It was revoked on that **d,** 3427
12: 3 On that **d,** when all the nations of 3427
12: 4 that **d** I will strike every horse with panic 3427
12: 6 "On that **d** I will make the leaders of Judah 3427
12: 8 that **d** the LORD will shield those who live 3427
12: 9 On that **d** I will set out to destroy all 3427
12:11 On that **d** the weeping in Jerusalem will 3427
13: 1 "On that **d** a fountain will be opened to 3427
13: 2 that **d,** I will banish the names of the idols 3427
13: 4 "On that **d** every prophet will be ashamed 3427
14: 1 A **d** of the LORD is coming 3427
14: 3 as he fights in the **d** *of* battle. 3427
14: 4 On that **d** his feet will stand on the Mount 3427
14: 6 On that **d** there will be no light, 3427
14: 7 It will be a unique **d,** 3427
14: 7 a **d** known to the LORD. NIH
14: 8 On that **d** living water will flow out 3427
14: 9 On that **d** there will be one LORD, 3427
14:13 that **d** men will be stricken by the LORD 3427
14:20 On that **d** HOLY TO THE LORD will 3427
14:21 that **d** there will no longer be a Canaanite in 3427
Mal 3: 2 But who can endure the **d** *of* his coming? 3427
3:17 "in the **d** when I make 3427
4: 1 the **d** is coming; it will burn like a furnace. 3427
4: 1 that **d** that is coming will set them on fire," 3427
4: 3 under the soles of your feet on the **d** 3427
4: 5 and dreadful **d** *of* the LORD comes. 3427
Mt 6:34 Each **d** has enough trouble of its own. *2465*
7:22 Many will say to me on that **d,** 'Lord, Lord, *2465*
10:15 and Gomorrah on the **d** of judgment than *2465*
11:22 and Sidon on the **d** of judgment than *2465*
11:23 it would have remained to this **d.** *4958*
11:24 be more bearable for Sodom on the **d** *2465*
12: 5 the priests in the temple desecrate the **d** and *NIG*
12:36 that men will have to give account on the **d** *2465*
13: 1 That same **d** Jesus went out of the house *2465*
16:21 be killed and *on* the third **d** be raised to life. *2465*
17:23 and *on* the third **d** he will be raised to life." *2465*
20: 2 He agreed to pay them a denarius *for* the **d** *2465*
20: 6 'Why have you been standing here all **d** *long* doing nothing?' *2465*
20:12 of the work and the **heat of the d.'** *3014*
20:19 *On* the third **d** he will be raised to life!" *2465*
22:23 That same **d** the Sadducees, *2465*
22:46 and from that **d** on no one dared *2465*
24:36 "No one knows about that **d** or hour, *2465*
24:38 up to the **d** Noah entered the ark; *2465*
24:42 not know *on* what **d** your Lord will come. *2465*
24:50 The master of that servant will come on a **d** *2465*

Mt 25:13 because you do not know the **d** or the hour. 2465
26:17 On the first **d** of the Feast NIG
26:29 until that **d** when I drink it anew with you 2465
26:55 **Every d** I sat in the temple courts teaching, 2465+2848
27: 8 the Field of Blood to this **d.** 4958
27:62 The **next d,** the one after Preparation Day, 2069
27:62 The next day, the one after **Preparation D,** 4187
27:64 to be made secure until the third **d.** 2465
28: 1 at dawn on the first **d** of the week, NIG
28:15 among the Jews to this **very d.** 2465+4958
Mk 2:20 and on that **d** they will fast. 2465
4:27 Night and **d,** whether he sleeps or gets up, 2465
4:35 That **d** when evening came, 2465
5: 5 Night and **d** among the tombs and in 2465
6:35 By this time it was **late in the d,** 4498+6052
11:12 The **next d** as they were leaving Bethany, 2069
13:32 "No one knows about that **d** or hour, 2465
14:12 *On* the first **d** of the Feast 2465
14:25 of the vine until that **d** when I drink it anew 2465
14:49 **Every d** I was with you, 2465+2848
15:42 It was **Preparation D** (that is, 4187
15:42 **d before the Sabbath).** 4640
16: 2 Very early on the first **d** of the week, NIG
16: 9 on the first **d of the week,** 4879
Lk 1:20 not able to speak until the **d** this happens, 2465
1:59 On the eighth **d** they came to circumcise 2465
2:21 On the eighth **d,** when it was time 2465
2:37 the temple but worshiped night and **d,** 2465
2:44 they traveled on *for* a **d.** 2465
4:16 the Sabbath **d** he went into the synagogue, 2465
5: 1 **One d** as Jesus was standing by the Lake of Gennesaret, 1181+1254
5:17 One **d** as he was teaching, 2465
6:23 "Rejoice in that **d** and leap for joy, 2465
8:22 One **d** Jesus said to his disciples, 2465
9:22 and he must be killed and *on* the third **d** 2465
9:37 The next **d,** when they came down from 2465
10:12 be more bearable on that **d** for Sodom than 2465
10:35 The **next d** he took out two silver coins 892
11: 1 **One d** Jesus was praying in a certain place. 1181+2779
11: 3 Give us each **d** our daily bread. 2465
12:46 The master of that servant will come on a **d** 2465
13:16 *on* the Sabbath **d** from what bound her?" 2465
13:32 and on the third **d** I will reach my goal.' NIG
13:33 and tomorrow and the **next d—** 2400
14: 5 that falls into a well on the Sabbath **d,** 2465
16:19 and fine linen and lived in luxury every **d.** 2465
17: 4 If he sins against you seven times *in* a **d,** 2465
17:24 of Man in his **d** will be like the lightning, 2465
17:27 in marriage up to the **d** Noah entered 2465
17:29 But the **d** Lot left Sodom, 2465
17:30 "It will be just like this on the **d** the Son 2465
17:31 On that **d** no one who is on the roof 2465
18: 7 who cry out to him **d** and night? 2465
18:33 *On* the third **d** he will rise again." 2465
19:42 on this **d** what would bring you peace— 2465
19:47 Every **d** he was teaching at the temple. 2465
20: 1 One **d** as he was teaching the people in 2465
21:34 that **d** will close on you unexpectedly like 2465
21:37 **Each d** Jesus was teaching at the temple, 2465+3836
22: 7 Then came the **d** of Unleavened Bread 2465
22:53 Every **d** I was with you in 2465
23:12 That **d** Herod and Pilate became friends— 2465
23:54 It was Preparation **D,** 2465
24: 1 *On* the **first d** of the week, 1651
24: 7 and *on* the third **d** be raised again.' " 2465
24:13 Now that same **d** two of them were going to 2465
24:21 it is the third **d** since all this took place. 2465
24:29 the **d** is almost over." 2465
24:46 and rise from the dead *on* the third **d,** 2465
Jn 1:29 The **next d** John saw Jesus coming 2069
1:35 The **next d** John was there again with two 2069
1:39 and spent that **d** with him. 2465
1:43 **next d** Jesus decided to leave for Galilee. 2069
2: 1 the third **d** a wedding took place at Cana 2465
5: 9 The **d** on which this took place was 2465
5:17 at his work to **this very d,** 785
6:22 The **next d** the crowd that had stayed on 2069
6:39 but raise them up at the last **d.** 2465
6:40 and I will raise him up at the last **d."** 2465
6:44 and I will raise him up at the last **d.** 2465
6:54 and I will raise him up *at* the last **d.** 2465
7:37 On the last and greatest **d** of the Feast, 2465
8:56 at the thought of seeing my **d;** 2465
9: 4 As long as it is **d,** 2465
9:14 the **d** on which Jesus had made the mud 2465
11: 9 A man who walks by **d** will not stumble, 2465
11:24 in the resurrection at the last **d."** 2465
11:53 from that **d** on they plotted to take his life. 2465
12: 7 that she should save this perfume for the **d** 2465
12:12 The **next d** the great crowd that had come 2069
12:48 will condemn him at the last **d.** 2465
14:20 On that **d** you will realize that I am 2465
16:23 that **d** you will no longer ask me anything. 2465
16:26 In that **d** you will ask in my name. 2465
19:14 the **d of Preparation** of Passover Week, 4187
19:31 Now it was the **d of Preparation,** 4187
19:31 and the next **d** was to be a special Sabbath. 2465
19:42 the Jewish **d of Preparation** and since 4187
20: 1 Early on the first **d** of the week, NIG
20:19 On the evening *of* that first **d** of the week, 2465
Ac 1: 2 until the **d** he was taken up to heaven, 2465
2: 1 When the **d** of Pentecost came, 2465
2:20 the coming of the great and glorious **d** of 2465
2:29 and his tomb is here to this **d.** 2465
2:41 to their number that **d.** 2465
2:46 Every **d** they continued to meet together in 2465
3: 1 One **d** Peter and John were going up to NIG
3: 2 where he was put every **d** to beg 2465
4: 3 they put them in jail until the **next d.** 892
4: 5 The **next d** the rulers, 892
5:42 **D after day,** in the temple courts and 2465+4246
5:42 **Day after d,** in the temple courts and 2465+4246
7:26 The next **d** Moses came 2465
8: 1 that **d** a great persecution broke out against 2465
9:24 **D** and night they kept close watch on 2465
10: 3 One **d** at about three in the afternoon he had NIG
10: 9 About noon the **following d** as they were 2069
10:23 The **next d** Peter started out with them, 2069
10:24 The **following d** he arrived in Caesarea. 2069
10:40 the dead on the third **d** and caused him to 2465
12:21 *On* the appointed **d** Herod, 2465
14:20 The **next d** he and Barnabas left for Derbe. 2069
16:11 and the **next d** on to Neapolis. 2079
17:11 and examined the Scriptures every **d** to see 2465
17:17 in the marketplace **d by day** 2465+2848+4246
17:17 in the marketplace **day by d** 2465+2848+4246
17:31 For he has set a **d** when he will judge 2465
19:15 [One **d**] the evil spirit answered them, NIG
20: 7 On the first **d** of the week we came together NIG
20: 7 because he intended to leave the **next d,** 2069
20:15 The **next d** we set sail from there 2079
20:15 The **d after** that we crossed over to Samos, 2283
20:15 and on the following **d** arrived at Miletus. NIG
20:16 if possible, by the **d** of Pentecost. 2465
20:18 the first **d** I came into the province of Asia. 2465
20:31 of you night and **d** with tears. 2465
21: 1 The next **d** we went to Rhodes and NIG
21: 7 the brothers and stayed with them *for* a **d.** 2465
21: 8 Leaving the **next d,** 2069
21:18 The **next d** Paul and the rest of us went 2079
21:26 The next **d** Paul took the men 2465
22:30 The **next d,** since the commander wanted 2069
23: 1 to God in all good conscience to this **d."** 2465
23:32 The **next d** they let the cavalry go on 2069
25: 6 and the **next d** he convened the court 2069
25:17 the court the next **d** and ordered the man to NIG
25:23 The **next d** Agrippa and Bernice came 2069
26: 7 as they earnestly serve God **d** and night. 2465
26:22 But I have had God's help to this very **d,** 2465
27: 3 The next **d** we landed at Sidon; NIG
27:18 from the storm that the next **d** they began NIG
27:19 On the third **d,** they threw the ship's NIG
28:13 **The next d** the south wind came up, 1651+2465+3552
28:13 **on the following d** we reached Puteoli. 1308
28:23 They arranged to meet Paul on a certain **d,** 2465
Ro 2: 5 against yourself for the **d** of God's wrath, 2465
2:16 on the **d** when God will judge men's secrets 2465
8:36 "For your sake we face death all **d** *long;* 2465
10:21 "All **d** long I have held out my hands to 2465
11: 8 so that they could not hear, to this **very d."** 2465+4958
13:12 night is nearly over; the **d** is almost here. 2465
14: 5 One man considers one **d** more sacred than another; 2465
14: 5 another man considers every **d** alike. 2465
14: 6 He who regards one **d** as special, 2465
1Co 1: 8 so that you will be blameless on the **d** 2465
3:13 because the **D** will bring it to light. 2465
5: 5 be destroyed and his spirit saved on the **d** of 2465
10: 8 and *in* one **d** twenty-three thousand 2465
15: 4 that he was raised *on* the third **d** according 2465
15:31 I die every **d—** 2465
16: 2 On the first **d** of every week, NIG
2Co 1:14 of us just as we will boast of you in the **d** of 2465
3:14 for to **this d** the same veil remains when 2465+3836+4958
3:15 Even to **this d** when Moses is read, 4958
4:16 inwardly we are being renewed **d** by day. 2465
4:16 inwardly we are being renewed day by **d.** 2465
6: 2 and in the **d** of salvation I helped you." 2465
6: 2 now is the **d** of salvation. 2465
11:25 **a night and a d** in the open sea, 3819
Eph 4:30 with whom you were sealed for the **d** 2465
6:13 so that when the **d** of evil comes, 2465
Php 1: 5 in the gospel from the first **d** until now, 2465
1: 6 on to completion until the **d** of Christ Jesus. 2465
1:10 be pure and blameless until the **d** of Christ, 2465
2:16 that I may boast on the **d** of Christ that I did 2465
3: 5 circumcised on the **eighth d,** of the people 3892
Col 1: 6 among you since the **d** you heard it 2465
1: 9 since the **d** we heard about you, 2465
2:16 a New Moon celebration or a **Sabbath d.** 4879
1Th 2: 9 and **d** in order not to be a burden to anyone 2465
3:10 Night and **d** we pray most earnestly 2465
5: 2 that the **d** of the Lord will come like a thief 2465
5: 4 that this **d** should surprise you like a thief. 2465
5: 5 of the light and sons *of* the **d.** 2465
5: 8 But since we belong *to* the **d,** 2465
2Th 1:10 on the **d** he comes to be glorified 2465
2: 2 that the **d** of the Lord has already come. 2465
2: 3 for [that **d** will not come] until NIG
3: 8 On the contrary, we worked night and **d,** 2465
1Ti 5: 5 in God and continues night and **d** to pray 2465
2Ti 1: 3 as night and **d** I constantly remember you 2465
1:12 I have entrusted to him for that **d.** 2465
1:18 from the Lord on that **d!** 2465
4: 8 will award to me on that **d—** 2465
Heb 4: 4 about the seventh **d** in these words: NIG
4: 4 "And on the seventh **d** God rested 2465
4: 7 Therefore God again set a certain **d,** 2465
4: 8 not have spoken later about another **d.** 2465
7:27 not need to offer sacrifices **d after day** 2465+2848
7:27 not need to offer sacrifices **day after d** 2465+2848
10:11 **D after day** every priest stands 2465+2848
10:11 **Day after d** every priest stands 2465+2848
10:25 all the more as you see the **D** approaching. 2465
Jas 5: 5 You have fattened yourselves in the **d** 2465
1Pe 2:12 and glorify God on the **d** he visits us. 2465
2Pe 1:19 until the **d** dawns and the morning star rises 2465
2: 8 living among them **d** after day, 2465
2: 8 living among them day after **d,** 2465
2: 9 the unrighteous for the **d** of judgment, 2465
3: 7 for the **d** of judgment and destruction 2465
3: 8 With the Lord a **d** is like a thousand years, 2465
3: 8 and a thousand years are like a **d.** 2465
3:10 But the **d** of the Lord will come like a thief. 2465
3:12 to the **d** of God and speed its coming. 2465
3:12 **That d** will bring about the destruction of 4005[S]
1Jn 4:17 so that we will have confidence on the **d** 2465
Jude 1: 6 for judgment on the great **D.** 2465
Rev 1:10 On the Lord's **D** I was in the Spirit, 2465
4: 8 **D** and night they never stop saying: 2465
6:17 For the great **d** of their wrath has come, 2465
7:15 before the throne of God and serve him **d** 2465
8:12 A third of the **d** was without light, 2465
9:15 and **d** and month and year were released 2465
12:10 who accuses them before our God **d** 2465
14:11 There is no rest **d** or night 2465
16:14 to gather them for the battle *on* the great **d** 2465
18: 8 in one **d** her plagues will overtake her: 2465
20:10 They will be tormented **d** and night for ever 2465
21:25 On no **d** will its gates ever be shut, 2465

DAY'S (9) [DAY]

Nu 11:31 as far as a **d** walk in any direction. 3427
1Ki 8:59 according to **each d** need, 3427+3427
19: 4 he himself went a **d** journey into the desert. 3427
1Ch 16:37 according to **each d** requirements. 928+2257+3427+3427
2Ch 8:14 the priests according to **each d** requirement. 928+3427+3427
Est 9:13 to carry out this **d** edict tomorrow also, 3427
Ac 1:12 a **Sabbath d walk from** the city. 1584+2400+3847+4879
Rev 6: 6 saying, "A quart of wheat *for* **a d wages,** 1324
6: 6 and three quarts of barley *for* **a d wages,** 1324

DAYBREAK (14) [DAY]

Ge 32:24 and a man wrestled with him till **d.** 8840
32:26 Then the man said, "Let me go, for it is **d."** 8840
Ex 14:27 and at **d** the sea went back to its place. 1332+7155
Jos 6:15 they got up at **d** and marched around 2021+6590+8840
Jdg 19:26 At **d** the woman went back to the house 1332+2021+7155
1Sa 9:26 about **d** and Samuel called to Saul on 2021+6590+8840
25:34 to Nabal would have been left alive by **d."** 240+1332+2021
25:36 So she told him nothing until **d.** 240+1332+2021
2Sa 2:32 and arrived at Hebron *by* **d.** 239
17:22 By **d,** no one was left who had not crossed 240+1332+2021
Ne 8: 3 from **d** till noon as he faced the square 240
Lk 4:42 **At d** Jesus went out to a solitary place. 1181+2002+2465
22:66 At **d** the council of the elders of the people, 1181+2465
Ac 5:21 At **d** they entered the temple courts, 3986

DAYLIGHT (17) [DAY, LIGHT]

Nu 25: 4 kill them and expose them in **broad d** 9087
Jdg 19:26 fell down at the door and lay there until **d.** 240
2Sa 12:11 and he will lie with your wives **in broad d.** 2021+2021+2296+4200+6524+9087
12:12 I will do this thing **in broad d** 2021+5584+9087
2Ki 7: 9 If we wait until **d,** 240+1332+2021
Job 3: 9 for **d** in vain and not see the first rays 240
24:14 When **d** is gone, the murderer rises up 240
Jer 6: 4 But, alas, the **d** is fading, 3427
Am 8: 9 noon and darken the earth in **broad d.** 240+3427
Mt 10:27 What I tell you in the dark, speak in the **d;** 5890
Lk 12: 3 in the dark will be heard in the **d,** 5890
Jn 11: 9 "Are there not twelve hours *of* **d?** 2465
Ac 16:35 When it was **d,** 2465
20:11 After talking until **d,** he left. 879
27:29 from the stern and prayed for **d.** 2465
27:39 When **d** came, they did not recognize 2465
2Pe 2:13 of pleasure is to carouse in **broad d.** 2465

DAYS (619) [DAY]

Ge 1:14 as signs to mark seasons and **d** and years, 3427
3:14 on your belly and you will eat dust all the **d** 3427
3:17 you will eat of it all the **d** *of* your life. 3427
6: 3 his **d** will be a hundred and twenty years." 3427
6: 4 The Nephilim were on the earth in those **d** 3427
7: 4 Seven **d** from now I will send rain on 3427
7: 4 now I will send rain on the earth for forty **d** 3427
7:10 And after the seven **d** the floodwaters came 3427
7:12 on the earth forty **d** and forty nights. 3427
7:17 For forty **d** the flood kept coming on 3427
7:24 the earth for a hundred and fifty **d.** 3427
8: 3 the hundred and fifty **d** the water had gone 3427

Ge 8: 6 After forty **d** Noah opened 3427
8:10 He waited seven more **d** and again sent out 3427
8:12 He waited seven more **d** and sent 3427
17:12 among you who is eight **d** old must 3427
21: 4 When his son Isaac was eight **d** old, 3427
24:55 "Let the girl remain with us ten **d** or so; 3427
27:41 "The **d** *of* mourning for my father are near; 3427
29:20 like only a few **d** to him because of his love 3427
31:23 he pursued Jacob for seven **d** and caught up 3427
34:25 Three **d** later, while all of them were still 3427
37:34 and mourned for his son many **d.** 3427
40:12 "The three branches are three **d.** 3427
40:13 Within three **d** Pharaoh will lift 3427
40:18 "The three baskets are three **d.** 3427
40:19 Within three **d** Pharaoh will lift off your head 3427
42:17 And he put them all in custody for three **d.** 3427
49: 1 to you in **d** to come. 3427
50: 3 taking a full forty **d,** 3427
50: 3 the Egyptians mourned for him seventy **d.** 3427
50: 4 When the **d** *of* mourning had passed, 3427
Ex 7:25 Seven **d** passed after the LORD struck 3427
10:22 and total darkness covered all Egypt *for* three **d.** 3427
10:23 or leave his place *for* three **d.** 3427
12:15 *For* seven **d** you are to eat bread made 3427
12:16 Do no work at all on **these d,** 2157S
12:19 *For* seven **d** no yeast is to be found 3427
13: 6 *For* seven **d** eat bread made without yeast 3427
13: 7 *during* those seven **d;** 3427
13:14 "*In* **d to come,** when your son asks you, 4737
15:22 *For* three **d** they traveled in the desert 3427
16: 5 as much as they gather *on* the **other d.** 3427+3427
16:26 Six **d** you are to gather it, 3427
16:29 the sixth day he gives you bread *for two* **d.** 3427
20: 9 Six **d** you shall labor and do all your work, 3427
20:11 *in* six **d** the LORD made the heavens and 3427
22:30 with their mothers *for* seven **d,** 3427
23:12 "Six **d** do your work, 3427
23:15 *for* seven **d** eat bread made without yeast, 3427
24:16 *For* six **d** the cloud covered the mountain, 3427
24:18 on the mountain forty **d** and forty nights. 3427
29:30 in the Holy Place is to wear them seven **d.** 3427
29:35 taking seven **d** to ordain them. 3427
29:37 *For* seven **d** make atonement for the altar 3427
31:15 *For* six **d,** work is to be done, 3427
31:17 *in* six **d** the LORD made the heavens and 3427
34:18 *For* seven **d** eat bread made without yeast, 3427
34:21 "Six **d** you shall labor, 3427
34:28 Moses was there with the LORD forty **d** 3427
35: 2 *For* six **d,** work is to be done, but 3427
Lev 8:33 to the Tent of Meeting *for* seven **d,** 3427
8:33 the **d** *of* your ordination are completed, 3427
8:33 for your ordination will last seven **d.** 3427
8:35 of Meeting day and night *for* seven **d** 3427
12: 2 be ceremonially unclean *for* seven **d,** 3427
12: 4 Then the woman must wait thirty-three **d** to 3427
12: 4 until the **d** *of* her purification are over. 3427
12: 5 Then she must wait sixty-six **d** to 3427
12: 6 " 'When the **d** *of* her purification for a son 3427
13: 4 the infected person in isolation *for* seven **d.** 3427
13: 5 to keep him in isolation another seven **d.** 3427
13:21 priest is to put him in isolation *for* seven **d.** 3427
13:26 priest is to put him in isolation *for* seven **d.** 3427
13:31 the infected person in isolation *for* seven **d.** 3427
13:33 to keep him in isolation another seven **d.** 3427
13:50 and isolate the affected article *for* seven **d.** 3427
13:54 Then he is to isolate it *for* another seven **d.** 3427
14: 8 he must stay outside his tent *for* seven **d.** 3427
14:38 of the house and close it up *for* seven **d.** 3427
15:13 he is to count off seven **d** 3427
15:19 of her monthly period will last seven **d,** 3427
15:24 he will be unclean *for* seven **d;** 3427
15:25 a discharge of blood *for* many **d** at 3427
15:25 just as in the **d** *of* her period. 3427
15:28 she must count off seven **d,** 3427
22:27 it is to remain with its mother *for* seven **d.** 3427
23: 3 " 'There are six **d** when you may work, 3427
23: 6 *for* seven **d** you must eat bread made 3427
23: 8 *For* seven **d** present an offering made to 3427
23:16 Count off fifty **d** up to the day after 3427
23:34 and it lasts *for* seven **d.** 3427
23:36 *For* seven **d** present offerings made to 3427
23:39 the festival to the LORD *for* seven **d;** 3427
23:40 before the LORD your God *for* seven **d.** 3427
23:41 to the LORD *for* seven **d** each year. 3427
23:42 Live in booths *for* seven **d:** 3427
Nu 6:12 The previous **d** do not count, 3427
9:20 over the tabernacle only a few **d;** 3427
9:22 over the tabernacle *for two* **d** or a month or 3427
10:33 of the LORD and traveled for three **d.** 3427
10:33 *during* those three **d** to find them a place 3427
11:19 or *two* **d,** or five, ten or twenty days, 3427
11:19 or two days, or five, ten or twenty **d,** 3427
12:14 not have been in disgrace *for* seven **d?** 3427
12:14 Confine her outside the camp *for* seven **d;** 3427
12:15 was confined outside the camp *for* seven **d,** 3427
13:25 of forty **d** they returned from exploring 3427
14:34 of the forty **d** you explored the land— 3427
19:11 of anyone will be unclean *for* seven **d.** 3427
19:12 on the third and seventh **d,** 3427
19:14 in it will be unclean *for* seven **d,** 3427
19:16 will be unclean *for* seven **d.** 3427
19:19 on the third and seventh **d,** 3427
20:29 of Israel mourned for him thirty **d.** 3427
24:14 to your people in **d** to come." 3427
28:17 *for* seven **d** eat bread made without yeast. 3427
Nu 28:24 *for* seven **d** as an aroma pleasing to 3427
29:12 a festival to the LORD *for* seven **d.** 3427
31:19 stay outside the camp seven **d.** 3427
31:19 and seventh **d** you must purify yourselves 3427
33: 8 and when they had traveled *for* three **d** in 3427
Dt 1: 2 (It takes eleven **d** to go from Horeb 3427
1:46 And so you stayed in Kadesh many **d—** 3427
4:30 then in later **d** you will return to 3427
4:32 Ask now about the former **d,** 3427
5:13 Six **d** you shall labor and do all your work, 3427
5:33 and prosper and prolong your **d** in the land 3427
9: 9 on the mountain forty **d** and forty nights; 3427
9:11 At the end of the forty **d** and forty nights, 3427
9:18 the LORD *for* forty **d** and forty nights; 3427
9:25 the LORD those forty **d** and forty nights 3427
10:10 Now I had stayed on the mountain forty **d** 3427
11:21 so that your **d** and the days 3427
11:21 and the **d** *of* your children may be many in 3427
11:21 as many as the **d** that the heavens are above 3427
16: 3 but *for* seven **d** eat unleavened bread, 3427
16: 3 the **d** *of* your life you may remember 3427
16: 4 in all your land *for* seven **d.** 3427
16: 8 *For* six **d** eat unleavened bread and on 3427
16:13 the Feast of Tabernacles *for* seven **d** 3427
16:15 *For* seven **d** celebrate the Feast to 3427
17:19 and he is to read it all the **d** *of* his life so 3427
28:33 but cruel oppression all your **d.** 3427
31:29 In **d** to come, disaster will fall upon you 3427
32: 7 Remember the **d** of old; 3427
33:25 and your strength will equal your **d.** 3427
34: 8 for Moses in the plains of Moab thirty **d,** 3427
Jos 1: 5 be able to stand up against you all the **d** 3427
1:11 Three **d** from now you will cross 3427
2:16 Hide yourselves there three **d** 3427
2:22 into the hills and stayed there three **d,** 3427
3: 2 After three **d** the officers went throughout 3427
4:14 and they revered him all the **d** *of* his life, 3427
6: 3 Do this *for* six **d.** 3427
6:14 They did this *for* six **d.** 3427
9:16 Three **d** after they made the treaty with 3427
Jdg 5: 6 "In the **d** *of* Shamgar son of Anath, 3427
5: 6 in the **d** *of* Jael, the roads were abandoned; 3427
11:40 of Israel go out *for* four **d** to commemorate 3427
14:12 the answer *within* the seven **d** *of* the feast, 3427
14:14 *For* three **d** they could not give the answer. 3427
14:17 She cried the whole seven **d** of the feast. 3427
15:20 for twenty years in the **d** *of* the Philistines. 3427
17: 6 In those **d** Israel had no king; 3427
18: 1 In those **d** Israel had no king. 3427
18: 1 And in those **d** the tribe of the Danites 3427
19: 1 In those **d** Israel had no king. 3427
19: 4 so he remained with him three **d,** 3427
20:27 (In those **d** the ark of the covenant 3427
21:25 In those **d** Israel had no king; 3427
Ru 1: 1 In the **d** *when* the judges ruled, 3427
1Sa 1:11 to the LORD *for* all the **d** *of* his life, 3427
3: 1 In those **d** the word of the LORD was rare; 3427
7:15 as judge over Israel all the **d** *of* his life. 3427
9:20 As for the donkeys you lost three **d** ago, 3427
10: 8 but you must wait seven **d** until I come 3427
11: 3 "Give us seven **d** so we can send 3427
13: 8 He waited seven **d,** the time set by Samuel; 3427
14:52 All the **d** *of* Saul there was bitter war with 3427
17:16 *For* forty **d** the Philistine came forward every morning 3427
18:29 he remained his enemy the rest of his **d.** 3427
25:10 from their masters these **d.** 3427
25:38 About ten **d** later, 3427
27: 1 of these **d** I will be destroyed by the hand 3427
28: 1 In those **d** the Philistines gathered their 3427
30:12 or drunk any water *for* three **d** 3427
30:13 when I became ill three **d** ago. 3427
31:13 and they fasted seven **d.** 3427
2Sa 1: 1 the Amalekites and stayed in Ziklag two **d.** 3427
7:12 When your **d** are over and you rest 3427
14: 2 a woman who has spent many **d** grieving 3427
16:23 in those **d** the advice Ahithophel gave was 3427
20: 4 of Judah to come to me *within* three **d,** 3427
21: 9 they were put to death during the first **d** *of* 3427
24: 8 at the end of nine months and twenty **d.** 3427
24:13 Or three **d** of plague in your land? 3427
1Ki 8:65 before the LORD our God for seven **d** 3427
8:65 for seven days and seven **d** more, 3427
8:65 fourteen **d** in all. 3427
10:21 of little value in Solomon's **d.** 3427
11:34 I have made him ruler all the **d** *of* his life 3427
12: 5 "Go away for three **d** and then come back 3427
12:12 Three **d** later Jeroboam and all 3427
12:12 "Come back to me in three **d."** 3427
15: 5 of the LORD's commands all the **d** 3427
16:15 Zimri reigned in Tirzah seven **d.** 3427
19: 8 he traveled forty **d** and forty nights 3427
20:29 *For* seven **d** they camped opposite each other, 3427
21:29 but I will bring it on his house in the **d** 3427
2Ki 2:17 who searched *for* three **d** but did 3427
3: 9 After a roundabout march of seven **d,** 3427
10:32 In those **d** the LORD began to reduce 3427
15:37 (In those **d** the LORD began 3427
19:25 In **d** of old I planned it; 3427
20: 1 In those **d** Hezekiah became ill and was at 3427
23:22 since the **d** *of* the judges who led Israel, 3427
23:22 throughout the **d** *of* the kings of Israel and 3427
1Ch 4:41 in the **d** *of* Hezekiah king of Judah. 3427
7:22 Ephraim mourned for them many **d,** 3427
10:12 and they fasted seven **d.** 3427
12:39 The men spent three **d** there with David, 3427
1Ch 17:11 When your **d** are over and you go to be 3427
21:12 or three **d** of the sword of the LORD— 3427
21:12 **d** of plague in the land, NIH
29:15 Our **d** on earth are like a shadow, 3427
2Ch 7: 8 *for* seven **d,** and all Israel with him— 3427
7: 9 the dedication of the altar *for* seven **d** and 3427
7: 9 and the festival *for* seven **d** more. 3427
10: 5 "Come back to me in three **d."** 3427
10:12 Three **d** later Jeroboam and all 3427
10:12 "Come back to me in three **d."** 3427
14: 1 and in his **d** the country was at peace 3427
15: 5 In those **d** it was not safe to travel about, 6961
20:25 so much plunder that it took three **d** 3427
26: 5 He sought God during the **d** *of* Zechariah, 3427
29:17 For eight more **d** they consecrated 3427
30:21 the Feast of Unleavened Bread *for* seven **d** 3427
30:22 the seven **d** they ate their assigned portion 3427
30:23 to celebrate the festival seven more **d;** 3427
30:23 another seven **d** they celebrated joyfully. 3427
30:26 since the **d** *of* Solomon son of David king 3427
32:24 In those **d** Hezekiah became ill and was at 3427
32:26 upon them during the **d** *of* Hezekiah. 3427
35:17 the Feast of Unleavened Bread *for* seven **d.** 3427
35:18 in Israel since the **d** *of* the prophet Samuel; 3427
36: 9 in Jerusalem three months and ten **d.** 3427
Ezr 4: 7 And in the **d** *of* Artaxerxes king of Persia, 3427
6:22 *For* seven **d** they celebrated with joy 3427
8:15 and we camped there three **d.** 3427
8:32 where we rested three **d.** 3427
9: 7 From the **d** *of* our forefathers until now, 3427
10: 8 within three **d** would forfeit all his property, 3427
10: 9 Within the three **d,** 3427
Ne 1: 4 *For some* **d** I mourned and fasted 3427
2:11 and after staying there three **d** 3427
5:18 and every ten **d** an abundant supply of wine 3427
6:15 on the twenty-fifth of Elul, in fifty-two **d.** 3427
6:17 in those **d** the nobles 3427
8:17 the **d** *of* Joshua son of Nun until that day, 3427
8:18 They celebrated the feast *for* seven **d,** 3427
9:32 and all your people, from the **d** *of* the kings 3427
12: 7 of the priests and their associates in the **d** 3427
12:12 In the **d** *of* Joiakim, 3427
12:22 The family heads of the Levites in the **d** 3427
12:26 They served in the **d** *of* Joiakim son 3427
12:26 and in the **d** *of* Nehemiah the governor and 3427
12:46 For long ago, in the **d** *of* David and Asaph, 3427
12:47 in the **d** *of* Zerubbabel and of Nehemiah, 3427
13:15 In those **d** I saw men 3427
13:23 in those **d** I saw men 3427
Est 1: 4 a full 180 **d** he displayed the vast wealth 3427
1: 5 When these **d** were over, 3427
1: 5 the king gave a banquet, lasting seven **d,** 3427
4:11 But thirty **d** have passed since I was called 3427
4:16 Do not eat or drink *for* three **d,** 3427
9:21 the fourteenth and fifteenth **d** of the month 3427
9:22 to observe **the d** as days of feasting and joy 4392S
9:22 as **d** *of* feasting and joy and giving presents 3427
9:26 (Therefore these **d** were called Purim, 3427
9:27 without fail observe these two **d** every year, 3427
9:28 These **d** should be remembered 3427
9:28 And these **d** *of* Purim should never cease to 3427
9:31 to establish these **d** *of* Purim 3427
Job 2:13 with him *for* seven **d** and seven nights. 3427
3: 6 the **d** *of* the year nor be entered in any of 3427
3: 8 May those who curse **d** curse that day, 3427
7: 1 Are not his **d** like those of a hired man? 3427
7: 6 "My **d** are swifter than a weaver's shuttle, 3427
7:16 Let me alone; my **d** have no meaning. 3427
8: 9 and our **d** on earth are but a shadow. 3427
9:25 "My **d** are swifter than a runner; 3427
10: 5 Are your **d** like those of a mortal 3427
10:20 Are not my few **d** almost over? 3427
14: 1 "Man born of woman is of few **d** and full 3427
14: 5 Man's **d** are determined; 3427
14:14 All the **d** *of* my hard service I will wait 3427
15:20 All his **d** the wicked man suffers torment, 3427
17: 1 My spirit is broken, my **d** are cut short, 3427
17:11 My **d** have passed, my plans are shattered, 3427
24: 1 in vain for such **d?** 3427
29: 2 for the **d** when God watched over me, 3427
29: 4 Oh, for the **d** when I was in my prime, 3427
29:18 my **d** as numerous as the grains of sand. 3427
30:16 my life ebbs away; **d** *of* suffering grip me. 3427
30:27 **d** *of* suffering confront me. 3427
33:25 it is restored as in the **d** *of* his youth. 3427
36:11 of their **d** in prosperity and their years 3427
38:23 for **d** *of* war and battle? 3427
Ps 21: 4 length of **d,** for ever and ever. 3427
23: 6 and love will follow me all the **d** 3427
25:13 He *will* **spend** *his* **d** in prosperity, 4328
27: 4 in the house of the LORD all the **d** 3427
34:12 and desires to see *many* good **d,** 3427
37:18 The **d** *of* the blameless are known to 3427
37:19 in **d** *of* famine they will enjoy plenty. 3427
39: 4 my life's end and the number of my **d;** 3427
39: 5 You have made my **d** a mere handbreadth; 3427
44: 1 our fathers have told us what you did in their **d,** 3427
44: 1 in their days, in **d** long ago. 3427
49: 5 Why should I fear when evil **d** come, 3427
55:23 not live out half their **d.** 3427
61: 6 **d of** the king's **life,** 3427
72: 7 In his **d** the righteous will flourish; 3427
77: 5 I thought about the former **d,** 3427
78:33 So he ended their **d** in futility 3427
89:45 You have cut short the **d** *of* his youth; 3427
90: 9 All our **d** pass away under your wrath; 3427

Ps 90:10 The **length of** our **d** is seventy years— 3427+9102
90:12 Teach us to number our **d** aright, 3427
90:14 we may sing for joy and be glad all our **d.** 3427
90:15 *for* as many **d as** you have afflicted us, 3427
93:5 holiness adorns your house for endless **d,** 3427
94:13 you grant him relief from **d** *of* trouble, 3427
102:3 For my **d** vanish like smoke; 3427
102:11 My **d** are like the evening shadow; 3427
102:23 he cut short my **d.** 3427
102:24 O my God, in the midst of my **d;** 3427
103:15 As for man, his **d** are like grass, 3427
109:8 May his **d** be few; 3427
128:5 the LORD bless you from Zion all the **d** 3427
139:16 All the **d** ordained for me were written 3427
143:5 I remember the **d** of long ago; 3427
144:4 his **d** are like a fleeting shadow. 3427
Pr 9:11 For through me your **d** will be many, 3427
15:15 All the **d** *of* the oppressed are wretched, 3427
31:12 not harm, all the **d** *of* her life. 3427
31:25 she can laugh at the **d** to come. 3427
Ecc 2:3 to do under heaven during the few **d** 3427
2:16 in **d** to come both will be forgotten. 3427
2:23 All his **d** his work is pain and grief; 3427
5:17 All his **d** he eats in darkness, 3427
5:18 the few **d** *of* life God has given him— 3427
5:20 He seldom reflects on the **d** *of* his life, 3427
6:12 during the few and meaningless **d** he passes 3427
7:10 "Why were the old **d** better than these?" 3427
8:13 and their **d** will not lengthen like a shadow. 3427
8:15 the **d** *of* the life God has given him under 3427
9:9 all the **d** *of* this meaningless life 3427
9:9 all your meaningless **d.** 3427
11:1 for after many **d** you will find it again. 3427
11:8 But let him remember the **d** *of* darkness, 3427
11:9 and let your heart give you joy in the **d** 3427
12:1 in the **d** *of* your youth, before the days 3427
12:1 before the **d** *of* trouble come and 3427
Isa 1:26 I will restore your judges as in **d of old,** 8037
2:2 In the last **d** the mountain of the LORD's 3427
13:22 and her **d** will not be prolonged. 3427
24:22 up in prison and be punished after many **d.** 3427
27:6 In **d** to come Jacob will take root, NIH
30:8 **d** to come it may be an everlasting witness. 3427
30:26 like the light of seven *full* **d,** 3427
37:26 In **d** of old I planned it; 3427
38:1 In those **d** Hezekiah became ill and was at 3427
38:20 with stringed instruments all the **d** 3427
43:13 Yes, and from ancient **d** I am he. 3427
51:9 awake, as in **d** gone by, 3427
53:10 he will see his offspring and prolong his **d,** 3427
54:9 "To me this is like the **d** *of* Noah, 3427
60:20 and your **d** *of* sorrow will end. 3427
63:9 he lifted them up and carried them all the **d** 3427
63:11 Then his people recalled the **d** of old, 3427
63:11 the **d** of Moses and his people— NIH
65:20 be in it an infant who lives but a *few* **d,** or 3427
65:22 For as the **d** *of* a tree, 3427
65:22 so will be the **d** *of* my people; 3427
Jer 2:32 Yet my people have forgotten me, **d** 3427
3:16 In those **d,** when your numbers have increased greatly in the land," 3427
3:18 In those **d** the house of Judah will join 3427
5:18 "Yet even in those **d,**" declares the LORD, 3427
7:32 So beware, the **d** are coming, 3427
9:25 "The **d** are coming," declares the LORD, 3427
13:6 Many **d** later the LORD said to me, 3427
16:9 Before your eyes and in your **d** I will bring 3427
16:14 "However, the **d** are coming," 3427
19:6 So beware, the **d** are coming, 3427
20:18 to see trouble and sorrow and to end my **d** 3427
23:5 "The **d** are coming," declares the LORD, 3427
23:6 In his **d** Judah will be saved 3427
23:7 "So then, the **d** are coming," 3427
23:20 In **d** to come you will understand it clearly. 3427
26:18 "Micah of Moresheth prophesied in the **d** 3427
30:3 The **d** are coming,' declares the LORD, 3427
30:20 Their children will be as in **d of old,** 7710
30:24 In **d** to come you will understand this. 3427
31:27 "The **d** are coming," declares the LORD, 3427
31:29 "In those **d** people will no longer say, 3427
31:38 "The **d** are coming," declares the LORD, 3427
33:14 " 'The **d** are coming,' declares the LORD, 3427
33:15 " 'In those **d** and at that time I will make 3427
33:16 In those **d** Judah will be saved 3427
42:7 Ten **d** later the word of the LORD came 3427
48:12 But **d** are coming," declares the LORD, 3427
48:47 the fortunes of Moab in **d** to come," 3427
49:2 But the **d** are coming," 3427
49:39 "Yet I will restore the fortunes of Elam in **d** 3427
50:4 "In those **d,** at that time," 3427
50:20 In those **d,** at that time," 3427
51:52 "But **d** are coming," declares the LORD, 3427
La 1:7 In the **d** *of* her affliction 3427
1:7 the treasures that were hers in **d** of old. 3427
4:18 Our end was near, our **d** were numbered, 3427
5:21 renew our **d** as of old 3427
Eze 3:15 I sat among them *for* seven **d—** 3427
3:16 of seven **d** the word of the LORD came 3427
4:4 to bear their sin *for* the number of **d** you lie 3427
4:5 I have assigned you the same number of **d** 3427
4:5 *for* 390 **d** you will bear the sin of the house 3427
4:6 I have assigned you 40 **d,** 3427
4:8 until you have finished the **d** *of* your siege. 3427
4:9 You are to eat it during the 390 **d** you lie 3427
5:2 When the **d** *of* your siege come to an end, 3427
12:22 'The **d** go by and every vision comes 3427
12:23 'The **d** are near when every vision will 3427
Eze 12:25 For in your **d,** you rebellious house, 3427
16:22 not remember the **d** *of* your youth, 3427
16:43 " 'Because you did not remember the **d** 3427
16:60 the covenant I made with you in the **d** 3427
22:4 You have brought your **d** to a close, 3427
23:19 and more promiscuous as she recalled the **d** 3427
38:8 After many **d** you will be called to arms. 3427
38:16 In **d** to come, O Gog, 3427
38:17 of in former **d** by my servants the prophets 3427
43:25 "*For* seven **d** you are to provide 3427
43:26 *For* seven **d** they are to make atonement for 3427
43:27 At the end of these **d,** 3427
44:26 After he is cleansed, he must wait seven **d.** 3427
45:21 a feast lasting seven **d,** 3427
45:23 during the seven **d** *of* the Feast he is 3427
45:25 " 'During the seven **d** of the Feast, 3427
46:1 to be shut on the six working **d,** 3427
Da 1:12 "Please test your servants *for* ten **d:** 3427
1:14 he agreed to this and tested them *for* ten **d.** 3427
1:15 the end of the ten **d** they looked healthier 3427
2:28 what will happen in **d** to come. 10317
5:26 the **d** of your reign and brought it to an end. NIH
6:7 to any god or man during the next thirty **d,** 10317
6:12 during the next thirty **d** anyone who prays 10317
7:9 and the Ancient of **D** took his seat. 10317
7:13 of **D** and was led into his presence. 10317
7:22 of **D** came and pronounced judgment 10317
8:27 was exhausted and lay ill *for several* **d.** 3427
10:13 Persian kingdom resisted me twenty-one **d.** 3427
11:6 In those **d** she will be handed over, 6961
12:11 there will be 1,290 **d.** 3427
12:12 for and reaches the end of the 1,335 **d.** 3427
12:13 and then at the end of the **d** you will rise 3427
Hos 2:11 her **Sabbath d**—all her appointed feasts. 8701
2:13 for the **d** she burned incense to the Baals; 3427
2:15 There she will sing as in the **d** *of* her youth, 3427
3:3 "You are to live with me many **d;** 3427
3:4 the Israelites will live many **d** without king 3427
3:5 and to his blessings in the last **d.** 3427
6:2 After *two* **d** he will revive us; 3427
9:5 on the festival **d** *of* the LORD? 3427
9:7 The **d** *of* punishment are coming, 3427
9:7 the **d** *of* reckoning are at hand. 3427
9:9 as in the **d** *of* Gibeah. 3427
10:9 "Since the **d** *of* Gibeah, you have sinned, 3427
12:9 as in the **d** *of* your appointed feasts. 3427
Joel 1:2 in your **d** or in the days of your forefathers? 3427
1:2 or in the **d** *of* your forefathers? 3427
2:29 I will pour out my Spirit in those **d.** 3427
3:1 "In those **d** and at that time, 3427
Am 8:11 "The **d** are coming," declares 3427
9:13 "The **d** are coming," declares the LORD, 3427
Jnh 1:17 inside the fish three **d** and three nights. 3427
3:3 a visit required three **d.** 3427
3:4 "Forty more **d** and Nineveh will 3427
Mic 4:1 In the last **d** the mountain of 3427
7:14 in Bashan and Gilead as in **d** long ago. 3427
7:15 "As in the **d** *when* you came out of Egypt, 3427
7:20 on oath to our fathers in **d** long ago. 3427
Hab 1:5 to do something in your **d** that you would 3427
Zec 8:23 "In those **d** ten men from all languages 3427
14:5 as you fled from the earthquake in the **d** 3427
Mal 3:4 as in **d** gone by, as in former years. 3427
Mt 3:1 In those **d** John the Baptist came, 2465
4:2 After fasting forty **d** and forty nights, 2465
11:12 From the **d** of John the Baptist until now, 2465
12:40 For as Jonah was three **d** and three nights in 2465
12:40 of Man will be three **d** and three nights in 2465
15:32 with me three **d** and have nothing to eat. 2465
17:1 After six **d** Jesus took with him Peter, 2465
23:30 'If we had lived in the **d** of our forefathers, 2465
24:19 How dreadful it will be in those **d** 2465
24:22 If those **d** had not been cut short, 2465
24:22 sake of the elect those **d** will be shortened. 2465
24:29 *of* those **d** " 'the sun will be darkened, and 2465
24:37 As it was in the **d** of Noah, 2465
24:38 For in the **d** before the flood, 2465
26:2 the Passover is two **d** away— 2465
26:61 of God and rebuild it in three **d.'** " 2465
27:40 to destroy the temple and build it in three **d,** 2465
27:63 'After three **d** I will rise again.' 2465
Mk 1:13 and he was in the desert forty **d,** 2465
2:1 A few **d** later, when Jesus again 1328+2465
2:26 **In the d of** Abiathar the high priest, 2093
8:1 those **d** another large crowd gathered. 2465
8:2 with me three **d** and have nothing to eat. 2465
8:31 be killed and after three **d** rise again. 2465
9:2 After six **d** Jesus took Peter, 2465
9:31 and after three **d** he will rise." 2465
10:34 Three **d** later he will rise." 2465
13:17 How dreadful it will be in those **d** 2465
13:19 be **d** of distress unequaled from 2465
13:20 If the Lord had not cut short those **d,** 2465
13:24 "But in those **d,** following that distress, 2465
14:1 Feast of Unleavened Bread were only two **d** away, 2465
14:58 and in three **d** will build another, 2465
15:29 to destroy the temple and build it in three **d,** 2465
Lk 1:25 "In these **d** he has shown his favor 2465
1:75 and righteousness before him all our **d.** 2465
2:1 In those **d** Caesar Augustus issued a decree 2465
2:46 After three **d** they found him in 2465
4:2 *for* forty **d** he was tempted by the devil. 2465
4:2 He ate nothing during those **d,** 2465
5:35 in those **d** they will fast." 2465
6:12 of those **d** Jesus went out to a mountainside 2465
9:28 About eight **d** after Jesus said this, 2465
Lk 13:14 "There are six **d** for work. 2465
13:14 So come and be healed on those **d,** NIG
17:22 when you will long to see one *of* the **d** of 2465
17:26 "Just as it was in the **d** of Noah, 2465
17:26 so also will it be in the **d** of the Son of Man. 2465
17:28 "It was the same in the **d** of Lot. 2465
19:43 The **d** will come upon you 2465
21:23 How dreadful it will be in those **d** 2465
24:18 that have happened there in these **d?"** 2465
Jn 2:12 There they stayed *for* a few **d.** 2465
2:19 and I will raise it again in three **d."** 2465
2:20 and you are going to raise it in three **d?"** 2465
4:40 and he stayed two **d.** 2465
4:43 After the two **d** he left for Galilee. 2465
10:40 John had been baptizing **in the early d.** 4754
11:6 he stayed where he was two more **d.** 2465
11:17 in the tomb *for* four **d.** 2465
11:39 for he has been there **four d."** 5479
12:1 Six **d** before the Passover, 2465
Ac 1:3 to them over a period *of* forty **d** and spoke 2465
1:5 but in a few **d** you will be baptized with 2465
1:15 In those **d** Peter stood up among 2465
2:17 " 'In the last **d,** I will pour out my Spirit 2465
2:18 I will pour out my Spirit in those **d,** 2465
3:24 have foretold these **d.** 2465
5:37 the **d** of the census and led a band of people 2465
6:1 In those **d** when the number 2465
7:8 and circumcised him eight **d** after his birth. 2465
9:9 *For* three **d** he was blind, 2465
9:19 Saul spent several **d** with the disciples 2465
9:23 After many **d** had gone by, 2465
10:30 "Four **d** ago I was in my house praying 2465
10:48 to stay with them *for* a few **d.** 2465
13:31 and for many **d** he was seen 2465
13:41 for I am going to do something in your **d** 2465
16:12 And we stayed there several **d.** 2465
16:18 She kept this up for many **d.** 2465
17:2 on three **Sabbath d** he reasoned with them 4879
20:6 and five **d** later joined the others at Troas, 2465
20:6 where we stayed seven **d.** 2465
21:4 we stayed with them seven **d.** 2465
21:10 After we had been there a number of **d,** 2465
21:26 when the **d** of purification would end and 2465
21:27 When the seven **d** were nearly over, 2465
24:1 Five **d** later the high priest Ananias went 2465
24:11 that no more than twelve **d** ago I went up 2465
24:24 Several **d** later Felix came 2465
25:1 Three **d** after arriving in the province, 2465
25:6 After spending eight or ten **d** with them, 2465
25:13 A few **d** later King Agrippa 2465
25:14 Since they were spending many **d** there, 2465
27:7 We made slow headway for many **d** 2465
27:20 for many **d** and the storm continued raging, 2465
27:33 "For the last fourteen **d,"** he said, 4958
28:7 and *for* three **d** entertained us hospitably. 2465
28:12 in at Syracuse and stayed there three **d.** 2465
28:17 Three **d** later he called together the leaders 2465
Gal 1:18 with Peter and stayed with him fifteen **d.** 2465
4:10 You are observing special **d** and months 2465
Eph 5:16 because the **d** are evil. 2465
Php 4:15 in the early **d** of your acquaintance with NIG
2Ti 3:1 There will be terrible times in the last **d.** 2465
Heb 1:2 but in these last **d** he has spoken to us 2465
5:7 During the **d** of Jesus' life on earth, 2465
7:3 without beginning *of* **d** or end of life, 2465
10:32 Remember those earlier **d** 2465
11:30 around them for seven **d.** 2465
Jas 5:3 You have hoarded wealth in the last **d.** 2465
1Pe 3:10 and see good **d** must keep his tongue 2465
3:20 the **d** of Noah while the ark was being built. 2465
2Pe 3:3 that in the last **d** scoffers will come, 2465
Rev 2:10 and you will suffer persecution *for* ten **d.** 2465
2:13 even in the **d** of Antipas, 2465
9:6 During those **d** men will seek death, 2465
10:7 in the **d** when the seventh angel is about 2465
11:3 and they will prophesy *for* 1,260 **d,** 2465
11:9 and a half **d** men from every people, 2465
11:11 after the three and a half **d** a breath of life 2465
12:6 be taken care of *for* 1,260 **d.** 2465

DAYSMAN (KJV) See ARBITRATE

DAYSPRING (KJV) See DAWN, RISING SUN

DAYTIME (7) [DAY]

Ge 31:40 The heat consumed me in the **d** and 3427
Jdg 6:27 he did it at night rather than **in the d.** 3429
Job 5:14 Darkness comes upon them **in the d;** 3429
Eze 12:3 pack your belongings for exile and **in the d,** 3429
12:4 **During the d,** while they watch, 3429
Zec 14:7 without **d** or nighttime— 3427
Ro 13:13 Let us behave decently, as in the **d,** 2465

DAZZLING (2)

Da 2:31 an enormous, **d** statue, 10228
Mk 9:3 His clothes became **d** white, 5118

DEACON (1) [DEACONS]

1Ti 3:12 A **d** must be the husband of but one wife 1356

DEACONS (3) [DEACON]

Php 1:1 together with the overseers and **d:** 1356

1Ti 3: 8 **D**, likewise, are to be men worthy *1356*
3:10 *let them* **serve as d.** *1354*

DEAD (314) [DIE]

Ge 20: 3 "You *are* **as good as d** because of 4637
23: 3 Then Abraham rose from beside his **d** *wife* 4637
23: 4 for a burial site here so I can bury my **d."** 4637
23: 6 Bury your **d** in the choicest of our tombs. 4637
23: 6 for burying your **d."** 4637
23: 8 "If you are willing to let me bury my **d,** 4637
23:11 Bury your **d."** 4637
23:13 from me so I can bury my **d** there." 4637
23:15 Bury your **d."** 4637
34:27 of Jacob came upon the **d bodies** and looted 2728
42:38 his brother *is* **d** and he is the only one left. 4637
44:20 His brother *is* **d,** 4637
50:15 that their father *was* **d,** 4637
Ex 4:19 all the men who wanted to kill you *are* **d."** 4637
12:30 there was not a house without *someone* **d.** 4637
14:30 and Israel saw the Egyptians *lying* **d** on 4637
21:34 and the **d** *animal* will be his. 4637
21:35 both the money and the **d** *animal* equally. 4637
21:36 and the **d** *animal* will be his. 4637
Lev 7:24 The fat of an **animal found d** or torn 5577
11:31 when they *are* **d** will be unclean 4637
14:51 the blood of the **d** bird and the fresh water, 8821
17:15 who eats **anything found d** or torn 5577
19:28 for the **d** or put tattoo marks on yourselves. 5883
21:11 not enter a place where there is a **d** body. 4637
22: 8 He must not eat **anything found d** or torn 5577
26:30 and pile your **d bodies** on the lifeless forms 7007
Nu 3: 4 **fell d** before the LORD when they made 4637
5: 2 because of a **d body.** 5883
6: 6 he must not go near a **d** body. 4637
6:11 by being in the presence of the **d body.** 5883
9: 6 on account of a **d** body. 5883
9: 7 because of a **d** body, 5883
9:10 of a **d body** or are away on a journey, 5883
16:48 He stood between the living and the **d,** 4637
19:11 the **d** body of anyone will be unclean 4637
19:13 Whoever touches the **d** body of anyone 4637
20: 3 when our brothers **fell d** before 1588
Dt 14: 1 or shave the front of your heads for the **d,** 4637
14:21 Do not eat anything you find **already d.** 5577
18:11 a medium or spiritist or who consults the **d.** 4637
25: 6 of the **d** brother so that his name will not 4637
26:14 nor have I offered any of it to the **d.** 4637
Jos 1: 2 "Moses my servant *is* **d.** 4637
Jdg 3:25 they saw their lord fallen to the floor, **d.** 4637
4:22 through his temple—**d.** 4637
5:27 where he sank, there he fell—**d.** 8720
9:55 the Israelites saw that Abimelech *was* **d,** 4637
Ru 1: 8 as you have shown to your **d** and to me. 4637
2:20 to the living and the **d."** 4637
4: 5 you acquire the **d** *man's* widow, 4637
4: 5 in order to maintain the name of the **d** 4637
4:10 in order to maintain the name of the **d** 4637
1Sa 4:17 Hophni and Phinehas, *are* **d,** 4637
4:19 and her husband *were* **d,** 4637
17:51 the Philistines saw that their hero *was* **d,** 4637
17:52 Their **d** were strewn along 2728
24:14 A **d** dog? A flea? 4637
25:39 When David heard that Nabal *was* **d,** 4637
28: 3 Now Samuel *was* **d,** 4637
31: 5 the armor-bearer saw that Saul *was* **d,** 4637
31: 8 when the Philistines came to strip the **d,** 2728
2Sa 1: 4 And Saul and his son Jonathan *are* **d."** 4637
1: 5 that Saul and his son Jonathan *are* **d?"** 4637
2: 7 for Saul your master *is* **d,** 4637
4:10 when a man told me, 'Saul *is* **d,'** 4637
9: 8 that you should notice a **d** dog like me?" 4637
11:21 'Also, your servant Uriah the Hittite *is* **d.' "** 4637
11:24 your servant Uriah the Hittite *is* **d."** 4637
11:26 Uriah's wife heard that her husband *was* **d,** 4637
12:18 to tell him that the child *was* **d,** 4637
12:18 How can we tell him the child *is* **d?** 4637
12:19 and he realized the child *was* **d.** 4637
12:19 *"Is* the child **d?"** 4637
12:19 "Yes," they replied, *"he is* **d."** 4637
12:21 but now that the child *is* **d,** 4637
12:23 But now that *he is* **d,** why should I fast? 4637
13:32 only Amnon *is* **d.** 4637
13:33 the report that all the king's sons *are* **d.** 4637
13:33 Only Amnon *is* **d."** 4637
14: 2 like a woman who has spent many days
grieving for the **d.** 4637
14: 5 my husband *is* **d.** 4637
16: 9 "Why should this **d** dog curse my lord 4637
18:20 because the king's son *is* **d."** 4637
19: 6 and all of us *were* **d.** 4637
23:10 but only to **strip the d.** 7320
1Ki 3:20 She put him by her breast and put her **d** son 4637
3:21 and *he was* **d!** 4637
3:22 the **d** *one* is yours." 4637
3:22 The **d** *one* is yours; the living one is mine." 4637
3:23 'My son is alive and your son *is* **d,'** 4637
3:23 Your son *is* **d** and mine is alive.' " 4637
11:15 who had gone up to bury the **d,** 2728
11:21 the commander of the army *was* also **d.** 4637
21:14 "Naboth has been stoned and *is* **d."** 4637
21:15 He is no longer alive, but **d."** 4637
21:16 When Ahab heard that Naboth *was* **d,** 4637
2Ki 4: 1 "Your servant my husband *is* **d,** 4637
4:32 there was the boy lying **d** on his couch. 4637
8: 5 the king how Elisha had restored the **d** 4637
11: 1 of Ahaziah saw that her son *was* **d,** 4637

2Ki 19:35 there were all the **d** bodies! 4637
1Ch 10: 5 the armor-bearer saw that Saul *was* **d,** 4637
10: 8 when the Philistines came to strip the **d,** 2728
21:14 seventy thousand men of Israel **fell d.** 5877
2Ch 20:24 they saw only **d bodies** lying on the ground; 7007
22:10 of Ahaziah saw that her son *was* **d,** 4637
Job 1:19 It collapsed on them and *they are* **d,** 4637
26: 5 "The **d** are in deep anguish, 8327
Ps 6: 5 No one remembers you when he is **d.** 4638
31:12 I am forgotten by them as though I *were* **d;** 4637
79: 2 the **d bodies** *of* your servants as food to 5577
79: 3 and there is no one to bury the **d.** NIH
88: 5 I am set apart with the **d,** 4637
88:10 Do you show your wonders to the **d?** 4637
88:10 Do *those who* are **d** rise up and praise you? 8327
110: 6 heaping up the **d** and crushing the rulers of 1581
115:17 It is not the **d** who praise the LORD, 4637
143: 3 in darkness like *those* long **d.** 4637
Pr 2:18 and her paths to the **spirits of the d.** 8327
9:18 But little do they know that the **d** are there, 8327
21:16 to rest in the company of the **d.** 8327
Ecc 4: 2 And I declared that the **d,** 4637
9: 3 and afterward they join the **d.** 4637
9: 4 even a live dog is better off than a **d** lion! 4637
9: 5 but the **d** know nothing; 4637
10: 1 As **d** flies give perfume a bad smell, 4638
Isa 5:25 the **d bodies** are like refuse in the streets. 5577
8:19 Why consult the **d** on behalf of the living? 4637
19: 3 the idols and the **spirits of the d,** 356
26:14 *They are now* **d,** they live no more; 4637
26:19 But your **d** will live; their bodies will rise. 4637
26:19 the earth will give birth to her **d.** 8327
34: 3 their **d bodies** will send up a stench; 7007
37:36 there were all the **d** bodies! 4637
59:10 among the strong, we *are* like the **d.** 4637
66:24 upon the **d bodies** *of* those who rebelled 7007
Jer 7:32 for they will bury the **d** in Topheth NIH
9:22 " 'The **d bodies** *of* men will lie like refuse 5577
16: 4 and their **d bodies** will become food for 5577
16: 7 to comfort those who mourn for the **d—** 4637
19:11 They will bury the **d** in Topheth NIH
22:10 not weep for the **d** [king] or mourn his loss; 4637
31:40 where **d bodies** and ashes are thrown, 7007
33: 5 'They will be filled with the **d bodies** *of* 7007
34:20 Their **d bodies** will become food for 5577
41: 9 of Nethaniah filled it with the **d.** 2728
La 3: 6 in darkness like *those* long **d.** 4637
Eze 4:14 now I have never eaten **anything found d** 5577
6: 5 I will lay the **d bodies** *of* the Israelites 7007
11: 6 in this city and filled its streets with the **d.** 2728
24:17 Groan quietly; do not mourn for the **d.** 4637
44:25 not defile himself by going near a **d** person; 4637
44:25 if the **d** person was his father or mother, NIH
44:31 **found d** or torn by wild animals. 5577
Am 1: 8 till the last of the Philistines *is* **d,"** 6
Na 3: 3 Many casualties, piles of **d,** 7007
Hag 2:13 with a **d body** touches one of these things, 5883
Mt 2:20 to take the child's life *are* **d."** *2569*
8:22 and let the **d** bury their own dead." *3738*
8:22 and let the dead bury their own **d."** *3738*
9:24 The girl *is* not **d** but asleep." *633*
10: 8 Heal the sick, raise the **d,** *3738*
11: 5 the deaf hear, the **d** are raised, *3738*
14: 2 he has risen from the **d!** *3738*
17: 9 the Son of Man has been raised from the **d."** *3738*
22:31 But about the resurrection *of* the **d—** *3738*
22:32 not the God *of* the **d** but of the living." *3738*
23:27 but on the inside are full *of* **d** *men's* bones *3738*
27:64 that he has been raised from the **d.** *3738*
28: 4 that they shook and became like **d** *men.* *3738*
28: 7 'He has risen from the **d** and is going ahead *3738*
Mk 5:35 "Your daughter *is* **d,"** they said. *633*
5:39 The child *is* not **d** but asleep." *633*
6:14 the Baptist has been raised from the **d,** *3738*
6:16 has been raised from the **d!"** *3738*
9: 9 until the Son of Man had risen from the **d.** *3738*
9:10 discussing what "rising from the **d"** meant. *3738*
9:26 like a corpse that many said, *"He's* **d."** *633*
12:25 When the **d** rise, they will neither marry nor *3738*
12:26 Now about the **d** rising— *3738*
12:27 He is not the God *of* the **d,** *3738*
15:44 to hear that *he was* already **d.** *2569*
Lk 7:12 a **d** *person* was being carried out— *2569*
7:15 The **d** *man* sat up and began to talk, *3738*
7:22 the deaf hear, the **d** are raised, *3738*
8:49 "Your daughter *is* **d,"** he said. *2569*
8:52 *"She is* not **d** but asleep." *633*
8:53 knowing that *she was* **d.** *633*
9: 7 that John had been raised from the **d,** *3738*
9:60 "Let the **d** bury their own dead, *3738*
9:60 "Let the dead bury their own **d,** *3738*
10:30 leaving him **half d.** *2467*
15:24 this son of mine was **d** and is alive again; *3738*
15:32 because this brother of yours was **d** *3738*
16:30 'but if someone from the **d** goes to them, *3738*
16:31 even if someone rises from the **d.' "** *3738*
17:37 He replied, "Where there is a **d body,** *5393*
20:35 from the **d** will neither marry nor be given *3738*
20:37 even Moses showed that the **d** rise, *3738*
20:38 He is not the God *of* the **d,** *3738*
24: 5 for the living among the **d?** *3738*
24:46 The Christ will suffer and rise from the **d** *3738*
Jn 2:22 After he was raised from the **d,** *3738*
5:21 the Father raises the **d** and gives them life, *3738*
5:25 now come when the **d** will hear the voice of *3738*
11:14 then he told them plainly, "Lazarus *is* **d,** *633*
11:39 Lord," said Martha, the sister *of* the **d** *man,* *5462*

Jn 11:44 The **d** *man* came out, *2569*
12: 1 whom Jesus had raised from the **d.** *3738*
12: 9 whom he had raised from the **d.** *3738*
12:17 from the **d** continued to spread the word. *3738*
19:33 to Jesus and found that he *was* already **d,** *2569*
20: 9 that Jesus had to rise from the **d.)** *3738*
21:14 after he was raised from the **d.** *3738*
Ac 2:24 **raised** him **from the d,** *482*
3:15 but God raised him from the **d.** *3738*
4: 2 in Jesus the resurrection of the **d.** *3738*
4:10 but whom God raised from the **d,** *3738*
5:10 the young men came in and, finding her **d,** *3738*
5:30 **raised** Jesus **from the d—** *1586*
9:40 Turning toward the **d** *woman,* he said, *5393*
10:40 **raised** him **from the d** *1586*
10:41 with him after he rose from the **d.** *3738*
10:42 as judge *of* the living and the **d.** *3738*
13:30 But God raised him from the **d,** *3738*
13:34 The fact that God raised him from the **d,** *3738*
13:37 But the one whom God **raised from the d** *1586*
14:19 thinking he *was* **d.** *2569*
17: 3 the Christ had to suffer and rise from the **d.** *3738*
17:31 this to all men by raising him from the **d."** *3738*
17:32 about the resurrection *of* the **d,** *3738*
20: 9 from the third story and was picked up **d.** *3738*
23: 6 of my hope in the resurrection *of* the **d."** *3738*
24:21 the **d** that I am on trial before you today.' " *3738*
25:19 about a **d** *man* named Jesus who Paul
claimed was alive. *2569*
26: 8 that God raises the **d?** *3738*
26:23 as the first to rise *from* the **d,** *3738*
28: 6 to swell up or suddenly fall **d,** *3738*
Ro 1: 4 of God by his resurrection *from* the **d:** *3738*
4:17 *to* the **d** and calls things that are not as *3738*
4:19 fact that his body was **as good as d—** *2453+3739*
4:19 and that Sarah's womb was also **d.** *3740*
4:24 him who raised Jesus our Lord from the **d.** *3738*
6: 4 just as Christ was raised from the **d** through *3738*
6: 9 that since Christ was raised from the **d,** *3738*
6:11 count yourselves **d** to sin but alive to God *3738*
7: 4 to him who was raised from the **d,** *3738*
7: 8 For apart from law, sin is **d.** *3738*
8:10 your body is **d** because of sin, *3738*
8:11 of him who raised Jesus from the **d** is living *3738*
8:11 he who raised Christ from the **d** will *3738*
10: 7 (that is, to bring Christ up from the **d).** *3738*
10: 9 that God raised him from the **d,** *3738*
11:15 be but life from the **d?** *3738*
14: 9 that he might be the Lord *of* both the **d** and *3738*
1Co 6:14 **raised** the Lord **from the d,** *1586*
15:12 that Christ has been raised from the **d,** *3738*
15:12 that there is no resurrection *of* the **d?** *3738*
15:13 If there is no resurrection *of* the **d,** *3738*
15:15 **raised** Christ **from the d.** *1586*
15:15 But he did not raise him if in fact the **d** are *3738*
15:16 For if the **d** are not raised, *3738*
15:20 Christ has indeed been raised from the **d,** *3738*
15:21 the resurrection *of* the **d** comes also *3738*
15:29 will those do who are baptized for the **d?** *3738*
15:29 If the **d** are not raised at all, *3738*
15:32 If the **d** are not raised, *3738*
15:35 someone may ask, "How are the **d** raised? *3738*
15:42 So will it be with the resurrection *of* the **d.** *3738*
15:52 the **d** will be raised imperishable, *3738*
2Co 1: 9 who raises the **d.** *3738*
4:14 **raised** the Lord Jesus **from the d** *1586*
Gal 1: 1 who raised him from the **d—** *3738*
Eph 1:20 from the **d** and seated him at his right hand *3738*
2: 1 you were **d** in your transgressions and sins, *3738*
2: 5 even when we were **d** in transgressions— *3738*
5:14 "Wake up, O sleeper, rise from the **d,** *3738*
Php 3:11 to attain to the resurrection from the **d.** *3738*
Col 1:18 and the firstborn from among the **d,** *3738*
2:12 who raised him from the **d.** *3738*
2:13 When you were **d** in your sins and in *3738*
1Th 1:10 whom he raised from the **d—** *3738*
4:16 and the **d** in Christ will rise first. *3738*
1Ti 5: 6 the widow who lives for pleasure *is* **d** even *2569*
2Ti 2: 8 Remember Jesus Christ, raised from the **d,** *3738*
4: 1 who will judge the living and the **d,** *3738*
Heb 6: 2 the resurrection *of* the **d,** *3738*
11: 4 by faith he still speaks, *even though he is* **d.** *633*
11:12 so from this one man, and he as good as **d,** *3739*
11:19 that God could raise the **d,** *3738*
11:35 Women received back their **d,** *3738*
13:20 from the **d** our Lord Jesus, *3738*
Jas 2:17 if it is not accompanied by action, is **d.** *3738*
2:26 As the body without the spirit is **d,** *3738*
2:26 so faith without deeds is **d.** *3738*
1Pe 1: 3 the resurrection of Jesus Christ from the **d,** *3738*
1:21 from the **d** and glorified him, *3738*
4: 5 to judge the living and the **d.** *3738*
4: 6 even *to* those who are now **d,** *3738*
Jude 1:12 and uprooted—twice **d.** *633*
Rev 1: 5 the firstborn *from* the **d,** *3738*
1:17 I fell at his feet as though **d.** *3738*
1:18 I am the Living One; I was **d,** *3738*
2:23 *I will* **strike** her children **d.** *650*
3: 1 a reputation of being alive, but you are **d.** *3738*
11:18 The time has come for judging the **d,** *3738*
14:13 Blessed are the **d** who die in the Lord from *3738*
16: 3 and it turned into blood like that of a **d** *man,* *3738*
20: 5 (The rest *of* the **d** did not come to life until *3738*
20:12 And I saw the **d,** great and small, *3738*
20:12 The **d** were judged according *3738*
20:13 The sea gave up the **d** that were in it, *3738*
20:13 and Hades gave up the **d** that were in them, *3738*

DEADENED (1) [DIE]
Jn 12:40 and **d** their hearts, so they can neither see *4800*

DEADLY (16) [DIE]
Ex 10:17 to take this **d plague** away from me." 4638
Dt 32:24 consuming pestilence and **d** plague; 5321
32:33 the **d** poison of cobras. 425
Ps 7:13 He has prepared his **d** weapons; 4638
64: 3 and aim their words like **d** arrows. 5253
91: 3 and from the **d** pestilence. 2095
144:10 from the **d** sword. 8273
Pr 21: 6 a fleeting vapor and a **d** snare. 4638
26:18 a madman shooting firebrands or **d** arrows 4638
Jer 9: 8 Their tongue is a **d** arrow; 8821
16: 4 "They will die of **d** diseases. 4926
Eze 5:16 at you with my **d** and destructive arrows 8273
9: 2 each with a **d** weapon in his hand. 5150
Mk 16:18 and when they drink **d poison,** *2503+5516*
2Co 1:10 He has delivered us from such a **d** peril, *2505*
Jas 3: 8 It is a restless evil, full *of* **d** poison. *2504*

DEAF (18)
Ex 4:11 Who makes him **d** or mute? 3094
Lev 19:14 " 'Do not curse the **d** or 3094
Dt 1:45 weeping and **turned a d ear** to you. 263+4202
Ps 28: 1 *do* not **turn a d ear** to me. 3087
38:13 I am like a **d** *man,* who cannot hear, 3094
39:12 *be* not **d** to my weeping. 3087
Pr 28: 9 If anyone turns a **d** ear *to* the law, 4946+9048
Isa 29:18 In that day the **d** will hear the words of 3094
35: 5 be opened and the ears of the **d** unstopped. 3094
42:18 "Hear, you **d;** look, you blind, and see! 3094
42:19 and **d** like the messenger I send? 3094
43: 8 who have ears but are **d.** 3094
Mic 7:16 and their ears *will become* **d.** 3087
Mt 11: 5 the **d** hear, the dead are raised, *3273*
Mk 7:32 a *man* who was **d** and could hardly talk, *3273*
7:37 even makes the **d** hear and the mute speak." *3273*
9:25 *"You* **d** and mute spirit," he said, *3273*
Lk 7:22 the **d** hear, the dead are raised, *3273*

DEAL (51) [DEALER, DEALING, DEALINGS, DEALS, DEALT]
Ge 21:23 before God that *you will* not **d falsely** 9213
Ex 1:10 *we must* **d shrewdly** with them 2681
8:22 " 'But on that day *I will* **d differently** 7111
Ru 1:17 *May* the LORD **d** with me, 6913
1Sa 3:17 *May* God **d** with you, be it ever so severely, 6913
14:44 Saul said, *"May* God **d** with me, 6913
20:13 *may* the LORD **d** with me, 6913
24: 4 into your hands *for you to* **d** with 6913
25:22 *May* God **d** with David, 6913
2Sa 3: 9 *May* God **d** with Abner, 6913
3:22 a raid and brought with them a **great d** 8041
3:35 *"May* God **d** with me, be it ever so severely, 6913
19:13 *May* God **d** with me, be it ever so severely, 6913
1Ki 2: 6 **D with** him according to your wisdom, 6913
2:23 *"May* God **d** with me, be it ever so severely, 6913
8:39 **d** with each man according to all he does, 5989
19: 2 *"May* the gods **d with** me, 6913
20:10 *"May* the gods **d** with me, 6913
2Ki 6:31 He said, *"May* God **d** with me, 6913
2Ch 6:30 **d** with each man according to all he does, 5989
12:15 of Iddo the seer *that* **d with genealogies?** 3509
28: 8 They also took a **great d** of plunder, 8041
Ne 5: 7 a large meeting to **d with** them 6584
9:24 to **d** with them as they pleased. 6913
Job 42: 8 and not **d** with you according to your folly. 6913
Ps 109:21 **d** well with me for your name's sake; 6913
119:124 **D** with your servant according to your love 6913
Isa 10:11 not **d** with Jerusalem and her images 6913
23:17 the LORD *will* **d** *with* Tyre. 7212
Jer 2: 8 *Those who* **d with** the law did not know me; 9530
7: 5 and **d** with each other justly, 6913+6913
18:23 **d** with them in the time of your anger. 6913
24: 8 'so *will I* **d** with Zedekiah king of Judah, 5989
32: 5 where he will remain until I **d** *with* him, 7212
La 1:22 **d** with them as you have dealt with me 6618
Eze 7:27 *I will* **d with** them according 6913
8:18 Therefore I *will* **d with** them in anger; 6913
16:59 *I will* **d with** you as you deserve, 6913
20:44 when I **d** with you for my name's sake and 6913
22:14 or your hands be strong in the day I **d** 6913
23:25 and *they will* **d** with you in fury. 6913
23:29 *They will* **d** with you in hatred 6913
25:14 and *they will* **d** with Edom in accordance 6913
31:11 for *him to* **d** with according to its wickedness. 6913+6913
Zep 3:19 At that time I *will* **d** 6913
Zec 8:11 But now I will not **d** with the remnant NIH
Mt 27:19 a **great d** today in a dream because of him." *4498*
Mk 5:26 She had suffered a **great d** under the care *4498*
Ac 16:16 She earned **a great d of** money *4498*
2Ti 4:14 the metalworker did me **a great d of** harm. *4498*
Heb 5: 2 *to* **d gently** with those who are ignorant *3584*

DEALER (1) [DEAL]
Ac 16:14 a **d in purple cloth** from the city *4527*

DEALING (4) [DEAL]
2Sa 7:19 Is this your **usual way of d** *with* man, 9368
Ezr 10:17 of the first month they finished **d with** all 928
Lk 16: 8 in **d** with their own kind than are the people *NIG*
2Co 13: 3 He is not weak **in d with** you, *1650*

DEALINGS (1) [DEAL]
1Sa 25: 3 a Calebite, was surly and mean in his **d.** 5095

DEALS (3) [DEAL]
Dt 25:16 anyone *who* **d** dishonestly. 6913
Jer 5: 1 but one person *who* **d** honestly and seeks 6913
1Th 2:11 that we dealt with each of you as a father **d** *NIG*

DEALT (9) [DEAL]
Ex 10: 2 and grandchildren how *I* **d harshly** with 6618
1Sa 6:19 of the heavy blow the LORD *had* **d** them, 5782
2Sa 22:21 "The LORD *has* **d with** me according 1694
Ps 18:20 The LORD *has* **d with** me according 1694
Isa 10:11 with Jerusalem and her images as *I* **d** 6913
La 1:22 with them as *you have* **d** with me because 6618
Eze 39:24 *I* **d** with them according 6913
Ac 7:19 He **d treacherously with** our people *2947*
1Th 2:11 For you know that we **d** with each of you as *NIG*

DEAR (62) [DEARER, DEARLY]
2Sa 1:26 *you were* very **d** to me. 5838
Ps 102:14 For her stones *are* **d** to your servants; 8354
Jer 31:20 Is not Ephraim my **d** son, 3692
Jn 2: 4 **"D woman,** why do you involve me?" *1222*
19:26 he said to his mother, **"D woman,** *1222*
Ac 15:25 with our **d friends** Barnabas and Paul— *28*
Ro 16: 5 Greet my **d friend** Epenetus, *28*
16: 9 and my **d friend** Stachys. *28*
16:12 Greet my **d friend** Persis, *28*
1Co 4:14 but to warn you, as my **d** children. *28*
10:14 Therefore, my **d friends,** flee from idolatry. *28*
15:58 Therefore, my **d** brothers, stand firm. *28*
2Co 7: 1 Since we have these promises, **d friends,** *28*
12:19 and everything we do, **d friends,** *28*
Gal 4:19 My **d children,** for whom I am again in *5451*
Eph 6:21 the **d** brother and faithful servant in *28*
Php 2:12 my **d friends,** as you have always obeyed— *28*
4: 1 in the Lord, **d friends!** *28*
Col 1: 7 Epaphras, our **d** fellow servant, *28*
4: 7 He is a **d** brother, *28*
4: 9 Onesimus, our faithful and **d** brother, *28*
4:14 Our **d friend** Luke, the doctor, *28*
1Th 2: 8 because you had become **so d** to us. *28*
1Ti 6: 2 and **d** to them. *28*
2Ti 1: 2 *To* Timothy, my **d** son: *28*
Phm 1: 1 *To* Philemon our **d friend** *28*
1:16 but better than a slave, as a **d** brother. *28*
1:16 He is very **d** to me but even dearer to you, *NIG*
Heb 6: 9 Even though we speak like this, **d friends,** *28*
Jas 1:16 Don't be deceived, my **d** brothers. *28*
1:19 My **d** brothers, take note of this: *28*
2: 5 Listen, my **d** brothers: *28*
1Pe 2:11 **D friends,** I urge you, *28*
4:12 **D friends,** do not be surprised at *28*
2Pe 3: 1 **D friends,** this is now my second letter *28*
3: 8 But do not forget this one thing, **d friends:** *28*
3:14 **d friends,** since you are looking forward *28*
3:15 as our **d** brother Paul also wrote you with *28*
3:17 **d friends,** since you already know this, *28*
1Jn 2: 1 My **d children,** I write this to you so *5448*
2: 7 **D friends,** I am not writing you *28*
2:12 I write to you, **d children,** *5448*
2:13 I write to you, **d children,** *4086*
2:18 **D children,** this is the last hour; *4086*
2:28 And now, **d children,** continue in him, *5448*
3: 2 **D friends,** now we are children of God, *28*
3: 7 **D children,** do not let anyone lead you astray. *5448*
3:18 **D children,** let us not love with words *5448*
3:21 **D friends,** if our hearts do not condemn us, *28*
4: 1 **D friends,** do not believe every spirit, *28*
4: 4 **d children,** are from God *5448*
4: 7 **D friends,** let us love one another, *28*
4:11 **D friends,** since God so loved us, *28*
5:21 **D children,** keep yourselves from idols. *5448*
2Jn 1: 5 And now, **d lady,** I am not writing you *3257*
3Jn 1: 1 The elder, *To* my **d friend** Gaius, *28*
1: 2 **D friend,** I pray that you may enjoy *28*
1: 5 **D friend,** you are faithful *28*
1:11 **D friend,** do not imitate what is evil *28*
Jude 1: 3 **D friends,** although I was very eager *28*
1:17 But, **d friends,** remember what the apostles *28*
1:20 But you, **d friends,** build yourselves up *28*

DEARER (1) [DEAR]
Phm 1:16 He is very dear to me but even **d** to you, *NIG*

DEARLY (3) [DEAR]
Hos 4:18 their rulers **d** love shameful ways. 170
Eph 5: 1 as **d loved** children *28*
Col 3:12 as God's chosen people, holy and **d** loved, *5073*

DEARTH (KJV) See DROUGHT, FAMINE

DEATH (450) [DIE]
Ge 24:67 Isaac was comforted **after** his mother's *d.* AIT
25:11 After Abraham's **d,** God blessed his son Isaac, 4638
26:11 **surely be put to d."** 4637+4637
27: 2 and don't know the day of my **d.** 4638
38: 7 so the LORD **put** him **to d.** 4637
38:10 so *he* **put** him **to d** also. 4637
38:24 "Bring her out and *have her* **burned** *to* **d!"** 8596
42:37 **put** both of my sons **to d** 4637
Ex 16: 3 to starve this entire assembly *to* **d."** 4637
19:12 **surely be put to d.** 4637+4637
21:12 **surely be put to d.** 4637+4637
21:14 from my altar and *put* him *to* **d.** 4637
21:15 **must be put to d.** 4637+4637
21:16 **must be put to d.** 4637+4637
21:17 **must be put to d.** 4637+4637
21:28 "If a bull gores a man or a woman *to* **d,** 4637
21:28 **must be stoned to d,** 6232+6232
21:29 and the owner also *must* **be put to d.** 4637
22:19 **must be put to d.** 4637+4637
23: 7 **put** an innocent or honest person **to d,** 2222
31:14 **must be put to d;** 4637+4637
31:15 **must be put to d.** 4637+4637
35: 2 on it *must* **be put to d.** 4637
Lev 16: 1 The LORD spoke to Moses after the **d** *of* 4638
19:20 Yet *they are* not *to* **be put to d,** 4637
20: 2 **must be put to d.** 4637+4637
20: 4 to Molech and they fail to **put him to d,** 4637
20: 9 **must be put to d.** 4637+4637
20:10 **must be put to d.** 4637+4637
20:11 **must be put to d;** 4637+4637
20:12 **must be put to d.** 4637+4637
20:13 **must be put to d;** 4637+4637
20:15 **must be put to d,** 4637+4637
20:16 **must be put to d;** 4637+4637
20:27 **must be put to d.** 4637+4637
24:16 **must be put to d.** 4637+4637
24:16 **must be put to d.** 4637
24:17 **must be put to d.** 4637+4637
24:21 but whoever kills a man *must* **be put to d.** 4637
27:29 **must be put to d.** 4637+4637
Nu 1:51 near it *shall* **be put to d.** 4637
3:10 the sanctuary *must* **be put to d."** 4637
3:38 the sanctuary *was to* **be put to d.** 4637
11:15 **put** me **to d** right now— 2222+2222
14:15 **put** these people **to d** 4637
15:36 the camp and stoned him *to* **d,** 4637
16:29 If these men die a natural **d** 4638
18: 7 near the sanctuary *must* **be put to d."** 4637
19:16 or *someone who has* **died a natural d,** 4637
19:18 or someone *who has* **died a natural d.** 4637
23:10 Let me die the **d** *of* the righteous, 4638
25: 5 "Each of *you must* **put to d** those 2222
25:15 Midianite woman who **was put to d** was Cozbi 5782
35:16 **shall be put to d.** 4637+4637
35:17 **shall be put to d.** 4637+4637
35:18 **shall be put to d.** 4637+4637
35:19 **put** the murderer **to d;** 4637
35:19 when he meets him, he *shall* **put** him **to d.** 4637
35:21 **shall be put to d;** 4637+4637
35:21 **put** the murderer **to d** 4637
35:25 He must stay there until the **d** *of* 4637
35:28 of refuge until the **d** *of* the high priest; 4638
35:28 after the **d** *of* the high priest may he return 4638
35:30 *to be* **put to d** as a murderer only on 8357
35:30 But no one *is to be* **put to d** on 4637
35:31 **must** surely **be put to d.** 4637+4637
35:32 and live on his own land before the **d** *of* 4638
Dt 9:28 he brought them out to **put them to d** in 4637
13: 5 That prophet or dreamer *must* **be put to d,** 4637
13: 9 **must certainly put** him **to d.** 2222+2222
13: 9 be the first in **putting** him **to d,** 4637
13:10 Stone him *to* **d,** 4637
17: 5 to your city gate and stone that person *to* **d.** 4637
17: 6 or three witnesses a man *shall* **be put to d,** 4637
17: 6 but no *one shall* **be put to d** on 4637
17: 7 be the first in **putting** him **to d,** 4637
17:12 to the LORD your God *must be* **put to d.** 4637
18:20 *must be* **put to d."** 4637
19: 6 even though he is not deserving of **d,** 4638
21:21 the men of his town shall stone him *to* **d.** 4637
21:22 a man guilty of a capital offense **is put to d** 4637
22:21 the men of her town shall stone her *to* **d.** 4637
22:24 the gate of that town and stone them *to* **d—** 4637
22:26 she has committed no sin deserving **d.** 4638
24:16 not **be put to d** for their children, 4637
24:16 nor children **put to d** for their fathers; 4637
30:15 before you today life and prosperity, **d** 4638
30:19 that I have set before you life and **d,** 4638
31:14 "Now the day of your **d** is near. 4637
31:29 For I know that after my **d** you are sure 4638
32:22 one that burns to the **realm of d** below. 8619
32:39 **I put to d** and I bring to life, 4637
33: 1 on the Israelites before his **d.** 4638
Jos 1: 1 the **d** *of* Moses the servant of the LORD, 4638
1:18 *will* **be put to d.** 4637
2:13 and that you will save us from **d."** 4638
11:17 **putting** them **to d.** 4637
20: 6 until the **d** *of* the high priest who is serving 4638
Jdg 1: 1 After the **d** *of* Joshua, 4638
6:31 Whoever fights for him *shall* **be put to d** 4637
13: 7 of God from birth until the day of his **d.' "** 4638
14:15 **burn** you and your father's household **to d.** 836+928+2021+8596
15: 6 **burned** her and her father **to d.** 836+928+2021+8596
16:16 day after day until he was tired to **d.** 4637
20:13 so that *we may* **put** them **to d** and purge 4637
21: 5 **certainly be put to d.** 4637+4637
Ru 1:17 if anything but **d** separates you and me." 4638
2:11 for your mother-in-law since the **d** 4638

1Sa 2: 6 "The LORD brings d and makes alive; 4637
2:25 it was the LORD's will to put them to d. 4637
5:11 For d had filled the city with panic; 4638
6:19 putting seventy of them to d 5782
11:12 to us and we will put them to d." 4637
11:13 Saul said, "No one shall be put to d today, 4637
14:45 and he was not put to d. 4637
15: 3 put to d men and women, 4637
15:32 "Surely the bitterness of d is past." 4638
15:33 And Samuel put Agag to d before 9119
19: 6 LORD lives, David will not be put to d." 4637
20: 3 there is only a step between me and d." 4638
20:32 "Why should he be put to d? 4637
22:22 for the d of your father's whole family. 5883
28: 9 a trap for my life to bring about my d?" 4637
2Sa 1: 1 After the d of Saul, 4638
1: 9 I am in the throes of d, but I'm still alive.' 8688
1:23 and in d they were not parted. 4638
4:10 I seized him and put him to d in Ziklag. 2222
6:23 of Saul had no children to the day of her d. 4638
8: 2 Every two lengths of them were put to d, 4637
13:39 he was consoled concerning Amnon's d. 4638
14: 7 so that we may put him to d for the life 4637
14:32 let him put me to d." 4637
15:21 whether it means life or d, 4638
17: 3 The d of the man you seek will mean NIH
19:21 "Shouldn't Shimei be put to d for this? 4637
19:22 Should anyone be put to d in Israel today? 4637
19:28 but d from my lord the king, 4638
20: 3 in confinement till the day of their d, 4637
21: 1 put the Gibeonites to d." 4637
21: 4 put anyone in Israel to d." 4637
21: 9 they were put to d during the first days of 4637
22: 5 "The waves of d swirled about me; 4638
22: 6 the snares of d confronted me. 4638
1Ki 1:51 put his servant to d 4637
2: 8 'I will not put you to d by the sword.' 4637
2:24 Adonijah shall be put to d today!" 4637
2:26 but I will not put you to d now, 4637
3:11 the d of your enemies but for discernment 5883
11:40 and stayed there until Solomon's d. 4638
12:18 but all Israel stoned him to d. 4637
18: 9 over to Ahab to be put to d? 4637
19:10 put your prophets to d 2222
19:14 put your prophets to d 2222
19:17 Jehu will put to d any who escape 4637
19:17 and Elisha will put to d any who escape 4637
21:10 Then take him out and stone him to d." 4637
21:13 the city and stoned him to d. 4637
21:15 that Naboth had been stoned to d, 4637
22:20 and going to his d there?' 5877
2Ki 1: 1 Ahab's d, Moab rebelled against Israel. 4638
2:21 Never again will it cause d or make 4638
4:40 "O man of God, there is d in the pot!" 4638
11: 8 Anyone who approaches your ranks must be put to d. 4637
11:15 "She must not be put to d in the temple of 4637
11:16 and there she was put to d. 4637
14: 6 put the sons of the assassins to d, 4637
14: 6 not be put to d for their children, 4637
14: 6 nor children put to d for their fathers; 4637
14:17 after the d of Jehoash son of Jehoahaz king 4638
16: 9 to Kir and put Rezin to d. 4637
18:32 Choose life and not d! 4638
19:35 of the LORD went out and put to d 5782
20: 1 and was at the point of d. 4637
1Ch 2: 3 so the LORD put him to d. 4637
10:14 So the LORD put him to d and turned 4637
22: 5 So David made extensive preparations before his d. 4638
2Ch 1:11 nor for the d of your enemies, 5883
10:18 but the Israelites stoned him to d. 4637
15:13 the God of Israel, were to be put to d, 4637
18:19 and going to his d there?' 5877
22: 4 his father's d they became his advisers, 4638
22: 9 He was brought to Jehu and put to d. 4637
23: 7 the temple must be put to d. 4637
23:14 "Do not put her to d at the temple of 4637
23:15 and there they put her to d. 4637
24:17 After the d of Jehoiada, 4638
24:21 order of the king they stoned him to d 74+8083
25: 4 put their sons to d, 4637
25: 4 to d for their children, nor children put 4637
25: 4 nor children put to d for their fathers; 4637
25:25 after the d of Jehoash son of Jehoahaz king 4638
32:24 and was at the point of d. 4637
Ezr 7:26 of the king must surely be punished by d, 10409
Est 4:11 that he be put to d. 4637
9:15 they put to d in Susa three hundred men, 2222
Job 3:21 to those who long for d that does not come, 4638
5:20 In famine he will ransom you from d, 4638
7:15 so that I prefer strangling and d, 4638
9:23 When a scourge brings sudden d, 4637
17:16 Will it go down to the gates of d? 8619
26: 6 D is naked before God; 8619
28:22 Destruction and D say, 4638
30:23 I know you will bring me down to d, 4638
33:22 and his life to the messengers of d. 4637
38:17 Have the gates of d been shown to you? 4638
38:17 the gates of the shadow of d? 7516
Ps 9: T To [the tune of] "The D of the Son." 4637
9:13 and lift me up from the gates of d, 4638
13: 3 Give light to my eyes, or I will sleep in d; 4638
18: 4 The cords of d entangled me; 4638
18: 5 the snares of d confronted me. 4638
22:15 you lay me in the dust of d. 4638
23: 4 through the valley of the shadow of d, 7516

Ps 33:19 to deliver them from d and keep them alive 4638
44:22 Yet for your sake we face d all day long; 2222
49:14 and d will feed on them. 4638
55: 4 the terrors of d assail me. 4638
55:15 Let d take my enemies by surprise; 4638
56:13 from d and my feet from stumbling, 4638
68:20 from the Sovereign LORD comes escape from d. 4638
72:13 and the needy and save the needy from d. 5883
78:31 he put to d the sturdiest among them, 2222
78:50 he did not spare them from d but gave them 4638
88:15 and close to d; 1588
89:48 What man can live and not see d, 4638
90: 5 You sweep men away in the sleep of d; 9104
94:17 in the silence of d. 1872
94:21 and condemn the innocent to d. 1947
102:20 and release those condemned to d." 9456
107:18 and drew near the gates of d. 4638
109:16 but hounded to d the poor and the needy 4637
116: 3 The cords of d entangled me, 4638
116: 8 O LORD, have delivered my soul from d, 4638
116:15 Precious in the sight of the LORD is the d 4638
118:18 but he has not given me over to d. 4638
141: 8 give me over to d. 6867
Pr 2:18 to d and her paths to the spirits of the dead. 4638
5: 5 Her feet go down to d; 4638
7:27 leading down to the chambers of d. 4638
8:36 all who hate me love d." 4638
10: 2 but righteousness delivers from d. 4638
11: 4 but righteousness delivers from d. 4638
11:19 but he who pursues evil goes to his d. 4638
13:14 turning a man from the snares of d. 4638
14:12 but in the end it leads to d. 4638
14:27 turning a man from the snares of d. 4638
14:32 but even in d the righteous have a refuge. 4638
15:11 D and Destruction lie open before 8619
16:14 A king's wrath is a messenger of d, 4638
16:25 but in the end it leads to d. 4638
18:21 The tongue has the power of life and d, 4638
19:18 do not be a willing party to his d. 4637
21:25 sluggard's craving will be the d of him, 4637
23:14 with the rod and save his soul from d. 8619
24:11 Rescue those being led away to d; 4638
27:20 D and Destruction are never satisfied, 8619
28:17 the guilt of murder will be a fugitive till d; 1014
Ecc 7: 1 and the day of d better than the day of birth. 4638
7: 2 for d is the destiny of every man; 2085[S]
7:26 I find more bitter than d the woman who is 4638
8: 8 so no one has power over the day of his d. 4638
SS 8: 6 for love is as strong as d, 4638
Isa 9: 2 land of the shadow of d a light has dawned. 7516
25: 8 he will swallow up d forever. 4638
28:15 "We have entered into a covenant with d, 4638
28:18 Your covenant with d will be annulled; 4638
37:36 of the LORD went out and put to d 5782
38: 1 and was at the point of d. 4637
38:10 of d and be robbed of the rest of my years?" 8619
38:18 d cannot sing your praise; 4638
53: 9 and with the rich in his d, 4638
53:12 because he poured out his life unto d, 4638
57: 2 they find rest as they lie in d. 5435
65:15 the Sovereign LORD will put you to d, 4637
Jer 8: 3 of this evil nation will prefer d to life, 4638
9:21 D has climbed in through our windows 4638
15: 2 " 'Those destined for d, to death; 4638
15: 2 " 'Those destined for death, to d; 4638
18:21 let their men be put to d, 2222+4638
21: 8 before you the way of life and the way of d. 4638
26:11 "This man should be sentenced to d 4638
26:15 however, that if you put me to d, 4637
26:16 "This man should not be sentenced to d! 4638
26:19 or anyone else in Judah put him to d? 4637+4637
26:21 the king sought to put him to d. 4637
26:24 over to the people to be put to d. 4637
29:21 of Babylon, and he will put them to d 5782
38: 4 "This man should be put to d. 4637
38: 9 to d when there is no longer any bread in 4637
43:11 bringing d to those destined for death, 4638
43:11 bringing death to those destined for d, 4638
52:11 in prison till the day of his d. 4638
52:34 till the day of his d. 4638
La 1:20 inside, there is only d. 4638
Eze 18:13 surely be put to d 4637+4637
18:23 Do I take any pleasure in the d of 4638
18:32 For I take no pleasure in the d of anyone, 4638
28: 8 and you will die a violent d in the heart of 4926
28:10 You will die the d of the uncircumcised at 4638
31:14 they are all destined for d, 4638
33:11 I take no pleasure in the d of the wicked, 4638
Da 2:13 put the wise men to d, 10625
2:13 for Daniel and his friends to put them to d. 10625
2:14 had gone out to put to d the wise men 10625
5:19 Those the king wanted to put to d, NIH
5:19 he put to d; 10625
Hos 13:14 I will redeem them from d. 4638
13:14 Where, O d, are your plagues? 4638
Hab 2: 5 as the grave and like d is never satisfied, 4638
Mt 2:15 where he stayed until the d of Herod. 5463
4:16 land of the shadow of d a light has dawned. 2505
10:21 "Brother will betray brother to d, 2505
10:21 and have them put to d. 2506
15: 4 or mother must be put to d.' 2505+5462
16:28 some who are standing here will not taste d 2505
20:18 They will condemn him to d 2505
24: 9 over to be persecuted and put to d, 650
26:38 with sorrow to the point of d. 2505
26:59 so that they could put him to d. 2506

Mt 26:66 "He is worthy of d," they answered. 2505
27: 1 to the decision to put Jesus to d. 2506
Mk 7:10 or mother must be put to d.' 2505+5462
9: 1 some who are standing here will not taste d 2505
10:33 condemn him to d and will hand him over 2505
13:12 "Brother will betray brother to d, 2505
13:12 and have them put to d. 2506
14:34 with sorrow to the point of d," 2505
14:55 so that they could put him to d, 2506
14:64 They all condemned him as worthy of d. 2505
Lk 1:79 in darkness and in the shadow of d, 2505
9:27 some who are standing here will not taste d 2505
15:17 and here I am starving to d! 660+3350
21:16 put some of you to d. 2506
22:33 to go with you to prison and to d." 2505
23:15 he has done nothing to deserve d. 2505
23:22 grounds for the d penalty. 165+2505
24:20 be sentenced to d, and they crucified him; 2505
Jn 4:47 who was close to d. 633
5:24 he has crossed over from d to life. 2505
8:51 he will never see d." 2505
8:52 he will never taste d. 2505
11: 4 Jesus said, "This sickness will not end in d. 2505
11:13 Jesus had been speaking of his d, 2505
12:33 to show the kind of d he was going to die. 2505
18:32 of d he was going to die would be fulfilled. 2505
21:19 of d by which Peter would glorify God. 2505
Ac 2:23 put him to d by nailing him to the cross. 359
2:24 freeing him from the agony of d, 2505
2:24 because it was impossible for d 899[S]
5:33 and wanted to put them to d. 359
7: 4 After the d of his father, 633
8: 1 Saul was there, giving approval to his d. 358
12: 2 put to d with the sword. 359
13:28 found no proper ground for a d sentence, 2505
22: 4 the followers of this Way to their d, 2505
23:29 that deserved d or imprisonment. 2505
25:11 I am guilty of doing anything deserving d, 2505
25:25 of d, but because he made his appeal to 2505
26:10 and when they were put to d, 359
26:31 not doing anything that deserves d 2505
28:18 not guilty of any crime deserving d. 2505
Ro 1:32 that those who do such things deserve d, 2505
4:25 over to d for our sins and was raised to life NIG
5:10 we were reconciled to him through the d 2505
5:12 and d through sin, and 2505
5:12 and in this way d came to all men, 2505
5:14 d reigned from the time of Adam to 2505
5:17 d reigned through that one man, 2505
5:21 just as sin reigned in d, 2505
6: 3 into Christ Jesus were baptized into his d? 2505
6: 4 with him through baptism into d in order 2505
6: 5 with him like this in his d, 2505
6: 9 d no longer has mastery over him. 2505
6:10 The d he died, he died to sin once for all; 4005[S]
6:13 those who have been brought from d to life; 3738
6:16 which leads to d, or to obedience, 2505
6:21 Those things result in d! 2505
6:23 For the wages of sin is d, 2505
7: 5 so that we bore fruit for d. 2505
7:10 to bring life actually brought d. 2505
7:11 through the commandment put me to d. 650
7:13 which is good, then, become d to me? 2505
7:13 it produced d in me through what was good, 2505
7:24 Who will rescue me from this body of d? 2505
8: 2 from the law of sin and d. 2505
8: 6 The mind of sinful man is d, 2505
8:13 by the Spirit you put to d the misdeeds of 2506
8:36 "For your sake we face d all day long; 2506
8:38 For I am convinced that neither d nor life, 2505
1Co 3:22 or the world or life or d or the present or 2505
11:26 you proclaim the Lord's d until he comes. 2505
15:21 For since d came through a man, 2505
15:26 The last enemy to be destroyed is d. 2505
15:54 "D has been swallowed up in victory." 2505
15:55 "Where, O d, is your victory? 2505
15:55 Where, O d, is your sting?" 2505
15:56 The sting of d is sin, 2505
2Co 1: 9 in our hearts we felt the sentence of d. 2505
2:16 To the one we are the smell of d; 2505
3: 7 Now if the ministry that brought d, 2505
4:10 We always carry around in our body the d 3740
4:11 given over to d for Jesus' sake, 2505
4:12 d is at work in us, but life is at work in you. 2505
7:10 but worldly sorrow brings d. 2505
11:23 and been exposed to d again and again. 2505
Eph 2:16 by which he put to d their hostility. 650
Php 1:20 whether by life or by d. 2505
2: 8 and became obedient to d— 2505
2: 8 even d on a cross! 2505
3:10 becoming like him in his d, 2505
Col 1:22 through d to present you holy in his sight, 2505
3: 5 Put to d, therefore, whatever belongs 3739
2Ti 1:10 who has destroyed d and has brought life 2505
Heb 2: 9 and honor because he suffered d, 2505
2: 9 so that by the grace of God he might taste d 2505
2:14 by his d he might destroy him who holds 2505
2:14 the power of d—that is, the devil— 2505
2:15 in slavery by their fear of d. 2505
5: 7 to the one who could save him from d, 2505
6: 1 of repentance from acts that lead to d, 3738
7:23 since d prevented them from continuing 2505
9:14 from acts that lead to d, 3738
9:16 to prove the d of the one who made it, 2505
11: 5 so that he did not experience d; 2505
11:19 he did receive Isaac back from d. 3854[S]
11:37 they were put to d by the sword. 633+1877+5840

Jas 1:15 sin, when it is full-grown, gives birth to **d.** *2505*
5:20 of his way will save him from **d** and cover *2505*
1Pe 3:18 *He was* **put to d** in the body but made alive *2506*
1Jn 3:14 We know that we have passed from **d** *2505*
3:14 Anyone who does not love remains in **d.** *2505*
5:16 a sin that does not lead to **d,** *2505*
5:16 to those whose sin does not lead to **d.** *2505*
5:16 There is a sin that leads to **d.** *2505*
5:17 and there is sin that does not lead to **d.** *2505*
Rev 1:18 And I hold the keys *of* **d** and Hades. *2505*
2:10 Be faithful, even to the point of **d,** *2505*
2:11 not be hurt at all by the second **d.** *2505*
2:13 who *was* **put to d** in your city— *650*
6:8 Its rider was named **D,** *2505*
9:6 During those days men will seek **d,** *2505*
9:6 they will long to die, but **d** will elude them. *2505*
12:11 so much as to shrink from **d.** *2505*
18:8 **d,** mourning and famine. *2505*
20:6 The second **d** has no power over them, *2505*
20:13 and **d** and Hades gave up the dead that were *2505*
20:14 Then **d** and Hades were thrown into *2505*
20:14 The lake of fire is the second **d.** *2505*
21:4 There will be no more **d** or mourning *2505*
21:8 This is the second **d.**" *2505*

DEATH'S (1) [DIE]

Job 18:13 **d** firstborn devours his limbs. 4638

DEATHLY (2) [DIE]

Jer 30:6 every face turned **d pale?** 3766
Da 10:8 my face turned **d pale** and I was helpless. 5422

DEATHS (1) [DIE]

1Sa 4:21 the **d** of her father-in-law and her husband. NIH

DEBAR See LO DEBAR

DEBASE (KJV) See DESCENDED

DEBATE (2) [DEBATED, DEBATING]

Ac 15:2 and Barnabas into sharp dispute and **d** *2428*
18:28 he vigorously refuted the Jews in public **d,** *NIG*

DEBATED (1) [DEBATE]

Ac 9:29 He talked and **d** with the Grecian Jews, *5184*

DEBATING (1) [DEBATE]

Mk 12:28 of the law came and heard them **d.** *5184*

DEBAUCHERY (5)

Ro 13:13 not in sexual immorality and **d,** *816*
2Co 12:21 and **d** in which they have indulged. *816*
Gal 5:19 sexual immorality, impurity and **d;** *816*
Eph 5:18 Do not get drunk on wine, which leads to **d.** *861*
1Pe 4:3 living in **d,** lust, drunkenness, orgies, *816*

DEBIR (12) [KIRIATH SANNAH]

Jos 10:3 Japhia king of Lachish and **D** king 1809
10:38 with him turned around and attacked **D.** 1810
10:39 They did to **D** and its king as they had done 1810
11:21 from Hebron, **D** and Anab, 1810
12:13 the king of **D** one the king of Geder one 1810
13:26 and from Mahanaim to the territory of **D;** 1810
15:7 then went up to **D** from the Valley of Achor 1810
15:15 in **D** (formerly called Kiriath Sepher). 1810
15:49 Dannah, Kiriath Sannah (that is, **D**), 1810
21:15 Holon, **D,** 1810
Jdg 1:11 in **D** (formerly called Kiriath Sepher). 1810
1Ch 6:58 Hilen, **D,** 1810

DEBORAH (11)

Ge 35:8 Now **D,** Rebekah's nurse, 1806
Jdg 4:4 **D,** a prophetess, the wife of Lappidoth, 1806
4:5 the Palm of **D** between Ramah and Bethel 1806
4:9 "Very well," **D** said, "I will go with you. NIH
4:9 So **D** went with Barak to Kedesh, 1806
4:10 and **D** also went with him. 1806
4:14 Then **D** said to Barak, "Go! 1806
5:1 On that day **D** and Barak son 1806
5:7 **D,** arose, arose a mother in Israel. 1806
5:12 'Wake up, wake up, **D!** 1806
5:15 The princes of Issachar were with **D;** 1806

DEBT (11) [DEBTOR, DEBTORS, DEBTS]

Dt 15:3 *must* **cancel** *any* **d** your brother owes you. 9023
24:6 **take** a pair of millstones—not even the upper one—**as security for a d,** 2471
1Sa 22:2 in distress or **in d** or discontented 4200+5957
Job 24:9 the infant of the poor *is* **seized for a d.** 2471
Mt 18:25 and all that he had be sold *to* **repay the d.** *625*
18:27 canceled the **d** and let him go. *1245*
18:30 into prison until he could pay the **d.** *4053*
18:32 that **d** of yours because you begged me to. *4051*
Lk 7:43 the one who had the bigger **d** canceled." *NIG*
Ro 13:8 *Let* no **d remain outstanding,** except *4053*
13:8 except the continuing **d** to love one another, *NIG*

DEBTOR (1) [DEBT]

Isa 24:2 for **d** as for creditor. 928+5957

DEBTORS (3) [DEBT]

Hab 2:7 Will not your **d** suddenly arise? 5967
Mt 6:12 as we also have forgiven our **d.** *4050*
Lk 16:5 "So he called in each one *of* his master's **d.** *5971*

DEBTS (9) [DEBT]

Dt 15:1 every seven years *you must* **cancel d.** 6913+9024
15:2 LORD's **time for canceling d** has been proclaimed. 9024
15:9 the year for **canceling d,** is near," 9024
31:10 in the year for **canceling d,** 9024
2Ki 4:7 "Go, sell the oil and pay your **d.** 5963
Ne 10:31 the land and will cancel all **d.** 3338+5391
Pr 22:26 in pledge or puts up security for **d;** 5391
Mt 6:12 Forgive us our **d,** *4052*
Lk 7:42 so he canceled the **d** of both. *NIG*

DECAPOLIS (3)

Mt 4:25 Large crowds from Galilee, the **D,** *1279*
Mk 5:20 in the **D** how much Jesus had done for him. *1279*
7:31 of Galilee and into the region *of* the **D.** *1279*

DECAY (12) [DECAYED]

Ps 16:10 nor will you let your Holy One see **d.** 8846
49:9 that he should live on forever and not see **d.** 8846
49:14 their forms *will* **d** in the grave, 1162
Pr 12:4 but a disgraceful wife is like **d** in his bones. 8373
Isa 5:24 so their roots will **d** 5215
Hab 3:16 **d** crept into my bones, 8373
Ac 2:27 nor will you let your Holy One see **d.** *1426*
2:31 nor did his body see **d.** *1426*
13:34 God raised him from the dead, never *to* **d,** *1426+1650+5715*
13:35 " 'You will not let your Holy One see **d.**' *1426*
13:37 from the dead did not see **d.** *1426*
Ro 8:21 *to* **d** and brought into the glorious freedom *5785*

DECAYED (2) [DECAY]

Jer 49:7 *Has* their wisdom **d?** 6244
Ac 13:36 with his fathers and *his* **body d.** *1426+3972*

DECEASED (KJV) See DEPARTED SPIRITS, DIED

DECEIT (32) [DECEIVE]

Job 15:35 their womb fashions **d.**" 5327
27:4 and my tongue will utter no **d.** 8245
31:5 in falsehood or my foot has hurried after **d** 5327
Ps 5:9 *with* their tongue *they* **speak d.** 2744
32:2 against him and in whose spirit is no **d.** 8245
50:19 for evil and harness your tongue to **d.** 5327
52:2 like a sharpened razor, you who practice **d.** 8245
101:7 No one who practices **d** will dwell 8245
Pr 6:14 who plots evil with **d** in his heart— 9337
12:20 There is **d** in the hearts 5327
26:24 but in his heart he harbors **d.** 5327
Isa 5:18 along with cords of **d,** 8736
30:12 relied on oppression and depended on **d,** 4279
53:9 nor was any **d** in his mouth. 5327
Jer 5:27 their houses are full of **d;** 5327
6:13 prophets and priests alike, all practice **d.** 9214
8:5 They cling to **d;** they refuse to return. 9567
8:10 prophets and priests alike, all practice **d.** 9214
9:6 in their **d** they refuse to acknowledge me," 5327
9:8 it speaks with **d.** 5327
Da 8:25 He will cause **d** to prosper, 5327
Hos 7:1 They practice **d,** thieves break into houses, 9214
11:12 the house of Israel with **d.** 5327
Zep 1:9 of their gods with violence and **d.** 5327
3:13 nor will **d** be found in their mouths. 4383+9567
Zec 10:2 The idols speak **d,** diviners see visions 224
Mk 7:22 malice, **d,** lewdness, envy, slander, *1515*
Ac 13:10 You are full of all kinds of **d** and trickery. *1515*
Ro 1:29 murder, strife, **d** and malice. *1515*
3:13 their tongues **practice d.**" *1514*
1Pe 2:1 rid yourselves of all malice and all **d,** *1515*
2:22 and no **d** was found in his mouth." *1515*

DECEITFUL (26) [DECEIVE]

Job 11:11 Surely he recognizes **d** men; 8736
Ps 5:6 bloodthirsty and **d** men the LORD abhors. 5327
17:1 it does not rise from **d** lips. 5327
26:4 I do not sit with **d** men, 8736
36:3 The words of his mouth are wicked and **d;** 5327
43:1 rescue me from **d** and wicked men. 5327
52:4 O you **d** tongue! 5327
55:23 and **d** men will not live out half their days. 5327
109:2 and **d** *men* have opened their mouths 5327
119:29 Keep me from **d** ways; 9214
120:2 from lying lips and from **d** tongues. 8245
120:3 and what more besides, O **d** tongue? 8245
144:8 whose right hands are **d.** 9214
144:11 whose right hands are **d.** 9214
Pr 12:5 but the advice of the wicked is **d.** 5327
14:25 but a false witness is **d.** 5327
15:4 but a **d** tongue crushes the spirit. 6157
17:20 *he* whose tongue *is* **d** falls into trouble. 2200
Isa 30:9 These are rebellious people, **d** children, 3952
Jer 17:9 heart is **d** above all things and beyond cure. 6815
Hos 10:2 Their heart *is* **d,** 2744
2Co 11:13 such men are false apostles, **d** workmen, *1513*
Eph 4:14 and craftiness of men in their **d** scheming. *4415*
4:22 which is being corrupted by its **d** desires; *573*
1Pe 3:10 from evil and his lips from **d** speech. *1515*
Rev 21:27 anyone who does what is shameful or **d,** *6022*

DECEITFULLY (6) [DECEIVE]

Ge 27:35 "Your brother came **d** 928+5327
34:13 Jacob's sons replied **d** as they spoke 928+5327
Ex 8:29 not **act d** again by not letting the people go 9438
Job 13:7 Will you speak **d** for him? 8245
Da 11:23 he will act **d,** 5327
Mic 6:12 and their tongues speak **d.** 8245

DECEITFULNESS (4) [DECEIVE]

Ps 119:118 for their **d** is in vain. 9567
Mt 13:22 of this life and the **d** of wealth choke it, *573*
Mk 4:19 the **d** of wealth and the desires *573*
Heb 3:13 none of you may be hardened *by* sin's **d.** *573*

DECEIVE (32) [DECEIT, DECEITFUL, DECEITFULLY, DECEITFULNESS, DECEIVED, DECEIVER, DECEIVERS, DECEIVES, DECEIVING, DECEPTION, DECEPTIVE, DECEPTIVELY]

Ge 31:27 Why did you run off secretly and **d** me? 1704
Lev 19:11 " 'Do not **d** one another. 9213
Jos 9:22 "Why *did you* **d** us by saying, 8228
1Sa 19:17 "Why *did you* **d** me like this 8228
2Sa 3:25 to **d** you and observe your movements 7331
2Ki 18:29 *Do* not **let** Hezekiah **d** you. 5958
19:10 **let** the god you depend on **d** 5958
2Ch 32:15 not *let* Hezekiah **d** you and mislead you 5958
Job 13:9 *Could you* **d** him 9438
13:9 as you *might* **d** men? 9438
15:31 not **d himself** by trusting what is worthless, 9494
Pr 14:5 A truthful witness *does* not **d,** 3941
24:28 or use your lips *to* **d.** 7331
Isa 36:14 *Do* not **let** Hezekiah **d** you. 5958
37:10 the god you depend on **d** you when he says, 5958
Jer 29:8 the prophets and diviners among you **d** you. 5958
37:9 *Do* not **d** yourselves, thinking, 5958
Ob 1:7 your friends *will* **d** and overpower you; 5958
Zec 13:4 on a prophet's garment of hair in order to **d.** 3950
Mt 24:5 'I am the Christ,' and *will* **d** many. *4414*
24:11 and **d** many people. *4414*
24:24 and perform great signs and miracles to **d** *4414*
Mk 13:6 claiming, 'I am he,' and *will* **d** many. *4414*
13:22 and perform signs and miracles to **d** *675*
Ro 16:18 By smooth talk and flattery *they* **d** *1987*
1Co 3:18 *Do* not **d** yourselves. *1987*
Eph 5:6 *Let* no one **d** you with empty words, *572*
Col 2:4 I tell you this so that no one *may* **d** you *4165*
2Th 2:3 Don't *let* anyone **d** you in any way, *1987*
Jas 1:22 and so **d** yourselves. *4165*
1Jn 1:8 *we* **d** ourselves and the truth is not in us. *4414*
Rev 20:8 *to* **d** the nations in the four corners of *4414*

DECEIVED (29) [DECEIVE]

Ge 3:13 The woman said, "The serpent **d** me, 5958
27:36 *He has* **d** me these two times: 6810
29:25 Why *have you* **d** me?" 8228
31:20 Jacob **d** Laban the Aramean by 1704+4213
31:26 "What have you done? *You've* **d** me, 1704+4222
Nu 25:18 when they **d** you in the affair 928+5792+5793
1Sa 28:12 "Why *have you* **d** me? 8228
Job 12:16 both **d** and deceiver are his. 8704
Isa 19:13 the leaders of Memphis **are d;** 5958
Jer 4:10 how **completely** *you have* **d** 5958+5958
20:7 O LORD, *you* **d** me, and I was deceived; 7331
20:7 O LORD, you deceived me, and *I* **was d;** 7331
20:10 saying, "Perhaps *he will* **be d;** 7331
49:16 and the pride of your heart *have* **d** you, 5958
Hos 7:11 **easily d** and senseless— 7331
Ob 1:3 The pride of your heart *has* **d** you, 5958
Lk 21:8 He replied: "Watch out that *you are* not **d.** *4414*
Jn 7:47 "You mean he *has* **d** you also?" *4414*
Ro 7:11 by the commandment, **d** me, and through *1987*
1Co 6:9 *Do not be* **d:** Neither the sexually immoral *4414*
2Co 11:3 But I am afraid that just as Eve was **d** by *1987*
Gal 6:7 *Do* not *be* **d:** God cannot be mocked. *4414*
1Ti 2:14 And Adam *was* not the one **d;** *572*
2:14 the woman who *was* **d** and became a sinner. *1987*
2Ti 3:13 deceiving and *being* **d.** *4414*
Tit 3:3 **d** and enslaved by all kinds of passions *4414*
Jas 1:16 Don't **be d,** my dear brothers. *4414*
Rev 13:14 *he* **d** the inhabitants of the earth. *4414*
20:10 And the devil, who **d** them, *4414*

DECEIVER (5) [DECEIVE]

Job 12:16 both deceived and **d** are his. 8706
Jer 9:4 For every brother *is a* **d,** 6810+6810
Mic 2:11 If a liar and **d** comes and says, 9214
Mt 27:63 that while he was still alive that **d** said, *4418*
2Jn 1:7 Any such person is the **d** and the antichrist. *4418*

DECEIVERS (3) [DECEIVE]

Ps 49:5 when wicked **d** surround me— 6812
Tit 1:10 mere talkers and **d,** *5855*
2Jn 1:7 Many **d,** who do *4418*

DECEIVES (8) [DECEIVE]

Pr 26:19 is a man *who* **d** his neighbor and says, 8228
Jer 9: 5 Friend **d** friend, and no one speaks 9438
Mt 24: 4 "Watch out that no one **d** you. *4414*
Mk 13: 5 "Watch out that no one **d** you. *4414*
Jn 7:12 Others replied, "No, *he* **d** the people." *4414*
Gal 6: 3 when he is nothing, *he* **d** himself. *5854*
2Th 2:10 of evil that **d** those who are perishing. *573*
Jas 1:26 *he* **d** himself and his religion is worthless. *572*

DECEIVING (4) [DECEIVE]

Lev 6: 2 to the LORD *by* **d** his neighbor 3950
1Ti 4: 1 and follow **d** spirits and things taught *4418*
2Ti 3:13 **d** and being deceived. *4414*
Rev 20: 3 to keep *him* from **d** the nations anymore *4414*

DECENCY (1) [DECENTLY]

1Ti 2: 9 with **d** and propriety, *133*

DECENTLY (1) [DECENCY]

Ro 13:13 Let us behave **d,** as in the daytime, *2361*

DECEPTION (9) [DECEIVE]

Ps 12: 2 flattering lips speak with **d.** 2256+4213+4213
38:12 all day long they plot **d.** 5327
Pr 14: 8 but the folly of fools is **d.** 5327
26:26 His malice may be concealed by **d,** 5396
Jer 3:23 on the hills and mountains is a **d;** 9214
9: 6 You live in the midst of **d;** 5327
Hos 10:13 you have eaten the fruit of **d.** 3951
Mt 27:64 This last **d** will be worse than the first." *4415*
2Co 4: 2 *we do* not **use d,** *1877+4111+4344*

DECEPTIVE (8) [DECEIVE]

Pr 11:18 The wicked man earns **d** wages, 9214
23: 3 for that food is **d.** 3942
31:30 Charm is **d,** and beauty is fleeting; 9214
Jer 7: 4 Do not trust in **d** words and say, 9214
7: 8 in **d** words that are worthless. 9214
15:18 Will you be to me like a **d** brook, 423
Mic 1:14 The town of Aczib will prove **d** to the kings 423
Col 2: 8 through hollow and **d** philosophy, *573*

DECEPTIVELY (1) [DECEIVE]

2Ki 10:19 Jehu was acting **d** in order to destroy 928+6817

DECIDE (16) [DECIDED, DECISION, DECISIONS]

Ex 18:16 and *I* **d** between the parties 9149
18:22 the simple cases *they can* **d** themselves. 9149
33: 5 and *I will* **d** what to do with you.' " 3359
Dt 21: 5 and to **d** all cases of dispute 2118+6584+7023
25: 1 to take it to court and *the* **judges** *will* **d** 9149
Jdg 11:27 **d the dispute** this day between the Israelites 9149
1Sa 24:15 the LORD be our judge and **d** between us. 9149
2Sa 24:13 think it over and **d** how I should answer 8011
1Ch 21:12 **d** how I should answer 8011
Job 22:28 What *you* **d** *on* will be done, 1615
34:33 You *must* **d,** not I; 1047
Isa 11: 3 or **d** by what he hears with his ears; 3519
Eze 44:24 the priests are to serve as judges and **d** it 9149
Jn 19:24 *"Let's* **d by lot** who will get it." *3275*
Ac 4:21 *They* could not **d** how to punish them, *2351*
24:22 he said, *"I will* **d** your case." *1336*

DECIDED (29) [DECIDE]

Ge 41:32 that the matter *has* **been firmly d** by God, 3922
Ex 18:26 but the simple ones *they* **d** themselves. 9149
Jdg 4: 5 to her to have their **disputes d.** 5477
2Ch 24: 4 Joash **d** to restore the temple 2118+4213+6640
30: 2 in Jerusalem **d** to celebrate the Passover in 3619
30: 5 *They* **d** to send a proclamation 1821+6641
Est 7: 7 Haman, realizing that the king *had already* **d** his fate, 3983
Jer 4:28 *I have* **d** and will not turn back." 2372
Da 2: 5 "This is what I have firmly **d:** 10418
2: 8 that this is what I have firmly **d:** 10418
Zep 3: 8 I have **d** to assemble the nations, 5477
Mt 27: 7 So they **d to** use the money to buy *3284+5206*
Lk 23:24 So Pilate **d** to grant their demand. *2137*
Jn 1:43 The next day Jesus **d** to leave for Galilee. *2527*
9:22 for already the Jews *had* **d** *5338*
Ac 3:13 *though he had* **d** to let him go. *3212*
4:28 and will *had* **d beforehand** should happen. *4633*
7:23 *he* **d** to visit his fellow Israelites. *326+2093+2840+3836*
11:29 **d** to provide help for the brothers living *3988*
15:22 **d** to choose some of their own men *1506*
19:21 Paul **d** to go to Jerusalem, *5502*
20: 3 *he* **d** to go back through Macedonia. *1181+1191*
20:16 Paul *had* **d** to sail past Ephesus *3212*
25:25 to the Emperor *I* **d** to send him to Rome. *3212*
27: 1 When *it was* **d that** we would sail *3212*
27:12 the majority **d that** we should sail on, *1087+5502*
27:39 where *they* **d** to run the ship aground *1086*
2Co 9: 7 Each man should give what *he has* **d** *4576*
Tit 3:12 because *I have* **d** to winter there. *3212*

DECIMATED (1)

2Sa 21: 5 plotted against us so that *we have* **been d** 9012

DECISION (15) [DECIDE]

Ex 28:29 over his heart on the breastpiece of **d** as 5477
2Sa 15: 2 to be placed before the king for a **d,** 5477
Ezr 5:17 let the king send us his **d** in this matter. 10668
10: 8 in accordance with the **d** *of* the officials 6783
Pr 16:33 but its every **d** is from the LORD. 5477
Isa 16: 3 "Give us counsel, render a **d.** 7131
Da 4:17 " 'The **d** is announced by messengers, 10601
Joel 3:14 Multitudes, multitudes in the valley of **d!** 3025
3:14 day of the LORD is near in the valley of **d.** 3025
Mt 27: 1 the elders of the people came **to the d** *3284+5206*
Mk 15: 1 and the whole Sanhedrin, reached a **d.** *5206*
Lk 23:51 not consented *to* their **d** and action. *1087*
Jn 1:13 nor of human **d** or a husband's will, *2525*
Ac 21:25 to them *our* **d that** they should abstain *3212*
25:21 to be held over for the Emperor's **d,** *1338*

DECISIONS (10) [DECIDE]

Ex 28:15 "Fashion a breastpiece for **making d—** 5477
28:30 the **means of making d** *for* the Israelites 5477
Nu 27:21 *who will* **obtain d** for him by inquiring of 8626
Dt 17:10 according to the **d** they give you at 1821
17:11 and the **d** they give you. 5477
Isa 11: 4 with justice *he will* **give d** for the poor of 3519
28: 7 they stumble when **rendering d.** 7133
58: 2 for just **d** and seem eager for God to come 5477
Jn 8:16 But if I do judge, my **d** are right, *3213*
Ac 16: 4 they delivered the **d** reached by the apostles *3212*

DECK (2) [DECKED, DECKS]

Eze 27: 6 the coasts of Cyprus they made your **d,** 7983
Jnh 1: 5 But Jonah had gone **below d,** 2021+3752+6208

DECKED (1) [DECK]

Hos 2:13 *she* **d** herself *with* rings and jewelry, 6335

DECKEDST, DECKEST (KJV) See DRESS, MAKE GAUDY, PUT ON

DECKS (1) [DECK]

Ge 6:16 middle and **upper** *d.* AIT

DECLARE (46) [DECLARED, DECLARES, DECLARING]

Ex 22: 9 the judges **d guilty** must pay back double 8399
Dt 5: 1 Hear, O Israel, the decrees and laws I **d** 1819
5: 5 and to **d** to you the word of the LORD 5583
21: 7 and *they shall* **d:** "Our hands did not shed 6699
26: 3 *"I* **d** today to the LORD your God 5583
26: 5 *you shall* **d** before the LORD your God: 6699
30:18 *I* **d** to you this day that you will certainly 5583
32:40 I lift my hand to heaven and **d:** 606
1Ki 1:36 the God of my lord the king, so **d** it. 606
8:32 **D** the innocent **not guilty,** 7405
2Ki 9: 3 the flask and pour the oil on his head and **d,** 606
1Ch 16:24 **D** his glory among the nations, 6218
17:10 " *'I* **d** to you that the LORD will build 5583
2Ch 6:23 **D** the innocent **not guilty** 7405
Job 34:34 "Men of understanding **d,** NIH
Ps 5:10 **D** them **guilty,** O God! 870
9:14 that *I may* **d** your praises in the gates of 6218
19: 1 The heavens **d** the glory of God; 6218
22:22 *I will* **d** your name to my brothers; 6218
40: 5 they would be too many *to* **d.** 6218
51:15 and my mouth *will* **d** your praise. 5583
71:17 and to this day *I* **d** your marvelous deeds. 5583
71:18 till *I* **d** your power to the next generation, 5583
75: 9 As for me, *I will* **d** this forever; 5583
89: 2 *I will* **d** that your love stands firm forever, 606
96: 3 **D** his glory among the nations, 6218
106: 2 of the LORD or fully **d** his praise? 9048
Isa 41:22 Or **d** *to* us the things to come, 9048
42: 9 and new things *I* **d;** 5583
44: 7 *Let him* **d** and lay out 5583
45:19 I **d** what is right. 5583
45:21 **D** what is to be, present it— 5583
58: 1 **D** to my people their rebellion and to 5583
Jer 23:31 against the prophets who wag their own tongues and yet **d,** 5535
Eze 38:19 In my zeal and fiery wrath *I* **d** that at 1819
Da 4:17 the holy ones **d** the verdict, 10397
Joel 1:14 **D** *a* **holy** fast; call a sacred assembly. 7727
2:15 Blow the trumpet in Zion, **d** a **holy** fast, 7727
Mic 3: 8 to **d** to Jacob his transgression, 5583
Ac 20:26 *I* **d** to you today that I am innocent of *3458*
1Co 15:50 *I* **d** to you, brothers, *5774*
Gal 5: 3 Again *I* **d** to every man who lets himself *3458*
Eph 6:20 Pray that I **may d** it fearlessly, as I should. *3281*
Heb 2:12 *"I will* **d** your name to my brothers; *550*
1Pe 2: 9 that *you may* **d** the praises *1972*
1Jn 1: 5 the message we have heard from him and **d** *334*

DECLARED (50) [DECLARE]

Nu 14:17 just as *you have* **d:** 1819
Dt 4:13 *He* **d** to you his covenant, 5583
26:17 *You have* **d** this day that 606
26:18 And the LORD *has* **d** this day 606
26:19 He has **d** that he will set you in praise, NIH
32:46 to heart all the words I *have* **solemnly d** 6386
1Ki 1:24 **d** that Adonijah shall be king after you, 606
8:53 just as *you* **d** through your servant Moses 1819
1Ki 13: 3 "This is the sign the LORD *has* **d:** 1819
13:32 the message *he* **d** by the word of the LORD 7924
22:11 of Kenaanah had made iron horns and *he* **d,** 606
22:28 Micaiah **d,** "If you ever return safely, 606
22:38 as the word of the LORD *had* **d.** 1819
2Ki 9: 6 the oil on Jehu's head and **d,** "This is what 606
13:17 arrow of victory over Aram!" Elisha **d.** 606
24:13 As the LORD *had* **d,** 1819
2Ch 18:10 and *he* **d,** "This is what the LORD says: 606
18:27 Micaiah **d,** "If you ever return safely, 606
Job 15:18 what wise men *have* **d,** 5583
Ps 88:11 **Is** your love **d** in the grave, 6218
95:11 So *I* **d on oath** in my anger, 8678
102:21 the name of the LORD *will be* **d** in Zion 6218
Pr 30: 1 This man **d** to Ithiel, to Ithiel and to Ucal: 5536
Ecc 4: 2 And I **d** that the dead, 8655
Isa 5: 9 The LORD Almighty has **d** in my hearing: NIH
45:21 *who* **d** it from the distant past? 5583
Jnh 3: 5 *They* **d** a fast, and all of them, 7924
Mt 26:35 But Peter **d,** "Even if I have to die *3306*
26:61 and **d,** "This fellow said, 'I am able *3306*
Mk 7:19 (In saying this, Jesus **d** all foods "clean.") *NIG*
10:20 he **d,** "all these I have kept since I was *5774*
12:36 speaking by the Holy Spirit, **d:** *3306*
14:29 Peter **d,** "Even if all fall away, I will not." *5774*
Jn 1:49 Then Nathanael **d,** "Rabbi, *646*
3: 3 In reply Jesus **d,** "I tell you the truth, *3306*
4:21 Jesus **d,** "Believe me, woman, *3306*
4:26 Then Jesus **d,** "I who speak to you am he." *3306*
6:35 Then Jesus **d,** "I am the bread of life. *3306*
7:46 the way this man does," the guards **d.** *646*
8:11 "Then neither do I condemn you," Jesus **d.** *3306*
Ac 20:21 *I have* **d** to both Jews and Greeks *1371*
25:12 *he* **d:** "You have appealed to Caesar. *646*
28:23 and **d** to them the kingdom of God and tried *1371*
Ro 1: 4 of holiness *was* **d** with power *to be* the Son *3988*
2:13 the law who *will be* **d righteous.** *1467*
3:20 *be* **d righteous** in his sight by observing *1467*
Heb 3:11 So *I* **d on oath** in my anger, *3923*
4: 3 "So *I* **d on oath** in my anger, *3923*
7: 8 by *him who is* **d** to be living. *3455*
7:17 For *it is* **d:** "You are a priest forever, *3455*

DECLARES (371) [DECLARE]

Ge 22:16 "I swear by myself, **d** the LORD, 5536
Ex 21: 5 "But if the servant **d,** 'I love my master 606+606
Nu 14:28 'As surely as I live, **d** the LORD, 5536
1Sa 2:30 the LORD, the God of Israel, **d:** 5536
2:30 But now the LORD **d:** 'Far be it from me! 5536
2Sa 7:11 " 'The LORD **d** to you that 5583
2Ki 9:26 and the blood of his sons, **d** the LORD, 5536
9:26 for it on this plot of ground, **d** the LORD.' 5536
19:33 he will not enter this city, **d** the LORD. 5536
22:19 I have heard you, **d** the LORD. 5536
2Ch 34:27 I have heard you, **d** the LORD. 5536
Isa 1:24 the Mighty One of Israel, **d:** 5536
3:15 **d** the Lord, the LORD Almighty. 5536
14:22 **d** the LORD Almighty. 5536
14:22 and descendants," **d** the LORD. 5536
14:23 **d** the LORD Almighty. 5536
17: 3 **d** the LORD Almighty. 5536
17: 6 **d** the LORD, the God of Israel. 5536
19: 4 **d** the Lord, the LORD Almighty. 5536
22:25 "In that day," **d** the LORD Almighty, 5536
30: 1 **d** the LORD, "to those who carry out plans 5536
31: 9 **d** the LORD, whose fire is in Zion, 5536
37:34 he will not enter this city," **d** the LORD. 5536
41:14 for I myself will help you," **d** the LORD, 5536
43:10 "You are my witnesses," **d** the LORD, 5536
43:12 You are my witnesses," **d** the LORD, 5536
49:18 As surely as I live," **d** the LORD, 5536
52: 5 **d** the LORD. 5536
52: 5 and those who rule them mock," **d** 5536
54:17 and this is their vindication from me," **d** 5536
55: 8 neither are your ways my ways," **d** the LORD. 5536
56: 8 The Sovereign LORD **d—** 5536
59:20 in Jacob who repent of their sins," **d** 5536
66: 2 **d** the LORD. 5536
66:17 they will meet their end together," **d** 5536
66:22 that I make will endure before me," **d** 5536
Jer 1: 8 for I am with you and will rescue you," **d** 5536
1:15 of the northern kingdoms," **d** the LORD. 5536
1:19 for I am with you and will rescue you," **d** 5536
2: 3 and disaster overtook them,' " **d** 5536
2: 9 against you again," **d** the LORD. 5536
2:12 and shudder with great horror," **d** 5536
2:19 **d** the Lord, the LORD Almighty. 5536
2:22 **d** the Sovereign LORD. 5536
2:29 against me," **d** the LORD. 5536
3: 1 **d** the LORD. 5536
3:10 but only in pretense," **d** the LORD. 5536
3:12 " 'Return, faithless Israel,' **d** the LORD, 5536
3:12 **d** the LORD, 'I will not be angry forever. 5536
3:13 and have not obeyed me,' " **d** the LORD. 5536
3:14 "Return, faithless people," **d** the LORD, 5536
3:16 **d** the LORD, "men will no longer say, 5536
3:20 O house of Israel," **d** the LORD. 5536
4: 1 O Israel, return to me," **d** the LORD. 5536
4: 9 "In that day," **d** the LORD, 5536
4:17 she has rebelled against me,' " **d** the LORD. 5536
5: 9 **d** the LORD. 5536
5:11 to me," **d** the LORD. 5536
5:15 O house of Israel," **d** the LORD, 5536
5:18 "Yet even in those days," **d** the LORD, 5536
5:22 **d** the LORD. 5536

Jer 5:29 **d** the LORD. 5536
6:12 against those who live in the land," **d** 5536
7:11 **d** the LORD. 5536
7:13 **d** the LORD, I spoke to you again 5536
7:19 **d** the LORD. 5536
7:30 of Judah have done evil in my eyes, **d** 5536
7:32 the days are coming, **d** the LORD, 5536
8: 1 " 'At that time, **d** the LORD, 5536
8: 3 **d** the LORD Almighty.' 5536
8:13 'I will take away their harvest, **d** the LORD. 5536
8:17 and they will bite you," **d** the LORD. 5536
9: 3 not acknowledge me," **d** the LORD. 5536
9: 6 to acknowledge me," **d** the LORD. 5536
9: 9 **d** the LORD. 5536
9:22 Say, "This is what the LORD **d:** 5536
9:24 for in these I delight," **d** the LORD. 5536
9:25 "The days are coming," **d** the LORD, 5536
12:17 and destroy it," **d** the LORD. 5536
13:11 and the whole house of Judah to me," **d** 5536
13:14 fathers and sons alike, **d** the LORD. 5536
13:25 the portion I have decreed for you," **d** 5536
15: 3 of destroyers against them," **d** the LORD, 5536
15: 6 You have rejected me," **d** the LORD. 5536
15: 9 to the sword before their enemies," **d** 5536
15:20 to rescue and save you," **d** the LORD. 5536
16: 5 from this people," **d** the LORD. 5536
16:11 **d** the LORD, 'and followed other gods 5536
16:14 the days are coming," **d** the LORD, 5536
16:16 **d** the LORD, "and they will catch them. 5536
17:24 **d** the LORD, and bring no load through 5536
18: 6 **d** the LORD. 5536
19: 6 the days are coming, **d** the LORD, 5536
19:12 to this place and to those who live here, **d** 5536
21: 7 After that, **d** the LORD, 5536
21:10 to do this city harm and not good, **d** 5536
21:13 above this valley on the rocky plateau, **d** 5536
21:14 as your deeds deserve, **d** the LORD. 5536
22: 5 But if you do not obey these commands, **d** 5536
22:16 **d** the LORD. 5536
22:24 "As surely as I live," **d** the LORD, 5536
23: 1 **d** the LORD. 5536
23: 2 for the evil you have done," **d** the LORD. 5536
23: 4 nor will any be missing," **d** the LORD. 5536
23: 5 "The days are coming," **d** the LORD, 5536
23: 7 the days are coming," **d** the LORD, 5536
23:11 in my temple I find their wickedness," **d** 5536
23:12 the year they are punished," **d** the LORD. 5536
23:23 "Am I only a God nearby," **d** the LORD, 5536
23:24 **d** the LORD. 5536
23:24 **d** the LORD. 5536
23:28 **d** the LORD. 5536
23:29 "Is not my word like fire," **d** the LORD, 5536
23:30 "Therefore," **d** the LORD, 5536
23:31 **d** the LORD, "I am against 5536
23:31 and yet declare, 'The LORD **d.**' 5536
23:32 who prophesy false dreams," **d** the LORD. 5536
23:32 not benefit these people in the least," **d** 5536
23:33 I will forsake you, **d** the LORD.' 5536
25: 7 you did not listen to me," **d** the LORD, 5536
25: 9 **d** the LORD, "and I will bring them 5536
25:12 for their guilt," **d** the LORD, 5536
25:29 **d** the LORD Almighty.' 5536
25:31 the wicked to the sword,' " **d** the LORD. 5536
27: 8 **d** the LORD, until I destroy it by his hand. 5536
27:11 to till it and to live there, **d** the LORD." ' " 5536
27:15 'I have not sent them,' **d** the LORD. 5536
27:22 the day I come for them,' **d** the LORD. 5536
28: 4 to Babylon,' **d** the LORD, 'for I will break 5536
29: 9 I have not sent them," **d** the LORD. 5536
29:11 **d** the LORD, "plans to prosper you and 5536
29:14 I will be found by you," **d** the LORD, 5536
29:14 where I have banished you," **d** the LORD, 5536
29:19 For they have not listened to my words," **d** 5536
29:19 And you exiles have not listened either," **d** 5536
29:23 and am a witness to it," **d** the LORD. 5536
29:32 the good things I will do for my people, **d** 5536
30: 3 The days are coming,' **d** the LORD, 5536
30: 8 " 'In that day,' **d** the LORD Almighty, 5536
30:10 O Israel,' **d** the LORD. 5536
30:11 with you and will save you,' **d** the LORD. 5536
30:17 and heal your wounds,' **d** the LORD, 5536
30:21 **d** the LORD. 5536
31: 1 "At that time," **d** the LORD, 5536
31:14 be filled with my bounty," **d** the LORD. 5536
31:16 for your work will be rewarded," **d** 5536
31:17 So there is hope for your future," **d** 5536
31:20 I have great compassion for him," **d** 5536
31:27 "The days are coming," **d** the LORD, 5536
31:28 to build and to plant," **d** the LORD. 5536
31:31 "The time is coming," **d** the LORD, 5536
31:32 though I was a husband to them," **d** 5536
31:33 with the house of Israel after that time," **d** 5536
31:34 from the least of them to the greatest," **d** 5536
31:36 if these decrees vanish from my sight," **d** 5536
31:37 of Israel because of all they have done," **d** 5536
31:38 "The days are coming," **d** the LORD, 5536
32: 5 until I deal with him, **d** the LORD. 5536
32:30 with what their hands have made, **d** 5536
32:44 because I will restore their fortunes, **d** 5536
33:14 " 'The days are coming,' **d** the LORD, 5536
34: 5 I myself make this promise, **d** the LORD.' " 5536
34:17 So I now proclaim 'freedom' for you, **d** 5536
34:22 I am going to give the order, **d** the LORD, 5536
35:13 **d** the LORD. 5536
39:17 I will rescue you on that day, **d** the LORD; 5536
39:18 because you trust in me, **d** the LORD.' " 5536
42:11 Do not be afraid of him, **d** the LORD, 5536
Jer 44:29 that I will punish you in this place,' **d** 5536
45: 5 For I will bring disaster on all people, **d** 5536
46: 5 and there is terror on every side," **d** 5536
46:18 "As surely as I live," **d** the King, 5536
46:23 **d** the LORD, "dense though it be. 5536
46:26 be inhabited as in times past," **d** 5536
46:28 for I am with you," **d** the LORD. 5536
48:12 But days are coming," **d** the LORD, 5536
48:15 down in the slaughter," **d** the King, 5536
48:25 her arm is broken," **d** the LORD. 5536
48:30 but it is futile," **d** the LORD, 5536
48:35 and burn incense to their gods," **d** 5536
48:38 like a jar that no one wants," **d** the LORD. 5536
48:43 O people of Moab," **d** the LORD. 5536
48:44 the year of her punishment," **d** the LORD. 5536
48:47 of Moab in days to come," **d** the LORD. 5536
49: 2 But the days are coming," **d** the LORD, 5536
49: 5 **d** the Lord, the LORD Almighty. 5536
49: 6 of the Ammonites," **d** the LORD. 5536
49:13 I swear by myself," **d** the LORD, 5536
49:16 I will bring you down," **d** the LORD. 5536
49:26 **d** the LORD Almighty. 5536
49:30 you who live in Hazor," **d** the LORD. 5536
49:31 which lives in confidence," **d** the LORD, 5536
49:32 on them from every side," **d** the LORD. 5536
49:37 even my fierce anger," **d** the LORD. 5536
49:38 and destroy her king and officials," **d** 5536
49:39 of Elam in days to come," **d** the LORD. 5536
50: 4 "In those days, at that time," **d** the LORD, 5536
50:10 all who plunder her will have their fill," **d** 5536
50:20 In those days, at that time," **d** the LORD, 5536
50:21 and completely destroy them," **d** 5536
50:30 be silenced in that day," **d** the LORD. 5536
50:31 **d** the Lord, the LORD Almighty, 5536
50:35 against the Babylonians!" **d** the LORD— 5536
50:40 **d** the LORD, "so no one will live there; 5536
51:24 the wrong they have done in Zion," **d** 5536
51:25 the whole earth," **d** the LORD. 5536
51:26 be desolate forever," **d** the LORD. 5536
51:39 then sleep forever and not awake," **d** 5536
51:48 of the north destroyers will attack her," **d** 5536
51:52 "But days are coming," **d** the LORD, 5536
51:53 against her," **d** the LORD. 5536
51:57 they will sleep forever and not awake," **d** 5536
Eze 5:11 **d** the Sovereign LORD, 5536
11: 8 **d** the Sovereign LORD. 5536
11:21 **d** the Sovereign LORD." 5536
12:25 **d** the Sovereign LORD.' " 5536
12:28 **d** the Sovereign LORD.' " 5536
13: 6 They say, "The LORD **d,"** 5536
13: 7 "The LORD **d,"** though I have not spoken? 5536
13: 8 I am against you, **d** the Sovereign LORD. 5536
13:16 **d** the Sovereign LORD." ' 5536
14:11 **d** the Sovereign LORD.' " 5536
14:14 **d** the Sovereign LORD. 5536
14:16 **d** the Sovereign LORD, 5536
14:18 **d** the Sovereign LORD, 5536
14:20 **d** the Sovereign LORD, even if Noah, 5536
14:23 **d** the Sovereign LORD." 5536
15: 8 **d** the Sovereign LORD." 5536
16: 8 **d** the Sovereign LORD, 5536
16:14 **d** the Sovereign LORD. 5536
16:19 **d** the Sovereign LORD. 5536
16:23 Woe to you, **d** the Sovereign LORD. 5536
16:30 **d** the Sovereign LORD, 5536
16:43 **d** the Sovereign LORD. 5536
16:48 As surely as I live, **d** the Sovereign LORD, 5536
16:58 and your detestable practices, **d** 5536
16:63 **d** the Sovereign LORD.' " 5536
17:16 surely as I live, **d** the Sovereign LORD, 5536
18: 3 surely as I live, **d** the Sovereign LORD, 5536
18: 9 he will surely live, **d** the Sovereign LORD. 5536
18:23 **d** the Sovereign LORD. 5536
18:30 **d** the Sovereign LORD. 5536
18:32 **d** the Sovereign LORD. 5536
20: 3 **d** the Sovereign LORD.' 5536
20:31 As surely as I live, **d** the Sovereign LORD, 5536
20:33 As surely as I live, **d** the Sovereign LORD, 5536
20:36 **d** the Sovereign LORD. 5536
20:40 **d** the Sovereign LORD, 5536
20:44 **d** the Sovereign LORD.' " 5536
21: 7 **d** the Sovereign LORD." 5536
21:13 **d** the Sovereign LORD.' 5536
22:12 **d** the Sovereign LORD. 5536
22:31 **d** the Sovereign LORD." 5536
23:34 I have spoken, **d** the Sovereign LORD. 5536
24:14 **d** the Sovereign LORD.' " 5536
25:14 **d** the Sovereign LORD.' " 5536
26: 5 for I have spoken, **d** the Sovereign LORD. 5536
26:14 **d** the Sovereign LORD. 5536
26:21 **d** the Sovereign LORD." 5536
28:10 I have spoken, **d** the Sovereign LORD.' " 5536
29:20 **d** the Sovereign LORD. 5536
30: 6 **d** the Sovereign LORD. 5536
31:18 **d** the Sovereign LORD.' " 5536
32: 8 **d** the Sovereign LORD. 5536
32:14 **d** the Sovereign LORD. 5536
32:16 **d** the Sovereign LORD." 5536
32:31 **d** the Sovereign LORD. 5536
32:32 **d** the Sovereign LORD." 5536
33:11 **d** the Sovereign LORD, 5536
34: 8 **d** the Sovereign LORD, 5536
34:15 **d** the Sovereign LORD. 5536
34:30 are my people, **d** the Sovereign LORD. 5536
34:31 **d** the Sovereign LORD.' " 5536
35: 6 **d** the Sovereign LORD, 5536
35:11 **d** the Sovereign LORD, 5536
Eze 36:14 **d** the Sovereign LORD. 5536
36:15 **d** the Sovereign LORD.' " 5536
36:23 **d** the Sovereign LORD, 5536
36:32 **d** the Sovereign LORD. 5536
37:14 and I have done it, **d** the LORD.' " 5536
38:18 **d** the Sovereign LORD. 5536
38:21 **d** the Sovereign LORD. 5536
39: 5 for I have spoken, **d** the Sovereign LORD. 5536
39: 8 **d** the Sovereign LORD. 5536
39:10 **d** the Sovereign LORD. 5536
39:13 **d** the Sovereign LORD. 5536
39:20 **d** the Sovereign LORD. 5536
39:29 **d** the Sovereign LORD." 5536
43:19 **d** the Sovereign LORD. 5536
43:27 I will accept you, **d** the Sovereign LORD." 5536
44:12 **d** the Sovereign LORD. 5536
44:15 **d** the Sovereign LORD. 5536
44:27 **d** the Sovereign LORD. 5536
45: 9 **d** the Sovereign LORD. 5536
45:15 **d** the Sovereign LORD. 5536
47:23 **d** the Sovereign LORD. 5536
48:29 **d** the Sovereign LORD. 5536
Hos 2:13 but me she forgot," **d** the LORD. 5536
2:16 "In that day," **d** the LORD, 5536
2:21 that day I will respond," **d** the LORD— 5536
11:11 in their homes," **d** the LORD. 5536
Joel 2:12 "Even now," **d** the LORD, 5536
Am 2:11 **d** the LORD. 5536
2:16 on that day," **d** the LORD. 5536
3:10 **d** the LORD, "who hoard plunder and loot 5536
3:13 **d** the Lord, the LORD God Almighty. 5536
3:15 and the mansions will be demolished," **d** 5536
4: 3 and you will be cast out toward Harmon," **d** 5536
4: 5 **d** the Sovereign LORD. 5536
4: 6 yet you have not returned to me," **d** 5536
4: 8 yet you have not returned to me," **d** 5536
4: 9 yet you have not returned to me," **d** 5536
4:10 yet you have not returned to me," **d** 5536
4:11 the fire, yet you have not returned to me," **d** 5536
6: 8 the LORD God Almighty **d:** 5536
6:14 For the LORD God Almighty **d,** 5536
8: 3 "In that day," **d** the Sovereign LORD, 5536
8: 9 "In that day," **d** the Sovereign LORD, 5536
8:11 **d** the Sovereign LORD, 5536
9: 7 **d** the LORD. 5536
9: 8 not totally destroy the house of Jacob," **d** 5536
9:12 **d** the LORD, who will do these things. 5536
9:13 "The days are coming," **d** the LORD, 5536
Ob 1: 4 from there I will bring you down," **d** 5536
1: 8 "In that day," **d** the LORD, 5536
Mic 4: 6 "In that day," **d** the LORD, 5536
5:10 "In that day," **d** the LORD, 5536
Na 2:13 **d** the LORD Almighty. 5536
3: 5 **d** the LORD Almighty. 5536
Zep 1: 2 from the face of the earth," **d** the LORD. 5536
1: 3 from the face of the earth," **d** the LORD. 5536
1:10 "On that day," **d** the LORD, 5536
2: 9 as surely as I live," **d** the LORD Almighty, 5536
3: 8 Therefore wait for me," **d** the LORD, 5536
Hag 1: 9 **d** the LORD Almighty. 5536
1:13 "I am with you," **d** the LORD. 5536
2: 4 be strong, O Zerubbabel,' **d** the LORD. 5536
2: 4 all you people of the land,' **d** the LORD, 5536
2: 4 I am with you,' **d** the LORD Almighty. 5536
2: 8 **d** the LORD Almighty. 5536
2: 9 **d** the LORD Almighty." 5536
2:14 and this nation in my sight,' **d** the LORD. 5536
2:17 yet you did not turn to me,' **d** the LORD. 5536
2:23 " 'On that day,' **d** the LORD Almighty, 5536
2:23 **d** the LORD, 'and I will make you 5536
2:23 **d** the LORD Almighty." 5536
Zec 1: 3 'Return to me,' **d** the LORD Almighty, 5536
1: 4 or pay attention to me, **d** the LORD. 5536
1:16 **d** the LORD Almighty. 5536
2: 5 of fire around it,' **d** the LORD, 'and I will 5536
2: 6 from the land of the north," **d** the LORD, 5536
2: 6 to the four winds of heaven," **d** the LORD. 5536
2:10 and I will live among you," **d** the LORD. 5536
3:10 **d** the LORD Almighty." 5536
5: 4 The LORD Almighty **d,** 'I will send it out, 5536
8: 6 **d** the LORD Almighty. 5536
8:11 **d** the LORD Almighty. 5536
8:17 I hate all this," **d** the LORD. 5536
10:12 in his name they will walk," **d** the LORD. 5536
11: 6 on the people of the land," **d** the LORD. 5536
12: 1 the spirit of man within him, **d:** 5536
12: 4 and its rider with madness," **d** the LORD. 5536
13: 2 **d** the LORD Almighty. 5536
13: 7 **d** the LORD Almighty. 5536
13: 8 In the whole land," **d** the LORD, 5536
Lk 20:42 David himself **d** in the Book of Psalms: *3306*
Ro 2:16 as my gospel **d.** *NIG*
Gal 3:22 But the Scripture **d** that the whole world is *NIG*
Heb 8: 8 "The time is coming, **d** the Lord, *3306*
8: 9 and I turned away from them, **d** the Lord. *3306*
8:10 with the house of Israel after that time, **d** *3306*

DECLARING (3) [DECLARE]

Ps 71: 8 **d** your splendor all day long. NIH
Jer 50:28 the fugitives and refugees from Babylon **d** 5583
Ac 2:11 we hear them **d** the wonders of God *3281*

DECLINED (1)

Ac 18:20 to spend more time with them, *he* **d.** *2153+4024*

DECORATE (2) [DECORATED, DECORATES, DECORATING, DECORATIONS]

1Ki 7:18 in two rows encircling each network to **d** 4059
Mt 23:29 You build tombs for the prophets and **d** *3175*

DECORATED (9) [DECORATE]

2Ki 25:17 and was **d with** a network and pomegranates 6584
2Ch 3: 5 and **d** it *with* palm tree and chain designs. 6590
SS 5:14 like polished ivory **d** *with* sapphires. 6634
Jer 52:22 was **d with** a network and pomegranates 6584
Eze 40:16 the projecting walls were **d with** palm trees. 448
40:31 palm trees **d** its jambs, 448
40:34 palm trees **d** the jambs on either side, 448
40:37 palm trees **d** the jambs on either side, 448
Rev 21:19 The foundations of the city walls *were* **d** *3175*

DECORATES (1) [DECORATE]

Jer 22:14 panels it with cedar and **d** it in red. 5417

DECORATING (4) [DECORATE]

1Ki 7:41 of network **d** the two bowl-shaped capitals 4059
7:42 **d** the bowl-shaped capitals on top of 4059
2Ch 4:12 of network **d** the two bowl-shaped capitals 4059
4:13 **d** the bowl-shaped capitals on top of 4059

DECORATIONS (2) [DECORATE]

Eze 40:22 its portico and its **palm tree d** had 9474
40:26 it had **palm tree d** on the faces of 9474

DECREASE (2) [DECREASED]

Lev 25:16 *you are to* **d** the price, 5070
Jer 29: 6 Increase in number there; *do* not **d**. 5070

DECREASED (2) [DECREASE]

Ps 107:39 Then *their* **numbers d**, 5070
Jer 30:19 and *they will* not *be* **d**; 5070

DECREE (41) [DECREED, DECREES]

Ex 15:25 the LORD made a **d** and a law for them, 2976
1Ch 16:17 He confirmed it to Jacob as a **d**, 2976
Ezr 5:13 King Cyrus issued a **d** to rebuild this house 10302
5:17 to see if King Cyrus did in fact issue a **d** 10302
6: 3 the king issued a **d** *concerning* the temple 10302
6: 8 I hereby **d** what you are to do 10302+10682
6:11 I **d** that if anyone changes this edict, 10302+10682
6:12 or people who lifts a hand to change this **d** NIH
6:13 because of the **d** King Darius had sent, NIH
7:13 I **d** that any of the Israelites in my kingdom, 10302+10682
Est 1:19 let him issue a royal **d** and let it be written 1821
3: 9 *let a* **d be issued** to destroy them, 4180
8: 8 Now write another **d** in the king's name NIH
9:32 Esther's **d** confirmed these regulations 4411
Job 23:14 He carries out his **d** *against* me, 2976
28:26 when he made a **d** for the rain and a path 2976
Ps 2: 7 I will proclaim the **d** *of* the LORD: 2976
7: 6 Awake, my God; **d** justice. 7422
81: 4 this is a **d** for Israel, 2976
105:10 He confirmed it to Jacob as a **d**, 2976
148: 6 he gave a **d** that will never pass away. 2976
Jer 51:12 *his* **d** against the people of Babylon. 1819
Da 2:13 **d** was issued to put the wise men to death, 10186
2:15 "Why did the king issue such a harsh **d**?" 10186
3:10 You have issued a **d**, O king, 10302
3:29 I **d** that the people of any nation 10302+10682
4:24 and this is the **d** the Most High has issued 10141
6: 7 and enforce the **d** that anyone who prays 10057
6: 8 the **d** and put it in writing so that it cannot 10057
6: 9 So King Darius put the **d** in writing. 10057
6:10 that the **d** had been published, 10375
6:12 the king and spoke to him about his royal **d** 10057
6:12 "Did you not publish a **d** that during 10057
6:12 The king answered, "The **d** stands— 10418
6:13 O king, or to the **d** you put in writing. 10057
6:15 of the Medes and Persians no **d** or edict that 10057
6:26 "I issue a **d** that in every part 10302
9:25 the **d** to restore and rebuild Jerusalem until 1821
Jnh 3: 7 "By the **d** *of* the king and his nobles: 3248
Lk 2: 1 In those days Caesar Augustus issued a **d** *1504*
Ro 1:32 Although they know God's **righteous d** *1468*

DECREED (24) [DECREE]

1Ki 22:23 The LORD *has* **d** disaster for you." 1819
2Ki 8: 1 the LORD *has* **d** a famine in the land 7924
2Ch 18:22 The LORD *has* **d** disaster for you." 1819
Ezr 6:12 I Darius *have* **d** it. 10302+10682
Est 2: 1 and what she had done and what *he had* **d** 1615
9:31 Mordecai the Jew and Queen Esther *had* **d** 7756
Job 14: 5 you have **d** the number of his months 907
Ps 78: 5 *He* **d** statutes for Jacob and established 7756
Isa 10:22 Destruction *has* **been d**, 3076
10:23 the destruction **d** upon the whole land. 3076
28:22 of the destruction **d** against the whole land. 3076
Jer 11:17 who planted you, *has* **d** disaster for you, 1819
13:25 the portion I have **d** *for* you," 4496
16:10 the LORD **d** such a great disaster 1819
40: 2 "The LORD your God **d** this disaster 1819
La 1:17 The LORD *has* **d** for Jacob 7422
La 2:17 which *he* **d** long ago. 7422
3:37 and have it happen if the Lord *has* not **d** it? 7422
Da 4:31 "This is what *is* **d** for you, 10042
9:24 "Seventy 'sevens' **are d** for your people 3155
9:26 and desolations *have* **been d**. 3076
9:27 the end *that* **is d** is poured out on him." 3076
Na 2: 7 *It is* **d** that [the city] be exiled 5893
Lk 22:22 The Son of Man will go as *it has been* **d**, *3988*

DECREES (132) [DECREE]

Ge 26: 5 my commands, my **d** and my laws." 2978
Ex 15:26 to his commands and keep all his **d**, 2976
18:16 and inform them of God's **d** and laws." 2976
18:20 Teach them the **d** and laws, 2976
Lev 10:11 and you must teach the Israelites all the **d** 2976
18: 4 and be careful to follow my **d**. 2978
18: 5 Keep my **d** and laws, 2978
18:26 But you must keep my **d** and my laws. 2978
19:19 " 'Keep my **d**. 2978
19:37 " 'Keep all my **d** and all my laws 2978
20: 8 Keep my **d** and follow them. 2978
20:22 " 'Keep all my **d** and laws and follow them, 2978
25:18 " 'Follow my **d** and be careful 2978
26: 3 " 'If you follow my **d** and are careful 2978
26:15 and if you reject my **d** and abhor my laws 2978
26:43 and abhorred my **d**. 2978
26:46 These are the **d**, the laws and 2976
Dt 4: 1 the **d** and laws I am about to teach you. 2976
4: 5 I have taught you **d** and laws as 2976
4: 6 who will hear about all these **d** and say, 2976
4: 8 as to have such righteous **d** and laws 2976
4:14 the **d** and laws you are to follow in the land 2976
4:40 Keep his **d** and commands, 2976
4:45 **d** and laws Moses gave them 2976
5: 1 Hear, O Israel, the **d** and laws I declare 2976
5:31 **d** and laws you are to teach them to follow 2976
6: 1 the commands, **d** and laws 2976
6: 2 as long as you live by keeping all his **d** 2978
6:17 and the stipulations and **d** he has given you. 2976
6:20 the meaning of the stipulations, **d** and laws 2976
6:24 to obey all these **d** and to fear 2976
7:11 **d** and laws I give you today. 2976
8:11 and his **d** that I am giving you this day. 2978
10:13 to observe the LORD's commands and **d** 2978
11: 1 his **d**, his laws and his commands always. 2978
11:32 be sure that you obey all the **d** 2976
12: 1 the **d** and laws you must be careful 2976
16:12 and follow carefully these **d**. 2976
17:19 the words of this law and these **d** 2976
26:16 to follow these **d** and laws; 2976
26:17 that you will keep his **d**, 2976
27:10 and follow his commands and **d** 2976
28:15 and **d** I am giving you today, 2978
28:45 the commands and **d** he gave you. 2978
30:10 and **d** that are written in this Book of 2978
30:16 and to keep his commands, **d** and laws; 2978
Jos 24:25 at Shechem he drew up for them **d** 2976
2Sa 22:23 I have not turned away from his **d**. 2978
1Ki 2: 3 and keep his **d** and commands, 2978
6:12 if you follow my **d**, 2978
8:58 **d** and regulations he gave our fathers. 2976
8:61 to live by his **d** and obey his commands, 2976
9: 4 and do all I command and observe my **d** 2976
9: 6 the commands and **d** I have given you 2978
11:11 not kept my covenant and my **d**, 2978
2Ki 17:13 Observe my commands and **d**, 2978
17:15 They rejected his **d** and 2976
17:34 nor adhere to the **d** and ordinances, 2978
17:37 You must always be careful to keep the **d** 2976
23: 3 and keep his commands, regulations and **d** 2978
1Ch 22:13 the **d** and laws that the LORD gave Moses 2976
29:19 requirements and **d** and to do everything 2976
2Ch 7:17 and observe my **d** and laws, 2976
7:19 "But if you turn away and forsake the **d** 2978
19:10 commands, **d** or ordinances— 2976
33: 8 **d** and ordinances given through Moses." 2976
34:31 and keep his commands, regulations and **d** 2976
Ezr 6:14 the command of the God of Israel and the **d** 10302
7:10 and to teaching its **d** and laws in Israel. 2976
7:11 in matters concerning the commands and **d** 2976
Ne 1: 7 **d** and laws you gave your servant Moses. 2976
9:13 and **d** and commands that are good. 2976
9:14 **d** and laws through your servant Moses. 2976
10:29 regulations and **d** *of* the LORD our Lord. 2976
Ps 18:22 I have not turned away from his **d**. 2978
44: 4 *who* **d** victories for Jacob. 7422
89:31 if they violate my **d** and fail 2978
94:20 one that brings on misery by its **d**? 2976
99: 7 and the **d** he gave them. 2976
119: 5 my ways were steadfast in obeying your **d**! 2976
119: 8 I will obey your **d**; 2976
119:12 teach me your **d**. 2976
119:16 I delight in your **d**; 2978
119:23 your servant will meditate on your **d**. 2976
119:26 teach me your **d**. 2976
119:33 Teach me, O LORD, to follow your **d**; 2976
119:48 which I love, and I meditate on your **d**. 2976
119:54 Your **d** are the theme 2976
119:64 teach me your **d**. 2976
119:68 teach me your **d**. 2976
119:71 to be afflicted so that I might learn your **d**. 2976
119:80 May my heart be blameless toward your **d**, 2976
119:83 I do not forget your **d**. 2976
119:112 My heart is set on keeping your **d** to 2976
119:117 I will always have regard for your **d**. 2976
119:118 You reject all who stray from your **d**, 2976
Ps 119:124 to your love and teach me your **d**. 2976
119:135 upon your servant and teach me your **d**. 2976
119:145 O LORD, and I will obey your **d**. 2976
119:155 for they do not seek out your **d**. 2976
119:171 for you teach me your **d**. 2976
147:19 his laws and **d** to Israel. 2976
Pr 31: 5 lest they drink and forget what the law **d**, 2980
Isa 10: 1 to *those who* **issue** oppressive **d**, 4180+4180
Jer 31:35 who **d** the moon and stars to shine by night, 2978
31:36 "Only if these **d** vanish from my sight," 2976
44:10 and the **d** I set before you and your fathers. 2978
44:23 not obeyed him or followed his law or his **d** 2978
Eze 5: 6 and **d** more than the nations and countries 2978
5: 6 and has not followed my **d**. 2978
5: 7 around you and have not followed my **d** 2978
11:12 not followed my **d** or kept my laws 2976
11:20 Then they will follow my **d** and be careful 2978
18: 9 He follows my **d** and faithfully keeps 2978
18:17 He keeps my laws and follows my **d**. 2978
18:19 and has been careful to keep all my **d**, 2978
18:21 and keeps all my **d** and does what is just 2978
20:11 I gave them my **d** and made known 2978
20:13 not follow my **d** but rejected my laws— 2978
20:16 and did not follow my **d** 2978
20:19 follow my **d** and be careful 2978
20:21 They did not follow my **d**, 2978
20:24 not obeyed my laws but had rejected my **d** 2978
33:15 follows the **d** *that give* life, 2978
36:27 in you and move you to follow my **d** and 2976
37:24 and be careful to keep my **d**. 2978
44:24 and my **d** for all my appointed feasts, 2978
Am 2: 4 of the LORD and have not kept his **d**, 2976
Zec 1: 6 But did not my words and my **d**, 2976
Mal 3: 7 from my **d** and have not kept them. 2976
4: 4 the **d** and laws I gave him at Horeb 2976
Ac 17: 7 They are all defying Caesar's **d**, *1504*

DEDAN (10) [DEDANITES]

Ge 10: 7 The sons of Raamah: Sheba and **D**. 1847
25: 3 Jokshan was the father of Sheba and **D**; 1847
25: 3 the descendants of **D** were the Asshurites, 1847
1Ch 1: 9 The sons of Raamah: Sheba and **D**. 1847
1:32 The sons of Jokshan: Sheba and **D**. 1847
Jer 25:23 **D**, Tema, Buz and all who are 1847
49: 8 hide in deep caves, you who live in **D**, 1847
Eze 25:13 and from Teman to **D** they will fall by 1847
27:20 " '**D** traded in saddle blankets with you. 1847
38:13 Sheba and **D** and the merchants of Tarshish 1847

DEDANITES (1) [DEDAN]

Isa 21:13 You caravans of **D**, 1848

DEDICATE (7) [DEDICATED, DEDICATES, DEDICATION]

Lev 27: 2 a special vow to **d** persons to the LORD NIH
27:26 however, *may* **d** the firstborn of an animal, 7727
Nu 6:12 *He must* **d** *himself* to the LORD for 5693
Dt 20: 5 in battle and someone else *may* **d** it. 2852
2Ch 2: 4 the Name of the LORD my God and to **d** it 7727
Pr 20:25 a man to **d** something rashly and only later 7731
Eze 43:26 thus *they will* **d** it. 3338+4848

DEDICATED (30) [DEDICATE]

Lev 21:12 because he has been **d** *by* the anointing oil 5694
Nu 6: 9 thus defiling the hair he has **d**, 5694
6:18 Nazirite must shave off the hair that he **d**. 5694
18: 6 **d** to the LORD to do the work at the Tent 5989
Dt 20: 5 a new house and not **d** it? 2852
2Sa 8:11 King David **d** these articles to the LORD, 7727
8:12 He also **d** the plunder taken NIH
1Ki 7:51 **things** his father David had **d**— 7731
8:63 the king and all the Israelites **d** the temple 2852
15:15 and the articles that he and his father had **d**. 7731
2Ki 12:18 of Judah took all the sacred objects **d** 7727
12:18 **gifts** he himself had **d** 7731
23:11 the horses that the kings of Judah *had* **d** to 5989
23:11 then burned the **chariots** *d to* the sun. AIT
1Ch 18:11 King David **d** these articles to the LORD, 7727
26:20 of God and the treasuries for the **d things**. 7731
26:26 of all the treasuries for the things **d** 7727
26:27 in battle *they* **d** for the repair of the temple 7727
26:28 And everything **d** *by* Samuel the seer and 7727
26:28 and all the other **d** *things* were in the care 7727
28:12 and for the treasuries for the **d things**. 7731
2Ch 5: 1 **things** his father David had **d**— 7731
7: 5 So the king and all the people **d** the temple 2852
15:18 and the articles that he and his father had **d**. 7731
29:31 *"You have* now **d** yourselves to the LORD. 3338+4848
31: 6 the holy things **d** to the LORD their God, 7727
31:12 tithes and **d gifts**. 7731
Ne 3: 1 They **d** it and set its doors in place, 7727
3: 1 as the Tower of the Hundred, which *they* **d**, 7727
Lk 21: 5 and *with* **gifts d to God**. *356*

DEDICATES (7) [DEDICATE]

Lev 27:14 " 'If a man **d** his house as something holy 7727
27:15 If the *man who* **d** his house redeems it, 7727
27:16 " 'If a man **d** to the LORD part 7727
27:17 If *he* **d** his field during the Year of Jubilee, 7727
27:18 But if *he* **d** his field after the Jubilee, 7727
27:19 the *man who* **d** the field wishes to redeem it, 7727
27:22 a *man* **d** to the LORD a field he has bought, 7727

DEDICATION (15) [DEDICATE]

Nu 6:19 the Nazirite has shaved off the hair of his **d,** 5694
7:10 the leaders brought their offerings for its **d** 2853
7:11 to bring his offering for the **d** *of* the altar." 2853
7:84 **offerings** of the Israelite leaders **for** the **d** 2853
7:88 These were the **offerings for** the **d** *of* 2853
2Ch 7:9 for they had celebrated the **d** *of* the altar 2853
Ezr 6:16 celebrated the **d** *of* the house of God 10273
6:17 For the **d** *of* this house of God they offered 10273
Ne 12:27 At the **d** *of* the wall of Jerusalem, 2853
12:27 the **d** with songs of thanksgiving and with 2853
Ps 30:T For the **d** *of* the temple. 2853
Da 3:2 to the **d** *of* the image he had set up. 10273
3:3 for the **d** *of* the image 10273
Jn 10:22 Then came the **Feast of D** at Jerusalem. *1589*
1Ti 5:11 *their* **sensual desires overcome their d to** *2952*

DEED (12) [DEEDED, DEEDS]

Dt 17:5 the man or woman who has done this evil **d** 1821
Ecc 3:17 a time for every **d."** 5126
12:14 For God will bring every **d** into judgment, 5126
Jer 32:10 I signed and sealed the **d,** had it witnessed, 6219
32:11 I took the **d** *of* purchase— 6219
32:12 and I gave this **d** to Baruch son of Neriah, 6219
32:12 of the witnesses who had signed the **d** and 6219
32:14 both the sealed and unsealed copies of the **d** 6219
32:16 the **d** *of* purchase to Baruch son of Neriah, 6219
Lk 24:19 powerful in word and **d** before God and all *2240*
Col 3:17 whatever you do, whether in word or **d,** *2240*
2Th 2:17 and strengthen you in every good **d** *2240*

DEEDED (2) [DEED]

Ge 23:17 within the borders of the field—*was* **d** 7756
23:20 in it *were* **d** to Abraham by the Hittites as 7756

DEEDS (110) [DEED]

Dt 3:24 in heaven or on earth who can do the **d** 5126
4:34 or by great and **awesome d,** 4616
34:12 or performed the awesome **d** that Moses did 1524
1Sa 2:3 and by him **d** are weighed. 6613
2:23 the people about these wicked **d** *of* yours. 1821
24:13 'From evildoers come **evil d,'** 8400
2Sa 3:39 the evildoer according to his **evil d!"** 8288
1Ch 16:24 his **marvelous** *d* among all peoples. AIT
Ezr 9:13 a result of our evil **d** and our great guilt, 5126
Ne 6:19 they kept reporting to me his **good d** and 3208
Job 34:25 Because he takes note of their **d,** 5042
Ps 14:1 They are corrupt, their **d** are vile; 6613
17:4 As for the **d** *of* men— 7190
26:7 and telling of all your **wonderful** *d.* AIT
28:4 for their **d** and for their evil work; 7189
45:4 let your right hand display **awesome** *d.* AIT
65:5 with **awesome d** of righteousness, 3707
66:3 Say to God, "How awesome are your **d!** 5126
71:17 and to this day I declare your **marvelous** *d.* AIT
72:18 who alone does **marvelous** *d.* AIT
73:28 I will tell of all your **d.** 4856
75:1 men tell of your **wonderful** *d.* AIT
77:11 I will remember the **d** of the LORD; 5095
77:12 and consider all your **mighty d.** 6613
78:4 the next generation the **praiseworthy d** *of* 9335
78:7 in God and would not forget his **d** 5095
86:8 no **d** can compare with yours. 5126
86:10 For you are great and do **marvelous** *d;* AIT
88:12 or your **righteous d** in the land of oblivion? 7407
90:16 May your **d** be shown to your servants, 7189
92:4 you make me glad by your **d,** O LORD; 7189
96:3 his **marvelous** *d* among all peoples. AIT
101:3 The **d** *of* faithless men I hate; 6913
103:7 his **d** to the people of Israel: 6613
106:22 miracles in the land of Ham and **awesome** *d* AIT
106:29 the LORD to anger by their **wicked d,** 5095
106:39 by their **d** they prostituted themselves. 5095
107:8 for his unfailing love and his **wonderful** *d* AIT
107:15 for his unfailing love and his **wonderful** *d* AIT
107:21 for his unfailing love and his **wonderful** *d* AIT
107:24 his **wonderful** *d* in the deep. AIT
107:31 for his unfailing love and his **wonderful** *d* AIT
111:3 Glorious and majestic are his **d,** 7189
141:4 in wicked **d** with men who are evildoers; 6613
141:5 against the **d of evildoers;** 8288
145:6 and I will proclaim your **great d.** 1525
Pr 5:22 The **evil d** *of* a wicked man ensnare him; 6411
8:22 before his **d** of old; 5148
Isa 1:16 Take your evil **d** out of my sight! 5095
3:8 their words and **d** are against the LORD, 5095
3:10 for they will enjoy the fruit of their **d.** 5095
5:12 but they have no regard for the **d** *of* 7189
32:8 and by **noble** *d* he stands. AIT
41:29 Their **d** amount to nothing; 5126
59:6 Their **d** are evil deeds, 5126
59:6 Their deeds are evil **d,** 5126
63:7 *d for which* he is to be **praised,** AIT
65:7 the full payment for their former **d."** 7190
Jer 5:28 Their evil **d** have no limit; 1821
17:10 according to what his **d** deserve." 5095
21:14 I will punish you as your **d** deserve, 5095
23:22 from their evil ways and from their evil **d.** 5095
25:14 I will repay them according to their **d** and 7189
32:19 and mighty are your **d.** 6614
32:19 to his conduct and as his **d** deserve. 5095
32:44 and **d** will be signed, 6219
48:7 Since you trust in your **d** and riches, 5126
50:29 Repay her for her **d;** 7189
Eze 22:28 Her prophets whitewash these **d** for them NIH
36:31 Then you will remember your evil ways and wicked **d,** 5095
Hos 4:9 for their ways and repay them for their **d.** 5095
5:4 "Their **d** do not permit them to return 5095
7:2 not realize that I remember all their **evil d.** 8288
9:15 Because of their sinful **d,** 5095
12:2 and repay him according to his **d.** 5095
Ob 1:15 your **d** will return upon your own head. 1691
Mic 7:13 as the result of their **d.** 5095
Hab 3:2 I stand in awe of your **d,** O LORD. 7189
Mt 5:16 that they may see your good **d** *2240*
Lk 1:51 He has performed **mighty d** with his arm; *3197*
23:41 for we are getting what our **d** deserve. *4556*
Jn 3:19 of light because their **d** were evil. *2240*
3:20 the light for fear that his **d** will be exposed. *2240*
Ac 19:18 and openly confessed their evil **d.** *4552*
26:20 and prove their repentance by their **d.** *2240*
Ro 13:12 So let us put aside the **d** of darkness and put *2240*
Eph 5:11 Have nothing to do with the fruitless **d** *2240*
1Ti 2:10 but with good **d,** *2240*
5:10 and is well known for her good **d,** *2240*
5:10 and devoting herself *to* all kinds of good **d.** *2240*
5:25 In the same way, good **d** are obvious, *2240*
6:18 to be rich in good **d,** *2240*
Heb 10:24 on toward love and good **d.** *2240*
Jas 2:14 if a man claims to have faith but has no **d?** *2240*
2:18 "You have faith; I have **d."** *2240*
2:18 Show me your faith without **d,** *2240*
2:20 that faith without **d** is useless? *2240*
2:26 so faith without **d** is dead. *2240*
3:13 by **d** done in the humility that comes *2240*
1Pe 2:12 they may see your good **d** and glorify God *2240*
2Pe 2:8 *by* the lawless **d** he saw and heard)— *2240*
Rev 2:2 I know your **d,** your hard work and *2240*
2:19 I know your **d,** your love and faith, *2240*
2:23 repay each of you according to your **d.** *2240*
3:1 I know your **d;** you have a reputation *2240*
3:2 for I have not found your **d** complete in *2240*
3:8 I know your **d.** *2240*
3:15 I know your **d,** that you are neither cold *2240*
14:13 for their **d** will follow them." *2240*
15:3 "Great and marvelous are your **d,** *2240*

DEEP (107) [ANKLE-DEEP, DEEPER, DEEPEST, DEEPLY, DEEPS, DEPTH, DEPTHS]

Ge 1:2 darkness was over the surface of the **d,** 9333
2:21 the man to fall into a **d sleep;** 9554
7:11 the springs of the great **d** burst forth, 9333
8:2 Now the springs of the **d** and the floodgates 9333
15:12 Abram fell into a **d sleep,** 9554
49:25 blessings of the **d** that lies below, 9333
Ex 15:5 The **d waters** have covered them; 9333
15:8 **d waters** congealed in the heart of the sea. 9333
Lev 13:3 the sore appears to be more than skin **d,** 6678
13:4 to be more than skin **d** and the hair in it has 6678
13:20 and if it appears to be more than skin **d** and 9166
13:21 not more than skin **d** and has faded, 9166
13:25 and it appears to be more than skin **d,** 6678
13:26 in the spot and if it is not more than skin **d** 9166
13:30 and if it appears to be more than skin **d** and 6678
13:31 it does not seem to be more than skin **d** 6678
13:32 not appear to be more than skin **d,** 6678
13:34 and appears to be no more than skin **d,** 6678
Dt 4:11 with black clouds and **d darkness.** 6906
5:22 the cloud and the **d darkness;** 6906
33:13 above and with the **d waters** that lie below; 9333
1Sa 26:12 the LORD had put them into a **d sleep.** 9554
2Sa 22:17 he drew me out of **d** waters. 8041
24:14 David said to Gad, "I am in **d** distress. 4394
1Ki 7:31 that had a circular frame one cubit **d.** 2025+5087
7:35 a circular band half a cubit **d.** 7757
18:27 Perhaps *he is* **d in thought,** or busy, 8488
1Ch 21:13 David said to Gad, "I am in **d** distress. 4394
Job 3:5 and **d shadow** claim it once more; 7516
4:13 when **d sleep** falls on men, 9554
7:12 Am I the sea, or the **monster of the d,** 9490
10:21 to the land of gloom and **d shadow,** 7516
10:22 of **d shadow** and disorder, 7516
12:22 He reveals the **d** *things* of darkness 6678
12:22 of darkness and brings **d shadows** into 7516
16:16 **d shadows** ring my eyes; 7516
24:17 For all of them, **d darkness** is their morning 7516
26:5 "The dead *are* **in d anguish,** 2655
28:14 The **d** says, 'It is not in me'; 9333
33:15 when **d sleep** falls on men as they slumber 9554
34:22 There is no dark place, no **d shadow,** 7516
38:16 the sea or walked in the recesses of the **d?** 9333
38:30 when the surface of the **d** is frozen? 9333
41:32 one would think the **d** had white hair. 9333
Ps 18:16 he drew me out of **d** waters. 8041
33:7 he puts the **d** into storehouses. 9333
36:6 your justice like the great **d.** 9333
42:7 **D** calls to deep in the roar 9333
42:7 to **d** in the roar of your waterfalls; 9333
44:19 and covered us over with **d darkness.** 7516
69:2 I have come into the **d** waters; 5099
69:14 from those who hate me, from the **d** waters. 5099
104:6 You covered it with the **d** as with 9333
107:24 his wonderful deeds in the **d.** 5185
Pr 4:19 the way of the wicked is like **d darkness;** 696
7:18 Come, *let's* **drink d** of love till morning; 8115
8:27 the horizon on the face of the **d,** 9333
8:28 and fixed securely the fountains of the **d,** 9333
Pr 18:4 The words of a man's mouth are **d** waters, 6678
19:15 Laziness brings on **d sleep,** 9554
20:5 The purposes of a man's heart are **d** waters, 6678
22:14 The mouth of an adulteress is a **d** pit; 6678
23:27 a prostitute is a **d** pit and a wayward wife is 6678
25:3 As the heavens are high and the earth is **d,** 6679
Isa 29:10 over you a **d sleep:** 8120+9554
30:33 Its fire pit *has been* **made d** and wide, 6676
44:27 who says to the **watery d,** 7425
51:10 the waters of the great **d,** 9333
54:7 with **d** compassion I will bring you back. 1524
59:9 for brightness, but we walk in **d shadows.** 696
Jer 13:16 to thick darkness and change it to **d gloom.** 6906
49:8 Turn and flee, hide in **d** caves, 6676
49:30 Stay in **d** caves, you who live in Hazor," 6676
La 2:13 Your wound is as **d** as the sea. 1524
Eze 23:32 a cup large and **d;** 6678
31:4 **d springs** made it grow tall; 9333
31:15 down to the grave I covered the **d springs** 9333
40:6 it was one rod **d.** 8145
40:7 the portico facing the temple was one rod **d.** NIH
40:9 it was eight cubits **d** NIH
40:30 and five cubits **d.)** 8145
43:13 Its gutter is a cubit **d** and a cubit wide, NIH
47:5 **d enough to swim in—** 8467
Da 2:22 He reveals **d** and hidden things; 10555
8:18 *I was* **in a d sleep,** 8101
10:9 *I* **fell into a d sleep,** 8101
Hos 5:2 The rebels *are* **d** *in* slaughter. 6676
9:9 *They have* **sunk d** *into* corruption, 6676
Am 7:4 up the great **d** and devoured the land. 9333
Jnh 1:5 he lay down and **fell into a d sleep.** 8101
2:3 You hurled me into the **d,** 5185
2:5 *the* **d** surrounded me; 9333
Hab 3:10 the **d** roared and lifted its waves on high. 9333
Mk 7:34 up to heaven and **with a d sigh** said to him, *5100*
Lk 5:4 he said to Simon, "Put out into **d** water, *958*
6:48 who dug **down d** and laid the foundation *959*
Jn 4:11 to draw with and the well is **d.** *960*
Ac 20:9 *into* a **d** sleep as Paul talked on and on. *960*
27:28 **a hundred and twenty feet d.** *1633+3976*
27:28 and found it was **ninety feet d.** *1278+3976*
Ro 10:7 "or 'Who will descend into the **d?'** " *12*
1Co 2:10 even the **d** *things* of God. *958*
2Co 7:7 your **d sorrow,** your ardent concern for me, *3851*
Eph 3:18 how wide and long and high and **d** is *958*
1Th 1:5 with the Holy Spirit and with **d** conviction. *4498*
1Ti 3:9 They must keep hold of the **d truths** of *3696*
Rev 2:24 learned Satan's so-called **d** secrets *960*

DEEPER (2) [DEEP]

Lev 14:37 that appear to be **d** than the surface of 9166
Job 11:8 They are **d** than the depths of the grave— 6678

DEEPEST (4) [DEEP]

Job 10:22 to the land of **d night,** 694+4017+6547
Ps 107:10 Some sat in darkness and the **d gloom,** 7516
107:14 the **d gloom** and broke away their chains. 7516
Isa 7:11 in the **d** depths or in the highest heights." 6676

DEEPLY (12) [DEEP]

Ge 43:30 **D moved** at the sight of his brother, 4023+8171
1Sa 1:15 "I am a woman who is **d troubled.** 7997+8120
Isa 66:11 *you will* **drink d** and delight 5209
Da 7:28 I, Daniel, was **d** troubled by my thoughts, 10678
Mk 3:5 **d distressed** at their stubborn hearts, *5200*
8:12 *He* **sighed d** and said, "Why *417+3836+4460*
14:33 he began *to be* **d distressed** and troubled. *1701*
Jn 11:33 *he was* **d moved** in spirit and troubled. *1839*
11:38 Jesus, once more **d moved,** *1839*
Ac 8:2 Godly men buried Stephen and **mourned d** *3157+3489+4472*
1Pe 1:22 love one another **d,** from the heart. *1757*
4:8 Above all, love each other **d,** *1756*

DEEPS (1) [DEEP]

Pr 3:20 by his knowledge the **d** were divided, 9333

DEER (14)

Dt 12:15 as if it were gazelle or **d,** 385
12:22 Eat them as you would gazelle or **d.** 385
14:5 the **d,** the gazelle, the roe deer, 385
14:5 the gazelle, the **roe d,** the wild goat, 3502
15:22 as if it were gazelle or **d.** 385
2Sa 22:34 He makes my feet like the feet of a **d;** 387
1Ki 4:23 as well as **d,** gazelles, 385
Ps 18:33 He makes my feet like the feet of a **d;** 387
42:1 As the **d** pants for streams of water, 385
Pr 5:19 A loving doe, a graceful **d—** 3607
7:22 like a **d** stepping into a noose 385
Isa 35:6 Then will the lame leap like a **d,** 385
La 1:6 Her princes are like **d** that find no pasture; 385
Hab 3:19 he makes my feet like the feet of a **d,** 387

DEFAMED (1)

Isa 48:11 How *can* I *let* myself **be d?** 2725

DEFEAT (9) [DEFEATED, DEFEATING]

Ex 32:18 it is not the sound of **d;** 2711
Nu 22:6 be able *to* **d** them and drive them out of 5782
Jdg 2:15 of the LORD was against them to **d** them, 8288
1Sa 4:3 "Why *did* the LORD **bring d upon** us today 5597

2Ki 13:19 But now *you will* **d** it only three times." 5782
Ps 92:11 My eyes have seen the **d** of my adversaries; NIH
Isa 9:4 For as in the day of Midian's **d**, NIH
Jer 37:10 *to* **d** the entire Babylonian army 5782
Heb 7:1 He met Abraham returning from the **d** of *3158*

DEFEATED (53) [DEFEAT]

Ge 14:5 and **d** the Rephaites in Ashteroth Karnaim, 5782
36:35 who **d** Midian in the country of Moab, 5782
Lev 26:17 so that *you will* **be d** by your enemies; 5597
Nu 14:42 *You will* **be d** by your enemies, 5597
Dt 1:4 after he *had* **d** Sihon king of the Amorites, 5782
1:4 and at Edrei had **d** Og king of Bashan, NIH
1:42 *You will* **be d** by your enemies.' " 5597
4:46 and *was* **d** *by* Moses and the Israelites 5782
7:2 over to you and *you have* **d** them, 5782
28:7 up against you *will* **be d** before you. 5597
28:25 The LORD will cause you *to* **be d** 5597
29:7 but *we* **d** them. 5782
Jos 10:10 *who* **d** them in a great victory at Gibeon. 5782
10:33 but Joshua **d** him and his army— 5782
11:8 *They* **d** them and pursued them all the way 5782
12:1 of the land whom the Israelites *had* **d** 5782
13:12 Moses *had* **d** them and taken over their land. 5782
13:21 Moses *had* **d** him and the Midianite chiefs, 5782
Jdg 1:10 and **d** Sheshai, Ahiman 5782
11:21 and *they* **d** them. 5782
20:35 The LORD **d** Benjamin before Israel, 5597
1Sa 4:2 Israel **was d** by the Philistines, 5597
4:10 and the Israelites **were d** and every man fled 5597
14:48 He fought valiantly and **d** the Amalekites, 5782
2Sa 2:17 the men of Israel **were d** by David's men. 5597
5:20 and there he **d** them. 5782
8:1 David **d** the Philistines and subdued them, 5782
8:2 David also **d** the Moabites. 5782
8:9 of Hamath heard that David *had* **d** 5782
10:19 of Hadadezer saw that *they had* **been d** 5597
18:7 the army of Israel **was d** by David's men, 5597
1Ki 8:33 "When your people Israel *have* **been d** by 5597
2Ki 13:19 then *you would have* **d** Aram 5782
13:25 Three times Jehoash **d** him, 5782
14:7 the *one who* **d** ten thousand Edomites in 5782
14:10 *You have* **indeed d** Edom and 5782+5782
18:8 he **d** the Philistines, 5782
1Ch 1:46 who **d** Midian in the country of Moab, 5782
5:10 *who were* **d** at their hands; 5877
14:11 and there *he* **d** them. 5782
18:1 David **d** the Philistines and subdued them, 5782
18:2 David also **d** the Moabites, 5782
18:9 of Hamath heard that David *had* **d** 5782
19:19 of Hadadezer saw that *they had* **been d** 5597
2Ch 6:24 "When your people Israel *have* **been d** by 5597
20:22 and *they* **were d.** 5597
25:19 You say to yourself that *you have* **d** Edom, 5782
28:5 The Arameans **d** him and took many 5782
28:23 who *had* **d** him; 5782
Jer 46:2 of Egypt, which was **d** at Carchemish on 5782
46:5 they are retreating, their warriors **are d.** 4198
Da 11:11 army, but it *will* **be d.** 928+3338+5989
1Co 6:7 lawsuits among you means you have been completely **d** already. *2488*

DEFEATING (5) [DEFEAT]

Ge 14:17 After Abram returned from **d** Kedorlaomer 5782
Jdg 20:32 "We *are* **d** them as before," 5597
20:39 "We *are* **d** them as in the first battle." 5597+5597
2Sa 1:1 David returned from **d** the Amalekites 5782
Da 7:21 against the saints and **d** them, 10321

DEFECT (58) [DEFECTED, DEFECTS]

Ex 12:5 be year-old males **without d**, 9459
29:1 Take a young bull and two rams **without d.** 9459
Lev 1:3 he is to offer a male **without d.** 9459
1:10 he is to offer a male **without d.** 9459
3:1 before the LORD an animal **without d.** 9459
3:6 he is to offer a male or female **without d.** 9459
4:3 a young bull **without d** as a sin offering for 9459
4:23 as his offering a male goat **without d.** 9459
4:28 a female goat **without d.** 9459
4:32 he is to bring a female **without d.** 9459
5:15 one **without d** and of the proper value 9459
5:18 one **without d** and of the proper value. 9459
6:6 one **without d** and of the proper value, 9459
9:2 *both* **without d,** and present them before 9459
9:3 both a year old and **without d—** 9459
14:10 each **without d,** along with three-tenths of 9459
21:17 of your descendants who has a **d** may come 4583
21:18 No man who has any **d** may come near: 4583
21:20 or who has any eye **d,** 9319
21:21 the priest who has any **d** is to come near 4583
21:21 He has a **d;** 4583
21:23 yet because of his **d,** 4583
22:19 you must present a male **without d** from 9459
22:20 Do not bring anything with a **d,** 4583
22:21 be **without d** or blemish to be acceptable. 9459
23:12 to the LORD a lamb a year old **without d,** 9459
23:18 each a year old and **without d,** 9459
Nu 6:14 a year-old male lamb **without d** for 9459
6:14 a year-old ewe lamb **without d** for 9459
6:14 a ram **without d** for a fellowship offering, 9459
19:2 a red heifer **without d** or blemish and 9459
28:3 two lambs a year old **without d,** 9459
28:9 of two lambs a year old **without d,** 9459
28:11 a year old, *all* **without d.** 9459
28:19 a year old, *all* **without d.** 9459
28:31 Be sure the animals are **without d.** 9459
29:2 male lambs a year old, *all* **without d.** 9459
29:8 male lambs a year old, *all* **without d.** 9459
29:13 male lambs a year old, *all* **without d.** 9459
29:17 male lambs a year old, *all* **without d.** 9459
29:20 male lambs a year old, *all* **without d.** 9459
29:23 male lambs a year old, *all* **without d.** 9459
29:26 male lambs a year old, *all* **without d.** 9459
29:29 male lambs a year old, *all* **without d.** 9459
29:32 male lambs a year old, *all* **without d.** 9459
29:36 male lambs a year old, *all* **without d.** 9459
Dt 15:21 If an animal has a **d,** is lame or blind, 4583
17:1 an ox or a sheep that has any **d** or flaw in it, 4583
Eze 43:22 a male goat **without d** for a sin offering, 9459
43:23 and a ram from the flock, both **without d.** 9459
43:25 and a ram from the flock, *both* **without d.** 9459
45:18 to take a young bull **without d** and purify 9459
45:23 and seven rams **without d** as 9459
46:4 and a ram, *all* **without d.** 9459
46:6 six lambs and a ram, *all* **without d.** 9459
46:13 to provide a year-old lamb **without d** for 9459
Da 1:4 young men without any **physical d,** 4583
1Pe 1:19 a lamb **without** blemish or **d.** *834*

DEFECTED (3) [DEFECT]

1Ch 12:8 Some Gadites **d** to David at his stronghold 976
12:19 of Manasseh **d** to David when he went with 5877
12:20 these were *the men* of Manasseh *who* **d** 5877

DEFECTS (1) [DEFECT]

Lev 22:25 because they are deformed and have **d.' "** 4583

DEFEND (23) [DEFENDED, DEFENDER, DEFENDERS, DEFENDING, DEFENDS, DEFENSE, DEFENSES]

Jdg 6:31 *he can* **d** himself when someone breaks 8189
2Ki 19:34 *I will* **d** this city and save it, 1713
20:6 *I will* **d** this city for my sake and for 1713
Job 13:15 *I will* surely **d** my ways to his face. 3519
Ps 72:4 *He will* **d** the afflicted among the people 9149
74:22 Rise up, O God, and **d** your cause; 8189
82:2 "How long *will you* **d** the unjust 9149
82:3 **D** *the* **cause** *of* the weak and fatherless; 9149
119:154 **D** my cause and redeem me; 8189
Pr 31:9 **d** the **rights** *of* the poor and needy." 1906
Ecc 4:12 two *can* **d** *themselves.* 5584+6641
Isa 1:17 **D the cause** *of* the fatherless, 9149
1:23 *They do* not **d the cause** *of* the fatherless, 9149
37:35 "*I will* **d** this city and save it, 1713
38:6 *I will* **d** this city. 1713
Jer 5:28 *they do* not **d** the rights of the poor. 9149
50:34 *He will* **vigorously d** their cause so 8189+8189
51:36 "See, I *will* **d** your cause and avenge you; 8189
Da 3:16 *we* do not need to **d** ourselves *before* you 10601+10754
Zec 9:8 But *I will* **d** my house 2837
Lk 12:11 about how *you will* **d yourselves** *664*
21:14 how *you will* **d yourselves.** *664*
Ac 25:16 and has had an opportunity to **d** himself *665*

DEFENDED (3) [DEFEND]

2Sa 23:12 *He* **d** it and struck the Philistines down, 5911
1Ch 11:14 *They* **d** it and struck the Philistines down, 5911
Jer 22:16 *He* **d** the cause of the poor and needy, 1906

DEFENDER (6) [DEFEND]

Ex 22:2 **the d** is not guilty of bloodshed; 2257[S]
Job 5:4 crushed in court without a **d.** 5911
Ps 68:5 A father to the fatherless, a **d** *of* widows, 1908
Pr 23:11 for their **D** is strong; 1457
Isa 19:20 he will send them a savior and **d,** 8189
29:21 who ensnare the **d** in court and 3519

DEFENDERS (1) [DEFEND]

2Sa 11:16 where he knew the **strongest d** were. 408+2657

DEFENDING (5) [DEFEND]

2Ki 9:14 and all Israel had been **d** Ramoth Gilead 9068
Ps 10:18 **d** the fatherless and the oppressed, 9149
Ro 2:15 now even **d** them.) *664*
2Co 12:19 that *we have been* **d ourselves** to you? *664*
Php 1:7 in chains or **d** and confirming the gospel, *665*

DEFENDS (3) [DEFEND]

Dt 10:18 *He* **d** the cause of the fatherless and 6913
33:7 With his own hands *he* **d** his **cause.** 8189
Isa 51:22 your God, *who* **d** his people: 8189

DEFENSE (17) [DEFEND]

2Ch 11:5 in Jerusalem and built up towns for **d** 5190
Job 31:35 I sign now my **d—** NIH
Ps 35:23 Awake, and rise to my **d!** 5477
Jer 41:9 of his **d against** Baasha king of Israel. 4946+7156
Na 3:8 The river was her **d,** the waters her wall. 2658
Ac 7:24 so he **went to** *his* **d** and avenged him *310*
19:33 *in order to* **make a d** before the people. *664+2527*
22:1 "Brothers and fathers, listen now to my **d."** *665*
24:10 so *I* gladly **make** *my* **d.** *664*
25:8 Then Paul **made** *his* **d:** *664*
26:1 with his hand and *began his* **d:** *664*
Ac 26:2 as *I* **make** *my* **d** against all the accusations *664*
26:24 At this point Festus interrupted Paul's **d.** *664*
1Co 9:3 This is my **d** to those who sit in judgment *665*
Php 1:16 that I am put here for the **d** of the gospel. *665*
2Ti 4:16 At my first **d,** no one came to my support, *665*
1Jn 2:1 **one who speaks** to the Father **in** *our* **d—** *4156*

DEFENSES (8) [DEFEND]

2Ch 11:11 He strengthened their **d** 5193
26:15 for use on the towers and on the **corner d** 7157
Job 13:12 your **d** are defenses of clay. 1462
13:12 your defenses are **d** *of* clay. 1462
Isa 22:8 the **d** *of* Judah are stripped away. 5009
22:9 of David had many **breaches in** its **d;** 1323
Joel 2:8 through **d** without breaking ranks. 8939
Na 3:14 for the siege, strengthen your **d!** 4448

DEFERENCE (1) [DEFERRED]

2Ki 16:18 **in d to** the king of Assyria. 4946+7156

DEFERRED (1) [DEFERENCE]

Pr 13:12 Hope **d** makes the heart sick, 5432

DEFIANCE (1) [DEFY]

1Sa 17:23 from his lines and shouted his usual **d,** 1821

DEFIANT (1) [DEFY]

Pr 7:11 (She is loud and **d,** 6253

DEFIANTLY (2) [DEFY]

Nu 15:30 " 'But anyone who **sins d,** 928+3338+6913+8123
Job 15:26 **d** charging against him with a thick, 928+7418

DEFIED (9) [DEFY]

1Sa 17:36 *he has* **d** the armies of the living God. 3070
17:45 whom *you have* **d.** 3070
1Ki 13:21 '*You have* **d** the word of the LORD 5286
13:26 "It is the man of God who **d** the word of 5286
Isa 65:7 on the mountains and **d** me on the hills, 3070
Jer 48:26 "Make her drunk, for *she has* **d** the LORD. 1540+6584
48:42 be destroyed as a nation because *she* **d** 1540+6584
50:29 For *she has* **d** the LORD, 2326
Da 3:28 **d** the king's command and were willing 10731

DEFIES (1) [DEFY]

Pr 18:1 *he* **d** all sound judgment. 1679

DEFILE (32) [DEFILED, DEFILEMENT, DEFILES, DEFILING]

Ex 20:25 for *you will* **d** it if you use a tool on it. 2725
Lev 11:43 not **d** yourselves by any of these creatures. 9210
18:20 with your neighbor's wife and **d** *yourself* 3237
18:23 with an animal and **d** *yourself* with it. 3237
18:24 not **d yourselves** in any of these ways, 3237
18:28 And if you **d** the land, 3237
18:30 before you came and *do* not **d yourselves** 3237
20:25 *Do* not **d** yourselves by any animal or bird 9210
21:4 and so **d** himself. 2725
21:15 not **d** his offspring among his people. 2725
Nu 5:3 the camp so *they will* not **d** their camp, 3237
18:32 then *you will* not **d** the holy offerings of 2725
35:34 *Do* not **d** the land where you live and 3237
2Ki 23:16 from them and burned on the altar *to* **d** it, 3237
Isa 30:22 Then *you will* **d** your idols overlaid 3237
Eze 7:21 and *they will* **d** it. 2725
9:7 "**D** the temple and fill the courts with 3237
14:11 nor *will they* **d themselves** anymore 3237
18:6 *He does* not **d** his neighbor's wife or lie 3237
18:15 *He does* not **d** his neighbor's wife. 3237
20:7 *do* not **d yourselves** with the idols of Egypt. 3237
20:18 or keep their laws or **d yourselves** 3237
20:30 *Will* you **d yourselves** 3237
20:31 *to* **d yourselves** with all your idols 3237
37:23 *They will* no longer **d themselves** 3237
43:7 of Israel *will* never again **d** my holy name— 3237
44:25 not **d** *himself* by going near a dead person; 3237
44:25 then *he may* **d himself.** 3237
Da 1:8 *to* **d himself** with the royal food and wine, 1458
1:8 for permission not *to* **d himself** this way. 1458
Heb 12:15 up to cause trouble and **d** many. *3620*
Rev 14:4 These are those who *did* not **d** *themselves* *3662*

DEFILED (70) [DEFILE]

Ge 34:5 that his daughter Dinah *had been* **d,** 3237
34:13 Because their sister Dinah *had been* **d,** 3237
34:27 the city where their sister *had been* **d.** 3237
49:4 onto my couch and **d** it. 2725
Lev 18:24 to drive out before you **became d.** 3237
18:25 Even the land *was* **d;** 3237
18:27 and the land *became* **d.** 3237
19:31 for you *will be* **d** by them. 3237
20:3 to Molech, *he has* **d** my sanctuary 3237
21:7 not marry women **d** *by* prostitution 2729
21:14 or a *woman* **d** *by* prostitution, 2729
22:4 also be unclean if he touches something **d** 3238
Nu 5:20 and *you have* **d yourself** by sleeping with 3237
5:27 If *she has* **d herself** and been unfaithful 3237
5:28 not **d herself** and is free from impurity, 3237
6:12 because *he became* **d** during his separation. 3237

Nu 19:20 he has d the sanctuary of the LORD. 3237
Dt 22: 9 but also the fruit of the vineyard will be d. 7727
24: 4 to marry her again after she has been d. 3237
Jos 22:19 If the land you possess is d, 3238
2Sa 1:21 For there the shield of the mighty was d, 1718
2Ki 23:19 and d all the shrines at the high places that 6913S
1Ch 5: 1 but when he d his father's marriage bed, 2725
Ne 13:29 because they d the priestly office and 1459
Job 31: 7 or if my hands have been d, 1815+4583
Ps 74: 7 they d the dwelling place of your Name. 2725
79: 1 they have d your holy temple, 3237
89:39 with your servant and have d his crown in 2725
106:39 They d themselves by what they did; 3237
Isa 24: 5 The earth is d by its people; 2866
52: 1 and d will not enter you again. 3238
Jer 2: 7 But you came and d my land 3237
2:23 "How can you say, 'I am not d; 3237
3: 1 Would not the land be completely d? 2866+2866
3: 2 You have d the land with your prostitution 2866
3: 9 she d the land and committed adultery 2866
7:30 the house that bears my Name and have d it. 3237
16:18 because they have d my land with 2725
19:13 the kings of Judah will be d like this place, 3238
32:34 in the house that bears my Name and d it. 3237
La 4:14 They are so d with blood that no one dares 1458
Eze 4:13 of Israel will eat d food among the nations 3238
4:14 I have never d myself. 3237
5:11 because you have d my sanctuary 3237
20:26 I let them become d through their gifts— 3237
20:43 by which you have d yourselves, 3237
22: 4 the blood you have shed and have become d 3237
22:16 you have been d in the eyes of the nations, 2725
23: 7 the elite of the Assyrians and d herself 3237
23:13 I saw that she too d herself; 3237
23:17 and in their lust they d her. 3237
23:17 After she had been d by them, 3237
23:30 the nations and d yourself with their idols. 3237
23:38 At that same time they d my sanctuary 3237
36:17 they d it by their conduct and their actions. 3237
36:18 and because they had d it with their idols. 3237
43: 8 they d my holy name 3237
Hos 6:10 to prostitution and Israel is d. 3237
Mic 2:10 because it is d, it is ruined, 3237
4:11 They say, "Let her be d, 2866
Zep 3: 1 to the city of oppressors, rebellious and d! 1458
Hag 2:13 "If a person d by contact with a dead body 3238
2:13 does it become d?" 3237
2:13 "Yes," the priests replied, "it becomes d." 3237
2:14 and whatever they offer there is d. 3238
Mal 1: 7 "You place d food on my altar. 1458
1: 7 "But you ask, 'How have we d you?' 1458
1:12 'It is d,' and of its food, 1458
Ac 21:28 into the temple area and d this holy place." 3124
1Co 8: 7 and since their conscience is weak, it is d. 3662

DEFILEMENT (1) [DEFILE]
2Ch 29: 5 Remove all d from the sanctuary. 5614

DEFILES (7) [DEFILE]
Lev 21: 9 a priest's daughter d herself by becoming 2725
Nu 5:29 and d herself while married to her husband, 3237
19:13 and fails to purify himself d the LORD's 3237
Eze 18:11 He d his neighbor's wife. 3237
22: 3 in her midst and d herself by making idols, 3237
22:11 another shamefully d his daughter-in-law, 3237
33:26 and each of you d his neighbor's wife. 3237

DEFILING (3) [DEFILE]
Lev 15:31 for d my dwelling place, 3237
Nu 6: 9 thus d the hair he has dedicated, 3237
2Ch 36:14 and d the temple of the LORD, 3237

DEFINITE (2) [DEFINITELY]
1Sa 23:23 and come back to me with d information. 3922
Ac 25:26 But I have nothing d to write 855

DEFINITELY (2) [DEFINITE]
1Sa 23:10 servant has heard d that Saul plans 9048+9048
26: 4 and learned that Saul had d arrived. 448+3922

DEFORMED (3) [FORM]
Lev 21:18 or lame, disfigured or d; 8594
22:23 an ox or a sheep that is d or stunted, 8594
22:25 because they are d and have defects.' " 5426

DEFRAUD (5) [FRAUD]
Lev 19:13 " 'Do not d your neighbor or rob him. 6943
Hos 12: 7 he loves to d. 6943
Mic 2: 2 They d a man of his home, 6943
Mal 3: 5 against those who d laborers of their wages, 6943
Mk 10:19 do not d, honor your father and mother.' " 691

DEFY (3) [DEFIANCE, DEFIANT, DEFIANTLY, DEFIED, DEFIES, DEFYING]
1Sa 17:10 "This day I d the ranks of Israel! 3070
17:25 He comes out to d Israel. 3070
17:26 that he should d the armies of 3070

DEFYING (2) [DEFY]
Isa 3: 8 d his glorious presence. 5286
Ac 17: 7 They are all d Caesar's decrees, 595+4556

DEGENERATE (KJV) See CORRUPT

DEGRADE (1) [DEGRADED, DEGRADING]
Lev 19:29 " 'Do not d your daughter by making her 2725

DEGRADED (2) [DEGRADE]
Dt 25: 3 your brother will be d in your eyes. 7829
Eze 16:25 and d your beauty, 9493

DEGRADING (1) [DEGRADE]
Ro 1:24 to sexual impurity for the d of their bodies 869

DEGREE (KJV) See CIRCUMSTANCES, EXALTED, HIGHBORN, HUMBLE, LOWBORN, RANK, STANDING

DEHAVITES (KJV) See OF (Ezr 4:9)

DEITY (1)
Col 2: 9 For in Christ all the fullness of the D lives 2540

DEJECTED (2)
Ge 40: 6 he saw that they were d. 2407
Isa 19:10 The workers in cloth will be d, 1917

DEKAR (KJV) See BEN-DEKER

DELAIAH (7)
1Ch 3:24 Pelaiah, Akkub, Johanan, D and Anani— 1933
24:18 the twenty-third to D and the twenty-fourth 1934
Ezr 2:60 The descendants of D, 1933
Ne 6:10 to the house of Shemaiah son of D, 1933
7:62 the descendants of D, 1933
Jer 36:12 Elishama the secretary, D son of Shemaiah, 1934
36:25 D and Gemariah urged the king not to burn 1934

DELAY (15) [DELAYED]
Ge 45: 9 Come down to me; don't d. 6641
2Ki 9: 3 Then open the door and run; don't d!" 2675
Ps 40:17 O my God, do not d. 336
70: 5 O LORD, do not d. 336
119:60 and not d to obey your commands. 4538
Ecc 5: 4 do not d in fulfilling it. 336
Isa 48: 9 For my own name's sake I d my wrath; 799
Jer 4: 6 Flee for safety without d! 6641
Eze 12:25 and it shall be fulfilled without d. 5432
Da 9:19 For your sake, O my God, do not d, 336
Hab 2: 3 it will certainly come and will not d. 336
Mk 1:20 Without d he called them, 2317
Ac 25:17 I did not d the case, 332+4472
Heb 10:37 and will not d. 5988
Rev 10: 6 and said, "There will be no more d! 5989

DELAYED (6) [DELAY]
Ge 43:10 As it is, if we had not d, 4538
Jos 10:13 and d going down about a full day. 237+4202
Jdg 5:28 Why is the clatter of his chariots d?' 336
Isa 46:13 and my salvation will not be d. 336
Eze 12:28 None of my words will be d any longer; 5432
1Ti 3:15 if I am d, you will know how people ought 1094

DELEGATION (5)
Jos 9: 4 as a d whose donkeys were loaded 7493
2Sa 10: 2 So David sent a d to express his 928+3338+6269
1Ch 19: 2 So David sent a d to express his sympathy 4855
Lk 14:32 a d while the other is still a long way off 4561
19:14 "But his subjects hated him and sent a d 4561

DELIBERATELY (3)
Ex 21:14 a man schemes and kills another man d, 928+6893
Heb 10:26 If we d keep on sinning 1731
2Pe 3: 5 But they d forget that long ago 2527

DELICACIES (6) [DELICATE]
Ge 49:20 he will provide d fit for a king. 5052
Ps 141: 4 let me not eat of their d. 4982
Pr 23: 3 Do not crave his d, 4761
23: 6 do not crave his d; 4761
Jer 51:34 and filled his stomach with our d, 6358
La 4: 5 Those who once ate d are destitute in 5052

DELICACY (1) [DELICATE]
SS 7:13 and at our door is every d, 4458

DELICATE (2) [DELICACIES, DELICACY]
Isa 47: 1 No more will you be called tender or d. 6697
Jer 6: 2 so beautiful and d. 6695

DELICIOUS (1)
Pr 9:17 food eaten in secret is d!" 5838

DELIGHT (69) [DELIGHTED, DELIGHTFUL, DELIGHTING, DELIGHTS]
Lev 26:31 and I will take no d in the pleasing aroma 8193
Dt 30: 9 The LORD will again d in you 8464
1Sa 2: 1 for I d in your deliverance. 8523
15:22 "Does the LORD d in burnt offerings 2914
Ne 1:11 and to the prayer of your servants who d 2913
Job 22:26 then you will find d in the Almighty 6695
27:10 Will he find d in the Almighty? 6695
Ps 1: 2 But his d is in the law of the LORD, 2914
16: 3 the glorious ones in whom is all my d. 2914
35: 9 in the LORD and d in his salvation. 8464
35:27 May those who d in my vindication shout 2913
37: 4 D yourself in the LORD 6695
43: 4 to God, my joy and my d. 1637
51:16 You do not d in sacrifice, 2911
51:19 whole burnt offerings to d you; 2911
62: 4 they take d in lies. 8354
68:30 Scatter the nations who d in war. 2911
111: 2 they are pondered by all who d in them. 2913
112: 1 who finds great d in his commands. 2911
119:16 I d in your decrees; 9130
119:24 Your statutes are my d; 9141
119:35 for there I find d. 2911
119:47 for I d in your commands 9130
119:70 but I d in your law. 9130
119:77 for your law is my d. 9141
119:92 If your law had not been my d, 9141
119:143 but your commands are my d. 9141
119:174 O LORD, and your law is my d. 9141
147:10 nor his d in the legs of a man; 8354
149: 4 For the LORD takes d in his people; 8354
Pr 1:22 How long will mockers d in mockery 2773
2:14 who d in doing wrong and rejoice in 8524
8:30 I was filled with d day after day, 9141
11: 1 but accurate weights are his d. 8356
29:17 he will bring d to your soul. 5052
Ecc 2:10 My heart took d in all my work, 8524
SS 1: 4 We rejoice and d in you; 8523
2: 3 I d to sit in his shade, 2773
Isa 5: 7 the men of Judah are the garden of his d. 9141
11: 3 and he will d in the fear of the LORD. 8193
13:17 not care for silver and have no d in gold. 2911
32:14 the d of donkeys, a pasture for flocks, 5375
42: 1 my chosen one in whom I d; 8354
55: 2 and your soul will d in the richest of fare. 6695
58:13 a d and the LORD's holy day honorable, 6696
61:10 I d greatly in the LORD; 8464+8464
62: 4 for the LORD will take d in you, 2911
65:18 for I will create Jerusalem to be a d 1638
65:19 over Jerusalem and take d in my people; 8464
66: 3 and their souls d in their abominations; 2911
66:11 and d in her overflowing abundance." 6695
Jer 9:24 for in these I d," declares the LORD. 2911
15:16 they were my joy and my heart's d, 8525
31:20 the child in whom I d? 9141
49:25 the town in which I d? 5375
Eze 24:16 to take away from you the d of your eyes. 4718
24:21 the d of your eyes, 4718
24:25 the d of their eyes, their heart's desire, 4718
Hos 7: 3 "They d the king with their wickedness, 8523
Mic 1:16 for the children in whom you d; 9503
7:18 not stay angry forever but d to show mercy. 2911
Zep 3:17 He will take great d in you, 928+8464+8525
Mt 12:18 the one I love, in whom I d; 2305
Mk 12:37 The large crowd listened to him with d. 2452
Lk 1:14 He will be a joy and d to you, 21
Ro 7:22 For in my inner being I d in God's law; 5310
1Co 13: 6 Love does not d in evil but rejoices with 5897
2Co 12:10 I d in weaknesses, in insults, in hardships, 2305
Col 2: 5 I am present with you in spirit and d to see 5897

DELIGHTED (15) [DELIGHT]
Ge 34:19 because he was d with Jacob's daughter. 2911
Ex 18: 9 Jethro was d to hear about all 2525
Dt 30: 9 just as he d in your fathers, 8464
2Sa 22:20 he rescued me because he d in me. 2911
1Ki 10: 9 who has d in you and placed you on 2911
2Ch 9: 8 who has d in you and placed you 2911
Est 5:14 This suggestion d Haman, 3512
Ps 18:19 he rescued me because he d in me. 2911
Isa 1:29 of the sacred oaks in which you have d; 2773
Mk 14:11 They were d to hear this and promised 5897
Lk 13:17 but the people were d with all 5897
22: 5 They were d and agreed to give him money. 5897
2Co 7:13 we were especially d to see how 4359+5897
1Th 2: 8 so much that we were d to share with you 2305
2Th 2:12 the truth but have d in wickedness. 2305

DELIGHTFUL (4) [DELIGHT]
Ps 16: 6 surely I have a d inheritance. 9182
SS 1: 2 for your love is more d than wine. 3202
4:10 How d is your love, my sister, my bride! 3636
Mal 3:12 for yours will be a d land," 2914

DELIGHTING (1) [DELIGHT]
Pr 8:31 in his whole world and d in mankind. 9141

DELIGHTS (21) [DELIGHT]
Est 6: 6 be done for the man the king d to honor?" 2911
6: 7 "For the man the king d to honor, 2911
6: 9 Let them robe the man the king d to honor, 2911
6: 9 'This is what is done for the man the king d 2911
6:11 "This is what is done for the man the king d 2911
Ps 22: 8 Let him deliver him, since he d in him." 2911
35:27 who d in the well-being of his servant." 2913
36: 8 you give them drink from your river of d. 6358

Ps 37:23 If the LORD **d in** a man's way, 2911
147:11 the LORD **d in** those who fear him, 8354
Pr 3:12 as a father the son *he* **d in.** 8354
10:23 but a man of understanding **d** in wisdom. NIH
11:20 but he **d** in those whose ways are blameless. 8356
12:22 but he **d** *in* men who are truthful. 8356
14:35 A king **d** in a wise servant, 8356
15:21 Folly **d** a man who lacks judgment, 8525
18:2 but **d** in airing his own opinions. NIH
23:24 he who has a wise son **d** in him. 8523
Ecc 2:8 the **d of the heart** *of* man. 9503
SS 7:6 O love, with your **d!** 9503
Col 2:18 not let anyone *who* **d** in false humility and *2527*

DELILAH (7)

Jdg 16:4 in the Valley of Sorek whose name was **D.** 1935
16:6 So **D** said to Samson, 1935
16:10 Then **D** said to Samson, 1935
16:12 **D** took new ropes and tied him with them. 1935
16:13 **D** then said to Samson, "Until now, 1935
16:13 **D** took the seven braids of his head, NIH
16:18 **D** saw that he had told her everything, 1935

DELIVER (79) [DELIVERANCE, DELIVERED, DELIVERER, DELIVERERS, DELIVERING, DELIVERS, DELIVERY]

Nu 21:2 "If *you will* **d** these people into our hands, 5989+5989
Dt 1:27 so he brought us out of Egypt to **d** us into 5989
2:31 **d** Sihon and his country **over** 5989
7:23 the LORD your God *will* **d** them **over** 5989
23:14 to protect you and to **d** your enemies 5989
31:5 The LORD *will* **d** them to you, 5989
32:39 and no *one can* **d** out of my hand. 5911
Jos 7:7 across the Jordan to **d** us into the hands of 5989
8:18 for into your hand *I will* **d** the city." 5989
Jdg 7:2 for me *to* **d** Midian into their hands. 5989
1Sa 4:8 Who *will* **d** us from the hand 5911
7:3 and *he will* **d** you out of the hand of 5911
9:16 *he will* **d** my people from the hand of 3828
12:10 now **d** us from the hands of our enemies, 5911
17:37 the lion and the paw of the bear *will* **d** me 5911
26:24 so may the LORD value my life and **d** me 5911
2Sa 14:16 Perhaps the king will agree to **d** his servant 5911
1Ki 20:28 *I will* **d** this vast army into your hands, 5989
2Ki 17:39 it is he *who will* **d** you from the hand 5911
18:29 He cannot **d** you from my hand. 5911
18:30 'The LORD *will* **surely d** us; 5911+5911
18:32 'The LORD *will* **d** us.' 5911
18:35 the LORD **d** Jerusalem from my hand?" 5911
19:3 of birth and there is no strength to **d** them. 4256
19:12 by my forefathers **d** them: 5911
19:19 O LORD our God, **d** us from his hand, 3828
20:6 And *I will* **d** you and this city from 5911
1Ch 16:35 gather us and **d** us from the nations, 5911
2Ch 32:13 of those nations ever able to **d** their land 5911
32:14 then can your god **d** you from my hand? 5911
32:15 to **d** his people from my hand or the hand 5911
32:15 How much less *will* your god **d** you 5911
Ezr 7:19 **D** to the God of Jerusalem all 10719
Job 6:23 **d** me from the hand of the enemy, 4880
22:30 *He will* **d** even one who is not innocent, 4880
Ps 3:2 "God *will* not **d** him." 3802
3:7 **D** me, O my God! 3828
6:4 Turn, O LORD, and **d** me; 2740
7:1 save and **d** me from all who pursue me, 5911
22:8 *Let him* **d** him, since he delights in him." 5911
22:20 **D** my life from the sword, 5911
31:1 **d** me in your righteousness. 7117
31:15 **d** me from my enemies and 5911
33:19 to **d** them from death and keep them alive 5911
50:15 *I will* **d** you, and you will honor me." 2740
59:1 **D** me from my enemies, O God; 5911
59:2 **D** me from evildoers and save me 5911
69:14 **d** *me* from those who hate me, 5911
71:2 Rescue me and **d** me in your righteousness; 7117
71:4 **D** me, O my God, 7117
72:12 For *he will* **d** the needy who cry out, 5911
79:9 **d** us and forgive our sins 5911
82:4 **d** them from the hand of the wicked. 5911
91:15 *I will* **d** him and honor him. 2740
109:21 out of the goodness of your love, **d** me. 5911
119:153 Look upon my suffering and **d** me, 2740
119:170 **d** me according to your promise. 5911
144:7 **d** me and rescue me from 7198
144:11 **D** me and rescue me from the hands 7198
Pr 20:22 Wait for the LORD, and *he will* **d** you. 3828
Isa 31:5 he will shield it and **d** it, 5911
36:14 He cannot **d** you! 5911
36:15 'The LORD *will* **surely d** us; 5911+5911
36:18 'The LORD *will* **d** us.' 5911
36:20 the LORD **d** Jerusalem from my hand?" 5911
37:3 of birth and there is no strength to **d** them. 4256
37:12 by my forefathers **d** them— 5911
37:20 O LORD our God, **d** us from his hand, 3828
38:6 And *I will* **d** you and this city from 5911
43:13 No *one can* **d** out of my hand. 5911
Jer 15:11 "Surely *I will* **d** you for a good purpose; 9223
42:11 with you and will save you and **d** you 5911
Am 6:8 *I will* **d up** the city and everything in it." 6037
Mic 5:6 *He will* **d** us from the Assyrian 5911
Hab 3:13 You came out to **d** your people, 3829
Mt 6:13 but **d** us from the evil one.' *4861*
Lk 21:12 *They will* **d** you to synagogues *4140*
2Co 1:10 and *he will* **d** us. *4861*
1:10 that *he will* continue to **d** us, *4861*

DELIVERANCE (19) [DELIVER]

Ge 45:7 on earth and to save your lives by a great **d.** 7129
49:18 "I look for your **d,** O LORD. 3802
Ex 14:13 the **d** the LORD will bring you today. 3802
Jdg 13:5 and he will begin the **d** *of* Israel from 3828
1Sa 2:1 for I delight in your **d.** 3802
14:45 he who has brought about this great **d** 3802
2Ch 12:7 not destroy them but will soon give them **d.** 7129
20:17 and see the **d** the LORD will give you, 3802
Est 4:14 relief and **d** for the Jews will arise 2208
Job 13:16 Indeed, this will turn out for my **d,** 3802
Ps 3:8 From the LORD comes **d.** 3802
32:7 and surround me with songs of **d.** 7119
33:17 A horse is a vain hope for **d;** 9591
78:22 they did not believe in God or trust in his **d.** 3802
Isa 20:6 to for help and **d** from the king of Assyria! 5911
59:11 for **d,** but it is far away. 3802
Joel 2:32 and in Jerusalem there will be **d,** 7129
Ob 1:17 But on Mount Zion will be **d;** 7129
Php 1:19 to me will turn out for my **d.** *5401*

DELIVERED (71) [DELIVER]

Ge 14:20 who **d** your enemies into your hand." 4481
48:16 the Angel who *has* **d** me from all harm— 1457
Dt 2:33 the LORD our God **d** him **over** to us 5989
7:2 the LORD your God *has* **d** them **over** 5989
Jos 6:2 "See, *I have* **d** Jericho into your hands, 5989
8:1 *I have* **d** into your hands the king of Ai, 5989
24:10 and *I* **d** you out of his hand. 5911
Jdg 13:1 so the LORD **d** them into the hands of 5989
16:23 saying, "Our god *has* **d** Samson, our enemy, 5989
16:24 "Our god *has* **d** our enemy into our hands, 5989
1Sa 7:14 and Israel **d** the neighboring territory from 5911
10:18 of Egypt, and *I* **d** you from the power 5911
11:9 tomorrow, you will be **d.'** " 9591
12:11 and *he* **d** you from the hands 5911
17:37 The LORD who **d** me from the paw of 5911
24:10 with your own eyes how the LORD **d** you 5989
24:18 the LORD **d** me into your hands, 6037
26:8 "Today God *has* **d** your enemy 6037
26:23 The LORD **d** you into my hands today, 5989
2Sa 4:9 who *has* **d** me out of all trouble, 7009
12:7 and I **d** you from the hand of Saul. 5911
18:19 to the king that the LORD *has* **d** him from 9149
18:28 *He has* **d up** the men who lifted their hands 6037
18:31 The LORD *has* **d** you today 9149
19:9 king **d** us from the hand of our enemies; 5911
22:1 of this song when the LORD **d** him from 5911
22:44 "*You have* **d** me from the attacks 7117
1Ki 1:29 who *has* **d** me out of every trouble, 7009
9:28 which *they* **d** to King Solomon. 995
2Ki 17:13 and that *I* **d** to you through my servants 8938
18:33 the god of any nation **ever d** his land 5911+5911
19:11 And *will* you **be d?** 5911
2Ch 8:18 which *they* **d** to King Solomon. 995
13:16 and God **d** them into their hands. 5989
16:8 *he* **d** them into your hand. 5989
24:24 the LORD **d** into their hands 5989
Ezr 8:36 also **d** the king's orders to the royal satraps 5989
Ne 9:28 and in your compassion *you* **d** them time 5911
Est 1:12 the attendants **d** the king's command, 928+3338
Job 21:30 that *he* **is d** from the day of wrath? 3297
22:30 *who will* **be d** through the cleanness 4880
23:7 and *I would be* **d** forever from my judge. 7117
Ps 18:T of this song when the LORD **d** him from 5911
18:43 *You have* **d** me from the attacks of 7117
22:4 they trusted and *you* **d** them. 7117
34:4 *he* **d** me from all my fears. 5911
54:7 For *he has* **d** me from all my troubles, 5911
56:13 For *you have* **d** me from death and my feet 5911
60:5 that those you love *may* **be d.** 2740
86:13 *you have* **d** me from the depths of 5911
106:43 Many times *he* **d** them, 5911
107:6 and *he* **d** them from their distress. 5911
108:6 that those you love *may* **be d.** 2740
116:8 *you,* O LORD, *have* **d** my soul from death, 2740
119:117 Uphold me, and *I will* **be d;** 3828
Isa 36:18 Has the god of any nation *ever* **d** his land 5911
37:11 And *will* you **be d?** 5911
Eze 35:5 an ancient hostility and **d** the Israelites **over** 5599
Da 1:2 And the Lord **d** Jehoiakim king of Judah 5989
11:41 Moab and the leaders of Ammon *will* **be d** 4880
12:1 found written in the book—*will* **be d.** 4880
Lk 24:7 'The Son of Man must *be* **d** into the hands *4140*
Ac 12:21 sat on his throne and **d a public address** to *1319*
15:30 the church together and **d** the letter. *2113*
16:4 *they* **d** the decisions reached by the apostles *4140*
23:33 they **d** the letter to the governor *347*
Ro 4:25 He *was* **d over** to death for our sins *4140*
2Co 1:10 He *has* **d** us from such a deadly peril, *4861*
2Th 3:2 that *we may be* **d** from wicked and evil men, *4861*
2Ti 4:17 And *I was* **d** from the lion's mouth. *4861*
Jude 1:5 that the Lord **d** his people out of Egypt, *5392*

DELIVERER (11) [DELIVER]

Jdg 3:9 he raised up for them a **d,** 4635
3:15 and he gave them a **d—** 4635
2Sa 22:2 LORD is my rock, my fortress and my **d;** 7117
2Ki 13:5 The LORD provided a **d** for Israel, 4635
Ps 18:2 LORD is my rock, my fortress and my **d;** 7117
40:17 You are my help and my **d;** 7117
70:5 You are my help and my **d;** 7117
140:7 O Sovereign LORD, my strong **d,** 3802
144:2 my stronghold and my **d,** my shield, 7117
Ac 7:35 to be their ruler and **d** by God himself, *3392*
Ro 11:26 "The **d** will come from Zion; *4861*

DELIVERERS (2) [DELIVER]

Ne 9:27 in your great compassion you gave them **d,** 4635
Ob 1:21 **D** will go up on Mount Zion to govern 4635

DELIVERING (2) [DELIVER]

1Sa 14:48 Amalekites, **d** Israel from the hands 5911
24:15 may he vindicate me by **d** me NIH

DELIVERS (15) [DELIVER]

Dt 20:13 the LORD your God **d** it into your hand, 5989
21:10 and the LORD your God **d** them 5989
Job 36:15 But those who suffer *he* **d** in their suffering; 2740
Ps 34:7 and *he* **d** them. 2740
34:17 *he* **d** them from all their troubles. 5911
34:19 but the LORD **d** him from them all; 5911
37:40 The LORD helps them and **d** them; 7117
37:40 *he* **d** them from the wicked and saves them, 7117
41:1 the LORD **d** him in times of trouble. 4880
97:10 and **d** them from the hand of the wicked. 5911
144:10 who **d** his servant David from 7198
Pr 10:2 but righteousness **d** from death. 5911
11:4 but righteousness **d** from death. 5911
11:6 The righteousness of the upright **d** them, 5911
Isa 66:7 before the pains come upon her, *she* **d** 4880

DELIVERY (4) [DELIVER]

Ex 1:16 and observe them on the **d stool,** if it is 78
1Sa 4:19 pregnant and **near the time of d.** 3528
Isa 66:9 to the moment of birth and not **give d?"** 3528
66:9 up the womb when I **bring to d?"** 3528

DELUDED (2) [DELUSION]

Isa 44:20 He feeds on ashes, a **d** heart misleads him; 9438
Rev 19:20 With these signs *he had* **d** those who had received the mark of the beast *4414*

DELUGED (1)

2Pe 3:6 the world of that time was **d** and destroyed. *2885+5623*

DELUSION (1) [DELUDED, DELUSIONS]

2Th 2:11 a powerful **d** so that they will believe the lie *4415*

DELUSIONS (3) [DELUSION]

Ps 4:2 long will you love **d** and seek false gods? 8198
Jer 14:14 idolatries and the **d** *of* their own minds. 9567
23:26 who prophesy the **d** *of* their own minds? 9567

DEMAND (15) [DEMANDED, DEMANDING, DEMANDS]

Ge 9:5 lifeblood *I will* surely **d an accounting.** 2011
9:5 *I will* **d an accounting** from every animal 2011
9:5 *I will* **d an accounting** *for* the life 2011
Dt 23:21 the LORD your God *will* **certainly d** it 2011+2011
2Sa 3:13 But I **d** one thing of you: 8626
4:11 not now **d** his blood from your hand and rid 1335
21:4 to **d** silver or gold from Saul or his family, NIH
1Ki 20:5 'I sent to **d** your silver and gold, 606
20:9 but this **d** I cannot meet.' " 1821
2Ki 18:14 and I will pay whatever *you* **d** of me." 5989
Ne 5:12 *we will* not **d** anything more from them. 1335
Job 17:3 "Give me, O God, the pledge you **d.** 6640
Lk 6:30 *do* not **d it back.** *555*
23:24 So Pilate decided to grant their **d.** *161*
1Co 1:22 Jews **d** miraculous signs and Greeks look *160*

DEMANDED (18) [DEMAND]

Ge 31:39 And *you* **d payment** from me 1335
Ex 21:30 However, if payment **is d** of him, 8883
21:30 by paying whatever **is d.** 8883
Jdg 6:30 The men of the town **d of** Joash, 606
1Ki 20:9 'Your servant will do all *you* **d** 8938
2Ki 6:11 He summoned his officers and **d of** them, 606
23:35 the silver and gold he **d.** 6584+7023
Ne 5:18 *I* never **d** the food allotted to the governor, 1335
Job 22:6 *You* **d security** *from* your brothers 2471
Ps 137:3 our tormentors **d** songs of joy; NIH
Mt 18:28 'Pay back what you owe me!' *he* **d.** *3306*
Lk 12:20 This very night your life *will be* **d from** *555*
12:48 much *will be* **d;** *2426*
22:64 *They* blindfolded him and **d,** "Prophesy! *2089*
23:23 But with loud shouts they insistently **d** that *160*
Jn 2:18 Then the Jews **d** of him, *646*
9:10 then were your eyes opened?" *they* **d.** *3306*
18:22 "Is this the way you answer the high priest?" *he* **d.** *3306*

DEMANDING (3) [DEMAND]

2Sa 3:14 **d,** "Give me my wife Michal, 606
Ps 78:18 They willfully put God to the test by **d** 8626
2Co 13:3 since *you are* **d** proof *2426*

DEMANDS (6) [DEMAND]

Ex 21:22 be fined whatever the woman's husband **d** 8883
1Ki 20:8 "Don't listen to him or **agree to** his **d."** 14

Ne 5:18 because the d were heavy on these people. 6275
Ps 25:10 for those who keep the d of his covenant. 6343
Isa 43:23 with grain offerings nor wearied you with d NIH
Mic 7: 3 the ruler d gifts, the judge accepts bribes, 8626

DEMAS (3)

Col 4:14 the doctor, and D send greetings. *1318*
2Ti 4:10 for D, because he loved this world, *1318*
Phm 1:24 And so do Mark, Aristarchus, D and Luke, *1318*

DEMETRIUS (3)

Ac 19:24 A silversmith named D, *1320*
19:38 D and his fellow craftsmen have *1320*
3Jn 1:12 D is well spoken of by everyone— *1320*

DEMOLISH (11) [DEMOLISHED]

Ex 23:24 *You* must d them 2238+2238
Nu 33:52 and d all their high places. 9012
Jer 43:13 in Egypt *he will* d the sacred pillars 8689
Eze 26: 9 against your walls and d your towers 5997
26:12 down your walls and d your fine houses 5997
Hos 10: 2 The LORD *will* d their altars 6904
Mic 5:10 from among you and d your chariots. 6
5:14 and d your cities. 9012
Mal 1: 4 "They may build, but I *will* d. 2238
2Co 10: 4 they have divine power to d strongholds. *2746*
10: 5 *We* d arguments and every pretension *2747*

DEMOLISHED (11) [DEMOLISH]

Nu 21:30 *We have* d them as far as Nophah, 9037
Jdg 6:28 there was Baal's altar, d, 5997
2Ki 10:27 *They* d the sacred stone of Baal and tore 5997
23:15 even that altar and high place *he* d. 5997
2Ch 33: 3 the high places his father Hezekiah *had* d; 5997
Jer 31:40 The city will never again be uprooted or d." 2238
Eze 6: 4 Your altars *will* be d 9037
6: 6 be laid waste and the high places d, 9037
Am 3:15 be destroyed and the mansions *will be* d," 6066
Zep 1:13 be plundered, their houses d. 9039
3: 6 their strongholds are d. 9037

DEMON (16) [DEMONS, DEMON-POSSESSED, DEMON-POSSESSION]

Mt 9:33 And when the d was driven out, *1228*
11:18 and they say, 'He has a d.' *1228*
17:18 Jesus rebuked the d, *1228*
Mk 7:26 She begged Jesus to drive the d out *1228*
7:29 the d has left your daughter." *1228*
7:30 and the d gone. *1228*
Lk 4:33 a man possessed by a d, *1228*
4:35 the d threw the man down before them all *1228*
7:33 and you say, 'He has a d.' *1228*
8:29 and had been driven by the d *1228*
9:42 d threw him to the ground in a convulsion. *1228*
11:14 Jesus was driving out a d that was mute. *1228*
11:14 When the d left, *1228*
Jn 8:49 "I am not possessed by a d," said Jesus, *1228*
10:21 not the sayings *of a man* possessed by a d. *1227*
10:21 Can a d open the eyes of the blind?" *1228*

DEMON-POSSESSED (16) [DEMON, POSSESS]

Mt 4:24 those suffering severe pain, the d, *1227*
8:16 many *who were* d were brought to him, *1227*
8:28 two d *men* coming from the tombs met him. *1227*
8:33 including what had happened to the d *men*. *1227*
9:32 a man *who was* d and could *1227*
12:22 a d *man* who was blind and mute, *1227*
Mk 1:32 to Jesus all the sick and d. *1227*
5:16 the people what had happened *to* the d *man* *1227*
5:18 man who *had been* d begged to go with him. *1227*
Lk 8:27 he was met by a d man from the town. *1228+2400*
8:36 the people how the d *man* had been cured. *1227*
Jn 7:20 "*You are* d," the crowd answered. *1228+2400*
8:48 saying that you are a Samaritan and d? *1228+2400*
8:52 "Now we know that *you are* d! *1228+2400*
10:20 "*He is* d and raving mad. *1228+2400*
Ac 19:13 of the Lord Jesus over those who *were* d. *2400+3836+3836+4460+4505*

DEMON-POSSESSION (1) [DEMON, POSSESS]

Mt 15:22 suffering terribly from d." *1227*

DEMONS (49) [DEMON]

Dt 32:17 They sacrificed to d, which are not God— 8717
Ps 106:37 and their daughters to d. 8717
Mt 7:22 and in your name drive out d *1228*
8:31 The d begged Jesus, "If you drive us out, *1230*
9:34 the prince *of* d that he drives out demons." *1228*
9:34 the prince of demons that he drives out d." *1228*
10: 8 cleanse those who have leprosy, drive out d. *1228*
12:24 "It is only by Beelzebub, the prince *of* d, *1228*
12:24 that this fellow drives out d." *1228*
12:27 And if I drive out d by Beelzebub, *1228*
12:28 But if I drive out d by the Spirit of God, *1228*
Mk 1:34 He also drove out many d, *1228*
1:34 the d speak because they knew who he was. *1228*
1:39 in their synagogues and driving out d. *1228*
3:15 and to have authority to drive out d. *1228*
Mk 3:22 the prince *of* d he is driving out demons." *1228*
3:22 the prince of demons he is driving out d." *1228*
5:12 The d begged Jesus, "Send us among *NIG*
5:15 possessed by the legion of d, *1227*
6:13 They drove out many d *1228*
9:38 "we saw a man driving out d in your name *1228*
16: 9 out of whom he had driven seven d. *1228*
16:17 In my name they will drive out d; *1228*
Lk 4:41 Moreover, d came out of many people, *1228*
8: 2 from whom seven d had come out; *1228*
8:30 because many d had gone into him. *1228*
8:32 The d begged Jesus to let them go *NIG*
8:33 When the d came out of the man, *1228*
8:35 the man from whom the d had gone out, *1228*
8:38 the d had gone out begged to go with him, *1228*
9: 1 to drive out all d and to cure diseases, *1228*
9:49 "we saw a man driving out d in your name *1228*
10:17 even the d submit to us in your name." *1228*
11:15 the prince *of* d, he is driving out demons." *1228*
11:15 the prince of demons, he is driving out d." *1228*
11:18 because you claim that I drive out d *1228*
11:19 Now if I drive out d by Beelzebub, *1228*
11:20 But if I drive out d by the finger of God, *1228*
13:32 'I will drive out d and heal people today *1228*
Ro 8:38 neither angels nor d, *794*
1Co 10:20 the sacrifices of pagans are offered *to* d, *1228*
10:20 I do not want you to be participants *with* d. *1228*
10:21 the cup of the Lord and the cup *of* d too; *1228*
10:21 in both the Lord's table and the table *of* d. *1228*
1Ti 4: 1 and things taught *by* d. *1228*
Jas 2:19 Even the d believe that—and shudder. *1228*
Rev 9:20 they did not stop worshiping d, *1228*
16:14 *of* d performing miraculous signs, *1228*
18: 2 She has become a home *for* d and a haunt *1228*

DEMONSTRATE (2) [DEMONSTRATES, DEMONSTRATION]

Ro 3:25 He did this to d his justice, *1893*
3:26 he did it to d his justice at the present time, *1893*

DEMONSTRATES (1) [DEMONSTRATE]

Ro 5: 8 But God d his own love for us in this: *5319*

DEMONSTRATION (1) [DEMONSTRATE]

1Co 2: 4 but with a d of the Spirit's power, *618*

DEN (16) [DENS]

Jer 7:11 become a d *of* robbers to you? 5117
Da 6: 7 O king, shall be thrown into the lions' d. 10129
6:12 O king, would be thrown into the lions' d?" 10129
6:16 and threw him into the lions' d. 10129
6:17 and placed over the mouth of the d, 10129
6:19 the king got up and hurried to the lions' d. 10129
6:20 When he came near the d, 10129
6:23 and gave orders to lift Daniel out of the d. 10129
6:23 And when Daniel was lifted from the d, 10129
6:24 in and thrown into the lions' d, 10129
6:24 And before they reached the floor of the d, 10129
Am 3: 4 in his d when he has caught nothing? 5104
Na 2:11 Where now is the lions' d, 5061
Mt 21:13 but you are making it a 'd of robbers.' " *5068*
Mk 11:17 But you have made it 'a d of robbers.' " *5068*
Lk 19:46 but you have made it 'a d of robbers.' " *5068*

DENARII (2) [DENARIUS]

Mt 18:28 fellow servants who owed him a hundred d. *1324*
Lk 7:41 One owed him five hundred d, *1324*

DENARIUS (7) [DENARII]

Mt 20: 2 to pay them a d for the day and sent them *1324*
20: 9 and each received a d. *1324*
20:10 But each one of them also received a d. *1324*
20:13 Didn't you agree to work for a d? *1324*
22:19 They brought him a d, *1324*
Mk 12:15 "Bring me a d and let me look at it." *1324*
Lk 20:24 "Show me a d. *1324*

DENIED (17) [DENY]

Job 6:10 that *I had* not d the words of the Holy One. 3948
27: 2 *who has* d me justice, the Almighty, 6073
31:13 "If *I have* d justice *to* my menservants 4415
31:16 "If *I have* d the desires of the poor or let 4979
38:15 The wicked are d their light, 4979
Ecc 2:10 *I* d *myself* nothing my eyes desired; 724
5: 8 and justice and rights d, 1609
Mt 26:70 But he d it before them all. *766*
26:72 *He* d it again, with an oath: "I don't know *766*
Mk 14:68 But he d it. "I don't know *766*
14:70 Again he d it. *766*
Lk 8:45 *When they* all d it, Peter said, "Master, *766*
22:57 But he d it. *766*
Jn 18:25 He d it, saying, "I am not." *766*
18:27 Again Peter d it, and at that moment *766*
1Ti 5: 8 *he has* d the faith and is worse than *766*
Rev 3: 8 kept my word and *have* not d my name. *766*

DENIES (4) [DENY]

Job 34: 5 'I am innocent, but God d me justice. 6073
1Jn 2:22 It is the man who d that Jesus is the Christ. *766*
2:22 he d the Father and the Son. *766*
2:23 No one who d the Son has the Father; *766*

DENOUNCE (5) [DENOUNCED, DENOUNCES]

Nu 5:21 and d you when he causes your thigh 8652
23: 7 for me; come, d Israel.' 2404
23: 8 How *can I* d those whom the LORD has 2404
Pr 24:24 peoples will curse him and nations d him. 2404
Mt 11:20 Then Jesus began *to* d the cities *3943*

DENOUNCED (3) [DENOUNCE]

Nu 23: 8 the LORD *has* not d? 2404
Da 3: 8 and d the Jews. 10030+10642
1Co 10:30 why *am I* d because *1059*

DENOUNCES (2) [DENOUNCE]

Job 17: 5 If *a man* d his friends for reward, 5583
21:31 Who d his conduct to his face? 5583

DENS (6) [DEN]

Job 37: 8 they remain in their d. 5104
38:40 when they crouch in their d or lie in wait in 5104
Ps 104:22 they return and lie down in their d. 5104
SS 4: 8 from the lions' d and the mountain haunts 5104
Mic 7:17 They will come trembling out of their d; 4995
Na 2:12 filling his lairs with the kill and his d with 5104

DENSE (6)

Ge 19:28 and he saw d smoke rising *from* the land, 7798
Ex 8:24 D swarms of flies poured 3878
19: 9 "I am going to come to you in a d cloud, 6295
Isa 30:27 with burning anger and d clouds of smoke; 3880
Jer 46:23 declares the LORD, "d though *it be*. 2983+4202
Zec 11: 2 the d forest has been cut down! 1293

DENY (20) [DENIED, DENIES, DENYING]

Ex 23: 6 "*Do* not d justice to your poor people 5742
Lev 16:29 the seventh month *you must* d yourselves 6700
16:31 and *you must* d yourselves; 6700
23:27 Hold a sacred assembly and d yourselves, 6700
23:29 not d himself on that day must be cut off 6700
23:32 and *you must* d yourselves. 6700
Nu 29: 7 *You must* d yourselves and do no work. 6700
30:13 or any sworn pledge to d herself. 6700
Job 27: 5 till I die, *I will* not d my integrity. 6073
Isa 5:23 but d justice to the innocent. 6073
La 3:35 to d a man his rights before the Most High, 5742
Am 2: 7 as upon the dust of the ground and d justice 5742
Mt 16:24 *he must* d himself and take up his cross *565*
Mk 8:34 *he must* d himself and take up his cross *565*
Lk 9:23 after me, *he must* d himself and take *766*
22:34 *you will* d three times that you know me." *565*
Ac 4:16 and we cannot d it. *766*
Tit 1:16 but by their actions *they* d him. *766*
Jas 3:14 not boast about it or d the truth. *237+2848+6017*
Jude 1: 4 and d Jesus Christ our only Sovereign *766*

DENYING (3) [DENY]

Eze 22:29 and mistreat the alien, d them justice. 4202
2Ti 3: 5 having a form of godliness but d its power. *766*
2Pe 2: 1 d the sovereign Lord who bought them— *766*

DEPART (12) [DEPARTED, DEPARTING, DEPARTS, DEPARTURE]

Ge 49:10 The scepter *will* not d from Judah, 6073
Jos 1: 8 *Do* not *let* this Book of the Law d 4631
2Sa 12:10 the sword *will* never d from your house, 6073
Job 1:21 and naked *I will* d. 8740
Ps 39:13 that I may rejoice again before *I* d 2143
Isa 49:17 and those who laid you waste d from you. 3655
52:11 D, depart, go out from there! 6073
52:11 Depart, d, go out from there! 6073
59:21 in your mouth *will* not d from your mouth, 4631
Jer 43:12 so will he wrap Egypt around himself and d 3655
Mt 25:41 he will say to those on his left, 'D from me, *4513*
Php 1:23 I desire to d and be with Christ, *386*

DEPARTED (11) [DEPART]

Jos 2:21 So she sent them away and *they* d. 2143
1Sa 4:21 saying, "The glory *has* d from Israel"— 1655
4:22 She said, "The glory *has* d from Israel, 1655
16:14 the Spirit of the LORD *had* d from Saul, 6073
Job 23:12 *I have* not d *from* the commands of his lips; 4631
Ps 119:102 *I have* not d from your laws, 6073
Isa 14: 9 it rouses the spirits of the d to greet you— 8327
26:14 *those* d spirits do not rise. 8327
La 1: 6 All the splendor *has* d from the Daughter 3655
Eze 10:18 of the LORD d from over the threshold of 3655
Jn 4:50 The man took Jesus at his word and d. *4513*

DEPARTING (1) [DEPART]

Hos 1: 2 the vilest adultery *in* d from the LORD." 339+4946

DEPARTS (4) [DEPART]

Ps 146: 4 their spirit d, they return to the ground; 3655
Ecc 5:15 and as he comes, so *he* d. 8740
5:16 As a man comes, so *he* d, 2143
6: 4 *it* d in darkness, and in darkness 2143

DEPARTURE (6) [DEPART]

Dt 16: 3 the time of your d from Egypt. 3655

Dt 16: 6 on the anniversary of your **d** from Egypt. 3655
SS 5: 6 My heart sank at his **d.** 1818
Lk 9:31 They spoke about his **d,** *2016*
2Ti 4: 6 and the time has come *for* my **d.** *385*
2Pe 1:15 that after my **d** you will always be able *2016*

DEPEND (6) [DEPENDED, DEPENDENT, DEPENDING, DEPENDS]

2Ki 18:21 Such is Pharaoh king of Egypt to all who **d** 1053
19:10 Do not let the god you **d** on deceive you 1053
Ps 62: 7 My salvation and my honor **d on** God; 6584
Isa 36: 6 Such is Pharaoh king of Egypt to all who **d** 1053
37:10 **let** the god you **d** 1053
Ro 9:16 therefore, **d** on man's desire or effort, *NIG*

DEPENDED (3) [DEPEND]

Isa 30:12 relied on oppression and **d** on deceit, 9128
Hos 10:13 Because *you have* **d** on your own strength 1053
Ac 12:20 because they **d** on the king's country *NIG*

DEPENDENT (2) [DEPEND]

Lev 21: 3 or an unmarried sister who is **d** on him 7940
1Th 4:12 so that *you will* not **be d on** anybody. 2400+*5970*

DEPENDING (8) [DEPEND]

2Ki 18:20 On whom *are you* **d,** 1053
18:21 Look now, *you are* **d** on Egypt, 1053
18:22 *"We are* **d** on the LORD our God"— 1053
18:24 though *you are* **d** on Egypt for chariots 1053
Isa 36: 5 On whom *are you* **d,** 1053
36: 6 Look now, *you are* **d** on Egypt, 1053
36: 7 *"We are* **d** on the LORD our God"— 1053
36: 9 though *you are* **d** on Egypt for chariots 1053

DEPENDS (5) [DEPEND]

Jer 17: 5 the one who trusts in man, *who* **d on** flesh 8492
Ro 12:18 If it is possible, *as far as* **it d on you,** 1666+3836+*5148*
Gal 3:18 For if the inheritance **d on** the law, *1666*
3:18 then it no longer **d on** a promise; *1666*
Col 2: 8 which **d on** human tradition and *2848*

DEPLOYED (5)

1Sa 4: 2 The Philistines **d** *their* **forces** 6885
2Sa 10: 9 the best troops in Israel and **d** them against 6885
10:10 of Abishai his brother and **d** them against 6885
1Ch 19:10 the best troops in Israel and **d** them against 6885
19:11 and *they were* **d** against the Ammonites. 6885

DEPORTED (11)

2Ki 15:29 and **d** the people to Assyria. 1655
16: 9 *He* **d** its inhabitants to Kir and put Rezin 1655
17: 6 the king of Assyria captured Samaria and **d** 1655
17:26 "The people *you* **d** and resettled in 1655
18:11 The king of Assyria **d** Israel to Assyria 1655
24:16 The king of Babylon also **d** to Babylon 995+1583
1Ch 6:15 Jehozadak *was* **d** when 2143
8: 6 of those living in Geba and *were* **d** 1655
8: 7 who **d** them and who was the father 1655
Ezr 4:10 and honorable Ashurbanipal **d** and settled 10144
5:12 who destroyed this temple and **d** the people 10144

DEPOSE (1) [DEPOSED, DEPOSES]

Isa 22:19 *I will* **d** you from your office, 2074

DEPOSED (3) [DEPOSE]

1Ki 15:13 *He* even **d** his grandmother Maacah 6073
2Ch 15:16 King Asa also **d** his grandmother Maacah 6073
Da 5:20 *he* **was d** from his royal throne and stripped 10474

DEPOSES (1) [DEPOSE]

Da 2:21 he sets up kings and **d** them. 10528

DEPOSIT (10) [DEPOSITED]

Ezr 5:15 'Take these articles and go and **d** them in 10474
Eze 24: 6 whose **d** will not go away! 2689
24:11 be melted and its **d** burned away. 2689
24:12 its heavy **d** has not been removed, 2689
Mt 25:27 you should have put my money on **d** with *NIG*
Lk 19:23 Why then didn't you put my money on **d,** *5544*
2Co 1:22 and put his Spirit in our hearts as a **d,** *775*
5: 5 the Spirit as a **d, guaranteeing** what is *775*
Eph 1:14 who is a **d guaranteeing** our inheritance *775*
2Ti 1:14 the good **d** that was **entrusted** to you— *4146*

DEPOSITED (2) [DEPOSIT]

1Sa 10:25 He wrote them down on a scroll and **d** it 5663
Ezr 6: 5 they *are to be* **d** in the house of God. 10474

DEPRAVED (5) [DEPRAVITY]

Eze 16:47 ways *you* soon *became* more **d** than they. 8845
23:11 prostitution *she was* more **d** than her sister. 8845
Ro 1:28 he gave them over to a **d** mind, *99*
Php 2:15 without fault in a crooked and **d** generation, *1406*
2Ti 3: 8 men oppose the truth—men of **d** minds, *2967*

DEPRAVITY (2) [DEPRAVED]

Ro 1:29 of wickedness, evil, greed and **d.** *2798*
2Pe 2:19 while they themselves are slaves *of* **d**— *5785*

DEPRESSIONS (1)

Lev 14:37 if it has greenish or reddish **d** that appear to 9206

DEPRIVE (13) [DEPRIVED, DEPRIVES, DEPRIVING]

Ex 21:10 *he must* not **d** the first one *of* her food, 1757
Dt 24:17 not **d** the alien or the fatherless *of* justice, 5742
Pr 18: 5 be partial to the wicked or to **d** the innocent 5742
31: 5 and **d** all the oppressed *of* their rights. 9101
Isa 10: 2 to **d** the poor of their rights 5742
29:21 and with false testimony **d** the innocent 5742
La 3:36 to **d** a man of justice— 6430
Eze 36:12 **d** them of their **children.** 8897
36:13 **d** your nation **of** *its* **children,"** 8897
Am 5:12 **d** the poor **of justice** 5742
Mal 3: 5 and **d** aliens **of justice,** 5742
1Co 7: 5 not **d** each other except by mutual consent *691*
9:15 I would rather die than have anyone **d** me *3033*

DEPRIVED (5) [DEPRIVE]

Ge 42:36 **d** me **of** my **children.** 8897
Jer 5:25 your sins *have* **d** you of good. 4979
La 3:17 I *have been* **d** of peace; 2396
Mic 7:16 **d of** all their power. 4946
Ac 8:33 In his humiliation he *was* **d** of justice. *149*

DEPRIVES (1) [DEPRIVE]

Job 12:24 *He* **d** the leaders of the earth *of* their reason; 6073

DEPRIVING (1) [DEPRIVE]

Ecc 4: 8 "and why *am* I **d** myself of enjoyment?" 2893

DEPTH (6) [DEEP]

Ge 7:20 covered the mountains to a **d** 2025+4200+5087
La 3:60 You have seen the **d** *of* their vengeance, 3972
Ro 8:39 neither height nor **d,** *958*
11:33 the **d** of the riches of the wisdom *958*
2Co 2: 4 not to grieve you but to let you know the **d** *4359*
Php 1: 9 and more in knowledge and **d** of insight, *4246*

DEPTHS (39) [DEEP]

Ex 15: 5 they sank to the **d** like a stone. 5185
Ne 9:11 but you hurled their pursuers into the **d,** 5185
Job 11: 8 They are deeper than the **d of the grave**— 8619
36:30 bathing the **d** *of* the sea. 9247
41:31 He makes the **d** churn like a boiling caldron 5185
Ps 30: 1 **lifted** me **out of the d** 1926
63: 9 they will go down to the **d** *of* the earth. 9397
68:22 I will bring them from the **d** *of* the sea, 5185
69: 2 I sink in the miry **d,** 5185
69:15 or the **d** swallow me up or 5185
71:20 from the **d** *of* the earth you will again bring 9333
77:16 the very **d** were convulsed. 9333
86:13 you have delivered me from the **d** of 9397
88: 6 in the darkest **d.** 5185
95: 4 In his hand are the **d** *of* the earth, 4736
106: 9 he led them through the **d** as through 9333
107:26 up to the heavens and went down to the **d;** 9333
130: 1 Out of the **d** I cry to you, O LORD; 5099
135: 6 in the seas and all their **d.** 9333
139: 8 if I make my bed in the **d,** you are there. 8619
139:15 I was woven together in the **d** *of* the earth, 9397
148: 7 you great sea creatures and all **ocean d,** 9333
Pr 9:18 that her guests are in the **d** *of* the grave. 6679
Isa 7:11 in the deepest **d** or in the highest heights." 8619
14:15 to the **d** *of* the pit. 3752
29:15 Woe to those *who* **go to great d** 6676
51:10 who made a road in the **d** *of* the sea so that 5099
63:13 who led them through the **d?** 9333
La 3:55 O LORD, from the **d** of the pit 9397
Eze 26:19 and when I bring the **ocean d** over you 9333
27:34 Now you are shattered by the sea in the **d** 5099
32:23 in the **d** *of* the pit and her army lies 3752
Am 9: 2 they dig down to the **d of the grave,** 8619
Jnh 2: 2 From the **d** *of* the grave I called for help, 1061
Mic 7:19 and hurl all our iniquities into the **d** *of* 5185
Zec 10:11 and all the **d** *of* the Nile will dry up. 5185
Mt 11:23 No, you will go down to the **d.** *87*
18: 6 around his neck and to be drowned in the **d** *4283*
Lk 10:15 No, you will go down to the **d.** *87*

DEPUTED (KJV) See REPRESENTATIVE

DEPUTY (2)

Jdg 9:28 and isn't Zebul his **d?** 7224
1Ki 22:47 There was then no king in Edom; a **d** ruled. 5893

DERBE (4)

Ac 14: 6 the Lycaonian cities of Lystra and **D** and to *1292*
14:20 The next day he and Barnabas left for **D.** *1292*
16: 1 He came to **D** and then to Lystra, *1292*
20: 4 Gaius **from D,** Timothy also, *1291*

DERIDE (1) [DERIDES, DERISION]

Hab 1:10 They **d** kings and scoff at rulers. 7840

DERIDED (KJV) See SNEERED

DERIDES (1) [DERIDE]

Pr 11:12 A man who lacks judgment **d** his neighbor, 996

DERISION (5) [DERIDE]

Job 27:23 **claps** its hands **in d** 8562
Ps 44:13 the scorn and **d** of those around us. 7841
79: 4 of scorn and **d** to those around us. 7841
Eze 23:32 it will bring scorn and **d,** 4353
Mic 6:16 over to ruin and your people to **d;** 9240

DERIVES (1)

Eph 3:15 in heaven and on earth **d** *its* **name.** *3951*

DESCEND (7) [DESCENDANT, DESCENDANTS, DESCENDED, DESCENDING, DESCENDS, DESCENT]

Dt 32: 2 like rain and my words **d** like dew, 5688
Job 17:16 *Will we* **d** together into the dust?" 5737
Ps 49:17 his splendor *will* not **d** with him. 3718
SS 4: 8 **D** from the crest of Amana, 8801
Isa 5:14 into it *will* **d** their nobles and masses 3718
14:19 *those who* **d** to the stones of the pit. 3718
Ro 10: 7 "or 'Who *will* **d** into the deep?' " *2849*

DESCENDANT (25) [DESCEND]

Lev 6:18 Any male **d** of Aaron may eat it. 1201
21:21 No **d** *of* Aaron 2446
22: 4 a **d** *of* Aaron has an infectious skin disease 408+2446+4946
Nu 16:40 a **d** *of* Aaron should come to burn incense 2446
26:59 Amram's wife was Jochebed, a **d** *of* Levi, 1426
32:41 Jair, a **d** *of* Manasseh, 1201
Dt 3:14 Jair, a **d** *of* Manasseh, 1201
2Sa 14: 7 leaving my husband neither name nor **d** on 8642
1Ch 7:14 Asriel *was his* **d** 3528
7:15 Another **d** was named Zelophehad, NIH
9: 4 the son of Bani, a **d** *of* Perez son of Judah. 1201
24: 3 a **d** *of* Eleazar and Ahimelech a descendant 1201
24: 3 a descendant of Eleazar and Ahimelech a **d** 1201
26:24 Shubael, a **d** *of* Gershom son of Moses, 1201
27: 3 He was a **d** *of* Perez and chief of all 1201
2Ch 20:14 a Levite and **d** *of* Asaph, 1201
Ezr 5: 1 Zechariah the prophet, a **d** *of* Iddo, 10120
6:14 Zechariah, a **d** *of* Iddo. 10120
Ne 11: 4 the son of Mahalalel, a **d** *of* Perez; 1201
11: 5 the son of Zechariah, a **d** of Shelah. 1201
Jer 33:21 and David will no longer have a **d** to reign 1201
Lk 1: 5 his wife Elizabeth was also a **d** of Aaron. *1666+2588+3836*
1:27 a man named Joseph, a **d** of David. *1666+3875*
Ro 1: 3 as to his human nature was a **d** of David, *5065*
11: 1 I am an Israelite myself, a **d** of Abraham, *5065*

DESCENDANTS (364) [DESCEND]

Ge 9: 9 with you and with your **d** after you 2446
15:13 for certain that your **d** will be strangers in 2446
15:16 In the fourth generation your **d** will come NIH
15:18 "To your **d** I give this land, 2446
16:10 "I will so increase your **d** that they will 2446
17: 7 between me and you and your **d** after you 2446
17: 7 to be your God and the God of your **d** 2446
17: 8 an everlasting possession to you and your **d** 2446
17: 9 you and your **d** after you for the generations 2446
17:10 and your **d** after you, the covenant you are 2446
17:19 an everlasting covenant for his **d** after him. 2446
21:23 with me or my children or my **d.** 5781
22:17 and make your **d** as numerous as the stars 2446
22:17 Your **d** will take possession of the cities 2446
25: 3 the **d** *of* Dedan were the Asshurites, 1201
25: 4 All these were **d** *of* Keturah. 1201
25:18 His **d** settled in the area from Havilah NIH
26: 3 to you and your **d** I will give all these lands 2446
26: 4 I will make your **d** as numerous as the stars 2446
26:24 and will increase the number of your **d** for 2446
28: 4 and your **d** the blessing given to Abraham, 2446
28:13 and your **d** the land on which you are lying 2446
28:14 Your **d** will be like the dust of the earth, 2446
32:12 and will make your **d** like the sand of 2446
35:12 I will give this land to your **d** after you." 2446
36:15 These were the chiefs among Esau's **d:** 1201
46: 8 of Israel (Jacob and his **d**) who went 1201
46:26 *those who were* his **direct d,** 3655+3751
48: 4 as an everlasting possession to your **d** 2446
48:19 and his **d** will become a group of nations." 2446
Ex 1: 5 The **d** *of* Jacob numbered seventy in all; 3655+3751+5883
12:24 as a lasting ordinance for you and your **d.** 1201
28:43 be a lasting ordinance for Aaron and his **d.** 2446
29:29 to his **d** so that they can be anointed 1201
30:21 a lasting ordinance for Aaron and his **d** for 2446
32:13 'I will make your **d** as numerous as 2446
32:13 I will give your **d** all this land I promised 2446
33: 1 saying, 'I will give it to your **d.'** 2446
Lev 21:17 of your **d** who has a defect may come near 2446
22: 3 if any of your **d** is ceremonially unclean 2446
23:43 so your **d** will know that I had 1887
25:30 to the buyer and his **d.** 1887
Nu 1:20 the **d** *of* Reuben the firstborn son of Israel: 1201
1:22 From the **d** *of* Simeon: 1201
1:24 From the **d** *of* Gad: 1201
1:26 From the **d** *of* Judah: 1201
1:28 From the **d** *of* Issachar: 1201

Nu 1:30 From the **d** *of* Zebulun: 1201
1:32 From the **d** *of* Ephraim: 1201
1:34 From the **d** *of* Manasseh: 1201
1:36 From the **d** *of* Benjamin: 1201
1:38 From the **d** *of* Dan: 1201
1:40 From the **d** *of* Asher: 1201
1:42 From the **d** *of* Naphtali: 1201
9:10 'When any of you or your **d** are unclean 1887
13:22 Sheshai and Talmai, the **d** *of* Anak, lived. 3535
13:28 We even saw **d** *of* Anak there. 3535
13:33 (the **d** *of* Anak come from the Nephilim). 1201
14:24 and his **d** will inherit it. 2446
25:13 He and his **d** will have a covenant of 2446
26:5 The **d** *of* Reuben, the firstborn son 1201
26:12 The **d** *of* Simeon by their clans were: 1201
26:15 The **d** *of* Gad by their clans were: 1201
26:20 The **d** *of* Judah by their clans were: 1201
26:21 The **d** *of* Perez were: 1201
26:23 The **d** *of* Issachar by their clans were: 1201
26:26 The **d** *of* Zebulun by their clans were: 1201
26:28 The **d** *of* Joseph by their clans 1201
26:29 The **d** *of* Manasseh: 1201
26:30 These were the **d** *of* Gilead: 1201
26:35 the **d** *of* Ephraim by their clans: 1201
26:36 These were the **d** *of* Shuthelah: 1201
26:37 These were the **d** *of* Joseph by their clans. 1201
26:38 The **d** *of* Benjamin by their clans were: 1201
26:40 The **d** *of* Bela through Ard 1201
26:42 These were the **d** *of* Dan by their clans: 1201
26:44 The **d** *of* Asher by their clans were: 1201
26:45 and through the **d** *of* Beriah: 1201
26:48 The **d** *of* Naphtali by their clans were: 1201
32:39 The **d** *of* Makir son of Manasseh went 1201
32:40 the **d** *of* Manasseh, and they settled there. 1201
36:1 from the clans of the **d** *of* Joseph, 1201
36:5 of the **d** *of* Joseph is saying is right. 1201
36:12 within the clans of the **d** *of* Manasseh son 1201
Dt 1:8 and to their **d** after them." 2446
1:36 and his **d** the land he set his feet on, 1201
2:4 the territory of your brothers the **d** *of* Esau, 1201
2:8 we went on past our brothers the **d** *of* Esau, 1201
2:9 I have given Ar to the **d** *of* Lot as 1201
2:12 but the **d** *of* Esau drove them out. 1201
2:19 I have given it as a possession to the **d** 1201
2:22 The LORD had done the same for the **d** 1201
2:29 as the **d** *of* Esau, who live in Seir, and 1201
4:37 and chose their **d** after them, 2446
10:15 their **d**, above all the nations, as it is today. 2446
11:9 to give to them and their **d**, 2446
17:20 Then he and his **d** will reign a long time 1201
18:5 and their **d** out of all your tribes to stand 1201
23:2 nor any of **his d** may enter the assembly of 2257S
23:3 or any of **his d** may enter the assembly of 2157S
28:46 and a wonder to you and your **d** forever. 2446
28:59 on you and your **d**, 2446
30:6 and the hearts of your **d**, 2446
31:21 because it will not be forgotten by their **d**. 2446
34:4 'I will give it to your **d**.' 2446
Jos 4:21 "In the future when your **d** ask their fathers, 1201
13:29 to half the family of the **d** *of* Manasseh, 1201
13:31 for the **d** *of* Makir son of Manasseh— 1201
15:14 and Talmai—**d** *of* Anak. 3535
16:4 Manasseh and Ephraim, the **d** *of* Joseph, 1201
17:2 the other male **d** *of* Manasseh son 1201
17:6 of Gilead belonged to the rest of the **d** 1201
21:4 The Levites who were **d** *of* Aaron 1201
21:5 of Kohath's **d** were allotted ten towns from 1201
21:6 The **d** *of* Gershon were allotted thirteen
towns 1201
21:7 The **d** *of* Merari, clan by clan, 1201
21:10 (these towns were assigned to the **d** 1201
21:13 the **d** *of* Aaron the priest they gave Hebron 1201
21:19 the **d** *of* Aaron, were thirteen, 1201
22:24 that some day your **d** might say to ours, 1201
22:25 So your **d** might cause ours to stop fearing 1201
22:27 in the future your **d** will not be able to say 1201
22:28 'If they ever say this to us, or to our **d**, 1887
24:3 throughout Canaan and gave him many **d**. 2446
24:32 This became the inheritance of Joseph's **d**. 1201
Jdg 1:16 The **d** *of* Moses' father-in-law, the Kenite, 1201
3:2 (he did this only to teach warfare to the **d** 1887
4:11 the **d** *of* Hobab, Moses' brother-in-law, 1201
1Sa 2:33 all your **d** will die in the prime of life. 1074+5270
20:42 and between your **d** 2446
20:42 and my **d** forever.' " 2446
24:21 the LORD that you will not cut off my **d** 2446
2Sa 19:28 All my grandfather's **d** deserved nothing 1074
21:6 let seven of his male **d** be given to us to 1201
21:16 And Ishbi-Benob, one of the **d** *of* Rapha, 3535
21:18 one of the **d** *of* Rapha. 3535
21:22 These four *were* **d** of Rapha in Gath, 3528
22:51 to David and his **d** forever." 2446
1Ki 2:4 'If your **d** watch how they live, 1201
2:33 on the head of Joab and his **d** forever. 2446
2:33 But on David and his **d**, 2446
9:21 their **d** remaining in the land, 1201
11:39 I will humble David's **d** because of this, 2446
21:21 I will consume your **d** and cut off 339
2Ki 5:27 to you and to your **d** forever." 2446
8:19 a lamp for David and his **d** forever. 1201
10:30 your **d** will sit on the throne of Israel to 1201
15:12 "Your **d** will sit on the throne of Israel to 1201
17:34 and commands that the LORD gave the **d** 1201
20:18 And some of your **d**, 1201
1Ch 1:29 These were their **d**: 9352
1:33 All these were **d** *of* Keturah. 1201
2:23 All these were **d** *of* Makir the father 1201

1Ch 2:33 These were the **d** *of* Jerahmeel. 1201
2:50 These were the **d** *of* Caleb. 1201
2:52 The **d** of Shobal the father 1201
2:54 The **d** *of* Salma: 1201
3:17 The **d** *of* Jehoiachin the captive: 1201
3:21 The **d** *of* Hananiah: 1201
3:22 The **d** *of* Shecaniah: 1201
4:1 The **d** *of* Judah: 1201
4:4 These were the **d** *of* Hur, 1201
4:6 These were the **d** *of* Naarah. 1201
4:20 The **d** *of* Ishi: Zoheth and Ben-Zoheth. 1201
4:24 The **d** *of* Simeon: 1201
4:26 The **d** *of* Mishma: 1201
5:4 The **d** *of* Joel: 1201
6:22 The **d** *of* Kohath: 1201
6:25 The **d** *of* Elkanah: Amasai, Ahimoth, 1201
6:29 The **d** *of* Merari: 1201
6:49 But Aaron and his **d** were 1201
6:50 These were the **d** *of* Aaron: 1201
6:54 to the **d** *of* Aaron who were from 1201
6:57 the **d** *of* Aaron were given Hebron (a city 1201
6:61 of Kohath's **d** were allotted ten towns from 1201
6:62 The **d** *of* Gershon, clan by clan, 1201
6:63 The **d** *of* Merari, clan by clan, 1201
7:2 the **d** of Tola listed as fighting men NIH
7:12 The Shuppites and Huppites were the **d** 1201
7:12 and the Hushites the **d** *of* Aher. 1201
7:13 the **d** *of* Bilhah. 1201
7:14 The **d** *of* Manasseh: 1201
7:20 The **d** *of* Ephraim: 1201
7:29 The **d** *of* Joseph son of Israel lived 1201
7:40 All these were **d** *of* Asher— 1201
8:6 These were the **d** *of* Ehud, 1201
8:40 All these were the **d** *of* Benjamin. 1201
9:23 They and their **d** were in charge of guarding 1201
15:4 He called together the **d** *of* Aaron and 1201
15:5 From the **d** *of* Kohath, Uriel the leader 1201
15:6 from the **d** *of* Merari, Asaiah the leader 1201
15:7 from the **d** *of* Gershon, Joel the leader 1201
15:8 the **d** *of* Elizaphan, Shemaiah the leader 1201
15:9 from the **d** *of* Hebron, Eliel the leader 1201
15:10 from the **d** *of* Uzziel, 1201
16:13 O **d** *of* Israel his servant, 2446
20:4 one of the **d** *of* the Rephaites, 3535
20:8 These *were* **d** of Rapha in Gath, 3528
23:13 Aaron was set apart, he and his **d** forever, 1201
23:16 The **d** *of* Gershom: Shubael was the first. 1201
23:17 The **d** *of* Eliezer: Rehabiah was the first. 1201
23:24 the **d** *of* Levi by their families— 1201
23:28 of the Levites was to help Aaron's **d** in 1201
23:32 under their brothers the **d** *of* Aaron, 1201
24:4 among Eleazar's **d** than among Ithamar's, 1201
24:4 sixteen heads of families from Eleazar's **d** 1201
24:4 of families from Ithamar's **d**. 1201
24:5 among the **d** *of* both Eleazar and Ithamar. 1201
24:20 As for the rest of the **d** *of* Levi: 1201
24:31 just as their brothers the **d** *of* Aaron did, 1201
26:8 All these were **d** *of* Obed-Edom; 1201
26:8 **d** of Obed-Edom, 62 in all. NIH
26:19 the divisions of the gatekeepers who were **d** 1201
26:21 The **d** *of* Ladan, 1201
28:8 on as an inheritance to your **d** forever. 1201
2Ch 8:8 their **d** remaining in the land, 1201
13:5 to David and his **d** forever by a covenant 1201
13:8 which is in the hands of David's **d**. 1201
20:7 to the **d** *of* Abraham your friend? 2446
21:7 a lamp for him and his **d** forever. 1201
23:3 as the LORD promised concerning the **d** 1201
26:18 That is for the priests, the **d** *of* Aaron 1201
29:13 from the **d** *of* Elizaphan, Shimri and Jeiel; 1201
29:13 from the **d** *of* Asaph, 1201
29:14 from the **d** *of* Heman, Jehiel and Shimei; 1201
29:14 from the **d** *of* Jeduthun, 1201
29:21 the **d** *of* Aaron, 1201
31:19 As for the priests, the **d** *of* Aaron, 1201
32:33 the hill where the tombs of David's **d** are. 1201
35:14 because the priests, the **d** *of* Aaron, 1201
35:15 The musicians, the **d** *of* Asaph, 1201
Ezr 2:3 the **d** *of* Parosh 2,172 1201
2:36 the **d** *of* Jedaiah (through the family 1201
2:40 the **d** *of* Jeshua and Kadmiel (through 1201
2:41 The singers: the **d** *of* Asaph 128 1201
2:42 the **d** *of* Shallum, Ater, Talmon, Akkub, 1201
2:43 the **d** *of* Ziha, Hasupha, Tabbaoth, 1201
2:55 The **d** *of* the servants of Solomon: 1201
2:55 the **d** *of* Sotai, Hassophereth, Peruda, 1201
2:58 and the **d** *of* the servants of Solomon 392 1201
2:60 The **d** *of* Delaiah, Tobiah and Nekoda 652 1201
2:61 The **d** *of* Hobaiah, 1201
3:9 and Kadmiel and his sons (**d** *of* Hodaviah) 1201
8:2 of the **d** *of* Phinehas, Gershom; 1201
8:2 of the **d** *of* Ithamar, Daniel; 1201
8:2 of the **d** *of* David, 1201
8:3 of the **d** *of* Shecaniah; 1201
8:3 of the **d** *of* Parosh, Zechariah, 1201
8:4 of the **d** *of* Pahath-Moab, Eliehoenai son 1201
8:5 the **d** *of* Zattu, Shecaniah son of Jahaziel, 1201
8:6 of the **d** *of* Adin, Ebed son of Jonathan, and 1201
8:7 of the **d** *of* Elam, Jeshaiah son of Athaliah, 1201
8:8 of the **d** *of* Shephatiah, Zebadiah son 1201
8:9 of the **d** *of* Joab, Obadiah son of Jehiel, and 1201
8:10 the **d** *of* Bani, Shelomith son of Josiphiah, 1201
8:11 the **d** *of* Bebai, Zechariah son of Bebai, and 1201
8:12 the **d** *of* Azgad, Johanan son of Hakkatan, 1201
8:13 of the **d** *of* Adonikam, 1201
8:14 of the **d** *of* Bigvai, 1201
8:18 from the **d** *of* Mahli son of Levi, 1201

Ezr 8:19 with Jeshaiah from the **d** *of* Merari, 1201
10:2 one of the **d** *of* Elam, said to Ezra, 1201
10:18 Among the **d** *of* the priests, 1201
10:18 From the **d** *of* Jeshua son of Jozadak, 1201
10:20 From the **d** *of* Immer: 1201
10:21 From the **d** *of* Harim: 1201
10:22 From the **d** *of* Pashhur: 1201
10:25 From the **d** *of* Parosh: 1201
10:26 From the **d** *of* Elam: 1201
10:27 From the **d** *of* Zattu: 1201
10:28 From the **d** *of* Bebai: 1201
10:29 From the **d** *of* Bani: 1201
10:30 From the **d** *of* Pahath-Moab: 1201
10:31 From the **d** *of* Harim: 1201
10:33 From the **d** *of* Hashum: 1201
10:34 From the **d** *of* Bani: Maadai, Amram, Uel, 1201
10:38 From the **d** *of* Binnui: Shimei, 1201
10:43 From the **d** *of* Nebo: 1201
Ne 7:8 the **d** *of* Parosh 2,172 1201
7:39 the **d** *of* Jedaiah (through the family 1201
7:43 the **d** *of* Jeshua (through Kadmiel through 1201
7:44 The singers: the **d** *of* Asaph 148 1201
7:45 the **d** *of* Shallum, Ater, Talmon, Akkub, 1201
7:46 the **d** *of* Ziha, Hasupha, Tabbaoth, 1201
7:57 The **d** *of* the servants of Solomon: 1201
7:57 the **d** *of* Sotai, Sophereth, Perida, 1201
7:60 and the **d** *of* the servants of Solomon 392 1201
7:62 the **d** *of* Delaiah, Tobiah and Nekoda 642 1201
7:63 the **d** *of* Hobaiah, 1201
9:8 to give to his **d** the land of the Canaanites, 2446
11:3 and **d** *of* Solomon's servants lived in 1201
11:4 From the **d** *of* Judah: 1201
11:6 The **d** *of* Perez who lived 1201
11:7 From the **d** *of* Benjamin: 1201
11:22 Uzzi was one of Asaph's **d**, 1201
11:24 one of the **d** *of* Zerah son of Judah, 1201
11:31 The **d** *of* the Benjamites from Geba lived 1201
12:23 the **d** *of* Levi up to the time of Johanan son 1201
12:47 the Levites set aside the portion for the **d** 1201
Est 9:27 to establish the custom that they and their **d** 2446
9:28 the memory of them die out among their **d**. 2446
9:31 for themselves and their **d** in regard 2446
Job 5:25 and your **d** like the grass of the earth. 7368
18:19 He has no offspring or **d** among his people, 5781
Ps 18:50 to David and his **d** forever. 2446
21:10 You will destroy their **d** from the earth, 7262
22:23 All you **d** *of* Jacob, honor him! 2446
22:23 Revere him, all you **d** *of* Israel! 2446
25:13 and his **d** will inherit the land. 2446
77:15 the **d** *of* Jacob and Joseph. 1201
83:8 to lend strength to the **d** *of* Lot. 1201
102:28 their **d** will be established before you." 2446
105:6 O **d** *of* Abraham his servant, 2446
106:27 make their **d** fall among the nations 2446
109:13 May his **d** be cut off, 344
132:11 "One of your own **d** I will place on your
throne— 1061+7262
Isa 14:22 her offspring and **d**," declares the LORD. 5781
39:7 And some of your **d**, 1201
41:8 you **d** *of* Abraham my friend, 2446
44:3 and my blessing on your **d**. 7368
45:19 I have not said to Jacob's **d**, 2446
45:25 But in the LORD all the **d** *of* Israel will 2446
48:19 Your **d** would have been like the sand, 2446
53:8 And who can speak of his **d**? 1887
54:3 your **d** will dispossess nations and settle 2446
59:21 or from the mouths of their **d** from this time 2446
61:9 Their **d** will be known among the nations 2446
65:9 I will bring forth **d** from Jacob, 2446
65:23 they and their **d** with them. 7368
66:22 "so will your name and **d** endure. 2446
Jer 23:8 who brought the **d** *of* Israel up out of 2446
29:32 the Nehelamite and his **d**. 2446
30:10 your **d** from the land of their exile. 2446
31:36 the **d** *of* Israel ever cease to be a nation 2446
31:37 be searched out will I reject all the **d** 2446
33:22 I will make the **d** *of* David my servant and 2446
33:26 the **d** *of* Jacob and David my servant 2446
33:26 of his sons to rule over the **d** *of* Abraham, 2446
35:6 nor your **d** must ever drink wine. 1201
35:16 The **d** *of* Jonadab son 1201
46:27 your **d** from the land of their exile. 2446
Eze 20:5 with uplifted hand to the **d** *of* the house 2446
44:15 who are Levites and **d** *of* Zadok 1201
46:16 it will also belong to his **d**; 1201
Da 11:4 It will not go to his **d**, 344
Na 1:14 *"You will* **have** no **d** to bear your name. 2445
Mal 2:3 "Because of you I will rebuke your **d**; 2446
3:6 So you, O **d** *of* Jacob, are not destroyed. 1201
Mt 23:31 the **d** of those who murdered the prophets. *5626*
Lk 1:55 *to* Abraham and his **d** forever, *5065*
Jn 8:33 "We are Abraham's **d** *5065*
8:37 I know you are Abraham's **d**. *5065*
Ac 2:30 he would place one of his **d** on his throne.
2843+3836+4019
7:5 and his **d** after him would possess the land, *5065*
7:6 'Your **d** will be strangers in a country *5065*
8:33 Who can speak of his **d**? *1155*
13:23 "From this man's **d** God has brought *5065*
Ro 9:7 Nor because they are his **d** are they all
Abraham's children. *5065*
9:29 "Unless the Lord Almighty had left us **d**, *5065*
2Co 11:22 Are they Abraham's **d**? *5065*
Heb 2:16 it is not angels he helps, but Abraham's **d**. *5065*
6:14 bless you and **give you many d**." *4437+4437*
7:5 the **d** of Levi who become priests to collect *5626*
11:12 **came d** as numerous as the stars in the sky *1164*

DESCENDED (24) [DESCEND]

Ge 36:16 These were the **chiefs** *d from* Eliphaz AIT
36:17 These were the **chiefs** *d from* Reuel AIT
36:18 These were the **chiefs** *d from* Esau's wife AIT
36:40 These were the **chiefs** *d from* Esau, AIT
Ex 19:18 because the LORD **d** on it in fire. 3718
19:20 The LORD **d** to the top of Mount Sinai 3718
Jos 16: 3 **d** westward to the territory of 3718
2Sa 21:20 He also **was d** from Rapha. 3528
1Ki 18:31 one for each of the tribes **d** *from* Jacob, 1201
1Ch 2:53 From these **d** the Zorathites and Eshtaolites. 3655
20: 6 He also **was d** from Rapha. 3528
2Ch 34:12 Levites **d** from Merari, 1201
34:12 and Zechariah and Meshullam, **d** 1201
Ezr 2:59 that their families were **d** from Israel: 2446
Ne 7:61 that their families were **d** from Israel: 2446
10:38 A priest **d** *from* Aaron is to accompany 1201
Isa 57: 9 *you* **d** to the grave itself! 9164
Lk 3:22 the Holy Spirit **d** on him in bodily form like *2849*
Ro 9: 6 For not all who are **d from** Israel are Israel. *1666*
Eph 4: 9 that *he* also **d** to the lower, *2849*
4:10 He who **d** is the very one who ascended *2849*
2Ti 2: 8 raised from the dead, **d from** David. *1666+5065*
Heb 7: 5 their brothers *are* **d from** Abraham. *2002+4019*
7:14 For it is clear that our Lord **d** from Judah, *422*

DESCENDING (7) [DESCEND]

Ge 28:12 the angels of God were ascending and **d** 3718
1Sa 25:20 there were David and his men **d** toward her, 3718
SS 4: 1 like a flock of goats **d** from Mount Gilead. 1683
6: 5 like a flock of goats **d** from Gilead. 1683
Mt 3:16 the Spirit of God **d** like a dove and lighting *2849*
Mk 1:10 and the Spirit **d** on him like a dove. *2849*
Jn 1:51 and the angels of God ascending and **d** on *2849*

DESCENDS (1) [DESCEND]

Isa 34: 5 see, *it* **d** in judgment on Edom, 3718

DESCENT (7) [DESCEND]

Ge 10:32 according to their **lines of d,** 9352
Ne 9: 2 of Israelite **d** had separated themselves 2446
13: 3 from Israel all who were **of foreign d.** 6850
Eze 44:22 they may marry only virgins of Israelite **d** 2446
Da 9: 1 (a Mede by **d**), who was made ruler over 2446
Jn 1:13 children born not of **natural d,** *135*
Heb 7: 6 however, *did* not **trace** *his* **d** from Levi, *1156*

DESCRIBE (2) [DESCRIBED, DESCRIBES, DESCRIPTION, DESCRIPTIONS]

Eze 43:10 **d** the temple *to* the people of Israel, 5583
Mk 4:30 or what parable shall we use to **d** it? *NIG*

DESCRIBED (5) [DESCRIBE]

1Ki 4:33 *He* **d** plant life, from the cedar 1819
Ac 12:17 and **d** how the Lord had brought him out *1455*
15:14 Simon *has* **d** to us how God *2007*
Rev 22:18 to them, God will add to him the plagues **d** *1211*
22:19 which *are* **d** in this book. *1211*

DESCRIBES (1) [DESCRIBE]

Ro 10: 5 Moses **d** in this way the righteousness *1211*

DESCRIPTION (3) [DESCRIBE]

Jos 18: 4 a survey of the land and *to* **write a d** *of* it, 4180
18: 8 and make a survey of the land and **write a d** 4180
18: 9 *They* **wrote** its **d** on a scroll, town by town, 4180

DESCRIPTIONS (1) [DESCRIBE]

Jos 18: 6 After you *have* **written d** *of* the seven parts 4180

DESCRY (KJV) See SPY OUT

DESECRATE (10) [DESECRATED, DESECRATES, DESECRATING]

Lev 21:12 nor leave the sanctuary of his God or **d** it, 2725
21:23 and so **d** my sanctuary. 2725
22:15 The priests *must* not **d** the sacred offerings 2725
Dt 21:23 *You must* not **d** the land 3237
Eze 7:22 and *they will* **d** my treasured place; 2725
7:22 robbers will enter it and **d** it. 2725
24:21 I *am about to* **d** my sanctuary— 2725
Da 11:31 up *to* **d** the temple fortress and will abolish 2725
Mt 12: 5 the temple **d** the day and yet are innocent? *1014*
Ac 24: 6 and even tried *to* **d** the temple; *1014*

DESECRATED (17) [DESECRATE]

Lev 19: 8 because *he has* **d** what is holy to 2725
2Ki 23: 8 the priests from the towns of Judah and **d** 3237
23:10 *He* **d** Topheth, which was in the Valley 3237
23:13 also **d** the high places that were east 3237
Ps 106:38 and the land *was* **d** by their blood. 2866
Isa 47: 6 with my people and **d** my inheritance; 2725
Eze 7:24 and their sanctuaries *will* **be d.** 2725
20:13 and *they* utterly **d** my Sabbaths. 2725
20:16 not follow my decrees and **d** my Sabbaths. 2725
20:21 and *they* **d** my Sabbaths. 2725
20:24 and **d** my Sabbaths, 2725
22: 8 and **d** my Sabbaths. 2725
23:38 and **d** my Sabbaths. 2725
Eze 23:39 they entered my sanctuary and **d** it. 2725
25: 3 over my sanctuary when *it* **was d** and over 2725
28:18 dishonest trade you *have* **d** your sanctuaries. 2725
Mal 2:11 Judah *has* **d** the sanctuary the LORD loves, 2725

DESECRATES (1) [DESECRATE]

Ex 31:14 *Anyone who* **d** it must be put to death; 2725

DESECRATING (5) [DESECRATE]

Ne 13:17 **d** the Sabbath day? 2725
13:18 up more wrath against Israel by **d** 2725
Isa 56: 2 who keeps the Sabbath without **d** it, 2725
56: 6 the Sabbath without **d** it and who hold fast 2725
Eze 44: 7 **d** my temple while you offered me food, 2725

DESERT (312) [DESERTED, DESERTING, DESERTS]

Ge 14: 6 as far as El Paran near the **d.** 4497
16: 7 near a spring in the **d;** 4497
21:14 She went on her way and wandered in the **d** 4497
21:20 He lived in the **d** and became an archer. 4497
21:21 While he was living in the **D** *of* Paran, 4497
36:24 in the **d** while he was grazing the donkeys 4497
37:22 Throw him into this cistern here in the **d,** 4497
Ex 3: 1 and he led the flock to the far side of the **d** 4497
3:18 Let us take a three-day journey into the **d** 4497
4:27 "Go into the **d** to meet Moses." 4497
5: 1 a festival to me in the **d.'** " 4497
5: 3 into the **d** to offer sacrifices to 4497
7:16 so that they may worship me in the **d.** 4497
8:27 We must take a three-day journey into the **d** 4497
8:28 to the LORD your God in the **d,** 4497
13:18 So God led the people around by the **d** road 4497
13:20 at Etham on the edge of the **d.** 4497
14: 3 hemmed in by the **d.'** 4497
14:11 in Egypt that you brought us to the **d** 4497
14:12 to serve the Egyptians than to die in the **d!"** 4497
15:22 from the Red Sea and they went into the **D** 4497
15:22 For three days they traveled in the **d** 4497
16: 1 from Elim and came to the **D** *of* Sin, 4497
16: 2 In the **d** the whole community grumbled 4497
16: 3 into this **d** to starve this entire assembly 4497
16:10 they looked toward the **d,** 4497
16:14 on the ground appeared on the **d** floor. 4497
16:32 the **d** when I brought you out of Egypt.' " 4497
17: 1 from the **D** *of* Sin, 4497
18: 5 came to him in the **d,** 4497
19: 1 they came to the **D** *of* Sinai. 4497
19: 2 they entered the **D** *of* Sinai, 4497
19: 2 and Israel camped there in the **d** in front of 4497
23:31 and from the **d** to the River. 4497
Lev 7:38 in the **D** *of* Sinai. 4497
11:18 the white owl, the **d owl,** the osprey, 7684
16:10 by sending it into the **d** as a scapegoat. 4497
16:21 into the **d** in the care of a man appointed for 4497
16:22 and the man shall release it in the **d.** 4497
Nu 1: 1 in the Tent of Meeting in the **D** *of* Sinai on 4497
1:19 And so he counted them in the **D** *of* Sinai: 4497
3: 4 with unauthorized fire before him in the **D** 4497
3:14 The LORD said to Moses in the **D** 4497
9: 1 in the **D** *of* Sinai in the first month of 4497
9: 5 and they did so in the **D** *of* Sinai at twilight 4497
10:12 from the **D** *of* Sinai and traveled from place 4497
10:12 the cloud came to rest in the **D** *of* Paran. 4497
10:31 You know where we should camp in the **d,** 4497
12:16 and encamped in the **D** *of* Paran. 4497
13: 3 from the **D** *of* Paran. 4497
13:21 up and explored the land from the **D** *of* Zin 4497
13:26 at Kadesh in the **D** *of* Paran. 4497
14: 2 Or in this **d!** 4497
14:16 so he slaughtered them in the **d.'** 4497
14:22 and in the **d** but who disobeyed me 4497
14:25 and set out toward the **d** along the route to 4497
14:29 In this **d** your bodies will fall— 4497
14:32 But you—your bodies will fall in this **d.** 4497
14:33 until the last of your bodies lies in the **d.** 4497
14:35 They will meet their end in this **d;** 4497
15:32 While the Israelites were in the **d,** 4497
16:13 with milk and honey to kill us in the **d?** 4497
20: 1 at the **D** *of* Zin, 4497
20: 4 the LORD's community into this **d,** 4497
21: 5 up out of Egypt to die in the **d?** 4497
21:11 in the **d** that faces Moab toward the sunrise. 4497
21:13 in the **d** extending into Amorite territory. 4497
21:18 Then they went from the **d** to Mattanah, 4497
21:23 and marched out into the **d** against Israel. 4497
24: 1 but turned his face toward the **d.** 4497
26:64 when they counted the Israelites in the **D** 4497
26:65 surely die in the **d,** 4497
27: 3 "Our father died in the **d.** 4497
27:14 at the waters in the **D** *of* Zin, 4497
27:14 in the **D** *of* Zin.) 4497
32:13 in the **d** forty years, 4497
32:15 he will again leave all this people in the **d,** 4497
33: 6 on the edge of the **d.** 4497
33: 8 and passed through the sea into the **d,** 4497
33: 8 for three days in the **D** *of* Etham, 4497
33:11 They left the Red Sea and camped in the **D** 4497
33:12 the **D** *of* Sin and camped at Dophkah. 4497
33:15 They left Rephidim and camped in the **D** 4497
33:16 They left the **D** *of* Sinai and camped 4497
33:36 in the **D** *of* Zin. 4497
34: 3 of the **D** *of* Zin along the border of Edom. 4497
Dt 1: 1 to all Israel in the **d** east of the Jordan— 4497
Dt 1:19 that vast and dreadful **d** that you have seen, 4497
1:31 and in the **d.** There you saw 4497
1:40 turn around and set out toward the **d** along 4497
2: 1 toward the **d** along the route to the Red Sea, 4497
2: 7 over your journey through this vast **d.** 4497
2: 8 and traveled along the **d** road of Moab. 4497
2:26 From the **d** *of* Kedemoth I sent messengers 4497
4:43 Bezer in the **d** plateau, for the Reubenites; 4497
8: 2 the way in the **d** these forty years, 4497
8:15 He led you through the vast and dreadful **d,** 4497
8:16 He gave you manna to eat in the **d,** 4497
9: 7 the LORD your God to anger in the **d.** 4497
9:28 to put them to death in the **d.'** 4497
11: 5 in the **d** until you arrived at this place, 4497
11:24 Your territory will extend from the **d** 4497
14:17 the **d owl,** the osprey, the cormorant, 7684
29: 5 the forty years that I led you through the **d,** 4497
32:10 In a **d** land he found him, 4497
32:51 at the waters of Meribah Kadesh in the **D** 4497
Jos 1: 4 the **d** to Lebanon, and from the great river, 4497
5: 4 in the **d** on the way after leaving Egypt. 4497
5: 5 the people born in the **d** during the journey 4497
5: 6 the **d** forty years until all the men who were 4497
8:15 and they fled toward the **d.** 4497
8:20 toward the **d** had turned back 4497
8:24 and in the **d** where they had chased them, 4497
12: 8 the mountain slopes, the **d** and the Negev— 4497
14:10 while Israel moved about in the **d.** 4497
15: 1 to the **D** *of* Zin in the extreme south. 4497
15:61 In the **d:** Beth Arabah, Middin, Secacah, 4497
16: 1 and went up from there through the **d** into 4497
18:12 coming out at the **d** *of* Beth Aven. 4497
20: 8 of Jericho they designated Bezer in the **d** on 4497
24: 7 Then you lived in the **d** for a long time. 4497
Jdg 1:16 to live among the people of the **D** *of* Judah 4497
8: 7 I will tear your flesh with **d** thorns 4497
8:16 by punishing them with **d** thorns and briers. 4497
11:16 Israel went through the **d** to the Red Sea 4497
11:18 "Next they traveled through the **d,** 4497
11:22 to the Jabbok and from the **d** to the Jordan. 4497
20:42 the Israelites in the direction of the **d,** 4497
20:45 As they turned and fled toward the **d** to 4497
20:47 and fled into the **d** to the rock of Rimmon, 4497
1Sa 4: 8 with all kinds of plagues in the **d.** 4497
13:18 the Valley of Zeboim facing the **d.** 4497
17:28 with whom did you leave those few sheep in the **d?** 4497
23:14 David stayed in the **d** strongholds and in 4497
23:14 and in the hills of the **D** *of* Ziph 4497
23:15 David was at Horesh in the **D** *of* Ziph, 4497
23:24 David and his men were in the **D** *of* Maon, 4497
23:25 to the rock and stayed in the **D** *of* Maon. 4497
23:25 into the **D** *of* Maon in pursuit of David. 4497
24: 1 "David is in the **D** *of* En Gedi." 4497
25: 1 David moved down into the **D** *of* Maon. 4497
25: 4 While David was in the **d,** 4497
25:14 from the **d** to give our master his greetings, 4497
25:21 in the **d** so that nothing of his was missing. 4497
26: 2 So Saul went down to the **D** *of* Ziph, 4497
26: 3 but David stayed in the **d.** 4497
2Sa 15:23 and all the people moved on toward the **d.** 4497
15:28 at the fords in the **d** until word comes 4497
16: 2 to refresh those who become exhausted in the **d."** 4497
17:16 not spend the night at the fords in the **d;** 4497
17:29 and tired and thirsty in the **d."** 4497
1Ki 2:34 and he was buried on his own land in the **d.** 4497
9:18 and Tadmor in the **d,** within his land, 4497
19: 4 he himself went a day's journey into the **d.** 4497
19:15 and go to the **D** *of* Damascus. 4497
2Ki 3: 8 "Through the **D** *of* Edom," he answered. 4497
1Ch 5: 9 of the **d** that extends to the Euphrates River, 4497
6:78 of Jericho they received Bezer in the **d,** 4497
12: 8 to David at his stronghold in the **d.** 4497
21:29 which Moses had made in the **d,** 4497
2Ch 1: 3 the LORD's servant had made in the **d.** 4497
8: 4 in the **d** and all the store cities he had built 4497
20:16 at the end of the gorge in the **D** *of* Jeruel. 4497
20:20 in the morning they left for the **D** *of* Tekoa. 4497
20:24 to the place that overlooks the **d** and looked 4497
24: 9 of God had required of Israel in the **d.** 4497
26:10 in the **d** and dug many cisterns, 4497
Ne 9:17 Therefore *you did* not **d** them, 6440
9:19 not abandon them in the **d.** 4497
9:21 For forty years you sustained them in the **d;** 4497
Job 1:19 in from the **d** and struck the four corners of 4497
24: 5 Like wild donkeys in the **d,** 4497
38:26 a **d** with no one in it, 4497
Ps 29: 8 The voice of the LORD shakes the **d;** 4497
29: 8 the LORD shakes the **D** *of* Kadesh. 4497
55: 7 I would flee far away and stay in the **d;** 4497
63: T When he was in the **D** *of* Judah. 4497
65:12 The grasslands of the **d** overflow; 4497
72: 9 The **d tribes** will bow before him 7470
74:14 as food to the **creatures of the d.** 7470
75: 6 the east or the west or from the **d** can exalt 4497
78:15 the **d** and gave them water as abundant as 4497
78:17 rebelling in the **d** against the Most High. 7480
78:19 saying, "Can God spread a table in the **d?** 4497
78:40 in the **d** and grieved him in the wasteland! 4497
78:52 he led them like sheep through the **d.** 4497
95: 8 as you did that day at Massah in the **d,** 4497
102: 6 I am like a **d** owl, 4497
105:41 like a river it flowed in the **d.** 7480
106: 9 through the depths as through a **d.** 4497
106:14 In the **d** they gave in to their craving; 4497
106:26 that he would make them fall in the **d,** 4497

Ps 107: 4 Some wandered in **d** wastelands, 4497
107:33 He turned rivers into a **d**, 4497
107:35 He turned the **d** into pools of water and 4497
136:16 to him who led his people through the **d**, 4497
Pr 21:19 Better to live in a **d** than with 824+4497
SS 3: 6 up from the **d** like a column of smoke, 4497
8: 5 Who is this coming up from the **d** leaning 4497
Isa 13:21 But **d creatures** will lie there, 7470
14:17 the man who made the world a **d**, 4497
16: 1 from Sela, across the **d**, 4497
16: 8 and spread toward the **d**. 4497
21: 1 An oracle concerning the **D** *by* the Sea: 4497
21: 1 an invader comes from the **d**, 4497
23:13 a place for **d creatures**; 7470
25: 5 and like the heat of the **d**. 7481
27:10 forsaken like the **d**; 4497
32: 2 in the **d** and the shadow of a great rock in 7481
32:15 and the **d** becomes a fertile field, 4497
32:16 in the **d** and righteousness live in 4497
34:11 The **d owl** and screech owl will possess it; 7684
34:14 **D creatures** will meet with hyenas, 7470
35: 1 The **d** and the parched land will be glad; 4497
35: 6 in the wilderness and streams in the **d**. 6858
40: 3 "In the **d** prepare the way for the LORD; 4497
41:18 I will turn the **d** into pools of water, 4497
41:19 I will put in the **d** the cedar and the acacia, 4497
42:11 Let the **d** and its towns raise their voices; 4497
43:19 a way in the **d** and streams in the wasteland. 4497
43:20 in the **d** and streams in the wasteland, 4497
49:10 the **d heat** or the sun beat upon them. 9220
50: 2 I turn rivers into a **d**; 4497
64:10 Your sacred cities have become a **d**; 4497
64:10 even Zion is a **d**, Jerusalem a desolation. 4497
Jer 2: 2 and followed me through the **d**, 4497
2:24 a wild donkey accustomed to the **d**, sniffing 4497
2:31 a **d** to Israel or a land of great darkness? 4497
3: 2 sat like a nomad in the **d**, 4497
4:11 in the **d** blows toward my people, but not 4497
4:26 I looked, and the fruitful land was a **d**; 4497
5: 6 a wolf from the **d** will ravage them, 6858
9: 2 in the **d** a lodging place for travelers, so 4497
9:10 up a lament concerning the **d** pastures. 4497
9:12 the land been ruined and laid waste like a **d** 4497
9:26 and all who live in the **d** in distant places. 4497
12:12 the **d** destroyers will swarm, for the sword 4497
13:24 like chaff driven by the **d** wind. 4497
17: 6 in the parched places of the **d**, 4497
17:11 his life is half gone, *they will* **d** him, 6440
22: 6 I will surely make you like a **d**, 4497
23:10 and the pastures in the **d** are withered. 4497
25:24 of the foreign people who live in the **d**; 4497
31: 2 the sword will find favor in the **d**; 4497
48: 6 become like a bush in the **d**. 4497
50:12 a wilderness, a dry land, a **d**. 6858
50:39 "So **d creatures** and hyenas will live there, 7470
51:43 a dry and **d** land, a land where no one lives, 6858
La 4: 3 like ostriches in the **d**. 4497
4:19 and lay in wait for us in the **d**. 4497
5: 9 of our lives because of the sword in the **d**. 4497
Eze 6:14 a desolate waste from the **d** to Diblah— 4497
19:13 Now it is planted in the **d**, 4497
20:10 of Egypt and brought them into the **d**. 4497
20:13 of Israel rebelled against me in the **d**. 4497
20:13 on them and destroy them in the **d**. 4497
20:15 to them in the **d** that I would not bring them 4497
20:17 or put an end to them in the **d**. 4497
20:18 I said to their children in the **d**, 4497
20:21 and spend my anger against them in the **d**. 4497
20:23 to them in the **d** that I would disperse them 4497
20:35 I will bring you into the **d** *of* the nations 4497
20:36 As I judged your fathers in the **d** *of* 4497
23:42 from the **d** along with men from the rabble, 4497
29: 5 I will leave you in the **d**, 4497
34:25 of wild beasts so that they may live in the **d** 4497
Hos 2: 3 I will make her like a **d**, 4497
2:14 I will lead her into the **d** and speak tenderly 4497
9:10 it was like finding grapes in the **d**; 4497
13: 5 I cared for you in the **d**, 4497
13:15 blowing in from the **d**; 4497
Joel 2: 3 a **d** waste—nothing escapes them. 4497
3:19 Egypt will be desolate, Edom a **d** waste, 4497
Am 2:10 the **d** to give you the land of the Amorites. 4497
5:25 and offerings forty years in the **d**, 4497
Hab 1: 9 like a **d wind** and gather prisoners like sand. 7708
Zep 2:13 and dry as the **d**. 4497
2:14 The **d owl** and the screech owl will roost 7684
Mal 1: 3 and left his inheritance to the **d** jackals." 4497
Mt 3: 1 preaching in the **D** of Judea 2245
3: 3 "A voice of one calling in the **d**, 2245
4: 1 Then Jesus was led by the Spirit into the **d** 2245
11: 7 "What did you go out into the **d** to see? 2245
24:26 anyone tells you, 'There he is, out in the **d**,' 2245
Mk 1: 3 "a voice of one calling in the **d**, 2245
1: 4 in the **d region** and preaching a baptism 2245
1:12 At once the Spirit sent him out into the **d**, 2245
1:13 and he was in the **d** forty days, 2245
Lk 1:80 in the **d** until he appeared publicly to Israel. 2245
3: 2 to John son of Zechariah in the **d**. 2245
3: 4 "A voice of one calling in the **d**, 2245
4: 1 and was led by the Spirit in the **d**, 2245
7:24 "What did you go out into the **d** to see? 2245
Jn 1:23 "I am the voice of one calling in the **d**, 2245
3:14 Just as Moses lifted up the snake in the **d**, 2245
6:31 Our forefathers ate the manna in the **d**; 2245
6:49 Your forefathers ate the manna in the **d**, 2245
11:54 Instead he withdrew to a region near the **d**, 2245
Ac 7:30 a burning bush in the **d** near Mount Sinai. 2245
Ac 7:36 at the Red Sea and for forty years in the **d**. 2245
7:38 He was in the assembly in the **d**, 2245
7:42 and offerings forty years in the **d**, 2245
7:44 of the Testimony with them in the **d**. 2245
8:26 to the road—the **d** road— 2245
13:18 for about forty years in the **d**, 2245
21:38 into the **d** some time ago?" 2245
1Co 10: 5 their bodies were scattered over the **d**. 2245
Heb 3: 8 during the time of testing in the **d**, 2245
3:17 whose bodies fell in the **d**? 2245
Rev 12: 6 the **d** to a place prepared for her by God, 2245
12:14 to the place prepared for her in the **d**, 2245
17: 3 angel carried me away in the Spirit into a **d**. 2245

DESERTED (34) [DESERT]

Lev 26:22 in number that your roads *will be* **d**. 9037
26:43 *be* **d** by them and will enjoy its sabbaths 6440
Dt 32:18 *You* **d** the Rock, who fathered you; 8861
Jos 22: 3 not **d** your brothers but have carried out 6440
2Sa 20: 2 Israel **d** David to follow Sheba 339+4946+6590
Ezr 9: 9 our God *has* not **d** us in our bondage. 6440
Ps 69:25 May their place be **d**; 9037
Isa 6:11 the houses are left **d** and the fields ruined 132+401+4946
17: 2 cities of Aroer *will be* **d** and left to flocks, 6440
32:14 the noisy city **d**; 6440
33: 8 The highways *are* **d**, 9037
54: 6 as if you were a wife **d** and distressed 6440
62: 4 No longer will they call you **D**, 6440
62:12 the City No *Longer* **D**. 6440
Jer 2:15 his towns are burned and **d**. 1172+3782+4946
4:29 All the towns *are* **d**; no one lives in them. 6440
26: 9 this city will be desolate and **d**?" 401+3782+4946
33:10 and the streets of Jerusalem that *are* **d**, 9037
38:22 your friends *have* **d** you.' 294+6047
44: 2 Today they *lie* **d** and in ruins 401+3782
La 1: 1 How **d** lies the city, once so full of people! 970
Eze 14: 5 who *have* all **d** me for their idols.' 2319
36: 4 and the **d** towns that have been plundered 6440
Hos 4:10 but not increase, because *they have* **d** 6440
Am 5: 2 never to rise again, **d** in her own land, 5759
Zep 3: 6 *I have* **left** their streets **d**, 2990
Zec 9: 5 and Ashkelon *will be* **d**. 3782+4202
Mt 26:56 Then all the disciples **d** him and fled. 918
Mk 14:50 Then everyone **d** him and fled. 918
Ac 1:20 " 'May his place be **d**; 2245
15:38 *because he had* **d** them in Pamphylia 918
2Ti 1:15 in the province of Asia *has* **d** me, 695
4:10 *has* **d** me and has gone to Thessalonica. 1593
4:16 but everyone **d** me. 1593

DESERTING (3) [DESERT]

Jer 37:13 "You *are* **d** to the Babylonians!" 5877
37:14 "I *am* not **d** to the Babylonians." 5877
Gal 1: 6 I am astonished that *you are* so quickly **d** the one who called you 608+3572

DESERTS (8) [DESERT]

1Ch 12:19 "It will cost us our heads *if he* **d** 5877
Pr 19: 4 but a poor man's friend **d** him. 7233
Isa 48:21 not thirst when he led them through the **d**; 2999
51: 3 he will make her **d** like Eden, 4497
Jer 2: 6 through a land of **d** and rifts, 6858
14: 5 the doe in the field **d** her newborn fawn 6440
Zec 11:17 *who* **d** the flock! 6440
Heb 11:38 They wandered in **d** and mountains, 2244

DESERVE (30) [DESERVED, DESERVES, DESERVING]

Ge 40:15 *to d being* **put** in a dungeon." AIT
Lev 26:21 seven times over, **as** your sins **d**. 3869
Jdg 20:10 it can give them **what** they **d for** 3869
1Sa 26:16 LORD lives, you and your men **d to** die, 1201
1Ki 2:26 You **d to** die, 408
Ps 28: 4 and bring back upon them **what** they **d**. 1691
94: 2 pay back to the proud **what** they **d**. 1691
103:10 he does not treat **us** as our sins **d** 5646
Pr 3:27 Do not withhold good from **those who d** it, 1251
Ecc 8:14 righteous men who get **what** the wicked **d**, 3869+5126
8:14 and wicked men who get **what** the righteous **d**. 3869+5126
Isa 66: 6 LORD repaying his enemies *all* they **d**. 1691
Jer 14:16 on them the **calamity** they *d*. AIT
17:10 according to **what** his deeds **d**." 7262
21:14 I will punish you as your deeds **d**, 7262
32:19 according to his conduct and as his deeds **d**. 7262
49:12 not **d** to drink the cup must drink it, 5477
La 3:64 Pay them back **what** they **d**, O LORD, 1691
Eze 16:59 I will deal with you as *you* **d**, 6913
Zec 1: 6 **what** our ways and practices **d**, 3869
Mt 8: 8 not **d** to have you come under my roof 1639+2653
22: 8 but those I invited *did* not **d** to come. 545+1639
Lk 7: 6 "Lord, don't trouble yourself, for *I do* not **d** to have you come 1639+2653
23:15 he has done nothing *to* **d** death. 545
23:41 for we are getting what our deeds **d**. 545
Ro 1:32 that those who do such things **d** death, 545+1639
1Co 15: 9 the apostles and do not even **d** to be called 2653
16:18 Such men *d* **recognition**. AIT
2Co 11:15 Their end will be *what* their **actions d**. 2240+2848
Rev 16: 6 given them blood to drink as *they* **d**." 545+1639

DESERVED (5) [DESERVE]

2Sa 19:28 All my grandfather's descendants **d** nothing 408
Ezr 9:13 punished us less **than** our sins have **d** 4946
Job 33:27 but I *did* not **get what** I **d**. 8750
Ac 23:29 against him that **d** death or imprisonment. 545
Ro 3: 8 Their condemnation is **d**. 1899

DESERVES (14) [DESERVE]

Nu 35:31 who **d** to die. 8401
Dt 25: 2 If the guilty man **d** to be beaten, 1201
25: 2 with the number of lashes his crime **d**, 1896+3869
Jdg 9:16 and if you have treated him as he **d**— 1691+3338
2Sa 12: 5 the man who did this **d to** die! 1201
Job 34:11 he brings upon him **what** his conduct **d**. 3869
Jer 51: 6 he will pay her **what** she **d**. 1691
Lk 7: 4 "This *man* **d** to have you do this, 545+1639
10: 7 for the worker **d** his wages. 545
Ac 26:31 not doing anything that **d** death 545
1Ti 1:15 a trustworthy saying that **d** full acceptance: 545
4: 9 a trustworthy saying that **d** full acceptance 545
5:18 and "The worker **d** his wages." 545
Heb 10:29 a *man* **d** to be punished who has trampled 546

DESERVING (7) [DESERVE]

Dt 19: 6 kill him even though he is not **d** *of* death, 5477
22:26 she has committed no **sin d** death. AIT
Mt 10:13 If the home is **d**, let your peace rest on it; 545
Lk 12:48 and does *things* **d** punishment will 545
Ac 25:11 I am guilty of doing anything **d** death, 545
25:25 I found he had done nothing **d** of death, 545
28:18 not guilty of any crime **d** death. NIG

DESIGN (7) [DESIGNED, DESIGNER, DESIGNERS, DESIGNS]

1Ki 7: 8 set farther back, was similar in **d**. 5126
2Ch 2:14 of engraving and can execute any **d** given 4742
24:13 of God according to its **original d** 5504
Eze 43:11 make known to them the **d** *of* the temple— 7451
43:11 its whole **d** and all its regulations and laws. 7451
43:11 to its **d** and follow all its regulations. 7451
Ac 17:29 an image made by man's **d** and skill. 1927

DESIGNATE (3) [DESIGNATED, DESIGNATING]

Ex 21:13 he is to flee to a place *I will* **d**. 8492
Dt 23:12 **D** a place outside the camp 2118
Jos 20: 2 "Tell the Israelites *to* **d** the cities of refuge, 5989

DESIGNATED (14) [DESIGNATE]

Jos 20: 8 of the Jordan of Jericho *they* **d** Bezer in 5989
20: 9 to these **d** cities and not be killed by 4597
2Sa 24:15 that morning until the end of the time **d**, 4595
1Ch 12:31 **d** by name to come and make David king— 5918
16:41 and the rest of those chosen and **d** by name 5918
28:14 He **d** the weight of gold for all NIH
2Ch 28:15 The men **d** by name took the prisoners, 5918
31:19 men **were d** by name to distribute portions 5918
Ezr 10:16 and all of them **d** by name. NIH
Ne 13:31 for contributions of wood at **d** times, 2374
Est 9:31 of Purim at their **d times**, 2375
Eze 43:21 for the sin offering and burn it in the **d part** 5152
Lk 6:13 whom *he* also **d** apostles: 3951
Heb 5:10 **d** by God **to be** high priest in the order 4641

DESIGNATING (1) [DESIGNATE]

Mk 3:14 He appointed twelve—**d** them apostles— 3951

DESIGNED (1) [DESIGN]

2Ch 26:15 In Jerusalem he made machines **d** 4742

DESIGNER (1) [DESIGN]

Ex 38:23 a craftsman and **d**, 3110

DESIGNERS (2) [DESIGN]

Ex 35:35 **d**, embroiderers in blue, 3110
35:35 all of them master craftsmen and **d**. 3110+4742

DESIGNS (3) [DESIGN]

Ex 31: 4 to make **artistic d** for work in gold, 4742
35:32 to make **artistic d** for work in gold, 4742
2Ch 3: 5 **palm tree** and chain **d**. 9474

DESIRABLE (3) [DESIRE]

Ge 3: 6 and also **d** for gaining wisdom, 2773
Pr 22: 1 A good name *is* more **d** than great riches; 1047
Jer 3:19 like sons and give you a **d** land, 2775

DESIRE (56) [DESIRABLE, DESIRED, DESIRES]

Ge 3:16 Your **d** will be for your husband, 9592
Dt 5:21 not **set** *your* **d on** your neighbor's house 203
1Sa 9:20 And to whom is all the **d** *of* Israel turned, 2775
2Sa 19:38 anything *you* **d** from me I will do for you." 1047
23: 5 and grant me my every **d**? 2914
1Ch 29:18 keep this **d** *in* the hearts 3671+4742
2Ch 1:11 "Since this is your heart's **d** and you have 6640
9: 8 for Israel and his **d** to uphold them forever, NIH
Job 13: 3 But I **d** to speak to the Almighty and 2911

Job 21:14 *We* **have** no **d** to know your ways. 2911
Ps 10:17 You hear, O LORD, the **d** *of* the afflicted; 9294
20: 4 May he give you the **d** *of* your heart 3869
21: 2 You have granted him the **d** *of* his heart 9294
27:12 Do not turn me over to the **d** *of* my foes, 5883
40: 6 Sacrifice and offering *you did* not **d**, 2911
40: 8 *I* **d** to do your will, O my God; 2911
40:14 may *all who* **d** my ruin be turned back 2913
41: 2 and not surrender him to the **d** *of* his foes. 5883
51: 6 Surely *you* **d** truth in the inner parts; 2911
70: 2 may *all who* **d** my ruin be turned back 2913
73:25 And earth has nothing *I* **d** besides you. 2911
Pr 3:15 nothing you **d** can compare with her. 2914
8:11 and nothing you **d** can compare with her. 2914
10:24 *what* the righteous **d** will be granted. 9294
11:23 The **d** *of* the righteous ends only in good, 9294
12:12 The wicked **d** the plunder of evil men, 2773
17:16 since he has no **d** to get wisdom? 4213
24: 1 *do* not **d** their company; 203
Ecc 12: 5 along and **d** no longer is stirred. 37
SS 6:12 my **d** set me among the royal chariots 5883
7:10 I belong to my lover, and his **d** is for me. 9592
Isa 26: 8 and renown are the **d** *of* our hearts. 9294
53: 2 in his appearance that *we should* **d** him. 2773
55:11 to me empty, but will accomplish what *I* **d** 2911
Eze 24:25 the delight of their eyes, their heart's **d**, 5362
Hos 6: 6 For *I* **d** mercy, not sacrifice, 2911
Mic 7: 3 the powerful dictate what they **d**— 2094
Mal 3: 1 whom you **d**, will come," 2913
Mt 9:13 '*I* **d** mercy, not sacrifice.' *2527*
12: 7 '*I* **d** mercy, not sacrifice,' *2527*
Jn 8:44 and you want to carry out your father's **d**. *2123*
Ro 7: 8 produced in me every kind of **covetous d**. *2123*
7:18 For I have the **d** to do what is good, *2527*
9:16 therefore, depend on man's **d** or effort, *2527*
10: 1 my heart's **d** and prayer to God for *2306*
1Co 12:31 But **eagerly d** the greater gifts. *2420*
14: 1 of love and **eagerly d** spiritual gifts, *2420*
2Co 8:10 to give but also *to* **have** the **d** to do so. *2527*
8:13 Our **d** is not that others might be relieved *NIG*
Php 1:23 I **d** to depart and be with Christ, *2123+2400*
Heb 10: 5 "Sacrifice and offering *you did* not **d**, *2527*
10: 8 and sin offerings *you did* not **d**, *2527*
13:18 a clear conscience and **d** to live honorably *2527*
Jas 1:14 by his own **evil d**, he is dragged away *2123*
1:15 after **d** has conceived, it gives birth to sin; *2123*
2Pe 2:10 of those who follow the corrupt **d** of *2123*

DESIRED (13) [DESIRE]

1Ki 9: 1 and had achieved all he had **d** to do, 2911+3139
9:19 whatever he **d** to build in Jerusalem, 3137+3139
10:13 the queen of Sheba all she **d** and asked for, 2914
2Ch 8: 6 whatever he **d** to build in Jerusalem, 3137+3139
9:12 the queen of Sheba all she **d** and asked for; 2914
Ps 107:30 and he guided them to their **d** haven. 2914
132:13 *he has* **d** it for his dwelling. 203
132:14 here I will sit enthroned, for *I have* **d** it— 203
Ecc 2:10 I denied myself nothing my eyes **d**; 8626
Jer 17:16 you know *I have* not **d** the day of despair. 203
Da 11:37 for the gods of his fathers or for the *one* **d** 2775
Hag 2: 7 and the **d** *of* all nations will come, 2775
Lk 22:15 "*I have* **eagerly d** to eat this Passover *2121+2123*

DESIRES (49) [DESIRE]

Ge 4: 7 it **d** to have you, but you must master it." 9592
41:16 the answer he **d**." 8934
2Sa 3:21 that you may rule over all that your heart **d**. 203
1Ki 11:37 and you will rule over all that your heart **d**; 203
Job 17:11 and so are the **d** *of* my heart. 4626
31:16 "If I have denied the **d** *of* the poor or let 2914
Ps 34:12 Whoever of you loves life and **d** 170
37: 4 and he will give you the **d** of you heart. 5399
103: 5 who satisfies your **d** with good things so 6344
140: 8 do not grant the wicked their **d**, O LORD; 4397
145:16 and satisfy the **d** of every living thing. 8356
145:19 He fulfills the **d** *of* those who fear him; 8356
Pr 11: 6 but the unfaithful are trapped by **evil d**. 2094
13: 4 but the **d** *of* the diligent are fully satisfied. 5883
19:22 *What* a man **d** is unfailing love; 9294
Ecc 6: 2 so that he lacks nothing his heart **d**, 203
SS 2: 7 Do not arouse or awaken love until *it so* **d**. 2911
3: 5 Do not arouse or awaken love until *it so* **d**. 2911
8: 4 Do not arouse or awaken love until *it so* **d**. 2911
Hab 2: 4 his **d** are not upright— 5883
Mk 4:19 of wealth and the **d** for other things come in *2123*
Ro 1:24 over in the **sinful d** of their hearts *2123*
6:12 so that you obey its **evil d**. *2123*
8: 5 on what that nature **d**; *NIG*
8: 5 on what the Spirit **d**. *NIG*
13:14 and do not think about how to gratify the **d** *2123*
Gal 5:16 not gratify the **d** of the sinful nature. *2123*
5:17 For the sinful nature **d** what is contrary to *2121*
5:24 the sinful nature with its passions and **d**. *2123*
Eph 2: 3 of our sinful nature and following its **d** *2525*
4:22 which is being corrupted by its deceitful **d**; *2123*
Col 3: 5 lust, evil **d** and greed, which is idolatry. *2123*
1Ti 3: 1 *he* **d** a noble task. *2121*
5:11 **sensual d overcome their dedication to** *2952*
6: 9 a trap and into many foolish and harmful **d** *2123*
2Ti 2:22 Flee the **evil d** of youth, *2123*
3: 6 and are swayed by all kinds of **evil d**, *2123*
4: 3 Instead, to suit their own **d**, *2123*
Jas 1:20 about the righteous life that God **d**. *NIG*
4: 1 Don't they come from your **d** that battle *2454*
1Pe 1:14 do not conform *to* the **evil d** you had *2123*
2:11 to abstain from sinful **d**, *2123*
4: 2 of his earthly life *for* **evil** human **d**, *2123*
2Pe 1: 4 in the world caused by **evil d**. *2123*
2:18 to the **lustful d** of sinful human nature, *816+2123*
3: 3 scoffing and following their own **evil d**. *2123*
1Jn 2:17 The world and its **d** pass away, *2123*
Jude 1:16 they follow their own **evil d**; *2123*
1:18 there will be scoffers who will follow their own ungodly **d**." *2123*

DESOLATE (83) [DESOLATION, DESOLATIONS]

Ge 47:19 and that the land *may* not *become* **d**." 9037
Ex 23:29 because the land would become **d** and 9039
Lev 26:34 that *it* **lies d** and you are in the country 9037
26:35 All the time *that it* **lies d**, 9037
26:43 and will enjoy its sabbaths while *it* **lies d** 9037
Jos 8:28 a **d place** to this day. 9039
2Sa 13:20 in her brother Absalom's house, a **d** *woman*. 9037
Job 30: 3 the parched land in **d** wastelands at night. 8739
38:27 to satisfy a **d** wasteland and make it sprout 8739
Isa 1: 7 Your country is **d**, your cities burned 9039
5: 9 "Surely the great houses will become **d**, 9014
13: 9 the land **d** and destroy the sinners within it. 9014
24:10 The ruined city *lies* **d**; 8689
27:10 The fortified city stands **d**, 970
34:10 to generation *it will lie* **d**; 2990
49: 8 the land and to reassign its **d** inheritances, 9037
49:19 "Though you were ruined and **made d** 9037
54: 1 of the **d** *woman* than of her who has 9037
54: 3 and settle in their **d** cities. 9037
62: 4 or name your land **D**. 9039
Jer 6: 8 and make your land **d** so no one can live 9039
7:34 for the land will become **d**. 2999
9:10 *They are* **d** and untraveled, 5898
10:22 It will make the towns of Judah **d**, 9039
12:10 into a **d** wasteland. 9039
12:11 parched and **d** before me; 9038
25:11 a **d** wasteland, and these nations will serve 2999
25:12 "and will make it **d** forever. 9039
25:38 and their land will become **d** because of 9014
26: 9 and this city *will be* **d** and deserted?" 2990
32:43 'It is a **d waste**, without men or animals, 9039
33:10 'You say about this place, "It is a **d waste**, 2992
33:12 **d** and without men or animals— 2992
44: 6 and made them the **d** ruins they are today. 2999
44:22 and a **d** waste without inhabitants, 2999
48: 9 her towns will become **d**, 9014
49:33 a **d place** forever. 9039
50:13 not be inhabited but will be completely **d**. 9039
50:23 How **d** is Babylon among the nations! 9014
51:26 for you will be **d** forever," 9039
51:43 Her towns will be **d**, a dry and desert land, 9014
51:62 it will be **d** forever.' 9039
La 1: 4 All her gateways are **d**, her priests groan, 9037
1:13 He made me **d**, faint all the day long. 9037
5:18 which **lies d**, with jackals prowling over it. 9037
Eze 6:14 and make the land a **d** waste from the desert 9039
12:20 be laid waste and the land will be **d**. 9039
14:15 and they leave it childless and it becomes **d** 9039
14:16 but the land would be **d**. 9039
15: 8 I will make the land **d** 9039
26:19 When I make you a **d** city, 2990
29: 9 Egypt will become a **d** wasteland. 9039
29:10 of Egypt a ruin and a **d** waste from Migdol 9039
29:12 of Egypt **d** among devastated lands, 9039
29:12 and her cities will lie **d** forty years 9039
30: 7 " '*They will be* **d** among desolate lands, 9037
30: 7 " 'They will be desolate among **d** lands, 9037
32:15 When I make Egypt **d** and strip the land 9039
33:28 I will make the land a **d** waste, 9039
33:28 and the mountains of Israel *will become* **d** 9037
33:29 when I have made the land a **d** waste 9039
35: 3 against you and make you a **d** waste. 9039
35: 4 into ruins and you will be **d**. 9039
35: 7 a **d** waste and cut off from it all who come 9040
35: 9 I will make you **d** forever; 9039
35:14 the whole earth rejoices, I will make you **d**. 9039
35:15 of the house of Israel *became* **d**, 9037
35:15 You will be **d**, O Mount Seir, 9039
36: 4 the ravines and valleys, to the **d** ruins and 9037
36:34 The **d** land will be cultivated instead 9037
36:34 be cultivated instead of lying **d** in the sight 9039
36:35 that were lying in ruins, **d** and destroyed, 9037
36:36 and have replanted what *was* **d**. 9037
38: 8 which had long been **d**. 2999
Da 9:17 look with favor on your **d** sanctuary. 9038
Joel 3:19 But Egypt will be **d**, Edom a desert waste, 9039
Mic 7:13 The earth will become **d** because 9039
Zep 2:13 leaving Nineveh **utterly d** and dry as 9039
Zec 7:14 The land **was left so d** behind them 9037
7:14 how they made the pleasant land **d**.' " 9014
Mt 23:38 Look, your house is left to you **d**. *2245*
Lk 13:35 Look, your house is left to you **d**. *2245*
Gal 4:27 *of* the **d** *woman* than of her who has *2245*

DESOLATION (14) [DESOLATE]

2Ch 36:21 all the time of its **d** it rested, 9014
Isa 17: 9 And all will be **d**. 9039
34:11 of chaos and the plumb line of **d**. 983
64:10 even Zion is a desert, Jerusalem a **d**. 9039
Eze 23:33 the cup of ruin and **d**, 9039
Da 8:13 the rebellion *that* **causes d**, 9037
9: 2 **d** *of* Jerusalem would last seventy years. 2999
9:18 open your eyes and see the **d** *of* the city 9037
9:27 set up an abomination *that* **causes d**, 9037
11:31 set up the abomination *that* **causes d**. 9037
12:11 and the abomination *that* **causes d** is set up, 9037
Mt 24:15 'the abomination that *causes* **d**,' spoken of *2247*
Mk 13:14 'the abomination that *causes* **d**' standing *2247*
Lk 21:20 you will know that its **d** is near. *2247*

DESOLATIONS (2) [DESOLATE]

Ps 46: 8 the **d** he has brought on the earth. 9014
Da 9:26 and **d** have been decreed. 9037

DESPAIR (12) [DESPAIRED, DESPAIRING, DESPAIRS]

1Sa 4:20 "Don't **d**; you have given birth to a son." 3707
Job 9:23 he mocks the **d** *of* the innocent. 5000
Ps 88:15 I have suffered your terrors and *am* **in d**. 7041
Ecc 2:20 to **d** over all my toilsome labor under 3286
Isa 19: 9 Those who work with combed flax *will* **d**, 1017
61: 3 a garment of praise instead of a spirit of **d**. 3910
Jer 17:16 you know I have not desired the day of **d**. 631
Eze 4:16 in anxiety and drink rationed water in **d**, 9041
7:27 the prince will be clothed with **d**, 9039
12:19 in anxiety and drink their water in **d**, 9041
Joel 1:11 **D**, you farmers, wail, you vine growers; 1017
2Co 4: 8 perplexed, but not **in d**; *1989*

DESPAIRED (1) [DESPAIR]

2Co 1: 8 so that we **d** even of life. *1989*

DESPAIRING (4) [DESPAIR]

Dt 28:65 eyes weary with longing, and a **d** heart. 1792
Job 6:14 "A **d man** should have the devotion 4988
6:26 and treat the words of a **d** *man* as wind? 3286
Jer 14: 3 dismayed and **d**, they cover their heads. 4007

DESPAIRS (1) [DESPAIR]

Job 15:22 *He* **d** *of* escaping the darkness; 586+4202

DESPERATE (4)

2Sa 12:18 He may do **something d**." 8288
Ps 60: 3 You have shown your people **d times**; 7997
79: 8 for we are in **d** need. 4394
142: 6 Listen to my cry, for I am in **d** need; 4394

DESPISE (34) [DESPISED, DESPISES]

Ge 16: 4 *she began to* **d** her mistress. 928+6524+7837
1Sa 2:30 but *those who* **d** me will be disdained. 1022
2Sa 12: 9 Why *did you* **d** the word of the LORD 1022
Est 1:17 and so they *will* **d** their husbands 928+1022+6524
Job 5:17 so *do* not **d** the discipline of the Almighty. 4415
7:16 *I* **d** my life; I would not live forever. 4415
9:21 *I* **d** my own life. 4415
36: 5 "God is mighty, but *does* not **d** men; 4415
42: 6 Therefore *I* **d** *myself* and repent in dust 4415
Ps 51:17 O God, *you will* not **d**. 1022
69:33 and *does* not **d** his captive people. 1022
73:20 O Lord, *you will* **d** them as fantasies. 1022
102:17 *he will* not **d** their plea. 1022
Pr 1: 7 but fools **d** wisdom and discipline. 1022
3:11 *do* not **d** the LORD's discipline and do 4415
6:30 *Men do* not **d** a thief if he steals 996
23:22 and *do* not **d** your mother when she is old. 996
SS 8: 1 I would kiss you, and no *one would* **d** me. 996
Isa 60:14 all *who* **d** you will bow down at your feet 5540
Jer 4:30 Your lovers **d** you; they seek your life. 4415
14:19 *Do* you **d** Zion? 1718
14:21 For the sake of your name *do* not **d** us; 5540
23:17 They keep saying to *those who* **d** me, 5540
33:24 So *they* **d** my people 5540
La 1: 8 All who honored her **d** her, 2361
Eze 16:57 all those around you who **d** you. 8764
Am 5:10 in court and **d** him who tells the truth. 9493
5:21 "I hate, *I* **d** your religious feasts; 4415
Mic 3: 9 who **d** justice and distort all that is right; 9493
Mt 6:24 be devoted to the one and **d** the other. *2969*
Lk 16:13 be devoted to the one and **d** the other. *2969*
1Co 11:22 Or *do you* **d** the church of God *2969*
Tit 2:15 *Do* not *let* anyone **d** you. *4368*
2Pe 2:10 of the sinful nature and **d** authority. *2969*

DESPISED (37) [DESPISE]

Ge 25:34 So Esau **d** his birthright. 1022
Nu 15:31 Because *he has* **d** the LORD's word 1022
1Sa 10:27 *They* **d** him and brought him no gifts. 1022
15: 9 *that* **was d** and weak they totally destroyed. 1022
17:42 ruddy and handsome, and *he* **d** him. 1022
2Sa 6:16 *she* **d** him in her heart. 1022
12:10 because *you* **d** me and took the wife 1022
1Ch 15:29 *she* **d** him in her heart. 1022
2Ch 36:16 **d** his words and scoffed at his prophets 1022
Ne 4: 4 Hear us, O our God, for we are **d**. 999
Ps 22: 6 scorned by men and **d** *by* the people. 1022
22:24 For *he has* not **d** or disdained the suffering 1022
53: 5 you put them to shame, for God **d** them. 4415
106:24 Then *they* **d** the pleasant land; 4415
107:11 of God and **d** the counsel of the Most High. 5540
119:141 Though I am lowly and **d**, 1022
Pr 12: 8 but men with warped minds are **d**. 997
Ecc 9:16 But the poor man's wisdom is **d**, 1022
Isa 16:14 and all her many people *will* **be d**, 7829
33: 8 The treaty is broken, its witnesses *are* **d**, 4415

Isa 49: 7 to him *who was* **d** and abhorred by 1022
53: 3 *He* **was d** and rejected by men, 1022
53: 3 from whom men hide their faces *he* **was d,** 1022
Jer 22:28 *Is* this man Jehoiachin *a* **d**, broken pot, 1022
49:15 among the nations, **d** among men. 1022
La 1:11 "Look, O LORD, and consider, for I am **d.**" 2361
Eze 16: 5 for on the day you were born you were **d.** 1719
16:45 *who* **d** her husband and her children; 1718
16:45 who **d** their husbands and their children. 1718
16:59 because *you have* **d** my oath by breaking 1022
17:16 whose oath *he* **d** and whose treaty he broke. 1022
17:18 *He* **d** the oath by breaking the covenant. 1022
17:19 that *he* **d** and my covenant that he broke. 1022
22: 8 *You have* **d** my holy things 1022
Ob 1: 2 you *will* **be** utterly **d.** 1022
Mal 2: 9 *to* **be d** and humiliated before all 1022
1Co 1:28 of this world and the **d** *things*— *2024*

DESPISES (11) [DESPISE]

Ge 16: 5 knows she is pregnant, she **d** *me.* 928+6524+7837
2Ki 19:21 " 'The Virgin Daughter of Zion **d** you 996
Ps 15: 4 *who* **d** a vile man but honors those who fear the LORD, 928+1022+6524
Pr 14: 2 but he whose ways are devious **d** him. 1022
14:21 *He who* **d** his neighbor sins, 996
15:20 but a foolish man **d** his mother. 1022
15:32 He who ignores discipline **d** himself, 4415
Isa 37:22 Virgin Daughter of Zion **d** and mocks you. 996
Eze 21:10 The sword **d** every such stick. 4415
21:13 which the sword **d**, does not continue? 4415
Zec 4:10 "Who **d** the day of small things? 996

DESPITE (9)

Ezr 3: 3 **D** their fear of the peoples around them, 3954
Ps 33:17 **d** all its great strength it cannot save. 928
49:12 But man, **d** his riches, does not endure; 928
Ecc 8:17 **D** all his efforts to search it out, 928+4200+8611
Isa 25:11 God will bring down their pride **d** 6640
Eze 21:29 **D** false visions concerning you 928
32:29 **d** their power, they are laid 928
32:30 they went down with the slain in disgrace **d** 928
Hos 7:10 but **d** all this he does not return to 928

DESPITE (KJV) See also INSULTED, MALICE

DESPOIL (1) [SPOIL]

Jer 30:16 who make spoil of you *I will* **d.** 1020+4200+5989

DESTINATION (1)

2Sa 16:14 with him arrived at their **d** exhausted. NIH

DESTINE (1) [DESTINED, DESTINY, PREDESTINED]

Isa 65:12 *I will* **d** you for the sword, 4948

DESTINED (13) [DESTINE]

Ps 49:14 Like sheep *they are* **d** for the grave, 9286
Isa 9: 5 in blood will be **d for** burning, 4200
Jer 15: 2 " 'Those **d for** death, to death; 4200
43:11 bringing death to those **d for** death, 4200
43:11 captivity to those **d for** captivity, 4200
43:11 and the sword to those **d for** the sword. 4200
Eze 31:14 they *are* all **d** for death, for the earth below, 5989
Lk 2:34 "This child *is* **d** to cause the falling *3023*
1Co 2: 7 that God **d** for our glory before time began. *4633*
Col 2:22 These are all **d** to perish with use, *NIG*
1Th 3: 3 You know quite well that *we were* **d** *3023*
Heb 9:27 Just as man *is* **d** to die once, *641*
1Pe 2: 8 which is also what *they were* **d** for. *5502*

DESTINY (7) [DESTINE]

Job 8:13 Such is the **d** *of* all who forget God; 784
Ps 73:17 then I understood their **final d.** 344
Ecc 7: 2 for death is the **d** *of* every man; 6067
9: 2 All share a common **d—** 5247
9: 3 The same **d** overtakes all. 5247
Isa 65:11 and fill bowls of mixed wine for **D,** 4972
Php 3:19 Their **d** is destruction, *5465*

DESTITUTE (8)

Ge 45:11 and all who belong to you *will become* **d.'** 3769
Job 20:19 the poor and **left** them **d;** 6440
Ps 102:17 He will respond to the prayer of the **d;** 6899
Pr 31: 8 for the rights of all *who* are **d.** 1201+2710
Isa 3:26 **d,** she will sit on the ground. 5927
La 1:16 My children are **d** because 9037
4: 5 Those who once ate delicacies *are* **d** in 9037
Heb 11:37 **d**, persecuted and mistreated— *5728*

DESTROY (247) [DESTROYED, DESTROYER, DESTROYERS, DESTROYING, DESTROYS, DESTRUCTION, DESTRUCTIVE]

Ge 6:13 surely *going to* **d** both them and the earth. 8845
6:17 on the earth to **d** all life under the heavens, 8845
8:21 And never again *will I* **d** all living creatures, 5782
9:11 never again will there be a flood to **d** 8845
9:15 the waters become a flood to **d** all life. 8845
Ge 18:28 *Will you* **d** the whole city because 8845
18:28 he said, *"I will* not **d** it." 8845
18:31 "For the sake of twenty, *I will* not **d** it." 8845
18:32 "For the sake of ten, *I will* not **d** it." 8845
19:13 because we *are going to* **d** this place. 8845
19:13 so great that he has sent us to **d** it." 8845
19:14 the LORD *is about to* **d** the city!" 8845
20: 4 "Lord, *will you* **d** an innocent nation? 2222
Ex 15: 9 and my hand *will* **d** them.' 3769
32:10 against them and that *I may* **d** them. 3983
33: 3 a stiff-necked people and *I might* **d** you on 3983
33: 5 *I might* **d** you. 3983
Lev 23:30 *I will* **d** from his people 6
26:16 and fever *that will* **d** your sight 3983
26:22 **d** your cattle and make you so few 4162
26:30 *I will* **d** your high places, 9012
26:44 so as to **d** them **completely,** 3983
Nu 14:12 down with a plague and **d** them, 3769
21: 2 *we will* **totally d** their cities." 3049
24:19 of Jacob and **d** the survivors of the city." 6
33:52 **D** all their carved images 6
Dt 1:27 into the hands of the Amorites to **d** us. 9012
4:31 not abandon or **d** you or forget the covenant 8845
6:15 and *he will* **d** you from the face of the land. 9012
7: 2 **must d** them **totally.** 3049+3049
7: 4 against you and *will* quickly **d** you. 9012
7:16 *You must* **d** all the peoples 430
7:24 you *will* **d** them. 9012
9: 3 He *will* **d** them; 9012
9: 8 so that he was angry enough to **d** you. 9012
9:14 that *I may* **d** them and blot out their name 9012
9:19 for he was angry enough with you to **d** you. 9012
9:20 with Aaron to **d** him, 9012
9:25 the LORD had said *he would* **d** you. 9012
9:26 *do* not **d** your people, 8845
10:10 It was not his will *to* **d** you. 8845
12: 2 **D completely** all the places on 6+6
13:15 **D** it **completely,** both its people 3049
20:17 **Completely d** them— 3049+3049
20:19 *do* not **d** its trees by putting an ax to them, 8845
28:63 so it will please him to ruin and **d** you. 9012
31: 3 He *will* **d** these nations before you, 9012
33:27 before you, saying, **'D** him!' 9012
Jos 7: 7 into the hands of the Amorites to **d** us? 6
7:12 with you anymore unless *you* **d** whatever 9012
11:20 so that *he might* **d** them **totally,** 3049
1Sa 15: 3 the Amalekites and **totally d** everything 3049
15: 6 the Amalekites so that *I do* not **d** you along 3578
15: 9 *to* **d completely,** but everything 3049
15:18 and **completely d** those wicked people, 3049
23:10 to Keilah and **d** the town on account of me. 8845
26: 9 But David said to Abishai, "Don't **d** him! 8845
26:15 Someone came to **d** your lord the king. 8845
2Sa 1:14 not afraid to lift your hand to **d** 8845
11:25 Press the attack against the city and **d** it.' 2238
20:19 You are trying to **d** a city that is a mother 4637
20:20 "Far be it from me to swallow up or **d!** 8845
24:16 angel stretched out his hand to **d** Jerusalem, 8845
2Ki 8:19 the LORD was not willing to **d** Judah. 8845
9: 7 *to* **d** the house of Ahab your master, 5782
10:19 in order to **d** the ministers of Baal. 6
11: 1 she proceeded *to* **d** the whole royal family. 6
13:17 *"You will* completely **d** the Arameans 5782
13:23 *to* **d** them or banish them 8845
18:25 to attack and **d** this place without word 8845
18:25 to march against this country and **d** it.' " 8845
24: 2 He sent them to **d** Judah, 6
1Ch 21:15 And God sent an angel to **d** Jerusalem. 8845
2Ch 12: 7 *I will* not **d** them 8845
20:10 from them and *did* not **d** them. 9012
20:23 from Mount Seir to **d** and annihilate them. 3049
20:23 they helped to **d** one another. 8845
20:37 the LORD *will* **d** what you have made." 7287
21: 7 the LORD was not willing to **d** the house 8845
22: 7 the LORD had anointed to **d** the house 4162
22:10 she proceeded *to* **d** the whole royal family 1818
25:16 "I know that God has determined to **d** you, 8845
35:21 who is with me, or *he will* **d** you." 8845
Ezr 6:12 to change this decree or to **d** this temple 10243
9:14 not be angry enough with us *to* **d** us, 3983
Est 3: 6 for a way to **d** all Mordecai's people, 9012
3: 9 let a decree be issued to **d** them, 6
3:13 with the order to **d,** kill and annihilate all 9012
8: 5 to **d** the Jews in all the king's provinces. 6
8:11 to **d,** kill and annihilate any armed force 9012
9:24 against the Jews to **d** them and had cast 6
Job 10: 8 Will *you* now turn and **d** me? 1180
14:19 so *you* **d** man's hope. 6
Ps 5: 6 *You* **d** those who tell lies; 6
21:10 *You will* **d** their descendants from 6
54: 5 in your faithfulness **d** them. 7551
57: T [To the tune of] *"Do* Not **D."** 8845
58: T [To the tune of] *"Do* Not **D."** 8845
59: T [To the tune of] *"Do* Not **D."** 8845
69: 4 *those who* **seek to d** me. 7551
73:27 *you* **d** all who are unfaithful to you. 7551
74:11 from the folds of your garment and **d** them! 3983
75: T [To the tune of] *"Do* Not **D."** 8845
78:38 and *did* not **d** them. 8845
83: 4 they say, *"let us* **d** them as a nation, 3948
94:23 and **d** them for their wickedness; 7551
94:23 the LORD our God *will* **d** them. 7551
106:23 So he said *he would* **d** them— 9012
106:34 *They did* not **d** the peoples as 9012
119:95 The wicked are waiting to **d** me, 6
143:12 **d** all my foes, for I am your servant. 6
145:20 but all the wicked *he will* **d.** 9012
Pr 1:32 and the complacency of fools *will* **d** them; 6
Ecc 5: 6 be angry at what you say and **d** the work 2472
7:16 be overwise—why **d yourself?** 9037
Isa 10: 7 his purpose is to **d,** 9012
10:18 and fertile fields *it will* completely **d,** 3983
11: 9 nor **d** on all my holy mountain, 8845
13: 5 to **d** the whole country. 2472
13: 9 the land desolate and **d** the sinners within it. 9012
14:30 But your root *I will* **d** by famine; 4637
25: 7 On this mountain *he will* **d** the shroud 1180
32: 7 he makes up evil schemes to **d** the poor 2472
34: 2 *He will* **totally d** them, 3049
36:10 have I come to attack and **d** this land 8845
36:10 to march against this country and **d** it.' " 8845
65: 8 'Don't **d** it, there is yet some good in it,' 8845
65: 8 *I will* not **d** them all. 8845
65:25 nor **d** on all my holy mountain," 8845
Jer 1:10 to **d** and overthrow, to build and to plant." 6
4:27 though *I will* not **d** it **completely.** 3986+6913
5:10 but *do* not **d** them **completely.** 3986+6913
5:17 the sword *they will* **d** the fortified cities 8406
5:18 *"I will* not **d** you **completely.** 3986+6913
6: 2 *I will* **d** the Daughter of Zion, 1950
6: 5 let us attack at night and **d** her fortresses!" 8845
11:19 saying, *"Let us* **d** the tree and its fruit; 8845
12:17 I will completely uproot and **d** it," 6
14:12 Instead, I *will* **d** them with the sword, 3983
15: 3 and the beasts of the earth to devour and **d.** 8845
15: 6 So I will lay hands on you and **d** you; 8845
17:18 **d** them *with* double destruction. 8689
21:10 and *he will* **d** it with fire.' 8596
25: 9 *I will* **completely d** them 3049
27: 8 until I **d** it by his hand. 9462
30:11 Though *I* **completely d** all the nations 3986+6913
30:11 *I will* not **completely d** you. 3986+6913
31:28 and to overthrow, **d** and bring disaster, 6
36:29 and **d** this land and cut off both men 8845
44: 8 You *will* **d** yourselves 4162
44:11 to bring disaster on you and to **d** all Judah. 4162
46: 8 *I will* **d** cities and their people.' 6
46:28 "Though *I* **completely d** all the nations 3986+6913
46:28 *I will* not **completely d** you. 3986+6913
47: 4 the day has come to **d** all the Philistines and 8720
47: 4 The LORD *is about to* **d** the Philistines, 8720
49:20 *he will* **completely d** their pasture 9037
49:28 attack Kedar and **d** the people of the East. 8720
49:38 I will set my throne in Elam and **d** her king 6
50:21 Pursue, kill and **completely d** them," 3049
50:26 **Completely d** her and leave her no 3049
50:45 *he will* **completely d** their pasture 9037
51: 3 **completely d** her army. 3049
51:11 because his purpose is to **d** Babylon. 8845
51:20 with you *I* **d** kingdoms, 8845
51:25 you who **d** the whole earth," 8845
51:55 The LORD *will* **d** Babylon; 8720
51:62 you have said you *will* **d** this place, 4162
La 3:66 in anger and **d** them from under the heavens 9012
Eze 5:16 I will shoot to **d** you. 8845
6: 3 and *I will* **d** your high places. 6
9: 8 *Are* you *going to* **d** the entire remnant 8845
11:13 *Will* you **completely d** the remnant 3986+6913
14: 9 and **d** him from among my people Israel. 9012
16:39 and **d** your lofty shrines. 5997
17:17 and siege works erected to **d** many lives. 4162
20:13 on them and **d** them in the desert. 3983
20:17 on them with pity and *did* not **d** them or put 8845
22:30 of the land so I *would* not *have to* **d** it, 8845
25: 7 *I will* **d** you, and you will know that 9012
25:15 with ancient hostility sought to **d** Judah, 5422
25:16 the Kerethites and **d** those remaining along 6
26: 4 *They will* **d** the walls of Tyre and pull 8845
30:11 will be brought in to **d** the land. 8845
30:13 " *'I will* **d** the idols and put an end to 6
32:13 *I will* **d** all her cattle from 6
34:16 but the sleek and the strong *I will* **d.** 9012
43: 3 to **d** the city and like the visions I had seen 8845
Da 4:23 'Cut down the tree and **d** it, 10243
8:24 *He will* **d** the mighty men and 8845
8:25 *he will* **d** many and take his stand against 8845
9:26 the ruler who will come *will* **d** the city and 8845
11:16 and will have the **power to d** it. 3986
11:26 the king's provisions *will try to* **d** him; 8689
11:44 in a great rage to **d** and annihilate many. 9012
Hos 4: 5 So *I will* **d** your mother— 1950
10: 2 and **d** their sacred stones. 8720
11: 6 *will* **d** the bars of their gates and put 3983
Am 1: 5 *I will* **d** the king who is in the Valley 4162
1: 8 *I will* **d** the king of Ashdod and 4162
2: 3 *I will* **d** her ruler and kill all her officials 4162
3:14 *I will* **d** the altars of Bethel; 7212
9: 8 *I will* **d** it from the face of the earth— 9012
9: 8 yet *I will* not **totally d** the house 9012+9012
Ob 1: 8 *"will I* not **d** the wise men of Edom, 6
Mic 1: 7 *I will* **d** all her images. 8492+9039
5:10 *"I will* **d** your horses from among you 4162
5:11 *I will* **d** the cities of your land and tear 4162
5:12 *I will* **d** your witchcraft 4162
5:13 *I will* **d** your carved images 4162
6:13 Therefore, I have begun *to* **d** you, 5782
Na 1:14 *I will* **d** the carved images and cast idols 4162
Zep 2: 5 *"I will* **d** you, and none will be left." 6
2:13 against the north and **d** Assyria, 6
Zec 5: 4 It will remain in his house and **d** it, 3983
9: 4 and **d** her power on the sea, 5782
9:15 *They will* **d** and overcome 430
12: 9 On that day I will set out to **d** all the nations 9012
Mt 6:19 where moth and rust **d,** *906*

Mt 6:20 where moth and rust *do* not **d**, *906*
10:28 of the One who can **d** both soul and body *660*
26:61 *to* **d** the temple of God and rebuild it *2907*
27:40 *to* **d** the temple and build it in three days, *2907*
Mk 1:24 Have you come *to* **d** us? *660*
14:58 'I *will* **d** this man-made temple and *2907*
15:29 *to* **d** the temple and build it in three days, *2907*
Lk 4:34 Have you come *to* **d** us? *660*
6: 9 to save life or *to* **d** it?" *660*
9:54 to call fire down from heaven *to* **d** them?" *384*
Jn 2:19 Jesus answered them, "**D** this temple, *3395*
10:10 thief comes only to steal and kill and **d**; *660*
Ac 6:14 that this Jesus of Nazareth *will* **d** this place *2907*
8: 3 But Saul **began** *to* **d** the church. *3381*
Ro 14:15 *Do* not by your eating **d** your brother *660*
14:20 not **d** the work of God for the sake of food. *2907*
1Co 1:19 *"I will* **d** the wisdom of the wise; *660*
3:17 destroys God's temple, God *will* **d** him; *5780*
6:13 but God *will* **d** them both. *2934*
Gal 1:13 the church of God and *tried to* **d** it. *4514*
1:23 now preaching the faith *he* once **tried** *to* **d**." *4514*
2Th 2: 8 with the breath of his mouth and **d** by *2934*
2Ti 2:18 and *they* **d** the faith of some. *426*
Heb 2:14 that by his death *he might* **d** him who holds *2934*
Jas 4:12 the one who is able *to* save and **d**. *660*
1Jn 3: 8 of God appeared was to **d** the devil's work. *3395*
Jude 1:10 these are the very things that **d** *them.* *5780*
Rev 11:18 and for destroying those who **d** the earth." *1425*

DESTROYED (216) [DESTROY]

Ge 13:10 (This was before the LORD **d** Sodom 8845
19:29 So when God **d** the cities of the plain, 8845
34:30 I and my household *will* **be d.**" 9012
Ex 9:31 (The flax and barley **were d,** 5782
9:32 The wheat and spelt, however, **were** not **d,** 5782
22:20 the LORD *must* **be d.** 3049
Lev 10: 6 for those the LORD *has* **d by fire.** 8596
Nu 21: 3 *They* **completely d** them and their towns; 3049
21:29 *You are* **d,** O people of Chemosh! 6
21:30 Heshbon *is* **d** all the way to Dibon. 6
24:22 be **d** when Asshur takes you captive." 1278
Dt 2:12 *They* **d** the Horites from before them 9012
2:21 The LORD **d** them from before 9012
2:22 when *he* **d** the Horites from before them. 9012
2:23 from Caphtor **d** them and settled 9012
2:34 and **completely d** them— 3049
3: 6 *We* **completely d** them, 3049
4: 3 The LORD your God **d** from 9012
4:26 but *will* **certainly be d.** 9012+9012
7:23 into great confusion until they **are d.** 9012
8:19 that *you will* **surely be d.** 6+6
8:20 Like the nations the LORD **d** before you, 6
8:20 so *you will* **be d** for not obeying 6
12:30 and after they *have* **been d** before you, 9012
19: 1 When the LORD your God *has* **d** 4162
28:20 until you **are d** and come to sudden ruin 9012
28:21 with diseases until he *has* **d** you from 3983
28:24 down from the skies until you **are d.** 9012
28:45 and overtake you until you *are* **d,** 9012
28:48 on your neck until he *has* **d** you. 9012
28:51 and the crops of your land until you **are d.** 9012
28:61 until you **are d.** 9012
30:18 that *you will* **certainly be d.** 6+6
31: 4 whom *he* **d** along with their land. 9012
31:17 and they will be **d.** 430
Jos 2:10 whom *you* **completely d.** 3049
6:21 **devoted** the city to the LORD **and d** 3049
7:15 with the devoted things *shall* **be d** by fire, 8596
8:26 until *he had* **d** all who lived in Ai. 3049
10: 1 that Joshua had taken Ai and **totally d** it, 3049
10:20 and the Israelites **d** them completely— 1524+4394+4804+5782
10:28 the sword and **totally d** everyone in it. 3049
10:35 the sword and **totally d** everyone in it, 3049
10:37 *they* **totally d** it and everyone in it. 3049
10:39 Everyone in it *they* **totally d.** 3049
10:40 *He* **totally d** all who breathed, 3049
11:11 *They* **totally d** them, 3049
11:12 *He* **totally d** them, 3049
11:14 the sword until they **completely d** them, 9012
11:21 that time Joshua went and **d** the Anakites 4162
11:21 Joshua **totally d** them and their towns. 3049
23:15 until he *has* **d** you from this good land 9012
24: 8 *I* **d** them from before you, 9012
Jdg 1:17 and *they* **totally d** the city. 3049
4:24 the Canaanite king, until *they* **d** him. 4162
9:45 Then *he* **d** the city and scattered salt over it. 5997
21:16 "With the women of Benjamin **d,** 9012
1Sa 15: 8 and all his people *he* **totally d** with 3049
15: 9 and weak *they* **totally d.** 3049
15:15 but *we* **totally d** the rest." 3049
15:20 *I* **completely d** the Amalekites 3049
27: 1 "One of these days *I will* **be d** by the hand 6200
30: 3 they found *it* **d** by fire and their wives 8596
2Sa 11: 1 *They* **d** the Ammonites 8845
14:11 so that my son *will* not *be* **d.**" 9012
21: 5 for the man who **d** us and plotted against us 3983
22:38 I did not turn back till they *were* **d.** 3983
22:41 and *I* **d** my foes. 7551
1Ki 11:16 until *they had* **d** all the men in Edom. 4162
11:24 of a band of rebels when David **d** the forces 2222
15:29 but **d** them all, according to the word of 9012
16: 7 and also because *he* **d** it. 5782
16:12 So Zimri **d** the whole family of Baasha, 9012
22:11 the Arameans until they *are* **d.**' " 3983
2Ki 3:25 *They* **d** the towns, 2238
10:17 *he* **d** them, according to the word of 9012
10:28 So Jehu **d** Baal worship in Israel. 9012
13: 7 of Aram *had* **d** the rest and made them like 6
13:19 and **completely d** it. 3983+6330
19:12 that *were* **d** *by* my forefathers deliver them: 8845
19:18 into the fire and **d** them, 6
21: 3 the high places his father Hezekiah *had* **d;** 6
21: 9 the LORD *had* **d** before the Israelites. 9012
1Ch 4:41 and **completely d** them, 3049
5:25 whom God *had* **d** before them. 9012
2Ch 8: 8 whom the Israelites *had* not **d**— 3983
12:12 and he *was* not totally **d.** 8845
14:14 *They* **d** all the villages around Gerar, 5782
18:10 the Arameans until they *are* **d.**' " 3983
31: 1 *They* **d** the high places and the altars 5997
31: 1 After they *had* **d** all of them, 3983
32:14 that my fathers **d** has been able 3049
33: 9 the LORD *had* **d** before the Israelites. 9012
36:19 the palaces and **d** everything of value there. 8845
Ezr 4:15 That is why this city **was d.** 10281
5:12 *who* **d** this temple and deported the people 10520
Ne 2: 3 and its gates *have* **been d** by fire?" 430
2:13 and its gates, *which had* **been d** by fire. 430
Est 9: 6 the Jews killed and **d** five hundred men. 6
9:12 and **d** five hundred men and the ten sons 6
Job 4: 7 **were** the upright *ever* **d?** 3948
4: 9 At the breath of God *they are* **d;** 6
19:26 And after my skin *has been* **d,** 5937
22:20 'Surely our foes **are d,** 3948
Ps 2:12 lest he be angry and *you be* **d** in your way, 6
9: 5 You have rebuked the nations and **d** 6
11: 3 When the foundations *are* **being d,** 2238
18:37 I did not turn back till they *were* **d.** 3983
18:40 and *I* **d** my foes. 7551
37:38 But all sinners *will* **be d;** 9012
48: 7 *You* **d** them like ships of Tarshish shattered 8689
63: 9 They who seek my life will be **d;** 8739
73:19 How suddenly are they **d,** 9014
78:47 *He* **d** their vines with hail 2222
79: 7 and **d** his homeland. 9037
88:16 your terrors *have* **d** me. 7551
92: 7 they *will* **be** forever **d.** 9012
105:16 on the land and **d** all their supplies of food; 8689
Pr 6:15 *he will* suddenly **be d**—without remedy. 8689
11: 3 but the unfaithful *are* **d** *by* their duplicity. 8720
11:11 but by the mouth of the wicked *it* **is d.** 2238
14:11 The house of the wicked *will* **be d,** 9012
21:28 whoever listens to him *will be* **d** forever. 1818
22: 8 and the rod of his fury *will be* **d.** 3983
29: 1 after many rebukes *will* suddenly **be d**— 8689
Isa 5: 5 I will take away its hedge, and it will be **d;** 1278
14:20 for *you have* **d** your land 8845
15: 1 Ar in Moab is ruined, **d** in a night! 8720
15: 1 Kir in Moab is ruined, **d** in a night! 8720
23: 1 Tyre *is* **d** and left without house or harbor. 8720
23:11 that her fortresses *be* **d.** 9012
23:14 your fortress *is* **d!** 8720
33: 1 O destroyer, you *who have* not **been d!** 8720
33: 1 When you stop destroying, *you will* **be d;** 8720
34: 5 the people I have **totally d.** 3051
37:12 Did the gods of the nations that *were* **d** 8845
37:19 into the fire and **d** them, 6
48:19 their name would never be cut off nor **d** 9012
55:13 an everlasting sign, *which will* not **be d.**" 4162
Jer 4:20 In an instant my tents **are d,** 8720
9:16 with the sword until *I have* **d** them." 3983
10:20 My tent **is d;** all its ropes are snapped. 8720
10:25 and **d** his homeland. 9037
18: 7 torn down and **d,** 6
24:10 and plague against them until they *are* **d** 9462
44:27 by sword and famine until they *are* all **d.** 3983
48: 8 The valley will be ruined and the plateau **d,** 9012
48:15 Moab *will* **be d** and her towns invaded; 8720
48:20 Announce by the Arnon that Moab **is d.** 8720
48:42 Moab *will* **be d** as a nation 9012
48:46 The people of Chemosh *are* **d;** 6
49: 3 "Wail, O Heshbon, for Ai **is d!** 8720
51: 6 *Do* not **be d** because of her sins. 1959
La 2: 5 up all her palaces and **d** her strongholds. 8845
2: 6 *he has* **d** his place of meeting. 8845
2: 9 their bars he has broken and **d.** 6
2:11 on the ground because my people are **d,** 8691
2:22 for and reared, my enemy *has* **d.**" 3983
3:48 from my eyes because my people are **d.** 8691
4:10 when my people were **d.** 8691
Eze 13:14 When it falls, *you will be* **d** in it; 3983
26:17 " 'How *you are* **d,** O city of renown, 6
36:35 that were lying in ruins, desolate and **d,** 2238
36:36 that I the LORD have rebuilt what **was d** 2238
43: 8 So *I* **d** them in my anger. 430
Da 2:44 up a kingdom that *will* never **be d,** 10243
6:26 his kingdom *will* not **be d,** 10243
7:11 until the beast was slain and its body **d** 10005
7:14 his kingdom is one that *will* never **be d.** 10243
7:26 and **completely d** forever. 10005+10221+10722
8:25 Yet *he will* **be d,** but not by human power. 8689
11:20 In a few years, however, *he will* **be d,** 8689
11:22 *it* and a prince of the covenant *will* **be d.** 8689
Hos 4: 6 my people **are d** from lack of knowledge. 1950
10: 8 The high places of wickedness *will* **be d**— 9012
10:15 king of Israel *will* **be completely d.** 1950+1950
13: 9 "You *are* **d,** O Israel, 8845
Joel 1:10 the grain *is* **d,** the new wine is dried up, 8720
1:11 because the harvest of the field *is* **d.** 6
Am 2: 9 "I **d** the Amorite before them, 9012
2: 9 *I* **d** his fruit above and his roots below. 9012
3:15 *be* **d** and the mansions will be demolished," 6
Am 7: 9 "The high places of Isaac *will* **be d** and 9037
Ob 1:10 *you will* **be d** forever. 4162
Mic 5: 9 and all your foes *will* **be d.** 4162
Na 1:15 they *will* **be** completely **d.** 4162
Hab 2: 8 you have **d** lands and cities and everyone 2805
2:17 you have **d** lands and cities and everyone 2805
Zep 3: 6 Their cities **are d;** 7400
Zec 11: 3 their rich pastures **are d!** 8720
14:11 It will be inhabited; never again will it be **d.** 3051
Mal 3: 6 So you, O descendants of Jacob, *are* not **d.** 3983
Mt 22: 7 *He* sent his army and **d** those murderers *660*
Lk 17:27 Then the flood came and **d** them all. *660*
17:29 down from heaven and **d** them all. *660*
Ac 27:22 only the ship will be **d.** *NIG*
1Co 5: 5 be **d** and his spirit saved on the day of *3897*
8:11 *is* **d** by your knowledge. *660*
15:24 the Father after *he has* **d** all dominion, *2934*
15:26 The last enemy *to be* **d** is death. *2934*
2Co 4: 9 struck down, but not **d.** *660*
5: 1 that if the earthly tent we live in *is* **d,** *2907*
Gal 2:18 If I rebuild what *I* **d,** *2907*
5:15 watch out or *you will be* **d** by each other. *384*
Eph 2:14 who has made the two one and *has* **d** *3395*
Php 1:28 This is a sign to them that they will be **d,** *724*
2Ti 1:10 *who has* **d** death and has brought life *2934*
Heb 10:39 not of those who shrink back and are **d,** *724+1650*
Jas 1:11 its blossom falls and its beauty *is* **d.** *660*
2Pe 2:12 born only to *be* caught and **d,** *5785*
3: 6 the world of that time *was* deluged and **d.** *660*
3:10 the elements *will be* **d** by fire, *3395*
3:11 *Since* everything *will be* **d** in this way, *3395*
Jude 1: 5 but later **d** those who did not believe. *660*
1:11 *they have been* **d** in Korah's rebellion. *660*
Rev 8: 9 and a third of the ships *were* **d.** *1425*

DESTROYER (12) [DESTROY]

Ex 12:23 not permit the **d** to enter your houses 5422
Isa 16: 4 be their shelter from the **d.**" 8720
33: 1 Woe to you, O **d,** 8720
54:16 And it is I who have created the **d** 5422
Jer 4: 7 a **d** *of* nations has set out. 5422
6:26 for suddenly the **d** will come upon us. 8720
15: 8 a **d** against the mothers of their young men; 8720
48: 8 The **d** will come against every town, 8720
48:32 The **d** has fallen on your ripened fruit 8720
51: 1 up the spirit of a **d** against Babylon and 5422
51:56 A **d** will come against Babylon; 8720
Heb 11:28 that the **d** *of* the firstborn would not touch *3905*

DESTROYERS (6) [DESTROY]

Jer 12:12 in the desert **d** will swarm, for the sword of 8720
15: 3 "I will send four kinds of **d** against them," NIH
22: 7 I will send **d** against you, 5422
51:48 for out of the north **d** will attack her," 8720
51:53 I will send **d** against her," 8720
Na 2: 2 though **d** have laid them waste 1327

DESTROYING (20) [DESTROY]

Dt 3: 6 **d** every city—men, women and children. 3049
1Sa 6: 5 of the tumors and of the rats that *are* **d** 8845
2Ki 19:11 to all the countries, **d** them **completely.** 3049
1Ch 21:15 and said to the angel who *was* **d** the people, 8845
Est 9: 5 killing and **d** them, 12
Job 30:13 they succeed in **d** me— 2095
Ps 52: 7 and grew strong by **d** others!" 2095
78:49 a band of **d** angels. 8273
106:23 before him to keep his wrath from **d** them. 8845
Isa 33: 1 When you stop **d,** you will be destroyed; 8720
37:11 to all the countries, **d** them **completely.** 3049
Jer 13:14 or compassion *to* keep me from **d** them.' " 8845
23: 1 to the shepherds *who are* **d** and scattering 6
25:36 for the LORD *is* **d** their pasture. 8720
51:25 "I am against you, O **d** mountain, 8845
La 2: 8 and did not withhold his hand from **d.** 1180
Hab 1:17 **d** nations without mercy? 2222
Lk 9:39 It scarcely ever leaves him and *is* **d** him. *5341*
1Co 10:10 and were killed by the **d** angel. *3904*
Rev 11:18 and *for* **d** those who destroy the earth." *1425*

DESTROYS (13) [DESTROY]

Ex 21:26 or maidservant in the eye and **d** it, 8845
Job 9:22 'He **d** both the blameless and the wicked.' 3983
12:23 He makes nations great, and **d** them; 6
Ps 91: 6 nor the plague *that* **d** at midday. 8720
Pr 6:32 whoever does so **d** himself. 8845
11: 9 With his mouth the godless **d** his neighbor, 8845
18: 9 in his work is brother to **one who d.** 1251+5422
28:24 he is partner to him who **d.** 5422
Ecc 9:18 but one sinner **d** much good. 6
Jer 48:18 *he who* **d** Moab will come up against you 8720
Zep 2:11 be awesome to them when *he* **d** all the gods 8135
Lk 12:33 where no thief comes near and no moth **d.** *1425*
1Co 3:17 If anyone **d** God's temple, *5780*

DESTRUCTION (96) [DESTROY]

Lev 27:29 " 'No person **devoted to d** may 3049+3051
Nu 32:15 and *you will be* the **cause** of their **d.**" 8845
Dt 7:10 to their face by **d;** 6
7:26 like it, will be **set apart for d.** 3051
7:26 for it is **set apart for d.** 3051
29:23 be like the **d** *of* Sodom and Gomorrah, 4550
30:15 and prosperity, death and **d.** 8273
Jos 6:18 **bring about** *your own* **d** 3049
6:18 of Israel liable to **d** and bring trouble on it. 3051

Jos 7:12 because they have been made liable to **d.** 3051
7:12 among you is **devoted to d.** 3051
2Sa 14:11 the avenger of blood from adding to the **d,** 8845
22: 5 the torrents of **d** overwhelmed me. 1175
1Ki 13:34 to its downfall and to its **d** from the face of 9012
Est 4: 7 into the royal treasury for *the* **d** of the Jews. 6
7: 4 For I and my people have been sold for **d** 9012
8: 6 How can I bear to see the **d** *of* my family?" 13
9: 2 to attack those seeking their **d.** 8288
9:24 the lot) for their ruin and **d.** 6
Job 5:21 and need not fear when **d** comes. 8719
5:22 You will laugh at **d** and famine, 8719
21:20 Let his own eyes see his **d;** 3957
26: 6 before God; **D** lies uncovered. 11
28:22 **D** and Death say, 'Only a rumor of it 11
31:12 It is a fire that burns to **D;** 11
31:23 For I dreaded **d** *from* God, 369
Ps 5: 9 their heart is filled with **d.** 2095
18: 4 the torrents of **d** overwhelmed me. 1175
30: 9 "What gain is there in my **d,** 1947
52: 2 Your tongue plots **d;** 2095
74: 3 **d** the enemy *has* **brought** 8317
88:11 your faithfulness in **D?** 11
137: 8 O Daughter of Babylon, **doomed to d,** 8720
Pr 15:11 Death and **D** lie open before the LORD— 11
16:18 Pride goes before **d,** 8691
17:19 he who builds a high gate invites **d.** 8691
24:22 those two will send sudden **d** upon them, 369
27:20 Death and **D** are never satisfied, 9
Isa 10:22 **D** has been decreed, 4001
10:23 the **d** decreed upon the whole land. 3986
10:25 and my wrath will be directed to their **d."** 9318
13: 6 it will come like **d** from the Almighty. 8719
14:23 I will sweep her with the broom of **d,"** 9012
15: 5 the road to Horonaim they lament their **d.** 8691
16: 4 and **d** will cease; 8719
19:18 One of them will be called the City of **D.** 2239
22: 4 to console me over the **d** *of* my people." 8719
28:22 of the **d** decreed against the whole land. 3986
30:28 He shakes the nations in the sieve of **d;** 8736
38:17 In your love you kept me from the pit of **d;** 1172
43:28 and I will consign Jacob to **d** and Israel 3051
51:13 who is bent on **d?** 8845
51:19 ruin and **d,** famine and sword— 8691
59: 7 ruin and **d** mark their ways. 8691
60:18 nor ruin or **d** within your borders, 8691
Jer 4: 6 from the north, even terrible **d."** 8691
6: 1 of the north, even terrible **d.** 8691
6: 7 Violence and **d** resound in her; 8719
15: 7 I will bring bereavement and **d** 6
17:18 destroy them with double **d.** 8695
20: 8 I cry out proclaiming violence and **d.** 8719
48: 3 cries of great havoc and **d.** 8691
48: 5 over the **d** are heard. 8691
50:22 the noise of great **d!** 8691
51:54 of great **d** from the land of the Babylonians. 8691
La 1: 7 at her and laughed at her **d.** 5404
3:47 and pitfalls, ruin and **d."** 8691
Eze 21:31 over to brutal men, men skilled in **d.** 5422
32: 9 of many peoples when I bring about your **d** 8691
Hos 7:13 **D** to them, because they have rebelled 8719
8: 4 for themselves to *their own* **d.** 4162
9: 6 Even if they escape from **d,** 8719
13:14 Where, O grave, is your **d?** 7776
Joel 1:15 it will come like **d** from the Almighty. 8719
Am 5: 9 he flashes **d** on the stronghold and brings 8719
Ob 1:12 the people of Judah in the day of their **d,** 6
Jnh 3:10 upon them the **d** he had threatened. 8288
Hab 1: 3 **D** and violence are before me; 8719
2:17 and your **d** *of* animals will terrify you. 8719
Mt 7:13 and broad is the road that leads to **d,** 724
Lk 6:49 it collapsed and its **d** was complete." *4837*
Jn 17:12 been lost except the one **doomed to d** 724
Ro 9:22 of his wrath—prepared for **d?** 724
Gal 6: 8 from that nature will reap **d;** *5785*
Php 3:19 Their destiny is **d,** 724
1Th 5: 3 **d** will come on them suddenly, *3897*
2Th 1: 9 be punished with everlasting **d** and shut out *3897*
2: 3 the man **doomed to d.** 724
1Ti 6: 9 that plunge men into ruin and **d.** 724
2Pe 2: 1 bringing swift **d** on themselves. 724
2: 3 and their **d** has not been sleeping. 724
3: 7 the day *of* judgment and **d** of ungodly men. 724
3:12 That day *will* bring about the **d** of *3395*
3:16 Scriptures, to their own **d.** 724
Rev 17: 8 up out of the Abyss and go to his **d.** 724
17:11 to the seven and is going to his **d.** 724

DESTRUCTIVE (9) [DESTROY]

Ex 12:13 No **d** plague will touch you 5422
Lev 13:51 it is a **d** mildew; the article is unclean. 4421
13:52 because the mildew *is* **d;** 4421
14:44 it *is* a **d** mildew; the house is unclean. 4421
Ps 55:11 **D forces** are at work in the city; 2095
Isa 28: 2 Like a hailstorm and a **d** wind, 7776
Eze 5:16 with my deadly and **d** arrows of famine, 5422
13:13 and torrents of rain will fall with **d** fury. 3986
2Pe 2: 1 They will secretly introduce **d** heresies, 724

DETACHMENT (4) [DETACHMENTS]

1Sa 13:23 a **d** *of* Philistines had gone out to the pass 5163
Jn 18: 3 guiding a **d of soldiers** and some officials *5061*
18:12 Then the **d of soldiers** with its commander *5061*
Ac 23:23 "Get ready a **d** of two hundred soldiers, *NIG*

DETACHMENTS (1) [DETACHMENT]

1Sa 13:17 from the Philistine camp in three **d.** 8031

DETAIL (3) [DETAILED, DETAILS]

Ac 21:19 and reported in **d** what God had done *1651+1667*
Col 2:18 **goes into great d about** what he has seen, *1836*
Heb 9: 5 we cannot discuss these things in **d** now. *3538*

DETAILED (1) [DETAIL]

2Ki 16:10 with **d** plans for its construction. 3972

DETAILS (3) [DETAIL]

1Ki 6:38 in all its **d** according to its specifications. 1821
1Ch 28:19 and he gave me understanding in all the **d** 4856
29:30 together with the **d** *of* his reign and power, 3972

DETAIN (2) [DETAINED]

Ge 24:56 But he said to them, *"Do* not **d** me, 336
Jdg 13:16 "Even though *you* **d** me, 6806

DETAINED (2) [DETAIN]

1Sa 21: 7 **d** before the LORD; 6806
Da 10:13 I **was d** there with the king of Persia. 3855

DETECT (3)

Job 39:29 his eyes **d** it from afar. 5564
Ps 36: 2 to **d** or hate his sin. 5162
Ob 1: 7 but you will not **d** it. 9312

DETER (1) [DETRIMENT]

Mt 3:14 But John *tried to* **d** him, saying, *1361*

DETERMINATE (KJV) See SET

DETERMINE (8) [DETERMINED, DETERMINES]

Ex 12: 4 **d** the **amount** *of* lamb **needed** 4082
22: 8 to **d** whether he has laid his hands on NIH
Lev 14:57 to **d** when something is clean or unclean. 3723
25:27 *he is to* **d the value** *for* the years 3108
27:18 the priest *will* **d** the value according to 3108
27:23 the priest *will* **d** its value up to the Year 3108
Ne 10:34 to **d** when each of our families is to bring to NIH
Da 11:17 *He will* **d** to come with the might 7156+8492

DETERMINED (33) [DETERMINE]

Jos 17:12 the Canaanites *were* **d** to live in that region. 3283
Jdg 1:27 the Canaanites *were* **d** to live in that land. 3283
1:35 And the Amorites *were* **d** also to hold out 3283
Ru 1:18 When Naomi realized that Ruth *was* **d** to go 599
1Sa 20: 7 you can be sure that he *is* **d** *to* harm me. 3983
20: 9 the least inkling that my father *was* **d** 3983
2Sa 17:14 For the LORD *had* **d** to frustrate 7422
1Ki 7:47 the weight of the bronze **was** not **d.** 2983
20:42 a man I had **d should die.** 3051
2Ki 12:11 When the **amount** *had* **been d,** 9419
1Ch 12:38 **fully d** to make David king 928+4222+8969
2Ch 4:18 that the weight of the bronze **was** not **d.** 2983
25:16 "I know that God *has* **d** to destroy you, 3619
Job 14: 5 Man's days *are* **d;** 3076
Ecc 7:23 *"I am d to be* **wise"**—but this was beyond me. AIT
Isa 14:26 This is the plan **d** for the whole world; 3619
Jer 21:10 *I have* **d** to do this city harm and not good, 7156+8492
42:15 'If you *are* **d** to go to Egypt 7156+8492+8492
42:17 all who *are* **d** to go to Egypt 7156+8492
44:11 I *am* **d** to bring disaster on you and 7156+8492
44:12 the remnant of Judah who *were* **d** to go 7156+8492
La 2: 8 The LORD **d** to tear down the wall around 3108
Da 6:14 *he was* **d** to rescue Daniel 10104+10682
11:36 for *what has* **been d** must take place. 3076
Hos 11: 7 My people *are* **d** to turn from me. 9428
Hab 2:13 Has not the LORD Almighty **d** that 907+4946
Zec 1: 6 just as *he* **d** to do.' " 2372
8:14 "Just as *I had* **d** to bring disaster upon you 2372
8:15 "so now *I have* **d** to do good again 2372
Jn 8:40 As it is, *you are* **d** to kill me, *2426*
Ac 5:28 with your teaching and *are* **d** *1089*
17:26 and *he* **d** the times set for them and *3988*
1Co 15:38 But God gives it a body as *he has* **d,** *2527*

DETERMINES (3) [DETERMINE]

Ps 147: 4 *He* **d** the number of the stars 4948
Pr 16: 9 but the LORD **d** his steps. 3922
1Co 12:11 and he gives them to each one, just as *he* **d.** *1089*

DETEST (17) [DETESTABLE, DETESTED, DETESTS]

Lev 11:10 you are to **d.** 9211
11:11 And since you are to **d** them, 9211
11:11 and *you must* **d** their carcasses. 9210
11:13 " 'These are the birds *you are to* **d** and 9210
11:23 that have four legs you are to **d.** 9211
Nu 21: 5 And we **d** this miserable food!" 7762
Dt 7:26 Utterly abhor and **d** it, 9493+9493
Job 9:31 so that even my clothes *would* **d** me. 9493
19:19 All my intimate friends **d** me; 9493
30:10 *They* **d** me and keep their distance; 9493
Pr 8: 7 for my lips **d** wickedness. 9359
13:19 but fools **d** turning from evil. 9359
16:12 Kings **d** wrongdoing, for 9359
24: 9 and men **d** a mocker. 9359
29:27 The righteous **d** the dishonest; 9359
29:27 the wicked **d** the upright. 9359
Am 6: 8 the pride of Jacob and **d** his fortresses; 8533

DETESTABLE (111) [DETEST]

Ge 43:32 for that is **d** to Egyptians. 9359
46:34 for all shepherds are **d** *to* the Egyptians." 9359
Ex 8:26 the LORD our God would be **d** *to* 9359
8:26 if we offer sacrifices that are **d** in their eyes, 9359
Lev 7:21 an unclean animal or any unclean, **d** *thing*— 9211
11:12 that does not have fins and scales is to be **d** 9211
11:13 to detest and not eat because they are **d:** 9211
11:20 that walk on all fours are to be **d** to you. 9211
11:41 that moves about on the ground is **d;** 9211
11:42 on many feet; it is **d.** 9211
18:22 with a woman; that is **d.** 9359
18:26 not do any of these **d things,** 9359
18:29 " 'Everyone who does any of these **d things** 9359
18:30 and do not follow any of the **d** customs 9359
20:13 both of them have done **what** is **d.** 9359
Dt 7:25 for it is **d** to the LORD your God. 9359
7:26 not bring a **d thing** into your house or you, 9359
12:31 of **d things** the LORD hates. 9359
13:14 that this **d thing** has been done among you, 9359
14: 3 Do not eat any **d thing.** 9359
17: 1 for that would be **d** *to* him. 9359
17: 4 that this **d thing** has been done in Israel, 9359
18: 9 to imitate the **d ways** *of* the nations there. 9359
18:12 Anyone who does these things is **d** *to* 9359
18:12 and because of these **d practices** 9359
20:18 to follow all the **d things** they do 9359
24: 4 That would be **d** in the eyes of the LORD. 9359
27:15 a **thing d** *to* the LORD, 9359
29:17 among them their **d images** and idols 9199
32:16 and angered him with their **d idols.** 9359
1Ki 11: 5 and Molech the **d god** *of* the Ammonites. 9199
11: 7 a high place for Chemosh the **d god** 9199
11: 7 for Molech the **d god** *of* the Ammonites. 9199
14:24 the people engaged in all the **d practices** *of* 9359
2Ki 16: 3 following the **d ways** *of* the nations 9359
21: 2 following the **d practices** *of* the nations 9359
21:11 of Judah has committed these **d sins.** 9359
23:13 Molech the **d god** *of* the people of Ammon. 9359
23:24 the idols and all the other **d things** seen 9199
2Ch 15: 8 the **d idols** from the whole land of Judah 9199
28: 3 following the **d ways** *of* the nations 9359
33: 2 following the **d practices** *of* the nations 9359
34:33 the **d idols** from all the territory belonging 9359
36: 8 the **d things** he did and all that was found 9359
36:14 following all the **d practices** *of* the nations 9359
Ezr 9: 1 with their **d practices,** 9359
9:11 By their **d practices** they have filled it 9359
9:14 the peoples who commit such **d practices?** 9359
Pr 6:16 seven that are **d** *to* him: 9359
21:27 The sacrifice of the wicked is **d—** 9359
28: 9 even his prayers are **d.** 9359
Isa 1:13 Your incense is **d** to me. 9359
41:24 he who chooses you is **d.** 9359
44:19 Shall I make a **d thing** from what is left? 9359
Jer 2: 7 and made my inheritance **d.** 9359
4: 1 "If you put your **d idols** out of my sight 9199
7:10 safe to do all these **d things?** 9359
7:30 They have set up their **d idols** in the house 9199
13:27 I have seen your **d acts** on the hills and in 9199
16:18 with their **d idols."** 9359
32:35 that they should do such a **d thing** and 9359
44: 4 'Do not do this **d** thing that I hate!' 9359
44:22 and the **d things** you did, 9359
Eze 5: 9 Because of all your **d idols,** 9359
5:11 with all your vile images and **d practices,** 9359
6: 9 and for all their **d practices.** 9359
6:11 because of all the wicked and **d practices** 9359
7: 3 and repay you for all your **d practices.** 9359
7: 4 for your conduct and the **d practices** 9359
7: 8 and repay you for all your **d practices.** 9359
7: 9 with your conduct and the **d practices** 9359
7:20 to make their **d** idols and vile images. 9359
8: 6 the utterly **d things** the house 9359
8: 6 **things** *that* are even more **d."** 9359
8: 9 and **d things** they are doing here." 9359
8:10 and **d** animals and all the idols of the house 9211
8:13 **things** *that* are even more **d."** 9359
8:15 **things** *that* are even more **d** 9359
8:17 to do the **d things** they are doing here? 9359
9: 4 over all the **d things** that are done in it." 9359
11:18 and remove all its vile images and **d idols.** 9359
11:21 to their vile images and **d idols,** 9359
12:16 they may acknowledge all their **d practices.** 9359
14: 6 and renounce all your **d practices!** 9359
16: 2 confront Jerusalem with her **d practices** 9359
16:22 In all your **d practices** 9359
16:36 and because of all your **d** idols, 9359
16:43 to all your other **d practices?** 9359
16:47 in their ways and copied their **d practices,** 9359
16:50 They were haughty and did **d things** 9359
16:51 You have done more **d things** than they, 9359
16:58 of your lewdness and your **d practices,** 9359
18:12 He does **d things.** 9359
18:13 Because he has done all these **d things,** 9359
18:24 and commits sin and does the same **d things** 9359
20: 4 Then confront them with the **d practices** 9359

Eze 22: 2 Then confront her with all her **d practices** 9359
22:11 a **d offense** with his neighbor's wife, 9359
23:36 Then confront them with their **d practices,** 9359
33:26 You rely on your sword, you do **d things,** 9359
33:29 because of all the **d things** they have done.' 9359
36:31 for your sins and **d practices.** 9359
43: 8 defiled my holy name by their **d practices.** 9359
44: 6 Enough of your **d practices,** 9359
44: 7 In addition to all your other **d practices,** 9359
44:13 the shame of their **d practices.** 9359
Mal 2:11 A **d thing** has been committed in Israel and 9359
Lk 16:15 What is highly valued among men is **d** *1007*
Tit 1:16 They are **d,** disobedient and unfit *1008*
1Pe 4: 3 orgies, carousing and **d** idolatry. *116*
Rev 18: 2 a haunt *for* every unclean and **d** bird. *3631*

DETESTED (1) [DETEST]
Zec 11: 8 The flock **d** me, 1041

DETESTS (13) [DETEST]
Dt 22: 5 LORD your God **d** anyone who does this. 9359
23:18 because the LORD your God **d** them both. 9359
25:16 the LORD your God **d** anyone who does these things, 9359
Pr 3:32 for the LORD **d** a perverse man but takes 9359
11:20 The LORD **d** men of perverse heart 9359
12:22 The LORD **d** lying lips, 9359
15: 8 The LORD **d** the sacrifice of the wicked, 9359
15: 9 The LORD **d** the way of the wicked 9359
15:26 The LORD **d** the thoughts of the wicked, 9359
16: 5 The LORD **d** all the proud of heart. 9359
17:15 the LORD **d** them both. 9359
20:10 differing measures—the LORD **d** them both. 9359
20:23 The LORD **d** differing weights, 9359

DETHRONED (1) [THRONE]
2Ch 36: 3 of Egypt **d** him in Jerusalem and imposed 6073

DETRIMENT (1) [DETER]
Ezr 4:22 to the **d** *of* the royal interests? 10472

DEUEL (5)
Nu 1:14 from Gad, Eliasaph son of **D;** 1979
2:14 of the people of Gad is Eliasaph son of **D.** 1979
7:42 On the sixth day Eliasaph son of **D,** 1979
7:47 This was the offering of Eliasaph son of **D.** 1979
10:20 and Eliasaph son of **D** was over the division 1979

DEVASTATE (6) [DEVASTATED, DEVASTATION]
Jos 22:33 to war against them to **d** the country where 8845
Job 12:15 if he lets them loose, *they* **d** the land. 2200
Isa 24: 1 to lay waste the earth and **d** it, 1191
Jer 19: 8 I will **d** this city and make it an object 9014
51: 2 to winnow her and *to* **d** her land; 1327
Hos 11: 9 nor will I turn and **d** Ephraim. 8845

DEVASTATED (11) [DEVASTATE]
Jdg 11:33 *He* **d** twenty towns from 1524+4394+4804+5782
Job 16: 7 *you have* **d** my entire household. 9037
Ps 78:45 and frogs that **d** them. 8845
Isa 61: 4 and restore the *places* long **d;** 9037
61: 4 *that have been* **d** *for* generations. 9037
Jer 4:30 What are you doing, O **d** *one?* 8720
Eze 6: 6 so that your altars will be laid waste and **d,** 870
19: 7 down their strongholds and **d** their towns. 2990
29:12 the land of Egypt desolate among **d** lands, 9037
Hos 10:14 so that all your fortresses *will* **be d—** 8720
10:14 Shalman **d** Beth Arbel on the day of battle, 8720

DEVASTATION (2) [DEVASTATE]
1Sa 5: 6 *he* **brought d** *upon* them and afflicted them 9037
Da 8:24 *He will* **cause** astounding **d** 8845

DEVELOPED (2) [DEVELOPS]
Eze 16: 7 up and **d** and became the most beautiful 1540
Jn 3:25 An argument **d** between some *1181*

DEVELOPS (1) [DEVELOPED]
Jas 1: 3 that the testing of your faith **d** perseverance. *2981*

DEVIATE (1)
2Ch 8:15 *They did* not **d** *from* the king's commands to 6073

DEVICES (1) [DEVISE]
Ps 81:12 to follow their own **d.** 4600

DEVIL (33) [DEVIL'S]
Mt 4: 1 into the desert to be tempted by the **d.** *1333*
4: 5 Then the **d** took him to the holy city *1333*
4: 8 the **d** took him to a very high mountain *1333*
4:11 Then the **d** left him, *1333*
13:39 and the enemy who sows them is the **d.** *1333*
25:41 into the eternal fire prepared *for* the **d** *1333*
Lk 4: 2 for forty days he was tempted by the **d.** *1333*
4: 3 **d** said to him, "If you are the Son of God, *1333*
4: 5 The **d** led him up to a high place *1333*
4: 9 The **d** led him to Jerusalem *NIG*
4:13 When the **d** had finished all this tempting, *1333*
8:12 then the **d** comes and takes away the word *1333*
Jn 6:70 Yet one of you is a **d!"** *1333*
8:44 You belong to your father, the **d,** *1333*
13: 2 the **d** had already prompted Judas Iscariot, *1333*
Ac 10:38 under the power of the **d,** *1333*
13:10 a child *of* the **d** and an enemy of everything *1333*
Eph 4:27 and do not give the **d** a foothold. *1333*
1Ti 3: 6 and fall under the same judgment *as* the **d.** *1333*
2Ti 2:26 and escape from the trap *of* the **d,** *1333*
Heb 2:14 holds the power of death—that is, the **d—** *1333*
Jas 3:15 but is earthly, unspiritual, **of the d.** *1229*
4: 7 Resist the **d,** and he will flee from you. *1333*
1Pe 5: 8 Your enemy the **d** prowls around like *1333*
1Jn 3: 8 He who does what is sinful is of the **d,** *1333*
3: 8 the **d** has been sinning from the beginning. *1333*
3:10 and who the children *of* the **d** are: *1333*
Jude 1: 9 when he was disputing *with* the **d** about *1333*
Rev 2:10 **d** will put some of you in prison to test you, *1333*
12: 9 that ancient serpent called the **d,** or Satan, *1333*
12:12 because the **d** has gone down to you! *1333*
20: 2 that ancient serpent, who is the **d,** or Satan, *1333*
20:10 And the **d,** who deceived them, *1333*

DEVIL'S (3) [DEVIL]
Eph 6:11 take your stand against the **d** schemes. *1333*
1Ti 3: 7 not fall into disgrace and into the **d** trap. *1333*
1Jn 3: 8 of God appeared was to destroy the **d** work. *1333*

DEVILS (KJV) See DEMONS, GOAT IDOLS

DEVIOUS (3) [DEVISE]
Pr 2:15 whose paths are crooked and *who are* **d** 4279
14: 2 but *he* whose ways *are* **d** despises him. 4279
21: 8 The way of the guilty is **d,** 2203

DEVISE (7) [DEVICES, DEVISED, DEVISES, DEVISING]
Ps 21:11 against you and **d** wicked schemes, 3108
35:20 but **d** false accusations 3108
58: 2 No, in your heart *you* **d** injustice, 7188
119:150 *Those who* **d** wicked schemes are near, 8103
140: 2 who **d** evil **plans** in their hearts and stir 3108
Isa 8:10 **D** your strategy, but it will be thwarted; 6418
Eze 38:10 and *you will* **d** an evil scheme. 3108

DEVISED (8) [DEVISE]
2Sa 14:13 then *have you* **d** a thing like this against 3108
Est 8: 3 which *he had* **d** against the Jews. 3108
8: 5 **d** and wrote to destroy the Jews in all 4742
9:25 that the evil scheme Haman *had* **d** against 3108
Ps 64: 6 "We have **d** a perfect plan!" 2924
Jer 49:30 *he has* **d** a plan against you. 3108
Da 11:25 to stand because of the plots **d** against him. 3108
Mt 28:12 with the elders and **d a plan,** 3284+5206

DEVISES (3) [DEVISE]
2Sa 14:14 *he* **d** ways so that a banished person may 3108
Ps 10: 2 who are caught in the schemes *he* **d.** 3108
Pr 6:18 a heart *that* **d** wicked schemes, 3086

DEVISING (1) [DEVISE]
Jer 18:11 a disaster for you and **d** a plan against you. 3108

DEVOTE (11) [DEVOTED, DEVOTES, DEVOTING, DEVOTION, DEVOUT]
1Ch 22:19 Now **d** your heart and soul to seeking 5989
2Ch 31: 4 and Levites so *they could* **d** *themselves* to 2616
Job 11:13 "Yet if you **d** your heart to him 3922
Jer 30:21 for who is he who *will* **d** himself to 6842
Mic 4:13 *You will* **d** their ill-gotten gains to 3049
1Co 7: 5 so that *you may* **d** *yourselves* to prayer. *5390*
Col 4: 2 **D** *yourselves* to prayer, *4674*
1Ti 1: 4 nor *to* **d** themselves to myths *4668*
4:13 **d** *yourself* to the public reading *4668*
Tit 3: 8 in God may be careful *to* **d** *themselves* *4613*
3:14 Our people must learn *to* **d** *themselves* **to** *4613*

DEVOTED (35) [DEVOTE]
Lev 27:21 like a field **d** to the LORD; 3051
27:28 everything so **d** is most holy to the LORD. 3051
27:29 " 'No person **d to destruction** may 3049+3051
Nu 18:14 in Israel that is **d to the LORD** is yours. 3051
Jos 6:17 The city and all that is in it are to be **d** to 3051
6:18 But keep away from the **d things,** 3051
6:21 **d** the city to the LORD **and destroyed** 3049
7: 1 in regard to the **d things;** 3051
7:11 They have taken some of the **d things;** 3051
7:12 among you is **d to destruction.** 3051
7:13 **That which is d** is among you, O Israel. 3051
7:15 with the **d things** shall be destroyed by fire, 3051
22:20 the **d things,** did not watch come upon 3051
1Sa 15:21 the best of what was **d to God,** 3051
1Ki 11: 4 not **fully d** to the LORD his God, 8969
15: 3 not **fully d** to the LORD his God, 8969
1Ch 2: 7 by violating the ban on taking **d things.** 3051
2Ch 17: 6 His heart *was* **d** to the ways of the LORD; 1467
Ezr 7:10 For Ezra *had* **d** himself to the study 3922
Ne 5:16 *I* **d** *myself* to the work on this wall. 2616
Ps 86: 2 Guard my life, for I am **d** to you. 2883
Ecc 1:13 *I* **d** myself to study and to explore 5989
Eze 11:21 But as for those whose hearts *are* **d to** 2143
20:16 For their hearts *were* **d to** their idols. 339+2143
44:29 in Israel **d** to the LORD will belong 3051
Mt 6:24 or *he will be* **d to** the one and despise *504*
15: 5 from me *is* a gift **d** to God,' *6067*
Mk 7:11 Corban' (that is, a **gift d to God),** *1565*
Lk 16:13 or *he will be* **d to** the one and despise *504*
Ac 2:42 *They* **d** *themselves* to the apostles' *1639+4674*
18: 5 Paul **d** *himself exclusively* to preaching, *5309*
Ro 12:10 Be **d** to one another in brotherly love. *5816*
1Co 7:34 Her aim is to be **d** to the Lord in both body *41*
16:15 and *they have* **d** themselves to the service of *5435*
2Co 7:12 for yourselves how **d** to us you *are.* *5082*

DEVOTES (1) [DEVOTE]
Lev 27:28 " 'But nothing that a man owns and **d** to 3049

DEVOTING (1) [DEVOTE]
1Ti 5:10 and **d** *herself* to all kinds of good deeds. *2051*

DEVOTION (13) [DEVOTE]
2Ki 20: 3 and with **wholehearted d** 4222+8969
1Ch 28: 9 and serve him with **wholehearted d** 4213+8969
29: 3 in my **d** to the temple of my God I 8354
29:19 the **wholehearted d** to keep your commands, 4222+8969
2Ch 32:32 and his **acts of d** are written in the vision 2876
35:26 of Josiah's reign and his **acts of d,** 2876
Job 6:14 "A despairing man should have the **d** 2876
15: 4 But you even undermine piety and hinder **d** 8491
Isa 38: 3 and with **wholehearted d** 4213+8969
Jer 2: 2 " 'I remember the **d** *of* your youth, 2876
Eze 33:31 With their mouths they express **d,** 6313
1Co 7:35 in a right way in undivided **d** to the Lord. *2339*
2Co 11: 3 be led astray from your **sincere** and pure **d** *605*

DEVOUR (53) [DEVOURED, DEVOURING, DEVOURS]
Ex 10: 5 *They will* **d** what little you have left after 430
10:12 over the land and **d** everything growing in 430
Lev 26:38 the land of your enemies *will* **d** you. 430
Nu 24: 8 *They* **d** hostile nations 430
Dt 28:38 because locusts *will* **d** it. 2887
28:51 *They will* **d** the young of your livestock 430
32:22 *It will* **d** the earth and its harvests 430
2Sa 2:26 *"Must* the sword **d** forever? 430
1Ki 21:23 'Dogs *will* **d** Jezebel by the wall 430
2Ki 9:10 dogs *will* **d** her on the plot of ground 430
9:36 at Jezreel dogs *will* **d** Jezebel's flesh. 430
2Ch 7:13 or command locusts to **d** the land or send 430
Job 20:21 Nothing is left for him to **d,** 430
20:26 and **d** what is left in his tent. 8286
Ps 14: 4 *those who* **d** my people as men eat bread 430
27: 2 evil men advance against me to **d** my flesh, 430
53: 4 *those who* **d** my people as men eat bread 430
Pr 30:14 with knives to **d** the poor from the earth, 430
Isa 9:20 On the right *they will* **d,** 1616
31: 8 a sword, not of mortals, *will* **d** them. 430
51: 8 the worm *will* **d** them like wool. 430
56: 9 come and **d,** all you beasts of the forest! 430
Jer 5:17 *They will* **d** your harvests and food, 430
5:17 **d** your sons and daughters; 430
5:17 *they will* **d** your flocks and herds, 430
5:17 **d** your vines and fig trees. 430
8:16 *to* **d** the land and everything in it, 430
12: 9 bring them to **d.** 430
12:12 of the LORD *will* **d** from one end of 430
15: 3 and the beasts of the earth to **d** and destroy. 430
30:16 " 'But all *who* **d** you will be devoured; 430
46:10 The sword *will* **d** till it is satisfied, 430
50:17 The first *to* **d** him was the king of Assyria; 430
Eze 22:25 *they* **d** people, take treasures 430
34:28 nor *will* wild animals **d** them. 430
35:12 and have been given over to us to **d."** 433
36:13 Because people say to you, "You **d** men 430
36:14 therefore *you will* no longer **d** men 430
Da 7:23 from all the other kingdoms and *will* **d** 10030
Hos 2:12 and wild animals *will* **d** them. 430
5: 7 their New Moon festivals *will* **d** them 430
7: 7 *they* **d** their rulers. 430
13: 8 Like a lion *I will* **d** them; 430
Am 5: 6 *it will* **d,** and Bethel will have no one 430
Na 2:13 and the sword *will* **d** your young lions. 430
3:15 There the fire *will* **d** you; 430
Hab 1: 8 They fly like a vulture swooping to **d;** 430
3:14 though about to **d** the wretched who were 430
Zec 11: 1 O Lebanon, so that fire *may* **d** your cedars! 430
Mk 12:40 *They* **d** widows' houses and for *2983*
Lk 20:47 They **d** widows' houses and for *2983*
1Pe 5: 8 a roaring lion looking for someone *to* **d.** *2927*
Rev 12: 4 so that *he might* **d** her child the moment it was born. *2983*

DEVOURED (29) [DEVOUR]
Ge 37:20 and say that a ferocious animal **d** him. 430
37:33 Some ferocious animal *has* **d** him. 430
Ex 10:15 *They* **d** all that was left after the hail— 430
Nu 26:10 whose followers died when the fire **d** 430
Job 31:39 if *I have* **d** its yield without payment 430
Ps 44:11 up to be **d** like sheep and have scattered us 4407
78:45 He sent swarms of flies that **d** them, 430
79: 7 for *they have* **d** Jacob 430

Isa 1:20 *you will* **be d** *by* the sword." 430
9:12 and Philistines from the west *have* **d** Israel 430
49:19 and *those who* **d** you will be far away. 1180
Jer 2:3 all *who* **d** her were held guilty, 430
2:30 Your sword *has* **d** your prophets like 430
10:25 For *they have* **d** Jacob; 430
10:25 *they have* **d** him completely 430
30:16 " 'But all who devour you *will* **be d;** 430
50:7 Whoever found them **d** them; 430
51:34 "Nebuchadnezzar king of Babylon *has* **d** us, 430
Eze 7:15 in the city *will* **be d** *by* famine and plague. 430
19:3 He learned to tear the prey and *he* **d** men. 430
19:6 He learned to tear the prey and *he* **d** men. 430
33:27 to the wild animals to *be* **d,** 430
Da 7:7 it crushed and **d** its victims 10030
7:19 the beast that crushed and **d** its victims 10030
Joel 1:19 for fire *has* **d** the open pastures 430
1:20 of water have dried up and fire *has* **d** 430
Am 4:9 Locusts **d** your fig and olive trees, 430
7:4 it dried up the great deep and **d** the land. 430
Rev 20:9 fire came down from heaven and **d** them. *2983*

DEVOURING (4) [DEVOUR]

Dt 9:3 across ahead of you like a **d** fire. 430
Isa 29:6 and tempest and flames of a **d** fire. 430
Mal 3:11 I will prevent pests from **d** your crops, 8845
Gal 5:15 If *you keep on* biting and **d** each other, *2983*

DEVOURS (12) [DEVOUR]

Ge 49:27 in the morning *he* **d** the prey, 430
Nu 13:32 "The land we explored **d** those living in it. 430
23:24 a lion that does not rest till *he* **d** his prey 430
Dt 32:42 while my sword **d** flesh: 430
2Sa 11:25 the sword **d** one as well as another. 430
Job 18:13 death's firstborn **d** his limbs. 430
22:20 and fire **d** their wealth.' 430
Ps 50:3 a fire **d** before him, 430
Pr 21:20 but a foolish man **d** all he has. 1180
Jer 46:14 for the sword **d** those around you.' 430
Joel 2:3 Before them fire **d,** 430
Rev 11:5 from their mouths and **d** their enemies. *2983*

DEVOUT (7) [DEVOTE]

1Ki 18:3 (Obadiah was a **d** believer in the LORD. 4394
Isa 57:1 **d** men are taken away, 2876
Lk 2:25 who was righteous and **d.** *2327*
Ac 10:2 and all his family were **d** and God-fearing; *2356*
10:7 of his servants and a **d** soldier who was one *2356*
13:43 and **d** converts to Judaism followed Paul *4936*
22:12 He was a **d** observer of the law *2327*

DEW (36)

Ge 27:28 of heaven's **d** and of earth's richness— 3228
27:39 away from the **d** *of* heaven above. 3228
Ex 16:13 the morning there was a layer of **d** around 3228
16:14 When the **d** was gone, 3228
Nu 11:9 When the **d** settled on the camp at night, 3228
Dt 32:2 like rain and my words descend like **d,** 3228
33:13 the precious **d** from heaven above and with 3228
33:28 where the heavens drop **d.** 3228
Jdg 6:37 If there is **d** only on the fleece and all 3228
6:38 he squeezed the fleece and wrung out the **d** 3228
6:39 and the ground covered with **d."** 3228
6:40 all the ground was covered with **d.** 3228
2Sa 1:21 may you have neither **d** nor rain, 3228
17:12 and we will fall on him as **d** settles on 3228
1Ki 17:1 there will be neither **d** nor rain in 3228
Job 29:19 and the **d** will lie all night on my branches. 3228
38:28 Who fathers the drops of **d?** 3228
Ps 110:3 of the dawn you will receive the **d** 3228
133:3 It is as if the **d** *of* Hermon were falling 3228
Pr 3:20 and the clouds let drop the **d.** 3228
19:12 but his favor is like **d** on the grass. 3228
SS 5:2 My head is drenched with **d,** 3228
Isa 18:4 like a cloud of **d** in the heat of harvest." 3228
26:19 Your **d** is like the dew of the morning; 3228
26:19 Your dew is like the **d** *of* the morning; 3228
Da 4:15 be drenched with the **d** *of* heaven, 10299
4:23 Let him be drenched with the **d** *of* heaven; 10299
4:25 and be drenched with the **d** *of* heaven. 10299
4:33 with the **d** *of* heaven until his hair grew 10299
5:21 and his body was drenched with the **d** 10299
Hos 6:4 like the early **d** that disappears. 3228
13:3 like the early **d** that disappears, 3228
14:5 I will be like the **d** to Israel; 3228
Mic 5:7 be in the midst of many peoples like **d** from 3228
Hag 1:10 of you the heavens have withheld their **d** 3228
Zec 8:12 and the heavens will drop their **d.** 3228

DIADEM (4)

Ex 29:6 on his head and attach the sacred **d** to 5694
39:30 They made the plate, the sacred **d,** 5694
Lev 8:9 the sacred **d,** on the front of it, 5694
Isa 62:3 a royal **d** in the hand of your God. 7565

DIAMETER (1)

1Ki 7:32 The **d** of each wheel was a cubit and a half. 7757

DIAMOND (KJV) See EMERALD, FLINT

DIANA (KJV) See ARTEMIS

DIBLAH (1)

Eze 6:14 a desolate waste from the desert to **D—** 1812

DIBLAIM (1)

Hos 1:3 So he married Gomer daughter of **D,** 1813

DIBLATH (KJV) See DIBLAH

DIBLATHAIM See ALMON DIBLATHAIM, BETH DIBLATHAIM

DIBON (9) [DIBON GAD]

Nu 21:30 Heshbon is destroyed all the way to **D.** 1897
32:3 **D,** Jazer, Nimrah, Heshbon, Elealeh, 1897
32:34 The Gadites built up **D,** Ataroth, Aroer, 1897
Jos 13:9 the whole plateau of Medeba as far as **D,** 1897
13:17 including **D,** Bamoth Baal, 1897
Ne 11:25 in **D** and its settlements, 1897
Isa 15:2 **D** goes up to its temple, 1897
Jer 48:18 O inhabitants of the Daughter of **D,** 1897
48:22 to **D,** Nebo and Beth Diblathaim, 1897

DIBON GAD (2) [DIBON, GAD]

Nu 33:45 They left Iyim and camped at **D.** 1898
33:46 They left **D** and camped 1898

DIBRI (1)

Lev 24:11 Shelomith, the daughter of **D** the Danite.) 1828

DICTATE (2) [DICTATED, DICTATING, DICTATION, EDICT]

Jer 36:17 Did Jeremiah **d** it?" 4946+7023
Mic 7:3 the powerful **d** what they desire— 1819

DICTATED (4) [DICTATE]

Jer 36:4 and while Jeremiah **d** all the words 4946+7023
36:6 of the LORD that you wrote as I **d.** 4946+7023
36:18 Baruch replied, "he **d** all these words to me, 4946+7023+7924
36:32 and as Jeremiah **d,** Baruch wrote 7023

DICTATING (1) [DICTATE]

Jer 45:1 written on a scroll the words Jeremiah was then **d:** 4946+7023

DICTATION (1) [DICTATE]

Jer 36:27 Baruch had written *at* Jeremiah's **d,** 4946+7023

DID (1316) [DO]

Ge 3:1 He said to the woman, *"D* God really **say,** AIT
3:3 but God *d* **say,** "You must not eat AIT
4:5 *d* not **look with favor.** AIT
6:22 Noah **d** everything just as God commanded 6913
7:5 And Noah **d** all that the LORD commanded 6913
8:12 but this time *it d* not **return** to him. AIT
12:19 Why *d you* **say,** 'She is my sister,' AIT
15:10 *d* not **cut in half.** AIT
18:13 "Why *d* Sarah **laugh** and say, AIT
18:15 so she lied and said, *"I d* not **laugh."** AIT
18:15 But he said, "Yes, *you d* **laugh."** AIT
19:3 But he insisted so strongly that *they d* **go** AIT
20:5 *D* he not **say** to me, 'She is my sister,' AIT
20:6 I know *you* **d** this with a clear conscience, 6913
20:6 That is why *I d* not **let** you touch her. AIT
21:1 LORD **d** for Sarah what he had promised. 6913
21:26 You *d* not **tell** me, AIT
26:9 Why *d you* **say,** 'She is my sister'?" AIT
26:29 just as *we d* not **molest** you AIT
27:20 "How *d you* **find** it so quickly, my son?" AIT
27:23 *He d* not **recognize** him, AIT
27:45 with you and forgets what *you* **d** to him, 6913
29:28 And Jacob **d** so. 6913
30:40 and *d* not **put** them with Laban's animals. AIT
31:27 Why *d you* **run off** secretly AIT
31:30 But why *d you* **steal** my gods?" AIT
31:32 Now Jacob *d* not **know** AIT
31:39 *I d* not **bring** you animals torn AIT
38:10 What *he* **d** was wicked in 6913
38:20 but *he d* not **find** her. AIT
38:23 After all, *I d* **send** her this young goat, AIT
38:26 And *he d* not **sleep with** her again. AIT
39:3 in everything he **d,** 6913
39:6 in charge, *he d* not **concern** *himself* AIT
39:23 and gave him success in whatever he **d.** 6913
40:23 *d* not **remember** Joseph; he forgot him. AIT
42:4 But Jacob *d* not **send** Benjamin, AIT
42:8 they *d* not **recognize** him. AIT
42:23 They *d* not **realize** AIT
43:6 *d you* **bring** *this* **trouble** AIT
43:17 The man **d** as Joseph told him and took 6913
44:2 And *he* **d** as Joseph said. 6913
45:21 So the sons of Israel **d** this. 6913
45:26 Jacob was stunned; *he d* not **believe** them. AIT
46:34 just as our fathers **d.'** NIH
47:22 *he d* not **buy** the land of the priests, AIT
47:22 That is why *they d* not **sell** their land. AIT
Ge 47:26 of the priests that *d* not **become** Pharaoh's. AIT
50:12 Jacob's sons **d** as he had commanded them: 6913
50:15 and pays us back for all the wrongs *we* **d** 1694
Ex 1:8 a new king, who *d* not **know about** Joseph, AIT
1:17 feared God and *d* not **do** what the king AIT
2:14 "What I **d** must have become known." NIH
2:20 "Why *d you* **leave** him? AIT
3:2 the bush was on fire it *d* not **burn up.** AIT
4:1 'The LORD *d* not **appear** to you'?" AIT
6:3 *d* not **make myself known** AIT
6:9 but *they d* not **listen** to him because AIT
7:6 Moses and Aaron **d** just as the LORD 6913
7:10 and Aaron went to Pharaoh and **d** just as 6913
7:11 also **d** the same things by their secret arts: 6913
7:20 Moses and Aaron **d** just as the LORD 6913
7:22 the Egyptian magicians **d** the same things 6913
7:23 and *d* not **take** even this *to* heart. AIT
8:7 But the magicians **d** the same things 6913
8:13 And the LORD **d** what Moses asked. 6913
8:17 *They* **d** this, and when Aaron 6913
8:24 And the LORD **d** this. 6913
8:31 and the LORD **d** what Moses asked: 6913
9:6 And the next day the LORD **d** it: 6913
9:26 The only place *it* **d** not hail was the land 2118
12:28 The Israelites **d** just what the LORD 6913
12:35 The Israelites **d** as Moses instructed 6913
12:39 and *d* not **have time** to prepare food AIT
12:50 All the Israelites **d** just what the LORD 6913
13:8 'I do this because of what the LORD **d** 6913
13:17 God *d* not **lead** them *on* the road through AIT
14:4 So the Israelites **d** this. 6913
16:15 For *they d* not **know** what it was. AIT
16:17 The Israelites **d** as they were told; 6913
16:18 *d* not **have too much,** AIT
16:18 *d* not **have too little.** AIT
16:24 and *it d* not **stink** or get maggots in it. AIT
17:3 *d you* **bring** us **up** AIT
17:6 So Moses **d** this in the sight of the elders 6913
18:11 for he **d** this to those who had treated Israel NIH
18:24 and **d** everything he said. 6913
19:4 'You yourselves have seen what *I* **d** 6913
21:36 *d* not **keep** it **penned up,** AIT
22:11 that the neighbor *d* not **lay** hands on AIT
24:11 But God *d* not **raise** his hand AIT
32:14 Then the LORD **relented and d not** bring 5714
32:21 "What *d* these people **do** to you, AIT
32:28 The Levites **d** as Moses commanded, 6913
32:35 with a plague because of what *they* **d** *with* 6913
33:11 of Nun *d* not **leave** the tent. AIT
36:10 and **d the same** *with* 285+285+448+2489^{S}
39:32 The Israelites **d** everything just as the LORD 6913
40:16 Moses **d** everything just as the LORD 6913
40:37 the cloud *d* not **lift,** they did not set out— AIT
40:37 *they d* not **set out**—until the day it lifted. AIT
Lev 4:20 with this bull just as *he* **d** with the bull for 6913
6:7 of these things *he* **d** that made him guilty." 6913
8:4 Moses **d** as the LORD commanded him, 6913
8:36 So Aaron and his sons **d** everything 6913
9:15 and offered it for a sin offering as he **d** with NIH
10:7 So *they* **d** as Moses said. 6913
16:15 and do with it as *he* **d** with the bull's blood: 6913
20:23 *they* **d** all these things, I abhorred them. 6913
24:23 The Israelites **d** as the LORD 6913
26:35 the land will have the rest *it d* not **have** AIT
Nu 1:54 The Israelites **d** all this just as the LORD 6913
2:34 So the Israelites **d** everything the LORD 6913
5:4 The Israelites **d** this; 6913
5:4 They **d** just as the LORD 6913
7:9 But Moses *d* not **give** any to the Kohathites, AIT
8:3 Aaron **d** so; he set up the 6913
8:20 Aaron and the whole Israelite community **d** 6913
8:22 *They* **d** with the Levites just as 6913
9:5 and *they* **d** so in the Desert of Sinai 906+2021+6913+7175^{S}
9:5 The Israelites **d** everything just as the LORD 6913
9:13 from his people because *he d* not **present** AIT
9:19 the LORD's order and *d* not **set out.** AIT
11:12 *D* I **conceive** all these people? AIT
11:12 *D* I **give** them **birth?** AIT
11:20 saying, "Why *d we ever* **leave** Egypt?" '" AIT
11:25 *d* not **do** *so* **again.** AIT
11:26 but *d* not **go out** to the Tent. AIT
12:15 and the people *d* not **move on** AIT
16:47 So Aaron **d** as Moses said, 4374^{S}
17:11 Moses **d** just as the LORD commanded 6913
20:4 Why *d you* **bring** the LORD's community AIT
20:5 *d you* **bring** us **up** AIT
20:12 "Because *you d* not **trust** in me enough AIT
20:27 Moses **d** as the LORD commanded: 6913
21:34 Do to him what *you* **d** to Sihon king of 6913
22:19 Now stay here tonight as the others **d,** NIH
22:34 *I d* not **realize** you were standing in AIT
22:37 *"D I* not **send** you an **urgent** AIT
23:2 Balak **d** as Balaam said, 6913
23:17 "What *d* the LORD **say?"** AIT
23:26 *"D I* not **tell** you I must do whatever AIT
23:30 Balak **d** as Balaam had said, 6913
24:1 *he d* not **resort to** sorcery as at other times, AIT
24:12 *"D I* not **tell** the messengers you sent me, AIT
25:11 *I d* not **put an end** to them. AIT
26:11 The line of Korah, however, *d* not **die out.** AIT
27:22 Moses **d** as the LORD commanded him. 6913
31:31 So Moses and Eleazar the priest **d** as 6913
32:8 This is what your fathers **d** 6913
35:23 not his enemy and *he d* not **intend** AIT
36:10 So Zelophehad's daughters **d** as the LORD 6913
Dt 1:30 will fight for you, as *he* **d** for you in Egypt, 6913

Dt 1:32 you *d* not **trust** in the LORD your God, AIT
2:12 just as Israel **d** in the land 6913
2:29 who live in Ar, **d** for us— 6913
2:37 *you d* not **encroach** on any of the land of AIT
3:2 Do to him what *you* **d** to Sihon king of 6913
3:4 not one of the sixty cities that *we d* not **take** AIT
4:3 with your own eyes what the LORD **d** 6913
4:34 the things the LORD your God **d** for you 6913
5:5 of the fire and *d* not **go up** the mountain.) AIT
6:10 flourishing cities *you d* not **build,** AIT
6:11 of good things *you d* not **provide,** AIT
6:11 wells *you d* not **dig,** AIT
6:11 and olive groves *you d* not **plant—** AIT
6:16 Do not test the LORD your God as *you* **d** 5814^S
7:7 *d* not **set** *his* **affection** AIT
7:18 the LORD your God **d** to Pharaoh and 6913
8:4 Your clothes *d* not **wear out** AIT
8:4 not wear out and your feet *d* not **swell** AIT
9:23 *You d* not **trust** him or obey him. AIT
10:10 as I **d** the first time, NIH
11:3 the signs he performed and the **things** he **d** 5126
11:4 what *he* **d** to the Egyptian army, 6913
11:5 It was not your children who saw what *he* **d** 6913
11:6 and what *he* **d** to Dathan and Abiram, 6913
19:6 since he **d** it to his neighbor NIH
21:7 "Our hands *d* not **shed** this blood, AIT
21:7 nor *d* our eyes **see** it done. AIT
22:14 *I d* not **find** proof of her virginity," AIT
22:17 '*I d* not **find** your daughter to be a virgin.' AIT
22:24 *d* not **scream for help,** AIT
23:4 *d* not **come to meet** AIT
24:9 Remember what the LORD your God **d** 6913
25:17 Remember what the Amalekites **d** to you 6913
28:45 because *you d* not **obey** AIT
28:47 Because *you d* not **serve** AIT
28:62 because *you d* not **obey** AIT
29:2 Your eyes have seen all that the LORD **d** 6913
29:5 your clothes *d* not **wear out,** AIT
29:5 nor **d** the sandals on your feet. 1162^S
29:6 I **d** this so that you might know that I am NIH
29:26 gods *they d* not **know,** AIT
31:4 And the LORD will do to them what *he* **d** 6913
32:17 gods your fathers *d* not **fear.** AIT
32:51 *d* not **uphold** my **holiness** AIT
33:9 *He d* not **recognize** his brothers AIT
34:9 So the Israelites listened to him and **d** what 6913
34:11 who **d** all those miraculous signs NIH
34:12 that Moses **d** in the sight of all Israel. 6913
Jos 2:4 *I d* not **know** where they had come from. AIT
2:10 and what *you* **d** to Sihon and Og, 6913
4:8 the Israelites **d** as Joshua commanded them. 6913
4:23 The LORD your God **d** to the Jordan NIH
4:24 He **d** this so that all the peoples of NIH
5:4 Now this is why he **d so:** 4576^S
5:15 And Joshua **d** so. 6913
6:14 *They* **d** this for six days. 6913
7:6 The elders of Israel **d** the same, NIH
7:7 *d you ever* **bring** this **people across** AIT
8:2 You shall do to Ai and its king as *you* **d** 6913
8:5 as they **d** before, we will flee from them. NIH
8:6 from us as they **d** before.' NIH
8:14 But he *d* not **know** that AIT
8:17 in Ai or Bethel who *d* not **go** after Israel. AIT
8:19 As soon as *he* **d this,** 2257+3338+5742^S
8:26 For Joshua *d* not **draw back** the hand AIT
8:27 But Israel *d* **carry off** for themselves AIT
8:35 that Joshua *d* not **read** to AIT
9:9 all that *he* **d** in Egypt, 6913
9:10 and all that *he* **d** to the two kings of 6913
9:14 but *d* not **inquire of** the LORD. AIT
9:18 But the Israelites *d* not **attack** them, AIT
9:22 "Why *d you* **deceive** us by saying, AIT
9:24 and that is why *we* **d** this. 6913
9:26 and *they d* not **kill** them. AIT
10:28 And *he* **d** to the king of Makkedah 6913
10:30 And *he* **d** to its king as he had done to 6913
10:39 *They* **d** to Debir and its king 6913
11:9 Joshua **d** to them as the LORD had directed: 6913
11:13 Yet Israel *d* not **burn** any of the cities built AIT
11:15 and Joshua **d** it; 6913
11:22 Gath and Ashdod *d any* **survive.** AIT
13:13 But the Israelites *d* not **drive out** the people AIT
16:10 *They d* not **dislodge** the Canaanites living AIT
17:13 *d* not **drive** them **out completely.** AIT
22:20 *d* not wrath **come** upon AIT
22:24 *We* **d** it for fear that some day 6913
24:5 I afflicted the Egyptians by what *I* **d** there, 6913
24:7 You saw with your own eyes what *I* **d** to 6913
24:11 as **d** also the Amorites, Perizzites, NIH
24:12 You **d** not do it with your own sword NIH
24:13 on which *you d* not **toil** and cities you did AIT
24:13 not toil and cities *you d* not **build;** AIT
24:13 and olive groves that you *d* not **plant.'** AIT
Jdg 1:7 Now God has paid me back for what *I* **d** 6913
1:27 But Manasseh *d* not **drive out** the people AIT
1:29 Nor *d* Ephraim **drive out** AIT
1:30 Neither *d* Zebulun **drive out** AIT
1:30 but they **d** subject them to forced labor. NIH
1:31 Nor *d* Asher **drive out** those living in Acco AIT
1:33 Neither *d* Naphtali **drive out** those living AIT
2:11 Then the Israelites **d** evil in the eyes of 6913
2:22 and walk in it as their forefathers **d."** 9068^S
2:23 *d* not **drive** them **out** AIT
3:2 (he **d** this only to teach warfare to NIH
3:7 The Israelites **d** evil in the eyes of 6913
3:12 Once again the Israelites **d** evil in the eyes 6913
3:12 and because *they* **d** this evil 6913

Jdg 3:22 *d* not **pull** the sword **out,** AIT
3:25 when he *d* not **open** the doors of the room, AIT
4:1 the Israelites once again **d** evil in the eyes 6913
5:16 Why *d you* **stay** among the campfires AIT
5:17 And Dan, why *d he* **linger** *by* the ships? AIT
5:18 so **d** Naphtali on the heights of the field. NIH
5:23 because *they d* not **come** to help the LORD, AIT
6:1 Again the Israelites **d** evil in the eyes of 6913
6:4 and *d* not **spare** a living thing for Israel, AIT
6:13 '*D* not the LORD **bring** us **up** AIT
6:20 And Gideon **d** so. 6913
6:27 So Gideon took ten of his servants and **d** as 6913
6:27 *he* **d** it at night rather than in the daytime. 6913
6:29 They asked each other, "Who **d** this?" 6913
6:29 they were told, "Gideon son of Joash **d** it." 6913
6:40 That night God **d** so. 6913
8:18 "What kind of men *d you* **kill** at Tabor?" AIT
8:20 But Jether *d* not **draw** his sword, AIT
8:28 the Israelites and *d* not **raise** its head again. AIT
8:34 and *d* not **remember** the LORD their God, AIT
9:24 God **d** this in order that the crime NIH
10:6 Again the Israelites **d** evil in the eyes of 6913
10:12 *d I* not **save** you from their hands? AIT
11:15 Israel *d* not **take** the land of Moab or AIT
11:18 *They d* not **enter** the territory of Moab, AIT
11:20 *d* not **trust** Israel to pass AIT
11:25 *D he ever* **quarrel** with Israel or fight AIT
11:39 she returned to her father and *he* **d** to her 6913
12:1 "Why *d you* **go** to fight the Ammonites AIT
13:1 Again the Israelites **d** evil in the eyes of 6913
13:16 (Manoah *d* not **realize** that it was the angel AIT
13:19 And the LORD **d** an amazing thing 6913
13:21 *d* not show himself **again** AIT
14:4 (His parents *d* not **know** that this was from AIT
14:9 But *he d* not **tell** them that he had taken AIT
14:15 *D you* **invite** us here to rob us?" AIT
15:6 When the Philistines asked, "Who **d** this?" 6913
15:10 they answered, "to do to him as *he* **d** to us." 6913
15:11 "*I* merely **d** to them what they did to me." 6913
15:11 "I merely did to them what *they* **d** to me." 6913
16:20 he *d* not **know** that the LORD had left him. AIT
17:6 everyone **d** as he saw fit. 6913
18:8 "How **d** you find things?" NIH
19:17 Where *d you* **come** from?" AIT
20:34 so heavy that the Benjamites *d* not **realize** AIT
21:22 *we d* not **get** wives for them during the war, AIT
21:22 you *d* not **give** your daughters to them.' " AIT
21:23 So that is what the Benjamites **d.** 6913
21:25 everyone **d** as he saw fit. 6913
Ru 2:11 to live with a people *you d* not **know** before. AIT
2:19 "Where *d you* **glean** today? AIT
2:19 Where *d you* **work?** AIT
3:6 and **d** everything her mother-in-law told her 6913
3:15 When *she* **d so,** 296^S
3:16 Naomi asked, **"How d it go,** my daughter?" 905+4769
4:2 "Sit here," and *they* **d so.** 3782^S
1Sa 1:22 Hannah *d* not **go.** AIT
2:25 *d* not **listen** to their father's rebuke, AIT
2:27 '*D I* not **clearly reveal myself** AIT
3:5 But Eli said, "*I d* not **call;** AIT
3:6 "My son," Eli said, "*I d* not **call;** AIT
3:7 Now Samuel *d* not yet **know** the LORD: AIT
4:3 *d* the LORD **bring defeat upon** AIT
4:20 But *she d* not **respond** or pay any attention. AIT
5:12 Those who *d* not **die** were afflicted AIT
6:6 harden your hearts as the Egyptians and Pharaoh **d?** 906+3877+4213+4392^S
6:6 *d they* not **send** the Israelites **out** AIT
6:10 So they **d** this. 6913
6:12 *they d* not **turn** *to* the right or *to* the left. AIT
7:13 and *d* not **invade** Israelite territory again. AIT
8:3 But his sons *d* not **walk** in his ways. AIT
9:4 but *they d* not **find** them. AIT
9:4 but *they d* not **find** them. AIT
9:27 and the servant **d so—** 6296^S
10:16 *he d* not **tell** his uncle what Samuel had said AIT
12:17 an evil thing *you* **d** in the eyes of 6913
13:8 but Samuel *d* not **come** *to* Gilgal, AIT
13:11 and that you *d* not **come** at the set time, AIT
14:1 But *he d* not **tell** his father. AIT
14:17 When *they* **d,** it was Jonathan 7212^S
14:37 But God *d* not **answer** him that day. AIT
14:45 for *he* **d** this today with God's help." 6913
15:2 the Amalekites for what *they* **d** to Israel 6913
15:17 **d** you not become the head of the tribes NIH
15:19 Why *d you* not **obey** the LORD? AIT
15:19 Why *d you* **pounce** on the plunder AIT
15:20 "But *I d* **obey** the LORD," Saul said. AIT
15:35 *d* not go to **see** AIT
16:4 Samuel **d** what the LORD said. 6913
17:28 with whom *d you* **leave** those few sheep AIT
18:2 with him and *d* not **let** him return AIT
18:5 David **d** it so successfully 3655^S
18:10 as he **usually d.** 928+3427+3427+3869
18:14 In everything he **d** he had great success, 2006
18:30 and as often as they **d,** 3655^S
19:17 "Why *d you* **deceive** me like this AIT
20:34 that second day of the month *he d* not **eat,** AIT
22:17 yet *they d* not **tell** me." AIT
23:13 *he d* not **go** there. AIT
23:14 but God *d* not **give** David into his hands. AIT
24:7 and *d* not **allow** them to attack Saul. AIT
24:11 the corner of your robe but *d* not **kill** you. AIT
24:18 now told me of the good *you* **d** to me; 6913
24:18 but *you d* not **kill** me. AIT
25:7 *we d* not **mistreat** them, AIT

1Sa 25:15 They *d* not **mistreat** *us,* AIT
25:19 But *she d* not **tell** her husband Nabal. AIT
25:25 *I d* not **see** the men my master sent. AIT
26:12 nor *d anyone* **wake up.** AIT
26:16 because *you d* not **guard** your master, AIT
27:9 *d* not **leave** a man or woman **alive,** AIT
27:10 "Where *d you* **go raiding** today?" AIT
27:11 *d* not **leave** a man or woman **alive** AIT
27:11 'This is what David **d.'** " 6913
28:6 but the LORD *d* not **answer** him by dreams AIT
28:18 Because *you d* not **obey** the LORD AIT
28:21 in my hands and **d** what you told me to do. 9048
30:22 "Because *they d* not **go out** with us, AIT
2Sa 1:22 the bow of Jonathan *d* not **turn** back, AIT
1:22 the sword of Saul *d* not **return** unsatisfied. AIT
2:28 nor *d they* fight **anymore.** AIT
3:7 "Why *d you* **sleep with** AIT
3:11 Ish-Bosheth *d* not **dare** to say another word AIT
3:24 *d you* **let** him **go?** AIT
3:26 But David *d* not **know** it. AIT
3:36 indeed, everything the king **d** pleased them. 6913
5:25 So David **d** as the LORD commanded him, 6913
7:7 *d I* **ever say** *to* any AIT
7:10 as they **d** at the beginning NIH
11:9 and *d* not **go down** to his house. AIT
11:10 David was told, "Uriah *d* not **go** home," AIT
11:13 *he d* not **go** home. AIT
11:20 *d you* **get so close** AIT
11:21 *d you* **get so close** AIT
12:5 the man who **d** this deserves to die! 6913
12:6 because *he* **d** such a thing and had no pity." 6913
12:9 Why *d you* **despise** the word of the LORD AIT
12:12 You **d** it in secret, 6913
12:31 *He* **d** this to all the Ammonite towns. 6913
13:29 So Absalom's men **d** 6913
14:20 Your servant Joab **d** this to change 6913
14:24 to his own house and *d* not **see** the face of AIT
14:31 Then Joab *d* **go** to Absalom's house AIT
19:19 not remember how your servant **d wrong** on 6390
19:41 *d* our brothers, the men of Judah, **steal** the king **away** AIT
19:42 "We **d** this because the king is closely NIH
20:3 but *d* not **lie with** them. AIT
20:6 will do us more harm than Absalom **d.** NIH
21:10 *she d* not **let** the birds of AIT
21:14 and **d** everything the king commanded. 6913
22:38 *I d* not **turn back** till they were destroyed. AIT
22:42 to the LORD, but *he d* not **answer.** AIT
22:44 People *I d* not **know** are subject to me, AIT
1Ki 1:8 Shimei and Rei and David's special guard **d** 2118
1:10 but *he d* not **invite** Nathan the prophet AIT
1:13 *d* you not **swear** to me your servant: AIT
1:26 and your servant Solomon *he d* not **invite.** AIT
2:5 what Joab son of Zeruiah **d** to me— 6913
2:5 what *he* **d** to the two commanders 6913
2:42 "*D I* not **make** you **swear** AIT
2:43 then *d you* not **keep** your oath to the LORD AIT
2:44 the wrong *you* **d** to my father David. 6913
3:14 and commands as David your father **d,** 2143^S
7:14 He came to King Solomon and **d** all 6913
7:18 *He* **d** the same for each capital. 6913
8:18 *you* **d well** to have this in your heart. 3201
9:4 as David your father **d,** 2143^S
9:22 But Solomon *d* not make **slaves** of any of AIT
9:23 550 officials supervising the men who **d** 6913
10:7 But *I d* not **believe** these things AIT
11:6 Solomon **d** evil in the eyes of the LORD; 6913
11:6 **d** not follow the LORD **completely,** 4848
11:8 *He* **d** the same for all his foreign wives, 6913
11:10 Solomon *d* not **keep** the LORD's command. AIT
11:28 how well the young man **d** his work, 6913
11:33 and laws as David, Solomon's father, **d.** NIH
11:38 as David my servant **d,** I will be with you. 6913
11:41 all *he* **d** and the wisdom he displayed— 6913
12:15 So the king *d* not **listen** to the people, AIT
12:32 This *he* **d** in Bethel, 6913
13:10 So he took another road and *d* not **return** by AIT
13:12 "Which way *d he* **go?"** AIT
13:27 "Saddle the donkey for me," and *they* **d so.** 2502^S
13:33 this, Jeroboam *d* not **change** his evil ways, AIT
14:4 So Jeroboam's wife **d** what he said 6913
14:22 Judah **d** evil in the eyes of the LORD. 6913
14:29 events of Rehoboam's reign, and all *he* **d,** 6913
15:7 other events of Abijah's reign, and all *he* **d,** 6913
15:11 Asa **d** what was right in the eyes of 6913
15:14 Although *he d* not **remove** the high places, AIT
15:23 all *he* **d** and the cities he built, 6913
15:26 *He* **d** evil in the eyes of the LORD, 6913
15:29 *He d* not **leave** Jeroboam anyone AIT
15:31 other events of Nadab's reign, and all *he* **d,** 6913
15:34 *He* **d** evil in the eyes of the LORD, 6913
16:5 what *he* **d** and his achievements, 6913
16:7 provoking him to anger by the **things** he **d,** 3338+5126
16:11 *He d* not **spare** a single male, AIT
16:14 other events of Elah's reign, and all *he* **d,** 6913
16:25 But Omri **d** evil in the eyes of the LORD 6913
16:27 what *he* **d** and the things he achieved, 6913
16:30 Ahab son of Omri **d** more evil in the eyes 6913
16:33 an Asherah pole and **d** more to provoke 6913
16:33 to anger than **d** all the kings of Israel NIH
17:5 So *he* **d** what the LORD had told him. 6913
17:15 She went away and **d** as Elijah had told her. 6913
17:16 not used up and the jug of oil *d* not **run dry,** AIT
17:18 *D you* **come** to remind me of my sin AIT
18:13 what *I* **d** while Jezebel was killing 6913
18:34 "Do it again," he said, and *they* **d** *it* **again.** 9101

1Ki 18:34 **d** *it* **the third time.** 8992
20: 7 my silver and my gold, *I d* not **refuse** him." AIT
20:34 as my father **d** in Samaria." 8492S
21:11 and nobles who lived in Naboth's city **d** 6913
22:24 *d* the spirit from the LORD **go** AIT
22:39 events of Ahab's reign, including all *he* **d,** 6913
22:43 of his father Asa and *d* not **stray** from them; AIT
22:43 he **d** what was right in the eyes of 6913
22:52 *He* **d** evil in the eyes of the LORD, 6913
2Ki 1:18 events of Ahaziah's reign, and what *he* **d,** 6913
2:17 for three days but *d* not **find** him. AIT
3: 2 *He* **d** evil in the eyes of the LORD, 6913
3: 3 *he d* not **turn away** from them. AIT
3:14 *d* not **have respect for** AIT
4:28 "*D I* **ask** you for a son, my lord?" AIT
4:36 And *he* **d.** 7924S
6: 6 "Where *d it* **fall?"** AIT
8:14 "What *d* Elisha **say** to you?" AIT
8:18 *He* **d** evil in the eyes of the LORD. 6913
8:23 events of Jehoram's reign, and all *he* **d,** 6913
8:27 the ways of the house of Ahab and **d** evil in 6913
9:11 Why *d* this madman **come** to you?" AIT
10:15 So *he* **d,** and Jehu helped him 2257+3338+5989S
10:29 he *d* not **turn away** from the sins AIT
10:31 *He d* not **turn away** from the sins AIT
10:34 for the other events of Jehu's reign, all *he* **d,** 6913
11: 9 of units of a hundred **d** just as Jehoiada 6913
12: 2 Joash **d** what was right in the eyes of 6913
12:15 *d* not **require an accounting** AIT
12:19 of the reign of Joash, and all *he* **d,** 6913
13: 2 *He* **d** evil in the eyes of the LORD 6913
13: 2 and *he d* not **turn away** from them. AIT
13: 6 But *they d* not **turn away** from the sins of AIT
13: 8 all *he* **d** and his achievements, 6913
13:11 *He* **d** evil in the eyes of the LORD and did 6913
13:11 the eyes of the LORD and *d* not **turn away** AIT
13:12 all *he* **d** and his achievements, 6913
13:15 "Get a bow and some arrows," and *he* **d so.** 2256+2932+4374+8008S
14: 3 *He* **d** what was right in the eyes of 6913
14: 6 *d* not **put** the sons of the assassins **to death,** AIT
14:15 what *he* **d** and his achievements, 6913
14:24 *He* **d** evil in the eyes of the LORD and did 6913
14:24 the eyes of the LORD and *d* not **turn away** AIT
14:28 other events of Jeroboam's reign, all *he* **d,** 6913
15: 3 *He* **d** what was right in the eyes of 6913
15: 6 events of Azariah's reign, and all *he* **d,** 6913
15: 9 *He* **d** evil in the eyes of the LORD, 6913
15: 9 *He d* not **turn away** from the sins AIT
15:18 *He* **d** evil in the eyes of the LORD. 6913
15:18 During his entire reign *he d* not **turn away** AIT
15:21 events of Menahem's reign, and all *he* **d,** 6913
15:24 Pekahiah **d** evil in the eyes of the LORD. 6913
15:24 *He d* not **turn away** from the sins AIT
15:26 events of Pekahiah's reign, and all *he* **d,** 6913
15:28 *He* **d** evil in the eyes of the LORD. 6913
15:28 *He d* not **turn away** from the sins AIT
15:31 other events of Pekah's reign, and all *he* **d,** 6913
15:34 *He* **d** what was right in the eyes of 6913
15:36 events of Jotham's reign, and what *he* **d,** 6913
16: 2 *he d* not **do** what was right in the eyes of AIT
16:16 the priest **d** just as King Ahaz had ordered. 6913
16:19 events of the reign of Ahaz, and what *he* **d,** 6913
17: 2 *He* **d** evil in the eyes of the LORD, 6913
17: 9 The Israelites **secretly d** things against 2901
17:11 *They* **d** wicked things that provoked 6913
17:14 who *d* not **trust** in the LORD their God. AIT
17:15 and they **d** the things NIH
17:19 and even Judah *d* not **keep** the commands of AIT
17:22 the sins of Jeroboam and *d* not **turn away** AIT
17:25 *they d* not **worship** the LORD; AIT
17:41 to do as their fathers **d.** 6913
18: 3 *He* **d** what was right in the eyes of 6913
18: 6 He held fast to the LORD and *d* not **cease** AIT
18: 7 the king of Assyria and *d* not **serve** him. AIT
19:12 *D* the gods of the nations that were destroyed by my forefathers **deliver** AIT
20: 7 *They* **d so** and applied it to the boil, 4374S
20:13 that Hezekiah *d* not **show** them. AIT
20:14 "What *d* those men **say,** AIT
20:14 and where *d they* **come** from?" AIT
20:15 "What *d they* **see** in your palace?" AIT
20:15 that *I d* not **show** them." AIT
21: 2 *He* **d** evil in the eyes of the LORD, 6913
21: 6 He **d** much evil in the eyes of the LORD, 6913
21: 9 But *the people d* not **listen.** AIT
21: 9 so that they **d** more evil than the nations 6913
21:16 to commit, so that they **d** evil in the eyes of 6913
21:17 events of Manasseh's reign, and all *he* **d,** 6913
21:20 *He* **d** evil in the eyes of the LORD, 6913
21:22 and *d* not **walk** in the way of the LORD. AIT
21:25 events of Amon's reign, and what *he* **d,** 6913
22: 2 *He* **d** what was right in the eyes of 6913
23: 5 *He* **d away with** the pagan priests appointed 8697
23: 7 and where women **d weaving** 755+1428
23: 9 of the high places *d* not **serve** at the altar of AIT
23:24 This he **d** to fulfill the requirements of NIH
23:25 like him who turned to the LORD as he **d—** NIH
23:26 the LORD *d* not **turn away** from the heat AIT
23:28 other events of Josiah's reign, and all *he* **d,** 6913
23:32 *He* **d** evil in the eyes of the LORD, 6913
23:37 And *he* **d** evil in the eyes of the LORD, 6913
24: 5 events of Jehoiakim's reign, and all *he* **d,** 6913
24: 7 The king of Egypt *d* not **march out** AIT
24: 9 *He* **d** evil in the eyes of the LORD, 6913
24:19 *He* **d** evil in the eyes of the LORD, 6913
1Ch 4:27 but his brothers **d** not have many children; NIH
1Ch 4:27 *d* not *become* as **numerous** AIT
10:13 *he d* not **keep** the word of the LORD and AIT
10:14 and *d* not **inquire of** the LORD. AIT
12:19 (*He and his men d* not **help** the Philistines AIT
13: 3 for *we d* not **inquire of** it during the reign AIT
13:13 He *d* not **take** the ark to be with him in AIT
14:16 So David **d** as God commanded him, 6913
15:13 *d* not **bring** it up the first time that AIT
15:13 *We d* not **inquire of** him *about* how to do it AIT
17: 6 *d I ever* **say** *to* any AIT
17: 9 as they **d** at the beginning NIH
20: 3 David **d** this to all the Ammonite towns. 6913
21: 6 *d* not include Levi and Benjamin *in the* **numbering,** AIT
23:11 but Jeush and Beriah *d* not **have many** sons; AIT
24: 2 Nadab and Abihu died before their father **d,** NIH
24:31 the descendants of Aaron **d,** NIH
27:23 David *d* not **take** the number of AIT
27:24 to count the men but *d* not **finish.** AIT
2Ch 2: 3 "Send me cedar logs as *you* **d** 6913
6: 8 *you* **d well** to have this in your heart. 3201
7: 6 as **d** the Levites with NIH
7:17 you walk before me as David your father **d,** 2143S
8: 9 But Solomon *d* not **make** slaves of AIT
8:15 *They d* not **deviate** *from* AIT
9: 6 But *I d* not **believe** what they said AIT
10:15 So the king *d* not **listen** to the people, AIT
12:14 *He* **d** evil because he had not set his heart 6913
13:20 Jeroboam *d* not **regain** power during AIT
13:22 **what** he **d** and what he said, 2006
14: 2 Asa **d** what was good and right in the eyes 6913
15:17 Although *he d* not **remove** the high places AIT
16:12 even in his illness *he d* not **seek help** *from* AIT
17: 3 *He d* not **consult** the Baals AIT
17:10 that *they d* not **make war** with Jehoshaphat. AIT
18:23 *d* the spirit from the LORD **go** AIT
20: 7 *d* you not **drive out** AIT
20:10 from them and *d* not **destroy** them. AIT
20:32 of his father Asa and *d* not **stray** from them; AIT
20:32 *he* **d** what was right in the eyes of 6913
21: 6 *He* **d** evil in the eyes of the LORD. 6913
21:13 just as the house of Ahab **d.** 2388S
22: 4 *He* **d** evil in the eyes of the LORD, 6913
23: 8 The Levites and all the men of Judah **d** just 6913
24: 2 Joash **d** what was right in the eyes of 6913
24: 5 *d* not **act at once.** AIT
24:11 *They* **d** this regularly and collected 6913
24:22 King Joash *d* not **remember** AIT
25: 2 *He* **d** what was right in the eyes of 6913
25: 4 *d* not **put** their sons **to death,** AIT
26: 4 *He* **d** what was right in the eyes of 6913
27: 2 *He* **d** what was right in the eyes of 6913
27: 2 but unlike him *he d* not **enter** the temple of AIT
27: 3 and **d** extensive **work** on the wall at the hill 1215
27: 7 and the other **things** he **d,** 2006
28: 1 *he d* not **do** what was right in the eyes of AIT
28:21 but that **d** not help him. NIH
29: 2 *He* **d** what was right in the eyes of 6913
29: 6 *they* **d** evil in the eyes of 6913
29: 7 *They d* not **burn** incense AIT
31:20 This is what Hezekiah **d** throughout Judah, 6913
32:12 *D* not Hezekiah himself **remove** AIT
32:17 of the other lands *d* not **rescue** their people AIT
32:19 about the God of Jerusalem as they **d** about NIH
32:25 and he *d* not **respond** to AIT
32:26 as **d** the people of Jerusalem; NIH
32:26 the LORD's wrath *d* not **come** upon them AIT
33: 2 *He* **d** evil in the eyes of the LORD, 6913
33: 6 He **d** much evil in the eyes of the LORD, 6913
33: 9 so that they **d** more evil than the nations 6913
33:22 *He* **d** evil in the eyes of the LORD, 6913
33:23 *he d* not **humble himself** before the LORD; AIT
34: 2 *He* **d** what was right in the eyes of 6913
34:12 The men **d** the work faithfully. 6913
34:32 of Jerusalem **d** this in accordance with 6913
34:33 *they d* not **fail** to follow the LORD, AIT
35:12 They **d** the same with the cattle. NIH
35:15 *d* not *need to* **leave** AIT
35:18 a Passover as **d** Josiah, 6913
36: 5 *He* **d** evil in the eyes of the LORD his God. 6913
36: 8 the detestable things *he* **d** and all 6913
36: 9 *He* **d** evil in the eyes of the LORD. 6913
36:12 *He* **d** evil in the eyes of the LORD his God 6913
36:12 and *d* not **humble himself** before Jeremiah AIT
Ezr 5:17 to see if King Cyrus *d* in fact **issue** a decree AIT
10:16 So the exiles **d** as was proposed. 6913
Ne 2:16 The officials *d* not **know** where I had gone AIT
4:16 half of my men **d** the work, 6913
4:17 Those who carried materials **d** their work 6913
5:13 And the people **d** as they had promised. 6913
5:15 of reverence for God I *d* not **act** like that. AIT
5:16 *we d* not **acquire** any land. AIT
9:16 and *d* not **obey** your commands. AIT
9:17 Therefore *you d* not **desert** them, AIT
9:19 great compassion you *d* not **abandon** them AIT
9:19 the pillar of cloud *d* not **cease** to guide them AIT
9:20 *You d* not **withhold** your manna AIT
9:21 their clothes *d* not **wear out** AIT
9:21 *d* their feet *become* **swollen.** AIT
9:28 they again **d** what was evil in your sight. 6913
9:31 in your great mercy *you d* not **put** an end AIT
9:33 while we **d wrong.** 8399
9:34 and our fathers *d* not **follow** your law; AIT
9:34 *they d* not **pay attention** AIT
9:35 *they d* not **serve** you or turn AIT
12:40 so **d** I, together with half the officials, NIH
12:45 as **d** also the singers and gatekeepers, NIH
Ne 13:24 and *d* not **know how** to speak the language AIT
Est 1:21 so the king **d** as Memucan proposed. 6913
9: 5 and *they* **d** what they pleased 6913
9:10 *they d* not **lay** their hands on the plunder. AIT
9:15 *they d* not **lay** their hands on the plunder. AIT
9:16 but *they d* not **lay** their hands on the plunder. AIT
Job 1:22 Job *d* not **sin** by charging God AIT
2:10 In all this, Job *d* not **sin** in what he said. AIT
3:10 for *it d* not **shut** the doors of the womb AIT
3:11 "Why *d I* not **perish** at birth, AIT
10:10 *D you* not **pour** me **out** AIT
10:18 *d you* **bring** me **out** AIT
20:19 he has seized houses *he d* not **build.** AIT
31:15 *D* not he who made me in the womb **make** AIT
31:15 *D* not the same one **form** AIT
31:20 and his heart *d* not **bless** me AIT
33:27 *d* not **get what I deserved.** AIT
39:17 for God *d* **not endow** her *with* wisdom AIT
42: 3 of things *I d* not **understand,** AIT
42: 9 and Zophar the Naamathite **d** what 6913
Ps 18:37 *I d* not **turn back** till they were destroyed. AIT
18:41 to the LORD, but *he d* not **answer.** AIT
18:43 people *I d* not **know** are subject to me. AIT
30: 1 *d* not **let** my enemies **gloat** AIT
32: 5 to you and *d* not **cover up** my iniquity. AIT
40: 6 Sacrifice and offering *you d* not **desire,** AIT
40: 6 and sin offerings *you d* not **require.** AIT
44: 1 our fathers have told us what *you* **d** 7188
44: 3 *d* their arm **bring** them **victory;** AIT
52: 7 man *who d* not **make** God his stronghold AIT
69: 4 I am forced to restore what *I d* not **steal.** AIT
78:10 *they d* not **keep** God's covenant and refused AIT
78:12 *He* **d** miracles in the sight of their fathers in 6913
78:22 for *they d* not **believe** in God or trust AIT
78:32 in spite of his wonders, *they d* not **believe.** AIT
78:38 and *d* not **destroy** them. AIT
78:38 and *d* not **stir up** his full wrath. AIT
78:42 *They d* not **remember** his power— AIT
78:50 *he d* not **spare** them from death AIT
78:56 *they d* not **keep** his statutes. AIT
78:67 *he d* not **choose** the tribe of Ephraim; AIT
81: 5 we heard a language *we d* not **understand.** AIT
83: 9 Do to them as you **d** to Midian, NIH
83: 9 as you **d** to Sisera and Jabin at NIH
95: 8 not harden your hearts as you **d** at Meribah, NIH
95: 8 as you **d** that day at Massah in the desert, NIH
95: 9 though they had seen **what I d.** 7189
106: 6 We have sinned, even as our fathers **d;** NIH
106: 7 *they d* not **remember** your many kindnesses AIT
106:13 and *d* not **wait** for his counsel. AIT
106:24 *they d* not **believe** his promise. AIT
106:25 They grumbled in their tents and *d* not **obey** AIT
106:34 *They d* not **destroy** the peoples as AIT
106:39 They defiled themselves by **what** they **d;** 5126
107:38 *d* not **let** their herds **diminish.** AIT
137: 7 the Edomites **d** on the day Jerusalem fell. NIH
Pr 1:29 and *d* not **choose** to fear the LORD, AIT
24:29 I'll pay that man back for what he **d."** 7189
Ecc 8:10 in the city where *they* **d** this. 6913
SS 3: 1 I looked for him but *d* not **find** him. AIT
3: 2 So I looked for him but *d* not **find** him. AIT
5: 6 I looked for him but *d* not **find** him. AIT
5: 6 I called him but *he d* not **answer.** AIT
6: 1 Which way *d* your lover **turn,** AIT
Isa 5: 4 why *d it* **yield** only bad? AIT
10:24 and lift up a club against you, as Egypt **d.** NIH
10:26 as he **d** in Egypt. NIH
20: 2 *he* **d** so, going around stripped and barefoot. 6913
22: 2 nor *d they* **die** *in* battle. AIT
22:11 but *you d* not **look** to the One who made it, AIT
28:21 The LORD will rise up as he **d** NIH
29:16 "*He d* not **make** me"? AIT
37:12 *D* the gods of the nations that were destroyed by my forefathers **deliver** AIT
39: 2 that Hezekiah *d* not **show** them. AIT
39: 3 "What *d* those men **say,** AIT
39: 3 and where *d they* **come** from?" AIT
39: 4 "What *d they* **see** in your palace?" AIT
39: 4 that *I d* not **show** them." AIT
40:14 *d* the LORD **consult** AIT
42:24 *they d* not **obey** his law. AIT
42:25 yet *they d* not **understand;** AIT
42:25 but *they d* not **take** it to heart. AIT
44: 8 *D I* not **proclaim** this AIT
45:18 *he d* not **create** it to be empty, AIT
47: 7 But *you d* not **consider** these things AIT
48: 5 that you could not say, 'My idols **d** them; 6913
48:21 *They d* not **thirst** when he led them through AIT
50: 1 Or to which of my creditors *d I* **sell** you? AIT
50: 6 *I d* not **hide** my face from mocking AIT
53: 7 yet *he d* not **open** his mouth; AIT
53: 7 so *he d* not **open** his mouth. AIT
57:10 and so *you d* not **faint.** AIT
63:13 *they d* not **stumble;** AIT
64: 3 when you **d** awesome things that we did 6913
64: 3 that *we d* not **expect,** AIT
65: 1 "I revealed myself to *those who d* not **ask** AIT
65: 1 I was found by *those who d* not **seek** me. AIT
65: 1 To a nation *that d* not **call** on my name, AIT
65:12 for I called but *you d* not **answer,** AIT
65:12 I spoke but *you d* not **listen.** AIT
65:12 *You* **d** evil in my sight 6913
66: 4 *They* **d** evil in my sight 6913
Jer 2: 5 "What fault *d* your fathers **find** in me, AIT
2: 6 *They d* not **ask,** 'Where is the LORD, AIT
2: 8 priests *d* not **ask,** 'Where is the LORD?' AIT
2: 8 Those who deal with the law *d* not **know** me AIT

Jer	2:21	*d you* **turn** against me **into** a corrupt	AIT
	2:30	*they d* not **respond to** correction.	AIT
	2:34	though *you d* not **catch** them breaking in.	AIT
	3: 7	to me but *she* **d** not,	8740S
	3:10	her unfaithful sister Judah *d* not **return**	AIT
	7:12	and see what *I* **d** to it because of	6913
	7:13	but *you d* not **listen;**	AIT
	7:13	I called you, but *you d* not **answer.**	AIT
	7:14	what *I* **d** to Shiloh I will now do to	6913
	7:15	just as *I* **d** all your brothers,	8959S
	7:22	*d* not *just* **give** them **commands**	AIT
	7:24	But *they d* not **listen** or pay attention;	AIT
	7:26	*they d* not **listen** to me or pay attention.	AIT
	7:26	and **d** more **evil** than their forefathers.'	8317
	7:31	something *I d* not **command,**	AIT
	7:31	nor *d it* **enter** my mind.	AIT
	10:11	who *d* not **make** the heavens and the earth,	AIT
	11: 8	But *they d* not **listen** or pay attention;	AIT
	11: 8	to follow but that *they d* not **keep.'"**	AIT
	11:19	*I d* not **realize** that they had plotted	AIT
	14:15	*I d* not **send** them, yet they are saying,	AIT
	15: 4	of Hezekiah king of Judah **d** in Jerusalem.	6913
	16:11	They forsook me and *d* not **keep** my law.	AIT
	16:19	worthless idols *that* **d** them no **good.**	3603
	17:11	that hatches eggs *it d* not **lay** is	AIT
	17:23	Yet *they d* not **listen** or pay attention;	AIT
	19: 5	something *I d* not **command** or mention,	AIT
	19: 5	nor *d it* **enter** my mind.	AIT
	20:17	For *he d* not **kill** me in the womb,	AIT
	20:18	*d I ever* **come out**	AIT
	22:15	*D* not your father **have food**	AIT
	22:15	*He* **d** what was right and just,	6913
	23:21	*I d* not **send** these prophets,	AIT
	23:21	*I d* not **speak** to them,	AIT
	23:32	yet I *d* not **send** or appoint them.	AIT
	25: 7	"But *you d* not **listen** to me,"	AIT
	26:19	"*D* Hezekiah king of Judah or anyone else in Judah **put him to death?**	AIT
	26:19	*D* not Hezekiah **fear** the LORD	AIT
	26:19	*d* not the LORD **relent, so that** he *did* **not bring** the disaster	AIT
	26:19	**relent, so that** he *d* **not bring** the disaster	AIT
	26:20	and this land as Jeremiah **d.**	NIH
	27:20	of Babylon *d* not **take away**	AIT
	29:16	your countrymen who *d* not **go** with you	AIT
	29:23	which *I d* not **tell** them to do.	AIT
	29:31	even though I *d* not **send** him,	AIT
	32:23	but *they d* not **obey** you or follow your law;	AIT
	32:23	*they d* not **do** what you commanded them	AIT
	32:35	nor *d it* **enter** my mind,	AIT
	34:14	*d* not **listen** to me or pay attention to me.	AIT
	34:15	Recently you repented and **d** what is right	6913
	35:17	I spoke to them, but *they d* not **listen;**	AIT
	35:17	I called to them, but *they d* not **answer.'"**	AIT
	36: 8	of Neriah **d** everything Jeremiah	6913
	36:17	how *d you come to* **write** all this?	AIT
	36:17	**D** Jeremiah dictate it?"	NIH
	36:24	nor *d they* **tear** their clothes.	AIT
	36:29	that scroll and said, "Why *d you* **write** on it	AIT
	38:12	to pad the ropes." Jeremiah **d** so,	6913
	38:15	Even if *I d* **give** you **counsel,**	AIT
	38:27	All the officials *d* **come** to Jeremiah	AIT
	40: 3	against the LORD and *d* not **obey** him.	AIT
	40:14	of Ahikam *d* not **believe** them.	AIT
	41: 8	So he let them alone and *d* not **kill** them	AIT
	44: 5	But *they d* not **listen** or pay attention;	AIT
	44: 5	they *d* not **turn** from their wickedness	AIT
	44:17	our kings and our officials **d** in the towns	6913
	44:19	**d** not our husbands know	NIH
	44:21	"*D* not the LORD **remember**	AIT
	44:22	and the detestable things *you* **d,**	6913
	48:11	So she tastes as she **d,**	6641S
	52: 2	*He* **d** evil in the eyes of the LORD,	6913
La	1: 9	*she d* not **consider** her future.	AIT
	2: 8	and *d* not **withhold** his hand	AIT
	2:14	*they d* not **expose** your sin	AIT
	4:12	The kings of the earth *d* not **believe,**	AIT
	4:12	nor **d** any of the world's people,	NIH
Eze	1: 9	*they d* not **turn** as they moved.	AIT
	1:17	the wheels *d* not **turn about** as	AIT
	3:20	*you d* not **warn** him, he will die for his sin.	AIT
	3:20	The righteous things *he* **d** will not	6913
	6:10	*I d* not **threaten** in vain	AIT
	10:11	the wheels *d* not **turn about** as	AIT
	10:16	the wheels *d* not **leave** their side.	AIT
	12: 7	So *I* **d** as I was commanded.	6913
	12: 9	*d* not that rebellious house of Israel **ask**	AIT
	16:22	and your prostitution *you d* not **remember**	AIT
	16:43	"'Because *you d* not **remember** the days	AIT
	16:43	*D you* not **add** lewdness	AIT
	16:48	and her daughters never **d** what you	6913
	16:49	*they d* not **help** the poor and needy.	AIT
	16:50	They were haughty and **d** detestable things	6913
	16:50	*I* **d away with** them as you have seen.	6073
	16:51	Samaria *d* not **commit** half the sins you did.	AIT
	16:51	Samaria did not commit half the sins you **d.**	NIH
	17:18	in pledge and yet **d** all these things,	6913
	18:18	robbed his brother and **d** what was wrong	6913
	20: 8	*d* not **get rid of**	AIT
	20: 8	nor *d they* **forsake** the idols of Egypt.	AIT
	20: 9	of my name *I* **d** what would keep it	6913
	20:13	*They d* not **follow** my decrees	AIT
	20:14	of my name *I* **d** what would keep it	6913
	20:16	and *d* not **follow** my decrees	AIT
	20:17	on them with pity and *d* not **destroy** them	AIT
	20:21	*They d* not **follow** my decrees,	AIT
	20:22	of my name *I* **d** what would keep it	6913
Eze	20:30	the way your fathers **d** and lust	NIH
	23: 8	*She d* not **give up** the prostitution she began	AIT
	23:39	That is what *they* **d** in my house.	6913
	24: 7	*she d* not **pour** it on the ground,	AIT
	24:18	The next morning *I* **d** as	6913
	27:12	"'Tarshish **d business with** you because	6086
	27:16	"'Aram **d business with** you because	6086
	27:18	**d business with** you in wine from Helbon	6086
	27:21	*they* **d business with** you in lambs,	6086
	29:20	for his efforts because *he and his army* **d** it	6913
	33: 5	of the trumpet but *d* not **take warning,**	AIT
	34: 8	and because my shepherds *d* not **search for**	AIT
	35: 6	Since *you d* not **hate** bloodshed,	AIT
	40:36	as **d** its alcoves,	NIH
	48:11	and *d* not **go astray** as the Levites did when	AIT
	48:11	and did not go astray as the Levites **d** when	9494S
Da	2:15	"Why **d** the king issue such	NIH
	5:23	But *you d* not **honor** the God who holds	AIT
	6:12	"*D you* not **publish** a decree that during	AIT
	8: 4	*He* **d** as he pleased and became great.	6913
	8:12	It prospered in everything *it* **d,**	6913
	9:14	The LORD **d not hesitate** to bring	9193
	10: 7	the men with me *d* not **see** it,	AIT
	11:24	nor his forefathers **d.**	6913
	12: 8	I heard, but *I d* not **understand.**	AIT
Hos	10: 3	"We have no king because *we d* not **revere**	AIT
	10: 9	*D* not war **overtake** the evildoers	AIT
	11: 3	*they d* not **realize** it was I who healed them.	AIT
Am	4: 8	for water but *d* not **get enough** to drink,	AIT
	4:10	"I sent plagues among you as I **d** to Egypt.	NIH
	5:25	"*D you* **bring** me sacrifices	AIT
	6:13	"*D we* not **take** Karnaim	AIT
	9: 7	"*D I* not **bring** Israel **up**	AIT
Jnh	1:13	*d their best to* **row**	AIT
	3:10	When God saw **what** they **d** and	5126
	3:10	he had compassion and *d* not **bring**	AIT
	4:10	though *you d* not **tend** it or make it grow.	AIT
Hab	3: 8	**D** you rage against the sea when you rode	NIH
Zep	3: 7	to act corruptly in all they **d.**	6613
Hag	2:17	mildew and hail, yet you **d** not turn to me,'	NIH
Zec	1: 6	*d* not my words and my decrees, which I commanded my servants the prophets, **overtake** your forefathers?	AIT
	7:13	"'When I called, *they d* not **listen;**	AIT
	8:11	with the remnant of this people as I **d** in the	NIH
Mal	2:10	*D* not one God **create** us?	AIT
	3:14	What **d** we gain by carrying out his	NIH
Mt	1:19	a righteous man and **d** not want	*NIG*
	1:24	*he* **d** what the angel of the Lord	*4472*
	7:22	Lord, *d we* not **prophesy** in your name,	*AIT*
	7:25	yet *it d* not **fall,**	*AIT*
	9:19	and so **d** his disciples.	*NIG*
	10:34	*I d* not **come** to bring peace, but a sword.	*AIT*
	11: 7	"What *d you* **go out** into the desert to see?	*AIT*
	11: 8	If not, what *d you* **go out** to see?	*AIT*
	11: 9	Then what *d you* **go out** to see?	*AIT*
	11:17	and *you d* not **dance;**	*AIT*
	11:17	we sang a dirge, and *you d* not **mourn.'**	*AIT*
	11:20	because *they d* not **repent.**	*AIT*
	12: 3	"Haven't you read what David **d** when he	*4472*
	13: 5	where *it d* not **have** much soil.	*AIT*
	13:17	to see what you see but *d* not **see** it,	*AIT*
	13:17	and to hear what you hear but *d* not **hear** it.	*AIT*
	13:27	Where then **d** the weeds come from?'	*NIG*
	13:28	"'An enemy **d** this,' he replied.	*4472*
	13:34	*he d* not **say** anything to them without using	*AIT*
	13:54	"Where **d** this man get this wisdom	*NIG*
	13:56	then **d** this man get all these things?"	*NIG*
	13:58	And *he d* not **do** many miracles there	*AIT*
	14:31	he said, "why *d you* **doubt?"**	*AIT*
	15:23	Jesus *d* not **answer** a word.	*AIT*
	17:12	and *they d* not **recognize** him,	*AIT*
	18:13	about the ninety-nine that *d* not **wander off.**	*AIT*
	19: 7	"*d* Moses **command** that a man give his wife a certificate of divorce	*AIT*
	20: 5	and the ninth hour and **d** the same thing.	*4472*
	20:28	as the Son of Man *d* not **come** to be served,	*AIT*
	21: 6	and **d** as Jesus had instructed them.	*4472*
	21:15	the law saw the wonderful things *he* **d** and	*4472*
	21:20	*d* the fig tree **wither**	*AIT*
	21:25	John's baptism—where **d** it come from?	*NIG*
	21:30	He answered, 'I will, sir,' but *he d* not **go.**	*AIT*
	21:31	of the two **d** what his father wanted?"	*4472*
	21:32	and *you d* not **believe** him,	*AIT*
	21:32	but the tax collectors and the prostitutes **d.**	*4409S*
	21:32	*you d* not **repent** and believe him.	*AIT*
	22: 8	but those I invited *d* not **deserve** to come.	*AIT*
	22:12	'how *d you* **get in** here	*AIT*
	25: 3	but *d* not **take** any oil with them.	*AIT*
	25:37	when *d we* **see** you hungry and feed you,	*AIT*
	25:38	When *d we* **see** you a stranger and invite you	*AIT*
	25:39	When *d we* **see** you sick or in prison and go	*AIT*
	25:40	whatever *you* **d** for one of the least	*4472*
	25:40	*you* **d** for me.'	*4472*
	25:43	*d* not **invite** me **in,**	*AIT*
	25:43	I needed clothes and *you d* not **clothe** me,	*AIT*
	25:43	in prison and *you d* not **look after** me.'	*AIT*
	25:44	when *d we* **see** you hungry or thirsty or	*AIT*
	25:44	and *d* not **help** you?'	*AIT*
	25:45	whatever *you d* not **do** for one of the least	*AIT*
	25:45	*you d* not **do** for me.'	*AIT*
	26:12	*she* **d** it to prepare me for burial.	*4472*
	26:19	the disciples **d** as Jesus had directed them	*4472*
	26:55	and *you d* not **arrest** me.	*AIT*
	26:60	But *they d* not **find** any,	*AIT*
	28:15	the money and **d** as they were instructed.	*4472*
Mk	2:25	"Have you never read what David **d**	*4472*
Mk	4: 5	where *it d* not **have** much soil.	*AIT*
	4: 7	so that *they d* not **bear** grain.	*AIT*
	4:34	*He d* not **say** anything to them without using	*AIT*
	5:19	Jesus *d* not **let** him, but said,	*AIT*
	5:37	*He d* not **let** anyone follow him except	*AIT*
	6: 2	"Where **d** this man get these things?"	*NIG*
	6:17	He **d** this because of Herodias,	*NIG*
	6:26	*he d* not **want** to refuse her.	*AIT*
	6:31	that they **d** not even have a chance to eat,	*NIG*
	7:24	a house and *d* not **want** anyone to know it;	*AIT*
	7:36	But the more *he* **d so,**	*1403S*
	8: 6	and *they* **d so.**	*4192S*
	8:19	many basketfuls of pieces *d you* **pick up?"**	*AIT*
	8:20	many basketfuls of pieces *d you* **pick up?"**	*AIT*
	9: 6	(*He d* not **know** what to say,	*AIT*
	9:30	Jesus *d* not **want** anyone to know	*AIT*
	9:32	But they *d* **not understand** what he meant	*AIT*
	10: 3	"What *d* Moses **command** you?" he replied.	*AIT*
	10:45	the Son of Man *d* not **come** to be served,	*AIT*
	14: 8	*She* **d** what she could.	*4472*
	14:40	*They d* not **know** what to say to him.	*AIT*
	14:49	and *you d* not **arrest** me.	*AIT*
	14:55	but *they d* not **find** any.	*AIT*
	14:56	but their statements **d** not agree.	*1639*
	14:59	Yet even then their testimony **d** not agree.	*1639*
	15: 8	to do for them what he usually **d.**	*NIG*
	15:23	but he *d* not **take** it.	*AIT*
	16:11	*they d* **not believe** it.	*AIT*
	16:13	but *they d* not **believe** them either.	*AIT*
Lk	1:20	because *you d* not **believe** my words,	*AIT*
	2:45	*When they d* not **find** him,	*AIT*
	2:50	they *d* not **understand** what he was saying	*AIT*
	4:23	that you **d** in Capernaum.'"	*1181*
	6: 3	"Have you never read what David **d**	*4472*
	6:10	"Stretch out your hand." He **d** so,	*4472*
	7: 7	*d* not even **consider** myself **worthy**	*AIT*
	7:24	"What *d you* **go out** into the desert to see?	*AIT*
	7:25	If not, what *d you* **go out** to see?	*AIT*
	7:26	But what *d you* **go out** to see?	*AIT*
	7:32	and *you d* not **dance;**	*AIT*
	7:32	we sang a dirge, and *you d* not **cry.'**	*AIT*
	7:44	*You d* not **give** me any water for my feet,	*AIT*
	7:45	*You d* not **give** me a kiss, but this woman,	*AIT*
	7:46	*d* not **put** oil **on** my head,	*AIT*
	8:51	*he d* not **let** anyone go in	*AIT*
	9:15	The disciples **d** so,	*4472*
	9:33	(*He d* not **know** what he was saying.)	*AIT*
	9:43	at all that Jesus **d,**	*4472*
	9:45	But they *d* **not understand** what this meant.	*AIT*
	9:45	so that *they d* not **grasp** it,	*AIT*
	9:53	but the *people* there *d* not **welcome** him,	*AIT*
	10:24	to see what you see but *d* not **see** it,	*AIT*
	10:24	and to hear what you hear but *d* not **hear** it."	*AIT*
	11:38	that Jesus *d* not first **wash** before the meal,	*AIT*
	11:40	*D* not the one who made the outside **make**	*AIT*
	11:48	of what your forefathers **d;**	*2240*
	13: 6	but *d* not **find** any.	*AIT*
	17: 9	the servant because *he* **d** what he was told	*4472*
	18:34	The disciples *d* not **understand** any of this.	*AIT*
	18:34	*they d* not **know** what he was talking about.	*AIT*
	19:21	You take out what *you d* not **put in**	*AIT*
	19:21	not put in and reap what *you d* not **sow.'**	*AIT*
	19:22	You knew, **d** you, that I am a hard man,	*NIG*
	19:22	taking out what *I d* not **put in,**	*AIT*
	19:22	and reaping what *I d* not **sow?**	*AIT*
	19:27	of mine who *d* not **want** me to be king	*AIT*
	19:44	because *you d* not **recognize** the time	*AIT*
	22:35	bag or sandals, *d you* **lack** anything?"	*AIT*
	22:53	and *you d* not **lay** a hand on me.	*AIT*
	24: 3	*they d* not **find** the body of the Lord Jesus.	*AIT*
	24:11	But *they d* **not believe** the women,	*AIT*
	24:24	but him *they d* not **see."**	*AIT*
	24:26	*D* not the Christ **have** to suffer these things	*AIT*
	24:41	*while* they still *d* **not believe** it because	*AIT*
Jn	1:10	the world *d* not **recognize** him.	*AIT*
	1:11	but his own *d* not **receive** him.	*AIT*
	1:20	*d* not fail *to* **confess,**	*AIT*
	1:31	I myself *d* not **know** him,	*AIT*
	1:41	The first thing Andrew **d** was	*NIG*
	2: 8	of the banquet." They **d so,**	*5770S*
	2: 9	*He d* not **realize** where it had come from,	*AIT*
	2:25	*He d* not **need** man's testimony about man,	*AIT*
	3:17	For God *d* not **send** his Son into the world	*AIT*
	4:12	**d** also his sons and his flocks and herds?"	*NIG*
	4:29	a man who told me everything *I* ever **d.**	*4472*
	4:39	"He told me everything *I* ever **d."**	*4472*
	6:11	He **d** the same with the fish.	*NIG*
	6:14	the miraculous sign that Jesus **d,**	*4472*
	6:25	"Rabbi, when *d you* **get** here?"	*AIT*
	6:64	the beginning which of them *d* not **believe**	*AIT*
	7: 5	even his own brothers *d* not **believe** in him.	*AIT*
	7:14	the Feast *d* Jesus **go up** to the temple courts	*AIT*
	7:15	*d* this man **get such learning**	*AIT*
	7:21	Jesus said to them, "*I* **d** one miracle,	*4472*
	7:22	(though actually *it d* not **come** from Moses,	*AIT*
	7:36	What *d* he **mean** when he said,	*AIT*
	8:27	*They d* not **understand**	*AIT*
	8:39	"then you would do the things Abraham **d.**	*NIG*
	8:40	Abraham *d* not **do** such things.	*AIT*
	8:52	Abraham died and so **d** the prophets,	*NIG*
	8:53	He died, and so **d** the prophets.	*NIG*
	8:55	If I said I **d** not, I would be a liar like you,	*NIG*
	9:18	The Jews still *d* not **believe**	*AIT*
	9:26	they asked him, "What *d he* **do** to you?	*AIT*
	9:26	How *d he* **open** your eyes?"	*AIT*
	9:27	and *you d* not **listen.**	*AIT*
	10: 6	*d* not **understand** what he was telling them.	*AIT*

Jn 10: 8 but the sheep d not listen to them. AIT
10:25 Jesus answered, "I d tell you, AIT
11:40 "D I not tell you that if you believed, AIT
11:45 and had seen what Jesus d, 4472
11:51 He d not say this on his own, AIT
12: 6 He d not say this because he cared about AIT
12:16 At first his disciples d not understand all this. AIT
12:16 after Jesus was glorified d they realize AIT
12:47 For I d not come to judge the world, AIT
12:49 For I d not speak of my own accord, AIT
15:16 You d not choose me, AIT
15:24 not done among them what no one else d, 4472
16: 4 I d not tell you this at first AIT
18:23 if I spoke the truth, why d you strike me?" AIT
18:28 the Jews d not enter the palace; AIT
18:34 "or d others talk to you about me?" AIT
19:24 So this is what the soldiers d. 4472
19:31 Because the Jews d not want the bodies left NIG
19:33 they d not break his legs. AIT
20: 5 of linen lying there but d not go in. AIT
20: 9 (They still d not understand from Scripture AIT
20:14 but she d not realize that it was Jesus. AIT
20:30 Jesus d many other miraculous signs in 4472
21: 4 the disciples d not realize that it was Jesus. AIT
21: 6 When they d, they were unable to haul 965S
21:13 and d the same with the fish. NIG
21:23 But Jesus d not say that he would not die; AIT
21:25 Jesus d many other things as well. 4472
Ac 2:22 which God d among you through him, 4472
2:31 nor d his body see decay. AIT
2:34 For David d not ascend to heaven, AIT
3: 4 Peter looked straight at him, as d John. NIG
3:17 as d your leaders. NIG
4: 7 or what name d you do this?" AIT
4:28 They d what your power 4472
5:22 the officers d not find them there. AIT
5:26 They d not use force, NIG
6: 8 d great wonders and miraculous signs 4472
7:25 but they d not. 5317S
7:32 Moses trembled with fear and d not dare AIT
7:36 He led them out of Egypt and d wonders 4472
7:42 " 'D you bring me sacrifices AIT
7:52 a prophet your fathers d not persecute? AIT
8: 6 and saw the miraculous signs he d, 4472
8:32 so he d not open his mouth. AIT
8:39 and the eunuch d not see him again, AIT
9: 7 they heard the sound but d not see anyone. AIT
9: 9 and d not eat or drink anything. AIT
10:39 "We are witnesses of everything he d in 4472
11:30 This they d, sending their gift to the elders 4472
12: 8 And Peter d so. 4472
12:19 for him and d not find him, AIT
12:23 because Herod d not give praise to God, AIT
13:27 and their rulers d not recognize Jesus, AIT
13:37 from the dead d not see decay. AIT
15: 8 just as he d to us. NIG
15:38 Paul d not think it wise to take him, AIT
17: 4 as d a large number of God-fearing Greeks NIG
17: 6 But when they d not find them, AIT
17:12 as d also a number NIG
17:27 God d this so that men would seek him NIG
19: 2 "D you receive the Holy Spirit AIT
19: 3 baptism d you receive?" AIT
19:11 God d extraordinary miracles through Paul, 4472
19:32 d not even know why they were there. AIT
20:35 In everything I d, I showed you that NIG
22: 9 but they d not understand the voice AIT
23: 5 I d not realize that he was the high priest; AIT
24:12 My accusers d not find me arguing AIT
25:17 d not delay the case, but convened the court the next day and ordered AIT
25:18 they d not charge him with any of AIT
26:10 And that is just what I d in Jerusalem. 4472
27: 7 d not allow us to hold our course, AIT
27:39 they d not recognize the land, AIT
Ro 1:28 d not think it worthwhile AIT
3: 3 What if some d not have faith? AIT
3:25 He d this to demonstrate his justice, NIG
3:26 he d it to demonstrate his justice at NIG
4:20 Yet he d not waver AIT
5:14 even over those who d not sin by breaking AIT
5:14 a command, as d Adam, who was a pattern NIG
5:15 d God's grace and the gift that came by the grace of the one man, Jesus Christ, overflow AIT
6:21 What benefit d you reap at that time from AIT
7:13 D that which is good, then, become AIT
8: 3 God d by sending his own Son in NIG
8:15 For you d not receive a spirit AIT
8:32 He who d not spare his own Son, AIT
9:20 'Why d you make me like this?' " AIT
9:23 What if he d this to make the riches NIG
9:30 Gentiles, who d not pursue righteousness, AIT
10: 3 Since they d not know the righteousness AIT
10: 3 they d not submit to God's righteousness. AIT
10:18 But I ask: D they not hear? AIT
10:18 Of course they d: NIG
10:19 D Israel not understand? AIT
10:20 "I was found by those who d not seek me; AIT
10:20 to those who d not ask for me." AIT
11: 1 I ask then: D God reject his people? AIT
11: 2 God d not reject his people, AIT
11: 7 so earnestly it d not obtain, AIT
11: 7 but the elect d. NIG
11:11 D they stumble so as to fall AIT
11:21 For if God d not spare the natural branches, AIT
15: 3 For even Christ d not please himself but, AIT
1Co 1:14 I am thankful that I d not baptize any AIT
1:17 For Christ d not send me to baptize, AIT
1:21 through its wisdom d not know him, AIT
2: 1 I d not come with eloquence AIT
4: 7 What do you have that you d not receive? AIT
4: 7 And if you d receive it, AIT
4: 7 why do you boast as though you d not? NIG
5: 2 of your fellowship the man who d this? 4556
5: 3 on the one who d this, 2981
7:30 as if they d not; NIG
9:12 But we d not use this right. AIT
10: 6 on evil things as they d. 2121S
10: 8 as some of them d— 4519S
10: 9 as some of them d— 4279S
10:10 And do not grumble, as some of them d— 1197S
11: 8 For man d not come from woman, AIT
14:36 D the word of God originate AIT
15:15 But he d not raise him if in fact the dead are AIT
15:46 The spiritual d not come first, NIG
2Co 1:17 When I planned this, d I do it lightly? AIT
1:23 to spare you that I d not return to Corinth. AIT
2: 3 I wrote as I d so that when I came 899+4047
2:13 because I d not find my brother Titus there. AIT
7: 8 Though I d regret it— AIT
7:12 not on account of the one who d the wrong 92
8: 5 And they d not do as we expected, NIG
8:15 d not have too much, AIT
8:15 d not have too little." AIT
10:14 for we d get as far as you with the gospel AIT
12:17 D I exploit you through any of AIT
12:18 Titus d not exploit you, did he? AIT
12:18 Titus did not exploit you, d he? NIG
12:18 D we not act in the same spirit and follow AIT
Gal 1:12 I d not receive it from any man, AIT
1:16 I d not consult any man, AIT
1:17 nor d I go up to Jerusalem AIT
2: 2 But I d this privately to those who seemed NIG
2: 5 We d not give in to them for a moment, AIT
3: 2 D you receive the Spirit by observing AIT
4: 8 Formerly, when you d not know God, AIT
4:14 d not treat me with contempt or scorn. AIT
5:21 I warn you, as I d before, 4625S
Eph 4:20 d not come to know AIT
Php 2: 6 d not consider equality with God something AIT
2:16 the day of Christ that I d not run or labor AIT
1Th 2: 5 nor d we put on a mask to cover up greed— NIG
2:18 certainly I, Paul, d, again and again— NIG
4: 7 For God d not call us to be impure, AIT
5: 9 For God d not appoint us to suffer wrath AIT
2Th 3: 8 nor d we eat anyone's food without paying AIT
3: 9 We d this, not because we do not have NIG
2Ti 1: 3 whom I serve, as my forefathers d, NIG
1: 7 For God d not give us a spirit of timidity, AIT
4:14 the metalworker d me a great deal of harm. 1892
Phm 1:14 But I d not want to do anything AIT
Heb 1: 5 For to which of the angels d God ever say, AIT
1:13 To which of the angels d God ever say, AIT
3: 8 do not harden your hearts as you d in NIG
3: 9 and for forty years saw what I d. 2240+3836
3:15 do not harden your hearts as you d in NIG
3:18 And to whom d God swear AIT
4: 2 gospel preached to us, just as they d; NIG
4: 2 d not combine it with AIT
4: 6 the gospel preached to them d not go in, AIT
4:10 just as God d from his. NIG
5: 5 d not take upon himself the glory AIT
6:18 God d this so that, NIG
7: 6 d not trace his descent AIT
8: 9 d not remain faithful to AIT
9:12 He d not enter by means of the blood AIT
9:24 For Christ d not enter a man-made AIT
9:25 Nor d he enter heaven to offer himself NIG
10: 5 "Sacrifice and offering you d not desire, AIT
10: 8 and sin offerings you d not desire, AIT
11: 4 a better sacrifice than Cain d. NIG
11: 5 d not experience death; AIT
11: 8 though he d not know where he was going. AIT
11: 9 he lived in tents, as d Isaac and Jacob, NIG
11:13 They d not receive the things promised; AIT
11:19 he d receive Isaac back from death. AIT
12:25 If they d not escape AIT
Jas 2:21 for what he d when he offered his son Isaac 2240
2:22 his faith was made complete by what he d. 2240
2:25 for what she d when she gave lodging to 2240
5:17 and it d not rain on the land for three and AIT
1Pe 2:23 he d not retaliate; AIT
2Pe 1:16 We d not follow cleverly invented stories AIT
2: 4 if God d not spare angels when they sinned, AIT
2: 5 if he d not spare the ancient world AIT
1Jn 2: 6 to live in him must walk as Jesus d. 4344S
2:19 d not really belong to AIT
3: 1 not know us is that it d not know him. AIT
3:12 And why d he murder him? AIT
5: 6 He d not come by water only, NIG
Jude 1: 5 later destroyed those who d not believe. AIT
1: 6 the angels who d not keep their positions AIT
1: 9 d not dare to bring a slanderous accusation AIT
Rev 2: 5 Repent and do the things you d at first. NIG
2:13 You d not renounce your faith in me, AIT
2:19 that you are now doing more than you d NIG
7:13 and where d they come from?" AIT
9: 4 but only those people who d not have AIT
9:20 not killed by these plagues still d not repent AIT
9:20 they d not stop worshiping demons, AIT
9:21 Nor d they repent of their murders, AIT
12:11 they d not love their lives so much as AIT
14: 4 These are those who d not defile themselves AIT
Rev 20: 5 d not come to life AIT
21:22 I d not see a temple in the city, AIT

DIDN'T (44) [DO, NOT]

Ge 12:18 "Why d you tell me she was your wife? 4202
20: 5 and d she also say, 'He is my brother'? AIT
29:25 I served you for Rachel, d I? 4202
31:27 Why d you tell me, 4202
31:28 You d even let me kiss my grandchildren 4202
38:22 "I d find her. 4202
38:23 but you d find her." 4202
42:22 "D I tell you not to sin against the boy? 4202
Ex 5:14 "Why d you meet your quota 4202
14:12 D we say to you in Egypt, 'Leave us alone; 4202
Lev 10:17 "Why d you eat the sin offering in 4202
Nu 22:37 Why d you come to me? 4202
Jdg 8: 1 Why d you call us when you went 1194
11: 7 "D you hate me and drive me 4202
11:26 Why d you retake them during that time? 4202
12: 2 you d save me out of their hands. 4202
13: 6 I d ask him where he came from, 4202
13: 6 and he d tell me his name. 4202
1Sa 26:15 Why d you guard your lord the king? 4202
2Sa 11:10 Why d you go home?" 4202
11:20 D you know they would shoot arrows from 4202
11:21 D a woman throw an upper millstone 4202
16:17 Why d you go with your friend?" 4202
18:11 Why d you strike him to 4202
19:25 "Why d you go with me, Mephibosheth?" 4202
1Ki 22:18 "D I tell you that he never prophesies 4202
2Ki 2:18 he said to them, "D I tell you not to go?" 4202
4:28 "D I tell you, 'Don't raise my hopes'?" 4202
5:25 "Your servant d go anywhere," 4202
2Ch 13: 9 But d you drive out the priests of 4202
18:17 "D I tell you that he never prophesies 4202
Ne 13:18 D your forefathers do the same things, 4202
Mt 13:27 'Sir, d you sow good seed in your field? 4049
16: 7 "It is because we d bring any bread." 4024
20:13 D you agree to work for a denarius? 4049
21:25 he will ask, 'Then why d you believe him?' 4024
Mk 11:31 he will ask, 'Then why d you believe him?' 4024
Lk 2:49 "D you know I had to be 4024
19:23 Why then d you put my money on deposit, 4024
20: 5 he will ask, 'Why d you believe him?' 4024
24:23 but d find his body. 3590
Jn 7:45 "Why d you bring him in?" 4024
18:26 "D I see you with him in the olive grove?" 4024
Ac 5: 4 D it belong to you before it was sold? 4049

DIDYMUS (3)

Jn 11:16 Then Thomas (called D) said to the rest of 1441
20:24 Now Thomas (called D), 1441
21: 2 Thomas (called D), Nathanael from Cana 1441

DIE (300) [DEAD, DEADENED, DEADLY, DEATH, DEATH'S, DEATHLY, DEATHS, DIED, DIES, DYING]

Ge 2:17 when you eat of it you will surely d." 4637+4637
3: 3 and you must not touch it, or you will d.' " 4637
3: 4 "You will not surely d," 4637+4637
19:19 this disaster will overtake me, and I'll d. 4637
20: 7 be sure that you and all yours will d." 4637+4637
21:16 for she thought, "I cannot watch the boy d." 4638
25:32 "Look, I am about to d," Esau said. 4637
27: 4 I may give you my blessing before I d." 4637
27: 7 in the presence of the LORD before I d.' 4638
30: 1 "Give me children, or I'll d!" 4637
33:13 all the animals will d. 4637
38:11 For he thought, "He may d too, 4637
42: 2 so that we may live and not d." 4637
42:20 be verified and that you may not d." 4637
43: 8 and our children may live and not d. 4637
44: 9 to have it, he will d; 4637
44:22 if he leaves him, his father will d.' 4637
44:31 that the boy isn't there, he will d. 4637
45:28 I will go and see him before I d." 4637
46:30 "Now I am ready to d, 4637
47:15 Why should we d before your eyes? 4637
47:19 Give us seed so that we may live and not d, 4637
47:29 When the time drew near for Israel to d, 4637
48:21 Israel said to Joseph, "I am about to d, 4637
50: 5 "I am about to d; 4637
50:24 "I am about to d. 4637
Ex 7:18 The fish in the Nile will d, 4637
9: 4 to the Israelites will d.' " 4637
9:19 and they will d.' " 4637
10:28 The day you see my face you will d." 4637
11: 5 Every firstborn son in Egypt will d, 4637
12:33 "For otherwise," they said, "we will all d!" 4637
14:11 that you brought us to the desert to d? 4637
14:12 for us to serve the Egyptians than to d in 4637
17: 3 make us and our children and livestock d 4637
20:19 do not have God speak to us or we will d." 4637
21:18 and he does not d but is confined to bed, 4637
28:35 so that he will not d. 4637
28:43 so that they will not incur guilt and d. 4637
30:20 with water so that they will not d. 4637
30:21 and feet so that they will not d. 4637
Lev 8:35 so you will not d; 4637
10: 6 or you will d and the LORD will 4637
10: 7 to the Tent of Meeting or you will d, 4637
10: 9 or you will d. 4637
15:31 so they will not d in their uncleanness 4637
16: 2 or else he will d, 4637

Lev 16:13 so that *he will* not **d**. 4637
20:20 *they will* **d** childless. 4637
21: 1 for any of his people who **d**, 5883
22: 9 not become guilty and **d** for treating them 4637
Nu 4:15 not touch the holy things or *they will* **d**. 4637
4:19 and not **d** when they come near 4637
4:20 even for a moment, or *they will* **d**." 4637
14:35 here *they will* **d**." 4637
15:35 the LORD said to Moses, "The man **must d**. 4637+4637
16:29 If these men **d** a natural death 4637
17:10 so that *they will* not **d**." 4637
17:12 The Israelites said to Moses, "*We will* **d**! 1588
17:13 near the tabernacle of the LORD *will* **d**. 4637
17:13 Are we all *going to* **d**?" 1588
18: 3 or both they and you *will* **d**. 4637
18:22 the consequences of their sin and *will* **d**. 4637
18:32 and *you will* not **d**.' " 4637
20: 4 that we and our livestock *should* **d** here? 4637
20:26 *he will* **d** there." 4637
21: 5 up out of Egypt to **d** in the desert? 4637
23:10 *Let* me **d** the death of the righteous, 4637
26:11 The line of Korah, however, *did* not **d out**. 4637
26:65 the LORD had told those Israelites *they would* **surely d** in the desert, 4637+4637
35:12 that a person accused of murder *may* not **d** 4637
35:31 who deserves to **d**. 4637
Dt 4:22 I *will* **d** in this land; 4637
5:25 But now, why *should we* **d**? 4637
5:25 and *we will* **d** if we hear the voice of 4637
18:16 or *we will* **d**." 4637
19:12 hand him over to the avenger of blood *to* **d**. 4637
20: 5 or *he may* **d** in battle 4637
20: 6 or *he may* **d** in battle 4637
20: 7 or *he may* **d** in battle 4637
22:22 with her and the woman *must* **d**. 4637
22:25 only the man who has done this *shall* **d**. 4637
24: 7 the kidnapper *must* **d**. 4637
24:16 each *is to* **d** for his own sin. 4637
31:27 how much more will you rebel after I **d**! 4638
32:50 that you have climbed *you will* **d** and 4637
33: 6 "Let Reuben live and not **d**, 4637
Jdg 6:23 *You are* not *going to* **d**." 4637
6:30 *He must* **d**, because he has broken 4637
13:22 "*We are* **doomed to d**!" 4637+4637
15:18 now **d** of thirst and fall into the hands of 4637
16:30 "*Let* me **d** with the Philistines!" 4637
Ru 1:17 Where *you* **d** I will die, 4637
1:17 Where you die *I will* **d**, 4637
1Sa 2:33 and all your descendants *will* **d** in 4637
2:34 they *will* both **d** on the same day. 4637
5:12 Those who *did* not **d** were afflicted 4637
12:19 for your servants so that *we will* not **d**, 4637
14:39 with my son Jonathan, *he* **must d**." 4637+4637
14:43 And now *must* I **d**?" 4637
14:44 be it ever so severely, if *you do* not **d**, 4637+4637
14:45 the men said to Saul, "*Should* Jonathan **d**— 4637
20: 2 "*You are* not *going to* **d**! 4637
20:31 for he **must d**!" 1201+4638
22:16 But the king said, "*You will* **surely d**, 4637+4637
26:10 either his time will come and *he will* **d**, 4637
26:16 you and your men deserve to **d**, 4638
2Sa 3:33 "Should Abner have died as the lawless **d**? 4638
11:15 from him so he will be struck down and **d**." 4637
12: 5 the man who did this deserves to **d**! 4638
12:13 *You are* not *going to* **d**. 4637
12:14 the son born to you *will* **d**." 4637+4637
14:14 cannot be recovered, so *we* **must d**. 4637+4637
18: 3 Even if half of us **d**, they won't care; 4637
19:23 the king said to Shimei, "*You shall* not **d**." 4637
19:37 that *I may* **d** in my own town near the tomb 4637
1Ki 1:52 but if evil is found in him, *he will* **d**." 4637
2: 1 When the time drew near for David to **d**, 4637
2:26 You deserve to **d**, 4638
2:30 But he answered, "No, *I will* **d** here." 4637
2:37 you can be sure *you will* **d**; 4637+4637
2:42 you can be sure *you will* **d**'? 4637+4637
13:31 he said to his sons, "When I **d**, 4638
14:11 to Jeroboam *who* **d** in the city, 4637
14:11 the birds of the air will feed on those *who* **d** 4637
14:12 the boy *will* **d**. 4637
16: 4 to Baasha *who* **d** in the city, 4637
16: 4 the birds of the air will feed on those *who* **d** 4637
17:12 that we may eat it—and **d**." 4637
17:20 **causing** her son **to d**?" 4637
19: 4 down under it and prayed that he *might* **d**. 4637
20:42 a man I had **determined should d**. 3051
21:24 to Ahab *who* **d** in the city, 4637
21:24 the birds of the air will feed on those *who* **d** 4637
2Ki 1: 4 *You will* **certainly d**!' " 4637+4637
1: 6 *You will* **certainly d**!" ' " 4637+4637
1:16 *You will* **certainly d**!" 4637+4637
7: 3 "Why stay here until we **d**? 4637
7: 4 the famine is there, and *we will* **d**. 4637
7: 4 And if we stay here, *we will* **d**. 4637
7: 4 if they kill us, then *we* **d**." 4637
8:10 to me that *he will* **in fact d**." 4637+4637
14: 6 each *is to* **d** for his own sins." 4637
20: 1 because you *are going to* **d**; 4637
2Ch 25: 4 each *is to* **d** for his own sins." 4637
32:11 to let you **d** of hunger and thirst. 4637
Est 9:28 of them **d out** among their descendants. 6066
Job 2: 9 Curse God and **d**!" 4637
3:11 and **d** as I came from the womb? 1588
4:21 so that *they* **d** without wisdom?' 4637
12: 2 and wisdom *will* **d** with you! 4637
13:19 If so, I will be silent and **d**. 1588
Job 14: 8 in the ground and its stump **d** in the soil, 4637
27: 5 till *I* **d**, I will not deny my integrity. 1588
29:18 "I thought, '*I will* **d** in my own house, 1588
34:20 *They* **d** in an instant, 4637
36:12 by the sword and **d** without knowledge. 1588
36:14 They **d** in their youth, 4637
Ps 37: 2 like green plants *they will* soon **d away**. 5570
41: 5 "When *will he* **d** and his name perish?" 4637
49:10 For all can see that wise men **d**; 4637
79:11 of your arm preserve those condemned to **d**. 9456
82: 7 But *you will* **d** like mere men; 4637
104:29 *they* **d** and return to the dust. 1588
105:29 **causing** their fish **to d**. 4637
118:17 *I will* not **d** but live, 4637
Pr 5:23 He *will* **d** for lack of discipline, 4637
10:21 but fools **d** for lack of judgment. 4637
15:10 he who hates correction *will* **d**. 4637
19:16 of his ways *will* **d**. 4637
23:13 you punish him with the rod, *he will* not **d**. 4637
30: 7 do not refuse me before *I* **d**: 4637
Ecc 2:16 Like the fool, the wise man too *must* **d**! 4637
3: 2 a time to be born and a time to **d**, 4637
7:17 why **d** before your time? 4637
9: 5 For the living know that *they will* **d**, 4637
Isa 5:13 their men of rank *will* **d** *of* hunger 4637
22: 2 nor *did they* **d** *in* battle. 4637
22:13 you say, "for tomorrow *we* **d**!" 4637
22:18 There *you will* **d** 4637
38: 1 because you *are going to* **d**; 4637
50: 2 their fish rot for lack of water and **d** 4637
51: 6 a garment and its inhabitants **d** like flies. 4637
51:14 *they will* not **d** in their dungeon, 4637
59: 5 Whoever eats their eggs *will* **d**, 4637
66:24 their worm *will* not **d**, 4637
Jer 11:21 the LORD or *you will* **d** by our hands'— 4637
11:22 Their young men *will* **d** by the sword, 4637
16: 4 "*They will* **d** *of* deadly diseases. 4637
16: 6 "Both high and low *will* **d** in this land. 4637
20: 6 There *you will* **d** and be buried, 4637
21: 6 and *they will* **d** of a terrible plague. 4637
21: 9 Whoever stays in this city *will* **d** by 4637
22:12 *He will* **d** in the place 4637
22:26 and there *you both will* **d**. 4637
26: 8 seized him and said, "*You* **must d**! 4637+4637
27:13 Why *will* you and your people **d** by 4637
28:16 This very year you *are going to* **d**, 4637
31:30 Instead, everyone *will* **d** for his own sin; 4637
34: 4 *You will* not **d** by the sword; 4637
34: 5 *you will* **d** peacefully. 4637
37:20 or *I will* **d** there." 4637
38: 2 'Whoever stays in this city *will* **d** by 4637
38:24 or *you may* **d**. 4637
38:26 to Jonathan's house to **d** there.' " 4637
42:16 and there *you will* **d**. 4637
42:17 to settle there *will* **d** by the sword, famine 4637
42:22 *You will* **d** by the sword, 4637
44:12 by the sword or **d** from famine. 9462
44:12 *they will* **d** by sword or famine. 4637
La 4: 9 better off than *those who* **d** of famine; 2728
Eze 3:18 '*You will* **surely d**,' 4637+4637
3:18 that wicked man *will* **d** for his sin, 4637
3:19 he *will* **d** for his sin; 4637
3:20 a stumbling block before him, he *will* **d**. 4637
3:20 you did not warn him, *he will* **d** for his sin. 4637
5:12 A third of your people *will* **d** of the plague 4637
6:12 He that is far away *will* **d** of the plague, 4637
6:12 and he that survives and is spared *will* **d** 4637
7:15 those in the country *will* **d** by the sword, 4637
12:13 but he will not see it, and there *he will* **d**. 4637
17:16 *he shall* **d** in Babylon. 4637
18: 4 The soul who sins is the one *who will* **d**. 4637
18:17 He *will* not **d** for his father's sin; 4637
18:18 But his father *will* **d** for his own sin, 4637
18:20 The soul who sins is the one *who will* **d**. 4637
18:21 *he will* not **d**. 4637
18:24 of the sins he has committed, *he will* **d**. 4637
18:26 *he will* **d** for it; 4637
18:26 of the sin he has committed *he will* **d**. 4637
18:28 *he will* not **d**. 4637
18:31 Why *will you* **d**, O house of Israel? 4637
28: 8 and *you will* **d** a violent death in the heart 4637
28:10 *You will* **d** the death of the uncircumcised 4637
33: 8 'O wicked man, *you will* **surely d**,' 4637+4637
33: 8 that wicked man *will* **d** for his sin, 4637
33: 9 he *will* **d** for his sin, 4637
33:11 Why *will you* **d**, O house of Israel?' 4637
33:13 *he will* **d** for the evil he has done. 4637
33:14 '*You will* **surely d**,' but he 4637+4637
33:15 *he will* not **d**. 4637
33:18 *he will* **d** for it. 4637
33:27 and those in strongholds and caves *will* **d** 4637
Am 6: 9 *they* too *will* **d**. 4637
7:11 " 'Jeroboam *will* **d** by the sword, 4637
7:17 and *you* yourself *will* **d** in 4637
9:10 All the sinners among my people *will* **d** by 4637
Jnh 1:14 not *let us* **d** for taking this man's life. 6
4: 3 for it is better for me to **d** than to live." 4638
4: 8 He wanted to **d**, and said, 4637
4: 8 "It would be better for me to **d** than 4638
4: 9 "I am angry enough to **d**." 4638
Hab 1:12 My God, my Holy One, *we will* not **d**. 4637
Zec 11: 9 *Let* the dying **d**, and the perishing perish. 4637
13: 3 will say to him, '*You must* **d**, 2649+4202
Mt 26:35 "Even if I have *to* **d** with you, *633*
26:52 "for all who draw the sword *will* **d** by *660*
Mk 9:48 where " 'their worm *does* not **d**, *5462*
14:31 "Even if I have *to* **d with** you, *5271*
Lk 2:26 he *would* not **d** before he had seen the Lord's Christ. *2505+3972*
7: 2 was sick and about to **d**. *5462*
13:33 surely no prophet can **d** outside Jerusalem! *660*
20:36 and they can no longer **d**; *633*
Jn 6:50 which a man may eat and not **d**. *633*
8:21 and *you will* **d** in your sin. *633*
8:24 I told you that *you would* **d** in your sins; *633*
8:24 *you will* indeed **d** in your sins." *633*
11:16 "Let us also go, that *we may* **d** with him." *633*
11:26 and believes in me *will* never **d**. *633*
11:50 for you that one man **d** for the people than *633*
11:51 that year he prophesied that Jesus would **d** *633*
12:33 the kind of death he was going to **d**. *633*
18:32 the kind of death he was going to **d** *633*
19: 7 and according to that law he must **d**, *633*
21:23 the brothers that this disciple *would* not **d**. *633*
21:23 But Jesus did not say that *he would* not **d**; *633*
Ac 7:19 so that they *would* **d**. *2441+3590*
21:13 but also *to* **d** in Jerusalem for the name of *633*
25:11 I do not refuse *to* **d**. *633*
Ro 5: 7 Very rarely *will* anyone **d** for a righteous *633*
5: 7 for a good man someone might possibly dare *to* **d**. *633*
6: 9 *he* cannot **d** again; *633*
8:13 according to the sinful nature, you will **d**; *633*
14: 8 and if *we* **d**, we die to the Lord. *633*
14: 8 and if we die, *we* **d** to the Lord. *633*
14: 8 So, whether *we* live or **d**, *633*
1Co 4: 9 like *men* **condemned to d** in the arena. *2119*
9:15 I *would* rather **d** than have anyone deprive me of this boast. *633*
15:22 For as in Adam all **d**, so in Christ all will be made alive. *633*
15:31 *I* **d** every day—I mean that, brothers— *633*
15:32 "Let us eat and drink, for tomorrow *we* **d**." *633*
2Co 7: 3 in our hearts that we *would* live or **d with** *5271*
Php 1:21 For to me, to live is Christ and *to* **d** is gain. *633*
Heb 7: 8 the tenth is collected by men **who d**; *633*
9:27 Just as man is destined *to* **d** once, *633*
1Pe 2:24 so that we might **d** to sins and live *614*
Rev 3: 2 Strengthen what remains and is about to **d**, *633*
9: 6 they will long *to* **d**, but death will elude them *633*
11: 5 anyone who wants to harm them must **d**. *650*
14:13 the dead who **d** in the Lord from now on." *633*

DIED (257) [DIE]

Ge 5: 5 Adam lived 930 years, and then *he* **d**. 4637
5: 8 Seth lived 912 years, and then *he* **d**. 4637
5:11 Enosh lived 905 years, and then *he* **d**. 4637
5:14 Kenan lived 910 years, and then *he* **d**. 4637
5:17 Mahalalel lived 895 years, and then *he* **d**. 4637
5:20 Jared lived 962 years, and then *he* **d**. 4637
5:27 Methuselah lived 969 years, and then *he* **d**. 4637
5:31 Lamech lived 777 years, and then *he* **d**. 4637
7:22 that had the breath of life in its nostrils **d**. 4637
9:29 Noah lived 950 years, and then *he* **d**. 4637
11:28 Haran **d** in Ur of the Chaldeans, 4637
11:32 Terah lived 205 years, and he **d** in Haran. 4637
23: 2 She **d** at Kiriath Arba (that is, Hebron) 4637
25: 8 and **d** at a good old age, an old man and full 4637
25:17 He breathed his last and **d**, 4637
26:18 had stopped up after Abraham **d**, 4638
35: 8 Deborah, Rebekah's nurse, **d** and 4637
35:19 So Rachel **d** and was buried on the way 4637
35:29 and **d** and was gathered to his people, 4637
36:33 When Bela **d**, Jobab son of Zerah 4637
36:34 When Jobab **d**, Husham from the land of 4637
36:35 When Husham **d**, Hadad son of Bedad, 4637
36:36 When Hadad **d**, Samlah 4637
36:37 When Samlah **d**, Shaul from Rehoboth on 4637
36:38 When Shaul **d**, Baal-Hanan son 4637
36:39 When Baal-Hanan son of Acbor **d**, 4637
38:12 the daughter of Shua, **d**. 4637
46:12 Perez and Zerah (but Er and Onan *had* **d** in 4637
48: 7 to my sorrow Rachel **d** in the land 4637
50:16 "Your father left these instructions before he **d**: 4638
50:26 So Joseph **d** at the age of a hundred and ten. 4637
Ex 1: 6 and all that generation **d**, 4637
2:23 the king of Egypt **d**. 4637
7:21 The fish in the Nile **d**, 4637
8:13 The frogs **d** in the houses, 4637
9: 6 All the livestock of the Egyptians **d**, 4637
9: 6 not one animal belonging to the Israelites **d**. 4637
9: 7 of the animals of the Israelites *had* **d**. 4637
16: 3 "If only we *had* **d** by the LORD's hand 4637
32:28 about three thousand of the people **d**. 5877
Lev 10: 2 and *they* **d** before the LORD. 4637
16: 1 the death of the two sons of Aaron *who* **d** 4637
Nu 11: 2 to the LORD and the fire **d down**. 9205
14: 2 "If only *we had* **d** in Egypt! 4637
14:37 *were* **struck down and d** of a plague 4637
16:49 But 14,700 *people* **d** from the plague, 4637
16:49 in addition to those *who had* **d** because 4637
19:16 or *someone who has* **d a natural death**, 4637
19:18 or someone *who has* **d a natural death**. 4637
20: 1 There Miriam **d** and was buried. 4637
20: 3 "If only *we had* **d** when our brothers fell 1588
20:28 And Aaron **d** there on top of the mountain. 4637
20:29 whole community learned that Aaron *had* **d**, 1588
21: 6 they bit the people and many Israelites **d**. 4637
25: 9 those *who* **d** in the plague numbered 24,000. 4637
26:10 whose followers **d** when the fire devoured 4637
26:19 but *they* **d** in Canaan. 4637
26:61 and Abihu **d** when they made an offering 4637

Nu 27: 3 "Our father **d** in the desert. 4637
27: 3 but *he* **d** for his own sin and left no sons. 4637
33:38 where *he* **d** on the first day of 4637
33:39 and twenty-three years old when he **d** 4637
Dt 2:16 among the people *had* **d**, 4637
10: 6 There Aaron **d** and was buried, 4637
32:50 just as your brother Aaron **d** on Mount Hor 4637
34: 5 the servant of the LORD **d** there in Moab, 4637
34: 7 a hundred and twenty years old when he **d**, 4637
Jos 5: 4 **d** in the desert on the way 4637
5: 6 of military age when they left Egypt *had* **d**, 9462
10:11 and more of them **d** from 4637
22:20 He was not the only one *who* **d** for his sin.' 1588
24:29 **d** at the age of a hundred and ten. 4637
24:33 And Eleazar son of Aaron **d** and was buried 4637
Jdg 1: 7 Jerusalem, and *he* **d** there. 4637
2: 8 **d** at the age of a hundred and ten. 4637
2:19 But when the judge **d**, 4638
2:21 of the nations Joshua left when *he* **d**. 4637
3:11 until Othniel son of Kenaz **d**. 4637
4: 1 After Ehud **d**, the Israelites once again did
evil in the eyes of the LORD. 4637
4:21 into the ground, and *he* **d**. 4637
8:32 of Joash **d** at a good old age and was buried 4637
8:33 No sooner *had* Gideon **d** than 4637
9:49 about a thousand men and women, also **d**. 4637
9:54 So his servant ran him through, and *he* **d**. 4637
10: 2 then *he* **d**, and was buried in Shamir. 4637
10: 5 When Jair **d**, he was buried in Kamon. 4637
12: 7 Then Jephthah the Gileadite **d**, 4637
12:10 Ibzan **d**, and was buried in Bethlehem. 4637
12:12 Then Elon **d**, and was buried in Aijalon in 4637
12:15 Then Abdon son of Hillel **d**, 4637
16:30 Thus he killed many more when he **d** than 4638
20: 5 They raped my concubine, and *she* **d**. 4637
Ru 1: 3 Now Elimelech, Naomi's husband, **d**, 4637
1: 5 both Mahlon and Kilion also **d**, 4637
1Sa 4:11 Hophni and Phinehas, **d**. 4637
4:18 His neck was broken and *he* **d**, 4637
15:35 Until the day Samuel **d**, 4638
25: 1 Now Samuel **d**, and all Israel assembled 4637
25:38 the LORD struck Nabal and *he* **d**. 4637
31: 5 he too fell on his sword and **d** with him. 4637
31: 6 and all his men **d** together that same day. 4637
31: 7 and that Saul and his sons *had* **d**, 4637
2Sa 1: 4 Many of them fell and **d**. 4637
1:15 So he struck him down, and *he* **d**. 4637
2:23 He fell there and **d** on the spot. 4637
2:23 to the place where Asahel had fallen and **d**. 4637
3:27 Joab stabbed him in the stomach, and *he* **d**. 4637
3:33 "*Should* Abner *have* **d** as the lawless die? 4637
4: 1 of Saul heard that Abner *had* **d** in Hebron, 4637
6: 7 down and *he* **d** there beside the ark of God. 4637
10: 1 the king of the Ammonites **d**, 4637
10:18 and *he* **d** there. 4637
11:17 moreover, Uriah the Hittite **d**. 4637
11:21 so that *he* **d** in Thebez? 4637
11:24 and some of the king's men **d**. 4637
12:18 On the seventh day the child **d**. 4637
17:23 So *he* **d** and was buried in his father's tomb. 4637
18:33 If only I *had* **d** instead of you— 4637
19:10 *has* **d** in battle. 4637
20:10 Without being stabbed again, Amasa **d**. 4637
24:15 of the people from Dan to Beersheba **d**. 4637
1Ki 2:25 and he struck down Adonijah and *he* **d**. 4637
3:19 "During the night this woman's son **d** 4637
14:17 over the threshold of the house, the boy **d**. 4637
16:18 palace on fire around him. So *he* **d**, 4637
16:22 So Tibni **d** and Omri became king. 4637
22:35 and that evening *he* **d**. 4637
22:37 So the king **d** and was brought to Samaria, 4637
2Ki 1:17 So *he* **d**, according to the word of 4637
3: 5 But after Ahab **d**, 4638
4:20 and then *he* **d**. 4637
7:17 in the gateway, and *he* **d**, just as the man 4637
7:20 in the gateway, and *he* **d**. 4637
8:15 so that *he* **d**. 4637
9:27 but he escaped to Megiddo and **d** there. 4637
12:21 *He* **d** and was buried with his fathers in 4637
13:14 from the illness from which *he* **d**. 4637
13:20 Elisha **d** and was buried. 4637
13:24 Hazael king of Aram **d**, 4637
15: 5 the king with leprosy until the day he **d**, 4637
23:34 and there *he* **d**. 4637
1Ch 1:44 When Bela **d**, Jobab son of Zerah 4637
1:45 When Jobab **d**, Husham from the land of 4637
1:46 When Husham **d**, Hadad son of Bedad, 4637
1:47 When Hadad **d**, Samlah 4637
1:48 When Samlah **d**, Shaul from Rehoboth on 4637
1:49 When Shaul **d**, Baal-Hanan son 4637
1:50 When Baal-Hanan **d**, Hadad succeeded him 4637
1:51 Hadad also **d**. 4637
2:19 When Azubah **d**, Caleb married Ephrath, 4637
2:24 After Hezron **d** in Caleb Ephrathah, 4638
2:30 Seled **d** without children. 4637
2:32 Jether **d** without children. 4637
10: 5 he too fell on his sword and **d**. 4637
10: 6 So Saul and his three sons **d**, 4637
10: 6 and all his house **d** together. 4637
10: 7 and that Saul and his sons *had* **d**, 4637
10:13 Saul **d** because he was unfaithful to 4637
13:10 So *he* **d** there before God. 4637
19: 1 Nahash king of the Ammonites **d**, 4637
23:22 Eleazar **d** without having sons: 4637
24: 2 Nadab and Abihu **d** before their father did, 4637
29:28 *He* **d** at a good old age, 4637
2Ch 13:20 And the LORD struck him down and *he* **d**. 4637
2Ch 16:13 in the forty-first year of his reign Asa **d** 4637
18:34 Then at sunset *he* **d**. 4637
21:19 and *he* **d** in great pain. 4637
24:15 and *he* **d** at the age of a hundred and thirty. 4637
24:25 *he* **d** and was buried in the City of David, 4637
26:21 King Uzziah had leprosy until the day he **d**. 4638
32:33 of Jerusalem honored him when he **d**. 4637
35:24 and brought him to Jerusalem, where *he* **d**. 4637
Est 2: 7 when her father and mother **d**. 4638
Job 10:18 *I wish I had* **d** before any eye saw me. 1588
42:17 And so he **d**, old and full of years. 4637
Ps 118:12 but *they* **d out** as quickly as burning thorns; 1980
Ecc 4: 2 I declared that the dead, who *had* already **d**, 4637
Isa 6: 1 In the year that King Uzziah **d**, 4638
14:28 This oracle came in the year King Ahaz **d**: 4638
Jer 28:17 Hananiah the prophet **d**. 4637
Eze 11:13 Pelatiah son of Benaiah **d**. 4637
13:19 have killed those who *should* not *have* **d** 4637
24:18 and in the evening my wife **d**. 4637
Hos 13: 1 he became guilty of Baal worship and **d**. 4637
Jnh 4:10 It sprang up overnight and **d** overnight. 6
Mt 2:19 *After* Herod **d**, an angel of the Lord 5462
8:32 down the steep bank into the lake and **d** in 633
9:18 "My daughter *has* just **d**. 5462
14:32 the wind **d down**. 3156
22:25 The first one married and **d**, 5462
22:27 Finally, the woman **d**. 633
27:52 of many holy people who *had* **d** were raised 3121
Mk 4:39 wind **d down** and it was completely calm. 3156
6:51 and the wind **d down**. 3156
12:20 and **d** without leaving any children. 633
12:21 but *he* also **d**, leaving no child. 633
12:22 Last of all, the woman **d** too. 633
15:39 heard his cry and saw how *he* **d**, he said, 1743
15:44 he asked him if Jesus *had* already **d**. 633
Lk 13: 4 Or those eighteen who **d** when the tower 650
16:22 the beggar **d** and the angels carried him 633
16:22 The rich man also **d** and was buried. 633
20:29 a woman and **d** childless. 633
20:31 and in the same way the seven **d**, 633
20:32 Finally, the woman **d** too. 633
Jn 6:49 the manna in the desert, yet *they* **d**. 633
6:58 Your forefathers ate manna and **d**, 633
8:52 Abraham **d** and so did the prophets, 633
8:53 He **d**, and so did the prophets. 633
11:21 my brother would not *have* **d**. 633
11:32 my brother would not *have* **d**." 633
18:14 that it would be good *if* one man **d** for 633
Ac 2:29 that the patriarch David **d** and was buried, 5462
5: 5 *he* fell down and **d**. 1775
5:10 that moment she fell down at his feet and **d**. 1775
7:15 where he and our fathers **d**. 5462
9:37 About that time she became sick and **d**, 633
12:23 and he was eaten by worms and **d**. 1775
Ro 5: 6 Christ **d** for the ungodly. 633
5: 8 While we were still sinners, Christ **d** for us. 633
5:15 the many **d** by the trespass of the one man, 633
6: 2 We **d** to sin; how can we live in it 633
6: 7 anyone who *has* **d** has been freed from sin. 633
6: 8 Now if *we* **d** with Christ, 633
6:10 The death *he* **d**, he died to sin once for all; 633
6:10 The death he died, *he* **d** to sin once for all; 633
7: 4 you also **d** to the law through the body 2506
7: 9 sin sprang to life and I **d**. 633
8:34 that condemns? Christ Jesus, who **d**— 633
14: 9 Christ **d** and returned to life so 633
14:15 your brother for whom Christ **d**. 633
1Co 8:11 So this weak brother, for whom Christ **d**, 633
10: 8 in one day twenty-three thousand of them **d**. 4406
15: 3 that Christ **d** for our sins according to 633
2Co 5:14 because we are convinced that one **d** for all, 633
5:14 and therefore all **d**. 633
5:15 And *he* **d** for all, that those who live 633
5:15 for themselves but for him who **d** for them 633
Gal 2:19 I **d** to the law so that I might live for God. 633
2:21 Christ **d** for nothing!" 633
Php 2:27 Indeed he was ill, and almost **d**. 2505
2:30 because he almost **d** for the work of Christ, 2505
Col 2:20 Since *you* **d** with Christ to the basic 633
3: 3 For *you* **d**, and your life is now hidden 633
1Th 4:14 We believe that Jesus **d** and rose again and 633
5:10 He **d** for us so that, whether we are awake or 633
2Ti 2:11 If *we* **d with** him, we will also live with him 5271
Heb 9:15 *that he has* **d** as a ransom to set them free
from the sins 1181+2505
9:17 because a will is in force only when
somebody has **d**; 2093+3738
10:28 **d** without mercy on the testimony of two 633
11:13 still living by faith when *they* **d**. 633
1Pe 3:18 For Christ **d** for sins once for all, 633
2Pe 3: 4 Ever since our fathers **d**, 3121
Rev 2: 8 who **d** and came to life again. 1181+3738
8: 9 a third of the living creatures in the sea **d**, 633
8:11 and many people **d** from the waters 633
16: 3 and every living thing in the sea **d**. 633

DIES (43) [DIE]

Ge 27:10 he may give you his blessing before he **d**." 4638
Ex 21:20 with a rod and the slave **d** as a direct result, 4637
21:35 the bull of another and *it* **d**, 4637
22: 2 in and is struck so that *he* **d**, the defender is 4637
22:10 to his neighbor for safekeeping and *it* **d** 4637
22:14 and it is injured or **d** while the owner is 4637
Lev 11:32 of them **d** and falls on something, 4637
11:39 an animal that you are allowed to eat **d**, 4637
Nu 6: 7 or mother or brother or sister **d**, 4637
Nu 6: 9 " 'If someone **d** suddenly in his presence, 4637
19:14 the law that applies when a person **d** in 4637
27: 8 'If a man **d** and leaves no son, 4637
35:16 an iron object so that *he* **d**, he is a murderer; 4637
35:17 and he strikes someone so that *he* **d**, 4637
35:18 and he hits someone so that *he* **d**, 4637
35:20 at him intentionally so that *he* **d** 4637
35:21 that *he* **d**, that person shall be put to death; 4637
35:23 a stone on him that could kill him, and *he* **d**, 4637
Dt 24: 3 sends her from his house, or if he **d**, 4637
25: 5 and one of them **d** without a son, 4637
Job 14:10 But man **d** and is laid low; 4637
14:14 If a man **d**, will he live again? 4637
21:23 One man **d** in full vigor, 4637
21:25 Another man **d** in bitterness of soul, 4637
Ps 49:17 he will take nothing with him when he **d**, 4638
Pr 11: 7 When a wicked man **d**, his hope perishes; 4638
26:20 without gossip a quarrel **d down**. 9284
Ecc 3:19 As one **d**, so dies the other. 4638
3:19 As one dies, so **d** the other. 4638
Isa 65:20 *he who* **d** at a hundred will be thought 4637
Jer 38:10 the prophet out of the cistern before *he* **d**." 4637
Mt 22:24 that if a man **d** without having children, 633
Mk 12:19 that if a man's brother **d** and leaves a wife 633
Lk 20:28 that if a man's brother **d** and leaves a wife 633
Jn 4:49 "Sir, come down before my child **d**." 633
11:25 believes in me will live, even though *he* **d**; 633
12:24 a kernel of wheat falls to the ground and **d**, 633
12:24 But if it **d**, it produces many seeds. 633
Ro 7: 2 but if her husband **d**, she is released 633
7: 3 But if her husband **d**, she is released 633
14: 7 and none of us **d** to himself alone. 633
1Co 7:39 But if her husband **d**, she is free to marry 3121
15:36 you sow does not come to life unless *it* **d**. 633

DIFFERENCE (7) [DIFFERENT]

2Sa 19:35 *Can I* **tell the d** between what is good 3359
2Ch 12: 8 so that *they may* **learn the d between** 3359
Eze 22:26 that there is no **d between** the unclean and 1068
44:23 They are to teach my people **the d between** 1068
Ro 3:22 to all who believe. There is no **d**, 1405
10:12 there is no **d** between Jew and Gentile— 1405
Gal 2: 6 whatever they were **makes** no **d** to me; 1422

DIFFERENCES (1) [DIFFERENT]

1Co 11:19 No doubt there have to be **d** among you 146

DIFFERENT (25) [DIFFERENCE, DIFFERENCES, DIFFERENTLY, DIFFERING, DIFFERS]

Lev 19:19 " 'Do not mate **d kinds** *of* animals. 3977
Nu 14:24 But because my servant Caleb has a **d** spirit 337
1Sa 10: 6 and you will be changed into a **d** person. 337
Est 1: 7 each one **d** from the other, 9101
3: 8 of your kingdom whose customs *are* **d** 9101
Da 7: 3 Four great beasts, each **d** from the others, 10731
7: 7 It *was* **d** from all the former beasts, 10731
7:19 which was **d** from all the others 10731
7:23 *It will be* **d** from all the other kingdoms 10731
7:24 **d** from the earlier ones; 10731
11:29 but this time the **outcome** will be **d** 3869+4202
Mk 16:12 Afterward Jesus appeared in a **d** form 2283
Ro 12: 6 We have **d** gifts, according to the grace 1427
1Co 4: 7 For who **makes** you **d** from anyone else? 1359
12: 4 There are **d** *kinds* of gifts, 1348
12: 5 There are **d** *kinds* of service, 1348
12: 6 There are **d** *kinds* of working, 1348
12:10 to another speaking in **d** kinds of tongues, NIG
12:28 and those speaking in **d** kinds of tongues. NIG
2Co 11: 4 a **d** spirit **from** the one you received, 2283
11: 4 or a **d** gospel **from** the one you accepted, 2283
Gal 1: 6 of Christ and are turning to a **d** gospel— 2283
4: 1 *he is* no **d from** a slave, 1422
Heb 7:13 belonged to a **d** tribe, 2283
Jas 2:25 and sent them off *in* a **d** direction? 2283

DIFFERENTLY (2) [DIFFERENT]

Ex 8:22 on that day *I will* **deal d** *with* the land 7111
Php 3:15 And if on some point you think **d**, 2284

DIFFERING (5) [DIFFERENT]

Dt 25:13 Do not have **two d weights** in your bag— 74+74+2256
25:14 Do not have **two d measures** in your
house— 406+406+2256
Pr 20:10 **D weights** and differing measures— 74+74+2256
20:10 Differing weights and **d measures**— 406+406+2256
20:23 The LORD detests **d weights**, 74+74+2256

DIFFERS (1) [DIFFERENT]

1Co 15:41 and star **d** from star in splendor. 1422

DIFFICULT (13) [DIFFICULTIES, DIFFICULTY]

Ge 47: 9 My years have been few and **d**, 8273
Ex 18:22 but have them bring every **d** case to you; 1524
18:26 The **d** cases they brought to Moses, 7997
Dt 17: 8 before your courts *that are* too **d** for you 7098
30:11 not too **d** for you or beyond your reach. 7098
2Ki 2:10 "You have asked a **d** *thing*," Elijah said, 7996

Eze 3: 5 and **d** language, but to the house of Israel— 3878
3: 6 of obscure speech and **d** language, 3878
Da 2:11 What the king asks is **too d.** 10330
4: 9 and no mystery is *too* **d** for you. 10048
5:12 explain riddles and solve **d problems.** 10626
5:16 and to solve **d problems.** 10626
Ac 15:19 that *we should* not **make it d for** *4214*

DIFFICULTIES (3) [DIFFICULT]
Dt 31:17 Many disasters and **d** will come upon them, 7650
31:21 And when many disasters and **d** come 7650
2Co 12:10 in hardships, in persecutions, *in* **d.** *5103*

DIFFICULTY (7) [DIFFICULT]
Ge 35:16 Rachel began to give birth and *had* **great d.** 7996
35:17 as she *was* **having great d** in childbirth, 7996
Ex 14:25 so that they had **d** driving. 3881
Jos 19:47 Danites **had d taking possession of** 3655+4946
Ac 14:18 they had **d** keeping the crowd from *3660*
27: 7 and had **d** arriving off Cnidus. *3660*
27: 8 We moved along the coast **with d** and came *3660*

DIG (10) [DIGGING, DIGS, DUG, GRAVEDIGGERS]
Dt 6:11 wells *you did* not **d,** 2933
8: 9 the rocks are iron and *you can* **d** copper out 2933
23:13 your equipment have **something to d with,** 3845
23:13 **d a hole** and cover up your excrement. 2916
Ps 119:85 The arrogant **d** pitfalls for me, 4125
Eze 8: 8 "Son of man, now **d** into the wall." 3168
12: 5 **d** through the wall 3168
Am 9: 2 *they* **d down** to the depths of the grave, 3168
Lk 13: 8 and *I'll* **d** around it and fertilize it. *4999*
16: 3 I'm not strong enough *to* **d,** *4999*

DIGGING (1) [DIG]
Mk 2: 4 *after* **d through** it, *2021*

DIGNITARIES (3) [DIGNITY]
Ge 50: 7 the **d** *of* his court and all the dignitaries 2418
50: 7 the dignitaries of his court and all the **d** 2418
Isa 43:28 So I will disgrace the **d** *of* your temple, 8569

DIGNITY (4) [DIGNITARIES]
Ex 28: 2 to give him **d** and honor. 3883
28:40 to give them **d** and honor. 3883
Job 30:15 my **d** is driven away as by the wind, 5619
Pr 31:25 She is clothed with strength and **d;** 2077

DIGS (4) [DIG]
Ex 21:33 a pit or **d one** and fails to cover it and an ox 4125
Ps 7:15 *He who* **d** a hole and scoops it out falls into 4125
Pr 26:27 If a *man* **d** a pit, he will fall into it; 4125
Ecc 10: 8 *Whoever* **d** a pit may fall into it; 2916

DIKLAH (2)
Ge 10:27 Hadoram, Uzal, **D,** 1989
1Ch 1:21 Hadoram, Uzal, **D,** 1989

DILEAN (1)
Jos 15:38 **D,** Mizpah, Joktheel, 1939

DILIGENCE (6) [DILIGENT]
Ezr 5: 8 on *with* **d** and is making rapid progress 10056
6:12 Let it be carried out **with d.** 10056
6:13 and their associates carried it out **with d.** 10056
7:21 to provide **with d** whatever Ezra the priest, 10056
7:23 be done **with d** for the temple of the God 10012
Heb 6:11 of you to show this same **d** to the very end, *5082*

DILIGENT (7) [DILIGENCE, DILIGENTLY]
2Ch 24:13 The men in charge of the work *were* **d,** 6913
Pr 10: 4 but **d** hands bring wealth. 3026
12:24 **D** hands will rule, 3026
12:27 but the **d** man prizes his possessions. 3026
13: 4 but the desires of the **d** are fully satisfied. 3026
21: 5 the **d** lead to profit as surely as haste leads 3026
1Ti 4:15 **Be d** in these matters; *1639*

DILIGENTLY (3) [DILIGENT]
Zec 6:15 if *you* **d obey** the LORD your God." 928+7754+9048+9048
Jn 5:39 *You* **d study** the Scriptures *2236*
Ro 12: 8 if it is leadership, let him govern **d;** *1877+5082*

DILL (1)
Mt 23:23 mint, **d** and cummin. *464*

DILUTED (1)
Isa 1:22 your choice wine *is* **d** with water. 4543

DIM (4)
Job 17: 7 My eyes *have* **grown d** with grief; 3908
Ps 88: 9 my eyes *are* **d** with grief. 1790
Ecc 12: 3 those looking through the windows *grow* **d;** 3124
La 5:17 because of these things our eyes *grow* **d** 3124

DIMENSIONS (2)
Job 38: 5 Who marked off its **d?** 4924
Eze 42:11 with similar exits and **d.** 5477

DIMINISH (1)
Ps 107:38 and *he did* not **let** their herds **d.** 5070

DIMNAH (1)
Jos 21:35 **D** and Nahalal, together 1962

DIMON (1) [DIMON'S]
Isa 15: 9 but I will bring still more upon **D—** 1904

DIMON'S (1) [DIMON]
Isa 15: 9 **D** waters are full of blood, 1904

DIMONAH (1)
Jos 15:22 Kinah, **D,** Adadah, 1905

DIN (1)
Jer 51:55 he will silence her **noisy d.** 1524+7754

DINAH (7) [DINAH'S]
Ge 30:21 to a daughter and named her **D.** 1909
34: 1 Now **D,** the daughter Leah had borne 1909
34: 3 His heart was drawn to **D** daughter 1909
34: 5 that his daughter **D** had been defiled, 1909
34:13 Because their sister **D** had been defiled, 1909
34:26 and took **D** from Shechem's house and left. 1909
46:15 besides his daughter **D.** 1909

DINAH'S (2) [DINAH]
Ge 34:11 Shechem said to **D** father and brothers, 2023S
34:25 Simeon and Levi, **D** brothers, 1909

DINAITES (KJV) See JUDGES

DINE (4) [DINED, DINNER]
1Sa 20: 5 *am* **supposed to d** with the king; 430+3782+3782
Est 7: 1 and Haman went to **d** with Queen Esther, 9272
Pr 23: 1 When you sit to **d** with a ruler, 4310
Am 6: 4 *You* **d on** choice lambs and fattened calves. 430

DINED (1) [DINE]
1Sa 9:24 And Saul **d** with Samuel that day. 430

DINHABAH (2)
Ge 36:32 His city was named **D.** 1973
1Ch 1:43 Bela son of Beor, whose city was named **D.** 1973

DINNER (11) [DINE]
Ge 43:16 slaughter an animal and prepare **d;** NIH
Est 5:14 go with the king to the **d** and be happy." 5492
Mt 9:10 *While* Jesus *was* **having d** *367*
14: 9 but because of his oaths and his **d guests,** *5263*
22: 4 that I have prepared my **d:** *756*
Mk 2:15 While Jesus was *having* **d** at Levi's house, *2879*
6:22 she pleased Herod and his **d guests.** *5263*
6:26 but because of his oaths and his **d guests,** *367*
Lk 7:36 of the Pharisees invited Jesus to **have d** *2266*
14:12 "When you give a luncheon or **d,** *1270*
Jn 12: 2 Here a **d** was given in Jesus' honor. *1270*

DIONYSIUS (1)
Ac 17:34 Among them was **D,** a member of *1477*

DIOTREPHES (1)
3Jn 1: 9 I wrote to the church, but **D,** *1485*

DIP (9) [DIPPED, DIPPING, DIPS]
Ex 12:22 **d** it into the blood in the basin and put some 3188
Lev 4: 6 He *is to* **d** his finger into the blood 3188
4:17 He *shall* **d** his finger into the blood 3188
14: 6 He is then to take the live bird and **d** it, 3188
14:16 **d** his right forefinger into the oil 3188
14:51 **d** them into the blood of the dead bird and 3188
Nu 19:18 **d** it in the water and sprinkle the tent 3188
Ru 2:14 and **d** it in the wine vinegar." 3188
Lk 16:24 and send Lazarus to **d** the tip of his finger *970*

DIPPED (7) [DIP]
Ge 37:31 slaughtered a goat and **d** the robe in 3188
Lev 9: 9 and *he* **d** his finger into the blood and put it 3188
1Sa 14:27 of the staff that was in his hand and **d** it into 3188
2Ki 5:14 and **d** *himself* in the Jordan seven times, 3188
Mt 26:23 "The one who *has* **d** his hand into the bowl *1835*
Jn 13:26 of bread when I *have* **d** it in the dish." *970*
Rev 19:13 He is dressed in a robe **d** in blood, *970*

DIPPING (1) [DIP]
Jn 13:26 Then, **d** the piece of bread, *970*

DIPS (1) [DIP]
Mk 14:20 "one who **d** bread into the bowl with me. *1835*

DIRE (2)
Dt 28:48 in nakedness and **d** poverty, 3972
Isa 21: 2 A **d** vision has been shown to me: 7997

DIRECT (12) [DIRECTED, DIRECTING, DIRECTION, DIRECTIONS, DIRECTIVES, DIRECTLY, DIRECTOR, DIRECTORS, DIRECTS]
Ge 18:19 so that *he will* **d** his children 7422
46:26 *those who were* his **d descendants,** 3655+3751
Ex 21:20 a rod and the slave dies **as a d result,** 3338+9393
Dt 17:10 Be careful to do everything *they* **d** you 3723
2Ch 34:12 to **d** them were Jahath and Obadiah, 5904
Ps 119:35 **D** me in the path of your commands, 2005
119:133 **D** my footsteps according to your word; 3922
Jer 10:23 it is not for man *to* **d** his steps. 3922
Eze 23:25 *I will* **d** my jealous anger against you, 5989
26: 9 *He will* **d** the blows of his battering rams 5989
2Th 3: 5 *May* the Lord **d** your hearts into God's love *2985*
1Ti 5:17 The elders who **d** the affairs of the church *4613*

DIRECTED (25) [DIRECT]
Ge 24:51 as the LORD *has* **d.**" 1819
45:19 "You **are** also **d** to tell them, 'Do this: 7422
47:11 the district of Rameses, as Pharaoh **d.** 7422
50: 2 Then Joseph **d** the physicians in his service 7422
Nu 16:40 as the LORD **d** him through Moses. 1819
Dt 2: 1 as the LORD *had* **d** me. 1819
4:14 the LORD **d** me at that time to teach you 7422
6: 1 the LORD your God **d** me to teach you 7422
Jos 4:10 just as Moses *had* **d** Joshua. 7422
4:12 as Moses *had* **d** them. 1819
11: 9 Joshua did to them as the LORD *had* **d:** 606
11:23 just as the LORD *had* **d** Moses, 1819
1Sa 17:20 loaded up and set out, as Jesse *had* **d.** 7422
1Ki 5:16 the project and **d** the workmen. 8097
21:11 as Jezebel **d** in the letters she had written 8938
Job 21: 4 "Is my complaint **d to** man? 4200
Pr 20:24 A man's steps are **d by** the LORD. 4946
Isa 10:25 and my wrath will be **d to** 6584
Jer 13: 2 So I bought a belt, as the LORD **d,** 1821
Mt 14:19 *he* **d** the people to sit down on the grass. *3027*
26:19 So the disciples did as Jesus *had* **d** them *5332*
Mk 6:39 Then Jesus **d** them to have all the people sit *2199*
Ac 7:44 It had been made as God **d** Moses, *1411*
22:24 *He* **d** that he be flogged and questioned *3306*
Tit 1: 5 appoint elders in every town, as I **d** you. *1411*

DIRECTING (1) [DIRECT]
1Ch 15:21 **d** according to sheminith. 5904

DIRECTION (24) [DIRECT]
Ex 38:21 by the Levites under the **d** *of* Ithamar son 3338
Nu 4:27 be done under the **d** *of* Aaron and his sons. 7023
4:28 to be under the **d** *of* Ithamar son of Aaron, 3338
4:33 of Meeting under the **d** *of* Ithamar son 3338
7: 8 They were all under the **d** *of* Ithamar son 3338
11:31 as far as a day's walk **in any d.** 2256+3907+3907
Dt 28: 7 They will come at you from one **d** but flee 2006
28:25 You will come at them from one **d** but flee 2006
Jos 8:20 no chance to escape **in any d,** 2178+2178+2256
Jdg 9:37 and a company is coming from the **d** *of* 2006
20:42 So they fled before the Israelites in the **d** *of* 2006
2Sa 13:34 "I see men in the **d** *of* Horonaim, 2006
1Ki 18: 6 Ahab going in one **d** and Obadiah 2006
2Ki 3:20 water flowing from the **d** *of* Edom! 2006
2Ch 26:11 and Maaseiah the officer under the **d** 3338
34: 4 **Under** his **d** the altars of the Baals 4200+7156
Ezr 5: 8 and is making rapid progress under their **d.** 10311
Ne 12:38 in the **opposite d.** 4578
12:42 The choirs sang under the **d** of Jezrahiah. 7224
Job 37:12 At his **d** they swirl around over the face of 9374
Pr 7: 8 walking along in the **d** *of* her house 2006
Eze 9: 2 And I saw six men coming from the **d** *of* 2006
10:11 The cherubim went in whatever **d** 5226
Jas 2:25 and sent them off *in* a different **d?** *3847*

DIRECTIONS (7) [DIRECT]
Ge 46:28 ahead of him to Joseph to **get d** to Goshen. 3723
1Sa 14:16 the army melting away **in all d.** 2151
2Ch 35: 4 to the **d written** *by* David king of Israel and 4181
Eze 1:17 in any one of the four **d** the creatures faced; 8063
10:11 in any one of the four **d** the cherubim faced; 8063
Ac 21:30 and the people came running from all **d.** *NIG*
1Co 11:34 And when I come *I will* **give** further **d.** *1411*

DIRECTIVES (1) [DIRECT]
1Co 11:17 In the following **d** I have no praise for you, *4133*

DIRECTLY (7) [DIRECT]
Ge 30:38 be **d in front of** the flocks 4200+5790
Ex 14: 2 sea, **d opposite** Baal Zephon. 4200+5790+7156
Lev 25:12 eat only what is taken **d from** the fields. 4946
Ne 12:37 At the Fountain Gate they continued **d** up 5584
Pr 4:25 **fix** your gaze **d** before you. 3837
Lk 20:17 Jesus **looked d at** them and asked, *1838*
Ac 14: 9 Paul **looked d at** him, *867*

DIRECTOR (58) [DIRECT]
Ne 11:17 the **d** who led in thanksgiving and prayer; 8031

Ps 4: T For the **d of music.** 5904
5: T For the **d of music.** 5904
6: T For the **d of music.** 5904
8: T For the **d of music.** 5904
9: T For the **d of music.** 5904
11: T For the **d of music.** Of David. 5904
12: T For the **d of music.** 5904
13: T For the **d of music.** A psalm of David. 5904
14: T For the **d of music.** Of David. 5904
18: T For the **d of music.** 5904
19: T For the **d of music.** A psalm of David. 5904
20: T For the **d of music.** A psalm of David. 5904
21: T For the **d of music.** A psalm of David. 5904
22: T For the **d of music.** 5904
31: T For the **d of music.** A psalm of David. 5904
36: T For the **d of music.** 5904
39: T For the **d of music.** 5904
40: T For the **d of music.** Of David. A psalm. 5904
41: T For the **d of music.** A psalm of David. 5904
42: T For the **d of music.** 5904
44: T For the **d of music.** 5904
45: T For the **d of music.** 5904
46: T For the **d of music.** 5904
47: T For the **d of music.** 5904
49: T For the **d of music.** 5904
51: T For the **d of music.** 5904
52: T For the **d of music.** 5904
53: T For the **d of music.** 5904
54: T For the **d of music.** 5904
55: T For the **d of music.** 5904
56: T For the **d of music.** 5904
57: T For the **d of music.** 5904
58: T For the **d of music.** 5904
59: T For the **d of music.** 5904
60: T For the **d of music.** 5904
61: T For the **d of music.** 5904
62: T For the **d of music.** 5904
64: T For the **d of music.** A psalm of David. 5904
65: T For the **d of music.** 5904
66: T For the **d of music.** A song. A psalm. 5904
67: T For the **d of music.** 5904
68: T For the **d of music.** 5904
69: T For the **d of music.** 5904
70: T For the **d of music.** Of David. A petition. 5904
75: T For the **d of music.** 5904
76: T For the **d of music.** 5904
77: T For the **d of music.** 5904
80: T For the **d of music.** 5904
81: T For the **d of music.** 5904
84: T For the **d of music.** 5904
85: T For the **d of music.** 5904
88: T For the **d of music.** 5904
109: T For the **d of music.** Of David. A psalm. 5904
139: T For the **d of music.** Of David. A psalm. 5904
140: T For the **d of music.** A psalm of David. 5904
Hab 3:19 For the **d of music.** 5904
Ro 16:23 who is the city's **d of public works,** *3874*

DIRECTORS (1) [DIRECT]
Ne 12:46 there had been **d** *for* the singers and for 8031

DIRECTS (4) [DIRECT]
Jdg 20: 9 We'll go up against it **as** the lot **d.** 928
Ps 42: 8 By day the LORD **d** his love, 7422
Pr 21: 1 *he* **d** it like 5742
Isa 48:17 *who* **d** you in the way you should go. 2005

DIRGE (2)
Mt 11:17 *we* **sang a d,** and you did not mourn.' *2577*
Lk 7:32 *we* **sang a d,** and you did not cry.' *2577*

DIRT (3)
2Sa 16:13 at him and showering him with **d.** 6760
Zec 9: 3 and gold like the **d** *of* the streets. 3226
1Pe 3:21 not the removal *of* **d** from the body but *4866*

DISABLED (2) [ABLE]
Jn 5: 3 a great number *of* **d** *people* used to lie— *820*
Heb 12:13 so that the lame *may* not *be* **d,** *1762*

DISAGREED (1) [AGREE, DISAGREEMENT]
Ac 28:25 *They* **d** among themselves and began *851+1639*

DISAGREEMENT (1) [AGREE, DISAGREED]
Ac 15:39 a **sharp d** that they parted company. *4237*

DISALLOW (KJV) See FORBID

DISANNUL, DISANNULLED (KJV) See DISCREDIT, THWART, SET ASIDE

DISAPPEAR (10) [DISAPPEARED, DISAPPEARS]
Nu 27: 4 Why *should* our father's name **d** 1757
Ru 4:10 not **d** from among his family or from 4162
Isa 2:18 and the idols *will* totally **d.** 2736
17: 3 The fortified city *will* **d** from Ephraim, 8697
Isa 29:20 the mockers *will* **d,** and all who have 3983
Mt 5:18 until heaven and earth **d,** *4216*
5:18 *will* by any means **d** from the Law *4216*
Lk 16:17 It is easier for heaven and earth *to* **d** than *4216*
Heb 8:13 what is obsolete and aging *will* soon **d.** *907*
2Pe 3:10 The heavens *will* **d** with a roar; *4216*

DISAPPEARED (3) [DISAPPEAR]
Jdg 6:21 And the angel of the LORD **d.** 2143+4946+6524
1Ki 20:40 and there, the man **d."** 401
Lk 24:31 and he **d** from their sight. *908+1181*

DISAPPEARS (4) [DISAPPEAR]
Job 14:11 As water **d** from the sea or 261
Hos 6: 4 like the early dew *that* **d.** 2143
13: 3 like the early dew *that* **d,** 2143
1Co 13:10 when perfection comes, the imperfect **d.** *2934*

DISAPPOINT (1) [DISAPPOINTED]
Ro 5: 5 And hope *does* not **d** us, *2875*

DISAPPOINTED (4) [DISAPPOINT]
Job 6:20 they arrive there, only *to be* **d.** 2917
Ps 22: 5 in you they trusted and *were* not **d.** 1017
Isa 49:23 those who hope in me *will* not *be* **d."** 1017
Jer 2:36 *be* **d** by Egypt as you were by Assyria. 1017

DISAPPROVE (1)
Pr 24:18 and **d** and turn his wrath away from him. 928+6524+8317

DISARMED (1) [DISARMS]
Col 2:15 And *having* **d** the powers and authorities, *588*

DISARMS (1) [DISARMED]
Job 12:21 contempt on nobles and **d** the mighty. 4653+8332

DISASTER (119) [DISASTERS, DISASTROUS]
Ge 19:19 this **d** will overtake me, and I'll die. 8288
Ex 32:12 relent and do not bring **d** on your people. 8288
32:14 on his people the **d** he had threatened. 8288
Dt 28:61 and **d** not recorded in this Book of the Law, 4804
29:19 This *will* **bring d** *on* the watered land 6200
29:21 from all the tribes of Israel for **d,** 8288
31:29 **d** will fall upon you 8288
32:35 their day of **d** is near and their doom rushes 369
Jos 24:20 he will turn and **bring d** on you and make 8317
Jdg 20:34 not realize how near **d** was. 8288
20:41 they realized that **d** had come upon them. 8288
1Sa 6: 9 the LORD has brought this great **d** on us. 8288
25:17 because **d** is hanging over our master 8288
2Sa 17:14 of Ahithophel in order to bring **d** 8288
22:19 They confronted me in the day of my **d,** 369
1Ki 5: 4 and there is no adversary or **d.** 7004+8273
8:37 whatever **d** or disease may come, 5596
9: 9 the LORD brought all this **d** on them.' " 8288
14:10 to bring **d** on the house of Jeroboam. 8288
21:21 'I am going to bring **d** on you. 8288
21:29 I will not bring this **d** in his day, 8288
22:23 The LORD has decreed **d** for you." 8288
2Ki 6:33 [the king] said, "This **d** is from the LORD. 8288
21:12 to bring such **d** on Jerusalem and Judah that 8288
22:16 to bring **d** on this place and its people, 8288
22:20 Your eyes will not see all the **d** I am going 8288
2Ch 6:28 whatever **d** or disease may come, 5596
7:22 that is why he brought all this **d** on them.' " 8288
18:22 The LORD has decreed **d** for you." 8288
34:24 to bring **d** on this place and its people— 8288
34:28 Your eyes will not see all the **d** I am going 8288
Est 8: 6 how can I bear to see **d** fall on my people? 8288
Job 18:12 **d** is ready for him when he falls. 369
31: 3 **d** for those who do wrong? 5798
Ps 18:18 They confronted me in the day of my **d,** 369
37:19 In times of **d** they will not wither; 8288
57: 1 of your wings until the **d** has passed. 2095
91:10 no **d** will come near your tent. 5596
140:11 may **d** hunt down men of violence. 8273
Pr 1:26 I in turn will laugh at your **d;** 369
1:27 when **d** sweeps over you like a whirlwind, 369
3:25 of sudden **d** or of the ruin that overtakes 7065
6:15 Therefore **d** will overtake him in an instant; 369
16: 4 even the wicked for a day of **d.** 8288
17: 5 over **d** will not go unpunished. 369
27:10 when **d** strikes you— 369
Ecc 11: 2 not know what **d** may come upon the land. 8288
Isa 3: 9 They have brought **d** upon themselves. 8288
3:11 **D** is upon them! 8273
10: 3 when **d** comes from afar? 8739
31: 2 Yet he too is wise and can bring **d;** 8273
45: 7 I bring prosperity and create **d;** 8273
47:11 **D** will come upon you, 8288
Jer 1:14 "From the north **d** will be poured out 8288
2: 3 and **d** overtook them,' " 8288
4: 6 For I am bringing **d** from the north, 8288
4:15 proclaiming **d** from the hills of Ephraim. 224
4:20 **D** follows disaster; the whole land lies in ruins. 8691
4:20 Disaster follows **d;** the whole land lies in ruins. 8691
6: 1 For **d** looms out of the north, 8288
Jer 6:19 I am bringing **d** on this people, 8288
11:11 on them a **d** they cannot escape. 8288
11:12 not help them at all when **d** strikes. 8288
11:17 who planted you, has decreed **d** for you, 8288
11:23 because I will bring **d** on the men 8288
15:11 with you in times of **d** and times of distress. 8288
16:10 the LORD decreed such a great **d** 8288
17:17 you are my refuge in the day of **d.** 8288
17:18 Bring on them the day of **d;** 8288
18: 8 and not inflict on it the **d** I had planned. 8288
18:11 a **d** for you and devising a plan against you. 8288
18:17 and not my face in the day of their **d."** 369
19: 3 to bring a **d** on this place that will make 8288
19:15 the villages around it every **d** I pronounced 8288
23:12 I will bring **d** on them in 8288
25:29 to **bring d** on the city that bears my Name, 8317
25:32 **D** is spreading from nation to nation; 8288
26: 3 and not bring on them the **d** I was planning 8288
26:13 and not bring the **d** he has pronounced 8288
26:19 that he did not bring the **d** he pronounced 8288
26:19 about to bring a terrible **d** on ourselves!" 8288
28: 8 **d** and plague against many countries 8288
31:28 and to overthrow, destroy and **bring d,** 8317
32:23 So you brought all this **d** upon them. 8288
35:17 in Jerusalem every **d** I pronounced 8288
36: 3 about every **d** I plan to inflict on them, each 8288
36:31 the people of Judah every **d** I pronounced 8288
39:16 against this city through **d,** 8288
40: 2 "The LORD your God decreed this **d** 8288
42:10 for I am grieved over the **d** I have inflicted 8288
42:17 or escape the **d** I will bring on them.' 8288
44: 2 You saw the great **d** I brought on Jerusalem 8288
44: 7 Why bring such great **d** on yourselves 8288
44:11 to bring **d** on you and to destroy all Judah. 8288
44:23 this **d** has come upon you, as you now see." 8288
45: 5 For I will bring **d** on all people, 8288
46:21 for the day of **d** is coming upon them, 369
49: 8 for I will bring **d** on Esau at 369
49:32 and will bring **d** on them from every side," 369
49:37 I will bring **d** upon them, 8288
51: 2 on every side in the day of her **d.** 8288
51:64 to rise no more because of the **d** I will bring 8288
Eze 7: 5 "This is what the Sovereign LORD says: **D!** 8288
7: 5 An unheard-of **d** is coming. 8288
14:22 be consoled regarding the **d** I have brought 8288
14:22 every **d** I have brought upon it. 889[S]
Da 9:12 by bringing upon us great **d.** 8288
9:13 all this **d** has come upon us, 8288
9:14 The LORD did not hesitate to bring the **d** 8288
Am 3: 6 When **d** comes to a city, 8288
9:10 '**D** will not overtake or meet us.' 8288
Ob 1: 5 Oh, what a **d awaits** *you*— 1950
1:13 the gates of my people in the day of their **d,** 369
1:13 in their calamity in the day of their **d,** 369
1:13 nor seize their wealth in the day of their **d.** 369
Mic 1:12 because **d** has come from the LORD, 8273
2: 3 "I am planning **d** against this people, 8288
3:11 No **d** will come upon us." 8288
Zec 8:14 as I had determined to **bring d** upon you 8317

DISASTERS (5) [DISASTER]
Dt 28:59 harsh and prolonged **d,** 4804
31:17 Many **d** and difficulties will come 8288
31:17 'Have not these **d** come upon us 8288
31:21 And when many **d** and difficulties come 8288
Jer 51:60 on a scroll about all the **d** that would come 8288

DISASTROUS (1) [DISASTER]
Ac 27:10 voyage is going to be **d** and bring great loss to ship and cargo, *3552+5615*

DISCARD (1) [DISCARDED]
Ps 119:119 the wicked of the earth *you* **d** like dross; 8697

DISCARDED (1) [DISCARD]
Ps 102:26 and *they will be* **d.** 2736

DISCERN (6) [DISCERNED, DISCERNING, DISCERNMENT]
Dt 32:29 and **d** what their end will be! 1067
Job 6:30 *Can* my mouth not **d** malice? 1067
34: 4 *Let us* **d** for ourselves what is right; 1047
Ps 19:12 Who *can* **d** his errors? 1067
139: 3 *You* **d** my going out and my lying down; 2431
Php 1:10 *be able to* **d** what is best and may be pure *1507*

DISCERNED (1) [DISCERN]
1Co 2:14 because *they are* spiritually **d.** *373*

DISCERNING (19) [DISCERN]
Ge 41:33 for a **d** and wise man and put him in charge 1067
41:39 there is no *one so* **d** and wise as you. 1067
2Sa 14:17 the king is like an angel of God in **d** good 9048
1Ki 3: 9 a **d** heart to govern your people and 9048
3:12 I will give you a wise and **d** heart, 1067
Pr 1: 5 and let the **d** get guidance— 1067
8: 9 To the **d** all of them are right; 1067
10:13 Wisdom is found on the lips of the **d,** 1067
14: 6 but knowledge comes easily to the **d.** 1067
14:33 the **d** and even among fools she lets herself 1067
15:14 The **d** heart seeks knowledge, 1067
16:21 The wise in heart are called **d,** 1067

Pr 17:24 A **d** *man* keeps wisdom in view, 1067
17:28 and **d** if he holds his tongue. 1067
18:15 The heart of the **d** acquires knowledge; 1067
19:25 rebuke a **d** *man,* and he will gain knowledge 1067
28: 7 He who keeps the law *is* a **d** son, 1067
Da 2:21 to the wise and knowledge to the **d.** 10100+10313
Hos 14: 9 Who *is* **d?** He will understand them. 1067

DISCERNMENT (8) [DISCERN]

Dt 32:28 there is no **d** in them. 9312
1Ki 3:11 for the death of your enemies but for **d** 1067
2Ch 2:12 endowed with intelligence and **d,** 1069
Job 12:20 of trusted advisers and takes away the **d** 3248
Ps 119:125 me **d** that I may understand your 1067
Pr 3:21 My son, preserve sound judgment and **d,** 4659
17:10 A rebuke impresses a *man of* **d** more than 1067
28:11 but a poor man *who has* **d** sees through him. 1067

DISCHARGE (21) [DISCHARGED, DISCHARGING]

Lev 15: 2 'When any man has a bodily **d,** 2307
15: 2 a bodily discharge, the **d** is unclean. 2308
15: 3 how his **d** will bring about uncleanness: 2308
15: 4 the *man with a* **d** lies on will be unclean, 2307
15: 6 anything the *man with a* **d** sat on 2307
15: 7 the *man who has a* **d** must wash his clothes 2307
15: 8 *with the* **d** spits on someone who is clean, 2307
15:11 *with a* **d** touches without rinsing his hands 2307
15:13 " 'When a man is cleansed from his **d,** 2308
15:15 the LORD for the man because of his **d.** 2308
15:25 woman **has a d** *of* blood for many days 2307+2308
15:25 or *has a* **d** that continues beyond her period, 2307
15:25 be unclean as long as she has the **d,** 2308+3240
15:26 on while her **d** continues will be unclean, 2308
15:28 " 'When she is cleansed from her **d,** 2308
15:30 the LORD for the uncleanness of her **d.** 2308
15:32 the regulations for a *man with a* **d,** 2307
15:33 for a man or a woman *with a* **d,** 2307+2308
22: 4 an infectious skin disease or a **bodily d,** 2307
Nu 5: 2 an infectious skin disease or a **d** 2307
2Ti 4: 5 **d all** the duties of your ministry. *4442*

DISCHARGED (1) [DISCHARGE]

Ecc 8: 8 As no one is **d** in time of war, 5449

DISCHARGING (1) [DISCHARGE]

1Co 9:17 I am simply **d** the trust committed to me. *NIG*

DISCIPLE (29) [DISCIPLES, DISCIPLES']

Isa 19:11 a **d** *of* the ancient kings"? 1201
Mt 8:21 Another **d** said to him, "Lord, *3412*
10:42 of these little ones because he is my **d,** *3412*
27:57 who *had* himself **become a d** of Jesus. *3411*
Lk 14:26 he cannot be my **d.** *3412*
14:27 and follow me cannot be my **d.** *3412*
14:33 up everything he has cannot be my **d.** *3412*
Jn 9:28 "You are this fellow's **d!** *3412*
13:23 One of them, the **d** whom Jesus loved, *NIG*
13:24 Simon Peter motioned to this **d** and said, *NIG*
18:15 and another **d** were following Jesus. *3412*
18:15 this **d** was known to the high priest, *3412*
18:16 The other **d,** who was known to *3412*
19:26 and the **d** whom he loved standing nearby, *3412*
19:27 and *to* the **d,** "Here is your mother." *3412*
19:27 this **d** took her into his home. *3412*
19:38 Now Joseph was a **d** of Jesus, *3412*
20: 2 to Simon Peter and the other **d,** *3412*
20: 3 Peter and the other **d** started for the tomb. *3412*
20: 4 but the other **d** outran Peter and reached *3412*
20: 8 Finally the other **d,** who had reached *3412*
21: 7 Then the **d** whom Jesus loved said to Peter, *3412*
21:20 **d** whom Jesus loved was following them. *3412*
21:23 the brothers that this **d** would not die. *3412*
21:24 This is the **d** who testifies to these things *3412*
Ac 9:10 In Damascus there was a **d** named Ananias. *3412*
9:26 not believing that he really was a **d.** *3412*
9:36 In Joppa there was a **d** named Tabitha *3413*
16: 1 where a **d** named Timothy lived, *3412*

DISCIPLES (266) [DISCIPLE]

Isa 8:16 and seal up the law among my **d.** 4341
Mt 5: 1 His **d** came to him, *3412*
8:23 he got into the boat and his **d** followed him. *3412*
8:25 The **d** went and woke him, saying, "Lord, *NIG*
9:10 and ate with him and his **d.** *3412*
9:11 they asked his **d,** *3412*
9:14 Then John's **d** came and asked him, *3412*
9:14 but your **d** do not fast?" *3412*
9:19 and so did his **d.** *3412*
9:37 Then he said *to* his **d,** "The harvest is *3412*
10: 1 He called his twelve **d** to him *3412*
11: 1 After Jesus had finished instructing his twelve **d,** *3412*
11: 2 what Christ was doing, he sent his **d** *3412*
11: 7 As **John's d** were leaving, *4047S*
12: 1 His **d** were hungry and began *3412*
12: 2 Your **d** are doing what is unlawful on *3412*
12:49 Pointing to his **d,** he said, *3412*
13:10 The **d** came to him and asked, *3412*
13:36 His **d** came to him and said, *3412*
14:12 John's **d** came and took his body *3412*
14:15 the **d** came to him and said, *3412*
14:19 Then he gave them *to* the **d,** *3412*
Mt 14:19 and the **d** gave them to the people. *3412*
14:20 and the **d** picked up twelve basketfuls *NIG*
14:22 the **d** get into the boat and go on ahead *3412*
14:26 When the **d** saw him walking on the lake, *3412*
15: 2 "Why do your **d** break the tradition of *3412*
15:12 Then the **d** came to him and asked, *3412*
15:23 So his **d** came to him and urged him, *3412*
15:32 Jesus called his **d** to him and said, *3412*
15:33 His **d** answered, "Where could we get *3412*
15:36 he broke them and gave them *to* the **d,** *3412*
15:37 Afterward the **d** picked up seven basketfuls *NIG*
16: 5 the **d** forgot to take bread. *3412*
16:13 he asked his **d,** "Who do people say *3412*
16:20 Then he warned his **d** not to tell anyone *3412*
16:21 that time on Jesus began to explain *to* his **d** *3412*
16:24 Then Jesus said *to* his **d,** *3412*
17: 6 When the **d** heard this, they fell facedown *3412*
17:10 The **d** asked him, "Why then do the *3412*
17:13 Then the **d** understood that he was talking *3412*
17:16 I brought him *to* your **d,** *3412*
17:19 the **d** came to Jesus in private and asked, *3412*
17:23 And the **d** were filled with grief. *NIG*
17:24 **Jesus and his d** arrived in Capernaum, *899S*
18: 1 At that time the **d** came to Jesus and asked, *3412*
19:10 The **d** said to him, *3412*
19:13 But the **d** rebuked those who brought them. *3412*
19:23 Then Jesus said *to* his **d,** *3412*
19:25 When the **d** heard this, *3412*
20:17 he took the twelve **d** aside and said to them, *3412*
20:29 As **Jesus and his d** were leaving Jericho, *899S*
21: 1 Jesus sent two **d,** *3412*
21: 6 The **d** went and did as Jesus had instructed *3412*
21:20 When the **d** saw this, they were amazed. *3412*
22:16 They sent their **d** to him along with *3412*
23: 1 Then Jesus said to the crowds and *to* his **d:** *3412*
24: 1 and was walking away when his **d** came up *3412*
24: 3 the **d** came to him privately. *3412*
26: 1 all these things, he said *to* his **d,** *3412*
26: 8 When the **d** saw this, they were indignant. *3412*
26:17 the **d** came to Jesus and asked, *3412*
26:18 the Passover with my **d** at your house.' " *3412*
26:19 So the **d** did as Jesus had directed them *3412*
26:26 and gave it *to* his **d,** saying, "Take and eat; *3412*
26:35 And all the other **d** said the same. *3412*
26:36 with **his d** to a place called Gethsemane, *899S*
26:40 to his **d** and found them sleeping. *3412*
26:45 Then he returned to the **d** and said to them, *3412*
26:56 Then all the **d** deserted him and fled. *3412*
27:64 his **d** may come and steal the body and tell *3412*
28: 7 Then go quickly and tell his **d:** *3412*
28: 8 and ran to tell his **d.** *3412*
28:13 'His **d** came during the night *3412*
28:16 Then the eleven **d** went to Galilee, *3412*
28:19 Therefore go and **make d** of all nations, *3411*
Mk 2:15 with him and his **d,** *3412*
2:16 they asked his **d:** "Why does he eat *3412*
2:18 John's **d** and the Pharisees were fasting. *3412*
2:18 "How is it that John's **d** and the disciples of *3412*
2:18 "How is it that John's disciples and the **d** of *3412*
2:23 and as his **d** walked along, *3412*
3: 7 Jesus withdrew with his **d** to the lake, *3412*
3: 9 Because of the crowd he told his **d** to have *3412*
3:20 that **he and his d** were not even able to eat. *899*
4:34 But when he was alone *with* his own **d,** *3412*
4:35 he said *to* **his d,** "Let us go over *899S*
4:38 The **d** woke him and said to him, "Teacher, *NIG*
4:40 He said *to* **his d,** "Why are you so afraid? *899S*
5:31 his **d** answered, "and yet you can ask, *3412*
5:40 and mother and the **d** who were with him, *NIG*
6: 1 accompanied by his **d.** *3412*
6:29 John's **d** came and took his body and laid it *3412*
6:35 so his **d** came to him. *3412*
6:41 Then he gave them *to* his **d** to set before *3412*
6:43 and the **d** picked up twelve basketfuls *NIG*
6:45 Immediately Jesus made his **d** get into *3412*
6:48 He saw **the d** straining at the oars, *899S*
7: 2 saw some *of* his **d** eating food with hands *3412*
7: 5 "Why don't your **d** live according to *3412*
7:17 his **d** asked him about this parable. *3412*
8: 1 Jesus called his **d** to him and said, *3412*
8: 4 His **d** answered, "But where *3412*
8: 6 he broke them and gave them *to* his **d** *3412*
8: 7 he gave thanks for them also and told the **d** *NIG*
8: 8 Afterward the **d** picked up seven basketfuls *NIG*
8:10 he got into the boat with his **d** and went to *3412*
8:14 The **d** had forgotten to bring bread, *NIG*
8:27 Jesus and his **d** went on to the villages *3412*
8:33 But when Jesus turned and looked at his **d,** *3412*
8:34 the crowd to him along with his **d** and said: *3412*
9:14 When they came to the other **d,** *3412*
9:18 I asked your **d** to drive out the spirit, *3412*
9:28 his **d** asked him privately, *3412*
9:31 because he was teaching his **d.** *3412*
10:10 the **d** asked Jesus about this. *3412*
10:13 but the **d** rebuked them. *3412*
10:23 Jesus looked around and said *to* his **d,** *3412*
10:24 The **d** were amazed at his words. *3412*
10:26 **The d** were even more amazed, *1254+3836S*
10:32 and the **d** were astonished, *NIG*
10:46 As Jesus and his **d,** *3412*
11: 1 Jesus sent two *of* his **d,** *3412*
11:14 And his **d** heard him say it. *3412*
12:43 Calling his **d** to him, Jesus said, *3412*
13: 1 one *of* his **d** said to him, "Look, Teacher! *3412*
14:12 Jesus' **d** asked him, "Where do you want *3412*
14:13 So he sent two *of* his **d,** telling them, *3412*
14:14 where I may eat the Passover with my **d?'** *3412*
Mk 14:16 The **d** left, went into the city *3412*
14:22 and gave it *to* **his d,** saying, "Take it; *899S*
14:32 and Jesus said *to* his **d,** *3412*
14:37 to his **d** and found them sleeping. *NIG*
16: 7 But go, tell his **d** and Peter, *3412*
16:20 **the d** went out and preached everywhere, *1697S*
Lk 5:30 to their sect complained to his **d,** *3412*
5:33 "John's **d** often fast and pray, *3412*
5:33 and so do the **d** of the Pharisees, *NIG*
6: 1 his **d** began to pick some heads of grain, *3412*
6:13 he called his **d** to him and chose twelve *3412*
6:17 *of* his **d** was there and a great number *3412*
6:20 Looking at his **d,** he said: *3412*
7:11 and his **d** and a large crowd went along *3412*
7:18 John's **d** told him about all these things. *3412*
8: 9 His **d** asked him what this parable meant. *3412*
8:22 One day Jesus said to **his d,** *899S*
8:24 The **d** went and woke him, saying, "Master, *NIG*
8:25 "Where is your faith?" he asked **his d.** *899S*
9:14 But he said to his **d,** "Have them sit *3412*
9:15 The **d** did so, and everybody sat down. *NIG*
9:16 Then he gave them *to* the **d** to set before *3412*
9:17 and the **d** picked up twelve basketfuls *NIG*
9:18 in private and his **d** were with him, *3412*
9:36 **The d** kept this to themselves, *899S*
9:40 I begged your **d** to drive it out, *3412*
9:43 he said to his **d,** *3412*
9:46 among **the d** as to which of them would be *899S*
9:54 When the **d** James and John saw this, *3412*
10:23 Then he turned to his **d** and said privately, *3412*
10:38 As **Jesus and his d** were on their way, *899S*
11: 1 When he finished, one *of* his **d** said to him, *3412*
11: 1 teach us to pray, just as John taught his **d."** *3412*
12: 1 Jesus began to speak first to his **d,** saying: *3412*
12:22 Then Jesus said to his **d:** *3412*
16: 1 Jesus told his **d:** "There was a rich man *3412*
17: 1 Jesus said to his **d:** "Things that *3412*
17:22 Then he said to his **d,** "The time is coming *3412*
18: 1 Then Jesus told **his d** a parable to show *899S*
18:15 When the **d** saw this, they rebuked them. *3412*
18:34 **The d** did not understand any of this. *899S*
19:29 he sent two *of* his **d,** saying to them, *3412*
19:37 the whole crowd *of* **d** began joyfully *3412*
19:39 "Teacher, rebuke your **d!"** *3412*
20:45 people were listening, Jesus said *to* his **d,** *3412*
21: 5 Some of his **d** were remarking about how *NIG*
22:11 where I may eat the Passover with my **d?'** *3412*
22:38 **The d** said, "See, Lord, *1254+3836S*
22:39 and his **d** followed him. *3412*
22:45 from prayer and went back to the **d,** *3412*
Jn 1:35 John was there again with two of his **d.** *3412*
1:37 When the two **d** heard him say this, *3412*
2: 2 and Jesus and his **d** had also been invited to *3412*
2:11 and his **d** put their faith in him. *3412*
2:12 with his mother and brothers and his **d.** *3412*
2:17 His **d** remembered that it is written: *3412*
2:22 his **d** recalled what he had said. *3412*
3:22 Jesus and his **d** went out into *3412*
3:25 between some of John's **d** and a certain Jew *3412*
4: 1 and baptizing more **d** than John, *3412*
4: 2 not Jesus who baptized, but his **d.** *3412*
4: 8 (His **d** had gone into the town to buy food.) *3412*
4:27 Just then his **d** returned and were surprised *3412*
4:31 Meanwhile his **d** urged him, "Rabbi, *3412*
4:33 Then his **d** said to each other, *3412*
6: 3 on a mountainside and sat down with his **d.** *3412*
6: 8 Another of his **d,** Andrew, *3412*
6:12 he said *to* his **d,** "Gather the pieces *3412*
6:16 evening came, his **d** went down to the lake, *3412*
6:22 and that Jesus had not entered it *with* his **d,** *3412*
6:24 that neither Jesus nor his **d** were there, *3412*
6:60 On hearing it, many of his **d** said, *3412*
6:61 that his **d** were grumbling about this, *3412*
6:66 From this time many of his **d** turned back *3412*
7: 3 so that your **d** may see the miracles you do. *3412*
8:31 hold to my teaching, you are really my **d.** *3412*
9: 2 His **d** asked him, "Rabbi, who sinned, *3412*
9:27 Do you want to become his **d,** too?" *3412*
9:28 We are **d** of Moses! *3412*
11: 7 he said *to* his **d,** "Let us go back to Judea." *3412*
11:12 His **d** replied, "Lord, if he sleeps, *3412*
11:13 but **his d** thought he meant natural sleep. *1697S*
11:16 said *to* the **rest of the d,** *5209*
11:54 where he stayed with his **d.** *3412*
12: 4 But one of his **d,** Judas Iscariot, *3412*
12:16 At first his **d** did not understand all this. *3412*
13:22 His **d** stared at one another, *3412*
13:35 all men will know that you are my **d,** *3412*
15: 8 showing yourselves to be my **d.** *3412*
16:17 Some of his **d** said to one another, *3412*
16:29 Then Jesus' **d** said, *3412*
18: 1 with his **d** and crossed the Kidron Valley. *3412*
18: 1 and he and his **d** went into it. *3412*
18: 2 Jesus had often met there with his **d.** *3412*
18:17 "You are not one of his **d,** are you?" *3412*
18:19 the high priest questioned Jesus about his **d** *3412*
18:25 he was asked, "You are not one of his **d,** *3412*
20:10 Then the **d** went back to their homes, *3412*
20:18 Mary Magdalene went *to* the **d** with *3412*
20:19 when the **d** were together, *3412*
20:20 The **d** were overjoyed when they saw *3412*
20:24 was not with **the d** when Jesus came. *899S*
20:25 other **d** told him, "We have seen the Lord!" *3412*
20:26 A week later his **d** were in the house again, *3412*
20:30 miraculous signs in the presence of his **d,** *3412*
21: 1 Afterward Jesus appeared again *to* his **d,** *3412*
21: 2 and two other **d** were together. *3412*

Jn 21: 4 but the **d** did not realize that it was Jesus. *3412*
21: 8 The other **d** followed in the boat, *3412*
21:12 None *of* the **d** dared ask him, *3412*
21:14 now the third time Jesus appeared *to* his **d** *3412*
Ac 6: 1 when the number of **d** was increasing, *3412*
6: 2 So the Twelve gathered all the **d** together *3412+3836*
6: 7 number *of* **d** in Jerusalem increased rapidly, *3412*
9: 1 murderous threats against the Lord's **d**. *3412*
9:19 Saul spent several days with the **d** *3412*
9:26 he tried to join the **d**, *3412*
9:38 when the **d** heard that Peter was in Lydda, *3412*
11:26 The **d** were called Christians first *3412*
11:29 The **d**, each according to his ability, *3412*
13:52 And the **d** were filled with joy and with *3412*
14:20 But after the **d** had gathered around him, *3412*
14:21 **won** a large number of **d**. *3411*
14:22 the **d** and encouraging them to remain true *3412*
14:28 they stayed there a long time with the **d**. *3412*
15:10 on the necks *of* the **d** a yoke that neither we *3412*
18:23 strengthening all the **d**. *3412*
18:27 and wrote *to* the **d** there to welcome him. *3412*
19: 1 There he found some **d** *3412*
19: 9 the **d** with him and had discussions daily in *3412*
19:30 but the **d** would not let him. *3412*
20: 1 Paul sent for the **d** and, *3412*
20:30 in order to draw away **d** after them. *3412*
21: 4 Finding the **d** there, he stayed with them *3412*
21: 5 All the **d** and their wives *NIG*
21:16 *of* the **d** from Caesarea accompanied us *3412*
21:16 a man from Cyprus and one of the early **d**. *3412*

DISCIPLES' (1) [DISCIPLE]
Jn 13: 5 into a basin and began to wash his **d'** feet, *3412*

DISCIPLINE (36) [DISCIPLINED, DISCIPLINES, SELF-DISCIPLINE]
Dt 4:36 From heaven he made you hear his voice to **d** you. 3579
11: 2 not the ones who saw and experienced the **d** 4592
21:18 not listen to them when *they* **d** him, 3579
Job 5:17 so do not despise the **d** *of* the Almighty. 4592
Ps 6: 1 do not rebuke me in your anger or **d** me 3579
38: 1 do not rebuke me in your anger or **d** me 3579
39:11 *You* rebuke and **d** men for their sin; 3579
94:12 Blessed is the man *you* **d**, O LORD, 3579
Pr 1: 2 for attaining wisdom and **d**; 4592
1: 7 but fools despise wisdom and **d**. 4592
3:11 do not despise the LORD's **d** and do 4592
5:12 You will say, "How I hated **d**! 4592
5:23 He will die for lack of **d**, 4592
6:23 and the corrections of **d** are the way to life, 4592
10:17 He who heeds **d** shows the way to life, 4592
12: 1 Whoever loves **d** loves knowledge, 4592
13:18 He who ignores **d** comes to poverty 4592
13:24 but he who loves him is careful to **d** him. 4592
15: 5 A fool spurns his father's **d**, 4592
15:10 Stern **d** awaits him who leaves the path; 4592
15:32 He who ignores **d** despises himself, 4592
19:18 **D** your son, for in that there is hope; 3579
22:15 but the rod of **d** will drive it far from him. 4592
23:13 Do not withhold **d** from a child; 4592
23:23 get wisdom, **d** and understanding. 4592
29:17 **D** your son, and he will give you peace; 3579
Jer 17:23 and would not listen or respond to **d**. 4592
30:11 *I will* **d** you but only with justice; 3579
32:33 they would not listen or respond to **d**. 4592
46:28 *I will* **d** you but only with justice; 3579
Hos 5: 2 I will **d** all of them. 4592
Heb 12: 5 "My son, do not make light of the Lord's **d**, *4082*
12: 7 Endure hardship as **d**; *4082*
12: 8 (and everyone undergoes **d**), *4005S*
12:11 No **d** seems pleasant at the time, *4082*
Rev 3:19 Those whom I love I rebuke and **d**. *4084*

DISCIPLINED (10) [DISCIPLINE]
Pr 1: 3 a **d** and prudent life, doing what is right 4592
Isa 26:16 when you **d** them, 4592
Jer 31:18 *'You* **d** me like an unruly calf, 3579
31:18 and *I have* **been d**. 3579
1Co 11:32 *we are being* **d** so that we will not *4084*
Tit 1: 8 who is self-controlled, upright, holy and **d**. *1604*
Heb 12: 7 For what son *is* not **d** by his father? *4084*
12: 8 not **d** (and everyone undergoes discipline), *4082*
12: 9 we have all had human fathers who **d** us *4083*
12:10 Our fathers **d** us for a little while *4084*

DISCIPLINES (6) [DISCIPLINE]
Dt 8: 5 then in your heart that as a man **d** his son, 3579
8: 5 so the LORD your God **d** you. 3579
Ps 94:10 Does he *who* **d** nations not punish? 3579
Pr 3:12 because the LORD **d** those he loves, 3519
Heb 12: 6 because the Lord **d** those he loves, *4084*
12:10 but God **d** us for our good, *NIG*

DISCLOSE (2) [DISCLOSED]
Job 11: 6 and **d** to you the secrets of wisdom, 5583
Isa 26:21 The earth *will* **d** the blood shed upon her; 1655

DISCLOSED (6) [DISCLOSE]
Mt 10:26 nothing concealed that *will* not *be* **d**, *636*
Mk 4:22 For whatever is hidden is meant to be **d**, *5746*
Lk 8:17 there is nothing hidden that will not be **d**, *5745*
Lk 12: 2 nothing concealed that *will* not *be* **d**, *636*
Col 1:26 but *is* now **d** to the saints. *5746*
Heb 9: 8 into the Most Holy Place *had* not yet *been* **d** *5746*

DISCOMFITED, DISCOMFITURE (KJV)
See BEAT, CONFUSION, FORCED LABOR, OVERCAME, PANIC, ROUTED, ROUTING

DISCOMFORT (1)
Jnh 4: 6 to give shade for his head to ease his **d**, 8288

DISCONTENTED (1)
1Sa 22: 2 or in debt or **d** gathered around him, 5253+5883

DISCORD (2)
Est 1:18 There will be no end of disrespect and **d**. 7912
Gal 5:20 hatred, **d**, jealousy, fits of rage, *2251*

DISCOURAGE (2) [DISCOURAGED, DISCOURAGEMENT, DISCOURAGING]
Nu 32: 7 Why *do you* **d** the Israelites from going over into the land 4213+5648
Ezr 4: 4 the peoples around them *set out to* **d** 3338+8332

DISCOURAGED (15) [DISCOURAGE]
Nu 32: 9 *they* **d** the Israelites from entering the land 4213+5648
Dt 1:21 Do not be afraid; *do* not *be* **d**." 3169
31: 8 Do not be afraid; *do* not *be* **d**." 3169
Jos 1: 9 Do not be terrified; *do* not *be* **d**, 3169
8: 1 Do not be afraid; *do* not *be* **d**. 3169
10:25 Do not be afraid; *do* not *be* **d**. 3169
1Ch 22:13 Do not be afraid or **d**. 3169
28:20 Do not be afraid or **d**, for the LORD God, 3169
2Ch 20:15 not be afraid or **d** because of this vast army. 3169
20:17 Do not be afraid; *do* not *be* **d**. 3169
32: 7 Do not be afraid or **d** because of the king 3169
Job 4: 5 now trouble comes to you, and *you are* **d**; 4206
Isa 42: 4 not falter or *be* **d** till he establishes justice 8368
Eph 3:13 *to be* **d** because of my sufferings for you, *1591*
Col 3:21 or *they will* **become d**. *126*

DISCOURAGEMENT (1) [DISCOURAGE]
Ex 6: 9 because of their **d** and cruel bondage. 7919+8120

DISCOURAGING (1) [DISCOURAGE]
Jer 38: 4 He *is* **d** the soldiers who are left 3338+8332

DISCOURSE (2) [DISCOURSED]
Job 27: 1 And Job continued his **d**: 5442
29: 1 Job continued his **d**: 5442

DISCOURSED (1) [DISCOURSE]
Ac 24:25 *As* Paul **d** on righteousness, *1363*

DISCOVER (5) [DISCOVERED]
Ecc 7:14 a man cannot **d** anything *about* his future. 5162
7:24 and most profound—who *can* **d** it? 5162
7:27 to another to **d** the scheme of things— 5162
8:17 man cannot **d** *its* **meaning**. 5162
2Co 13: 6 And I trust that *you will* **d** that we have *1182*

DISCOVERED (12) [DISCOVER]
Ge 26:19 the valley and **d** a well of fresh water there. 5162
36:24 This is the Anah who **d** the hot springs in 5162
Dt 22:28 to be married and rapes her and *they are* **d**, 5162
Jdg 16: 9 So the secret of his strength **was** not **d**. 3359
21: 8 They **d** that no one from Jabesh Gilead 2180
Ru 3: 8 he turned and **d** a woman lying at his feet. 2180
1Sa 22: 6 that David and his men *had* **been d**. 3359
2Ki 17: 4 king of Assyria **d** that Hoshea was a traitor, 5162
23:24 the priest *had* **d** *in* the temple of the LORD. 5162
Ps 44:21 *would* not God *have* **d** it, 2983
Ecc 7:27 says the Teacher, "this is what *I have* **d**: 5162
Ro 4: 1 our forefather, **d** in this matter? *2351*

DISCREDIT (2) [DISCREDITED]
Ne 6:13 they would give me a bad name to **d** me. 3070
Job 40: 8 *"Would you* **d** my justice? 7296

DISCREDITED (2) [DISCREDIT]
Ac 19:27 temple of the great goddess Artemis *will be* **d**, *1650+3357+4029*
2Co 6: 3 so that our ministry *will* not *be* **d**. *3699*

DISCREETLY (1) [DISCRETION]
Pr 26:16 than seven men who answer **d**. 3248

DISCRETION (6) [DISCREETLY]
1Ch 22:12 the LORD give you **d** and understanding 8507
Pr 1: 4 knowledge and **d** to the young— 4659
2:11 **D** will protect you, 4659
5: 2 that you may maintain **d** 4659
8:12 I possess knowledge and **d**. 4659
Pr 11:22 a beautiful woman who shows no **d**. 3248

DISCRIMINATED (1)
Jas 2: 4 not **d** among yourselves and become judges *1359*

DISCUSS (2) [DISCUSSED, DISCUSSING, DISCUSSION, DISCUSSIONS]
Lk 6:11 *to* **d** with one another what they might do *1362*
Heb 9: 5 But we cannot **d** these things in detail now. *3306*

DISCUSSED (9) [DISCUSS]
1Sa 20:23 And about the matter you and I **d**— 1819
Mt 16: 7 They **d** this among themselves and said, *1368*
21:25 They **d** it among themselves and said, *1368*
Mk 8:16 *They* **d** this with one another and said, *1368*
11:31 *They* **d** it among themselves and said, *1368*
Lk 20: 5 They **d** it among themselves and said, *5199*
22: 4 and **d with** them how he might betray Jesus. *5196*
24:15 and **d** these things with each other, *5184*
Ac 25:14 Festus **d** Paul's case with the king. *423*

DISCUSSING (2) [DISCUSS]
Mk 9:10 **d** what "rising from the dead" meant. *5184*
Lk 24:17 "What *are you* **d** together *506*

DISCUSSION (3) [DISCUSS]
Mt 16: 8 Aware of their **d**, Jesus asked, *NIG*
Mk 8:17 Aware of their **d**, Jesus asked them: *NIG*
Ac 15: 7 After much **d**, Peter got up *2428*

DISCUSSIONS (1) [DISCUSS]
Ac 19: 9 with him and *had* **d** daily in the lecture hall *1363*

DISDAINED (4) [DISDAINFUL]
1Sa 2:30 but those who despise me *will be* **d**. 7837
Job 30: 1 whose fathers *I would have* **d** to put 4415
Ps 22:24 For he has not despised or **d** the suffering 9210
Jer 30:19 and *they will* not *be* **d**. 7592

DISDAINFUL (1) [DISDAINED]
Pr 30:13 whose glances *are* so **d**; 5951

DISEASE (39) [DISEASED, DISEASES]
Lev 13: 2 that may become an infectious **skin d**, 7669
13: 3 it is an infectious **skin d**. 7669
13: 8 it is an **infectious d**. 7669
13: 9 "When anyone has an infectious **skin d**, 7669
13:11 it is a chronic **skin d** and 7669
13:12 "If the **d** breaks out all over his skin and, 7669
13:13 and if the **d** has covered his whole body, 7669
13:15 he has an **infectious d**. 7669
13:20 It is an infectious **skin d** that has broken out 7669
13:25 it is an **infectious d** that has broken out in 7669
13:25 it is an infectious **skin d**. 7669
13:27 it is an infectious **skin d**. 7669
13:30 an **infectious d** *of* the head or chin. 7669
13:42 an **infectious d** breaking out on his head 7669
13:43 like an **infectious** skin **d**, 7669
13:45 an infectious **d** must wear torn clothes, 7665
14: 3 of his infectious **skin d**, 7669
14: 7 the **infectious d** and pronounce him clean. 7669
14:32 an infectious **skin d** and who cannot afford 7669
14:54 the regulations for any infectious **skin d**, 7669
22: 4 **has an infectious skin d** or a bodily 7665
Nu 5: 2 anyone who **has an infectious skin d** 7665
Dt 7:15 The LORD will keep you free from every **d**. 2716
28:22 The LORD will strike you with **wasting d**, 8831
1Ki 8:37 whatever disaster or **d** may come, 4701
2Ch 6:28 whatever disaster or **d** may come, 4701
16:12 of his reign Asa *was* **afflicted with a d** 2688
16:12 Though his **d** was severe, 2716
21:15 be very ill with a lingering **d** *of* the bowels, 4700
21:15 the **d** causes your bowels to come out.' " 2716
21:18 with an incurable **d** of the bowels. 2716
21:19 his bowels came out because of the **d**, 2716
Ps 41: 8 "A vile **d** has beset him; 1821
106:15 but sent a **wasting d** upon them. 8137
Isa 10:16 a **wasting d** upon his sturdy warriors; 8137
17:11 in the day of **d** and incurable pain. 5710
Mt 4:23 and healing every **d** and sickness among *3798*
9:35 of the kingdom and healing every **d** *3798*
10: 1 to drive out evil spirits and to heal every **d** *3798*

DISEASED (6) [DISEASE]
Lev 13:33 he must be shaved except for the **d area**, 5999
13:44 the man *is* **d** and is unclean. 7665
14: 2 "These are the regulations for the **d** *person* 7665
1Ki 15:23 In his old age, however, his feet *became* **d**. 2703
Mal 1: 8 When you sacrifice crippled or **d** *animals*, 2703
1:13 or **d** *animals* and offer them as sacrifices, 2703

DISEASES (19) [DISEASE]
Ge 12:17 the LORD inflicted serious **d** on Pharaoh 5596
Ex 15:26 not bring on you any of the **d** I brought on 4701
Lev 14:57 **infectious skin d and mildew**. 7669
26:16 upon you sudden terror, **wasting d** 8831
Dt 7:15 not inflict on you the horrible **d** you knew 4504
24: 8 of leprous **d** be very careful to do exactly as 5596
28:21 with **d** until he has destroyed you from 1822

Dt 28:60 He will bring upon you all the **d** *of* Egypt 4504
29:22 that have fallen on the land and the **d** 9377
Ps 103: 3 and heals all your **d,** 9377
Jer 16: 4 "They will die of deadly **d.** 9377
Mt 4:24 to him all who were ill *with* various **d,** *3798*
8:17 up our infirmities and carried our **d."** *3798*
Mk 1:34 Jesus healed many who had various **d.** *2809+3798*
3:10 with **d** were pushing forward to touch him. *3465*
Lk 6:18 to hear him and to be healed of their **d.** *3798*
7:21 very time Jesus cured many who had **d,** *3798*
8: 2 of evil spirits and **d:** *819*
9: 1 to drive out all demons and to cure **d,** *3798*

DISFIGURE (1) [DISFIGURED]

Mt 6:16 for *they* **d** their faces *906*

DISFIGURED (2) [DISFIGURE]

Lev 21:18 no man who is blind or lame, **d** 3050
Isa 52:14 his appearance *was* so **d** beyond that 5425

DISGRACE (61) [DISGRACED, DISGRACEFUL, DISGRACES]

Ge 30:23 "God has taken away my **d."** 3075
34:14 That would be a **d** to us. 3075
Lev 20:17 and they have sexual relations, it is a **d.** 2875
Nu 12:14 not *have* **been in d** for seven days? 4007
1Sa 11: 2 of you and so bring **d** on all Israel." 3075
17:26 and removes this **d** from Israel? 3075
2Sa 13:13 Where could I get rid of my **d?** 3075
2Ki 19: 3 a day of distress and rebuke and **d,** 5541
2Ch 32:21 So he withdrew to his own land in **d.** 1425+7156
Ne 1: 3 in the province are in great trouble and **d.** 3075
2:17 and we will no longer be *in* **d."** 3075
Ps 6:10 they will turn back *in* sudden **d.** 1017
35:26 over me be clothed with shame and **d.** 4009
40:14 be turned back *in* **d.** 4007
44:15 My **d** is before me all day long, 4009
52: 1 you who are a **d** *in the eyes of* God? 2875
70: 2 be turned back **in d.** 4007
71:13 to harm me be covered with scorn and **d.** 4009
74:21 Do not let the oppressed retreat *in* **d;** 4007
83:17 may they perish *in* **d.** 2917
109:29 with **d** and wrapped in shame as in a cloak. 4009
119:39 Take away the **d** I dread, 3075
Pr 6:33 Blows and **d** are his lot, 7830
11: 2 When pride comes, then comes **d,** 7830
13: 5 but the wicked bring shame and **d.** 2917
14:34 but sin is a **d** *to* any people. 2875
18: 3 so does contempt, and with shame comes **d.** 3075
19:26 a son who brings shame and **d.** 2917
Isa 4: 1 Take away our **d!"** 3075
22:18 you **d** *to* your master's house! 7830
25: 8 he will remove the **d** *of* his people from all 3075
30: 3 Egypt's shade will bring you **d.** 4009
30: 5 but only shame and **d."** 3075
37: 3 a day of distress and rebuke and **d,** 5541
43:28 So *I will* **d** the dignitaries of your temple, 2725
45:16 they will go off into **d** together. 4009
54: 4 *Do* not **fear d;** you will not be humiliated. 4007
61: 7 of **d** they will rejoice in their inheritance; 4009
Jer 3:25 and let our **d** cover us. 4009
23:40 I will bring upon you everlasting **d—** 3075
31:19 and humiliated because I bore the **d** 3075
La 3:30 and let him be filled with **d.** 3075
5: 1 look, and see our **d.** 3075
Eze 16:52 Bear your **d,** for you have furnished some justification for 4009
16:52 So then, be ashamed and bear your **d,** 4009
16:54 that you may bear your **d** and be ashamed 4009
28:16 *I* **drove** you **in d** from the mount of God, 2725
32:30 with the slain *in* **d** despite the terror caused 1017
36:30 so that you will no longer suffer **d** among 3075
Hos 2: 5 and has conceived them *in* **d.** 1017
Mic 2: 6 **d** will not overtake us." 4009
Hab 2:16 and **d** will cover your glory. 7814
Mt 1:19 **expose** her **to public d,** *1258*
Lk 1:25 and taken away my **d** among the people." *3945*
Ac 5:41 *of* **suffering d** for the Name. *869*
1Co 11: 6 if it is a **d** for a woman to have her hair cut *156*
11:14 if a man has long hair, it is a **d** to him, *871*
1Ti 3: 7 not fall into **d** and into the devil's trap. *3944*
Heb 6: 6 **subjecting** him **to public d.** *4136*
11:26 He regarded **d** for the sake of Christ as *3944*
13:13 bearing the **d** he bore. *3944*

DISGRACED (24) [DISGRACE]

2Sa 13:22 because *he had* **d** his sister Tamar. 6700
Ezr 9: 6 "O my God, I am too ashamed and **d** to lift 4007
Ps 35: 4 *May* those who seek my life *be* **d** and put 1017
69: 6 in you not *be* **d** because of me, O Lord, 1017
69:19 how I am scorned, **d** and shamed; 1425
Isa 1:29 *you will be* **d** because of the gardens 2917
41:11 against you will surely be ashamed and **d;** 4007
45:16 of idols will be put to shame and **d;** 4007
45:17 you will never be put to shame or **d,** 4007
50: 7 *I will* not **be d.** 4007
Jer 2:26 "As a thief is **d** when he is caught, 1425
2:26 so the house of Israel *is* **d—** 1017
15: 9 *she will be* **d** and humiliated. 1017
20:11 They will fail and *be* thoroughly **d;** 1017
22:22 Then you will be ashamed and **d** because 4007
48: 1 Kiriathaim *will* **be d** and captured; 1017
48: 1 the stronghold *will* **be d** and shattered. 1017
48:20 Moab *is* **d,** for she is shattered. 1017

Jer 50:12 she who gave you birth *will be* **d.** 2917
51:47 **be d** and her slain will all lie fallen 1017
51:51 *"We are* **d,** for we have been insulted 1017
Eze 36:32 Be ashamed and **d** for your conduct, 4007
Hos 10: 6 Ephraim *will be* **d;** 1423+4374
Mic 3: 7 be ashamed and the diviners **d.** 2917

DISGRACEFUL (11) [DISGRACE]

Ge 34: 7 because Shechem had done a **d thing** 5576
Dt 22:21 a **d thing** in Israel by being promiscuous 5576
Jos 7:15 of the LORD and has done a **d thing** 5576
Jdg 19:23 don't do this **d thing.** 5576
19:24 But to this man, don't do such a **d** thing." 5576
20: 6 because they committed this lewd and **d** act 5576
Pr 10: 5 he who sleeps during harvest *is* a **d** son. 1017
12: 4 but a **d** wife is like decay in his bones. 1017
17: 2 A wise servant will rule over a **d** son, 1017
Hos 4: 7 they exchanged their Glory for *something* **d.** 7830
1Co 14:35 it is **d** for a woman to speak in the church. *156*

DISGRACES (3) [DISGRACE]

Lev 21: 9 she **d** her father; 2725
Pr 28: 7 but a companion of gluttons **d** his father. 4007
29:15 but a child left to himself **d** his mother. 1017

DISGUISE (4) [DISGUISED, DISGUISES]

Ge 38:14 covered herself with a veil *to* **d herself,** 6634
1Ki 14: 2 **d yourself,** so you won't be recognized as 9101
22:30 "I will enter the battle **in d,** 2924
2Ch 18:29 "I will enter the battle **in d,** 2924

DISGUISED (5) [DISGUISE]

1Sa 28: 8 So Saul **d himself,** putting on other clothes, 2924
1Ki 20:38 *He* **d himself** with his headband down 2924
22:30 So the king of Israel **d himself** and went 2924
2Ch 18:29 So the king of Israel **d himself** and went 2924
35:22 but **d himself** to engage him in battle. 2924

DISGUISES (1) [DISGUISE]

Pr 26:24 A malicious man **d himself** with his lips, 5795

DISGUST (4) [DISGUSTED]

Eze 23:17 **turned away** from them **in d.** 3697
23:18 **turned away** from her **in d,** 3697
23:22 **turned away** from in **d,** 5936
23:28 **turned away** from **in d.** 5936

DISGUSTED (1) [DISGUST]

Ge 27:46 *"I'm* **d** with living because 7762

DISH (22) [DISHES]

Nu 7:14 one gold **d** weighing ten shekels, filled 4090
7:20 one gold **d** weighing ten shekels, filled 4090
7:26 one gold **d** weighing ten shekels, filled 4090
7:32 one gold **d** weighing ten shekels, filled 4090
7:38 one gold **d** weighing ten shekels, filled 4090
7:44 one gold **d** weighing ten shekels, filled 4090
7:50 one gold **d** weighing ten shekels, filled 4090
7:56 one gold **d** weighing ten shekels, filled 4090
7:62 one gold **d** weighing ten shekels, filled 4090
7:68 one gold **d** weighing ten shekels, filled 4090
7:74 one gold **d** weighing ten shekels, filled 4090
7:80 one gold **d** weighing ten shekels, filled 4090
2Ki 21:13 I will wipe out Jerusalem as one wipes a **d,** 7505
1Ch 28:17 weight of gold for **each** gold **d;** 2256+4094+4094
28:17 of silver for **each** silver **d;** 2256+4094+4094
Pr 19:24 The sluggard buries his hand in the **d;** 7505
26:15 The sluggard buries his hand in the **d;** 7505
Mt 23:25 You clean the outside of the cup and **d,** *4243*
23:26 First clean the inside of the cup and **d,** *4243*
Lk 11:39 clean the outside *of* the cup and **d,** *4402*
11:41 But give what is inside [the **d**] to the poor, *NIG*
Jn 13:26 of bread when I have dipped it in the **d."** *NIG*

DISHAN (5)

Ge 36:21 Dishon, Ezer and **D.** These sons of Seir 1915
36:28 The sons of **D:** Uz and Aran. 1915
36:30 Dishon, Ezer and **D.** These were the Horite chiefs, 1915
1Ch 1:38 Shobal, Zibeon, Anah, Dishon, Ezer and **D.** 1915
1:42 The sons of **D:** Uz and Aran. 1914

DISHEARTENED (3) [HEART]

Dt 20: 8 so that his brothers *will* not *become* **d** too." 906+4222+5022
Jer 49:23 *They are* **d,** troubled like the restless sea. 4570
Eze 13:22 Because you **d** the righteous with your lies, 3874+4213

DISHES (15) [DISH]

Ex 25:29 And make its plates and **d** of pure gold, 4090
37:16 its plates and **d** and bowls and its pitchers 4090
Nu 4: 7 **d** and bowls, and the jars 4090
7:84 and twelve gold **d.** 4090
7:85 the silver **d** weighed two thousand four hundred shekels, 3998
7:86 The twelve gold **d** filled 4090
7:86 the gold **d** weighed a hundred and twenty shekels. 4090
1Ki 7:50 sprinkling bowls, **d** and censers; 4090

2Ki 25:14 **d** and all the bronze articles used in 4090
2Ch 4:22 sprinkling bowls, **d** and censers; 4090
24:14 also **d** and other objects of gold and silver. 4090
Ezr 1: 9 gold **d** 30 silver dishes 1,000 113
1: 9 gold dishes 30 silver **d** 1,000 113
Jer 52:18 **d** and all the bronze articles used in 4090
52:19 **d** and bowls used for drink offerings— 4090

DISHES (Anglicized) See also BASINS

DISHON (7)

Ge 36:21 **D,** Ezer and Dishan. These sons of Seir 1914
36:25 **D** and Oholibamah daughter of Anah. 1914
36:26 The sons of **D:** 1914
36:30 **D,** Ezer and Dishan. These were the Horite chiefs, 1914
1Ch 1:38 Lotan, Shobal, Zibeon, Anah, **D,** 1914
1:41 The son of Anah: **D.** 1914
1:41 The sons of **D:** 1914

DISHONEST (18) [DISHONESTLY]

Ex 18:21 trustworthy men who hate **d gain—** 1299
Lev 19:35 not use **d** standards when measuring length, 6404
1Sa 8: 3 after **d gain** and accepted bribes 1299
Pr 11: 1 The LORD abhors **d** scales, 5327
13:11 **D** money dwindles away, 2039
20:23 and **d** scales do not please him. 5327
29:27 The righteous detest the **d;** 6404
Jer 22:17 and your heart are set only on **d gain,** 1299
Eze 28:18 **d** trade you have desecrated your sanctuaries. 6404
Hos 12: 7 merchant uses **d** scales; he loves to defraud. 5327
Am 8: 5 the price and cheating with **d** scales, 5327
Mic 6:11 Shall I acquit a man with **d** scales, 8400
Lk 16: 8 "The master commended the **d** manager *94*
16:10 and whoever is **d** with very little will also *96*
16:10 with very little will also be **d** with much. *96*
1Ti 3: 8 and not **pursuing d gain.** *153*
Tit 1: 7 not violent, not **pursuing d gain.** *153*
1:11 and that for the sake of **d** gain. *156*

DISHONESTLY (1) [DISHONEST]

Dt 25:16 anyone who deals **d.** 6404

DISHONOR (16) [DISHONORED, DISHONORS]

Lev 18: 7 **d** your father **by having sexual relations with** your mother. 1655+6872
18: 8 that would **d** your father. 6872
18:10 that would **d** you. 6872
18:14 **d** your father's brother **by approaching** his wife **to have sexual relations;** 1655+6872
18:16 that would **d** your brother. 6872
20:19 for *that would* **d** a close relative; 6867
Dt 22:30 *he must* not **d** his father's **bed.** 1655+4053
Pr 30: 9 and so **d** the name of my God. 9530
Jer 14:21 *do* not **d** your glorious throne. 5571
20:11 their **d** will never be forgotten. 4009
La 2: 2 and its princes down to the ground *in* **d.** 2725
Eze 22:10 In you are *those who* **d** their fathers' **bed;** 1655+6872
Jn 8:49 "but I honor my Father and you **d** me. *869*
Ro 2:23 *do* you **d** God by breaking the law? *869*
1Co 15:43 it is sown in **d,** it is raised in glory; *871*
2Co 6: 8 glory and **d,** bad report and good report; *871*

DISHONORED (7) [DISHONOR]

Lev 20:11 *he has* **d** his father. 1655+6872
20:17 *He has* **d** his sister and will 1655+6872
20:20 If a man sleeps with his aunt, *he has* **d** his uncle. 1655+6872
20:21 *he has* **d** his brother. 1655+6872
Dt 21:14 since *you have* **d** her. 6700
Ezr 4:14 and it is not proper for us to see the king **d,** 10571
1Co 4:10 You are honored, we are **d!** *872*

DISHONORS (6) [DISHONOR]

Dt 27:16 the man *who* **d** his father or his mother." 7829
27:20 for *he* **d** his father's **bed."** 1655+4053
Job 20: 3 I hear a rebuke that **d** me, 4009
Mic 7: 6 For a son **d** his father, 5571
1Co 11: 4 with his head covered **d** his head. *2875*
11: 5 with her head uncovered **d** her head— *2875*

DISILLUSIONMENT (1)

Ps 7:14 and conceives trouble gives birth to **d.** 9214

DISLIKES (3)

Dt 22:13 a wife and, after lying with her, **d** her 8533
22:16 but *he* **d** her. 8533
24: 3 and her second husband **d** her 8533

DISLODGE (3)

Jos 15:63 Judah could not **d** the Jebusites, 3769
16:10 not **d** the Canaanites living in Gezer; 3769
Jdg 1:21 however, failed *to* **d** the Jebusites, 3769

DISLOYAL (1)

Ps 78:57 Like their fathers *they were* **d** and faithless, 6047

DISMAY (3) [DISMAYED]
Job 41:22 **d** goes before him. 1791
Ps 35: 4 be turned back *in* **d**. 2917
116:11 And in my **d** I said, "All men are liars." 2905

DISMAYED (18) [DISMAY]
1Sa 17:11 and all the Israelites *were* **d** and terrified. 3169
2Ki 19:26 drained of power, *are* **d** and put to shame. 3169
Job 4: 5 it strikes you, and *you are* **d**. 987
32:15 *"They are* **d** and have no more to say; 3169
Ps 6:10 All my enemies will be ashamed and **d**; 987+4394
30: 7 but when you hid your face, I was **d**. 987
83:17 May they ever be ashamed and **d**; 987
143: 4 my heart within me *is* **d**. 9037
Isa 28:16 the one who trusts *will* never *be* **d**. 2591
37:27 drained of power, *are* **d** and put to shame. 3169
41:10 *do* not *be* **d**, for I am your God. 9283
41:23 so that *we will be* **d** and filled with fear. 9283
Jer 8: 9 *they will be* **d** and trapped. 3169
14: 3 **d** and despairing, they cover their heads. 1017
14: 4 the farmers *are* **d** and cover their heads. 1017
30:10 *do* not *be* **d**, O Israel,' declares the LORD. 3169
46:27 *do* not *be* **d**, O Israel. 3169
49:23 "Hamath and Arpad *are* **d**, 1017

DISMISS (1) [DISMISSED]
Lk 2:29 *you* now **d** your servant in peace. *668*

DISMISSED (9) [DISMISS]
Jdg 2: 6 After Joshua *had* **d** the Israelites, 8938
1Sa 10:25 Then Samuel **d** the people, 8938
2Ch 25:10 So Amaziah **d** the troops who had come 976
Mt 14:22 while *he* **d** the crowd. *668*
14:23 *After he had* **d** them, *668*
Mk 6:45 while he **d** the crowd. *668*
Ac 13:43 When the congregation *was* **d**, *3395*
19:41 After he had said this, *he* **d** the assembly. *668*
23:22 The commander **d** the young man *668*

DISOBEDIENCE (9) [DISOBEY]
Jos 22:22 If this has been in rebellion or **d** to 5086
Jer 43: 7 So they entered Egypt *in* **d** *to* the LORD 928+4202+7754+9048
Ro 5:19 For just as through the **d** of the one man *4157*
11:30 received mercy *as a result of* their **d**, *577*
11:32 to **d** so that he may have mercy on them all. *577*
2Co 10: 6 we will be ready to punish every **act of d**, *4157*
Heb 2: 2 and **d** received its just punishment, *4157*
4: 6 did not go in, because of their **d**. *577*
4:11 by following their example *of* **d**. *577*

DISOBEDIENT (14) [DISOBEY]
Ne 9:26 "But *they were* **d** and rebelled against you; 5286
Lk 1:17 to their children and the **d** to the wisdom of *579*
Ac 26:19 I was not **d** to the vision from heaven. *579*
Ro 10:21 to a **d** and obstinate people." *578*
11:30 as you who *were* at one time **d** to God have *578*
11:31 now *become* **d** in order that they too may *578*
Eph 2: 2 now at work in those who are **d**. *577*
5: 6 God's wrath comes on those who are **d**. *577*
5:12 even to mention what the **d** do in secret. *NIG*
2Ti 3: 2 boastful, proud, abusive, **d** to their parents, *579*
Tit 1: 6 not open to the charge of being wild and **d**. *538*
1:16 **d** and unfit for doing anything good. *579*
3: 3 At one time we too were foolish, **d**, *579*
Heb 11:31 was not killed with those who *were* **d**. *578*

DISOBEY (6) [DISOBEDIENCE, DISOBEDIENT, DISOBEYED, DISOBEYING, DISOBEYS]
Dt 11:28 the curse if *you* **d** the commands of 4202+9048
2Ch 24:20 'Why *do* you **d** the LORD's commands? 6296
Est 3: 3 "Why *do* you **d** the king's command?" 6296
Jer 42:13 so **d** the LORD your God, 928+1194+7754+9048
Ro 1:30 they **d** their parents; *579*
1Pe 2: 8 *because they* **d** the message— *578*

DISOBEYED (9) [DISOBEY]
Nu 14:22 but *who* **d** me and tested me ten times— 928+4202+7754+9048
27:14 *both of you* **d** my command to honor me 5286
Jdg 2: 2 Yet *you have* **d** me. 928+4202+7754+9048
Ne 9:29 and **d** your commands. 4202+9048
Isa 24: 5 *they have* **d** the laws, 6296
Jer 43: 4 the army officers and all the people **d** 4202+9048
Lk 15:29 for you and never **d** your orders. *4216*
Heb 3:18 if not *to* those who **d**? *578*
1Pe 3:20 *who* **d** long ago when God waited patiently *578*

DISOBEYING (1) [DISOBEY]
Nu 14:41 "Why *are* you **d** the LORD's command? 6296

DISOBEYS (1) [DISOBEY]
Eze 33:12 not save him when he **d**, 7322

DISORDER (4)
Job 10:22 of deep shadow and **d**, 4202+6043
1Co 14:33 For God is not a God *of* **d** but of peace. *189*
2Co 12:20 factions, slander, gossip, arrogance and **d**. *189*
Jas 3:16 there you find **d** and every evil practice. *189*

DISOWN (13) [DISOWNED, DISOWNS]
Pr 30: 9 I may have too much and **d** you and say, 3950
Mt 10:33 I *will* **d** him before my Father in heaven. *766*
26:34 rooster crows, *you will* **d** me three times." *565*
26:35 *I will* never **d** you." *565*
26:75 rooster crows, *you will* **d** me three times." *565*
Mk 14:30 before the rooster crows twice you yourself *will* **d** me three times." *565*
14:31 *I will* never **d** you." *565*
14:72 "Before the rooster crows twice *you will* **d** me three times." *565*
Lk 22:61 "Before rooster crows today, *you will* **d** me three times." *565*
Jn 13:38 rooster crows, *you will* **d** me three times! *766*
2Ti 2:12 If *we* **d** him, he will also disown us; *766*
2:12 If we disown him, he *will* also **d** us; *766*
2:13 for he cannot **d** himself. *766*

DISOWNED (3) [DISOWN]
Lk 12: 9 before men *will be* **d** before the angels *766*
Ac 3:13 and *you* **d** him before Pilate, *766*
3:14 You **d** the Holy and Righteous One *766*

DISOWNS (3) [DISOWN]
Job 8:18 that place **d** it and says, 'I never saw you.' 3950
Mt 10:33 But whoever **d** me before men, *766*
Lk 12: 9 But he who **d** me before men will *766*

DISPATCH (1) [DISPATCHED, DISPATCHES]
Isa 10: 6 *I* **d** him against a people who anger me, 7422

DISPATCHED (1) [DISPATCH]
1Ki 20:17 Ben-Hadad *had* **d** scouts, who reported, 8938

DISPATCHES (4) [DISPATCH]
Est 1:22 He sent **d** to all parts of the kingdom, 6219
3:13 **D** were sent by couriers to all 6219
8: 5 be written overruling the **d** that Haman son 6219
8:10 sealed the **d** with the king's signet ring, 6219

DISPENSATION (KJV) See ADMINISTRATION, COMMISSION, TRUST

DISPENSES (1)
Zep 3: 5 Morning by morning *he* **d** his justice, 5989

DISPERSE (7) [DISPERSED, DISPERSES, DISPERSING]
Ge 49: 7 I will scatter them in Jacob and **d** them 7046
Eze 12:15 when I **d** them among the nations 7046
20:23 to them in the desert that I *would* **d** them 7046
22:15 *I will* **d** you among the nations 7046
29:12 And *I will* **d** the Egyptians among 7046
30:23 *I will* **d** the Egyptians among the nations 7046
30:26 *I will* **d** the Egyptians among the nations 7046

DISPERSED (6) [DISPERSE]
2Sa 20:22 and his men **d** from the city, 7046
1Ki 1:49 all Adonijah's guests rose in alarm and **d**. 2006+2143+4200
Est 3: 8 "There is a certain people **d** and scattered 7061
Job 38:24 to the place where the lightning **is d**, 2745
Eze 36:19 *I* **d** them among the nations, 7046
Ac 5:36 He was killed, all his followers *were* **d**, *1370*

DISPERSES (2) [DISPERSE]
Dt 30: 1 the LORD your God **d** you among 5615
Job 12:23 he enlarges nations, and **d** them. 5697

DISPERSING (1) [DISPERSE]
2Ch 11:23 **d** some of his sons throughout the districts 7287

DISPLACES (1)
Pr 30:23 and a maidservant *who* **d** her mistress. 3769

DISPLAY (13) [DISPLAYED, DISPLAYS]
Dt 22:17 Then her parents *shall* **d** the cloth before 7298
Est 1:11 to **d** her beauty to the people and nobles, 8011
Job 10:16 again **d** *your* **awesome power** against me. 7098
Ps 19: 2 night after night *they* **d** knowledge. 2555
45: 4 *let* your right hand **d** awesome deeds. 3723
77:14 *you* **d** your power among the peoples. 3359
Isa 49: 3 Israel, in whom *I will* **d** *my* **splendor."** 6995
60:21 for *the* **d** *of* my **splendor.** 6995
61: 3 of the LORD for *the* **d** *of* his **splendor.** 6995
Eze 39:21 *"I will* **d** my glory among the nations, 5989
Ro 9:17 that *I might* **d** my power in you and *1892*
1Co 4: 9 **put** us apostles **on d** *617*
1Ti 1:16 Christ Jesus *might* **d** his unlimited patience *1892*

DISPLAYED (8) [DISPLAY]
Ex 14:31 saw the great power the LORD **d** against 6913
Nu 14:17 "Now *may* the Lord's strength *be* **d**, 1540
1Ki 11:41 all he did and the wisdom he **d**— NIH
Est 1: 4 For a full 180 days he **d** the vast wealth 8011
Job 26: 3 And what great insight *you have* **d**! 3359
Ps 78:43 the day *he* **d** his miraculous signs in Egypt, 8492
Jn 9: 3 that the work of God *might be* **d** in his life. *5746*
2Th 2: 9 be in accordance with the work of Satan **d** *NIG*

DISPLAYS (2) [DISPLAY]
Pr 14:29 but a quick-tempered man **d** folly. 8123
Isa 44:23 *he* **d** *his* **glory** in Israel. 6995

DISPLEASE (3) [DISPLEASED, DISPLEASES, DISPLEASING, DISPLEASURE]
Nu 11:11 What *have I done to* **d** you that you put the burden 928+2834+4202+5162+6524
1Sa 29: 7 do nothing to **d** the Philistine rulers." 928+6524+8273
1Th 2:15 *They* **d** God and are hostile to all men *743+3590*

DISPLEASED (7) [DISPLEASE]
Ge 48:17 on Ephraim's head he *was* **d**; 928+6524+8317
Nu 22:34 Now if you *are* **d**, I will go back. 928+6524+8317
1Sa 8: 6 this **d** Samuel; so he prayed to the LORD. 928+6524+8317
2Sa 11:27 the thing David had done **d** the LORD. 928+6524+8317
Ne 13: 8 I *was* greatly **d** and threw all 8317
Isa 59:15 *was* **d** that there was no justice. 928+6524+8317
Jnh 4: 1 But Jonah *was* greatly **d** and became angry. 8288+8317

DISPLEASES (2) [DISPLEASE]
Isa 65:12 in my sight and chose what **d** *me*." 2911+4202
66: 4 in my sight and chose what **d** *me*." 2911+4202

DISPLEASING (2) [DISPLEASE]
Ge 28: 8 how **d** the Canaanite women were to his father 928+6524+8273
Dt 24: 1 If a man marries a woman who becomes **d** to him 928+2834+4202+5162+6524

DISPLEASURE (1) [DISPLEASE]
Ps 85: 4 and put away your **d** toward us. 4088

DISPOSAL (2) [DISPOSED]
Mt 26:53 at once **put at** my **d** more than twelve legions of angels? *4225*
Ac 5: 4 it was sold, wasn't the money at your **d**? *2026*

DISPOSED (5) [DISPOSAL]
Ex 3:21 the Egyptians **favorably d toward** this people, 928+2834+6524
11: 3 the Egyptians **favorably d toward** the people, 928+2834+6524
12:36 the Egyptians **favorably d toward** the people, 928+2834+6524
Dt 31:21 I know what they are **d** to do, 3671
1Sa 20:12 If *he* is **favorably d** toward you, 3201

DISPOSSESS (5) [DISPOSSESSING]
Dt 9: 1 and **d** nations greater and stronger than you, 3769
11:23 and *you will* **d** nations larger 3769
12:29 the nations you are about to invade and **d**. 3769
18:14 The nations you *will* **d** listen 3769
Isa 54: 3 your descendants *will* **d** nations and settle 3769

DISPOSSESSED (KJV) See DRIVEN OUT, DROVE OUT

DISPOSSESSING (2) [DISPOSSESS]
Dt 12: 2 the nations you *are* **d** worship their gods. 3769
Eze 45: 9 Stop **d** my people, 1766

DISPUTABLE (1) [DISPUTE]
Ro 14: 1 without passing judgment *on* **d** *matters*. *1369*

DISPUTE (18) [DISPUTABLE, DISPUTED, DISPUTES, DISPUTING]
Ex 18:16 Whenever they have a **d**, 1821
24:14 anyone involved in a **d** can go to them." 1821
Dt 19:17 the two men involved in the **d** must stand in 8190
21: 5 of the LORD and to decide all **cases of d** 8190
25: 1 When men have a **d**, 8190
Jdg 11:27 **decide** *the* **d** this day between the Israelites 9149
Job 9: 3 Though one wished to **d** with him, 8189
9:14 "How then *can* I **d** *with* him? 6699
Pr 17:14 so drop the matter before a **d** breaks out. 8190
Eze 44:24 " 'In any **d**, the priests are to serve 8190
Lk 22:24 Also a **d** arose among them as to which *5808*
Ac 15: 2 and Barnabas into sharp **d** and debate *5087*
17:18 and Stoic philosophers *began to* **d with** him. *5202*
23: 7 a **d** broke out between the Pharisees and *5087*
23:10 The **d** became so violent that *5087*
25:19 they had some **points of d** with him *2427*
1Co 6: 1 If any of you has a **d** with another, *4547*
6: 5 among you wise enough *to* **judge a d** *1359*

DISPUTED (1) [DISPUTE]
Ge 26:20 because *they* **d** with him. 6921

DISPUTES (10) [DISPUTE]
Ex 18:19 before God and bring their **d** to him. 1821
Dt 1:12 and your burdens and your **d** all by myself? 8190
1:16 Hear the **d** between your brothers NIH
Jdg 4:5 to her to have their **d decided.** 5477
2Ch 19:8 the law of the LORD and to settle **d.** 8190
Pr 18:18 Casting the lot settles **d** 4506
18:19 and **d** are like the barred gates of a citadel. 4506
Isa 2:4 between the nations and *will* **settle d** 3519
Mic 4:3 between many peoples and *will* **settle d** 3519
1Co 6:4 if you have **d** about such matters, *3215*

DISPUTING (2) [DISPUTE]
1Ti 2:8 without anger or **d.** *1369*
Jude 1:9 when *he was* **d** with the devil about the body of Moses, *1359+1363*

DISQUALIFIED (1) [DISQUALIFY]
1Co 9:27 I myself will not be **d** for the prize. *99*

DISQUALIFY (1) [DISQUALIFIED]
Col 2:18 **d** you **for the prize.** *2857*

DISQUIETING (1)
Job 4:13 Amid **d** dreams in the night, 8546

DISREGARDED (2) [DISREGARDING]
Ezr 9:10 For *we have* **d** the commands 6440
Isa 40:27 my cause *is* **d** by my God"? 6296

DISREGARDING (1) [DISREGARDED]
Am 1:9 **d** a treaty of brotherhood, 2349+4202

DISREPUTE (1)
2Pe 2:2 **bring** the way of truth **into d.** *1059*

DISRESPECT (1)
Est 1:18 There will be no end of **d** and discord. 1025

DISROBING (1)
2Sa 6:20 **d** in the sight of the slave girls 1655

DISSEMBLED, DISSIMULATION (KJV)
See LIED, FATAL MISTAKE, JOINED IN HYPOCRISY

DISSENSION (8) [DISSENSIONS]
Pr 6:14 he always stirs up **d.** 4506
6:19 and a man who stirs up **d** among brothers. 4506
10:12 Hatred stirs up **d,** 4506
15:18 A hot-tempered man stirs up **d,** 4506
16:28 A perverse man stirs up **d,** 4506
28:25 A greedy man stirs up **d,** 4506
29:22 An angry man stirs up **d,** 4506
Ro 13:13 not *in* **d** and jealousy. *2251*

DISSENSIONS (1) [DISSENSION]
Gal 5:20 jealousy, fits of rage, selfish ambition, **d,** *1496*

DISSIPATION (2)
Lk 21:34 be weighed down with **d,** *3190*
1Pe 4:4 with them into the same flood *of* **d,** *861*

DISSOLVED (1)
Isa 34:4 the heavens *will* **be d** and the sky rolled up 5245

DISSUADE (2) [DISSUADED]
Eze 3:18 or speak out to **d** him from his evil ways 2302
33:8 not speak out to **d** him from his ways, 2302

DISSUADED (1) [DISSUADE]
Ac 21:14 *When* he *would* not *be* **d,** *4275*

DISTAFF (1)
Pr 31:19 In her hand she holds the **d** and grasps 3969

DISTANCE (50) [DISTANT]
Ge 22:4 up and saw the place in the **d.** 8158
35:16 While they were still **some d** from Ephrath, 824+2021+3896
36:6 a land **some d from** his brother Jacob. 4946+7156
37:18 But they saw him in the **d,** 8158
48:7 a **little d** from Ephrath. 824+3896
Ex 2:4 at a **d** to see what would happen to him. 8158
20:18 They stayed at a **d** 8158
20:21 The people remained at a **d,** 8158
24:1 You are to worship at a **d,** 8158
33:7 outside the camp **some d away,** 4946+8178
Nu 2:2 to camp around the Tent of Meeting **some d** 5584
16:37 and scatter the coals **some d away,** for 2134
Dt 19:6 overtake him if the **d** is too great, 2006
20:15 cities that are **at a d** from you 4394+8158
21:2 and judges shall go out and **measure** *the* **d** 4499
32:52 you will see the land only from a **d;** 5584
Jos 3:4 a **d** of about a thousand yards between you 8158
3:16 It piled up in a heap a great **d away,** 8178
Jdg 18:22 they *had* **gone some d** from Micah's house, 8178
1Sa 26:13 stood on top of the hill **some d away;** 4946+8158
2Sa 11:10 "Haven't you just come from a **d?** 2006
15:17 and they halted at a place **some d away.** 5305
16:1 When David had gone a **short d** beyond 5071
18:13 you *would have* **kept** *your* **d** *from* me." 3656+4946+5584
19:36 over the Jordan with the king for a **short d,** 5071
2Ki 2:7 of the prophets went and stood at a **d,** 8158
4:25 When he saw her in the **d,** 5584
5:19 After Naaman had traveled **some d,** 824+3896
Job 2:12 When they saw him from a **d,** 8158
30:10 They detest me and **keep** *their* **d;** 8178
Isa 59:14 and righteousness stands at a **d;** 8158
Eze 40:13 the **d** was twenty-five cubits 8145
40:15 The **d** from the entrance of the gateway to NIH
40:19 Then he measured the **d** from the inside of 8145
48:35 "The **d** all around will be 18,000 cubits. NIH
Mt 8:30 **Some d** from them a large herd *3426*
14:24 but the boat was already a considerable **d** *5084*
26:58 But Peter followed him at a **d,** *3427*
27:55 women were there, watching from **a d.** *3427*
Mk 5:6 When he saw Jesus from a **d,** *3427*
8:3 some of them have come a **long d."** *3427*
11:13 Seeing in the **d** a fig tree in leaf, *3427*
14:54 Peter followed him at a **d,** *3427*
15:40 Some women were watching from a **d.** *3427*
Lk 17:12 They stood **at a d** *4523*
18:13 "But the tax collector stood **at a d.** *3427*
22:54 Peter followed **at a d.** *3427*
23:49 stood at a **d,** watching these things. *3427*
Heb 11:13 and welcomed them **from a d.** *4523*
Rev 14:20 as high as the horses' bridles **for a d of** *608*

DISTANT (37) [DISTANCE]
Dt 14:24 But if that place *is* too **d** 2006+2021+8049
29:22 from **d** lands will see the calamities 8158
30:4 to the **most d land** *under* the heavens, 7895
Jos 9:6 "We have come from a **d** country; 8158
9:9 from a very **d** country because of the fame 8158
1Ki 8:41 from a **d** land because of your name— 8158
2Ki 20:14 "From a **d** land," Hezekiah replied. 8158
2Ch 6:32 from a **d** land because of your great name 8158
Est 10:1 throughout the empire, to its **d shores,** 362+3542
Ps 56:T To [the tune of] "A Dove on **D** Oaks." 8158
72:10 and of **d shores** will bring tribute to him; 362
97:1 let the **d** shores rejoice. 8041
Pr 25:25 to a weary soul is good news from a **d** land. 5305
Isa 5:26 He lifts up a banner for the **d** nations, 4946+8158
7:18 the **d** streams of Egypt and for bees from 7895
8:9 Listen, all you **d** lands. 5305
39:3 "From a **d** land," Hezekiah replied. 8158
45:21 who declared it from the **d past?** 255
49:1 hear this, you **d** nations: 4946+8158
66:19 and Greece, and to the **d** islands that have 8158
Jer 4:16 'A besieging army is coming from a **d** land, 5305
5:15 "I am bringing a **d** nation against you 4946+5305
6:20 or sweet calamus from a **d** land? 5305
9:26 and all who live in the desert in **d** places. 7899
18:14 Do its cool waters from **d sources** ever cease 2424
25:23 Tema, Buz and all who are in **d places;** 6991+7899
30:10 'I will surely save you out of a **d place,** 8158
31:10 proclaim it in **d** coastlands: 4946+5305
46:27 I will surely save you out of a **d place,** 8158
49:32 those who are in **d places** 6991+7899
51:50 Remember the LORD in a **d** *land,* 8158
Eze 12:27 and he prophesies about the **d** future.' 8158
Da 4:22 and your dominion extends to **d parts** *of* 10509
8:26 for it concerns the **d future."** 3427+8041
Zec 10:9 yet in **d lands** they will remember me. 5305
Lk 15:13 a **d** country and there squandered his wealth *3431*
19:12 a **d** country to have himself appointed king *3431*

DISTILL (1)
Job 36:27 *which* **d** as rain to the streams; 2423

DISTINCTION (7) [DISTINCTLY]
Ex 8:23 a **d** between my people and your people. 7151
9:4 But the LORD *will* **make a d** between 7111
11:7 that the LORD **makes a d** between Egypt 7111
Lev 20:25 therefore **make a d** between clean 976
Mal 3:18 the **d between** the righteous and the wicked, 1068
Ac 15:9 *He* **made** no **d** between us and them, *1359*
1Co 14:7 unless there is a **d** in the notes? *1405*

DISTINCTLY (1) [DISTINCTION]
Ac 10:3 He **d** saw an angel of God, *5747*

DISTINGUISH (8) [DISTINGUISHED, DISTINGUISHING]
Ex 33:16 What else *will* **d** me and your people 7111
Lev 10:10 You *must* **d** between the holy and the common, 976
11:47 You *must* **d** between the unclean and the clean, 976
1Ki 3:9 and to **d** between right and wrong. 1067
Ezr 3:13 No one *could* **d** the sound of the shouts 5795
Eze 22:26 not **d** between the holy and the common; 976
44:23 **show** them **how to d** between 3359
Heb 5:14 to **d** good **from** evil. *1360*

DISTINGUISHED (4) [DISTINGUISH]
Nu 22:15 more numerous and more **d** than the first. 3877
2Sa 6:20 How the king of Israel *has* **d himself** today, 3877
Da 6:3 so **d himself** among the administrators and 10488
Lk 14:8 a **person more d than** you may have been invited. *1952*

DISTINGUISHING (2) [DISTINGUISH]
1Co 12:10 to another **d between** spirits, *1360*
2Th 3:17 which is **the d mark** in all my letters. *4956*

DISTORT (5) [DISTORTED]
Jer 23:36 and so *you* **d** the words of the living God, 2200
Mic 3:9 who despise justice and **d** all that is right; 6835
Ac 20:30 and **d the truth** in order *1406+3281*
2Co 4:2 nor *do we* **d** the word of God. *1516*
2Pe 3:16 which ignorant and unstable people **d,** *5137*

DISTORTED (1) [DISTORT]
Eze 27:35 with horror and their faces *are* **d with fear.** 8307

DISTRACTED (1)
Lk 10:40 But Martha *was* **d** by all the preparations *4352*

DISTRAUGHT (1)
Ps 55:2 My thoughts trouble me and *I am* **d** 2101

DISTRESS (84) [DISTRESSED, DISTRESSES, DISTRESSING]
Ge 32:7 and **d** Jacob divided the people who were 7674
35:3 who answered me in the day of my **d** 7650
42:21 that's why this **d** has come upon us." 7650
Dt 4:30 in **d** and all these things have happened 7639
28:57 in the **d** that your enemy will inflict on you 5186
Jdg 2:15 They *were* **in** great **d.** 7674
10:9 and Israel *was* **in** great **d.** 7674
1Sa 2:32 and you will see **d** *in* my dwelling. 7639
14:24 Now the men of Israel *were* **in d** that day, 5601
22:2 in **d** or in debt or discontented gathered 5186
28:15 "I am in great **d,"** Saul said. 7639
2Sa 16:12 that the LORD will see my **d** and repay me 6715
22:7 In my **d** I called to the LORD; 7639
24:14 David said to Gad, "I am in deep **d.** 7639
2Ki 4:27 She *is* **in bitter d,** 5352
19:3 a day of **d** and rebuke and disgrace, 7639
1Ch 21:13 David said to Gad, "I am in deep **d.** 7639
2Ch 15:4 But in their **d** they turned to the LORD, 7639
15:6 with every kind of **d.** 7650
20:9 and will cry out to you in our **d,** 7650
33:12 In his **d** he sought the favor of 7674
Ne 9:37 We are in great **d.** 7650
Est 4:4 she *was* **in** great **d.** 2655
7:4 because no such **d** would justify disturbing 7639
Job 15:24 **D** and anguish fill him with terror; 7639
20:22 **d** *will* overtake him; 7674
27:9 Does God listen to his cry when **d** comes 7650
30:24 when he cries for help in his **d.** 7085
33:19 a bed of pain with constant **d** *in* his bones, 8190
36:16 from the jaws of **d** to a spacious place free 7639
36:19 so you would not be in **d?** 7639
Ps 4:1 Give me relief from my **d;** 7639
18:6 In my **d** I called to the LORD; 7639
20:1 the LORD answer you when you are in **d;** 7650
25:18 and my **d** and take away all my sins. 6662
31:9 O LORD, for I am in **d;** 7639
35:26 over my **d** be put to shame and confusion; 8288
55:17 Evening, morning and noon I cry out **in d,** 8488
57:6 I *was* **bowed down in d.** 4104
69:29 I am in pain and **d;** 6714
77:2 When I was *in* **d,** I sought the Lord; 7650
81:7 In your **d** you called and I rescued you, 7650
102:2 from me when I am *in* **d.** 7639
106:44 of their **d** when he heard their cry; 7639
107:6 and he delivered them from their **d.** 5188
107:13 and he saved them from their **d.** 5188
107:19 and he saved them from their **d.** 5188
107:28 and he brought them out of their **d.** 5188
119:143 Trouble and **d** have come upon me, 5186
120:1 I call on the LORD in my **d,** 7650
144:14 no **cry of d** in our streets. 7424
Pr 1:27 when **d** and trouble overwhelm you. 7650
Isa 5:7 for righteousness, but heard **cries of d.** 7591
5:30 he will see darkness and **d;** 7639
8:22 the earth and see only **d** and darkness 7650
9:1 be no more gloom for those who were *in* **d.** 4608
25:4 a refuge for the needy in his **d,** 7639
26:16 LORD, they came to you in their **d;** 7639
30:6 Through a land of hardship and **d,** 7442
33:2 our salvation in time of **d.** 7650
37:3 a day of **d** and rebuke and disgrace, 7650
63:9 In all their **d** he too was distressed, 7650
Jer 10:18 *I will* **bring d** on them so that they may 7674
11:14 when they call to me in the time of their **d.** 8288
14:8 O Hope of Israel, its Savior in times of **d,** 7650
15:11 with you in times of disaster and times of **d.** 7650
16:19 my refuge in time of **d,** 7650
La 1:3 in the midst of her **d.** 5210
1:21 All my enemies have heard of my **d;** 8288

Eze 30:16 Memphis will be *in* constant **d.** 7639
Da 12: 1 a time of **d** such as has not happened from 7650
Jnh 2: 2 He said: "In my **d** I called to the LORD, 7650
Hab 3: 7 I saw the tents of Cushan in **d,** 224
Zep 1:15 a day of **d** and anguish, 7650
1:17 *I will* **bring d** on the people 7674
Mt 24:21 For then there will be great **d,** *2568*
24:29 after the **d** of those days " 'the sun will *2568*
Mk 13:19 be days of **d** unequaled from the beginning, *2568*
13:24 "But in those days, following that **d,** *2568*
Lk 21:23 There will be great **d** in the land and wrath *340*
Ro 2: 9 There will be trouble and **d** *5103*
2Co 2: 4 For I wrote you out of great **d** and anguish *2568*
1Th 3: 7 in all our **d** *340*
Jas 1:27 to look after orphans and widows in their **d** *2568*

DISTRESSED (24) [DISTRESS]

Ge 21:11 The matter **d** Abraham greatly 928+6524+8317
21:12 *Do* not *be so* **d** about the boy and your maidservant. 928+6524+8317
42:21 We saw *how* **d** he was when he pleaded 7650
45: 5 *be* **d** and do not be angry with yourselves 6772
1Sa 30: 6 David *was* greatly **d** because 7674
Ezr 10: 9 **greatly d** by the occasion and because of 8283
Job 6:20 *They are* **d,** because they had been confident 1017
Isa 8:21 **D** and hungry, they will roam through 7996
54: 6 as if you were a wife deserted and **d** 6772
63: 9 In all their distress he too was **d,** 7639
La 1:20 "See, O LORD, how **d** I am! 7639
Da 6:14 When the king heard this, he *was* greatly **d;** 10091
Mt 14: 9 The king *was* **d,** but because of his oaths *3382*
18:31 *they were* greatly **d** and went *3382*
Mk 3: 5 **deeply d** at their stubborn hearts, *5200*
6:26 The king was **greatly d,** *4337*
14:33 and he began *to be* **deeply d** and troubled. *1701*
Lk 12:50 and how **d** *I am* until it is completed! *5309*
Ac 17:16 he *was* **greatly d** to see that *4236*
Ro 14:15 If your brother *is* **d** because *3382*
2Co 1: 6 If *we are* **d,** it is for your comfort *2567*
2: 3 so that when I came *I should* not *be* **d** *2400+3383*
Php 2:26 and *is* **d** because you heard he was ill. *86*
2Pe 2: 7 *who was* **d** by the filthy lives of lawless men *2930*

DISTRESSES (2) [DISTRESS]

1Sa 10:19 of all your calamities and **d.** 7650
2Co 6: 4 in troubles, hardships and **d;** *5103*

DISTRESSING (1) [DISTRESS]

Ex 33: 4 When the people heard these **d** words, 8273

DISTRIBUTE (7) [DISTRIBUTED, DISTRIBUTES, DISTRIBUTING, DISTRIBUTION]

Nu 33:54 **D** the land by lot, according to your clans. 5706
33:54 **D** it according to your ancestral tribes. 5706
2Ch 31:19 men were designated by name to **d** portions 5989
Eze 47:21 *to* **d** this land among yourselves according 2745
Da 11:24 *He will* **d** plunder, 1029
11:39 over many people and *will* **d** the land at 2745
Mk 8: 7 also and told the disciples *to* **d** them. *4192*

DISTRIBUTED (10) [DISTRIBUTE]

Nu 26:55 Be sure that the land **is d** by lot. 2745
26:56 Each inheritance *is to* **be d** by lot among 2745
Jos 18:10 and there he **d** the land to the Israelites 2745
1Ch 6:60 which were **d among** the Kohathite clans, 928
2Ch 31:16 they **d** to the males three years old NIH
31:17 And they **d** to the priests enrolled NIH
Est 2:18 throughout the provinces and **d** gifts 5989
Jn 6:11 and **d** to those who were seated as much *1443*
Ac 4:35 and *it was* **d** to anyone as he had need. *1344*
Heb 2: 4 and **gifts** of the Holy Spirit **d** *3536*

DISTRIBUTES (1) [DISTRIBUTE]

Isa 34:17 his hand **d** them by measure. 2745

DISTRIBUTING (3) [DISTRIBUTE]

2Ch 31:14 **d** the contributions made to the LORD and 5989
31:15 **d** to their fellow priests according 5989
Ne 13:13 for **d** *the* **supplies** to their brothers. 2745

DISTRIBUTION (1) [DISTRIBUTE]

Ac 6: 1 overlooked in the daily **d** of food. *1355*

DISTRICT (23) [DISTRICTS, HALF-DISTRICT]

Ge 47:11 the **d** *of* Rameses, as Pharaoh directed. 824
1Sa 9: 4 They went on into the **d** *of* Shaalim, 824
9: 5 When they reached the **d** *of* Zuph, 824
1Ki 4: 5 in charge of the **d officers;** 5893
4: 7 also had twelve **d governors** over all Israel, 5893
4:13 as well as the **d** *of* Argob in Bashan 2475
4:19 He was the only governor over the **d.** 824
4:27 The **d officers,** each in his month, 5893
2Ki 22:14 She lived in Jerusalem, in the **Second D.** 5467
2Ch 34:22 She lived in Jerusalem, in the **Second D.** 5467
Ezr 5: 8 king should know that we went to the **d** 10406
Ne 3:14 ruler of the **d** *of* Beth Hakkerem. 7135
3:15 ruler of the **d** *of* Mizpah, 7135
3:17 Hashabiah, ruler of half the **d** *of* Keilah, 7135
Ne 3:17 carried out repairs for his **d.** 7135
11: 9 was over the **Second D** of the city. 5467
Ecc 5: 8 If you see the poor oppressed in a **d,** 4519
Eze 45: 1 of the land as a **sacred** *d,* 25,000 cubits long AIT
45: 3 In the sacred **d,** measure off 4500
45: 7 by the sacred **d** and the property of the city. 9556
Zep 1:11 Wail, you who live in the **market d;** 4847
Mt 2:22 he withdrew to the **d** of Galilee, *3538*
Ac 16:12 the leading city *of* that **d** of Macedonia. *3535*

DISTRICTS (5) [DISTRICT]

Jdg 5:15 the **d** *of* Reuben there was much searching 7106
5:16 the **d** *of* Reuben there was much searching 7106
1Ch 27:25 of the storehouses in the **outlying d,** 8441
2Ch 11:13 The priests and Levites from all their **d** 1473
11:23 throughout the **d** *of* Judah and Benjamin, 824

DISTURB (1) [DISTURBANCE, DISTURBED, DISTURBING]

2Ki 23:18 "Don't *let* anyone **d** his bones." 5675

DISTURBANCE (2) [DISTURB]

Ac 19:23 About that time there arose a **great d** about *3900+4024+5431*
24:18 nor was I involved in any **d.** *2573*

DISTURBED (14) [DISTURB]

1Sa 28:15 "Why *have you* **d** me by bringing me up?" 8074
2Sa 7:10 a home of their own and no longer *be* **d.** 8074
1Ch 17: 9 a home of their own and no longer *be* **d.** 8074
Ne 2:10 they *were* **very** much **d** 8288+8317
Job 20: 2 to answer because I am **greatly d.** 2591
Ps 42: 5 Why *so* **d** within me? 2159
42:11 Why *so* **d** within me? 2159
43: 5 Why *so* **d** within me? 2159
Isa 31: 4 he is not frightened by their shouts or **d** 6700
La 1:20 and in my heart *I am* **d,** 2200
Da 7:15 that passed through my mind **d** me. 10097
Mt 2: 3 When King Herod heard this *he was* **d,** *5429*
Ac 4: 2 *They were* **greatly d** because *1387*
15:24 without our authorization and **d** you, *5429*

DISTURBING (1) [DISTURB]

Est 7: 4 no such distress would justify **d** the king." 5691

DITCHES (1)

2Ki 3:16 Make this valley **full of d.** 1463+1463

DIVERS, DIVERSE (KJV) See COLORFUL, DIFFERENT, EMBROIDERED, KINDS, RICHLY ORNAMENTED, SOME, SWARMS, VARIED

DIVIDE (23) [DIVIDED, DIVIDES, DIVIDING, DIVISION, DIVISIONS, DIVISIVE, SUBDIVISION, SUBDIVISIONS]

Ex 14:16 and stretch out your hand over the sea *to* **d** 1324
15: 9 *I will* **d** the spoils; 2745
21:35 **d** both the money and the dead animal **equally.** 2936
Nu 31:27 **D** the spoils between the soldiers 2936
Dt 19: 3 Build roads to them and **d into three** parts 8992
31: 7 **d** it *among* them **as** their **inheritance.** 5706
Jos 13: 7 and **d** it as an inheritance among 2745
18: 5 *You are to* **d** the land into seven parts. 2745
22: 8 and **d** with your brothers the plunder 2745
2Sa 19:29 I order you and Ziba *to* **d** the fields." 2745
Job 27:17 and the innocent *will* **d** his silver. 2745
41: 6 *Will they* **d** him **up** among the merchants? 2936
Ps 22:18 *They* **d** my garments among them 2745
68:12 in the camps *men* **d** the plunder. 2745
Isa 7: 6 let us tear it apart and **d** it among ourselves, 1324
53:12 and *he will* **d** the spoils with the strong, 2745
Eze 5: 1 Then take a set of scales and **d up** the hair. 2745
47:13 **d** the land **for an inheritance** 5706
47:14 *You are to* **d** it equally among them. 5706
Mic 2: 5 in the assembly of the LORD *to* **d** the land 8959
Lk 12:13 tell my brother *to* **d** the inheritance *3532*
22:17 "Take this and **d** it among you. *1374*
Jude 1:19 These are the men who **d** you, *626*

DIVIDED (58) [DIVIDE]

Ge 10:25 because in his time the earth **was d;** 7103
14:15 the night Abram **d** his men to attack them 2745
32: 7 and distress Jacob **d** the people who were 2936
33: 1 so *he* **d** the children among Leah, 2936
Ex 14:21 The waters **were d,** 1324
Lev 11: 3 a split hoof **completely d** and that chews the cud. 9117+9118
11: 7 it has a split hoof **completely d,** 9117+9118
11:26 a split hoof not **completely d** or 9117+9118
Dt 14: 6 a split hoof **d** *in* two and that chews 9117+9118
14: 7 a split hoof **completely d** you may not eat 9117
32: 8 when he **d** all mankind, 7233
Jos 14: 5 So the Israelites **d** the land, 2745
Jdg 9:43 **d** them into three companies and set 2936
1Ki 18: 6 So *they* **d** the land they were to cover, 2745
2Ki 2: 8 The water **d** to the right and to the left, 2936
2:14 *it* **d** to the right and to the left, 2936
1Ch 1:19 because in his time the earth **was d;** 7103
23: 6 David **d** the Levites into groups 2745
24: 4 and they *were* **d** *accordingly:* 2745
24: 5 *They* **d** them impartially by drawing lots, 2745
Ne 9:11 *You* **d** the sea before them, 1324
Ps 78:13 *He* **d** the sea and led them through; 1324
136:13 to *him who* **d** the Red Sea asunder 1615
Pr 3:20 by his knowledge the deeps **were d,** 1324
Isa 18: 2 whose land *is* **d** *by* rivers, 1021
18: 7 whose land *is* **d** *by* rivers— 1021
33:23 Then an abundance of spoils *will* **be d** and 2745
63:12 *who* **d** the waters before them, 1324
Eze 37:22 be two nations or **be d** into two kingdoms. 2936
Da 2:41 so this will be a **d** kingdom; 10583
5:28 Your kingdom **is d** and given to the Medes 10592
Joel 3: 2 among the nations and **d up** my land. 2745
Am 7:17 **be** measured and **d up,** 2745
Mic 2: 4 my people's possession *is* **d up.** 4614
Zec 14: 1 when your plunder *will* **be d** among you. 2745
Mt 12:25 "Every kingdom **d** against itself will *3532*
12:25 or household **d** against itself will not stand. *3532*
12:26 *he is* **d** against himself. *3532*
27:35 *they* **d up** his clothes by casting lots. *1374*
Mk 3:24 If a kingdom *is* **d** against itself, *3532*
3:25 If a house *is* **d** against itself, *3532*
3:26 And if Satan opposes himself and *is* **d,** *3532*
6:41 *He* also **d** the two fish among them all. *3532*
Lk 11:17 "Any kingdom **d** against itself will *1374*
11:17 and a house **d** against itself will fall. *NIG*
11:18 If Satan *is* **d** against himself, *1374*
12:52 be five in one family **d** against each other, *1374*
12:53 *They will* be **d,** father against son *1374*
15:12 So he **d** his property **between** them. *1349*
23:34 And they **d up** his clothes by casting lots. *1374*
Jn 7:43 Thus the people were **d** because of Jesus. *5388*
9:16 So they were **d.** *5388*
10:19 At these words the Jews were again **d.** *5388*
19:24 *"They* **d** my garments **among** them *1374*
Ac 14: 4 The people of the city *were* **d;** *5387*
23: 7 and the assembly *was* **d.** *5387*
1Co 1:13 *Is* Christ **d?** Was Paul crucified for you? *3532*
7:34 and his interests *are* **d.** *3532*

DIVIDES (2) [DIVIDE]

Ge 49:27 in the evening *he* **d** the plunder." 2745
Lk 11:22 the man trusted and **d up** the spoils. *1344*

DIVIDING (9) [DIVIDE]

Jos 19:49 When they had finished **d** the land 5706
19:51 And so they finished **d** the land. 2745
Jdg 5:30 'Are they not finding and **d** the spoils: 2745
7:16 **D** the three hundred men 2936
Isa 9: 3 as men rejoice when **d** the plunder. 2745
Mk 15:24 **D up** his clothes, *1374*
Jn 19:23 **d** them **into** four **shares,** *3538+4472*
Eph 2:14 the **d wall** of hostility, *3546*
Heb 4:12 it penetrates even to **d** soul and spirit, *3536*

DIVINATION (16) [DIVINATIONS, DIVINE, DIVINER, DIVINERS]

Ge 30:27 *I have* **learned by d** that 5727
44: 5 from and also **uses for d?** 5727+5727
44:15 **find things out by d?"** 5727+5727
Lev 19:26 " *'Do* not **practice d** or sorcery. 5727
Nu 22: 7 taking with them the **fee for d.** 7877
23:23 no **d** against Israel. 7877
Dt 18:10 *who* **practices d** or sorcery, 7876+7877
18:14 to those who practice sorcery or **d.** 7876
Jos 13:22 of Beor, who **practiced d.** 7876
1Sa 15:23 For rebellion is like the sin of **d,** 7877
2Ki 17:17 *They* **practiced d** and sorcery 7876+7877
21: 6 practiced sorcery and **d,** 5727
2Ch 33: 6 practiced sorcery, **d** and witchcraft, 5727
Isa 2: 6 *they* **practice d** like the Philistines 6726
Eze 13:23 therefore you will no longer see false visions or **practice d.** 7876+7877
Mic 3: 6 without visions, and darkness, without **d.** 7876

DIVINATIONS (7) [DIVINATION]

Jer 14:14 to you false visions, **d,** idolatries and 7877
Eze 12:24 or flattering **d** among the people of Israel. 5241
13: 6 Their visions are false and their **d** a lie. 7877
13: 7 not seen false visions and uttered lying **d** 5241
13: 9 and **utter** lying **d.** 7876
21:29 concerning you and lying **d** about you, 7876
22:28 for them by false visions and lying **d.** 7876

DIVINE (9) [DIVINATION]

Isa 35: 4 with **d** retribution he will come 466
Ac 8:10 the **d** power known as the Great Power." *2536*
17:29 the **d being** is like gold or silver or stone— *2521*
19:27 will be robbed *of* her **d majesty."** *3484*
Ro 1:20 his eternal power and **d nature—** *2522*
9: 4 theirs the **d** glory, the covenants, *NIG*
2Co 10: 4 they have **d** power to demolish strongholds. *2536*
2Pe 1: 3 His **d** power has given us everything we need for life and godliness *2521*
1: 4 you may participate in the **d** nature and *2521*

DIVINER (1) [DIVINATION]

Da 2:27 magician or **d** can explain to the king 10140

DIVINERS (9) [DIVINATION]

1Sa 6: 2 for the priests and the **d** and said, 7876
Isa 44:25 of false prophets and makes fools of **d**, 7876
Jer 27: 9 So do not listen to your prophets, your **d**, 7876
29: 8 the prophets and **d** among you deceive you. 7876
Da 4: 7 enchanters, astrologers and **d** came, 10140
5: 7 astrologers and **d** to be brought and said 10140
5:11 enchanters, astrologers and **d**. 10140
Mic 3: 7 be ashamed and the **d** disgraced. 7876
Zec 10: 2 **d** see visions that lie; 7876

DIVISION (43) [DIVIDE]

Nu 2: 4 His **d** numbers 74,600. 7372
2: 6 His **d** numbers 54,400. 7372
2: 8 His **d** numbers 57,400. 7372
2:11 His **d** numbers 46,500. 7372
2:13 His **d** numbers 59,300. 7372
2:15 His **d** numbers 45,650. 7372
2:19 His **d** numbers 40,500. 7372
2:21 His **d** numbers 32,200. 7372
2:23 His **d** numbers 35,400. 7372
2:26 His **d** numbers 62,700. 7372
2:28 His **d** numbers 41,500. 7372
2:30 His **d** numbers 53,400. 7372
10:15 Nethanel son of Zuar was over the **d** *of* 7372
10:16 and Eliab son of Helon was over the **d** *of* 7372
10:19 of Zurishaddai was over the **d** *of* the tribe 7372
10:20 of Deuel was over the **d** *of* the tribe of Gad. 7372
10:23 Gamaliel son of Pedahzur was over the **d** 7372
10:24 and Abidan son of Gideoni was over the **d** 7372
10:26 Pagiel son of Ocran was over the **d** *of* 7372
10:27 and Ahira son of Enan was over the **d** *of* 7372
Jos 22:14 of a family **d** among the Israelite clans. 1074
1Ch 27: 1 Each **d** consisted of 24,000 men. 4713
27: 2 In charge of the first **d**, for the first month, 4713
27: 2 There were 24,000 men in his **d**. 4713
27: 4 of the **d** *for* the second month was Dodai 4713
27: 4 Mikloth was the leader of his **d**. 4713
27: 4 There were 24,000 men in his **d**. 4713
27: 5 and there were 24,000 men in his **d**. 4713
27: 6 His son Ammizabad was in charge of his **d**. 4713
27: 7 There were 24,000 men in his **d**. 4713
27: 8 There were 24,000 men in his **d**. 4713
27: 9 There were 24,000 men in his **d**. 4713
27:10 There were 24,000 men in his **d**. 4713
27:11 There were 24,000 men in his **d**. 4713
27:12 There were 24,000 men in his **d**. 4713
27:13 There were 24,000 men in his **d**. 4713
27:14 There were 24,000 men in his **d**. 4713
27:15 There were 24,000 men in his **d**. 4713
Ezr 10:16 one from each family **d**, 1074
Lk 1: 5 who belonged to the **priestly d** of Abijah; *2389*
1: 8 Once when Zechariah's **d** was on duty *2389*
12:51 No, I tell you, but **d**. *1375*
1Co 12:25 so that there should **be no d** in the body, *5388*

DIVISIONS (51) [DIVIDE]

Ge 36:30 according to their **d**, in the land of Seir. 477
Ex 6:26 the Israelites out of Egypt by their **d**." 7372
7: 4 of judgment I will bring out my **d**, 7372
12:17 on this very day that I brought your **d** out 7372
12:41 all the LORD's **d** left Egypt. 7372
12:51 the Israelites out of Egypt by their **d**. 7372
Nu 1: 3 You and Aaron are to number by their **d** all 7372
1:52 The Israelites are to set up their tents by **d**, 7372
2: 3 the **d** *of* the camp of Judah are to encamp 7372
2: 9 according to their **d**, number 186,400. 7372
2:10 On the south will be the **d** *of* the camp 7372
2:16 according to their **d**, number 151,450. 7372
2:18 On the west will be the **d** *of* the camp 7372
2:24 according to their **d**, number 108,100. 7372
2:25 the north will be the **d** *of* the camp of Dan, 7372
2:32 All those in the camps, by their **d**, 7372
10:14 The **d** *of* the camp of Judah went first, 7372
10:18 The **d** *of* the camp of Reuben went next, 7372
10:22 The **d** *of* the camp of Ephraim went next, 7372
10:25 the **d** *of* the camp of Dan set out, 7372
10:28 of march for the Israelite **d** as they set out. 7372
33: 1 when they came out of Egypt by **d** under 7372
Jos 11:23 to Israel according to their tribal **d**. 4713
12: 7 of Israel according to their **tribal d**— 4713
18:10 to the Israelites according to their **tribal d**. 4713
1Sa 11:11 The next day Saul separated his men into three **d**; 8031
1Ch 24: 1 These were the **d** of the sons of Aaron: 4713
24: 3 David **separated** them **into d** 2745
26: 1 The **d** of the gatekeepers: 4713
26:12 These **d** *of* the gatekeepers, 4713
26:19 These were the **d** *of* 4713
27: 1 in all that concerned the **army d** that were 4713
28: 1 over the tribes, the commanders of the **d** in 4713
28:13 He gave him instructions for the **d** *of* 4713
28:21 The **d** *of* the priests and Levites are ready 4713
2Ch 5:11 regardless of their **d**. 4713
8:14 the **d** *of* the priests for their duties, 4713
8:14 He also appointed the gatekeepers by **d** for 4713
23: 8 the priest had not released any of the **d**. 4713
26:11 to go out by **d** according to their numbers 1522
31: 2 the priests and Levites to **d**— 4713
31:15 to their fellow priests according to their **d**, 4713
31:16 to their responsibilities and their **d**. 4713
31:17 to their responsibilities and their **d**. 4713
35: 4 Prepare yourselves by families in your **d**, 4713
35:10 in their places with the Levites in their **d** as 4713
Ezr 6:18 the priests in their **d** and the Levites 10585
Ne 11:36 of the **d** *of* the Levites of Judah settled 4713
Ro 16:17 for those who cause **d** and put obstacles *1496*
1Co 1:10 with one another so that there may be no **d** *5388*
11:18 there are **d** among you, *5388*

DIVISIVE (1) [DIVIDE]

Tit 3:10 Warn a **d** person once, *148*

DIVORCE (18) [DIVORCED, DIVORCES]

Dt 22:19 he must not **d** her as long as he lives. 8938
22:29 He can never **d** her as long as he lives. 8938
24: 1 and he writes her a certificate of **d**, 4135
24: 3 and writes her a certificate of **d**, 4135
Isa 50: 1 "Where is your mother's certificate of **d** 4135
Jer 3: 8 I gave faithless Israel her certificate of **d** 4135
Mal 2:16 "I hate **d**," says the LORD God of Israel, 8938
Mt 1:19 he had in mind to **d** her quietly. *668*
5:31 must give her a **certificate of d.'** *687*
19: 3 "Is it lawful for a man *to* **d** his wife for any *668*
19: 7 that a man give his wife a certificate *of* **d** *687*
19: 8 "Moses permitted you *to* **d** your wives *668*
Mk 10: 2 "Is it lawful for a man *to* **d** his wife?" *668*
10: 4 a certificate *of* **d** and send her away." *687*
1Co 7:11 And a husband *must* not **d** his wife. *918*
7:12 *he must* not **d** her. *918*
7:13 *she must* not **d** him. *918*
7:27 Are you married? Do not seek a **d**. *3386*

DIVORCED (9) [DIVORCE]

Lev 21: 7 by prostitution or **d** from their husbands, 1763
21:14 He must not marry a widow, a **d** *woman*, 1763
22:13 priest's daughter becomes a widow or *is* **d**, 1763
Nu 30: 9 a widow or **d** *woman* will be binding on her. 1763
Dt 24: 4 then her first husband, who **d** her, is 8938
1Ch 8: 8 after he *had* **d** his wives Hushim and Baara. 8938
Eze 44:22 They must not marry widows or **d** *women;* 1763
Mt 5:32 the **d** *woman* commits adultery. *668*
Lk 16:18 a **d** *woman* commits adultery. *467+608+668*

DIVORCES (7) [DIVORCE]

Jer 3: 1 "If a man **d** his wife and she leaves him 8938
Mt 5:31 'Anyone who **d** his wife must give her *668*
5:32 But I tell you that anyone who **d** his wife, *668*
19: 9 I tell you that anyone who **d** his wife, *668*
Mk 10:11 "Anyone who **d** his wife and marries *668*
10:12 she **d** her husband and marries another man, *668*
Lk 16:18 "Anyone who **d** his wife and marries *668*

DIZAHAB (1)

Dt 1: 1 Laban, Hazeroth and **D**. 1903

DIZZINESS (1)

Isa 19:14 LORD has poured into them a spirit of **d**; 6413

DO (2715) [DID, DIDN'T, DO-NOTHING, DOES, DOESN'T, DOING, DONE, DON'T]

Ge 4: 7 If *you* **d what is right**, 3512
4: 7 *d* not **do what is right**, AIT
4: 7 But if *you do* not **d what is right**, 3512
11: 6 to **d** this, then nothing they plan to do will 6913
11: 6 to **d** will be impossible for them. 6913
15: 1 *"D* not *be* **afraid**, Abram. AIT
16: 6 **"D** with her whatever you think best." 6913
18: 3 my lord, *d* not **pass** your servant by. AIT
18: 5 they answered, **"d** as you say." 6913
18:17 from Abraham what I *am about to* **d?** 6913
18:25 Far be it from you *to* **d** such a thing— 6913
18:25 not the Judge of all the earth **d** right?" 6913
18:29 "For the sake of forty, *I will* not **d** it." 6913
18:30 *"I will* not **d** it if I find thirty there." 6913
19: 7 Don't **d** *this* **wicked thing.** 8317
19: 8 and *you can* **d** what you like with them. 6913
19: 8 But don't **d** anything to these men, 6913
19:12 **"D** you have anyone else here— NIH
19:22 I cannot **d** anything until you reach it." 6913
20: 7 But if you *d* not **return** her, AIT
21:12 *"D* not *be so* **distressed** AIT
21:17 *D* not *be* **afraid;** AIT
21:22 "God is with you in everything you **d**. 6913
22:12 *"D* not **lay** a hand on the boy," he said. AIT
22:12 *"D* not **do** anything to him. AIT
22:12 *"Do* not **d** anything to him. 6913
24: 6 *d* not **take** my son **back** AIT
24: 8 *d* not **take** my son **back** AIT
24:56 But he said to them, *"D* not **detain** me, AIT
26: 2 *"D* not **go down** to Egypt; AIT
26:24 *D* not *be* **afraid**, for I am with you; AIT
26:29 that *you will* **d** us no harm, 6913
27: 8 listen carefully and **d** what I tell you: NIH
27:13 Just **d** what I say; go and get them for me." 9048
27:37 So what *can I possibly* **d** for you, 6913
27:38 **"D** you have only one blessing, my father? NIH
27:43 Now then, my son, **d** what I say: 9048
28: 1 *"D* not **marry** a Canaanite woman. AIT
28: 6 *"D* not **marry** a Canaanite woman," AIT
29: 5 He said to them, *"D you* **know** Laban, AIT
30:30 *may* I **d** *something* for my own household?" 6913
30:31 "But if *you will* **d** this one thing for me, 6913
31:14 *D* we still **have** any share in the inheritance AIT
31:16 So **d** whatever God has told you." 6913
31:43 Yet what *can I* **d** today 6913
32:17 'To whom **d** you belong, NIH
Ge 32:29 But he replied, "Why *d you* **ask** my name?" AIT
32:32 Therefore to this day the Israelites *d* not **eat** AIT
33: 8 "What **d** you mean NIH
33:15 "But why **d** that?" NIH
34:14 "We can't **d** such a thing; 6913
37: 8 *"D you* **intend to reign** AIT
39: 9 then *could I* **d** such a wicked thing and sin 6913
40: 8 **"D** not interpretations belong to God? NIH
40:13 to **d** when you were his cupbearer. 5477
41:16 "I cannot **d** it," Joseph replied to Pharaoh, NIH
41:25 to Pharaoh what *he is about to* **d**. 6913
41:28 God has shown Pharaoh what *he is about to* **d**. 6913
41:32 and God *will* **d** it soon. 6913
41:55 "Go to Joseph and **d** what he tells you." 6913
42: 1 *d you just keep* **looking at each other?"** AIT
42: 7 "Where *d you* **come** from?" AIT
42:18 **"D** this and you will live, for I fear God: 6913
42:20 This *they proceeded to* **d**. 6913
42:37 *d* not **bring** him **back** AIT
43: 7 *'D* you **have** another brother?' AIT
43: 9 *d* not **bring** him **back** AIT
43:11 "If it must be, then **d** this: 6913
44: 7 from your servants *to* **d** anything like that! 6913
44:17 "Far be it from me *to* **d** such a thing! 6913
44:18 *D* not *be* **angry** with your servant, AIT
44:19 *'D* you **have** a father or a brother?' AIT
44:32 *d* not **bring** him **back** AIT
44:34 *D* not *let me* **see** AIT
45: 5 *d* not *be* **distressed** and do not be angry AIT
45: 5 do not be distressed and *d* not *be* **angry** AIT
45:17 "Tell your brothers, **'D** this: 6913
45:19 "You are also directed to tell them, **'D** this: 6913
46: 3 *"D* not *be* **afraid** to go down to Egypt, AIT
47: 9 and *they d* not **equal** the years of AIT
47:29 *D* not **bury** me in Egypt, AIT
47:30 "I *will* **d** as you say," he said. 6913
50: 6 **made** you **swear** *to d."* AIT
Ex 1:17 not **d** what the king of Egypt had told them 6913
1:17 the king of Egypt had told them to **d**; NIH
3: 5 *"D* not **come** *any* **closer,"** AIT
4: 1 "What if *they d* not **believe** me or listen AIT
4: 8 "If *they d* not **believe** you or pay attention AIT
4: 9 But if *they d* not **believe** these two signs AIT
4:13 "O Lord, please send someone else to **d** it." NIH
4:15 of you speak and will teach you what *to* **d**. 6913
4:21 wonders I have given you the power to **d**. NIH
5: 2 *I d* not **know** the LORD and I will AIT
6: 1 you will see what *I will* **d** to Pharaoh: 6913
8:21 *d* not **let** my people **go**, AIT
9: 5 "Tomorrow the LORD *will* **d** this in 6913
9:30 that you and your officials still *d* not **fear** AIT
10: 7 *D you* not yet **realize** AIT
10:28 Make sure *you d* not **appear** AIT
12: 9 *D* **not eat** the meat raw or cooked in water, AIT
12:10 *D* not **leave** any of it till morning; AIT
12:16 **D** no work at all on these days, 6913
12:16 that is all you *may* **d**. 6913
12:46 *D* not **break** any of the bones. AIT
13: 8 **'I d** this because of what the LORD did NIH
13:13 but if *you d* not **redeem** it, break its neck. AIT
14:13 *"D* not *be* **afraid.** AIT
15:26 of the LORD your God and **d** what is right 6913
17: 2 "Why *d you* **quarrel** with me? AIT
17: 2 *d you* **put** the **LORD to the test?"** AIT
17: 4 "What *am I to* **d** with these people? 6913
18:14 *d* you alone **sit as judge,** AIT
18:23 If *you* **d** this and God so commands, 6913
19: 8 *"We will* **d** everything 6913
19:12 that you *d* not **go up** the mountain or touch AIT
19:21 *d* not **force** *their* **way through** AIT
20: 9 and **d** all your work, 6913
20:10 On it *you shall* not **d** any work, 6913
20:19 *d* not *have* God **speak** AIT
20:20 Moses said to the people, *"D* not *be* **afraid.** AIT
20:23 *D* not **make** any gods to be alongside me; AIT
20:23 *d* not **make** for yourselves gods of silver AIT
20:25 *d* not **build** it *with* dressed stones, AIT
20:26 And *d* not **go up** to my altar on steps, AIT
21: 5 *d* not *want to* **go** AIT
21: 7 she is not to go free as menservants **d**. 3655[S]
21:13 if he *does* not **d** it **intentionally,** 7399
22:18 *"D* not **allow** a sorceress **to live.** AIT
22:21 *"D* not **mistreat** an alien or oppress him, AIT
22:22 *"D* not **take advantage** *of* a widow or AIT
22:23 If *you* **d** and they cry out to me, 6700+6700[S]
22:25 *d* not **be** like a moneylender; AIT
22:28 *"D* not **blaspheme** God or curse the ruler AIT
22:29 *"D* not **hold back** offerings AIT
22:30 **D** the same with your cattle and your sheep. 6913
22:31 So *d* not **eat** the meat of an animal torn AIT
23: 1 *"D* not **spread** false reports. AIT
23: 1 *D* not **help** a wicked man by being AIT
23: 2 *"D* not **follow** the crowd in doing wrong. AIT
23: 2 *d* not **pervert** justice by siding with AIT
23: 3 and *d* not **show favoritism** *to* a poor man AIT
23: 5 **d not** leave it there; 2532
23: 6 *"D* not **deny** justice to your poor people AIT
23: 7 **Have nothing to d** with a false charge 8178
23: 7 *d* not **put** an innocent or honest person **to death,** AIT
23: 8 *"D* not **accept** a bribe, AIT
23: 9 *"D* not **oppress** an alien; AIT
23:11 **D** the same with your vineyard 6913
23:12 "Six days **d** your work, 6913
23:12 but on the seventh day **d not work,** 8697
23:13 *"Be* **careful to d** everything I have said 9068

Ex 23:13 *D* not **invoke** the names of other gods; AIT
23:13 *d* not *let them* **be heard** AIT
23:15 **D** this at the appointed time in the month NIH
23:18 "*D* not **offer** the blood of a sacrifice to me AIT
23:19 "*D* not **cook** a young goat in its mother's AIT
23:21 *D* not **rebel** against him; AIT
23:22 to what he says and **d** all that I say, 6913
23:24 *D* not **bow down** before their gods AIT
23:32 *D* not **make** a covenant with them or AIT
23:33 *D* not *let them* **live** AIT
24:3 the LORD has said *we will* **d.**" 6913
24:7 "*We will* **d** everything the LORD has said; 6913
26:3 and **d the same** *with* the other five. 2489S
26:4 and **d** the same with the end curtain in 6913
29:1 "This is what *you are to* **d** 6913
29:35 "**D** for Aaron and his sons everything I have commanded you, 6913
30:9 *D* not **offer** on this altar any other incense AIT
30:9 and *d* not **pour** a drink offering on it. AIT
30:32 *D* not **pour** it on men's bodies and do AIT
30:32 *d* not **make** any oil with the same formula. AIT
30:37 *D* not **make** any incense with this formula AIT
32:12 **relent and d not bring** disaster 5714
32:21 "What *did* these people **d** to you, 6913
32:22 "*D* not *be* **angry,** my lord," Aaron answered. AIT
33:5 and I will decide what *to* **d** with you.' " 6913
33:15 *d* not **send** us **up** AIT
33:17 "*I will* **d** the very thing you have asked, 6913
34:10 all your people *I will* **d** wonders never 6913
34:10 the LORD, *will* **d** for you. 6913
34:14 *D* not **worship** any other god, for the LORD, AIT
34:16 *they will* **lead** your sons **to d the same.** 339+466+2177+2388S
34:17 "*D* not **make** cast idols. AIT
34:18 **D** this at the appointed time in the month NIH
34:20 but if *you d* not **redeem** it, break its neck. AIT
34:25 "*D* not **offer** the blood of a sacrifice to me AIT
34:25 *d* not *let* any of the sacrifice from the Passover Feast **remain** until morning. AIT
34:26 "*D* not **cook** a young goat inits mother's AIT
35:1 the LORD has commanded you to **d:** 6913
35:3 *D* not **light** a fire in any of your dwellings AIT
35:29 through Moses had commanded them to **d.** 6913
35:35 He has filled them with skill to **d** all kinds 6913
36:1 the sanctuary *are to* **d** *the* **work** just as 6913
36:2 and who was willing to come and **d** 6913
36:7 to **d** all the work. 6913
Lev 2:13 *D* not **leave** the salt of the covenant AIT
4:20 and **d** with this bull just as he did with 6913
5:4 **d** anything, whether **good** 3512
5:16 for what *he has* **failed** to **d** in regard to 2627
6:3 he commits any such sin that people *may* **d** 6913
7:23 '*D* not **eat** any of the fat of cattle, AIT
8:33 *D* not **leave** the entrance to the Tent AIT
8:35 and night for seven days and **d** what 9068
9:6 the LORD has commanded you *to* **d,** 6913
10:6 "*D* not *let* your hair *become* **unkempt,** AIT
10:6 and *d* not **tear** your clothes, AIT
10:7 *D* not **leave** the entrance to the Tent AIT
11:10 or streams that **d** not have fins and scales— NIH
11:43 *D* not **defile** yourselves by any AIT
11:43 *D* not **make yourselves unclean** AIT
11:44 *D* not **make** yourselves **unclean** AIT
16:15 and take its blood behind the curtain and **d** 6913
16:16 *to* **d** the same for the Tent of Meeting, 6913
16:29 and not **d** any work— 6913
18:3 *You must* not **d** as they do in Egypt, 6913
18:3 You must not do as they **d** *in* Egypt, 5126
18:3 and *you must* not **d** as they do in the land 6913
18:3 and you must not do as they **d** *in* the land 5126
18:3 *D* not **follow** their practices. AIT
18:7 " '*D* not **dishonor** your father **by having sexual relations with** your mother. AIT
18:7 *d* not **have relations with** her. AIT
18:8 " '*D* not **have sexual relations with** AIT
18:9 " '*D* not **have sexual relations with** AIT
18:10 " '*D* not **have sexual relations with** AIT
18:11 " '*D* not **have sexual relations with** AIT
18:12 " '*D* not **have sexual relations with** AIT
18:13 " '*D* not **have sexual relations with** AIT
18:14 " '*D* not **dishonor** your father's brother **by** approaching his wife **to have sexual relations;** AIT
18:15 " '*D* not **have sexual relations with** AIT
18:15 *d* not **have relations with** AIT
18:16 " '*D* not **have sexual relations with** AIT
18:17 " '*D* not **have sexual relations with** AIT
18:17 *D* not **have sexual relations with** AIT
18:18 " '*D* not **take** your wife's sister as AIT
18:19 " '*D* not **approach** a woman AIT
18:20 " '*D* not **have sexual relations** AIT
18:21 " '*D* not **give** any of your children to AIT
18:22 " '*D* not **lie with** a man as one lies with a woman; AIT
18:23 " '*D* not **have sexual relations** AIT
18:24 " '*D* not **defile yourselves** AIT
18:26 the aliens living among you *must* not **d** any 6913
18:30 and *d* not **follow** any of the detestable AIT
18:30 *d* not **defile yourselves** AIT
19:4 " '*D* not **turn** to idols or make gods AIT
19:9 *d* not **reap** *to* the very edges of your field AIT
19:10 *D* not **go over** your vineyard **a second time** AIT
19:11 " '*D* not **steal.** AIT
19:11 " '*D* not **lie.** AIT
19:11 " '*D* not **deceive** one another. AIT
19:12 " '*D* not **swear** falsely by my name and AIT
19:13 " '*D* not **defraud** your neighbor or rob him. AIT
Lev 19:13 " '*D* not **hold back** the wages of a hired man **overnight.** AIT
19:14 " '*D* not **curse** the deaf or put AIT
19:15 " '*D* not **pervert** justice; AIT
19:15 *d* not **show partiality** *to* the poor AIT
19:16 " '*D* not **go about** spreading slander AIT
19:16 " '*D* not **do anything that endangers** your neighbor's **life.** AIT
19:16 " '*D* not **d anything that endangers** your neighbor's **life.** 1947+6584+6641
19:17 " '*D* not **hate** your brother in your heart. AIT
19:18 " '*D* not **seek revenge** or bear a grudge AIT
19:19 " '*D* not **mate** different kinds of animals. AIT
19:19 " '*D* not **plant** your field **with** two kinds of **seed.** AIT
19:19 " '*D* not **wear** clothing woven of two kinds AIT
19:26 " '*D* not **eat** any meat with the blood still AIT
19:26 " '*D* not **practice divination** AIT
19:27 " '*D* not **cut the hair** AIT
19:28 " '*D* not **cut** your bodies for the dead AIT
19:29 " '*D* not **degrade** your daughter AIT
19:31 " '*D* not **turn** to mediums AIT
19:33 *d* not **mistreat** him. AIT
19:35 " '*D* not **use** dishonest standards AIT
20:19 " '*D* not **have sexual relations with** AIT
20:25 *D* not **defile** yourselves by any animal AIT
22:9 so that they *d* not **become guilty** and die AIT
22:20 *D* not **bring** anything with a defect, AIT
22:22 *D* not **offer** to the LORD the blind, AIT
22:22 *D* not **place** any of these on the altar as AIT
22:24 *You must* not **d** this in your own land, 6913
22:28 *D* not **slaughter** a cow or a sheep AIT
22:32 *D* not **profane** my holy name. AIT
23:3 *You are* not *to* **d** any work; 6913
23:7 a sacred assembly and **d** no regular work. 6913
23:8 a sacred assembly and **d** no regular work.' " 6913
23:21 a sacred assembly and **d** no regular work. 6913
23:22 *d* not **reap** *to* the very edges of your field AIT
23:25 **D** no regular work, 6913
23:28 **D** no work on that day, 6913
23:31 *You shall* **d** no work at all. 6913
23:35 **d** no regular work. 6913
23:36 **d** no regular work. 6913
25:4 *D* not **sow** your fields AIT
25:5 *D* not **reap** what grows of itself or harvest AIT
25:11 *d* not **sow** and do not reap what grows AIT
25:11 not sow and *d* not **reap** what grows of itself AIT
25:14 *d* not **take advantage of** each other. AIT
25:17 *D* not **take advantage of** each other, AIT
25:20 if *we d* not **plant** or harvest our crops?" AIT
25:36 *D* not **take** interest of any kind from him, AIT
25:39 *d* not **make** him **work** as a slave. AIT
25:43 *D* not **rule** over them ruthlessly, AIT
26:1 " '*D* not **make** idols or set up an image or AIT
26:1 and *d* not **place** a carved stone in your land AIT
26:16 then I *will* **d** this to you: 6913
26:23 *d* not **accept** my **correction** AIT
26:27 " 'If in spite of this *you still d* not **listen** AIT
Nu 1:51 the Levites *shall* **d** it. 7756S
4:15 to come to *d the* **carrying.** AIT
4:19 **d** this for them: 6913
4:26 The Gershonites *are to* **d** all that needs to 6268
4:47 of age who came to **d** the work of serving 6268
6:12 The previous days **d not count,** 5877
8:7 To purify them, **d** this: 6913
8:11 so that they may be ready to **d** the work of 6268
8:15 they are to come to **d** *their* **work** at the Tent 6268
8:19 as gifts to Aaron and his sons to **d** the work 6268
8:22 the Levites came to **d** their work at the Tent 6268
8:26 but *they themselves must* not **d** the work. 6268
9:14 to celebrate the LORD's Passover *must* **d** 6913
10:31 But Moses said, "Please *d* not **leave** us. AIT
11:12 Why *d you* **tell** me to carry them AIT
11:15 *d* not *let me* **face** my own ruin." AIT
11:25 but *they did* not **d** *so* **again.** 3578
12:11 *d* not **hold** against us the sin we have AIT
12:12 *D* not *let her* **be** like a stillborn infant AIT
13:19 What kind of land *d* they **live** in? AIT
13:19 What kind of towns *d* they **live** in? AIT
13:20 **D** *your* **best** to bring back some of the fruit 2616
13:30 for **we can certainly d** it." 3523+3523
14:9 Only *d* not **rebel** against the LORD. AIT
14:9 *d* not *be* **afraid** *of* the people of the land, AIT
14:9 *D* not **be afraid** *of* them." AIT
14:28 *I will* **d** to you the very things 6913
14:35 and *I will* surely **d** these things 6913
14:42 **D** not **go up,** AIT
15:12 **D** this for each one, 6913
15:13 " 'Everyone who is native-born *must* **d** these things 6913
15:14 *he must* **d** exactly as you do. 6913
15:14 he must do exactly as *you* **d.** 6913
16:3 Why then *d you* **set yourselves** above AIT
16:6 Korah, and all your followers *are to* **d** this: 6913
16:9 and brought you near himself to **d** the work 6268
16:15 "*D* not **accept** their offering. AIT
16:26 *D* not **touch** anything belonging to them, AIT
16:28 the LORD has sent me to **d** all these things 6913
18:6 dedicated to the LORD to **d** the work at 6268
18:21 in return for the work they **d** while serving 6268
18:23 It is the Levites *who are to* **d** the work at 6268
21:34 "*D* not **be afraid** *of* him, AIT
21:34 **D** to him what you did to Sihon king of 6913
22:12 God said to Balaam, "*D* not **go** with them. AIT
22:16 *D* not *let anything* **keep** AIT
22:17 and **d** whatever you say. 6913
22:18 not **d** anything great or small to go beyond 6913
Nu 22:20 go with them, but **d** only what I tell you." 6913
23:9 *d* not **consider themselves** AIT
23:26 "Did I not tell you *I must* **d** whatever 6913
24:13 I could not **d** anything of my own accord, 6913
24:14 let me warn you of what this people *will* **d** 6913
28:18 a sacred assembly and **d** no regular work. 6913
28:25 a sacred assembly and **d** no regular work. 6913
28:26 a sacred assembly and **d** no regular work. 6913
29:1 a sacred assembly and **d** no regular work. 6913
29:7 You must deny yourselves and **d** no work. 6913
29:12 a sacred assembly and **d** no regular work. 6913
29:35 an assembly and **d** no regular work. 6913
30:2 but *must* **d** everything he said. 6913
32:5 *D* not **make us cross** AIT
32:7 Why *d you* **discourage** the Israelites AIT
32:20 Moses said to them, "If *you will* **d** this— 6913
32:23 "But if *you* fail *to* **d** this, 6913
32:24 but **d** what you have promised." 6913
32:25 "*We* your servants *will* **d** 6913
32:30 if *they d* not **cross over** with you armed, AIT
32:31 "Your servants *will* **d** what 6913
33:55 if *you d* not **drive out** the inhabitants of AIT
33:56 And then *I will* **d** to you what I plan to do 6913
33:56 I will do to you what I plan to **d** to them.' " 6913
35:31 " '*D* not **accept** a ransom for the life of AIT
35:32 " '*D* not **accept** a ransom for anyone AIT
35:33 " '*D* not **pollute** the land where you are. AIT
35:34 *D* not **defile** the land where you live and AIT
Dt 1:14 "What you propose to **d** is good." 6913
1:17 *D* not **show partiality** AIT
1:17 *D* not *be* **afraid** of any man, AIT
1:18 I told you everything *you were to* **d.** 6913
1:21 *D* not *be* **afraid;** do not be discouraged." AIT
1:21 Do not be afraid; *d* not *be* **discouraged."** AIT
1:29 Then I said to you, "*D* not *be* **terrified;** AIT
1:29 *d* not *be* **afraid** of them. AIT
1:39 your children who *d* not yet **know** good AIT
1:42 "Tell them, '*D* not **go up** and fight, AIT
2:5 *D* not **provoke** them **to war,** AIT
2:9 "*D* not **harass** the Moabites or provoke them to war, AIT
2:19 *d* not **harass** them or provoke them to war, AIT
3:2 "*D* not *be* **afraid** *of* him, AIT
3:2 **D** to him what you did to Sihon king of 6913
3:21 The LORD *will* **d** the same to all 6913
3:22 *D* not *be* **afraid** *of* them; AIT
3:24 in heaven or on earth who *can* **d** the deeds 6913
3:24 the deeds and mighty works you **d?** NIH
3:26 "*D* not **speak** to me anymore AIT
4:2 *D* not **add** to what I command you and do AIT
4:2 to what I command you and *d* not **subtract** AIT
4:9 so that *you d* not **forget** AIT
4:16 so that *you d* not *become* **corrupt** and make AIT
4:19 *d* not **be enticed** *into* bowing down to them AIT
4:23 *d* not **make** for yourselves an idol in the form of anything AIT
5:13 and **d** all your work, 6913
5:14 On it *you shall* not **d** any work, 6913
5:14 and maidservant may rest, as you **d.** NIH
5:32 So be careful to **d** what 6913
5:32 *d* not **turn aside** *to* the right or to the left. AIT
6:12 that *you d* not **forget** the LORD, AIT
6:14 *D* not **follow** other gods, AIT
6:16 *D* not **test** the LORD your God as you did AIT
6:18 **D** what is right and good in 6913
7:3 *D* not **intermarry** with them. AIT
7:3 *D* not **give** your daughters to their sons AIT
7:5 This is what *you are to* **d** to them: 6913
7:16 *D* not **look** on them **with pity** AIT
7:16 with pity and *d* not **serve** their gods, AIT
7:18 But *d* not *be* **afraid** of them; AIT
7:19 The LORD your God *will* **d** the same 6913
7:21 *D* not *be* **terrified** by them, AIT
7:25 *D* not **covet** the silver and gold on them, AIT
7:25 and *d* not **take** it for yourselves, AIT
7:26 *D* not **bring** a detestable thing AIT
8:11 Be careful that *you d* not **forget** AIT
9:4 *d* not **say** to yourself, AIT
9:26 *d* not **destroy** your people, AIT
10:8 as they still **d** today. NIH
10:16 and *d* not **be stiff-necked** any longer. AIT
12:8 *You are* not *to* **d** as we do here today, 6913
12:8 You are not to do as we **d** here today, 6913
12:23 But be sure you *d* not **eat** the blood, AIT
12:25 *D* not **eat** it, so that it may go well AIT
12:30 "How *d* these nations **serve** their gods? AIT
12:30 We *will* **d** the same." 6913
12:31 *they* **d** all kinds of detestable things 6913
12:32 See that *you* **d** all I command you; 6913
12:32 *d* not **add** to it or take away from it. AIT
13:8 *d* not **yield** to him or listen to him. AIT
13:8 *D* not **spare** him or shield him. AIT
13:11 among you *will* **d** such an evil thing again. 6913
14:1 *D* not **cut yourselves** or shave the front AIT
14:3 *D* not **eat** any detestable thing. AIT
14:7 *d* not *have a* **split** hoof; AIT
14:19 *d* not **eat** *them.* AIT
14:21 *D* not **eat** anything you find already dead. AIT
14:21 *D* not **cook** a young goat in its mother's AIT
14:27 And *d* not **neglect** the Levites living AIT
15:7 *d* not **be hardhearted** or tightfisted AIT
15:9 *d* not **show ill will** AIT
15:10 to him and **d so** without a grudging heart; 5989S
15:13 *d* not **send** him away empty-handed. AIT
15:16 *I d* not *want to* **leave** AIT
15:17 **D** the same for your maidservant. 6913
15:18 *D* not **consider** it a hardship AIT

Dt 15:18 God will bless you in everything *you* **d.** 6913
15:19 *D* not **put** the firstborn of your oxen **to work,** AIT
15:19 and *d* not **shear** the firstborn of your sheep. AIT
16: 3 *D* not **eat** it with bread made with yeast, AIT
16: 4 *D* not *let* any of the meat you sacrifice on the evening of the first day **remain** AIT
16: 8 to the LORD your God and **d** no work. 6913
16:19 *D* not **pervert** justice or show partiality. AIT
16:19 *D* not **accept** a bribe, AIT
16:21 *D* not **set up** any wooden Asherah pole AIT
16:22 and *d* not **erect** a sacred stone, AIT
17: 1 *D* not **sacrifice** to the LORD your God AIT
17:10 Be careful to **d** everything they direct you 6913
17:10 to do everything they direct you to **d.** NIH
17:11 *D* not **turn aside** from what they tell you, AIT
17:15 *D* not **place** a foreigner over you, AIT
18: 9 *d* not **learn** to imitate the detestable ways AIT
18:14 not **permitted** you **to d** so. 5989
18:22 *D* not *be* **afraid** of him. AIT
19:10 **D** this so that innocent blood will not NIH
19:14 *D* not **move** your neighbor's boundary stone AIT
19:19 **d** to him as he intended to do to his brother. 6913
19:19 do to him as he intended to **d** to his brother. 6913
20: 1 *d* not *be* **afraid** of them, AIT
20: 3 *D* not *be* **fainthearted** or afraid; AIT
20: 3 *d* not *be* **terrified** or give way to panic AIT
20:15 at a distance from you and **d** not belong to NIH
20:16 *d* not **leave alive** anything that breathes. AIT
20:18 to follow all the detestable things *they* **d** 6913
20:19 *d* not **destroy** its trees by putting an ax AIT
20:19 *D* not **cut** them **down.** AIT
21: 8 and *d* not **hold** your people guilty of AIT
22: 1 *d* not **ignore** it but be sure to take it back AIT
22: 2 near you or if *you d* not **know** who he is, AIT
22: 3 **D** the same if you find your brother's donkey 6913
22: 3 *D* not **ignore** it. AIT
22: 4 *d* not **ignore** it. AIT
22: 6 *d* not **take** the mother with the young. AIT
22: 9 *D* not **plant** two kinds of **seed** AIT
22: 9 if you **d,** not only the crops you plant but NIH
22:10 *D* not **plow** with an ox and AIT
22:11 *D* not **wear clothes** of wool and linen AIT
22:26 **D** nothing to the girl; 6913
23: 6 *D* not **seek** a treaty of friendship with them AIT
23: 7 *D* not **abhor** an Edomite, AIT
23: 7 *D* not **abhor** an Egyptian, AIT
23:15 *d* not **hand** him **over** AIT
23:16 *D* not **oppress** him. AIT
23:19 *D* not **charge** your brother **interest,** AIT
23:21 *d* not *be* **slow** to pay it, AIT
23:23 be sure *to* **d,** 6913
23:24 but *d* not **put** any in your basket. AIT
24: 4 *D* not **bring sin** *upon* the land AIT
24: 6 *D* not **take** a pair of millstones—not even the upper one—**as security for a debt,** AIT
24: 8 be very careful to **d** exactly as the priests, 6913
24:10 *d* not **go** into his **house** AIT
24:12 *d* not **go to sleep** with his pledge in your AIT
24:14 *D* not **take advantage** *of* a hired man AIT
24:17 *D* not **deprive** the alien or the fatherless AIT
24:18 That is why I command you to **d** this. 6913
24:19 *d* not **go back** to get it. AIT
24:20 *d* not **go over the branches a second time.** AIT
24:21 *d* not **go over the vines again.** AIT
24:22 That is why I command you to **d** this. 6913
25: 4 *D* not **muzzle** an ox while it is treading out AIT
25: 8 *"I d* not **want** to marry her," AIT
25:13 *D* not **have** two differing weights AIT
25:14 *D* not **have** two differing measures AIT
25:19 *D* not **forget!** AIT
27: 5 *D* not **use** any iron tool upon them. AIT
28:14 *D* not **turn aside** from any of the commands AIT
28:15 if *you d* not **obey** the LORD your God AIT
28:15 *d* not carefully **follow** all his commands AIT
28:29 be unsuccessful in **everything** you **d;** 2006
28:33 that *you d* not **know** will eat what your land AIT
28:58 If *you d* not **carefully** follow all AIT
28:58 and *d* not **revere** this glorious AIT
29: 9 that you may prosper in everything *you* **d.** 6913
31: 4 the LORD *will* **d** to them what he did 6913
31: 5 and *you must* **d** to them all 6913
31: 6 *D* not *be* **afraid** or terrified because AIT
31: 8 *D* not *be* **afraid; d**o not be discouraged." AIT
31: 8 Do not be afraid; *d* not *be* **discouraged."** AIT
31:13 Their children, who *d* not **know** this law, AIT
31:21 I know what they are disposed *to* **d,** 6913
31:29 because *you will* **d** evil in the sight of 6913
34:11 and wonders the LORD sent him to **d** 6913
Jos 1: 7 *d* not **turn** from it to the right or to the left, AIT
1: 8 *D* not *let* this Book of the Law **depart** AIT
1: 8 be careful to **d** everything written in it. 6913
1: 9 *D* not *be* **terrified;** AIT
1: 9 Do not be terrified; *d* not *be* **discouraged,** AIT
1:16 "Whatever you have commanded us *we will* **d,** 6913
3: 4 *d* not **go near** it." AIT
3: 5 the LORD *will* **d** amazing things 6913
4: 6 'What **d** these stones mean?' NIH
4:21 'What **d** these stones mean?' NIH
6: 3 **D** this for six days. 6913
6:10 *"D* not **give a war cry,** AIT
6:10 *d* not **raise** your voices, AIT
6:10 *d* not **say** a word until the day I tell you AIT
7: 3 to take it and *d* not **weary** all the people, AIT
7: 9 What then *will you* **d** 6913
Jos 7:19 *d* not **hide** it from me." AIT
8: 1 LORD said to Joshua, *"D* not *be* **afraid;** AIT
8: 1 *d* not *be* **discouraged.** AIT
8: 2 *You shall* **d** to Ai and its king as you did 6913
8: 8 **D** what the LORD has commanded. 6913
9: 8 and where *d you* **come** from?" AIT
9:20 This is what *we will* **d** to them: 6913
9:25 **D** to us whatever seems good and right 6913
10: 6 *"D* not **abandon** your servants. AIT
10: 8 *"D* not *be* **afraid** of them; AIT
10:25 Joshua said to them, *"D* not *be* **afraid;** AIT
10:25 *d* not *be* **discouraged.** AIT
10:25 This is what the LORD *will* **d** to all 6913
11: 6 *"D* not *be* **afraid** of them, AIT
15:18 Caleb asked her, "What can I **d for** you?" 4200
15:19 She replied, **"D** me a special favor. 5989
16:10 but are required to **d** forced labor. 6268
18: 7 however, **d** not get a portion among you, NIH
22:19 But *d* not **rebel** against the LORD or AIT
22:22 *d* not **spare** us this day. AIT
22:24 'What **d** you have to do with the LORD, NIH
22:24 'What do you **have to d with** the LORD, 4200
23: 7 *D* not **associate with** these nations AIT
23: 7 *d* not **invoke** the names of their gods AIT
24:12 not **d** it with your own sword and bow. NIH
Jdg 1:14 Caleb asked her, "What can I **d for** you?" 4200
1:15 She replied, **"D** me a special favor. 2035
6:10 *d* not **worship** the gods of the Amorites, AIT
6:18 Please *d* not **go away** until I come back AIT
6:23 *D* not *be* **afraid.** AIT
6:39 *"D* not *be* **angry** with me. AIT
7:17 **d** exactly as I do. 6913
7:17 do exactly as *I* **d.** 6913
8: 3 What was I able *to* **d** compared to you?" 6913
8: 6 **"D** you already have the hands of Zebah NIH
8:15 **'D** you already have the hands of Zebah NIH
8:21 "Come, **d** *it* yourself. 7003[S]
8:24 And he said, *"I d* **have** *one* **request,** AIT
9:33 **d** whatever your hand finds to do." 6913
9:33 do whatever your hand finds to **d."** NIH
9:48 **D** what you have seen me do!" 6913
9:48 Do what you have seen me **d!"** 6913
10:15 **D** with us whatever you think best, 6913
11: 7 Why *d you* **come** to me now, AIT
11:10 *we will* certainly **d** as you say." 6913
11:12 "What **d** you have against us NIH
11:36 **D** to me just as you promised, 6913
13: 4 and that *you d* not **eat** anything unclean, AIT
13: 7 and *d* not **eat** anything unclean, AIT
13:13 "Your wife *must* **d** all that I have told her. 9068
13:14 *She must* **d** everything I have commanded her." 9068
13:18 He replied, "Why *d you* **ask** my name? AIT
15:10 "to **d** to him as he did to us." 6913
18: 9 **Aren't** you *going to* **d something?** 3120
18:14 *"D you* **know** that one of these houses has AIT
18:14 Now you know what *to* **d."** 6913
18:24 What else **d** I have? NIH
19:23 don't **d** this disgraceful thing. 6913
19:24 and **d** to them whatever you wish. 6913
19:24 don't **d** such a disgraceful thing." 6913
19:30 Tell us what to **d!"** NIH
20: 9 But now this is what *we'll* **d** to Gibeah: 6913
21:11 "This is what *you are to* **d,"** they said. 6913
21:22 **'D** us **a kindness** by helping them, 2858
Ru 2:13 though *I d* not **have** the standing of one AIT
3: 4 He will tell you what *to* **d."** 6913
3: 5 *"I will* **d** whatever you say," 6913
3: 6 everything her mother-in-law told her to **d.** NIH
3:11 *I will* **d** for you all you ask. 6913
3:13 as surely as the LORD lives I *will* **d it.** 1457[S]
4: 4 If you will redeem it, **d so.** 1457[S]
4: 4 no one **has the right to d it** 1457[S]
4: 6 I cannot **d it."** 1457[S]
1Sa 1:16 *D* not **take** your servant **for** AIT
1:23 **"D** what seems best to you," 6913
2: 3 *"D* not **keep** talking so proudly AIT
2:23 "Why *d you* **do** such things? AIT
2:23 "Why *do you* **d** such things? 6913
2:29 Why *d you* **scorn** my sacrifice and offering AIT
2:29 Why *d you* **honor** your sons more than me AIT
2:33 that *I d* not **cut off** from my altar will AIT
2:35 *who will* **d** according to what is in my heart 6913
3:11 "See, I *am about to* **d** something in Israel 6913
3:17 *"D* not **hide** it from me. AIT
3:18 *let him* **d** what is good in his eyes." 6913
5: 8 "What *shall we* **d** with the ark of the god 6913
6: 2 "What *shall we* **d** with the ark of 6913
6: 3 *d* not **send it away** AIT
6: 6 Why *d you* **harden** your hearts as AIT
7: 8 *"D* not **stop** crying out to AIT
8: 5 and your sons *d* not **walk** in your ways; AIT
8: 9 **what** the king who will reign over them **will d."** 5477[S]
8:11 **what** the king who will reign over you will **d:** 5477[S]
9: 7 What **d** we have?" NIH
9:20 *d* not **worry** about them; AIT
9:21 Why *d you* **say** such a thing to me?" AIT
10: 2 'What *shall I* **d** about my son?" ' 6913
10: 7 **d** whatever your hand finds to do, 6913
10: 7 do whatever your hand finds to **d,** NIH
10: 8 to you and tell you what *you are to* **d."** 6913
10:24 *"D you* **see** the man the LORD has chosen? AIT
11:10 and *you can* **d** to us whatever seems good 6913
12:14 and *d* not **rebel** against his commands, and AIT
12:15 But if *you d* not **obey** the LORD, AIT
1Sa 12:16 *about to* **d** before your eyes! 6913
12:20 *"D* not *be* **afraid,"** Samuel replied. AIT
12:20 yet *d* not **turn away** from the LORD, AIT
12:21 *D* not **turn away** after useless idols. AIT
12:21 *They can* **d** you no **good,** 3603
14: 7 **"D** all that you have in mind," 6913
14:34 *D* not **sin** against the LORD by eating meat AIT
14:36 **"D** whatever seems best to you," 6913
14:40 **"D** what seems best to you," 6913
14:44 be it ever so severely, if *you d* not **die,** AIT
15: 3 *D* not **spare** them; AIT
15: 6 the Amalekites so that *I d* not **destroy** you AIT
15:19 on the plunder and **d** evil in the eyes of 6913
16: 3 and I will show you what *to* **d.** 6913
16: 4 They asked, *"D you* **come** in peace?" AIT
16: 7 *D* not **consider** his appearance or his height, AIT
17: 8 "Why *d you* **come out** and line up AIT
17:25 *D you* **see** how this man keeps coming out? AIT
18: 5 Whatever Saul sent him to **d,** NIH
18:17 *Let* the Philistines **d that!** 928+2118+2257+3338[S]
18:23 *"D* you think *it is a* **small** AIT
19: 4 not the king **d wrong** to his servant David; 2627
19: 5 Why then *would you* **d wrong** to 2627
20: 2 Look, my father doesn't **d** anything, 6913
20: 4 "Whatever you want me to **d,** NIH
20: 4 *I'll* **d** for you." 6913
20:13 *d* not **let** you **know** AIT
20:15 *d* not ever **cut off** your kindness AIT
21: 3 *d* you **have on hand?** AIT
22: 3 with you until I learn what God *will* **d** 6913
22: 5 *"D* not **stay** in the stronghold. AIT
23:20 down whenever it pleases you to **d so,** 3718[S]
24: 6 that *I should* **d** such a thing to my master, 6913
24: 9 "Why *d you* **listen** when men say, AIT
25:17 Now think it over and see what *you can* **d,** 6913
26:20 *d* not *let* my blood **fall** to the ground AIT
26:25 *you will* **d great things** and 6913+6913
27: 1 The best thing I can **d** is to escape to NIH
28: 2 for yourself what your servant *can* **d."** 6913
28:13 What *d you* **see?"** AIT
28:15 I have called on you to tell me what *to* **d."** 6913
28:16 Samuel said, "Why *d you* **consult** me, AIT
28:21 in my hands and did what you told me to **d.** NIH
29: 7 **d** nothing to displease the Philistine rulers." 6913
30:13 David asked him, "To whom **d** you belong, NIH
30:13 and where **d** you come from?" NIH
30:23 *you must* not **d** that with what 6913
31: 4 and would not **d** it; NIH
2Sa 1: 5 "How *d you* **know** that Saul AIT
1: 7 and I said, **'What can I d?'** 2180
2:14 **"All right,** *let them* **d it,"** 7756[S]
3: 9 if *I d* not **do** for David what AIT
3: 9 if *I do* not **d** for David what 6913
3:13 *D* not **come into** my **presence** AIT
3:18 Now **d** *it!* 6913
3:19 the whole house of Benjamin **wanted to d.** 928+3202+6524
3:38 *"D you* not **realize** that a prince and AIT
5:23 *"D* not **go straight up,** AIT
7: 3 go ahead and **d** it, 6913
7:25 **D** as you promised, 6913
9:11 "Your servant *will* **d** whatever my lord 6913
9:11 the king commands his servant to **d."** NIH
10: 3 **"D** you think David is honoring your father NIH
10:12 The LORD *will* **d** what is good 6913
11:11 as you live, *I will* not **d** such a thing!" 6913
12:12 but I *will* **d** this thing in broad daylight 6913
12:18 *He may* **d** something desperate." 6913
13: 2 for him to **d** anything to her. 6913
13: 4 He asked Amnon, "Why **d** you, NIH
13:12 Don't **d** this wicked thing. 6913
14:15 perhaps he *will* **d** what his servant asks. 6913
14:18 *"D* not **keep** from me the answer AIT
14:19 to **d** this and who put all these words into NIH
14:21 "Very well, *I will* **d** it. 6913
15:15 "Your servants are **ready to d** whatever our lord the king chooses." 2180
15:20 **d not know where** I **am going?** 889+2143+2143+6584
15:26 *let him* **d** to me whatever seems good 6913
16:10 "What **d** you and I have in common, NIH
16:10 who can ask, 'Why *d you* **do** this?' " AIT
16:10 who can ask, 'Why *do you* **d** this?' " 6913
16:20 What *should we* **d?"** 6913
17: 6 *Should we* **d** what he says? 6913
17:15 and the elders of Israel to **d** such and such, NIH
17:15 but I have advised them to **d** so and so. NIH
17:16 *'D* not **spend** the night at the fords in AIT
18: 4 *"I will* **d** whatever seems best to you." 6913
18:20 but *you must* not **d so** today, 1413[S]
18:22 *d* you *want to* **go?** AIT
19:10 So why *d* you **say nothing** *about* bringing AIT
19:18 over and to **d** whatever he wished. 6913
19:19 *D* not **remember** how your servant did wrong AIT
19:22 "What **d** you and I have in common, NIH
19:22 *D I* not **know** that today I am king AIT
19:27 so **d** whatever pleases you. 6913
19:28 So what right **d** I have NIH
19:37 **D** for him whatever pleases you." 6913
19:38 and I *will* **d** for him whatever pleases you. 6913
19:38 And anything you desire from me *I will* **d** 6913
19:43 *d you* **treat** us **with contempt?** AIT
20: 6 *will* **d** us more **harm** than Absalom did. 8317
20:19 *d you want to* **swallow up** AIT
21: 3 "What *shall I* **d** for you? 6913
21: 4 nor **d** we have the right to put anyone NIH

2Sa 21: 4 “What *d* you **want** me to do for you?” AIT
21: 4 “What do you want *me to* **d** for you?” 6913
22:37 so that my ankles *d* not **turn.** AIT
23:17 “Far be it from me, O LORD, *to* **d** this!” 6913
24: 3 the king want to **d** such a thing?” NIH
24:14 *d* not *let me* **fall** into the hands AIT
1Ki 1: 6 “Why *d you* **behave** as you do?” AIT
1: 6 “Why do you behave as you **d?”** NIH
1:18 my lord the king, *d* not **know about** it. AIT
2: 3 so that you may prosper in all *you* **d** 6913
2: 6 *d* not **let** his gray head **go down** AIT
2: 9 *d* not **consider** him **innocent.** AIT
2: 9 you will know what *to* **d** to him. 6913
2:13 *“D* you **come** peacefully?” AIT
2:16 *D* not **refuse** me.” AIT
2:20 *“D* not **refuse** me.” AIT
2:22 “Why *d* you **request** Abishag AIT
2:31 king commanded Benaiah, **“D** as he says. 6913
2:36 but *d* not **go** anywhere else. AIT
2:38 Your servant *will* **d** as my lord 6913
3: 7 and *d* not **know how** to carry out my duties. AIT
3:12 *I will* **d** what you have asked. 6913
3:27 *D* not **kill** him; she is his mother.” AIT
5: 8 and *will* **d** all you want in providing 6913
5:11 *to* **d** this for Hiram year after year. 5989^S
8:25 if only your sons are careful in **all** they **d** 2006
8:43 and **d** whatever the foreigner asks of you, 6913
8:43 as **d** your own people Israel, NIH
9: 1 and had achieved all he had desired to **d,** 6913
9: 4 and **d** all I command, 6913
9: 6 from me and *d* not **observe** the commands AIT
11:12 *I will* not **d** it during your lifetime. 6913
11:22 Hadad replied, “but **d let me go!”** 8938+8938
11:33 I will **d** this because they have forsaken me NIH
11:38 If *you* **d** whatever I command you 9048
11:38 in my ways and **d** what is right in my eyes 6913
12:16 “What share **d** we have in David, NIH
12:24 *D* not **go up** to fight against your brothers, AIT
17:13 Go home and **d** as you have said. 6913
17:18 “What **d** you have against me, man of God? NIH
18:25 but *d* not **light** the fire.” AIT
18:34 **“D** *it* **again,”** he said, and they did it again. 9101
18:34 **“D** *it* **a third time,”** 8992
19: 2 if by this time tomorrow *I d* not **make** your life AIT
20: 9 ‘Your servant *will* **d** all you demanded 6913
20:13 *‘D you* **see** this vast army? AIT
20:14 “But who will **d** this?” 928
20:14 of the provincial commanders will **d** it.’ ” 928
20:24 **D** this: Remove all the kings from their 6913
21:20 “because you have sold yourself to **d** evil in 6913
21:25 who sold himself to **d** evil in the eyes of 6913
22:22 ‘Go and **d** it.’ 6913
22:31 *“D* not **fight** *with* anyone, small or great, AIT
2Ki 1:15 *d* not *be* **afraid** of him.” AIT
2: 3 *“D you* **know** that the LORD is going AIT
2: 3 Elisha replied, “but *d* **not speak** *of* it.” AIT
2: 5 *“D you* **know** that the LORD is going AIT
2: 5 I know,” he replied, “but *d* **not speak** *of* it.” AIT
2: 9 what *can I* **d** for you before I am taken 6913
2:16 “No,” Elisha replied, *“d* not **send** them.” AIT
3:13 “What **d** we have to do with each other? NIH
3:13 “What do we **have to d with** each other? 2256+4200+4200
4: 2 Tell me, what **d** you have in your house?” NIH
4:29 If you meet anyone, *d* not **greet** him, AIT
4:29 and if anyone greets you, *d* not **answer.** AIT
5:13 prophet had told you to **d** some great thing, NIH
6:15 “Oh, my lord, what *shall we* **d?”** 6913
6:22 *“D* not **kill** them,” he answered. AIT
8: 2 The woman proceeded *to* **d** as the man 6913
8:12 “Because I know the harm *you will* **d** to 6913
9:17 **‘D** you come in peace?’ ” NIH
9:18 **‘D** you come in peace?’ ” NIH
9:18 “What **d** you have to do with peace?” NIH
9:18 “What do you **have to d with** peace?” 4200
9:19 **‘D** you come in peace?’ ” NIH
9:19 “What **d** you have to do with peace? NIH
9:19 “What do you **have to d with** peace? 4200
10: 5 and *we will* **d** anything you say. 6913
10: 5 *you* **d** whatever you think best.” 6913
10:30 to the house of Ahab all I had in mind to **d,** NIH
11: 5 saying, “This is what *you are to* **d:** 6913
16: 2 *he did* not **d** what was right in the eyes of 6913
17:12 *“You shall* not **d** this.” 6913
17:15 *“D* not **do** as they do,” AIT
17:15 *“Do* not **d** as they do,” 6913
17:15 “Do not do as they **d,”** NIH
17:15 the LORD had forbidden them to **d.** NIH
17:17 and sorcery and sold themselves to **d** evil in 6913
17:26 in the towns of Samaria *d* not **know** what AIT
17:26 the people *d* not **know** what he requires.” AIT
17:35 *“D* not **worship** any other gods or bow AIT
17:37 *D* not **worship** other gods. AIT
17:38 *D* not **forget** the covenant I have made AIT
17:38 and *d* not **worship** other gods. AIT
17:41 and grandchildren *continue to* **d** 6913
18:29 *D* not **let** Hezekiah **deceive** AIT
18:30 *D* not **let** Hezekiah **persuade** you **to trust** AIT
18:31 *“D* not **listen** to Hezekiah. AIT
18:32 *“D* not **listen** to Hezekiah, AIT
18:36 *“D* not **answer** him.” AIT
19: 6 *D* not *be* **afraid** of what you have heard— AIT
19:10 *D* not **let** the god you depend on **deceive** AIT
20: 9 the LORD *will* **d** what he has promised: 6913
21: 8 to **d** everything I commanded them 6913
23:35 In order to **d so,** 5989^S

2Ki 25:24 *“D* not *be* **afraid** of AIT
1Ch 10: 4 and would not **d** it; NIH
11:19 “God forbid that I *should* **d** this!” 6913
12:32 the times and knew what Israel *should* **d—** 6913
13: 4 The whole assembly agreed to **d** this, 6913
14:14 *“D* not **go straight up,** AIT
15:13 We did not inquire of him about how to **d** it NIH
16:22 *“D* not **touch** my anointed ones; AIT
16:22 *d* my prophets no **harm.”** AIT
17: 2 “Whatever you have in mind, **d** it, 6913
17:23 **D** as you promised, 6913
19: 3 **“D** you think David is honoring your father NIH
19:13 The LORD *will* **d** what is good 6913
21: 3 Why *does* my lord **want to d** this? 1335
21:13 *d* not *let me* **fall** into the hands AIT
21:17 but **d** not let this plague remain NIH
21:23 the king **d** whatever pleases him. 6913
22:13 *D* not *be* **afraid** or discouraged. AIT
23:30 They were to **d** the same in the evening NIH
26: 8 with the strength to **d** the work— NIH
28:10 Be strong and **d** *the* **work.”** 6913
28:20 “Be strong and courageous, and **d** *the* **work.** 6913
28:20 *D* not *be* **afraid** or discouraged, AIT
29:19 and decrees and to **d** everything to build 6913
2Ch 6:16 in **all** they **d** to walk before me according 2006
6:33 and **d** whatever the foreigner asks of you, 6913
6:33 as **d** your own people Israel, NIH
6:42 *d* not **reject** your anointed one. AIT
7:11 in mind to **d** in the temple of the LORD 6913
7:17 and **d** all I command, 6913
10:16 “What share **d** we have in David, NIH
11: 4 *D* not **go up** to fight against your brothers. AIT
13: 9 as the peoples of other lands **d?** NIH
13:12 *d* not **fight** against the LORD, AIT
14:11 *d* not *let* man **prevail** AIT
15: 7 But as for you, be strong and *d* not **give up,** AIT
18:21 ‘Go and **d** it.’ 6913
18:30 *“D* not **fight** *with* anyone, small or great, AIT
19: 6 “Consider carefully wha. you **d,** 6913
19:10 **D** this, and you will not sin. 6913
19:11 may the LORD be with those who **d** well.” NIH
20:12 We *d* not **know** what to do, AIT
20:12 We do not know what *to* **d,** 6913
20:15 *‘D* not *be* **afraid** or discouraged because AIT
20:17 *D* not *be* **afraid;** do not be discouraged. AIT
20:17 Do not be afraid; *d* not *be* **discouraged.** AIT
23: 4 Now this is what *you are to* **d:** 6913
23:14 *“D* not **put** her **to death** AIT
24: 5 **D** it **now.”** 4554
24:20 ‘Why *d* you **disobey** AIT
25:15 “Why *d you* **consult** this people’s gods, AIT
28: 1 *he did* not **d** what was right in the eyes of 6913
28:13 *D you* **intend** to add to our sin and guilt? AIT
29:11 My sons, *d* not *be* **negligent** now, AIT
30: 7 *D* not **be** like your fathers and brothers, AIT
30: 8 *D* not *be* **stiff-necked,** as your fathers were; AIT
32: 7 *D* not *be* **afraid** or discouraged because of AIT
32:13 *“D you* not **know** what I AIT
32:15 *d* not *let* Hezekiah **deceive** AIT
32:15 *D* not **believe** him, AIT
33: 8 to **d** everything I commanded them 6913
Ezr 6: 7 *D* **not interfere** with the work AIT
6: 8 *to* **d** for these elders of the Jews in 10522
7:18 then **d** whatever seems best with the rest of 10522
7:25 you are to teach any who *d* not **know** them. AIT
9:12 *d* not **give** your daughters **in marriage** AIT
9:12 *D* not **seek** a treaty of friendship with them AIT
10: 4 so take courage and **d** it.” 6913
10: 5 under oath to **d** what had been suggested. 6913
10:11 the God of your fathers, and **d** his will. 6913
10:12 We *must* **d** as you say. 6913
Ne 2:12 in my heart to **d** for Jerusalem. 6913
4: 5 *D* not **cover up** their guilt AIT
5:12 *We will* **d** as you say.” 6913
5:12 an oath to **d** what they had promised. 6913
7: 2 and feared God more than most men **d.** NIH
8: 9 *D* not **mourn** or weep.” AIT
8:10 *D* not **grieve,** for the joy of AIT
8:11 *D* not **grieve.”** AIT
9:32 *d* not *let* all this hardship *seem* **trifling** AIT
13:14 and *d* not **blot out** what I have AIT
13:18 Didn’t your forefathers **d** the same things, 6913
13:21 *d* you **spend the night** AIT
13:21 you **d** *this* **again,** I will lay hands on you.” 9101
Est 2:10 Mordecai had forbidden her *to* **d so.** 5583^S
2:20 as Mordecai had told her to **d,** NIH
3: 3 “Why *d* you **disobey** the king’s command?” AIT
3: 8 of all other people and who *d* not **obey** AIT
3:11 “and **d** with the people as you please.” 6913
4:13 *“D* not **think** that because you are in AIT
4:16 *D* not **eat** or drink for three days, AIT
4:16 I and my maids will fast as you **d.** NIH
5: 5 “so that we **may d** what Esther asks.” 6913
6:10 the horse and **d** just as you have suggested 6913
6:10 *D* not **neglect** anything you have recommended.” AIT
7: 5 the man who has dared to **d** such a thing?” 6913
8: 5 with favor and thinks it the right thing to **d,** NIH
8:12 for the Jews to **d** this in all the provinces NIH
Job 1:12 but on the man himself *d* not **lay** a finger.” AIT
5:17 *d* not **despise** the discipline of the Almighty. AIT
6:11 “What strength **d** I have, NIH
6:12 **D** I have the strength of stone? NIH
6:13 **D** I have any power to help myself, NIH
6:25 *d* your arguments **prove?** AIT
6:26 *D you* **mean** to correct what I say, AIT
6:29 Relent, *d* not **be** unjust; AIT

Job 7:21 Why *d you* not **pardon** my offenses AIT
9:16 *I d* not **believe** he would give me AIT
10: 2 I will say to God: *D* not **condemn** me, AIT
10: 4 **D** you have eyes of flesh? NIH
10: 4 *D you* **see** as a mortal sees? AIT
11: 8 what *can you* **d?** 7188
13:14 *d I* **put** myself **in jeopardy** AIT
13:24 Why *d you* **hide** your face AIT
14: 3 *D you* **fix** your eye on such a one? AIT
15: 8 *D you* **listen in** on God’s council? AIT
15: 8 *D you* **limit** wisdom to yourself? AIT
15: 9 What *d you* **know** that we do not know? AIT
15: 9 What do you know that *we d* not **know?** AIT
15: 9 What **insights** *d you* **have** that we do AIT
15: 9 What insights do you have that we **d** NIH
15:12 and why *d* your eyes **flash,** AIT
16:18 “O earth, *d* not **cover** my blood; AIT
19:22 Why *d you* **pursue** me as God does? AIT
21: 7 *d* the wicked **live on,** AIT
21:10 their cows calve and *d* not **miscarry.** AIT
22:17 What *can* the Almighty **d** to us?’ 7188
23: 8 if I go to the west, *I d* not **find** him. AIT
23: 9 he is at work in the north, *I d* not **see** him; AIT
24:13 *who d* not **know** its ways or stay in its paths. AIT
24:16 **want** nothing **to d with** the light. 3359
26: 8 the clouds *d* not **burst** under their weight. AIT
27: 6 but *will* **d** it so **no more;** 665
28: 8 *d* not **set foot on** it, AIT
30:10 *they d* not **hesitate** to spit in my face. AIT
30:20 O God, but *you d* not **answer;** AIT
31: 3 disaster for *those who* **d** wrong? 7188
31:14 what *will I* **d** when God confronts me? 6913
31:23 of his splendor *I* **could** not **d** such things. 3523
31:33 if I have concealed my sin as men **d,** NIH
32:13 *D* not **say,** ‘We have found wisdom; AIT
33:13 Why *d you* **complain** to him AIT
34:10 Far be it from God to **d** evil, NIH
34:10 from the Almighty to **d** wrong. NIH
34:12 It is unthinkable that God *would* **d wrong,** 8399
34:32 I have done wrong, *I will* not **d** so **again.’** 3578
35: 2 *“D you* **think** this is just? AIT
35: 3 and what *d I* **gain** by not sinning?’ AIT
35: 6 what *does that* **d** to him? 6913
35: 7 you are righteous, what *d you* **give** to him, AIT
35:14 when you say that *you d* not **see** him, AIT
36:12 But if *they d* not **listen,** AIT
36:13 *d* not **cry for help.** AIT
36:18 *d* not *let* a large bribe **turn** you **aside.** AIT
36:20 *D* not **long for** the night, AIT
37:12 to **d** whatever he commands them. 7188
37:15 *D you* **know** how God controls the clouds AIT
37:16 *D you* **know** how the clouds hang poised, AIT
38:20 *D you* **know** the paths to their dwellings? AIT
38:33 *D you* **know** the laws of the heavens? AIT
38:35 *D you* **send** the lightning bolts on their way? AIT
38:35 *D they* **report** to you, ‘Here we are’? AIT
38:39 *“D you* **hunt** the prey for the lioness AIT
39: 1 *“D you* **know** when the mountain goats AIT
39: 1 *D you* **watch** when the doe bears her fawn? AIT
39: 2 *D you* **count** the months till they bear? AIT
39: 2 *D you* **know** the time they give birth? AIT
39: 4 they leave and *d* not **return.** AIT
39:19 *“D you* **give** the horse his strength AIT
39:20 *D you* **make** him **leap** AIT
40: 9 **D** you have an arm like God’s, NIH
41: 8 the struggle and never **d** *it* **again!** 3578
41:28 *d* not **make** him **flee;** AIT
42: 2 “I know that you **can d** all things; 3523
Ps 2: 1 Why *d* the nations **conspire** and AIT
4: 4 In your anger *d* not **sin;** AIT
5: 5 you hate all *who* **d** wrong. 7188
6: 1 *d* not **rebuke** me in your anger AIT
6: 8 Away from me, all you *who* **d** evil, 7188
10: 1 O LORD, *d you* **stand** far off? AIT
10: 1 *Why d you* **hide** *yourself* in times AIT
10:12 *D* not **forget** the helpless. AIT
10:14 But you, O God, *d* **see** trouble and grief; AIT
11: 3 what *can* the righteous **d?”** 7188
14: 4 as men eat bread and *who d* not **call on** AIT
18:36 so that my ankles *d* not **turn.** AIT
22: 2 I cry out by day, but *you d* not **answer,** AIT
22:11 *D* not *be* **far** from me, AIT
25: 2 *D* not *let me be* **put to shame,** AIT
26: 4 *I d* not **sit** with deceitful men, AIT
26: 4 nor *d I* **consort** with hypocrites; AIT
26: 9 *D* not **take away** my soul along with sinners, AIT
27: 9 *D* not **hide** your face from me, AIT
27: 9 *d* not **turn** your servant **away** AIT
27: 9 *D* not **reject** me or forsake me, AIT
27:12 *D* not **turn** me **over** AIT
28: 1 *d* not **turn a deaf ear** AIT
28: 3 *D* not **drag** me **away** AIT
28: 3 with *those who* **d** evil, 7188
32: 9 *D* not **be** like the horse or the mule, AIT
33:15 who considers everything they **d.** 5126
34:14 Turn from evil and **d** good; 6913
34:16 of the LORD is against *those who* **d** evil, 6913
35:20 *They d* not **speak** peaceably, AIT
35:22 *D* not *be* **far** from me, O Lord. AIT
35:24 *d* not *let them* **gloat** AIT
35:25 *D* not *let them* **think,** AIT
36: 3 he has ceased to be wise and to **d good.** 3512
37: 1 *D* not **fret** because of evil men or AIT
37: 1 or be envious of *those who* **d** wrong; 6913
37: 3 Trust in the LORD and **d** good; 6913
37: 5 trust in him and he *will* **d** this: 6913

Ps 37: 7 *d* not **fret** when men succeed in their ways, AIT
37: 8 *d* not **fret**—it leads only to evil. AIT
37:21 The wicked borrow and *d* not **repay,** AIT
37:27 Turn from evil and **d** good; 6913
37:31 his feet *d* not **slip.** AIT
38: 1 *d* not **rebuke** me in your anger AIT
38:16 "*D* not *let them* **gloat** AIT
38:21 O LORD, *d* not **forsake** me; AIT
39: 7 "But now, Lord, what *d I* **look for?** AIT
39: 8 *d* not **make** me the scorn of fools. AIT
40: 8 I desire to **d** your will, O my God; 6913
40: 9 *I d* not **seal** my lips, as you know, AIT
40:10 *I d* not **hide** your righteousness in my heart; AIT
40:10 *I d* not **conceal** your love and your truth AIT
40:11 *D* not **withhold** your mercy from me, AIT
40:17 O my God, *d* not **delay.** AIT
44: 6 *I d* not **trust** in my bow, AIT
44:23 Why *d you* **sleep?** AIT
44:23 *D* not **reject** us forever. AIT
44:24 Why *d you* **hide** your face AIT
49:16 *D* not *be* **overawed** when a man grows rich, AIT
50: 8 *I d* not **rebuke** you for your sacrifices AIT
50:13 *D I* **eat** the flesh of bulls or drink the blood AIT
51:11 *D* not **cast** me from your presence AIT
51:16 *You d* not **delight in** sacrifice, AIT
51:16 *d* not **take pleasure in** burnt offerings. AIT
52: 1 Why *d you* **boast** of evil, you mighty man? AIT
52: 1 Why **d** you boast all day long, NIH
53: 4 as men eat bread and *who d* not **call on** AIT
55: 1 O God, *d* not **ignore** my plea; AIT
56: 4 What *can* mortal man **d** to me? 6913
56:11 What *can* man **d** to me? 6913
57: T [To the tune of] "*D* Not **Destroy."** AIT
58: T [To the tune of] "*D* Not **Destroy."** AIT
58: 1 *D you* rulers indeed **speak** AIT
58: 1 *D you* **judge** uprightly among men? AIT
59: T [To the tune of] "*D* Not **Destroy."** AIT
59:11 But *d* not **kill** them, O Lord our shield, AIT
62:10 *D* not **trust** in extortion or take pride AIT
62:10 *d* not **set** your heart on them. AIT
69:14 *d* not *let me* **sink;** AIT
69:15 *D* not *let* the floodwaters **engulf** AIT
69:17 *D* not **hide** your face from your servant; AIT
69:27 *d* not *let them* **share** AIT
70: 5 O LORD, *d* not **delay.** AIT
71: 9 *D* not **cast** me **away** AIT
71: 9 *d* not **forsake** me when my strength is gone. AIT
71:18 *d* not **forsake** me, O God, AIT
74:11 Why *d you* **hold back** your hand, AIT
74:19 *D* not **hand over** the life of your dove AIT
74:19 *d* not **forget** the lives of your afflicted AIT
74:21 *D* not *let* the oppressed **retreat** AIT
74:23 *D* not **ignore** the clamor of your adversaries, AIT
75: T [To the tune of] "*D* Not **Destroy."** AIT
75: 4 '*D* not **lift up** your horns. AIT
75: 5 *D* not **lift** your horns against heaven; AIT
75: 5 *d* not **speak** with outstretched neck.' " AIT
79: 6 the nations that *d* not **acknowledge** you, on AIT
79: 6 on the kingdoms that *d* not **call** AIT
79: 8 *D* not **hold** against us the sins of AIT
83: 1 O God, **d** not keep silent; NIH
83: 9 **D** to them as you did to Midian, 6913
86:10 For you are great and **d** marvelous deeds; 6913
88:10 *D you* **show** your wonders to the dead? AIT
88:10 *D* those who are dead **rise up** AIT
88:14 *d you* **reject** me and hide your face AIT
89:30 and *d* not **follow** my statutes, AIT
92: 6 fools *d* not **understand,** AIT
95: 8 *d* not **harden** your hearts as you did AIT
101: 4 *I will* **have** nothing *to* **d with** evil. 3359
102: 2 *D* not **hide** your face from me when I am AIT
102:24 "*D* not **take** me **away,** AIT
103:20 you mighty ones *who* **d** his bidding, 6913
103:21 you his servants *who* **d** his will. 6913
105:15 "*D* not **touch** my anointed ones; AIT
105:15 **d** my prophets no **harm."** 8317
106: 3 *who* constantly **d** what is right. 6913
109: 1 O God, whom I praise, *d* not *remain* **silent,** AIT
115: 2 Why *d* the nations **say,** AIT
118: 6 What *can* man **d** to me? 6913
119: 3 *They* **d** nothing wrong; 7188
119: 8 *d* not utterly **forsake** me. AIT
119:10 *d* not **let** me **stray** AIT
119:17 **D good** to your servant, and I will live; 1694
119:19 *d* not **hide** your commands from me. AIT
119:31 *d* not **let** me **be put to shame.** AIT
119:43 *D* not **snatch** the word of truth AIT
119:51 but *I d* not **turn** from your law. AIT
119:65 **D** good to your servant according 6913
119:68 You are good, and *what you* **d** *is* **good;** 3512
119:83 *I d* not **forget** your decrees. AIT
119:116 *d* not **let** my hopes **be dashed.** AIT
119:121 *d* not **leave** me to my oppressors. AIT
119:132 you **always d** to those who love your name. 5477
119:141 *I d* not **forget** your precepts. AIT
119:155 for *they d* not **seek out** your decrees. AIT
119:158 for *they d* not **obey** your word. AIT
120: 3 What *will he* **d** to you, 5989
125: 3 **use** their hands **to d** evil. 8938
125: 4 **D good,** O LORD, to those who are good, 3512
131: 1 *I d* not **concern** *myself* with great matters AIT
132:10 *d* not **reject** your anointed one. AIT
137: 6 of my mouth if *I d* not **remember** you, AIT
137: 6 *I d* not **consider** Jerusalem my highest joy. AIT
138: 8 *d* not **abandon** the works of your hands. AIT
139:21 *D I* not **hate** those who hate you, AIT
140: 8 *d* not **grant** the wicked their desires, AIT

Ps 140: 8 *d* not **let** their plans **succeed,** AIT
141: 8 *d* not **give** me **over to death.** AIT
143: 2 *D* not **bring** your servant into judgment, AIT
143: 7 *D* not **hide** your face from me or I will be AIT
143:10 Teach me to **d** your will, 6913
146: 3 *D* not **put** *your* **trust** in mortal men, AIT
147:20 *they d* not **know** his laws. AIT
148: 8 stormy winds *that* **d** his bidding, 6913
Pr 1: 8 and *d* not **forsake** your mother's teaching. AIT
1:10 if sinners entice you, *d* not **give in** *to* them. AIT
1:15 *d* not **go** along with them, AIT
1:15 *d* **not set** foot on their paths; AIT
3: 1 My son, *d* not **forget** my teaching, AIT
3: 7 *D* not **be** wise in your own eyes; AIT
3:11 *d* not **despise** the LORD's discipline and do AIT
3:11 and *d* not **resent** his rebuke, AIT
3:21 *d* not **let** *them* **out** of your sight; AIT
3:27 *D* not **withhold** good AIT
3:28 *D* not **say** to your neighbor, AIT
3:29 *D* not **plot** harm against your neighbor, AIT
3:30 *D* not **accuse** a man for no reason— AIT
3:31 *D* not **envy** a violent man or choose any AIT
4: 2 so *d* not **forsake** my teaching. AIT
4: 5 *d* **not** forget my words or swerve AIT
4: 6 *D* not **forsake** wisdom, AIT
4:13 *d* not **let** it **go;** AIT
4:14 *D* not **set foot** on the path of the wicked AIT
4:15 Avoid it, *d* not **travel** on it; AIT
4:16 For they cannot sleep till *they* **d evil;** 8317
4:19 *they d* not **know** what makes them stumble. AIT
4:21 *D* not **let** *them* **out** of your sight, AIT
4:27 *D* not **swerve** *to* the right or the left; AIT
5: 7 *d* not **turn aside** from what I say. AIT
5: 8 *d* not **go near** the door of her house, AIT
6: 3 then **d** this, my son, to free yourself, 6913
6:20 and *d* not **forsake** your mother's teaching. AIT
6:25 *D* not **lust** in your heart **after** AIT
6:30 *Men d* not **despise** a thief if he steals AIT
7:25 *D* not *let* your heart **turn** AIT
8:33 *d* not **ignore** it. AIT
9: 8 *D* not **rebuke** a mocker or he will hate you; AIT
9:18 little *d they* **know** that the dead are there, AIT
10:29 but it is the ruin of *those who* **d** evil. 7188
14:22 *D* not those who plot evil **go astray?** AIT
16: 3 Commit to the LORD **whatever** you **d,** 5126
19: 7 how much more *d* his friends **avoid** him! AIT
19:18 *d* not **be a willing party** AIT
19:19 *you will have to* **d** it **again.** 3578+6388
20:13 *D* not **love** sleep or you will grow poor; AIT
20:22 *D* not **say,** "I'll pay you back AIT
20:23 and dishonest scales **d** not please him. NIH
21: 3 *To* **d** what is right 6913
21: 7 for they refuse to **d** what is right. 6913
22:22 *D* not **exploit** the poor AIT
22:22 because they are poor and *d* not **crush** AIT
22:24 *D* not **make friends** with a hot-tempered man, AIT
22:24 *d* not **associate** with one easily angered, AIT
22:26 *D* not **be** a man who strikes hands in pledge AIT
22:28 *D* not **move** an ancient boundary stone set AIT
22:29 *D you* **see** a man skilled in his work? AIT
23: 3 *D* not **crave** his delicacies, AIT
23: 4 *D* not **wear** *yourself* **out** AIT
23: 6 *D* not **eat** the food of a stingy man, AIT
23: 6 *d* not **crave** his delicacies; AIT
23: 9 *D* not **speak** to a fool, AIT
23:10 *D* not **move** an ancient boundary stone AIT
23:13 *D* not **withhold** discipline from a child; AIT
23:17 *D* not *let* your heart **envy** AIT
23:20 *D* not **join** those who drink too much wine AIT
23:22 *d* not **despise** your mother when she is old. AIT
23:23 Buy the truth and *d* not **sell** it; AIT
23:31 *D* not **gaze** *at* wine when it is red, AIT
24: 1 *D* not **envy** wicked men, AIT
24: 1 *d* not **desire** their company; AIT
24:15 *D* not **lie in wait** AIT
24:15 *d* not **raid** his dwelling place; AIT
24:17 *D* not **gloat** when your enemy falls; AIT
24:17 *d* not *let* your heart **rejoice,** AIT
24:19 *D* not **fret** because of evil men or AIT
24:21 my son, and *d* not **join** with the rebellious, AIT
24:28 *D* not **testify** against your neighbor AIT
24:29 *D* not **say,** "I'll do to him as he has done AIT
24:29 "*I'll* **d** to him as he has done to me; 6913
25: 6 *D* not **exalt yourself** AIT
25: 6 and *d* not **claim** a place among great men; AIT
25: 8 *d* not **bring** hastily to court, AIT
25: 8 for what *will you* **d** in the end 6913
25: 9 *d* not **betray** another man's confidence, AIT
26: 4 *D* not **answer** a fool according to his folly, AIT
26:12 *D you* **see** a man wise in his own eyes? AIT
26:25 his speech is charming, *d* not **believe** him, AIT
27: 1 *D* not **boast** about tomorrow, AIT
27: 1 *you d* not **know** what a day may bring forth. AIT
27:10 *D* not **forsake** your friend and the friend AIT
27:10 and *d* not **go** *to* your brother's house AIT
27:24 for riches **d** not endure forever, NIH
28: 5 Evil men *d* not **understand** justice, AIT
28:21 a man *will* **d wrong** for a piece of bread. 7321
29:20 *D you* **see** a man who speaks in haste? AIT
30: 2 I **d** not have a man's understanding. NIH
30: 6 *D* not **add** to his words, AIT
30: 7 *d* not **refuse** me before I die: AIT
30:10 "*D* not **slander** a servant to his master, AIT
30:11 and *d* not **bless** their mothers; AIT
30:18 four *that I d* not **understand:** AIT
31: 3 *d* not **spend** your strength on women, AIT

Pr 31:29 "Many women **d** noble things, 6913
Ecc 2: 3 to see what was worthwhile for men *to* **d** 6913
2:12 king's successor **d** than what has already been done? NIH
2:15 What then **d** I gain by being wise?" NIH
2:21 For a man *may* **d** his work with wisdom, 3780
2:24 A man can **d** nothing better than to eat NIH
3:12 to be happy and **d** good while they live. 6913
5: 1 who *d* not **know** that they do wrong. AIT
5: 1 who do not know that they **d** wrong. 6913
5: 2 *D* not *be* **quick** with your mouth, AIT
5: 2 *d* not *be* **hasty** in your heart AIT
5: 4 *d* not **delay** in fulfilling it. AIT
5: 6 *D* not **let** your mouth lead you into sin. AIT
5: 6 And *d* not **protest** to AIT
5: 8 *d* not *be* **surprised** at such things; AIT
5:11 so **d** those who consume them. 8045[S]
6: 6 *D* not all **go** to the same place? AIT
7: 9 *D* not *be* quickly **provoked** AIT
7:10 *D* not **say,** "Why were AIT
7:16 *D* not **be** overrighteous, neither be overwise AIT
7:17 *D* not *be* **overwicked,** and do not be a fool AIT
7:17 Do not be overwicked, and *d* not **be** a fool AIT
7:21 *D* not pay **attention** AIT
8: 3 *D* not *be* **in a hurry** AIT
8: 3 *D* not **stand up** for a bad cause, AIT
8: 3 for *he will* **d** whatever he pleases. 6913
8:11 with schemes to **d** wrong. 6913
8:13 Yet because the wicked **d** not fear God, NIH
9: 1 and **what** they **d** are in God's hands, 6271
9: 2 and *those* who **d** not. 2284[S]
9: 7 for it is now that God favors **what** you **d.** 5126
9:10 Whatever your hand finds to **d,** 6913
9:10 **d** it with all your might, for in the grave, 6913
10: 4 *d* not **leave** your post; AIT
10:20 *D* not **revile** the king even AIT
11: 2 for *you d* not **know** what disaster may come AIT
11: 5 As you *d* not **know** the path of the wind, AIT
11: 6 for you *d* not **know** which will succeed, AIT
11: 6 or whether both will **d** equally well. NIH
SS 1: 6 *D* not **stare** *at* me because I am dark, AIT
1: 8 If *you d* not **know,** AIT
2: 7 *D* not **arouse** or awaken love until it AIT
3: 5 *D* not **arouse** or awaken love until it AIT
8: 4 *D* not **arouse** or awaken love until it AIT
8: 8 What *shall we* **d** for our sister for 6913
Isa 1: 3 my people *d* not **understand."** AIT
1: 5 Why *d you* **persist** *in* rebellion? AIT
1:17 learn *to* **d right!** 3512
1:23 *d* not **defend the cause** of the fatherless AIT
2: 9 *d* not **forgive** them. AIT
3: 7 *d* not **make** me the leader of the people." AIT
3: 9 *they d* not **hide** it. AIT
3:15 What **d** you mean by crushing my people NIH
5: 5 Now I will tell you what *I am going to* **d** 6913
7: 4 *D* not **lose** heart because AIT
7: 9 *d* not **stand firm** in *your* **faith,** AIT
8:12 "*D* not **call** conspiracy everything AIT
8:12 *d* not **fear** what they fear, AIT
8:12 and *d* not **dread** it. AIT
8:20 If *they d* not **speak** according to this word, AIT
10: 3 What *will you* **d** on the day of reckoning, 6913
10:24 *d* not *be* **afraid** of the Assyrians, AIT
13:17 who *d* not **care for** silver AIT
14:29 *D* not **rejoice,** all you Philistines, that AIT
16: 3 *d* not **betray** the refugees. AIT
19:15 There is nothing Egypt *can* **d—** 6913
22: 4 *D* not **try** to console me over AIT
24: 9 No longer *d they* **drink** wine with a song; AIT
26:10 *they d* not **learn** righteousness; AIT
26:11 your hand is lifted high, but *they d* not **see** it. AIT
26:13 but your name alone *d we* **honor.** AIT
26:14 those departed spirits *d* not **rise.** AIT
28:10 For it is: **D** and do, do and do, rule on rule, 7422
28:10 For it is: Do and **d,** do and do, rule on rule, 7422
28:10 For it is: Do and do, **d** and do, rule on rule, 7422
28:10 For it is: Do and do, do and **d,** rule on rule, 7422
28:13 **D** and do, do and do, rule on rule, 7422
28:13 Do and **d,** do and do, rule on rule, 7422
28:13 Do and do, **d** and do, rule on rule, 7422
28:13 Do and do, do and **d,** rule on rule, 7422
28:21 to **d** his work, his strange work, 6913
28:28 his horses *d* not **grind** it. AIT
29:15 *who* **d** their work in darkness and think, 2118
31: 1 but *d* not **look** to the Holy One of Israel, AIT
31: 4 down to **d battle** on Mount Zion and 7371
35: 4 "Be strong, *d* not **fear;** AIT
36:14 *D* not **let** Hezekiah **deceive** AIT
36:15 *D* not **let** Hezekiah **persuade** you **to trust** AIT
36:16 "*D* not **listen** to Hezekiah. AIT
36:18 "*D* not **let** Hezekiah **mislead** AIT
36:21 "*D* not **answer** him." AIT
37: 6 *D* not *be* **afraid** of what you have heard— AIT
37:10 *D* not **let** the god you **depend** AIT
38: 7 the LORD *will* **d** what he has promised: 6913
40: 9 lift it up, *d* not *be* **afraid;** AIT
40:21 *D you* not **know?** AIT
40:24 no sooner *d they* **take root** in the ground, AIT
40:27 Why *d you* **say,** O Jacob, and complain, AIT
40:28 *D you* not **know?** AIT
41:10 So *d* not **fear,** for I am with you; AIT
41:10 *d* not *be* **dismayed,** for I am your God. AIT
41:13 *D* not **fear;** I will help you. AIT
41:14 *D* not *be* **afraid,** O worm Jacob, AIT
41:23 **D** *something,* whether **good** 3512
42:16 These are the things *I will* **d;** 6913

Isa 43: 5 *D* not *be* **afraid,** for I am with you; AIT
43: 6 '*D* not **hold** them **back.'** AIT
43:18 *d* not **dwell on** the past. AIT
43:19 Now it springs up; *d you* not **perceive** it? AIT
44: 2 *D* not *be* **afraid,** O Jacob, my servant, AIT
44: 8 *D* not **tremble,** do not be afraid. AIT
44: 8 Do not tremble, *d* not be **afraid.** AIT
45: 4 though *you d* not **acknowledge** me. AIT
45: 7 I, the LORD, **d** all these things. 6913
45:11 *d you* **question** me about my children, AIT
46:10 and *I will* **d** all that I please. 6913
46:11 what I have planned, that *will I* **d.** 6913
47:15 That is all *they can* **d** for you— 2118
48: 8 Well *d I* **know** how treacherous you are; AIT
48:11 my own sake, for my own sake, *I* **d** this. 6913
50: 2 **D** I lack the strength to rescue you? NIH
51: 7 *D* not **fear** the reproach of men or AIT
52: 5 "And now what **d** I have here?" NIH
54: 2 *d* not **hold back;** AIT
54: 4 *D* not *be* **afraid;** you will not suffer shame. AIT
54: 4 *D* not **fear disgrace;** AIT
55: 5 and nations *that d* not **know** you will hasten AIT
55:10 and *d* not **return** to it without watering AIT
56: 1 "Maintain justice and **d** what is right, 6913
57: 4 At whom *d you* **sneer** AIT
57:11 that *you d* not **fear** me? AIT
58: 1 "Shout it aloud, *d* not **hold back.** AIT
58: 3 *you* **d** as you please 5162
58: 4 as you **d** today and expect your voice to NIH
58: 9 "If *you* **d away with** the yoke of oppression, 4946+6073+9348
59: 8 The way of peace *they d* not **know;** AIT
60:22 in its time *I will* **d** this **swiftly."** 2590
63:17 *d you* **make** us **wander** AIT
63:17 and harden our hearts so we **d** NIH
64: 5 to the help of those who gladly **d** right, 6913
64: 9 *D* not *be* **angry** beyond measure, O LORD; AIT
64: 9 *d* not **remember** our sins forever. AIT
65: 8 so *will I* **d** in behalf of my servants; 6913
65:16 a blessing in the land *will* **d so** by the God 1385S
66: 9 *D* I **bring to the moment of birth** AIT
66: 9 "*D I* **close up** the womb when I bring AIT
Jer 1: 6 I said, "*I d* not **know how** to speak; AIT
1: 7 But the LORD said to me, "*D* not **say,** AIT
1: 8 *D* not *be* **afraid** of them, AIT
1:11 "What *d* you **see,** Jeremiah?" AIT
1:13 "What *d* you **see?"** AIT
1:17 *D* not *be* **terrified** by them, AIT
2:25 **D not run** until your feet are bare 4979
2:29 "Why *d you* **bring charges** against me? AIT
2:31 Why *d* my people **say,** AIT
2:36 Why *d you* **go about** so much, AIT
3: 5 but *you* **d** all the evil you can." 6913
4: 3 up your unplowed ground and *d* not **sow** AIT
4:22 "My people are fools; *they d* not **know** me. AIT
4:22 they know not how to **d good."** 3512
5: 3 O LORD, **d** not your eyes look for truth? NIH
5: 4 for *they d* not **know** the way of the LORD, AIT
5:10 *d* not **destroy** them **completely.** AIT
5:10 these people **d** not belong to the LORD. NIH
5:12 they said, "He will **d** nothing! NIH
5:15 a people whose language *you d* not **know,** AIT
5:15 whose speech *you d* not **understand.** AIT
5:21 who have eyes but *d* not **see,** AIT
5:21 who have ears but *d* not **hear:** AIT
5:24 *They d* not **say** to themselves, AIT
5:28 *they d* not **plead** the case of the fatherless AIT
5:28 *they d* not **defend** the rights of the poor. AIT
5:31 But what *will you* **d** in the end? 6913
6:15 *d* not even **know how** AIT
6:20 **What d I care about** incense from Sheba 2296+3276+4200+4200+4537
6:20 your sacrifices *d* not **please** me." AIT
6:25 *D* not **go out** *to* the fields or walk on AIT
7: 4 *D* not **trust** in deceptive words and say, AIT
7: 6 if *you d* not **oppress** the alien, AIT
7: 6 or the widow and *d* not **shed** innocent blood AIT
7: 6 and if *you d* not **follow** other gods AIT
7:10 safe to **d** all these detestable things? 6913
7:14 *now* **d** to the house that bears my Name, 6913
7:16 "So *d* not **pray** for this people AIT
7:16 *d* not **plead** with me, AIT
7:17 *D* you not **see** what they are doing in AIT
8: 4 *d they* not **get up?** AIT
8: 6 but *they d* not **say** what is right. AIT
8: 7 But my people *d* not **know** the requirements AIT
8: 9 what kind of wisdom **d** they have? NIH
8:12 *d* not even **know how** to blush. AIT
9: 3 *they d* not **acknowledge** me," AIT
9: 4 *d* not **trust** your brothers. AIT
9: 7 for what else *can I* **d** because of the sin 6913
10: 2 "*D* not **learn** the ways of the nations or AIT
10: 5 *D* not **fear** them; AIT
10: 5 *they can* **d** no **harm** 8317
10: 5 nor *can* they **d** *any* **good."** 3512
10:21 and *d* not **inquire of** the LORD; AIT
10:21 so *they d* not **prosper** AIT
10:25 on the nations that *d* not **acknowledge** you, AIT
10:25 the peoples who *d* not **call** on your name. AIT
11: 4 and **d** everything I command you, 6913
11:14 "*D* not **pray** for this people AIT
11:21 '*D* not **prophesy** in the name of the LORD AIT
12: 1 *d* all the faithless **live at ease?** AIT
12: 6 *D* not **trust** them, AIT
13: 1 *d* not **let** it **touch** water." AIT
13:15 Hear and pay attention, *d* not *be* **arrogant,** AIT
13:17 But if *you d* not **listen,** AIT

Jer 13:23 Neither can you **d good** who are accustomed to doing evil. 3512
14: 7 **d something** for the sake of your name. 6913
14: 9 *d* not **forsake** us! AIT
14:10 *they d* not **restrain** their feet. AIT
14:11 *D* not **pray** for the well-being of this people. AIT
14:19 *D* you **despise** Zion? AIT
14:21 For the sake of your name *d* not **despise** us; AIT
14:21 *d* not **dishonor** your glorious throne. AIT
14:21 with us and *d* not **break** it. AIT
14:22 *D* any of the worthless idols of the nations **bring rain?** AIT
14:22 *D* the skies *themselves* **send down** AIT
15:14 to your enemies in a land *you d* not **know,** AIT
15:15 *d* not **take** me **away;** AIT
16: 5 "*D* not **enter** a house where there is AIT
16: 5 *d* not **go** to mourn or show sympathy, AIT
16: 8 "And *d* not **enter** a house AIT
16:20 *D* men **make** their own gods? AIT
17: 4 to your enemies in a land *you d* not **know,** AIT
17:17 *D* not **be** a terror to me; AIT
17:22 *D* not **bring** a load **out** AIT
17:22 a load out of your houses or **d** any work on 6913
17:27 But if *you d* not **obey** me to keep AIT
18: 6 can I not **d** with you as this potter does?" 6913
18:10 **good** I had intended to **d** 3208+3512
18:14 *D* its cool waters from distant sources *ever* **cease** AIT
18:23 *D* not **forgive** their crimes AIT
19:12 This is what *I will* **d** to this place and 6913
21:10 I have determined to **d** this city harm and NIH
22: 3 **D** what is just and right. 6913
22: 3 **D** no **wrong** or violence to the alien, 3561
22: 3 and *d* not **shed** innocent blood in this place. AIT
22: 5 But if *you d* not **obey** these commands, AIT
22:10 *D* not **weep** for the dead [king] AIT
22:28 cast into a land *they d* not **know?** AIT
23: 5 and **d** what is just and right in the land. 6913
23:16 "*D* not **listen** to what the prophets AIT
23:24 "*D* not I **fill** heaven and earth?" AIT
23:28 what **has** straw **to d with** grain?" 4200
23:32 *d* not **benefit** these people **in the least,"** AIT
24: 3 the LORD asked me, "What *d* you **see,** AIT
25: 6 *D* not **follow** other gods to serve AIT
25: 6 *d* not **provoke** me **to anger** AIT
26: 2 *d* not **omit** a word. AIT
26: 4 *you d* not **listen** to me and follow my law, AIT
26: 5 and if you *d* not **listen** to the words AIT
26: 9 Why *d you* **prophesy** in the LORD's name AIT
26:14 **d** with me whatever you think is good 6913
27: 9 So *d* not **listen** to your prophets, AIT
27:14 *D* not **listen** to the words of the prophets AIT
27:16 *D* not **listen** to the prophets who say, AIT
27:17 *D* not **listen** to them. AIT
28: 6 *May* the LORD **d** so! 6913
29: 6 Increase in number there; *d* not **decrease.** AIT
29: 8 "*D* not *let* the prophets and diviners among you **deceive** you. AIT
29: 8 *D* not **listen** to the dreams AIT
29:23 which I did not tell them to **d.** NIH
29:32 the good things I *will* **d** for my people, 6913
30: 6 Then why *d I* **see** every strong man AIT
30:10 " 'So *d* not **fear,** O Jacob my servant; AIT
30:10 *d* not *be* **dismayed,** O Israel,' AIT
30:15 Why *d you* **cry out** over your wound, AIT
32: 3 saying, "Why *d* you **prophesy** as you do? AIT
32: 3 saying, "Why do you prophesy as you **d?** NIH
32:23 *they did* not **d** what you commanded them 6913
32:23 not do what you commanded them to **d.** 6913
32:35 that they *should* **d** such a detestable thing 6913
33: 3 and unsearchable things *you d* not **know.'** AIT
33: 9 on earth that hear of all the good things I **d** 6913
33:15 *he will* **d** what is just and right in the land. 6913
35: 6 But they replied, "*We d* not **drink** wine, AIT
35:14 To this day *they d* not **drink** wine, AIT
35:15 *d* not **follow** other gods to serve them. AIT
36: 8 the prophet told him to **d;** NIH
37: 9 *D* not **deceive** yourselves, thinking, AIT
37:20 *D* not **send** me **back** AIT
38: 5 "The king **can d** nothing to oppose you." 3523
38:14 "*D* not **hide** anything from me." AIT
38:24 "*D* not *let* anyone **know** AIT
38:25 *d* not **hide** it from us or we will kill you,' AIT
39:12 but **d** for him whatever he asks." 6913
40: 4 but if you **d** not want to, then don't come. NIH
40: 9 "*D* not *be* **afraid** to serve the Babylonians," AIT
40:16 "Don't **d** such a thing! 6913
42: 3 where we should go and what *we should* **d."** 6913
42: 5 against us if we *d* not **act** in accordance AIT
42:11 *D* not *be* **afraid** of the king of Babylon, AIT
42:11 *D* not *be* **afraid** of him, AIT
42:15 to go to Egypt and *you d* **go** to settle there, AIT
42:19 '*D* not **go** *to* Egypt.' AIT
42:20 tell us everything he says and *we will* **d** it.' 6913
44: 4 '*D* not **do** this detestable thing that I hate!' AIT
44: 4 '*Do* not **d** this detestable thing that I hate!' 6913
44:17 *We will* **certainly d** everything we said we would: 6913+6913
44:25 *Go ahead* then, **d** what you promised! 6913+6913
46: 5 What *d I* **see?** AIT
46:27 "*D* not **fear,** O Jacob my servant; AIT
46:27 *d* not *be* **dismayed,** O Israel. AIT
46:28 *D* not **fear,** O Jacob my servant, AIT
49: 1 Why *d* his people **live** in its towns? AIT
49: 4 Why *d you* **boast** of your valleys, AIT
49:12 "If those who **d** not deserve to drink NIH
49:36 be a nation where Elam's exiles *d* not **go.** AIT

Jer 50: 9 like skilled warriors *who d* not **return** empty-handed. AIT
50:15 **d** to her as she has done to others. 6913
50:21 **"D** everything I have commanded you. 6913
50:25 to **d** in the land of the Babylonians. NIH
50:29 **d** to her as she has done. 6913
51: 3 *D* not **spare** her young men; AIT
51: 6 *D* not **be destroyed** because of her sins. AIT
51:46 *D* not **lose** heart or be afraid AIT
51:50 leave and *d* not **linger!** AIT
La 3:56 "*D* not **close** your ears to my cry for relief." AIT
3:57 and you said, "*D* not **fear."** AIT
5:20 Why *d you* always **forget** us? AIT
5:20 Why *d you* **forsake** us so long? AIT
Eze 2: 6 *d* not *be* **afraid** of them or their words. AIT
2: 6 *D* not *be* **afraid,** AIT
2: 6 *D* not *be* **afraid** of what they say AIT
2: 8 *D* not **rebel** like that rebellious house; AIT
3: 9 *D* not *be* **afraid** *of* them or terrified AIT
3:18 and *you d* not **warn** him or speak out AIT
3:19 if you *d* **warn** the wicked man and he does AIT
3:21 if you *d* **warn** the righteous man not to sin AIT
5: 9 *I will* **d** to you what I have never done 6913
5: 9 before and *will* never **d** again. 6913
8: 6 *d* you **see** what they are doing— AIT
8:15 He said to me, "*D you* **see** this, son of man? AIT
8:17 a trivial matter for the house of Judah *to* **d** 6913
9: 6 but *d* not **touch** anyone who has the mark. AIT
12: 2 They have eyes to see but *d* not **see** and ears AIT
12: 2 not see and ears to hear but *d* not **hear,** AIT
14: 5 I will **d** this to recapture the hearts of NIH
15: 3 *D they* **make** pegs from it to hang things on? AIT
16: 5 or had compassion enough to **d** any 6913
16:30 when you **d** all these things, 6913
17:12 '*D you* not **know** what these things mean?' AIT
17:24 and *I will* **d** it.' " 6913
18: 2 **"What d you** people **mean** 4013+4200+4537
18:14 *he does* not **d** such things: 6913
18:23 *D I* **take any pleasure in** the death of AIT
20: 7 *d* not **defile yourselves** AIT
20:18 "*D* not **follow** the statutes of your fathers AIT
21:24 revealing your sins in all *that* you **d—** 6613
22:14 I the LORD have spoken, and *I will* **d** it. 6913
22:26 Her priests **d violence** *to* my law 2803
22:26 *they d* not **distinguish** between the holy and AIT
24:16 *d* not **lament** or weep or shed any tears. AIT
24:17 Groan quietly; **d** not mourn for the dead. 6913
24:17 *d* not **cover** the lower part of your face AIT
24:19 "Won't you tell us what these things **have to d with** us?" 4200
24:22 And *you will* **d** as I have done. 6913
24:24 *you will* **d** just as he has done. 6913
32:27 *D they* not **lie** with AIT
33: 8 and *you d* not **speak out** to dissuade him AIT
33: 9 But if you *d* **warn** the wicked man to turn AIT
33: 9 to turn from his ways and *he does* not **d so,** 2006+4946+8740S
33:26 *you* **d** detestable things, 6913
33:31 My people come to you, as they usually **d,** 4427S
33:31 *d* not **put** them **into practice.** AIT
33:32 *d* not **put** them **into practice.** AIT
34: 3 *d* not **take care of** the flock. AIT
36:22 that I *am going to* **d** these things, 6913
36:36 and *I will* **d** it.' 6913
36:37 to the plea of the house of Israel and **d** this 6913
44:19 so that *they d* not **consecrate** the people AIT
45: 9 and oppression and **d** what is just and right. 6913
45:20 *You are to* **d** the same on the seventh day 6913
47: 6 He asked me, "Son of man, *d you* **see** this?" AIT
Da 2: 5 If *you d* not **tell** me what my dream was AIT
2: 9 If *you d* not **tell** me the dream, AIT
2:10 on earth who can **d** what the king asks! 10252S
2:11 and they **d** not live among men." 10029
2:24 "*D* not **execute** the wise men of Babylon. AIT
3: 4 "This is what you are commanded to **d,** NIH
3:14 that you *d* not **serve** my gods or worship AIT
3:15 But if *you d* not **worship** it, AIT
3:16 we *d* not **need** to defend ourselves AIT
4:19 *d* not *let* the dream or its meaning **alarm** AIT
6: 4 they were unable to **d so.** 10353+10544+10708S
6: 5 unless it has **something to d with** the law 10089
9:18 We *d* not **make** requests of you AIT
9:19 For your sake, O my God, *d* not **delay,** AIT
10:12 he continued, "*D* not *be* **afraid,** Daniel. AIT
10:19 "*D* not *be* **afraid,** O man highly esteemed," AIT
10:20 "*D you* **know** why I have come to you? AIT
11: 3 with great power and **d** as he pleases. 6913
11:16 The invader *will* **d** as he pleases; 6913
11:36 "The king *will* **d** as he pleases. 6913
Hos 4:15 "*D* not **go** *to* Gilgal; AIT
4:15 *d* not **go up** *to* Beth Aven. AIT
4:15 And *d* not **swear,** AIT
5: 4 "Their deeds *d* not **permit** them to return AIT
5: 4 *they d* not **acknowledge** the LORD. AIT
6: 4 "What *can I* **d** with you, Ephraim? 6913
6: 4 What *can I* **d** with you, Judah? 6913
6: 9 so **d** bands of priests; NIH
7: 2 but they *d* not **realize** AIT
7:14 *They d* not **cry out** to me from their hearts AIT
7:16 *They d* not **turn** *to* the Most High; AIT
9: 1 *D* not **rejoice,** O Israel; AIT
9: 1 *d* not *be* **jubilant** like the other nations. AIT
9: 5 What *will you* **d** on the day 6913
10: 3 if we had a king, what *could he* **d** for us?" 6913
12:11 *D they* **sacrifice** bulls in Gilgal? AIT
14: 8 **have I to d with** with idols? 4200
Joel 2: 8 *They d* not **jostle** each other; AIT

Joel 2:17 *D* not **make** your inheritance an object AIT
Am 3: 3 *D* two **walk** together unless they have AIT
3: 3 unless they have agreed to **d** so? NIH
3: 6 *d* not the people **tremble?** AIT
3:10 *"They d* not **know how** to do right," AIT
3:10 "They do not know how *to* **d** right," 6913
4: 5 for this is what you love to **d,"** NIH
4:12 "Therefore this is what *I will* **d** to you, 6913
4:12 Israel, and because *I will* **d** this to you, 6913
5: 5 *d* not **seek** Bethel, AIT
5: 5 *d* not **go** *to* Gilgal, AIT
5: 5 *d* not **journey** *to* Beersheba. AIT
5:18 Why *d* you **long for** the day of AIT
6: 6 *you d* not **grieve** over the ruin of Joseph. AIT
6:12 *D* horses **run** on the rocky crags? AIT
7: 8 And the LORD asked me, "What *d* you **see,** AIT
7:12 and *d your* **prophesying** there. AIT
7:16 You say, " *'D* not **prophesy** against Israel, AIT
8: 2 "What *d* you **see,** Amos?" AIT
8: 4 you who trample the needy and **d away with** the poor of the land, 8697
9:12 *who will* **d** these things. 6913
Jnh 1: 8 What **d** you do? NIH
1: 8 What do you **d?** 4856
1: 8 Where *d you* **come** from? AIT
1:11 "What *should we* **d** to you to make 6913
1:14 *d* not *let us* **die** AIT
1:14 *D* not **hold** us **accountable** AIT
3: 7 *D* not *let* any man or beast, herd or flock, **taste** anything; AIT
3: 7 *d* not *let them* **eat** or drink. AIT
4: 9 *"D* you **have a right** AIT
4: 9 "I **d,"** he said. 3512S
Mic 2: 1 because it is in their power to **d** it. NIH
2: 6 *"D* not **prophesy,"** their prophets say. AIT
2: 6 *"D* not **prophesy** about these things; AIT
2: 7 Does he **d** such things?" 5095
2: 7 *"D* not my words **do good** AIT
2: 7 *"Do* not my words **d good** 3512
4: 9 *d you* now **cry aloud—** AIT
4:12 they *d* not **know** the thoughts of the LORD; AIT
4:12 *they d* not **understand** his plan, AIT
5: 7 which *d* not **wait** for man or linger AIT
7: 5 *D* not **trust** a neighbor; AIT
7: 8 *D* not **gloat** over me, my enemy! AIT
7:18 *You d* not **stay** angry forever but delight AIT
Hab 1: 2 must I call for help, but *you d* not **listen?** AIT
1: 2 but *you d* not **save?** AIT
1: 3 *d you* **make** me **look** AIT
1: 3 Why *d you* **tolerate** wrong? AIT
1: 5 For *I am going to* **d** something in your days 7188
1:13 Why then *d you* **tolerate** the treacherous? AIT
Zep 1:12 'The LORD *will d* nothing, either **good** AIT
2: 3 *you who* **d** what he commands. 7188
3: 4 the sanctuary and **d violence** *to* the law. 2803
3:13 The remnant of Israel *will* **d** no wrong; 6913
3:16 *"D* not **fear,** O Zion; AIT
3:16 *d* not *let* your hands **hang limp.** AIT
Hag 2: 5 *D* not **fear.'** AIT
2:14 'Whatever they **d** and whatever they offer there is defiled. 3338+5126
Zec 1: 4 *D* not **be** like your forefathers, AIT
1: 5 And the prophets, *d they* **live** forever? AIT
1: 6 just as he determined to **d.' "** 6913
1:21 I asked, "What are these coming to **d?"** 6913
4: 2 He asked me, "What *d you* **see?"** AIT
4: 5 *"D you* not **know** what these are?" AIT
4:13 *"D you* not **know** what these are?" AIT
5: 2 He asked me, "What *d* you **see?"** AIT
7:10 *D* not **oppress** the widow or the fatherless, AIT
7:10 In your hearts *d* not **think** evil of each other.' AIT
8:13 *D* not *be* **afraid,** AIT
8:15 "so now I have determined to **d good** again 3512
8:15 *D* not *be* **afraid.** AIT
8:16 These are the things *you are to* **d:** 6913
8:17 *d* not **plot** evil **against** AIT
8:17 and *d* not **love** to swear falsely. AIT
11: 5 Their own shepherds *d* not **spare** them. AIT
14:17 of the peoples of the earth *d* not **go up** AIT
14:18 If the Egyptian people *d* not **go up** AIT
14:18 on the nations that *d* not **go up** to celebrate AIT
14:19 the nations that *d* not **go up** to celebrate AIT
Mal 2: 2 If *you d* not **listen,** AIT
2: 2 and if *you d* not **set** your heart AIT
2:10 Why *d we* **profane** the covenant AIT
2:13 Another thing *you* **d:** 6913
2:15 and *d* not **break faith** with the wife AIT
2:16 and *d* not **break faith.** AIT
2:17 "All *who* **d** evil are good in the eyes of 6913
3: 5 but *d* not **fear** me," AIT
3: 6 "I the LORD *d* not **change.** AIT
3: 8 "But you ask, 'How *d we* **rob** you?' AIT
3:18 and *those* who **d** not. 6268S
4: 3 on the day when I **d** these things," 6913
Mt 1:20 *d* not **be afraid** to take Mary home AIT
3: 9 And *d* not **think** you can say to yourselves, AIT
3:14 and *d* you **come** to me?" AIT
3:15 for us to **d** this to fulfill all righteousness." NIG
4: 7 *'D* not **put** the Lord your God **to the test.' "** AIT
5:15 Neither *d people* **light** a lamp and put it AIT
5:17 *"D* not **think** that I have come to abolish AIT
5:19 and teaches others to **d** the same will NIG
5:21 to the people long ago, *'D* not **murder,** AIT
5:25 **D** it while you are still with him on NIG
5:27 *'D* not **commit adultery.'** AIT
5:33 *'D* not **break** *your* **oath,** AIT
5:34 But I tell you, *D* not **swear** at all: AIT
Mt 5:36 And *d* not **swear** by your head, AIT
5:39 But I tell you, *D* not **resist** an evil person. AIT
5:42 *d* not **turn away from** the one who wants AIT
5:47 *D* not even pagans **do** that? AIT
5:47 *Do* not even pagans **d** that? 4472
6: 1 not *to* **d** your 'acts of righteousness' 4472
6: 1 If you **d,** you will have no reward 1145+3590S
6: 2 *d* not **announce** it **with trumpets,** AIT
6: 2 the hypocrites **d** in the synagogues and on 4472
6: 3 *d* not *let* your left hand **know** AIT
6: 5 when you pray, *d* not **be** like the hypocrites, AIT
6: 7 *d* not *keep on* **babbling** AIT
6: 8 *D* not *be* **like** them, AIT
6:15 But if *you d* not **forgive** men their sins, AIT
6:16 *d* not **look somber** as the hypocrites do, AIT
6:16 do not look somber as the hypocrites **d,** NIG
6:19 *"D* not **store up** for yourselves treasures AIT
6:20 where moth and rust *d* not **destroy,** AIT
6:20 and where thieves *d* not **break in** and steal. AIT
6:25 I tell you, *d* not **worry about** your life, AIT
6:26 they *d* not **sow** or reap or store away AIT
6:28 "And why *d you* **worry** about clothes? AIT
6:28 *They d* not **labor** or spin. AIT
6:31 *d* not **worry,** saying, 'What shall we eat?' AIT
6:34 Therefore *d* not **worry** about tomorrow, AIT
7: 1 *"D* not **judge,** or you too will be judged. AIT
7: 3 "Why *d you* **look at** the speck of sawdust AIT
7: 6 *"D* not **give** dogs what is sacred; AIT
7: 6 *d* not **throw** your pearls to pigs. AIT
7: 6 **If you d,** they may trample them 3607
7:12 **d** to others what you would have them do 4472
7:12 do to others what you would have *them* **d** 4472
7:16 *D people* **pick** grapes from thornbushes, AIT
8: 8 *I d* not **deserve** to have you come AIT
8: 9 I say to my servant, **'D** this,' 4472
8:29 **"What d** you **want with** us, 2779+5515
9: 4 *d you* **entertain** evil **thoughts** AIT
9:14 but your disciples *d* not **fast?"** AIT
9:17 Neither *d men* **pour** new wine AIT
9:17 If they **d,** the skins will burst, 1145+3590S
9:28 *"D you* **believe** that I am able to do this?" AIT
9:28 "Do you believe that I am able *to* **d** this?" 4472
10: 5 *"D* not **go** among the Gentiles AIT
10: 9 *D* not **take along** any gold or silver AIT
10:19 *d* not **worry about** what to say or how AIT
10:26 *d* not *be* **afraid of** them. AIT
10:28 *D* not *be* **afraid** of those who kill the body AIT
10:34 *"D* not **suppose** that I have come AIT
12: 4 which was not lawful for them *to* **d,** 2266S
12:12 it is lawful *to* **d** good on the Sabbath." 4472
12:27 *d* your people **drive** them **out?** AIT
13:10 "Why *d you* **speak** to the people AIT
13:13 "Though seeing, *they d* not **see;** AIT
13:13 *d* not **hear** or **understand.** AIT
13:28 *'D you* **want** us to go and pull them up?' AIT
13:41 that causes sin and all who **d** evil. 4472
13:58 And *he did* not **d** many miracles there 4472
14:16 Jesus replied, *"They d* not **need** to go away. AIT
15: 2 "Why *d* your disciples **break** the tradition AIT
15: 3 "And why *d* you **break** the command of God AIT
15:12 *"D you* **know** that the Pharisees AIT
15:32 *I d* not **want** to send them away hungry, AIT
15:34 "How many loaves *d you* **have?"** AIT
16: 9 *D* you still not **understand?** AIT
16:13 "Who *d* people **say** the Son of Man is?" AIT
16:15 "Who *d you* **say** I am?" AIT
16:23 *d* not **have in mind** the things of God, AIT
17:10 "Why then *d* the teachers of the law **say** AIT
17:25 "What *d* you **think,** Simon?" AIT
17:25 *d* the kings of the earth **collect** duty AIT
18:10 *d* not **look down on** one of these little ones. AIT
18:12 "What *d* you **think?** AIT
19:14 and *d* not **hinder** them, AIT
19:16 what good thing *must I* **d** 4472
19:17 "Why *d you* **ask** me about what is good?" AIT
19:18 Jesus replied, " *'D* not **murder,** AIT
19:18 *d* not **commit adultery,** AIT
19:18 *d* not **steal,** do not give false testimony, AIT
19:18 *d* not **give false testimony,** AIT
19:20 "What *d I* still **lack?"** AIT
20:15 *to* **d** what I want with my own money? 4472
20:32 "What *d you* **want** me to do for you?" AIT
20:32 "What do you want *me to* **d** for you?" 4472
21:16 *D you* **hear** what these children are saying?" AIT
21:21 if you have faith and *d* not **doubt,** AIT
21:21 not only *can you* **d** what was done to 4472
21:28 "What *d* you **think?** AIT
21:40 what *will he* **d** to those tenants?" 4472
22:29 "You are in error *because you d* not **know** AIT
22:42 "What *d* you **think** about the Christ? AIT
23: 3 and **d** everything they tell you. 4472
23: 3 But *d* not **do** what they do, AIT
23: 3 But *do* not **d** what they do, 4472
23: 3 But do not do what they **d,** 2240
23: 3 for *they d* not **practice** what they preach. AIT
23: 5 "Everything they **d** is done for men to see: 2240
23: 9 And *d* not **call** anyone on earth 'father,' AIT
23:13 You yourselves *d* not **enter,** AIT
24: 2 *"D you* **see** all these things?" AIT
24:23 *d* not **believe** it. AIT
24:26 out in the desert,' *d* not **go out;** AIT
24:26 in the inner rooms,' *d* not **believe** it. AIT
24:42 because *you d* not **know** AIT
24:44 at an hour when *you d* not **expect** him. AIT
25:13 because *you d* not **know** the day or the hour. AIT
25:45 whatever *you did* not **d** for one of the least 4472
25:45 *you did* not **d** for me.' 4472
Mt 26:17 "Where *d you* **want** us AIT
26:50 *d* what *you* **came for."** AIT
26:53 *D you* **think** I cannot call on my Father, AIT
26:65 Why *d we* **need** any more witnesses? AIT
26:66 What *d* you **think?"** AIT
27:17 "Which one *d you* **want** me to release AIT
27:19 "Don't have anything to **d** with NIG
27:21 the two *d you* **want** me to release to you?" AIT
27:22 "What *shall I* **d,** then, **with** 4472
28: 5 *"D* not *be* **afraid,** AIT
28:10 Then Jesus said to them, *"D* not *be* **afraid.** AIT
Mk 1:24 **"What d** you **want with** 2779+5515
3: 4 *to* **d** good or to do evil, 4472
3: 4 to do good or *to* **d evil,** 2803
4:21 *D you* **bring** in a lamp to put it under a bowl AIT
4:40 *D you* still **have** no faith?" AIT
5: 7 **"What d** you **want with** 2779+5515
6: 5 He could not **d** any miracles there, 4472
6:38 "How many loaves *d you* **have?"** AIT
7: 3 (The Pharisees and all the Jews *d* not **eat** AIT
7: 4 from the marketplace *they d* not **eat** AIT
7:12 then you no longer let him **d** anything 4472
7:13 And *you* **d** many things like that." 4472
8: 5 "How many loaves *d you* **have?"** AIT
8:17 *D you* still not **see** AIT
8:18 *D you* have eyes but fail to **see,** AIT
8:21 *"D you* still not **understand?"** AIT
8:23 Jesus asked, *"D you* **see** anything?" AIT
8:27 "Who *d* people **say** I am?" AIT
8:29 "Who *d* you **say** I am?" AIT
8:33 *d* not **have in mind** AIT
9:11 *d* the teachers of the law **say** AIT
9:22 But if *you* **can d** anything, 1538
9:24 the boy's father exclaimed, *"I d* **believe;** AIT
9:39 *"D* not **stop** him," Jesus said. AIT
10:14 and *d* not **hinder** them, AIT
10:17 "what *must I* **d** to inherit eternal life?" 4472
10:18 "Why *d you* **call** me good?" AIT
10:19 *'D* not **murder,** do not commit adultery, AIT
10:19 *d* not **commit adultery,** AIT
10:19 *d* not **steal,** do not give false testimony, AIT
10:19 *d* not **give false testimony,** AIT
10:19 do not give false testimony, *d* not **defraud,** AIT
10:35 *to* **d** for us whatever we ask." 4472
10:36 "What *d you* **want** me to do for you?" AIT
10:36 "What do you want *me to* **d** for you?" 4472
10:51 "What *d you* **want** me to do for you?" AIT
10:51 "What do you want *me to* **d** for you?" 4472
11:28 "And who gave you authority to **d** this?" 4472
12: 9 then *will* the owner of the vineyard **d?** 4472
12:24 because *you d* not **know** the Scriptures or AIT
13: 2 *"D you* **see** all these great buildings?" AIT
13: 7 *d* not *be* **alarmed.** AIT
13:11 *d* not **worry beforehand about** AIT
13:21 *d* not **believe** it. AIT
13:33 *You d* not **know** when that time will come. AIT
13:35 because *you d* not **know** when the owner of AIT
13:36 **d** not let him find you sleeping. NIG
14:12 "Where *d you* **want** us to go AIT
14:63 "Why *d we* **need** any more witnesses?" AIT
14:64 What *d* you **think?"** AIT
15: 8 The crowd came up and asked Pilate *to* **d** 4472
15: 9 *"D you* **want** me to release to you the king AIT
15:12 "What *shall I* **d,** then, **with** 4472
Lk 1:13 *"D* not **be afraid,** Zechariah; AIT
1:30 But the angel said to her, *"D* not *be* **afraid,** AIT
2:10 But the angel said to them, *"D* not *be* **afraid.** AIT
2:27 the parents brought in the child Jesus *to* **d** 4472
3: 8 And *d* not **begin** to say to yourselves, AIT
3:10 "What *should we* **d** then?" the crowd asked. 4472
3:11 the one who has food *should* **d** the same." 4472
3:12 they asked, "what *should we* **d?"** 4472
3:14 "And what *should* we **d?"** 4472
4:12 *'D* not **put** the Lord your God **to the test.' "** AIT
4:23 **D** here in your hometown what we have heard that you did in Capernaum.' " 4472
4:34 **What d** you **want with** 2779+5515
5:19 When they could not find a way *to* **d this** 1662S
5:30 "Why *d you* **eat** and drink AIT
5:33 and **so d** the disciples of the Pharisees, 3931
6: 9 *to* **d good** or to do evil, 16
6: 9 to do good or *to* **d evil,** 2803
6:11 with one another what *they* might **d** 4472
6:27 **d** good to those who hate you, 4472
6:29 *d* not **stop** him **from taking** AIT
6:30 *d* not **demand** it **back.** AIT
6:31 **D** to others as you would have them do 4472
6:31 to others as you would **have** them **d** to you. 4472
6:33 And if *you* **d good** to those who are good 16
6:33 Even 'sinners' **d** that. 4472
6:35 But love your enemies, **d good** to them, 16
6:37 *"D* not **judge,** and you will not be judged. AIT
6:37 *D* not **condemn,** and you will not AIT
6:41 "Why *d you* **look at** the speck of sawdust AIT
6:44 *People d* not **pick** figs from thornbushes, AIT
6:46 "Why *d you* **call** me, 'Lord, Lord,' AIT
6:46 'Lord, Lord,' and *d* not **do** what I say? AIT
6:46 'Lord, Lord,' and *do* not **d** what I say? 4472
7: 4 "This man deserves *to have you* **d** this, 4218
7: 6 for *I d* not **deserve** to have you come AIT
7: 8 I say to my servant, **'D** this,' 4472
7:44 *"D you* **see** this woman? AIT
8:14 riches and pleasures, and *they d* not **mature.** AIT
8:28 **"What d** you **want with** 2779+5515
9: 5 If people *d* not **welcome** you, AIT
9:18 "Who *d* the crowds **say** I am?" AIT

Lk 9:20 "Who *d you* say I am?" *AIT*
9:50 "*D* not **stop** him," Jesus said, *AIT*
9:54 *d you* **want** us to call fire down *AIT*
10: 4 *D* not **take** a purse or bag or sandals; *AIT*
10: 4 and *d* not **greet** anyone on the road. *AIT*
10: 7 *D* not **move around** from house to house. *AIT*
10:20 *d* not **rejoice** that the spirits submit to you, *AIT*
10:25 "what *must I* **d** to inherit eternal life?" *4472*
10:26 "How *d you* **read** it?" *AIT*
10:28 **"D** this and you will live." *4472*
10:36 of these three *d you* **think** was a neighbor to *AIT*
10:37 Jesus told him, "Go and **d** likewise." *4472*
10:40 that my sister has left me *to* **d the work** *1354*
11:19 *d* your followers **drive** them **out?** *AIT*
12: 4 *d* not *be* **afraid** of those who kill the body *AIT*
12: 4 the body and after that can **d** no more. *4472*
12:11 *d* not **worry about** how you will defend *AIT*
12:17 He thought to himself, 'What *shall I* **d?** *4472*
12:18 "Then he said, 'This is what *I'll* **d.** *4472*
12:22 *d* not **worry about** your life, *AIT*
12:24 Consider the ravens: *They d* not **sow** or reap, *AIT*
12:26 *you* **cannot d** this very little thing, *1538+4028*
12:26 why *d you* **worry** about the rest? *AIT*
12:27 *They d* not **labor** or spin. *AIT*
12:29 *d* not **set** *your* **heart on** what you will eat *AIT*
12:29 *d* not **worry about** it. *AIT*
12:32 "*D* not **be afraid,** little flock, *AIT*
12:40 at an hour when *you d* not **expect** him." *AIT*
12:47 not **d** what his master wants will be beaten *4472*
12:51 *D you* **think** I came to bring peace on earth? *AIT*
13: 2 Jesus answered, "*D you* **think** *AIT*
13: 4 *d you* **think** they were more guilty than all *AIT*
14: 8 *d* not **take** the place of honor, *AIT*
14:12 *d* not **invite** your friends, *AIT*
14:12 **if you d,** they may invite you back and *3607*
15: 7 over ninety-nine righteous persons who *d*
not **need** to repent. *AIT*
16: 3 'What *shall I* **d** now? *4472*
16: 4 I know what *I'll* **d** so that, *4472*
16: 5 'How much *d you* **owe** my master?' *AIT*
16: 7 'And how much *d you* **owe?'** *AIT*
16:31 'If *they d* not **listen** *to* Moses and *AIT*
17: 9 because he did what *he was* **told to d?** *1411*
17:10 you have done everything you *were*
told to d, *1411*
17:23 *D* not **go running off after** them. *AIT*
18:16 and *d* not **hinder** them, *AIT*
18:18 what *must I* **d** to inherit eternal life?" *4472*
18:19 "Why *d you* **call** me good?" *AIT*
18:20 '*D* not **commit adultery,** *AIT*
18:20 'Do not commit adultery, *d* not **murder,** *AIT*
18:20 *d* not **steal,** do not give false testimony, *AIT*
18:20 *d* not **give false testimony,** *AIT*
18:41 "What *d you* **want** me to do for you?" *AIT*
18:41 "What do you want *me to* **d** for you?" *4472*
19:48 Yet they could not find any way *to* **d** it, *4472*
20:13 'What *shall I* **d?** *4472*
20:15 then *will* the owner of the vineyard **d** *4472*
20:21 that *you d* not **show partiality** but teach *AIT*
21: 8 *D* not **follow** them. *AIT*
21: 9 *d* not *be* **frightened.** *AIT*
22: 9 "Where *d you* **want** us to prepare for it?" *AIT*
22:19 **d** this in remembrance of me." *4472*
22:23 of them it might be who would **d** this. *4556*
22:71 "Why *d we* **need** any more testimony? *AIT*
23:28 Daughters of Jerusalem, *d* not **weep** for me; *AIT*
23:31 if *men* **d** these things when the tree is green, *4472*
23:34 for *they d* not **know** what they are doing." *AIT*
24: 5 "Why *d you* **look for** the living among *AIT*
24:18 to Jerusalem and *d* not **know** the things *AIT*
24:38 and why *d* doubts **rise** in your minds? *AIT*
24:41 "*D you* **have** anything here to eat?" *AIT*
Jn 1:22 What *d you* **say** about yourself?" *AIT*
1:25 "Why then *d you* **baptize** if you are not *AIT*
1:26 "but among you stands one you *d* not **know.** *AIT*
1:38 "What *d you* **want?"** *AIT*
1:48 "How *d you* **know** me?" *AIT*
2: 4 Dear woman, **why d** you **involve** me? *2779+5515*
2: 5 **"D** whatever he tells you." *4472*
2:18 to prove your authority *to* **d** all this?" *4472*
3:10 "and *d you* not **understand** these things? *AIT*
3:11 still *you people d* not **accept** our testimony. *AIT*
3:12 of earthly things and *you d* not **believe;** *AIT*
4: 9 (For Jews *d* not **associate with** Samaritans.) *AIT*
4:22 Samaritans worship what *you d* not **know;** *AIT*
4:22 we worship what *we d* **know,** *AIT*
4:27 But no one asked, "What *d you* **want?"** *AIT*
4:34 "is to **d** the will of him who sent me and *4472*
4:35 *D* you not **say,** 'Four months more *AIT*
5: 6 he asked him, "*D you* **want** to get well?" *AIT*
5:19 the Son can **d** nothing by himself; *4472*
5:19 he can **d** only what he sees his Father doing, *NIG*
5:28 "*D* not *be* **amazed at** this, *AIT*
5:30 By myself I can **d** nothing; *4472*
5:38 for you *d* not **believe** the one he sent. *AIT*
5:41 "*I d* not **accept** praise from men, *AIT*
5:42 I know that *you d* not **have** the love of God *AIT*
5:43 and *you d* not **accept** me; *AIT*
5:45 "But *d* not **think** I will accuse you before *AIT*
5:47 But since *you d* not **believe** what he wrote, *AIT*
6: 6 in mind what he was going to **d.** *4472*
6:27 *D* not **work for** food that spoils, but **for** *AIT*
6:28 "What *must we* **d** to do *4472*
6:28 to **d** the works God requires?" *2237*
6:30 What *will you* **d?** *2237*
6:36 and still *you d* not **believe.** *AIT*
6:38 down from heaven not to **d** my will but *4472*
Jn 6:38 from heaven not to do my will but to **d** *NIG*
6:64 there are some of you who *d* not **believe."** *AIT*
6:67 "You *d* not **want** to leave too, do you?" *AIT*
6:67 "You do not want to leave too, **d** you?" *NIG*
7: 3 disciples may see the miracles *you* **d.** *4472*
7:17 If anyone chooses *to* **d** God's will, *4472*
7:28 You *d* not **know** him, *AIT*
7:31 *will he* **d** more miraculous signs than this
man?" *4472*
8: 5 Now what *d* you **say?"** *AIT*
8:11 neither *d* I **condemn** you," Jesus declared. *AIT*
8:16 But if I *d* **judge,** my decisions are right, *AIT*
8:19 "*You d* not **know** me or my Father," *AIT*
8:24 if *you d* not **believe** that I am *AIT*
8:28 and that *I* **d** nothing on my own *4472*
8:29 for I always **d** what pleases him." *4472*
8:38 and you **d** what you have heard *4472*
8:39 "then *you would* **d** the things Abraham did. *4472*
8:40 Abraham *did* not **d** such things. *4472*
8:45 I tell the truth, *you d* not **believe** me! *AIT*
8:47 The reason you *d* not **hear** is that you do *AIT*
8:47 not hear is that *you d* not **belong** *to* God." *AIT*
8:53 **Who d you think you are?"** *4472+4932+5515*
8:55 Though *you d* not **know** him, I know him. *AIT*
8:55 but *I d* **know** him and keep his word. *AIT*
9: 4 we must **d** the work of him who sent me. *2237*
9:16 can a sinner **d** such miraculous signs?" *4472*
9:25 One thing *I d* **know.** *AIT*
9:26 they asked him, "What *did he* **d** to you? *4472*
9:27 Why *d you* **want** to hear it again? *AIT*
9:27 *D* you **want** to become his disciples, too?" *AIT*
9:33 he could **d** nothing." *4472*
9:35 "*D* you **believe** in the Son of Man?" *AIT*
10: 5 from him because *they d* not **recognize** *AIT*
10:25 "I did tell you, but *you d* not **believe.** *AIT*
10:25 The miracles I **d** in my Father's name speak *4472*
10:26 but you *d* not **believe** because you are *AIT*
10:32 For which of these *d you* **stone** me?" *AIT*
10:36 Why then *d you* **accuse** me of blasphemy *AIT*
10:37 *D* not **believe** me *AIT*
10:37 unless *I* **d** what my Father does. *4472*
10:38 But if *I* **d** it, even though you do not believe *4472*
10:38 I do it, even though *you d* not **believe** me, *AIT*
11:26 *D you* **believe** this?" *AIT*
11:50 *You d* not **realize** that it is better for you *AIT*
11:56 "What *d* you **think?** *AIT*
12:15 "*D* not *be* **afraid,** O Daughter of Zion; *AIT*
12:47 I *d* not **judge** him. *AIT*
13: 7 "You *d* not **realize** now what I am doing, *AIT*
13:12 "*D you* **understand** what I have done *AIT*
13:15 that you *should* **d** as I have done for you. *4472*
13:17 you will be blessed if *you* **d** them. *4472*
13:27 "What *you are about to* **d,** do quickly," *4472*
13:27 "What you are about to do, **d** quickly," *4472*
14: 1 "*D* not *let* your hearts *be* **troubled.** *AIT*
14: 7 *you d* **know** him and have seen him." *AIT*
14:12 in me *will* **d** what I have been doing. *4472*
14:12 *He will* **d** even greater things than these, *4472*
14:13 *I will* **d** whatever you ask in my name, *4472*
14:14 and I *will* **d** it. *4472*
14:22 why *d you* **intend** to show yourself to us *AIT*
14:27 I *d* not **give** to you as the world gives. *AIT*
14:27 *D* not *let* your hearts *be* **troubled** *AIT*
14:27 be troubled and *d* not *be* **afraid.** *AIT*
14:31 *I* **d** exactly what my Father has commanded
me. *4472*
15: 5 apart from me you can **d** nothing. *4472*
15:14 if *you* **d** what I command. *4472*
15:19 As it is, *you d* not **belong to** the world, *AIT*
15:21 for *they d* not **know** the One who sent me. *AIT*
16: 3 *They will* **d** such things because they have *4472*
16: 9 because *men d* not **believe** in me; *AIT*
16:30 and that *you d* not even **need** *AIT*
17: 4 by completing the work you gave me to **d.** *4472*
18:39 *D you* **want** me to release 'the king of *AIT*
19: 9 "Where *d* you **come** from?" *AIT*
19:10 "*D you* refuse to **speak** *AIT*
19:21 "*D* not **write** 'The King of the Jews,' *AIT*
20:17 "*D* not **hold on to** me, *AIT*
20:23 if you *d* **not forgive** them, *AIT*
21:15 *d you* **truly love** me more than these?" *AIT*
21:16 "Simon son of John, *d you* **truly love** me?" *AIT*
21:17 "Simon son of John, *d you* **love** me?" *AIT*
21:17 "*D you* **love** me?" *AIT*
21:18 and lead you where *you d* not **want** to go." *AIT*
Ac 1: 1 about all that Jesus began *to* **d** and to teach *4472*
1: 4 "*D* not **leave** Jerusalem, *AIT*
1:11 "why *d you* **stand** here looking into *AIT*
2:37 "Brothers, what *shall we* **d?"** *4472*
3: 6 Peter said, "Silver or gold I *d* not **have,** *AIT*
3:12 Why *d you* **stare at** us as if *AIT*
4: 7 or what name *did* you **d** this?" *4472*
4:16 "What *are we going to* **d with** these men?" *4472*
4:25 " 'Why *d* the nations **rage** and *AIT*
5:35 consider carefully what you intend *to* **d** *4556*
7:26 why *d you* want to **hurt** each other?' *AIT*
7:28 *D* you **want** to kill me as you killed *AIT*
7:60 "Lord, *d* not **hold** this sin against them." *AIT*
8:30 "*D you* **understand** what you are reading?" *AIT*
9: 4 "Saul, Saul, why *d you* **persecute** me?" *AIT*
9: 6 and you will be told what you must **d."** *4472*
10:15 "*D* not **call** anything **impure** *AIT*
10:20 *D* not **hesitate** to go with them, *AIT*
10:35 and **d** what is right. *2237*
11: 9 '*D* not **call** anything **impure** *AIT*
13:22 he *will* **d** everything I want him to do.' *4472*
13:22 he will do everything I want him to **d.'** *NIG*
Ac 13:25 'Who *d you* **think** I am? *AIT*
13:41 for I *am going to* **d** something in your days *2237*
13:46 and *d* not **consider** yourselves worthy *AIT*
14: 3 by enabling them *to* **d** miraculous signs *1181*
15:10 *d you try to* **test** God *AIT*
15:29 You *will* **d** well to avoid these things. *4556*
16:30 "Sirs, what must I **d** to be saved?" *4472*
16:37 *d they want to* **get rid of** us quietly? *AIT*
18: 9 "*D* not be **afraid;** *AIT*
18: 9 keep on speaking, *d* not *be* **silent.** *AIT*
19:36 to be quiet and not **d** anything rash. *4556*
21:22 **What shall we d?** *1639+4036+5515*
21:23 so **d** what we tell you. *4472*
21:37 "*D you* **speak** Greek?" *AIT*
22: 7 Why *d you* **persecute** me?' *AIT*
22:10 " 'What *shall I* **d,** Lord?' *4472*
22:10 that you have been assigned *to* **d.'** *4472*
22:26 "What are you going to **d?"** *4472*
23: 5 '*D* not **speak** evil **about** the ruler *AIT*
23:29 that the accusation had **to d with** questions *4309*
25: 9 Festus, wishing *to* **d** the Jews a favor, *2960*
25:11 *I d* not **refuse** to die. *AIT*
26: 9 "I too was convinced that I ought *to* **d** all *4556*
26:14 'Saul, Saul, why *d you* **persecute** me? *AIT*
26:27 King Agrippa, *d you* **believe** the prophets? *AIT*
26:27 I know *you* **d."** *4409S*
26:28 **"D** you think that in such a short time *NIG*
27:24 '*D* not **be afraid,** Paul. *AIT*
Ro 1:13 *I d* not **want** you to be unaware, brothers, *AIT*
1:28 *to* **d** what ought not to be done. *4472*
1:32 that those who **d** such things deserve death, *4556*
1:32 not only *continue to* **d** these very things *4472*
2: 1 you who pass judgment **d** the same things. *4556*
2: 2 against those who **d** such things is based *4556*
2: 3 on them and yet **d** the same things, *4472*
2: 3 *d you* **think** you will escape God's
judgment? *AIT*
2: 4 *d you* **show contempt for** *AIT*
2:14 when Gentiles, who *d* not **have** the law, *AIT*
2:14 **d** by nature things required by the law, *4472*
2:14 *even though they d* not **have** the law, *AIT*
2:21 who teach others, *d you* not **teach** yourself? *AIT*
2:21 against stealing, *d you* **steal?** *AIT*
2:22 *d you* **commit adultery?** *AIT*
2:22 You who abhor idols, *d you* **rob temples?** *AIT*
2:23 *d* you **dishonor** God by breaking the law? *AIT*
3: 8 "*Let us* **d** evil that good may result"? *4472*
3:17 and the way of peace *they d* not **know.** *AIT*
3:31 *D we*, then, **nullify** the law by this faith? *AIT*
4:21 *to* **d** what he had promised. *4472*
6:12 *d* not *let* sin **reign** in your mortal body *AIT*
6:13 *D* not **offer** the parts of your body to sin, *AIT*
7: 1 *D you* **not know,** brothers— *AIT*
7: 7 if the law had not said, "*D* not **covet."** *AIT*
7:15 *I d* not **understand** what I do. *AIT*
7:15 I do not understand what *I* **d.** *2981*
7:15 For what I want to **d** I do not do, *NIG*
7:15 For what I want to do *I d* not **do,** *AIT*
7:15 For what I want to do *I do not* **d,** *4556*
7:15 but what I hate *I* **d.** *4472*
7:16 And if *I* **d** what I do not want to do, *4472*
7:16 And if I do what *I d* not **want** to do, *AIT*
7:16 And if I do what I do not want to **d,** *NIG*
7:17 As it is, it is no longer I myself who **d** it, *2981*
7:18 For I have the desire to **d** what is good, *NIG*
7:19 For what *I* **d** is not the good I want to do; *4472*
7:19 For what I do is not the good I want to **d;** *NIG*
7:19 no, the evil *I d* not **want** to do— *AIT*
7:19 no, the evil I do not want to **d—** *NIG*
7:20 Now if I **d** what I do not want to do, *4472*
7:20 Now if I do what *I d* not **want** to do, *AIT*
7:20 Now if I do what I do not want to **d,** *NIG*
7:20 it is no longer I who **d** it, *2981*
7:21 When I want to **d** good, *4472*
8: 3 For what the law was powerless to **d** in *NIG*
8: 4 who *d* not **live** according to *AIT*
8: 7 nor can it **d** so. *NIG*
8:25 But if we hope for what *we d* not yet **have,** *AIT*
8:26 *We d* not **know** what we ought to pray for, *AIT*
10: 6 "*D* not **say** in your heart, *AIT*
11:18 *d* not **boast over** those branches. *AIT*
11:18 If you **d,** consider this: *NIG*
11:18 You *d* not **support** the root, *AIT*
11:20 *D* not *be* **arrogant,** but be afraid. *AIT*
11:23 And if they *d* not **persist in** unbelief, *AIT*
11:25 *I d* not **want** you to be ignorant *AIT*
12: 2 *D* not **conform** *any longer* **to the pattern of** *AIT*
12: 3 *D* not **think** of yourself more **highly** *AIT*
12: 4 and these members *d* not all **have** *AIT*
12: 8 it is showing mercy, let him **d** it cheerfully. *NIG*
12:14 bless and *d* not **curse.** *AIT*
12:16 *D* not **be proud,** *AIT*
12:16 *D* not **be** conceited. *AIT*
12:17 *D* not **repay** anyone evil for evil. *AIT*
12:17 to **d** what is right in the eyes of everybody. *NIG*
12:19 *D* not **take revenge,** my friends, *AIT*
12:21 *D* not *be* **overcome** by evil, *AIT*
13: 2 and those who **d so** will bring judgment *468S*
13: 3 rulers hold no terror *for* those who **d** right, *2240*
13: 3 but *for* those who **d** wrong. *NIG*
13: 3 *D you* **want** to be free from fear of the one *AIT*
13: 3 **d** what is right and he will commend you. *4472*
13: 4 For he is God's servant to **d** you good. *NIG*
13: 4 But if *you* **d** wrong, be afraid, *4472*
13: 9 "*D* not **commit adultery,"** *AIT*
13: 9 "*D* not **murder,"** *AIT*
13: 9 "*D* not **steal,"** *AIT*

Ro 13: 9 "Do not steal," *"D* not **covet,"** *AIT*
13:11 And **d** this, understanding the present time. *NIG*
13:14 and *d* not **think about** how to gratify *AIT*
14:10 You, then, why *d you* **judge** your brother? *AIT*
14:10 *d you* **look down on** *AIT*
14:15 *D* not by your eating **destroy** *AIT*
14:16 *D* not *allow* what you consider good *to be* **spoken of as evil.** *AIT*
14:19 therefore make every effort to **d** what leads *NIG*
14:20 *D* not **destroy** the work of God for the sake *AIT*
14:21 or drink wine or to **d** anything else *NIG*
15:24 I plan to **d** so when I go to Spain. *NIG*
15:27 They were pleased to **d** it, *NIG*
16:21 **sends** *his* **greetings to** you, as *d* *AIT*
1Co 1: 7 Therefore you *d* not **lack** any spiritual gift *AIT*
2: 6 *We d*, however, **speak** a message of wisdom *AIT*
3:18 *D* not **deceive** yourselves. *AIT*
4: 3 indeed, *I d* not even **judge** myself. *AIT*
4: 6 **"D** not go beyond what is written." *NIG*
4: 7 What *d you* **have** that you did not receive? *AIT*
4: 7 why *d you* **boast** as though you did not? *AIT*
4:15 you **d** not have many fathers, *NIG*
4:21 What *d you* **prefer?** *AIT*
5:11 **With** such a man *d* not even **eat.** *AIT*
6: 2 *D you* not **know** that the saints will judge *AIT*
6: 3 *D you* not **know** that we will judge angels? *AIT*
6: 8 Instead, *you* yourselves cheat and **d wrong,** *92*
6: 8 and you **d** this to your brothers. *NIG*
6: 9 *D you* not **know** that the wicked will *AIT*
6: 9 *D* not *be* **deceived:** *AIT*
6:15 *D you* not **know** that the wicked will not *AIT*
6:16 *D you* not **know** that he who unites himself *AIT*
6:19 *D you* not **know** that your body is a temple *AIT*
7: 5 *D* not **deprive** each other except *AIT*
7:15 But if the unbeliever leaves, *let him* **d so.** *6004S*
7:16 How *d you* **know,** wife, *AIT*
7:16 Or, how *d you* **know,** husband, *AIT*
7:21 if you can gain your freedom, **d so.** *3437+5968*
7:23 *d* not **become** slaves of men. *AIT*
7:27 Are you married? *D* not **seek** a divorce. *AIT*
7:27 Are you unmarried? *D* not **look for** a wife. *AIT*
7:28 But if *you d* **marry,** you have not sinned; *AIT*
7:36 *he should d* as he wants. *4472*
8: 8 we are no worse if *we d* not **eat,** *AIT*
8: 8 and no better if *we* **d.** *2266S*
9: 5 as **d** the other apostles and *NIG*
9: 8 *D I* **say** this merely from a human point *AIT*
9: 9 *"D* not **muzzle** an ox while it is treading out *AIT*
9:10 to **d** so in the hope of sharing in the harvest. *NIG*
9:15 in the hope that you *will* **d** such things *1181*
9:16 Woe to me if *I d* not **preach the gospel!** *AIT*
9:23 *I* **d** all this for the sake of the gospel, *4472*
9:24 *D you* not **know** that in a race all *AIT*
9:25 They **d** it to get a crown that will not last; *NIG*
9:25 we **d** it to get a crown that will last forever. *NIG*
9:26 I *d* not **run** like a man running aimlessly; *AIT*
9:26 *I d* not **fight** like a man beating the air. *AIT*
10: 1 *I d* not **want** you to be ignorant of the fact, *AIT*
10: 7 *D* not **be** idolaters, as some of them were; *AIT*
10:10 And *d* not **grumble,** as some of them did— *AIT*
10:18 *D* not those who eat the sacrifices **participate** in the altar? *AIT*
10:19 *D I* **mean** then that a sacrifice offered to *AIT*
10:20 and *I d* not **want** you to be participants *AIT*
10:28 then *d* not **eat it,** *AIT*
10:31 or drink or whatever *you* **d,** *4472*
10:31 **d** it all for the glory of God. *4472*
10:32 **D** not cause anyone to stumble, *1181*
11:16 nor **d** the churches of God. *NIG*
11:17 for your meetings **d** more harm than good. *NIG*
11:22 Or *d you* **despise** the church of God *AIT*
11:24 **d** this in remembrance of me." *4472*
11:25 **d** this, whenever you drink it, *4472*
12: 1 brothers, *I d* not **want** you to be ignorant. *AIT*
12:15 *I* **d** not belong to the body," *1639*
12:16 *I* **d** not belong to the body," *1639*
12:29 **D** all work miracles? *NIG*
12:30 **D** all have gifts of healing? *NIG*
12:30 **D** all speak in tongues? *NIG*
12:30 **D** all interpret? *NIG*
14:11 If then *I d* not **grasp the meaning** *AIT*
14:15 So what *shall I* **d?** *1639*
14:16 **among those who d not understand** *2626*
14:23 and **some who d not understand** *2626*
14:39 and *d* not **forbid** speaking in tongues. *AIT*
15: 9 For I am the least of the apostles and **d** not *1639*
15:29 what *will* those **d** who are baptized for *4472*
15:30 why *d we* **endanger** ourselves every hour? *AIT*
15:33 *D* not *be* **misled:** *AIT*
15:37 *you d* not **plant** the body that will be, *AIT*
16: 1 **D** what I told the Galatian churches to do. *4472*
16: 1 Do what I told the Galatian churches to **d.** *NIG*
16: 7 *I d* not **want** to see you now and make only *AIT*
16:14 **D** everything in love. *1181*
2Co 1: 8 *We d* not **want** you to be uninformed, *AIT*
1:13 *we d* not **write** you anything you cannot read *AIT*
1:17 When I planned this, *did I* **d** it lightly? *5968*
1:17 Or *d I* **make** *my* **plans** in a worldly manner *AIT*
2:17 *we* **d** not peddle the word of God for profit. *1639*
3: 1 Or *d we* **need,** like some people, *AIT*
4: 1 *we d* not **lose heart.** *AIT*
4: 2 *we d* not **use deception,** *AIT*
4: 2 nor *d we* **distort** the word of God. *AIT*
4: 5 For *we d* not **preach** ourselves, *AIT*
4:16 Therefore *we d* not **lose heart.** *AIT*
5: 4 because *we d* not **wish** to be unclothed but *AIT*
5:16 *we* **d so** no longer. *1182S*
2Co 6:14 *D* not **be** yoked together with unbelievers. *AIT*
6:14 For what **d** righteousness *NIG*
7: 3 *I d* not **say** this to condemn you; *AIT*
7: 8 *I d* not **regret** it. *AIT*
8: 5 And they did not **d** as we expected, *NIG*
8:10 to give but also to have the desire to **d** so. *NIG*
8:11 to **d** it may be matched by your completion *NIG*
8:21 For we are taking pains to **d** what is right, *NIG*
10: 3 *we d* not **wage war** as the world does. *AIT*
10: 9 *I d* not want *to* **seem** *AIT*
10:12 *We d* not **dare** to classify *AIT*
10:15 Neither **d** we go beyond our limits *NIG*
10:16 *d* not *want to* **boast about** *AIT*
11: 5 But *I d* not **think** I am in the least inferior *AIT*
11: 6 but I **d** have knowledge. *NIG*
11: 9 and *will continue to* **d so.** *5498S*
11:11 Because *I d* not **love** you? *AIT*
11:11 God knows I **d!** *NIG*
11:16 But if you **d,** *1145+3590S*
11:16 so that I *may d* a little **boasting.** *AIT*
11:29 Who is weak, and *I d* not **feel weak?** *AIT*
11:29 and *I d* not inwardly **burn?** *AIT*
12: 2 in the body or out of the body *I d* not **know** *AIT*
12: 3 the body *I d* not **know,** but God knows— *AIT*
12: 6 of me than is warranted by what I **d** or say. *1063S*
12:19 and everything we **d,** dear friends, *NIG*
13: 5 *D you* not **realize** that Christ Jesus is *AIT*
13: 7 to God that you *will* not **d** anything wrong. *4472*
13: 7 the test but that you *will* **d** what is right *4472*
13: 8 For *we* **cannot d** anything against the truth, *1538+4024*
Gal 2:10 the very thing I was eager *to* **d.** *4472*
2:21 *I d* not **set aside** the grace of God, *AIT*
3:10 not continue *to* **d** everything written in *4472*
3:17 by God and thus **d away with** the promise. *2934*
4: 9 *D you* **wish** to be enslaved by them all *AIT*
5: 1 *d* not *let yourselves be* **burdened** *AIT*
5:13 But **d** not use your freedom to indulge *NIG*
5:17 so that *you d* not **do** what you want. *AIT*
5:17 so that *you do* not **d** what you want. *4472*
6: 7 *D* not *be* **deceived:** God cannot be mocked. *AIT*
6: 9 a harvest *if we d* not **give up.** *AIT*
6:10 **let** *us* **d** good to all people, *2237*
6:12 The only reason they **d** this is *NIG*
Eph 2:10 created in Christ Jesus to **d** good works, *NIG*
2:10 God prepared in advance for *us to* **d.** *4344*
3:20 *to* **d** immeasurably more than all we ask *4472*
4:17 you must no longer live as the Gentiles **d,** *NIG*
4:26 "In your anger *d* not **sin":** *AIT*
4:26 *D* not *let* the sun **go down** *AIT*
4:27 and *d* not **give** the devil a foothold. *AIT*
4:29 *D* not *let* any unwholesome talk **come out** *AIT*
4:30 And *d* not **grieve** the Holy Spirit of God, *AIT*
5: 7 Therefore *d* not **be** partners with them. *AIT*
5:11 *Have* nothing **to d with** the fruitless deeds *5170*
5:12 to mention what the disobedient **d** in secret. *1181*
5:17 Therefore *d* not **be** foolish, *AIT*
5:18 *D* not **get drunk** on wine, *AIT*
6: 4 Fathers, *d* not **exasperate** your children; *AIT*
6: 9 *D* **not** threaten them, *AIT*
Php 1:16 The latter **d** so in love, *NIG*
1:22 *I d* not **know!** *AIT*
2: 3 **D** nothing out of selfish ambition *NIG*
2:14 **D** everything without complaining *4472*
3: 2 those men who **d** evil, *2239*
3:13 *I d* not **consider** myself yet *AIT*
3:13 But one thing I **d:** *NIG*
4: 6 *D* not *be* **anxious about** *AIT*
4:13 *I* **can d** everything through him who gives *2710*
Col 2:16 *d* not *let* anyone **judge** you by what *AIT*
2:18 *D* not *let* anyone who delights in false humility and the worship of angels **disqualify** you **for the prize.** *AIT*
2:20 *d you* **submit** to its **rules:** *AIT*
2:21 *"D* not **handle!** *AIT*
2:21 *D* not **taste!** *AIT*
2:21 *D* not **touch!"?** *AIT*
3: 9 *D* not **lie** to each other, *AIT*
3:17 And whatever *you* **d,** *4472*
3:17 **d** it all in the name of the Lord Jesus, *NIG*
3:19 love your wives and *d* not **be harsh** *AIT*
3:21 Fathers, *d* not **embitter** your children, *AIT*
3:22 and **d** it, not only when their eye is on you *NIG*
3:23 Whatever *you* **d,** work at it *4472*
1Th 1: 8 *we d* not **need** to say anything about it, *AIT*
4: 1 **d this more and more.** *3437+4355*
4: 5 who *d* not **know** God; *AIT*
4: 9 about brotherly love *we d* not **need** to write *AIT*
4:10 you **d** love all the brothers *4472*
4:10 **d so more and more.** *3437+4355*
4:13 *we d* not **want** you to be ignorant *AIT*
5: 1 about times and dates *we d* not **need** to write *AIT*
5: 5 *d* not **belong to** the night or **to** *AIT*
5:19 *D* not **put out** the Spirit's fire; *AIT*
5:20 *d* not **treat** prophecies **with contempt.** *AIT*
5:24 and he *will* **d** it. *4472*
2Th 1: 8 He will punish those who *d* not **know** God *AIT*
1: 8 and *d* not **obey** the gospel of our Lord Jesus. *AIT*
2: 7 now holds it back will continue to **d** so *NIG*
3: 4 *to* **d** the things we command. *4472*
3: 9 *we d* not **have** the right to such help, *AIT*
3:14 *D* not **associate with** him, *AIT*
3:15 Yet *d* not **regard** him as an enemy, *AIT*
1Ti 1: 7 but *they d* not **know** what they are talking *AIT*
2:12 *I d* not **permit** a woman to teach or *AIT*
4: 7 *Have* **nothing to d with** godless myths *4148*
4:14 *D* not **neglect** your gift, *AIT*
1Ti 4:16 Persevere in them, because *if you* **d,** *4472*
5: 1 *D* not **rebuke** an older man **harshly,** *AIT*
5:11 *d* **not put** them **on such a list.** *AIT*
5:13 And not only **d** they become idlers, *NIG*
5:18 *"D* not **muzzle** the ox while it is treading *AIT*
5:19 *D* not **entertain** an accusation against *AIT*
5:21 and *to* **d** nothing out of favoritism. *4472*
5:22 *D* not be hasty in the **laying on of** *AIT*
5:22 and *d* not **share in** the sins of others. *AIT*
6:18 Command them *to* **d good,** *14*
2Ti 1: 8 *d* not *be* **ashamed** to testify about our Lord, *AIT*
2:15 **D** *your* **best** to present yourself to God *5079*
2:21 and prepared **to d** any good work. *1650*
2:23 **Don't have anything to d with** foolish *4148*
2:26 who has taken them captive **to d** his will. *1650*
3: 5 **Have nothing to d with** them. *706*
4: 5 **d** the work of an evangelist, *4472*
4: 9 **D** *your* **best** to come to me quickly, *5079*
4:21 **D** *your* **best** to get here before winter. *5079*
4:21 Eubulus greets you, and so **d** Pudens, *NIG*
Tit 1:15 who are corrupted and **d** not believe, *NIG*
2:14 eager *to* **d** what is good. *2240*
2:15 *D* not *let* anyone **despise** you. *AIT*
3: 1 to be ready to **d** whatever is good, *2240*
3:10 After that, *have* **nothing to d with** him. *4148*
3:12 **d** *your* **best** to come to me at Nicopolis, *5079*
3:13 *D* everything you can to **help** Zenas the lawyer and Apollos **on** *their* **way** *AIT*
Phm 1: 8 be bold and order you to **d** what you ought *NIG*
1: 8 to do **what you ought to d,** *465+3836*
1:14 *to* **d** anything without your consent, *4472*
1:14 so that any favor you **d** will be spontaneous *NIG*
1:20 *I d wish,* brother, *that I may have* some **benefit** from you *AIT*
1:21 that *you will* **d** even more than I ask. *4472*
1:24 And so **d** Mark, Aristarchus, *NIG*
Heb 2: 1 so that *we d* not **drift away.** *AIT*
2: 8 at present *we d* not **see** everything subject *AIT*
3: 8 *d* not **harden** your hearts as you did in *AIT*
3:15 *d* not **harden** your hearts as you did in *AIT*
4: 7 *d* not **harden** your hearts." *AIT*
4:15 For *we d* not **have** a high priest who is *AIT*
6: 3 And God permitting, *we will* **d** so. *4472*
6:12 We **d** not want you to become lazy, *NIG*
8: 1 *We d* **have** such a high priest, *AIT*
9:26 at the end of the ages to **d away** with sin by *120*
10: 7 I have come to **d** your will, O God.' " *4472*
10: 9 "Here I am, I have come to **d** your will." *4472*
10:29 How much more severely *d you* **think** *AIT*
10:35 So *d* not **throw away** your confidence; *AIT*
11: 1 for and certain of what *we d* not **see.** *AIT*
11:29 but *when* the Egyptians **tried to d** so, *3284+4278*
11:32 I *d* **not have** time to tell about Gideon, *AIT*
12: 5 *d* not **make light of** the Lord's discipline, *AIT*
12: 5 and *d* not **lose heart** when he rebukes you, *AIT*
12:25 to it that *you d* not **refuse** him who speaks. *AIT*
13: 2 *D* not **forget** to entertain strangers, *AIT*
13: 6 What *can* man **d** to me?" *4472*
13: 9 *D* not *be* **carried away** *AIT*
13:14 For here *we d* not **have** an enduring city, *AIT*
13:16 And *d* not **forget** to do good and to share *AIT*
13:16 And do not forget to **d good** and to share *2343*
Jas 1:22 **D** not merely listen to the word, *NIG*
1:22 **D** what it says. *1181+4475*
1:23 the word but does not **d** what it says is like *4475*
1:25 and continues to **d** this, *NIG*
2:11 *"D* not **commit adultery,"** *AIT*
2:11 also said, *"D* not **murder."** *AIT*
2:11 *d* not **commit adultery** *AIT*
2:11 not commit adultery but *d* **commit murder,** *AIT*
2:18 and I will show you my faith by what I **d.** *2240*
2:20 *d you* **want** evidence that faith *AIT*
3:14 *d* not **boast** about it or deny the truth. *AIT*
4: 2 *You d* not **have,** *AIT*
4: 2 because you *d* not **ask** God. *AIT*
4: 3 When you ask, *you d* not **receive,** *AIT*
4: 5 Or *d you* **think** Scripture says *AIT*
4:11 Brothers, *d* not **slander** one another. *AIT*
4:14 you *d* not even **know** what will happen tomorrow. *AIT*
4:15 we will live and **d** this or that." *4472*
4:17 the good *he ought to* **d** and doesn't do it, *4472*
4:17 the good he ought to do and doesn't **d** it, *4472*
5:12 *d* not **swear—**not **by** heaven *AIT*
1Pe 1: 8 and *even though you d* not **see** him now, *AIT*
1:14 *d* not **conform** to the evil desires you had *AIT*
1:15 so be holy in all you **d;** *419*
2: 7 But to those who **d** not believe, *NIG*
2:14 by him to punish *those who* **d wrong** and *2804*
2:14 and to commend *those who* **d right.** *18*
2:16 *d* not *use* your freedom as a **cover-up** *AIT*
3: 1 if any of them **d not believe** the word, *578*
3: 6 *if you* **d what is right** and do not give way *16*
3: 6 *d* not give way to **fear.** *AIT*
3: 9 *D* not **repay** evil with evil or insult *AIT*
3:11 He must turn from evil and **d** good; *4472*
3:12 the face of the Lord is against **those who d** evil." *4472*
3:13 to harm you if you are eager to **d** good? *NIG*
3:14 *"D* not **fear** what they fear; *AIT*
3:14 *d* not *be* **frightened."** *AIT*
3:15 But **d** this with gentleness and respect, *NIG*
4: 3 in the past doing what pagans choose to **d—** *NIG*
4: 4 that you *d* not **plunge with** them into *AIT*
4:11 he should **d** it as one speaking *NIG*
4:11 he should **d** it with the strength God *NIG*
4:12 *d* not *be* **surprised** at the painful trial *AIT*

1Pe 4:16 you suffer as a Christian, *d* not *be* **ashamed,** AIT
4:17 the outcome be *for* those who *d* **not obey** AIT
4:19 and continue to **d good.** 17
2Pe 1:10 For *if you* **d** these things, 4472
1:19 and you *will* **d** well to pay attention to it, 4472
2:11 *d* not **bring** slanderous accusations AIT
2:12 in matters *they d* **not understand.** AIT
3:8 *d* not **forget** this one thing, dear friends: AIT
3:16 as they **d** the other Scriptures, NIG
1Jn 1:6 we lie and *d* not **live by** the truth. AIT
2:4 but *does* not **d** what he commands is a liar, 5498
2:15 *D* not **love** the world or anything in AIT
2:21 *I d* not **write** to you because you do AIT
2:21 to you because *you d* not **know** the truth, AIT
2:21 but because *you d* **know** it and AIT
2:27 and *you d* not **need** anyone to teach you. AIT
3:7 *d* not *let* anyone **lead** you **astray.** AIT
3:10 Anyone who *does* not **d** what is right is not 4472
3:12 **D** not be like Cain, NIG
3:13 *D* not *be* **surprised,** my brothers, AIT
3:21 Dear friends, if our hearts *d* not **condemn** us, AIT
3:22 and **d** what pleases him. 4472
4:1 Dear friends, *d* not **believe** every spirit, AIT
4:18 because fear has to **d** with punishment. NIG
2Jn 1:7 who *d* not **acknowledge** Jesus Christ AIT
1:8 that *you d* not **lose** what you have worked AIT
1:10 *d* not **take** him into your house AIT
1:12 but *I d* not **want** to use paper and ink. AIT
3Jn 1:6 *You will* **d** well to send them on their way 4472
1:9 *will* **have** nothing *to d with* us. AIT
1:10 to **d** so and puts them out of the church. NIG
1:11 *d* not **imitate** what is evil but what is good. AIT
1:13 but *I d* not **want** to do so with pen and ink. AIT
1:13 but I do not want *to* **d** so with pen and ink. 1211[S]
Jude 1:10 against whatever *they d* not **understand;** AIT
1:10 what things *they d* **understand** by instinct, AIT
1:19 and *d* not **have** the Spirit. AIT
Rev 1:17 *"D* not *be* **afraid.** AIT
2:5 Repent and **d** the things you did at first. 4472
2:5 If *you d* not **repent,** AIT
2:10 *D* not *be* **afraid of** what you are about to suffer. AIT
2:24 to you who *d* not **hold to** her teaching AIT
3:3 But if *you d* not **wake up,** AIT
3:17 I have acquired wealth and *d* not **need** AIT
3:17 *you d* not **realize** that you are wretched, AIT
5:5 one of the elders said to me, *"D* not **weep!** AIT
6:6 and *d* not **damage** the oil and the wine!" AIT
7:3 **"D** not **harm** the land or the sea or the trees 92
10:4 *d* not **write** it **down."** AIT
11:2 exclude the outer court; *d* not **measure** it, AIT
13:14 of the signs he was given power *to* **d** 4472
19:10 But he said to me, *"D* not **do it!** AIT
19:10 But he said to me, *"Do* not **d it!** 3972[S]
22:9 But he said to me, *"D* not **do it!** AIT
22:9 But he said to me, *"Do* not **d it!** 3972[S]
22:10 *"D* not **seal up** the words of the prophecy AIT
22:11 *Let* him who does wrong continue *to* **d wrong;** 92
22:11 *let* him who does right continue *to* **d** right; 4472

DO-NOTHING (1) [DO, NOTHING]

Isa 30:7 Therefore I call her Rahab the **D.** 8700

DOCTOR (4) [DOCTORS]

Mt 9:12 "It is not the healthy who need a **d,** 2620
Mk 2:17 "It is not the healthy who need a **d,** 2620
Lk 5:31 "It is not the healthy who need a **d,** 2620
Col 4:14 Our dear friend Luke, the **d,** 2620

DOCTORS (1) [DOCTOR]

Mk 5:26 a great deal under the care *of* many **d** 2620

DOCTRINE (5) [DOCTRINES]

1Ti 1:10 for whatever else is contrary *to* the sound **d** 1436
4:16 Watch your life and **d** closely. 1436
2Ti 4:3 when men will not put up with sound **d.** 1436
Tit 1:9 so that he can encourage others by sound **d** 1436
2:1 in accord *with* sound **d.** 1436

DOCTRINES (2) [DOCTRINE]

1Ti 1:3 not *to* **teach false d** any longer 2281
6:3 If anyone **teaches false d** and does 2281

DOCUMENT (1) [DOCUMENTS]

Est 8:8 for no **d** written in the king's name 4181

DOCUMENTS (1) [DOCUMENT]

Jer 32:14 Take these **d,** both the sealed 6219

DODAI (3)

2Sa 23:9 to him was Eleazar son of **D** the Ahohite. 1862
1Ch 11:12 to him was Eleazar son of **D** the Ahohite, 1862
27:4 of the division for the second month was **D** 1862

DODAVAHU (1)

2Ch 20:37 Eliezer son of **D** of Mareshah prophesied 1845

DODO (3)

Jdg 10:1 the son of **D,** rose to save Israel. 1861
2Sa 23:24 Elhanan son of **D** *from* Bethlehem, 1861
1Ch 11:26 Elhanan son of **D** from Bethlehem, 1861

DOE (5) [DOES]

Ge 49:21 a **d** set free that bears beautiful fawns. 387
Job 39:1 Do you watch when the **d** bears her fawn? 387
Ps 22:T To [the tune of] "The **D** *of* the Morning." 387
Pr 5:19 A loving **d,** a graceful deer— 387
Jer 14:5 the **d** in the field deserts her newborn fawn 387

DOEG (6)

1Sa 21:7 he was **D** the Edomite, 1795
22:9 But **D** the Edomite, 1795
22:18 The king then ordered **D,** 1795
22:18 So **D** the Edomite turned 1795
22:22 "That day, when **D** the Edomite was there, 1795
Ps 52:T When **D** the Edomite had gone to Saul 1795

DOES (582) [DO, DOE]

Ge 31:15 *D* he not **regard** *us as* foreigners? AIT
39:8 "my master *d* not **concern** *himself* AIT
44:7 "Why *d* my lord **say** such things? AIT
Ex 3:3 why the bush *d* not **burn up."** AIT
8:29 *d* not **act deceitfully** AIT
11:1 and when he **d,** he will drive you out 8938[S]
12:26 'What **d** this ceremony mean to you?' NIH
13:14 'What **d** this mean?' NIH
21:8 If *she d* **not please** the master AIT
21:11 If *he d* not **provide** her with these three AIT
21:13 *d* not **do** it **intentionally,** AIT
21:18 with his fist and *he d* not **die** but is confined AIT
31:14 whoever **d** any work on that day must 6913
31:15 Whoever **d** any work on 6913
33:15 "If your Presence *d* not **go** with us, AIT
34:7 *d* not **leave the guilty unpunished;** AIT
35:2 Whoever **d** any work on it must be put 6913
Lev 4:2 and **d** what is forbidden in any of 6913
4:13 and **d** what is forbidden in any of 6913
4:22 and **d** what is forbidden in any of 6913
4:27 and **d** what is forbidden in any of 6913
5:1 'If a person sins because *he d* not **speak up** AIT
5:17 a person sins and **d** what is forbidden in any 6913
5:17 even though *he d* not **know** it, AIT
11:4 *d* not *have* a **split** hoof; AIT
11:5 *d* not *have* a **split** hoof; AIT
11:6 *d* not *have* a **split** hoof; AIT
11:7 *d* not **chew** the cud; it is unclean for you. AIT
11:12 the water that **d** not have fins and scales is NIH
11:26 *that d* not **chew** the cud is unclean for you; AIT
13:4 but **d** not appear to be more than skin deep NIH
13:7 But if the rash *d* **spread** in his skin AIT
13:31 it **d** not seem to be more than skin deep NIH
13:32 and there is no yellow hair in it and it **d** NIH
13:35 But if the itch *d* **spread** in the skin AIT
13:36 *d* not *need to* **look** for yellow hair AIT
17:9 and *d* not **bring** it to the entrance to the Tent AIT
17:16 *he d* not **wash** his clothes and bathe himself, AIT
18:29 " 'Everyone who **d** any of these 6913
23:29 Anyone who *d* not **deny himself** on AIT
23:30 among his people anyone who **d** any work 6913
25:28 if he *d* not **acquire** the means to repay him, AIT
25:53 to it that his owner *d* not **rule over** AIT
27:20 If, however, *he d* not **redeem** the field, AIT
27:27 If he *d* not **redeem** *it,* AIT
27:33 If *he d* **make a substitution,** AIT
Nu 14:8 and it *d* **flow** *with* milk and honey! AIT
14:18 *d* not **leave the guilty unpunished;** AIT
19:12 But if *he d* not **purify himself** on the third AIT
19:20 person who is unclean *d* not **purify himself,** AIT
23:19 *D* he **speak** and then not act? AIT
23:19 *D he* **promise** and not fulfill? AIT
23:24 a lion *that d* not **rest** till he devours his prey AIT
24:23 "Ah, who can live when God **d** this? 8492
30:11 but says nothing to her and *d* not **forbid** her, AIT
Dt 8:3 that man *d* not **live** on bread alone but AIT
10:12 what *d* the LORD your God **ask** of you AIT
14:8 it **d** not chew the cud. NIH
14:10 that **d** not have fins and scales you may NIH
18:12 Anyone *who* **d** these things is detestable to 6913
18:19 If anyone *d* not **listen** to my words that AIT
18:22 in the name of the LORD *d* not **take place** AIT
21:15 the son of the wife *he d* **not love,** AIT
21:16 the son of the wife *he d* **not love.** AIT
21:18 and rebellious son who *d* not **obey** his father AIT
22:2 the brother **d** not live near you or if you do NIH
22:5 LORD your God detests anyone *who* **d** this. 6913
25:7 man *d* not **want** to marry his brother's wife, AIT
25:16 LORD your God detests anyone *who* **d** these 6913
27:26 "Cursed is the man who *d* not **uphold** AIT
32:4 A faithful God who **d** no wrong, NIH
Jos 1:18 and *d* not **obey** your words, AIT
5:14 "What **message** *d* my Lord *have* AIT
1Sa 6:9 But if it **d** not, NIH
11:7 of anyone who *d* not **follow** Saul AIT
15:22 **"D** the LORD delight in burnt offerings NIH
15:29 He who is the Glory of Israel *d* not **lie** AIT
16:7 The LORD **d** not look at the things man looks NIH
22:8 as he **d** today." NIH
22:13 as he **d** today?" NIH
24:19 *d he* **let** him **get away** AIT
28:14 "What **d** he look like?" NIH
2Sa 7:14 When he **d wrong,** I will punish him 6390
14:13 **d** he not convict himself, NIH
14:14 But God *d* not **take away** life; AIT
24:3 *d* my lord the king **want** AIT
1Ki 2:23 be it ever so severely, if Adonijah **d** not pay NIH
8:39 deal with each man according to all he **d,** 2006
8:41 "As for the foreigner who **d** not belong NIH
8:46 for there is no one who *d* not **sin—** AIT
2Ki 5:7 Why *d* this fellow **send** someone to me to AIT
6:27 "If the LORD *d* not **help** you, AIT
1Ch 21:3 *Why d* my lord **want to do** this? AIT
2Ch 6:30 deal with each man according to all he **d,** 2006
6:32 "As for the foreigner who **d** not belong NIH
6:36 for there is no one who *d* not **sin—** AIT
Ezr 7:26 Whoever *d* not **obey** the law of your God AIT
Ne 2:2 "Why **d** your face look so sad when you are NIH
5:13 every man who *d* not **keep** this promise. AIT
Job 1:9 *"D* Job **fear** God for nothing?" Satan replied. AIT
3:21 who long for death that **d** not come, NIH
5:6 For hardship *d* not **spring** from the soil, AIT
5:6 nor *d* trouble **sprout** from the ground. AIT
6:5 *D* a wild donkey **bray** AIT
7:1 **"D** not man have hard service on earth? NIH
7:9 down to the grave *d* not **return.** AIT
8:3 *D* God **pervert** justice? AIT
8:3 *D* the Almighty **pervert** AIT
8:15 he clings to it, but *it d* not **hold.** AIT
8:20 "Surely God *d* not **reject** a blameless man AIT
9:7 He speaks to the sun and *it d* not **shine;** AIT
9:13 God *d* not **restrain** his anger; AIT
10:3 **D** it please you to oppress me, NIH
11:11 *d he* not **take note?** AIT
12:3 Who **d** not know all these things? NIH
12:9 Which of all these *d* not **know** that the hand AIT
12:11 *D* not the ear **test** words AIT
12:12 **D** not long life bring understanding? NIH
14:2 like a fleeting shadow, *he d* not **endure.** AIT
14:12 so man lies down and *d* not **rise;** AIT
14:21 If his sons are honored, *he d* not **know** it; AIT
14:21 if they are brought low, *he d* not **see** it. AIT
16:6 and if I refrain, *it d* not **go** away. AIT
19:16 I summon my servant, but *he d* not **answer,** AIT
19:22 Why do you pursue me as God **d?** NIH
21:17 How often *d* calamity **come** upon them, AIT
21:21 For what **d** he care about the family NIH
22:13 Yet you say, 'What *d* God **know?** AIT
22:13 *D he* **judge** through such darkness? AIT
22:14 so *he d* not **see** us as he goes about in AIT
23:13 *He* **d** whatever he pleases. 6913
24:1 *d* the Almighty not **set** times for judgment? AIT
25:3 *d* his light not **rise?** AIT
27:9 *D* God **listen** *to* his cry AIT
28:12 Where **d** understanding dwell? NIH
28:13 Man *d* not **comprehend** its worth; AIT
28:20 "Where then *d* wisdom **come** from? AIT
28:20 Where **d** understanding dwell? NIH
31:4 *D* he not **see** my ways AIT
33:14 For God *d* **speak—** AIT
33:29 "God **d** all these things to a man— 7188
34:19 to princes and *d* not **favor** the rich over AIT
35:6 If you sin, how *d that* **affect** him? AIT
35:6 your sins are many, what *d that* **do** to him? AIT
35:7 or what *d he* **receive** from your hand? AIT
35:12 *He d* not **answer** when men cry out because AIT
35:13 God *d* not **listen** *to* their empty plea; AIT
35:15 *d* not **take** the least **notice** AIT
36:5 "God is mighty, but *d* not **despise** men; AIT
36:6 *d* not **keep** the wicked **alive** AIT
36:7 *He d* not **take** his eyes off the righteous; AIT
37:5 *he* **d** great things beyond our understanding. 6913
37:23 and great righteousness, *he d* not **oppress.** AIT
37:24 *d he* not **have regard for** AIT
38:19 And where **d** darkness reside? NIH
38:28 *D* the rain **have** a father? AIT
39:7 *he d* not **hear** a driver's shout. AIT
39:22 *he d* not **shy away** from the sword. AIT
39:26 *"D* the hawk **take flight** AIT
39:27 *D* the eagle **soar** at your command AIT
41:26 nor **d** the spear or the dart or the javelin. NIH
Ps 1:1 the man who *d* not **walk** in the counsel of AIT
1:3 in season and whose leaf *d* not **wither.** AIT
1:3 Whatever *he* **d** prospers. 6913
7:12 *he d* not **relent,** he will sharpen his sword; AIT
9:12 *he d* not **ignore** the cry of the afflicted. AIT
10:4 In his pride the wicked *d* not **seek** him; AIT
10:13 *d* the wicked man **revile** AIT
10:13 Why *d he* **say** to himself, AIT
14:1 there is no *one who* **d** good. 6913
14:3 there is no *one who* **d** good, not even one. 6913
15:2 and *who* **d** what is righteous, 7188
15:3 *who* **d** his neighbor no wrong 6913
15:5 without usury and *d* not **accept** a bribe AIT
15:5 *He who* **d** these things will never be shaken. 6913
17:1 it **d** not rise from deceitful lips. NIH
24:4 who *d* not **lift up** his soul to an idol AIT
32:2 the man whose sin the LORD *d* not **count** AIT
33:4 he is faithful in all he **d.** 5126
36:4 and *d* not **reject** what is wrong. AIT
38:14 I have become like a man who *d* not **hear,** AIT
40:4 *who d* not **look** to the proud, AIT
41:11 for my enemy *d* not **triumph** over me. AIT
44:6 *d* not **bring** me **victory;** AIT
49:12 But man, despite his riches, *d* not **endure;** AIT
53:1 there is no *one who* **d** good. 6913
53:3 there is no *one who* **d** good, not even one. 6913
69:33 and *d* not **despise** his captive people. AIT
72:18 *who* alone **d** marvelous deeds. 6913

Ps 73:11 **D** the Most High have knowledge?" NIH
74: 1 Why *d* your anger **smolder** against AIT
78:39 a passing breeze *that d* not **return.** AIT
84:11 no good thing *d he* **withhold** AIT
92: 6 The senseless man *d* not **know,** AIT
94: 7 They say, "The LORD *d* not **see;** AIT
94: 9 *D he* who implanted the ear not **hear?** AIT
94: 9 *D he* who formed the eye not **see?** AIT
94:10 *D he* who disciplines nations not **punish?** AIT
94:10 **D** he who teaches man lack knowledge? NIH
103:10 *he d* not **treat** us as our sins deserve AIT
115: 3 *he* **d** whatever pleases him. 6913
121: 1 where *d* my help **come** from? AIT
135: 6 The LORD **d** whatever pleases him, 6913
136: 4 to *him who* alone **d** great wonders, 6913
Pr 6:32 whoever **d** so destroys himself. 6913
8: 1 *D* not wisdom **call out?** AIT
8: 1 *D* not understanding **raise** her voice? AIT
10: 3 *d* not **let** the righteous **go hungry** AIT
12:27 The lazy man *d* not **roast** his game, AIT
13: 1 but a mocker *d* not **listen** *to* rebuke. AIT
14: 5 A truthful witness *d* not **deceive,** AIT
14:17 A quick-tempered man **d** foolish things, 6913
17:20 A man of perverse heart *d* not **prosper;** AIT
18: 3 When wickedness comes, so **d** contempt, 995[S]
20: 4 A sluggard *d* not **plow** in season; AIT
20:16 in pledge if he **d** it for a wayward woman. NIH
24:12 *d* not he who weighs the heart **perceive** AIT
24:12 *D* not he who guards your life **know** AIT
25:14 boasts of **gifts he d not give.** 5522+9214
26: 2 an undeserved curse *d* not **come to rest.** AIT
27:13 in pledge if he **d** it for a wayward woman. NIH
28:13 He who conceals his sins *d* not **prosper,** AIT
29:16 When the wicked thrive, **so d** sin, 8049[S]
31:18 and her lamp *d* not **go out** at night. AIT
31:27 the affairs of her household and *d* not **eat** AIT
Ecc 1: 3 What **d** man gain from all his labor NIH
2: 2 *d* pleasure **accomplish?"** AIT
2:22 What *d* a man **get** for all the toil AIT
2:23 even at night his mind *d* not **rest.** AIT
3: 9 What **d** the worker gain from his toil? NIH
3:14 that everything God **d** will endure forever; 6913
3:14 God **d** it so that men will revere him. 6913
5:16 so he departs, and what **d** he gain, NIH
6: 2 but God *d* not **enable** him to enjoy them, AIT
6: 3 and *d* not **receive** proper burial, AIT
6: 5 it has more rest than **d** that man— NIH
6: 8 What **d** a poor man gain by knowing how NIH
6:11 and how **d** that profit anyone? NIH
7:20 on earth who **d** what is right and never sins. 6913
9:11 or the battle to the strong, nor **d** food come NIH
10:15 *he d* not **know** the way to town. AIT
SS 2: 7 I charge you by the gazelles and by the **d** *of* 387
3: 5 I charge you by the gazelles and by the **d** *of* 387
Isa 1: 3 but Israel *d* not **know,** AIT
1:23 the widow's case *d* not **come** before them. AIT
10:15 *D* the ax **raise itself** AIT
19:14 they make Egypt stagger in all **that** she **d,** 5126
28:24 **d** he plow continually? NIH
28:24 *D he keep on* **breaking up** AIT
28:25 *d he* not **sow** caraway and scatter cummin? AIT
28:25 *D he* not **plant** wheat in its place, AIT
28:28 *d* not **go on threshing** AIT
31: 2 *he d* not **take back** his words. AIT
45: 9 *D* the clay **say** to the potter, AIT
45: 9 **D** your work say, 'He has no hands'? NIH
46: 7 Though one cries out to it, *it d* not **answer;** AIT
54:15 If *anyone d* **attack** you, AIT
55: 2 and your labor on what **d** not satisfy? NIH
56: 2 Blessed is the man *who* **d** this, 6913
58: 2 as if they were a nation that **d** what is right 6913
59: 9 and righteousness *d* not **reach** us. AIT
63:16 though Abraham *d* not **know** us AIT
65:20 an old man who *d* not **live out** his years; AIT
Jer 2:32 *D* a maiden **forget** her jewelry, AIT
8: 4 When a man turns away, *d he* not **return?** AIT
8: 5 Why **d** Jerusalem **always** turn away? 5904
11: 3 'Cursed is the man who *d* not **obey** the terms of this covenant— AIT
12: 1 Why *d* the way of the wicked **prosper?** AIT
12:17 But if any nation *d* not **listen,** AIT
14:10 So the LORD *d* not **accept** them; AIT
14:22 for you are the *one who* **d** all this. 6913
17: 8 *It d* not **fear** when heat comes; AIT
18: 6 can I not do with you as this potter **d?"** NIH
18:10 *it* **d** evil in my sight and does not obey me, 6913
18:10 if it does evil in my sight and *d* not **obey** me, AIT
18:14 *D* the snow of Lebanon *ever* **vanish** AIT
22:15 "*D it make you a* **king** AIT
La 3:33 *d* not willingly **bring affliction** AIT
Eze 3:19 and *he d* not **turn** from his wickedness or AIT
3:20 from his righteousness and **d** evil, 6913
3:21 not to sin and he *d* not **sin,** AIT
8:12 They say, 'The LORD *d* not **see** us; AIT
9: 9 the LORD *d* not **see.'** AIT
17:15 Will he who **d** such things escape? 6913
18: 5 a righteous man *who* **d** what is just and right. 6913
18: 6 *He d* not **eat** at the mountain shrines or look AIT
18: 6 *He d* not **defile** his neighbor's wife or lie AIT
18: 7 *He d* not **oppress** anyone, AIT
18: 7 *He d* not **commit robbery** but gives his food to the hungry AIT
18: 8 *He d* not **lend** at usury AIT
18:10 or **d** any of these other things 6913
18:12 *He d* not **return** what he took in pledge. AIT
Eze 18:12 *He* **d** detestable things. 6913
18:14 *he d* not **do** such things: AIT
18:15 "*He d* not **eat** at the mountain shrines AIT
18:15 *He d* not **defile** his neighbor's wife. AIT
18:16 *He d* not **oppress** anyone or require a pledge AIT
18:16 *He d* not **commit robbery** but gives his food to the hungry AIT
18:19 *d* the son not **share** AIT
18:21 and keeps all my decrees and **d** what is just 6913
18:24 and **d** the same detestable things 6913
18:24 detestable things the wicked man **d,** 6913
18:27 and **d** what is just and right, 6913
21:13 which the sword despises, *d* not **continue?** AIT
33: 4 *d* not **take warning** and the sword comes AIT
33: 6 and *d* not **blow** the trumpet to warn AIT
33: 9 to turn from his ways and *he d* not **do so,** AIT
33:13 in his righteousness and **d** evil, none of 6913
33:14 from his sin and **d** what is just and right— 6913
33:15 and **d** no evil, he will surely live; 6913
33:18 from his righteousness and **d** evil, 6913
33:19 from his wickedness and **d** what is just 6913
46:12 or his fellowship offerings as *he* **d** on 6913
Da 3: 6 Whoever *d* not **fall down** AIT
3:11 and that whoever *d* not **fall down** AIT
3:18 But even if he **d** not, we want you to know, NIH
4:35 *He* **d** as he pleases with the powers 10522
4:37 because everything he **d** is right 10434
8:24 and will succeed in whatever *he* **d.** 6913
9:14 God is righteous in everything *he* **d;** 6913
Hos 7: 9 but he *d* not **realize** it. AIT
7: 9 but he *d* not **notice.** AIT
7:10 but despite all this *he d* not **return** to AIT
13:13 *he d* not **come** to the opening of the womb. AIT
Am 3: 4 *D* a lion **roar** in the thicket AIT
3: 4 *D* he **growl** in his den AIT
3: 5 *D* a bird **fall** into a trap on the ground AIT
3: 5 *D* a trap **spring up** AIT
3: 7 Surely the Sovereign LORD **d** nothing 6913
6:12 *D one* **plow** there with oxen? AIT
Mic 2: 7 **D** he do such things?" NIH
3: 5 if *he* **d** not, they prepare to wage war 5989
6: 8 And what *d* the LORD **require** of you? AIT
Hab 3:17 Though the fig tree *d* not **bud** AIT
Zep 3: 2 *She d* not **trust** in the LORD, AIT
3: 2 *she d* not **draw near** to her God. AIT
3: 5 *he* **d** no wrong. 6913
3: 5 and every new day *he d* not **fail,** AIT
Hag 2: 3 How *d* it **look** to you now? AIT
2: 3 **D** it not seem to you like nothing? NIH
2:12 *d it become* **consecrated?"** " AIT
2:13 *d it become* **defiled?"** AIT
Mal 2:12 As for the man who **d** this, 6913
Mt 3:10 that *d* not **produce** good fruit will be cut *AIT*
4: 4 'Man *d* not **live** on bread alone, *AIT*
7:19 Every tree that *d* not **bear** good fruit is cut *AIT*
7:21 but only he who **d** the will *4472*
7:26 *d* not **put** them **into practice** *AIT*
8: 9 I say to my servant, 'Do this,' and *he* **d** it." *4472*
9:11 "Why *d* your teacher **eat** with tax collectors *AIT*
10:38 and anyone who *d* not **take** his cross *AIT*
11: 6 the man who *d* not **fall away** on account *AIT*
12:30 and he who *d* not **gather** with me scatters, *AIT*
12:43 and *d* not **find** it. *AIT*
12:50 For whoever **d** the will of my Father *4472*
13:12 Whoever *d* not **have,** *AIT*
13:19 about the kingdom and *d* not **understand** it, *AIT*
15:11 *d* not **make** him **'unclean,'** *AIT*
15:20 *d* not **make** him **'unclean.'** " *AIT*
17:25 "Yes, he **d,"** he replied. *NIG*
24:50 on a day when *he d* not **expect** him and at *AIT*
25:29 Whoever *d* not **have,** *AIT*
Mk 2: 7 "Why *d* this fellow **talk** like that? *AIT*
2:16 "Why *d he* **eat** with tax collectors *AIT*
2:21 **If he d,** the new piece will pull away from the old, *1254+1623+3590*
2:22 **If he d,** the wine will burst the skins, *1254+1623+3590*
3:35 Whoever **d** God's will is my brother *4472*
4:25 whoever *d* not **have,** *AIT*
4:27 though he *d* not **know** how. *AIT*
6: 2 that he even **d** miracles! *1181*
8:12 *d* this generation **ask for** *AIT*
9:12 Elijah *d* **come** first, and restores all things. *AIT*
9:37 whoever welcomes me *d* not **welcome** me *AIT*
9:39 "No one who **d** a miracle in my name can *4472*
9:48 where " 'their worm *d* not **die,** *AIT*
11:23 and *d* not **doubt** in his heart but believes *AIT*
13:14 where *it d* not **belong—** *AIT*
16:16 whoever *d* not **believe** will be condemned. *AIT*
Lk 3: 9 *that d* not **produce** good fruit will be cut *AIT*
4: 4 'Man *d* not **live** on bread alone.' " *AIT*
5:36 If he **d,** he will have torn the new garment, *1145+3590[S]*
5:37 If he **d,** the new wine will burst the skins, *1145+3590[S]*
6:43 nor *d* a bad tree **bear** good fruit. *AIT*
6:49 *d* not **put** them **into practice** *AIT*
7: 8 I say to my servant, 'Do this,' and *he* **d** it." *4472*
7:23 the man who *d* not **fall away** on account *AIT*
8:18 whoever *d* not **have,** *AIT*
11:23 and he who *d* not **gather** with me, scatters. *AIT*
11:24 and *d* not **find** it. *AIT*
12:15 a man's life *d* not **consist** in the abundance *AIT*
12:46 on a day when *he d* not **expect** him and at *AIT*
12:47 and *d* not **get ready** or does *AIT*
12:47 or *d* not **do** what his master wants will *AIT*
Lk 12:48 But the one who *d* not **know** *AIT*
12:48 and **d** things deserving punishment will *4472*
12:54 'It's going to rain,' and *it* **d.** *1181+4048[S]*
14:26 to me and *d* not **hate** his father and mother, *AIT*
14:27 And anyone who *d* not **carry** his cross *AIT*
14:33 any of you who *d* not **give up** *AIT*
15: 4 *D he* not **leave** the ninety-nine in *AIT*
15: 8 *D she* not **light** a lamp, *AIT*
17:20 "The kingdom of God *d* not **come** *AIT*
24:39 a ghost *d* not **have** flesh and bones, *AIT*
Jn 3:18 whoever *d* not **believe** stands condemned already *AIT*
3:20 Everyone who **d** evil hates the light, *4556*
5:19 whatever the Father **d** the Son also does. *4472*
5:19 whatever the Father does the Son also **d.** *4472*
5:20 the Son and shows him all he **d.** *4472*
5:23 He who *d* not **honor** the Son does not honor *AIT*
5:23 He who does not honor the Son *d* not **honor** *AIT*
5:38 nor *d* his word **dwell** in you, *AIT*
6:61 Jesus said to them, "*D* this **offend** you? *AIT*
7: 7 because I testify that what it **d** is evil. *2240*
7:18 on his own **d** so to gain honor for himself, *NIG*
7:35 "Where *d* this man **intend** to go *AIT*
7:42 *D* not the Scripture **say** *AIT*
7:46 "No one ever spoke the way this man **d,"** *NIG*
7:51 "*D* our law **condemn** anyone without first *AIT*
7:52 that a prophet *d* not **come** out of Galilee." *AIT*
8:41 You are doing the things your own father **d."** *NIG*
9:16 for *he d* not **keep** the Sabbath." *AIT*
9:31 We know that God *d* not **listen** *to* sinners. *AIT*
9:31 He listens to the godly man who **d** his will. *4472*
10: 1 the man who *d* not **enter** the sheep pen by *AIT*
10:37 unless I do what my Father **d.** *NIG*
12:35 The man who walks in the dark *d* not **know** *AIT*
12:44 *he d* not **believe** in me only, *AIT*
12:47 but *d* not **keep** them, *AIT*
12:48 and *d* not **accept** my words; *AIT*
13:19 *it d* **happen** you will believe that I am He. *AIT*
14:24 He who *d* not **love** me will *AIT*
14:29 so that when *it d* **happen** you will believe. *AIT*
15: 2 that *d* **bear** fruit he prunes so that it will be *AIT*
15: 6 If anyone *d* not **remain** in me, *AIT*
15:15 a servant *d* not **know** his master's business. *AIT*
16:17 "What *d he* **mean** by saying, *AIT*
16:18 "What *d he* **mean** by 'a little while'? *AIT*
17:25 though the world *d* not **know** you, *AIT*
Ac 2:12 "What *d* this **mean?"** *AIT*
3:12 "Men of Israel, why *d* this **surprise** *you?* *AIT*
3:23 Anyone who *d* not **listen** *to* him will *AIT*
7:48 the Most High *d* not **live** in houses made *AIT*
10:34 that God *d* not **show favoritism** *AIT*
13:40 the prophets have said *d* not **happen** to you: *AIT*
15:17 says the Lord, *who* **d** these things' *4472*
17:24 and *d* not **live** in temples built by hands. *AIT*
Ro 2: 9 for every human being who **d** evil: *2981*
2:10 honor and peace *for* everyone who **d** good: *2237*
2:11 For God *d* not **show favoritism.** *AIT*
3:12 there is no one who **d** good, not even one." *4472*
4: 3 What *d* the Scripture **say?** *AIT*
4: 5 *to* the man who *d* not **work** *AIT*
5: 5 And hope *d* not **disappoint** us, *AIT*
7:20 but it is sin living in me that **d** it. *NIG*
8: 7 *It d* not **submit** to God's law, *AIT*
8: 9 if anyone *d* not **have** the Spirit of Christ, *AIT*
8: 9 he **d** not **belong to** Christ. *1639*
9:16 It **d** not, therefore, depend on man's desire *NIG*
9:19 "Then why *d* God still **blame** us? *AIT*
9:21 *D* not the potter **have** the right *AIT*
10: 5 "The man who **d** these things will live *4472*
10: 8 But what *d it* **say?** *AIT*
13: 4 for *he d* not **bear** the sword for nothing. *AIT*
13:10 Love **d** no harm to its neighbor. *2237*
14: 3 not look down on him who **d** not, *NIG*
14: 3 and the man who *d* not **eat** everything must *AIT*
14: 3 not condemn the man who **d,** *NIG*
14: 6 one day as special, **d so** to the Lord. *5858[S]*
14: 6 who abstains, **d so** to the Lord and gives thanks to God. *2266+4024[S]*
14:22 the man who *d* not **condemn** himself *AIT*
14:23 everything that **d** not come from faith is sin. *NIG*
1Co 2:14 the Spirit *d* not **accept** the things that come *AIT*
4: 4 but that *d* not **make** *me* **innocent.** *AIT*
5: 1 a kind that **d** not occur even among pagans: *NIG*
7: 4 The wife's body *d* not **belong** to her alone *AIT*
7: 4 *d* not **belong to** him alone but also **to** *AIT*
7:11 But if *she* **d,** she must remain unmarried *6004[S]*
7:37 this *man* also **d** the right thing. *4472*
7:38 So then, he who marries the virgin **d** right, *4472*
7:38 he who *d* not **marry** her does even better. *AIT*
7:38 he who does not marry her **d** even better. *4472*
8: 2 The man who thinks he knows something *d* not yet **know** *AIT*
8: 8 food *d* not **bring** us **near** to God; *AIT*
8: 9 the exercise of your freedom *d* not **become** *AIT*
9: 7 a vineyard and *d* not **eat** of its grapes? *AIT*
9: 7 Who tends a flock and *d* not **drink** of *AIT*
11: 6 If a woman *d* not **cover** her head, *AIT*
11:14 *D* not the very nature of things **teach** *AIT*
13: 4 *It d* not **envy,** it does not boast, *AIT*
13: 4 It does not envy, it *d* not **boast,** *AIT*
13: 6 Love *d* not **delight** in evil but rejoices with *AIT*
14: 2 in a tongue *d* not **speak** to men but to God. *AIT*
14: 8 if the trumpet *d* not **sound** a clear call, *AIT*
14:16 since he *d* not **know** what you are saying? *AIT*
14:24 **someone who d not understand** *2626*
15:27 that this **d** not include God himself, *NIG*
15:36 *d* not **come to life** unless it dies. *AIT*

1Co 15:50 nor *d* the perishable **inherit** *AIT*
16:19 so **d** the church that meets at their house. *NIG*
16:22 If anyone *d* not **love** the Lord— *AIT*
2Co 6:15 What **d** a believer have in common with *NIG*
8:12 not according to what *he d* not **have.** *AIT*
10: 3 we do not wage war **as** the world **d.** *2848*
11:18 **in the way** the world **d,** *2848*
Gal 2: 6 *d* not **judge by external appearance—** *AIT*
2:17 **d that mean that** Christ promotes sin? *727*
3: 5 *D* God **give** you his Spirit *AIT*
3:10 "Cursed is everyone who *d* not **continue** *AIT*
3:12 man who **d** these things will live by them." *4472*
3:16 The Scripture *d* not **say** "and to seeds," *AIT*
3:17 *d* not **set aside** the covenant *AIT*
3:20 however, **d** not represent just one party; *NIG*
4:30 But what *d* the Scripture **say?** *AIT*
5: 8 That kind of persuasion **d** not come from *NIG*
Eph 4: 9 (What *d* "he ascended" **mean** except that he *AIT*
4:16 as each part **d** its work. *NIG*
5:29 just as Christ **d** the church— *NIG*
6: 8 for whatever good *he* **d,** *4472*
Php 1:18 But **what d it matter?** *1142+5515*
Col 3:25 Anyone who **d wrong** will be repaid *92*
4:10 as **d** Mark, the cousin of Barnabas. *NIG*
1Th 2: 3 the appeal we make **d** not spring from error *NIG*
3:12 just as ours **d** for you. *NIG*
4: 8 he who rejects this instruction *d* not **reject** man but God, *AIT*
2Th 3: 6 and *d* not **live** according to the teaching *AIT*
3:14 If anyone *d* not **obey** our instruction *AIT*
1Ti 3: 5 (If anyone *d* not **know** how to manage *AIT*
5: 8 *d* not **provide for** his relatives, *AIT*
6: 3 and *d* not **agree to** the sound instruction *AIT*
2Ti 2: 5 *he d* not **receive the victor's crown** *AIT*
2:15 a workman *who* **d not need to be ashamed** *454*
Tit 1: 2 which God, who *d* **not lie,** *AIT*
Heb 7:27 he *d* not **need** to offer sacrifices day *AIT*
Jas 1: 8 unstable in all he **d.** *NIG*
1:13 nor *d* he **tempt** anyone; *AIT*
1:17 who *d* not **change** like shifting shadows. *AIT*
1:20 for man's anger *d* not **bring about** *AIT*
1:23 to the word but **d** not do what it says is like *NIG*
1:25 he will be blessed in what he **d.** *4474*
1:26 *d* not **keep a tight rein on** his tongue, *AIT*
2:16 but **d** nothing about his physical needs, *1443*
2:24 that a person is justified by **what he d** and *2240*
3:15 Such "wisdom" *d* not **come down** *AIT*
1Pe 4: 2 *he d* not **live** the rest of his earthly life *AIT*
5:13 and so **d** my son Mark. *NIG*
2Pe 1: 9 But *if* anyone *d* not **have** them, *AIT*
1Jn 2: 1 But if anybody *d* **sin,** we have one who *AIT*
2: 4 but *d* not **do** what he commands is a liar, *AIT*
2:11 *he d* not **know** where he is going, *AIT*
2:16 **what he has and d—** *1050*
2:17 man who **d** the will of God lives forever. *4472*
2:24 If it **d,** you also will remain in the Son *1877+3531+5148*[S]
2:29 everyone who **d** what is right has been born *4472*
3: 1 The reason the world *d* not **know** us is *AIT*
3: 7 He who **d** what is right is righteous, *4472*
3: 8 He who **d** what is sinful is of the devil, *4472*
3:10 Anyone who *d* not **do** what is right is not *AIT*
3:10 nor is anyone who *d* not **love** his brother. *AIT*
3:14 Anyone *who d* not **love** remains in death. *AIT*
4: 3 that *d* not **acknowledge** Jesus is not *AIT*
4: 6 but whoever is not from God *d* not **listen** *AIT*
4: 8 Whoever *d* not **love** does not know God, *AIT*
4: 8 Whoever does not love *d* not **know** God, *AIT*
4:20 For anyone who *d* not **love** his brother, *AIT*
5:10 Anyone who *d* not **believe** God has made him out to be a liar, *AIT*
5:12 he who *d* not **have** the Son of God does *AIT*
5:12 not have the Son of God *d* not **have** life. *AIT*
5:16 a sin that **d** not lead to death, *NIG*
5:16 to those whose sin **d** not lead to death. *NIG*
5:17 and there is sin that **d** not lead to death. *NIG*
5:18 *d* not *continue to* **sin;** *AIT*
2Jn 1: 9 Anyone who runs ahead and *d* not **continue** *AIT*
1: 9 in the teaching of Christ *d* not **have** God; *AIT*
1:10 to you and *d* not **bring** this teaching, *AIT*
3Jn 1:11 Anyone who **d what is good** is from God. *16*
1:11 Anyone who **d what is evil** has *2803*
Rev 2:26 To him who overcomes and **d** my will to *5498*
17:10 *he d* **come,** he must remain for a little while. *AIT*
21:23 The city *d* not **need** the sun or the moon *AIT*
21:27 nor will anyone who **d** what is shameful *4472*
22:11 Let him who **d wrong** continue to do wrong; *92*
22:11 let him who *d* **right** continue to do right; *AIT*

DOESN'T (9) [DO]

1Sa 20: 2 Look, my father **d** do anything, 4202
1Ki 18:12 If I go and tell Ahab and he **d** find you, 4202
Mt 17:24 **"D** your teacher pay the temple tax?" *4024*
Mk 7:19 it **d** go into his heart but into his stomach, *4024*
Lk 13:15 **D** each of you on the Sabbath untie his ox *4024*
Ac 19:35 "Men of Ephesus, **d** all the world know that *4024*
1Co 9: 8 **D** the Law say the same thing? *4024*
9:10 Surely he says this for us, **d** he? *3590*
Jas 4:17 the good he ought to do and **d** do it, *3590*

DOG (12) [DOG'S, DOGS]

Ex 11: 7 But among the Israelites not a **d** will bark 3978
Jdg 7: 5 a **d** from those who kneel down to drink." 3978
1Sa 17:43 He said to David, "Am I a **d,** 3978
24:14 A dead **d?** A flea? 3978
2Sa 9: 8 that you should notice a dead **d** like me?" 3978
16: 9 "Why should this dead **d** curse my lord 3978
2Ki 8:13 "How could your servant, a mere **d,** 3978
Job 18:11 on every side and **d** his every step. 7046
Pr 26:11 As a **d** returns to its vomit, 3978
26:17 Like one who seizes a **d** by the ears 3978
Ecc 9: 4 even a live **d** is better off than a dead lion! 3978
2Pe 2:22 "A **d** returns to its vomit," and, *3264*

DOG'S (2) [DOG]

2Sa 3: 8 "Am I a **d** head—on Judah's side? 3978
Isa 66: 3 like one who breaks a **d** neck; 3978

DOGS (27) [DOG]

Ex 22:31 throw it to the **d.** 3978
1Ki 14:11 **D** will eat those belonging to Jeroboam 3978
16: 4 **D** will eat those belonging to Baasha 3978
21:19 where **d** licked up Naboth's blood, 3978
21:19 **d** will lick up your blood—yes, yours!' " 3978
21:23 **'D** will devour Jezebel by the wall 3978
21:24 **"D** will eat those belonging to Ahab 3978
22:38 and the **d** licked up his blood, 3978
2Ki 9:10 **d** will devour her on the plot of ground 3978
9:36 at Jezreel **d** will devour Jezebel's flesh. 3978
Job 30: 1 to put with my sheep **d.** 3978
Ps 22:16 **D** have surrounded me; 3978
22:20 my precious life from the power of the **d.** 3978
59: 6 snarling like **d,** and prowl about the city. 3978
59:14 snarling like **d,** and prowl about the city. 3978
68:23 the tongues of your **d** have their share." 3978
Isa 56:10 they are all mute **d,** they cannot bark; 3978
56:11 They are **d** *with* mighty appetites; 3978
Jer 15: 3 to kill and the **d** to drag away and the birds 3978
Mt 7: 6 "Do not give **d** what is sacred; *3264*
15:26 the children's bread and toss it *to* their **d."** *3249*
15:27 "but even the **d** eat the crumbs that fall *3249*
Mk 7:27 the children's bread and toss it *to* their **d."** *3249*
7:28 "but even the **d** under the table eat *3249*
Lk 16:21 Even the **d** came and licked his sores. *3264*
Php 3: 2 Watch out for those **d,** those men who do evil, *3264*
Rev 22:15 Outside are the **d,** those who practice magic arts, *3264*

DOING (183) [DO]

Ge 2: 2 the work *he had been* **d;** 6913
18:19 of the LORD by **d** what is right and just, 6913
20:10 "What was your reason for **d** this?" 6913
31:12 for I have seen all that Laban *has been* **d** 6913
34:19 lost no time in **d** what they said, 6913
Ex 18:14 that Moses *was* **d** for the people, 6913
18:14 "What is this you *are* **d** for the people? 6913
18:17 "What you *are* **d** is not good. 6913
23: 2 "Do not follow the crowd in *d* **wrong.** AIT
36: 4 So all the skilled craftsmen who *were* **d** all 6913
36: 5 for **d** the work the LORD commanded to 6275
Nu 3: 7 of Meeting by **d** the work of the tabernacle. 6268
3: 8 **fulfilling** the obligations of the Israelites **by d** the work 6268
4:27 whether carrying or **d** other **work,** 6275
22:30 Have I been in the habit of **d** this to you?" 6913
Dt 4:25 **d** evil in the eyes of the LORD your God 6913
9:18 the sin you had committed, **d** what was evil 6913
12:25 because *you will be* **d** what is right in 6913
12:28 *be* **d** what is good and right in the eyes of 6913
13:18 and **d** what is right in his eyes. 6913
17: 2 the LORD gives you is found **d** evil in 6913
Jos 2:14 "If you don't tell what we are **d,** 1821
2:20 But if you tell what we are **d,** 1821
7:10 What *are* you *d* **down** on your face? AIT
10: 1 **d** to Ai and its king as he had done 6913
Jdg 11:27 but you *are* **d** me wrong by waging war 6913
18: 3 What *are* you **d** in this place? 6913
18:18 the priest said to them, "What *are* you **d?"** 6913
1Sa 2:22 heard about everything his sons *were* **d** 6913
8: 8 so they *are* **d** to you. 6913
12:25 Yet if *you* **persist in d evil,** 8317+8317
25:39 He has kept his servant from **d** wrong NIH
2Sa 3:25 and find out everything you *are* **d."** 6913
8:15 **d** what was just and right for all his people. 6913
12: 9 of the LORD by **d** what is evil in his eyes? 6913
12:14 by **d** this you have made the enemies of NIH
1Ki 12:24 every one of you, for this is my **d.' "** 907+4946
14: 8 **d** only what was right in my eyes. 6913
16:19 **d** evil in the eyes of the LORD 6913
19: 9 **"What are you d** here, Elijah?" 3870+4200+4537
19:13 a voice said to him, **"What are you d** here, 3870+4200+4537
22: 3 and yet we *are* **d nothing** to retake it from 3120
2Ki 7: 9 they said to each other, "We're not **d** right. 6913
1Ch 18:14 **d** what was just and right for all his people. 6913
21: 8 "I have sinned greatly *by* **d** this. 6913
21:15 But as the angel *was* **d so,** 8845[S]
2Ch 11: 4 every one of you, for this is my **d.' "** 907+4946
22: 3 for his mother encouraged him in **d wrong.** 8399
31: 7 They began **d this** in the third month 2021+3569+6894[S]
31:20 **d** what was good and right and faithful 6913
34:16 "Your officials *are* **d** everything 6913
35: 6 **d** what the LORD commanded 6913
Ne 2:16 not know where I had gone or what I *was* **d,** 6913
2:16 or officials or any others *who would be* **d** 6913
2:19 "What is this you *are* **d?"** 6913
4: 2 he said, "What are those feeble Jews **d?** 6913
5: 9 I continued, "What you *are* **d** is not right. 6913
6:13 so that I would commit a sin *by* **d** this, 6913
13:17 "What is this wicked thing you *are* **d—** 6913
13:27 you too *are* **d** all this terrible wickedness 6913
Est 9:23 **d** what Mordecai had written to them. NIH
Job 9:12 Who can say to him, 'What *are you* **d?'** 6913
Ps 109:16 For he never thought of **d** a kindness, 6913
Pr 1: 3 *d* what is **right** and just and fair; AIT
2:14 in **d** wrong and rejoice in the perverseness 6913
25:22 **In d this,** you will heap burning coals 3954
Ecc 8: 4 who can say to him, "What *are you* **d?"** 6913
Isa 1:16 of my sight! Stop **d wrong,** 8317
22:16 **What are you d** here 3870+4200+4537
26:10 of uprightness *they go on* **d evil** and regard 6401
38:19 they praise you, as I am **d** today; NIH
43:19 See, I *am* **d** a new thing! 6913
54:15 it will not be my **d;** 907+4946
56: 2 and keeps his hand from **d** any evil." 6913
58:13 and from **d** as you please on my holy day, 6913
58:13 not **d** as you please or speaking idle words, 5162
Jer 4:22 They are skilled in **d evil;** 8317
4:30 What *are* you **d,** O devastated one? 6913
7:13 While you *were* **d** all these things, 6913
7:17 Do you not see what they *are* **d** in the towns 6913
11:15 **"What is** my beloved **d** 4200+4537
11:18 that time he showed me **what** they were **d.** 5095
13:23 Neither can you do good who are accustomed to **d evil.** 8317
17:24 the Sabbath day holy by not **d** any work 6913
32:40 I will never stop **d good** *to* them, 3512
32:41 I will rejoice in **d** them **good** 3201
38:20 "Obey the LORD by **d** what I tell you. NIH
48:10 on *him who is* lax *in* **d** the LORD's work! 6913
Eze 8: 6 "Son of man, do you see what they *are* **d—** 6913
8: 6 the house of Israel *is* **d** here, 6913
8: 9 and detestable things they *are* **d** here." 6913
8:12 of the house of Israel *are* **d** in the darkness, 6913
8:13 "You will see them **d** things that are 6913
8:17 to do the detestable things *they are* **d** here? 6913
12: 9 'What *are* you **d?'** 6913
18: 8 He withholds his hand from **d wrong** 6404
25:12 of Judah and became very guilty *by* **d so,** 5933
33:19 he will live by **d so.** 2157[S]
36:32 to know that I *am* not **d** this for your sake, 6913
Da 4:27 Renounce your sins by **d** what is right, NIH
Mic 7: 3 Both hands are skilled in **d** evil; NIH
Mt 5:46 *Are* not even the tax collectors **d** that? *4472*
5:47 what *are you* **d** more than others? *4472*
6: 3 do not let your left hand know what your right hand *is* **d,** *4472*
11: 2 John heard in prison what Christ was **d,** *2240*
12: 2 Your disciples *are* **d** what is unlawful on *4472*
20: 3 in the marketplace **d nothing.** *734*
20: 6 'Why have you been standing here all day long **d nothing?'** *734*
21:23 "By what authority *are you* **d** these things?" *4472*
21:24 by what authority *I am* **d** these things. *4472*
21:27 by what authority *I am* **d** these things. *4472*
24:46 for that servant whose master finds him **d** *4472*
Mk 2:24 why *are they* **d** what is unlawful on *4472*
3: 8 When they heard all *he was* **d,** *4472*
11: 3 If anyone asks you, 'Why *are you* **d** this?' *4472*
11: 5 "What *are you* **d,** untying that colt?" *4472*
11:28 "By what authority *are you* **d** these things?" *4472*
11:29 by what authority *I am* **d** these things. *4472*
11:33 by what authority *I am* **d** these things." *4472*
Lk 6: 2 "Why *are you* **d** what is unlawful on *4472*
12:43 for that servant whom the master finds **d** so *4472*
13:17 with all the wonderful things he *was* **d.** *1181*
20: 2 by what authority *you are* **d** these things," *4472*
20: 8 by what authority *I am* **d** these things." *4472*
23:34 for they do not know what *they are* **d."** *4472*
Jn 2:23 the miraculous signs *he was* **d** and believed *4472*
3: 2 the miraculous signs you *are* **d** if God were *4472*
5:16 Jesus *was* **d** these things on the Sabbath, *4472*
5:19 he can do only what he sees his Father **d,** *4472*
5:36 and which *I am* **d,** *4472*
7: 4 Since *you are* **d** these things, *4472*
7:51 to find out what *he is* **d?"** *4472*
8:41 You *are* **d** the things your own father does." *4472*
13: 7 "You do not realize now what I *am* **d,** *4472*
14:10 living in me, who *is* **d** his work. *4472*
14:12 in me will do what I *have been* **d.** *4472*
Ac 5: 4 What made you think of **d** such a thing? *NIG*
9:36 who was always **d** good and helping *2240*
10:38 around **d good** and healing all who were *2308*
12: 9 the angel was **d** was really happening; *NIG*
14:15 why *are you* **d** this? *4472*
15:36 of the Lord and see how *they are* **d."** *2400*
17:21 foreigners who lived there spent their time **d** nothing *1650*
19:14 a Jewish chief priest, were **d** this. *4472*
24:18 in the temple courts **d** this. *NIG*
25:11 I am guilty of **d** anything deserving death, *4556*
26:31 not **d** anything that deserves death *4556*
Ro 1:13 (but have been prevented from **d** so *NIG*
1:30 they invent ways of **d** evil; *NIG*
2: 7 by persistence in **d** good seek glory, *2240*
7:19 this *I keep on* **d.** *4556*
12:20 *In* **d** this, you will heap burning coals *4472*
2Co 11: 1 but *you are already* **d that.** *462*[S]
11:12 And *I will keep on* **d** what I am doing *4472*
11:12 And I will keep on doing what *I am* **d** *4472*
Gal 6: 9 Let us not become weary *in* **d** good, *2237*
Eph 4:28 **d** something useful with his own hands, *2237*
6: 6 **d** the will of God from your heart. *4472*
6:21 also may know how I am and what *I am* **d.** *4556*
Col 1: 6 just as it has been **d** among you since *NIG*

1Th 5:11 just as in fact *you are* **d.** *4472*
2Th 3: 4 in the Lord that *you are* **d** and will continue *4472*
3:13 you, brothers, never tire of **d what is right.** *2818*
1Ti 6:21 and in so **d** have wandered from the faith. *NIG*
Tit 1:16 disobedient and unfit for **d** anything good. *2240*
2: 7 an example *by* **d** what is good. *2240*
3: 8 to devote themselves *to* **d** what is good. *2240*
3:14 to devote themselves to **d** what is good, *2240*
Heb 10:25 as some are in the habit of **d,** *NIG*
13: 2 by **so d** some people have entertained angels *4047S*
13:21 with everything good for **d** his will, *4472*
Jas 1:25 not forgetting what he has heard, but **d** it— *4475*
2: 8 *you are* **d** right. *4472*
1Pe 2:12 though they accuse you of **d wrong,** *2804*
2:15 that *by* **d good** you should silence *16*
2:20 a beating *for* **d wrong** and endure it? *279*
2:20 if you suffer *for* **d good** and you endure it, *16*
3:17 to suffer *for* **d good** than for doing evil. *16*
3:17 to suffer for doing good than *for* **d evil.** *2803*
4: 3 in the past **d** what pagans choose to do— *2981*
3Jn 1: 5 you are faithful in what *you are* **d** for *2237*
1:10 I will call attention to what *he is* **d,** *4472*
Rev 2:19 and that you are now **d** more than you did *2240*

DOLE (1)

Lev 26:26 and *they will* **d out** the bread by weight. 8740

DOLEFUL (KJV) See MOURNFUL

DOMAIN (2) [DOMINION]

Dt 33:20 "Blessed is he who enlarges Gad's **d!** NIH
Eze 27: 4 Your **d** was on the high seas; 1473

DOMINION (18) [DOMAIN]

Job 25: 2 "**D** and awe belong to God; 5440
38:33 Can you set up [God's] **d** over the earth? 5428
Ps 22:28 for **d** belongs to the LORD and he rules 4867
103:22 all his works everywhere in his **d.** 4939
114: 2 Judah became God's sanctuary, Israel his **d.** 4939
145:13 and your **d** endures through all generations. 4939
Da 2:37 of heaven has given you **d** and power 10424
4: 3 his **d** endures from generation 10717
4:22 your **d** extends to distant parts of the earth. 10717
4:34 His **d** is an eternal dominion; 10717
4:34 His dominion is an eternal **d;** 10717
6:26 his **d** will never end. 10717
7:14 His **d** is an everlasting dominion that will 10717
7:14 His dominion is an everlasting **d** that will 10717
Mic 4: 8 the former **d** will be restored to you; 4939
1Co 15:24 the Father after he has destroyed all **d,** *794*
Eph 1:21 and authority, power and **d,** and every title *3262*
Col 1:13 from the **d** of darkness and brought us into *2026*

DOMINIONS (KJV) See RULERS

DON'T (213) [DO, NOT]

Ge 4: 9 "I **d** know," he replied. 4202
19: 7 **D** do this wicked thing. 440
19: 8 But **d** do anything to these men, 440
19:17 **D** look back, and don't stop anywhere in 440
19:17 and **d** stop anywhere in the plain! 440
21:26 "I **d** know who has done this. 4202
27: 2 "I am now an old man and **d** know the day 4202
30:31 "**D** give me anything," Jacob replied. 4202
31:35 Rachel said to her father, "**D** be angry, 440
35:17 "**D** be afraid, for you have another son." 440
37:22 "**D** shed any blood. 440
37:22 but **d** lay a hand on him." 440
42:23 We **d** know who put our silver 4202
43:23 "**D** be afraid. 440
44:15 **D** you know that a man 4202
45: 9 Come down to me; **d** delay. 440
45:24 "**D** quarrel on the way!" 440
50:19 But Joseph said to them, "**D** be afraid. 440
50:21 So then, **d** be afraid. 440
Ex 5: 8 **d** reduce the quota. 4202
9:28 you **d** have to stay any longer." 4202
32: 1 we **d** know what has happened to him." 4202
32:23 we **d** know what has happened to him.' 4202
Jos 2: 5 I **d** know which way they went. 4202
2:14 "If you **d** tell what we are doing, 4202
8: 4 **D** go very far from it. 440
10:19 But **d** stop! 440
10:19 the rear and **d** let them reach their cities, 440
Jdg 4: 8 but if you **d** go with me, I won't go." 4202
4:18 **D** be afraid." 440
14:16 You **d** really love me. 4202
15:11 "**D** you realize that the Philistines are rulers 4202
18: 9 **D** hesitate to go there and take it over. 440
18:19 **D say a word.** 3338+6584+7023+8492
18:25 The Danites answered, "**D** argue with us, 440
19:19 We **d** need anything." 401
19:20 Only **d** spend the night in the square." 440
19:23 "No, my friends, **d** be so vile. 440
19:23 **d** do this disgraceful thing. 440
19:24 **d** do such a disgraceful thing." 4202
Ru 1:16 "**D** urge me to leave you or to turn back 440
1:20 "**D** call me Naomi," she told them. 440
2: 8 **D** go and glean in another field 440
2: 8 in another field and **d** go away from here. 4202
2:15 among the sheaves, **d** embarrass her. 4202
2:16 and **d** rebuke her." 4202
3: 3 but **d** let him know you are there 440
Ru 3:11 And now, my daughter, **d** be afraid. 440
3:14 "**D** let it be known that a woman came to 440
3:17 of barley, saying, '**D** go back 440
1Sa 1: 8 Why **d** you eat? 4202
1: 8 **D** I mean more to you than ten sons?" 4202
2:16 if you **d,** I'll take it by force." 4202
4:20 "**D** despair; you have given birth to a son." 440
17:55 "As surely as you live, O king, I **d** know." 561
19:11 "If you **d** run for your life tonight, 401
20:30 **D** I know that you have sided with the son 4202
20:38 "Hurry! Go quickly! **D** stop!" 440
21: 4 "I **d** have any ordinary bread on hand; 401
21: 8 "**D** you have a spear or a sword here? 403
22:23 Stay with me; **d** be afraid; 440
23:17 "**D** be afraid," he said. 440
26: 9 But David said to Abishai, "**D** destroy him! 440
28:13 The king said to her, "**D** be afraid. 440
29: 6 but the rulers **d** approve of you. 4202
2Sa 2:26 **D** you realize that this will end 4202
9: 7 "**D** be afraid," David said to him, 440
11:25 '**D** let this upset you; 440
13:12 "**D,** my brother!" 440
13:12 "**D** force me. 440
13:12 **D** do this wicked thing. 440
13:20 **D** take this thing to heart." 440
13:28 **D** be afraid. 440
14: 2 and **d** use any cosmetic lotions. 440
18:22 You **d** have any news that will bring you 401
18:29 your servant, but I **d** know what it was." 4202
19: 7 I swear by the LORD that if you **d** go out, 401
1Ki 3:26 **D** kill him!" 440
17:12 she replied, "I **d** have any bread— 561
17:13 Elijah said to her, "**D** be afraid. 440
18:12 I **d** know where the Spirit of 4202
18:40 **D** let anyone get away!" 440
20: 8 "**D** listen to him or agree to his demands." 440
22: 3 "**D** you know that Ramoth Gilead belongs 2022
2Ki 4: 3 **D** ask for just a few. 440
4:16 "**D** mislead your servant, O man of God!" 440
4:24 **d** slow down for me unless I tell you." 440
4:28 "Didn't I tell you, '**D** raise my hopes'?" 4202
6:16 "**D** be afraid," the prophet answered. 440
6:32 to the elders, "**D** you see 2022
9: 3 Then open the door and run; **d** delay!" 4202
9:15 **d** let anyone slip out of the city to go 440
18:26 **D** speak to us in Hebrew in the hearing of 440
23:18 "**D** let anyone disturb his bones." 440
2Ch 13: 5 **D** you know that the LORD, 4202
Ne 4:14 "**D** be afraid of them. 440
Pr 23:35 They beat me, but I **d** feel it! 1153
Isa 7: 4 'Be careful, keep calm and **d** be afraid. 440
29:12 he will answer, "I **d** know how to read." 4202
36:11 **D** speak to us in Hebrew in the hearing of 440
65: 5 **d** come near me, 440
65: 8 '**D** destroy it, there is yet some good in it,' 440
Jer 13:12 '**D** we know that every wineskin should 4202
36:19 **D** let anyone know where you are." 440
39:12 **d** harm him but do 440
40: 4 but if you do not want to, then **d** come. 2532
40:14 "**D** you know that Baalis king of 2022
40:16 "**D** do such a thing! 440
41: 8 But ten of them said to Ishmael, "**D** kill us! 440
La 4:15 **D** touch us!" 440
Da 5:10 "**D** be alarmed! 10031
5:10 **D** look so pale! 10031
Am 7:13 **D** prophesy anymore at Bethel, 4202
Mt 8: 4 "See that you **d** tell **anyone.** *3594*
10:31 So **d** be afraid; *3590*
14:27 **D** be afraid." *3590*
15: 2 They **d** wash their hands before they eat!" *4024*
15:17 "**D** you see that whatever enters *4024*
16: 9 **D** you remember the five loaves for *4028*
16:11 How is it you **d** understand that I was *4024*
17: 7 "**D** be afraid." *3590*
17: 9 "**D** tell **anyone** what you have seen, *3594*
20:15 **D** I have the right to do what I want *4024*
20:22 "You **d** know what you are asking," *4024*
21:27 So they answered Jesus, "We **d** know." *4024*
25:12 'I tell you the truth, I **d** know you.' *4024*
26:70 "I **d** know what you're talking about," *4024*
26:72 "I **d** know the man!" *4024*
26:74 "I **d** know the man!" *4024*
27:13 "**D** you hear the testimony they are bringing *4024*
27:19 "**D** have **anything** to do with *3594*
Mk 1:44 "See that you **d** tell **this** to anyone. *3594*
4:13 "**D** you understand this parable? *4024*
4:21 Instead, **d** you put it on its stand? *4024*
4:38 "Teacher, **d** you care if we drown?" *4024*
5:36 "**D** be afraid; just believe." *3590*
6:50 **D** be afraid." *3590*
7: 5 "Why **d** your disciples live according to *4024*
7:18 "**D** you see that nothing that enters a man *4024*
8:18 And **d** you remember? *4024*
8:26 saying, "**D** go into the village." *3593*
10:38 "You **d** know what you are asking," *4024*
11:33 So they answered Jesus, "We **d** know." *4024*
14:68 "I **d** know or understand what you're talking *4046*
14:71 "I **d** know this man you're talking about." *4024*
16: 6 "**D** be alarmed," he said. *3590*
Lk 3:13 "**D** collect any more than you are required *3594*
3:14 He replied, "**D** extort money *3594*
3:14 "Don't extort money **and d** accuse people falsely— *3593*
5:10 Then Jesus said to Simon, "**D** be afraid; *3590*
5:14 Then Jesus ordered him, "**D** tell **anyone,** *3594*
7: 6 "Lord, **d** trouble yourself, *3590*
7:13 to her and he said, "**D** cry." *3590*
Lk 8:28 I beg you, **d** torture me!" *3590*
8:49 "**D** bother the teacher **any more.**" *3600*
8:50 Jesus said to Jairus, "**D** be afraid; *3590*
10:40 **d** you care that my sister has left me to do *4024*
11: 7 the one inside answers, '**D** bother me. *3590*
12: 7 of your head are all numbered. **D** be afraid; *3590*
12:56 How is it that you **d** know how *4024*
12:57 "Why **d** you judge for yourselves *4024*
13:25 'I **d** know you or where you come from.' *4024*
13:27 'I **d** know you or where you come from. *4024*
18: 4 though I **d** fear God or care about men, *4024*
19:14 'We **d** want this man to be our king.' *4024*
20: 7 "We **d** know where it was from." *3590*
22:36 and if you **d** have a sword, *3590*
22:57 "Woman, I **d** know him," he said. *4024*
22:60 I **d** know what you're talking about!" *4024*
23:40 "**D** you fear God," he said, *4028*
Jn 6:20 But he said to them, "It is I; **d** be afraid." *3590*
8:46 why **d** you believe me? *4024*
9:12 "I **d** know," he said. *4024*
9:21 or who opened his eyes, we **d** know. *4024*
9:25 "Whether he is a sinner or not, I **d** know. *4024*
9:29 we **d** even know where he comes from." *4024*
9:30 You **d** know where he comes from, *4024*
14: 5 "Lord, we **d** know where you are going, *4024*
14: 9 Jesus answered: "**D** you know me, Philip, *4024*
14:10 **D** you believe that I am in the Father, *4024*
16:18 We **d** understand what he is saying." *4024*
19:10 "**D** you realize I have power either *4024*
20: 2 and we **d** know where they have put him!" *4024*
20:13 "and I **d** know where they have put him." *4024*
Ac 7:40 we **d** know what has happened to him!' *4024*
16:28 But Paul shouted, "**D** harm yourself! *3594*
20:10 "**D** be alarmed," he said. *3590*
23:21 **D** give in to them, *3590*
23:22 "**D** tell **anyone** that you have reported this *3594*
Ro 6: 3 Or **d** *you* **know** that all *51*
6:16 **D** you know that when you offer yourselves *4024*
11: 2 **D** you know what the Scripture says in *4024*
1Co 1:16 I **d** remember if I baptized anyone else.) *4024*
3:16 **D** you know that you yourselves are God's temple *4024*
5: 6 **D** you know that a little yeast works *4024*
7:21 **D** let it trouble you— *3590*
9: 4 **D** we have the right to food and drink? *3590+4024*
9: 5 **D** we have the right to take a believing wife *3590+4024*
9:13 **D** you know that those who work in *4024*
10:12 be careful that you **d** fall! *3590*
11:22 **D** you have homes to eat and drink in? *3590+4024*
12:21 "I **d** need you!" *4024*
12:21 "I **d** need you!" *4024*
2Th 2: 3 **D** let anyone deceive you in any way, *3590*
2: 5 **D** you remember that when I was *4024*
1Ti 4:12 **D** let **anyone** look down on you *3594*
2Ti 2:23 **D have anything to do with** *4148*
Jas 1:16 **D** be deceived, my dear brothers. *3590*
2: 1 **d** show favoritism. *3590*
4: 1 **D** they come from your desires that battle *4024*
4: 2 You want something but **d** get it. *4024*
4: 4 **d** you know that friendship with *4024*
5: 9 **D** grumble against each other, brothers, *3590*

DONATED (1)

Ezr 8:25 and all Israel present there *had* **d** for the house of our God. 8123

DONE (549) [DO]

Ge 2: 3 from all the work of creating that he *had* **d.** 6913
3:13 "What is this *you have* **d?"** 6913
3:14 "Because *you have* **d** this, 6913
4:10 The LORD said, "What *have you* **d?** 6913
8:21 as *I have* **d.** 6913
9:24 and found out what his youngest son *had* **d** 6913
12:18 "What *have you* **d** to me?" 6913
18:21 down and see if *what they have* **d** is as bad 6913
20: 5 *I have* **d** this with a clear conscience 6913
20: 9 "What *have you* **d** to us? 6913
20: 9 *You have* **d** things to me that should not 6913
20: 9 to me that *should* not **be d."** 6913
21:26 "I don't know who *has* **d** this. 6913
22:16 that because *you have* **d** this and have 6913
24:66 Then the servant told Isaac all *he had* **d.** 6913
26:10 "What is this *you have* **d** to us? 6913
27:19 *I have* **d** as you told me. 6913
28:15 until *I have* **d** what I have promised you." 6913
29:25 "What is this *you have* **d** to me? 6913
30:26 You know how much work I've **d** *for* you." 6268
31:26 Laban said to Jacob, "What *have you* **d?** 6913
31:28 *You have* **d** a foolish thing. 6913
34: 7 because Shechem *had* **d** a disgraceful thing 6913
34: 7 a *thing that should* not **be d.** 6913
39:22 for all that *was* **d** there. 6913
40:15 and even here *I have* **d** nothing 6913
41:21 no one could tell that they *had* **d so;** 448+995+7931S
42:25 After this *was* **d** for them, 6913
42:28 "What is this that God *has* **d** to us?" 6913
44: 5 This is a wicked thing *you have* **d.' "** 6913
44:15 "What is this *you have* **d?** 6913
45: 4 When *they had* **d so,** he said, 5602S
50:20 to accomplish what is now being **d,** NIH
Ex 1:18 "Why *have you* **d** this? 6913
3:16 over you and have seen what *has* **been d** 6913
14: 5 "What *have we* **d?** 6913

Ex 14:11 What *have you* **d** to us by bringing us out 6913
18: 1 heard of everything God *had* **d** for Moses 6913
18: 8 about everything the LORD *had* **d** 6913
18: 9 the LORD *had* **d** for Israel in rescuing them 6913
31:15 For six days, work *is to* **be d,** 6913
34:10 before **d** in any nation in all the world. 1343
35: 2 For six days, work *is to* **be d,** 6913
36: 5 the work the LORD commanded to *be* **d."** 6913
36:11 and the same *was* **d** with the end curtain in 6913
39:42 The Israelites *had* **d** all the work just as 6913
39:43 the work and saw that *they had* **d** it just as 6913
Lev 8: 5 the LORD has commanded to *be* **d."** 6913
8:34 What *has been* **d** today was commanded by 6913
16:34 And *it was* **d,** as the LORD commanded 6913
18:27 for all these things *were* **d** *by* 6913
20:12 What *they have* **d** is a perversion; 6913
20:13 both of them *have* **d** what is detestable. 6913
24:19 whatever *he has* **d** must be done to him: 6913
24:19 whatever he has done *must* **be d** to him: 6913
Nu 4:26 that *needs to* **be d** with these things. 6913
4:27 *is to be* **d** under the direction of Aaron 2118
11:11 What *have I* **d** *to* **displease** you AIT
15:24 and if *this is* **d** unintentionally without 6913
15:34 it was not clear what *should* **be d** to him. 6913
22: 2 of Zippor saw all that Israel *had* **d** to 6913
22:28 "What *have I* **d** to you 6913
23:11 "What *have you* **d** to me? 6913
23:11 *you have* **d nothing but bless** them!" 1385+1385
23:23 'See what God *has* **d!'** 7188
32:13 whole generation of those *who had* **d** evil in his sight was gone. 6913
Dt 2:22 The LORD *had* **d** the same for 6913
2:30 as he has now **d.** NIH
3: 6 as *we had* **d** with Sihon king of Heshbon, 6913
3:21 that the LORD your God *has* **d** 6913
11: 7 the LORD *has* **d.** 6913
13:14 that this detestable thing *has* **been d** 6913
15: 2 This is how it is to be **d:** NIH
17: 4 this detestable thing *has* **been d** in Israel, 6913
17: 5 the man or woman who *has* **d** this evil deed 6913
19:20 an evil thing *be* **d** among you. 6913
21: 7 nor did our eyes see it **d.** NIH
21: 9 since *you have* **d** what is right in the eyes of 6913
22:21 *She has* **d** a disgraceful thing in Israel 6913
22:25 the man who *has* **d this** shall die. 6640+8886[S]
25: 9 "This is what **is d** to the man who will 6913
26:14 *I have* **d** everything you commanded me. 6913
28:20 of the evil you have **d** in forsaking him. 5095
29:24 "Why *has* the LORD **d** this to this land? 6913
32:27 the LORD *has* not **d** all this.' " 7188
Jos 1:15 as he has **d** for you, NIH
4:10 the LORD had commanded Joshua *was* **d** 9462
4:23 the Jordan just what *he had* **d** to the Red Sea 6913
6:23 young men who *had* **d** the **spying** went in AIT
7:15 of the LORD and *has* **d** a disgraceful thing 6913
7:19 Tell me what *you have* **d;** 6913
7:20 This is what *I have* **d:** 6913
9: 3 of Gibeon heard what Joshua *had* **d** 6913
10: 1 to Ai and its king as *he had* **d** to Jericho 6913
10:28 to the king of Makkedah as *he had* **d** to the king of Jericho. 6913
10:30 And he did to its king as *he had* **d** to the king of Jericho. 6913
10:32 just as *he had* **d** to Libnah. 6913
10:35 just as *they had* **d** to Lachish. 6913
10:39 to Debir and its king as *they had* **d** to Libnah 6913
22: 2 "You *have* **d** all that Moses the servant of 9068
23: 3 the LORD your God *has* **d** 6913
24:31 the LORD *had* **d** for Israel. 6913
Jdg 2: 2 Why *have you* **d** this? 6913
2: 7 the great things the LORD *had* **d** for Israel. 6913
2:10 the LORD nor what *he had* **d** for Israel. 6913
8:35 for all the good things *he had* **d** for them. 6913
9:56 the wickedness that Abimelech *had* **d** 6913
14: 6 nor his mother what *he had* **d.** 6913
15:11 What *have you* **d** to us?" 6913
18: 4 He told them what Micah *had* **d** for him, 6913
19:30 "Such a thing has never been seen or **d,** 2118
20:10 for all this vileness **d** in Israel." 6913
20:30 **as** they had **d before.** 928+3869+7193+7193
Ru 2:11 "I've been told all about what *you have* **d** 6913
2:12 the LORD repay you for **what** you have **d.** 7189
3:16 she told her everything Boaz *had* **d** for her 6913
1Sa 2:32 Although **good** *will be* **d** *to* Israel, 3512
8: 8 As *they have* **d** from the day I brought them 6913
11: 7 "This is what *will* **be d** to the oxen 6913
12: 3 If I have **d** any of these, NIH
12:20 "You *have* **d** all this evil; 6913
12:24 **great things** *he has* **d** 1540
13:11 "What *have you* **d?"** 6913
14:35 it was the first time *he had* **d this.** 1215+3378+4200+4640[S]
14:43 "Tell me what *you have* **d."** 6913
17:26 "What *will* **be d** for 6913
17:27 "This is what *will* **be d** for 6913
17:29 "Now what *have I* **d?"** 6913
19: 4 **what** he has **d** has benefited you greatly. 5126
19:18 at Ramah and told him all that Saul *had* **d** 6913
20: 1 "What *have I* **d?** 6913
20:32 What *has he* **d?"** 6913
24:12 **avenge** *the* **wrongs** you have *d* AIT
25:30 When the LORD *has* **d** 6913
26:16 What *you have* **d** is not good. 6913
26:18 What *have I* **d,** 6913
26:19 If, however, men have **d** it, NIH
28: 9 "Surely you know what Saul *has* **d.** 6913
1Sa 28:17 The LORD *has* **d** what he predicted 6913
28:18 the LORD *has* **d** this to you today. 6913
29: 8 "But what *have I* **d?"** 6913
31:11 of what the Philistines *had* **d** to Saul, 6913
2Sa 2: 6 the same favor because *you have* **d** this. 6913
3:24 "What *have you* **d?** 6913
7:11 and have **d** ever since NIH
7:21 *you have* **d** this great thing 6913
8:11 as *he had* **d** with the silver and gold 7727[S]
11:27 thing David *had* **d** displeased the LORD. 6913
13:12 Such a thing *should* not **be d** in Israel! 6913
13:16 greater wrong than what *you have already* **d** 6913
21:11 Saul's concubine, *had* **d,** 6913
22:22 not **d evil** by turning from my God. 8399
24:10 "I have sinned greatly in what *I have* **d.** 6913
24:10 **d** a very **foolish thing."** 6118
24:17 "I am the one who has sinned and **d wrong.** 6390
24:17 What *have they* **d?** 6913
1Ki 1:27 *Is* this something my lord the king *has* **d** 2118
7:51 work King Solomon *had* **d** for the temple 6913
8:25 to walk before me as *you have* **d.'** 2143[S]
8:32 down on his own head **what** he has **d.** 2006
8:47 *we have* **d wrong,** we have acted wickedly'; 6390
8:66 for all the good things the LORD *had* **d** 6913
9: 8 the LORD **d** such a thing to this land and 6913
11: 6 as David his father had **d.** NIH
11:33 nor **d** what is right in my eyes, 6913
13:11 the man of God *had* **d** there that day. 5126+6913
14: 9 You have **d** more evil than all who lived 6913
14:22 stirred up his jealous anger more than their fathers *had* **d.** 6913
15: 3 He committed all the sins his father *had* **d** 6913
15: 5 For David *had* **d** what was right in the eyes 6913
15:11 as his father David had **d.** NIH
16: 7 because of all the evil *he had* **d** 6913
18: 9 "What *have I* **d wrong,"** asked Obadiah, 2627
18:36 and *have* **d** all these things 6913
19: 1 Ahab told Jezebel everything Elijah *had* **d** 6913
19:20 "What *have I* **d** to you?" 6913
20:22 and see what *must be* **d,** 6913
22:53 to anger, just as his father *had* **d.** 6913
2Ki 1:16 Because you have **d** this, NIH
3: 2 but not as his father and mother had **d.** NIH
4:13 Now what *can be* **d** for you? 6913
4:14 "What *can be* **d** for her?" 6913
5:13 *would* you not *have* **d** it? 6913
7:12 "I will tell you what the Arameans *have* **d** 6913
8: 4 about all the great things Elisha *has* **d."** 6913
8:18 as the house of Ahab *had* **d,** 6913
8:27 as the house of Ahab had **d,** NIH
10:10 The LORD *has* **d** what he promised 6913
10:30 "Because *you have* **d well** 3201
10:30 and *have* **d** to the house of Ahab all I had 6913
12: 7 "Why aren't you repairing the **damage** *d to* AIT
14: 3 but not as his father David had **d.** NIH
15: 3 just as his father Amaziah *had* **d.** 6913
15: 9 as his fathers *had* **d.** 6913
15:34 just as his father Uzziah *had* **d.** 6913
17: 4 as he had **d** year by year. NIH
17:11 before them had **d.** NIH
18: 3 just as his father David *had* **d.** 6913
18:14 *"I have* **d wrong.** 2627
19:11 of Assyria *have* **d** to all the countries, 6913
20: 3 and *have* **d** what is good in your eyes." 6913
21: 3 as Ahab king of Israel *had* **d.** 6913
21:11 *He has* **d** more **evil** than 8317
21:15 because *they have* **d** evil in my eyes 6913
21:20 as his father Manasseh *had* **d.** 6913
23:17 of Bethel the very things *you have* **d** to it." 6913
23:19 Just as *he had* **d** at Bethel, 5126+6913
23:26 *d to* **provoke** him **to anger.** AIT
23:32 just as his fathers *had* **d.** 6913
23:37 just as his fathers *had* **d.** 6913
24: 3 of the sins of Manasseh and all *he had* **d,** 6913
24: 9 just as his father *had* **d.** 6913
24:19 just as Jehoiakim *had* **d.** 6913
1Ch 6:49 of incense in connection with all that was **d** 4856
10:11 of everything the Philistines *had* **d** to Saul, 6913
16: 8 among the nations **what** he has **d.** 6613
16:12 Remember the wonders *he has* **d,** 6913
17:10 and have **d** ever since NIH
17:19 *you have* **d** this great thing 6913
18:11 as he had **d** with the silver NIH
21: 8 **d** a very **foolish thing."** 6118
21:17 I am the one who has sinned and **d wrong.** 8317+8317
21:17 What *have they* **d?** 6913
28: 7 as is being **d** at this time.' NIH
29: 5 all the work to be **d by** the craftsmen. 928+3338
2Ch 5: 1 the work Solomon *had* **d** for the temple of 6913
6:16 as *you have* **d.'** 2143[S]
6:23 down on his own head **what** he has **d.** 2006
6:37 *we have* **d wrong** and acted wickedly'; 6390
7:10 the good things the LORD *had* **d** for David 6913
7:21 the LORD **d** such a thing to this land and 6913
16: 9 . You *have* **d a foolish thing,** 6118
21: 6 as the house of Ahab *had* **d,** 6913
22: 4 as the house of Ahab had **d,** NIH
24:16 because of the good *he had* **d** in Israel 6913
25:16 because *you have* **d** this and have 6913
26: 4 just as his father Amaziah *had* **d.** 6913
27: 2 just as his father Uzziah *had* **d,** 6913
29: 2 just as his father David *had* **d.** 6913
29:36 because it *was* **d** so quickly. 2118
31:11 and *this was* **d.** 3922[S]
32: 1 After *all* that Hezekiah had so faithfully **d,** 1821
32:13 and my fathers *have* **d** to all the peoples of 6913
2Ch 33:22 as his father Manasseh *had* **d.** 6913
Ezr 7:23 *let it* **be d** with diligence for the temple of 10522
9: 1 After these things *had been* **d,** 3983
10: 3 *Let it* **be d** according to the Law. 6913
Ne 5:19 for all *I have* **d** for these people. 6913
6:14 O my God, because of what they have **d;** 5126
6:16 that this work *had* **been d** with the help 6913
13: 7 about the evil thing Eliashib *had* **d** 6913
13:14 not blot out what I *have* so faithfully **d** for 6913
Est 1:15 what *must be* **d** to Queen Vashti?" 6913
1:16 "Queen Vashti *has* **d wrong,** 6390
2: 1 what *she had* **d** and what he had decreed 6913
2:20 as *she had* **d** when he was bringing her up. 2118
4: 1 Mordecai learned of all that *had* **been d,** 6913
4:16 When this is **d,** I will go to the king, NIH
6: 3 "Nothing *has* **been d** for him," 6913
6: 6 *be* **d** for the man the king delights 6913
6: 9 'This is what **is d** for the man 6913
6:11 "This is what **is d** for the man 6913
9:12 What *have they* **d** in the rest of 6913
9:14 So the king commanded that this **be d.** 6913
Job 7:20 If I have sinned, what *have I* **d** to you, 7188
12: 9 that the hand of the LORD *has* **d** this? 6913
21:31 Who repays him for what *he has* **d?** 6913
22:28 What you decide on *will be* **d,** 7756
34:11 He repays a man for **what** he has **d;** 7189
34:32 if *I have* **d** wrong, I will not do so again.' 7188
36: 9 he tells them **what** they have **d—** 7189
36:23 or said to him, *'You have* **d** wrong'? 7188
Ps 7: 3 if *I have* **d** this and there is guilt 6913
7: 4 if *I have* **d** evil *to* him who is at peace 1694
9:11 proclaim among the nations **what** he has **d.** 6613
18:21 not **d evil** by turning from my God. 8399
22:31 for *he has* **d** it. 6913
28: 4 **what** their hands have **d** 5126
28: 5 **what** his hands have **d,** 5126
39: 9 for you are the *one who has* **d** this. 6913
40: 5 are the wonders you *have* **d.** 6913
50:21 These things *you have* **d** and I kept silent; 6913
51: 4 have I sinned and **d** what is evil 6913
52: 9 for *what you have* **d;** 6913
59: 4 I have **d** no wrong, NIH
62:12 according to **what** he has **d.** 5126
64: 9 works of God and ponder **what** he has **d.** 5126
66: 5 Come and see **what** God has **d,** 5149
66:16 let me tell you what *he has* **d** for me. 6913
68:28 O God, as *you have* **d** before. 7188
71:19 O God, *you* who *have* **d** great things. 6913
78: 4 his power, and the wonders *he has* **d.** 6913
78:11 They forgot **what** he had **d,** 6613
98: 1 for *he has* **d** marvelous things; 6913
99: 4 in Jacob *you have* **d** what is just and right. 6913
105: 1 among the nations **what** he has **d.** 6613
105: 5 Remember the wonders *he has* **d,** 6913
106: 6 *we have* **d wrong** and acted wickedly. 6390
106:13 But they soon forgot **what** he had **d** and did 5126
106:21 *who had* **d** great things in Egypt, 6913
109:27 that you, O LORD, *have* **d** it. 6913
111: 8 **d** in faithfulness and uprightness. 6913
118:15 LORD's right hand *has* **d** mighty things! 6913
118:16 the LORD's right hand *has* **d** mighty things!" 6913
118:17 **what** the LORD has **d.** 5126
118:23 the LORD *has* **d** this, 2118
119:121 *I have* **d** what is righteous and just; 6913
126: 2 "The LORD *has* **d** great things for them." 6913
126: 3 The LORD *has* **d** great things for us, 6913
137: 8 for what *you have* **d** to us— 1694
143: 5 **what** your hands have **d.** 5126
147:20 *He has* **d** this for no other nation; 6913
Pr 3:30 when *he has* **d** you no harm. 1694
19:17 and he will reward him for **what** he has **d.** 1691
21:15 *When* justice *is* **d,** it brings joy 6913
24:12 according to **what** he has **d?** 7189
24:29 "I'll do to him as *he has* **d** to me; 6913
30:20 *'I've* **d** nothing wrong.' 7188
Ecc 1: 9 what *has* **been d** will be done again; 6913
1: 9 what has been done *will* **be d** *again;* 6913
1:13 and to explore by wisdom all that **is d** 6913
1:14 I have seen all the things that **are d** under 6913
2:11 when I surveyed all that my hands *had* **d** 6913
2:12 What more can king's successor do than what *has* already *been* **d?** 6913
2:17 that **is d** under the sun was grievous to me. 6913
3:11 yet they cannot fathom what God *has* **d** 6913
4: 3 has not seen the evil that **is d** under 5126+6913
7:13 Consider **what** God has **d:** 5126
8: 9 as I applied my mind to everything **d** under 6913
8:17 then I saw all **that** God has **d.** 5126
Isa 3:11 **what** their hands have **d.** 1691
5: 4 What more *could have been* **d** 6913
5: 4 for my vineyard than *I have* **d** for it? 6913
10:13 " 'By the strength of my hand *I have* **d** this, 6913
12: 4 among the nations **what** he has **d,** 6613
12: 5 for *he has* **d** glorious things; 6913
25: 1 in perfect faithfulness *you have* **d** marvelous things, 6913
26:12 all that we have accomplished *you have* **d** 7188
33:13 You who are far away, hear what *I have* **d;** 6913
37:11 of Assyria *have* **d** to all the countries, 6913
38: 3 and *have* **d** what is good in your eyes." 6913
38:15 and *he* himself *has* **d** this. 6913
41: 4 Who *has* **d** this and carried it through, 7188
41:20 that the hand of the LORD *has* **d** this, 6913
44:23 O heavens, for the LORD *has* **d** this; 6913
53: 9 though *he had* **d** no violence, 6913
59:18 According to **what** they have **d,** 1692
63: 7 according to all the LORD *has* **d** *for* us— 1694

Isa 63: 7 the many good things *he has* **d** for the house 1694
Jer 2:23 consider what *you have* **d.** 6913
3: 6 "Have you seen what faithless Israel *has* **d?** 6913
3: 7 that after she *had* **d** all this she would return 6913
4: 4 like fire because of the evil you have **d—** 5095
5:13 so *let* what they say **be d** to them." 6913
5:19 'Why *has* the LORD our God **d** all this 6913
7:30 " 'The people of Judah *have* **d** evil 6913
8: 6 saying, "What *have I* **d?"** 6913
11:17 of Israel and the house of Judah *have* **d** evil 6913
16:10 What wrong have we **d?** NIH
18:13 A most horrible thing *has been* **d** 6913
21:12 like fire because of the evil you have **d—** 5095
22: 8 'Why *has* the LORD **d** such a thing 6913
23: 2 on you for the evil you have **d,"** 5095
26: 3 because of the evil they have **d.** 5095
29:23 For *they have* **d** outrageous things in Israel; 6913
30:15 and many sins *I have* **d** these things to you. 6913
31:37 of Israel because of all *they have* **d,"** 6913
32:30 of Israel and Judah *have* **d** nothing but evil 6913
32:30 indeed, the people of Israel have **d** nothing NIH
32:32 by all the evil *they have* **d—** 6913
35:18 and *have* **d** everything he ordered.' 6913
38: 9 in all *they have* **d** to Jeremiah the prophet. 6913
40: 3 *he has* **d** just as he said he would. 6913
44: 3 because of the evil *they have* **d.** 6913
50:15 do to her as *she has* **d** to others. 6913
50:29 do to her as *she has* **d.** 6913
51:10 **what** the LORD our God has **d.'** 5126
51:24 in Babylonia for all the wrong *they have* **d** 6913
51:35 May the violence **d** to our flesh be NIH
52: 2 just as Jehoiakim *had* **d.** 6913
La 1:21 they rejoice at what you *have* **d.** 6913
2:17 The LORD *has* **d** what he planned; 6913
3:59 O LORD, the **wrong** *d to* me. 6432
3:64 **what** their hands have **d.** 5126
Eze 5: 9 I will do to you what *I have* never **d** *before* 6913
6: 9 for the evil *they have* **d** and 6913
9: 4 over all the detestable things that **are d** 6913
9:10 bring down on their own heads **what** they have **d."** 2006
9:11 saying, *"I have* **d** as you commanded." 6913
11:21 down on their own heads **what** they have **d,** 2006
12:11 "As *I have* **d,** so it will be done to them. 6913
12:11 "As I have done, so *it will* **be d** to them. 6913
14:23 that *I have* **d** nothing in it without cause, 6913
16:43 down on your head **what** you have **d,** 2006
16:48 and your daughters *have* **d.** 6913
16:51 *You have* **d more** detestable things than they, 8049
16:51 by all these things *you have* **d.** 6913
16:54 of all *you have* **d** in giving them comfort. 6913
16:63 for you for all *you have* **d,** 6913
18:11 (though the father *has* **d** none of them): 6913
18:13 Because *he has* **d** all these detestable things, 6913
18:19 Since the son *has* **d** what is just and right 6913
18:22 of the righteous things *he has* **d,** he will live. 6913
18:24 None of the righteous things *he has* **d** will 6913
20:43 for all the evil *you have* **d.** 6913
21:24 you *have* **d this,** you will be taken captive. 2349[S]
22:31 down on their own heads *all* they have **d,** 2006
23:38 *They have* also **d** this to me: 6913
24:22 And you will do as *I have* **d.** 6913
24:24 you will do just as *he has* **d.** 6913
33:13 none of the righteous things he has **d** will NIH
33:13 he will die for the evil *he has* **d.** 6913
33:16 *He has* **d** what is just and right; 6913
33:29 of all the detestable things *they have* **d.'** 6913
37:14 and *I have* **d** it, declares the LORD.' " 6913
43:11 and if they are ashamed of all *they have* **d,** 6913
44:14 the temple and all the work that *is to* **be d** 6913
Da 4:35 "What *have you* **d?"** 10522
6:10 just as *he had* **d** before. 10522
6:22 Nor *have I ever* **d** any wrong before you, 10522
9: 5 we have sinned and **d wrong.** 6390
9:12 the whole heaven nothing *has ever* **been d** 6913
9:12 like what has **been d** to Jerusalem. 6913
9:15 we have sinned, *we have* **d wrong.** 8399
Joel 2:20 Surely *he has* **d** great things. 6913
2:21 Surely the LORD *has* **d** great things. 6913
3: 4 for **something** I have **d?** 1691
3: 4 on your own heads **what** you have **d.** 1691
3: 7 on your own heads **what** you have **d.** 1691
3:19 of **violence** *d to* the people of Judah, AIT
Am 8: 7 "I will never forget anything they have **d.** 5126
Ob 1:15 As *you have* **d,** it will be done to you; 6913
1:15 As you have done, *it will* **be d** to you; 6913
Jnh 1:10 "What *have you* **d?"** 6913
1:14 for you, O LORD, *have* **d** as you pleased." 6913
Mic 3: 4 from them because of the evil they have **d.** 5095
6: 3 "My people, what *have I* **d** to you? 6913
Hab 2:17 The violence you have **d** NIH
Zep 3:11 to shame for all the wrongs you have **d** 6613
Zec 1: 6 'The LORD Almighty *has* **d** 6913
7: 3 as *I have* **d** for so many years?" 6913
Mt 6: 4 your Father, who sees what is **d** in secret, NIG
6: 6 your Father, who sees what is **d** in secret, NIG
6:10 your will **be d** on earth as it is in heaven. 1181
6:18 your Father, who sees what is **d** in secret, NIG
8:13 *It will* **be d** just as you believed it would." 1181
9:29 "According to your faith *will it* **be d** 1181
16:27 according to what he **has d.** 4552
17:12 but *have* **d** to him everything they wished. 4472
18:19 *be* **d** for you by my Father in heaven. 1181
21:21 only can you do what was **d** to the fig tree, NIG
21:21 and *it will* **be d.** 1181
21:42 the Lord *has* **d** this, 1181
Mt 23: 5 "Everything they do *is* **d** for men to see: 4472
25:21 "His master replied, **'Well d,** 2292
25:23 "His master replied, **'Well d,** 2292
26:10 *She has* **d** a beautiful thing to me. 2237
26:13 what she *has* **d** will also be told, 4472
26:42 *may* your will *be* **d."** 1181
Mk 5:19 and tell them how much the Lord *has* **d** 4472
5:20 in the Decapolis how much Jesus *had* **d** 4472
5:32 around to see who *had* **d** it. 4472
6:30 and reported to him all *they had* **d** 4472
7:37 *"He has* **d** everything well," they said. 4472
9:13 *they have* **d** to him everything they wished, 4472
11:23 it will be **d** for him. NIG
12:11 the Lord *has* **d** this, 1181
14: 6 *She has* **d** a beautiful thing to me. 2237
14: 9 what she *has* **d** will also be told, 4472
Lk 1:25 "The Lord *has* **d** this for me," she said. 4472
1:49 the Mighty One *has* **d** great things for me— 4472
2:39 and Mary *had* **d** everything required by 5464
3:19 and all the other evil things *he had* **d,** 4472
5: 6 *When they had* **d** so, 4472
8:39 "Return home and tell how much God *has* **d** 4472
8:39 over town how much Jesus *had* **d** for him. 4472
9:10 they reported to Jesus what *they had* **d.** 4472
14:22 'what you ordered *has been* **d,** 1181
17:10 *you have* **d** everything you were told to do, 4472
17:10 *we have* only **d** our duty.' " 4472
19:17 " **'Well d,** my good servant!' 2301
22:42 yet not my will, but yours *be* **d."** 1181
23:15 he *has* **d** nothing to deserve death. 1639+4556
23:41 But this man *has* **d** nothing wrong." 4556
Jn 3:21 that what he has **d** has been done 2240
3:21 that what he has done *has been* **d** 1639+2237
4:38 Others *have d* the **hard work,** AIT
4:45 They had seen all that *he had* **d** in Jerusalem 4472
5:29 those who *have* **d** good will rise to live, 4472
5:29 to live, and those who *have* **d** evil will rise 4556
11:46 and told them what Jesus *had* **d.** 4472
12:16 about him and that *they had* **d** these things 4472
12:37 *after* Jesus *had* **d** all these miraculous signs 4472
13:12 "Do you understand what I *have* **d** for you?" 4472
13:15 an example that you should do as *I have* **d** 4472
15:24 not **d** among them what no one else did, 4472
18:35 What is it *you have* **d?"** 4472
Ac 2:43 and miraculous signs *were* **d** by 1181
4:16 in Jerusalem knows they *have* **d** 1181
9:13 about this man and all the harm *he has* **d** 4472
14:11 When the crowd saw what Paul *had* **d,** 4472
14:27 that God *had* **d** through them and 4472
15: 4 they reported everything God *had* **d** 4472
15:12 miraculous signs and wonders God *had* **d** 4472
21:14 "The Lord's will *be* **d."** 1181
21:19 what God *had* **d** among the Gentiles 4472
21:33 asked who he was and what *he had* **d.** 1639+4472
25: 5 if he *has* **d** anything wrong." 1639
25: 8 *"I have* **d** nothing **wrong** against the law of 270
25:10 *I have* not **d** any **wrong** *to* the Jews, 92
25:25 I found he *had* **d** nothing deserving of death, 4556
26:26 because it was not **d** in a corner. 4556
28:17 "My brothers, *although* I *have* **d** nothing 4472
Ro 1:28 to do what **ought** not **to be d.** 2763
2: 6 to each person according to what he *has* **d."** 2240
6: 6 so that the body of sin *might be* **d away with,** 2934
9:11 the twins were born or *had* **d** anything good 4556
15:18 to obey God *by* what I have said and **d—** 2240
1Co 14:26 of these *must be* **d** for the strengthening of 1181
14:40 But everything *should be* **d** in a fitting 1181
15:28 When *he has* **d** this, 5718[S]
2Co 1:12 We have **d** so not according NIG
5:10 for the things **d** while in the body, 4556
7:11 **readiness to see justice d.** 1689
10:15 beyond our limits by boasting of work **d by** 1877
10:16 not want to boast about **work already d** 2289
12:12 *were* **d** among you with great perseverance. 2981
Gal 4:12 *You have* **d** me no **wrong.** 92
4:15 I can testify that, if you **could have d so,** 1543
Eph 2:11 **d** in the body **by the hands** 5935
6:13 and *after you have* **d** everything, to stand. 2981
Col 2:11 **not** with a circumcision **d by the hands of men** 942
2:11 but with the circumcision **d** by Christ, NIG
2Ti 1: 9 because of anything we have **d** but because 2240
4:14 The Lord will repay him for what he has **d.** 2240
Tit 3: 5 not because of righteous things we *had* **d,** 4472
Phm 1:18 If *he has* **d** you any **wrong** 92
Heb 10:36 so that *when you have* **d** the will of God, 4472
Jas 3:13 by deeds **d** in the humility that comes NIG
1Pe 4: 1 in his body *is* **d with** sin. 4264
2Pe 2:13 with harm for the **harm** *they have* **d.** 92
Jude 1:15 **d in** the **ungodly way,** 814
Rev 16:11 they refused to repent of what they **had d.** 2240
16:17 from the throne, saying, *"It is* **d!"** 1181
18: 6 pay her back double for what she *has* **d.** 2240
20:12 to what they *had* **d** as recorded in the books. 2240
20:13 according to what he *had* **d.** 2240
21: 6 He said to me: *"It is* **d.** 1181
22:12 to everyone according to what he has **d.** 2240

DONKEY (74) [DONKEY'S, DONKEYS, DONKEYS']

Ge 16:12 He will be a **wild d** of a man; 7230
22: 3 up and saddled his **d.** 2789
22: 5 the **d** while I and the boy go over there. 2789
42:27 to get feed for his **d,** 2789
49:11 He will tether his **d** to a vine, 6554
49:14 "Issachar is a rawboned **d** lying down 2789
Ex 4:20 put them on a **d** and started back to Egypt. 2789
13:13 Redeem with a lamb every firstborn **d,** 2789
20:17 his ox or **d,** or anything that belongs 2789
21:33 and fails to cover it and an ox or a **d** falls 2789
22: 4 whether ox or **d** or sheep— 2789
22: 9 a **d,** a sheep, a garment, 2789
22:10 "If a man gives a **d,** an ox, 2789
23: 4 across your enemy's ox or **d** wandering off, 2789
23: 5 the **d** *of* someone who hates you fallen 2789
23:12 so that your ox and your **d** may rest and 2789
34:20 Redeem the firstborn **d** with a lamb, 2789
Nu 16:15 I have not taken so much as a **d** from them, 2789
22:21 saddled his **d** and went with the princes 912
22:22 Balaam was riding on his **d,** 912
22:23 the **d** saw the angel of the LORD standing 912
22:25 When the **d** saw the angel of the LORD, 912
22:27 When the **d** saw the angel of the LORD, 912
22:29 Balaam answered the **d,** 912
22:30 The **d** said to Balaam, 912
22:30 "Am I not your own **d,** 912
22:32 "Why have you beaten your **d** these three times? 912
22:33 The **d** saw me and turned away 912
Dt 5:14 nor your ox, your **d** or any of your animals, 2789
5:21 his manservant or maidservant, his ox or **d,** 2789
22: 3 Do the same if you find your brother's **d** 2789
22: 4 If you see your brother's **d** or his ox fallen 2789
22:10 with an ox and a **d** yoked together. 2789
28:31 Your **d** will be forcibly taken from you 2789
Jos 15:18 When she got off her **d,** Caleb asked her, 2789
Jdg 1:14 When she got off her **d,** Caleb asked her, 2789
15:15 Finding a fresh jawbone of a **d,** 2789
19:28 man put her on his **d** and set out for home. 2789
1Sa 12: 3 Whose **d** have I taken? 2789
16:20 So Jesse took a **d** *loaded with* bread, 2789
25:20 As she came riding her **d** into 2789
25:23 she quickly got off her **d** and bowed down 2789
25:42 Abigail quickly got on a **d** and, 2789
2Sa 17:23 he saddled his **d** and set out for his house 2789
19:26 'I will have my **d** saddled and will ride 2789
1Ki 2:40 he saddled his **d** and went to Achish at Gath 2789
13:13 he said to his sons, "Saddle the **d** for me." 2789
13:13 And when they had saddled the **d** for him, 2789
13:23 the prophet who had brought him back saddled his **d** 2789
13:24 both the **d** and the lion standing beside it. 2789
13:27 "Saddle the **d** for me," and they did so. 2789
13:28 with the **d** and the lion standing beside it. 2789
13:28 the body nor mauled the **d.** 2789
13:29 laid it on the **d,** 2789
2Ki 4:22 "Please send me one of the servants and a **d** 912
4:24 She saddled the **d** and said to her servant, 912
Job 6: 5 Does a **wild d** bray when it has grass, 7230
24: 3 They drive away the orphan's **d** and take 2789
39: 5 "Who let the **wild d** go free? 7230
Pr 26: 3 A whip for the horse, a halter for the **d,** 2789
Isa 1: 3 the **d** his owner's manger, 2789
Jer 2:24 a **wild d** accustomed to the desert, sniffing 7241
22:19 He will have the burial of a **d—** 2789
Hos 8: 9 to Assyria like a **wild d** wandering alone. 7230
Zec 9: 9 gentle and riding on a **d,** on a colt, 2789
9: 9 on a colt, the foal of a **d.** 912
Mt 21: 2 and at once you will find a **d** tied there, 3952
21: 5 gentle and riding on a **d,** on a colt, 3952
21: 5 on a colt, the foal *of* a **d.'** " 5689
21: 7 They brought the **d** and the colt, 3952
Lk 10:34 Then he put the man on his own **d,** 3229
13:15 the Sabbath untie his ox or **d** from the stall 3952
Jn 12:14 Jesus found a **young d** and sat upon it, 3942
2Pe 2:16 for his wrongdoing by a **d—a beast** 5689

DONKEY'S (6) [DONKEY]

Nu 22:28 Then the LORD opened the **d** mouth, 912
Jdg 15:16 a **d** jawbone I have made donkeys of them. 2789
15:16 a **d** jawbone I have killed a thousand men." 2789
2Ki 6:25 so long that a **d** head sold for eighty shekels 2789
Job 11:12 a **wild d** colt can be born a man. 7230
Jn 12:15 your king is coming, seated on a **d** colt." 3952

DONKEYS (71) [DONKEY]

Ge 12:16 **male** and female **d,** 2789
24:35 and camels and **d.** 2789
30:43 and camels and **d.** 2789
32: 5 I have cattle and **d,** sheep and goats, 2789
32:15 and twenty **female d** and ten male donkeys. 912
32:15 and twenty female donkeys and ten **male d.** 6555
34:28 They seized their flocks and herds and **d** 2789
36:24 in the desert while he was grazing the **d** 2789
42:26 they loaded their grain on their **d** and left. 2789
43:18 and seize us as slaves and take our **d."** 2789
43:24 and provided fodder for their **d.** 2789
44: 3 on their way with their **d.** 2789
44:13 Then they all loaded their **d** and returned to 2789
45:23 ten **d** loaded with the best things of Egypt, 2789
45:23 and ten **female d** loaded with grain 912
47:17 their sheep and goats, their cattle and **d.** 2789
Ex 9: 3 on your horses and **d** and camels and 2789
Nu 31:28 whether persons, cattle, **d,** sheep or goats. 2789
31:30 cattle, **d,** sheep, goats or other animals. 2789
31:34 61,000 **d** 2789
31:39 **d,** of which the tribute for the LORD was 61; 2789
31:45 30,500 **d** 2789
Jos 6:21 young and old, cattle, sheep and **d.** 2789
7:24 **d** and sheep, his tent and all that he had, 2789

Jos 9: 4 as a delegation whose **d** were loaded 2789
Jdg 5: 10 "You who ride on white **d**, 912
6: 4 neither sheep nor cattle nor **d**. 2789
10: 4 He had thirty sons, who rode thirty **d**. 6555
12: 14 who rode on seventy **d**. 6555
15: 16 "With a donkey's jawbone I have made **d** of them. 2789+2789
19: 3 He had with him his servant and two **d**. 2789
19: 10 with his two saddled **d** and his concubine. 2789
19: 19 both straw and fodder for our **d** and bread 2789
19: 21 So he took him into his house and fed his **d**. 2789
1Sa 8: 16 the best of your cattle and **d** he will take 2789
9: 3 **d** belonging to Saul's father Kish were lost, 912
9: 3 with you and go and look for the **d**." 912
9: 4 but the **d** were not there. NIH
9: 5 or my father will stop thinking about the **d** 912
9: 20 As for the **d** you lost three days ago, 912
10: 2 **d** you set out to look for have been found. 912
10: 14 "Looking for the **d**," he said. 912
10: 16 "He assured us that the **d** had been found." 912
15: 3 cattle and sheep, camels and **d**.' " 2789
22: 19 and its cattle, **d** and sheep. 2789
25: 18 and loaded them on **d**. 2789
27: 9 but took sheep and cattle, **d** and camels, 2789
2Sa 16: 1 He had a string of **d** saddled and loaded 2789
16: 2 **d** are for the king's household to ride on, 2789
2Ki 7: 7 and their horses and **d**. 2789
7: 10 only tethered horses and **d**, 2789
1Ch 5: 21 and two thousand **d**. 2789
12: 40 and Naphtali came bringing food on **d**, 2789
27: 30 the Meronothite was in charge of the **d**. 912
2Ch 28: 15 All those who were weak they put on **d**. 2789
Ezr 2: 67 435 camels and 6,720 **d**. 2789
Ne 7: 69 435 camels and 6,720 **d**. 2789
13: 15 and bringing in grain and loading it on **d**, 2789
Job 1: 3 of oxen and five hundred **d**, 912
1: 14 and the **d** were grazing nearby, 912
24: 5 Like **wild d** in the desert, 7230
42: 12 a thousand yoke of oxen and a thousand **d**. 912
Ps 104: 11 the **wild d** quench their thirst. 7230
Isa 21: 7 riders on **d** or riders on camels, 2789
30: 24 and **d** that work the soil will eat fodder 6555
32: 14 the delight of **d**, a pasture for flocks, 7230
32: 20 and letting your cattle and **d** range free. 2789
Jer 14: 6 **Wild d** stand on the barren heights 7230
Eze 23: 20 like those of **d** and whose emission was like 2789
Da 5: 21 with the **wild d** and ate grass like cattle; 10570
Zec 14: 15 the camels and **d**, 2789

DONKEYS' (1) [DONKEY]

Isa 30: 6 the envoys carry their riches on **d'** backs, 6555

DOOM (7) [DOOMED]

Dt 32: 35 of disaster is near and their **d** rushes 6969
Eze 7: 7 **D** has come upon you— 7619
7: 10 **D** has burst forth, the rod has budded, 7619
22: 3 on herself **d** by shedding blood in her midst 6961
30: 3 a day of clouds, a time of **d** for the nations. NIH
30: 9 of them on the day of Egypt's **d**, NIH
Rev 18: 10 In one hour your **d** has come!' *3213*

DOOMED (7) [DOOM]

Jdg 13: 22 *"We are* **d to die!"** 4637+4637
2Ki 7: 13 be like all these Israelites who *are* **d**. 9462
Ps 137: 8 O Daughter of Babylon, **d to destruction**, 8720
Isa 65: 23 in vain or bear children **d to** misfortune; 4200
Jer 8: 14 For the LORD our God *has* **d** us **to perish** 1959
Jn 17: 12 the one **d to destruction** *724*
2Th 2: 3 the man **d to destruction**. *724*

DOOR (71) [DOORFRAME, DOORFRAMES, DOORKEEPER, DOORKEEPERS, DOORPOST, DOORPOSTS, DOORS, DOORWAY, DOORWAYS]

Ge 4: 7 sin is crouching at your **d**; 7339
6: 16 a **d** in the side of the ark and make lower, 7339
19: 6 to meet them and shut the **d** behind him 1946
19: 9 and moved forward to break down the **d**. 1946
19: 10 into the house and shut the **d**. 1946
19: 11 Then they struck the men who were at the **d** 7339
19: 11 so that they could not find the **d**. 7339
Ex 12: 22 of you shall go out the **d** *of* his house 7339
21: 6 the **d** or the doorpost and pierce his ear with 1946
Dt 15: 17 and push it through his ear lobe into the **d**, 1946
22: 21 be brought to the **d** *of* her father's house 7339
Jdg 11: 31 whatever comes out of the **d** *of* my house 1946
19: 22 Pounding on the **d**, 1946
19: 26 down at the **d** and lay there until daylight. 7339
19: 27 the morning and opened the **d** *of* the house 1946
2Sa 13: 17 "Get this woman out of here and bolt the **d** 1946
13: 18 So his servant put her out and bolted the **d** 1946
1Ki 14: 6 the sound of her footsteps at the **d**, 7339
2Ki 4: 4 Then go inside and shut the **d** behind you 1946
4: 5 She left him and afterward shut the **d** 1946
4: 21 then shut the **d** and went out. NIH
4: 33 shut the **d** on the two of them and prayed to 1946
5: 9 and stopped at the **d** of Elisha's house. 7339
6: 32 shut the **d** and hold it shut against him. 1946
9: 3 Then open the **d** and run; don't delay!" 1946
9: 10 Then he opened the **d** and ran. 1946
Job 31: 9 or if I have lurked at my neighbor's **d**, 7339
31: 32 for my **d** was always open to the traveler— 1946
Ps 141: 3 keep watch over the **d** *of* my lips. 1923
Pr 5: 8 do not go near the **d** *of* her house, 7339
9: 14 She sits at the **d** *of* her house, 7339
26: 14 As a **d** turns on its hinges, 1946
SS 7: 13 and at our **d** is every delicacy, 7339
8: 9 If she is a **d**, we will enclose her 1946
Eze 41: 24 Each **d** had two leaves— 1946
41: 24 two hinged leaves for each **d**. 1946
42: 2 The building whose **d** faced north was 7339
Hos 2: 15 will make the Valley of Achor a **d** *of* hope. 7339
Mt 6: 6 close the **d** and pray to your Father, *2598*
7: 7 knock and the **d** will be opened to you. *NIG*
7: 8 to him who knocks, the **d** will be opened. *NIG*
24: 33 you know that it is near, right at the **d**. *2598*
25: 10 And the **d** was shut. *2598*
25: 11 'Open the **d** for us!' *NIG*
Mk 1: 33 The whole town gathered at the **d**, *2598*
2: 2 not even outside the **d**, *2598*
13: 29 you know that it is near, right at the **d**. *2598*
13: 34 and tells the **one at the d** to keep watch. *2601*
Lk 11: 7 The **d** is already locked, *2598*
11: 9 knock and the **d** will be opened to you. *NIG*
11: 10 to him who knocks, the **d** will be opened. *NIG*
12: 36 they can immediately open the **d** for him. *NIG*
13: 24 to enter through the narrow **d**, *2598*
13: 25 of the house gets up and closes the **d**, *2598*
13: 25 'Sir, open the **d** for us.' *2598*
Jn 18: 16 but Peter had to wait outside at the **d**. *2598*
18: 17 the girl *at* the **d** asked Peter. *2601*
Ac 5: 9 men who buried your husband are at the **d**, *2598*
12: 13 to answer the **d**. *NIG*
12: 14 "Peter is at the **d**!" *4784*
12: 16 and when they opened the **d** and saw him, *NIG*
14: 27 through them and how he had opened the **d** *2598*
18: 7 the synagogue and went **next d** to the house *5327*
1Co 16: 9 a great **d** for effective work has opened *2598*
2Co 2: 12 and found that the Lord had opened a **d** *2598*
Col 4: 3 that God may open a **d** for our message, *2598*
Jas 5: 9 The Judge is standing at the **d**! *2598*
Rev 3: 8 before you an open **d** that no one can shut. *2598*
3: 20 I stand at the **d** and knock. *2598*
3: 20 If anyone hears my voice and opens the **d**, *2598*
4: 1 before me was a **d** standing open in heaven. *2598*

DOORFRAME (3) [DOOR, FRAME]

Ex 12: 22 on the top and on both sides of the **d**. 4647
12: 23 the top and sides of the **d** and will pass over 4647
Eze 41: 21 The outer sanctuary had a rectangular **d**, 4647

DOORFRAMES (4) [DOOR, FRAME]

Ex 12: 7 on the sides and tops of the **d** of the houses 4647
Dt 6: 9 on the **d** *of* your houses and on your gates. 4647
11: 20 on the **d** *of* your houses and on your gates, 4647
2Ch 3: 7 He overlaid the ceiling beams, **d**, 6197

DOORKEEPER (2) [DOOR, KEEP]

Ps 84: 10 be *a* **d** in the house of my God than dwell in 6214
Jer 35: 4 of Maaseiah son of Shallum the **d**. 6197+9068

DOORKEEPERS (9) [DOOR, KEEP]

2Ki 22: 4 the **d** have collected from the people. 6197+9068
23: 4 and the **d** to remove from the temple 6197+9068
25: 18 the priest next in rank and the three **d**. 6197+9068
1Ch 15: 23 Berekiah and Elkanah were to be **d** for 8788
15: 24 Obed-Edom and Jehiah were also to be **d** 8788
2Ch 23: 19 He also stationed **d** at the gates of 8788
34: 9 Levites *who were* the **d** had collected 6197+9068
34: 13 the Levites were secretaries, scribes and **d**. 8788
Jer 52: 24 the priest next in rank and the three **d**. 6197+9068

DOORPOST (2) [DOOR, POST]

Ex 21: 6 to the door or the **d** and pierce his ear with 4647
1Sa 1: 9 on a chair by the **d** *of* the LORD's temple. 4647

DOORPOSTS (6) [DOOR, POST]

2Ki 18: 16 with which he had covered the doors and **d** 595
Isa 6: 4 of their voices the **d** and thresholds shook 564
57: 8 your **d** you have put your pagan symbols. 4647
Eze 43: 8 and their **d** beside my doorposts, 4647
43: 8 and their doorposts beside my **d**, 4647
45: 19 of the sin offering and put it on the **d** *of* 4647

DOORS (59) [DOOR]

Jdg 3: 23 he shut the **d** *of* the upper room behind him 1946
3: 24 and found the **d** *of* the upper room locked. 1946
3: 25 when he did not open the **d** *of* the room, 1946
16: 3 up and took hold of the **d** *of* the city gate, 1946
1Sa 3: 15 down until morning and then opened the **d** 1946
21: 13 like a madman, making marks on the **d** *of* 1946
1Ki 6: 31 of the inner sanctuary he made **d** 1946
6: 32 the two olive wood **d** he carved cherubim, 1946
6: 34 He also made two pine **d**, 1946
7: 50 and the gold sockets for the **d** *of* 1946
7: 50 also for the **d** of the main hall of the temple. 1946
2Ki 18: 16 the gold with which he had covered the **d** 1946
1Ch 22: 3 to make nails for the **d** *of* the gateways and 1946
2Ch 3: 7 walls and **d** *of* the temple with gold, 1946
4: 9 and the large court and the **d** for the court, 1946
4: 9 and overlaid the **d** with bronze. 1946
4: 22 and the gold **d** *of* the temple: 7339
4: 22 the inner **d** to the Most Holy Place and 1946
4: 22 Most Holy Place and the **d** of the main hall. 1946
2Ch 23: 4 on the Sabbath are to keep watch at the **d**, 6197
28: 24 He shut the **d** *of* the LORD's temple 1946
29: 3 the **d** *of* the temple of the LORD 1946
29: 7 the **d** *of* the portico and put out the lamps. 1946
Ne 3: 1 They dedicated it and set its **d** in place, 1946
3: 3 They laid its beams and put its **d** and bolts 1946
3: 6 They laid its beams and put its **d** and bolts 1946
3: 13 and put its **d** and bolts and bars in place. 1946
3: 14 He rebuilt it and put its **d** and bolts and bars 1946
3: 15 roofing it over and putting its **d** and bolts 1946
6: 1 though up to that time I had not set the **d** in 1946
6: 10 and let us close the temple **d**, 1946
7: 1 the wall had been rebuilt and I had set the **d** 1946
7: 3 have them shut the **d** and bar them. 1946
13: 19 I ordered the **d** to be shut and not opened 1946
Job 3: 10 for it did not shut the **d** *of* the womb on me 1946
38: 8 up the sea behind **d** when it burst forth from 1946
38: 10 when I fixed limits for it and set its **d** 1946
41: 14 Who dares open the **d** *of* his mouth, 1946
Ps 24: 7 be lifted up, you ancient **d**, 7339
24: 9 lift them up, you ancient **d**, 7339
78: 23 above and opened the **d** *of* the heavens; 1946
Pr 8: 34 watching daily at my **d**, 1946
Ecc 12: 4 the **d** to the street are closed and the sound 1946
Isa 26: 20 enter your rooms and shut the **d** 1946
45: 1 to open **d** before him so that gates will not 1946
57: 8 Behind your **d** and your doorposts you have put your pagan symbols. 1946
Eze 26: 2 and its **d** have swung open to me; NIH
33: 30 by the walls and at the **d** *of* the houses, 7339
41: 23 and the Most Holy Place had double **d**. 1946
41: 25 And on the **d** *of* the out sanctuary 1946
42: 4 Their **d** were on the north. 7339
Zec 11: 1 Open your **d**, O Lebanon, 1946
Mal 1: 10 that one of you would shut the temple **d**, 1946
Jn 20: 19 with the **d** locked for fear of the Jews, *2598*
20: 26 Though the **d** were locked, *2598*
Ac 5: 19 an angel of the Lord opened the **d** of the jail *2598*
5: 23 with the guards standing at the **d**; *2598*
16: 26 At once all the prison **d** flew open, *2598*
16: 27 and when he saw the prison **d** open, *2598*

DOORWAY (13) [DOOR, WAY]

Ex 12: 23 of the doorframe and will pass over that **d**, 7339
35: 15 for the **d** at the entrance to the tabernacle; 7339
Lev 14: 38 the priest shall go out the **d** *of* the house 7339
Jdg 4: 20 "Stand in the **d** *of* the tent," he told her. 7339
19: 27 fallen in the **d** *of* the house, 7339
2Ki 4: 15 So he called her, and she stood in the **d**. 7339
Est 2: 21 of the king's officers who guarded the **d**, 6197
6: 2 of the king's officers who guarded the **d**, 6197
Pr 8: 34 waiting at my **d**. 4647+7339
Eze 8: 8 So I dug into the wall and saw a **d** there. 7339
40: 38 A room with a **d** was by the portico in each 7339
42: 12 a **d** at the beginning of the passageway 7339
Mk 11: 4 a colt outside in the street, tied at a **d**. *2598*

DOORWAYS (4) [DOOR, WAY]

1Ki 7: 5 All the **d** had rectangular frames; 4647+7339
Eze 42: 11 Similar to the **d** on the north 7339
42: 12 were the **d** *of* the rooms on the south. 7339
Zep 2: 14 rubble will be in the **d**, 6197

DOPHKAH (2)

Nu 33: 12 the Desert of Sin and camped at **D**. 1986
33: 13 They left **D** and camped at Alush. 1986

DOR (4) [HAMMOTH DOR, NAPHOTH DOR]

Jos 12: 23 the king of **D** (in Naphoth Dor) one 1888
17: 11 Ibleam and the people of **D**, Endor, 1799
Jdg 1: 27 the people of Beth Shan or Taanach or **D** 1888
1Ch 7: 29 Taanach, Megiddo and **D**, 1888

DORCAS (2) [TABITHA]

Ac 9: 36 Tabitha (which, when translated, is **D**), *1520*
9: 39 that **D** had made while she was still *1520*

DOTED (KJV) See LUSTED AFTER

DOTHAN (3)

Ge 37: 17 "I heard them say, 'Let's go to **D**.' " 2019
37: 17 after his brothers and found them near **D**. 2019
2Ki 6: 13 The report came back: "He is in **D**." 2019

DOUBLE (24) [DOUBLE-EDGED, DOUBLE-MINDED, DOUBLE-PRONGED, DOUBLY]

Ge 43: 12 Take **d** *the amount of* silver with you, 5467
43: 15 So the men took the gifts and **d** *the amount* 5467
Ex 22: 4 he must pay back **d**. 9109
22: 7 the thief, if he is caught, must pay back **d**. 9109
22: 9 the judges declare guilty must pay back **d** 9109
26: 9 **Fold** the sixth curtain **d** 4100
26: 24 be **d** from the bottom all the way to the top, 9339
28: 16 and a span wide—and **folded d**. 4100
36: 29 At these two corners the frames were **d** 9339
39: 9 and a span wide—and **folded d**. 4100
Dt 21: 17 as the firstborn by giving him a **d** share 9109
1Sa 1: 5 But to Hannah he gave a **d** portion 678
2Ki 2: 9 "Let me inherit a **d** portion of your spirit," 9109
Isa 40: 2 from the LORD's hand **d** for all her sins. 4101

Isa 51:19 These **d** calamities have come upon you— 9109
61: 7 Instead of their shame my people will receive a **d portion,** 5467
61: 7 and so they will inherit a **d portion** 5467
Jer 16:18 I will repay them **d** for their wickedness 5467
17:18 destroy them with **d** destruction. 5467
Eze 41:23 and the Most Holy Place had **d** doors. 9109
Hos 10:10 to put them in bonds for their **d** sin. 9109
1Ti 5:17 of the church well are worthy *of* **d** honor, *1486*
Rev 18: 6 **pay** her **back d** for what she has done. *1486+1488*
18: 6 Mix her a **d** *portion* from her own cup. *1486*

DOUBLE-EDGED (6) [DOUBLE, EDGE]

Jdg 3:16 Now Ehud had made a **d** sword 7023+9109
Ps 149: 6 and a **d** sword in their hands, 7092
Pr 5: 4 sharp as a **d** sword. 7023
Heb 4:12 Sharper than any **d** sword, *1492*
Rev 1:16 and out of his mouth came a sharp **d** sword. *1492*
2:12 of him who has the sharp, **d** sword. *1492*

DOUBLE-MINDED (3) [DOUBLE, MIND]

Ps 119:113 I hate **d** *men,* but I love your law. 6189
Jas 1: 8 he is a **d** man, unstable in all he does. *1500*
4: 8 you sinners, and purify your hearts, you **d.** *1500*

DOUBLE-PRONGED (1) [DOUBLE]

Eze 40:43 And **d hooks,** each a handbreadth long, 9191

DOUBLY (1) [DOUBLE]

1Ch 11:21 He was **d** honored above the Three 928+2021+9109

DOUBT (8) [DOUBTED, DOUBTING, DOUBTLESS, DOUBTS]

Mt 14:31 he said, "why *did you* **d?"** *1491*
21:21 if you have faith and *do* not **d,** *1359*
Mk 11:23 and *does* not **d** in his heart but believes *1359*
Ac 12:11 "Now I know **without a d** that *242*
1Co 11:19 No **d** there have to be differences *NIG*
Heb 7: 7 And without **d** the lesser person is blessed *517*
Jas 1: 6 when he asks, he must believe and not **d,** *1359*
Jude 1:22 Be merciful to those who **d;** *1359*

DOUBTED (1) [DOUBT]

Mt 28:17 they worshiped him; but some **d.** *1491*

DOUBTING (1) [DOUBT]

Jn 20:27 Stop **d** and believe." *603+1181*

DOUBTLESS (1) [DOUBT]

Job 12: 2 **"D** you are the people, 597

DOUBTS (3) [DOUBT]

Lk 24:38 and why do **d** rise in your minds? *1369*
Ro 14:23 the man who *has* **d** is condemned if he eats, *1359*
Jas 1: 6 because he who **d** is like a wave of the sea, *1359*

DOUGH (11)

Ex 12:34 So the people took their **d** before 1302
12:39 *With* the **d** they had brought from Egypt, 1302
12:39 The **d** was without yeast NIH
2Sa 13: 8 She took some **d,** kneaded it, 1302
Jer 7:18 and the women knead the **d** and make cakes 1302
Hos 7: 4 from the kneading of the **d** till it rises. 1302
Mt 13:33 until it **worked** all **through the d."** *2435*
Lk 13:21 until it **worked** all **through the d."** *2435*
Ro 11:16 of the **d** offered as firstfruits is holy, then *NIG*
1Co 5: 6 works through the whole **batch of d?** *5878*
Gal 5: 9 works through the whole **batch of d."** *5878*

DOVE (24) [DOVES]

Ge 8: 8 a **d** to see if the water had receded from 3433
8: 9 But the **d** could find no place to set its feet 3433
8: 9 He reached out his hand and took **the d** 2023S
8:10 and again sent out the **d** from the ark. 3433
8:11 When the **d** returned to him in the evening, 3433
8:12 and sent the **d** out again, 3433
15: 9 along with a **d** and a young pigeon." 9367
Lev 1:14 he is to offer a **d** or a young pigeon. 9367
12: 6 a burnt offering and a young pigeon or a **d** 9367
Ps 55: 6 I said, "Oh, that I had the wings of a **d!** 3433
56: T To [the tune of] "A **D** *on* Distant Oaks." 3433
68:13 wings of [my] **d** are sheathed with silver, 3433
74:19 over the life of your **d** to wild beasts; 9367
SS 2:14 My **d** in the clefts of the rock, 3433
5: 2 "Open to me, my sister, my darling, my **d,** 3433
6: 9 but my **d,** my perfect one, is unique, 3433
Isa 38:14 I moaned like a mourning **d.** 3433
Jer 8: 7 and the **d,** the swift and the thrush observe 9367
48:28 Be like a **d** that makes its nest at the mouth 3433
Hos 7:11 "Ephraim is like a **d,** 3433
Mt 3:16 of God descending like a **d** and lighting *4361*
Mk 1:10 and the Spirit descending on him like a **d.** *4361*
Lk 3:22 on him in bodily form like a **d.** *4361*
Jn 1:32 the Spirit come down from heaven as a **d** *4361*

DOVES (23) [DOVE]

Lev 5: 7 he is to bring two **d** or two young pigeons 9367
5:11 " 'If, however, he cannot afford two **d** 9367
12: 8 she is to bring two **d** or two young pigeons, 9367
14:22 and two **d** or two young pigeons, 9367
14:30 Then he shall sacrifice the **d** or 9367
15:14 On the eighth day he must take two **d** 9367
15:29 On the eighth day she must take two **d** 9367
Nu 6:10 Then on the eighth day he must bring two **d** 9367
SS 1:15 Your eyes are **d.** 3433
2:12 the cooing of **d** is heard in our land. 9367
4: 1 Your eyes behind your veil are **d.** 3433
5:12 His eyes are like **d** by the water streams, 3433
Isa 59:11 we moan mournfully like **d.** 3433
60: 8 like **d** to their nests? 3433
Eze 7:16 moaning like **d** *of* the valleys, 3433
Hos 11:11 like **d** from Assyria. 3433
Na 2: 7 Its slave girls moan like **d** and beat 3433
Mt 10:16 as shrewd as snakes and as innocent as **d.** *4361*
21:12 and the benches of those selling **d.** *4361*
Mk 11:15 and the benches of those selling **d,** *4361*
Lk 2:24 "a pair of **d** or two young pigeons." *5583*
Jn 2:14 sheep and **d,** and others sitting *4361*
2:16 To those who sold **d** he said, *4361*

DOWN (1207) [DOWNCAST, DOWNFALL, DOWNHEARTED, DOWNPOUR, DOWNSTAIRS, DOWNSTREAM]

Ge 8: 3 and fifty days the water *had* **gone d,** 2893
11: 5 But the LORD **came d** to see the city and 3718
11: 7 *let us* **go d** and confuse their language 3718
12:10 and Abram **went d** to Egypt to live there for 3718
15:11 Then birds of prey **came d** on the carcasses, 3718
18:16 *they* **looked d** toward Sodom, 9207
18:21 that *I will* **go d** and see 3718
19: 1 up to meet them and **bowed d** *with* his face 2556
19: 9 and moved forward to **break d** the door. 8689
19:24 Then the LORD **rained d** burning sulfur 4763
19:28 *He* **looked d** toward Sodom and Gomorrah, 9207
19:33 He was not aware of it when she **lay d** or 8886
19:35 of it when she **lay d** or when she got up. 8886
21:16 Then she went off and **sat d** nearby, 3782
23: 7 and **bowed d** before the people of the land, 2556
23:12 Again Abraham **bowed d** before the people 2556
24:11 **had** the camels **kneel d** 1384
24:14 'Please **let d** your jar that I may have 5742
24:16 *She* **went d** to the spring, 3718
24:26 the man **bowed d** and worshiped the LORD, 7702
24:45 *She* **went d** to the spring and drew water, 3718
24:48 and *I* **bowed d** and worshiped the LORD, 7702
24:52 *he* **bowed d** to the ground before the LORD. 2556
24:64 *She* **got d** from her camel 5877
26: 2 "*Do* not **go d** to Egypt; 3718
26: 8 Abimelech king of the Philistines **looked d** 9207
27:12 be tricking him and *would* **bring d** a curse 995
27:29 May nations serve you and peoples **bow d** 2556
27:29 *may* the sons of your mother **bow d** to you. 2556
28:11 under his head and **lay d to sleep.** 8886
31:36 that *you* **hunt** me **d?** 1944
33: 3 He himself went on ahead and **bowed d** to 2556
33: 6 and their children approached and **bowed d.** 2556
33: 7 Leah and her children came and **bowed d.** 2556
33: 7 and *they* too **bowed d.** 2556
37: 7 around mine and **bowed d** to it." 2556
37: 9 and moon and eleven stars *were* **bowing d** 2556
37:10 and your brothers actually come and **bow d** 2556
37:25 As *they* **sat d** to eat their meal, 3782
37:25 and they were on their way to **take** them **d** 3718
37:35 "in mourning *will I* **go d** to the grave 3718
38: 1 Judah left his brothers and **went d** to stay 3718
38:14 and then **sat d** at the entrance to Enaim, 3782
39: 1 Now Joseph *had* **been taken d** to Egypt. 3718
42: 2 **Go d** there and buy some for us, 3718
42: 3 of Joseph's brothers **went d** to buy grain 3718
42: 6 *they* **bowed d** to him *with* their faces to 2556
42:38 "My son *will* not **go d** there with you; 3718
42:38 **bring** my gray head **d** 3718
43: 4 *we will* **go d** and buy food for you. 3718
43: 5 if you will not send him, *we will* not **go d,** 3718
43: 7 '**Bring** your brother **d** here'?" 3718
43:11 in your bags and **take** them **d** to the man *as* 3718
43:15 They hurried **d** *to* Egypt 3718
43:20 "*we* **came d** here the first time to buy food. 3718+3718
43:26 and *they* **bowed d** before him to the ground. 2556
44:21 '**Bring** him **d** to me so I can see him 3718
44:23 your youngest brother **comes d** with you, 3718
44:26 But we said, 'We cannot **go d.** 3718
44:29 **bring** my gray head **d** 3718
44:31 **bring** the gray head of our father **d** 3718
45: 9 **Come d** to me; don't delay. 3718
45:13 And **bring** my father **d** here quickly." 3718
46: 3 "Do not be afraid *to* **go d** to Egypt, 3718
46: 4 I *will* **go d** to Egypt with you, 3718
48:12 and **bowed d** *with* his face to the ground. 2556
49: 8 your father's sons *will* **bow d** to you. 2556
49: 9 Like a lion he crouches and **lies d,** 8069
49:14 "Issachar is a rawboned donkey **lying d** 8069
50:18 and **threw** *themselves* **d** before him. 5877
Ex 2: 5 Then Pharaoh's daughter **went d** to the Nile 3718
2:15 where he **sat d** by a well. 3782
3: 8 So *I have* **come d** to rescue them from 3718
4:31 *they* **bowed d** and worshiped. 7702
7: 9 and **throw** it **d** before Pharaoh,' 8959
7:10 Aaron **threw** his staff **d** in front of Pharaoh 8959
7:12 Each one **threw d** his staff and it became 8959
9:23 and lightning **flashed d** to the ground. 2143
9:25 it **beat d** everything growing in the fields 5782
9:33 the rain no *longer* **poured d** on the land. 5988
10:14 and **settled d** in every area of the country 5663
11: 8 **bowing d** before me and saying, 'Go, 2556
12:12 and **strike d** every firstborn— 5782
12:23 the LORD goes through the land to **strike d** 5597
12:23 to enter your houses and **strike** you **d.** 5597
12:27 and spared our homes when he **struck d** 5597
12:27 Then the people **bowed d** and worshiped. 7702
12:29 the LORD **struck d** all the firstborn 5782
14:24 the LORD **looked d** from the pillar of fire 9207
15: 7 the greatness of your majesty *you* **threw d** 2238
16: 4 "I *will* **rain d** bread from heaven for you. 4763
18: 7 to meet his father-in-law and **bowed d** 2556
19:11 the LORD *will* **come d** on Mount Sinai in 3718
19:14 After Moses *had* **gone d** the mountain to 3718
19:21 **"Go d** and warn the people so they do 3718
19:24 "Go **d** and bring Aaron up with you. 3718
19:25 Moses **went d** to the people and told them. 3718
20: 5 not **bow d** to them or worship them; 2556
23: 5 of someone who hates you **fallen d** 8069
23:24 not **bow d** before their gods or worship 2556
24: 4 Moses then **wrote d** everything 4180
26:12 that is left over *is to* **hang d** at the rear of 6243
32: 1 that Moses was so long in **coming d** from 3718
32: 6 Afterward *they* **sat d** to eat and drink 3782
32: 7 Then the LORD said to Moses, "Go **d,** 3718
32: 8 *They have* **bowed d** to it and sacrificed to it 2556
32:15 Moses turned and **went d** the mountain with 3718
33: 9 the pillar of cloud *would* **come d** and stay at 3718
34: 5 Then the LORD **came d** in the cloud 3718
34:13 **Break d** their altars, 5997
34:13 sacred stones and **cut d** their Asherah poles 4162
34:27 **"Write d** these words, 4180
34:29 When Moses **came d** from Mount Sinai 3718
Lev 9:22 and the fellowship offering, *he* **stepped d.** 3718
14:45 It *must be* **torn d**— 5997
22: 7 When the sun **goes d,** he will be clean, 995
26: 1 a carved stone in your land to **bow d** 2556
26: 6 and *you will* **lie d** 8886
26:19 *I will* **break d** your stubborn pride 8689
26:30 **cut d** your incense altars 4162
Nu 1:51 the Levites *are to* **take** it **d,** 3718
3:13 When I **struck d** all the firstborn in Egypt, 5782
4: 5 Aaron and his sons are to go in and **take d** 3718
8:17 When I **struck d** all the firstborn in Egypt, 5782
10:17 Then the tabernacle **was taken d,** 3718
11: 2 he prayed to the LORD and the fire **died d.** 9205
11: 9 the manna also **came d.** 3718
11:17 *I will* **come d** and speak with you there, 3718
11:25 the LORD **came d** in the cloud and spoke 3718
11:31 *It* **brought** them **d** all around the camp to 5759
12: 5 the LORD **came d** in a pillar of cloud; 3718
14:12 *I will* **strike** them **d** with a plague 5782
14:37 *were* **struck d and died** of a plague 4637
14:45 that hill country **came d** and attacked them 3718
14:45 down and attacked them and **beat** them **d** 4198
16:30 and *they* **go d** alive into the grave, 3718
16:33 They **went d** alive into the grave, 3718
20:15 Our forefathers **went d** into Egypt, 3718
20:28 and Eleazar **came d** from the mountain, 3718
21:35 So *they* **struck** him **d,** 5782
22:27 *she* **lay d** under Balaam, 8069
24: 9 Like a lion they crouch and **lie d,** 8886
25: 2 and **bowed d** before these gods. 2556
33: 4 whom the LORD *had* **struck d** among them; 5782
34:11 The boundary *will* **go d** from Shepham 3718
34:12 the boundary *will* **go d** along the Jordan 3718
Dt 1:25 *they* **brought** it **d** to us and reported, 3718
1:44 and **beat** you **d** from Seir all the way 5782
2:33 over to us and *we* **struck** him **d,** 5782
3: 3 *We* **struck** them **d,** leaving no survivors. 5782
3:16 the territory extending from Gilead **d to** 6330
4:19 do not be enticed into **bowing d** to them 2556
5: 9 not **bow d** to them or worship them; 2556
6: 7 when you **lie d** and when you get up. 8886
7: 5 **Break d** their altars, 5997
7: 5 **cut d** their Asherah poles 1548
8:12 when you build fine houses and **settle d,** 3782
8:19 and worship and **bow d** to them, 2556
9:12 LORD told me, **"Go d** from here at once, 3718
9:15 So I turned and **went d** from the mountain 3718
9:21 into a stream that **flowed d** the mountain. 3718
10: 5 Then I came back **d** the mountain and put 3718
10:22 Your forefathers *who* **went d** 3718
11:16 and worship other gods and **bow d** to them. 2556
11:19 when you **lie d** and when you get up. 8886
12: 3 **Break d** their altars, 5997
12: 3 **cut d** the idols of their gods 1548
16: 6 when the sun **goes d,** 995
17: 3 **bowing d** to them or to the sun or the moon 2556
20:19 *Do* not **cut** them **d.** 4162
20:20 *you may* **cut d** trees that you know are 4162
21: 4 and **lead** her **d** to a valley that has 3718
23: 2 even **d** to the tenth generation. NIH
23: 3 even **d** to the tenth generation. NIH
25: 2 the judge *shall* **make** him **lie d** 5877
26: 4 from your hands and **set** it **d** in front of 5663
26: 5 and *he* **went d** into Egypt with a few people 3718
26:10 before the LORD your God and **bow d** 2556
26:15 **Look d** from heaven, 9207
28:24 *it will* **come d** from the skies 3718
28:49 like an eagle **swooping d,** 1797
28:52 in which you trust **fall d.** 3718
29:26 and worshiped other gods and **bowed d** 2556
30:17 *to* **bow d** to other gods and worship them, 2556
31: 9 So Moses **wrote d** this law and gave it to 4180
31:19 "Now **write d** for yourselves this song 4180

Dt 31:22 So Moses **wrote d** this song that day 4180
33: 3 At your feet they all **bow d,** 9413
33:29 and you *will* **trample d** their high places." 2005
Jos 2: 8 Before the spies **lay d** for the night, 8886
2:15 So *she* **let** them **d** by a rope through 3718
2:18 the window through which *you* **let** us **d,** 3718
2:23 *They* **went d** out of the hills, 3718
3:16 while the water **flowing d** to the Sea of 3718
4: 3 to carry them over with you and **put** them **d** 5663
4: 8 where *they* **put** them **d.** 5663
7: 5 as the stone quarries and **struck** them **d** on 5782
7:10 What *are* you *doing* **d** on your face? 5877
8:22 Israel **cut** them **d,** 5782
8:29 take his body from the tree and **throw** it **d** 8959
10:10 to Beth Horon and **cut** them **d** all the way 5782
10:11 Israel on the **road d** *from* Beth Horon 4618
10:11 **hurled** large hailstones **d** 8959
10:13 the middle of the sky and delayed **going d** 995
10:27 the order and *they* **took** them **d** from 3718
11:17 and **struck** them **d,** 5782
15: 1 extended **d to** the territory of Edom, 448
15: 9 of Mount Ephron and **went d** *toward* Baalah 9305
15:10 **continued d** *to* Beth Shemesh and crossed 3718
16: 7 Then *it* **went d** from Janoah to Ataroth 3718
18:13 and **went d** *to* Ataroth Addar on 3718
18:16 The boundary **went d** to the foot of 3718
18:16 *It* **continued d** the Hinnom Valley along 3718
18:17 and **ran d** *to* the Stone of Bohan son 3718
18:18 the northern slope of Beth Arabah and *on* **d** 3718
23: 7 You must not serve them or **bow d** to them. 2556
23:16 go and serve other gods and **bow d** to them, 2556
24: 4 but Jacob and his sons **went d** *to* Egypt. 3718
Jdg 1: 4 and *they* **struck d** ten thousand men 5782
1: 9 the men of Judah **went d** to fight against 3718
1:34 not allowing them to **come d** into the plain. 3718
2: 2 but *you shall* **break d** their altars.' 5997
2:20 that *I* **laid d** *for* their forefathers and has 7422
3:27 Israelites **went d** with him from the hills, 3718
3:28 So *they* followed him **d** and, 3718
3:29 At that time *they* **struck d** 5782
3:31 *who* **struck d** six hundred Philistines with 5782
4:14 So Barak **went d** Mount Tabor, 3718
5: 4 the clouds **poured d** water. 5752
5:11 "Then the people of the LORD **went d** to 3718
5:13 the men who were left **came d** to the nobles; 3718
5:14 From Makir captains **came d,** 3718
6:11 the LORD came and **sat d** under the oak 3782
6:16 and *you will* **strike d** all 5782
6:25 **Tear d** your father's altar to Baal and cut 2238
6:25 down your father's altar to Baal and **cut d** 4162
6:26 of the Asherah pole that *you* **cut d,** 4162
6:28 with the Asherah pole beside it **cut d** and 4162
6:30 because *he has* **broken d** Baal's altar and 5997
6:30 and **cut d** the Asherah pole beside it." 4162
6:31 when *someone* **breaks d** his altar." 5997
6:32 because *he* **broke d** Baal's altar. 5997
7: 4 **Take** them **d** to the water, 3718
7: 5 So Gideon **took** the men **d** to the water. 3718
7: 5 a dog from those who kneel **d** to drink." 4156
7: 6 All the rest **got d** on their knees to drink. 4156
7: 9 "Get up, **go d** against the camp, 3718
7:10 **go d** to the camp with your servant Purah 3718
7:11 and Purah his servant **went d** to the outposts 3718
7:24 **"Come d** against the Midianites and seize 3718
8: 9 *I will* **tear d** this tower." 5997
8:14 the young man **wrote d** for him the names 4180
8:17 *He* also **pulled d** the tower of Peniel 5997
9:36 people *are* **coming d** from the tops of 3718
9:37 "Look, people *are* **coming d** from the center 3718
9:44 upon those in the fields and **struck** them **d.** 5782
12: 1 *to* **burn d** your house over your head."
836+928+2021+8596
12: 4 The Gileadites **struck** them **d** because 5782
14: 1 Samson **went d** to Timnah and saw there 3718
14: 5 Samson **went d** to Timnah together 3718
14: 7 Then *he* **went d** and talked with the woman, 3718
14:10 Now his father **went d** to see the woman. 3718
14:19 *He* **went d** *to* Ashkelon, 3718
14:19 **struck d** thirty of their men, 5782
15: 8 Then *he* **went d** and stayed in a cave in 3718
15:11 from Judah **went d** to the cave in the rock 3718
15:15 he grabbed it and **struck d** a thousand men. 5782
16:21 gouged out his eyes and **took** him **d** 3718
16:30 and **d came** the temple on the rulers and all 5877
16:31 and his father's whole family **went d** 3718
18:27 with the sword and **burned d** their city.
836+928+2021+8596
19: 6 two of them **sat d** to eat and drink together. 3782
19:26 **fell d** *at* the door and lay there 5877
20:21 and **cut d** twenty-two thousand Israelites 8845
20:25 from Gibeah to oppose them, *they* **cut d** 8845
20:35 on that day the Israelites **struck d** 25,100 8845
20:42 of the towns **cut** them **d** there. 8845
20:45 the Israelites **cut d** five thousand men 6618
20:45 as Gidom and **struck d** two thousand more. 5782
Ru 2:10 she bowed **d** with her face to the ground. 5877
2:14 When *she* **sat d** with the harvesters, 3782
3: 3 Then **go d** to the threshing floor, 3718
3: 4 When he **lies d,** 8886
3: 4 Then go and uncover his feet and **lie d.** 8886
3: 6 So *she* **went d** *to* the threshing floor 3718
3: 7 over to **lie d** at the far end of the grain pile. 8886
3: 7 uncovered his feet and **lay d.** 8886
4: 1 "Come over here, my friend, and **sit d."** 3782
4: 1 So he went over and **sat d.** 3782
1Sa 2: 6 *he* **brings d** *to* the grave and raises up. 3718
2:36 and **bow d** before him for a piece of silver 2556

1Sa 3: 2 *was* **lying d** in his usual place. 8886
3: 3 and Samuel *was* **lying d** in the temple of 8886
3: 5 Eli said, "I did not call; go back and **lie d."** 8886
3: 5 So he went and **lay d.** 8886
3: 6 go back and **lie d."** 8886
3: 9 So Eli told Samuel, "Go and **lie d,** 8886
3: 9 So Samuel went and **lay d** in his place. 8886
3:15 Samuel **lay d** until morning and 8886
6:15 The Levites **took d** the ark of the LORD, 3718
6:19 But God **struck d** some of the men 5782
6:21 **Come d** and take it up to your place." 3718
9:25 After *they* **came d** from the high place to 3718
9:27 they *were* **going d** to the edge of the town, 3718
10: 5 of prophets **coming d** from the high place 3718
10: 8 **"Go d** ahead of me *to* Gilgal. 3718
10: 8 I *will* surely **come d** to you 3718
10:25 *He* **wrote** them **d** on a scroll and deposited it before the LORD. 4180
13:12 the Philistines *will* **come d** against me 3718
13:20 So all Israel **went d** *to* the Philistines 3718
14:31 the Israelites *had* **struck d** the Philistines 5782
14:36 *"Let us* **go d** after the Philistines by night 3718
14:37 *"Shall I* **go d** after the Philistines? 3718
15:12 and has turned and gone on **d** *to* Gilgal." 3718
16:11 *we will* not **sit d** until he arrives." 6015
17: 8 Choose a man and *have him* **come d** to me. 3718
17:28 "Why *have you* **come d** here? 3718
17:28 *you* **came d** only to watch the battle." 3718
17:46 *I'll* **strike** you **d** and cut off your head. 5782
17:50 without a sword in his hand *he* **struck d** 5782
19:12 So Michal **let** David **d** through a window, 3718
20:24 the king **sat d** to eat. 3782
20:41 and bowed **d** before Jonathan three times, 5877
21:13 the gate and **letting** saliva **run d** his beard. 3718
22: 1 *they* **went d** to him there. 3718
22:18 "You turn and **strike d** the priests." 7003
22:18 the Edomite turned and **struck** them **d.** 7003
23: 4 **"Go d** *to* Keilah, 3718
23: 6 of Ahimelech *had* **brought** the ephod **d** 3718
23: 8 to **go d** *to* Keilah to besiege David 3718
23:11 *Will* Saul **come d,** 3718
23:20 **come d** whenever it pleases you to do so, 3718
23:23 in the area, *I will* **track** him **d** among all 2924
23:25 *he* **went d** *to* the rock and stayed in 3718
24: 8 David **bowed d** and prostrated himself 7702
24:11 but you *are* **hunting** me **d** to take my life. 7399
25: 1 David **moved d** into the Desert of Maon. 3718
25:23 and bowed **d** before David with her face to 5877
25:39 **brought** Nabal's wrongdoing **d** 8740
25:41 *She* **bowed d** with her face to the ground 2556
26: 2 So Saul **went d** to the Desert of Ziph, 3718
26: 5 the commander of the army, *had* **lain d.** 8886
26: 6 "Who *will* **go d** into the camp with me 3718
28:14 and *he* **bowed d** and prostrated himself 7702
30:15 *"Can you* **lead** me **d** to this raiding party?" 3718
30:15 and *I will* **take** you **d** to them." 3718
30:16 *He* **led** David **d,** and there they were, 3718
30:24 to be the same as that of him *who* **went d** to 3718
31:12 *They* **took d** the bodies of Saul and his sons 4374
2Sa 1:15 of his men and said, "Go, **strike** him **d!"** 7003
1:15 So *he* **struck** him **d,** and he died. 5782
2:13 One group **sat d** on one side of the pool 3782
2:16 and *they* **fell d** together. 5877
2:22 Why should I strike you **d?** 824+2025
5:17 but David heard about it and **went d** to 3718
5:25 and *he* **struck d** the Philistines all the way 5782
6: 7 therefore God **struck** him **d** 5782
6:12 So David **went d** and brought up the ark 2143
8: 2 *He* **made** them **lie d** on the ground 8886
8: 5 David **struck d** twenty-two thousand 5782
8:13 from **striking d** eighteen thousand Edomites 5782
9: 6 *he* **bowed d** to pay him honor. 5877+6584+7156
9: 8 Mephibosheth **bowed d** and said, 2556
10:18 *He* also **struck d** Shobach the commander 5782
11: 8 **"Go d** to your house and wash your feet." 3718
11: 9 and *did* not **go d** to his house. 3718
11:15 from him so *he will* **be struck d** and die." 5782
12: 9 *You* **struck d** Uriah the Hittite with 5782
13: 6 So Amnon **lay d** and pretended to be ill. 8886
13: 8 who *was* **lying d.** 8886
13:28 **'Strike** Amnon **d,'** then kill him. 5782
13:30 "Absalom *has* **struck d** all the king's sons; 5782
13:31 tore his clothes and **lay d** on the ground; 8886
13:34 coming **d** the side of the hill. 4946
14: 7 over the *one who* **struck** his brother **d,** so 5782
14:33 and **bowed d** with his face to the ground 2556
15: 5 whenever anyone approached him to **bow d** 2556
15:24 *They* **set d** the ark of God, 3668
17: 2 *I would* **strike d** only the king 5782
17:13 and *we will* **drag** it **d** to the valley until 6079
17:18 and *they* **climbed d** *into* it. 3718
18:21 The Cushite **bowed d** before Joab 2556
18:26 and he called **d to** the gatekeeper, "Look, 448
18:28 *He* **bowed d** before the king with his face to 2556
19:16 hurried **d** with the men of Judah 3718
19:20 of the whole house of Joseph to **come d** 3718
19:24 also **went d** to meet the king. 3718
19:31 the Gileadite also **came d** from Rogelim 3718
20:15 they were battering the wall to **bring** it **d,** 5877
21:10 till the rain **poured d** from the heavens on 5988
21:12 after they **struck** Saul **d** on Gilboa.) 5782
21:15 David **went d** with his men to fight against 3718
21:17 *he* **struck** the Philistine **d** and killed him. 5782
22:10 He parted the heavens and **came d;** 3718
22:17 *"He* **reached d** from on high and took hold 8938
22:36 you **stoop d** to make me great. 6700
23:10 but he stood his ground and **struck d** 5782

2Sa 23:12 **struck** the Philistines **d,** 5782
23:13 of the thirty chief men came **d** to David at 3718
23:20 He **struck d** two of Moab's best men. 5782
23:20 He also **went d** into a pit on a snowy day 3718
23:21 And he **struck d** a huge Egyptian. 5782
24:17 the angel who *was* **striking d** the people, 5782
24:20 and **bowed d** before the king with his face to the ground. 2556
1Ki 1:25 Today *he has* **gone d** 3718
1:33 on my own mule and **take** him **d** to Gihon. 3718
1:38 and the Pelethites **went d** and put Solomon 3718
1:53 and *they* **brought** him **d** from the altar. 3718
1:53 And Adonijah came and **bowed d** 2556
2: 6 **let** his gray head **go d** 3718
2: 8 **called d** bitter **curses** 7837+7839
2: 8 When he **came d** to meet me at the Jordan, 3718
2: 9 **Bring** his gray head **d** 3718
2:19 **bowed d** to her and sat down on his throne. 2556
2:19 bowed down to her and **sat d** on his throne. 3782
2:19 and *she* **sat d** at his right hand. 3782
2:25 and *he* **struck d** Adonijah and he died. 7003
2:29 of Jehoiada, "Go, **strike** him **d!"** 7003
2:31 **Strike** him **d** and bury him, 7003
2:34 of Jehoiada went up and **struck d** Joab 7003
2:46 and he went out and **struck** Shimei **d** 7003
5: 9 My men *will* **haul** them **d** from Lebanon 3718
8:32 condemning the guilty and **bringing d** 5989
11:15 *had* **struck d** all the men in Edom. 5782
13:24 and his body was **thrown d** on the road, 8959
13:25 saw the body **thrown d** there, 8959
13:28 and found the body **thrown d** on the road, 8959
15:13 Asa **cut** the pole **d** and burned it in 4162
15:27 and he **struck** him **d** at Gibbethon, 5782
16:10 **struck** him **d** and killed him in 5782
17:23 the child and **carried** him **d** from the room 3718
18: 7 **bowed d to the ground,** 5877+6584+7156
18:35 The water **ran d** around the altar and 2143
18:40 and Elijah *had* them **brought d** to 3718
18:42 **bent d** to the ground and put his face 1566
18:44 'Hitch up your chariot and **go d** before 3718
19: 4 **sat d** under it and prayed that he might die. 3782
19: 5 *he* **lay d** under the tree and fell asleep. 8886
19: 6 He ate and drank and then **lay d** again. 8886
19:10 **broken d** your altars, 2238
19:14 **broken d** your altars, 2238
19:18 all whose knees *have* not **bowed d** to Baal 4156
20:20 and each one **struck d** his opponent. 5782
20:38 He disguised himself with his headband **d** NIH
21:16 he got up and **went d** to take possession 3718
21:18 "Go **d** to meet Ahab king of Israel, 3718
22: 2 of Judah **went d** to see the king of Israel. 3718
2Ki 1: 9 "Man of God, the king says, **'Come d!'** " 3718
1:10 *may* fire **come d** from heaven 3718
1:11 **'Come d** at once!' " 3718
1:12 *"may* fire **come d** from heaven 3718
1:15 **"Go d** with him; do not be afraid of him." 3718
1:15 So Elijah got up and **went d** with him to 3718
2: 2 So *they* **went d** *to* Bethel. 3718
2:16 up and **set** him **d** on some mountain or 8959
2:24 and **called d a curse** *on* them in the name 7837
3:12 and the king of Edom **went d** to him. 3718
3:19 *You will* **cut d** every good tree, 5877
3:25 They stopped up all the springs and **cut d** 5877
4:11 he went up to his room and **lay d** there. 8886
4:24 don't **slow d** for me unless I tell you."
4200+6806+8206
5:14 So *he* **went d** and dipped himself in 3718
5:18 of Rimmon to **bow d** and he is leaning 2556
5:18 when I **bow d** *in* the temple of Rimmon, 2556
5:21 *he* **got d** from the chariot to meet him. 5877
5:26 not my spirit with you when the man **got d** 2200
6: 4 They went to the Jordan and *began to* **cut d** 1615
6: 5 As one of them was **cutting d** a tree, 5877
6: 9 because the Arameans are **going d** there." 5741
6:18 As the enemy **came d** toward him, 3718
6:33 the messenger **came d** to him. 3718
7:17 of God had foretold when the king **came d** 3718
8:29 of Judah **went d** to Jezreel to see Joram son 3718
9:16 and Ahaziah king of Judah *had* **gone d** 3718
9:24 and *he* **slumped d** in his chariot. 4156
9:32 Two or three eunuchs **looked d** at him. 9207
9:33 **"Throw** her **d!"** 9023
9:33 So *they* **threw** her **d,** 9023
10:13 and *we have* **come d** to greet the families of 3718
10:25 So *they* **cut** them **d** with the sword. 5782
10:27 of Baal and **tore d** the temple of Baal, 5997
11:18 to the temple of Baal and **tore** it **d.** 5997
11:19 and *together they* **brought** the king **d** from 3718
12:20 on the **road d** *to* Silla. 3718
13:14 Jehoash king of Israel **went d** to see him 3718
14:13 Then Jehoash went to Jerusalem and **broke d** the wall 7287
17:16 *They* **bowed d** to all the starry hosts, 2556
17:35 "Do not worship any other gods or **bow d** 2556
17:36 To him *you shall* **bow d** and 2556
18: 4 smashed the sacred stones and **cut d** 4162
19: 7 and there *I will* **have** him **cut d** with 5877
19:23 *I have* **cut d** its tallest cedars, 4162
19:37 and Sharezer **cut** him **d** with the sword, 5782
20:11 ten steps *it had* **gone d** on the stairway 345+3718
21: 3 *He* **bowed d** to all the starry hosts 2556
21:13 wiping it and turning it **upside d.** 6584+7156
21:21 and **bowed d** to them. 2556
23: 7 *He* also **tore d** the quarters of 5997
23: 8 *He* **broke d** the shrines at the gates— 5997
23:12 *He* **pulled d** the altars the kings 5997
23:14 Josiah smashed the sacred stones and **cut d** 4162

2Ki 25: 9 Every important building *he* **burned d.** 836+928+2021+8596
25:10 **broke d** the walls around Jerusalem. 5997
25:24 **"Settle d** in the land and serve the king 3782
1Ch 6:32 according to the **regulations** *laid d* AIT
7:21 when *they* **went d** to seize their livestock. 3718
11:14 **struck** the Philistines **d,** 5782
11:15 Three of the thirty chiefs **came d** to David 3718
11:22 He **struck d** two of Moab's best men. 5782
11:22 He also **went d** into a pit on a snowy day 3718
11:23 And he **struck d** an Egyptian 5782
13:10 and *he* **struck** him **d** 5782
14:16 and *they* **struck d** the Philistine army, 5782
18: 5 David **struck d** twenty-two thousand 5782
18:12 Abishai son of Zeruiah **struck d** 5782
21:21 and **bowed d** before David with his face to 2556
2Ch 2:16 **float** them in rafts by sea *d* to Joppa. AIT
6:13 He stood on the platform and then **knelt d** 1384+1386+6584
6:23 repaying the guilty by **bringing d** 5989
7: 1 fire **came d** from heaven and consumed 3718
7: 3 the Israelites saw the fire **coming d** and 3718
13:20 And the LORD **struck** him **d** and he died. 5597
14: 3 smashed the sacred stones and **cut d** 1548
14:12 The LORD **struck d** the Cushites 5597
15:16 Asa **cut** the pole **d,** 4162
18: 2 Some years later *he* **went d** to visit Ahab 3718
20:16 Tomorrow **march d** against them. 3718
20:18 of Judah and Jerusalem **fell d** in worship 5877
22: 6 of Judah **went d** to Jezreel to see Joram son 3718
23:17 to the temple of Baal and **tore** it **d.** 5997
23:20 and **brought** the king **d** from the temple of 3718
25:12 threw them **d** so that all were dashed 4946+8031
25:14 **bowed d** to them and burned sacrifices 2556
25:16 Why *be* **struck d?"** 5782
25:23 and **broke d** the wall of Jerusalem from 7287
26: 6 against the Philistines and **broke d** the walls 7287
29:29 and everyone present with him **knelt d** 4156
31: 1 smashed the sacred stones and **cut d** 1548
32:21 some of his sons **cut** him **d** with the sword. 5877
32:30 spring and channeled the water **d** 4200+4752
33: 3 *He* **bowed d** to all the starry hosts 2556
34: 4 the altars of the Baals *were* **torn d;** 5997
34: 7 *he* **tore d** the altars and the Asherah poles 5997
36:19 They set fire to God's temple and **broke d** 5997
Ezr 4: 5 and **d to** the reign of Darius king of Persia. 6330
5:10 so that *we could* **write d** the names 10374
9: 3 from my head and beard and **sat d** 3782
10: 1 and **throwing himself d** before the house 5877
10:16 of the tenth month *they* **sat d** to investigate 3782
Ne 1: 3 The wall of Jerusalem *is* **broken d,** 7287
1: 4 *I* **sat d** and wept. 3782
2:13 which *had been* **broken d,** and its gates, 7287
3:15 as the steps **going d** from the City of David. 3718
4: 3 *he would* **break d** their wall of stones!" 7287
6: 3 on a great project and cannot **go d.** 3718
6: 3 the work stop while I leave it and **go d** 3718
8: 6 Then *they* **bowed d** and worshiped 7702
9:13 *"You* **came d** on Mount Sinai, 3718
13: 2 but had hired Balaam to **call a curse d** 7837
13:25 I rebuked them and **called curses d** 7837
Est 3: 2 the royal officials at the king's gate **knelt d** 4156
3: 2 But Mordecai *would* not **kneel d** 4156
3: 5 that Mordecai *would* not **kneel d** 4156
3:15 The king and Haman **sat d** to drink, 3782
9: 5 The Jews **struck d** all their enemies *with* the sword, 4804+5782
9:32 and *it* **was written d** in the records. 4180
Job 1:17 and **swept d** on your camels 7320
3:13 For now *I would be* **lying d** in peace; 8886
7: 4 When *I* **lie d** I think, 8886
7: 9 *he who* **goes d** to the grave does not return. 3718
7:21 For *I will* soon **lie d** in the dust; 8886
9:26 like eagles **swooping d** on their prey. 3216
11:19 *You will* **lie d,** 8069
12:14 What *he* **tears d** cannot be rebuilt; 2238
13:26 For *you* **write d** bitter things against me 4180
14: 7 If *it* **is cut d,** it will sprout again, 4162
14:12 so man **lies d** and does not rise; 8886
17:16 *Will it* **go d** *to* the gates of death? 3718
18: 7 his own schemes **throw** him **d.** 8959
19:10 *He* **tears** me **d** on every side till I am gone; 5997
20:23 against him and **rain d** his blows upon him. 4763
21:13 in prosperity and **go d** *to* the grave 5737
27:19 *He* **lies d** wealthy, but will do so no more; 8886
30:23 I know *you will* **bring** me **d** *to* death, 8740
33:24 'Spare him from **going d** to the pit; 3718
33:28 He redeemed my soul from **going d** to 6296
36:28 the clouds **pour d** *their* **moisture** 5688
39: 3 *They* **crouch d** and bring forth their young; 4156
41: 1 a fishhook or **tie d** his tongue with a rope? 9205
41:34 *He* **looks d on** all that are haughty; 8011
Ps 3: 5 I **lie d** and sleep; 8886
4: 8 *I will* **lie d** and sleep in peace, 8886
5: 7 in reverence *will I* **bow d** 2556
7:16 his violence **comes d** on his own head. 3718
10: 2 In his arrogance the wicked man **hunts d** 1944
14: 2 The LORD **looks d** from heaven on 9207
17:11 *They have* **tracked** me **d,** 892
17:13 O LORD, confront them, **bring** them **d;** 4156
18: 9 He parted the heavens and **came d;** 3718
18:16 *He* **reached d** from on high and took hold 8938
18:35 you **stoop d** to make me great. 6708
22:27 the families of the nations *will* **bow d** 2556
22:29 all *who* **go d** *to* the dust will kneel 3718
23: 2 *He* **makes** me **lie d** in green pastures, 8069
28: 1 be like *those who have* **gone d** *to* the pit. 3718
Ps 28: 5 *he will* **tear** them **d** and never build them 2238
30: 3 you spared me from **going d** *into* the pit. 3718
30: 9 in my **going d** into the pit? 3718
33:13 the LORD **looks d** and sees all mankind; 5564
36:12 **thrown d,** not able to rise! 1890
37:14 the bow to **bring d** the poor and needy, 5877
38: 2 and your hand *has* **come d** upon me. 5737
38: 6 *I am* **bowed d** and brought very low; 6390
44:25 We *are brought* **d** to the dust; 8863
52: 5 **bring** you **d** to everlasting **ruin:** 5997
53: 2 God **looks d** from heaven on the sons 9207
55: 3 for *they* **bring d** suffering upon me 4572
55:15 *let them* **go d** alive *to* the grave, 3718
55:23 *will* **bring d** the wicked into the pit 3718
56: 7 in your anger, O God, **bring d** the nations. 3718
57: 6 I *was* **bowed d in distress.** 4104
59:11 and **bring** them **d.** 3718
60: T and **struck d** twelve thousand Edomites in 5782
60:12 and he *will* **trample d** our enemies. 1008
62: 3 *Would* all of you **throw** him **d—** 8357
63: 9 *they will* **go d** to the depths of the earth. 995
64: 7 suddenly they will be **struck d.** 4804
66: 4 All the earth **bows d** to you; 2556
68: 8 the heavens **poured d rain,** before God, 5752
72:11 All kings *will* **bow d** to him 2556
73:18 *you* **cast** them **d** to ruin. 5877
75: 7 *He* **brings** one **d,** he exalts another. 9164
75: 8 and all the wicked of the earth **drink** it **d** 5172
77:17 The clouds **poured d** water, 2442
78:16 of a rocky crag and **made** water **flow d** 3718
78:24 *he* **rained d** manna for the people to eat, 4763
78:27 *He* **rained** meat **d** on them like dust, 4763
78:28 *He* **made** them **come d** inside their camp, 5877
78:31 **cutting d** the young men of Israel. 4156
78:51 *He* **struck d** all the firstborn of Egypt, 5782
80:12 Why *have you* **broken d** its walls so 7287
80:14 **Look d** from heaven and see! 5564
80:16 Your vine **is cut d,** it is burned with fire; 4065
81: 9 *you shall* not **bow d** to an alien god. 2556
85:11 and righteousness **looks d** from heaven. 9207
88: 4 I am counted among *those who* **go d** *to* 3718
89:23 I will crush his foes before him and **strike d** 5597
95: 6 Come, *let us* **bow d** in worship, 4156
102:19 "The LORD **looked d** from his sanctuary 9207
104: 8 *they* **went d** *into* the valleys, 3718
104:19 and the sun knows when to **go d.** 4427
104:22 they return and **lie d** in their dens. 8069
105:16 *He* **called d** famine on the land 7924
105:33 *he* **struck d** their vines and fig trees 5782
105:36 *he* **struck d** all the firstborn in their land, 5782
107:16 for *he* **breaks d** gates of bronze and cuts 8689
107:26 They mounted up to the heavens and **went d** 3718
108:13 and he *will* **trample d** our enemies. 1008
113: 6 who **stoops d** to look on the heavens and 9164
115:17 those *who* **go d** *to* silence; 3718
119: 4 You *have* **laid d** precepts that are to 7422
119:138 The statutes *you have* **laid d** are righteous; 7422
133: 2 **running d** on the beard, 3718
133: 2 running **d** on Aaron's beard, NIH
133: 2 **d** upon the collar of his robes. 3718
135: 8 He **struck d** the firstborn of Egypt, 5782
135:10 He **struck d** many nations 5782
136:10 to *him who* **struck d** the firstborn 5782
136:17 *who* **struck d** great kings, 5782
137: 7 **"Tear it d,"** they cried, 6867
137: 7 they cried, **"tear it d** to its foundations!" 6867
138: 2 *I will* **bow d** toward your holy temple 2556
139: 3 and my **lying d;** 8061
140:11 *may* disaster **hunt d** men of violence. 4200+4511+7421
141: 6 their rulers *will* **be thrown d** from the cliffs, 9023
143: 7 from me or I will be like *those who* **go d** *to* 3718
144: 5 Part your heavens, O LORD, and **come d;** 3718
144: 7 **Reach d** your hand from on high; 8938
145:14 and lifts up all who **are bowed d.** 4104
146: 8 the LORD lifts up *those who* **are bowed d,** 4104
147:17 *He* **hurls d** his hail like pebbles. 8959
Pr 1:12 and whole, like *those who* **go d** *to* the pit; 3718
2:18 For her house **leads d** to death 8755
3:24 when *you* **lie d,** you will not be afraid; 8886
3:24 when *you* **lie d,** your sleep will be sweet. 8886
5: 5 Her feet **go d** *to* death; 3718
7: 8 *He was* **going d** the street near her corner, 6296
7:26 Many are the victims *she has* **brought d;** 5877
7:27 **leading d** to the chambers of death. 3718
11: 5 but the wicked *are* **brought d** 5877
12:25 An anxious heart **weighs** a man **d,** 8817
14: 1 the foolish one **tears** hers **d.** 2238
14:19 Evil men *will* **bow d** in the presence of 8820
14:32 calamity comes, the wicked **are brought d,** 1890
15:24 for the wise to keep him from **going d to** 4752
15:25 The LORD **tears d** the proud man's house 5815
16:29 and leads him **d** a path that is not good. 928
18: 8 they **go d** *to* a man's inmost parts. 3718
19:28 and the mouth of the wicked **gulps d** evil. 1180
21:22 of the mighty and **pulls d** the stronghold 3718
23:31 when *it* **goes d** smoothly! 2143
24:16 but the wicked **are brought d** by calamity. 4173
25:28 Like a city whose walls **are broken d** is 7287
26:20 without gossip a quarrel **dies d.** 9284
26:22 they **go d** *to* a man's inmost parts. 3718
29: 4 but one who is greedy for bribes **tears** it **d.** 2238
30: 4 Who has gone up to heaven and **come d?** 3718
Ecc 3: 3 a time to **tear d** and a time to build, 7287
3:21 and if the spirit of the animal **goes d** into the earth? 3718+4200+4752
4:10 If one **falls d,** his friend can help him up. 5877
Ecc 4:11 if two **lie d** *together,* they will keep warm. 8886
SS 4:15 a well of flowing water **streaming d** 5688
6: 2 My lover *has* **gone d** to his garden, 3718
6:11 *I* **went d** to the grove of nut trees to look at 3718
Isa 2: 8 *they* **bow d** to the work of their hands, 2556
5: 5 I *will* **break d** its wall, 7287
5:24 of fire lick up straw and as dry grass **sinks d** 8332
5:25 his hand is raised and *he* **strikes** them **d.** 5782
6:13 and oak leave stumps when they are **cut d,** 8961
9:10 "The bricks *have* **fallen d,** 5877
10: 6 **trample** them **d** like mud in the streets 5330+8492
10:19 be so few that a child *could* **write** them **d.** 4180
10:20 no longer rely on *him who* **struck** them **d** 5782
10:26 he **struck d** Midian at the rock of Oreb; 4804
10:34 *He will* **cut d** the forest thickets with 5937
11: 6 the leopard *will* **lie d** with the goat, 8069
11: 7 their young *will* **lie d** together, 8069
11:14 *They will* **swoop d** on the slopes of Philistia 6414
13:18 Their bows *will* **strike d** the young men; 8187
14: 6 *which* in anger **struck d** peoples 5782
14: 8 no *woodsman* comes *to* **cut** us **d."** 4162
14:11 All your pomp *has* **been brought d** *to* 3718
14:12 *You have* **been cast d** to the earth, 1548
14:15 But *you* **are brought d** to the grave, 3718
14:25 on my mountains *I will* **trample** him **d.** 1008
14:30 and the needy *will* **lie d** in safety. 8069
16: 8 The rulers of the nations *have* **trampled d** 2150
17: 2 *which will* **lie d,** 8069
18: 5 and **cut d** and take away 9372
22: 5 of **battering d** walls and of crying out to 7982
22:10 and **tore d** houses to strengthen the wall. 5997
22:25 and the load hanging on it *will* **be cut d."** 4162
25:10 as straw **is trampled d** in the manure. 1889
25:11 God *will* **bring d** their pride despite 9164
25:12 *He will* **bring d** your high fortified walls 8820
25:12 *he will* **bring** them **d** to the ground, 5595
26: 5 he levels it to the ground and **casts** it **d** to 5595
26: 6 Feet **trample** it **d—** 8252
27: 7 Has [the LORD] struck her as he **struck d** 4804
27:10 there the calves graze, there *they* **lie d;** 8069
28:18 you will be **beaten d** by it. 5330
29:16 You **turn** things **upside d,** 2201
29:20 all who have an eye for evil *will* **be cut d—** 4162
30: 2 who go **d** *to* Egypt without consulting me; 3718
30:30 and will make them see his arm **coming d** 5738
30:31 with his scepter *he will* **strike** them **d.** 5782
31: 1 Woe to those *who* **go d** *to* Egypt for help, 3718
31: 4 so the LORD Almighty *will* **come d** 3718
37: 7 and there *I will* **have** him **cut d** with 5877
37:24 *I have* **cut d** its tallest cedars, 4162
37:38 and Sharezer **cut** him **d** with the sword, 5782
38: 8 the sun go back the ten steps *it has* **gone d** 3718
38: 8 the ten steps *it had* **gone d.** 3718
38:12 shepherd's tent my house *has* **been pulled d** 5825
38:18 *those who* **go d** *to* the pit cannot hope 3718
41: 7 *He* **nails d** the idol so it will not topple. 928+2616+5021
42:10 you *who* **go d** *to* the sea, and all that is in it, 3718
43:14 to Babylon and **bring d** as fugitives all 3718
44:11 *be* **brought d to terror** and infamy. 7064
44:14 He **cut d** cedars, 4162
44:15 he makes an idol and **bows d** to it. 6032
44:17 *he* **bows d** to it and worships. 6032
44:19 *Shall I* **bow d** to a block of wood?" 6032
45: 2 *I will* **break d** gates of bronze and cut 8689
45: 8 *"You* heavens above, **rain d** righteousness; 8319
45: 8 *let* the clouds **shower** it **d.** 5688
45:14 *They will* **bow d** before you and plead 2556
46: 1 Bel **bows d,** Nebo stoops low; 4156
46: 2 They stoop and **bow d** together; 4156
46: 6 and *they* **bow d** and worship it. 6032
47: 1 **"Go d,** sit in the dust, 3718
49: 7 princes will see and **bow d,** 2556
49:23 *They will* **bow d** before you 2556
50:11 *You will* **lie d** in torment. 8886
52: 4 "At first my people **went d** *to* Egypt to live; 3718
55:10 the rain and the snow **come d** from heaven, 3718
60:14 all who despise you *will* **bow d** at your feet 2556
63: 3 in my anger and **trod** them **d** in my wrath; 8252
63:14 like cattle *that* **go d** to the plain, 3718
63:15 **Look d** from heaven and see 5564
63:18 but now our enemies *have* **trampled d** 1008
64: 1 you would rend the heavens and **come d,** 3718
64: 2 come **d** to make your name known NIH
64: 3 *you* **came d,** and the mountains trembled 3718
65:12 and you *will* all **bend d** for the slaughter; 4156
66:15 *he will* **bring d** his anger with fury, 8740
66:23 all mankind will come and **bow d** 2556
Jer 1: 3 **d to** the fifth month of the eleventh year of Zedekiah 6330+9462
1:10 and kingdoms to uproot and **tear d,** 5997
2:20 and under every spreading tree you **lay d** 7579
3:25 *Let us* **lie d** in our shame, 8886
5: 1 **"Go up and d** the streets of Jerusalem, 8763
6: 6 **"Cut d** the trees and build siege ramps 4162
6:11 and the old, *those* **weighed d** *with* years. 4849
6:15 *they will* **be brought d** 4173
8: 4 " 'When *men* **fall d,** do they not get up? 5877
8:12 *they will* **be brought d** 4173
12:10 and **trample d** my field; 1008
13:18 **"Come d** from your thrones, 9164
14:22 *Do* the skies *themselves* **send d** showers? 5989
15: 8 suddenly *I will* **bring d** on them anguish 5877
16: 8 a house where there is feasting and **sit d** 3782
16:16 and *they will* **hunt** them **d** 7421
18: 2 **"Go d** *to* the potter's house, 3718
18: 3 So *I* **went d** *to* the potter's house, 3718

Jer 18: 7 **torn d** and destroyed, 5997
21: 6 *I will* **strike d** those who live in this city— 5782
22: 1 **"Go d** *to* the palace of the king of Judah 3718
23:19 a whirlwind **swirling d** on the heads of 2565
24: 6 I will build them up and not **tear** them **d;** 2238
25:29 for I *am* **calling d** a sword 7924
26:23 *who* **had** him **struck d** with a sword 5782
29: 5 "Build houses and **settle d;** 3782
29:28 Therefore build houses and **settle d;** 3782
30:23 a driving wind **swirling d** on the heads of 2565
31:28 over them to uproot and **tear d,** 5997
32:29 *they will* **burn** it **d,** 8596
33: 4 of Judah that *have* **been torn d** to be used 5997
34: 2 and *he will* **burn** it **d.** 836+928+2021+8596
34:22 take it and **burn** it **d.** 836+928+2021+8596
36:12 *he* **went d** to the secretary's room in 3718
36:15 They said to him, **"Sit d,** please, 3782
37: 8 they will capture it and **burn** it **d.'** 836+928+2021+8596
37:10 they would come out and **burn** this city **d."** 836+928+2021+8596
38: 6 and Jeremiah **sank d** into the mud. 3190
38:11 and **let** them **d** with ropes to Jeremiah in 8938
38:17 and this city *will* not **be burned d;** 836+928+2021+8596
38:18 the Babylonians and *they will* **burn** it **d;** 836+928+2021+8596
38:23 and this city *will be* **burned d."** 836+928+2021+8596
39: 8 and the houses of the people and **broke d** 5997
40: 9 **"Settle d** in the land and serve the king 3782
41: 2 with him got up and **struck d** Gedaliah son 5782
42:10 I will build you up and not **tear** you **d;** 2238
43:13 and *will* **burn d** the temples of the gods 836+928+2021+8596
46:12 both *will* **fall d** together." 5877
46:15 for the LORD *will* **push** them **d.** 2074
46:22 like *men who* **cut d** trees. 2634
46:23 *They will* **chop d** her forest," 4162
48: 5 on the **road d** *to* Horonaim anguished cries 4618
48:15 her finest young men *will* **go d** in 3718
48:18 **"Come d** from your glory and sit on 3718
48:40 An eagle *is* **swooping d,** 1797
49:16 from there *I will* **bring** you **d,"** 3718
49:22 An eagle will soar and **swoop d,** 1797
50:15 her towers fall, her walls **are torn d.** 2238
50:27 *let them* **go d** *to* the slaughter! 3718
51: 4 *They will* **fall d** slain in Babylon, 5877
51:40 *"I will* **bring** them **d** like lambs to 3718
52:13 Every important building *he* **burned d.** 836+928+2021+8596
52:14 of the imperial guard **broke d** all the walls 5997
La 1:13 **sent** it **d** into my bones. 3718
2: 1 *He has* **hurled d** the splendor of Israel 8959
2: 2 in his wrath *he has* **torn d** the strongholds 2238
2: 2 **brought** her kingdom and its princes **d** 5595
2: 8 The LORD determined to **tear d** the wall 8845
3: 7 *he has* **weighed** me **d** *with* chains. 3877
3:50 the LORD **looks d** from heaven and sees. 9207
Eze 1:27 that from there **d** he looked like fire; 4200+4752
4: 6 "After you have finished this, **lie d** again, 8886
6: 6 your incense altars **broken d,** 1548
8: 2 From what appeared to be his waist **d** 4200+4752
8:16 they *were* **bowing d** to the sun in the east. 2556
9:10 but *I will* **bring d** 5989
11:21 *I will* **bring d** 5989
13:11 and I will send hailstones **hurtling d,** 5877
13:14 *I will* **tear d** the wall you have covered 2238
14: 1 of the elders of Israel came to me and **sat d** 3782
16:39 and *they will* **tear d** your mounds 2238
16:41 *They will* **burn d** your houses 836+928+2021+8596
16:43 I *will* surely **bring d** 5989
17:19 *I will* **bring d** on his head my oath 5989
17:24 the LORD **bring d** the tall tree and make 9164
19: 2 *She* **lay d** among the young lions 8069
19: 7 *He* **broke d** their strongholds 1548
20: 1 and *they* **sat d** in front of me. 3782
22:31 with my fiery anger, **bringing d** 5989
23:47 The mob will stone them and **cut** them **d** 1345
23:47 **burn d** their houses. 836+928+2021+8596
26: 4 the walls of Tyre and **pull d** her towers; 2238
26:12 *they will* **break d** your walls 2238
26:16 of the coast *will* **step d** from their thrones 3718
26:20 then *I will* **bring** you **d** with those who go 3718
26:20 down with *those who* **go d** *to* the pit, 3718
26:20 with *those who* **go d** *to* the pit, 3718
27:34 all your company *have* **gone d** with you. 5877
28: 8 *They will* **bring** you **d** to the pit, 3718
30: 4 and her foundations **torn d.** 2238
31: 7 for its roots went *d* to abundant waters. AIT
31:12 the most ruthless of foreign nations **cut** it **d** 4162
31:14 with *those who* **go d** *to* the pit. 3718
31:15 On the day it *was* **brought d** to 3718
31:16 the sound of its fall when I **brought** it **d** to 3718
31:16 to the grave with *those who* **go d** *to* the pit. 3718
31:17 *had* also **gone d** to the grave with it, 3718
31:18 *will* **be brought d** with the trees of Eden to 3718
32:15 when I **strike d** all who live there, 5782
32:18 with *those who* **go d** *to* the pit. 3718
32:19 **Go d** and be laid among the uncircumcised. 3718
32:21 *'They have* **come d** and they lie with 3718
32:24 the land of the living **went d** uncircumcised 3718
32:24 They bear their shame with *those who* **go d** 3718
32:25 they bear their shame with *those who* **go d** 3718
32:27 who **went d** *to* the grave 3718
32:29 with *those who* **go d** *to* the pit. 3718
32:30 *they* **went d** with the slain in disgrace 3718
Eze 32:30 and bear their shame with *those who* **go d** 3718
33:10 "Our offenses and sins **weigh** us **d,** 6584
34:14 There *they will* **lie d** 8069
34:15 and **have** them **lie d,** 8069
34:26 *I will* **send d** showers in season; 3718
38:22 *I will* **pour d** torrents of rain, 4763
43:11 **Write** these **d** before them so that they may 4180
47: 1 The water *was* **coming d** from under 3718
47: 8 toward the eastern region and **goes d** into 3718
Da 3: 5 *you must* **fall d** and worship the image 10484
3: 6 not **fall d** and worship will immediately 10484
3: 7 nations and men of every language **fell d** 10484
3:10 pipes and all kinds of music *must* **fall d** 10484
3:11 not **fall d** and worship will be thrown 10484
3:15 *to* **fall d** and worship the image I made, 10484
4:13 a holy one, **coming d** from heaven. 10474
4:14 **'Cut d** the tree and trim off its branches; 10134
4:23 **coming d** from heaven and saying, 10474
4:23 **'Cut d** the tree and destroy it, 10134
6:10 Three times a day he **got d** on his knees 10121
7: 1 *He* **wrote d** the substance of his dream. 10374
7:23 **trampling** it **d** and crushing it. 10165
8:10 **threw** some of the starry host **d** 5877
Hos 2:18 so that all *may* **lie d** in safety. 8886
7:12 *I will* **pull** them **d** like birds of the air. 3718
11: 4 from their neck and **bent d** to feed them. 5742
14: 5 a cedar of Lebanon *he will* **send d** his roots; 5782
Joel 1:17 the granaries *have* **been broken d,** 2238
3: 2 I will gather all nations and **bring** them **d** to 3718
3:11 **Bring d** your warriors, O LORD! 5737
Am 1: 5 *I will* **break d** the gate of Damascus; 8689
2: 2 Moab *will* **go d** 4637
2: 8 *They* **lie d** beside every altar 5742
3:11 *he will* **pull d** your strongholds 3718
3:15 *I will* **tear d** the winter house along with 5782
6: 2 and then **go d** *to* Gath in Philistia. 3718
8: 9 **make** the sun **go d** 995
9: 1 **Bring** them **d** on the heads of all the people; 1298
9: 2 *they* **dig d** to the depths of the grave, 3168
9: 2 from there *I will* **bring** them **d.** 3718
9: 3 there *I will* **hunt** them **d** and seize them. 2924
Ob 1: 3 'Who *can* **bring** me **d** to the ground?' 3718
1: 4 from there *I will* **bring** you **d,"** 3718
1: 9 in Esau's mountains *will* **be cut d** in 4162
1:12 *You should* not **look d** on your brother in 8011
1:13 nor **look d on** them in their calamity in 8011
1:14 at the crossroads to **cut d** their fugitives, 4162
Jnh 1: 3 *He* **went d** *to* Joppa, 3718
1: 5 where *he* **lay d** and fell into a deep sleep. 8886
1:11 to you *to make* the sea **calm d** for us?" 9284
2: 6 To the roots of the mountains *I* **sank d;** 3718
3: 6 covered himself with sackcloth and **sat d** in 3782
4: 5 Jonah went out and **sat d** at a place east of 3782
Mic 1: 3 *he* **comes d** and treads the high places of 3718
1: 4 like water rushing **d** a slope. 928
5:11 the cities of your land and **tear d** 2238
5:13 *you will* no longer **bow d** to the work 2556
6: 6 before the LORD and **bow d** before 4104
Na 3:15 the sword *will* **cut** you **d** and, 4162
3:18 your nobles **lie d to rest.** 8905
Hab 2: 2 **"Write d** the revelation and make it plain 4180
Zep 1: 5 **bow d** on the roofs **to worship** 2556
1: 5 those *who* **bow d** and swear by the LORD 2556
2: 7 the evening *they will* **lie d** in the houses 8069
2:14 Flocks and herds *will* **lie d** there, 8069
3:13 They will eat and **lie d** 8069
Hag 1: 8 the mountains and **bring d** timber and build 995
Zec 1:21 to terrify them and **throw d** these horns of 3343
5: 8 **pushed** the lead cover **d** 8959
10:11 Assyria's pride *will* **be brought d** 3718
11: 2 the dense forest *has been* **cut d!** 3718
13: 8 "two-thirds *will* **be struck d** and perish; 4162
Mal 4: 3 Then *you will* **trample d** the wicked; 6748
Mt 2:11 and they **bowed d** and worshiped him. *4406*
3:10 not produce good fruit *will be* **cut d** *1716*
4: 6 he said, "throw yourself **d.** *3004*
4: 9 "if you will **bow d** and worship me." *4406*
5: 1 he went up on a mountainside and **sat d.** *2767*
7:19 not bear good fruit *is* **cut d** and thrown *1716*
7:25 The rain **came d,** the streams rose, *2849*
7:27 The rain **came d,** the streams rose, *2849*
8: 1 *When* he **came d** from the mountainside, *2849*
8:32 the whole herd rushed **d** the steep bank into *2848*
11:23 No, *you will* **go d** to the depths. *2849*
13:47 of heaven is like a net that *was* **let d** into *965*
13:48 Then they **sat d** and collected the good fish *2767*
14:19 he directed the people *to* **sit d** on the grass. *369*
14:29 Then Peter **got d** out of the boat, *2849*
14:32 they climbed into the boat, the wind **died d.** *3156*
15:29 *he* went up on a mountainside and **sat d.** *2764*
15:35 He told the crowd *to* **sit d** on the ground. *404*
17: 9 *As* they *were* **coming d** the mountain, *2849*
18:10 not **look d on** one of these little ones. *2969*
20:20 **kneeling d,** asked a favor of him. *4686*
22:26 **right on d** to the seventh. *2401*
24: 2 every one *will be* **thrown d."** *2907*
24:17 *Let* no one on the roof of his house **go d** *2849*
26:58 *He* entered and **sat d** with the guards to see *2764*
26:74 *to* **call d curses** on himself and he swore *2874*
27:36 **sitting d,** they kept watch over him there. *2764*
27:40 **Come d** from the cross, *2849*
27:42 *Let him* **come d** now from the cross, *2849*
28: 2 angel of the Lord **came d** from heaven and, *2849*
Mk 1: 7 not worthy to **stoop d** and untie. *3252*
3:11 *they* **fell d before** him and cried out, *4700*
3:22 of the law who **came d** from Jerusalem said, *2849*
4:39 the wind **died d** and it was completely calm. *3156*
Mk 5:13 rushed **d** the steep bank into the lake *2848*
6:39 **have** all the people **sit d** *369*
6:40 *they* **sat d** in groups of hundreds and fifties. *404*
6:51 and the wind **died d.** *3156*
7:13 by your tradition that *you have* **handed d.** *4140*
7:31 **d** to the Sea of Galilee and into the region *NIG*
8: 6 He told the crowd *to* **sit d** on the ground. *404*
9: 9 *As* they *were* **coming d** the mountain, *2849*
9:35 **Sitting d,** Jesus called the Twelve *2767*
12:41 Jesus **sat d** opposite the place where *2767*
13: 2 every one *will be* **thrown d."** *2907*
13:15 *Let* no one on the roof of his house **go d** *2849*
14:71 He began *to* **call d curses** on himself, *354*
14:72 And he **broke d** and wept. *2095*
15:30 **come d** from the cross and save yourself!" *2849*
15:32 **come d** now from the cross, *2849*
15:36 Let's see if Elijah comes *to* **take** him **d,"** *2747*
15:46 **took d** the body, wrapped it in the linen, *2747*
Lk 1: 2 as *they were* **handed d** to us by those who *4140*
1:52 *He has* **brought d** rulers from their thrones *2747*
2:51 Then *he* **went d** to Nazareth with them *2849*
3: 9 not produce good fruit *will be* **cut d** *1716*
4: 9 he said, "throw yourself **d** from here. *3004*
4:20 gave it back to the attendant and **sat d.** *2767*
4:29 **throw** him **d the cliff.** *2889*
4:31 Then *he* **went d** to Capernaum, *2982*
4:35 the demon **threw** the man **d** before them all *4849*
5: 3 Then he **sat d** and taught the people from *2767*
5: 4 and **let d** the nets for a catch." *5899*
5: 5 you say so, *I will* **let d** the nets." *5899*
6:17 He **went d** with them and stood on *2849*
6:38 A good measure, **pressed d,** *4390*
6:48 who dug **d deep** and laid the foundation *959*
8:23 A squall **came d** on the lake, *2849*
8:33 and the herd rushed **d** the steep bank into *2848*
9:14 *"Have* them **sit d** in groups of *2884*
9:15 The disciples did so, and everybody **sat d.** *2884*
9:37 *when* they **came d** from the mountain, *2982*
9:54 to call fire **d** from heaven to destroy them?" *2849*
10:15 No, *you will* **go d** to the depths. *2849*
10:30 man *was* **going d** from Jerusalem to Jericho, *2849*
10:31 A priest happened *to be* **going d** *2849*
11:46 because *you* **load** people **d** *5844*
12:18 *I will* **tear d** my barns *2747*
13: 7 **Cut** it **d!** *1716*
13: 9 If not, then **cut** it **d.' "** *1716*
14:28 Will he not first **sit d** and estimate the cost *2767*
14:31 Will he not first **sit d** and consider *2767*
16: 6 **sit d** quickly, and make it four hundred.' *2767*
17: 7 'Come along now and **sit d to eat'?** *404*
17:29 fire and sulfur rained **d from** heaven *608*
17:31 *should* **go d** to get them. *2849*
18: 9 of their own righteousness and **looked d on** *2024*
19: 5 "Zacchaeus, **come d** immediately. *2849*
19: 6 *he* **came d** at once and welcomed him gladly. *2849*
19:37 **place where the road goes d** *2853*
21: 6 every one of them *will be* **thrown d."** *2907*
21:34 or your hearts *will be* **weighed d** *976*
22:41 **knelt d** and prayed, *1205+5502*
22:55 of the courtyard and *had* **sat d together,** *5154*
22:55 Peter **sat d** with them. *2764*
23:53 Then he **took** it **d,** *2747*
24: 5 the *women* **bowed d** with their faces to *3111*
Jn 1:32 the Spirit **come d** from heaven as a dove *2849*
1:33 on whom you see the Spirit **come d** *2849*
2:12 After this *he* **went d** to Capernaum *2849*
4: 6 **sat d** by the well. *2757*
4:49 "Sir, **come d** before my child dies." *2849*
5: 7 someone else **goes d** ahead of me." *2849*
6: 3 a mountainside and **sat d** with his disciples. *2764*
6:10 Jesus said, "Have the people **sit d."** *404*
6:10 and the men **sat d,** *404*
6:16 his disciples **went d** to the lake, *2849*
6:33 For the bread of God is he who **comes d** *2849*
6:38 For *I have* **come d** from heaven not *2849*
6:41 "I am the bread that **came d** from heaven." *2849*
6:42 can he now say, *'I* **came d** from heaven'?" *2849*
6:50 here is the bread that **comes d** from heaven, *2849*
6:51 the living bread that **came d** from heaven. *2849*
6:58 This is the bread that **came d** from heaven. *2849*
8: 2 and *he* **sat d** to teach them. *2767*
8: 6 But Jesus bent **d** and started to write on *3004*
8: 8 Again *he* **stooped d** and wrote on *2893*
10:11 good shepherd **lays d** his life for the sheep. *5502*
10:15 and *I* **lay d** my life for the sheep. *5502*
10:17 that I **lay d** my life— *5502*
10:18 but I **lay** it **d** of my own accord. *5502*
10:18 I have authority *to* **lay** it **d** and authority *5502*
13:37 *I will* **lay d** my life for you." *5502*
13:38 *"Will you* really **lay d** your life for me? *5502*
15:13 that he **lay d** his life for his friends. *5502*
19:13 he brought Jesus out and **sat d** on *2767*
19:31 the legs broken and the bodies **taken d.** *149*
21:24 to these things and who **wrote** them **d.** *1211*
21:25 If every one of them *were* **written d,** *1211*
Ac 5: 5 he **fell d** and died. *4406*
5:10 At that moment *she* **fell d** at his feet *4406*
6:14 and change the customs Moses **handed d** *4140*
7:15 Then Jacob **went d** to Egypt, *2849*
7:34 I have heard their groaning and *have* **come d** to set them free. *2849*
8: 5 Philip **went d** to a city in Samaria *2982*
8:26 that **goes d** from Jerusalem to Gaza." *2849*
8:38 Then both Philip and the eunuch **went d** *2849*
9:30 *they* **took** him **d** to Caesarea *2864*
9:40 then *he* **got d** on his knees and prayed. *5502*

Ac 10:11 like a large sheet *being* **let d** to earth *2768*
10:21 Peter **went d** and said to the men, *2849*
11: 5 like a large sheet *being* **let d** from heaven *2768*
11: 5 and it came **d** to where I was. *2849*
11:27 During this time some prophets **came d** *2982*
12:23 an angel of the Lord **struck** him **d,** *4250*
13: 4 **went d** to Seleucia and sailed from there *2982*
13:14 the synagogue and **sat d.** *2767*
13:29 they **took** him **d** from the tree and laid him *2747*
14:11 "The gods *have* **come d** to us *2849*
14:25 *they* **went d** to Attalia. *2849*
15: 1 Some men **came d** from Judea to Antioch *2982*
15:30 The men were sent off and **went d** *2982*
16: 8 they passed by Mysia and **went d** to Troas. *2849*
16:13 We **sat d** and began to speak to *2767*
18:22 up and greeted the church and then **went d** *2849*
20:10 Paul **went d,** threw himself on *2849*
20:36 he **knelt d** with all of them and prayed. *1205+3836+5502*
21:10 prophet named Agabus **came d** from Judea. *2982*
21:32 and soldiers and **ran d** to the crowd. *2963*
23:10 to **go d** and take him away from them *2849*
24: 1 the high priest Ananias **went d** to Caesarea *2849*
25: 6 *he* **went d** to Caesarea, *2849*
25: 7 the Jews *who had* **come d** *2849*
27:14 swept **d from** the island. *2848*
27:30 the sailors **let** the lifeboat **d** into the sea, *5899*
Ro 10: 6 *to* **bring** Christ **d)** *2864*
11: 3 they have killed your prophets and **torn d** *2940*
14: 3 not **look d on** him who does not, *2024*
14:10 Or why *do* you **look d on** your brother? *2024*
16:22 I, Tertius, who **wrote d** this letter, *1211*
1Co 7:17 **the rule** *I* **lay d** in all the churches. *1411*
10: 7 "The people **sat d** to eat and drink and got *2767*
10:11 examples and *were* **written d** as warnings *1211*
14:25 So he will **fall d** and worship God, *4406*
14:30 to someone *who is* **sitting d,** *2764*
2Co 4: 9 **struck d,** but not destroyed. *2850*
10: 8 up rather than **pulling** you **d,** *2746*
13:10 not for **tearing** you **d.** *2746*
Eph 4:26 the sun **go d** while you are still angry, *2115*
1Th 4:16 the Lord himself *will* **come d** from heaven, *2849*
2Th 3:12 to **settle d** and earn the bread they eat. *2484+3552*
1Ti 4:12 Don't *let* anyone **look d on** you *2969*
2Ti 3: 6 *who are* **loaded d** with sins and are swayed *5397*
Heb 1: 3 *he* **sat d** at the right hand of the Majesty *2767*
8: 1 We do have such a high priest, who **sat d** at *2767*
10:12 *he* **sat d** at the right hand of God. *2767*
12: 2 **sat d** at the right hand of the throne of God. *2767*
Jas 1:17 **coming d** from the Father of *2849*
3:15 not **come d** from heaven but is earthly, *2982*
1Pe 1:18 **handed d** to you **from** your **forefathers,** *4261*
1Jn 3:16 Jesus Christ laid **d** his life for us. *5502*
3:16 *to* **lay d** our lives for our brothers. *5502*
Rev 1:13 **a robe reaching d to** his **feet** *4468*
3: 9 and **fall d** at your feet and acknowledge *4686*
3:12 which *is* **coming d** out of heaven *2849*
3:21 just as I overcame and **sat d** with my Father *2767*
4:10 the twenty-four elders **fall d** before him *4406*
5: 8 and the twenty-four elders **fell d** before *4406*
5:14 and the elders **fell d** and worshiped. *4406*
7:11 *They* **fell d** on their faces before *4406*
8: 7 and it was hurled **d upon** the earth. *1650*
9: 3 of the smoke locusts came **d upon** the earth *1650*
10: 1 Then I saw another mighty angel **coming d** *2849*
10: 4 and *do* not **write** it **d."** *1211*
12: 9 The great dragon *was* **hurled d—** *965*
12:10 *has been* **hurled d.** *965*
12:12 because the devil *has* **gone d** to you! *2849*
13:13 *to* **come d** from heaven to earth in full view *2849*
18: 1 After this I saw another angel **coming d** *2849*
18:21 the great city of Babylon *will be* **thrown d,** *965*
19: 4 and the four living creatures **fell d** *4406*
19:15 a sharp sword with which to **strike d** *4250*
20: 1 And I saw an angel **coming d** out of heaven, *2849*
20: 9 But fire **came d** from heaven *2849*
21: 2 **coming d** out of heaven from God, *2849*
21: 5 Then he said, **"Write** this **d,** *1211*
21:10 **coming d** out of heaven from God. *2849*
22: 2 **d** the middle of the great street of the city. *1877*
22: 8 *I* **fell d** to worship at the feet of the angel *4406*

DOWNCAST (11) [DOWN, CAST]

Ge 4: 5 So Cain was very angry, and his face *was* **d.** 5877
4: 6 Why *is* your face **d?** 5877
1Sa 1:18 and her face *was* no longer **d.** 2118+4200
Job 22:29 then he will save the **d.** 6524+8814
Ps 42: 5 Why *are you* **d,** O my soul? 8863
42: 6 My soul *is* **d** within me; 8863
42:11 Why *are you* **d,** O my soul? 8863
43: 5 Why *are you* **d,** O my soul? 8863
La 3:20 and my soul *is* **d** within me. 8820
Lk 24:17 They stood still, their faces **d.** *5034*
2Co 7: 6 But God, who comforts the **d,** *5424*

DOWNFALL (16) [DOWN, FALL]

1Ki 13:34 the house of Jeroboam that **led to** its **d** and 3948
2Ki 14:10 Why ask for trouble and *cause* your own **d** 5877
2Ch 22: 7 God brought about Ahaziah's **d.** 9313
25:19 Why ask for trouble and *cause* your own **d** 5877
26:16 his pride led to his **d.** 8845
28:23 But they were his **d** and the downfall 4173
28:23 But they were his downfall and the **d** NIH
Est 6:13 before whom your **d** has started, 5877
Ps 5:10 *Let* their intrigues *be their* **d.** 5877
Pr 18:12 Before his **d** a man's heart is proud, 8691
29:16 but the righteous will see their **d.** 5147
Jer 48: 2 in Heshbon men will plot her **d:** 8288
Eze 18:30 then sin will not be your **d.** 4842
32:10 On the day of your **d** each 5147
Hos 14: 1 Your sins *have been your* **d!** 4173
Mic 7:10 My eyes will see her **d;** NIH

DOWNHEARTED (1) [DOWN, HEART]

1Sa 1: 8 Why *are* you **d?** 4222+8317

DOWNPOUR (2) [DOWN, POUR]

Job 37: 6 to the rain shower, 'Be a mighty **d.'** 1773+4764
Isa 28: 2 like a driving rain and a **flooding d,** 3888+8851

DOWNSITTING (KJV) See SIT

DOWNSTAIRS (1) [DOWN, STAIRS]

Ac 10:20 So get up and **go d.** *2849*

DOWNSTREAM (1) [DOWN, STREAM]

Jos 3:13 in the Jordan, its waters flowing **d** will be cut off 2025+4200+4946+5087

DOWNWARD (KJV) See BELOW, DOWN

DOWRY (KJV) See BRIDE-PRICE, GIFT, PRICE FOR THE BRIDE

DRACHMAS (5) [FOUR-DRACHMA, TWO-DRACHMA]

Ezr 2:69 for this work 61,000 **d** of gold, 5,000 minas 2007
Ne 7:70 The governor gave to the treasury 1,000 **d** 2007
7:71 20,000 **d** of gold and 2,200 minas of silver. 2007
7:72 the rest of the people was 20,000 **d** of gold, 2007
Ac 19:19 the total came to fifty thousand **d.** *736*

DRAG (8) [DRAGGED, DRAGGING, DRAGS]

2Sa 17:13 and *we will* **d** it **down** to the valley until not 6079
Job 36:20 to **d** people **away** *from* their homes. 6590
Ps 28: 3 *Do* not **d** me **away** with the wicked, 5432
Pr 21: 7 violence of the wicked *will* **d** them **away,** 1760
Jer 12: 3 **D** them **off** like sheep to be butchered! 5998
15: 3 to kill and the dogs to **d away** and the birds 6079
Eze 39: 2 I will turn you around and **d** you **along.** 9255
Lk 12:58 or *he may* **d** you **off** to the judge, *2955*

DRAGGED (14) [DRAG]

2Sa 20:12 *he* **d** him from the road *into* a field 6015
Jer 22:19 **d away** and thrown outside the gates 6079
49:20 The young of the flock *will be* **d away;** 6079
50:45 The young of the flock *will be* **d away;** 6079
La 3:11 *he* **d** me *from* the path and mangled me 6073
Eze 32:20 *let* her *be* **d off** with all her hordes. 5432
Jn 21:11 Simon Peter climbed aboard and **d** *1816*
Ac 7:58 **d** him out of the city and began *1675*
8: 3 *he* **d off** men and women and put them *5359*
14:19 *They* stoned Paul and **d** him outside *5359*
16:19 *they* seized Paul and Silas and **d** them into *1816*
17: 6 *they* **d** Jason and some other brothers *5359*
21:30 Seizing Paul, *they* **d** him from the temple, *1816*
Jas 1:14 *he is* **d away** and enticed. *1999*

DRAGGING (1) [DRAG]

Jas 2: 6 not the ones who *are* **d** you into court? *1816*

DRAGNET (2) [NET]

Hab 1:15 he gathers them up in his **d;** 4823
1:16 to his net and burns incense to his **d,** 4823

DRAGON (14)

Rev 12: 3 an enormous red **d** with seven heads *1532*
12: 4 The **d** stood in front of the woman who was *1532*
12: 7 and his angels fought against the **d,** *1532*
12: 7 and the **d** and his angels fought back. *1532*
12: 9 The great **d** was hurled down— *1532*
12:13 When the **d** saw that he had been hurled to *1532*
12:16 that the **d** had spewed out of his mouth. *1532*
12:17 Then the **d** was enraged at the woman *1532*
13: 1 And the **d** stood on the shore of the sea. *NIG*
13: 2 The **d** gave the beast his power *1532*
13: 4 the **d** because he had given authority to *1532*
13:11 but he spoke like a **d.** *1532*
16:13 they came out of the mouth *of* the **d,** *1532*
20: 2 He seized the **d,** that ancient serpent, *1532*

DRAGONS (KJV) See JACKAL WELL, SERPENT

DRAGS (4) [DRAG]

Job 7: 4 The night **d on,** and I toss till dawn. 4499
24:22 But God **d away** the mighty by his power; 5432
Ps 10: 9 he catches the helpless and **d** them **off** 5432
Ecc 12: 5 and the grasshopper **d himself along** 6022

DRAIN (3) [DRAINED, DRAINING]

Lev 17:13 be eaten *must* **d out** the blood and cover it 9161
26:16 and **d away** your life. 1853
Eze 23:34 You will drink it and **d** it **dry;** 5172

DRAINED (5) [DRAIN]

Lev 1:15 its blood *shall* **be d out** on the side of 5172
5: 9 of the blood *must* **be d out** at the base of 5172
2Ki 19:26 Their people, **d** *of* power, 7920
Isa 37:27 Their people, **d** *of* power, 7920
51:17 *you who have* **d to** its **dregs** the goblet 5172+9272

DRAINING (1) [DRAIN]

Na 2: 8 and its water *is* **d away.** 5674

DRAMS (KJV) See DARICS, DRACHMAS

DRANK (40) [DRINK]

Ge 9:21 When *he* **d** some of its wine, 9272
24:46 So *I* **d,** and she watered the camels also. 9272
24:54 and the men who were with him ate and **d** 9272
25:34 He ate and **d,** and then got up and left. 9272
26:30 and they ate and **d.** 9272
27:25 and he brought some wine and *he* **d.** 9272
43:34 So they feasted and **d freely** with him. 8910
Ex 24:11 they saw God, and they ate and **d.** 9272
Nu 20:11 and the community and their livestock **d.** 9272
Dt 9: 9 I ate no bread and **d** no water. 9272
9:18 I ate no bread and **d** no water, 9272
29: 6 and **d** no wine or other fermented drink. 9272
32:14 *You* **d** the foaming blood of the grape. 9272
32:38 the fat of their sacrifices and **d** the wine 9272
Jdg 15:19 When Samson **d,** his strength returned 9272
2Sa 11:13 he ate and **d** with him, 9272
12: 3 **d** from his cup and even slept in his arms. 9272
1Ki 4:20 they ate, *they* **d** and they were happy. 9272
13:19 returned with him and ate and **d** in his house. 9272
13:22 and **d** water in the place where he told you 9272
17: 6 and *he* **d** from the brook. 9272
19: 6 He ate and **d** and then lay down again. 9272
19: 8 So he got up and ate and **d.** 9272
2Ki 7: 8 They ate and **d,** and carried away silver, 9272
9:34 Jehu went in and ate and **d.** 9272
1Ch 29:22 and **d** with great joy in the presence of 9272
Ezr 10: 6 he ate no food and **d** no water, 9272
Job 29:23 and **d in** my words as the spring rain. 7023+7196
Jer 51: 7 The nations **d** her wine; 9272
Da 5: 1 for a thousand of his nobles and **d** wine 10748
5: 3 his wives and his concubines **d** from them. 10748
5: 4 *As they* **d** the wine, 10748
5:23 and your concubines **d** wine from them 10748
Ob 1:16 Just as *you* **d** on my holy hill, 9272
Mk 14:23 and *they* all **d** from it. *4403*
Lk 13:26 you will say, *'We* ate and **d** with you, *4403*
Jn 4:12 who gave us the well and **d** from it himself, *4403*
Ac 10:41 and **d** with him after he rose from the dead. *5228*
1Co 10: 4 and **d** the same spiritual drink; *4403*
10: 4 for *they* **d** from the spiritual rock *4403*

DRAUGHT (KJV) See CATCH, LATRINE, OUT OF BODY

DRAW (48) [DRAWING, DRAWN, DRAWS, DREW]

Ge 24:11 the time the *women* go out *to* **d water.** 8612
24:13 the townspeople are coming out to **d** water. 8612
24:19 she said, *"I'll* **d water** for your camels too, 8612
24:20 ran back to the well to **d** *more* **water,** 8612
24:43 if a maiden comes out to **d water** and I say 8612
24:44 and *I'll* **d water** for your camels too," 8612
Ex 2:16 and they came *to* **d water** and fill 1926
15: 9 *I will* **d** my sword 8197
Lev 26:33 and *will* **d out** my sword and pursue you. 8197
Nu 5:15 reminder offering *to* **d attention** to guilt. 2349
Jos 8:26 not **d back** the hand that held out his javelin 8740
Jdg 8:20 But Jether *did* not **d** his sword, 8990
9:54 **"D** your sword and kill me, 8990
20:32 Let's retreat and **d** them **away** from the city 5998
1Sa 9:11 they met some girls coming out to **d** water, 8612
31: 4 **"D** your sword and run me through, 8990
1Ch 10: 4 **"D** your sword and run me through, 8990
Job 37:19 *we* cannot **d up** our **case** because 6885
Ps 37:14 The wicked **d** the sword and bend the bow 7337
58: 7 *when they* **d the bow,** 2005
144:14 our oxen *will* **d heavy loads.** 6022
Isa 5:18 Woe to *those who* **d** sin **along** with cords 5432
12: 3 With joy *you will* **d** water from the wells 8612
Jer 46: 9 men of Lydia *who* **d** the bow. 2005
50:14 all you *who* **d** the bow. 2005
50:29 all *those who* **d** the bow. 2005
Eze 4: 1 in front of you and **d** the city of Jerusalem 2980
21: 3 *I will* **d** my sword from its scabbard 3655
28: 7 *they will* **d** their swords 8197
30:11 *They will* **d** their swords against Egypt 8197
40:46 who are the only Levites who may **d near** to 7929
45: 4 in the sanctuary and who **d near** to minister 7929
Joel 3: 9 *Let* all the fighting men **d near** and attack. 5602
Na 3:14 **D** water for the siege, 8612
Zep 3: 2 *she does* not **d near** to her God. 7928
Hag 2:16 to a wine vat to **d** fifty measures, 3106
Mt 26:52 all who **d** the sword will die by the sword. *3284*
Lk 1: 1 Many have undertaken *to* **d up** an account *421*

Jn 2: 8 "Now d some out and take it to the master 533
4: 7 a Samaritan woman came to d water, 533
4: 11 "you have nothing to d with and 534
4: 15 and have to keep coming here to d water." 533
12: 32 will d all men to myself." 1816
Ac 20: 30 in order to d away disciples after them. 685
Gal 2: 12 he began to d back and separate himself 5713
Heb 7: 19 by which we d near to God. 1581
10: 1 make perfect those who d near to worship. 4665
10: 22 let us d near to God with a sincere heart 4665

DRAWING (3) [DRAW]

1Sa 17: 21 Israel and the Philistines were d up 6885
1Ch 24: 5 They divided them impartially by d lots, 1598
Lk 21: 28 because your redemption is d near." 1581

DRAWN (24) [DRAW]

Ge 34: 3 His heart was d to Dinah daughter of Jacob, 1815
Nu 22: 23 in the road with a d sword in his hand, 8990
22: 31 in the road with his sword d. 8990
Dt 30: 17 and if you are d away to bow down 5615
Jos 5: 13 in front of him with a d sword in his hand. 8990
Jdg 20: 31 meet them and were d away from the city. 5998
1Ch 21: 16 with a d sword in his hand extended 8990
Job 19: 6 that God has wronged me and d his net 5938
Ps 3: 6 of thousands d up against me on every side. 8883
21: 12 when you aim at them with d bow. 4798
55: 21 yet they are d swords. 7347
141: 4 Let not my heart be d to what is evil, 5742
Isa 21: 15 from the d sword, 5759
50: 5 I have not d back. 294+6047
Jer 31: 3 I have d you with loving-kindness. 5432
Eze 5: 2 For I will pursue them with d sword. 8197
5: 12 to the winds and pursue with d sword. 8197
12: 14 and I will pursue them with d sword. 8197
21: 5 that I the LORD have d my sword 3655
21: 28 " 'A sword, a sword, d for the slaughter, 7337
32: 20 The sword is d; 5989
Joel 2: 5 like a mighty army d up for battle. 6885
Mic 5: 6 the land of Nimrod with d sword. 7347
Jn 2: 9 the servants who had d the water knew. 533

DRAWS (7) [DRAW]

Job 33: 22 His soul d near to the pit, 7928
36: 27 "He d up the drops of water, 1758
Ps 88: 3 of trouble and my life d near the grave. 5595
Pr 20: 5 but a man of understanding d them out. 1926
Isa 51: 5 My righteousness d near speedily, AIT
Jn 4: 36 Even now the reaper d his wages, 3284
6: 44 to me unless the Father who sent me d him, 1816

DREAD (22) [DREADED, DREADFUL, DREADS]

Ge 9: 2 and d of you will fall upon all the beasts of 3145
Ex 1: 12 so the Egyptians came to d the Israelites 7762
15: 16 terror and d will fall upon them. 7065
Nu 22: 3 Moab was filled with d because of 7762
Dt 28: 66 filled with d both night and day, 7064
2Ch 29: 8 an object of d and horror and scorn, 2317
Job 9: 28 I still d all my sufferings, 3336
13: 11 Would not the d of him fall on you? 7065
Ps 14: 5 There they are, overwhelmed with d, 7064+7065
31: 11 I am a d to my friends— 7065
53: 5 they were, overwhelmed with d, 7064+7065
53: 5 where there was nothing to d. 7065
105: 38 because d of Israel had fallen on them. 7065
119: 39 Take away the disgrace I d, 3336
Isa 2: 10 hide in the ground from d of the LORD 7065
2: 19 the rocks and to holes in the ground from d 7065
2: 21 and to the overhanging crags from d of 7065
7: 16 of the two kings you d will be laid waste. 7762
8: 12 do not fear what they fear, and do not d it. 6907
8: 13 he is the one you are to d, 6907
66: 4 and will bring upon them what they d. 4475
Jer 42: 16 and the famine you d will follow you 1793

DREADED (8) [DREAD]

Dt 28: 60 the diseases of Egypt that you d, 3336
32: 27 but I d the taunt of the enemy, lest 1593
Job 3: 25 what I d has happened to me. 3336
31: 23 For I d destruction from God, 7065
31: 34 so feared the crowd and so d the contempt 3169
Isa 57: 11 so d and feared that you have been false 1793
Da 5: 19 and nations and men of every language d 10227
Hab 1: 7 They are a feared and d people; 3707

DREADFUL (12) [DREAD]

Ge 15: 12 and a thick and d darkness came over him. 399
Dt 1: 19 that vast and d desert that you have seen, 3707
8: 15 He led you through the vast and d desert, 3707
Job 6: 21 you see something d and are afraid. 3170
Eze 14: 21 against Jerusalem my four d judgments— 8273
Joel 2: 11 The day of the LORD is great; it is d. 3707+4394
2: 31 coming of the great and d day of the LORD. 3707
Mal 4: 5 that great and d day of the LORD comes. 3707
Mt 24: 19 How d it will be in those days 4026
Mk 13: 17 How d it will be in those days 4026
Lk 21: 23 How d it will be in those days 4026
Heb 10: 31 It is a d thing to fall into the hands of 5829

DREADS (1) [DREAD]

Pr 10: 24 What the wicked d will overtake him; 4475

DREAM (77) [DREAMED, DREAMER, DREAMERS, DREAMING, DREAMS]

Ge 20: 3 in a d one night and said to him, "You are 2706
20: 6 Then God said to him in the d, "Yes, 2706
28: 12 He had a d in which he saw 2731
31: 10 a d in which I looked up and saw that 2706
31: 11 The angel of God said to me in the d, 2706
31: 24 to Laban the Aramean in a d at night 2706
37: 5 Joseph had a d, 2706+2731
37: 6 said to them, "Listen to this d I had: 2706+2731
37: 8 because of his d and what he had said. 2706
37: 9 Then he had another d, 2706+2731
37: 9 "Listen," he said, "I had another d, 2706+2731
37: 10 "What is this d you had? 2706+2731
40: 5 had a d the same night, 2706+2731
40: 5 and each d had a meaning of its own. 2706
40: 9 So the chief cupbearer told Joseph his d. 2706
40: 9 "In my d I saw a vine in front of me, 2706
40: 16 he said to Joseph, "I too had a d: 2706
41: 1 Pharaoh had a d: 2731
41: 5 He fell asleep again and had a second d: 2731
41: 7 Then Pharaoh woke up; it had been a d. 2706
41: 11 Each of us had a d the same night, 2706+2731
41: 11 and each d had a meaning of its own. 2706
41: 12 giving each man the interpretation of his d. 2706
41: 15 Pharaoh said to Joseph, "I had a d, 2706+2731
41: 15 that when you hear a d you can interpret it." 2706
41: 17 "In my d I was standing on the bank of 2706
41: 26 it is one and the same d. 2706
41: 32 the d was given to Pharaoh in two forms is 2706
Jdg 7: 13 as a man was telling a friend his d. 2706
7: 13 "I had a d," he was saying. 2706+2731
7: 15 the d and its interpretation, 2706
1Ki 3: 5 to Solomon during the night in a d, 2706
3: 15 and he realized it had been a d. 2706
Job 20: 8 Like a d he flies away, 2706
33: 15 In a d, in a vision of the night, 2706
Ps 73: 20 As a d when one awakes, 2706
Ecc 5: 3 As a d comes when there are many cares, 2706
Isa 29: 7 will be as it is with a d, 2706
56: 10 they lie around and d, they love to sleep. 2111
Jer 23: 25 They say, 'I had a d! 2731
23: 25 I had a d!' 2731
23: 28 Let the prophet who has a d tell his dream, 2706
23: 28 Let the prophet who has a dream tell his d, 2706
Da 2: 3 "I have had a d that troubles me 2706+2731
2: 4 Tell your servants the d, 10267
2: 5 not tell me what my d was and interpret it, 10267
2: 6 But if you tell me the d and explain it, 10267
2: 6 So tell me the d and interpret it for me." 10267
2: 7 "Let the king tell his servants the d, 10267
2: 9 If you do not tell me the d, 10267
2: 9 So then, tell me the d, 10267
2: 16 so that he might interpret the d for him. NIH
2: 23 of you, you have made known to us the d 10418[S]
2: 24 and I will interpret his d for him." NIH
2: 25 the king what his d means." NIH
2: 26 Are you able to tell me what I saw in my d 10267
2: 28 Your d and the visions that passed 10267
2: 36 "This was the d, 10267
2: 45 The d is true and 10267
4: 5 I had a d that made me afraid. 10267
4: 6 be brought before me to interpret the d 10267
4: 7 I told them the d, 10267
4: 8 into my presence and I told him the d. 10267
4: 9 Here is my d; interpret it for me. 10256+10267
4: 18 "This is the d that I, King Nebuchadnezzar, 10267
4: 19 do not let the d or its meaning alarm you." 10267
4: 19 if only the d applied to your enemies 10267
7: 1 Daniel had a d, 10267
7: 1 He wrote down the substance of his d. 10267
Joel 2: 28 your old men will d dreams, 2731
Mt 1: 20 of the Lord appeared to him in a d and said, 3941
2: 12 And having been warned in a d not 3941
2: 13 of the Lord appeared to Joseph in a d. 3941
2: 19 the Lord appeared in a d to Joseph in Egypt 3941
2: 22 Having been warned in a d, 3941
27: 19 for I have suffered a great deal today in a d 3941
Ac 2: 17 your old men will d dreams. 1965

DREAMED (2) [DREAM]

Ps 126: 1 we were like men who d. 2731
Da 2: 2 and astrologers to tell him what he had d. 2706

DREAMER (3) [DREAM]

Ge 37: 19 "Here comes that d!" they said 1251+2021+2706
Dt 13: 3 you must not listen to the words of that prophet or d. 2706+2731
13: 5 That prophet or d must be put to death 2706+2731

DREAMERS (1) [DREAM]

Jude 1: 8 these d pollute their own bodies, 1965

DREAMING (1) [DREAM]

Ecc 5: 7 Much d and many words are meaningless. 2706

DREAMS (26) [DREAM]

Ge 37: 20 Then we'll see what comes of his d." 2706
40: 8 "We both had d," they answered, 2706+2731
40: 8 Tell me your d." NIH
41: 8 Pharaoh told them his d, 2706
41: 12 We told him our d, 2706
41: 22 "In my d I also saw seven heads of grain, 2706
41: 25 "The d of Pharaoh are one and the same. 2706
42: 9 Then he remembered his d about them 2706+2731
Nu 12: 6 I speak to him in d. 2706
Dt 13: 1 If a prophet, or one who foretells by d 2706+2731
1Sa 28: 6 not answer him by d or Urim or prophets. 2706
28: 15 either by prophets or by d. 2706
Job 4: 13 Amid disquieting d in the night, 2612
7: 14 then you frighten me with d and terrify me 2706
Isa 29: 8 as when a hungry man d that he is eating, 2731
29: 8 as when a thirsty man d that he is drinking, 2731
Jer 23: 27 d they tell one another will make my people forget my name, 2706
23: 32 I am against those who prophesy false d," 2706
27: 9 your diviners, your interpreters of d, 2706
29: 8 d you encourage them to have. 2706+2731
Da 1: 17 And Daniel could understand visions and d 2706
2: 1 Nebuchadnezzar had d; 2706+2731
5: 12 and also the ability to interpret d, 10267
Joel 2: 28 your old men will dream d, 2706
Zec 10: 2 they tell d that are false, 2706
Ac 2: 17 your old men will dream d. 1966

DREGS (4)

Ps 75: 8 of the earth drink it down to its very d. 9069
Isa 51: 17 you who have drained to its d the goblet 5172+9272
Jer 48: 11 like wine left on its d, 9069
Zep 1: 12 who are like wine left on its d, who think, 9069

DRENCH (4) [DRENCHED]

Ps 6: 6 with weeping and d my couch with tears. 4998
65: 10 You d its furrows and level its ridges; 8115
Isa 16: 9 O Heshbon, O Elealeh, I d you with tears! 8115
Eze 32: 6 I will d the land with your flowing blood 9197

DRENCHED (9) [DRENCH]

Job 24: 8 They are d by mountain rains and hug 8182
29: 6 when my path was d with cream and 8175
SS 5: 2 My head is d with dew, 4848
Isa 34: 7 Their land will be d with blood, 8115
Da 4: 15 " 'Let him be d with the dew of heaven, 10607
4: 23 Let him be d with the dew of heaven; 10607
4: 25 like cattle and be d with the dew of heaven. 10607
4: 33 His body was d with the dew of heaven 10607
5: 21 and his body was d with the dew of heaven, 10607

DRESS (13) [DRESSED, DRESSING, WELL-DRESSED]

Ex 29: 5 the garments and d Aaron with the tunic, 4252
29: 8 Bring his sons and d them in tunics 4252
40: 13 Then d Aaron in the sacred garments, 4252
40: 14 Bring his sons and d them in tunics. 4252
2Sa 14: 2 D in mourning clothes, 4252
Jer 4: 30 Why d yourself in scarlet and put 4252
6: 14 They d the wound of my people as 8324
8: 11 They d the wound of my people as 8324
Eze 16: 10 an embroidered d and put leather sandals 8391
23: 12 warriors in full d, mounted horsemen, 4229
Lk 12: 37 he will d himself to serve, 4322
Jn 21: 18 and someone else will d you and lead you 2439
1Ti 2: 9 I also want women to d modestly, 3175

DRESSED (43) [DRESS]

Ge 41: 42 He d him in robes of fine linen and put 4252
Ex 20: 25 do not build it with d stones, 1607
1Sa 17: 38 Then Saul d David in his own tunic. 4252
25: 18 five d sheep, five seahs of roasted grain, 6913
1Ki 5: 17 a foundation of d stone for the temple. 1607
6: 7 only blocks d at the quarry were used, 8969
6: 36 of three courses of d stone and one course 1607
7: 12 of three courses of d stone and one course 1607
22: 10 D in their royal robes, 4252
2Ki 12: 12 and d stone for the repair of the temple of 4732
22: 6 and d stone to repair the temple. 4732
1Ch 22: 2 to prepare d stone for building the house 1607
2Ch 5: 12 d in fine linen and playing cymbals, 4252
18: 9 D in their royal robes, 4252
34: 11 and builders to purchase d stone, 4732
Pr 7: 10 d like a prostitute and with crafty intent. 8884
Isa 9: 10 but we will rebuild with d stone; 1607
Jer 10: 9 and goldsmith have made is then d in blue 4230
Eze 16: 10 I d you in fine linen and covered you 2502
40: 42 There were also four tables of d stone for 1607
Da 10: 5 and there before me was a man d in linen, 4229
Zec 3: 3 Now Joshua was d in filthy clothes 4252
Mt 6: 29 not even Solomon in all his splendor was d 4314
11: 8 A man d in fine clothes? 314
Mk 5: 15 sitting there, d and in his right mind; 2667
16: 5 a young man d in a white robe sitting on 4314
Lk 7: 25 A man d in fine clothes? 314
8: 35 d and in his right mind; 2667
12: 27 not even Solomon in all his splendor was d 4314
12: 35 "Be d ready for service 3836+4019+4322
16: 19 "There was a rich man who was d in purple 1898
Jn 21: 18 when you were younger you d yourself 2439
Ac 1: 10 when suddenly two men d in white stood 2264
Rev 1: 13 d in a robe reaching down to his feet and 1907
3: 4 They will walk with me, d in white, NIG
3: 5 like them, be d in white. 2668+4314
4: 4 They were d in white and had crowns 2668+4314
15: 6 They were d in clean, shining linen 1907
17: 4 The woman was d in purple and scarlet, 4314
18: 16 Woe, O great city, d in fine linen, 4314

Rev 19:13 He is d in a robe dipped in blood, 4314
19:14 riding on white horses and d in fine linen, 1907
21: 2 as a bride beautifully d for her husband. 3175

DRESSING (1) [DRESS]
Lk 23:11 D him in an elegant robe, 4314

DREW (37) [DRAW]
Ge 14: 8 d up their battle lines 6885
24:20 and d enough for all his camels. 8612
24:45 She went down to the spring and d water, 8612
38:29 But when he d back his hand, 8740
47:29 When the time d near for Israel to die, 7928
49:33 he d his feet up into the bed, 665
Ex 2:10 saying, "I d him out of the water." 5406
2:19 He even d water for us and watered the flock." 1926+1926
Jos 24:25 at Shechem he d up for them decrees 8492
Jdg 3:21 d the sword from his right thigh 4374
20:24 Then the Israelites d near to Benjamin 7928
1Sa 7: 6 they d water and poured it out before 8612
7:10 the Philistines d near to engage Israel 5602
17: 2 d up their battle line 6885
17:51 of the Philistine's sword and d it from 8990
2Sa 10: 8 The Ammonites came out and d up 6885
22:17 he d me out of deep waters. 5406
23:16 d water from the well near the gate 8612
1Ki 2: 1 When the time d near for David to die, 7928
22:34 But someone d his bow at random and hit 5432
2Ki 9:24 Jehu d his bow and shot Joram 928+3338+4848
1Ch 11:18 d water from the well near the gate 8612
19: 9 The Ammonites came out and d up 6885
2Ch 13: 3 d up a battle line 6885
18:31 God d them away from him, 6077
18:33 But someone d his bow at random and hit 5432
Ps 18:16 he d me out of deep waters. 5406
107:18 They loathed all food and d near the gates 5595
Isa 43:17 who d out the chariots and horses, 3655
La 3:12 He d his bow and made me the target 2005
Mt 26:51 d it out and struck the servant of 685
Mk 14:47 near d his sword and struck the servant of 5060
Jn 18: 6 they d back and fell to the ground. 599
18:10 d it and struck the high priest's servant, 1816
Ac 7:17 "As the time d near for God 1581
16:27 he d his sword and was about to kill himself 5060
23:19 d him aside and asked, 432

DRIED (27) [DRY]
Ge 8: 7 until the water had d up from the earth. 3312
8:13 the water had d up from the earth. 2990
Jos 2:10 the LORD d up the water of the Red Sea 3312
4:23 For the LORD your God d up the Jordan 3312
4:23 to the Red Sea when he d it up before us 3312
5: 1 how the LORD had d up the Jordan before 3312
Jdg 16: 7 that have not been d, 2990
16: 8 that had not been d, 2990
1Ki 17: 7 Some time later the brook d up 3312
2Ki 19:24 With the soles of my feet I have d up all 2990
Ps 22:15 My strength is d up like a potsherd, 3312
74:15 you d up the ever flowing rivers. 3312
106: 9 He rebuked the Red Sea, and it d up; 2990
Isa 15: 6 The waters of Nimrim are d up and 5457
37:25 With the soles of my feet I have d up all 2990
51:10 Was it not you who d up the sea, 2990
Jer 48:34 for even the waters of Nimrim are d up. 5457
Eze 37:11 'Our bones are d up and our hope is gone; 3312
Joel 1:10 The fields are ruined, the ground is d up; 62
1:10 the new wine is d up, the oil fails. 3312
1:12 vine is d up and the fig tree is withered; 3312
1:12 of the field—are d up. 3312
1:17 for the grain has d up. 3312
1:20 of water have d up and fire has devoured 3312
Am 4: 7 another had none and d up. 3312
7: 4 it d up the great deep and devoured 430
Rev 16:12 and its water was d up to prepare the way 3830

DRIES (4) [DRY]
Pr 17:22 but a crushed spirit d up the bones. 3312
Isa 24: 4 The earth d up and withers, 62
24: 7 The new wine d up and the vine withers; 62
Na 1: 4 He rebukes the sea and d it up; 3312

DRIFT (1)
Heb 2: 1 so that we do not d away. 4184

DRINK (320) [DRANK, DRINKERS, DRINKING, DRINKS, DRUNK, DRUNKARD, DRUNKARD'S, DRUNKARDS, DRUNKEN, DRUNKENNESS]
Ge 19:32 get our father to d wine 9197
19:33 got their father to d wine, 9197
19:34 Let's get him to d wine again tonight, 9197
19:35 got their father to d wine that night also, 9197
21:19 gave the boy a d. 9197
24:14 that I may have a d,' and she says, 'Drink, 9272
24:14 'D, and I'll water your camels too'— 9272
24:18 "D, my lord," she said, 9272
24:18 the jar to her hands and gave him a d. 9197
24:19 After she had given him a d, she said, 9197
24:43 to her, "Please let me d a little water 9197
Ge 24:44 if she says to me, "D, and I'll draw water 9272
24:45 and I said to her, 'Please give me a d.' 9197
24:46 'D, and I'll water your camels too.' 9272
30:38 in front of the flocks when they came to d. 9272
30:38 the flocks were in heat and came to d, 9272
35:14 and he poured out a d offering on it; 5821
Ex 7:18 not be able to d its water.' " 9272
7:21 that the Egyptians could not d its water. 9272
7:24 they could not d the water of the river. 9272
15:23 not d its water because it was bitter. 9272
15:24 saying, "What are we to d?" 9272
17: 1 but there was no water for the people to d. 9272
17: 2 "Give us water to d." 9272
17: 6 of it for the people to d." 9272
29:40 a quarter of a hin of wine as a d offering. 5821
29:41 the same grain offering and its d offering 5821
30: 9 and do not pour a d offering on it. 5821
32: 6 down to eat and d and got up to indulge 9272
32:20 on the water and made the Israelites d it. 9197
37:16 pouring out of d offerings. 5818
Lev 10: 9 "You and your sons are not to d wine 9272
10: 9 or other fermented d whenever you go into 8911
23:13 its d offering of a quarter of a hin of wine. 5821
23:18 with their grain offerings and d offerings— 5821
23:37 and d offerings required for each day. 5821
Nu 4: 7 and the jars for d offerings; 5821
5:24 He shall have the woman d the bitter water 9197
5:26 he is to have the woman d the water. 9197
5:27 when she is made to d the water that brings 9197
6: 3 from wine and other fermented d and must 8911
6: 3 and must not d vinegar made from wine or 9272
6: 3 from wine or from other fermented d. 8911
6: 3 not d grape juice or eat grapes or raisins. 9272
6:15 with their grain offerings and d offerings, 5821
6:17 with its grain offering and d offering. 5821
6:20 After that, the Nazirite may d wine. 9272
15: 5 a quarter of a hin of wine as a d offering. 5821
15: 7 and a third of a hin of wine as a d offering. 5821
15:10 bring half a hin of wine as a d offering. 5821
15:24 and d offering, and a male goat for 5821
20: 5 And there is no water to d!" 9272
20: 8 so they and their livestock can d." 9197
20:17 or d water from any well. 9272
20:19 if we or our livestock d any of your water, 9272
21:22 or d water from any well. 9272
28: 7 The accompanying d offering is to be 5821
28: 7 of a hin of fermented d with each lamb. 8911
28: 7 Pour out the d offering to the LORD at 5821
28: 8 and d offering that you prepare in 5821
28: 9 with its d offering and a grain offering 5821
28:10 and its d offering. 5821
28:14 With each bull there is to be a d offering 5821
28:15 with its d offering, 5821
28:24 and its d offering. 5821
28:31 with their d offerings, 5821
29: 6 with their grain offerings and d offerings 5821
29:11 and their d offerings. 5821
29:16 with its grain offering and d offering 5821
29:18 and d offerings according to 5821
29:19 and their d offerings. 5821
29:21 and d offerings according to 5821
29:22 with its grain offering and d offering. 5821
29:24 and d offerings according to 5821
29:25 with its grain offering and d offering. 5821
29:27 and d offerings according to 5821
29:28 with its grain offering and d offering. 5821
29:30 and d offerings according to 5821
29:31 with its grain offering and d offering. 5821
29:33 and d offerings according to 5821
29:34 with its grain offering and d offering. 5821
29:37 and d offerings according to 5821
29:38 with its grain offering and d offering. 5821
29:39 d offerings and fellowship offerings.' " 5821
33:14 no water for the people to d. 9272
Dt 2: 6 for the food you eat and the water you d.' " 9272
2:28 and water to d for their price in silver. 9272
14:26 cattle, sheep, wine or other fermented d, 8911
28:39 and cultivate them but you will not d 9272
29: 6 and drank no wine or other fermented d. 8911
32:38 and drank the wine of their d offerings? 5816
Jdg 4:19 She opened a skin of milk, gave him a d, 9197
7: 5 from those who kneel down to d." 9272
7: 6 All the rest got down on their knees to d. 9272
13: 4 Now see to it that you d no wine 9272
13: 4 that you drink no wine or other fermented d nor eat anything unclean. 8911
13: 7 d no wine or other fermented drink and do 9272
13: 7 drink no wine or other fermented d and do 8911
13:14 nor d any wine or other fermented drink 9272
13:14 nor drink any wine or other fermented d 8911
19: 6 two of them sat down to eat and d together. 9272
19:21 they had something to eat and d. 9272
Ru 2: 9 go and get a d from the water jars 9272
1Sa 30:11 They gave him water to d and food 9197
2Sa 11:11 How could I go to my house to eat and d 9272
23:15 that someone would get me a d of water 9197
23:16 But he refused to d it; 9272
23:17 And David would not d it. 9272
1Ki 13: 8 nor would I eat bread or d water here. 9272
13: 9 not eat bread or d water or return by 9272
13:16 nor can I eat bread or d water with you 9272
13:17 not eat bread or d water there or return by 9272
13:18 so that he may eat bread and d water.' " 9272
13:22 the place where he told you not to eat or d. 9272
17: 4 You will d from the brook, 9272
17:10 a little water in a jar so I may have a d?" 9272
18:41 And Elijah said to Ahab, "Go, eat and d, 9272
1Ki 18:42 So Ahab went off to eat and d, 9272
2Ki 3:17 your cattle and your other animals will d. 9272
6:22 so that they may eat and d and then go back 9272
16:13 poured out his d offering, 5821
16:15 their grain offering and their d offering. 5821
18:27 and d their own urine?" 9272
18:31 from his own vine and fig tree and d water 9272
1Ch 11:17 that someone would get me a d of water 9197
11:18 But he refused to d it; 9272
11:19 "Should I d the blood these men who 9272
11:19 David would not d it. 9272
29:21 together with their d offerings, 5821
2Ch 28:15 food and d, and healing balm. 9197
29:35 the fellowship offerings and the d offerings 5821
Ezr 3: 7 and gave food and d and oil to the people 5492
7:17 with their grain offerings and d offerings, 10483
Ne 8:12 Then all the people went away to eat and d, 9272
Est 1: 8 was allowed to d in his own way, 9276
3:15 The king and Haman sat down to d, 9272
4:16 Do not eat or d for three days, night or day. 9272
Job 1: 4 to eat and d with them. 9272
21:20 let him d of the wrath of the Almighty. 9272
Ps 36: 8 you give them d from your river 9197
50:13 the flesh of bulls or d the blood of goats? 9272
73:10 to them and d up waters in abundance. 5172
75: 8 and all the wicked of the earth d it down 5172
78:44 they could not d from their streams. 9272
80: 5 you have made them d tears by the bowlful. 9197
102: 9 For I eat ashes as my food and mingle my d 9198
110: 7 He will d from a brook beside the way; 9272
Pr 4:17 of wickedness and d the wine of violence. 9272
5:15 D water from your own cistern, 9272
7:18 Come, let's d deep of love till morning; 8115
9: 5 eat my food and d the wine I have mixed. 9272
23: 7 "Eat and d," he says to you, 9272
23:20 Do not join those who d too much wine 6010
23:35 will I wake up so I can find another d?" 5647S
25:21 give him water to d. 9197
31: 4 not for kings to d wine, 9272
31: 5 lest they d and forget what the law decrees, 9272
31: 7 let them d and forget their poverty 9272
Ecc 2:24 and d and find satisfaction in his work. 9272
3:13 That everyone may eat and d, 9272
5:18 a man to eat and d, and to find satisfaction 9272
8:15 under the sun than to eat and d and be glad. 9272
9: 7 and d your wine with a joyful heart, 9272
SS 5: 1 Eat, O friends, and d; 9272
5: 1 d your fill, O lovers. 8910
8: 2 give you spiced wine to d, 9197
Isa 21: 5 they spread the rugs, they eat, they d! 9272
22:13 "Let us eat and d," you say, 9272
24: 9 No longer do they d wine with a song; 9272
36:12 and d their own urine?" 9272
36:16 from his own vine and fig tree and d water 9272
43:20 to give d to my people, my chosen, 9197
51:22 you will never d again. 9272
56:12 Let us d our fill of beer! 6010
57: 6 to them you have poured out d offerings 5821
60:16 You will d the milk of nations and 3567
62: 8 and never again will foreigners d 9272
62: 9 and those who gather the grapes will d it 9272
65:13 my servants will d, but you will go thirsty; 9272
66:11 you will d deeply and delight 5209
Jer 2:18 Now why go to Egypt to d water from 9272
2:18 And why go to Assyria to d water from 9272
7:18 They pour out d offerings to other gods 5821
8:14 given us poisoned water to d, 9197
9:15 and d poisoned water. 9197
16: 7 nor will anyone give them a d 3926+9197
16: 8 and sit down to eat and d. 9272
19:13 and poured out d offerings to other gods.' " 5821
22:15 Did not your father have food and d? 9272
23:15 and d poisoned water, 9197
25:15 make all the nations to whom I send you d 9197
25:16 When they d it, 9272
25:17 made all the nations to whom he sent me d 9197
25:26 the king of Sheshach will d it too. 9272
25:27 D, get drunk and vomit, 9272
25:28 to take the cup from your hand and d, 9272
25:28 You must d it! 9272+9272
32:29 by pouring out d offerings to other gods. 5821
35: 2 give them wine to d." 9197
35: 5 and said to them, "D some wine." 9272
35: 6 But they replied, "We do not d wine, 9272
35: 6 nor your descendants must ever d wine. 9272
35:14 to d wine and this command has been kept. 9272
35:14 To this day they do not d wine, 9272
44:17 and will pour out d offerings to her 5821
44:18 and pouring out d offerings to her, 5821
44:19 and poured out d offerings to her, 5821
44:19 like her image and pouring out d offerings 5821
44:25 to burn incense and pour out d offerings to 5821
49:12 not deserve to d the cup must drink it, 9272
49:12 not deserve to drink the cup must d it, 9272+9272
49:12 You will not go unpunished, but must d it. 9272+9272
52:19 bowls used for d offerings— 4984
La 5: 4 We must buy the water we d; 9272
Eze 4:11 of a hin of water and d it at set times. 9272
4:16 in anxiety and d rationed water in despair, 9272
12:18 and shudder in fear as you d your water. 9272
12:19 in anxiety and d their water in despair. 9272
20:28 and poured out their d offerings. 5821
23:32 "You will d your sister's cup, 9272
23:34 You will d it and drain it dry; 9272
25: 4 they will eat your fruit and d your milk. 9272
34:18 Is it not enough for you to d clear water? 9272

Eze 34:19 and **d** what you have muddied 9272
39:17 There you will eat flesh and **d** blood. 9272
39:18 You will eat the flesh of mighty men and **d** 9272
39:19 till you are glutted and **d** blood 9272
44:21 *to* **d** wine when he enters the inner court. 9272
45:17 grain offerings and **d offerings** at 5821
Da 1:10 who has assigned your food and **d.** 5492
1:12 but vegetables to eat and water *to* **d.** 9272
1:16 to **d** and gave them vegetables instead. 5492
5:2 and his concubines *might* **d** from them. 10748
Hos 2:5 my wool and my linen, my oil and my **d.'** 9198
Joel 1:9 Grain offerings and **d offerings** are cut off 5821
1:13 and **d offerings** are withheld from 5821
2:14 and **d offerings** for the LORD your God. 5821
3:3 they sold girls for wine that *they might* **d.** 9272
Am 2:8 In the house of their god *they* **d** wine taken 9272
2:12 "But *you* **made** the Nazirites **d** wine 9197
4:8 for water but did not get enough *to* **d,** 9272
5:11 *you will* not **d** their wine. 9272
6:6 *You* **d** wine by the bowlful and use 9272
9:14 They will plant vineyards and **d** their wine; 9272
Ob 1:16 so all the nations *will* **d** continually; 9272
1:16 *they will* **d** and drink and be as 9272
1:16 and **d** and be as if they had never been. 4363
Jnh 3:7 do not let them eat or **d.** 9272
Mic 6:15 you will crush grapes but not **d** the wine. 9272
Hab 2:15 "Woe to *him who* **gives d** *to* his neighbors, 9197
2:16 **D** and be exposed! 9272
Zep 1:13 they will plant vineyards but not **d** 9272
Hag 1:6 *You* **d,** but never have your fill. 9272
Zec 9:15 *They will* **d** and roar as with wine; 9272
Mt 6:25 what you will eat or **d;** *4403*
6:31 or 'What *shall we* **d?'** *4403*
20:22 "Can you **d** the cup I am going to drink?" *4403*
20:22 "Can you drink the cup I am going to **d?"** *4403*
20:23 *"You will* indeed **d from** my cup, *4403*
24:49 to beat his fellow servants and to eat and **d** *4403*
25:35 **gave** me something **to d,** *4540*
25:37 **give** you something **to d?** *4540*
25:42 **gave** me nothing **to d,** *4540*
26:27 saying, "**D** from it, all of you. *4403*
26:29 *I will* not **d** of this fruit of the vine from *4403*
26:29 until that day when *I* **d** it anew with you *4403*
26:42 for this cup to be taken away unless *I* **d** it, *4403*
27:34 There they offered Jesus wine *to* **d,** *4403*
27:34 but after tasting it, he refused *to* **d** it. *4403*
27:48 **offered** it to Jesus **to d.** *4540*
Mk 10:38 "Can you **d** the cup I drink or be baptized *4403*
10:38 "Can you drink the cup I **d** or be baptized *4403*
10:39 *"You will* **d** the cup I drink and be baptized *4403*
10:39 "You will drink the cup I **d** and be baptized *4403*
14:25 *I will* not **d** again of the fruit of the vine *4403*
14:25 when *I* **d** it anew in the kingdom of God." *4403*
15:36 **offered** it to Jesus **to d.** *4540*
16:18 and when *they* **d** deadly poison, *4403*
Lk 1:15 to take wine or other **fermented d,** *4975*
5:30 "Why do you eat and **d** with tax collectors *4403*
12:19 Take life easy; eat, **d** and be merry." ' *4403*
12:29 on what you will eat or **d;** *4403*
12:45 and maidservants and *to* eat and **d** *4403*
17:8 and wait on me while *I* eat and **d;** *4403*
17:8 after that you *may* eat and **d'?** *4403*
22:18 not **d** again of the fruit of the vine until *4403*
22:30 and **d** at my table in my kingdom and sit *4403*
Jn 2:10 guests *have* **had too much to d;** *3499*
4:7 Jesus said to her, "Will you give me a **d?"** *4403*
4:9 How can you ask me for a **d?"** *4403*
4:10 of God and who it is that asks you for a **d,** *4403*
6:53 the flesh of the Son of Man and **d** his blood, *4403*
6:55 and my blood is real **d.** *4530*
7:37 let him come to me and **d.** *4403*
18:11 not **d** the cup the Father has given me?" *4403*
19:30 When he had received the **d,** Jesus said, *NIG*
Ac 9:9 and did not eat or **d** anything. *4403*
23:12 not *to* eat or **d** until they had killed Paul. *4403*
23:21 not to eat or **d** until they have killed him. *4403*
Ro 12:20 **give** him something **to d.** *4540*
14:21 to eat meat or **d** wine or to do anything else *4403*
1Co 9:4 Don't we have the right *to* food and **d?** *4403*
9:7 Who tends a flock and *does* not **d** of *2266*
10:4 and drank the same spiritual **d;** *4503*
10:7 "The people sat down *to* eat and **d** and got *4403*
10:21 You cannot **d** the cup of the Lord and *4403*
10:31 whether you eat or **d** or whatever you do, *4403*
11:22 Don't you have homes to eat and **d** in? *4403*
11:25 do this, whenever *you* **d** it, *4403*
11:26 whenever you eat this bread and **d** this cup, *4403*
12:13 *we were* all **given** the one Spirit **to d.** *4540*
15:32 the dead are not raised, *"Let us* eat and **d,** *4403*
Php 2:17 **poured out like a d offering** *5064*
Col 2:16 by what you eat or **d,** *4530*
2Ti 4:6 **poured out like a d offering,** *5064*
Heb 9:10 and **d** and various ceremonial washings— *4503*
Rev 14:8 **made** all the nations **d** *4540*
14:10 too, *will* **d** of the wine of God's fury, *4403*
16:6 and you have given them blood *to* **d** *4403*
21:6 To him who is thirsty I will give to **d** *NIG*

DRINKERS (2) [DRINK]

Isa 24:9 the beer is bitter to its **d.** 9272
Joel 1:5 Wail, all you **d** *of* wine; 9272

DRINKING (39) [DRINK]

Ge 24:19 until they have finished **d."** 9272
24:22 When the camels had finished **d,** 9272
Ex 7:24 along the Nile to *get* **d** water, 9272
34:28 without eating bread or **d** water. 9272
Jdg 9:27 While they were eating and **d,** 9272
19:4 eating and **d,** and sleeping there. 9272
Ru 3:3 until he has finished eating and **d.** 9272
3:7 When Boaz had finished eating and **d** 9272
1Sa 1:9 Once when they had finished eating and **d** 9272
1:15 *I have* not *been* **d** wine or beer; 9272
30:16 **d** and reveling because of the great amount 9272
2Sa 13:28 in high spirits from **d** wine and I say to you, NIH
1Ki 1:25 Right now they are eating and **d** with him 9272
13:23 the man of God had finished eating and **d,** 9272
20:12 while he and the kings *were* **d** in their tents, 9272
2Ki 6:23 and after they had finished eating and **d,** 9272
1Ch 12:39 with David, eating and **d,** 9272
Est 5:6 As they were **d** wine, 5492
7:2 and as they were **d** wine on that second day, 5492
Job 1:13 and daughters were feasting and **d** wine at 9272
1:18 and daughters were feasting and **d** wine at 9272
Pr 26:6 Like cutting off one's feet or **d** violence is 9272
Isa 5:22 at **d** wine and champions at mixing drinks, 9272
22:13 eating of meat and **d** *of* wine! 9272
29:8 as when a thirsty man dreams that *he is* **d,** 9272
Da 5:2 While Belshazzar was **d** his wine, 10302
Zec 7:6 And when you were eating and **d,** 9272
Mt 11:18 For John came neither eating nor **d,** *4403*
11:19 The Son of Man came eating and **d,** *4403*
24:38 people were eating and **d,** *4403*
Lk 5:33 but yours *go on* eating and **d."** *4403*
5:39 no one *after* **d** old wine wants the new, *4403*
7:33 nor **d** wine, and you say, 'He has *4403*
7:34 The Son of Man came eating and **d,** *4403*
10:7 eating and **d** whatever they give you, *4403*
17:27 *People were* eating, **d,** *4403*
17:28 People were eating and **d,** *4403*
Ro 14:17 of God is not a matter of eating and **d,** *4530*
1Ti 5:23 Stop **d only water,** *5621*

DRINKS (22) [DRINK]

Ge 44:5 the cup my master **d** from and also uses 9272
Nu 23:24 till he devours his prey and **d** the blood 9272
Dt 11:11 a land of mountains and valleys that **d** rain 9272
2Sa 19:35 Can your servant taste what he eats and **d?** 9272
Ne 8:10 "Go and enjoy choice food and sweet **d,** 9272
Job 6:4 my spirit **d in** their poison; 9272
15:16 *who* **d up** evil like water! 9272
34:7 *who* **d** scorn like water? 9272
Isa 5:11 in the morning to run after their **d,** 8911
5:22 and champions at mixing **d,** 8911
44:12 *he* **d** no water and grows faint. 9272
Hos 4:18 Even when their **d** are gone, 6011
Am 4:1 "Bring us *some* **d!"** 9272
Jn 4:13 "Everyone who **d** this water will be thirsty *4403*
4:14 but whoever **d** the water I give him will never thirst. *4403*
6:54 and **d** my blood has eternal life, *4403*
6:56 and **d** my blood remains in me, *4403*
1Co 11:27 whoever eats the bread or **d** the cup of *4403*
11:28 before he eats of the bread and **d** of the cup. *4403*
11:29 and **d** without recognizing the body of *4403*
11:29 of the Lord eats and **d** judgment on himself. *4403*
Heb 6:7 Land that **d in** the rain often falling on it *4403*

DRIP (3) [DRIPPED, DRIPPING]

Pr 5:3 For the lips of an adulteress **d** honey, 5752
Joel 3:18 that day the mountains *will* **d** new wine, 5752
Am 9:13 New wine *will* **d** *from* the mountains 5752

DRIPPED (1) [DRIP]

SS 5:5 and my hands **d** *with* myrrh, 5752

DRIPPING (3) [DRIP]

Pr 19:13 quarrelsome wife is like a **constant d.** 1942+3265
27:15 quarrelsome wife is like a **constant d** 1942+3265
SS 5:13 His lips are like lilies **d** *with* myrrh. 5752

DRIVE (89) [DRIVEN, DRIVER, DRIVER'S, DRIVERS, DRIVES, DRIVING, DROVE]

Ex 6:1 of my mighty hand *he will* **d** them **out** 1763
11:1 *he will* **d** you **out** completely. 1763+1763
23:28 the hornet ahead of you *to* **d** the Hivites, 1763
23:29 But *I will* not **d** them **out** in a single year, 1763
23:30 by little *I will* **d** them out before you, 1763
23:31 and *you will* **d** them out before you. 1763
33:2 I will send an angel before you and **d out** 1763
34:11 I *will* **d out** before you the Amorites, 1763
34:24 *I will* **d out** nations before you 3769
Lev 18:24 how the nations that I *am going to* **d out** 8938
20:23 the nations I *am going to* **d out** before you. 8938
Nu 22:6 be able to defeat them and **d** them **out** of 1763
22:11 be able to fight them and **d** them **away.'** " 1763
33:52 **d out** all the inhabitants of the land 3769
33:55 " 'But if *you do* not **d out** the inhabitants of 3769
Dt 4:27 to which the LORD *will* **d** you. 5627
4:38 to **d out** before you nations greater 3769
7:17 How can we **d** them **out?"** 3769
7:22 The LORD your God *will* **d out** those nations 5970
9:3 And *you will* **d** them **out** 3769
9:4 that the LORD *is going to* **d** them **out** 3769
9:5 the LORD your God *will* **d** them **out** 3769
11:23 the LORD *will* **d out** all these nations 3769
18:12 LORD your God *will* **d out** those nations 3769
28:34 The sights you see will **d** you **mad.** 8713
Dt 28:36 The LORD *will* **d** you and the king 2143
28:37 the nations where the LORD *will* **d** you. 5627
33:27 *He will* **d out** your enemy before you, 1763
Jos 3:10 that *he will* **certainly d out** before you 3769+3769
13:6 *I* myself *will* **d** them **out** before 3769
13:13 But the Israelites *did* not **d out** the people 3769
14:12 *I will* **d** them **out** just as he said." 3769
17:13 **d** them **out completely.** 3769+3769
17:18 *you can* **d** them **out."** 3769
23:5 The LORD your God himself *will* **d** them **out** 2074
23:13 LORD your God will no longer **d out** these nations 3769
Jdg 1:19 but *they were* unable to **d** the people **from** 3769
1:27 But Manasseh *did* not **d out** the people 3769
1:29 Nor *did* Ephraim **d out** the Canaanites 3769
1:30 Neither *did* Zebulun **d out** the Canaanites 3769
1:31 Nor *did* Asher **d out** those living in Acco 3769
1:33 Neither *did* Naphtali **d out** those living 3769
2:3 that *I will* not **d** them **out** before you; 1763
2:21 I will no longer **d out** before them any of 3769
2:23 not **d** them **out** at once by giving them into 3769
11:7 and **d** me from my father's house? 1763
2Ch 13:9 But didn't *you* **d out** the priests of 5615
20:7 not **d out** the inhabitants of this land 3769
20:11 to **d** us **out** of the possession you gave us 1763
Job 24:3 *They* **d away** the orphan's donkey and take 5627
30:22 You snatch me up and **d** me before 8206
Ps 36:11 nor the hand of the wicked **d** me **away.** 5653
Pr 22:10 **D out** the mocker, and out goes strife; 1763
22:15 rod of discipline *will* **d** it **far** from him. 8178
Isa 22:23 *I will* **d** him like a peg into a firm place; 9546
Jer 22:22 **d** all your shepherds **away,** 8286
29:18 among all the nations where *I* **d** them. 5615
46:9 **D furiously,** O charioteers! 2147
49:2 Israel *will* **d out** those who drove her out," 3769
Eze 4:13 among the nations where *I will* **d** them." 5615
8:6 that *will* **d** me **far** from my sanctuary? 8178
11:7 but *I will* **d** you **out** of it. 3655
11:9 *I will* **d** you **out** of the city and hand you 3655
Hos 9:15 *I will* **d** them out of my house. 1763
10:11 *I will* **d** Ephraim, Judah must plow, 8206
Joel 2:20 **d** the northern army **far** 8178
Mic 2:9 *You* **d** the women of my people 1763
Mt 7:22 and in your name **d out** demons *1675*
8:31 "If *you* **d** us **out,** *1675*
10:1 to **d out** evil spirits and *1675*
10:8 cleanse those who have leprosy, **d out** demons. *1675*
12:27 And if I **d out** demons by Beelzebub, *1675*
12:27 by whom *do* your people **d** them **out?** *1675*
12:28 But if I **d out** demons by the Spirit of God, *1675*
17:19 "Why couldn't we **d** it **out?"** *1675*
Mk 3:15 and to have authority *to* **d out** demons. *1675*
3:23 "How can Satan **d out** Satan? *1675*
7:26 She begged Jesus to **d** the demon **out** *1675*
9:18 I asked your disciples to **d out** the spirit, *1675*
9:28 "Why couldn't we **d** it **out?"** *1675*
16:17 In my name *they will* **d out** demons; *1675*
Lk 9:1 *to* **d out** all demons and to cure diseases, *2093*
9:40 I begged your disciples to **d** it **out,** *1675*
11:18 because you claim that I **d out** demons *1675*
11:19 Now if I **d out** demons by Beelzebub, *1675*
11:19 by whom *do* your followers **d** them **out?** *1675*
11:20 But if I **d out** demons by the finger of God, *1675*
13:32 *'I will* **d out** demons *1675*
Jn 6:37 to me *I will* never **d** away. *1675*

DRIVEN (49) [DRIVE]

Ge 4:11 Now you are under a curse and **d from** 4946
33:13 If they *are* **d hard** just one day, 1985
Ex 10:11 Then Moses and Aaron *were* **d** out 1763
12:39 without yeast because *they had* **been d out** 1763
Nu 32:21 until he *has* **d** his enemies out before him— 3769
Dt 9:4 After the LORD your God has **d** them **out** 2074
12:29 But when *you have* **d** them **out** and settled 3769
19:1 and when *you have* **d** them **out** and settled 3769
Jos 8:15 **let themselves be d back** before them, 5595
23:9 "The LORD *has* **d out** before you great 3769
Jdg 11:23 *has* **d** the Amorites **out** 3769
1Sa 26:19 *They have* now **d** me from my share in 1763
1Ki 14:24 of the nations the LORD *had* **d out** before 3769
2Ki 16:3 of the nations the LORD *had* **d out** before 3769
17:8 of the nations the LORD *had* **d out** before 3769
17:11 the LORD *had* **d out** before them had done. 1655
21:2 of the nations the LORD *had* **d out** before 3769
2Ch 28:3 of the nations the LORD *had* **d out** before 3769
33:2 of the nations the LORD *had* **d out** before 3769
Job 6:13 now that success *has* **been d** from me? 5615
18:18 He *is* **d** from light into darkness 2074
30:8 *they* **were d out** of the land. 5777
30:15 my dignity *is* **d away** as *by* the wind, 8103
Ps 109:10 *may they* **be d** from their ruined homes. 1763
Isa 17:13 **d** before the wind like chaff on the hills, 8103
22:25 peg **d** into the firm place will give way; 9546
59:14 So justice **is d back,** 294+6047
Jer 13:24 scatter you like chaff **d** by the desert wind. 6296
23:2 and **d** them **away** and have 5615
23:3 of all the countries where *I have* **d** them 5615
49:5 "Every one of *you will* **be d away,** 5615
La 3:2 *He has* **d** me **away** and made me walk 5627
Eze 34:21 until *you have* **d** them away, 7046
Da 4:25 *be* **d away** from people and will live with 10304
4:32 *be* **d away** from people and will live with 10304
4:33 *He* **was d away** from people and ate grass 10304
5:21 *He* **was d away** from people and given 10304
Am 9:4 Though *they are* **d** into exile 2143

Mic 4: 7 those d away a strong nation. 2133
Mt 9:33 And when the demon was d out, 1675
Mk 16: 9 out of whom he had d seven demons. 1675
Lk 8:29 he had broken his chains and had been d by 1785
Jn 12:31 now the prince of this world will be d out. 1675
Ac 27:15 so we gave way to it and were d along. 5770
27:17 let the ship be d along. 5770
27:27 the fourteenth night we were still being d 1422
28: 3 a viper, d out by the heat, 2002
Jas 3: 4 they are so large and are d by strong winds, 1785
2Pe 2:17 without water and mists d by a storm. 1785

DRIVER (3) [DRIVE]
1Ki 22:34 The king told his chariot d, 8208
2Ch 18:33 The king told the chariot d, 8208
Jer 51:21 with you I shatter chariot and d, 8206

DRIVER'S (2) [DRIVE]
Job 3:18 they no longer hear the slave d shout. 5601
39: 7 he does not hear a d shout. 5601

DRIVERS (7) [DRIVE]
Ex 3: 7 because of their slave d, 5601
5: 6 to the slave d and foremen in charge of 5601
5:10 Then the slave d and the foremen went out 5601
5:13 The slave d kept pressing them, saying, 5601
5:14 by Pharaoh's slave d were beaten 5601
2Ki 7:14 He commanded the d, NIH
Hag 2:22 I will overthrow chariots and their d; 8206

DRIVES (12) [DRIVE]
Dt 7: 1 and d out before you many nations— 5970
2Ki 9:20 he d like a madman." 5627
Pr 16:26 his hunger d him on. 436
19:26 and d out his mother is 1368
20:26 he d the threshing wheel over them. 8740
Isa 27: 8 with his fierce blast he d her out, 2048
28:28 d the wheels of his threshing cart over 2169
59:19 that the breath of the LORD d along. 5674
Mt 9:34 of demons that he d out demons." 1675
12:24 that this fellow d out demons." 1675
12:26 If Satan d out Satan, 1675
1Jn 4:18 But perfect love d out fear, 965

DRIVING (24) [DRIVE]
Ge 4:14 Today you are d me from the land, 1763
Ex 14:25 so that they had difficulty d. 5627
2Sa 7:23 and awesome wonders by d out nations 1763
1Ki 19:19 and he himself was d the twelfth pair. 928
2Ki 9:20 The d is like that of Jehu son of Nimshi— 4952
16: 6 of Aram recovered Elath for Aram by d out 5970
1Ch 17:21 by d out nations from before your people, 1763
Job 37: 9 the cold from the d winds. 4668
Ps 35: 5 with the angel of the LORD d them away; 1890
Pr 28: 3 like a d rain that leaves no crops. 6085
Isa 25: 4 the ruthless is like a storm d against a wall AIT
28: 2 like a d rain and a flooding downpour, 2443+4784
Jer 30:23 a d wind swirling down on the heads of 1760
Eze 46:18 d them off their property. 3561
Mk 1:39 in their synagogues and d out demons. 1675
3:22 the prince of demons he is d out demons." 1675
9:38 "we saw a man d out demons in your name 1675
11:15 and began d out those who were buying 1675
Lk 9:49 "we saw a man d out demons in your name 1675
11:14 Jesus was d out a demon that was mute. 1675
11:15 the prince of demons, he is d out demons." 1675
19:45 and began d out those who were selling. 1675
Ac 19:13 around d out evil spirits tried to invoke 2020
26:24 "Your great learning is d you insane." 4365

DROMEDARIES, DROMEDARY (KJV)
See CAMELS, CAMEL

DROP (11) [DROPPED, DROPPING, DROPS]
Dt 28:40 because the olives will d off. 5970
33:28 where the heavens d dew. 6903
Pr 3:20 and the clouds let d the dew. 8319
17:14 so d the matter before a dispute breaks out. 5759
SS 4:11 Your lips d sweetness as the honeycomb, 5752
Isa 33: 9 and Bashan and Carmel d their leaves. 5850
40:15 Surely the nations are like a d in a bucket; 5254
Eze 39: 3 your left hand and make your arrows d 5877
Zec 8:12 and the heavens will d their dew. 5989
Lk 16:17 for the least stroke of a pen to d out of 4406
Rev 6:13 as late figs d from a fig tree when shaken 965

DROPPED (4) [DROP]
Jdg 9:53 a woman d an upper millstone on his head 8959
15:14 and the bindings d from his hands. 5022
2Sa 20: 8 he stepped forward, it d out of its sheath. 5877
Ac 27:29 they d four anchors from the stern 4849

DROPPING (1) [DROP]
2Ch 24:10 d them into the chest until it was full. 8959

DROPS (4) [DROP]
Nu 35:23 d a stone on him that could kill him, 5877
Job 36:27 "He draws up the d of water, 5754
38:28 Who fathers the d of dew? 103
Lk 22:44 and his sweat was like d of blood falling to 2584

DROPSY (1)
Lk 14: 2 in front of him was a man suffering from d. 5622

DROSS (7)
Ps 119:119 the wicked of the earth you discard like d; 6092
Pr 25: 4 Remove the d from the silver, 6092
Isa 1:22 Your silver has become d, 6092
1:25 I will thoroughly purge away your d 6092
Eze 22:18 the house of Israel has become d to me; 6092
22:18 They are but the d of silver. 6092
22:19 'Because you have all become d, 6092

DROUGHT (8)
Dt 28:22 with scorching heat and d, 2996
Job 12:15 If he holds back the waters, there is d; 3312
24:19 heat and d snatch away the melted snow, 7480
Jer 2: 6 a land of d and darkness, 7480
14: 1 the LORD to Jeremiah concerning the d: 1314
17: 8 in a year of d and never fails to bear fruit." 1316
50:38 A d on her waters! 2996
Hag 1:11 for a d on the fields and the mountains, 2996

DROVE (43) [DRIVE]
Ge 3:24 After he d the man out, 1763
15:11 but Abram d them away. 5959
31:18 d all his livestock ahead 5627
Ex 2:17 along and d them away, 1763
14:21 and all that night the LORD d the sea back 2143
Nu 11:31 the LORD and d quail in from the sea. 1577
21:32 and d out the Amorites who were there. 3769
25: 8 He d the spear through both of them— 1991
32:39 and d out the Amorites who were there. 3769
Dt 2:12 but the descendants of Esau d them out. 3769
2:21 who d them out and settled in their place. 3769
2:22 They d them out and have lived 3769
Jos 15:14 From Hebron Caleb d out 3769
24:12 which d them out before you— 1763
24:18 the LORD d out before us all the nations, 1763
Jdg 1:20 who d from it the three sons of Anak. 3769
1:28 d them out completely. 3769+3769
4:21 She d the peg through his temple into 9546
6: 9 I d them from before you 1763
9:41 and Zebul d Gaal and his brothers out 1763
11: 2 they d Jephthah away. 1763
1Sa 19:10 but David eluded him as Saul d the spear 5782
30:20 and his men d them ahead of 5627
2Sa 11:23 but we d them back to the entrance to 2118+6584
1Ki 21:26 like the Amorites the LORD d out 3769
1Ch 8:13 in Aijalon and who d out the inhabitants 1368
Ne 13:28 And I d him away from me. 1368
Ps 34: T who d him away, and he left. 1763
44: 2 With your hand you d out the nations 3769
78:55 He d out nations before them 1763
80: 8 you d out the nations and planted it. 1763
Jer 49: 2 Israel will drive out those who d her out," 3769
Eze 28:16 I d you in disgrace from the mount of God, 2725
29:18 of Babylon d his army in a hard campaign 6268
Mt 8:16 and he d out the spirits with a word 1675
21:12 and d out all who were buying 1675
Mk 1:34 He also d out many demons, 1675
6:13 They d out many demons 1675
Lk 4:29 They got up, d him out of the town, 1675
Jn 2:15 and d all from the temple area, 1675
Ac 7:45 from the nations God d out before them. 2034
2Co 12:11 but you d me to it. 337
1Th 2:15 and the prophets and also d us out. 1691

DROVES (4)
Ge 33: 8 "What do you mean by all these d I met?" 4722
33:14 along slowly at the pace of the d before me 4856
Ex 12:38 as well as large d of livestock, 5238
2Ch 14:15 and carried off d of sheep and goats 4200+8044

DROWN (3) [DROWNED]
Mt 8:25 We're going to d!" 660
Mk 4:38 "Teacher, don't you care if we d?" 660
Lk 8:24 saying, "Master, Master, we're going to d!" 660

DROWNED (6) [DROWN]
Ex 15: 4 of Pharaoh's officers are d in the Red Sea. 3190
Job 10:15 I am full of shame and d in my affliction. 8116
Mt 18: 6 around his neck and to be d in the depths 2931
Mk 5:13 the steep bank into the lake and were d. 4464
Lk 8:33 the steep bank into the lake and was d. 678
Heb 11:29 the Egyptians tried to do so, they were d. 2927

DROWSINESS (1) [DROWSY]
Pr 23:21 and d clothes them in rags. 5671

DROWSY (1) [DROWSINESS]
Mt 25: 5 and they all became d and fell asleep. 3818

DRUNK (38) [DRINK]
Ge 9:21 he became d and lay uncovered 8910
Lev 11:34 that could be d from it is unclean. 9272
Dt 32:42 I will make my arrows d with blood, 8910
1Sa 1:13 Eli thought she was d 8893
1:14 "How long will you keep on getting d? 8910
25:36 He was in high spirits and very d. 8893
30:12 not eaten any food or d any water 9272
2Sa 11:13 and David made him d. 8910
1Ki 16: 9 getting d in the home of Arza, 8893+9272
20:16 with him were in their tents getting d. 8893+9272
2Ki 19:24 I have dug wells in foreign lands and d 9272
SS 5: 1 I have d my wine and my milk. 9272
Isa 29: 9 be d, but not from wine, stagger, 8910
34: 5 My sword has d its fill in the heavens; 8115
37:25 I have dug wells in foreign lands and d 9272
49:26 they will be d on their own blood, 8910
51:17 you who have d from the hand of 9272
51:21 made d, but not with wine. 8912
63: 6 in my wrath I made them d 8910
Jer 25:27 Drink, get d and vomit, 8910
35: 8 and daughters have ever d wine 9272
48:26 "Make her d, for she has defied the LORD. 8910
51: 7 made the whole earth d. 8910
51:39 make them d, so that they shout 8910
51:57 make her officials and wise men d, 8910
La 4:21 you will be d and stripped naked. 8910
Eze 39:19 and drink blood till you are d. 8913
Na 1:10 They will be entangled among thorns and d 6010
3:11 You too will become d; 8910
Hab 2:15 pouring it from the wineskin till they are d, 8910
Lk 12:45 and to eat and drink and get d. 3499
Ac 2:15 These men are not d, as you suppose. 3501
1Co 11:21 One remains hungry, another gets d. 3501
Eph 5:18 Do not get d on wine, 3499
1Th 5: 7 and those who get d, get drunk at night. 3499
5: 7 and those who get drunk, get d at night. 3501
Rev 17: 6 I saw that the woman was d with the blood 3501
18: 3 the nations have d the maddening wine 4540

DRUNKARD (6) [DRINK]
Dt 21:20 He is a profligate and a d." 6010
Isa 19:14 as a d staggers around in his vomit. 8893
24:20 The earth reels like a d, 8893
Mt 11:19 and they say, 'Here is a glutton and a d, 3884
Lk 7:34 and you say, 'Here is a glutton and a d, 3884
1Co 5:11 an idolater or a slanderer, a d or a swindler. 3500

DRUNKARD'S (1) [DRINK]
Pr 26: 9 a d hand is a proverb in the mouth of a fool. 8893

DRUNKARDS (8) [DRINK]
Job 12:25 he makes them stagger like d. 8893
Ps 69:12 and I am the song of the d. 8911+9272
Pr 23:21 for d and gluttons become poor, 6010
Isa 28: 1 the pride of Ephraim's d, 8893
28: 3 That wreath, the pride of Ephraim's d, 8893
Joel 1: 5 Wake up, you d, and weep! 8893
Mt 24:49 and to eat and drink with d. 3501
1Co 6:10 nor the greedy nor d nor slanderers 3500

DRUNKEN (2) [DRINK]
Ps 107:27 They reeled and staggered like d men; 8893
Jer 23: 9 I am like a d man, 8893

DRUNKENNESS (9) [DRINK]
Ecc 10:17 for strength and not for d. 9275
Jer 13:13 to fill with d all who live in this land, 8913
Eze 23:33 You will be filled with d and sorrow, 8913
Lk 21:34 d and the anxieties of life, 3494
Ro 13:13 as in the daytime, not in orgies and d, 3494
Gal 5:21 d, orgies, and the like. 3494
1Ti 3: 3 not given to d, not violent but gentle, 4232
Tit 1: 7 not quick-tempered, not given to d, 4232
1Pe 4: 3 living in debauchery, lust, d, orgies, 3886

DRUSILLA (1)
Ac 24:24 Felix came with his wife D, 1537

DRY (77) [DRIED, DRIES, DRYING]
Ge 1: 9 and let d ground appear." 3317
1:10 God called the d ground "land," 3317
7:22 Everything on d land that had the breath 3000
8:13 that the surface of the ground was d. 2990
8:14 the earth was completely d. 3312
Ex 4: 9 from the Nile and pour it on the d ground. 3317
14:16 through the sea on d ground. 3317
14:21 and turned it into d land. 3000
14:22 Israelites went through the sea on d ground, 3317
14:29 Israelites went through the sea on d ground, 3317
15:19 through the sea on d ground. 3317
Lev 7:10 whether mixed with oil or d, 2992
Dt 29:19 on the watered land as well as the d. 7534
Jos 3:17 of the LORD stood firm on d ground in 3000
3:17 the crossing on d ground. 3000
4:18 on the d ground than the waters of 3000
4:22 'Israel crossed the Jordan on d ground.' 3317
9: 5 All the bread of their food supply was d 3312
9:12 But now see how d and moldy it is. 3312
Jdg 6:37 If there is dew only on the fleece and all the ground is d, 2996
6:39 the fleece d and the ground covered 2996
6:40 Only the fleece was d; 2996
1Ki 17:14 be used up and the jug of oil will not run d 2893
17:16 not used up and the jug of oil did not run d, 2893
2Ki 2: 8 the two of them crossed over on d ground. 3000
Ne 9:11 so that they passed through it on d ground, 3317
Job 6:17 but that cease to flow in the d season, 2427

Job 13:25 Will you chase after **d** chaff? 3313
14:11 or a riverbed becomes parched and **d,** 3312
18:16 His roots **d up** below 3312
30: 6 to live in the **d** stream beds, 6877
Ps 58: 9 whether they be green or **d**— 3019
63: 1 a **d** and weary land where there is no water. 7480
66: 6 He turned the sea into **d land,** 3317
90: 6 by evening *it is* **d** and withered. 4908
95: 5 and his hands formed the **d land.** 3318
Pr 17: 1 Better a **d** crust with peace and quiet than 2992
Isa 5:24 and as **d grass** sinks down in the flames, 3143
11:15 The LORD *will* **d up** the gulf of 2990
19: 5 The waters of the river *will* **d up,** 5980
19: 5 and the riverbed will be parched and **d.** 3312
19: 6 the streams of Egypt will dwindle and **d up.** 2990
27:11 When its twigs *are* **d,** 3312
42:15 and hills and **d up** all their vegetation; 3312
42:15 I will turn rivers into islands and **d up** 3312
44: 3 and streams on the **d ground;** 3317
44:27 *'Be* **d,** and I will dry up your streams,' 2990
44:27 'Be dry, and *I will* **d up** your streams,' 3312
50: 2 By a mere rebuke *I* **d up** the sea, 2990
53: 2 and like a root out of **d** ground. 7480
56: 3 "I am only a **d** tree." 3313
Jer 2:25 until your feet are bare and your throat is **d.** 7535
50:12 a wilderness, a **d land,** a desert. 7480
50:38 *They will* **d up.** 3312
51:36 *I will* **d up** her sea 2990
51:36 I will dry up her sea and **make** her springs **d** 3312
51:43 a **d** and desert land, 7480
La 4: 8 it has become as **d** as a stick. 3313
Eze 17:24 *I* **d up** the green tree and make 3312
17:24 the green tree and make the **d** tree flourish. 3313
19:13 in a **d** and thirsty land. 7480
20:47 both green and **d.** 3313
23:34 You will drink it and **drain** it **d;** 5172
30:12 *I will* **d up** the streams of the Nile 3000+5989
37: 2 bones *that* were very **d.** 3313
37: 4 **'D** bones, hear the word of the LORD! 3313
Hos 9:14 that miscarry and breasts *that are* **d.** 7546
13:15 his spring will fail and his well **d up.** 2990
Am 1: 2 the pastures of the shepherds **d up,** 62
Jnh 2:10 and it vomited Jonah onto **d land.** 3317
Na 1: 4 **makes** all the rivers **run d.** 2990
1:10 they will be consumed like **d** stubble. 3313
Zep 2:13 leaving Nineveh utterly desolate and **d** as 7480
Hag 2: 6 the sea and the **d land.** 3000
Zec 10:11 and all the depths of the Nile *will* **d up.** 3312
Lk 23:31 what will happen when it is **d?"** *3831*
Heb 11:29 through the Red Sea as on **d** land; *3831*

DRYING (1) [DRY]

Jn 13: 5 **d** them with the towel that was wrapped *1726*

DRYSHOD (KJV) See IN SANDALS

DUE (20) [DULY]

Lev 19:20 there must be **d punishment.** 1334
Dt 18: 3 This is the **share** *d* the priests from AIT
32:35 In **d time** their foot will slip; 6961
1Ch 16:29 to the LORD the **glory** *d* his name. AIT
2Ch 24: 5 the money **d annually** from all Israel, 928+1896+4946+9102+9102
31: 4 to give the **portion** *d* the priests and Levites AIT
Job 36:17 But now you are laden with the **judgment** *d* AIT
Ps 29: 2 to the LORD the **glory** *d* his name; AIT
90:11 as great as the **fear** *that is d* you. AIT
96: 8 to the LORD the **glory** *d* his name; AIT
Pr 11:31 If the righteous **receive** *their* **d** on earth, 8966
Isa 49: 4 Yet *what* is **d** me is in the LORD's hand, 5477
59:18 he will repay the islands their **d.** 1691
Jer 10: 7 This is your **d.** 3278
Mal 1: 6 If I am a father, where is the **honor** *d* me? AIT
1: 6 where is the **respect** *d* me?" AIT
Ro 1:27 and received in themselves the **d** penalty *1256*
2Co 5:10 that each one may receive what is **d** him for *NIG*
Eph 4:18 in them **d to** the hardening of their hearts. *1328*
1Pe 5: 6 that he may lift you up in **d time.** *2789*

DUG (32) [DIG]

Ge 21:30 as a witness that *I* **d** this well." 2916
26:15 the wells that his father's servants *had* **d** in 2916
26:18 Isaac reopened the wells that *had been* **d** in 2916
26:19 Isaac's servants **d** in the valley 2916
26:21 Then *they* **d** another well, 2916
26:22 on from there and **d** another well, 2916
26:25 and there his servants **d** a well. 4125
26:32 and told him about the well *they had* **d.** 2916
50: 5 bury me in the tomb *I* **d** for myself in 4125
Ex 7:24 And all the Egyptians **d** along the Nile 2916
Nu 21:18 the well that the princes **d,** that the nobles 2916
1Ki 18:32 and *he* **d** a trench around it large enough 6913
2Ki 19:24 I *have* **d wells** in foreign lands and drunk 7769
2Ch 26:10 in the desert and **d** many cisterns, 2933
Ne 9:25 wells *already* **d,** vineyards, 2933
Ps 9:15 nations have fallen into the pit *they have* **d;** 6913
35: 7 for me without cause and without cause **d** 2916
57: 6 *They* **d** a pit in my path— 4125
94:13 till a pit **is d** for the wicked. 4125
Isa 5: 2 *He* **d** it **up** and cleared it of stones 6466
37:25 I *have* **d wells** in foreign lands and drunk 7769
Jer 2:13 and *have* **d** their own cisterns, 2933
13: 7 to Perath and **d up** the belt and took it from 2916
18:20 Yet *they have* **d** a pit for me. 4125
18:22 for *they have* **d** a pit to capture me 4125
Eze 8: 8 *I* **d** into the wall and saw a doorway there. 3168
12: 7 Then in the evening *I* **d** through the wall 3168
12:12 and a hole *will be* **d** in the wall for him 3168
Mt 21:33 **d** a winepress in it and built a watchtower. *4002*
25:18 **d a hole** in the ground *4002*
Mk 12: 1 **d** a pit for the winepress and built *4002*
Lk 6:48 who **d** down deep and laid the foundation *4999*

DUKE, DUKES (KJV) See CHIEF, CHIEFS

DULCIMER (KJV) See PIPES

DULL (8)

Lev 13:39 and if the spots are **d** white, 3910
Ecc 10:10 If the ax *is* **d** and its edge unsharpened, 7733
Isa 6:10 **make** their ears **d** and close their eyes. 3877
59: 1 nor his ear too **d** to hear. 3877
La 4: 1 the fine gold *become* **d!** 9096
Mt 15:16 "Are you still so **d?"** Jesus asked them. *852*
Mk 7:18 "Are you so **d?"** *852*
2Co 3:14 But their minds *were* **made d,** *4800*

DULY (1) [DUE]

Gal 3:15 *that has been* **d established,** *3263*

DUMAH (4)

Ge 25:14 Mishma, **D,** Massa, 1874
Jos 15:52 Arab, **D,** Eshan, 1873
1Ch 1:30 Mishma, **D,** Massa, Hadad, Tema, 1874
Isa 21:11 An oracle concerning **D:** 1874

DUMB (KJV) See CANNOT SPEAK, COULD NOT TALK, LIFELESS, MUTE, ROBBED OF SPEECH, SILENT, SPEECHLESS, WITHOUT SPEECH

DUMPED (1)

Lev 14:41 and the material that is scraped off **d** into 9161

DUNG (6)

1Ki 14:10 up the house of Jeroboam as one burns **d,** 1672
Ne 2:13 toward the Jackal Well and the **D** Gate, 883
3:13 of the wall as far as the **D** Gate. 883
3:14 The **D** Gate was repaired by Malkijah son 883
12:31 toward the **D** Gate. 883
Job 20: 7 he will perish forever, like his own **d;** 1645

DUNGEON (7) [DUNGEONS]

Ge 40:15 to deserve being put in a **d."** 1014
41:14 and he was quickly brought from the **d.** 1014
Ex 12:29 who was in the **d,** 1014+1074
Isa 24:22 like prisoners bound in a **d;** 1014
42: 7 and to release from the **d** those who sit 1074+3975
51:14 they will not die in their **d,** 8846
Jer 37:16 Jeremiah was put into a vaulted cell in a **d,** 1014+1074

DUNGEONS (1) [DUNGEON]

2Pe 2: 4 into gloomy **d** to be held for judgment; *4987*

DUNGHILL (KJV) See ASH HEAP, MANURE PILE, PILE OF RUBBLE,

DUPLICITY (2)

Pr 11: 3 but the unfaithful are destroyed by their **d.** 6157
Lk 20:23 He saw through their **d** and said to them, *4111*

DURA (1)

Da 3: 1 the plain of **D** in the province of Babylon. 10164

DURETH (KJV) See LASTS

DURING (133)

Ge 14:15 *D the* **night** Abram divided his men AIT
30:14 **D** wheat harvest, Reuben went out into 928+3427
41:34 of Egypt **d** the seven years of abundance. 928
41:36 to be used **d** the seven years of famine 4200
41:47 **D** the seven years of abundance 928
Ex 2:23 **D** that long period, the king of Egypt died. 928
12:30 and all the Egyptians got up *d* **the night,** AIT
12:31 *D* **the night** Pharaoh summoned Moses AIT
13: 7 Eat unleavened bread *d* those seven **days;** AIT
14:24 **D** the last watch of the night 928
23:11 but **d** the seventh year let NIH
34:21 even **d** the plowing season 928
40:38 of all the house of Israel **d** all their travels. 928
Lev 12: 2 just as she is unclean **d** her monthly period. 3427
12: 5 unclean, as **d** her period. NIH
15:20 " 'Anything she lies on **d** her period will 928
15:26 unclean, as is her bed **d** her monthly period, NIH
15:26 unclean, as **d** her period. NIH
18:19 to have sexual relations **d** the uncleanness 928
20:18 with a woman **d** her monthly period NIH
25: 6 the land yields **d** the sabbath year will NIH
25:22 While you plant **d** the eighth year, NIH
25:29 **D that time** he may redeem it. 3427
26:35 the land will have the rest it did not have **d** 928
27:17 he dedicates his field **d** the Year of Jubilee, 4946
Nu 3: 4 and Ithamar served as priests **d** the lifetime 6584
6: 5 " '*D* the entire **period** *of* his vow AIT
6:12 because he became defiled **d** his separation. NIH
10:33 before them *d* those three **days** to find them AIT
28:14 to be made at each **new moon** *d* the year. AIT
28:26 to the LORD an offering of new grain **d** 928
Dt 8: 4 not swell *d* these forty **years.** AIT
28:53 that your enemy will inflict on you **d** 928
28:55 on you **d** the siege of all your cities. 928
28:57 to eat them secretly **d** the siege and in 928
29: 5 *D* the forty **years** that I led you through AIT
31:10 **d** the Feast of Tabernacles, 928
Jos 3:15 the Jordan is at flood stage all **d** harvest. 3427
5: 5 the people born in the desert **d** the journey 928
Jdg 7: 9 **D** that night the LORD said to Gideon, 928
8:28 **D** Gideon's lifetime, the land enjoyed peace 928
9:32 *d* the **night** you and your men should come AIT
11:26 Why didn't you retake them **d** that time? 928
16: 2 They made no move **d** the night, saying, 3972
20: 5 *D* the **night** the men of Gibeah came AIT
21:22 we did not get wives for them **d** the war, 928
1Sa 11:11 **d** the last watch of the night they broke into 928
29: 4 or he will turn against us **d** the fighting. 928
2Sa 3: 6 **D** the war between the house of Saul and 928
18:18 **D** his lifetime Absalom had taken a pillar 928
19:32 He had provided for the king **d** his stay 928
21: 1 **D** the reign of David, there was a famine 928
21: 9 they were put to death **d** the first days of 928
23:13 **D** harvest time, three of the thirty chief men 448
1Ki 3: 5 to Solomon *d* the **night** in a dream, AIT
3:19 "*D* the **night** this woman's son died AIT
4:25 **D** Solomon's lifetime Judah and Israel, 3972
9:10 *d* **which** Solomon built these two buildings AIT
11:12 I will not do it **d** your lifetime. 928
12: 6 elders who had served his father Solomon **d** 928
2Ki 15:18 *D* his entire **reign** he did not turn away from AIT
24: 1 **D** Jehoiakim's reign, Nebuchadnezzar king 928
1Ch 5:10 **D** Saul's reign they waged war against 928
5:17 in the genealogical records **d** the reigns 928
5:20 because they cried out to him **d** the battle. 928
7: 2 **D** the reign of David, 928
13: 3 we did not inquire of it **d** the reign of Saul." 928
22: 9 and I will grant Israel peace and quiet **d** 928
2Ch 8: 1 *d* **which** Solomon built the temple of AIT
10: 6 elders who had served his father Solomon **d** 928
11:17 the ways of David and Solomon **d** this time. 4200
13:20 Jeroboam did not regain power **d** the time 928
14: 6 No one was at war with him **d** those years, 928
26: 5 He sought God **d** the days of Zechariah, 928
32:26 upon them **d** the days of Hezekiah. 928
Ezr 4: 5 and frustrate their plans **d** the entire reign NIH
7: 1 **d** the reign of Artaxerxes king of Persia, 928
8: 1 up with me from Babylon **d** the reign 928
Ne 2:12 I set out *d* the **night** with a few men. AIT
5: 3 our vineyards and our homes to get grain **d** 928
8:14 in booths **d** the feast of the seventh month 928
Est 1: 1 This is what happened **d** the time 928
2:21 **D** the time Mordecai was sitting at 928
Pr 10: 5 but he who sleeps **d** harvest is 928
Ecc 2: 3 for men to do under heaven **d** the few days NIH
5:18 in his toilsome labor under the sun **d** NIH
6:12 **d** the few and meaningless days he passes NIH
Isa 1: 1 that Isaiah son of Amoz saw **d** the reigns 928
49:20 The **children** *born d* your bereavement will AIT
Jer 3: 6 **D** the reign of King Josiah, 928
19: 9 and they will eat one another's flesh **d** 928
35: 1 that came to Jeremiah from the LORD **d** 928
49: 9 If thieves came **d** the night, 928
Eze 4: 9 to eat it **d** the 390 days you lie on your side. 5031
12: 4 **D the daytime,** while they watch, 3429
12: 7 **D the day** I brought out my things packed 3429
18: 6 or lie with a woman *d* her **period.** AIT
22:10 in you are those who violate women **d** NIH
23: 8 when **d** her youth men slept with her, 928
36:38 as the flocks for offerings at Jerusalem **d** 928
45:21 **d** which you shall eat bread made NIH
45:23 Every **day** *d* the seven days of AIT
45:25 " '**D** the seven days of the Feast, 928
Da 2:19 **D** the night the mystery was revealed 10168
6: 7 that anyone who prays to any god or man **d** 10527
6:12 "Did you not publish a decree that **d** 10527
6:28 So Daniel prospered **d** the reign of Darius 10089
Hos 1: 1 to Hosea son of Beeri **d** the reigns 928
1: 1 and **d** the reign of Jeroboam son 928
Mic 1: 1 of Moresheth **d** the reigns of Jotham, Ahaz 928
Zep 1: 1 **d** the reign of Josiah son of Amon king 928
Zec 1: 8 **D** the night I had a vision— NIH
Mt 2: 1 **d** the time of King Herod, *1877*
2:14 the child and his mother *d* **the night** and left *AIT*
14:25 *D* the **fourth watch** of the night *AIT*
26: 5 "But not **d** the Feast," they said, *1877*
28:13 'His disciples came *d* the **night** *AIT*
Mk 8: 1 **D** those days another large crowd gathered. *1877*
14: 2 "But not **d** the Feast," they said, *1877*
Lk 3: 2 **d** the high priesthood of Annas *2093*
4: 2 He ate nothing **d** those days, *1877*
Jn 19:31 the bodies left on the crosses **d** the Sabbath, *1877*
Ac 5:19 But **d** the night an angel of the Lord opened *1328*
11:27 **D** this time some prophets came down *1877*
11:28 (This happened **d** the reign of Claudius.) *2093*
12: 3 This happened **d** the Feast *2465*
13:17 the people prosper **d** their stay in Egypt, *1877*
16: 9 **D** the night Paul had a vision of a man *1328*
23:31 with them **d** the night and brought him *1328*

Heb 3: 8 **d** the time of testing in the desert, *2848*
5: 7 **D** the days of Jesus' life on earth, *1877*
Rev 9: 6 **D** those days men will seek death, *1877*
11: 6 not rain *d* **the time** they are prophesying; *AIT*

DURST (KJV) See DARE, DARED, DARING

DUSK (10)

Jos 2: 5 At **d,** when it was time to close 3125
1Sa 30:17 David fought them from **d** until the evening 5974
2Ki 7: 5 At **d** they got up and went to the camp of 5974
7: 7 and fled in the **d** and abandoned their tents 5974
Job 4:20 Between dawn and **d** they are broken 6847
24:15 The eye of the adulterer watches for **d;** 5974
Eze 12: 6 and carry them out at **d.** 6602
12: 7 I took my belongings out at **d,** 6602
12:12 on his shoulder at **d** and leave, 6602
Hab 1: 8 fiercer than wolves at **d.** 6847

DUST (109)

Ge 2: 7 the LORD God formed the man from the **d** 6760
3:14 on your belly and you will eat **d** all the days 6760
3:19 for **d** you are and to dust you will return." 6760
3:19 for dust you are and to **d** you will return." 6760
13:16 I will make your offspring like the **d** *of* 6760
13:16 so that if anyone could count the **d,** 6760
18:27 though I am nothing but **d** and ashes, 6760
28:14 Your descendants will be like the **d** *of* 6760
Ex 8:16 'Stretch out your staff and strike the **d** *of* 6760
8:16 the land of Egypt the **d** will become gnats." NIH
8:17 the staff and struck the **d** *of* the ground, 6760
8:17 All the **d** throughout the land 6760
9: 9 It will become **fine d** over the whole land 85
Nu 5:17 and put some **d** from the tabernacle floor 6760
23:10 Who can count the **d** *of* Jacob or number 6760
Dt 9:21 as fine as **d** and threw the dust into a stream 6760
9:21 as fine as dust and threw the **d** into a stream 6760
28:24 the rain of your country into **d** and powder; 6760
32:24 the venom of vipers that glide in the **d.** 6760
Jos 7: 6 and sprinkled **d** on their heads. 6760
1Sa 2: 8 the poor from the **d** and lifts the needy from 6760
4:12 his clothes torn and **d** on his head. 141
2Sa 1: 2 with his clothes torn and with **d** 141
15:32 his robe torn and **d** on his head. 141
22:43 I beat them as fine as the **d** *of* the earth; 6760
1Ki 16: 2 up from the **d** and made you leader 6760
20:10 be it ever so severely, if enough **d** remains 6760
2Ki 13: 7 and made them like the **d** at threshing time. 6760
23: 6 He ground it to powder and scattered the **d** 6760
2Ch 1: 9 over a people who are as numerous as the **d** 6760
Ne 9: 1 fasting and wearing sackcloth and having **d** 141
Job 2:12 and they tore their robes and sprinkled **d** 6760
4:19 whose foundations are in the **d,** 6760
7:21 For I will soon lie down in the **d;** 6760
10: 9 Will you now turn me to **d** again? 6760
16:15 over my skin and buried my brow in the **d.** 6760
17:16 Will we descend together into the **d?"** 6760
20:11 with him in the **d.** 6760
21:26 Side by side they lie in the **d,** 6760
22:24 and assign your nuggets to the **d,** 6760
27:16 Though he heaps up silver like **d** 6760
28: 6 and its **d** contains nuggets of gold. 6760
30:19 and I am reduced to **d** and ashes. 6760
34:15 and man would return to the **d.** 6760
38:38 when the **d** becomes hard and the clods 6760
40:13 Bury them all in the **d** together; 6760
42: 6 Therefore I despise myself and repent in **d** 6760
Ps 7: 5 to the ground and make me sleep in the **d.** 6760
18:42 I beat them as fine as **d** borne on the wind; 6760
22:15 you lay me in the **d** *of* death. 6760
22:29 down to the **d** will kneel before him— 6760
30: 9 Will the **d** praise you? 6760
44:25 We are brought down to the **d;** 6760
72: 9 before him and his enemies will lick the **d.** 6760
78:27 He rained meat down on them like **d,** 6760
89:39 and have defiled his crown in the **d.** 824
90: 3 You turn men back to **d,** saying, 1919
90: 3 saying, "Return to **d,** O sons of men." NIH
102:14 her very **d** moves them to pity. 6760
103:14 he remembers that we are **d.** 6760
104:29 they die and return to the **d.** 6760
113: 7 the poor from the **d** and lifts the needy from 6760
119:25 I am laid low in the **d;** 6760
Pr 8:26 or its fields or any of the **d** *of* the world. 6760
Ecc 3:20 all come from **d,** and to dust all return. 6760
3:20 all come from dust, and to **d** all return. 6760
12: 7 the **d** returns to the ground it came from, 6760
Isa 5:24 and their flowers blow away like **d;** 85
25:12 down to the ground, to the very **d.** 6760
26: 5 to the ground and casts it down to the **d.** 6760
26:19 You who dwell in the **d,** 6760
29: 4 your speech will mumble out of the **d.** 6760
29: 4 out of the **d** your speech will whisper. 6760
29: 5 like fine **d,** the ruthless hordes 85
34: 7 and the **d** will be soaked with fat. 6760
34: 9 her **d** into burning sulfur; 6760
40:12 Who has held the **d** *of* the earth in a basket, 6760
40:15 they are regarded as **d** *on* the scales; 8836
40:15 the islands as though they were fine **d.** NIH
41: 2 He turns them to **d** with his sword, 6760
47: 1 "Go down, sit in the **d,** 6760
49:23 they will lick the **d** *at* your feet. 6760
52: 2 Shake off your **d;** 6760
65:25 but **d** will be the serpent's food. 6760
Jer 17:13 in the **d** because they have forsaken 824
25:34 roll in the **d,** you leaders of the flock. NIH
La 2:10 they have sprinkled **d** on their heads 6760
2:21 and old lie together in the **d** of the streets; 824
3:16 he has trampled me in the **d.** 709
3:29 Let him bury his face in the **d—** 6760
Eze 24: 7 where the **d** would cover it. 6760
26:10 be so many that they will cover you with **d.** 85
27:30 they will sprinkle **d** on their heads and roll 6760
Da 12: 2 Multitudes who sleep in the **d** *of* 6760
Am 2: 7 upon the **d** *of* the ground and deny justice 6760
Jnh 3: 6 with sackcloth and sat down in the **d.** 709
Mic 1:10 In Beth Ophrah roll in the **d.** 6760
7:17 They will lick **d** like a snake, 6760
Na 1: 3 and clouds are the **d** *of* his feet. 85
Zep 1:17 be poured out like **d** and their entrails 6760
Zec 9: 3 she has heaped up silver like **d,** 6760
Mt 10:14 shake the **d** off your feet when you leave *3155*
Mk 6:11 shake the **d** off your feet when you leave, *5967*
Lk 9: 5 shake the **d** off your feet when you leave *3155*
10:11 'Even the **d** of your town that sticks *3155*
Ac 13:51 the **d** from their feet in protest against them *3155*
22:23 and throwing off their cloaks and flinging **d** *3155*
1Co 15:47 The first man was of the **d** of the earth, *5954*
Rev 18:19 They will throw **d** on their heads, *5967*

DUTIES (25) [DUTY]

Ge 39:11 into the house to attend to his **d,** 4856
Ex 18:20 to live and the **d** they are to perform. 5126
Nu 3: 7 They are to perform **d** *for* him and for 5466
4:28 Their **d** are to be under the direction 5466
8:26 in performing their **d** at the Tent 5466
18: 3 and are to perform all the **d** *of* the Tent, 5466
1Ki 3: 7 and do not know how *to* **carry out** *my* **d.** 995+2256+3655
1Ch 6:32 They performed their **d** according to 6275
6:48 to all the other **d** *of* the tabernacle, 6275
9:25 from time to time and **share their d** 465+6640
9:33 **were exempt from** *other* **d** 7080
23:28 and the performance of *other* **d** *at* the house 6275
25: 8 cast lots *for* their **d.** 5466
26:12 had **d** for ministering in the temple of 5466
26:29 and his sons were assigned **d** away from 4856
2Ch 8:14 the divisions of the priests for their **d,** 6275
31: 2 each of them according to their **d** as priests 6275
31:16 to perform the daily **d** of their various tasks, 1821
35: 2 the priests to their **d** and encouraged them 5466
Ne 10:33 and for all the **d** *of* the house of our God. 4856
13:30 and assigned them **d,** each to his own task. 5466
Eze 44:14 the **d** *of* the temple and all the work that is 5466
44:15 and who faithfully carried out the **d** 5466
2Ti 4: 5 discharge all the **d** of your ministry. *NIG*
Heb 10:11 **performs** his **religious d;** *3310*

DUTY (32) [DUTIES]

Ge 38: 8 **fulfill** *your* **d** *to* her **as a brother-in-law** 3302
Nu 4:31 This is their **d** as they perform service at 5466
Dt 24: 5 not be sent to war or have any other **d** laid 1821
25: 5 **fulfill the d of a brother-in-law** 3302
25: 7 **fulfill the d of a brother-in-law** 3302
1Ki 14:27 to the commanders of the guard **on d** at 9068
2Ki 11: 5 the three companies *that are* **going on d** *on* 995
11: 7 *that* normally **go off** Sabbath **d** are all 3655
11: 9 *those who were* **going on d** *on* the Sabbath 995
11: 9 and *those who were* **going off d—** 3655
1Ch 23:28 The **d** *of* the Levites was 5096
27: 1 that *were* **on d** month by month 995+2256+3655
2Ch 12:10 to the commanders of the guard **on d at** 9068
23: 4 and Levites *who are* **going on d** *on* 995
23: 6 the priests and Levites **on d;** 9250
23: 8 *those who were* **going on d** *on* the Sabbath 995
23: 8 and *those who were* **going off d—** 3655
Ezr 4:13 no more taxes, tribute or **d** will be paid, 10208
4:20 and taxes, tribute and **d** were paid to them. 10208
7:24 tribute or **d** on any of the priests, Levites, 10208
Ne 7: 3 While the gatekeepers *are still* **on d,** 6641
Ecc 12:13 for this is the whole [**d**] of man. NIH
Jer 32: 7 **as nearest relative** it is your right and **d** 1460
Eze 44: 8 Instead of carrying out your **d** *in regard* 5466
45:17 It will be **the d of** the prince to provide 6584
Mt 17:25 the kings of the earth collect **d** and taxes— *5465*
Lk 1: 8 Once when Zechariah's division was on **d** *NIG*
17:10 we have only done *our* **d,'** " *4005+4053+4472*
Jn 18:16 to the **girl on d** there and brought Peter in. *2601*
Ac 23: 1 I *have* **fulfilled** *my* **d** to God *4488*
Ro 15:16 the **priestly d** of proclaiming the gospel *2646*
1Co 7: 3 The husband should fulfill his marital **d** *4051*

DWARFED (1)

Lev 21:20 or who is hunchbacked or **d,** 1987

DWELL (79) [DWELLERS, DWELLING, DWELLINGS, DWELLS, DWELT, TENT-DWELLING]

Ex 25: 8 and *I will* **d** among them. 8905
29:45 Then *I will* **d** among the Israelites and 8905
29:46 of Egypt so that I *might* **d** among them. 8905
Nu 5: 3 where I **d** among them." 8905
35:34 the land where you live and where I **d,** 8905
35:34 for I, the LORD, **d** among the Israelites.' " 8905
2Sa 7: 5 the one to build me a house to **d in?** 3782
1Ki 8:12 "The LORD has said that he *would* **d** in 8905
8:13 a place for you to **d** forever." 3782
8:27 "But *will* God really **d** on earth? 3782
1Ch 17: 4 not the one to build me a house to **d in.** 3782
23:25 and *has* **come to d** in Jerusalem forever, 8905
2Ch 6: 1 "The LORD has said that he *would* **d** in 8905
6: 2 a place for you to **d** forever." 3782
6:18 "But *will* God really **d** on earth with men? 3782
Ezr 6:12 who *has* **caused** his Name **to d** there, 10709
Job 11:14 **allow** no evil **to d** 8905
17: 2 my eyes *must* **d** *on* their hostility. 4328
28: 4 Far from where *people* **d** he cuts a shaft, 1591
28:12 Where does understanding **d?** 5226
28:20 Where does understanding **d?** 5226
Ps 4: 8 O LORD, **make** me **d** in safety. 3782
5: 4 *with* you the wicked cannot **d.** 1591
15: 1 LORD, who *may* **d** in your sanctuary? 1591
23: 6 and *I will* **d** in the house of 8740
27: 4 that I *may* **d** in the house of the LORD all 3782
37: 3 **d in** the land and enjoy safe pasture. 8905
37:27 then *you will* **d in** the land forever. 8905
37:29 the righteous will inherit the land and **d** 8905
39:12 For I **d with** you as an alien, a stranger, 6640
43: 3 to the **place where** you **d.** 5438
61: 4 *to* **d** in your tent forever and take refuge in 1591
68:16 where the LORD himself *will* **d** forever? 8905
68:18 that you, O LORD God, *might* **d** there. 8905
69:25 let there be no *one to* **d** in their tents. 3782
69:36 and those who love his name *will* **d** there. 8905
84: 4 Blessed are *those who* **d in** your house; 3782
84:10 a doorkeeper in the house of my God than **d** 1884
85: 9 that his glory *may* **d** in our land. 8905
101: 6 that they *may* **d** with me; 3782
101: 7 No one who practices deceit *will* **d** 3782
120: 5 Woe to me that *I* **d** *in* Meshech, 1591
143: 3 *he* **makes** me **d** in darkness 3782
Pr 8:12 "I, wisdom, **d** *together with* prudence; 8905
SS 8:13 You who **d** in the gardens with friends 3782
Isa 1:21 righteousness *used to* **d** in her— 4328
13:21 there the owls *will* **d,** 8905
26: 5 He humbles *those who* **d** on high, 3782
26:19 *You who* **d in** the dust, 8905
32:16 Justice *will* **d** in the desert 8905
33:14 "Who of us *can* **d** *with* the consuming fire? 1591
33:14 Who of us *can* **d** *with* everlasting burning?" 1591
33:16 this is the *man who will* **d** on the heights, 8905
33:24 sins of those who **d** there will be forgiven. 3782
34:17 and **d** there from generation to generation. 8905
38:11 or be with *those who now* **d in** this world. 3782
43:18 *do* not **d on** the past. 1067
44:13 that it *may* **d in** a shrine. 3782
65:21 They will build houses and **d in** them; 3782
Jer 17: 6 *He will* **d in** the parched places of 8905
47: 2 all *who* **d in** the land will wail 3782
48:28 Abandon your towns and **d** among 8905
49:18 no man *will* **d** in it. 1591
49:33 no man *will* **d** in it." 1591
50:39 and there the owl *will* **d.** 3782
50:40 no man *will* **d** in it. 1591
La 3: 6 *He has* **made** me **d** in darkness 3782
Eze 7: 7 you *who* **d in** the land. 3782
26:20 *I will* **make** you **d** in the earth below, 3782
Hos 14: 7 *Men will* **d** again in his shade. 3782
Joel 3:17 the LORD your God, **d** in Zion, 8905
Zep 2: 6 The land by the sea, *where* the Kerethites **d,** 5661
Zec 8: 3 "I will return to Zion and **d** in Jerusalem. 8905
Jn 5:38 nor *does* his word **d** in you, *2400+3531*
Ac 1:20 let there be no one *to* **d** in it,' and, *2997*
Eph 3:17 Christ *may* **d** in your hearts through faith. *2997*
Col 1:19 *to have* all his fullness **d** in him, *2997*
3:16 *Let* the word of Christ **d in** you richly *1940*
Rev 12:12 you heavens and you who **d** in them! *5012*

DWELLERS (1) [DWELL]

Isa 5: 3 "Now you **d** *in* Jerusalem and men 3782

DWELLING (72) [DWELL]

Ge 27:39 "Your **d** will be away from the earth's 4632
Ex 15:13 guide them to your holy **d.** 5659
15:17 the place, O LORD, you made for your **d,** 3782
Lev 15:31 for defiling my **d place,** 5438
26:11 I will put my **d place** among you, 5438
Nu 24: 5 O Jacob, your **d places,** O Israel! 5438
24:21 "Your **d place** is secure, 4632
Dt 12: 5 to put his Name there for his **d.** 8905
12:11 the LORD your God will choose as a **d** 8905
14:23 at the place he will choose as a **d** 8905
16: 2 at the place the LORD will choose as a **d** 8905
16: 6 except in the place he will choose as a **d** 8905
16:11 at the place he will choose as a **d** 8905
26: 2 the LORD your God will choose as a **d** 8905
26:15 your holy **d place,** 5061
1Sa 2:29 and offering that I prescribed for my **d?** 5061
2:32 and you will see distress in my **d.** 5061
2Sa 7: 6 from place to place with a tent as my **d.** 5438
15:25 and let me see it and his **d place** again. 5659
1Ki 8:30 Hear from heaven, your **d** place, 3782
8:39 then hear from heaven, your **d** place. 3782
8:43 from heaven, your **d** place, and do whatever 3782
8:49 from heaven, your **d** place, hear their prayer 3782
1Ch 9:19 for guarding the entrance to the **d** *of* 4722
16:27 strength and joy in his **d place.** 5226
17: 5 from one **d place** to another. 5438
2Ch 6:21 Hear from heaven, your **d** place; 3782
6:30 then hear from heaven, your **d** place. 3782
6:33 from heaven, your **d** place, and do whatever 3782
6:39 from heaven, your **d** place, hear their prayer 3782
29: 6 from the LORD's **d place** 5438

2Ch 30:27 his holy **d place.** 5061
31: 2 at the gates of the LORD's **d.** 4722
36:15 on his people and on his **d place.** 5061
Ezr 7:15 whose **d** is in Jerusalem, 10445
Ne 1: 9 to the place I have chosen as a **d** 8905
Job 18:15 burning sulfur is scattered over his **d.** 5659
18:21 Surely such is the **d** *of* an evil man; 5438
23: 3 if only I could go to his **d!** 9414
Ps 27: 5 of trouble he will keep me safe in his **d;** 6108
31:20 in your **d** you keep them safe 6109
33:14 from his **d** place he watches all who live 3782
68: 5 a defender of widows, is God in his holy **d.** 5061
74: 7 they defiled the **d place** *of* your Name. 5438
76: 2 His tent is in Salem, his **d place** in Zion. 5104
84: 1 How lovely is your **d place,** 5438
90: 1 you have been our **d place** 5061
91: 9 If you make the Most High your **d**— 5061
132: 5 a **d** for the Mighty One of Jacob." 5438
132: 7 "Let us go to his **d place;** 5438
132:13 he has desired it for his **d:** 4632
Pr 24:15 do not raid his **d place;** 8070
Isa 18: 4 and will look on from my **d place,** 4806
26:21 the LORD is coming out of his **d** to punish 5226
32:18 My people will live in peaceful **d places,** 5659
Jer 7:12 to the place in Shiloh where *I* first **made a d** 8905
25:30 from his holy **d** and roar mightily 5061
31:23 'The LORD bless you, O righteous **d,** 5659
La 2: 6 He has laid waste his **d** like a garden; 8494
Eze 3:12 of the LORD be praised in his **d place!**— 5226
37:27 My **d place** will be with them; 5438
Mic 1: 3 The LORD is coming from his **d place;** 5226
Hab 1: 6 across the whole earth to seize **d places** 5438
Zep 3: 7 Then her **d** would not be cut off, 5061
Zec 2:13 he has roused himself from his holy **d."** 5061
Jn 1:14 The Word became flesh and **made his d** *5012*
Ac 7:46 and asked that he might provide a **d place** *5013*
2Co 5: 2 longing to be clothed with our heavenly **d,** *3863*
5: 4 but to be clothed with our heavenly **d,** *NIG*
Eph 2:22 a **d** in which God lives by his Spirit. *2999*
Rev 13: 6 and to slander his name and his **d place** *5008*
21: 3 "Now the **d** of God is with men, *5008*

DWELLINGS (13) [DWELL]

Ex 35: 3 a fire in any of your **d** on the Sabbath day." 4632
1Ch 4:41 They attacked the Hamites in their **d** and 185
5:10 they occupied the **d** *of* the Hagrites 185
Job 38:20 Do you know the paths to their **d?** 1074
Ps 49:11 their **d** for endless generations, 5438
87: 2 of Zion more than all the **d** *of* Jacob. 5438
Isa 58:12 Restorer of Streets with **D.** 3782
Jer 30:18 and have compassion on his **d;** 5438
51:30 Her **d** are set on fire; 5438
La 2: 2 the Lord has swallowed up all the **d** 5661
Hab 3: 7 the **d** *of* Midian in anguish. 3749
Zec 12: 7 "The LORD will save the **d** *of* Judah first, 185
Lk 16: 9 you will be welcomed into eternal **d.** *5008*

DWELLS (12) [DWELL]

Job 28:23 the way to it and he alone knows **where** it **d,** 5226
39:28 *He* **d** *on* a cliff and stays there at night; 8905
Ps 26: 8 O LORD, the place **where** your glory **d.** 5438
46: 4 **where** the Most High **d.** 5438
91: 1 *He who* **d** in the shelter of the Most High 3782
135:21 to *him who* **d** in Jerusalem. 8905
Isa 8:18 who **d** on Mount Zion. 8905
33: 5 The LORD is exalted, for *he* **d** on high; 8905
La 1: 3 She **d** among the nations; 3782
Da 2:22 and light **d** with him. 10742
Joel 3:21 The LORD **d** in Zion! 8905
Mt 23:21 by it and by the one who **d in** it. *2997*

DWELT (6) [DWELL]

Dt 33:16 the favor of *him who* **d in** the burning bush. 8905
2Sa 7: 6 not **d** in a house from the day I brought 3782
1Ch 17: 5 *I have* not **d** in a house from 3782
Job 29:25 *I* **d** as a king among his troops; 8905
Ps 74: 2 Mount Zion, where *you* **d.** 8905
94:17 I *would* soon *have* **d in** the silence of death. 8905

DWINDLE (1) [DWINDLES]

Isa 19: 6 the streams of Egypt *will* **d** and dry up. 1937

DWINDLES (1) [DWINDLE]

Pr 13:11 Dishonest money **d away,** 5070

DYED (6)

Ex 25: 5 ram skins **d red** and hides of sea cows; 131
26:14 for the tent a covering of ram skins **d red,** 131
35: 7 ram skins **d red** and hides of sea cows; 131
35:23 ram skins **d red** or hides of sea cows 131
36:19 for the tent a covering of ram skins **d red,** 131
39:34 of ram skins **d red,** the covering of hides 131

DYING (15) [DIE]

Ge 35:18 for *she was* **d**—she named her son Ben-Oni. 4637
1Sa 4:20 As she *was* **d,** the women attending her 4637
2Ch 24:22 who said as he lay **d,** 4638
Job 11:20 their hope will become a **d** gasp." 5883
24:12 The groans of the **d** rise from the city, 4637
29:13 The *man who was* **d** blessed me; 6
Isa 22:14 "Till *your* **d** day this sin will not be atoned 4637
Hos 4: 3 of the air and the fish of the sea *are* **d.** 665
Zec 11: 9 Let the **d** die, and the perishing perish. 4637
Mk 5:23 "My little daughter is **d.** *2275*
Lk 8:42 a girl of about twelve, *was* **d.** *633*
Jn 11:37 the blind man have kept this man from **d?"** *633*
Ro 7: 6 But now, *by* **d** to what once bound us, *633*
2Co 6: 9 **d,** and yet we live on; *633*
Heb 11:21 By faith Jacob, *when he was* **d,** *633*

DYNASTY (3)

1Sa 25:28 the LORD will certainly make a lasting **d** 1074
1Ki 2:24 of my father David and has founded a **d** 1074
11:38 a **d** as enduring as the one I built for David 1074

DYSENTERY (1)

Ac 28: 8 suffering from fever and **d.** *1548*

E

EACH (628)

Ge 1:24 and wild animals, **e** according to its kind." NIH
2:19 whatever the man called **e** living creature, 2257
9: 5 And from **e** man, too, 278+408+2257
10: 5 **e** with its own language.) 408
11: 3 They said to **e** other, "Come, 408
11: 7 so they will not understand **e** other." 408
15: 9 a goat and a ram, **e** three years old, NIH
15:10 and arranged the halves opposite **e** other; 408
25:22 The babies **jostled e other** within her, 8368
26:31 the men swore an oath to **e** other. 408
31:49 and me when we are away from **e** other. 408
32:16 care of his servants, **e herd** by itself, 6373+6373
37:19 they said to **e** other. 408
40: 5 **e** of the two men— 408
40: 5 and **e** dream had a meaning of its own. 408
41:11 **E of us** had a dream the same night, 638+2085+2256
41:11 and **e** dream had a meaning of its own. 408
41:12 giving *e* **man** the interpretation AIT
41:48 In **e** city he put the food grown in 2021
42: 1 "Why *do you just keep* **looking at e other?"** 8011
42:25 to put **e** man's silver back in his sack, 408
42:28 and they turned to **e** other trembling 408
42:35 in **e** man's sack was his pouch of silver! 408
43:21 for the night we opened our sacks and **e** 408
43:33 and they looked at **e** other in astonishment. 408
44: 1 put *e* **man's** silver in the mouth of his sack. AIT
44:11 **E** of them quickly lowered his sack to 408
45:22 To **e** *of* them he gave new clothing, 3972
49:28 giving **e** the blessing appropriate to him. 408
Ex 1: 1 **e** with his family: 408
5:13 the work required of you **for e day,** 928+1821+3427+3427
5:19 number of bricks required of you **for e day."** 928+1821+3427+3427
7:12 **E** *one* threw down his staff and it became 408
12: 3 that on the tenth day of this month *e* **man** is AIT
12: 3 one for **e** household. 2021
12: 4 in accordance with what **e** *person* will eat. 408
13:15 and redeem **e** *of* my firstborn sons.' 3972
16: 4 to go out **e** day and gather enough for NIH
16:15 the Israelites saw it, they said to **e** other, 408
16:16 '**E** *one* is to gather as much as he needs. 408
16:16 for **e** person you have in your tent.' " 1653+5031
16:18 **E** *one* gathered as much as he needed. 408
16:21 **E morning** everyone gathered as much as he needed, 928+928+1332+1332+2021+2021
16:22 two omers for **e** *person*— 285
18: 7 They greeted **e** other and then went into 408
25: 2 from **e** man whose heart prompts him 3972
25:20 The cherubim are to face **e** other, 408
26: 5 with the loops opposite **e** other. 851
26:16 **E** frame is to be ten cubits long and a cubit 285
26:17 with two projections set parallel to **e** other. 851
26:19 two bases for **e** frame, 285
26:19 one under **e** projection. 9109
26:21 and forty silver bases—two under **e** frame. 285
26:25 two under **e** frame. 285
27: 2 Make a horn at **e** of the four corners, NIH
27: 4 a bronze ring at **e** of the four corners of NIH
28:21 one for **e** of the names of the sons of Israel, NIH
28:21 **e** engraved like a seal with the name of one 408
29:36 Sacrifice a bull **e** day as a sin offering 4200
29:38 to offer on the altar regularly **e** day: 4200
30:12 **e** *one* must pay the LORD a ransom 408
30:13 **E** one who crosses over 3972
32:27 '**E** *man* strap a sword to his side. 408
32:27 **e** killing his brother and friend 408
33:10 **e** at the entrance to his tent. 408
34:24 up three times **e** year to appear before 2021
36:12 with the loops opposite **e** other. 285
36:21 **E** frame was ten cubits long and a cubit and 285
36:22 with two projections set parallel to **e** other. 285
36:24 two bases for **e** frame, 285
36:24 one under **e** projection. 9109
36:26 and forty silver bases—two under **e** frame. 285
36:30 two under **e** frame. 285
Ex 37: 9 The cherubim faced **e** other, 408
38: 2 They made a horn at **e** of the four corners, NIH
38:27 one talent for **e** base. 2021
39:14 one for **e** of the names of the sons of Israel, NIH
39:14 **e** engraved like a seal with the name of one 408
Lev 7:14 He is to bring one of **e** *kind* as an offering, 3972
14:10 **e** without defect, along with three-tenths of NIH
19: 3 " '**E** of you must respect his mother 408
23:18 **e** a year old and without defect, NIH
23:19 **e** a year old, for a fellowship offering. NIH
23:37 offerings required for **e day.** 928+3427+3427
23:41 to the LORD for seven days **e** year. 928
24: 5 using two-tenths of an ephah for **e** loaf. 285
24: 6 Set them in two rows, six in **e** row, 2021
24: 7 Along **e** row put some pure incense as 2021
25:10 **e** *one* of you is to return 408
25:10 to return to his family property and **e** 408
25:14 do not take advantage of **e** other. 408
25:17 Do not take advantage of **e** other, 408
Nu 1: 4 One man from **e** tribe, 2021
1: 4 **e** the head of his family, is to help you. 408
1:44 **e** one representing his family. 408+408
1:52 **e man** in his own camp AIT
2: 2 *e* **man** under his standard with the banners AIT
2:17 **e** in his own place under his standard. 408
2:34 **e** with his clan and family. 408
3:47 collect five shekels for **e one,** 1653
4:19 and assign to **e** man his work and what he is 408
4:32 Assign **to e man** the specific things he 928+9005
4:49 **e** was assigned his work and told what 408+408
5:10 *E* **man's** sacred gifts are his own, AIT
7: 3 ox from **e** leader and a cart from every two. 285
7: 5 to the Levites as *e* **man's** work requires." AIT
7:11 **"E day** one leader is to bring his offering 2021+2021+3427+3427+4200+4200
7:13 **e** filled with fine flour mixed with oil as 9109
7:19 **e** filled with fine flour mixed with oil as 9109
7:25 **e** filled with fine flour mixed with oil as 9109
7:31 **e** filled with fine flour mixed with oil as 9109
7:37 **e** filled with fine flour mixed with oil as 9109
7:43 **e** filled with fine flour mixed with oil as 9109
7:49 **e** filled with fine flour mixed with oil as 9109
7:55 **e** filled with fine flour mixed with oil as 9109
7:61 **e** filled with fine flour mixed with oil as 9109
7:67 **e** filled with fine flour mixed with oil as 9109
7:73 **e** filled with fine flour mixed with oil as 9109
7:79 **e** filled with fine flour mixed with oil as 9109
7:85 **E** silver plate weighed a hundred 285
7:85 and **e** sprinkling bowl seventy shekels. 285
7:86 with incense weighed ten shekels **e,** 2021+4090S
11:10 **e** at the entrance to his tent. 408
13: 2 From **e** ancestral tribe send one 3972
14: 4 And they said to **e** other, 408
14:34 for **e** *of* the forty days you explored 3427S
15: 5 With **e** lamb for the burnt offering or 285
15:11 **E** bull or ram, each lamb or young goat, 285
15:11 Each bull or ram, **e** lamb or young goat, 2021
15:12 Do this for **e one,** 285
15:38 with a blue cord on **e** tassel. 2021
16:17 *E* **man** is to take his censer and put incense AIT
16:18 So *e* **man** took his censer, AIT
17: 2 from the leader of **e** of their ancestral tribes. 3972
17: 2 Write the name of *e* **man** on his staff. AIT
17: 3 one staff for the head of **e** ancestral tribe. 4392S
17: 6 for the leader of **e** of their ancestral tribes, NIH
17: 9 and *e* **man** took his own staff. AIT
23: 2 of them offered a bull and a ram on **e** altar. 2021
23: 4 on **e** altar I have offered a bull and a ram." 2021
23:14 and offered a bull and a ram on **e** altar. 2021
23:30 and offered a bull and a ram on **e** altar. 2021
25: 5 **"E** of you must put to death those 408
26:54 **e** is to receive its inheritance according to 408
26:55 What **e** group inherits will be according to NIH
26:56 **E** inheritance is to be distributed by lot 2257
28: 3 as a regular burnt offering **e** day. 2021
28: 7 of a hin of fermented drink with **e** lamb. 285
28:12 With **e** bull there is to be a grain offering 285
28:13 and with **e** lamb, 285
28:14 With **e** bull there is to be a drink offering 2021
28:14 and with **e** lamb, a quarter of a hin. 2021
28:14 to be made at **e** new moon during the year. NIH
28:20 With **e** bull prepare a grain offering 2021
28:21 and with **e** of the seven lambs, one-tenth. 285
28:28 With **e** bull there is to be a grain offering 285
28:29 and with **e** *of* the seven lambs, one-tenth. 285
29: 4 and with **e** of the seven lambs, one-tenth. 285
29:10 and with **e** of the seven lambs, one-tenth. 285
29:14 With **e** of the thirteen bulls prepare 285
29:14 with **e** of the two rams, two-tenths; 285
29:15 and with **e** of the fourteen lambs, one-tenth. 285
31: 4 Send into battle a thousand men from **e** *of* 3972
31: 5 a thousand from **e** tribe, 2021
31: 6 a thousand from **e** tribe, 2021
31:50 an offering to the LORD the gold articles **e** 408
31:53 **E** soldier had taken plunder for himself. 408
34:18 And appoint one leader from **e** tribe 285
35: 8 in proportion to the inheritance of **e** tribe: 408
36: 9 for **e** Israelite tribe is to keep 408
Dt 1:13 understanding and respected men from **e** NIH
1:23 one man from **e** tribe. 2021
3:20 **e** of you may go back to 408
14:22 of all that your fields produce **e year.** 9102+9102
15:20 **E year** you and your family are to eat them 928+9102+9102
16:17 **E** of you must bring a gift in proportion to 408
16:18 Appoint judges and officials for **e** NIH
24:15 Pay him his wages **e** day before sunset, 928

Dt 24:16 e is to die for his own sin. 408
Jos 3:12 one from e tribe. 2021
4: 2 one from e tribe, NIH
4: 4 one from e tribe, NIH
4: 5 E of you is to take up a stone 408
18: 4 Appoint three men from e tribe. 2021
18: 4 according to the inheritance of e. 4392
21:42 E of these **towns** had pasturelands surrounding it; 6551+6551
22:14 one for e *of* the tribes of Israel, 3972
22:14 e the head of a family division among 408
24:28 e to his own inheritance. 408
Jdg 1:18 e city with its territory. NIH
2: 6 e to his own inheritance. 408
5:30 a girl or two for e man, 8031
6:29 They asked e other, "Who did this?" 408
7: 7 e to his own place." 408
7:21 *e* **man** held his position around the camp, AIT
7:22 throughout the camp to turn on e other 2084
8:18 "*e* **one** with the bearing of a prince." AIT
8:24 that e of you give me an earring 408
8:25 *e* **man** threw a ring from his plunder onto it. AIT
10:18 of the people of Gilead said to e other, 408
11:40 **e year** the young women 2025+3427+3427+4946
16: 5 E *one* of us will give you eleven hundred shekels of silver." 408
20: 6 into pieces and sent one piece to e region 3972
20:16 e *of* whom could sling a stone at a hair and 3972
21:21 and e of you seize a wife from the girls 408
21:23 e man caught one and carried her off 4200+5031S
21:24 e to his own inheritance. 408
Ru 1: 8 "Go back, e of you, to your mother's home. 851
1: 9 the LORD grant that e of you will find rest 851
1Sa 2:19 **E year** his mother made him a little robe 2025+3427+3427+4946
6:17 **one** *e* for Ashdod, Gaza, Ashkelon, AIT
10:11 they asked e other, 408
10:25 e to his own home. 408
14: 4 **On e side** *of* the pass 2021+2021+2296+2296 +4946+4946+4946+4946+6298+6298
14:20 striking e other with their swords. 408
14:34 'E of you bring me your cattle and sheep, 408
17:10 Give me a man and let us fight **e other.**" 3480
17:21 up their lines **facing e other.** 5120+7925
20:41 they kissed e other and wept together— 408
20:42 we have sworn friendship with **e other** 5646+9109
27: 3 *E* **man** had his family with him, AIT
30: 6 e one was bitter in spirit because of his sons 3972
30:22 *e* **man** may take his wife and children AIT
2Sa 2: 3 e with his family, 408
2:16 Then *e* **man** grabbed his opponent by AIT
6:19 to **e** person in the whole crowd of Israelites, 3972
10: 4 shaved off half of *e* **man's** beard, AIT
14: 6 They got into a fight with **e other** in 2157+9109S
18: 5 concerning Absalom to e *of* 3972
19: 9 the people *were* all **arguing with e other,** 1906
20:22 e returning to his home. 408
21:20 with six fingers on e hand and six toes 2257
21:20 on each hand and six toes on e foot— 2257
1Ki 4: 7 E one had to provide supplies 2021
4:25 *e* **man** under his own vine and fig tree. AIT
4:27 The district officers, e *in* his month, 408
6:10 The height of e was five cubits, 2257
6:23 e ten cubits high. 2257
6:26 The height of e cherub was ten cubits. 285
6:27 and their wings touched e other in 4053S
6:34 e having two leaves that turned in sockets 285
7: 4 in sets of three, **facing e other.** 448+4691+4691
7: 5 in sets of three, **facing e other.** 448+4691+4691
7:15 e eighteen cubits high and twelve cubits 285
7:16 e capital was five cubits high. 285
7:17 seven for e capital. 285
7:18 in two rows encircling e network 285
7:18 He did the same for e capital. 9108
7:27 e was four cubits long, 285
7:30 E stand had four bronze wheels 285
7:30 and e had a basin resting on four supports, 2157
7:30 cast with wreaths on e side. 408
7:32 The diameter of e wheel was a cubit and 285
7:34 E stand had four handles, 285
7:34 one on e corner, projecting from the stand. 752S
7:38 e holding forty baths 285
7:38 one basin to go on e of the ten stands. 285
7:42 of pomegranates for e network, decorating 285
8:38 e *one* aware of the afflictions 408
8:39 deal with e man according to all he does, 2021
8:59 according to **e day's** need, 3427+3427
10:16 of gold went into e shield. 285
10:17 with three minas of gold in e shield. 285
10:19 with a lion standing beside e of them. 9109
10:20 one at either end of e step. NIH
18: 4 fifty in e, and had supplied them with food NIH
18:13 in two caves, fifty in e, and supplied them NIH
18:31 **one for e** *of* the tribes descended 3869+5031
20:10 in Samaria to give e *of* my men a handful." 3972
20:20 and e *one* struck down his opponent. 408
20:29 seven days they camped opposite **e other,** 465
22:17 Let e *one* go home in peace.'" 408
2Ki 3:13 "What do we have to do with **e other?** 3870S
3:23 and slaughtered e other. 408
3:25 and *e* **man** threw a stone AIT
4: 4 Pour oil into all the jars, and as e is filled, 2021
6: 2 where e of us can get a pole; 408
7: 3 They said to e other, 408
7: 9 they said to e other, "We're not doing right. 408
9:21 e in his own chariot, to meet Jehu. 408
11: 8 *e* **man** with his weapon in his hand. AIT
2Ki 11: 9 E *one* took his men— 408
11:11 The guards, e with his weapon in his hand, 408
14: 6 e is to die for his own sins." 408
14:11 Amaziah king of Judah **faced e other** 7156+8011
17:29 **e national group** made its own gods 1580+1580
25:17 E pillar was twenty-seven feet high. 285
1Ch 9:27 charge of the key for opening it **e morning.** 1332+1332+2021+2021+4200+4200
13: 1 David conferred with e *of* his officers, 3972
16: 3 of raisins to e Israelite man and woman. 3972
16:37 according to **e day's** requirements. 928+2257+3427+3427
16:43 all the people left, e for his own home, 408
20: 6 with six fingers on e hand and six toes NIH
20: 6 on each hand and six toes on e foot— NIH
26:13 Lots were cast for **e gate,** 2256+9133+9133
27: 1 E division consisted of 24,000 men. 285
28:15 the weight for **e lampstand** and its lamps; 2256+4963+4963
28:15 the weight of silver for e silver **lampstand** 4963+4963
28:15 according to the use of **e lampstand;** 2256+4963+4963
28:16 of gold for **e table** for consecrated bread; 2256+8947+8947
28:17 weight of gold for **e** gold **dish;** 2256+4094+4094
28:17 weight of silver for e silver **dish** 2256+4094+4094
2Ch 3:15 e with a capital on top measuring five cubits 2257
4:13 of pomegranates for e network, decorating 285
6:29 e *one* aware of his afflictions and pains, 408
6:30 deal with e man according to all he does, 2021
8:14 according to **e day's** requirement 928+3427+3427
9:15 of hammered gold went into e shield. 285
9:16 of gold in e shield. 285
9:18 with a lion standing beside e of them. 9109
9:19 one at either end of e step. NIH
18:16 Let e *one* go home in peace.'" 408
19: 5 in e *of* the fortified cities of Judah. 3972
23: 7 *e* **man** with his weapons in his hand. AIT
23: 8 E *one* took his men— 408
23:10 e with his weapon in his hand, 408
25: 4 e is to die for his own sins." 408
25:21 Amaziah king of Judah **faced e other** 7156+8011
31: 2 e of them according to their duties 408
35: 5 with a group of Levites for *e* **subdivision** *of* AIT
35:15 The gatekeepers at **e gate** 2256+9133+9133
Ezr 2: 1 e to his own town, 408
3: 4 offerings prescribed for **e day.** 928+3427+3427
6:17 one for e of the tribes of Israel. 10433
10:14 the elders and judges of **e town,** 2256+6551+6551
10:16 one from e family division, 4392
10:19 for their guilt they e presented a ram from NIH
Ne 3:28 e in front of his own house. 408
4:15 e to his own work. 408
4:18 and e of the builders wore his sword 408
4:19 and we are widely separated from e other 408
4:23 e had his weapon, 408
5:18 E day one ox, 285
6: 4 and e time I gave them the same answer. NIH
7: 6 e to his own town, 408
10:32 a shekel e year for the service of the house 2021
10:34 to determine when e of our families is NIH
10:34 at set times **e year** a contribution 928+9102+9102
10:35 of the LORD **e year** the firstfruits 928+9102+9102
11: 3 e on his own property in the various towns, 408
11:20 e on his ancestral property. 408
13:30 and assigned them duties, e to his own task. 408
Est 1: 7 *e* **one** different from the other, AIT
1: 8 the king's command e guest was allowed NIH
1: 8 to serve *e* **man** what he wished. AIT
1:22 to **e province** in its own script 2256+4519+4519
1:22 to **e people** in its own language, 2256+6639+6639
1:22 in e people's tongue that every man should 2257
3:12 the script of **e province** and 2256+4519+4519
3:12 of **e people** all Haman's orders 2256+6639+6639
8: 9 in the script of **e province** 2256+4519+4519
8: 9 and the language of **e people** 2256+6639+6639
9:19 a day for giving presents to e other. 408
Job 1: 5 a burnt offering for e *of* them, 3972
9:32 that we might confront **e other** in court. 3481
41:16 e is so close to the next 285
42:11 and e *one* gave him a piece of silver and 408
Ps 39: 5 E man's life is but a breath. 3972
39:11 e man is but a breath. 3972
62:12 Surely you will reward *e* **person** according AIT
64: 5 They encourage **e other** in evil plans, 4564S
84: 7 till *e* **appears** before God in Zion. AIT
85:10 righteousness and peace **kiss** *e other.* AIT
147: 4 the number of the stars and calls them e 3972
Pr 14:10 *E* **heart** knows its own bitterness, AIT
24:12 Will he not repay *e* **person** according AIT
SS 3: 8 e with his sword at his side, 408
4: 2 E has its twin; not one of them is alone. 3972
6: 6 E has its twin, not one of them is alone. 3972
8:11 E was to bring for its fruit 408
Isa 3: 5 People *will* **oppress e other—** 5601
6: 2 Above him were seraphs, e with six wings: 285
9:20 E will feed on the flesh 408
13: 8 They will look aghast at e other, 408
13:14 e will return to his own people, 408
13:14 e will flee to his native land. 408
14:18 e in his own tomb. 408
32: 2 *E* **man** will be like a shelter from the wind AIT
34:14 and wild goats will bleat to **e other;** 8276S
34:15 also the falcons will gather, e with its mate. 851
40:26 and calls them e by name. 3972
41: 6 e helps the other and says to his brother, 408
Isa 47:15 E of them goes on in his error; 408
50: 8 Let us face **e other!** 3480
53: 6 e of us has turned to his own way; 408
56:11 e seeks his own gain. 408
56:12 "Come," e one cries, "let me get wine! NIH
58: 4 and *in* **striking** *e other* with wicked fists. AIT
Jer 5: 8 e neighing for another man's wife. 408
6: 3 e tending his own portion." 408
7: 5 and deal with e other justly, 408
8: 6 E pursues his own course like 3972
9: 8 With his mouth *e* **speaks** cordially AIT
12:15 and will bring e of them back 408
16:12 how e of you is following the stubbornness 408
18:11 So turn from your evil ways, e *one* of you, 408
18:12 e of us will follow the stubbornness 408
22: 7 *e* **man** with his weapons, AIT
23:35 This is what e of you keeps on saying 408
25: 5 They said, "Turn now, e of you, 408
26: 3 Perhaps they will listen and e will turn 408
34:14 'Every seventh year e of you must free any 408
34:15 E of you proclaimed freedom 408
34:16 e of you has taken back the male 408
35:15 "E of you must turn 408
36: 3 e of them will turn from his wicked way; 408
36: 7 and e will turn from his wicked ways, 408
36:16 they looked at e other in fear and said 408
37:21 the street of the bakers **e day** 2021+3427+4200
46:16 they will fall over e other. 408
51: 9 let us leave her and e go to his own land, 408
52:21 E of the pillars was eighteen cubits high 285
52:21 e was four fingers thick, and hollow. 2257
Eze 1: 6 e of them had four faces and four wings. 285
1: 9 E *one* went straight ahead; 408
1:10 E *of* the four had the face of a man, 4392
1:10 on the right side e had the face of a lion, 5527
1:10 e also had the face of an eagle. 5527
1:11 e had two wings, 408
1:12 E *one* went straight ahead. 408
1:15 a wheel on the ground beside e creature 2021
1:16 E appeared to be made like 2157
1:23 and e had two wings covering its body. 408
3:13 the living creatures brushing against e other 851
4: 6 a day for e year. 2021
4:10 of food to eat e day and eat it at set times. 2021
4:17 They will be appalled at the sight of e other 408
7:16 e because of his sins. 408
8:11 E had a censer in his hand, 408
8:12 e at the shrine of his own idol? 408
9: 1 e with a weapon in his hand." 408
9: 2 e with a deadly weapon in his hand. 408
10: 9 one beside e of the cherubim; 285
10:10 *e* **was** like a wheel intersecting a wheel. AIT
10:14 E of the cherubim had four faces: 285
10:21 E had four faces and four wings, 285
10:22 E *one* went straight ahead. 408
18:30 e *one* according to his ways, 408
20: 7 And I said to them, "E of you, 408
22: 6 how e of the princes of Israel who are 408
32:10 On the day of your downfall e 408
33:20 But I will judge e of you according 408
33:26 and e of you defiles his neighbor's wife. 408
33:30 saying to e other, 2522
40: 5 e of which was a cubit and a handbreadth. NIH
40:10 the east gate were three alcoves **on e side;** 2256+4946+4946+7024+7024
40:10 of the projecting walls **on e side** had 2256+4946+4946+7024+7024
40:12 of e alcove was a wall one cubit high, 2021
40:21 Its alcoves—three **on e side—** 2256+4946+4946+7024+7024
40:26 the faces of the projecting walls **on e side.** 2256+4946+4946+7024+7024
40:38 with a doorway was by the portico in e of NIH
40:39 of the gateway were two tables **on e side,** 2256+4946+4946+7024+7024
40:42 e a cubit and a half long, NIH
40:43 e a handbreadth long, NIH
40:49 and there were pillars **on e side** of the jambs. 2256+4946+4946+7024+7024
41: 1 width of the jambs was six cubits **on e side.** 2256+4946+4946+7024+7024
41: 2 and the projecting walls **on e side** 2256+4946+4946+7024+7024
41: 3 e was two cubits wide. NIH
41: 3 on e side of it were seven cubits wide. NIH
41: 5 it was six cubits thick, and e side room 2021
41: 6 one above another, thirty on *e* **level.** AIT
41: 7 wider **at e successive level.** 2025+2025+4200+4200+5087+5087
41:15 including its galleries **on e side;** 2256+4946+4946+7024+7024
41:18 E cherub had two faces: 2021
41:24 E door had two leaves— 9109S
41:24 two hinged leaves for e door. 285
41:26 with palm trees carved **on e side.** 2256+4946+4946+7024+7024
45: 7 the land **bordering e side** of the area formed 2256+2296+2296+4946+4946S
45:13 an ephah from e homer of wheat and a sixth NIH
45:13 a sixth of an ephah from e homer of barley. NIH
45:14 a tenth of a bath from e cor (which consists 2021
45:24 as a grain offering an ephah for e bull and 2021
45:24 for each bull and an ephah for e ram, 2021
45:24 along with a hin of oil for e ephah. 2021
46: 5 along with a hin of oil for e ephah. 2021
46: 7 along with a hin of oil with e ephah. 2021
46: 9 *e is to* **go out** AIT

Eze 46:11 along with a hin of oil for e ephah. 2021
46:21 and I saw **in e corner** another court. 928+928+5243+5243
46:22 *e of the* **courts** in the four corners was AIT
46:23 *e of the* four **courts** AIT
47: 7 I saw a great number of trees **on e side** *of* 2256+2296+2296+4946+4946S
48:20 25,000 cubits **on e side.** 928
Da 7: 3 e different from the others, 10154
11:27 at the same table and **lie** *to e other,* AIT
Joel 2: 8 They do not jostle e other; 408
2: 8 e marches straight ahead. 1505S
Am 4: 3 You will e go straight out through breaks in 851
Jnh 1: 5 All the sailors were afraid and e cried out 408
1: 7 Then the sailors said to e other, "Come, 408
Mic 7: 2 e hunts his brother with a net. 408
Hag 1: 9 while e of you is busy with his own house. 408
2:22 e by the sword of his brother. 408
Zec 3:10 that day e of you will invite his neighbor 408
7:10 In your hearts do not think evil of e other.' 408
8: 4 e with cane in hand because of his age. 408
8:16 Speak the truth to e other, 408
12:12 The land will mourn, **e clan** by itself, 5476+5476
14:13 *E* **man** will seize the hand of another, AIT
14:13 and they will attack e other. 2084
Mal 3:16 the LORD talked with e other, 408
Mt 6:34 **E** day has enough trouble of its own. *3836*
16:27 and then he will reward e *person* according *1667*
18:35 how my heavenly Father will treat e of you *1667*
20: 9 the eleventh hour came and e received *324*
20:10 **e one** of them also received a denarius. *324+3836*
21:38 the tenants saw the son, they said to **e other,** *1571*
24:10 the faith and will betray and hate **e other,** *253*
25:15 e according to his ability. *1667*
Mk 1:27 so amazed that they asked **e other,** *1571*
4:41 They were terrified and asked **e other,** *253*
9:50 and be at peace with **e other."** *253*
10:26 and said to **e other,** *1571*
13:34 e with his assigned task, *1667*
15:24 they cast lots to see what **e** would get. *5515*
16: 3 and they asked **e other,** *1571*
Lk 4:36 the people were amazed and said to **e other,** *253*
4:40 and laying his hands on e one, *1667*
6:44 **E** tree is recognized by its own fruit. *1667*
7:32 the marketplace and calling out *to* **e other:** *253*
9:14 down in groups of about fifty **e."** *324*
11: 3 Give us e day our daily bread. *2848*
12:52 in one family divided against e other, *NIG*
13:15 Doesn't e of you on *1667*
16: 5 he called in e one of his master's debtors. *1667*
21:37 **E day** Jesus was teaching at the temple, *2465+3836*
21:37 and **e evening** he went out to spend *3816+3836*
24:14 They were talking with **e other** *253*
24:15 and discussed these things with e other, *NIG*
24:32 They asked **e other,** *253*
Jn 2: 6 **e** holding from twenty to thirty gallons. *NIG*
4:33 Then his disciples said to **e other,** *253*
6: 7 not buy enough bread for **e one** to have *1667*
7:53 Then **e** went to his own home. *1667*
15:12 Love **e other** as I have loved you. *253*
15:17 This is my command: Love **e other.** *253*
16:32 **e** to his own home. *1667*
19:18 **one on e side** and Jesus in the middle. *1949+1949+2779*
19:23 one *for* e of them, *1667*
Ac 2: 3 tongues of fire that separated and came to rest on e of them. *1651+1667*
2: 6 because e one heard them speaking *1667*
2: 8 Then how is it that e of us hears them *1667*
3:26 to you to bless you by turning **e** of you *1667*
7:26 why do you want to hurt **e other?'** *253*
11:29 The disciples, e according to his ability, *1667*
12: 4 by four squads of four soldiers **e.** *NIG*
14:23 for them **in e** church and, *2848*
17:27 though he is not far from e one of us. *1667*
20:31 three years I never stopped warning e *1651+1667*
21: 6 After saying good-by to **e other,** *253*
21:26 offering would be made for e of them. *1651+1667*
28: 4 they said to **e other,** *253*
Ro 1:12 be mutually encouraged by **e other's** faith. *253*
2: 6 *to* **e** *person* according to what he has done." *1667*
12: 4 Just as e of us has one body *NIG*
12: 5 and **e** member belongs to all the others. *1651*
14: 5 **E** *one* should be fully convinced *1667*
14:12 **e** of us will give an account of himself *1667*
15: 2 **E** of us should please his neighbor *1667*
1Co 3: 5 as the Lord has assigned *to* **e** his task. *1667*
3: 8 and **e** will be rewarded according *1667*
3:10 But **e** *one* should be careful how he builds. *1667*
3:13 fire will test the quality *of* **e** *man's* work. *1667*
4: 5 that time **e** will receive his praise from God. *1667*
7: 2 **e** *man* should have his own wife, *1667*
7: 2 and **e** *woman* her own husband. *1667*
7: 5 Do not deprive **e other** except *253*
7: 7 But **e** *man* has his own gift from God; *1667*
7:17 **e** *one* should retain the place in life that *1667*
7:20 **E** *one* should remain in the situation *1667*
7:24 Brothers, **e** *man,* as responsible to God, *1667*
11:21 **e** of you goes ahead without waiting *1667*
11:33 wait for **e other.** *253*
12: 7 Now *to* **e** *one* the manifestation of *1667*
12:11 and he gives them *to* **e** *one,* *1667*
12:25 parts should have equal concern for **e other.** *253*
12:27 and **e one** of you is a part of it. *3517S*
15:23 But **e** in his own turn: *1667*
15:38 *to* **e** *kind* of seed he gives its own body. *1667*
1Co 16: 2 **e** *one* of you should set aside a sum *1667*
2Co 5:10 that **e** *one* may receive what is due him for *1667*
9: 7 **E** man should give what he has decided *1667*
Gal 5:15 on biting and devouring **e other,** *253*
5:15 or you will be destroyed by **e other.** *253*
5:17 They are in conflict *with* **e other,** *253*
5:26 provoking and envying **e other.** *253*
6: 2 Carry **e other's** burdens, *253*
6: 4 **E** *one* should test his own actions. *1667*
6: 5 for **e** *one* should carry his own load. *1667*
Eph 4: 7 But *to* **e** one of us grace has been given *1667*
4:16 as **e** part does its work. *1651+1667*
4:25 Therefore **e of** you must put off falsehood *1667*
4:32 to one another, forgiving **e other,** just as *4932*
5:33 **e** one of you also must love his wife *1667*
Php 2: 4 **E** of you should look not only to your own *1667*
4: 2 with Syntyche to agree with **e** other in *NIG*
Col 3: 9 Do not lie to **e other,** *253*
3:13 Bear with **e other** and forgive *253*
1Th 2:11 you know that we dealt with **e** of you *1651+1667*
3:12 for **e other** and for everyone else, *253*
4: 4 that **e** of you should learn *1667*
4: 9 by God to love **e other.** *253*
4:18 encourage **e other** with these words. *253*
5:11 encourage one another and build **e other** up, *1651+1651+3836*
5:13 Live in peace with **e other.** *4932*
5:15 to be kind to **e other** and to everyone else. *253*
2Th 1: 3 of you has for **e other** is increasing. *253*
Heb 6:11 We want **e** of you to show this same *1667*
11:21 blessed **e** of Joseph's sons, *1667*
13: 1 Keep on **loving e other as brothers.** *5789*
Jas 1:14 but **e** *one* is tempted when, *1667*
5: 9 Don't grumble against **e other,** brothers, *253*
5:16 Therefore confess your sins *to* **e other** *253*
5:16 for **e other** so that you may be healed. *253*
1Pe 1:17 Father who judges **e** *man's* work impartially *1667*
4: 8 Above all, love **e other** deeply, *4932*
4:10 **E** *one* should use whatever gift he has received *1667*
Rev 2:23 and I will repay **e** of you according *1667*
4: 8 **E** of the four living creatures had six wings *1651+1651+2848*
5: 8 **E** *one* had a harp *1667*
6: 4 the earth and to make men slay **e other.** *253*
6:11 Then **e** of them was given a white robe, *1667*
11:10 and will celebrate by sending **e other** gifts, *253*
13: 1 and on **e** head a blasphemous name. *3836*
16:21 of about a hundred pounds **e** fell upon men. *NIG*
20:13 and **e** *person* was judged according *1667*
21:21 **e** gate made of a single pearl. *324+1651+1667*
22: 2 **On e side** of the river stood the tree of life, *1696+1949+2779*

EAGER (21) [EAGERLY, EAGERNESS]

2Ch 26:20 Indeed, *he* himself *was* **e** to leave, 1894
Ps 56: 6 they watch my steps, **e** to take my life. 7747
Pr 28:20 *one* **e** to get rich will not go unpunished. 237
28:22 A stingy man *is* **e** to get rich 987
31:13 and flax and works with **e** hands. 2914
Isa 58: 2 *they seem* **e** to know my ways, 2911
58: 2 and *seem* **e** for God to come near them. 2911
Zep 3: 7 But *they were still* **e** to act corruptly 8899
Ro 1:15 That is why I am so **e** to preach the gospel *4609*
8:19 The creation waits in **e expectation for** *638*
1Co 14:12 Since you are **e** to have spiritual gifts, *2421*
14:39 Therefore, my brothers, *be* **e** to prophesy, *2420*
2Co 8:11 so that your **e** willingness to do it may *4608*
Gal 2:10 the very thing *I was* **e** to do. *5079*
Php 2:28 Therefore I am **all the more e** to send him, *5081*
1Ti 6:10 Some people, **e for** money, *3977*
Tit 2:14 **e** to do what is good. *2421*
1Pe 3:13 Who is going to harm you if you are **e** *2421*
5: 2 not greedy for money, but **e** to serve; *4610*
2Pe 1:10 *be* all the more **e** to make your calling *5079*
Jude 1: 3 although I was very **e** to write to you about *5082*

EAGERLY (11) [EAGER]

2Ch 15:15 They sought God **e,** 928+3972+8356
Job 7: 2 or a hired man **waiting e** *for* his wages, 7747
Ps 78:34 they **e** turned to him again. 8838
Lk 22:15 *"I have* **e desired** to eat this Passover *2121+2123*
Ro 8:23 *as we* **wait e for** our adoption as sons, *587*
1Co 1: 7 not lack any spiritual gift *as you* **e wait for** *587*
12:31 But **e desire** the greater gifts. *2420*
14: 1 the way of love and **e desire** spiritual gifts, *2420*
Gal 5: 5 **e await** through the Spirit the righteousness **for** which we hope. *587*
Php 1:20 I **e expect** and hope that I will in no way *638*
3:20 And *we* **e await** a Savior from there, *587*

EAGERNESS (4) [EAGER]

Ac 17:11 for they received the message with great **e** *4608*
2Co 7:11 what **e** to **clear** yourselves, *665*
8:19 to honor the Lord himself and to show our **e** *4608*
9: 2 For I know your **e** to help, *4608*

EAGLE (20) [EAGLE'S, EAGLES, EAGLES']

Lev 11:13 the **e,** the vulture, the black vulture, 5979
Dt 14:12 the **e,** the vulture, the black vulture, 5979
28:49 like an **e** swooping down, 5979
32:11 like an **e** that stirs up its nest and hovers 5979
Job 39:27 Does the **e** soar at your command 5979
Pr 23: 5 and fly off to the sky like an **e.** 5979
Pr 30:19 the way of an **e** in the sky, 5979
Jer 48:40 An **e** is swooping down, 5979
49:22 An **e** will soar and swoop down, 5979
Eze 1:10 each also had the face of an **e.** 5979
10:14 and the fourth the face of an **e.** 5979
17: 3 A great **e** with powerful wings, 5979
17: 7 " 'But there was another great **e** 5979
Da 4:33 of an **e** and his nails like the claws of a bird. 10495
7: 4 and it had the wings of an **e.** 10495
Hos 8: 1 An **e** is over the house of the LORD 5979
Ob 1: 4 the **e** and make your nest among the stars, 5979
Rev 4: 7 the fourth was like a flying **e.** *108*
8:13 an **e** that was flying in midair call out in *108*
12:14 the two wings *of* a great **e,** *108*

EAGLE'S (2) [EAGLE]

Ps 103: 5 so that your youth is renewed like the **e.** 5979
Jer 49:16 you build your nest as high as the **e,** 5979

EAGLES (5) [EAGLE]

2Sa 1:23 They were swifter than **e,** 5979
Job 9:26 like **e** swooping down on their prey. 5979
Isa 40:31 They will soar on wings like **e;** 5979
Jer 4:13 his horses are swifter than **e.** 5979
La 4:19 Our pursuers were swifter than **e** *in* 5979

EAGLES' (1) [EAGLE]

Ex 19: 4 on **e'** wings and brought you to myself. 5979

EAR (56) [EARS]

Ex 21: 6 to the door or the doorpost and pierce his **e** 265
Lev 8:23 and put it on the lobe of Aaron's right **e,** 265
14:14 of the right **e** of the one to be cleansed, 265
14:17 in his palm on the lobe of the right **e** *of* 265
14:25 of the right **e** *of* the one to be cleansed, 265
14:28 of the right **e** *of* the one to be cleansed, 265
Dt 1:45 and **turned a deaf e** to you. 263+4202
15:17 an awl and push it through his **e lobe** into 265
2Ki 19:16 **Give e,** O LORD, and hear; 265+5742
Ne 1: 6 let your **e** be attentive and your eyes open 265
1:11 let your **e** be attentive to the prayer 265
Job 12:11 the **e** test words as the tongue tastes food? 265
34: 3 the **e** tests words as the tongue tastes food. 265
Ps 5: 1 **Give e** *to* my words, O LORD, 263
17: 1 **Give e** *to* my prayer— 263
17: 6 **give e** to me and hear my prayer. 265+5742
28: 1 *do* not **turn a deaf e** to me. 3087
31: 2 Turn your **e** to me, 265
45:10 Listen, O daughter, consider and **give e:** 265+5742
49: 4 I will turn my **e** to a proverb; 265
71: 2 turn your **e** to me and save me. 265
88: 2 turn your **e** to my cry. 265
94: 9 Does he who implanted the **e** not hear? 265
102: 2 Turn your **e** to me; 265
116: 2 Because he turned his **e** to me, 265
Pr 2: 2 turning your **e** to wisdom 265
25:12 a wise man's rebuke to a listening **e.** 265
28: 9 If anyone turns a deaf **e** to the law, 265
Ecc 1: 8 nor the **e** its fill of hearing. 265
Isa 37:17 **Give e,** O LORD, and hear; 265+5742
48: 8 from of old your **e** has not been open. 265
50: 4 wakens my **e** to listen like one being taught. 265
55: 3 **Give e** and come to me; 265+5742
59: 1 nor his **e** too dull to hear. 265
64: 4 no **e** *has* **perceived,** 263
Da 9:18 **Give e,** O God, and hear; 265+5742
Am 3:12 or a piece of an **e,** 265
Mt 10:27 what is whispered in your **e,** *4044*
26:51 servant of the high priest, cutting off his **e.** *6065*
Mk 14:47 servant of the high priest, cutting off his **e.** *6064*
Lk 12: 3 the **e** in the inner rooms will be proclaimed *4044*
22:50 of the high priest, cutting off his right **e.** *4044*
22:51 he touched the man's **e** and healed him. *6065*
Jn 18:10 high priest's servant, cutting off his right **e.** *6064*
18:26 of the man whose **e** Peter had cut off, *6065*
1Co 2: 9 "No eye has seen, no **e** has heard, *4044*
12:16 And if the **e** should say, *4044*
12:17 If the whole body were an **e,** *198*
Rev 2: 7 He who has an **e,** let him hear *4044*
2:11 He who has an **e,** let him hear *4044*
2:17 He who has an **e,** let him hear *4044*
2:29 He who has an **e,** let him hear *4044*
3: 6 He who has an **e,** let him hear *4044*
3:13 He who has an **e,** let him hear *4044*
3:22 He who has an **e,** let him hear *4044*
13: 9 He who has an **e,** let him hear. *4044*

[IN THE] EAR (Anglicized) See HEADED

EARED, EARING (KJV) PLOW, PLOWED

EARLIER (18) [EARLY]

Ge 13: 3 and Ai where his tent had been **e** 928+2021+9378
26: 1 besides the **e** famine of Abraham's time— 8037
Ru 3:10 that which you showed **e:** 8037
4: 7 (Now **in e times** in Israel, 7156
1Ki 11:15 **E** when David was fighting with Edom, 2118
1Ch 9:20 **In e times** Phinehas son of Eleazar 4200+7156
Ne 5:15 But the **e** governors— 8037
Da 7:24 different from the **e** *ones;* 10623
9:21 Gabriel, the man I had seen in the **e** vision, 928+2021+9378

Zec 1: 4 to whom the **e** prophets proclaimed: 8037
7: 7 through the **e** prophets when Jerusalem 8037
7:12 by his Spirit through the **e** prophets. 8037
Jn 7:50 who had gone to Jesus **e** and who was one *4728*
19:39 the man who **e** had visited Jesus at night. *4754*
2Co 8: 6 since *he had* **e made a beginning,** *4599*
12:21 be grieved over many who *have* **sinned e** *4579*
13: 2 not spare those who **sinned e** or any of *4579*
Heb 10:32 Remember those **e** days *4728*

EARLIEST (1) [EARLY]

Ac 15:21 in every city from the **e** times and is read in *792*

EARLY (69) [EARLIER, EARLIEST]

Ge 19: 2 then go on your way **e in the morning."** 8899
19:27 **E** the next morning Abraham **got up** 8899
20: 8 **E** the next morning Abimelech summoned all his officials, 8899
21:14 **E** the next morning Abraham took some 8899
22: 3 **E** the next morning Abraham **got up** 8899
26:31 **E** the next morning the men swore an oath 8899
28:18 **E** the next morning Jacob took 8899
31:55 **E** the next morning Laban kissed his grandchildren and his daughters 8899
Ex 2:18 "Why have you returned *so* **e** today?" 4554
8:20 **"Get up e** in the morning 8899
9:13 **"Get up e** in the morning, 8899
24: 4 *He* **got up e** the next morning and built 8899
32: 6 So the next day the people **rose e** 8899
34: 4 the first ones and went up Mount Sinai **e** in 8899
Nu 14:40 **E** the next morning they went up toward 8899
Jos 3: 1 **E** in the morning Joshua and all 8899
6:12 Joshua **got up e** the next morning and 8899
7:16 **E** the next morning Joshua had Israel come forward by tribes, 8899
8:10 **E** the next morning Joshua mustered his men, 8899
8:14 of the city hurried out **e in the morning** 8899
Jdg 6:38 Gideon **rose e** the next day; 8899
7: 1 **E in the morning,** Jerub-Baal 8899
19: 5 On the fourth day *they* **got up e** 8899
19: 9 **E** tomorrow **morning** *you can* **get up** 8899
21: 4 **E** the next day the people built an altar 8899
1Sa 1:19 **E** the next morning *they* **arose** 8899
5: 3 the people of Ashdod **rose e** the next day, 8899
15:12 **E** in the morning Samuel **got up** 8899
17:20 **E** in the morning David left the flock with 8899
29:10 Now **get up e,** 8899
29:11 and his men **got up e** in the morning 8899
2Sa 15: 2 He *would* **get up e** and stand by the side of 8899
2Ki 3:22 When *they* **got up e** in the morning, 8899
6:15 up and went out **e the next morning,** 8899
2Ch 17: 3 because in his **e** years he walked in 8037
20:20 **E** in the morning they left for the Desert 8899
29:20 **E the next morning** King Hezekiah 8899
Job 1: 5 **E** in the morning he would sacrifice 8899
Ps 127: 2 In vain you rise **e** and stay up late, 8899
Pr 27:14 If a man loudly blesses his neighbor **e** in 8899
SS 2:13 The fig tree forms its **e fruit;** 7001
7:12 *Let us* **go e** to the vineyards to see if 8899
Isa 5:11 to *those who* **rise e** in the morning to run 8899
Jer 24: 2 like those that **ripen e;** 1136
26: 1 **E** *in* the reign of Jehoiakim son 928+8040
27: 1 **E** *in* the reign of Zedekiah son 928+8040
28: 1 **e** *in* the reign of Zedekiah king of Judah 928+8040
28: 8 From **e times** the prophets who preceded 6409
49:34 **e** in the reign of Zedekiah king of Judah: 8040
Hos 6: 4 like the **e** dew that disappears. 8899
9:10 it was like seeing the **e fruit** on the fig tree. 1136
13: 3 like the **e** dew that disappears, 8899
Mic 7: 1 none of the **e figs** that I crave. 1136
Mt 20: 1 a landowner who went out **e in the morning** *275+4745*
21:18 **E in the morning,** as he was on his way *4745*
27: 1 **E in the morning,** all the chief priests *4746*
Mk 1:35 Very **e in the morning,** *4745*
15: 1 **Very e in the morning,** *2317+4745*
16: 2 Very **e** on the first day of the week, *4745*
16: 9 When Jesus rose **e** on the first day of *4745*
Lk 21:38 the people **came e in the morning** *3983*
24: 1 **very e in the morning,** *960+3986*
24:22 They went to the tomb **e** this **morning** *3984*
Jn 10:40 John had been baptizing **in the e days.** *4754*
18:28 By now it was **e morning,** *4745*
20: 1 **E** on the first day of the week, *4745*
21: 4 **E in the morning,** Jesus stood on the shore, *1181+4746*
Ac 21:16 from Cyprus and one of the **e** disciples. *792*
Php 4:15 in the **e** days of your acquaintance with *794*

EARN (5) [EARNED, EARNERS, EARNINGS, EARNS]

Dt 23:19 or food or anything else that *may* **e interest.** 5967
Am 7:12 **E** your bread there 430
Hag 1: 6 You **e wages,** only to put them in a purse with holes in it." 8509+8509
2Th 3:12 settle down and **e** the bread they eat. *2237*
Rev 18:17 and all who **e** *their* **living** from the sea, *2237*

EARNED (4) [EARN]

Pr 31:31 Give her the **reward** she has **e,** 3338+7262
Lk 19:16 'Sir, your mina *has* **e** ten **more.'** *4664*
19:18 'Sir, your mina *has* **e** five more.' *4472*
Ac 16:16 She **e** a great deal of money for her owners *4218*

EARNERS (1) [EARN]

Isa 19:10 and all the wage **e** will be sick at heart. 6913

EARNEST (2) [EARNESTNESS, EARNESTLY]

Pr 27: 9 of one's friend springs from his **e** counsel. 5883
Rev 3:19 So *be* **e,** and repent. *2418*

EARNESTLY (13) [EARNEST]

1Sa 20: 6 'David **e asked** my **permission** to hurry to Bethlehem, 8626+8626
20:28 **e asked** me **for permission** 8626+8626
Ps 63: 1 O God, you are my God, **e** *I* **seek** you; 8838
Hos 5:15 in their misery *they will* **e seek** me." 8838
Mk 5:23 and pleaded **e** with him, *4498*
Lk 7: 4 they pleaded **e** with him, *5081*
22:44 And being in anguish, he prayed *more* **e,** *1757*
Ac 12: 5 the church was **e** praying to God for him. *1757*
26: 7 to see fulfilled as they **e** serve God day *1755+1877*
Ro 11: 7 What Israel **sought so e** it did not obtain, *2118*
1Th 3:10 Night and day we pray **most e** *5655*
Heb 11: 6 and that he rewards those who **e seek** him. *1699*
Jas 5:17 *He* **prayed e** that it would not rain, *4666+4667*

EARNESTNESS (4) [EARNEST]

Dt 18: 6 all **e** to the place the LORD will choose, 205+5883
2Co 7:11 what **e,** what eagerness to clear yourselves, *5082*
8: 7 *in* complete **e** and in your love for us— *5082*
8: 8 of your love by comparing it with the **e** *5082*

EARNINGS (3) [EARN]

Dt 23:18 not bring the **e** *of* a female prostitute or of 924
Pr 31:16 out of her **e** she plants a vineyard. 4090+7262
Isa 23:18 Yet her profit and her **e** will be set apart for 924

EARNS (1) [EARN]

Pr 11:18 The wicked man **e** deceptive wages, 6913

EARRING (2) [EARRINGS]

Jdg 8:24 you give me an **e** *from* your share of 5690
Pr 25:12 an **e** *of* gold or an ornament of fine gold is 5690

EARRINGS (9) [EARRING]

Ex 32: 2 "Take off the gold **e** that your wives, 5690
32: 3 So all the people took off their **e** 5690
35:22 brooches, **e,** rings and ornaments. 5690
Nu 31:50 bracelets, signet rings, **e** and necklaces— 6316
Jdg 8:24 of the Ishmaelites to wear gold **e.)** 5690
SS 1:10 Your cheeks are beautiful with **e,** 9366
1:11 We will make you **e** *of* gold, 9366
Isa 3:19 the **e** and bracelets and veils, 5755
Eze 16:12 **e** on your ears and a beautiful crown 6316

EARS (84) [EAR]

Ge 35: 4 and the rings in their **e,** 265
Ex 29:20 of the right **e** *of* Aaron and his sons, 265
Lev 8:24 of the blood on the lobes of their right **e,** 265
Dt 29: 4 that understands or eyes that see or **e** 265
1Sa 3:11 that will make the **e** *of* everyone who hears 265
15:14 then is this bleating of sheep in my **e?** 265
2Sa 7:22 as we have heard with our own **e.** 265
22: 7 my cry came to his **e.** 265
2Ki 19:28 and your insolence has reached my **e,** 265
21:12 and Judah that the **e** *of* everyone who hears 265
1Ch 17:20 as we have heard with our own **e.** 265
2Ch 6:40 may your eyes be open and your **e** attentive 265
7:15 and my **e** attentive to the prayers offered 265
Job 4:12 my **e** caught a whisper of it. 265
13: 1 my **e** have heard and understood it. 265
13:17 let your **e** take in what I say. 265
15:21 Terrifying sounds fill his **e;** 265
28:22 'Only a rumor of it has reached our **e.'** 265
29:22 my words fell gently on their **e.** NIH
33:16 in their **e** and terrify them with warnings, 265
42: 5 My **e** had heard of you but 265
Ps 18: 6 my cry came before him, into his **e.** 265
34:15 on the righteous and his **e** are attentive 265
40: 6 but my **e** you have pierced; 265
44: 1 We have heard with our **e,** O God; 265
58: 4 like that of a cobra that has stopped its **e,** 265
92:11 my **e** have heard the rout 265
115: 6 they have **e,** but cannot hear, noses, 265
130: 2 Let your **e** be attentive to my cry for mercy. 265
135:17 they have **e,** but cannot hear, 265
Pr 18:15 the **e** *of* the wise seek it out. 265
20:12 **E** that hear and eyes that see— 265
21:13 If a man shuts his **e** to the cry of the poor, 265
23:12 Apply your heart to instruction and your **e** 265
26:17 a dog by the **e** is a passer-by who meddles 265
Isa 6:10 make their **e** dull and close their eyes. 265
6:10 hear with their **e,** 265
11: 3 or decide by what he hears with his **e;** 265
30:21 your **e** will hear a voice behind you, saying, 265
32: 3 and the **e** *of* those who hear will listen. 265
33:15 who stops his **e** against plots of murder 265
35: 5 the eyes of the blind be opened and the **e** *of* 265
37:29 because your insolence has reached my **e,** 265
42:20 your **e** are open, but you hear nothing." 265
43: 8 who have **e** but are deaf. 265
50: 5 The Sovereign LORD has opened my **e,** 265
Jer 5:21 who have **e** but do not hear: 265
6:10 Their **e** are closed so they cannot hear. 265
9:20 open your **e** to the words of his mouth. 265
19: 3 that will make the **e** *of* everyone who hears 265
26:11 You have heard it with your own **e!"** 265
La 3:56 "Do not close your **e** to my cry for relief." 265
Eze 8:18 Although they shout in my **e,** 265
12: 2 but do not see and **e** to hear but do not hear, 265
16:12 earrings on your **e** and a beautiful crown 265
23:25 They will cut off your noses and your **e,** 265
40: 4 look with your eyes and hear with your **e** 265
Mic 7:16 and their **e** will become deaf. 265
Zec 7:11 and stopped up their **e.** 265
Mt 11:15 He who has **e,** let him hear. *4044*
13: 9 He who has **e,** let him hear." *4044*
13:15 they hardly hear *with* their **e,** *4044*
13:15 hear *with* their **e,** *4044*
13:16 and your **e** because they hear. *4044*
13:43 He who has **e,** let him hear. *4044*
Mk 4: 9 Then Jesus said, "He who has **e** to hear, *4044*
4:23 If anyone has **e** to hear, let him hear." *4044*
7:33 Jesus put his fingers into the man's **e.** *4044*
7:35 At this, the man's **e** were opened, *198*
8:18 and **e** but fail to hear? *4044*
Lk 1:44 as the sound of your greeting reached my **e,** *4044*
8: 8 "He who has **e** to hear, let him hear." *4044*
14:35 "He who has **e** to hear, let him hear." *4044*
Ac 7:51 with uncircumcised hearts and **e!** *4044*
7:57 At this they covered their **e** and, *4044*
11:22 News of this reached the **e** of the church *4044*
17:20 to our **e,** and we want *198*
28:27 they hardly hear *with* their **e,** *4044*
28:27 hear *with* their **e,** *4044*
Ro 11: 8 not see and **e** so that they could not hear, *4044*
2Ti 4: 3 to say **what** their itching **e want to hear.** *198*
4: 4 They will turn their **e** away from the truth *198*
Jas 5: 4 of the harvesters have reached the **e** of *4044*
1Pe 3:12 on the righteous and his **e** are attentive *4044*

EARS OF CORN (Anglicized) See HEADS OF GRAIN

EARTH (738) [EARTH'S, EARTHEN, EARTHLY]

Ge 1: 1 God created the heavens and the **e.** 824
1: 2 Now the **e** was formless and empty, 824
1:15 of the sky to give light on the **e."** 824
1:17 of the sky to give light on the **e,** 824
1:20 above the **e** across the expanse of the sky." 824
1:22 and let the birds increase on the **e."** 824
1:26 over the livestock, over all the **e,** 824
1:28 fill the **e** and subdue it. 824
1:29 of the whole **e** and every tree that has fruit 824
1:30 to all the beasts of the **e** and all the birds of 824
2: 1 Thus the heavens and the **e** were completed 824
2: 4 This is the account of the heavens and the **e** 824
2: 4 When the LORD God made the **e** and 824
2: 5 of the field had yet appeared on the **e** 824
2: 5 not sent rain on the **e** and there was no man 824
2: 6 but streams came up from the **e** and watered 824
4:12 You will be a restless wanderer on the **e."** 824
4:14 I will be a restless wanderer on the **e,** 824
6: 1 in number on the **e** and daughters were born 141
6: 4 Nephilim were on the **e** in those days— 824
6: 5 on the **e** had become, 824
6: 6 that he had made man on the **e,** 824
6: 7 whom I have created, from the face of the **e** 141
6:11 Now the **e** was corrupt in God's sight 824
6:12 God saw how corrupt the **e** had become, 824
6:12 the people on **e** had corrupted their ways. 824
6:13 **e** is filled with violence because of them. 824
6:13 surely going to destroy both them and the **e.** 824
6:17 the **e** to destroy all life under the heavens. 824
6:17 Everything on **e** will perish. 824
7: 3 to keep their various kinds alive throughout the **e.** 824
7: 4 now I will send rain on the **e** for forty days 824
7: 4 of the **e** every living creature I have made." 141
7: 6 when the floodwaters came on the **e.** 824
7:10 the floodwaters came on the **e.** 824
7:12 on the **e** forty days and forty nights. 824
7:17 the flood kept coming on the **e,** 824
7:17 the ark high above the **e.** 824
7:18 and increased greatly on the **e,** 824
7:19 They rose greatly on the **e,** 824
7:21 that moved on the **e** perished— 824
7:21 all the creatures that swarm over the **e,** 824
7:23 on the face of the **e** was wiped out; 141
7:23 the birds of the air were wiped from the **e.** 824
7:24 The waters flooded the **e** for a hundred 824
8: 1 and he sent a wind over the **e,** 824
8: 3 The water receded steadily from the **e.** 824
8: 7 until the water had dried up from the **e.** 824
8: 9 over all the surface of the **e;** 824
8:11 that the water had receded from the **e.** 824
8:13 the water had dried up from the **e.** 824
8:14 the second month the **e** was completely dry. 824
8:17 so they can multiply on the **e** and be fruitful 824
8:19 everything that moves on the **e**— 824
8:22 "As long as the **e** endures, 824
9: 1 and increase in number and fill the **e.** 824
9: 2 upon all the beasts of the **e** and all the birds 824
9: 7 multiply on the **e** and increase upon it." 824
9:10 every living creature on **e.** 824
9:11 be a flood to destroy the **e."** 824
9:13 sign of the covenant between me and the **e.** 824

Ge 9:14 the e and the rainbow appears in the clouds, 824
9:16 of every kind on the e." 824
9:17 between me and all life on the e." 824
9:19 the people who were scattered over the e. 824
10: 8 who grew to be a mighty warrior on the e. 824
10:25 because in his time the e was divided; 824
10:32 the nations spread out over the e after 824
11: 4 be scattered over the face of the whole e." 824
11: 8 from there over all the e, 824
11: 9 over the face of the whole e. 824
12: 3 and all peoples on e will be blessed 141
13:16 like the dust of the e, 824
14:19 Creator of heaven and e. 824
14:22 God Most High, Creator of heaven and e, 824
18:18 and all nations on e will be blessed 824
18:25 Will not the Judge of all the e do right?" 824
19:31 as is the custom all over the e. 824
22:18 through your offspring all nations on e will 824
24: 3 the God of heaven and the God of e, 824
26: 4 through your offspring all nations on e will 824
26:15 stopped up, filling them with e. 6760
28:12 in which he saw a stairway resting on the e, 824
28:14 be like the dust of the e, 824
28:14 on e will be blessed through you 141
45: 7 of you to preserve for you a remnant on e 824
48:16 and may they increase greatly upon the e." 824
Ex 9:14 that there is no one like me in all the e. 824
9:15 that would have wiped you off the e. 824
9:16 be proclaimed in all the e. 824
9:29 you may know that the e is the LORD's. 824
15:12 and the e swallowed them. 824
19: 5 Although the whole e is mine, 824
20: 4 or on the e beneath or in the waters below. 824
20:11 the LORD made the heavens and the e, 824
20:24 " 'Make an altar of e for me and sacrifice 141
31:17 the LORD made the heavens and the e, 824
32:12 and to wipe them off the face of the e'? 141
33:16 the other people on the face of the e?" 141
Lev 17:13 the blood and cover it with e, 6760
Nu 12: 3 on the face of the e.) 141
14:21 as the glory of the LORD fills the whole e, 824
16:30 the e opens its mouth and swallows them, 141
16:32 e opened its mouth and swallowed them, 824
16:33 the e closed over them, 824
16:34 "The e is going to swallow us too!" 824
26:10 The e opened its mouth 824
Dt 3:24 in heaven or on e who can do the deeds 824
4:17 or like any animal on e or any bird that flies 824
4:26 and e as witnesses against you this day 824
4:32 from the day God created man on the e; 824
4:36 On e he showed you his great fire, 824
4:39 in heaven above and on the e below. 824
5: 8 or on the e beneath or in the waters below. 824
7: 6 of all the peoples on the face of the e to 141
10:14 the e and everything in it. 824
11: 6 the e opened its mouth right in the middle 824
11:21 as the days that the heavens are above the e. 824
14: 2 Out of all the peoples on the face of the e, 141
28: 1 above all the nations on e. 824
28:10 the peoples on e will see that you are called 824
28:25 a thing of horror to all the kingdoms on e. 824
28:26 the birds of the air and the beasts of the e, 824
28:49 from the ends of the e, 824
28:64 from one end of the e to the other. 824
30:19 This day I call heaven and e as witnesses 824
31:28 in their hearing and call heaven and e 824
32: 1 hear, O e, the words of my mouth. 824
32:22 It will devour the e and its harvests 824
33:16 with the best gifts of the e and its fullness 824
33:17 even those at the ends of the e. 824
Jos 2:11 in heaven above and on the e below. 824
3:11 the covenant of the Lord of all the e will go 824
3:13 the Lord of all the e— 824
4:24 that all the peoples of the e might know that 824
7: 9 and wipe out our name from the e. 824
23:14 "Now I am about to go the way of all the e. 824
Jdg 5: 4 the e shook, the heavens poured, 824
1Sa 2: 8 the foundations of the e are the LORD's; 824
2:10 the LORD will judge the ends of the e. 824
17:46 the birds of the air and the beasts of the e, 824
20:15 of David's enemies from the face of the e." 141
20:31 As long as the son of Jesse lives on this e, 141
2Sa 4:11 from your hand and rid the e of you!" 824
7: 9 like the names of the greatest men of the e. 824
7:23 the one nation on e that God went out 824
14: 7 nor descendant on the face of the e." 141
22: 8 "The e trembled and quaked, 824
22:16 the e laid bare at the rebuke of the LORD, 9315
22:43 I beat them as fine as the dust of the e; 824
23: 4 after rain that brings the grass from the e.' 824
1Ki 2: 2 "I am about to go the way of all the e," 824
8:23 like you in heaven above or on e below— 824
8:27 "But will God really dwell on e? 824
8:43 of the e may know your name and fear you, 824
8:60 the e may know that the LORD is God and 824
10:23 the other kings of the e. 824
13:34 and to its destruction from the face of the e. 141
2Ki 5:17 as much e as a pair of mules can carry, 141
19:15 over all the kingdoms of the e. 824
19:15 You have made heaven and e. 824
19:19 so that all kingdoms on e may know 824
1Ch 1:10 who grew to be a mighty warrior on e. 824
1:19 because in his time the e was divided; 824
16:14 his judgments are in all the e. 824
16:23 Sing to the LORD, all the e; 824
16:30 Tremble before him, all the e! 824
16:31 Let the heavens rejoice, let the e be glad; 824
1Ch 16:33 for he comes to judge the e. 824
17: 8 like the names of the greatest men of the e. 824
17:21 the one nation on e whose God went out 824
21:16 the LORD standing between heaven and e, 824
22: 8 because you have shed much blood on the e 824
29:11 for everything in heaven and e is yours. 824
29:15 Our days on e are like a shadow, 824
2Ch 1: 9 as numerous as the dust of the e. 824
2:12 the God of Israel, who made heaven and e! 824
6:14 there is no God like you in heaven or on e— 824
6:18 "But will God really dwell on e with men? 824
6:33 of the e may know your name and fear you, 824
9:22 the other kings of the e. 824
9:23 the e sought audience with Solomon to hear 824
16: 9 of the LORD range throughout the e 824
36:23 of the e and he has appointed me to build 824
Ezr 1: 2 of the e and he has appointed me to build 824
5:11 the servants of the God of heaven and e, 10075
Ne 9: 6 the e and all that is on it, 824
Job 1: 7 through the e and going back and forth 824
1: 8 There is no one on e like him; 824
2: 2 through the e and going back and forth 824
2: 3 There is no one on e like him; 824
3:14 with kings and counselors of the e, 824
5:10 He bestows rain on the e; 824
5:22 and need not fear the beasts of the e. 824
5:25 your descendants like the grass of the e. 824
7: 1 "Does not man have hard service on e? 824
8: 9 and our days on e are but a shadow. 824
9: 6 He shakes the e from its place 824
11: 9 Their measure is longer than the e 824
12: 8 or speak to the e, 824
12:24 the leaders of the e of their reason; 824
16:18 "O e, do not cover my blood; 824
18: 4 is the e to be abandoned for your sake? 824
18:17 The memory of him perishes from the e; 824
19:25 and that in the end he will stand upon the e. 6760
20: 4 ever since man was placed on the e, 824
20:27 the e will rise up against him. 824
26: 7 he suspends the e over nothing. 824
28: 2 Iron is taken from the e, 6760
28: 5 The e, from which food comes, 824
28:24 the ends of the e and sees everything under 824
34:13 Who appointed him over the e? 824
35:11 the beasts of the e and makes us wiser than 824
37: 3 and sends it to the ends of the e. 824
37: 6 He says to the snow, 'Fall on the e,' 824
37:12 around over the face of the **whole e** 824+9315
37:13 or to water his e and show his love. 824
38:13 the e by the edges and shake the wicked out 824
38:14 The e takes shape like clay under a seal; NIH
38:18 the vast expanses of the e? 824
38:24 the east winds are scattered over the e? 824
38:33 you set up [God's] dominion over the e? 824
38:38 and the **clods of e** stick together? 8073
41:33 Nothing on e is his equal— 6760
Ps 2: 2 The kings of the e take their stand and 824
2: 8 the ends of the e your possession. 824
2:10 be warned, you rulers of the e. 824
8: 1 how majestic is your name in all the e! 824
8: 9 how majestic is your name in all the e! 824
10:18 who is of the e, may terrify no more. 824
18: 7 The e trembled and quaked, 824
18:15 and the foundations of the e laid bare 9315
19: 4 Their voice goes out into all the e, 824
21:10 from the e, their posterity 824
22:27 the ends of the e will remember and turn to 824
22:29 All the rich of the e will feast and worship; 824
24: 1 The e is the LORD's, and everything in it, 824
33: 5 the e is full of his unfailing love. 824
33: 8 Let all the e fear the LORD; 824
33:14 from his dwelling place he watches all who live on e— 824
34:16 to cut off the memory of them from the e. 824
46: 2 the e give way and the mountains fall into 824
46: 6 he lifts his voice, the e melts. 824
46: 8 the desolations he has brought on the e. 824
46: 9 He makes wars cease to the ends of the e; 824
46:10 I will be exalted in the e." 824
47: 2 the great King over all the e! 824
47: 7 For God is the King of all the e; 824
47: 9 for the kings of the e belong to God; 824
48: 2 the joy of the whole e. 824
48:10 your praise reaches to the ends of the e; 824
50: 1 the e from the rising of the sun to the place 824
50: 4 He summons the heavens above, and the e, 824
57: 5 let your glory be over all the e. 824
57:11 let your glory be over all the e. 824
58: 2 and your hands mete out violence on the e. 824
58:11 surely there is a God who judges the e." 824
59:13 the ends of the e that God rules over Jacob. 824
61: 2 From the ends of the e I call to you, 824
63: 9 they will go down to the depths of the e. 824
65: 5 the ends of the e and of the farthest seas, 824
66: 1 Shout with joy to God, all the e! 824
66: 4 All the e bows down to you; 824
67: 2 that your ways may be known on e, 824
67: 4 and guide the nations of the e. 824
67: 7 and all the ends of the e will fear him. 824
68: 8 the e shook, the heavens poured down rain, 824
68:32 Sing to God, O kingdoms of the e, 824
69:34 Let heaven and e praise him, 824
71:20 of the e you will again bring me up. 824
72: 6 like showers watering the e. 824
72: 8 and from the River to the ends of the e. 824
72:19 may the whole e be filled with his glory. 824
73: 9 and their tongues take possession of the e. 824
Ps 73:25 And e has nothing I desire besides you. 824
74:12 you bring salvation upon the e. 824
74:17 the boundaries of the e; 824
75: 3 When the e and all its people quake, 824
75: 8 and all the wicked of the e drink it down 824
76:12 he is feared by the kings of the e. 824
77:18 the e trembled and quaked. 824
78:69 like the e that he established forever. 824
79: 2 flesh of your saints to the beasts of the e. 824
82: 5 all the foundations of the e are shaken. 824
82: 8 Rise up, O God, judge the e, 824
83:18 you alone are the Most High over all the e. 824
85:11 Faithfulness springs forth from the e, 824
89:11 heavens are yours, and yours also the e; 824
89:27 the most exalted of the kings of the e. 824
90: 2 or you brought forth the e and the world, 824
94: 2 Rise up, O Judge of the e; 824
95: 4 In his hand are the depths of the e, 824
96: 1 sing to the LORD, all the e. 824
96: 9 tremble before him, all the e. 824
96:11 Let the heavens rejoice, let the e be glad; 824
96:13 for he comes, he comes to judge the e. 824
97: 1 The LORD reigns, let the e be glad; 824
97: 4 the e sees and trembles. 824
97: 5 before the Lord of all the e. 824
97: 9 are the Most High over all the e; 824
98: 3 of the e have seen the salvation of our God. 824
98: 4 Shout for joy to the LORD, all the e, 824
98: 9 for he comes to judge the e. 824
99: 1 between the cherubim, let the e shake. 824
100: 1 Shout for joy to the LORD, all the e. 824
102:15 all the kings of the e will revere your glory. 824
102:19 from heaven he viewed the e, 824
102:25 the foundations of the e, 824
103:11 For as high as the heavens are above the e, 824
104: 5 He set the e on its foundations; 824
104: 9 never again will they cover the e. 824
104:13 the e is satisfied by the fruit of his work. 824
104:14 bringing forth food from the e: 824
104:24 the e is full of your creatures. 824
104:30 and you renew the face of the e. 141
104:32 he who looks at the e, 824
104:35 But may sinners vanish from the e and 824
105: 7 his judgments are in all the e. 824
106:17 The e opened up and swallowed Dathan; 824
108: 5 and let your glory be over all the e. 824
109:15 the memory of them from the e. 824
110: 6 and crushing the rulers of the whole e. 824
113: 6 down to look on the heavens and the e? 824
114: 7 Tremble, O e, at the presence of the Lord, 824
115:15 the Maker of heaven and e. 824
115:16 but the e he has given to man. 824
119:19 I am a stranger on e; 824
119:64 The e is filled with your love, O LORD; 824
119:87 They almost wiped me from the e, 824
119:90 you established the e, and it endures. 824
119:119 the wicked of the e you discard like dross; 824
121: 2 the Maker of heaven and e. 824
124: 8 the Maker of heaven and e. 824
134: 3 the Maker of heaven and e, 824
135: 6 in the heavens and on the e, 824
135: 7 from the ends of the e; 824
136: 6 who spread out the e upon the waters, 824
138: 4 May all the kings of the e praise you, 824
139:15 I was woven together in the depths of the e, 824
141: 7 "As one plows and breaks up the e, 824
146: 6 and e, the sea, and everything in them— 824
147: 8 the e with rain and makes grass grow on 824
147:15 He sends his command to the e; 824
148: 7 Praise the LORD from the e, 824
148:11 kings of the e and all nations, 824
148:11 you princes and all rulers on e, 824
148:13 his splendor is above the e and the heavens. 824
Pr 8:16 and all nobles who rule on e. 824
8:26 before he made the e or its fields or any of 824
8:29 he marked out the foundations of the e. 824
11:31 If the righteous receive their due on e, 824
17:24 a fool's eyes wander to the ends of the e. 824
25: 3 As the heavens are high and the e is deep, 824
30: 4 Who has established all the ends of the e? 824
30:14 with knives to devour the poor from the e, 824
30:21 "Under three things the e trembles, 824
30:24 "Four things on e are small, 824
Ecc 1: 4 but the e remains forever. 824
3:21 of the animal goes down into the e?" 824
5: 2 God is in heaven and you are on e, 824
7:20 a righteous man on e who does what is right 824
8:14 meaninglessness that occurs on e: 824
8:16 and to observe man's labor on e— 824
11: 3 they pour rain upon the e. 824
SS 2:12 Flowers appear on the e; 824
Isa 1: 2 Listen, O e! 824
2:19 when he rises to shake the e. 824
2:21 when he rises to shake the e. 824
5:26 he whistles for those at the ends of the e. 824
6: 3 the whole e is full of his glory." 824
8:22 the e and see only distress and darkness 824
11: 4 for the poor of the e. 824
11: 4 He will strike the e with the rod 824
11: 9 for the e will be full of the knowledge of 824
11:12 of Judah from the four quarters of the e. 824
13:13 the e will shake from its place at the wrath 824
14:12 You have been cast down to the e, 824
14:16 the e and made kingdoms tremble, 824
14:21 the land and cover the e with their cities. 9315
18: 3 you who live on the e, 824
19:24 a blessing on the e. 824

Isa 23: 8 whose traders are renowned in the e? 824
23: 9 to humble all who are renowned on the e. 824
23:17 with all the kingdoms on the face of the e. 141
24: 1 the LORD is going to lay waste the e 824
24: 3 The e will be completely laid waste 824
24: 4 The e dries up and withers, 824
24: 4 the exalted of the e languish. 824
24: 5 The e is defiled by its people; 824
24: 6 Therefore a curse consumes the e; 824
24:11 all gaiety is banished from the e. 824
24:13 be on the e and among the nations, 824
24:16 From the ends of the e we hear singing: 824
24:17 O people of the e. 824
24:18 the foundations of the e shake. 824
24:19 The e is broken up, 824
24:19 earth is broken up, the e is split asunder, 824
24:19 the e is thoroughly shaken. 824
24:20 The e reels like a drunkard, 824
24:21 above and the kings on the e below. 141
25: 8 the disgrace of his people from all the e. 824
26: 9 When your judgments come upon the e, 824
26:18 We have not brought salvation to the e; 824
26:19 the e will give birth to her dead. 824
26:21 of his dwelling to punish the people of the e 824
26:21 The e will disclose the blood shed 824
29: 4 Your voice will come ghostlike from the e; 824
34: 1 Let the e hear, and all that is in it, 824
37:16 over all the kingdoms of the e. 824
37:16 You have made heaven and e. 824
37:20 so that all kingdoms on e may know 824
40:12 Who has held the dust of the e in a basket, 824
40:21 not understood since the e was founded? 824
40:22 He sits enthroned above the circle of the e, 824
40:28 the Creator of the ends of the e. 824
41: 5 the ends of the e tremble. 824
41: 9 I took you from the ends of the e, 824
42: 4 till he establishes justice on e. 824
42: 5 who spread out the e and all that comes out 824
42:10 his praise from the ends of the e, 824
43: 6 and my daughters from the ends of the e— 824
44:23 shout aloud, O e beneath. 824
44:24 who spread out the e by myself, 824
45: 8 Let the e open wide, let salvation spring up, 824
45:12 It is I who made the e and created mankind 824
45:18 he who fashioned and made the e, 824
45:22 all you ends of the e; 824
48:13 My own hand laid the foundations of the e, 824
48:20 Send it out to the ends of the e; 824
49: 6 to the ends of the e." 824
49:13 rejoice, O e; burst into song, O mountains! 824
51: 6 look at the e beneath; 824
51: 6 like smoke, the e will wear out like 824
51:13 and laid the foundations of the e, 824
51:16 who laid the foundations of the e, 824
52:10 of the e will see the salvation of our God. 824
54: 5 he is called the God of all the e. 824
54: 9 of Noah would never again cover the e, 824
55: 9 "As the heavens are higher than the e, 824
55:10 without watering the e and making it bud 824
60: 2 the e and thick darkness is over the peoples, 824
62: 7 and makes her the praise of the e. 824
62:11 to the ends of the e: 824
65:17 I will create new heavens and a new e. 824
66: 1 and the e is my footstool. 824
66:22 and the new e that I make will endure 824
Jer 4:23 I looked at the e, 824
4:28 Therefore the e will mourn and the heavens 824
6:19 O e: I am bringing disaster on 824
6:22 up from the ends of the e. 824
7:33 the birds of the air and the beasts of the e, 824
9:24 justice and righteousness on e, 824
10:10 When he is angry, the e trembles; 824
10:11 who did not make the heavens and the e, 10077
10:11 from the e and from under the heavens.' " 10075
10:12 But God made the e by his power; 824
10:13 he makes clouds rise from the ends of the e. 824
15: 3 of the air and the beasts of the e to devour 824
15: 4 of the e because of what Manasseh son 824
16: 4 the birds of the air and the beasts of the e." 824
16:19 the nations will come from the ends of the e 824
19: 7 the birds of the air and the beasts of the e. 824
23:24 "Do not I fill heaven and e?" 824
24: 9 and an offense to all the kingdoms of the e, 824
25:26 all the kingdoms on the face of the e. 141
25:29 down a sword upon all who live on the e, 824
25:30 shout against all who live on the e. 824
25:31 tumult will resound to the ends of the e, 824
25:32 from the ends of the e." 824
25:33 from one end of the e to the other. 824
26: 6 of cursing among all the nations of the e.' " 824
27: 5 the e and its people and the animals that are 824
28:16 about to remove you from the face of the e. 141
29:18 of the e and an object of cursing and horror, 824
31: 8 and gather them from the ends of the e. 824
31:22 The LORD will create a new thing on e— 824
31:37 the e below be searched out will I reject all 824
32:17 the heavens and the e by your great power 824
33: 2 he who made the e, 2023S
33: 9 and honor before all nations on e that hear 824
33:25 and the fixed laws of heaven and e, 824
34:17 to all the kingdoms of the e. 824
34:20 the birds of the air and the beasts of the e. 824
44: 8 and reproach among all the nations on e. 824
46: 8 She says, 'I will rise and cover the e; 824
46:12 your cries will fill the e. 824
49:21 At the sound of their fall the e will tremble; 824
50:23 and shattered is the hammer of the whole e! 824
Jer 50:41 up from the ends of the e. 824
50:46 of Babylon's capture the e will tremble; 824
51: 7 she made the whole e drunk. 824
51:15 "He made the e by his power; 824
51:16 he makes clouds rise from the ends of the e. 824
51:25 you who destroy the whole e," 824
51:41 the boast of the whole e seized! 824
51:48 and e and all that is in them will shout 824
51:49 in all the e have fallen because of Babylon. 824
La 2: 1 the splendor of Israel from heaven to e; 824
2:15 the joy of the whole e?" 824
4:12 The kings of the e did not believe, 824
Eze 7:21 and as loot to the wicked of the e, 824
8: 3 up between e and heaven and in visions 824
26:20 I will make you dwell in the e below, 824
27:33 the kings of the e. 824
28:17 So I threw you to the e; 824
29: 5 I will give you as food to the beasts of the e 824
31:12 of the e came out from under its shade 824
31:14 for the e below, among mortal men, 824
31:16 were consoled in the e below. 824
31:18 down with the trees of Eden to the e below; 824
32: 4 the beasts of the e gorge themselves on you. 824
32:18 to the e below both her and the daughters 824
32:24 down uncircumcised to the e below. 824
34: 6 They were scattered over the whole e, 824
35:14 whole e rejoices, I will make you desolate. 824
38:20 the people on the face of the e will tremble 141
39:18 the e as if they were rams and lambs, goats 824
Da 2:10 a man on e who can do what the king asks! 10309
2:35 a huge mountain and filled the whole e. 10075
2:39 one of bronze, will rule over the whole e. 10075
4:11 it was visible to the ends of the e. 10075
4:15 with the animals among the plants of the e. 10075
4:20 visible to the whole e, 10075
4:22 to distant parts of the e. 10075
4:35 the peoples of the e are regarded as nothing. 10075
4:35 of heaven and the peoples of the e. 10075
6:27 and wonders in the heavens and on the e. 10075
7:17 that will rise from the e. 10075
7:23 a fourth kingdom that will appear on e. 10075
7:23 and will devour the whole e, 10075
8: 5 the whole e without touching the ground. 824
8:10 the starry host down to the e and trampled 824
12: 2 in the dust of the e will awake: 141
Hos 2:21 and they will respond to the e; 824
2:22 and the e will respond to the grain, 824
6: 3 like the spring rains that water the e." 824
Joel 2:10 Before them the e shakes, the sky trembles, 824
2:30 in the heavens and on the e, 824
3:16 the e and the sky will tremble. 824
Am 3: 2 of all the families of the e; 141
3: 5 from the e when there is nothing to catch? 141
4:13 and treads the high places of the e— 824
8: 9 at noon and darken the e in broad daylight. 824
9: 5 he who touches the e and it melts, 824
9: 6 on the e, who calls for the waters of the sea 824
9: 8 I will destroy it from the face of the e— 141
Jnh 2: 6 the e beneath barred me in forever. 824
Mic 1: 2 all of you, listen, O e and all who are in it, 824
1: 3 down and treads the high places of the e. 824
4:13 their wealth to the Lord of all the e. 824
5: 4 his greatness will reach to the ends of the e. 824
6: 2 listen, you everlasting foundations of the e. 824
7:13 The e will become desolate because 824
Na 1: 5 The e trembles at his presence, 824
2:13 I will leave you no prey on the e. 824
Hab 1: 6 across the whole e to seize dwelling places 824
2:14 For the e will be filled with the knowledge 824
2:20 let all the e be silent before him." 824
3: 3 the heavens and his praise filled the e. 824
3: 6 He stood, and shook the e; 824
3: 9 Selah You split the e with rivers; 824
3:12 the e and in anger you threshed the nations. 824
Zep 1: 2 from the face of the e," 141
1: 3 when I cut off man from the face of the e," 141
1:18 a sudden end of all who live in the e." 824
3:20 and praise among all the peoples of the e 824
Hag 1:10 and the e its crops. 824
2: 6 the heavens and the e, 824
2:21 that I will shake the heavens and the e. 824
Zec 1:10 the LORD has sent to go throughout the e." 824
1:11 throughout the e and found the whole world 824
4:10 which range throughout the e.)" 824
4:14 to serve the Lord of all the e." 824
5: 9 up the basket between heaven and e. 824
6: 7 they were straining to go throughout the e. 824
6: 7 And he said, "Go throughout the e!" 824
6: 7 So they went throughout the e. 824
9:10 and from the River to the ends of the e. 824
12: 1 who lays the foundation of the e, 824
12: 3 the nations of the e are gathered against her, 824
14: 9 The LORD will be king over the whole e. 824
14:17 the e do not go up to Jerusalem to worship 824
Mt 5: 5 for they will inherit the e. 1178
5:13 "You are the salt *of* the e. 1178
5:18 until heaven and e disappear, 1178
5:35 or by the e, for it is his footstool; 1178
6:10 your will be done on e as it is in heaven. 1178
6:19 not store up for yourselves treasures on e, 1178
9: 6 Son of Man has authority on e to forgive sins...." 1178
10:34 that I have come to bring peace to the e. 1178
11:25 "I praise you, Father, Lord of heaven and e, 1178
12:40 and three nights in the heart *of* the e. 1178
12:42 *of* the e to listen to Solomon's wisdom, 1178
16:19 whatever you bind on e will be bound 1178
Mt 16:19 in heaven, and whatever you loose on e will 1178
17:25 the kings *of* the e collect duty and taxes— 1178
18:18 whatever you bind on e will be bound 1178
18:18 and whatever you loose on e will be loosed 1178
18:19 of you on e agree about anything you ask 1178
23: 9 And do not call anyone on e 'father,' 1178
23:35 the righteous blood that has been shed on e, 1178
24:30 and all the nations *of* the e will mourn. 1178
24:35 Heaven and e will pass away, 1178
27:51 The e shook and the rocks split. 1178
28:18 in heaven and on e has been given to me. 1178
Mk 2:10 Son of Man has authority on e to forgive sins...." 1178
13:27 the ends *of* the e to the ends of the heavens. 1178
13:31 Heaven and e will pass away, 1178
Lk 2:14 and on e peace to men 1178
5:24 Son of Man has authority on e to forgive sins...." 1178
10:21 Father, Lord *of* heaven and e, 1178
11:31 *of* the e to listen to Solomon's wisdom, 1178
12:49 "I have come to bring fire on the e, 1178
12:51 Do you think I came to bring peace on e? 1178
12:56 how to interpret the appearance *of* the e 1178
16:17 and e to disappear than for the least stroke 1178
18: 8 will he find faith on the e?" 1178
21:25 On the e, nations will be in anguish 1178
21:33 Heaven and e will pass away, 1178
21:35 on the face *of* the whole e. 1178
Jn 3:31 one who is from the e belongs to the earth, 1178
3:31 one who is from the earth belongs to the e, 1178
3:31 and speaks as one from the e. 1178
12:32 But I, when I am lifted up from the e, 1178
17: 4 on e by completing the work you gave me 1178
Ac 1: 8 and to the ends *of* the e." 1178
2:19 the heaven above and signs on the e below, 1178
3:25 *on* e will be blessed.' 1178
4:24 "you made the heaven and the e and 1178
4:26 The kings *of* the e take their stand and 1178
7:49 and the e is my footstool. 1178
8:33 For his life was taken from the e." 1178
10:11 like a large sheet being let down to e 1178
10:12 as well as reptiles *of* the e and birds of 1178
11: 6 and saw four-footed animals *of* the e, 1178
13:47 to the ends *of* the e.' " 1178
14:15 and e and sea and everything in them. 1178
17:24 the Lord *of* heaven and e and does not live 1178
17:26 that they should inhabit the whole e; 1178
22:22 "Rid the e of him! 1178
Ro 9:17 my name might be proclaimed in all the e." 1178
9:28 the Lord will carry out his sentence on e 1178
10:18 "Their voice has gone out into all the e, 1178
1Co 4:13 we have become the scum *of* the e, 3180
8: 5 or on e (as indeed there are many "gods" 1178
10:26 "The e is the Lord's, and everything in it," 1178
15:47 The first man was of the dust of the e, 1178
15:48 so are those who are *of the* e; 5954
Eph 1:10 in heaven and on e together under one head, 1178
3:15 in heaven and on e derives its name. 1178
6: 3 and that you may enjoy long life on the e." 1178
Php 2:10 in heaven and on e and under the earth, 2103
2:10 in heaven and on earth and under the e, 2973
Col 1:16 things in heaven and on e, 1178
1:20 whether things on e or things in heaven, 1178
Heb 1:10 O Lord, you laid the foundations of the e, 1178
5: 7 During the days of Jesus' life on e, 4922
8: 4 If he were on e, he would not be a priest, 1178
11:13 that they were aliens and strangers on e. 1178
12:25 they refused him who warned them on e, 1178
12:26 At that time his voice shook the e, 1178
12:26 "Once more I will shake not only the e but 1178
Jas 5: 5 on e in luxury and self-indulgence. 1178
5:12 not by heaven or by e or by anything else. 1178
5:18 and the e produced its crops. 1178
2Pe 3: 5 the e was formed out of water and by water. 1178
3: 7 the present heavens and e are reserved 1178
3:10 the e and everything in it will be laid bare. 1178
3:13 to a new heaven and a new e, 1178
Rev 1: 5 and the ruler of the kings *of* the e. 1178
1: 7 the peoples *of* the e will mourn because 1178
3:10 to test those who live on the e. 1178
5: 3 on e or under the earth could open the scroll 1178
5: 3 on earth or under the e could open the scroll 1178
5: 6 of God sent out into all the e. 1178
5:10 and they will reign on the e." 1178
5:13 and on e and under the earth and on the sea, 1178
5:13 and on earth and under the e and on the sea, 1178
6: 4 the e and to make men slay each other. 1178
6: 8 over a fourth *of* the e to kill by sword, 1178
6: 8 and by the wild beasts *of* the e. 1178
6:10 until you judge the inhabitants of the e 1178
6:13 and the stars in the sky fell to e, 1178
6:15 Then the kings *of* the e, the princes, 1178
7: 1 at the four corners *of* the e, 1178
7: 1 the four winds of the e to prevent any wind 1178
8: 5 and hurled it on the e; 1178
8: 7 and it was hurled down upon the e. 1178
8: 7 A third *of* the e was burned up, 1178
8:13 Woe to the inhabitants of the e, 1178
9: 1 a star that had fallen from the sky to the e. 1178
9: 3 down upon the e and were given power like 1178
9: 3 like that of scorpions *of* the e. 1178
9: 4 not to harm the grass *of* the e or any plant 1178
10: 6 the e and all that is in it, 1178
11: 4 that stand before the Lord *of* the e. 1178
11: 6 and to strike the e with every kind of plague 1178
11:10 the e will gloat over them and will celebrate 1178
11:10 had tormented those who live on the e. 1178

Rev 11:18 and for destroying those who destroy the e." *1178*
12: 4 of the sky and flung them to the e. *1178*
12: 9 He was hurled to the e, *1178*
12:12 But woe *to* the e and the sea, *1178*
12:13 that he had been hurled to the e, *1178*
12:16 But the e helped the woman *1178*
13: 8 All inhabitants of the e will worship *1178*
13:11 I saw another beast, coming out of the e. *1178*
13:12 and made the e and its inhabitants worship *1178*
13:13 to come down from heaven to e in full view *1178*
13:14 he deceived the inhabitants of the e. *1178*
14: 3 who had been redeemed from the e. *1178*
14: 6 to proclaim to those who live on the e— *1178*
14: 7 Worship him who made the heavens, the e, *1178*
14:15 for the harvest *of* the e is ripe." *1178*
14:16 on the cloud swung his sickle over the e, *1178*
14:16 and the e was harvested. *1178*
14:19 The angel swung his sickle on the e, *1178*
16: 1 the seven bowls of God's wrath on the e." *1178*
16:18 since man has been on e, *1178*
17: 2 the kings *of* the e committed adultery and *1178*
17: 2 the inhabitants of the e were intoxicated *1178*
17: 5 THE MOTHER OF PROSTITUTES AND OF THE ABOMINATIONS OF THE E. *1178*
17: 8 of the e whose names have not been written *1178*
17:18 that rules over the kings *of* the e." *1178*
18: 1 and the e was illuminated by his splendor. *1178*
18: 3 The kings *of* the e committed adultery *1178*
18: 3 and the merchants *of* the e grew rich *1178*
18: 9 the kings *of* the e who committed adultery *1178*
18:11 *of* the e will weep and mourn over her *1178*
18:24 and of all who have been killed on the e." *1178*
19: 2 the great prostitute who corrupted the e *1178*
19:19 Then I saw the beast and the kings *of* the e *1178*
20: 8 the nations in the four corners *of* the e— *1178*
20: 9 across the breadth *of* the e and surrounded *1178*
20:11 E and sky fled from his presence, *1178*
21: 1 Then I saw a new heaven and a new e, *1178*
21: 1 first heaven and the first e had passed away, *1178*
21:24 the kings *of* the e will bring their splendor *1178*

EARTH'S (6) [EARTH]

Ge 27:28 of heaven's dew and of e richness— 824
27:39 be away from the e richness, 824
Job 38: 4 were you when I laid the e foundation? 824
Pr 3:19 By wisdom the LORD laid the e foundations, 824
Isa 24: 6 Therefore e inhabitants are burned up, 824
Rev 14:18 the clusters of grapes *from* the e vine, *1178*

EARTHEN (1) [EARTH, EARTHENWARE]

Hab 1:10 they build e **ramps** and capture them. 6760

EARTHENWARE (1) [EARTHEN]

Pr 26:23 over e are fervent lips with an evil heart. 3084

EARTHLY (15) [EARTH]

Jn 3:12 I have spoken to you of e **things** and you do *2103*
1Co 15:40 also heavenly bodies and there are e bodies; *2103*
15:40 and the splendor *of* the e bodies is another. *2103*
15:48 As was the e *man*, *5954*
15:49 as we have borne the likeness *of* the e *man*, *5954*
2Co 5: 1 that if the e tent we live in is destroyed, *2103*
Eph 4: 9 also descended to the lower, e regions? *1178*
6: 5 Slaves, obey your e masters with respect and fear, *2848+4922*
Php 3:19 Their mind is on e **things.** *2103*
Col 3: 2 not on e things. *1178*
3: 5 whatever belongs to your e nature: *1178*
3:22 Slaves, obey your e masters in everything; *2848+4922*
Heb 9: 1 for worship and also an e sanctuary. *3176*
Jas 3:15 not come down from heaven but is e, *2103*
1Pe 4: 2 the rest of his e life for evil human desires, *4922*

EARTHQUAKE (17) [QUAKE]

1Ki 19:11 After the wind there was an e, 8323
19:11 but the LORD was not in the e. 8323
19:12 After the e came a fire, 8323
Isa 29: 6 with thunder and e and great noise, 8323
Eze 38:19 that time there shall be a great e in the land 8323
Am 1: 1 concerning Israel two years before the e, 8323
Zec 14: 5 the e in the days of Uzziah king of Judah. 8323
Mt 27:54 the e and all that had happened, *4939*
28: 2 There was a violent e, *4939*
Ac 16:26 Suddenly there was such a violent e that *4939*
Rev 6:12 There was a great e. *4939*
8: 5 rumblings, flashes of lightning and an e. *4939*
11:13 a severe e and a tenth of the city collapsed. *4939*
11:13 Seven thousand people were killed in the e, *4939*
11:19 peals of thunder, an e and a great hailstorm. *4939*
16:18 rumblings, peals of thunder and a severe e. *4939*
16:18 No e like it has ever occurred *NIG*

EARTHQUAKES (3) [QUAKE]

Mt 24: 7 be famines and e in various places. *4939*
Mk 13: 8 There will be e in various places, *4939*
Lk 21:11 There will be great e, *4939*

EASE (9) [EASIER, EASILY, EASY]

Job 3:18 Captives also **enjoy** *their* e; 8631
7:13 and my couch *will* e my complaint, 5951
12: 5 *Men* **at** e have contempt for misfortune as 8633
Job 21:23 completely secure and **at** e, 8929
Pr 1:33 to me will live in safety and *be* **at** e, 8631
Jer 12: 1 Why *do* all the faithless **live at** e? 8922
49:31 "Arise and attack a nation **at** e, 8929
La 1: 5 her enemies *are* **at** e. 8922
Jnh 4: 6 for his head to e his discomfort, 5911

EASIER (7) [EASE]

Mt 9: 5 Which is e: to say, 'Your sins are forgiven,' *2324*
19:24 it is e for a camel to go through the eye of *2324*
Mk 2: 9 Which is e: to say to the paralytic, *2324*
10:25 It is e for a camel to go through the eye of *2324*
Lk 5:23 Which is e: to say, 'Your sins are forgiven,' *2324*
16:17 It is e for heaven and earth to disappear *2324*
18:25 it is e for a camel to go through the eye of *2324*

EASILY (10) [EASE]

Jdg 16: 9 he snapped the thongs **as** e **as** a piece 889+3869
20:43 chased them and e overran them in 4957
Pr 14: 6 but knowledge **comes** e to the discerning. 7837
22:24 do not associate with one e **angered,** 2779
Hos 7:11 e **deceived** and senseless— 7331
Ac 24:11 You can e verify that *NIG*
1Co 13: 5 it is not self-seeking, *it is* not e **angered,** *4236*
2Co 11: 4 you put up with it e enough. *2822*
2Th 2: 2 not to become e unsettled or alarmed *5441*
Heb 12: 1 and the sin that so e **entangles,** *2342*

EAST (188) [EASTERN, EASTWARD, NORTHEASTER, SOUTHEAST]

Ge 2: 8 LORD God had planted a garden in the e, 7710
2:14 it runs along the e *side of* Asshur. 7713
3:24 the e *side* of the Garden of Eden cherubim 7710
4:16 and lived in the land of Nod, e *of* Eden. 7713
12: 8 there he went on toward the hills e 4946+7710
12: 8 with Bethel on the west and Ai on the e. 7710
13:11 of the Jordan and set out toward the e. 7710
13:14 and look north and south, e and west. 2025+7711
25: 6 from his son Isaac to the land of the e. 7710
28:14 you will spread out to the west and to the e, 7711
41: 6 thin and scorched by the e **wind.** 7708
41:23 and thin and scorched by the e **wind.** 7708
41:27 of grain scorched by the e **wind:** 7708
Ex 10:13 an e wind blow across the land all that day 7708
14:21 a strong e wind and turned it into dry land. 7708
27:13 On the e end, toward the sunrise, 2025+7711
38:13 The e end, toward the sunrise, 2025+7711
Lev 1:16 with its contents and throw it to the e side 7711
Nu 2: 3 On the e, toward the sunrise, 7711
3:38 and his sons were to camp to the e *of* 7711
10: 5 the tribes camping on the e are to set out. 7711
32:19 to us on the e side of the Jordan." 4667
33: 7 to the e *of* Baal Zephon, 7156
34: 3 On the e, your southern boundary will start 7711
34:11 to Riblah on the e *side* of Ain and continue 7710
34:11 the slopes e of the Sea of Kinnereth. 2025+7711
34:15 on the e side of the Jordan of Jericho, 7711
35: 5 measure three thousand feet on the e side, 7711
Dt 1: 1 all Israel in the desert e *of* the Jordan— 928+6298
1: 5 E *of* the Jordan in the territory of Moab, 928+6298
3: 8 Amorites the territory e *of* the Jordan, 928+6298
3:27 look west and north and south and e. 2025+4667
4:41 Moses set aside three cities e *of* the Jordan, 928+2025+4667+6298+9087
4:46 were in the valley near Beth Peor e *of* 928+6298
4:47 the two Amorite kings e *of* the Jordan. 928+4667+6298+9087
4:49 and included all the Arabah e *of* the Jordan, 2025+4667+6298
Jos 1:14 that Moses gave you e *of* the Jordan, 928+6298
1:15 the servant of the LORD gave you e *of* 928+6298
2:10 the two kings of the Amorites e *of* 928+6298
7: 2 which is near Beth Aven to the e of Bethel, 7710
9:10 to the two kings of the Amorites e *of* 928+6298
11: 3 to the Canaanites in the e and west; 4667
11: 8 and to the Valley of Mizpah on the e, 4667
12: 1 over e *of* the Jordan, 2021+2025+4667+9087
13: 3 from the Shihor River on the e *of* Egypt to 7156
13: 5 and all Lebanon to the e, 2021+4667+9087
13: 8 the inheritance that Moses had given them e of the Jordan, 928+2025+4667+6298
13:27 of Sihon king of Heshbon (the e side of 4667
13:32 in the plains of Moab across the Jordan e of Jericho. 2025+4667
14: 3 the two-and-a-half tribes their inheritance e of the Jordan 4946+6298
16: 1 e of the waters of Jericho, 2025+4667
16: 5 in the e to Upper Beth Horon 4667
16: 6 passing by it to Janoah on the e. 4667
17: 5 of land besides Gilead and Bashan e of 4946+6298
17: 7 Asher to Micmethath e *of* Shechem. 6584+7156
17:10 on the north and Issachar on the e. 4667
18: 7 on the e side of the Jordan. 4667
19:12 It turned e from Sarid toward the sunrise to 2025+7711
19:27 turned e toward Beth Dagon, 2021+4667+9087
19:34 and the Jordan on the e. 4667+9087
20: 8 On the e side of the Jordan 2025+4667
24: 8 the Amorites who lived e *of* the Jordan. 928+6298
Jdg 8:11 the route of the nomads e of Nobah 4946+7710
10: 8 the Israelites on the e **side** *of* the Jordan 6298
20:43 in the vicinity of Gibeah on the e. 4667+9087
21:19 and e of the road that goes from Bethel 2021+2025+4667+9087
1Sa 13: 5 e *of* Beth Aven. 7713
15: 7 to the e *of* Egypt. 7156
1Ki 4:30 the wisdom of all the men of the E, 7710
7:25 three facing south and three facing e. 2025+4667
11: 7 On a hill e *of* Jerusalem, 6584+7156
17: 3 e *of* the Jordan. 6584+7156
17: 5 e *of* the Jordan, and stayed there. 6584+7156
2Ki 10:33 e of the Jordan in all the land of Gilead 2021+4667+9087
13:17 "Open the e window," he said, 2025+7711
23:13 high places that were e *of* Jerusalem 6584+7156
1Ch 4:39 the outskirts of Gedor to the e *of* the valley 4667
5: 9 the e they occupied the land up to the edge 4667
5:10 the Hagrites throughout the entire region e 4667
6:78 the Jordan e *of* Jericho they received Bezer 4667
7:28 Naaran to the e, 4667
9:18 being stationed at the King's Gate on the e, 4667
9:24 e, west, north and south. 4667
12:15 to the e and to the west. 4667
12:37 from e of the Jordan, men of Reuben, Gad 6298
26:14 The lot for the E Gate fell to Shelemiah. 4667
26:17 There were six Levites a day on the e, 4667
2Ch 4: 4 three facing south and three facing e. 2025+4667
5:12 stood on the e *side* of the altar, 4667
29: 4 assembled them in the square on the e *side* 4667
31:14 keeper of the E Gate, 2025+4667
Ne 3:26 toward the e and the projecting tower. 4667
3:29 the guard at the E Gate, made repairs. 4667
12:37 of David to the Water Gate *on* the e. 4667
Job 1: 3 among all the people of the E. 7710
15: 2 or fill his belly with the **hot** e **wind?** 7708
18:20 *men of the* e are seized with horror. 7719
23: 8 "But if I go to the e, he is not there; 7710
27:21 The e **wind** carries him off, and he is gone; 7708
38:24 or the place where the e **winds** are scattered 7708
Ps 48: 7 of Tarshish shattered by an e wind. 7708
75: 6 No one from the e or the west or from 4604
78:26 the e **wind** from the heavens and led forth 7708
103:12 as far as the e is from the west, 4667
107: 3 from e and west, from north and south. 4667
Isa 2: 6 They are full of superstitions from the E; 7710
9:12 Arameans from the e and Philistines from 7710
11:14 the people to the e. 7710
24:15 Therefore in the e give glory to the LORD; 241
27: 8 as on a day the e **wind** blows. 7708
41: 2 "Who has stirred up one from the e, 4667
43: 5 from the e and gather you from the west. 4667
46:11 From the e I summon a bird of prey; 4667
Jer 18:17 Like a wind from the e, 7708
31:40 the e as far as the corner of the Horse Gate, 4667
49:28 and destroy the people of the E. 7710
Eze 8:16 of the LORD and their faces toward the e, 7711
8:16 they were bowing down to the sun in the e. 7711
10:19 They stopped at the entrance to the e gate 7719
11: 1 of the house of the LORD that faces e. 2025+7708
11:23 and stopped above the mountain e 4946+7710
17:10 when the e wind strikes it— 7708
19:12 The e wind made it shrivel, 7708
25: 4 to the people of the E as a possession. 7710
25:10 with the Ammonites to the people of the E 7710
27:26 But the e wind will break you to pieces in 7708
39:11 in the valley of those who travel e *toward* 7713
40: 6 Then he went to the gate facing e. 2025+7708
40:10 the e gate were three alcoves on each side; 7708
40:19 a hundred cubits on the e *side* as well as on 7708
40:22 as those of the gate facing e. 7708
40:23 just as there was on the e. 7708
40:32 on the e side, and he measured the gateway; 7708
41:14 The width of the temple courtyard on the e, 7708
42: 9 on the e *side* as one enters them from 7708
42:15 the e gate and measured the area all around: 7708
42:16 the e side with the measuring rod; 7708
43: 1 the man brought me to the gate facing e, 7708
43: 2 of the God of Israel coming from the e. 7708
43: 4 the temple through the gate facing e. 7708
43:17 The steps of the altar face e." 7708
44: 1 the one facing e, and it was shut. 7708
45: 7 and eastward from the e side, 2025+7711
46: 1 of the inner court facing e is to be shut on 7708
46:12 the gate facing e is to be opened for him. 7708
47: 1 the threshold of the temple toward the e (for 7708
47: 1 toward the east (for the temple faced e). 7708
47: 2 the outside to the outer gate facing e, 7708
47:18 "On the e side the boundary will run 7708
47:18 This will be the e boundary. 2025+7708
48: 1 be part of its border from the e *side* to 7708
48: 2 it will border the territory of Dan from e 7708
48: 3 border the territory of Asher from e 2025+7708
48: 4 territory of Naphtali from e to west. 2025+7708
48: 5 territory of Manasseh from e to west. 2025+7708
48: 6 the territory of Ephraim from e to west. 7708
48: 7 it will border the territory of Reuben from e 7708
48: 8 the territory of Judah from e to west will be 7708
48: 8 its length from e to west will equal 2025+7708
48:10 10,000 cubits wide on the e *side* and 7708
48:16 the south side 4,500 cubits, the e side 4,500 7708
48:17 250 cubits on the e, 7708
48:18 cubits on the e *side* and 10,000 7708
48:23 from the e side to the west side. 2025+7708
48:24 territory of Benjamin from e to west. 2025+7708
48:25 border the territory of Simeon from e 2025+7708
48:26 territory of Issachar from e to west. 2025+7708
48:27 territory of Zebulun from e to west. 2025+7708
48:32 "On the e side, which is 4,500 cubits 2025+7708
Da 8: 9 and to the e and toward the Beautiful Land. 4667
11:44 from the e and the north will alarm him, 4667
Hos 12: 1 he pursues the e **wind** all day 7708

Hos 13:15 An e wind from the LORD will come, 7708
Am 8:12 from sea to sea and wander from north to e, 4667
Jnh 4: 5 Jonah went out and sat down at a place e of 7710
4: 8 God provided a scorching e wind, 7708
Zec 8: 7 from the countries of the e and the west. 4667
14: 4 Mount of Olives, e of Jerusalem 6584+7156+7710
14: 4 of Olives will be split in two from e 4667
Mt 2: 1 Magi from the e came to Jerusalem *424*
2: 2 in the e and have come to worship him." *424*
2: 9 in the e went ahead of them until it stopped *424*
8:11 I say to you that many will come from the e *424*
24:27 as lightning that comes from the e is visible *424*
Lk 13:29 from e and west and north and south, *424*
Rev 7: 2 another angel coming up from the e, *424+2463*
16:12 the way for the kings from the E. *424+2463*
21:13 There were three gates on the e, *424*

EASTER (KJV) PASSOVER

EASTERN (20) [EAST]

Ge 10:30 in the e hill country. 7710
29: 1 and came to the land of the e peoples. 7710
Nu 23: 7 the king of Moab from the e mountains. 7710
34:10 " 'For your e boundary, 2025+7711
Jos 4:19 and camped at Gilgal on the e border 4667
12: 1 including all the e *side of* the Arabah: 2025+4667
12: 3 e Arabah from the Sea of Kinnereth to 2025+4667
15: 5 The e boundary is the Salt Sea as far 2025+7711
18:20 the boundary on the e side. 2025+7711
Jdg 6: 3 and other e peoples invaded the country. 7710
6:33 and other e peoples joined forces 7710
7:12 the other e peoples had settled in the valley, 7710
8:10 that were left of the armies of the e peoples; 7710
11:18 the e side of the country of Moab, 4667+9087
Eze 45: 7 the western to the e border parallel to 2025+7708
47: 8 toward the e region and goes down into 7716
47:18 to the e sea and as far as Tamar. 7719
48:21 cubits of the sacred portion to the e border, NIH
Joel 2:20 with its front columns going into the e sea 7719
Zec 14: 8 half to the e sea and half to the western sea, 7719

EASTWARD (8) [EAST]

Ge 11: 2 As men moved **e,** 4946+7710
Jos 16: 6 north it curved e to Taanath Shiloh, 2025+4667
19:13 Then it continued e to Gath Hepher 2025+2025+4667+7711
1Ki 17: 3 turn e and hide in the Kerith Ravine, 2025+7711
Eze 42:12 to the corresponding wall extending **e,** 7708
45: 7 the west side and e from the east side, 2025+7708
47: 3 As the man went e with a measuring line 7708
48:21 It will **extend** e from the 25,000 2025+7708

EASY (5) [EASE]

Dt 1:41 **thinking it** e to go up into the hill country, 2103
2Ki 3:18 *an* e *thing* in the eyes of the LORD; 7837
5:20 "My master *was* **too** e **on** Naaman, 3104
Mt 11:30 For my yoke is e and my burden is light." *5982*
Lk 12:19 **Take life** e; eat, drink and be merry." ' *399*

EAT (514) [ATE, EATEN, EATER, EATING, EATS]

Ge 2:16 *"You are* **free to** e from any tree in 430+430
2:17 not e from the tree of the knowledge 430
2:17 for when you e of it you will surely die." 430
3: 1 not e from any tree in the garden'?" 430
3: 2 *"We may* e fruit from the trees in the garden, 430
3: 3 not e fruit from the tree that is in the middle 430
3: 5 when you e of it your eyes will be opened, 430
3:11 that I commanded you not *to* e from?" 430
3:14 on your belly and *you will* e dust all 430
3:17 *'You must* not e of it,' 430
3:17 through painful toil *you will* e *of* it all 430
3:18 and *you will* e the plants of the field. 430
3:19 of your brow *you will* e your food 430
3:22 and take also from the tree of life and e, 430
9: 4 not e meat that has its lifeblood still in it. 430
18: 5 Let me get you **something to e,** 4312+7326
24:33 not e until I have told you what I have 430
27: 4 of tasty food I like and bring it to me *to* e, 430
27: 7 and prepare me some tasty food *to* e, 430
27:10 Then take it to your father *to* e, 430
27:19 Please sit up and e some of my game so 430
27:25 bring me some of your game *to* e, 430
27:31 "My father, sit up and e some of my game, 430
28:20 and will give me food to e and clothes 430
32:32 the Israelites *do* not e the tendon attached to 430
37:25 As they sat down to e their meal, 430
40:19 And the birds *will* **e away** your flesh." 430
43:16 they *are to* e with me at noon." 430
43:25 they had heard that *they were to* e there. 430
43:32 because Egyptians could not e 430
Ex 2:20 Invite him *to have* something *to* **e."** 430
12: 4 with what each person *will* **e.** 430
12: 7 the doorframes of the houses where *they* e 430
12: 8 *to* e the meat roasted over the fire, 430
12: 9 *Do* not e the meat raw or cooked in water, 430
12:11 This is how *you are to* e it: 430
12:11 E it in haste; it is the LORD's Passover. 430
12:15 For seven days *you are to* e bread made 430
12:16 **prepare food** for everyone **to e—** 430
12:18 In the first month *you are to* e bread made 430
12:20 E nothing made with yeast. 430
Ex 12:20 *you must* e unleavened bread." 430
12:43 "No foreigner *is to* e of it. 430
12:44 Any slave you have bought *may* e of it 430
12:45 and a hired worker *may* not e of it. 430
12:48 No uncircumcised male *may* e of it. 430
13: 3 E nothing containing yeast. 430
13: 6 For seven days e bread made without yeast 430
13: 7 E unleavened bread during those 430
16: 8 when he gives you meat to e in the evening 430
16:12 Tell them, 'At twilight *you will* e meat, 430
16:15 the bread the LORD has given you to **e.** 433
16:25 **"E** it today," Moses said, 430
16:32 so they can see the bread *I* **gave** you **to e** 430
18:12 to e bread with Moses' father-in-law in 430
22:31 So *do* not e the meat of an animal torn 430
23:11 and the wild animals *may* e what they leave. 430
23:15 for seven days e bread made without yeast, 430
29:32 and his sons *are to* e the meat of the ram 430
29:33 *They are to* e these offerings 430
29:33 But no *one* else *may* e them, 430
32: 6 down to e and drink and got up to indulge 430
34:15 and *you will* e their sacrifices. 430
34:18 For seven days e bread made without yeast, 430
Lev 3:17 *You must* not e any fat or any blood.' " 430
6:16 Aaron and his sons *shall* e the rest of it, 430
6:16 *they are to* e it in the courtyard of the Tent 430
6:18 Any male descendant of Aaron *may* e it. 430
6:26 The priest who offers it *shall* e it; 430
6:29 Any male in a priest's family *may* e it; 430
7: 6 Any male in a priest's family *may* e it, 430
7:19 anyone ceremonially clean *may* e it. 430
7:23 *'Do* not e any of the fat of cattle, 430
7:24 but *you* **must** not e it. 430+430
7:26 *you must* not e the blood of any bird 430
8:31 and e it there with the bread from the basket 430
8:31 saying, 'Aaron and his sons *are to* e it.' 430
10:12 to the LORD by fire and e it prepared 430
10:13 E it in a holy place, 430
10:14 and your sons and your daughters *may* e 430
10:14 E them in a ceremonially clean place; NIH
10:17 "Why didn't *you* e the sin offering in 430
11: 2 these are the ones *you may* **e:** 430
11: 3 *You may* e any animal that has 430
11: 4 but *you must* not e them. 430
11: 8 not e their meat or touch their carcasses; 430
11: 9 *you may* e any that have fins and scales. 430
11:11 *you must* not e their meat 430
11:13 and not e because they are detestable: 430
11:21 that walk on all fours that *you may* **e:** 430
11:22 Of these *you may* e any kind of locust, 430
11:39 an animal that you are allowed to e dies, 433
11:42 not *to* e any creature that moves about on 430
17:12 "None of you *may* e blood, 430
17:12 nor *may* an alien living among you e blood." 430
17:14 *"You must* not e the blood of any creature, 430
19:25 But in the fifth year *you may* e its fruit. 430
19:26 " *'Do* not e any meat with the blood still 430
21:22 *He may* e the most holy food of his God, 430
22: 4 *he may* not e the sacred offerings 430
22: 6 *He must* not e any of the sacred offerings 430
22: 7 and after that *he may* e the sacred offerings, 430
22: 8 *He must* not e anything found dead or torn 430
22:10 a priest's family *may* e the sacred offering, 430
22:10 the guest of a priest or his hired worker e it. 430
22:11 that slave *may* e his food. 430
22:12 not e any of the sacred contributions. 430
22:13 *she may* e of her father's food. 430
22:13 however, *may* e any of it. 430
22:16 by *allowing* them *to* e the sacred offerings 430
23: 6 for seven days *you must* e bread made 430
23:14 *You must* not e any bread, 430
24: 9 *who are to* e it in a holy place, 430
25:12 e only what is taken directly from 430
25:19 and *you will* e your fill and live there 430
25:20 "What *will we* e in the seventh year 430
25:22 *you will* e from the old crop 430
25:22 from the old crop and *will continue to* e 430
26: 5 and *you will* e all the food you want 430
26:16 because your enemies *will* e it. 430
26:26 *You will* e, but you will not be satisfied. 430
26:29 *You will* e the flesh of your sons and 430
Nu 6: 3 not drink grape juice or e grapes or raisins, 430
6: 4 *he must* not e anything that comes from 430
9:11 *They are to* e the lamb, 430
11: 4 "If only we **had** meat **to e!** 430
11:13 'Give us meat *to* **e!'** 430
11:18 when *you will* e meat. 430
11:18 "If only we **had** meat **to e!** 430
11:18 and *you will* e it. 430
11:19 *You will* not e it for just one day, 430
11:21 'I will give them meat *to* e for 430
15:19 and you e the food of the land, 430
18:10 E it as something most holy; 430
18:10 every male *shall* e it. 430
18:11 who is ceremonially clean *may* e it. 430
18:13 who is ceremonially clean *may* e it. 430
18:31 You and your households *may* e the rest 430
28:17 for seven days e bread made without yeast. 430
Dt 2: 6 to pay them in silver for the food *you* e and 430
2:28 *to* e and water to drink for their price 430
4:28 which cannot see or hear or e or smell. 430
6:11 then when *you* e and are satisfied, 430
8:12 Otherwise, when *you* e and are satisfied, 430
8:16 He **gave** you manna **to** e in the desert, 430
11:15 and *you will* e and be satisfied. 430
12: 7 and your families *shall* e and shall rejoice 430
12:15 of your towns and e as much of the meat 430
Dt 12:15 ceremonially unclean and the clean *may* e it. 430
12:16 But *you must* not e the blood; 430
12:17 You must not e in your own towns the tithe 430
12:18 *you are to* e them in the presence of 430
12:20 then *you may* e as much of it as you want. 430
12:21 and in your own towns *you may* e as much 430
12:22 E them as you would gazelle or deer. 430
12:22 ceremonially unclean and the clean *may* **e.** 430
12:23 But be sure you *do* not e the blood, 430
12:23 and *you must* not e the life with the meat. 430
12:24 *You must* not e the blood; 430
12:25 *Do* not e it, so that it may go well with you 430
12:27 but *you may* e the meat. 430
14: 3 *Do* not e any detestable thing. 430
14: 4 These are the animals *you may* **e:** 430
14: 6 *You may* e any animal that has 430
14: 7 not e the camel, 430
14: 8 not *to* e their meat or touch their carcasses. 430
14: 9 *you may* e any that has fins and scales. 430
14:10 not have fins and scales *you may* not **e;** 430
14:11 *You may* e any clean bird. 430
14:12 But these *you may* not **e:** 430
14:19 *do* not e *them.* 430
14:20 that is clean *you may* **e.** 430
14:21 *Do* not e anything you find already dead. 430
14:21 and *he may* e it, 430
14:23 E the tithe of your grain, new wine and oil, 430
14:26 Then you and your household *shall* e there 430
14:29 in your towns may come and e and 430
15:20 and your family *are to* e them in 430
15:22 *You are to* e it in your own towns. 430
15:22 and the clean may e it, NIH
15:23 But *you must* not e the blood; 430
16: 3 *Do* not e it with bread made with yeast, 430
16: 3 but for seven days e unleavened bread, 430
16: 7 Roast it and e it at the place 430
16: 8 For six days e unleavened bread and on 430
20:19 because *you can* e their fruit. 430
23:24 *you may* e all the grapes you want, 430
26:12 *they may* e in your towns and be satisfied. 430
28:31 but *you will* e none of it. 430
28:33 not know *will* e what your land 430
28:39 because worms *will* e them. 430
28:53 *you will* e the fruit of the womb, 430
28:57 For *she intends to* e them secretly during 430
31:20 and when *they* e their fill and thrive, 430
Jos 24:13 and you live in them and e *from* vineyards 430
Jdg 13: 4 and that *you do* not e anything unclean, 430
13: 7 and *do* not e anything unclean, 430
13:14 *She must* not e anything that comes from 430
13:14 nor e anything unclean. 430
13:16 *I will* not e any of your food. 430
14:14 "Out of the eater, **something to e;** 4407
19: 5 Refresh yourself with **something to e;** 4312+7326
19: 6 of them sat down *to* e and drink together, 430
19:21 *they had something to* e and drink. 430
1Sa 1: 7 till she wept and *would* not **e.** 430
1: 8 Why don't *you* **e?** 430
2:36 so *I can have* food *to* **e." ' "** 430
9:13 before he goes up to the high place to **e.** 430
9:13 afterward, those who are invited *will* **e.** 430
9:19 for today *you are to* e with me, 430
9:24 **E,** because it was set aside for you 430
14:34 and slaughter them here and e them. 430
20:24 the king sat down to **e.** 430
20:34 that second day of the month *he did* not **e,** 430
28:22 so *you may* e and have the strength to go 430
28:23 He refused and said, *"I will* not **e."** 430
30:11 They gave him water to drink and food *to* e 430
2Sa 3:35 and **urged** David **to** e something 1356
9: 7 and you *will* always e at my table." 430
9:10 *will* always e at my table." 430
11:11 How could I go to my house to e and drink 430
12:17 and *he would* not e any food with them. 1356
12:21 you get up and **e!"** 430
13: 5 **give** me something **to e.** 1356
13: 5 in my sight so I may watch her and then e it 430
13: 6 so *I may* e from her hand." 1356
13: 9 but he refused to **e.** 430
13:10 the food here into my bedroom so *I may* e 1356
13:11 But when she took it to him to e, 430
16: 2 the bread and fruit are for the men to e, 430
17:29 for David and his people to e. 430
1Ki 2: 7 be among *those who* e *at* your table. 430
13: 7 with me and **have something to e,** 6184
13: 8 nor *would I* e bread or drink water here. 430
13: 9 not e bread or drink water or return by 430
13:15 "Come home with me and **e."** 430
13:16 nor *can I* e bread or drink water with you 430
13:17 not e bread or drink water there or return by 430
13:18 so that *he may* e bread and drink water.' " 430
13:22 in the place where he told you not *to* e 430
14:11 Dogs *will* e those belonging to Jeroboam 430
16: 4 Dogs *will* e those belonging to Baasha 430
17:12 that *we may* e it—and die." 430
18:19 *who* e *at* Jezebel's table." 430
18:41 And Elijah said to Ahab, "Go, e and drink, 430
18:42 So Ahab went off to e and drink, 430
19: 5 "Get up and **e."** 430
19: 7 "Get up and **e,** 430
21: 4 He lay on his bed sulking and refused *to* **e.** 430
21: 5 Why won't you **e?"** 430
21: 7 Get up and **e!** 430
21:24 "Dogs *will* e those belonging to Ahab 430
2Ki 4: 8 he stopped there to **e.** 430
4:40 but as they *began to* e it, they cried out, 430
4:40 And they could not e it. 430

2Ki 4:41 "Serve it to the people *to* **e.**" 430
4:42 "Give it to the people *to* **e,**" Elisha said. 430
4:43 "Give it to the people *to* **e.** 430
4:43 'They *will* **e** and have some left over.' " 430
6:22 that *they may* **e** and drink and then go back 430
6:28 'Give up your son so *we may* **e** him today, 430
6:28 and tomorrow *we'll* **e** my son.' 430
6:29 'Give up your son so *we may* **e** him,' 430
7: 2 "but *you will* not **e** any of it!" 430
7:19 but *you will* not **e** any of it!" 430
18:27 like you, *will have to* **e** their own filth 430
18:31 of you *will* **e** *from* his own vine 430
19:29 "This year you *will* **e** what grows by itself, 430
19:29 plant vineyards and **e** their fruit. 430
25: 3 that there was no food for the people to **e.** NIH
2Ch 31:10 we have had enough *to* **e** and plenty 430
Ezr 2:63 The governor ordered them not *to* **e** any of 430
9:12 be strong and **e** the good things of the land 430
Ne 5: 2 in order for *us to* **e** and stay alive, 430
7:65 not *to* **e** any of the most sacred food 430
8:12 all the people went away to **e** and drink, 430
9:36 so they *could* **e** its fruit and 430
Est 4:16 *Do* not **e** or drink for three days, 430
Job 1: 4 and they would invite their three sisters to **e** 430
27:14 his offspring will never have enough to **e.** 4312
31: 8 then *may* others **e** what I have sown, 430
Ps 14: 4 those who devour my people as *men* **e** bread 430
22:26 The poor *will* **e** and be satisfied; 430
50:13 *Do I* **e** the flesh of bulls or drink the blood 430
53: 4 those who devour my people as *men* **e** bread 430
78:24 he rained down manna for the people to **e,** 430
78:25 **all** the food they **could e.** 8427
102: 4 I forget *to* **e** my food. 430
102: 9 For *I* **e** ashes as my food 430
127: 2 toiling for food *to* **e—** 430
128: 2 *You will* **e** the fruit of your labor; 430
141: 4 *let me* not **e** of their delicacies. 4310
Pr 1:31 *they will* **e** the fruit of their ways and 430
4:17 *They* **e** the bread of wickedness and drink 4310
9: 5 **e** my food and drink the wine I have mixed. 4310
13:25 The righteous **e** to their hearts' content, 430
18:21 and those who love it *will* **e** its fruit. 430
23: 6 *Do* not **e** the food of a stingy man, 4310
23: 7 **"E** and drink," he says to you, 430
24:13 **E** honey, my son, for it is good; 430
25:16 If you find honey, **e** just enough— 430
25:21 **give** him food **to e;** 430
25:27 It is not good *to* **e** too much honey, 430
27:18 He who tends a fig tree *will* **e** its fruit, 430
31:27 the affairs of her household and *does* not **e** 430
Ecc 2:24 A man can do nothing better than *to* **e** 430
2:25 who *can* **e** or find enjoyment? 430
3:13 That everyone *may* **e** and drink, 430
5:18 and proper for a man to **e** and drink, and 430
8:15 a man under the sun than to **e** and drink and 430
9: 7 Go, **e** your food with gladness, 430
10:17 and whose princes **e** at a proper time— 430
SS 5: 1 **E,** O friends, and drink; 430
Isa 1:19 *you will* **e** the best from the land; 430
4: 1 *"We will* **e** our own food 430
7:15 *He will* **e** curds and honey 430
7:22 *he will have* curds *to* **e.** 430
7:22 All who remain in the land *will* **e** curds 430
9:20 on the left *they will* **e,** but not be satisfied. 430
11: 7 and the lion *will* **e** straw like the ox. 430
21: 5 they spread the rugs, they **e,** they drink! 430
22:13 *"Let* us **e** and drink," you say, 430
30:24 that work the soil *will* **e** fodder and mash, 430
36:12 like you, *will have to* **e** their own filth 430
36:16 of you *will* **e** *from* his own vine 430
37:30 "This year you *will* **e** what grows by itself, 430
37:30 plant vineyards and **e** their fruit. 430
49:26 **make** your oppressors **e** their own flesh; 430
50: 9 the moths *will* **e** them **up.** 430
51: 8 the moth *will* **e** them **up** like a garment; 430
55: 1 you who have no money, come, buy and **e!** 430
55: 2 Listen, listen to me, and **e** what is good, 430
62: 9 but those who harvest it *will* **e** it and praise 430
65: 4 who **e** the flesh of pigs, 430
65:13 "My servants *will* **e,** 430
65:21 they will plant vineyards and **e** their fruit. 430
65:22 or plant and others **e.** 430
65:25 and the lion *will* **e** straw like the ox, 430
66:17 the one in the midst of *those who* **e** the flesh 430
Jer 2: 7 I brought you into a fertile land to **e** its fruit 430
7:21 to your other sacrifices and **e** 430
9:15 **make** this people **e** bitter **food** 430
16: 8 where there is feasting and sit down to **e** 430
19: 9 *I will* **make** them **e** the flesh of their sons 430
19: 9 and *they will* **e** one another's flesh during 430
23:15 **make** them **e** bitter **food** 430
29: 5 plant gardens and **e** what they produce. 430
29:28 plant gardens and **e** what they produce.' " 430
52: 6 that there was no food for the people to **e.** NIH
La 2:20 *Should* women **e** their offspring, 430
Eze 2: 8 open your mouth and **e** what I give you." 430
3: 1 **e** what is before you, eat this scroll; 430
3: 1 eat what is before you, **e** this scroll; 430
3: 2 **gave** me the scroll **to e.** 430
3: 3 **e** this scroll I am giving you 430
4: 9 *You are to* **e** it during the 390 days you lie 430
4:10 of food *to* **e** each day and eat it at set times. 430
4:10 of food to eat each day and **e** it at set times. 430
4:12 **E** the food as you would a barley cake; 430
4:13 the people of Israel *will* **e** defiled food 430
4:16 *The people will* **e** rationed food in anxiety 430
5:10 in your midst fathers *will* **e** their children, 430
Eze 5:10 and children *will* **e** their fathers. 430
12:18 tremble *as you* **e** your food, 430
12:19 *They will* **e** their food in anxiety 430
16:19 olive oil and honey *I* **gave** you **to e—** 430
18: 2 " 'The fathers **e** sour grapes, 430
18: 6 not **e** at the mountain shrines or look to 430
18:15 not **e** at the mountain shrines or look to 430
22: 9 in you are *those who* **e** at 430
24:17 do not cover the lower part of your face or **e** 430
24:22 not cover the lower part of your face or **e** 430
25: 4 they *will* **e** your fruit and drink your milk. 430
33:25 Since *you* **e** meat with the blood still in it 430
34: 3 *You* **e** the curds, 430
39:17 *There you will* **e** flesh and drink blood. 430
39:18 *You will* **e** the flesh of mighty men 430
39:19 *you will* **e** fat till you are glutted 430
39:20 At my table *you will* **e** *your* **fill** 8425
42:13 the LORD *will* **e** the most holy offerings. 430
44: 3 inside the gateway to **e** in the presence of 430
44:29 They *will* **e** the grain offerings, 430
44:31 The priests *must* not **e** anything, 430
45:21 during which you *shall* **e** bread made 430
Da 1:12 but vegetables *to* **e** and water to drink. 430
1:13 that of the young men who **e** the royal food, 430
4:25 you *will* **e** grass like cattle and 10301
4:32 you *will* **e** grass like cattle. 10301
7: 5 It was told, 'Get up and **e** your fill of flesh!' 10030
11:26 *Those who* **e** *from* 430
Hos 4:10 *"They will* **e** but not have enough; 430
8:13 They offer sacrifices given to me and *they* **e** 430
9: 3 to Egypt and **e** unclean food in Assyria. 430
9: 4 all *who* **e** them will be unclean. 430
Joel 2:26 *You will* **have plenty to e,** 430+430
Am 9:14 they will make gardens and **e** their fruit. 430
Ob 1: 7 those who **e** your bread will set a trap NIH
Jnh 3: 7 *do* not *let them* **e** or drink. 8286
Mic 3: 3 who **e** my people's flesh, strip off their skin 430
6:14 You *will* **e** but not be satisfied; 430
7: 1 there is no cluster of grapes to **e,** 430
Zep 3:13 They *will* **e** and lie down 8286
Hag 1: 6 *You* **e,** but never have enough. 430
Zec 11: 9 *Let* those who are left **e** one another's flesh. 430
11:16 but *will* **e** the meat of the choice sheep, 430
Mt 6:25 what *you will* **e** or drink; *2266*
6:31 do not worry, saying, 'What *shall we* **e?'** *2266*
9:11 "Why *does* your teacher **e** *2266*
12: 1 *to* pick some heads of grain and **e** them. *2266*
14:16 You give them something *to* **e."** *2266*
15: 2 They don't wash their hands before *they* **e!"** *2266*
15:27 "but even the dogs **e** the crumbs that fall *2266*
15:32 with me three days and have nothing *to* **e.** *2266*
24:49 to beat his fellow servants and *to* **e** *2266*
25:35 and you gave me something *to* **e,** *2266*
25:42 and you gave me nothing *to* **e,** *2266*
26:17 to make preparations for you *to* **e** *2266*
26:26 saying, "Take and **e;** this is my body." *2266*
Mk 2:16 "Why *does he* **e** with tax collectors *2266*
2:26 which is lawful only for priests *to* **e.** *2266*
3:20 and his disciples were not even able *to* **e.** *2266*
5:43 and told them to give her something *to* **e.** *2266*
6:31 that they did not even have a chance *to* **e,** *2266*
6:36 and buy themselves something *to* **e."** *2266*
6:37 "You give them something *to* **e."** *2266*
6:37 on bread and give it to them *to* **e?"** *2266*
7: 3 (The Pharisees and all the Jews *do* not **e** *2266*
7: 4 from the marketplace *they do* not **e** *2266*
7:27 "First let the children **e all they want,"** *5963*
7:28 under the table **e** the children's crumbs." *2266*
8: 1 Since they had nothing *to* **e,** *2266*
8: 2 with me three days and have nothing *to* **e.** *2266*
11:14 *"May* no one ever **e** fruit from you again." *2266*
14:12 to go and make preparations for *you to* **e** *2266*
14:14 *I may* **e** the Passover with my disciples?' *2266*
Lk 5:30 "Why *do you* **e** and drink *2266*
6: 1 rub them in their hands and **e** the kernels. *2266*
6: 4 he ate what is lawful only for priests *to* **e.** *2266*
8:55 Jesus told them to give her something *to* **e.** *2266*
9:13 "You give them something *to* **e."** *2266*
10: 8 **e** what is set before you. *2266*
11:37 a Pharisee invited him *to* **e** with him; *753*
12:19 Take life easy; **e,** drink and be merry." ' *2266*
12:22 about your life, what *you will* **e;** *2266*
12:29 not set your heart on what *you will* **e** *2266*
12:45 the menservants and maidservants and *to* **e** *2266*
14: 1 *to* **e** in the house of a prominent Pharisee, *2266*
14:15 "Blessed is the man who *will* **e** at the feast *2266*
16:21 *to* **e** what fell from the rich man's table. *5963*
17: 7 'Come along now and **sit down to e'?** *404*
17: 8 and wait on me while *I* **e** and drink; *2266*
17: 8 after that you *may* **e** and drink'? *2266*
22: 8 "Go and make preparations for us to **e** *2266*
22:11 *I may* **e** the Passover with my disciples?' *2266*
22:15 *to* **e** this Passover with you before I suffer. *2266*
22:16 not **e** it again until it finds fulfillment in *2266*
22:30 so that *you may* **e** and drink at my table *2266*
24:41 "Do you have anything here **to e?"** *1110*
Jn 4:31 "Rabbi, **e** something." *2266*
4:32 *to* **e** that you know nothing about." *2266*
6: 5 shall we buy bread for these people *to* **e?"** *2266*
6:12 When they had all had enough to **e,** *NIG*
6:31 'He gave them bread from heaven *to* **e.' "** *2266*
6:50 which a man *may* **e** and not die. *2266*
6:52 "How can this man give us his flesh *to* **e?"** *2266*
6:53 unless *you* **e** the flesh of the Son of Man *2266*
18:28 *they wanted to be able to* **e** the Passover. *2266*
Ac 9: 9 and *did* not **e** or drink anything. *2266*
10:10 and wanted something *to* **e,** *1174*
Ac 10:13 "Get up, Peter. Kill and **e."** *2266*
11: 7 'Get up, Peter. Kill and **e.'** *2266*
23:12 and bound themselves with an oath not *to* **e** *2266*
23:14 not *to* **e** anything until we have killed Paul. *1174*
23:21 not *to* **e** or drink until they have killed him. *2266*
27:33 before dawn Paul urged them all *to* **e.** *3561+5575*
27:35 Then he broke it and began *to* **e.** *2266*
Ro 14: 2 One man's faith allows him *to* **e** everything, *2266*
14: 3 the man who *does* not **e** everything must *2266*
14:15 because of **what** *you* **e,** *1109*
14:20 *to* **e** anything that causes someone else *2266*
14:21 It is better not *to* **e** meat or drink wine or *2266*
1Co 5:11 **With** such a man *do* not even **e.** *5303*
8: 7 that when *they* **e** such food they think of it *2266*
8: 8 we are no worse if *we do* not **e,** *2266*
8:10 *to* **e** what has been sacrificed to idols? *2266*
8:13 if **what** I **e** causes my brother to fall into sin, *1109*
8:13 *I will* never **e** meat again, *2266*
9: 7 a vineyard and *does* not **e** of its grapes? *2266*
10: 7 down *to* **e** and drink and got up to indulge *2266*
10:18 not those who **e** the sacrifices participate in *2266*
10:25 **E** anything sold in the meat market *2266*
10:27 **e** whatever is put before you *2266*
10:28 then *do* not **e** it, *2266*
10:31 whether *you* **e** or drink or whatever you do, *2266*
11:20 it is not the Lord's Supper *you* **e,** *2266*
11:21 for as *you* **e,** *2266*
11:22 Don't you have homes to **e** and drink in? *2266*
11:26 For whenever *you* **e** this bread *2266*
11:33 my brothers, when you come together to **e,** *2266*
11:34 If anyone is hungry, *he should* **e** at home, *2266*
15:32 dead are not raised, *"Let us* **e** and drink, *2266*
Gal 2:12 *he used to* **e** with the Gentiles. *5303*
Col 2:16 not let anyone judge you by what you **e** *1111*
2Th 3: 8 nor *did we* **e** anyone's food without paying *2266*
3:10 "If a man will not work, *he shall* not **e."** *2266*
3:12 to settle down and earn the bread they **e.** *2266*
Heb 13: 9 which are of no value to those who **e** them. *4344*
13:10 at the tabernacle have no right *to* **e.** *2266*
Jas 5: 3 against you and **e** your flesh like fire. *2266*
Rev 2: 7 I will give the right *to* **e** from the tree *2266*
3:20 I will come in and **e** with him, *1268*
10: 9 He said to me, "Take it and **e** it. *2983*
17:16 *they will* **e** her flesh and burn her with fire. *2266*
19:18 so that *you may* **e** the flesh of kings, *2266*

EATEN (66) [EAT]

Ge 3:11 *Have you* **e** from the tree 430
6:21 to take every kind of food that *is to* **be e** 430
14:24 but what my men *have* **e** and the share 430
31:38 nor *have I* **e** rams from your flocks. 430
31:54 After *they had* **e,** they spent the night there. 430
43: 2 So when *they had* **e** all 430
Ex 12:46 *"It must* **be e** inside one house; 430
21:28 and its meat *must* not **be e.** 430
29:34 *It must* not **be e,** because it is sacred. 430
Lev 6:16 *it is to* **be e** without yeast in a holy place; 430
6:23 *it must* not **be e."** 430
6:26 *it is to* **be e** in a holy place, 430
6:30 in the Holy Place *must* not **be e;** 430
7: 6 but *it must* **be e** in a holy place; 430
7:15 of thanksgiving *must* **be e** on 430
7:16 sacrifice *shall* **be e** on the day he offers it, 430
7:16 but anything left over *may* **be e** on 430
7:18 If any meat of the fellowship offering *is* **e** 430+430
7:19 that touches anything ceremonially unclean *must* not **be e;** 430
10:18 *you should have* **e** the goat in 430+430
10:19 the LORD have been pleased if *I had* **e** 430
11:34 Any food that *could* **be e** but has water on it 430
11:41 it *is* not *to* **be e.** 430
11:47 between living creatures that *may* **be e** 430
11:47 be eaten and those that *may* not **be e.' "** 430
17:13 that *may* **be e** must drain out the blood 430
19: 6 *It shall* **be e** on the day you sacrifice it or 430
19: 7 If *any of it* **is e** on the third day, 430+430
19:23 *it must* not **be e.** 430
22:30 *It must* **be e** that same day; 430
25: 7 Whatever the land produces may be **e.** 430
Nu 12:12 with its flesh half **e away."** 430
Dt 8:10 When *you have* **e** and are satisfied, 430
26:14 not **e** any of the sacred portion while I was 430
Ru 2:18 over after she *had* **e enough.** 8425
1Sa 14:30 if the men *had* **e** today some of 430+430
28:20 for *he had* **e** nothing all that day and night. 430
30:12 for *he had* not **e** any food or drunk any water 430
2Sa 19:42 **e** any of the king's **provisions?** 430+430
1Ki 13:28 The lion *had* neither **e** the body nor mauled 430
Job 6: 6 **Is** tasteless food **e** without salt, 430
13:28 like a garment **e** *by* moths. 430
Pr 9:17 food **e** in secret is delicious!" NIH
23: 8 You will vomit up the little *you have* **e** 430
30:17 *will be* **e** *by* the vultures. 430
SS 5: 1 *I have* **e** my honeycomb and my honey; 430
Jer 24: 2 so bad *they could* not **be e.** 430
24: 3 the poor ones are so bad *they* cannot **be e."** 430
24: 8 which are so bad *they* cannot **be e,'** 430
29:17 that are so bad *they* cannot **be e.** 430
31:29 'The fathers *have* **e** sour grapes, 430
Eze 4:14 now *I have* never **e** anything found dead 430
Hos 10:13 *you have* **e** the fruit of deception. 430
Joel 1: 4 the great locusts *have* **e;** 430
1: 4 the young locusts *have* **e;** 430
1: 4 young locusts have left other locusts *have* **e.** 430
2:25 for the years the locusts *have* **e—** 430

Mk 6:44 of the men who *had* **e** was five thousand. *2266*
Jn 6:13 over *by* those who *had* **e.** *1048*
6:23 the place where the people *had* **e** the bread *2266*
Ac 10:14 *"I have* never **e** anything impure *2266*
12:23 and he was **e by worms** and died. *5037*
27:33 *you* haven't **e** anything. *4689*
27:38 **e as much as** *they* **wanted,** *3170*
Jas 5:2 and **moths have e** your clothes. *1181+4963*
Rev 10:10 but when *I had* **e** it, *2266*

EATER (3) [EAT]

Jdg 14:14 He replied, "Out of the **e,** something to eat; 430
Isa 55:10 for the sower and bread for the **e,** 430
Na 3:12 the figs fall into the mouth of the **e.** 430

EATING (56) [EAT]

Ge 40:17 but the birds *were* **e** them out of the basket 430
Ex 34:28 without **e** bread or drinking water. 430
Lev 26:10 *be* **e** last year's harvest when you will have 430
Dt 27:7 **e** them and rejoicing in the presence of 430
28:55 of the flesh of his children that *he is* **e.** 430
Jdg 9:27 While *they were* **e** and drinking, 430
19:4 **e** and drinking, and sleeping there. 430
Ru 3:3 until he has finished **e** and drinking. 430
3:7 When Boaz *had finished* **e** and drinking 430
1Sa 1:9 Once when *they had* finished **e** and drinking 430
9:13 The people *will* not *begin* **e** 430
14:33 against the LORD by **e** meat that has blood 430
14:34 Do not sin against the LORD by **e** meat 430
30:16 scattered over the countryside, **e,** 430
1Ki 1:25 Right now they *are* **e** and drinking with him 430
13:23 When the man of God had finished **e** 430
2Ki 6:23 and after *they had finished* **e** and drinking, 430
1Ch 12:39 with David, **e** and drinking, 430
Isa 22:13 **e** *of* meat and drinking of wine! 430
29:8 as when a hungry man dreams that *he is* **e,** 430
Jer 41:1 While *they were* **e** together there, 430
Da 6:18 to his palace and spent the night **without e** 10297
Zec 7:6 And when *you were* **e** and drinking, 430
Mt 11:18 For John came neither **e** nor drinking, *2266*
11:19 The Son of Man came **e** and drinking, *2266*
15:20 but **e** with unwashed hands does *2266*
24:38 people were **e** and drinking, *5592*
26:21 And *while* they *were* **e,** he said, *2266*
26:26 *While* they were **e,** Jesus took bread, *2266*
Mk 2:15 and "sinners" *were* **e with** him *5263*
2:16 the law who were Pharisees saw *him* **e** with *2266*
7:2 saw some of his disciples **e** food with hands *2266*
7:5 of **e** their food with 'unclean' hands?" *2266*
14:18 *While* they were reclining at the table **e,** *2266*
14:18 one who *is* **e** with me." *2266*
14:22 *While* they were **e,** Jesus took bread, *2266*
16:14 to the Eleven *as they were* **e;** *367*
Lk 5:29 of tax collectors and others were **e** *2879*
5:33 but yours *go on* **e** and drinking." *2266*
7:33 For John the Baptist came neither **e** bread *2266*
7:34 The Son of Man came **e** and drinking, *2266*
7:37 that Jesus *was* **e** at the Pharisee's house, *2879*
10:7 **e** and drinking whatever they give you, *2266*
15:16 with the pods that the pigs *were* **e,** *2266*
17:27 *People were* **e,** drinking, *2266*
17:28 *People were* **e** and drinking, *2266*
Jn 21:15 When *they had finished* **e,** *753*
Ac 1:4 On one occasion, *while he was* **e** with them, *5259*
Ro 14:15 Do not *by* your **e** destroy your brother *1109*
14:17 For the kingdom of God is not a matter of **e** *1111*
14:23 because his **e** is not from faith; *NIG*
1Co 8:4 So then, about **e** food sacrificed to idols: *NIG*
8:10 weak conscience sees you who have this knowledge **e** in an idol's temple, *2879*
Jude 1:12 **e with** you without the slightest qualm— *5307*
Rev 2:14 the Israelites to sin by **e** food sacrificed *2266*
2:20 and the **e of** food sacrificed to idols. *2266*

EATS (41) [EAT]

Ex 12:15 for whoever **e** anything with yeast in it 430
12:19 And whoever **e** anything with yeast 430
Lev 7:18 the person who **e** any of it will 430
7:20 But if anyone who is unclean **e** any meat of 430
7:21 and then **e** any of the meat of 430
7:25 Anyone *who* **e** the fat of an animal 430
7:27 If anyone **e** blood, 430
11:40 Anyone *who* **e** some of 430
14:47 or **e** in the house must wash his clothes. 430
17:10 among them who **e** any blood— 430
17:10 against that person who **e** blood 430
17:14 anyone *who* **e** it must be cut off." 430
17:15 who **e** anything found dead or torn 430
19:8 *Whoever* **e** it will be held responsible 430
22:14 " 'If anyone **e** a sacred offering by mistake, 430
1Sa 14:24 "Cursed be any man who **e** food before 430
14:28 'Cursed be any man who **e** food today!' 430
2Sa 19:35 Can your servant taste what *he* **e** 430
Job 18:13 *It* **e away** parts of his skin; 430
39:24 In frenzied excitement *he* **e up** the ground; 1686
Ps 106:20 for an image of a bull, *which* **e** grass. 430
Pr 30:20 *She* **e** and wipes her mouth and says, 430
Ecc 5:12 whether *he* **e** little or much, 430
5:17 All his days *he* **e** in darkness, 430
Isa 44:16 he roasts his meat and **e** *his* **fill.** 8425
59:5 Whoever **e** their eggs will die, 430
Jer 31:30 whoever **e** sour grapes— 430
Eze 18:11 *"He* **e** at the mountain shrines. 430
Lk 15:2 "This man welcomes sinners and **e with** *5303*
Jn 6:51 anyone **e** of this bread, he will live forever. *2266*
6:54 Whoever **e** my flesh and drinks my blood *5592*
6:56 Whoever **e** my flesh and drinks my blood *5592*
Ro 14:2 whose faith is weak, **e** only vegetables. *2266*
14:3 The man who **e** everything must not look *2266*
14:6 He who **e** meat, eats to the Lord, *2266*
14:6 He who eats meat, **e** to the Lord, *2266*
14:23 man who has doubts is condemned if *he* **e,** *2266*
1Co 11:27 whoever **e** the bread or drinks the cup of *2266*
11:28 to examine himself before he **e** of the bread *2266*
11:29 For anyone who **e** and drinks without *2266*
11:29 the body of the Lord **e** and drinks judgment *2266*

EAVES (1)

1Ki 7:9 and from foundation to **e,** 3258

EBAL (7)

Ge 36:23 Alvan, Manahath, **E,** Shepho and Onam. 6507
Dt 11:29 and on Mount **E** the curses. 6506
27:4 set up these stones on Mount **E,** 6506
27:13 And these tribes shall stand on Mount **E** 6506
Jos 8:30 Then Joshua built on Mount **E** an altar to 6506
8:33 and half of them in front of Mount **E,** 6506
1Ch 1:40 Alvan, Manahath, **E,** Shepho and Onam. 6507

EBB (1) [EBBED, EBBING, EBBS]

La 2:12 as their lives **e away** in their mothers' arms. 9161

EBBED (1) [EBB]

Ps 107:5 and their lives **e away.** 6494

EBBING (1) [EBB]

Jnh 2:7 "When my life *was* **e away,** 6494

EBBS (1) [EBB]

Job 30:16 my life **e away;** days of suffering grip me. 9161

EBED (6)

Jdg 9:26 of **E** moved with his brothers 6270
9:28 Then Gaal son of **E** said, 6270
9:30 of the city heard what Gaal son of **E** said, 6270
9:31 "Gaal son of **E** and his brothers have come 6270
9:35 of **E** had gone out and was standing at 6270
Ezr 8:6 **E** son of Jonathan, and with him 50 men; 6270

EBED-MELECH (6)

Jer 38:7 But **E,** a Cushite, an official in 6283
38:8 **E** went out of the palace and said to him, 6283
38:10 Then the king commanded **E** the Cushite, 6283
38:11 So **E** took the men with him and went to 6283
38:12 **E** the Cushite said to Jeremiah, 6283
39:16 "Go and tell **E** the Cushite, 'This is what 6283

EBENEZER (3)

1Sa 4:1 The Israelites camped at **E,** 75
5:1 they took it from **E** to Ashdod. 75
7:12 He named it **E,** saying, 75

EBER (16)

Ge 10:21 Shem was the ancestor of all the sons of **E.** 6299
10:24 and Shelah the father of **E.** 6299
10:25 Two sons were born to **E:** 6299
11:14 he became the father of **E.** 6299
11:15 And after he became the father of **E,** 6299
11:16 When **E** had lived 34 years, 6299
11:17 **E** lived 430 years and had other sons 6299
Nu 24:24 they will subdue Asshur and **E,** 6299
1Ch 1:18 and Shelah the father of **E.** 6299
1:19 Two sons were born to **E:** 6299
1:25 **E,** Peleg, Reu, 6299
5:13 Sheba, Jorai, Jacan, Zia and **E**—seven in all. 6299
8:12 The sons of Elpaal: **E,** Misham, 6299
8:22 Ishpan, **E,** Eliel, 6299
Ne 12:20 of Sallu's, Kallai; of Amok's, **E;** 6299
Lk 3:35 the son *of* **E,** the son of Shelah, *1576*

EBEZ (1)

Jos 19:20 Rabbith, Kishion, **E,** 82

EBIASAPH (3)

1Ch 6:23 Elkanah his son, **E** his son, Assir his son, 47
6:37 the son of **E,** the son of Korah, 47
9:19 Shallum son of Kore, the son of **E,** 47

EBONY (1)

Eze 27:15 they paid you with ivory tusks and **e.** 2041

EBRONAH (KJV) ABRONAH

ECBATANA (1)

Ezr 6:2 in the citadel of **E** in the province of Media, 10020

ECHO (2) [ECHOES]

Hab 2:11 and the beams of the woodwork *will* **e** it. 6699
Zep 2:14 Their calls *will* **e** through the windows, 8876

ECHOES (1) [ECHO]

Isa 15:8 Their outcry **e along** the border of Moab; 5938

ED (KJV) WITNESS

EDEN (19) [BETH EDEN]

Ge 2:8 a garden in the east, in **E;** 6359
2:10 the garden flowed from **E;** 6359
2:15 in the Garden of **E** to work it and take care 6359
3:23 from the Garden of **E** to work the ground 6359
3:24 the east side of the Garden of **E** cherubim 6359
4:16 and lived in the land of Nod, east of **E.** 6359
2Ki 19:12 and the people of **E** who were in Tel Assar? 6361
2Ch 29:12 Joah son of Zimmah and **E** son of Joah; 6360
31:15 **E,** Miniamin, Jeshua, Shemaiah, 6360
Isa 37:12 and the people of **E** who were in Tel Assar? 6361
51:3 he will make her deserts like **E,** 6359
Eze 27:23 Canneh and **E** and merchants of Sheba, 6361
28:13 You were in **E,** the garden of God; 6359
31:9 the envy of all the trees of **E** in the garden 6359
31:16 Then all the trees of **E,** 6359
31:18 " 'Which of the trees of **E** can be compared 6359
31:18 down with the trees of **E** to the earth below; 6359
36:35 like the garden of **E;** 6359
Joel 2:3 garden of **E,** behind them, a desert waste— 6359

EDER (4) [MIDGAL EDER]

Jos 15:21 of Edom were: Kabzeel, **E,** 6375
1Ch 8:15 Zebadiah, Arad, **E,** 6376
23:23 Mahli, **E** and Jerimoth—three in all. 6374
24:30 the sons of Mushi: Mahli, **E** and Jerimoth. 6374

EDGE (35) [DOUBLE-EDGED, EDGES]

Ex 13:20 at Etham on the **e** *of* the desert. 7895
26:4 Make loops of blue material along the **e** *of* 8557
26:10 along the **e** *of* the end curtain in one set and 8557
26:10 and also along the **e** *of* the end curtain in 8557
28:26 of the breastpiece on the inside **e** next to 8557
28:32 a woven **e** like a collar around this opening, 8557
36:11 along the **e** *of* the end curtain in one set, 8557
36:17 along the **e** *of* the end curtain in one set and 8557
36:17 and also along the **e** *of* the end curtain in 8557
39:19 of the breastpiece on the inside **e** next to 8557
Nu 20:16 a town on the **e** *of* your territory. 7895
22:36 at the **e** *of* his territory. 7895
33:6 on the **e** *of* the desert. 7895
Jos 3:8 the **e** *of* the Jordan's waters, 7895
3:15 and their feet touched the water's **e,** 7895
Jdg 7:17 When I get to the **e** *of* the camp, 7895
7:19 the hundred men with him reached the **e** *of* 7895
1Sa 9:27 they were going down to the **e** *of* the town, 7895
2Ki 7:5 When they reached the **e** *of* the camp, 7895
7:8 The men who had leprosy reached the **e** *of* 7895
1Ch 5:9 the east they occupied the land up to the **e** 995
Ps 89:43 You have turned back the **e** *of* his sword 7644
Ecc 10:10 If the ax is dull and its **e** unsharpened, 7156
Jer 31:29 and the children's teeth *are* **set on e.'** 7733
31:30 his own teeth *will be* **set on e.** 7733
Eze 18:2 and the children's teeth *are* **set on e'?** 7733
43:13 with a rim of one span around the **e,** 8557
Am 3:12 be saved, those who sit in Samaria on the **e** 6991
Mt 9:20 behind him and touched the **e** of his cloak. *3192*
14:36 to let the sick just touch the **e** of his cloak, *3192*
Mk 4:1 along the shore at the **water's e.** *2498*
6:56 to let them touch even the **e** of his cloak, *3192*
Lk 5:2 he saw at the water's **e** two boats, *NIG*
8:44 She came up behind him and touched the **e** *3192*
Heb 11:34 and escaped the **e** *of* the **sword;** *3479+5125*

EDGE (Anglicized) See also LEDGE

EDGES (5) [EDGE]

Lev 19:9 do not reap to the very **e** *of* your field 6991
19:27 of your head or clip off the **e** *of* your beard. 6991
21:5 the **e** *of* their beards or cut their bodies. 6991
23:22 do not reap to the very **e** *of* your field 6991
Job 38:13 the earth by the **e** and shake the wicked out 4053

EDICT (17) [DICTATE]

Ezr 6:11 I decree that if anyone changes this **e,** 10601
Est 1:20 Then when the king's **e** is proclaimed 7330
2:8 the king's order and **e** had been proclaimed, 2017
3:14 A copy of the text of the **e** was to be issued NIH
3:15 and the **e** was issued in the citadel of Susa. 2017
4:3 In every province to which the **e** and order 1821
4:8 He also gave him a copy of the text of the **e** 2017
8:11 The king's **e** granted the Jews in every city 889S
8:13 A copy of the text of the **e** was to be issued NIH
8:14 the **e** was also issued in the citadel of Susa. 2017
8:17 wherever the **e** *of* the king went, 2017
9:1 the **e** commanded by the king was to 2017
9:13 to carry out this day's **e** tomorrow also, 2017
9:14 An **e** was issued in Susa, 2017
Da 6:7 that the king should issue an **e** and enforce 10628
6:15 the Medes and Persians no decree or **e** that 10628
Heb 11:23 and they were not afraid of the king's **e.** *1409*

EDIFICATION (1) [EDIFIED, EDIFIES]

Ro 14:19 to do what leads to peace and to mutual **e.** *3869*

EDIFIED (2) [EDIFICATION]

1Co 14: 5 so that the church *may* be e. 3284+3869
14: 17 but the other man *is* not e. 3868

EDIFIES (2) [EDIFICATION]

1Co 14: 4 He who speaks in a tongue e himself, 3868
14: 4 but he who prophesies e the church. 3868

EDOM (92) [EDOM'S, EDOMITE, EDOMITES, ESAU]

Ge 25: 30 (That is why he was also called E.) 121
32: 3 the country of E. 121
36: 1 This is the account of Esau (that is, E). 121
36: 8 (that is, E) settled in the hill country of Seir. 121
36: 16 the chiefs descended from Eliphaz in E; 121+824
36: 17 the chiefs descended from Reuel in E; 121+824
36: 19 These were the sons of Esau (that is, E), 121
36: 21 sons of Seir in E were Horite chiefs. 121+824
36: 31 These were the kings who reigned in E 121+824
36: 32 Bela son of Beor became king of E. 121
36: 43 These were the chiefs of E, 121
Ex 15: 15 The chiefs of E will be terrified, 121
Nu 20: 14 from Kadesh to the king of E, saying: 121
20: 18 But E answered: "You may 121
20: 20 Then E came out against them with a large 121
20: 21 Since E refused to let them go 121
20: 23 At Mount Hor, near the border of E, 121+824
21: 4 to go around E. 121+824
24: 18 E will be conquered; 121
33: 37 on the border of E. 121+824
34: 3 of the Desert of Zin along the border of E. 121
Jos 15: 1 extended down to the territory of E, 121
15: 21 the Negev toward the boundary of E were: 121
Jdg 5: 4 when you marched from the land of E, 121
11: 17 Israel sent messengers to the king of E, 121
11: 17 but the king of E would not listen. 121
11: 18 skirted the lands of E and Moab, 121
1Sa 14: 47 Moab, the Ammonites, E, 121
2Sa 8: 12 E and Moab, the Ammonites and 121
8: 14 He put garrisons throughout E, 121
1Ki 9: 26 which is near Elath in E, 121+824
11: 14 from the royal line of E. 121
11: 15 Earlier when David was fighting with E, 121
11: 15 had struck down all the men in E. 121
11: 16 until they had destroyed all the men in E. 121
22: 47 There was then no king in E; 121
2Ki 3: 8 "Through the Desert of E," he answered. 121
3: 9 with the king of Judah and the king of E. 121
3: 12 and Jehoshaphat and the king of E went 121
3: 20 water flowing from the direction of E! 121
3: 26 to break through to the king of E, 121
8: 20 E rebelled against Judah and set 121
8: 22 To this day E has been in rebellion 121
14: 10 You have indeed defeated E and 121
1Ch 1: 43 These were the kings who reigned in E 121+824
1: 51 The chiefs of E were: 121
1: 54 These were the chiefs of E. 121
18: 11 E and Moab, the Ammonites and 121
18: 13 He put garrisons in E, 121
2Ch 8: 17 Ezion Geber and Elath on the coast of E. 121+824
20: 2 against you from E, 121
21: 8 E rebelled against Judah and set 121
21: 10 To this day E has been in rebellion 121
25: 19 to yourself that you have defeated E, 121
25: 20 because they sought the gods of E. 121
Ps 60: 8 upon E I toss my sandal; 121
60: 9 Who will lead me to E? 121
83: 6 the tents of E and the Ishmaelites, 121
108: 9 upon E I toss my sandal; 121
108: 10 Who will lead me to E? 121
Isa 11: 14 They will lay hands on E and Moab, 121
34: 5 see, it descends in judgment on E, 121
34: 6 in Bozrah and a great slaughter in E. 121+824
34: 11 over E the measuring line of chaos and 2023S
63: 1 Who is this coming from E, from Bozrah, 121
Jer 9: 26 E, Ammon, Moab and all who live in 121
25: 21 E, Moab and Ammon; 121
27: 3 Then send word to the kings of E, Moab, 121
40: 11 E and all the other countries heard that 121
49: 7 Concerning E: This is what the LORD Almighty says: 121
49: 17 "E will become an object of horror; 121
49: 19 I will chase E from its land in an instant. 5647S
49: 20 the LORD has planned against E, 121
La 4: 21 Rejoice and be glad, O Daughter of E, 121
4: 22 But, O Daughter of E, 121
Eze 16: 57 by the daughters of E and all her neighbors 121
25: 12 'Because E took revenge on the house 121
25: 13 against E and kill its men and their animals. 121
25: 14 I will take vengeance on E by the hand 121
25: 14 and they will deal with E in accordance 121
32: 29 "E is there, her kings and all her princes; 121
35: 15 O Mount Seir, you and all of E. 121
36: 5 the rest of the nations, and against all E, 121
Da 11: 41 Many countries will fall, but E, 121
Joel 3: 19 Egypt will be desolate, E a desert waste, 121
Am 1: 6 and sold them to E, 121
1: 9 sold whole communities of captives to E, 121
1: 11 "For three sins of E, even for four, 121
9: 12 so that they may possess the remnant of E 121
Ob 1: 1 the Sovereign LORD says about E— 121
1: 8 "will I not destroy the wise men of E, 121
Mal 1: 4 E may say, "Though we have been crushed, 121

EDOM'S (3) [EDOM]

Isa 34: 9 E streams will be turned into pitch, 2023S
Jer 49: 22 that day the hearts of E warriors will be like 121
Am 2: 1 as if to lime, the bones of E king, 121

EDOMITE (8) [EDOM]

Dt 23: 7 Do not abhor an E, for he is your brother. 122
1Sa 21: 7 he was Doeg the E, Saul's head shepherd. 122
22: 9 But Doeg the E, 122
22: 18 Doeg the E turned and struck them down. 122
22: 22 "That day, when Doeg the E was there, 122
1Ki 11: 14 Hadad the E, from the royal line of Edom. 122
11: 17 some E officials who had served his father. 122
Ps 52: T Doeg the E had gone to Saul and told him: 122

EDOMITES (15) [EDOM]

Ge 36: 9 the account of Esau the father of the E in 121
36: 43 This was Esau the father of the E. 121
2Sa 8: 13 from striking down eighteen thousand E in 121
8: 14 and all the E became subject to David. 121
1Ki 11: 1 Moabites, Ammonites, E, 122
2Ki 8: 21 The E surrounded him 121
14: 7 the one who defeated ten thousand E in 121
16: 6 E then moved into Elath 122
1Ch 18: 12 down eighteen thousand E in the Valley 121
18: 13 and all the E became subject to David. 121
2Ch 21: 9 The E surrounded him 121
25: 14 from slaughtering the E, 122
28: 17 The E had again come and attacked Judah 122
Ps 60: T and struck down twelve thousand E in 121
137: 7 the E did on the day Jerusalem fell. 121+1201

EDREI (8)

Nu 21: 33 to meet them in battle at E. 167
Dt 1: 4 and at E had defeated Og king of Bashan, 167
3: 1 to meet us in battle at E. 167
3: 10 and all Bashan as far as Salecah and E, 167
Jos 12: 4 who reigned in Ashtaroth and E. 167
13: 12 and E and had survived as one of the last of 167
13: 31 and Ashtaroth and E (the royal cities of Og 167
19: 37 Kedesh, E, En Hazor, 167

EDUCATED (1)

Ac 7: 22 Moses *was* e in all the wisdom of 4084

EFFECT (8) [EFFECTIVE, EFFECTIVELY, EFFECTS]

Job 41: 26 The sword that reaches him has no e, 7756
Isa 32: 17 the e *of* righteousness will be quietness 6275
Ac 7: 53 that was put into e through angels but have 1408
1Co 15: 10 and his grace to me was not without e. 3031
Gal 3: 19 The law *was* put into e through angels by 1411
Eph 1: 10 to be put into e when the times 3873
Heb 9: 17 it never takes e while the one who made it 2710
9: 18 even the first covenant *was* not put into e 1590

EFFECTIVE (2) [EFFECT]

1Co 16: 9 a great door for e work has opened to me, 1921
Jas 5: 16 of a righteous man is powerful and e. 1919

EFFECTIVELY (1) [EFFECT]

Ac 14: 1 There they spoke so e that a great number NIG

EFFECTS (1) [EFFECT]

Ac 28: 5 into the fire and suffered no ill e. 2805

EFFEMINATE (KJV) MALE PROSTITUTES

EFFORT (15) [EFFORTS]

Ecc 2: 19 the work into which *I have* poured *my* e 6661
Da 6: 14 to rescue Daniel and made every e 10700
Lk 13: 24 "Make every e to enter through the narrow 76
Jn 5: 44 make no e to obtain the praise that 2426
Ro 9: 16 therefore, depend on man's desire or e, 5556
14: 19 therefore make every e to do what leads 1503
Gal 3: 3 now trying to attain your goal *by* human e? 4922
Eph 4: 3 Make every e to keep the unity of the Spirit 5079
1Th 2: 16 in their e to keep us from speaking to NIG
2: 17 intense longing *we* made every e to see you. 5079
Heb 4: 11 therefore, make every e to enter that rest, 5079
12: 14 Make every e to live in peace with all men 1503
2Pe 1: 5 make every e to add to your faith goodness; 5082
1: 15 And *I will* make every e to see that 5079
3: 14 make every e to be found spotless, 5079

EFFORTS (7) [EFFORT]

Job 36: 19 or even all your mighty e sustain you 4410
Ecc 6: 7 All man's e are for his mouth, 6662
8: 17 Despite *all his* e to search it out, 6661
Eze 24: 12 It has frustrated *all* e; 9303
29: 20 for *his* e because he and his army did it 6268
Gal 4: 11 that somehow *I have* wasted *my* e on you. 3159
1Th 3: 5 and our e might have been useless. 3160

EGG (2) [EGGS]

Job 6: 6 or is there flavor in the white of an e? 2733
Lk 11: 12 Or if he asks for an e, 6051

EGGS (7) [EGG]

Dt 22: 6 on the young or on the e, 1070
Job 39: 14 She lays her e on the ground 1070
Isa 10: 14 as men gather abandoned e, 1070
34: 15 The owl will nest there and lay e, 4880
59: 5 the e *of* vipers and spin a spider's web. 1070
59: 5 Whoever eats their e will die, 1070
Jer 17: 11 a partridge *that* hatches e it did not lay is 1842

EGLAH (2)

2Sa 3: 5 Ithream the son of David's wife E. 6321
1Ch 3: 3 and the sixth, Ithream, by his wife E. 6321

EGLAIM (1) [EN EGLAIM]

Isa 15: 8 their wailing reaches as far as E, 104

EGLATH SHELISHIYAH (2)

Isa 15: 5 as far as E. 6326
Jer 48: 34 as far as Horonaim and E, 6326

EGLON (13)

Jos 10: 3 Japhia king of Lachish and Debir king of E. 6324
10: 5 Jarmuth, Lachish and E—joined forces. 6324
10: 23 Hebron, Jarmuth, Lachish and E. 6324
10: 34 with him moved on from Lachish to E; 6324
10: 36 and all Israel with him went up from E 6324
10: 37 Just as at E, they totally destroyed it 6324
12: 12 the king of E one the king of Gezer one 6324
15: 39 Lachish, Bozkath, E, 6324
Jdg 3: 12 the LORD gave E king of Moab power 6323
3: 13 E came and attacked Israel, NIH
3: 14 to E king of Moab for eighteen years. 6323
3: 15 with tribute to E king of Moab. 6323
3: 17 He presented the tribute to E king of Moab, 6323

EGYPT (609) [EGYPT'S, EGYPTIAN, EGYPTIAN'S, EGYPTIANS]

Ge 12: 10 and Abram went down to E to live there for 5213
12: 11 As he was about to enter E, 5213
12: 14 When Abram came to E, 5213
13: 1 So Abram went up from E to the Negev, 5213
13: 10 like the land of E, toward Zoar. 5213
15: 18 from the river of E to the great river, 5213
21: 21 his mother got a wife for him from E. 824+5213
25: 18 near the border of E, 5213
26: 2 "Do not go down to E; 5213
37: 25 on their way to take them down to E. 5213
37: 28 who took him to E. 5213
37: 36 the Midianites sold Joseph in E to Potiphar, 5213
39: 1 Now Joseph had been taken down to E. 5213
40: 1 of the king of E offended their master, 5213
40: 1 their master, the king of E. 5213
40: 5 cupbearer and the baker of the king of E, 5213
41: 8 for all the magicians and wise men of E. 5213
41: 19 in all the land of E. 5213
41: 29 throughout the land of E, 5213
41: 30 all the abundance in E will be forgotten, 824+5213
41: 33 and put him in charge of the land of E. 5213
41: 34 E during the seven years of abundance. 824+5213
41: 36 of famine that will come upon E, 824+5213
41: 41 in charge of the whole land of E." 5213
41: 43 in charge of the whole land of E. 5213
41: 44 or foot in all E." 824+5213
41: 45 And Joseph went throughout the land of E. 5213
41: 46 the service of Pharaoh king of E. 5213
41: 46 and traveled throughout E. 824+5213
41: 48 in E and stored it in the cities. 824+5213
41: 53 The seven years of abundance in E 824+5213
41: 54 but in the whole land of E there was food. 5213
41: 55 When all E began to feel the famine, 824+5213
41: 56 for the famine was severe throughout E. 824+5213
41: 57 the countries came to E to buy grain 5213
42: 1 Jacob learned that there was grain in E, 5213
42: 2 "I have heard that there is grain in E. 5213
42: 3 down to buy grain from E. 5213
43: 2 the grain they had brought from E, 5213
43: 15 to E and presented themselves to Joseph. 5213
45: 4 the one you sold into E! 5213
45: 8 his entire household and ruler of all E. 824+5213
45: 9 God has made me lord of all E. 5213
45: 13 in E and about everything you have seen. 5213
45: 18 of E and you can enjoy the fat of the land.' 5213
45: 19 some carts from E for your children 824+5213
45: 20 because the best of all E will be yours.' 824+5213
45: 23 with the best things of E, 5213
45: 25 up out of E and came to their father Jacob 5213
45: 26 In fact, he is ruler of all E." 824+5213
46: 3 "Do not be afraid to go down to E, 5213
46: 4 I will go down to E with you, 5213
46: 6 and Jacob and all his offspring went to E. 5213
46: 7 with him to E his sons and grandsons 5213
46: 8 and his descendants) who went to E: 5213
46: 20 In E, Manasseh and Ephraim were born 824+5213
46: 26 All those who went to E with Jacob— 5213
46: 27 two sons who had been born to Joseph in E, 5213
46: 27 which went to E, were seventy in all. 5213
47: 6 and the land of E is before you; 5213
47: 11 in E and gave them property in the best 824+5213
47: 13 both E and Canaan wasted away 824+5213
47: 14 found in E and Canaan in payment for 824+5213
47: 15 the people of E and Canaan was gone, 824+5213
47: 15 all E came to Joseph and said, 5213
47: 20 Joseph bought all the land in E for Pharaoh. 5213

Ge 47:21 from one end of E to the other. 5213
47:26 as a law concerning land in E— 5213
47:27 Now the Israelites settled in E in the region of Goshen. 824+5213
47:28 Jacob lived in E seventeen years, 824+5213
47:29 Do not bury me in E, 5213
47:30 of E and bury me where they are buried." 5213
48: 5 in E before I came to you here 824+5213
50: 7 his court and all the dignitaries of E— 824+5213
50:14 burying his father, Joseph returned to E, 5213
50:22 Joseph stayed in E, 5213
50:26 he was placed in a coffin in E. 5213
Ex 1: 1 of Israel who went to E with Jacob, each 5213
1: 5 Joseph was already in E. 5213
1: 8 came to power in E. 5213
1:15 of E said to the Hebrew midwives, 5213
1:17 not do what the king of E had told them 5213
1:18 the king of E summoned the midwives 5213
2:23 During that long period, the king of E died. 5213
3: 7 the misery of my people in E. 5213
3:10 to bring my people the Israelites out of E." 5213
3:11 and bring the Israelites out of E?" 5213
3:12 you have brought the people out of E, 5213
3:16 done to you in E. 5213
3:17 to bring you up out of your misery in E into 5213
3:18 the elders are to go to the king of E and say 5213
3:19 that the king of E will not let you go unless 5213
4:18 in E to see if any of them are still alive." 5213
4:19 "Go back to E, 5213
4:20 on a donkey and started back to E. 824+5213
4:21 "When you return to E, 5213
5: 4 But the king of E said, "Moses and Aaron, 5213
5:12 E to gather stubble to use for straw. 824+5213
6:11 of E to let the Israelites go out 5213
6:13 about the Israelites and Pharaoh king of E, 5213
6:13 to bring the Israelites out of E. 824+5213
6:26 Israelites out of E by their divisions." 824+5213
6:27 the ones who spoke to Pharaoh king of E 5213
6:27 about bringing the Israelites out of E. 5213
6:28 when the LORD spoke to Moses in E, 824+5213
6:29 of E everything I tell you." 5213
7: 3 and wonders in E, 824+5213
7: 4 Then I will lay my hand on E and 5213
7: 5 against E and bring the Israelites out of it." 5213
7:19 over the waters of E— 5213
7:19 Blood will be everywhere in E, 824+5213
7:21 Blood was everywhere in E. 824+5213
8: 5 and make frogs come up on the land of E.' " 5213
8: 6 over the waters of E, 5213
8: 7 also made frogs come up on the land of E. 5213
8:16 the land of E the dust will become gnats," 5213
8:17 throughout the land of E became gnats. 5213
8:24 and throughout E the land was ruined 824+5213
9: 4 the livestock of Israel and that of E, 5213
9: 9 over the whole land of E, 5213
9:18 that has ever fallen on E, 5213
9:22 the sky so that hail will fall all over E 824+5213
9:22 everything growing in the fields of E." 824+5213
9:23 So the LORD rained hail on the land of E; 5213
9:24 the land of E since it had become a nation. 5213
9:25 Throughout E hail struck everything in 824+5213
10: 7 Do you not yet realize that E is ruined?" 5213
10:12 over E so that locusts will swarm over 824+5213
10:13 So Moses stretched out his staff over E, 824+5213
10:14 they invaded all E and settled down 824+5213
10:15 on tree or plant in all the land of E. 5213
10:19 Not a locust was left anywhere in E. 1473+5213
10:21 so that darkness will spread over E— 824+5213
10:22 total darkness covered all E for three days. 824+5213
11: 1 on Pharaoh and on E. 5213
11: 3 in E by Pharaoh's officials and by 824+5213
11: 4 'About midnight I will go throughout E. 5213
11: 5 Every firstborn son in E will die, 824+5213
11: 6 will be loud wailing throughout E— 824+5213
11: 7 the LORD makes a distinction between E 5213
11: 9 so that my wonders may be multiplied in E." 824+5213
12: 1 LORD said to Moses and Aaron in E, 824+5213
12:12 that same night I will pass through E 824+5213
12:12 I will bring judgment on all the gods of E. 5213
12:13 when I strike E. 824+5213
12:17 that I brought your divisions out of E. 824+5213
12:27 of the Israelites in E and spared our homes 5213
12:29 down all the firstborn in E, 824+5213
12:30 and there was loud wailing in E, 5213
12:39 With the dough they had brought from E, 5213
12:39 of E and did not have time to prepare food 5213
12:40 Israelite people lived in E was 430 years. 5213
12:41 all the LORD's divisions left E. 824+5213
12:42 that night to bring them out of E, 824+5213
12:51 the LORD brought the Israelites out of E 824+5213
13: 3 the day you came out of E, 5213
13: 8 for me when I came out of E.' 5213
13: 9 For the LORD brought you out of E 5213
13:14 the LORD brought us out of E, 5213
13:15 the LORD killed every firstborn in E, 824+5213
13:16 that the LORD brought us out of E 5213
13:17 and return to E." 5213
13:18 The Israelites went up out of E armed 824+5213
14: 5 king of E was told that the people had fled, 5213
14: 7 along with all the other chariots of E, 5213
14: 8 the heart of Pharaoh king of E, 5213
14:11 "Was it because there were no graves in E 5213
14:11 to us by bringing us out of E? 5213
14:12 Didn't we say to you in E, 'Leave us alone; 5213
14:20 coming between the armies of E and Israel. 5213
Ex 14:25 The LORD is fighting for them against E." 5213
16: 1 after they had come out of E. 824+5213
16: 3 by the LORD's hand in E! 824+5213
16: 6 the LORD who brought you out of E, 824+5213
16:32 in the desert when I brought you out of E.' " 824+5213
17: 3 up out of E to make us and our children 5213
18: 1 the LORD had brought Israel out of E. 5213
19: 1 In the third month after the Israelites left E— 824+5213
19: 4 'You yourselves have seen what I did to E, 5213
20: 2 who brought you out of E, 824+5213
22:21 for you were aliens in E. 824+5213
23: 9 because you were aliens in E. 824+5213
23:15 for in that month you came out of E. 5213
29:46 of E so that I might dwell among them. 824+5213
32: 1 Moses who brought us up out of E, 824+5213
32: 4 O Israel, who brought you up out of E. 824+5213
32: 7 whom you brought up out of E, 824+5213
32: 8 O Israel, who brought you up out of E. 824+5213
32:11 E with great power and a mighty hand? 824+5213
32:23 Moses who brought us up out of E, 824+5213
33: 1 and the people you brought up out of E, 824+5213
34:18 for in that month you came out of E. 5213
Lev 11:45 the LORD who brought you up out of E 824+5213
18: 3 You must not do as they do in E, 824+5213
19:34 for you were aliens in E. 824+5213
19:36 who brought you out of E. 824+5213
22:33 brought you out of E to be your God. 824+5213
23:43 booths when I brought them out of E. 824+5213
25:38 of E to give you the land of Canaan 824+5213
25:42 whom I brought out of E, 824+5213
25:55 whom I brought out of E. 824+5213
26:13 E so that you would no longer be slaves 824+5213
26:45 of E in the sight of the nations to 824+5213
Nu 1: 1 after the Israelites came out of E. 824+5213
3:13 I struck down all the firstborn in E, 824+5213
8:17 I struck down all the firstborn in E, 824+5213
9: 1 second year after they came out of E. 824+5213
11: 5 We remember the fish we ate in E 5213
11:18 We were better off in E!" 5213
11:20 saying, "Why did we ever leave E?" '" 5213
13:22 before Zoan in E.) 5213
14: 2 "If only we had died in E! 824+5213
14: 3 be better for us to go back to E?" 5213
14: 4 a leader and go back to E." 5213
14:19 from the time they left E until now." 5213
14:22 the miraculous signs I performed in E and 5213
15:41 brought you out of E to be your God. 824+5213
20: 5 Why did you bring us up out of E 5213
20:15 Our forefathers went down into E, 5213
20:16 and sent an angel and brought us out of E. 5213
21: 5 "Why have you brought us up out of E 5213
22: 5 Balak said: "A people has come out of E; 5213
22:11 that has come out of E covers the face of 5213
23:22 God brought them out of E; 5213
24: 8 "God brought them out of E; 5213
26: 4 the Israelites who came out of E: 824+5213
26:59 who was born to the Levites in E. 5213
32:11 of E will see the land I promised on oath 5213
33: 1 the Israelites when they came out of E 824+5213
33:38 after the Israelites came out of E. 824+5213
34: 5 join the Wadi of E and end at the Sea. 5213
Dt 1:27 so he brought us out of E to deliver us 824+5213
1:30 will fight for you, as he did for you in E, 5213
4:20 of the iron-smelting furnace, out of E, 5213
4:34 the LORD your God did for you in E 5213
4:37 of E by his Presence and his great strength, 5213
4:45 when they came out of E 5213
4:46 and the Israelites as they came out of E. 5213
5: 6 who brought you out of E, 824+5213
5:15 Remember that you were slaves in E 824+5213
6:12 who brought you out of E, 824+5213
6:21 tell him: "We were slaves of Pharaoh in E, 5213
6:21 but the LORD brought us out of E with 5213
6:22 great and terrible—upon E and Pharaoh 5213
7: 8 from the power of Pharaoh king of E. 5213
7:15 on you the horrible diseases you knew in E, 5213
7:18 to Pharaoh and to all E. 5213
8:14 who brought you out of E, 824+5213
9: 7 day you left E until you arrived here, 824+5213
9:12 of E have become corrupt. 5213
9:26 by your great power and brought out of E 5213
10:19 for you yourselves were aliens in E. 824+5213
10:22 down into E were seventy in all, 5213
11: 3 and the things he did in the heart of E, both 5213
11: 3 of E and to his whole country; 5213
11:10 to take over is not like the land of E, 5213
13: 5 of E and redeemed you from the land 824+5213
13:10 who brought you out of E, 824+5213
15:15 Remember that you were slaves in E and824+5213
16: 1 the month of Abib he brought you out of E 5213
16: 3 because you left E in haste— 824+5213
16: 3 the time of your departure from E. 824+5213
16: 6 the anniversary of your departure from E. 5213
16:12 Remember that you were slaves in E, 5213
17:16 the people return to E to get more of them, 5213
20: 1 who brought you up out of E, 824+5213
23: 4 on your way when you came out of E, 5213
24: 9 along the way after you came out of E. 5213
24:18 Remember that you were slaves in E and 5213
24:22 Remember that you were slaves in E. 824+5213
25:17 along the way when you came out of E. 5213
26: 5 and he went down into E with a few people 5213
26: 8 So the LORD brought us out of E with 5213
28:27 with the boils of E and with tumors, 5213
28:60 He will bring upon you all the diseases of E 5213
Dt 28:68 in ships to E on a journey 5213
29: 2 that the LORD did in E to Pharaoh, 824+5213
29:16 yourselves know how we lived in E 824+5213
29:25 when he brought them out of E. 824+5213
34:11 the LORD sent him to do in E— 824+5213
Jos 2:10 for you when you came out of E, 5213
5: 4 All those who came out of E— 5213
5: 4 in the desert on the way after leaving E. 5213
5: 5 during the journey from E had not. 5213
5: 6 of military age when they left E had died, 5213
5: 9 the reproach of E from you." 5213
9: 9 all that he did in E, 5213
13: 3 on the east of E to the territory of Ekron on 5213
15: 4 along to Azmon and joined the Wadi of E, 5213
15:47 as far as the Wadi of E and the coastline of 5213
24: 4 but Jacob and his sons went down to E. 5213
24: 6 When I brought your fathers out of E, 5213
24:14 beyond the River and in E, 5213
24:17 and our fathers up out of E, 824+5213
24:32 which the Israelites had brought up from E, 5213
Jdg 2: 1 "I brought you up out of E and led you into 5213
2:12 who had brought them out of E. 824+5213
6: 8 I brought you up out of E, 5213
6: 9 I snatched you from the power of E and 5213
6:13 not the LORD bring us up out of E?' 5213
11:13 "When Israel came up out of E, 5213
11:16 But when they came up out of E, 5213
19:30 the day the Israelites came up out of E. 824+5213
1Sa 2:27 to your father's house when they were in E 5213
8: 8 from the day I brought them up out of E 5213
10:18 'I brought Israel up out of E, 5213
10:18 from the power of E and all the kingdoms 5213
12: 6 brought your forefathers up out of E. 824+5213
12: 8 "After Jacob entered E, 5213
12: 8 who brought your forefathers out of E 5213
15: 2 as they came up from E. 5213
15: 6 the Israelites when they came up out of E." 5213
15: 7 to the east of E. 5213
27: 8 in the land extending to Shur and E.) 824+5213
2Sa 7: 6 the day I brought the Israelites up out of E 5213
7:23 whom you redeemed from E? 5213
1Ki 3: 1 an alliance with Pharaoh king of E 5213
4:21 as far as the border of E. 5213
4:30 and greater than all the wisdom of E. 5213
6: 1 after the Israelites had come out of E, 824+5213
8: 9 the Israelites after they came out of E. 824+5213
8:16 the day I brought my people Israel out of E, 5213
8:21 when he brought them out of E." 824+5213
8:51 whom you brought out of E, 5213
8:53 brought our fathers out of E." 5213
8:65 from Lebo Hamath to the Wadi of E. 5213
9: 9 who brought their fathers out of E, 824+5213
9:16 of E had attacked and captured Gezer. 5213
10:28 Solomon's horses were imported from E 5213
10:29 from E for six hundred shekels of silver, 5213
11:17 But Hadad, still only a boy, fled to E 5213
11:18 they went to E, to Pharaoh king of Egypt, 5213
11:18 they went to Egypt, to Pharaoh king of E, 5213
11:21 While he was in E, 5213
11:40 but Jeroboam fled to E, 5213
12: 2 of Nebat heard this (he was still in E, 5213
12: 2 he returned from E. 5213
12:28 O Israel, who brought you up out of E." 824+5213
14:25 Shishak king of E attacked Jerusalem. 5213
2Ki 17: 4 for he had sent envoys to So king of E, 5213
17: 7 of E from under the power of Pharaoh 824+5213
17: 7 from under the power of Pharaoh king of E. 5213
17:36 up out of E with mighty power 824+5213
18:21 Look now, you are depending on E, 5213
18:21 of E to all who depend on him. 5213
18:24 though you are depending on E for chariots 5213
19: 9 the Cushite king [of E], NIH
19:24 up all the streams of E." 5191
21:15 from the day their forefathers came out of E 5213
23:29 of E went up to the Euphrates River to help 5213
23:34 he took Jehoahaz and carried him off to E, 5213
24: 7 The king of E did not march out 5213
24: 7 from the Wadi of E to the Euphrates River. 5213
25:26 fled to E for fear of the Babylonians. 5213
1Ch 13: 5 the Shihor River in E to Lebo Hamath, 5213
17: 5 from the day I brought Israel up out of E NIH
17:21 whom you redeemed from E? 5213
2Ch 1:16 Solomon's horses were imported from E 5213
1:17 from E for six hundred shekels of silver, 5213
5:10 with the Israelites after they came out of E. 5213
6: 5 the day I brought my people out of E, 824+5213
7: 8 from Lebo Hamath to the Wadi of E. 5213
7:22 who brought them out of E, 824+5213
9:26 as far as the border of E. 5213
9:28 Solomon's horses were imported from E 5213
10: 2 of Nebat heard this (he was in E, 5213
10: 2 he returned from E. 5213
12: 2 Shishak king of E attacked Jerusalem in 5213
12: 3 and Cushites that came with him from E, 5213
12: 9 Shishak king of E attacked Jerusalem, 5213
20:10 to invade when they came from E; 824+5213
26: 8 his fame spread as far as the border of E, 5213
35:20 of E went up to fight at Carchemish on 5213
36: 3 The king of E dethroned him in Jerusalem 5213
36: 4 The king of E made Eliakim, 5213
36: 4 and carried him off to E. 5213
Ne 9: 9 the suffering of our forefathers in E; 5213
9:18 who brought you up out of E,' 5213
Ps 68:31 Envoys will come from E; 5213
78:12 in the sight of their fathers in the land of E, 5213
78:43 day he displayed his miraculous signs in E, 5213
78:51 He struck down all the firstborn of E, 5213

Ps 80: 8 You brought a vine out of E; 5213
81: 5 for Joseph when he went out against E, 824+5213
81: 10 who brought you up out of E. 824+5213
105: 23 Then Israel entered E; 5213
105: 38 E was glad when they left, 5213
106: 7 When our fathers were in E, 5213
106: 21 who had done great things in E, 5213
114: 1 When Israel came out of E, 5213
135: 8 He struck down the firstborn of E, 5213
135: 9 O E, against Pharaoh and all his servants. 5213
136: 10 who struck down the firstborn of E 5213
Pr 7: 16 with colored linens from E. 5213
Isa 7: 18 of E and for bees from the land of Assyria. 5213
10: 24 and lift up a club against you, as E did. 5213
10: 26 as he did in E. 5213
11: 11 from **Lower** E, from Upper Egypt, 5213
11: 11 from **Upper** E, from Cush, from Elam, 7356
11: 16 for Israel when they came up from E. 824+5213
19: 1 An oracle concerning E: 5213
19: 1 on a swift cloud and is coming to E. 5213
19: 1 The idols of E tremble before him, 5213
19: 6 the streams of E will dwindle and dry up. 5191
19: 12 and make known what the LORD Almighty has planned against E. 5213
19: 13 of her peoples have led E astray. 5213
19: 14 they make E stagger in all that she does, 5213
19: 15 There is nothing E can do— 5213
19: 18 in E will speak the language of Canaan 824+5213
19: 19 an altar to the LORD in the heart of E, 824+5213
19: 20 to the LORD Almighty in the land of E. 5213
19: 22 The LORD will strike E with a plague; 5213
19: 23 In that day there will be a highway from E 5213
19: 23 to E and the Egyptians to Assyria. 5213
19: 24 along with E and Assyria, 5213
19: 25 saying, "Blessed be E my people, 5213
20: 3 as a sign and portent against E and Cush, 5213
20: 5 in Cush and boasted in E will be afraid 5213
23: 5 When word comes to E, 5213
27: 12 the flowing Euphrates to the Wadi of E, 5213
27: 13 in E will come and worship the LORD 824+5213
30: 2 who go down to E without consulting me; 5213
30: 7 to E, whose help is utterly useless. 5213
31: 1 Woe to those who go down to E for help, 5213
36: 6 Look now, you are depending on E, 5213
36: 6 of E to all who depend on him. 5213
36: 9 though you are depending on E for chariots 5213
37: 9 the Cushite king [of E], NIH
37: 25 up all the streams of E.' 5191
43: 3 I give E for your ransom, 5213
45: 14 products of E and the merchandise of Cush, 5213
52: 4 "At first my people went down to E to live; 5213
Jer 2: 6 who brought us up out of E and led us 824+5213
2: 18 Now why go to E to drink water from 5213
2: 36 You will be disappointed by E as you were 5213
7: 22 I brought your forefathers out of E 824+5213
7: 25 the time your forefathers left E until 824+5213
9: 26 E, Judah, Edom, Ammon, Moab 5213
11: 4 when I brought them out of E, 824+5213
11: 7 up from E until today, 824+5213
16: 14 who brought the Israelites up out of E,' 824+5213
23: 7 who brought the Israelites up out of E,' 824+5213
24: 8 in this land or live in E. 824+5213
25: 19 Pharaoh king of E, 5213
26: 21 But Uriah heard of it and fled in fear to E. 5213
26: 22 however, sent Elnathan son of Acbor to E, 5213
26: 23 They brought Uriah out of E and took him 5213
31: 32 by the hand to lead them out of E, 824+5213
32: 20 signs and wonders in E and 5213
32: 21 You brought your people Israel out of E 824+5213
34: 13 when I brought them out of E, 824+5213
37: 5 Pharaoh's army had marched out of E, 5213
37: 7 will go back to its own land, to E. 5213
41: 17 near Bethlehem on their way to E 5213
42: 14 'No, we will go and live in E, 824+5213
42: 15 to go to E and you do go to settle there, 5213
42: 16 famine you dread will follow you into E, 5213
42: 17 to E to settle there will die by the sword, 5213
42: 18 be poured out on you when you go to E. 5213
42: 19 the LORD has told you, 'Do not go to E.' 5213
43: 2 'You must not go to E to settle there.' 5213
43: 7 So they entered E in disobedience to 824+5213
43: 11 He will come and attack E, 824+5213
43: 12 to the temples of the gods of E; 5213
43: 12 so will he wrap E around himself 824+5213
43: 13 temple of the sun in E he will demolish 824+5213
43: 13 down the temples of the gods of E.' " 5213
44: 1 concerning all the Jews living in **Lower** E— 824+5213
44: 1 and in **Upper** E: 824+7356
44: 8 burning incense to other gods in E, 824+5213
44: 12 Judah who were determined to go to E 824+5213
44: 12 They will all perish in E; 824+5213
44: 13 I will punish those who live in E with 824+5213
44: 14 in E will escape or survive to return 824+5213
44: 15 people living in **Lower** and Upper E, 824+5213
44: 24 all you people of Judah in E. 824+5213
44: 26 all Jews living in E: 824+5213
44: 26 in E will ever again invoke my name 824+5213
44: 27 in E will perish by sword and famine 824+5213
44: 28 return to the land of Judah from E will 824+5213
44: 28 in E will know whose word will stand 824+5213
44: 30 of E over to his enemies who seek his life, 5213
46: 2 Concerning E: This is the message against 5213
46: 2 of E, which was defeated at Carchemish on 5213
46: 8 E rises like the Nile, 5213
46: 11 O Virgin Daughter of E. 5213
46: 13 of Babylon to attack E: 824+5213
Jer 46: 14 "Announce this in E, and proclaim it 5213
46: 17 'Pharaoh king of E is only a loud noise; 5213
46: 19 you who live in E, 1426+5213
46: 20 "E is a beautiful heifer, 5213
46: 22 E will hiss like a fleeing serpent as 2023^S
46: 24 The Daughter of E will be put to shame, 5213
46: 25 on E and her gods and her kings, 5213
46: 26 E will be inhabited as in times past," NIH
La 5: 6 to E and Assyria to get enough bread. 5213
Eze 17: 15 by sending his envoys to E to get horses 5213
19: 4 They led him with hooks to the land of E. 5213
20: 5 and revealed myself to them in E. 824+5213
20: 6 them that I would bring them out of E 824+5213
20: 7 do not defile yourselves with the idols of E. 5213
20: 8 nor did they forsake the idols of E. 5213
20: 8 and spend my anger against them in E. 824+5213
20: 9 the Israelites by bringing them out of E. 824+5213
20: 10 of E and brought them into the desert. 824+5213
20: 36 in the desert of the land of E, 5213
23: 3 They became prostitutes in E, 5213
23: 8 not give up the prostitution she began in E, 5213
23: 19 when she was a prostitute in E. 824+5213
23: 21 when in E your bosom was caressed 5213
23: 27 and prostitution you began in E. 824+5213
23: 27 with longing or remember E anymore. 5213
27: 7 from E was your sail and served 5213
29: 2 against Pharaoh king of E and prophesy 5213
29: 2 and prophesy against him and against all E. 5213
29: 3 " 'I am against you, Pharaoh king of E, 5213
29: 6 Then all who live in E will know that I am 5213
29: 9 E will become a desolate wasteland. 824+5213
29: 10 the land of E a ruin and a desolate waste 5213
29: 12 of E desolate among devastated lands, 5213
29: 14 captivity and return them to **Upper** E, 824+7356
29: 16 E will no longer be a source of confidence NIH
29: 19 to give E to Nebuchadnezzar king 824+5213
29: 20 I have given him E as a reward 824+5213
30: 4 A sword will come against E, 5213
30: 4 When the slain fall in E, 5213
30: 5 by the sword along with E. 4392^S
30: 6 " 'The allies of E will fall 5213
30: 8 to E and all her helpers are crushed. 5213
30: 10 of E by the hand of Nebuchadnezzar king 5213
30: 11 against E and fill the land with the slain. 5213
30: 13 No longer will there be a prince in E, 824+5213
30: 14 I will lay waste **Upper** E, 7356
30: 15 the stronghold of E, 5213
30: 16 I will set fire to E; 5213
30: 18 at Tahpanhes when I break the yoke of E; 5213
30: 19 So I will inflict punishment on E, 5213
30: 21 the arm of Pharaoh king of E. 5213
30: 22 I am against Pharaoh king of E. 5213
30: 25 and he brandishes it against E. 824+5213
31: 2 say to Pharaoh king of E and to his hordes: 5213
32: 2 up a lament concerning Pharaoh king of E 5213
32: 12 They will shatter the pride of E, 5213
32: 15 I make E desolate and strip the land 824+5213
32: 16 for E and all her hordes they will chant it, 5213
32: 18 wail for the hordes of E and consign to 5213
32: 21 the grave the mighty leaders will say of E 2257^S
47: 19 along the Wadi [of E] to the Great Sea. NIH
48: 28 along the Wadi [of E] to the Great Sea. NIH
Da 9: 15 of E with a mighty hand and who made 824+5213
11: 8 of silver and gold and carry them off to E. 5213
11: 42 E will not escape. 824+5213
11: 43 of gold and silver and all the riches of E, 5213
Hos 2: 15 as in the day she came up out of E. 824+5213
7: 11 now calling to E, now turning to Assyria. 5213
7: 16 this they will be ridiculed in the land of E. 5213
8: 13 They will return to E. 5213
9: 3 to E and eat unclean food in Assyria. 5213
9: 6 E will gather them, 5213
11: 1 I loved him, and out of E I called my son. 5213
11: 5 to E and will not Assyria rule over them 824+5213
11: 11 like birds from E, 5213
12: 1 with Assyria and sends olive oil to E. 5213
12: 9 [who brought you] out of E; 824+5213
12: 13 a prophet to bring Israel up from E, 5213
13: 4 [who brought you] out of E. 824+5213
Joel 3: 19 But E will be desolate, 5213
Am 2: 10 "I brought you up out of E, 824+5213
3: 1 the whole family I brought up out of E: 824+5213
3: 9 of Ashdod and to the fortresses of E: 824+5213
4: 10 "I sent plagues among you as I did to E. 5213
8: 8 up and then sink like the river of E. 5213
9: 5 then sinks like the river of E— 5213
9: 7 "Did I not bring Israel up from E, 824+5213
Mic 6: 4 of E and redeemed you from the land 824+5213
7: 12 to you from Assyria and the cities of E, 5191
7: 12 from E to the Euphrates and from sea to sea 5191
7: 15 As in the days when you came out of E, 824+5213
Na 3: 9 Cush and E were her boundless strength; 5213
Hag 2: 5 with you when you came out of E. 5213
Zec 10: 10 from E and gather them from Assyria. 824+5213
14: 19 be the punishment of E and the punishment 5213
Mt 2: 13 the child and his mother and escape to E. *131*
2: 14 during the night and left for E, *131*
2: 15 "Out of E I called my son." *131*
2: 19 in a dream to Joseph in E *131*
Ac 2: 10 E and the parts of Libya near Cyrene; *131*
7: 9 they sold him as a slave into E. *131*
7: 10 to gain the goodwill of Pharaoh king *of* E; *131*
7: 10 he made him ruler over E and all his palace. *131*
7: 11 "Then a famine struck all E and Canaan, *131*
7: 12 that there was grain in E, *131*
7: 15 Then Jacob went down to E, *131*
7: 17 of our people in E greatly increased. *131*
Ac 7: 18 became ruler of E. *131*
7: 34 the oppression of my people in E. *131*
7: 34 Now come, I will send you back to E.' *131*
7: 36 of E and did wonders and miraculous signs *NIG*
7: 36 did wonders and miraculous signs in E, *131+1178*
7: 39 and in their hearts turned back to E. *131*
7: 40 this fellow Moses who led us out of E *131+1178*
13: 17 people prosper during their stay in E, *131+1178*
Heb 3: 16 not all those Moses led out of E? *131*
8: 9 by the hand to lead them out of E, *131+1178*
11: 22 **exodus** of the Israelites **from** E *2016*
11: 26 as of greater value than the treasures *of* E, *131*
11: 27 By faith he left E, *131*
Jude 1: 5 the Lord delivered his people out of E, *131+1178*
Rev 11: 8 which is figuratively called Sodom and E, *131*

EGYPT'S (5) [EGYPT]

Isa 20: 4 with buttocks bared—to E shame. 5213
30: 2 to E shade for refuge. 5213
30: 3 E shade will bring you disgrace. 5213
Eze 30: 9 of them on the day of E doom, 5213
Zec 10: 11 down and E scepter will pass away. 5213

EGYPTIAN (35) [EGYPT]

Ge 16: 1 she had an E maidservant named Hagar; 5212
16: 3 Sarai his wife took her E maidservant Hagar 5212
21: 9 the E had borne to Abraham was mocking, 5212
25: 12 whom Sarah's maidservant, Hagar the E, 5212
39: 1 an E who was one of Pharaoh's officials, 5212
39: 2 and he lived in the house of his E master. 5212
39: 5 the LORD blessed the household of the E 5212
Ex 1: 19 "Hebrew women are not like E women; 5212
2: 11 He saw an E beating a Hebrew, 5212
2: 12 he killed the E and hid him in the sand. 5212
2: 14 of killing me as you killed the E?" 5212
2: 19 "An E rescued us from the shepherds. 5212
7: 11 the E magicians also did the same things 5213
7: 22 But the E magicians did the same things 5213
14: 24 of fire and cloud at the E army and threw it 5213
Lev 24: 10 an Israelite mother and an E father went out 5212
Dt 11: 4 what he did to the E army, 5213
23: 7 Do not abhor an E, 5212
1Sa 30: 11 They found an E in a field and brought him 5212
30: 13 He said, "I am an E, 5212
2Sa 23: 21 And he struck down a huge E. 5212
23: 21 Although the E had a spear in his hand, 5212
2Ki 7: 6 of Israel has hired the Hittite and E kings 5213
1Ch 2: 34 He had an E servant named Jarha. 5212
11: 23 And he struck down an E who was seven 5212
11: 23 the E had a spear like a weaver's rod 5212
Isa 11: 15 up the gulf of the E sea; 5213
19: 2 "I will stir up E against Egyptian— 5213
19: 2 "I will stir up Egyptian against E— 5213
20: 4 the E captives and Cushite exiles, young 5213
Zec 14: 18 If the E people do not go up and take part, 5213
Ac 7: 24 of them being mistreated by an E, *NIG*
7: 24 and avenged him by killing the E. *130*
7: 28 to kill me as you killed the E yesterday?' *130*
21: 38 "Aren't you the E who started a revolt *130*

EGYPTIAN'S (2) [EGYPT]

2Sa 23: 21 the spear from the E hand and killed him 5212
1Ch 11: 23 the spear from the E hand and killed him 5212

EGYPTIANS (91) [EGYPT]

Ge 12: 12 When the E see you, they will say, 5213
12: 14 the E saw that she was 5213
41: 55 Then Pharaoh told all the E, 5213
41: 56 the storehouses and sold grain to the E, 5213
43: 32 and the E who ate with him by themselves, 5213
43: 32 because E could not eat with Hebrews, 5213
43: 32 for that is detestable to E. 5213
45: 2 he wept so loudly that the E heard him, 5213
46: 34 for all shepherds are detestable to the E." 5213
47: 20 The E, one and all, sold their fields, 5213
50: 3 And the E mourned for him seventy days. 5213
50: 11 "The E are holding a solemn ceremony 5213
Ex 1: 12 so the E came to dread the Israelites NIH
1: 14 the E used them ruthlessly. NIH
3: 8 down to rescue them from the hand of the E 5213
3: 9 the way the E are oppressing them. 5213
3: 20 and strike the E with all the wonders 5213
3: 21 "And I will make the E favorably disposed 5213
3: 22 And so you will plunder the E." 5213
6: 5 whom the E are enslaving, 5213
6: 6 from under the yoke of the E. 5213
6: 7 from under the yoke of the E. 5213
7: 5 And the E will know that I am the LORD 5213
7: 18 the E will not be able to drink its water.' " 5213
7: 21 so bad that the E could not drink its water. 5213
7: 24 And all the E dug along the Nile 5213
8: 21 The houses of the E will be full of flies, 5213
8: 26 be detestable to the E. 5213
9: 6 All the livestock of the E died, 5213
9: 11 that were on them and on all the E. 5213
10: 2 with the E and how I performed my signs 5213
10: 6 those of all your officials and all the E— 5213
11: 3 the E favorably disposed toward the people, 5213
12: 23 through the land to strike down the E, 5213
12: 27 when he struck down the E.' " 5213
12: 30 and all his officials and all the E got up 5213
12: 33 The E urged the people to hurry and leave 5213
12: 35 as Moses instructed and asked **the** E 5213
12: 36 the E favorably disposed toward the people, 5213

Ex 12:36 so they plundered the **E.** 5213
14: 4 and the **E** will know that I am the LORD." 5213
14: 9 The **E**—all Pharaoh's horses 5213
14:10 and there were the **E,** marching after them. 5213
14:12 let us serve the **E**'? 5213
14:12 to serve the **E** than to die in the desert!" 5213
14:13 **E** you see today you will never see again. 5213
14:17 of the **E** so that they will go in after them. 5213
14:18 The **E** will know that I am the LORD 5213
14:23 The **E** pursued them, 5213
14:25 And the **E** said, 5213
14:26 so that the waters may flow back over the **E** 5213
14:27 The **E** were fleeing toward it, 5213
14:30 from the hands of the **E,** 5213
14:30 Israel saw the **E** lying dead on the shore. 5213
14:31 the LORD displayed against the **E,** 5213
15:26 of the diseases I brought on the **E,** 5213
18: 8 the LORD had done to Pharaoh and the **E** 5213
18: 9 in rescuing them from the hand of the **E.** 5213
18:10 who rescued you from the hand of the **E** 5213
18:10 the people from the hand of the **E.** 5213
32:12 Why should the **E** say, 5213
Lev 26:13 be slaves to **the E;** 2157[S]
Nu 14:13 "Then the **E** will hear about it! 5213
20:15 The **E** mistreated us and our fathers, 5213
33: 3 in full view of all the **E,** 5213
Dt 26: 6 But the **E** mistreated us and made us suffer, 5213
Jos 24: 5 and I afflicted the **E** by what I did there, 5213
24: 6 and the **E** pursued them with chariots 5213
24: 7 he put darkness between you and the **E;** 5213
24: 7 with your own eyes what I did to the **E.** 5213
Jdg 10:11 The LORD replied, "When the **E,** 5213
1Sa 4: 8 the **E** with all kinds of plagues in the desert. 5213
6: 6 Why do you harden your hearts as the **E** 5213
Ezr 9: 1 Ammonites, Moabites, **E** and Amorites. 5212
Ne 9:10 how arrogantly the **E** treated them. NIH
Isa 19: 1 and the hearts of the **E** melt within them. 5213
19: 3 The **E** will lose heart, 5213
19: 4 the **E** over to the power of a cruel master, 5213
19:16 In that day the **E** will be like women. 5213
19:17 the land of Judah will bring terror to the **E;** 5213
19:21 LORD will make himself known to the **E,** 5213
19:23 The Assyrians will go to Egypt and the **E** 5213
19:23 The **E** and Assyrians will worship together. 5213
31: 3 But the **E** are men and not God; 5213
Eze 16:26 engaged in prostitution with the **E,** 1201+5213
29:12 And I will disperse the **E** among the nations 5213
29:13 At the end of forty years I will gather the **E** 5213
30:23 the **E** among the nations and scatter them 5213
30:26 the **E** among the nations and scatter them 5213
Ac 7:22 the wisdom *of* the **E** and was powerful *130*
Heb 11:29 the **E** tried to do so, they were drowned. *130*

EHI (1)

Ge 46:21 Bela, Beker, Ashbel, Gera, Naaman, **E,** 305

EHUD (12)

Jdg 3:15 **E,** a left-handed man, the son of Gera 179
3:16 Now **E** had made a double-edged sword 179
3:18 After **E** had presented the tribute, NIH
3:20 **E** then approached him 179
3:21 **E** reached with his left hand, 179
3:22 **E** did not pull the sword out, NIH
3:23 Then **E** went out to the porch; 179
3:26 While they waited, **E** got away. 179
3:31 After **E** came Shamgar son of Anath, 2257[S]
4: 1 After **E** died, the Israelites once again did evil in the eyes of the LORD. 179
1Ch 7:10 The sons of Bilhan: Jeush, Benjamin, **E,** 179
8: 6 These were the descendants of **E,** 287

EIGHT (38) [EIGHTH]

Ge 17:12 among you who is **e** days old must 9046
21: 4 When his son Isaac was **e** days old, 9046
22:23 Milcah bore these **e** sons 9046
Ex 26:25 be **e** frames and sixteen silver bases— 9046
36:30 So there were **e** frames 9046
Nu 7: 8 and he gave four carts and **e** oxen to 9046
29:29 " 'On the sixth day prepare **e** bulls, 9046
Jdg 3: 8 the Israelites were subject for **e** years. 9046
12:14 He led Israel **e** years. 9046
1Sa 17:12 Jesse had **e** sons, 9046
2Sa 23: 8 he raised his spear against **e** hundred men, 9046
24: 9 In Israel there were **e** hundred thousand able-bodied men who could handle 9046
1Ki 7:10 some measuring ten cubits and some **e.** 9046
2Ki 8:17 and he reigned in Jerusalem **e** years. 9046
22: 1 Josiah was **e** years old 9046
1Ch 24: 4 from Eleazar's descendants and **e** heads 9046
2Ch 13: 3 with **e** hundred thousand able troops. 9046
21: 5 and he reigned in Jerusalem **e** years. 9046
21:20 and he reigned in Jerusalem **e** years. 9046
29:17 For **e** more days they consecrated 9046
34: 1 Josiah was **e** years old 9046
Ecc 11: 2 Give portions to seven, yes to **e,** 9046
Jer 41:15 and **e** *of* his men escaped from Johanan 9046
Eze 40: 9 it was **e** cubits deep 9046
40:31 and **e** steps led up to it. 9046
40:34 and **e** steps led up to it. 9046
40:37 and **e** steps led up to it. 9046
40:41 **e** tables in all— 9046
Mic 5: 5 even **e** leaders of men. 9046
Mk 6:37 **e months of a man's wages!** *1324+1357*
Lk 9:28 About **e** days after Jesus said this, *3893*
16: 6 " '**E hundred gallons** of olive oil,' *1004+1669*
Lk 16: 7 'Take your bill and make it **e hundred.'** *3837*
Jn 6: 7 **"E months' wages** would not buy *1324+1357*
Ac 7: 8 and circumcised him **e** days after his birth. *3838*
9:33 a paralytic who had been bedridden for **e** years. *3893*
25: 6 After spending **e** or ten days with them, *3893*
1Pe 3:20 In it only a few people, **e** in all, *3893*

EIGHTEEN (15) [EIGHTEENTH, 18]

Jdg 3:14 to Eglon king of Moab for **e** years. 6926+9046
10: 8 For **e** years they oppressed all the Israelites 6926+9046
20:25 they cut down another **e** thousand Israelites, 6925+9046
20:44 **E** thousand Benjamites fell, 6925+9046
2Sa 8:13 striking down **e** thousand Edomites in 6925+9046
1Ki 7:15 each **e** cubits high and twelve cubits 6926+9046
2Ki 24: 8 Jehoiachin was **e** years old 6926+9046
1Ch 18:12 struck down **e** thousand Edomites in 6925+9046
29: 7 **e thousand** talents of bronze and 547+2256+8052+9046
2Ch 11:21 he had **e** wives and sixty concubines, 6926+9046
36: 9 Jehoiachin was **e** years old 6926+9046
Jer 52:21 Each of the pillars was **e** cubits high 6926+9046
Lk 13: 4 Or those **e** who died when the tower *1277*
13:11 crippled by a spirit *for* **e** years. *1277*
13:16 kept bound *for* **e** long years, *1274+2779+3893*

EIGHTEENTH (11) [EIGHTEEN]

1Ki 15: 1 In the **e** year of the reign of Jeroboam 6926+9046
2Ki 3: 1 in the **e** year of Jehoshaphat king of 6926+9046
22: 3 In the **e** year of his reign, 6926+9046
23:23 But in the **e** year of King Josiah, 6926+9046
1Ch 24:15 the **e** to Happizzez, 6925+9046
25:25 the **e** to Hanani, his sons and relatives, 6925+9046
2Ch 13: 1 In the **e** year of the reign of Jeroboam, 6926+9046
34: 8 In the **e** year of Josiah's reign, 6926+9046
35:19 Passover was celebrated in the **e** year 6926+9046
Jer 32: 1 the **e** year of Nebuchadnezzar. 6926+9046
52:29 Nebuchadnezzar's **e** year, 832 people 6926+9046

EIGHTH (35) [EIGHT]

Ex 22:30 but give them to me on the **e** day. 9029
Lev 9: 1 On the **e** day Moses summoned Aaron 9029
12: 3 On the **e** day the boy is to be circumcised. 9029
14:10 the **e** day he must bring two male lambs 9029
14:23 "On the **e** day he must bring them 9029
15:14 On the **e** day he must take two doves 9029
15:29 On the **e** day she must take two doves 9029
22:27 From the **e** day on, 9029
23:36 and on the **e** day hold a sacred assembly 9029
23:39 and the **e** day also is a day of rest. 9029
25:22 While you plant during the **e** year, 9029
Nu 6:10 Then on the **e** day he must bring two doves 9029
7:54 On the **e** day Gamaliel son of Pedahzur, 9029
29:35 " 'On the **e** day hold an assembly 9029
1Ki 6:38 the **e** month, the temple was finished 9029
12:32 on the fifteenth day of the **e** month, 9029
12:33 On the fifteenth day of the **e** month, 9029
2Ki 24:12 In the **e** year of the reign of the king 9046
1Ch 12:12 Johanan the **e,** Elzabad the ninth, 9029
24:10 the seventh to Hakkoz, the **e** to Abijah, 9029
25:15 the **e** to Jeshaiah, his sons and relatives, 12 9029
26: 5 Issachar the seventh and Peullethai the **e.** 9029
27:11 The **e,** for the eighth month, 9029
27:11 The eighth, for the **e** month, 9029
2Ch 7: 9 On the **e** day they held an assembly, 9029
29:17 and by the **e** day of the month they reached 9046
34: 3 In the **e** year of his reign, 9046
Ne 8:18 and on the **e** day, 9029
Eze 43:27 At the end of these days, from the **e** day on, 9029
Zec 1: 1 In the **e** month of the second year of Darius, 9029
Lk 1:59 the **e** day they came to circumcise the child, *3838*
2:21 the **e** day, when it was time to circumcise *3893*
Php 3: 5 circumcised on the **e day,** of the people *3892*
Rev 17:11 and now is not, is an **e** king. *3838*
21:20 the seventh chrysolite, the **e** beryl, *3838*

EIGHTIETH (1) [EIGHTY]

1Ki 6: 1 and **e** year after the Israelites had come out 9046

EIGHTY (16) [EIGHTIETH, 80]

Ge 35:28 Isaac lived a hundred and **e** years. 9046
Ex 7: 7 Moses was **e** years old 9046
Jdg 3:30 and the land had peace for **e** years. 9046
2Sa 19:32 Barzillai was a very old man, **e** years of age. 9046
19:35 I am now **e** years old. 9046
1Ki 5:15 and **e** thousand stonecutters in the hills, 9046
12:21 a hundred and **e** thousand fighting men— 9046
2Ki 6:25 a donkey's head sold for **e** shekels of silver, 9046
10:24 Now Jehu had posted **e** men outside 9046
2Ch 2: 2 as carriers and **e** thousand as stonecutters in 9046
11: 1 a hundred and **e** thousand fighting men— 9046
14: 8 and two hundred and **e** thousand 9046
26:17 the priest with **e** other courageous priests of 9046
Ps 90:10 or **e,** if we have the strength; 9046
SS 6: 8 **e** concubines, and virgins beyond number; 9046
Jer 41: 5 **e** men who had shaved off their beards, 9046

EIGHTY-FIVE (4)

Jos 14:10 So here I am today, **e** years old! 2256+2822+9046
1Sa 22:18 he killed **e** men who wore 2256+2822+9046
2Ki 19:35 a hundred and **e** thousand men 2256+2822+9046
Isa 37:36 a hundred and **e** thousand men 2256+2822+9046

EIGHTY-FOUR (1)

Lk 2:37 was a widow until she was **e.** *2291+3837+5475*

EIGHTY-SIX (1)

Ge 16:16 Abram was **e** years old 2256+9046+9252

EIGHTY-THREE (1)

Ex 7: 7 and Aaron **e** when they spoke to Pharaoh. 2256+8993+9046

EITHER (41)

Ge 31:24 not to say anything to Jacob, **e** good or bad. 4946
31:29 not to say anything to Jacob, **e** good or bad. 4946
Ex 21:16 "Anyone who kidnaps another **and e** 2256
Lev 1: 2 an animal from **e** the herd **or** the flock. 2256
1:10 from **e** the sheep **or** the goats, 196
18: 9 **e** your father's daughter **or** 196
18:17 **e** her son's daughter **or** 2256
20:17 the daughter of **e** his father **or** his mother, 196
20:19 the sister of **e** your mother **or** your father, 2256
22:18 **e** an Israelite **or** an alien living in Israel— 2256
22:18 **e** to fulfill a vow **or** as a freewill offering, 2256
Nu 22:26 **e** to the right **or** to the left 2256
Dt 1:37 "You shall not enter it, **e.** 1685
22: 6 **e** in a tree **or** on the ground, 196
1Sa 16: 8 "The LORD has not chosen this one **e."** 1685
20:27 **e** yesterday or today?" 1685
26:10 **e** his time will come and he will die, 196
28:15 **e** by prophets or by dreams. 1685
2Sa 13:22 **e** good or bad; 4946
1Ki 10:20 one **at e end** of each step. 2256+2296+2296+4946+4946[S]
2Ki 9:20 but he isn't coming back **e.** NIH
18: 5 **e** before him **or** after him. 2256
2Ch 9:19 one **at e end** of each step. 2256+2296+2296+4946+4946[S]
Jer 29:19 And you exiles have not listened **e,"** NIH
Eze 1:11 the wing of another creature on **e** side, NIH
40:34 palm trees decorated the jambs **on e side,** 2256+4946+4946+7024+7024
40:37 palm trees decorated the jambs **on e side,** 2256+4946+4946+7024+7024
40:48 they were five cubits wide **on e side.** 2256+4946+4946+7024+7024
40:48 its projecting walls were three cubits wide **on e side.** 2256+4946+4946+7024+7024
Am 7: 6 "This will not happen **e,"** 1685
Zep 1:12 'The LORD will do nothing, **e** good or bad.' 4202
Mt 5:34 **e** by heaven, for it is God's throne; *3612*
6:24 **E** he will hate the one and love the other, *2445*
12:32 **e** in this age or in the age to come. *4046*
Mk 16:13 but they did **not** believe them **e.** *NIG*
Lk 16:13 **E** he will hate the one and love the other, *2445*
Jn 19:10 "Don't you realize I have power **e** *NIG*
Ro 11:21 he will **not** spare you **e.** *4028*
1Co 15:16 then Christ has **not** been raised **e.** *4028*
1Jn 3: 6 No one who continues to sin has **e** seen him *NIG*
Rev 3:15 I wish you were **e** one or the other! *NIG*

EJECTED (1)

Ac 18:16 So *he* **had** them **e from** the court. *590*

EKED See BETH EKED

EKER (1)

1Ch 2:27 Maaz, Jamin and **E.** 6831

EKRON (24)

Jos 13: 3 on the east of Egypt to the territory of **E** on 6833
13: 3 Ashdod, Ashkelon, Gath and **E**— 6834
15:11 It went to the northern slope of **E,** 6833
15:45 **E,** with its surrounding settlements 6833
15:46 west of **E,** all that were in the vicinity 6833
19:43 Elon, Timnah, **E,** 6833
Jdg 1:18 and **E**—each city with its territory. 6833
1Sa 5:10 So they sent the ark of God to **E.** 6833
5:10 As the ark of God was entering **E,** 6833
5:10 the **people of E** cried out, 6834
6:16 and then returned that same day to **E.** 6833
6:17 Gaza, Ashkelon, Gath and **E.** 6833
7:14 The towns from **E** to Gath that 6833
17:52 the entrance of Gath and to the gates of **E.** 6833
17:52 along the Shaaraim road to Gath and **E.** 6833
2Ki 1: 2 "Go and consult Baal-Zebub, the god of **E,** 6833
1: 3 consult Baal-Zebub, the god of **E?'** 6833
1: 6 to consult Baal-Zebub, the god of **E?** 6833
1:16 to consult Baal-Zebub, the god of **E?** 6833
Jer 25:20 Gaza, **E,** and the people left at Ashdod); 6833
Am 1: 8 I will turn my hand against **E,** 6833
Zep 2: 4 be emptied and **E** uprooted. 6833
Zec 9: 5 Gaza will writhe in agony, and **E** too, 6833
9: 7 and **E** will be like the Jebusites. 6833

EL See IPHTAH EL, MIGDAL EL

EL BETHEL (1) [BETHEL]

Ge 35: 7 and he called the place **E,** 450

EL ELOHE ISRAEL (1) [ISRAEL]
Ge 33:20 up an altar and called it **E.** 449

EL PARAN (1) [PARAN]
Ge 14: 6 as far as **E** near the desert. 386

EL-BERITH (1)
Jdg 9:46 into the stronghold of the temple of **E.** 451

ELA (1)
1Ki 4:18 Shimei son of **E**—in Benjamin; 452

ELAH (16) [ELAH'S]
Ge 36:41 Oholibamah, **E,** Pinon, 462
1Sa 17: 2 the Valley of **E** and drew up their battle line 463
17:19 and all the men of Israel in the Valley of **E,** 463
21: 9 whom you killed in the Valley of **E,** 463
1Ki 16: 6 And **E** his son succeeded him as king. 462
16: 8 **E** son of Baasha became king of Israel, 462
16: 9 **E** was in Tirzah at the time, 2085S
16:13 and his son **E** had committed 462
2Ki 15:30 of **E** conspired against Pekah son 462
17: 1 Hoshea son of **E** became king of Israel 462
18: 1 In the third year of Hoshea son of **E** king 462
18: 9 the seventh year of Hoshea son of **E** king 462
1Ch 1:52 Oholibamah, **E,** Pinon, 462
4:15 Iru, **E** and Naam. 462
4:15 The son of **E:** Kenaz. 462
9: 8 **E** son of Uzzi, the son of Micri; 462

ELAH'S (1) [ELAH]
1Ki 16:14 As for the other events of **E** reign, 462

ELAM (27) [ELAM'S, ELAMITES]
Ge 10:22 **E,** Asshur, Arphaxad, Lud and Aram. 6520
14: 1 Kedorlaomer king of **E** and Tidal king 6520
14: 9 against Kedorlaomer king of **E,** Tidal king 6520
1Ch 1:17 **E,** Asshur, Arphaxad, Lud and Aram. 6521
8:24 Hananiah, **E,** Anthothijah, 6521
26: 3 **E** the fifth, Jehohanan the sixth 6521
Ezr 2: 7 of **E** 1,254 6521
2:31 of the other **E** 1,254 6521
8: 7 of the descendants of **E,** Jeshaiah son 6521
10: 2 one of the descendants of **E,** said to Ezra, 6521
10:26 From the descendants of **E:** 6521
Ne 7:12 of **E** 1,254 6521
7:34 of the other **E** 1,254 6521
10:14 Parosh, Pahath-Moab, **E,** Zattu, Bani, 6521
12:42 Uzzi, Jehohanan, Malkijah, **E** and Ezer. 6521
Isa 11:11 from Upper Egypt, from Cush, from **E,** 6520
21: 2 the looter takes loot. **E,** 6520
22: 6 **E** takes up the quiver, 6520
Jer 25:25 all the kings of Zimri, **E** and Media; 6520
49:34 to Jeremiah the prophet concerning **E,** early 6520
49:35 "See, I will break the bow of **E,** 6520
49:36 I will bring against **E** the four winds from 6520
49:37 I will shatter **E** before their foes, 6520
49:38 in **E** and destroy her king and officials," 6520
49:39 "Yet I will restore the fortunes of **E** in days 6520
Eze 32:24 "**E** is there, with all her hordes 6520
Da 8: 2 in the citadel of Susa in the province of **E;** 6520

ELAM'S (1) [ELAM]
Jer 49:36 not be a nation where **E** exiles do not go. 6520

ELAMITES (2) [ELAM]
Ezr 4: 9 Persia, Erech and Babylon, the **E** of Susa, 10551
Ac 2: 9 Parthians, Medes and **E;** *1780*

ELAPSED (1)
1Sa 18:26 **before** the allotted time **e,** 4202+4848

ELASAH (2)
Ezr 10:22 Ishmael, Nethanel, Jozabad and **E.** 543
Jer 29: 3 He entrusted the letter to **E** son of Shaphan 543

ELATED (1) [ELATION]
1Sa 11: 9 to the men of Jabesh, *they were* **e.** 8523

ELATH (7)
Dt 2: 8 which comes up from **E** and Ezion Geber, 397
1Ki 9:26 which is near **E** in Edom, 393
2Ki 14:22 the one who rebuilt **E** and restored it 397
16: 6 Rezin king of Aram recovered **E** for Aram 397
16: 6 then moved into **E** and have lived there 397
2Ch 8:17 Then Solomon went to Ezion Geber and **E** 393
26: 2 the one who rebuilt **E** and restored it 393

ELATION (1) [ELATED]
Pr 28:12 the righteous triumph, there is great **e;** 9514

ELDAAH (2)
Ge 25: 4 Epher, Hanoch, Abida and **E.** 456
1Ch 1:33 Ephah, Epher, Hanoch, Abida and **E.** 456

ELDAD (2)
Nu 11:26 two men, whose names were **E** and Medad, 455
11:27 "**E** and Medad are prophesying in 455

ELDER (6) [ELDERLY, ELDERS]
Isa 3: 2 the soothsayer and **e,** 2418
1Ti 5:19 Do not entertain an accusation against an **e** *4565*
Tit 1: 6 An **e** must be blameless, *NIG*
1Pe 5: 1 I appeal as a **fellow e,** *5236*
2Jn 1: 1 The **e,** To the chosen lady and her children, *4565*
3Jn 1: 1 The **e,** To my dear friend Gaius, *4565*

ELDER, ELDEST (Anglicized) See also OLDER, OLDEST

ELDERLY (1) [ELDER]
Lev 19:32 show respect for the **e** and revere your God. 2418

ELDERS (188) [ELDER]
Ex 3:16 assemble the **e** *of* Israel and say to them, 2418
3:18 "The **e** *of* Israel will listen to you. 2418
3:18 the **e** are to go to the king of Egypt and say NIH
4:29 Moses and Aaron brought together all the **e** 2418
12:21 Then Moses summoned all the **e** *of* Israel 2418
17: 5 with you some of the **e** *of* Israel and take 2418
17: 6 So Moses did this in the sight of the **e** 2418
18:12 and Aaron came with all the **e** *of* Israel 2418
19: 7 and summoned the **e** *of* the people and set 2418
24: 1 and seventy of the **e** *of* Israel. 2418
24: 9 and the seventy **e** *of* Israel went up 2418
24:14 He said to the **e,** 2418
Lev 4:15 The **e** *of* the community are 2418
9: 1 and his sons and the **e** *of* Israel. 2418
Nu 11:16 of Israel's **e** who are known to you 2418
11:24 He brought together seventy of their **e** 2418
11:25 on him and put the Spirit on the seventy **e.** 2418
11:26 They were listed among the **e,** NIH
11:30 Then Moses and the **e** *of* Israel returned to 2418
16:25 and the **e** *of* Israel followed him. 2418
22: 4 The Moabites said to the **e** *of* Midian, 2418
22: 7 The **e** *of* Moab and Midian left, 2418
Dt 5:23 of your tribes and your **e** came to me. 2418
19:12 the **e** *of* his town shall send for him, 2418
21: 2 your **e** and judges shall go out and measure 2418
21: 3 Then the **e** *of* the town nearest 2418
21: 6 Then all the **e** *of* the town nearest 2418
21:19 of him and bring him to the **e** at the gate 2418
21:20 They shall say to the **e,** 2418
22:15 that she was a virgin to the town **e** at 2418
22:16 The girl's father will say to the **e,** 2418
22:17 the cloth before the **e** *of* the town, 2418
22:18 the **e** shall take the man and punish him. 2418
25: 7 she shall go to the **e** at the town gate 2418
25: 8 Then the **e** *of* his town shall summon him 2418
25: 9 up to him in the presence of the **e,** 2418
27: 1 and the **e** *of* Israel commanded the people: 2418
29:10 and chief men, your **e** and officials, 2418
31: 9 and to all the **e** *of* Israel. 2418
31:28 Assemble before me all the **e** *of* your tribes 2418
32: 7 Ask your father and he will tell you, your **e,** 2418
Jos 7: 6 The **e** *of* Israel did the same, 2418
8:33 aliens and citizens alike, with their **e,** 2418
9:11 And our **e** and all those living 2418
20: 4 the city gate and state his case before the **e** 2418
23: 2 their **e,** leaders, judges and officials— 2418
24: 1 He summoned the **e,** leaders, 2418
24:31 of Joshua and of the **e** who outlived him 2418
Jdg 2: 7 of Joshua and of the **e** who outlived him 2418
8:14 the **e** *of* the town. 2418
8:16 He took the **e** *of* the town and taught 2418
11: 5 the **e** *of* Gilead went to get Jephthah from 2418
11: 8 The **e** *of* Gilead said to him, "Nevertheless, 2418
11:10 The **e** *of* Gilead replied, 2418
11:11 So Jephthah went with the **e** *of* Gilead, 2418
21:16 And the **e** *of* the assembly said, 2418
Ru 4: 2 Boaz took ten of the **e** *of* the town and said, 2418
4: 4 and in the presence of the **e** *of* my people. 2418
4: 9 Boaz announced to the **e** and all the people, 2418
4:11 Then the **e** and all those at the gate said, 2418
1Sa 4: 3 the **e** *of* Israel asked, 2418
8: 4 the **e** *of* Israel gathered together and came 2418
11: 3 The **e** *of* Jabesh said to him, 2418
15:30 before the **e** *of* my people and before Israel; 2418
16: 4 the **e** *of* the town trembled 2418
30:26 he sent some of the plunder to the **e** 2418
2Sa 3:17 Abner conferred with the **e** *of* Israel 2418
5: 3 the **e** *of* Israel had come to King David 2418
12:17 The **e** *of* his household stood beside him 2418
17: 4 to Absalom and to all the **e** *of* Israel. 2418
17:15 "Ahithophel has advised Absalom and the **e** 2418
19:11 "Ask the **e** *of* Judah, 2418
1Ki 8: 1 into his presence at Jerusalem the **e** 2418
8: 3 When all the **e** *of* Israel had arrived, 2418
12: 6 the **e** who had served his father Solomon 2418
12: 8 the advice the **e** gave him and consulted 2418
12:13 Rejecting the advice given him by the **e,** 2418
20: 7 The king of Israel summoned all the **e** *of* 2418
20: 8 The **e** and the people all answered, 2418
21: 8 and sent them to the **e** and nobles who lived 2418
21:11 So the **e** and nobles who lived 2418
2Ki 6:32 and the **e** were sitting with him. 2418
6:32 but before he arrived, Elisha said to the **e,** 2418
10: 1 to the officials of Jezreel, to the **e** and to 2418
10: 5 the **e** and the guardians sent this message 2418
23: 1 the king called together all the **e** *of* Judah 2418
1Ch 11: 3 the **e** *of* Israel had come to King David 2418
15:25 the **e** *of* Israel and the commanders of units 2418
21:16 Then David and the **e,** clothed in sackcloth, 2418
2Ch 5: 2 to Jerusalem the **e** *of* Israel, 2418
5: 4 When all the **e** *of* Israel had arrived, 2418
10: 6 the **e** who had served his father Solomon 2418
10: 8 the advice the **e** gave him and consulted 2418
10:13 Rejecting the advice of the **e,** 2418
34:29 the king called together all the **e** *of* Judah 2418
Ezr 5: 5 of their God was watching over the **e** *of* 10675
5: 9 We questioned the **e** and asked them, 10675
6: 7 the Jews and the Jewish **e** rebuild this house 10675
6: 8 for these **e** *of* the Jews in the construction 10675
6:14 So the **e** *of* the Jews continued to build 10675
10: 8 with the decision of the officials and **e,** 2418
10:14 along with the **e** and judges of each town, 2418
Job 12:20 and takes away the discernment of **e.** 2418
Ps 105:22 as he pleased and teach his **e** wisdom. 2418
107:32 and praise him in the council of the **e.** 2418
119:100 I have more understanding than the **e,** 2418
Pr 31:23 he takes his seat among the **e** *of* the land. 2418
Isa 3:14 into judgment against the **e** and leaders 2418
9:15 the **e** and prominent men are the head, 2418
24:23 and before its **e,** gloriously. 2418
Jer 19: 1 Take along some of the **e** *of* the people and 2418
26:17 Some of the **e** *of* the land stepped forward 2418
29: 1 to the surviving **e** *among* the exiles and to 2418
La 1:19 My priests and my **e** perished in the city 2418
2:10 The **e** *of* the Daughter of Zion sit on 2418
4:16 priests are shown no honor, the **e** no favor. 2418
5:12 **e** are shown no respect. 2418
5:14 The **e** are gone from the city gate; 2418
Eze 7:26 as will the counsel of the **e.** 2418
8: 1 in my house and the **e** *of* Judah were sitting 2418
8:11 of them stood seventy **e** *of* the house 2418
8:12 the **e** *of* the house of Israel are doing in 2418
9: 6 So they began with the **e** who were in front 2418
14: 1 Some of the **e** *of* Israel came to me and sat 2418
20: 1 some of the **e** *of* Israel came to inquire of 2418
20: 3 speak to the **e** *of* Israel and say to them, 2418
Joel 1: 2 you **e;** listen, all who live in the land. 2418
1:14 Summon the **e** and all who live in the land 2418
2:16 bring together the **e,** gather the children, 2418
Mt 15: 2 the tradition *of* the **e?** *4565*
16:21 at the hands of the **e,** *4565*
21:23 and the **e** of the people came to him. *4565*
26: 3 the **e** of the people assembled in the palace *4565*
26:47 the chief priests and the **e** of the people. *4565*
26:57 of the law and the **e** had assembled. *4565*
27: 1 and the **e** of the people came to the decision *4565*
27: 3 to the chief priests and the **e.** *4565*
27:12 by the chief priests and the **e,** *4565*
27:20 But the chief priests and the **e** persuaded *4565*
27:41 of the law and the **e** mocked him. *4565*
28:12 When the chief priests had met with the **e** *4565*
Mk 7: 3 holding to the tradition *of* the **e.** *4565*
7: 5 according to the tradition *of* the **e** instead *4565*
8:31 and be rejected by the **e,** *4565*
11:27 the teachers of the law and the **e** came *4565*
14:43 the teachers of the law, and the **e.** *4565*
14:53 **e** and teachers of the law came together. *4565*
15: 1 the chief priests, with the **e,** *4565*
Lk 7: 3 of Jesus and sent some **e** of the Jews to him, *4565*
9:22 and be rejected by the **e,** *4565*
20: 1 together with the **e,** came up to him. *4565*
22:52 the officers of the temple guard, and the **e,** *4565*
22:66 the **council of** the **e** of the people *4564*
Ac 4: 5 **e** and teachers of the law met in Jerusalem. *4565*
4: 8 "Rulers and **e** of the people! *4565*
4:23 that the chief priests and **e** had said to them. *4565*
5:21 the full **assembly of** the **e** of Israel— *1172*
6:12 So they stirred up the people and the **e** and *4565*
11:30 sending their gift to the **e** by Barnabas *4565*
14:23 Paul and Barnabas appointed **e** for them *4565*
15: 2 up to Jerusalem to see the apostles and **e** *4565*
15: 4 by the church and the apostles and **e,** *4565*
15: 6 and **e** met to consider this question. *4565*
15:22 Then the apostles and **e,** *4565*
15:23 The apostles and **e,** your brothers, *4565*
16: 4 the decisions reached by the apostles and **e** *4565*
20:17 Paul sent to Ephesus for the **e** of the church. *4565*
21:18 and all the **e** were present. *4565*
23:14 They went to the chief priests and **e** *4565*
24: 1 down to Caesarea with some *of* the **e** and *4565*
25:15 and **e** of the Jews brought charges *4565*
1Ti 4:14 when the **body of e** laid their hands on you. *4564*
5:17 The **e** who direct the affairs of *4565*
Tit 1: 5 and appoint **e** in every town, *4565*
Jas 5:14 He should call the **e** of the church to pray *4565*
1Pe 5: 1 To the **e** among you, *4565*
Rev 4: 4 and seated on them were twenty-four **e.** *4565*
4:10 the twenty-four **e** fall down *4565*
5: 5 one of the **e** said to me, "Do not weep! *4565*
5: 6 by the four living creatures and the **e.** *4565*
5: 8 and the twenty-four **e** fell down before *4565*
5:11 and the living creatures and the **e.** *4565*
5:14 and the **e** fell down and worshiped. *4565*
7:11 around the **e** and the four living creatures. *4565*
7:13 Then one of the **e** asked me, *4565*
11:16 And the twenty-four **e,** *4565*
14: 3 before the four living creatures and the **e.** *4565*
19: 4 The twenty-four **e** and the four living *4565*

ELEAD (1)
1Ch 7:21 and **E** were killed by the native-born men 537

ELEADAH (1)
1Ch 7:20 Tahath his son, E his son, Tahath his son, 538

ELEALEH (5)
Nu 32: 3 Dibon, Jazer, Nimrah, Heshbon, E, Sebam, 542
32:37 And the Reubenites rebuilt Heshbon, E 541
Isa 15: 4 Heshbon and E cry out, 542
16: 9 O Heshbon, O E, I drench you with tears! 542
Jer 48:34 of their cry rises from Heshbon to E 542

ELEASAH (4)
1Ch 2:39 Helez the father of E, 543
2:40 E the father of Sismai, 543
8:37 E his son and Azel his son. 543
9:43 E his son and Azel his son. 543

ELEAZAR (74) [ELEAZAR'S]
Ex 6:23 and she bore him Nadab and Abihu, E 540
6:25 E son of Aaron married one of 540
28: 1 along with his sons Nadab and Abihu, E 540
Lev 10: 6 Then Moses said to Aaron and his sons E 540
10:12 E and Ithamar, "Take the grain offering left 540
10:16 he was angry with E and Ithamar, 540
Nu 3: 2 the firstborn and Abihu, E and Ithamar. 540
3: 4 so only E and Ithamar served as priests 540
3:32 The chief leader of the Levites was E son 540
4:16 "E son of Aaron, the priest, 540
16:37 "Tell E son of Aaron, the priest, to take 540
16:39 So E the priest collected 540
19: 3 Give it to E the priest; 540
19: 4 Then E the priest is to take some 540
20:25 and his son E and take them up Mount Hor. 540
20:26 and put them on his son E, for Aaron will 540
20:28 and put them on his son E. 540
20:28 and E came down from the mountain, 540
25: 7 When Phinehas son of E, the son of Aaron, 540
25:11 "Phinehas son of E, the son of Aaron, 540
26: 1 the LORD said to Moses and E son 540
26: 3 and E the priest spoke with them and said, 540
26:60 of Nadab and Abihu, E and Ithamar. 540
26:63 These are the ones counted by Moses and E 540
27: 2 before Moses, E the priest, the leaders and 540
27:19 before E the priest and the entire assembly 540
27:21 He is to stand before E the priest, 540
27:22 before E the priest and the whole assembly. 540
31: 6 along with Phinehas son of E, the priest, 540
31:12 and E the priest and the Israelite assembly 540
31:13 E the priest and all the leaders of 540
31:21 Then E the priest said to the soldiers 540
31:26 "You and E the priest and the family heads 540
31:29 from their half share and give it to E 540
31:31 So Moses and E the priest did as 540
31:41 Moses gave the tribute to E the priest as 540
31:51 Moses and E the priest accepted from them 540
31:52 of hundreds that Moses and E presented as NIH
31:54 Moses and E the priest accepted the gold 540
32: 2 So they came to Moses and E the priest and 540
32:28 to E the priest and Joshua son of Nun and 540
34:17 E the priest and Joshua son of Nun. 540
Dt 10: 6 and E his son succeeded him as priest. 540
Jos 14: 1 which E the priest, 540
17: 4 They went to E the priest, 540
19:51 These are the territories that E the priest, 540
21: 1 of the Levites approached E the priest, 540
22:13 So the Israelites sent Phinehas son of E, 540
22:31 And Phinehas son of E, the priest, 540
22:32 Then Phinehas son of E, the priest, 540
24:33 And E son of Aaron died and was buried 540
Jdg 20:28 with Phinehas son of E, 540
1Sa 7: 1 the hill and consecrated E his son to guard 540
2Sa 23: 9 to him was E son of Dodai the Ahohite. 540
23:10 The troops returned to E, 2257[S]
1Ch 6: 3 Nadab, Abihu, E and Ithamar. 540
6: 4 E was the father of Phinehas, 540
6:50 E his son, Phinehas his son, 540
9:20 In earlier times Phinehas son of E was 540
11:12 to him was E son of Dodai the Ahohite, 540
23:21 The sons of Mahli: E and Kish. 540
23:22 E died without having sons: 540
24: 1 Abihu, E and Ithamar. 540
24: 2 so E and Ithamar served as the priests. 540
24: 3 of Zadok a descendant of E and Ahimelech 540
24: 5 of God among the descendants of both E 540
24: 6 from E and then one from Ithamar. 540
24:28 From Mahli: E, who had no sons. 540
Ezr 7: 5 the son of Phinehas, the son of E, 540
8:33 E son of Phinehas was with him, 540
10:25 Ramiah, Izziah, Malkijah, Mijamin, E, 540
Ne 12:42 Shemaiah, E, Uzzi, Jehohanan, Malkijah, 540
Mt 1:15 Eliud the father of E, *1789*
1:15 E the father of Matthan, *1789*

ELEAZAR'S (2) [ELEAZAR]
1Ch 24: 4 among E descendants than 540
24: 4 from E descendants and eight heads 540

ELECT (11) [ELECTION]
Mt 24:22 sake of the e those days will be shortened. *1723*
24:24 and miracles to deceive even the e— *1723*
24:31 they will gather his e from the four winds, *1723*
Mk 13:20 But for the sake of the e, *1723*
13:22 and miracles to deceive the e— *1723*
13:27 And he will send his angels and gather his e *1723*
Ro 11: 7 it did not obtain, but the e did. *1724*
1Ti 5:21 of God and Christ Jesus and the e angels, *1723*
2Ti 2:10 for the sake of the e, *1723*
Tit 1: 1 of Jesus Christ for the faith of God's e and *1723*
1Pe 1: 1 an apostle of Jesus Christ, *To* God's e, *1723*

ELECTION (3) [ELECT]
Ro 9:11 that God's purpose in e might stand: *1724*
11:28 but as far as e is concerned, *1724*
2Pe 1:10 to make your calling and e sure. *1724*

ELEGANCE (1) [ELEGANT]
SS 4: 4 like the tower of David, built with e; 9444

ELEGANT (2) [ELEGANCE]
Eze 23:41 You sat on an e couch, 3884
Lk 23:11 Dressing him in an e robe, *3287*

ELEMENTARY (2) [ELEMENTS]
Heb 5:12 you need someone to teach you the e **truths** *794+3836+5122*
6: 1 the e teachings about Christ and go on *794*

ELEMENTS (2) [ELEMENTARY]
2Pe 3:10 the e will be destroyed by fire, *5122*
3:12 and the e will melt in the heat. *5122*

ELEVATE (1) [ELEVATED, ELEVATING]
2Co 11: 7 in order to e you by preaching the gospel *5738*

ELEVATED (1) [ELEVATE]
Est 5:11 how *he had* e him above the other nobles 5951

ELEVATING (1) [ELEVATE]
Est 3: 1 e him and giving him a seat 5951

ELEVEN (23) [ELEVENTH]
Ge 32:22 and his e sons and crossed the ford of 285+6925
37: 9 sun and moon and e stars were bowing 285+6925
Ex 26: 7 over the tabernacle—e altogether. 6926+6954
26: 8 All e curtains are to be the same size 6926+6954
36:14 over the tabernacle—e altogether. 6926+6954
36:15 All e curtains were the same size— 6926+6954
Nu 29:20 " 'On the third day prepare e bulls, 6925+6954
Dt 1: 2 (It takes e days to go from Horeb 285+6925
Jos 15:51 e towns and their villages. 285+6926
Jdg 16: 5 will give you e **hundred** shekels 547+2256+4395
17: 2 "The e **hundred** shekels of silver 547+2256+4395
17: 3 the e **hundred** shekels of silver to his mother, 547+2256+4395
2Ki 23:36 and he reigned in Jerusalem e years. 285+6926
24:18 and he reigned in Jerusalem e years. 285+6926
2Ch 36: 5 and he reigned in Jerusalem e years. 285+6926
36:11 and he reigned in Jerusalem e years. 285+6926
Jer 52: 1 and he reigned in Jerusalem e years. 285+6926
Mt 28:16 Then the e disciples went to Galilee, *1894*
Mk 16:14 Later Jesus appeared *to* the E *1894*
Lk 24: 9 they told all these things *to* the E and to all *1894*
24:33 There they found the E and those *1894*
Ac 1:26 so he was added to the e apostles. *1894*
2:14 Then Peter stood up with the E, *1894*

ELEVENTH (20) [ELEVEN]
Nu 7:72 On the e day Pagiel son of Ocran, 6925+6954
Dt 1: 3 on the first day of the e month, 6925+6954
1Ki 6:38 In the e year in the month of Bul, 285+6926
2Ki 9:29 (In the e year of Joram son of Ahab, 285+6926
25: 2 until the e year of King Zedekiah. 6926+6954
1Ch 12:13 and Macbannai the e. 6925+6954
24:12 the e to Eliashib, the twelfth to Jakim, 6925+6954
25:18 the e to Azarel, his sons and relatives, 6925+6954
27:14 The e, for the eleventh month, 6925+6954
27:14 The eleventh, for the e month, 6925+6954
Jer 1: 3 the e year of Zedekiah son of Josiah 6926+6954
39: 2 the fourth month of Zedekiah's e year, 6926+6954
52: 5 until the e year of King Zedekiah. 6926+6954
Eze 26: 1 e year, on the first day of the month, 6926+6954
30:20 In the e year, in the first month on 285+6926
31: 1 In the e year, in the third month on 285+6926
Zec 1: 7 the twenty-fourth day of the e month, 6925+6954
Mt 20: 6 About the e hour he went out *1895*
20: 9 about the e hour came and each received *1895*
Rev 21:20 the e jacinth, and the twelfth amethyst. *1895*

ELHANAN (4)
2Sa 21:19 E son of Jaare-Oregim 481
23:24 E son of Dodo from Bethlehem, 481
1Ch 11:26 E son of Dodo from Bethlehem, 481
20: 5 E son of Jair killed Lahmi the brother 481

ELI (33) [ELI'S]
1Sa 1: 3 the two sons of E, 6603
1: 9 Now E the priest was sitting on a chair by 6603
1:12 E observed her mouth. 6603
1:13 E thought she was drunk 6603
1:17 E answered, "Go in peace, 6603
1:25 they brought the boy to E, 6603
2:11 before the LORD under E the priest. 6603
2:20 E would bless Elkanah and his wife, 6603
2:22 Now E, who was very old, 6603
2:27 a man of God came to E and said to him, 6603
3: 1 The boy Samuel ministered before the LORD under E. 6603
3: 2 One night E, whose eyes were becoming 6603
3: 5 And he ran to E and said, "Here I am; 6603
3: 5 But E said, "I did not call; NIH
3: 6 And Samuel got up and went to E and said, 6603
3: 6 "My son," E said, "I did not call; NIH
3: 8 and Samuel got up and went to E and said, 6603
3: 8 Then E realized that the LORD was calling 6603
3: 9 So E told Samuel, "Go and lie down, 6603
3:12 carry out against E everything I spoke 6603
3:14 Therefore, I swore to the house of E, 6603
3:15 He was afraid to tell E the vision, 6603
3:16 but E called him and said, 6603
3:17 "What was it he said to you?" E asked. NIH
3:18 Then E said, "He is the LORD; NIH
4:13 there was E sitting on his chair by the side 6603
4:14 E heard the outcry and asked, 6603
4:14 The man hurried over to E, 6603
4:16 He told E, "I have just come from 6603
4:16 E asked, "What happened, my son?" NIH
4:18 E fell backward off his chair by the side of NIH
14: 3 the son of E, the LORD's priest in Shiloh. 6603
1Ki 2:27 at Shiloh about the house of E. 6603

ELI'S (4) [ELI]
1Sa 2:12 E sons were wicked men; 6603
3:14 'The guilt of E house will never be atoned 6603
4: 4 And E two sons, Hophni and Phinehas, 6603
4:11 and E two sons, Hophni and Phinehas, 6603

ELIAB (20)
Nu 1: 9 from Zebulun, E son of Helon; 482
2: 7 of the people of Zebulun is E son of Helon. 482
7:24 On the third day, E son of Helon, 482
7:29 This was the offering of E son of Helon. 482
10:16 and E son of Helon was over the division of 482
16: 1 Dathan and Abiram, sons of E, 482
16:12 the sons of E. 482
26: 8 The son of Pallu was E, 482
26: 9 and the sons of E were Nemuel, 482
Dt 11: 6 sons of E the Reubenite, 482
1Sa 16: 6 Samuel saw E and thought, 482
17:13 The firstborn was E; 482
17:28 When E, David's oldest brother, 482
1Ch 2:13 Jesse was the father of E his firstborn; 482
6:27 E his son, Jeroham his son, Elkanah his son 482
12: 9 the second in command, E the third, 482
15:18 Unni, E, Benaiah, Maaseiah, Mattithiah, 482
15:20 Aziel, Shemiramoth, Jehiel, Unni, E, 482
16: 5 Shemiramoth, Jehiel, Mattithiah, E, 482
2Ch 11:18 the daughter of Jesse's son E. 482

ELIADA (4)
2Sa 5:16 Elishama, E and Eliphelet. 486
1Ki 11:23 Rezon son of E, 486
1Ch 3: 8 Elishama, E and Eliphelet—nine in all. 486
2Ch 17:17 From Benjamin: E, a valiant soldier, 486

ELIAH (KJV) ELIJAH

ELIAHBA (2)
2Sa 23:32 E the Shaalbonite, the sons 494
1Ch 11:33 the Baharumite, E the Shaalbonite, 494

ELIAKIM (15) [ELIAKIM'S, JEHOIAKIM]
2Ki 18:18 E son of Hilkiah the palace administrator, 509
18:26 Then E son of Hilkiah, 509
18:37 E son of Hilkiah the palace administrator, 509
19: 2 He sent E the palace administrator, 509
23:34 Pharaoh Neco made E son of Josiah king 509
2Ch 36: 4 The king of Egypt made E, 509
Ne 12:41 E, Maaseiah, Miniamin, Micaiah, Elioenai, 509
Isa 22:20 E son of Hilkiah. 509
36: 3 E son of Hilkiah the palace administrator, 509
36:11 Then E, Shebna and Joah said to 509
36:22 E son of Hilkiah the palace administrator, 509
37: 2 He sent E the palace administrator, 509
Mt 1:13 Abiud the father of E, *1806*
1:13 E the father of Azor, *1806*
Lk 3:30 the son of Jonam, the son *of* E, *1806*

ELIAKIM'S (3) [ELIAKIM]
2Ki 23:34 and changed E name to Jehoiakim. 2257[S]
2Ch 36: 4 and changed E name to Jehoiakim. 2257[S]
36: 4 But Neco took E brother Jehoahaz 2257[S]

ELIAM (2)
2Sa 11: 3 the daughter of E and the wife of Uriah 500
23:34 E son of Ahithophel the Gilonite, 500

ELIAS (KJV) ELIJAH

ELIASAPH (6)
Nu 1:14 from Gad, E son of Deuel; 498
2:14 The leader of the people of Gad is E son 498
3:24 the families of the Gershonites was E son 498
7:42 On the sixth day E son of Deuel, 498

Nu 7:47 This was the offering of **E** son of Deuel. 498
10:20 and **E** son of Deuel was over the division of 498

ELIASHIB (15) [ELIASHIB'S]
1Ch 3:24 The sons of Elioenai: Hodaviah, **E**, Pelaiah, 513
24:12 the eleventh to **E**, the twelfth to Jakim, 513
Ezr 10:6 to the room of Jehohanan son of **E**. 513
10:24 From the singers: **E**. 513
10:27 From the descendants of Zattu: Elioenai, **E**, 513
10:36 Vaniah, Meremoth, **E**, 513
Ne 3:1 **E** the high priest and his fellow priests went 513
3:20 the angle to the entrance of the house of **E** 513
12:10 Joiakim the father of **E**, 513
12:10 **E** the father of Joiada, 513
12:22 of the Levites in the days of **E**, 513
12:23 the time of Johanan son of **E** were recorded 513
13:4 **E** the priest had been put in charge of 513
13:7 about the evil thing **E** had done 513
13:28 of **E** the high priest was son-in-law 513

ELIASHIB'S (1) [ELIASHIB]
Ne 3:21 from the entrance of **E** house to the end 513

ELIATHAH (2)
1Ch 25:4 Hanani, **E**, Giddalti and Romamti-Ezer; 484
25:27 the twentieth to **E**, his sons and relatives, 517

ELIDAD (1)
Nu 34:21 **E** son of Kislon, from the tribe 485

ELIEHOENAI (2)
1Ch 26:3 Jehohanan the sixth and **E** the seventh. 492
Ezr 8:4 **E** son of Zerahiah, and with him 200 men; 492

ELIEL (10)
1Ch 5:24 Epher, Ishi, **E**, Azriel, Jeremiah, 483
6:34 the son of Jeroham, the son of **E**, 483
8:20 Elienai, Zillethai, **E**, 483
8:22 Ishpan, Eber, **E**, 483
11:46 **E** the Mahavite, Jeribai and Joshaviah 483
11:47 **E**, Obed and Jaasiel the Mezobaite. 483
12:11 Attai the sixth, **E** the seventh, 483
15:9 **E** the leader and 80 relatives; 483
15:11 Shemaiah, **E** and Amminadab the Levites. 483
2Ch 31:13 Asahel, Jerimoth, Jozabad, **E**, Ismakiah, 483

ELIENAI (1)
1Ch 8:20 **E**, Zillethai, Eliel, 501

ELIEZER (15)
Ge 15:2 and the one who will inherit my estate is **E** 499
Ex 18:4 and the other was named **E**, 499
1Ch 7:8 The sons of Beker: Zemirah, Joash, **E**, 499
15:24 and **E** the priests were to blow trumpets 499
23:15 The sons of Moses: Gershom and **E**. 499
23:17 The descendants of **E**: 499
23:17 **E** had no other sons, 499
26:25 His relatives through **E**: 499
27:16 **E** son of Zicri; 499
2Ch 20:37 **E** son of Dodavahu 499
Ezr 8:16 So I summoned **E**, Ariel, Shemaiah, 499
10:18 Maaseiah, **E**, Jarib and Gedaliah. 499
10:23 Kelita), Pethahiah, Judah and **E**. 499
10:31 From the descendants of Harim: **E**, Ishijah, 499
Lk 3:29 the son *of* **E**, the son of Jorim, *1808*

ELIHOENAI (KJV) ELIEHOENAI

ELIHOREPH (1)
1Ki 4:3 **E** and Ahijah, sons of Shisha— 495

ELIHU (10)
1Sa 1:1 the son of **E**, the son of Tohu, 491
1Ch 12:20 Jediael, Michael, Jozabad, **E** and Zillethai, 491
26:7 his relatives **E** and Semakiah were 490
27:18 **E**, a brother of David; 490
Job 32:2 But **E** son of Barakel the Buzite, 491
32:4 Now **E** had waited before speaking to Job 490
32:6 So **E** son of Barakel the Buzite said: 491
34:1 Then **E** said: 491
35:1 Then **E** said: 490
36:1 **E** continued: 491

ELIJAH (111) [ELIJAH'S]
1Ki 17:1 Now **E** the Tishbite, from Tishbe in Gilead, 489
17:2 Then the word of the LORD came to **E**: 2257[S]
17:13 **E** said to her, "Don't be afraid. 489
17:15 She went away and did as **E** had told her. 489
17:15 So there was food every day for **E** and for 2085[S]
17:16 with the word of the LORD spoken by **E**. 489
17:18 She said to **E**, "What do you have against 489
17:19 "Give me your son," **E** replied. NIH
17:23 **E** picked up the child and carried him down 489
17:24 Then the woman said to **E**, 489
18:1 the word of the LORD came to **E**: 489
18:2 So **E** went to present himself to Ahab. 489
18:7 As Obadiah was walking along, **E** met him. 489
18:7 and said, "Is it really you, my lord **E**?" 489
18:8 "Go tell your master, '**E** is here.' " 489
1Ki 18:11 to go to my master and say, '**E** is here.' 489
18:14 to go to my master and say, '**E** is here.' 489
18:15 **E** said, "As the LORD Almighty lives, 489
18:16 and Ahab went to meet **E**. 489
18:17 When he saw **E**, he said to him, 489
18:18 not made trouble for Israel," **E** replied. NIH
18:21 **E** went before the people and said, 489
18:22 Then **E** said to them, 489
18:25 **E** said to the prophets of Baal, 489
18:27 At noon **E** began to taunt them. 489
18:30 Then **E** said to all the people, 489
18:31 **E** took twelve stones, 489
18:36 the prophet **E** stepped forward and prayed: 489
18:40 Then **E** commanded them, 489
18:40 and **E** had them brought down to 489
18:41 And **E** said to Ahab, "Go, eat and drink, 489
18:42 but **E** climbed to the top of Carmel, 489
18:43 Seven times **E** said, "Go back." NIH
18:44 So **E** said, "Go and tell Ahab, NIH
18:46 The power of the LORD came upon **E** 489
19:1 Ahab told Jezebel everything **E** had done 489
19:2 So Jezebel sent a messenger to **E** to say, 489
19:3 **E** was afraid and ran for his life. NIH
19:9 "What are you doing here, **E**?" 489
19:13 When **E** heard it, 489
19:13 "What are you doing here, **E**?" 489
19:19 So **E** went from there and found Elisha son NIH
19:19 **E** went up to him and threw his cloak 489
19:20 Elisha then left his oxen and ran after **E**. 489
19:20 "Go back," **E** replied. NIH
19:21 to follow **E** and became his attendant. 489
21:17 word of the LORD came to **E** the Tishbite: 489
21:20 Ahab said to **E**, "So you have found me, 489
21:28 word of the LORD came to **E** the Tishbite: 489
2Ki 1:3 angel of the LORD said to **E** the Tishbite, 488
1:4 So **E** went. 488
1:8 The king said, "That was **E** the Tishbite." 488
1:9 to **E** a captain with his company 2257[S]
1:9 The captain went up to **E**, 2257[S]
1:10 **E** answered the captain, 489
1:11 At this the king sent to **E** another captain 2257[S]
1:12 "If I am a man of God," **E** replied, 488
1:13 up and fell on his knees before **E**. 489
1:15 The angel of the LORD said to **E**, 489
1:15 So **E** got up and went down with him to NIH
1:17 the word of the LORD that **E** had spoken. 489
2:1 When the LORD was about to take **E** up 489
2:1 **E** and Elisha were on their way 489
2:2 **E** said to Elisha, "Stay here; 489
2:4 Then **E** said to him, "Stay here, Elisha; 489
2:6 Then **E** said to him, "Stay here; 489
2:7 where **E and Elisha** had stopped 2157+9109[S]
2:8 **E** took his cloak, rolled it up and struck 489
2:9 When they had crossed, **E** said to Elisha, 489
2:10 "You have asked a difficult thing," **E** said, NIH
2:11 and **E** went up to heaven in a whirlwind. 489
2:13 that had fallen from **E** and went back 489
2:14 "Where now is the LORD, the God of **E**?" 489
2:15 said, "The spirit of **E** is resting on Elisha." 489
3:11 He used to pour water on the hands of **E**." 489
9:36 that he spoke through his servant **E** 489
10:10 through his servant **E**." 489
10:17 to the word of the LORD spoken to **E**. 489
1Ch 8:27 **E** and Zicri were the sons of Jeroham. 488
2Ch 21:12 a letter from **E** the prophet, which said: 489
Ezr 10:21 Maaseiah, **E**, Shemaiah, Jehiel and Uzziah. 488
10:26 Zechariah, Jehiel, Abdi, Jeremoth and **E**. 488
Mal 4:5 I will send you the prophet **E** before 489
Mt 11:14 he is the **E** who was to come. *2460*
16:14 "Some say John the Baptist; others say **E**; *2460*
17:3 before them Moses and **E**, *2460*
17:4 one for you, one for Moses and one *for* **E**." *2460*
17:10 of the law say that **E** must come first?" *2460*
17:11 **E** comes and will restore all things. *2460*
17:12 But I tell you, **E** has already come, *2460*
27:47 they said, "He's calling **E**." *2460*
27:49 Let's see if **E** comes to save him." *2460*
Mk 6:15 Others said, "He is **E**." *2460*
8:28 "Some say John the Baptist; others say **E**; *2460*
9:4 there appeared before them **E** and Moses, *2460*
9:5 one for you, one for Moses and one *for* **E**." *2460*
9:11 of the law say that **E** must come first?" *2460*
9:12 **E** does come first, and restores all things. *2460*
9:13 But I tell you, **E** has come, *2460*
15:35 they said, "Listen, he's calling **E**." *2460*
15:36 Let's see if **E** comes to take him down," *2460*
Lk 1:17 in the spirit and power *of* **E**, *2460*
4:26 Yet **E** was not sent to any of them, *2460*
9:8 others that **E** had appeared, *2460*
9:19 "Some say John the Baptist; others say **E**; *2460*
9:30 Two men, Moses and **E**, *2460*
9:33 one for you, one for Moses and one *for* **E**." *2460*
Jn 1:21 Are you **E**?" *2460*
1:25 nor **E**, nor the Prophet?" *2460*
Ro 11:2 the Scripture says in the passage about **E**— *2460*
Jas 5:17 **E** was a man just like us. *2460*

ELIJAH'S (2) [ELIJAH]
1Ki 17:22 The LORD heard **E** cry, 489
Lk 4:25 in Israel in **E** time, *2460*

ELIKA (1)
2Sa 23:25 Shammah the Harodite, **E** the Harodite, 508

ELIM (5) [BEER ELIM]
Ex 15:27 Then they came to **E**, 396
16:1 from **E** and came to the Desert of Sin, 396
16:1 which is between **E** and Sinai, 396
Nu 33:9 They left Marah and went to **E**, 396
33:10 They left **E** and camped by the Red Sea. 396

ELIMELECH (6)
Ru 1:2 The man's name was **E**, 497
1:3 Now **E**, Naomi's husband, died, 497
2:1 from the clan of **E**, a man of standing, 497
2:3 who was from the clan of **E**. 497
4:3 of land that belonged to our brother **E**. 497
4:9 from Naomi all the property of **E**, 497

ELIMINATE (1) [ELIMINATED]
Dt 7:22 You will not be allowed to **e** them all 3983

ELIMINATED (1) [ELIMINATE]
Dt 2:15 against them until he *had* completely **e** them 2169

ELIOENAI (7)
1Ch 3:23 **E**, Hizkiah and Azrikam—three in all. 493
3:24 The sons of **E**: 493
4:36 also **E**, Jaakobah, Jeshohaiah, 493
7:8 Zemirah, Joash, Eliezer, **E**, Omri, 493
Ezr 10:22 From the descendants of Pashhur: **E**, 493
10:27 From the descendants of Zattu: **E**, Eliashib, 493
Ne 12:41 Eliakim, Maaseiah, Miniamin, Micaiah, **E**, 493

ELIPHAL (1)
1Ch 11:35 **E** son of Ur, 503

ELIPHAZ (14)
Ge 36:4 Adah bore **E** to Esau, Basemath bore Reuel, 502
36:10 **E**, the son of Esau's wife Adah, and Reuel, 502
36:11 The sons of **E**: 502
36:12 Esau's son **E** also had 502
36:15 The sons of **E** the firstborn of Esau: 502
36:16 These were the chiefs descended from **E** 502
1Ch 1:35 **E**, Reuel, Jeush, Jalam and Korah. 502
1:36 The sons of **E**: 502
Job 2:11 When Job's three friends, **E** the Temanite, 502
4:1 Then **E** the Temanite replied: 502
15:1 Then **E** the Temanite replied: 502
22:1 Then **E** the Temanite replied: 502
42:7 he said to **E** the Temanite, 502
42:9 So **E** the Temanite, Bildad the Shuhite 502

ELIPHELEHU (2)
1Ch 15:18 Eliab, Benaiah, Maaseiah, Mattithiah, **E**, 504
15:21 **E**, Mikneiah, Obed-Edom, 504

ELIPHELET (8)
2Sa 5:16 Elishama, Eliada and **E**. 505
23:34 **E** son of Ahasbai the Maacathite, 505
1Ch 3:6 There were also Ibhar, Elishua, **E**, 505
3:8 Elishama, Eliada and **E**—nine in all. 505
8:39 Jeush the second son and **E** the third. 505
14:7 Elishama, Beeliada and **E**. 505
Ezr 8:13 whose names were **E**, Jeuel and Shemaiah, 505
10:33 Mattenai, Mattattah, Zabad, **E**, Jeremai, 505

ELISABETH (KJV) ELIZABETH

ELISEUS (KJV) ELISHA

ELISHA (90) [ELISHA'S]
1Ki 19:16 and anoint **E** son of Shaphat 515
19:17 and **E** will put to death any who escape 515
19:19 So Elijah went from there and found **E** son 515
19:20 **E** then left his oxen and ran after Elijah. NIH
19:21 So **E** left him and went back. NIH
2Ki 2:1 Elijah and **E** were on their way from Gilgal. 515
2:2 Elijah said to **E**, "Stay here; 515
2:2 But **E** said, "As surely as the LORD lives 515
2:3 of the prophets at Bethel came out to **E** 515
2:3 "Yes, I know," **E** replied, NIH
2:4 Then Elijah said to him, "Stay here, **E**; 515
2:5 at Jericho went up to **E** and asked him, 515
2:7 where **Elijah and E** had stopped 2157+9109[S]
2:9 When they had crossed, Elijah said to **E**, 515
2:9 a double portion of your spirit," **E** replied. 515
2:12 **E** saw this and cried out, "My father! 515
2:12 And **E** saw him no more. NIH
2:15 said, "The spirit of Elijah is resting on **E**." 515
2:16 "No," **E** replied, "do not send them." NIH
2:18 When they returned to **E**, 2257[S]
2:19 The men of the city said to **E**, "Look, 515
2:22 according to the word **E** had spoken. 515
2:23 From there **E** went up to Bethel. NIH
3:11 "**E** son of Shaphat is here. 515
3:13 **E** said to the king of Israel, 515
3:14 **E** said, "As surely as 515
3:15 the hand of the LORD came upon **E** 2257[S]
4:1 the company of the prophets cried out to **E**, 515
4:2 **E** replied to her, "How can I help you? 515
4:3 **E** said, "Go around NIH
4:8 One day **E** went to Shunem. 515

2Ki 4:11 One day when **E** came, NIH
4:13 **E** said to him, "Tell her, NIH
4:14 be done for her?" **E** asked. NIH
4:15 Then **E** said, "Call her." NIH
4:16 "About this time next year," **E** said, NIH
4:17 just as **E** had told her. 515
4:29 **E** said to Gehazi, NIH
4:31 Gehazi went back to meet **E** and told him, 2257[S]
4:32 When **E** reached the house, 515
4:35 **E** turned away and walked back and forth NIH
4:36 **E** summoned Gehazi and said, NIH
4:38 **E** returned to Gilgal and there was a famine 515
4:41 **E** said, "Get some flour." NIH
4:42 "Give it to the people to eat," **E** said. NIH
4:43 **E** answered, "Give it to the people to eat. NIH
5:8 When **E** the man of God heard that the king 515
5:10 **E** sent a messenger to say to him, "Go, 515
5:19 "Go in peace," **E** said. NIH
5:20 the servant of **E** the man of God, 515
5:25 he went in and stood before his master **E**. NIH
5:25 "Where have you been, Gehazi?" **E** asked. 515
5:26 But **E** said to him, NIH
6:1 The company of the prophets said to **E**, 515
6:3 "I will," **E** replied. NIH
6:6 **E** cut a stick and threw it there, NIH
6:10 Time and again **E** warned the king, NIH
6:12 "but **E**, the prophet who is in Israel, 515
6:17 And **E** prayed, "O LORD, 515
6:17 of horses and chariots of fire all around **E**. 515
6:18 **E** prayed to the LORD, 515
6:18 as **E** had asked. 515
6:19 **E** told them, "This is not the road 515
6:20 After they entered the city, **E** said, 515
6:21 he asked **E**, "Shall I kill them, my father? 515
6:31 if the head of **E** son of Shaphat remains 515
6:32 Now **E** was sitting in his house, 515
6:32 but before he arrived, **E** said to the elders, 2085[S]
7:1 **E** said, "Hear the word of the LORD. 515
7:2 answered **E**, "but you will not eat any NIH
8:1 Now **E** had said to the woman 515
8:4 about all the great things **E** has done." 515
8:5 the king how **E** had restored the dead NIH
8:5 the woman whose son **E** had brought back NIH
8:5 this is her son whom **E** restored to life." 515
8:7 **E** went to Damascus, 515
8:9 Hazael went to meet **E**, 2257[S]
8:10 **E** answered, "Go and say to him, 515
8:13 of Aram," answered **E**. 515
8:14 Hazael left **E** and returned to his master. 515
8:14 "What did **E** say to you?" 515
9:1 The prophet **E** summoned a man from 515
13:14 Now **E** was suffering from the illness 515
13:15 **E** said, "Get a bow and some arrows," 515
13:16 **E** put his hands on the king's hands. 515
13:17 **E** said, and he shot. 515
13:17 arrow of victory over Aram!" **E** declared. NIH
13:18 **E** told him, "Strike the ground." NIH
13:20 **E** died and was buried. 515
Lk 4:27 with leprosy in the time of **E** the prophet, *1811*

ELISHA'S (4) [ELISHA]

2Ki 5:9 and stopped at the door of **E** house. 515
5:27 from **E** presence and he was leprous. 2257[S]
13:21 so they threw the man's body into **E** tomb. 515
13:21 When the body touched **E** bones, 515

ELISHAH (3)

Ge 10:4 **E**, Tarshish, the Kittim and the Rodanim. 511
1Ch 1:7 **E**, Tarshish, the Kittim and the Rodanim. 511
Eze 27:7 of blue and purple from the coasts of **E**. 511

ELISHAMA (16)

Nu 1:10 from Ephraim, **E** son of Ammihud; 514
2:18 of Ephraim is **E** son of Ammihud. 514
7:48 On the seventh day **E** son of Ammihud, 514
7:53 the offering of **E** son of Ammihud. 514
10:22 **E** son of Ammihud was in command. 514
2Sa 5:16 **E**, Eliada and Eliphelet 514
2Ki 25:25 Ishmael son of Nethaniah, the son of **E**, 514
1Ch 2:41 and Jekamiah the father of **E**. 514
3:8 **E**, Eliada and Eliphelet—nine in all. 514
7:26 Ladan his son, Ammihud his son, **E** his son, 514
14:7 **E**, Beeliada and Eliphelet. 514
2Ch 17:8 and the priests **E** and Jehoram. 514
Jer 36:12 **E** the secretary, Delaiah son of Shemaiah, 514
36:20 After they put the scroll in the room of **E** 514
36:21 from the room of **E** the secretary and read it 514
41:1 the son of **E**, 514

ELISHAPHAT (1)

2Ch 23:1 and **E** son of Zicri. 516

ELISHEBA (1)

Ex 6:23 Aaron married **E**, daughter of Amminadab 510

ELISHUA (3)

2Sa 5:15 Ibhar, **E**, Nepheg, Japhia, 512
1Ch 3:6 There were also Ibhar, **E**, Eliphelet, 512
14:5 Ibhar, **E**, Elpelet, 512

ELITE (1)

Eze 23:7 as a prostitute to all the **e** *of* the Assyrians 4436

ELIUD (2)

Mt 1:14 Akim the father of **E**, *1809*
1:15 **E** the father of Eleazar, *1809*

ELIZABETH (10)

Lk 1:5 his wife **E** was also a descendant of Aaron. *1810*
1:7 they had no children, because **E** was barren; *1810*
1:13 Your wife **E** will bear you a son, *1810*
1:24 After this his wife **E** became pregnant and *1810*
1:36 Even **E** your relative is going to have *1810*
1:40 where she entered Zechariah's home and greeted **E**. *1810*
1:41 When **E** heard Mary's greeting, *1810*
1:41 and **E** was filled with the Holy Spirit. *1810*
1:56 Mary stayed with **E** for about three months *899*[S]
1:57 When it was time *for* **E** to have her baby, *1810*

ELIZAPHAN (4)

Nu 3:30 of the Kohathite clans was **E** son of Uzziel. 507
34:25 **E** son of Parnach, the leader from the tribe 507
1Ch 15:8 the descendants of **E**, Shemaiah the leader 507
2Ch 29:13 the descendants of **E**, Shimri and Jeiel; 507

ELIZUR (5)

Nu 1:5 from Reuben, **E** son of Shedeur; 506
2:10 The leader of the people of Reuben is **E** son 506
7:30 On the fourth day **E** son of Shedeur, 506
7:35 This was the offering of **E** son of Shedeur. 506
10:18 **E** son of Shedeur was in command. 506

ELKANAH (20)

Ex 6:24 of Korah were Assir, **E** and Abiasaph. 555
1Sa 1:1 whose name was **E** son of Jeroham, 555
1:4 Whenever the day came for **E** to sacrifice, 555
1:8 **E** her husband would say to her, "Hannah, 555
1:19 **E** lay with Hannah his wife, 555
1:21 the man **E** went up with all his family 555
1:23 **E** her husband told her. 555
2:11 Then **E** went home to Ramah, 555
2:20 Eli would bless **E** and his wife, saying, 555
1Ch 6:23 **E** his son, Ebiasaph his son, Assir his son, 555
6:25 The descendants of **E**: Amasai, Ahimoth, 555
6:26 **E** his son, Zophai his son, Nahath his son, 555
6:27 **E** his son and Samuel his son. 555
6:34 the son of **E**, the son of Jeroham, 555
6:35 the son of **E**, the son of Mahath, 555
6:36 the son of **E**, the son of Joel, 555
9:16 and Berekiah son of Asa, the son of **E**, 555
12:6 **E**, Isshiah, Azarel, Joezer and Jashobeam 555
15:23 Berekiah and **E** were to be doorkeepers for 555
2Ch 28:7 and **E**, second to the king. 555

ELKOSHITE (1)

Na 1:1 The book of the vision of Nahum the **E**. 556

ELLASAR (2)

Ge 14:1 Arioch king of **E**, 536
14:9 of Shinar and Arioch king of **E**— 536

ELMADAM (1)

Lk 3:28 the son of Cosam, the son *of* **E**, *1825*

ELNAAM (1)

1Ch 11:46 Jeribai and Joshaviah the sons of **E**, 534

ELNATHAN (7)

2Ki 24:8 mother's name was Nehushta daughter of **E**; 535
Ezr 8:16 I summoned Eliezer, Ariel, Shemaiah, **E**, 535
8:16 Shemaiah, Elnathan, Jarib, **E**, Nathan, 535
8:16 who were leaders, and Joiarib and **E**, 535
Jer 26:22 however, sent **E** son of Acbor to Egypt, 535
36:12 **E** son of Acbor, Gemariah son of Shaphan, 535
36:25 though **E**, Delaiah and Gemariah urged 535

ELOHE See EL ELOHE ISRAEL

ELOI (4)

Mt 27:46 "**E**, Eloi, lama sabachthani?"— *1830*
27:46 "Eloi, **E**, lama sabachthani?"— *1830*
Mk 15:34 "**E**, Eloi, lama sabachthani?"— *1830*
15:34 "Eloi, **E**, lama sabachthani?"— *1830*

ELON (7) [ELONITE]

Ge 26:34 also Basemath daughter of **E** the Hittite. 390
36:2 Adah daughter of **E** the Hittite, 390
46:14 The sons of Zebulun: Sered, **E** and Jahleel. 472
Nu 26:26 through **E**, the Elonite clan; 472
Jos 19:43 **E**, Timnah, Ekron, 391
Jdg 12:11 **E** the Zebulunite led Israel ten years. 390
12:12 Then **E** died, and was buried in Aijalon in 390

ELON BETHHANAN (1)

1Ki 4:9 Beth Shemesh and **E**; 392

ELONITE (1) [ELON]

Nu 26:26 through Elon, the **E** clan; 533

ELOQUENCE (1) [ELOQUENT]

1Co 2:1 with **e** or superior wisdom as I proclaimed *3364*

ELOQUENT (1) [ELOQUENCE]

Ex 4:10 "O Lord, I have never been **e**, 408+1821

ELOTH (KJV) ELATH

ELPAAL (3)

1Ch 8:11 By Hushim he had Abitub and **E**. 551
8:12 The sons of **E**: 551
8:18 Izliah and Jobab were the sons of **E**. 551

ELPELET (1)

1Ch 14:5 Ibhar, Elishua, **E**, 550

ELSE (92) [ELSE'S, ELSEWHERE]

Ge 19:12 "Do you have anyone **e** here— 6388
19:12 or anyone **e** in the city who belongs to you? NIH
34:28 and donkeys and **everything e** of theirs in 889
Ex 4:13 "O Lord, please send **someone e** to do it." 928+3338[S]
10:23 No one could see **anyone e** 278[S]
22:27 **What** *e* will he sleep in? AIT
29:33 But no one **e** may eat them, 2424
33:16 What **e** will distinguish me and your people NIH
36:6 "No man or woman is to make anything **e** 6388
Lev 16:2 or **e** he will die, 4202
27:20 or if he has sold it to someone **e**, 337
Nu 1:51 **Anyone e** who goes near it shall be put 2424
3:10 **anyone e** who approaches 2424
3:38 **Anyone e** who approached 2424
6:21 in addition to **whatever** *e* he can afford. AIT
12:3 more humble than anyone **e** on the face of 132[S]
15:14 or **anyone** *e* living among you presents AIT
18:4 and no one **e** may come near where you are. 2424
18:7 **Anyone e** who comes near 2424
20:19 to pass through on foot—nothing **e**." 1821
22:19 and I will find out what **e** 3578
31:23 and anything **e** that can withstand fire must NIH
Dt 20:5 in battle and someone **e** may dedicate it. 337
20:6 in battle and someone **e** enjoy it. 337
20:7 in battle and someone **e** marry her." 337
20:14 the livestock and everything **e** in the city, 889[S]
23:19 or food or anything **e** that may earn interest. NIH
Jdg 18:7 and had no relationship with anyone **e**. NIH
18:24 What **e** do I have? 6388
18:28 and had no relationship with anyone **e**. NIH
20:48 the animals and everything **e** they found. NIH
1Sa 17:30 then turned away to **someone e** and brought 337
30:19 plunder or **anything** *e* they had taken. AIT
2Sa 3:35 so severely, if I taste bread or **anything** *e* AIT
1Ki 2:36 but do not go **anywhere e**. 625+625+2025+2025+2256
2:42 'On the day you leave to go **anywhere e**, 625+625+2025+2025+2256
14:5 **pretend to be someone e**." 5796
Ezr 7:20 And **anything e** needed for the temple 10692
Est 1:19 to **someone e** who is better than she. 8295
Job 17:3 Who **e** will put up security for me? 2085
Pr 4:23 Above all **e**, guard your heart, 5464[S]
14:10 and no *one* **e** can share its joy. 2424
27:2 **someone e**, and not your own lips. 5799
Ecc 3:16 And I saw **something e** under the sun: 6388
8:14 There is something **e** meaningless NIH
9:11 I have seen **something e** under the sun: 8740
Isa 27:5 **Or e** let them come to me for refuge; 196
Jer 9:7 and test them, for **what e** can I do because 375
23:34 If a prophet or a priest or **anyone e** claims, 6639[S]
26:19 "Did Hezekiah king of Judah or **anyone** *e* AIT
40:5 or go **anywhere** *e* you please." AIT
Eze 27:27 and **everyone e** on board will sink into 3972+7736
Da 5:17 and give your rewards to **someone e**. 10025
Mal 4:6 **or e** I will come and strike the land with 7153
Mt 11:3 or should we expect **someone e**?" *2283*
Mk 1:38 Jesus replied, "Let us go **somewhere e**— *250*
Lk 7:19 or should we expect **someone e**?" *257*
7:20 or should we expect **someone e**?' " *257*
13:31 "Leave this place and go somewhere **e**. *NIG*
18:9 and looked down on **everybody e**, *3370*
22:58 A little later *someone* **e** saw him and said, *2283*
Jn 5:7 **someone e** goes down ahead of me." *257*
5:43 but if **someone e** comes in his own name, *257*
15:24 not done among them what no one **e** did, *257*
21:18 and **someone e** will dress you and lead you *257*
Ac 4:12 Salvation is found in no one **e**, *257*
5:13 No one **e** dared join them, *3370*
8:34 prophet talking himself or someone **e**?" *2283*
17:25 and breath and everything **e**. *NIG*
24:12 in the synagogues or **anywhere e in** the city. *2848*
Ro 2:1 you who pass judgment on someone **e**, *NIG*
8:39 nor anything **e** in all creation, *2283*
14:20 to eat anything that causes someone **e** *NIG*
14:21 or drink wine or to do anything **e** *NIG*
1Co 1:16 I don't remember if I baptized anyone **e**.) *257*
3:10 and **someone e** is building on it. *257*
4:7 who makes you different from anyone **e**? *NIG*
7:11 or **e** be reconciled to her husband. *NIG*
11:21 ahead without waiting for anybody **e**. *NIG*
15:37 perhaps of wheat or *of* something **e**. *3370*
2Co 9:13 in sharing with them and with everyone **e**. *NIG*
11:21 What anyone **e** dares to boast about— *NIG*

2Co 11:28 **Besides everything e,** I face daily the pressure of my concern *3836+4211+6006*
Gal 6: 4 without comparing himself to **somebody e,** *2283*
Php 1:13 *to* everyone **e** that I am in chains for Christ. *3370*
2:20 I have no one **e** like him, *NIG*
3: 4 If anyone **e** thinks he has reasons *257*
1Th 2: 6 not from you or **anyone e.** *257*
3:12 for each other and for everyone **e,** *NIG*
5:15 to be kind to each other and to everyone **e.** *NIG*
1Ti 1:10 whatever **e** is contrary to the sound doctrine *2283*
Jas 5:12 not by heaven or by earth or by anything **e.** *257*

ELSE'S (5) [ELSE]

Ge 43:34 as much as anyone **e.** 4392
Ru 2:22 in **someone e** field you might be harmed." 337
Lk 16:12 with **someone e** property, *259*
Ro 14: 4 Who are you to judge **someone e** servant? *259*
15:20 not be building on **someone e** foundation. *259*

ELSEWHERE (7) [ELSE, WHERE]

Lev 18: 9 in the same home or **e.** 2575
2Ch 26: 6 near Ashdod and **e** among the Philistines. NIH
Ezr 4:10 and settled in the city of Samaria and **e** 10692
4:17 of their associates living in Samaria and **e** 10692
Ps 84:10 in your courts than a thousand **e;** NIH
Jn 12:39 because, as Isaiah says **e:** *4099*
Ac 13:35 So it is stated **e:** *1877+2283*

ELTEKEH (2)

Jos 19:44 **E,** Gibbethon, Baalath, 559
21:23 Also from the tribe of Dan they received **E,** 558

ELTEKON (1)

Jos 15:59 Beth Anoth and **E—** 560

ELTOLAD (2)

Jos 15:30 **E,** Kesil, Hormah, 557
19: 4 **E,** Bethul, Hormah, 557

ELUDE (2) [ELUDED]

Job 11:20 and escape *will* **e** them; 6
Rev 9: 6 but death *will* **e** them. *608+5771*

ELUDED (2) [ELUDE]

1Sa 18:11 But David **e** him twice. 4946+6015+7156
19:10 but David **e** him as Saul drove the spear 7080

ELUL (1)

Ne 6:15 on the twenty-fifth of **E,** 469

ELUZAI (1)

1Ch 12: 5 **E,** Jerimoth, Bealiah, Shemariah 539

ELYMAS (2)

Ac 13: 8 But **E** the sorcerer (for *1829*
13: 9 looked straight at **E** and said, *899*[S]

ELZABAD (2)

1Ch 12:12 Johanan the eighth, **E** the ninth, 479
26: 7 Othni, Rephael, Obed and **E;** 479

ELZAPHAN (2)

Ex 6:22 of Uzziel were Mishael, **E** and Sithri. 553
Lev 10: 4 Moses summoned Mishael and **E,** 553

EMASCULATE (1) [EMASCULATED]

Gal 5:12 the whole way and **e** *themselves!* *644*

EMASCULATED (1) [EMASCULATE]

Dt 23: 1 No *one who has* **been e** *by* crushing 7205

EMBALM (1) [EMBALMED, EMBALMING]

Ge 50: 2 in his service to **e** his father Israel. 2846

EMBALMED (2) [EMBALM]

Ge 50: 2 So the physicians **e** him, 2846
50:26 And after *they* **e** him, 2846

EMBALMING (1) [EMBALM]

Ge 50: 3 for that was the time required for **e.** 2847

EMBANKMENT (1) [BANK]

Lk 19:43 when your enemies will build an **e** *5918*

EMBARRASS (1) [EMBARRASSED, EMBARRASSMENT]

Ru 2:15 among the sheaves, don't **e** her. 4007

EMBARRASSED (1) [EMBARRASS]

2Co 7:14 and you *have* not **e** *me.* *2875*

EMBARRASSMENT (1) [EMBARRASS]

Jdg 3:25 They waited to the point of **e,** 1017

EMBEDDED (1)

Ecc 12:11 words of the wise are like **firmly e** nails— 5749

EMBERS (2)

Ps 102: 3 my bones burn like **glowing e.** 4611
Pr 26:21 As charcoal to **e** and as wood to fire, 1624

EMBITTER (1) [BITTER]

Col 3:21 Fathers, *do* not **e** your children, *2241*

EMBITTERED (1) [BITTER]

Ps 73:21 my heart was grieved and my spirit **e,** 9111

EMBODIMENT (1) [BODY]

Ro 2:20 in the law the **e** of knowledge and truth— *3673*

EMBOLDENED (1) [BOLD]

1Co 8:10 *be* **e** to eat what has been sacrificed *3868*

EMBRACE (5) [EMBRACED, EMBRACES, EMBRACING]

Pr 3:18 She is a tree of life to those *who* **e** her; 2616
4: 8 **e** her, and she will honor you. 2485
5:20 Why **e** the bosom of another man's wife? 2485
Ecc 3: 5 a time to **e** and a time to refrain, 2485
Mic 7: 5 Even with her who lies in your **e** be careful 2668

EMBRACED (7) [EMBRACE]

Ge 29:13 *He* **e** him and kissed him and brought him 2485
33: 4 But Esau ran to meet Jacob and **e** him; 2485
45:14 and Benjamin **e** him, weeping. 6584+7418
48:10 and his father kissed them and **e** them. 2485
1Ki 9: 9 and *have* **e** other gods, 2616
2Ch 7:22 and *have* **e** other gods, 2616
Ac 20:37 They all wept as *they* **e** him and kissed him. *2093+2158+3836+5549*

EMBRACES (2) [EMBRACE]

SS 2: 6 and his right arm **e** me. 2485
8: 3 under my head and his right arm **e** me. 2485

EMBRACING (1) [EMBRACE]

Ecc 2: 3 with wine, and **e** folly— 296

EMBROIDERED (10) [EMBROIDERER, EMBROIDERERS]

Jdg 5:30 as plunder for Sisera, colorful garments **e,** 8391
5:30 **highly e** garments for my neck— 8391
Ps 45:14 In **e garments** she is led to the king; 8391
Eze 16:10 an **e dress** and put leather sandals on you. 8391
16:13 of fine linen and costly fabric and **e cloth.** 8391
16:18 you took your **e** clothes to put on them, 8391
26:16 and take off their **e** garments. 8391
27: 7 Fine **e** linen from Egypt was your sail 8391
27:16 purple fabric, **e work,** fine linen, 8391
27:24 **e work** and multicolored rugs 8391

EMBROIDERER (7) [EMBROIDERED]

Ex 26:36 the work of an **e.** 8387
27:16 the work of an **e—** 8387
28:39 The sash is to be the work of an **e.** 8387
36:37 the work of an **e;** 8387
38:18 the work of an **e.** 8387
38:23 a craftsman and designer, and an **e** in blue, 8387
39:29 the work of an **e—** 8387

EMBROIDERERS (1) [EMBROIDERED]

Ex 35:35 **e** in blue, purple and scarlet yarn 8387

EMEK See BETH EMEK, EMEK KEZIZ

EMEK KEZIZ (1)

Jos 18:21 Jericho, Beth Hoglah, **E,** 6681

EMERALD (5)

Ex 28:18 a sapphire and an **e;** 3402
39:11 a sapphire and an **e;** 3402
Eze 28:13 ruby, topaz and **e,** chrysolite, 3402
Rev 4: 3 A rainbow, resembling an **e,** *5039*
21:19 the third chalcedony, the fourth **e,** *5040*

EMERODS (KJV) TUMORS

EMERGE (1)

Da 8:22 *that will* **e** from his nation but will 6641

EMINENT (KJV) MOUND, MOUNDS, LOFTY

EMISSION (6)

Lev 15:16 " 'When a man has an **e** *of* semen, 8887
15:18 with a woman and there is an **e** *of* semen, 8887
15:32 for anyone made unclean by an **e** *of* semen, 8887
Lev 22: 4 by a corpse or by anyone who has an **e** 8887
Dt 23:10 unclean because of a nocturnal **e,** 7937
Eze 23:20 like those of donkeys and whose **e** was like 2444

EMITES (3)

Ge 14: 5 the **E** in Shaveh Kiriathaim 400
Dt 2:10 (The **E** used to live there— 400
2:11 but the Moabites called them **E.** 400

EMMANUEL (KJV) IMMANUEL

EMMOR (KJV) HAMOR

EMMAUS (1)

Lk 24:13 of them were going to a village called **E,** *1843*

EMPEROR (1) [EMPIRE]

Ac 25:25 to the **E** I decided to send him to Rome. *4935*

EMPEROR'S (1) [EMPIRE]

Ac 25:21 to be held over for the **E** decision, *4935*

EMPHATICALLY (1)

Mk 14:31 But Peter insisted **e,** *1735*

EMPIRE (4) [EMPEROR, EMPEROR'S, IMPERIAL]

Est 10: 1 King Xerxes imposed tribute throughout the **e,** 824
Jer 34: 1 and peoples in the **e** he ruled were fighting 824
Da 11: 4 his **e** will be broken up and parceled out 4895
11: 4 his **e** will be uprooted and given to others. 4895

EMPLOYED (1)

Eze 39:14 " 'Men *will be* regularly **e** to cleanse 976

EMPTIED (5) [EMPTY]

Ge 24:20 So she quickly **e** her jar into the trough, 6867
Lev 14:36 to order the house *to be* **e** before he goes in 7155
Ne 5:13 So may such a man be shaken out and **e!"** 8199
Zep 2: 4 At midday Ashdod *will be* **e** 1763
1Co 1:17 lest the cross of Christ *be* **e** of its power. *3033*

EMPTIES (1) [EMPTY]

Eze 47: 8 *When* it **e** into the Sea, 3655

EMPTY (33) [EMPTY-HANDED, EMPTIED, EMPTIES, EMPTYING]

Ge 1: 2 Now the earth was formless and **e,** 983
37:24 the cistern was **e;** there was no water in it. 8199
Jdg 7:16 he placed trumpets and **e** jars in the hands 8199
Ru 1:21 but the LORD has brought me back **e.** 8200
1Sa 6: 3 do not send it away **e,** 8200
20:18 because your seat *will be* **e.** 7212
20:25 but David's place *was* **e.** 7212
20:27 David's place *was* **e** again. 7212
2Ki 4: 3 around and ask all your neighbors for **e** jars. 8199
18:20 but you speak only **e words.** 1821+8557
2Ch 24:11 the chief priest would come and **e** the chest 6867
Job 15: 2 "Would a wise man answer with **e** notions 8120
26: 7 the northern [skies] over **e space;** 9332
35:13 God does not listen to their **e plea;** 8736
35:16 So Job opens his mouth with **e talk;** 2039
Pr 14: 4 Where there are no oxen, the manger is **e,** 1338
Isa 16: 6 but her boasts are **e.** 4027+4202
32: 6 the hungry he **leaves e** and from 8197
36: 5 but you speak only **e words.** 1821+8557
45:18 he did not create it to be **e,** 9332
55:11 It will not return to me **e,** 8200
59: 4 They rely on **e** arguments and speak lies; 9332
Jer 4:23 and it was formless and **e;** 983
48:12 *they will* **e** her jars and smash her jugs. 8197
51:34 he has made us an **e** jar. 8198
Eze 24: 6 **E** it piece by piece without casting lots 3655
24:11 the **e** pot on the coals till it becomes hot 8199
Am 4: 6 "I gave you **e stomachs** in every city 5931+9094
Mic 6:14 your stomach will still be **e.** 3803
Lk 1:53 but has sent the rich away **e.** *3031*
Eph 5: 6 Let no one deceive you *with* **e** words, *3031*
1Pe 1:18 from the **e** way of life handed down to you *3469*
2Pe 2:18 For they mouth **e,** boastful words and, *3470*

EMPTY-HANDED (12) [EMPTY, HAND]

Ge 31:42 you would surely have sent me away **e.** 8200
Ex 3:21 so that when you leave you will not go **e.** 8200
23:15 "No one is to appear before me **e.** 8200
34:20 "No one is to appear before me **e.** 8200
Dt 15:13 you release him, do not send him away **e.** 8200
16:16 No man should appear before the LORD **e:** 8200
Ru 3:17 'Don't go back to your mother-in-law **e.'** " 8200
Job 22: 9 And you sent widows away **e** and broke 8200
Jer 50: 9 be like skilled warriors who do not return **e.** 8200
Mk 12: 3 beat him and sent him away **e.** *3031*
Lk 20:10 the tenants beat him and sent him away **e.** *3031*
20:11 and treated shamefully and sent away **e.** *3031*

EMPTYING (2) [EMPTY]
Ge 42:35 As they were **e** their sacks, 8197
Hab 1:17 *Is he to* keep on **e** his net, 8197

EMULATION (KJV) ENVY

EN EGLAIM (1) [EGLAIM]
Eze 47:10 from En Gedi to **E** there will 6536

EN GANNIM (3)
Jos 15:34 Zanoah, **E,** Tappuah, Enam, 6528
19:21 **E,** En Haddah and Beth Pazzez. 6528
21:29 Jarmuth and **E,** together 6528

EN GEDI (6) [HAZAZON TAMAR]
Jos 15:62 the City of Salt and **E**— 6527
1Sa 23:29 and lived in the strongholds of **E.** 6527
24: 1 "David is in the Desert of **E.**" 6527
2Ch 20: 2 in Hazazon Tamar" (that is, **E**). 6527
SS 1:14 from the vineyards of **E.** 6527
Eze 47:10 from **E** to En Eglaim there will 6527

EN HADDAH (1)
Jos 19:21 En Gannim, **E** and Beth Pazzez. 6532

EN HAKKORE (1)
Jdg 15:19 So the spring was called **E,** 6530

EN HAZOR (1) [HAZOR]
Jos 19:37 Kedesh, Edrei, **E,** 6533

EN MISHPAT (1) [KADESH]
Ge 14: 7 and went to **E** (that is, 6535

EN RIMMON (1) [RIMMON]
Ne 11:29 in **E,** in Zorah, in Jarmuth, 6538

EN ROGEL (4)
Jos 15: 7 of En Shemesh and came out at **E.** 6537
18:16 of the Jebusite city and so to **E.** 6537
2Sa 17:17 and Ahimaaz were staying at **E.** 6537
1Ki 1: 9 at the Stone of Zoheleth near **E.** 6537

EN SHEMESH (1)
Jos 15: 7 It continued along to the waters of **E** 6539
Jos 18:17 It then curved north, went to **E,** 6539

EN TAPPUAH (1) [TAPPUAH]
Jos 17: 7 to include the people living at **E.** 6540

ENABLE (3) [ABLE]
Ecc 6: 2 but God *does* not **e** him to enjoy them, 8948
Lk 1:74 and *to* **e** us to serve him without fear *1443*
Ac 4:29 consider their threats and **e** your servants *1443*

ENABLED (6) [ABLE]
Lev 26:13 and **e** you **to walk** with heads held high. 2143
Ru 4:13 and the LORD **e** her to conceive, 5989
Jn 6:65 to me unless the Father *has* **e** him." *1443+1639*
Ac 2: 4 in other tongues as the Spirit **e** them. *1443*
7:10 He gave Joseph wisdom and **e** him to gain *NIG*
Heb 11:11 was **e** to become a father *1539*

ENABLES (5) [ABLE]
2Sa 22:34 *he* **e** me **to stand** on the heights. 6641
Ps 18:33 *he* **e** me **to stand** on the heights. 6641
Ecc 5:19 and **e** him to enjoy them, 8948
Hab 3:19 he **e** me **to go** on the heights. 2005
Php 3:21 by the power that **e** him to bring everything *1538*

ENABLING (1) [ABLE]
Ac 14: 3 the message of his grace *by* **e** them to do miraculous signs and *1328+1443+3836+5931*

ENAIM (2)
Ge 38:14 and then sat down at the entrance to **E,** 6542
38:21 beside the road at **E?"** 6542

ENAM (1)
Jos 15:34 Zanoah, En Gannim, Tappuah, **E,** 6543

ENAN (5) [HAZAR ENAN]
Nu 1:15 from Naphtali, Ahira son of **E."** 6544
2:29 of the people of Naphtali is Ahira son of **E.** 6544
7:78 On the twelfth day Ahira son of **E,** 6544
7:83 This was the offering of Ahira son of **E.** 6544
10:27 and Ahira son of **E** was over the division of 6544

ENCAMP (9) [CAMP]
Ex 14: 2 "Tell the Israelites to turn back and **e** 2837
14: 2 *They are to* **e** by the sea, 2837
Nu 1:50 they are to take care of it and **e** around it. 2837
2: 3 the divisions of the camp of Judah *are to* **e** 2837
2:17 in the same order as *they* **e,** 2837
9:20 at the LORD's command *they would* **e,** 2837
Job 19:12 they build a siege ramp against me and **e** 2837
Isa 29: 3 *I will* **e** against you all around; 2837
Jer 50:29 **E** all around her; let no one escape. 2837

ENCAMPED (14) [CAMP]
Ge 26:17 So Isaac moved away from there and **e** in 2837
Nu 2:34 that is the way *they* **e** under their standards, 2837
9:17 wherever the cloud settled, the Israelites **e.** 2837
9:18 and at his command *they* **e.** 2837
9:23 At the LORD's command *they* **e,** 2837
12:16 the people left Hazeroth and **e** in the Desert 2837
24: 2 and saw Israel **e** tribe by tribe, 8905
Dt 23: 9 When *you are* **e** against your enemies, 3655+4722
Jdg 11:20 He mustered all his men and **e** at Jahaz 2837
1Sa 26: 5 with the army **e** around him. 2837
2Sa 23:13 a band of Philistines *was* **e** in the Valley 2837
1Ki 16:15 The army *was* **e** near Gibbethon, 2837
2Ki 25: 1 *He* **e** outside the city 2837
1Ch 11:15 a band of Philistines *was* **e** in the Valley 2837

ENCAMPS (1) [CAMP]
Ps 34: 7 of the LORD **e** around those who fear him, 2837

ENCHANTER (4) [ENCHANTERS]
Ps 58: 5 however skillful the **e** *may be.* 2489+2490
Isa 3: 3 skilled craftsman and clever **e.** 4318
Da 2:10 a thing of any magician or **e** or astrologer. 10081
2:27 Daniel replied, "No wise man, **e,** 10081

ENCHANTERS (6) [ENCHANTER]
Da 1:20 the magicians and **e** in his whole kingdom. 879
2: 2 So the king summoned the magicians, **e,** 879
4: 7 When the magicians, **e,** 10081
5: 7 The king called out for the **e,** 10081
5:11 appointed him chief of the magicians, **e,** 10081
5:15 The wise men and **e** were brought 10081

ENCIRCLE (3) [CIRCLE]
Ps 22:12 strong bulls of Bashan **e** me. 4193
Isa 29: 3 *I will* **e** you *with* towers and set 6584+7443
Lk 19:43 and **e** you and hem you in on every side. *4333*

ENCIRCLED (7) [CIRCLE]
1Ki 7:24 Below the rim, gourds **e** it— 6015+6017
2Ch 4: 3 figures of bulls **e** it— 6015+6017+6017
Ps 22:16 a band of evil men *has* **e** me, 5938
SS 7: 2 Your waist is a mound of wheat **e** by lilies. 6048
Rev 4: 3 resembling an emerald, **e** the throne. *3239*
5: 6 **e** by the four living creatures and the elders. *NIG*
5:11 They **e** the throne and the living creatures *3241*

ENCIRCLING (2) [CIRCLE]
1Ki 7:18 in two rows **e** each network to decorate 6017
2Ch 33:14 as far as the entrance of the Fish Gate and **e** 6015

ENCLOSE (1) [CLOSE]
SS 8: 9 *we will* **e** her *with* panels of cedar. 7443

ENCLOSED (3) [CLOSE]
Est 1: 5 in the **e** garden of the king's palace, 2958
SS 4:12 you are a spring **e,** a sealed fountain. 3159
Eze 46:22 of the outer court were **e** courts, 7788

ENCOUNTER (3)
Ex 23:27 into confusion every nation *you* **e.** 928+995
2Sa 23: 8 whom he killed in one **e.** 7193
1Ch 11:11 whom he killed in one **e.** 7193

ENCOURAGE (24) [ENCOURAGED, ENCOURAGEMENT, ENCOURAGES, ENCOURAGING, ENCOURAGINGLY]
Dt 1:38 **E** him, because he will lead Israel 2616
3:28 and **e** and strengthen him, 2616
2Sa 11:25 Say this *to* **e** Joab." 2616
19: 7 Now go out and **e** your men. 1819+4213+6584
Job 16: 5 But my mouth *would* **e** you; 599
Ps 10:17 *you* **e** them, and you listen to their cry, 3922+4213
64: 5 *They* **e** each other in evil plans, 2616
Isa 1:17 Seek justice, **e** the oppressed. 887
Jer 29: 8 **dreams** you **e** them **to have.** 2706+2731
Ac 15:32 said much *to* **e** and strengthen the brothers. *4151*
Ro 12: 8 if it is encouraging, let him **e;** *4155*
Eph 6:22 and that *he may* **e** you. *4151*
Col 4: 8 and that *he may* **e** your hearts. *4151*
1Th 3: 2 to strengthen and **e** you in your faith, *4151*
4:18 Therefore **e** each other with these words. *4151*
5:11 **e** one another and build each other up, *4151*
5:14 warn those who are idle, **e** the timid, *4170*
2Th 2:17 **e** your hearts and strengthen you *4151*
2Ti 4: 2 correct, rebuke and **e**— *4151*
Tit 1: 9 so that he can **e** others by sound doctrine *4151*
2: 6 **e** the young men to be self-controlled. *4151*
2:15 **E** and rebuke with all authority. *4151*
Heb 3:13 But **e** one another daily, *4151*
10:25 but let us **e** one another— *4151*

ENCOURAGED (20) [ENCOURAGE]
Jdg 7:11 you *will be* **e** to attack the camp." 2616+3338
20:22 of Israel **e** one another and again took 2616
2Ch 22: 3 for his mother **e** him in doing wrong. 3446
32: 6 and **e** them with these words: 1819+4222+6584
35: 2 to their duties and **e** them in the service of 2616
Eze 13:22 because you **e** the wicked not to turn 2616+3338
Ac 9:31 and **e** by the Holy Spirit, *4155*
11:23 he was glad and **e** them all to remain true to *4151*
16:40 they met with the brothers and **e** them. *4151*
18:27 the brothers **e** him and wrote to *4730*
27:36 They were all **e** and ate some food *2314*
28:15 Paul thanked God and **was e.** *2511+3284*
Ro 1:12 *be* **mutually e** by each other's faith. *5220*
1Co 14:31 so that everyone *may be* instructed and **e.** *4151*
2Co 7: 4 *I am* **greatly e;** *4155+4444*
7:13 By all this *we are* **e.** *4151*
Php 1:14 most of the brothers in the Lord *have been* **e** *4275*
Col 2: 2 My purpose is that they *may be* **e** in heart *4151*
1Th 3: 7 in all our distress and persecution *we were* **e** *4151*
Heb 6:18 hope offered to us *may* **be** greatly **e.** *2400+4155*

ENCOURAGEMENT (11) [ENCOURAGE]
Ac 4:36 called Barnabas (which means Son *of* **E**), *4155*
13:15 if you have a message *of* **e** for the people, *4155*
20: 2 **speaking** many words of **e to** *4151*
Ro 15: 4 the **e** of the Scriptures we might have hope. *4155*
15: 5 and **e** give you a spirit of unity *4155*
1Co 14: 3 for their strengthening, **e** and comfort. *4155*
2Co 7:13 In addition *to* our own **e,** *4155*
Php 2: 1 If you have any **e** from being united *4155*
2Th 2:16 and by his grace gave us eternal **e** *4155*
Phm 1: 7 Your love has given me great joy and **e,** *4155*
Heb 12: 5 that word *of* **e** that addresses you as sons: *4155*

ENCOURAGES (1) [ENCOURAGE]
Isa 41: 7 The craftsman **e** the goldsmith, 2616

ENCOURAGING (6) [ENCOURAGE]
Ac 14:22 the disciples and **e** them to remain true to *4151*
15:31 and were glad for its **e message.** *4155*
20: 1 and, *after* **e** them, said good-by and set out *4151*
Ro 12: 8 if it is **e,** let him encourage; *4151*
1Th 2:12 **e,** comforting and urging you *4151*
1Pe 5:12 **e** you and testifying that this is *4151*

ENCOURAGINGLY (1) [ENCOURAGE]
2Ch 30:22 Hezekiah spoke **e** to all the Levites, 4213+6584

ENCROACH (2)
Dt 2:37 not **e** on any of the land of the Ammonites, 7928
Pr 23:10 not move an ancient boundary stone or **e** on 995

ENCRUSTED (1) [CRUST]
Eze 24: 6 to the pot now **e,** 2689

END (268) [ENDED, ENDING, ENDS, ENDLESS, ENDLESSLY]
Ge 6:13 "I am going to put an **e** to all people, 7891
8: 3 At the **e** *of* the hundred and fifty days 7895
23: 9 which belongs to him and is at the **e** 7895
41:53 of abundance in Egypt **came to an e,** 3983
47:21 from *one* **e** *of* Egypt to the other. 1473+7895
Ex 12:41 At the **e** *of* the 430 years, to the very day, 7891
23:16 the Feast of Ingathering at the **e** *of* the year, 3655
25:19 on one **e** and the second cherub on 7896
26: 4 along the edge of the **e** curtain in one set, 7896
26: 4 the same with the **e** curtain in the other set. 7812
26: 5 and fifty loops on the **e** curtain of 7895
26:10 the edge of the **e** curtain in one set and also 7812
26:10 and also along the edge of the **e** curtain in NIH
26:22 Make six frames for the **far e,** that is, 3752
26:22 that is, the west **e** of the tabernacle, NIH
26:23 for the corners at the **far e.** 3752
26:27 at the **far e** *of* the tabernacle 3752
26:28 from **e** to end at the middle of the frames. 7895
26:28 from end to **e** at the middle of the frames. 7895
27:12 "The west **e** *of* the courtyard shall 6991
27:13 On the east **e,** toward the sunrise, 6991
32:27 through the camp from *one* **e** to the other, 9133S
36:11 along the edge of the **e** curtain in one set, 7896
36:11 and the same was done with the **e** curtain in 7812
36:12 and fifty loops on the **e** curtain of 7895
36:17 the edge of the **e** curtain in one set and also 7812
36:17 and also along the edge of the **e** curtain in NIH
36:27 They made six frames for the **far e,** that is, 3752
36:27 that is, the west **e** of the tabernacle, NIH
36:28 the corners of the tabernacle at the **far e.** 3752
36:32 at the **far e** *of* the tabernacle. 3752
36:33 that it extended from **e** to end at the middle 7895
36:33 that it extended from end to **e** at the middle 7895
37: 8 on one **e** and the second cherub on 7896
38:12 The west **e** was fifty cubits wide 6991
38:13 The east **e,** toward the sunrise, 6991
Nu 13:25 At the **e** *of* forty days they returned 7891
14:35 *They will* **meet** their **e** in this desert; 9462
16:21 from this assembly so *I can* **put an e** 3983
16:45 from this assembly so *I can* **put an e** 3983
17:10 *This will* **put an e** *to* their grumbling 3983
23:10 and may my **e** be like theirs!" 344
25:11 that in my zeal *I did* not **put an e** *to* them. 3983
34: 3 from the **e** *of* the Salt Sea, 7895
34: 5 the Wadi of Egypt and **e** at the Sea. 2118+9362
34: 9 to Ziphron and **e** *at* Hazar Enan. 2118+9362

Nu 34:12 along the Jordan and e *at* the Salt Sea. 2118+9362
Dt 4:32 ask from *one* e *of* the heavens to the other. 7895
8:16 to test you so that in the e it might go well 344
9:11 At the e *of* the forty days and forty nights, 7891
11:12 on it from the beginning of the year to its **e.** 344
13:7 from one e of the land to the other), 7895
14:28 At the e *of* every three years, 7895
15:1 At the e *of* every seven years 7891
28:64 from one e *of* the earth to the other. 7895
31:10 "At the e *of* every seven years, 7891
31:24 the words of this law from beginning to **e,** 9462
31:30 the words of this song from beginning to e 9462
32:20 he said, "and see what their e will be; 344
32:29 and discern what their e will be! 344
Jos 13:27 up to the e *of* the Sea of Kinnereth). 7895
15:2 the bay at the southern e *of* the Salt Sea, 7895
15:8 at the northern e *of* the Valley of Rephaim. 7895
24:20 and bring disaster on you and **make an e** 3983
Ru 3:7 to lie down at the **far** e *of* the grain pile. 7895
1Sa 3:12 from beginning to **e.** 3983
14:27 so he reached out the e *of* the staff that was 7895
14:43 "I merely tasted a little honey with the e 7895
2Sa 2:26 Don't you realize that *this will* e in bitterness? 340+928+2021+2118
15:7 At the e *of* four years, 7891
24:8 at the e *of* nine months and twenty days. 7895
24:15 on Israel from that morning **until the e of** 6330
1Ki 9:10 At the e *of* twenty years, 7895
10:20 one **at either** e of each step. 2256+2296+2296+4946+4946[S]
2Ki 8:3 At the e *of* the seven years she came back 7895
10:21 until it was full from *one* e to the other. 7023
18:10 the e *of* three years the Assyrians took it. 7895
21:16 that he filled Jerusalem from e to end— 7023
21:16 that he filled Jerusalem from end to **e—** 7023
24:20 **in the e** he thrust them from his presence. 6330
1Ch 29:29 from beginning to **e,** 340
2Ch 8:1 At the e *of* twenty years, 7891
9:19 one **at either** e of each step. 2256+2296+2296+4946+4946[S]
9:29 of Solomon's reign, from beginning to **e,** 340
12:15 of Rehoboam's reign, from beginning to **e,** 340
16:11 events of Asa's reign, from beginning to **e,** 340
20:16 and you will find them at the e *of* the gorge 6067
20:34 Jehoshaphat's reign, from beginning to **e,** 340
21:19 at the e of the second year, 7891
25:26 of Amaziah's reign, from beginning to **e,** 340
26:22 of Uzziah's reign, from beginning to **e,** 340
28:26 and all his ways, from beginning to **e,** 340
35:27 all the events, from beginning to **e,** 340
Ezr 9:11 with their impurity from *one* e to the other. 7023
Ne 3:21 the entrance of Eliashib's house to the e 9417
4:11 and will kill them and **put an e** *to* 8697
9:31 in your great mercy you did not put an e 3986
Est 1:18 be **no e** *of* disrespect and discord. 1896+3869
8:3 She begged him to **put an e** *to* the evil plan 6296
Job 4:15 and the hair on my body **stood on e.** 6169
7:6 and *they* **come to an e** without hope. 3983
16:3 Will your long-winded speeches never **e?** 7891
18:2 "When *will you* e these speeches? 7874+8492
19:25 that *in the* e he will stand upon the earth. 340
21:21 when his allotted months **come to an e?** 2951
28:3 Man puts an e to the darkness; 7891
Ps 7:9 **bring to an e** the violence of the wicked 1698
19:6 It rises at *one* e *of* the heavens 7895
39:4 my life's e and the number of my days; 7891
48:14 he will be our guide even to the **e.** 4637
89:44 *You have* **put an e** to his splendor 8697
102:27 and your years *will* never **e.** 9462
107:27 they *were* **at** their **wits' e.** 1182+2683+3972
112:8 **in the e** he will look in triumph on his foes. 889+6330
119:33 then I will keep them **to the e.** 6813
119:112 My heart is set on keeping your decrees **to the very e.** 4200+6409+6813
Pr 1:19 the e *of* all who go after ill-gotten gain; 784
5:4 but *in the* e she is bitter as gall, 344
5:11 At the **e of** your **life** you will groan, 344
14:12 but *in the* e it leads to death. 344
14:13 and joy may e in grief. 344
16:25 but *in the* e it leads to death. 344
19:20 and in the e you will be wise. 344
20:21 at the beginning will not be blessed at the **e.** 344
23:32 the e it bites like a snake and poisons like 344
25:8 in the e if your neighbor puts you to shame? 344
28:23 He who rebukes man will **in the e** gain more favor than 343
29:21 he will bring grief *in* the **e.** 344
Ecc 3:11 what God has done from beginning to **e.** 6067
4:8 There was no **e** to his toil, 7891
4:16 There was no **e** to all the people who were 7891
7:8 **e** *of* a matter is better than its beginning, 344
10:13 at the **e** they are wicked madness— 344
12:12 Of making many books there is no **e,** 7891
Isa 2:7 there is no e to their treasures. 7897
2:7 there is no e to their chariots. 7897
7:3 at the e *of* the aqueduct of the Upper Pool, 7895
9:7 and peace there will be no **e.** 7891
10:7 to **put an** e to many nations. 4162
10:25 Very soon my anger against you *will* e 3983
13:11 *I will* **put an e** *to* the arrogance of 8697
14:4 How the oppressor *has* **come to an e!** 8697
16:4 The oppressor *will* **come to an e,** 699
16:10 for *I have* **put an e** *to* the shouting. 8697
21:2 *I will* **bring to an e** all 8697
21:16 all the pomp of Kedar *will* **come to an e.** 3983
23:15 But at the e *of* these seventy years, 7891
Isa 23:17 At the e *of* seventy years, 7891
38:12 day and night *you* **made an e** *of* me. 8966
38:13 day and night *you* **made an e** *of* me. 8966
46:10 I make known the e from the beginning, 344
60:20 and your days of sorrow *will* **e.** 8966
66:17 *they will* **meet** *their* e together," 6066
Jer 5:31 But what will you do in the **e?** 344
7:34 *I will* **bring an e** *to* the sounds of joy 8697
12:12 of the LORD will devour from *one* e *of* 7895
16:9 and in your days I *will* **bring an e** *to* 8697
17:11 and in the e he will prove to be a fool. 344
20:18 to see trouble and sorrow and *to* e my days 3983
25:33 from *one* e *of* the earth to the other. 7895
48:2 'Come, *let us* **put an e** to that nation.' 4162
48:35 In Moab *I will* **put an e** 8697
49:37 the sword until I *have* **made an e** *of* them. 3983
51:13 your **e** has come, 7891
51:64 The words of Jeremiah **e** here. 6330
52:3 **in the e** he thrust them from his presence. 6330
La 3:53 *to* e my life in a pit and threw stones at me; 7551
4:18 Our e was near, our days were numbered, 7891
4:18 for our e had come. 7891
4:22 your punishment *will* **e;** 9462
Eze 3:16 At the e *of* seven days the word of 7895
5:2 When the days of your siege **come to an e,** 4848
7:2 to the land of Israel: The **e!** 7891
7:2 The e has come upon the four corners of 7891
7:3 The e is now upon you 7891
7:6 The e has come! 7891
7:6 The e has come! 7891
7:24 *I will* **put an e** *to* the pride of the mighty, 8697
12:23 *I am going to* **put an e** *to* this proverb, 8697
20:17 not destroy them or put an e to them in 3986
22:4 and the e *of* your years has come. 6961
22:15 and *I will* **put an e** *to* your uncleanness. 9462
23:48 *I will* **put an e** *to* lewdness in the land, 8697
26:13 *I will* **put an e** *to* your noisy songs, 8697
26:21 I will bring you to a **horrible** e and you will 1166
27:36 you have come to a **horrible** e and will 1166
28:19 you have come to a **horrible** e and will 1166
29:13 At the e *of* forty years I will gather 7891
30:10 " '*I will* **put an e** *to* the hordes of Egypt 8697
30:13 " 'I will destroy the idols and **put an e** *to* 8697
30:18 there her proud strength *will* **come to an e.** 8697
33:28 and her proud strength *will* **come to an e,** 8697
39:14 At the e *of* the seven months 7895
40:15 to the **far** e of its portico was fifty cubits. 7164
41:4 and its width was twenty cubits across the e 7156
43:27 *At the* e *of* these days, 3983
46:19 and showed me a place at the western e. 3752
Da 1:15 the e *of* the ten days they looked healthier 7921
1:18 At the e *of* the time set by the king 7921
2:44 **bring** them **to an e,** 10508
4:34 At the e *of* that time, I, Nebuchadnezzar, 10636
5:26 **brought** it **to an e.** 10719
6:26 his dominion will **never e.** 10002+10509+10527
7:28 "This is the e of the matter. 10509
8:17 that the vision concerns the time of the **e."** 7891
8:19 vision concerns the appointed time of the **e.** 7891
9:24 to **put an e** *to* sin, to atone for wickedness, 9462
9:26 The e will come like a flood: 7891
9:26 War will continue until the **e,** 7891
9:27 of the 'seven' *he will* **put an e** *to* sacrifice 8697
9:27 the e that is decreed is poured out on him." 3986
11:18 but a commander *will* **put an e** 8697
11:27 an e will still come at the appointed time. 7891
11:35 and made spotless until the time of the **e,** 7891
11:40 the e the king of the South will engage him 7891
11:45 Yet he will come to his **e,** 7891
12:4 of the scroll until the time of the **e.** 7891
12:9 up and sealed until the time of the **e.** 7891
12:12 the one who waits for and reaches the e of NIH
12:13 "As for you, go your way till the **e.** 7891
12:13 and then at the e *of* the days you will rise 7891
Hos 1:4 *I will* **put an e** *to* the kingdom of Israel. 8697
11:6 of their gates and **put an e** to their plans. 430
Am 6:7 your feasting and lounging *will* **e.** 6073
8:10 an only son and the e *of* it like a bitter day. 344
Na 1:8 an overwhelming flood he will make an e 3986
1:9 against the LORD he will bring to an **e;** 3986
Hab 2:3 it speaks of the e and will not prove false. 7891
Zep 1:18 for he will make a sudden e of all who live 3986
Mt 10:22 he who stands firm to the e will be saved. *5465*
13:39 The harvest is the e of the age, *5333*
13:40 so it will be at the e of the age. *5333*
13:49 This is how it will be at the e of the age. *5333*
21:41 **bring** those wretches **to** a wretched **e,"** *660*
24:3 be the sign of your coming and *of* the e of *5333*
24:6 but the e is still to come. *5465*
24:13 he who stands firm to the e will be saved. *5465*
24:14 and then the e will come. *5465*
24:31 from one e of the heavens to the other. *216*
28:20 to the **very** e of the age." *5333*
Mk 3:26 his **e** has come. *5465*
13:7 but the e is still to come. *5465*
13:13 he who stands firm to the e will be saved. *5465*
Lk 1:33 his kingdom will never **e."** *5465*
4:2 and *at the* e of them he was hungry. *5334*
17:24 and lights up the sky from one e to *NIG*
21:9 but the e will not come right away." *5465*
Jn 11:4 "This sickness *will* not e in death. *1639+4639*
Ac 21:26 when the days of purification *would* e and *1741*
Ro 10:4 Christ is the e of the law so that there may *5465*
1Co 1:8 He will keep you strong to the **e,** *5465*
4:9 on display at the e of the procession, *2274*
15:24 Then the e will come, *5465*
2Co 11:15 Their **e** will be what their actions deserve. *5465*
Col 1:29 **To this e** I labor, *1650+4005*
Heb 1:12 and your years *will* never **e."** *1722*
3:14 to share in Christ if we hold firmly till the e *5465*
6:8 In the e it will be burned. *5465*
6:11 to show this same diligence to the very **e,** *5465*
6:16 the oath confirms what is said and puts an e *4306*
7:3 without beginning of days or e of life, *2400+5465*
9:26 now he has appeared once for all at the e of *5333*
11:22 By faith Joseph, *when his* **e was near,** *5462*
1Pe 4:7 The e of all things is near. *5465*
2Pe 2:20 they are worse off at the e than they were at *2274*
Rev 2:26 does my will to the **e,** I will give authority *5465*
21:6 the Beginning and the **E.** *5465*
22:13 the Beginning and the **E.** *5465*

ENDANGER (2) [DANGER]

Ru 4:6 because *I might* e my own estate. 8845
1Co 15:30 for us, why *do we* e ourselves every hour? *3073*

ENDANGERED (1) [DANGER]

Ecc 10:9 whoever splits logs *may* **be e** by them. 6124

ENDANGERS (1) [DANGER]

Lev 19:16 **do anything that** e your neighbor's **life.** 1947+6584+6641

ENDEAVOUR (KJV) MAKE EVERY EFFORT

ENDED (16) [END]

Jos 15:11 The boundary e at the sea. 2118+9362
16:8 to the Kanah Ravine and e at the sea. 2118+9362
17:9 the northern side of the ravine and e at 2118+9362
19:14 and e at the Valley of Iphtah El. 2118+9362
19:22 and e at the Jordan. 2118+9362
2Ch 31:1 When all this *had* **e,** 3983
Job 31:40 The words of Job *are* **e.** 9462
39:3 their labor pains *are* **e.** 8938
Ps 78:33 So *he* e their days in futility and their years 3983
Pr 22:10 quarrels and insults *are* **e.** 8697
Isa 14:4 How his fury *has* **e!** 8697
Jer 8:20 "The harvest is past, the summer *has* **e,** 3983
Am 8:5 be e that we may market wheat?"— NIH
Ac 20:1 When the uproar *had* **e,** *4264*
Rev 20:3 until the thousand years *were* **e.** *5464*
20:5 to life until the thousand years *were* **e.)** *5464*

ENDING (4) [END]

Ge 44:12 with the oldest and e with the youngest. 3983
Jos 15:4 e at the sea. 2118+9362
16:3 e at the sea. 2118+9362
19:33 to Lakkum and e *at* the Jordan. 2118+9362

ENDLESS (8) [END]

Job 22:5 Are not your sins **e?** 401+7891
Ps 9:6 **E** ruin has overtaken the enemy, 4200+5905
49:11 dwellings for **e generations,** 1887+1887+2256
93:5 holiness adorns your house for e days, 802
106:31 credited to him as righteousness for **e** generations to come. 6330+6409
Na 2:9 The supply is **e,** 401+7897
3:19 for who has not felt your e cruelty? 9458
1Ti 1:4 *to* myths and e genealogies. *596*

ENDLESSLY (1) [END]

Heb 10:1 same sacrifices repeated **e** year *1457+1650+3836*

ENDOR (3)

Jos 17:11 Ibleam and the people of Dor, **E,** 6529
1Sa 28:7 "There is one in **E,"** they said. 6529
Ps 83:10 at **E** and became like refuse on the ground. 6529

ENDOW (2) [ENDOWED]

Job 39:17 for God *did* **not e** her *with* wisdom 5960
Ps 72:1 **E** the king *with* your justice, O God, 5989

ENDOWED (4) [ENDOW]

2Ch 2:12 **e with** intelligence and discernment, 3359
Job 38:36 Who **e** the heart *with* wisdom 8883
Isa 55:5 for *he has* **e** you **with splendor."** 6995
60:9 for *he has* **e** you **with splendor.** 6995

ENDS (66) [END]

Ex 25:18 of hammered gold at the e *of* the cover. 7896
25:19 of one piece with the cover, at the two **e.** 7896
28:25 the other e *of* the chains to the two settings, 7896
37:7 of hammered gold at the e *of* the cover. 7896
37:8 at the two e he made them of one piece with 7896
39:18 the other e *of* the chains to the two settings, 7896
Dt 28:49 from the e *of* the earth, 7895
33:17 even those at the e *of* the earth. 700
1Sa 2:10 the LORD will judge the e *of* the earth. 700
1Ki 8:8 These poles were so long that their e could 8031
2Ch 5:9 These poles were so long that their **e,** 8031
Job 28:24 the e *of* the earth and sees everything under 7896
37:3 the whole heaven and sends it to the e *of* 4053
Ps 2:8 the e *of* the earth your possession. 700
19:4 their words to the e *of* the world. 7895
22:27 the e *of* the earth will remember and turn to 700

Ps 46: 9 He makes wars cease to the e *of* the earth; 7895
48:10 your praise reaches to the e *of* the earth; 7898
59:13 the e *of* the earth that God rules over Jacob. 700
61: 2 From the e *of* the earth I call to you, 7895
65: 5 the e *of* the earth and of the farthest seas, 7898
67: 7 and all the e *of* the earth will fear him. 700
72: 8 from sea to sea and from the River to the e 700
98: 3 all the e *of* the earth have seen the salvation 700
135: 7 He makes clouds rise from the e *of* 7895
Pr 11:23 The desire of the righteous e only in good, NIH
12:24 but laziness e in slave labor. 2118
16: 4 LORD works out everything for his own e— 5102
17:24 a fool's eyes wander to the e *of* the earth. 7895
18: 1 An unfriendly man pursues **selfish e;** 9294
20:17 but he **e up** with a mouth full of gravel. 339
30: 4 Who has established all the e *of* the earth? 700
Isa 5:26 he whistles for those at the e *of* the earth. 7895
13: 5 from the e *of* the heavens— 7895
24:16 From the e *of* the earth we hear singing: 4053
40:28 the Creator of the e *of* the earth. 7896
41: 5 the e *of* the earth tremble. 7896
41: 9 I took you from the e *of* the earth, 7896
42:10 his praise from the e *of* the earth, 7895
43: 6 and my daughters from the e *of* the earth— 7895
45:22 all you e *of* the earth; 700
48:20 Send it out to the e *of* the earth; 7895
49: 6 that you may bring my salvation to the e *of* 7895
52:10 the e *of* the earth will see the salvation 700
58: 4 Your fasting e in quarreling and strife, NIH
62:11 The LORD has made proclamation to the e 7895
Jer 6:22 a great nation is being stirred up from the e 3752
10:13 he makes clouds rise from the e *of* 7895
16:19 to you the nations will come from the e *of* 700
25:31 tumult will resound to the e *of* the earth, 7895
25:32 a mighty storm is rising from the e *of* 3752
31: 8 of the north and gather them from the e *of* 3752
48:47 Here e the judgment on Moab. 6330
50:41 up from the e *of* the earth. 3752
51:16 he makes clouds rise from the e *of* 7895
Eze 15: 4 on the fire as fuel and the fire burns both e 7896
Da 4:11 it was visible to the e *of* the earth. 10509
Mic 5: 4 for then his greatness will reach to the e *of* 700
Zec 9:10 from sea to sea and from the River to the e 700
Mt 12:42 for she came from the e of the earth *4306*
Mk 13:27 the e of the earth to the ends of the heavens. *216*
13:27 the ends of the earth to the e of the heavens. *216*
Lk 11:31 for she came from the e of the earth *4306*
Ac 1: 8 and to the e of the earth." *2274*
13:47 that you may bring salvation to the e of *2274*
Ro 10:18 their words to the e of the world." *4306*

ENDUED (1)

Ps 89:13 Your arm is **e with** power; 6640

ENDURANCE (12) [ENDURE]

Ro 15: 4 so that through e and the encouragement of *5705*
15: 5 May the God who *gives* e *5705*
2Co 1: 6 which produces in you **patient** e of *5705*
6: 4 in every way: in great **e;** *5705*
Col 1:11 you may have **great** e and patience, *4246+5705*
1Th 1: 3 and your e inspired by hope *5705*
1Ti 6:11 godliness, faith, love, e and gentleness. *5705*
2Ti 3:10 my purpose, faith, patience, love, **e,** *5705*
Tit 2: 2 and sound in faith, in love and *in* **e.** *5705*
Rev 1: 9 in the suffering and kingdom and **patient e** *5705*
13:10 for **patient** e and faithfulness on the part of *5705*
14:12 This calls for **patient** e on the part of *5705*

ENDURE (40) [ENDURANCE, ENDURED, ENDURES, ENDURING]

1Sa 13:14 But now your kingdom *will* not **e;** 7756
2Sa 7:16 and your kingdom *will* e forever 586
Job 14: 2 like a fleeting shadow, *he does* not **e.** 6641
15:29 be rich and his wealth *will* not **e,** 7756
20:21 his prosperity *will* not **e.** 2656
Ps 37:18 and their inheritance *will* e forever. 2118
49:12 But man, despite his riches, *does* not **e;** 4328
55:12 *I could* e it; 5951
69: 7 For *I* e scorn for your sake, 5951
69:10 When I weep and fast, I *must* e scorn; 2118+4200
72: 5 *He will* e as long as the sun, 799
72:17 *May* his name e forever; 2118
89:29 **as long as** the heavens **e.** 3427+3869
89:36 and his throne e before me like the sun; NIH
101: 5 him *will I* not **e.** 3523
104:31 *May* the glory of the LORD e forever; 2118
119:91 Your laws e to this day, 6641
Pr 12:19 Truthful lips e forever, 3922
27:24 for riches do not e forever, NIH
Ecc 3:14 that everything God does *will* e forever; 2118
Isa 66:22 and the new earth that I make *will* e 6641
66:22 "so *will* your name and descendants **e.** 6641
Jer 10:10 the nations cannot e his wrath. 3920
10:19 "This is my sickness, and *I must* e it." 5951
44:22 LORD could no longer e your wicked actions 5951
Eze 22:14 *Will* your courage e or your hands 6641
Da 2:44 but *it will* itself e forever. 10624
Joel 2:11 Who *can* e it? 3920
Na 1: 6 Who *can* e his fierce anger? 7756
Mal 3: 2 But who *can* e the day of his coming? 3920
1Co 4:12 when we are persecuted, *we* e it; *462*
2Co 1: 8 far beyond our ability to **e,** *NIG*
2Ti 2: 3 **E** hardship **with** us like a good soldier *5155*
2:10 Therefore *I* e everything for the sake of *5702*
2Ti 2:12 if *we* **e,** we will also reign *5702*
4: 5 keep your head in all situations, **e hardship,** *2802*
Heb 12: 7 E hardship as discipline; *5702*
1Pe 2:20 a beating for doing wrong and e it? *5702*
2:20 if you suffer for doing good and *you* e it, *5702*
Rev 3:10 you have kept my command **to e patiently,** *5705*

ENDURED (8) [ENDURE]

Ps 123: 3 for *we have* e much contempt. 8425
123: 4 We *have* e much ridicule from the proud, 8425
132: 1 remember David and all *the* **hardships** he **e.** 6700
Ac 13:18 *he* e their conduct for about forty years in *5574*
2Ti 3:11 Iconium and Lystra, the persecutions *I* **e.** *5722*
Heb 12: 2 who for the joy set before him e the cross, *5702*
12: 3 Consider him who e such opposition *5702*
Rev 2: 3 You have persevered and *have* e **hardships** *1002*

ENDURES (60) [ENDURE]

Ge 8:22 "As long as the earth **e,** 3427
1Ch 16:34 his love e forever. NIH
16:41 "for his love e forever." NIH
2Ch 5:13 his love e forever." NIH
7: 3 his love e forever." NIH
7: 6 saying, "His love e forever." NIH
20:21 for his love e forever." NIH
Ezr 3:11 his love to Israel e forever." NIH
Ps 100: 5 the LORD is good and his love e forever; NIH
102:12 your renown e through all generations. NIH
106: 1 his love e forever. NIH
107: 1 his love e forever. NIH
111: 3 and his righteousness e forever. 6641
112: 3 and his righteousness e forever. 6641
112: 9 his righteousness e forever; 6641
117: 2 the faithfulness of the LORD e forever. NIH
118: 1 his love e forever. NIH
118: 2 Let Israel say: "His love e forever." NIH
118: 3 "His love e forever." NIH
118: 4 "His love e forever." NIH
118:29 his love e forever. NIH
119:90 you established the earth, and *it* **e.** 6641
125: 1 which cannot be shaken but e forever. 3782
135:13 Your name, O LORD, e forever, NIH
136: 1 His love e forever. NIH
136: 2 His love e forever. NIH
136: 3 His love e forever. NIH
136: 4 His love e forever. NIH
136: 5 His love e forever. NIH
136: 6 His love e forever. NIH
136: 7 His love e forever. NIH
136: 8 His love e forever. NIH
136: 9 His love e forever. NIH
136:10 the firstborn of Egypt His love e forever. NIH
136:11 from among them His love e forever. NIH
136:12 His love e forever. NIH
136:13 the Red Sea asunder His love e forever. NIH
136:14 His love e forever. NIH
136:15 His love e forever. NIH
136:16 His love e forever. NIH
136:17 His love e forever. NIH
136:18 killed mighty kings—His love e forever. NIH
136:19 of the Amorites His love e forever. NIH
136:20 Og king of Bashan—His love e forever. NIH
136:21 His love e forever. NIH
136:22 His love e forever. NIH
136:23 in our low estate His love e forever. NIH
136:24 His love e forever. NIH
136:25 His love e forever. NIH
136:26 His love e forever. NIH
138: 8 your love, O LORD, e forever— NIH
145:13 your dominion e through all generations. NIH
Jer 33:11 his love e forever." NIH
La 5:19 your throne e from generation NIH
Da 4: 3 his dominion e from generation NIH
4:34 his kingdom e from generation NIH
6:26 "For he is the living God and he e forever; 10629
9:15 and who made for yourself a name that e NIH
Jn 6:27 but for food that e to eternal life, *3531*
2Co 9: 9 his righteousness e forever." *3531*

ENDURING (7) [ENDURE]

1Ki 11:38 a dynasty as e as the one I built for David 586
Ps 19: 9 The fear of the LORD is pure, e forever. 6641
Pr 8:18 e wealth and prosperity. 6982
Jer 5:15 an ancient and e nation, 419
2Th 1: 4 in all the persecutions and trials *you are* **e.** *462*
Heb 13:14 For here we do not have an e city, *3531*
1Pe 1:23 through the living and e word of God. *3531*

ENEMIES (275) [ENEMY]

Ge 14:20 who delivered your e into your hand." 7640
22:17 take possession of the cities of their **e,** 367
24:60 offspring possess the gates of their **e."** 8533
49: 8 your hand will be on the neck of your **e;** 367
Ex 1:10 if war breaks out, will join our **e,** 8533
23:22 I will be an enemy to your e 367
23:27 I will make all your e turn their backs 367
32:25 and so become a laughingstock to their **e.** 7756
Lev 26: 7 You will pursue your **e,** 367
26: 8 your e will fall by the sword before you. 367
26:16 because your e will eat it. 367
26:17 so that you will be defeated by your **e;** 367
26:32 that your e who live there will be appalled. 367
26:34 and you are in the country of your **e;** 367
26:36 in the lands of their e that the sound of 367
Lev 26:37 you will not be able to stand before your **e.** 367
26:38 the land of your e will devour you. 367
26:39 in the lands of their e because of their sins; 367
26:41 so that I sent them into the land of their **e—** 367
26:44 when they are in the land of their **e,** 367
Nu 10: 9 and rescued from your **e.** 367
10:35 May your e be scattered; 367
14:42 You will be defeated by your **e,** 367
23:11 I brought you to curse my **e,** 367
24:10 "I summoned you to curse my **e,** 367
25:17 **"Treat** the Midianites **as e** and kill them, 7675
25:18 because they **treated** you **as e** 7675
32:21 until he has driven his e out before him— 367
Dt 1:42 You will be defeated by your **e.' "** 367
6:19 thrusting out all your e before you, 367
12:10 and he will give you rest from all your e 367
20: 1 against your e and see horses and chariots 367
20: 3 into battle against your **e.** 367
20: 4 for you against your e to give you victory." 367
20:14 And you may use the plunder the LORD your God gives you from your **e.** 367
21:10 When you go to war against your e and 367
23: 9 When you are encamped against your **e,** 367
23:14 to protect you and to deliver your e to you. 367
25:19 from all the e around you in 367
28: 7 The LORD will grant that the e who rise 367
28:25 to be defeated before your **e.** 367
28:31 Your sheep will be given to your **e,** 367
28:48 you will serve the e the LORD sends 367
28:68 for sale to your e as male and female slaves, 367
30: 7 on your e who hate and persecute you. 367
32:31 as even our e concede. 367
32:43 on his e and make atonement for his land 7640
33:29 Your e will cower before you, 367
Jos 5:13 "Are you for us or for our **e?"** 7640
7: 8 now that Israel has been routed by its **e?** 367
7:12 the Israelites cannot stand against their **e;** 367
7:13 against your e until you remove it. 367
10:13 till the nation avenged itself on its **e,** 367
10:19 Pursue your **e,** attack them from the rear 367
10:25 to all the e you are going to fight." 367
21:44 Not one of their e withstood them; 367
21:44 the LORD handed all their e over to them. 367
22: 8 divide with your brothers the plunder from your **e."** 367
23: 1 from all their e around them, 367
Jdg 2:14 He sold them to their e all around, 367
2:18 and saved them out of the hands of their e 367
5:31 "So may all your e perish, O LORD! 367
8:34 from the hands of all their e on every side. 367
11:36 that the LORD has avenged you of your **e,** 367
1Sa 2: 1 My mouth boasts over my **e,** 367
4: 3 with us and save us from the hand of our **e."** 367
12:10 But now deliver us from the hands of our **e,** 367
12:11 from the hands of your e on every side, 367
14:24 before I have avenged myself on my **e!"** 367
14:30 of the plunder they took from their **e.** 367
14:47 he fought against their e on every side: 367
18:25 to take revenge on his **e.' "** 367
20:15 of David's e from the face of the earth." 367
20:16 the LORD call David's e to account." 367
25:26 may your e and all who intend 367
25:29 But the lives of your e he will hurl away as 367
29: 8 Why can't I go and fight against the e 367
30:26 for you from the plunder of the LORD's **e."** 367
2Sa 3:18 and from the hand of all their **e.' "** 367
5: 8 and blind' *who are* David's **e."** 5883+8533
5:20 the LORD has broken out against my e 367
7: 1 from all his e around him, 367
7: 9 I have cut off all your e from before you. 367
7:11 I will also give you rest from all your **e.** 367
12:14 because by doing this you have made the e 367
18:19 from the hand of his **e."** 367
18:32 the e *of* my lord the king and all who rise 367
19: 9 king delivered us from the hand of our **e;** 367
22: 1 from the hand of all his e and from the hand 367
22: 4 and I am saved from my **e.** 367
22:15 He shot arrows and scattered **[the e],** 4392[S]
22:38 "I pursued my e and crushed them; 367
22:41 You made my e turn their backs in flight, 367
22:49 who sets me free from my **e.** 367
24:13 Or three months of fleeing from your e 7640
1Ki 3:11 for the death of your e but for discernment 367
5: 3 until the LORD put **his e** under his feet. 4392[S]
8:44 your people go to war against their **e,** 367
8:48 of their e who took them captive, and pray 367
2Ki 17:39 from the hand of all your **e."** 367
21:14 and hand them over to their **e.** 367
1Ch 12:17 But if you have come to betray me to my e 7640
14:11 God has broken out against my e 367
17: 8 I have cut off all your e from before you. 367
17:10 I will also subdue all your **e.** 367
21:12 of being swept away before your **e,** 7640
22: 9 and I will give him rest from all his e 367
2Ch 1:11 riches or honor, nor for the death of your **e,** 8533
6:28 when e besiege them in any of their cities, 367
6:34 your people go to war against their **e,** 367
20:27 to rejoice over their **e.** 367
20:29 how the LORD had fought against the e 367
26:13 to support the king against his **e.** 367
Ezr 4: 1 When the e *of* Judah and Benjamin heard 7640
8:22 and horsemen to protect us from e on 367
8:31 and he protected us from e and bandits 367
Ne 4:11 Also our e said, 7640
4:15 When our e heard that we were aware 367
5: 9 to avoid the reproach of our Gentile **e?** 367
6: 1 of our e that I had rebuilt the wall and not 367

Ne 6:16 When all our e heard about this, 367
9:27 So you handed them over to their e, 7640
9:27 who rescued them from the hand of their e. 7640
9:28 to the hand of their e so that they ruled 367
Est 8:11 and to plunder the property of **their e.** 4392S
8:13 on that day to avenge themselves on their e. 367
9:1 On this day the e *of* the Jews had hoped 367
9:5 The Jews struck down all their e with 367
9:16 and get relief from their e. 367
9:22 time when the Jews got relief from their e, 367
Job 8:22 Your e will be clothed in shame, 8533
19:11 he counts me among his e. 7640
27:7 "May my e be like the wicked, 367
Ps 3:7 Strike all my e on the jaw; 367
5:8 in your righteousness because of my e— 8806
6:10 All my e will be ashamed and dismayed; 367
7:6 rise up against the rage of my e. 7675
8:2 because of your e, 7675
9:3 My e turn back; 367
9:13 O LORD, see how my e persecute me! 8533
10:5 he sneers at all his e. 7675
17:9 from my mortal e who surround me. 367
18:T from the hand of all his e and from the hand 367
18:3 and I am saved from my e. 367
18:14 He shot his arrows and scattered **[the e],** 4392
18:37 I pursued my e and overtook them; 367
18:40 You made my e turn their backs in flight, 367
18:48 who saves me from my e. 367
21:8 Your hand will lay hold on all your e; 367
23:5 a table before me in the presence of my e. 7675
25:2 nor let my e triumph over me. 367
25:19 See how my e have increased and 367
27:2 when my e and my foes attack me, 7640
27:6 be exalted above the e who surround me; 367
30:1 of the depths and did not let my e gloat 367
31:11 Because of all my e, 7675
31:15 from my e and from those who pursue me. 367
35:19 Let not those gloat over me *who* are my e 367
37:20 The LORD's e will be like the beauty of 367
38:19 Many are *those who* are my vigorous e; 367
41:5 My e say of me in malice, 367
41:7 All my e whisper together against me; 8533
44:5 Through you we push back our e; 7640
44:7 but you give us victory over our e, 7640
45:5 the hearts of the king's e; 367
55:15 Let death take **my e** by surprise; 4564S
56:9 my e will turn back when I call for help. 367
59:1 Deliver me from my e, O God; 367
60:12 and he will trample down our e. 7640
66:3 So great is your power that your e cringe 367
68:1 May God arise, may his e be scattered; 367
68:21 Surely God will crush the heads of his e, 367
69:4 many are my e without cause, 367
69:19 all my e are before you. 7675
71:10 For my e speak against me; 367
72:9 before him and his e will lick the dust. 367
74:23 the uproar of your e, 7756
78:53 but the sea engulfed their e. 367
78:66 He beat back his e; 7640
80:6 and our e mock us. 367
81:14 how quickly would I subdue their e 367
83:2 See how your e are astir, 367
86:17 that my e may see it and be put to shame, 8533
89:10 with your strong arm you scattered your e. 367
89:42 you have made all his e rejoice. 367
89:51 the taunts with which your e have mocked, 367
92:9 For surely your e, O LORD, 367
92:9 O LORD, surely your e will perish; 367
102:8 All day long my e taunt me; 367
106:42 Their e oppressed them and subjected them 367
108:13 and he will trample down our e. 7640
110:1 "Sit at my right hand until I make your e 367
110:2 you will rule in the midst of your e. 367
118:7 I will look in triumph on my e. 8533
119:98 Your commands make me wiser than my e, 367
119:139 for my e ignore your words. 7640
127:5 to shame when they contend with their e in 367
132:18 I will clothe his e with shame, 367
136:24 and freed us from our e, 7640
139:22 I count them my e. 367
143:9 Rescue me from my e, O LORD, 367
143:12 In your unfailing love, silence my e; 367
144:6 Send forth lightning and scatter **[the e];** 4392S
Pr 16:7 he makes even his e live at peace with him. 367
Isa 1:24 from my foes and avenge myself on my e. 367
9:11 against them and has spurred their e on. 367
11:13 and Judah's e will be cut off; 7675
26:11 the fire reserved for your e consume them. 7640
29:5 But your many e will become like fine dust, 2424
41:12 Though you search for your e, 408+5194
42:13 the battle cry and will triumph over his e. 367
59:18 to his e and retribution to his foes; 7640
62:8 as food for your e, 367
63:18 our e have trampled down your sanctuary. 7640
64:2 down to make your name known to your e 7640
66:6 the LORD repaying his e all they deserve. 367
Jer 12:7 the one I love into the hands of her e. 367
15:9 the survivors to the sword before their e," 367
15:11 surely I will make your e plead with you 367
15:14 I will enslave you to your e in a land you do 367
17:4 I will enslave you to your e in a land you do 367
18:17 I will scatter them before their e; 367
19:7 by the sword before their e, 367
19:9 on them by the e who seek their lives.' 367
20:4 by the sword of their e. 367
20:5 over to their e all the wealth of this city— 367
21:7 and to their e who seek their lives. 367
Jer 30:16 all your e will go into exile. 7640
34:20 over to their e who seek their lives. 367
34:21 over to their e who seek their lives, 367
44:30 of Egypt over to his e who seek his life, 367
50:7 their e said, 'We are not guilty, 7640
51:55 Waves [of e] will rage like great waters; 2157S
La 1:2 they have become her e. 367
1:5 her e are at ease. 367
1:7 Her e looked at her and laughed 7640
1:21 All my e have heard of my distress; 367
2:16 All your e open their mouths wide 367
3:46 "All our e have opened their mouths wide 367
3:52 *Those who* were my e 367
3:62 what my e whisper and mutter 7756
4:12 that e and foes could enter the gates 367
Eze 16:27 I gave you over to the greed of your e, 8533
39:23 from them and handed them over to their e, 7640
39:27 from the countries of their e, 367
Da 4:19 the dream applied to your e and its meaning 10686
Am 9:4 into exile by their e, 367
Mic 4:10 of the hand of your e. 367
5:9 be lifted up in triumph over your e, 7640
7:6 a man's e are the members 367
Na 1:2 and maintains his wrath against his e. 367
3:13 gates of your land are wide open to your e; 367
Mt 5:44 Love your e and pray *2398*
10:36 a man's e will be the members *2398*
22:44 "Sit at my right hand until I put your e *2398*
Mk 12:36 "Sit at my right hand until I put your e *2398*
Lk 1:71 salvation from our e and from the hand *2398*
1:74 to rescue us from the hand *of* our e, *2398*
6:27 "But I tell you who hear me: Love your e, *2398*
6:35 But love your e, do good to them, *2398*
19:27 But those e of mine who did not want me to *2398*
19:43 when your e will build an embankment *2398*
20:43 until I make your e a footstool *2398*
23:12 before this they had been e. *1877+2397*
Ac 2:35 until I make your e a footstool *2398*
Ro 5:10 For if, when we were God's e, *2398*
11:28 they are e on your account; *2398*
1Co 15:25 For he must reign until he has put all his e *2398*
Php 3:18 many live as e of the cross of Christ. *2398*
Col 1:21 from God and were e in your minds *2398*
Heb 1:13 "Sit at my right hand until I make your e *2398*
10:13 Since that time he waits for his e to *2398*
10:27 and of raging fire that will consume the e *5641*
Rev 11:5 from their mouths and devours their e. *2398*
11:12 while their e looked on. *2398*

ENEMY (107) [ENEMIES, ENEMY'S, ENMITY]

Ex 15:6 Your right hand, O LORD, shattered the e. 367
15:9 "The e boasted, 'I will pursue, 367
23:22 *I will be an* e *to* your enemies 366
Lev 26:25 and you will be given into e hands. 367
Nu 10:9 against an e who is oppressing you, 7640
24:18 Edom will be conquered; Seir, his e, 367
35:23 not his e and he did not intend to harm him, 367
Dt 28:53 the suffering that your e will inflict on you 367
28:55 because of the suffering your e will inflict 367
28:57 in the distress that your e will inflict on you 367
32:27 of the e, lest the adversary misunderstand 367
32:42 the heads of the e leaders." 367
33:27 He will drive out your e before you, saying, 367
Jdg 3:28 "for the LORD has given Moab, your e, 367
16:23 "Our god has delivered Samson, our e, 367
16:24 "Our god has delivered our e 367
1Sa 18:29 and he remained his e the rest of his days. 367
19:17 and send my e away so that he escaped?" 367
24:4 'I will give your e into your hands for you 367
24:19 When a man finds his e, 367
26:8 "Today God has delivered your e 367
28:16 from you and become your e? 6839
2Sa 4:8 your e, who tried to take your life. 367
22:18 He rescued me from my powerful e, 367
1Ki 8:33 an e because they have sinned against you, 367
8:37 an e besieges them in any of their cities, 367
8:46 with them and give them over to the e, 367
21:20 "So you have found me, my e!" 367
2Ki 6:18 As the e came down toward him, NIH
2Ch 6:24 an e because they have sinned against you 367
6:36 over to the e, who takes them captive to 367
25:8 God will overthrow you before the e, 367
Est 3:10 the Agagite, the e *of* the Jews. 7675
7:6 "The adversary and e is this vile Haman." 367
8:1 Haman, the e *of* the Jews. 7675
9:10 Haman son of Hammedatha, the e *of* the Jews. 7675
9:24 the Agagite, the e *of* all the Jews, 7675
Job 6:23 deliver me from the hand of the e, 7640
13:24 and consider me your e? 367
33:10 he considers me his e. 367
Ps 7:5 then let my e pursue and overtake me; 367
9:6 Endless ruin has overtaken the e, 367
13:2 How long will my e triumph over me? 367
13:4 my e will say, 367
18:17 He rescued me from my powerful e, 367
31:8 You have not handed me over to the e 367
41:11 for my e does not triumph over me. 367
42:9 oppressed by the e?" 367
43:2 oppressed by the e?" 367
44:10 You made us retreat before the e, 7640
44:16 because of the e, who is bent on revenge. 367
55:3 of the e, at the stares of the wicked; 367
55:12 If an e were insulting me, I could endure it; 367
60:11 Give us aid against the e, 7640
Ps 64:1 protect my life from the threat of the e. 367
74:3 all this destruction the e has brought on 367
74:10 How long will the e mock you, O God? 7640
74:18 Remember how the e has mocked you, 367
78:61 his splendor into the hands of the e. 7640
89:22 No e will subject him to tribute; 367
106:10 from the hand of the e he redeemed them. 367
108:12 Give us aid against the e, 7640
143:3 The e pursues me, he crushes me to 367
Pr 24:17 Do not gloat when your e falls; 367
25:21 If your e is hungry, give him food to eat; 8533
27:6 but an e multiplies kisses. 8533
29:24 The accomplice of a thief is his own e; 8533
Isa 22:3 having fled while the e was still far away. NIH
63:10 and became their e and he himself fought 367
Jer 6:25 for the e has a sword, 367
30:14 as an e would and punished you as would 367
31:16 "They will return from the land of the e. 367
44:30 the e who was seeking his life.'" 367
46:22 a fleeing serpent as the e advances in force; NIH
47:3 of e chariots and the rumble of their wheels. 2257S
La 1:7 When her people fell into e hands, 7640
1:9 on my affliction, for the e has triumphed." 367
1:10 The e laid hands on all her treasures; 7640
1:16 because the e has prevailed." 367
2:3 at the approach of the e. 367
2:4 Like an e he has strung his bow; 367
2:5 The Lord is like an e; 367
2:7 He has handed over to the e the walls 367
2:17 he has let the e gloat over you, 367
2:22 for and reared, my e has destroyed." 367
Eze 36:2 The e said of you, "Aha! 367
Hos 8:3 an e will pursue him. 367
Am 3:11 "An e will overrun the land; 7640
Mic 2:8 Lately my people have risen up like an e. 367
7:8 Do not gloat over me, my e! 367
7:10 Then my e will see it and will be covered 367
Na 3:11 into hiding and seek refuge from the e. 367
Zep 3:15 he has turned back your e. 367
Zec 8:10 about his business safely because of his e, 7640
Mt 5:43 'Love your neighbor and hate your e.' *2398*
13:25 his e came and sowed weeds among *2398*
13:28 "'An e did this,' he replied. *476+2398*
13:39 and the e who sows them is the devil. *2398*
Lk 10:19 and to overcome all the power *of* the e; *2398*
Ac 13:10 a child of the devil and an e of everything *2398*
Ro 12:20 "If your e is hungry, feed him; *2398*
1Co 15:26 The last e to be destroyed is death. *2398*
Gal 4:16 Have I now become your e by telling you *2398*
2Th 3:15 Yet do not regard him as an e, *2398*
1Ti 5:14 and to give the e no opportunity for slander. *512*
Jas 4:4 a friend of the world becomes an e of God. *2398*
1Pe 5:8 Your e the devil prowls around like *508*

ENEMY'S (3) [ENEMY]

Ex 23:4 across your e ox or donkey wandering off, 367
Job 31:29 "If I have rejoiced at my e misfortune 8533
Jer 8:16 snorting of **the e** horses is heard from Dan; 2257S

ENERGY (1)

Col 1:29 struggling with all his e, *1918*

ENFOLDS (1) [FOLD]

Isa 25:7 the shroud that e all peoples, the sheet 4286

ENFORCE (1) [FORCE]

Da 6:7 that the king should issue an edict and e 10772

ENGAGE (9) [ENGAGED, ENGAGES, ENGAGING]

Ex 31:5 and to e in all kinds of craftsmanship. 6913
35:33 to e in all kinds of artistic craftsmanship. 6913
Dt 2:24 to take possession of it and e him *in* battle. 1741
20:12 If they refuse to make peace and *they* e you 6913
1Sa 7:10 the Philistines drew near to e Israel NIH
2Ch 35:22 but disguised himself to e him **in battle.** 4309
Jer 11:15 When you e in your wickedness, NIH
Da 11:40 of the South *will* e him **in battle,** 5590
Hos 4:10 *they will* e **in prostitution** but 2388

ENGAGED (7) [ENGAGE]

Jdg 12:2 "I and my people *were* e **in** a great struggle 2118
1Ki 14:24 the people e **in** all the detestable practices 6913
Eze 16:17 and e **in prostitution** with them. 2388
16:26 *You* e **in prostitution** with the Egyptians, 2388
16:28 *You* e **in prostitution** with the Assyrians 2388
23:5 "Oholah e **in prostitution** 2388
1Co 7:36 improperly toward the virgin he is e to, *NIG*

ENGAGES (1) [ENGAGE]

Dt 18:10 interprets omens, e **in witchcraft,** 4175

ENGAGING (1) [ENGAGE]

Eze 23:3 e **in prostitution** from their youth. 2388

ENGRAFTED (KJV) PLANTED

ENGRAVE (4) [ENGRAVED, ENGRAVES, ENGRAVING]

Ex 28:9 "Take two onyx stones and e on them 7338

Ex 28:11 E the names of the sons of Israel on 7338
28:36 "Make a plate of pure gold and e on it 7334+7338
Zec 3: 9 and I will e an inscription on it,' 7338

ENGRAVED (10) [ENGRAVE]
Ex 28:21 each e like a seal with the name of one of 7334
32:16 the writing was the writing of God, e on 3100
39: 6 and e them like a seal with the names 7334+7338
39:14 each e like a seal with the name of one of 7334
39:30 out of pure gold and e on it, 4180
1Ki 7:36 He e cherubim, lions and palm trees on 7338
Job 19:24 or e in rock forever! 2933
Isa 49:16 I have e you on the palms of my hands; 2980
Jer 17: 1 "Judah's sin is e with an iron tool, 4180
2Co 3: 7 which was e in letters on stone, 1963

ENGRAVES (1) [ENGRAVE]
Ex 28:11 on the two stones the way a gem cutter e 7334

ENGRAVING (3) [ENGRAVE]
1Ki 7:31 Around its opening there was e. 5237
2Ch 2: 7 and experienced in the art of e, 7334+7338
2:14 experienced in all kinds of e 7334+7338

ENGROSSED (1)
1Co 7:31 as if not e in them. 2974

ENGULF (3) [ENGULFED, ENGULFING]
Ps 69: 2 the floods e me. 8851
69:15 Do not let the floodwaters e me or 8851
Hos 7: 2 Their sins e them; 6015

ENGULFED (3) [ENGULF]
Ps 78:53 but the sea e their enemies. 4059
88:17 they have completely e me. 5938
124: 4 the flood would have e us, 8851

ENGULFING (1) [ENGULF]
Jnh 2: 5 The e waters threatened me, 705

ENHANCES (1)
Ro 3: 7 "If my falsehood e God's truthfulness and 4355

ENJOIN, ENJOINED (KJV) ORDER, ORDERED

ENJOY (39) [JOY]
Ge 45:18 of Egypt and you can e the fat of the land.' 430
Ex 30:38 like it to e its fragrance must be cut off 8193
Lev 26:34 Then the land will e its sabbath years all 8354
26:34 then the land will rest and e its sabbaths. 8354
26:43 be deserted by them and will e its sabbaths 8354
Nu 14:31 in to e the land you have rejected. 3359
Dt 6: 2 and so that you may e long life. 799+3427
20: 6 a vineyard and not begun to e it? 2725
20: 6 in battle and someone else e it. 2725
28:30 but you will not even begin to e its fruit. 2725
Jdg 19: 6 "Please stay tonight and e yourself." 3512
19: 9 Stay and e yourself. 3512
Ne 8:10 "Go and e choice food and sweet drinks, 430
Job 3:18 Captives also e their ease; 8631
20:17 He will not e the streams, 8011
20:18 he will not e the profit from his trading. 6632
33:28 and I will live to e the light.' 8011
Ps 37: 3 dwell in the land and e safe pasture. 8286
37:11 the land and e great peace. 6695
37:19 in days of famine they will e plenty. 8425
106: 5 I may e the prosperity of your chosen ones, 8011
Pr 7:18 let's e ourselves with love! 6632
28:16 he who hates ill-gotten gain will e a long life. 799+3427
Ecc 3:22 for a man than to e his work, 8523
5:19 and enables him to e them, 430
6: 2 but God does not enable him to e them, 430
6: 3 if he cannot e his prosperity and does 8425
6: 6 over but fails to e his prosperity. 8011
9: 9 E life with your wife, whom you love, 8011
11: 8 let him e them all. 8523
Isa 3:10 for they will e the fruit of their deeds. 430
65:22 my chosen ones will long e the works 1162
Jer 31: 5 the farmers will plant them and e their fruit. 2725
33: 6 and will let them e abundant peace 1655
Jn 5:35 and you chose for a time to e his light. 22
Ro 16:23 and the whole church here e, NIG
Eph 6: 3 and that you may e long life on 1639+3432
Heb 11:25 of God rather than to e the pleasures of sin 2400
3Jn 1: 2 I pray that you may e good health and 5617

ENJOYED (9) [JOY]
Jdg 8:28 the land e peace forty years. 9200
1Ch 29:28 having e long life, wealth and honor. 3427+8428
2Ch 36:21 The land e its sabbath rests; 8354
Job 21:25 never having e anything good. 430
Ps 55:14 with whom I once e sweet fellowship 5517
Ac 7:46 who e God's favor and asked 2351
9:31 Galilee and Samaria e a time of peace. 2400
24: 2 "We have e a long period of peace under you, 5593
Ro 15:24 after I have e your company for a while. 1855

ENJOYING (3) [JOY]
Jdg 19:22 While they were e themselves, 3512
Ne 9:35 e your great goodness to them in NIH
Ac 2:47 praising God and e the favor of all 2400+5921

ENJOYMENT (4) [JOY]
Ecc 2:25 for without him, who can eat or find e? 2591
4: 8 "and why am I depriving myself of e?" 3208
8:15 So I commend the e of life, 8525
1Ti 6:17 with everything for our e. 656

ENJOYS (3) [JOY]
Pr 13: 2 the fruit of his lips a man e good things, 430
Ecc 6: 2 and a stranger e them instead. 430
Hab 1:16 for by his net he lives in luxury and e NIH

ENLARGE (4) [LARGE]
Ex 34:24 before you and e your territory, 8143
1Ch 4:10 that you would bless me and e my territory! 8049
Isa 54: 2 "E the place of your tent, 8143
2Co 9:10 and increase your store of seed and will e 889

ENLARGED (5) [LARGE]
Dt 12:20 the LORD your God has e your territory 8143
Isa 9: 3 You have e the nation 8049
26:15 You have e the nation, O LORD; 3578
26:15 you have e the nation. 3578
Jer 20:17 her womb e forever. 2226

ENLARGES (4) [LARGE]
Dt 19: 8 If the LORD your God e your territory, 8143
33:20 "Blessed is he who e Gad's domain! 8143
Job 12:23 he e nations, and disperses them. 8848
Isa 5:14 the grave e its appetite and opens its mouth 8143

ENLIGHTEN (1) [LIGHT]
Isa 40:14 Whom did the LORD consult to e him, 1067

ENLIGHTENED (2) [LIGHT]
Eph 1:18 be e in order that you may know the hope 5894
Heb 6: 4 for those who have once been e, 5894

ENMITY (1) [ENEMY]
Ge 3:15 I will put e between you and the woman, 368

ENOCH (13)
Ge 4:17 she became pregnant and gave birth to E. 2840
4:17 and he named it after his son E. 2840
4:18 To E was born Irad, 2840
5:18 he became the father of E. 2840
5:19 And after he became the father of E, 2840
5:21 When E had lived 65 years, 2840
5:22 E walked with God 300 years 2840
5:23 Altogether, E lived 365 years. 2840
5:24 E walked with God; 2840
1Ch 1: 3 E, Methuselah, Lamech, Noah. 2840
Lk 3:37 the son of E, the son of Jared, 1970
Heb 11: 5 By faith E was taken from this life, 1970
Jude 1:14 E, the seventh from Adam, 1970

ENORMOUS (3)
Da 2:31 e, dazzling statue, awesome in appearance. 10647
4:10 Its height was e. 10678
Rev 12: 3 an e red dragon with seven heads 3489

ENOS (KJV) ENOSH

ENOSH (8)
Ge 4:26 Seth also had a son, and he named him E. 633
5: 6 he became the father of E. 633
5: 7 And after he became the father of E, 633
5: 9 When E had lived 90 years, 633
5:10 E lived 815 years and had other sons 633
5:11 Altogether, E lived 905 years, 633
1Ch 1: 1 Adam, Seth, E, 633
Lk 3:38 the son of E, 1968

ENOUGH (98)
Ge 19:20 Look, here is a town near e to run to, AIT
22: 3 he had cut e wood for the burnt offering, AIT
24:20 and drew e for all his camels. AIT
30:15 But she said to her, "Wasn't it e 5071
47:22 from Pharaoh and had food e from 430
Ex 9:28 for we have had e thunder and hail. 8041
16: 4 to go out each day and gather e for that day. 1821
23:30 until you have increased e AIT
36: 5 "The people are bringing more than e 1896
36: 7 what they already had was more than e 1896
Lev 25:21 in the sixth year that the land will yield e 9311
Nu 11:22 Would they have e if flocks 5162
11:22 Would they have e if all the fish in 5162
16: 9 Isn't it e for you that the God 5071
16:13 Isn't it e that you have brought us up out of 5071
20:12 in me e to honor me as holy in the sight of NIH
Dt 1: 6 "You have stayed long e at this mountain. 8041
2: 3 around this hill country long e; 8041
2: 5 not even e to put your foot on. 6330
3:26 "That is e," the LORD said. 8041
Dt 9: 8 the LORD's wrath so that he was angry e AIT
9:19 for he was angry e with you to destroy you. AIT
9:20 And the LORD was angry e with Aaron 4394
19:15 One witness is not e to convict AIT
Jos 17:16 "The hill country is not e for us, 5162
22:17 Was not the sin of Peor e for us? 5071
Jdg 21:14 But there were not e for all of them. 4027
Ru 2:18 over after she had eaten e. 8425
2Sa 7:19 And as if this were not e in your sight, 6388+7781
24:16 the angel who was afflicting the people, "E! 8041
1Ki 18:32 around it large e to hold two seahs of seed. 3869
19: 4 "I have had e, LORD," he said. 8041
20:10 if e dust remains in Samaria to give each 8563
1Ch 17:17 And as if this were not e in your sight, 7781
21:15 to the angel who was destroying the people, "E! 8041
2Ch 13: 7 and indecisive and not strong e AIT
22: 9 the house of Ahaziah powerful e to retain AIT
30: 3 not e priests had consecrated themselves 1896+4200+4537
31:10 we have had e to eat and plenty to spare, 8425
Ezr 9:14 not be angry e with us to destroy us, 6330
Ne 2:14 not e room for my mount to get through; NIH
Job 15:11 Are God's consolations not e for you, 5071
19:22 Will you never get e of my flesh? 8425
27:14 his offspring will never have e to eat. 8425
41:10 No one is fierce e to rouse him. AIT
Ps 49: 8 no payment is ever e— 2532
78:29 They ate till they had more than e, 8425
Pr 25:16 If you find honey, eat just e— 1896
30:15 four that never say, 'E!': 2104
30:16 and fire, which never says, 'E!' 2104
Ecc 1: 8 The eye never has e of seeing, 8425
5:10 Whoever loves money never has money e; 8425
Isa 1:11 "I have more than e of burnt offerings, 8425
7:13 Is it not e to try the patience of men? 5071
7:15 and honey when he knows e to reject AIT
7:16 before the boy knows e to reject the wrong AIT
40:16 nor its animals e for burnt offerings. 1896
56:11 they never have e. 8429
Jer 9:12 What man is wise e to understand this? AIT
La 5: 6 to Egypt and Assyria to get e bread. 8425
Eze 16: 5 with pity or had compassion e to do any AIT
16: 8 and saw that you were old e for love, AIT
16:20 Was your prostitution not e? 5071
30:21 in a splint so as to become strong e to hold AIT
34:18 Is it not e for you to feed on 5071
34:18 Is it not e for you to drink clear water? NIH
44: 6 E of your detestable practices, 8041
45: 9 You have gone far e, O princes of Israel! 8041
47: 5 deep e to swim in— 8467
Hos 4:10 "They will eat but not have e; 8425
Joel 2:19 e to satisfy you fully; AIT
Am 4: 8 to town for water but did not get e to drink, 8425
Jnh 4: 9 "I am angry e to die." 6330
Na 2:12 The lion killed e for his cubs and strangled 1896
Hag 1: 6 You eat, but never have e. 8425
Zec 10:10 and there will not be room e for them. 5162
Mal 3:10 that you will not have room e for it. 1896
Mt 6:34 Each day has e trouble of its own. 757
10:25 It is e for the student to be like his teacher, 757
15:33 "Where could we get e bread 5537
25: 9 'there may not be e for both us and you. 758
Mk 5: 4 No one was strong e to subdue him. NIG
8: 4 in this remote place can anyone get e bread NIG
14:41 "Are you still sleeping and resting? E! 600
Lk 14:28 to see if he has e money to complete it? 1650+2400
16: 3 I'm not strong e to dig, NIG
22:38 "That is e," he replied. 2653
Jn 6: 7 not buy e bread for each one to have 758
6:12 When they had all had e to eat, 1855
14: 8 show us the Father and that will be e 758
Ac 24: 4 that you be kind e to hear us briefly. NIG
24:25 "That's e for now! NIG
1Co 6: 5 that there is nobody among you wise e NIG
14:17 You may be giving thanks well e, NIG
2Co 11: 4 you put up with it easily e. NIG
1Th 3: 9 How can we thank God e for you in return NIG
1Pe 4: 3 For you have spent e time in the 757
Rev 12: 8 But he was not strong e, NIG

ENQUIRE, ENQUIRED, ENQUIREST, ENQUIRY (Anglicized, KJV) ASK, ASKS, ASKING, BRING UP, FIND OUT, GREET, INQUIRE, INQUIRED, INQUIRING, QUESTION, SEEKING

ENRAGED (8) [RAGE]
2Ki 6:11 This e the king of Aram. 4213+6192
2Ch 16:10 he was so e that he put him in prison. 2408
Est 3: 5 or pay him honor, he was e. 2779+4848
Isa 8:21 they will become e and, looking upward, 7911
57:17 I was e by his sinful greed; 7911
Eze 16:43 the days of your youth but e me 8074
Mt 22: 7 The king was e. 3974
Rev 12:17 the dragon was e at the woman and went off 3974

ENRICH (2) [RICH]
Ps 65: 9 you e it abundantly. 6947
Pr 5:10 and your toil e another man's house. NIH

ENRICHED (3) [RICH]
Isa 23: 2 whom the seafarers have e. 4848

Eze 27:33 and your wares *you* e the kings of 6947
1Co 1: 5 For in him *you have been* e in every way— *4457*

ENROLL (2) [ENROLLED, ENROLLMENT]
2Sa 24: 2 of Israel from Dan to Beersheba and e 7212
24: 4 of the king to e the fighting men of Israel. 7212

ENROLLED (1) [ENROLL]
2Ch 31:17 e by their families **in the genealogical records** 3509

ENROLLMENT (1) [ENROLL]
2Ch 17:14 Their e by families was as follows: 7213

ENSAMPLE (KJV) EXAMPLE, MODEL, PATTERN

ENSLAVE (3) [SLAVE]
Jer 15:14 *I will* e you *to* your enemies in 6268
17: 4 *I will* e you *to* your enemies in 6268
30: 8 no longer *will* foreigners e them. 6268

ENSLAVED (9) [SLAVE]
Ge 15:13 *be* e and mistreated four hundred years. 6268
Ne 5: 5 Some of our daughters *have already* **been e,** 3899
Jer 25:14 *be* e by many nations and great kings; 6268
34:11 the slaves they had freed and e them again. 2256+3899+4200+4200+6269+9148
Eze 34:27 from the hands of those *who* e them. 6268
Na 3: 4 who e nations by her prostitution 4835
Ac 7: 6 a country not their own, and *they will* **be e** *1530*
Gal 4: 9 Do you wish *to be* e by them all *1526*
Tit 3: 3 deceived and e by all kinds of passions *1526*

ENSLAVES (1) [SLAVE]
2Co 11:20 up with anyone who e you or exploits you *2871*

ENSLAVING (1) [SLAVE]
Ex 6: 5 whom the Egyptians *are* e, 6268

ENSNARE (7) [SNARE]
Pr 5:22 The evil deeds of a wicked man e him; 4334
Ecc 7:26 but the sinner she *will* e. 4334
Isa 29:21 *who* e the defender in court and 7772
Eze 13:18 for their heads in order to e people. 7421
13:18 *Will you* e the lives of my people 7421
13:20 with which you e people like birds 7421
13:20 I will set free the people that you e 7421

ENSNARED (5) [SNARE]
Dt 7:25 or *you will* **be** e by it, 3704
12:30 not *to* **be** e by inquiring about their gods, 5943
Ps 9:16 the wicked **are** e by the work of their hands. 3704
Pr 6: 2 e by the words of your mouth, 4334
22:25 you may learn his ways and get yourself **e.** 4613

ENSUE (KJV) PURSUE

ENSURE (1)
Ps 119:122 **E** your servant's well-being; 6842

ENTANGLE (1) [ENTANGLED, ENTANGLES]
Ps 35: 8 *may* the net they hid e them, 4334

ENTANGLED (4) [ENTANGLE]
Ps 18: 4 The cords of death e me; 705
116: 3 The cords of death e me, 705
Na 1:10 *They will be* e among thorns and drunk 6018
2Pe 2:20 and Savior Jesus Christ and *are* again e **in** it *1861*

ENTANGLES (1) [ENTANGLE]
Heb 12: 1 that hinders and the sin that so **easily e,** *2342*

ENTER (168) [ENTERED, ENTERING, ENTERS, ENTRANCE, ENTRANCES, ENTRYWAY, REENTERED]
Ge 6:18 and *you will* e the ark— 448+995
12:11 As he was about to e Egypt, 995
49: 6 *Let* me not e their council, 928+995
Ex 12:23 not permit the destroyer to e your houses 448+995
12:25 When *you* e the land that 448+995
28:43 his sons must wear them whenever they e 448+995
30:20 Whenever they e the Tent of Meeting, 448+995
40:35 Moses could not e the Tent of Meeting 448+995
Lev 14:34 "When *you* e the land of Canaan, 448+995
16: 3 how Aaron *is to* e the sanctuary area: 448+995
19:23 'When *you* e the land and plant any kind 448+995
21:11 not e a place where there is a dead body 995+6584
23:10 'When *you* e the land I am going 448+995
25: 2 *you* e the land I am going to give you, 448+995
Nu 5:22 that brings a curse e your body so 928+995
5:24 and this water *will* e her 928+995
14:30 Not one of you *will* e the land I swore 448+995
15: 2 *you* e the land I am giving you as a home 448+995
Nu 15:18 you e the land to which I am taking you 448+995
20:24 *He will* not e the land I give the Israelites, 448+995
34: 2 'When you e Canaan, the land that will 448+995
Dt 1:37 "You *shall* not e it, either. 995
1:38 your assistant, Joshua son of Nun, *will* e it. 995
1:39 they *will* e the land. 995
4:21 not cross the Jordan and e the good land 448+995
8: 1 and increase and *may* e and possess the land 995
10:11 so that *they may* e and possess the land 995
11:31 to cross the Jordan to e and take possession 995
17:14 When *you* e the land 448+995
18: 9 When you e the land 448+995
23: 1 crushing or cutting *may* e the assembly 928+995
23: 2 of his descendants *may* e the assembly of 928+995
23: 3 Moabite or any of his descendants *may* e 928+995
23: 8 born to them *may* e the assembly of 928+995
23:24 If *you* e your neighbor's vineyard, 928+995
23:25 If *you* e your neighbor's grainfield, 928+995
27: 3 when you have crossed over to e 448+995
29:12 You are standing here in order to e into 6296
30:18 in the land you are crossing the Jordan to e 995
32:52 not e the land I am giving to the people 448+995
Jos 2:18 *when* we e the land, 928+995
Jdg 11:18 *They did* not e the territory of Moab, 928+995
1Sa 5: 5 nor any *others* who e Dagon's temple 995
9:13 As soon as you e the town, 995
2Sa 5: 8 'blind and lame' *will* not e the palace." 448+995
1Ki 22:30 "*I will* e the battle in disguise, 928+995
2Ki 11:16 as she reached the place where the horses e 4427
13:20 Now Moabite raiders *used to* e 928+995
19:32 not e this city or shoot an arrow here. 448+995
19:33 *he will* not e this city, declares the LORD. 448+995
2Ch 7: 2 not e the temple of the LORD because 448+995
18:29 "*I will* e the battle in disguise, 928+995
23: 6 *to* e the temple of the LORD except 995
23: 6 they *may* e because they are consecrated, 995
23:19 in any way unclean *might* e. 995
27: 2 but unlike him *he did* not e the temple of 448+995
31:16 all who *would* e the temple of the LORD 995+4200
Ne 9:23 into the land that you told their fathers to e 995
Est 1:19 that Vashti *is* never again *to* e the presence 995
4: 2 in sackcloth was allowed to e it. 448+995
Ps 45:15 *they* e the palace of the king. 928+995
95:11 "*They shall* never e my rest." 448+995
100: 4 **E** his gates with thanksgiving and his courts 995
118:19 *I will* e and give thanks to the LORD. 928+995
118:20 through which the righteous *may* **e.** 995
132: 3 "*I will* not e my house or go to my bed 928+995
Pr 2:10 For wisdom *will* e your heart, 928+995
Isa 10:28 *They* e Aiath; they pass 995+6584
13: 2 beckon to them *to* e the gates of the nobles. 995
26: 2 the gates that the righteous nation *may* **e,** 995
26:20 e your rooms and shut the doors 928+995
35:10 *They will* e Zion with singing; 995
37:33 not e this city or shoot an arrow here. 448+995
37:34 *he will* not e this city," 448+995
51:11 *They will* e Zion with singing; 995
52: 1 and defiled *will* not e you again. 928+995
57: 2 Those who walk uprightly e *into* peace; 995
59:14 in the streets, honesty cannot **e.** 995
Jer 3:16 *It will* never e their minds or 6584+6590
7:31 nor *did it* e my mind. 6584+6590
16: 5 not e a house where there is a funeral meal; 995
16: 8 not e a house where there is feasting and sit 995
19: 5 nor *did it* e my mind. 6584+6590
21:13 Who *can* e our refuge?" 928+995
32:35 nor *did it* e my mind, 6584+6590
La 1:10 she saw pagan nations e her sanctuary— 995
1:10 *to* e your assembly. 928+995
4:12 and foes *could* e the gates of Jerusalem. 928+995
Eze 7:22 robbers *will* e it and desecrate it. 928+995
13: 9 nor *will they* e the land of Israel. 448+995
20:38 yet *they will* not e the land of Israel. 448+995
26:10 when he enters your gates as *men* e 4427
37: 5 I *will* **make** breath e you, 928+995
42:14 Once the priests e the holy precincts, 995
44: 2 no one *may* e through it. 995
44: 3 *to* e by way of the portico of the gateway 995
44: 9 in heart and flesh *is to* e my sanctuary, 448+995
44:16 They alone *are to* e my sanctuary; 448+995
44:17 When they e the gates of the inner court, 448+995
46: 2 *to* e from the outside through the portico of 995
Da 1: 5 after that *they were to* e the king's **service.** 4200+6641+7156
11: 7 the king of the North and e his fortress; 928+995
Joel 2: 9 like thieves *they* e through the windows. 995
3: 2 There *I will* **e into judgment** against them 9149
Zec 5: 4 and *it will* e the house of the thief and 448+995
Mt 5:20 *you will* certainly not e the kingdom *1656*
7:13 "**E** through the narrow gate. *1656*
7:13 and many e through it. *1639+1656*
7:21 Lord,' *will* e the kingdom of heaven, *1656*
10: 5 not go among the Gentiles or e any town of *1656*
10:11 "Whatever town or village *you* **e,** *1656*
10:12 *As you* e the home, give it your greeting. *1656*
12:29 how can anyone e a strong man's house *1656*
18: 3 *you will* never e the kingdom of heaven. *1656*
18: 8 for you *to* e life maimed or crippled than *1656*
18: 9 *to* e life with one eye than to have two eyes *1656*
19:17 If you want *to* e life, *1656*
19:23 for a rich man *to* e the kingdom of heaven. *1656*
19:24 the eye of a needle than for a rich man *to* e *1656*
23:13 You yourselves *do* not **e,** *1656*
23:13 nor will you let those e who are trying to. *1656*
Mk 1:45 Jesus could no longer e a town openly *1656*
3:27 no one can **e** a strong man's house *1656*
6:10 Whenever *you* e a house, *1656*
Mk 9:25 come out of him and never e him again." *1656*
9:43 *to* e life maimed than with two hands to go *1656*
9:45 *to* e life crippled than to have two feet and *1656*
9:47 It is better for you *to* e the kingdom of God *1656*
10:15 of God like a little child *will* never e it." *1656*
10:23 for the rich *to* e the kingdom of God!" *1656*
10:24 how hard it is *to* e the kingdom of God! *1656*
10:25 the eye of a needle than for a rich man *to* e *1656*
11: 2 and just as *you* e it, *1660*
13:15 down or e the house to take anything out. *1656*
Lk 9: 4 Whatever house *you* **e,** *1656*
10: 5 "When *you* e a house, first say, *1656*
10: 8 "When *you* e a town and are welcomed, *1656*
10:10 when *you* e a town and are not welcomed, *1656*
13:24 "Make every effort *to* e through *1656*
13:24 will try *to* e and will not be able to. *1656*
18:17 of God like a little child *will* never e it." *1656*
18:24 for the rich *to* e the kingdom of God! *1660*
18:25 the eye of a needle than for a rich man *to* e *1656*
19:30 and *as you* e it, *1660*
21:21 and *let* those in the country not e the city. *1656*
22:10 He replied, "*As you* e the city, *1656*
24:26 to suffer these things and then e his glory?" *1656*
Jn 3: 4 e a second time **into** his mother's womb *1656*
3: 5 no one can e the kingdom of God *1656*
10: 1 the man who *does* not e the sheep pen by *1656*
18:28 the Jews *did* not e the palace; *1656*
Ac 3: 3 When he saw Peter and John about to **e,** *1655*
14:22 "We must go through many hardships *to* e *1656*
16: 7 they tried *to* e Bithynia, *1650+4513*
Heb 3:11 '*They shall* never e my rest.' " *1656*
3:18 that they would never e his rest if not *1656*
3:19 So we see that they were not able *to* **e,** *1656*
4: 3 Now we who have believed e that rest, *1656*
4: 3 '*They shall* never e my rest.' " *1656*
4: 5 "*They shall* never e my rest." *1656*
4: 6 It still remains that some *will* e that rest, *1656*
4:11 therefore, make every effort *to* e that rest, *1656*
9:12 *He did* not e by means of the blood of goats *1656*
9:24 For Christ *did* not e a man-made sanctuary *1656*
9:25 Nor did he e heaven to offer himself again *NIG*
10:19 to e the Most Holy Place by the blood *1658*
Rev 15: 8 and no one could e the temple until *1656*
21:27 Nothing impure will ever e it, *1656*

ENTERED (107) [ENTER]
Ge 7: 7 his wife and his sons' wives e the ark 448+995
7: 9 came to Noah and e the ark, NIH
7:13 and the wives of his three sons, e the ark. 448+995
7:15 of life in them came to Noah and e the ark. NIH
19: 3 they did go with him and e his house. 448+995
31:33 *he* e Rachel's tent. 928+995
41:46 when he e **the service** *of* Pharaoh king of Egypt. 4200+6641+7156
Ex 19: 2 *they* e the Desert of Sinai, 995
24:18 Then Moses e the cloud as he went on up 928+995+9348
33: 8 watching Moses until he e the tent. 995+2025
34:34 But whenever he e the LORD's presence 995
40:32 They washed whenever they e the Tent 448+995
Lev 16:23 the linen garments he put on before he e 448+995
Nu 7:89 When Moses e the Tent of Meeting 448+995
17: 8 The next day Moses e the Tent of 448+995
Dt 26: 1 When *you have* e the land 448+995
Jos 2: 1 So they went and e the house of 995
2: 3 men who came to you and e your house, 995+4200
8:19 *They* e the city and captured it 995
Jdg 4:18 So *he* e her tent, 448+6073
18: 2 The men e the hill country of Ephraim 995
1Sa 4:13 When the man e the town 928+995
12: 8 "After Jacob e Egypt, 995
14:25 The entire army e the woods, 928+995
16:21 David came to Saul and e his **service.** 4200+6641+7156
19:16 But when the men **e,** 995
1Ki 2:30 So Benaiah e the tent of the LORD 448+995
2Ki 6:20 After they e the city, Elisha said, "LORD, 995
7: 8 edge of the camp and e one of the tents. 448+995
7: 8 and e another tent and took some things 448+995
9:31 As Jehu e the gate, she asked, 928+995
10:25 and then e the inner shrine of 2143+6330
1Ch 5:17 **were e in the genealogical records** 3509
24:19 ministering when they e the temple of 995+4200
27:24 and the number *was* not e in the book of 6590
2Ch 8:11 the ark of the LORD *has* e are holy." 448+995
15:12 *They* e into a covenant to seek the LORD, 995
20:28 *They* e Jerusalem **and went** to the temple of 995
26:16 and e the temple of the LORD 448+995
Est 6: 4 Now Haman *had just* e the outer court 995+4200
6: 6 When Haman **e,** the king asked him, 995
Job 3: 6 among the days of the year nor *be* e in any 995
38:22 "*Have you* e the storehouses of the snow 448+995
Ps 73:17 till *I* e the sanctuary of God; 448+995
105:23 Then Israel e Egypt; 995
109:18 *it* e into his body like water, 995
Isa 28:15 "*We have* e *into* a covenant with death, 4162
Jer 9:21 and *has* e our fortresses; 928+995
34:10 and people who e into this covenant agreed 995
43: 7 So *they* e Egypt in disobedience to 995
51:51 foreigners *have* e the holy places of 995+6584
Eze 4:14 No unclean meat *has ever* e my mouth." 928+995
16: 8 I gave you my solemn oath and e into 995
23:39 *they* e my sanctuary and desecrated it. 448+995
37:10 and breath e them; 928+995
43: 4 The glory of the LORD e the temple 448+995
44: 2 the God of Israel, *has* e through it. 995

Eze 46: 9 to return through the gate by which he e, 928+995
Da 1:19 so they e the king's service. 4200+6641+7156
Am 5:19 as though he e his house and rested his hand 995
Ob 1:11 and foreigners e his gates and cast lots 995
Mt 8: 5 When Jesus had e Capernaum, 1656
9:23 When Jesus e the ruler's house and saw 1650+2262
12: 4 He e the house of God, 1656
21:10 When Jesus e Jerusalem, 1656
21:12 Jesus e the temple area 1656
21:23 Jesus e the temple courts, and, 1650+2262
24:38 up to the day Noah e the ark; 1656
26:58 He e and sat down with the guards to see 1656
Mk 2: 1 when Jesus again e Capernaum, 1656
2:26 he e the house of God and ate 1656
3:20 Then Jesus e a house, 1650+2262
7:17 After he had left the crowd and e the house, 1656
7:24 He e a house and did not want anyone 1656
11:11 Jesus e Jerusalem and went to the temple. 1656
11:15 Jesus e the temple area 1656
16: 5 As they e the tomb, 1656
Lk 1:40 where she e Zechariah's home 1656
6: 4 He e the house of God, 1656
7: 1 the hearing of the people, he e Capernaum. 1656
7:45 but this woman, from the time I e, 1656
9:34 and they were afraid as they e the cloud. 1656
11:52 You yourselves have not e, 1656
17:27 in marriage up to the day Noah e the ark. 1656
19: 1 Jesus e Jericho and was passing through. 1656
19:45 Then he e the temple area 1656
22: 3 Then Satan e Judas, called Iscariot, 1656
24: 3 but when they e, 1656
Jn 6:22 and that Jesus had not e it with his disciples, 5291
11:30 Now Jesus had not yet e the village, 2262
13:27 Satan e into him. 1656
16:28 I came from the Father and e the world 1650+2262
Ac 5:21 At daybreak they e the temple courts, 1656
9:17 Then Ananias went to the house and e it. 1656
10:25 As Peter e the house, 1181+1656
11: 8 or unclean has ever e my mouth.' 1656
11:12 and we e the man's house. 1656
13:14 On the Sabbath they e the synagogue 1656
19: 8 Paul e the synagogue 1656
25:23 with great pomp and e the audience room 1656
Ro 5:12 just as sin e the world through one man, 1656
Heb 6:20 who went before us, has e on our behalf. 1656
9: 6 the priests e regularly into the outer room 1655
9: 7 But only the high priest e the inner room, NIG
9:12 but he e the Most Holy Place once for all NIG
9:24 he e heaven itself, NIG
Rev 11:11 a breath of life from God e them, 1656

ENTERING (24) [ENTER]

Nu 32: 9 e the land the LORD had given them. 448+995
Dt 4: 5 the land you are e to take possession of it. 995
7: 1 the land you are e to possess and drives out 995
11:10 The land you are e to take over is not like 995
11:29 into the land you are e to possess, 995
23:20 to in the land you are e to possess. 995
28:21 from the land you are e to possess. 995
28:63 be uprooted from the land you are e 995
30:16 in the land you are e to possess. 995
31:16 to the foreign gods of the land they are e. 928+995+7931
1Sa 5:10 As the ark of God was e Ekron, 995
9:14 and as they were e it, there was Samuel, 928+995+9348
23: 7 for David has imprisoned himself by e 928+995
2Sa 6:16 As the ark of the LORD was e the City 995
15:37 at Jerusalem as Absalom was e the city. 995
17:17 they could not risk being seen e the city. 995+2025
1Ki 15:17 leaving or e the territory of Asa king 995+4200
2Ki 11:19 e by way of the gate of the guards. NIH
1Ch 15:29 the ark of the covenant of the LORD was e the City of David, 995+6330
2Ch 16: 1 leaving or e the territory of Asa king 995+4200
Ezr 9:11 'The land you are e to possess is 995
Mt 21:31 e the kingdom of God ahead of 4575
Lk 11:52 and you have hindered those who were e." 1656
Heb 4: 1 since the promise of e his rest still stands, 1656

ENTERS (25) [ENTER]

Ex 28:29 "Whenever Aaron e the Holy Place, 448+995
28:30 be over Aaron's heart whenever he e 995
28:35 be heard when he e the Holy Place 448+995
Nu 19:14 Anyone who e the tent and anyone who 448+995
2Ki 5:18 When my master e the temple of Rimmon 995
12: 9 on the right side as one e the temple of 995
2Ch 23: 7 Anyone who e the temple must be put 448+995
Isa 3:14 The LORD e into judgment against 995
Eze 26:10 and chariots when he e your gates 928+995
42: 9 entrance on the east side as one e them 995+4200
42:12 by which one e the rooms. 995
44:21 to drink wine when he e the inner court. 448+995
46: 8 When the prince e, 995
46: 9 whoever e by the north gate to worship is 995
46: 9 and whoever e by the south gate is to go out 995
47: 8 where it e the Sea. 995+2025
Mt 15:17 that whatever e the mouth goes into 1660
Mk 7:18 "Don't you see that nothing that e a man 1660
14:14 Say to the owner of the house he e, 1656
Lk 22:10 Follow him to the house that he e, 1660
Jn 10: 2 The man who e by the gate is the shepherd 1656
10: 9 whoever e through me will be saved. 1656
Heb 4:10 for anyone who e God's rest also rests 1656
6:19 It e the inner sanctuary behind the curtain, 1656

Heb 9:25 the way the high priest e 1656

ENTERTAIN (4) [ENTERTAINED, ENTERTAINMENT]

Jdg 16:25 they shouted, "Bring out Samson to e us." 8471
Mt 9: 4 Why do you e evil thoughts in your hearts? 1926
1Ti 5:19 Do not e an accusation against an elder 4138
Heb 13: 2 Do not forget to e strangers, 5810

ENTERTAINED (2) [ENTERTAIN]

Ac 28: 7 and for three days e us hospitably. 3826
Heb 13: 2 for by so doing some people have e angels 3826

ENTERTAINMENT (1) [ENTERTAIN]

Da 6:18 and without any e being brought to him. 10166

ENTHRALLED (1)

Ps 45:11 The king is e by your beauty; 203

ENTHRONED (20) [THRONE]

1Sa 4: 4 who is e between the cherubim. 3782
2Sa 6: 2 who is e between the cherubim that are on 3782
2Ki 19:15 God of Israel, e between the cherubim, 3782
1Ch 13: 6 who is e between the cherubim— 3782
Ps 2: 4 The One e in heaven laughs; 3782
9:11 Sing praises to the LORD, e in Zion; 3782
22: 3 Yet you are e as the Holy One; 3782
29:10 The LORD sits e over the flood; 3782
29:10 the LORD is e as King forever. 3782
55:19 God, who is e forever, 3782
61: 7 May he be e in God's presence forever; 3782
80: 1 you who sit e between the cherubim, 3782
99: 1 he sits e between the cherubim, 3782
102:12 But you, O LORD, sit e forever; 3782
113: 5 the One who sits e on high, 3782
132:14 here I will sit e, for I have desired it— 3782
Isa 14:13 I will sit e on the mount of assembly, 3782
37:16 God of Israel, e between the cherubim, 3782
40:22 He sits e above the circle of the earth, 3782
52: 2 rise up, sit e, O Jerusalem. 3782

ENTHRONES (1) [THRONE]

Job 36: 7 he e them with kings 2021+3782+4058+4200

ENTHUSIASM (2)

2Co 8:17 but he is coming to you with much e and 5080
9: 2 your e has stirred most of them to action. 2419

ENTICE (7) [ENTICED, ENTICES, ENTICING]

1Ki 22:20 'Who will e Ahab into attacking 7331
22:21 'I will e him.' 7331
2Ch 18:19 'Who will e Ahab king of Israel 7331
18:20 'I will e him.' 7331
Pr 1:10 My son, if sinners e you, 7331
2Pe 2:18 they e people who are just escaping 1284
Rev 2:14 who taught Balak to e the Israelites to sin 965+1967+4998

ENTICED (8) [ENTICE]

Dt 4:19 do not be e into bowing down to them 5615
11:16 be e to turn away and worship other gods 4222+7331
2Ki 17:21 Jeroboam e Israel away from following 5615
Job 31: 9 "If my heart has been e by a woman, 7331
31:27 so that my heart was secretly e 7331
Eze 14: 9 if the prophet is e to utter a prophecy, 7331
14: 9 I the LORD have e that prophet, 7331
Jas 1:14 he is dragged away and e. 1284

ENTICES (3) [ENTICE]

Dt 13: 6 or your closest friend secretly e you, 6077
Job 36:18 Be careful that no one e you by riches; 6077
Pr 16:29 A violent man e his neighbor and leads him 7331

ENTICING (2) [ENTICE]

1Ki 22:22 " 'You will succeed in e him,' 7331
2Ch 18:21 " 'You will succeed in e him,' 7331

ENTIRE (89) [ENTIRELY]

Ge 2:11 it winds through the e land of Havilah, 3972
2:13 it winds through the e land of Cush. 3972
7:19 under the e heavens were covered. 3972
19:25 and the e plain, including all those living in 3972
45: 8 of his e household and ruler of all Egypt. 3972
Ex 14:28 the e army of Pharaoh that had followed 3972
16: 3 into this desert to starve this e assembly 3972
16: 9 "Say to the e Israelite community, 3972
29:18 Then burn the e ram on the altar. 3972
Lev 3: 9 the e fat tail cut off close to the backbone, 9459
8: 3 and gather the e assembly at the entrance to 3972
9: 5 the e assembly came near and stood before 3972
19: 2 to the e assembly of Israel and say to them: 3972
24:14 and the e assembly is to stone him. 3972
24:16 The e assembly must stone him. 3972
27:32 The e tithe of the herd and flock— 3972
Nu 4:16 in charge of the e tabernacle and everything 3972
5:30 the LORD and is to apply this e law to her. 3972
6: 5 " 'During the e period of his vow 3972
14: 7 and said to the e Israelite assembly, 3972
16:19 of the LORD appeared to the e assembly. 3972
16:22 the e assembly when only one man sins?" 3972
20:29 the e house of Israel mourned 3972
21:23 He mustered his e army and marched out 3972
27:19 before Eleazar the priest and the e assembly 3972
27:21 At his command he and the e community of 3972
Dt 2:14 By then, that e generation 3972
Jos 6:23 They brought out her e family and put them 3972
8:11 The e force that was with him marched up 3972
9: 1 and along the e coast of the Great Sea as far 3972
9:21 and water carriers for the e community." 3972
10: 7 up from Gilgal with his e army, 3972
11:16 So Joshua took this e land: 3972
11:23 So Joshua took the e land, 3972
13:21 the plateau and the e realm of Sihon king of 3972
13:30 the e realm of Og king of Bashan— 3972
24:17 on our e journey and among all the nations 3972
Jdg 8:12 routing their e army. 3972
1Sa 14:25 The e army entered the woods, 3972
2Sa 6:11 LORD blessed him and his e household. 3972
6:15 and the e house of Israel brought up the ark 3972
7:17 to David all the words of this e revelation. 3972
8: 9 that David had defeated the e army 3972
10: 7 David sent Joab out with the e army 3972
12:29 So David mustered the e army and went 3972
12:31 David and his e army returned to Jerusalem. 3972
15:16 with his e household following him; 3972
20:14 and through the e region of the Berites, 3972
20:23 Joab was over Israel's e army; 3972
24: 8 After they had gone through the e land, 3972
1Ki 8: 5 the e assembly of Israel that had gathered 3972
20: 1 of Aram mustered his e army. 3972
2Ki 6:24 of Aram mobilized his e army and marched 3972
15:18 During his e reign he did not turn away 3972
17: 5 The king of Assyria invaded the e land, 3972
17:13 the e Law that I commanded your fathers 3972
24:16 also deported to Babylon the e force 3972
1Ch 4:27 so their e clan did not become as numerous 3972
5:10 of the Hagrites throughout the e region east 3972
17:15 to David all the words of this e revelation. 3972
18: 9 the e army of Hadadezer king of Zobah, 3972
19: 8 David sent Joab out with the e army 3972
20: 3 David and his e army returned to Jerusalem. 3972
2Ch 5: 6 the e assembly of Israel that had gathered 3972
26:14 bows and slingstones for the e army. 3972
29:18 "We have purified the e temple of 3972
30:25 The e assembly of Judah rejoiced, 3972
34: 9 Ephraim and the e remnant of Israel and 3972
35:16 the e service of the LORD was carried out 3972
Ezr 4: 5 and frustrate their plans during the e reign 3972
8:34 and the e weight was recorded at that time. 3972
Job 16: 7 you have devastated my e household. 3972
Isa 39: 2 the spices, the fine oil, his e armory 3972
Jer 26:17 and said to the e assembly of people, 3972
36:23 until the e scroll was burned in the fire. 3972
37:10 if you were to defeat the e Babylonian army 3972
42: 2 to the LORD your God for this e remnant. 3972
51:31 of Babylon that his e city is captured, 4946+7895
Eze 9: 8 the e remnant of Israel in this outpouring 3972
10:12 Their e bodies, including their backs, 3972
20:40 the land the e house of Israel will serve me, 3972
45: 1 the e area will be holy. 3972
48:20 The e portion will be a square, 25,000 3972
Da 2:48 the e province of Babylon and placed him 10353
11:17 of his e kingdom and will make an alliance 3972
Lk 2: 1 be taken of the e Roman world. 4246
Ac 11:28 over the e Roman world. 3910
18: 8 and his e household believed in the Lord; 3910
Gal 5:14 The e law is summed up in 4246

ENTIRELY (5) [ENTIRE]

Ex 28:31 the robe of the ephod e of blue cloth, 4003
39:22 the robe of the ephod e of blue cloth— 4003
Jer 30:11 let you go e unpunished.' 5927+5927
46:28 let you go e unpunished." 5927+5927
2Co 8: 3 E on their own, 882

ENTRAILS (1)

Zep 1:17 be poured out like dust and their e like filth. 4302

ENTRANCE (144) [ENTER]

Ge 18: 1 while he was sitting at the e to his tent in 7339
18: 2 from the e of his tent to meet them 7339
18:10 Sarah was listening at the e to the tent, 7339
38:14 and then sat down at the e to Enaim, 7339
43:19 and spoke to him at the e to the house. 7339
Ex 26:36 the e to the tent make a curtain of blue, 7339
27:14 to be on one side of the e, NIH
27:16 "For the e to the courtyard, 9133
29: 4 the e to the Tent of Meeting and wash them 7339
29:11 the LORD's presence at the e to the Tent 7339
29:32 At the e to the Tent of Meeting, 7339
29:42 to be made regularly at the e to the Tent 7339
32:26 So he stood at the e to the camp and said, 9133
33: 9 down and stay at the e, 7339
33:10 the pillar of cloud standing at the e to 7339
33:10 each at the e to his tent. 7339
35:15 for the doorway at the e to the tabernacle; 7339
35:17 and the curtain for the e to the courtyard; 9133
36:37 For the e to the tent they made a curtain 7339
38: 8 the women who served at the e to the Tent 7339
38:14 on one side of the e, NIH
38:15 on the other side of the e to the courtyard, 9133
38:18 The curtain for the e to the courtyard was 9133

Ex 38:30 They used it to make the bases for the **e** *to* 7339
38:31 and those for its **e** and all the tent pegs for 9133
39:38 and the curtain for the **e** *to* the tent; 7339
39:40 and the curtain for the **e** *to* the courtyard; 9133
40: 5 the Testimony and put the curtain at the **e** *to* 7339
40: 6 in front of the **e** *to* the tabernacle, the Tent 7339
40: 8 around it and put the curtain at the **e** *to* 9133
40:12 the **e** *to* the Tent of Meeting and wash them 7339
40:28 up the curtain at the **e** to the tabernacle. 7339
40:29 He set the altar of burnt offering near the **e** 7339
40:33 and altar and put up the curtain at the **e** *to* 9133
Lev 1: 3 the **e** *to* the Tent of Meeting so that it will 7339
1: 5 on all sides at the **e** *to* the Tent of Meeting. 7339
3: 2 of his offering and slaughter it at the **e** *to* 7339
4: 4 He is to present the bull at the **e** *to* the Tent 7339
4: 7 of the altar of burnt offering at the **e** *to* 7339
4:18 of the altar of burnt offering at the **e** *to* 7339
8: 3 and gather the entire assembly at the **e** *to* 7339
8: 4 the assembly gathered at the **e** *to* the Tent 7339
8:31 the **e** *to* the Tent of Meeting and eat it there 7339
8:33 Do not leave the **e** *to* the Tent of Meeting 7339
8:35 the **e** *to* the Tent of Meeting day and night 7339
10: 7 Do not leave the **e** *to* the Tent of Meeting 7339
12: 6 to the priest at the **e** *to* the Tent of Meeting 7339
14:11 and his offerings before the LORD at the **e** 7339
14:23 to the priest at the **e** *to* the Tent of Meeting, 7339
15:14 the **e** *to* the Tent of Meeting and give them 7339
15:29 to the priest at the **e** *to* the Tent of Meeting. 7339
16: 7 and present them before the LORD at the **e** 7339
17: 4 the **e** *to* the Tent of Meeting to present it as 7339
17: 5 at the **e** *to* the Tent of Meeting 7339
17: 6 the LORD at the **e** *to* the Tent of Meeting 7339
17: 9 not bring it to the **e** *to* the Tent of Meeting 7339
19:21 a ram to the **e** *to* the Tent of Meeting for 7339
Nu 3:25 the curtain at the **e** *to* the Tent of Meeting, 7339
3:26 at the **e** *to* the courtyard surrounding 7339
4:25 for the **e** *to* the Tent of Meeting, 7339
4:26 the curtain for the **e,** 7339+9133
6:10 to the priest at the **e** *to* the Tent of Meeting. 7339
6:13 be brought to the **e** *to* the Tent of Meeting. 7339
6:18 " 'Then at the **e** *to* the Tent of Meeting, 7339
10: 3 to assemble before you at the **e** *to* the Tent 7339
11:10 each at the **e** *to* his tent. 7339
12: 5 at the **e** *to* the Tent and summoned Aaron 7339
16:18 and stood with Moses and Aaron at the **e** *to* 7339
16:19 in opposition to them at the **e** *to* the Tent 7339
16:50 Then Aaron returned to Moses at the **e** *to* 7339
20: 6 and Aaron went from the assembly to the **e** 7339
25: 6 of Israel while they were weeping at the **e** 7339
27: 2 the **e** *to* the Tent of Meeting and stood 7339
Dt 31:15 and the cloud stood over the **e** *to* the Tent. 7339
Jos 8:29 from the tree and throw it down at the **e** *of* 7339
19:51 the LORD at the **e** *to* the Tent of Meeting. 7339
20: 4 in the **e** *of* the city gate and state his case 7339
Jdg 9:35 at the **e** *to* the city gate just as Abimelech 7339
9:40 all the way to the **e** *to* the gate. 7339
9:44 to a position at the **e** *to* the city gate. 7339
9:52 as he approached the **e** *to* the tower to set it 7339
18:16 armed for battle, stood at the **e** *to* the gate. 7339
18:17 the six hundred armed men stood at the **e** 7339
1Sa 2:22 the women who served at the **e** *to* the Tent 7339
17:52 and pursued the Philistines to the **e** *of* Gath 995
2Sa 10: 8 and drew up in battle formation at the **e** 7339
11: 9 But Uriah slept at the **e** *to* the palace 7339
11:23 but we drove them back to the **e** *to* 7339
1Ki 6: 8 The **e** *to* the lowest floor was on 7339
6:31 the **e** *of* the inner sanctuary he made doors 7339
6:33 of olive wood for the **e** *to* the main hall. 7339
14:27 on duty at the **e** *to* the royal palace. 7339
22:10 at the threshing floor by the **e** *of* the gate 7339
2Ki 7: 3 with leprosy at the **e** *of* the city gate. 7339
10: 8 at the **e** *of* the city gate until morning." 7339
12: 9 The priests who guarded the **e** put into 6197
23: 8 at the **e** to the Gate of Joshua, 7339
23:11 He removed from the **e** *to* the temple of 995
1Ch 9:19 for guarding the **e** to the dwelling of 4427
9:21 of Meshelemiah was the gatekeeper at the **e** 7339
19: 9 up in battle formation at the **e** *to* their city, 7339
2Ch 12:10 on duty at the **e** *to* the royal palace. 7339
18: 9 at the threshing floor by the **e** *to* the gate 7339
23:13 standing by his pillar at the **e.** 4427
23:15 So they seized her as she reached the **e** *of* 4427
33:14 the **e** of the Fish Gate and encircling the hill 995
Ne 3:20 the angle to the **e** *of* the house of Eliashib 7339
3:21 from the **e** *of* Eliashib's house to the end 7339
Est 5: 1 on his royal throne in the hall, facing the **e.** 7339
Isa 24:10 the **e** *to* every house is barred. 995
Jer 1:15 and set up their thrones in the **e** *of* the gates 7339
19: 2 near the **e** *of* the Potsherd Gate. 7339
26:10 the LORD and took their places at the **e** *of* 7339
36:10 which was in the upper courtyard at the **e** 7339
38:14 to the third **e** to the temple of the LORD. 4427
43: 9 at the **e** *to* Pharaoh's palace in Tahpanhes. 7339
Eze 8: 3 to the **e** *to* the north gate of the inner court, 7339
8: 5 and in the **e** north of the gate of 929
8: 7 Then he brought me to the **e** *to* the court. 7339
8:14 to the **e** to the north gate of the house of 7339
8:16 and there at the **e** *to* the temple, 7339
10:19 They stopped at the **e** *to* the east gate of 7339
11: 1 at the **e** *to* the gate were twenty-five men, 7339
40:11 Then he measured the width of the **e** *to* 7339
40:15 The distance from the **e** *of* the gateway to 415
40:40 the **e** *to* the north gateway were two tables, 7339
40:48 The width of the **e** was fourteen cubits 9133
41: 2 The **e** was ten cubits wide, 7339
41: 3 and measured the jambs of the **e;** 7339
41: 3 The **e** was six cubits wide, 7339
Eze 41:17 the **e** to the inner sanctuary and on the walls 7339
41:20 From the floor to the area above the **e,** 7339
42: 9 The lower rooms had an **e** on the east side 4427
44: 5 Give attention to the **e** *of* the temple and all 4427
46: 3 in the presence of the LORD at the **e** *to* 7339
46:19 Then the man brought me through the **e** at 4427
47: 1 The man brought me back to the **e** *of* 7339
Mt 27:60 in front of the **e** to the tomb and went away. *2598*
Mk 15:46 he rolled a stone against the **e** of the tomb. *2598*
16: 3 "Who will roll the stone away from the **e** of *2598*
Jn 11:38 It was a cave with a stone laid across the **e.** *NIG*
20: 1 that the stone had been removed from the **e.** *NIG*
Ac 12: 6 and sentries stood guard at the **e.** *2598*
12:13 Peter knocked at the **outer e,** *2598+4784*

ENTRANCE (Anglicized) See also ENTRYWAY

ENTRANCES (5) [ENTER]

Ex 33: 8 all the people rose and stood at the **e** 7339
Nu 16:27 and little ones at the **e** *to* their tents. 7339
Pr 8: 3 at the **e,** she cries aloud: 4427+7339
Eze 41:11 There were **e** *to* the side rooms from 7339
43:11 its arrangement, its exits and **e**— 4569

ENTREAT (3) [ENTREATY]

Zec 7: 2 to **e** the LORD 906+2704+7156
8:21 'Let us go at once to **e** the LORD and seek 906+2704+7156
8:22 to seek the LORD Almighty and to **e** him." 906+2704+7156

ENTREATY (2) [ENTREAT]

2Ch 33:13 the LORD **was moved by** his **e** 6983
33:19 God **was moved by** his **e,** 6983

ENTRIES, ENTRY (KJV) DOORS, ENTRANCE, ENTRANCES, ENTRYWAY, GATEWAY

ENTRUST (4) [TRUST]

Ge 42:37 **E** him to my care, 5989
2Ki 22: 5 *Have them* **e** it to the men appointed 5989
Jn 2:24 But Jesus *would* not **e** himself to them, *4409*
2Ti 2: 2 in the presence of many witnesses **e** *4192*

ENTRUSTED (35) [TRUST]

Ge 39: 4 and *he* **e** to his care everything he owned. 5989
39: 8 everything he owns *he has* **e** to my care. 5989
Lev 6: 2 deceiving his neighbor about **something e** 7214
6: 4 or what **was e** to him, 7212+7214
1Ki 15:18 *He* **e** it to his officials and sent them 5989
2Ki 22: 7 But they need not account for the money **e** 5989
22: 9 and *have* **e** it to the workers and supervisors 5989
1Ch 9:26 **e with** the responsibility for the rooms 575+928
9:31 was **e with** the responsibility for baking 575+928
2Ch 34:10 Then *they* **e** it to the men appointed 5989
34:17 in the temple of the LORD and *have* **e** it to 5989
Ezr 7:19 to the God of Jerusalem all the articles **e** 10314
Est 2: 8 was taken to the king's palace and **e to** 448+3338
6: 9 Then *let* the robe and horse *be* **e** to one of 5989
Jer 13:20 Where is the flock *that* **was e** to you, 5989
29: 3 He **e** the letter **to** Elasah son of Shaphan 928+3338
Mt 25:14 who called his servants and **e** his property *4140*
25:20 he said, *'you* **e** me with five talents. *4140*
25:22 he said, *'you* **e** me with two talents; *4140*
Lk 12:48 from the one who *has been* **e with** much, *4192*
Jn 5:22 but *has* **e** all judgment to the Son, *1443*
Ro 3: 2 *they have been* **e with** the very words *4409*
6:17 the form of teaching to which *you were* **e.** *4140*
1Co 4: 1 as **those e with** the secret things of God. *3874*
Gal 2: 7 that *I had been* **e with** the task of preaching *4409*
1Th 2: 4 as men approved by God *to be* **e with** *4409*
1Ti 1:11 which he **e** to me. *4409*
6:20 **what has been e** to *your* **care.** *4146*
2Ti 1:12 that he is able to guard what I have **e** to him *4146*
1:14 Guard the good **deposit** that was **e** to you— *4146*
Tit 1: 3 to light through the preaching **e** to me by *4409*
1: 7 Since an overseer is **e with** God's **work,** *3874*
1Pe 2:23 *he* **e** *himself* to him who judges justly. *4140*
5: 3 not lording it over those **e** to you, *NIG*
Jude 1: 3 the faith that was once for all **e** to the saints. *4140*

ENTRYWAY (2) [ENTER]

2Ki 16:18 and removed the royal **e** outside the temple 4427
Mk 14:68 he said, and went out into the **e.** *4580*

ENTWINES (1)

Job 8:17 *it* **e** its roots around a pile of rocks 6018

ENVELOPED (4)

Isa 42:25 It **e** them in flames, 4946+6017
Mt 17: 5 he was still speaking, a bright cloud **e** them, *2173*
Mk 9: 7 Then a cloud appeared and **e** them, *2173*
Lk 9:34 a cloud appeared and **e** them, *2173*

ENVIED (2) [ENVY]

Ge 26:14 and servants that the Philistines **e** him. 7861
Ps 73: 3 For *I* **e** the arrogant when I saw 7861

ENVIES (1) [ENVY]

Jas 4: 5 the spirit he caused to live in us **e** intensely? *5784*

ENVIOUS (7) [ENVY]

Dt 32:21 I *will* **make** them **e** by those who are not 7861
Ps 37: 1 of evil men or *be* **e** of those who do wrong; 7861
106:16 In the camp *they grew* **e** of Moses and 7861
Pr 24:19 because of evil men or *be* **e** of the wicked, 7861
Mt 20:15 Or are you **e** because I am generous?' *1639+3836+4057+4505*
Ro 10:19 "I *will* **make** you **e** by those who are not *4143*
11:11 to the Gentiles to **make** Israel **e.** *4143*

ENVOY (3) [ENVOYS]

Pr 13:17 but a trustworthy **e** brings healing. 7495
Jer 49:14 An **e** was sent to the nations to say, 7495
Ob 1: 1 An **e** was sent to the nations to say, "Rise, 7495

ENVOYS (12) [ENVOY]

1Ki 5: 1 he sent his **e** to Solomon, 6269
2Ki 17: 4 for he had sent **e** to So king of Egypt, 4855
2Ch 32:31 when **e** were sent *by* the rulers of Babylon 4885
Ps 68:31 **E** will come from Egypt; 3134
Isa 14:32 What answer shall be given to the **e** *of* 4855
18: 2 which sends **e** by sea in papyrus boats over 7495
30: 4 in Zoan and their **e** have arrived in Hanes, 4855
30: 6 the **e** carry their riches on donkeys' backs, NIH
33: 7 the **e** *of* peace weep bitterly. 4855
39: 2 Hezekiah received **the e** gladly 2157S
Jer 27: 3 through the **e** who have come to Jerusalem 4855
Eze 17:15 by sending his **e** to Egypt to get horses and 4855

ENVY (21) [ENVIED, ENVIES, ENVIOUS, ENVYING]

Job 5: 2 and **e** slays the simple. 7863
Ps 68:16 Why **gaze in e,** O rugged mountains, 8353
Pr 3:31 *Do* not **e** a violent man or choose any 7861
14:30 but **e** rots the bones. 7863
23:17 *Do* not *let* your heart **e** sinners, 7861
24: 1 *Do* not **e** wicked men, 7861
Ecc 4: 4 and all achievement spring from man's **e** 7863
Eze 31: 9 *the* **e** *of* all the trees of Eden in the garden 7861
Mt 27:18 of **e** that they had handed Jesus over to him. *5784*
Mk 7:22 **e,** slander, arrogance and folly. *4057+4505*
15:10 of **e** that the chief priests had handed Jesus *5784*
Ro 1:29 They are full of **e,** murder, strife, *5784*
11:14 **arouse** my own people **to e** *4143*
1Co 13: 4 *It does* not **e,** it does not boast, *2420*
Gal 5:21 and **e;** drunkenness, orgies, *5784*
Php 1:15 that some preach Christ out of **e** and rivalry, *5784*
1Ti 6: 4 and quarrels about words that result in **e,** *5784*
Tit 3: 3 We lived in malice and **e,** *5784*
Jas 3:14 if you harbor bitter **e** and selfish ambition *2419*
3:16 For where you have **e** and selfish ambition, *2419*
1Pe 2: 1 hypocrisy, **e,** and slander of every kind. *5784*

ENVYING (1) [ENVY]

Gal 5:26 provoking and **e** each other. *5783*

EPAENETUS (KJV) EPENETUS

EPAPHRAS (3)

Col 1: 7 You learned it from **E,** *2071*
4:12 **E,** who is one of you and a servant *2071*
Phm 1:23 **E,** my fellow prisoner in Christ Jesus, *2071*

EPAPHRODITUS (2)

Php 2:25 to send back to you **E,** *2073*
4:18 I have received from **E** the gifts you sent. *2073*

EPENETUS (1)

Ro 16: 5 Greet my dear friend **E,** *2045*

EPHAH (52)

Ge 25: 4 The sons of Midian were **E,** Epher, 6549
Ex 16:36 (An omer is one tenth of an **e.**) 406
29:40 of an **e** of fine flour mixed with a quarter of NIH
Lev 5:11 for his sin a tenth of an **e** *of* fine flour for 406
6:20 a tenth of an **e** *of* fine flour as 406
14:10 with three-tenths of an **e** of fine flour mixed NIH
14:21 a tenth of an **e** of fine flour mixed with oil NIH
19:36 an honest **e** and an honest hin. 406
23:13 with its grain offering of two-tenths of an **e** NIH
23:17 bring two loaves made of two-tenths of an **e** NIH
24: 5 using two-tenths of an **e** for each loaf. NIH
Nu 5:15 a tenth of an **e** *of* barley flour on her behalf. 406
15: 4 of an **e** of fine flour mixed with a quarter of NIH
15: 6 an **e** of fine flour mixed with a third of a hin NIH
15: 9 of an **e** of fine flour mixed with half a hin NIH
28: 5 of an **e** *of* fine flour mixed with a quarter of 406
28: 9 and a grain offering of two-tenths of an **e** NIH
28:12 to be a grain offering of three-tenths of an **e** NIH
28:12 of two-tenths of an **e** of fine flour mixed NIH
28:13 a tenth of an **e** of fine flour mixed with oil. NIH
28:20 of three-tenths of an **e** of fine flour mixed NIH
28:28 to be a grain offering of three-tenths of an **e** NIH
29: 3 of three-tenths of an **e** of fine flour mixed NIH
29: 9 of three-tenths of an **e** of fine flour mixed NIH
29:14 of three-tenths of an **e** of fine flour mixed NIH
Jdg 6:19 an **e** *of* flour he made bread without yeast. 406

Ru 2:17 and it amounted to about an **e**. 406
1Sa 1:24 an **e** of flour and a skin of wine, 406
17:17 "Take this **e** *of* roasted grain 406
1Ch 1:33 **E**, Epher, Hanoch, Abida and Eldaah. 6549
2:46 Caleb's concubine **E** was the mother 6549
2:47 Jotham, Geshan, Pelet, **E** and Shaaph. 6549
Isa 5:10 a homer of seed only an **e** of grain." 406
60:6 young camels of Midian and **E**. 6548
Eze 45:10 an accurate **e** and an accurate bath. 406
45:11 The **e** and the bath are to be the same size, 406
45:11 of a homer and the **e** a tenth of a homer; 406
45:13 an **e** from each homer of wheat and a sixth 406
45:13 a sixth of an **e** from each homer of barley. 406
45:24 as a grain offering an **e** for each bull and 406
45:24 for each bull and an **e** for each ram, 406
45:24 along with a hin of oil for each **e**. 406
46:5 with the ram is to be an **e**, 406
46:5 along with a hin of oil for each **e**. 406
46:7 He is to provide as a grain offering *one* **e** 406
46:7 *one* **e** with the ram, 406
46:7 along with a hin of oil with each **e**. 406
46:11 the grain offering is to be an **e** with a bull, 406
46:11 an **e** with a ram, 406
46:11 along with a hin of oil for each **e**. 406
46:14 of a sixth of an **e** with a third of a hin of oil 406
Mic 6:10 your ill-gotten treasures and the short **e**, 406

EPHAI (1)

Jer 40:8 the sons of **E** the Netophathite, 6550

EPHER (4)

Ge 25:4 The sons of Midian were Ephah, **E**, 6761
1Ch 1:33 Ephah, **E**, Hanoch, Abida and Eldaah. 6761
4:17 Jether, Mered, **E** and Jalon. 6761
5:24 These were the heads of their families: **E**, 6761

EPHES DAMMIM (1)

1Sa 17:1 They pitched camp at **E**, 702

EPHESIAN (1) [EPHESUS]

Ac 21:29 (They had previously seen Trophimus the **E** *2386*

EPHESIANS (2) [EPHESUS]

Ac 19:28 "Great is Artemis *of* the **E**!" *2386*
19:34 "Great is Artemis *of* the **E**!" *2386*

EPHESUS (18) [EPHESIAN, EPHESIANS]

Ac 18:19 They arrived at **E**, *2387*
18:21 Then he set sail from **E**. *2387*
18:24 a native of Alexandria, came to **E**. *1650*
19:1 through the interior and arrived at **E**. *2387*
19:17 to the Jews and Greeks living in **E**, *2387*
19:26 *in* **E** and in practically the whole province *2387*
19:35 "Men of **E**, doesn't all the world know that *2386*
19:35 the city of **E** is the guardian of the temple *2386*
20:16 to sail past **E** to avoid spending time in *2387*
20:17 Paul sent to **E** for the elders of the church. *2387*
1Co 15:32 in **E** for merely human reasons, *2387*
16:8 But I will stay on at **E** until Pentecost, *2387*
Eph 1:1 To the saints in **E**, *2387*
1Ti 1:3 in **E** so that you may command certain men *2387*
2Ti 1:18 in how many ways he helped me in **E**. *2387*
4:12 I sent Tychicus to **E**. *2387*
Rev 1:11 to **E**, Smyrna, Pergamum, Thyatira, Sardis, *2387*
2:1 "To the angel of the church in **E** write: *2387*

EPHLAL (2)

1Ch 2:37 Zabad the father of **E**, 697
2:37 **E** the father of Obed, 697

EPHOD (50)

Ex 25:7 to be mounted on the **e** and breastpiece. 680
28:4 a breastpiece, an **e**, a robe, a woven tunic, 680
28:6 "Make the **e** of gold, and of blue, 680
28:8 of one piece with **the e** and made with gold, 5647[S]
28:12 of the **e** as memorial stones for the sons 680
28:15 Make it like the **e**: 680
28:25 to the shoulder pieces of the **e** at the front. 680
28:26 on the inside edge next to the **e**. 680
28:27 of the shoulder pieces on the front of the **e**, 680
28:27 the seam just above the waistband of the **e**. 680
28:28 be tied to the rings of the **e** with blue cord, 680
28:28 not swing out from the **e**. 680
28:31 the robe of the **e** entirely of blue cloth, 680
29:5 the robe of the **e**, 680
29:5 the **e** itself and the breastpiece. 680
29:5 Fasten the **e** on him 680
35:9 to be mounted on the **e** and breastpiece. 680
35:27 to be mounted on the **e** and breastpiece. 680
39:2 They made the **e** of gold, and of blue, 680
39:4 They made shoulder pieces for **the e**, 2257[S]
39:5 of one piece with **the e** and made with gold, 5647[S]
39:7 of the **e** as memorial stones for the sons 680
39:8 They made it like the **e**: 680
39:18 to the shoulder pieces of the **e** at the front. 680
39:19 on the inside edge next to the **e**. 680
39:20 of the shoulder pieces on the front of the **e**, 680
39:20 the seam just above the waistband of the **e**. 680
39:21 of the **e** with blue cord, connecting it to 680
39:21 not swing out from the **e**— 680
39:22 the robe of the **e** entirely of blue cloth— 680
Lev 8:7 clothed him with the robe and put the **e** 680
Lev 8:7 He also tied the **e** to him 680
Nu 34:23 Hanniel son of **E**, the leader from the tribe 681
Jdg 8:27 Gideon made the gold into an **e**, 680
17:5 an **e** and some idols and installed one 680
18:14 that one of these houses has an **e**, 680
18:17 inside and took the carved image, the **e**, 680
18:18 the **e**, the other household gods and 680
18:20 He took the **e**, the other household gods 680
1Sa 2:18 a boy wearing a linen **e**. 680
2:28 and to wear an **e** in my presence. 680
14:3 who was wearing an **e**. 680
21:9 it is wrapped in a cloth behind the **e**. 680
22:18 That day he killed eighty-five men who wore the linen **e**. 680
23:6 the **e** down with him when he fled to David 680
23:9 he said to Abiathar the priest, "Bring the **e**." 680
30:7 the son of Ahimelech, "Bring me the **e**." 680
2Sa 6:14 David, wearing a linen **e**, 680
1Ch 15:27 David also wore a linen **e**. 680
Hos 3:4 without **e** or idol. 680

EPHPHATHA (1)

Mk 7:34 and with a deep sigh said to him, "**E**!" *2395*

EPHRAIM (157) [EPHRAIM'S, EPHRAIMITE, EPHRAIMITES]

Ge 41:52 The second son he named **E** and said, 713
46:20 Manasseh and **E** were born to Joseph 713
48:1 So he took his two sons Manasseh and **E** 713
48:5 **E** and Manasseh will be mine, 713
48:13 **E** on his right toward Israel's left hand 713
48:20 'May God make you like **E** 713
48:20 So he put **E** ahead of Manasseh. 713
Nu 1:10 from **E**, Elishama son of Ammihud; 713
1:32 From the descendants of **E**: 713
1:33 number from the tribe of **E** was 40,500. 713
2:18 of the camp of **E** under their standard. 713
2:18 of **E** is Elishama son of Ammihud. 713
2:24 All the men assigned to the camp of **E**, 713
7:48 the leader of the people of **E**, 713
10:22 divisions of the camp of **E** went next, 713+1201
13:8 from the tribe of **E**, Hoshea son of Nun; 713
26:28 through Manasseh and **E** were: 713
26:35 the descendants of **E** by their clans: 713
26:37 These were the clans of **E**; 713+1201
34:24 leader from the tribe of **E** son of Joseph; 713+1201
Dt 33:17 Such are the ten thousands of **E**; 713
34:2 the territory of **E** and Manasseh, 713
Jos 14:4 sons of Joseph had become two tribes—Manasseh and **E**. 713
16:4 So Manasseh and **E**, 713
16:5 This was the territory of **E**, clan by clan: 713+1201
16:10 the Canaanites live among the people of **E** 713
17:9 to **E** lying among the towns of Manasseh, 713
17:10 On the south the land belonged to **E**, 713
17:15 if the hill country of **E** is too small for you, 713
17:17 to **E** and Manasseh— 713
19:50 Timnath Serah in the hill country of **E**. 713
20:7 Shechem in the hill country of **E**, 713
21:5 from the clans of the tribes of **E**, 713
21:20 from the tribe of **E**: 713
21:21 of **E** they were given Shechem (a city 713
24:30 at Timnath Serah in the hill country of **E**, 713
24:33 to his son Phinehas in the hill country of **E**. 713
Jdg 1:29 Nor did **E** drive out the Canaanites living 713
2:9 at Timnath Heres in the hill country of **E**, 713
3:27 he blew a trumpet in the hill country of **E**, 713
4:5 and Bethel in the hill country of **E**, 713
5:14 Some came from **E**, whose roots were 713
7:24 throughout the hill country of **E**, 713
7:24 the men of **E** were called out and they took 713
10:1 He lived in Shamir, in the hill country of **E**. 713
10:9 Benjamin and the house of **E**; 713
12:1 The men of **E** called out their forces, 713
12:4 the men of Gilead and fought against **E**. 713
12:4 "You Gileadites are renegades from **E** 713
12:5 the fords of the Jordan leading to **E**, 713
12:5 and whenever a survivor of **E** said, 713
12:15 and was buried at Pirathon in **E**, 713+824
17:1 from the hill country of **E** 713
17:8 to Micah's house in the hill country of **E**. 713
18:2 the hill country of **E** and came to the house 713
18:13 on to the hill country of **E** and came 713
19:1 a remote area in the hill country of **E** took 713
19:16 an old man from the hill country of **E**, 713
19:18 to a remote area in the hill country of **E** 713
1Sa 1:1 a Zuphite from the hill country of **E**, 713
9:4 of **E** and through the area around Shalisha, 713
14:22 of **E** heard that the Philistines were on 713
2Sa 2:9 and also over **E**, Benjamin and all Israel. 713
13:23 at Baal Hazor near the border of **E**, 713
18:6 and the battle took place in the forest of **E**. 713
20:21 from the hill country of **E**, 713
1Ki 4:8 in the hill country of **E**; 713
12:25 in the hill country of **E** and lived there. 713
2Ki 5:22 to me from the hill country of **E**. 713
14:13 the wall of Jerusalem from the **E** Gate to 713
1Ch 6:66 as their territory towns from the tribe of **E**. 713
6:67 of **E** they were given Shechem (a city 713
7:20 The descendants of **E**: 713
7:22 Their father **E** mourned 713
9:3 and from **E** and Manasseh who lived 713+1201
12:30 men of **E**, brave warriors, famous 713
2Ch 13:4 in the hill country of **E**, and said, 713
15:8 the towns he had captured in the hills of **E**. 713
2Ch 15:9 and Benjamin and the people from **E**, 713
17:2 of **E** that his father Asa had captured. 713
19:4 the hill country of **E** and turned them back 713
25:7 not with any of the people of **E**. 713
25:10 the troops who had come to him from **E** 713
25:23 the wall of Jerusalem from the **E** Gate to 713
28:12 Then some of the leaders in **E**— 713+1201
30:1 and also wrote letters to **E** and Manasseh, 713
30:10 couriers went from town to town in **E** 713+824
30:18 of the many people who came from **E**, 713
31:1 throughout Judah and Benjamin and in **E** 713
34:6 In the towns of Manasseh, **E** and Simeon, 713
34:9 **E** and the entire remnant of Israel and 713
Ne 8:16 and the one by the Gate of **E**. 713
12:39 over the Gate of **E**, 713
Ps 60:7 **E** is my helmet, Judah my scepter. 713
78:9 The men of **E**, though armed with bows, 713
78:67 he did not choose the tribe of **E**; 713
80:2 before **E**, Benjamin 713
108:8 **E** is my helmet, Judah my scepter. 713
Isa 7:2 "Aram has allied itself with **E**"; 713
7:5 Aram, **E** and Remaliah's son have plotted your ruin, 713
7:8 Within sixty-five years **E** will 713
7:9 The head of **E** is Samaria, 713
7:17 a time unlike any since **E** broke away 713
9:9 **E** and the inhabitants of Samaria— 713
9:21 Manasseh will feed on **E**, and Ephraim 713
9:21 and **E** on Manasseh; 713
11:13 **E** will not be jealous of Judah, 713
11:13 nor Judah hostile toward **E**. 713
17:3 The fortified city will disappear from **E**, 713
Jer 4:15 proclaiming disaster from the hills of **E**. 713
7:15 the people of **E**.' 713
31:6 when watchmen cry out on the hills of **E**, 713
31:9 and **E** is my firstborn son. 713
31:20 Is not **E** my dear son, 713
50:19 be satisfied on the hills of **E** and Gilead. 713
Eze 48:5 "**E** will have one portion; 713
48:6 it will border the territory of **E** from east 713
Hos 4:17 **E** is joined to idols; leave him alone! 713
5:3 I know all about **E**; 713
5:3 **E**, you have now turned to prostitution; 713
5:5 the Israelites, even **E**, stumble in their sin; 713
5:9 **E** will be laid waste on the day 713
5:11 **E** is oppressed, trampled in judgment, 713
5:12 I am like a moth to **E**, 713
5:13 "When **E** saw his sickness, 713
5:13 then **E** turned to Assyria, 713
5:14 For I will be like a lion to **E**, 713
6:4 "What can I do with you, **E**? 713
6:10 There **E** is given to prostitution 713
7:1 the sins of **E** are exposed and the crimes 713
7:8 "**E** mixes with the nations; 713
7:8 **E** is a flat cake not turned over. 713
7:11 "**E** is like a dove, 713
8:9 **E** has sold herself to lovers. 713
8:11 **E** built many altars for sin offerings, 713
9:3 **E** will return to Egypt and eat unclean food 713
9:8 is the watchman over **E**, 713
9:13 I have seen **E**, like Tyre, 713
9:13 But **E** will bring out their children to 713
9:16 **E** is blighted, their root is withered, 713
10:6 **E** will be disgraced; 713
10:11 **E** is a trained heifer that loves to thresh; 713
10:11 I will drive **E**, Judah must plow, 713
11:3 It was I who taught **E** to walk, 713
11:8 "How can I give you up, **E**? 713
11:9 nor will I turn and devastate **E**. 713
11:12 **E** has surrounded me with lies, 713
12:1 **E** feeds on the wind; 713
12:8 **E** boasts, "I am very rich; 713
12:14 But **E** has bitterly provoked him to anger; 713
13:1 When **E** spoke, men trembled; 713
13:12 The guilt of **E** is stored up, 713
14:8 O **E**, what more have I to do with idols? 713
Ob 1:19 They will occupy the fields of **E** 713
Zec 9:10 from **E** and the war-horses from Jerusalem, 713
9:13 as I bend my bow and fill it with **E**. 713
Jn 11:54 to a village called **E**, *2394*

EPHRAIM'S (12) [EPHRAIM]

Ge 48:14 and put it on **E** head, 713
48:17 on **E** head he was displeased; 713
48:17 of his father's hand to move it from **E** head 713
50:23 and saw the third generation of **E** children. 713
Jdg 8:2 Aren't the gleanings of **E** grapes better than 713
Isa 11:13 **E** jealousy will vanish, 713
28:1 the pride of **E** drunkards, 713
28:3 That wreath, the pride of **E** drunkards, 713
Jer 31:18 "I have surely heard **E** moaning: 713
Eze 37:16 and write on it, '**E** stick, 713
37:19 which is in **E** hand— 713
Hos 9:11 **E** glory will fly away like a bird— 713

EPHRAIMITE (6) [EPHRAIM]

Jdg 12:5 "Are you an **E**?" 718
1Sa 1:1 the son of Tohu, the son of Zuph, an **E**. 718
1Ki 11:26 an **E** from Zeredah, 718
1Ch 27:10 was Helez the Pelonite, an **E**. 713+1201
27:14 was Benaiah the Pirathonite, an **E**. 713+1201
2Ch 28:7 an **E** warrior, killed Maaseiah 713

EPHRAIMITES (8) [EPHRAIM]

Jos 16:8 the inheritance of the tribe of the **E**, 713+1201

Jos 16: 9 that were set aside for the E within 713+1201
17: 8 belonged to the E.) 713+1201
Jdg 8: 1 Now the E asked Gideon, 408+713
12: 4 down because the E had said, 713
12: 6 Forty-two thousand E were killed at 713+4946
1Ch 27:20 over the E: Hoshea son of Azaziah; 713+1201
Zec 10: 7 The E will become like mighty men, 713

EPHRAIN (KJV) EPHRON

EPHRATH (5) [EPHRATHITE, EPHRATHITES]

Ge 35:16 from E, Rachel began to give birth 714
35:19 and was buried on the way to E (that is, 714
48: 7 a little distance from E. 714
48: 7 So I buried her there beside the road to E" 714
1Ch 2:19 When Azubah died, Caleb married E, 715

EPHRATHAH (5) [BETHLEHEM, CALEB EPHRATHAH]

Ru 4:11 May you have standing in E and be famous 716
1Ch 2:50 The sons of Hur the firstborn of E: 717
4: 4 the firstborn of E and father of Bethlehem. 717
Ps 132: 6 We heard it in E, 716
Mic 5: 2 "But you, Bethlehem E, 716

EPHRATHITE (1) [EPHRATH]

1Sa 17:12 David was the son of an E named Jesse, 718

EPHRATHITES (1) [EPHRATH]

Ru 1: 2 They were E from Bethlehem, Judah. 718

EPHRON (10) [EPHRON'S]

Ge 23: 8 then listen to me and intercede with E son 6766
23:10 E the Hittite was sitting among his people 6766
23:13 and he said to E in their hearing, 6766
23:14 E answered Abraham, 6766
25: 9 in the field of E son of Zohar the Hittite, 6766
49:29 with my fathers in the cave in the field of E 6766
49:30 as a burial place from E the Hittite, 6766
50:13 as a burial place from E the Hittite, 6766
Jos 15: 9 came out at the towns of Mount E and went 6767
2Ch 13:19 the towns of Bethel, Jeshanah and E, 6767

EPHRON'S (2) [EPHRON]

Ge 23:16 to E terms and weighed out for him 6766
23:17 So E field in Machpelah near Mamre— 6766

EPICUREAN (1)

Ac 17:18 A group *of* E and Stoic philosophers began *2134*

EPISTLE (KJV) LETTER

EQUAL (18) [EQUALED, EQUALITY, EQUALLY, EQUITY, EQUIVALENT]

Ge 44:18 though you are e to Pharaoh himself. 4017
47: 9 not e the years of the pilgrimage 5952
Ex 30:34 frankincense, all **in e amounts,** 928+963+963
Dt 33:25 and your strength will e your days. 3869
1Sa 9: 2 an impressive young man **without** e among the Israelites— 401+3202+4946
1Ki 3:13 so that in your lifetime you will have no e 4017
Job 41:33 Nothing on earth is his e— 5444
Isa 40:25 Or who *is my* e?" 8750
46: 5 or **count** me e? 8750
Eze 31: 8 nor *could* the pine trees e its boughs, 1948
45:12 Twenty shekels plus twenty-five shekels plus fifteen shekels e one mina. NIH
48: 8 and its length from east to west will e one 3869
Da 1:19 and he found none e to Daniel, Hananiah, 3869
Mt 20:12 'and you have made them e *2698*
Jn 5:18 making himself e with God. *2698*
1Co 12:25 but that its parts should have e concern *899+3836*
2Co 2:16 And who *is* e to such a task? *2653*
11:12 an opportunity to be considered **e with us** in the things they boast about. *1609+2777+2779*

EQUALED (2) [EQUAL]

Mt 24:21 and never to be e again. *NIG*
Mk 13:19 and never to be e again. *NIG*

EQUALITY (3) [EQUAL]

2Co 8:13 but that there might be e. *2699*
8:14 Then there will be e, *2699*
Php 2: 6 did not consider e with God something to be grasped, *1639+2698+3836*

EQUALLY (5) [EQUAL]

Ex 21:35 **divide** both the money and the dead animal e. 2936
Lev 7:10 belongs e to all the sons of Aaron. 278+408+2257+3869
Dt 18: 8 He is to share e in their benefits, 3869
Ecc 11: 6 or whether both will do e well. 285+3869
Eze 47:14 You are to divide it **e among them.** 278+408+2257+3869

EQUIP (1) [EQUIPMENT, EQUIPPED]

Heb 13:21 e you with everything good *2936*

EQUIPMENT (10) [EQUIP]

Nu 3:36 all its e, and everything related to their use, 3998
4:26 the ropes and all the e *used in* its service. 3998
4:32 all their e and everything related 3998
Dt 23:13 As part of your e have something to dig 266
1Sa 8:12 to make weapons of war and e 3998
1Ki 19:21 the plowing e to cook the meat and gave it 3998
2Ki 7:15 and e the Arameans had thrown away 3998
2Ch 20:25 a great amount of e and clothing and 8214
Ne 13: 9 then I put back into them the e *of* the house 3998
Zec 11:15 "Take again the e *of* a foolish shepherd. 3998

EQUIPPED (4) [EQUIP]

2Ch 14: 8 e *with* large shields and *with* spears, 5951
Ne 4:16 while the other half *were* e *with* spears, 2616
Da 11:13 he will advance with a huge army fully e. 8214
2Ti 3:17 so that the man of God may be thoroughly e *1992*

EQUITY (3) [EQUAL]

Ps 96:10 he will judge the peoples with e. 4797
98: 9 in righteousness and the peoples with e. 4797
99: 4 you have established e; 4797

EQUIVALENT (2) [EQUAL]

Lev 27: 2 to the LORD by giving e **values,** 6886
Eze 45:14 for ten baths are e to a homer). NIH

ER (10)

Ge 38: 3 who was named E. 6841
38: 6 Judah got a wife for E, his firstborn, 6841
38: 7 But E, Judah's firstborn, 6841
46:12 The sons of Judah: E, Onan, Shelah, 6841
46:12 Perez and Zerah (but E and Onan had died 6841
Nu 26:19 E and Onan were sons of Judah, 6841
1Ch 2: 3 The sons of Judah: E, Onan and Shelah. 6841
2: 3 E, Judah's firstborn, was wicked in 6841
4:21 E the father of Lecah, 6841
Lk 3:28 the son of Elmadam, the son *of* E, *2474*

ERAN (1) [ERANITE]

Nu 26:36 through E, the Eranite clan. 6896

ERANITE (1) [ERAN]

Nu 26:36 through Eran, the E clan. 6897

ERASTUS (3)

Ac 19:22 He sent two of his helpers, Timothy and E, *2235*
Ro 16:23 E, who is the city's director *2235*
2Ti 4:20 E stayed in Corinth, *2235*

ERECH (2)

Ge 10:10 E, Akkad and Calneh, in Shinar. 804
Ezr 4: 9 E and Babylon, the Elamites of Susa, 10074

ERECT (3) [ERECTED]

Dt 16:22 and *do* not e a sacred stone, 7756
Eze 4: 2 E siege works against it, 1215
21:22 to build a ramp and to e siege works. 1215

ERECTED (9) [ERECT]

Ex 40:18 he put the bases in place, e the frames, 8492
2Sa 18:18 e it in the King's Valley **as a monument** 5893
1Ki 7:21 *He* e the pillars at the portico of the temple. 7756
2Ki 21: 3 *he* also e altars to Baal and made 7756
23:12 down the altars the kings of Judah *had* e on 6913
2Ch 3:17 *He* e the pillars in the front of the temple, 7756
33: 3 *he* also e altars to the Baals 7756
Est 6: 4 on the gallows *he had* e for him. 3922
Eze 17:17 and siege works e to destroy many lives. 1215

ERI (2) [ERITE]

Ge 46:16 Zephon, Haggi, Shuni, Ezbon, E, 6878
Nu 26:16 through E, the Erite clan; 6878

ERITE (1) [ERI]

Nu 26:16 through Eri, the E clan; 6879

ERODES (1)

Job 14:18 "But as a mountain e and crumbles and as 5877

ERRAND (KJV) HAVE TO SAY, MESSAGE

ERRED (2) [ERROR]

Nu 15:28 the one who e by sinning unintentionally, 8704
1Sa 26:21 I have acted like a fool and *have* e greatly." 8706

ERROR (12) [ERRED, ERRORS]

Job 4:18 if he charges his angels with e, 9334
19: 4 my e remains my concern alone. 5413
Ecc 10: 5 the sort of e that arises from a ruler: 8705
Isa 32: 6 He practices ungodliness and spreads e 9360
47:15 Each of them goes on in his e; 9494
Mt 22:29 *"You are* **in** e because you do not know *4414*
Mk 12:24 *"Are you* not **in** e because you do not know *4414*
1Th 2: 3 the appeal we make does not spring from e *4415*
Jas 5:20 a sinner from the e of his way will save him *4415*
2Pe 2:18 from those who live in e. *4415*
3:17 not be carried away *by* the e of lawless men *4415*
Jude 1:11 for profit *into* Balaam's e; *4415*

ERRORS (2) [ERROR]

Ps 19:12 Who can discern his e? 8709
Ecc 10: 4 calmness can lay great e to rest. 2628

ESARHADDON (3)

2Ki 19:37 And E his son succeeded him as king. 675
Ezr 4: 2 to him since the time of E king of Assyria, 675
Isa 37:38 And E his son succeeded him as king. 675

ESAU (87) [EDOM, ESAU'S]

Ge 25:25 so they named him E. 6916
25:27 and E became a skillful hunter, 6916
25:28 who had a taste for wild game, loved E, 6916
25:29 E came in from the open country, famished. 6916
25:32 "Look, I am about to die," E said. 6916
25:34 Then Jacob gave E some bread 6916
25:34 So E despised his birthright. 6916
26:34 When E was forty years old, 6916
27: 1 he called for E his older son and said 6916
27: 5 as Isaac spoke to his son E. 6916
27: 5 When E left for the open country 6916
27: 6 to your brother E, 6916
27:11 "But my brother E is a hairy man, 6916
27:15 the best clothes of E her older son, 6916
27:19 "I am E your firstborn. 6916
27:21 to know whether you really are my son E 6916
27:22 but the hands are the hands of E." 6916
27:23 like those of his brother E; 6916
27:24 "Are you really my son E?" 6916
27:30 his brother E came in from hunting. 6916
27:32 he answered, "your firstborn, E." 6916
27:34 When E heard his father's words, 6916
27:36 E said, "Isn't he rightly named Jacob? NIH
27:37 Isaac answered E, "I have made him lord 6916
27:38 E said to his father, 6916
27:38 Then E wept aloud. 6916
27:41 E held a grudge against Jacob because of 6916
27:42 Rebekah was told what her older son E had said, 6916
27:42 "Your brother E is consoling himself with 6916
28: 5 who was the mother of Jacob and E. 6916
28: 6 Now E learned that Isaac had blessed Jacob 6916
28: 8 E then realized how displeasing 6916
32: 3 of him to his brother E in the land of Seir, 6916
32: 4 to say to my master E: 6916
32: 6 they said, "We went to your brother E, 6916
32: 8 "If E comes and attacks one group, 6916
32:11 I pray, from the hand of my brother E, 6916
32:13 a gift for his brother E: 6916
32:17 "When my brother E meets you and asks, 6916
32:18 They are a gift sent to my lord E, 6916
32:19 the same thing to E when you meet him. 6916
33: 1 Jacob looked up and there was E, 6916
33: 4 But E ran to meet Jacob and embraced him; 6916
33: 5 Then E looked up and saw the women NIH
33: 8 E asked, "What do you mean NIH
33: 9 E said, "I already have plenty, my brother. 6916
33:11 And because Jacob insisted, E accepted it. NIH
33:12 Then E said, "Let us be on our way; NIH
33:15 E said, "Then let me leave some of my men 6916
33:16 that day E started on his way back to Seir. 6916
35: 1 from your brother E." 6916
35:29 And his sons E and Jacob buried him. 6916
36: 1 This is the account of E (that is, Edom). 6916
36: 2 E took his wives from the women 6916
36: 4 Adah bore Eliphaz to E, 6916
36: 5 These were the sons of E, 6916
36: 6 E took his wives and sons and daughters 6916
36: 8 So E (that is, Edom) settled in the hill 6916
36: 9 the account of E the father of the Edomites 6916
36:14 whom she bore to E: 6916
36:15 The sons of Eliphaz the firstborn of E: 6916
36:19 These were the sons of E (that is, Edom), 6916
36:40 These were the chiefs descended from E, 6916
36:43 This was E the father of the Edomites. 6916
Dt 2: 4 of your brothers the descendants of E, 6916
2: 5 I have given E the hill country of Seir 6916
2: 8 on past our brothers the descendants of E, 6916
2:12 but the descendants of E drove them out. 6916
2:22 the same for the descendants of E, 6916
2:29 the descendants of E, who live in Seir, and 6916
Jos 24: 4 and to Isaac I gave Jacob and E. 6916
24: 4 I assigned the hill country of Seir to E, 6916
1Ch 1:34 The sons of Isaac: E and Israel. 6916
1:35 The sons of E: 6916
Jer 49: 8 for I will bring disaster on E at 6916
49:10 But I will strip E bare; 6916
Ob 1: 6 But how E will be ransacked, 6916
1: 8 of understanding in the mountains of E? 6916
1:18 the house of E will be stubble, 6916
1:18 be no survivors from the house of E." 6916
1:19 the Negev will occupy the mountains of E, 6916
1:21 to govern the mountains of E. 6916
Mal 1: 2 "Was not E Jacob's brother?" 6916
1: 3 but E I have hated, 6916
Ro 9:13 "Jacob I loved, but E I hated." *2481*
Heb 11:20 By faith Isaac blessed Jacob and E *2481*
12:16 or is godless like E, *2481*

ESAU'S (14) [ESAU]

Ge 25:26 with his hand grasping **E** heel; 6916
36:10 These are the names of **E** sons: 6916
36:10 Eliphaz, the son of **E** wife Adah, and Reuel, 6916
36:10 and Reuel, the son of **E** wife Basemath. 6916
36:12 **E** son Eliphaz also had a concubine 6916
36:12 These were grandsons of **E** wife Adah. 6916
36:13 These were grandsons of **E** wife Basemath. 6916
36:14 The sons of **E** wife Oholibamah daughter 6916
36:15 the chiefs among **E** descendants: 6916
36:17 The sons of **E** son Reuel: 6916
36:17 they were grandsons of **E** wife Basemath. 6916
36:18 The sons of **E** wife Oholibamah: 6916
36:18 from **E** wife Oholibamah daughter of Anah. 6916
Ob 1:9 and everyone in **E** mountains will be cut 6916

ESCAPE (66) [ESCAPED, ESCAPES, ESCAPING]

Ge 7:7 entered the ark *to* **e** the waters of the flood. 4946+7156
32:8 the group that is left may **e.**" 7129
Jos 8:20 they had no chance to **e** in any direction, 5674
Jdg 20:42 but they *could* **not e** the battle. 1815
1Sa 19:10 That night David **made good** *his* **e.** 2256+4880+5674
19:18 When David had fled and **made** *his* **e,** 4880
27:1 The best thing I can do *is to* **e** to the land of the Philistines. 4880+4880
2Sa 15:14 or none of us will **e** from Absalom. 7129
20:6 he will find fortified cities and **e** *from* us." 5911
1Ki 12:18 to get into his chariot and **e** *to* Jerusalem. 5674
19:17 Jehu will put to death any *who* **e** the sword 4880
19:17 and Elisha will put to death any *who* **e** 4880
2Ki 10:24 of the men I am placing in your hands **e,** 4880
10:25 *let* no one **e."** 3655
2Ch 10:18 to get into his chariot and **e** *to* Jerusalem. 5674
Est 4:13 you alone of all the Jews *will* **e.** 4880
Job 11:20 and **e** will elude them; 4960
15:30 *He will* not **e** the darkness; 6073
Ps 56:7 On no account **let** them **e;** 7117
68:20 comes **e** from death. 9362
88:8 *I* am confined and cannot **e;** 3655
Pr 11:9 but through knowledge the righteous **e.** 2740
Ecc 7:26 The man who pleases God *will* **e** her, 4880
Isa 20:6 How then *can* we **e?'** " 4880
Jer 11:11 on them a disaster they cannot **e.** 3655
21:9 he will **e with** his life. 4200+8965
25:35 the leaders of the flock no **place to e.** 7129
32:4 Zedekiah king of Judah *will* not **e** out of 4880
34:3 You *will* not **e** from his grasp but will 4880
35:11 **e** the Babylonian and Aramean armies 4946+7156
38:2 He will **e with** his life; he will live.' 4200+8965
38:18 not **e** from their hands.' " 4880
38:23 not **e** from their hands but will be captured 4880
39:18 by the sword but will **e with** your life, 4200+8965
41:18 to **e** the Babylonians. 4946+7156
42:17 or **e** the disaster I will bring on them.' 7127
44:14 to live in Egypt will **e** or survive to return 7127
44:28 *Those who* **e** the sword and return to 7127
45:5 wherever you go I will let you **e with** 4200+8965
46:6 "The swift cannot flee nor the strong **e.** 4880
48:8 and not a town *will* **e.** 4880
50:29 Encamp all around her; let no *one* **e.** 7129
La 3:7 He has walled me in so *I* cannot **e;** 3655
Eze 6:8 for some of you will **e** the sword 7127
6:9 *those who* **e** will remember me 7127
7:16 All who survive and **e** will be in 7127
17:15 *Will he* who does such things **e?** 4880
17:15 Will he break the treaty and yet **e?** 4880
17:18 *he shall* not **e.** 4880
Da 11:42 Egypt will not **e.** 7129
Hos 9:6 Even if *they* **e** from destruction, 2143
Am 2:14 The swift *will* **not e,** 6+4960
9:1 Not one will get away, none *will* **e.** 4880+7127
Hab 2:9 to **e** the clutches of ruin! 5911
Zec 2:7 **E,** you who live in the Daughter 4880
Mal 3:15 and even those who challenge God **e.'** " 4880
Mt 2:13 the child and his mother and **e** to Egypt. *5771*
23:33 How *will you* **e** being condemned to hell? *5771*
Lk 21:36 that you may be able *to* **e** all that is about *1767*
Ac 27:30 In an attempt *to* **e** from the ship, *5771*
Ro 2:3 do you think you *will* **e** God's judgment? *1767*
1Th 5:3 and *they will* not **e.** *1767*
2Ti 2:26 that they will come to their senses and **e** *NIG*
Heb 2:3 how *shall* we **e** if we ignore such *1767*
12:25 If they *did* not **e** when they refused him *1767*
2Pe 1:4 and **e** the corruption in the world *709*

ESCAPED (38) [ESCAPE]

Ge 14:13 One who *had* **e** came and reported this 7127
Jdg 3:26 He passed by the idols and **e** to Seirah. 4880
3:29 not a man **e.** 4880
9:5 the youngest son of Jerub-Baal, **e** by hiding. 3855
1Sa 19:12 and he fled and **e.** 4880
19:17 and send my enemy away so that *he* **e?"** 4880
22:1 David left Gath and **e** to the cave 4880
22:20 **e** and fled to join David. 4880
23:13 When Saul was told that David *had* **e** 4880
2Sa 1:3 *"I have* **e** from the Israelite camp." 4880
1Ki 20:20 of Aram **e** on horseback with some 4880
20:30 The rest of them **e** to the city of Aphek, 5674
2Ki 9:27 but *he* **e** *to* Megiddo and died there. 5674
13:5 and *they* **e** from the power of Aram. 3655
19:37 and they **e** *to* the land of Ararat. 4880
1Ch 4:43 the remaining Amalekites who had **e,** 7129
2Ch 16:7 of the king of Aram *has* **e** from your hand. 4880
20:24 no one had **e.** 7129
30:6 who have **e** from the hand of the kings 7129
36:20 who **e from** the sword, 4946
Job 1:15 I am the only one *who has* **e** to tell you!" 4880
1:16 I am the only one *who has* **e** to tell you!" 4880
1:17 I am the only one *who has* **e** to tell you!" 4880
1:19 I am the only one *who has* **e** to tell you!" 4880
19:20 *I have* **e** with only the skin of my teeth. 4880
Ps 124:7 We *have* **e** like a bird out of 4880
124:7 the snare has been broken, and we *have* **e.** 4880
Isa 37:38 and they **e** *to* the land of Ararat. 4880
Jer 41:15 of his men **e** from Johanan and fled to 4880
51:50 You *who* have **e** the sword, 7128
La 2:22 of the LORD's anger no one **e** or survived; 7127
Eze 33:21 **man who** *had* **e** from Jerusalem came to me 7127
Jn 10:39 but *he* **e** their grasp. *2002*
Ac 16:27 because he thought the prisoners *had* **e.** *1767*
26:26 that none of this *has* **e** his **notice,** *3291*
28:4 for *though he* **e** from the sea, *1407*
Heb 11:34 and **e** the edge of the sword; *5771*
2Pe 2:20 If *they have* **e** the corruption of the world *709*

ESCAPES (3) [ESCAPE]

Ps 33:16 no warrior **e** by his great strength. 5911
Pr 12:13 but a righteous man **e** trouble. 3655
Joel 2:3 a desert waste—nothing **e** them. 2118+7129

ESCAPING (7) [ESCAPE]

Jdg 9:21 Then Jotham fled, **e** to Beer, 1368
Job 15:22 He despairs of **e** the darkness; 8740
Jer 48:19 Ask the man fleeing and the *woman* **e,** 4880
Hos 13:3 like smoke **e** through a window. NIH
Ac 27:42 of them from swimming away and **e.** *1423*
1Co 3:15 but only as one **e** through the flames. *NIG*
2Pe 2:18 they entice people who *are* just **e from** *709*

ESCORT (2) [ESCORTED]

Da 11:6 together with her royal **e** and her father and 995
Ac 16:37 *Let them* come themselves and **e** us **out."** *1974*

ESCORTED (4) [ESCORT]

1Ki 1:38 on King David's mule and **e** him to Gihon. 2143
SS 3:7 **e by** sixty warriors, the noblest of Israel, 6017
Ac 16:39 They came to appease them and **e** them *1974*
17:15 The men who **e** Paul brought him to Athens *2770*

ESAIAS (KJV) ISAIAH

ESCHEW (KJV) TURN FROM

ESEK (1)

Ge 26:20 So he named the well **E,** 6922

ESH-BAAL (2) [BAAL, ISH-BOSHETH]

1Ch 8:33 Malki-Shua, Abinadab and **E.** 843
9:39 Malki-Shua, Abinadab and **E.** 843

ESHAN (1)

Jos 15:52 Arab, Dumah, **E,** 878

ESHBAN (2)

Ge 36:26 Hemdan, **E,** Ithran and Keran. 841
1Ch 1:41 Hemdan, **E,** Ithran and Keran. 841

ESHCOL (6)

Ge 14:13 a brother of **E** and Aner, 866
14:24 to Aner, **E** and Mamre. 866
Nu 13:23 When they reached the Valley of **E,** 865
13:24 the Valley of **E** because of the cluster 865
32:9 up to the Valley of **E** and viewed the land, 865
Dt 1:24 came to the Valley of **E** and explored it. 865

ESHEAN (KJV) ESHAN

ESHEK (1)

1Ch 8:39 The sons of his brother **E:** 6944

ESHKALONITES (KJV) ASHKELON

ESHTAOL (7) [ESHTAOLITES]

Jos 15:33 In the western foothills: **E,** Zorah, Ashnah, 900
19:41 Zorah, **E,** Ir Shemesh, 900
Jdg 13:25 between Zorah and **E.** 900
16:31 and **E** in the tomb of Manoah his father. 900
18:2 and **E** to spy out the land and explore it. 900
18:8 When they returned to Zorah and **E,** 900
18:11 armed for battle, set out from Zorah and **E.** 900

ESHTAOLITES (1) [ESHTAOL]

1Ch 2:53 From these descended the Zorathites and **E.** 901

ESHTARAH See BE ESHTARAH

ESHTEMOA (5)

Jos 21:14 Jattir, **E,** 904
1Sa 30:28 to those in Aroer, Siphmoth, **E** 904
1Ch 4:17 Shammai and Ishbah the father of **E.** 904
4:19 the father of Keilah the Garmite, and **E** 904
6:57 (a city of refuge), and Libnah, Jattir, **E,** 904

ESHTEMOH (1)

Jos 15:50 Anab, **E,** Anim, 903

ESHTON (2)

1Ch 4:11 who was the father of **E.** 902
4:12 **E** was the father of Beth Rapha, 902

ESLI (1)

Lk 3:25 the son of Nahum, the son *of* **E,** *2268*

ESPECIALLY (15) [SPECIAL]

Jos 2:1 look over the land," he said, "**e** Jericho." 2256
Est 8:10 who rode fast horses **e bred** for the king. 1201+2021+8247
Ac 25:26 and **e** before you, King Agrippa, *3436*
26:3 and **e so** because you are well acquainted *3436*
1Co 14:1 **e** the gift of prophecy. *3437*
2Co 1:12 and **e** in our relations with you, *4359*
7:13 we were **e** delighted to see *3437*
Gal 6:10 **e** to those who belong to the family *3436*
Php 4:22 **e** those who belong to Caesar's household. *3436*
1Ti 4:10 and **e** of those who believe. *3436*
5:8 and **e** for his immediate family, *3436*
5:17 **e** those whose work is preaching *3436*
2Ti 4:13 and my scrolls, **e** the parchments. *3436*
Tit 1:10 **e** those of the circumcision group. *3436*
2Pe 2:10 This is **e** true of those who follow *3436*

ESPIED, ESPY (KJV) EXPLORE, SAW, SEARCHED OUT, WATCHED

ESPOUSALS, ESPOUSED (KJV) BETROTHED, PLEDGED TO BE MARRIED, PROMISED

ESROM (KJV) HEZRON

ESTABLISH (37) [ESTABLISHED, ESTABLISHES, ESTABLISHING, REESTABLISHED]

Ge 6:18 But *I will* **e** my covenant with you, 7756
9:9 "I now **e** my covenant with you and 7756
9:11 *I* **e** my covenant with you: 7756
17:7 *I will* **e** my covenant as 7756
17:19 *I will* **e** my covenant with him as 7756
17:21 But my covenant *I will* **e** with Isaac, 7756
Ex 23:31 *"I will* **e** your borders from the Red Sea to 8883
Dt 28:9 The LORD *will* **e** you as his holy people, 7756
1Sa 2:35 *I will* firmly **e** his house, 1215
2Sa 3:10 and **e** David's throne over Israel and Judah 7756
7:11 that the LORD *himself will* **e** a house 6913
7:12 and *I will* **e** his kingdom. 3922
7:13 *I will* **e** the throne of his kingdom forever. 3922
1Ki 8:32 and so **e** his innocence. 5989
9:5 *I will* **e** your royal throne 7756
1Ch 17:11 and *I will* **e** his kingdom. 3922
17:12 and *I will* **e** his throne forever. 3922
18:3 to **e** his control along the Euphrates River. 5893
22:10 And *I will* **e** the throne of his kingdom 3922
28:7 *I will* **e** his kingdom forever 3922
2Ch 6:23 not guilty and so **e** his innocence. 5989
7:18 *I will* **e** your royal throne, 7756
Est 9:27 upon themselves *to* **e the custom** that they 7756
9:31 to **e** these days of Purim 7756
Ps 87:5 and the Most High himself *will* **e** her." 3922
89:4 *'I will* **e** your line forever 3922
89:29 *I will* **e** his line forever, 8492
90:17 **e** the work of our hands for us— 3922
90:17 yes, **e** the work of our hands. 3922
Isa 26:12 LORD, *you* **e** peace for us; 9189
Eze 16:60 *I will* **e** an everlasting covenant with you. 7756
16:62 So I *will* **e** my covenant with you, 7756
37:26 *I will* **e** them and increase their numbers, 5989
Da 11:16 *He will* **e** *himself* in the Beautiful Land 6641
Ro 10:3 from God and sought *to* **e** their own, *2705*
16:25 *to* him who is able *to* **e** you by my gospel *5114*
Heb 10:9 He sets aside the first to **e** the second. *2705*

ESTABLISHED (75) [ESTABLISH]

Ge 9:17 "This is the sign of the covenant *I have* **e** 7756
47:26 So Joseph **e** it as a law concerning land 8492
Ex 6:4 also **e** my covenant with them to give them 7756
15:17 the sanctuary, O Lord, your hands **e.** 3922
Lev 26:46 and the regulations that the LORD **e** 5989
Dt 19:15 A matter *must be* **e** by the testimony 7756
1Sa 13:13 if you had, he *would have* **e** your kingdom 3922
20:31 neither you nor your kingdom *will* **be e.** 3922
24:20 and that the kingdom of Israel *will be* **e** 7756
2Sa 5:12 And David knew that the LORD *had* **e** him 3922
7:16 your throne will be **e** forever.' " 3922
7:24 *You have* **e** your people Israel 3922
7:26 of your servant David will be **e** before you. 3922

1Ki 2:12 and his rule **was firmly e.** 3922
2:24 *he* who *has* e me securely on the throne 3922
2:46 The kingdom **was** now **firmly e** 3922
1Ch 14: 2 And David knew that the LORD *had* e him 3922
16:30 The world **is firmly e**; it cannot be moved. 3922
17:14 his throne will be e forever.' " 3922
17:23 and his house **be e** forever. 586
17:24 so that *it will* **be e** and that your name will 586
17:24 of your servant David *will* **be e** before you. 3922
2Ch 1: 1 Solomon son of David **e himself firmly** 2616
12: 1 After Rehoboam's position as king *was* e 3922
12:13 King Rehoboam **e himself firmly** 2616
17: 5 The LORD e the kingdom 3922
21: 4 When Jehoram e *himself* firmly 7756
Ezr 8:20 and the officials *had* e to assist the Levites. 5989
Est 9:31 and as *they had* e for themselves 7756
Job 12:19 and overthrows *men* **long e.** 419
21: 8 They see their children e around them, 3922
24:22 though *they become* e, 7756
28:25 When he e the force of the wind 6913
Ps 9: 7 *he has* e his throne for judgment. 3922
24: 2 for he founded it upon the seas and e it 3922
74:16 you e the sun and moon. 3922
78: 5 He decreed statutes for Jacob and e the law 8492
78:69 like the earth that *he* e forever. 3569
81: 5 *He* e it as a statute for Joseph 8492
89: 2 you e your faithfulness in heaven itself. 3922
89:37 *it will* **be e** forever like the moon, 3922
93: 1 The world **is firmly e**; it cannot be moved. 3922
93: 2 Your throne **was e** long ago; 3922
96:10 The world **is firmly e**, it cannot be moved; 3922
99: 4 you *have* e equity; 3922
102:28 their descendants *will* **be e** before you." 3922
103:19 The LORD *has* e his throne in heaven, 3922
119:90 *you* e the earth, and it endures. 3922
119:152 from your statutes that *you* e them 3569
140:11 *Let* slanderers not **be e** in the land; 3922
Pr 8:28 when he e the clouds above 599
12: 3 A man cannot **be e** through wickedness, 3922
16:12 for a throne **is e** through righteousness. 3922
24: 3 and through understanding *it* **is e**; 3922
25: 5 his throne *will* **be e** through righteousness. 3922
30: 4 Who *has* e all the ends of the earth? 7756
Isa 2: 2 of the LORD's temple will be e as chief 3922
14:32 "The LORD *has* e Zion, 3569
16: 5 In love a throne *will* **be e**; 3922
44: 7 since I e my ancient people, and what is yet 8492
54:14 In righteousness *you will* **be e**: 3922
Jer 12:16 then *they will* **be e** among my people. 1215
30:20 and their community *will* **be e** before me; 3922
33: 2 the LORD who formed it and e it— 3922
33:25 not e my covenant *with* day and night and 8492
Mic 4: 1 of the LORD's temple will be e as chief 3922
Mt 18:16 that 'every matter *may be* e by the testimony *2705*
Ro 13: 1 that which God has **e.** *5679*
13: 1 The authorities that exist *have* been e *5435*
2Co 13: 1 "Every matter *must be* e by the testimony *2705*
Gal 3:15 to a human covenant *that has been* **duly e,** *3263*
3:17 not set aside the covenant **previously e** *4623*
Eph 3:17 I pray that you, *being* rooted and e in love, *2530*
Col 1:23 in your faith, e and firm, not moved from *2530*
2Pe 1:12 and *are* **firmly e** in the truth you now have. *5114*

ESTABLISHES (5) [ESTABLISH]

Job 25: 2 *he* e order in the heights of heaven. 6913
Isa 42: 4 not falter or be discouraged till *he* e justice 8492
62: 7 till *he* e Jerusalem and makes her the praise 3922
Mic 7: 9 until he pleads my case and e my right. 6913
Hab 2:12 with bloodshed and e a town by crime! 3922

ESTABLISHING (1) [ESTABLISH]

Isa 9: 7 **e** and upholding it with justice 3922

ESTATE (10)

Ge 15: 2 and the one who will inherit my e is Eliezer 1074
31:14 in the inheritance of our father's **e?** 1074
Ru 4: 6 because I might endanger my own **e.** 5709
Est 8: 1 the e *of* Haman, 1074
8: 2 And Esther appointed him over Haman's **e.** 1074
8: 7 I have given his e to Esther, 1074
Ps 136:23 in our **low e** His love endures forever. 9165
Lk 15:12 'Father, give me my share *of* the **e.'** *4045*
Ac 28: 7 an e nearby that belonged to Publius, *6005*
Gal 4: 1 although he owns **the whole** *e*. *AIT*

ESTEEM (3) [ESTEEMED]

Est 10: 3 and **held in high e** by his many fellow Jews, 8354
Pr 4: 8 E her, and she will exalt you; 6147
Isa 66: 2 "This is the one *I* **e**: 5564

ESTEEMED (5) [ESTEEM]

Pr 22: 1 to **be e** is better than silver or gold. 2834
Isa 53: 3 and *we* e him not. 3108
Da 9:23 for you are **highly e.** 2776
10:11 He said, "Daniel, you who are **highly e,** 2776
10:19 "Do not be afraid, O man **highly e,"** he said. 2776

ESTHER (42) [ESTHER'S]

Est 2: 7 This girl, who was also known as **E,** 676
2: 8 **E** also was taken to the king's palace 676
2:10 **E** had not revealed her nationality 676
2:11 how **E** was and what was happening to her. 676
2:15 for **E** (the girl Mordecai had adopted, 676
2:15 And **E** won the favor of everyone 676
2:17 Now the king was attracted to **E** more than 676
2:20 **E** had kept secret her family background 676
2:22 about the plot and told Queen **E,** 676
4: 5 Then **E** summoned Hathach, 676
4: 8 to show to **E** and explain it to her, 676
4: 9 and reported to **E** what Mordecai had said. 676
4:15 Then **E** sent this reply to Mordecai: 676
5: 1 On the third day **E** put on her royal robes 676
5: 2 When he saw Queen **E** standing in 676
5: 2 So **E** approached and touched the tip of 676
5: 3 the king asked, "What is it, Queen **E?** 676
5: 4 "If it pleases the king," replied **E,** 676
5: 5 "so that we may do what **E** asks." 676
5: 5 to the banquet **E** had prepared. 676
5: 6 the king again asked **E,** 676
5: 7 **E** replied, "My petition 676
5:12 "I'm the only person Queen **E** invited 676
6:14 to the banquet **E** had prepared. 676
7: 1 and Haman went to dine with Queen **E,** 676
7: 2 "Queen **E,** what is your petition? 676
7: 3 Then Queen **E** answered, 676
7: 5 King Xerxes asked Queen **E,** "Who is he? 676
7: 6 **E** said, "The adversary and enemy 676
7: 7 stayed behind to beg Queen **E** for his life. 676
7: 8 on the couch where **E** was reclining. 676
8: 1 That same day King Xerxes gave Queen **E** 676
8: 1 for **E** had told how he was related to her. 676
8: 2 And **E** appointed him over Haman's estate. 676
8: 3 **E** again pleaded with the king, 676
8: 4 to **E** and she arose and stood before him. 676
8: 7 to Queen **E** and to Mordecai the Jew, 676
8: 7 I have given his estate to **E,** 676
9:12 The king said to Queen **E,** 676
9:13 "If it pleases the king," **E** answered, 676
9:29 So Queen **E,** daughter of Abihail, 676
9:31 the Jew and Queen **E** had decreed for them, 676

ESTHER'S (5) [ESTHER]

Est 2:18 the king gave a great banquet, **E** banquet, 676
4: 4 When **E** maids and eunuchs came 676
4:12 When **E** words were reported to Mordecai, 676
4:17 and carried out all of **E** instructions. 676
9:32 **E** decree confirmed these regulations 676

ESTIMATE (1)

Lk 14:28 *Will he* not first sit down and e the cost *6028*

ESTRANGED (2) [STRANGE]

2Sa 14:14 so that a banished person *may* not *remain* e 5615
Job 19:13 my acquaintances *are* completely e 2319

ETAM (5)

Jdg 15: 8 down and stayed in a cave in the rock of **E.** 6515
15:11 down to the cave in the rock of **E** and said 6515
1Ch 4: 3 These were the sons of **E:** 6515
4:32 Their surrounding villages were **E,** Ain, 6515
2Ch 11: 6 Bethlehem, **E,** Tekoa, 6515

ETERNAL (81) [ETERNALLY, ETERNITY]

Ge 21:33 upon the name of the LORD, the E God. 6409
Dt 33:27 The e God is your refuge, 7710
1Ki 10: 9 the LORD's e love for Israel, 4200+6409
Ps 16:11 with e pleasures at your right hand. 5905
21: 6 you have granted him e blessings 4200+6329
111:10 To him belongs e praise. 4200+6329
119:89 Your word, O LORD, is **e;** 4200+6409
119:160 all your righteous laws are **e.** 4200+6409
Ecc 12: 5 to his e home and mourners go about 6409
Isa 26: 4 for the LORD, the LORD, is the Rock **e.** 6409
47: 7 'I will continue forever—the e queen!' 6329
Jer 10:10 he is the living God, the e King. 6409
Da 4: 3 His kingdom is an e kingdom; 10550
4:34 His dominion is an e dominion; 10550
Hab 3: 6 His ways are **e.** 6409
Mt 18: 8 or two feet and be thrown into e fire. *173*
19:16 what good thing must I do to get e life?" *173*
19:29 as much and will inherit e life. *173*
25:41 into the e fire prepared for the devil *173*
25:46 "Then they will go away to e punishment, *173*
25:46 but the righteous to e life." *173*
Mk 3:29 he is guilty *of* an e sin." *173*
10:17 he asked, "what must I do to inherit e life?" *173*
10:30 persecutions) and in the age to come, e life. *173*
Lk 10:25 he asked, "what must I do to inherit e life?" *173*
16: 9 you will be welcomed into e dwellings. *173*
18:18 what must I do to inherit e life?" *173*
18:30 in the age to come, e life." *173*
Jn 3:15 in him may have e life. *173*
3:16 in him shall not perish but have e life. *173*
3:36 Whoever believes in the Son has e life, *173*
4:14 a spring of water welling up to e life." *173*
4:36 even now he harvests the crop for e life, *173*
5:24 and believes him who sent me has e life *173*
5:39 that by them you possess e life. *173*
6:27 but for food that endures to e life, *173*
6:40 and believes in him shall have e life, *173*
6:54 and drinks my blood has e life, *173*
6:68 You have the words *of* e life. *173*
10:28 I give them e life, and they shall never perish *173*
12:25 in this world will keep it for e life. *173*
12:50 I know that his command leads to e life. *173*
17: 2 over all people that he might give e life *173*
17: 3 Now this is e life: that they may know you, *173*
Ac 13:46 not consider yourselves worthy *of* e life, *173*
13:48 all who were appointed for e life believed. *173*
Ro 1:20 his e power and divine nature— *132*
2: 7 honor and immortality, he will give e life. *173*
5:21 through righteousness to bring e life *173*
6:22 and the result is e life. *173*
6:23 of God is e life in Christ Jesus our Lord. *173*
16:26 the e God, so that all nations might believe *173*
2Co 4:17 an e glory that far outweighs them all. *173*
4:18 but what is unseen is **e.** *173*
5: 1 an e house in heaven, *173*
Gal 6: 8 from the Spirit will reap e life. *173*
Eph 3:11 to his e purpose which he accomplished *172*
2Th 2:16 and by his grace gave us e encouragement *173*
1Ti 1:16 on him and receive e life. *173*
1:17 Now to the King **e,** immortal, invisible, *172*
6:12 *of* the e life to which you were called *173*
2Ti 2:10 that is in Christ Jesus, with e glory. *173*
Tit 1: 2 on the hope *of* e life, *173*
3: 7 the hope *of* e life. *173*
Heb 5: 9 he became the source *of* e salvation *173*
6: 2 of the dead, and e judgment. *173*
9:12 having obtained e redemption. *173*
9:14 the e Spirit offered himself unblemished *173*
9:15 the promised e inheritance— *173*
13:20 the blood *of* the e covenant brought back *173*
1Pe 5:10 who called you to his e glory in Christ, *173*
2Pe 1:11 a rich welcome into the e kingdom *173*
1Jn 1: 2 and we proclaim to you the e life, *173*
2:25 this is what he promised us—even e life. *173*
3:15 and you know that no murderer has e life *173*
5:11 God has given us e life, *173*
5:13 so that you may know that you have e life. *173*
5:20 He is the true God and e life. *173*
Jude 1: 7 the punishment *of* e fire. *173*
1:21 to bring you to e life. *173*
Rev 14: 6 the e gospel to proclaim to those who live *173*

ETERNALLY (2) [ETERNAL]

Gal 1: 8 let him be **e condemned!** *353*
1: 9 let him be **e condemned!** *353*

ETERNITY (3) [ETERNAL]

Ps 93: 2 you are from **all e.** 6409
Pr 8:23 I was appointed from **e,** 6409
Ecc 3:11 He has also set e in the hearts of men; 6409

ETH KAZIN (1)

Jos 19:13 to Gath Hepher and **E;** 6962

ETHAM (4)

Ex 13:20 After leaving Succoth they camped at **E** on 918
Nu 33: 6 They left Succoth and camped at **E,** 918
33: 7 They left **E,** turned back to Pi Hahiroth, 918
33: 8 for three days in the Desert of **E,** 918

ETHAN (8)

1Ki 4:31 including **E** the Ezrahite— 420
1Ch 2: 6 Zimri, **E,** Heman, Calcol and Darda— 420
2: 8 The son of **E:** Azariah. 420
6:42 the son of **E,** the son of Zimmah, 420
6:44 **E** son of Kishi, the son of Abdi, 420
15:17 and from their brothers the Merarites, **E** son 420
15:19 and **E** were to sound the bronze cymbals; 420
Ps 89: T A maskil of **E** the Ezrahite. 420

ETHANIM (1)

1Ki 8: 2 at the time of the festival in the month of **E,** 923

ETHBAAL (1)

1Ki 16:31 also married Jezebel daughter of **E** king of 909

ETHER (2)

Jos 15:42 Libnah, **E,** Ashan, 6987
19: 7 Rimmon, **E** and Ashan— 6987

ETHIOPIA (KJV) CUSH

ETHIOPIAN (2) [ETHIOPIANS]

Jer 13:23 Can the **E** change his skin or 3934
Ac 8:27 and on his way he met an **E** eunuch, *134+467*

ETHIOPIANS (1) [ETHIOPIAN]

Ac 8:27 treasury of Candace, queen *of* the **E.** *134*

ETHNAN (1)

1Ch 4: 7 The sons of Helah: Zereth, Zohar, **E,** 925

ETHNI (1)

1Ch 6:41 the son of **E,** the son of Zerah, 922

EUBULUS (1)

2Ti 4:21 **E** greets you, and so do Pudens, Linus, *2300*

EUNICE (1)

2Ti 1: 5 grandmother Lois and in your mother **E** *2332*

EUNUCH (10) [EUNUCHS]

Est 2: 3 king's **e**, who is in charge of the women; 6247
2:14 the king's **e** who was in charge of 6247
2:15 king's **e** who was in charge of the harem, 6247
Isa 56: 3 And let not any **e** complain, 6247
Ac 8:27 and on his way he met an Ethiopian **e**, *2336*
8:32 The **e** was reading this passage of Scripture: *NIG*
8:34 The **e** asked Philip, "Tell me, please, *2336*
8:36 they came to some water and the **e** said, *2336*
8:38 Then both Philip and the **e** went down into *2336*
8:39 and the **e** did not see him again, *2336*

EUNUCHS (11) [EUNUCH]

2Ki 9:32 Two or three **e** looked down at him. 6247
20:18 and they will become **e** in the palace of 6247
Est 1:10 the seven **e** who served him— 6247
1:15 of King Xerxes that the **e** have taken 6247
4: 4 and **e** came and told her about Mordecai, 6247
4: 5 one of the king's **e** assigned to attend her, 6247
6:14 the king's **e** arrived 6247
7: 9 Harbona, one of the **e** attending the king, 6247
Isa 39: 7 and they will become **e** in the palace of 6247
56: 4 "To the **e** who keep my Sabbaths, 6247
Mt 19:12 For some are **e** because they were born *2336*

EUODIA (1)

Php 4: 2 with **E** and I plead with Syntyche to agree *2337*

EUPHRATES (20) [TRANS-EUPHRATES]

Ge 2:14 And the fourth river is the **E**. 7310
15:18 the river of Egypt to the great river, the **E**— 7310
Dt 1: 7 as far as the great river, the **E**. 7310
11:24 and from the **E** River to the western sea. 7310
Jos 1: 4 and from the great river, the **E**— 7310
2Sa 8: 3 to restore his control along the **E** River. 7310
2Ki 23:29 to the **E** River to help the king of Assyria. 7310
24: 7 from the Wadi of Egypt to the **E** River. 7310
1Ch 5: 9 of the desert that extends to the **E** River. 7310
18: 3 to establish his control along the **E** River. 7310
2Ch 35:20 up to fight at Carchemish on the **E**, 7310
Isa 11:15 over the **E** River. NIH
27:12 the LORD will thresh from the flowing **E** 5643S
Jer 46: 2 on the **E** River by Nebuchadnezzar king 7310
46: 6 In the north by the River **E** they stumble 7310
46:10 in the land of the north by the River **E**. 7310
51:63 tie a stone to it and throw it into the **E**. 7310
Mic 7:12 from Egypt to the **E** and from sea to sea 5643S
Rev 9:14 at the great river **E**." *2371*
16:12 on the great river **E**, *2371*

EUROCLYDON (KJV) NORTHEASTER

EUTYCHUS (1)

Ac 20: 9 in a window was a young man named **E**, *2366*

EVANGELIST (2) [EVANGELISTS]

Ac 21: 8 and stayed at the house *of* Philip the **e**, *2296*
2Ti 4: 5 endure hardship, do the work *of* an **e**, *2296*

EVANGELISTS (1) [EVANGELIST]

Eph 4:11 some to be prophets, some to be **e**, *2296*

EVE (4)

Ge 3:20 Adam named his wife **E**, 2558
4: 1 Adam lay with his wife **E**, 2558
2Co 11: 3 But I am afraid that just as **E** was deceived *2293*
1Ti 2:13 For Adam was formed first, then **E**. *2293*

EVEN (565) [EVENLY]

Ge 8:21 because of man, **e though** every inclination 3954
14:23 **not e** a thread or the thong of a sandal, 561
24:41 be released from my oath **e** if they refuse 2256
31:28 You didn't **e** let me kiss my grandchildren 2256
31:50 **e** though no one is with us, NIH
39:10 he refused to go to bed with her or **e** be NIH
40:15 and **e** here I have done nothing 1685
41:21 **But e** after they ate them, 2256
44: 8 We **e** brought back to you from the land 2176
48:14 **e though** Manasseh was the firstborn. 3954
Ex 1:10 or *they will become e more* **numerous** and, AIT
1:20 and became **e more** numerous. 4394
2:19 He **e** drew water for us and watered 1685
7:19 **e** in the wooden buckets and stone jars." 2256
7:23 and did not take **e** this to heart. 1685
8:21 and **e** the ground where they are. 1685
9: 7 and found that not **e** one of the animals of 6330
10:24 **E** your women and children may go 1685
19:22 **E** the priests, who approach the LORD, 1685+2256
33: 5 If I were to go with you **e** for a moment, NIH
34: 3 not **e** the flocks and herds may graze 1685
34:21 **e** during the plowing season NIH
Lev 4:13 **e though** the community is unaware of 2256
5: 2 **e though** he is unaware of it, 2256
5: 3 **e though** he is unaware of it, 2256
5: 4 **e though** he is unaware of it, 2256
5:17 **e though** he does not know it, 2256
13:55 **e though** it has not spread, it is unclean. 2256
18:25 **E** the land was defiled; 2256
21:11 **e** for his father or mother, NIH
25:54 " '**E if** he is not redeemed in any 2256
26:17 you will flee **e when** no one is pursuing you 2256
26:36 **e though** no one is pursuing them. 2256
26:37 **e though** no one is pursuing them. 2256
Nu 4:20 **e for** a moment, or they will die." 3869
5:14 or if he is jealous and suspects her **e though** 2256
6: 4 not **e** the seeds or skins. 6330
6: 7 **E if** his own father or mother or brother 928
13:28 We **e** saw descendants of Anak there. 1685+2256
17:13 Anyone who **e comes near** the tabernacle
of the LORD will die. 7929+7929
22:18 "**E if** Balak gave me his palace filled 561
24:13 '**E if** Balak gave me his palace filled 561
32:14 making the LORD **e** more angry with Israel. 6388
Dt 1:28 We **e** saw the Anakites there.' " 1685
2: 5 not **e enough** to put your foot on. 6330
2:36 **e** as far as Gilead, 2256
5:24 a man can live **e** if God speaks with him. NIH
7:20 among them until **e** the survivors who hide 2256
10:14 **e** the highest heavens, 2256
12:31 They **e** burn their sons and daughters 1685+3954
18: 8 **e though** he has received money from 963+4200
19: 6 and kill him **e though** he is not deserving 2256
23: 2 **e** down to the tenth generation. 1685
23: 3 **e** down to the tenth generation. 1685
24: 6 not **e** the upper one— 2256
28:30 but *you will* not *e begin to* **enjoy** its fruit. AIT
28:54 **E** the most gentle and sensitive man NIH
29:19 **e though** I persist in going my own way." 3954
30: 4 **E if** you have been banished to 561
31:21 **e** before I bring them into NIH
32:31 as **e** our enemies concede. 2256
33:17 **e** those at the ends of the earth. 3481
Jos 22:17 **e though** a plague fell on the community of 2256
Jdg 2:19 to ways **e more** corrupt **than** those 4946
3:22 **E** the handle sank in after the blade, 1685
13:16 "**E though** you detain me, 561
14:16 "I haven't **e** explained it to my father 2180
15: 3 **have a right to get e** 5927
Ru 1:12 **E if** I thought there was still hope for me— 3954
1:12 **e** if I had a husband tonight and 1685
2:15 "**E if** she gathers among the sheaves, 1685
2:21 Ruth the Moabitess said, "He **e** said to me, 3954
1Sa 2:15 But **e** before the fat was burned, NIH
12:12 **e though** the LORD your God was your king 2256
13: 7 Some Hebrews **e** crossed the Jordan to 2256
14:30 the slaughter of the Philistines have been **e** 3954
14:39 **e** if it lies with my son Jonathan, 3954
17:29 "Can't I **e** speak?" NIH
18: 4 and **e** his sword, his bow and his belt. 6330
19:23 But the Spirit of God came **e** upon him, 1685
20:15 from my family—not **e** when 2256
21: 5 The men's things are holy **e** on missions 2256
23:17 **E** my father Saul knows this." 1685+2256
25:29 **E though** someone is pursuing you 2256
2Sa 5: 6 **e** the blind and the lame can ward you 561+3954
6:22 I will become **e** more undignified than this, 6388
12: 3 drank from his cup **and e** slept in his arms. 2256
12: 8 *I would have* **given** you **e more.**
2179+2179+2256+3578+3869+3869
17: 9 **E** now, he is hidden in a cave 2180
17:10 Then **e** the bravest soldier, 1685
17:13 to the valley until not **e** a piece of it can 1685
18: 3 **E** if half of us die, they won't care; 2256
18:12 "**E** if a thousand shekels were weighed out 2256
19:43 of Judah responded **e more** harshly **than** 4946
23:19 **e though** he was not included among them. 2256
1Ki 1: 1 not keep warm **e when** they put covers 2256
1:37 **make** his throne *e* **greater** AIT
1:42 **E as** he was speaking, 6388
8:27 The heavens, **e** the highest heaven, 2256
10: 7 Indeed, **not e** half was told me; AIT
12:11 I *will* **make** it **e heavier.** 3578
12:14 I *will* **make** it **e heavier.** 3578
12:30 the people went **e as far as** Dan to worship 6330
12:31 **e though** they were not Levites. 889
13: 8 "**E if** you were to give me half 561
13:33 **E** after this, Jeroboam did not change NIH
14:14 Yes, **e** now. 1685
14:24 There were **e** male shrine prostitutes in 1685+2256
15:13 He **e** deposed his grandmother Maacah 1685+2256
18:35 The water ran down around the altar and **e** 1685
22:46 male shrine prostitutes who remained there
e after the reign 928
2Ki 3:14 I would not look at you **or e** notice you. 2256
5:16 **And e though** Naaman urged him, 2256
7: 2 *e if* the LORD *should* **open** AIT
7:19 *e if* the LORD *should* **open** AIT
16: 3 of Israel and **e** sacrificed his son in the fire, 1685
17:19 **and e** Judah did not keep the commands of 1685
17:41 **E while** these people were worshiping 2256
18:24 **e though** you are depending on Egypt 2256
23:15 **E** the altar at Bethel, 1685+2256
23:15 **e** that altar and high place he demolished. 1685
1Ch 10:13 of the LORD and **e** consulted a medium 1685
11: 2 In the past, **e** while Saul was king, 1685
11:21 **e though** he was not included among them. 2256
2Ch 2: 6 **e** the highest heavens, cannot contain him? 2256
6:18 The heavens, **e** the highest heavens, 2256
9: 6 **not** *e* half the greatness AIT
10:11 I *will* **make** it **e heavier.** 3578
10:14 I *will* **make** it **e heavier.** 3578
11:14 The Levites **e** abandoned their pasturelands 3954
16:12 **e** in his illness he did not seek help from
the LORD, 1685+2256
24: 7 of God and had used **e** its sacred objects for 1685
25: 8 **E** if you go and fight courageously 3954
28:22 King Ahaz became **e** more unfaithful 2256
30:19 **e if** he is not clean according to the rules of 2256
Ezr 5:14 He **e** removed from the temple of Babylon
10059+10221
Ne 1: 9 then **e if** your exiled people are at 561
4: 3 **if e** a fox climbed up on it, 561
4:23 **e** when he went for water. NIH
6: 7 and have **e** appointed prophets 1685
9: 6 **e** the highest heavens, NIH
9:18 **e** when they cast for themselves an image 677
9:22 allotting to them **e** the remotest frontiers. NIH
9:35 **E** while they were in their kingdom, 2256
13:26 **but e** he was led into sin 1685
Est 4:16 **e though** it is against the law. 889
5: 3 **E** up to half the kingdom, NIH
5: 6 **E** up to half the kingdom, NIH
7: 2 **E** up to half the kingdom, NIH
7: 8 "Will he **e** molest the queen while she is 1685
Job 5: 5 taking it **e** from among thorns, 2256
6:14 **e though** he forsakes the fear of 2256
6:27 You would **e** cast lots for the fatherless 677
7:14 **e then** you frighten me with dreams 2256
7:19 or let me alone **e** for an instant? NIH
8: 6 **e** now he will rouse himself on your behalf 3954
9:13 **e** the cohorts of Rahab cowered at his feet. NIH
9:16 **E if** I summoned him and he responded, 561
9:20 **E if** I were innocent, 561
9:30 **E if** I washed myself with soap 561
9:31 so that **e** my clothes would detest me. NIH
10:15 **E if** I am innocent, I cannot lift my head, 2256
10:22 where **e** the light is like darkness." 2256
11: 6 God has **e** forgotten some of your sin. 3954
15: 4 **But** you **e** undermine piety 677
15:10 *men e* **older** than your father. AIT
15:15 if **e** the heavens are not pure in his eyes, 2256
16:19 **E** now my witness is in heaven; 1685
19:18 **E** the little boys scorn me; 1685
21:22 since he judges **e** the highest? NIH
22: 2 Can **e** a wise man benefit him? 3954
22:30 He will deliver **e** one who is not innocent, NIH
23: 2 "**E** today my complaint is bitter; 1685
25: 5 If **e** the moon is not bright and the stars are 6330
28:21 concealed **e** from the birds of the air. 2256
33:29 twice, **e** three times— NIH
36:13 **e when** he fetters them, 3954
36:19 Would your wealth **or** *e* AIT
36:33 **e** the cattle make known its approach. 677
Ps 9: 6 **e** the memory of them has perished. NIH
14: 3 there is no one who does good, not **e** one. 1685
15: 4 who keeps his oath **e** when it hurts, NIH
16: 7 **e** at night my heart instructs me. 677
22: 9 in you **e** at my mother's breast. NIH
23: 4 **E** though I walk through the valley of 1685
27: 3 **e** then will I be confident. NIH
33:22 O LORD, **e as** we put our hope in you. 889+3869
36: 4 **E** on his bed he plots evil; NIH
38:10 **e** the light has gone from my eyes. 2256
39: 2 **not** *e* **saying** anything good, AIT
41: 9 **E** my close friend, whom I trusted, 1685
48:14 he will be our guide **e** to the end. NIH
53: 3 there is no one who does good, not **e** one. 1685
55:18 **e though** many oppose me. 3954
58: 3 **E** from birth the wicked go astray; NIH
68:13 **E** while you sleep among the campfires, NIH
68:18 **e** from the rebellious— 677+2256
71:18 **E** when I am old and gray, 1685+2256
78: 6 **e** the children yet to be born, NIH
78:30 **e** while it was still in their mouths, NIH
83: 8 **E** Assyria has joined them to lend strength 1685
84: 2 My soul yearns, **e** faints, 1685+2256
84: 3 **E** the sparrow has found a home, 1685
91: 9 **e** the LORD, who is my refuge— NIH
106: 6 We have sinned, **e as** our fathers did; 6640
112: 4 **E** in darkness light dawns for the upright, NIH
133: 3 the LORD bestows his blessing, **e** NIH
139:10 **e** there your hand will guide me, 1685
139:12 **e** the darkness will not be dark to you; 1685
Pr 11:24 One man gives freely, yet gains **e more;** 6388
14:13 **E** in laughter the heart may ache, 1685
14:20 The poor are shunned **e** by their neighbors, 1685
14:32 **but e** in death the righteous have a refuge. 2256
14:33 in the heart of the discerning **and e** 2256
16: 4 **e** the wicked for a day of disaster. 1685+2256
16: 7 he makes **e** his enemies live at peace 1685
17:28 **E** a fool is thought wise if he keeps silent, 1685
19:24 he will not **e** bring it back to his mouth! 1685
20:11 **E** a child is known by his actions, 1685
22:19 I teach you today, **e** you. 677
27: 7 to the hungry **e** what is bitter tastes sweet. 3972
28: 9 **e** his prayers are detestable. 1685
Ecc 1:11 and **e** those who are yet to come will not 1685
2:23 **e** at night his mind does not rest. 1685
6: 6 **e** if he lives a thousand years twice over 2256
8:17 **E** if a wise man claims he knows, 1685+2256
9: 4 **e** a live dog is better off than a dead lion! 3954
9: 5 and **e** the memory of them is forgotten. 3954
10: 3 **E** as he walks along the road, 1685+2256
10:20 Do not revile the king **e** in your thoughts, 1685
Isa 1:15 **e** if you offer many prayers, 1685
5:30 **e** the light will be darkened by the clouds. 2256
14: 8 **E** the pine trees and the cedars 1685
23:12 **e** there you will find no rest." 1685
26:10 **e** in a land of uprightness they go NIH
32: 7 **e** when the plea of the needy is just. 2256
33:23 and **e** the lame will carry off plunder. NIH
36: 9 **e though** you are depending on Egypt 2256
40:30 **E** youths grow tired and weary, 2256
43:11 I, **e** I, am the LORD, NIH
43:25 **e** I, am he who blots out your transgressions NIH

Isa 44:19 I e baked bread over its coals, 677
46: 4 E to your old age and gray hairs I am he, 2256
47: 6 E on the aged you laid a very heavy yoke. NIH
47:14 They cannot e save themselves from NIH
48:15 I, e I, have spoken; yes, I have called him. NIH
51:12 "I, e I, am he who comforts you. NIH
56:12 or e **far** better." 3856+4394
64:10 e Zion is a desert, Jerusalem a desolation. NIH
Jer 2:33 E the worst of women can learn 1685
4: 6 e terrible destruction." 2256
5:18 "Yet e in those days," declares the LORD, 1685
6: 1 For disaster looms out of the north, e 2256
6:15 they do not e know how to blush. 1685
8: 7 E the stork in the sky knows 1685
8:12 they do not e know how to blush. 2256
9:26 **and** e the whole house 2256
11:23 Not e a remnant will be left to them, 2256
12: 6 e they have betrayed you; 1685
12:16 e **as** they once taught my people to swear by Baal— 889+3869
14: 5 E the doe in the fields deserts her 1685+3954
15: 1 **"E if** Moses and Samuel were to stand 561
16: 7 not e for a father or a mother— 2256
17: 2 E their children remember their altars 3869
22:24 as I live," declares the LORD, **"e if** you, 3954
23:11 e in my temple I find their wickedness," 1685
23:38 e **though** I told you that you must not claim, 2256
27: 6 I will make e the wild animals subject 1685
28:14 I will e give him control over 1685
29:31 e **though** I did not send him, 2256
34:15 You e made a covenant before me in 2256
36:25 E though Elnathan, Delaiah 1685
37:10 E if you were to defeat 3954
38:15 E if I did give you counsel, 2256
48:34 for e the waters of Nimrim are dried up. 1685
49:37 e my fierce anger," declares the LORD. NIH
51:53 E **if** Babylon reaches the sky 3954
La 3: 8 E when I call out or cry for help, 1685
4: 3 E jackals offer their breasts 1685
Eze 5: 7 You have not e conformed to the standards 2256
8: 6 that are e **more** detestable." 1524
8:13 that are e **more** detestable." 1524
8:15 that are e **more** detestable than this." 1524
14:14 e **if** these three men— 2256
14:16 e if these three men were in it, NIH
14:18 e **if** these three men were in it, 2256
14:20 declares the Sovereign LORD, **e if** Noah, 2256
16:28 **and e after** that, 2256
16:29 **but** e with this you were not satisfied. 1685+2256
16:56 not e mention your sister Sodom in the day 2256
16:57 E **so,** you are now scorned by the daughters 4017
17:10 E if it is transplanted, will it thrive? 2256
21:14 Let the sword strike twice, e three times. NIH
23:37 they e sacrificed their children, 1685+2256
23:40 "They e sent messengers for 677+2256+3954
24:12 not been removed, not e by fire. NIH
35:10 e **though** I the LORD was there, 2256
36:10 e the whole house of Israel. NIH
44: 9 and flesh is to enter my sanctuary, not e 3972
Da 2:41 e **as** you saw iron mixed with clay. 10168+10353+10619
3:18 But e **if** he does not, we want you to know, 10213
4:36 and **became e greater** than before. 10323+10339+10650
5: 9 King Belshazzar became e **more** terrified 10678
9: 9 e **though** we have rebelled against him; 3954
11: 5 one of his commanders *will become e* **stronger** than he AIT
11:15 e their best troops will not have the strength 2256
Hos 4:18 E when their drinks are gone, NIH
5: 5 the Israelites, e Ephraim, 2256
9: 6 E if they escape from destruction, 2180
9:12 E if they rear children, 3954
9:16 E if they bear children, 1685
10: 3 But e if we had a king, NIH
11: 7 E if they call to the Most High, 2256
11:12 e against the faithful Holy One. 2256
13:15 e **though** he thrives among his brothers. 3954
Joel 1:18 e the flocks of sheep are suffering. 1685
1:20 E the wild animals pant for you; 1685
2:12 **"E** now," declares the LORD, 1685+2256
2:29 E on my servants, both men and women, I will pour out my Spirit 1685+2256
Am 1: 3 "For three sins of Damascus, e for four, 2256
1: 6 "For three sins of Gaza, **e** for four, 2256
1: 9 "For three sins of Tyre, e for four, 2256
1:11 "For three sins of Edom, e for four, 2256
1:13 "For three sins of Ammon, e for four, 2256
2: 1 "For three sins of Moab, e for four, 2256
2: 4 "For three sins of Judah, e for four, 2256
2: 6 "For three sins of Israel, e for four, 2256
2:16 E the bravest warriors will flee naked on 2256
5:22 E though you bring me burnt offerings 3954
8: 6 selling e the sweepings with the wheat. 2256
Jnh 1:13 for the sea **grew e wilder** than before. 2143+2256+6192
Mic 1: 9 e to Jerusalem itself. NIH
1:12 e to the gate of Jerusalem. NIH
5: 5 e eight leaders of men. 2256
7: 5 E with her who lies in your embrace NIH
7:10 e now she will be trampled underfoot NIH
7:12 e from Egypt to the Euphrates and from sea 2256
Hab 1: 5 e **if** you were told. 3954
Zec 9:12 e now I announce that I will restore twice 1685
Mal 1: 5 e **beyond** the borders of Israel!' 4946+6584
2:12 e **though** he brings offerings to 2256
3:15 and e those who challenge God escape.'" 1685

Mt 5:36 you cannot make e one hair white or black. *NIG*
5:46 Are not e the tax collectors doing that? *2779*
5:47 Do not e pagans do that? *2779*
6:29 Yet I tell you that **not e** Solomon *4028*
8:27 E the winds and the waves obey him!" *2779*
10:30 And e the very hairs of your head are all numbered. *2779*
10:42 if anyone gives **e** a cup of cold water to one *3668*
13:12 e what he has will be taken from him. *2779*
15:27 "but e the dogs eat the crumbs that fall *2779*
18:17 and if he refuses to listen e to the church, *2779*
21:32 And e after you saw this, *NIG*
24:24 and miracles to deceive e the elect— *2779*
24:27 that comes from the east is visible e in *2401*
24:33 E so, when you see all these things, *2779*
24:36 **not** e the angels in heaven, nor the Son, *4028*
25:29 e what he has will be taken from him. *2779*
26:33 **"E** if all fall away on account of you, *NIG*
26:35 Peter declared, **"E** if I have to die with you, *2779*
27:14 **not** e to a single charge— *4028*
Mk 1:27 He e gives orders to evil spirits *2779*
2: 2 **not** e outside the door, *3593*
2:28 the Son of Man is Lord e of the Sabbath." *2779*
3:20 he and his disciples were **not e** able to eat. *3593*
4: 8 sixty, or e a hundred times." *2779*
4:20 sixty **or** e a hundred times what was sown." *2779*
4:24 measured to you—**and e more.** *2779+4707+5148*
4:25 e what he has will be taken from him." *2779*
4:41 E the wind and the waves obey him!" *2779*
5: 3 **not** e with a chain. *4028*
6: 2 that he e does miracles! *2779*
6:31 and going that they did not e have a chance *2779*
6:56 let them touch e the edge of his cloak, *1569+2779*
7:28 "but e the dogs under the table eat *2779*
7:37 "He e makes the deaf hear and *2779*
10:26 The disciples were **e more** amazed, *4360*
10:45 For e the Son of Man did not come to *2779*
13:29 E so, when you see these things happening, *2779*
13:32 **not** e the angels in heaven, nor the Son, *4028*
14:29 Peter declared, **"E** if all fall away, *2779*
14:31 **"E** if I have to die with you, *NIG*
14:59 Yet e then their testimony did not agree. *2779*
Lk 1:15 and he will be filled with the Holy Spirit e *2285*
1:36 E Elizabeth your relative is going to have *2779*
1:55 e **as** he said to our fathers." *2777*
6:32 E 'sinners' love those who love them. *2779*
6:33 E 'sinners' do that. *2779*
6:34 E 'sinners' lend to 'sinners,' *2779*
7: 7 not e consider myself worthy to come *NIG*
7: 9 not found such great faith e in Israel." *NIG*
7:29 (All the people, e the tax collectors, *2779*
7:49 "Who is this who e forgives sins?" *2779*
8:18 not have, e what he thinks he has will *2779*
8:25 He commands e the winds and the water, *2779*
9:42 E while the boy was coming, *2285*
10:11 'E the dust of your town that sticks *2779*
10:17 e the demons submit to us in your name." *2779*
12:27 Yet I tell you, **not e** Solomon *4028*
12:38 e if he comes in the second or third watch *2779*
14:26 yes, e his own life— *2779*
15:29 **Yet** you never gave me e *2779*
16:21 E the dogs came and licked his sores. *2779*
16:31 they will **not** be convinced e *4028*
18: 4 'E though I don't fear God or care *2779*
18:11 or e like this tax collector. *2779*
18:13 He would **not** e look up to heaven, *4024+4028*
19:26 e what he has will be taken away. *2779*
19:42 e you, had only known *2779*
20:37 e Moses showed that the dead rise, *2779*
21:16 You will be betrayed e by parents, brothers, *2779*
21:31 E so, when you see these things happening, *2779*
23:35 and the rulers e sneered at him. *2779*
Jn 4:36 E **now** the reaper draws his wages, *2453*
4:36 e now he harvests the crop for eternal life, *2779*
5:18 but he was e calling God his own Father, *2779*
5:20 to your amazement he will show him **e** *2779*
5:21 e so the Son gives life to whom *2779*
7: 5 e his own brothers did **not** believe in him. *4028*
8:14 **"E** if I testify on my own behalf, *2779*
8:30 *E as* he **spoke,** many put their faith in him. *AIT*
9:29 we don't e know where he comes from." *NIG*
10:38 if I do it, e though you do not believe me, *2779*
11:22 But I know that e now God will give you *2779*
11:25 believes in me will live, e though he dies; *2779*
12:37 E after Jesus had done all these miraculous signs in their presence, *1254*
12:42 Yet at the same time many e among *2779*
14: 9 e after I have been among you such *2779*
14:12 He will do e greater things than these, *2779*
15: 2 so that it will be e more fruitful. *NIG*
16:30 and that you do not e need *NIG*
17:16 not of the world, e **as** I am not of it. *2777*
17:23 that you sent me and have loved them **e as** *2777*
19: 8 he was e more afraid, *NIG*
21:11 **but** e with so many the net was not torn. *2779*
21:25 e the whole world would **not** *4028*
Ac 2:18 E on my servants, both men and women, *2779*
3:20 who has been appointed for you—e Jesus. *NIG*
5:13 e **though** they were highly regarded by *247*
7: 5 **not** e a foot of ground. *4028*
7: 5 e though at that time Abraham had no child. *NIG*
7:52 They e killed those who predicted *2779*
10:45 of the Holy Spirit had been poured out e on *2779*
11:18 God has granted e the Gentiles repentance *2779*
13:41 e if someone told you.'" *NIG*
14:18 E with these words, *2779*
16:37 *e though we* **are** Roman citizens, *AIT*

Ac 17:23 I e found an altar with this inscription: *2779*
19: 2 we have **not** e heard that there is *4028*
19:12 so that e handkerchiefs and aprons *2779*
19:31 E some of the officials of the province, *2779*
19:32 not e know why they were there. *NIG*
20:30 E from your own number men will arise *2779*
22: 5 I e obtained letters from them *2779*
22:25 to flog a Roman citizen who hasn't e *2779*
24: 6 **and e** tried to desecrate the temple; *2779*
26:11 I e went to foreign cities to persecute them. *2779*
28:23 and came in e larger numbers to the place *NIG*
Ro 1:26 E their women exchanged natural relations *5445*
2:14 *e though they do* not **have** *AIT*
2:15 now e defending them.) *2779*
2:27 e though you have the written code *NIG*
3:10 "There is no one righteous, **not** e one; *4028*
3:12 there is no one who does good, not e one." *2401*
5:14 e over those who did not sin by breaking *2779*
7: 3 *e though she* **marries** another man. *AIT*
9:24 e us, whom he also called, not only from *NIG*
15: 3 For e Christ did not please himself but, *2779*
1Co 2:10 e the deep things of God. *2779*
4: 3 indeed, I do **not** e judge myself. *4028*
4:15 **E though** you have ten thousand guardians *1142+1569*
5: 1 a kind that does **not** occur e among pagans: *4028*
5: 3 **E though** I am not physically present, *1142+3525*
5:11 With such a man do **not** e eat. *3593*
6: 4 appoint as judges e men of little account in *NIG*
7:38 he who does not marry her does e better. *NIG*
8: 5 For e if there are so-called gods, *2779*
9: 2 **E though** I may not be an apostle to others, *1623*
10:33 e **as** I try to please everybody in every way. *2777*
13:12 I shall know fully, e as I am fully known. *2779*
14: 7 **E in the case of** lifeless things *3940*
14:21 **but** e then they will not listen to me," *2779*
15: 9 and do not e deserve to be called an apostle, *NIG*
15:13 then **not** e Christ has been raised. *4028*
16: 6 or e spend the winter, *2779*
2Co 1: 8 so that we despaired e of life. *2779*
3: 8 will not the ministry of the Spirit be e *4802*
3:15 E to this day when Moses is read, *247*
4: 3 And e if our gospel is veiled, *2779*
7: 8 E if I caused you sorrow by my letter, *2779*
7:12 So e though I wrote to you, *2779*
8: 3 **and** e beyond their ability. *2779*
8:22 and now **e more so** because *4498+5080S*
10: 8 For e if I boast somewhat freely about *5445*
10:13 a field that reaches e to you. *2779*
11:20 you e put up with anyone who enslaves you *NIG*
12: 6 **E if** I should choose to boast, *1569*
12:11 e though I am nothing. *2779*
13: 7 the test but that you will do what is right **e** *1254*
Gal 1: 8 But e if we or an angel from heaven *2779*
2: 3 Yet **not e** Titus, who was with me, *4028*
2: 3 *e though he* **was** a Greek. *AIT*
2:13 so that by their hypocrisy e *2779*
4:14 **E though** my illness was a trial to you, *2779*
6:13 **Not** e those who are circumcised obey *4028*
6:16 e to the Israel of God. *2779*
Eph 1:10 on earth together under one head, e Christ. *NIG*
2: 5 with Christ e when we were dead *2779*
5: 3 But among you there must **not** be e a hint *3593*
5:12 For it is shameful e to mention what *2779*
Php 2: 8 e death on a cross! *1254*
2:17 But e if I am being poured out like *2779*
3:18 before and now say again e with tears, *2779*
4:16 for e when I was in Thessalonica, *2779*
4:18 I have received full payment and e more; *NIG*
2Th 3:10 For e when we were with you, *2779*
1Ti 1:13 *E though I* **was** once a blasphemer and *AIT*
5: 6 for pleasure is dead *e while she* **lives.** *AIT*
5:25 **and** e those that are not cannot be hidden. *2779*
6: 2 Instead, they are to serve them e better, *NIG*
2Ti 2: 9 **e to the point of** being chained *3588*
Tit 1:12 E one of their own prophets has said, *NIG*
Phm 1:16 He is very dear to me but e dearer to you, *NIG*
1:21 knowing that you will do e more than I ask. *2779*
Heb 4:12 it penetrates **e to** dividing soul and spirit, *948*
6: 9 E though we speak like this, dear friends, *2779*
7: 4 E the patriarch Abraham gave him a tenth *NIG*
7: 5 **e though** their brothers are descended *2788*
7: 9 **One might e say** that Levi, *2229+3306+6055*
7:15 And what we have said is e more clear *2285*
9:18 This is why e the first covenant was not put *NIG*
11: 4 *e though he is* **dead.** *AIT*
11: 8 *e though he did* not **know** *AIT*
11:11 **e though** he was past age— *2779*
11:18 e though God had said to him, *NIG*
12:20 "If e an animal touches the mountain, *2779*
Jas 1:11 the rich man will fade away e while he goes *NIG*
2:19 E the demons believe that—and shudder. *2779*
2:25 was not e Rahab the prostitute *2779*
4:14 not e know what will happen tomorrow. *NIG*
1Pe 1: 7 which perishes **e** though refined by fire— *1254*
1: 8 *e though you do* not **see** *AIT*
1:12 E angels long to look into these things. *NIG*
3:14 But e if you should suffer for what is right, *2779*
4: 6 the gospel was preached e to those who are *2779*
4:15 or e as a meddler. *NIG*
2Pe 1:12 **e though** you know them *2788*
2: 1 They will secretly introduce destructive heresies, e denying the sovereign Lord *2779*
2:11 **yet** e angels, although they are stronger *3963*
1Jn 2:18 e now many antichrists have come. *2779*
2:25 this is what he promised us—e eternal life. *NIG*
4: 3 which you have heard is coming **and e** *2779*

1Jn 5: 4 the victory that has overcome the world, **e** *NIG*
5:20 **e** in his Son Jesus Christ. *NIG*
3Jn 1: 2 **e as** your soul is getting along well. *2777*
1: 5 **e though** they are strangers to you. *2779*
1:12 **and e** by the truth itself. *2779*
Jude 1: 9 But **e** the archangel Michael, *NIG*
1:23 hating **e** the clothing stained by corrupted *2779*
Rev 1: 7 **e** those who pierced him; *2779*
2:10 **e to the point of** death, *948*
2:13 **e** in the days of Antipas, *2779*
4: 8 eyes all around, **e** under his wings. *2779*
5: 3 could open the scroll **or e** look inside it. *4046*
13:13 **e** causing fire to come down from heaven *2779*

EVEN-TEMPERED (1) [TEMPER]

Pr 17:27 and a man of understanding is **e.** 7922+8120

EVENING (142) [EVENINGS]

Ge 1: 5 And there was **e,** and there was morning— 6847
1: 8 And there was **e,** and there was morning— 6847
1:13 And there was **e,** and there was morning— 6847
1:19 And there was **e,** and there was morning— 6847
1:23 And there was **e,** and there was morning— 6847
1:31 And there was **e,** and there was morning— 6847
8:11 When the dove returned to him in the **e,** 6847
19: 1 The two angels arrived at Sodom in the **e,** 6847
24:11 it was toward **e,** 6847
24:63 He went out to the field one **e** to meditate, 6847
29:23 But when **e** came, 6847
30:16 when Jacob came in from the fields that **e,** 6847
49:27 in the **e** he divides the plunder." 6847
Ex 12:18 the **e** of the fourteenth day until the evening 6847
12:18 the evening of the fourteenth day until the **e** 6847
16: 6 *"In* the **e** you will know that it was 6847
16: 8 to eat in the **e** and all the bread you want in 6847
16:13 That **e** quail came and covered the camp, 6847
18:13 they stood around him from morning till **e.** 6847
18:14 around you from morning till **e?"** 6847
27:21 before the LORD from **e** till morning. 6847
Lev 6:20 half of it in the morning and half in the **e.** 6847
11:24 be unclean till **e.** 6847
11:25 and he will be unclean till **e.** 6847
11:27 be unclean till **e.** 6847
11:28 and he will be unclean till **e.** 6847
11:31 will be unclean till **e.** 6847
11:32 Put it in water; it will be unclean till **e,** 6847
11:39 the carcass will be unclean till **e.** 6847
11:40 and he will be unclean till **e.** 6847
11:40 and he will be unclean till **e.** 6847
14:46 while it is closed up will be unclean till **e.** 6847
15: 5 and he will be unclean till **e.** 6847
15: 6 and he will be unclean till **e.** 6847
15: 7 and he will be unclean till **e.** 6847
15: 8 and he will be unclean till **e.** 6847
15:10 that were under him will be unclean till **e;** 6847
15:10 and he will be unclean till **e.** 6847
15:11 and he will be unclean till **e.** 6847
15:16 and he will be unclean till **e.** 6847
15:17 and it will be unclean till **e.** 6847
15:18 and they will be unclean till **e.** 6847
15:19 be unclean till **e.** 6847
15:21 and he will be unclean till **e.** 6847
15:22 and he will be unclean till **e.** 6847
15:23 he will be unclean till **e.** 6847
15:27 and he will be unclean till **e.** 6847
17:15 and he will be ceremonially unclean till **e;** 6847
22: 6 be unclean till **e.** 6847
23:32 From the **e** of the ninth day of the month 6847
23:32 of the month until the following **e** you are 6847
24: 3 to tend the lamps before the LORD from **e** 6847
Nu 9:15 From **e** till morning the cloud above 6847
9:21 the cloud stayed only from **e** till morning, 6847
19: 7 but he will be ceremonially unclean till **e.** 6847
19: 8 and he too will be unclean till **e.** 6847
19:10 and he too will be unclean till **e.** 6847
19:19 and that **e** he will be clean. 6847
19:21 the water of cleansing will be unclean till **e.** 6847
19:22 who touches it becomes unclean till **e."** 6847
Dt 16: 4 the **e** of the first day remain until morning. 6847
16: 6 the Passover in the **e,** 6847
23:11 But as **e** approaches he is to wash himself, 6847
28:67 "If only it were **e!"** 6847
28:67 and in the **e,** "If only it were morning!"— 6847
Jos 5:10 On the **e** of the fourteenth day of the month, 6847
7: 6 remaining there till **e.** 6847
8:29 a tree and left him there until **e.** 2021+6847+6961
10:26 they were left hanging on the trees until **e.** 6847
Jdg 19: 9 said, "Now look, it's almost **e.** 6845
19:16 That **e** an old man from the hill country 6847
20:23 up and wept before the LORD until **e,** 6847
20:26 until **e** and presented burnt offerings 6847
21: 2 where they sat before God until **e,** 6847
Ru 2:17 So Ruth gleaned in the field until **e.** 6847
1Sa 14:24 be any man who eats food before **e** comes, 6847
17:16 and **e** and took his stand. 6845
20: 5 and hide in the field until the **e** of the day 6847
20:19 The day after tomorrow, **toward e,** 3718+4394
30:17 David fought them from dusk until the **e** of 6847
2Sa 1:12 They mourned and wept and fasted till **e** 6847
11: 2 One **e** David got up from his bed 6847
11:13 in the **e** Uriah went out to sleep on his mat 6847
1Ki 17: 6 in the morning and bread and meat in the **e,** 6847
18:29 until the time for the **e sacrifice.** 4966+6590
22:35 and that **e** he died. 6847
2Ki 16:15 and the **e** grain offering, 6847
1Ch 16:40 of burnt offering regularly, morning and **e,** 6847
23:30 They were to do the same in the **e** 6847
2Ch 2: 4 and **e** and on Sabbaths and New Moons and 6847
13:11 and **e** they present burnt offerings 928+928+2021+2021+6847+6847
13:11 the lamps on the gold lampstand **every e.** 928+928+2021+2021+6847+6847
18:34 in his chariot facing the Arameans until **e.** 6847
31: 3 the morning and **e** burnt offerings and for 6847
Ezr 3: 3 both the morning and **e** sacrifices. 6847
9: 4 I sat there appalled until the **e** sacrifice. 6847
9: 5 Then, at the **e** sacrifice, 6847
Ne 13:19 When **e shadows fell** *on* the gates 7511
Est 2:14 In the **e** she would go there and in 6847
Job 7: 2 Like a slave longing for the **e shadows,** 7498
Ps 55:17 **E,** morning and noon I cry out in distress, 6847
59: 6 They return at **e,** 6847
59:14 They return at **e,** 6847
65: 8 and **e** fades you call forth songs of joy. 6847
90: 6 by **e** it is dry and withered. 6847
102:11 My days are like the **e** shadow; 5742
104:23 to his labor until **e.** 6847
109:23 I fade away like an **e** shadow; 5742
141: 2 up of my hands be like the **e** sacrifice. 6847
Ecc 11: 6 and at **e** let not your hands be idle, 6847
Isa 17:14 In the **e,** sudden terror! 6847
Jer 6: 4 and the shadows of **e** grow long. 6847
Eze 12: 4 Then in the **e,** while they are watching, 6847
12: 7 the **e** I dug through the wall with my hands. 6847
24:18 and in the **e** my wife died. 6847
33:22 Now the **e** before the man arrived, 6847
46: 2 but the gate will not be shut until **e.** 6847
Da 9:21 about the time of the **e** sacrifice. 6847
Zep 2: 7 In the **e** they will lie down in the houses 6847
3: 3 her rulers are **e** wolves, 6847
Zec 14: 7 When **e** comes, there will be light. 6847
Mt 8:16 When **e** came, many who were demon-possessed were brought to him, *4070*
14:15 As **e** approached, the disciples came to him *4070*
14:23 When **e** came, he was there alone, *4070*
16: 2 He replied, "When **e** comes, you say, *4070*
20: 8 "When **e** came, the owner of *4070*
26:20 When **e** came, Jesus was reclining at *4070*
27:57 As **e** approached, there came a rich man *4070*
Mk 1:32 **That e** after sunset the people brought *1181+4070*
4:35 That day when **e** came, *4070*
6:47 When **e** came, the boat was in the middle of *4070*
11:19 When **e** came, they went out of the city. *4067*
13:35 whether **in the e,** or at midnight, *4067*
14:17 When **e** came, Jesus arrived with *4070*
15:42 So as **e** approached, *4070*
Lk 21:37 and **each e** he went out to spend the night on the hill *3816+3836*
24:29 for it is nearly **e;** the day is almost over." *2270*
Jn 6:16 When **e** came, his disciples went down to *4070*
13: 2 The **e meal** was being served, *1270*
20:19 **On the e** of that first day of the week, *1639+4070*
Ac 4: 3 and because it was **e,** *2270*
28:23 till **e** he explained and declared to them *2270*

EVENINGS (2) [EVENING]

Da 8:14 "It will take 2,300 **e** and mornings; 6847
8:26 "The vision of the **e** and mornings 6847

EVENLY (1) [EVEN]

1Ki 6:35 and overlaid them with gold **hammered e** over the carvings. 3837

EVENT (KJV) DESTINY, FATE

EVENTS (56)

1Ki 11:41 As for the other **e** *of* Solomon's reign— 1821
12:15 for this **turn of e** was from the LORD, 6016
14:19 The other **e** *of* Jeroboam's reign, 1821
14:29 As for the other **e** *of* Rehoboam's reign, 1821
15: 7 As for the other **e** *of* Abijah's reign, 1821
15:23 As for all the other **e** *of* Asa's reign, 1821
15:31 As for the other **e** *of* Nadab's reign, 1821
16: 5 As for the other **e** *of* Baasha's reign, 1821
16:14 As for the other **e** *of* Elah's reign, 1821
16:20 As for the other **e** *of* Zimri's reign, 1821
16:27 As for the other **e** *of* Omri's reign, 1821
22:39 As for the other **e** *of* Ahab's reign, 1821
22:45 As for the other **e** *of* Jehoshaphat's reign, 1821
2Ki 1:18 As for all the other **e** *of* Ahaziah's reign, 1821
8:23 As for the other **e** *of* Jehoram's reign, 1821
10:34 As for the other **e** *of* Jehu's reign, 1821
12:19 As for the other **e** *of* the reign of Joash, 1821
13: 8 As for the other **e** *of* the reign of Jehoahaz, 1821
13:12 As for the other **e** *of* the reign of Jehoash, 1821
14:15 As for the other **e** *of* the reign of Jehoash, 1821
14:18 As for the other **e** *of* Amaziah's reign, 1821
14:28 As for the other **e** *of* Jeroboam's reign, 1821
15: 6 As for the other **e** *of* Azariah's reign, 1821
15:11 The other **e** *of* Zechariah's reign are written 1821
15:15 The other **e** *of* Shallum's reign, 1821
15:21 As for the other **e** *of* Menahem's reign, 1821
15:26 The other **e** *of* Pekahiah's reign, 1821
15:31 As for the other **e** *of* Pekah's reign, 1821
15:36 As for the other **e** *of* Jotham's reign, 1821
16:19 As for the other **e** *of* the reign of Ahaz, 1821
20:20 As for the other **e** *of* Hezekiah's reign, 1821
21:17 As for the other **e** *of* Manasseh's reign, 1821
21:25 As for the other **e** *of* Amon's reign, 1821
2Ki 23:28 As for the other **e** *of* Josiah's reign, 1821
24: 5 As for the other **e** *of* Jehoiakim's reign, 1821
1Ch 29:29 As for the **e** *of* King David's reign, 1821
2Ch 9:29 As for the other **e** *of* Solomon's reign, 1821
10:15 for this **turn of e** was from God, 5813
12:15 As for the **e** *of* Rehoboam's reign, 1821
13:22 The other **e** *of* Abijah's reign, 1821
16:11 The **e** *of* Asa's reign, 1821
20:34 The other **e** *of* Jehoshaphat's reign, 1821
25:26 As for the other **e** *of* Amaziah's reign, 1821
26:22 The other **e** *of* Uzziah's reign, 1821
27: 7 The other **e** *in* Jotham's reign, 1821
28:26 The other **e** *of* his reign and all his ways, 1821
32:32 The other **e** *of* Hezekiah's reign 1821
33:18 The other **e** *of* Manasseh's reign, 1821
35:26 The other **e** *of* Josiah's reign and his acts 1821
35:27 all the **e,** from beginning to end, are written 1821
36: 8 The other **e** *of* Jehoiakim's reign, 1821
Est 3: 1 After these **e,** King Xerxes honored Haman 1821
9:20 Mordecai recorded these **e,** 1821
Lk 21:11 **fearful e** and great signs from heaven. *5831*
Ac 5:11 and all who heard about **these** *e.* *AIT*
19:40 with rioting because of today's **e.** *NIG*

EVENTUALLY (1)

Lk 18: 5 so that she won't **e** wear me out *1650+5465*

EVER (248) [EVERLASTING, FOREVER, FOREVERMORE]

Ge 24:16 no man *had e* **lain with** her. AIT
Ex 5:23 **E since** I went to Pharaoh to speak 255+4946
9:18 the worst hailstorm that has **e** fallen 4202
10: 6 nor your forefathers *have e* **seen** from AIT
10:14 nor *will there e* **be** again. AIT
11: 6 worse than *there has e* **been** or ever will AIT
11: 6 or *e will be* **again.** AIT
15:18 The LORD will reign for **e** and ever." 6409
15:18 The LORD will reign for ever and **e."** 6329
Nu 11:20 saying, "Why *did we e* **leave** Egypt?" '" AIT
14:23 of them *will e* **see** the land I promised AIT
14:23 with contempt *will e* **see** it. AIT
35:26 if the accused **e goes outside** the limits 3655+3655
Dt 4:32 *Has* anything so great as this *e* **happened,** AIT
4:32 or *has* anything like it *e* **been heard of?** AIT
4:34 *Has* any god *e* **tried** to take for himself AIT
5:26 For what mortal man has **e** heard the voice 3972
8:19 If *you* **e forget** the LORD your God 8894+8894
9:24 the LORD **e since** I have known you. 3427+4946
34:12 For no one has **e** shown the mighty power NIH
Jos 7: 7 *e* **bring** this people **across** AIT
7:26 called the Valley of Achor **e since.** 2021+2021+2296+3427+6330
14:14 belonged to Caleb son of Jephunneh the Kenizzite **e since,** 2021+2021+2296+3427+6330
22:28 "And we said, 'If they **e** say this to us, 4737
Jdg 11:25 *Did he e* **quarrel** with Israel or fight AIT
16:17 "No razor *has e been* **used** on my head," AIT
Ru 1:17 LORD deal with me, be it **e so** severely, 3907
1Sa 1:11 and no razor *will e be* **used** on his head." AIT
3:17 May God deal with you, be it **e so** severely, 3907
14:44 "May God deal with me, be it **e so** severely, 3907
20:13 LORD deal with me, be it **e so** severely, 3907
20:15 and do not **e** cut off your kindness 6330+6409
25:22 God deal with David, be it **e so** severely, 3907
27: 6 belonged to the kings of Judah **e since.** 2021+2021+2296+3427+6330
2Sa 3: 9 God deal with Abner, be it **e so** severely, 3907
3:35 "May God deal with me, be it **e so** severely, 3907
6: 9 *can* the ark of the LORD *e* **come** to me?" AIT
7: 7 *did I* **e say** *to* any of their rulers 1819+1821
7:11 and have done **e since** 4946
13:32 This has been Absalom's expressed intention **e since** 4946
19:13 May God deal with me, be it **e so** severely, 3907
1Ki 2:23 "May God deal with me, be it **e so** severely, 3907
3:12 nor will there **e** be. 339
10:20 Nothing like it *had e* **been made** AIT
19: 2 the gods deal with me, be it **e so** severely, 3907
20:10 the gods deal with me, be it **e so** severely, 3907
22:28 Micaiah declared, "If *you* **e return** safely, 8740+8740
2Ki 6:31 "May God deal with me, be it **e so** severely, 3907
18:33 god of any nation **e delivered** his land 5911+5911
1Ch 13:12 "How *can I e* **bring** the ark of God to me?" AIT
17: 6 *did I* **e say** *to* any of their leaders AIT
17:10 and have done **e since** 4946
29:25 as no king over Israel **e** had before. 3972
2Ch 1:12 such as no king who was before you *e* **had** AIT
9:11 like them had **e** been seen in Judah.) 4200+7156
9:19 Nothing like it *had e* **been made** AIT
18:27 Micaiah declared, "If *you* **e return** safely, 8740+8740
32:13 the gods of those nations **e able** to deliver their land 3523+3523
35:18 of the kings of Israel *had e* **celebrated** such AIT
Ne 13: 1 that no Ammonite or Moabite should **e** 6330+6409
Job 4: 7 Who, being innocent, *has e* **perished?** AIT
4: 7 **were** the upright *e* **destroyed?** AIT
6:22 Have I **e** said, 'Give something 3954
15: 7 "Are you the **first** man *e* born? AIT
20: 4 **e since** man was placed on the earth, 4974
29:20 the bow *e* **new** in my hand.' AIT
38:12 "Have you **e** given orders to the morning, 3427+4946
Ps 5:11 let them **e** sing for joy. 4200+6409

Ps 9: 5 you have blotted out their name for e 6409
9: 5 blotted out their name for ever and **e.** 6329
9: 18 nor the hope of the afflicted e perish. 4200+6329
10: 16 The LORD is King **for** e and ever; 6409
10: 16 The LORD is King for ever and **e;** 6329
21: 4 length of days, **for** e and ever. 6409
21: 4 length of days, for ever and **e.** 6329
25: 3 No one whose hope is in you will e be put 1685
25: 15 My eyes are e on the LORD, 9458
26: 3 for your love is e before me, NIH
38: 17 and my pain is e with me. 9458
45: 6 O God, will last **for** e and ever; 6409
45: 6 O God, will last for ever and **e;** 6329
45: 17 the nations will praise you for e and ever. 6409
45: 17 the nations will praise you for ever and **e.** 6329
48: 14 For this God is our God **for** e and ever; 6409
48: 14 For this God is our God for ever and **e;** 6329
49: 8 no payment is e enough— 4200+6409
50: 8 which are e before me. 9458
52: 8 in God's unfailing love **for** e and ever. 6409
52: 8 in God's unfailing love for ever and **e.** 6329
61: 8 Then will I e sing praise to your name 4200+6329
71: 6 I will e praise you. 9458
72: 15 May people e pray for him 9458
74: 15 you dried up the e **flowing** rivers. 419
83: 17 May they e be ashamed and dismayed; 6329+6330
84: 4 they are e praising you. 6388
89: 33 nor *will I* e **betray** my faithfulness. AIT
111: 8 They are steadfast for e and ever, 6329
111: 8 They are steadfast for ever and **e,** 4200+6409
119: 44 I will always obey your law, for e and ever. 6409
119: 44 I will always obey your law, for ever and **e.** 6329
119: 98 for they are e with me. 4200+6409
132: 12 on your throne for **e and ever."** 6329
132: 12 on your throne for **ever and e."** 6329
132: 14 "This is my resting place for **e and ever;** 6329
132: 14 "This is my resting place for **ever and e;** 6329
132: 16 and her saints *will* e **sing for joy.** 8264+8264
141: 5 Yet my prayer is e against the deeds 6388
145: 1 I will praise your name for e and ever. 6409
145: 1 I will praise your name for ever and **e.** 6329
145: 2 and extol your name for e and ever. 6409
145: 2 and extol your name for ever and **e.** 6329
145: 21 praise his holy name for e and ever. 6409
145: 21 praise his holy name for ever and **e.** 6329
148: 6 He set them in place for e and ever; 6329
148: 6 He set them in place for ever and **e;** 4200+6409
Pr 4: 18 **shining** e **brighter** till the full light of day. 239+2143+2256
5: 19 may you e be captivated by her love. 9458
30: 13 those whose eyes are e **so** haughty, 4537
Ecc 1: 6 *e* **returning** on its course. AIT
Isa 6: 9 *Be* e **hearing,** but never understanding 9048+9048
6: 9 *be* e **seeing,** but never perceiving.' 8011+8011
34: 10 e pass through it **again.** 4200+5905+5905
36: 18 the god of any nation *e* **delivered** his land AIT
49: 16 your walls are e before me. 9458
59: 12 Our offenses are e with us, NIH
66: 8 Who *has e* **heard** *of* such a thing? AIT
66: 8 Who *has e* **seen** such things? AIT
Jer 2: 10 see if *there has e* **been** anything like this: AIT
2: 11 Has a nation *e* **changed** its gods? AIT
6: 7 her sickness and wounds are e before me. 9458
7: 7 in the land I gave your forefathers for e 4946+6409
7: 7 for ever and **e.** 6330+6409
18: 13 Who *has e* **heard** anything like this? AIT
18: 14 of Lebanon *e* **vanish** from its rocky slopes? AIT
18: 14 from distant sources *e* **cease** to flow? AIT
19: 4 nor the kings of Judah *e* **knew,** AIT
20: 18 Why *did I e* **come out** of the womb AIT
25: 5 to you and your fathers for e and ever. 4946+6409
25: 5 to you and your fathers for ever and **e.** 6330+6409
31: 36 "will the descendants of Israel e cease to be a nation before me." 2021+3427+3972
33: 18 *e* **fail to have** a man to stand AIT
35: 6 your descendants must e drink wine. 6330+6409
35: 8 and daughters have e drunk wine 3427+3972
44: 3 nor you nor your fathers *e* **knew.** AIT
44: 18 But e **since** we stopped burning incense 255+4946
44: 26 in Egypt will e **again** invoke my name 6388
La 2: 20 Whom *have you e* **treated** like this? AIT
Eze 4: 14 No unclean meat *has e* **entered** my mouth." AIT
15: 3 **Is** wood *e* **taken** from it AIT
16: 16 nor *should they e* **occur.** AIT
27: 32 "Who was e silenced like Tyre, NIH
31: 14 the waters *are e to* **tower proudly** on high, AIT
31: 14 so well-watered *are e to* **reach** such AIT
Da 2: 10 *has e* **asked** such a thing of any magician AIT
2: 20 to the name of God for e and ever; 10002+10550
2: 20 name of God for ever and **e;** 10002+10527+10550
6: 22 Nor *have I e* **done** any wrong before you, AIT
7: 18 yes, for e and ever.' 10550
7: 18 yes, for ever and **e.'** 10002+10550
9: 12 the whole heaven nothing *has e* **been done** AIT
12: 3 like the stars for e and ever. 6409
12: 3 like the stars for ever and **e.** 6329
Joel 1: 2 like this *e* **happened** in your days or in AIT
2: 2 as never was of old nor e *will be* in ages 3578
Mic 4: 5 in the name of the LORD our God for e 6409
4: 5 of the LORD our God for ever and **e.** 6329
Mal 3: 7 **E since** the time of your forefathers 4200+4946
Mt 9: 33 **"Nothing** like this has e *4030*
13: 14 *be* **e hearing** but never understanding; *198+201*
13: 14 *you will be* **e seeing** but never perceiving. *1063+1063*
Mk 4: 12 " *'they may be* **e seeing** but never perceiving, *1063+1063*
4: 12 and **e hearing** but never understanding; *201+201*
11: 2 which no one has e ridden. *4037*
11: 14 "May no one e eat fruit from you again." *172+1650+3836*
Lk 9: 39 It **scarcely** e leaves him *3653*
19: 30 which no one has e ridden. *4799*
Jn 1: 18 No one has e seen God, *4799*
3: 13 No one has e gone into heaven except *NIG*
4: 29 see a man who told me everything I e did. *4012*
4: 39 "He told me everything I e did." *NIG*
7: 46 **"No one** e spoke the way this man does," *4030*
9: 32 Nobody has e heard of opening the eyes of a man born blind. *172+1666+3836*
10: 8 All **who** e came before me were thieves *4012*
19: 41 in which no one had e been laid. *4031*
Ac 7: 52 **Was there** e a prophet your fathers did *5515*
11: 8 **Nothing** impure or unclean has e *4030*
20: 25 the kingdom will e see me **again.** *4033*
26: 4 "The Jews all know the way I have lived e *NIG*
28: 26 *be* **e hearing** but never understanding; *198+201*
28: 26 *you will be* **e seeing** but never perceiving." *1063+1063*
Ro 11: 35 "Who has e given to God, *NIG*
2Co 7: 7 so that my joy was **greater than e.** *3437*
Gal 1: 5 to whom be glory for e and ever. Amen. *172*
1: 5 to whom be glory for ever and **e.** Amen. *172*
Eph 1: 15 *e since* I **heard about** *AIT*
3: 21 throughout all generations, for e and ever! *172*
3: 21 throughout all generations, for ever and **e!** *172*
5: 29 After all, no one e hated his own body, *4537*
Php 4: 20 To our God and Father be glory for e *172*
4: 20 and Father be glory for ever and **e.** *172*
1Ti 1: 17 be honor and glory for e and ever. *172*
1: 17 be honor and glory for ever and **e.** *172*
2Ti 4: 18 To him be glory for e and ever. *172*
4: 18 To him be glory for ever and **e.** *172*
Heb 1: 5 For to which of the angels did God e say, *4537*
1: 8 O God, will last for e and ever, *172*
1: 8 O God, will last for ever and **e,** *172*
1: 13 To which of the angels did God e say, *4537*
7: 13 and no one from that tribe *has e* **served at** *AIT*
13: 21 to whom be glory for e and ever. *172*
13: 21 to whom be glory for ever and **e.** *172*
1Pe 4: 11 be the glory and the power for e and ever. *172*
4: 11 be the glory and the power for ever and **e.** *172*
5: 11 To him be the power for e and ever. Amen. *172*
5: 11 To him be the power for ever and **e.** Amen. *172*
2Pe 3: 4 **E since** our fathers died, *608+4005*
1Jn 4: 12 No one has e seen God; *4799*
Rev 1: 6 to him be glory and power for e and ever! *172*
1: 6 to him be glory and power for ever and **e!** *172*
1: 18 and behold I am alive for e and ever! *172*
1: 18 and behold I am alive for ever and **e!** *172*
4: 9 on the throne and who lives for e and ever, *172*
4: 9 on the throne and who lives for ever and **e,** *172*
4: 10 and worship him who lives for e and ever. *172*
4: 10 and worship him who lives for ever and **e.** *172*
5: 13 and glory and power, for e and ever!" *172*
5: 13 and glory and power, for ever and **e!"** *172*
7: 12 and power and strength be to our God for e *172*
7: 12 and strength be to our God for ever and **e.** *172*
10: 6 he swore by him who lives for e and ever, *172*
10: 6 he swore by him who lives for ever and **e,** *172*
11: 15 and he will reign for e and ever." *172*
11: 15 and he will reign for ever and **e."** *172*
14: 11 smoke of their torment rises for e and ever. *172*
14: 11 smoke of their torment rises for ever and **e.** *172*
15: 7 who lives for e and ever. *172*
15: 7 who lives for ever and **e.** *172*
16: 18 No earthquake like it has e occurred **since** man has been *608+4005*
18: 18 **'Was there e** a city like this great city?' *5515*
18: 22 No workman of any trade will e be found *3590*
19: 3 smoke from her goes up for e and ever." *172*
19: 3 smoke from her goes up for ever and **e."** *172*
20: 10 They will be tormented day and night for e *172*
20: 10 be tormented day and night for ever and **e.** *172*
21: 25 **e** be shut, for there will be **no** *3590+4024*
21: 27 **Nothing** impure will e enter it, *3590*
22: 5 And they will reign for e and ever. *172*
22: 5 And they will reign for ever and **e.** *172*

EVER-INCREASING (2) [INCREASE]

Ro 6: 19 in slavery to impurity and *to* e **wickedness,** *490+490+1650+3836*
2Co 3: 18 being transformed into his likeness **with e glory,** *608+1518+1518+1650*

EVER-PRESENT (1) [PRESENT]

Ps 46: 1 an e help in trouble. 4394+5162

EVERLASTING (71) [EVER]

Ge 9: 16 and remember the e covenant between God 6409
17: 7 as an e covenant between me and you 6409
17: 8 I will give as an e possession to you 6409
17: 13 in your flesh is to be an e covenant. 6409
17: 19 an e covenant for his descendants after him. 6409
48: 4 and I will give this land as an e possession 6409
Nu 18: 19 It is an e covenant of salt before the LORD 6409
Dt 33: 15 and the fruitfulness of the e hills; 6409
33: 27 and underneath are the e arms. 6409
2Sa 23: 5 Has he not made with me an e covenant, 6409
1Ch 16: 17 to Israel as an e covenant: 6409
16: 36 the God of Israel, from e to everlasting. 6409
16: 36 the God of Israel, from everlasting to **e.** 6409
1Ch 29: 10 from e to everlasting. 6409
29: 10 from everlasting to **e.** 6409
Ezr 9: 12 to your children as an e inheritance.' 6330+6409
Ne 9: 5 who is from e to everlasting." 6409
9: 5 who is from everlasting to **e."** 6409
Ps 41: 13 the God of Israel, from e to everlasting. 6409
41: 13 the God of Israel, from everlasting to **e.** 6409
52: 5 God will bring you down to e ruin: 4200+5905
74: 3 Turn your steps toward these e ruins, 5905
78: 66 he put them to e shame. 6409
90: 2 from e to everlasting you are God. 6409
90: 2 from everlasting to e you are God. 6409
103: 17 from e to everlasting the LORD's love is 6409
103: 17 from everlasting to e the LORD's love is 6409
105: 10 to Israel as an e covenant: 6409
106: 48 the God of Israel, from e to everlasting. 6409
106: 48 the God of Israel, from everlasting to **e.** 6409
119: 142 Your righteousness is e 4200+6409
139: 24 and lead me in the way **e.** 6409
145: 13 Your kingdom is an e kingdom, 3972+6409
Isa 9: 6 Mighty God, E Father, Prince of Peace. 6329
24: 5 the statutes and broken the e covenant. 6409
30: 8 days to come it may be an e witness. 6330+6409
33: 14 Who of us can dwell with e burning?" 6409
35: 10 e joy will crown their heads. 6409
40: 28 The LORD is the e God, 6409
45: 17 be saved by the LORD with an e salvation; 6409
45: 17 be put to shame or disgraced, to ages **e.** 6329
51: 11 e joy will crown their heads. 6409
54: 8 but with e kindness I will have compassion 6409
55: 3 I will make an e covenant with you, 6409
55: 13 for an e sign, which will not be destroyed." 6409
56: 5 I will give them an e name that will not 6409
60: 15 the e pride and the joy of all generations. 6409
60: 19 for the LORD will be your e light, 6409
60: 20 the LORD will be your e light, 6409
61: 7 and e joy will be theirs. 6409
61: 8 and make an e covenant with them. 6409
63: 12 to gain for himself e renown, 6409
Jer 5: 22 an e barrier it cannot cross. 6409
23: 40 I will bring upon you e disgrace— 6409
23: 40 e shame that will not be forgotten." 6409
25: 9 object of horror and scorn, and an e ruin. 6409
31: 3 "I have loved you with an e love; 6409
32: 40 I will make an e covenant with them: 6409
50: 5 to the LORD in an e covenant that will not 6409
Eze 16: 60 and I will establish an e covenant with you. 6409
37: 26 it will be an e covenant. 6409
Da 7: 14 His dominion is an e dominion that will 10550
7: 27 His kingdom will be an e kingdom, 10550
9: 24 to bring in e righteousness, 6409
12: 2 some to e life, 6409
12: 2 others to shame and e contempt. 6409
Mic 6: 2 listen, you e foundations of the earth. 419
Hab 1: 12 O LORD, are you not from **e?** 7710
Jn 6: 47 he who believes has e life. *173*
2Th 1: 9 be punished with e destruction and shut out *173*
Jude 1: 6 bound *with* e chains for judgment on *132*

EVERY (628) [EVERYBODY, EVERYBODY'S, EVERYDAY, EVERYONE, EVERYONE'S, EVERYTHING, EVERYWHERE]

Ge 1: 21 and e living and moving thing with which 3972
1: 21 and e winged bird according to its kind. 3972
1: 28 the air and over e living creature that moves 3972
1: 29 "I give you e seed-bearing plant on the face 3972
1: 29 of the whole earth and e tree that has fruit 3972
1: 30 I give e green plant for food." 3972
6: 5 and that e inclination of the thoughts 3972
6: 17 e creature that has the breath of life in it. NIH
6: 20 Two of e kind of bird, NIH
6: 20 of e kind of animal and of every kind NIH
6: 20 and of e kind of creature that moves along 3972
6: 21 to take e *kind of* food that is to be eaten 3972
7: 2 with you seven of e *kind of* clean animal, 3972
7: 2 and two of e kind of unclean animal, NIH
7: 3 and also seven of e kind of bird, NIH
7: 4 of the earth e living creature I have made." 3972
7: 14 with them e wild animal according 3972
7: 14 e creature that moves along the ground 3972
7: 14 the ground according to its kind and e bird 3972
7: 16 in were male and female of e living thing, 3972
7: 21 **E** living thing that moved on 3972
7: 23 **E** living thing on the face of 3972
8: 17 Bring out e *kind of* living creature that is 3972
8: 21 even though e inclination of his heart is evil NIH
9: 2 upon e creature that moves along 3972
9: 5 I will demand an accounting from e animal. 3972
9: 10 with e living creature that was with you— 3972
9: 10 e living creature on earth. 3972
9: 12 and e living creature with you, a covenant 3972
9: 15 and you and all living creatures of e kind. 3972
9: 16 and all living creatures of e kind on 3972
17: 10 **E** male among you shall be circumcised. 3972
17: 12 For the generations to come e male 3972
17: 23 e male in his household, 3972
17: 27 And e male in Abraham's household, 3972
19: 4 from e **part** of the city of Sodom— 7895
20: 18 up e womb in Abimelech's household 3972
24: 1 and the LORD had blessed him in e **way.** 3972
30: 32 from them e speckled or spotted sheep, 3972
30: 32 e dark-colored lamb and every spotted 3972
30: 32 every dark-colored lamb and e spotted 928
34: 24 and e male in the city was circumcised. 3972

Ge 34:25 the unsuspecting city, killing e male. 3972
Ex 1:22 **"E** boy that is born you must throw into 3972
1:22 but let e girl live." 3972
3:22 *E* **woman** is to ask her neighbor AIT
9:19 the hail will fall on e man and animal 3972
9:25 in the fields and stripped e tree. 3972
10:5 including e tree that is growing 3972
10:14 in e area of the country in great numbers. 3972
11:5 E firstborn son in Egypt will die, 3972
12:12 and strike down e firstborn— 3972
13:2 "Consecrate to me e firstborn male. 3972
13:2 of e womb among the Israelites belongs 3972
13:12 to the LORD the first offspring of e womb. 3972
13:13 Redeem with a lamb e firstborn donkey, 3972
13:13 Redeem e firstborn among your sons. 3972
13:15 the LORD killed e firstborn in Egypt, 3972
13:15 the first male offspring of e womb 3972
18:22 but have them bring e difficult case to you; 3972
23:27 into confusion e nation you encounter. 3972
30:7 burn fragrant incense on the altar **e morning** 928+928+1332+1332+2021+2021
34:19 first offspring of e womb belongs to me, 3972
35:25 E skilled woman spun with her hands 3972
36:1 Oholiab and e skilled person to whom 3972
36:2 and Oholiab and e skilled person to whom 3972
Lev 2:11 " 'E grain offering you bring to 3972
6:12 **E morning** the priest is to add firewood 928+928+1332+1332+2021+2021
6:23 E grain offering of a priest shall 3972
7:9 E grain offering baked in an oven 3972
7:10 and e grain offering, 3972
11:26 " 'E animal that has a split hoof 3972
11:41 " 'E creature that moves about on 3972
11:46 e living thing that moves in the water 3972
11:46 in the water and e creature that moves about 3972
17:14 because the life of e creature is its blood. 3972
17:14 because the life of e creature is its blood; 3972
27:25 E value is to be set according to 3972
27:32 e tenth animal that passes under 3972
Nu 1:2 listing e man by name, one by one. 3972
3:12 first male offspring of e Israelite woman. 3972
3:13 I set apart for myself e firstborn in Israel, 3972
3:15 Count e male a month old or more." 3972
3:39 including e male a month old or more, 3972
7:3 ox from each leader and a cart from e two. NIH
8:16 first male offspring from e Israelite woman. 3972
8:17 E firstborn male in Israel, 3972
11:10 Moses heard the people of e family wailing, 2257S
14:29 e *one of* you twenty years old 3972
16:3 e *one of* them, 3972
18:10 e male shall eat it. 3972
18:15 The first offspring of e womb, 3972
18:15 But you must redeem e firstborn son NIH
18:15 and e firstborn male of unclean animals. NIH
19:15 and e open container without a lid fastened 3972
28:10 the burnt offering for **e Sabbath,** 928+8701+8701
28:11 " 'On the first of **e** month, 4013S
28:24 the food for the offering made by fire e day 4200
30:4 then all her vows and e pledge 3972
31:7 and killed e man. 3972
31:17 And kill e woman who has slept with 3972
31:18 for yourselves e girl who has never slept 3972
31:20 Purify e garment as well 3972
31:28 for the LORD one out of e five hundred, 2021
31:30 select one out of e fifty, whether persons, 2021
31:47 Moses selected one out of e fifty persons 2021
32:18 until e Israelite has received his inheritance. 408
32:27 But your servants, e man armed for battle, 3972
32:29 e man armed for battle, 3972
34:12 with its boundaries **on e side.' "** 6017
36:7 for e Israelite shall keep 408
36:8 E daughter who inherits land 3972
36:8 that e Israelite will possess the inheritance 408
Dt 1:41 So e *one* of you put on his weapons, 408
3:6 of Heshbon, destroying e city— 3972
7:15 The LORD will keep you free from e disease. 3972
8:1 to follow e command I am giving you today, 3972
8:3 but on e word that comes from the mouth of 3972
11:6 their tents and e living thing that belonged 3972
11:24 E place where you set your foot will 3972
12:2 and on the hills and under e spreading tree 3972
14:28 At the end of e three years, NIH
15:1 of e seven years you must cancel debts. NIH
15:2 E creditor shall cancel the loan he has made 3972
15:19 for the LORD your God e firstborn male 3972
16:18 for each of your tribes in e town 3972
28:61 The LORD will also bring on you e *kind* 3972
31:10 "At the end of e seven years, NIH
Jos 1:3 I will give you e place 3972
6:5 the people will go up, e man straight in." 2257
6:20 so e man charged straight in, 408
6:21 and destroyed with the sword e living thing 3972
8:24 and when e *one of* them had been put to 3972
21:44 The LORD gave them rest on **e side,** 6017
21:45 e *one* was fulfilled. 3972
23:14 E promise has been fulfilled; 3972
23:15 But just as e good promise of the LORD 3972
Jdg 8:34 hands of all their enemies **on e side.** 4946+6017
15:4 He then fastened a torch to e pair of tails, NIH
20:10 of e hundred from all the tribes of Israel, 2021
21:11 "Kill e male and every woman who is not 3972
21:11 "Kill every male and e woman who is not 3972
1Sa 2:29 of e offering made by my people Israel?' 3972
2:33 E *one* of you that I do not cut off 408
4:10 the Israelites were defeated and *e* **man** fled AIT
11:2 that I gouge out the right eye of e *one* 3972
12:11 from the hands of your enemies on **e side,** 6017
1Sa 14:47 he fought against their enemies **on e side:** 6017
17:16 the Philistine came forward *e* **morning** AIT
20:15 not even when the LORD has cut off e *one* 408
25:12 When they arrived, they reported e word. 3972
25:30 for my master e good thing he promised 3972
26:23 The LORD rewards e man for his 2021
2Sa 2:23 And e *man* stopped when he came to 3972
8:2 E two lengths of them were put to death, NIH
13:37 But King David mourned for his son e day. 3972
20:1 *E* **man** to his tent, O Israel!" AIT
23:5 arranged and secured in e *part?* 3972
23:5 and grant me my e desire? 3972
1Ki 1:29 who has delivered me out of e trouble, 3972
5:4 on **e side,** and there is no adversary 6017
7:36 in e available space, 408
10:22 Once e three years it returned, 4200
12:24 Go home, e *one* of you, 408
14:10 I will cut off from Jeroboam **e last male** 928+7815+8874
14:23 and Asherah poles on e high hill and 3972
14:23 and under e spreading tree. 3972
17:15 So there was food **e day** for Elijah and for 3427
21:21 cut off from Ahab **e last male** 928+7815+8874
22:36 *"E* **man** to his town; everyone to his land!" AIT
2Ki 3:19 You will overthrow e fortified city 3972
3:19 and e major town. 3972
3:19 You will cut down e good tree, 3972
3:19 and ruin e good field with stones." 3972
3:21 so e *man,* young and old, 3972
3:25 a stone on e good field until it was covered. 3972
3:25 up all the springs and cut down e good tree. 3972
9:8 cut off from Ahab **e last male** 928+7815+8874
12:5 Let e priest receive the money from one of 408
13:20 to enter the country **e spring.** 995+9102
14:12 and *e* **man** fled to his home. AIT
15:20 E wealthy man had to contribute fifty 3972
16:4 on the hilltops and under e spreading tree. 3972
17:10 and Asherah poles on e high hill and 3972
17:10 and under e spreading tree. 3972
17:11 At e high place they burned incense, 3972
18:31 Then e *one* of you will eat 408
25:9 E important building he burned down. 3972
1Ch 9:32 preparing *for* **e Sabbath** the bread set out on the table. 8701+8701
12:33 with e *type of* weapon, to help David 3972
12:37 armed with e *type of* weapon—120,000. 3972
14:17 So David's fame spread throughout e land, 3972
21:12 of the LORD ravaging e part of Israel.' 3972
22:9 from all his enemies **on e side.** 4946+6017
22:15 as well as men skilled in e *kind of* work 3972
22:18 has he not granted you rest **on e side?** 4946+6017
23:30 They were also to stand **e morning** to thank 928+928+1332+1332+2021+2021
26:32 of Manasseh for e matter pertaining to God 3972
28:9 for the LORD searches e heart 3972
28:9 and understands e motive behind 3972
28:21 and e willing man skilled 3972
28:21 the people will obey your e command." 3972
2Ch 2:4 and for making burnt offerings e morning 4200
9:21 Once e three years it returned, 4200
11:4 Go home, e *one* of you, 408
11:16 from e tribe of Israel who set their hearts 3972
13:11 **E morning** and evening they present burnt offerings 928+928+1332+1332+2021+2021
13:11 light the lamps on the gold lampstand **e evening.** 928+928+2021+2021+6847+6847
14:5 the high places and incense altars in e town 3972
14:7 and he has given us rest **on e side."** 4946+6017
15:6 with e *kind of* distress. 3972
15:15 So the LORD gave them rest **on e side.** 4946+6017
19:10 *In* e case that comes before you 3972
20:4 indeed, they came from e town in Judah 3972
20:30 his God had given him rest **on e side.** 4946+6017
25:22 and *e* **man** fled to his home. AIT
28:4 on the hilltops and under e spreading tree. 3972
28:24 up altars at e street corner in Jerusalem. 3972
28:25 In e town in Judah he built high places 3972
30:21 priests sang to the LORD **e day,** 928+3427+3427
31:19 to distribute portions to e male among them 3972
32:22 He took care of them **on e side.** 4946+6017
Ne 4:22 "Have *e* **man** and his helper stay AIT
5:13 and possessions e man who does 3972
5:18 and e ten days an abundant supply of wine 1068
10:31 E seventh year we will forgo working 2021
10:35 of our crops and of e fruit tree. 3972
11:1 the people cast lots to bring one out of e ten 2021
Est 1:22 in each people's tongue that e man should 3972
2:3 in e province of his realm 3972
2:11 **E day** he walked back and forth near the courtyard 2256+3427+3427+3972
3:14 as law in e province and made known to 3972
3:14 to the people of e nationality so they would 3972
4:3 In e province to which the edict and order 3972
8:11 The king's edict granted the Jews in e city 3972
8:13 as law in e province and made known to 3972
8:13 of e nationality so that the Jews would 3972
8:17 In e province and in every city, 3972
8:17 In every province and in e city, 3972
9:27 without fail observe these two days e year, 3972
9:28 in e generation by every family, 3972
9:28 in every generation by **e family,** 2256+5476+5476
9:28 in **e province** and in every city, 2256+4519+4519
9:28 in every province and in **e city.** 2256+6551+6551
Job 7:18 that you examine him e morning 4200
7:18 and test him e moment? 4200
12:10 of e creature and the breath of all mankind. 3972
18:11 Terrors startle him **on e side** 6017
Job 18:11 on every side and dog his *e* **step.** AIT
19:10 He tears me down **on e side** till I am gone; 6017
28:21 It is hidden from the eyes of e living thing, 3972
31:4 not see my ways and count my e step? 3972
31:37 I would give him an account of my *e* **step;** AIT
34:21 he sees their e step. 3972
37:7 he stops e man from his labor. 3972
40:11 look at e proud man and bring him low, 3972
40:12 look at e proud man and humble him, 3972
Ps 3:6 of thousands drawn up against me **on e side.** 6017
7:11 a God who expresses his wrath e day. 3972
12:3 all flattering lips and e boastful tongue NIH
13:2 with my thoughts and **e day** have sorrow 3429
31:13 there is terror **on e side;** 4946+6017
50:10 for e animal of the forest is mine, 3972
50:11 I know e bird in the mountains, 3972
52:4 You love e harmful word, 3972
73:14 I have been punished e morning. 4200
74:8 They burned e place 3972
82:7 you will fall like *e* **other** ruler." AIT
88:9 I call to you, O LORD, e day; 3972
89:51 with which they have mocked *e* **step** AIT
97:3 before him and consumes his foes **on e side.** 6017
101:8 E morning I will put to silence all 4200
101:8 I will cut off e evildoer from the city of 3972
105:35 they ate up e green thing in their land, 3972
118:11 They surrounded me **on e side,** 6015
119:101 I have kept my feet from e evil path so 3972
119:104 therefore I hate e wrong path. 3972
119:128 I hate e wrong path. 3972
136:25 and who gives food to e creature. 3972
140:2 in their hearts and stir up war e day. 3972
144:13 Our barns will be filled with **e kind** of provision. 448+2385+2385+4946
145:2 E day I will praise you and extol your name 3972
145:16 and satisfy the desires of e living thing. 3972
145:21 Let e creature praise his holy name for ever 3972
Pr 2:9 right and just and fair—e good path. 3972
7:12 now in the squares, at e corner she lurks.) 3972
13:16 E prudent man acts out of knowledge, 3972
16:33 but its e decision is from the LORD. 3972
20:3 but e fool is quick to quarrel. 3972
30:5 **"E** word of God is flawless; 3972
Ecc 3:1 and a season for e activity under heaven: 3972
3:17 for there will be a time for e activity, 3972
3:17 a time for e deed." 3972
7:2 for death is the destiny of e man; 3972
7:21 Do not pay attention to e word people say, 3972
8:6 a proper time and procedure for e matter, 3972
12:14 For God will bring e deed into judgment, 3972
12:14 including e hidden thing, 3972
SS 4:14 with e *kind of* incense tree, 3972
7:13 and at our door is e delicacy, 3972
Isa 2:15 for e lofty tower and every fortified wall, 3972
2:15 for every lofty tower and e fortified wall, 3972
2:16 for e trading ship and every stately vessel. 3972
2:16 for every trading ship and e stately vessel. 3972
7:23 in e place where there were 3972
9:5 E warrior's boot used in battle 3972
9:5 in battle and e garment rolled in blood will NIH
9:17 e mouth speaks vileness. 3972
13:7 e man's heart will melt. 3972
15:2 E head is shaved and every beard cut off. 3972
15:2 Every head is shaved and e beard cut off. 3972
19:7 E sown field along 3972
21:8 e night I stay at my post. 3972
24:10 the entrance to e house is barred. 3972
30:25 on e high mountain and every lofty hill. 3972
30:25 on every high mountain and e lofty hill. 3972
30:32 E stroke the LORD lays on them 3972
31:7 in that day e *one* of you will reject the idols 408
32:20 sowing your seed by e stream, 3972
33:2 Be our strength e morning, 4200
36:16 Then e *one of* you will eat 408
40:4 E valley shall be raised up, 3972
40:4 e mountain and hill made low; 3972
45:23 Before me e knee will bow; 3972
45:23 by me e tongue will swear. 3972
49:9 the roads and find pasture on e barren hill. 3972
51:13 that you live in constant terror e day 3972
51:20 they lie at the head of e street, 3972
54:17 you will refute e tongue that accuses you. 3972
57:5 among the oaks and under e spreading tree; 3972
58:6 to set the oppressed free and break e yoke? 3972
Jer 2:20 Indeed, on e high hill and 3972
2:20 and under e spreading tree you lay down as 3972
3:6 She has gone up on e high hill and 3972
3:6 and under e spreading tree 3972
3:13 to foreign gods under e spreading tree, 3972
4:25 e bird in the sky had flown away. 3972
4:29 of horsemen and archers e town takes 3972
6:25 and there is terror **on e side.** 4946+6017
9:4 For e brother is a deceiver, 3972
9:4 and e friend a slanderer. 3972
10:14 e goldsmith is shamed by his idols. 3972
12:4 the land lie parched and the grass in e field 3972
13:12 E wineskin should be filled with wine.' 3972
13:12 that e wineskin should be filled with wine?' 3972
16:16 down on e mountain and hill and from 3972
19:15 around it e disaster I pronounced 3972
20:10 many whispering, "Terror **on e side!** 4946+6017
21:12 " 'Administer justice e morning; 4200
23:36 *e* **man's** *own* word becomes his oracle AIT
30:6 Then why do I see e strong man 3972
30:6 e face turned deathly pale? 3972
34:14 'E seventh year each of you must 4946+7891
35:17 in Jerusalem e disaster I pronounced 3972

Jer 36: 3 about e disaster I plan to inflict on them, 3972
36:31 the people of Judah e disaster I pronounced 3972
46: 5 and there is terror **on e side,"** 4946+6017
48: 8 The destroyer will come against e town, 3972
48:37 E head is shaved and every beard cut off; 3972
48:37 Every head is shaved and e beard cut off; 3972
48:37 e hand is slashed and every waist is covered 3972
48:37 every hand is slashed and e waist is covered NIH
49: 5 "E *one* of you will be driven away. 408
49:29 will shout to them, 'Terror **on e side!'** 4946+6017
49:32 on them from e side," 3972
50:15 Shout against her **on e side!** 6017
51: 2 will oppose her **on e side** in the day 4946+6017
51:17 "E man is senseless and without knowledge 3972
51:17 e goldsmith is shamed by his idols. 3972
52:13 E important building he burned down. 3972
La 2: 3 In fierce anger he has cut off e horn 3972
2:19 faint from hunger at the head of e street. 3972
2:22 you summoned against me terrors **on e side.** 4946+6017
3:23 They are new e morning; 4200
4: 1 scattered at the head of e street. 3972
4:18 Men stalked us at *e* **step,** AIT
Eze 6:13 on e high hill and on all the mountaintops, 3972
6:13 under e spreading tree 3972
6:13 and e leafy oak— 3972
7:17 E hand will go limp, 3972
7:17 and e knee will become as weak as water. 3972
12:22 'The days go by and e vision comes 3972
12:23 'The days are near when e vision will 3972
14:22 e disaster I have brought upon it. 3972
16:24 and made a lofty shrine in e public square. 3972
16:25 of e street you built your lofty shrines 3972
16:31 of e street and made your lofty shrines 3972
16:31 made your lofty shrines in e public square, 3972
16:33 E prostitute receives a fee, 3972
17:23 Birds *of* e *kind* will nest in it; 3972
18: 4 For e living soul belongs to me, 3972
20:26 the sacrifice of e firstborn— 3972
20:39 Go and serve your idols, e *one* of you! 408
20:47 and e face from south to north will 3972
21: 7 E heart will melt and every hand go limp; 3972
21: 7 Every heart will melt and e hand go limp; 3972
21: 7 e spirit will become faint 3972
21: 7 and e knee become as weak as water.' 3972
21:10 The sword despises e such stick. 3972
21:14 **closing in** on them **from e side.** 2539
23:22 against you from **e side—** 6017
23:24 take up positions against you **on e side** with 6017
26:16 trembling e moment, appalled at you. 4200
27:11 and Helech manned your walls **on e side;** 6017
28:13 e precious stone adorned you: 3972
28:23 with the sword against her **on e side.** 4946+6017
29:18 e head was rubbed bare 3972
29:18 and e shoulder made raw. 3972
32:10 of them will tremble e moment for his life. 4200
34: 6 over all the mountains and on e high hill. 3972
36: 3 and hounded you **from e side** so 4946+6017
38:20 e creature that moves along the ground, 3972
38:20 the cliffs will crumble and e wall will fall to 3972
38:21 *E* **man's** sword will be against his brother. AIT
39:17 to e kind of bird and all the wild animals: 3972
39:20 mighty men and soldiers of e *kind,*' 3972
45:15 be taken from e flock of two hundred from 2021
45:23 E day during the seven days of 4200
46:13 " '**E day** you are to provide a year-old lamb 2021+3427+4200
47:12 E month they will bear, 4200
Da 1: 4 showing aptitude for e *kind of* learning, 3972
1:20 In e matter of wisdom and understanding 3972
3: 4 O peoples, nations and **men of e language:** 10392
3: 7 nations and **men of e language** fell down 10392
4: 1 nations and **men of e language,** 10392
4:12 from it e creature was fed. 10353
5:19 nations and **men of e language** dreaded 10392
6:14 to rescue Daniel and **made e effort** 10700
6:25 nations and **men of e language** throughout 10392
6:26 in e part of my kingdom people must fear 10353
7:14 and **men of e language** worshiped him. 10392
11:36 above e god and will say unheard-of things 3972
Hos 9: 1 of a prostitute at e threshing floor. 3972
9:12 I will bereave them of e *one.* 132
Joel 2: 6 e face turns pale. 3972
3:11 all you nations **from e side,** 4946+6017
3:12 to judge all the nations **on e side.** 4946+6017
Am 2: 8 beside e altar on garments taken in pledge. 3972
4: 4 Bring your sacrifices e morning, 4200
4: 4 your tithes e three years. 4200
4: 6 in e city and lack of bread in every town, 3972
4: 6 in every city and lack of bread in e town, 3972
5:16 and cries of anguish in e public square. 3972
Mic 4: 4 *E* **man** will sit under his own vine and AIT
Na 2:10 bodies tremble, e face grows pale. 3972
3:10 to pieces at the head of e street. 3972
Zep 1: 4 I will cut off from this place *e* **remnant** AIT
2:11 The nations on e shore will worship him, 3972
2:11 e *one* in its own land. 408
2:14 creatures of e kind. 3972
3: 5 and e new day he does not fail, 4200
3:19 I will give them praise and honor in e land 3972
Zec 5: 3 e thief will be banished, 3972
8:10 for I had turned e man against his neighbor. 3972
10: 4 from him the battle bow, from him e ruler. 3972
12: 4 On that day I will strike e horse with panic 3972
13: 4 "On that day e prophet will be ashamed 408
14:21 E pot in Jerusalem and Judah will be holy 3972
Mal 1:11 In e place incense and pure offerings will 3972

Mal 4: 1 the arrogant and e evildoer will be stubble, 3972
Mt 3:10 and e tree that does not produce good fruit *4246*
4: 4 but on e word that comes from the mouth *4246*
4:23 and healing e disease and sickness among *4246*
7:17 Likewise e good tree bears good fruit, *4246*
7:19 E tree that does not bear good fruit is cut *4246*
9:35 of the kingdom and healing e disease *4246*
10: 1 to drive out evil spirits and to heal e disease *4246*
12:25 "E kingdom divided against itself will *4246*
12:25 and e city or household divided *4246*
12:31 e sin and blasphemy will be forgiven men, *4246*
12:36 for e careless word they have spoken. *4246*
13:52 "Therefore e teacher of the law *4246*
15:13 "E plant that my heavenly Father has *4246*
18:16 so that 'e matter may be established by *4246*
19: 3 to divorce his wife for **any and e** reason?" *4246*
24: 2 e one will be thrown down." *NIG*
26:55 **E day** I sat in the temple courts *2465+2848*
Mk 13: 2 e one will be thrown down." *NIG*
14:49 **E day** I was with you, *2465+2848*
Lk 2:23 "E firstborn male is to be consecrated to *4246*
2:41 E year his parents went to Jerusalem for *2848*
3: 5 E valley shall be filled in, *4246*
3: 5 e mountain and hill made low. *4246*
3: 9 and e tree that does not produce good fruit *4246*
5:17 who had come from e village of Galilee and *4246*
10: 1 of him to e town and place where he was *4246*
13:24 "**Make e effort** to enter through *76*
16:19 and fine linen and lived in luxury e day. *2848*
19:43 and encircle you and hem you in **on e side.** *4119*
19:47 E day he was teaching at the temple. *2848*
21: 6 e one of them will be thrown down." *NIG*
22:53 E day I was with you in the temple courts, *2848*
Jn 1: 9 that gives light to e man was coming into *4246*
13:10 you are clean, though not e *one* of you." *4246*
13:11 that was why he said not e *one* was clean. *4246*
15: 2 He cuts off e branch in me that bears no *4246*
15: 2 in me that bears no fruit, while e branch *4246*
21:25 If e one of them were written down, *2848*
Ac 2: 5 from e nation under heaven. *4246*
2:38 "Repent and be baptized, **e one** of you, *1667*
2:46 E day they continued to meet together in *2848*
3: 2 where he was put e day to beg *2848*
10:35 but accepts men from e nation who fear him *4246*
13:27 of the prophets that are read e Sabbath. *2848+4246*
15:21 For Moses has been preached **in** e city from *2848*
15:21 in the synagogues on e Sabbath." *4246*
17:11 and examined the Scriptures e day to see *2848*
17:22 I see that in e *way* you are very religious. *4246*
17:26 From one man *he* made e nation of men, *4246*
18: 4 E Sabbath he reasoned in the synagogue, *2848+4246*
20:23 that **in** e city the Holy Spirit warns me *2848*
24: 3 Everywhere and *in* e *way,* *4118*
Ro 1:29 They have become filled *with* e *kind* *4246*
2: 9 for e human being who does evil: *4246*
3: 2 Much in e way! *4246*
3: 4 Let God be true, and e man a liar. *4246*
3:19 so that e mouth may be silenced and *4246*
7: 8 produced in me e *kind* of covetous desire. *4246*
12: 3 the grace given me I say *to* e *one* of you: *4246*
14: 5 another man considers e day alike. *4246*
14:11 says the Lord, 'e knee will bow before me; *4246*
14:11 e tongue will confess to God.' " *4246*
14:19 therefore **make e effort** to do what leads *1503*
1Co 1: 5 For in him you have been enriched in e *way* *4246*
4:17 with what I teach everywhere in e church. *4246*
10:33 even as I try to please everybody *in* e *way.* *4246*
11: 3 to realize that the head *of* e man is Christ, *4246*
11: 4 E man who prays or prophesies *4246*
11: 5 And e woman who prays or prophesies *4246*
12:18 e one of them, just as he wanted them to be. *1667*
12:26 If one part suffers, e part suffers with it; *4246*
12:26 one part is honored, e part rejoices with it. *4246*
14: 5 like e *one* of you to speak in tongues, *4246*
15:30 us, why do we endanger ourselves e hour? *4246*
15:31 I die e day— *2848*
16: 2 On the first day of e week, *NIG*
2Co 4: 2 to e man's conscience in the sight of God. *4246*
4: 8 We are hard pressed on e *side,* *4246*
6: 4 of God we commend ourselves in e *way:* *4246*
7: 5 but we were harassed at e turn— *4246*
7:11 At e *point* you have proved yourselves to *4246*
9: 8 you will abound in e good work. *4246*
9:11 be made rich in e *way* so that you can *4246*
9:11 so that you can be generous on e *occasion,* *4246*
10: 5 and e pretension that sets itself up against *4246*
10: 5 and we take captive e thought *4246*
10: 6 be ready to punish e act of disobedience, *4246*
11: 6 perfectly clear to you in e *way.* *4246*
13: 1 "E matter must be established by *4246*
Gal 5: 3 Again I declare *to* e man who lets himself *4246*
Eph 1: 3 with e spiritual blessing in Christ. *4246*
1:21 and e title that can be given, *4246*
1:23 of him who fills everything in e *way.* *4246*
4: 3 **Make e effort** to keep the unity of the Spirit *5079*
4:14 *by* e wind of teaching and by the cunning *4246*
4:16 and held together by e supporting ligament, *4246*
4:19 over to sensuality so as to indulge in e *kind* *4246*
4:31 along with e *form* of malice. *4246*
5:16 making the most of e opportunity, *NIG*
Php 1: 3 I thank my God e time I remember you. *4246*
1:18 The important thing is that *in* e way, *4246*
2: 9 the name that is above e name, *4246*
2:10 at the name of Jesus e knee should bow, *4246*
2:11 e tongue confess that Jesus Christ is Lord, *4246*
4:12 of being content in any and e *situation,* *4246*

Col 1:10 of the Lord and may please him in e *way:* *4246*
1:10 bearing fruit in e good work, *4246*
1:23 and that has been proclaimed to e creature *4246*
2:10 who is the head *over* e power and authority. *4246*
4: 5 make the most of e opportunity. *NIG*
1Th 2:17 out of our intense longing we made e effort *4359*
5:22 Avoid e kind of evil. *4246*
2Th 1: 3 and the love e one of you has *1667*
1:11 by his power he may fulfill e good purpose *4246*
1:11 of yours and e act prompted by your faith. *NIG*
2:10 and in e *sort* of evil that deceives *4246*
2:17 and strengthen you in e good deed *4246*
3: 6 from e brother who is idle and does not live *4246*
3:16 at all times and in e way. *4246*
2Ti 3:17 be thoroughly equipped for e good work. *4246*
4:18 The Lord will rescue me from e evil attack *4246*
Tit 1: 5 and appoint elders **in** e town, *2848*
2:10 so that in e *way* they will make the teaching *4246*
Phm 1: 6 *of* e good thing we have in Christ. *4246*
Heb 2: 2 by angels was binding, and e violation *4246*
2:17 to be made like his brothers in e *way,* *4246*
3: 4 For e house is built by someone, *4246*
4:11 therefore, **make e effort** to enter that rest, *5079*
4:15 in e *way,* just as we are— *4246*
5: 1 E high priest is selected from among men *4246*
8: 3 E high priest is appointed to offer both gifts *4246*
9:19 Moses had proclaimed e commandment *4246*
9:25 the Most Holy Place e year with blood *2848*
10:11 Day after day e priest stands *4246*
12:14 **Make e effort** to live in peace with all men *1503*
13:18 and desire to live honorably in e *way.* *4246*
Jas 1:17 E good and perfect gift is from above, *4246*
3:16 there you find disorder and e evil practice. *4246*
1Pe 2: 1 hypocrisy, envy, and slander of e *kind.* *4246*
2:13 for the Lord's sake *to* e authority instituted *4246*
2Pe 1: 5 make e effort to add to your faith goodness; *4246*
1:15 And *I will* **make e effort** to see that *5079*
3:14 **make e effort** to be found spotless, *5079*
1Jn 4: 1 Dear friends, do not believe e spirit, *4246*
4: 2 E spirit that acknowledges that Jesus Christ *4246*
4: 3 but e spirit that does not acknowledge *4246*
Rev 1: 7 and e eye will see him, *4246*
5: 9 from e tribe and language and people *4246*
5:13 Then I heard e creature in heaven and *4246*
6:14 and e mountain and island was removed *4246*
6:15 and e slave and every free man hid in caves *4246*
6:15 and every slave and e free man hid in caves *NIG*
7: 9 from e nation, tribe, people and language, *4246*
7:17 God will wipe away e tear from their eyes." *4246*
11: 6 to strike the earth with e *kind* of plague *4246*
11: 9 and a half days men from e people, *NIG*
13: 7 And he was given authority over e tribe, *4246*
14: 6 to e nation, tribe, language and people. *4246*
16: 3 and e living thing in the sea died. *4246*
16:20 E island fled away and the mountains could *4246*
18: 2 for demons and a haunt *for* e evil spirit, *4246*
18: 2 a haunt *for* e unclean and detestable bird. *4246*
18:12 e *sort* of citron wood, *4246*
18:12 and articles of e kind made of ivory, *4246*
18:17 "E sea captain, and all who travel by ship, *4246*
21: 4 He will wipe e tear from their eyes. *4246*
21:19 the city walls were decorated *with* e *kind* *4246*
22: 2 yielding its fruit e month. *1667*

EVERYBODY (8) [BODY, EVERY]

Lk 9:15 The disciples did so, and e sat down. *570*
18: 9 and looked down on e **else,** *3370*
Ac 4:16 "E living in Jerusalem knows they have done an outstanding miracle, *4246*
21:24 Then e will know there is no truth *4246*
Ro 12:17 to do what is right in the eyes *of* e. *476+4246*
1Co 10:33 even as I try to please e in every way. *4246*
14:24 in while e is prophesying, *4246*
2Co 3: 2 written on our hearts, known and read by **e.** *476+4246*

EVERYBODY'S (1) [BODY, EVERY]

Ac 16:26 and e chains came loose. *4246*

EVERYDAY (1) [DAY, EVERY]

Gal 3:15 let me take an example **from e life.** *476+2848*

EVERYONE (216) [EVERY, ONE]

Ge 16:12 against e and everyone's hand against him, 3972
21: 6 e who hears about this will laugh with me." 3972
45: 1 "Have e leave my presence!" 408+3972
Ex 12:16 except to prepare food for e to eat— 3972+5883
16:21 Each morning e gathered as much 408
16:29 E is to stay where he is on the seventh day; 408
19:16 E in the camp trembled. 2021+3972+6639
35: 5 E *who* is willing is to bring to the LORD 3972
35:21 and e who was willing 408+3972
35:23 E who had blue, purple or scarlet yarn 408+3972
35:24 and e who had acacia wood for any part of 3972
38:26 from e who had crossed over 3972
Lev 18:29 " 'E who does any of these detestable 3972
25:13 of Jubilee e is to return to his own property. 408
Nu 15:13 'E who is native-born must do these things 3972
15:29 to e who sins unintentionally, 2021[S]
18:11 E in your household *who* is ceremonially clean may eat it. 3972
18:13 E in your household *who* is ceremonially clean may eat it. 3972
Dt 4: 3 e who followed the Baal of Peor, 408+2021+3972

Dt 12: 8 e as he sees fit, 408
Jos 10:28 and totally destroyed e in it. 2021+3972+5883
10:30 The city and e in it Joshua put to the sword.
2021+3972+5883
10:32 The city and e in it he put to the sword,
2021+3972+5883
10:35 to the sword and totally destroyed e in it,
2021+3972+5883
10:37 its villages and e in it. 2021+3972+5883
10:37 totally destroyed it and e in it. 2021+3972+5883
10:39 E in it they totally destroyed. 3972+5883
11:11 E in it they put to the sword. 2021+3972+5883
Jdg 9:25 to ambush and rob e who passed by, 3972
17: 6 e did as he saw fit. 408
19:30 E who saw it said, 3972
21:25 e did as he saw fit. 408
1Sa 2:36 Then e left in your family line will come 3972
3:11 that will make the ears of e who hears 3972
8:22 "E go back to his town." 408
14:34 So e brought his ox that night 2021+3972+6639
2Sa 13: 9 "Send e out of here," Amnon said. 408+3972
13: 9 So e left him. 408+3972
15: 4 Then e who has a complaint 408+3972
16:21 hands of e with you will be strengthened." 3972
20:12 that e who came up to Amasa stopped, 3972
1Ki 10:25 e who came brought a gift— 408
22:36 e to his land!" 408
2Ki 10:11 So Jehu killed e in Jezreel who remained of 3972
14:26 how bitterly e in Israel, whether slave NIH
15:16 attacked Tiphsah and e in the city 3972
21:12 that the ears of e who hears of it will tingle. 3972
1Ch 12:15 and they put to flight e *living in* 3972
2Ch 9:24 e who came brought a gift— 408
29:29 the king and e present with him knelt down 3972
30:18 the LORD, who is good, pardon e 3972
34:32 Then he had e in Jerusalem 3972
Ezr 1: 5 e whose heart God had moved— 3972
8:22 of our God is on e who looks to him, 3972
9: 4 Then e who trembled at the words of 3972
10:14 Then let e in our towns who has married 3972
Est 2:15 And Esther won the favor of e who saw her. 3972
Job 17: 6 "God has made me a byword to e, 6639
34:26 for their wickedness where *e can* see them, AIT
42:11 and e who had known him before came 3972
Ps 12: 2 E lies to his neighbor; 408
32: 6 Therefore let e who is godly pray to you 3972
53: 3 E has turned away, 3972
Pr 19: 6 and e is the friend of a man who gives gifts. 3972
Ecc 3:13 That e may eat and drink, 132+2021+3972
10: 3 the fool lacks sense and shows e 3972
Isa 6:12 until the LORD has sent e far away and 132
9:17 for e is ungodly and wicked, 3972
19:17 e to whom Judah is mentioned will 3972
30: 5 e will be put to shame because of 3972
43: 7 e who is called by my name, 3972
Jer 1: 7 You must go to e I send you to 3972
10:14 E is senseless and without knowledge; 132+3972
15:10 yet e curses me. 3972
17:20 and e living in Jerusalem who come 3972
19: 3 that will make the ears of e who hears 3972
20: 7 I am ridiculed all day long; e mocks me. 3972
31:30 Instead, e will die for his own sin; 408
32:19 you reward e according to his conduct and 408
34: 9 E was to free his Hebrew slaves, 408
35:17 to bring on Judah and on e living 3972
50:16 the oppressor let e return to his own people, 408
50:16 let e flee to his own land. 408
Eze 16:44 " 'E who quotes proverbs will quote this
proverb 3972
20:48 E will see that I the LORD have kindled it;
1414+3972
21: 4 my sword will be unsheathed against e 1414+3972
23: 7 with all the idols of e she lusted after. 3972
27:27 and e else on board will sink into 3972+7736
Da 3:10 e who hears the sound of the horn, 10050+10353
11: 2 he will stir up e against the kingdom 3972
12: 1 e whose name is found written in 3972
Joel 2:32 And e who calls on the name of 3972
Ob 1: 9 and e in Esau's mountains will be cut down 408
Jnh 3: 8 *Let e* call urgently on God. AIT
Na 3:19 E who hears the news 3972
Hab 2: 8 have destroyed lands and cities and e 3782+3972
2:17 have destroyed lands and cities and e 3782+3972
Zec 5: 3 e who swears falsely will be banished. 3972
10: 1 and plants of the field to e. 408
11: 6 "I will hand e over to his neighbor 132
Mt 5:15 and it gives light *to* e in the house. *4246*
7: 8 For e who asks receives; *4246*
7:21 "Not e who says to me, 'Lord, Lord,' *4246*
7:24 "Therefore e who hears these words *4246*
7:26 But e who hears these words of mine *4246*
13:25 But while e was sleeping, *476*
19:11 Jesus replied, "Not e can accept this word, *4246*
19:29 And e who has left houses or brothers *4246*
25:29 For e who has will be given more, *4246*
Mk 1:37 "E is looking for you!" *4246*
2:12 This amazed e and they praised God, *4246*
3: 3 "Stand up in front of e." *3545+3836*
7:14 "Listen to me, e, and understand this. *4246*
9:49 E will be salted with fire. *4246*
11:32 for e held that John really was a prophet.) *570*
13:37 What I say to you, I say *to* e: 'Watch!' " *4246*
14:50 Then e deserted him and fled. *4246*
Lk 1:66 E who heard this wondered about it, asking, *4246*
2: 3 e went to his own town to register. *1667+4246*
2:47 E who heard him was amazed *4246*
4:15 and e praised him. *4246*
4:20 *of* e in the synagogue were fastened *4246*
5:26 E was amazed and gave praise to God. *570*
6: 8 "Get up and stand in front of e." *3545+3836*
6:30 Give *to* e who asks you, *4246*
6:40 but e who is fully trained will be *4246*
9:43 While e was marveling at all that Jesus did, *4246*
11: 4 for we also forgive e who sins against us. *4246*
11:10 For e who asks receives; *4246*
12:10 And e who speaks a word against the Son *4246*
12:41 are you telling this parable to us, or to e?" *4246*
12:48 *From* e who has been given much, *4246*
14:11 For e who exalts himself will be humbled, *4246*
14:29 e who sees it will ridicule him, *4246*
16:16 and e is forcing his way into it. *4246*
18:14 For e who exalts himself will be humbled, *4246*
19:26 "He replied, 'I tell you that *to* e who has, *4246*
20:18 E who falls on that stone will be broken *4246*
Jn 2:10 "E brings out the choice wine first and *476+4246*
3: 8 So it is with e born of the Spirit." *3836+4246*
3:15 that e who believes in him may have eternal
life. *4246*
3:20 E who does evil hates the light, *4246*
3:26 he is baptizing, and e is going to him." *4246*
4:13 "E who drinks this water will *4246*
6:40 For my Father's will is that e who looks to *4246*
6:45 E who listens to the Father and learns *4246*
8:34 e who sins is a slave to sin. *4246*
11:48 e will believe in him, *4246*
18:37 E on the side of truth listens to me." *4246*
Ac 1:19 E in Jerusalem heard about this, *4246*
2:21 And e who calls on the name of *323+4246*
2:43 E was filled with awe, *4246+6034*
8:19 that e on whom I lay my hands may receive *1569*
10:43 about him that e who believes *4246*
13:39 Through him e who believes is justified *4246*
27:44 In this way e reached land in safety. *4246*
Ro 1:16 of God for the salvation *of* e who believes: *4246*
2:10 honor and peace *for* e who does good: *4246*
10: 4 be righteousness *for* e who believes. *4246*
10:13 "E who calls on the name of the Lord will *4246*
12:18 live at peace with e. *476+4246*
13: 1 E must submit himself to *4246+6034*
13: 7 Give e what you owe him: *4246*
16:19 E has heard about your obedience, *4246*
1Co 8: 7 But not e knows this. *4246*
9:19 I make myself a slave *to* e, *4246*
9:25 E who competes in the games goes *4246*
14: 3 But e who prophesies speaks to men *3836*
14:23 and e speaks in tongues, *4246*
14:26 When you come together, e has a hymn, *1667*
14:31 so that e may be instructed and encouraged. *4246*
16:16 as these and *to* e who joins in the work, *4246*
2Co 9:13 in sharing with them and with e else. *4246*
Gal 3:10 "Cursed is e who does not continue *4246*
3:13 "Cursed is e who is hung on a tree." *4246*
Eph 3: 9 and to make plain to e the administration *4246*
6: 8 that the Lord will reward e *1667*
Php 1:13 and *to* e else that I am in chains for Christ. *4246*
2:21 For e looks out for his own interests, *4246*
Col 1:28 and teaching e with all wisdom, *476+4246*
1:28 that we may present e perfect in Christ. *476+4246*
4: 6 that you may know how to answer e. *1651+1667*
1Th 3:12 and overflow for each other and for e else, *4246*
5:14 help the weak, be patient with e. *4246*
5:15 to be kind to each other and to e else. *4246*
2Th 3: 2 for not e has faith. *4246*
1Ti 2: 1 and thanksgiving be made for e— *476+4246*
4:15 so that e may see your progress. *4246*
2Ti 1:15 You know that e in the province *4246*
2:19 and, "E who confesses the name of *4246*
2:24 instead, he must be kind to e, able to teach, *4246*
3: 9 their folly will be clear *to* e. *4246*
3:12 e who wants to live a godly life *4246*
4:16 but e deserted me. *4246*
Tit 3: 8 and profitable *for* e. *476*
3:15 E with me sends you greetings. *4246*
Heb 2: 9 the grace of God he might taste death for e. *4246*
12: 6 and he punishes e he accepts as a son." *4246*
12: 8 (and e undergoes discipline), *4246*
Jas 1:19 E should be quick to listen, *476+4246*
1Pe 2:17 Show proper respect to e: *4246*
3:15 *to* e who asks you to give the reason for *4246*
2Pe 3: 9 to perish, but e to come to repentance. *4246*
1Jn 2:29 that e who does what is right has been born *4246*
3: 3 E who has this hope *4246*
3: 4 E who sins breaks the law; *4246*
4: 7 E who loves has been born of God *4246*
5: 1 E who believes that Jesus is *4246*
5: 1 and e who loves the father loves his child *4246*
5: 4 for e born of God overcomes the world. *4246*
3Jn 1:12 Demetrius is well spoken of by e— *4246*
Jude 1:15 judge e, and to convict all the ungodly *2848+4246*
Rev 13:16 He also forced e, small and great, *4246*
22:12 *to* e according to what he has done. *1667*
22:15 and e who loves and practices falsehood. *4246*
22:18 I warn e who hears the words of *4246*

EVERYONE'S (4) [EVERY, ONE]

Ge 16:12 against everyone and e hand against him, 3972
Jos 2:11 our hearts melted and e courage failed 408+928
Lk 1:63 and to e astonishment he wrote, *4246*
Ac 1:24 Then they prayed, "Lord, you know e heart. *4246*

EVERYTHING (386) [EVERY, THING]

Ge 1:30 e that has the breath of life in it— NIH
6:17 E on earth will perish. 3972
6:22 Noah did e just as God commanded him. 3972
7:14 and every bird according to its kind, e 3972
7:22 E on dry land that had the breath of life 3972
8:19 e that moves on the earth— 3972
9: 3 E that lives and moves will be food for you. 3972
9: 3 I now give you e. 3972
12:20 with his wife and e he had. 3972
13: 1 with his wife and e he had, 3972
14:20 Then Abram gave him a tenth of e. 3972
21:22 "God is with you in e you do. 3972
24:36 and he has given him e he owns. 3972
25: 5 Abraham left e he owned to Isaac. 3972
31: 1 "Jacob has taken e our father owned 3972
31:34 through e *in* the tent but found nothing. 3972
34:28 and donkeys and e else of theirs in the city 889
34:29 taking as plunder e in the houses. 3972
39: 3 the LORD gave him success in e he did, 3972
39: 4 and he entrusted to his care e he owned. 3972
39: 5 of the LORD was on e Potiphar had, 3972
39: 6 So he left in Joseph's care e he had; 3972
39: 8 e he owns he has entrusted to my care. 3972
42:36 E is against me!" 3972+5626
45:13 in Egypt and about e you have seen. 3972
45:27 told him e Joseph had said to them, 1821+3972
46:32 and herds and e they own.' 3972
47: 1 with their flocks and herds and e they own, 3972
Ex 4:28 Then Moses told Aaron e the LORD 3972
4:30 Aaron told them e the LORD had said 1821+3972
6:29 Tell Pharaoh king of Egypt e I tell you." 3972
7: 2 You are to say e I command you, 3972
9:19 now to bring your livestock and e you have 3972
9:22 and animals and on e growing in the fields 3972
9:25 Throughout Egypt hail struck e in 3972
9:25 it beat down e growing in the fields 3972
10:12 the land and devour e growing in the fields, 3972
10:12 e left by the hail." 3972
10:15 e growing in the fields and the fruit on 3972
18: 1 heard of e God had done for Moses and 3972
18: 8 about e the LORD had done to Pharaoh 3972
18:24 to his father-in-law and did e he said. 3972
19: 8 "We will do e the LORD has said." 3972
23:13 "Be careful to do e I have said to you. 3972
24: 3 "E the LORD has said we will do."
1821+2021+3972
24: 4 then wrote down e the LORD had said. 3972
24: 7 "We will do e the LORD has said; 3972
29:35 and his sons e I have commanded you, 3972
31: 6 to make e I have commanded you: 3972
35:10 and make e the LORD has commanded: 3972
38:22 made e the LORD commanded Moses; 3972
39:32 The Israelites did e just as the LORD 3972
40: 9 and anoint the tabernacle and e in it; 3972
40:16 Moses did e just as the LORD 3972
Lev 8:10 and anointed the tabernacle and e in it, 3972
8:36 and his sons did e the LORD commanded
1821+2021+3972
11:33 e in it will be unclean, 3972
15: 9 " 'E the man sits on when riding will 3972
27:28 e so devoted is most holy to the LORD. 3972
27:30 " 'A tithe of e *from* the land, 3972
Nu 1:50 over all its furnishings and e belonging 3972
2:34 So the Israelites did e the LORD 3972
3:26 and e related to their use. 3972
3:31 the curtain, and e *related to* their use. 3972
3:36 and e *related to* their use, 3972
4:16 in charge of the entire tabernacle and e in it, 3972
4:32 all their equipment and e related 3972
9: 5 The Israelites did e just as the LORD 3972
16:30 with e that belongs to them, 3972
16:33 with e they owned; 3972
18: 7 in connection with e *at* the altar 1821+3972
18:14 "E in Israel that is devoted to 3972
18:29 the best and holiest part of e given to you.' 3972
22: 4 "This horde is going to lick up e around us, 3972
30: 2 not break his word but must do e he said. 3972
31:20 Purify every garment as well as e 3972+3998
Dt 1:18 at that time I told you e you were to do.
1821+2021+3972
5:28 E they said was good. 3972
10:14 the earth and e in it. 3972
12: 7 in e you have put your hand to, 3972
12:11 there you are to bring e I command you: 3972
12:14 and there observe e I command you. 3972
12:18 in e you put your hand to. 3972
15:10 and in e you put your hand to. 3972
15:18 your God will bless you in e you do. 3972
17:10 Be careful to do e they direct you to do. 3972
18:18 and he will tell them e I command him. 3972
20:14 the livestock and e else in the city, 3972
23: 9 keep away from e impure. 1821+3972
23:20 in e you put your hand to in 3972
26:14 I have done e you commanded me. 3972
28: 8 and on e you put your hand to. 3972
28:20 and rebuke in e you put your hand to, 3972
28:29 You will be unsuccessful in e you do; 2006
29: 9 so that you may prosper in e you do. 3972
30: 2 according to e I command you today, 3972
Jos 1: 8 that you may be careful to do e written in it. 3972
2:23 and told him e that had happened to them. 3972
4:10 in the middle of the Jordan until e the LORD
1821+2021+3972
6:24 Then they burned the whole city and e in it, 3972
22: 2 and you have obeyed me in e I commanded. 3972
23: 3 You yourselves have seen e 3972
24:31 and who had experienced e 3972+5126
Jdg 13:14 She must do e I have commanded her." 3972

Jdg 16:17 So he told her e. 3972+4213
16:18 Delilah saw that he had told her e, 3972+4213
16:18 he has told me e." 3972+4213
20:48 including the animals and e else they found. 3972
Ru 3: 6 and did e her mother-in-law told her to do. 3972
3:16 Then she told her e Boaz had done for her 3972
1Sa 2:22 about e his sons were doing to all Israel and 3972
3:12 against Eli e I spoke against his family— 3972
3:18 So Samuel told him e, 1821+2021+3972
9: 6 and e he says comes true. 3972
12: 1 to e you said to me and have set a king 3972
15: 3 attack the Amalekites and totally destroy e 3972
15: 9 e that was good. 3972
15: 9 but e that was despised 2021+3972+4856
18:14 In e he did he had great success, 3972
30:18 David recovered e the Amalekites had taken 3972
30:19 David brought e back. 2021+3972
2Sa 3:19 to Hebron to tell David e that Israel and 3972
3:25 and find out e you are doing." 3972
3:36 indeed, e the king did pleased them. 3972
6:12 the household of Obed-Edom and e he has, 3972
9: 9 "I have given your master's grandson e 3972
11:22 he arrived he told David e Joab had sent him 3972
14:20 he knows e that happens in the land." 3972
19:30 "Let him take e, 3972
21:14 and did e the king commanded. 3972
1Ki 6:18 E was cedar; no stone was to be seen. 3972
14:26 He took e, including all 3972
19: 1 Now Ahab told Jezebel e Elijah had done 3972
20: 6 They will seize e you value 3972
22:43 In e he walked in the ways of his father Asa 3972
2Ki 4:26 "E is all right," she said. NIH
5:21 "Is e all right?" NIH
5:22 "E is all right," Gehazi answered. NIH
8: 6 "Give back e that belonged to her, 3972
9:11 one of them asked him, "Is e all right? NIH
14: 3 *In* e he followed the example 3972
20:13 and e found among his treasures. 3972
20:15 "They saw e in my palace," Hezekiah said. 3972
20:17 surely come when e in your palace, 3972
21: 8 to do e I commanded them and will keep 3972
22:16 according to e written in the book the king 3972
1Ch 10:11 the inhabitants of Jabesh Gilead heard of e 3972
13:14 LORD blessed his household and e he had. 3972
16:32 let the fields be jubilant, and e in them! 3972
16:40 in accordance with e written in the Law of 3972
26:28 And e dedicated by Samuel the seer and 3972
29: 3 over and above e I have provided 3972
29:11 for e in heaven and earth is yours. 3972
29:14 E comes from you, 3972
29:19 and to do e to build the palatial structure 3972
2Ch 12: 9 took e, including the gold shields Solomon had made. 3972
21:14 sons, your wives and e *that* is yours, 3972+8214
29:16 of the LORD's temple e unclean 3972
31: 5 They brought a great amount, a tithe of e. 3972
31:21 In e that he undertook in the service 3972+5126
32:30 He succeeded in e he undertook. 3972
32:31 God left him to test him and to know e 3972
33: 8 to do e I commanded them concerning all 3972
34:16 "Your officials are doing e 3972
36:19 they burned all the palaces and destroyed e of value there. 3972+3998
Ezr 7: 6 The king had granted him e he asked, 3972
8:34 E was accounted for by number 3972
Ne 9: 6 You give life to e, 3972
13:30 the priests and the Levites of e foreign, 3972
Est 4: 7 Mordecai told him e that had happened 3972
6:13 and all his friends e that had happened 3972
9:26 Because of e written in this letter and 3972
Job 1:10 and his household and e he has? 3972
1:11 and strike e he has, 3972
1:12 "Very well, then, e he has is in your hands, 3972
28:24 for he views the ends of the earth and sees e 3972
33: 1 pay attention to e I say. 3972
41:11 E under heaven belongs to me. 3972
Ps 8: 6 you put e under his feet: 3972
24: 1 The earth is the LORD's, and e in it, 4850
33:15 who considers e they do. 3972
96:12 and e in them. 3972
98: 7 Let the sea resound, and e in it, the world, 4850
146: 6 the sea, and e in them— 3972
150: 6 Let e that has breath praise the LORD. 3972
Pr 16: 4 LORD works out e for his own ends— 3972
Ecc 1: 2 E is meaningless." 3972
2:11 e was meaningless, a chasing after the wind; 3972
3: 1 There is a time for e, 3972
3:11 He has made e beautiful in its time. 3972
3:14 I know that e God does will endure forever; 3972
3:19 E is meaningless. 3972
8: 9 as I applied my mind to e done under 3972+5126
9: 3 the evil in e that happens under the sun: 3972
10:19 but money is the answer for e. 3972
11: 8 E to come is meaningless. 3972
12: 8 "E is meaningless!" 3972
Isa 8:12 "Do not call conspiracy e that these people 3972
39: 2 the fine oil, his entire armory and e found 3972
39: 4 "They saw e in my palace," Hezekiah said. 3972
39: 6 surely come when e in your palace, 3972
Jer 8:16 They have come to devour the land and e in 4850
11: 4 I said, 'Obey me and do e I command you, 3972
21:14 a fire in your forests that will consume e 3972
26: 2 Tell them e I command you; 1821+2021+3972
26: 8 as Jeremiah finished telling all the people e 3972
35: 8 We have obeyed e our forefather Jonadab 3972
35:10 have fully obeyed e our forefather Jonadab commanded us. 3972
Jer 35:18 and have done e he ordered.' 3972
36: 8 Baruch son of Neriah did e Jeremiah 3972
36:13 Micaiah told them e he had heard Baruch read 1821+2021+3972
36:20 to the king in the courtyard and reported e to him. 1821+2021+3972
38:27 and he told them e the king had ordered 3972
42: 4 I will tell you e the LORD says 1821+2021+3972
42: 5 with e the LORD your God sends you to tell us. 1821+2021+3972
42:20 tell us e he says and we will do it.' 3972
43: 1 e the LORD had sent him to tell them— 465+1821+2021+2021+3972
44:17 We will certainly do e we said we would: 1821+2021+3972
47: 2 They will overflow the land and e in it, 4850
50:21 "Do e I have commanded you. 3972
La 2: 3 like a flaming fire that consumes e around 6017
Eze 7:14 they blow the trumpet and get e ready, 3972
11:25 the exiles e the LORD had shown me. 1821+3972
12:19 be stripped of e in it because of the violence 4850
23:29 and take away e you have worked for. 3972
30:12 the land and e in it. 4850
32:15 and strip the land of e in it, 4850
40: 4 and pay attention to e I am going 3972
40: 4 Tell the house of Israel e you see." 3972
41:16 e beyond and including NIH
44: 5 and give attention to e I tell you 3972
44:29 and e in Israel devoted to 3972
47: 9 so where the river flows e will live. 3972
Da 2:40 for iron breaks and smashes e— 10353
4:37 e he does is right and all his ways are just. 10353
8:12 It prospered in e it did, NIH
9:14 for the LORD our God is righteous in e he does; 3972+5126
Am 6: 8 I will deliver up the city and e in it." 4850
Zep 1: 2 "I will sweep away e from the face of 3972
Mt 5:18 from the Law until e is accomplished. *4246*
7:12 So in e, do to others *4246*
13:41 and they will weed out of his kingdom e *4246*
13:46 and sold e he had and bought it. *4012+4246*
17:12 but have done to him e they wished. *4012*
18:26 he begged, 'and I will pay back e.' *4246*
18:31 and told their master e that had happened. *4246*
19:27 "We have left e to follow you! *4246*
22: 4 and e is ready. *4246*
23: 3 you must obey them and do e they tell you. *1569+4012+4246*
23: 5 "E they do is done for men to see: *4246*
23:20 by the altar swears by it and by e on it. *4246*
23:27 of dead men's bones and e unclean. *4246*
28:11 the city and reported to the chief priests e *570*
28:20 to obey e I have commanded you. *4012+4246*
Mk 4:11 to those on the outside e is said in parables *3836+4246*
4:34 with his own disciples, he explained e. *4246*
7:37 "He has done e well," they said. *4246*
8:25 his sight was restored, and he saw e clearly. *570*
9:13 and they have done to him e they wished, *4012*
9:23 "E is possible for him who believes." *4246*
10:21 "Go, sell e you have and give to the poor, *4012*
10:28 "We have left e to follow you!" *4246*
11:11 He looked around at e, *4246*
12:44 but she, out of her poverty, put in e— *4246*
13:23 I have told you e ahead of time. *4246*
14:36 Father," he said, "e is possible for you. *4246*
Lk 1: 3 since I myself have carefully investigated e *4246*
2:39 When Joseph and Mary had done e required *4246*
5:11 left e and followed him. *4246*
5:28 and Levi got up, left e and followed him. *4246*
11:41 and e will be clean for you. *4246*
14:17 'Come, for e is now ready.' *NIG*
14:33 not give up e he has cannot be my disciple. *4246*
15:14 After he had spent e, *4246*
15:31 and e I have is yours. *4246*
17:10 when you have done e you were told to do, *4246*
18:22 Sell e you have and give to the poor, *4012+4246*
18:31 and e that is written by the prophets about *4246*
24:14 with each other about e that had happened. *4246*
24:44 E must be fulfilled that is written about me *4246*
Jn 3:35 The Father loves the Son and has placed e *4246*
4:25 When he comes, he will explain e to us." *570*
4:29 see a man who told me e I ever did. *4246*
4:39 "He told me e I ever did." *4246*
14:26 and will remind you of e I have said to you. *4246*
15:15 for e that I learned from my Father *4246*
17: 7 e you have given me comes from you. *4012+4246*
Ac 2:44 All the believers were together and had e in common. *570*
3:21 until the time comes for God to restore e, *4246*
3:22 you must listen to e he tells you. *323+4012+4246*
4:24 the earth and the sea, and e in them. *4246*
4:32 but they shared e they had. *570*
10: 8 He told them e that had happened *570*
10:33 to listen to e the Lord has commanded you *4246*
10:39 *of* e he did in the country of the Jews and *4246*
11: 4 and explained e to them precisely *NIG*
12:11 from Herod's clutches and from e *4246*
13:10 of the devil and an enemy *of* e that is right! *4246*
13:22 he will do e I want him to do.' *4246*
13:39 from e you could not be justified from by *4246*
14:15 who made heaven and earth and sea and e *4246*
15: 4 to whom they reported e God had done *4012*
17:24 "The God who made the world and e in it is *4246*
17:25 gives all men life and breath and e else. *4246*
20:35 In e I did, I showed you that by this kind *4246*
24:14 I believe e that agrees with the Law and *4246*
Ro 14: 2 One man's faith allows him to eat e, *4246*
14: 3 The man who eats e must not look down *NIG*
14: 3 and the man who does not eat e must *NIG*
14:23 and e that does not come from faith is sin. *4246*
15: 4 For e that was written in the *4012*
1Co 6:12 "E is permissible for me"— *4246*
6:12 but not e is beneficial. *4246*
6:12 "E is permissible for me"— *4246*
10:23 "E is permissible"— *4246*
10:23 but not e is beneficial. *4246*
10:23 "E is permissible"— *4246*
10:23 but not e is constructive. *4246*
10:26 for, "The earth is the Lord's, and e in it." *4445*
11: 2 for remembering me in e and for holding to *4246*
11:12 But e comes from God. *3836+4246*
14:40 But e should be done in a fitting *4246*
15:27 For he "has put e under his feet." *4246*
15:27 it says that "e" has been put under him, *4246*
15:27 who put e under Christ. *3836+4246*
15:28 be made subject to him who put e *3836+4246*
16:14 Do e in love. *4246*
2Co 2: 9 the test and be obedient in e. *4246*
6:10 having nothing, and yet possessing e. *4246*
7: 1 from e that contaminates body and spirit, *4246*
7:14 But just as e we said to you was true, *4246*
8: 7 But just as you excel in e— *4246*
11:28 Besides e else, I face daily the pressure of my concern *3836+4211+6006*
12:15 spend for you e I have and expend *1682*
12:19 and e we do, dear friends, *4246*
Gal 3:10 not continue to do e written in the Book of *4246*
Eph 1:11 of him who works out e in conformity with *4246*
1:22 and appointed him to be head over e for *4246*
1:23 of him who fills e in every way. *3836+4246*
5:13 But e exposed by the light becomes visible, *4246*
5:14 for it is light that makes e visible. *4246*
5:20 to God the Father for e, *4246*
5:24 wives should submit to their husbands in e. *4246*
6:13 and after you have done e, to stand. *570*
6:21 will tell you e, so that you also may know *4246*
Php 2:14 Do e without complaining or arguing, *4246*
3: 8 I consider e a loss compared to *4246*
3:21 by the power that enables him to bring e under his control, *3836+4246*
4: 6 Do not be anxious about anything, but in e, *4246*
4:13 I can do e through him who gives me strength. *4246*
Col 1:18 so that in e he might have the supremacy. *4246*
3:20 Children, obey your parents in e, *4246*
3:22 Slaves, obey your earthly masters in e; *4246*
4: 9 They will tell you e that is happening here. *4246*
1Th 5:21 Test e. Hold on to the good. *4246*
2Th 2: 4 over e that is called God or is worshiped, *4246*
1Ti 3:11 but temperate and trustworthy in e. *4246*
4: 4 For e God created is good, *4246*
6:13 In the sight of God, who gives life to e, *4246*
6:17 who richly provides us with e *4246*
2Ti 2:10 Therefore I endure e for the sake of *4246*
Tit 2: 7 In e set them an example *4246*
2: 9 to be subject to their masters in e, *4246*
3:13 Do e you can to help Zenas the lawyer *5081*
3:13 and see that they have e they need. *3309+3594*
Heb 2: 8 and put e under his feet." *4246*
2: 8 In putting e under him, *3836+4246*
2: 8 at present we do not see e subject to him. *4246*
2:10 for whom and through whom e exists, *3836+4246*
3: 4 but God is the builder of e. *4246*
4:13 E is uncovered and laid bare before the eyes *4246*
7: 2 and Abraham gave him a tenth of e. *4246*
8: 5 "See to it that you make e according to *4246*
9: 6 When e had been arranged like this, *4047*
9:21 the tabernacle and e used in its ceremonies. *4246*
9:22 the law requires that nearly e be cleansed *4246*
12: 1 let us throw off e that hinders and the sin *4246*
13:21 equip you with e good for doing his will, *4246*
2Pe 1: 3 His divine power has given us e we need *4246*
3: 4 e goes on as it has since the beginning *4246*
3:10 and the earth and e in it will be laid bare. *NIG*
3:11 Since e will be destroyed in this way, *4246*
1Jn 2:16 For e in the world— *4246*
3:20 and he knows e. *4246*
Rev 1: 2 who testifies to e he saw— *4012*
21: 5 "I am making e new!" *4246*

EVERYWHERE (25) [EVERY, WHERE]

Ge 20:13 E we go, say of me, "He is my brother."'" 2021+3972+5226
Ex 7:19 Blood will be e in Egypt, 3972
7:21 Blood was e in Egypt. 3972
Lev 25: 9 the trumpet sounded e on the tenth day of NIH
1Ch 18: 6 LORD gave David victory e he went. 928+3972
18:13 LORD gave David victory e he went. 928+3972
Ps 103:22 all his works e in his dominion. 3972+5226
Pr 15: 3 The eyes of the LORD are e, 928+3972+5226
24:31 thorns had come up e, 3972
Jer 25:33 by the LORD will be e— NIH
Eze 16:33 to you from e for your illicit favors. 6017
Am 8: 3 Many, many bodies—flung e! 3972+5226
Mk 1:45 Yet the people still came to him from e. *4119*
16:20 Then the disciples went out and preached e, *4116*
Lk 9: 6 preaching the gospel and healing people e. *4116*
Ac 8:13 And *he* followed Philip e, *4674*
17:30 now he commands all people e to repent. *4116*
21:28 This is the man who teaches all men e *4114*
24: 3 E and in every way, most excellent Felix, *4116*
28:22 that people e are talking against this sect." *4116*

1Co 1: 2 all those e who call on the name *1877+4246+5536*
4: 17 with what I teach e in every church. *4116*
2Co 2: 14 through us spreads e the fragrance of the knowledge of him. *1877+4246+5536*
1Th 1: 8 your faith in God has become known **e.** *1877+4246+5536*
1Ti 2: 8 I want men e to lift up holy hands in prayer, *4246+5536*

EVI (2)

Nu 31: 8 Among their victims were **E,** Rekem, Zur, 209
Jos 13: 21 **E,** Rekem, Zur, Hur and Reba— 209

EVIDENCE (8) [EVIDENT]

Ex 22: 13 the remains as **e** and he will not be required 6332
1Sa 12: 7 because *I am going to* **confront** you **with e** 9149
Mt 26: 59 for **false e** against Jesus so *6019*
Mk 14: 55 and the whole Sanhedrin were looking for **e** *3456*
Jn 14: 11 at least believe **on the e of** the miracles *1328*
Ac 11: 23 When he arrived and saw the **e** of the grace *NIG*
2Th 1: 5 All this is **e** that God's judgment is right, *1891*
Jas 2: 20 do you want **e** that faith without works is useless? *1182*

EVIDENT (3) [EVIDENCE, EVIDENTLY]

1Ch 4: 41 as is **e** to this day. NIH
Gal 2: 17 *it becomes* **e** that we ourselves are sinners, *2351*
Php 4: 5 *Let* your gentleness *be* **e** to all. *1182*

EVIDENTLY (1) [EVIDENT]

Gal 1: 7 **E** some people are throwing you *1623+3590*

EVIL (454) [EVILDOER, EVILDOERS, EVILS]

Ge 2: 9 the tree of the knowledge of good and **e,** 8273
2: 17 the tree of the knowledge of good and **e,** 8273
3: 5 knowing good and **e."** 8273
3: 22 knowing good and **e.** 8273
6: 5 of the thoughts of his heart was only **e** all 8273
8: 21 though every inclination of his heart is **e** 8273
44: 4 'Why have you repaid good with **e?** 8288
Ex 10: 10 Clearly you are bent on **e.** 8288
32: 12 with **e intent** that he brought them out, 8288
32: 22 how prone these people are to **e.** 8273
Lev 5: 4 whether good or **e—** 8317
Nu 32: 13 of those who had done **e** 8273
Dt 1: 35 "Not a man of this **e** generation shall see 8273
4: 25 doing **e** in the eyes of the LORD your God 8273
9: 18 doing what was **e** in the LORD's sight and 8273
13: 5 You must purge the **e** from among you. 8273
13: 11 among you will do such an **e** thing again. 8273
17: 2 the LORD gives you is found doing **e** in 8273
17: 5 or woman who has done this **e** deed 8273
17: 7 You must purge the **e** from among you. 8273
17: 12 You must purge the **e** from Israel. 8273
19: 19 You must purge the **e** from among you. 8273
19: 20 and never again will such an **e** thing 8273
21: 21 You must purge the **e** from among you. 8273
22: 21 You must purge the **e** from among you. 8273
22: 22 You must purge the **e** from Israel. 8273
22: 24 You must purge the **e** from among you. 8273
24: 7 You must purge the **e** from among you. 8273
28: 20 of the **e** you have done in forsaking him. 8278
31: 29 upon you because you will do **e** in the sight 8273
Jos 23: 15 on you all the **e** he has threatened, 8273
Jdg 2: 11 Then the Israelites did **e** in the eyes of 8273
2: 19 They refused to give up their **e practices** 5095
3: 7 The Israelites did **e** in the eyes of 8273
3: 12 Once again the Israelites did **e** in the eyes 8273
3: 12 and because they did this **e** 8273
4: 1 the Israelites once again did **e** in the eyes of 8273
6: 1 Again the Israelites did **e** in the eyes of 8273
9: 23 God sent an **e** spirit between Abimelech 8273
10: 6 Again the Israelites did **e** in the eyes of 8273
13: 1 Again the Israelites did **e** in the eyes of 8273
20: 13 to death and purge the **e** from Israel." 8288
1Sa 12: 17 an **e thing** you did in the eyes of the LORD 8288
12: 19 for we have added to all our other sins the **e** 8288
12: 20 "You have done all this **e;** 8288
12: 25 Yet if *you* **persist in doing e,** 8317+8317
15: 19 on the plunder and do **e** in the eyes of 8273
15: 23 and arrogance like the **e** of idolatry. 224
16: 14 an **e** spirit from the LORD tormented him. 8273
16: 15 an **e** spirit from God is tormenting you. 8273
16: 16 the **e** spirit from God comes upon you, 8273
16: 23 and the **e** spirit would leave him. 8273
18: 10 an **e** spirit from God came forcefully 8273
19: 9 an **e** spirit from the LORD came upon Saul 8273
24: 13 'From evildoers come **e deeds,'** 8400
25: 21 He has paid me back **e** for good. 8288
30: 22 But all the **e** men and troublemakers 8273
2Sa 3: 39 the evildoer according to his **e deeds!"** 8288
12: 9 the LORD by doing what is **e** in his eyes? 8273
14: 17 an angel of God in discerning good and **e.** 8273
22: 22 *I have* not **done e** by turning from my God. 8399
23: 6 **e men** are all to be cast aside like thorns, 1175
1Ki 1: 52 but if **e** is found in him, he will die." 8288
11: 6 Solomon did **e** in the eyes of the LORD; 8273
13: 33 this, Jeroboam did not change his **e** ways, 8273
14: 9 *You have* done more **e** than all who lived 8317
14: 22 Judah did **e** in the eyes of the LORD. 8273
15: 26 He did **e** in the eyes of the LORD, 8273
15: 34 He did **e** in the eyes of the LORD, 8273
1Ki 16: 7 because of all the **e** he had done in the eyes 8288
16: 19 doing **e** in the eyes of the LORD 8273
16: 25 But Omri did **e** in the eyes of the LORD 8273
16: 30 Ahab son of Omri did more **e** in the eyes of 8273
21: 20 "because you have sold yourself to do **e** in 8273
21: 25 who sold himself to do **e** in the eyes of 8273
22: 52 He did **e** in the eyes of the LORD, 8273
2Ki 3: 2 He did **e** in the eyes of the LORD, 8273
8: 18 He did **e** in the eyes of the LORD. 8273
8: 27 the ways of the house of Ahab and did **e** in 8273
13: 2 He did **e** in the eyes of the LORD 8273
13: 11 He did **e** in the eyes of the LORD and did 8273
14: 24 He did **e** in the eyes of the LORD and did 8273
15: 9 He did **e** in the eyes of the LORD, 8273
15: 18 He did **e** in the eyes of the LORD. 8273
15: 24 Pekahiah did **e** in the eyes of the LORD. 8273
15: 28 He did **e** in the eyes of the LORD. 8273
17: 2 He did **e** in the eyes of the LORD, 8273
17: 13 "Turn from your **e** ways. 8273
17: 17 and sorcery and sold themselves to do **e** in 8273
21: 2 He did **e** in the eyes of the LORD, 8273
21: 6 He did much **e** in the eyes of the LORD, 8273
21: 9 so that they did more **e** than the nations 8273
21: 11 *He has* **done** more **e** than 8317
21: 15 because they have done **e** in my eyes 8273
21: 16 so that they did **e** in the eyes of the LORD. 8273
21: 20 He did **e** in the eyes of the LORD, 8273
23: 32 He did **e** in the eyes of the LORD, 8273
23: 37 And he did **e** in the eyes of the LORD, 8273
24: 9 He did **e** in the eyes of the LORD, 8273
24: 19 He did **e** in the eyes of the LORD, 8273
1Ch 21: 7 This command *was* also **e** in the sight 8317
2Ch 12: 14 He did **e** because he had not set his heart 8273
21: 6 He did **e** in the eyes of the LORD. 8273
22: 4 He did **e** in the eyes of the LORD, 8273
29: 6 they did **e** in the eyes of 8273
33: 2 He did **e** in the eyes of the LORD, 8273
33: 6 He did much **e** in the eyes of the LORD, 8273
33: 9 so that they did more **e** than the nations 8273
33: 22 He did **e** in the eyes of the LORD, 8273
36: 5 He did **e** in the eyes of the LORD his God. 8273
36: 9 He did **e** in the eyes of the LORD. 8273
36: 12 He did **e** in the eyes of the LORD his God 8273
Ezr 9: 13 a result of our **e** deeds and our great guilt, 8273
Ne 9: 28 they again did what was **e** in your sight. 8273
9: 35 not serve you or turn from their **e** ways. 8273
13: 7 about the **e thing** Eliashib had done 8288
Est 8: 3 an end to the **e** plan of Haman the Agagite, 8288
9: 25 the **e** scheme Haman had devised against 8288
Job 1: 1 he feared God and shunned **e.** 8273
1: 8 a man who fears God and shuns **e."** 8273
2: 3 a man who fears God and shuns **e.** 8273
4: 8 those who plow **e** and those who sow 224
11: 11 and when he sees **e,** does he not take note? 224
11: 14 that is in your hand and allow no **e** to dwell 6406
15: 16 who drinks up **e** like water! 6406
15: 35 They conceive trouble and give birth to **e;** 224
16: 11 to **e men** and thrown me into the clutches of 6397
18: 21 Surely such is the dwelling of an **e man;** 6405
20: 12 "Though **e** is sweet in his mouth 8288
21: 30 **e** *man* is spared from the day of calamity, 8273
22: 15 to the old path that **e** men have trod? 224
24: 20 **e** *men* are no longer remembered 6406
28: 28 and to shun **e** is understanding.' " 8273
30: 26 Yet when I hoped for good, **e** came; 8273
34: 10 Far be it from God to do **e,** 8400
36: 10 and commands them to repent of their **e.** 224
36: 21 Beware of turning to **e,** 224
Ps 5: 4 You are not a God who takes pleasure in **e;** 8400
6: 8 Away from me, all you who do **e,** 224
7: 4 if I have done **e** to him who is at peace 8273
7: 14 with **e** and conceives trouble gives birth 224
10: 7 trouble and **e** are under his tongue. 224
10: 15 Break the arm of the wicked and **e** *man;* 8273
18: 21 *I have* not **done e** by turning from my God. 8399
21: 11 Though they plot **e** against you 8288
22: 16 a band of **e** *men* has encircled me, 8317
23: 4 I will fear no **e,** for you are with me; 8273
27: 2 When **e** *men* advance against me 8317
28: 3 with those who do **e,** 224
28: 4 for their deeds and for their **e** work; 8278
34: 13 from **e** and your lips from speaking lies. 8273
34: 14 Turn from **e** and do good; 8273
34: 16 of the LORD is against those who do **e,** 8273
34: 21 **E** will slay the wicked; 8288
35: 12 They repay me **e** for good 8288
36: 4 Even on his bed he plots **e;** 224
37: 1 Do not fret because of **e** *men* or be envious 8317
37: 8 it **leads** only **to e.** 8317
37: 9 For **e** *men* will be cut off, 8317
37: 27 Turn from **e** and do good; 8273
38: 20 who repay my good with **e** slander me 8288
49: 5 Why should I fear when **e** days come, 8273
50: 19 for **e** and harness your tongue to deceit. 8288
51: 4 have I sinned and done what is **e** 8273
52: 1 Why do you boast of **e,** you mighty man? 8288
52: 3 You love **e** rather than good, 8273
54: 5 Let **e** recoil on those who slander me; 8273
55: 15 for **e** finds lodging among them. 8288
64: 5 They encourage each other in **e** plans, 8273
71: 4 from the grasp of **e** and cruel men. 6401
73: 7 the **e conceits** *of* their minds know no limits. 5381
97: 10 Let those who love the LORD hate **e,** 8273
101: 4 I will have nothing to do with **e.** 8273
109: 5 They repay me **e** for good, 8288
109: 6 Appoint an **e** *man* to oppose him; 8401
109: 20 to those who speak **e** of me. 8273
Ps 119: 101 I have kept my feet from every **e** path so 8273
125: 3 the righteous might use their hands to do **e.** 6406
139: 20 They speak of you with **e intent;** 4659
140: 1 Rescue me, O LORD, from **e** men; 8273
140: 2 who devise **e** plans in their hearts and stir 8273
141: 4 Let not my heart be drawn to what is **e,** 8273
Pr 2: 14 and rejoice in the perverseness of **e,** 8273
3: 7 fear the LORD and shun **e.** 8273
4: 14 of the wicked or walk in the way of **e** *men.* 8273
4: 16 For they cannot sleep till *they* **do e;** 8317
4: 27 keep your foot from **e.** 8273
5: 22 The **e deeds** *of* a wicked man ensnare him; 6411
6: 14 who plots **e** with deceit in his heart— 8273
6: 18 feet that are quick to rush into **e,** 8288
8: 13 To fear the LORD is to hate **e;** 8273
8: 13 **e** behavior and perverse speech. 8273
10: 23 A fool finds pleasure in **e** conduct, 2365
10: 29 but it is the ruin of those who do **e.** 224
11: 6 but the unfaithful are trapped by **e desires.** 2094
11: 19 but he who pursues **e** goes to his death. 8288
11: 27 but **e** comes to him who searches for it. 8288
12: 12 The wicked desire the plunder of **e** *men,* 8273
12: 13 An **e** *man* is trapped by his sinful talk, 8273
12: 20 in the hearts of those who plot **e,** 8273
13: 19 but fools detest turning from **e.** 8273
14: 16 A wise man fears the LORD and shuns **e,** 8273
14: 19 **E** *men* will bow down in the presence of 8273
14: 22 Do not those who plot **e** go astray? 8273
15: 28 but the mouth of the wicked gushes **e.** 8288
16: 6 the fear of the LORD a man avoids **e.** 8273
16: 17 The highway of the upright avoids **e;** 8273
16: 27 A scoundrel plots **e,** 8288
16: 30 he who purses his lips is bent on **e.** 8288
17: 4 A wicked man listens to **e** lips; 224
17: 11 An **e** *man* is bent only on rebellion; 8273
17: 13 If a man pays back **e** for good, 8288
17: 13 **e** will never leave his house. 8288
19: 28 and the mouth of the wicked gulps down **e.** 224
20: 8 he winnows out all **e** with his eyes. 8273
20: 30 Blows and wounds cleanse away **e,** 8273
21: 10 The wicked man craves **e;** 8273
21: 27 much more so when brought with **e intent!** 2365
24: 8 He who plots **e** will be known as a schemer. 8317
24: 19 Do not fret because of **e** *men* or be envious 8317
24: 20 for the **e** *man* has no future hope, 8273
26: 23 are fervent lips with an **e** heart. 8273
28: 5 **E** men do not understand justice, 8273
28: 10 along an **e** path will fall into his own trap, 8273
29: 6 An **e** man is snared by his own sin, 8273
30: 32 or if *you have* **planned e,** 2372
Ecc 4: 3 who has not seen the **e** that is done under 8273
5: 13 I have seen a grievous **e** under the sun: 8288
5: 16 This too is a grievous **e:** 8288
6: 1 I have seen another **e** under the sun, 8288
6: 2 This is meaningless, a grievous **e.** 2716
9: 3 This is the **e** in everything that happens 8273
9: 3 of **e** and there is madness in their hearts 8273
9: 12 in a snare, so men are trapped by **e** times 8288
10: 5 There is an **e** I have seen under the sun, 8288
12: 14 whether it is good or **e.** 8273
Isa 1: 13 I cannot bear your **e** assemblies. 224
1: 16 Take your **e** deeds out of my sight! 8278
5: 20 to those who call **e** good and good evil, 8273
5: 20 to those who call evil good and good **e,** 8273
13: 11 I will punish the world for its **e,** 8288
26: 10 land of uprightness *they go on* **doing e** 6401
29: 20 and all who have an eye for **e** will 224
32: 6 fool speaks folly, his mind is busy with **e:** 224
32: 7 he makes up **e schemes** to destroy the poor 2365
33: 15 shuts his eyes against contemplating **e—** 8273
55: 7 and the **e** man his thoughts. 224
56: 2 and keeps his hand from doing any **e."** 8273
57: 1 to be spared from **e.** 8288
59: 4 they conceive trouble and give birth to **e.** 224
59: 6 Their deeds are **e** deeds, 224
59: 7 Their thoughts are **e** thoughts; 224
59: 15 and whoever shuns **e** becomes a prey. 8273
65: 12 You did **e** in my sight 8273
66: 4 They did **e** in my sight 8273
Jer 2: 19 and realize how **e** and bitter it is for you 8273
3: 5 but you do *all* the **e** you can." 8273
3: 17 the stubbornness of their **e** hearts. 8273
4: 4 like fire because of the **e** you have done— 8278
4: 14 wash the **e** from your heart and be saved. 8288
4: 22 They are skilled in **doing e;** 8317
5: 28 Their **e** deeds have no limit; 8273
7: 24 the stubborn inclinations of their **e** hearts. 8273
7: 26 and **did** more **e** than their forefathers.' 8317
7: 30 " 'The people of Judah have done **e** 8273
8: 3 of this **e** nation will prefer death to life, 8273
11: 8 the stubbornness of their **e** hearts. 8273
11: 15 doing in my temple as she works out her **e schemes** 4659
11: 17 of Judah have done **e** and provoked me 8288
13: 23 Neither can you do good who are accustomed to **doing e.** 8317
16: 12 the stubbornness of his **e** heart instead 8273
18: 8 and if that nation I warned repents of its **e,** 8288
18: 10 it does **e** in my sight and does not obey me, 8273
18: 11 So turn from your **e** ways, each one of you, 8273
18: 12 the stubbornness of his **e** heart.' " 8273
18: 20 Should good be repaid with **e?** 8288
21: 12 like fire because of the **e** you have done— 8278
23: 2 on you for the **e** you have done," 8278
23: 10 an **e** course and use their power unjustly. 8288
23: 22 from their **e** ways and from their evil deeds. 8273
23: 22 from their evil ways and from their **e** deeds. 8278

Jer 25: 5 from your e ways and your evil practices, 8273
25: 5 from your evil ways and your e practices, 8278
26: 3 and each will turn from his e way. 8273
26: 3 because of the e they have done. 8278
32:30 of Israel and Judah have done nothing but e 8273
32:32 by all the e they have done— 8288
44: 3 because of the e they have done. 8288
52: 2 He did e in the eyes of the LORD, 8273
Eze 3:18 to dissuade him from his e ways in order 8401
3:19 or from his e ways, he will die for his sin; 8401
3:20 from his righteousness and does e, 6404
6: 9 for the e they have done and 8288
11: 2 these are the men who are plotting e 224
13:22 from their e ways and so save their lives, 8273
20:43 for all the e you have done. 8288
20:44 to your e ways and your corrupt practices, 8288
30:12 of the Nile and sell the land to e *men;* 8273
33:11 Turn from your e ways! 8273
33:13 in his righteousness and does e, none of 6404
33:13 he will die for the e he has done. 6404
33:15 and does no e, he will surely live; 6404
33:18 from his righteousness and does e, 6404
36:31 Then you will remember your e ways 8273
38:10 and you will devise an e scheme. 8273
Da 11:27 The two kings, with their hearts bent on e, 5334
Hos 7: 2 not realize that I remember all their e **deeds.** 8288
7:15 but they plot e against me. 8273
10:13 planted wickedness, you have reaped e, 6406
Am 5:13 quiet in such times, for the times are e. 8273
5:14 Seek good, not e, that you may live. 8273
5:15 Hate e, love good; 8273
6: 3 You put off the e day and bring near a reign 8273
9: 4 I will fix my eyes upon them for e and not 8288
Jnh 3: 8 up their e ways and their violence. 8273
3:10 and how they turned from their e ways, 8273
Mic 2: 1 to those who plot e on their beds! 8273
3: 2 you who hate good and love e; 8273
3: 4 from them because of the e they have done. 8317
7: 3 Both hands are skilled in doing e; 8273
Na 1:11 has one come forth who plots e against 8288
Hab 1:13 Your eyes are too pure to look on e; 8273
Zec 1: 4 from your e ways and your evil practices.' 8273
1: 4 from your evil ways and your e practices.' 8273
7:10 In your hearts do not think e *of* each other.' 8288
8:17 do not plot e against your neighbor, 8288
Mal 2:17 "All who do e are good in the eyes of 8273
Mt 5:11 persecute you and falsely say all kinds of e 4505
5:37 beyond this comes from the e one. 4505
5:39 But I tell you, Do not resist an e *person.* 4505
5:45 He causes his sun to rise on the e and 4505
6:13 but deliver us from the e *one.'* 4505
7:11 If you, then, though you are e, 4505
9: 4 "Why do you entertain e thoughts 4505
10: 1 to drive out e spirits and 176
12:34 how can you who are e say anything good? 4505
12:35 and the e man brings evil things out of 4505
12:35 and the evil man brings e *things* out of 4505
12:35 of the e stored up in him. 4505
12:43 "When an e spirit comes out of a man, 176
13:19 the e *one* comes and snatches away 4505
13:38 The weeds are the sons *of* the e *one,* 4505
13:41 that causes sin and all who do e. 490
15:19 For out of the heart come e thoughts, 4505
22:18 But Jesus, knowing their e intent, said, 4504
Mk 1:23 by an e spirit cried out, 176
1:26 The e spirit shook the man violently 176
1:27 He even gives orders *to* e spirits 176
3: 4 to do good or *to* **do e,** 2803
3:11 Whenever the e spirits saw him, 176
3:30 "He has an e spirit." 176
5: 2 a man with an e spirit came from the tombs 176
5: 8 "Come out of this man, *you* e spirit!" 176
5:13 e spirits came out and went into the pigs. 176
6: 7 and gave them authority over e spirits. 176
7:21 come e thoughts, sexual immorality, theft, 2805
7:25 by an e spirit came and fell at his feet. 176
9:25 he rebuked the e spirit. 176
Lk 3:19 and all the other e *things* he had done, 4505
4:33 a man possessed by a demon, an e spirit. 176
4:36 and power he gives orders *to* e spirits 176
6: 9 to do good or *to* **do e,** 2803
6:18 Those troubled by e spirits were cured, 176
6:22 and insult you and reject your name as e, 4505
6:45 and the e *man* brings evil things out of 4505
6:45 and the evil man brings e things out of 4505
6:45 of the e stored up in his heart. 4505
7:21 sicknesses and e spirits, 4505
8: 2 of e spirits and diseases: 4505
8:29 For Jesus had commanded the e spirit 176
9:42 But Jesus rebuked the e spirit, 176
11:13 If you then, though you are e, 4505
11:24 "When an e spirit comes out of a man, 176
Jn 3:19 of light because their deeds were e. 4505
3:20 Everyone who does e hates the light, 5765
5:29 to live, and those who have done e will rise 5765
7: 7 because I testify that what it does is e. 4505
17:15 but that you protect them from the e *one.* 4505
Ac 5:16 and those tormented by e spirits, 176
8: 7 With shrieks, e spirits came out of many, 176
19:12 and the e spirits left them. 4505
19:13 around **driving out** e **spirits** tried to invoke 2020
19:15 [One day] the e spirit answered them, 4505
19:16 Then the man who had the e spirit jumped 4505
19:18 and openly confessed their e deeds. *NIG*
23: 5 'Do not speak e about the ruler 2809
Ro 1:29 e, greed and depravity. 4504
1:30 they invent ways of doing e; 2805

Ro 2: 8 and who reject the truth and follow e, *94*
2: 9 for every human being who does e: *2805*
3: 8 "Let us do e that good may result"? *2805*
6:12 so that you obey its e **desires.** *2123*
7:19 no, the e I do not want to do— *2805*
7:21 I want to do good, e is right there with me. *2805*
12: 9 Hate what is e; cling to what is good. *4505*
12:17 Do not repay anyone e for evil. *2805*
12:17 Do not repay anyone evil for e. *2805*
12:21 Do not be overcome by e, *2805*
12:21 but overcome e with good. *2805*
14:16 *to be* **spoken of as** e. *1059*
16:19 and innocent about what is e. *2805*
1Co 10: 6 from setting our hearts on e *things* *2805*
13: 6 Love does not delight in e but rejoices with *94*
14:20 *In regard to* e be infants, *2798*
Gal 1: 4 to rescue us from the present e age, *4505*
Eph 5:16 because the days are e. *4505*
6:12 and against the spiritual forces *of* e in *4504*
6:13 so that when the day *of* e comes, *4505*
6:16 the flaming arrows *of* the **e one.** *4505*
Php 3: 2 those men who do e, *2805*
Col 1:21 in your minds because of your e behavior. *4505*
3: 5 lust, e desires and greed, which is idolatry. *2805*
1Th 5:22 Avoid every kind *of* e. *4505*
2Th 2:10 *of* e that deceives those who are perishing. *94*
3: 2 be delivered from wicked and e men, *4505*
3: 3 and protect you from the e *one.* *4505*
1Ti 6: 4 in envy, strife, malicious talk, e suspicions *4505*
6:10 love of money is a root of all kinds *of* e. *2805*
2Ti 2:22 Flee the e **desires** of youth, *2123*
3: 6 and are swayed by all kinds of e **desires,** *2123*
3:13 while e men and impostors will go *4505*
4:18 from every e attack *4505*
Tit 1:12 "Cretans are always liars, e brutes, *2805*
Heb 5:14 to distinguish good from e. *2805*
Jas 1:13 For God cannot be tempted *by* e, *2805*
1:14 is tempted when, by his own e **desire,** *2123*
1:21 the e that is so prevalent and humbly accept *2798*
2: 4 and become judges *with* e thoughts? *4505*
3: 6 a world *of* e among the parts of the body. *94*
3: 8 It is a restless e, full of deadly poison. *2805*
3:16 there you find disorder and every e practice. *5765*
4:16 All such boasting is e. *4505*
1Pe 1:14 do not conform *to* the e **desires** you had *2123*
2:16 do not use your freedom as a cover-up *for* e; *2798*
3: 9 not repay e with evil or insult with insult, *2805*
3: 9 not repay evil with e or insult with insult, *2805*
3:10 from e and his lips from deceitful speech. *2805*
3:11 He must turn from e and do good; *2805*
3:12 face of the Lord is against those who do e." *2805*
3:17 to suffer for doing good than *for* **doing** e. *2803*
4: 2 of his earthly life *for* e human **desires,** *2123*
2Pe 1: 4 in the world caused by e **desires.** *2123*
3: 3 scoffing and following their own e **desires.** *2123*
1Jn 2:13 because you have overcome the e *one.* *4505*
2:14 and you have overcome the e *one.* *4505*
3:12 to the e *one* and murdered his brother. *4505*
3:12 Because his own actions were e *4505*
5:18 and the e *one* cannot harm him. *4505*
5:19 under the control of the e *one.* *4505*
3Jn 1:11 do not imitate what is e but what is good. *2805*
1:11 Anyone who **does what is** e has *2803*
Jude 1:16 they follow their own e **desires;** *2123*
Rev 16:13 I saw three e spirits that looked like frogs; *176*
18: 2 for demons and a haunt *for* every e spirit, *176*

EVIL-MERODACH (2)

2Ki 25:27 in the year E became king of Babylon, 213
Jer 52:31 in the year E became king of Babylon, 213

EVILDOER (3) [EVIL]

2Sa 3:39 May the LORD repay the e according 6913+8288
Ps 101: 8 I will cut off every e from the city of 224+7188
Mal 4: 1 arrogant and every e will be stubble, 6913+8402

EVILDOERS (29) [EVIL]

1Sa 24:13 'From e come evil deeds,' 8401
Job 8:20 or strengthen the hands of e. 8317
34: 8 He keeps company with e; 224+7188
34:22 no deep shadow, where e can hide. 224+7188
Ps 14: 4 Will e never learn— 224+7188
14: 6 You e frustrate the plans of the poor, NIH
26: 5 I abhor the assembly of e and refuse to sit 8317
36:12 See how the e lie fallen— 224+7188
53: 4 Will the e never learn— 224+7188
59: 2 Deliver me from e and save me from 224+7188
64: 2 from that noisy crowd of e. 224+7188
92: 7 up like grass and all e flourish, 224+7188
92: 9 all e will be scattered. 224+7188
94: 4 all the e are full of boasting. 224+7188
94:16 Who will take a stand for me against e? 224+7188
119:115 Away from me, you e, 8317
125: 5 the LORD will banish with the e. 224+7188
141: 4 in wicked deeds with men *who are* e; 224+7188
141: 5 my prayer is ever against the **deeds of e;** 8288
141: 9 from the traps set by e. 224+7188
Pr 21:15 joy to the righteous but terror to e. 224+7188
Isa 1: 4 a brood of e, children given to corruption! 8317
31: 2 against those who help e. 224+7188
Jer 23:14 They strengthen the hands of e, 8317
Hos 10: 9 Did not war overtake the e in Gibeah? 1201+6594
Mal 3:15 Certainly the e prosper, 6913+8402
Mt 7:23 Away from me, *you* e!' *490+2237+3836*
Lk 13:27 Away from me, all *you* e!' *94+2239*

Lk 18:11 robbers, e, adulterers— *96*

EVILS (1) [EVIL]

Mk 7:23 All these e come from inside and make *4505*

EWE (6) [EWES]

Ge 21:28 Abraham set apart seven e **lambs** *from* 3898
21:29 of these seven e **lambs** you have set apart 3898
Lev 14:10 and one e **lamb** a year old, 3898
Nu 6:14 for a burnt offering, a year-old e **lamb** 3898
2Sa 12: 3 poor man had nothing except one little e **lamb** he had bought. 3898
12: 4 the e **lamb** *that belonged to* the poor man 3898

EWES (2) [EWE]

Ge 32:14 two hundred e and twenty rams, 8161
33:13 the e and cows that are nursing their young. 7366

EXACT (6) [EXACTED, EXACTING, EXACTLY]

Ge 43:21 the e **weight**—in the mouth of his sack. 5486
Est 4: 7 including the e **amount** 7308
Mt 2: 7 **found out** from them the e *208*
Jn 4:53 the father realized that this was the e time *NIG*
Ac 17:26 and the e **places** where they should live. *3999*
Heb 1: 3 of God's glory and the e **representation** *5917*

EXACTED (3) [EXACT]

2Ki 15:20 Menahem e this money from Israel. 3655
18:14 The king of Assyria e from Hezekiah king 8492
23:35 and e the silver and gold *from* the people of 5601

EXACTING (2) [EXACT]

Ne 5: 7 You *are* e usury from your own countrymen 5957
5:10 But let the e **of usury** stop! 5391

EXACTLY (9) [EXACT]

Ge 41:13 And things turned out e 4027
Ex 25: 9 all its furnishings e **like** 889+3869+3972+4027
Nu 8: 4 lampstand was made e **like** the pattern 3869+4027
15:14 he must do e **as** you do. 889+3869+4027
Dt 24: 8 careful to do e **as** the priests, 889+3869+3972
Jdg 7:17 do e **as** I do. 889+3869+4027
2Ki 7:20 And that is e what happened to him, 4027
Jn 14:31 I do e what my Father has commanded me. *4048*
Ac 22:30 to find out e why Paul was being accused *855*

EXALT (28) [EXALTED, EXALTS]

Ex 15: 2 my father's God, and *I will* e him. 8123
Jos 3: 7 "Today I will begin *to* e you in the eyes 1540
1Sa 2:10 to his king and e the horn of his anointed." 8123
1Ch 25: 5 through the promises of God to e him. 8123
29:12 In your hands are strength and power to e 1540
Job 19: 5 If indeed *you would* e *yourselves* 1540
Ps 30: 1 *I will* e you, O LORD, 8123
34: 3 *let us* e his name together. 8123
35:26 may *all* who e *themselves* over me 1540
37:34 *He will* e you to inherit the land; 8123
38:16 not let them gloat or e *themselves* over me 1540
75: 6 the east or the west or from the desert *can* e 8123
89:17 and by your favor *you* e our horn. 8123
99: 5 E the LORD our God and worship 8123
99: 9 E the LORD our God and worship 8123
107:32 *Let them* e him in the assembly of 8123
118:28 you are my God, and *I will* e you. 8123
145: 1 *I will* e you, my God the King; 8123
Pr 4: 8 Esteem her, and *she will* e you; 8123
25: 6 Do not e **yourself** in the king's presence, 2075
Isa 24:15 e the name of the LORD, NIH
25: 1 *I will* e you and praise your name, 8123
Eze 29:15 of kingdoms and *will* never again e **itself** 5951
Da 4:37 praise and e and glorify the King of heaven, 10659
11:36 e and magnify **himself** above every god 8123
11:37 but *will* e **himself** above them all. 1540
Hos 11: 7 *he will* by no means e them. 8123
2Th 2: 4 and will e **himself** over everything *5643*

EXALTED (67) [EXALT]

Ex 15: 1 for *he is* **highly** e. 1448+1448
15:21 "Sing to the LORD, for *he is* **highly** e. 1448+1448
Nu 24: 7 their kingdom *will* **be** e. 5951
Jos 4:14 That day the LORD e Joshua in the sight 1540
2Sa 5:12 as king over Israel and *had* e his kingdom 5951
22:47 E *be* God, the Rock, my Savior! 8123
22:49 *You* e me above my foes; 8123
23: 1 the oracle of the man e *by* the Most High, 7756
1Ch 14: 2 and that his kingdom *had* **been** highly e for 5951
17:17 as though I were the **most** e *of* men, 5092+9366
29:11 you *are* e as head over all. 5951
29:25 The LORD highly e Solomon in the sight 1540
Ne 9: 5 *may it* **be** e above all blessing and praise. 8123
Job 24:24 For a little while *they are* e, 8250
36:22 "God *is* e in his power. 8435
37:23 The Almighty is beyond our reach and e 8438
Ps 18:46 E *be* God my Savior! 8123
18:48 *You* e me above my foes; 8123
21:13 *Be* e, O LORD, in your strength; 8123
27: 6 *be* e above the enemies who surround me; 8123
35:27 may they always say, "The LORD *be* e, 1540
40:16 "The LORD *be* e!" 1540
46:10 *I will be* e among the nations, 8123

Ps 46:10 *I will be* e in the earth." 8123
47: 9 *he is* greatly **e.** 6590
57: 5 *Be* **e,** O God, above the heavens; 8123
57:11 *Be* **e,** O God, above the heavens; 8123
70: 4 *"Let* God *be* **e!"** 1540
89:13 your hand is strong, your right hand **e.** 8123
89:19 *I have* e a young man from among 8123
89:24 and through my name his horn *will be* **e.** 8123
89:27 the **most** e of the kings of the earth. 6609
89:42 *You have* e the right hand of his foes; 8123
92: 8 But you, O LORD, are e forever. 5294
92:10 *You have* e my horn like that of a wild ox; 8123
97: 9 *you* **are** e far above all gods. 6590
99: 2 he *is* e over all the nations. 8123
108: 5 *Be* **e,** O God, above the heavens, 8123
113: 4 The LORD *is* e over all the nations, 8123
138: 2 for *you have* e above all things your name 1540
148:13 for his name alone **is e;** 8435
Pr 11:11 the blessing of the upright a city *is* **e,** 8123
30:32 you have played the fool and **e yourself,** 5951
Isa 2:11 the LORD alone *will* **be** e in that day. 8435
2:12 for all *that* **is** e (and they will be humbled), 5951
2:17 the LORD alone *will* **be** e in that day, 8435
5:16 LORD Almighty *will be* e by his justice, 1467
6: 1 the Lord seated on a throne, high and **e,** and 5951
12: 4 and proclaim that his name *is* **e.** 8435
24: 4 the e *of* the earth languish. 5294+6639
33: 5 The LORD **is e,** for he dwells on high; 8435
33:10 "Now *will I* **be e;** now will I be lifted up. 8123
52:13 he will be raised and lifted up and highly **e.** 1467
Jer 17:12 A glorious throne, e from the beginning, 5294
La 2:17 *he has* e the horn of your foes. 8123
Eze 21:26 The lowly *will be* e and the exalted will 1467
21:26 be exalted and the e will be brought low. 1469
Hos 13: 1 he *was* e in Israel. 5951
Mic 6: 6 and bow down before the e God? 5294
Mt 23:12 and whoever humbles himself *will be* **e.** *5738*
Lk 14:11 and he who humbles himself *will be* **e."** *5738*
18:14 and he who humbles himself *will be* **e."** *5738*
Ac 2:33 **E** to the right hand of God, *5738*
5:31 God e him to his own right hand as Prince *5738*
Php 1:20 as always Christ *will be* e in my body, *3486*
2: 9 Therefore God e him **to the highest place** *5671*
Heb 7:26 set apart from sinners, e **above** the heavens. *5734*

EXALTS (7) [EXALT]

1Sa 2: 7 he humbles and *he* **e.** 8123
Job 36: 7 with kings and e *them* forever. 1467
Ps 75: 7 He brings one down, *he* e another. 8123
Pr 14:34 Righteousness e a nation, 8123
Mt 23:12 For whoever e himself will be humbled, *5738*
Lk 14:11 everyone who e himself will be humbled, *5738*
18:14 everyone who e himself will be humbled, *5738*

EXAMINE (36) [CROSS-EXAMINED, EXAMINED, EXAMINES, EXAMINING]

Ge 37:32 **E** it **to see** whether it is your son's robe." 5795
Lev 13: 3 The priest *is to* e the sore on his skin, 8011
13: 5 On the seventh day the priest *is to* e him, 8011
13: 6 *to* e him again, and if the sore has faded 8011
13: 8 The priest *is to* e him, 8011
13:10 The priest *is to* e him, 8011
13:13 the priest *is to* e him, 8011
13:17 The priest *is to* e him, 8011
13:20 The priest *is to* e it, 8011
13:25 the priest *is to* e the spot, 8011
13:27 On the seventh day the priest *is to* e him, 8011
13:30 the priest *is to* e the sore, and if it appears 8011
13:32 the seventh day the priest *is to* e the sore, 8011
13:34 the seventh day the priest *is to* e the itch, 8011
13:36 *to* e him, and if the itch has spread in 8011
13:39 the priest *is to* e them, and if 8011
13:43 The priest *is to* e him, 8011
13:50 The priest *is to* e the mildew and isolate 8011
13:51 On the seventh day *he is to* e it, 8011
13:55 the priest *is to* e it, 8011
14: 3 to go outside the camp and e him. 8011
14:36 to be emptied before he goes in to e 8011
14:37 *He is to* e the mildew on the walls, 8011
14:44 to go and e it and, if the mildew has spread 8011
14:48 the priest comes *to* e it and the mildew has 8011
Job 7:18 that *you* e him every morning 7212
34:23 God *has* no *need to* e men further, 8492
Ps 11: 4 his eyes e them. 1043
17: 3 you probe my heart and e me at night, 7212
26: 2 and try me, e my heart and my mind; 7671
Jer 17:10 the LORD search the heart and e the mind, 1043
20:12 you *who* e the righteous and probe the heart 1043
La 3:40 *Let us* e our ways and test them, 2924
Eze 21:21 he will consult his idols, *he will* e the liver. 8011
1Co 11:28 A man *ought to* e himself before he eats of *1507*
2Co 13: 5 **E** yourselves to see whether you are in the faith; *4279*

EXAMINED (5) [EXAMINE]

Job 5:27 *"We have* e this, and it is true. 2983
13: 9 Would it turn out well if *he* e you? 2983
Lk 23:14 I *have* e him in your presence *373*
Ac 17:11 the message with great eagerness and e *373*
28:18 They e me and wanted to release me, *373*

EXAMINES (8) [EXAMINE]

Lev 13: 3 When the priest e him, 8011
13:21 But if, when the priest e it, 8011
13:26 if the priest e it and there is no white hair in 8011
13:31 But if, when the priest e this kind of sore, 8011
13:53 "But if, when the priest e it, 8011
13:56 If, when the priest e it, 8011
Ps 11: 5 The LORD e the righteous, 1043
Pr 5:21 and *he* e all his paths. 7143

EXAMINING (3) [EXAMINE]

Ne 2:13 e the walls of Jerusalem, 8431
2:15 so I went up the valley by night, e the wall. 8431
Ac 24: 8 *By* e him yourself you will be able to learn *373*

EXAMPLE (19) [EXAMPLES]

2Ki 14: 3 In everything *he* **followed the** e 3869+6913+6913
Ecc 9:13 I also saw under the sun **this** e *of* wisdom AIT
Eze 14: 8 that man and make him an e and a byword. 253
Jn 13:15 an e that you should do as I have done *5682*
Ro 7: 2 **For e,** by law a married woman is bound *1142*
1Co 11: 1 **Follow** my **e,** as I follow the example *1181+3629*
11: 1 as I follow the e of Christ. *NIG*
Gal 3:15 *let me* **take an e** from everyday life. *3306*
Php 3:17 **Join with others** in **following** my **e,** *1181+5213*
2Th 3: 7 how you ought *to* **follow** our **e.** *3628*
1Ti 1:16 as an e for those who would believe on him *5721*
4:12 but set an e for the believers in speech, *5596*
Tit 2: 7 an e by doing what is good. *5596*
Heb 4:11 so that no one will fall by following their **e** *5682*
Jas 3: 4 Or take ships as an **e.** *NIG*
5:10 as an e of patience in the face of suffering, *5682*
1Pe 2:21 leaving you an **e,** that you should follow *5681*
2Pe 2: 6 and made them an e of what is going *5682*
Jude 1: 7 as an e of those who suffer the punishment *1257*

EXAMPLES (3) [EXAMPLE]

1Co 10: 6 Now these things occurred as e to keep us *5596*
10:11 as e and were written down as warnings *5595*
1Pe 5: 3 but being e to the flock. *5596*

EXASPERATE (1)

Eph 6: 4 Fathers, *do* not e your children; *4239*

EXCEED (2) [EXCEEDED, EXCEEDINGLY, EXCESSIVE]

Nu 3:46 273 firstborn Israelites who e the **number** 6369
Job 14: 5 and have set limits *he* cannot **e.** 6296

EXCEEDED (3) [EXCEED]

Nu 3:49 from those *who* e the **number** redeemed by 6369
1Ki 10: 7 in wisdom and wealth *you have* **far e** 3578
2Ch 9: 6 *you have* **far** e the report I heard. 3578

EXCEEDINGLY (6) [EXCEED]

Ge 30:43 In this way the man grew e prosperous 4394+4394
Ex 1: 7 and became e numerous, 928+4394+4394
Nu 11:10 The LORD became e angry, 4394
14: 7 through and explored is e good. 4394+4394
2Ch 1: 1 with him and made him e great. 2025+4200+5087
Eze 9: 9 of Israel and Judah is e great; 928+4394+4394

EXCEL (4) [EXCELLED, EXCELLENCY, EXCELLENT, EXCELLING]

Ge 49: 4 *you will* no longer **e,** 3855
1Co 14:12 try to e in gifts that build up the church. *4355*
2Co 8: 7 But just as *you* e in everything— *4355*
8: 7 *see* that *you* also e in this grace of giving. *4355*

EXCELLED (1) [EXCEL]

Isa 10:10 kingdoms whose images e those 4946

EXCELLENCY (1) [EXCEL]

Ac 23:26 *To* His **E,** Governor Felix: Greetings. *3196*

EXCELLENT (8) [EXCEL]

Ps 45: 2 *You are the* **most** e of men 3636
Lk 1: 3 for you, **most** e Theophilus, *3196*
Ac 24: 3 Everywhere and in every way, **most** e Felix, *3196*
26:25 "I am not insane, **most** e Festus," *3196*
1Co 12:31 now I will show you the **most** e way. *2848+5651*
Php 4: 8 if anything is e or praiseworthy— *746*
1Ti 3:13 an e standing and great assurance *2819*
Tit 3: 8 These things are e and profitable *2819*

EXCELLING (2) [EXCEL]

Ge 49: 3 the first sign of my strength, e *in* honor, 3856
49: 3 excelling in honor, e *in* power. 3856

EXCEPT (94) [EXCEPTION, EXCEPTIONAL]

Ge 39: 6 did not concern himself with anything e 561+3954
39: 9 withheld nothing from me e you, 561+3954
47:18 for our lord e our bodies and our land. 561+1194
Ex 8: 9 e *for* those that remain in the Nile." 8370
12:16 e to prepare food for everyone to eat— 421
Lev 13:33 be shaved **e for** the diseased area, 2256+4202
21: 2 e for a close relative, 561+3954
Nu 14:30 e Caleb son of Jephunneh and Joshua son of Nun. 561+3954
16:40 that no one e a descendant of Aaron 889+4202
26:65 was left e Caleb son of Jephunneh 561+3954
32:12 not one e Caleb son of Jephunneh 1194
35:33 e by the blood of the one who shed it. 561+3954
Dt 1:36 e Caleb son of Jephunneh. 2314
16: 6 e in the place he will choose as a dwelling for his Name. 561+3954
Jos 6:15 **e that** on that day they circled 8370
8: 2 **e that** you may carry off their plunder 8370
11:13 e Hazor, which Joshua burned. 2314
11:19 **E for** the Hivites living in Gibeon, 1194
Jdg 11:34 **E for** her he had neither son nor daughter. 4946
Ru 2: 7 **e for** a short rest in the shelter." 2296
4: 4 For no one has the right to do it e you, 2314
1Sa 21: 6 there was no bread there e the bread 561+3954
30:17 e four hundred young men who rode off 561+3954
2Sa 12: 3 poor man had nothing e one little ewe lamb he had bought. 561+3954
22:32 And who is the Rock e our God? 1187+4946
1Ki 3: 3 e that he offered sacrifices 8370
8: 9 in the ark e the two stone tablets 8370
15: 5 e in the case of Uriah the Hittite. 8370
17: 1 in the next few years e at my word." 561+3954
22:31 small or great, e the king of Israel." 561+3954
2Ki 4: 2 she said, **"e** a little oil." 561+3954
5:15 that there is no God in all the world e 561+3954
9:35 they found nothing e her skull, 561+3954
13: 7 the army of Jehoahaz e fifty horsemen, 561+3954
2Ch 2: 6 e as a place to burn sacrifices before him? 561+3954
5:10 There was nothing in the ark e 8370
18:30 small or great, e the king of Israel." 561+3954
21:17 Not a son was left to him e Ahaziah, 561+3954
23: 6 of the LORD e the priests and Levites 561+3954
Ne 2:12 with me e the one I was riding on. 561+3954
Ps 18:31 And who is the Rock e our God? 2314
Ecc 5:11 what benefit are they to the owner e 561+3954
Jer 44:14 none will return e a few fugitives." 561+3954
Da 2:11 No one can reveal it to the king e the gods, 10386
3:28 or worship any god e their own God. 10386
6: 7 e to you, O king, 10386
6:12 who prays to any god or man e to you, 10386
10:21 supports me against them e Michael, 561+3954
Hos 13: 4 no God but me, no Savior e me. 1194
Mt 5:13 e to be thrown out and trampled by men. *1623+3590*
5:32 **e for** marital unfaithfulness, *4211*
11:27 No one knows the Son e the Father, *1623+3590*
11:27 no one knows the Father e the Son and *1623+3590*
12:39 e the sign of the prophet Jonah. *1623+3590*
16: 4 will be given it e the sign of Jonah." *1623+3590*
17: 8 they saw no one e Jesus. *1623+3590*
19: 9 e for marital unfaithfulness, *3590*
21:19 but found nothing on it e leaves. *1623+3590*
Mk 5:37 follow him e Peter, James and John *1623+3590*
6: 5 e lay his hands on a few sick people *1623+3590*
6: 8 "Take nothing for the journey e a staff *1623+3590*
8:14 **e for** one loaf they had with them in *1623+3590*
9: 8 no longer saw anyone with them e Jesus. *247*
10:18 "No one is good—e God alone. *1623+3590*
Lk 8:51 not let anyone go in with him e Peter, *1623+3590*
10:22 No one knows who the Son is e the Father, *1623+3590*
10:22 knows who the Father is e the Son and *1623+3590*
11:29 will be given it e the sign of Jonah. *1623+3590*
17:18 give praise to God e this foreigner?" *1623+3590*
18:19 "No one is good—e God alone. *1623+3590*
Jn 1:33 **e that** the one who sent me to baptize *247*
3:13 No one has ever gone into heaven e *1623+3590*
6:46 No one has seen the Father e the one *1623+3590*
14: 6 No one comes to the Father e through me. *1623+3590*
17:12 None has been lost e the one doomed *1623+3590*
Ac 8: 1 and all e the apostles were scattered *4440*
26:29 to me today may become what I am, **e for** *4211*
Ro 7: 7 not have known what sin was e through the law. *1623+3590*
13: 1 for there is no authority e that which *1623+3590*
13: 8 e the continuing debt to love one another, *1623+3590*
15:18 of anything e what Christ has accomplished *NIG*
1Co 1:14 I did not baptize any of you e Crispus and Gaius, *1623+3590*
2: 2 e Jesus Christ and him crucified. *1623+3590*
2:11 knows the thoughts of a man e the man's spirit *1623+3590*
2:11 no one knows the thoughts of God e the Spirit of God. *1623+3590*
7: 5 not deprive each other e by mutual consent *323+1623+3614*
10:13 No temptation has seized you e what is common to man. *1623+3590*
12: 3 "Jesus is Lord," e by the Holy Spirit. *1623+3590*
2Co 12: 5 e about my weaknesses. *1623+3590*
12:13 e that I was never a burden to you? *1623+3590*
Gal 6:14 May I never boast e in the cross *1623+3590*
Eph 4: 9 (What does "he ascended" mean e that *1623+3590*
Php 4:15 of giving and receiving, e you only; *1623+3590*
Rev 14: 3 No one could learn the song e the 144,000 who had been redeemed *1623+3590*

EXCEPTION (1) [EXCEPT]

Est 4:11 The **only** e to this is for the king to 963+4200

EXCEPTIONAL (1) [EXCEPT]

Da 6: 3 by his e qualities that the king planned 10339

EXCESSIVE (6) [EXCEED]

Eze 18: 8 He does not lend at usury or take e **interest.** 9552
18:13 He lends at usury and takes **e interest.** 9552
18:17 from sin and takes no usury or e **interest.** 9552
22:12 and e **interest** and make unjust gain 9552
2Co 2: 7 he will not be overwhelmed *by* e sorrow. *4358*
Rev 18: 3 of the earth grew rich from her e luxuries." *1539*

EXCHANGE (13) [EXCHANGED, EXCHANGING]

Ge 47:16 "I will sell you food **in e for** your livestock, 928
47:17 and he gave them food **in e for** their horses, 928
47:17 with food **in e for** all their livestock. 928
47:19 Buy us and our land **in e for** food, 928
Lev 27:10 *He must* not e it or substitute a good one for 2736
Dt 14:25 then e your tithe for silver, 5989
1Ki 21: 2 **In e** I will give you a better vineyard or, 9393
Isa 43: 4 I will give men **in e for** you, 9393
43: 4 and people **in e for** your life. 9393
Eze 48:14 They must not sell or e any of it. 4614
Mt 16:26 Or what can a man give **in e for** his soul? *498*
Mk 8:37 Or what can a man give **in e for** his soul? *498*
2Co 6:13 As a fair **e**—I speak as to my children— *521*

EXCHANGED (13) [EXCHANGE]

Ps 106:20 *They* e their Glory for an image of a bull, 4614
Jer 2:11 But my people *have* e their Glory 4614
Eze 27:12 *they* e silver, iron, tin and lead 5989
27:13 *they* e slaves and articles of bronze 5989
27:14 " 'Men of Beth Togarmah e work horses, 5989
27:16 *they* e turquoise, purple fabric, 5989
27:17 *they* e wheat from Minnith and confections, 5989
27:19 *they* e wrought iron, 5989
27:22 for your merchandise *they* e the finest 5989
Hos 4: 7 *they* e their Glory for something disgraceful 4614
Ro 1:23 and e the glory of the immortal God *248*
1:25 They e the truth of God for a lie, *3563*
1:26 Even their women e natural relations *3563*

EXCHANGING (1) [EXCHANGE]

Jn 2:14 and others sitting at tables **e money.** *3048*

EXCITEMENT (1)

Job 39:24 In frenzied e he eats up the ground; 8075

EXCLAIM (3) [EXCLAIMED, EXCLAIMING]

Ps 35:10 My whole being *will* e, "Who is like you, 606
Jer 46:17 There *they will* e, 'Pharaoh king 7924
Rev 18:18 the smoke of her burning, *they will* e, *3189*

EXCLAIMED (12) [EXCLAIM]

Jdg 6:22 he e, "Ah, Sovereign LORD! 606
Ru 1:19 and *the women* e, "Can this be Naomi?" 606
2:10 *She* e, "Why have I found such favor 606
2Ki 3:10 "What!" e the king of Israel. 606
Est 7: 8 The king e, "Will he even molest the queen 606
Mt 27:54 and e, "Surely he was the Son of God!" *3306*
Mk 1:37 *they* e: "Everyone is looking for you!" *3306*
9:24 Immediately the boy's father e, *3189*
Lk 1:42 In a loud voice *she* e: "Blessed are you *430*
Jn 8:52 At this the Jews e, "Now we know *3306*
Ac 8:10 gave him their attention and e, *3306*
12:14 without opening it and e, *550*

EXCLAIMING (1) [EXCLAIM]

1Co 14:25 So he will fall down and worship God, e, *550*

EXCLUDE (4) [EXCLUDED, EXCLUSIVELY]

Isa 56: 3 "The LORD *will* **surely** e me 976+976
66: 5 and e you because of my name, have said, 5612
Lk 6:22 when *they* e you and insult you *928*
Rev 11: 2 But e the outer court; *1675*

EXCLUDED (6) [EXCLUDE]

2Ch 26:21 and e from the temple of the LORD. 1615
Ezr 2:62 so were **e from** the priesthood as unclean. 4946
Ne 7:64 so were **e from** the priesthood as unclean. 4946
13: 3 *they* e from Israel all who were 976
Ro 3:27 *It is* e. *1710*
Eph 2:12 e from citizenship in Israel and foreigners *558*

EXCLUSIVELY (1) [EXCLUDE]

Ac 18: 5 Paul **devoted** *himself e* to preaching, *AIT*

EXCREMENT (3)

Dt 23:13 dig a hole and cover up your **e.** 7362
Eze 4:12 using human e for fuel." 1645+7362
4:15 over cow manure instead of human **e."** 1645

EXCUSE (6) [EXCUSES]

Ps 25: 3 to shame who are treacherous **without e.** 8200
Lk 14:18 Please e me.' *2400+4148*
14:19 Please e me.' *2400+4148*
Jn 15:22 Now, however, they have no e for their sin. *4733*
Ro 1:20 so that men are **without e.** *406*
2: 1 You, therefore, have **no e,** *406*

EXCUSES (1) [EXCUSE]

Lk 14:18 "But they all alike began *to* **make e.** *4148*

EXECRATION (KJV) OBJECT OF CURSING

EXECUTE (11) [EXECUTED, EXECUTING, EXECUTION, EXECUTIONER]

2Ch 2:14 of engraving and *can* e any design given 3108
Isa 66:16 the LORD *will* **e judgment** *upon* all men, 9149
Eze 11:10 and *I will* **e judgment** *on* you at 9149
11:11 *I will* **e judgment** *on* you at the borders 9149
17:20 I will bring him to Babylon and **e judgment** 9149
20:35 face to face, *I will* **e judgment** upon you. 9149
38:22 *I will* **e judgment** upon him with plague 9149
Da 2:24 the king had appointed to e the wise men 10005
2:24 *"Do* not e the wise men of Babylon. 10005
Hab 1:12 you have appointed them to e judgment; NIH
Jn 18:31 "But we have no right *to* e anyone," *650*

EXECUTED (10) [EXECUTE]

2Ki 14: 5 the kingdom was firmly in his grasp, *he* e 5782
25:21 the king *had* them e. 2256+4637+5782
2Ch 24:24 judgment *was* e *on* Joash. 6913
25: 3 the kingdom was firmly in his control, *he* e 2222
Jer 52:27 the king **had** them e. 2256+4637+5782
Da 2:18 and his friends *might* not *be* e with the rest 10005
Mt 27:20 to ask for Barabbas and to *have* Jesus **e.** *660*
Lk 23:32 were also led out with him *to be* **e.** *359*
Ac 12:19 the guards and ordered that *they be* **e.** *552*
13:28 they asked Pilate *to have* him **e.** *359*

EXECUTING (1) [EXECUTE]

2Ch 22: 8 While Jehu was **e judgment** on the house 9149

EXECUTION (1) [EXECUTE]

Da 2:12 so angry and furious that he ordered the e 10005

EXECUTIONER (1) [EXECUTE]

Mk 6:27 So he immediately sent an e with orders *5063*

EXEMPT (4)

1Sa 17:25 **e** his father's family **from taxes** 2930+6913
1Ki 15:22 an order to all Judah—no one was **e**— 5929
1Ch 9:33 **were e from** *other* **duties** 7080
Mt 17:26 "Then the sons are **e,"** Jesus said to him. *1801*

EXERCISE (5) [EXERCISED, EXERCISES, EXERTED]

Mt 20:25 their high officials **e authority over** them. *2980*
Mk 10:42 their high officials **e authority over** them. *2980*
Lk 22:25 and those who **e authority over** *2027*
1Co 8: 9 that the **e** *of* your **freedom** does not become *2026*
Rev 13: 5 and *to* e his authority for forty-two months. *4472*

EXERCISED (2) [EXERCISE]

Da 11: 4 nor will it have the power *he* e, 5440
Rev 13:12 *He* e all the authority of the first beast *4472*

EXERCISES (1) [EXERCISE]

Jer 9:24 that I am the LORD, *who* e kindness, 6913

EXERTED (1) [EXERCISE]

Eph 1:20 which *he* **e in** Christ when he raised him *1919*

EXHAUST (2) [EXHAUSTED]

Jer 51:58 the peoples **e** *themselves* for nothing, 3333
Hab 2:13 that the nations **e** *themselves* for nothing? 3615

EXHAUSTED (13) [EXHAUST]

Jdg 4:21 to him while he lay fast asleep, **e.** 6545
8: 4 **e** yet keeping up the pursuit, 6546
8:15 give bread to your **e** men?' " 6546
1Sa 14:31 from Micmash to Aijalon, *they were* **e.** 4394+6545
30:10 for two hundred men *were* too e to cross 7006
30:21 to the two hundred men who *had been* too e 7006
2Sa 16: 2 the wine is to refresh those who become e 3617
16:14 with him arrived at their destination **e.** 6546
21:15 and he *became* **e.** 6545
Jer 51:30 Their strength *is* **e;** 5980
Da 8:27 I, Daniel, *was* e and lay ill for several days. 2118
Lk 12:33 a treasure in heaven that will **not be e,** *444*
22:45 he found them asleep, e from sorrow. *NIG*

EXHORT (1) [EXHORTATION, EXHORTED]

1Ti 5: 1 but e him as if he were your father. *4151*

EXHORTATION (1) [EXHORT]

Heb 13:22 I urge you to bear with my word *of* **e,** *4155*

EXHORTED (1) [EXHORT]

Lk 3:18 with many other words John e the people *4151*

EXILE (78) [EXILED, EXILES]

2Sa 15:19 an e from your homeland. 1655
2Ki 17:23 *taken* from their homeland **into e** 1655
24:14 **He carried into e** all Jerusalem: 1655+1655
25:11 the commander of the guard **carried into e** 1655
25:27 of the e *of* Jehoiachin king of Judah, 1661
1Ch 5: 6 of Assyria **took into e.** 1655
5:22 And they occupied the land until the **e.** 1583
5:26 **took** the Reubenites, the Gadites and the half-tribe of Manasseh **into e.** 1655
6:15 **sent** Judah and Jerusalem **into e** 1655
2Ch 36:20 *He* **carried into e** to Babylon the remnant, 1655
Ezr 6:21 Israelites who had returned from the e ate it, 1583
Ne 1: 2 the Jewish remnant that survived the **e,** 8660
1: 3 "Those who survived the e and are back in 8660
8:17 from e built booths and lived in them. 8660
Est 2: 6 who *had* **been carried into e** from Jerusalem 1655
Isa 5:13 Therefore my people *will* **go into e** 1655
27: 8 By warfare and e you contend with her— 8938
Jer 1: 3 when the people of Jerusalem **went into e.** 1655
13:19 All Judah *will* **be carried into e,** 1655
20: 6 in your house will go into e to Babylon. 8660
22:22 and your allies will go into e. 8660
24: 1 the artisans of Judah *were* **carried into e** 1655
27:20 **carried** Jehoiachin son of Jehoiakim king of Judah **into e** 1655
29: 1 other people Nebuchadnezzar *had* **carried into e** 1655
29: 2 and the artisans had gone into e NIH
29: 4 to all those *I* **carried into e** from Jerusalem 1655
29: 7 the city to which *I have* **carried** you **into e.** 1655
29:14 the place from which *I* **carried** you **into e."** 1655
29:16 not go with you into e— 1583
30:10 your descendants from the land of their **e.** 8660
30:16 all your enemies will go into e. 8660
39: 9 of the imperial guard **carried into e** 1655
40: 1 and Judah who *were* **being carried into e** 1655
40: 7 and who *had* not **been carried into e** 1655
43: 3 so they may kill us or **carry** us **into e** 1655
46:19 Pack your belongings for **e,** 1583
46:27 your descendants from the land of their **e.** 8660
48: 7 and Chemosh will go into **e,** 1583
48:11 she has not gone into **e.** 1583
48:46 into e and your daughters into captivity. 8660
49: 3 for Molech will go into **e,** 1583
52:15 of the guard **carried into e** some of 1655
52:28 the people Nebuchadnezzar **carried into e:** 1655
52:30 745 Jews **taken into e** *by* Nebuzaradan 1655
52:31 of the e *of* Jehoiachin king of Judah, 1661
La 1: 3 Judah *has* **gone into e.** 1655
1: 5 Her children have gone into **e,** 8660
1:18 and maidens have gone into **e.** 8660
4:22 he will not prolong your **e.** 1655
Eze 1: 2 the fifth year of the e *of* King Jehoiachin— 1661
3:11 to your countrymen in e and speak to them. 1583
12: 3 pack your belongings for e and in 1583
12: 4 bring out your belongings packed for **e.** 1583
12: 4 go out like those who go into **e.** 1583
12: 7 During the day I brought out my things packed for **e.** 1583
12:11 They will go into e as captives. 1583
25: 3 the people of Judah when they went into **e,** 1583
33:21 In the twelfth year of our **e,** 1661
39:23 the people of Israel **went into e** for their sin, 1655
39:28 I **sent** them **into e** among the nations, 1655
40: 1 In the twenty-fifth year of our **e,** 1661
Hos 10: 5 **taken** from them **into e.** 1655
Am 1: 5 The people of Aram *will* **go into e** to Kir," 1655
1:15 Her king will go into **e,** 1583
5: 5 For Gilgal *will* **surely go into e,** 1655+1655
5:27 *I will* **send** you **into e** beyond Damascus," 1655
6: 7 be among the first to **go into e;** 1655+1655
7:11 and Israel *will* **surely go into e,** 1655+1655
7:17 And Israel *will* **certainly go into e,** 1655+1655
9: 4 Though they are driven into e 8660
Mic 1:16 **go** from you **into e.** 1655
Na 3:10 Yet she was taken captive and went into e. 8660
Zec 14: 2 Half of the city will go into **e,** 1583
Mt 1:11 and his brothers at the time *of* the e *3578*
1:12 After the e to Babylon: *3578*
1:17 fourteen from David to the e to Babylon, *3578*
1:17 and fourteen from the e to the Christ. *3578*
Ac 7:43 Therefore *I will* **send** you **into e'** *3579*

EXILED (8) [EXILE]

2Ki 17:28 So one of the priests who *had been* **e** 1655
Ne 1: 9 if your **e** *people* are at the farthest horizon, 5615
Isa 27:13 and those *who* **were e** in Egypt will come 5615
49:21 I *was* e and rejected. 1655
Jer 22:10 rather, weep bitterly for him *who is* **e,** 2143
La 2: 9 and her princes are e among the nations, NIH
Am 9:14 I will bring back my e people Israel; 8654
Na 2: 7 that [the city] **be e** and carried away. 1655

EXILES (38) [EXILE]

Ezr 1:11 the e came up from Babylon to Jerusalem. 1583
2: 1 up from the captivity of the **e,** 1583
4: 1 that the e were building a temple for 1201+1583
6:16 the priests, the Levites and the rest of the e— 10120+10145
6:19 the e celebrated the Passover. 1201+1583
6:20 the Passover lamb for all the **e,** 1201+1583
8:35 Then the e who had returned 1201+1583
9: 4 because of this unfaithfulness of the **e.** 1583
10: 6 to mourn over the unfaithfulness of the **e.** 1583
10: 7 and Jerusalem for all the e to assemble 1201+1583

Ezr 10: 8 be expelled from the assembly of the **e.** 1583
10:16 So the e did as was proposed. 1201+1583
Ne 7: 6 of the **e** whom Nebuchadnezzar king 1583
Ps 147: 2 he gathers the **e** *of* Israel. 5615
Isa 11:12 for the nations and gather the **e** *of* Israel; 5615
20: 4 the Egyptian captives and Cushite **e,** young 1661
45:13 He will rebuild my city and set my **e** free, 1661
56: 8 he who gathers the **e** *of* Israel: 5615
Jer 24: 5 I regard as good the **e** *from* Judah, 1661
28: 4 and all the other **e** *from* Judah who went 1661
28: 6 of the LORD's house and all the **e** back 1583
29: 1 to the surviving elders among the **e** and to 1583
29:19 And you **e** have not listened either," NIH
29:20 all you **e** whom I have sent away 1583
29:22 all the **e** *from* Judah who are 1661
29:31 "Send this message to all the **e:** 1583
49:36 not be a nation where Elam's **e** do not go. 5615
Eze 1: 1 I was among the **e** by the Kebar River, 1583
3:15 I came to the **e** who lived at Tel Abib near 1583
11:24 to the **e** in Babylonia in the vision given by 1583
11:25 the **e** everything the LORD had shown me. 1583
Da 2:25 a man among the **e** from Judah who can tell the king what his dream means." 10120+10145
5:13 Daniel, one of the **e** my father the king brought from Judah? 10120+10145
6:13 "Daniel, who is one of the **e** from Judah, 10120+10145
Ob 1:20 This company of Israelite **e** who are 1661
1:20 the **e** *from* Jerusalem who are 1661
Mic 4: 6 the **e** and those I have brought to grief. 5615
Zec 6:10 "Take [silver and gold] from the **e** Heldai, 1583

EXIST (1) [EXISTED, EXISTS]
Ro 13: 1 The authorities that **e** have been established *1639*

EXISTED (1) [EXIST]
2Pe 3: 5 the heavens **e** and the earth was formed out *1639*

EXISTS (3) [EXIST]
Ecc 6:10 Whatever **e** has already been named, 2118
Heb 2:10 for whom and through whom everything **e,** *NIG*
11: 6 to him must believe that *he* **e** and *1639*

EXITS (4)
Eze 42:11 with similar **e** and dimensions. 4604
43:11 its arrangement, its **e** and entrances— 4604
44: 5 of the temple and all the **e** *of* the sanctuary. 4604
48:30 "These will be the **e** *of* the city: 9362

EXODUS (1)
Heb 11:22 **e** of the Israelites **from Egypt** *2016*

EXORBITANT (1)
Pr 28: 8 by **e interest** amasses it for 2256+5968+9552

EXORCISTS (KJV) DRIVING OUT EVIL SPIRITS

EXPAND (1) [EXPANSE]
2Co 10:15 of activity among you *will* greatly **e,** *3486*

EXPANSE (13) [EXPAND, EXPANSES]
Ge 1: 6 an **e** between the waters to separate water 8385
1: 7 So God made the **e** and separated the water 8385
1: 7 and separated the water under the **e** from 8385
1: 8 God called the **e** "sky." 8385
1:14 in the **e** *of* the sky to separate the day from 8385
1:15 be lights in the **e** *of* the sky to give light on 8385
1:17 in the **e** *of* the sky to give light on the earth, 8385
1:20 and let birds fly above the earth across the **e** 8385
Eze 1:22 like an **e,** sparkling like ice, 8385
1:23 the **e** their wings were stretched out one 8385
1:25 Then there came a voice from above the **e** 8385
1:26 the **e** over their heads was what looked like 8385
10: 1 of a throne of sapphire above the **e** that was 8385

EXPANSES (1) [EXPANSE]
Job 38:18 Have you comprehended the **vast e** *of* 8144

EXPECT (13) [EXPECTANT, EXPECTANTLY, EXPECTATION, EXPECTED, EXPECTING]
Isa 58: 4 **e** your voice **to be heard** 9048
64: 3 you did awesome things that *we did* not **e,** 7747
Eze 13: 6 yet *they* **e** their words to be fulfilled. 3498
Mt 11: 3 or *should* we **e** someone else?" *4659*
24:44 at an hour when *you do* not **e** him. *1506*
24:50 when *he does* not **e** him and at an hour he is *4659*
Lk 6:34 to those from whom *you* **e** repayment, *1827*
7:19 or *should* we **e** someone else?" *4659*
7:20 or *should* we **e** someone else?' " *4659*
12:40 at an hour when *you do* not **e** him." *1506*
12:46 when *he does* not **e** him and at an hour he is *4659*
2Co 10: 2 as *I* **e** to be toward some people who think *3357*
Php 1:20 I **eagerly e** and hope that I will in no way *638*

EXPECTANT (1) [EXPECT]
Jer 31: 8 **e mothers** and women in labor; 2226

EXPECTANTLY (2) [EXPECT]
Job 29:21 "Men listened to me **e,** 3498
Lk 3:15 The people *were* **waiting e** *4659*

EXPECTATION (4) [EXPECT]
Ps 5: 3 before you and **wait in e.** 7595
Eze 19: 5 she saw her hope unfulfilled, her **e** gone, 9536
Ro 8:19 The creation waits in **eager e for** the sons *638*
Heb 10:27 a fearful **e** of judgment and of raging fire *1693*

EXPECTED (8) [EXPECT]
Ge 48:11 *"I* never **e** to see your face again, 7136
Pr 11: 7 *all* he **e** *from* his power comes to nothing. 9347
Hag 1: 9 *"You* **e** much, but see, 7155
Mt 20:10 *they* **e** to receive more. *3787*
Ac 16:13 where *we* **e** to find a place of prayer. *3787*
25:18 with any of the crimes I *had* **e.** *5706*
28: 6 The people **e** him to swell up *4659*
2Co 8: 5 And they did not do as *we* **e,** *1827*

EXPECTING (7) [EXPECT]
Lk 2: 5 to be married to him and was **e a child.** *1607*
6:34 **e to** be repaid in full. *2671*
6:35 without **e to get** anything **back.** *594*
8:40 for they were all **e** him. *4659*
Ac 3: 5 **e** to get something from them. *4659*
10:24 Cornelius was **e** them *4659*
1Co 16:11 *I am* **e** him along with the brothers. *1683*

EXPEDIENT (KJV) BENEFICIAL, BEST, BETTER, GAINED, GOOD

EXPEL (1) [EXPELLED]
1Co 5:13 **"E** the wicked man from among you." *1976*

EXPELLED (5) [EXPEL]
1Sa 28: 3 Saul *had* **e** the mediums and spiritists from 6073
1Ki 15:12 *He* **e** the male shrine prostitutes from 6296
Ezr 10: 8 and *would* himself **be e** from the assembly 976
Eze 28:16 and *I* **e** you, O guardian cherub, 6
Ac 13:50 and **e** them from their region. *1675*

EXPEND (1) [EXPENSE]
2Co 12:15 spend for you **everything I have** and **e** *1682*

EXPEND (Anglicized) See also SPEND

EXPENSE (2) [EXPEND, EXPENSES, EXPENSIVE]
Lk 10:35 for any **extra e** you may have.' *4655*
1Co 9: 7 Who serves as a soldier *at* his own **e?** *4072*

EXPENSES (3) [EXPENSE]
2Ki 12:12 **met** all *the other* **e** 3655
Ezr 6: 8 The **e** of these men are to be fully paid out 10486
Ac 21:24 in their purification rites and **pay** their **e,** *1251*

EXPENSIVE (5) [EXPENSE]
Mt 26: 7 with an alabaster jar *of* **very e** perfume, *988*
Mk 14: 3 with an alabaster jar *of* **very e** perfume, *4500*
Lk 7:25 those who wear **e** clothes and indulge *1902*
Jn 12: 3 about a pint of pure nard, an **e** perfume; *4501*
1Ti 2: 9 or gold or pearls or **e** clothes, *4500*

EXPERIENCE (3) [EXPERIENCED]
Nu 16:29 and **e** only what usually happens to men, 7212
Jdg 3: 2 not **had** previous battle **e):** 3359
Heb 11: 5 so that he did not **e** death; *3972*

EXPERIENCED (13) [EXPERIENCE]
Dt 11: 2 not the ones who saw and **e** the discipline 3359
Jos 24:31 and who *had* **e** everything 3359
Jdg 3: 1 to test all those Israelites who *had* not **e** any 3359
2Sa 17: 8 Besides, your father is an **e fighter;** 408+4878
1Ki 7:14 Huram was highly skilled and **e** 1981+2256+9312
1Ch 12:33 **e soldiers** prepared for battle 3655+7372
12:36 **e soldiers** prepared for battle— 3655+7372
2Ch 2: 7 and **e** in the art of engraving, 3359
2:14 **e** in all kinds of **engraving** 7334+7338
17:13 He also kept **e fighting men** in Jerusalem. 408+1475+2657+4878
Ecc 1:16 I *have* **e** much of wisdom and knowledge." 8011
SS 3: 8 all of them wearing the sword, all **e** *in* battle 4340
Ro 11:25 Israel *has* **e** a hardening in part until *1181*

EXPERT (4) [EXPERTS]
Mt 22:35 One of them, an **e in the law,** *3788*
Lk 10:25 On one occasion an **e in the law** stood up *3788*
10:37 **The e in the law** replied, *1254+3836*[S]
1Co 3:10 I laid a foundation as an **e** builder, *5055*

EXPERTS (7) [EXPERT]
Est 1:13 for the king to consult **e** *in* matters of law 3359
Lk 7:30 and **e in the law** rejected God's purpose *3788*
11:45 One *of* the **e in the law** answered him, *3788*
11:46 Jesus replied, "And you **e in the law,** *3788*
11:52 "Woe to you **e in the law,** *3788*
14: 3 Jesus asked the Pharisees and **e in the law,** *3788*
2Pe 2:14 are **e** in greed—an accursed brood! *1214+2840*

EXPIRED (KJV) ELAPSED, END, OVER, PASSED, SPRING

EXPLAIN (20) [EXPLAINED, EXPLAINING, EXPLAINS, EXPLANATION]
Ge 41:24 but none *could* **e** it to me." 5583
Dt 32: 7 your elders, and *they will* **e** to you. 606
Jdg 14:16 he replied, "so *why should I* **e** it to you?" 5583
1Ki 10: 3 nothing was too hard for the king *to* **e** 5583
2Ch 9: 2 nothing was too hard for him *to* **e** to her. 5583
Est 4: 8 to show to Esther and **e** it to her, 5583
Job 15:17 "Listen to me and *I will* **e** *to* you; 2555
Jer 9:12 by the LORD and *can* **e** it? 5583
Da 2: 6 But if you tell me the dream and **e** it, 10600
2:27 magician or diviner can **e** to the king 10252
5:12 **e** riddles and solve difficult problems. 10252
5:15 but they could not **e** it. 10252+10600
10:14 to **e** *to* you what will happen to your people 1067
Mt 13:36 **"E** to us the parable of the weeds in *1397*
15:15 Peter said, **"E** the parable to us." *5851*
16:21 *to* **e** to his disciples that he must go *1259*
Jn 4:25 he comes, he *will* **e** everything to us." *334*
Ac 2:14 *let* me **e** this to you; *1196+1639*
Heb 5:11 but *it is* **hard to e** because you are slow *1549*
Rev 17: 7 I *will* **e** to you the mystery of the woman *3306*

EXPLAINED (12) [EXPLAIN]
Jdg 14:16 *"I* haven't even **e** it to my father or mother," 5583
14:17 *She* in turn **e** the riddle to her people. 5583
14:19 and gave their clothes to *those* who *had* **e** 5583
1Sa 10:25 Samuel **e** to the people the regulations of 1819
Da 2:15 Arioch then **e** the matter to Daniel. 10313
2:17 and **e** the matter to his friends Hananiah, 10313
Zec 1:10 the man standing among the myrtle trees **e,** 6699
Mk 4:34 with his own disciples, *he* **e** everything. *2147*
Lk 24:27 **e** to them **what** *was* **said** *1450*
Ac 11: 4 and **e** everything to them precisely *1758*
18:26 they invited him to their home and **e** to him *1758*
28:23 From morning till evening *he* **e** and declared *1758*

EXPLAINING (3) [EXPLAIN]
Jdg 14:15 "Coax your husband into **e** the riddle for us, 5583
Isa 28: 9 *To* whom *is he* **e** his message? 1067
Ac 17: 3 **e** and proving that the Christ had to suffer *1380*

EXPLAINS (1) [EXPLAIN]
Ac 8:31 he said, "unless someone **e** it **to me?"** *3842*

EXPLANATION (2) [EXPLAIN]
Ecc 8: 1 Who knows the **e** *of* things? 7323
Da 7:23 *"He* **gave** me this **e:** 10042

EXPLOIT (5) [EXPLOITED, EXPLOITING, EXPLOITS]
Pr 22:22 Do not **e** the poor because they are poor 1608
Isa 58: 3 you as you please and **e** all your workers. 5601
2Co 12:17 *Did I* **e** you through any of the men I sent *4430*
12:18 Titus *did* not **e** you, did he? *4430*
2Pe 2: 3 In their greed *these* teachers *will* **e** you *1864*

EXPLOITED (1) [EXPLOIT]
2Co 7: 2 *we have* **e** no one. *4430*

EXPLOITING (1) [EXPLOIT]
Jas 2: 6 Is it not the rich who *are* **e** you? *2872*

EXPLOITS (8) [EXPLOIT]
2Sa 23:17 Such *were the* **e** of the three mighty men. 6913
23:20 who **performed** great **e.** 7189
23:22 *the* **e** *of* Benaiah son of Jehoiada; 6913
1Ki 22:45 the things he achieved and *his* **military e,** 1369
1Ch 11:19 Such *were the* **e** *of* the three mighty men. 6913
11:22 who **performed** great **e.** 7189
11:24 *the* **e** *of* Benaiah son of Jehoiada; 6913
2Co 11:20 up with anyone who enslaves you or **e** you *2983*

EXPLORE (11) [EXPLORED, EXPLORING]
Nu 13: 2 "Send some men *to* **e** the land of Canaan, 9365
13:16 the names of the men Moses sent to **e** 9365
13:17 When Moses sent them to **e** Canaan, 9365
14:36 So the men Moses had sent to **e** the land, 9365
14:38 Of the men who went to **e** the land, 9365
Jos 14: 7 from Kadesh Barnea to **e** the land. 8078
Jdg 18: 2 and Eshtaol to spy out the land and **e** it. 2983
18: 2 They told them, "Go, **e** the land." 2983
2Sa 10: 3 Hasn't David sent them to you to **e** the city 2983
1Ch 19: 3 to you to **e** and spy out the country 2983
Ecc 1:13 to study and to **e** by wisdom all that is done 9365

EXPLORED (7) [EXPLORE]
Nu 13:21 and **e** the land from the Desert of Zin as far 9365
13:32 a bad report about the land *they had* **e.** 9365
13:32 "The land *we* **e** devours those living in it. 6296+9365

Nu 14: 6 who were among those *who had* e the land, 9365
14: 7 through and e is exceedingly good. 9365
14:34 for each of the forty days *you* e the land— 9365
Dt 1:24 and came to the Valley of Eshcol and e it. 8078

EXPLORING (1) [EXPLORE]
Nu 13:25 of forty days they returned from e the land. 9365

EXPORTED (2)
1Ki 10:29 also e *them* to all the kings of the Hittites 3655
2Ch 1:17 also e them to all the kings of the Hittites 3655

EXPOSE (10) [EXPOSED, EXPOSES, EXPOSING]
Nu 25: 4 **kill** them **and** e them in broad daylight 3697
Job 20:27 The heavens *will* e his guilt; 1655
Isa 57:12 I *will* e your righteousness 5583
La 2:14 not e your sin to ward off your captivity. 1655
4:22 and e your wickedness. 1655
Eze 25: 9 therefore I *will* e the flank of Moab, 7337
Hos 2:10 now *I will* e her lewdness before the eyes 1655
Mt 1:19 did not want to e her **to public disgrace,** *1258*
1Co 4: 5 and *will* e the motives of men's hearts. *5746*
Eph 5:11 but rather e them. *1794*

EXPOSED (24) [EXPOSE]
Ex 20:26 lest your nakedness **be** e on it.' 1655
Lev 20:18 *he has* e the source of her flow, 6867
2Sa 21: 6 to us *to be* **killed and** e before the LORD 3697
21: 9 *who* **killed and** e them on a hill before 3697
21:13 *who had* **been killed and** e were gathered up 3697
22:16 of the sea **were** e and the foundations of 8011
Ne 4:13 of the wall at the e **places,** 7460
Est 6: 2 that Mordecai *had* e Bigthana and Teresh, 5583
Ps 18:15 of the sea **were** e and the foundations of 8011
Pr 26:26 his wickedness *will* **be** e in the assembly. 1655
Isa 47: 3 Your nakedness *will* **be** e 1655
Jer 8: 2 They *will be* e to the sun and the moon 8848
36:30 be thrown out and e to the heat by day and NIH
Eze 16:36 and e your nakedness in your promiscuity 1655
23:18 and e her nakedness, 1655
23:29 the shame of your prostitution *will* **be** e. 1655
Hos 7: 1 the sins of Ephraim *are* e and the crimes 1655
Hab 2:16 Drink and **be** e! 6887
Zep 2:14 the beams of cedar *will be* e. 6867
Jn 3:20 the light for fear that his deeds *will be* e. *1794*
2Co 11:23 and been e **to death** again and again. *2505*
Eph 5:13 everything e by the light becomes visible, *1794*
Heb 10:33 Sometimes *you were* **publicly** e to insult *2518*
Rev 16:15 he may not go naked and *be* shamefully e." *1063*

EXPOSES (1) [EXPOSE]
Pr 13:16 but a fool e his folly. 7298

EXPOSING (1) [EXPOSE]
Ge 30:37 and e the white inner wood of the branches. 4741

EXPOUND (2)
Dt 1: 5 Moses began *to* e this law, saying: 930
Ps 49: 4 with the harp *I will* e my riddle: 7337

EXPRESS (8) [EXPRESSED, EXPRESSES, EXPRESSING, EXPRESSION, EXPRESSIONS]
2Sa 10: 2 David sent a delegation to e his **sympathy** 5714
10: 3 by sending men to you *to* e **sympathy?** 5714
1Ch 19: 2 David sent a delegation to e his **sympathy** 5714
19: 2 in the land of the Ammonites to e **sympathy** 5714
19: 3 by sending men to you *to* e **sympathy?** 5714
Eze 33:31 With their mouths they e devotion, 6913
Ro 8:26 for us with groans *that* **words cannot** e. *227*
Col 4: 8 I am sending him to you **for the** e **purpose** that you may know *899+1650+4047*

EXPRESSED (2) [EXPRESS]
2Sa 13:32 This has been Absalom's e intention 6584+7023
Eph 2: 7 grace, e in his kindness to us in Christ Jesus. *NIG*

EXPRESSES (1) [EXPRESS]
Ps 7:11 a God *who* e his **wrath** every day. 2404

EXPRESSING (2) [EXPRESS]
1Co 2:13 e spiritual truths in spiritual words. *5173*
Gal 5: 6 The only thing that counts is faith e *itself* *1919*

EXPRESSION (2) [EXPRESS]
Lev 7:12 " 'If he offers it as an e **of thankfulness,** 9343
Job 9:27 I will change my e, and smile,' 7156

EXPRESSIONS (1) [EXPRESS]
2Co 9:12 but is also overflowing in many e **of thanks** *2374*

EXTEND (20) [EXTENDED, EXTENDING, EXTENDS, EXTENSIVE, EXTENT]
Ge 9:27 *May* God e **the territory** of Japheth; 7332
49:13 his border will e **toward** Sidon. 6584
Ex 25:32 Six branches *are to* e from the sides of 3655
26:28 The center crossbar *is to* e from end to end 1368
Nu 35: 4 will e **out** fifteen hundred feet 2025+2575
Dt 11:24 Your territory *will* e from the desert 2118
Jos 1: 4 Your territory *will* e from the desert 2118
1Ch 11:10 gave his kingship strong support to e it over 4887
Est 4:11 to this is for the king *to* e the gold scepter 3804
Ps 109:12 *May* no *one* e kindness to him or take pity 5432
110: 2 The LORD *will* e your mighty scepter 8938
Isa 66:12 "I *will* e peace to her like a river, 5742
Eze 45: 7 It will e **westward** from the west side 2025+3542
47:17 The boundary *will* e from the sea 2118
48:21 It will e **eastward** from the 25,000 2025+7708
48:23 it will e **from** the east side to the west side. 4946
Da 11:42 *He will* e his power over many countries; 8938
Am 1:13 of Gilead in order to e his borders, 8143
Zec 9:10 His rule will e **from** sea to sea and from 4946
14: 5 for it *will* e to Azel. 5595

EXTENDED (16) [EXTEND]
Ex 36:33 They made the center crossbar so that *it* e 1368
37:18 Six branches e from the sides of 3655
Dt 4:48 This land e **from** Aroer on the rim of 4946
Jos 13: 9 It e **from** Aroer on the rim of 4946
15: 1 e down to the territory of Edom, 2118
17: 7 The territory of Manasseh e from Asher 2118
19:11 and e to the ravine near Jokneam. 7003
1Ki 6: 3 main hall of the temple e the width of 6584+7156
6:21 and *he* e gold chains across the front of 6296
1Ch 5:16 the pasturelands of Sharon as far as they e. 9362
21:16 with a drawn sword in his hand e 5742
2Ch 3:13 wings of these cherubim e twenty cubits. 7298
Ezr 7:28 and *who has* e his good favor to me before 5742
Est 8: 4 Then the king e the gold scepter to Esther 3804
Isa 26:15 *you have* e all the borders of the land. 8178
Eze 42: 7 it e in front of the rooms for fifty cubits. 802

EXTENDING (11) [EXTEND]
Ex 25:33 for all six branches e from the lampstand. 3655
25:35 be under the first pair of branches e from 3655
37:19 for all six branches e from the lampstand. 3655
37:21 under the first pair of branches e from 3655
Nu 21:13 in the desert e into Amorite territory. 3655
Dt 3:16 and the Gadites I gave the territory e **from** 4946
Jos 13:30 The territory e from Mahanaim 2118
1Sa 27: 8 in the land e to Shur and Egypt.) 995
2Ch 5: 9 e **from** the ark, could be seen from in front 4946
Eze 42:12 to the corresponding wall e eastward, 2006
Mic 7:11 the day *for* e your boundaries. 8178

EXTENDS (5) [EXTEND]
Nu 21:30 which e **to** Medeba." 6330
1Ch 5: 9 desert that e **to** the Euphrates River, 4200+4946
Pr 31:20 to the poor and e her hands to the needy. 8938
Da 4:22 and your dominion e **to** distant parts of 10378
Lk 1:50 His mercy e to those who fear him, *NIG*

EXTENSIVE (3) [EXTEND]
1Ch 22: 5 David made e preparations before his death. 4200+8044
2Ch 27: 3 and did e work on the wall at 4200+8044
Ne 4:19 "The work is e and spread out, 2221

EXTENT (3) [EXTEND]
Jn 13: 1 showed them **the full** e **of** his love. *1650+5465*
1Co 11:18 and to some e I believe it. *3538*
2Co 2: 5 grieved all of you, **to some** e— *247+608+3538*

EXTERMINATE (2) [EXTERMINATING]
1Ki 9:21 whom the Israelites could not e— 3049
Eze 25: 7 the nations and e you from the countries. 6

EXTERMINATING (1) [EXTERMINATE]
Jos 11:20 e them without mercy, 9012

EXTERNAL (2)
Gal 2: 6 not **judge by** e **appearance—** *476+3284+4725*
Heb 9:10 e regulations applying until the time of *4922*

EXTINCT (KJV) CUT SHORT, EXTINGUISHED

EXTINGUISH (1) [EXTINGUISHED]
Eph 6:16 with which you can e all the flaming arrows *4931*

EXTINGUISHED (2) [EXTINGUISH]
2Sa 21:17 so that the lamp of Israel *will* not *be* e." 3882
Isa 43:17 and they lay there, never to rise again, e, 1980

EXTOL (11)
Job 36:24 Remember *to* e his work, 8434
Ps 34: 1 *I will* e the LORD at all times; 1385
68: 4 e him who rides on the clouds— 6148
95: 2 with thanksgiving and e him with music 8131
109:30 With my mouth *I will* greatly e 3344
111: 1 *I will* e the LORD with all my heart in 3344
115:18 it is we *who* e the LORD, 1385
117: 1 e him, all *you* peoples. 8655
145: 2 and e your name for ever and ever. 2146
145:10 your saints *will* e you. 1385
Ps 147:12 **E** the LORD, O Jerusalem; 8655

EXTORT (1) [EXTORTION]
Lk 3:14 He replied, "Don't e **money** *1398*

EXTORTION (9) [EXTORT]
Lev 6: 4 stolen or **taken by** e, 6943+6945
Ps 62:10 not trust in e or take pride in stolen goods; 6945
Ecc 7: 7 E turns a wise man into a fool, 6945
Isa 33:15 who rejects gain from e and keeps his hand 5131
Jer 22:17 and on oppression and e." 5298
Eze 18:18 because *he* **practiced** e, 6943+6945
22:12 from your neighbors by e. 6945
22:29 The people of the land **practice** e and 6943+6945
Hab 2: 6 and makes himself wealthy *by* e! 6294

EXTRA (4)
Mt 10:10 or e tunic, or sandals or a staff; *1545*
Mk 6: 9 Wear sandals but not an e tunic. *1545*
Lk 9: 3 no bag, no bread, no money, no e tunic. *324+1545*
10:35 for any e **expense** you may have.' *4655*

EXTRAORDINARY (1)
Ac 19:11 God did e miracles through Paul *3836+4024+5593*

EXTREME (2) [EXTREMES, EXTREMELY]
Jos 15: 1 to the Desert of Zin in the e south. 7895
2Co 8: 2 and their e poverty welled up *958+2848*

EXTREMELY (2) [EXTREME]
Pr 30:24 yet they *are* e **wise:** 2681+2682
Gal 1:14 of my own age and was e zealous for *4359*

EXTREMES (1) [EXTREME]
Ecc 7:18 The man who fears God will avoid all [e]. 4392S

EXULT (3)
Ps 89:16 *they* e in your righteousness. 8123
Isa 14: 8 the cedars of Lebanon e over you and say, 8523
45:25 be found righteous and *will* e. 2146

EYE (72) [EYEBROWS, EYED, EYELIDS, EYES, EYESIGHT]
Ge 2: 9 trees that were pleasing to the e and good 5260
3: 6 good for food and pleasing to the e, 6524
Ex 21:24 e for eye, tooth for tooth, hand 6524
21:24 eye for e, tooth for tooth, hand for hand, 6524
21:26 or maidservant in the e and destroys it, 6524
21:26 the servant go free to compensate for the e. 6524
Lev 21:20 or who has any e defect, 6524
24:20 e for eye, tooth for tooth. 6524
24:20 eye for e, tooth for tooth. 6524
Nu 24: 3 the oracle of one whose e sees clearly, 6524
24:15 the oracle of one whose e sees clearly, 6524
Dt 19:21 life for life, e for eye, tooth for tooth, 6524
19:21 life for life, eye for e, tooth for tooth, 6524
32:10 he guarded him as the apple of his e, 6524
1Sa 11: 2 on the condition that I gouge out the right e 6524
18: 9 Saul **kept a jealous** e **on** David. 6523
Ezr 5: 5 But the e *of* their God was watching over 10540
Job 7: 8 e that now sees me will see me no longer; 6524
10:18 I wish I had died before any e saw me. 6524
14: 3 Do you fix your e on such a one? 6524
20: 9 The e that saw him will not see him again; 6524
24:15 The e *of* the adulterer watches for dusk; 6524
24:15 he thinks, 'No e will see me,' 6524
28: 7 no falcon's e has seen it. 6524
Ps 17: 8 Keep me as the apple of your e; 6524
35:19 without reason maliciously wink the e. 6524
94: 9 Does he who formed the e not see? 6524
Pr 6:13 who winks with his e, 6524
7: 2 guard my teachings as the apple of your e. 6524
16:30 with his e is plotting perversity; 6524
30:17 "The e that mocks a father, 6524
Ecc 1: 8 The e never has enough of seeing, 6524
6: 9 the e sees than the roving of the appetite. 6524
Isa 29:20 and all *who* **have an** e **for** evil will 9193
64: 4 no e has seen any God besides you, 6524
La 2: 4 Like a foe he has slain all who were pleasing to the e; 6524
Zec 2: 8 touches you touches the apple of his e— 6524
11:17 the sword strike his arm and his right e! 6524
11:17 his right e totally blinded!" 6524
12: 4 "I will keep a watchful e over the house 6524
Mt 5:29 If your right e causes you to sin, *4057*
5:38 '**E** for eye, and tooth for tooth.' *4057*
5:38 'Eye for e, and tooth for tooth.' *4057*
6:22 "The e is the lamp of the body. *4057*
7: 3 at the speck of sawdust in your brother's e *4057*
7: 3 to the plank in your own e? *4057*
7: 4 'Let me take the speck out *of* your e,' *4057*
7: 4 the time there is a plank in your own e? *4057*
7: 5 first take the plank out *of* your own e, *4057*
7: 5 to remove the speck from your brother's e. *4057*
18: 9 And if your e causes you to sin, *4057*
18: 9 with **one** e than to have two eyes and *3669*
19:24 a camel to go through the e of a needle than *5585*
Mk 9:47 if your e causes you to sin, pluck it out. *4057*
9:47 to enter the kingdom of God with **one** e than *3669*
10:25 a camel to go through the e of a needle than *5584*
Lk 6:41 at the speck of sawdust in your brother's e *4057*

Lk 6:41 to the plank in your own e? 4057
6:42 let me take the speck out of your e,' 4057
6:42 to see the plank in your own e? 4057
6:42 first take the plank out of your e, 4057
6:42 to remove the speck from your brother's e. 4057
11:34 Your e is the lamp of your body. 4057
18:25 a camel to go through the e of a needle than 5557
1Co 2:9 However, as it is written: "No e has seen, 4057
12:16 the ear should say, "Because I am not an e, 4057
12:17 If the whole body were an e, 4057
12:21 The e cannot say to the hand, 4057
15:52 in the twinkling of an e, at the last trumpet. 4057
Eph 6:6 win their favor when their e is on you, 4056
Col 3:22 and do it, not only when their e is on you 4056
Rev 1:7 and every e will see him, 4057

EYEBROWS (1) [EYE]

Lev 14:9 his beard, his e and the rest of his hair. 1461+6524

EYED (1) [EYE]

Ecc 5:8 for one official is e by a higher one, 9068

EYELIDS (3) [EYE]

Ps 132:4 no slumber to my e, 6757
Pr 6:4 no slumber to your e. 6757
Jer 9:18 with tears and water streams from our e. 6757

EYES (522) [EYE]

Ge 3:5 when you eat of it your e will be opened, 6524
3:7 Then the e of both of them were opened, 6524
6:8 Noah found favor in the e of the LORD. 6524
13:14 "Lift up your e from where you are 6524
18:3 He said, "If I have found favor in your e, 6524
19:19 Your servant has found favor in your e, 6524
21:19 Then God opened her e and she saw a well 6524
27:1 When Isaac was old and his e were so weak 6524
29:17 Leah had weak e, 6524
30:27 "If I have found favor in your e, 6524
31:40 and sleep fled from my e. 6524
32:5 that I may find favor in your e.' " 6524
33:8 "To find favor in your e, my lord," he said. 6524
33:10 "If I have found favor in your e, 6524
33:15 "Just let me find favor in the e of my lord." 6524
34:11 "Let me find favor in your e, 6524
39:4 in his e and became his attendant. 6524
39:21 and granted him favor in the e of 6524
42:24 from them and bound before their e. 6524
46:4 And Joseph's own hand will close your e." 6524
47:15 Why should we die before your e? NIH
47:19 Why should we perish before your e— 6524
47:25 "May we find favor in the e of our lord; 6524
47:29 "If I have found favor in your e, 6524
48:10 Israel's e were failing because of old age, 6524
49:12 His e will be darker than wine, 6524
50:4 "If I have found favor in your e, 6524
Ex 8:26 that are detestable in their e, 6524
15:26 and do what is right in his e, 6524
34:9 "O Lord, if I have found favor in your e," 6524
Lev 20:4 If the people of the community close their e 6524
20:17 be cut off before the e of their people. 6524
Nu 10:31 and you can be our e. 6524
11:15 if I have found favor in your e— 6524
13:33 We seemed like grasshoppers in our own e, 6524
15:39 after the lusts of your own hearts and e. 6524
16:14 Will you gouge out the e of these men? 6524
20:8 before their e and it will pour out its water. 6524
22:31 Then the LORD opened Balaam's e, 6524
24:4 and whose e are opened: 6524
24:16 and whose e are opened: 6524
25:6 the e of Moses and the whole assembly 6524
27:14 to honor me as holy before their e." 6524
32:5 If we have found favor in your e," they said, 6524
33:55 to remain will become barbs in your e 6524
Dt 1:30 before your very e, 6524
3:21 "You have seen with your own e all that 6524
3:27 Look at the land with your own e, 6524
4:3 with your own e what the LORD did 6524
4:9 the things your e have seen or let them slip 6524
4:25 doing evil in the e of the LORD your God 6524
4:34 for you in Egypt before your very e? 6524
6:22 Before our e the LORD sent miraculous signs 6524
7:19 You saw with your own e the great trials, 6524
9:17 breaking them to pieces before your e. 6524
10:21 with your own e. 6524
11:7 But it was your own e 6524
11:12 the e of the LORD your God are continually 6524
12:25 be doing what is right in the e of the LORD 6524
12:28 and right in the e of the LORD your God. 6524
13:18 and doing what is right in his e. 6524
16:19 a bribe blinds the e of the wise and twists 6524
17:2 the e of the LORD your God in violation 6524
21:7 nor did our e see it done. 6524
21:9 since you have done what is right in the e 6524
24:4 be detestable in the e of the LORD. 4200+7156
25:3 your brother will be degraded in your e. 6524
28:31 Your ox will be slaughtered before your e, 6524
28:32 and you will wear out your e watching 6524
28:65 e weary with longing, 6524
28:67 and the sights that your e will see. 6524
29:2 Your e have seen all that the LORD did 6524
29:3 With your own e you saw those great trials, 6524
29:4 a mind that understands or e that see or ears 6524
34:4 I have let you see it with your e, 6524
34:7 his e were not weak nor his strength gone. 6524
Jos 3:7 "Today I will begin to exalt you in the e 6524
23:13 whips on your backs and thorns in your e, 6524
24:7 You saw with your own e what I did to 6524
24:17 performed those great signs before our e. 6524
Jdg 2:11 the Israelites did evil in the e of the LORD 6524
3:7 The Israelites did evil in the e of the LORD; 6524
3:12 Once again the Israelites did evil in the e of 6524
4:1 the Israelites once again did evil in the e of 6524
6:1 Again the Israelites did evil in the e of 6524
6:17 "If now I have found favor in your e, 6524
10:6 Again the Israelites did evil in the e of 6524
13:1 Again the Israelites did evil in the e of 6524
16:21 gouged out his e and took him down 6524
16:28 on the Philistines for my two e." 6524
Ru 2:2 behind anyone in whose e I find favor." 6524
2:10 "Why have I found such favor in your e 6524
2:13 "May I continue to find favor in your e, 6524
1Sa 1:18 "May your servant find favor in your e." 6524
2:33 be spared only to blind your e with tears 6524
3:2 whose e were becoming so weak 6524
3:18 let him do what is good in his e." 6524
4:15 and whose e were set so that he could 6524
12:3 a bribe to make me shut my e? 6524
12:16 the LORD is about to do before your e! 6524
12:17 an evil thing you did in the e of the LORD 6524
14:27 and his e brightened. 6524
14:29 how my e brightened when I tasted a little 6524
15:17 you were once small in your own e, 6524
15:19 on the plunder and do evil in the e of 6524
20:3 that I have found favor in your e, 6524
20:29 If I have found favor in your e, 6524
24:10 This day you have seen with your own e 6524
27:5 "If I have found favor in your e, 6524
29:9 that you have been as pleasing in my e as 6524
2Sa 6:22 and I will be humiliated in my own e. 6524
12:9 the LORD by doing what is evil in his e? 6524
12:11 Before your very e I will take your wives 6524
14:22 that he has found favor in your e, 6524
15:25 If I find favor in the LORD's e, 6524
16:4 "May I find favor in your e, 6524
22:28 but your e are on the haughty 6524
24:3 and may the e of my lord the king see it. 6524
1Ki 1:20 the e of all Israel are on you, 6524
1:48 who has allowed my e to see a successor 6524
8:29 May your e be open toward this temple 6524
8:52 "May your e be open to your servant's plea 6524
9:3 My e and my heart will always be there. 6524
10:7 until I came and saw with my own e. 6524
11:6 Solomon did evil in the e of the LORD; 6524
11:33 nor done what is right in my e, 6524
11:38 in my ways and do what is right in my e 6524
14:8 doing only what was right in my e. 6524
14:22 Judah did evil in the e of the LORD. 6524
15:5 For David had done what was right in the e 6524
15:11 Asa did what was right in the e of the LORD 6524
15:26 He did evil in the e of the LORD, 6524
15:34 He did evil in the e of the LORD, 6524
16:7 the evil he had done in the e of the LORD, 6524
16:19 in the e of the LORD and walking in 6524
16:25 But Omri did evil in the e of the LORD 6524
16:30 Ahab son of Omri did more evil in the e of 6524
20:38 with his headband down over his e. 6524
20:41 the headband from his e, 6524
21:20 to do evil in the e of the LORD. 6524
21:25 who sold himself to do evil in the e of 6524
22:43 he did what was right in the e of the LORD 6524
22:52 He did evil in the e of the LORD, 6524
2Ki 3:2 He did evil in the e of the LORD, 6524
3:18 an easy thing in the e of the LORD, 6524
4:34 mouth to mouth, e to eyes, hands to hands. 6524
4:34 mouth to mouth, eyes to e, hands to hands. 6524
4:35 and opened his e. 6524
6:17 "O LORD, open his e so he may see." 6524
6:17 Then the LORD opened the servant's e, 6524
6:20 open the e of these men so they can see." 6524
6:20 the LORD opened their e and they looked, 6524
7:2 "You will see it with your own e," 6524
7:19 "You will see it with your own e, 6524
8:18 He did evil in the e of the LORD. 6524
8:27 the house of Ahab and did evil in the e of 6524
9:30 Jezebel heard about it, she painted her e, 6524
10:30 in accomplishing what is right in my e 6524
12:2 the e of the LORD all the years Jehoiada 6524
13:2 the e of the LORD by following the sins 6524
13:11 the e of the LORD and did not turn away 6524
14:3 He did what was right in the e of the LORD 6524
14:24 the e of the LORD and did not turn away 6524
15:3 He did what was right in the e of the LORD 6524
15:9 He did evil in the e of the LORD, 6524
15:18 He did evil in the e of the LORD. 6524
15:24 Pekahiah did evil in the e of the LORD. 6524
15:28 He did evil in the e of the LORD. 6524
15:34 He did what was right in the e of the LORD 6524
16:2 he did not do what was right in the e of 6524
17:2 He did evil in the e of the LORD, 6524
17:17 and sold themselves to do evil in the e of 6524
18:3 He did what was right in the e of the LORD 6524
19:16 open your e, O LORD, and see; 6524
19:22 and lifted your e in pride? 6524
20:3 and have done what is good in your e." 6524
21:2 He did evil in the e of the LORD, 6524
21:6 He did much evil in the e of the LORD, 6524
21:15 in my e and have provoked me to anger 6524
21:16 so that they did evil in the e of the LORD. 6524
21:20 He did evil in the e of the LORD, 6524
22:2 in the e of the LORD and walked in all 6524
22:20 Your e will not see all 6524
2Ki 23:32 He did evil in the e of the LORD, 6524
23:37 And he did evil in the e of the LORD, 6524
24:9 He did evil in the e of the LORD, 6524
24:19 He did evil in the e of the LORD, 6524
25:7 the sons of Zedekiah before his e. 6524
25:7 Then they put out his e, 6524
2Ch 6:20 May your e be open toward this temple day 6524
6:40 may your e be open and your ears attentive 6524
7:15 Now my e will be open 6524
7:16 My e and my heart will always be there. 6524
9:6 until I came and saw with my own e. 6524
14:2 Asa did what was good and right in the e of 6524
16:9 For the e of the LORD range throughout 6524
20:12 but our e are upon you." 6524
20:32 he did what was right in the e of the LORD 6524
21:6 He did evil in the e of the LORD. 6524
22:4 He did evil in the e of the LORD, 6524
24:2 Joash did what was right in the e of 6524
25:2 He did what was right in the e of the LORD 6524
26:4 He did what was right in the e of the LORD 6524
27:2 He did what was right in the e of the LORD 6524
28:1 he did not do what was right in the e of 6524
29:2 He did what was right in the e of the LORD 6524
29:6 in the e of the LORD our God 6524
29:8 as you can see with your own e. 6524
33:2 He did evil in the e of the LORD, 6524
33:6 He did much evil in the e of the LORD, 6524
33:22 He did evil in the e of the LORD, 6524
34:2 the e of the LORD and walked in the ways 6524
34:28 Your e will not see all 6524
36:5 He did evil in the e of the LORD his God. 6524
36:9 He did evil in the e of the LORD. 6524
36:12 He did evil in the e of the LORD his God 6524
Ezr 9:8 to our e and a little relief in our bondage. 6524
Ne 1:6 let your ear be attentive and your e open 6524
9:32 do not let all this hardship seem trifling in your e— 4200+7156
Job 3:10 the womb on me to hide trouble from my e. 6524
4:16 A form stood before my e, 6524
7:7 my e will never see happiness again. 6524
10:4 Do you have e of flesh? 6524
11:20 But the e of the wicked will fail, 6524
13:1 "My e have seen all this, 6524
15:12 and why do your e flash, 6524
15:15 if even the heavens are not pure in his e, 6524
16:9 my opponent fastens on me his piercing e. 6524
16:16 deep shadows ring my e; 6757
16:20 as my e pour out tears to God; 6524
17:2 my e must dwell on their hostility. 6524
17:5 the e of his children will fail. 6524
17:7 My e have grown dim with grief; 6524
19:27 I myself will see him with my own e— 6524
21:8 their offspring before their e. 6524
21:20 Let his own e see his destruction; 6524
24:23 but his e are on their ways. 6524
25:5 and the stars are not pure in his e, 6524
27:19 when he opens his e, all is gone. 6524
28:10 his e see all its treasures. 6524
28:21 from the e of every living thing, 6524
29:15 I was e to the blind and feet to the lame. 6524
31:1 a covenant with my e not to look lustfully 6524
31:7 if my heart has been led by my e, 6524
31:16 or let the e of the widow grow weary, 6524
32:1 because he was righteous in his own e. 6524
34:21 "His e are on the ways of men; 6524
36:7 He does not take his e off the righteous; 6524
39:29 his e detect it from afar. 6524
40:24 Can anyone capture him by the e, 6524
41:18 his e are like the rays of dawn. 6524
42:5 of you but now my e have seen you. 6524
Ps 6:7 My e grow weak with sorrow; 6524
11:4 his e examine them. 6757
13:3 Give light to my e, or I will sleep in death; 6524
17:2 may your e see what is right. 6524
17:11 with e alert, to throw me to the ground. 6524
18:27 but bring low those whose e are haughty. 6524
19:8 giving light to the e. 6524
25:15 My e are ever on the LORD, 6524
31:9 my e grow weak with sorrow, 6524
33:18 e of the LORD are on those who fear him, 6524
34:15 The e of the LORD are on the righteous 6524
35:21 With our own e we have seen it." 6524
36:1 There is no fear of God before his e. 6524
36:2 in his own e he flatters himself too much 6524
38:10 even the light has gone from my e. 6524
52:1 you who are a disgrace in the e of God? AIT
54:7 my e have looked in triumph on my foes. 6524
66:7 his e watch the nations— 6524
69:3 My e fail, looking for my God. 6524
69:23 May their e be darkened so they cannot see, 6524
77:4 You kept my e from closing; 6524
79:10 Before our e, make known among 6524
88:9 my e are dim with grief. 6524
91:8 You will only observe with your e and see 6524
92:11 My e have seen the defeat 6524
101:3 I will set before my e no vile thing. 6524
101:5 whoever has haughty e and a proud heart, 6524
101:6 My e will be on the faithful in the land, 6524
115:5 They have mouths, but cannot speak, e, 6524
116:8 my e from tears, my feet from stumbling, 6524
118:23 and it is marvelous in our e. 6524
119:18 Open my e that I may see wonderful things 6524
119:37 Turn my e away from worthless things; 6524
119:82 My e fail, looking for your promise; 6524
119:123 My e fail, looking for your salvation, 6524
119:136 Streams of tears flow from my e, 6524
119:148 My e stay open through the watches of 6524

Ps 121: 1 I lift up my e to the hills— 6524
123: 1 I lift up my e to you, 6524
123: 2 As the e *of* slaves look to the hand 6524
123: 2 as the e *of* a maid look to the hand 6524
123: 2 so our e look to the LORD our God, 6524
131: 1 O LORD, my e are not haughty; 6524
132: 4 I will allow no sleep to my e, 6524
135: 16 They have mouths, but cannot speak, e, 6524
139: 16 your e saw my unformed body. 6524
141: 8 But my e are fixed on you, 6524
145: 15 The e *of* all look to you, 6524
Pr 3: 7 Do not be wise in your own e; 6524
4: 25 Let your e look straight ahead, 6524
6: 4 Allow no sleep to your e, 6524
6: 17 haughty e, a lying tongue, hands 6524
6: 25 or let her captivate you with her e, 6757
10: 26 As vinegar to the teeth and smoke to the e, 6524
15: 3 The e *of* the LORD are everywhere, 6524
17: 24 a fool's e wander to the ends of the earth. 6524
20: 8 he winnows out all evil with his e. 6524
20: 12 Ears that hear and e that see— 6524
21: 4 Haughty e and a proud heart, 6524
22: 12 The e *of* the LORD keep watch 6524
23: 26 give me your heart and let your e keep 6524
23: 29 Who has bloodshot e? 6524
23: 33 Your e will see strange sights 6524
25: 7 What you have seen with your e 6524
26: 5 or he will be wise in his own e. 6524
26: 12 Do you see a man wise in his own e? 6524
26: 16 The sluggard is wiser in his own e than seven men who answer discreetly. 6524
27: 20 and neither are the e *of* man. 6524
28: 11 A rich man may be wise in his own e, 6524
28: 27 but he who closes his e 6524
29: 13 The LORD gives sight to the e *of* both. 6524
30: 12 in their own e and yet are not cleansed 6524
30: 13 those whose e are ever so haughty, 6524
Ecc 2: 10 I denied myself nothing my e desired; 6524
2: 14 The wise man has e in his head, 6524
4: 8 yet his e were not content with his wealth. 6524
5: 11 to the owner except to feast his e on them? 6524
8: 16 his e not seeing sleep day or night— 6524
11: 7 and it pleases the e to see the sun. 6524
11: 9 of your heart and whatever your e see, 6524
SS 1: 15 Your e are doves. 6524
4: 1 Your e behind your veil are doves. 6524
4: 9 with one glance of your e, 6524
5: 12 His e are like doves by the water streams, 6524
6: 5 Turn your e from me; they overwhelm me. 6524
7: 4 Your e are the pools of Heshbon by the gate 6524
8: 10 in his e like one bringing contentment. 6524
Isa 1: 15 I will hide my e from you; 6524
2: 11 The e *of* the arrogant man will be humbled 6524
3: 16 flirting with their e, 6524
5: 15 the e *of* the arrogant humbled. 6524
5: 21 in their own e and clever in their own sight. 6524
6: 5 and my e have seen the King, 6524
6: 10 make their ears dull and close their e. 6524
6: 10 Otherwise they might see with their e, 6524
10: 12 of his heart and the haughty look in his e. 6524
11: 3 with his e, or decide by what he hears 6524
13: 16 be dashed to pieces before their e; 6524
17: 7 and turn their e to the Holy One of Israel. 6524
29: 10 He has sealed your e (the prophets); 6524
29: 18 and darkness the e *of* the blind will see. 6524
30: 20 with your own e you will see them. 6524
32: 3 Then the e *of* those who see will no longer 6524
33: 15 against plots of murder and shuts his e 6524
33: 17 Your e will see the king in his beauty 6524
33: 20 your e will see Jerusalem, a peaceful abode, 6524
35: 5 the e *of* the blind be opened and the ears of 6524
37: 17 open your e, O LORD, and see; 6524
37: 23 and lifted your e in pride? 6524
38: 3 and have done what is good in your e." 6524
38: 14 My e grew weak as I looked to the heavens. 6524
40: 26 Lift your e and look to the heavens: 6524
42: 7 to open e that are blind, 6524
43: 8 Lead out those who have e but are blind, 6524
44: 18 their e are plastered over 6524
49: 5 for I am honored in the e *of* the LORD 6524
49: 18 Lift up your e and look around; 6524
51: 6 Lift up your e to the heavens, 6524
52: 8 they will see it with their own e. 6524
59: 10 feeling our way like men without e. 6524
60: 4 "Lift up your e and look about you: 6524
65: 16 be forgotten and hidden from my e. 6524
Jer 4: 30 Why shade your e with paint? 6524
5: 3 O LORD, do not your e look for truth? 6524
5: 21 who have e but do not see, 6524
7: 30 of Judah have done evil in my e, 6524
9: 1 of water and my e a fountain of tears! 6524
9: 18 over us till our e overflow with tears 6524
13: 17 my e will weep bitterly, 6524
13: 20 up your e and see those who are coming 6524
14: 17 " 'Let my e overflow with tears night 6524
16: 9 Before your e and in your days I will bring 6524
16: 17 My e are on all their ways; 6524
16: 17 nor is their sin concealed from my e. 6524
20: 4 with your own e you will see them fall by 6524
22: 17 "But your e and your heart are set only 6524
24: 6 My e will watch over them for their good, 6524
29: 21 to death before your very e. 6524
31: 16 from weeping and your e from tears, 6524
32: 4 to face and see him with his own e. 6524
32: 19 Your e are open to all the ways of men; 6524
34: 3 the king of Babylon with your own e, 6524
39: 6 of Zedekiah before his e and also killed all 6524
Jer 39: 7 Then he put out Zedekiah's e 6524
39: 16 be fulfilled **before** your e. 4200+7156
51: 24 "Before your e I will repay Babylon 6524
52: 2 He did evil in the e *of* the LORD, 6524
52: 10 the sons of Zedekiah before his e; 6524
52: 11 Then he put out Zedekiah's e, 6524
La 1: 16 "This is why I weep and my e overflow 6524
2: 11 My e fail from weeping, 6524
2: 18 give yourself no relief, your e no rest. 1426+6524
3: 48 Streams of tears flow from my e 6524
3: 49 My e will flow unceasingly, without relief, 6524
4: 17 our e failed, looking in vain for help; 6524
5: 17 because of these things our e grow dim 6524
Eze 1: 18 and all four rims were full of e all around. 6524
6: 9 from me, and by their e, 6524
10: 12 were completely full of e, 6524
12: 2 They have e to see but do not see and ears 6524
20: 7 of the vile images you have set your e on, 6524
20: 8 of the vile images they had set their e on, 6524
20: 9 the e *of* the nations they lived among and 6524
20: 14 from being profaned in the e *of* the nations 6524
20: 22 from being profaned in the e *of* the nations 6524
20: 24 and their e [lusted] after their fathers' idols. 6524
22: 16 When you have been defiled in the e *of* 6524
22: 26 and they shut their e to the keeping 6524
23: 40 painted your e and put on your jewelry. 6524
24: 16 to take away from you the delight of your e. 6524
24: 21 the delight of your e, the object of your 6524
24: 25 the delight of their e, their heart's desire, 6524
36: 23 through you before their e. 6524
37: 20 before their e the sticks you have written on 6524
38: 16 through you before their e. 6524
40: 4 look with your e and hear with your ears 6524
Da 4: 34 raised my e toward heaven, 10540
7: 8 This horn had e like the eyes of a man and 10540
7: 8 This horn had eyes like the e *of* a man and 10540
7: 20 the others and that had e and a mouth 10540
8: 5 a prominent horn between his e came from 6524
8: 21 large horn between his e is the first king. 6524
9: 18 open your e and see the desolation of 6524
10: 6 his e like flaming torches, 6524
Hos 2: 10 now I will expose her lewdness before the e 6524
Joel 1: 16 not the food been cut off before our very e 6524
Am 9: 4 I will fix my e upon them for evil and not 6524
9: 8 "Surely the e *of* the Sovereign LORD are 6524
Mic 4: 11 let our e gloat over Zion!" 6524
7: 10 My e will see her downfall; 6524
Hab 1: 13 Your e are too pure to look on evil; 6524
Zep 3: 20 before your very e," 6524
Zec 3: 9 There are seven e on that one stone, 6524
4: 10 "(These seven are the e *of* the LORD, 6524
9: 1 the e *of* men and all the tribes of Israel are 6524
14: 12 their e will rot in their sockets, 6524
Mal 1: 5 You will see it with your own e and say, 6524
2: 17 "All who do evil are good in the e *of* 6524
Mt 6: 22 If your e are good, *4057*
6: 23 But if your e are bad, *4057*
9: 29 Then he touched their e and said, *4057*
13: 15 and they have closed their e. *4057*
13: 15 Otherwise they might see *with* their e, *4057*
13: 16 But blessed are your e because they see, *4057*
18: 9 to enter life with one eye than to have two e *4057*
20: 34 on them and touched their e. *3921*
21: 42 and it is marvelous in our e'? *4057*
26: 43 because their e were heavy. *4057*
Mk 8: 18 Do you have e but fail to see, *4057*
8: 23 spit on the man's e and put his hands on him *3921*
8: 25 put his hands on the man's e. *4057*
8: 25 Then *his* e *were* **opened,** *1332*
9: 47 of God with one eye than to have two e and *4057*
12: 11 and it is marvelous in our e'?" *4057*
14: 40 because their e were heavy. *4057*
Lk 2: 30 For my e have seen your salvation, *4057*
4: 20 The e of everyone in the synagogue *4057*
10: 23 "Blessed are the e that see what you see. *4057*
11: 34 When your e are good, *4057*
16: 15 the ones who justify yourselves **in the** e of *1967*
19: 42 but now it is hidden from your e. *4057*
24: 31 Then their e were opened *4057*
Jn 4: 35 **open** your e and look at the fields! *2048+4057*
9: 6 and put it on the man's e. *4057*
9: 10 "How then were your e opened?" *4057*
9: 11 and put it on my e. *4057*
9: 14 and opened the man's e was a Sabbath. *4057*
9: 15 "He put mud on my e," the man replied, *4057*
9: 17 It was your e he opened." *4057*
9: 21 how he can see now, or who opened his e, *4057*
9: 26 How did he open your e?" *4057*
9: 30 yet he opened my e. *4057*
9: 32 Nobody has ever heard of opening the e of *4057*
10: 21 Can a demon open the e of the blind?" *4057*
11: 37 the e of the blind man have kept this man *4057*
12: 40 "He has blinded their e *4057*
12: 40 so they can neither see *with* their e, *4057*
Ac 1: 9 he was taken up **before their very** e, *899+1063*
9: 8 when he opened his e he could see nothing. *4057*
9: 18 something like scales fell from Saul's e, *4057*
9: 40 She opened her e, *4057*
26: 18 to open their e and turn them from darkness *4057*
28: 27 and they have closed their e. *4057*
28: 27 Otherwise they might see *with* their e, *4057*
Ro 3: 18 "There is no fear of God before their e." *4057*
11: 8 e so that they could not see and ears so *4057*
11: 10 May their e be darkened so they cannot see, *4057*
12: 17 to do what is right **in the** e of everybody. *1967*
2Co 4: 18 **fix** our e not **on** what is seen, but on *5023*
8: 21 not only **in the** e of the Lord but also in *1967*
2Co 8: 21 in the eyes of the Lord but also **in the** e *1967*
Gal 3: 1 Before your very e Jesus Christ was clearly portrayed as crucified. *4057*
4: 15 you would have torn out your e *4057*
Eph 1: 18 that the e of your heart may be enlightened *4057*
Heb 4: 13 and laid bare *before* the e of him *4057*
12: 2 *Let us* **fix** *our* e on Jesus, *927*
Jas 2: 5 not God chosen those who are poor in the e *NIG*
1Pe 3: 12 For the e of the Lord are on the righteous *4057*
2Pe 2: 14 With e full of adultery, *4057*
1Jn 1: 1 which we have seen *with* our e, *4057*
2: 16 the cravings of sinful man, the lust *of* his e *4057*
Rev 1: 14 and his e were like blazing fire. *4057*
2: 18 the Son of God, whose e are like blazing fire *2400+4057*
3: 18 and salve to put on your e, so you can see. *4057*
4: 6 and they were covered with e, *4057*
4: 8 and was covered with e all around, *4057*
5: 6 He had seven horns and seven e, *4057*
7: 17 God will wipe away every tear from their e. *4057*
19: 12 His e are like blazing fire, *4057*
21: 4 He will wipe every tear from their e. *4057*

EYESIGHT (1) [EYE]

Jer 14: 6 their e fails for lack of pasture." 6524

EYEWITNESSES (2) [WITNESS]

Lk 1: 2 the first were e and servants of the word. *898*
2Pe 1: 16 but we were e of his majesty. *2228*

EZBAI (1)

1Ch 11: 37 Hezro the Carmelite, Naarai son of E, 256

EZBON (2)

Ge 46: 16 The sons of Gad: Zephon, Haggi, Shuni, E, 719
1Ch 7: 7 The sons of Bela: E, Uzzi, Uzziel, 719

EZEKIEL (2)

Eze 1: 3 word of the LORD came to E the priest, 3489
24: 24 E will be a sign to you; 3489

EZEKIAS (KJV) HEZEKIAH

EZEL (1) [BETH EZEL]

1Sa 20: 19 and wait by the stone E. 262

EZEM (3)

Jos 15: 29 Baalah, Iim, E, 6796
19: 3 Hazar Shual, Balah, E, 6796
1Ch 4: 29 Bilhah, E, Tolad, 6796

EZER (10)

Ge 36: 21 Dishon, E and Dishan. 733
36: 27 The sons of E: Bilhan, Zaavan and Akan. 733
36: 30 Dishon, E and Dishan. 733
1Ch 1: 38 Zibeon, Anah, Dishon, E and Dishan. 733
1: 42 The sons of E: Bilhan, Zaavan and Akan. 733
4: 4 and E the father of Hushah. 6470
7: 21 E and Elead were killed by 6470
12: 9 E was the chief, 6470
Ne 3: 19 Next to him, E son of Jeshua, 6470
12: 42 Uzzi, Jehohanan, Malkijah, Elam and E. 6472

EZION GEBER (7) [GEBER]

Nu 33: 35 They left Abronah and camped at E. 6787
33: 36 They left E and camped at Kadesh, 6787
Dt 2: 8 which comes up from Elath and E, 6787
1Ki 9: 26 King Solomon also built ships at E, 6787
22: 48 they were wrecked at E. 6787
2Ch 8: 17 to E and Elath on the coast of Edom. 6787
20: 36 After these were built at E, 6787

EZRA (26) [EZRA'S]

Ezr 7: 1 E son of Seraiah, the son of Azariah, 6474
7: 6 this E came up from Babylon. 6474
7: 8 E arrived in Jerusalem in the fifth month of NIH
7: 10 For E had devoted himself to the study 6474
7: 11 the letter King Artaxerxes had given to E 6474
7: 12 king of kings, To E the priest, 10537
7: 21 to provide with diligence whatever E 10537
7: 25 E, in accordance with the wisdom 10537
10: 1 While E was praying and confessing, 6474
10: 2 one of the descendants of Elam, said to E, 6474
10: 5 So E rose up and put the leading priests 6474
10: 6 Then E withdrew from before the house 6474
10: 10 E the priest stood up and said to them, 6474
10: 16 E the priest selected men who were family heads, 6474
Ne 8: 1 They told E the scribe to bring out 6474
8: 2 So on the first day of the seventh month E 6474
8: 4 E the scribe stood on 6474
8: 5 E opened the book. 6474
8: 6 E praised the LORD, the great God; 6474
8: 9 E the priest and scribe, 6474
8: 13 around E the scribe to give attention to 6474
8: 18 E read from the Book of the Law of God. NIH
12: 1 with Jeshua: Seraiah, Jeremiah, E, 6474
12: 26 the governor and of E the priest and scribe. 6474
12: 33 along with Azariah, E, Meshullam, 6474
12: 36 E the scribe led the procession. 6474

EZRA'S (1) [EZRA]

Ne 12:13 of E, Meshullam; of Amariah's, 6474

EZRAH (1) [EZRAHITE]

1Ch 4:17 The sons of E: 6477

EZRAHITE (3) [EZRAH]

1Ki 4:31 including Ethan the E— 276
Ps 88: T A maskil of Heman the E. 276
89: T A maskil of Ethan the E. 276

EZRI (1)

1Ch 27:26 E son of Kelub was in charge of 6479

F

FABLES (KJV) See MYTHS, STORIES

FABRIC (6)

Jdg 16:13 into the f [on the loom] and tighten it with 5018
16:13 wove them into the f 5018
16:14 up the pin and the loom, with the f. 5018
Eze 16:13 and **costly** f and embroidered cloth. 5429
27:16 they exchanged turquoise, purple f, NIH
27:24 with you beautiful garments, blue f, 1659

FACE (313) [FACED, FACEDOWN, FACES, FACING, STERN-FACED]

Ge 1:29 on the f *of* the whole earth and every tree 7156
4:5 and his f was downcast. 7156
4:6 Why is your f downcast? 7156
6:7 from the f *of* the earth— 7156
7:4 and I will wipe from the f *of* 7156
7:23 on the f *of* the earth was wiped out; 7156
11:4 be scattered over the f *of* the whole earth." 7156
11:9 the LORD scattered them over the f *of* 7156
19:1 to meet them and bowed down with his f to 678
30:40 but **made** the rest f the streaked 5989+7156
32:30 saying, "It is because I saw God f to face, 7156
32:30 saying, "It is because I saw God face to f, 7156
33:10 to see your f is like seeing the face of God, 7156
33:10 to see your face is like seeing the f *of* God, 7156
38:15 for she had covered her f. 7156
43:3 not see my f again unless your brother is 7156
43:5 not see my f again unless your brother is 7156
43:31 After he had washed his f, 7156
44:23 you will not see my f again.' 7156
44:26 the man's f unless our youngest brother is 7156
48:11 "I never expected to see your f again, 7156
48:12 and bowed down with his f to the ground. 678
Ex 3:6 At this, Moses hid his f, 7156
10:5 They will cover the f *of* the ground so 6524
10:28 The day you see my f you will die." 7156
13:17 For God said, "If they f war, 8011
25:20 The cherubim are to f each other, 7156
32:12 in the mountains and to wipe them off the f 7156
33:11 The LORD would speak to Moses f 7156
33:11 to Moses face to f, 7156
33:16 the other people on the f *of* the earth?" 7156
33:20 But," he said, "you cannot see my f, 7156
33:23 but my f must not be seen." 7156
34:29 he was not aware that his f was radiant 6425+7156
34:30 his f was radiant, 6425+7156
34:33 he put a veil over his f. 7156
34:35 they saw that his f was radiant. 6425+7156
34:35 over his f until he went in to speak with 7156
Lev 13:45 **lower part of** his f 8559
17:10 I will set my f against 7156
20:3 I will set my f against that man 7156
20:5 I will set my f against that man 7156
20:6 " 'I will set my f against 7156
26:17 I will set my f against you so that you will 7156
Nu 6:25 the LORD make his f shine upon you and 7156
6:26 the LORD turn his f toward you 7156
11:15 and *do* not *let me* f my own ruin." 8011
12:3 more humble than anyone else on the f *of* 7156
12:8 With him I speak f to face, 7023
12:8 With him I speak face to f, 7023
12:14 "If her father had spit in her f, 7156
14:14 O LORD, have been seen f to face, 6524
14:14 O LORD, have been seen face to f, 6524
14:43 and Canaanites will f you there. 4200+7156
22:5 the f *of* the land and have settled next 6524
22:11 that has come out of Egypt covers the f *of* 6524
24:1 but turned his f toward the desert. 7156
Dt 5:4 The LORD spoke to you f to face out of 7156
5:4 The LORD spoke to you face to f out of 7156
6:15 he will destroy you from the f *of* the land. 7156
7:6 of all the peoples on the f *of* the earth to 7156
7:10 he will repay to their f by destruction; 7156
7:10 to repay to their f those who hate him. 7156
14:2 Out of all the peoples on the f *of* the earth, 7156
25:9 spit in his f and say, 7156
Dt 31:17 I will hide my f from them, 7156
31:18 And I will certainly hide my f on that day 7156
32:20 "I will hide my f from them," he said, 7156
34:10 Moses, whom the LORD knew f to face, 7156
34:10 Moses, whom the LORD knew face to f, 7156
Jos 5:1 they no longer had the courage to f 4946+7156
7:10 What are you doing down on your f? 7156
Jdg 6:22 I have seen the angel of the LORD f 7156
6:22 the angel of the LORD face to f!" 7156
Ru 2:10 she bowed down with her f to the ground. 7156
1Sa 1:18 and her f was no longer downcast. 7156
5:3 fallen on his f on the ground before the ark 7156
5:4 fallen on his f on the ground before the ark 7156
20:15 of David's enemies from the f *of* 7156
20:41 with his f to the ground. 678
24:8 down and prostrated himself with his f to 678
25:23 and bowed down before David with her f 7156
25:41 She bowed down with her f to the ground 678
28:14 down and prostrated himself with his f to 678
2Sa 2:22 **look** your brother Joab **in the f**?" 448+5951+7156
14:4 with her f to the ground to pay him honor, 678
14:7 nor descendant on the f *of* the earth." 7156
14:22 with his f to the ground to pay him honor, 7156
14:24 he must not see my f." 7156
14:24 to his own house and did not see the f *of* 7156
14:28 in Jerusalem without seeing the king's f. 7156
14:32 Now then, I want to see the king's f, 7156
14:33 and he came in and bowed down with his f 678
18:28 He bowed down before the king with his f 678
19:4 The king covered his f and cried aloud, 7156
21:1 so David sought the f *of* the LORD. 7156
24:20 and bowed down before the king with his f 678
1Ki 1:23 before the king and bowed with his f to 678
1:31 Then Bathsheba bowed low with her f to 678
13:34 to its destruction from the f *of* the earth. 7156
18:42 the ground and put his f between his knees. 7156
19:13 he pulled his cloak over his f and went out 7156
22:24 up and slapped Micaiah in the f. 4305
2Ki 4:29 Lay my staff on the boy's f." 7156
4:31 on ahead and laid the staff on the boy's f, 7156
8:15 in water and spread it over the king's f, 7156
14:8 "Come, meet me **f to face.**" 7156
14:8 "Come, meet me **face to f.**" 7156
20:2 Hezekiah turned his f to the wall 7156
1Ch 16:11 seek his f always. 7156
21:21 and bowed down before David with his f 678
2Ch 7:14 and pray and seek my f and turn 7156
18:23 up and slapped Micaiah in the f. 4305
20:12 we have no power to f this vast army 4200+7156
20:17 Go out to f them tomorrow, 4200+7156
20:18 Jehoshaphat bowed with his f to 678
25:17 "Come, meet me **f to face.**" 7156
25:17 "Come, meet me **face to f.**" 7156
30:9 not turn his f from you if you return 7156
Ezr 9:6 and disgraced to lift up my f to you, 7156
Ne 2:2 "Why does your f look so sad 7156
2:3 Why should my f not look sad when 7156
4:5 they have thrown insults **in the f of** 4200+5584
Est 7:8 they covered Haman's f. 7156
Job 1:11 and he will surely curse you to your f." 7156
2:5 and he will surely curse you to your f." 7156
4:15 A spirit glided past my f, 7156
6:28 Would I lie to your f? 7156
11:15 then you will lift up your f without shame; 7156
13:15 I will surely defend my ways to his f. 7156
13:24 Why do you hide your f 7156
15:27 "Though his f is covered with fat 7156
16:16 My f is red with weeping, 7156
17:6 a man in whose f people spit. 7156
17:12 in the f *of* darkness they say, 7156
21:31 Who denounces his conduct to his f? 7156
22:26 in the Almighty and will lift up your f 7156
23:17 by the thick darkness that covers my f. 7156
24:15 and he keeps his f concealed. 7156
26:9 He covers the f *of* the full moon, 7156
26:10 the horizon on the f *of* the waters for 7156
29:24 the light of my f was precious to them. 7156
30:10 they do not hesitate to spit in my f. 7156
33:26 he sees God's f and shouts for joy; 7156
34:29 If he hides his f, who can see him? 7156
37:12 around over the f *of* the whole earth 7156
Ps 4:6 Let the light of your f shine upon us, 7156
10:11 he covers his f and never sees." 7156
11:7 upright men will see his f. 7156
13:1 How long will you hide your f from me? 7156
17:15 And I—in righteousness I will see your f; 7156
22:24 not hidden his f from him but has listened 7156
24:6 who seek your f, O God of Jacob. 7156
27:8 My heart says of you, "Seek his f!" 7156
27:8 Your f, LORD, I will seek. 7156
27:9 Do not hide your f from me, 7156
30:7 but when you hid your f, I was dismayed. 7156
31:16 Let your f shine on your servant; 7156
34:16 the f *of* the LORD is 7156
44:3 and the light of your f, for you loved them. 7156
44:15 and my f is covered with shame 7156
44:22 Yet for your sake *we* **f death** all day long; 2222
44:24 Why do you hide your f 7156
50:21 I will rebuke you and accuse you to your f. 6524
51:9 Hide your f from my sins 7156
67:1 and bless us and make his f shine upon us, 7156
69:7 and shame covers my f. 7156
69:17 Do not hide your f from your servant; 7156
80:3 make your f shine upon us, 7156
80:7 make your f shine upon us, 7156
80:19 make your f shine upon us, 7156
88:14 do you reject me and hide your f from me? 7156
Ps 102:2 Do not hide your f from me when I am 7156
104:15 oil to make his f shine, 7156
104:29 When you hide your f, they are terrified; 7156
104:30 and you renew the f *of* the earth. 7156
105:4 seek his f always. 7156
119:58 I have sought your f with all my heart; 7156
119:135 Make your f shine upon your servant 7156
143:7 Do not hide your f from me or I will be 7156
Pr 7:13 and with a brazen f she said: 7156
8:27 when he marked out the horizon on the f 7156
15:13 A happy heart makes the f cheerful, 7156
16:15 When a king's f brightens, it means life; 7156
27:19 water **reflects a f,** 2021+2021+4200+7156+7156
Ecc 7:3 because a sad f is good for the heart. 7156
8:1 a man's f and changes its hard appearance. 7156
SS 2:14 show me your f, let me hear your voice; 5260
2:14 your voice is sweet, and your f is lovely. 5260
Isa 8:17 who is hiding his f from the house 7156
23:17 with all the kingdoms on the f *of* the earth. 7156
24:1 he will ruin its f and scatter its inhabitants— 7156
38:2 Hezekiah turned his f to the wall 7156
50:6 not hide my f from mocking and spitting. 7156
50:7 Therefore have I set my f like flint, 7156
50:8 *Let us* f each other! 6641
54:8 of anger I hid my f from you for a moment, 7156
57:17 I punished him, and hid my f in anger, NIH
59:2 your sins have hidden his f from you, 7156
64:7 for you have hidden your f from us 7156
65:3 to my very f, offering sacrifices in gardens 7156
Jer 13:26 over your f that your shame may be seen— 7156
18:17 I will show them my back and not my f in 7156
25:26 all the kingdoms on the f *of* the earth. 7156
28:16 'I am about to remove you from the f *of* 7156
30:6 every f turned deathly pale? 7156
32:4 and will speak with him f to face 7023
32:4 to f and see him with his own eyes. 7023
33:5 I will hide my f from this city because 7156
34:3 and he will speak with you f to face. 7023
34:3 and he will speak with you face to f. 7023
La 3:29 Let him bury his f in the dust— 7023
Eze 1:10 Each of the four had the f *of* a man, 7156
1:10 on the right side each had the f *of* a lion, 7156
1:10 and on the left the f *of* an ox; 7156
1:10 each also had the f *of* an eagle. 7156
4:3 between you and the city and turn your f 7156
4:7 Turn your f toward the siege of Jerusalem 7156
6:2 set your f against the mountains of Israel; 7156
7:22 I will turn my f away from them, 7156
10:14 One f was that of a cherub, 7156
10:14 the second the f *of* a man, 7156
10:14 the third the f *of* a lion, 7156
10:14 and the fourth the f *of* an eagle. 7156
12:6 Cover your f so that you cannot see 7156
12:12 He will cover his f so that he cannot see 7156
13:17 set your f against the daughters 7156
14:4 a wicked stumbling block before his f and 7156
14:7 a wicked stumbling block before his f and 7156
14:8 I will set my f against that man 7156
15:7 I will set my f against them. 7156
15:7 And when I set my f against them, 7156
20:35 into the desert of the nations and there, f 7156
20:35 of the nations and there, face to f, 7156
20:46 set your f toward the south; 7156
20:47 and every f from south to north will 7156
21:2 set your f against Jerusalem and preach 7156
24:17 **lower part of** your f 8559
24:22 **lower part of** your f 8559
25:2 set your f against the Ammonites 7156
28:21 set your f against Sidon; 7156
29:2 set your f against Pharaoh king of Egypt 7156
35:2 set your f against Mount Seir; 7156
38:2 set your f against Gog, 7156
38:20 on the f *of* the earth will tremble 7156
39:23 So I hid my f from them and handed them 7156
39:24 and I hid my f from them. 7156
39:29 I will no longer hide my f from them, 7156
41:19 the f *of* a man toward the palm tree 7156
41:19 and the f *of* a lion toward the palm tree on 7156
47:1 The steps of the altar f east." 7155
Da 5:6 His f turned **pale** and he was so frightened 10228
5:9 and his f grew more **pale.** 10228
7:28 and my f turned **pale,** 10228
8:18 with my f to the ground. 7156
10:6 his f like lightning, 7156
10:8 my f turned deathly pale 2086
10:9 I fell into a deep sleep, my f to the ground. 7156
10:15 I bowed with my f toward the ground 7156
Hos 2:2 from her f and the unfaithfulness from 7156
5:15 And they will seek my f; 7156
Joel 2:6 every f turns pale. 7156
Am 5:8 of the sea and pours them out over the f *of* 7156
9:6 of the sea and pours them out over the f *of* 7156
9:8 I will destroy it from the f *of* the earth— 7156
Mic 3:4 At that time he will hide his f from them 7156
Na 2:10 bodies tremble, every f grows pale. 7156
3:5 "I will lift your skirts over your f. 7156
Zep 1:2 "I will sweep away everything from the f 7156
1:3 of rubble when I cut off man from the f *of* 7156
Mt 6:17 put oil on your head and wash your f, *4725*
17:2 His f shone like the sun, *4725*
18:10 that their angels in heaven always see the f *4725*
26:39 he fell with his f to the ground and prayed, *4725*
26:67 in his f and struck him with their fists. *4725*
Mk 10:22 At this the man's **f fell.** *5145*
Lk 5:12 with his f to the ground and begged him, *4725*
9:29 the appearance *of* his f changed, *4725*
21:35 upon all those who live on the f of *4725*

Jn 11:44 and a cloth around his **f.** *4071*
18:22 **struck** him **in the f.** *1443+4825*
19: 3 **struck** him **in the f.** *1443+4825*
Ac 6:15 and they saw that his **f** was like the face of *4725*
6:15 and they saw that his face was like the **f** of *4725*
16:19 into the marketplace to **f** the authorities. *2093*
20:38 that they would never see his **f** again. *4725*
Ro 8:36 "For your sake *we* **f death** all day long; *2506*
1Co 7:28 But those who marry will **f** many troubles *2400*
13:12 then we shall see **f** to face. *4725*
13:12 then we shall see face to **f.** *4725*
2Co 3: 7 not look steadily at the **f** of Moses because *4725*
3:13 over his **f** to keep the Israelites from gazing *4725*
4: 6 the knowledge of the glory of God in the **f** *4725*
10: 1 am "timid" **when f to face** with you, *2848+4725*
10: 1 am "timid" **when face to f** with you, *2848+4725*
11:20 or slaps you in the **f.** *4725*
11:28 I **f** daily the pressure of my concern for all *NIG*
Gal 2:11 I opposed him to his **f,** *4725*
Heb 9:27 and after that to **f** judgment, *NIG*
10:32 in a great contest in the **f** of suffering. *NIG*
Jas 1: 2 whenever *you* **f** trials of many kinds, *4346*
1:23 like a man who looks at his **f** in a mirror *4725*
5:10 example of patience in the **f** of suffering, *NIG*
1Pe 3:12 **f** of the Lord is against those who do evil." *4725*
2Jn 1:12 to visit you and talk with you **f** to face, *5125*
1:12 to visit you and talk with you face to **f,** *5125*
3Jn 1:14 and we will talk **f** to face. *5125*
1:14 and we will talk face to **f.** *5125*
Rev 1:16 His **f** was like the sun shining *4071*
4: 7 the third had a **f** like a man, *4725*
6:16 and hide us from the **f** of him who sits on *4725*
10: 1 his **f** was like the sun, *4725*
22: 4 They will see his **f,** *4725*

FACED (20) [FACE]

Ex 37: 9 The cherubim **f** each other, 7156
Nu 8: 3 the lamps so that they **f forward** 448+4578+7156
2Ki 14:11 He and Amaziah king of Judah **f each other** 7156+8011
23:29 but Neco **f** him and killed him at Megiddo. 8011
2Ch 25:21 He and Amaziah king of Judah **f each other** 7156+8011
Ne 8: 3 he **f** the square before the Water Gate 4200+7156
Eze 1:17 of the four directions the creatures **f;** NIH
10:11 of the four directions the cherubim **f;** NIH
10:11 in whatever direction the head **f,** 7155
40: 9 The portico of the gateway **f** the temple. 4946
40:16 the openings all around **f** inward. 4200
40:31 Its portico **f** the outer court; 448
40:34 Its portico **f** the outer court; 4200
40:37 Its portico **f** the outer court; 4200
42: 2 The building whose door **f** north was 448+7156
42: 3 gallery **f** gallery at the three levels. 448+7156
47: 1 toward the east (for the temple **f** east). 7156
Ac 25:16 any man before he has **f** his accusers *2848+4725*
Ro 4:19 *he* **f the fact** that his body was as good *2917*
Heb 11:36 Some **f** jeers and flogging, *3284+4278*

FACEDOWN (20) [FACE]

Ge 17: 3 Abram fell **f,** and God said to him, 6584+7156
17:17 Abraham fell **f;** he laughed 6584+7156
Lev 9:24 they shouted for joy and fell **f.** 6584+7156
Nu 14: 5 Moses and Aaron fell **f** in front of 6584+7156
16: 4 When Moses heard this, he fell **f.** 6584+7156
16:22 Moses and Aaron fell **f** and cried out, 6584+7156
16:45 And they fell **f.** 6584+7156
20: 6 to the Tent of Meeting and fell **f,** 6584+7156
22:31 So he bowed low and **fell f.** 678+2556+4200
Jos 5:14 Joshua fell **f** to the ground in reverence, 448+7156
7: 6 Joshua tore his clothes and fell **f** to 6584+7156
1Sa 17:49 and he fell **f** on the ground. 6584+7156
1Ch 21:16 clothed in sackcloth, fell **f.** 6584+7156
Eze 1:28 When I saw it, I fell **f,** 6584+7156
3:23 and I fell **f.** 6584+7156
9: 8 I fell **f,** crying out, "Ah, 6584+7156
11:13 I fell **f** and cried out in a loud voice, 6584+7156
43: 3 and I fell **f.** 448+7156
44: 4 and I fell **f.** 448+7156
Mt 17: 6 they fell **f** to the ground, terrified. *2093+4725*

FACES (61) [FACE]

Ge 9:23 Their **f** were turned the other way so 7156
40: 7 "Why are your **f** so sad today?" 7156
42: 6 they bowed down to him with their **f** to 678
Nu 21:11 desert that **f** Moab toward the sunrise. 6584+7156
Jos 15: 7 which **f** the Pass of Adummim south of 5790
18:17 which **f** the Pass of Adummim, 5790
Jdg 13:20 and his wife fell with their **f** to the ground. 7156
16: 3 to the top of the hill that **f** Hebron. 6584+7156
1Sa 26: 1 the hill of Hakilah, which **f** Jeshimon? 6584+7156
1Ki 7: 9 with a saw on their inner and **outer** *f.* AIT
1Ch 12: 8 Their **f** were the faces of lions, 7156
12: 8 Their faces were the **f** *of* lions, 7156
2Ch 7: 3 on the pavement with their **f** to the ground, 678
29: 6 They turned their **f** away from 7156
Ne 8: 6 and worshiped the LORD with their **f** to 678
Job 40:13 shroud their **f** in the grave. 7156
Ps 34: 5 their **f** are never covered with shame. 7156
83:16 Cover their **f** with shame so 7156
Isa 3: 9 The look on their **f** testifies against them; 7156
3:15 by crushing my people and grinding the **f** 7156
6: 2 With two wings they covered their **f,** 7156
13: 8 at each other, their **f** aflame. 7156
25: 8 LORD will wipe away the tears from all **f;** 7156
Isa 29:22 no longer will their **f** grow pale. 7156
49:23 down before you with their **f** to the ground; 678
53: 3 Like one from whom men hide their **f** 7156
Jer 2:27 to me and not their **f;** 7156
5: 3 They made their **f** harder than stone 7156
32:33 to me and not their **f;** 7156
50: 5 the way to Zion and turn their **f** toward it. 7156
51:51 and shame covers our **f,** 7156
Eze 1: 6 each of them had four **f** and four wings. 7156
1: 8 All four of them had **f** and wings, 7156
1:10 Their **f** looked like this: 7156
1:11 Such were their **f.** 7156
1:15 beside each creature with its four **f.** 7156
7:18 Their **f** will be covered with shame 7156
8:16 of the LORD and their **f** toward the east, 7156
9: 2 of the upper gate, which **f** north, each with 7155
10:14 Each of the cherubim had four **f:** 7156
10:21 Each had four **f** and four wings, 7156
10:22 Their **f** had the same appearance 7156
11: 1 of the house of the LORD that **f** east. 7155
14: 3 put wicked stumbling blocks before their **f.** 7156
27:35 with horror and their **f** are distorted 7156
40:10 the same measurements, and the **f** of NIH
40:14 the **f** of the projecting walls all around the NIH
40:16 The **f** of the projecting walls were decorated with palm trees. NIH
40:26 it had palm tree decorations **on the f of** 448
41:18 Each cherub had two **f:** 7156
Mic 3: 7 They will all cover their **f** 8559
Mal 2: 3 I will spread on your **f** the offal 7156
Mt 6:16 for they disfigure their **f** *4725*
23:13 the kingdom of heaven **in** men's **f.** *1869*
Lk 24: 5 the women bowed down with their **f** to *4725*
24:17 They stood still, their **f** downcast. *NIG*
2Co 3:18 with unveiled **f** all reflect the Lord's glory, *4725*
Rev 7:11 They fell down on their **f** before the throne *4725*
9: 7 and their **f** resembled human faces. *4725*
9: 7 and their faces resembled human **f.** *4725*
11:16 fell on their **f** and worshiped God, *4725*

FACING (48) [FACE]

Jos 8:33 **f** those who carried it— 5584
18:14 the hill **f** Beth Horon on the south 6584+7156
18:16 to the foot of the hill **f** the Valley 6584+7156
19:46 with the area **f** Joppa. 4578
1Sa 13:18 the Valley of Zeboim **f** the desert. 2025
17:21 up their lines **f each other.** 5120+7925
26: 3 on the hill of Hakilah **f** Jeshimon, 6584+7156
1Ki 7: 4 in sets of three, **f each other.** 448+4691+4691
7: 5 in sets of three, **f each other.** 448+4691+4691
7:25 Sea stood on twelve bulls, three **f** north, 7155
7:25 three facing north, three **f** west, 7155
7:25 three **f** south and three facing east. 7155
7:25 three facing south and three **f** east. 7155
22:35 the king was propped up in his chariot **f** 5790
2Ki 2: 7 **f** the place where Elijah 4946+5584
2Ch 3:13 They stood on their feet, **f** the main hall. 7156
4: 4 Sea stood on twelve bulls, three **f** north, 7155
4: 4 three facing north, three **f** west, 7155
4: 4 three **f** south and three facing east. 7155
4: 4 three facing south and three **f** east. 7155
18:34 in his chariot **f** the Arameans until evening. 5790
Ne 3:19 a point **f** the ascent to the armory as far as 5584
Est 5: 1 on his royal throne in the hall, **f** 5790
Eze 40: 6 Then he went to the gate **f** east. 7156
40: 7 the portico **f** the temple was one rod deep. 4946
40:14 The measurement was up to the **portico** *f* AIT
40:20 the length and width of the gate **f** north, 7156
40:22 as those of the gate **f** east. 7156
40:23 a gate to the inner court **f** the north gate, 5584
40:24 to the south side and I saw a gate **f** south. 2006
40:27 The inner court also had a gate **f** south, 2006
40:44 at the side of the north gate and **f** south, 7156
40:44 at the side of the south gate and **f** north. 7156
40:45 "The room **f** south is for 7156
40:46 and the room **f** north is for 7156
41:12 The building **f** the temple courtyard on 448+7156
41:15 the building **f** the courtyard at the rear 448+7156
41:15 inner sanctuary and the **portico** *f* the court, AIT
42:13 south rooms **f** the temple courtyard are 448+7156
43: 1 the man brought me to the gate **f** east, 7155
43: 4 the temple through the gate **f** east. 7156
44: 1 the *one* **f** east, and it was shut. 7155
46: 1 of the inner court **f** east is to be shut on 7155
46:12 the gate **f** east is to be opened for him. 7155
46:19 of the gate to the sacred rooms **f** north, 7155
47: 2 around the outside to the outer gate **f** east, 7155
Ac 20:23 that prison and hardships *are* **f** me. *3531*
27:12 **f** both southwest and northwest. *1063*

FACT (33) [FACTS]

Ge 45:26 **In f,** he is ruler of all Egypt." 3954
47:18 "We cannot hide from our lord *the f* **that** AIT
2Sa 13:15 with intense hatred. **In f,** 3954
2Ki 8:10 to me that *he will* **in f die."** 4637+4637
Ezr 5:17 to see if King Cyrus did **in f** issue a decree 10029
Mk 3:27 **In f,** no one can enter a strong man's house *247*
7:25 **In f,** as soon as she heard about him, *247*
12:22 **In f,** none of the seven left any children. *2779*
Jn 4: 2 **although in f** it was not Jesus who baptized, *2793*
4:18 **The f is,** you have had five husbands, *1142*
9:37 **in f,** he is the one speaking with you." *2779*
10: 5 But they will never follow a stranger; **in f,** *247*
16: 2 **in f,** a time is coming *247*
18:37 In **f,** for this reason I was born, *NIG*
Ac 2:32 and we are all witnesses *of* **the f.** *4005*[S]
13:34 **The f that** God raised him from the dead, *4022*
Ro 4: 2 If, **in f,** Abraham was justified by works, *1142*
4:19 *he* **faced the f** that his body was as good *2917*
1Co 6: 7 The very **f** that you have lawsuits among you *NIG*
10: 1 I do not want you to be ignorant of the **f,** *NIG*
12:18 **in f** God has arranged the parts in the body, *3815*
15:15 But he did not raise him **if in f** the dead *726+1642*
2Co 11:20 **In f,** you even put up anyone who enslaves *1142*
1Th 3: 4 **In f,** when we were with you, *1142+2779*
4: 1 to please God, as **in f** you are living. *2779*
4:10 And **in f,** you do love all the brothers *1142*
5:11 just as **in f** you are doing. *2779*
1Ti 5:15 Some have **in f** already turned away *1142*
2Ti 3:12 **In f,** everyone who wants to live *1254+2779*
Tit 1:15 **In f,** both their minds and consciences *247*
Heb 5:12 **In f,** though by this time you ought to *1142+2779*
9:22 **In f,** the law requires that nearly everything *2779*
1Jn 3: 4 **in f,** sin is lawlessness. *2779*

FACTIONS (3)

1Ki 16:21 the people of Israel were split into **two** *f:* AIT
2Co 12:20 **f,** slander, gossip, arrogance and disorder. *2249*
Gal 5:20 of rage, selfish ambition, dissensions, **f** *146*

FACTS (1) [FACT]

Ac 19:36 Therefore, since **these** *f* are undeniable, *AIT*

FADE (6) [FADED, FADES, FADING]

Ps 109:23 *I* **f away** like an evening shadow; 2143
Isa 17: 4 "In that day the glory of Jacob *will* **f;** 1937
Na 1: 4 and the blossoms of Lebanon **f.** 581
Jas 1:11 the rich man *will* **f away** even *3447*
1Pe 1: 4 that can never perish, spoil or **f**— *278*
5: 4 the crown of glory that will **never f away.** *277*

FADED (5) [FADE]

Lev 13: 6 sore *has* **f** and has not spread in the skin, 3908
13:21 and it is not more than skin deep and *has* **f,** 3908
13:26 if it is not more than skin deep and *has* **f,** 3908
13:28 in the skin but *has* **f,** it is a swelling from 3908
13:56 the mildew *has* **f** after 3908

FADES (2) [FADE]

Ps 65: 8 and evening **f** you call forth songs of joy. NIH
Ecc 12: 4 and the sound of grinding **f;** 9164

FADING (8) [FADE]

Pr 7: 9 as the day was **f,** as the dark of night set in. 6847
Isa 1:30 You will be like an oak with **f** leaves, 5570
28: 1 to the **f** flower, his glorious beauty, 5570
28: 4 That **f** flower, his glorious beauty, 5570
Jer 6: 4 But, alas, the daylight *is* **f,** 7155
2Co 3: 7 because of its glory, **f** *though it was,* *2934*
3:11 And if what *was* **f away** came with glory, *2934*
3:13 at it *while* the radiance *was* **f away.** *2934*

FAIL (55) [FAILED, FAILING, FAILINGS, FAILS, FAILURE]

Lev 20: 4 to Molech and they **f** to put him to death, 1194
26:15 and **f** to carry out all my commands and 1194
Nu 15:22 " 'Now if you unintentionally **f** to keep any 4202
32:23 "But if you **f** to do this, 4202
2Sa 17:16 **cross over without f,** 6296+6296
1Ki 2: 4 you *will* never **f to have** a man on the 4162+4200
8:25 'You *shall* never **f to have** a man to sit 4162+4200
9: 5 *'You shall* never **f to have** a man on 4162+4200
2Ki 10:10 against the house of Ahab *will* **f.** 824+2025+5877
1Ch 28:20 not **f** you or forsake you until all the work 8332
2Ch 6:16 'You *shall* never **f to have** a man to sit 4162+4200
7:18 'You *shall* never **f to have** a man to 4162+4200
34:33 *they did* not **f** to follow the LORD, 4946+6073
Ezr 6: 9 must be given them daily without **f,** 10712
Est 9:27 without **f** observe these two days every year, 6296
Job 11:20 But the eyes of the wicked *will* **f,** 3983
14: 7 and its new shoots *will* not **f.** 2532
17: 5 the eyes of his children *will* **f.** 3983
21:10 Their bulls never **f** to breed; 1718
41:12 *"I will* not **f to speak** *of* his limbs, 3087
Ps 6: 7 *they* **f** because of all my foes. 6980
69: 3 My eyes **f,** looking for my God. 3983
73:26 My flesh and my heart *may* **f,** 3983
89:28 and my covenant with him *will* **never f.** 586
89:31 if they violate my decrees and **f** 4202
119:82 My eyes **f,** looking for your promise; 3983
119:123 My eyes **f,** looking for your salvation, 3983
Pr 15:22 Plans **f** for lack of counsel, 7296
Isa 32:10 the grape harvest *will* **f,** 3983
33:16 and water *will* **not f** him. 586
51: 6 my righteousness *will* never **f.** 3169
58:11 like a spring whose waters never **f.** 3941
Jer 20:11 *They will* **f** and be thoroughly disgraced; 4202+8505
33:17 David *will* never **f to have** a man to sit 4162+4200
33:18 Levites, *ever* **f to have** a man to stand 4162+4200
35:19 Recab *will* never **f to have** a man to 4162+4200
La 2:11 My eyes **f** from weeping, 3983
3:22 for his compassions never **f.** 3983
Eze 2: 5 And whether they listen or **f** to listen— 2532
2: 7 whether they listen or **f** to listen, 2532
3:11 whether they listen or **f** to listen." 2532
30: 6 and her proud strength *will* **f.** 3718

Eze 47:12 nor *will* their fruit **f**. 9462
Hos 9: 2 the new wine *will* **f** them. 3950
13:15 his spring *will* **f** and his well dry up. 3312
Zep 3: 5 and every new day *he does* not **f**, 6372
Mk 8:18 Do you have eyes but **f** to see, *4024*
8:18 and ears but **f** to hear? *4024*
10:30 **f** to receive a hundred times as much *1569+3590*
Lk 6:42 when you yourself **f** to see the plank *4024*
18:30 will **f** to receive many times as much *3590+4049*
22:32 Simon, that your faith *may* not **f**. *1722*
Jn 1:20 He did not **f** to confess, *766*
Ac 5:38 or activity is of human origin, *it will* **f**. *2907*
2Co 13: 5 unless, of course, *you* **f the test?** *99+1639*

FAILED (24) [FAIL]

Lev 5:16 for what *he has* **f to do** in regard to 2627
Jos 2:11 our hearts melted and everyone's courage **f** 4202+6388+7756
21:45 good promises to the house of Israel **f**; 5877
23:14 the LORD your God gave you *has* **f**. 5877
23:14 has been fulfilled; not one *has* **f**. 5877
Jdg 1:21 however, **f** to dislodge the Jebusites, 4202
8:35 They also **f** to show kindness to the family 4202
21: 5 the tribes of Israel has **f** to assemble before 4202
21: 5 that anyone who **f** to assemble before 4202
21: 8 of the tribes of Israel **f** to assemble before 4202
1Sa 3:13 and he **f** to restrain them. 4202
25:37 his heart **f** him and he became like a stone. 4637
1Ki 8:56 Not one word *has* **f** of all 5877
15: 5 *had* not **f to keep** any of the LORD's commands all the days of his life— 4946+6073
2Ki 3:26 to the king of Edom, but *they* **f**. 3523+4202
Ezr 10: 8 Anyone who **f** to appear within three days 4202
Ne 9:17 They refused to listen and **f** to remember 4202
Job 32:15 words *have* **f** them. 4946+6980
Ps 77: 8 *Has* his promise **f** for all time? 1698
La 4:17 our eyes **f**, looking in vain for help; 3983
Ro 9: 6 It is not as though God's word *had* **f**. *1738*
2Co 13: 6 that we *have* not **f the test.** *99+1639*
13: 7 even though we *may* seem **to have f.** *99+1639*
Jas 5: 4 The wages *you* **f to pay** the workmen *691*

FAILING (3) [FAIL]

Ge 48:10 Israel's eyes *were* **f** because of old age, 3877
Dt 8:11 **f** to observe his commands, 1194
1Sa 12:23 that I should sin against the LORD by **f** 2532

FAILINGS (1) [FAIL]

Ro 15: 1 We who are strong ought to bear with the **f** *821*

FAILS (17) [FAIL]

Ex 21:33 a pit or digs one and **f** to cover it and an ox 4202
Nu 9:13 on a journey **f** to celebrate the Passover, 2532
19:13 of anyone and **f** to purify himself defiles 4202
2Ki 10:19 Anyone who **f to come** will no longer live." 7212
Ps 31:10 my strength **f** because of my affliction, 4173
38:10 My heart pounds, my strength **f** me; 6440
40:12 and my heart **f** *within* me. 6440
143: 7 O LORD; my spirit **f**. 3983
Pr 8:36 But *whoever* **f to find** me harms himself; 2627
Ecc 6: 6 over but **f** to enjoy his prosperity. 4202
Isa 65:20 he *who* **f to reach** a hundred will 2627
Jer 14: 6 their eyesight **f** for lack of pasture." 3983
15:18 like a spring *that* **f**? 586+4202
17: 8 a year of drought and never **f** to bear fruit." 4631
Joel 1:10 the new wine is dried up, the oil **f**. 581
Hab 3:17 olive crop **f** and the fields produce no food, 3950
1Co 13: 8 Love never **f**. *4406*

FAILURE (1) [FAIL]

1Th 2: 1 brothers, that our visit to you was not a **f**. *3031*

FAIN (KJV) See LONGED

FAINT (31) [FAINTED, FAINTHEARTED, FAINTING, FAINTS]

1Sa 14:28 That is why the men *are* **f**." 6545
Job 23:16 God *has* **made** my heart **f**; 8216
26:14 how **f** the whisper we hear of him! 9066
Ps 6: 2 Be merciful to me, LORD, for I *am* **f**; 583
61: 2 I call as my heart *grows* **f**; 6494
77: 3 I mused, and my spirit *grew* **f**. 6494
102: T When *he is* **f** and pours out his lament 6494
142: 3 When my spirit *grows* **f** within me, 6494
143: 4 So my spirit *grows* **f** within me; 6494
Ecc 12: 4 but all their songs *grow* **f**; 8820
SS 2: 5 refresh me with apples, for I *am* **f** *with* love. 2703
5: 8 Tell him I *am* **f** *with* love. 2703
Isa 15: 4 and their hearts *are* **f**. 3760
29: 8 that he is drinking, but he awakens **f**, 6546
40:31 they will walk and not *be* **f**. 3615
44:12 he drinks no water and *grows* **f**. 3615
57:10 and so *you did* not **f**. 2703
57:16 the spirit of man *would grow* **f** before me— 6494
Jer 8:18 my heart is **f** within me. 1868
15: 9 of seven *will grow* **f** and breathe her last. 581
31:25 I will refresh the weary and satisfy the **f**." 1790+5883
La 1:13 He made me desolate, **f** all the day long. 1865
1:22 My groans are many and my heart is **f**." 1868
2:11 because children and infants **f** in the streets 6494
2:12 as they **f** like wounded men in the streets 6494
La 2:19 who **f** from hunger at the head 6488
5:17 Because of this our hearts are **f**, 1865
Eze 21: 7 every spirit *will become* **f** 3908
Am 8:13 and strong young men *will* **f** because 6634
Jnh 4: 8 on Jonah's head so that *he grew* **f**. 6634
Lk 21:26 Men *will* **f** from terror, *715*

FAINTED (1) [FAINT]

Isa 51:20 Your sons *have* **f**; 6634

FAINTHEARTED (2) [FAINT, HEART]

Dt 20: 3 *Do* not *be* **f** or afraid; 4222+8216
20: 8 shall add, "Is any man afraid or **f**? 4222+8205

FAINTING (1) [FAINT]

Jer 4:31 I *am* **f**; my life is given over to murderers." 6545

FAINTS (2) [FAINT]

Ps 84: 2 My soul yearns, even **f**, for the courts of 3983
119:81 My soul **f with longing** for your salvation, 3983

FAIR (9) [FAIR HAVENS, FAIRLY, FAIRNESS]

Jdg 9:16 and if you have been **f** to Jerub-Baal 3208
Job 26:13 By his breath the skies became **f**; 9185
Pr 1: 3 doing what is right and just and **f**; 4797
2: 9 understand what is right and just and **f**— 4797
SS 6:10 **f** as the moon, bright as the sun, 3637
Hos 10:11 so I will put a yoke on her **f** neck. 3206
Mt 16: 2 'It will be **f weather,** for the sky is red,' *2304*
2Co 6:13 As a **f** exchange— *NIG*
Col 4: 1 with what is right and **f**, 2699

FAIR HAVENS (1)

Ac 27: 8 and came to a place called **F**, *2816*

FAIRLY (5) [FAIR]

Lev 19:15 but judge your neighbor **f**. 928+7406
Dt 1:16 between your brothers and judge **f**, 7406
16:18 and they shall judge the people **f**. 7406
Pr 31: 9 Speak up and judge **f**; 7406
Eze 18: 8 and judges **f** between man and man. 622

FAIRNESS (1) [FAIR]

Pr 29:14 If a king judges the poor with **f**, 622

FAIRS (KJV) See MERCHANDISE, WARES

FAITH (270) [FAITHFUL, FAITHFULLY, FAITHFULNESS, FAITHLESS]

Ex 21: 8 because he *has* **broken f** with her. 953
Dt 32:51 *of you* **broke f** with me in the presence of 5085
Jos 22:16 'How *could you* **break f** with the God 5085+5086
Jdg 9:16 in **good f** when you made Abimelech king, 9459
9:19 and in **good f** toward Jerub-Baal 9459
1Sa 14:33 *"You have* **broken f,"** he said. 953
2Ch 20:20 **Have f** in the LORD your God 586
20:20 **have f** in his prophets and you will 586
Isa 7: 9 **stand firm in** *your* **f**, 586
26: 2 the nation that keeps **f**. 574
Hab 2: 4 but the righteous will live by his **f**— 575
Mal 2:10 the covenant of our fathers *by* **breaking f** 953
2:11 Judah *has* **broken f**. 953
2:14 because you *have* **broken f** with her, 953
2:15 *do* not **break f** with the wife of your youth. 953
2:16 and *do* not **break f**. 953
Mt 6:30 *O you* **of little f**? *3899*
8:10 found anyone in Israel with such great **f**. *4411*
8:26 He replied, *"You* **of little f**, *3899*
9: 2 When Jesus saw their **f**, he said *4411*
9:22 he said, "your **f** has healed you." *4411*
9:29 "According to your **f** will it be done *4411*
13:58 miracles there because of their **lack of f**. *602*
14:31 *"You* **of little f,"** he said, *3899*
15:28 "Woman, you have great **f**! *4411*
16: 8 Jesus asked, *"You* **of little f**, *3899*
17:20 "Because you have so **little f**. *3898*
17:20 if you have **f** as small as a mustard seed, *4411*
21:21 if you have **f** and do not doubt, *4411*
24:10 the **f** and will betray and hate each other, *NIG*
Mk 2: 5 When Jesus saw their **f**, he said *4411*
4:40 Do you still have no **f**?" *4411*
5:34 "Daughter, your **f** has healed you. *4411*
6: 6 And he was amazed at their **lack of f**. *602*
10:52 "Go," said Jesus, "your **f** has healed you." *4411*
11:22 "Have **f** in God," Jesus answered. *4411*
16:14 he rebuked them for their **lack of f** *602*
Lk 5:20 When Jesus saw their **f**, he said, "Friend, *4411*
7: 9 not found such great **f** even in Israel." *4411*
7:50 "Your **f** has saved you; go in peace." *4411*
8:25 "Where is your **f**?" *4411*
8:48 "Daughter, your **f** has healed you. *4411*
12:28 *O you* **of little f**! *3899*
17: 5 to the Lord, "Increase our **f**!" *4411*
17: 6 "If you have **f** as small as a mustard seed, *4411*
17:19 your **f** has made you well." *4411*
18: 8 will he find **f** on the earth?" *4411*
18:42 your **f** has healed you." *4411*
22:32 Simon, that your **f** may not fail. *4411*
Jn 2:11 and his disciples **put** *their* **f** in him. *4409*
Jn 7:31 Still, many in the crowd **put** *their* **f** in him. *4409*
8:30 Even as he spoke, many **put** *their* **f** in him. *4409*
11:45 **put** *their* **f** in him. *4409*
12:11 over to Jesus and **putting** *their* **f** in him. *4409*
12:42 not confess their **f** for fear they would *NIG*
14:12 anyone who *has* **f** in me will do what I *4409*
Ac 3:16 By **f** in the name of Jesus, *4411*
3:16 It is Jesus' name and the **f** that comes *4411*
6: 5 a man full *of* **f** and of the Holy Spirit; *4411*
6: 7 of priests became obedient *to* the **f**. *4411*
11:24 full of the Holy Spirit and **f**, *4411*
13: 8 and tried to turn the proconsul from the **f**. *4411*
14: 9 saw that he had **f** to be healed *4411*
14:22 to remain true to the **f**. *4411*
14:27 and how he had opened the door *of* **f** to *4411*
15: 9 for he purified their hearts *by* **f**. *4411*
16: 5 So the churches were strengthened *in* the **f** *4411*
20:21 in repentance and have **f** in our Lord Jesus. *4411*
24:24 to him as he spoke about **f** in Christ Jesus. *4411*
26:18 among those who are sanctified *by* **f** *4411*
27:25 for *I have* **f** in God that it will happen just *4409*
Ro 1: 5 to the obedience that comes *from* **f**. *4411*
1: 8 your **f** is being reported all over the world. *4411*
1:12 be mutually encouraged by each other's **f**. *4411*
1:17 **f from first to last,** *1650+4411+4411*
1:17 "The righteous will live by **f**." *4411*
3: 3 What if some *did* **not have f**? *601*
3: 3 Will their **lack of f** nullify God's faithfulness? *602*
3:22 from God comes through **f** in Jesus Christ *4411*
3:25 atonement, through **f** in his blood. *4411*
3:26 one who justifies those who **have f** *1666+4411*
3:27 No, but on that *of* **f**. *4411*
3:28 is justified *by* **f** apart from observing the law. *4411*
3:30 who will justify the circumcised by **f** and *4411*
3:30 and the uncircumcised through that same **f**. *4411*
3:31 Do we, then, nullify the law by this **f**? *4411*
4: 5 his **f** is credited as righteousness. *4411*
4: 9 that Abraham's **f** was credited to him *4411*
4:11 a seal of the righteousness that he had *by* **f** *4411*
4:12 but who also walk in the footsteps *of* the **f** *4411*
4:13 through the righteousness that comes *by* **f**. *4411*
4:14 **f** has no value and the promise is worthless, *4411*
4:16 Therefore, the promise comes by **f**, *4411*
4:16 of the law but also to those who are of the **f** *4411*
4:19 Without weakening *in* his **f**, *4411*
4:20 strengthened *in* his **f** and gave glory to God, *4411*
5: 1 since we have been justified through **f**, *4411*
5: 2 *by* **f** into this grace in which we now stand. *4411*
9:30 a righteousness that is by **f**; *4411*
9:32 Because they pursued it not by **f** but as *4411*
10: 6 But the righteousness that is by **f** says: *4411*
10: 8 that is, the word *of* **f** we are proclaiming: *4411*
10:17 **f** comes from hearing the message, *4411*
11:20 and you **stand** *by* **f**. *4411*
12: 3 with the measure *of* **f** God has given you *4411*
12: 6 let him use it in proportion to his **f**. *4411*
14: 1 Accept him whose **f** is weak, *4411*
14: 2 One man's **f** allows him to eat everything, *4409*
14: 2 whose **f** is weak, eats only vegetables. *NIG*
14:23 because his eating is not from **f**; *4411*
14:23 that does not come from **f** is sin. *4411*
1Co 2: 5 your **f** might not rest on men's wisdom, *4411*
12: 9 to another **f** by the same Spirit, *4411*
13: 2 and if I have a **f** that can move mountains, *4411*
13:13 now these three remain: **f**, hope and love. *4411*
15:14 our preaching is useless and so is your **f**. *4411*
15:17 if Christ has not been raised, your **f** is futile; *4411*
16:13 Be on your guard; stand firm in the **f**; *4411*
2Co 1:24 Not that we lord it over your **f**, *4411*
1:24 because it is *by* **f** you stand firm. *4411*
4:13 With that same spirit *of* **f** we also believe *4411*
5: 7 We live by **f**, not by sight. *4411*
8: 7 But just as you excel in everything—*in* **f**, *4411*
10:15 as your **f** continues to grow, *4411*
13: 5 to see whether you are in the **f**; *4411*
Gal 1:23 now preaching the **f** he once tried *4411*
2:16 but by **f** in Jesus Christ. *4411*
2:16 *have* **put** *our* **f** in Christ Jesus that we may *4409*
2:16 that we may be justified by **f** in Christ and *4411*
2:20 I live by **f** in the Son of God, *4411*
3: 8 by **f**, and announced the gospel in advance *4411*
3: 9 So those who **have f** are blessed along *1666+4411*
3: 9 Abraham, the man *of* **f**. *4412*
3:11 because, "The righteous will live by **f**." *4411*
3:12 The law is not based on **f**; *4411*
3:14 so that by **f** we might receive the promise *4411*
3:22 being given through **f** in Jesus Christ, *4411*
3:23 Before this **f** came, we were held prisoners *4411*
3:23 locked up until **f** should be revealed. *4411*
3:24 to Christ that we might be justified by **f**. *4411*
3:25 Now that **f** has come, *4411*
3:26 You are all sons of God through **f** *4411*
5: 5 by **f** we eagerly await through the Spirit *4411*
5: 6 that counts is **f** expressing itself *4411*
Eph 1:15 since I heard about your **f** in the Lord Jesus *4411*
2: 8 by grace you have been saved, through **f**— *4411*
3:12 through **f** in him we may approach God *4411*
3:17 Christ may dwell in your hearts through **f**. *4411*
4: 5 one Lord, one **f**, one baptism; *4411*
4:13 *in* the **f** and in the knowledge of the Son *4411*
6:16 take up the shield *of* **f**, *4411*
6:23 and love with **f** from God the Father and *4411*
Php 1:25 of you for your progress and joy *in* the **f**, *4411*
1:27 contending as one man *for* the **f** of *4411*
2:17 and service *coming from* your **f**, *4411*
3: 9 but that which is through **f** in Christ— *4411*

Php 3: 9 that comes from God and is by **f**. *4411*
Col 1: 4 because we have heard of your **f** *4411*
1: 5 the **f** and love that spring from the hope *NIG*
1:23 if you continue in your **f**, *4411*
2: 5 how orderly you are and how firm your **f** *4411*
2: 7 strengthened *in* the **f** as you were taught, *4411*
2:12 and raised with him through your **f** in *4411*
1Th 1: 3 and Father your work *produced by* **f**, *4411*
1: 8 **f** in God has become known everywhere. *4411*
3: 2 to strengthen and encourage you in your **f**, *4411*
3: 5 I sent to find out about your **f**. *4411*
3: 6 and has brought good news about your **f** *4411*
3: 7 about you because of your **f**. *4411*
3:10 and supply what is lacking *in* your **f**. *4411*
5: 8 putting on **f** and love as a breastplate, *4411*
2Th 1: 3 because your **f** is growing more and more, *4411*
1: 4 about your perseverance and **f** in all *4411*
1:11 of yours and every act *prompted by* your **f**. *4411*
3: 2 for not everyone has **f**. *4411*
1Ti 1: 2 To Timothy my true son in the **f**: *4411*
1: 4 God's work—which is by **f**. *4411*
1: 5 and a good conscience and a sincere **f**. *4411*
1:14 with the **f** and love that are in Christ Jesus. *4411*
1:19 holding on to **f** and a good conscience. *4411*
1:19 and so have shipwrecked their **f**. *4411*
2: 7 and a teacher of the true **f** to the Gentiles. *4411*
2:15 if they continue in **f**, *4411*
3: 9 *of* the **f** with a clear conscience. *4411*
3:13 and great assurance in their **f** *4411*
4: 1 that in later times some will abandon the **f** *4411*
4: 6 the truths *of* the **f** and of the good teaching *4411*
4:12 in life, in love, in **f** and in purity. *4411*
5: 8 the **f** and is worse than an unbeliever. *4411*
6:10 from the **f** and pierced themselves *4411*
6:11 and pursue righteousness, godliness, **f**, *4411*
6:12 Fight the good fight *of* the **f**. *4411*
6:21 and in so doing have wandered from the **f**. *4411*
2Ti 1: 5 I have been reminded *of* your sincere **f**, *4411*
1:13 with **f** and love in Christ Jesus. *4411*
2:18 and they destroy the **f** of some. *4411*
2:22 and pursue righteousness, **f**, *4411*
3: 8 as far as the **f** is concerned, are rejected. *4411*
3:10 my purpose, **f**, patience, love, endurance, *4411*
3:15 to make you wise for salvation through **f** *4411*
4: 7 I have finished the race, I have kept the **f**. *4411*
Tit 1: 1 of Jesus Christ for the **f** of God's elect and *4411*
1: 2 a **f** and knowledge resting on the hope *NIG*
1: 4 my true son in our common **f**: *4411*
1:13 so that they will be sound in the **f** *4411*
2: 2 and sound *in* **f**, in love and in endurance. *4411*
3:15 Greet those who love us in the **f**. *4411*
Phm 1: 5 I hear *about* your **f** in the Lord Jesus *4411*
1: 6 that you may be active in sharing your **f**, *4411*
Heb 4: 2 those who heard did not combine it with **f**. *4411*
4:14 let us hold firmly to the **f** we profess. *NIG*
6: 1 and *of* **f** in God, *4411*
6:12 but to imitate those who through **f** *4411*
10:22 with a sincere heart in full assurance *of* **f**, *4411*
10:38 But my righteous one will live by **f**. *4411*
11: 1 Now **f** is being sure of what we hope for *4411*
11: 3 *By* **f** we understand that the universe *4411*
11: 4 *By* **f** Abel offered God a better sacrifice *4411*
11: 4 By **f** he was commended as *4005*[S]
11: 4 by **f** he still speaks, even though he is dead. *899*[S]
11: 5 *By* **f** Enoch was taken from this life, *4411*
11: 6 without **f** it is impossible to please God, *4411*
11: 7 *By* **f** Noah, when warned about things not *4411*
11: 7 By **his f** he condemned the world *4005*[S]
11: 7 of the righteousness that comes by **f**. *4411*
11: 8 *By* **f** Abraham, when called to go to *4411*
11: 9 *By* **f** he made his home in the promised land *4411*
11:11 *By* **f** Abraham, even though he was past age *4411*
11:13 All these people were still living by **f** *4411*
11:17 *By* **f** Abraham, when God tested him, *4411*
11:20 *By* **f** Isaac blessed Jacob and Esau *4411*
11:21 *By* **f** Jacob, when he was dying, *4411*
11:22 *By* **f** Joseph, when his end was near, *4411*
11:23 *By* **f** Moses' parents hid him *4411*
11:24 *By* **f** Moses, when he had grown up, *4411*
11:27 *By* **f** he left Egypt, *4411*
11:28 *By* **f** he kept the Passover and *4411*
11:29 *By* **f** the people passed through the Red Sea *4411*
11:30 *By* **f** the walls of Jericho fell, *4411*
11:31 *By* **f** the prostitute Rahab, *4411*
11:33 who through **f** conquered kingdoms, *4411*
11:39 These were all commended for their **f**, *4411*
12: 2 the author and perfecter *of* our **f**, *4411*
13: 7 of their way of life and imitate their **f**. *4411*
Jas 1: 3 *of* your **f** develops perseverance. *4411*
2: 5 in the eyes of the world to be rich in **f** and *4411*
2:14 if a man claims to have **f** but has no deeds? *4411*
2:14 Can such **f** save him? *4411*
2:17 In the same way, **f** by itself, *4411*
2:18 But someone will say, "You have **f**; *4411*
2:18 Show me your **f** without deeds, *4411*
2:18 and I will show you my **f** by what I do. *4411*
2:20 that **f** without deeds is useless? *4411*
2:22 You see that his **f** and his actions were *4411*
2:22 his **f** was made complete by what he did. *4411*
2:24 by what he does and not by **f** alone. *4411*
2:26 so **f** without deeds is dead. *4411*
5:15 And the prayer offered *in* **f** will make *4411*
1Pe 1: 5 through **f** are shielded by God's power *4411*
1: 7 These have come so that your **f**— *4411*
1: 9 for you are receiving the goal *of* your **f**, *4411*
1:21 and so your **f** and hope are in God. *4411*
5: 9 Resist him, standing firm *in* the **f**, *4411*
2Pe 1: 1 have received a **f** as precious as ours: *4411*
1: 5 to add to your **f** goodness; *4411*
1Jn 5: 4 that has overcome the world, even our **f**. *4411*
Jude 1: 3 *for* the **f** that was once for all entrusted to *4411*
1:20 build yourselves up *in* your most holy **f** *4411*
Rev 2:13 You did not renounce your **f** in me, *4411*
2:19 I know your deeds, your love and **f**, *4411*

FAITHFUL (83) [FAITH]

Nu 12: 7 he *is* **f** in all my house. 586
Dt 7: 9 he is the **f** God, 586
32: 4 A **f** God who does no wrong, 575
1Sa 2:35 I will raise up for myself a **f** priest, 586
2Sa 20:19 We are the peaceful and **f** *in* Israel. 573
22:26 "To the **f** you show yourself faithful, 2883
22:26 "To the faithful *you* **show yourself f**, 2874
1Ki 3: 6 *he was* **f** to you and righteous 622+928+2143
2Ch 31:18 they were **f** *in* consecrating themselves. 575
31:20 and right and **f** before the LORD his God. 622
Ne 9: 8 You found his heart **f** to you, 586
Ps 12: 1 the **f** have vanished from among men. 574
18:25 To the **f** you show yourself faithful, 2883
18:25 To the faithful *you* **show yourself f**, 2874
25:10 the ways of the LORD are loving and **f** 622
31:23 The LORD preserves the **f**, 573
33: 4 he is **f** in all he does. 575
37:28 the just and will not forsake his **f** *ones*. 2883
78: 8 whose spirits *were* not **f** to him. 586
78:37 *they were* not **f** to his covenant. 586
89:19 to your **f** *people* you said: 2883
89:24 My **f** love will be with him, 575
89:37 the **f** witness in the sky." 586
97:10 the lives of his **f** *ones* and delivers them 2883
101: 6 My eyes will be on the **f** *in* the land, 586
111: 7 The works of his hands are **f** and just; 622
145:13 The LORD *is* **f** to all his promises 586
146: 6 the LORD, who remains **f** forever. 622
Pr 2: 8 the just and protects the way of his **f** *ones*. 2883
20: 6 but a **f** man who can find? 574
28:20 A **f** man will be richly blessed, 575
31:26 and **f** instruction is on her tongue. 2876
Isa 1:21 See how the **f** city has become a harlot! 586
1:26 the City of Righteousness, the **F** City." 586
49: 7 because of the LORD, who *is* **f**, 586
55: 3 my **f** love promised to David. 586
Jer 42: 5 be a true and **f** witness against us if we do 586
Eze 43:11 down before them so that *they may be* **f** 9068
48:11 who *were* **f** *in* serving me and did 9068
Hos 11:12 even against the **f** Holy One. 586
Zec 8: 8 be my people, and I will be **f** and righteous 622
Mt 24:45 "Who then is the **f** and wise servant, *4412*
25:21 'Well done, good and **f** servant! *4412*
25:21 You have been **f** with a few things; *4412*
25:23 'Well done, good and **f** servant! *4412*
25:23 You have been **f** with a few things; *4412*
Lk 12:42 "Who then is the **f** and wise manager, *4412*
Ro 12:12 patient in affliction, **f** in prayer. *4674*
1Co 1: 9 with his Son Jesus Christ our Lord, is **f**. *4412*
4: 2 a trust must prove **f**. *4412*
4:17 my son whom I love, who is **f** in the Lord. *4412*
10:13 God is **f**; he will not let you be tempted
beyond what you can bear. *4412*
2Co 1:18 But as surely as God is **f**, *4412*
Eph 1: 1 the **f** in Christ Jesus: *4412*
6:21 the dear brother and **f** servant in the Lord, *4412*
Col 1: 2 *To* the holy and **f** brothers in Christ *4412*
1: 7 who is a **f** minister of Christ on our behalf, *4412*
4: 7 a **f** minister and fellow servant in the Lord. *4412*
4: 9 our **f** and dear brother, who is one of you. *4412*
1Th 5:24 one who calls you is **f** and he will do it. *4412*
2Th 3: 3 But the Lord is **f**, and he will strengthen *4412*
1Ti 1:12 that he considered me **f**, *4412*
5: 9 has been **f to her husband**, *467+1222+1651*
2Ti 2:13 if we are faithless, he will remain **f**, *4412*
Heb 2:17 a merciful and **f** high priest in service *4412*
3: 2 He was **f** to the one who appointed him, *4412*
3: 2 just as Moses was **f** in all God's house. *NIG*
3: 5 Moses was **f** as a servant in all God's house, *4412*
3: 6 But Christ is **f** as a son over God's house. *NIG*
8: 9 they *did* not **remain f to** my covenant, *1844*
10:23 for he who promised is **f**. *4412*
11:11 he considered him **f** who had made *4412*
1Pe 4:19 *to* their **f** Creator and continue to do good. *4412*
5:12 whom I regard as a **f** brother, *4412*
1Jn 1: 9 he is **f** and just and will forgive us our sins *4412*
3Jn 1: 5 you are **f** in what you are doing for *4412*
Rev 1: 5 who is the **f** witness, *4412*
2:10 Be **f**, even to the point of death, *4412*
2:13 even in the days of Antipas, my **f** witness, *4412*
3:14 the **f** and true witness, *4412*
14:12 and remain **f** to Jesus. *4411*
17:14 chosen and **f** *followers*." *4412*
19:11 whose rider is called **F** and True. *4412*

FAITHFULLY (18) [FAITH]

Dt 11:13 So if *you* **f obey** the commands 9048+9048
Jos 2:14 and **f** when the LORD gives us the land." 622
1Sa 12:24 be sure to fear the LORD and serve him **f** 622+928
1Ki 2: 4 they live, and if they walk **f** before me 622+928
2Ki 20: 3 how I have walked before you **f** and 622+928
22: 7 because they are acting **f**." 575+928
2Ch 19: 9 "You must serve **f** and wholeheartedly in 575+928
31:12 Then they **f** brought in the contributions, 575+928
31:15 Shecaniah assisted him **f** in the towns 575+928
32: 1 After all that Hezekiah had *so* **f** done, 622
2Ch 34:12 The men did the work **f**. 575+928
Ne 9:33 you have acted **f**, while we did wrong. 622
13:14 and do not blot out what I have *so* **f** done 2876
Isa 38: 3 how I have walked before you **f** and 622+928
Jer 23:28 but let the one who has my word speak it **f**. 622
Eze 18: 9 and **f** keeps my laws. 622+6913
44:15 of Zadok and who **f carried out** the duties 9068
1Pe 4:10 **f** administering God's grace *2819+6055*

FAITHFULNESS (59) [FAITH]

Ge 24:27 who has not abandoned his kindness and **f** 622
24:49 Now if you will show kindness and **f** 622
32:10 and **f** you have shown your servant. 622
47:29 that you will show me kindness and **f**. 622
Ex 34: 6 slow to anger, abounding in love and **f**, 622
Jos 24:14 the LORD and serve him with all **f**. 622
1Sa 26:23 for his righteousness and **f**. 575
2Sa 2: 6 the LORD now show you kindness and **f**, 622
15:20 May kindness and **f** be with you." 622
Ps 30: 9 Will it proclaim your **f**? 622
36: 5 reaches to the heavens, your **f** to the skies. 575
40:10 I speak of your **f** and salvation. 575
54: 5 in your **f** destroy them. 622
57: 3 God sends his love and his **f**. 622
57:10 your **f** reaches to the skies. 622
61: 7 appoint your love and **f** to protect him. 622
71:22 I will praise you with the harp for your **f**, 622
85:10 Love and **f** meet together; 622
85:11 **F** springs forth from the earth, 622
86:15 slow to anger, abounding in love and **f**. 622
88:11 your **f** in Destruction? 575
89: 1 with my mouth I will make your **f** known 575
89: 2 that you established your **f** in heaven itself. 575
89: 5 O LORD, your **f** too, 575
89: 8 O LORD, and your **f** surrounds you. 575
89:14 love and **f** go before you. 622
89:33 nor will I ever betray my **f**. 575
89:49 which in your **f** you swore to David? 575
91: 4 his **f** will be your shield and rampart. 622
92: 2 in the morning and your **f** at night, 575
98: 3 He has remembered his love and his **f** to 575
100: 5 his **f** continues through all generations. 575
108: 4 your **f** reaches to the skies. 622
111: 8 done in **f** and uprightness. 622
115: 1 because of your love and **f**. 622
117: 2 and the **f** *of* the LORD endures forever. 622
119:75 and in **f** you have afflicted me. 575
119:90 Your **f** continues through all generations; 575
138: 2 for your love and your **f**, 622
143: 1 in your **f** and righteousness come 575
Pr 3: 3 Let love and **f** never leave you; 622
14:22 those who plan what is good find love and **f**. 622
16: 6 Through love and **f** sin is atoned for; 622
20:28 Love and **f** keep a king safe; 622
Isa 11: 5 be his belt and **f** the sash around his waist. 575
16: 5 in **f** a man will sit on it— 622
25: 1 in perfect **f** you have done marvelous things, 575
38:18 down to the pit cannot hope for your **f**. 622
38:19 fathers tell their children about your **f**. 622
42: 3 In **f** he will bring forth justice; 622
61: 8 In my **f** I will reward them and make 622
La 3:23 They are new every morning; great is your **f**. 575
Hos 2:20 I will betroth you in **f**, 575
4: 1 "There is no **f**, no love, 622
Mt 23:23 more important matters of the law—justice,
mercy and **f**. *4411*
Ro 3: 3 Will their lack of faith nullify God's **f**? *4411*
Gal 5:22 joy, peace, patience, kindness, goodness, **f**, *4411*
3Jn 1: 3 and tell about your **f** to the truth and *NIG*
Rev 13:10 for patient endurance and **f** on the part of *4411*

FAITHLESS (13) [FAITH]

Ps 78:57 Like their fathers they were disloyal and **f**, 953
101: 3 The deeds of **f** *men* I hate; 6091
119:158 I look on the **f** with loathing, 953
Pr 14:14 **f** will be fully repaid for their ways, 4213+6047
Jer 3: 6 "Have you seen what **f** Israel has done? 5412
3: 8 I gave **f** Israel her certificate of divorce 5412
3:11 "**F** Israel is more righteous than unfaithful
Judah. 5412
3:12 " 'Return, **f** Israel,' declares the LORD, 5412
3:14 "Return, **f** people," declares the LORD, 8743
3:22 **f** people; I will cure you of backsliding." 8743
12: 1 Why do all the **f** live at ease? 953+954
Ro 1:31 they are senseless, **f**, heartless, ruthless. *853*
2Ti 2:13 if *we are* **f**, he will remain faithful, *601*

FALCON (1) [FALCON'S, FALCONS]

Dt 14:13 the red kite, the black kite, any kind of **f**, 1901

FALCON'S (1) [FALCON]

Job 28: 7 no **f** eye has seen it. 370

FALCONS (1) [FALCON]

Isa 34:15 there also the **f** will gather, 1901

FALL (228) [FALLEN, FALLING, FALLS, FELL, FELLED, FELLING]

Ge 2:21 **caused** the man **to f** into a deep sleep; 5877
9: 2 and dread of you *will* **f** upon all the beasts 2118
27:13 "My son, let the curse **f** on me. NIH
Ex 9:19 the hail *will* **f** on every man and animal 3718
9:22 the sky so that hail *will* **f** all over Egypt— 2118

Ex 15:16 terror and dread *will* **f** upon them. 5877
Lev 26: 7 and *they will* **f** by the sword before you. 5877
26: 8 and your enemies *will* **f** by the sword 5877
26:36 and *they will* **f**, 5877
Nu 1:53 the Testimony so that wrath *will* not **f** on 2118
14: 3 to this land only to *let us* **f** by the sword? 5877
14:29 In this desert your bodies *will* **f**— 5877
14:32 you—your bodies *will* **f** in this desert. 5877
14:43 be with you and *you will* **f** by the sword." 5877
18: 5 wrath *will* not **f** on the Israelites again. 2118
Dt 28:52 in which you trust **f down.** 3718
29:20 All the curses written in this book *will* **f** 8069
31:29 disaster *will* **f upon** you 7925
32: 2 *Let* my teaching **f** like rain 6903
Jos 9:20 so that wrath *will* not **f** on us for breaking 2118
Jdg 15:18 now die of thirst and **f** into the hands of 5877
1Sa 3:19 **let** none of his words **f** 5877
14:45 not a hair of his head *will* **f** to the ground, 5877
18:25 Saul's plan was to **have** David **f** by 5877
26:20 not *let* my blood **f** to the ground far from 5877
2Sa 3:29 *May* his blood **f** upon the head of Joab and 2565
14:11 "not one hair of your son's head *will* **f** to 5877
17:12 and we will **f** on him as dew settles on NIH
24:14 *Let us* **f** into the hands of the LORD, 5877
24:14 but *do* not *let me* **f** into the hands of men." 5877
24:17 *Let* your hand **f** upon me and my family." 2118
1Ki 1:52 not a hair of his head *will* **f** to the ground; 5877
2Ki 6: 6 The man of God asked, "Where *did it* **f?**" 5877
9:18 **"F in** behind me." 448+6015
9:19 **F in** behind me." 448+6015
1Ch 21:13 *Let me* **f** into the hands of the LORD, 5877
21:13 but *do* not *let me* **f** into the hands of men." 5877
21:17 *let* your hand **f** upon me and my family, 2118
2Ch 34:11 kings of Judah *had* **allowed to f into ruin.** 8845
Est 8: 6 can I bear to see disaster **f on** my people? 5162
Job 13:11 *Would* not the dread of him **f** on you? 5877
31:22 then *let* my arm **f** from the shoulder, 5877
36:28 and abundant **showers f** on mankind. 8319
37: 6 He says to the snow, '**F** *on* the earth,' 2092
Ps 10:10 *they* **f** under his strength. 5877
13: 4 and my foes will rejoice when *I* **f.** 4572
20: 8 They are brought to their knees and **f,** 5877
27: 2 they will stumble and **f.** 5877
35: 8 *may they* **f** into the pit, to their ruin. 5877
37:24 *he will* not **f,** 3214
38:17 For I am about to **f,** 7520
45: 5 *let* the nations **f** beneath your feet. 5877
46: 2 the earth give way and the mountains **f** into 4572
46: 5 God is within her, *she will* not **f;** 4572
46: 6 Nations are in uproar, kingdoms **f;** 4572
55:22 he will never let the righteous **f.** 4572
69: 9 the insults of those who insult you **f** on me. 5877
82: 7 *you will* **f** like every other ruler." 5877
91: 7 A thousand *may* **f** at your side, 5877
106:26 that he *would* **make** them **f** in the desert, 5877
106:27 **make** their descendants **f** 5877
118:13 I was pushed back and *about to* **f,** 5877
140:10 *Let* burning coals **f** upon them; 4572
141:10 *Let* the wicked **f** into their own nets, 5877
145:14 The LORD upholds all those *who* **f** 5877
Pr 4:16 of slumber till *they* **make** someone **f.** 4173
11:28 Whoever trusts in his riches *will* **f,** 5877
16:18 a haughty spirit before a **f.** 4174
22:14 under the LORD's wrath *will* **f** *into* it. 5877
26:27 If a man digs a pit, *he will* **f** into it; 5877
28:10 along an evil path *will* **f** into his own trap, 5877
28:18 he whose ways are perverse *will* suddenly **f.** 5877
Ecc 9:12 by evil times that **f unexpectedly** 5877
10: 8 Whoever digs a pit *may* **f** into it; 5877
Isa 3:25 Your men *will* **f** by the sword, 5877
8:14 to stumble and a rock that **makes** them **f.** 4842
8:15 *they will* **f** and be broken, 5877
9: 8 *it will* **f** on Israel. 5877
10: 4 among the captives or **f** among the slain. 5877
10:34 Lebanon *will* **f** before the Mighty One. 5877
13:15 all who are caught *will* **f** by the sword. 5877
22:25 it will be sheared off and *will* **f,** 5877
24:18 Whoever flees at the sound of terror *will* **f** 5877
28:13 so that they will go and **f** backward, 4173
30:25 when the towers **f,** 5877
31: 3 he who is helped *will* **f;** 5877
31: 8 "Assyria *will* **f** by a sword that is not 5877
31: 9 Their stronghold *will* **f** because of terror; 6296
34: 4 the starry host *will* **f** like withered leaves 5570
34: 7 And the wild oxen *will* **f** with them, 3718
40: 7 The grass withers and the flowers **f,** 5570
40: 8 The grass withers and the flowers **f,** 5570
40:30 and young men **stumble and f;** 4173+4173
47:11 A calamity *will* **f** upon you 5877
51:23 '**F prostrate** that we may walk over you.' 8817
Jer 6:15 So *they will* **f** among the fallen; 5877
8: 4 " 'When *men* **f down,** do they not get up? 5877
8:12 So *they will* **f** among the fallen; 5877
13:18 for your glorious crowns *will* **f** 3718
19: 7 *I will* **make** them **f** by the sword 5877
20: 4 with your own eyes you will see *them* **f** by 5877
23:12 to darkness and there *they will* **f.** 5877
25:27 and vomit, and **f** to rise no more because of 5877
25:34 you *will* **f** and be shattered 5877
34:17 'freedom' to **f** by the sword, NIH
39:18 not **f** by the sword but will escape 5877
44:12 *they will* **f** by the sword or die 5877
46: 6 by the River Euphrates they stumble and **f.** 5877
46:12 both *will* **f down** together." 5877
46:16 *they will* **f** over each other. 5877
48:16 "The **f** *of* Moab is at hand; 369
48:44 "Whoever flees from the terror *will* **f** into 5877
Jer 49:21 the sound of their **f** the earth will tremble; 5877
49:26 her young men *will* **f** in the streets; 5877
50:15 She surrenders, her towers **f,** 5877
50:30 her young men *will* **f** in the streets; 5877
50:32 The arrogant one will stumble and **f** 5877
51: 4 *They will* **f down** slain in Babylon, 5877
51: 8 Babylon *will* suddenly **f** and be broken. 5877
51:44 And the wall of Babylon *will* **f.** 5877
51:49 "Babylon *must* **f** because of Israel's slain, 5877
51:64 And *her people will* **f.**' " 3615
La 1: 9 *Her* **f** was astounding; 3718
Eze 5:12 a third *will* **f** by the sword 5877
6: 7 Your *people will* **f** slain among you, 5877
6:11 for *they will* **f** by the sword, 5877
6:12 and he that is near *will* **f** by the sword, 5877
11:10 *You will* **f** by the sword, 5877
13:11 with whitewash that *it is going to* **f.** 5877
13:13 of rain *will* **f** with destructive fury. 2118
13:21 *they will* no longer **f** prey to your power. 2118
17:21 All his fleeing troops *will* **f** by the sword, 5877
23:25 of you who are left *will* **f** by the sword. 5877
24:21 and daughters you left behind *will* **f** by 5877
25:13 and from Teman to Dedan *they will* **f** by 5877
26:11 your strong pillars *will* **f** to the ground. 3718
26:15 at the sound of your **f,** 5147
26:18 coastlands tremble on the day of your **f;** 5147
28:23 The slain *will* **f** within her, 5877
29: 5 *You will* **f** on the open field and not 5877
30: 4 When the slain **f** in Egypt, 5877
30: 5 and the people of the covenant land *will* **f** 5877
30: 6 " 'The allies of Egypt *will* **f** 5877
30: 6 From Migdol to Aswan *they will* **f** by 5877
30:17 of Heliopolis and Bubastis *will* **f** by 5877
30:22 and **make** the sword **f** from his hand. 5877
30:25 but the arms of Pharaoh *will* **f limp.** 5877
31:16 at the sound of its **f** when I brought it down 5147
32:12 **cause** your hordes **to f** 5877
32:20 *They will* **f** among those killed by 5877
33:12 not *cause him to* **f** when he turns from it. 4173
33:27 those who are left in the ruins *will* **f** by 5877
35: 8 by the sword *will* **f** on your hills and 5877
36:15 **cause** your nation **to f,** 4173
38:20 and every wall *will* **f** to the ground. 5877
39: 4 On the mountains of Israel *you will* **f,** 5877
39: 5 *You will* **f** in the open field, 5877
40: 1 the fourteenth year after the **f** *of* the city— 5782
44:12 **made** the house of Israel **f** 2118+4200+4842
Da 3: 5 *you must* **f down** and worship the image 10484
3: 6 not **f down** and worship will immediately 10484
3:10 pipes and all kinds of music *must* **f down** 10484
3:11 not **f down** and worship will be thrown into 10484
3:15 *to* **f down** and worship the image I made, 10484
11:19 of his own country but will stumble and **f,** 5877
11:26 and many *will* **f in battle.** 2728+5877
11:33 though for a time *they will* **f** by the sword 4173
11:34 When they **f,** they will receive a little help, 4173
11:41 Many countries *will* **f,** but Edom, 4173
Hos 7: 7 All their kings **f,** and none of them calls on 5877
7:16 Their leaders *will* **f** by the sword because 5877
10: 8 and to the hills, "**F** on us!" 5877
13:16 *They will* **f** by the sword; 5877
Am 3: 5 *Does* a bird **f** into a trap on the ground 5877
3:14 the altar will be cut off and **f** to the ground. 5877
7:17 and your sons and daughters *will* **f** by 5877
8:14 *they will* **f,** never to rise again." 5877
Na 3:12 the figs **f** into the mouth of the eater. 5877
3:19 about you claps his hands at your **f,** NIH
Hag 2:22 horses and their riders *will* **f,** 3718
Mt 7:25 beat against that house; yet *it did* not **f,** *4406*
10:29 not one of them *will* **f** to the ground apart *4406*
11: 6 the man who *does* not **f away** on account *4997*
15:14 both *will* **f** into a pit." *4406*
15:27 "but even the dogs eat the crumbs that **f** *4406*
24:29 the stars *will* **f** from the sky, *4406*
26:31 "This very night you *will* all **f away** *4997*
26:33 "Even if all **f away** on account of you, *4997*
26:41 so that *you will* not **f into** temptation. *1656*
Mk 4:17 *they* quickly **f away.** *4997*
13:25 the stars *will* **f** from the sky, *1639+4406*
14:27 "*You will* all **f away,"** Jesus told them, *4997*
14:29 Peter declared, "Even if all **f away,** *4997*
14:38 so that *you will* not **f** into temptation. *2262*
Lk 6:39 *Will they* not both **f** into a pit? *1860*
7:23 the man who *does* not **f away** on account *4997*
8:13 but in the time of testing *they* **f away.** *923*
10:18 "I saw Satan **f** like lightning from heaven. *4406*
11:17 and a house divided against itself *will* **f.** *4406*
21:24 *They will* **f** by the sword and will be taken *4406*
22:40 that *you will* not **f into** temptation." *1656*
22:46 so that *you will* not **f into** temptation." *1656*
23:30 Then " 'they will say to the mountains, "**F** *4406*
Ac 5:15 so that at least Peter's shadow *might* **f on** *2173*
27:32 that held the lifeboat and let it **f away.** *1738*
28: 6 to swell up or suddenly **f** dead, *2928*
Ro 3:23 for all have sinned and **f short** of the glory *5728*
9:33 to stumble and a rock *that* **makes** them **f,** *4998*
11:11 so as to **f** beyond recovery? *4406*
14:21 that *will* **cause** your brother *to* **f.** *4684*
1Co 8:13 **causes** my brother *to* **f into sin,** *4997*
8:13 so that *I will* not **cause** him **to f.** *4997*
10:12 be careful that *you* don't **f!** *4406*
14:25 So he will **f down** and worship God, *4406*
1Th 4:13 to be ignorant about those who **f asleep,** *3121*
1Ti 3: 6 or he may become conceited and **f** under *1860*
3: 7 not **f** into disgrace and into the devil's trap. *1860*
6: 9 want to get rich **f** into temptation and a trap *1860*
Heb 4:11 so that no one *will* **f** by following their *4406*
Heb 6: 6 *if they* **f away,** to be brought back *4178*
10:31 It is a dreadful thing *to* **f** into the hands of the living God. *1860*
1Pe 1:24 the grass withers and the flowers **f,** *1738*
2: 8 to stumble and a rock *that* **makes** them **f.**" *4998*
2Pe 1:10 if you do these things, *you will* never **f,** *4760*
3:17 by the error of lawless men and **f from** *1738*
Rev 3: 9 and **f down** at your feet and acknowledge *4686*
4:10 the twenty-four elders **f down** *4406*
6:16 "**F** on us and hide us from the face *4406*

FALLEN (77) [FALL]

Ge 15:17 When the sun had set and darkness *had* **f,** 2118
Ex 9:18 the worst hailstorm that *has* ever **f** 2118
23: 5 of someone who hates you **f down** 8069
Lev 19:10 or pick up the **grapes that have f.** 7261
Dt 22: 4 or his ox **f** on the road, 5877
29:22 the calamities that have **f** on the land and NIH
Jos 2: 9 to you and that a great fear of you *has* **f** 5877
Jdg 3:25 There they saw their lord **f** to the floor, 5877
8:10 and twenty thousand swordsmen *had* **f.** 5877
19:27 concubine, **f** *in* the doorway of the house, 5877
1Sa 5: 3 **f** on his face on the ground before the ark 5877
5: 4 **f** on his face on the ground before the ark 5877
20:37 to the place where Jonathan's arrow *had* **f,** 3721
31: 8 and his three sons **f** on Mount Gilboa. 5877
2Sa 1:10 because I knew that after he *had* **f** he could 5877
1:12 because *they had* **f** by the sword. 5877
1:19 How the mighty *have* **f!** 5877
1:25 "How the mighty *have* **f** in battle! 5877
1:27 "How the mighty *have* **f!** 5877
2:23 to the place where Asahel *had* **f** and died. 5877
3:38 and a great man *has* **f** in Israel this day? 5877
2Ki 1: 2 Now Ahaziah *had* **f** through the lattice 5877
1:14 fire *has* **f** from heaven and consumed 3718
2:13 that *had* **f** from Elijah and went back 5877
2:14 Then he took the cloak that *had* **f** from him 5877
1Ch 10: 8 and his sons **f** on Mount Gilboa. 5877
2Ch 14:14 the terror of the LORD *had* **f** upon them. 2118
29: 8 the LORD *has* **f** on Judah and Jerusalem; 2118
29: 9 This is why our fathers *have* **f** by the sword 5877
Ps 9:15 nations *have* **f** into the pit they have dug; 3190
16: 6 The boundary lines *have* **f** for me 5877
36:12 See how the evildoers **lie f—** 5877
57: 6 but *they have* **f** into it *themselves.* 5877
68:14 *it was like* **snow f** on Zalmon. 8919
105:38 because dread of Israel *had* **f** on them. 5877
Pr 6: 3 *you have* **f** into your neighbor's hands: 995
Isa 9:10 "The bricks *have* **f down,** 5877
14:12 How *you have* **f** from heaven, 5877
21: 9 'Babylon *has* **f,** has fallen! 5877
21: 9 'Babylon has fallen, *has* **f!** 5877
Jer 3: 3 and no spring rains *have* **f.** 2118
6:15 So they will fall among the **f;** 5877
8:12 So they will fall among the **f;** 5877
48:32 The destroyer *has* **f** on your ripened fruit 5877
51:47 be disgraced and her slain *will* all **lie f** 5877
51:49 in all the earth *have* **f** because of Babylon. 5877
La 2:21 my young men and maidens *have* **f** by 5877
5:16 The crown *has* **f** from our head. 5877
Eze 21:15 So that hearts may melt and the **f** be many, 4842
31:13 All the birds of the air settled on the **f** tree, 5147
32:22 all who *have* **f** by the sword. 5877
32:23 **f** by the sword. 5877
32:24 All of them are slain, **f** by the sword. 5877
32:27 other uncircumcised warriors *who have* **f,** 5877
33:21 "The city *has* **f!"** 5782
Am 5: 2 **"F** *is* Virgin Israel, 5877
9:11 "In that day I will restore David's **f** tent. 5877
Mic 7: 8 Though *I have* **f,** I will rise. 5877
Zec 11: 2 Wail, O pine tree, for the cedar *has* **f;** 5877
Jn 11:11 "Our friend Lazarus *has* **f asleep;** *3121*
Ac 15:16 this I will return and rebuild David's **f** tent. *4406*
Ro 15: 3 of those who insult you *have* **f on** me." *2158*
1Co 11:30 and a number of you *have* **f asleep.** *3121*
15: 6 though some *have* **f asleep.** *3121*
15:18 also who *have* **f asleep** in Christ are lost. *3121*
15:20 the firstfruits *of* those who *have* **f asleep.** *3121*
Gal 5: 4 *you have* **f away from** grace. *1738*
1Th 4:14 with Jesus those who *have* **f asleep** in him. *3121*
4:15 not precede those who *have* **f asleep.** *3121*
Heb 4: 1 that none of you be found *to have* **f short** *5728*
Rev 2: 5 the height from which *you have* **f!** *4406*
9: 1 and I saw a star *that had* **f** from the sky to *4406*
14: 8 A second angel followed and said, **"F!** *4406*
14: 8 **F** is Babylon the Great, *4406*
17:10 Five *have* **f,** one is, the other has not yet come; *4406*
18: 2 With a mighty voice he shouted: **"F!** *4406*
18: 2 **F** is Babylon the Great! *4406*

FALLING (11) [FALL]

Ge 8: 2 and the rain *had* **stopped f** from the sky. 3973
Est 7: 8 Haman *was* **f** on the couch 5877
8: 3 **f** at his feet and weeping. 5877
Ps 72: 6 He will be like rain **f** on a mown field, 3718
133: 3 the dew of Hermon *were* **f** on Mount Zion. 3718
Isa 3: 8 Jerusalem staggers, Judah *is* **f;** 5877
Mk 15:19 **F on** their knees, they paid homage to him. *5502*
Lk 2:34 to cause the **f** and rising of many in Israel, *4774*
22:44 and his sweat was like drops of blood **f** to *2849*
Heb 6: 7 in the rain often **f** on it and that produces *2262*
Jude 1:24 To him who is able to keep you from **f** and *720*

FALLOW (KJV) See UNPLOWED

FALLOWDEER (KJV) See ROE DEER

FALLS (42) [FALL]

Ex 21:33 to cover it and an ox or a donkey **f** into it, 5877
Lev 11:32 of them dies and **f** on something, 5877
11:33 If one of them **f** into a clay pot, 5877
11:35 of their carcasses **f** on becomes unclean; 5877
11:37 If a carcass **f** on any seeds that are to 5877
11:38 on the seed and a carcass **f** on it, 5877
16: 9 Aaron shall bring the goat whose lot **f** to 6590
Nu 24: 4 from the Almighty, *who* **f prostrate,** 5877
24:16 from the Almighty, *who* **f prostrate,** 5877
33:54 Whatever **f** to them by lot will be theirs. 3655
Dt 20:20 until the city at war with you **f.** 3718
22: 8 on your house if someone **f** from the roof. 5877
2Sa 3:29 or leprosy or who leans on a crutch or *who* **f** 5877
3:34 You fell as *one* **f** before wicked men." 5877
Job 4:13 when deep sleep **f** on men, 5877
9:24 a land **f** into the hands of the wicked, 5989
18:12 disaster is ready for him when he **f.** 7520
33:15 when deep sleep **f** on men as they slumber 5877
Ps 7:15 and scoops it out **f** into the pit he has made. 5877
Pr 11:14 For lack of guidance a nation **f,** 5877
13:17 A wicked messenger **f** into trouble, 5877
17:20 he whose tongue is deceitful **f** into trouble. 5877
24:16 for though a righteous man **f** seven times, 5877
24:17 Do not gloat when your enemy **f;** 5877
28:14 but he who hardens his heart **f** into trouble. 5877
Ecc 4:10 If one **f down,** his friend can help him up. 5877
4:10 But pity the man who **f** and has no one 5877
11: 3 a tree **f** to the south or to the north, 5877
11: 3 in the place where it **f,** there will it lie. 5877
Isa 24:20 upon it is the guilt of its rebellion that *it* **f**— 5877
Eze 13:14 When *it* **f,** you will be destroyed in it; 5877
Mt 12:11 "If any of you has a sheep and it **f** into a pit *1860*
13:21 *he* quickly **f away.** *4997*
17:15 *He* often **f** into the fire or into the water. *4406*
21:44 He who **f** on this stone will be broken *4406*
21:44 but he on whom *it* **f** will be crushed." *4406*
Lk 14: 5 "If one of you has a son or an ox that **f** into *4406*
20:18 Everyone who **f** on that stone will *4406*
20:18 but he on whom *it* **f** will be crushed." *4406*
Jn 12:24 a kernel of wheat **f** to the ground and dies, *4406*
Ro 14: 4 To his own master he stands or **f.** *4406*
Jas 1:11 its blossom **f** and its beauty is destroyed. *1738*

FALSE (85) [FALSEHOOD, FALSELY]

Ex 20:16 not give **f** testimony against your neighbor. 9214
23: 1 "Do not spread **f** reports. 8736
23: 7 Have nothing to do with a **f** charge and do 9214
Dt 5:20 not give **f** testimony against your neighbor. 8736
19:18 giving **f** testimony against his brother, 9214
Job 24:25 who *can* **prove** me **f** and reduce my words 3941
36: 4 Be assured that my words are not **f;** 9214
41: 9 Any hope of subduing him *is* **f;** 3941
Ps 4: 2 and seek **f gods?** 3942
24: 4 up his soul to an idol or swear by *what* is **f.** 5327
27:12 for **f** witnesses rise up against me, 9214
35:20 but devise **f** accusations 5327
40: 4 to those who turn aside to **f gods.** 3942
44:17 though we had not forgotten you or *been* **f** 9213
Pr 6:19 a **f** witness who pours out lies and 9214
12:17 but a **f** witness tells lies. 9214
13: 5 The righteous hate what is **f,** 9214
14: 5 but a **f** witness pours out lies. 9214
14:25 but a **f** witness is deceitful. 3942
19: 5 A **f** witness will not go unpunished, 9214
19: 9 A **f** witness will not go unpunished, 9214
21:28 A **f** witness will perish, 3942
25:18 the man who gives **f** testimony 9214
Isa 29:21 and with **f** testimony deprive the innocent 9332
41:29 See, they are all **f!** 224
44:25 of **f prophets** and makes fools of diviners, 967
57:11 so dreaded and feared that *you have been* **f** 3941
63: 8 sons *who will* not *be* **f** to me"; 9213
Jer 13:25 and trusted in **f gods.** 9214
14:14 They are prophesying to you **f** visions, 9214
16:19 "Our fathers possessed nothing but **f gods,** 9214
23:16 **fill** you **with f hopes.** 2038
23:32 against those who prophesy **f** dreams," 9214
50:36 A sword against her **f prophets!** 967
La 2:14 of your prophets were **f** and worthless; 8736
2:14 The oracles they gave you were **f** 8736
Eze 12:24 For there will be no more **f** visions 8736
13: 6 Their visions are **f** and their divinations 8736
13: 7 Have you not seen **f** visions 8736
13: 8 Because of your **f** words and lying visions, 8736
13: 9 be against the prophets who see **f** visions 8736
13:23 therefore you will no longer see **f** visions 8736
21:23 It will seem like a **f** omen 8736
21:29 Despite **f** visions concerning you 8736
22:28 for them by **f** visions and lying divinations. 8736
Hos 10: 4 take **f** oaths and make agreements; 8736
Am 2: 4 they have been led astray by **f gods,** 3942
Mic 6:11 with a bag of **f** weights? 5327
Hab 2: 3 it speaks of the end and *will* not **prove f.** 3941
Zec 10: 2 they tell dreams that are **f,** 8736
Mal 2: 6 in his mouth and nothing **f** was found 6406
Mt 7:15 "Watch out for **f prophets.** *6021*
15:19 sexual immorality, theft, **f testimony,** *6019*
19:18 do not steal, *do* not **give f testimony,** *6018*
24:11 and many **f prophets** will appear *6021*
24:24 For **f Christs** and false prophets will appear *6023*
24:24 For false Christs and **f prophets** will appear *6021*
26:59 looking for **f evidence** against Jesus so *6019*
26:60 though many **f witnesses** came forward. *6019*
Mk 10:19 *do* not **give f testimony,** do not defraud, *6018*
13:22 For **f Christs** and false prophets will appear *6023*
13:22 For false Christs and **f prophets** will appear *6021*
14:57 up and **gave** this **f testimony** against him: *6018*
Lk 6:26 how their fathers treated the **f prophets.** *6021*
18:20 do not steal, *do* not **give f testimony,** *6018*
Jn 1:47 in whom there is nothing **f."** *1515*
7:18 there is **nothing f** about him. *94+4024*
Ac 6:13 They produced **f** witnesses, who testified, *6014*
13: 6 and **f prophet** named Bar-Jesus, *6021*
1Co 15:15 then found to be **f witnesses** about God, *6020*
2Co 11:13 For such men are **f apostles,** *6013*
11:26 and in danger from **f brothers.** *6012*
Gal 2: 4 some **f brothers** had infiltrated our ranks *6012*
Php 1:18 whether *from* **f motives** or true, *4733*
Col 2:18 not let anyone who delights in **f** humility *NIG*
2:23 their **f** humility and their harsh treatment of *NIG*
1Ti 1: 3 not *to* **teach f doctrines** any longer *2281*
6: 3 If anyone **teaches f doctrines** and does *2281*
2Pe 2: 1 But there were also **f prophets** among *6021*
2: 1 just as there will be **f teachers** among you. *6015*
1Jn 4: 1 because many **f prophets** have gone out *6021*
Rev 2: 2 and have found them **f.** *6014*
16:13 and out of the mouth *of* the **f prophet.** *6021*
19:20 with him the **f prophet** who had performed *6021*
20:10 and the **f prophet** had been thrown. *6021*

FALSEHOOD (10) [FALSE]

Job 21:34 Nothing is left of your answers but **f!"** 5086
31: 5 in **f** or my foot has hurried after deceit— 8736
Ps 52: 3 **f** rather than speaking the truth. 9214
119:163 I hate and abhor **f** but I love your law. 9214
Pr 30: 8 Keep **f** and lies far from me; 8736
Isa 28:15 a lie our refuge and **f** our hiding place." 9214
Ro 3: 7 "If my **f** enhances God's truthfulness and *6025*
Eph 4:25 of you must put off **f** and speak truthfully *6022*
1Jn 4: 6 the Spirit of truth and the spirit *of* **f.** *4415*
Rev 22:15 and everyone who loves and practices **f.** *6022*

FALSELY (16) [FALSE]

Ge 21:23 before God that *you will* not **deal f** 9213
Lev 6: 3 or if he swears **f,** 6584+9214
6: 5 he swore **f** about. 2021+4200+9214
19:12 " 'Do not swear **f** by my name 2021+4200+9214
Ps 41: 6 to see me, he speaks **f,** 8736
101: 7 no one who speaks **f** will stand 9214
Jer 5: 2 still they are swearing **f."** 2021+4200+9214
8: 8 of the scribes has handled it **f?** 2021+4200+9214
Da 6:24 the men who *had* **f accused** Daniel were brought 10030+10642
Zec 5: 3 everyone who **swears f** will be banished. 8678
5: 4 and the house of him who swears **f** 9214
8:17 and do not love to swear **f.** 9214
Mt 5:11 persecute you and **f** say all kinds of evil *6017*
Mk 14:56 Many **testified f** against him, *6018*
Lk 3:14 and don't **accuse** people **f**— *5193*
1Ti 6:20 *of* what *is* **f called** knowledge, *6024*

FALTER (2) [FALTERED, FALTERING, FALTERS]

Pr 24:10 If *you* **f** in times of trouble, 8332
Isa 42: 4 *he will* not **f** or be discouraged 3908

FALTERED (1) [FALTER]

Ps 105:37 and from among their tribes no *one* **f.** 4173

FALTERING (3) [FALTER]

Ex 6:12 since I speak with **f** lips?" 6888
6:30 "Since I speak with **f** lips, 6888
Job 4: 4 you have strengthened **f** knees. 4156

FALTERS (1) [FALTER]

Isa 21: 4 My heart **f,** fear makes me tremble; 9494

FAME (16) [FAMOUS]

Dt 26:19 in praise, **f** and honor high above all 9005
Jos 6:27 and his **f** spread throughout the land. 9053
9: 9 because of the **f** *of* the LORD your God. 9005
1Ki 4:31 his **f** spread to all the surrounding nations. 9005
10: 1 When the queen of Sheba heard about the **f** 9051
1Ch 14:17 So David's **f** spread throughout every land, 9005
22: 5 of great magnificence and **f** and splendor 9005
2Ch 9: 1 the queen of Sheba heard of Solomon's **f,** 9051
26: 8 his **f** spread as far as the border of Egypt, 9005
26:15 His **f** spread far and wide, 9005
Isa 66:19 not heard of my **f** or seen my glory. 9051
Jer 48:17 all who know her **f;** 9005
Eze 16:14 And your **f** spread among the nations 9005
16:15 in your beauty and used your **f** to become 9005
Hos 14: 7 his **f** will be like the wine from Lebanon. 2352
Hab 3: 2 LORD, I have heard of your **f;** 9051

FAMILIAR (3)

Ps 139: 3 *you are* **f with** all my ways. 6122
Isa 53: 3 a man of sorrows, and **f with** suffering. 3359
Ac 26:26 The king *is* **f** with these things, *2179*

FAMILIES (109) [FAMILY]

Ge 45:18 bring your father and your **f** back to me. 1074
Ex 1:21 he gave them **f** of their own. 1074
6:14 These were the heads of their **f:** 3+1074
6:25 These were the heads of the Levite **f,** 3
12:21 for your **f** and slaughter the Passover lamb. 5476
Nu 1: 2 by their clans and **f,** 3+1074
1:18 by their clans and **f,** 3+1074
1:20 to the records of their clans and **f.** 3+1074
1:22 to the records of their clans and **f.** 3+1074
1:24 to the records of their clans and **f.** 3+1074
1:26 to the records of their clans and **f.** 3+1074
1:28 to the records of their clans and **f.** 3+1074
1:30 to the records of their clans and **f.** 3+1074
1:32 to the records of their clans and **f.** 3+1074
1:34 to the records of their clans and **f.** 3+1074
1:36 to the records of their clans and **f.** 3+1074
1:38 to the records of their clans and **f.** 3+1074
1:40 to the records of their clans and **f.** 3+1074
1:42 to the records of their clans and **f.** 3+1074
1:45 according to their **f.** 3+1074
1:47 The **f** of the tribe of Levi, however, 3
2:32 counted according to their **f.** 3+1074
3:15 "Count the Levites by their **f** and clans. 3+1074
3:20 according to their **f.** 3+1074
3:24 the **f** of the Gershonites was Eliasaph son 3+1074
3:30 The leader of the **f** of the Kohathite clans 3+1074
3:35 the **f** of the Merarite clans was Zuriel son 3+1074
4: 2 of the Levites by their clans and **f.** 3+1074
4:22 of the Gershonites by their **f** and clans. 3+1074
4:29 "Count the Merarites by their clans and **f.** 3+1074
4:34 the Kohathites by their clans and **f.** 3+1074
4:38 by their clans and **f.** 3+1074
4:40 counted by their clans and **f,** were 2,630. 3+1074
4:42 by their clans and **f.** 3+1074
4:46 the Levites by their clans and **f.** 3+1074
7: 2 the heads of **f** who were the tribal leaders 3+1074
26: 2 of the whole Israelite community by **f**— 3+1074
34:14 because the **f** *of* the tribe of Reuben, 3+1074
36: 1 the heads of the Israelite **f.** 3
Dt 12: 7 you and your **f** shall eat and shall rejoice 1074
Jos 7:17 of the Zerahites come forward by **f.** 1505
21: 1 and the heads of the other tribal **f** of Israel 3
2Sa 15:22 on with all his men and the **f** that were 3251
1Ki 8: 1 the tribes and the chiefs of the Israelite **f,** 3
2Ki 10:13 the **f** *of* the king and of the queen mother." 1201
1Ch 4:38 Their **f** increased greatly, 3+1074
5:13 Their relatives, by **f,** were: 3+1074
5:24 These were the heads of their **f:** 3+1074
5:24 famous men, and heads of their **f.** 3+1074
7: 2 heads of their **f.** 3+1074
7: 7 Uzzi, Uzziel, Jerimoth and Iri, heads of **f**— 3+1074
7: 9 the heads of **f** and 20,200 3+1074
7:11 All these sons of Jediael were heads of **f.** 3
7:40 heads of **f,** choice men, 3+1074
8: 6 who were heads of **f** of those living 3
8:10 These were his sons, heads of **f.** 3
8:13 who were heads of **f** of those living 3
8:28 All these were heads of **f,** 3
9: 9 All these men were heads of their **f.** 3+1074
9:13 The priests, who were heads of **f,** 3+1074
9:33 heads of Levite **f,** 3
9:34 All these were heads of Levite **f,** 3
12:39 their **f** had supplied provisions for them. 278
15:12 "You are the heads of the Levitical **f;** 3
16:28 Ascribe to the LORD, O **f** *of* nations, 5476
23: 9 These were the heads of the **f** of Ladan. 3
23:24 the descendants of Levi by their **f**— 3+1074
23:24 the heads of **f** as they were registered 3
24: 4 of **f** from Eleazar's descendants 3+1074
24: 4 of **f** from Ithamar's descendants. 3+1074
24: 6 of Abiathar and the heads of **f** of the priests 3
24:30 according to their **f.** 3+1074
24:31 heads of **f** of the priests and of the Levites. 3
24:31 The **f** *of* the oldest brother were treated 3
26:13 according to their **f,** young and old alike. 3+1074
26:21 of **f** belonging to Ladan the Gershonite, 3
26:26 the heads of **f** who were the commanders 3
26:31 to the genealogical records of their **f.** 3
26:32 who were able men and heads of **f,** 3
27: 1 heads of **f,** commanders of thousands 3
29: 6 Then the leaders of **f,** 3
2Ch 1: 2 to all the leaders in Israel, the heads of **f**— 3
5: 2 the tribes and the chiefs of the Israelite **f,** 3
17:14 Their enrollment by **f** was as follows: 3+1074
19: 8 of Israelite **f** to administer the law of 3
23: 2 the heads of Israelite **f** from all the towns. 3
25: 5 and assigned them according to their **f** 3+1074
31:17 by their **f** in the genealogical records 3+1074
35: 4 Prepare yourselves by **f** in your divisions, 3+1074
35: 5 of Levites for each subdivision of the **f** 3+1074
35:12 to give them to the subdivisions of the **f** 3+1074
Ezr 2:59 that their **f** were descended from Israel: 3+1074
2:68 of the heads of the **f** gave freewill offerings 3
4: 2 to Zerubbabel and to the heads of the **f** 3
4: 3 of the heads of the **f** of Israel answered, 3
Ne 4:13 posting them by **f,** with their swords, 5476
7: 5 the common people for **registration by f.** 3509
7:61 that their **f** were descended from Israel: 3+1074
7:70 the heads of the **f** contributed to the work. 3
7:71 the heads of the **f** gave to the treasury for 3
8:13 the heads of all the **f,** 3
10:34 to determine when each of our **f** is to bring 3+1074
11:13 who were heads of **f**— 3
12:12 these were the heads of the priestly **f:** 3
Ps 22:27 and all the **f** *of* the nations will bow down 5476
68: 6 God sets the lonely in **f,** 1074
96: 7 Ascribe to the LORD, O **f** *of* nations, 5476
107:41 of their affliction and increased their **f** 5476
Am 3: 2 "You only have I chosen of all the **f** *of* 5476

FAMILY (177) [FAMILIES]

Ge 7: 1 "Go into the ark, you and your whole f, 1074
16: 2 perhaps *I can* **build a** f through her." 1215
19:32 then lie with him and preserve our f **line** 2446
19:34 with him so we can preserve our f **line** 2446
24:38 but go to my father's f and to my own clan, 1074
24:40 from my own clan and from my father's f. 1074
30: 3 and that through her I too *can* **build a** f." 1215
43: 7 about ourselves and our f. 4580
46:27 the members of Jacob's f, 1074
50:22 along with all his father's f. 1074
Ex 1: 1 each with his f: 1074
12: 3 to take a lamb for his f, 3+1074
Lev 6:29 Any male in a priest's f may eat it; NIH
7: 6 Any male in a priest's f may eat it, NIH
20: 5 and his f and will cut off from their people 5476
22:10 " 'No one **outside a priest's** f may eat 2424
25:10 to his f **property** and each to his own clan. 299
27:16 the LORD part of his f **land,** its value is 299+8441
27:22 which is not part of his f **land,** 299+8441
27:28 whether man or animal or f **land—** 299+8441
Nu 1: 4 each the head of his f, is to help you. 3+1074
1:44 each one representing his f. 3+1074
2: 2 with the banners of his f." 3+1074
2:34 each with his clan and f. 3+1074
3: 1 the **account of the** f *of* Aaron and Moses 9352
11:10 Moses heard the people of every f wailing, 5476
18: 1 your sons and your father's f are to bear 1074
25: 6 to his f a Midianite woman right before 278
25:14 the leader of a Simeonite f. 3+1074
25:15 a tribal chief of a Midianite f. 3+1074
31:26 "You and Eleazar the priest and the f heads 3
32:28 and Joshua son of Nun and to the f heads 3
36: 1 The f heads of the clan of Gilead son 3
Dt 15:16 and your f and is well off with you, 1074
15:20 Each year you and your f are to eat them in 1074
18: 8 from the sale of f **possessions.** 3
25: 5 his widow must not marry **outside the** f. 2021+2025+2424+2575
25: 9 not build up his brother's f **line."** 1074
25:10 in Israel as The F *of* the Unsandaled. 1074
Jos 2:12 that you will show kindness to my f, 3+1074
2:18 and all your f into your house. 3+1074
6:23 They brought out her entire f and put them 5476
6:25 with her f and all who belonged to her, 3+1074
7:14 that the LORD takes shall come forward f NIH
7:14 that the LORD takes shall come forward family by f; 1074
7:14 the f that the LORD takes shall come forward 1074
7:18 Joshua had his f come forward man 1074
13:29 the f *of* the descendants of Manasseh, clan 4751
21: 1 Now the f heads of the Levites 3
22:14 of a f division among the Israelite clans. 3
Jdg 1:25 but spared the man and his whole f. 5476
6:15 and I am the least in my f." 3+1074
6:27 because he was afraid of his f and the men 3+1074
8:27 and it became a snare to Gideon and his f. 1074
8:35 They also failed to show kindness to the f 1074
9:16 and his f, and if you have treated him 1074
9:18 revolted against my father's f, 1074
9:19 toward Jerub-Baal and his f today, 1074
11: 2 not going to get any inheritance in our f," 3+1074
16:31 and his father's whole f went down 1074
18:25 and you and your f will lose your lives." 1074
Ru 4:10 from among his f or from the town records. 278
4:12 may your f be like that of Perez, 1074
4:18 This, then, is the f **line** *of* Perez: 9352
1Sa 1:21 with all his f to offer the annual sacrifice to 1074
2:31 there will not be an old man in your f **line** 1074
2:32 in your f **line** there will never be 1074
2:36 in your f **line** will come and bow down 1074
3:12 against Eli everything I spoke against his f 1074
3:13 that I would judge his f forever because of 1074
9:20 if not to you and all your father's f?" 1074
17:25 in marriage and will exempt his father's f 1074
18:18 what is my f or my father's clan in Israel, 2646
20:15 not ever cut off your kindness from my f— 1074
20:29 because our f is observing a sacrifice in 5476
22:11 of Ahitub and his father's whole f, 1074
22:15 or any of his father's f, 1074
22:16 Ahimelech, you and your father's whole f." 1074
22:22 for the death of your father's whole f. 1074
24:21 or wipe out my name from my father's f." 1074
27: 3 Each man had his f with him, 1074
2Sa 2: 3 men who were with him, each with his f, 1074
3: 8 to the house of your father Saul and to his f 278
7:18 O Sovereign LORD, and what is my f, 1074
9: 9 that belonged to Saul and his f. 1074
14: 9 the blame rest on me and on my father's f, 1074
16: 5 from the same clan as Saul's f came out 1074
21: 4 or gold from Saul or his f, 1074
24:17 Let your hand fall upon me and my f." 3+1074
1Ki 14:14 a king over Israel who will cut off the f 1074
15:29 he killed Jeroboam's whole f. 1074
16:11 he killed off Baasha's whole f. 1074
16:12 So Zimri destroyed the whole f *of* Baasha, 1074
17:15 for Elijah and for the woman and her f. 1074
18:18 "But you and your father's f have. 1074
2Ki 8: 1 "Go away with your f and stay for a 1074
8: 2 and her f went away and stayed in the land 1074
8:27 for he was related by marriage to Ahab's f. 1074
10:17 he killed all who were left there of Ahab's f; NIH
11: 1 she proceeded to destroy the whole royal f. 2446
1Ch 5:15 the son of Guni, was head of their f. 3+1074
7: 4 According to their f genealogy, 3+1074
7:23 because there had been misfortune in his f. 1074
1Ch 9:19 his f (the Korahites) were responsible for 3+1074
12:27 leader of the f **of Aaron,** with 3,700 men, 195
12:28 with 22 officers from his f; 3+1074
13:14 of God remained with the f *of* Obed-Edom 1074
16:43 and David returned home to bless his f. 1074
17:16 O LORD God, and what is my f, 1074
21:17 let your hand fall upon me and my f, 3+1074
23:11 as one f with one assignment. 3+1074
24: 6 one f being taken from Eleazar and 3+1074
26: 6 who were leaders in their father's f 1074
27:15 from the f of Othniel. NIH
28: 4 chose me from my whole f to be king 3+1074
28: 4 from the house of Judah he chose my f, 3+1074
2Ch 22:10 she proceeded to destroy the whole royal f 2446
26:12 The total number of f leaders over 3
31:10 from the f *of* Zadok, answered, 1074
Ezr 1: 5 Then the f heads of Judah and Benjamin, 3
2:36 the descendants of Jedaiah (through the f 1074
2:62 These searched for their f records, 3509
3:12 the older priests and Levites and f heads, 3
8: 1 These are the f heads and those registered 3
8:29 and the Levites and the f heads of Israel." 3
10:16 the priest selected men who were f heads, 3
10:16 one from each f division, 3
Ne 7:39 the descendants of Jedaiah (through the f 1074
7:64 These searched for their f records, 3509
12:12 of Seraiah's f, Meraiah; NIH
12:22 The f heads of the Levites in the days 3
12:23 The f heads among the descendants of Levi 3
Est 2:10 Esther not revealed her nationality and f **background,** 4580
2:20 Esther had kept secret her f **background** 4580
4:14 but you and your father's f will perish. 1074
8: 6 to see the destruction of my f?" 4580
9:28 in every generation by **every** f, 2256+5476+5476
Job 21:21 For what does he care about the f he leaves 1074
32: 2 the Buzite, of the f *of* Ram, 5476
Pr 11:29 on his f will inherit only wind, 1074
15:27 A greedy man brings trouble to his f, 1074
27:27 of goats' milk to feed you and your f and 1074
31:15 for her f and portions for her servant girls. 1074
Isa 22:24 All the glory of his f will hang on him: 3+1074
Jer 12: 6 Your brothers, your own f— 3+1074
35: 2 to the Recabite f and invite them to come 1074
35: 3 the whole f *of* the Recabites. 1074
35: 5 the men of the Recabite f and said to them, 1074
35:18 Jeremiah said to the f *of* the Recabites, 1074
38:17 you and your f will live. 1074
Eze 17:13 a member of the royal f and made a treaty 2446
43:19 who are Levites, of the f *of* Zadok, 2446
Da 1: 3 in some of the Israelites from the royal f 2446
11: 7 her f **line** will arise to take her place. 5916+9247
Am 3: 1 the whole f I brought up out of Egypt: 5476
Mk 3:21 When his f heard about this, *3836+4123*
5:19 to **your** f and tell them how much *3836+5050*
Lk 9:61 and say good-by to my f." *3875*
12:52 be five in one f divided against each other, *3875*
Jn 7:42 that the Christ will come from David's f *5065*
8:35 a slave has no permanent place in the f, *3864*
Ac 4: 6 and the other men of the high priest's f. *1169*
7:13 and Pharaoh learned about Joseph's f. *1169*
7:14 for his father Jacob and his whole f, *5149*
10: 2 and all his f were devout and God-fearing; *3875*
16:33 immediately he and all his f were baptized. *3836*
16:34 believe in God—he and his **whole** f. *4109*
Gal 6:10 to those who **belong to** the f of believers. *3858*
Eph 3:15 from whom his whole f in heaven and *4255*
1Ti 3: 4 He must manage his own f well and see *3875*
3: 5 not know how to manage his own f, *3875*
5: 4 into practice by caring for their own f and *3875*
5: 8 and especially for his **immediate** f, *3858*
5:16 a believer has widows in her f, *NIG*
Heb 2:11 those who are made holy are of the same f. *NIG*
11: 7 in holy fear built an ark to save his f. *3836+3875*
1Pe 4:17 for judgment to begin with the f of God; *3875*

FAMINE (102) [FAMINES]

Ge 12:10 Now there was a f in the land, 8280
12:10 for a while because the f was severe. 8280
26: 1 Now there was a f in the land— 8280
26: 1 besides the earlier f of Abraham's time— 8280
41:27 They are seven years of f. 8280
41:30 but seven years of f will follow them. 8280
41:30 and the f will ravage the land. 8280
41:31 the f that follows it will be so severe. 8280
41:36 during the seven years of f that will come 8280
41:36 that the country may not be ruined by the f." 8280
41:50 Before the years of f came, 8280
41:54 and the seven years of f began, 8280
41:54 There was f in all the other lands, 8280
41:55 When all Egypt *began to* **feel the** f, 8279
41:56 the f had spread over the whole country, 8280
41:56 for the f was severe throughout Egypt. 8280
41:57 because the f was severe in all the world. 8280
42: 5 for the f was in the land of Canaan also. 8280
43: 1 Now the f was still severe in the land. 8280
45: 6 two years now there has been f in the land, 8280
45:11 because five years of f are still to come. 8280
47: 4 because the f is severe in Canaan 8280
47:13 the whole region because the f was severe; 8280
47:13 and Canaan wasted away because of the f. 8280
47:20 because the f was too severe for them. 8280
Dt 32:24 I will send wasting f against them, 8280
Ru 1: 1 there was a f in the land, 8280
2Sa 21: 1 there was a f for three successive years; 8280
24:13 upon you three years of f in your land? 8280
1Ki 8:37 "When f or plague comes to the land, 8280
18: 2 Now the f was severe in Samaria, 8280
2Ki 4:38 Elisha returned to Gilgal and there was a f 8280
6:25 There was a great f in the city; 8280
7: 4 the f is there, and we will die. 8280
8: 1 a f in the land that will last seven years." 8280
25: 3 the ninth day of the [fourth] month the f in 8280
1Ch 21:12 three years of f, three months of being 8280
2Ch 6:28 "When f or plague comes to the land, 8280
20: 9 sword of judgment, or plague or f, 8280
Ne 5: 3 and our homes to get grain during the f." 8280
Job 5:20 In f he will ransom you from death, 8280
5:22 You will laugh at destruction and f, 4103
Ps 33:19 from death and keep them alive in f. 8280
37:19 in days of f they will enjoy plenty. 8282
105:16 He called down f on the land 8280
Isa 14:30 But your root I will destroy by f; 8280
51:19 ruin and destruction, f and sword— 8280
Jer 5:12 we will never see sword or f. 8280
11:22 their sons and daughters by f. 8280
14:12 with the sword, f and plague." 8280
14:13 'You will not see the sword or suffer f. 8280
14:15 'No sword or f will touch this land.' 8280
14:15 same prophets will perish by sword and f. 8280
14:16 of Jerusalem because of the f and sword. 8280
14:18 if I go into the city, I see the ravages of f. 8280
16: 4 They will perish by sword and f, 8280
18:21 So give their children over to f; 8280
21: 7 and f, to Nebuchadnezzar king of Babylon 8280
21: 9 in this city will die by the sword, f 8280
24:10 sword, f and plague against them 8280
27: 8 sword, f and plague, declares the LORD, 8280
27:13 sword, f and plague with which 8280
29:17 the sword, f and plague against them 8280
29:18 sword, f and plague and will make them 8280
32:24 Because of the sword, f and plague, 8280
32:36 sword, f and plague it will be handed over 8280
34:17 to fall by the sword, plague and f. 8280
38: 2 in this city will die by the sword, f 8280
42:16 the f you dread will follow you into Egypt, 8280
42:17 to settle there will die by the sword, f 8280
42:22 You will die by the sword, f and plague in 8280
44:12 they will fall by the sword or die from f. 8280
44:12 they will die by sword or f. 8280
44:13 f and plague, as I punished Jerusalem. 8280
44:18 and have been perishing by sword and f." 8280
44:27 by sword and f until they are all destroyed. 8280
52: 6 By the ninth day of the fourth month the f 8280
La 4: 9 sword are better off than those who die of f; 8280
Eze 5:12 of the plague or perish by f inside you; 8280
5:16 and destructive arrows of f, 8280
5:16 I will bring more and more f upon you 8280
5:17 I will send f and wild beasts against you, 8280
6:11 of Israel, for they will fall by the sword, f 8280
6:12 he that survives and is spared will die of f. 8280
7:15 inside are plague and f; 8280
7:15 and those in the city will be devoured by f 8280
12:16 of them from the sword, f and plague, so 8280
14:13 to cut off its food supply and send f upon it 8280
14:21 sword and f and wild beasts and plague— 8280
34:29 be victims of f in the land or bear the scorn 8280
36:29 and make it plentiful and will not bring f 8280
36:30 among the nations because of f. 8280
Am 8:11 "when I will send a f through the land— 8280
8:11 not a f of food or a thirst for water, 8280
8:11 but a f of hearing the words of the LORD. NIH
Lk 4:25 and a half years and there was a severe f *3350*
15:14 there was a severe f in that whole country, *3350*
Ac 7:11 "Then a f struck all Egypt and Canaan, *3350*
11:28 that a severe f would spread over *3350*
Ro 8:35 or persecution or f or nakedness or danger *3350*
Rev 6: 8 over a fourth of the earth to kill by sword, f *3350*
18: 8 death, mourning and f. *3350*

FAMINES (3) [FAMINE]

Mt 24: 7 be f and earthquakes in various places. *3350*
Mk 13: 8 be earthquakes in various places, and f. *3350*
Lk 21:11 f and pestilences in various places, *3350*

FAMISHED (3) [FAMISH]

Ge 25:29 Esau came in from the open country, f. 6546
25:30 let me have some of that red stew! I'm f!" 6546
Isa 8:21 when *they are* f, they will become enraged 8279

FAMOUS (11) [FAME]

Ru 4:11 in Ephrathah and *be* f in Bethlehem. 7924+9005
4:14 *May* he *become* f throughout Israel! 7924+9005
2Sa 8:13 And David **became** f after he returned 6913+9005
23:18 and so he became as f as the Three. 9005
23:22 he too was as f as the three mighty men. 9005
1Ki 1:47 **make** Solomon's name more f 3512
1Ch 5:24 They were brave warriors, f men, 9005
11:20 and so he became as f as the Three. 9005
11:24 he too was as f as the three mighty men. 9005
12:30 brave warriors, f in their own clans— 408+9005
Isa 66:19 to the Libyans and Lydians (f as archers), NIH

FAN (1) [FANS]

2Ti 1: 6 *to* f **into flame** the gift of God, *351*

FANGS (5) [FANG]

Dt 32:24 against them the f *of* wild beasts, 9094
Job 20:16 the f *of* an adder will kill him. 4383
29:17 I broke the f *of* the wicked and snatched 5506

Ps 58: 6 tear out, O LORD, the f *of* the lions! 4922
Joel 1: 6 it has the teeth of a lion, the f *of* a lioness. 5506

FANNERS (KJV) See FOREIGNERS

FANS (1) [FAN]

Isa 54:16 the blacksmith *who* f the coals *into* flame 5870

FANTASIES (3)

Ps 73:20 O Lord, you will despise them as f. 7513
Pr 12:11 but he who chases f lacks judgment. 8199
28:19 but the one who chases f will have his fill 8199

FAR (244) [AFAR, FAR-OFF, FARAWAY, FARTHER, FARTHEST]

Ge 10:19 from Sidon toward Gerar **as f as** Gaza, 6330
10:19 Admah and Zeboiim, **as f as** Lasha. 6330
12: 6 Abram traveled through the land **as f as** 6330
14: 6 **as f as** El Paran near the desert. 6330
14:14 in his household and went in pursuit **as f as** 6330
14:15 pursuing them **as f as** Hobah, 6330
18:25 **F be it** from you to do such a thing— 2721
18:25 **F be it** from you! 2721
44: 4 not gone f from the city when Joseph said 8178
44: 7 **F be it** from your servants to do anything 2721
44:17 **"F be it** from me to do such a thing! 2721
Ex 3: 1 the **f side** *of* the desert and came to Horeb, 339
8:28 **must** not go **very f.** 8178+8178
26:22 Make six frames for the **f end,** that is, 3752
26:23 for the corners at the **f end.** 3752
26:27 at the **f end** *of* the tabernacle. 3752
36:27 They made six frames for the **f end,** that is, 3752
36:28 the corners of the tabernacle at the **f end.** 3752
36:32 at the **f end** *of* the tabernacle. 3752
Lev 13:12 **so f as** the priest can see, 3972+4200
Nu 11:31 **as f as** a day's walk in any direction. 3869
13:21 the land from the Desert of Zin **as f as** 6330
16: 3 "You have **gone too f!** 8041
16: 7 You Levites have **gone too f!"** 8041
21:24 but only **as f as** the Ammonites, 6330
21:26 and had taken from him all his land **as f as** 6330
21:30 We have demolished them **as f as** Nophah, 6330
Dt 1: 7 **as f as** the great river, the Euphrates. 6330
2:23 Avvites who lived in villages **as f as** Gaza, 6330
2:36 even **as f as** Gilead, 6330
3: 8 the Arnon Gorge **as f as** Mount Hermon. 6330
3:10 and all Bashan **as f as** Salecah and Edrei. 6330
3:14 took the whole region of Argob **as f as** 6330
4:49 **as f as** the Sea of the Arabah, 6330
12:21 to put his Name *is too* **f away** from you, 8178
13: 7 whether near or f, 8158
14:24 to put his Name *is so* **f away),** 8178
28:49 a nation against you from **f away,** 8158
34: 2 all the land of Judah **as f as** the western sea, 6330
34: 3 the City of Palms, **as f as** Zoar. 6330
Jos 7: 5 from the city gate **as f as** the stone quarries 6330
8: 4 Don't **go** very f from it. 8178
9: 1 the Great Sea **as f as** Lebanon 448+4578
13: 4 from Arah of the Sidonians **as f as** Aphek, 6330
13: 9 the whole plateau of Medeba **as f as** Dibon, 6330
13:11 all of Mount Hermon and all Bashan **as f as** 6330
13:25 and half the Ammonite country **as f as** 6330
15: 5 the Salt Sea **as f as** the mouth of the Jordan. 6330
15:47 and villages, **as f as** the Wadi of Egypt and 6330
16: 3 to the territory of the Japhletites **as f as** 6330
19: 8 the villages around these towns **as f as** 6330
19:10 of their inheritance went **as f as** Sarid. 6330
19:28 Hammon and Kanah, **as f as** Greater Sidon. 6330
22:29 **"F be it** from us to rebel against 2721
24: 6 with chariots and horsemen as f as NIH
24:16 **"F be it** from us to forsake the LORD 2721
Jdg 4:16 and army **as f as** Harosheth Haggoyim. 6330
7:22 to Beth Shittah toward Zererah **as f as** 6330
7:24 of the Jordan ahead of them **as f as** 6330
7:24 the waters of the Jordan **as f as** Beth Barah. 6330
11:33 **as f as** Abel Keramim. 6330
20:45 the Benjamites **as f as** Gidom and struck 6330
Ru 3: 7 to lie down at the **f end** *of* the grain pile. 7895
1Sa 2:30 the LORD declares: **'F be it** from me! 2721
6:12 of the Philistines followed them **as f as** 6330
7:12 **"Thus f** has the LORD helped us." 2178+6330
12:23 **f be it** from me that I should sin against 2721
24: 3 David and his men were **f back in** the cave. 928+3752
26:20 not let my blood fall to the ground **f from** the presence of the LORD. 4946+5584
2Sa 7:18 that you have brought me **this f?** 2151+6330
19:15 king returned and went **as f as** the Jordan. 6330
20:20 **"F be it** from me!" 2721
20:20 **"F be it** from me to swallow up or destroy! 2721
23:17 **"F be it** from me, O LORD, to do this!" 2721
1Ki 4:21 **as f as** the border of Egypt. 6330
8:46 to his own land, **f away** or near; 8158
10: 7 in wisdom and wealth *you have* **f exceeded** 3578
12:30 the people went **even as f as** Dan 6330
2Ki 7:15 They followed them **as f as** the Jordan, 6330
18: 8 **as f as** Gaza and its territory. 6330
1Ch 4:33 the villages around these towns **as f as** 6330
5:11 **as f as** Salecah: 6330
5:16 on all the pasturelands of Sharon **as f as** 6584
12:40 their neighbors from **as f away** as Issachar, 6330
13: 2 let us send word **f and wide** to the rest 7287
17:16 that you have brought me **this f?** 2151+6330
18: 3 **as f as** Hamath, 2025
2Ch 6:36 who takes them captive to a land **f away** 8158
9: 6 *you have* **f exceeded** the report I heard. 3578
9:26 **as f as** the border of Egypt. 6330
12: 4 of Judah and came **as f as** Jerusalem. 6330
14: 9 and came **as f as** Mareshah. 6330
14:13 and Asa and his army pursued them **as f as** 6330
26: 8 his fame spread **as f as** the border of Egypt, 6330
26:15 fame spread **f and wide,** 4200+4946+6330+8158
30:10 **as f as** Zebulun, 6330
33:14 **as f as** the entrance of the Fish Gate 2256
34: 6 Ephraim and Simeon, **as f as** Naphtali, 6330
Ezr 3:13 And the sound was heard **f away.** 4200+4946+6330+8158
Ne 3: 1 building **as f as** the Tower of the Hundred, 6330
3: 1 and **as f as** the Tower of Hananel. 6330
3: 8 They restored Jerusalem **as f as** 6330
3:13 of the wall **as f as** the Dung Gate. 6330
3:15 **as f as** the steps going down from the City 6330
3:16 **as f as** the artificial pool and the House of 6330
3:19 point facing the ascent to the armory as f as NIH
3:31 made repairs **as f as** the house of 6330
3:31 and **as f as** the room above the corner; 6330
5: 8 **"As f as possible,** 1896+3869
12:39 **as f as** the Sheep Gate. 6330
12:43 in Jerusalem could be heard **f away.** 4946+8158
Est 4: 2 But he went only **as f as** the king's gate, 6330
9:20 the provinces of King Xerxes, near and **f,** 8158
Job 5: 4 His children *are* f from safety, 8178
13:21 **Withdraw** your hand f from me, 8178
22:23 If *you* **remove** wickedness f from your tent 8178
28: 4 **F from** where people dwell he cuts a shaft, 4946
28: 4 **f from** men he dangles and sways. 4946
34:10 **F be it** from God to do evil, 2721
38:11 **'This f** you may come and no farther; 6330+7024
Ps 10: 1 O LORD, do you stand **f off?** 928+8158
10: 5 haughty and your laws are **f from** him; 4946+5584
22: 1 Why are you *so* f from saving me, 8158
22: 1 so f from the words of my groaning? NIH
22:11 *Do* not *be* f from me, 8178
22:19 But you, O LORD, *be* not **f off;** 8178
35:22 *Do* not *be* f from me, O Lord. 8178
38:11 my neighbors stay **f away.** 4946+8158
38:21 *be* not f from me, O my God. 8178
49:14 **f from** their princely mansions. 4946
55: 7 *I would* flee **f away** and stay in the desert; 8178
55: 8 **f from** the tempest and storm." 4946
65: 8 Those living **f away** fear your wonders; 7921
71:12 *Be* not f from me, O God; 8178
73:27 *Those who are* f *from* you will perish; 8179
80:11 its shoots **as f as** the River. 448
97: 9 you are exalted **f above** all gods. 4394
101: 4 Men of perverse heart *shall be* f from me; 6073
103:12 as f as the east *is* from the west, 8178
103:12 *so* f *has he* **removed** our transgressions 8178
109:17 *may it be* f from him. 8178
119:150 but *they are* f from your law. 8178
119:155 Salvation is f from the wicked, 8158
139: 9 if I settle on the **f side** *of* the sea, 344
Pr 4:24 **keep** corrupt talk f from your lips. 8178
5: 8 **Keep** *to* a path f from her, 8178
15:29 The LORD is f from the wicked 8158
22: 5 he who guards his soul **stays** f from them. 8178
22:15 rod of discipline *will* **drive** it f from him. 8178
27:10 a neighbor nearby than a brother **f away.** 8158
30: 8 **Keep** falsehood and lies f from me; 8178
31:10 She is worth f more than rubies. 8158
Ecc 2: 9 I became greater **by** f than anyone 3578
7:24 it is **f off** and most profound— 8158
Isa 6:12 until the LORD *has* **sent** everyone **f away** 8178
15: 5 her fugitives flee **as f as** Zoar, 6330
15: 5 as f as Eglath Shelishiyah. NIH
15: 8 their wailing reaches **as f as** Eglaim, 6330
15: 8 their lamentation as f as Beer Elim. NIH
16: 8 Their shoots spread out and **went as f as** 6296
17:13 he rebukes them they flee **f away,** 4946+5305
18: 2 people feared **f and wide,** 2085+2134+2256+4946
18: 7 people feared **f and wide,** 2085+2134+2256+4946
22: 3 while the enemy was still **f away.** 4946+8158
29:13 but their hearts *are* f from me. 8178
33:13 You *who are* **f away,** hear what I have done; 8158
46:12 you who are f from righteousness. 8158
46:13 *it is* not **f away;** 8178
49:19 those who devoured you *will be* **f away.** 8178
54:14 Tyranny *will be* f from *you;* 8178
54:14 Terror will be f removed; NIH
56:12 or **even f** better." 3856+4394
57: 9 You sent your ambassadors **f away;** 4946+8158
57:19 Peace, peace, to those f and near," 8158
59: 9 So justice *is* f from us, 8178
59:11 for deliverance, but *it is* **f away.** 8178
Jer 2: 5 that *they* **strayed** so f from me? 8178
8:19 to the cry of my people from a land **f away:** 5305
12: 2 on their lips but f from their hearts. 8158
23:23 "and not a God **f away?** 4946+8158
25:26 near and **f,** one after the other— 8158
27:10 that *will only serve to* **remove** you f 8178
31:40 to the Kidron Valley on the east **as f as** 6330
43: 7 to the LORD and went **as f as** Tahpanhes. 6330
48:24 to all the towns of Moab, f and near. 8158
48:32 Your branches spread as f as the sea; NIH
48:32 they reached **as f as** the sea of Jazer. 6330
48:34 from Zoar **as f as** Horonaim 6330
Eze 6:12 He *that* is **f away** will die of the plague, 8158
8: 6 that *will* **drive** me f from my sanctuary? 8178
10: 5 the cherubim could be heard **as f away as** 6330
11:15 *'They are* **f away** from the LORD; 8178
11:16 Although *I* **sent** them **f away** among 8178
22: 5 and those *who* are **f away** will mock you, 8158
23:40 for men who came from **f away,** 5305
29:10 **as f as** the border of Cush. 6330
38: 6 from the **f north** with all its troops— 3752
38:15 from your place in the **f north,** 3752
39: 2 from the **f north** and send you against 3752
40:15 to the **f end** of its portico was fifty cubits. 7164
44:10 " 'The Levites who **went** f from me 8178
45: 9 You have **gone f enough,** 8041
47:16 as f as Hazer Hatticon, NIH
47:18 to the eastern sea and as f as Tamar. NIH
47:19 from Tamar **as f as** the waters 6330
Da 9: 7 of Jerusalem and all Israel, both near and **f,** 8158
11: 2 who will be f richer than all the others. 1524
11:10 and carry the battle **as f as** his fortress. 6330
Joel 2:20 **drive** the northern army f 8178
3: 6 *you might* **send** them f from their homeland. 8178
3: 8 a nation **f away."** 8158
Ob 1:20 in Canaan will possess [the land] **as f as** 6330
Mic 4: 3 for strong nations **f and wide.** 6330+8158
Zec 6:15 *Those who are* **f away** will come and help 8158
Mt 15: 8 but their hearts are f from me. *4522*
Mk 7: 6 but their hearts are f from me. *4522*
12:34 "You are not f from the kingdom of God." *3426*
Lk 7: 6 He was not f from the house when *3426*
16:23 he looked up and saw Abraham **f away,** *608+3427*
Jn 6: 1 **to the f shore** of the Sea of Galilee (that is, *4305*
6: 9 but **how f will they go** among *1639+4047+5515*
21: 8 for they were not f from shore, *3426*
Ac 2:39 children and for all who are **f off—** *1650+3426*
11:19 in connection with Stephen traveled **as f as** *2401*
17:27 though he is not f from each one of us. *3426*
22:21 I will send you **f away** to the Gentiles.' " *3426*
23:31 during the night and brought him **as f as** *1650*
28:15 and they traveled **as f as** the Forum *948*
Ro 11:28 **As f as** the gospel is concerned, *3525*
11:28 **but as f as** election is concerned, *1254*
12:18 *f as* **it depends on you,** *AIT*
2Co 1: 8 f beyond our ability to endure, *NIG*
4:17 **that f outweighs them all.** *983+1650+2848+5651+5651*
10:14 *We are* not **going too f** in our boasting, *5657*
10:14 for we did get **as f as** you with the gospel *948*
Eph 1:21 **f above** all rule and authority, *5645*
2:13 in Christ Jesus you who once were **f away** have been brought near *3426*
2:17 peace to you who were **f away** and peace *3426*
Php 1:23 which is better **by f;** *4498*
2Ti 3: 8 as f as the faith is concerned, are rejected. *NIG*
3: 9 But *they will* not **get very f** *2093+4498+4621*
Rev 18:10 they will stand **f off** and cry: " 'Woe! *608+3427*
18:15 will stand **f off,** terrified at her torment. *608+3427*
18:17 from the sea, will stand **f off.** *608+3427*

FAR-OFF (2) [FAR]

Isa 23: 7 to settle in f lands? 8158
46:11 from a f land, a man to fulfill my purpose. 5305

FARAWAY (1) [FAR]

Isa 13: 5 They come from f lands, 5305

FARE (2) [FARED]

Isa 55: 2 your soul will delight in the **richest of f.** 2016
Jnh 1: 3 After paying the f, he went aboard 8510

FARED (2) [FARE]

Ge 30:29 how your livestock *has* f under my care. 2118
Isa 10: 9 'Has not Calno **f like** Carchemish? 3869

FAREWELL (1)

Ac 15:29 do well to avoid these things. **F.** *4874*

FARM (3) [FARMED, FARMER, FARMERS]

2Sa 9:10 and your servants *are to* f the land for him 6268
2Ch 31:19 on the f lands *around* their towns or 4494
Eze 48:19 from the city *who* f it will come from all 6268

FARMED (2) [FARM]

1Ch 27:26 in charge of the field workers who f 6275
Heb 6: 7 for whom *it is* f receives the blessing *1175*

FARMER (9) [FARM]

Isa 28:24 When a f plows for planting, 3086
Jer 51:23 with you I shatter f and oxen, 438
Zec 13: 5 I am not a prophet. I am a **f;** 141+408+6268
Mt 13: 3 "A f went out to sow his seed. *5062*
Mk 4: 3 "Listen! A f went out to sow his seed. *5062*
4:14 The f sows the word. *5062*
Lk 8: 5 "A f went out to sow his seed. *5062*
2Ti 2: 6 The hardworking f should be the first *1177*
Jas 5: 7 See how the f waits for the land *1177*

FARMERS (8) [FARM]

Jer 14: 4 the f are dismayed and cover their heads. 438
31: 5 the f will plant them and enjoy their fruit. 5749
31:24 f and those who move about 438
Joel 1:11 Despair, you f, wail, you vine growers; 438
Am 5:16 The f will be summoned to weep and 438
Mt 21:33 the vineyard *to* some f and went away on *1177*
Mk 12: 1 the vineyard *to* some f and went away on *1177*
Lk 20: 9 *to* some f and went away for a long time. *1177*

FARTHER (6) [FAR]
1Ki 7: 8 palace in which he was to live, **set f back,** 337+2021+2958
Job 38:11 'This far you may come and no **f;** 3578
Mt 26:39 **Going** a little **f,** *4601*
Mk 1:19 *When he had* **gone** a little **f,** *4581*
14:35 **Going** a little **f,** *4601*
Lk 24:28 Jesus acted as if he were going **f.** *4522*

FARTHEST (5) [FAR]
Jos 17:18 Clear it, and its **f limits** will be yours; 9362
Ne 1: 9 if your exiled people are at the **f** horizon, 7895
Job 28: 3 he searches the **f recesses** for ore in 3972+9417
Ps 65: 5 the ends of the earth and of the **f** seas, 8158
Isa 41: 9 from its **f corners** I called you. 721

FARTHING (KJV) See PENNY

FASHION (1) [FASHIONED, FASHIONING, FASHIONS]
Ex 28:15 **"F** a breastpiece for making decisions— 6913

FASHIONED (5) [FASHION]
Ex 39: 8 *They* **f** the breastpiece— 6913
2Ki 19:18 **f** *by* men's hands. 5126
Isa 37:19 **f** *by* human hands. 5126
45:18 *he who* **f** and made the earth, he founded it; 3670
Hos 13: 2 from their silver, **cleverly f** images, 9312

FASHIONING (1) [FASHION]
Ex 32: 4 cast in the shape of a calf, **f** it with a tool. 7445

FASHIONS (3) [FASHION]
Job 15:35 their womb **f** deceit." 3922
Isa 40:19 with gold and **f** silver chains for it. 7671
44:15 But *he* also **f** a god and worships it; 7188

FAST (50) [FASTED, FASTING, FASTS]
Dt 4: 4 but all of you who **held f** to 1816
10:20 **Hold f** to him and take your oaths 1815
11:22 in all his ways and to **hold f** to him— 1815
13: 4 serve him and **hold f** to him. 1815
30:20 listen to his voice, and **hold f** to him. 1815
Jos 22: 5 to obey his commands, to **hold f** to him 1815
23: 8 *to* **hold f** to the LORD your God, 1815
Jdg 4:21 to him while he **lay f asleep,** 8101
2Sa 12:23 But now that he is dead, why *should* I **f?** 7426
1Ki 11: 2 Solomon **held f** to them in love. 1815
21:12 a **f** and seated Naboth in a prominent place 7427
2Ki 18: 6 *He* **held f** to the LORD and did not cease 1815
2Ch 20: 3 and he proclaimed a **f** for all Judah. 7427
Ezr 8:21 by the Ahava Canal, I proclaimed a **f,** 7427
Est 4:16 all the Jews who are in Susa, and **f** for me. 7426
4:16 I and my maids *will* **f** as you do. 7426
8:10 who rode **f horses** especially bred for 8224
Job 18: 9 a snare **holds** him **f.** 2616
36: 8 **held f** by cords of affliction, 4334
41:17 *They* **are joined f** to one another; 1815
Ps 69:10 When I weep and **f,** I must endure scorn; 7427
119:31 *I* **hold f** to your statutes, O LORD; 1815
139:10 your right hand *will* **hold** me **f.** 296
Pr 5:22 the cords of his sin **hold** *him* **f.** 9461
Isa 56: 2 the man *who* **holds** it **f,** 2616
56: 4 who choose what pleases me and **hold f** 2616
56: 6 without desecrating it and *who* **hold f** 2616
58: 4 *You* cannot **f** as you do today 7426
58: 5 Is this the kind of **f** I have chosen, 7427
58: 5 Is that what you call a **f,** 7427
Jer 14:12 *they* **f,** I will not listen to their cry; 7426
50:33 All their captors **hold** them **f,** 2616
Joel 1:14 Declare a holy **f;** call a sacred assembly. 7427
2:15 Blow the trumpet in Zion, declare a holy **f,** 7427
Jnh 3: 5 They declared a **f,** and all of them, 7427
Zec 7: 3 "Should I mourn and **f** in the fifth month, 5692
Mt 6:16 "When *you* **f,** do not look somber as *3764*
6:17 But *when* you **f,** put oil on your head *3764*
9:14 "How is it that we and the Pharisees **f,** *3764*
9:14 but your disciples *do* not **f?"** *3764*
9:15 then *they will* **f.** *3764*
Mk 2:19 of the bridegroom **f** while he is with them? *3764*
2:20 and on that day *they will* **f.** *3764*
Lk 5:33 "John's disciples often **f** and pray, *3764*
5:34 of the bridegroom **f** while he is with them? *3764*
5:35 in those days *they will* **f."** *3764*
18:12 *I* **f** twice a week and give a tenth *3764*
Ac 27: 9 because by now it was after the **F.** *3763*
27:41 The bow **stuck f** and would not move, *2242*
1Pe 5:12 **Stand f** in it. *2705*

FASTED (15) [FAST]
Jdg 20:26 *They* **f** that day until evening 7426
1Sa 7: 6 that day *they* **f** and there they confessed, 7426
31:13 and *they* **f** seven days. 7426
2Sa 1:12 They mourned and wept and **f** till evening 7426
12:16 He **f** and went into his house and spent 7426+7427
12:21 While the child was alive, *you* **f** and wept, 7426
12:22 *I* **f** and wept. 7426
1Ki 21:27 he tore his clothes, put on sackcloth and **f.** 7426
1Ch 10:12 and *they* **f** seven days. 7426
Ezr 8:23 So *we* **f** and petitioned our God about this, 7426
Ne 1: 4 and **f** and prayed before the God of heaven. 7426
Isa 58: 3 'Why *have we* **f,**' they say, 7426
Zec 7: 5 'When *you* **f** and mourned in the fifth 7426
7: 5 was it really *for* me that *you* **f?** 7426+7426
Ac 13: 3 So *after they had* **f** and prayed, *3764*

FASTEN (15) [FASTENED, FASTENS]
Ex 25:12 Cast four gold rings for it and **f** them 5989
25:26 for the table and **f** them to the four corners, 5989
26: 6 and use them *to* **f** the curtains together so 2489
26:11 in the loops *to* **f** the tent **together** as a unit. 2489
28:12 and **f** them on the shoulder pieces of 8492
28:23 Make two gold rings for it and **f** them 5989
28:24 **F** the two gold chains to the rings at 5989
28:37 **F** a blue cord to it to attach it to the turban; 8492
29: 5 **F** the ephod on him 679
36:13 *to* **f** the two sets of curtains together so 2489
36:18 to **f** the tent **together** as a unit. 2489
Job 13:27 *You* **f** my feet in shackles; 8492
Pr 6:21 **f** them around your neck. 6698
Isa 22:21 with your robe and **f** your sash *around* him 2616
Jer 10: 4 *they* **f** it with hammer and nails so it will 2616

FASTENED (19) [FASTEN]
Ex 28: 7 so *it can* **be f.** 2489
37: 3 He cast four gold rings for it and **f** them NIH
37:13 for the table and **f** them to the four corners, 5989
39: 4 so *it could* **be f.** 2489
39: 7 Then *they* **f** them on the shoulder pieces of 8492
39:16 and **f** the rings to two of the corners of 5989
39:17 *They* **f** the two gold chains to the rings at 5989
39:31 Then *they* **f** a blue cord to it to attach it to 5989
Lev 8: 7 so it *was* **f** on him. 679
Nu 19:15 and every open container without a lid **f** 7348
Jdg 15: 4 *He* then **f** a torch to every pair of tails, 8492
1Sa 17:39 David **f on** his sword over the tunic 2520
31:10 of the Ashtoreths and **f** his body to the wall 9546
Est 1: 6 **f** with cords of white linen 296
Eze 24:17 *Keep* your turban **f** and your sandals 2502
Lk 4:20 of everyone in the synagogue were **f** *867*
Jn 19:19 Pilate had a notice prepared and **f** to *5502*
Ac 16:24 he put them in the inner cell and **f** their feet *856*
28: 3 **f** *itself* on his hand. *2750*

FASTENS (2) [FASTEN]
Job 16: 9 my opponent **f** on me his **piercing** eyes. 4323
33:11 *He* **f** my feet in shackles; 8492

FASTING (21) [FAST]
1Ki 21: 9 "Proclaim a **day of f** and seat Naboth in 7427
Ne 9: 1 **f** and wearing sackcloth and having dust 7427
Est 4: 3 with **f,** weeping and wailing. 7427
9:31 to their times of **f** and lamentation. 7427
Ps 35:13 on sackcloth and humbled myself with **f.** 7427
109:24 My knees give way from **f;** 7427
Isa 58: 3 "Yet on the day of your **f,** 7427
58: 4 *Your* **f** ends in quarreling and strife, 7426
58: 6 "Is not this the kind of **f** I have chosen: 7427
Jer 36: 6 of **f** and read to the people from the scroll 7427
36: 9 a **time of f** before the LORD 7427
Da 9: 3 in **f,** and in sackcloth and ashes. 7427
Joel 2:12 with **f** and weeping and mourning." 7427
Mt 4: 2 *After* **f** forty days and forty nights, *3764*
6:16 to show men *they are* **f.** *3764*
6:18 be obvious to men that *you are* **f,** but only *3764*
Mk 2:18 John's disciples and the Pharisees were **f.** *3764*
2:18 and the disciples of the Pharisees *are* **f,** *3764*
Lk 2:37 the temple but worshiped night and day, **f** *3763*
Ac 13: 2 they were worshiping the Lord and **f,** *3764*
14:23 with prayer and **f,** committed them *3763*

FASTS (1) [FAST]
Zec 8:19 "The **f** *of* the fourth, fifth, seventh and tenth 7427

FAT (93) [FATTENED, FATTENING]
Ge 4: 4 But Abel brought **f portions** from some of 2693
41: 2 sleek and **f,** and they grazed among 1374+1414
41: 4 and gaunt ate up the seven sleek, **f** cows. 1374
41:18 the river there came up seven cows, **f** 1374+1414
41:20 up the seven **f** cows that came up first. 1374
45:18 the land of Egypt and you can enjoy the **f** 2693
Ex 23:18 "The **f** *of* my festival offerings must not 2693
29:13 Then take all the **f** around the inner parts, 2693
29:13 and both kidneys with the **f** on them, 2693
29:22 "Take from this ram the **f,** the fat tail, 2693
29:22 "Take from this ram the fat, the **f tail,** 487
29:22 the fat tail, the **f** around the inner parts, 2693
29:22 both kidneys with the **f** on them, 2693
Lev 1: 8 including the head and the **f,** 7022
1:12 including the head and the **f,** 7022
3: 3 all the **f** that covers the inner parts 2693
3: 4 both kidneys with the **f** on them near 2693
3: 9 its **f,** the entire fat tail cut off close to 2693
3: 9 entire **f tail** cut off close to the backbone, 487
3: 9 to the backbone, all the **f** that covers 2693
3:10 both kidneys with the **f** on them near 2693
3:14 all the **f** that covers the inner parts 2693
3:15 both kidneys with the **f** on them near 2693
3:16 All the **f** is the LORD's. 2693
3:17 You must not eat any **f** or any blood.' " 2693
4: 8 He shall remove all the **f** from the bull of 2693
4: 8 the **f** that covers the inner parts 2693
4: 9 with the **f** on them near the loins, and 2693
4:10 the **f** is removed from the ox sacrificed as NIH
Lev 4:19 the **f** from it and burn it on the altar, 2693
4:26 the **f** on the altar as he burned the fat of 2693
4:26 the fat on the altar as he burned the **f** *of* 2693
4:31 He shall remove all the **f,** 2693
4:31 just as the **f** is removed from 2693
4:35 He shall remove all the **f,** 2693
4:35 just as the **f** is removed from the lamb of 2693
6:12 the burnt offering on the fire and burn the **f** 2693
7: 3 All its **f** shall be offered: 2693
7: 3 the **f tail** and the fat that covers 487
7: 3 and the **f** that covers the inner parts, 2693
7: 4 both kidneys with the **f** on them near 2693
7:23 'Do not eat any of the **f** *of* cattle, 2693
7:24 The **f** *of* an animal found dead or torn 2693
7:25 the **f** of an animal from which an offering 2693
7:30 he is to bring the **f,** 2693
7:31 The priest shall burn the **f** on the altar, 2693
7:33 of Aaron who offers the blood and the **f** *of* 2693
8:16 also took all the **f** around the inner parts, 2693
8:16 and both kidneys and their **f,** 2693
8:20 the pieces and the **f.** 7022
8:25 He took the **f,** the fat tail, 2693
8:25 He took the fat, the **f tail,** 487
8:25 the fat tail, all the **f** around the inner parts, 2693
8:25 both kidneys and their **f** and the right thigh. 2693
8:26 on the **f portions** and on the right thigh. 2693
9:10 On the altar he burned the **f,** 2693
9:19 But the **f portions** of the ox and the ram— 2693
9:19 the **f tail,** the layer of fat, 487
9:19 the fat tail, the **layer of f,** 4833
9:20 and then Aaron burned the **f** on the altar. 2693
9:24 the burnt offering and the **f portions** on 2693
10:15 with the **f portions** *of* the offerings made 2693
16:25 He shall also burn the **f** *of* the sin offering 2693
17: 6 the **f** as an aroma pleasing to the LORD. 2693
Nu 18:17 and burn their **f** as an offering made 2693
Dt 32:15 Jeshurun **grew f** and kicked; 9042
32:38 the **f** *of* their sacrifices and drank the wine 2693
Jdg 3:17 Eglon king of Moab, who was a very **f** man. 1374
3:22 and the **f** closed in over it. 2693
1Sa 2:15 But even before the **f** was burned, 2693
2:16 "Let the **f** be burned up first, 2693
15: 9 the **f** *calves* and lambs— 5458
15:22 and to heed is better than the **f** *of* rams. 2693
1Ki 8:64 and the **f** *of* the fellowship offerings, 2693
8:64 and the **f** *of* the fellowship offerings. 2693
2Ch 7: 7 and the **f** *of* the fellowship offerings, 2693
7: 7 the grain offerings and the **f portions.** 2693
29:35 with the **f** *of* the fellowship offerings and 2693
35:14 the burnt offerings and the **f portions** 2693
Job 15:27 with **f** and his waist bulges with flesh, 2693
Ps 66:15 I will sacrifice **f animals** to you and 4671
Isa 1:11 of rams and the **f** *of* fattened animals; 2693
10:27 be broken because you have grown so **f.** 9043
17: 4 the **f** *of* his body will waste away. 5458
34: 6 it is covered with **f—** 2693
34: 6 **f** *from* the kidneys of rams. 2693
34: 7 and the dust will be soaked with **f.** 2693
43:24 or lavished on me the **f** *of* your sacrifices. 2693
Jer 5:28 and *have grown* **f** and sleek. 9042
Eze 34:20 between the **f** sheep and the lean sheep. 1374
39:19 you will eat **f** till you are glutted 2693
44: 7 **f** and blood, and you broke my covenant. 2693
44:15 to stand before me to offer sacrifices of **f** 2693

FATAL (5)
Jer 42:20 that *you* **made a f mistake** when you sent
me to the LORD your God 928+5883+9494
Na 3:19 your injury *is* **f.** 2703
Rev 13: 3 of the beast seemed to have had a **f** wound, *2505*
13: 3 but the **f** wound had been healed. *2505*
13:12 whose **f** wound had been healed. *2505*

FATALLY (1)
Jer 51: 4 **f wounded** in her streets. 1991

FATE (13)
Est 7: 7 that the king had already decided his **f,** 8288
Job 12: 5 as the **f** of those whose feet are slipping. 5787
18:20 Men of the west are appalled at his **f;** 3427
20:29 Such is the **f** God allots the wicked, 2750
21:17 the **f** God allots in his anger? 2475
27:13 "Here is the **f** God allots to the wicked, 2750
27:14 their **f** is the sword; NIH
Ps 49:13 the **f** *of* those who trust in themselves, 2006
Ecc 2:14 that the same **f** overtakes them both. 5247
2:15 "The **f** *of* the fool will overtake me also. 5247
3:19 Man's **f** is like that of the animals; 5247
3:19 the same **f** awaits them both: 5247
Isa 14:16 they ponder your **f:** NIH

FATFLESHED (KJV) See FAT

FATHER (1082) [FATHER-IN-LAW, FATHER'S, FATHERED, FATHERLESS, FATHERS, FATHERS', FOREFATHER, FOREFATHER'S, FOREFATHERS, GRANDFATHER, GRANDFATHER'S]
Ge 2:24 a man will leave his **f** and mother and 3
4:18 and Irad *was the* **f** *of* Mehujael, 3528
4:18 and Mehujael *was the* **f** *of* Methushael, 3528
4:18 and Methushael *was the* **f** *of* Lamech. 3528

Ge 4:20 he was the **f** *of* those who live in tents 3
4:21 the **f** *of* all who play the harp and flute. 3
5: 6 *he became the* **f** *of* Enosh. 3528
5: 7 And after he *became the* **f** *of* Enosh, 3528
5: 9 *he became the* **f** *of* Kenan. 3528
5:10 And after he *became the* **f** *of* Kenan, 3528
5:12 *he became the* **f** *of* Mahalalel. 3528
5:13 And after he *became the* **f** *of* Mahalalel, 3528
5:15 *he became the* **f** *of* Jared. 3528
5:16 And after he *became the* **f** *of* Jared, 3528
5:18 *he became the* **f** *of* Enoch. 3528
5:19 And after he *became the* **f** *of* Enoch, 3528
5:21 *he became the* **f** *of* Methuselah. 3528
5:22 And after he *became the* **f** *of* Methuselah, 3528
5:25 *he became the* **f** *of* Lamech. 3528
5:26 And after he *became the* **f** *of* Lamech, 3528
5:32 he *became the* **f** *of* Shem, 3528
9:18 (Ham was the **f** *of* Canaan.) 3
9:22 Ham, the **f** *of* Canaan, 3
10: 8 Cush *was the* **f** *of* Nimrod, 3528
10:13 Mizraim *was the* **f** *of* the Ludites, 3528
10:15 Canaan *was the* **f** *of* Sidon his firstborn, 3528
10:24 Arphaxad *was the* **f** *of* Shelah, 3528
10:24 and Shelah *the* **f** *of* Eber. 3528
10:26 Joktan *was the* **f** *of* Almodad, Sheleph, 3528
11:10 *he became the* **f** *of* Arphaxad. 3528
11:11 And after he *became the* **f** *of* Arphaxad, 3528
11:12 *he became the* **f** *of* Shelah. 3528
11:13 And after he *became the* **f** *of* Shelah, 3528
11:14 *he became the* **f** *of* Eber. 3528
11:15 And after he *became the* **f** *of* Eber, 3528
11:16 *he became the* **f** *of* Peleg. 3528
11:17 And after he *became the* **f** *of* Peleg, 3528
11:18 *he became the* **f** *of* Reu. 3528
11:19 And after he *became the* **f** *of* Reu, 3528
11:20 *he became the* **f** *of* Serug. 3528
11:21 And after he *became the* **f** *of* Serug, 3528
11:22 *he became the* **f** *of* Nahor. 3528
11:23 And after he *became the* **f** *of* Nahor, 3528
11:24 *he became the* **f** *of* Terah. 3528
11:25 And after he *became the* **f** *of* Terah, 3528
11:26 *he became the* **f** *of* Abram, 3528
11:27 Terah *became the* **f** *of* Abram, 3528
11:27 And Haran *became the* **f** *of* Lot. 3528
11:28 While his **f** Terah was still alive, 3
11:29 the **f** *of* both Milcah and Iscah. 3
17: 4 You will be the **f** *of* many nations. 3
17: 5 for I have made you a **f** *of* many nations. 3
17:20 *He will be the* **f** *of* twelve rulers, 3528
19:31 "Our **f** is old, and there is no man around 3
19:32 Let's get our **f** to drink wine and then lie 3
19:32 and preserve our family line through our **f.**" 3
19:33 That night they got their **f** to drink wine, 3
19:34 "Last night I lay with my **f.** 3
19:34 can preserve our family line through our **f.**" 3
19:35 So they got their **f** to drink wine that night 3
19:36 both of Lot's daughters became pregnant by their **f.** 3
19:37 he is the **f** *of* the Moabites of today. 3
19:38 he is the **f** *of* the Ammonites of today. 3
20:12 daughter of my **f** though not of my mother; 3
22: 7 Isaac spoke up and said to his **f** Abraham, 3
22: 7 up and said to his father Abraham, "**F?**" 3
22:21 Buz his brother, Kemuel (the **f** *of* Aram), 3
22:23 Bethuel *became the* **f** *of* Rebekah. 3528
25: 3 Jokshan *was the* **f** *of* Sheba and Dedan; 3528
25:19 Abraham *became the* **f** *of* Isaac, 3528
26: 3 the oath I swore to your **f** Abraham. 3
26:15 in the time of his **f** Abraham, 3
26:18 in the time of his **f** Abraham, 3
26:18 the same names his **f** had given them. 3
26:24 "I am the God of your **f** Abraham. 3
27: 6 I overheard your **f** say 3
27: 9 so I can prepare some tasty food for your **f,** 3
27:10 Then take it to your **f** to eat, 3
27:12 What if my **f** touches me? 3
27:14 just the way his **f** liked it. 3
27:18 He went to his **f** and said, "My father." 3
27:18 He went to his father and said, "My **f.**" 3
27:19 Jacob said to his **f,** 3
27:22 Jacob went close to his **f** Isaac, 3
27:26 Then his **f** Isaac said to him, "Come here, 3
27:31 and brought it to his **f.** 3
27:31 Then he said to him, "My **f,** 3
27:32 His **f** Isaac asked him, "Who are you?" 3
27:34 with a loud and bitter cry and said to his **f,** 3
27:34 "Bless me—me too, my **f!**" 3
27:38 Esau said to his **f,** 3
27:38 "Do you have only one blessing, my **f?** 3
27:38 Bless me too, my **f!**" 3
27:39 His **f** Isaac answered him, 3
27:41 of the blessing his **f** had given him. 3
27:41 "The days of mourning for my **f** are near; 3
28: 2 to the house of your mother's **f** Bethuel. 3
28: 7 and that Jacob had obeyed his **f** and mother 3
28: 8 the Canaanite women were to his **f** Isaac; 3
28:13 of your **f** Abraham and the God of Isaac. 3
29:12 a relative of her **f** and a son of Rebekah. 3
29:12 So she ran and told her **f.** 3
31: 1 "Jacob has taken everything our **f** owned 3
31: 1 from what belonged to our **f.**" 3
31: 5 but the God of my **f** has been with me. 3
31: 6 You know that I've worked for your **f** 3
31: 7 yet your **f** has cheated me 3
31:16 from our **f** belongs to us and our children. 3
31:18 to go to his **f** Isaac in the land of Canaan. 3
31:29 but last night the God of your **f** said to me, 3

Ge 31:35 Rachel said to her **f,** "Don't be angry, 3
31:42 If the God of my **f,** 3
31:53 the God of their **f,** judge between us." 3
31:53 in the name of the Fear of his **f** Isaac. 3
32: 9 Jacob prayed, "O God of my **f** Abraham, 3
32: 9 God of my **f** Isaac, O LORD, 3
33:19 Hamor, the **f** *of* Shechem, 3
34: 4 And Shechem said to his **f** Hamor, 3
34: 6 Then Shechem's **f** Hamor went out to talk 3
34:11 Shechem said to Dinah's **f** and brothers, 3
34:13 as they spoke to Shechem and his **f** Hamor. 3
35:18 But his **f** named him Benjamin. 3
35:27 Jacob came home to his **f** Isaac in Mamre, 3
36: 9 the account of Esau the **f** *of* the Edomites 3
36:24 the donkeys of his **f** Zibeon. 3
36:43 This was Esau the **f** *of* the Edomites. 3
37: 1 in the land where his **f** had stayed, 3
37: 2 he brought their **f** a bad report about them. 3
37: 4 that their **f** loved him more than any 3
37:10 When he told his **f** as well as his brothers, 3
37:10 his **f** rebuked him and said, 3
37:11 but his **f** kept the matter in mind. 3
37:22 from them and take him back to his **f.** 3
37:32 the ornamented robe back to their **f** 3
37:35 So his **f** wept for him. 3
42:13 The youngest is now with our **f,** 3
42:29 to their **f** Jacob in the land of Canaan, 3
42:32 We were twelve brothers, sons of one **f.** 3
42:32 the youngest is now with our **f** in Canaan.' 3
42:35 they and their **f** saw the money pouches, 3
42:36 Their **f** Jacob said to them, 3
42:37 Then Reuben said to his **f,** 3
43: 2 their **f** said to them, 3
43: 7 'Is your **f** still living?' 3
43: 8 Then Judah said to Israel his **f,** 3
43:11 Then their **f** Israel said to them, 3
43:23 Your God, the God of your **f,** 3
43:27 "How is your aged **f** you told me about? 3
43:28 "Your servant our **f** is still alive and well." 3
44:17 go back to your **f** in peace." 3
44:19 'Do you have a **f** or a brother?' 3
44:20 And we answered, 'We have an aged **f,** 3
44:20 and his **f** loves him.' 3
44:22 'The boy cannot leave his **f;** 3
44:22 if he leaves him, his **f** will die.' 3
44:24 When we went back to your servant my **f,** 3
44:25 "Then our **f** said, 3
44:27 "Your servant my **f** said to us, 3
44:30 when I go back to your servant my **f** and 3
44:30 to your servant my father and if my **f,** NIH
44:31 the gray head of our **f** down to the grave 3
44:32 the boy's safety to my **f.** 3
44:32 I will bear the blame before you, my **f,** 3
44:34 How can I go back to my **f** if the boy is not 3
44:34 the misery that would come upon my **f.**" 3
45: 3 Is my **f** still living?" 3
45: 8 He made me **f** to Pharaoh, 3
45: 9 Now hurry back to my **f** and say to him, 3
45:13 Tell my **f** about all the honor accorded me 3
45:13 And bring my **f** down here quickly." 3
45:18 bring your **f** and your families back to me. 3
45:19 and get your **f** and come. 3
45:23 And this is what he sent to his **f:** 3
45:25 up out of Egypt and came to their **f** Jacob 3
45:27 the spirit of their **f** Jacob revived. 3
46: 1 to the God of his **f** Isaac. 3
46: 3 "I am God, the God of your **f,**" he said. 3
46: 5 and Israel's sons took their **f** Jacob 3
46:29 and went to Goshen to meet his **f** Israel. 3
46:29 he threw his arms around **his f** and wept for 2257^S
47: 1 "My **f** and brothers, 3
47: 5 "Your **f** and your brothers have come 3
47: 6 settle your **f** and your brothers in 3
47: 7 Then Joseph brought his **f** Jacob in 3
47:11 So Joseph settled his **f** and his brothers 3
47:12 Joseph also provided his **f** and his brothers 3
48: 1 "Your **f** is ill." 3
48: 9 Joseph said to his **f.** 3
48:10 and his **f** kissed them and embraced them. NIH
48:17 Joseph saw his **f** placing his right hand 3
48:18 Joseph said to him, "No, my **f,** 3
48:19 But his **f** refused and said, "I know, 3
49: 2 listen to your **f** Israel. 3
49:28 and this is what their **f** said to them 3
50: 1 Joseph threw himself upon his **f** and wept 3
50: 2 in his service to embalm his **f** Israel. 3
50: 5 'My **f** made me swear an oath and said, 3
50: 5 Now let me go up and bury my **f;** 3
50: 6 Pharaoh said, "Go up and bury your **f,** 3
50: 7 So Joseph went up to bury his **f.** 3
50:10 a seven-day period of mourning for his **f.** 3
50:14 After burying his **f,** 3
50:14 with him to bury his **f.** 3
50:15 Joseph's brothers saw that their **f** was dead, 3
50:16 "Your **f** left these instructions 3
50:17 of the servants of the God of your **f.**" 3
Ex 2:18 When the girls returned to Reuel their **f,** 3
3: 6 Then he said, "I am the God of your **f,** 3
20:12 "Honor your **f** and your mother, 3
21:15 "Anyone who attacks his **f** or mother must 3
21:17 "Anyone who curses his **f** or mother must 3
22:17 her **f** absolutely refuses to give her to him, 3
40:15 Anoint them just as you anointed their **f,** 3
Lev 16:32 to succeed his **f** as high priest is 3
18: 7 " 'Do not dishonor your **f** 3
18: 8 that would dishonor your **f.** 3
18:11 born to your **f;** she is your sister. 3

Lev 19: 3 of you must respect his mother and **f,** 3
20: 9 " 'If anyone curses his **f** or mother, 3
20: 9 He has cursed his **f** or his mother, 3
20:11 he has dishonored his **f.** 3
20:17 the daughter of either his **f** or his mother, 3
20:19 the sister of either your mother or your **f,** 3
21: 2 such as his mother or **f,** 3
21: 9 she disgraces her **f;** 3
21:11 even for his **f** or mother, 3
24:10 and an Egyptian **f** went out among 408
Nu 3: 4 during the lifetime of their **f** Aaron. 3
6: 7 Even if his own **f** or mother or brother 3
12:14 "If her **f** had spit in her face, 3
26:29 Makirite clan (Makir *was the* **f** *of* Gilead); 3528
26:60 Aaron *was the* **f** *of* Nadab and Abihu, 3528
27: 3 "Our **f** died in the desert. 3
27:11 If his **f** had no brothers, 3
30: 4 and her **f** hears about her vow or pledge 3
30: 5 if her **f** forbids her when he hears about it, 3
30: 5 because her **f** has forbidden her. 3
30:16 a **f** and his young daughter still living 3
36: 6 within the tribal clan of their **f.** 3
Dt 1:31 as a **f** carries his son, 408
5:16 "Honor your **f** and your mother, 3
21:13 and mourned her **f** and mother for 3
21:18 and rebellious son who does not obey his **f** 3
21:19 his **f** and mother shall take hold of him 3
22:15 the girl's **f** and mother shall bring proof 3
22:16 The girl's **f** will say to the elders, 3
22:19 of silver and give them to the girl's **f,** 3
22:29 he shall pay the girl's **f** fifty shekels 3
26: 5 "My **f** was a wandering Aramean, 3
27:16 "Cursed is the man who dishonors his **f** 3
27:22 of his **f** or the daughter of his mother." 3
32: 6 Is he not your **F,** your Creator, 3
32: 7 Ask your **f** and he will tell you, 3
33: 9 He said of his **f** and mother, 3
Jos 2:13 that you will spare the lives of my **f** 3
2:18 you have brought your **f** and mother, 3
6:23 her **f** and mother and brothers 3
15:18 she urged him to ask her **f** for a field. 3
17: 4 along with the brothers of their **f,** 3
24: 2 including Terah the **f** *of* Abraham 3
24: 3 But I took your **f** Abraham from the land 3
24:32 Hamor, the **f** *of* Shechem. 3
Jdg 1:14 she urged him to ask her **f** for a field. 3
8:32 of his **f** Joash in Ophrah of the Abiezrites. 3
9:17 and to think that my **f** fought for you, 3
9:28 Serve the men of Hamor, Shechem's **f!** 3
9:56 to his **f** by murdering his seventy brothers. 3
11: 1 His **f** *was* Gilead; 3528
11:36 "My **f,**" she replied, "you have given your word to the LORD. 3
11:39 to her **f** and he did to her as he had vowed. 3
14: 2 he returned, he said to his **f** and mother, 3
14: 3 His **f** and mother replied, 3
14: 3 But Samson said to his **f,** "Get her for me. 3
14: 5 to Timnah together with his **f** and mother. 3
14: 6 But he told neither his **f** 3
14:10 Now his **f** went down to see the woman. 3
14:16 even explained it to my **f** or mother," 3
15: 1 But her **f** would not let him go in. 3
15: 6 up and burned her and her **f** to death. 3
16:31 and Eshtaol in the tomb of Manoah his **f.** 3
17:10 "Live with me and be my **f** and priest, 3
18:19 Come with us, and be our **f** and priest. 3
19: 3 and when her **f** saw him, 3
19: 4 His father-in-law, the girl's **f,** 3
19: 5 but the girl's **f** said to his son-in-law, 3
19: 6 Afterward the girl's **f** said, 3
19: 8 when he rose to go, the girl's **f** said, 3
19: 9 his father-in-law, the girl's **f,** said, 3
Ru 2:11 how you left your **f** and mother 3
4:17 He was the **f** *of* Jesse, the father of David. 3
4:17 He was the father of Jesse, the **f** *of* David. 3
4:18 Perez *was the* **f** *of* Hezron, 3528
4:19 Hezron *the* **f** *of* Ram, 3528
4:19 Ram *the* **f** *of* Amminadab, 3528
4:20 Amminadab *the* **f** *of* Nahshon, 3528
4:20 Nahshon *the* **f** *of* Salmon, 3528
4:21 Salmon *the* **f** *of* Boaz, 3528
4:21 Boaz *the* **f** *of* Obed, 3528
4:22 Obed *the* **f** *of* Jesse, 3528
4:22 and Jesse *the* **f** *of* David. 3528
1Sa 2:28 I chose **your f** out of all the tribes of Israel 2257^S
9: 3 to Saul's **f** Kish were lost, 3
9: 5 or my **f** will stop thinking about 3
10: 2 And now your **f** has stopped thinking 3
10:12 "And who is their **f?**" 3
14: 1 But he did not tell his **f.** 3
14:27 not heard that his **f** had bound the people 3
14:28 "Your **f** bound the army under a strict oath, 3
14:29 "My **f** has made trouble for the country. 3
14:51 Saul's **f** Kish and Abner's father Ner were sons of Abiel. 3
14:51 and Abner's **f** Ner were sons of Abiel. 3
19: 2 "My **f** Saul is looking for a chance 3
19: 3 with my **f** in the field where you are. 3
19: 4 of David to Saul his **f** and said to him, "Let 3
20: 1 How have I wronged your **f,** 3
20: 2 Look, my **f** doesn't do anything, 3
20: 3 "Your **f** knows very well 3
20: 6 If your **f** misses me at all, tell him, 3
20: 8 Why hand me over to your **f?**" 3
20: 9 the least inkling that my **f** was determined 3
20:10 if your **f** answers you harshly?" 3
20:12 surely sound out my **f** by this time the day 3

1Sa 20:13 But if my **f** is inclined to harm you, 3
20:13 be with you as he has been with my **f.** 3
20:32 Jonathan asked his **f.** 3
20:33 Then Jonathan knew that his **f** intended 3
22: 3 "Would you let my **f** and mother come 3
23:17 "My **f** Saul will not lay a hand on you. 3
23:17 Even my **f** Saul knows this." 3
24:11 my **f,** look at this piece of your robe 3
2Sa 3: 8 the house of your **f** Saul and to his family 3
6:21 who chose me rather than your **f** or anyone 3
7:14 I will be his **f,** and he will be my son. 3
9: 7 for the sake of your **f** Jonathan. 3
10: 2 just as his **f** showed kindness to me." 3
10: 2 to Hanun concerning his **f.** 3
10: 3 "Do you think David is honoring your **f** 3
13: 5 "When your **f** comes to see you, 3
16:19 Just as I served your **f,** 3
17: 8 You know your **f** and his men; 3
17: 8 Besides, your **f** is an experienced fighter; 3
17:10 for all Israel knows that your **f** is a fighter 3
19:37 in my own town near the tomb of my **f** 3
21:14 in the tomb of Saul's **f** Kish, 3
1Ki 1: 6 (His **f** had never interfered with him 3
2:12 Solomon sat on the throne of his **f** David, 3
2:24 the throne of my **f** David and has founded 3
2:26 the Sovereign LORD before my **f** David 3
2:32 of my **f** David he attacked two men 3
2:44 the wrong you did to my **f** David. 3
3: 3 according to the statutes of his **f** David, 3
3: 6 my **f** David, because he was faithful to you 3
3: 7 in place of my **f** David. 3
3:14 and commands as David your **f** did, 3
5: 1 to succeed his **f** David, 3
5: 3 of the wars waged against my **f** David 3
5: 5 as the LORD told my **f** David, 3
6:12 the promise I gave to David your **f.** 3
7:14 of Naphtali and whose **f** was a man of Tyre 3
7:51 in the things his **f** David had dedicated— 3
8:15 with his own mouth to my **f** David. 3
8:17 "My **f** David had it in his heart to build 3
8:18 But the LORD said to my **f** David, 3
8:20 I have succeeded David my **f** and now I sit 3
8:24 to your servant David my **f;** 3
8:25 keep for your servant David my **f** 3
8:26 let your word that you promised your
servant David my **f** come true. 3
9: 4 as David your **f** did, 3
9: 5 as I promised David your **f** when I said, 3
11: 4 as the heart of David his **f** had been. 3
11: 6 as David his **f** had done. 3
11:12 Nevertheless, for the sake of David your **f,** 3
11:17 Edomite officials who had served his **f.** 3
11:27 in the wall of the city of David his **f.** 3
11:33 and laws as David, Solomon's **f,** 3
11:43 and was buried in the city of David his **f.** 3
12: 4 "Your **f** put a heavy yoke on us, 3
12: 6 the elders who had served his **f** Solomon 3
12: 9 'Lighten the yoke your **f** put on us'?" 3
12:10 'Your **f** put a heavy yoke on us, 3
12:11 My **f** laid on you a heavy yoke; 3
12:11 My **f** scourged you with whips; 3
12:14 "My **f** made your yoke heavy; 3
12:14 My **f** scourged you with whips; 3
13:11 They also told their **f** what he had said to 3
13:12 Their **f** asked them, 3
15: 3 He committed all the sins his **f** had done 3
15:11 as his **f** David had done. 3
15:15 the articles that he and his **f** had dedicated. 3
15:19 there was between my **f** and your father. 3
15:19 there was between my father and your **f.** 3
15:24 with them in the city of his **f** David. 3
15:26 walking in the ways of his **f** and in his sin, 3
19:20 "Let me kiss my **f** and mother good-by," 3
20:34 the cities my **f** took from your father," 3
20:34 the cities my father took from your **f,"** 3
20:34 as my **f** did in Samaria." 3
22:43 in the ways of his **f** Asa and did not stray 3
22:46 even after the reign of his **f** Asa. 3
22:50 with them in the city of David his **f.** 3
22:52 because he walked in the ways of his **f** 3
22:53 to anger, just as his **f** had done. 3
2Ki 2:12 Elisha saw this and cried out, "My **f!** 3
2:12 and cried out, "My father! My **f!** 3
3: 2 but not as his **f** and mother had done. 3
3: 2 of Baal that his **f** had made. 3
3:13 of your **f** and the prophets of your mother." 3
4:18 and one day he went out to his **f,** 3
4:19 he said to his **f.** 3
4:19 His **f** told a servant, NIH
5:13 "My **f,** if the prophet had told you 3
6:21 he asked Elisha, "Shall I kill them, my **f?** 3
9:25 in chariots behind Ahab his **f** when 3
13:14 and wept over him. "My **f!** 3
13:14 over him. "My father! My **f!"** 3
13:25 in battle from his **f** Jehoahaz. 3
14: 3 but not as his **f** David had done. 3
14: 3 the example of his **f** Joash. 3
14: 5 the officials who had murdered his **f** 3
14:21 in place of his **f** Amaziah. 3
15: 3 just as his **f** Amaziah had done. 3
15:34 just as his **f** Uzziah had done. 3
15:38 the city of his **f.** 3
16: 2 Unlike David his **f,** 3
18: 3 just as his **f** David had done. 3
20: 5 the God of your **f** David, says: 3
21: 3 high places his **f** Hezekiah had destroyed; 3
21:20 as his **f** Manasseh had done. 3

2Ki 21:21 He walked in all the ways of his **f;** 3
21:21 the idols his **f** had worshiped, 3
22: 2 and walked in all the ways of his **f** David, 3
23:30 and made him king in place of his **f.** 3
23:34 of Josiah king in place of his **f** Josiah 3
24: 9 just as his **f** had done. 3
1Ch 1:10 Cush *was the* **f** *of* Nimrod, 3528
1:11 Mizraim *was the* **f** *of* the Ludites, 3528
1:13 Canaan *was the* **f** *of* Sidon his firstborn, 3528
1:18 Arphaxad *was the* **f** *of* Shelah, 3528
1:18 and Shelah *the* **f** *of* Eber. 3528
1:20 Joktan *was the* **f** *of* Almodad, Sheleph, 3528
1:34 Abraham *was the* **f** *of* Isaac. 3528
2:10 Ram *was the* **f** *of* Amminadab, 3528
2:10 and Amminadab *the* **f** *of* Nahshon, 3528
2:11 Nahshon *was the* **f** *of* Salmon, 3528
2:11 Salmon *the* **f** *of* Boaz, 3528
2:12 *the* **f** *of* Obed and Obed the father of Jesse. 3528
2:12 the father of Obed and Obed *the* **f** *of* Jesse. 3528
2:13 Jesse *was the* **f** *of* Eliab his firstborn; 3528
2:17 whose **f** was Jether the Ishmaelite. 3
2:20 Hur *was the* **f** *of* Uri, 3528
2:20 and Uri *the* **f** *of* Bezalel. 3528
2:21 Makir the **f** *of* Gilead 3
2:22 Segub *was the* **f** *of* Jair, 3528
2:23 All these were descendants of Makir the **f** 3
2:24 of Hezron bore him Ashhur the **f** *of* Tekoa. 3
2:31 Ishi, who was the **f** *of* Sheshan. 1201S
2:31 Sheshan was the **f** *of* Ahlai. 1201S
2:36 Attai *was the* **f** *of* Nathan, 3528
2:36 Nathan *the* **f** *of* Zabad, 3528
2:37 Zabad *the* **f** *of* Ephlal, 3528
2:37 Ephlal *the* **f** *of* Obed, 3528
2:38 Obed *the* **f** *of* Jehu, 3528
2:38 Jehu *the* **f** *of* Azariah, 3528
2:39 Azariah *the* **f** *of* Helez, 3528
2:39 Helez *the* **f** *of* Eleasah, 3528
2:40 Eleasah *the* **f** *of* Sismai, 3528
2:40 Sismai *the* **f** *of* Shallum, 3528
2:41 Shallum *the* **f** *of* Jekamiah, 3528
2:41 and Jekamiah *the* **f** *of* Elishama. 3528
2:42 who was the **f** *of* Ziph, 3
2:42 who was the **f** *of* Hebron. 3
2:44 Shema *was the* **f** *of* Raham, 3528
2:44 and Raham the **f** *of* Jorkeam. 3
2:44 Rekem *was the* **f** *of* Shammai. 3528
2:45 and Maon was the **f** *of* Beth Zur. 3
2:46 Haran *was the* **f** *of* Gazez. 3528
2:49 to Shaaph the **f** *of* Madmannah and 3
2:49 to Sheva the **f** *of* Macbenah and Gibea. 3
2:50 Shobal the **f** *of* Kiriath Jearim, 3
2:51 Salma the **f** *of* Bethlehem, 3
2:51 and Hareph the **f** *of* Beth Gader. 3
2:52 of Shobal the **f** *of* Kiriath Jearim were: 3
2:55 the **f** *of* the house of Recab. 3
4: 2 Reaiah son of Shobal *was the* **f** *of* Jahath, 3528
4: 2 and Jahath *the* **f** *of* Ahumai and Lahad. 3528
4: 4 Penuel was the **f** *of* Gedor, 3
4: 4 and Ezer the **f** *of* Hushah. 3
4: 4 firstborn of Ephrathah and **f** *of* Bethlehem. 3
4: 5 Ashhur the **f** *of* Tekoa had two wives, 3
4: 8 *who was the* **f** *of* Anub and Hazzobebah 3528
4:11 Shuhah's brother, *was the* **f** *of* Mehir, 3528
4:11 who was the **f** *of* Eshton. 3
4:12 Eshton *was the* **f** *of* Beth Rapha, 3528
4:12 Paseah and Tehinnah the **f** *of* Ir Nahash. 3
4:14 Meonothai *was the* **f** *of* Ophrah. 3528
4:14 Seraiah *was the* **f** *of* Joab, 3528
4:14 the **f** *of* Ge Harashim. 3
4:17 Shammai and Ishbah the **f** *of* Eshtemoa. 3
4:18 (His Judean wife gave birth to Jered the **f** 3
4:18 Heber the **f** *of* Soco, 3
4:18 and Jekuthiel the **f** *of* Zanoah.) 3
4:19 the **f** *of* Keilah the Garmite, 3
4:21 Er the **f** *of* Lecah, 3
4:21 Laadah the **f** *of* Mareshah and the clans of 3
6: 4 Eleazar *was the* **f** *of* Phinehas, 3528
6: 4 Phinehas *the* **f** *of* Abishua, 3528
6: 5 Abishua *the* **f** *of* Bukki, 3528
6: 5 Bukki *the* **f** *of* Uzzi, 3528
6: 6 Uzzi *the* **f** *of* Zerahiah, 3528
6: 6 Zerahiah *the* **f** *of* Meraioth, 3528
6: 7 Meraioth *the* **f** *of* Amariah, 3528
6: 7 Amariah *the* **f** *of* Ahitub, 3528
6: 8 Ahitub *the* **f** *of* Zadok, 3528
6: 8 Zadok *the* **f** *of* Ahimaaz, 3528
6: 9 Ahimaaz *the* **f** *of* Azariah, 3528
6: 9 Azariah *the* **f** *of* Johanan, 3528
6:10 Johanan *the* **f** *of* Azariah (it was he who 3528
6:11 Azariah *the* **f** *of* Amariah, 3528
6:11 Amariah *the* **f** *of* Ahitub, 3528
6:12 Ahitub *the* **f** *of* Zadok, 3528
6:12 Zadok *the* **f** *of* Shallum, 3528
6:13 Shallum *the* **f** *of* Hilkiah, 3528
6:13 Hilkiah *the* **f** *of* Azariah, 3528
6:14 Azariah *the* **f** *of* Seraiah, 3528
6:14 and Seraiah *the* **f** *of* Jehozadak. 3528
7:14 She gave birth to Makir the **f** *of* Gilead. 3
7:22 Their **f** Ephraim mourned 3
7:31 who was the **f** *of* Birzaith. 3
7:32 Heber *was the* **f** *of* Japhlet, 3528
8: 1 Benjamin *was the* **f** *of* Bela his firstborn, 3528
8: 7 and *who was the* **f** *of* Uzza and Ahihud. 3528
8:29 Jeiel the **f** *of* Gibeon lived in Gibeon. 3
8:32 *who was the* **f** *of* Shimeah. 3528
8:33 Ner *was the* **f** *of* Kish, 3528
8:33 Kish *the* **f** *of* Saul, 3528

1Ch 8:33 and Saul *the* **f** *of* Jonathan, Malki-Shua, 3528
8:34 Merib-Baal, who *was the* **f** *of* Micah. 3528
8:36 Ahaz *was the* **f** *of* Jehoaddah, 3528
8:36 Jehoaddah *was the* **f** *of* Alemeth, 3528
8:36 and Zimri *was the* **f** *of* Moza. 3528
8:37 Moza *was the* **f** *of* Binea; 3528
9:35 Jeiel the **f** *of* Gibeon lived in Gibeon. 3
9:38 Mikloth *was the* **f** *of* Shimeam. 3528
9:39 Ner *was the* **f** *of* Kish, 3528
9:39 Kish *the* **f** *of* Saul, 3528
9:39 and Saul *the* **f** *of* Jonathan, Malki-Shua, 3528
9:40 Merib-Baal, who *was the* **f** *of* Micah. 3528
9:42 Ahaz *was the* **f** *of* Jadah, 3528
9:42 Jadah *was the* **f** *of* Alemeth, 3528
9:42 and Zimri *was the* **f** *of* Moza. 3528
9:43 Moza *was the* **f** *of* Binea; 3528
14: 3 *the* **f** *of* more sons and daughters. 3528
17:13 I will be his **f,** and he will be my son. 3
19: 2 because his **f** showed kindness to me." 3
19: 2 to Hanun concerning his **f.** 3
19: 3 "Do you think David is honoring your **f** 3
22:10 He will be my son, and I will be his **f.** 3
24: 2 Nadab and Abihu died before their **f** did, 3
25: 3 under the supervision of their **f** Jeduthun, 3
26:10 his **f** had appointed him the first), 3
28: 6 and I will be his **f.** 3
28: 9 acknowledge the God of your **f,** 3
29:10 O LORD, God of our **f** Israel, 3
29:23 the LORD as king in place of his **f** David. 3
2Ch 1: 8 to David my **f** and have made me king 3
1: 9 let your promise to my **f** David 3
2: 3 for my **f** David when you sent him cedar 3
2: 7 whom my **f** David provided. 3
2:14 from Dan and whose **f** was from Tyre. 3
2:14 and with those of my lord, David your **f.** 3
2:17 after the census his **f** David had taken; 3
3: 1 the LORD had appeared to his **f** David. 3
5: 1 in the things his **f** David had dedicated— 3
6: 4 with his mouth to my **f** David. 3
6: 7 "My **f** David had it in his heart to build 3
6: 8 But the LORD said to my **f** David, 3
6:10 I have succeeded David my **f** and now I sit 3
6:15 to your servant David my **f;** 3
6:16 keep for your servant David my **f** 3
7:17 if you walk before me as David your **f** did, 3
7:18 as I covenanted with David your **f** 3
8:14 with the ordinance of his **f** David, 3
9:31 and was buried in the city of David his **f.** 3
10: 4 "Your **f** put a heavy yoke on us, 3
10: 6 the elders who had served his **f** Solomon 3
10: 9 'Lighten the yoke your **f** put on us'?" 3
10:10 'Your **f** put a heavy yoke on us, 3
10:11 My **f** laid on you a heavy yoke; 3
10:11 My **f** scourged you with whips; 3
10:14 "My **f** made your yoke heavy; NIH
10:14 My **f** scourged you with whips; 3
15:18 the articles that he and his **f** had dedicated. 3
16: 3 there was between my **f** and your father. 3
16: 3 there was between my father and your **f.** 3
17: 2 of Ephraim that his **f** Asa had captured. 3
17: 3 in the ways his **f** David had followed. 3
17: 4 but sought the God of his **f** 3
20:32 He walked in the ways of his **f** Asa and did 3
21: 3 Their **f** had given them many gifts of silver 3
21:12 the God of your **f** David, says: 3
21:12 of your **f** Jehoshaphat or of Asa king 3
24:22 kindness Zechariah's **f** Jehoiada had shown 3
25: 3 the officials who had murdered his **f** 3
26: 1 made him king in place of his **f** Amaziah. 3
26: 4 just as his **f** Amaziah had done. 3
27: 2 just as his **f** Uzziah had done, 3
28: 1 Unlike David his **f,** 3
29: 2 just as his **f** David had done. 3
33: 3 high places his **f** Hezekiah had demolished; 3
33:22 as his **f** Manasseh had done. 3
33:23 But unlike his **f** Manasseh, 3
34: 2 and walked in the ways of his **f** David, 3
34: 3 he began to seek the God of his **f** David. 3
36: 1 in Jerusalem in place of his **f.** 3
Ne 12:10 Jeshua *was the* **f** *of* Joiakim, 3528
12:10 Joiakim *the* **f** *of* Eliashib, 3528
12:10 Eliashib the **f** *of* Joiada, NIH
12:11 Joiada *the* **f** *of* Jonathan, 3528
12:11 and Jonathan *the* **f** *of* Jaddua. 3528
Est 2: 7 up because she had neither **f** nor mother. 3
2: 7 as his own daughter when her **f** 3
Job 15:10 men even older than your **f.** 3
17:14 'You are my **f,'** and to the worm, 3
29:16 I was a **f** to the needy; 3
31:18 from my youth I reared him as would a **f,** 3
38:28 Does the rain have a **f?** 3
42:15 and their **f** granted them an inheritance 3
Ps 2: 7 today I *have become* your **F.** 3528
27:10 Though my **f** and mother forsake me, 3
68: 5 A **f** *to* the fatherless, 3
89:26 He will call out to me, 'You are my **F,** 3
103:13 As a **f** has compassion on his children, 3
Pr 3:12 as a **f** the son he delights in. 3
10: 1 A wise son brings joy to his **f,** 3
15:20 A wise son brings joy to his **f,** 3
17:21 there is no joy for the **f** *of* a fool. 3
17:25 A foolish son brings grief to his **f** 3
19:26 He who robs his **f** 3
20:20 If a man curses his **f** or mother, 3
23:22 Listen to your **f,** who gave you life, 3
23:24 The **f** *of* a righteous man has great joy; 3
23:25 May your **f** and mother be glad; 3

Pr 27:10 and the friend of your **f**, and do not go 3
28: 7 a companion of gluttons disgraces his **f**. 3
28:24 He who robs his **f** or mother and says, 3
29: 3 man who loves wisdom brings joy to his **f**, 3
30:17 "The eye that mocks a **f**, 3
Isa 7:17 on your people and on the house of your **f** 3
8: 4 Before the boy knows how to say 'My **f**' 3
9: 6 Everlasting **F**, Prince of Peace. 3
22:21 be a **f** to those who live in Jerusalem and to 3
22:23 be a seat of honor for the house of his **f**. 3
38: 5 the God of your **f** David, says: 3
43:27 Your first **f** sinned; 3
45:10 Woe to him who says to his **f**, 3
51: 2 your **f**, and to Sarah, who gave you birth. 3
58:14 to feast on the inheritance of your **f** Jacob." 3
63:16 But you are our **F**, 3
63:16 you, O LORD, are our **F**, 3
64: 8 Yet, O LORD, you are our **F**. 3
Jer 2:27 They say to wood, 'You are my **f**,' 3
3: 4 Have you not just called to me: 'My **F**, 3
3:19 I thought you would call me '**F**' and 3
16: 7 not even for a **f** or a mother— 3
20:15 be the man who brought my **f** the news, 3
22:11 who succeeded his **f** as king of Judah 3
22:15 Did not your **f** have food and drink? 3
31: 9 because I am Israel's **f**, 3
Eze 16: 3 your **f** was an Amorite and your mother 3
16:45 Your mother was a Hittite and your **f** 3
18: 4 the **f** as well as the son— 3
18:11 (though **the f** has done none of them): 2085S
18:14 a son who sees all the sins his **f** commits, 3
18:18 But his **f** will die for his own sin, 3
18:19 the son not share the guilt of his **f**?' 3
18:20 The son will not share the guilt of the **f**, 3
18:20 nor will the **f** share the guilt of the son. 3
22: 7 In you they have treated **f** and mother 3
44:25 if the dead person was his **f** or mother, 3
Da 5: 2 that Nebuchadnezzar his **f** had taken from 10003
5:11 of your **f** he was found to have insight 10003
5:11 King Nebuchadnezzar your **f**— 10003
5:11 your **f** the king, I say— 10003
5:13 one of the exiles my **f** the king brought 10003
5:18 the Most High God gave your **f**
Nebuchadnezzar sovereignty 10003
11: 6 together with her royal escort and her **f** and 3528
Am 2: 7 **F** and son use the same girl and 3
Mic 7: 6 For a son dishonors his **f**, 3
Zec 13: 3 if anyone still prophesies, his **f** and mother, 3
Mal 1: 6 son honors his **f**, and a servant his master. 3
1: 6 If I am a **f**, where is the honor due me? 3
2:10 Have we not all one **F**? 3
Mt 1: 2 Abraham *was the* **f** *of* Isaac, *1164*
1: 2 Isaac *the* **f** *of* Jacob, *1164*
1: 2 Jacob *the* **f** *of* Judah and his brothers, *1164*
1: 3 Judah *the* **f** *of* Perez and Zerah, *1164*
1: 3 Perez *the* **f** *of* Hezron, *1164*
1: 3 Hezron *the* **f** *of* Ram, *1164*
1: 4 Ram *the* **f** *of* Amminadab, *1164*
1: 4 Amminadab *the* **f** *of* Nahshon, *1164*
1: 4 Nahshon *the* **f** *of* Salmon, *1164*
1: 5 Salmon *the* **f** *of* Boaz, *1164*
1: 5 Boaz *the* **f** *of* Obed, *1164*
1: 5 Obed *the* **f** *of* Jesse, *1164*
1: 6 and Jesse *the* **f** *of* King David. *1164*
1: 6 David *was the* **f** *of* Solomon, *1164*
1: 7 Solomon *the* **f** *of* Rehoboam, *1164*
1: 7 Rehoboam *the* **f** *of* Abijah, *1164*
1: 7 Abijah *the* **f** *of* Asa, *1164*
1: 8 Asa *the* **f** *of* Jehoshaphat, *1164*
1: 8 Jehoshaphat *the* **f** *of* Jehoram, *1164*
1: 8 Jehoram *the* **f** *of* Uzziah, *1164*
1: 9 Uzziah *the* **f** *of* Jotham, *1164*
1: 9 Jotham *the* **f** *of* Ahaz, *1164*
1: 9 Ahaz *the* **f** *of* Hezekiah, *1164*
1:10 Hezekiah *the* **f** *of* Manasseh, *1164*
1:10 Manasseh *the* **f** *of* Amon, *1164*
1:10 Amon *the* **f** *of* Josiah, *1164*
1:11 Josiah *the* **f** *of* Jeconiah and his brothers at *1164*
1:12 Jeconiah *was the* **f** *of* Shealtiel, *1164*
1:12 Shealtiel *the* **f** *of* Zerubbabel, *1164*
1:13 Zerubbabel *the* **f** *of* Abiud, *1164*
1:13 Abiud *the* **f** *of* Eliakim, *1164*
1:13 Eliakim *the* **f** *of* Azor, *1164*
1:14 Azor *the* **f** *of* Zadok, *1164*
1:14 Zadok *the* **f** *of* Akim, *1164*
1:14 Akim *the* **f** *of* Eliud, *1164*
1:15 Eliud *the* **f** *of* Eleazar, *1164*
1:15 Eleazar *the* **f** *of* Matthan, *1164*
1:15 Matthan *the* **f** *of* Jacob, *1164*
1:16 and Jacob *the* **f** *of* Joseph, *1164*
2:22 in Judea in place of his **f** Herod, *4252*
3: 9 'We have Abraham as our **f**.' *4252*
4:21 They were in a boat with their **f** Zebedee, *4252*
4:22 the boat and their **f** and followed him. *4252*
5:16 and praise your **F** in heaven. *4252*
5:45 that you may be sons *of* your **F** in heaven. *4252*
5:48 therefore, as your heavenly **F** is perfect. *4252*
6: 1 you will have no reward from your **F** *4252*
6: 4 Then your **F**, who sees what is done *4252*
6: 6 close the door and pray *to* your **F**, *4252*
6: 6 Then your **F**, who sees what is done *4252*
6: 8 for your **F** knows what you need *4252*
6: 9 " 'Our **F** in heaven, *4252*
6:14 your heavenly **F** will also forgive you. *4252*
6:15 your **F** will not forgive your sins. *4252*
6:18 but only *to* your **F**, who is unseen; *4252*
6:18 and your **F**, who sees what is done *4252*
Mt 6:26 and yet your heavenly **F** feeds them. *4252*
6:32 your heavenly **F** knows that you need *4252*
7:11 how much more will your **F** in heaven give *4252*
7:21 the will *of* my **F** who is in heaven. *4252*
8:21 "Lord, first let me go and bury my **f**." *4252*
10:20 the Spirit *of* your **F** speaking through you. *4252*
10:21 and a **f** his child; *4252*
10:29 the ground apart from the will *of* your **F**. *4252*
10:32 I will also acknowledge him before my **F** *4252*
10:33 I will disown him before my **F** in heaven. *4252*
10:35 I have come to turn " 'a man against his **f**, *4252*
10:37 "Anyone who loves his **f** or mother more *4252*
11:25 At that time Jesus said, "I praise you, **F**, *4252*
11:26 Yes, **F**, for this was your good pleasure. *4252*
11:27 committed to me by my **F**. *4252*
11:27 No one knows the Son except the **F**, *4252*
11:27 no one knows the **F** except the Son and *4252*
12:50 does the will *of* my **F** in heaven is my
brother and sister *4252*
13:43 like the sun in the kingdom *of* their **F**. *4252*
15: 4 'Honor your **f** and mother' *4252*
15: 4 and 'Anyone who curses his **f** or mother *4252*
15: 5 But you say that if a man says *to* his **f** *4252*
15: 6 he is not to 'honor his **f**' with it. *4252*
15:13 that my heavenly **F** has not planted will *4252*
16:17 but by my **F** in heaven. *4252*
18:10 in heaven always see the face *of* my **F** *4252*
18:14 In the same way your **F** in heaven is *4252*
18:19 it will be done for you by my **F** in heaven. *4252*
18:35 "This is how my heavenly **F** will treat each *4252*
19: 5 'For this reason a man will leave his **f** *4252*
19:19 honor your **f** and mother,' *4252*
19:29 or sisters or **f** or mother or children *4252*
20:23 for whom they have been prepared by my **F**. *4252*
21:30 "Then the **f** went to the other son and said *NIG*
21:31 "Which of the two did what his **f** wanted?" *4252*
23: 9 And do not call anyone on earth '**f**,' *4252*
23: 9 for you have one **F**, and he is in heaven. *4252*
24:36 nor the Son, but only the **F**. *4252*
25:34 'Come, you who are blessed *by* my **F**; *4252*
26:39 "My **F**, if it is possible, may this cup be *4252*
26:42 "My **F**, if it is not possible for this cup to *4252*
26:53 Do you think I cannot call on my **F**, *4252*
28:19 the **F** and of the Son and of the Holy Spirit, *4252*
Mk 1:20 and they left their **f** Zebedee in the boat *4252*
5:40 he took the child's **f** and mother and *4252*
7:10 'Honor your **f** and your mother,' and, *4252*
7:10 'Anyone who curses his **f** or mother must *4252*
7:11 But you say that if a man says *to* his **f** *4252*
7:12 let him do anything *for* his **f** or mother. *4252*
9:21 Jesus asked the boy's **f**, *4252*
9:24 Immediately the boy's **f** exclaimed, *4252*
10: 7 'For this reason a man will leave his **f** *4252*
10:19 honor your **f** and mother.' " *4252*
10:29 or mother or **f** or children or fields for me *4252*
11:10 the coming kingdom *of* our **f** David!" *4252*
11:25 so that your **F** in heaven may forgive you *4252*
13:12 and a **f** his child. *4252*
13:32 nor the Son, but only the **F**. *4252*
14:36 **F**," he said, "everything is possible for you. *4252*
15:21 Simon, the **f** of Alexander and Rufus, *4252*
Lk 1:32 the throne *of* his **f** David, *4252*
1:59 to name him after his **f** Zechariah, *4252*
1:62 Then they made signs *to* his **f**, *4252*
1:67 His **f** Zechariah was filled with *4252*
1:73 the oath he swore to our **f** Abraham: *4252*
2:33 The child's **f** and mother marveled *4252*
2:48 Your **f** and I have been anxiously searching *4252*
3: 8 'We have Abraham as our **f**.' *4252*
6:36 Be merciful, just as your **F** is merciful. *4252*
8:51 and the child's **f** and mother. *4252*
9:26 the glory *of* the **F** and of the holy angels. *4252*
9:42 healed the boy and gave him back *to* his **f**. *4252*
9:59 "Lord, first let me go and bury my **f**." *4252*
10:21 "I praise you, **F**, Lord of heaven and earth, *4252*
10:21 Yes, **F**, for this was your good pleasure. *4252*
10:22 committed to me by my **F**. *4252*
10:22 No one knows who the Son is except the **F**, *4252*
10:22 no one knows who the **F** is except the Son *4252*
11: 2 " '**F**, hallowed be your name, *4252*
11:13 how much more will your **F** in heaven give *4252*
12:30 and your **F** knows that you need them. *4252*
12:32 for your **F** has been pleased to give you *4252*
12:53 **f** against son and son against father, *4252*
12:53 father against son and son against **f**, *4252*
14:26 to me and does not hate his **f** and mother, *4252*
15:12 The younger one said *to* his **f**, 'Father, *4252*
15:12 The younger one said to his father, '**F**, *4252*
15:18 I will set out and go back to my **f** and say *4252*
15:18 **F**, I have sinned against heaven and *4252*
15:20 So he got up and went to his **f**. *4252*
15:20 his **f** saw him and was filled *4252*
15:21 "The son said to him, '**F**, *4252*
15:22 "But the **f** said to his servants, 'Quick! *4252*
15:27 'and your **f** has killed the fattened calf *4252*
15:28 So his **f** went out and pleaded with him. *4252*
15:29 But he answered his **f**, 'Look! *4252*
15:31 " 'My son,' **the f** said, *1254+3836S*
16:24 So he called to him, '**F** Abraham, *4252*
16:27 "He answered, 'Then I beg you, **f**, *4252*
16:30 " 'No, **f** Abraham,' he said, *4252*
18:20 honor your **f** and mother.' " *4252*
22:29 just as my **F** conferred one on me, *4252*
22:42 "**F**, if you are willing, take this cup *4252*
23:34 Jesus said, "**F**, forgive them, *4252*
23:46 Jesus called out with a loud voice, "**F**, *4252*
24:49 to send you what my **F** has promised; *4252*
Jn 1:14 the One and Only, who came from the **F**, *4252*
3:35 The **F** loves the Son and has placed *4252*
4:12 Are you greater than our **f** Jacob, *4252*
4:21 when you will worship the **F** neither *4252*
4:23 the true worshipers will worship the **F** *4252*
4:23 the kind of worshipers the **F** seeks. *4252*
4:53 the **f** realized that this was the exact time *4252*
5:17 "My **F** is always at his work *4252*
5:18 but he was even calling God his own **F**, *4252*
5:19 he can do only what he sees his **F** doing, *4252*
5:19 whatever **the F** does the Son also does. *1697S*
5:20 **F** loves the Son and shows him all he does. *4252*
5:21 as the **F** raises the dead and gives them life, *4252*
5:22 Moreover, the **F** judges no one, *4252*
5:23 the Son just as they honor the **F**. *4252*
5:23 not honor the Son does not honor the **F**, *4252*
5:26 For as the **F** has life in himself, *4252*
5:36 For the very work that the **F** has given me *4252*
5:36 testifies that the **F** has sent me. *4252*
5:37 the **F** who sent me has himself testified *4252*
5:45 do not think I will accuse you before the **F**. *4252*
6:27 the **F** has placed his seal of approval." *4252*
6:32 but it is my **F** who gives you the true bread *4252*
6:37 All that the **F** gives me will come to me, *4252*
6:42 whose **f** and mother we know? *4252*
6:44 to me unless the **F** who sent me draws him, *4252*
6:45 to the **F** and learns from him comes to me. *4252*
6:46 the **F** except the one who is from God; *4252*
6:46 only he has seen the **F**. *4252*
6:57 the living **F** sent me and I live because of *4252*
6:57 and I live because of the **F**, *4252*
6:65 to me unless the **F** has enabled him." *4252*
8:16 I stand with the **F**, **who** sent me. *4252*
8:18 my other witness is the **F**, who sent me." *4252*
8:19 Then they asked him, "Where is your **f**?" *4252*
8:19 "You do not know me or my **F**," *4252*
8:19 you would know my **F** also." *4252*
8:27 that he was telling them about his **F**. *4252*
8:28 but speak just what the **F** has taught me. *4252*
8:38 you do what you have heard from your **f**." *4252*
8:39 "Abraham is our **f**," they answered. *4252*
8:41 You are doing the things your own **f** does." *4252*
8:41 "The only **F** we have is God himself." *4252*
8:42 Jesus said to them, "If God were your **F**, *4252*
8:44 You belong to your **f**, the devil, *4252*
8:44 for he is a liar and the **f** of lies. *4252*
8:49 "but I honor my **F** and you dishonor me. *4252*
8:53 Are you greater than our **f** Abraham? *4252*
8:54 My **F**, whom you claim as your God, *4252*
8:56 Your **f** Abraham rejoiced at the thought *4252*
10:15 the **F** knows me and I know the Father— *4252*
10:15 as the Father knows me and I know the **F**— *4252*
10:17 The reason my **F** loves me is that I lay *4252*
10:18 This command I received from my **F**." *4252*
10:29 My **F**, who has given them to me, *4252*
10:30 I and the **F** are one." *4252*
10:32 "I have shown you many great miracles
from the **F**. *4252*
10:36 what about the one whom the **F** set apart *4252*
10:37 not believe me unless I do what my **F** does. *4252*
10:38 and understand that the **F** is in me, *4252*
10:38 the Father is in me, and I in the **F**." *4252*
11:41 Then Jesus looked up and said, "**F**, *4252*
12:26 My **F** will honor the one who serves me. *4252*
12:27 '**F**, save me from this hour'? *4252*
12:28 **F**, glorify your name!" *4252*
12:49 the **F** who sent me commanded me what *4252*
12:50 the **F** has told me to say." *4252*
13: 1 for him to leave this world and go to the **F**. *4252*
13: 3 the **F** had put all things under his power, *4252*
14: 6 No one comes to the **F** except through me. *4252*
14: 7 you would know my **F** as well. *4252*
14: 8 show us the **F** and that will be enough *4252*
14: 9 Anyone who has seen me has seen the **F**. *4252*
14: 9 How can you say, 'Show us the **F**'? *4252*
14:10 Don't you believe that I am in the **F**, *4252*
14:10 and that the **F** is in me? *4252*
14:10 Rather, it is the **F**, living in me, *4252*
14:11 that I am in the **F** and the Father is in me; *4252*
14:11 that I am in the Father and the **F** is in me; *4252*
14:12 because I am going to the **F**. *4252*
14:13 so that the Son may bring glory to the **F**. *4252*
14:16 And I will ask the **F**, and he will give you *4252*
14:20 that day you will realize that I am in my **F**, *4252*
14:21 He who loves me will be loved by my **F**, *4252*
14:23 My **F** will love him, *4252*
14:24 they *belong to* the **F** who sent me. *4252*
14:26 whom the **F** will send in my name, *4252*
14:28 be glad that I am going to the **F**, *4252*
14:28 for the **F** is greater than I. *4252*
14:31 the world must learn that I love the **F** and *4252*
14:31 I do exactly what my **F** has commanded me. *4252*
15: 1 and my **F** is the gardener. *4252*
15: 9 the **F** has loved me, so have I loved you. *4252*
15:15 from my **F** I have made known to you. *4252*
15:16 Then the **F** will give you whatever you ask *4252*
15:23 He who hates me hates my **F** as well. *4252*
15:24 and yet they have hated both me and my **F**. *4252*
15:26 whom I will send to you from the **F**, *4252*
15:26 the Spirit of truth who goes out from the **F**, *4252*
16: 3 because they have not known the **F** or me. *4252*
16:10 because I am going to the **F**, *4252*
16:15 All that belongs to the **F** is mine. *4252*
16:17 and 'Because I am going to the **F**'?" *4252*
16:23 my **F** will give you whatever you ask *4252*
16:25 but will tell you plainly about my **F**. *4252*
16:26 I am not saying that I will ask the **F** *4252*

Jn 16:27 the F himself loves you 4252
16:28 I came from the F and entered the world; 4252
16:28 the world and going back to the F." 4252
16:32 Yet I am not alone, for my F is with me. 4252
17: 1 "F, the time has come. 4252
17: 5 now, F, glorify me in your presence with 4252
17:11 Holy F, protect them by the power 4252
17:21 F, just as you are in me and I am in you. 4252
17:24 "F, I want those you have given me to be 4252
17:25 "Righteous F, though the world does 4252
18:11 not drink the cup the F has given me?" 4252
20:17 for I have not yet returned to the F. 4252
20:17 'I am returning to my F and your Father, 4252
20:17 'I am returning to my Father and your F, 4252
20:21 As the F has sent me, I am sending you." 4252
Ac 1: 4 but wait for the gift my F promised, 4252
1: 7 or dates the F has set by his own authority. 4252
2:33 from the F the promised Holy Spirit 4252
4:25 the mouth of your servant, our f David: 4252
7: 2 of glory appeared *to* our f Abraham 4252
7: 4 After the death of his f, 4252
7: 8 And Abraham **became the f of** Isaac *1164*
7: 8 Later Isaac became the f of Jacob, *NIG*
7: 8 the f of the twelve patriarchs. *NIG*
7:14 for his f Jacob and his whole family, 4252
13:33 today I *have* **become** your F.' *1164*
16: 1 but whose f was a Greek. 4252
16: 3 for they all knew that his f was a Greek. 4252
28: 8 His f was sick in bed, 4252
Ro 1: 7 and peace to you from God our F and from 4252
4:11 he is the f of all who believe but have 4252
4:12 And he is also the f of the circumcised who 4252
4:12 of the faith that our f Abraham had 4252
4:16 He is the f of us all. 4252
4:17 "I have made you a f of many nations." 4252
4:17 He is our f in the sight of God, *NIG*
4:18 and so became the f of many nations, 4252
6: 4 from the dead through the glory *of* the F, 4252
8:15 And by him we cry, "Abba, F." 4252
9:10 Rebekah's children had one and the same f, *NIG*
9:10 and the same father, our f Isaac. 4252
15: 6 and mouth you may glorify the God and F 4252
1Co 1: 3 from God our F and the Lord Jesus Christ. 4252
4:15 for in Christ Jesus I **became** your f through *1164*
8: 6 the F, from whom all things came and 4252
15:24 the F after he has destroyed all dominion, 4252
2Co 1: 2 from God our F and the Lord Jesus Christ. 4252
1: 3 to the God and F of our Lord Jesus Christ, 4252
1: 3 the F of compassion and the God 4252
6:18 "I will be a F to you, 4252
11:31 The God and F of the Lord Jesus, 4252
Gal 1: 1 but by Jesus Christ and God the F, 4252
1: 3 from God our F and the Lord Jesus Christ, 4252
1: 4 according to the will *of* our God and F, 4252
4: 2 and trustees until the time set *by* his f. 4252
4: 6 the Spirit who calls out, "Abba, F." 4252
Eph 1: 2 from God our F and the Lord Jesus Christ. 4252
1: 3 to the God and F of our Lord Jesus Christ, 4252
1:17 of our Lord Jesus Christ, the glorious F, 4252
2:18 through him we both have access to the F 4252
3:14 For this reason I kneel before the F, 4252
4: 6 one God and F of all, 4252
5:20 always giving thanks *to* God the F 4252
5:31 "For this reason a man will leave his f 4252
6: 2 "Honor your f and mother"— 4252
6:23 from God the F and the Lord Jesus Christ. 4252
Php 1: 2 from God our F and the Lord Jesus Christ. 4252
2:11 to the glory of God the F. 4252
2:22 as a son *with* his f he has served with me in 4252
4:20 To our God and F be glory for ever 4252
Col 1: 2 Grace and peace to you from God our F. 4252
1: 3 the F of our Lord Jesus Christ, 4252
1:12 giving thanks *to* the F, 4252
3:17 giving thanks *to* God the F through him. 4252
1Th 1: 1 in God the F and the Lord Jesus Christ: 4252
1: 3 before our God and F your work produced 4252
2:11 that we dealt with each of you as a f deals 4252
3:11 our God and F himself and our Lord Jesus 4252
3:13 and holy in the presence of our God and F 4252
2Th 1: 1 in God our F and the Lord Jesus Christ: 4252
1: 2 from God the F and the Lord Jesus Christ. 4252
2:16 and God our F, who loved us 4252
1Ti 1: 2 from God the F and Christ Jesus our Lord. 4252
5: 1 but exhort him as if he were your f. 4252
2Ti 1: 2 from God the F and Christ Jesus our Lord. 4252
Tit 1: 4 the F and Christ Jesus our Savior. 4252
Phm 1: 3 from God our F and the Lord Jesus Christ. 4252
Heb 1: 5 today I *have* **become** your F"? *1164*
1: 5 Or again, "I will be his F, 4252
5: 5 today I *have* **become** your F." *1164*
7: 3 **Without** f or mother, without genealogy, 574
11:11 was enabled to **become a f** 2856+3284+5065
12: 7 For what son is not disciplined by his f? 4252
12: 9 *to* the F of our spirits and live! 4252
Jas 1:17 down from the F of the heavenly lights, 4252
1:27 Religion that God our F accepts as pure 4252
3: 9 With the tongue we praise our Lord and F, 4252
1Pe 1: 2 the foreknowledge *of* God the F, through 4252
1: 3 to the God and F of our Lord Jesus Christ! 4252
1:17 F who judges each man's work impartially, 4252
2Pe 1:17 the F when the voice came to him from 4252
1Jn 1: 2 which was with the F and has appeared 4252
1: 3 And our fellowship is with the F and 4252
2: 1 we have one who speaks to the F 4252
2:13 because you have known the F. 4252
2:15 the love *of* the F is not in him. 4252
2:16 comes not from the F but from the world. 4252
1Jn 2:22 he denies the F and the Son. 4252
2:23 No one who denies the Son has the F; 4252
2:23 the Son has the F also. 4252
2:24 also will remain in the Son and in the F. 4252
3: 1 How great is the love the F has lavished 4252
4:14 and testify that the F has sent his Son to be 4252
5: 1 the f loves his child as well. *1164*
2Jn 1: 3 from God the F and from Jesus Christ, 4252
1: 4 just as the F commanded us. 4252
1: 9 in the teaching has both the F and the Son. 4252
Jude 1: 1 by God the F and kept by Jesus Christ: 4252
Rev 1: 6 and priests to serve his God and F— 4252
2:27 as I have received authority from my F. 4252
3: 5 before my F and his angels. 4252
3:21 just as I overcame and sat down with my F 4252

FATHER'S (149) [FATHER]

Ge 9:22 the father of Canaan, saw his f nakedness 3
9:23 in backward and covered their f nakedness. 3
9:23 that they would not see their f nakedness. 3
12: 1 your people and your f household and go 3
20:13 from my f household, I said to her, 'This is 3
24: 7 who brought me out of my f household 3
24:23 in your f house for us to spend the night?" 3
24:38 but go to my f family and to my own clan, 3
24:40 from my own clan and from my f family. 3
26:15 So all the wells that his f servants had dug 3
27:30 and Jacob had scarcely left his f presence, 3
27:34 When Esau heard his f words, 3
28:21 so that I return safely to my f house, 3
29: 9 Rachel came with her f sheep, 3+4200
31: 5 "I see that your f attitude toward me is 3
31: 9 So God has taken away your f livestock 3
31:14 in the inheritance of our f estate? 3
31:19 Rachel stole her f household gods. 3+4200
31:30 to return to your f house. 3
34:19 the most honored of all his f household, 3
35:22 in and slept with his f concubine Bilhah, 3
37: 2 his f wives, and he brought their father 3
37:12 to graze their f flocks near Shechem, 3
38:11 "Live as a widow in your f house 3
38:11 So Tamar went to live in her f house. 3
41:51 and all my f household." 3
46:31 to his brothers and to his f household, 3
46:31 'My brothers and my f household, 3
47:12 and his brothers and all his f household 3
48:17 so he took hold of his f hand to move it 3
49: 4 for you went up onto your f bed, 3
49: 8 your f sons will bow down to you. 3
49:25 because of your f God, 3
49:26 Your f blessings are greater than 3
50: 8 and those belonging to his f household. 3
50:22 along with all his f family. 3
Ex 2:16 and fill the troughs to water their f flock. 3
6:20 Amram married his f **sister** Jochebed, 1860
15: 2 and I will praise him, my f God, 3
18: 4 for he said, "My f God was my helper; 3
Lev 18: 8 not have sexual relations with your f wife; 3
18: 9 your f daughter or your mother's daughter, 3
18:11 with the daughter of your f wife, born 3
18:12 not have sexual relations with your f sister; 3
18:12 she is your f close relative. 3
18:14 " 'Do not dishonor your f brother 3
20:11 " 'If a man sleeps with his f wife, 3
22:13 and she returns to live in her f house as 3
22:13 she may eat of her f food. 3
Nu 18: 1 your sons and your f family are to bear 3
27: 4 Why should our f name disappear 3
27: 4 Give us property among our f relatives." 3
27: 7 as an inheritance among their f relatives 3
27: 7 and turn their f inheritance over to them. 3
27:10 give his inheritance to his f brothers. 3
30: 3 in her f house makes a vow to the LORD 3
36: 8 in her f tribal clan, 3
36:11 married their **cousins on their f side.** 1201+1856
36:12 in their f clan and tribe. 3
Dt 21:17 That son is the first sign of **his** f strength. 2257[S]
22:21 the door of her f house and there the men 3
22:21 while still in her f house. 3
22:30 A man is not to marry his f wife; 3
22:30 he must not dishonor his f bed. 3
27:20 the man who sleeps with his f wife, 3
27:20 for he dishonors his f bed." 3
Jdg 6:25 "Take the second bull from your f herd, 3
6:25 down your f altar to Baal and cut down 3+4200
9: 5 He went to his f home in Ophrah and 3
9:18 revolted against my f family, 3
11: 7 and drive me from my f house? 3
14:15 or we will burn you and your f household 3
14:19 he went up to his f house. 3
16:31 and his f whole family went down 3
19: 2 and went back to her f house in Bethlehem, 3
19: 3 She took him into her f house, 3
1Sa 2:25 however, did not listen to their f rebuke, 3
2:27 to your f house when they were in Egypt 3
2:28 I also gave your f house all 3
2:30 and your f house would minister 3
2:31 and the strength of your f house, 3
9:20 if not to you and all your f family?" 3
17:15 from Saul to tend his f sheep at Bethlehem. 3
17:25 in marriage and will exempt his f family 3
17:34 Your servant has been keeping his f sheep 3+4200
18: 2 and did not let him return to his f house. 3
18:18 what is my family or my f clan in Israel, 3
20:34 at his f shameful treatment of David. 3
22: 1 and his f household heard about it, 3
1Sa 22:11 of Ahitub and his f whole family, 3
22:15 or any of his f family, 3
22:16 Ahimelech, you and your f whole family." 3
22:22 for the death of your f whole family. 3
24:21 or wipe out my name from my f family." 3
2Sa 2:32 and buried him in his f tomb at Bethlehem. 3
3: 7 "Why did you sleep with my f concubine?" 3
3:29 the head of Joab and upon all his f house! 3
14: 9 the blame rest on me and on my f family, 3
15:34 I was your f servant in the past, 3
16:21 "Lie with your f concubines whom he left 3
16:21 a stench in your f nostrils, 3
16:22 and he lay with his f concubines in 3
17:23 So he died and was buried in his f tomb. 3
1Ki 2:26 and shared all my f hardships." 3
2:31 and so clear me and my f house of the guilt 3
12:10 'My little finger is thicker than my f waist. 3
18:18 "But you and your f family have. 3
2Ki 10: 3 and set him on his f throne. 3
1Ch 5: 1 but when he defiled his f marriage bed, 3
26: 6 who were leaders in their f family 3
28: 4 and from my f sons he was pleased 3
2Ch 10:10 'My little finger is thicker than my f waist. 3
21: 4 over his f kingdom, 3
21:13 members of your f house, 3
22: 4 after his f death they became his advisers, 3
Ne 1: 6 including myself and my f house, 3
Est 4:14 but you and your f family will perish. 3
Ps 45:10 Forget your people and your f house. 3
Pr 1: 8 to your f instruction and do 3
4: 1 Listen, my sons, to a f instruction; 3
4: 3 When I was a boy in my f house, 3
6:20 keep your f commands and do 3
13: 1 A wise son heeds his f instruction, 3
15: 5 A fool spurns his f discipline, 3
19:13 A foolish son is his f ruin, 3
Isa 3: 6 at his f home, and say, "You have 3
Eze 18:17 He will not die for his f sin; 3
22:11 his own f daughter. 3
Mt 16:27 of Man is going to come in his F glory 4252
26:29 with you in my F kingdom." 4252
Mk 8:38 of him when he comes in his F glory with 4252
Lk 2:49 "Didn't you know I had to be in my F house?" 4252
15:17 'How many *of* my f hired men have food 4252
16:27 father, send Lazarus to my f house, 4252
Jn 1:18 who is at the F side, has made him known. 4252
2:16 How dare you turn my F house into 4252
5:43 I have come in my F name, 4252
6:40 For my F will is that everyone who looks 4252
8:38 what I have seen in the F presence, 4252
8:44 and you want to carry out your f desire. 4252
10:25 miracles I do in my F name speak for me, 4252
10:29 no one can snatch them out of my F hand. 4252
14: 2 In my F house are many rooms; 4252
15: 8 This is to my F glory, 4252
15:10 just as I have obeyed my F commands 4252
Ac 7:20 he was cared for in his f house. 4252
1Co 5: 1 A man has his f wife. 4252
2Jn 1: 3 the F Son, will be with us in truth and love. 4252
Rev 14: 1 and his F name written on their foreheads. 4252

FATHER-IN-LAW (24) [FATHER]

Ge 38:13 "Your f is on his way to Timnah 2767
38:25 she sent a message to her f. 2767
Ex 3: 1 the flock of Jethro his f, 3162
4:18 Then Moses went back to Jethro his f 3162
18: 1 the priest of Midian and f *of* Moses, 3162
18: 2 his f Jethro received her 3162
18: 5 Moses' f, together with Moses' sons 3162
18: 6 to him, "I, your f Jethro, am coming to you 3162
18: 7 So Moses went out to meet his f 3162
18: 8 Moses told his f about everything 3162
18:12 Then Jethro, Moses' f, 3162
18:12 to eat bread with Moses' f in the presence 3162
18:14 When his f saw all that Moses was doing 3162
18:17 Moses' f replied, "What you are doing is 3162
18:24 to his f and did everything he said. 3162
18:27 Then Moses sent his f on his way, 3162
Nu 10:29 Moses' f, "We are setting out for the place 3162
Jdg 1:16 The descendants of Moses' f, the Kenite, 3162
19: 4 His f, the girl's father, 3162
19: 7 the man got up to go, his f persuaded him, 3162
19: 9 got up to leave, his f, the girl's father, said, 3162
1Sa 4:19 and that her f and her husband were dead, 2767
4:21 of the ark of God and the deaths of her f 2767
Jn 18:13 Annas, who was the f of Caiaphas, *4290*

FATHERED (1) [FATHER]

Dt 32:18 You deserted the Rock, *who* f you; 3528

FATHERLESS (39) [FATHER]

Ex 22:24 will become widows and your children f. 3846
Dt 10:18 He defends the cause of the f and 3846
14:29 the aliens, the f and the widows who live 3846
16:11 the f and the widows living among you. 3846
16:14 the aliens, the f and the widows who live 3846
24:17 Do not deprive the alien or the f of justice, 3846
24:19 Leave it for the alien, the f and the widow, 3846
24:20 the alien, the f and the widow. 3846
24:21 the alien, the f and the widow. 3846
26:12 the alien, the f and the widow, 3846
26:13 the alien, the f and the widow, 3846
27:19 the alien, the f or the widow." 3846
Job 6:27 for the f and barter away your friend. 3846

Job 22: 9 and broke the strength of the f. 3846
24: 9 The f child is snatched from the breast; 3846
29:12 and the f who had none to assist him. 3846
31:17 not sharing it with the f— 3846
31:21 if I have raised my hand against the f, 3846
Ps 10:14 you are the helper of the f. 3846
10:18 defending the f and the oppressed, 3846
68: 5 A father to the f, a defender of widows, 3846
82: 3 Defend the cause of the weak and f; 3846
94: 6 they murder the f. 3846
109: 9 May his children be f and his wife 3846
109:12 or take pity on his f children. 3846
146: 9 the alien and sustains the f and the widow, 3846
Pr 23:10 or encroach on the fields of the f, 3846
Isa 1:17 Defend the cause of the f, 3846
1:23 They do not defend the cause of the f; 3846
9:17 nor will he pity the f and widows, 3846
10: 2 and robbing the f. 3846
Jer 5:28 they do not plead the case of the f to win it, 3846
7: 6 not oppress the alien, the f or the widow 3846
22: 3 violence to the alien, the f or the widow, 3846
La 5: 3 We have become orphans and f, 3+401
Eze 22: 7 and mistreated the f and the widow. 3846
Hos 14: 3 for in you the f find compassion." 3846
Zec 7:10 Do not oppress the widow or the f, 3846
Mal 3: 5 who oppress the widows and the f, 3846

FATHERS (312) [FATHER]

Ge 15:15 will go to your f in peace and be buried at 3
31: 3 to the land of your f and to your relatives, 3
46:34 just as our f did.' 3
47: 3 "just as our f were." 3
47: 9 the years of the pilgrimage of my f." 3
47:30 but when I rest with my f, 3
48:15 "May the God before whom my f Abraham 3
48:16 and the names of my f Abraham and Isaac, 3
48:21 and take you back to the land of your f. 3
49:29 with my f in the cave in the field of Ephron 3
Ex 3:13 'The God of your f has sent me to you,' 3
3:15 'The LORD, the God of your f— 3
3:16 'The LORD, the God of your f— 3
4: 5 the LORD, the God of their f— 3
10: 6 something neither your f 3
20: 5 the children for the sin of the f to the third 3
34: 7 of the f to the third and fourth generation." 3
Lev 26:40 and the sins of their f— 3
Nu 14:18 he punishes the children for the sin of the f 3
20:15 The Egyptians mistreated us and our f, 3
32: 8 This is what your f did when I sent them 3
32:14 the place of your f and making the LORD 3
36: 8 the inheritance of his f. 3
Dt 1: 8 the LORD swore he would give to your f— 3
1:11 May the LORD, the God of your f, 3
1:21 the LORD, the God of your f, told you. 3
4: 1 the LORD, the God of your f, is giving you. 3
5: 3 It was not with our f that 3
5: 9 the children for the sin of the f to the third 3
6: 3 just as the LORD, the God of your f, 3
6:10 to your f, to Abraham, Isaac and Jacob, 3
8: 3 which neither you nor your f had known, 3
8:16 something your f had never known, 3
9: 5 to accomplish what he swore to your f, 3
10:11 and possess the land that I swore to their f 3
12: 1 the LORD, the God of your f, 3
13: 6 that neither you nor your f have known, 3
24:16 F shall not be put to death 3
24:16 nor children put to death for their f; 3
26: 7 the LORD, the God of our f, 3
27: 3 just as the LORD, the God of your f, 3
28:36 to a nation unknown to you or your f. 3
28:64 which neither you nor your f have known. 3
29:13 and as he swore to your f, 3
29:25 the LORD, the God of their f, 3
30: 5 to the land that belonged to your f, 3
30: 5 and numerous than your f. 3
30: 9 just as he delighted in your f, 3
30:20 in the land he swore to give to your f, 3
31:16 "You are going to rest with your f, 3
32:17 gods your f did not fear. 3
Jos 4:21 when your descendants ask their f, 3
5: 6 that he had solemnly promised their f 3
18: 3 the LORD, the God of your f, has given you? 3
22:28 of the LORD's altar, which our f built, 3
24: 6 When I brought your f out of Egypt, 3
24:17 and our f up out of Egypt, 3
Jdg 2:10 to their f, another generation grew 3
2:12 the LORD, the God of their f, 3
2:17 Unlike their f, they quickly turned from NIH
2:17 from the way in which their f had walked, 3
2:19 even more corrupt than those of their f, 3
6:13 Where are all his wonders that our f told us 3
21:22 When their f or brothers complain to us, 3
1Sa 12: 7 by the LORD for you and your f. 3
12:15 as it was against your f. 3
2Sa 7:12 over and you rest with your f, 3
1Ki 1:21 the king is laid to rest with his f, 3
2:10 David rested with his f and was buried in 3
8:21 of the LORD that he made with our f 3
8:34 to the land you gave to their f. 3
8:40 in the land you gave our f. 3
8:48 toward the land you gave their f, toward 3
8:53 brought our f out of Egypt." 3
8:57 be with us as he was with our f; 3
8:58 decrees and regulations he gave our f. 3
9: 9 who brought their f out of Egypt, 3
11:21 with his f and that Joab the commander of 3
1Ki 11:43 Then he rested with his f and was buried in 3
13:22 not be buried in the tomb of your f.' " 3
14:20 and then rested with his f. 3
14:22 stirred up his jealous anger more than their f had done. 3
14:31 Rehoboam rested with his f and was buried 3
15: 8 Abijah rested with his f and was buried 3
15:12 and got rid of all the idols his f had made. 3
15:24 Then Asa rested with his f and was buried 3
16: 6 Baasha rested with his f and was buried 3
16:28 Omri rested with his f and was buried 3
21: 3 the inheritance of my f." 3
21: 4 not give you the inheritance of my f." 3
22:40 Ahab rested with his f. 3
22:50 with his f and was buried with them in 3
2Ki 8:24 Jehoram rested with his f and was buried 3
9:28 with his f in his tomb in the City of David. 3
10:35 with his f and was buried in Samaria. 3
12:18 the sacred objects dedicated by his f— 3
12:21 and was buried with his f in the City 3
13: 9 Jehoahaz rested with his f and was buried 3
13:13 Jehoash rested with his f. 3
14: 6 "F shall not be put to death 3
14: 6 nor children put to death for their f; 3
14:16 with his f and was buried in Samaria with 3
14:20 and was buried in Jerusalem with his f, 3
14:22 to Judah after Amaziah rested with his f. 3
14:29 Jeroboam rested with his f, 3
15: 7 Azariah rested with his f and was buried 3
15: 9 as his f had done. 3
15:22 Menahem rested with his f. 3
15:38 Jotham rested with his f and was buried 3
16:20 with his f and was buried with them in 3
17:13 the entire Law that I commanded your f 3
17:14 and were as stiff-necked as their f, 3
17:15 the covenant he had made with their f and 3
17:41 to do as their f did. 3
20:17 all that your f have stored up until this day, 3
20:21 Hezekiah rested with his f. 3
21:18 Manasseh rested with his f and was buried 3
21:22 He forsook the LORD, the God of his f, 3
22:13 against us because our f have not obeyed 3
22:20 Therefore I will gather you to your f, 3
23:32 just as his f had done. 3
23:37 just as his f had done. 3
24: 6 Jehoiakim rested with his f. 3
1Ch 5:25 of their f and prostituted themselves to 3
6:19 of the Levites listed according to their f: 3
9:19 as their f had been responsible for guarding 3
12:17 may the God of our f see it and judge you." 3
17:11 over and you go to be with your f, 3
25: 6 the supervision of their f for the music of 3
29:18 O LORD, God of our f Abraham, 3
29:20 the LORD, the God of their f; 3
2Ch 6:25 to the land you gave to them and their f. 3
6:31 in the land you gave our f. 3
6:38 and pray toward the land you gave their f, 3
7:22 the LORD, the God of their f, 3
9:31 Then he rested with his f and was buried in 3
11:16 the LORD, the God of their f. 3
12:16 Rehoboam rested with his f and was buried 3
13:12 the LORD, the God of your f, 3
13:18 the LORD, the God of their f. 3
14: 1 Abijah rested with his f and was buried in 3
14: 4 the LORD, the God of their f, 3
15:12 the LORD, the God of their f, 3
16:13 of his reign Asa died and rested with his f. 3
19: 4 the LORD, the God of their f. 3
20: 6 "O LORD, God of our f, 3
20:33 not set their hearts on the God of their f. 3
21: 1 Jehoshaphat rested with his f and was 3
21:10 the LORD, the God of his f. 3
21:19 as they had for his f. 3
24:18 the LORD, the God of their f, 3
24:24 the LORD, the God of their f, 3
25: 4 "F shall not be put to death 3
25: 4 nor children put to death for their f; 3
25:28 by horse and was buried with his f in 3
26: 2 to Judah after Amaziah rested with his f. 3
26:23 Uzziah rested with his f and was buried 3
27: 9 Jotham rested with his f and was buried 3
28: 6 the LORD, the God of their f. 3
28: 9 the LORD, the God of your f, was angry with Judah, 3
28:25 provoked the LORD, the God of his f, to anger. 3
28:27 Ahaz rested with his f and was buried in 3
29: 5 the LORD, the God of your f. 3
29: 6 Our f were unfaithful; 3
29: 9 This is why our f have fallen by the sword 3
30: 7 Do not be like your f and brothers, 3
30: 7 the LORD, the God of their f, 3
30: 8 Do not be stiff-necked, as your f were; 3
30:19 the LORD, the God of his f— 3
30:22 praised the LORD, the God of their f. 3
32:13 not know what I and my f have done to all 3
32:14 that my f destroyed has been able 3
32:15 from my hand or the hand of my f. 3
32:33 with his f and was buried on the hill where 3
33:12 before the God of his f. 3
33:20 Manasseh rested with his f and was buried 3
34:21 on us because our f have not kept the word 3
34:28 Now I will gather you to your f, 3
34:32 covenant of God, the God of their f. 3
34:33 follow the LORD, the God of their f. 3
35:24 He was buried in the tombs of his f, 3
36:15 The LORD, the God of their f, 3
Ezr 5:12 because our f angered the God of heaven, 10003
7:27 Praise be to the LORD, the God of our f, 3
8:28 offering to the LORD, the God of your f. 3
10:11 the LORD, the God of your f, and do his will. 3
Ne 2: 3 the city where my f are buried lies in ruins, 3
2: 5 the city in Judah where my f are buried so 3
9: 2 and the wickedness of their f. 3
9:23 into the land that you told their f to enter 3
9:32 upon our f and all your people, 3
9:34 and our f did not follow your law; 3
Job 8: 8 and find out what their f learned, 3
15:18 hiding nothing received from their f 3
30: 1 whose f I would have disdained to put 3
38:28 Who f the drops of dew? 3528
Ps 22: 4 In you our f put their trust; 3
39:12 a stranger, as all my f were. 3
44: 1 our f have told us what you did 3
44: 2 the nations and planted our f; 4392S
44: 2 the peoples and made our f flourish. 4392S
45:16 Your sons will take the place of your f; 3
49:19 he will join the generation of his f, 3
78: 3 what our f have told us. 3
78:12 in the sight of their f in the land of Egypt, 3
78:57 Like their f they were disloyal 3
79: 8 Do not hold against us the sins of the f; 8037
95: 9 where your f tested and tried me, 3
106: 6 We have sinned, even as our f did; 3
106: 7 When our f were in Egypt, 3
109:14 of his f be remembered before the LORD; 3
Pr 30:11 "There are those who curse their f and do 3
Isa 38:19 f tell their children about your faithfulness. 3
39: 6 all that your f have stored up until this day, 3
49:23 Kings will be your foster f, 587
64:11 where our f praised you, 3
65: 7 both your sins and the sins of your f," 3
Jer 2: 5 "What fault did your f find in me, 3
3:25 both we and our f; 3
6:21 F and sons alike will stumble over them; 3
7:14 the place I gave to you and your f. 3
7:18 children gather wood, the f light the fire, 3
9:14 as their f taught them." 3
9:16 that neither they nor their f have known, 3
13:14 f and sons alike, declares the LORD. 3
14:20 and the guilt of our f; 3
16: 3 and the men who are their f: 3
16:11 'It is because your f forsook me,' 3
16:12 you have behaved more wickedly than your f 3
16:13 a land neither you nor your f have known, 3
16:19 "Our f possessed nothing but false gods, 3
19: 4 in it to gods that neither they nor their f nor 3
23:27 just as their f forgot my name 3
23:39 with the city I gave to you and your f. 3
24:10 from the land I gave to them and their f.' " 3
25: 5 the land the LORD gave to you and your f 3
31:29 'The f have eaten sour grapes, 3
34: 5 a funeral fire in honor of your f, 3
34:14 Your f, however, did not listen to me 3
35:15 in the land I have given to you and your f." 3
44: 3 nor you nor your f ever knew. 3
44: 9 the wickedness committed by your f and 3
44:10 and the decrees I set before you and your f. 3
44:17 to her just as we and our f, 3
44:21 the streets of Jerusalem by you and your f, 3
47: 3 F will not turn to help their children; 3
50: 7 the LORD, the hope of their f.' 3
La 5: 7 Our f sinned and are no more, 3
Eze 2: 3 and their f have been in revolt against me 3
5:10 in your midst f will eat their children, 3
5:10 and children will eat their f. 3
18: 2 " 'The f eat sour grapes, 3
20: 4 with the detestable practices of their f 3
20:18 the statutes of your f or keep their laws 3
20:27 In this also your f blasphemed me 3
20:30 the way your f did and lust 3
20:36 As I judged your f in the desert of the land 3
20:42 with uplifted hand to give to your f. 3
37:25 the land where your f lived. 3
Da 2:23 I thank and praise you, O God of my f: 10003
9: 6 our princes and our f, 3
9: 8 and our f are covered with shame 3
9:16 the iniquities of our f have made Jerusalem 3
11:24 and will achieve what neither his f 3
11:37 for the gods of his f or for the one desired 3
11:38 to his f he will honor with gold and silver, 3
Hos 9:10 when I saw your f, 3
Mic 7:20 on oath to our f in days long ago. 3
Zec 8:14 when your f angered me," 3
Mal 2:10 Why do we profane the covenant of our f 3
4: 6 of the f to their children, and the hearts of 3
4: 6 and the hearts of the children to their f; 3
Lk 1:17 to turn the hearts *of* the f to their children 4252
1:55 even as he said to our f." 4252
1:72 to show mercy to our f and 4252
6:23 For that is how their f treated the prophets. 4252
6:26 how their f treated the false prophets. 4252
11:11 "Which of you f, if your son asks for 4252
Jn 4:20 Our f worshiped on this mountain, 4252
Ac 3:13 Isaac and Jacob, the God *of* our f, 4252
3:25 and of the covenant God made with your f. 4252
5:30 God *of* our f raised Jesus from the dead— 4252
7: 2 "Brothers and f, listen to me! 4252
7:11 and our f could not find food. 4252
7:12 he sent our f on their first visit. 4252
7:15 where he and our f died. 4252
7:32 'I am the God *of* your f, 4252
7:38 on Mount Sinai, and *with* our f; 4252
7:39 "But our f refused to obey him. 4252

Ac 7:45 our f under Joshua brought it with them 4252
7:51 You are just like your f: 4252
7:52 Was there ever a prophet your f did 4252
13:17 God of the people of Israel chose our f; 4252
13:32 What God promised our f 4252
13:36 with his f and his body decayed. 4252
15:10 that neither we nor our f have been able 4252
22: 1 "Brothers and f, listen now 4252
22: 3 in the law *of* our f and was just as zealous 4262
22:14 *of* our f has chosen you to know his will 4252
24:14 the God *of* our f as a follower of the Way, 4262
26: 6 of my hope in what God *has* promised our f 4252
1Co 4:15 you do not have many f, 4252
Gal 1:14 for the traditions *of* my f. 4257
Eph 6: 4 F, do not exasperate your children; 4252
Col 3:21 F, do not embitter your children, 4252
1Ti 1: 9 *for those who* **kill their** f or mothers, 4260
Heb 3: 9 where your f tested and tried me and 4252
12: 9 we have all had human f who disciplined us 4252
12:10 **Our** f disciplined us for a little while 3525+3836S
2Pe 3: 4 Ever since our f died, 4252
1Jn 2:13 I write to you, f, 4252
2:14 I write to you, f, 4252

FATHERS' (5) [FATHER]
Lev 26:39 of their f' sins they will waste away. 3
Jer 3:24 the fruits of our f' labor— 3
32:18 for the f' sins into the laps of their children 3
Eze 20:24 and their eyes [lusted] after their f' idols. 3
22:10 In you are those who dishonor their f' bed; 3

FATHOM (5) [FATHOMED]
Job 11: 7 *"Can you* f the mysteries of God? 5162
Ps 145: 3 his greatness no one can f. 2984
Ecc 3:11 yet they cannot f what God has done 5162
Isa 40:28 and his understanding no one can f. 2984
1Co 13: 2 the gift of prophecy and can f all mysteries 3857

FATHOMED (2) [FATHOM]
Job 5: 9 He performs wonders that cannot be f, 2984
9:10 He performs wonders that cannot be f, 2984

FATLING (KJV) See YEARLING

FATTED (KJV) See FATTENED

FATTENED (16) [FAT]
Dt 32:14 and flock and with f lambs and goats, 2693
1Sa 28:24 The woman had a f calf at the house, 5272
2Sa 6:13 he sacrificed a bull and a **f calf.** 5309
1Ki 1: 9 and **f calves** at the Stone of Zoheleth 5309
1:19 **f calves,** and sheep, and has invited all 5309
1:25 sacrificed great numbers of cattle, **f calves,** 5309
Pr 15:17 where there is love than a f calf 80
Isa 1:11 of rams and the fat of **f animals;** 5309
Jer 46:21 in her ranks are like f calves. 5272
Eze 39:18 all of them **f animals** *from* Bashan. 5309
Am 6: 4 You dine on choice lambs and f calves. 5272
Mt 22: 4 and **f cattle** have been butchered, 4990
Lk 15:23 Bring the f calf and kill it. 4988
15:27 the f calf because he has him back safe 4988
15:30 you kill the f calf for him!' 4988
Jas 5: 5 *You have* f yourselves in the day 5555

FATTENING (1) [FAT]
1Sa 2:29 by f yourselves on the choice parts 1344

FAULT (13) [FAULTFINDERS, FAULTLESS, FAULTS, FAULTY]
Ex 5:16 but *the* f *is with* your own people." 2627
1Sa 29: 3 I have found no f in him." 4399
29: 6 I have found no f in you, 8288
Job 33:10 Yet God has found f with me, 9481
Jer 2: 5 "What f did your fathers find in me, 6404
17: 4 **Through** your own f you will lose 928
Jnh 1:12 I know that it is my f 928+4200+8611
Mt 18:15 go and **show** him his f, 1794
Php 2:15 children of God **without** f in a crooked 320
Heb 8: 8 But God **found** f **with** the people and said: 3522
Jas 1: 5 to all without **finding** f, 3943
3: 2 If anyone *is* never **at** f in what he says, 4760
Jude 1:24 before his glorious presence **without** f and 320

FAULTFINDERS (1) [FAULT, FIND]
Jude 1:16 These men are grumblers and f; 3523

FAULTLESS (3) [FAULT]
Pr 8: 9 they are f to those who have knowledge. 3838
Php 3: 6 as for legalistic righteousness, f. 289+1181
Jas 1:27 as pure and f is this: 299

FAULTS (2) [FAULT]
Job 10: 6 that you must search out my f and probe 6411
Ps 19:12 Forgive my **hidden** *f.* AIT

FAULTY (2) [FAULT]
Ps 78:57 as unreliable as a f bow. 8244
Hos 7:16 they are like a f bow. 8244

FAVOR (117) [FAVORABLE, FAVORABLY, FAVORED, FAVORITE, FAVORITISM, FAVORS]
Ge 4: 4 The LORD **looked with** f on Abel 9120
4: 5 and his offering *he did* not **look with** f. 9120
6: 8 Noah found f in the eyes of the LORD. 2834
18: 3 He said, "If I have found f in your eyes, 2834
19:19 Your servant has found f in your eyes, 2834
30:27 "If I have found f in your eyes, please stay. 2834
32: 5 that I may find f in your eyes.' " 2834
33: 8 "To find f in your eyes, my lord," he said. 2834
33:10 "If I have found f in your eyes, 2834
33:15 "Just let me find f in the eyes of my lord." 2834
34:11 "Let me find f in your eyes, 2834
39: 4 Joseph found f in his eyes 2834
39:21 he showed him kindness and granted him f 2834
47:25 "May we find f in the eyes of our lord; 2834
47:29 "If I have found f in your eyes, 2834
50: 4 "If I have found f in your eyes, 2834
Ex 32:11 Moses **sought the** f **of** the LORD his God. 906+2704+7156
33:12 'I know you by name and you have found f 2834
33:13 so I may know you and continue to find f 2834
34: 9 "O Lord, if I have found f in your eyes," 2834
Lev 26: 9 *I will* **look** on you **with** f 7155
Nu 11:15 if I have found f in your eyes— 2834
32: 5 If we have found f in your eyes," they said, 2834
Dt 33:16 and its fullness and the f *of* him who dwelt 8356
33:23 "Naphtali is abounding with the f of 8356
Jos 15:19 She replied, "Do me a **special** f. 1388
Jdg 1:15 She replied, "Do me a **special** f. 1388
6:17 "If now I have found f in your eyes, 2834
Ru 2: 2 behind anyone in whose eyes I find f." 2834
2:10 "Why have I found such f in your eyes 2834
2:13 "May I continue to find f in your eyes, 2834
1Sa 1:18 "May your servant find f in your eyes." 2834
2:26 and *in* f with the LORD and with men. 3202
13:12 not **sought** the LORD's f.' 2704+7156
20: 3 that I have found f in your eyes, 2834
20:29 If I have found f in your eyes, 2834
27: 5 "If I have found f in your eyes, 2834
29: 4 How better *could* he **regain** his master's f than by taking the heads 8354
2Sa 2: 6 the same f because you have done this. 3208
14:22 that he has found f in your eyes, 2834
15:25 If I find f in the LORD's eyes, 2834
16: 4 "May I find f in your eyes, 2834
2Ki 13: 4 Jehoahaz **sought** the LORD's f, 906+2704+7156
2Ch 33:12 In his distress *he* **sought the** f **of** 906+2704+7156
Ezr 7:28 and who has extended his **good** f to me 2876
Ne 1:11 by granting him f in the presence 8171
2: 5 and if your servant *has* **found** f in his sight, 3512
5:19 Remember me with f, O my God, 3208
13:31 Remember me with f, O my God. 3208
Est 2: 9 The girl pleased him and won his f. 2876
2:15 the f of everyone who saw her. 2834
2:17 and she won his f and approval 2834
5: 8 the king regards me with f and if it pleases 2834
7: 3 "If I have found f with you, O king, 2834
8: 5 "and if he regards me with f and thinks it 2834
Job 11:19 and many *will* **court** your f. 2704+7156
33:26 He prays to God and **finds** f **with** him, 8354
34:19 to princes and *does* not f the rich over 5795
Ps 5:12 you surround them with your f as with 8356
30: 5 but his f lasts a lifetime; 8356
45:12 men of wealth *will* **seek** your f. 2704+7156
69:13 O LORD, in the time of your f; 8356
77: 7 *Will* he never **show** his f again? 8354
84: 9 **look with** f *on* your anointed one. 5564+7156
84:11 the LORD bestows f and honor; 2834
85: 1 *You* **showed** f *to* your land, O LORD; 8354
89:17 and by your f you exalt our horn. 8356
90:17 the f *of* the Lord our God rest upon us; 5840
102:13 for it is time to **show** f *to* her; 2858
106: 4 when you show f *to* your people, 8356
Pr 3: 4 Then you will win f and a good name in 2834
8:35 and receives f from the LORD. 8356
12: 2 A good man obtains f from the LORD, 8356
13:15 Good understanding wins f, 2834
16:15 his f is like a rain cloud in spring. 8356
18:22 a wife finds what is good and receives f 8356
19: 6 Many **curry** f **with** a ruler, 2704+7156
19:12 but his f is like dew on the grass. 8356
28:23 in the end gain more f than he who has 2834
Ecc 9:11 or wealth to the brilliant or f to the learned; 2834
Isa 27:11 and their Creator **shows** them no f. 2858
49: 8 "In the time of my f I will answer you, 8356
60:10 in f I will show you compassion. 8356
61: 2 to proclaim the year of the LORD's f and 8356
Jer 16:13 for I will show you no f.' 2850
26:19 the LORD and **seek** his f? 906+2704+7156
31: 2 the sword will find f in the desert; 2834
La 4:16 priests are shown no honor, the elders no f. 2858
Eze 5:11 *I myself will* **withdraw** *my* f; 1757
36: 9 and *will* **look** on you **with** f; 7155
Da 1: 9 Now God had caused the official to show f 2876
7:22 and pronounced judgment **in** f **of** the saints 10378
9:13 not **sought the** f **of** the LORD our God 906+2704+7156
9:17 **look with** f on your desolate sanctuary. 239+7156
11:30 and **show** f to those who forsake 1067
Hos 12: 4 he wept and **begged for** his f. 2858
Zec 11: 7 Then I took two staffs and called one F and 5840
11:10 Then I took my staff called F and broke it, 5840
Mt 20:20 kneeling down, **asked** a f of him. 160
Lk 1:25 "In these days *he has* **shown** *his* f 2078
1:30 Mary, you have found f with God. 5921
2:14 peace to men **on whom** his f **rests."** 2306
2:52 and *in* f with God and men. 5921
4:19 to proclaim the year of the Lord's f." 1283
Jn 5:32 There is another who testifies **in** my f, 4309
Ac 2:47 praising God and **enjoying** the f of all 2400+5921
7:46 who enjoyed God's f and asked 5921
24:27 Felix wanted to grant a f to the Jews, 5921
25: 3 as a f to them, 5921
25: 9 Festus, wishing to do the Jews a f, 5921
2Co 1:11 on our behalf for the **gracious** f **granted** us 5922
6: 2 he says, *"In* the time of my f I heard you, 1283
6: 2 I tell you, now is the time of God's f, 2347
Eph 6: 6 not only to **win** their f when their eye is 473
Col 3:22 when their eye is on you and to **win** their f, 473
Phm 1:14 that any f you do will be spontaneous and 19
Rev 2: 6 But you have this in your f: NIG

FAVORABLE (5) [FAVOR]
Ge 40:16 that Joseph had given a f interpretation, 3202
1Sa 25: 8 Therefore *be* f **toward** my young men, 928+2834+5162+6524
1Ki 12: 7 and serve them and give them a f answer, 3202
2Ch 10: 7 and please them and give them a f answer, 3202
Jer 42: 6 Whether it is f or unfavorable, 3202

FAVORABLY (7) [FAVOR]
Ge 33:10 now that *you have* **received** me f. 8354
Ex 3:21 I will make the Egyptians f **disposed toward** this people, 928+2834+6524
11: 3 The LORD made the Egyptians f **disposed toward** the people, 928+2834+6524
12:36 The LORD had made the Egyptians f **disposed toward** the people, 928+2834+6524
1Sa 20:12 If *he is* f **disposed** toward you, 3201
1Ki 22:13 with theirs, and speak f." 3202
2Ch 18:12 with theirs, and speak f." 3202

FAVORED (6) [FAVOR]
Dt 33: 8 and Urim belong to the man you f. 2883
33:24 let him be f *by* his brothers, 8354
Ps 30: 7 O LORD, when you f me, 8356
Eze 32:19 Say to them, *'Are you* **more** f than others? 5838
Lk 1:28 "Greetings, *you* who *are* **highly** f! 5923
1:43 But why am I so f, NIG

FAVORITE (1) [FAVOR]
SS 6: 9 the f of the one who bore her. 1338

FAVORITISM (9) [FAVOR]
Ex 23: 3 *do* not **show** f *to* a poor man in his lawsuit. 2075
Lev 19:15 do not show partiality to the poor or f 2075+7156
Ac 10:34 how true it is that God *does* not **show** f 1639+4720
Ro 2:11 For God *does* not **show** f. 1639+4721
Eph 6: 9 and there is no f with him. 4721
Col 3:25 and there is no f. 4721
1Ti 5:21 and to do nothing **out of** f. 2848+4680
Jas 2: 1 as believers in our glorious Lord Jesus Christ, don't **show** f. 1877+4721
2: 9 But if *you* **show** f, you sin 4719

FAVORS (6) [FAVOR]
2Sa 20:11 and said, "Whoever f Joab, and whoever is 2911
Ecc 9: 7 for it is now that God f what you do. 8354
Jer 3:13 you have scattered your f to foreign gods 2006
Eze 16:15 You lavished your f on anyone who passed 9373
16:33 from everywhere for your **illicit** f. 9373
16:34 **runs after** you **for** your f. 339+2388

FAWN (2) [FAWNS]
Job 39: 1 Do you watch when the doe bears her f? NIH
Jer 14: 5 the doe in the field deserts *her* **newborn** *f* AIT

FAWNS (4) [FAWN]
Ge 49:21 a doe set free that bears beautiful f. 611
SS 4: 5 Your two breasts are like two f, 6762
4: 5 like twin f of a gazelle that browse among NIH
7: 3 Your breasts are like two f, 6762

FEAR (260) [AFRAID, FEARED, FEARFUL, FEARFULLY, FEARING, FEARLESSLY, FEARS, FEARSOME, FRIGHT, FRIGHTEN, FRIGHTENED, FRIGHTENING, GOD-FEARING]
Ge 9: 2 The f and dread of you will fall upon all 4616
20:11 'There is surely no f *of* God in this place, 3711
22:12 Now I know that you f God, 3710
31:42 the God of Abraham and the F *of* Isaac, 7065
31:53 So Jacob took an oath in the name of the F 7065
32: 7 *In* great f and distress Jacob divided 3707
42:18 "Do this and you will live, for I f God: 3710
Ex 9:30 that you and your officials still *do* not f 3707
18:21 *men who* f God, 3710
20:18 they trembled *with* f. 3707
20:20 the f *of* God will be with you to keep you 3711
Lev 19:14 but f your God. 3707
25:17 but f your God. 3707
25:36 but f your God, 3707
25:43 but f your God. 3707

Dt 2:25 the terror and f of you on all the nations 3711
5:29 to f me and keep all my commands always, 3707
6: 2 after them may f the LORD your God 3707
6:13 F the LORD your God, 3707
6:24 to obey all these decrees and to f 3707
7:19 the same to all the peoples you now f. 3707
10:12 the LORD your God ask of you but to f 3707
10:20 F the LORD your God and serve him. 3707
11:25 the terror and f of you on the whole land, 4616
25:18 they had no f of God. 3707
28:10 and they will f you. 3707
31:12 and learn to f the LORD your God 3707
31:13 and learn to f the LORD your God as long 3707
32:17 gods your fathers did not f. 8549
Jos 2: 9 to you and that a great f of you has fallen 399
2: 9 in this country are melting in f because 4570
2:24 the people are melting in f because of us." 4570
4:24 and so that you might always f 3707
14: 8 made the hearts of the people melt with f. 4998
22:24 We did it for f that some day 1796
24:14 "Now f the LORD and serve him 3707
Jdg 7: 3 with f may turn back 3710
1Sa 12:14 If you f the LORD and serve him 3707
12:24 to f the LORD and serve him faithfully 3707
13: 7 the troops with him were quaking with f. 3006
17:24 they all ran from him in great f. 3707
28:20 filled with f because of Samuel's words. 3707+4394
2Sa 17:10 will melt with f, for all Israel knows 5022+5022
23: 3 when he rules in the f of God, 3711
1Ki 1:50 But Adonijah, in f of Solomon, 3707
8:40 that they will f you all the time they live 3707
8:43 the earth may know your name and f you, 3707
2Ki 25:26 fled to Egypt for f of the Babylonians. 3707
1Ch 14:17 and the LORD made all the nations f him. 7065
2Ch 6:31 so that they will f you and walk 3707
6:33 the earth may know your name and f you, 3707
12: 5 in Jerusalem for f of Shishak, 4946+7156
17:10 The f of the LORD fell on all 7065
19: 7 Now let the f of the LORD be upon you. 7065
19: 9 and wholeheartedly in the f of the LORD. 3711
20:29 The f of God came upon all the kingdoms 7065
26: 5 who instructed him in the f of God. 3711
Ezr 3: 3 Despite their f of the peoples around them, 399
10: 3 of those who f the commands of our God. 3007
Ne 5: 9 in the f of our God to avoid the reproach 3711
Est 5: 9 that he neither rose nor showed f 2316
8:17 because f of the Jews had seized them. 7065
9: 3 because f of Mordecai had seized them. 7065
Job 1: 9 "Does Job f God for nothing?" 3707
4:14 f and trembling seized me 7065
5:21 and need not f when destruction comes. 3707
5:22 and need not f the beasts of the earth. 3707
6:14 though he forsakes the f of the Almighty. 3711
9:35 Then I would speak up without f of him, 3707
11:15 you will stand firm and without f. 3707
19:29 you should f the sword yourselves; 1593
21: 9 Their homes are safe and free from f; 7065
23:15 when I think of all this, I f him. 7064
28:28 And he said to man, 'The f of the Lord— 3711
31:23 and for f of his splendor I could 4946
33: 7 No f of me should alarm you, 399
39:22 He laughs at f, afraid of nothing; 7065
41:33 a creature without f. 3145
Ps 2:11 Serve the LORD with f and rejoice 3711
3: 6 I will not f the tens of thousands drawn 3707
15: 4 but honors those who f the LORD, 3710
19: 9 f of the LORD is pure, enduring forever. 3711
22:23 You who f the LORD, praise him! 3710
22:25 those who f you will I fulfill my vows. 3710
23: 4 I will f no evil, for you are with me; 3707
25:14 The LORD confides in those who f him; 3710
27: 1 my salvation—whom shall I f? 3707
27: 3 an army besiege me, my heart will not f; 3707
31:19 up for those who f you, 3710
33: 8 Let all the earth f the LORD; 3707
33:18 eyes of the LORD are on those who f him, 3710
34: 7 around those who f him, 3710
34: 9 F the LORD, you his saints, 3707
34: 9 for those who f him lack nothing. 3710
34:11 I will teach you the f of the LORD. 3711
36: 1 There is no f of God before his eyes. 7065
40: 3 Many will see and f and put their trust in 3707
46: 2 Therefore we will not f, 3707
49: 5 Why should I f when evil days come, 3707
52: 6 The righteous will see and f; 3707
55: 5 F and trembling have beset me; 3711
55:19 and have no f of God. 3707
60: 4 But for those who f you, 3710
61: 5 the heritage of those who f your name. 3710
64: 4 they shoot at him suddenly, without f. 3707
64: 9 All mankind will f; 3707
65: 8 Those living far away f your wonders; 3707
66:16 all you who f God; 3710
67: 7 and all the ends of the earth will f him. 3707
85: 9 his salvation is near those who f him, 3710
86:11 that I may f your name. 3707
90:11 For your wrath is as great as the f 3711
91: 5 You will not f the terror of night, 3707
102:15 The nations will f the name of 3707
103:11 so great is his love for those who f him; 3710
103:13 on those who f him; 3710
103:17 with those who f him, and his righteousness 3710
111: 5 He provides food for those who f him; 3710
111:10 The f of the LORD is the beginning 3711
112: 7 He will have no f of bad news; 3707
112: 8 His heart is secure, he will have no f; 3707
Ps 115:11 You who f him, trust in the LORD— 3710
115:13 he will bless those who f the LORD— 3710
118: 4 Let those who f the LORD say: 3710
119:63 I am a friend to all who f you, 3707
119:74 May those who f you rejoice 3710
119:79 May those who f you turn to me, 3710
119:120 My flesh trembles in f of you; 7065
128: 1 Blessed are all who f the LORD, 3710
135:20 you who f him, praise the LORD. 3710
145:19 He fulfills the desires of those who f him; 3710
147:11 the LORD delights in those who f him, 3710
Pr 1: 7 The f of the LORD is the beginning 3711
1:29 and did not choose to f the LORD, 3711
1:33 be at ease, without f of harm." 7065
2: 5 you will understand the f of the LORD 3711
3: 7 f the LORD and shun evil. 3707
3:25 Have no f of sudden disaster or of the ruin 3707
8:13 To f the LORD is to hate evil; 3711
9:10 "The f of the LORD is the beginning 3711
10:27 The f of the LORD adds length to life, 3711
14:27 The f of the LORD is a fountain of life, 3711
15:16 with the f of the LORD than great wealth 3711
15:33 f of the LORD teaches a man wisdom, 3711
16: 6 the f of the LORD a man avoids evil. 3711
19:23 The f of the LORD leads to life: 3711
22: 4 and the f of the LORD bring wealth 3711
23:17 always be zealous for the f of the LORD. 3711
24:21 F the LORD and the king, my son, 3707
29:25 F of man will prove to be a snare, 3010
31:21 it snows, she has no f for her household; 3707
Ecc 8:13 Yet because the wicked do not f God, 3710
12:13 F God and keep his commandments, 3707
Isa 7:25 you will no longer go there for f of 3711
8:12 do not f what they fear, and do not dread it. 3707
8:12 do not fear what they f, and do not dread it. 4616
8:13 he is the one you are to f, 4616
11: 2 of knowledge and of the f of the LORD— 3711
11: 3 and he will delight in the f of the LORD. 3711
19:16 with f at the uplifted hand that 7064
21: 4 My heart falters, f makes me tremble; 7146
33: 6 f of the LORD is the key to this treasure. 3711
35: 4 "Be strong, do not f; 3707
41: 5 The islands have seen it and f; 3707
41:10 So do not f, for I am with you; 3707
41:13 Do not f; I will help you. 3707
41:23 we will be dismayed and filled with f. 3707
43: 1 "F not, for I have redeemed you; 3707
51: 7 Do not f the reproach of men or be terrified 3707
51:12 Who are you that you f mortal men, 3707
54: 4 Do not f disgrace; 4007
54:14 you will have nothing to f. 3707
57:11 that you do not f me? 3707
59:19 men will f the name of the LORD, 3707
Jer 3: 8 that her unfaithful sister Judah had no f; 3707
5:22 Should you not f me?" 3707
5:24 'Let us f the LORD our God, 3707
10: 5 Do not f them; 3707
17: 8 It does not f when heat comes; 3707
22:25 to those who seek your life, those you f— 3328
26:19 Did not Hezekiah f the LORD 3707
26:21 Uriah heard of it and fled in f to Egypt. 3707
30: 5 " 'Cries of f are heard—terror, not peace. 3010
30:10 " 'So do not f, O Jacob my servant; 3707
32:39 so that they will always f me 3707
32:40 and I will inspire them to f me, 3711
36:16 looked at each other in f 7064
36:24 all his attendants who heard all these words showed no f, 7064
39:17 you will not be handed over to those you f. 3328
42:11 king of Babylon, whom you now f. 3710
42:16 the sword you f will overtake you there, 3710
46:27 "Do not f, O Jacob my servant; 3707
46:28 Do not f, O Jacob my servant, 3707
La 3:57 and you said, "Do not f." 3707
Eze 11: 8 You f the sword, and the sword 3707
12:18 and shudder in f as you drink your water. 1796
27:35 and their faces are distorted with f. 8307
30:13 and I will spread f throughout the land. 3711
Da 6:26 in every part of my kingdom people must f 10227
Hos 10: 5 in Samaria f for the calf-idol of Beth Aven. 1593
Am 3: 8 The lion has roared—who will not f? 3707
Mic 6: 9 and to f your name is wisdom— 3707
7:17 they will turn in f to the LORD our God 7064
Na 2:11 and the cubs, with nothing to f? 3006
Zep 3: 7 you will f me and accept correction!' 3707
3:15 never again will you f any harm. 3707
3:16 "Do not f, O Zion; 3707
Hag 2: 5 my Spirit remains among you. Do not f.' 3707
Zec 9: 5 Ashkelon will see it and f; 3707
Mal 3: 5 but do not f me," says the LORD 3707
Mt 14:26 "It's a ghost," they said, and cried out in f. 5832
Mk 5:33 trembling with f, told him the whole truth. 5828
Lk 1:12 was startled and was gripped with f. 2158+5832
1:50 His mercy extends to those who f him, 5828
1:74 and to enable us to serve him without f 925
8:25 In f and amazement they asked one 5828
8:37 because they were overcome with f. 3489+5832
12: 5 But I will show you whom you should f: 5828
12: 5 F him who, after the killing of the body, 5828
12: 5 Yes, I tell you, f him. 5828
18: 4 though I don't f God or care about men, 5828
23:40 "Don't you f God," he said, 5828
Jn 3:20 will not come into the light for f that 2671+3590
7:13 about him for f of the Jews. 5832
12:42 not confess their faith for f they would NIG
20:19 with the doors locked for f of the Jews, 5832
Ac 5: 5 And great f seized all who heard 5832
Ac 5:11 Great f seized the whole church 5832
7:32 Moses trembled with f and did not 1181+1958
9:31 living in the f of the Lord. 5832
10: 4 Cornelius stared at him in f. 1181+1873
10:35 from every nation who f him 5828
19:17 they were all seized with f, 2158+5832
Ro 3:18 "There is no f of God before their eyes." 5832
8:15 a spirit that makes you a slave again to f, 5832
13: 3 Do you want to be free from f of the one in authority? 3590+5828
1Co 2: 3 I came to you in weakness and f, 5832
16:10 see to it that he has nothing to f while he is 925
2Co 5:11 then, we know what it is to f the Lord, 5832
7:15 receiving him with f and trembling. 5832
12:20 I f that there may be quarreling, jealousy, NIG
Gal 2: 2 for f that I was running or had run 3590+4803
4:11 I f for you, that somehow I have wasted my 5828
Eph 6: 5 Slaves, obey your earthly masters with respect and f, 5571
Php 2:12 continue to work out your salvation with f 5832
Heb 2:15 in slavery by their f of death. 5832
11: 7 in holy f built an ark to save his family. 2326
12:21 "I am trembling with f." 1769
1Pe 1:17 as strangers here in reverent f. 5832
2:17 Love the brotherhood of believers, f God, 5828
3: 6 and do not give way to f. 5828
3:14 "Do not f what they fear; 5828
3:14 "Do not fear what they f; 5832
1Jn 4:18 There is no f in love. 5832
4:18 But perfect love drives out f, 5832
4:18 because f has to do with punishment. 5832
Jude 1:23 to others show mercy, mixed with f— 5832
Rev 14: 7 "F God and give him glory, 5828
15: 4 Who will not f you, O Lord, 5828
19: 5 you who f him, both small and great!" 5828

FEARED (37) [FEAR]

Ex 1:17 f God and did not do what the king 3707
1:21 And because the midwives f God, 3707
9:20 Those officials of Pharaoh who f the word 3707
14:31 the people f the LORD and put their trust 3707
Dt 9:19 I f the anger and wrath of the LORD, 3336
Jos 9:24 So we f for our lives because of you, 3707
1Sa 4:13 because his heart f for the ark of God. 2118+3007
14:26 because they f the oath. 3707
1Ch 16:25 he is to be f above all gods. 3707
Ne 7: 2 and f God more than most men do. 3707
Job 1: 1 he f God and shunned evil. 3710
3:25 What I f has come upon me; 7064
31:34 because I so f the crowd and so dreaded 6907
Ps 76: 7 You alone are to be f. 3707
76: 8 and the land f and was quiet— 3707
76:11 to the One to be f. 4616
76:12 he is f by the kings of the earth. 3707
89: 7 of the holy ones God is greatly f; 6907
96: 4 he is to be f above all gods. 3707
119:38 so that you may be f. 3711
130: 4 therefore you are f. 3707
Isa 18: 2 to a people f far and wide, 3707
18: 7 from a people f far and wide, 3707
57:11 so dreaded and f that you have been false 3707
Da 5:19 of every language dreaded and f him. 10167
Jnh 1:16 At this the men greatly f the LORD, 3707+3711
Hab 1: 7 They are a f and dreaded people; 398
Hag 1:12 And the people f the LORD. 3707
Mal 1:14 my name is to be f among the nations. 3707
3:16 Then those who f the LORD talked 3710
3:16 in his presence concerning those who f 3710
Mk 6:20 because Herod f John and protected him, 5828
11:18 for a way to kill him, for they f him, 5828
11:32 (They f the people, 5828
Lk 18: 2 a judge who neither f God nor cared 5828
Jn 19:38 but secretly because he f the Jews. 5832
Ac 5:26 they f that the people would stone them. 5828

FEARFUL (7) [FEAR]

Lev 26:36 I will make their hearts so f in the lands 5322
Dt 28:59 the LORD will send f plagues on you 7098
Job 32: 6 that is why I was f, 2324
Isa 8:22 and darkness and f gloom, 7442
35: 4 say to those with f hearts, "Be strong, do 4554
Lk 21:11 and f events and great signs from heaven. 5831
Heb 10:27 but only a f expectation of judgment and 5829

FEARFULLY (1) [FEAR]

Ps 139:14 because I am f and wonderfully made; 3707

FEARING (4) [FEAR]

Jos 22:25 might cause ours to stop f the LORD. 3707
Ac 27:17 F that they would run aground on 3590+5828
27:29 F that we would be dashed against 3590+5828
Heb 11:27 not f the king's anger; 5828

FEARLESSLY (4) [FEAR]

Ac 9:27 in Damascus he had preached f in the name 4245
Eph 6:19 so that I will f make known the mystery of 4244
6:20 Pray that I may declare it f, as I should. 4245
Php 1:14 the word of God more courageously and f. 925

FEARS (15) [FEAR]

Job 1: 8 a man who f God and shuns evil." 3710
2: 3 a man who f God and shuns evil. 3710
Ps 25:12 Who, then, is the man that f the LORD? 3710

Ps 34: 4 he delivered me from all my **f.** 4475
112: 1 Blessed is the man *who* **f** the LORD, 3707
128: 4 Thus is the man blessed *who* **f** the LORD. 3710
Pr 14: 2 He whose walk is upright **f** the LORD, 3707
14:16 A wise man **f** the LORD and shuns evil, 3707
14:26 *He who* **f** the LORD has a secure fortress, 3711
28:14 the man *who* always **f** the LORD, 7064
31:30 a woman *who* **f** the LORD is to be praised. 3710
Ecc 7:18 *man who* **f** God will avoid all [extremes]. 3710
Isa 50:10 Who among you **f** the LORD and obeys 3710
2Co 7: 5 conflicts on the outside, **f** within. 5832
1Jn 4:18 The one who **f** is not made perfect in love. 5828

FEARSOME (1) [FEAR]

Job 41:14 ringed about with his **f** teeth? 399

FEAST (97) [FEASTED, FEASTING, FEASTS]

Ge 21: 8 on the day Isaac was weaned Abraham held a great **f.** 5492
26:30 Isaac then made a **f** for them, 5492
29:22 the people of the place and gave a **f.** 5492
40:20 and he gave a **f** for all his officials. 5492
Ex 12:17 **F of Unleavened Bread,** 5174
23:15 "Celebrate the **F** of Unleavened Bread; 2504
23:16 the **F** *of* Harvest with the firstfruits of 2504
23:16 the **F** *of* Ingathering at the end of the year, 2504
34:18 "Celebrate the **F** *of* Unleavened Bread. 2504
34:22 the **F** *of* Weeks with the firstfruits of 2504
34:22 the **F** *of* Ingathering at the turn of the year. 2504
34:25 of the sacrifice from the Passover **F** remain 2504
Lev 23: 6 the LORD's **F** *of* Unleavened Bread 2504
23:34 the LORD's **F** *of* Tabernacles begins, 2504
Nu 28:26 of new grain during the **F of Weeks,** 8651
Dt 16:10 the **F** *of* Weeks to the LORD your God 2504
16:13 the **F** of Tabernacles for seven days 2504
16:14 Be joyful at your **F—** 2504
16:15 For seven days **celebrate the F** to 2510
16:16 at the **F** *of* Unleavened Bread, 2504
16:16 of Unleavened Bread, the **F** *of* Weeks and 2504
16:16 of Weeks and the **F** *of* Tabernacles. 2504
31:10 during the **F** *of* Tabernacles, 2504
33:19 *they will* **f on** the abundance of the seas, 3567
Jdg 14:10 And Samson made a **f** there, 5492
14:12 the answer within the seven days of the **f,** 5492
14:17 She cried the whole seven days of the **f.** 5492
2Sa 3:20 David prepared a **f** for him and his men. 5492
1Ki 1:41 as they were finishing their **f.** 430
3:15 Then he gave a **f** for all his court. 5492
2Ki 6:23 So *he* **prepared** a great **f** for them, 4127+4130
2Ch 8:13 the **F** *of* Unleavened Bread, 2504
8:13 of Unleavened Bread, the **F** *of* Weeks and 2504
8:13 of Weeks and the **F** *of* Tabernacles. 2504
30:13 to celebrate the **F** *of* Unleavened Bread in 2504
30:21 the **F** *of* Unleavened Bread for seven days 2504
35:17 the **F** *of* Unleavened Bread for seven days. 2504
Ezr 3: 4 they celebrated the **F** *of* Tabernacles with 2504
6:22 with joy the **F** *of* Unleavened Bread, 2504
Ne 8:14 in booths during the **f** of the seventh month 2504
8:18 They celebrated the **f** for seven days, 2504
Job 39:30 His young ones **f on** blood, 6633
Ps 22:29 the rich of the earth *will* **f** and worship; 430
36: 8 *They* **f** on the abundance of your house; 8115
81: 3 on the day of our **F;** 2504
Pr 5:10 lest strangers **f on** your wealth 8425
15:15 but the cheerful heart has a continual **f.** 5492
Ecc 5:11 to the owner except to **f** his eyes **on** them? 8021
10:16 and whose princes **f** in the morning. 430
10:19 A **f** is made for laughter, 4312
Isa 25: 6 a **f** *of* rich food for all peoples, a banquet 5492
58:14 of the land and *to* **f on** the inheritance 430
Jer 51:39 a **f** *for* them and make them drunk, so 5492
La 2: 7 as on the day of an **appointed f.** 4595
2:22 "As you summon to a **f** day, 4595
Eze 45:21 a **f** *lasting* seven days, 2504
45:23 of the **F** he is to provide seven bulls 2504
45:25 " 'During the seven days of the **F,** 2504
Zec 14:16 and to celebrate the **F** *of* Tabernacles. 2504
14:18 up to celebrate the **F** *of* Tabernacles. 2504
14:19 up to celebrate the **F** *of* Tabernacles. 2504
Mt 8:11 **take** *their* **places at the f** with Abraham, 369
26: 5 "But not during the **F,"** they said, 2038
26:17 **F of Unleavened Bread,** 109
27:15 Now it was the governor's custom at the **F** 2038
Mk 14: 1 **F of Unleavened Bread** 109
14: 2 "But not during the **F,"** they said, 2038
14:12 **F of Unleavened Bread,** 109
15: 6 Now it was the custom at the **F** to release 2038
Lk 2:41 to Jerusalem *for* the **F** of the Passover. 2038
2:42 they went up to the **F,** 2038
2:43 After the **F** was over, NIG
13:29 **take** *their* **places at the f** in the kingdom 369
14: 8 "When someone invites you to a **wedding f,** 1141
14:15 "Blessed is the man who will eat at the **f** in 756
15:23 Let's **have a f** and celebrate. 2266
22: 1 Now the **F** of Unleavened Bread, 2038
Jn 2:23 he was in Jerusalem at the Passover **F,** 2038
4:45 in Jerusalem at the **Passover F,** 2038
5: 1 Jesus went up to Jerusalem for a **f** of 2038
6: 4 The Jewish Passover **F** was near. 2038
7: 2 the Jewish **F** of Tabernacles was near, 2038
7: 8 You go to the **F.** 2038
7: 8 I am not yet going up to this **F,** 2038
7:10 after his brothers had left for the **F,** 2038
7:11 at the **F** the Jews were watching for him 2038
Jn 7:14 until halfway through the **F** did Jesus go up 2038
7:37 On the last and greatest day *of* the **F,** 2038
10:22 came the **F of Dedication** at Jerusalem. 1589
11:56 Isn't he coming to the **F** at all?" 2038
12:12 the great crowd that had come for the **F** 2038
12:20 up to worship at the **F.** 2038
13: 1 It was just before the Passover **F.** 2038
13:29 to buy what was needed for the **F,** 2038
Ac 12: 3 **F of Unleavened Bread.** 109
20: 6 **F of Unleavened Bread,** 109+2465
2Pe 2:13 reveling in their pleasures *while they* **f with** 5307

FEASTED (1) [FEAST]

Ge 43:34 So *they* **f** and drank freely with him. 9272

FEASTING (13) [FEAST]

Est 8:17 with **f** and celebrating. 5492
9:17 and made it a day of **f** and joy. 5492
9:18 and made it a day of **f** and joy. 5492
9:19 of the month of Adar as a day of joy and **f,** 5492
9:22 of **f** and joy and giving presents of food 5492
Job 1: 5 When a period of **f** had run its course, 5492
1:13 and daughters *were* **f** and drinking wine at 430
1:18 and daughters *were* **f** and drinking wine at 430
Pr 17: 1 with peace and quiet than a house full of **f,** 2285
Ecc 7: 2 of **f,** for death is the destiny of every man; 5492
Jer 16: 8 a house where there is **f** and sit down to eat 5492
Am 6: 7 your **f** and lounging will end. 5301
Zec 7: 6 *were* you not *just* **f** *for* yourselves? 430+2256+9272

FEASTS (30) [FEAST]

Lev 23: 2 'These are my **appointed f,** 4595
23: 2 the **appointed f** *of* the LORD, 4595
23: 4 " 'These are the LORD's **appointed f,** 4595
23:37 (" 'These are the LORD's **appointed f,** 4595
23:44 to the Israelites the **appointed f** *of* 4595
Nu 10:10 your **appointed f** and New Moon 4595
29:39 for the LORD at your **appointed f:** 4595
1Ch 23:31 at New Moon festivals and at **appointed f.** 4595
2Ch 2: 4 at the **appointed f** *of* the LORD our God. 4595
8:13 New Moons and the three annual **f—** 4595
31: 3 New Moons and **appointed f** as written in 4595
Ezr 3: 5 the sacrifices for all the **appointed** sacred **f** 4595
Ne 10:33 New Moon festivals and **appointed f;** 4595
Job 1: 4 to take turns holding **f** in their homes, 5492
24:20 womb forgets them, the worm **f on** them; 5517
Isa 1:14 and your **appointed f** my soul hates. 4595
La 1: 4 for no one comes to her **appointed f.** 4595
2: 6 LORD has made Zion forget her **appointed f** 4595
Eze 36:38 at Jerusalem during her **appointed f.** 4595
44:24 and my decrees for all my **appointed f,** 4595
45:17 the **appointed f** *of* the house of Israel. 4595
46: 9 before the LORD at the **appointed f,** 4595
46:11 " 'At the festivals and the **appointed f,** 4595
Hos 2:11 all her **appointed f.** 4595
9: 5 on the day of your **appointed f,** 4595
12: 9 as in the days of your **appointed f.** 4595
Am 5:21 "I hate, I despise your **religious f;** 2504
8:10 I will turn your **religious f** into mourning 2504
Zep 3:18 the **appointed f** I will remove from you; 4595
Jude 1:12 These men are blemishes at your **love f,** 27

FEAT (1)

2Ki 8:13 a mere dog, accomplish such a **f?"** 1524+1821

FEATHERS (6)

Job 39:13 with the pinions and **f** of the stork. 5681
39:18 **spreads** *her* **f to run,** 928+2021+5257+5294
Ps 68:13 its **f** with shining gold." 89
91: 4 He will cover you with his **f,** 89
Eze 17: 3 A great eagle with powerful wings, long **f** 88
Da 4:33 until his hair grew like the **f** of an eagle NIH

FEATURES (3)

1Sa 16:12 with a fine appearance and handsome **f.** 8024
Est 2: 7 Esther, was lovely in form and **f,** 5260
Job 38:14 its **f** stand out like those of a garment. NIH

FED (10) [FEED]

Dt 32:13 on the heights of the land and **f** him *with* 430
Jdg 19:21 into his house and **f** his donkeys. 1176
Ps 80: 5 *You have* **f** them *with* the bread of tears; 430
81:16 you *would be* **f** with the finest of wheat; 430
Da 4:12 from it every creature **was f.** 10226
Hos 13: 6 When I **f** them, they were satisfied; 5338
Na 2:11 the **place where** they **f** their young, 5337
Lk 6:25 Woe to you who *are* **well f** now, 1855
Php 4:12 whether **well f** or hungry, 5963
Jas 2:16 *keep* warm and **well f,"** 5963

FEE (2)

Nu 22: 7 taking with them the **f for divination.** 7877
Eze 16:33 Every prostitute receives a **f,** 5613

FEEBLE (8) [FEEBLEST]

Ne 4: 2 he said, "What are those **f** Jews doing? 584
Job 4: 3 how you have strengthened **f** hands. 8333
26: 2 How you have saved the arm that is **f!** 4202+6437
Ps 38: 8 *I am* **f** and utterly crushed; 7028
Isa 16:14 her survivors will be very few and **f."** 3888+4202
Isa 35: 3 Strengthen the **f** hands, 8333
Jer 49:24 Damascus *has become* **f,** 8332
Heb 12:12 strengthen your **f** arms and weak knees. 4223

FEEBLEMINDED (KJV) See TIMID

FEEBLEST (1) [FEEBLE]

Zec 12: 8 that the **f** among them will be like David, 4173

FEED (33) [FED, FEEDING, FEEDS, OVERFED, PASTURE-FED, STALL-FED, WELL-FED]

Ge 42:27 of them opened his sack to get **f** 5028
1Ki 14:11 the birds of the air *will* **f on** those who die 430
16: 4 the birds of the air *will* **f on** those who die 430
17: 4 I have ordered the ravens to **f** you there." 3920
21:24 the birds of the air *will* **f on** those who die 430
Ps 49:14 and death *will* **f on** them. 8286
80:13 and the creatures of the field **f on** it. 8286
Pr 27:27 of goats' milk to **f** you and your family and 4312
Isa 5:17 lambs *will* **f** *among* the ruins of the rich. 430
9:20 Each *will* **f on** the flesh 430
9:21 Manasseh will **f** on Ephraim, and Ephraim NIH
11: 7 The cow *will* **f** with the bear, 8286
18: 6 the birds will **f on** them all summer, 6584
49: 9 *"They will* **f** beside the roads 8286
61: 6 *You will* **f on** the wealth of nations, 430
65:25 The wolf and the lamb *will* **f** together, 8286
Eze 34:10 the shepherds *can* no longer **f** themselves. 8286
34:14 and there *they will* **f** *in* a rich pasture on 8286
34:18 for you *to* **f on** the good pasture? 8286
34:19 *Must* my flock **f on** 8286
Hos 4: 8 *They* **f on** the sins of my people 430
9: 2 and winepresses *will* not **f** the people; 8286
11: 4 from their neck and bent down *to* **f** them. 430
Mic 7:14 *Let them* **f** in Bashan and Gilead as 8286
Zec 11:16 or heal the injured, or **f** the healthy, 3920
Mt 15:33 in this remote place to **f** such a crowd?" 5963
25:37 when did we see you hungry and **f** you, 5555
Mk 8: 4 in this remote place can anyone get enough bread *to* **f** them?" 5963
Lk 15:15 who sent him to his fields *to* **f** pigs. 1081
Jn 21:15 Jesus said, **"F** my lambs." 1081
21:17 Jesus said, **"F** my sheep. 1081
Ro 12:20 "If your enemy is hungry, **f** him; 6039
Jude 1:12 shepherds who **f** only themselves. NIG

FEEDING (4) [FEED]

Dt 8: 3 to hunger and then **f** you *with* manna, 430
Mt 8:30 from them a large herd of pigs was **f,** 1081
Mk 5:11 of pigs was **f** on the nearby hillside. 1081
Lk 8:32 A large herd of pigs was **f** there on 1081

FEEDS (10) [FEED]

Job 40:15 with you and *which* **f on** grass like an ox. 430
Pr 15:14 but the mouth of a fool **f on** folly. 8286
Isa 44:20 *He* **f on** ashes, 8286
Hos 12: 1 Ephraim **f on** the wind; 8286
Mic 3: 5 if one **f** them, they proclaim 'peace'; 928+5966+9094
Mt 6:26 and yet your heavenly Father **f** them. 5555
Lk 12:24 no storeroom or barn; yet God **f** them. 5555
Jn 6:57 one who **f on** me will live because of me. 5592
6:58 he who **f on** this bread will live forever." 5592
Eph 5:29 but *he* **f** and cares for it, 1763

FEEL (19) [FEELING, FEELINGS, FEELS, FELT]

Ge 41:55 When all Egypt *began to* **f the famine,** 8279
Jdg 16:26 where I *can* **f** the pillars that support 4630
1Sa 16:16 and you *will* **f better."** 3201
16:23 he *would* **f better,** 3201
2Ki 9:15 Jehu said, "If this is the way you **f,** 5883
Ps 58: 9 Before your pots *can* **f** [the heat of] 1067
115: 7 but cannot **f,** feet, but they cannot walk; 4630
Pr 23:35 They beat me, but *I* don't **f** it! 3359
Isa 32: 9 you daughters *who* **f secure,** 1053
32:10 a year you *who* **f secure** will tremble; 1053
32:11 shudder, you daughters *who* **f secure!** 1053
Da 8:25 When they **f secure,** 8932
11:21 the kingdom when its people **f secure,** 8932
11:24 When the richest provinces **f secure,** 8932
Am 6: 1 and to *you who* **f secure** on Mount Samaria, 1053
Zec 1:15 with the nations that **f secure.** 8633
2Co 11:29 Who is weak, and *I do* not **f weak?** 820
Php 1: 7 It is right for me *to* **f** this way about all 5858
2Th 3:14 in order that *he may* **f ashamed.** 1956

FEELING (2) [FEEL]

Job 24:23 He may let them rest in a **f of security,** 1055
Isa 59:10 **f** *our* **way** like men without eyes. 1779

FEELINGS (2) [FEEL]

Nu 5:14 and if **f** *of* jealousy come over her husband 8120
5:30 or when **f** *of* jealousy come over a man 8120

FEELS (3) [FEEL]

Ex 23: 9 you yourselves know **how it f** to be aliens, 5883
Job 14:22 *He* **f** but *the* **pain** of his own body 3872
1Co 7:36 along in years and he **f** he ought to marry, NIG

FEET (281) [FOOT]

Ge 6:15 The ark is to be **450 f** long, 564+4395+8993
6:15 **75 f** wide and 45 feet high. 564+2822
6:15 75 feet wide and **45 f** high. 564+8993
7:20 to a depth of more than **twenty f.** 564+2822+6926
8:9 dove could find no place to set its **f** 4090+8079
18:4 and then you may all wash your **f** and rest 8079
19:2 You can wash your **f** and spend the night 8079
24:32 water for him and his men to wash their **f.** 8079
43:24 to wash their **f** and provided fodder 8079
49:10 nor the ruler's staff from between his **f,** 8079
49:33 he drew his **f** up into the bed, 8079
Ex 4:25 and touched [Moses'] **f** with it. 8079
12:11 on your **f** and your staff in your hand. 8079
24:10 Under his **f** was something like 8079
25:12 for it and fasten them to its four **f,** 7193
29:20 and on the big toes of their right **f.** 8079
30:19 and his sons are to wash their hands and **f** 8079
30:21 they shall wash their hands and **f** so 8079
37:3 for it and fastened them to its four **f,** 7193
40:31 to wash their hands and **f.** 8079
Lev 8:24 and on the big toes of their right **f.** 8079
11:42 or walks on all fours or on many **f;** 8079
Nu 11:31 the camp to about **three f** above the ground, 564
35:4 will extend out **fifteen hundred f** 547+564
35:5 **three thousand f** on the east side, 547+564
Dt 1:36 and his descendants the land *he* **set** *his* **f** 2005
3:11 and was **more than thirteen f** long 564+9596
3:11 and **six f** wide. 564+752
8:4 not wear out and your **f** did not swell 8079
22:4 **get it to its f.** 7756+7756
28:35 the soles of your **f** to the top of your head. 8079
29:5 nor did the sandals on your **f.** 8079
33:3 At your **f** they all bow down, 8079
33:24 and let him bathe his **f** in oil. 8079
Jos 3:15 and their **f** touched the water's edge, 8079
4:18 No sooner had they set their **f** on 4090+8079
9:5 on their **f** and wore old clothes. 8079
10:24 "Come here and put your **f** on the necks 8079
10:24 So they came forward and placed their **f** 8079
14:9 on which your **f** have walked will 8079
Jdg 5:27 At her **f** he sank, he fell; there he lay. 8079
5:27 At her **f** he sank, he fell; 8079
19:21 After they had washed their **f,** 8079
Ru 3:4 Then go and uncover his **f** and lie down. 5274
3:7 uncovered his **f** and lay down. 5274
3:8 and discovered a woman lying at his **f.** 5274
3:14 So she lay at his **f** until morning, 5274
1Sa 2:9 He will guard the **f** *of* his saints, 8079
14:13 using his hands and **f,** 8079
17:4 He was **over nine f** tall. 564+2256+2455+9252
25:24 She fell at his **f** and said: 8079
25:41 and wash the **f** *of* my master's servants." 8079
2Sa 3:34 your **f** were not fettered. 8079
4:4 of Saul had a son who was lame in *both* **f.** 8079
4:12 They cut off their hands and **f** and hung 8079
9:3 he is crippled in *both* **f.**" 8079
9:13 and he was crippled in both **f.** 8079
11:8 "Go down to your house and wash your **f.**" 8079
19:24 of his **f** or trimmed his mustache 8079
22:10 dark clouds were under his **f.** 8079
22:34 He makes my **f** like the feet of a deer; 8079
22:34 He makes my feet like the **f** of a deer; NIH
22:39 they fell beneath my **f.** 8079
22:40 you made my adversaries bow **at** my **f.** 9393
1Ki 2:5 around his waist and the sandals on his **f.** 8079
5:3 the LORD put his enemies under his **f.** 4090+8079
15:23 however, his **f** became diseased. 8079
2Ki 4:27 she took hold of his **f.** 8079
4:37 fell at his **f** and bowed to the ground. 8079
9:35 her **f** and her hands. 8079
13:21 the man came to life and stood up on his **f.** 8079
14:13 section **about six hundred f** long. 564+752+4395
19:24 With the soles of my **f** I have dried up all 7193
21:8 the **f** *of* the Israelites wander from 8079
25:17 Each pillar was **twenty-seven f** high. 564+6926+9046
25:17 **four and a half f** high 564+8993
1Ch 11:23 **seven and a half f** tall. 564+928+2021+2822
28:2 King David rose to his **f** and said: 8079
2Ch 3:13 They stood on their **f,** facing the main hall. 8079
16:12 with a disease in his **f.** 8079
25:23 section **about six hundred f** long. 564+752+4395
33:8 not again make the **f** *of* the Israelites leave 8079
Ezr 6:3 **ninety f** high and ninety feet wide, 10039+10749
6:3 ninety feet high and **ninety f** wide, 10039+10749
Ne 9:21 nor did their **f** become swollen. 8079
Est 5:14 "Have a gallows built, **seventy-five f** high, 564+2822
7:9 "A gallows **seventy-five f** high stands 564+2822
8:3 falling at his **f** and weeping. 8079
Job 2:7 with painful sores from the soles of his **f** to 8079
9:13 the cohorts of Rahab cowered **at** his **f.** 9393
12:5 as the fate of those whose **f** are slipping. 8079
13:27 You fasten my **f** in shackles; 8079
13:27 by putting marks on the soles of my **f.** 8079
18:8 His **f** thrust him into a net and he wanders 8079
23:11 My **f** have closely followed his steps; 8079
29:8 and the old men rose **to** *their* **f;** 6641
29:15 I was eyes to the blind and **f** to the lame. 8079
30:12 they lay snares for my **f,** 8079
33:11 He fastens my **f** in shackles; 8079
Ps 8:6 you put everything under his **f:** 8079
9:15 **f** are caught in the net they have hidden. 8079
17:5 my **f** have not slipped. 7193
18:9 dark clouds were under his **f.** 8079
18:33 He makes my **f** like the feet of a deer; 8079
18:33 He makes my feet like the **f** of a deer; NIH
18:38 they fell beneath my **f.** 8079
18:39 you made my adversaries bow **at** my **f.** 9393
22:16 they have pierced my hands and my **f.** 8079
25:15 only he will release my **f** from the snare. 8079
26:12 My **f** stand on level ground; 8079
31:8 over to the enemy but have set my **f** in 8079
37:31 his **f** do not slip. 892
40:2 he set my **f** on a rock and gave me 8079
44:18 our **f** had not strayed from your path. 892
45:5 let the nations fall beneath your **f.** NIH
47:3 peoples under our **f.** 8079
56:13 from death and my **f** from stumbling, 8079
57:6 They spread a net for my **f**— 7193
58:10 when they bathe their **f** in the blood of 7193
66:9 he has preserved our lives and kept our **f** 8079
68:23 that you may plunge your **f** in the blood 8079
73:2 But as for me, my **f** had almost slipped; 8079
105:18 They bruised his **f** with shackles, 8079
110:1 a footstool for your **f.**" 8079
115:7 but cannot feel, **f,** but they cannot walk; 8079
116:8 my eyes from tears, my **f** from stumbling, 8079
119:101 I have kept my **f** from every evil path so 8079
119:105 Your word is a lamp to my **f** and a light 8079
122:2 Our **f** are standing in your gates, 8079
140:4 of violence who plan to trip my **f.** 7193
Pr 1:16 for their **f** rush into sin, 8079
4:26 for your **f** and take only ways that are firm. 8079
5:5 Her **f** go down to death; 8079
6:13 with his **f** and motions with his fingers, 8079
6:18 **f** that are quick to rush into evil, 8079
6:28 on hot coals without his **f** being scorched? 8079
7:11 her **f** never stay at home; 8079
26:6 Like cutting off one's **f** 8079
29:5 a net for his **f.** 7193
SS 5:3 I have washed my **f**— 8079
7:1 How beautiful your sandaled **f,** 7193
Isa 6:2 with two they covered their **f,** 8079
20:2 and the sandals from your **f.**" 8079
23:7 whose **f** have taken her to settle 8079
26:6 **F** trample it down— 8079
26:6 the **f** *of* the oppressed, 8079
37:25 With the soles of my **f** I have dried up all 7193
41:3 by a path his **f** have not traveled before. 8079
49:23 they will lick the dust at your **f.** 8079
52:7 How beautiful on the mountains are the **f** 8079
58:13 "If you keep your **f** from breaking 8079
59:7 Their **f** rush into sin; 8079
60:13 and I will glorify the place of my **f.** 8079
60:14 will bow down at your **f** and 4090+8079
Jer 2:25 until your **f** are bare and your throat is dry. 8079
13:16 before your **f** stumble on 8079
14:10 they do not restrain their **f.** 8079
18:22 and have hidden snares for my **f.** 8079
38:22 Your **f** are sunk in the mud; 8079
La 1:13 a net for my **f** and turned me back. 8079
Eze 1:7 their **f** were like those of a calf 4090+8079
2:1 stand up on your **f** and I will speak to you." 8079
2:2 into me and raised me to my **f,** 8079
3:24 Spirit came into me and raised me to my **f.** 8079
6:11 and stamp your **f** and cry out "Alas!" 8079
24:17 and your sandals on your **f;** 8079
24:23 on your heads and your sandals on your **f.** 8079
25:6 and stamped your **f,** 8079
32:2 with your **f** and muddying the streams. 8079
34:18 the rest of your pasture with your **f?** 8079
34:18 also muddy the rest with your **f?** 8079
34:19 and drink what you have muddied with your **f?** 8079
37:10 they came to life and stood up on their **f**— 8079
43:7 and the place for the soles of my **f.** 8079
Da 2:33 its **f** partly of iron and partly of baked clay. 10655
2:34 on its **f** of iron and clay and smashed them. 10655
2:41 as you saw that the **f** and toes were partly 10655
3:1 **ninety f** high and nine feet wide, 10039+10749
3:1 ninety feet high and **nine f** wide, 10039+10747
3:24 King Nebuchadnezzar **leaped to** *his* **f** 10624
7:4 from the ground so that it stood on *two* **f** 10655
8:18 Then he touched me and raised me to my **f.** 6642
Na 1:3 and clouds are the dust of his **f.** 8079
1:15 the **f** *of* one who brings good news, 8079
Hab 3:19 he makes my **f** like the feet of a deer, 8079
3:19 he makes my feet like the **f** of a deer, NIH
Zec 5:2 **thirty f** long and fifteen feet wide." 564+928+2021+6929
5:2 thirty feet long and **fifteen f** wide." 564+928+2021+6924
14:4 On that day his **f** will stand on the Mount 8079
14:12 while they are still standing on their **f,** 8079
Mal 4:3 they will be ashes under the soles of your **f** 8079
Mt 7:6 they may trample them under their **f,** *4546*
10:14 shake the dust off your **f** when you leave *4546*
15:30 and laid them at his **f;** and he healed them. *4546*
18:8 or crippled than to have two hands or two **f** *4546*
22:44 until I put your enemies under your **f.**" ' *4546*
28:9 clasped his **f** and worshiped him. *4546*
Mk 5:4 and broke the **irons on** his **f.** *4267*
5:22 he fell at his **f** *4546*
5:33 came and **fell at** his **f** and, *4700*
6:11 shake the dust off your **f** when you leave, *4546*
7:25 by an evil spirit came and fell at his **f.** *4546*
9:27 by the hand and lifted him to his **f,** *NIG*
9:45 to enter life crippled than to have two **f** and *4546*
10:49 **On your f!** He's calling you." *1586*
10:50 he **jumped to his f** and came to Jesus. *403*
12:36 until I put your enemies under your **f.**" ' *4546*
Lk 1:79 to guide our **f** into the path of peace." *4546*
7:38 as she stood behind him at his **f** weeping, *4546*
7:38 she began to wet his **f** with her tears. *4546*
7:44 You did not give me any water for my **f,** *4546*
7:44 but she wet my **f** with her tears *4546*
7:45 has not stopped kissing my **f.** *4546*
7:46 but she has poured perfume on my **f.** *4546*
8:28 he cried out and **fell at** his **f,** *4700*
8:35 at Jesus' **f,** dressed and in his right mind; *4546*
8:41 came and fell at Jesus' **f,** *4546*
8:47 came trembling and **fell at** his **f.** *4700*
9:5 shake the dust off your **f** *4546*
10:11 that sticks to our **f** we wipe off against you. *4546*
10:39 at the Lord's **f** listening to what he said. *4546*
15:22 a ring on his finger and sandals on his **f.** *4546*
17:16 at Jesus' **f** and thanked him— *4546*
20:43 a footstool *for* your **f.**" ' *4546*
24:39 Look at my hands and my **f.** *4546*
24:40 he showed them his hands and **f.** *4546*
Jn 11:2 on the Lord and wiped his **f** with her hair. *4546*
11:32 she fell at his **f** and said, "Lord, *4546*
11:44 his hands and **f** wrapped with strips *4546*
12:3 she poured it on Jesus' **f** and wiped his feet *4546*
12:3 she poured it on Jesus' feet and wiped his **f** *4546*
13:5 a basin and began to wash his disciples' **f,** *4546*
13:6 "Lord, are you going to wash my **f?**" *4546*
13:8 said Peter, "you shall never wash my **f.**" *4546*
13:9 "not just my **f** but my hands and my head *4546*
13:10 who has had a bath needs only to wash his **f** *4546*
13:12 When he had finished washing their **f,** *4546*
13:14 have washed your **f,** *4546*
13:14 you also should wash one another's **f.** *4546*
Ac 2:35 a footstool *for* your **f.**" ' *4546*
3:7 the man's **f** and ankles became strong. *1000*
3:8 *He* jumped *to his* **f** and began to walk. *2705*
4:35 and put it at the apostles' **f,** *4546*
4:37 the money and put it at the apostles' **f.** *4546*
5:2 the rest and put it at the apostles' **f.** *4546*
5:9 **f** of the men who buried your husband are at the door, *4546*
5:10 At that moment she fell down at his **f** *4546*
7:58 the witnesses laid their clothes at the **f** of *4546*
9:41 **helped** her to **her f.** *482*
10:25 Cornelius met him and fell at his **f** *4546*
13:51 the dust from their **f** in protest against them *4546*
14:8 In Lystra there sat a man crippled *in* his **f,** *4546*
14:10 "Stand up on your **f!**" *4546*
16:24 in the inner cell and fastened their **f** in *4546*
21:11 tied his own hands and **f** with it and said, *4546*
26:16 'Now get up and stand on your **f.** *4546*
27:28 **a hundred and twenty f deep.** *1633+3976*
27:28 and found it was **ninety f deep.** *1278+3976*
Ro 3:15 "Their **f** are swift to shed blood; *4546*
10:15 the **f** of those who bring good news!" *4546*
16:20 of peace will soon crush Satan under your **f.** *4546*
1Co 12:21 And the head cannot say *to* the **f,** *4546*
15:25 until he has put all his enemies under his **f.** *4546*
15:27 For he "has put everything under his **f.**" *4546*
Eph 1:22 under his **f** and appointed him to be head *4546*
6:15 and with your **f** fitted with the readiness *4546*
1Ti 5:10 washing the **f** of the saints, *4546*
Heb 1:13 a footstool *for* your **f**"? *4546*
2:8 and put everything under his **f.**" *4546*
12:13 "Make level paths *for* your **f,**" *4546*
Jas 2:3 or "Sit on the floor by my **f,**" *5711*
Rev 1:13 **a robe reaching down to** his **f** *4468*
1:15 His **f** were like bronze glowing in *4546*
1:17 I fell at his **f** as though dead. *4546*
2:18 and whose **f** are like burnished bronze. *4546*
3:9 and fall down at your **f** and acknowledge *4546*
11:11 and they stood on their **f,** *4546*
12:1 with the sun, with the moon under her **f** *4546*
13:2 but had **f** like those of a bear and a mouth *4546*
19:10 At this I fell at his **f** to worship him. *4546*
22:8 I fell down to worship at the **f** of *4546*

FEIGN, FEIGNED (Anglicized, KJV) See PRETEND, PRETENDED

FELIX (10)

Ac 23:24 that he may be taken safely to Governor **F.**" *5772*
23:26 *To* His Excellency, Governor **F:** Greetings. *5772*
24:2 Tertullus presented his case before **F:** *NIG*
24:3 most excellent **F,** we acknowledge this *5772*
24:22 Then **F,** who was well acquainted with *5772*
24:24 Several days later **F** came *5772*
24:25 **F** was afraid and said, *5772*
24:27 **F** was succeeded by Porcius Festus, *5772*
24:27 **F** wanted to grant a favor to the Jews, *5772*
25:14 a man here whom **F** left as a prisoner. *5772*

FELL (186) [FALL]

Ge 7:12 And rain **f** on the earth forty days 2118
14:10 *of the men* **f** into them and the rest fled to 5877
15:12 Abram **f** *into* a deep sleep, 5877
17:3 Abram **f** facedown, and God said to him, 5877
17:17 Abraham **f** facedown; 5877
35:5 and the terror of God **f** upon the towns all 2118
41:5 *He* **f asleep** again and had a second dream: 3822
Ex 9:24 hail **f** and lightning flashed back and forth. 2118
Lev 9:24 they shouted for joy and **f** facedown. 5877
Nu 3:4 **f dead** before the LORD when they made 4637
14:5 Then Moses and Aaron **f** facedown in front 5877
16:4 When Moses heard this, *he* **f** facedown. 5877

Nu 16:22 and Aaron **f** facedown and cried out, 5877
16:45 And *they* **f** facedown. 5877
20: 3 when our brothers **f dead** before 1588
20: 6 to the Tent of Meeting and **f** facedown, 5877
22:31 he bowed low and **f facedown.** 678+2556+4200
Dt 9:18 Then once again *I* **f prostrate** before 5877
19: 5 and as he swings his ax to **f** a tree, 4162
Jos 5:14 Then Joshua **f** facedown to the ground 5877
7: 6 and **f** facedown to the ground before 5877
8:25 Twelve thousand men and women **f** 5877
21:10 because the first lot **f** to them): 2118
22:17 plague **f** on the community of the LORD! 2118
Jdg 4:16 All the troops of Sisera **f** by the sword; 5877
5:27 At her feet he sank, *he* **f**; there he lay. 5877
5:27 At her feet he sank, *he* **f**; 5877
5:27 where he sank, there *he* **f**—dead. 5877
8:11 of Nobah and Jogbehah and **f upon** 5782
9:40 and many **f** wounded in the flight— 5877
13:20 Manoah and his wife **f** with their faces to 5877
16: 4 *he* **f in love with** a woman in the Valley 170
19:26 **f down** *at* the door and lay there 5877
20:31 about thirty men **f** in the open field and on NIH
20:44 Eighteen thousand Benjamites **f**, 5877
20:46 On that day twenty-five thousand Benjamite swordsmen **f**, 5877
1Sa 4:18 Eli **f** backward off his chair by the side of 5877
11: 7 the terror of the LORD **f** on the people, 5877
14:13 The Philistines **f** before Jonathan, 5877
17:49 and *he* **f** facedown on the ground. 5877
25:24 *She* **f** at his feet and said: 5877
28:20 Immediately Saul **f** full length on 5877
31: 1 and *many* **f** slain on Mount Gilboa. 5877
31: 4 so Saul took his own sword and **f** on it. 5877
31: 5 he too **f** on his sword and died with him. 5877
2Sa 1: 2 *he* **f** to the ground to pay him honor. 5877
1: 4 Many of them **f** and died. 5877
2:16 and *they* **f down** together. 5877
2:23 *He* **f** there and died on the spot. 5877
3:34 *You* **f** as one falls before wicked men." 5877
4: 4 *he* **f** and became crippled. 5877
11:17 some of the men in David's army **f**; 5877
13: 1 Amnon son of David **f in love with** 170
14: 4 *she* **f** with her face to the ground 5877
14:22 Joab **f** with his face to the ground 5877
19:18 *he* **f prostrate** before the king 5877
21: 9 All seven of them **f** together; 5877
21:22 *they* **f** at the hands of David and his men. 5877
22:39 *they* **f** beneath my feet. 5877
1Ki 18:38 the LORD **f** and burned up the sacrifice, 5877
18:39 *they* **f** prostrate and cried, "The LORD— 5877
19: 5 he lay down under the tree and **f asleep.** 3822
2Ki 1:10 Then fire **f** from heaven and consumed 3718
1:12 of God **f** from heaven and consumed him 3718
1:13 up and **f** on his knees before Elijah. 4156
4:37 **f** at his feet and bowed to the ground. 5877
6: 5 the iron axhead **f** into the water. 5877
1Ch 5:22 and many others **f** slain, 5877
10: 1 and *many* **f** slain on Mount Gilboa. 5877
10: 4 so Saul took his own sword and **f** on it. 5877
10: 5 he too **f** on his sword and died. 5877
20: 8 *they* **f** at the hands of David and his men. 5877
21:14 and seventy thousand men of Israel **f dead.** 5877
21:16 clothed in sackcloth, **f** facedown. 5877
24: 7 The first lot **f** to Jehoiarib, 3655
25: 9 **f** to Joseph, his sons and relatives, 3655
26:14 The lot for the East Gate **f** to Shelemiah. 5877
26:14 and the lot for the North Gate **f** *to* him. 3655
26:15 lot for the South Gate **f** to Obed-Edom, NIH
26:15 and the lot for the storehouse **f** to his sons. NIH
26:16 on the upper road **f** to Shuppim and Hosah. NIH
29:20 they bowed low and **f prostrate** before 2556
2Ch 14:13 of Cushites **f** that they could not recover; 5877
17:10 of the LORD **f** on all the kingdoms of 2118
20:18 of Judah and Jerusalem **f down** in worship 5877
Ezr 9: 5 and **f** on my knees 4156
Ne 13:19 When **evening shadows f** *on* the gates 7511
Est 3: 7 And the lot **f** on the twelfth month, NIH
Job 1:16 "The fire of God **f** from the sky and burned 5877
1:20 Then *he* **f** to the ground in worship 5877
29:22 my words **f gently** on their ears. 5752
Ps 18:38 *they* **f** beneath my feet. 5877
105:44 *they* **f heir** *to* what others had toiled for— 3769
137: 7 the Edomites did on the day Jerusalem **f**. NIH
La 1: 7 When her people **f** into enemy hands, 5877
Eze 1:28 When I saw it, *I* **f** facedown, 5877
3:23 and *I* **f** facedown. 5877
9: 8 *I* **f** facedown, crying out, "Ah, 5877
11:13 *I* **f** facedown and cried out in a loud voice, 5877
31:12 Its boughs **f** on the mountains and in all 5877
39:23 and they all **f** by the sword. 5877
43: 3 and *I* **f** facedown. 5877
44: 4 and *I* **f** facedown. 5877
Da 2:46 Then King Nebuchadnezzar **f** prostrate 10484
3: 7 nations and men of every language **f down** 10484
3:23 firmly tied, **f** into the blazing furnace. 10484
7:20 before which three of *them* **f**— 10484
8:17 I was terrified and **f** prostrate. 5877
10: 9 *I* **f into a deep sleep,** 8101
Jnh 1: 5 he lay down and **f into a deep sleep.** 8101
1: 7 They cast lots and the lot **f** on Jonah. 5877
Mt 7:27 and *it* **f** with a great crash." *4406*
13: 4 some **f** along the path, *4406*
13: 5 Some **f** on rocky places, *4406*
13: 7 Other seed **f** among thorns, *4406*
13: 8 Still other seed **f** on good soil, *4406*
13:20 The one who **received** the **seed that f** *5062*
13:22 The one who **received** the **seed that f** *5062*
Mt 13:23 the one who **received** the **seed that f** *5062*
17: 6 *they* **f** facedown to the ground, terrified. *4406*
18:26 "The servant **f** on his knees before him. *4406*
18:29 "His fellow servant **f** to his knees *4406*
25: 5 and they all became drowsy and **f asleep.** *2761*
26:39 **f** with his face **to the ground** *4406*
Mk 3:11 *they* **f down before** him and cried out, *4700*
4: 4 some **f** along the path, *4406*
4: 5 Some **f** on rocky places, *4406*
4: 7 Other seed **f** among thorns, *4406*
4: 8 Still other seed **f** on good soil. *4406*
5: 6 **f on** his **knees in front of** *4686*
5:22 *he* **f** at his feet *4406*
5:33 came and **f at** his **feet** and, *4700*
7:25 by an evil spirit came and **f** at his feet. *4700*
9:20 He **f** to the ground and rolled around, *4406*
10:17 **f on** his **knees before** *1206*
10:22 At this the man's **face f.** *5145*
14:35 *he* **f** to the ground and prayed that *4406*
Lk 5: 8 *he* **f at** Jesus' knees and said, *4700*
5:12 he **f** with his face to the ground *4406*
8: 5 some **f** along the path; *4406*
8: 6 Some **f** on rock, and when it came up, *2928*
8: 7 Other seed **f** among thorns, *4406*
8: 8 Still other seed **f** on good soil. *4406*
8:14 The seed that **f** among thorns stands *4406*
8:23 As they sailed, *he* **f asleep.** *934*
8:28 he cried out and **f at** his **feet,** *4700*
8:41 came and **f** at Jesus' feet, *4406*
8:47 came trembling and **f at** his **feet.** *4700*
10:30 **f into the hands of** robbers. *4346*
10:36 a neighbor to the man who **f** into the hands *1860*
13: 4 when the tower in Siloam **f** on them— *4406*
16:21 to eat what **f** from the rich man's table. *4406*
Jn 11:32 *she* **f** at his feet and said, "Lord, *4406*
18: 6 they drew back and **f** to the ground. *4406*
Ac 1:18 there *he* **f headlong,** *1181+4568*
1:26 they cast lots, and the lot **f** to Matthias; *4406*
5: 5 he **f down** and died. *4406*
5:10 At that moment *she* **f down** at his feet *4406*
7:60 Then he **f on** his knees and cried out, *5502*
7:60 When he had said this, *he* **f asleep.** *3121*
9: 4 He **f** to the ground and heard a voice say *4406*
9:18 something like scales **f** from Saul's eyes, *674*
10:10 he **f into a trance.** *1181+1749+2093*
10:25 Cornelius met him and **f** at his feet *4406*
12: 7 he said, and the chains **f off** Peter's wrists. *1738*
13:36 in his own generation, *he* **f asleep;** *3121*
16:29 in and **f** trembling **before** Paul and Silas. *4700*
19:35 **image, which f from heaven?** *1479*
20: 9 *he* **f** to the ground from the third story *4406*
22: 7 *I* **f** to the ground and heard a voice say *4406*
22:17 I **f** into a trance *1181*
26:14 We all **f** to the ground, *2928*
Ro 11:22 sternness to those who **f**, *4406*
Heb 3:17 whose bodies **f** in the desert? *4406*
11:30 By faith the walls of Jericho **f**, *4406*
Rev 1:17 *I* **f** at his feet as though dead. *4406*
5: 8 and the twenty-four elders **f down** before *4406*
5:14 and the elders **f down** and worshiped. *4406*
6:13 and the stars in the sky **f** to earth, *4406*
7:11 *They* **f down** on their faces before *4406*
8:10 **f** from the sky on a third of the rivers and *4406*
11:16 **f** on their faces and worshiped God, *4406*
16:21 about a hundred pounds each **f** upon men. *2849*
19: 4 and the four living creatures **f down** *4406*
19:10 At this *I* **f** at his feet to worship him. *4406*
22: 8 *I* **f down** to worship at the feet of *4406*

FELLED (2) [FALL]

Isa 9:10 the fig trees *have* **been f**, 1548
10:33 The lofty trees *will* **be f**, 1548

FELLER (KJV) See WOODSMAN

FELLING (1) [FALL]

1Ki 5: 6 that we have no one so skilled in **f** timber 4162

FELLOW (91) [FELLOW'S, FELLOWMAN, FELLOWS, FELLOWSHIP]

Ge 9: 5 an accounting for the life of his *f* **man.** AIT
19: 9 they said, "This **f** came here as an alien, 285[S]
34:20 their city to speak to their **f townsmen.** 408+6551
Ex 2:13 "Why are you hitting your **f** Hebrew?" 8276
32: 1 As for this **f** Moses who brought us up out 408
32:23 As for this **f** Moses who brought us up out 408
Lev 25:46 not rule over your **f** Israelites ruthlessly. 278
Nu 16:10 He has brought you and all your **f** Levites 278
18: 2 Bring your **f** Levites 278
18: 6 I myself have selected your **f** Levites from 278
Dt 15: 2 the loan he has made to his **f Israelite.** 8276
15: 2 not require payment from his **f Israelite** 8276
15:12 If a **f** Hebrew, a man or a woman, 278
18: 7 like all his **f** Levites who serve there in 278
Jdg 20:13 not listen to their **f** Israelites. 278
Ru 3:11 All my **f townsmen** know that you 6639+9133
1Sa 10:27 "How can **this** *f* save us?" AIT
21:15 that you have to bring **this** *f* here to carry AIT
2Sa 6:20 of his servants as any **vulgar** *f* would!" AIT
1Ki 22:27 Put **this** *f* in prison and give him nothing AIT
2Ki 5: 7 Why does **this** *f* send someone to me to AIT
9:11 When Jehu went out to his **f officers,** 123+6269
23: 9 with their **f** priests. 278
1Ch 6:48 Their **f** Levites were assigned to all 278
1Ch 9:19 and his **f** gatekeepers from his family 278
15:12 you and your **f Levites** are 278
16:39 David left Zadok the priest and his **f** priests 278
26:20 Their **f** Levites were in charge of 278
2Ch 18:26 Put **this** *f* in prison and give him nothing AIT
19:10 from your **f countrymen** who live in 278
28:11 Send back your **f countrymen** you have 278
28:15 to their **f countrymen** at Jericho, 278
31:15 distributing to their **f** priests according 278
35: 5 of the families of your **f countrymen,** 278
35: 6 [the lambs] for your **f countrymen,** 278
35:15 because their **f** Levites made 278
Ezr 3: 2 and his **f** priests and Zerubbabel son 278
6: 6 their **f** officials of that province, 10360
Ne 3: 1 and his **f** priests went to work and rebuilt 278
Est 10: 3 held in high esteem by his many **f Jews,** 278
Job 30: 5 They were banished from their **f men,** 1569
Jer 34: 9 no one was to hold a **f** Jew in bondage. 278
34:14 of you must free any **f** Hebrew who has sold himself 278
34:17 for your **f** countrymen. 278
Mt 9: 3 **"This** *f* is blaspheming!" *AIT*
12:24 that **this** *f* drives out demons." *AIT*
18:28 *of* his **f servants** who owed him *5281*
18:29 "His **f servant** fell to his knees *5281*
18:33 on your **f servant** just as I had on you?' *5281*
24:49 to beat his **f servants** and to eat and drink *5281*
26:61 and declared, **"This** *f* said, 'I am able *AIT*
26:71 **"This** *f* was with Jesus of Nazareth." *AIT*
Mk 2: 7 "Why does **this** *f* talk like that? *AIT*
14:69 **"This** *f* is one of them." *AIT*
Lk 5:21 "Who is **this** *f* who speaks blasphemy? *AIT*
14:10 in the presence of all your **f guests.** *5263*
14:30 'This **f** began to build and was not able *476*
22:59 "Certainly **this** *f* was with him, *AIT*
Jn 5:12 "Who is this **f** who told you to pick it up *476*
9:29 but as for **this** *f*, *AIT*
Ac 2:14 **"F** Jews and all of you who live *NIG*
6:13 "This **f** never stops speaking *476*
7:23 he decided to visit his **f** Israelites. *81*
7:40 for **this** *f* Moses who led us out of Egypt— *AIT*
19:26 and hear how **this** *f* Paul has convinced *AIT*
19:38 Demetrius and **his f** craftsmen have a grievance *899+3836+5250*
Ro 16: 3 my **f workers** in Christ Jesus. *5301*
16: 9 Greet Urbanus, our **f worker** in Christ, *5301*
16:21 Timothy, my **f worker,** *5301*
1Co 3: 9 For we are God's **f workers;** *5301*
2Co 6: 1 As God's **f workers** we urge you not *5300*
8:23 he is my partner and **f worker** among you; *5301*
12:16 Yet, **crafty** *f* that I am, *AIT*
Eph 2:19 but **f citizens with** God's people *5232*
Php 2:25 my brother, **f worker** and fellow soldier, *5301*
2:25 my brother, fellow worker and **f soldier,** *5369*
4: 3 with Clement and the rest *of* my **f workers,** *5301*
Col 1: 7 Epaphras, our dear **f servant,** *5281*
4: 7 a faithful minister and **f servant** in *5281*
4:10 My **f prisoner** Aristarchus sends you his greetings, *5257*
4:11 the only Jews among my **f workers** for *5301*
1Th 3: 2 and God's **f worker** in spreading the gospel *5301*
Phm 1: 1 *To* Philemon our dear friend and **f worker,** *5301*
1: 2 *to* Archippus our **f soldier** and to *5369*
1:23 Epaphras, my **f prisoner** in Christ Jesus, *5257*
1:24 Demas and Luke, my **f workers.** *5301*
Heb 13: 3 in prison as if you were their **f prisoners,** *5279*
1Pe 5: 1 I appeal as a **f elder,** *5236*
Rev 6:11 of their **f servants** and brothers who were *5281*
19:10 I am a **f servant with** you and with *5281*
22: 9 I am a **f servant with** you and with *5281*

FELLOW'S (2) [FELLOW]

1Sa 25:21 all my watching over **this f** property 2296+4200[S]
Jn 9:28 "You are **this** *f* disciple! *AIT*

FELLOWCITIZENS (KJV) See FELLOW CITIZEN

FELLOWLABOURER (KJV) See FELLOW WORKERS

FELLOWMAN (3) [FELLOW, MAN]

Ps 15: 3 and casts no slur on his **f**, 7940
Mic 2: 2 a **f** of his inheritance. 408
Ro 13: 8 for he who loves **his f** has fulfilled the law. *2283+3836[S]*

FELLOWPRISONER (KJV) See FELLOW PRISONER

FELLOWS (3) [FELLOW]

1Sa 14: 6 to the outpost of those **uncircumcised** *f*. AIT
31: 4 or these **uncircumcised** *f* will come AIT
1Ch 10: 4 or these **uncircumcised** *f* will come AIT

FELLOWSERVANT (KJV) See FELLOW SERVANT

FELLOWSHIP (99) [FELLOW]

Ex 20:24 on it your burnt offerings and **f offerings,** 8968

Ex 24: 5 and sacrificed young bulls as **f** offerings to 8968
29:28 to the LORD from their **f** offerings. 8968
32: 6 and presented **f offerings.** 8968
Lev 3: 1 " 'If someone's offering is a **f** offering, 8968
3: 3 From the **f** offering he is to bring 8968
3: 6 an animal from the flock as a **f** offering to 8968
3: 9 From the **f** offering he is to bring 8968
4:10 from the ox sacrificed as a **f offering.** 8968
4:26 as he burned the fat of the **f** offering. 8968
4:31 as the fat is removed from the **f** offering, 8968
4:35 from the lamb of the **f** offering, 8968
6:12 the fire and burn the fat of the **f offerings** 8968
7:11 for the **f** offering a person may present to 8968
7:13 with his **f** offering of thanksgiving he is 8968
7:14 the blood of the **f offerings.** 8968
7:15 of his **f** offering of thanksgiving must 8968
7:18 of the **f** offering is eaten on the third day, 8968
7:20 of the **f** offering belonging to the LORD, 8968
7:21 of the **f** offering belonging to the LORD, 8968
7:29 a **f** offering to the LORD is to bring part 8968
7:32 to give the right thigh of your **f** offerings to 8968
7:33 of the **f offering** shall have the right thigh 8968
7:34 From the **f** offerings of the Israelites, 8968
7:37 the ordination offering and the **f** offering, 8968
9: 4 a **f offering** to sacrifice before the LORD, 8968
9:18 and the ram as the **f** offering for the people. 8968
9:22 the burnt offering and the **f offering,** 8968
10:14 as your share of the Israelites' **f** offerings. 8968
17: 5 and sacrifice them as **f** offerings. 8968
19: 5 " 'When you sacrifice a **f** offering to 8968
22:21 or flock a **f** offering to the LORD to fulfill 8968
23:19 each a year old, for a **f** offering. 8968
Nu 6:14 a ram without defect for a **f offering,** 8968
6:17 and is to sacrifice the ram as a **f** offering to 8968
6:18 that is under the sacrifice of the **f offering.** 8968
7:17 to be sacrificed as a **f offering.** 8968
7:23 to be sacrificed as a **f offering.** 8968
7:29 to be sacrificed as a **f offering.** 8968
7:35 to be sacrificed as a **f offering.** 8968
7:41 to be sacrificed as a **f offering.** 8968
7:47 to be sacrificed as a **f offering.** 8968
7:53 to be sacrificed as a **f offering.** 8968
7:59 to be sacrificed as a **f offering.** 8968
7:65 to be sacrificed as a **f offering.** 8968
7:71 to be sacrificed as a **f offering.** 8968
7:77 to be sacrificed as a **f offering.** 8968
7:83 to be sacrificed as a **f offering.** 8968
7:88 the **f offering** came to twenty-four oxen, 8968
10:10 over your burnt offerings and **f** offerings, 8968
15: 8 special vow or a **f offering** to the LORD, 8968
29:39 drink offerings and **f offerings.' "** 8968
Dt 27: 7 Sacrifice **f offerings** there, 8968
Jos 8:31 and sacrificed **f offerings.** 8968
22:23 or to sacrifice **f** offerings on it, 8968
22:27 sacrifices and **f offerings.** 8968
Jdg 20:26 and **f offerings** to the LORD. 8968
21: 4 presented burnt offerings and **f offerings.** 8968
1Sa 10: 8 to sacrifice burnt offerings and **f** offerings, 8968
11:15 There they sacrificed **f** offerings before 8968
13: 9 the burnt offering and the **f offerings."** 8968
2Sa 6:17 and **f offerings** before the LORD. 8968
6:18 the burnt offerings and **f offerings,** 8968
24:25 sacrificed burnt offerings and **f offerings.** 8968
1Ki 3:15 sacrificed burnt offerings and **f offerings.** 8968
8:63 Solomon offered a sacrifice of **f** offerings 8968
8:64 and the fat of the **f offerings,** 8968
8:64 and the fat of the **f offerings.** 8968
9:25 and **f offerings** on the altar he had built for 8968
2Ki 16:13 and sprinkled the blood of his **f offerings** 8968
1Ch 16: 1 and **f offerings** before God. 8968
16: 2 the burnt offerings and **f offerings,** 8968
21:26 sacrificed burnt offerings and **f offerings.** 8968
2Ch 7: 7 and the fat of the **f offerings,** 8968
29:35 together with the fat of the **f offerings** and 8968
30:22 and offered **f** offerings and praised 8968
31: 2 to offer burnt offerings and **f offerings,** 8968
33:16 of the LORD and sacrificed **f** offerings 8968
Ps 55:14 with whom I once enjoyed sweet **f** 6051
Pr 7:14 "I have **f** offerings at home; 8968
Eze 43:27 and **f offerings** on the altar. 8968
45:15 and **f offerings** to make atonement for 8968
45:17 and **f offerings** to make atonement for 8968
46: 2 and his **f offerings.** 8968
46:12 whether a burnt offering or **f offerings—** 8968
46:12 or his **f offerings** as he does on 8968
Am 5:22 Though you bring choice **f offerings,** 8968
Ac 2:42 to the apostles' teaching and to the **f,** *3126*
1Co 1: 9 into **f** with his Son Jesus Christ our Lord, *3126*
5: 2 with grief and have put out of your **f** *3545*
2Co 6:14 Or what **f** can light have with darkness? *3126*
13:14 and the **f** of the Holy Spirit be with you all. *3126*
Gal 2: 9 *of* **f** when they recognized the grace given *3126*
Php 2: 1 if any **f** with the Spirit, *3126*
3:10 of his resurrection and the **f of sharing** *3126*
1Jn 1: 3 so that you also may have **f** with us. *3126*
1: 3 And our **f** is with the Father and *3126*
1: 6 If we claim to have **f** with him yet walk in *3126*
1: 7 we have **f** with one another, *3126*

FELLOWSOLDIER (KJV) See FELLOW SOLDIER

FELLOWWORKERS (KJV) See FELLOW WORKERS

FELT (13) [FEEL]

Ge 2:25 both naked, and *they* **f** no **shame.** 1017
Ex 2: 6 He was crying, and *she* **f sorry** for him. 2798
10:21 darkness *that can be* **f."** 5491
1Sa 13:12 So *I* **f compelled** to offer 706
2Ki 8:11 with a fixed gaze until Hazael **f ashamed.** 1017
Ps 30: 6 I **f secure,** I said, "I will never be shaken." 8930
Jer 5: 3 You struck them, but *they* **f** no **pain;** 2655
22:21 I warned you when you **f secure,** 8932
Na 3:19 for who *has* not **f** your endless cruelty? 6296
Mk 5:29 and *she* **f** in her body that she was freed *1182*
2Co 1: 9 in our hearts we **f** the sentence of death. *2400*
Heb 10: 2 and would no longer have **f guilty** *5287*
Jude 1: 3 I **f** I had to write and urge you to contend *2400*

FEMALE (37) [FEMALES]

Ge 1:27 male and **f** he created them. 5922
5: 2 He created them male and **f** 5922
6:19 male and **f,** to keep them alive with you. 5922
7: 3 and **f,** to keep their various kinds alive 5922
7: 9 and **f,** came to Noah and entered the ark, 5922
7:16 were male and **f** of every living thing, 5922
12:16 male and **f** donkeys, 912
20:14 and **f** slaves and gave them to Abraham, 9148
30:35 and all the speckled or **spotted** *f* goats AIT
32:14 two hundred **f** goats NIH
32:15 thirty **f** camels with their young, 3567
32:15 twenty **f donkeys** and ten male donkeys. 912
45:23 and ten **f donkeys** loaded with grain 912
Ex 21:20 a man beats his male or **f** slave with a rod 563
21:32 If the bull gores a male or **f** slave, 563
Lev 3: 1 whether male or **f,** 5922
3: 6 he is to offer a male or **f** without defect. 5922
4:28 offering for the sin he committed a **f** goat 5922
4:32 he is to bring a **f** without defect. 5922
5: 6 the LORD a **f** lamb or goat from the flock 5922
25:44 " 'Your male and **f** slaves are to come from 563
27: 4 and if it is a **f,** 5922
27: 5 at twenty shekels and of a **f** at ten shekels. 5922
27: 6 and that of a **f** at three shekels of silver. 5922
27: 7 at fifteen shekels and of a **f** at ten shekels. 5922
Nu 5: 3 Send away male and **f** alike; 5922
15:27 a **year-old** *f* goat for a sin offering. AIT
Dt 23:18 not bring the earnings of a *f* **prostitute** or AIT
28:68 to your enemies as male and **f** slaves, 9148
Est 7: 4 as male and **f** slaves, 9148
Ecc 2: 7 I bought male and **f** slaves 9148
Jer 34: 9 both male and **f;** 9148
34:10 that they would free their male and **f** slaves 9148
34:16 the male and **f** slaves you had set free to go 9148
Mt 19: 4 the Creator 'made them male and **f,'** *2559*
Mk 10: 6 of creation God 'made them male and **f.'** *2559*
Gal 3:28 Jew nor Greek, slave nor free, male nor **f,** *2559*

FEMALES (1) [FEMALE]

Ge 30:41 Whenever the **stronger** *f* were in heat, AIT

FENCE (1)

Ps 62: 3 this leaning wall, this tottering **f?** 1555

FENCED (KJV) See BLOCKED, DUG UP, FORTIFIED, KNIT TOGETHER, WALLS

FERMENTED (10)

Lev 10: 9 or other **f drink** whenever you go into 8911
Nu 6: 3 he must abstain from wine and other **f drink** 8911
6: 3 from wine or from other **f drink.** 8911
28: 7 a quarter of a hin of **f drink** with each lamb. 8911
Dt 14:26 cattle, sheep, wine or other **f drink,** 8911
29: 6 and drank no wine or other **f drink.** 8911
Jdg 13: 4 to it that you drink no wine or other **f drink** 8911
13: 7 drink no wine or other **f drink** and do 8911
13:14 or other **f drink** nor eat anything unclean. 8911
Lk 1:15 He is never to take wine or other **f drink,** *4975*

FEROCIOUS (4)

Ge 37:20 and say that a **f** animal devoured him. 8273
37:33 Some **f** animal has devoured him. 8273
Isa 35: 9 nor will any **f** beast get up on it; 7264
Mt 7:15 but inwardly they are **f** wolves. *774*

FERTILE (16) [FERTILIZE]

Nu 13:20 Is it **f** or poor? 9045
2Ch 26:10 in the hills and in the **f lands,** 4149
Ne 9:25 They captured fortified cities and **f** land; 9045
9:35 in the spacious and **f** land you gave them, 9045
Isa 5: 1 a vineyard on a **f** hillside. 1201+9043
10:18 and **f fields** it will completely destroy, 4149
28: 1 set on the head of a **f** valley— 9043
28: 4 set on the head of a **f** valley, 9043
29:17 into a **f field** and the fertile field seem like 4149
29:17 into a fertile field and the **f field** seem like 4149
32:15 and the desert becomes a **f field,** 4149
32:15 and the **f field** seems like a forest. 4149
32:16 and righteousness live in the **f field.** 4149
Jer 2: 7 I brought you into a **f** land to eat its fruit 4149
Eze 17: 5 of the seed of your land and put it in **f** soil. 2446
Mic 7:14 by itself in a forest, in **f pasturelands.** 4149

FERTILIZE (1) [FERTILE]

Lk 13: 8 and I'll dig around it and **f** it. *965+3162*

FERVENT (1) [FERVOR]

Pr 26:23 of glaze over earthenware are **f** lips with 1944

FERVOR (2) [FERVENT]

Ac 18:25 and he spoke **with great f** and *2417+3836+4460*
Ro 12:11 but *keep* your spiritual **f,** serving the Lord. *2417*

FESTAL (1) [FESTIVAL]

Ps 118:27 the **f procession** up to the horns of the altar. 2504

FESTER (1) [FESTERING]

Ps 38: 5 My wounds **f** and are loathsome because 5245

FESTERING (6) [FESTER]

Ex 9: 9 and **f** boils will break out on men 81
9:10 and **f** boils broke out on men and animals. 81
Lev 21:20 or who has **f** or running sores 1734
22:22 anything with warts or **f** or running sores. 1734
Dt 28:27 **f sores** and the itch, 1734
Job 7: 5 my skin is broken and **f.** 4416

FESTIVAL (32) [FESTAL, FESTIVALS, FESTIVE]

Ex 5: 1 so that *they may* **hold a f** to me in 2510
10: 9 because we are to celebrate a **f** *to* 2504
12:14 to come you shall celebrate it as a **f** to 2504
13: 6 on the seventh day hold a **f** to the LORD. 2504
23:14 a year *you are to* **celebrate a f** to me. 2510
23:18 "The fat of my **f offerings** must not 2504
32: 5 "Tomorrow there will be a **f** to 2504
Lev 23:39 the **f** *to* the LORD for seven days; 2504
23:41 a **f** to the LORD for seven days each year. 2504
Nu 15: 3 or freewill offerings or **f offerings—** 4595
28:17 of this month there is to be a **f;** 2504
29:12 Celebrate a **f** to the LORD for seven days. 2504
Jdg 9:27 they held a **f** in the temple of their god. 2136
21:19 the annual **f** *of* the LORD in Shiloh, 2504
1Sa 20: 5 "Look, tomorrow is the **New Moon f,** 2544
20:18 "Tomorrow is the **New Moon f.** 2544
20:24 and when the **New Moon f** came, 2544
1Ki 8: 2 the time of the **f** in the month of Ethanim, 2504
8:65 So Solomon observed the **f** at that time, 2504
12:32 He instituted a **f** on the fifteenth day of 2504
12:32 like the **f** held in Judah, 2504
12:33 So he instituted the **f** for the Israelites 2504
2Ch 5: 3 at the time of the **f** in the seventh month. 2504
7: 8 So Solomon observed the **f** at that time 2504
7: 9 of the altar for seven days and the **f** 2504
30:23 to celebrate the **f** seven more days; NIH
Isa 30:29 as on the night you celebrate a holy **f;** 2504
Hos 7: 5 On the day of the **f** of our king NIH
9: 5 on the **f** days of the LORD? 2504
Mal 2: 3 the offal from your **f sacrifices,** 2504
1Co 5: 8 Therefore *let us* **keep the F,** *2037*
Col 2:16 or with regard to a **religious f,** *2038*

FESTIVALS (12) [FESTIVAL]

Nu 10:10 appointed feasts and **New Moon f—** 2544+8031
1Ch 23:31 the LORD on Sabbaths and at **New Moon f** 2544
Ne 10:33 **New Moon f** and appointed feasts; 2544
Isa 1:14 Your **New Moon f** 2544
29: 1 to year and let your cycle of **f** go on. 2504
33:20 Look upon Zion, the city of our **f;** 4595
Eze 45:17 grain offerings and drink offerings at the **f,** 2504
46:11 " 'At the **f** and the appointed feasts, 2504
Hos 2:11 her **yearly f,** her New Moons, 2504
5: 7 Now their **New Moon f** will devour them 2544
Na 1:15 Celebrate your **f,** O Judah, 2504
Zec 8:19 and glad occasions and happy **f** for Judah. 4595

FESTIVE (2) [FESTIVAL]

1Sa 25: 8 since we come at a **f** time. 3202
Ps 42: 4 and thanksgiving among the **f** throng. 2510

FESTOONED (1)

1Ki 7:17 of interwoven chains **f** the capitals on top 1544

FESTUS (14) [PORCIUS]

Ac 24:27 Felix was succeeded by Porcius **F,** *5776*
25: 1 **F** went up from Caesarea to Jerusalem, *5776*
25: 3 They urgently requested **F,** *899S*
25: 4 **F** answered, "Paul is being held *5776*
25: 9 **F,** wishing to do the Jews a favor, *5776*
25:12 After **F** had conferred with his council, *5776*
25:13 at Caesarea to pay their respects to **F.** *5776*
25:14 **F** discussed Paul's case with the king. *5776*
25:22 Then Agrippa said to **F,** *5776*
25:23 At the command *of* **F,** *5776*
25:24 **F** said: "King Agrippa, *5776*
26:24 At this point **F** interrupted Paul's defense. *5776*
26:25 "I am not insane, most excellent **F,"** *5776*
26:32 Agrippa said *to* **F,** *5776*

FETCH, FETCHED (KJV) See BRING, BROUGHT, CAPTURE, COME BACK, GET, ESCORT, TAKE

FETTERED (1) [FETTERS]

2Sa 3:34 your feet **were** not **f.** 4200+5602+5733

FETTERS (3) [FETTERED]

Job 36:13 when *he* **f** them, they do not cry for help. 673
Ps 2: 3 they say, "and throw off their **f.**" 6310
149: 8 to bind their kings with **f,** 2414

FEVER (11) [FEVERISH]

Lev 26:16 and **f** that will destroy your sight 7707
Dt 28:22 with **f** and inflammation, 7707
Job 30:30 my body burns with **f.** 2996
Mt 8:14 Peter's mother-in-law lying in bed **with a f.** *4789*
8:15 He touched her hand and the **f** left her, *4790*
Mk 1:30 Simon's mother-in-law was in bed **with a f,** *4789*
1:31 The **f** left her and she began to wait *4790*
Lk 4:38 suffering *from* a high **f,** *4790*
4:39 So he bent over her and rebuked the **f,** *4790*
Jn 4:52 "The **f** left him yesterday at *4790*
Ac 28: 8 suffering from **f** and dysentery. *4790*

FEVERISH (1) [FEVER]

La 5:10 Our skin is hot as an oven, **f** from hunger. 2363

FEW (76) [FEWEST]

Ge 29:20 but they seemed like **only a f** days to him 285
34:30 We are **f** *in* number, 5493
47: 9 My years have been **f** and difficult, 5071
Lev 25:16 and when the years *are* **f,** 5070
25:52 If **only a f** years remain until the Year 5071
26:22 **make** you *so* **f in number** 5070
Nu 9:20 over the tabernacle **only a f** days; 5031
13:18 or weak, **f** or many. 5071
35: 8 but **f** from one that has few." 5070
35: 8 but few from one that has **f.**" 5071
Dt 4:27 and **only a f** *of* you will survive 5031+5493
26: 5 with a **f** people and lived there and became 5071
28:62 in the sky will be left but **f in number,** 5071+5493
33: 6 nor his men be **f.**" 5031
Jos 7: 3 for **only a f** men are there." 5071
10:20 **f** who were left reached their fortified cities. 8586
1Sa 14: 6 whether by many or by **f.**" 5071
17:28 with whom did you leave those **f** sheep in 5071
1Ki 17: 1 in the **next** *f* years except at my word." AIT
17:12 a **f** sticks to take home and make a meal 9109
2Ki 4: 3 Don't ask for **just a f.** 5070
1Ch 16:19 When they were but **f** *in* number, 5493
16:19 they were but few in number, **f** indeed, 5071
2Ch 24:24 with **only a f** men, 5203
29:34 were **too f** to skin all the burnt offerings; 5071
Ne 2:12 I set out during the night with a **f** men. 5071
7: 4 but there were **f** people in it, 5071
Job 10:20 Are not my **f** days almost over? 5071
14: 1 "Man born of woman is of **f** days and full 7920
16:22 "Only a **f** years will pass before I go on 5031
Ps 105:12 When they were but **f** *in* number, 5493
105:12 they were but few in number, **f** indeed, 3869+5071
109: 8 May his days be **f;** 5071
Ecc 2: 3 to do under heaven during the **f** days 5031
5: 2 so let your words be **f.** 5071
5:18 the **f** days of life God has given him— 5031
6:12 the **f** and meaningless days he passes 5031
9:14 a small city with **only a f** people in it. 5071
12: 3 the grinders cease because *they are* **f,** 5070
Isa 10:19 be *so* **f** that a child could write them down. 5031
16:14 survivors will be **very f** and feeble." 4663+5071
21:17 the warriors of Kedar, *will be* **f.**" 5070
24: 6 and **very f** are left. 632+4663
65:20 be in it an infant who lives but a *f* **days,** AIT
Jer 42: 2 now **only a f** are left. 5071
44:14 none will return except a *f* **fugitives."** AIT
44:28 of Judah from Egypt will be **very f.** 5031+5493
49: 9 would they not leave a **f grapes?** 6622
Eze 5: 3 a **f** strands of hair and tuck them away in the folds of your garment. 928+5031+5071
5: 4 a **f** *of* these and throw them into the fire 4946
12:16 I will spare a **f** of them from the sword, 5031
13:19 a *f* **handfuls** *of* barley and scraps of bread. AIT
Da 11:20 In a **f** years, however, he will be destroyed, 285
11:23 with **only a f** people he will rise to power. 5071
Ob 1: 5 would they not leave a **f grapes?** 6622
Mt 7:14 and only a **f** find it. *3900*
9:37 but the workers are **f.** *3900*
15:34 "Seven," they replied, "and a **f** small fish." *3900*
22:14 "For many are invited, but **f** are chosen." *3900*
25:21 You have been faithful with a **f** *things;* *3900*
25:23 You have been faithful with a **f** *things;* *3900*
Mk 2: 1 A **f** days later, *NIG*
6: 5 except lay his hands on a **f** sick people *3900*
8: 7 They had a **f** small fish as well; *3900*
Lk 10: 2 but the workers are **f.** *3900*
12:48 be beaten with **f** blows. *3900*
13:23 are only a **f** people going to be saved?" *3900*
Jn 2:12 There they stayed *for* a **f** days. *4024+4498*
Ac 1: 5 in a **f** days you will be baptized with *4024+4498*
10:48 to stay with them *for* **a f** days. *5516*
17: 4 and not a **f** prominent women. *3900*
17:34 A *f* men became followers of Paul *AIT*
25:13 A *f* days later King Agrippa *AIT*
1Pe 3:20 In it only a **f** people, eight in all, *3900*
Rev 2:14 Nevertheless, I have a **f** *things* against you: *3900*
3: 4 a **f** people in Sardis who have *3900*

FEWEST (1) [FEW]

Dt 7: 7 for you were the **f** of all peoples. 5071

FIDELITY (KJV) See TRUSTED

FIELD (216) [BATTLEFIELD, FIELDS, FIELDSTONES, GRAINFIELD, GRAINFIELDS]

Ge 2: 5 and no shrub of the **f** had yet appeared on 8441
2: 5 and no plant of the **f** had yet sprung up, 8441
2:19 of the ground all the beasts of the **f** and all 8441
2:20 of the air and all the beasts of the **f.** 8441
3:18 and you will eat the plants of the **f.** 8441
4: 8 "Let's go out to the **f.**" 8441
4: 8 And while they were in the **f,** 8441
23: 9 to him and is at the end of his **f.** 8441
23:11 "Listen to me; I give you the **f,** 8441
23:13 I will pay the price of the **f.** 8441
23:17 Ephron's **f** in Machpelah near Mamre— 8441
23:17 both the **f** and the cave in it, 8441
23:17 all the trees within the borders of the **f**— 8441
23:19 the **f** *of* Machpelah near Mamre (which is 8441
23:20 So the **f** and the cave in it were deeded 8441
24:63 He went out to the **f** one evening 8441
24:65 that man in the **f** coming to meet us?" 8441
25: 9 in the **f** *of* Ephron son of Zohar the Hittite, 8441
25:10 **f** Abraham had bought from the Hittites. 8441
27:27 the smell of my son is like the smell of a **f** 8441
29: 2 There he saw a well in the **f,** 8441
37: 7 in the **f** when suddenly my sheaf rose 8441
39: 5 both in the house and in the **f.** 8441
49:29 in the cave in the **f** *of* Ephron the Hittite, 8441
49:30 the cave in the **f** *of* Machpelah, 8441
49:30 along with the **f.** NIH
49:32 The **f** and the cave in it were bought from 8441
50:13 and buried him in the cave in the **f** 8441
50:13 along with the **f.** 8441
Ex 9: 3 a terrible plague on your livestock in the **f**— 8441
9:19 and everything you have in the **f** to a place 8441
9:19 not been brought in and is still out in the **f,** 8441
9:21 and livestock in the **f.** 8441
22: 5 in a **f** or vineyard and lets them stray 8441
22: 5 and they graze in another man's **f,** 8441
22: 5 from the best of his own **f** or vineyard. 8441
22: 6 of grain or standing grain or the *whole* **f,** 8441
23:16 of the crops you sow in your **f.** 8441
23:16 when you gather in your crops from the **f.** 8441
Lev 19: 9 do not reap to the very edges of your **f** 8441
19:19 not plant your **f** with two kinds of seed. 8441
23:22 do not reap to the very edges of your **f** 8441
26: 4 and the trees of the **f** their fruit. 8441
27:17 If he dedicates his **f** during the Year 8441
27:18 But if he dedicates his **f** after the Jubilee, 8441
27:19 If the man who dedicates the **f** wishes 8441
27:19 and the **f** will again become his. NIH
27:20 If, however, he does not redeem the **f,** 8441
27:21 When the **f** is released in the Jubilee, 8441
27:21 like a **f** devoted to the LORD; 8441
27:22 to the LORD a **f** he has bought, 8441
27:24 In the Year of Jubilee the **f** will revert to 8441
Nu 20:17 We will not go through any **f** or vineyard, 8441
21:22 not turn aside into any **f** or vineyard, 8441
22: 4 as an ox licks up the grass of the **f.**" 8441
22:23 she turned off the road into a **f.** 8441
23:14 to the **f** *of* Zophim on the top of Pisgah, 8441
Dt 20:19 Are the trees of the **f** people, 8441
21: 1 lying in a **f** in the land 8441
24:19 in your **f** and you overlook a sheaf, 8441
28:38 in the **f** but you will harvest little, 8441
Jos 15:18 she urged him to ask her father for a **f.** 8441
Jdg 1:14 she urged him to ask her father for a **f.** 8441
5:18 so did Naphtali on the heights of the **f.** 8441
13: 9 to the woman while she was out in the **f;** 8441
20:31 that about thirty men fell in the **open f** and 8441
Ru 2: 3 she found herself working in a **f** belonging to Boaz, 2754+8441
2: 7 into the **f** and has worked steadily NIH
2: 8 in another **f** and don't go away from here. 8441
2: 9 Watch the **f** where the men are harvesting, 8441
2:17 So Ruth gleaned in the **f** until evening. 8441
2:22 in someone else's **f** you might be harmed." 8441
1Sa 6:14 to the **f** *of* Joshua of Beth Shemesh, 8441
6:18 is a witness to this day in the **f** *of* Joshua 8441
14:15 those in the camp and **f,** 8441
17:44 the birds of the air and the beasts of the **f!**" 8441
19: 3 with my father in the **f** where you are. 8441
20: 5 and hide in the **f** until the evening of 8441
20:11 Jonathan said, "let's go out into the **f.**" 8441
20:24 So David hid in the **f,** 8441
20:35 In the morning Jonathan went out to the **f** 8441
30:11 an Egyptian in a **f** and brought him 8441
2Sa 14: 6 into a fight with each other in the **f,** 8441
14:30 "Look, Joab's **f** is next to mine, 2754
14:30 So Absalom's servants set the **f** on fire. 2754
14:31 "Why have your servants set my **f** on fire?" 2754
18: 6 The army marched into the **f** to fight Israel, 8441
20:12 from the road into a **f** and threw a garment 8441
23:11 where there was a **f** full of lentils, 2754+8441
23:12 in the middle of the **f.** 2754
2Ki 3:19 and ruin every good **f** with stones." 2754
3:25 on every good **f** until it was covered. 2754
9:25 and throw him on the **f** *that belonged* 2754+8441
18:17 his chief officer and his **f commander** with 8072
18:17 on the road to the Washerman's **F.** 8441
2Ki 18:19 The **f commander** said to them, 8072
18:26 Shebna and Joah said to the **f commander,** 8072
18:37 told him what the **f commander** had said. 8072
19: 4 the words of the **f commander,** 8072
19: 8 When the **f commander** heard that the king 8072
19:26 They are like plants in the **f,** 8441
1Ch 11:13 where there was a **f** full of barley, 2754+8441
11:14 they took their stand in the middle of the **f.** 2754
27:26 in charge of the **f** workers who farmed 8441
2Ch 26:23 near them in a **f** *for* burial that belonged to 8441
Job 5:23 a covenant with the stones of the **f,** 8441
Ps 8: 7 and the beasts of the **f,** 8442
50:11 and the creatures of the **f** are mine. 8442
72: 6 He will be like rain falling on a **mown f,** 1600
72:16 let it thrive like the grass of the **f.** 824
80:13 and the creatures of the **f** feed on it. 8442
103:15 he flourishes like a flower of the **f;** 8441
104:11 They give water to all the beasts of the **f;** 8442
Pr 13:23 poor man's **f** may produce abundant food, 5776
24:30 I went past the **f** *of* the sluggard, 8441
27:26 and the goats with the price of a **f.** 8441
31:16 She considers a **f** and buys it; 8441
SS 2: 7 by the gazelles and by the does of the **f:** 8441
3: 5 by the gazelles and by the does of the **f:** 8441
Isa 1: 8 like a hut in a **f of melons,** 5252
5: 8 to you who add house to house and join **f** 8441
5: 8 to **f** till no space is left and you live alone 8441
7: 3 on the road to the Washerman's **F.** 8441
19: 7 Every **sown f** *along* 4669
28:25 barley in its plot, and spelt *in* its **f?** 1474
29:17 will not Lebanon be turned into a **fertile f** 4149
29:17 into a fertile field and the **fertile f** seem 4149
32:15 and the desert becomes a **fertile f,** 4149
32:15 and the **fertile f** seems like a forest. 4149
32:16 and righteousness live in the **fertile f.** 4149
36: 2 the king of Assyria sent his **f commander** 8072
36: 2 on the road to the Washerman's **F,** 8441
36: 4 The **f commander** said to them, 8072
36:11 Shebna and Joah said to the **f commander,** 8072
36:22 told him what the **f commander** had said. 8072
37: 4 the words of the **f commander,** 8072
37: 8 When the **f commander** heard that the king 8072
37:27 They are like plants in the **f,** 8441
40: 6 all their glory is like the flowers of the **f.** 8441
55:12 all the trees of the **f** will clap their hands. 8441
56: 9 Come, all you beasts of the **f,** 8442
Jer 4:17 They surround her like men guarding a **f,** 8442
7:20 on man and beast, on the trees of the **f** and 8441
9:22 of men will lie like refuse on the open **f,** 8441
12: 4 and the grass in every **f** be withered? 8441
12:10 and trample down my **f;** 2754
12:10 they will turn my pleasant **f** into 2754
14: 5 the doe in the **f** deserts her newborn fawn 8441
26:18 " 'Zion will be plowed like a **f,** 8441
32: 7 'Buy my **f** at Anathoth, 8441
32: 8 'Buy my **f** at Anathoth in the territory 8441
32: 9 the **f** at Anathoth from my cousin Hanamel 8441
32:25 'Buy the **f** with silver and have 8441
41: 8 oil and honey, hidden in a **f.**" 8441
La 4: 9 for lack of food from the **f.** 8442
Eze 16: 5 you were thrown out into the open **f,** 8441
16: 7 I made you grow like a plant of the **f.** 8441
17:24 of the **f** will know that I the LORD bring 8441
29: 5 You will fall on the open **f** and not 8441
31: 4 to all the trees of the **f.** 8441
31: 5 the trees of the **f;** 8441
31: 6 of the **f** gave birth under its branches; 8441
31:13 of the **f** were among its branches. 8441
31:15 and all the trees of the **f** withered away. 8441
32: 4 on the land and hurl you on the open **f.** 8441
34:27 The trees of the **f** will yield their fruit and 8441
36:30 the fruit of the trees and the crops of the **f,** 8441
38:20 the birds of the air, the beasts of the **f,** 8441
39: 5 You will fall in the open **f,** 7156
Da 2:38 the beasts of the **f** and the birds of the air. 10119
4:12 Under it the beasts of the **f** found shelter, 10119
4:15 remain in the ground, in the grass of the **f.** 10119
4:21 giving shelter to the beasts of the **f,** 10119
4:23 in the grass of the **f,** 10119
Hos 2:18 a covenant for them with the beasts of the **f** 8441
4: 3 the **f** and the birds of the air and the fish of 8441
10: 4 up like poisonous weeds in a plowed **f.** 8442
12:11 be like piles of stones on a plowed **f.** 8442
Joel 1:11 because the harvest of the **f** is destroyed. 8441
1:12 all the trees of the **f**—are dried up. 8441
1:19 up all the trees of the **f.** 8441
Am 4: 7 One **f** had rain; 2754
Mic 3:12 Zion will be plowed like a **f,** 8441
4:10 the city to camp in the **open f.** 8441
Zec 10: 1 and plants of the **f** to everyone. 8441
Mt 6:28 See how the lilies *of* the **f** grow. *69*
6:30 that is how God clothes the grass *of* the **f,** *69*
9:38 to send out workers into his **harvest f.**" *2546*
13:24 like a man who sowed good seed in his **f.** *69*
13:27 'Sir, didn't you sow good seed in your **f?** *69*
13:31 which a man took and planted in his **f.** *69*
13:36 to us the parable of the weeds *in* the **f.**" *69*
13:38 The **f** is the world, *69*
13:44 of heaven is like treasure hidden in a **f.** *69*
13:44 and sold all he had and bought that **f.** *69*
22: 5 one to his **f,** another to his business. *69*
24:18 Let no one in the **f** go back to get his cloak. *69*
24:40 Two men will be in the **f;** *69*
27: 7 to use the money to buy the potter's **f** as *69*
27: 8 That is why it has been called the **F** *69*
27:10 and they used them to buy the potter's **f,** *69*
Mk 13:16 Let no one in the **f** go back to get his cloak. *69*

Lk 10: 2 to send out workers into his harvest f. 2546
12:28 that is how God clothes the grass of the f, 69
14:18 The first said, 'I have just bought a f, 69
15:25 "Meanwhile, the older son was in the f. 69
17: 7 the servant when he comes in from the f, 69
17:31 in the f should go back for anything. 69
Ac 1:18 Judas bought a f; 6005
1:19 that f in their language Akeldama, 6005
1:19 that is, F of Blood.) 6005
4:37 sold a f he owned and brought the money 69
1Co 3: 9 you are God's f, God's building. 1176
2Co 10:13 to the f God has assigned to us, 2834+3586+3836
10:13 a f that reaches even to you. 3586
1Pe 1:24 all their glory is like the flowers of the f; 5965

FIELDS (107) [FIELD]

Ge 30:14 into the f and found some mandrake plants, 8441
30:16 Jacob came in from the f that evening, 8441
31: 4 to come out to the f where his flocks were. 8441
34: 5 his sons were in the f with his livestock; 8441
34: 7 Now Jacob's sons had come in from the f 8441
34:28 of theirs in the city and out in the f. 8441
37:15 around in the f and asked him, 8441
41:48 the food grown in the f surrounding it. 8441
47:20 The Egyptians, one and all, sold their f, 8441
47:24 as seed for the f and as food for yourselves 8441
Ex 1:14 and with all kinds of work in the f; 8441
8:13 in the courtyards and in the f. 8441
9:22 on everything growing in the f of Egypt." 8441
9:25 Throughout Egypt hail struck everything in the f— 8441
9:25 it beat down everything growing in the f 8441
10: 5 that is growing in your f. 8441
10:12 and devour everything growing in the f, 824
10:15 everything growing in the f and the fruit on 824
23:10 "For six years you are to sow your f 824
Lev 14: 7 he is to release the live bird in the open f. 8441
14:53 to release the live bird in the open f outside 8441
17: 5 now making in the open f. 8441
25: 3 For six years sow your f, 8441
25: 4 Do not sow your f or prune your vineyards. 8441
25:12 eat only what is taken directly from the f. 8441
Nu 16:14 and honey or given us an inheritance of f 8441
Dt 11:15 I will provide grass in the f for your cattle, 8441
14:22 a tenth of all that your f produce each year. 8441
32:13 the land and fed him with the fruit of the f. 8442
32:32 of Sodom and from the f of Gomorrah. 8727
Jos 8:24 the men of Ai in the f and in the desert 8441
21:12 But the f and villages around 8441
Jdg 9:27 After they had gone out into the f 8441
9:32 and lie in wait in the f. 8441
9:42 the people of Shechem went out to the f, 8441
9:43 and set an ambush in the f. 8441
9:44 upon those in the f and struck them down. 8441
19:16 came in from his work in the f. 8441
Ru 2: 2 to the f and pick up the leftover grain 8441
2: 3 So she went out and began to glean in the f 8441
1Sa 8:14 of your f and vineyards and olive groves 8441
11: 5 Just then Saul was returning from the f, 8441
22: 7 of Jesse give all of you f and vineyards? 8441
25:15 and the whole time we were out in the f 8441
2Sa 1:21 nor f that yield offerings [of grain]. 8441
11:11 are camped in the open f. 8441
19:29 I order you and Ziba to divide the f." 8441
1Ki 2:26 "Go back to your f in Anathoth. 8441
2Ki 4:39 the f to gather herbs and found a wild vine. 8441
23: 4 He burned them outside Jerusalem in the f 8727
25:12 of the land to work the vineyards and f. 3320
1Ch 6:56 But the f and villages around 8441
16:32 let the f be jubilant, 8441
2Ch 26:10 working his f and vineyards 4144
31: 5 oil and honey and all that the f produced. 8441
Ne 5: 3 "We are mortgaging our f, 8441
5: 4 the king's tax on our f and vineyards. 8441
5: 5 because our f and our vineyards belong 8441
5:11 Give back to them immediately their f, 8441
11:25 As for the villages with their f, 8441
11:30 in Lachish and its f, 8441
12:44 the f around the towns they were to bring 8441
13:10 the service had gone back to their own f. 8441
Job 24: 6 They gather fodder in the f and glean in 8441
Ps 37:20 like the beauty of the f, they will vanish— 4120
96:12 let the f be jubilant, 8442
107:37 They sowed f and planted vineyards 8441
132: 6 we came upon it in the f of Jaar: 8441
144:13 by tens of thousands in our f; 2575
Pr 8:26 before he made the earth or its f or any of 2575
23:10 or encroach on the f of the fatherless, 8441
24:27 and get your f ready; 8441
Ecc 5: 9 the king himself profits from the f. 8441
Isa 1: 7 your f are being stripped 141
6:11 the houses are left deserted and the f ruined 141
10:18 and fertile f it will completely destroy, 4149
16: 8 The f of Heshbon wither, 8727
32:12 Beat your breasts for the pleasant f, 8441
61: 5 foreigners will work your f and vineyards. 438
Jer 6:12 together with their f and their wives, 8441
6:25 Do not go out to the f or walk on the roads, 8441
8:10 to other men and their f to new owners. 8441
13:27 on the hills and in the f. 8441
32:15 f and vineyards will again be bought 8441
32:43 Once more f will be bought in this land 8441
32:44 F will be bought for silver, 8441
35: 9 to live in or had vineyards, f or crops. 8441
39:10 at that time he gave them vineyards and f. 3321
48:33 from the orchards and f of Moab. 824
Jer 52:16 of the land to work the vineyards and f. 3320
Eze 39:10 not need to gather wood from the f or cut it 8441
Hos 5: 7 Now their New Moon festivals will devour them and their f. 2750
Joel 1:10 The f are ruined, the ground is dried up; 8441
Ob 1:19 They will occupy the f of Ephraim 8441
Mic 2: 2 They covet f and seize them, and houses, 8441
2: 4 He assigns our f to traitors.' " 8441
Hab 3:17 olive crop fails and the f produce no food, 8727
Hag 1:11 for a drought on the f and the mountains, 824
Mal 3:11 the vines in your f will not cast their fruit," 8441
Mt 19:29 or children or f for my sake will receive 69
Mk 10:29 or mother or father or children or f for me 69
10:30 brothers, sisters, mothers, children and f— 69
11: 8 spread branches they had cut in the f. 69
Lk 2: 8 shepherds living out in the f nearby, 6001
15:15 who sent him to his f to feed pigs. 69
Jn 4:35 I tell you, open your eyes and look at the f! 6001
Jas 5: 4 workmen who mowed your f are crying out 6001

FIELDSTONES (1) [FIELD, STONE]

Dt 27: 6 the altar of the LORD your God with f 74+8969

FIERCE (49) [FIERCE-LOOKING, FIERCELY, FIERCER, FIERCEST]

Ge 49: 7 Cursed be their anger, so f, and their fury, 6434
Ex 32:12 Turn from your f anger; 3019
Nu 25: 4 that the LORD's f anger may turn away 3019
Dt 13:17 that the LORD will turn from his f anger; 3019
29:23 which the LORD overthrew in f anger. 2779
29:24 Why this f, burning anger?" 1524
Jos 7:26 Then the LORD turned from his f anger. 3019
1Sa 20:34 Jonathan got up from the table in f anger; 3034
28:18 the LORD or carry out his f wrath against 3019
31: 3 The fighting grew f around Saul, 3877
2Sa 2:17 The battle that day was very f, 7997
17: 8 as f as a wild bear robbed of her cubs. 5253+5883
2Ki 23:26 not turn away from the heat of his f anger, 1524
1Ch 10: 3 The fighting grew f around Saul, 3877
2Ch 28:11 for the LORD's f anger rests on you." 3019
28:13 and his f anger rests on Israel." 3019
29:10 so that his f anger will turn away from us. 3019
30: 8 so that his f anger will turn away from you. 3019
Ezr 10:14 until the f anger of our God 3019
Job 41:10 No one is f enough to rouse him. 425
Ps 59: 3 F men conspire against me for no offense 6434
69:24 let your f anger overtake them. 3019
85: 3 and turned from your f anger. 3019
Pr 26:13 a f lion roaming the streets!" 787
Isa 7: 4 because of the f anger of Rezin and Aram 3034
13: 9 a cruel day, with wrath and f anger— 3019
19: 4 and a f king will rule over them," 6434
27: 1 his f, great and powerful sword, 7997
27: 8 with his f blast he drives her out, 7997
49:24 or captives rescued from the f? 6883
49:25 and plunder retrieved from the f; 6883
Jer 4: 8 for the f anger of the LORD has 3019
4:26 before the LORD, before his f anger. 3019
12:13 because of the LORD's f anger." 3019
25:37 be laid waste because of the f anger of 3019
25:38 and because of the LORD's f anger. 3019
30:24 The f anger of the LORD will 3019
44: 6 Therefore, my f anger was poured out; 2779
49:37 even my f anger," declares the LORD. 3019
51:45 Run from the f anger of the LORD. 3019
La 1:12 on me in the day of his f anger? 3019
2: 3 In f anger he has cut off every horn 3034
2: 6 in his f anger he has spurned both king 2405
4:11 he has poured out his f anger. 3019
Hos 11: 9 I will not carry out my f anger, 3019
Jnh 3: 9 and with compassion turn from his f anger 3019
Na 1: 6 Who can endure his f anger? 3019
Zep 2: 2 the f anger of the LORD comes upon you, 3019
3: 8 all my f anger. 3019

FIERCE-LOOKING (1) [FIERCE]

Dt 28:50 a f nation without respect for the old 6434+7156

FIERCELY (4) [FIERCE]

Job 39:21 He paws f, rejoicing in his strength, 928+2021+6677
Ps 25:19 and how f they hate me! 2805
Jer 6:29 The bellows blow f to burn away the lead 5723
Lk 11:53 of the law began to oppose him f and 1267

FIERCER (1) [FIERCE]

Hab 1: 8 f than wolves at dusk. 2523

FIERCEST (1) [FIERCE]

2Sa 11:15 in the front line where the fighting is f. 2617

FIERY (16) [FIRE]

Ps 11: 6 On the wicked he will rain f coals 836
21: 9 like a f furnace. 836
Eze 21:31 and breathe out my f anger against you; 836
22:20 into a furnace to melt it with a f blast, 836
22:21 and I will blow on you with my f wrath, 836
22:31 and consume them with my f anger, 836
28:14 you walked among the f stones. 836
28:16 from among the f stones. 836
38:19 In my zeal and f wrath I declare that at 836
Mt 13:42 They will throw them into the f furnace, 4786
Mt 13:50 and throw them into the f furnace, 4786
Rev 6: 4 Then another horse came out, a f red one. 4794
9:17 Their breastplates were f red, dark blue, 4791
10: 1 and his legs were like f pillars. 4786
19:20 of them were thrown alive into the f lake 4786
21: 8 be in the f lake of burning sulfur. 4786

FIFTEEN (18) [FIFTEENTH]

Ex 27:14 Curtains f cubits long are to be on 2822+6926
27:15 and curtains f cubits long are to be on 2822+6926
38:14 Curtains f cubits long were on one 2822+6926
38:15 and curtains f cubits long were on 2822+6926
Lev 27: 7 set the value of a male at f shekels 2822+6925
Nu 35: 4 will extend out f hundred feet 547+564
Jdg 8:10 about f thousand men, all that were 2822+6925
2Sa 9:10 Ziba had f sons and twenty servants.) 2822+6925
19:17 and his f sons and twenty servants. 2822+6925
1Ki 7: 3 forty-five beams, f to a row. 2822+6925
2Ki 14:17 for f years after the death of Jehoash 2822+6926
20: 6 I will add f years to your life. 2822+6926
2Ch 25:25 for f years after the death of Jehoash 2822+6926
Isa 38: 5 I will add f years to your life. 2822+6926
Eze 45:12 Twenty shekels plus twenty-five shekels plus f shekels equal one mina. 2256+2822+6927
Hos 3: 2 So I bought her for f shekels of silver 2822+6925
Zec 5: 2 thirty feet long and f feet wide." 564+928+2021+6924
Gal 1:18 with Peter and stayed with him f days. 1278

FIFTEENTH (18) [FIFTEEN]

Ex 16: 1 on the f day of the second month 2822+6925
Lev 23: 6 the f day of that month the LORD's Feast of Unleavened Bread 2822+6925
23:34 'On the f day of the seventh month 2822+6925
23:39 with the f day of the seventh month, 2822+6925
Nu 28:17 On the f day of this month there is 2822+6925
29:12 " 'On the f day of the seventh month, 2822+6925
33: 3 on the f day of the first month, 2822+6925
1Ki 12:32 on the f day of the eighth month, 2822+6925
12:33 On the f day of the eighth month, 2822+6925
2Ki 14:23 In the f year of Amaziah son of Joash 2822+6926
1Ch 24:14 the f to Bilgah, the sixteenth to Immer, 2822+6925
25:22 the f to Jerimoth, his sons and 2822+6925
2Ch 15:10 in the third month of the f year 2822+6926
Est 9:18 on the f they rested and made it a day 2822+6925
9:21 the fourteenth and f days of the month 2822+6925
Eze 32:17 on the f day of the month, 2822+6925
45:25 in the seventh month on the f day, 2822+6925
Lk 3: 1 the f year of the reign of Tiberius Caesar— 4298

FIFTH (55) [FIVE]

Ge 1:23 and there was morning—the f day. 2797
30:17 and bore Jacob a f son. 2797
41:34 the land to take a f of the harvest of Egypt 2821
47:24 give a f of it to Pharaoh. 2797
47:26 that a f of the produce belongs to Pharaoh. 2823
Lev 5:16 add a f of the value to that and give it all 2797
6: 5 add a f of the value to it and give it all to 2797
19:25 But in the f year you may eat its fruit. 2797
22:14 to the priest for the offering and add a f of 2797
27:13 he must add a f to its value. 2797
27:15 he must add a f to its value, 2797
27:19 he must add a f to its value, 2797
27:27 adding a f of the value to it. 2797
27:31 he must add a f of the value to it. 2797
Nu 5: 7 add one f to it and give it all to 2797
7:36 On the f day Shelumiel son of Zurishaddai, 2797
29:26 " 'On the f day prepare nine bulls, 2797
33:38 of the f month of the fortieth year after 2797
Jos 19:24 The f lot came out for the tribe of Asher, 2797
Jdg 19: 8 On the morning of the f day, 2797
2Sa 3: 4 the f, Shephatiah the son of Abital; 2797
1Ki 14:25 In the f year of King Rehoboam, 2797
2Ki 8:16 In the f year of Joram son of Ahab king 2822
25: 8 On the seventh day of the f month, 2797
1Ch 2:14 the fourth Nethanel, the f Raddai, 2797
3: 3 the f, Shephatiah the son of Abital; 2797
8: 2 Nohah the fourth and Rapha the f. 2797
12:10 Mishmannah the fourth, Jeremiah the f, 2797
24: 9 the f to Malkijah, the sixth to Mijamin, 2797
25:12 the f to Nethaniah, 2797
26: 3 the f, Jehohanan the sixth and Eliehoenai 2797
26: 4 Sacar the fourth, Nethanel the f, 2797
27: 8 The f, for the fifth month, 2797
27: 8 The fifth, for the f month, 2797
2Ch 12: 2 of Egypt attacked Jerusalem in the f year 2797
Ezr 7: 8 the f month of the seventh year of the king. 2797
7: 9 on the first day of the f month, 2797
Ne 6: 5 Then, the f time, Sanballat sent his aide 2797
Jer 1: 3 down to the f month of the eleventh year 2797
28: 1 In the f month of that same year, 2797
36: 9 the f year of Jehoiakim son of Josiah king 2797
52:12 On the tenth day of the f month, 2797
Eze 1: 1 in the fourth month on the f day, 2822
1: 2 On the f of the month— 2822
1: 2 it was the f year of the exile 2797
8: 1 in the sixth month on the f day, 2822
20: 1 in the f month on the tenth day, 2797
33:21 in the tenth month on the f day, 2822
Zec 7: 3 "Should I mourn and fast in the f month, 2797
7: 5 and mourned in the f and seventh months 2797
8:19 "The fasts of the fourth, f, 2797
Rev 6: 9 When he opened the f seal, 4286
9: 1 The f angel sounded his trumpet, 4286
16:10 The f angel poured out his bowl on 4286

Rev 21:20 the **f** sardonyx, the sixth carnelian, *4286*

FIFTIES (5) [FIFTY]

Ex 18:21 as officials over thousands, hundreds, **f** 2822
18:25 over thousands, hundreds, **f** and tens. 2822
Dt 1:15 of **f** and of tens and as tribal officials. 2822
1Sa 8:12 of thousands and commanders of **f,** 2822
Mk 6:40 they sat down in groups of hundreds and **f.** *4299*

FIFTIETH (3) [FIFTY]

Lev 25:10 Consecrate the **f** year and proclaim liberty 2822
25:11 The **f** year shall be a jubilee for you; 2822
2Ki 15:23 In the **f** year of Azariah king of Judah, 2822

FIFTY (81) [FIFTIES, FIFTIETH, 50]

Ge 7:24 the earth for a hundred and **f** days. 2822
8:3 the hundred and **f** days the water had gone 2822
18:24 if there are **f** righteous people in the city? 2822
18:24 for the sake of the **f** righteous people in it? 2822
18:26 "If I find **f** righteous people in the city 2822
18:28 of the righteous is five less than **f?** 2822
Ex 26:5 Make **f** loops on one curtain and fifty loops 2822
26:5 Make fifty loops on one curtain and **f** loops 2822
26:6 Then make **f** gold clasps and use them 2822
26:10 Make **f** loops along the edge of 2822
26:11 Then make **f** bronze clasps and put them in 2822
27:12 of the courtyard shall be **f** cubits wide 2822
27:13 the courtyard shall also be **f** cubits wide. 2822
27:18 be a hundred cubits long and **f** cubits wide, 2822
36:12 They also made **f** loops on one curtain 2822
36:12 and **f** loops on the end curtain of 2822
36:13 Then they made **f** gold clasps 2822
36:17 Then they made **f** loops along the edge of 2822
36:18 They made **f** bronze clasps to fasten 2822
38:12 The west end was **f** cubits wide 2822
38:13 toward the sunrise, was also **f** cubits wide. 2822
Lev 23:16 Count off **f** days up to the day after 2822
27:3 and sixty at **f** shekels of silver, according 2822
27:16 **f** shekels of silver to a homer 2822
Nu 4:3 Count all the men from thirty to **f** years 2822
4:23 Count all the men from thirty to **f** years 2822
4:30 Count all the men from thirty to **f** years 2822
4:35 from thirty to **f** years of age who came 2822
4:39 from thirty to **f** years of age who came 2822
4:43 from thirty to **f** years of age who came 2822
4:47 to **f** years of age who came to do the work 2822
8:25 but at the age of **f,** 2822
31:30 select one out of every **f,** whether persons, 2822
31:47 Moses selected one out of every **f** persons 2822
Dt 22:29 he shall pay the girl's father **f** shekels 2822
Jos 7:21 and a wedge of gold weighing **f** shekels, 2822
2Sa 15:1 a chariot and horses and with **f** men to run 2822
24:24 and the oxen and paid **f** shekels of silver 2822
1Ki 1:5 with **f** men to run ahead of him. 2822
7:2 **f** wide and thirty high, 2822
7:6 a colonnade **f** cubits long and thirty wide. 2822
10:29 and a horse for a hundred and **f.** 2822
18:4 **f** in each, and had supplied them with food 2822
18:13 in two caves, **f** in each, and supplied them 2822
18:19 And bring the four hundred and **f** prophets 2822
18:22 but Baal has four hundred and **f** prophets. 2822
2Ki 1:9 a captain with his *company of* **f** *men.* 2822
1:10 and consume you and your **f** *men!"* 2822
1:11 to Elijah another captain with his **f** *men.* 2822
1:12 and consume you and your **f** *men!"* 2822
1:12 and consumed him and his **f** *men.* 2822
1:13 the king sent a third captain with his **f** *men.* 2822
1:13 for my life and the lives of these **f** *men,* 2822
2:7 **F** men of the company of the prophets 2822
2:16 "we your servants have **f** able men. 2822
2:17 And they sent **f** men, 2822
13:7 the army of Jehoahaz except **f** horsemen, 2822
15:20 to contribute **f** shekels of silver to be given 2822
15:25 Taking **f** men of Gilead with him, 2822
1Ch 5:21 of the Hagrites—**f** thousand camels, 2822
5:21 two hundred **f** thousand sheep 2822
2Ch 1:17 and a horse for a hundred and **f.** 2822
3:9 The gold nails weighed **f** shekels. 2822
8:10 two hundred and **f** officials supervising 2822
8:18 and **f** talents of gold, 2822
Ne 5:17 and **f** Jews and officials ate at my table, 2822
Isa 3:3 the captain of **f** and man of rank, 2822
Eze 40:15 to the far end of its portico was **f** cubits. 2822
40:21 It was **f** cubits long 2822
40:25 It was **f** cubits long 2822
40:29 It was **f** cubits long 2822
40:33 It was **f** cubits long 2822
40:36 It was **f** cubits long 2822
42:2 a hundred cubits long and **f** cubits wide. 2822
42:7 in front of the rooms for **f** cubits. 2822
42:8 to the outer court was **f** cubits long, 2822
Hag 2:16 to a wine vat to draw **f** measures, 2822
Lk 7:41 five hundred denarii, and the other **f.** *4299*
9:14 down in groups of about **f** each." *4299*
Jn 8:57 "You are not yet **f** years old," *4299*
Ac 19:19 total came to **f thousand** drachmas. *3689+4297*

FIFTY-FIVE (2)

2Ki 21:1 he reigned in Jerusalem **f** years. 2256+2822+2822
2Ch 33:1 he reigned in Jerusalem **f** years. 2256+2822+2822

FIFTY-SECOND (1) [FIFTY-TWO]

2Ki 15:27 In the **f** year of Azariah king of Judah, 2256+2822+9109

FIFTY-TWO (3) [FIFTY-SECOND, 52]

2Ki 15:2 he reigned in Jerusalem **f** years. 2256+2822+9109
2Ch 26:3 he reigned in Jerusalem **f** years. 2256+2822+9109
Ne 6:15 twenty-fifth of Elul, in **f** days. 2256+2822+9109

FIG (41) [FIGS, SYCAMORE-FIG, SYCAMORE-FIGS]

Ge 3:7 so they sewed **f** leaves together 9300
Dt 8:8 vines and **f trees,** pomegranates, 9300
Jdg 9:10 "Next, the trees said to the **f tree,** 9300
9:11 "But the **f tree** replied, 9300
1Ki 4:25 each man under his own vine and **f tree.** 9300
2Ki 18:31 from his own vine and **f tree** 9300
1Ch 12:40 **f cakes,** raisin cakes, wine, oil, 1811
Ps 105:33 down their vines and **f trees** and shattered 9300
Pr 27:18 He who tends a **f tree** will eat its fruit, 9300
SS 2:13 The **f tree** forms its early fruit; 9300
Isa 9:10 the **f trees** have been felled, 9204
28:4 will be like a **f ripe** before harvest— 1136
34:4 like shriveled figs from the **f tree.** 9300
36:16 from his own vine and **f tree** 9300
Jer 5:17 devour your vines and **f trees.** 9300
Hos 2:12 I will ruin her vines and her **f trees,** 9300
9:10 like seeing the early fruit on the **f tree.** 9300
Joel 1:7 and ruined my **f trees.** 9300
1:12 vine is dried up and the **f tree** is withered; 9300
2:22 the **f tree** and the vine yield their riches. 9300
Am 4:9 Locusts devoured your **f** and olive trees, 9300
Mic 4:4 and under his own **f tree,** 9300
Na 3:12 like **f trees** with their first ripe fruit; 9300
Hab 3:17 Though the **f tree** does not bud 9300
Hag 2:19 Until now, the vine and the **f tree,** 9300
Zec 3:10 to sit under his vine and **f tree,'** 9300
Mt 21:19 Seeing a **f tree** by the road, *5190*
21:20 "How did the **f tree** wither so quickly?" *5190*
21:21 do what was done *to* the **f tree,** *5190*
24:32 "Now learn this lesson from the **f tree:** *5190*
Mk 11:13 Seeing in the distance a **f tree** in leaf, *5190*
11:20 they saw the **f tree** withered from the roots. *5190*
11:21 The **f tree** you cursed has withered!" *5190*
13:28 "Now learn this lesson from the **f tree:** *5190*
Lk 13:6 "A man had a **f tree,** *5190*
13:7 on this **f tree** and haven't found any. *5190*
21:29 "Look at the **f tree** and all the trees. *5190*
Jn 1:48 under the **f tree** before Philip called you." *5190*
1:50 I saw you under the **f tree.** *5190*
Jas 3:12 My brothers, can a **f tree** bear olives, *5190*
Rev 6:13 as late figs drop *from* **a f tree** when shaken *899S*

FIGHT (111) [FIGHTER, FIGHTERS, FIGHTING, FIGHTS, FOUGHT]

Ex 1:10 **f** against us and leave the country." 4309
14:14 The LORD *will* **f** for you; 4309
17:9 of our men and go out *to* **f** the Amalekites. 4309
Lev 24:10 and a **f broke out** in the camp between him 5897
Nu 22:11 be able to **f** them and drive them away.' " 4309
32:27 will cross over to **f** before the LORD, 4878
Dt 1:30 *will* **f** for you, as he did for you in Egypt, 4309
1:41 We will go up and **f,** 4309
1:42 "Tell them, 'Do not go up and **f,** 4309
3:22 the LORD your God himself *will* **f** 4309
20:4 with you to **f** for you against your enemies 4309
29:7 and Og king of Bashan came out to **f** 4878
Jos 10:25 to all the enemies you *are going to* **f."** 4309
11:5 to **f** against Israel. 4309
24:9 prepared *to* **f** against Israel, 4309
Jdg 1:1 "Who will be the first to go up and **f** for us 4309
1:3 *to* **f** against the Canaanites. 4309
1:9 down to **f** against the Canaanites living in 4309
2:15 Whenever Israel went out to **f,** NIH
8:1 when you went to **f** Midian?" 4309
9:38 Go out and **f** them!" 4309
10:9 to **f** against Judah, Benjamin and the house 4309
11:6 so *we can* **f** the Ammonites." 4309
11:8 come with us *to* **f** the Ammonites, 4309
11:9 "Suppose you take me back to **f** 4309
11:25 Did he ever quarrel with Israel or **f** 4309+4309
11:32 Jephthah went over to **f** the Ammonites, 4309
12:1 to **f** the Ammonites without calling us 4309
12:3 and crossed over to **f** the Ammonites, NIH
12:3 why have you come up today to **f** me?" 4309
15:10 "Why have you come to **f** us?" 6584
18:23 **called out** your men to **f?"** 2410
20:14 to **f** against the Israelites. 2021+3655+4200+4878
20:18 "Who of us shall go first to **f** against 4878
20:20 of Israel went out to **f** the Benjamites 4878
1Sa 4:1 Now the Israelites went out to **f** against 4878
4:9 Be men, and **f!"** 4309
8:20 and to go out before us and **f** our battles." 4309
13:5 The Philistines assembled to **f** Israel, 4309
17:9 If he is able to **f** and kill me, 4309
17:10 Give me a man and *let us* **f** each other." 4309
17:32 your servant will go and **f** him." 4309
17:33 to go out against this Philistine and **f** him; 4309
18:17 only serve me bravely and **f** the battles of 4309
28:1 the Philistines gathered their forces to **f** 4309
29:8 Why can't I go and **f** against the enemies 4309
2Sa 2:14 the young men get up and **f hand to hand** 8471
2:28 nor did they **f** anymore. 4309
10:12 and *let us* **f bravely** for our people and 2616
10:13 with him advanced to **f** the Arameans, 4878
11:20 'Why did you get so close to the city to **f?** 4309
14:6 *They* **got into a f** *with* each other in 5897
18:6 The army marched into the field to **f** Israel, 7925
2Sa 21:15 with his men *to* **f** *against* the Philistines, 4309
1Ki 12:24 Do not go up *to* **f** against your brothers, 4309
20:23 But if *we* **f** them on the plains, 4309
20:25 so *we can* **f** Israel on the plains. 4309
20:26 and went up to Aphek to **f** against Israel. 4878
22:4 with me to **f** against Ramoth Gilead?" 4878
22:31 *"Do* not **f** *with* anyone, small or great, 4309
2Ki 3:7 Will you go with me to **f** against Moab?" 4878
3:21 that the kings had come to **f** against them; 4309
10:3 Then **f** for your master's house." 4309
16:5 of Israel marched up to **f** against Jerusalem 4878
19:9 was marching out to **f** against him. 4309
1Ch 12:19 when he went with the Philistines to **f** 4878
19:13 and *let us* **f bravely** for our people and 2616
19:14 with him advanced to **f** the Arameans, 4878
2Ch 11:4 Do not go up *to* **f** against your brothers. 4309
13:12 Men of Israel, *do* not **f** against the LORD, 4309
18:30 *"Do* not **f** *with* anyone, small or great, 4309
20:17 You *will* not *have* to **f** this **battle.** 4309
25:8 if you go and **f** courageously in battle, 6913
32:8 to help us and to **f** our battles." 4309
35:20 up to **f** at Carchemish on the Euphrates, 4309
35:22 but went to **f** him on the plain of Megiddo. 4309
Ne 4:8 and **f** against Jerusalem and stir up trouble 4309
4:14 and **f** for your brothers, 4309
4:20 Our God *will* **f** for us!" 4309
Ps 35:1 **f** against those who fight against me. 4309
35:1 fight against *those who* **f** *against* me. 4309
Isa 7:1 of Remaliah king of Israel marched up to **f** 4878
19:2 brother *will* **f** against brother, 4309
29:7 Then the hordes of all the nations that **f** 7371
29:8 be with the hordes of all the nations that **f** 7371
37:9 was marching out to **f** against him. 4309
Jer 1:19 *They will* **f** against you but will 4309
15:20 *they will* **f** against you but will 4309
21:4 in your hands, which you *are* using *to* **f** 4309
21:5 *I* myself *will* **f** against you with 4309
32:5 If *you* **f** against the Babylonians, 4309
33:5 *in the* **f** with the Babylonians: 4309
34:22 *They will* **f** against it, 4309
41:12 and went to **f** Ishmael son of Nethaniah. 4309
Da 10:20 Soon I will return to **f** against the prince 4309
11:7 *he will* **f** against them and be victorious. 6913
11:11 of the South will march out in a rage and **f** 4309
Zec 10:5 *they will* **f** and overthrow the horsemen. 4309
14:2 the nations to Jerusalem to **f** against it; 4878
14:3 Then the LORD will go out and **f** 4309
14:14 Judah too *will* **f** at Jerusalem. 4309
Jn 18:36 my servants would **f** to prevent my arrest *76*
1Co 9:26 *I do* not **f** like a man beating the air. *4782*
2Co 10:4 The **weapons** we **f with** are not the weapons of the world. *3836+3960+5127*
1Ti 1:18 so that by following them *you may* **f** *5129*
1:18 by following them you may fight the good **f,** *5127*
6:12 **F** the good fight of the faith. *76*
6:12 Fight the good **f** of the faith. *74*
2Ti 4:7 I have fought the good **f,** *74*
Jas 4:2 You quarrel and **f.** *4482*
Rev 2:16 and *will* **f** against them with the sword *4482*

FIGHTER (4) [FIGHT]

2Sa 17:8 your father is an **experienced f;** 408+4878
17:10 for all Israel knows that your father is a **f** 1475
23:20 Benaiah son of Jehoiada was a **valiant f** 408+1201+2657
1Ch 11:22 Benaiah son of Jehoiada was a **valiant f** 408+1201+2657

FIGHTERS (4) [FIGHT]

Jos 10:2 and all its men were **good f.** 1475
Jdg 20:44 all of them **valiant f.** 408+2657
20:46 all of them **valiant f.** 408+2657
2Sa 17:8 they are **f,** and as fierce as a wild bear 1475

FIGHTING (66) [FIGHT]

Ex 2:13 and saw two Hebrews **f.** 5897
14:25 The LORD *is* **f** for them against Egypt." 4309
21:22 "If men *who are* **f** hit a pregnant woman 5897
Nu 31:42 from that of the **f** men— 7371
Dt 2:14 of **f** men had perished from the camp, 4878
2:16 of these **f** men among the people had died, 4878
20:19 **f** against it to capture it, 4309
25:11 If two men *are* **f** and the wife of one 5897
Jos 1:14 but all your **f men,** fully armed, 1475+2657
6:2 along with its king and its **f men.** 1475+2657
8:3 of his **best f men** and sent them out 1475+2657
10:7 including all the **best f men.** 1475+2657
10:14 Surely the LORD *was* **f** for Israel! 4309
Jdg 20:17 all of them **f** men. 4878
20:34 The **f** was so heavy that the Benjamites did 4878
21:10 assembly sent twelve thousand **f** men 1201+2657
1Sa 17:19 **f** against the Philistines." 4309
17:33 and he has been a **f** man from his youth." 4878
23:1 the Philistines *are* **f** against Keilah 4309
28:15 "The Philistines *are* **f** against me, 4309
29:4 or he will turn against us during the **f.** 4878
31:3 The **f** grew fierce around Saul, 4878
2Sa 10:7 with the entire army of **f men.** 1475
10:14 So Joab returned from **f** the Ammonites 6584
11:15 in the front line where the **f** is fiercest. 4878
24:2 to Beersheba and enroll the **f men,** 6639
24:4 the presence of the king to enroll the **f men** 6639
24:9 Joab reported the number of the **f men** to 6639
24:10 after he had counted the **f men,** 6639
1Ki 9:22 they were his **f** men, 4878

1Ki 11:15 Earlier when David *was* **f with** Edom, 907+2118
12:21 a hundred and eighty thousand **f** men 4878+6913
22:34 "Wheel around and get me out of the **f.** 4722
2Ki 19: 8 and found the king **f** against Libnah. 4309
24:14 all the officers and **f men,** 1475+2657
24:16 the entire force of seven thousand **f** men, 2657
25:19 he took the officer in charge of the **f** men 4878
1Ch 5:20 They were helped in **f** them, 6584
7: 2 descendants of Tola listed as **f men** 1475+2657
7: 5 The relatives who were **f men** 1475+2657
7: 7 record listed 22,034 **f men.** 1475+2657
7: 9 heads of families and 20,200 **f men.** 1475+2657
7:11 **f men** ready to go out to war. 1475+2657
10: 3 The **f** grew fierce around Saul. 4878
12:38 All these were **f** men who volunteered 4878
19: 8 with the entire army of **f men.** 1475
21: 5 Joab reported the number of the **f men** 6639
21:17 not I who ordered the **f men** to be counted? 6639
2Ch 8: 9 they were his **f** men, 4878
11: 1 a hundred and eighty thousand **f** men 4878+6913
13: 3 of four hundred thousand able **f** men, 4878
14: 8 All these were **brave f men.** 1475+2657
17:13 He also kept **experienced f men** in Jerusalem. 408+1475+2657+4878
17:14 the commander, with 300,000 **f men;** 1475+2657
18:33 "Wheel around and get me out of the **f.** 4722
25: 6 a hundred thousand **f men** from Israel 1475+2657
26:12 leaders over the **f men** was 2,600. 1475+2657
32:21 the **f men** and the leaders and officers 1475+2657
Isa 37: 8 and found the king **f** against Libnah. 4309
Jer 34: 1 and peoples in the empire he ruled *were* **f** 4309
34: 7 of Babylon *was* **f** against Jerusalem and 4309
51:30 Babylon's warriors have stopped **f;** 4309
52:25 he took the officer in charge of the **f** men, 4878
Joel 3: 9 Let all the **f** men draw near and attack. 4878
Ac 5:39 you will only find yourselves **f against God** *2534*
7:26 upon two Israelites *who were* **f.** *3481*

FIGHTS (6) [FIGHT]

Jos 23:10 because the LORD your God **f** for you, 4309
Jdg 6:31 Whoever **f** for him shall be put to death 8189
1Sa 25:28 because he **f** the LORD's battles. 4309
Isa 30:32 *as he* **f** them in battle *with* the blows 4309
Zec 14: 3 as he **f** in the day of battle. 4309
Jas 4: 1 What causes **f** and quarrels among you? *4483*

FIGS (24) [FIG]

Nu 13:23 along with some pomegranates and **f.** 9300
20: 5 It has no grain or **f,** 9300
1Sa 25:18 and two hundred **cakes of pressed f,** 1811
30:12 a **cake of pressed f** and two cakes of raisins. 1811
2Sa 16: 1 a hundred **cakes of f** and a skin of wine. 7811
2Ki 20: 7 Then Isaiah said, "Prepare a poultice *of* **f.**" 9300
Ne 13:15 grapes, **f,** and all other kinds of loads. 9300
Isa 34: 4 like shriveled **f** from the fig tree. NIH
38:21 "Prepare a poultice of **f** and apply it to 9300
Jer 8:13 There will be no **f** on the tree, 9300
24: 1 of **f** placed in front of the temple of 9300
24: 2 One basket had very good **f,** 9300
24: 2 the other basket had very poor **f,** 9300
24: 3 **"F,"** I answered. 9300
24: 5 'Like these good **f,** 9300
24: 8 " 'But like the poor **f,** 9300
29:17 and I will make them like poor **f** that are 9300
Mic 7: 1 none of the **early f** that I crave. 1136
Na 3:12 the **f** fall into the mouth of the eater. NIH
Mt 7:16 or **f** from thistles? *5192*
Mk 11:13 because it was not the season *for* **f.** *5192*
Lk 6:44 People do not pick **f** from thornbushes, *5192*
Jas 3:12 or a grapevine bear **f?** *5192*
Rev 6:13 as late **f** drop from a fig tree when shaken *5190*

FIGURATIVELY (4) [FIGURE]

Jn 16:25 "Though I have been speaking **f,** *1877+4231*
Gal 4:24 These things may be **taken f,** *251*
Heb 11:19 **f speaking,** he did receive Isaac back *1877+4130*
Rev 11: 8 which is **f** called Sodom and Egypt, *4462*

FIGURE (4) [FIGURATIVELY, FIGURES]

Eze 1:26 and high above on the throne was a **f** like 1952
8: 2 I looked, and I saw a **f** like that of a man. 1952
Jn 7: 4 to become **a public f** acts in secret. *1877+4244*
10: 6 Jesus used this **f of speech,** *4231*

FIGUREHEAD (1) [HEAD]

Ac 28:11 the **f** of the twin gods Castor and Pollux. *4185*

FIGURES (3) [FIGURE]

2Ch 4: 3 Below the rim, **f** *of* bulls encircled it— 1952
Eze 23:14 **f** *of* Chaldeans portrayed in red, 7512
Jn 16:29 and without **f of speech.** *4231*

FILIGREE (6)

Ex 28:11 Then mount the stones in gold **f** settings 5401
28:13 Make gold **f settings** 5401
28:20 Mount them in gold **f settings.** 8687
39: 6 in gold **f** settings and engraved them like 5401
39:13 They were mounted in gold **f** settings. 5401
39:16 They made two gold **f settings** 5401

FILL (68) [FILLED, FILLING, FILLS, FULL, FULLNESS, FULLY]

Ge 1:22 and increase in number and **f** the water in 4848
1:28 **f** the earth and subdue it. 4848
9: 1 "Be fruitful and increase in number and **f** 4848
42:25 Joseph gave orders *to* **f** their bags 4848
44: 1 **"F** the men's sacks *with* as much food 4848
Ex 2:16 and they came to draw water and **f** 4848
10: 6 *They will* **f** your houses and those 4848
Lev 25:19 you will eat your **f** and live there in safety. 8427
Dt 28:67 of the terror that *will* **f** your hearts and 7064
31:20 and when they eat *their* **f** and thrive, 8425
1Sa 16: 1 **F** your horn *with* oil and be on your way; 4848
1Ki 18:33 **"F** four large jars *with* water and pour it on 4848
Job 8:21 *He will* yet **f** your mouth *with* laughter 4848
15: 2 with empty notions or **f** his belly *with* 4848
15:21 Terrifying sounds **f** his ears; 928
15:24 Distress and anguish **f** him **with terror;** 1286
23: 4 and **f** my mouth *with* arguments. 4848
31:31 'Who *has* not **had** *his* **f** of Job's meat?'— 8425
41: 7 *Can you* **f** his hide with harpoons 4848
Ps 16:11 you will **f** me *with* joy in your presence, 8427
74:20 of violence **f** the dark places of the land. 4848
81:10 Open wide your mouth and *I will* **f** it. 4848
129: 7 *with* it the reaper cannot **f** his hands, 4848
129: 7 nor the one who gathers **f** his arms. NIH
Pr 1:13 of valuable things and **f** our houses 4848
12:21 but the wicked **have** *their* **f** *of* trouble. 4848
26:25 for seven abominations **f** his heart. 928
28:19 one who chases fantasies *will* **have** *his* **f** 8425
Ecc 1: 8 nor the ear *its* **f** of hearing. 4848
SS 5: 1 **drink** *your* **f,** O lovers. 8910
Isa 13:21 jackals *will* **f** her houses; 4848
27: 6 and blossom and **f** all the world *with* fruit. 4848
33: 5 *he will* **f** Zion *with* justice 4848
34: 5 My sword *has* **drunk its f** in the heavens; 8115
44:16 he roasts his meat and **eats** *his* **f.** 8425
56:12 *Let us* **drink** *our* **f** *of* beer! 6010
65:11 who spread a table for Fortune and **f** bowls 4848
Jer 13:13 *to* **f** *with* drunkenness all who live 4848
23:16 **f** you **with false hopes.** 2038
23:24 *"Do* not I **f** heaven and earth?" 4848
46:12 your cries *will* **f** the earth. 4848
50:10 all who plunder her *will have their* **f,"** 8425
51:14 *I will* surely **f** you *with* men, 4848
Eze 3: 3 and **f** your stomach *with* it." 4848
7:19 not satisfy their hunger or **f** their stomachs 4848
8:17 *Must they* also **f** the land *with* violence 4848
9: 7 the temple and **f** the courts *with* the slain. 4848
10: 2 **F** your hands *with* burning coals from 4848
20:26 that *I might* **f** them **with horror** 9037
24: 4 **F** it *with* the best of these bones; 4848
30:11 against Egypt and **f** the land *with* the slain. 4848
32: 5 and **f** the valleys *with* your remains. 4848
35: 8 *I will* **f** your mountains *with* the slain; 4848
39:20 At my table *you will* **eat** *your* **f** *of* horses 8425
Da 7: 5 'Get up and eat your **f** of flesh!' 10678
Zep 1: 9 who **f** the temple of their gods 4848
Hag 1: 6 You drink, but never **have** *your* **f.** 8910
2: 7 and *I will* **f** this house *with* glory,' 4848
Zec 9:13 I will bend Judah as I bend my bow and **f** it 4848
Mt 23:32 **F up,** then, the measure of the sin *4444*
Lk 15:16 He longed *to* **f** his stomach with the pods *1153*
Jn 2: 7 **"F** the jars with water"; *1153*
6:26 because you ate the loaves and *had your* **f.** *5963*
Ac 2:28 *you will* **f** me with joy in your presence.' *4444*
Ro 15:13 *May* the God of hope **f** you with all joy *4444*
Eph 4:10 in order to **f** the whole universe.) *4444*
Col 1: 9 to **f** *you* **with** the knowledge of his will *4444*
1:24 and *I* **f up** in my flesh what is still lacking *499*

FILLED (184) [FILL]

Ge 6: 6 and his heart **was f with pain.** 6772
6:13 earth *is* **f** *with* violence because of them. 4848
21:19 and **f** the skin *with* water and gave the boy 4848
24:16 **f** her jar and came up again. 4848
34: 7 They *were* **f with grief** and fury, 6772
Ex 1: 7 so that the land **was f** *with* them. 4848
16:12 in the morning *you will be* **f** *with* bread. 8425
31: 3 and *I have* **f** him *with* the Spirit of God, 4848
35:31 and *he has* **f** him *with* the Spirit of God, 4848
35:35 *He has* **f** them *with* skill to do all kinds 4848
40:34 the glory of the LORD **f** the tabernacle. 4848
40:35 the glory of the LORD **f** the tabernacle. 4848
Lev 19:29 or the land will turn to prostitution and *be* **f** 4848
Nu 7:13 each **f** *with* fine flour mixed with oil as 4849
7:14 one gold dish weighing ten shekels, **f** *with* incense; 4849
7:19 each **f** *with* fine flour mixed with oil as 4849
7:20 one gold dish weighing ten shekels, **f** *with* incense; 4849
7:25 each **f** *with* fine flour mixed with oil as 4849
7:26 one gold dish weighing ten shekels, **f** *with* incense; 4849
7:31 each **f** *with* fine flour mixed with oil as 4849
7:32 one gold dish weighing ten shekels, **f** *with* incense; 4849
7:37 each **f** *with* fine flour mixed with oil as 4849
7:38 one gold dish weighing ten shekels, **f** *with* incense; 4849
7:43 each **f** *with* fine flour mixed with oil as 4849
7:44 one gold dish weighing ten shekels, **f** *with* incense; 4849
7:49 each **f** *with* fine flour mixed with oil as 4849
7:50 one gold dish weighing ten shekels, **f** *with* incense; 4849
7:55 each **f** *with* fine flour mixed with oil as 4849
Nu 7:56 one gold dish weighing ten shekels, **f** *with* incense; 4849
7:61 each **f** *with* fine flour mixed with oil as 4849
7:62 one gold dish weighing ten shekels, **f** *with* incense; 4849
7:67 each **f** *with* fine flour mixed with oil as 4849
7:68 one gold dish weighing ten shekels, **f** *with* incense; 4849
7:73 each **f** *with* fine flour mixed with oil as 4849
7:74 one gold dish weighing ten shekels, **f** *with* incense; 4849
7:79 each **f** *with* fine flour mixed with oil as 4849
7:80 one gold dish weighing ten shekels, **f** *with* incense; 4849
7:86 The twelve gold dishes **f** with incense 4849
22: 3 Moab *was* **f with dread** because of 7762
22:18 if Balak gave me his palace **f** *with* silver 4850
24:13 if Balak gave me his palace **f** *with* silver 4850
Dt 6:11 houses **f** *with* all kinds 4849
28:66 **f with dread** both night and day, 7064
32:15 **f with food,** he became heavy and sleek. 9042
32:32 Their **grapes** are *f with* poison, AIT
34: 9 of Nun *was* **f** *with* the spirit of wisdom 4848
Jos 9:13 And these wineskins that *we* **f** were new, 4848
Ru 2: 9 a drink from the water jars the men *have* **f."** 8612
1Sa 5:11 death *had* **f** the city *with* panic; 928+2118+3972
28: 5 **terror f** his heart. 3006+4394
28:20 **f with fear** because of Samuel's words. 3707+4394
1Ki 3:26 The woman whose son was alive *was* **f with** 4023
8:10 the cloud **f** the temple of the LORD. 4848
8:11 for the glory of the LORD **f** his temple. 4848
11:27 the supporting terraces and *had* **f in** the gap 6037
18:35 around the altar and even **f** the trench. 4848
2Ki 3:17 yet this valley *will* **be f** *with* water, 4848
3:20 And the land **was f** *with* water. 4848
4: 4 Pour oil into all the jars, and as each is **f,** 4849
4:39 of its gourds and **f** the fold of his cloak. 4850
21:16 so much innocent blood that *he* **f** Jerusalem 4848
24: 4 For *he had* **f** Jerusalem *with* innocent blood, 4848
2Ch 5:13 temple of the LORD *was* **f** *with* a cloud, 4848
5:14 glory of the LORD **f** the temple of God. 4848
7: 1 and the glory of the LORD **f** the temple. 4848
7: 2 because the glory of the LORD **f** it. 4848
Ezr 6:22 the LORD *had* **f** them **with joy** by changing 8523
9:11 By their detestable practices *they have* **f** it 4848
Ne 9:25 of houses **f** *with* all kinds of good things, 4849
Est 5: 9 he **was f** *with* rage against Mordecai. 4848
Job 3:15 who **f** their houses *with* silver. 4848
3:22 who are **f with gladness** and 448+1637+8524
20:23 When he has **f** his belly, 4848
22:18 Yet it was he *who* **f** their houses 4848
Ps 4: 7 *You have* **f** my heart *with* greater joy than 5989
5: 9 their heart is **f** with destruction. NIH
38: 7 My back *is* **f** *with* searing pain; 4848
48:10 your right hand *is* **f** *with* righteousness. 4848
65: 4 *We are* **f** with the good things 8425
65: 9 The streams of God *are* **f** *with* water 4848
71: 8 My mouth *is* **f** *with* your praise, 4848
72:19 *may* the whole earth **be f** *with* his glory. 4848
80: 9 and it took root and **f** the land. 4848
119:64 The earth *is* **f** *with* your love, O LORD; 4848
126: 2 Our mouths **were f** *with* laughter, 4848
126: 3 and we are **f with joy.** 8524
144:13 Our barns will be **f** *with* every kind 4849
Pr 1:31 and *be* **f** with the fruit of their schemes. 8425
3:10 then your barns *will* **be f** to overflowing, 4848
7:20 He took his **purse** *f with* money AIT
8:30 I was **f with delight** day after day, 9141
12:14 of his lips a man *is* **f** *with* good things as 8425
18:20 of his mouth a man's stomach *is* **f;** 8425
24: 4 through knowledge its rooms **are f** 4848
Ecc 8:11 the people *are* **f** *with* schemes to do wrong. 4848
Isa 6: 1 and the train of his robe **f** the temple. 4848
6: 4 and thresholds shook and the temple **was f** 4848
41:23 that we will be dismayed and *f with* **fear.** AIT
51:20 They are **f** *with* the wrath of the LORD 4849
Jer 6: 6 it is **f with** oppression. 928+7931
13:12 Every wineskin *should* **be f** *with* wine.' 4848
13:12 that every wineskin *should* **be f** 4848
15:17 on me and *you had* **f** me *with* indignation. 4848
16:18 and *have* **f** my inheritance 4848
19: 4 and *they have* **f** this place *with* the blood of 4848
25:15 from my hand this **cup** *f with* the wine AIT
31:14 and my people *will be* **f** *with* my bounty," 8425
33: 5 'They *will* **be f** *with* the dead bodies of 4848
41: 9 Ishmael son of Nethaniah **f** it *with* 4848
50: 2 be put to shame, Marduk **f with terror.** 3169
50: 2 to shame and her idols **f with terror.'** 3169
50:36 *They will* **be f with terror.** 3169
51:34 and **f** his stomach with our delicacies, 4848
La 3:15 *He has* **f** me with bitter herbs and sated me 8425
3:30 and *let him be* **f** with disgrace. 8425
Eze 10: 3 and a cloud **f** the inner court. 4848
10: 4 The cloud **f** the temple, 4848
11: 6 in this city and **f** its streets *with* the dead. 4848
23:33 *You will* **be f** *with* drunkenness 4848
27:25 *You are* **f** *with* heavy cargo in the heart of 4848
28:16 Through your widespread trade you *were* **f** 4848
32: 6 and the ravines *will* **be f** with your flesh. 4848
36:38 the ruined cities **be f** *with* flocks of people. 4849
43: 5 and the glory of the LORD **f** the temple. 4848
Da 2:35 the statue became a huge mountain and **f** 10416
11:12 king of the South *will be* **f with pride** 4222+8123
Joel 2:24 The threshing floors *will be* **f** *with* grain; 4848
Am 4:10 *I* **f** your nostrils *with* the stench 6590
Mic 3: 8 But as for me, *I am* **f** *with* power, 4848

Na 1: 2 the LORD takes vengeance and is **f with** 1251
Hab 2:14 For the earth *will* **be f** *with* the knowledge 4848
2:16 *You will be* **f** *with* shame instead of glory. 8425
3: 3 the heavens and his praise **f** the earth. 4848
Zec 8: 5 The city streets *will* **be f** *with* boys 4848
Mt 5: 6 for they *will be* **f.** *5963*
9: 8 *they were* **f with awe;** *5828*
17:23 And the disciples *were* **f with grief.** *3382+5379*
22:10 and the wedding hall *was* **f** with guests. *4398*
27:48 *He* **f** it with wine vinegar, put it on a stick, *4398*
28: 8 afraid yet **f with joy,** *3489+5915*
Mk 1:41 **F with compassion,** Jesus reached out his hand *5072*
15:36 **f** a sponge with wine vinegar, *1153*
Lk 1:15 and *he will be* **f** with the Holy Spirit even *4398*
1:41 and Elizabeth *was* **f** with the Holy Spirit. *4398*
1:53 *He has* **f** the hungry with good things *1855*
1:65 The neighbors were all **f** with awe, *NIG*
1:67 His father Zechariah *was* **f** with the Holy Spirit and prophesied: *4398*
2:40 *he was* **f** with wisdom, *4444*
3: 5 Every valley *shall be* **f in,** *4444*
5: 7 and **f** both boats so full that they began *4398*
5:26 *They were* **f** with awe and said, *4398*
7:16 They were all **f with awe** and praised God. *3284+5832*
15:20 and *was* **f with compassion for** him; *5072*
Jn 2: 7 so *they* **f** them to the brim. *1153*
6:13 So they gathered them and **f** twelve baskets *1153*
12: 3 And the house *was* **f** with the fragrance of *4444*
16: 6 you *are* **f with** grief. *4444*
Ac 2: 2 of a violent wind came from heaven and **f** *4444*
2: 4 All of them *were* **f** with the Holy Spirit *4398*
2:43 Everyone **was f with** awe, *1181*
3:10 and *they were* **f** with wonder *4398*
4: 8 Peter, **f** with the Holy Spirit, said to them: *4398*
4:31 And *they were* all **f** with the Holy Spirit *4398*
5: 3 how is it that Satan *has* so **f** your heart *4444*
5:17 *were* **f** with jealousy. *4398*
5:28 "Yet *you have* **f** Jerusalem *4444*
9:17 so that you may see again and *be* **f** with *4398*
13: 9 **f** with the Holy Spirit, *4398*
13:45 *they were* **f** with jealousy *4398*
13:52 And the disciples *were* **f** with joy and with *4444*
16:34 *he was* **f with joy** because he had come *22*
Ro 1:29 *They have become* **f** with every kind *4444*
1Co 5: 2 Shouldn't *you* rather *have been* **f with grief** *4291*
Eph 3:19 that *you may be* **f** to the measure of all *4444*
5:18 Instead, *be* **f** with the Spirit. *4444*
Php 1:11 **f with** the fruit of righteousness that comes *4444*
2Ti 1: 4 so that *I may be* **f** with joy. *4444*
1Pe 1: 8 **f with** an inexpressible and glorious **joy,** *22+5915*
Rev 8: 5 **f** it with fire from the altar, *1153*
12:12 *He is* **f with** fury, *2400*
15: 7 the seven angels seven golden bowls **f** with *1154*
15: 8 And the temple *was* **f** with smoke from *1153*
16:19 and gave her the cup **f** with the wine of *NIG*
17: 4 **f** with abominable things and the filth *1154*

FILLET, FILLETED (KJV) See BANDS

FILLING (3) [FILL]
Ge 26:15 Philistines stopped up, **f** them *with* earth. 4848
Eze 44: 4 I looked and saw the glory of the LORD **f** 4848
Na 2:12 **f** his lairs *with* the kill and his dens *with* 4848

FILLS (6) [FILL]
Nu 14:21 the glory of the LORD **f** the whole earth, 4848
Job 20:11 The youthful vigor *that* **f** his bones will lie 4848
36:32 *He* **f** his hands *with* lightning 4059
Ps 107: 9 for he satisfies the thirsty and **f** the hungry 4848
Ac 14:17 **f** your hearts **with joy."** *2372*
Eph 1:23 of him who **f** everything in every way. *4444*

FILTH (9) [FILTHINESS, FILTHY]
2Ki 18:27 who, like you, will have to eat their own **f** 2989
Pr 30:12 and yet are not cleansed of their **f;** 7363
Isa 4: 4 The Lord will wash away the **f** *of* 7363
28: 8 and there is not a spot without **f.** 7363
36:12 who, like you, will have to eat their own **f** 2989
Na 3: 6 I will pelt you with **f,** 9199
Zep 1:17 like dust and their entrails like **f.** 1672
Jas 1:21 get rid of all **moral f** and the evil that is *4864*
Rev 17: 4 filled with abominable things and the **f** *176*

FILTHINESS (1) [FILTH]
La 1: 9 Her **f** clung to her skirts; 3240

FILTHY (5) [FILTH]
Isa 64: 6 and all our righteous acts are like **f** rags; 6340
Zec 3: 3 in **f** clothes as he stood before the angel. 7364
3: 4 "Take off his **f** clothes." 7364
Col 3: 8 slander, and **f language** from your lips. *155*
2Pe 2: 7 who was distressed by the **f** lives *816*

FINAL (6) [FINALITY, FINALLY]
Ru 4: 7 and transfer of property to *become* **f,** 7756
Ps 73:17 then I understood their **f destiny.** 344
Isa 41:22 and know their **f outcome.** 344
Mt 12:45 the **f** *condition* of that man is worse than *2274*
Lk 11:26 the **f** *condition* of that man is worse than *2274*
Ac 28:25 after Paul had made this **f** statement: *NIG*

FINALITY (1) [FINAL]
Ro 9:28 on earth *with* speed and **f."** *5334*

FINALLY (36) [FINAL]
Nu 10:25 **F,** as the rear guard for all the units, 2256
Jdg 9:14 "**F** all the trees said to the thornbush, 2256
14:17 So on the seventh day he **f** told her, NIH
1Sa 10:21 **F** Saul son of Kish was chosen. 2256
19:22 **F,** he himself left for Ramah and went 1685+2256
2Sa 24: 7 **F,** they went on to Beersheba in the Negev 2256
1Ki 17:17 and **f** stopped breathing. 889+6330
22:21 **F,** a spirit came forward, 2256
2Ch 18:20 **F,** a spirit came forward, 2256
Ne 2:15 **F,** I turned back and reentered through 2256
Da 2:40 **F,** there will be a fourth kingdom, 10221
4: 8 **F,** Daniel came into my presence 10024+10221+10527
6: 5 **F** these men said, 10008
12: 7 power of the holy people has been **f** broken, 3983
Mt 22:27 **F,** the woman died. *4246+5731*
26:60 **F** two came forward *5731*
Mk 6:21 **F** the opportune time came. *NIG*
Lk 18: 4 But **f** he said to himself, *3552+4047*
20:32 **F,** the woman died too. *5731*
Jn 1:22 **F** they said, "Who are you? *4036*
7:45 **F** the temple guards went back to *4036*
9:17 **F** they turned again to the blind man, *4036*
19:16 **F** Pilate handed him over to them to *5538*
20: 8 **F** the other disciple, *4036+5538*
Ac 16:18 **F** Paul became so troubled that he turned *1254*
20: 2 and **f** arrived in Greece, *NIG*
27:20 we **f** gave up all hope of being saved. *3370*
2Co 13:11 **F,** brothers, good-by. *3370*
Gal 6:17 **F,** let no one cause me trouble, *3370+3836*
Eph 6:10 **F,** be strong in the Lord and *3370+3836*
Php 3: 1 **F,** my brothers, rejoice in the Lord! *3370+3836*
4: 8 **F,** brothers, whatever is true, *3370+3836*
1Th 4: 1 **F,** brothers, we instructed you how to live *3370*
2Th 3: 1 **F,** brothers, pray for us that *3370+3836*
Jas 5:11 have seen what the Lord **f** brought about. *5465*
1Pe 3: 8 **F,** all of you, live in harmony *3836+5465*

FINANCIAL (1)
1Ti 6: 5 think that godliness is a **means to f gain.** *4516*

FIND (230) [FINDING, FINDS, FOUND]
Ge 8: 9 the dove *could* **f** no place to set its feet 5162
18:26 "If *I* **f** fifty righteous people in the city 5162
18:28 "If *I* **f** forty-five there," he said, 5162
18:30 "I will not do it if *I* **f** thirty there." 5162
19:11 with blindness so that they could not **f** 5162
27:20 "How *did you* **f** it so quickly, my son?" 5162
31:32 But if *you* **f** anyone who has your gods, 5162
31:35 but *could* not **f** the household gods. 5162
32: 5 that I *may* **f** favor in your eyes.' " 5162
33: 8 "To **f** favor in your eyes, my lord," he said. 5162
33:15 *"Just let me* **f** favor in the eyes 5162
34:11 *"Let me* **f** favor in your eyes, 5162
38:20 but *he did* not **f** her. 5162
38:22 *"I* didn't **f** her. 5162
38:23 but you didn't **f** her." 5162
41:38 *"Can we* **f** anyone like this man, 5162
44:15 **f things out by divination?"** 5727+5727
47:25 *"May we* **f** favor in the eyes of our lord; 5162
Ex 5:11 get your own straw wherever *you can* **f** it, 5162
16:25 not **f** any of it on the ground today. 5162
33:13 and *continue to* **f** favor with you. 5162
Nu 9: 8 until *I* **f out** what the LORD commands 9048
10:33 during those three days to **f** them a place 9365
22:19 and *I will* **f out** what else 3359
32:23 be sure that your sin *will* **f** you **out.** 5162
Dt 4:29 *you will* **f** him if you look for him 5162
13: 3 to **f out** whether you love him 3359
14:21 Do not eat anything you **f** already dead. NIH
22: 3 Do the same if you **f** your brother's donkey NIH
22:14 *I did* not **f** proof of her virginity," 5162
22:17 *'I did* not **f** your daughter to be a virgin.' 5162
28:65 Among those nations *you will* **f** no **repose,** 8089
Jos 2:16 to the hills so the pursuers *will* not **f** you. 7003
20: 3 and **f** protection from the avenger of blood. 2118
Jdg 18: 8 **"How did you f things?"** 4537
18:10 *you will* **f** an unsuspecting people and 448+995
Ru 1: 9 that each of you *will* **f** rest in the home 5162
2: 2 behind anyone in whose eyes *I* **f** favor." 5162
2:13 *"May I continue to* **f** favor in your eyes, 5162
3: 1 *should I* not **try to f** a home for you, 1335
3:18 until *you* **f out** what happens. 3359
1Sa 1:18 *"May* your servant **f** favor in your eyes." 5162
9: 4 but *they did* not **f** them. 5162
9: 4 but *they did* not **f** them. 5162
9:13 *you will* **f** him before he goes up to 5162
9:13 *you should* **f** him about this time." 5162
14:38 *let us* **f out** what sin has been committed today. 2256+3359+8011
16:17 "**F** someone who plays well and bring him 8011
17:56 "**F out** whose son this young man is." 8626
19: 3 about you and will tell you what *I* **f out."** 8011
20:21 Then I will send a boy and say, 'Go, **f** 5162
20:36 "Run and **f** the arrows I shoot." 5162
21: 3 or whatever *you can* **f."** 5162
23:16 and **helped** him **f strength** 906+2616+3338
23:22 **F out** where David usually goes 2256+3359+8011
23:23 **F out** about all the hiding places he uses 2256+3359+8011
1Sa 25: 8 and your son David whatever you *can* **f** 5162
28: 7 "**F** me a woman who is a medium, 1335
2Sa 3:25 and **f out** everything you are doing." 3359
11: 3 David sent someone *to* **f out** about her. 2011
15:25 If *I* **f** favor in the LORD's eyes, 5162
16: 4 *"May I* **f** favor in your eyes, 5162
20: 6 or *he will* **f** fortified cities and escape 5162
1Ki 18: 5 Maybe *we can* **f** some grass to keep 5162
18:10 he made them swear *they could* not **f** you. 5162
18:12 If I go and tell Ahab and *he* doesn't **f** you, 5162
22:25 "You *will* **f out** on the day you go to hide 8011
2Ki 2:17 for three days but *did* not **f** him. 5162
6:13 "Go, **f out** where he is," the king ordered, 8011
7:13 let us send them *to* **f out** what happened." 8011
7:14 "Go and **f out** what has happened." 8011
2Ch 18:24 "You *will* **f out** on the day you go to hide 8011
20:16 and *you will* **f** them at the end of 5162
32: 4 of Assyria come and **f** plenty of water?" 5162
Ezr 2:62 not **f** *them* and so were excluded from 5162
4:15 In these records *you will* **f** that this city is 10708
Ne 5: 8 because *they could* **f** nothing to say. 5162
7:64 not **f** *them* and so were excluded from 5162
Est 2:11 near the courtyard of the harem to **f out** 3359
4: 5 to **f out** what was troubling Mordecai 3359
Job 5:24 of your property and **f** nothing **missing.** 2627
8: 8 and **f out** what their fathers learned, 3922
9:14 *How can I* **f** words to argue with him? 1047
17:10 *I will* not **f** a wise man among you. 5162
22:26 then *you will* **f delight** in the Almighty 6695
23: 3 If only I knew where *to* **f** him; 5162
23: 5 *I would* **f out** what he would answer me, 3359
23: 8 if I go to the west, *I do* not **f** him. 1067
27:10 *Will he* **f delight** in the Almighty? 6695
32:20 I must speak and **f relief;** 8118
Ps 17: 3 though you test me, *you will* **f** nothing; 5162
36: 7 and low among men **f refuge** in the shadow 2879
62: 5 **F rest,** O my soul, in God alone; 1957
91: 4 and under his wings *you will* **f refuge;** 2879
119:35 for there *I* **f delight.** 2911
119:52 O LORD, and *I* **f comfort** in them. 5714
132: 5 till *I* **f** a place for the LORD, 5162
Pr 1:28 they will look for me but *will* not **f** me. 5162
2: 5 of the LORD and **f** the knowledge of God. 5162
4:22 for they are life to *those who* **f** them 5162
8:17 and those who seek me **f** me. 5162
8:36 But *whoever* **fails to f** me harms himself; 2627
14: 7 for *you will* not **f** knowledge on his lips. 3359
14:22 But those who plan what is good **f** love NIH
20: 6 but a faithful man who *can* **f?** 5162
23:35 will I wake up so *I can* **f** another drink?" 1335
24:14 if *you* **f** it, there is a future hope for you, 5162
25:16 If *you* **f** honey, eat just enough— 5162
31:10 A wife of noble character who *can* **f?** 5162
Ecc 2: 1 with pleasure *to* **f out** what is good." 8011
2:24 and drink and **f** satisfaction in his work. 8011
2:25 who can eat or **f enjoyment?** 2591
3:13 and **f** satisfaction in all his toil— 8011
5:18 to **f** satisfaction in his toilsome labor under 8011
7:26 I **f** more bitter than death 5162
11: 1 for after many days *you will* **f** it *again.* 5162
12: 1 "I **f** no pleasure in them"— 4200
12:10 Teacher searched to **f** just the right words, 5162
SS 3: 1 I looked for him but *did* not **f** him. 5162
3: 2 So I looked for him but *did* not **f** him. 5162
5: 6 I looked for him but *did* not **f** him. 5162
5: 8 if *you* **f** my lover, what will you tell him? 5162
Isa 14:30 The poorest of the poor *will* **f pasture,** 8286
14:32 in her his afflicted people *will* **f refuge."** 2879
23:12 even there you *will* **f** no **rest."** 5663
34:14 the night creatures will also repose and **f** 5162
41:12 *you will* not **f** them. 5162
49: 9 and **f** pasture on every barren hill. NIH
57: 2 *they* **f rest** as they lie in death. 5663
58:14 then *you will* **f** *your* **joy** in the LORD, 6695
59:11 We look for justice, but **f** none; NIH
Jer 2: 5 "What fault *did* your fathers **f** in me, 5162
2:24 at mating time *they will* **f** her. 5162
2:34 On your clothes *men* **f** the lifeblood of 5162
5: 1 If *you can* **f** but one person 5162
6:10 *they* **f** no **pleasure** in it. 2911
6:16 and *you will* **f** rest for your souls. 5162
14: 3 they go to the cisterns but **f** no water. 5162
23:11 even in my temple *I* **f** their wickedness," 5162
29: 6 **f** wives for your sons 4374
29:13 and **f** me when you seek me 5162
31: 2 the sword *will* **f** favor in the desert; 5162
45: 3 with groaning and **f** no rest.' " 5162
La 1: 6 Her princes are like deer *that* **f** no pasture; 5162
2: 9 and her prophets no longer **f** visions from 5162
5: 5 we are weary and **f** no **rest.** 5663
Eze 17:23 *they will* **f shelter** in the shade 8905
Da 6: 4 the satraps tried to **f** grounds for charges 10708
6: 4 *They could* **f** no corruption in him, 10708
6: 5 *"We will* never **f** any basis for charges 10708
Hos 2: 6 in so that *she* cannot **f** her way. 5162
2: 7 she will look for them but not **f** them. 5162
5: 6 *they will* not **f** him; 5162
12: 8 With all my wealth *they will* not **f** 5162
14: 3 for in you the fatherless **f compassion."** 8163
Am 8:12 but *they will* not **f** it. 5162
Jnh 1: 7 let us cast lots *to* **f out** who is responsible 3359
Na 3: 7 Where *can I* **f** anyone to comfort you?" 1335
Zep 2: 7 there *they will* **f pasture.** 8286
Zec 2: 2 to **f out** how wide and how long it is." 8011
Mt 2: 8 As soon as *you* **f** him, report to me, *2351*
7: 7 seek and *you will* **f;** *2351*
7:14 that leads to life, and only a few **f** it. *1639+2351*

Mt 10:39 whoever loses his life for my sake *will* **f** it. *2351*
11:29 and *you will* **f** rest for your souls. *2351*
12:43 seeking rest and *does* not **f** it. *2351*
16:25 but whoever loses his life for me *will* **f** it. *2351*
17:27 and *you will* **f** a four-drachma coin. *2351*
21: 2 at once *you will* **f** a donkey tied there, *2351*
22: 9 and invite to the banquet anyone *you* **f.'** *2351*
22:10 and gathered all the people *they* could **f,** *2351*
26:60 But *they did* not **f** any, *2351*
Mk 11: 2 *you will* **f** a colt tied there, *2351*
11:13 he went *to* **f out** if it had any fruit. *2351*
13:36 do not let *him* **f** you sleeping. *2351*
14:55 but *they did* not **f** any. *2351*
Lk 1:62 to **f** out what he would like to name *NIG*
2:12 *You will* **f** a baby wrapped in cloths *2351*
2:45 *When they did* not **f** him, *2351*
5:19 *When they* could not **f** a way to do this *2351*
9:12 and countryside and **f** food and lodging, *2351*
11: 9 seek and *you will* **f;** *2351*
11:24 seeking rest and *does* not **f** it. *2351*
13: 6 to look for fruit on it, but *did* not **f** any. *2351*
18: 8 *will he* **f** faith on the earth?" *2351*
19:15 in order to **f out** what they had gained *1182*
19:30 *you will* **f** a colt tied there, *2351*
19:48 Yet *they could* not **f** any way to do it, *2351*
23: 4 *"I* **f** no basis for a charge against this man." *2351*
24: 3 *they did* not **f** the body of the Lord Jesus. *2351*
24:23 but didn't **f** his body. *2351*
Jn 1:41 *to* **f** his brother Simon and tell him, *2351*
4:27 and were surprised to **f** him talking with *NIG*
7:17 *he will* **f out** whether my teaching comes *1182*
7:34 but *you will* not **f** me; *2351*
7:35 to go that we cannot **f** him? *2351*
7:36 but *you will* not **f** me,' and 'Where I am, *2351*
7:51 to **f out** what he is doing?" *1182*
7:52 and *you will* **f** that a prophet does *3972*
10: 9 He will come in and go out, and **f** pasture. *2351*
18:38 "I **f** no basis for a charge against him. *2351*
19: 4 to you to let you know that *I* **f** no basis for *2351*
19: 6 *I* **f** no basis for a charge against him." *2351*
21: 6 of the boat and *you will* **f** some." *2351*
Ac 5:22 the officers *did* not **f** them there. *2351*
5:39 *you will* only **f** *yourselves* fighting *2351*
7:11 and our fathers *could* not **f** food. *2351*
12:19 for him and *did* not **f** him, *2351*
16:13 where we expected *to* **f** a place of prayer. *1639*
17: 6 But *when they did* not **f** them, *2351*
17:27 and perhaps reach out for him and **f** him, *2351*
22:24 to **f out** why the people were shouting *2105*
22:30 to **f out** exactly why Paul was being accused *1182*
23: 9 *"We* **f** nothing wrong with this man," *2351*
24:12 My accusers *did* not **f** me arguing *2351*
24:25 *When I* **f** it **convenient,** *2789+3561*
Ro 7:21 So *I* **f** this law at work: *2351*
1Co 4:19 and then *I will* **f out** not only *1182*
2Co 2:13 *because I did* not **f** my brother Titus there. *2351*
9: 4 with me and **f** you unprepared, we— *2351*
12:20 when I come *I may* not **f** you as I want you *2351*
12:20 and you *may* not **f** me as you want me *2351*
Eph 5:10 and **f out** what pleases the Lord. *1507*
1Th 3: 5 I sent to **f out about** your faith. *1182*
2Ti 1:18 the Lord grant that he *will* **f** mercy from *2351*
Heb 4:16 and **f** grace to help us in our time of need. *2351*
Jas 3:16 there you **f** disorder and every evil practice. *NIG*
1Pe 1:11 **trying to f out** the time and circumstances *2236*
2Jn 1: 4 to **f** some of your children walking in the truth, *2351*
Rev 9: 6 men will seek death, but *will* not **f** it; *2351*

FINDING (12) [FIND]

Ex 15:22 in the desert without **f** water. 5162
Jos 2:22 the road and returned without **f** them. 5162
Jdg 5:30 *'Are they* not **f** and dividing the spoils: 5162
15:15 **F** a fresh jawbone of a donkey, 5162
Job 36:26 The number of his years is past **f out.** 2984
Ps 107: 4 **f** no way to a city where they could settle. 5162
Ecc 7:28 while I was still searching but not **f—** 5162
Hos 9:10 it was like **f** grapes in the desert; NIH
Jn 1:43 **F** Philip, he said to him, "Follow me." *2351*
Ac 5:10 the young men came in and, **f** her dead, *2351*
21: 4 **F** the disciples there, *461*
Jas 1: 5 to all without **f fault,** *3943*

FINDS (45) [FIND]

Ge 4:14 and whoever **f** me will kill me." 5162
Lev 6: 3 or if *he* **f** lost property and lies about it, or 5162
Nu 35:27 the avenger of blood **f** him outside the city, 5162
Dt 24: 1 because *he* **f** something indecent about her, 5162
Jdg 9:33 do whatever your hand **f** to do." 5162
1Sa 10: 7 do whatever your hand **f** to do, 5162
24:19 When a man **f** his enemy, 5162
Job 33:20 so that his very being **f** food **repulsive** 2299
33:26 He prays to God and **f favor with** him, 8354
Ps 55:15 for evil **f** lodging among them. NIH
62: 1 My soul **f** rest in God alone; NIH
112: 1 *who* **f** great **delight** in his commands. 2911
119:162 in your promise like *one who* **f** great spoil. 5162
Pr 3:13 Blessed is the man *who* **f** wisdom, 5162
8:35 For *whoever* **f** me finds life 5162
8:35 For whoever finds me **f** life 5162
10:23 A fool **f** pleasure in evil conduct, 4200
11:27 He who seeks good **f** goodwill, 1335
14: 6 The mocker seeks wisdom and *f* **none,** AIT
15:23 A man **f** joy in giving an apt reply— NIH
18: 2 A fool **f** no **pleasure** in understanding 2911
18:22 *He who* **f** a wife finds what is good 5162
18:22 a wife **f** what is good and receives favor 5162
20: 4 so at harvest time he looks but **f** nothing. NIH
21:21 who pursues righteousness and love **f** life, 5162
28:13 and renounces them **f mercy.** 8163
Ecc 9:10 Whatever your hand **f** to do, 5162
Isa 38:16 and my spirit **f** life in them too. NIH
La 1: 3 *she* **f** no resting place. 5162
Mt 7: 8 he who seeks **f;** *2351*
10:39 Whoever **f** his life will lose it, *2351*
12:44 *it* **f** the house unoccupied, *2351*
18:13 And if *he* **f** it, I tell you the truth, *1181+2351*
24:46 for that servant whose master **f** him doing *2351*
Lk 11:10 he who seeks **f;** *2351*
11:25 *it* **f** the house swept clean and put *2351*
12:37 good for those servants whose master **f** them watching *2351*
12:38 those servants whose master **f** them ready, *2351*
12:43 for that servant whom the master **f** doing *2351*
15: 4 and go after the lost sheep until *he* **f** it? *2351*
15: 5 And *when he* **f** it, *2351*
15: 8 and search carefully until *she* **f** it? *2351*
15: 9 And *when she* **f** it, *2351*
22:16 not eat it again until *it* **f fulfillment** in the kingdom of God." *4444*
1Co 14:16 how can one who **f himself** among those *405*

FINE (123) [FINE-LOOKING, FINE-SOUNDING, FINED, FINELY, FINERY, FINES, FINEST]

Ge 18: 6 "get three seahs of **f** flour and knead it 6159
41:42 He dressed him in robes of **f linen** and put 9254
Ex 2: 2 When she saw that he was a **f** *child,* 3202
9: 9 It will become **f dust** over the whole land 85
25: 4 purple and scarlet yarn and **f linen;** 9254
28: 5 purple and scarlet yarn, and **f linen.** 9254
28:39 the tunic of **f linen** and make the turban 9254
28:39 and make the turban of **f linen.** 9254
29: 2 And from **f** wheat **flour,** without yeast, 6159
29:40 a tenth of an ephah of **f flour** mixed with 6159
30:23 "Take the following **f** spices: 8031
35: 6 purple and scarlet yarn and **f linen;** 9254
35:23 purple or scarlet yarn or **f linen,** 9254
35:25 blue, purple or scarlet yarn or **f linen.** 9254
35:35 purple and scarlet yarn and **f linen,** 9254
38:23 purple and scarlet yarn and **f linen.)** 9254
39: 3 purple and scarlet yarn and **f linen—** 9254
39:27 they made tunics of **f linen—** 9254
39:28 and the turban of **f linen,** 9254
Lev 2: 1 his offering is to be of **f flour.** 6159
2: 2 a handful of the **f flour** and oil, 6159
2: 4 it is to consist of **f flour:** 6159
2: 5 it is to be made of **f flour** mixed with oil, 6159
2: 7 it is to be made of **f flour** and oil. 6159
5:11 of an ephah of **f flour** for a sin offering. 6159
6:15 The priest is to take a handful of **f flour** 6159
6:20 of **f flour** as a regular grain offering, 6159
7:12 of **f flour** well-kneaded and mixed 6159
14:10 of an ephah of **f flour** mixed with oil *for* 6159
14:21 with a tenth of an ephah of **f flour** mixed 6159
23:13 of an ephah of **f flour** mixed with oil— 6159
23:17 of two-tenths of an ephah of **f flour,** 6159
24: 5 "Take **f flour** and bake twelve loaves 6159
Nu 6:15 cakes made of **f flour** mixed with oil, 6159
7:13 each filled with **f flour** mixed with oil as 6159
7:19 each filled with **f flour** mixed with oil as 6159
7:25 each filled with **f flour** mixed with oil as 6159
7:31 each filled with **f flour** mixed with oil as 6159
7:37 each filled with **f flour** mixed with oil as 6159
7:43 each filled with **f flour** mixed with oil as 6159
7:49 each filled with **f flour** mixed with oil as 6159
7:55 each filled with **f flour** mixed with oil as 6159
7:61 each filled with **f flour** mixed with oil as 6159
7:67 each filled with **f flour** mixed with oil as 6159
7:73 each filled with **f flour** mixed with oil as 6159
7:79 each filled with **f flour** mixed with oil as 6159
8: 8 with its grain offering of **f flour** mixed 6159
15: 4 a tenth of an ephah of **f flour** mixed with 6159
15: 6 an ephah of **f flour** mixed with a third of 6159
15: 9 an ephah of **f flour** mixed with half a hin 6159
28: 5 a tenth of an ephah of **f flour** mixed with 6159
28: 9 of an ephah of **f flour** mixed with oil. 6159
28:12 of an ephah of **f flour** mixed with oil; 6159
28:12 of an ephah of **f flour** mixed with oil; 6159
28:13 of a tenth of an ephah of **f flour** mixed 6159
28:20 of an ephah of **f flour** mixed with oil; 6159
28:28 of an ephah of **f flour** mixed with oil; 6159
29: 3 of an ephah of **f flour** mixed with oil; 6159
29: 9 of an ephah of **f flour** mixed with oil; 6159
29:14 of an ephah of **f flour** mixed with oil; 6159
Dt 3:25 that **f** hill country and Lebanon." 3202
8:12 when you build **f** houses and settle down, 3202
9:21 to powder as **f** as dust and threw the dust 1990
22:19 *They shall* **f** him a hundred shekels 6740
1Sa 16:12 a **f** appearance and handsome features. 3637
2Sa 22:43 *I* **beat** them as **f** as the dust of the earth; 8835
1Ki 4:22 of **f flour** and sixty cors of meal, 6159
10:18 with ivory and overlaid with **f** gold. 7059
2Ki 20:13 silver, the gold, the spices and the **f** oil— 3202
1Ch 15:27 David was clothed in a robe of **f linen,** 1009
29: 2 and all kinds of **f** stone and marble— 3701
2Ch 2:14 and blue and crimson yarn and **f linen.** 1009
3: 5 with **f** gold and decorated it with palm tree 3202
3: 8 inside with six hundred talents of **f** gold. 3202
3:14 purple and crimson yarn and **f linen,** 1009
5:12 dressed in **f linen** and playing cymbals, 1009
Ezr 8:27 and two **f** articles of polished bronze, 3202
Est 8:15 of gold and a purple robe of **f linen.** 1009
Job 16: 4 *I could* **make f speeches** against you 928+2488+4863
Ps 18:42 *I* **beat** them as **f** as dust borne on the wind; 8835
92:10 **f** oils have been poured upon me. 8316
Pr 8:19 My fruit is better than **f gold;** 7058
25:12 of **f gold** is a wise man's rebuke to 4188
31:22 she is clothed in **f linen** and purple. 9254
Ecc 7: 1 A good name is better than **f perfume,** 9043
Isa 3:22 the **f robes** and the capes and cloaks, 4711
3:24 instead of **f clothing,** sackcloth; 7345
5: 9 the **f** mansions left without occupants. 1524+2256+3202
19: 9 the weavers of **f linen** will lose hope. 2583
23:18 for abundant food and **f** clothes. 6971
29: 5 your many enemies will become like **f** dust, 1987
39: 2 the silver, the gold, the spices, the **f** oil, 3202
40:15 the islands as though they were **f** dust. 1987
Jer 22: 7 up your **f** cedar beams and throw them into 4436
25:34 you will fall and be shattered like **f** pottery. 2775
La 4: 1 the **f** gold become dull! 3202
Eze 16:10 I dressed you in **f linen** and covered you 9254
16:13 your clothes were of **f linen** 9254
16:13 Your food was **f flour,** 6159
16:17 You also took the **f** jewelry I gave you, 9514
16:19 the **f flour,** olive oil 6159
16:39 of your clothes and take your **f** jewelry 9514
23:26 of your clothes and take your **f** jewelry. 9514
26:12 and demolish your **f** houses 2775
27: 7 **F** embroidered **linen** from Egypt 9254
27:16 purple fabric, embroidered work, **f linen,** 1009
Mt 11: 8 A man dressed in **f clothes?** *3434*
11: 8 who wear **f clothes** are in kings' palaces. *3434*
13:45 like a merchant looking for **f** pearls. *2819*
Mk 7: 9 a **f way** of setting aside the commands *2822*
Lk 7:25 A man dressed in **f** clothes? *3434*
13: 9 If it bears fruit next year, **f!** *NIG*
16:19 and **f linen** and lived in luxury every day. *1116*
Gal 4:18 It is **f** to be zealous, *2819*
Jas 2: 2 a gold ring and **f** clothes, *3287*
2: 3 to the man wearing **f** clothes and say, *3287*
1Pe 3: 3 the wearing of gold jewelry and **f** clothes. *NIG*
Rev 18:12 **f linen,** purple, silk and scarlet cloth; *1115*
18:13 of **f flour** and wheat; *4947*
18:16 Woe, O great city, dressed in **f linen,** *1115*
19: 8 **F linen,** bright and clean, *1115*
19: 8 **(F linen** stands for the righteous acts of *1115*
19:14 on white horses and dressed in **f linen,** *1115*

FINE-LOOKING (1) [FINE, LOOK]

1Sa 16:18 He speaks well and is a **f** man. 9307

FINE-SOUNDING (1) [FINE, SOUND]

Col 2: 4 no one may deceive you by **f arguments.** *4391*

FINED (1) [FINE]

Ex 21:22 the offender **must be f** whatever 6740+6740

FINELY (22) [FINE]

Ex 26: 1 with ten curtains of **f twisted** linen 8813
26:31 purple and scarlet yarn and **f twisted** linen, 8813
26:36 and scarlet yarn and **f twisted** linen— 8813
27: 9 and is to have curtains of **f twisted** linen, 8813
27:16 and scarlet yarn and **f twisted** linen— 8813
27:18 of **f twisted** linen five cubits high, 8813
28: 6 and of **f twisted** linen— 8813
28: 8 and with **f twisted** linen. 8813
28:15 and of **f twisted** linen. 8813
36: 8 with ten curtains of **f twisted** linen 8813
36:35 purple and scarlet yarn and **f twisted** linen, 8813
36:37 and scarlet yarn and **f twisted** linen— 8813
38: 9 and had curtains of **f twisted** linen, 8813
38:16 the courtyard were of **f twisted** linen. 8813
38:18 and scarlet yarn and **f twisted** linen— 8813
39: 2 and of **f twisted** linen. 8813
39: 5 and with **f twisted** linen, 8813
39: 8 and of **f twisted** linen. 8813
39:24 and scarlet yarn and **f twisted** linen around 8813
39:28 and the undergarments of **f twisted** linen. 8813
39:29 The sash was of **f twisted** linen and blue, 8813
Lev 16:12 of **f ground** fragrant incense and take them 1987

FINER (KJV) See SILVERSMITH

FINERY (2) [FINE]

2Sa 1:24 who clothed you in scarlet and **f,** 6358
Isa 3:18 that day the Lord will snatch away their **f:** 9514

FINES (1) [FINE]

Am 2: 8 of their god they drink wine taken as **f.** 6711

FINEST (19) [FINE]

Nu 18:12 the **f** olive oil and all the finest new wine 2693
18:12 and all the **f** new wine and grain they give 2693
Dt 32:14 of Bashan and the **f** kernels of wheat. 2693
33:14 with the best the sun brings forth and the **f** 4458
Jdg 20:34 Then ten thousand of Israel's **f** men made 1047
2Ki 8: 9 as a gift forty camel-loads of all the **f wares** 3206
19:23 the **f** of its **forests.** 3623+4149
Job 28:15 It cannot be bought with the **f gold,** 6034

Ps 81:16 But you would be fed with the **f** *of* wheat; 2693
147:14 to your borders and satisfies you with the **f** 2693
SS 4:14 with myrrh and aloes and all the **f** spices. 8031
Isa 17:10 the **f** plants and plant imported vines, 5846
25: 6 the best of meats and the **f** of wines. 2423
37:24 the **f of** its **forests.** 3623+4149
Jer 48:15 her **f** young men will go down in 4436
Eze 27:22 for your merchandise they exchanged the **f** 8031
Da 10: 5 a belt of the **f gold** around his waist. 233+4188
Joel 3: 5 and my gold and carried off my **f** treasures 3202
Am 6: 6 by the bowlful and use the **f** lotions, 8040

FINGER (31) [FINGERS]

Ge 41:42 from his **f** and put it on Joseph's finger. 3338
41:42 from his finger and put it on Joseph's **f.** 3338
Ex 8:19 "This is the **f** *of* God." 720
29:12 on the horns of the altar with your **f,** 720
31:18 tablets of stone inscribed by the **f** *of* God. 720
Lev 4: 6 He is to dip his **f** into the blood 720
4:17 He shall dip his **f** into the blood 720
4:25 of the sin offering with his **f** and put it on 720
4:30 the blood with his **f** and put it on the horns 720
4:34 of the sin offering with his **f** and put it on 720
8:15 and with his **f** he put it on all the horns of 720
9: 9 and he dipped his **f** into the blood 720
14:16 and with his **f** sprinkle some of it before 720
16:14 of the bull's blood and with his **f** sprinkle it 720
16:14 of it with his **f** seven times before 720
16:19 of the blood on it with his **f** seven times 720
Nu 19: 4 on his **f** and sprinkle it seven times toward 720
Dt 9:10 inscribed by the **f** *of* God. 720
1Ki 12:10 'My **little f** is thicker than my father's waist. 7782
2Ch 10:10 'My **little f** is thicker than my father's waist. 7782
Est 3:10 So the king took his signet ring from his **f** 3338
Job 1:12 but on the man himself do not lay a **f.**" 3338
Isa 58: 9 with the pointing **f** and malicious talk, 720
Mt 23: 4 not willing to **lift a f** to move them. *1235*
Lk 11:20 But if I drive out demons by the **f** of God, *1235*
11:46 and you yourselves will not lift one **f** *1235*
15:22 Put a ring on his **f** and sandals on his feet. *5931*
16:24 and send Lazarus to dip the tip *of* his **f** *1235*
Jn 8: 6 to write on the ground *with* his **f.** *1235*
20:25 the nail marks in his hands and put my **f** *1235*
20:27 Then he said to Thomas, "Put your **f** here; *1235*

FINGERS (14) [FINGER]

2Sa 21:20 with six **f** *on* each hand and six toes 720
1Ch 20: 6 with six **f** on each hand and six toes 720
Ps 8: 3 the work of your **f,** the moon and the stars, 720
144: 1 trains my hands for war, my **f** for battle. 720
Pr 6:13 with his feet and motions with his **f,** 720
7: 3 Bind them on your **f;** 720
31:19 and grasps the spindle with her **f.** 4090
SS 5: 5 my **f** with flowing myrrh, 720
Isa 2: 8 to what their **f** have made. 720
17: 8 and the incense altars their **f** have made. 720
59: 3 stained with blood, your **f** with guilt. 720
Jer 52:21 each was four **f** thick, and hollow. 720
Da 5: 5 the **f** of a human hand appeared and wrote 10064
Mk 7:33 Jesus put his **f** into the man's ears. *1235*

FINING POT (KJV) See CRUCIBLE

FINISH (18) [FINISHED, FINISHING]

Ge 6:16 and **f** the ark to within 18 inches of the top. 3983
29:27 **F** this daughter's bridal week; 4848
Ru 2:21 until *they* **f** harvesting all my grain.' " 3983
1Ch 27:24 to count the men but *did* not **f.** 3983
Ne 4: 2 *Will they* **f** in a day? 3983
Ps 90: 9 *we* **f** our years with a moan. 3983
Pr 24:27 **F** your outdoor work 3922
Jer 51:63 When you **f** reading this scroll, 3983
Da 9:24 and your holy city to **f** transgression, 3974
Mt 10:23 *you will* not **f** going through the cities *5464*
Lk 14:29 the foundation and is not able *to* **f** it, *1754*
14:30 to build and was not able *to* **f.**' *1754*
Jn 4:34 of him who sent me and *to* **f** his work. *5457*
5:36 that the Father has given me to **f,** *5457*
Ac 20:24 if only *I may* **f** the race and complete *5457*
2Co 8:11 Now **f** the work, *2200*
9: 5 **f the arrangements for** the generous gift *4616*
Jas 1: 4 Perseverance *must* **f** its work so *2400+5455*

FINISHED (90) [FINISH]

Ge 2: 2 By the seventh day God *had* **f** the work 3983
17:22 When *he had* **f** speaking with Abraham, 3983
18:33 the LORD *had* **f** speaking with Abraham, 3983
24:15 Before he *had* **f** praying, 3983
24:19 until *they have* **f** drinking." 3983
24:22 When the camels *had* **f** drinking, 3983
24:45 "Before I **f** praying in my heart, 3983
27:30 After Isaac **f** blessing him 3983
29:28 *He* **f** the week with Leah, 4848
49:33 Jacob *had* **f** giving instructions to his sons, 3983
Ex 31:18 When the LORD **f** speaking to Moses 3983
34:33 When Moses **f** speaking to them, 3983
40:33 And so Moses **f** the work. 3983
Lev 16:20 "When Aaron *has* **f** making atonement for 3983
Nu 4:15 "After Aaron and his sons *have* **f** covering 3983
7: 1 When Moses **f** setting up the tabernacle, 3983
16:31 As soon as he **f** saying all this, 3983
Dt 20: 9 the officers *have* **f** speaking to the army, 3983
26:12 When *you have* **f** setting aside a tenth 3983
31:24 After Moses **f** writing in a book the words 3983
32:45 When Moses **f** reciting all these words 3983
Jos 4: 1 the whole nation *had* **f** crossing the Jordan, 9462
8:24 When Israel *had* **f** killing all the men of Ai 3983
19:49 When *they had* **f** dividing the land 3983
19:51 And so *they* **f** dividing the land. 3983
Jdg 15:17 When he **f** speaking, he threw away 3983
Ru 2:23 until the barley and wheat harvests *were* **f.** 3983
3: 3 until he *has* **f** eating and drinking. 3983
3: 7 When Boaz *had f* **eating** and drinking AIT
1Sa 1: 9 Once when they had **f** eating and drinking 339
13:10 Just as he **f** making the offering, 3983
18: 1 After David *had* **f** talking with Saul, 3983
24:16 When David **f** saying this, Saul asked, 3983
2Sa 6:18 After he *had* **f** sacrificing the burnt offerings 3983
11:19 "When you *have* **f** giving the king this 3983
13:36 As he **f** speaking, the king's sons came in, 3983
15:24 until all the people *had* **f** leaving the city. 9462
1Ki 3: 1 of David until he **f** building his palace and 3983
6:38 the temple *was* **f** in all its details according 3983
7:40 So Huram **f** all the work he had undertaken 3983
7:51 the temple of the LORD *was* **f,** he brought 8966
8:54 When Solomon *had* **f** all these prayers 3983
9: 1 When Solomon *had* **f** building the temple of 3983
13:23 the man of God had **f** eating and drinking, 339
2Ki 6:23 and after *they had f* **eating** and drinking, AIT
10:25 as Jehu *had* **f** making the burnt offering, 3983
16:11 and **f** it before King Ahaz returned. 6913
1Ch 16: 2 After David *had* **f** sacrificing 3983
28:20 of the temple of the LORD *is* **f.** 3983
2Ch 4:11 So Huram **f** the work he had undertaken 3983
5: 1 the temple of the LORD *was* **f,** he brought 8966
7: 1 When Solomon **f** praying, 3983
7:11 When Solomon *had* **f** the temple of 3983
8:16 So the temple of the LORD *was* **f.** 8966
20:23 After they **f** slaughtering the men 3983
24:14 When they *had* **f,** they brought the rest of 3983
29:29 When the offerings *were* **f,** 3983
29:34 the Levites helped them until the task *was* **f** 3983
31: 7 the third month and **f** in the seventh month. 3983
Ezr 5:11 one that a great king of Israel built and **f.** 10354
5:16 under construction but *is* not yet **f.**" 10719
6:14 *They* **f** building the temple according to 10354
10:17 of the first month *they* **f** dealing with all 3983
Isa 10:12 When the Lord *has* **f** all his work 1298
Jer 26: 8 But as soon as Jeremiah **f** telling all 3983
43: 1 When Jeremiah had **f** telling the people all 3983
Eze 4: 6 "After *you have* **f** this, lie down again, 3983
4: 8 from one side to the other until you *have* **f** 3983
42:15 When he *had* **f** measuring what was inside 3983
43:23 When you *have* **f** purifying it, 3983
Mt 7:28 When Jesus *had* **f** saying these things, *5464*
11: 1 After Jesus *had* **f** instructing his twelve disciples, *5464*
13:53 When Jesus *had* **f** these parables, *5464*
19: 1 When Jesus *had* **f** saying these things, *5464*
26: 1 When Jesus *had* **f** saying all these things, *5464*
Lk 4:13 *When* the devil *had* **f** all this tempting, *5334*
5: 4 When *he had* **f** speaking, he said to Simon, *4264*
7: 1 When Jesus *had* **f** saying all this in *4444*
11: 1 When *he* **f,** one of his disciples said to him, *4264*
11:37 When Jesus had **f** speaking, *NIG*
Jn 12:36 When he *had f* **speaking,** *AIT*
13:12 When *he had f* **washing** their feet, *AIT*
18: 1 *When he had f* **praying,** *AIT*
19:30 Jesus said, *"It is* **f."** *5464*
21:15 When *they had f* **eating,** *AIT*
Ac 12:25 Barnabas and Saul *had* **f** their mission, *4444*
15:13 When they **f,** James spoke up: *4967*
2Ti 4: 7 *I have* **f** the race, I have kept the faith. *5464*
Heb 4: 3 yet his work *has been* **f** since the creation *1181*
Rev 11: 7 Now when *they have* **f** their testimony, *5464*

FINISHING (2) [FINISH]

1Ki 1:41 with him heard it as they *were* **f** their feast. 3983
2Ch 29:17 **f** on the sixteenth day of the first month. 3983

FINS (5)

Lev 11: 9 you may eat any that have **f** and scales. 6181
11:10 or streams that do not have **f** and scales— 6181
11:12 the water that does not have **f** and scales is 6181
Dt 14: 9 you may eat any that has **f** and scales. 6181
14:10 that does not have **f** and scales you may 6181

FIR (2) [FIRS]

Isa 41:19 the **f** and the cypress together, 9329
60:13 the pine, the **f** and the cypress together, 9329

FIRE (459) [AFIRE, CAMPFIRES, FIERY, FIREBRANDS, FIRELIGHT, FIREPANS, FIREPOT, FIRES, FIREWOOD]

Ge 22: 6 and he himself carried the **f** and the knife. 836
22: 7 "The **f** and wood are here," Isaac said, 836
Ex 3: 2 the LORD appeared to him in flames of **f** 836
3: 2 though the bush *was* **on f** it did not burn up. 836+928+1277+2021
12: 8 to eat the meat roasted over the **f,** 836
12: 9 but roast it over the **f**— 836
13:21 by night in a pillar of **f** to give them light, 836
13:22 the pillar of **f** by night left its place in front 836
14:24 down from the pillar of **f** and cloud at 836
19:18 because the LORD descended on it in **f.** 836
22: 6 a **f** breaks out and spreads into thornbushes 836
22: 6 who started the **f** must make restitution. 1282
24:17 like a consuming **f** on top of the mountain. 836
29:18 **offering made** to the LORD **by f.** 852
29:25 **offering made** to the LORD **by f.** 852
29:41 **offering made** to the LORD **by f.** 852
30:20 **offering made** to the LORD **by f,** 852
32:20 and burned it in the **f;** 836
32:24 and I threw it into the **f,** 836
35: 3 Do not light a **f** in any of your dwellings 836
40:38 and **f** was in the cloud by night, 836
Lev 1: 7 The sons of Aaron the priest are to put **f** on 836
1: 7 on the altar and arrange wood on the **f.** 836
1: 9 It is a burnt offering, an **offering made by f,** 852
1:13 It is a burnt offering, an **offering made by f,** 852
1:17 on the wood that is on the **f** on the altar. 836
1:17 It is a burnt offering, an **offering made by f,** 852
2: 2 an **offering made by f,** 852
2: 3 **offerings made** *to* the LORD **by f.** 852
2: 9 on the altar as an **offering made by f,** 852
2:10 **offerings made** *to* the LORD **by f.** 852
2:11 **offering made** to the LORD **by f.** 852
2:14 of new grain roasted in the **f.** 836
2:16 **offering made** to the LORD **by f.** 852
3: 3 **sacrifice made** to the LORD **by f:** 852
3: 5 as an **offering made by f,** 852
3: 9 **sacrifice made** to the LORD **by f:** 852
3:11 **offering made** to the LORD **by f.** 852
3:14 **offering** to the LORD **by f:** 852
3:16 an **offering made by f,** a pleasing aroma. 852
4:12 and burn it in a wood **f** on the ash heap. 836
4:35 **offerings made** *to* the LORD **by f.** 852
5:12 **offerings made** *to* the LORD **by f.** 852
6: 9 and the **f** must be kept burning on the altar. 836
6:10 the burnt offering that the **f** has consumed 836
6:12 The **f** on the altar must be kept burning; 836
6:12 the burnt offering on *the* **f** and burn the fat 1277
6:13 The **f** must be kept burning on 836
6:17 **offerings made** *to* me **by f.** 852
6:18 **offerings made** *to* the LORD **by f** 852
7: 5 **offering made** to the LORD **by f.** 852
7:25 from which an **offering by f** may be made 852
7:30 **offering made** *to* the LORD **by f;** 852
7:35 **offerings made** *to* the LORD **by f** 852
8:21 **offering made** to the LORD **by f,** 852
8:28 **offering made** to the LORD **by f.** 852
9:24 **F** came out from the presence of the LORD 836
10: 1 put **f** in them and added incense; 836
10: 1 and they offered unauthorized **f** before 836
10: 2 **f** came out from the presence of the LORD 836
10: 6 for those the LORD *has* **destroyed by f.** 8596
10:12 **offerings made** *to* the LORD **by f** 852
10:13 **offerings made** *to* the LORD **by f;** 852
10:15 the fat portions of the **offerings made by f,** 852
13:55 Burn it with **f,** 836
13:57 the mildew must be burned with **f.** 836
16:13 the incense on the **f** before the LORD, 836
20:14 Both he and they must be burned in the **f,** 836
21: 6 **offerings made** *to* the LORD **by f,** 852
21: 9 she must be burned in the **f.** 836
21:21 **offerings made** *to* the LORD **by f.** 852
22:22 **offering made** to the LORD **by f.** 852
22:27 **offering made** to the LORD **by f.** 852+7933
23: 8 **offering made** to the LORD **by f.** 852
23:13 **offering made** to the LORD **by f,** 852
23:18 an **offering made by f,** 852
23:25 **offering made** to the LORD **by f.'** " 852
23:27 **offering made** to the LORD **by f.** 852
23:36 **offerings made** to the LORD **by f,** 852
23:36 **offering made** to the LORD **by f.** 852
23:37 **offerings made** to the LORD **by f**— 852
24: 7 **offering made** to the LORD **by f.** 852
24: 9 **offerings made** *to* the LORD **by f."** 852
Nu 3: 4 an offering with unauthorized **f** before him 836
6:18 and put it in the **f** that is under the sacrifice 836
9:15 above the tabernacle looked like **f.** 836
9:16 and at night it looked like **f.** 836
11: 1 Then **f** *from* the LORD burned 836
11: 2 to the LORD and the **f** died down. 836
11: 3 **f** *from* the LORD had burned among them. 836
14:14 in a pillar of cloud by day and a pillar of **f** 836
15: 3 to the LORD **offerings made by f,** from 852
15:10 It will be an **offering made by f,** 852
15:13 an **offering made by f** as an aroma pleasing 852
15:14 an **offering made by f** as an aroma pleasing 852
15:25 for their wrong an offering **made by f** and 852
16: 7 and tomorrow put **f** and incense in them 836
16:18 put **f** and incense in it, 836
16:35 And **f** came out from the LORD 836
16:46 along with **f** from the altar, 836
18: 9 that is kept from the **f.** 836
18:17 and burn their fat as an **offering made by f,** 852
21:28 "**F** went out from Heshbon, 836
26:10 whose followers died when the **f** devoured 836
26:61 before the LORD with unauthorized **f.**) 836
28: 2 the food for my offerings **made by f,** 852
28: 3 'This is the **offering made by f** that you are 852
28: 6 **offering made** to the LORD **by f.** 852
28: 8 This is an **offering made by f,** 852
28:13 **offering made** to the LORD **by f.** 852
28:19 to the LORD an **offering made by f,** 852
28:24 for the **offering made by f** every day 852
29: 6 **offerings made** to the LORD **by f**— 852
29:13 an **offering made by f** as an aroma pleasing 852
29:36 an **offering made by f** as an aroma pleasing 852
31:23 and anything else that can withstand **f** must 836
31:23 be put through the **f,** 836
31:23 And whatever cannot withstand **f** must 836
Dt 1:33 in **f** by night and in a cloud by day, 836

Dt 4:11 while it blazed with **f** to the very heavens, 836
4:12 Then the LORD spoke to you out of the **f**. 836
4:15 to you at Horeb out of the **f**. 836
4:24 the LORD your God is a consuming **f**, 836
4:33 the voice of God speaking out of **f**, 836
4:36 On earth he showed you his great **f**, 836
4:36 and you heard his words from out of the **f**. 836
5:4 to face out of the **f** on the mountain. 836
5:5 of the **f** and did not go up the mountain.) 836
5:22 of the **f**, the cloud and the deep darkness; 836
5:23 while the mountain was ablaze with **f**, 836
5:24 and we have heard his voice from the **f**. 836
5:25 This great **f** will consume us, 836
5:26 of the living God speaking out of **f**, 836
7:5 and burn their idols in the **f**. 836
7:25 of their gods you are to burn in the **f**. 836
9:3 across ahead of you like a devouring **f**. 836
9:10 to you on the mountain out of the **f**, 836
9:15 the mountain while it was ablaze with **f**. 836
9:21 and burned it in the **f**. 836
10:4 out of the **f**, on the day of the assembly. 836
12:3 and burn their Asherah poles in the **f**; 836
12:31 even burn their sons and daughters in the **f** 836
18:1 **offerings made** *to* the LORD **by f**, 852
18:10 or daughter in the **f**, 836
18:16 nor see this great **f** anymore, 836
32:22 For a **f** has been kindled by my wrath, 836
Jos 7:15 the devoted things shall be destroyed by **f**, 836
8:8 When you have taken the city, **set** it **on f**. 836+928+2021+3675
8:19 and captured it and quickly **set** it **on f**. 836+928+2021+3675
13:14 the **offerings made by f** *to* the LORD, 852
Jdg 1:8 the city to the sword and set it on **f**. 836
6:21 **F** flared from the rock, 836
9:15 if not, then let **f** come out of the thornbush 836
9:20 let **f** come out from Abimelech 836
9:20 and let **f** come out from you, 836
9:49 and **set** it **on f** over the people inside. 836+928+2021+3675
9:52 the entrance to the tower to **set** it **on f**, 836+928+2021+8596
20:48 the towns they came across they set on **f**. 836
1Sa 2:28 the **offerings made with f** *by* the Israelites. 852
30:3 by **f** and their wives and sons 836
2Sa 14:30 Go and **set** it **on f**." 836+928+2021+3675
14:30 **set** the field **on f**. 836+928+2021+3675
14:31 **set** my field **on f**?" 836+928+2021+3675
22:9 consuming **f** came from his mouth, 836
1Ki 9:16 *He had* **set** it **on f**. 836+928+2021+8596
16:18 **set** the palace **on f** 836+928+2021+8596
18:23 and put it on the wood but not set **f** to it. 836
18:23 and put it on the wood but not set **f** to it. 836
18:24 The god who answers by **f**—he is God." 836
18:25 but do not light the **f**." 836
18:38 Then the **f** *of* the LORD fell and burned 836
19:12 After the earthquake came a **f**, 836
19:12 but the LORD was not in the **f**. 836
19:12 And after the **f** came a gentle whisper. 836
2Ki 1:10 may **f** come down from heaven 836
1:10 Then **f** fell from heaven and consumed 836
1:12 "may **f** come down from heaven 836
1:12 Then the **f** *of* God fell from heaven 836
1:14 **f** has fallen from heaven and consumed 836
2:11 a chariot of **f** and horses of fire appeared 836
2:11 a chariot of fire and horses of **f** appeared 836
6:17 the hills full of horses and chariots of **f** all 836
8:12 *"You will* **set f** to their fortified places, 836+928+2021+8938
16:3 and even sacrificed his son in the **f**, 836
17:17 and daughters in the **f**. 836
17:31 in the **f** as sacrifices to Adrammelech 836
19:18 They have thrown their gods into the **f** 836
21:6 He sacrificed his own son in the **f**, 836
23:10 to sacrifice his son or daughter in the **f** 836
25:9 *He* **set f to** the temple of the LORD, 8596
1Ch 14:12 David gave orders to burn them in the **f**. 836
21:26 and the LORD answered him with **f** 836
2Ch 7:1 **f** came down from heaven and consumed 836
7:3 the Israelites saw the **f** coming down and 836
16:14 and they made a huge **f** in his honor. 8599
21:19 His people made no **f** in his honor, 8599
28:3 and sacrificed his sons in the **f**, 836
33:6 He sacrificed his sons in the **f** in the Valley 836
35:13 the Passover animals over the **f** 836
36:19 *They* **set f to** God's temple and broke 8596
Ne 1:3 and its gates have been burned with **f**." 836
2:3 and its gates have been destroyed by **f**?" 836
2:13 which had been destroyed by **f**. 836
2:17 and its gates have been burned with **f**. 836
9:12 with a pillar of **f** to give them light on 836
9:19 of **f** by night to shine on the way they were 836
Job 1:16 "The **f** *of* God fell from the sky 836
15:34 and **f** will consume the tents 836
18:5 the flame of his **f** stops burning. 836
18:15 **F** resides in his tent; 4442
20:26 A **f** unfanned will consume him 836
22:20 and **f** devours their wealth.' 836
28:5 is transformed below as by **f**; 836
31:12 It is a **f** that burns to Destruction; 836
41:19 sparks of **f** shoot out. 836
41:20 as from a boiling pot over a **f** of reeds. NIH
Ps 18:8 consuming **f** came from his mouth, 836
21:9 and his **f** will consume them. 836
39:3 and as I meditated, the **f** burned; 836
46:9 he burns the shields with **f**. 836
50:3 a **f** devours before him, 836
66:12 we went through **f** and water, 836
68:2 as wax melts before the **f**, 836
78:14 by day and with light from the **f** all night. 836
78:21 his **f** broke out against Jacob, 836
78:63 **F** consumed their young men, 836
79:5 How long will your jealousy burn like **f**? 836
80:16 Your vine is cut down, it is burned with **f**; 836
83:14 As **f** consumes the forest or a flame sets 836
89:46 How long will your wrath burn like **f**? 836
97:3 **F** goes before him and consumes his foes 836
104:4 flames of **f** his servants. 836
105:39 and a **f** to give light at night. 836
106:18 **F** blazed among their followers; 836
140:10 may they be thrown into the **f**, 836
Pr 6:27 Can a man scoop **f** into his lap 836
16:27 and his speech is like a scorching **f**. 836
26:20 Without wood a **f** goes out; 836
26:21 As charcoal to embers and as wood to **f**, 836
30:16 which is never satisfied with water, and **f**, 836
SS 8:6 It burns like blazing **f**, like a mighty flame. 836
Isa 1:7 your cities burned with **f**; 836
1:31 with no *one to* **quench** *the* **f**." 3882
4:4 by a spirit of judgment and a spirit of **f**. 1277
4:5 of smoke by day and a glow of flaming **f** 836
5:24 of **f** lick up straw and as dry grass sinks 836
9:5 will be fuel for the **f**. 836
9:18 Surely wickedness burns like a **f**; 836
9:19 and the people will be fuel for the **f**; 836
10:16 a **f** will be kindled like a blazing flame. 3679
10:17 The Light of Israel will become a **f**, 836
26:11 let the **f** *reserved* for your enemies 836
27:4 **set** them all **on f**. 7455
29:6 and tempest and flames of a devouring **f**. 836
30:27 and his tongue is a consuming **f**. 836
30:30 with raging anger and consuming **f**, 836+4258
30:33 Its **f pit** has been made deep and wide, 4509
30:33 with an abundance of **f** and wood; 836
31:9 declares the LORD, whose **f** is in Zion, 241
33:11 your breath is a **f** that consumes you. 836
33:14 of us can dwell with the consuming **f**? 836
37:19 They have thrown their gods into the **f** 836
43:2 When you walk through the **f**, 836
44:15 *he* **kindles a f** and bakes bread. 5956
44:16 Half of the wood he burns in the **f**; 836
44:16 I am warm; I see the **f**." 241
47:14 the **f** will burn them up. 836
47:14 here is no **f** to sit by. 241
64:2 when **f** sets twigs ablaze and causes water 836
64:11 has been burned with **f**, 836
65:5 a **f** that keeps burning all day. 836
66:15 See, the LORD is coming with **f**, 836
66:15 and his rebuke with flames of **f**. 836
66:16 For with **f** and with his sword 836
66:24 nor will their **f** be quenched, 836
Jer 4:4 like **f** because of the evil you have done— 836
5:14 a **f** and these people the wood it consumes. 836
6:29 the lead with **f**, but the refining goes on 836
7:18 the fathers light the **f**, 836
7:31 to burn their sons and daughters in the **f**— 836
11:16 of a mighty storm *he will* **set** it **on f**, 836+3675
15:14 for my anger will kindle a **f** that will burn 836
17:27 then I will kindle an unquenchable **f** in 836
19:5 to burn their sons in the **f** as offerings 836
20:9 his word is in my heart like a **f**, 836
20:9 a **f** shut up in my bones. 1277
21:10 and he will destroy it with **f**.' 836
21:12 like **f** because of the evil you have done— 836
21:14 I will kindle a **f** in your forests 836
22:7 and throw them into the **f**. 836
23:29 "Is not my word like **f**," 836
29:22 the king of Babylon burned in the **f**.' 836
32:29 come in and **set** it **on f**; 836+928+2021+3675
34:5 As people made a **funeral f** *in honor* 5386
34:5 so *they will* **make a f** in your honor 8596
36:22 a **f** burning *in* the firepot in front of him. 836
36:23 until the entire scroll was burned in the **f**. 836
36:32 of Judah had burned in the **f**. 836
39:8 The Babylonians **set f to** the royal palace 836+928+2021+8596
43:12 *He will* **set f** to the temples of the gods 836+3675
48:45 for a **f** has gone out from Heshbon, 836
49:2 its surrounding villages *will be* **set on f**. 836+928+2021+3675
49:27 *"I will* **set f** to the walls of Damascus; 836+3675
50:32 I will kindle a **f** in her towns 836
51:30 Her dwellings *are* **set on f**; 3675
51:32 the marshes **set on f**, 836+928+2021+8596
51:58 be leveled and her high gates **set on f**; 836+928+2021+3675
52:13 *He* **set f to** the temple of the LORD, 8596
La 1:13 "From on high he sent **f**, 836
2:3 like a flaming **f** that consumes everything 836
2:4 like **f** on the tent of the Daughter of Zion. 836
4:11 a **f** in Zion that consumed her foundations. 836
Eze 1:4 of the **f** looked like glowing metal, 836
1:5 and in **the f** was what looked 2023[S]
1:13 like burning coals of **f** or like torches. 836
1:13 **F** moved back and forth among 2085[S]
1:27 like glowing metal, as if full of **f**, 836
1:27 and that from there down he looked like **f**; 836
5:2 a third of the hair with **f** inside the city. 241
5:4 a few of these and throw them into the **f** 836
5:4 A **f** will spread from there to 836
8:2 to be his waist down he was like **f**, 836
10:6 "Take **f** from among the wheels, 836
10:7 the cherubim reached out his hand to the **f** 836
15:4 on the **f** as fuel and the fire burns both ends 836
Eze 15:4 on the fire as fuel and the **f** burns both ends 836
15:5 when the **f** has burned it and it is charred? 836
15:6 the trees of the forest as fuel for the **f**, 836
15:7 Although they have come out of the **f**, 836
15:7 the **f** will yet consume them. 836
19:12 and **f** consumed them. 836
19:14 **F** spread from one of its main branches 836
20:31 the sacrifice of your sons in the **f**— 836
20:47 I *am about to* **set f** to you, 836+3675
21:32 You will be fuel for the **f**, 836
23:25 of you who are left will be consumed by **f**. 836
24:10 So heap on the wood and kindle the **f**. 836
24:12 not been removed, not even by **f**. 836
28:18 So I made a **f** come out from you, 836
30:8 when I set **f** to Egypt 836
30:14 set **f** to Zoan and inflict punishment 836
30:16 I will set **f** to Egypt; 836
39:6 I will send **f** on Magog and 836
46:23 with **places for f** built all around under 4453
Da 3:22 flames of the **f** killed the soldiers who took 10471
3:24 that we tied up and threw into the **f**?" 10471
3:25 I see four men walking around in the **f**, 10471
3:26 Meshach and Abednego came out of the **f**, 10471
3:27 the **f** had not harmed their bodies, nor was 10471
3:27 and there was no smell of **f** on them. 10471
7:9 His throne was flaming with **f**, 10471
7:10 A river of **f** was flowing, 10471
7:11 and thrown into the blazing **f**. 10080
Hos 7:4 an oven whose **f** the baker need not stir NIH
7:6 in the morning it blazes like a flaming **f**. 836
8:14 But I will send **f** upon their cities 836
Joel 1:19 for **f** has devoured the open pastures 836
1:20 of water have dried up and **f** has devoured 836
2:3 Before them **f** devours, 836
2:5 like a crackling **f** consuming stubble, 836+4258
2:30 blood and **f** and billows of smoke. 836
Am 1:4 I will send **f** upon the house of Hazael 836
1:7 I will send **f** upon the walls of Gaza 836
1:10 I will send **f** upon the walls of Tyre 836
1:12 I will send **f** upon Teman 836
1:14 *I will* **set f** to the walls of Rabbah 836+3675
2:2 I will send **f** upon Moab that will consume 836
2:5 I will send **f** upon Judah that will consume 836
4:11 like a burning stick snatched from the **f**, 8599
5:6 through the house of Joseph like a **f**; 836
7:4 for judgment by **f**; 836
Ob 1:18 be a **f** and the house of Joseph a flame; 836
1:18 and *they will* **set** it **on f** and consume it. 1944
Mic 1:4 like wax before the **f**, 836
1:7 all her temple gifts will be burned with **f**; 836
Na 1:6 His wrath is poured out like **f**; 836
3:13 **f** has consumed their bars. 836
3:15 There the **f** will devour you; 836
Hab 2:13 the people's labor is only **fuel for** the **f**, 836+928+1896
Zep 1:18 the **f** *of* his jealousy the whole world will 836
3:8 be consumed by the **f** *of* my jealous anger. 836
Zec 2:5 And I myself will be a wall of **f** around it,' 836
3:2 a burning stick snatched from the **f**?" 836
9:4 and she will be consumed by **f**. 836
11:1 so that **f** may devour your cedars! 836
13:9 This third I will bring into the **f**; 836
Mal 3:2 be like a refiner's **f** or a launderer's soap. 836
4:1 that day that is coming *will* **set** them **on f**," 4265
Mt 3:10 be cut down and thrown into the **f**. *4786*
3:11 with the Holy Spirit and with **f**. *4786*
3:12 up the chaff *with* unquenchable **f**." *4786*
5:22 will be in danger *of* the **f** of hell. *4786*
6:30 and tomorrow is thrown into the **f**, *3106*
7:19 down and thrown into the **f**. *4786*
13:40 up and burned *in* the **f**, *4786*
17:15 He often falls into the **f** or into the water. *4786*
18:8 or two feet and be thrown into eternal **f**. *4786*
18:9 to have two eyes and be thrown into the **f** *4786*
25:41 into the eternal **f** prepared for the devil *4786*
Mk 9:22 "It has often thrown him into **f** or water *4786*
9:43 where the **f** never goes out. *4786*
9:48 and the **f** is not quenched.' *4786*
9:49 Everyone will be salted *with* **f**. *4786*
14:54 the guards and warmed himself at the **f**. *5890*
Lk 3:9 be cut down and thrown into the **f**." *4786*
3:16 with the Holy Spirit and with **f**. *4786*
3:17 up the chaff *with* unquenchable **f**." *4786*
9:54 do you want us to call **f** down from heaven *4786*
12:28 and tomorrow is thrown into the **f**, *3106*
12:49 "I have come to bring **f** on the earth, *4786*
16:24 because I am in agony in this **f**.' *5825*
17:29 **f** and sulfur rained down from heaven *4786*
22:55 when they had kindled a **f** in the middle of *4786*
Jn 15:6 thrown into the **f** and burned. *4786*
18:18 around a **f** they had made to keep warm. *471*
21:9 a **f of burning coals** there with fish on it, *471*
Ac 2:3 to be tongues *of* **f** that separated and came *4786*
2:19 blood and **f** and billows of smoke. *4786*
28:2 They built a **f** and welcomed us all *4787*
28:3 as he put it on the **f**, a viper, *4787*
28:5 But Paul shook the snake off into the **f** *4786*
1Co 3:13 It will be revealed with **f**, *4786*
3:13 **f** will test the quality of each man's work. *4786*
1Th 5:19 Do not put out the Spirit's **f**; *NIG*
2Th 1:7 in blazing **f** with his powerful angels. *4786*
Heb 1:7 his servants flames *of* **f**." *4786*
10:27 *of* raging **f** that will consume the enemies *4786*
12:18 be touched and that is burning *with* **f**; *4786*
12:29 for our "God is a consuming **f**." *4786*
Jas 3:5 Consider what a great forest *is* **set on f** by *409*
3:6 The tongue also is a **f**, *4786*

Jas 3: 6 sets the whole course of his life on f, 5824
3: 6 and is itself set on f by hell. 5824
5: 3 against you and eat your flesh like f. 4786
1Pe 1: 7 which perishes even though refined by f— 4786
2Pe 3: 7 and earth are reserved for f, 4786
3:10 the elements will be destroyed by f, 3012
3:12 about the destruction of the heavens by f, 4792
Jude 1: 7 the punishment of eternal f. 4786
1:23 snatch others from the f and save them; 4786
Rev 1:14 and his eyes were like blazing f. 4786
2:18 of God, whose eyes are like blazing f 4786
3:18 to buy from me gold refined in the f, 4786
8: 5 filled it with f from the altar, 4786
8: 7 there came hail and f mixed with blood, 4786
9:17 and out of their mouths came f, 4786
9:18 by the three plagues of f, 4786
11: 5 f comes from their mouths 4786
13:13 even causing f to come down from heaven 4786
14:18 who had charge of the f, 4786
15: 2 like a sea of glass mixed with f and, 4786
16: 8 to scorch people with f. 4786
17:16 they will eat her flesh and burn her with f. 4786
18: 8 She will be consumed by f, 4786
19:12 His eyes are like blazing f, 4786
20: 9 But f came down from heaven 4786
20:14 and Hades were thrown into the lake of f. 4786
20:14 The lake of f is the second death. 4786
20:15 he was thrown into the lake of f. 4786

FIREBRANDS (2) [FIRE]

Job 41:19 F stream from his mouth; 4365
Pr 26:18 a madman shooting f or deadly arrows 2415

FIRELIGHT (1) [FIRE]

Lk 22:56 A servant girl saw him seated there in the f. 5890

FIREPANS (3) [FIRE]

Ex 27: 3 sprinkling bowls, meat forks and f. 4746
38: 3 sprinkling bowls, meat forks and f. 4746
Nu 4:14 including the f, meat forks, 4746

FIREPOT (4) [FIRE]

Ge 15:17 a smoking f with a blazing torch appeared 9486
Jer 36:22 with a fire burning in the f in front of him. 279
36:23 a scribe's knife and threw them into the f, 279
Zec 12: 6 leaders of Judah like a f in a woodpile, 836+3963

FIRES (5) [FIRE]

Isa 27:11 and women come and make f with them. 239
40:16 Lebanon is not sufficient for altar f, 1277
50:11 all you who light f and provide yourselves 836
50:11 walk in the light of your f and of 836
Mal 1:10 so that you would not light useless f 239

FIREWOOD (2) [FIRE]

Lev 6:12 to add f and arrange the burnt offering on 6770
Isa 7: 4 because of these two smoldering stubs of f 202

FIRKINS (KJV) See GALLONS

FIRM (54) [FIRMLY]

Ex 14:13 Stand f and you will see the deliverance 3656
15: 8 The surging waters stood f like a wall; 5893
Jos 3:17 of the LORD stood f on dry ground in 3922
2Ch 20:17 stand f and see the deliverance 6641
Ezr 9: 8 and giving us a f place in his sanctuary, 3845
Job 11:15 you will stand f and without fear. 3668
36: 5 he is mighty, and f in his purpose. 3946
41:23 they are f and immovable. 3668
Ps 20: 8 but we rise up and stand f. 6386
30: 7 you made my mountain stand f; 6437
33: 9 he commanded, and it stood f. 6641
33:11 the plans of the LORD stand f forever, 6641
37:23 he makes his steps f; 3922
40: 2 on a rock and gave me a f place to stand. 3922
75: 3 it is I who hold its pillars f. 9419
78:13 made the water stand f 5893
89: 2 that your love stands f forever, 1215
89: 4 and make your throne f 1215
93: 5 Your statutes stand f; 586+4394
119:89 it stands f in the heavens. 5893
Pr 4:26 for your feet and take only ways that are f. 3922
10:25 but the righteous stand f forever. 3572
12: 7 but the house of the righteous stands f. 6641
Isa 7: 9 stand f in your faith, 586
22:17 to take f hold of you and hurl you away, 6487+6487
22:23 I will drive him like a peg into a f place; 586
22:25 peg driven into the f place will give way; 586
Eze 13: 5 the house of Israel so that it will stand f 6641
Zec 8:23 and nations will take f hold of one Jew 2616
Mt 10:22 he who stands f to the end will be saved. 5702
24:13 he who stands f to the end will be saved. 5702
Mk 13:13 he who stands f to the end will be saved. 5702
Lk 21:19 By standing f you will gain life. 5705
1Co 10:12 So, if you think you are standing f, 2705
15:58 Therefore, my dear brothers, stand f. 1181+1612
16:13 Be on your guard; stand f in the faith; 2705
2Co 1: 7 And our hope for you is f, 1010
1:21 makes both us and you stand f 1011
1:24 because it is by faith you stand f. 2705
Gal 5: 1 Stand f, then, and do not let yourselves 2705
Eph 6:14 Stand f then, with the belt of truth buckled 2705
Php 1:27 I will know that you stand f in one spirit, 2705
4: 1 is how you should stand f in the Lord, 2705
Col 1:23 and f, not moved from the hope held out in 1612
2: 5 how orderly you are and how f your faith 5106
4:12 that you may stand f in all the will of God, 2705
1Th 3: 8 since you are standing f in the Lord. 2705
2Th 2:15 stand f and hold to the teachings 2705
1Ti 6:19 as a f foundation for the coming age, 2819
2Ti 2:19 God's solid foundation stands f, 2705
Heb 6:19 as an anchor for the soul, f and secure. 855
Jas 5: 8 You too, be patient and stand f, 2840+3836+5114
1Pe 5: 9 Resist him, standing f in the faith, 5104
5:10 and make you strong, f and steadfast. 4964

FIRMAMENT (KJV) See EXPANSE

FIRMLY (22) [FIRM]

Ge 41:32 that the matter has been f decided by God, 3922
1Sa 2:35 I will f establish his house, 586
1Ki 2:12 and his rule was f established. 4394
2:46 The kingdom was now f established 3922
2Ki 14: 5 After the kingdom was f in his grasp, 2616
1Ch 16:30 The world is f established; 3922
2Ch 1: 1 of David established himself f 2616
12:13 King Rehoboam established himself f 2616
21: 4 When Jehoram established himself f 2616
25: 3 After the kingdom was f in his control, 2616
Ps 93: 1 The world is f established; 3922
96:10 The world is f established, 3922
Ecc 12:11 like f embedded nails— 5749
Da 2: 5 "This is what I have f decided: 10014
2: 8 that this is what I have f decided: 10014
3:23 f tied, fell into the blazing furnace. 10366
11:32 who know their God will f resist him. 2616
1Co 15: 2 you hold f to the word I preached to you. 2988
Tit 1: 9 He must hold f to the trustworthy message 504
Heb 3:14 to share in Christ if we hold f till the end 1010
4:14 let us hold f to the faith we profess. 3195
2Pe 1:12 and are f established in the truth you 5114

FIRS (1) [FIR]

SS 1:17 our rafters are f. 1361

FIRST (377) [FIRSTBORN, FIRSTFRUITS]

Ge 1: 5 and there was morning—the f day. 285
2:11 The name of the f is the Pishon; 285
8: 5 on the f day of the tenth month the tops of 285
8:13 By the f day of the first month 285
8:13 of the f month of Noah's six hundred 8037
8:13 of Noah's six hundred and f year, 285
10:10 The f centers of his kingdom 8040
13: 4 and where he had f built an altar. 8037
25:25 The f to come out was red, 8037
25:31 Jacob replied, "F sell me your birthright." 2021+3427+3869
25:33 But Jacob said, "Swear to me f." 3427+3869
38:28 "This one came out f." 8037
41:20 up the seven fat cows that came up f. 8037
43:18 that was put back into our sacks the f time. 9378
43:20 down here the f time to buy food. 9378
49: 3 my might, the f sign of my strength, 8040
Ex 4: 8 or pay attention to the f miraculous sign, 8037
12: 2 "This month is to be for you the f month, 8031
12: 2 the f month of your year. 8037
12:15 On the f day remove the yeast 8037
12:15 from the f day through the seventh must 8037
12:16 On the f day hold a sacred assembly, 8037
12:18 In the f month you are to eat bread made 8037
13: 2 The f offspring of every womb among 7081
13:12 to give over to the LORD the f offspring 7081
13:15 the f male offspring of every womb 7081
21:10 he must not deprive the f one of her food, NIH
25:35 be under the f pair of branches extending NIH
28:17 In the f row there shall be a ruby, 285
29:40 With the f lamb offer a tenth of an ephah 285
34: 1 two stone tablets like the f ones, 8037
34: 1 the words that were on the f tablets, 8037
34: 4 the f ones and went up Mount Sinai early 8037
34:19 f offspring of every womb belongs to me, 7081
37:21 under the f pair of branches extending NIH
39:10 In the f row there was a ruby, 285
40: 2 on the f day of the first month. 285
40: 2 on the first day of the f month. 8037
40:17 So the tabernacle was set up on the f day 285
40:17 up on the first day of the f month in 8037
Lev 4:21 and burn it as he burned the f bull. 8037
5: 8 who shall f offer the one for 8037
9:15 for a sin offering as he did with the f one. 8037
23: 5 on the fourteenth day of the f month. 8037
23: 7 On the f day hold a sacred assembly 8037
23:10 the priest a sheaf of the f grain you harvest. 8040
23:24 'On the f day of the seventh month you are 285
23:35 The f day is a sacred assembly; 8037
23:39 the f day is a day of rest, 8037
23:40 the f day you are to take choice fruit from 8037
Nu 1: 1 of Sinai on the f day of the second month 285
1:18 the whole community together on the f day 285
2: 9 They will set out f. 8037
3:12 in place of the f male offspring 1147+7081+8167
7:12 the f day was Nahshon son of Amminadab 8037
8:16 the f male offspring from every Israelite 1147
9: 1 of Sinai in the f month of the second year 8037
9: 5 on the fourteenth day of the f month. 8037
Nu 10:13 They set out, this f time, 8037
10:14 The divisions of the camp of Judah went f, 8037
13:20 (It was the season for the f ripe grapes.) 1137
15:20 the f of your ground meal and present it as 8040
15:21 from the f of your ground meal. 8040
18:15 The f offspring of every womb, 7081
20: 1 In the f month the whole Israelite 8037
22:15 and more distinguished than the f. 465[S]
24:20 "Amalek was f among the nations, 8040
28:11 " 'On the f of every month, 8031
28:16 day of the f month the LORD's Passover 8037
28:18 On the f day hold a sacred assembly 8037
29: 1 " 'On the f day of the seventh month hold 285
33: 3 on the fifteenth day of the f month, 8037
33:38 on the f day of the fifth month of 285
Dt 1: 3 on the f day of the eleventh month, 285
10: 1 like the f ones and come up to me on 8037
10: 2 the words that were on the f tablets, 8037
10: 3 two stone tablets like the f ones, 8037
10:10 as I did the f time, 8037
13: 9 Your hand must be the f in putting him 8037
16: 4 on the evening of the f day remain 8037
17: 7 the witnesses must be the f in putting him 8037
18: 4 the f wool from the shearing of your sheep, 8040
21:17 the f sign of his father's strength. 8040
24: 4 then her f husband, who divorced her 8037
25: 6 The f son she bears shall carry on 1147
Jos 4:19 of the f month the people went up from 8037
21: 4 The f lot came out for the Kohathites, NIH
21:10 because the f lot fell to them): 8037
Jdg 1: 1 "Who will be the f to go up and fight for us 9378
20:18 "Who of us shall go f to fight against the Benjamites?" 928+2021+9378
20:18 LORD replied, "Judah shall go f." 928+2021+9378
20:22 they had stationed themselves the f day. 8037
20:39 "We are defeating them as in the f battle." 8037
1Sa 2:16 "Let the fat be burned up f, 2021+3427+3869
14:14 In that f attack Jonathan 8037
14:35 it was the f time he had done this. 2725
22:15 Was that day the f time I inquired of God 2725
2Sa 17: 9 If he should attack your troops f, 928+2021+9378
18:27 the f one runs like Ahimaaz son of Zadok." 8037
19:20 the f of the whole house of Joseph to come 8037
19:43 the f to speak of bringing back our king?" 8037
21: 9 they were put to death during the f days of 8037
1Ki 3:22 But the f one insisted, "No! 2296[S]
3:27 "Give the living baby to the f woman. 2023[S]
6:24 of the f cherub was five cubits long, and 285
17:13 But f make a small cake of bread for me 928+2021+8037
18:25 "Choose one of the bulls and prepare it f, 8037
20: 9 'Your servant will do all you demanded the f time, 8037
20:17 of the provincial commanders went out f. 8037
22: 5 F seek the counsel of the LORD. 2021+3427+3869
2Ki 1:14 the f two captains and all their men. 8037
4:42 from the f ripe grain, 1137
17:25 When they f lived there, 9378
1Ch 6:54 because the f lot was for them): NIH
9: 2 Now the f to resettle on their own property 8037
11: 6 Joab son of Zeruiah went up f, 8037
12:15 the Jordan in the f month 8037
15:13 did not bring it up the f time that 8037
16: 7 That day David f committed to Asaph 8031
23: 8 Jehiel the f, Zetham and Joel—three in all. 8031
23:11 Jahath was the f and Ziza the second, 8031
23:16 Shubael was the f. 8031
23:17 Rehabiah was the f. 8031
23:18 The sons of Izhar: Shelomith was the f. 8031
23:19 Jeriah the f, Amariah the second, 8031
23:20 Micah the f and Isshiah the second. 8031
24: 7 The f lot fell to Jehoiarib, 8037
24:21 Rehabiah, from his sons: Isshiah was the f. 8031
24:23 Jeriah the f, Amariah the second, 8031
25: 9 The f lot, which was for Asaph, 8037
26:10 the f (although he was not the firstborn, 8031
26:10 his father had appointed him the f), 8031
27: 2 In charge of the f division, 8037
27: 2 for the f month, was Jashobeam 8037
27: 3 of all the army officers for the f month. 8037
2Ch 3:11 of the f cherub was five cubits long NIH
3:12 touched the wing of the f cherub. 285
18: 4 F seek the counsel of the LORD. 2021+3427+3869
29: 3 In the f month of the first year of his reign, 8037
29: 3 In the first month of the f year of his reign, 8037
29:17 They began the consecration on the f day 285
29:17 on the first day of the f month, 8037
29:17 on the sixteenth day of the f month. 8037
35: 1 on the fourteenth day of the f month. 8037
36:22 In the f year of Cyrus king of Persia, 285
Ezr 1: 1 In the f year of Cyrus king of Persia, 285
3: 6 the f day of the seventh month they began 285
5:13 in the f year of Cyrus king of Babylon, 10248
6: 3 In the f year of King Cyrus, the king issued 10248
6:19 On the fourteenth day of the f month, 8037
7: 9 on the f day of the first month, 285
7: 9 on the first day of the f month, 8037
7: 9 and he arrived in Jerusalem on the f day of 285
8:31 the twelfth day of the f month we set out 8037
10:16 the f day of the tenth month they sat down 285
10:17 and by the f day of the first month 285
10:17 the f month they finished dealing with all 8037
Ne 4:21 from the f light of dawn till the stars came out. 6590+8840
7: 5 of those who had been the f to return. 8037
8: 2 So on the f day of the seventh month Ezra 285
8:18 Day after day, from the f day to the last, 8037

Ne 10:37 to the priests, the f of our ground meal, 8040
Est 3: 7 in the f month, the month of Nisan, 8037
3:12 Then on the thirteenth day of the f month 8037
Job 3: 9 for daylight in vain and not see the f rays 6757
15: 7 "Are you the f man ever born? 8037
40:19 He ranks f among the works of God, 8040
42:12 the latter part of Job's life more than the f. 8040
42:14 The f daughter he named Jemimah, 285
Pr 4:18 the righteous is like the f gleam of dawn, AIT
8:22 the f of his works, before his deeds of old; 8040
18:17 The f to present his case seems right, 8037
Isa 41: 4 with the f of them and with the last— 8037
41:27 I was the f to tell Zion, 'Look, 8037
43:27 Your f father sinned; 8037
44: 6 I am the f and I am the last; 8037
48:12 I am the f and I am the last. 8037
48:16 the f announcement I have not spoken 8031
52: 4 "At f my people went down to Egypt 8037
Jer 4:31 a groan as of one bearing her f child— 1144
7:12 now to the place in Shiloh where I f made a dwelling 928+2021+8037
25: 1 the f year of Nebuchadnezzar king 8038
36:28 on it all the words that were on the f scroll, 8037
50:17 f to devour him was the king of Assyria; 8037
Eze 26: 1 on the f day of the month, 285
29:17 in the f month on the first day, 8037
29:17 in the first month on the f day, 285
30:20 in the f month on the seventh day, 8037
31: 1 in the third month on the f day, 285
32: 1 in the twelfth month on the f day, 285
40:21 as those of the f gateway. 8037
44:30 the f portion of your ground meal so that 8040
45:18 the f month on the first day you are to take 8037
45:18 the first month on the f day you are to take 285
45:21 the f month on the fourteenth day you are 8037
Da 1:21 And Daniel remained there until the f year 285
6:19 At the f light of dawn, 10459
7: 1 the f year of Belshazzar king of Babylon, 10248
7: 4 "The f was like a lion, 10623
7: 8 and three of the f horns were uprooted 10623
8:21 large horn between his eyes is the f king. 8037
9: 1 the f year of Darius son of Xerxes (a Mede 285
9: 2 in the f year of his reign, 285
10: 4 On the twenty-fourth day of the f month, 8037
10:12 Since the f day that you set your mind 8037
10:21 but f I will tell you what is written in NIH
11: 1 And in the f year of Darius the Mede, 285
11:13 larger than the f; 8037
Hos 2: 7 'I will go back to my husband as at f, 8037
Am 6: 7 Therefore you will be among the f to go 8031
Jnh 3: 4 On the f day, Jonah started into the city. 285
Na 3:12 like fig trees with their f ripe fruit; 1137
Hag 1: 1 on the f day of the sixth month, 285
Zec 6: 2 The f chariot had red horses, 8037
12: 7 the dwellings of Judah f, 8037
14:10 the Benjamin Gate to the site of the F Gate, 8037
Mt 5:24 F go and be reconciled to your brother; 4754
6:33 seek f his kingdom and his righteousness, 4754
7: 5 f take the plank out of your own eye, 4754
8:21 "Lord, f let me go and bury my father." 4754
10: 2 f, Simon (who is called Peter) 4755
12:29 unless he f ties up the strong man? 4754
12:45 of that man is worse than the f. 4755
13:30 F collect the weeds and tie them in bundles 4754
17:10 of the law say that Elijah must come f?" 4754
17:25 Jesus was the f to speak. 4740
17:27 Take the f fish you catch; 4755
19:30 But many who are f will be last, 4755
19:30 and many who are last will be f. 4755
20: 8 the last ones hired and going on to the f.' 4755
20:10 So when those came who were hired f, 4755
20:16 the last will be f, and the first will be last." 4755
20:16 the last will be first, and the f will be last." 4755
20:27 and whoever wants to be f must 4755
21:28 He went to the f and said, 'Son, 4755
21:31 "The f," they answered. 4755
21:36 more than the f time, 4755
22:25 The f one married and died, 4755
22:38 This is the f and greatest commandment. 4755
23:26 F clean the inside of the cup and dish, 4754
26:17 On the f day of the Feast of Unleavened 4755
27:64 be worse than the f." 4755
28: 1 at dawn on the f day of the week, 1651
Mk 3:27 unless he f ties up the strong man. 4754
4:28 f the stalk, then the head, 4754
7:27 "F let the children eat all they want," 4754
9:11 of the law say that Elijah must come f?" 4754
9:12 Elijah does come f, and restores all things. 4754
9:35 "If anyone wants to be f, 4755
10:31 But many who are f will be last, 4755
10:31 and the last f." 4755
10:44 whoever wants to be f must be slave of all. 4755
12:20 The f one married and died 4755
13:10 gospel must f be preached to all nations. 4754
14:12 On the f day of the Feast of Unleavened 4755
16: 2 Very early on the f day of the week, 1651
16: 9 When Jesus rose early on the f day of 4755
16: 9 he appeared f to Mary Magdalene, 4754
Lk 1: 2 by those who from the f were eyewitnesses 794
2: 2 (This was the f census that took place 4755
6:42 f take the plank out of your eye, 4754
9:59 "Lord, f let me go and bury my father." 4754
9:61 but f let me go back and say good-by 4754
10: 5 "When you enter a house, f say, 4754
11:26 of that man is worse than the f." 4755
11:38 that Jesus did not f wash before the meal, 4754
12: 1 Jesus began to speak f to his disciples, 4754
Lk 13:30 be f, and first who will 4755
13:30 and f who will be last." 4755
14:18 The f said, 'I have just bought a field, 4755
14:28 Will he not f sit down and estimate the cost 4754
14:31 Will he not f sit down 4754
16: 5 He asked the f, 4755
17:25 But f he must suffer many things and 4754
19:16 "The f one came and said, 'Sir, 4755
20:29 The f one married a woman 4755
21: 9 These things must happen f, 4754
24: 1 On the f day of the week, 1651
Jn 1:41 The f thing Andrew did was 4754
2:10 "Everyone brings out the choice wine f and 4754
2:11 This, the f of his miraculous signs, 794
7:51 without f hearing him 4754
8: 7 let him be the f to throw a stone at her." 4755
8: 9 the older ones f, until only Jesus was left, 806
12:16 At f his disciples did 4754
15:18 keep in mind that it hated me f. 4754
16: 4 I did not tell you this at f because I was 794
18:13 and brought him f to Annas, 4754
19:32 of the f man who had been crucified 4755
20: 1 Early on the f day of the week, 1651
20: 4 and reached the tomb f. 4755
20: 8 who had reached the tomb f, 4755
20:19 On the evening of that f day of the week, 1651
Ac 3:26 he sent him f to you to bless you 4754
7:12 he sent our fathers on their f visit. 4755
11:26 The disciples were called Christians f 4759
12:10 They passed the f and second guards 4755
13:46 to speak the word of God to you f. 4754
15:14 at f showed his concern by taking from 4754
20: 7 On the f day of the week we came together 1651
20:18 the f day I came into the province of Asia. 4755
26:20 F to those in Damascus, 4754
26:23 as the f to rise from the dead, 4755
27:43 to jump overboard f and get to land. 4755
Ro 1: 8 F, I thank my God through Jesus Christ 4754
1:16 f for the Jew, then for the Gentile. 4754
1:17 by faith from f to last, 1650+4411+4411
2: 9 f for the Jew, then for the Gentile; 4754
2:10 f for the Jew, then for the Gentile. 4754
3: 2 F of all, they have been entrusted with 4754
10:19 F, Moses says, "I will make you envious 4755
13:11 now than when we f believed. NIG
16: 5 the f convert to Christ in the province 569
1Co 11:18 In the f place, I hear that when you come 4754
12:28 church God has appointed f of all apostles, 4754
14:30 the f speaker should stop. 4755
15: 3 on to you as of f importance: 1877+4755
15:45 "The f man Adam became a living being"; 4755
15:46 The spiritual did not come f, 4754
15:47 The f man was of the dust of the earth, 4755
16: 2 On the f day of every week, 1651
16:15 of Stephanas were the f converts in Achaia, 569
2Co 1:15 I planned to visit you f so 4728
8: 5 but they gave themselves f to the Lord and 4754
8:10 Last year you were the f not only to give 4599
Gal 4:13 of an illness that I f preached the gospel 4728
Eph 1:12 who were the f to hope in Christ, 4598
6: 2 the f commandment with a promise— 4755
Php 1: 5 in the gospel from the f day until now, 4755
1Th 4:16 and the dead in Christ will rise f. 4754
1Ti 2: 1 I urge, then, f of all, that requests, prayers, 4754
2:13 For Adam was formed f, then Eve. 4755
3:10 They must f be tested; 4754
5: 4 these should learn f of all 4754
5:12 because they have broken their f pledge. 4755
2Ti 1: 5 which f lived in your grandmother Lois 4754
2: 6 The hardworking farmer should be the f 4755
4:16 At my f defense, 4755
Heb 2: 3 which was f announced by the Lord, 794
3:14 till the end the confidence we had at f. 794
7: 2 F, his name means "king of righteousness" 4754
7:27 f for his own sins, 4728
8: 7 with that f covenant, 4755
8:13 he has made the f one obsolete; 4755
9: 1 the f covenant had regulations for worship 4755
9: 2 In its f room were the lampstand, 4755
9: 8 as the f tabernacle was still standing. 4755
9:15 the sins committed under the f covenant. 4755
9:18 even the f covenant was not put into effect 4755
10: 8 F he said, "Sacrifices and offerings, 542
10: 9 He sets aside the f to establish the second. 4755
10:15 about this. F he says: 3552+3836
Jas 3:17 that comes from heaven is f of all pure; 4754
2Pe 3: 3 F of all, you must understand that in 4047+4754
1Jn 4:19 We love because he f loved us. 4755
3Jn 1: 9 but Diotrephes, who loves to be f, 5812
Rev 1:17 I am the F and the Last. 4755
2: 4 You have forsaken your f love. 4755
2: 5 Repent and do the things you did at f. 4755
2: 8 the words of him who is the F and the Last, 4755
2:19 now doing more than you did at f. 4755
4: 1 And the voice I had f heard speaking to me 4755
4: 7 The f living creature was like a lion, 4755
6: 1 the Lamb opened the f of the seven seals. 1651
8: 7 The f angel sounded his trumpet, 4755
9:12 The f woe is past; 1651
13:12 He exercised all the authority of the f beast 4755
13:12 and its inhabitants worship the f beast, 4755
13:14 to do on behalf of the f beast, NIG
13:15 to give breath to the image of the f beast, NIG
16: 2 The f angel went and poured out his bowl 4755
20: 5 This is the f resurrection. 4755
20: 6 who have part in the f resurrection. 4755
21: 1 for the f heaven and the first earth 4755
Rev 21: 1 heaven and the f earth had passed away, 4755
21:19 The f foundation was jasper, 4755
22:13 the F and the Last, 4755

FIRSTBEGOTTEN (KJV) See FIRSTBORN

FIRSTBORN (132) [FIRST, BEAR]

Ge 4: 4 from some of the f of his flock. 1147
10:15 Canaan was the father of Sidon his f, 1147
22:21 the f, Buz his brother, Kemuel (the father 1147
25:13 Nebaioth the f of Ishmael, Kedar, Adbeel, 1147
27:19 Jacob said to his father, "I am Esau your f. 1147
27:32 "I am your son," he answered, "your f, 1147
35:23 Reuben the f of Jacob, Simeon, Levi, 1147
36:15 The sons of Eliphaz the f of Esau: 1147
38: 6 Judah got a wife for Er, his f, 1147
38: 7 Judah's f, was wicked in 1147
41:51 Joseph named his f Manasseh and said, 1147
43:33 from the f to the youngest; 1147
46: 8 Reuben the f of Jacob. 1147
48:14 even though Manasseh was the f. 1147
48:18 "No, my father, this one is the f; 1147
49: 3 "Reuben, you are my f, my might, 1147
Ex 4:22 Israel is my f son, 1147
4:23 so I will kill your f son.' " 1147
6:14 of Reuben the f son of Israel were Hanoch 1147
11: 5 Every f son in Egypt will die, 1147
11: 5 from the f son of Pharaoh, 1147
11: 5 to the f son of the slave girl, 1147
11: 5 and all the f of the cattle as well. 1147
12:12 through Egypt and strike down every f— 1147
12:29 the LORD struck down all the f in Egypt, 1147
12:29 from the f of Pharaoh, 1147
12:29 to the f of the prisoner, 1147
12:29 and the f of all the livestock as well. 1147
13: 2 "Consecrate to me every f male. 1147
13:12 All the f males of your livestock belong to the LORD. 7081+8715
13:13 Redeem with a lamb every f donkey, 7081
13:13 Redeem every f among your sons. 1147
13:15 the LORD killed every f in Egypt, 1147
13:15 and redeem each of my f sons.' 1147
22:29 "You must give me the f of your sons. 1147
34:19 including all the f males of your livestock, 7081
34:20 Redeem the f donkey with a lamb, 7081
34:20 Redeem all your f sons. 1147
Lev 27:26 however, may dedicate the f of an animal, 1147
27:26 the f already belongs to the LORD; 1144+4200
Nu 1:20 From the descendants of Reuben the f son 1147
3: 2 of Aaron were Nadab the f and Abihu, 1147
3:13 for all the f are mine. 1147
3:13 When I struck down all the f in Egypt, 1147
3:13 I set apart for myself every f in Israel, 1147
3:40 the f Israelite males who are a month old 1147
3:41 Take the Levites for me in place of all the f 1147
3:41 of all the f of the livestock of the Israelites. 1147
3:42 So Moses counted all the f of the Israelites, 1147
3:43 The total number of f males a month old 1147
3:45 the Levites in place of all the f of Israel, 1147
3:46 the 273 f Israelites who exceed the number 1147
3:50 From the f of the Israelites 1147
8:16 as my own in place of the f, 7082
8:17 Every f male in Israel, 1147
8:17 When I struck down all the f in Egypt, 1147
8:18 the Levites in place of all the f sons 1147
18:15 But you must redeem every f son 1147
18:15 and every f male of unclean animals. 1147
18:17 "But you must not redeem the f of an ox, 1147
26: 5 Reuben, the f son of Israel, were: 1147
33: 4 who were burying all their f, whom 1147
Dt 12: 6 and the f of your herds and flocks. 1147
12:17 or the f of your herds and flocks, 1147
14:23 and the f of your herds and flocks in 1147
15:19 for the LORD your God every f male 1147
15:19 Do not put the f of your oxen to work, 1147
15:19 and do not shear the f of your sheep. 1147
21:15 and both bear him sons but the f is the son 1147
21:16 not give the rights of the f to the son 1144
21:16 in preference to his actual f, 1147
21:17 of his unloved wife as the f by giving him 1147
21:17 The right of the f belongs to him. 1148
33:17 In majesty he is like a f bull; 1147
Jos 6:26 of his f son will he lay its foundations; 1147
17: 1 for the tribe of Manasseh as Joseph's f, 1147
17: 1 that is, for Makir, Manasseh's f. 1147
1Sa 8: 2 The name of his f was Joel and the name 1147
17:13 The f was Eliab; 1147
2Sa 3: 2 His f was Amnon the son of Ahinoam 1147
1Ki 16:34 at the cost of his f son Abiram, 1147
2Ki 3:27 Then he took his f son, 1147
1Ch 1:13 Canaan was the father of Sidon his f, 1147
1:29 Nebaioth the f of Ishmael, Kedar, Adbeel, 1147
2: 3 Judah's f, was wicked in the LORD's sight 1147
2:13 Jesse was the father of Eliab his f; 1147
2:25 The sons of Jerahmeel the f of Hezron: 1147
2:25 Ram his f, Bunah, Oren, 1147
2:27 The sons of Ram the f of Jerahmeel: 1147
2:42 Mesha his f, who was the father of Ziph, 1147
2:50 The sons of Hur the f of Ephrathah: 1147
3: 1 The f was Amnon the son of Ahinoam 1147
3:15 Johanan the f, Jehoiakim the second son, 1147
4: 4 f of Ephrathah and father of Bethlehem. 1147
5: 1 The sons of Reuben the f of Israel (he was 1147
5: 1 the firstborn of Israel (he was the f, but 1147

1Ch 5: 1 his **rights as** f were given to the sons 1148
5: 2 the **rights of the** f belonged to Joseph)— 1148
5: 3 the sons of Reuben the f *of* Israel: 1147
6:28 Joel the f and Abijah the second son. 1147
8: 1 Benjamin was the father of Bela his f, 1147
8:30 and his f son was Abdon, 1147
8:39 The sons of his brother Eshek: Ulam his f, 1147
9: 5 Asaiah the f and his sons. 1147
9:31 the f son of Shallum the Korahite, 1147
9:36 and his f son was Abdon, 1147
26: 2 Meshelemiah had sons: Zechariah the f, 1147
26: 4 Obed-Edom also had sons: Shemaiah the f, 1147
26:10 Shimri the first (although he was not the f, 1147
2Ch 21: 3 to Jehoram because he was his f *son.* 1147
Ne 10:36 we will bring the f *of* our sons and 1147
Job 18:13 death's f devours his limbs. 1147
Ps 78:51 He struck down all the f of Egypt, 1147
89:27 I will also appoint him my f, 1147
105:36 Then he struck down all the f in their land, 1147
135: 8 He struck down the f *of* Egypt, 1147
135: 8 the f of men and animals. NIH
136:10 the f *of* Egypt His love endures forever. 1147
Jer 31: 9 and Ephraim is my f *son.* 1147
Eze 20:26 the sacrifice of every f— 7081+8167
Mic 6: 7 Shall I offer my f for my transgression, 1147
Zec 12:10 for him as one grieves for a f *son.* 1147
Lk 2: 7 and she gave birth to her f, *4758*
2:23 "Every f male is to be consecrated to *1380+3616*
Ro 8:29 be the f among many brothers. *4758*
Col 1:15 the f over all creation. *4758*
1:18 he is the beginning and the f from among *4758*
Heb 1: 6 when God brings his f into the world, *4758*
11:28 that the destroyer of the f would not touch *4758*
11:28 of the firstborn would not touch **the** f *899S*
12:23 to the church *of* the f, *4758*
Rev 1: 5 the f from the dead, *4758*

FIRSTFRUITS (29) [FIRST]

Ex 23:16 of Harvest with the f *of* the crops you sow 1137
23:19 the best of the f *of* your soil to the house 1137
34:22 of Weeks with the f *of* the wheat harvest, 1137
34:26 the best of the f *of* your soil to the house 1137
Lev 2:12 to the LORD as an offering of the f, 8040
2:14 " 'If you bring a grain offering of f to 1137
23:17 as a wave offering of f to the LORD. 1137
23:20 together with the bread of the f. 1137
Nu 18:12 the LORD as the f **of** their **harvest.** 8040
18:13 All the land's f that they bring to 1137
28:26 " 'On the day of f, 1137
Dt 18: 4 You are to give them the f *of* your grain, 8040
26: 2 f *of* all that you produce from the soil 7262+8040
26:10 now I bring the f *of* the soil that you, 7262+8040
2Ch 31: 5 the Israelites generously gave the f 8040
Ne 10:35 of the LORD each year the f *of* our crops 1137
12:44 of the storerooms for the contributions, f 8040
13:31 and for the f. 1137
Ps 78:51 the f *of* manhood in the tents of Ham. 8040
105:36 the f of all their manhood. 8040
Pr 3: 9 with the f *of* all your crops; 8040
Jer 2: 3 the f *of* his harvest; 8040
Eze 44:30 The best of all the f and 1137
Ro 8:23 who have the f of the Spirit, *569*
11:16 If the part of the dough offered as f is holy, *569*
1Co 15:20 the f of those who have fallen asleep. *569*
15:23 But each in his own turn: Christ, the f; *569*
Jas 1:18 be a kind of f of all he created. *569*
Rev 14: 4 from among men and offered as f to God *569*

FIRSTLING (KJV) See FIRSTBORN

FISH (64) [FISHERMEN, FISHERS, FISHHOOK, FISHHOOKS, FISHING]

Ge 1:26 and let them rule over the f *of* the sea and 1836
1:28 over the f *of* the sea and the birds of the air 1836
9: 2 and upon all the f *of* the sea; 1834
Ex 7:18 The f in the Nile will die, 1836
7:21 The f in the Nile died, 1836
Nu 11: 5 We remember the f we ate in Egypt 1836
11:22 the f *in* the sea were caught for them?" 1834
Dt 4:18 the ground or any f in the waters below. 1836
1Ki 4:33 about animals and birds, reptiles and f. 1834
2Ch 33:14 as the entrance of the F Gate and encircling 1834
Ne 3: 3 The F Gate was rebuilt by the sons 1834
12:39 the Jeshanah Gate, the F Gate, 1834
13:16 in f and all kinds of merchandise 1794
Job 12: 8 or let the f *of* the sea inform you. 1834
Ps 8: 8 and the f *of* the sea, 1834
105:29 causing their f to die. 1836
Ecc 9:12 As f are caught in a cruel net, 1834
Isa 50: 2 their f rot for lack of water and die 1836
Eze 29: 4 the f *of* your streams stick to your scales. 1836
29: 4 with all the f sticking to your scales. 1836
29: 5 you and all the f *of* your streams. 1836
38:20 The f *of* the sea, the birds of the air, 1834
47: 9 There will be large numbers of f, 1836
47:10 The f will be of many kinds— 1836
47:10 like the f *of* the Great Sea. 1836
Hos 4: 3 the field and the birds of the air and the f 1834
Jnh 1:17 But the LORD provided a great f 1834
1:17 inside the f three days and three nights. 1834
2: 1 the f Jonah prayed to the LORD his God. 1836
2:10 And the LORD commanded the f, 1834
Hab 1:14 You have made men like f *in* the sea, 1834
Zep 1: 3 the birds of the air and the f *of* the sea. 1834
Zep 1:10 "a cry will go up from the F Gate, 1834
Mt 7:10 Or if he asks for a f, will give him a snake? *2716*
12:40 and three nights in the belly *of* a **huge** f, *3063*
13:47 into the lake and caught all kinds of f. *NIG*
13:48 down and collected the good f in baskets, *NIG*
14:17 of bread and two f," *2716*
14:19 the five loaves and the two f and looking *2716*
15:34 "Seven," they replied, "and a few **small** f." *2715*
15:36 Then he took the seven loaves and the f, *2716*
17:27 Take the first f you catch; *2716*
Mk 6:38 they said, "Five—and two f." *2716*
6:41 the five loaves and the two f and looking *2716*
6:41 He also divided the two f among them all. *2716*
6:43 of broken pieces of bread and f. *2716*
8: 7 They had a few **small** f as well; *2715*
Lk 5: 6 a large number *of* f that their nets began *2716*
5: 9 at the catch *of* f they had taken, *2716*
9:13 of bread and two f— *2716*
9:16 the five loaves and the two f and looking *2716*
11:11 if your son asks for a f, *2716*
24:42 They gave him a piece *of* broiled f, *2716*
Jn 6: 9 and two **small** f, *4066*
6:11 He did the same with the f. *4066*
21: 3 "I'm going out *to* f," *244*
21: 5 "Friends, haven't you any f?" *4709*
21: 6 the net in because of the large number *of* f. *2716*
21: 8 towing the net full *of* f, *2716*
21: 9 a fire of burning coals there with f on it, *4066*
21:10 "Bring some *of* the f you have just caught." *4066*
21:11 It was full of large f, 153, *2716*
21:13 and did the same with the f. *4066*
1Co 15:39 birds another and f another. *2716*

FISHERMEN (7) [FISH]

Isa 19: 8 The f will groan and lament, 1900
Jer 16:16 "But now I will send for many f," 1900
Eze 47:10 F will stand along the shore; 1854
Mt 4:18 for they were f. *243*
13:48 it was full, the f pulled it up on the shore. *NIG*
Mk 1:16 for they were f. *243*
Lk 5: 2 left there by the f, *243*

FISHERS (2) [FISH]

Mt 4:19 Jesus said, "and I will make you f of men." *243*
Mk 1:17 Jesus said, "and I will make you f of men." *243*

FISHHOOK (1) [FISH, HOOK]

Job 41: 1 a f or tie down his tongue with a rope? 2676

FISHHOOKS (1) [FISH, HOOK]

Am 4: 2 the last of you with f. 1855+6106

FISHING (1) [FISH]

Job 41: 7 with harpoons or his head with f spears? 1834

FISHING NETS (Anglicized) See FISHNETS

FISHNETS (2) [NET]

Eze 26: 5 the sea she will become a place to spread f, 3052
26:14 and you will become a place to spread f. 3052

FISHPOOL (KJV) See POOL

FIST (4) [FISTS, TIGHTFISTED]

Ex 21:18 a stone or with his f and he does not die 114
Nu 35:21 with his f so that he dies, that person shall 3338
Job 15:25 because he shakes his f at God 3338
Isa 10:32 they will shake their f at the mount of 3338

FISTS (4) [FIST]

Isa 58: 4 and in striking each other with wicked f. 114
Zep 2:15 by her scoff and shake their f. 3338
Mt 26:67 **struck** him **with** *their* f. *3139*
Mk 14:65 **struck** him **with** their f, *3139*

FIT (13) [FITS, FITTED, FITTING, FITTINGS]

Ge 49:20 he will provide **delicacies** *f for* a king. AIT
Dt 12: 8 everyone as he sees f, 3838
Jdg 5:25 in a **bowl** *f* for nobles AIT
17: 6 everyone did as he saw f. 3838
21:25 everyone did as he saw f. 3838
2Ki 24:16 strong and f **for** war, 6913
Isa 54:16 into flame and forges a weapon f **for** 4200
Eze 19:11 f **for** a ruler's scepter. 448
19:14 No strong branch is left on it f for NIH
Mt 3:11 whose sandals I am not f to carry. *2653*
Lk 9:62 the plow and looks back is f **for service** in *2310*
14:35 It is f neither for the soil nor for *2310*
Ac 22:22 He's not f to live!" *2763*

FITCHES (KJV) See CARAWAY

FITS (1) [FIT]

Gal 5:20 hatred, discord, jealousy, f **of rage,** *2596*

FITTED (3) [FIT]

Ex 26:24 and f into a single ring; 3481+9447
Ex 36:29 the top and f into a single ring; 3481+9447
Eph 6:15 and with your feet f with the readiness *5686*

FITTING (8) [FIT]

Ps 33: 1 it is f for the upright to praise him. 5534
147: 1 how pleasant and f to praise him! 5534
Pr 10:32 The lips of the righteous know *what* is f, 8356
19:10 It is not f for a fool to live in luxury— 5534
26: 1 honor is not f for a fool. 5534
1Co 14:40 But everything should be done in a f *2361*
Col 3:18 as *is* f in the Lord. *465*
Heb 2:10 *it was* f that God, *4560*

FITTINGS (1) [FIT]

1Ch 22: 3 for the doors of the gateways and for the f, 4677

FIVE (209) [FIFTH, FIVE-SIDED, FOUR-FIFTHS]

Ge 14: 9 four kings against f. 2822
18:28 of the righteous is f less than fifty? 2822
18:28 the whole city because of f *people?"* 2822
43:34 Benjamin's portion was f times as much 2822
45: 6 the next f years there will not be plowing 2822
45:11 because f years of famine are still to come. 2822
45:22 of silver and f sets of clothes. 2822
47: 2 He chose f of his brothers 2822
Ex 22: 1 he must pay back f head of cattle for the ox 2822
26: 3 Join f *of* the curtains together, 2822
26: 3 and do the same with the other f. 2822
26: 9 Join f *of* the curtains together into one set 2822
26:26 f for the frames on one side of 2822
26:27 f for those on the other side, 2822
26:27 and f for the frames on the west, 2822
26:37 and f posts of acacia wood overlaid 2822
26:37 And cast f bronze bases for them. 2822
27: 1 f cubits long and five cubits wide. 2822
27: 1 five cubits long and f cubits wide. 2822
27:18 of finely twisted linen f cubits high, 2822
36:10 They joined f *of* the curtains together 2822
36:10 and did the same with the other f. 2822
36:16 They joined f *of* the curtains into one set 2822
36:31 f for the frames on one side of 2822
36:32 f for those on the other side, 2822
36:32 and f for the frames on the west, 2822
36:38 and they made f posts with hooks for them. 2822
36:38 with gold and made their f bases of bronze. 2822
38: 1 f cubits long and five cubits wide. 2822
38: 1 five cubits long and f cubits wide. 2822
38:18 the curtains of the courtyard, f cubits high, 2822
Lev 26: 8 F of you will chase a hundred, 2822
27: 5 a person between the ages of f and twenty, 2822
27: 6 a person between one month and f years, 2822
27: 6 set the value of a male at f shekels of silver 2822
Nu 3:47 collect f shekels for each one, 2822
7:17 and two oxen, f rams, five male goats 2822
7:17 f male goats and five male lambs 2822
7:17 five male goats and f male lambs 2822
7:23 and two oxen, f rams, five male goats 2822
7:23 f male goats and five male lambs 2822
7:23 five male goats and f male lambs 2822
7:29 and two oxen, f rams, five male goats 2822
7:29 f male goats and five male lambs 2822
7:29 five male goats and f male lambs 2822
7:35 and two oxen, f rams, five male goats 2822
7:35 f male goats and five male lambs 2822
7:35 five male goats and f male lambs 2822
7:41 and two oxen, f rams, five male goats 2822
7:41 f male goats and five male lambs 2822
7:41 five male goats and f male lambs 2822
7:47 and two oxen, f rams, five male goats 2822
7:47 f male goats and five male lambs 2822
7:47 five male goats and f male lambs 2822
7:53 and two oxen, f rams, five male goats 2822
7:53 f male goats and five male lambs 2822
7:53 five male goats and f male lambs 2822
7:59 and two oxen, f rams, five male goats 2822
7:59 f male goats and five male lambs 2822
7:59 five male goats and f male lambs 2822
7:65 and two oxen, f rams, five male goats 2822
7:65 f male goats and five male lambs 2822
7:65 five male goats and f male lambs 2822
7:71 and two oxen, f rams, five male goats 2822
7:71 f male goats and five male lambs 2822
7:71 five male goats and f male lambs 2822
7:77 and two oxen, f rams, five male goats 2822
7:77 f male goats and five male lambs 2822
7:77 five male goats and f male lambs 2822
7:83 and two oxen, f rams, five male goats 2822
7:83 f male goats and five male lambs 2822
7:83 five male goats and f male lambs 2822
11:19 or two days, or f, ten or twenty days, 2822
18:16 at the redemption price set at f shekels 2822
31: 8 the f kings of Midian. 2822
31:28 for the LORD one out of every f hundred, 2822
Jos 8:12 Joshua had taken about f thousand men 2822
10: 5 Then the f kings of the Amorites— 2822
10:16 the f kings had fled and hidden in the cave 2822
10:17 that the f kings had been found hiding in 2822
10:22 of the cave and bring those f kings out 2822
10:23 they brought the f kings out of the cave— 2822
10:26 the kings and hung them on f trees, 2822
13: 3 (the territory of the f Philistine rulers 2822
Jdg 3: 3 the f rulers of the Philistines, 2822
18: 2 So the Danites sent f warriors from Zorah 2822

Jdg 18: 7 So the **f** men left and came to Laish, 2822
18:14 Then the **f** men who had spied out the land 2822
18:17 The **f** men who had spied out the land went 2822
20:45 the Israelites cut down **f** thousand men 2822
1Sa 6: 4 "**F** gold tumors and five gold rats, 2822
6: 4 "Five gold tumors and **f** gold rats, 2822
6:16 The **f** rulers of the Philistines saw all this 2822
6:18 to the **f** rulers— 2822
17: 5 of bronze weighing **f** thousand shekels; 2822
17:40 chose **f** smooth stones from the stream, 2822
21: 3 Give me **f** loaves of bread, 2822
25:18 **f** dressed sheep, five seahs of roasted grain, 2822
25:18 five dressed sheep, **f** seahs of roasted grain, 2822
25:42 attended by her **f** maids, 2822
2Sa 4: 4 He was **f** years old when the news 2822
21: 8 with the **f** sons of Saul's daughter Merab, 2822
24: 9 and in Judah **f** hundred thousand. 2822
1Ki 4:32 and his songs numbered a thousand and **f.** 2822
6: 6 The lowest floor was **f** cubits wide, 2822
6:10 The height of each was **f** cubits, 2822
6:24 of the first cherub was **f** cubits long, and 2822
6:24 and the other wing **f** cubits— 2822
7:16 each capital was **f** cubits high. 2822
7:23 from rim to rim and **f** cubits high. 2822
7:39 He placed **f** of the stands on the south side 2822
7:39 on the south side of the temple and **f** on 2822
7:49 the lampstands of pure gold (**f** on the right 2822
7:49 on the right and **f** on the left, in front of 2822
2Ki 6:25 quarter of a cab of seed pods for **f** shekels. 2822
7:13 "Have some men take **f** of the horses 2822
13:19 "You should have struck the ground **f** 2822
25:19 of the fighting men and **f** royal advisers. 2822
1Ch 2: 4 Judah had **f** sons in all. 2822
2: 6 and Darda—**f** in all. 2822
3:20 There were also **f** others: 2822
4:32 and Ashan—**f** towns— 2822
4:42 And **f** hundred of these Simeonites, 2822
7: 3 All **f** of them were chiefs. 2822
7: 7 of families—**f** in all. 2822
29: 7 on the temple of God **f** thousand talents 2822
2Ch 3:11 of the first cherub was **f** cubits long 2822
3:11 while its other wing, also **f** cubits long, 2822
3:12 of the second cherub was **f** cubits long 2822
3:12 and its other wing, also **f** cubits long, 2822
3:15 with a capital on top measuring **f** cubits. 2822
4: 2 from rim to rim and **f** cubits high. 2822
4: 6 for washing and placed **f** on the south side 2822
4: 6 and placed five on the south side and **f** on 2822
4: 7 **f** on the south side and five on the north. 2822
4: 7 five on the south side and **f** on the north. 2822
4: 8 **f** on the south side and five on the north. 2822
4: 8 five on the south side and **f** on the north. 2822
6:13 a bronze platform, **f** cubits long, 2822
6:13 **f** cubits wide and three cubits high, 2822
13:17 there were **f** hundred thousand casualties 2822
35: 9 provided **f** thousand Passover offerings 2822
35: 9 and **f** hundred head of cattle for 2822
Ne 3:13 repaired **f hundred yards** of the wall 547+564
Est 9: 6 Jews killed and destroyed **f** hundred men. 2822
9:12 and destroyed **f** hundred men and 2822
Job 1: 3 **f** hundred yoke of oxen 2822
1: 3 of oxen and **f** hundred donkeys, 2822
Isa 17: 6 four or **f** on the fruitful boughs," 2822
19:18 In that day **f** cities in Egypt will speak 2822
30:17 at the threat of **f** you will all flee away, 2822
Jer 52:22 on top of the one pillar was **f** cubits high 2822
Eze 40: 7 between the alcoves were **f** cubits thick. 2822
40:30 and **f** cubits deep.) 2822
40:48 they were **f** cubits wide on either side. 2822
41: 2 on each side of it were **f** cubits wide. 2822
41: 9 of the side rooms was **f** cubits thick. 2822
41:11 the open area was **f** cubits wide all around. 2822
41:12 the building was **f** cubits thick all around, 2822
42:16 it was **f** hundred cubits. 2822
42:17 it was **f** hundred cubits by 2822
42:18 it was **f** hundred cubits by 2822
42:19 it was **f** hundred cubits by 2822
42:20 **f** hundred cubits long 2822
42:20 and **f** hundred cubits wide, 2822
Mt 14:17 "We have here only **f** loaves of bread *4297*
14:19 the **f** loaves and the two fish and looking *4297*
14:21 who ate was about **f thousand** men, *4295*
16: 9 Don't you remember the **f** loaves for *4297*
16: 9 the five loaves *for* the **f thousand,** *4295*
25: 2 **F** of them were foolish and five were wise. *4297*
25: 2 Five of them were foolish and **f** were wise. *4297*
25:15 To one he gave **f** talents of money, *4297*
25:16 the **f** talents went at once *4297*
25:16 to work and gained **f** more. *4297*
25:20 the **f** talents brought the other five. *4297*
25:20 the five talents brought the other **f.** *4297*
25:20 he said, 'you entrusted me with **f** talents. *4297*
25:20 See, I have gained **f** more.' *4297*
Mk 6:38 When they found out, they said, "**F**— *4297*
6:41 the **f** loaves and the two fish and looking *4297*
6:44 of the men who had eaten was **f thousand.** *4295*
8:19 I broke the **f** loaves for the five thousand, *4297*
8:19 I broke the five loaves for the **f thousand,** *4295*
Lk 1:24 and *for* **f** months remained in seclusion. *4297*
7:41 One owed him **f hundred** denarii, *4296*
9:13 "We have only **f** loaves of bread *4297*
9:14 (About **f thousand** men were there.) *4295*
9:16 the **f** loaves and the two fish and looking *4297*
12: 6 Are not **f** sparrows sold for two pennies? *4297*
12:52 on there will be **f** in one family divided *4297*
14:19 'I have just bought **f** yoke of oxen, *4297*
16:28 for I have **f** brothers. *4297*
Lk 19:18 'Sir, your mina has earned **f** more.' *4297*
19:19 'You take charge of **f** cities.' *4297*
Jn 4:18 The fact is, you have had **f** husbands, *4297*
5: 2 by **f** covered colonnades. *4297*
6: 9 "Here is a boy with **f** small barley loaves *4297*
6:10 men sat down, about **f thousand** of them. *4295*
6:13 with the pieces of the **f** barley loaves left *4297*
Ac 4: 4 number of men grew to about **f** thousand. *4297*
20: 6 and **f** days later joined the others at Troas, *4297*
24: 1 **F** days later the high priest Ananias went *4297*
1Co 14:19 in the church I would rather speak **f**
intelligible words to instruct others *4297*
15: 6 *to* more than **f hundred** of the brothers at *4296*
2Co 11:24 **F times** I received from the Jews *4294*
Rev 9: 5 but only to torture them *for* **f** months. *4297*
9:10 to torment people *for* **f** months. *4297*
17:10 **F** have fallen, one is, *4297*

FIVE-SIDED (1) [FIVE, SIDE]
1Ki 6:31 of olive wood with **f** jambs. 2797

FIX (8) [AFFIXING, FIXED]
Dt 11:18 **F** these words of mine in your hearts 8492
Job 14: 3 *Do you* **f** your eye on such a one? 7219
Pr 4:25 **f** your gaze **directly** before you. 3837
Isa 46: 8 "Remember this, **f it in mind,** 899
Am 9: 4 *I will* **f** my eyes upon them for evil and 8492
2Co 4:18 **f our eyes** not on what is seen, but on *5023*
Heb 3: 1 **f** *your* **thoughts on** Jesus, *2917*
12: 2 *Let us* **f** *our* **eyes** on Jesus, *927*

FIXED (6) [FIX]
2Ki 8:11 He **stared** *at* him **with a f gaze** until Hazael
906+2256+6641+7156+8492
Job 38:10 when *I* **f** limits for it and set its doors 8689
Ps 141: 8 But my eyes are **f on** you, 448
Pr 8:28 and **f securely** the fountains of the deep, 6451
Jer 33:25 and the **f laws** *of* heaven and earth, 2978
Lk 16:26 and you a great chasm *has been* **f,** *5114*

FLAG (KJV) See REED

FLAGSTAFF (1) [STAFF]
Isa 30:17 till you are left like a **f** on a mountaintop, 9568

FLAKES (1)
Ex 16:14 thin **f** like frost on the ground appeared on 2892

FLAME (16) [AFLAME, FLAMED, FLAMES, FLAMING]
Jdg 13:20 As the **f** blazed up from the altar 4258
13:20 the angel of the LORD ascended in the **f.** 4258
16: 9 of string snaps when it comes close to a **f.** 836
Job 15:30 a **f** will wither his shoots, 8927
18: 5 the **f** *of* his fire stops burning. 8663
Ps 83:14 the forest or a **f** sets the mountains ablaze, 4259
106:18 a **f** consumed the wicked. 4259
SS 8: 6 It burns like blazing fire, like a **mighty f.** 8928
Isa 10:16 a fire will be kindled like a blazing **f.** 836
10:17 their Holy One a **f;** 4259
47:14 from the power of the **f.** 4259
54:16 into **f** and forges a weapon fit for its work. 836
Eze 20:47 The blazing **f** will not be quenched, 8927
Joel 2: 3 behind them a **f** blazes. 4259
Ob 1:18 be a fire and the house of Joseph a **f;** 4259
2Ti 1: 6 For this reason I remind you *to* **fan into f** *351*

FLAMED (1) [FLAME]
Am 1:11 and his fury **f unchecked,** 5905+9068

FLAMES (16) [FLAME]
Ex 3: 2 of the LORD appeared to him in **f** *of* fire 4225
Job 41:21 and **f** dart from his mouth. 4258
Ps 104: 4 **f** *of* fire his servants. 4265
Isa 5:24 down in the **f,** so their roots will decay 4259
29: 6 and tempest and **f** *of* a devouring fire. 4258
42:25 *It* enveloped them **in f,** 4265
43: 2 the **f** will not set you ablaze. 4259
66:15 and his rebuke with **f** *of* fire. 4258
Jer 51:58 the nations' labor is only **fuel for the f."**
836+928+1896
Da 3:22 the **f** of the fire killed the soldiers who took 10695
Joel 1:19 the open pastures and **f** have burned up all 4259
Ac 7:30 an angel appeared to Moses in the **f** of *5825*
1Co 3:15 but only as one escaping through the **f.** *4786*
13: 3 to the poor and surrender my body to the **f,** *2794*
Heb 1: 7 his servants **f** of fire." *5825*
11:34 the fury *of* the **f,** and escaped the edge of *4786*

FLAMING (11) [FLAME]
Ge 3:24 a **f** sword flashing back and forth to guard 4267
Ps 7:13 he makes ready his **f** arrows. 1944
Isa 4: 5 of smoke by day and a glow of **f** fire 4259
50:11 and provide yourselves with **f torches,** 2338
La 2: 3 a **f** fire that consumes everything around it. 4259
Da 7: 9 His throne was **f** with fire, 10695
10: 6 his eyes like **f** torches, 836
Hos 7: 6 in the morning it blazes like a **f** fire. 4259
Na 2: 4 They look like **f torches;** 4365
Zec 12: 6 like a **f** torch among sheaves. 836
Eph 6:16 the **f** arrows of the evil one. *4792*

FLANK (2)
Eze 25: 9 therefore I will expose the **f** *of* Moab, 4190
34:21 Because you shove with **f** and shoulder, 7396

FLAP (1) [FLAPPED]
Job 39:13 "The wings of the ostrich **f joyfully,** 6632

FLAPPED (1) [FLAP]
Isa 10:14 not *one* **f** a wing, 5610

FLARE (2) [FLARED]
2Sa 11:20 the king's anger *may* **f up,** 6590
Ps 2:12 for his wrath *can* **f up** in a moment. 1277

FLARED (3) [FLARE]
Jdg 6:21 Fire **f** from the rock, 6590
1Sa 20:30 Saul's anger **f up** at Jonathan and he said 3013
Ps 124: 3 when their anger **f** against us, 3013

FLASH (9) [FLASHED, FLASHES, FLASHING]
Job 15:12 and why *do* your eyes **f,** 8141
37:15 **makes** his lightning **f?** 3649
Eze 21:10 polished to **f like lightning!** 1398
21:15 It is made to **f like lightning,** 1398
21:28 to consume and to **f like lightning!** 1398
Hos 11: 6 Swords *will* **f** in their cities, 2565
Zec 9:14 his arrow *will* **f** like lightning. 3655
Lk 9:29 as bright as a **f of lightning.** *1993*
1Co 15:52 in a **f,** in the twinkling of an eye, at *875*

FLASHED (8) [FLASH]
Ex 9:23 and lightning **f down** to the ground. 2143
9:24 and lightning **f back and forth.** 928+4374+9348
Ps 77:17 your arrows **f back and forth.** 2143
Eze 1:13 it was bright, and lightning **f out** of it. 3655
Hos 6: 5 my judgments **f** like lightning *upon* you. 3655
Hab 3: 4 rays **f** from his hand, NIH
Ac 9: 3 suddenly a light from heaven **f around** *4313*
22: 6 a bright light from heaven **f around** me. *4313*

FLASHES (10) [FLASH]
Job 41:18 His snorting **throws out f** *of* light; 2145
Ps 29: 7 of the LORD strikes with **f** *of* lightning. 4259
Eze 1:14 and forth like **f of lightning.** 1027
Am 5: 9 he **f** destruction on the stronghold 1158
Na 2: 3 The metal on the chariots **f** on 836+928
Lk 17:24 **which f** and lights up the sky from one end *848*
Rev 4: 5 From the throne came **f of lightning,** *847*
8: 5 **f of lightning** and an earthquake. *847*
11:19 And there came **f of lightning,** *847*
16:18 Then there came **f of lightning,** *847*

FLASHING (7) [FLASH]
Ge 3:24 a flaming sword **f back and forth** to guard 2200
Dt 32:41 when I sharpen my **f** sword 1398
Job 39:23 along with the **f** spear and lance. 4258
Ps 76: 3 There he broke the **f** arrows, 8404
Eze 1: 4 an immense cloud with **f** lightning 4374
Na 3: 3 **f** swords and glittering spears! 4258
Hab 3:11 at the lightning of your **f** spear. 5586

FLASK (3)
1Sa 10: 1 Then Samuel took a **f** *of* oil and poured it 7095
2Ki 9: 1 take this **f** *of* oil with you and go 7095
9: 3 the **f** and pour the oil on his head 7095

FLAT (1) [FLATS, FLATTENS]
Hos 7: 8 Ephraim is a **f cake** not turned over. 6314

FLATS (1) [FLAT]
Job 39: 6 the **salt f** as his habitat. 4877

FLATTENS (1) [FLAT]
Isa 32:19 Though hail **f** the forest and 3718

FLATTER (3) [FLATTERING, FLATTERS, FLATTERY]
Job 32:21 nor *will I* **f** any man; 4033
Ps 78:36 then *they would* **f** him with their mouths, 7331
Jude 1:16 they boast about themselves and **f** others
2513+4725

FLATTERING (5) [FLATTER]
Ps 12: 2 their **f** lips speak with deception. 2747
12: 3 May the LORD cut off all **f** lips 2747
Pr 26:28 and a **f** mouth works ruin. 2747
28:23 He who rebukes a man will in the end gain
more favor than *he who has a* **f** tongue. 2744
Eze 12:24 or **f** divinations among the people of Israel. 2728

FLATTERS (2) [FLATTER]
Ps 36: 2 For in his own eyes *he* **f** himself *too much* 2744
Pr 29: 5 Whoever **f** his neighbor is spreading a net 2744

FLATTERY (4) [FLATTER]

Job 32:22 for if I were skilled in f, 4033
Da 11:32 With f he will corrupt those who have violated the covenant, 2747
Ro 16:18 By smooth talk and f they deceive *2330*
1Th 2: 5 You know we never used f, *3135*

FLAVOR (1)

Job 6: 6 or is there f in the white of an egg? 3248

FLAW (3) [FLAWLESS]

Dt 15:21 is lame or blind, or has any serious f, 4583
17: 1 ox or a sheep that has any defect or f 1821+8273
SS 4: 7 there is no f in you. 4583

FLAWLESS (6) [FLAW]

2Sa 22:31 the word of the LORD *is* f. 7671
Job 11: 4 'My beliefs are f and I am pure 2341
Ps 12: 6 And the words of the LORD are f, 3196
18:30 the word of the LORD *is* f. 7671
Pr 30: 5 "Every word of God *is* f; 7671
SS 5: 2 my sister, my darling, my dove, my f *one*. 9447

FLAX (6)

Ex 9:31 (The f and barley were destroyed, 7325
9:31 barley had headed and the f was in bloom. 7325
Jos 2: 6 the stalks of f she had laid out on the roof.) 7324
Jdg 15:14 on his arms became like charred f, 7324
Pr 31:13 and f and works with eager hands. 7324
Isa 19: 9 with combed f will despair, 7324

FLAY (KJV) See SKIN, STRIP OFF

FLEA (2)

1Sa 24:14 A dead dog? A f? 7282
26:20 of Israel has come out to look for a f— 7282

FLED (118) [FLEE]

Ge 14:10 when the kings of Sodom and Gomorrah f, 5674
14:10 of the men fell into them and the rest f to 5674
16: 6 Sarai mistreated Hagar; so *she* f from her. 1368
31:21 So he f with all he had, 1368
31:22 that Jacob *had* f. 1368
31:40 and sleep f from my eyes. 5610
Ex 2:15 but Moses f from Pharaoh and went to live 1368
14: 5 of Egypt was told that the people *had* f, 1368
Nu 16:34 all the Israelites around them f, shouting, 5674
35:25 to the city of refuge to which *he* f. 5674
35:26 of the city of refuge to which *he has* f 5674
35:32 not accept a ransom for *anyone who has* f to 5674
Jos 8:15 and *they* f toward the desert. 5674
10:11 As they f before Israel on the road down 5674
10:16 the five kings *had* f and hidden in the cave 5674
20: 6 in the town from which *he* f." 5674
Jdg 1: 6 Adoni-Bezek f, but they chased him 5674
4:15 Sisera abandoned his chariot and f on foot. 5674
4:17 however, f on foot to the tent of Jael, 5674
7:21 all the Midianites ran, crying out as *they* f. 5674
7:22 The army f to Beth Shittah toward Zererah 5674
8:12 f, but he pursued them and captured them, 5674
9:21 Then Jotham f, escaping to Beer, 5674
9:51 all the people of the city—f. 5674
11: 3 So Jephthah f from his brothers and settled 1368
20:42 So *they* f before the Israelites in 7155
20:45 As they turned and f toward the desert to 5674
20:47 But six hundred men turned and f into 5674
1Sa 4:10 and every man f to his tent. 5674
4:16 I f from it this very day." 5674
4:17 "Israel f before the Philistines, 5674
19: 8 He struck them with such force that *they* f 5674
19:12 and *he* f and escaped. 1368
19:18 When David *had* f and made his escape, 1368
20: 1 Then David f from Naioth at Ramah 1368
21:10 That day David f from Saul and went 1368
22:20 escaped and f to join David. 1368
23: 6 with him when he f to David *at* Keilah.) 1368
27: 4 Saul was told that David *had* f *to* Gath, 1368
30:17 on camels and f. 5674
31: 1 the Israelites f before them, 5674
31: 7 the Jordan saw that the Israelite army *had* f 5674
31: 7 they abandoned their towns and f. 5674
2Sa 1: 4 He said, "The men f from the battle. 5674
4: 3 because the people of Beeroth f to Gittaim 1368
4: 4 His nurse picked him up and f, 5674
10:13 and *they* f before him. 5674
10:14 *they* f before Abishai and went inside 5674
10:18 But they f before Israel, 5674
13:29 mounted their mules and f. 5674
13:34 Meanwhile, Absalom *had* f. 1368
13:37 Absalom f and went to Talmai son 1368
13:38 After Absalom f and went to Geshur, 1368
18:17 all the Israelites f to their homes. 5674
19: 8 the Israelites *had* f to their homes. 5674
19: 9 *he has* f the country because of Absalom; 1368
23:11 Israel's troops f from them. 5674
1Ki 2: 7 when I f from your brother Absalom. 1368
2:28 he f to the tent of the LORD 5674
2:29 King Solomon was told that Joab *had* f to 5674
11:17 But Hadad, still only a boy, f to Egypt 1368
11:23 who *had* f from his master, 1368
11:40 but Jeroboam f to Egypt, 1368
12: 2 where *he had* f from King Solomon), 1368
1Ki 20:20 At that, the Arameans f, 5674
20:30 And Ben-Hadad f to the city and hid in 5674
2Ki 3:24 up and fought them until *they* f. 5674
7: 7 and f in the dusk and abandoned their tents 5674
8:21 his army, however, f back home. 5674
9:23 Joram turned about and f, 5674
9:27 *he* f up the road to Beth Haggan. 5674
14:12 and every man f to his home. 5674
14:19 and *he* f to Lachish, 5674
25: 4 the whole army f at night through the gate NIH
25: 4 *They* f toward the Arabah, 2143
25:26 f *to* Egypt for fear of the Babylonians. 995
1Ch 10: 1 the Israelites f before them, 5674
10: 7 in the valley saw that the army *had* f and 5674
10: 7 they abandoned their towns and f. 5674
11:13 the troops f from the Philistines. 5674
19:14 and *they* f before him. 5674
19:15 they too f before his brother Abishai 5674
19:18 But they f before Israel, 5674
2Ch 10: 2 where *he had* f from King Solomon), 1368
13:16 The Israelites f before Judah, 5674
14:12 and Judah. The Cushites f, 5674
25:22 and every man f to his home. 5674
25:27 against him in Jerusalem and *he* f 5674
Ps 3: T When he f from his son Absalom. 1368
48: 5 *they* f in terror. 2905
57: T When he *had* f from Saul into the cave. 1368
104: 7 But at your rebuke the waters f, 5674
114: 3 sea looked and f, the Jordan turned back; 5674
114: 5 Why was it, O sea, that *you* f, O Jordan, 5674
Isa 20: 6 those *we* f *to* for help and deliverance from 5674
22: 3 All your leaders *have* f together; 5610
22: 3 All you who were caught were taken prisoner together, *having* f while 1368
Jer 9:10 of the air *have* f and the animals are gone. 5610
26:21 Uriah heard of it and f in fear *to* Egypt. 1368
39: 4 and all the soldiers saw them, *they* f; 1368
41:15 of his men escaped from Johanan and f to 2143
52: 7 and the whole army f. 1368
52: 7 *They* f toward the Arabah, 2143
La 1: 6 in weakness *they have* f before the pursuer. 2143
Da 10: 7 that *they* f and hid themselves. 1368
Hos 12:12 Jacob f *to* the country of Aram; 1368
Am 5:19 as though a man f from a lion only to meet 5674
Zec 14: 5 You will flee as *you* f from the earthquake 5674
Mt 26:56 Then all the disciples deserted him and f. *5771*
Mk 14:50 Then everyone deserted him and f. *5771*
14:52 he f naked, leaving his garment behind. *5771*
16: 8 the women went out and f from the tomb. *5771*
Ac 7:29 When Moses heard this, *he* f to Midian, *5771*
14: 6 and f to the Lycaonian cities of Lystra *2966*
Heb 6:18 we who *have* f to take hold of the hope *2966*
Rev 12: 6 The woman f into the desert to a place *5771*
16:20 Every island f away and *5771*
20:11 Earth and sky f from his presence, *5771*

FLEE (89) [FLED, FLEEING, FLEES]

Ge 19:17 one of them said, "F for your lives! 4880
19:17 F to the mountains or you will 4880
19:19 But I can't f to the mountains; 4880
19:20 *Let me* f to it—it is very small, isn't it? 4880
19:22 But f there quickly, 4880
27:43 F at once to my brother Laban in Haran. 1368
Ex 21:13 *he is to* f to a place I will designate. 5674
Lev 26:17 over you, and *you will* f even 5674
Nu 10:35 *may* your foes f before you." 5674
35: 6 a person who has killed someone *may* f. 5674
35:11 person who has killed someone accidentally *may* f. 5674
35:15 anyone who has killed another accidentally *can* f there. 5674
Dt 4:42 a person *could* f if he had unintentionally 5674
4:42 *He could* f into one of these cities 5674
19: 3 so that anyone who kills a man *may* f there. 5674
19: 5 That man *may* f to one of these cities 5674
28: 7 from one direction but f from you in seven. 5674
28:25 at them from one direction but f from them 5674
Jos 8: 5 as they did before, *we will* f from them. 5674
8: 6 So when *we* f from them, 5674
20: 3 and unintentionally *may* f there 5674
20: 9 who killed someone accidentally *could* f 5674
2Sa 15:14 *We must* f, or none of us will escape 1368
17: 2 and then all the people with him *will* f. 5674
18: 3 if *we are* forced to f, 5674+5674
19: 3 in who are ashamed when they f 5674
2Ki 19:21 of Jerusalem tosses her head as you f. 339
Job 41:28 Arrows *do* not make him f; 1368
Ps 11: 1 "F like a bird *to* your mountain. 5653
31:11 those who see me on the street f from me. 5610
55: 7 I would f far away and stay in the desert; 5610
68: 1 *may* his foes f before him. 5674
68:12 "Kings and armies f in haste; 5610+5610
139: 7 Where *can I* f from your presence? 1368
SS 2:17 Until the day breaks and the shadows f, 5674
4: 6 Until the day breaks and the shadows f, 5674
Isa 2:19 *Men will* f to caves in the rocks and 995
2:21 They *will* f to caverns in the rocks and to 995
13:14 each *will* f to his native land. 5674
15: 5 her fugitives f as far as Zoar, NIH
17:13 when he rebukes them *they* f far away, 5674
21:15 *They* f from the sword, 5610
30:16 You said, 'No, *we will* f on horses.' 5674
30:16 Therefore *you will* f! 5674
30:17 A thousand will f at the threat of one; NIH
30:17 at the threat of five *you will all* f away, 5674
31: 8 *They will* f before the sword 5674
Isa 33: 3 the thunder of your voice, the peoples f; 5610
35:10 and sorrow and sighing *will* f away. 5674
37:22 of Jerusalem tosses her head as you f. 339
48:20 Leave Babylon, f from the Babylonians! 1368
51:11 and sorrow and sighing *will* f away. 5674
Jer 4: 5 *Let us* f to the fortified cities!' 995
4: 6 F for safety without delay! 6395
6: 1 "F for safety, people of Benjamin! 6395
6: 1 F from Jerusalem! NIH
8:14 *Let us* f to the fortified cities 995
25:35 The shepherds will have nowhere to f, 4960
46: 5 *They* f in haste without looking back, 4960+5674
46: 6 "The swift cannot f nor the strong escape. 5674
46:21 They too will turn and f together, 5674
48: 6 F! Run for your lives; 5674
49: 8 Turn and f, hide in deep caves, 5674
49:24 to f and panic has gripped her; 5674
49:30 "F quickly away! 5674
50: 3 both men and animals *will* f away. 5653
50: 8 "F out of Babylon; 5653
50:16 *let* everyone f to his own land. 5674
51: 6 "F from Babylon! 5674
La 4:15 When *they* f and wander about, 5680
Da 4:14 the animals f from under it and the birds 10469
Am 2:16 bravest warriors *will* f naked on that day," 5674
Jnh 1: 3 he went aboard and sailed for Tarshish to f NIH
4: 2 That is why I was so quick to f to Tarshish. 1368
Na 3: 7 All who see you *will* f from you and say, 5610
Zec 2: 6 F from the land of the north," 5674
14: 5 *You will* f *by* my mountain valley, 5674
14: 5 *You will* f as you fled from the earthquake 5674
Mt 3: 7 warned you *to* f from the coming wrath? *5771*
10:23 When you are persecuted in one place, f *5771*
24:16 then *let* those who are in Judea f to *5771*
Mk 13:14 then *let* those who are in Judea f to *5771*
Lk 3: 7 warned you *to* f from the coming wrath? *5771*
21:21 Then *let* those who are in Judea f to *5771*
1Co 6:18 F from sexual immorality. *5771*
10:14 Therefore, my dear friends, f from idolatry. *5771*
1Ti 6:11 But you, man of God, f from all this, *5771*
2Ti 2:22 F the evil desires of youth, *5771*
Jas 4: 7 Resist the devil, and *he will* f from you. *5771*

FLEE, FLEETH (KJV) See FLED, FLEE, FLEES, FLEETING, FLY, RUNS AWAY

FLEECE (7)

Jdg 6:37 I will place a wool f on the threshing floor. 1603
6:37 If there is dew only on the f and all 1603
6:38 he squeezed the f and wrung out the dew— 1603
6:39 Allow me one more test with the f. 1603
6:39 the f dry and the ground covered 1603
6:40 Only the f was dry; 1603
Job 31:20 for warming him with the f *from* my sheep, 1600

FLEEING (13) [FLEE]

Ge 35: 1 when you *were* f from your brother Esau." 1368
35: 7 to him when he *was* f from his brother. 1368
Ex 14:27 The Egyptians *were* f toward it, 5674
Lev 26:36 They will run as though f *from* the sword, 4961
26:37 over one another as though f from NIH
Jos 8:20 for the Israelites who *had been* f *toward* 5674
1Sa 22:17 They knew he *was* f, 1368
2Sa 10:14 Ammonites saw that the Arameans *were* f, 5674
24:13 Or three months of f from your enemies 5674
1Ch 19:15 Ammonites saw that the Arameans *were* f, 5674
Jer 46:22 a f serpent as the enemy advances in force; 2143
48:19 Ask the *man* f and the woman escaping, 5674
Eze 17:21 All his f troops will fall by the sword, 4451

FLEES (9) [FLEE]

Dt 19: 4 the man who kills another and f there 5674
19:11 and then f to one of these cities, 5674
Jos 20: 4 "When *he* f to one of these cities, 5674
Job 20:24 Though *he* f from an iron weapon, 1368
27:22 as *he* f headlong from its power. 1368+1368
Pr 28: 1 The wicked man f though no one pursues, 5674
Isa 10:29 Ramah trembles; Gibeah of Saul f. 5674
24:18 Whoever f at the sound of terror will fall 5674
Jer 48:44 "Whoever f from the terror will fall into 5674

FLEET (6) [FLEETING]

1Ki 9:27 to serve in the f with Solomon's men. 639
10:22 The king had a f of trading ships at sea 639+9576
22:48 a f of trading ships to go to Ophir for gold, 641+9576
2Ch 9:21 king had a f of trading ships 641+2143+9576
20:36 a f of trading ships. 641+2143+4200+9576
Da 11:40 and cavalry and a great f of ships. 641

FLEET-FOOTED (2) [FOOT]

2Sa 2:18 Now Asahel was as f as a wild gazelle. 928+7824+8079
Am 2:15 the f soldier will not get away, 928+7824+8079

FLEETING (6) [FLEET]

Job 14: 2 like a f shadow, he does not endure. 1368
Ps 39: 4 let me know how f is my life. 2534
89:47 Remember how f is my life. 2698
144: 4 his days are like a f shadow. 6296
Pr 21: 6 by a lying tongue is a f vapor and 5622
31:30 Charm is deceptive, and beauty is f; 2039

FLESH (130)

Ge 2:21 and closed up the place with **f.** 1414
2:23 now bone of my bones and **f** of my flesh; 1414
2:23 now bone of my bones and flesh of my **f;** 1414
2:24 and they will become one **f.** 1414
17:13 in your **f** is to be an everlasting covenant. 1414
17:14 who has not been circumcised in the **f,** 1414
29:14 "You are my own **f** and blood." 1414
37:27 all, he is our brother, our own **f and blood."** 1414
40:19 And the birds will eat away your **f."** 1414
Ex 4:7 it was restored, like the rest of his **f.** 1414
29:14 the bull's **f** and its hide and its offal outside 1414
Lev 4:11 But the hide of the bull and all its **f,** 1414
6:27 of the **f** will become holy, 1414
8:17 and its **f** and its offal he burned up outside 1414
9:11 the **f** and the hide he burned up outside 1414
13:10 the hair white and if there is raw **f** in 1414
13:14 But whenever raw **f** appears on him, 1414
13:15 When the priest sees the raw **f,** 1414
13:15 The raw **f** is unclean; 1414
13:16 Should the raw **f** change and turn white, 1414
13:24 or white spot appears in the **raw f** *of* 4695
16:27 their hides, **f** and offal are to be burned up. 1414
26:29 You will eat the **f** *of* your sons and 1414
26:29 of your sons and the **f** *of* your daughters. 1414
Nu 12:12 with its **f** half eaten away." 1414
19:5 its hide, **f,** blood and offal. 1414
Dt 28:53 the **f** *of* the sons and daughters 1414
28:55 to one of them any of the **f** *of* his children 1414
32:42 while my sword devours **f:** 1414
Jdg 8:7 I will tear your **f** with desert thorns 1414
9:2 Remember, I am your **f** and blood." 1414
1Sa 17:44 "and I'll give your **f** to the birds of the air 1414
2Sa 1:22 from the **f** *of* the mighty, 2693
5:1 "We are your own **f** and blood. 1414
16:11 "My son, who is of my own **f,** 5055
19:12 You are my brothers, my own **f** and blood. 1414
19:13 'Are you not my own **f** and blood? 1414
1Ki 8:19 who *is* your own **f and blood—** 2743+3655+4946
2Ki 5:10 and your **f** will be restored and you will 1414
5:14 and his **f** was restored and became clean 1414
9:36 at Jezreel dogs will devour Jezebel's **f.** 1414
20:18 **your own f and blood,** 3655+3870+4946
1Ch 11:1 "We are your own **f** and blood. 1414
2Ch 6:9 who *is* your own **f and blood—** 2743+3655+4946
32:8 With him is only the arm of **f,** 1414
Ne 5:5 Although we are of the same **f and blood** 1414
Job 2:5 But stretch out your hand and strike his **f** 1414
6:12 Is my **f** bronze? 1414
10:4 Do you have eyes of **f?** 1414
10:11 and **f** and knit me together with bones 1414
15:27 with fat and his waist **bulges with f,** 6913+7089
19:22 Will you never get enough of my **f?** 1414
19:26 yet in my **f** I will see God; 1414
33:21 His **f** wastes away to nothing, 1414
33:25 then his **f** is renewed like a child's; 1414
41:23 The folds of his **f** are tightly joined; 1414
Ps 27:2 against me to devour my **f,** 1414
50:13 the **f** *of* bulls or drink the blood of goats? 1414
73:26 My **f** and my heart may fail, 8638
78:39 He remembered that they were but **f,** 1414
79:2 **f** *of* your saints to the beasts of the earth. 1414
84:2 and my **f** cry out for the living God. 1414
119:120 My **f** trembles in fear of you; 1414
Pr 5:11 when your **f** and body are spent. 1414
Isa 9:20 on the **f** *of* his own offspring: 1414
31:3 their horses are **f** and not spirit. 1414
39:7 **your own f and blood** 3655+3870+4946
49:26 I will make your oppressors eat their own **f;** 1414
58:7 to turn away from your own **f and blood?** 1414
65:4 who eat the **f** *of* pigs, 1414
66:17 in the midst of those who eat the **f** *of* pigs 1414
Jer 9:25 "when I will punish all who are
circumcised only in the **f—** 6889
17:5 in man, who depends on **f** for his strength 1414
19:9 I will make them eat the **f** *of* their sons 1414
19:9 and they will eat one another's **f** during 1414
51:35 May the violence done to our **f** be 8638
La 3:4 He has made my skin and my **f** grow old 6425
Eze 11:19 of stone and give them a heart of **f.** 1414
32:5 I will spread your **f** on the mountains 1414
32:6 and the ravines will be filled with your **f.** NIH
36:26 of stone and give you a heart of **f.** 1414
37:6 and make **f** come upon you and cover you 1414
37:8 and tendons and **f** appeared on them 1414
39:17 There you will eat **f** and drink blood. 1414
39:18 You will eat the **f** *of* mighty men and drink 1414
40:43 The tables were for the **f** *of* the offerings. 1414
44:7 in heart and **f** into my sanctuary, 1414
44:9 in heart and **f** is to enter my sanctuary, 1414
Da 7:5 It was told, 'Get up and eat your fill of **f!'** 10125
Mic 3:2 from my people and the **f** from their bones; 8638
3:3 who eat my people's **f,** strip off their skin 8638
3:3 like **f** for the pot?" 1414
Zec 11:9 Let those who are left eat one another's **f."** 1414
14:12 Their **f** will rot while they are still standing 1414
Mal 2:15 *In* **f** and spirit they are his. 8638
Mt 19:5 and the two will become one **f'?** *4922*
Mk 10:8 and the two will become one **f.'** *4922*
Lk 24:39 a ghost does not have **f** and bones, *4922*
Jn 1:14 The Word became **f** and made his dwelling *4922*
3:6 **F** gives birth to flesh, *4922*
3:6 Flesh gives birth to **f,** *4922*
6:51 This bread is my **f,** *4922*
6:52 "How can this man give us his **f** to eat?" *4922*
6:53 unless you eat the **f** of the Son of Man *4922*
Jn 6:54 Whoever eats my **f** and drinks my blood *4922*
6:55 For my **f** is real food *4922*
6:56 Whoever eats my **f** and drinks my blood *4922*
6:63 Spirit gives life; the **f** counts for nothing. *4922*
1Co 6:16 For it is said, "The two will become one **f."** *4922*
15:39 All **f** is not the same: *4922*
15:39 Men have one kind of **f,** *4922*
15:50 that **f** and blood cannot inherit the kingdom *4922*
2Co 12:7 there was given me a thorn *in* my **f,** *4922*
Gal 6:13 that they may boast about your **f.** *4922*
Eph 2:15 in his **f** the law with its commandments *4922*
5:31 and the two will become one **f."** *4922*
6:12 For our struggle is not against **f** and blood, *4922*
Php 3:2 those mutilators of the **f.** *NIG*
3:3 and who put no confidence in the **f—** *4922*
3:4 to put confidence in the **f,** I have more: *4922*
Col 1:24 up in my **f** what is still lacking in regard *4922*
Heb 2:14 Since the children have **f** and blood, *4922*
Jas 5:3 against you and eat your **f** like fire. *4922*
1Jn 4:2 acknowledges that Jesus Christ has come in
the **f** is from God, *4922*
2Jn 1:7 Jesus Christ as coming in the **f,** *4922*
Jude 1:23 even the clothing stained by **corrupted f.** *4922*
Rev 17:16 they will eat her **f** and burn her with fire. *4922*
19:18 so that you may eat the **f** of kings, *4922*
19:18 and the **f** of all people, free and slave, *4922*
19:21 all the birds gorged themselves on their **f.** *4922*

FLESH (KJV) See also BIRTH, BODY, CREATURES, EARTHLY, HUMAN ANCESTRY, HUMAN EFFORT, HUMAN NATURE, HUMAN STANDARDS, KIND, LIFE, MAN, MANKIND, MEAT, MORTAL, ONE, ORDINARY, OUTWARDLY, NATURAL, PEOPLE, PHYSICAL, SINFUL NATURE, SENSUAL, WORLD, WORLDLY

FLESHHOOK (KJV) See HOOK

FLEW (4) [FLY]

2Sa 22:11 He mounted the cherubim and **f;** 6414
Ps 18:10 He mounted the cherubim and **f;** 6414
Isa 6:6 of the seraphs **f** to me with a live coal 6414
Ac 16:26 At once all the prison doors **f open,** *487*

FLIES (15) [FLY]

Ex 8:21 I will send **swarms of f** on you 6856
8:21 of the Egyptians will be full of **f,** 6856
8:22 no **swarms of f** will be there, 6856
8:24 Dense **swarms of f** poured 6856
8:24 the land was ruined by the **f.** 6856
8:29 the **f** will leave Pharaoh and his officials 6856
8:31 The **f** left Pharaoh and his officials 6856
Dt 4:17 like any animal on earth or any bird that **f** 6414
Job 20:8 Like a dream *he* **f away,** 6414
Ps 78:45 He sent **swarms of f** that devoured them, 6856
91:5 nor the arrow *that* **f** by day, 6414
105:31 He spoke, and there came **swarms of f,** 6856
Ecc 10:1 As dead **f** give perfume a bad smell, 2279
Isa 7:18 that day the LORD will whistle for **f** from 2279
51:6 like a garment and its inhabitants die like **f.** 4031

FLIGHT (15) [FLY]

Lev 26:36 of a windblown leaf *will* **put** them **to f.** 8103
Dt 32:30 **put** ten thousand **to f,** 5674
Jdg 9:40 and many fell wounded *in the* **f—** 5674
2Sa 22:41 You made my enemies turn their backs in **f,** NIH
2Ki 7:15 in their **headlong f.** 2905
1Ch 12:15 and *they* **put to f** everyone living in 1368
Job 39:26 *"Does* the hawk **take f** by your wisdom 87
Ps 18:40 You made my enemies turn their backs in **f,** NIH
104:7 the sound of your thunder *they* **took to f;** 2905
Isa 10:31 Madmenah *is* in **f;** 5610
52:12 But you will not leave in haste or go in **f;** 4961
Jer 4:29 and archers every town **takes to f.** 1368
Eze 40:49 It was reached by a **f of stairs,** 5092
Da 9:21 came to me in **swift f** about the time 3616+3618
Mt 24:20 that your **f** will not take place in winter or *5870*

FLIMSY (1)

Eze 13:10 and because, when a **f wall** is built, 2666

FLINGING (1) [FLUNG]

Ac 22:23 and throwing off their cloaks and **f** dust *965*

FLINT (8) [FLINTY]

Ex 4:25 But Zipporah took a **f knife,** 7644
Jos 5:2 "Make **f** knives and circumcise 7644
5:3 So Joshua made **f** knives and circumcised 7644
Isa 5:28 their horses' hoofs seem like **f,** 7641
50:7 Therefore have I set my face like **f,** 2734
Jer 17:1 inscribed with a **f** point, 9032
Eze 3:9 like the hardest stone, harder than **f.** 7644
Zec 7:12 They made their hearts **as hard as f** 9032

FLINTY (2) [FLINT]

Dt 32:13 and with oil from the **f** crag, 2734
Job 28:9 the **f rock** and lays bare the roots of 2734

FLIRTING (1)

Isa 3:16 **f** *with* their eyes, 8568

FLOAT (4) [FLOATED]

1Ki 5:9 and I *will* **f** them *in* rafts by sea to 8492
2Ki 6:6 and **made** the iron **f.** 7429
2Ch 2:16 that you need and *will* **f** them *in* rafts 995
Hos 10:7 and its king *will* **f away** like a twig on 1950

FLOATED (1) [FLOAT]

Ge 7:18 and the ark **f** on the surface of the water. 2143

FLOCK (99) [FLOCKING, FLOCKS]

Ge 4:4 from some of the firstborn of his **f.** 7366
21:28 set apart seven ewe lambs from the **f,** 7366
27:9 the **f** and bring me two choice young goats, 7366
30:40 the **young of the f** by themselves, 4166
31:10 with the **f** were streaked, 7366
31:12 with the **f** are streaked, 7366
38:17 "I'll send you a young goat from my **f,"** 7366
Ex 2:16 and fill the troughs to water their father's **f.** 7366
2:17 to their rescue and watered their **f.** 7366
2:19 even drew water for us and watered the **f."** 7366
3:1 the **f** *of* Jethro his father-in-law, 7366
3:1 and he led the **f** to the far side of the desert 7366
34:19 whether from herd or **f.** 8445
Lev 1:2 an animal from either the herd or the **f.** 7366
1:10 the offering is a burnt offering from the **f,** 7366
3:6 " 'If he offers an animal from the **f** as 7366
5:6 a female lamb or goat from the **f** as 7366
5:15 the LORD as a penalty a ram from the **f,** 7366
5:18 as a guilt offering a ram from the **f,** 7366
6:6 his guilt offering, a ram from the **f,** 7366
22:21 from the herd or **f** a fellowship offering to 7366
27:32 The entire tithe of the herd and **f—** 7366
Nu 15:3 from the herd or the **f,** 7366
Dt 15:14 Supply him liberally from your **f,** 7366
16:2 an **animal from** your **f** or herd at the place 7366
32:14 with curds and milk from herd and **f** and 7366
1Sa 17:20 Early in the morning David left the **f** with 7366
17:34 and carried off a sheep from the **f,** 6373
2Sa 7:8 from the pasture and from following the **f** 7366
1Ch 17:7 from the pasture and from following the **f,** 7366
Ezr 10:19 a ram from the **f** as a guilt offering.) 7366
Job 21:11 They send forth their children as a **f;** 7366
Ps 77:20 like a **f** by the hand of Moses and Aaron. 7366
78:52 But he brought his people out like a **f;** 7366
80:1 you who lead Joseph like a **f;** 7366
95:7 the **f** under his care. 7366
SS 1:7 where *you* **graze** *your* **f** and 8286
4:1 Your hair is like a **f** *of* goats descending 6373
4:2 Your teeth are like a **f** *of* sheep just shorn, 6373
6:5 like a **f** *of* goats descending from Gilead. 6373
6:6 Your teeth are like a **f** *of* sheep coming up 6373
Isa 40:11 He tends his **f** like a shepherd: 6373
63:11 with the shepherd of his **f?** 7366
Jer 10:21 not prosper and all their **f** is scattered. 5338
13:17 the LORD's **f** will be taken captive. 6373
13:20 Where is the **f** that was entrusted to you, 6373
23:2 "Because you have scattered my **f** 7366
23:3 the remnant of my **f** out of all the countries 7366
25:34 roll in the dust, you leaders of the **f.** 7366
25:35 the leaders of the **f** no place to escape. 7366
25:36 the wailing of the leaders of the **f,** 7366
31:10 and will watch over his **f** like a shepherd.' 6373
49:20 The young of the **f** will be dragged away; 7366
50:8 and be like the goats that lead the **f.** 7366
50:17 a scattered **f** that lions have chased away. 8445
50:45 The young of the **f** will be dragged away; 7366
51:23 with you I shatter shepherd and **f,** 6373
Eze 24:5 take the pick of the **f.** 7366
34:2 Should not shepherds take care of the **f?** 7366
34:3 but you do not take care of the **f.** 7366
34:8 because my **f** lacks a shepherd and 7366
34:8 not search for my **f** but cared 7366
34:8 for themselves rather than for my **f,** 7366
34:10 and will hold them accountable for my **f.** 7366
34:10 I will remove them from tending the **f** so 7366
34:10 I will rescue my **f** from their mouths, 7366
34:12 after his scattered **f** when he is with them, 6373
34:16 I will shepherd **the f** with justice. 5626[S]
34:17 " 'As for you, my **f,** 7366
34:19 Must my **f** feed on what you have trampled 7366
34:22 I will save my **f,** 7366
43:23 to offer a young bull and a ram from the **f,** 7366
43:25 a young bull and a ram from the **f,** 7366
45:15 be taken from every **f** of two hundred from 7366
Am 7:15 But the LORD took me from tending the **f** 7366
Jnh 3:7 Do not let any man or beast, herd or **f,** 7366
Mic 2:12 like a **f** in its pasture; 6373
4:8 As for you, O watchtower of the **f,** 6373
5:4 **shepherd** *his* **f** in the strength of the LORD, 8286
7:14 the **f** *of* your inheritance, 7366
Zec 9:16 on that day as the **f** *of* his people. 7366
10:3 the LORD Almighty will care for his **f,** 6373
11:4 "Pasture the **f** *marked for* slaughter. 7366
11:7 So I pastured the **f** *marked for* slaughter, 7366
11:7 particularly the oppressed of the **f.** 7366
11:7 and I pastured the **f.** 7366
11:8 **The f** detested me, 4392+5883[S]
11:11 the **f** who were watching me knew it was 7366
11:17 who deserts the **f!** 7366
Mal 1:14 an acceptable male in his **f** and vows 6373
Mt 26:31 and the sheep *of* the **f** will be scattered.' *4479*

Lk 12:32 "Do not be afraid, little **f**, *4480*
Jn 10:12 Then the wolf attacks **the f** and scatters it. *899S*
10:16 and there shall be one **f** and one shepherd. *4479*
Ac 20:28 Keep watch over yourselves and all the **f** *4480*
20:29 in among you and will not spare the **f.** *4480*
1Co 9: 7 Who tends a **f** and does not drink of *4479*
1Pe 5: 2 of God's **f** that is under your care, serving *4480*
5: 3 but being examples *to* the **f.** *4480*

FLOCKING (1) [FLOCK]

Hos 7:12 I hear them **f together,** I will catch them. 6337

FLOCKS (100) [FLOCK]

Ge 4: 2 Abel kept **f**, and Cain worked the soil. 7366
13: 5 also had **f** and herds and tents. 7366
26:14 He had so many **f** and herds and 5238+7366
29: 2 with three **f** *of* sheep lying near it because 6373
29: 2 because the **f** were watered from that well. 6373
29: 3 When all the **f** were gathered there, 6373
29: 7 it is not time for the **f** to be gathered. 5238
29: 8 "until all the **f** are gathered and 6373
30:31 on tending your **f** and watching over them: 7366
30:32 through all your **f** today and remove 7366
30:36 to tend the rest of Laban's **f.** 7366
30:38 be directly in front of the **f** when they came 7366
30:38 When the **f** were in heat and came to drink, 7366
30:40 Thus he made separate **f** for himself 6373
30:43 and came to own large **f**, 7366
31: 4 to come out to the fields where his **f** were. 7366
31: 8 then all the **f** gave birth to speckled young; 7366
31: 8 then all the **f** bore streaked young. 7366
31:38 nor have I eaten rams from your **f.** 7366
31:41 and six years for your **f**, 7366
31:43 and the **f** are my flocks. 7366
31:43 and the flocks are my **f.** 7366
32: 7 and the **f** and herds and camels as well. 7366
34:28 They seized their **f** and herds and donkeys 7366
37: 2 was tending the **f** with his brothers, 7366
37:12 to graze their father's **f** near Shechem, 7366
37:13 your brothers *are* **grazing the f** 8286
37:14 with your brothers and with the **f**, 7366
37:16 where they *are* **grazing** *their* **f?"** 8286
45:10 your **f** and herds, and all you have. 7366
46:32 and they have brought along their **f** 7366
47: 1 with their **f** and herds 7366
47: 4 and your servants' **f** have no pasture. 7366
50: 8 and their **f** and herds were left in Goshen. 7366
Ex 10: 9 and with our **f** and herds, 7366
10:24 only leave your **f** and herds behind." 7366
12:32 Take your **f** and herds, as you have said, 7366
12:38 both **f** and herds. 7366
34: 3 not even the **f** and herds may graze in front 7366
Nu 11:22 if **f** and herds were slaughtered for them? 7366
31: 9 **f** and goods as plunder. 5238
32: 1 who had very large **herds and f**, 5238
32:24 and pens for your **f**, 7366
32:26 our **f** and herds will remain here in 5238
32:36 and built pens for their **f.** 7366
35: 3 **f** and all their other livestock. 8214
Dt 7:13 of your herds and the lambs of your **f** in 7366
8:13 and when your herds and **f** grow large 7366
12: 6 and the firstborn of your herds and **f.** 7366
12:17 or the firstborn of your herds and **f**, 7366
12:21 the herds and **f** the LORD has given you, 7366
14:23 and the firstborn of your herds and **f** in 7366
15:19 of your herds and **f.** 7366
28: 4 of your herds and the lambs of your **f.** 7366
28:18 of your herds and the lambs of your **f.** 7366
28:51 or lambs of your **f** until you are ruined. 7366
Jos 14: 4 with pasturelands for their **f** and herds. 5238
Jdg 5:16 to hear the whistling for the **f?** 6373
1Sa 8:17 He will take a tenth of your **f**, 7366
30:20 He took all the **f** and herds, 7366
1Ki 20:27 like two **small f** *of* goats, 3105
2Ki 5:26 **f**, herds, or menservants and maidservants? 7366
1Ch 4:39 the valley in search of pasture for their **f.** 7366
4:41 because there was pasture for their **f.** 7366
27:31 Jaziz the Hagrite was in charge of the **f.** 7366
2Ch 17:11 and the Arabs brought him **f**: 7366
31: 6 also brought a tithe of their herds and **f** and 7366
32:28 and pens for the **f.** 6373
32:29 and acquired great numbers of **f** and herds, 7366
Ne 10:36 of our herds and of our **f** to the house 7366
Job 1:10 that his **f and herds** are spread throughout 5238
24: 2 they pasture **f** they have stolen. 6373
Ps 8: 7 all **f** and herds, and the beasts of the field, 7556
65:13 The meadows are covered with **f** and 7366
107:41 and increased their families like **f.** 7366
Pr 27:23 Be sure you know the condition of your **f**, 7366
Ecc 2: 7 I also owned more herds and **f** than anyone 7366
SS 1: 7 be like a veiled woman beside the **f** 6373
Isa 13:20 no shepherd *will* **rest** *his* **f** there. 8069
17: 2 of Aroer will be deserted and left to **f**, 6373
32:14 the delight of donkeys, a pasture for **f**, 6373
60: 7 All Kedar's **f** will be gathered to you, 7366
61: 5 Aliens will shepherd your **f**; 7366
65:10 Sharon will become a pasture for **f**, 7366
Jer 3:24 their **f** and herds, their sons and daughters. 7366
5:17 they will devour your **f** and herds, 7366
6: 3 with their **f** will come against her; 6373
31:12 the young of the **f** and herds. 7366
31:24 and those who move about with their **f.** 6373
33:12 be pastures for shepherds to rest their **f.** 7366
33:13 **f** will again pass under the hand of 7366
49:29 Their tents and their **f** will be taken; 7366
Eze 36:38 as numerous as the **f** *for* offerings 7366
36:38 the ruined cities be filled with **f** *of* people. 7366
Hos 5: 6 with their **f** and herds to seek the LORD, 7366
Joel 1:18 even the **f** *of* sheep are suffering. 6373
Mic 5: 8 like a young lion among **f** *of* sheep, 6373
Zep 2:14 **F and herds** will lie down there, 6373
Lk 2: 8 keeping watch over their **f** at night. *4479*
Jn 4:12 as did also his sons and his **f and herds?"** *2576*

FLOG (8) [FLOGGED, FLOGGING, FLOGGINGS]

Pr 17:26 or to **f** officials for their integrity. 5782
19:25 **F** a mocker, and the simple will learn 5782
Mt 10:17 over to the local councils and **f** you *3463*
23:34 others *you will* **f** in your synagogues *3463*
Mk 10:34 spit on him, **f** him and kill him. *3463*
Lk 18:32 insult him, spit on him, **f** him and kill him. *3463*
Ac 22:25 As they stretched him out *to* **f** him, *2666*
22:25 for you *to* **f** a Roman citizen who hasn't *3464*

FLOGGED (11) [FLOG]

Dt 25: 2 down and **have** him **f** in his presence with 5782
25: 3 If he *is* **f** more than that, 4804+5782
Mt 20:19 over to the Gentiles to *be* mocked and **f** *3463*
27:26 But he **had** Jesus **f**, *5849*
Mk 13: 9 the local councils and **f** in the synagogues. *1296*
15:15 He **had** Jesus **f**, *5849*
Jn 19: 1 Then Pilate took Jesus and had him **f.** *3463*
Ac 5:40 They called the apostles in and *had them* **f.** *1296*
16:23 *After they had been* severely **f**, *2202+4435*
22:24 He directed that he be **f** and questioned *3465*
2Co 11:23 been **f** more severely, *4435*

FLOGGING (2) [FLOG]

Ps 89:32 their iniquity with **f**; 5596
Heb 11:36 Some faced jeers and **f**, *3465*

FLOGGINGS (1) [FLOG]

2Sa 7:14 with **f** *inflicted by* men. 5596

FLOOD (33) [FLOODED, FLOODGATES, FLOODING, FLOODS, FLOODWATERS]

Ge 7: 7 the ark to escape the waters of the **f.** 4429
7:17 For forty days the **f** kept coming on 4429
9:11 be cut off by the waters of a **f**; 4429
9:11 never again will there be a **f** to destroy 4429
9:15 the waters become a **f** to destroy all life. 4429
9:28 After the **f** Noah lived 350 years. 4429
10: 1 who themselves had sons after the **f.** 4429
10:32 over the earth after the **f.** 4429
11:10 Two years after the **f**, 4429
Jos 3:15 the Jordan *is* **at f stage** all during harvest. 1536+3972+4848+6584
4:18 and ran **at f stage** as before. 1536+3972+6584
Job 20:28 A **f** will carry off his house, 4429
22:11 and why a **f** *of* water covers you. 9180
22:16 their foundations washed away by a **f.** 5643
27:20 Terrors overtake him like a **f**; 4784
38:34 to the clouds and cover yourself with a **f** 9180
Ps 6: 6 all night long *I* **f** my bed with weeping 8466
29:10 The LORD sits enthroned over the **f**; 4429
88:17 All day long they surround me like a **f**; 4784
124: 4 the **f** would have engulfed us, 4784
Isa 59:19 For he will come like a pent-up **f** that 5643
Da 9:26 The end will come like a **f**: 8852
11:10 on like an irresistible **f** and carry the battle 8851
11:40 and sweep through them like *a* **f.** 8851
Hos 5:10 I will pour out my wrath on them like a **f** NIH
Na 1: 8 but with an overwhelming **f** he will make 8852
Mal 2:13 *You* **f** the LORD's altar *with* tears. 4059
Mt 24:38 For in the days before the **f**, *2886*
24:39 about what would happen until the **f** came *2886*
Lk 6:48 When a **f** came, the torrent struck that house *4439*
17:27 Then the **f** came and destroyed them all. *2886*
1Pe 4: 4 with them into the same **f** of dissipation, *431*
2Pe 2: 5 the ancient world when he brought the **f** *2886*

FLOODED (1) [FLOOD]

Ge 7:24 The waters **f** the earth for a hundred 1504

FLOODGATES (6) [FLOOD]

Ge 7:11 and the **f** *of* the heavens were opened. 748
8: 2 and the **f** *of* the heavens had been closed, 748
2Ki 7: 2 LORD should open the **f** of the heavens, 748
7:19 LORD should open the **f** of the heavens, 748
Isa 24:18 The **f** of the heavens are opened, 748
Mal 3:10 if I will not throw open the **f** *of* heaven 748

FLOODING (2) [FLOOD]

Isa 28: 2 like a driving rain and a **f downpour,** 3888+8851
66:12 and the wealth of nations like a **f** stream; 8851

FLOODS (1) [FLOOD]

Ps 69: 2 the **f** engulf me. 8673

FLOODWATERS (5) [FLOOD]

Ge 6:17 bring **f** on the earth to destroy all life 4429+4784
7: 6 when the **f** came on the earth. 4429+4784
7:10 And after the seven days the **f** came on 4429+4784
Ps 69:15 the **f** engulf me or the depths swallow 4784+8673
Isa 8: 7 to bring against them the mighty **f** *of* 4784+8041

FLOOR (58) [FLOORS]

Ge 50:10 When they reached the **threshing f** *of* Atad, 1755
50:11 the mourning at the **threshing f** *of* Atad, 1755
Ex 16:14 on the ground appeared on the desert **f.** 7156
Nu 5:17 and put some dust from the tabernacle **f** 7977
15:20 as an offering from the **threshing f.** 1755
18:27 to you as grain from the **threshing f** or juice 1755
18:30 to you as the product of the **threshing f** or 1755
Dt 15:14 your **threshing f** and your winepress. 1755
16:13 of your **threshing f** and your winepress. 1755
Jdg 3:25 There they saw their lord fallen to the **f**, 824
6:37 I will place a wool fleece on the **threshing f** 1755
Ru 3: 2 be winnowing barley on the **threshing f.** 1755
3: 3 Then go down to the **threshing f**, 1755
3: 6 So she went down to the **threshing f** 1755
3:14 that a woman came to the **threshing f."** 1755
2Sa 6: 6 they came to the **threshing f** *of* Nacon, 1755
24:16 at the **threshing f** *of* Araunah the Jebusite. 1755
24:18 on the **threshing f** *of* Araunah the Jebusite." 1755
24:21 "To buy your **threshing f**," David answered 1755
24:24 So David bought the **threshing f** and 1755
1Ki 6: 6 The lowest **f** was five cubits wide, 3666
6: 6 the middle **f** six cubits and NIH
6: 6 and the third **f** seven. NIH
6: 8 to the lowest **f** was on the south side of 7521
6:15 paneling them from the **f** *of* the temple to 7977
6:15 the **f** *of* the temple with planks of pine. 7977
6:16 with cedar boards from **f** to ceiling to form 7977
7: 7 he covered it with cedar from **f** to ceiling. 7977
22:10 at the **threshing f** *by* the entrance of the gate 1755
22:35 The blood from his wound ran onto the **f** 2668
2Ki 6:27 From the **threshing f?** 1755
1Ch 13: 9 they came to the **threshing f** *of* Kidon, 1755
21:15 then standing at the **threshing f** *of* Araunah 1755
21:18 on the **threshing f** *of* Araunah the Jebusite. 1755
21:21 he left the **threshing f** and bowed down 1755
21:22 of your **threshing f** so I can build an altar to 1755
21:28 on the **threshing f** *of* Araunah the Jebusite, 1755
2Ch 3: 1 on the **threshing f** *of* Araunah the Jebusite, 1755
18: 9 at the **threshing f** *by* the entrance to the gate 1755
Job 39:12 and gather it to your **threshing f?** 1755
Isa 21:10 O my people, crushed on the **threshing f**, 1755
Jer 51:33 like a **threshing f** at the time it is trampled; 1755
Eze 37: 2 a great many bones on the **f** *of* the valley, 7156
41: 7 from the **lowest** *f* to the top floor through AIT
41: 7 from the lowest floor to the **top** *f* through AIT
41: 7 to the top floor through the **middle** *f.* AIT
41:16 The **f**, the wall up to the windows, 824
41:20 From the **f** to the area above the entrance, 824
42: 6 The rooms *on the* **third** *f* had no pillars, AIT
42: 6 so they were smaller in **f space** than those 824
Da 2:35 like chaff on a **threshing f** *in* the summer. 10010
6:24 And before they reached the **f** *of* the den, 10076
Hos 9: 1 of a prostitute at every **threshing f.** 1755+1841
13: 3 like chaff swirling from a **threshing f**, 1755
Mic 4:12 like sheaves to the **threshing f.** 1755
Mt 3:12 and he will clear his **threshing f**, *272*
Lk 3:17 in his hand to clear his **threshing f** and *272*
Jas 2: 3 "You stand there" or "Sit on the **f** *NIG*

FLOORS (6) [FLOOR]

1Sa 23: 1 and are looting the **threshing f**," 1755
1Ki 6:30 the **f** *of* both the inner and outer rooms of 7977
Eze 42: 5 on the lower and **middle** *f of* the building. AIT
42: 6 on the lower and **middle** *f.* AIT
Hos 9: 2 **Threshing f** and winepresses will not feed 1755
Joel 2:24 The **threshing f** will be filled with grain; 1755

FLORAL (2) [FLOWER]

1Ki 7:49 the gold **f work** and lamps and tongs; 7258
2Ch 4:21 the gold **f work** and lamps and tongs 7258

FLOUR (68)

Ge 18: 6 "get three seahs of fine **f** and knead it 7854
Ex 29: 2 And from **fine** wheat **f**, without yeast, 6159
29:40 an ephah of **fine f** mixed with a quarter of 6159
Lev 2: 1 his offering is to be of **fine f.** 6159
2: 2 The priest shall take a handful of the **fine f** 6159
2: 4 it is to consist of **fine f**: 6159
2: 5 it is to be made of **fine f** mixed with oil, 6159
2: 7 it is to be made of **fine f** and oil. 6159
5:11 for his sin a tenth of an ephah of **fine f** for 6159
6:15 The priest is to take a handful of **fine f** 6159
6:20 of **fine f** as a regular grain offering, 6159
7:12 of **fine f** well-kneaded and mixed with oil. 6159
14:10 of an ephah of **fine f** mixed with oil *for* 6159
14:21 a tenth of an ephah of **fine f** mixed with oil 6159
23:13 of two-tenths of an ephah of **fine f** mixed 6159
23:17 of two-tenths of an ephah of **fine f**, 6159
24: 5 "Take **fine f** and bake twelve loaves 6159
Nu 5:15 of an ephah of barley **f** on her behalf. 7854
6:15 cakes made of **fine f** mixed with oil, 6159
7:13 each filled with **fine f** mixed with oil as 6159
7:19 each filled with **fine f** mixed with oil as 6159
7:25 each filled with **fine f** mixed with oil as 6159
7:31 each filled with **fine f** mixed with oil as 6159
7:37 each filled with **fine f** mixed with oil as 6159
7:43 each filled with **fine f** mixed with oil as 6159
7:49 each filled with **fine f** mixed with oil as 6159
7:55 each filled with **fine f** mixed with oil as 6159
7:61 each filled with **fine f** mixed with oil as 6159
7:67 each filled with **fine f** mixed with oil as 6159

Nu 7:73 each filled with **fine f** mixed with oil as 6159
7:79 each filled with **fine f** mixed with oil as 6159
8: 8 with its grain offering of **fine f** mixed 6159
15: 4 of a tenth of an ephah of **fine f** mixed with 6159
15: 6 of an ephah of **fine f** mixed with a third of 6159
15: 9 of an ephah of **fine f** mixed with half a hin 6159
28: 5 of a tenth of an ephah of **fine f** mixed with 6159
28: 9 of two-tenths of an ephah of **fine f** mixed 6159
28:12 of three-tenths of an ephah of **fine f** mixed 6159
28:12 of two-tenths of an ephah of **fine f** mixed 6159
28:13 of a tenth of an ephah of **fine f** mixed 6159
28:20 of three-tenths of an ephah of **fine f** mixed 6159
28:28 of three-tenths of an ephah of **fine f** mixed 6159
29: 3 of three-tenths of an ephah of **fine f** mixed 6159
29: 9 of three-tenths of an ephah of **fine f** mixed 6159
29:14 of three-tenths of an ephah of **fine f** mixed 6159
Jdg 6:19 an ephah of **f** he made bread without yeast. 7854
1Sa 1:24 an ephah of **f** and a skin of wine, 7854
28:24 She took *some* **f**, kneaded it 7854
2Sa 17:28 **f** and roasted grain, beans and lentils, 7854
1Ki 4:22 of **fine f** and sixty cors of meal, 6159
17:12 only a handful of **f** in a jar and a little oil in 7854
17:14 'The jar of **f** will not be used up and 7854
17:16 For the jar of **f** was not used up and the jug 7854
2Ki 4:41 Elisha said, "Get *some* **f**." 7854
7: 1 of **f** will sell for a shekel and two seahs 6159
7:16 So a seah of **f** sold for a shekel, 6159
7:18 of **f** will sell for a shekel and two seahs 6159
1Ch 9:29 as well as the **f** and wine, and the oil, 6159
12:40 There were plentiful supplies of **f**, 7854
23:29 the **f** for the grain offerings, 6159
Isa 47: 2 Take millstones and grind **f**; 7854
Eze 16:13 Your food was **fine f**, honey and olive oil. 6159
16:19 the **fine f**, olive oil and honey I gave you 6159
46:14 with a third of a hin of oil to moisten the **f**. 6159
Hos 8: 7 The stalk has no head; it will produce no **f**. 7854
Mt 13:33 *of* **f** until it worked all through the dough." 236
Lk 13:21 mixed into a **large amount of f** 236+4929+5552
Rev 18:13 of wine and olive oil, of **fine f** and wheat; *4947*

FLOURISH (13) [FLOURISHES, FLOURISHING]

Ge 26:22 and *we will* **f** in the land." 7238
Job 15:32 and his branches *will* not **f**. 8315
Ps 44: 2 the peoples and **made** our fathers **f**. 8938
72: 7 In his days the righteous *will* **f**; 7255
72:16 *Let* its fruit **f** like Lebanon; 7437
92: 7 up like grass and all evildoers **f**, 7437
92:12 The righteous *will* **f** like a palm tree, 7255
92:13 *they will* **f** in the courts of our God. 7255
Pr 14:11 but the tent of the upright *will* **f**. 7255
Isa 55:10 the earth and making it bud and **f**, 7541
66:14 your heart will rejoice and you *will* **f** 7255
Eze 17:24 **make** the dry tree **f**. 7255
Hos 14: 7 *He will* **f** like the grain. 2649

FLOURISHES (2) [FLOURISH]

Ps 103:15 *he* **f** like a flower of the field; 7437
Pr 12:12 but the root of the righteous **f**. 5989

FLOURISHING (4) [FLOURISH]

Dt 6:10 a land with large, **f** cities you did not build, 3202
Ps 37:35 I have seen a wicked and ruthless man **f** 6590
52: 8 But I am like an olive tree **f** in the house 8316
Ecc 2: 6 to water groves of **f** trees. 7541

FLOW (31) [FLOWED, FLOWING, FLOWS]

Ex 14:26 the sea so that the waters *may* **f back** over 8740
Lev 12: 7 be ceremonially clean from her **f** *of* blood. 5227
15:19 When a woman has her **regular f** *of* blood, 928+1414+2307
15:24 with her and her **monthly f** touches him, 5614
20:18 he has exposed the source of her **f**, 1947
Nu 13:27 and it *does* **f** *with* milk and honey! 2307
24: 7 Water *will* **f** from their buckets; 5688
Jos 4: 7 that the **f** *of* the Jordan was cut off before 4784
Job 6:17 but that **cease to f** in the dry season, 7551
Ps 78:16 of a rocky crag and **made** water **f down** 3718
119:136 Streams of tears **f** *from* my eyes, 3718
147:18 he stirs up his breezes, and the waters **f**. 5688
Ecc 1: 7 All streams **f** into the sea, 2143
Isa 30:25 of water will **f** on every high mountain 3298
41:18 *I will* **make** rivers **f** on barren heights, 7337
48:21 *he* **made** water **f** for them from the rock; 5688
Jer 18:14 from distant sources ever cease *to* **f**? 5688
48:33 I have stopped the **f** of wine from NIH
La 2:18 **let** your tears **f** like a river day and night; 3718
3:48 Streams of tears **f from** my eyes 3718
3:49 My eyes *will* **f** unceasingly, 5599
Eze 28:23 upon her and make blood **f** in her streets. NIH
32:14 and **make** her streams **f** like oil, 2143
Joel 3:18 and the hills *will* **f** *with* milk; 2143
3:18 A fountain *will* **f out** of the LORD's house 3655
Am 9:13 from the mountains and **f** *from* all the hills. 4570
Zec 14: 8 On that day living water *will* **f out** from 3655
Jn 7:38 of living water *will* **f** from within him." *4835*
19:34 bringing a sudden **f** of blood and water. *NIG*
2Co 1: 5 For just as the sufferings of Christ **f over** *4355*
Jas 3:11 *Can* both fresh water and salt water **f** from *1108*

FLOWED (10) [FLOW]

Ge 2:10 A river watering the garden **f** from Eden; 3655
Ex 14:28 The water **f back** and covered the chariots 8740
Dt 9:21 and threw the dust into a stream that **f down** 3718
1Ki 18:28 as was their custom, until their blood **f**. 9161
2Ch 32: 4 the springs and the stream that **f** through 8851
Ps 78:20 and streams **f abundantly**. 8851
104: 8 *they* **f over** the mountains, 6590
105:41 like a river *it* **f** in the desert. 2143
Eze 31: 4 their streams **f** all around its base 2143
Rev 14:20 and blood **f out** of the press, *2002*

FLOWER (6) [FLORAL, FLOWERLIKE, FLOWERS]

Job 14: 2 He springs up like a **f** and withers away; 7488
Ps 103:15 he flourishes like a **f** *of* the field; 7488
Isa 18: 5 the blossom is gone and the **f** becomes 5900
28: 1 to the fading **f**, his glorious beauty, 7488
28: 4 That fading **f**, his glorious beauty, 7491
Jas 1:10 because he will pass away like a wild **f**. *470*

FLOWERLIKE (2) [FLOWER]

Ex 25:31 its **f** cups, buds and blossoms shall be NIH
37:17 its **f** cups, buds and blossoms were NIH

FLOWERS (15) [FLOWER]

Ex 25:33 Three cups **shaped like almond f** with buds 5481
25:34 to be four cups **shaped like almond f** 5481
37:19 Three cups **shaped like almond f** with buds 5481
37:20 were four cups **shaped like almond f** 5481
1Ki 6:18 carved with gourds and open **f**. 7488
6:29 he carved cherubim, palm trees and open **f**. 7488
6:32 palm trees and open **f**, 7488
6:35 and open **f** on them and overlaid them 7488
SS 2:12 **F** appear on the earth; 5890
Isa 5:24 and their **f** blow away like dust; 7258
40: 6 and all their glory is like the **f** *of* the field. 7488
40: 7 The grass withers and the **f** fall, 7488
40: 8 The grass withers and the **f** fall, 7488
1Pe 1:24 and all their glory is like the **f** of the field; *470*
1:24 the grass withers and the **f** fall, *470*

FLOWING (45) [FLOW]

Ex 3: 8 a land **f** *with* milk and honey— 2307
3:17 a land **f** *with* milk and honey.' 2307
13: 5 a land **f** *with* milk and honey— 2307
33: 3 Go up to the land **f** *with* milk and honey. 2307
Lev 15: 3 Whether it *continues* **f** *from* his body 8201
20:24 a land **f** *with* milk and honey." 2307
Nu 14: 8 a land **f** *with* milk and honey, 2307
16:13 of a land **f** *with* milk and honey to kill us in 2307
16:14 a land **f** *with* milk and honey or given us 2307
Dt 6: 3 that you may increase greatly in a land **f** 2307
8: 7 with springs **f** in the valleys and hills; 3655
11: 9 a land **f** *with* milk and honey. 2307
21: 4 or planted and where there is a **f stream.** 419
26: 9 a land **f** *with* milk and honey; 2307
26:15 a land **f** *with* milk and honey." 2307
27: 3 a land **f** *with* milk and honey, 2307
31:20 When I have brought them into the land **f** 2307
Jos 3:13 in the Jordan, its waters **f** downstream will 3718
3:16 the water from upstream stopped **f**. 3718
3:16 the water **f down** to the Sea of the Arabah 3718
5: 6 a land **f** *with* milk and honey. 2307
2Ki 3:20 water **f** from the direction of Edom! 995
4: 6 Then the oil stopped **f**. NIH
Job 20:17 the **rivers** *f with* honey and cream. AIT
39:19 or clothe his neck with a **f mane?** 8310
Ps 74:15 you dried up the **ever f** rivers. 419
107:33 **f springs** into thirsty ground, 4604+4784
107:35 and the parched ground into **f springs;** 4604+4784
SS 4:15 of **f** water streaming down from Lebanon. 2645
5: 5 my fingers with **f** myrrh, 6296
7: 9 **f gently** *over* lips and teeth. 1803
Isa 8: 6 the gently **f** waters of Shiloah and rejoices 2143
27:12 from the **f** Euphrates to the Wadi of Egypt, 8673
44: 4 like poplar trees by **f streams.** 3298+4784
Jer 11: 5 a land **f** *with* milk and honey'— 2307
32:22 a land **f** *with* milk and honey. 2307
Eze 20: 6 a land **f** *with* milk and honey, 2307
20:15 a land **f** *with* milk and honey, 2307
23:15 with belts around their waists and **f** turbans 6242
32: 6 I will drench the land with your **f** blood all 7597
47: 2 and the water *was* **f** from the south side. 7096
Da 7:10 A river of fire *was* **f**, 10457
Mk 12:38 to walk around in **f robes** and be greeted in *5124*
Lk 20:46 around in **f robes** and love to be greeted in *5124*
Rev 22: 1 **f from** the throne of God and of the Lamb *1744*

FLOWN (1) [FLY]

Jer 4:25 every bird in the sky *had* **f away.** 5610

FLOWS (8) [FLOW]

Ezr 8:15 I assembled them at the canal that **f** 995
Ps 58: 7 Let them vanish like water *that* **f away;** 2143
104:10 *it* **f** between the mountains. 2143
Eze 47: 8 "This water **f** toward the eastern region 3655
47: 9 creatures will live wherever the river **f**. 995
47: 9 because this water **f** there and makes 995
47: 9 so where the river **f** everything will live. 995
47:12 the water from the sanctuary **f** *to* them. 3655

FLUENT (1)

Isa 32: 4 stammering tongue *will be* **f** and clear. 1819+4200+4554

FLUNG (2) [FLINGING]

Am 8: 3 Many, many bodies—**f** everywhere! 8959
Rev 12: 4 of the stars out of the sky and **f** them to *965*

FLUTE (15) [FLUTES]

Ge 4:21 the father of all who play the harp and **f**. 6385
Job 21:12 they make merry to the sound of the **f**. 6385
30:31 and my **f** to the sound of wailing. 6385
Ps 150: 4 praise him with the strings and **f**, 6385
Jer 48:36 "So my heart laments for Moab like a **f**; 2720
48:36 like a **f** for the men of Kir Hareseth. 2720
Da 3: 5 **f**, zither, lyre, harp, pipes and all kinds 10446
3: 7 **f**, zither, lyre, harp and all kinds of music, 10446
3:10 **f**, zither, lyre, harp, pipes and all kinds 10446
3:15 when you hear the sound of the horn, **f**, 10446
Mt 9:23 and saw the **f players** and the noisy crowd, *886*
11:17 '*We* **played the f** for you, and you did not *884*
Lk 7:32 '*We* **played the f** for you, and you did not *884*
1Co 14: 7 such as the **f** or harp, *888*
Rev 18:22 **f players** and trumpeters, *886*

FLUTES (5) [FLUTE]

1Sa 10: 5 **f** and harps being played before them, 2720
1Ki 1:40 playing **f** and rejoicing greatly, 2720
Ps 5: T For the director of music. For **f**. 5704
Isa 5:12 tambourines and **f** and wine, 2720
30:29 when people go up with **f** to the mountain 2720

FLUTTERING (2)

Pr 26: 2 Like a **f** sparrow or a darting swallow, 5653
Isa 16: 2 Like **f** birds pushed from the nest, 5610

FLUX (KJV) See DYSENTERY

FLY (14) [FLEW, FLIES, FLIGHT, FLOWN, FLYING]

Ge 1:20 and *let* birds **f** above the earth across 6414
Ex 8:31 not a **f** remained. NIH
Dt 19: 5 the head *may* **f off** and hit his neighbor 5970
Job 5: 7 to trouble as surely as sparks **f** upward. 6414
9:25 *they* **f away** without a glimpse of joy. 1368
Ps 55: 6 *I would* **f away** and be at rest— 6414
90:10 for they quickly pass, and *we* **f away.** 6414
Pr 23: 5 for they will surely sprout wings and **f off** 6414
Isa 60: 8 "Who are these *that* **f along** like clouds, 6414
Hos 9:11 Ephraim's glory *will* **f away** like a bird— 6414
Na 3:16 the land and then **f away.** 6414
3:17 but when the sun appears *they* **f away,** 5610
Hab 1: 8 *They* **f** like a vulture swooping to devour; 6414
Rev 12:14 so that *she might* **f** to the place prepared *4375*

FLYING (13) [FLY]

Ge 8: 7 and *it kept* **f** back and forth until 3655
Lev 11:20 " 'All **f** insects that walk on all fours are to 6416
Dt 14:19 All **f** insects that swarm are unclean 6416
Ps 78:27 **f** birds like sand on the seashore. 4053
148:10 small creatures and **f** birds, 4053
Isa 6: 2 and with two *they were* **f**. 6414
Hab 3:11 in the heavens at the glint of your **f** arrows, 2143
Zec 5: 1 and there before me was a **f** scroll! 6414
5: 2 I answered, "I see a **f** scroll, 6414
Rev 4: 7 the fourth was like a **f** eagle. *4375*
8:13 an eagle *that was* **f** in midair call out in *4375*
14: 6 Then I saw another angel **f** in midair, *4375*
19:17 who cried in a loud voice *to* all the birds **f** *4375*

FOAL (2)

Zec 9: 9 on a colt, the **f** *of* a donkey. 1201
Mt 21: 5 on a colt, the **f** of a donkey.' " *5626*

FOAM (2) [FOAMING, FOAMS]

Job 24:18 "Yet they are **f** on the surface of the water; 7824
Ps 46: 3 though its waters roar and **f** and 2812

FOAMING (4) [FOAM]

Dt 32:14 You drank the **f** blood of the grape. 2815
Ps 75: 8 of the LORD is a cup full of **f** wine mixed 2812
Mk 9:20 **f at the mouth.** *930*
Jude 1:13 wild waves of the sea, **f** up their shame; *2072*

FOAMS (2) [FOAM]

Mk 9:18 *He* **f at the mouth,** *930*
Lk 9:39 into convulsions so that he **f at the mouth.** *931*

FODDER (7)

Ge 24:25 she added, "We have plenty of straw and **f**, 5028
24:32 Straw and **f** were brought for the camels, 5028
43:24 and provided **f** for their donkeys. 5028
Jdg 19:19 both straw and **f** for our donkeys and bread 5028
Job 6: 5 or an ox bellow when it has **f**? 1173
24: 6 They gather **f** in the fields and glean in 1173
Isa 30:24 and donkeys that work the soil will eat **f** 1173

FOE (10) [FOES]

Ps 7: 4 or without cause have robbed my **f**— 7675
8: 2 to silence the **f** and the avenger. 367
55:12 if a **f** were raising himself against me, 8533
61: 3 a strong tower against the **f**. 367

Ps 74:10 Will the **f** revile your name forever? 367
106:10 He saved them from the hand of the **f;** 8533
107: 2 those he redeemed from the hand of the **f,** 7640
La 1: 5 captive before the **f.** 7640
2: 4 Like a **f** he has slain all who were pleasing 7640
Hab 1:15 wicked **f** pulls all of them up with hooks, NIH

FOES (52) [FOE]

Nu 10:35 may your **f** flee before you." 8533
Dt 33: 7 Oh, be his help against his **f!**" 7640
33:11 strike his **f** till they rise no more." 8533
2Sa 22:18 from my **f,** who were too strong for me. 8533
22:41 and I destroyed my **f.** 8533
22:49 You exalted me above my **f;** 7756
2Ki 21:14 be looted and plundered by all their **f,** 367
Job 22:20 'Surely our **f** are destroyed, 7799
Ps 3: 1 O LORD, how many are my **f!** 7640
6: 7 they fail because of all my **f.** 7675
13: 4 and my **f** will rejoice when I fall. 7640
17: 7 in you from their **f.** 7756
18:17 from my **f,** who were too strong for me. 8533
18:40 and I destroyed my **f.** 8533
18:48 You exalted me above my **f;** 7756
21: 8 your right hand will seize your **f.** 8533
27: 2 when my enemies and my **f** attack me, 367
27:12 Do not turn me over to the desire of my **f,** 7640
34:21 the **f** *of* the righteous will be condemned. 8533
41: 2 and not surrender him to the desire of his **f.** 367
42:10 as my **f** taunt me, 7675
44: 5 through your name we trample our **f.** 7756
54: 7 my eyes have looked in triumph on my **f.** 367
68: 1 may his **f** flee before him. 8533
68:23 in the blood of your **f,** 367
69:18 redeem me because of my **f.** 367
74: 4 Your **f** roared in the place where you met 7675
81:14 and turn my hand against their **f!** 7640
83: 2 how your **f** rear their heads. 8533
89:23 I will crush his **f** before him and strike 7640
89:42 You have exalted the right hand of his **f;** 7640
92:11 the rout of my wicked **f.** 7756
97: 3 Fire goes before him and consumes his **f** 7640
105:24 he made them too numerous for their **f,** 7640
106:41 and their **f** ruled over them. 8533
112: 8 in the end he will look in triumph on his **f.** 7640
119:157 Many are the **f** who persecute me, 7640
138: 7 against the anger of my **f,** 367
143:12 destroy all my **f,** for I am your servant. 7675
Isa 1:24 "Ah, I will get relief from my **f** 7640
9:11 But the LORD has strengthened Rezin's **f** 7640
59:18 to his enemies and retribution to his **f;** 367
66:14 but his fury will be shown to his **f.** 367
Jer 46:10 a day of vengeance, for vengeance on his **f.** 7640
49:37 I will shatter Elam before their **f,** 367
La 1: 5 Her **f** have become her masters; 7640
1:17 for Jacob that his neighbors become his **f;** 7640
2:17 he has exalted the horn of your **f.** 7640
4:12 and **f** could enter the gates of Jerusalem. 7640
Mic 5: 9 and all your **f** will be destroyed. 367
Na 1: 2 The LORD takes vengeance on his **f** 7640
1: 8 he will pursue his **f** into darkness. 367

FOILS (2)

Ps 33:10 The LORD **f** the plans of the nations; 7296
Isa 44:25 *who* **f** the signs of false prophets 7296

FOLD (4) [ENFOLDS, FOLDED, FOLDING, FOLDS]

Ex 26: 9 **F** the sixth curtain **double** 4100
2Ki 4:39 of its gourds and filled the **f of** his **cloak.** 955
Hag 2:12 a person carries consecrated meat in the **f** 4053
2:12 and that **f** touches some bread or stew, 4053

FOLDED (3) [FOLD]

Ex 28:16 and a span wide—and **f double.** 4100
39: 9 and a span wide—and **f double.** 4100
Jn 20: 7 The cloth *was* **f up** by itself, *1962*

FOLDING (2) [FOLD]

Pr 6:10 a little **f** *of* the hands to rest— 2486
24:33 a little **f** *of* the hands to rest— 2486

FOLDS (5) [FOLD]

Ne 5:13 I also shook out the **f of** my **robe** and said, 2950
Job 41:23 The **f** *of* his flesh are tightly joined; 5139
Ps 74:11 the **f** *of* your garment and destroy them! 7931
Ecc 4: 5 The fool **f** his hands and ruins himself. 2485
Eze 5: 3 in the **f of** your **garment.** 4053

FOLIAGE (4)

Eze 19:11 It towered high above the **thick f,** 6291
31: 3 it towered on high, its top above the **thick f.** 6291
31:10 lifting its top above the **thick f,** 6291
31:14 lifting their tops above the **thick f.** 6291

FOLK (KJV) See MEN, CREATURES, PEOPLE

FOLLOW (189) [FOLLOWED, FOLLOWER, FOLLOWERS, FOLLOWING, FOLLOWS]

Ge 41:30 but seven years of famine *will* **f** them. 339+7756
Ex 11: 8 'Go, you and all the people who **f** you!' 928+8079
16: 4 see whether *they will* **f** my instructions. 928+2143
23: 2 *"Do* not **f** the crowd in doing wrong. 339+2118
23:24 or worship them or **f** their practices. 3869+6913
Lev 18: 3 *Do* not **f** their practices. 2143
18: 4 and be careful to **f** my decrees. 2143
18:30 Keep my requirements and *do* not **f** any of 6913
19:37 and all my laws and **f** them. 6913
20: 5 both him and all who **f** him 339
20: 8 Keep my decrees and **f** them. 6913
20:22 Keep all my decrees and laws and **f** them, 6913
22:31 "Keep my commands and **f** them. 6913
25:18 " '**F** my decrees and be careful 6913
26: 3 " 'If *you* **f** my decrees and are careful 2143
Nu 9:12 they must **f** all the regulations. 3869
Dt 4: 1 **F** them so that you may live and may go in 6913
4: 5 so that you *may* **f** them in 4027+6913
4:13 which he commanded you to **f** and 6913
4:14 *to* **f** in the land that you are crossing 6913
5: 1 Learn them and be sure to **f** them. 6913
5:31 and laws you are to teach them *to* **f** in 6913
6:14 *Do* not **f** other gods, 339+2143
7:11 Therefore, take care to **f** the commands, 6913
7:12 to these laws and are careful *to* **f** them, 6913
8: 1 to **f** every command I am giving you today, 6913
8:19 the LORD your God and **f** other gods 339+2143
11:22 If you carefully observe all these commands I am giving you to **f**— 6913
12: 1 be careful to **f** in the land that the LORD, 6913
13: 2 *"Let us* **f** other gods" (gods you have 339+2143
13: 4 It is the LORD your God *you must* **f,** 339+2143
13: 5 turn you from the way the LORD your God commanded you to **f.** 928+2143
15: 5 **f** all these commands I am giving you today. 6913
16:12 and **f** carefully these decrees. 6913
16:20 **F** justice and justice alone, 8103
17:19 and **f** carefully all the words of this law 6913
19: 9 carefully **f** all these laws I command you today— 6913
20:18 to **f** all the detestable things they do 3869+6913
24: 8 You *must* **f** carefully what I have commanded them. 6913
26:16 to **f** these decrees and laws; 6913
27:10 the LORD your God and **f** his commands 6913
28: 1 carefully **f** all his commands I give you today, 6913
28:13 and carefully **f** them, 6913
28:15 and *do* not carefully **f** all his commands 6913
28:58 not carefully **f** all the words of this law, 6913
29: 9 Carefully **f** the terms of this covenant, 6913
29:22 Your children who **f** you 339+4946+7756
29:29 that we *may* **f** all the words of this law. 6913
30: 8 **f** all his commands I am giving you today. 6913
31:12 and **f** carefully all the words of this law. 6913
Jos 3: 3 move out from your positions and **f** it 339+2143
22:27 and you and the generations that **f,** 339
Jdg 3:28 "**F** me," he ordered, "for the LORD 8103
6:34 summoning the Abiezrites to **f** him. 339
7:17 "**F** my **lead.** 4027+6913
9: 3 they were inclined to **f** Abimelech, 339
Ru 2: 9 and **f along** after the girls. 2143
1Sa 11: 7 of anyone who *does* not **f** Saul 339+3655
12:14 over you **f** the LORD your God— 339+2118
25:19 on ahead; I'll **f** you. 339+995
25:27 be given to the men who **f** you. 928+2143+8079
30:21 *to* **f** him and who were left behind at 339+2143
2Sa 17: 9 among the troops who **f** Absalom.' 339
20: 2 of Israel deserted David to **f** Sheba son 339
20:11 and whoever is for David, let him **f** Joab!" 339
1Ki 6:12 if *you* **f** my decrees, 928+2143
11: 6 he did not **f** the LORD completely, 339
11:10 had forbidden Solomon *to* **f** other gods, 339+2143
18:21 If the LORD is God, **f** him; 339+2143
18:21 but if Baal is God, **f** him." 339+2143
19:21 *to* **f** Elijah and became his attendant. 339+2143
2Ki 6:19 **F** me, and I will lead you to 339+2143
18: 6 to the LORD and did not cease to **f** him; 339
23: 3 to **f** the LORD and keep his commands, 339+2143
1Ch 28: 8 Be careful *to* **f** all the commands of 2011
2Ch 34:31 to **f** the LORD and keep his commands, 339+2143
34:33 they did not fail to **f** the LORD, 339
Ne 9:34 and our fathers *did* not **f** your law; 6913
10:29 **f** the Law of God given through Moses 928+2143
Est 2:20 *to* **f** Mordecai's instructions 6913
Job 21:33 all men **f** after him, 5432
Ps 23: 6 and love *will* **f** me all the days of my life, 8103
45:14 her virgin companions **f** her 339
81:12 *to* **f** their own devices. 928+2143
81:13 if Israel *would* **f** my ways, 928+2143
89:30 and *do* not **f** my statutes, 928+2143
94:15 and all the upright in heart will **f** it. 339
111:10 all *who* **f** his precepts have good understanding. 6913
119:33 Teach me, O LORD, to **f** your decrees; 2006
119:63 to *all who* **f** your precepts. 9068
119:106 that I *will* **f** your righteous laws. 9068
119:166 O LORD, and *I* **f** your commands. 6913
Ecc 1:11 not be remembered by those who **f.** 340
11: 9 **F** the ways of your heart 928+2143
SS 1: 8 **f** the tracks of the sheep 3655
Isa 8:11 not *to* **f** the way of this people. 928+2143
42:24 For they would not **f** his ways; 928+2143
Jer 3:17 No longer *will they* **f** the stubbornness 339+2143
7: 6 *do* not **f** other gods to your own harm, 339+2143
7: 9 and **f** other gods you have not known, 339+2143
11: 6 to the terms of this covenant and **f** them. 6913
11: 8 the covenant I had commanded them to **f** 6913
Jer 13:10 who **f** the stubbornness of their hearts 928+2143
18:12 each of *us will* **f** the stubbornness 6913
23:10 The [prophets] **f** an evil course 2118
23:17 And to all *who* **f** the stubbornness 928+2143
25: 6 *Do* not **f** other gods to serve 339+2143
26: 4 If you do not listen to me and **f** my law, 928+2143
32:23 but they did not obey you or **f** your law; 928+2143
35:15 *do* not **f** other gods to serve them. 339+2143
42:16 and the famine you dread *will* **f** you 339+1815
Eze 9: 5 "**F** him through the city and kill, 339+6296
11:20 Then *they will* **f** my decrees and 928+2143
13: 3 foolish prophets who **f** their own spirit 339+2143
20:13 not **f** my decrees but rejected my laws 928+2143
20:16 and *did* not **f** my decrees 928+2143
20:18 *"Do* not **f** the statutes of your fathers 928+2143
20:19 **f** my decrees and be careful 928+2143
20:21 *They did* not **f** my decrees, 928+2143
36:27 I will put my Spirit in you and move *you to* **f** my decrees 928+2143
37:24 *They will* **f** my laws and be careful 928+2143
43:11 to its design and **f** all its regulations. 6913
48: 1 **f** the Hethlon road to Lebo Hamath; 448+3338
Hos 11:10 *They will* **f** the LORD; 339+2143
Mt 4:19 "Come, **f** me," Jesus said, *3958*
8:19 "Teacher, *I will* **f** you wherever you go." *199*
8:22 But Jesus told him, "**F** me, *199*
9: 9 "**F** me," he told him, *199*
10:38 anyone who does not take his cross and **f** me is not worthy of me. *199+3958*
16:24 and take up his cross and **f** me. *199*
19:21 Then come, **f** me." *199*
19:27 "We have left everything to **f** you! *199*
Mk 1:17 "Come, **f** me," Jesus said, *3958*
2:14 "**F** me," Jesus told him, *199*
5:37 He did not let anyone **f** him except Peter, *5258*
8:34 and take up his cross and **f** me. *199*
10:21 Then come, **f** me." *199*
10:28 "We have left everything *to* **f** you!" *199*
14:13 of water will meet you. **F** him. *199*
Lk 5:27 "**F** me," Jesus said to him, *199*
9:23 and take up his cross daily and **f** me. *199*
9:57 *"I will* **f** you wherever you go." *199*
9:59 He said to another man, "**F** me." *199*
9:61 Still another said, *"I will* **f** you, Lord; *199*
14:27 not carry his cross and **f** me cannot *2262+3958*
18:22 Then come, **f** me." *199*
18:28 "We have left all we had *to* **f** you!" *199*
21: 8 *Do* not **f** them. *3958+4513*
22:10 **F** him to the house that he enters, *199*
Jn 1:43 Finding Philip, he said to him, "**F** me." *199*
10: 4 and his sheep **f** him *199*
10: 5 But *they will* never **f** a stranger; *199*
10:27 I know them, and *they* **f** me. *199*
12:26 Whoever serves me *must* **f** me; *199*
13:36 "Where I am going, you cannot **f** now, *199*
13:36 but *you will* **f** later." *199*
13:37 "Lord, why can't *I* **f** you now? *199*
21:19 Then he said to him, "**F** me!" *199*
21:22 You *must* **f** me." *199*
Ac 12: 8 "Wrap your cloak around you and **f** me," *199*
Ro 2: 8 and who reject the truth and **f** evil, *4275*
15: 5 among yourselves as you **f** Christ Jesus, *NIG*
1Co 1:12 One of you says, "I **f** Paul"; *1639*
1:12 another, "I **f** Apollos"; *NIG*
1:12 another, "I **f** Cephas"; *NIG*
1:12 still another, "I **f** Christ." *NIG*
3: 4 For when one says, "I **f** Paul," and another, *1639*
3: 4 "I follow Paul," and another, "I **f** Apollos," *NIG*
11: 1 **F** my **example,** as I follow the *1181+3629*
11: 1 as I **f** the example of Christ. *NIG*
14: 1 **F** the way of love *1503*
2Co 12:18 in the same spirit and **f the same course?** *2717*
Gal 2:14 you force Gentiles to **f Jewish customs?** *2678*
6:16 Peace and mercy to all who **f** this rule, *5123*
2Th 3: 7 how you ought *to* **f** our **example.** *3628*
3: 9 to make ourselves a model for you to **f.** *3628*
1Ti 4: 1 and **f** deceiving spirits and things taught *4668*
5:15 in fact already turned away to **f** Satan. *3958*
1Pe 1:11 of Christ and the glories **that would f.** *3552+4047*
2:21 that *you should* **f** in his steps. *2051*
2Pe 1:16 *We did* not **f** cleverly invented stories *1979*
2: 2 Many *will* **f** their shameful ways *1979*
2:10 This is especially true of those who **f** *3958+4513*
2:15 the straight way and wandered off *to* **f** *1979*
Jude 1:16 they **f** their own evil desires; *4513*
1:18 scoffers who will **f** their own ungodly desires." *4513*
1:19 who **f mere natural instincts** *6035*
Rev 14: 4 They **f** the Lamb wherever he goes. *199*
14:13 for their deeds *will* **f** them." *199*

FOLLOWED (134) [FOLLOW]

Ge 32:19 and all the *others who* **f** the herds: 339+2143
Ex 14:23 and chariots and horsemen **f** them into 339+995
14:28 of Pharaoh that *had* **f** the Israelites into 339+995
15:20 and all the women **f** her, 339+3655
Nu 16:25 and the elders of Israel **f** him. 339+2143
25: 8 and **f** the Israelite into the tent. 339+995
31:16 the ones who **f** Balaam's advice and were 928
32:11 not **f** me wholeheartedly, not one of 339
32:12 for they **f** the LORD wholeheartedly.' 339
Dt 1:36 because he **f** the LORD wholeheartedly." 339
4: 3 among you everyone who **f** the Baal 339+2143
Jos 6: 8 the ark of the LORD's covenant **f** them. 339+2143
6: 9 and the rear guard **f** the ark. 339+2143
6:13 and the rear guard **f** the ark of the LORD, 339+2143

Jos 14: 8 f the LORD my God wholeheartedly. 339
14: 9 because you have f 339
14:14 because he f the LORD, the God of Israel, 339
Jdg 2:12 They f and worshiped various gods of 339+2143
3:28 So they f him down and, 339
4:10 Ten thousand men f him, 928+6590+8079
4:14 f by ten thousand men. 339
5:14 Benjamin was with the people who f you. 339
9:49 the men cut branches and f Abimelech. 339+2143
10: 3 He was f by Jair of Gilead, 339+7756
11: 3 around him and f him. 3655+6640
13:11 Manoah got up and f his wife. 339+2143
1Sa 6:12 Philistines f them as far as the border 339+2143
14:13 his armor-bearer f and killed behind him. NIH
17:13 Jesse's three oldest sons had f Saul to 339+2143
17:14 The three oldest f Saul, 339+2143
26: 3 When he saw that Saul had f him there, 339+995
2Sa 2:10 The house of Judah, however, f David. 339+2118
17:23 that his advice had not been f, 6913
20:14 who gathered together and f him. 339+995
1Ki 11: 5 He f Ashtoreth the goddess of 339+2143
12:14 he f the advice of the young men and said, 3869
14: 8 who kept my commands and f me 339+2143
18:18 the LORD's commands and have f 339+2143
2Ki 4:30 So he got up and f her. 339+2143
7:15 They f them as far as the Jordan, 339+2143
14: 3 In everything he f the example 3869+6913+6913
17: 8 and f the practices of the nations 928+2143
17:15 They f worthless idols 339+2143
17:19 f the practices Israel had introduced. 928+2143
1Ch 8:30 f by Zur, Kish, Baal, Ner, Nadab, 2256
9:36 f by Zur, Kish, Baal, Ner, Nadab, 2256
2Ch 10:14 he f the advice of the young men and said, 3869
11:16 f the Levites to Jerusalem 339+995
17: 3 in the ways his father David had f. NIH
17: 4 and f his commands rather than 928+2143
22: 5 He also f their counsel when he went 928+2143
26:17 of the LORD f him in. 339+995
Ne 12:32 and half the leaders of Judah f them, 339+2143
12:38 I f them on top of the wall, 339
Est 2: 4 appealed to the king, and he f it. 4027+6913
Job 23:11 My feet have closely f his steps; 296
Pr 7:22 All at once he f her like an ox going to 339+2143
Ecc 4:15 and walked under the sun f the youth, 6640
Jer 2: 2 as a bride you loved me and f me 339+2143
2: 5 They f worthless idols 339+2143
7:24 instead, they f the stubborn inclinations 928+2143
8: 2 and which they have f and consulted 339+2143
9:13 they have not obeyed me or f my law. 928+2143
9:14 they have f the stubbornness of their hearts; 339+2143
9:14 they have f the Baals, 339
11: 8 f the stubbornness of their evil hearts. 928+2143
11:10 They have f other gods to serve them. 339+2143
16:11 'and f other gods and served 339+2143
35:18 and have f all his instructions 9068
44:10 nor have they f my law and 928+2143
44:23 not obeyed him or f his law or his decrees 928+2143
Eze 5: 6 and has not f my decrees. 2143
5: 7 and have not f my decrees or kept my laws. 2143
11:12 not f my decrees or kept my laws 2143
Am 2: 4 the gods their ancestors f, 339+2143
Mic 6:16 and you have f their traditions. 928+2143
Hab 3: 5 pestilence f his steps. 3655
Mal 2: 9 not f my ways but have shown partiality 9068
Mt 4:20 At once they left their nets and f him. 199
4:22 the boat and their father and f him. 199
4:25 and the region across the Jordan f him. 199
8: 1 large crowds f him. 199
8:23 he got into the boat and his disciples f him. 199
9: 9 and Matthew got up and f him. 199
9:27 two blind men f him, calling out, 199
12:15 Many f him, and he healed all their sick, 199
14:13 the crowds f him on foot from the towns. 199
19: 2 Large crowds f him, 199
19:28 you who have f me will also sit 199
20:29 a large crowd f him. 199
20:34 they received their sight and f him. 199
21: 9 ahead of him and those that f shouted, 199
26:58 But Peter f him at a distance, 199
27:55 They had f Jesus from Galilee to care 199
Mk 1:18 At once they left their nets and f him. 199
1:20 the boat with the hired men and f him. 599+3958
2:14 Jesus told him, and Levi got up and f him. 199
2:15 for there were many who f him. 199
3: 7 and a large crowd from Galilee f. 199
5:24 A large crowd f and pressed around him. 199
10:32 while those who f were afraid. 199
10:52 and f Jesus along the road. 199
11: 9 ahead and those who f shouted, 199
14:54 Peter f him at a distance, 199
15:41 In Galilee these women had f him 199
Lk 5:11 left everything and f him. 199
5:28 and Levi got up, left everything and f him. 199
9:11 but the crowds learned about it and f him. 199
18:43 he received his sight and f Jesus, 199
22:39 and his disciples f him. 199
22:54 Peter f at a distance. 199
23:27 A large number of people f him, 199
23:49 the women who had f him from Galilee, 5258
23:55 with Jesus from Galilee f Joseph and saw 2887
Jn 1:37 When the two disciples heard him say this, they f Jesus. 199
1:40 and who had f Jesus. 199
6: 2 and a great crowd of people f him 199
6:66 turned back and no longer f him. 3552+4344
Jn 11:31 they f her, supposing she was going to 199
21: 8 The other disciples f in the boat, 2262
Ac 8:11 They f him because he had amazed them 4668
8:13 And he f Philip everywhere, 4674
12: 9 Peter f him out of the prison, 199+2002
13:43 and devout converts to Judaism f Paul 199
16:17 This girl f Paul and the rest of us, shouting, 2887
21:36 The crowd that f kept shouting, 199
27:11 f the advice of the pilot and of the owner NIG
Ro 5:16 The judgment f one sin NIG
5:16 but the gift f many trespasses 1666
Eph 2: 2 to live when you f the ways of this world 2848
1Ti 4: 6 and of the good teaching that you have f. 4158
Rev 13: 3 The whole world was astonished and f 3958
14: 8 A second angel f and said, "Fallen! 199
14: 9 A third angel f them and said in 199

FOLLOWER (1) [FOLLOW]

Ac 24:14 the God of our fathers as a f of the Way, 2848

FOLLOWERS (24) [FOLLOW]

Nu 16: 5 Then he said to Korah and all his f: 6337
16: 6 You, Korah, and all your f are to do this: 6337
16:11 and all your f have banded together. 6337
16:16 "You and all your f are to appear before 6337
16:19 When Korah had gathered all his f 6337
16:40 or he would become like Korah and his f. 6337
26: 9 and Aaron and were among Korah's f 6337
26:10 whose f died when the fire devoured 6337
27: 3 He was not among Korah's f, 6337
Jdg 9: 4 who became his f. 339+2143
1Sa 30:22 and troublemakers among David's f said, 408+889+2143+6640
1Ki 16:22 But Omri's f proved stronger than those of Tibni 339+889+2021+6639
Ne 11: 8 and his f, Gabbai and Sallai—928 men. 339
Ps 49:13 and of their f, who approve their sayings. 339
106:18 Fire blazed among their f; 6337
Da 11:24 loot and wealth among his f. 2157S
Lk 11:19 by whom do your f drive them out? 5626
22:49 When Jesus' f saw what was going to happen, 1254+3836S
Ac 5:36 He was killed, all his f were dispersed, 4275
5:37 and all his f were scattered. 4275
9:25 But his f took him by night 3412
17:34 A few men became f of Paul and believed. 3140
22: 4 the f of this Way to their death, NIG
Rev 17:14 chosen and faithful f." AIT

FOLLOWING (64) [FOLLOW]

Ge 47:18 they came to him the f year and said, 9108
Ex 30:23 "Take the f fine spices: NIH
Lev 20: 6 to prostitute himself by f them, 339
23:32 of the month until the f evening you are NIH
Nu 32:15 If you turn away from f him, 339
Dt 7: 4 from f me to serve other gods, 339
11:28 I command you today by f other gods, 339+2143
28:14 f other gods and serving them. 339+2143
Jos 18:21 clan by clan, had the f cities: NIH
21: 3 the Israelites gave the Levites the f towns 465S
21: 9 and Simeon they allotted the f towns 465S
Jdg 2:19 f other gods and serving 339+2143
1Sa 5: 4 But the f morning when they rose, 4740
2Sa 7: 8 the pasture and from f the flock to be ruler 339
15:12 and Absalom's f kept on increasing. 907+6639
15:16 with his entire household f him; 928+8079
15:17 king set out, with all the people f him, 928+8079
1Ki 8:66 On the f day he sent the people away. 9029S
2Ki 13: 2 He did evil in the eyes of the LORD by f 339+2143
16: 3 f the detestable ways of the nations 3869
17:21 Jeroboam enticed Israel away from f 339
21: 2 f the detestable practices of the nations 3869
1Ch 6:71 The Gershonites received the f: NIH
6:77 (the rest of the Levites) received the f: NIH
17: 7 I took you from the pasture and from f 339
2Ch 25:27 the time that Amaziah turned away from f 339
28: 3 f the detestable ways of the nations 3869
29:15 f the word of the LORD. 928
30:12 f the word of the LORD. 928
33: 2 f the detestable practices of the nations 3869
36:14 f all the detestable practices of the nations 3869
Ezr 2:59 The f came up from the towns 465S
10:18 the f had married foreign women: 5162
Ne 7:61 The f came up from the towns 465S
Job 34:27 from f him and had no regard for any 339
Ps 119:14 I rejoice in f your statutes as one rejoices 2006
Isa 66:17 f the one in the midst of those who eat 339
Jer 2: 8 by Baal, f worthless idols. 339+2143
3:19 and not turn away from f me. 339
16:12 each of you is f the stubbornness 339+2143
Zep 1: 6 those who turn back from f the LORD 339
Mt 8:10 he was astonished and said to those f him, 199
10: 5 with the f instructions: NIG
Mk 13:24 "But in those days, f that distress, 3552
14:51 but a linen garment, was f Jesus. 5258
Lk 7: 9 and turning to the crowd f him, he said, 199
Jn 1:38 Jesus saw them f and asked, 199
18:15 and another disciple were f Jesus. 199
21:20 the disciple whom Jesus loved was f them. 199
Ac 10: 9 the f day as they were on their journey 2069
10:24 The f day he arrived in Caesarea. 2069
15:23 With them they sent the f letter: NIG
15:28 with anything beyond the f requirements: 4047
20:15 and on the f day arrived at Miletus. 2400
23:11 The f night the Lord stood near Paul 2079
Ac 28:13 and on the f day we reached Puteoli. 1308
1Co 11:17 In the f directives I have no praise for you, 4047
Eph 2: 3 of our sinful nature and f its desires 4472
Php 3:17 Join with others in f my example, 1181+5213
1Ti 1:18 by f them you may fight the good fight, NIG
Heb 4:11 so that no one will fall by f their example NIG
2Pe 3: 3 scoffing and f their own evil desires. 4513
Rev 6: 8 and Hades was f close behind him. 199
19:14 The armies of heaven were f him, 199

FOLLOWS (16) [FOLLOW]

Ge 41:31 the famine that f it will be so severe. 339+4027
Nu 14:24 a different spirit and f me wholeheartedly, 339
2Ki 11:15 and put to the sword anyone who f her." 339+995
2Ch 17:14 Their enrollment by families was as f: 465
23:14 and put to the sword anyone who f her." 339+995
Ezr 4: 8 to Artaxerxes the king as f: 10358
5: 7 The report they sent him read as f: 10180+10341
Jer 4:20 Disaster f disaster; the whole land lies in ruins. 6584+7925
51:31 One courier f another 7925
51:31 and messenger f messenger to announce to 7925
Eze 18: 9 He f my decrees and faithfully keeps 928+2143
18:17 He keeps my laws and f my decrees. 928+2143
33:15 f the decrees that give life, 928+2143
Hos 4: 2 and bloodshed f bloodshed. 5595
Jn 8:12 Whoever f me will never walk in darkness, 199
Ac 23:25 He wrote a letter as f: 2400+3836+4047+5596

FOLLY (37) [FOOL]

1Sa 25:25 his name is Fool, and f goes with him. 5576
Job 42: 8 and not deal with you according to your f. 5576
Ps 38: 5 and are loathsome because of my sinful f. 222
69: 5 You know my f, O God; 222
85: 8 but let them not return to f. 4074
Pr 5:23 led astray by his own great f. 222
9:13 The woman F is loud; 4070
12:23 but the heart of fools blurts out f. 222
13:16 but a fool exposes his f. 222
14: 8 but the f of fools is deception. 222
14:18 The simple inherit f, 222
14:24 but the f of fools yields folly. 222
14:24 but the folly of fools yields f. 222
14:29 but a quick-tempered man displays f. 222
15: 2 but the mouth of the fool gushes f. 222
15:14 but the mouth of a fool feeds on f. 222
15:21 F delights a man who lacks judgment, 222
16:22 but f brings punishment to fools. 222
17:12 of her cubs than a fool in his f. 222
18:13 that is his f and his shame. 222
19: 3 A man's own f ruins his life, 222
22:15 F is bound up in the heart of a child, 222
24: 9 The schemes of f are sin, 222
26: 4 Do not answer a fool according to his f, 222
26: 5 Answer a fool according to his f, 222
26:11 so a fool repeats his f. 222
27:22 you will not remove his f from him. 222
Ecc 1:17 and also of madness and f, 8508
2: 3 with wine, and embracing f— 6121
2:12 and also madness and f. 6121
2:13 I saw that wisdom is better than f, 6121
7:25 of wickedness and the madness of f. 6121
10: 1 so a little f outweighs wisdom and honor. 6121
10:13 At the beginning his words are f; 6121
Isa 32: 6 fool speaks f, his mind is busy with evil: 5576
Mk 7:22 lewdness, envy, slander, arrogance and f. 932
2Ti 3: 9 their f will be clear to everyone. 486

FOMENTING (1)

Isa 59:13 f oppression and revolt, 1819

FOND (1)

1Sa 19: 1 But Jonathan was very f of David 2911

FONDLED (2)

Eze 23: 3 In that land their breasts were f 5080
23:21 and your young breasts f. 5080

FOOD (317) [FOODS]

Ge 1:29 They will be yours for f. 433
1:30 I give every green plant for f." 433
2: 9 pleasing to the eye and good for f. 4407
3: 6 of the tree was good for f and pleasing to 4407
3:19 the sweat of your brow you will eat your f 4312
6:21 to take every kind of f that is to be eaten 4407
6:21 be eaten and store it away as f for you and 433
9: 3 Everything that lives and moves will be f; 433
14:11 of Sodom and Gomorrah and all their f; 431
21:14 the next morning Abraham took some f and 4312
24:33 Then f was set before him, but he said, 430
27: 4 the kind of tasty f I like and bring it to me 4761
27: 7 and prepare me some tasty f to eat, 4761
27: 9 I can prepare some tasty f for your father, 4761
27:14 and she prepared some tasty f, 4761
27:17 the tasty f and the bread she had made. 4761
27:31 He too prepared some tasty f 4761
28:20 and will give me f to eat and clothes 4312
39: 6 with anything except the f he ate. 4312
41:35 the f of these good years that are coming 431
41:35 to be kept in the cities for f. 431
41:36 This f should be held in reserve for 431
41:48 the f produced in those seven years 431
41:48 the f grown in the fields surrounding it. 431

Ge 41:54 but in the whole land of Egypt there was f. 4312
41:55 the people cried to Pharaoh for f. 4312
42: 7 they replied, "to buy f." 431
42:10 "Your servants have come to buy f. 431
42:33 take f for your starving households and go. NIH
43: 2 "Go back and buy us a little more f." 431
43: 4 we will go down and buy f for you. 431
43:20 down here the first time to buy f. 431
43:22 additional silver with us to buy f. 431
43:31 controlling himself, said, "Serve the f." 4312
44: 1 "Fill the men's sacks with as much f 431
44:25 'Go back and buy a little more f.' 431
47:12 and all his father's household with f, 4312
47:13 There was no f, however, 4312
47:15 to Joseph and said, "Give us f. 4312
47:16 "I will sell you f in exchange NIH
47:17 and he gave them f in exchange 4312
47:17 with f in exchange for all their livestock. 4312
47:19 Buy us and our land in exchange for f, 4312
47:22 from Pharaoh and **had f enough** *from* 430
47:24 as f *for* yourselves and your households 431
49:20 "Asher's f will be rich; 4312
Ex 12:16 **prepare** f for everyone **to eat**— 430
12:39 of Egypt and did not have time to prepare f 7476
16: 3 of meat and ate all the f we wanted, 4312
21:10 he must not deprive the first one of her f, 8638
23:11 the poor among your people *may* **get** f 430
23:25 his blessing will be on your f and water. 4312
Lev 3:11 The priest shall burn them on the altar as f, 4312
3:16 The priest shall burn them on the altar as f, 4312
11:34 Any f that could be eaten but has water 431
21: 6 the f *of* their God, they are to be holy. 4312
21: 8 because they offer up the f *of* your God. 4312
21:17 a defect may come near to offer the f 4312
21:21 not come near to offer the f *of* his God. 4312
21:22 He may eat the most holy f *of* his God, 4312
21:22 as well as the holy f; NIH
22: 7 for they are his f. 4312
22:11 that slave may eat his f. 4312
22:13 she may eat of her father's f. 4312
22:25 of a foreigner and offer them as the f 4312
25: 6 during the sabbath year will be f for you— 433
25:37 not lend him money at interest or sell him f 431
26: 5 and you will eat all the f you want and live 4312
Nu 11: 4 with them *began to* **crave other** f, 203+9294
11:34 the people who *had* **craved other** f. 203
15:19 and you eat the f *of* the land, 4312
21: 5 And we detest this miserable f!" 4312
28: 2 the f for my offerings made by fire, 4312
28:24 In this way prepare the f *for* 4312
Dt 2: 6 to pay them in silver for the f you eat and 431
2:28 Sell us f to eat and water to drink 431
10:18 giving him f and clothing. 4312
23:19 or f or anything else that may earn interest. 431
28:26 Your carcasses will be f for all the birds of 4407
32:15 **filled with** f, he became heavy and sleek. 9042
Jos 5:12 the day after they ate this f *from* the land, 6289
9: 5 All the bread of their f **supply** was dry 7474
Jdg 13:16 I will not eat any of your f. 4312
17:10 your clothes and your f." 4695
Ru 1: 6 to the aid of his people by providing f 4312
1Sa 2: 5 Those who were full hire themselves out for f, 4312
2:36 to some priestly office so I can have f 4312+7326
9: 7 The f in our sacks is gone. 4312
14:24 "Cursed be any man who eats f 4312
14:24 So none of the troops tasted f. 4312
14:28 'Cursed be any man who eats f today!' 4312
28:22 and let me give you some f so you may eat 4312
30:11 They gave him water to drink and f 4312
30:12 not eaten *any* f or drunk any water 4312
2Sa 3:29 or who falls by the sword or who lacks f." 4312
12: 3 It shared his f, 7326
12:17 and he would not eat any f with them. 4312
12:20 and at his request they served him f, 4312
13: 5 the f in my sight so I may watch her and 1376
13: 7 of your brother Amnon and prepare some f 1376
13:10 the f here into my bedroom so I may eat 1376
1Ki 5: 9 by providing f for my royal household." 4312
5:11 of wheat as f for his household, 4818
10: 5 the f *on* his table, 4407
11:18 a house and land and provided him with f. 4312
17: 9 a widow in that place to **supply** you **with** f. 3920
17:15 So *there was* f every day for Elijah and for 430
18: 4 and had supplied them with f and water.) 4312
18:13 and supplied them with f and water. 4312
19: 8 Strengthened by that f, 428
2Ki 6:22 Set f and water before them so 4312
25: 3 so severe that there was no f for the people 4312
1Ch 12:40 and Naphtali came bringing f on donkeys, 4312
2Ch 9: 4 the f *on* his table, 4407
11:11 with supplies of f, olive oil and wine. 4407
28:15 f and drink, and healing balm. 430
Ezr 2:63 of the **most sacred** *f* until there was AIT
3: 7 and gave f and drink and oil to the people 4407
10: 6 he ate no f and drank no water, 4312
Ne 5:14 nor my brothers ate the f *allotted to* 4312
5:15 from them in addition to f and wine. 4312
5:18 I never demanded the f *allotted to* 4312
7:65 the **most sacred** f until there should be 7731+7731
8:10 "Go and enjoy **choice** f and sweet drinks, 5460
8:12 to send **portions of** f and to celebrate 4950
13: 2 with f and water but had hired Balaam 4312
13:15 I warned them against selling f on that day. 7474
Est 2: 9 with her beauty treatments and **special** f. 4950
9:22 of feasting and joy and giving **presents of** f 4950
Job 3:24 For sighing comes to me instead of f; 4312
Job 6: 6 Is **tasteless** *f* eaten without salt, AIT
6: 7 I refuse to touch it; such f makes me ill. 4312
12:11 the ear test words as the tongue tastes f? 431
15:23 He wanders about—f for vultures; 4312
20:14 yet his f will turn sour in his stomach; 4312
22: 7 to the weary and you withheld f from 4312
24: 5 the poor go about their labor of foraging f; 3272
24: 5 the wasteland provides f for their children. 4312
28: 5 The earth, from which f comes, 4312
30: 4 and their f was the root of the broom tree. 4312
33:20 so that his very being finds f repulsive 4312
34: 3 the ear tests words as the tongue tastes f. 430
36:16 of your table laden with **choice** f. 2016
36:31 the nations and provides f in abundance. 431
38:41 Who provides f for the raven 7474
38:41 to God and wander about for lack of f? 431
39:29 From there he seeks out his f; 431
Ps 42: 3 My tears have been my f day and night, 4312
59:15 They wander about for f and howl if 430
63:10 be given over to the sword and become f 4987
69:21 They put gall in my f and gave me vinegar 1362
74:14 the heads of Leviathan and gave him as f 4407
78:18 to the test by demanding the f they craved. 431
78:20 But can he also give us f? 4312
78:25 he sent them all the f they could eat. 7476
78:30 before they turned from the f they craved, 431
79: 2 of your servants as f to the birds of the air, 4407
102: 4 I forget to eat my f. 4312
102: 9 as my f and mingle my drink with tears 4312
104:14 bringing forth f from the earth: 4312
104:21 for their prey and seek their f from God. 431
104:27 These all look to you to give them their f at 431
105:16 and destroyed all their supplies of f; 4312
107:18 They loathed all f and drew near the gates 431
111: 5 He provides f for those who fear him; 3272
127: 2 toiling for f to eat— 4312
132:15 her poor will I satisfy with f. 4312
136:25 and who gives f to every creature. 4312
145:15 you give them their f at the proper time. 431
146: 7 of the oppressed and gives f to the hungry. 4312
147: 9 He provides f for the cattle and for 4312
Pr 6: 8 in summer and gathers its f at harvest. 4407
9: 5 eat my f and drink the wine I have mixed. 4312
9:17 f eaten in secret is delicious!" 4312
12: 9 to be somebody and have no f. 4312
12:11 He who works his land will have abundant f 4312
13:23 poor man's field may produce abundant f, 431
20:13 stay awake and you will have f to spare. 4312
20:17 F *gained by* fraud tastes sweet to a man, 4312
21:20 the house of the wise are stores of **choice** *f* AIT
22: 9 for he shares his f with the poor. 4312
23: 3 for that f is deceptive. 4312
23: 6 Do not eat the f *of* a stingy man, 4312
25:21 If your enemy is hungry, give him f to eat; 4312
28:19 He who works his land will have abundant f 4312
30:22 a fool who is full of f, 4312
30:25 yet they store up their f in the summer; 4312
31:14 bringing her f from afar. 4312
31:15 she provides f for her family and portions 3272
Ecc 9: 7 Go, eat your f with gladness, 4312
9:11 or the battle to the strong, nor does f come 4312
Isa 3: 1 all supplies of f and all supplies of water, 4312
3: 7 I have no f or clothing in my house; 4312
4: 1 "We will eat our own f 4312
21:14 bring f *for* the fugitives. 4312
23:18 for abundant f and fine clothes. 430
25: 6 a feast of **rich** f for all peoples, a banquet 9043
30:23 the f that comes from the land will be rich 4312
58: 7 Is it not to share your f with the hungry 4312
62: 8 "Never again will I give your grain as f 4407
65:25 but dust will be the serpent's f. 4312
Jer 5:17 They will devour your harvests and f, 4312
7:33 the carcasses of this people will become f 4407
9:15 **make** this people **eat** bitter f 430
16: 4 and their dead bodies will become f for 4407
16: 7 No *one will* **offer** f to comfort 7271
19: 7 as f to the birds of the air and the beasts of 4407
22:15 *Did* not your father **have** f and drink? 430
23:15 *I will* **make** them **eat** bitter f 430
34:20 Their dead bodies will become f for 4407
44:17 At that time we had plenty of f 4312
52: 6 so severe that there was no f for the people 4312
La 1:11 they barter their treasures for f 431
1:19 in the city while they searched for f 431
4: 9 with hunger, they waste away for lack of f 9482
4:10 who became their f 1356
Eze 4:10 of f to eat each day and eat it at set times. 4407
4:12 Eat **the** f as you would a barley cake; 5626S
4:13 the people of Israel will eat defiled f 4312
4:16 I will cut off the supply of f in Jerusalem. 4312
4:16 The people will eat rationed f in anxiety 4312
4:17 for f and water will be scarce. 4312
5:16 upon you and cut off your supply of f. 4312
12:18 tremble as you eat your f, 4312
12:19 They will eat their f in anxiety 4312
14:13 to cut off its f supply and send famine 4312
16:13 *Your* f was fine flour, honey and olive oil. 430
16:19 Also the f I provided for you— 4312
16:20 to me and sacrificed them as f to the idols. 430
18: 7 He does not commit robbery but gives his f 4312
18:16 He does not commit robbery but gives his f 4312
23:37 whom they bore to me, as f for them. 433
24:17 or eat the customary f [of mourners]." 4312
24:22 or eat the customary f [of mourners]. 4312
29: 5 as f to the beasts of the earth and the birds 433
34: 5 when they were scattered they became f 433
34: 8 and has become f for all the wild animals, 433
Eze 34:10 and it will no longer be f for them. 433
39: 4 as f to all kinds of carrion birds and to 433
44: 7 while you offered me f, 4312
47:12 Their fruit will serve for f and their leaves 4407
48:18 Its produce will supply f for the workers of 4312
Da 1: 5 of f and wine *from* the king's table. 7329
1: 8 to defile himself with the royal f and wine, 7329
1:10 who has assigned your f and drink. 4407
1:13 that of the young men who eat the royal f, 7329
1:15 of the young men who ate the royal f. 7329
1:16 So the guard took away their **choice** f and 7329
4:12 its fruit abundant, and on it was f for all. 10410
4:21 providing f for all, giving shelter to 10410
10: 3 I ate no choice f; 4312
Hos 2: 5 who give me my f and my water, 4312
9: 3 to Egypt and eat unclean f in Assyria. NIH
9: 4 This f will be for themselves; 4312
Joel 1:16 the f been cut off before our very eyes— 431
Am 8:11 not a famine of f or a thirst for water, 4312
Hab 1:16 in luxury and enjoys the choicest f. 4407
3:17 olive crop fails and the fields produce no f, 431
Hag 2:12 some wine, oil or other f, 4407
Zec 9: 7 the **forbidden** f from between their teeth. 9199
Mal 1: 7 "You place defiled f on my altar. 4312
1:12 and of its f, 'It is contemptible.' 431
3:10 that there may be f in my house. 3272
Mt 3: 4 His f was locusts and wild honey. *5575*
6:25 Is not life more important than f, *5575*
14:15 to the villages and buy themselves some f." *1109*
24:45 in his household to give them their f at *5575*
Mk 7: 2 of his disciples eating f with hands *788*
7: 5 of eating their f with 'unclean' hands?" *788*
Lk 3:11 the one who has f should do the same." *1109*
9:12 and countryside and find f and lodging, *2169*
9:13 unless we go and buy f for all this crowd." *1109*
12:23 Life is more than f, *5575*
12:42 to give them their f **allowance** at *4991*
15:17 of my father's hired men have f to spare, *788*
Jn 4: 8 into the town to buy f.) *5575*
4:32 "I have f to eat that you know nothing about *1111*
4:33 "Could someone have brought him f?" *2266*
4:34 "My f," said Jesus, "is to do the will *1109*
6:27 Do not work for f that spoils, *1111*
6:27 but for f that endures to eternal life, *1111*
6:55 For my flesh is real f *1111*
Ac 6: 1 in the daily distribution of f. *NIG*
7:11 and our fathers could not find f. *5964*
9:19 and after taking some f, *5575*
12:20 on the king's country for their f **supply.** *5555*
14:17 with plenty *of* f and fills your hearts *5575*
15:20 telling them to abstain from f polluted *NIG*
15:29 abstain from f **sacrificed to idols,** *1628*
21:25 abstain from f **sacrificed to idols,** *1628*
27:21 the men had gone a long time **without** f, *826*
27:33 and have gone **without** f— *827*
27:34 Now I urge you to take some f. *5575*
27:36 and ate some f themselves. *5575*
Ro 14:14 I am fully convinced that no f is unclean *NIG*
14:20 the work of God for the sake *of* f. *1109*
14:20 All f is clean, but it is wrong for a man to *NIG*
1Co 3: 2 I gave you milk, not **solid** f, *1109*
6:13 "F for the stomach and the stomach *1109*
6:13 for the stomach and the stomach *for* f"— *1109*
8: 1 Now about f **sacrificed to idols:** *1628*
8: 4 So then, about eating f sacrificed to idols: *1111*
8: 7 to idols that when they eat **such** f they think *1628*
8: 8 But f does not bring us near to God; *1109*
9: 4 Don't we have the right *to* f and drink? *2266*
9:13 in the temple **get** *their* f from the temple, *2266*
10: 3 They all ate the same spiritual f *1109*
2Co 9:10 the sower and bread for f will also supply *1111*
11:27 and thirst and have often **gone without** f; *3763*
2Th 3: 8 did we eat anyone's f without paying for it. *788*
1Ti 6: 8 But if we have f and clothing, *1418*
Heb 5:12 You need milk, not solid f! *5575*
5:14 But solid f is for the mature, *5575*
9:10 They are only a matter of f and drink *1109*
Jas 2:15 or sister is without clothes and daily f. *5575*
Rev 2:14 to sin by eating f **sacrificed to idols** and *1628*
2:20 the eating of f **sacrificed to idols.** *1628*

FOODS (4) [FOOD]

Ps 63: 5 be satisfied as with the **richest of** f; 2016+2256+2693
Mk 7:19 Jesus declared all f "clean.") *1109*
1Ti 4: 3 and order them to abstain from certain f, *1109*
Heb 13: 9 not *by* ceremonial f, *1109*

FOOL (82) [FOLLY, FOOL'S, FOOLISH, FOOLISHLY, FOOLISHNESS, FOOLS]

Nu 22:29 *"You have* **made a** f **of** me! 6618
Jdg 16:10 *"You have* **made a** f **of** me; you lied to me. 9438
16:13 *you have been* **making a** f **of** me and lying 9438
16:15 This is the third time *you have* **made a** f **of** 9438
1Sa 25:25 his name is F, and folly goes with him. 5572
26:21 Surely *I have* **acted like a** f 6118
Job 5: 2 Resentment kills a f, 211
5: 3 I myself have seen a f taking root, 211
Ps 14: 1 The f says in his heart, "There is no God." 5572
53: 1 The f says in his heart, "There is no God." 5572
Pr 10: 8 but a chattering f comes to ruin. 211
10:10 and a chattering f comes to ruin. 211
10:14 but the mouth of a f invites ruin. 211
10:18 and whoever spreads slander is a f. 4067
10:23 A f finds pleasure in evil conduct, 4067

Pr 11:29 and the f will be servant to the wise. 211
12:15 The way of a f seems right to him, 211
12:16 A f shows his annoyance at once, 211
13:16 but a f exposes his folly. 4067
14:16 but a f is hotheaded and reckless. 4067
15: 2 but the mouth of the f gushes folly. 4067
15: 5 A f spurns his father's discipline, 211
15:14 but the mouth of a f feeds on folly. 4067
17: 7 Arrogant lips are unsuited to a f— 5572
17:10 a hundred lashes a f. 4067
17:12 to meet a bear robbed of her cubs than a f 4067
17:16 Of what use is money in the hand of a f, 4067
17:21 To have a f for a son brings grief; 4067
17:21 there is no joy for the father of a f. 5572
17:28 Even a f is thought wise if he keeps silent, 211
18: 2 A f finds no pleasure in understanding 4067
19: 1 a f whose lips are perverse. 4067
19:10 It is not fitting for a f to live in luxury— 4067
20: 3 but every f is quick to quarrel. 211
23: 9 Do not speak to a f, 4067
24: 7 Wisdom is too high for a f; 211
26: 1 honor is not fitting for a f. 4067
26: 4 Do not answer a f according to his folly, 4067
26: 5 Answer a f according to his folly, 4067
26: 6 of a message by the hand of a f. 4067
26: 7 a proverb in the mouth of a f. 4067
26: 8 in a sling is the giving of honor to a f. 4067
26: 9 a proverb in the mouth of a f. 4067
26:10 at random is he who hires a f 4067
26:11 so a f repeats his folly. 4067
26:12 There is more hope for a f than for him. 4067
27: 3 but provocation by a f is heavier than both. 211
27:22 Though you grind a f in a mortar, 211
28:26 He who trusts in himself is a f, 4067
29: 9 If a wise man goes to court with a f, 211
29: 9 the f rages and scoffs, NIH
29:11 A f gives full vent to his anger, 4067
29:20 There is more hope for a f than for him. 4067
30:22 a f who is full of food, 5572
30:32 "If *you have* **played the f** 5571
Ecc 2:14 while the f walks in the darkness; 4067
2:15 "The fate of the f will overtake me also. 4067
2:16 For the wise man, like the f, 4067
2:16 Like the f, the wise man too must die! 4067
2:19 whether he will be a wise man or a f? 6119
4: 5 The f folds his hands and ruins himself. 4067
5: 3 speech of a f when there are many words. 4067
6: 8 What advantage has a wise man over a f? 4067
7: 7 Extortion **turns** a wise man **into a f**, 2147
7:17 Do not be overwicked, and do not be a f— 6119
10: 2 but the heart of the f to the left. 4067
10: 3 the f lacks sense and shows everyone 6119
10:12 but a f is consumed by his own lips. 4067
10:14 and the f multiplies words. 6119
Isa 32: 5 No longer will the f be called noble nor 5572
32: 6 f speaks folly, his mind is busy with evil: 5572
Jer 17:11 and in the end he will prove to be a f. 5572
Hos 9: 7 the prophet is considered a f, 211
Mt 5:22 But anyone who says, *'You f!'* 3704
Lk 12:20 "But God said to him, *'You f!* 933
1Co 3:18 a "f" so that he may become wise. 3704
2Co 11:16 I repeat: Let no one take me for a f. 933
11:16 then receive me just as you would a f, 933
11:17 not talking as the Lord would, but as a f. 932
11:21 I am speaking **as a f**— 932+1877
12: 6 I would not be a f, 933
12:11 I have made a f of myself, 933

FOOL'S (5) [FOOL]

Pr 14: 3 A f talk brings a rod to his back, 211
17:24 a f eyes wander to the ends of the earth. 4067
18: 6 A f lips bring him strife, 4067
18: 7 A f mouth is his undoing, 4067
Ecc 10:15 A f work wearies him; 4067

FOOLISH (46) [FOOL]

Ge 31:28 You have done a f *thing*. 6118
Dt 32: 6 O f and unwise people? 5572
2Sa 24:10 *I have* **done** a very **f thing.**" 6118
1Ch 21: 8 *I have* **done** a very **f thing.**" 6118
2Ch 16: 9 *You have* **done a f thing**, 6118
Job 2:10 "You are talking like a f *woman*. 5572
Ps 49:10 the f and the senseless alike perish 4067
74:18 how f people have reviled your name. 5572
Pr 8: 5 you who are f, gain understanding. 4067
10: 1 but a f son grief to his mother. 4067
14: 1 the f *one* tears hers down. 222
14: 7 Stay away from a f man, 4067
14:17 A quick-tempered man does f *things*, 222
15:20 but a f man despises his mother. 4067
17:25 A f son brings grief to his father 4067
19:13 A f son is his father's ruin, 4067
21:20 but a f man devours all he has. 4067
Ecc 2: 2 "Laughter," I said, *"is* f. 2147
4:13 an old but f king who no longer knows 4067
Jer 5: 4 *they are* f, for they do not know the way of 3282
5:21 you f and senseless people, 6119
10: 8 They are all senseless and f; 4071
Eze 13: 3 the f prophets who follow their own spirit 5572
Zec 11:15 "Take again the equipment of a f shepherd. 216
Mt 7:26 like a f man who built his house on sand. 3704
25: 2 Five of them were f and five were wise. 3704
25: 3 The f *ones* took their lamps but did 3704
25: 8 The f *ones* said to the wise, 3704
Lk 11:40 *You* f *people!* 933
24:25 He said to them, **"How f you are,** 485+6043
Ro 1:14 both to the wise and the f. 485
1:21 and their f hearts were darkened. 852
2:20 an instructor *of* the f, a teacher of infants, 933
1Co 1:20 not God **made** f the wisdom of the world? 3701
1:27 But God chose the f *things* of the world 3704
15:36 How f! What you sow does 933
Gal 3: 1 You f Galatians! 485
3: 3 Are you so f? 485
Eph 5: 4 **f talk** or coarse joking, 3703
5:17 Therefore do not be f, 933
1Ti 6: 9 a trap and into many f and harmful desires 485
2Ti 2:23 to do with f and stupid arguments, 3704
Tit 3: 3 At one time we too were f, disobedient, 485
3: 9 But avoid f controversies and genealogies 3704
Jas 2:20 You f man, do you want evidence that faith 3031
1Pe 2:15 the ignorant talk *of* f men. 933

FOOLISHLY (2) [FOOL]

Nu 12:11 against us the sin we have *so* f committed. 3282
1Sa 13:13 *"You* **acted f,"** Samuel said. 6118

FOOLISHNESS (8) [FOOL]

2Sa 15:31 **turn** Ahithophel's counsel **into f.**" 6118
1Co 1:18 of the cross is f to those who are perishing, 3702
1:21 through the f of what was preached 3702
1:23 a stumbling block to Jews and f 3702
1:25 the f of God is wiser than man's wisdom, 3704
2:14 Spirit of God, for they are f to him, 3702
3:19 wisdom of this world is f in God's sight. 3702
2Co 11: 1 up with a little *of* my f; 932

FOOLS (41) [FOOL]

2Sa 13:13 You would be like one of the **wicked** f 5572
Job 12:17 and **makes** f of judges. 2147
Ps 39: 8 do not make me the scorn of f. 5572
74:22 remember how f mock you all day long. 5572
92: 6 f do not understand, 4067
94: 8 you f, when will you become wise? 4067
107:17 *Some* became f through their rebellious 211
Pr 1: 7 but f despise wisdom and discipline. 211
1:22 in mockery and f hate knowledge? 4067
1:32 the complacency of f will destroy them; 4067
3:35 but f he holds up to shame. 4067
10:21 but f die for lack of judgment. 211
12:23 but the heart of f blurts out folly. 4067
13:19 but f detest turning from evil. 4067
13:20 but a companion of f suffers harm. 4067
14: 8 but the folly of f is deception. 4067
14: 9 F mock at making amends for sin, 211
14:24 but the folly of f yields folly. 4067
14:33 even among f she lets herself be known. 4067
15: 7 not so the hearts of f. 4067
16:22 but folly brings punishment to f. 211
19:29 and beatings for the backs of f. 4067
26: 3 and a rod for the backs of f! 4067
Ecc 5: 1 to offer the sacrifice of f, 4067
5: 4 He has no pleasure in f; fulfill your vow. 4067
7: 4 the heart of f is in the house of pleasure. 4067
7: 5 to listen to the song of f. 4067
7: 6 so is the laughter of f. 4067
7: 9 for anger resides in the lap of f. 4067
9:17 to be heeded than the shouts of a ruler of f. 4067
10: 6 F are put in many high positions, 6120
Isa 19:11 The officials of Zoan are nothing but f; 211
19:13 The officials of Zoan *have* **become** f, 3282
35: 8 **wicked** f will not go about on it. 211
44:25 false prophets and **makes** f of diviners, 2147
Jer 4:22 "My people are f; they do not know me. 211
50:36 *They will* **become** f. 3282
Mt 23:17 *You* blind f! 3704
Ro 1:22 to be wise, *they became* f 3701
1Co 4:10 We are f for Christ, 3704
2Co 11:19 You gladly put up with f since you are 933

FOOT (86) [BAREFOOT, AFOOT, FEET, FLEET-FOOTED, FOOTHOLD, FOOTINGS, FOOTPRINTS, FOUR-FOOTED, UNDERFOOT]

Ge 41:44 will lift hand or f in all Egypt." 8079
Ex 12:37 about six hundred thousand men **on** f, 8081
19:12 not go up the mountain or touch the f *of* it. 7895
19:17 and they stood at the f *of* the mountain. 9397
21:24 tooth for tooth, hand for hand, f for foot, 8079
21:24 tooth for tooth, hand for hand, foot for f, 8079
24: 4 and built an altar **at the f of** the mountain 9393
32:19 breaking them to pieces **at the f of** 9393
Lev 8:23 and on the big toe of his right f. 8079
13:12 of the infected person from head to f, 8079
14:14 and on the big toe of his right f. 8079
14:17 and on the big toe of his right f, 8079
14:25 and on the big toe of his right f. 8079
14:28 and on the big toe of his right f. 8079
21:19 no man with a crippled f or hand, 8079
Nu 11:21 among six hundred thousand men **on** f, 8081
20:19 We only want to pass through on f— 8079
22:25 crushing Balaam's f against it. 8079
Dt 2: 5 not even enough to put your f on. 4090+8079
2:28 Only let us pass through on f— 8079
4:11 near and stood **at** the f of the mountain 9393
11:10 by f as in a vegetable garden. 8079
11:24 Every place where you set your f will 4090+8079
19:21 tooth for tooth, hand for hand, f for foot. 8079
19:21 tooth for tooth, hand for hand, foot for f. 8079
28:56 to touch the ground with the sole of her f— 8079
28:65 no resting place for the sole of your f. 8079
32:35 In due time their f will slip; 8079
Jos 1: 3 where you set your f, 4090+8079
3:13 set f in the Jordan, 4090+8079
18:16 down to the f *of* the hill facing the Valley 7895
Jdg 3:16 sword **about a f and a half** long, 1688
4:15 Sisera abandoned his chariot and fled on f. 8079
4:17 however, fled on f to the tent of Jael, 8079
1Sa 4:10 Israel lost thirty thousand **f soldiers.** 8081
15: 4 two hundred thousand **f soldiers** 8081
2Sa 8: 4 and twenty thousand **f soldiers.** 408+8081
10: 6 hired twenty thousand Aramean **f soldiers** 8081
10:18 and forty thousand of their **f soldiers.** 8081
14:25 to the sole of his f there was no blemish 8079
21:20 on each hand and six toes on each f— 8079
1Ki 14:12 When you set f in your city, 8079
20:29 on the Aramean **f soldiers** in one day. 8081
2Ki 13: 7 ten chariots and ten thousand **f soldiers,** 8081
1Ch 18: 4 and twenty thousand **f soldiers.** 408+8081
19:18 and forty thousand of their **f soldiers.** 408+8081
20: 6 on each hand and six toes on each f— NIH
Job 28: 4 in places forgotten by the f of man; 8079
28: 8 Proud beasts *do* **not set f on** it, 2005
31: 5 or my f has hurried after deceit— 8079
39:15 unmindful that a f may crush them, 8079
Ps 36:11 the f *of* the proud not come against me, 8079
38:16 over me when my f slips." 8079
66: 6 they passed through the waters on f— 8079
91:12 you will not strike your f against a stone. 8079
94:18 When I said, "My f is slipping," your love, 8079
121: 3 He will not let your f slip— 8079
Pr 1:15 do not set f on their paths; 8079
3:23 and your f will not stumble; 8079
3:26 be your confidence and will keep your f 8079
4:14 not **set** f on the path of the wicked or walk 995
4:27 keep your f from evil. 8079
25:17 Seldom set f in your neighbor's house— 8079
25:19 Like a bad tooth or a lame f is reliance on 8079
Ecc 10: 7 while princes go **on** f like slaves. 824+2021+6584
Isa 1: 6 From the sole of your f to the top 8079
Jer 12: 5 with men on f and they have worn you out, 8079
Eze 29:11 No f *of* man or animal will pass through it; 8079
32:13 be stirred by the f *of* man or muddied by 8079
Hab 3:13 you stripped him from head to f. 3572
Mt 4: 6 so that you will not strike your f against 4546
14:13 crowds followed him **on** f from the towns. 4270
18: 8 If your hand or your f causes you to sin, 4546
22:13 'Tie him hand and f, 4546
Mk 5: 4 For he had often been chained hand and f, 4267
6:33 and ran **on** f from all the towns 4270
9:45 And if your f causes you to sin, cut it off. 4546
Lk 4:11 so that you will not strike your f against 4546
8:29 though he was chained hand and f and kept 4267
Jn 20:12 one at the head and the other at the f. 4546
Ac 7: 5 not even **a f of ground.** 1037+4546
20:13 because he was going there **on** f. 4269
1Co 12:15 If the f should say, "Because I am not 4546
Heb 10:29 **trampled** the Son of God **under** f, 2922
Rev 10: 2 He planted his right f on the sea 4546
10: 2 on the sea and his left f on the land, NIG

FOOTHILLS (20) [HILL]

Dt 1: 7 in the mountains, in the **western** f, 9169
Jos 9: 1 those in the hill country, in the **western** f, 9169
10:40 the **western** f and the mountain slopes, 9169
11: 2 in the **western** f and in Naphoth Dor on 9169
11:16 the whole region of Goshen, the **western** f, 9169
11:16 and the mountains of Israel with their f, 9169
12: 8 the **western** f, the Arabah, 9169
15:33 In the **western** f: Eshtaol, Zorah, Ashnah, 9169
Jdg 1: 9 the Negev and the **western** f. 9169
1Ki 10:27 as plentiful as sycamore-fig trees in the f. 9169
1Ch 27:28 and sycamore-fig trees in the **western** f. 9169
2Ch 1:15 as plentiful as sycamore-fig trees in the f. 9169
9:27 as plentiful as sycamore-fig trees in the f. 9169
26:10 because he had much livestock in the f and 9169
28:18 the Philistines had raided towns in the f 9169
Jer 17:26 the territory of Benjamin and the **western** f, 9169
32:44 of the **western** f and of the Negev, 9169
33:13 of the **western** f and of the Negev, 9169
Ob 1:19 and people from the f will possess the land 9169
Zec 7: 7 Negev and the **western** f were settled?' " 9169

FOOTHOLD (3) [FOOT]

Ps 69: 2 where there is no f. 5097
73: 2 I had nearly lost my f. 892
Eph 4:27 and do not give the devil a f. 5536

FOOTINGS (1) [FOOT]

Job 38: 6 On what were its f set, 149

FOOTMEN (KJV) See MEN ON FOOT

FOOTPRINTS (2) [FOOT]

Ps 77:19 though your f were not seen. 6811
Hos 6: 8 *stained with* f of blood. 6814

FOOTSTEPS (5) [STEP]

1Ki 14: 6 So when Ahijah heard the sound of her f at 8079
2Ki 6:32 the sound of his master's f behind him?" 8079
Ps 119:133 Direct my f according to your word; 7193

Isa 26: 6 the feet of the oppressed, the f of the poor. 7193
Ro 4:12 but who also walk in the f of the faith 2717

FOOTSTOOL (13) [STOOL]

1Ch 28: 2 for the f of our God, 2071+8079
2Ch 9:18 and a f of gold was attached to it. 3900
Ps 99: 5 LORD our God and worship at his f; 2071+8079
110: 1 until I make your enemies a f 2071
132: 7 let us worship at his f— 2071+8079
Isa 66: 1 and the earth is my f. 2071+8079
La 2: 1 he has not remembered his f in the day of his anger. 2071+8079
Mt 5:35 or by the earth, for it is his f; 5711
Lk 20:43 until I make your enemies a f 5711
Ac 2:35 until I make your enemies a f 5711
7:49 and the earth is my f. 3836+4546+5711
Heb 1:13 until I make your enemies a f 5711
10:13 for his enemies to be made his f, 5711

FOR (7282) See Index of Articles Etc.

FORAGING (1)

Job 24: 5 the poor go about their labor of f food; 8838

FORBAD (KJV) See DETER, STOP

FORBEARANCE (1)

Ro 3:25 because in his f he had left the sins committed beforehand unpunished— 496

FORBID (7) [FORBIDDEN, FORBIDS]

Nu 30:11 but says nothing to her and does not f her, 5648
1Sa 24: 6 "The LORD f that I should do such 2721
26:11 But the LORD f that I should lay a hand 2721
1Ki 21: 3 "The LORD f that I should give you 2721
1Ch 11:19 "God f that I should do this!" 2721
1Co 14:39 and do not f speaking in tongues. 3266
1Ti 4: 3 They f people to marry and order them 3266

FORBIDDEN (15) [FORBID]

Lev 4: 2 and does what is f in any of 4202+6913
4:13 and does what is f in any of 4202+6913
4:22 and does what is f in any of 4202+6913
4:27 and does what is f in any of 4202+6913
5:17 a person sins and does what is f in any 4202+6913
19:23 regard its fruit as f. 6887+6889
19:23 For three years you are to consider it f; 6888
Nu 30: 5 because her father has f her. 5648
Dt 4:23 of anything the LORD your God has f. 7422
23: 2 one born of a f marriage 4927
1Ki 11:10 he had f Solomon to follow other gods 1194+7422
2Ki 17:15 the things the LORD had f them to do. NIH
Est 2:10 because Mordecai had f her to do so. 4202+7422
La 1:10 you had f to enter your assembly. 4202+7422
Zec 9: 7 the f food from between their teeth. 9199

FORBIDS (3) [FORBID]

Nu 30: 5 if her father f her when he hears about it, 5648
30: 8 if her husband f her when he hears about it, 5648
Jn 5:10 the law f you to carry your mat." 2003+4024

FORECAST (KJV) See PLOT

FORCE (37) [ENFORCE, FORCED, FORCEFUL, FORCEFULLY, FORCES, FORCIBLY, FORCING]

Ge 31:31 take your daughters away from me by f. 1608
47:26 still in f today— 6330
Ex 9:14 the full f of my plagues against you and 3972
19:21 not f their way through to see the LORD 2238
19:24 the people must not f their way through 2238
Jos 8:11 The entire f that was with him marched up 4878+6639
Jdg 7:13 the tent with such f that the tent overturned 5877[S]
8:10 with a f of about fifteen thousand men, all 4722
1Sa 2:16 if you don't, I'll take it by f." 2622
19: 8 He struck them with such f that they fled 4804
2Sa 5:17 they went up in full f to search for him, 3972
13:12 "Don't f me. Such a thing should not be 6700
1Ki 9:21 for his slave labor f, 4989
11:28 the whole labor f of the house of Joseph. 6023
2Ki 6:14 and chariots and a strong f there. 2657
24:16 also deported to Babylon the entire *f* AIT
1Ch 14: 8 they went up in full f to search for him, 3972
2Ch 8: 8 for his slave labor f, 4989
13: 3 Abijah went into battle with a f 2657
26:13 a powerful f to support the king 2657
32: 4 A large f of men assembled, 6639
Ezr 4:23 in Jerusalem and compelled them by f 10013
Est 8:11 to destroy, kill and annihilate any armed f 2657
Job 19:12 His troops advance in f; 3480
20:22 the full f of misery will come upon him. 3338
24: 4 f all the poor of the land into hiding. 2461
28:25 When he established the f of the wind 5486
Jer 46:22 as the enemy advances in f; 2657
Am 5:11 on the poor and f him to give you grain. 4374
Ob 1: 7 All your allies will f you to the border; 8938
Jn 6:15 to come and make him king by f, 773
Ac 5:26 They did not use f, 1040+3552
23:10 take him away from them by f 773

Ac 26:11 and I tried to f them to blaspheme. 337
27:14 Before very long, a wind of hurricane f, 5607
Gal 2:14 you f Gentiles to follow Jewish customs? 337
Heb 9:17 will is in f only when somebody has died; 1010

FORCED (24) [FORCE]

Ge 49:15 to the burden and submit to f labor. 4989
Ex 1:11 over them to oppress them with f labor, 6026
Dt 20:11 the people in it shall be subject to f labor 4989
Jos 16:10 of Ephraim but are required to do f labor. 4989
17:13 they subjected the Canaanites to f labor 4989
Jdg 1:28 they pressed the Canaanites into f labor 4989
1:30 but they did subject them to f labor. 4989
1:33 and Beth Anath became f laborers 4989
1:35 they too were pressed into f labor. 4989
2Sa 18: 3 if we are f to flee, 5674+5674
20:24 Adoniram was in charge of f labor; 4989
1Ki 4: 6 in charge of f labor. 4989
5:14 Adoniram was in charge of the f labor. 4989
9:15 of the f labor King Solomon conscripted 4989
12:18 who was in charge of f labor, 4989
2Ch 10:18 who was in charge of f labor, 4989
Job 30: 6 They were f to live in the dry stream beds, 4200
Ps 69: 4 I am f to restore what I did not steal. 8740
Isa 31: 8 be put to f labor. 4989
Jer 34:16 You have f them 3899
Mt 27:32 and they f him to carry the cross. 30
Mk 15:21 and they f him to carry the cross. 30
Phm 1:14 will be spontaneous and not f. 340+2848
Rev 13:16 He also f everyone, small and great, 4472

FORCEFUL (2) [FORCE]

Mt 11:12 and f men lay hold of it. 1043
2Co 10:10 some say, "His letters are weighty and f, 2708

FORCEFULLY (3) [FORCE]

1Sa 18:10 an evil spirit from God came f upon Saul. 7502
Isa 28: 2 he will throw it f to the ground. 928+3338
Mt 11:12 kingdom of heaven has been f advancing, 1041

FORCES (36) [FORCE]

Ge 14: 3 All these latter kings joined f in the Valley 2489
21:22 the commander of his f said to Abraham, 7372
21:32 and Phicol the commander of his f returned 7372
26:26 and Phicol the commander of his f. 7372
34:30 if they join f against me and attack me, 665
Jos 10: 5 Jarmuth, Lachish and Eglon—joined f. 665
10: 6 the hill country have joined f against us." 7695
11: 5 All these kings joined f 3585
Jdg 6:33 and other eastern peoples joined f 665+3481
12: 1 The men of Ephraim called out their f, NIH
1Sa 4: 2 The Philistines deployed their f 6885
14:17 "Muster the f and see who has left us." 7212
17: 1 Now the Philistines gathered their f for war 4722
23: 3 if we go to Keilah against the Philistine f!" 5120
23: 8 And Saul called up all his f for battle, 6639
23:26 As Saul and his f were closing in on David 408
28: 1 the Philistines gathered their f to fight 4722
29: 1 The Philistines gathered all their f 4722
30:23 and handed over to us the f that came 1522
1Ki 11:24 when David destroyed the f [of Zobah]; 4392[S]
15:20 the commanders of his f against the towns 2657
1Ch 20: 1 Joab led out the armed f. 2657+7372
2Ch 14:13 before the LORD and his f. 4722
16: 4 the commanders of his f against the towns 2657
32: 9 and all his f were laying siege to Lachish, 4939
Job 10:17 your f come against me wave upon wave. 7372
25: 3 Can his f be numbered? 1522
Ps 48: 4 When the kings joined f, 3585
55:11 Destructive f are at work in the city; 2095
Da 11: 7 He will attack the f of the king of 2657
11:15 The f of the South will be powerless 2432
11:31 "His armed f will rise up to desecrate 2432
Joel 2:11 his f are beyond number, 4722
Zec 9: 8 I will defend my house against marauding f. 7372
Mt 5:41 If someone f you to go one mile, 30
Eph 6:12 and against the spiritual f of evil in NIG

FORCIBLY (2) [FORCE]

Ge 40:15 For I was f carried off from the land 1704+1704
Dt 28:31 Your donkey will be f taken from you 1608

FORCING (2) [FORCE]

Lk 16:16 and everyone is f his way into it. 1041
Ac 7:19 and oppressed our forefathers by f them 4472

FORD (2) [FORDED, FORDS]

Ge 32:22 and his eleven sons and crossed the f of 5044
2Sa 19:18 the f to take the king's household over and 6302

FORDED (1) [FORD]

Jos 2:23 f the river and came to Joshua son of Nun 6296

FORDS (7) [FORD]

Jos 2: 7 on the road that leads to the f of the Jordan, 5045
Jdg 3:28 taking possession of the f of the Jordan 5045
12: 5 the f of the Jordan leading to Ephraim, 5045
12: 6 they seized him and killed him at the f of 5045
2Sa 15:28 at the f in the desert until word comes 6302
17:16 not spend the night at the f in the desert; 6302
Isa 16: 2 the women of Moab at the f of the Arnon. 5045

FOREFATHER (13) [FATHER]

Nu 26:58 (Kohath was the f of Amram; 3528
Jos 15:13 (Arba was the f of Anak.) 3
19:47 in Leshem and named it Dan after their f.) 3
21:11 (Arba was the f of Anak.) 3
Jdg 18:29 They named it Dan after their f Dan, 3
1Ki 15: 3 as the heart of David his f had been. 3
1Ch 24:19 for them by their f Aaron, 3
Jer 35: 6 because our f Jonadab son 3
35: 8 We have obeyed everything our f Jonadab 3
35:10 have fully obeyed everything our f Jonadab commanded us. 3
35:16 the command their f gave them, 3
35:18 the command of your f Jonadab 3
Ro 4: 1 Abraham, our f, discovered in this matter? 4635

FOREFATHER'S (1) [FATHER]

Jer 35:14 because they obey their f command. 3

FOREFATHERS (98) [FATHER]

Ex 10: 6 nor your f have ever seen from 3+3
13: 5 the land he swore to your f to give you, 3
13:11 as he promised on oath to you and your f, 3
Lev 25:41 to his own clan and to the property of his f. 3
Nu 11:12 the land you promised on oath to their f? 3
14:23 the land I promised on oath to their f. 3
20:15 Our f went down into Egypt, 3
36: 4 from the tribal inheritance of our f." 3
36: 7 the tribal land inherited from his f. 3
Dt 1:35 the good land I swore to give your f, 3
4:31 or forget the covenant with your f, 3
4:37 Because he loved your f 3
6:18 the LORD promised on oath to your f, 3
6:23 the land that he promised on oath to our f. 3
7: 8 to your f that he brought you out with 3
7:12 as he swore to your f. 3
7:13 that he swore to your f to give you. 3
8: 1 the LORD promised on oath to your f. 3
8:18 which he swore to your f, as it is today. 3
10:15 Yet the LORD set his affection on your f 3
10:22 Your f who went down into Egypt 3
11: 9 the LORD swore to your f to give to them 3
11:21 that the LORD swore to give your f, 3
13:17 as he promised on oath to your f, 3
19: 8 as he promised on oath to your f, 3
26: 3 the LORD swore to our f to give us." 3
26:15 as you promised on oath to our f, 3
28:11 in the land he swore to your f to give you. 3
31: 7 the LORD swore to their f to give them, 3
31:20 the land I promised on oath to their f, 3
Jos 1: 6 the land I swore to their f to give them. 3
21:43 the land he had sworn to give their f, 3
21:44 just as he had sworn to their f. 3
24: 2 'Long ago your f, 3
24:14 Throw away the gods your f worshiped 3
24:15 the gods your f served beyond the River, 3
Jdg 2: 1 into the land that I swore to give to your f. 3
2:20 down for their f and has not listened to me, 3
2:22 of the LORD and walk in it as their f did." 3
3: 4 which he had given their f through Moses. 3
1Sa 12: 6 and Aaron and brought your f up out 3
12: 8 who brought your f out of Egypt 3
1Ki 14:15 from this good land that he gave to their f 3
2Ki 19:12 that were destroyed by my f deliver them: 3
21: 8 from the land I gave their f, 3
21:15 from the day their f came out of Egypt 3
1Ch 29:15 as were all our f. 3
2Ch 33: 8 the land I assigned to your f, 3
Ezr 9: 7 From the days of our f until now, 3
Ne 9: 9 "You saw the suffering of our f in Egypt; 3
9:16 our f, became arrogant and stiff-necked, 3
9:36 slaves in the land you gave our f 3
13:18 Didn't your f do the same things, 3
Ps 78: 5 which he commanded our f 3
78: 8 They would not be like their f— 3
Pr 22:28 an ancient boundary stone set up by your f. 3
Isa 14:21 to slaughter his sons for the sins of their f; 3
37:12 by my f deliver them— 3
Jer 3:18 a northern land to the land I gave your f as 3
7: 7 in the land I gave your f for ever and ever 3
7:22 For when I brought your f out of Egypt 3
7:25 From the time your f left Egypt until now, 3
7:26 and did more evil than their f.' 3
11: 4 the terms I commanded your f 3
11: 5 I will fulfill the oath I swore to your f, 3
11: 7 the time I brought your f up from Egypt 3
11:10 They have returned to the sins of their f, 3+8037
11:10 the covenant I made with their f. 3
16:15 to the land I gave their f. 3
17:22 as I commanded your f. 3
30: 3 and restore them to the land I gave their f 3
31:32 not be like the covenant I made with their f 3
32:22 to give their f, 3
34:13 with your f when I brought them out 3
Eze 36:28 You will live in the land I gave your f; 3
47:14 with uplifted hand to give it to your f, 3
Da 11:24 nor his f did. 3+3
Joel 1: 2 in your days or in the days of your f? 3
Zec 1: 2 "The LORD was very angry with your f. 3
1: 4 Do not be like your f, 3
1: 5 Where are your f now? 3
1: 6 the prophets, overtake your f? 3
Mal 3: 7 the time of your f you have turned away 3
Mt 23:30 'If we had lived in the days of our f, 4252
23:32 then, the measure of the sin of your f! 4252

Lk 11:47 and it was your **f** who killed them. *4252*
11:48 that you approve of what your **f** did; *4252*
Jn 6:31 Our **f** ate the manna in the desert; *4252*
6:49 Your **f** ate the manna in the desert, *4252*
6:58 Your **f** ate manna and died, *4252*
Ac 7:19 and oppressed our **f** by forcing them *4252*
7:44 "Our **f** had the tabernacle of the Testimony *4252*
28:25 "The Holy Spirit spoke the truth to your **f** *4252*
1Co 10: 1 that our **f** were all under the cloud and *4252*
2Ti 1: 3 I thank God, whom I serve, as **my f** did, *4591*
Heb 1: 1 In the past God spoke *to* our **f** through *4252*
8: 9 not be like the covenant I made *with* their **f** *4252*
1Pe 1:18 **handed down** to you **from** your **f**, *4261*

FOREFINGER (2)

Lev 14:16 dip his right **f** into the oil in his palm, 720
14:27 and with his right **f** sprinkle some of the oil 720

FOREFRONT (KJV) See FRONT, INSIDE, OUTSIDE

FOREHEAD (17) [FOREHEADS]

Ex 13: 9 hand and a reminder **on** your **f** that 1068+6524
13:16 hand and a symbol **on** your **f** that 1068+6524
28:38 It will be on Aaron's **f**, 5195
28:38 on Aaron's **f** continually so that they will 5195
Lev 13:41 the front of his scalp and has a **bald f**, 1477
13:42 a reddish-white sore on his bald head or **f**, 1478
13:42 on his head or **f**. 1478
13:43 on his head or **f** is reddish-white like 1478
1Sa 17:49 and struck the Philistine on the **f**. 5195
17:49 The stone sank into his **f**, 5195
2Ch 26:19 leprosy broke out on his **f**. 5195
26:20 they saw that he had leprosy on his **f**, 5195
Isa 48: 4 of your neck were iron, your **f** was bronze. 5195
Eze 3: 9 I will make your **f** like the hardest stone, 5195
Rev 13:16 a mark on his right hand or on his **f**, *3587*
14: 9 and receives his mark on the **f** or on *3587*
17: 5 This title was written on her **f**: *3587*

FOREHEADS (10) [FOREHEAD]

Nu 24:17 He will crush the **f** *of* Moab, 6991
Dt 6: 8 your hands and bind them **on** your **f**. 1068+6524
11:18 your hands and bind them **on** your **f**. 1068+6524
Jer 48:45 it burns the **f** *of* Moab, 6991
Eze 9: 4 on the **f** *of* those who grieve and lament 5195
Rev 7: 3 a seal on the **f** of the servants of our God." *3587*
9: 4 not have the seal of God on their **f**. *3587*
14: 1 and his Father's name written on their **f**. *3587*
20: 4 and had not received his mark on their **f** *3587*
22: 4 and his name will be on their **f**. *3587*

FOREIGN (51) [FOREIGNER, FOREIGNERS, FOREIGNERS']

Ge 35: 2 "Get rid of the **f** gods you have with you, 5797
35: 4 So they gave Jacob all the **f** gods they had 5797
Ex 2:22 "I have become an alien in a **f** land." 5799
18: 3 "I have become an alien in a **f** land"; 5799
Dt 31:16 to the **f** gods of the land they are entering. 5797
32:12 no **f** god was with him. 5797
32:16 They made him jealous with their **f** gods 2424
Jos 24:20 you forsake the LORD and serve **f** gods, 5797
24:23 "throw away the **f** gods that are among you 5797
Jdg 10:16 of the **f** gods among them and served 5797
1Sa 7: 3 then rid yourselves of the **f** gods and 5797
1Ki 11: 1 Solomon, however, loved many **f** women besides Pharaoh's daughter— 5799
11: 8 He did the same for all his **f** wives, 5799
2Ki 19:24 I have dug wells in **f** *lands* and drunk 2424
2Ch 14: 3 the **f** altars and the high places, 5797
33:15 of the **f** gods and removed the image from 5797
Ezr 9: 7 and humiliation at the hand of **f** kings, 824
10: 2 by marrying **f** women from the peoples 5799
10:10 you have married **f** women, 5799
10:11 around you and from your **f** wives." 5799
10:14 a **f** woman come at a set time, 5799
10:17 the men who had married **f** women. 5799
10:18 the following had married **f** women: 5799
10:44 All these had married **f** women, 5799
Ne 13: 3 from Israel all who were **of f descent.** 6850
13:26 but even he was led into sin by **f** women. 5799
13:27 to our God by marrying **f** women?" 5799
13:30 the priests and the Levites of everything **f**, 5797
Ps 44:20 or spread out our hands to a **f** god, 2424
81: 9 You shall have no **f** god among you; 2424
114: 1 house of Jacob from a people of **f tongue,** 4357
137: 4 the songs of the LORD while in a **f** land? 5797
Isa 28:11 Very well then, with **f** lips 4353
37:25 I have dug wells in **f** lands and drunk NIH
43:12 I, and not *some* **f** god among you. 2424
Jer 2:25 I love **f** gods, and I must go after them.' 2424
3:13 you have scattered your favors to **f** gods 2424
5:19 and served **f** gods in your own land, 5797
8:19 with their worthless **f** idols?" 5797
19: 4 **made** this a place of **f** gods; 5796
25:20 and all the **f people** there; 6850
25:24 and all the kings of the **f people** who live 6850
Eze 31:12 the most ruthless of **f** nations cut it down 2424
Da 11:39 with the help of a **f** god 5797
Zep 1: 8 and all those clad in **f** clothes. 5799
Hag 2:22 and shatter the power of the **f** kingdoms. 1580
Mal 2:11 by marrying the daughter of a **f** god. 5797
Ac 17:18 "He seems to be advocating **f** gods." *3828*
Ac 26:11 I even went to **f** cities to persecute them. *2032*
Heb 11: 9 like a stranger in a **f** country; *NIG*
11:34 in battle and routed **f** armies. *259*

FOREIGNER (20) [FOREIGN]

Ge 17:12 or bought with money from a **f**— 1201+5797
17:27 in his household or bought from a **f**, 1201+5797
Ex 12:43 "No **f** is to eat of it. 1201+5797
Lev 22:25 such animals from the hand of a **f** 1201+5797
Dt 14:21 and he may eat it, or you may sell it to a **f**. 5799
15: 3 You may require payment from a **f**, 5799
17:15 Do not place a **f** over you, 5799
23:20 You may charge a **f** interest, 5799
Ru 2:10 that you notice me—a **f**?" 5799
2Sa 15:19 You are a **f**, an exile from your homeland. 5799
1Ki 8:41 "As for the **f** who does not belong 5799
8:43 and do whatever the **f** asks of you, 5799
2Ch 6:32 "As for the **f** who does not belong 5799
6:33 and do whatever the **f** asks of you, 5799
Isa 56: 3 Let no **f** who has bound himself 1201+2021+5797
Eze 44: 9 No **f** uncircumcised in heart and flesh 1201+5797
Lk 17:18 and give praise to God except this **f**?" *254*
Ac 7:29 where he **settled as** a **f** and had two sons. *4230*
1Co 14:11 I am a **f** to the speaker, *975*
14:11 and he is a **f** to me. *975*

FOREIGNERS (37) [FOREIGN]

Ge 31:15 Does he not regard us as **f**? 5799
Ex 21: 8 He has no right to sell her to **f**, 5799+6639
Dt 29:22 and **f** who come from distant lands will see 5799
2Sa 22:45 and **f** come cringing to me; 1201+5797
Ne 9: 2 Those of Israelite descent had separated themselves from all **f**. 1201+5797
Ps 18:44 **f** cringe before me. 1201+5797
144: 7 the mighty waters, from the hands of **f** 1201+5797
144:11 rescue me from the hands of **f** 1201+5797
Isa 1: 7 your fields are being stripped by **f** right 2424
25: 5 You silence the uproar of **f**; 2424
56: 6 **f** who bind themselves to the LORD to serve him, 1201+2021+5797
60:10 "**F** will rebuild your walls, 1201+5797
61: 5 **f** will work your fields and vineyards. 1201+5797
62: 8 never again will **f** drink the new wine 1201+5797
Jer 5:19 you will serve **f** in a land not your own.' 2424
30: 8 no longer will **f** enslave them. 2424
50:37 against her horses and chariots and all the **f** 6850
51: 2 I will send **f** to Babylon to winnow her and 2424
51:51 because **f** have entered the holy places of 2424
La 5: 2 our homes to **f**. 5799
Eze 7:21 as plunder to **f** and as loot to the wicked of 2424
11: 9 over to **f** and inflict punishment on you. 2424
28: 7 to bring **f** against you, the most ruthless 2424
28:10 of the uncircumcised at the hands of **f**. 2424
30:12 by the hand of **f** I will lay waste the land 2424
44: 7 you brought **f** uncircumcised in heart 1201+5797
44: 9 the **f** who live among the Israelites. 1201+5797
Hos 7: 9 **F** sap his strength, 2424
8: 7 **f** would swallow it up. 2424
Joel 3:17 never again will **f** invade her. 2424
Ob 1:11 and **f** entered his gates and cast lots 5799
Zec 9: 6 **F** will occupy Ashdod, 4927
Mt 27: 7 the potter's field as a burial place *for* **f**. *3828*
Ac 17:21 **f** who lived there spent their time doing nothing *3828*
1Co 14:21 the lips *of* **f** I will speak to this people, *2283*
Eph 2:12 excluded from citizenship in Israel and **f** to *3828*
2:19 you are no longer **f** and aliens, *3828*

FOREIGNERS' (1) [FOREIGN]

Isa 25: 2 the **f'** stronghold a city no more; 2424

FOREKNEW (2) [KNOW]

Ro 8:29 For those God **f** he also predestined to *4589*
11: 2 God did not reject his people, whom *he* **f**. *4589*

FOREKNOW (KJV) See FOREKNEW

FOREKNOWLEDGE (2) [KNOW]

Ac 2:23 over to you *by* God's set purpose and **f**; *4590*
1Pe 1: 2 who have been chosen according to the **f** *4590*

FOREMAN (3) [FOREMEN]

Ru 2: 5 Boaz asked the **f** of his harvesters, 5853+5893
2: 6 The **f** replied, "She is the Moabitess 5853+5893
Mt 20: 8 the owner of the vineyard said *to* his **f**, *2208*

FOREMEN (8) [FOREMAN]

Ex 5: 6 to the slave drivers and **f** in charge of 8853
5:10 and the **f** went out and said to the people, 8853
5:14 The Israelite **f** appointed by Pharaoh's 8853
5:15 Israelite **f** went and appealed to Pharaoh: 8853
5:19 The Israelite **f** realized they were in trouble 8853
1Ki 5:16 thirty-three hundred **f** who supervised 5893+8569
2Ch 2: 2 and thirty-six hundred as **f** over them. 5904
2:18 **f** over them to keep the people working. 5904

FOREMOST (2) [MOST]

Jer 31: 7 shout for the **f** *of* the nations. 8031
Am 6: 1 you notable men of the **f** nation, 8040

FOREORDAINED (KJV) See CHOSEN

FOREPART (KJV) See BOW, FRONT, INNER

FORERUNNER (KJV) See WENT BEFORE

FORESAIL (1) [SAIL]

Ac 27:40 the **f** to the wind and made for the beach. *784*

FORESAW (1) [FORESEE]

Gal 3: 8 The Scripture **f** that God would justify *4632*

FORESEE (1) [FORESAW, FORESIGHT]

Isa 47:11 catastrophe *you* cannot **f** will suddenly come 3359

FORESEETH (KJV) See SEES

FORESHIP (KJV) See BOW

FORESIGHT (1) [FORESEE]

Ac 24: 2 of peace under you, and your **f** has brought *4630*

FORESKIN (1) [FORESKINS]

Ex 4:25 Zipporah took a flint knife, cut off her son's **f** 6889

FORESKINS (3) [FORESKIN]

1Sa 18:25 for the bride than a hundred Philistine **f**, 6889
18:27 He brought their **f** and presented 6889
2Sa 3:14 for the price of a hundred Philistine **f**." 6889

FOREST (41) [FORESTED, FORESTS]

Dt 19: 5 a man may go into the **f** with his neighbor 3623
Jos 17:15 the **f** and clear land for yourselves there in 3623
1Sa 22: 5 So David left and went to the **f** *of* Hereth. 3623
2Sa 18: 6 the battle took place in the **f** *of* Ephraim. 3623
18: 8 and the **f** claimed more lives that day than 3623
18:17 a big pit in the **f** and piled up a large heap 3623
1Ki 7: 2 Palace of the **F** *of* Lebanon a hundred cubits 3623
10:17 The king put them in the Palace of the **F** 3623
10:21 Palace of the **F** *of* Lebanon were pure gold. 3623
1Ch 16:33 Then the trees of the **f** will sing, 3623
2Ch 9:16 The king put them in the Palace of the **F** 3623
9:20 Palace of the **F** *of* Lebanon were pure gold. 3623
Ne 2: 8 keeper of the king's **f**, 7236
Ps 50:10 for every animal of the **f** is mine, 3623
80:13 Boars from the **f** ravage it and the creatures 3623
83:14 the **f** or a flame sets the mountains ablaze, 3623
96:12 Then all the trees of the **f** will sing for joy; 3623
104:20 and all the beasts of the **f** prowl. 3623
SS 2: 3 among the trees of the **f** is my lover among 3623
Isa 7: 2 as the trees of the **f** are shaken by the wind. 3623
9:18 it sets the **f** thickets ablaze, 3623
10:34 He will cut down the **f** thickets with an ax; 3623
22: 8 to the weapons in the Palace of the **F**; 3623
29:17 and the fertile field seem like a **f**? 3623
32:15 and the fertile field seems like a **f**. 3623
32:19 the **f** and the city is leveled completely, 3623
44:14 He let it grow among the trees of the **f**, 3623
56: 9 come and devour, all you beasts of the **f**! 3623
Jer 5: 6 a lion from the **f** will attack them, 3623
10: 3 they cut a tree out of the **f**, 3623
12: 8 to me like a lion in the **f**. 3623
46:23 They will chop down her **f**," 3623
Eze 15: 2 of a branch on any of the trees in the **f**? 3623
15: 6 the vine among the trees of the **f** as fuel for 3623
20:46 the south and prophesy against the **f** *of* 3623
20:47 Say to the southern **f**: 3623
31: 3 beautiful branches overshadowing the **f**; 3091
Mic 5: 8 like a lion among the beasts of the **f**, 3623
7:14 which lives by itself in a **f**, 3623
Zec 11: 2 the dense **f** has been cut down! 3623
Jas 3: 5 Consider what a great **f** is set on fire by *5627*

FORESTED (1) [FOREST]

Jos 17:18 but the **f** hill country as well. 3623

FORESTS (9) [FOREST]

2Ki 19:23 the **finest of** its **f**. 3623+4149
Ps 29: 9 the oaks and strips the **f** bare. 3623
Isa 10:18 The splendor of his **f** 3623
10:19 the remaining trees of his **f** will be so few 3623
37:24 the **finest of** its **f**. 3623+4149
44:23 you mountains, you **f** and all your trees, 3623
Jer 21:14 in your **f** that will consume everything 3623
Eze 34:25 in the desert and sleep in the **f** in safety. 3623
39:10 from the fields or cut it from the **f**, 3623

FORETELL (2) [FORETELLS, FORETOLD]

Isa 44: 7 yes, *let him* **f** what will come. 5583
44: 8 Did I not proclaim this and **f** it long ago? 5583

FORETELLS (1) [FORETELL]

Dt 13: 1 If a prophet, or *one who* **f by dreams**, 2706+2731

FORETOLD (12) [FORETELL]

2Ki 7:17 the man of God *had* **f** when the king came 1819
23:16 by the man of God who **f** these things. 7924
Ps 105:19 till **what** he **f** came to pass, 1821
Isa 41:26 No one told of this, no *one* **f** it, 9048
43: 9 Which of them **f** this and proclaimed to us 5583
45:21 Who **f** this long ago, 9048
48: 3 *I* **f** the former things long ago, 5583
48:14 Which of [the idols] *has* **f** these things? 5583
52: 6 that day they will know that it is I who **f** it. 1819
Ac 3:18 how God fulfilled what *he had* **f** through all *4615*
3:24 as many as have spoken, *have* **f** these days. *2859*
Jude 1:17 the apostles of our Lord Jesus Christ **f**. *4625*

FOREVER (290) [EVER]

Ge 3:22 the tree of life and eat, and live **f**." 4200+6409
6: 3 My Spirit will not contend with man **f**, 4200+6409
13:15 to you and your offspring **f**. 6330+6409
Ex 3:15 This is my name **f**, 4200+6409
31:17 a sign between me and the Israelites **f**, 4200+6409
32:13 and it will be their inheritance **f**.' " 4200+6409
Dt 5:29 with them and their children **f**! 4200+6409
13:16 It is to remain a ruin **f**, never to be rebuilt. 6409
28:46 wonder to you and your descendants **f**. 6330+6409
29:29 to us and to our children **f**, 6330+6409
32:40 As surely as I live **f**, 4200+6409
Jos 4: 7 a memorial to the people of Israel **f**." 6330+6409
14: 9 and that of your children **f**, 6330+6409
1Sa 2:30 and your father's house would minister before me **f**.' 6330+6409
3:13 that I would judge his family **f** because 6330+6409
20:23 the LORD is witness between you and me **f**." 6330+6409
20:42 descendants and my descendants **f**.' " 6330+6409
27:12 the Israelites, that he will be my servant **f**." 6409
2Sa 2:26 "Must the sword devour **f**? 4200+5905
3:28 "I and my kingdom are **f** innocent 6330+6409
7:13 I will establish the throne of his kingdom **f**. 6330+6409
7:16 your kingdom will endure **f** before me; 6330+6409
7:16 your throne will be established **f**.' " 6330+6409
7:24 as your very own **f**, 6330+6409
7:25 keep **f** the promise you have made 6330+6409
7:26 so that your name will be great **f**. 6330+6409
7:29 that it may continue **f** in your sight; 4200+6409
7:29 house of your servant will be blessed **f** 4200+6409
22:51 to David and his descendants **f**." 6330+6409
1Ki 1:31 "May my lord King David live **f**!" 4200+6409
2:33 blood rest on the head of Joab and his descendants **f**. 4200+6409
2:33 may there be the LORD's peace **f**." 6330+6409
2:45 before the LORD **f**." 6330+6409
8:13 a place for you to dwell **f**." 6409
9: 3 by putting my Name there **f**. 6330+6409
9: 5 I will establish your royal throne over Israel **f**, 4200+6409
11:39 because of this, but not **f**.' " 2021+3427+3972
2Ki 5:27 to you and to your descendants **f**." 4200+6409
8:19 a lamp for David and his descendants **f**. 2021+3427+3972
21: 7 I will put my Name **f**. 4200+6409
1Ch 15: 2 and to minister before him **f**." 6330+6409
16:15 He remembers his covenant **f**, 4200+6409
16:34 his love endures **f**. 4200+6409
16:41 "for his love endures **f**." 4200+6409
17:12 and I will establish his throne **f**. 6330+6409
17:14 my house and my kingdom **f**; 2021+6330+6409
17:14 his throne will be established **f**.' " 6330+6409
17:22 You made your people Israel your very own **f**, 6330+6409
17:23 and his house be established **f**. 6330+6409
17:24 and that your name will be great **f**. 6330+6409
17:27 that it may continue **f** in your sight; 4200+6409
17:27 blessed it, and it will be blessed **f**." 4200+6409
22:10 throne of his kingdom over Israel **f**.' 6330+6409
23:13 he and his descendants **f**, 6330+6409
23:13 to pronounce blessings in his name **f**. 6330+6409
23:25 come to dwell in Jerusalem **f**, 4200+6330+6409
28: 4 to be king over Israel **f**. 4200+6409
28: 7 I will establish his kingdom **f** 4200+6330+6409
28: 8 an inheritance to your descendants **f**. 6330+6409
28: 9 if you forsake him, he will reject you **f** 4200+6329
29:18 in the hearts of your people **f**, 4200+6409
2Ch 5:13 his love endures **f**." 4200+6409
6: 2 a place for you to dwell **f**." 6409
7: 3 his love endures **f**." 4200+6409
7: 6 saying, "His love endures **f**." 4200+6409
7:16 so that my Name may be there **f**. 6330+6409
9: 8 Israel and his desire to uphold them **f**, 4200+6409
13: 5 Israel to David and his descendants **f** 4200+6409
20: 7 give it **f** to the descendants of Abraham your friend? 4200+6409
20:21 for his love endures **f**." 4200+6409
21: 7 a lamp for him and his descendants **f**. 2021+3427+3972
30: 8 which he has consecrated **f**. 4200+6409
33: 4 My Name will remain in Jerusalem **f**. 4200+6409
33: 7 I will put my Name **f**. 4200+6409
Ezr 3:11 his love to Israel endures **f**." 4200+6409
Ne 2: 3 "May the king live **f**! 4200+6409
Job 4:20 unnoticed, they perish **f**. 4200+5905
7:16 I despise my life; I would not live **f**. 4200+6409
19:24 or engraved in rock **f**! 4200+6329
20: 7 he will perish **f**, like his own dung; 4200+5905
23: 7 I would be delivered **f** from my judge. 4200+5905
Job 36: 7 with kings and exalts them **f**. 4200+5905
Ps 9: 7 The LORD reigns **f**; 4200+6409
12: 7 and protect us from such people **f**. 4200+6409
13: 1 Will you forget me **f**? 5905
18:50 to David and his descendants **f**. 6330+6409
19: 9 The fear of the LORD is pure, enduring **f**. 4200+6329
22:26 may your hearts live **f**! 4200+6329
23: 6 I will dwell in the house of the LORD **f**. 802+3427+4200
28: 9 their shepherd and carry them **f**. 2021+6330+6409
29:10 the LORD is enthroned as King **f**. 4200+6409
30:12 I will give you thanks **f**. 4200+6409
33:11 But the plans of the LORD stand firm **f**, 4200+6409
37:18 and their inheritance will endure **f**. 4200+6409
37:27 then you will dwell in the land **f**. 4200+6409
37:28 They will be protected **f**, 4200+6409
37:29 the land and dwell in it **f**. 4200+6329
41:12 and set me in your presence **f**. 4200+6409
44: 8 and we will praise your name **f**. 4200+6409
44:23 Do not reject us **f**. 4200+5905
45: 2 since God has blessed you **f**. 4200+6409
48: 8 God makes her secure **f**. 6330+6409
49: 9 he should live on **f** and not see decay. 4200+5905
49:11 Their tombs will remain their houses **f**, 4200+6409
52: 9 I will praise you **f** for what you have done; 4200+6409
55:19 God, who is enthroned **f**, 7710
61: 4 in your tent **f** and take refuge in the shelter 6409
61: 7 May he be enthroned in God's presence **f**; 6409
66: 7 He rules **f** by his power, 6409
68:16 where the LORD himself will dwell **f**? 4200+5905
69:23 and their backs be bent **f**. 9458
72:17 May his name endure **f**; 4200+6409
72:19 Praise be to his glorious name **f**; 4200+6409
73:26 strength of my heart and my portion **f**. 4200+6409
74: 1 Why have you rejected us **f**, O God? 4200+5905
74:10 Will the foe revile your name **f**? 4200+5905
74:19 the lives of your afflicted people **f**. 4200+5905
75: 9 As for me, I will declare this **f**; 4200+6409
77: 7 "Will the Lord reject **f**? 4200+6409
77: 8 Has his unfailing love vanished **f**? 4200+5905
78:69 like the earth that he established **f**. 4200+6409
79: 5 Will you be angry **f**? 4200+5905
79:13 will praise you **f**; 4200+6409
81:15 and their punishment would last **f**. 4200+6409
85: 5 Will you be angry with us **f**? 4200+6409
86:12 I will glorify your name **f**. 4200+6409
89: 1 I will sing of the LORD's great love **f**; 6409
89: 2 I will declare that your love stands firm **f**, 6409
89: 4 'I will establish your line **f** 6330+6409
89:28 I will maintain my love to him **f**, 4200+6409
89:29 I will establish his line **f**, 4200+6329
89:36 that his line will continue **f** 4200+6409
89:37 it will be established **f** like the moon, 6409
89:46 Will you hide yourself **f**? 4200+5905
89:52 Praise be to the LORD **f**! 4200+6409
92: 7 they will be **f** destroyed. 6329+6330
92: 8 But you, O LORD, are exalted **f**. 4200+6409
100: 5 LORD is good and his love endures **f**; 4200+6409
102:12 But you, O LORD, sit enthroned **f**; 4200+6409
103: 9 nor will he harbor his anger **f**; 4200+6409
104:31 May the glory of the LORD endure **f**; 4200+6409
105: 8 He remembers his covenant **f**, 4200+6409
106: 1 his love endures **f**. 4200+6409
107: 1 his love endures **f**. 4200+6409
109:19 like a belt tied **f** around him. 9458
110: 4 "You are a priest **f**, 4200+6409
111: 3 and his righteousness endures **f**. 4200+6329
111: 5 he remembers his covenant **f**. 4200+6409
111: 9 he ordained his covenant **f**— 4200+6409
112: 3 and his righteousness endures **f**. 4200+6329
112: 6 a righteous man will be remembered **f**. 6409
112: 9 his righteousness endures **f**; 4200+6329
117: 2 the faithfulness of the LORD endures **f**. 4200+6409
118: 1 his love endures **f**. 4200+6409
118: 2 Let Israel say: "His love endures **f**." 4200+6409
118: 3 "His love endures **f**." 4200+6409
118: 4 "His love endures **f**." 4200+6409
118:29 his love endures **f**. 4200+6409
119:111 Your statutes are my heritage **f**; 4200+6409
119:144 Your statutes are **f** right; 4200+6409
119:152 that you established them to last **f**. 4200+6409
125: 1 which cannot be shaken but endures **f**. 4200+6409
135:13 Your name, O LORD, endures **f**, 4200+6409
136: 1 His love endures **f**. 4200+6409
136: 2 His love endures **f**. 4200+6409
136: 3 His love endures **f**. 4200+6409
136: 4 His love endures **f**. 4200+6409
136: 5 His love endures **f**. 4200+6409
136: 6 His love endures **f**. 4200+6409
136: 7 His love endures **f**. 4200+6409
136: 8 His love endures **f**. 4200+6409
136: 9 His love endures **f**. 4200+6409
136:10 His love endures **f**. 4200+6409
136:11 His love endures **f**. 4200+6409
136:12 His love endures **f**. 4200+6409
136:13 His love endures **f**. 4200+6409
136:14 His love endures **f**. 4200+6409
136:15 His love endures **f**. 4200+6409
136:16 His love endures **f**. 4200+6409
136:17 His love endures **f**. 4200+6409
136:18 His love endures **f**. 4200+6409
136:19 His love endures **f**. 4200+6409
136:20 His love endures **f**. 4200+6409
136:21 His love endures **f**. 4200+6409
136:22 His love endures **f**. 4200+6409
Ps 136:23 His love endures **f**. 4200+6409
136:24 His love endures **f**. 4200+6409
136:25 His love endures **f**. 4200+6409
136:26 His love endures **f**. 4200+6409
138: 8 your love, O LORD, endures **f**— 4200+6409
146: 6 the LORD, who remains faithful **f**. 4200+6409
146:10 The LORD reigns **f**, your God, O Zion, 4200+6409
Pr 6:21 Bind them upon your heart **f**; 9458
10:25 but the righteous stand firm **f**. 6409
12:19 Truthful lips endure **f**, 4200+6329
21:28 listens to him will be destroyed **f**. 4200+5905
27:24 for riches do not endure **f**, 4200+6409
Ecc 1: 4 but the earth remains **f**. 4200+6409
3:14 everything God does will endure **f**; 4200+6409
Isa 9: 7 and righteousness from that time on and **f**. 6330+6409
25: 8 he will swallow up death **f**. 4200+5905
26: 4 Trust in the LORD **f**, for the LORD, 6329+6330
28:28 so one does not go on threshing it **f**. 4200+5905
32:14 watchtower will become a wasteland **f**, 6330+6409
32:17 be quietness and confidence **f**. 6330+6409
34:10 its smoke will rise **f**. 4200+6409
34:17 They will possess it **f** and dwell there 6330+6409
40: 8 but the word of our God stands **f**." 4200+6409
47: 7 You said, 'I will continue **f**— 4200+6409
51: 6 But my salvation will last **f**, 4200+6409
51: 8 But my righteousness will last **f**, 4200+6409
57:15 he who lives **f**, whose name is holy: 6329
57:16 I will not accuse **f**, 4200+6409
59:21 from this time on and **f**," 6330+6409
60:21 and they will possess the land **f**. 4200+6409
64: 9 do not remember our sins **f**. 4200+6329
65:18 and rejoice **f** in what I will create, 6329+6330
Jer 3: 5 Will your wrath continue **f**?' 4200+5905
3:12 the LORD, 'I will not be angry **f**. 4200+6409
17: 4 and it will burn **f**." 6330+6409
17:25 and this city will be inhabited **f**. 4200+6409
20:17 her womb enlarged **f**. 6409
25:12 "and will make it desolate **f**. 6409
33:11 his love endures **f**." 4200+6409
49:13 and all its towns will be in ruins **f**." 6409
49:33 a desolate place **f**. 6330+6409
51:26 for you will be desolate **f**," 6409
51:39 then sleep **f** and not awake," 6409
51:57 they will sleep **f** and not awake," 6409
51:62 it will be desolate **f**.' 6409
La 3:31 For men are not cast off by the Lord **f**. 4200+6409
5:19 You, O LORD, reign **f**; 4200+6409
Eze 35: 9 I will make you desolate **f**; 6409
37:25 children's children will live there **f**, 6330+6409
37:25 David my servant will be their prince **f** 4200+6409
37:26 I will put my sanctuary among them **f**. 4200+6409
37:28 when my sanctuary is among them **f**.' 4200+6409
43: 7 I will live among the Israelites **f**. 4200+6409
43: 9 and I will live among them **f**. 4200+6409
Da 2: 4 the king in Aramaic, "O king, live **f**! 10378+10550
2:44 but it will itself endure **f**. 10002+10378+10550
3: 9 Nebuchadnezzar, "O king, live **f**! 10378+10550
4:34 I honored and glorified him who lives **f**. 10002+10550
5:10 "O king, live **f**!" 10378+10550
6: 6 "O King Darius, live **f**! 10378+10550
6:21 Daniel answered, "O king, live **f**! 10378+10550
6:26 "For he is the living God and he endures **f**; 10378+10550
7:18 the kingdom and will possess it **f**— 10002+10527+10550
7:26 be taken away and completely destroyed **f**. 10002+10509+10527
12: 7 and I heard him swear by him who lives **f**, 6409
Hos 2:19 I will betroth you to me **f**; 4200+6409
Joel 3:20 Judah will be inhabited **f** and 4200+6409
Ob 1:10 you will be destroyed **f**. 4200+6409
Jnh 2: 6 the earth beneath barred me in **f**. 4200+6409
Mic 2: 9 from their children **f**. 4200+6409
4: 7 in Mount Zion from that day and **f**. 6330+6409
7:18 You do not stay angry **f** but delight to show mercy. 4200+6329
Zep 2: 9 weeds and salt pits, a wasteland **f**. 6330+6409
Zec 1: 5 And the prophets, do they live **f**? 4200+6409
Lk 1:33 he will reign over the house of Jacob **f**; *172+1650+3836*
1:55 Abraham and his descendants **f**, *172+1650+3836*
Jn 6:51 If anyone eats of this bread, he will live **f**. *172+1650+3836*
6:58 but he who feeds on this bread will live **f**." *172+1650+3836*
8:35 but a son belongs to it **f**. *172+1650+3836*
12:34 that the Christ will remain **f**, *172+1650+3836*
14:16 to be with you **f**— *172+1650+3836*
Ro 1:25 who is **f** praised. *172+1650+3836*
9: 5 who is God over all, **f** praised! *172+1650+3836*
11:10 and their backs be bent **f**." *1328+4246*
11:36 To him be the glory **f**! *172+1650+3836*
16:27 be glory **f** through Jesus Christ! *172+1650+3836*
1Co 9:25 we do it to get a crown that will **last f**. *915*
2Co 9: 9 his righteousness endures **f**." *172+1650+3836*
11:31 who is to be praised **f**, *172+1650+3836*
1Th 4:17 And so we will be with the Lord **f**. *4121*
1Ti 6:16 To him be honor and might **f**. *173*
Heb 5: 6 "You are a priest **f**, *172+1650+3836*
6:20 He has become a high priest **f**, *172+1650+3836*
7: 3 like the Son of God he remains a priest **f**. *1457+1650+3836*
7:17 it is declared: "You are a priest **f**, *172+1650+3836*
7:21 'You are a priest **f**.' " *172+1650+3836*
7:24 but because Jesus lives **f**, *172+1650+3836*

Heb 7:28 who has been made perfect f. 172+1650+3836
10:14 by one sacrifice he has made perfect f those who are being made holy. 1457+1650+3836
13: 8 Jesus Christ is the same yesterday and today and f. 172+1650+3836
1Pe 1:25 but the word of the Lord stands f. 172+1650+3836
2Pe 3:18 To him be glory both now and f! 172+1650+2465
1Jn 2:17 the man who does the will of God lives f. 172+1650+3836
2Jn 1: 2 the truth, which lives in us and will be with us f: 172+1650+3836
Jude 1:13 for whom blackest darkness has been reserved f. 172+1650

FOREVERMORE (7) [EVER]

Ps 113: 2 the LORD be praised, both now and f. 6330+6409
115:18 extol the LORD, both now and f. 6330+6409
121: 8 coming and going both now and f. 6330+6409
125: 2 surrounds his people both now and f. 6330+6409
131: 3 in the LORD both now and f. 6330+6409
133: 3 For there the LORD bestows his blessing, even life f. 2021+6330+6409
Jude 1:25 before all ages, now and f! 172+1650+3836+4246

FOREWARN (KJV) See SHOW

FORFEIT (4) [FORFEITING, FORFEITS]

Ezr 10: 8 within three days would f all his property, 3049
Jnh 2: 8 to worthless idols f the grace that could 6440
Mk 8:36 gain the whole world, yet f his soul? 2423
Lk 9:25 and yet lose or f his very self? 2423

FORFEITING (1) [FORFEIT]

Hab 2:10 shaming your own house and f your life. 2627

FORFEITS (2) [FORFEIT]

Pr 20: 2 he who angers him f his life. 2627
Mt 16:26 gains the whole world, yet f his soul? 2423

FORGAT (KJV) See FORGOT

FORGAVE (7) [FORGIVE]

Ps 32: 5 and you f the guilt of my sin. 5951
65: 3 you f our transgressions. 4105
78:38 he f their iniquities and did 4105
85: 2 You f the iniquity of your people 5951
Eph 4:32 just as in Christ God f you. 5919
Col 2:13 He f us all our sins, 5919
3:13 Forgive as the Lord f you. 5919

FORGED (2) [FORGES]

Ge 4:22 who f all kinds of tools out of bronze 4323
Isa 54:17 no weapon f against you will prevail, 3670

FORGES (2) [FORGED]

Isa 44:12 he f it with the might of his arm. 7188
54:16 into flame and f a weapon fit for its work. 3655

FORGET (58) [FORGETS, FORGETTING, FORGOT, FORGOTTEN]

Ge 41:51 because God has made me f all my trouble 5960
Dt 4: 9 not f the things your eyes have seen 8894
4:23 to f the covenant of the LORD your God 8894
4:31 or f the covenant with your forefathers, 8894
6:12 be careful that you do not f the LORD, 8894
8:11 that you do not f the LORD your God, 8894
8:14 and you will f the LORD your God, 8894
8:19 If you ever f the LORD your God 8894+8894
9: 7 and never f how you provoked 8894
25:19 Do not f! 8894
1Sa 1:11 and not f your servant but give her a son, 8894
2Ki 17:38 not f the covenant I have made with you, 8894
Job 8:13 Such is the destiny of all who f God; 8894
9:27 If I say, 'I will f my complaint, 8894
11:16 You will surely f your trouble, 8894
Ps 9:17 all the nations that f God. 8895
10:12 Do not f the helpless. 8894
13: 1 Will you f me forever? 8894
44:24 and f our misery and oppression? 8894
45:10 F your people and your father's house. 8894
50:22 "Consider this, you who f God, 8894
59:11 O Lord our shield, or my people will f. 8894
74:19 do not f the lives 8894
78: 7 in God and would not f his deeds 8894
102: 4 I f to eat my food. 8894
103: 2 O my soul, and f not all his benefits— 8894
119:61 I will not f your law. 8894
119:83 I do not f your decrees. 8894
119:93 I will never f your precepts, 8894
119:109 I will not f your law. 8894
119:141 I do not f your precepts. 8894
137: 5 If I f you, O Jerusalem, 8894
137: 5 may my right hand f [its skill]. 8894
Pr 3: 1 My son, do not f my teaching, 8894
4: 5 do not f my words or swerve from them. 8894
31: 5 lest they drink and f what the law decrees, 8894
31: 7 let them drink and f their poverty 8894
Isa 43:18 "F the former things; 440+2349
44:21 O Israel, I will not f you. 5960
49:15 "Can a mother f the baby at her breast 8894
49:15 Though she may f, I will not forget you! 8894
49:15 Though she may forget, I will not f you! 8894
51:13 that you f the LORD your Maker, 8894
54: 4 You will f the shame of your youth 8894
65:11 the LORD and f my holy mountain, 8895
Jer 2:32 Does a maiden f her jewelry, 8894
23:27 dreams they tell one another will make my people f my name, 8894
23:39 I will surely f you and cast you out 5960+5960
La 2: 6 LORD has made Zion f her appointed feasts 8894
5:20 Why do you always f us? 8894
Eze 39:26 They will f their shame and all 5960
Am 8: 7 "I will never f anything they have done. 8894
Mic 6:10 Am I still to f, O wicked house, 5960
Heb 6:10 he will not f your work and 2140
13: 2 Do not f to entertain strangers, 2140
13:16 not f to do good and to share with others, 2140
2Pe 3: 5 But they deliberately f that long ago 3291
3: 8 But do not f this one thing, dear friends: 3291

FORGETS (4) [FORGET]

Ge 27:45 with you and f what you did to him, 8894
Job 24:20 womb f them, the worm feasts on them; 8894
Jn 16:21 her baby is born she f the anguish 3648+4033
Jas 1:24 and immediately f what he looks like. 2140

FORGETTING (2) [FORGET]

Php 3:13 F what is behind and straining 2140
Jas 1:25 not f what he has heard, but doing it— 2144

FORGIVE (74) [FORGAVE, FORGIVEN, FORGIVENESS, FORGIVES, FORGIVING]

Ge 50:17 I ask you to f your brothers the sins and 5951
50:17 Now please f the sins of the servants of 5951
Ex 10:17 Now f my sin once more and pray to 5951
23:21 he will not f your rebellion, 5951
32:32 But now, please f their sin— 5951
34: 9 f our wickedness and our sin, 6142
Nu 14:19 f the sin of these people, 6142
Dt 29:20 The LORD will never be willing to f him; 6142
Jos 24:19 He will not f your rebellion and your sins. 5951
1Sa 15:25 f my sin and come back with me, 5951
25:28 Please f your servant's offense, 5951
1Ki 8:30 your dwelling place, and when you hear, f. 6142
8:34 then hear from heaven and f the sin 6142
8:36 from heaven and f the sin of your servants, 6142
8:39 your dwelling place. F and act; 6142
8:50 And f your people, who have sinned 6142
8:50 f all the offenses they have committed NIH
2Ki 5:18 But may the LORD f your servant 6142
5:18 may the LORD f your servant for this." 6142
24: 4 and the LORD was not willing to f. 6142
2Ch 6:21 and when you hear, f. 6142
6:25 then hear from heaven and f the sin 6142
6:27 from heaven and f the sin of your servants, 6142
6:30 F, and deal with each man according 6142
6:39 And f your people, 6142
7:14 from heaven and will f their sin 6142
Job 7:21 not pardon my offenses and f my sins? 6296
Ps 19:12 F my hidden faults. 5927
25:11 O LORD, f my iniquity, though it is great. 6142
79: 9 and f our sins for your name's sake. 4105
Isa 2: 9 do not f them. 5951
Jer 5: 1 I will f this city. 6142
5: 7 "Why should I f you? 6142
18:23 Do not f their crimes or blot out their sins 4105
31:34 "For I will f their wickedness 6142
33: 8 and will f all their sins of rebellion 6142
36: 3 I will f their wickedness and their sin." 6142
50:20 for I will f the remnant I spare. 6142
Da 9:19 O Lord, listen! O Lord, f! 6142
Hos 1: 6 that I should at all f them. 5951+5951
14: 2 "F all our sins and receive us graciously, 5951
Am 7: 2 I cried out, "Sovereign LORD, f! 6142
Mt 6:12 F us our debts, as we also have forgiven 918
6:14 if you f men when they sin against you, 918
6:14 your heavenly Father will also f you. 918
6:15 But if you do not f men their sins, 918
6:15 your Father will not f your sins. 918
9: 6 Son of Man has authority on earth to f sins 918
18:21 how many times shall I f my brother 918
18:35 of you unless you f your brother 918
Mk 2: 7 Who can f sins but God alone?" 918
2:10 Son of Man has authority on earth to f sins 918
11:25 if you hold anything against anyone, f him, 918
11:25 your Father in heaven may f you your sins." 918
Lk 5:21 Who can f sins but God alone?" 918
5:24 Son of Man has authority on earth to f sins 918
6:37 F, and you will be forgiven. 668
11: 4 F us our sins, for we also forgive 918
11: 4 for we also f everyone who sins against us. 918
17: 3 rebuke him, and if he repents, f him. 918
17: 4 to you and says, 'I repent,' f him." 918
23:34 Jesus said, "Father, f them, 918
Jn 20:23 If you f anyone his sins, they are forgiven; 918
20:23 if you do not f them, 3195
Ac 8:22 Perhaps he will f you for having such 918
2Co 2: 7 instead, you ought to f and comfort him, 5919
2:10 If you f anyone, I also forgive him. 5919
2:10 If you forgive anyone, I also f him. NIG
2:10 if there was anything to f— 5919
12:13 F me this wrong! 5919
Col 3:13 and f whatever grievances you may have 5919
3:13 F as the Lord forgave you. NIG
Heb 8:12 For I will f their wickedness 1639+2664
1Jn 1: 9 and will f us our sins and purify us 918

FORGIVEN (45) [FORGIVE]

Lev 4:20 and they will be f. 6142
4:26 and he will be f. 6142
4:31 and he will be f. 6142
4:35 and he will be f. 6142
5:10 and he will be f. 6142
5:13 and he will be f. 6142
5:16 and he will be f. 6142
5:18 and he will be f. 6142
6: 7 and he will be f for any 6142
19:22 and his sin will be f. 6142
Nu 14:20 The LORD replied, "I have f them, 6142
15:25 and they will be f, 6142
15:26 the aliens living among them will be f, 6142
15:28 he will be f. 6142
Ps 32: 1 Blessed is he whose transgressions are f, 5951
Isa 33:24 the sins of those who dwell there will be f. 5951
La 3:42 and rebelled and you have not f. 6142
Mt 6:12 as we also have f our debtors. 918
9: 2 "Take heart, son; your sins are f." 918
9: 5 Which is easier: to say, 'Your sins are f,' 918
12:31 every sin and blasphemy will be f men, 918
12:31 blasphemy against the Spirit will not be f. 918
12:32 a word against the Son of Man will be f, 918
12:32 against the Holy Spirit will not be f, 918
Mk 2: 5 "Son, your sins are f." 918
2: 9 to say to the paralytic, 'Your sins are f,' 918
3:28 and blasphemies of men will be f them. 918
3:29 against the Holy Spirit will never be f; 912+2400
4:12 otherwise they might turn and be f!' " 918
Lk 5:20 he said, "Friend, your sins are f." 918
5:23 Which is easier: to say, 'Your sins are f,' 918
6:37 Forgive, and you will be f. 668
7:47 I tell you, her many sins have been f— 918
7:47 But he who has been f little loves little." 918
7:48 Then Jesus said to her, "Your sins are f." 918
12:10 a word against the Son of Man will be f, 918
12:10 against the Holy Spirit will not be f. 918
Jn 20:23 If you forgive anyone his sins, they are f; 918
20:23 if you do not forgive them, they are not f." 3195
Ro 4: 7 Blessed are they whose transgressions are f, 918
2Co 2:10 And what I have f— 5919
2:10 I have f in the sight of Christ for your sake, NIG
Heb 10:18 And where these have been f, 912
Jas 5:15 If he has sinned, he will be f. 918
1Jn 2:12 because your sins have been f on account 918

FORGIVENESS (14) [FORGIVE]

Ps 130: 4 But with you there is f; 6145
Mt 26:28 which is poured out for many for the f 912
Mk 1: 4 a baptism of repentance for the f of sins. 912
Lk 1:77 the knowledge of salvation through the f 912
3: 3 preaching a baptism of repentance for the f 912
24:47 and f of sins will be preached in his name 912
Ac 2:38 of Jesus Christ for the f of your sins. 912
5:31 that he might give repentance and f of sins 912
10:43 in him receives f of sins 912
13:38 I want you to know that through Jesus the f 912
26:18 that they may receive f of sins and a place 912
Eph 1: 7 redemption through his blood, the f of sins, 912
Col 1:14 in whom we have redemption, the f of sins. 912
Heb 9:22 without the shedding of blood there is no f. 912

FORGIVES (3) [FORGIVE]

Ps 103: 3 who f all your sins 6142
Mic 7:18 who pardons sin and f the transgression of 6296
Lk 7:49 "Who is this who even f sins?" 918

FORGIVING (7) [FORGIVE]

Ex 34: 7 and f wickedness, rebellion and sin. 5951
Nu 14:18 abounding in love and f sin and rebellion. 5951
Ne 9:17 But you are a f God, 6145
Ps 86: 5 You are f and good, O Lord, 6143
99: 8 you were to Israel a f God, 5951
Da 9: 9 The Lord our God is merciful and f, 6145
Eph 4:32 to one another, f each other, just as 5919

FORGO (1)

Ne 10:31 Every seventh year we will f working 5759

FORGOT (12) [FORGET]

Ge 40:23 not remember Joseph; he f him. 8894
Dt 32:18 you f the God who gave you birth. 8894
Jdg 3: 7 they f the LORD their God and served 8894
1Sa 12: 9 "But they f the LORD their God; 8894
Ps 78:11 They f what he had done, 8894
106:13 But they soon f what he had done and did 8894
106:21 They f the God who saved them, 8894
Jer 23:27 just as their fathers f my name 8894
50: 6 and f their own resting place. 8894
Hos 2:13 and went after her lovers, but me she f," 8894
13: 6 then they f me. 8894
Mt 16: 5 the disciples f to take bread. 2140

FORGOTTEN (39) [FORGET]

Ge 41:30 Then all the abundance in Egypt will be f, 8894
Dt 26:13 from your commands nor have I f any 8894
31:21 it will not be f by their descendants. 8894
Job 11: 6 God has even f some of your sin. 5960

Job 19:14 my friends *have* f me. 8894
28:4 in places f by the foot of man; 8894
Ps 9:18 But the needy *will* not always **be f**, 8894
10:11 He says to himself, "God *has* f; 8894
31:12 *I* **am f** by them as though I were dead; 4213+4946+8894
42:9 "Why *have you* f me? 8894
44:17 not f you or been false to your covenant. 8894
44:20 If *we had* f the name of our God 8894
77:9 *Has* God f to be merciful? 8894
119:153 for *I have* not f your law. 8894
119:176 for *I have* not f your commands. 8894
Ecc 2:16 in days to come both *will* **be f**. 8894
9:5 and even the memory of them **is f**. 8894
Isa 17:10 *You have* f God your Savior; 8894
23:15 that time Tyre *will* **be f** for seventy years, 8894
23:16 walk through the city, O prostitute **f**; 8894
49:14 the Lord *has* f me." 8894
65:16 For the past troubles *will* **be f** and hidden 8894
Jer 2:32 Yet my people *have* f me, 8894
3:21 and *have* f the LORD their God. 8894
13:25 *you have* f me and trusted in false gods. 8894
18:15 Yet my people *have* f me; 8894
20:11 their dishonor *will* never **be f**. 8894
23:40 everlasting shame that *will* not **be f**." 8894
30:14 All your allies *have* f you; 8894
44:9 *Have you* f the wickedness committed 8894
50:5 an everlasting covenant *that will* not **be f**. 8894
La 3:17 *I have* f what prosperity is. 5960
Eze 22:12 And *you have* f me, 8894
23:35 Since *you have* f me and thrust me 8894
Hos 8:14 Israel *has* f his Maker and built palaces; 8894
Mk 8:14 The disciples *had* f to bring bread, *2140*
Lk 12:6 Yet not one of them is f by God. *2140*
Heb 12:5 And *you have* f that word *1720*
2Pe 1:9 and *has* **f that** he has been cleansed *3284+3330*

FORK (7) [FORKS]

1Sa 2:13 with a three-pronged f in his hand. 4657
2:14 for himself whatever the f brought up. 4657
Isa 30:24 spread out with f and shovel. 8181
Jer 15:7 a **winnowing** f at the city gates of the land. 4665
Eze 21:21 of Babylon will stop at the f *in* the road, at 562
Mt 3:12 His **winnowing** f is in his hand, *4768*
Lk 3:17 His **winnowing** f is in his hand *4768*

FORKS (6) [FORK]

Ex 27:3 sprinkling bowls, **meat** f and firepans 4657
38:3 sprinkling bowls, **meat** f and firepans, 4657
Nu 4:14 **meat** f, shovels and sprinkling bowls. 4657
1Sa 13:21 of a shekel for sharpening f and axes and 7849
1Ch 28:17 for the f, sprinkling bowls and pitchers; 4657
2Ch 4:16 shovels, **meat** f and all related articles. 4657

FORLORN (1)

Ps 35:12 for good and leave my soul f. 8890

FORM (30) [DEFORMED, FORMATION, FORMED, FORMING, FORMS]

Ge 29:17 but Rachel was lovely in f, and beautiful. 9307
Ex 20:4 in the f of anything in heaven above or on 9454
Nu 12:8 he sees the f *of* the LORD. 9454
Dt 4:12 the sound of words but saw no f; 9454
4:15 You saw no f of any kind the day 9454
4:23 do not make for yourselves an idol in the f 9454
5:8 in the f of anything in heaven above or on 9454
1Ki 6:16 with cedar boards from floor to ceiling *to* f 1215
Est 2:7 was lovely in f and features, 9307
Job 4:16 A f stood before my eyes, 9454
31:15 the same one f us both within our mothers? 3922
41:12 his strength and his graceful f. 6886
Ps 83:5 *they* f an alliance against you— 4162
Isa 44:13 He shapes it in the f *of* man, 9322
45:7 I f the light and create darkness, 3670
52:14 and his f marred beyond human likeness— 9307
Jer 11:16 with fruit beautiful in f. 9307
Eze 1:5 In appearance their f was that of a man, 1952
Mk 16:12 Afterward Jesus appeared in a different f *3671*
Lk 3:22 on him in bodily f like a dove. *1626*
Jn 5:37 have never heard his voice nor seen his f, *1626*
Ac 7:41 **made** an idol **in the f of a calf**. *3674*
14:11 down to us in human **f**!" *3929*
Ro 6:17 you wholeheartedly obeyed the f *5596*
12:5 so in Christ *we* who are many f one body, *1639*
1Co 7:31 this world in its present f is passing away. *5386*
12:12 all its parts are many, *they* f one body. *1639*
Eph 4:31 along with **every** *f* of malice. *AIT*
Col 2:9 the fullness of the Deity lives **in bodily f**, *5395*
2Ti 3:5 a f of godliness but denying its power. *3673*

FORMATION (4) [FORM]

2Sa 10:8 and drew up in **battle** f at the entrance 4878
1Ch 19:9 up in **battle** f at the entrance to their city, 4878
Jer 6:23 like men in battle f to attack you, 6885
50:42 like men **in** battle f to attack you, 6885

FORMED (43) [FORM]

Ge 2:7 the LORD God f the man *from* the dust of 3670
2:8 and there he put the man *he had* f. 3670
2:19 the LORD God *had* f out of the ground all 3670
Dt 4:16 whether f *like* a man or a woman, 9322
32:6 your Creator, who made you and f you? 3922
Jos 18:20 The Jordan **f the boundary** on 1487
2Sa 2:25 *They* f *themselves* into a group 2118
10:17 The Arameans f *their* **battle lines** 6885
1Ch 19:17 and f *his* **battle lines** opposite them. 6885
19:17 David f *his* **lines** to meet the Arameans 6885
Job 1:17 "The Chaldeans f three raiding parties 8492
Ps 65:6 *who* f the mountains by your power, 3922
94:9 Does he *who* f the eye not see? 3670
95:5 and his hands f the dry land. 3670
103:14 for he knows how we are f, 3671
104:26 which *you* f to frolic there. 3670
119:73 Your hands made me and f me; 3922
Ecc 11:5 or how the body is f in a mother's womb, NIH
Isa 29:16 Shall *what* is f say to him who formed it, 5126
29:16 Shall what is formed say to *him who* f it, 6913
43:1 he who created you, O Jacob, *he who* f you, 3670
43:7 whom *I* f and made." 3670
43:10 Before me no god **was f**, 3670
43:21 the people *I* f for myself 3670
44:2 he who made you, *who* f you in the womb, 3670
44:24 your Redeemer, *who* f you in the womb: 3670
45:18 but f it to be inhabited— 3670
49:5 *he who* f me in the womb to be his servant 3670
Jer 1:5 "Before *I* f you in the womb I knew you, 3670
18:4 so the potter f it *into* another pot, 6913
33:2 the LORD *who* f it and established it— 3670
Eze 16:7 Your breasts **were** f and your hair grew, 3922
45:7 the land bordering each side of the area f NIH
48:21 "What remains on both sides of the area f NIH
Mt 13:26 When the wheat sprouted and f heads, *4472*
Ac 17:5 **f a mob** and started a riot in the city. *4062*
23:12 The next morning the Jews f a conspiracy *4472*
Ro 9:20 "Shall what is f say to him who formed it, *4420*
9:20 "Shall what is formed say *to* him who f it, *4421*
Gal 4:19 in the pains of childbirth until Christ *is* f *3672*
1Ti 2:13 For Adam *was* f first, then Eve. *4421*
Heb 11:3 that the universe *was* f at God's command, *2936*
2Pe 3:5 the heavens existed and the earth *was* f out *5319*

FORMER (32) [FORMERLY]

Nu 21:26 who had fought against the f king of Moab 8037
Dt 4:32 Ask now about the f days, 8037
1Ki 16:24 the name of the f owner of the hill. NIH
2Ki 17:34 To this day they persist in their f practices. 8037
17:40 however, but persisted in their f practices. 8037
Ezr 3:12 who had seen the f temple, 8037
Job 8:8 "Ask the f generations 8037
Ps 77:5 I thought about the f days, 4946+7710
89:49 where is your f great love, 8037
Isa 33:18 In your thoughts you will ponder the f terror NIH
41:22 Tell us what the f *things* were, 8037
42:9 See, the f *things* have taken place, 8037
43:9 and proclaimed to us the f *things*? 8037
43:18 "Forget the f *things*; 8037
46:9 **Remember the** f *things*, those of long ago; 8037
48:3 I foretold the f *things* long ago, 8037
65:7 the full payment for their f deeds." 8037
65:17 The f *things* will not be remembered, 8037
Jer 34:5 the f kings who preceded you, 8037
Eze 33:12 to live because of **his f righteousness**.' 2023[S]
38:17 the one I spoke of in f days by my servants 7719
Da 7:7 It was different from all the f beasts, 10621
Mic 4:8 the f dominion will be restored to you; 8037
Hag 2:3 who saw this house in its f glory? 8037
2:9 be greater than the glory of the f house,' 8037
Mal 3:4 as in days gone by, as in f years. 7719
Mt 23:23 without neglecting the f. *1697[S]*
Lk 11:42 the latter without leaving **the** f undone. *1697[S]*
Ac 1:1 In my f book, Theophilus, *4755*
Eph 4:22 with regard to your f way of life, *4728*
Php 1:17 The f preach Christ out of selfish ambition, *1254*
Heb 7:18 The f regulation is set aside *4575*

FORMERLY (15) [FORMER]

Jos 8:33 of the LORD had f commanded 928+2021+8037
15:15 in Debir (f called Kiriath Sepher). 4200+7156
Jdg 1:10 in Hebron (f called Kiriath Arba) 4200+7156
1:11 in Debir (f called Kiriath Sepher). 4200+7156
1:23 to spy out Bethel (f called Luz), 4200+7156
1Sa 9:9 (F in Israel, if a man went to inquire 4200+7156
10:11 When all those who had f known him saw
him prophesying 919+4946+8997
1Ch 4:40 Some Hamites had lived there f. 4200+7156
Ne 13:5 with a large room f used to store 4200+7156
Jn 9:8 those who had f seen him begging asked, *4728*
Gal 1:23 "The man who f persecuted us is *4537*
4:8 F, when you did not know God, *5538*
Eph 2:11 remember that f you who are Gentiles *4537*
Phm 1:11 F he was useless to you, *4537*
Heb 4:6 and those who f had the gospel preached *4728*

FORMING (3) [FORM]

Isa 30:1 **f an alliance**, but not by my Spirit, 5011+5818
Eze 41:8 f the foundation of the side rooms. NIH
Zec 14:4 f a great valley, NIH

FORMLESS (2)

Ge 1:2 Now the earth was f and empty, 9332
Jer 4:23 and it was f and empty; 9332

FORMS (9) [FORM]

Ge 41:32 the dream was given to Pharaoh *in two* f is 7193
Lev 26:30 on the **lifeless** f *of* your idols, 7007
Ps 33:15 he *who* f the hearts of all, 3670
49:14 their f will decay in the grave, 7451
SS 2:13 The fig tree f its early fruit; 2845
Jer 16:18 with the **lifeless** f *of* their vile images 5577
Am 4:13 *He who* f the mountains, creates the wind, 3670
Zec 12:1 and *who* f the spirit of man within him, 3670
1Pe 4:10 God's grace in its various f. *NIG*

FORMULA (2)

Ex 30:32 and do not make any oil with the same f. 5504
30:37 Do not make any incense with this f 5504

FORNICATION (KJV) See MARITAL UNFAITHFULNESS, PROSTITUTE, SEXUAL IMMORALITY

FORSAKE (44) [FORSAKEN, FORSAKES, FORSAKING, FORSOOK]

Dt 31:6 he will never leave you nor f you." 6440
31:8 he will never leave you nor f you. 6440
31:16 *They will* f me and break 6440
31:17 with them and f them; 6440
Jos 1:5 I will never leave you nor f you. 6440
24:16 *to* f the LORD to serve other gods! 6440
24:20 *you* f the LORD and serve foreign gods, 6440
1Ki 8:57 may he never leave us nor f us. 5759
2Ki 21:14 *I will* f the remnant of my inheritance 5759
1Ch 28:9 but if *you* f him, he will reject you forever. 6440
28:20 or f you until all the work for the service of 6440
2Ch 7:19 "But if you turn away and f the decrees 6440
15:2 he will be found by you, but if *you* f him, 6440
15:2 but if you forsake him, *he will* f you. 6440
Ezr 8:22 but his great anger is against all *who* f him." 6440
Ps 27:9 Do not reject me or f me, 6440
27:10 Though my father and mother f me, 6440
37:28 the just and *will* not f his faithful ones. 6440
38:21 O LORD, *do* not f me; 6440
71:9 *do* not f me when my strength is gone. 6440
71:18 Even when I am old and gray, *do* not f me, 6440
89:30 "If his sons f my law and do 6440
94:14 *he will* never f his inheritance. 6440
119:8 *do* not utterly f me. 6440
Pr 1:8 and *do* not f your mother's teaching. 5759
4:2 so *do* not f my teaching. 6440
4:6 *Do* not f wisdom, and she will protect you; 6440
6:20 and *do* not f your mother's teaching. 5759
27:10 *Do* not f your friend and the friend 6440
28:4 *Those who* f the law praise the wicked, 6440
Isa 1:28 and *those who* f the LORD will perish. 6440
41:17 *I*, the God of Israel, *will* not f them. 6440
42:16 *I will* not f them. 6440
55:7 Let the wicked f his way and 6440
65:11 "But as for you *who* f the LORD 6440
Jer 2:19 how evil and bitter it is for you *when* you f 6440
12:7 "*I will* f my house, 6440
14:9 we bear your name; *do* not f us! 5663
17:13 all *who* f you will be put to shame. 6440
23:33 *I will* f you, declares the LORD.' 5759
La 5:20 Why *do you* f us so long? 6440
Eze 20:8 nor *did they* f the idols of Egypt. 6440
Da 11:30 to *those who* f the holy covenant. 6440
Heb 13:5 "Never will I leave you; never *will I* f you." *1593*

FORSAKEN (39) [FORSAKE]

Jdg 10:13 But you *have* f me and served other gods, 6440
1Sa 12:10 *we have* f the LORD and served the Baals 6440
1Ki 9:9 'Because *they have* f the LORD their God, 6440
11:33 I will do this because *they have* f me 6440
2Ki 22:17 Because *they have* f me and burned incense 6440
2Ch 7:22 'Because *they have* f the LORD, 6440
13:10 and *we have* not f him. 6440
13:11 But you *have* f him. 6440
21:10 because Jehoram *had* f the LORD, 6440
24:20 Because *you have* f the LORD, 6440
24:20 *he has* f you.' " 6440
24:24 Because Judah *had* f the LORD, 6440
28:6 because Judah *had* f the LORD, 6440
34:25 Because *they have* f me and burned incense 6440
Ps 9:10 LORD, *have* never f those who seek you. 6440
22:1 My God, my God, why *have you* f me? 6440
37:25 yet I have never seen the righteous f 6440
71:11 They say, "God *has* f him; 6440
119:53 *who have* f your law. 6440
119:87 but I *have* not f your precepts. 6440
Isa 1:4 *They have* f the LORD; 6440
6:12 and the land is utterly f. 6440
27:10 an abandoned settlement, f like the desert; 6440
49:14 But Zion said, "The LORD *has* f me, 6440
58:2 and *has* not f the commands of its God. 6440
60:15 "Although you have been f and hated, 6440
Jer 2:13 *They have* f me, the spring of living water, 6440
5:7 Your children *have* f me and sworn 6440
5:19 'As *you have* f me and served foreign gods 6440
9:13 "It is because they *have* f my law, 6440
17:13 in the dust because *they have* f the LORD, 6440
19:4 For *they have* f me and made this a place 6440
22:9 'Because *they have* f the covenant of 6440
51:5 and Judah have not been f by their God, 527
Eze 8:12 the LORD *has* f the land.' " 6440
9:9 They say, 'The LORD *has* f the land; 6440
Mt 27:46 "My God, my God, why *have you* f me?" *1593*
Mk 15:34 "My God, my God, why *have you* f me?" *1593*
Rev 2:4 You *have* f your first love. *918*

FORSAKES (1) [FORSAKE]
Job 6:14 even though *he* f the fear of the Almighty. 6440

FORSAKING (7) [FORSAKE]
Dt 28:20 of the evil you have done *in* f him. 6440
Jdg 10:10 f our God and serving the Baals." 6440
1Sa 8: 8 f me and serving other gods, 6440
Isa 57: 8 F me, you uncovered your bed, 907+4946
Jer 1:16 because of their wickedness *in* f me, 6440
2:17 *by* f the LORD your God when he led you 6440
Eze 20:27 your fathers blasphemed me by f me: 5085+5086

FORSOMUCH (KJV) See BECAUSE

FORSOOK (8) [FORSAKE]
Jdg 2:12 *They* f the LORD, 6440
2:13 because *they* f him and served Baal and 6440
10: 6 And because the Israelites f the LORD 6440
2Ki 17:16 *They* f all the commands of 6440
21:22 *He* f the LORD, the God of his fathers, 6440
2Ch 29: 6 the eyes of the LORD our God and f him. 6440
Jer 16:11 'It is because your fathers f me,' 6440
16:11 *They* f me and did not keep my law. 6440

FORSWEAR (KJV) See BREAK OATH

FORT (KJV) See FORTRESS

FORTH (64)
Ge 3:24 and a flaming sword **flashing back and f** 2200
4: 1 the help of the LORD *I have* **brought f** 7865
7:11 the springs of the great deep **burst f,** 1324
8: 7 and f until the water had dried up from 3655
Ex 9:24 lightning **flashed back and f.** 928+4374+9348
32:27 and f through the camp from one end to 6296
Dt 33: 2 *he* **shone f** from Mount Paran. 3649
33:14 with the best the sun **brings f** and the finest 9311
1Sa 17:15 but David **went** back and f from Saul 2143
2Sa 22:13 of his presence bolts of lightning **blazed f.** 1277
2Ki 4:35 Elisha turned away and walked **back and f** 285+285+2178+2178+2256
Est 2:11 Every day he **walked back and f** near 2143
Job 1: 7 through the earth and **going back and f** 2143
2: 2 through the earth and **going back and f** 2143
8:10 *Will they* not **bring f** words 3655
14: 9 of water it will bud and **put f** shoots like 6913
15: 7 **Were** *you* **brought f** before the hills? 2655
21:11 *They* **send f** their children as a flock; 8938
23:10 *I will* **come f** as gold. 3655
24:14 in the night *he* **steals f** like a thief. 2118
38: 8 the sea behind doors when it burst f from 3655
38:32 *Can you* **bring f** the constellations 3655
39: 3 They crouch down and **bring f** their young; 7114
Ps 19: 2 Day after day *they* **pour f** speech; 5580
19: 5 a bridegroom **coming f** from his pavilion, 3655
43: 3 **Send f** your light and your truth, 8938
45: 4 In your majesty **ride f** victoriously in behalf 8206
50: 2 From Zion, perfect in beauty, God **shines f.** 3649
60: 1 O God, and **burst f** *upon* us; 7287
65: 8 *you* **call f songs of joy.** 8264
68: 6 he **leads f** the prisoners with singing; 3655
71: 6 you **brought** me **f** from my mother's womb. 1602
77:17 your arrows **flashed back and f.** 2143
78:26 from the heavens and **led f** the south wind 5627
80: 1 enthroned between the cherubim, **shine f** 3649
85:11 Faithfulness **springs f** from the earth, 7541
90: 2 the mountains were born or *you* **brought f** 2655
94: 1 O God who avenges, **shine f.** 3649
104:14 **bringing f** food from the earth: 3655
107:20 *He* **sent f** his word and healed them; 8938
144: 6 **Send f lightning** and scatter 1397+1398
Pr 8:22 "The LORD **brought** me **f** as the first 7865
10:31 mouth of the righteous **brings f** wisdom, 5649
27: 1 you do not know what a day *may* **bring f.** 3528
Isa 35: 6 Water *will* **gush f** in the wilderness 1324
41: 4 **calling f** the generations from 7924
41:21 **"Set f** your arguments," 5602
42: 3 In faithfulness *he will* **bring f** justice; 3655
55:12 You will go out in joy and **be led f** 3297
58: 8 Then your light *will* **break f** like the dawn, 1324
65: 9 *I will* **bring f** descendants from Jacob, 3655
66: 8 or a nation **be brought f** in a moment? 3528
Eze 1:13 Fire **moved back and f** among the creatures; 2143
1:14 The creatures **sped** back and **f** like flashes 8351
7:10 Doom *has* **burst f,** the rod has budded, 3655
13:11 and violent winds *will* **burst f.** 1324
17: 2 **set f** an allegory and tell the house of Israel 2554
37: 2 He led me **back and f** among them, 6017+6017
Hos 10: 1 *he* **brought f** fruit for himself. 8751
Na 1:11 *has one* **come f** who plots evil against 3655
2: 4 **rushing back and f** through the squares. 9212
2Co 4: 2 **setting f** the truth **plainly** *5748*
Gal 4:27 **break f** and cry aloud, *4838*
Eph 4:14 **tossed back and f by the waves,** *3115*

FORTHWITH (KJV) See AS SOON AS, AT ONCE, IMMEDIATELY, SUDDEN, SUDDENLY, QUICKLY

FORTIETH (3) [FORTY]
Nu 33:38 the first day of the fifth month of the f year 752
Dt 1: 3 In the f year, on the first day of the eleventh 752
1Ch 26:31 In the f year of David's reign 752

FORTIFICATIONS (1) [FORTRESS]
2Sa 20:15 and it stood against the **outer f.** 2658

FORTIFIED (63) [FORTRESS]
Nu 13:19 Are they unwalled or f? 4448
13:28 and the cities are f and very large. 1290
21:24 because their border was f. 6434
32:17 and children will live in f cities, 4448
32:36 Beth Nimrah and Beth Haran as f cities, 4448
Dt 3: 5 All these cities were f with high walls and 1290
28:52 throughout your land until the high f walls 1290
Jos 10:20 the few who were left reached their f cities. 4448
14:12 and their cities were large and f, 1290
19:29 toward Ramah and went to the f city 4448
19:35 The f cities were Ziddim, Zer, Hammath, 4448
1Sa 6:18 the f towns with their country villages. 4448
2Sa 20: 6 or he will find f cities and escape from us." 1290
1Ki 12:25 Then Jeroboam f Shechem in 1215
15:17 and f Ramah to prevent anyone 1215
22:39 and the cities *he* f, 1215
2Ki 3:19 You will overthrow every f city 4448
8:12 "You will set fire to their f **places,** 4448
10: 2 a f city and weapons, 4448
17: 9 From watchtower to f city they built 4448
18: 8 From watchtower to f city, 4448
18:13 of Assyria attacked all the f cities of Judah 1290
19:25 you have turned f cities into piles of stone. 1290
2Ch 8: 5 and Lower Beth Horon as f cities, 5190
11:10 These were f cities in Judah and Benjamin. 5193
11:23 and to all the f cities. 5193
12: 4 he captured the f cities of Judah and came 5193
14: 6 He built up the f cities of Judah, 5193
16: 1 and f Ramah to prevent anyone 1215
17: 2 in all the f cities of Judah and put garrisons 1290
17:19 besides those he stationed in the f cities 4448
19: 5 in each of the f cities of Judah. 1290
21: 3 as well as f cities in Judah, 5193
26: 9 and *he* f them. 2616
32: 1 He laid siege to the f cities, 1290
33:14 in all the f cities in Judah. 1290
Ne 9:25 They captured f cities and fertile land; 1290
Ps 60: 9 Who will bring me to the f city? 5190
108:10 Who will bring me to the f city? 4448
Pr 10:15 The wealth of the rich is their f city, 6437
18:11 The wealth of the rich is their f city; 6437
18:19 a f city, and disputes are like 6437
Isa 2:15 for every lofty tower and every f wall, 1290
17: 3 The f city will disappear from Ephraim, 4448
25: 2 the f town a ruin, 1290
25:12 down your high f walls and lay them low; 4448
27:10 The f city stands desolate, 1290
36: 1 of Assyria attacked all the f cities of Judah 1290
37:26 you have turned f cities into piles of stone. 1290
Jer 1:18 Today I have made you a f city, 4448
4: 5 Let us flee to the f cities!' 4448
5:17 the sword they will destroy the f cities 4448
8:14 Let us flee to the f cities and perish there! 4448
15:20 a f wall of bronze; 1290
34: 7 These were the only f cities left in Judah. 4448
48:18 up against you and ruin your f **cities.** 4448
Eze 21:20 and another against Judah and f Jerusalem. 1290
36:35 are now f and inhabited." 1290
Da 11:15 up siege ramps and will capture a f city. 4448
Hos 8:14 Judah has f many towns. 1290
Am 5: 9 on the stronghold and brings the f **city** 4448
Hab 1:10 They laugh at all f **cities;** 4448
Zep 1:16 the f cities and against the corner towers. 1290

FORTIFIES (1) [FORTRESS]
Jer 51:53 the sky and f her lofty stronghold, 1307

FORTRESS (35) [FORTIFICATIONS, FORTIFIED, FORTIFIES, FORTRESSES, FORTS]
2Sa 5: 7 David captured the f *of* Zion, 5181
5: 9 then took up residence in the f and called it 5181
22: 2 LORD is my rock, my f and my deliverer; 5181
24: 7 toward the f *of* Tyre and all the towns of 4448
1Ch 11: 5 David captured the f *of* Zion, 5181
11: 7 David then took up residence in the f, 5171
Ps 18: 2 LORD is my rock, my f and my deliverer; 5181
28: 8 a f *of* salvation for his anointed one. 5057
31: 2 a **strong** f to save me. 1074+5181
31: 3 Since you are my rock and my f, 5181
46: 7 the God of Jacob is our f. 5369
46:11 the God of Jacob is our f. 5369
48: 3 he has shown himself to be her f. 5369
59: 9 you, O God, are my f, 5369
59:16 for you are my f, 5369
59:17 you, O God, are my f, my loving God. 5369
62: 2 he is my f, I will never be shaken. 5369
62: 6 he is my f, I will not be shaken. 5369
71: 3 for you are my rock and my f. 5181
91: 2 "He is my refuge and my f, my God, 5181
94:22 But the LORD has become my f, 5369
144: 2 He is my loving God and my f, 5181
Pr 14:26 He who fears the LORD has a secure f, 6437
Isa 17:10 not remembered the Rock, your f. 5057
Isa 23: 4 O f *of* the sea, for the sea has spoken: 5057
23:14 your f is destroyed! 5057
29: 7 that attack her and her f and besiege her, 5183
32:14 The f will be abandoned, 810
33:16 whose refuge will be the mountain f. 5171
Jer 16:19 O LORD, my strength and my f, 5057
Da 11: 7 of the king of the North and enter his f; 5057
11:10 and carry the battle as far as his f. 5057
11:31 to desecrate the temple f and will abolish 5057
Na 2: 1 Guard the f, watch the road, 5193
Zec 9:12 Return to your f, O prisoners of hope; 1315

FORTRESSES (26) [FORTRESS]
Isa 23:11 an order concerning Phoenicia that her f 5058
23:13 they stripped its f bare and turned it into 810
Jer 6: 5 let us attack at night and destroy her f!" 810
9:21 and has entered our f; 810
17:27 of Jerusalem that will consume her f.' " 810
49:27 it will consume the f *of* Ben-Hadad." 810
Da 11:19 the f *of* his own country but will stumble 5057
11:24 He will plot the overthrow of f— 4448
11:38 Instead of them, he will honor a god of f; 5057
11:39 He will attack the **mightiest** f with 4448+5057
Hos 8:14 upon their cities that will consume their f." 810
10:14 so that all your f will be devastated— 4448
Am 1: 4 the house of Hazael that will consume the f 810
1: 7 the walls of Gaza that will consume her f. 810
1:10 the walls of Tyre that will consume her f." 810
1:12 upon Teman that will consume the f 810
1:14 that will consume her f amid war cries on 810
2: 2 upon Moab that will consume the f 810
2: 5 that will consume the f *of* Jerusalem." 810
3: 9 to the f of Ashdod and to the fortresses 810
3: 9 to the fortresses of Ashdod and to the f 810
3:10 "who hoard plunder and loot in their f." 810
3:11 down your strongholds and plunder your f." 810
6: 8 the pride of Jacob and detest his f; 810
Mic 5: 5 and marches through our f, 810
Na 3:12 All your f are like fig trees 4448

FORTS (2) [FORTRESS]
2Ch 17:12 he built f and store cities in Judah 1072
27: 4 He built towns in the Judean hills and f 1072

FORTUNATE (1) [FORTUNE]
Ac 26: 2 I consider myself f to stand before you *3421*

FORTUNATUS (1)
1Co 16:17 F and Achaicus arrived, *5847*

FORTUNE (4) [FORTUNATE, FORTUNE-TELLING, FORTUNES]
Ge 30:11 Then Leah said, "What **good f!"** 1513
Job 31:25 the f my hands had gained, 3888
Pr 21: 6 A f made by a lying tongue is 238
Isa 65:11 a table for F and fill bowls of mixed wine 1513

FORTUNE-TELLING (1) [FORTUNE]
Ac 16:16 a great deal of money for her owners *by* f. *3446*

FORTUNES (19) [FORTUNE]
Dt 30: 3 the LORD your God will restore your f 8654
Ps 14: 7 the LORD restores the f *of* his people, 8654
53: 6 When God restores the f *of* his people, 8654
85: 1 you restored the f *of* Jacob. 8669
126: 4 Restore our f, O LORD, 8669
Jer 30:18 the f *of* Jacob's tents and have compassion 8654
32:44 because I will restore their f, 8654
33:11 the f *of* the land as they were before,' 8654
33:26 For I will restore their f 8654
48:47 "Yet I will restore the f *of* Moab in days 8654
49: 6 I will restore the f *of* the Ammonites," 8654
49:39 "Yet I will restore the f *of* Elam in days 8654
Eze 16:53 the f *of* Sodom and her daughters and 8669
16:53 and your f along with them, 8669
Hos 6:11 "Whenever I would restore the f 8654
Joel 3: 1 I restore the f *of* Judah and Jerusalem, 8654
Mic 3:11 and her prophets **tell** f for money. 7876
Zep 2: 7 he will restore their f. 8654
3:20 of the earth when I restore your f 8654

FORTY (95) [FORTIETH, 40]
Ge 7: 4 now I will send rain on the earth for f days 752
7: 4 on the earth for forty days and f nights, 752
7:12 on the earth f days and forty nights. 752
7:12 on the earth forty days and f nights. 752
7:17 For f days the flood kept coming on 752
8: 6 After f days Noah opened 752
18:29 "What if only f are found there?" 752
18:29 He said, "For the sake of f, 752
25:20 and Isaac was f years old 752
26:34 When Esau was f years old, 752
32:15 f cows and ten bulls, 752
50: 3 taking a full f days, 752
Ex 16:35 The Israelites ate manna f years, 752
24:18 on the mountain f days and forty nights. 752
24:18 on the mountain forty days and f nights. 752
26:19 make f silver bases to go under them— 752
26:21 and f silver bases—two under each frame. 752
34:28 Moses was there with the LORD f days 752
34:28 with the LORD forty days and f nights 752

Ex 36:24 made **f** silver bases to go under them— 752
36:26 and **f** silver bases—two under each frame. 752
Nu 13:25 of **f** days they returned from exploring 752
14:33 be shepherds here for **f** years, 752
14:34 For **f** years—one year 752
14:34 of the **f** days you explored the land— 752
32:13 in the desert **f** years, 752
Dt 2: 7 These **f** years the LORD your God has been with you, 752
8: 2 the way in the desert these **f** years, 752
8: 4 not swell during these **f** years. 752
9: 9 on the mountain **f** days and forty nights; 752
9: 9 on the mountain forty days and **f** nights; 752
9:11 At the end of the **f** days and forty nights, 752
9:11 At the end of the forty days and **f** nights, 752
9:18 the LORD for **f** days and forty nights; 752
9:18 the LORD for forty days and **f** nights; 752
9:25 the LORD those **f** days and forty nights 752
9:25 the LORD those forty days and **f** nights 752
10:10 Now I had stayed on the mountain **f** days 752
25: 3 he must not give him more than **f** lashes. 752
29: 5 During the **f** years that I led you through 752
Jos 4:13 About **f** thousand armed for battle crossed 752
5: 6 about in the desert **f** years until all 752
14: 7 I was **f** years old when Moses the servant 752
Jdg 3:11 So the land had peace for **f** years, 752
5: 8 or spear was seen among **f** thousand 752
5:31 Then the land had peace **f** years. 752
8:28 the land enjoyed peace **f** years. 752
12:14 He had **f** sons and thirty grandsons, 752
13: 1 into the hands of the Philistines for **f** years. 752
1Sa 4:18 He had led Israel **f** years. 752
17:16 For **f** days the Philistine came forward every morning 752
2Sa 2:10 Ish-Bosheth son of Saul was **f** years old 752
5: 4 and he reigned **f** years. 752
10:18 and **f** thousand of their foot soldiers. 752
1Ki 2:11 He had reigned **f** years over Israel— 752
6:17 in front of this room was **f** cubits long. 752
7:38 each holding **f** baths 752
11:42 in Jerusalem over all Israel **f** years. 752
19: 8 he traveled **f** days and forty nights 752
19: 8 and **f** nights until he reached Horeb, 752
2Ki 8: 9 a gift **f** camel-loads of all the finest wares 752
12: 1 and he reigned in Jerusalem **f** years. 752
1Ch 19:18 and **f** thousand of their foot soldiers. 752
29:27 He ruled over Israel **f** years— 752
2Ch 9:30 in Jerusalem over all Israel **f** years. 752
24: 1 and he reigned in Jerusalem **f** years. 752
Ne 5:15 on the people and took **f** shekels of silver 752
9:21 For **f** years you sustained them in 752
Job 42:16 After this, Job lived a hundred and **f** years; 752
Ps 95:10 **f** years I was angry with that generation; 752
Eze 29:11 no one will live there for **f** years. 752
29:12 and her cities will lie desolate **f** years 752
29:13 of **f** years I will gather the Egyptians from 752
41: 2 it was **f** cubits long and twenty cubits wide. 752
46:22 **f** cubits long and thirty cubits wide; 752
Am 2:10 and I led you **f** years in the desert 752
5:25 and offerings **f** years in the desert, 752
Jnh 3: 4 "**F** more days and Nineveh will 752
Mt 4: 2 After fasting **f** days and forty nights, *5477*
4: 2 After fasting forty days and **f** nights, *5477*
Mk 1:13 and he was in the desert **f** days, *5477*
Lk 4: 2 *for* **f** days he was tempted by the devil. *5477*
Ac 1: 3 to them over a period *of* **f** days and spoke *5477*
4:22 miraculously healed was over **f** years old. *5477*
7:23 "When Moses *was* **f years** old, *5478*
7:30 "After **f** years had passed, *5477*
7:36 at the Red Sea and *for* **f** years in the desert. *5477*
7:42 and offerings **f** years in the desert, *5477*
13:18 he endured their conduct *for* about **f years** *5478*
13:21 of the tribe of Benjamin, who ruled **f** years. *5477*
23:13 More than **f** *men* were involved in this plot. *5477*
23:21 because more than **f** of them are waiting *5477*
2Co 11:24 from the Jews the **f** lashes minus one. *5477*
Heb 3: 9 and *for* **f** years saw what I did. *5477*
3:17 And with whom was he angry *for* **f** years? *5477*

FORTY-EIGHT (2)

Nu 35: 7 In all you must give the Levites **f** towns, 752+2256+9046
Jos 21:41 held by the Israelites were **f** 752+2256+9046

FORTY-FIRST (1)

2Ch 16:13 in the **f** year of his reign Asa died 285+752+2256

FORTY-FIVE (3) [45]

Ge 18:28 "If I find **f** there," he said, 752+2256+2822
Jos 14:10 he has kept me alive for **f** years 752+2256+2822
1Ki 7: 3 **f** beams, fifteen to a row. 752+2256+2822

FORTY-NINE (1)

Lev 25: 8 amount to a period of **f** years. 752+2256+9596

FORTY-ONE (4)

1Ki 14:21 **f** years old when he became king, 285+752+2256
15:10 he reigned in Jerusalem **f** years. 285+752+2256
2Ki 14:23 and he reigned **f** years. 285+752+2256
2Ch 12:13 **f** years old when he became king, 285+752+2256

FORTY-SEVEN (1)

Ge 47:28 of his life were a hundred and **f**. 752+2256+8679

FORTY-SIX (1)

Jn 2:20 "It has taken **f** years to build this temple, *1971+2779+5477*

FORTY-TWO (6) [42]

Nu 35: 6 give them **f** other towns. 752+2256+9109
Jdg 12: 6 **F** thousand Ephraimites were killed at that time. 752+2256+9109
1Sa 13: 1 he reigned over Israel [**f**] years. 752+2256+9109
2Ki 2:24 and mauled **f** of the youths. 752+2256+9109
10:14 of Beth Eked—**f** men. 752+2256+9109
Rev 13: 5 to exercise his authority *for* **f** months. *1545+5477*

FORUM (1)

Ac 28:15 and they traveled as far as the **F** of Appius *5842*

FORWARD (55)

Ge 19: 9 and **moved f** to break down the door. 5602
Lev 8: 6 **brought** Aaron and his sons **f** 7928
8:13 **brought** Aaron's sons **f**, 7928
8:24 **brought** Aaron's sons **f** 7928
16:20 *he shall* **bring f** the live goat. 7928
Nu 8: 3 the lamps so that they **faced f** *on* 448+4578+7156
12: 5 When both of them **stepped f**, 3655
Dt 20: 2 the priest *shall* **come f** and address 5602
21: 5 The priests, the sons of Levi, *shall* **step f**, 5602
Jos 6: 8 before the LORD **went f**, 6296
6:13 the seven trumpets **went f**, 2143
7:14 the LORD takes *shall* **come f** clan by clan; 7928
7:14 that the LORD takes *shall* **come f** family 7928
7:14 that the LORD takes *shall* **come f** man 7928
7:16 the next morning Joshua **had** Israel **come f** 7928
7:17 The clans of Judah **came f**, 7928
7:17 **had** the clan of the Zerahites **come f** 7928
7:18 **had** his family **come f** 7928
8:19 from their position and **rushed f**. 8132
10:24 So *they* **came f** and placed their feet 7928
Jdg 8:21 So Gideon **stepped f** and killed them, 7756
9:44 and the companies with him **rushed f** to 7320
1Sa 10:21 Then *he* **brought f** the tribe of Benjamin, 7928
17:16 the Philistine **came f** every morning 5602
17:52 Then the men of Israel and Judah **surged f** 7756
2Sa 20: 8 he **stepped f**, it dropped out of its sheath. 3655
1Ki 1: 5 **put himself f** and said, "I will be king." 5951
18:36 the prophet Elijah **stepped f** and prayed: 5602
22:21 Finally, a spirit **came f**, 3655
2Ki 20: 9 *Shall* the shadow **go f** ten steps, 2143
20:10 for the shadow to **go f** ten steps," 5742
2Ch 18:20 Finally, a spirit **came f**, 3655
Ps 35:11 Ruthless witnesses **come f**; 7756
Pr 18:17 till another **comes** *f* and questions him. AIT
Isa 41: 1 *Let them* **come f** and speak; 5602
41: 5 They approach and **come f**; 910
47:13 *Let* your astrologers **come f**, 6641
63: 1 **striding f** in the greatness of his strength? 7579
Jer 7:24 They went backward and not **f**. 4200+7156
26:17 of the elders of the land **stepped f** and said 7756
Eze 39:22 that day **f** the house of Israel will know 2134
Da 3: 8 At this time some astrologers **came f** 10638
Zec 5: 5 the angel who was speaking to me **came f** 3655
Mt 26:50 Then the *men* **stepped f**, *4665*
26:60 *though* many false witnesses **came f**. *4665*
26:60 Finally two **came f** *4665*
Mk 3:10 with diseases *were* **pushing f** to touch him. *2158*
Lk 2:38 the child *to* all who *were* **looking f** to *4657*
13:12 *he* **called** her **f** and said to her, "Woman, *4715*
Ac 5: 6 Then the young men **came f**, *482*
2Co 11:20 or **pushes** *himself* **f** or slaps you in the face. *2048*
Heb 11:10 For *he* was **looking f** to the city *1683*
2Pe 3:12 *as you* **look f** to the day of God *4659*
3:13 with his promise *we are* **looking f** to *4659*
3:14 *since* you *are* **looking f** to this, *4659*

FORWARDNESS (KJV) See EAGERNESS, EARNESTNESS

FOSTER (1)

Isa 49:23 Kings will be your **f fathers**, 587

FOUGHT (46) [FIGHT]

Ex 17:10 So Joshua **f** the Amalekites 4309
Nu 21:23 When he reached Jahaz, *he* **f** with Israel. 4309
21:26 who *had* **f** against the former king of Moab 4309
31: 7 *They* **f** against Midian, 7371
31:28 From the soldiers who **f in** the battle, 3655+4200
31:36 of those *who* **f in** the battle was: 928+3655
Jos 10:42 the God of Israel, **f** for Israel. 4309
23: 3 it was the LORD your God who **f** for you. 4309
24: 8 *They* **f** against you, 4309
24:11 The citizens of Jericho **f** against you, 4309
Jdg 1: 5 that they found Adoni-Bezek and **f** 4309
5:19 "Kings came, *they* **f**; the kings of Canaan 4309
5:19 of Canaan **f** at Taanach by the waters 4309
5:20 From the heavens the stars **f**, 4309
5:20 from their courses *they* **f** against Sisera. 4309
9:17 and to think that my father **f** for you, 4309
9:39 the citizens of Shechem and **f** Abimelech. 4309
11:20 and encamped at Jahaz and **f** with Israel. 4309
12: 4 the men of Gilead and **f** against Ephraim. 4309
1Sa 4:10 So the Philistines **f**, 4309
12: 9 the Philistines and the king of Moab, *who* **f** 4309
14:47 *he* **f** against their enemies on every side: 4309
14:48 *He* **f** valiantly and defeated the Amalekites, 6913
19: 8 and David went out and **f** the Philistines. 4309
23: 5 So David and his men went to Keilah, **f** 4309
30:17 David **f** them from dusk until the evening 5782
31: 1 Now the Philistines **f** against Israel; 4309
2Sa 8: 3 David **f** Hadadezer son of Rehob, 5782
10:17 to meet David and **f** against him. 4309
11:17 the city came out and **f** against Joab, some 4309
12:26 Meanwhile Joab **f** against Rabbah of 4309
12:27 *"I have* **f** against Rabbah 4309
2Ki 3:23 "Those kings **must have f** 2991+2991
3:24 the Israelites rose up and **f** them 5782
1Ch 10: 1 Now the Philistines **f** against Israel; 4309
18: 3 David **f** Hadadezer king of Zobah, 5782
19:17 and *they* **f** against him. 4309
22: 8 and *have* **f** many wars. 6913
2Ch 20:29 how the LORD *had* **f** against the enemies 4309
Ps 60: T he **f** Aram Naharaim and Aram Zobah, 5897
Isa 63:10 and became their enemy and *he* himself **f** 4309
Zec 14:12 the LORD will strike all the nations that **f** 7371
1Co 15:32 If *I* **f wild beasts** in Ephesus *2562*
2Ti 4: 7 *I have* **f** the good fight, *76*
Rev 12: 7 and his angels **f** against the dragon, *4482*
12: 7 and the dragon and his angels **f** back. *4482*

FOUL (KJV) See EVIL, MUDDY, RED, STORMY

FOUND (336) [FIND]

Ge 2:20 But for Adam no suitable helper *was* **f**. 5162
4:15 so that no one *who* **f** him would kill him. 5162
6: 8 Noah **f** favor in the eyes of the LORD. 5162
7: 1 I *have* **f** you righteous in this generation. 4200+7156+8011
9:24 and **f out** what his youngest son had done 3359
11: 2 *they* **f** a plain in Shinar and settled there. 5162
16: 7 of the LORD **f** Hagar near a spring in 5162
18: 3 He said, "If *I have* **f** favor in your eyes, 5162
18:29 "What if only forty **are f** there?" 5162
18:30 What if only thirty *can* **be f** there?" 5162
18:31 what if only twenty *can* **be f** there?" 5162
18:32 What if only ten *can* **be f** there?" 5162
19:19 Your servant *has* **f** favor in your eyes, 5162
24:30 he went out to the man and **f** him standing 2180
26:32 They said, *"We've* **f** water!" 5162
30:14 into the fields and **f** some mandrake plants, 5162
30:27 "If *I have* **f** favor in your eyes, please stay. 5162
31:33 but *he* **f** nothing. 5162
31:34 in the tent but **f** nothing. 5162
31:37 what *have you* **f** that belongs 5162
33:10 "If *I have* **f** favor in your eyes, 5162
37:15 a man **f** him wandering around in the fields 5162
37:17 after his brothers and **f** them near Dothan. 5162
37:32 to their father and said, *"We* **f** this. 5162
39: 4 Joseph **f** favor in his eyes 5162
43:21 and each of us **f** his silver— 2180
44: 8 of Canaan the silver *we* **f** inside the mouths 5162
44: 9 If any of your servants **is f** to have *it*, 5162
44:10 **is f** to have *it* will become my slave; 5162
44:12 And the cup **was f** in Benjamin's sack. 5162
44:16 we ourselves and the one who **was f** to have 5162
44:17 Only the man who **was f** to have 5162
47:14 *to* **be f** in Egypt and Canaan in payment for 5162
47:29 "If *I have* **f** favor in your eyes, 5162
50: 4 "If *I have* **f** favor in your eyes, 5162
Ex 5:20 *they* **f** Moses and Aaron waiting 7003
9: 7 Pharaoh sent men to investigate and **f** *that* 2180
12:19 For seven days no yeast *is to* **be f** 5162
16:27 but *they* **f** none. 5162
22: 4 "If the stolen animal **is f** alive in his possession— 5162+5162
22: 8 But if the thief **is** not **f**, 5162
33:12 'I know you by name and *you have* **f** favor 5162
34: 9 "O Lord, if *I have* **f** favor in your eyes," 5162
Lev 6: 4 or the lost property *he* **f**, 5162
7:24 The fat of an **animal f dead** or torn 5577
10:16 about the goat of the sin offering and **f** 2180
17:15 who eats **anything f dead** or torn 5577
22: 8 He must not eat **anything f dead** or torn 5577
Nu 11:15 if *I have* **f** favor in your eyes— 5162
15:32 a man *was* **f** gathering wood on 5162
15:33 Those *who* **f** him gathering wood brought him to Moses and Aaron 5162
23: 6 So he went back to him and **f** him standing 2180
23:17 and **f** him standing beside his offering, 2180
32: 5 If *we have* **f** favor in your eyes," they said, 5162
Dt 13:17 of those condemned things *shall be* **f** 1815
15: 9 and you will be **f** guilty of sin. NIH
16: 4 *Let* no yeast **be f** in your possession 8011
17: 2 the LORD gives you **is f** doing evil in 5162
18:10 *Let* no *one* **be f** among you who 5162
21: 1 If a *man* **is f** slain, 5162
22:20 and no proof of the girl's virginity *can* **be f**, 5162
22:22 man **is f** sleeping with another man's wife, 5162
22:27 for the man **f** the girl out in the country, 5162
32:10 In a desert land *he* **f** him, 5162
Jos 10:17 the five kings *had* **been f** hiding in the cave 5162
Jdg 1: 5 It was there that *they* **f** Adoni-Bezek 5162
3:24 and **f** the doors of the upper room locked. 8011
6:17 "If now *I have* **f** favor in your eyes, 5162
20:48 the animals and everything else they **f**. 5162
21: 9 they **f** that none of the people 2180
21:12 *They* **f** among the people living 5162
Ru 2: 3 she **f** herself working in a field belonging NIH
2:10 "Why *have I* **f** such favor in your eyes 5162

1Sa 9:20 *they have* **been f.** 5162
10:2 donkeys you set out to look for *have* **been f.** 5162
10:14 "But when we saw they were not to be **f,** NIH
10:16 He assured us that the donkeys *had* **been f.** 5162
10:21 they looked for him, *he was* not *to* **be f.** 5162
12:5 that *you have* not **f** anything in my hand." 5162
13:19 a blacksmith *could* **be f** in the whole land 5162
14:20 They **f** the Philistines in total confusion, 2180
20:3 that *I have* **f** favor in your eyes, 5162
20:29 If *I have* **f** favor in your eyes, 5162
25:28 *Let* no wrongdoing **be f** in you as long 5162
27:5 "If *I have* **f** favor in your eyes, 5162
29:3 *I have* **f** no fault in him." 5162
29:6 *I have* **f** no fault in you, 5162
29:8 "What *have you* **f** against your servant 5162
30:3 they **f** it destroyed by fire and their wives 2180
30:6 But David **f strength** in 2616
30:11 *They* **f** an Egyptian in a field 5162
31:8 *they* **f** Saul and his three sons fallen 5162
2Sa 2:30 nineteen of David's men **were f missing.** 7212
7:27 So your servant *has* **f** courage 5162
14:22 that *he has* **f** favor in your eyes, 5162
17:12 we will attack him wherever *he may* **be f,** 5162
17:13 until not even a piece of it *can* **be f."** 5162
17:20 The men searched but **f** no one, 5162
1Ki 1:3 for a beautiful girl and **f** Abishag, 5162
1:52 but if evil **is f** in him, he will die." 5162
13:14 *He* **f** him sitting under an oak tree 5162
13:28 and **f** the body thrown down on the road, 5162
14:13 the God of Israel, *has* **f** anything good. 5162
19:19 So Elijah went from there and **f** Elisha son 5162
20:36 a lion **f** him and killed him. 5162
20:37 The prophet **f** another man and said, 5162
21:20 Ahab said to Elijah, "So *you have* **f** me, 5162
21:20 *"I have* **f** you," he answered, 5162
2Ki 4:39 the fields to gather herbs and **f** a wild vine. 5162
7:15 and they **f** the whole road strewn with 2180
9:5 he **f** the army officers sitting together. 2180
9:35 *they* **f** nothing except her skull, 5162
12:5 be used to repair whatever damage **is f** in 5162
12:18 the gold **f** in the treasuries of the temple of 5162
14:14 the gold and silver and all the articles **f** *in* 5162
16:8 and gold **f** *in* the temple of the LORD and 5162
18:15 that **was f** *in* the temple of the LORD and 5162
19:8 and **f** the king fighting against Libnah. 5162
20:13 and everything **f** among his treasures. 5162
22:8 *"I have* **f** the Book of the Law in the temple 5162
22:13 in this book that *has* **been f.** 5162
23:2 which *had* **been f** in the temple of 5162
25:19 of the land and sixty of his men who **were f** 5162
1Ch 4:40 *They* **f** rich, good pasture, 5162
10:8 *they* **f** Saul and his sons fallen 5162
17:25 So your servant *has* **f courage** to pray 5162
20:2 its weight *was* **f** to be a talent of gold, 5162
24:4 A larger number of leaders **were f** 5162
26:31 the Hebronites **were f** at Jazer in Gilead. 5162
28:9 If you seek him, *he will* **be f** by you; 5162
2Ch 2:17 and *they* **were f** to be 153,600. 5162
15:2 If you seek him, *he will* **be f** by you, 5162
15:4 and sought him, and *he* **was f** by them. 5162
15:15 and *he* **was f** by them. 5162
20:25 and *they* **f** among them a great amount 5162
21:17 invaded it and carried off all the goods **f** in 5162
22:8 *he* **f** the princes of Judah and the sons 5162
25:5 those twenty years old or more and **f** 5162
25:24 the gold and silver and all the articles **f** in 5162
29:16 that *they* **f** in the temple of the LORD. 5162
34:14 Hilkiah the priest **f** the Book of the Law of 5162
34:15 *"I have* **f** the Book of the Law in the temple 5162
34:21 in this book that *has* **been f.** 5162
34:30 which *had* **been f** in the temple of 5162
36:8 and all that **was f** against him, 5162
Ezr 4:19 and *it was* **f** that this city has 10708
6:2 A scroll **was f** in the citadel of Ecbatana in 10708
8:15 *I* **f** no Levites there. 5162
Ne 2:5 and if your servant *has* **f favor** in his sight, 3512
7:5 *I* **f** the genealogical record 5162
7:5 This is what *I* **f** written there: 5162
8:14 *They* **f** written in the Law, 5162
9:8 *You* **f** his heart faithful to you, 5162
13:1 of the people and there *it* **was f** written 5162
Est 2:22 But Mordecai **f** *out about* the plot 3359
2:23 report was investigated and **f to be true,** 5162
6:2 *It* **was f** recorded there 5162
7:3 "If *I have* **f** favor with you, O king, 5162
Job 9:29 Since I *am already f* **guilty,** AIT
12:12 Is not wisdom **f** among the aged? NIH
20:8 no more *to be* **f,** 5162
28:12 "But where *can* wisdom **be f?** 5162
28:13 *it* cannot **be f** in the land of the living. 5162
32:3 because *they had* **f** no way to refute Job, 5162
32:13 Do not say, *'We have* **f** wisdom; 5162
33:10 Yet God *has* **f** fault with me; 5162
33:24 *I have* **f** a ransom for him'— 5162
42:15 Nowhere in all the land **were** *there* **f** women 5162
Ps 10:15 *that would* not *be* **f out.** 5162
32:6 to you while you *may be* **f;** 5162
37:10 you look for them, they will not be **f.** NIH
37:36 though I looked for him, *he could* not **be f.** 5162
69:20 for comforters, but *I* **f** none. 5162
84:3 Even the sparrow *has* **f** a home, 5162
89:20 *I have* **f** David my servant; 5162
109:7 When he is tried, *let him be* **f** guilty, 3655
109:17 *he* **f** no **pleasure** in blessing— 2911
Pr 7:15 I looked for you and *have* **f** you! 5162
10:9 he who takes crooked paths *will* **be f out.** 3359
10:13 Wisdom **is f** on the lips of the discerning, 5162
13:10 but wisdom is **f** in those who take advice. NIH
14:9 but goodwill is **f** among the upright. NIH
19:7 they are nowhere to be **f.** NIH
30:28 yet it is **f** in kings' palaces. NIH
Ecc 7:28 *I* **f** one [upright] man among a thousand, 5162
7:29 This only *have I* **f:** 5162
SS 3:3 The watchmen **f** me as they made their 5162
3:4 Scarcely had I passed them when *I* **f** 5162
5:7 The watchmen **f** me as they made their 5162
8:1 Then, if *I* **f** you outside, I would kiss you, 5162
Isa 30:14 a fragment *will* **be f** for taking coals from 5162
35:9 *they will* not **be f** there. 5162
37:8 and **f** the king fighting against Libnah. 5162
39:2 and everything **f** among his treasures. 5162
45:25 of Israel *will be f* **righteous** and will exult. AIT
51:3 Joy and gladness *will* **be f** in her, 5162
55:6 Seek the LORD while he *may* **be f;** 5162
57:10 *You* **f** renewal of your strength, 5162
59:15 Truth is **nowhere to be f,** 6372
65:1 *I* **was f** by those who did not seek me. 5162
65:8 when juice is *still* **f** in a cluster of grapes 5162
Jer 29:14 *I will* **be f** by you," declares the LORD, 5162
40:1 He *had* **f** Jeremiah bound in chains 4374
40:2 the commander of the guard **f** Jeremiah, 4374
50:7 Whoever **f** them devoured them; 5162
50:20 but none *will* **be f,** 5162
50:24 *you* **were f** and captured 5162
52:25 of the land and sixty of his men who **were f** 5162
Eze 4:14 now I have never eaten **anything f dead** 5577
16:37 with whom *you* **f pleasure,** 6844
22:30 but *I* **f** none. 5162
26:21 but *you will* never again **be f,** 5162
28:15 till wickedness **was f** in you. 5162
44:31 **f dead** or torn by wild animals. 5577
Da 1:19 and he **f** none equal to Daniel, Hananiah, 5162
1:20 *he* **f** them ten times better than all 5162
2:25 *"I have* **f** a man among the exiles 10708
4:12 Under it the beasts of the field **f shelter,** 10300
5:11 of your father he **was f** to have insight 10708
5:12 **was f** to have a keen mind and knowledge 10708
5:27 on the scales and **f** wanting. 10708
6:11 and **f** Daniel praying and asking God 10708
6:22 because I **was f** innocent in his sight. 10708
6:23 no wound **was f** on him, 10708
12:1 everyone whose name **is f** written in 5162
Hos 9:10 "When *I* **f** Israel, it was like finding grapes 5162
12:4 *He* **f** him at Bethel and talked 5162
Jnh 1:3 where *he* **f** a ship bound for that port. 5162
Mic 1:13 the transgressions of Israel **were f** in you. 5162
Zep 3:13 nor *will* deceit **be f** in their mouths. 5162
Zec 1:11 and **f** the whole world at rest and in peace." 2180
Mal 2:6 in his mouth and nothing false **was f** 5162
Mt 1:18 but before they came together, *she was* **f** to 2351
2:7 **f out** from them the **exact** time 208
8:10 not **f** anyone in Israel with such great faith. 2351
13:44 **When** a man **f** it, he hid it again, 2351
13:46 *When he* **f** one of great value, 2351
18:28 "But when that servant went out, *he* **f** one 2351
20:6 and **f** still others standing around. 2351
21:19 up to it but **f** nothing on it except leaves. 2351
26:40 to his disciples and **f** them sleeping. 2351
26:43 *he* again **f** them sleeping, 2351
Mk 1:37 and when *they* **f** him, they exclaimed: 2351
6:38 *When they* **f out,** they said, "Five— 1182
7:30 *She* went home and **f** her child lying on 2351
11:4 They went and **f** a colt outside in the street, 2351
11:13 *he* **f** nothing but leaves, 2351
14:16 and **f** things just as Jesus had told them. 2351
14:37 to his disciples and **f** them sleeping. 2351
14:40 *he* again **f** them sleeping, 2351
Lk 1:30 Mary, *you have* **f** favor with God. 2351
2:16 So they hurried off and **f** Mary and Joseph, 461
2:46 After three days *they* **f** him in 2351
4:17 *he* **f** the place where it is written: 2351
7:9 not **f** such great faith even in Israel." 2351
7:10 to the house and **f** the servant well. 2351
8:35 they **f** the man from whom 2351
9:36 *they* **f** that Jesus was alone. 2351
13:7 for fruit on this fig tree and haven't **f** any. 2351
15:6 *I have* **f** my lost sheep.' 2351
15:9 *I have* **f** my lost coin.' 2351
15:24 he was lost and *is* **f.'** 2351
15:32 he was lost and *is* **f.' "** 2351
17:18 *Was* no *one* **f** to return and give praise 2351
19:32 and **f** it just as he had told them. 2351
22:13 and **f** things just as Jesus had told them. 2351
22:45 *he* **f** them asleep, exhausted from sorrow. 2351
23:2 *"We have* **f** this man subverting our nation. 2351
23:14 in your presence and *have* **f** no basis 2351
23:22 *I have* **f** in him no grounds for 2351
24:2 *They* **f** the stone rolled away from 2351
24:24 and **f** it just as the women had said, 2351
24:33 There *they* **f** the Eleven and those 2351
Jn 1:41 *"We have* **f** the Messiah" (that is, the Christ) 2351
1:45 Philip **f** Nathanael and told him, 2351
1:45 *"We have* **f** the one Moses wrote about in 2351
2:14 In the temple courts *he* **f** men selling cattle, 2351
5:14 Later Jesus **f** him at the temple and said 2351
6:25 *When they* **f** him on the other side of 2351
9:35 and *when he* **f** him, he said, 2351
11:17 Jesus **f that** Lazarus had already been in 2351
11:57 that if anyone **f out** where Jesus was, 1182
12:9 Meanwhile a large crowd of Jews **f out** 1182
12:14 Jesus **f** a young donkey and sat upon it, 2351
19:33 to Jesus and **f** that he was already dead, 3972
Ac 4:12 Salvation is **f** in no one else, NIG
5:23 *"We* **f** the jail securely locked, with 2351
5:23 when we opened them, *we* **f** no one inside." 2351
9:2 if *he* **f** any there who belonged to the Way, 2351
9:33 There *he* **f** a man named Aeneas, 2351
10:17 the men sent by Cornelius **f out** 1452
10:27 Peter went inside and **f** a large gathering 2351
11:26 and *when he* **f** him, 2351
13:22 *'I have* **f** David son of Jesse a man 2351
13:28 *Though they* **f** no proper ground for 2351
14:6 But *they* **f out about** it and fled to 5328
17:23 *I* even **f** an altar with this inscription: 2351
19:1 There *he* **f** some disciples 2351
21:2 We **f** a ship crossing over to Phoenicia, 2351
22:25 **hasn't even been f guilty?"** 185
23:29 *I* **f** that the accusation had to do 2351
24:5 *"We have* **f** this man to be a troublemaker, 2351
24:18 I was ceremonially clean when *they* **f** me 2351
24:20 who are here should state what crime *they* **f** 2351
25:25 I **f** he had done nothing deserving of death, 2898
27:6 the centurion **f** an Alexandrian ship sailing 2351
27:28 and **f** that the water was a hundred 2351
27:28 and **f** it was ninety feet deep. 2351
28:1 *we* **f out** that the island was called Malta. 2105
28:14 There *we* **f** some brothers who invited us 2351
Ro 7:10 *I* **f** that the very commandment 2351
10:20 *"I was* **f** by those who did not seek me; 2351
1Co 15:15 then **f** to be false witnesses about God, 2351
2Co 2:12 of Christ and **f** that the Lord had opened NIG
5:3 *we will* not *be* **f** naked. 2351
Php 2:8 And *being* **f** in appearance as a man, 2351
3:9 and *be* **f** in him, not having a righteousness 2351
Col 2:17 the reality, however, is **f** in Christ. NIG
2Ti 1:17 he searched hard for me until *he* **f** me. 2351
Heb 3:3 Jesus *has been* **f worthy of** greater honor 546
4:1 that none of you *be* **f** to have fallen short 1506
8:8 But God **f fault with** the people and said: 3522
11:5 he *could* not **be f,** 2351
Jas 2:8 If you really keep the royal law **f in** 2848
1Pe 2:22 and no deceit **was f** in his mouth." 2351
2Pe 3:14 make every effort *to be* **f** spotless, 2351
Rev 2:2 and *have* **f** them false. 2351
3:2 for *I have* not **f** your deeds complete in 2351
5:4 because no one *was* **f** who was worthy 2351
14:5 No lie *was* **f** in their mouths; 2351
16:20 and the mountains *could* not *be* **f.** 2351
18:21 never *to be* **f** again. 2351
18:22 No workman of any trade *will* ever *be* **f** 2351
18:24 In her *was* **f** the blood of prophets and of 2351
20:15 If anyone's name *was* not **f** written in 2351
21:16 He measured the city with the rod and **f** it NIG

FOUNDATION (39) [FOUNDATIONS, FOUNDED]

1Ki 5:17 to **provide a f** *of* dressed stone *for* 3569
6:37 **The f** of the temple of the LORD **was laid** 3569
7:9 to the great courtyard and from **f** to eaves, 4996
2Ch 3:3 **The f** Solomon **laid** for building 3569
8:16 **f** *of* the temple of the LORD was **laid** 4586
23:5 the royal palace and a third at the F Gate, 3572
Ezr 3:3 on its **f** and sacrificed burnt offerings on it 4807
3:6 **the f** of the LORD's temple *had* not *yet* **been laid.** 3569
3:10 When the builders **laid the f** *of* the temple 3569
3:11 **the f** *of* the house of the LORD **was laid.** 3569
3:12 **the f** *of* this temple *being* **laid,** 3569
Job 38:4 were you when I **laid the** earth's **f?** 3569
Ps 87:1 He has set his **f** on the holy mountain; 3573
89:14 and justice are the **f** *of* your throne; 4806
97:2 and justice are the **f** *of* his throne. 4806
Isa 28:16 a precious cornerstone for a sure **f;** 4586
33:6 He will be the **sure f** *for* your times, 575
Jer 51:26 nor any stone for a **f,** 4589
Eze 13:14 to the ground so that its **f** will be laid bare. 3572
41:8 forming the **f** *of* the side rooms. 4588
Am 9:6 in the heavens and sets its **f** on the earth, 99
Hag 2:18 **the f** of the LORD's temple **was laid.** 3569
Zec 4:9 "The hands of Zerubbabel *have* **laid the f** 3569
8:9 **when the f was laid** *for* the house of 3569
12:1 *who* **lays the f** *of* the earth, 3569
Mt 7:25 because *it had* its **f** on the rock. 2530
Lk 6:48 who dug down deep and laid the **f** on rock. 2529
6:49 a house on the ground without a **f.** 2529
14:29 if he lays the **f** and is not able to finish it, 2529
Ro 15:20 not be building on someone else's **f.** 2529
1Co 3:10 I laid a **f** as an expert builder, 2529
3:11 For no one can lay any **f** other than 2529
3:12 If any man builds on this **f** using gold, 2529
Eph 2:20 built on the **f** of the apostles and prophets, 2529
1Ti 3:15 the pillar and **f** of the truth. 1613
6:19 up treasure for themselves as a firm **f** for 2529
2Ti 2:19 Nevertheless, God's solid **f** stands firm, 2529
Heb 6:1 the **f** of repentance from acts that lead 2529
Rev 21:19 The first **f** was jasper, the second sapphire, 2529

FOUNDATIONS (38) [FOUNDATION]

Dt 32:22 the earth and its harvests and set afire the **f** 4587
Jos 6:26 of his firstborn son *will he* **lay** its **f;** 3569
1Sa 2:8 "For the **f** *of* the earth are the LORD's; 5187
2Sa 22:8 the **f** *of* the heavens shook; 4589
22:16 the **f** *of* the earth laid bare at the rebuke of 4589
1Ki 7:10 **The f were laid** *with* large stones 3569
16:34 *He* **laid** its **f** at the cost 3569
Ezr 4:12 the walls and repairing the **f.** 10079
5:16 So this Sheshbazzar came and laid the **f** of 10079
6:3 and let its **f** be laid. 10079
Job 4:19 whose **f** are in the dust, 3572

Job 22:16 their **f** washed away by a flood. 3572
Ps 11: 3 When the **f** are being destroyed, 9268
18: 7 and the **f** *of* the mountains shook; 4587
18:15 the **f** *of* the earth laid bare at your rebuke, 4589
82: 5 all the **f** *of* the earth are shaken. 4587
102:25 the beginning *you* **laid the f** *of* the earth, 3569
104: 5 He set the earth on its **f;** 4806
137: 7 they cried, "tear it down to its **f!"** 3572
Pr 3:19 By wisdom the LORD **laid the** earth's **f,** 3569
8:29 and when he marked out the **f** *of* the earth. 4587
Isa 24:18 the **f** *of* the earth shake. 4587
44:28 and of the temple, *"Let its* **f be laid."'** 3569
48:13 My own hand **laid the f** *of* the earth, 3569
51:13 the heavens and **laid the f** *of* the earth, 3569
51:16 *who* **laid the f** *of* the earth, 3569
54:11 your **f** with sapphires. 3569
58:12 and will raise up the age-old **f;** 4587
Jer 31:37 be measured and the **f** *of* the earth below 4587
La 4:11 a fire in Zion that consumed her **f.** 3572
Eze 30: 4 be carried away and her **f** torn down. 3572
Mic 1: 6 into the valley and lay bare her **f.** 3572
6: 2 listen, you everlasting **f** *of* the earth. 4587
Ac 16:26 that the **f** of the prison were shaken. *2528*
Heb 1:10 O Lord, you **laid the f of** the earth, *2530*
11:10 he was looking forward to the city with **f,** *2529*
Rev 21:14 The wall of the city had twelve **f,** *2529*
21:19 The **f** of the city walls were decorated *2529*

FOUNDED (11) [FOUNDATION]

Ex 9:18 from the day it **was f** till now. 3569
1Ki 2:24 on the throne of my father David and *has* **f** 6913
Ps 24: 2 for he **f** it upon the seas and established it 3569
89:11 you **f** the world and all that is in it. 3569
94:15 Judgment will again be **f on** righteousness, 6330
107:36 and *they* **f** a city where they could settle. 3922
Isa 40:21 not understood since the earth was **f?** 4589
45:18 and made the earth, he **f** it; 3922
Jer 10:12 *he* **f** the world by his wisdom 3922
51:15 *he* **f** the world by his wisdom 3922
Heb 8: 6 and it *is* **f** on better promises. *3793*

FOUNTAIN (15) [FOUNTAINS]

Ne 2:14 on toward the **F** Gate and the King's Pool, 6524
3:15 The **F** Gate was repaired by Shallun son 6524
12:37 At the **F** Gate they continued directly up 6524
Ps 36: 9 For with you is the **f** *of* life; 5227
Pr 5:18 May your **f** be blessed, 5227
10:11 The mouth of the righteous is a **f** *of* life, 5227
13:14 The teaching of the wise is a **f** *of* life, 5227
14:27 The fear of the LORD is a **f** *of* life, 5227
16:22 a **f** *of* life to those who have it, 5227
18: 4 but the **f** *of* wisdom is a bubbling brook. 5227
SS 4:12 you are a spring enclosed, a sealed **f.** 1644
4:15 You are a garden **f,** 5078
Jer 9: 1 a spring of water and my eyes a **f** *of* tears! 5227
Joel 3:18 A **f** will flow out of the LORD's house 5078
Zec 13: 1 a **f** will be opened to the house of David 5227

FOUNTAINS (2) [FOUNTAIN]

Ps 87: 7 "All my **f** are in you." 5078
Pr 8:28 and fixed securely the **f** *of* the deep, 6524

FOUR (225) [FOUR-DRACHMA, FOUR-FIFTHS, FOUR-FOOTED, FOUR-SIDED, FOURS, FOURTH]

Ge 2:10 from there it was separated into **f** headwaters. 752
14: 9 **f** kings against five. 752
14:11 The **f** kings seized all the goods of Sodom NIH
15:13 and mistreated **f** hundred years. 752
23:15 land is worth **f** hundred shekels of silver, 752
23:16 **f** hundred shekels of silver, 752
32: 6 and **f** hundred men are with him." 752
33: 1 coming with his **f** hundred men; 752
Ex 22: 1 for the ox and **f** sheep for the sheep 752
25:12 Cast **f** gold rings for it and fasten them 752
25:12 for it and fasten them to its **f** feet, 752
25:26 Make **f** gold rings for the table 752
25:26 the table and fasten them to the **f** corners, 752
25:26 where the **f** legs are. 752
25:34 the lampstand there are to be **f** cups shaped 752
26: 2 twenty-eight cubits long and **f** cubits wide. 752
26: 8 thirty cubits long and **f** cubits wide. 752
26:32 Hang it with gold hooks on **f** posts 752
26:32 with gold and standing on **f** silver bases. 752
27: 2 Make a horn at each of the **f** corners, 752
27: 4 a bronze ring at each of the **f** corners of 752
27:16 with **f** posts and four bases. 752
27:16 with four posts and **f** bases. 752
28:17 mount **f** rows of precious stones on it. 752
36: 9 twenty-eight cubits long and **f** cubits wide. 752
36:15 thirty cubits long and **f** cubits wide. 752
36:36 They made **f** posts of acacia wood for it 752
36:36 for them and cast their **f** silver bases. 752
37: 3 He cast **f** gold rings for it 752
37: 3 for it and fastened them to its **f** feet, 752
37:13 They cast **f** gold rings for the table 752
37:13 and fastened them to the **f** corners, 752
37:13 where the **f** legs were. 752
37:20 And on the lampstand were **f** cups shaped 752
38: 2 They made a horn at each of the **f** corners, 752
38: 5 for the **f** corners of the bronze grating. 752
38:19 with **f** posts and four bronze bases. 752
38:19 with four posts and **f** bronze bases. 752
Ex 39:10 Then they mounted **f** rows 752
Lev 11:23 that have **f** legs you are to detest. 752
Nu 7: 7 He gave two carts and **f** oxen to 752
7: 8 and he gave **f** carts and eight oxen to 752
7:85 silver dishes weighed two thousand **f** hundred shekels, 752
Dt 22:12 on the **f** corners of the cloak you wear. 752
Jos 19: 7 **f** towns and their villages— 752
21:18 with their pasturelands—**f** towns. 752
21:22 with their pasturelands—**f** towns. 752
21:24 with their pasturelands—**f** towns. 752
21:29 with their pasturelands—**f** towns; 752
21:31 with their pasturelands—**f** towns; 752
21:35 with their pasturelands—**f** towns; 752
21:37 with their pasturelands—**f** towns; 752
21:39 **f** towns in all. 752
Jdg 9:34 near Shechem in **f** companies. 752
11:40 of Israel go out for **f** days to commemorate 752
19: 2 After she had been there **f** months, 752
20: 2 **f** hundred thousand soldiers armed 752
20:17 mustered **f** hundred thousand swordsmen, 752
20:47 where they stayed **f** months. 752
21:12 in Jabesh Gilead **f** hundred young women who had never slept with a man, 752
1Sa 4: 2 about **f** thousand of them on the battlefield. 752
22: 2 About **f** hundred men were with him. 752
25:13 About **f** hundred men went up with David, 752
27: 7 in Philistine territory a year and **f** months. 752
30:10 and **f** hundred men continued the pursuit. 752
30:17 except **f** hundred young men who rode off 752
2Sa 12: 6 He must pay for that lamb **f** *times over,* 752
15: 7 At the end of **f** years, 752
21:22 These **f** were descendants of Rapha 752
1Ki 4:26 Solomon had **f** thousand stalls 752
6: 1 In the **f** hundred and eightieth year after 752
7: 2 and thirty high, with **f** rows 752
7:19 in the shape of lilies, **f** cubits high. 752
7:27 each was **f** cubits long, 752
7:27 **f** wide and three high. 752
7:30 Each stand had **f** bronze wheels 752
7:30 and each had a basin resting on **f** supports, 752
7:32 The **f** wheels were under the panels, 752
7:34 Each stand had **f** handles, 752
7:38 and measuring **f** cubits across, 752
7:42 the **f** hundred pomegranates for 752
18:19 And bring the **f** hundred and fifty prophets 752
18:19 and the **f** hundred prophets of Asherah, 752
18:22 but Baal has **f** hundred and fifty prophets. 752
18:33 "Fill **f** large jars with water and pour it on 752
22: 6 about **f** hundred men— 752
2Ki 7: 3 Now there were **f** men with leprosy at 752
25:17 pillar was **f and a half feet** high 564+8993
1Ch 3: 5 These **f** were by Bathsheba daughter 752
7: 1 and Shimron—**f** in all. 752
9:24 The gatekeepers were on the **f** sides: 752
9:26 But the **f** principal gatekeepers, 752
21: 5 including **f** hundred and seventy thousand 752
21:20 his **f** sons who were 752
23: 5 **F** thousand are to be gatekeepers 752
23: 5 be gatekeepers and **f** thousand are to praise 752
23:10 These were the sons of Shimei—**f** in all. 752
23:12 and Uzziel—**f** in all. 752
26:17 **f** a day on the north, 752
26:17 **f** a day on the south and two at a time at 752
26:18 there were **f** at the road and two at 752
2Ch 4:13 the **f** hundred pomegranates for 752
8:18 sailed to Ophir and brought back **f** hundred 752
9:25 Solomon had **f** thousand stalls for horses 752
13: 3 of **f** hundred thousand able fighting men, 752
18: 5 the prophets—**f** hundred men— 752
Ezr 6:17 **f** hundred male lambs and, 10065
Ne 6: 4 **F** times they sent me the same message, 752
Job 1:19 from the desert and struck the **f** corners of 752
Pr 30:15 **f** that never say, 'Enough!': 752
30:18 **f** that I do not understand: 752
30:21 under **f** it cannot bear up: 752
30:24 "**F** things on earth are small, 752
30:29 **f** that move with stately bearing: 752
Isa 11:12 of Judah from the **f** quarters of the earth. 752
17: 6 **f** or five on the fruitful boughs," 752
Jer 15: 3 "I will send **f** kinds of destroyers 752
36:23 or **f** columns of the scroll, 752
49:36 I will bring against Elam the **f** winds from 752
49:36 the four winds from the **f** quarters of 752
49:36 I will scatter them to the **f** winds, 3972[S]
52:21 each was **f** fingers thick, and hollow. 752
Eze 1: 5 like **f** living creatures. 752
1: 6 each of them had **f** faces and four wings. 752
1: 6 each of them had four faces and **f** wings. 752
1: 8 Under their wings on their **f** sides they had 752
1: 8 *All* **f** *of* them had faces and wings, 752
1:10 Each of the **f** had the face of a man, 752
1:15 beside each creature with its **f** faces. 752
1:16 and *all* **f** looked alike. 752
1:17 of the **f** directions the creatures faced; 752
1:18 and *all* **f** rims were full of eyes all around. 752
7: 2 The end has come upon the **f** corners of 752
10: 9 and I saw beside the cherubim **f** wheels, 752
10:10 the **f** *of* them looked alike; 752
10:11 of the **f** directions the cherubim faced; 752
10:12 as were their **f** wheels. 752
10:14 Each of the cherubim had **f** faces: 752
10:21 Each had **f** faces and four wings, 752
10:21 Each had four faces and **f** wings, 752
14:21 against Jerusalem my **f** dreadful judgments— 752
37: 9 Come from the **f** winds, O breath, 752
40:41 So there were **f** tables on one side of 752
Eze 40:41 on one side of the gateway and **f** on 752
40:42 There were also **f** tables of dressed stone 752
41: 5 around the temple was **f** cubits wide. 752
42:20 So he measured the area on *all* **f** sides. 752
43:14 up to the larger ledge it is **f** cubits high and 752
43:15 The altar hearth is **f** cubits high, 752
43:15 **f** horns project upward from the hearth. 752
43:20 and put it on the **f** horns of the altar and on 752
43:20 on the **f** corners of the upper ledge and all 752
45:19 the **f** corners of the upper ledge of the altar 752
46:21 and led me around to its **f** corners, 752
46:22 In the **f** corners of the outer court 752
46:22 each of the courts in the **f** corners was 752
46:23 of each of the **f** courts was a ledge of stone, 752
Da 1:17 To these **f** young men God gave knowledge 752
3:25 I see **f** men walking around in the fire, 10065
7: 2 and there before me were the **f** winds 10065
7: 3 **F** great beasts, each different from 10065
7: 6 And on its back it had **f** wings like those of 10065
7: 6 This beast had **f** heads, 10065
7:17 'The **f** great beasts are four kingdoms 10065
7:17 'The four great beasts are **f** kingdoms 10065
8: 8 and in its place **f** prominent horns grew up 752
8: 8 up toward the **f** winds of heaven. 752
8:22 The **f** horns that replaced the one 752
8:22 that was broken off represent **f** kingdoms 752
11: 4 up and parceled out toward the **f** winds 752
Am 1: 3 "For three sins of Damascus, even for **f,** 752
1: 6 "For three sins of Gaza, even for **f,** 752
1: 9 "For three sins of Tyre, even for **f,** 752
1:11 "For three sins of Edom, even for **f,** 752
1:13 "For three sins of Ammon, even for **f,** 752
2: 1 "For three sins of Moab, even for **f,** 752
2: 4 "For three sins of Judah, even for **f,** 752
2: 6 "For three sins of Israel, even for **f,** 752
Zec 1:18 and there before me were **f** horns! 752
1:20 Then the LORD showed me **f** craftsmen. 752
2: 6 "for I have scattered you to the **f** winds 752
6: 1 before me were **f** chariots coming out from 752
6: 5 "These are the **f** spirits of heaven, 752
Mt 15:38 of those who ate was **f thousand,** *5483*
16:10 Or the seven loaves *for* the **f thousand,** *5483*
24:31 they will gather his elect from the **f** winds, *5475*
Mk 2: 3 carried by **f** of them. *5475*
8: 9 About **f thousand** *men* were present. *5483*
8:20 I broke the seven loaves for the **f thousand,** *5483*
13:27 and gather his elect from the **f** winds, *5475*
Lk 16: 6 sit down quickly, and make it **f hundred.'** *4299*
19: 8 I will pay back **f times** the amount." *5486*
Jn 4:35 '**F months** more and then the harvest'? *5485*
11:17 in the tomb *for* **f** days. *5475*
11:39 for he has been there **f days."** *5479*
19:23 dividing them into **f** shares, *5475*
Ac 5:36 and about **f hundred** men rallied to him. *5484*
7: 6 enslaved and mistreated **f hundred** years. *5484*
10:11 down to earth *by* its **f** corners. *5475*
10:30 "**F** days ago I was in my house praying *5480*
11: 5 down from heaven *by* its **f** corners, *5475*
12: 4 handing him over to be guarded *by* **f squads** *5482*
12: 4 by four squads *of* **f** soldiers each. *5475*
21: 9 He had **f** unmarried daughters who prophesied. *5475*
21:23 There are **f** men with us who have made *5475*
21:38 a revolt and led **f thousand** terrorists out *5483*
27:29 they dropped **f** anchors from the stern *5475*
Rev 4: 6 around the throne, were **f** living creatures, *5475*
4: 8 Each of the **f** living creatures had six wings *5475*
5: 6 *by* the **f** living creatures and the elders. *5475*
5: 8 the **f** living creatures and the twenty-four *5475*
5:14 The **f** living creatures said, "Amen," *5475*
6: 1 of the **f** living creatures say in a voice *5475*
6: 6 like a voice among the **f** living creatures, *5475*
7: 1 After this I saw **f** angels standing at *5475*
7: 1 at the **f** corners of the earth, *5475*
7: 1 holding back the **f** winds of the earth *5475*
7: 2 *to* the **f** angels who had been given power *5475*
7:11 around the elders and the **f** living creatures. *5475*
9:14 "Release the **f** angels who are bound at *5475*
9:15 And the **f** angels who had been kept ready *5475*
14: 3 before the **f** living creatures and the elders. *5475*
15: 7 Then one of the **f** living creatures gave to *5475*
19: 4 and the **f** living creatures fell down *5475*
20: 8 the nations in the **f** corners of the earth— *5475*

FOUR-DRACHMA (1) [DRACHMAS, FOUR]

Mt 17:27 open its mouth and you will find a **f coin.** *5088*

FOUR-FIFTHS (1) [FIVE, FOUR]

Ge 47:24 The *other* **f** you may keep as seed for 752+3338

FOUR-FOOTED (2) [FOUR, FOOT]

Ac 10:12 It contained all kinds of **f animals,** *5488*
11: 6 into it and saw **f animals** of the earth, *5488*

FOUR-SIDED (1) [FOUR, SIDE]

1Ki 6:33 In the same way he made **f** jambs 8055

FOURFOLD (KJV) See FOUR TIMES

FOURS (4) [FOUR]

Lev 11:20 that walk on **all f** are to be detestable 752
11:21 some winged creatures that walk on **all f** 752

Lev 11:27 Of all the animals that walk on **all f**, 752
11:42 or walks on **all f** or on many feet; 752

FOURSCORE (KJV) See EIGHTY, EIGHT HUNDRED

FOURSQUARE (KJV) See SQUARE

FOURTEEN (27) [FOURTEENTH]

Ge 31:41 for you **f** years for your two daughters 752+6926
46:22 to Jacob—**f** in all. 752+6925
Nu 29:13 two rams and **f** male lambs a year old, 752+6925
29:15 and with each of the **f** lambs, one-tenth. 752+6925
29:17 two rams and **f** male lambs a year old, 752+6925
29:20 two rams and **f** male lambs a year old, 752+6925
29:23 two rams and **f** male lambs a year old, 752+6925
29:26 two rams and **f** male lambs a year old, 752+6925
29:29 two rams and **f** male lambs a year old, 752+6925
29:32 two rams and **f** male lambs a year old, 752+6925
Jos 15:36 **f** towns and their villages. 752+6926
18:28 **f** towns and their villages. 752+6926
1Ki 8:65 **f** days in all. 752+6925
10:26 he had **f hundred** chariots 547+752+2256+4395
1Ch 25:5 God gave Heman **f** sons 752+6925
2Ch 1:14 he had **f hundred** chariots 547+752+2256+4395
13:21 He married **f** wives 752+6926
Job 42:12 He had **f** thousand sheep, 752+6925
Eze 40:48 The width of the entrance was **f** cubits 752+6926
43:17 **f** cubits long and fourteen cubits wide, 752+6926
43:17 fourteen cubits long and **f** cubits wide, 752+6926
Mt 1:17 Thus there were **f** generations in all *1280*
1:17 **f** from David to the exile to Babylon, *1280*
1:17 and **f** from the exile to the Christ. *1280*
Ac 27:33 "For the last **f** days," he said, *5476*
2Co 12:2 in Christ who **f** years ago was caught up to *1280*
Gal 2:1 **F** years later I went up again to Jerusalem, *1280*

FOURTEENTH (24) [FOURTEEN]

Ge 14:5 In the **f** year, Kedorlaomer and 752+6926
Ex 12:6 of them until the **f** day of the month, 752+6925
12:18 evening of the **f** day until the evening 752+6925
Lev 23:5 twilight on the **f** day of the first month. 752+6925
Nu 9:3 at twilight on the **f** day of this month, 752+6925
9:5 Desert of Sinai at twilight on the **f** day 752+6925
9:11 **f** day of the second month at twilight. 752+6925
28:16 " 'On the **f** day of the first month 752+6925
Jos 5:10 the evening of the **f** day of the month, 752+6925
2Ki 18:13 In the **f** year of King Hezekiah's reign, 752+6926
1Ch 24:13 the **f** to Jeshebeab, 752+6925
25:21 the **f** to Mattithiah, 752+6925
2Ch 30:15 on the **f** day of the second month. 752+6925
35:1 on the **f** day of the first month. 752+6925
Ezr 6:19 On the **f** day of the first month, 752+6925
Est 9:15 in Susa came together on the **f** day of 752+6925
9:17 on the **f** they rested and made it a day 752+6925
9:18 had assembled on the thirteenth and **f**, 752+6925
9:19 observe the **f** of the month of Adar as 752+6925
9:21 to have them celebrate annually the **f** 752+6925
Isa 36:1 In the **f** year of King Hezekiah's reign, 752+6926
Eze 40:1 in the **f** year after the fall of the city— 752+6926
45:21 **f** day you are to observe the Passover, 752+6925
Ac 27:27 On the **f** night we were still being driven *5476*

FOURTH (72) [FOUR]

Ge 1:19 and there was morning—the **f** day. 8055
2:14 And the **f** river is the Euphrates. 8055
15:16 In the **f** generation your descendants will come back here, 8055
Ex 20:5 of the fathers to the third and **f generation** 8067
28:20 in the **f** row a chrysolite, 8055
34:7 of the fathers to the third and **f generation."** 8067
39:13 in the **f** row a chrysolite, 8055
Lev 19:24 In the **f** year all its fruit will be holy, 8055
Nu 7:30 On the **f** day Elizur son of Shedeur, 8055
14:18 the fathers to the third and **f generation.'** 8067
23:10 of Jacob or number the **f part** *of* Israel? 8065
29:23 " 'On the **f** day prepare ten bulls, 8055
Dt 5:9 of the fathers to the third and **f generation** 8067
Jos 19:17 **f** lot came out for Issachar, clan by clan. 8055
Jdg 14:15 On the **f** day, they said to Samson's wife, 8055
19:5 the **f** day they got up early and he prepared 8055
2Sa 3:4 the **f**, Adonijah the son of Haggith; 8055
1Ki 6:1 the **f** year of Solomon's reign over Israel, 8055
6:37 of the LORD was laid in the **f** year, 8055
22:41 of Asa became king of Judah in the **f** year 752
2Ki 10:30 on the throne of Israel to the **f generation."** 8055
15:12 on the throne of Israel to the **f generation."** 8055
18:9 In King Hezekiah's **f** year, 8055
25:3 the ninth day of the [**f**] month the famine NIH
1Ch 2:14 the **f** Nethanel, the fifth Raddai, 8055
3:2 the **f**, Adonijah the son of Haggith; 8055
3:15 Zedekiah the third, Shallum the **f**. 8055
8:2 Nohah the **f** and Rapha the fifth. 8055
12:10 Mishmannah the **f**, Jeremiah the fifth, 8055
23:19 Jahaziel the third and Jekameam the **f**. 8055
24:8 the third to Harim, the **f** to Seorim, 8055
24:23 Jahaziel the third and Jekameam the **f**. 8055
25:11 the **f** to Izri, his sons and relatives, 12 8055
26:2 Zebadiah the third, Jathniel the **f**, 8055
26:4 Sacar the **f**, Nethanel the fifth, 8055
26:11 Tabaliah the third and Zechariah the **f**. 8055
27:7 The **f**, for the fourth month, 8055
27:7 The fourth, for the **f** month, 8055
2Ch 3:2 the second month in the **f** year of his reign. 752
20:26 On the **f** day they assembled in the Valley 8055
Ezr 8:33 On the **f** day, in the house of our God, 8055
Job 42:16 and their children to the **f** generation. 752
Jer 25:1 the **f** year of Jehoiakim son of Josiah king 8055
28:1 the **f** year, early in the reign 8055
36:1 the **f** year of Jehoiakim son of Josiah king 8055
39:2 of the **f** month of Zedekiah's eleventh year, 8055
45:1 the **f** year of Jehoiakim son of Josiah king 8055
46:2 the **f** year of Jehoiakim son of Josiah king 8055
51:59 with Zedekiah king of Judah in the **f** year 8055
52:6 By the ninth day of the **f** month the famine 8055
Eze 1:1 in the **f** month on the fifth day, 8055
10:14 and the **f** the face of an eagle. 8055
Da 2:40 Finally, there will be a **f** kingdom, 10651
3:25 and the **f** looks like a son of the gods." 10651
7:7 and there before me was a **f** beast— 10651
7:19 of the **f** beast, which was different from all 10651
7:23 'The **f** beast is a fourth kingdom 10651
7:23 a **f** kingdom that will appear on earth. 10651
11:2 and then a **f**, who will be far richer 8055
Zec 6:3 and the **f** dappled—all of them powerful. 8055
7:1 In the **f** year of King Darius, 752
7:1 the LORD came to Zechariah on the **f** day 752
8:19 "The fasts of the **f**, fifth, 8055
Mt 14:25 the **f** watch of the night Jesus went out *5480*
Mk 6:48 About the **f** watch of the night he went out *5480*
Rev 4:7 the **f** was like a flying eagle. *5480*
6:7 When the Lamb opened the **f** seal, *5480*
6:7 the voice *of* the **f** living creature say, *5480*
6:8 over a **f** of the earth to kill by sword, *5480*
8:12 The **f** angel sounded his trumpet, *5480*
16:8 The **f** angel poured out his bowl on *5480*
21:19 the third chalcedony, the **f** emerald, *5480*

FOURTH (Anglicized) See also QUARTER

FOWL (1) [FOWLER, FOWLER'S]

1Ki 4:23 gazelles, roebucks and choice **f**. 1350

FOWLER (1) [FOWL]

Pr 6:5 like a bird from the snare of the **f**. 3687

FOWLER'S (2) [FOWL]

Ps 91:3 the **f** snare and from the deadly pestilence. 3687
124:7 like a bird out of the **f** snare; 3704

FOWLS (KJV) See BIRDS

FOX (2) [FOXES]

Ne 4:3 if even a **f** climbed up on it, 8785
Lk 13:32 He replied, "Go tell that **f**, *273*

FOXES (6) [FOX]

Jdg 15:4 So he went out and caught three hundred **f** 8785
15:5 and let the **f** loose in the standing grain of NIH
SS 2:15 Catch for us the **f**, 8785
2:15 the little **f** that ruin the vineyards, 8785
Mt 8:20 **"F** have holes and birds of the air have nests *273*
Lk 9:58 **"F** have holes and birds of the air have nests *273*

FRACTION (1)

Mk 12:42 copper coins, worth only **a f of a penny.** *3119*

FRACTURE (2) [FRACTURES]

Lev 24:20 **f** for fracture, eye for eye, tooth 8691
24:20 fracture for **f**, eye for eye, tooth 8691

FRACTURES (1) [FRACTURE]

Ps 60:2 mend its **f**, for it is quaking. 8691

FRAGILE (1)

Job 8:14 What he trusts in is **f**; 3684

FRAGMENT (1)

Isa 30:14 that among its pieces not a **f** will be found 3084

FRAGRANCE (14) [FRAGRANT]

Ex 30:38 like it to **enjoy** its **f** must be cut off 8193
SS 1:3 Pleasing is the **f** *of* your perfumes; 8194
1:12 my perfume spread its **f**. 8194
2:13 the blossoming vines spread their **f**. 8194
4:10 and the **f** *of* your perfume than any spice! 8194
4:11 The **f** *of* your garments is like that 8194
4:16 that its **f** may spread abroad. 1411
7:8 the **f** *of* your breath like apples, 8194
7:13 The mandrakes send out their **f**, 8194
Isa 3:24 Instead of **f** there will be a stench; 1411
Hos 14:6 his **f** like a cedar of Lebanon. 8194
Jn 12:3 house was filled with the **f** of the perfume. *4011*
2Co 2:14 and through us spreads everywhere the **f** of *4011*
2:16 to the other, the **f** of life. *4011*

FRAGRANT (28) [FRAGRANCE]

Ex 25:6 for the anointing oil and for the **f** incense; 6160
30:7 "Aaron must burn **f** incense on 6160
30:23 250 shekels) of **f** cinnamon, 1411
30:23 250 shekels of **f** cane, 1411
30:25 a **f** blend, the work of a perfumer. 5351
30:34 the LORD said to Moses, "Take **f spices**— 6160
30:35 and make a **f blend** *of* incense, 8381
31:11 and the anointing oil and **f** incense for 6160
35:8 for the anointing oil and for the **f** incense; 6160
35:15 the anointing oil and the **f** incense; 6160
35:28 for the anointing oil and for the **f** incense. 6160
37:29 **f** incense—the work of a perfumer. 6160
39:38 the anointing oil, the **f** incense, 6160
40:27 and burned **f** incense on it, 6160
Lev 4:7 on the horns of the altar of **f** incense that is 6160
16:12 of finely ground **f** incense and take them 6160
Nu 4:16 the **f** incense, the regular grain offering and 6160
2Ch 2:4 to dedicate it to him for burning **f** incense 6160
13:11 and **f** incense to the LORD. 6160
Ps 45:8 All your robes are **f** with myrrh and aloes NIH
Isa 43:24 You have not bought *any* **f calamus** 7866
Eze 6:13 places where they offered **f incense** 5767+8194
8:11 and a **f** cloud of incense was rising. 6986
16:19 you offered as **f incense** before them. 5767+8194
20:28 presented their **f incense** 5767+8194
20:41 as **f incense** when I bring you out from 5767+8194
Eph 5:2 as a **f** offering and sacrifice to God. *2380+4011*
Php 4:18 They are a **f** offering, *2380+4011*

FRAIL (KJV) See FLEETING

FRAME (14) [FRAMES]

Ex 26:16 Each **f** is to be ten cubits long and a cubit 7983
26:19 two bases for each **f**, 7983
26:21 and forty silver bases—two under each **f**. 7983
26:25 two under each **f**. 7983
36:21 Each **f** was ten cubits long and a cubit and 7983
36:24 two bases for each **f**, 7983
36:26 and forty silver bases—two under each **f**. 7983
36:30 two under each **f**. 7983
Nu 4:10 of sea cows and put it on a **carrying f**. 4573
4:12 of sea cows and put them on a **carrying f**. 4573
1Ki 7:31 that had a **circular f** one cubit deep. 4196
Job 17:7 my whole **f** is but a shadow. 3674
Ps 139:15 My **f** was not hidden from you 6798
Isa 58:11 and will strengthen your **f**. 6795

FRAMES (29) [FRAME]

Ex 26:15 "Make upright **f** of acacia wood for 7983
26:17 the **f** *of* the tabernacle in this way. 7983
26:18 Make twenty **f** for the south side of 7983
26:20 of the tabernacle, make twenty **f** 7983
26:22 Make six **f** for the far end, that is, 7983
26:23 make two **f** for the corners at the far end. 7983
26:25 be eight **f** and sixteen silver bases— 7983
26:26 five for the **f** *on* one side of the tabernacle, 7983
26:27 and five for the **f** on the west, 7983
26:28 from end to end at the middle of the **f**. 7983
26:29 the **f** with gold and make gold rings to hold 7983
35:11 clasps, **f**, crossbars, posts and bases; 7983
36:20 They made upright **f** of acacia wood for 7983
36:22 They made all the **f** *of* the tabernacle 7983
36:23 They made twenty **f** for the south side of 7983
36:25 they made twenty **f** 7983
36:27 They made six **f** for the far end, that is, 7983
36:28 and two **f** were made for the corners of 7983
36:29 At these two corners the **f** were double NIH
36:30 So there were eight **f** 7983
36:31 five for the **f** *on* one side of the tabernacle, 7983
36:32 and five for the **f** on the west, 7983
36:33 from end to end at the middle of the **f**. 7983
36:34 the **f** with gold and made gold rings to hold 7983
39:33 the tent and all its furnishings, its clasps, **f**, 7983
40:18 he put the bases in place, erected the **f**, 7983
Nu 3:36 to take care of the **f** *of* the tabernacle, 7983
4:31 to carry the **f** *of* the tabernacle, 7983
1Ki 7:5 All the doorways had rectangular **f**; 9208

FRANKINCENSE (2) [INCENSE]

Ex 30:34 and pure **f**, all in equal amounts, 4247
Rev 18:13 myrrh and **f**, of wine and olive oil, *3337*

FRANKLY (1)

Lev 19:17 **Rebuke** your neighbor **f** 3519+3519

FRANTIC (1)

1Ki 18:29 and *they continued their* **f prophesying** 5547

FRAUD (3) [DEFRAUD]

Pr 20:17 Food gained by **f** tastes sweet to a man, 9214
Jer 10:14 His images are a **f**; 9214
51:17 His images are a **f**; 9214

FRAY (1)

Job 39:21 and charges into the **f**. 5977

FRECKLED (KJV) See RASH

FREE (111) [FREED, FREEDMAN, FREEDMEN, FREEDOM, FREEING, FREELY]

Ge 2:16 *"You are* **f to eat** from any tree in 430+430
44:10 the rest of you will be **f from blame."** 5929
49:21 a doe **set f** that bears beautiful fawns. 8938

Ex 6: 6 *I will* **f** you from being slaves to them, 5911
21: 2 But in the seventh year, he shall go **f**, 2930
21: 3 If he comes alone, *he is to* **go f** alone; 3655
21: 4 and only the man *shall* **go f**. 3655
21: 5 and children and do not want to go **f**,' 2930
21: 7 *she is* not *to* **go f** as menservants do. 3655
21:11 *she is to* **go f**, 3655
21:26 the servant go **f** to compensate for the eye. 2930
21:27 he must let the servant go **f** to compensate 2930
Nu 5:28 not defiled herself and is **f from impurity,** 3196
32:22 **f from** your **obligation** to the LORD and 5929
Dt 7:15 The LORD *will* **keep** you **f** 6073
15:12 in the seventh year you must let him go **f**. 2930
15:18 a hardship *to* **set** your servant **f**, 2930+8938
24: 5 be **f** to stay at home and bring happiness to 5929
32:36 and no one is left, slave or **f**. 6440
Jdg 16:20 "I'll go out as before and **shake myself f."** 5850
2Sa 22:49 *who* **sets** me **f** from my enemies. 3655
1Ki 14:10 every last male in Israel—slave or **f**. 6440
20:34 "On the basis of a treaty I *will* **set** you **f."** 8938
20:42 *'You have* **set f** a man 3338+4946+8938
21:21 every last male in Israel—slave or **f**. 6440
2Ki 9: 8 every last male in Israel—slave or **f**. 6440
14:26 whether slave or **f**, was suffering; 6440
1Ch 4:10 from harm so that I will be **f from** pain." 1194
12:17 when my hands are **f from** violence 928+4202
Job 10: 1 therefore *I will* **give f rein** 6440
16:17 yet my hands have been **f of** violence 4202
21: 9 Their homes are safe and **f from** fear; 4946
33: 9 I am clean and **f from** guilt. 4202
36:16 to a spacious place **f from** restriction, 4202
39: 5 "Who let the wild donkey go **f?** 2930
Ps 25:17 **f** me from my anguish. 3655
31: 4 **F** me from the trap that is set for me, 3655
73: 5 They are **f from** the burdens common 401
81: 6 their hands *were* **set f** from the basket. 6296
105:20 the ruler of peoples **set** him **f**. 7337
118: 5 and he answered by **setting** me **f**. 5303
119:32 for *you have* **set** my heart **f**. 8143
129: 4 *he has* **cut** me **f** *from* the cords of 7915
142: 7 **Set** me **f** from my prison, 3655
146: 7 The LORD **sets** prisoners **f**, 6002
Pr 6: 3 my son, *to* **f yourself,** 5911
6: 5 **F yourself,** like a gazelle from the hand of 5911
11:21 but those who are righteous *will* **go f**. 4880
19: 5 and he who pours out lies *will* not **go f**. 4880
Isa 32:20 and **letting** your cattle and donkeys **range f**. 8079+8938
42: 7 to **f** captives from prison and to release 3655
45:13 and **set** my exiles **f**, 8938
49: 9 and to those in darkness, *'Be* **f!'** 1655
51:14 The cowering prisoners *will* soon **be set f;** 7337
52: 2 **F yourself** *from* the chains on your neck, 7337
58: 6 the cords of the yoke, to set the oppressed **f** 2930
Jer 2:31 *'We are* **f** *to* **roam;** AIT
34: 9 Everyone was to **f** his Hebrew slaves, 2930+8938
34:10 that they *would* **f** their male 2930+8938
34:10 They agreed, and **set** them **f**. 8938
34:14 each of *you must* **f** any fellow Hebrew who 8938
34:14 you must let him go **f**.' 2930
34:16 the male and female slaves you had set **f** 2930
37: 4 Now Jeremiah *was* **f** *to* **come** and go among AIT
La 5: 8 and there is none *to* **f** us from their hands. 7293
Eze 13:20 *I will* **set f** the people that you ensnare 8938
Zec 9:11 *I will* **f** your prisoners from 8938
Lk 13:12 *you are* **set f** from your infirmity." *668*
13:16 **be set f** on the Sabbath day *3395*
Jn 8:32 and the truth *will* **set** you **f."** *1802*
8:33 How can you say that we shall be **set f?"** *1801*
8:36 the Son **sets** you **f**, you will be free indeed. *1802*
8:36 the Son sets you free, you will be **f** indeed. *1801*
19:10 power either *to* **f** or to crucify you?" *668*
19:12 From then on, Pilate tried *to* **set** Jesus **f**, *668*
Ac 7:34 and have come down *to* **set** them **f**. *1975*
26:32 "This man could *have been* **set f** if he had *668*
Ro 6:18 *You have been* **set f** from sin *1802*
6:20 you were **f** from the control *1801*
6:22 But now *that you have been* **set f** from sin *1802*
8: 2 of the Spirit of life **set** me **f** from the law *1802*
13: 3 Do you want *to be* **f from fear of** the *3590+5828*
1Co 7:22 similarly, he who was a **f** *man* *1801*
7:32 I would like you to be **f from concern.** *291*
7:39 she is **f** to marry anyone she wishes, *1801*
9: 1 Am I not **f?** *1801*
9:18 the gospel I may offer it **f of charge,** *78*
9:19 I am **f and belong to no man,** *1666+1801+4246*
9:21 the law (though I am not **f from** God's **law** *491*
12:13 whether Jews or Greeks, slave or **f**— *1801*
2Co 11: 7 the gospel of God to you **f of charge?** *1562*
Gal 3:28 slave nor **f**, male nor female, *1801*
4:22 and the other by the **f** *woman*. *1801*
4:23 by the **f** *woman* was born as the result of *1801*
4:26 But the Jerusalem that is above is **f**, *1801*
4:30 in the inheritance with the **f** *woman's* son." *1801*
4:31 but *of* the **f** *woman*. *1801*
5: 1 It is for freedom that Christ *has* **set** us **f**. *1802*
5:13 You, my brothers, were called to **be f**. *1800*
Eph 6: 8 whether he is slave or **f**. *1801*
Col 1:22 without blemish and **f from accusation**— *441*
3:11 slave or **f**, but Christ is all, and is in all. *1801*
Heb 2:15 and **f** those who all their lives were held *557*
9:15 that he has died as a ransom to set them **f** *NIG*
13: 5 **f from the love of money** *921*
1Pe 2:16 Live as **f** *men*, but do not use your freedom *1801*
Rev 6:15 and every **f** *man* hid in caves and among *1801*
13:16 small and great, rich and poor, **f** and slave, *1801*
19:18 and the flesh *of* all people, **f** and slave, *1801*
20: 3 After that, he must *be* **set f** for a short time. *3395*
22:17 let him take the **f gift** of the water of life. *1562*

FREED (10) [FREE]

Lev 19:20 because *she had* not **been f**. 2926
Job 3:19 and the slave is **f** from his master. 2930
Ps 116:16 *you have* **f** me from my chains. 7337
136:24 and **f** us from our enemies, 7293
Jer 34:11 and took back the slaves *they had* **f** 2930+8938
52:31 of Judah and **f** him from prison on 3655
Mk 5:29 and she felt in her body that *she was* **f** *2615*
5:34 Go in peace and be **f** from your suffering." *5618*
Ro 6: 7 anyone who has died *has been* **f** from sin. *1467*
Rev 1: 5 and *has* **f** us from our sins by his blood, *3395*

FREEDMAN (1) [FREE]

1Co 7:22 by the Lord is the Lord's **f;** *592*

FREEDMEN (1) [FREE]

Ac 6: 9 from members of the Synagogue *of* the **F** *3339*

FREEDOM (24) [FREE]

Lev 19:20 not been ransomed or given her **f**, 2928
Ps 119:45 I will walk about in **f**, 8146
Isa 61: 1 to proclaim **f** for the captives and release 2002
Jer 34: 8 in Jerusalem to proclaim **f for** *the* **slaves.** 2002
34:15 of you proclaimed **f** to his countrymen. 2002
34:17 you have not proclaimed **f** 2002
34:17 So I now proclaim **'f'** for you, 2002
34:17 **'f'** to fall by the sword, plague and famine. NIH
Eze 46:17 the servant may keep it until the year of **f;** 2002
Lk 4:18 He has sent me to proclaim **f** for *912*
Ac 24:23 to give him some **f** and permit his friends *457*
Ro 8:21 to decay and brought into the glorious **f** of *1800*
1Co 7:21 although if you can **gain** *your* **f**, do so. *1181+1801*
8: 9 that the **exercise of** your **f** does not become *2026*
10:29 For why should my **f** be judged *1800*
2Co 3:17 where the Spirit of the Lord is, there is **f**. *1800*
Gal 2: 4 to spy on the **f** we have in Christ Jesus and *1800*
5: 1 It is *for* **f** that Christ has set us free. *1800*
5:13 not use your **f** to indulge the sinful nature; *1800*
Eph 3:12 in him we may approach God with **f** *4244*
Jas 1:25 the perfect law that *gives* **f**, and continues *1800*
2:12 to be judged by the law that *gives* **f**, *1800*
1Pe 2:16 but do not use your **f** as a cover-up for evil; *1800*
2Pe 2:19 They promise them **f**, *1800*

FREEING (2) [FREE]

Jer 40: 4 But today *I am* **f** you from the chains 7337
Ac 2:24 **f** him from the agony of death, *3395*

FREELY (22) [FREE]

Ge 43:34 So they feasted and **drank f** with him. 8910
Dt 15: 8 and **f lend** him whatever he needs. 6292+6292
23:23 because you made your vow **f** to 5607
1Ch 29: 9 for *they had* **given f** and wholeheartedly to 5605
Ezr 7:15 that the king and his advisers *have* **f given** 10461
Ps 12: 8 The wicked **f strut** about 2143
37:26 They are always generous and **lend f;** 4278
112: 5 to him who is generous and **lends f**, 4278
Pr 11:24 *One man* **gives f**, yet gains even more; 7061
Isa 55: 7 and to our God, for *he will* **f** pardon. 8049
Hos 14: 4 heal their waywardness and love them **f**, 5607
Mt 10: 8 **F** you have received, freely give. *1562*
10: 8 Freely you have received, **f** give. *1562*
Mk 1:45 Instead he went out and began to talk **f**, *4498*
Jn 1:20 He did not fail to confess, but confessed **f**, *NIG*
Ac 9:28 **moved about f** in Jerusalem, *1660+1744+2779*
26:26 and I can speak **f** to him. *4245*
Ro 3:24 and are justified **f** by his grace through *1562*
1Co 2:12 we may understand what God *has* **f given** us *5919*
2Co 6:11 We *have* **spoken f** to you, Corinthians, *487+3836+5125*
10: 8 if I boast somewhat **f** about the authority *4358*
Eph 1: 6 which *he has* **f given** us in the One he loves. *5923*

FREEMAN (KJV) See FREE MAN

FREEWILL (22) [WILL]

Ex 35:29 to the LORD **f offerings** for all the work 5607
36: 3 to bring **f offerings** morning after morning. 5607
Lev 7:16 the result of a vow or is a **f** offering, 5607
22:18 either to fulfill a vow or as a **f offering,** 5607
22:21 to fulfill a special vow or as a **f offering,** 5607
22:23 present as a **f offering** an ox or a sheep 5607
23:38 the **f offerings** you give to the LORD.) 5607
Nu 15: 3 or **f offerings** or festival offerings— 5607
29:39 and your **f offerings,** prepare these for 5607
Dt 12: 6 to give and your **f offerings,** 5607
12:17 or your **f offerings** or special gifts. 5607
16:10 a **f offering** in proportion to the blessings 5607
2Ch 31:14 in charge of the **f offerings** *given to* God, 5607
Ezr 1: 4 and with **f offerings** for the temple of God 5607
1: 6 in addition to all the **f offerings.** 5605
2:68 the heads of the families **gave f offerings** 5605
3: 5 **brought** as **f offerings** 5605+5607
7:16 as the **f offerings** *of* the people and priests 10461
8:28 and gold are a **f offering** to the LORD, 5607
Ps 54: 6 I will sacrifice a **f offering** to you; 5607
Eze 46:12 When the prince provides a **f offering** to 5607
Am 4: 5 and brag about your **f offerings**— 5607

FREEWOMAN (KJV) See FREE WOMAN

FRENZIED (1)

Job 39:24 In **f** excitement he eats up the ground; 8323

FREQUENT (1) [FREQUENTLY]

1Ti 5:23 of your stomach and your **f** illnesses. *4781*

FREQUENTLY (2) [FREQUENT]

Ac 24:26 so he sent for him **f** and talked with him. *4781*
2Co 11:23 been in prison **more f**, *4359*

FRESH (18) [FRESH-CUT, FRESHLY]

Ge 26:19 and discovered a well of **f** water there. 2645
Lev 14: 5 that one of the birds be killed over **f** water 2645
14: 6 of the bird that was killed over the **f** water. 2645
14:50 He shall kill one of the birds over **f** water 2645
14:51 the blood of the dead bird and the **f** water, 2645
14:52 the **f** water, the live bird, the cedar wood, 2645
15:13 and bathe himself with **f** water, 2645
Nu 19:17 into a jar and pour **f** water over them. 2645
Jdg 15:15 Finding a **f** jawbone of a donkey, 3269
16: 7 "If anyone ties me with seven **f** thongs 4300
16: 8 the Philistines brought her seven **f** thongs 4300
Job 29:20 My glory will remain **f** in me, 2543
Ps 92:14 they will stay **f** and green, 2015
Eze 47: 8 the water there *becomes* **f**. 8324
47: 9 **makes** the salt water **f;** 8324
47:11 swamps and marshes *will* not *become* **f;** 8324
Jas 3:11 Can both **f water** and salt water flow from *1184*
3:12 Neither can a salt spring produce **f** water. *1184*

FRESH-CUT (1) [CUT, FRESH]

Ge 30:37 however, took **f** branches from poplar, 4300

FRESHLY (1) [FRESH]

Ge 8:11 there in its beak was a **f plucked** olive leaf! 3273

FRET (4)

Ps 37: 1 *Do* not **f** because of evil men or be envious 3013
37: 7 *do* not **f** when men succeed in their ways, 3013
37: 8 *do* not **f**—it leads only to evil. 3013
Pr 24:19 *Do* not **f** because of evil men or be envious 3013

FRICTION (1)

1Ti 6: 5 **constant f between** men of corrupt mind, *1384*

FRIEND (70) [FRIENDLY, FRIENDS, FRIENDSHIP]

Ge 38:12 his **f** Hirah the Adullamite went with him. 8276
38:20 the young goat by his **f** the Adullamite 8276
Ex 32:27 each killing his brother and **f** 8276
33:11 as a man speaks with his **f**. 8276
Dt 13: 6 or your **closest f** secretly entices you, 889+3869+3870+5883+8276
Jdg 7:13 as a man was telling a **f** his dream. 8276
7:14 His **f** responded, "This can 8276
14:20 the **f** who had attended him at his wedding. 5335
15: 2 he said, "that I gave her to your **f**. 5335
15: 6 because his wife was given to his **f."** 5335
Ru 4: 1 "Come over here, my **f**, and sit down." 532+7141
2Sa 13: 3 Now Amnon had a **f** named Jonadab son 8276
15:37 So David's **f** Hushai arrived at Jerusalem 8291
16:16 Then Hushai the Arkite, David's **f**, 8291
16:17 "Is this the love you show your **f?** 8276
16:17 Why didn't you go with your **f?"** 8276
1Ki 16:11 whether relative or **f**. 8276
1Ch 27:33 Hushai the Arkite was the king's **f**. 8276
2Ch 20: 7 to the descendants of Abraham your **f?** 170
Job 6:27 for the fatherless and barter away your **f**. 8276
16:20 My intercessor is my **f** 8276
16:21 with God as a man pleads for his **f**. 8276
Ps 35:14 I went about mourning as though for my **f** 8276
41: 9 Even my **close f**, whom I trusted, 408+8934
55:13 my companion, my **close f**, 3359
88:18 the darkness *is* my **closest f**. 3359
119:63 I am a **f** to all who fear you, 2492
Pr 17:17 A **f** loves at all times, 8276
18:24 there is a **f** who sticks closer than a brother. 170
19: 4 but a poor man's **f** deserts him. 8276
19: 6 everyone is the **f** of a man who gives gifts. 8276
22:11 will have the king for his **f**. 8276
27: 6 Wounds from a **f** can be trusted, 170
27: 9 of one's **f** springs from his earnest counsel. 8276
27:10 Do not forsake your **f** and the friend 8276
27:10 and the **f** *of* your father, and do not go 8276
Ecc 4:10 his **f** can help him up. 2492
SS 5:16 This is my lover, this my **f**, 8276
Isa 41: 8 you descendants of Abraham my **f**, 170
Jer 3: 4 'My Father, my **f** *from* my youth, 476
9: 4 and every **f** a slanderer. 8276
9: 5 **F** deceives friend, and no one speaks 408[S]
9: 5 Friend deceives **f**, and no one speaks 8276
23:35 of you keeps on saying to his **f** or relative: 8276
Mic 7: 5 put no confidence in a **f**. 476
Mt 11:19 a **f** of tax collectors and "sinners." ' *5813*
20:13 "But he answered one of them, **'F,** *2279*
22:12 **'F,'** he asked, 'how did you get in here *2279*
26:50 Jesus replied, **"F,** do what you came for." *2279*
Lk 5:20 When Jesus saw their faith, he said, **"F,** *476*

Lk 7:34 a f of tax collectors and "sinners." ' *5813*
11: 5 "Suppose one of you has a f, *5813*
11: 5 '**F**, lend me three loaves of bread, *5813*
11: 6 a f of mine on a journey has come to me, *5813*
11: 8 and give him the bread because he is his **f**, *5813*
14:10 '**F**, move up to a better place.' *5813*
Jn 3:29 The **f** who attends the bridegroom waits *5813*
11:11 "Our **f** Lazarus has fallen asleep; *5813*
19:12 you are no **f** of Caesar. *5813*
Ro 16: 5 Greet my **dear f** Epenetus, *28*
16: 9 and my **dear f** Stachys. *28*
16:12 Greet my **dear f** Persis, *28*
Col 4:14 Our **dear f** Luke, the doctor, *28*
Phm 1: 1 *To* Philemon our **dear f** and fellow worker, *28*
Jas 2:23 and he was called God's **f**. *5813*
4: 4 a **f** of the world becomes an enemy of God. *5813*
3Jn 1: 1 The elder, *To* my **dear f** Gaius, *28*
1: 2 **Dear f**, I pray *28*
1: 5 **Dear f**, you are faithful *28*
1:11 **Dear f**, do not imitate what is evil *28*

FRIENDLY (3) [FRIEND]

Ge 34:21 "These men are **f** toward us," they said. 8969
Jdg 4:17 because there were **f relations** 8934
1Ki 5: 1 he had always been **on f terms** with David. 170

FRIENDS (91) [FRIEND]

Ge 19: 7 and said, "No, my **f**. Don't do this wicked 278
Jdg 11:37 to roam the hills and weep with my **f**, 8292
19:23 "No, my **f**, don't be so vile. 278
1Sa 30:26 who were his **f**, saying, 8276
2Sa 3: 8 of your father Saul and to his family and **f**. 5335
2Ki 10:11 his **close f** and his priests, 3359
Est 5:10 Calling together his **f** and Zeresh, his wife, 170
5:14 His wife Zeresh and all his **f** said to him, 170
6:13 and all his **f** everything that had happened 170
Job 2:11 When Job's three **f**, Eliphaz the Temanite, 8276
6:14 should have the devotion of his **f**, 5335
12: 4 "I have become a laughingstock to my **f**, 8276
17: 5 If a man denounces his **f** for reward, 8276
19:14 my **f** have forgotten me. 3359
19:19 All my intimate **f** detest me; 5493
19:21 "Have pity on me, my **f**, have pity, 8276
24:17 *they* **make f with** the terrors of darkness. 5795
32: 3 He was also angry with the three **f**, 8276
35: 4 like to reply to you and to your **f** with you. 8276
42: 7 "I am angry with you and your two **f**, 8276
42:10 After Job had prayed for his **f**, 8276
Ps 31:11 I am a dread to my **f**— 3359
38:11 My **f** and companions avoid me because 170
55:20 My companion attacks his **f**; 8934
88: 8 You have taken from me my **closest f** 3359
122: 8 For the sake of my brothers and **f**, 8276
Pr 14:20 but the rich have many **f**. 170
16:28 and a gossip separates **close f**. 476
17: 9 whoever repeats the matter separates **close f**. 476
19: 4 Wealth brings many **f**, 8276
19: 7 how much more do his **f** avoid him! 5335
22:24 *Do* not **make f** with a hot-tempered man, 8287
SS 1: 7 beside the flocks of your **f**? 2492
5: 1 Eat, O **f**, and drink; 8276
8:13 You who dwell in the gardens with **f** 2492
Jer 6:21 neighbors and **f** will perish." 8276
9: 4 "Beware of your **f**; 8276
20: 4 a terror to yourself and to all your **f**; 170
20: 6 and all your **f** to whom you prophesied lies.' 170
20:10 All my **f** are waiting for me to slip, 632+8934
38:22 those **trusted f** *of* yours. 408+8934
38:22 your **f** have deserted you.' NIH
La 1: 2 All her **f** have betrayed her; 8276
Da 2:13 for Daniel and his **f** to put them to death. 10245
2:17 and explained the matter to his **f** Hananiah, 10245
2:18 so that he and his **f** might not be executed 10245
Ob 1: 7 your **f** will deceive and overpower you; 408+8934
Zec 13: 6 wounds I was given at the house of my **f**.' 170
Lk 2:44 for him among their relatives and **f**. *1196*
7: 6 the house when the centurion sent **f** to say *5813*
12: 4 "I tell you, my **f**, *5813*
14:12 do not invite your **f**, *5813*
15: 6 Then he calls his **f** and neighbors together *5813*
15: 9 she calls her **f** and neighbors together *5813*
15:29 so I could celebrate with my **f**. *5813*
16: 9 use worldly wealth to gain **f** *5813*
21:16 brothers, relatives and **f**, *5813*
23:12 That day Herod and Pilate became **f**— *5813*
Jn 15:13 that he lay down his life for his **f**. *5813*
15:14 You are my **f** if you do what I command. *5813*
15:15 Instead, I have called you **f**, *5813*
21: 5 He called out to them, "**F**, *4086*
Ac 10:24 called together his relatives and close **f**. *5813*
15:25 to you with our **dear f** Barnabas and Paul— *28*
19:31 **f** of Paul, sent him a message begging him *5813*
24:23 to give him some freedom and permit his **f** *2625*
27: 3 to go to his **f** so they might provide *5813*
Ro 12:19 Do not take revenge, my **f**, *28*
1Co 10:14 Therefore, my **dear f**, flee from idolatry. *28*
2Co 7: 1 Since we have these promises, **dear f**, *28*
12:19 and everything we do, **dear f**, *28*
Php 2:12 my **dear f**, as you have always obeyed— *28*
4: 1 stand firm in the Lord, **dear f**! *28*
Heb 6: 9 Even though we speak like this, **dear f**, *28*
1Pe 2:11 **Dear f**, I urge you, as aliens and strangers *28*
4:12 **Dear f**, do not be surprised at *28*
2Pe 3: 1 **Dear f**, this is now my second letter to you. *28*
3: 8 But do not forget this one thing, **dear f**: *28*
2Pe 3:14 then, **dear f**, since you are looking forward *28*
3:17 **dear f**, since you already know this, *28*
1Jn 2: 7 **Dear f**, I am not writing you a new command *28*
3: 2 **Dear f**, now we are children of God, *28*
3:21 **Dear f**, if our hearts do not condemn us, *28*
4: 1 **Dear f**, do not believe every spirit, *28*
4: 7 **Dear f**, let us love one another, *28*
4:11 **Dear f**, since God so loved us, *28*
3Jn 1:14 The **f** here send their greetings. *5813*
1:14 Greet the **f** there by name. *5813*
Jude 1: 3 **Dear f**, although I was very eager to write *28*
1:17 But, **dear f**, remember what the apostles *28*
1:20 But you, **dear f**, build yourselves up *28*

FRIENDSHIP (8) [FRIEND]

Dt 23: 6 not seek a **treaty of f** *with* them 2256+3208+8934
1Sa 20:42 for we have sworn **f** with each other in NIH
Ezr 9:12 not seek a **treaty of f** *with* them 2256+3208+8934
Job 29: 4 when God's **intimate f** blessed my house, 6051
Ps 109: 4 In return for my **f** they accuse me, 173
109: 5 and hatred for my **f**. 173
Pr 12:26 A righteous man is cautious in **f**, 8276
Jas 4: 4 that **f** with the world is hatred toward God? *5802*

FRIGHT (1) [FEAR]

Lk 24: 5 *In* their **f** the women bowed down *1181+1873*

FRIGHTEN (7) [FEAR]

Dt 28:26 and there will be no *one to* **f** them **away**. 3006
Ne 6: 9 They *were* all *trying to* **f** us, thinking, 3707
Job 7:14 then *you* **f** me with dreams and terrify me 3169
9:34 so that his terror *would* **f** me no more. 1286
Jer 7:33 and there will be no *one to* **f** them **away**. 3006
Eze 30: 9 to **f** Cush *out of* her complacency. 3006
2Co 10: 9 I do not want to seem to be trying *to* **f** you *1768*

FRIGHTENED (9) [FEAR]

Ge 42:35 the money pouches, *they were* **f**. 3707
43:18 Now the men *were* **f** when they were taken 3707
Isa 31: 4 against him, *he is* not **f** by their shouts 3169
Da 5: 6 *so* **f** that his knees knocked together 10097
Mk 9: 6 did not know what to say, they were **so f**.) *1769*
Lk 21: 9 wars and revolutions, *do* not *be* **f**. *4765*
24:37 They were startled and **f**, *1873*
Php 1:28 without *being* **f** in any way *4769*
1Pe 3:14 "Do not fear what they fear; *do* not *be* **f**." *5429*

FRIGHTENING (2) [FEAR]

Job 13:21 and stop **f** me *with* your terrors. 1286
Da 7: 7 terrifying and **f** and very powerful. 10028

FRINGE (1)

Job 26:14 And these are but the **outer f** *of* his works; 7896

FRO (2)

Ps 39: 6 Man is a mere phantom *as he* **goes to and f**: 2143
104:26 There the ships **go to and f**, 2143

FROGS (14)

Ex 8: 2 I will plague your whole country with **f**. 7630
8: 3 The Nile will teem with **f**. 7630
8: 4 The **f** will go up on you and your people 7630
8: 5 make **f** come up on the land of Egypt.' " 7630
8: 6 and the **f** came up and covered the land. 7630
8: 7 also made **f** come up on the land of Egypt. 7630
8: 8 to take the **f** away from me and my people, 7630
8: 9 and your houses may be rid of the **f**, 7630
8:11 The **f** will leave you and your houses, 7630
8:12 to the LORD about the **f** he had brought 7630
8:13 The **f** died in the houses, 7630
Ps 78:45 and **f** that devastated them. 7630
105:30 Their land teemed with **f**, 7630
Rev 16:13 I saw three evil spirits that looked like **f**; *1005*

FROLIC (2)

Ps 104:26 which you formed to **f** there. 8471
Jer 50:11 because *you* **f** like a heifer threshing grain 7055

FROM (5013) See Index of Articles Etc.

FRONDS (1)

Lev 23:40 and palm **f**, leafy branches and poplars, 4093

FRONT (159) [FRONTAL]

Ge 30:38 so that they would be **directly in f of** 4200+5790
30:39 they mated **in f of** the branches. 448
30:41 the branches in the troughs **in f of** 4200+6524
31:37 Put it here **in f of** your relatives and mine, 5584
32:17 owns all these animals **in f of** you?' 4200+7156
33: 2 the maidservants and their children *in* **f**, 8037
40: 9 "In my dream I saw a vine **in f of** me, 4200+7156
Ex 7:10 Aaron threw his staff down **in f of** Pharaoh 4200+7156
13:22 night left its place **in f of** the people. 4200+7156
14:19 who had been traveling **in f of** 4200+7156
14:19 The pillar of cloud also moved from **in f** 7156
16:34 the manna **in f of** the Testimony, 4200+7156
19: 2 in the desert **in f of** the mountain. 5584
25:37 up on it so that they light the space **in f of** 7156
Ex 26: 9 the sixth curtain double at the **f** *of* the tent. 7156
27:21 the curtain that is **in f of** the Testimony, 6584
28:25 to the shoulder pieces of the ephod at the **f**. 7156
28:27 the shoulder pieces on the **f** *of* the ephod, 7156
28:37 it is to be on the **f** *of* the turban. 7156
29:10 the bull to the **f** *of* the Tent of Meeting, 7156
30: 6 altar **in f of** the curtain that is before 4200+7156
30:36 and place it **in f of** the Testimony in 4200+7156
32: 5 an altar **in f of** the calf and announced, 4200+7156
32:15 on both sides, **f** and back. 2296[S]
33:19 to pass **in f of** you, 6584+7156
34: 3 herds may graze **in f of** the mountain." 448+4578
34: 6 he passed **in f of** Moses, proclaiming, 6584+7156
39:18 to the shoulder pieces of the ephod at the **f**. 7156
39:20 the shoulder pieces on the **f** *of* the ephod, 7156
40: 5 altar of incense **in f of** the ark of the Testimony 4200+7156
40: 6 Place the altar of burnt offering **in f of** 4200+7156
40:26 the Tent of Meeting **in f of** the curtain 4200+7156
Lev 3: 8 of his offering and slaughter it **in f of** 4200+7156
3:13 and slaughter it **in f of** the Tent 4200+7156
4: 6 **in f of** the curtain of the sanctuary. 907+7156
4:17 sprinkle it before the LORD seven times **in f of** the curtain. 907+7156
6:14 **in f of** the altar. 448+7156
8: 9 the sacred diadem, on the **f** *of* it, 7156
9: 5 the things Moses commanded to the **f** *of* 7156
10: 4 away from the **f** *of* the sanctuary." 7156
13:41 the **f** *of* his scalp and has a bald forehead, 6991
16: 2 the curtain **in f of** the atonement cover 448+7156
16:14 and with his finger sprinkle it on the **f** *of* 7156
16:15 on the atonement cover and **in f of** it. 4200+7156
17: 4 to the LORD **in f of** the tabernacle of 4200+7156
19:14 put a stumbling block **in f of** the blind, 4200+7156
Nu 3:38 **in f of** the Tent of Meeting. 4200+7156
8: 2 to light the area **in f of** the lampstand.' " 448+4578+7156
8: 9 the Levites to the **f** *of* the Tent of Meeting 7156
8:13 Have the Levites stand **in f of** Aaron 4200+7156
14: 5 and Aaron fell facedown **in f of** 4200+7156
16:43 Then Moses and Aaron went to the **f** *of* 7156
17: 4 Tent of Meeting **in f of** the Testimony, 4200+7156
17:10 "Put back Aaron's staff **in f of** 4200+7156
19: 4 and sprinkle it seven times toward the **f** *of* 7156
20:10 the assembly together **in f of** the rock 448+7156
Dt 14: 1 shave the **f of** your **heads** for the dead, 1068+6524
26: 4 and set it down **in f of** the altar 4200+7156
Jos 4:12 armed, **in f of** the Israelites, 4200+7156
5:13 saw a man standing **in f of** him with 4200+5584
6: 4 of rams' horns **in f of** the ark. 4200+7156
6: 6 seven priests carry trumpets **in f of** 4200+7156
8:11 and approached the city and arrived **in f of** 5584
8:33 the people stood **in f of** Mount Gerizim 448+4578
8:33 and half of them **in f of** Mount Ebal, 448+4578
Jdg 18:21 livestock and their possessions **in f of** 4200+7156
1Sa 8:11 and they will run **in f of** his chariots. 4200+7156
9:24 what was on it and set it **in f of** Saul. 4200+7156
16: 8 and had him pass **in f of** Samuel. 4200+7156
17:41 with his shield bearer **in f of** him, 4200+7156
21:15 to carry on like this **in f of** me? 6584
2Sa 2:14 up and fight hand to hand **in f of** us." 4200+7156
3:31 and walk in mourning **in f of** 4200+7156
5:23 attack them **in f of** the balsam trees. 4578+4946
5:24 the LORD has gone out **in f of** you 4200+7156
6: 4 and Ahio was walking **in f of** it. 4200+7156
10: 9 Joab saw that there were battle lines **in f of** him and behind him; 4946+7156
11:15 "Put Uriah **in the f line** where 448+4578+7156
1Ki 6: 3 The portico at the **f** *of* the main hall of 7156
6: 3 and projected ten cubits from the **f** *of* 7156
6:17 The main hall **in f of** this room 4200+7156
6:21 and he extended gold chains across the **f** 7156
7: 5 they were **in the f part** in sets of three, 4578
7: 6 **In f of** it was a portico, 6584+7156
7: 6 and **in f of** that were pillars and 6584+7156
7:49 **in f of** the inner sanctuary); 4200+7156
8: 8 Holy Place **in f of** the inner sanctuary, 6584+7156
8:22 of the LORD **in f of** the whole assembly 5584
8:64 middle part of the courtyard **in f of** 4200+7156
2Ki 11:18 killed Mattan the priest of Baal **in f of** 4200+7156
15:10 He attacked him **in f of** the people, 7692
16:14 before the LORD he brought from the **f** 7156
1Ch 14:14 attack them **in f of** the balsam trees. 4578+4946
14:15 will mean God has gone out **in f of** 4200+7156
19:10 Joab saw that there were battle lines **in f of** 7156
2Ch 1: 5 in Gibeon **in f of** the tabernacle of 4200+7156
3: 4 the **f** *of* the temple was twenty cubits long 7156
3:15 **In** the **f of** the temple he made two pillars, 4200+7156
3:17 the pillars in the **f** *of* the temple, 7156
4:20 to burn **in f of** the inner sanctuary 4200+7156
5: 9 seen from **in f of** the inner sanctuary, 6584+7156
6:12 of the LORD **in f of** the whole assembly 5584
7: 7 middle part of the courtyard **in f of** 4200+7156
8:12 of the LORD that he had built **in f of** 4200+7156
13:13 while he was **in f of** Judah the ambush 4200+7156
13:14 that they were being attacked at both **f** 7156
15: 8 the LORD that was **in f of** the portico 4200+7156
20: 5 the LORD **in** the **f of** the new courtyard 4200+7156
23:17 killed Mattan the priest of Baal **in f of** 4200+7156
29:19 They are now **in f of** the LORD's altar. 4200+7156
Ne 3:23 and Hasshub made repairs **in f of** 5584
3:28 each **in f of** his own house. 4200+5584
Est 4: 6 in the open square of the city **in f of** 4200+7156
5: 1 **in f of** the king's hall. 5790
Ps 68:25 **In f** *are* the singers, 7709
Pr 21:29 A wicked man **puts up a bold f**, 928+6451+7156

Jer 24: 1 of figs placed **in f of** the temple of 4200+7156
36:22 fire burning in the firepot **in f of** him. 4200+7156
Eze 4: 1 put it **in f of** you and draw the city 4200+7156
6: 4 slay your people **in f of** your idols. 4200+7156
6: 5 the dead bodies of the Israelites **in f of** 4200+7156
8:11 **In f of** them stood seventy elders of 4200+7156
9: 6 the elders who were **in f of** the temple. 4200+7156
14: 1 Israel came to me and sat down **in f of** 4200+7156
16:37 from all around and will strip you **in f of** 448
20: 1 and they sat down **in f of** me. 4200+7156
40:12 **In f of** each alcove was 4200+7156
40:47 And the altar was **in f of** the temple. 4200+7156
40:49 and twelve cubits **from f to back.** 8145
41:14 including the **f** *of* the temple, 7156
41:21 the **f** *of* the Most Holy Place was similar. 7156
41:25 a wooden overhang on the **f** *of* the portico. 7156
42: 4 **In f of** the rooms was 4200+7156
42: 7 it extended **in f of** the rooms 448+7156
42:11 with a passageway **in f of** them. 4200+7156
44: 4 of the north gate to the **f** *of* the temple. 7156
Joel 2:20 with its **f columns** going into 7156
Zec 3: 9 See, the stone I have set **in f of** Joshua! 4200+7156
14:20 like the sacred bowls **in f of** the altar. 4200+7156
Mt 5:24 leave your gift there **in f of** the altar. *1869*
27:24 he took water and washed his hands **in f of** *595*
27:29 a staff in his right hand and knelt **in f of** *1869*
27:60 **rolled** a big stone **in f of** the entrance *4685*
Mk 3: 3 "Stand up in **f of everyone."** *3545+3836*
5: 6 **fell on** his **knees in f of** him. *4686*
15:39 who stood there **in f of** Jesus, *1666+1885*
Lk 5:19 right **in f of** Jesus. *1869*
5:25 Immediately he stood up **in f of** them, *1967*
6: 8 "Get up and stand **in f of everyone."** *3545+3836*
14: 2 There **in f of** him was a man suffering *1869*
19:27 bring them here and kill them **in f of** *1869*
Ac 18:17 the synagogue ruler and beat him **in f of** *1869*
19:33 **pushed** Alexander **to the f,** *4582*
27:35 and gave thanks to God **in f of** them all. *1967*
1Co 6: 6 and this **in f of** unbelievers! *2093*
Gal 2:14 I said to Peter **in f of** them all, *1869*
Rev 4: 6 covered with eyes, **in f** and in back. *1869*
7: 9 before the throne and **in f of** the Lamb. *1967*
12: 4 The dragon stood **in f of** the woman *1967*

FRONTAL (1) [FRONT]

Jdg 20:34 of Israel's finest men made a **f** attack 4946+5584

FRONTIER (2) [FRONTIERS]

Eze 25: 9 beginning at its **f** towns— 7895
48: 1 the northern **f,** Dan will have one portion, 7895

FRONTIERS (1) [FRONTIER]

Ne 9:22 allotting to them even the **remotest f.** 6992

FROST (5)

Ex 16:14 thin flakes like **f** on the ground appeared 4095
Job 38:29 Who gives birth to the **f** *from* the heavens 4095
Ps 147:16 like wool and scatters the **f** like ashes. 4095
Jer 36:30 and exposed to the heat by day and the **f** 7943
Zec 14: 6 there will be no light, no cold or **f.** 7885

FROWARD (KJV) See CORRUPT, CROOKED, DEVIOUS, HARSH, PERVERSE, WICKED, WILY

FROWN (1)

Jer 3:12 *'I will* **f** on you no longer, 5877+7156

FROZE (1) [FROZEN]

2Sa 23:10 the Philistines till his hand grew tired and **f** 1815

FROZEN (2) [FROZE]

Job 37:10 and the broad waters become **f.** 3668
38:30 when the surface of the deep *is* **f?** 4334

FRUIT (172) [FIRSTFRUITS, FRUITAGE, FRUITFUL, FRUITFULNESS, FRUITION, FRUITLESS, FRUITS]

Ge 1:11 and trees on the land that bear **f** with seed 7262
1:12 according to their kinds and trees bearing **f** 7262
1:29 of the whole earth and every tree that has **f** 7262
3: 2 "We may eat **f** from the trees in the garden, 7262
3: 3 'You must not eat **f** from the tree that is in 7262
3: 6 that the **f** of the tree was good for food 7262
3:12 she gave me some **f** from the tree, NIH
Ex 10:15 everything growing in the fields and the **f** 7262
Lev 19:23 the land and plant any kind of **f** tree, 4407
19:23 regard its **f** as forbidden. 7262
19:24 In the fourth year all its **f** will be holy, 7262
19:25 But in the fifth year you may eat its **f.** 7262
23:40 the first day you are to take choice **f** *from* 7262
25:19 Then the land will yield its **f,** 7262
26: 4 and the trees of the field their **f.** 7262
26:20 nor will the trees of the land yield their **f.** 7262
27:30 from the soil or **f** *from* the trees, belongs to 7262
Nu 13:20 Do your best to bring back some of the **f** 7262
13:26 the whole assembly and showed them the **f** 7262
13:27 Here is its **f.** 7262
Dt 1:25 with them some of the **f** *of* the land, 7262
7:13 He will bless the **f** *of* your womb, 7262
Dt 20:19 because you can eat their **f.** NIH
20:20 that you know are not **f** trees and use them 4407
22: 9 not only the crops you plant but also the **f** 9311
28: 4 The **f** *of* your womb will be blessed, 7262
28:11 in the **f** *of* your womb, 7262
28:18 The **f** *of* your womb will be cursed, 7262
28:30 but you will not even begin to enjoy its **f.** NIH
28:53 you will eat the **f** *of* the womb, 7262
30: 9 of your hands and in the **f** *of* your womb, 7262
32:13 of the land and fed him with the **f** *of* 9482
Jdg 9:11 the fig tree replied, 'Should I give up my **f,** 9482
2Sa 16: 2 the bread and **f** are for the men to eat, 7811
2Ki 19:29 plant vineyards and eat their **f.** 7262
19:30 and bear **f** above. 7262
Ne 9:25 olive groves and **f** trees in abundance. 4407
9:36 so they could eat its **f** and 7262
10:35 of our crops and of every **f** tree. 7262
10:37 the **f** *of* all our trees and of our new wine 7262
Ps 1: 3 which yields its **f** in season 7262
72: 3 the hills the **f** of righteousness. NIH
72:16 Let its **f** flourish like Lebanon; 7262
92:14 *They will* still **bear f** in old age, 5649
104:13 the earth is satisfied by the **f** *of* his work. 7262
128: 2 You will eat the **f** of your **labor;** 3330+4090
148: 9 **f** trees and all cedars, 7262
Pr 1:31 they will eat the **f** *of* their ways and 7262
1:31 and be filled with the **f** of their schemes. NIH
8:19 My **f** is better than fine gold; 7262
11:30 The **f** *of* the righteous is a tree of life, 7262
12:14 From the **f** *of* his lips a man is filled 7262
13: 2 the **f** *of* his lips a man enjoys good things, 7262
18:20 From the **f** *of* his mouth 7262
18:21 and those who love it will eat its **f.** 7262
27:18 He who tends a fig tree will eat its **f,** 7262
Ecc 2: 5 and parks and planted all kinds of **f** trees 7262
SS 2: 3 and his **f** is sweet to my taste. 7262
2:13 The fig tree forms its **early f;** 7001
7: 7 and your breasts like **clusters of f.** 864
7: 8 I will take hold of its **f."** 6180
8:11 for its **f** a thousand shekels of silver. 7262
8:12 two hundred are for those who tend its **f.** 7262
Isa 3:10 for they will enjoy the **f** *of* their deeds. 7262
4: 2 the **f** *of* the land will be the pride and glory 7262
5: 2 but it yielded only **bad f.** 946
11: 1 from his roots a Branch *will* **bear f.** 7238
14:29 its **f** will be a darting, venomous serpent. 7262
16: 9 The shouts of joy over your **ripened f** and 7811
27: 6 and blossom and fill all the world with **f.** 9482
32:10 and the **harvest of f** will not come. 668
32:17 The **f** *of* righteousness will be peace; 5126
37:30 plant vineyards and eat their **f.** 7262
37:31 and bear **f** above. 7262
65:21 they will plant vineyards and eat their **f.** 7262
Jer 2: 7 I brought you into a fertile land to eat its **f** 7262
6:19 the **f** *of* their schemes, 7262
7:20 on the trees of the field and on the **f** *of* 7262
11:16 a thriving olive tree with **f** beautiful 7262
11:19 saying, "Let us destroy the tree and its **f;** 4312
12: 2 they grow and bear **f.** 7262
17: 8 a year of drought and never fails to bear **f."** 7262
31: 5 farmers will plant them and enjoy their **f.** NIH
40:10 harvest the wine, **summer f** and oil, 7811
40:12 an abundance of wine and **summer f.** 7811
48:32 The destroyer has fallen on your **ripened f** 7811
Eze 17: 8 bear **f** and become a splendid vine.' 7262
17: 9 Will it not be uprooted and stripped of its **f** 7262
17:23 and bear **f** and become a splendid cedar. 7262
19:12 it was stripped of its **f;** 7262
19:14 of its main branches and consumed its **f.** 7262
25: 4 they will eat your **f** and drink your milk. 7262
34:27 The trees of the field will yield their **f** and 7262
36: 8 will produce branches and **f** 7262
36:30 the **f** *of* the trees and the crops of the field, 7262
47:12 **F** trees of all kinds will grow on 4407
47:12 nor will their **f** fail. 7262
47:12 Their **f** will serve for food and their leaves 7262
Da 4:12 Its leaves were beautiful, its **f** abundant, 10004
4:14 strip off its leaves and scatter its **f.** 10004
4:21 with beautiful leaves and abundant **f,** 10004
Hos 9:10 like seeing the **early f** on the fig tree. 1136
9:16 their root is withered, they yield no **f.** 7262
10: 1 he brought forth **f** for himself 7262
10: 1 As his **f** increased, he built more altars; 7262
10:12 reap the **f** *of* unfailing love, 7023
10:13 you have eaten the **f** *of* deception. 7262
14: 2 that we may offer the **f** *of* our lips. 7262
Joel 2:22 The trees are bearing their **f;** 7262
Am 2: 9 I destroyed his **f** above 7262
6:12 and the **f** *of* righteousness into bitterness— 7262
8: 1 a basket of **ripe f.** 7811
8: 2 "A basket of **ripe f,"** I answered. 7811
9:14 they will make gardens and eat their **f.** 7262
Mic 6: 7 the **f** *of* my body for the sin of my soul? 7262
7: 1 I am like one who gathers **summer f** at 7811
Na 3:12 like fig trees with their **first ripe f;** 1137
Hag 2:19 and the olive tree *have* not **borne f.** 5951
Zec 8:12 the vine will yield its **f,** 7262
Mal 3:11 in your fields *will* not **cast** *their* **f,"** 8897
Mt 3: 8 Produce **f** in keeping with repentance. *2843*
3:10 that does not produce good **f** will be cut *2843*
7:16 By their **f** you will recognize them. *2843*
7:17 Likewise every good tree bears good **f,** *2843*
7:17 but a bad tree bears bad **f.** *2843*
7:18 A good tree cannot bear bad **f,** *2843*
7:18 and a bad tree cannot bear good **f.** *2843*
7:19 Every tree that does not bear good **f** is cut *2843*
7:20 Thus, by their **f** you will recognize them. *2843*
Mt 12:33 "Make a tree good and its **f** will be good, *2843*
12:33 or make a tree bad and its **f** will be bad, *2843*
12:33 for a tree is recognized by its **f.** *2843*
21:19 "May you never bear **f** again!" *2843*
21:34 to the tenants to collect his **f.** *2843*
21:43 to a people who will produce its **f.** *2843*
26:29 not drink of this **f** of the vine from now on *1163*
Mk 11:13 he went to find out if it had any **f.** *NIG*
11:14 "May no one ever eat **f** from you again." *2843*
12: 2 from them some of the **f** of the vineyard. *2843*
14:25 I will not drink again of the **f** of the vine *1163*
Lk 3: 8 Produce **f** in keeping with repentance. *2843*
3: 9 that does not produce good **f** will be cut *2843*
6:43 "No good tree bears bad **f,** *2843*
6:43 nor does a bad tree bear good **f.** *2843*
6:44 Each tree is recognized by its own **f.** *2843*
13: 6 and he went to look for **f** on it, *2843*
13: 7 for **f** on this fig tree and haven't found any. *2843*
13: 9 If it bears **f** next year, fine! *2843*
20:10 so they would give him some of the **f** of *2843*
22:18 For I tell you I will not drink again of the **f** *1163*
Jn 15: 2 cuts off every branch in me that bears no **f,** *2843*
15: 2 that does bear **f** he prunes so that it will be *2843*
15: 4 No branch can bear **f** by itself; *2843*
15: 4 Neither can you bear **f** unless you remain *NIG*
15: 5 he will bear much **f;** *2843*
15: 8 that you bear much **f,** *2843*
15:16 and appointed you to go and bear **f**— *2843*
15:16 **f** that will last. *2843*
Ro 7: 4 in order that *we might* **bear f** to God. *2844*
7: 5 so that *we* **bore f** for death. *2844*
15:28 that they have received this **f,** *2843*
Gal 5:22 But the **f** of the Spirit is love, joy, peace, *2843*
Eph 5: 9 the **f** of the light consists in all goodness, *2843*
Php 1:11 with the **f** of righteousness that comes *2843*
Col 1: 6 All over the world this gospel is **bearing f** *2844*
1:10 **bearing f** in every good work, *2844*
Heb 13:15 the **f** of lips that confess his name. *2843*
Jas 3:17 submissive, full of mercy and good **f,** *2843*
Jude 1:12 autumn trees, **without f** and uprooted— *182*
Rev 18:14 'The **f** you longed for is gone from you. *3967*
22: 2 the tree of life, bearing twelve crops of **f,** *2843*
22: 2 yielding its **f** every month. *2843*

FRUITAGE (1) [FRUIT]

Isa 27: 9 and this will be the full **f** *of* the removal 7262

FRUITFUL (30) [FRUIT]

Ge 1:22 *"Be* **f** and increase in number and fill 7238
1:28 *"Be* **f** and increase in number; 7238
8:17 so they can multiply on the earth and *be* **f** 7238
9: 1 *"Be* **f** and increase in number and fill 7238
9: 7 As for you, *be* **f** and increase in number; 7238
17: 6 *I will* **make** you very **f;** 7238
17:20 *I will* **make** him **f** 7238
28: 3 and **make** you **f** and increase your numbers 7238
35:11 *be* **f** and increase in number. 7238
41:52 because God *has* **made** me **f** in the land 7238
47:27 They acquired property there and *were* **f** 7238
48: 4 'I *am going to* **make** you **f** 7238
49:22 "Joseph is a **f vine,** 1201+7238
49:22 a **f vine** near a spring, 1201+7238
Ex 1: 7 the Israelites *were* **f** and multiplied greatly 7238
Lev 26: 9 and **make** you **f** and increase your numbers, 7238
Ps 105:24 **made** his people very **f;** 7238
107:34 and **f** land into a salt waste, 7262
107:37 that yielded a **f** harvest; 7262
128: 3 *be* like a **f** vine within your house; 7238
Isa 17: 6 four or five on the **f** boughs," 7238
27: 2 In that day—"Sing about a **f** vineyard: 2774
32:12 for the **f** vines 7238
Jer 4:26 I looked, and the **f land** was a desert; 4149
23: 3 *they will be* **f** and increase in number. 7238
49: 4 boast of your valleys *so* **f?** 2307
Eze 19:10 it was **f** and full of branches because 7238
36:11 and *they will be* **f** and become numerous. 7238
Jn 15: 2 so that *it will be* even more **f.** *2843+5770*
Php 1:22 this will mean **f** labor for me. *2843*

FRUITFULNESS (2) [FRUITFUL]

Dt 33:15 and the **f** *of* the everlasting hills; 4458
Hos 14: 8 your **f** comes from me." 7262

FRUITION (1) [FRUIT]

2Sa 23: 5 *Will he* not **bring to f** my salvation 7541

FRUITLESS (1) [FRUIT]

Eph 5:11 Have nothing to do with the **f** deeds *182*

FRUITS (5) [FRUIT]

Ge 4: 3 Cain brought some of the **f** *of* the soil as 7262
Ps 109:11 may strangers plunder the **f of** his **labor.** 3330
SS 4:13 an orchard of pomegranates with choice **f,** 7262
4:16 into his garden and taste its choice **f.** 7262
Jer 3:24 consumed **f of** our fathers' **labor—** 3330

FRUSTRATE (4) [FRUSTRATED, FRUSTRATES, FRUSTRATING, FRUSTRATION]

2Sa 17:14 to **f** the good advice of Ahithophel in order 7296
Ezr 4: 5 and **f** their plans during the entire reign 7296
Ps 14: 6 *You* evildoers **f** the plans of the poor, 1017

1Co 1:19 the intelligence of the intelligent *I will* **f.**" *119*

FRUSTRATED (3) [FRUSTRATE]
2Sa 13: 2 Amnon *became* **f** to the point of illness 7674
Ne 4:15 of their plot and that God *had* **f** it, 7296
Eze 24:12 *It has* **f** all efforts; 4206

FRUSTRATES (2) [FRUSTRATE]
Ps 146: 9 but *he* **f** the ways of the wicked. 6430
Pr 22:12 but *he* **f** the words of the unfaithful. 6156

FRUSTRATING (1) [FRUSTRATE]
2Sa 15:34 *you can* help me *by* **f** Ahithophel's advice. 7296

FRUSTRATION (2) [FRUSTRATE]
Ecc 5:17 with great **f**, affliction and anger. 4088
Ro 8:20 For the creation was subjected *to* **f**, *3470*

FRYINGPAN (KJV) See PAN

FUEL (13)
Isa 9: 5 will be **f** *for* the fire. 4409
9:19 be scorched and the people will be **f** *for* 4409
44:15 It is man's **f** for burning; NIH
44:19 "Half of it *I* **used for f;** 836+1198+8596
Jer 51:58 the nations' labor is only **f for** the **flames."** 836+928+1896
Eze 4:12 using human excrement for **f."** NIH
15: 4 on the fire as **f** and the fire burns both ends 433
15: 6 the vine among the trees of the forest as **f** 433
21:32 You will be **f** for the fire, 433
39: 9 **use** the weapons **for f** 1277
39: 9 seven years *they will* **use** them **for f.** 836+1277
39:10 **use** the weapons **for f.** 836+1277
Hab 2:13 the people's labor is only **f for** the **fire,** 836+928+1896

FUGITIVE (2) [FUGITIVES]
Pr 28:17 the guilt of murder *will be a* **f** till death; 5674
Eze 24:26 that day a **f** will come to tell you the news. 7127

FUGITIVES (14) [FUGITIVE]
Nu 21:29 up his sons as **f** and his daughters 7129
Jos 8:22 leaving them neither survivors nor **f.** 7127
Isa 15: 5 her **f** flee as far as Zoar, 1371
15: 9 the **f** *of* Moab and upon those who remain 7129
16: 3 Hide the **f**, do not betray the refugees. 5615
16: 4 Let the Moabite **f** stay with you; 5615
21:14 you who live in Tema, bring food for the **f.** 5610
43:14 and bring down as **f** all the Babylonians, 1371
45:20 assemble, you **f** *from* the nations. 7127
Jer 44:14 none will return except a *few* **f."** 7128
48:45 the **f** stand helpless, for a fire has gone out 5674
49: 5 and no one will gather the **f.** 5610
50:28 the **f** and refugees from Babylon declaring 5674
Ob 1:14 at the crossroads to cut down their **f,** 7129

FULFILL (50) [FULFILLED, FULFILLING, FULFILLMENT, FULFILLS]
Ge 38: 8 **f** *your* **duty** *to* her **as a brother-in-law** 3302
Lev 22:18 either **to f** a vow or as a freewill offering, 4200
22:21 to the LORD **to f a special vow** or as 5624+7098
Nu 6:21 *He must* **f** the vow he has made, 3869+4027+6913+7023
23:19 Does he promise and not **f?** 7756
Dt 25: 5 **f the duty of a brother-in-law** *to* her. 3302
25: 7 *He will* not **f the duty of a brother-in-law** 3302
1Sa 1:21 to the LORD and to **f** his vow, NIH
2Sa 15: 7 "Let me go to Hebron and **f** a vow I made 8966
1Ki 6:12 *I will* **f** through you the promise I gave 7756
12:15 to **f** the word the LORD had spoken 7756
2Ki 23:24 to **f** the requirements of the law written in 7756
2Ch 10:15 to **f** the word the LORD had spoken 7756
36:22 to **f** the word of the LORD spoken 3983
Ezr 1: 1 to **f** the word of the LORD spoken 3983
Est 5: 8 to grant my petition and **f** my request, 6913
Job 22:27 and *you will* **f** your vows. 8966
Ps 22:25 those who fear you *will I* **f** my vows. 8966
50:14 **f** your vows to the Most High, 8966
61: 8 to your name and **f** my vows day after day. 8966
66:13 with burnt offerings and **f** my vows 8966
76:11 to the LORD your God and **f** them; 8966
116:14 *I will* **f** my vows to the LORD in 8966
116:18 *I will* **f** my vows to the LORD in 8966
119:38 **F** your promise to your servant, 7756
138: 8 The LORD *will* **f** [his purpose] for me; 1698
Ecc 5: 4 He has no pleasure in fools; **f** your vow. 8966
5: 5 not to vow than to make a vow and not **f** it. 8966
Isa 46:11 from a far-off land, a **man** *to* **f** my purpose. AIT
Jer 11: 5 Then *I will* **f** the oath I swore 7756
28: 6 *May* the LORD **f** the words 7756
29:10 to you and **f** my gracious promise 7756
33:14 'when *I will* **f** the gracious promise 7756
39:16 *I am about to* **f** my words against this city 995
Eze 12:25 *I will* **f** whatever I say, 6913
Na 1:15 O Judah, and **f** your vows. 8966
Mt 1:22 to **f** what the Lord had said through *4444*
3:15 for us to do this *to* **f** all righteousness." *4444*
4:14 to **f** what was said through *4444*
5:17 not come to abolish them but *to* **f** them. *4444*
8:17 This was to **f** what was spoken through *4444*
Mt 12:17 This was to **f** what was spoken through *4444*
21: 4 to **f** what was spoken through the prophet: *4444*
Jn 12:38 to **f** the word of Isaiah the prophet: *4444*
13:18 But this is to **f** the scripture: *4444*
15:25 But this is to **f** what is written in their Law: *4444*
Ac 7:17 the time drew near for God to **f** his promise *NIG*
1Co 7: 3 The husband *should* **f** his marital duty *625*
Gal 6: 2 in this way *you will* **f** the law of Christ. *405*
2Th 1:11 by his power *he may* **f** every good purpose *4444*

FULFILLED (60) [FULFILL]
Jos 21:45 every one *was* **f.** 995
23:14 Every promise *has been* **f;** 995
Jdg 13:12 "When your words *are* **f,** 995
1Sa 10: 7 Once these signs *are* **f,** 995
10: 9 and all these signs *were* **f** that day. 995
1Ki 8:15 with his own hand *has* **f** what he promised 4848
8:24 and with your hand *you have* **f** it— 4848
9:25 **f** the temple **obligations.** 8966
2Ki 15:12 of the LORD spoken to Jehu *was* **f:** 2118+4027
2Ch 6: 4 *who* with his hands *has* **f** what he promised 4848
6:15 and with your hand *you have* **f** it— 4848
Ps 65: 1 to you our vows *will* **be f.** 8966
Pr 7:14 today *I* **f** my vows. 8966
13:12 but a longing **f** is a tree of life. 995
13:19 A longing **f** is sweet to the soul, 2118
Jer 1:12 to *see that* my word *is* **f."** 6913
17:15 *Let it* now **be f!"** 995
25:12 "But when the seventy years *are* **f,** 4848
34:18 not **f** the terms of the covenant they made 7756
39:16 that time *they will be* **f** before your eyes. 2118
La 2:17 *he has* **f** his word, 1298
Eze 12:23 days are near when every vision will be **f.** 1821
12:25 and *it shall* **be f** without delay. 6913
12:28 whatever I say *will* **be f,** 6913
13: 6 yet they expect their words to *be* **f.** 7756
Da 4:33 about Nebuchadnezzar *was* **f.** 10508
8:13 "How long will it take for the vision to be **f** NIH
9:12 *You have* **f** the words spoken against us and 7756
12: 6 be before these astonishing things are **f?"** 7891
Mt 2:15 so *was* **f** what the Lord had said through *4444*
2:17 through the prophet Jeremiah *was* **f:** *4444*
2:23 *was* **f** what was said through the prophets: *4444*
13:14 In them *is* **f** the prophecy of Isaiah: *405*
13:35 So *was* **f** what was spoken through *4444*
26:54 the Scriptures *be* **f** that say it must happen *4444*
26:56 that the writings of the prophets *might be* **f."** *4444*
27: 9 by Jeremiah the prophet *was* **f:** *4444*
Mk 13: 4 be the sign that they are all about to *be* **f?"** *5334*
14:49 But the Scriptures *must be* **f."** *4444*
Lk 1: 1 an account of the things that *have been* **f** *4442*
4:21 "Today this scripture *is* **f** in your hearing." *4444*
18:31 about the Son of Man *will be* **f.** *5464*
21:24 until the times of the Gentiles *are* **f.** *4444*
22:37 and I tell you that this must *be* **f** in me. *5464*
24:44 *be* **f** that is written about me in the Law *4444*
Jn 17:12 to destruction so that Scripture *would be* **f.** *4444*
18: 9 that the words he had spoken *would be* **f:** *4444*
18:32 of death he was going to die *would be* **f.** *4444*
19:24 that the scripture *might be* **f** which said, *4444*
19:28 and so that the Scripture *would be* **f,** *5464*
19:36 so that the scripture *would be* **f:** *4444*
Ac 1:16 *be* **f** which the Holy Spirit spoke long ago *4444*
3:18 But this is how God **f** what he had foretold *4444*
13:27 yet in condemning him *they* **f** the words of *4444*
13:33 he *has* **f** for us, their children, *1740*
23: 1 *I have* **f** *my* **duty** to God *4488*
26: 7 *to* **see f** as they earnestly serve God day *2918*
Ro 13: 8 he who loves his fellowman *has* **f** the law. *4444*
Jas 2:23 And the scripture *was* **f** that says, *4444*
Rev 17:17 until God's words *are* **f.** *5464*

FULFILLING (3) [FULFILL]
Nu 3: 8 **f** the obligations of the Israelites **by doing** 6268
1Ki 2:27 **f** the word the LORD had spoken 4848
Ecc 5: 4 do not delay in **f** it. 8966

FULFILLMENT (10) [FULFILL]
Lev 22:23 but it will not be accepted **in f** of a vow. 4200
2Ch 36:21 the seventy years were completed *in* **f** *of* 4848
Da 11:14 among your own people will rebel in **f** *of* 6641
Lk 9:31 which he was about to **bring to f** *4444*
21:22 For this is the time of punishment *in* **f** *4398*
22:16 until *it* **finds f** in the kingdom of God." *4444*
22:37 what is written about me is reaching its **f."** *5465*
Ro 13:10 Therefore love is the **f** of the law. *4445*
1Co 10:11 on whom the **f** of the ages has come. *5465*
Eph 1:10 when the times will have reached their **f**— *4445*

FULFILLS (3) [FULFILL]
Ps 57: 2 to God, *who* **f** [his purpose] for me. 1698
145:19 *He* **f** the desires of those who fear him; 6913
Isa 44:26 and **f** the predictions of his messengers, 8966

FULL (200) [FILL]
Ge 6:11 in God's sight and *was* **f** *of* violence. 4848
14:10 the Valley of Siddim was **f of** tar **pits,** 931+931
15:16 not yet reached its **f measure."** 8969
23: 9 for the **f** price as a burial site among you." 4849
25: 8 an old man and **f** of years; 8428
35:29 old and **f** *of* years. 8428
41: 1 When *two* **f years** had passed, 3427+9102
41: 7 up the seven healthy, **f** heads. 4849
41:22 **f** and good, growing on a single stalk. 4849
Ge 50: 3 **taking** a **f** forty days, 4848
Ex 5:18 you must produce your **f quota** *of* bricks." 9420
8:21 The houses of the Egyptians *will be* **f** 4848
9:14 the **f force** *of* my plagues against you and 3972
16:20 *it was* **f** *of* maggots and began to smell. 8249
23:26 *I will* **give** you *a* **f** life span. 4848
Lev 6: 5 He must make restitution in **f,** 8031
16:12 a censer **f** *of* burning coals from the altar 4850
23:15 count off seven **f** weeks. 9459
25:29 he retains the right of redemption a **f** year 9448
25:30 not redeemed before a **f** year has passed, 9459
Nu 5: 7 *He must* **make f restitution** *for* his wrong, 928+8031+8740
33: 3 They marched out boldly in **f view** *of* all 6524
Dt 21:13 and mother for a **f** month, 3427
33:23 of the LORD and *is* **f** *of* his blessing; 4848
Jos 10:13 and delayed going down about a **f** day. 9459
Jdg 8: 2 the **f grape harvest** *of* Abiezer? 1292
Ru 1:21 I went away **f**, but the LORD has brought me 4849
1Sa 2: 5 *Those who were* **f** hire themselves out 8428
18:27 and **presented the f number** to the king so 4848
28:20 Immediately Saul fell **f** length on 4850
2Sa 5:17 they went up **in f force** to search for him, 3972
11:18 Joab sent David a **f** account of the battle. 3972
23:11 a place where there was a field **f** *of* lentils, 4849
2Ki 3:16 Make this valley **f of ditches.** 1463+1463
4: 6 When all the jars *were* **f,** 4848
6:17 and he looked and saw the hills **f** *of* horses 4848
10:21 until it *was* **f** from one end to the other. 4848
1Ch 11:13 a place where there was a field **f** *of* barley, 4849
14: 8 they went up **in f force** to search for him, 3972
21:22 Sell it to me at the **f** price." 4849
21:24 "No, I insist on paying the **f** price. 4849
23: 1 When David was old and **f** *of* years, 8425
2Ch 24:10 dropping them into the chest until it *was* **f.** 3983
24:15 Now Jehoiada was old and **f** *of* years, 8425
Ne 9:25 They ate *to the* **f** and were well-nourished; 8425
Est 1: 4 a **f** 180 days he displayed the vast wealth 8041
9:29 wrote with **f** authority to confirm this 3972
10: 2 together with a **f account** *of* the greatness 7308
Job 5:26 You will come to the grave in **f vigor,** 3995
10:15 for I am **f** *of* shame and drowned 8428
14: 1 "Man born of woman is of few days and **f** 8428
15:32 Before his time *he will* **be paid in f,** 4848
20:22 the **f** force of misery will come upon him. 3972
21:23 One man dies in **f** vigor, 9448
21:27 "I know **f well** what you are thinking, 2176
26: 9 He covers the face of the **f moon,** 4057
32:12 **gave** you *my* **f attention.** 1067
32:18 For *I am* **f** *of* words, 4848
42:17 And so he died, old and **f** *of* years. 8428
Ps 10: 7 His mouth *is* **f** *of* curses and lies 4848
26:10 whose right hands *are* **f** *of* bribes. 4848
31:23 but the proud he pays back in **f.** 3856
33: 5 the earth *is* **f** *of* his unfailing love. 4848
75: 8 In the hand of the LORD is a cup **f** 4848
78:38 and did not stir up his **f** wrath. 3972
81: 3 and when the **moon** is **f,** 4057
88: 3 For my soul *is* **f** of trouble 8425
94: 4 all the evildoers *are* **f of boasting.** 607
104:24 the earth *is* **f** *of* your creatures. 4848
116: 5 our God *is* **f of compassion.** 8163
127: 5 Blessed is the man whose quiver *is* **f** 4848
130: 7 and with him is **f** redemption. 2221
139:14 I know that **f well.** 4394
144: 8 whose mouths *are* **f of** lies, 1819
144:11 of foreigners whose mouths *are* **f of** lies, 1819
Pr 1:17 How useless to spread a net in **f view** *of* all 6524
4:18 shining ever brighter till the **f** light of day. 3922
5:21 man's ways are **in f view** *of* the LORD, 5790+6524
7:20 and will not be home till **f moon."** 3427+4057
8:21 **making** their treasuries **f.** 4848
17: 1 and quiet than a house **f** *of* feasting, 4849
20:17 but he ends up with a mouth **f** *of* gravel. 4848
27: 7 He who is **f** loathes honey, 8428
29:11 A fool gives **f** vent to his anger, 3972
30:22 a fool *who is* **f** *of* food, 8425
31:11 Her husband **has f confidence** in her 1053+4213
Ecc 1: 7 yet the sea is never **f.** 4849
9: 3 *are* **f** *of* evil and there is madness 4848
11: 3 If clouds *are* **f** *of* water, 4848
Isa 1:15 Your hands *are* **f** *of* blood; 4848
1:21 She once was **f** *of* justice; 4849
2: 6 *They are* **f** *of* superstitions from the East; 4848
2: 7 Their land *is* **f** *of* silver and gold; 4848
2: 7 Their land *is* **f** *of* horses; 4848
2: 8 Their land *is* **f** *of* idols; 4848
6: 3 the whole earth is **f** *of* his glory." 4850
11: 9 for the earth *will be* **f** *of* the knowledge 4848
15: 9 Dimon's waters *are* **f** *of* blood, 4848
22: 2 O town **f** *of* commotion, 4849
22: 7 Your choicest valleys *are* **f** *of* chariots, 4848
27: 9 be the **f** fruitage of the removal of his sin: 3972
30:26 like the light of seven *f* **days,** AIT
30:27 his lips *are* **f** *of* wrath, 4848
47: 9 They will come upon you in **f measure,** 9448
65: 6 not keep silent but *will* **pay back in f;** 8966
65: 7 **measure** into their laps **the f payment** 4499
Jer 5:27 Like cages **f** *of* birds, 4849
5:27 their houses are **f** *of* deceit; 4849
6:11 But *I am* **f** *of* the wrath of the LORD, 4848
23:10 The land *is* **f** *of* adulterers; 4848
35: 5 Then I set bowls **f** *of* wine and some cups 4849
51: 5 though their land *is* **f** *of* guilt before 4848
51:56 *he will* **repay in f.** 8966+8966
La 1: 1 deserted lies the city, once *so* **f** *of* people! 8041
4:11 The LORD *has* **given f vent** *to* his wrath; 3983

Eze 1:18 and all four rims were f of eyes all around. 4849
1:27 like glowing metal, as if f of fire, 1074+6017
7:23 because the land is f of bloodshed and 4848
7:23 of bloodshed and the city is f of violence. 4848
9: 9 the land is f of bloodshed and 4848
9: 9 of bloodshed and the city is f of injustice. 4848
10: 4 the court was f of the radiance of the glory 4848
10:12 were completely f of eyes, 4849
17: 3 and f plumage of varied colors came 4849
17: 7 with powerful wings and f plumage. 8041
19:10 it was fruitful and f of branches because 6734
22: 5 O infamous city, f of turmoil. 8041
23:12 warriors in f dress, mounted horsemen, 4814
28:12 f of wisdom and perfect in beauty. 4849
37: 1 it was f of bones. 4849
Joel 2:26 until you are f, and you will praise 8425
3:13 the winepress is f and the vats overflow— 4848
Na 3: 1 Woe to the city of blood, f of lies, 3972
3: 1 f of plunder, never without victims! 4849
Zec 9:15 be f like a bowl used for sprinkling 4848
Mt 6: 2 received their reward in f. 600
6: 5 received their reward in f. 600
6:16 received their reward in f. 600
6:22 your whole body will be f of light. 5893
6:23 your whole body will be f of darkness. 5027
13:48 When it was f, the fishermen pulled it up 4444
23:25 but inside they are f of greed 1154
23:27 but on the inside are f of dead men's bones 1154
23:28 but on the inside you are f of hypocrisy 3550
Mk 2:12 took his mat and walked out in f view of 1869
4:28 then the head, then the f kernel in the head. 4441
Lk 4: 1 Jesus, f of the Holy Spirit, 4441
5: 7 and filled both boats so f that they began NIG
6:34 expecting to be repaid in f. 2698+3836
10:21 Jesus, f of joy through the Holy Spirit, said, 22
11:34 your whole body also is f of light. 5893
11:34 your body also is f of darkness. 5027
11:36 if your whole body is f of light, 5893
11:39 inside you are f of greed and wickedness. 1154
14:23 so that my house will be f. 1153
Jn 1:14 came from the Father, f of grace and truth. 4441
3:29 and is f of joy when he hears 5897+5915
10:10 that they may have life, and have it to the f. 4356
13: 1 showed them the f extent of his love. 1650+5465
17:13 that they may have the f measure of my joy 4444
21: 8 towing the net f of fish, NIG
21:11 It was f of large fish, 153, 3550
Ac 5: 2 With his wife's f knowledge he kept back part of the money 5323
5:20 the people the f message of this new life." 4246
5:21 the f assembly of the elders of Israel— 4246
6: 3 from among you who are known to be f of 4441
6: 5 a man f of faith and of the Holy Spirit; 4441
6: 8 a man f of God's grace and power, 4441
7:55 But Stephen, f of the Holy Spirit, 4441
8:23 that you are f of bitterness and captive 1650
11:24 f of the Holy Spirit and faith, 4441
13:10 You are f of all kinds of deceit 4441
17:16 to see that the city was f of idols. 2977
Ro 1:29 They are f of envy, murder, strife, 3550
3:14 "Their mouths are f of cursing 1154
11:25 the f number of the Gentiles has come in. 4445
13: 6 who give their f time to governing. 4674
15:14 that you yourselves are f of goodness, 3550
15:29 I will come in the f measure of the blessing 4445
16:19 so I am f of joy over you; 5897
Gal 4: 5 that we might receive the f rights of sons. 5625
Eph 6:11 Put on the f armor of God so 4110
6:13 Therefore put on the f armor of God, 4110
Php 4:18 I have received f payment and even more; 4246
Col 2: 2 the f riches of complete understanding, 4246
4: 6 Let your conversation be always f of grace, NIG
1Ti 1:15 that deserves f acceptance: 4246
2:11 in quietness and f submission. 4246
4: 9 that deserves f acceptance 4246
6: 1 of f respect, so that God's name 4246
Phm 1: 6 so that you will have a f understanding 2106
Heb 10:22 with a sincere heart in f assurance of faith, 4443
Jas 3: 8 It is a restless evil, f of deadly poison. 3550
3:17 submissive, f of mercy and good fruit, 3550
5:11 The Lord is f of compassion and mercy. 4499
2Pe 2:14 With eyes f of adultery, 3550
Rev 5: 8 they were holding golden bowls f of incense 1154
13:13 down from heaven to earth in f view of 1967
14:10 which has been poured f strength into 204
21: 9 the seven bowls f of the seven last plagues 1154

FULL-GROWN (1) [GROW]

Jas 1:15 and sin, when it is f, gives birth to death. 699

FULLER (KJV) See SOAP

FULLER'S (KJV) See WASHERMAN'S

FULLNESS (10) [FILL]

Dt 33:16 and its f and the favor of him who dwelt in 4850
Jn 1:16 From the f of his grace we have all received 4445
Ro 11:12 how much greater riches will their f bring! 4445
Eph 1:23 f of him who fills everything in every way. 4445
3:19 be filled to the measure of all the f of God. 4445
4:13 to the whole measure of the f of Christ. 4445
Col 1:19 For God was pleased to have all his f dwell 4445
1:25 present to you the word of God in its f— 4444
2: 9 For in Christ all the f of the Deity lives 4445
2:10 and you have been given f in Christ, 1639+4444

FULLY (45) [FILL]

Ex 19: 5 if you obey me f and keep my covenant, 928+7754+9048+9048
Dt 15: 5 if only you f obey the LORD your God 928+7754+9048+9048
28: 1 If you f obey the LORD your God 928+7754+9048+9048
Jos 1:14 but all your fighting men, f armed, 2821
1:17 Just as we f obeyed Moses, 3972
1Ki 8:61 be f committed to the LORD our God, 8969
11: 4 not f devoted to the LORD his God, 8969
15: 3 not f devoted to the LORD his God, 8969
15:14 Asa's heart was f committed to the LORD 8969
1Ch 12:38 came to Hebron f determined to make David king 928+4222+8969
2Ch 15:17 Asa's heart was f committed 8969
16: 9 to strengthen those whose hearts are f committed to him. 8969
Ezr 6: 8 to be f paid out of the royal treasury, 10056
Ps 62: 4 They f intend to topple him 421
106: 2 of the LORD or f declare his praise? 3972
119: 4 down precepts that are to be f obeyed. 4394
119:138 they are f trustworthy. 4394
Pr 13: 4 the desires of the diligent are f satisfied. 2014
14:14 faithless will be f repaid for their ways, 8425
28: 5 those who seek the LORD understand it f. 3972
Isa 21: 7 let him be alert, f alert." 8041
Jer 23:20 not turn back until he f accomplishes the purposes of his heart. 2256+6913+7756
30:24 not turn back until he f accomplishes the purposes of his heart. 2256+6913+7756
35:10 have f obeyed everything our forefather Jonadab commanded us. 2256+6913+9048
Eze 38: 4 your horses, your horsemen f armed, 4814
Da 11:13 with a huge army f equipped. 8041
Joel 2:19 new wine and oil, enough to satisfy you f; 8425
Lk 6:40 but everyone who is f trained will be 2936
9:32 but when they became f awake, 1340
11:21 "When a strong man, f armed, 2774
Ro 4:21 being f persuaded that God had power 4442
8: 4 of the law might be f met in us, 4444
14: 5 Each one should be f convinced 4442
14:14 I am f convinced that no food is unclean 2779+3857+4275
15:19 I have f proclaimed the gospel of Christ. 4444
1Co 13:12 I shall know f, even as I am fully known. 2105
13:12 I shall know fully, even as I am f known. 2105
15:58 Always give yourselves f to the work of 4355
2Co 1:14 to understand f that you can boast 2401+5465
Gal 4: 4 But when the time had f come, 4445
Col 4:12 mature and f assured, 4442
2Ti 4:17 the message might be f proclaimed and all 4442
Tit 2:10 but to show that they can be f trusted, 4246
1Pe 1:13 set your hope f on the grace to be given you 5458
2Jn 1: 8 but that you may be rewarded f. 4441

FUN (1)

Ac 2:13 Some, however, made f of them and said, 1430

FUNCTION (2)

Ex 27:19 whatever their f, including all the tent pegs NIH
Ro 12: 4 these members do not all have the same f, 4552

FUNERAL (2)

Jer 16: 5 not enter a house where there is a f meal; 5301
34: 5 As people made a f fire in honor 5386

FURBISHED (KJV) See POLISHED

FURIOUS (16) [FURY]

Dt 29:28 In f anger and in great wrath 2779
2Sa 13:21 King David heard all this, he was f. 3013+4394
2Ch 25:10 They were f with Judah and left 678+3013+4394
Est 1:12 king became f and burned with anger. 4394+7911
Jer 32:37 where I banish them in my f anger 2779
Da 2:12 and f that he ordered the execution of all 10633
3:13 F with rage, Nebuchadnezzar summoned 10270
3:19 Then Nebuchadnezzar was f 10270+10416
Mt 2:16 outwitted by the Magi, he was f, and 2597+3336
8:24 a f storm came up on the lake, 3489
Mk 4:37 A f squall came up, 3489
Lk 4:28 the synagogue were f when they heard 2596+4398
6:11 But they were f and began to discuss 486+4398
Ac 5:33 they were f and wanted to put them 1391
7:54 they were f and gnashed their teeth at him. 1391
19:28 they were f and began shouting: 2596+4441

FURIOUSLY (2) [FURY]

Jer 46: 9 Drive f, O charioteers! 2147
Da 8: 7 I saw him attack the ram f, 5352

FURLONGS (KJV) See MILES, STADIA

FURNACE (31)

Ge 19:28 like smoke from a f. 3901
Ex 9: 8 of soot from a f and have Moses toss it into 3901
9:10 So they took soot from a f and stood 3901
19:18 up from it like smoke from a f, 3901
Dt 4:20 and brought you out of the iron-smelting f, 3929
1Ki 8:51 out of that iron-smelting f. 3929
Ps 12: 6 like silver refined in a f of clay, 6612
21: 9 like a fiery f. 9486
Pr 17: 3 The crucible for silver and the f for gold, 3929
27:21 The crucible for silver and the f for gold, 3929
Isa 31: 9 whose f is in Jerusalem. 9486
48:10 I have tested you in the f of affliction. 3929
Jer 11: 4 out of the iron-smelting f.' 3929
Eze 22:18 tin, iron and lead left inside a f. 3929
22:20 and tin into a f to melt it with a fiery blast, 3929
22:22 As silver is melted in a f, 3929
Da 3: 6 be thrown into a blazing f." 10086
3:11 be thrown into a blazing f. 10086
3:15 be thrown immediately into a blazing f. 10086
3:17 If we are thrown into the blazing f, 10086
3:19 the f heated seven times hotter than usual 10086
3:20 and throw them into the blazing f. 10086
3:21 were bound and thrown into the blazing f. 10086
3:22 so urgent and the f so hot that the flames of 10086
3:23 firmly tied, fell into the blazing f. 10086
3:26 the opening of the blazing f and shouted, 10086
Mal 4: 1 the day is coming; it will burn like a f. 9486
Mt 13:42 They will throw them into the fiery f, 2825
13:50 and throw them into the fiery f, 2825
Rev 1:15 His feet were like bronze glowing in a f, 2825
9: 2 from it like the smoke from a gigantic f. 2825

FURNISHED (4) [FURNISHINGS]

Eze 16:52 for you have f some justification 7136
Mk 14:15 a large upper room, f and ready. 5143
Lk 22:12 He will show you a large upper room, all f. 5143
Ac 28:10 they f us with the supplies we needed. 2202

FURNISHINGS (23) [FURNISHED]

Ex 25: 9 Make this tabernacle and all its f exactly 3998
31: 7 and all the other f of the tent— 3998
39:33 the tent and all its f, its clasps, frames, 3998
39:40 all the f for the tabernacle, 3998
40: 9 consecrate it and all its f, 3998
Nu 1:50 over all its f and everything belonging to it. 3998
1:50 to carry the tabernacle and all its f; 3998
3: 8 They are to take care of all the f of 3998
4:15 the holy f and all the holy articles, 7731
4:16 including its holy f and articles." 7731
7: 1 and consecrated it and all its f. 3998
18: 3 near the f of the sanctuary or the altar, 3998
19:18 the water and sprinkle the tent and all the f 3998
1Ki 7:48 Solomon also made all the f that were in 3998
7:51 the silver and gold and the f— 3998
8: 4 the Tent of Meeting and all the sacred f 3998
1Ch 9:29 Others were assigned to take care of the f 3998
2Ch 4:19 Solomon also made all the f that were 3998
5: 1 the silver and gold and all the f 3998
5: 5 the Tent of Meeting and all the sacred f 3998
28:24 Ahaz gathered together the f from 3998
Jer 27:18 the f remaining in the house of the LORD 3998
27:19 and the other f that are left in this city, 3998

FURNITURE (KJV) See ACCESSORIES, ARTICLES, FURNISHINGS, SADDLES, TREASURES, UTENSILS

FURROW (1) [FURROWS]

Job 39:10 Can you hold him to the f with a harness? 9439

FURROWS (3) [FURROW]

Job 31:38 against me and all its f are wet with tears, 9439
Ps 65:10 You drench its f and level its ridges; 9439
129: 3 and made their f long. 5103

FURTHER (17) [FURTHERMORE]

1Sa 10:22 So they inquired f of the LORD, 6388
23:22 Go and make f preparation. 6388
2Ch 32:16 Sennacherib's officers spoke f against 6388
Job 34:23 God has no need to examine men f, 6388
35:15 and f, that his anger never punishes 6964
Ecc 9: 5 they have no f reward, 6388
Eze 23:14 carried her prostitution still f. 3578
Hos 11: 2 the f they went from me. 4027
Zec 1:17 "Proclaim f: This is what the LORD Almighty says: 6388
Ac 4:17 stop this thing from spreading any f 2093+4498
4:21 After f threats they let them go. 4653
11:18 they had no f objections and praised God, NIG
13:42 the people invited them to speak f NIG
19:39 If there is anything f you want to bring up, 4304
24: 4 But in order not to weary you f, 4498
1Co 11:34 And when I come I will give f directions. 3370
Heb 12:19 that no f word be spoken to them, 3364+4707

FURTHER (Anglicized) See also FARTHER

FURTHERMORE (12) [FURTHER]

2Sa 16:19 F, whom should I serve? 2021+2256+9108
2Ki 18:25 F, have I come to attack 6964
23:24 F, Josiah got rid of the mediums 1685+2256
2Ch 17: 6 f, he removed the high places and 2256+6388
36:14 F, all the leaders of the priests and 1685
Ezr 4:13 F, the king should know that 10363
6:11 F, I decree that if anyone changes this 10221
Ne 5:17 F, a hundred and fifty Jews 2256

Isa 36:10 F, have I come to attack 2256+6964
Jer 21:8 "F, tell the people, 'This is what 2256
26:24 F, Ahikam son of Shaphan 421
Ro 1:28 F, since they did not think it worthwhile *2779*

FURY (24) [FURIOUS, FURIOUSLY]

Ge 27:44 for a while until your brother's f subsides. 2779
34:7 They were filled with grief and f, 3013+4394
49:7 so fierce, and their f, so cruel! 6301
2Ki 3:27 The f against Israel was great; 7912
Est 7:10 Then the king's f subsided. 2779
Job 40:11 Unleash the f *of* your wrath, 6301
Pr 6:34 for jealousy arouses a husband's f, 2779
22:8 and the rod of his f will be destroyed. 6301
27:4 Anger is cruel and f overwhelming, 678
Isa 14:4 How his f has ended! 4502
14:6 and in f subdued nations 678
66:14 but *his* f *will be* **shown** *to* his foes. 2404
66:15 he will bring down his anger with f, 2779
Jer 21:5 and a mighty arm in anger and f 2779
Eze 13:13 of rain will fall with destructive f. 2779
19:12 But it was uprooted in f and thrown to 2779
23:25 and they will deal with you in f. 2779
Da 11:30 and **vent** *his* f against the holy covenant. 2404
Am 1:11 and his f flamed unchecked, 6301
Heb 11:34 the f of the flames, and escaped the edge of *1539*
Rev 12:12 He is filled with f, *2596+3489*
14:10 too, will drink of the wine *of* God's f, *2596*
16:19 the cup filled with the wine *of* the f *2596*
19:15 *of* the f of the wrath of God Almighty. *2596*

FUTILE (6) [FUTILITY]

Ps 94:11 he knows that they are f. 2039
Jer 48:30 I know her insolence but it is f," 4027+4202
Mal 3:14 "You have said, 'It is f to serve God. 8736
Ro 1:21 but their thinking *became* f *3471*
1Co 3:20 that the thoughts of the wise are f." *3469*
15:17 Christ has not been raised, your faith is f; *3469*

FUTILITY (4) [FUTILE]

Job 7:3 so I have been allotted months of f, 8736
Ps 78:33 So he ended their days in f and their years 2039
89:47 For what f you have created all men! 8736
Eph 4:17 in the f of their thinking. *3470*

FUTURE (33)

Ge 30:33 my honesty will testify for me in the f, 3427+4737
Dt 6:20 **In the f,** when your son asks you, 4737
Jos 4:6 **In the f,** when your children ask you, 4737
4:21 to the Israelites, **"In the f** 4737
22:27 Then **in the f** your descendants will not 4737
2Sa 7:19 the f of the house of your servant. 4946+8158
1Ch 17:17 you have spoken about the f of the house of your servant. 4946+8158
Job 8:7 so prosperous will your f be. 344
Ps 22:30 f generations will be told about the Lord. 995
37:37 there is a f for the man of peace. 344
37:38 the f *of* the wicked will be cut off. 344
102:18 Let this be written for a f generation, 340
Pr 23:18 There is surely a **f hope** for you, 344
24:14 if you find it, there is a **f hope** for you, 344
24:20 for the evil man has no **f hope,** 344
Ecc 7:14 a man cannot discover anything about his f. 339
8:7 Since no man knows the f, 2118+4537+8611
Isa 9:1 the f he will honor Galilee of the Gentiles, 340
41:23 tell us what the f holds, 294
Jer 29:11 plans to give you hope and a f. 344
31:17 So there is hope for your f," 344
La 1:9 she did not consider her f. 344
Eze 12:27 and he prophesies about the distant f.' 6961
38:8 In f years you will invade a land 344
Da 2:45 God has shown the king what will take place **in the f.** 10021+10180
8:26 for it concerns the **distant f."** 3427+8041
10:14 to your people in the f, 344+3427
Mt 26:64 **In the** f you will see the Son of Man *608+785*
Ac 16:16 **spirit** by **which** she **predicted the f.** *4460+4780*
Ro 8:38 neither the present nor **the f,** *3516*
1Co 3:22 or life or death or the present or **the f—** *3516*
Heb 3:5 testifying *to* what *would be* **said** *in the f.* *AIT*
11:20 and Esau in regard to their f. *3516*

G

GAAL (10)

Jdg 9:26 Now G son of Ebed moved 1720
9:28 Then G son of Ebed said, 1720
9:30 of the city heard what G son of Ebed said, 1720
9:31 "G son of Ebed and his brothers have come 1720
9:33 When G and his men come out against you, 2085S
9:35 Now G son of Ebed had gone out 1720
9:36 When G saw them, he said to Zebul, 1720
9:37 But G spoke up again: 1720
9:39 So G led out the citizens of Shechem 1720
9:41 and Zebul drove G and his brothers out 1720

GAASH (4)

Jos 24:30 north of Mount G. 1724
Jdg 2:9 north of Mount G. 1724
2Sa 23:30 Hiddai from the ravines of G, 1724
1Ch 11:32 Hurai from the ravines of G, 1724

GABA (KJV) See GEBA

GABBAI (1)

Ne 11:8 and his followers, G and Sallai—928 men. 1480

GABBATHA (1)

Jn 19:13 Stone Pavement (which in Aramaic is G). *1119*

GABRIEL (4)

Da 8:16 a man's voice from the Ulai calling, "G, 1508
9:21 G, the man I had seen in the earlier vision, 1508
Lk 1:19 The angel answered, "I am G. *1120*
1:26 God sent the angel G to Nazareth, *1120*

GAD (55) [BAAL GAD, DIBON GAD, GAD'S, GADITES, MIGDAL GAD]

Ge 30:11 So she named him G. 1514
35:26 of Leah's maidservant Zilpah: G and Asher. 1514
46:16 The sons of G: 1514
49:19 "G will be attacked by a band of raiders, 1514
Ex 1:4 Dan and Naphtali; G and Asher. 1514
Nu 1:14 from G, Eliasaph son of Deuel; 1514
1:24 From the descendants of G: 1514
1:25 number from the tribe of G was 45,650. 1514
2:14 The tribe of G will be next. 1514
2:14 of the people of G is Eliasaph son of Deuel. 1514
7:42 the leader of the people of G, 1514
10:20 over the division of the tribe of G. 1201+1514
13:15 from the tribe of G, Geuel son of Maki. 1514
26:15 The descendants of G by their clans were: 1514
26:18 These were the clans of G; 1201+1514
34:14 the tribe of G and the half-tribe 1201+1532
Dt 27:13 Reuben, G, Asher, Zebulun, 1514
33:20 About G he said: 1514
33:20 G lives there like a lion, NIH
Jos 4:12 G and the half-tribe of Manasseh crossed 1514
13:24 to the tribe of G, clan by clan: 1514
18:7 And G, Reuben and the half-tribe 1514
20:8 Ramoth in Gilead in the tribe of G, 1514
21:7 from the tribes of Reuben, G and Zebulun. 1514
21:38 from the tribe of G, 1514
22:13 G and the half-tribe of Manasseh. 1201+1514
22:15 G and the half-tribe of Manasseh— 1201+1514
22:21 G and the half-tribe of Manasseh 1201+1514
22:30 G and Manasseh had to say, 1201+1514
22:31 said to Reuben, G and Manasseh, 1201+1514
1Sa 13:7 even crossed the Jordan to the land of G 1514
22:5 But the prophet G said to David, 1514
2Sa 24:5 and then went through G and on to Jazer. 1514
24:11 of the LORD had come to G the prophet, 1514
24:13 So G went to David and said to him, 1514
24:14 David said to G, "I am in deep distress. 1514
24:18 that day G went to David and said to him, 1514
24:19 as the LORD had commanded through G. 1514
2Ki 10:33 in all the land of Gilead (the region **of** G, 1532
1Ch 2:2 Joseph, Benjamin, Naphtali, G and Asher. 1514
6:63 from the tribes of Reuben, G and Zebulun. 1514
6:80 from the tribe of G they received Ramoth 1514
12:37 G and the half-tribe of Manasseh, 1532
21:9 The LORD said to G, David's seer, 1514
21:11 So G went to David and said to him, 1514
21:13 David said to G, "I am in deep distress. 1514
21:18 of the LORD ordered G to tell David to go 1514
21:19 in obedience to the word that G had spoken 1514
29:29 of Nathan the prophet and the records of G 1514
2Ch 29:25 by David and G the king's seer and Nathan 1514
Jer 49:1 then has Molech taken possession of G? 1514
Eze 48:27 "G will have one portion; 1514
48:28 of G will run south from Tamar to 1514
48:34 the gate of G, 1514
Rev 7:5 from the tribe *of* G 12,000, *1122*

GAD'S (1) [GAD]

Dt 33:20 "Blessed is he who enlarges G domain! 1514

GADARENES (1)

Mt 8:28 at the other side in the region *of* the G, *1123*

GADDAH See HAZAR GADDAH

GADDEST (KJV) See GO ABOUT

GADDI (1)

Nu 13:11 G son of Susi; 1534

GADDIEL (1)

Nu 13:10 from the tribe of Zebulun, G son of Sodi; 1535

GADER See BETH GADER

GADFLY (1)

Jer 46:20 a g is coming against her from the north. 7976

GADI (2)

2Ki 15:14 Then Menahem son of G went from Tirzah 1533
15:17 Menahem son of G became king of Israel, 1533

GADITES (29) [GAD]

Nu 32:1 The Reubenites and G, 1201+1514
32:6 Moses said to the G and Reubenites, 1201+1514
32:25 The G and Reubenites said to Moses, 1201+1514
32:29 to them, "If the G and Reubenites, 1201+1514
32:31 The G and Reubenites answered, 1201+1514
32:33 Then Moses gave to the G, 1201+1514
32:34 The G built up Dibon, Ataroth, Aroer, 1201+1514
Dt 3:12 the Reubenites and the G the territory north 1532
3:16 and the G I gave the territory extending 1532
4:43 Ramoth in Gilead, for the G; 1532
29:8 the G and the half-tribe of Manasseh. 1532
Jos 1:12 the G and the half-tribe of Manasseh, 1532
12:6 the G and the half-tribe of Manasseh to 1532
13:8 the Reubenites and the G had received 1532
13:28 the inheritance of the G, 1201+1514
22:1 the G and the half-tribe of Manasseh 1532
22:9 the G and the half-tribe of Manasseh 1201+1514
22:10 the G and the half-tribe of Manasseh 1201+1514
22:25 you Reubenites and G! 1201+1514
22:32 with the Reubenites and G in Gilead 1201+1514
22:33 where the Reubenites and the G lived. 1201+1514
22:34 And the Reubenites and the G gave 1201+1514
1Ch 5:11 The G lived next to them in Bashan, 1201+1514
5:16 The G lived in Gilead, NIH
5:18 the G and the half-tribe 1532
5:26 the G and the half-tribe of Manasseh 1532
12:8 Some G defected to David at his stronghold 1532
12:14 These G were army commanders; 1201+1514
26:32 the G and the half-tribe of Manasseh 1532

GAHAM (1)

Ge 22:24 Tebah, G, Tahash and Maacah. 1626

GAHAR (2)

Ezr 2:47 Giddel, G, Reaiah, 1627
Ne 7:49 Hanan, Giddel, G, 1627

GAIETY (2)

Isa 24:8 The g *of* the tambourines is stilled, 5375
24:11 all g is banished from the earth. 5375

GAIN (68) [GAINED, GAINING, GAINS, REGAIN, REGAINED]

Ge 15:8 how can I know that *I will* g **possession** 3769
37:26 "What will we g if we kill our brother 1299
Ex 14:4 But *I will* g **glory for myself** 3877
14:17 And *I will* g **glory** through Pharaoh 3877
14:18 that I am the LORD when I g **glory** 3877
18:21 trustworthy men who hate **dishonest g—** 1299
1Sa 8:3 after **dishonest** g and accepted bribes 1299
2Ki 15:19 a thousand talents of silver to g his **support** 907+2118+3338
Job 21:15 What *would we* g by praying to him?' 3603
22:3 would he g if your ways were blameless? 1299
35:3 and what *do I* g by not sinning?' 3603
Ps 30:9 "What g is there in my destruction, 1299
60:12 With God *we will* g the victory, 6913
90:12 that *we may* g a heart of wisdom. 995
108:13 With God *we will* g the victory, 6913
119:36 and not toward **selfish g.** 1299
119:104 *I* g **understanding** from your precepts; 1067
Pr 1:19 all *who* **go after ill-gotten g;** 1298+1299
4:1 pay attention and g understanding. 3359
8:5 You who are simple, g prudence; 1067
8:5 you who are foolish, g understanding. 1067
11:16 but ruthless men g only wealth. 9461
16:8 a little with righteousness than much g 9311
19:25 and *he will* g knowledge. 1067
21:11 a mocker is punished, the simple *g* **wisdom;** AIT
28:16 but he who hates **ill-gotten g** will enjoy 1299
28:23 He who rebukes a man will in the end g more favor than 5162
Ecc 1:3 What does man g from all his labor 3862
2:15 What then do I g by being wise?" 3463
3:9 What does the worker g from his toil? 3862
5:16 so he departs, and what does he g, 3862
6:8 What does a poor man g by knowing how 4200
Isa 29:24 wayward in spirit *will* g understanding; 3359
33:15 who rejects g *from* extortion 1299
56:11 each seeks his own g. 1299
63:12 to g for himself everlasting renown, 6913
Jer 6:13 all are greedy for g; 1299
8:10 all are greedy for g; 1299
12:13 they will wear themselves out but g nothing. 3603
22:17 and your heart are set only on **dishonest g,** 1299
Eze 22:12 and excessive interest and **make unjust g** 1298
22:13 at the **unjust g** you have made and at 1299
22:27 and kill people to **make unjust g.** 1298+1299
28:22 O Sidon, and *I will* g **glory** within you. 3877
33:31 but their hearts are greedy for **unjust g.** 1299
Da 2:8 "I am certain that you *are trying to* g time, 10223
10:12 to g **understanding** and to humble yourself 1067
11:43 *He will* g **control** of the treasures of gold 5440
Hab 2:9 to him who builds his realm by unjust g 1299
Mal 3:14 What did we g by carrying out his 1299
Mk 8:36 *to* g the whole world, yet forfeit is soul? *3045*
Lk 9:25 *to* g the whole world, and yet lose or forfeit his very self? *3045*

Lk 16: 9 use worldly wealth *to* g friends *4472*
21:19 By standing firm *you will* g life. *3227*
Jn 7:18 on his own does so *to* g honor for himself, *2426*
Ac 7:10 to g the goodwill of Pharaoh king of Egypt; *NIG*
1Co 7:21 if you can g *your* **freedom,** do so. *1181+1801*
13: 3 but have not love, *I* g nothing. *6067*
Php 1:21 For to me, to live is Christ and to die is **g.** *3046*
3: 8 I consider them rubbish, that *I may* g Christ *3045*
1Ti 3: 8 and not **pursuing dishonest g.** *153*
3:13 Those who have served well g *4347*
6: 5 that godliness is a **means to financial g.** *4516*
6: 6 But godliness with contentment is great **g.** *4516*
2Ti 3: 6 and g **control over** weak-willed women, *170*
Tit 1: 7 not violent, not **pursuing dishonest g.** *153*
1:11 and that for the sake of dishonest **g.** *3046*
Heb 11:35 so that *they might* g a better resurrection. *5593*

GAINED (23) [GAIN]

Ge 31: 1 and *has* g all this wealth 6913
2Sa 15:12 And so the conspiracy g strength, 2118
2Ch 32: 8 And the people g **confidence** 6164
Job 31:25 the fortune my hands *had* g, 5162
Ps 129: 2 but *they have* not g **the victory** over me. 3523
Pr 20:17 **Food** *g by* fraud tastes sweet to a man, AIT
20:21 An inheritance **quickly** g at 987
Ecc 2:11 nothing was g under the sun. 3862
Isa 26:15 **g glory for yourself;** 3877
Jer 32:20 and *have* g the renown that is still yours. 6913
Eze 28: 4 and understanding *you have* g wealth 6913
Da 11: 2 When he has g **power** by his wealth, 2621
Mt 25:16 and put his money to work and g five more. *3045*
25:17 the one with the two talents g two more. *3045*
25:20 See, *I have* g five more.' *3045*
25:22 see, *I have* g two more.' *3045*
Lk 19:15 in order to find out what *they had* g with it. *1390*
Ro 5: 2 through whom *we* **have** *g* access by faith *AIT*
1Co 15:32 what have I **g?** *4055*
2Co 12: 1 *Although* there is nothing *to be* **g,** *5237*
Gal 2:21 if righteousness could be g through the law, *NIG*
Heb 11:33 and g what was promised; *2209*
Rev 18:15 and g their **wealth** *4456*

GAINING (3) [GAIN]

Ge 3: 6 and also desirable for **g wisdom,** 8505
Ps 44:12 g nothing from their sale. 8049
Jn 4: 1 The Pharisees heard that Jesus *was* g *4472*

GAINS (8) [GAIN]

Pr 3:13 the man *who* g understanding, 7049
11:16 A kindhearted woman g respect, 9461
11:24 One man gives freely, yet g even more; 3578
15:32 whoever heeds correction g understanding. 7864
29:23 but a man of lowly spirit g honor. 9461
Jer 17:11 the *man who* g riches by unjust means. 6913
Mic 4:13 You will devote their **ill-gotten** g to 1299
Mt 16:26 What good will it be for a man if *he* g *3045*

GAINSAY, GAINSAYERS (KJV) See OPPOSE, RESIST

GAINSAYING (KJV) See OBSTINATE, RAISING OBJECTION, REBELLION

GAIUS (5)

Ac 19:29 The people seized G and Aristarchus, *1127*
20: 4 G from Derbe, Timothy also, *1127*
Ro 16:23 **G,** whose hospitality I and *1127*
1Co 1:14 of you except Crispus and **G,** *1127*
3Jn 1: 1 The elder, *To* my dear friend **G,** *1127*

GALAL (3)

1Ch 9:15 Heresh, G and Mattaniah son of Mica, 1674
9:16 the son of **G,** the son of Jeduthun; 1674
Ne 11:17 and Abda son of Shammua, the son of **G,** 1674

GALATIA (5) [GALATIAN, GALATIANS]

Ac 16: 6 throughout the region of Phrygia and **G,** *1131*
18:23 throughout the region of G and Phrygia, *1131*
Gal 1: 2 To the churches *in* **G:** *1130*
2Ti 4:10 Crescens has gone to **G,** *1130*
1Pe 1: 1 **G,** Cappadocia, Asia and Bithynia, *1130*

GALATIAN (1) [GALATIA]

1Co 16: 1 Do what I told the G churches to do. *1130*

GALATIANS (1) [GALATIA]

Gal 3: 1 You foolish **G!** *1129*

GALBANUM (1)

Ex 30:34 gum resin, onycha and **g—** 2697

GALE (3)

Job 21:18 like chaff swept away by a **g?** 6070
Isa 17:13 like tumbleweed before a **g.** 6070
41:16 and a g will blow them away. 6194

GALEED (2)

Ge 31:47 and Jacob called it **G.** 1681
Ge 31:48 That is why it was called **G.** 1681

GALILEAN (4) [GALILEE]

Mk 14:70 you are one of them, for you are a **G."** *1134*
Lk 22:59 this fellow was with him, for he is a **G."** *1134*
23: 6 Pilate asked if the man was a **G.** *1134*
Ac 5:37 Judas the G appeared in the days of the census *1134*

GALILEANS (5) [GALILEE]

Lk 13: 1 about the G whose blood Pilate had mixed *1134*
13: 2 that these G were worse sinners than all *1134*
13: 2 the other G because they suffered this way? *1134*
Jn 4:45 the G welcomed him. *1134*
Ac 2: 7 not all these men who are speaking **G?** *1134*

GALILEE (70) [GALILEAN, GALILEANS, TIBERIAS]

Jos 20: 7 in G in the hill country of Naphtali, 1665
21:32 in G (a city of refuge for one accused 1665
1Ki 9:11 King Solomon gave twenty towns in G 824+1665
2Ki 15:29 He took Gilead and **G,** 1665
1Ch 6:76 of Naphtali they received Kedesh in **G,** 1665
Isa 9: 1 the future he will honor G *of* the Gentiles, 1665
Mt 2:22 he withdrew to the district *of* **G,** *1133*
3:13 Then Jesus came from G to the Jordan to *1133*
4:12 he returned to **G.** *1133*
4:15 along the Jordan, G of the Gentiles— *1133*
4:18 As Jesus was walking beside the Sea *of* **G,** *1133*
4:23 Jesus went throughout **G,** *1133*
4:25 Large crowds from **G,** the Decapolis, *1133*
11: 1 to teach and preach in the towns of **G.** *NIG*
15:29 and went along the Sea *of* **G.** *1133*
17:22 When they came together in **G,** *1133*
19: 1 he left G and went into the region of Judea *1133*
21:11 the prophet from Nazareth in **G."** *1133*
26:32 I have risen, I will go ahead of you into **G."** *1133*
26:69 "You also were with Jesus *of* **G,"** she said. *1133*
27:55 They had followed Jesus from G to care *1133*
28: 7 the dead and is going ahead of you into **G.** *1133*
28:10 Go and tell my brothers to go to **G;** *1133*
28:16 Then the eleven disciples went to **G,** *1133*
Mk 1: 9 that time Jesus came from Nazareth *in* G *1133*
1:14 Jesus went into **G,** *1133*
1:16 As Jesus walked beside the Sea *of* **G,** *1133*
1:28 over the whole region *of* **G.** *1133*
1:39 So he traveled throughout **G,** *1133*
3: 7 and a large crowd from G followed. *1133*
6:21 and the leading men *of* **G.** *1133*
7:31 down to the Sea *of* G and into the region of *1133*
9:30 They left that place and passed through **G.** *1133*
14:28 I have risen, I will go ahead of you into **G."** *1133*
15:41 In G these women *had* followed him *1133*
16: 7 'He is going ahead of you into **G.** *1133*
Lk 1:26 Nazareth, a town *in* **G,** *1133*
2: 4 from the town of Nazareth *in* G to Judea, *1133*
2:39 they returned to G to their own town *1133*
3: 1 *of* **G,** his brother Philip tetrarch of Iturea *1133*
4:14 Jesus returned to G in the power of *1133*
4:31 he went down to Capernaum, a town *in* **G,** *1133*
5:17 who had come from every village *of* G and *1133*
8:26 which is across the lake *from* **G.** *1133*
17:11 along the border between Samaria and **G.** *1133*
23: 5 in G and has come all the way here." *1133*
23:49 the women who had followed him from **G,** *1133*
23:55 from G followed Joseph and saw the tomb *1133*
24: 6 while he was still with you in **G:** *1133*
Jn 1:43 The next day Jesus decided to leave for **G.** *1133*
2: 1 a wedding took place at Cana *in* **G.** *1133*
2:11 Jesus performed at Cana *in* **G.** *1133*
4: 3 and went back once more to **G.** *1133*
4:43 After the two days he left for **G.** *1133*
4:45 When he arrived in **G,** *1133*
4:46 Once more he visited Cana *in* **G,** *1133*
4:47 that Jesus had arrived in G from Judea, *1133*
4:54 having come from Judea to **G.** *1133*
6: 1 to the far shore of the Sea *of* G (that is, *1133*
7: 1 After this, Jesus went around in **G,** *1133*
7: 9 Having said this, he stayed in **G.** *1133*
7:41 "How can the Christ come from **G?** *1133*
7:52 They replied, "Are you from **G,** too? *1133*
7:52 that a prophet does not come out of **G."** *1133*
12:21 who was from Bethsaida *in* **G,** *1133*
21: 2 Nathanael from Cana *in* **G,** *1133*
Ac 1:11 "Men *of* **G,"** they said, *1134*
9:31 G and Samaria enjoyed a time of peace. *1133*
10:37 in G after the baptism that John preached— *1133*
13:31 by those who had traveled with him from G *1133*

GALL (6) [GALLED]

Job 16:13 he pierces my kidneys and spills my g on 5354
Ps 69:21 They put g in my food and gave me vinegar 8032
Pr 5: 4 but in the end she is bitter as **g,** 4360
La 3:15 with bitter herbs and sated me with **g.** 4360
3:19 the bitterness and the **g.** 4360
Mt 27:34 to drink, mixed with **g;** *5958*

GALLED (1) [GALL]

1Sa 18: 8 Saul was very angry; this refrain **g** him. 928+6524+8317

GALLERIES (3) [GALLERY]

Eze 41:15 including its g on each side; 916
41:16 the narrow windows and g around the three 916
42: 5 the g took more space from them than from 916

GALLERY (2) [GALLERIES]

Eze 42: 3 **g** faced gallery at the three levels. 916
42: 3 gallery faced **g** at the three levels. 916

GALLEY (1)

Isa 33:21 No g *with* oars will ride them, 639

GALLIM (2)

1Sa 25:44 to Paltiel son of Laish, who was from **G.** 1668
Isa 10:30 Cry out, O Daughter of **G!** 1668

GALLIO (3)

Ac 18:12 While G was proconsul of Achaia, *1136*
18:14 G said to the Jews, *1136*
18:17 But G showed no concern whatever. *1136*

GALLONS (2)

Lk 16: 6 " '**Eight hundred** g of olive oil,' *1004+1669*
Jn 2: 6 each holding from **twenty to thirty g.** *1545+2445+3583+5552*

GALLOP (1) [GALLOPING, GALLOPS]

Joel 2: 4 *they* **g along** like cavalry. 8132

GALLOPING (4) [GALLOP]

Jdg 5:22 **g,** galloping go his mighty steeds. 1852
5:22 galloping, **g** go his mighty steeds. 1852
Jer 47: 3 at the sound of the hoofs of **g** steeds, 9121
Na 3: 2 **g** horses and jolting chariots! 1851

GALLOPS (1) [GALLOP]

Hab 1: 8 Their cavalry **g headlong;** 7055

GALLOWS (9)

Est 2:23 the two officials were hanged on a **g.** 6770
5:14 "Have a **g** built, seventy-five feet high, 6770
5:14 and he had the **g** built. 6770
6: 4 on the **g** he had erected for him. 6770
7: 9 "A **g** seventy-five feet high stands 6770
7:10 on the **g** he had prepared for Mordecai. 6770
8: 7 and they have hanged him on the **g.** 6770
9:13 and let Haman's ten sons be hanged on **g."** 6770
9:25 he and his sons should be hanged on the **g.** 6770

GAMALIEL (7)

Nu 1:10 from Manasseh, G son of Pedahzur; 1697
2:20 of the people of Manasseh is G son 1697
7:54 On the eighth day G son of Pedahzur, 1697
7:59 This was the offering of G son of Pedahzur. 1697
10:23 G son of Pedahzur was over the division of 1697
Ac 5:34 But a Pharisee named **G,** *1137*
22: 3 Under G I was thoroughly trained in *1137*

GAME (10) [GAMES]

Ge 25:28 Isaac, who had a taste for **wild g,** 7473
27: 3 to the open country to hunt *some* **wild g** 7473
27: 5 for the open country to hunt **g** 7473
27: 7 'Bring me *some* **g** 7473
27:19 Please sit up and eat some of my **g** so 7473
27:25 "My son, bring me some of your **g** to eat, 7473
27:31 "My father, sit up and eat some of my **g,** 7473
27:33 then, that hunted **g** and brought it to me? 7473
Ps 76: 4 more majestic than mountains rich with **g.** 3272
Pr 12:27 The lazy man does not roast his **g,** 7473

GAMES (1) [GAME]

1Co 9:25 Everyone who **competes in the g** goes *76*

GAMMAD (1)

Eze 27:11 **men of G** were in your towers. 1689

GAMUL (1) [BETH GAMUL]

1Ch 24:17 the twenty-second to **G,** 1690

GANGRENE (1)

2Ti 2:17 Their teaching will spread like **g.** *1121*

GANNIM See EN GANNIM

GAP (4) [GAPS]

Jdg 21:15 LORD had made a **g** in the tribes of Israel. 7288
1Ki 11:27 and had filled in the **g in the wall** *of* 7288
Ne 6: 1 the wall and not a **g** was left in it— 7288
Eze 22:30 and stand before me in the **g** on behalf of 7288

GAPE (1) [GAPING]

Ps 35:21 *They* g at me and say, "Aha! 7023+8143

GAPING (1) [GAPE]

Job 30:14 They advance as through a **g** breach; 8146

GAPS (1) [GAP]

Ne 4: 7 ahead and that the **g** were being closed, 7287

GARDEN (53) [GARDENER, GARDENS]

Ge 2: 8 the LORD God had planted a **g** in the east, 1703
2: 9 the middle of the **g** were the tree of life and 1703
2: 10 A river watering the **g** flowed from Eden; 1703
2: 15 the **G** *of* Eden to work it and take care of it. 1703
2: 16 "You are free to eat from any tree in the **g**; 1703
3: 1 'You must not eat from any tree in the **g**'?" 1703
3: 2 "We may eat fruit from the trees in the **g**, 1703
3: 3 from the tree that is in the middle of the **g**, 1703
3: 8 the LORD God as he was walking in the **g** 1703
3: 8 the LORD God among the trees of the **g**. 1703
3: 10 He answered, "I heard you in the **g**, 1703
3: 23 the LORD God banished him from the **G** 1703
3: 24 on the east side of the **G** *of* Eden cherubim 1703
13: 10 like the **g** *of* the LORD, 1703
Dt 11: 10 and irrigated it by foot as in a vegetable **g**. 1703
1Ki 21: 2 to use for a vegetable **g**, 1703
2Ki 21: 18 and was buried in his palace **g**, 1703
21: 18 in his palace garden, the **g** *of* Uzza. 1703
21: 26 He was buried in his grave in the **g** 1703
25: 4 between the two walls near the king's **g**, 1703
Ne 3: 15 by the King's **G**, 1703
Est 1: 5 in the enclosed **g** *of* the king's palace, 1708
1: 6 **g** had hangings of white and blue linen, NIH
7: 7 left his wine and went out into the palace **g**. 1708
7: 8 Just as the king returned from the palace **g** 1708
Job 8: 16 spreading its shoots over the **g**; 1708
SS 4: 12 You are a **g** locked up, my sister, my bride; 1703
4: 15 You are a **g** fountain, 1703
4: 16 Blow on my **g**, 1703
4: 16 into his **g** and taste its choice fruits. 1703
5: 1 I have come into my **g**, my sister, 1703
6: 2 My lover has gone down to his **g**, 1703
Isa 1: 30 like a **g** without water. 1708
5: 7 the men of Judah are the **g** *of* his delight. 5750
51: 3 her wastelands like the **g** *of* the LORD. 1703
58: 11 You will be like a well-watered **g**, 1703
61: 11 the sprout come up and a **g** causes seeds 1708
Jer 31: 12 They will be like a well-watered **g**, 1703
39: 4 the city at night by way of the king's **g**, 1703
52: 7 between the two walls near the king's **g**, 1703
La 2: 6 He has laid waste his dwelling like a **g**; 1703
Eze 28: 13 You were in Eden, the **g** *of* God; 1703
31: 8 cedars in the **g** *of* God could not rival it, 1703
31: 8 in the **g** *of* God could match its beauty. 1703
31: 9 the envy of all the trees of Eden in the **g** 1703
36: 35 that was laid waste has become like the **g** 1703
Joel 2: 3 Before them the land is like the **g** *of* Eden, 1703
Mt 13: 32 it is the largest *of* **g plants** and becomes *3303*
Mk 4: 32 and becomes the largest of all **g plants**, *3303*
Lk 11: 42 rue and all other kinds of **g herbs**, *3303*
13: 19 which a man took and planted in his **g**. *3057*
Jn 19: 41 where Jesus was crucified, there was a **g**, *3057*
19: 41 and in the **g** a new tomb, *3057*

GARDENER (2) [GARDEN]

Jn 15: 1 "I am the true vine, and my Father is the **g**. *1177*
20: 15 Thinking he was the **g**, she said, "Sir, *3058*

GARDENS (11) [GARDEN]

Nu 24: 6 like **g** beside a river, 1708
Ecc 2: 5 I made **g** and parks and planted all kinds 1708
SS 6: 2 to browse in the **g** and to gather lilies. 1703
8: 13 You who dwell in the **g** with friends 1703
Isa 1: 29 because of the **g** that you have chosen. 1708
65: 3 offering sacrifices in **g** and burning incense 1708
66: 17 into the **g**, following the one in the midst 1708
Jer 29: 5 plant **g** and eat what they produce. 1708
29: 28 plant **g** and eat what they produce.' " 1708
Am 4: 9 "Many times I struck your **g** and vineyards, 1708
9: 14 they will make **g** and eat their fruit. 1708

GAREB (3)

2Sa 23: 38 Ira the Ithrite, **G** the Ithrite 1735
1Ch 11: 40 Ira the Ithrite, **G** the Ithrite, 1735
Jer 31: 39 from there straight to the hill of **G** and 1736

GARLAND (2)

Pr 1: 9 They will be a **g** to grace your head and 4292
4: 9 a **g** *of* grace on your head and present you 4292

GARLIC (1)

Nu 11: 5 melons, leeks, onions and **g**. 8770

GARMENT (47) [GARMENTS, UNDERGARMENT, UNDERGARMENTS]

Ge 9: 23 But Shem and Japheth took a **g** and laid it 8529
25: 25 and his whole body was like a hairy **g**; 168
Ex 22: 9 a donkey, a sheep, a **g**, 8515
Lev 6: 27 and if any of the blood is spattered on a **g**, 955
Nu 31: 20 Purify every **g** as well as everything made 955
Jdg 8: 25 So they spread out a **g**, 8529
Ru 3: 9 "Spread the **corner of** your **g** over me, 4053
1Sa 19: 13 with a **g** and putting some goats' hair at 955
2Sa 13: 18 of **g** the virgin daughters of the king wore. 5077
20: 12 from the road into a field and threw a **g** 955
2Ki 1: 8 "He was a man with a **g of hair** and with 8552
Job 13: 28 like a **g** eaten by moths. 955
Job 30: 18 he binds me like the neck of my **g**. 4189
31: 19 or a needy man without a **g**, 4064
38: 9 the clouds its **g** and wrapped it 4230
38: 14 its features stand out like those of a **g**. 4230
Ps 74: 11 from the folds of your **g** and destroy them! 2668
102: 26 they will all wear out like a **g**. 955
104: 2 He wraps himself in light as with a **g**; 8515
104: 6 You covered it with the deep as with a **g**; 4230
109: 18 He wore cursing as his **g**; 4496
Pr 20: 16 Take the **g** *of* one who puts up security for 955
25: 20 Like one who takes away a **g** on a cold day, 955
27: 13 Take the **g** *of* one who puts up security for 955
Isa 9: 5 and every **g** rolled in blood will be destined 8529
50: 9 They will all wear out like a **g**; 955
51: 6 like smoke, the earth will wear out like a **g** 955
51: 8 For the moth will eat them up like a **g**; 955
61: 3 a **g** *of* praise instead of a spirit of despair. 5073
Jer 43: 12 As a shepherd wraps his **g** around him, 4230
Eze 5: 3 in the **folds of** your **g**. 4053
16: 8 I spread the **corner of** my **g** over you 4053
44: 17 not wear any **woolen g** while ministering at 7547
Hag 2: 12 in the fold of his **g**, 955
Zec 13: 4 on a **prophet's g** *of* hair in order to deceive. 168
Mal 2: 16 with violence as well as with his **g**," 4230
Mt 9: 16 a patch of unshrunk cloth on an old **g**, *2668*
9: 16 for the patch will pull away from the **g**, *2668*
Mk 2: 21 a patch of unshrunk cloth on an old **g**. *2668*
14: 51 wearing nothing but a **linen g**, *4984*
14: 52 he fled naked, leaving his **g** behind. *4984*
Lk 5: 36 from a new **g** and sews it on an old one. *2668*
5: 36 If he does, he will have torn the new **g**, *NIG*
Jn 19: 23 This **g** was seamless, *5945*
21: 7 he wrapped his **outer g** around him *2087*
Heb 1: 11 they will all wear out like a **g**. *2668*
1: 12 like a **g** they will be changed. *2668*

GARMENTS (73) [GARMENT]

Ge 3: 21 The LORD God made **g** *of* skin for Adam 4189
49: 11 he will wash his **g** in wine, 4230
Ex 28: 2 Make sacred **g** for your brother Aaron, 955
28: 3 in such matters that they are to make **g** 955
28: 4 These are the **g** they are to make: 955
28: 4 They are to make these sacred **g** 955
29: 5 Take the **g** and dress Aaron with the tunic, 955
29: 21 and sprinkle it on Aaron and his **g** and 955
29: 21 and on his sons and their **g**. 955
29: 21 Then he and his sons and their **g** will 955
29: 29 "Aaron's sacred **g** will belong 955
31: 10 and also the woven **g**, 955
31: 10 both the sacred **g** for Aaron the priest and 955
31: 10 for Aaron the priest and the **g** *for* his sons 955
35: 19 the woven **g** worn for ministering in 955
35: 19 both the sacred **g** for Aaron the priest and 955
35: 19 for Aaron the priest and the **g** *for* his sons 955
35: 21 for all its service, and for the sacred **g**. 955
39: 1 purple and scarlet yarn they made woven **g** 955
39: 1 They also made sacred **g** for Aaron, 955
39: 41 and the woven **g** worn for ministering in 955
39: 41 both the sacred **g** for Aaron the priest and 955
39: 41 the **g** *for* his sons when serving as priests. 955
40: 13 Then dress Aaron in the sacred **g**, 955
Lev 8: 2 their **g**, the anointing oil, 955
8: 30 and sprinkled them on Aaron and his **g** and 955
8: 30 and on his sons and their **g**. 955
8: 30 and his **g** and his sons and their garments. 955
8: 30 and his garments and his sons and their **g**. 955
16: 4 These are sacred **g**; 955
16: 23 of Meeting and take off the linen **g** he put 955
16: 24 in a holy place and put on his regular **g**. 955
16: 32 He is to put on the sacred linen **g** 955
21: 10 to wear the priestly **g**, 955
Nu 15: 38 to make tassels on the corners of your **g**, 955
20: 26 Remove Aaron's **g** and put them 955
20: 28 Moses removed Aaron's **g** and put them 955
Jdg 5: 30 **colorful g** as plunder for Sisera, 7389
5: 30 **colorful g** embroidered, 7389
5: 30 highly embroidered **g** for my neck— 7389
8: 26 the purple **g** worn by the kings of Midian or 955
14: 12 I will give you thirty **linen g** and thirty sets 6041
14: 13 you must give me thirty **linen g** 6041
2Sa 1: 24 who adorned your **g** with ornaments 4230
10: 4 cut off their **g** in the middle at the buttocks, 4503
1Ch 19: 4 cut off their **g** in the middle at the buttocks, 4503
Ezr 2: 69 5,000 minas of silver and 100 priestly **g**. 4189
Ne 7: 70 50 bowls and 530 **g** *for* priests. 4189
7: 72 2,000 minas of silver and 67 **g** *for* priests. 4189
Est 8: 15 the king's presence wearing royal **g** *of* blue 4230
Ps 22: 18 They divide my **g** among them and cast lots 955
45: 14 In **embroidered g** she is led to the king; 8391
Pr 31: 24 She makes **linen g** and sells them, 6041
SS 4: 11 The fragrance of your **g** is like that 8515
Isa 3: 23 and the **linen g** and tiaras and shawls. 6041
52: 1 Put on your **g** *of* splendor, O Jerusalem, 955
59: 17 the **g** *of* vengeance and wrapped himself 955
61: 10 For he has clothed me with **g** *of* salvation 955
63: 1 from Bozrah, with his **g** stained crimson? 955
63: 2 Why are your **g** red, 4230
63: 3 their blood spattered my **g**, 955
La 4: 14 that no one dares to touch their **g**. 4230
Eze 16: 10 and covered you with **costly g**. 5429
16: 16 of your **g** to make gaudy high places, 955
26: 16 and take off their embroidered **g**. 955
27: 24 with you **beautiful g**, 4815
42: 14 the outer court until they leave behind the **g** 955
44: 19 the people by means of their **g**. 955
Joel 2: 13 Rend your heart and not your **g**. 955
Am 2: 8 They lie down beside every altar on **g** taken 955
Zec 3: 4 and I will put **rich g** on you." 4711
Mt 23: 5 and the tassels *on* their **g** long; *2668*
Jn 19: 24 "They divided my **g** among them *2668*

GARMITE (1)

1Ch 4: 19 the father of Keilah the **G**, 1753

GARNER, GARNERS (KJV) See BARN, BARNS, STOREHOUSES

GARRISON (2) [GARRISONS]

2Sa 23: 14 and the Philistine **g** was at Bethlehem. 5163
1Ch 11: 16 and the Philistine **g** was at Bethlehem. 5907

GARRISONS (5) [GARRISON]

2Sa 8: 6 He put **g** in the Aramean kingdom 5907
8: 14 He put **g** throughout Edom, 5907
1Ch 18: 6 He put **g** in the Aramean kingdom NIH
18: 13 He put **g** in Edom, 5907
2Ch 17: 2 in all the fortified cities of Judah and put **g** 5907

GASP (2) [GASPING]

Job 11: 20 their hope will become a dying **g**." 5134
Isa 42: 14 I cry out, *I* **g** and pant. 5971

GASPING (1) [GASP]

Jer 4: 31 cry of the Daughter of Zion **g for breath**, 3640

GAT (KJV) See ACQUIRED, CAME, CLIMBED, GET, LEFT, MOUNTED, MOVED, SET OUT, TRAVELED, WENT

GATAM (3)

Ge 36: 11 Teman, Omar, Zepho, **G** and Kenaz. 1725
36: 16 Korah, **G** and Amalek. 1725
1Ch 1: 36 Teman, Omar, Zepho, **G** and Kenaz; 1725

GATE (222) [GATEKEEPERS, GATEPOST, GATEPOSTS, GATES, GATEWAY, GATEWAYS]

Ge 23: 10 of all the Hittites who had come to the **g** *of* 9133
23: 18 of all the Hittites who had come to the **g** *of* 9133
28: 17 this is the **g** *of* heaven." 9133
34: 20 and his son Shechem went to the **g** 9133
34: 24 the men who went out of the city **g** agreed 9133
Dt 17: 5 to your **city g** and stone that person 9133
21: 19 of him and bring him to the elders at the **g** 9133
22: 15 a virgin to the town elders at the **g**. 9133
22: 24 you shall take both of them to the **g** *of* 9133
25: 7 she shall go to the elders at the **town g** 9133
Jos 2: 5 when it was time to close the **city g**, 9133
2: 7 the **g** was shut. 9133
7: 5 from the **city g** as far as the stone quarries 9133
8: 29 down at the entrance of the city **g**. 9133
20: 4 the entrance of the city **g** and state his case 9133
Jdg 9: 35 the entrance to the city **g** just as Abimelech 9133
9: 40 all the way to the entrance to the **g**. 9133
9: 44 to a position at the entrance to the city **g**. 9133
16: 2 in wait for him all night at the city **g**. 9133
16: 3 up and took hold of the doors of the city **g**, 9133
18: 16 stood at the entrance to the **g**. 9133
18: 17 at the entrance to the **g**. 9133
Ru 4: 1 Meanwhile Boaz went up to the **town g** 9133
4: 11 Then the elders and all those at the **g** said, 9133
1Sa 4: 18 by the side of the **g**. 9133
21: 13 the **g** and letting saliva run down his beard. 9133
2Sa 10: 8 at the entrance to their **city g**, 9133
11: 23 to the entrance to the **city g**. 9133
15: 2 the side of the road leading to the **city g**. 9133
18: 4 beside the **g** while all the men marched out 9133
23: 15 a drink of water from the well near the **g** 9133
23: 16 near the **g** of Bethlehem and carried it back 9133
1Ki 4: 13 with bronze **g bars**); 1378
17: 10 When he came to the town **g**, 7339
22: 10 the threshing floor by the entrance of the **g** 9133
2Ki 7: 1 and two seahs of barley for a shekel at the **g** 9133
7: 3 with leprosy at the entrance of the **city g**. 9133
7: 17 on whose arm he leaned in charge of the **g**, 9133
7: 18 and two seahs of barley for a shekel at the **g** 9133
9: 31 As Jehu entered the **g**, she asked, 9133
10: 8 at the entrance of the **city g** until morning." 9133
11: 6 at the Sur **G**, and a third at the gate behind 9133
11: 6 and a third at the **g** behind the guard, 9133
11: 19 entering by way of the **g** *of* the guards. 9133
14: 13 the wall of Jerusalem from the Ephraim **G** 9133
14: 13 from the Ephraim Gate to the Corner **G**— 9133
15: 35 the Upper **G** *of* the temple of the LORD. 9133
23: 8 at the entrance to the **G** *of* Joshua, 9133
23: 8 which is on the left of the city **g**. 9133
25: 4 the whole army fled at night through the **g** 9133
1Ch 9: 18 being stationed at the King's **G** on the east, 9133
11: 17 a drink of water from the well near the **g** 9133
11: 18 near the **g** of Bethlehem and carried it back 9133
16: 42 of Jeduthun were stationed at the **g**. 9133
26: 13 Lots were cast for **each g**, 2256+9133+9133
26: 14 The lot for the East **G** fell to Shelemiah. NIH
26: 14 and the lot for the North **G** fell to him. NIH
26: 15 The lot for the South **G** fell to Obed-Edom, NIH

1Ch 26:16 for the West **G** and the Shalleketh Gate on NIH
26:16 and the Shalleketh **G** on the upper road fell 9133
2Ch 18: 9 the threshing floor by the entrance to the **g** 9133
23: 5 and a third at the Foundation **G**, 9133
23:15 as she reached the entrance of the Horse **G** 9133
23:20 through the Upper **G** and seated the king on 9133
24: 8 at the **g** *of* the temple of the LORD. 9133
25:23 the wall of Jerusalem from the Ephraim **G** 9133
25:23 from the Ephraim Gate to the Corner **G**— 9133
26: 9 in Jerusalem at the Corner **G**, 9133
26: 9 at the Valley **G** and at the angle of the wall, 9133
27: 3 Jotham rebuilt the Upper **G** *of* the temple 9133
31:14 **keeper of** the East **G**, 8788
32: 6 before him in the square at the city **g** 9133
33:14 as the entrance of the Fish **G** and encircling 9133
35:15 The gatekeepers at **each g** 2256+9133+9133
Ne 2:13 By night I went out through the Valley **G** 9133
2:13 toward the Jackal Well and the Dung **G**, 9133
2:14 toward the Fountain **G** and the King's Pool, 9133
2:15 and reentered through the Valley **G**. 9133
3: 1 to work and rebuilt the Sheep **G**. 9133
3: 3 The Fish **G** was rebuilt by the sons 9133
3: 6 The Jeshanah **G** was repaired by Joiada son 9133
3:13 The Valley **G** was repaired by Hanun and 9133
3:13 of the wall as far as the Dung **G**. 9133
3:14 The Dung **G** was repaired by Malkijah son 9133
3:15 The Fountain **G** was repaired 9133
3:26 up to a point opposite the Water **G** toward 9133
3:28 Above the Horse **G**, 9133
3:29 the guard at the East **G**, made repairs. 9133
3:31 opposite the Inspection **G**, 9133
3:32 the room above the corner and the Sheep **G** 9133
8: 1 in the square before the Water **G**. 9133
8: 3 as he faced the square before the Water **G** 9133
8:16 the square by the Water **G** and the one by 9133
8:16 by the Water Gate and the one by the **G** 9133
12:31 toward the Dung **G**. 9133
12:37 the Fountain **G** they continued directly up 9133
12:37 above the house of David to the Water **G** 9133
12:39 over the **G** *of* Ephraim, 9133
12:39 the Jeshanah **G**, the Fish Gate, 9133
12:39 the Jeshanah Gate, the Fish **G**, 9133
12:39 as far as the Sheep **G**. 9133
12:39 At the **G** *of* the Guard they stopped. 9133
Est 2:19 Mordecai was sitting at the king's **g**. 9133
2:21 Mordecai was sitting at the king's **g**, 9133
3: 2 All the royal officials at the king's **g** knelt 9133
3: 3 at the king's **g** asked Mordecai, 9133
4: 2 But he went only as far as the king's **g**, 9133
4: 6 of the city in front of the king's **g**. 9133
5: 9 But when he saw Mordecai at the king's **g** 9133
5:13 that Jew Mordecai sitting at the king's **g**." 9133
6:10 Mordecai the Jew, who sits at the king's **g**. 9133
6:12 Mordecai returned to the king's **g**. 9133
Job 29: 7 to the **g** of the city and took my seat in 9133
Ps 69:12 Those who sit at the **g** mock me, 9133
118:20 This is the **g** *of* the LORD through which 9133
127: 5 with their enemies in the **g**. 9133
Pr 17:19 he who builds a high **g** invites destruction. 7339
24: 7 the **assembly at the g** he has nothing to say. 9133
31:23 Her husband is respected at the **city g**, 9133
31:31 her works bring her praise at the **city g**. 9133
SS 7: 4 of Heshbon by the **g** *of* Bath Rabbim. 9133
Isa 14:31 Wail, O **g**! 9133
24:12 its **g** is battered to pieces. 9133
28: 6 to those who turn back the battle at the **g**. 9133
Jer 7: 2 "Stand at the **g** *of* the LORD's house 9133
17:19 "Go and stand at the **g** *of* the people, 9133
19: 2 near the entrance of the Potsherd **G**. 9133
20: 2 in the stocks at the Upper **G** *of* Benjamin at 9133
26:10 of the New **G** *of* the LORD's house. 9133
31:38 the Tower of Hananel to the Corner **G**. 9133
31:40 the east as far as the corner of the Horse **G**, 9133
36:10 at the entrance of the New **G** *of* the temple, 9133
37:13 But when he reached the Benjamin **G**, 9133
38: 7 the king was sitting in the Benjamin **G**, 9133
39: 3 and took seats in the Middle **G**: 9133
39: 4 through the **g** between the two walls, 9133
52: 7 through the **g** between the two walls near 9133
La 5:14 The elders are gone from the **city g**; 9133
Eze 8: 3 to the north **g** *of* the inner court, 9133
8: 5 the **g** *of* the altar I saw this idol of jealousy. 9133
8:14 the entrance to the north **g** *of* the house of 9133
9: 2 from the direction of the upper **g**, 9133
10:19 They stopped at the entrance to the east **g** 9133
11: 1 up and brought me to the **g** *of* the house of 9133
11: 1 the entrance to the **g** were twenty-five men, 9133
26: 2 The **g** *to* the nations is broken, 1946
40: 6 Then he went to the **g** facing east. 9133
40: 6 and measured the threshold of the **g**; 9133
40: 7 And the threshold of the **g** next to 9133
40:10 the east **g** were three alcoves on each side; 9133
40:20 the length and width of the **g** facing north, 9133
40:22 as those of the **g** facing east. 9133
40:23 a **g** to the inner court facing the north gate, 9133
40:23 a gate to the inner court facing the north **g**, 9133
40:23 from one **g** to the opposite one; 9133
40:24 to the south side and I saw a **g** facing south. 9133
40:27 The inner court also had a **g** facing south, 9133
40:27 and he measured from this **g** to 9133
40:27 to the outer **g** *on* the south side; 9133
40:28 into the inner court through the south **g**, 9133
40:28 and he measured the south **g**; 9133
40:35 Then he brought me to the north **g** 9133
40:44 Outside the inner **g**, within the inner court, 9133
40:44 at the side of the north **g** and facing south, 9133
40:44 at the side of the south **g** and facing north. 9133
Eze 42:15 the east **g** and measured the area all around: 9133
43: 1 the man brought me to the **g** facing east, 9133
43: 4 the temple through the **g** facing east. 9133
44: 1 the man brought me back to the outer **g** *of* 9133
44: 2 "This **g** is to remain shut. 9133
44: 4 the man brought me by way of the north **g** 9133
46: 1 The **g** *of* the inner court facing east is to 9133
46: 2 but the **g** will not be shut until evening. 9133
46: 9 whoever enters by the north **g** to worship is 9133
46: 9 to worship is to go out the south **g**; 9133
46: 9 by the south **g** is to go out the north gate. 9133
46: 9 by the south gate is to go out the north **g**. 9133
46: 9 through the **g** by which he entered, 9133
46: 9 but each is to go out the opposite **g**. NIH
46:12 the **g** facing east is to be opened for him. 9133
46:12 the **g** will be shut. 9133
46:19 through the entrance at the side of the **g** to 9133
47: 2 He then brought me out through the north **g** 9133
47: 2 the outside to the outer **g** facing east, 9133
48:31 on the north side will be the **g** *of* Reuben, 9133
48:31 the **g** *of* Judah and the gate of Levi. 9133
48:31 the gate of Judah and the **g** *of* Levi. 9133
48:32 the **g** *of* Joseph, 9133
48:32 the **g** *of* Benjamin and the gate of Dan. 9133
48:32 the gate of Benjamin and the **g** *of* Dan. 9133
48:33 the **g** *of* Simeon, 9133
48:33 the **g** *of* Issachar and the gate of Zebulun. 9133
48:33 the gate of Issachar and the **g** *of* Zebulun. 9133
48:34 the **g** *of* Gad, 9133
48:34 the **g** *of* Asher and the gate of Naphtali. 9133
48:34 the gate of Asher and the **g** *of* Naphtali. 9133
Am 1: 5 I will break down the **g** *of* Damascus; 1378
Mic 1: 9 It has reached the very **g** *of* my people, 9133
1:12 even to the **g** *of* Jerusalem. 9133
2:13 they will break through the **g** and go out. 9133
Zep 1:10 "a cry will go up from the Fish **G**, 9133
Zec 14:10 the Benjamin **G** to the site of the First Gate, 9133
14:10 to the site of the First **G**, 9133
14:10 to the Corner **G**, and from the Tower 9133
Mt 7:13 "Enter through the narrow **g**. *4783*
7:13 For wide is the **g** and broad is the road *4783*
7:14 the **g** and narrow the road that leads to life, *4783*
Lk 7:12 As he approached the town **g**, *4783*
16:20 At his **g** was laid a beggar named Lazarus, *4784*
Jn 5: 2 Now there is in Jerusalem near the **Sheep G** *4583*
10: 1 who does not enter the sheep pen by the **g**, *2598*
10: 2 enters by the **g** is the shepherd of his sheep. *2598*
10: 3 The watchman opens the **g** for him, *NIG*
10: 7 I am the **g** for the sheep. *2598*
10: 9 I am the **g**; whoever enters through me will be saved. *2598*
Ac 3: 2 to the temple **g** called Beautiful, *2598*
3:10 at the temple **g** called Beautiful, *4783*
10:17 and stopped at the **g**. *4784*
12:10 and came to the iron **g** leading to the city. *4783*
16:13 On the Sabbath we went outside the **city g** *4783*
Heb 13:12 so Jesus also suffered outside the **city g** *4783*
Rev 21:21 each **g** made of a single pearl. *4784*

GATEKEEPER (2) [GATE, KEEP]

2Sa 18:26 and he called down to the **g**, "Look, 8788
1Ch 9:21 of Meshelemiah was the **g** *at* the entrance 8788

GATEKEEPERS (34) [GATE,KEEP]

2Ki 7:10 to the city **g** and told them, "We went into 8788
7:11 The **g** shouted the news, 8788
1Ch 9:17 The **g**: Shallum, Akkub, 8788
9:18 the **g** belonging to the camp of the Levites. 8788
9:19 and his fellow **g** from his family NIH
9:20 of Eleazar was in charge of **the g**, 2157[S]
9:22 to be **g** at the thresholds numbered 212. 8788
9:22 **The g** had been assigned to their positions 2156[S]
9:24 The **g** were on the four sides: 8788
9:26 But the four principal **g**, who were Levites, 8788
15:18 Mikneiah, Obed-Edom and Jeiel, the **g**. 8788
16:38 and also Hosah, were **g**. 8788
23: 5 to be **g** and four thousand are to praise 8788
26: 1 The divisions of the **g**: 8788
26:12 These divisions of the **g**, 8788
26:19 of the **g** who were descendants of Korah 8788
2Ch 8:14 He also appointed the **g** by divisions for 8788
35:15 The **g** at each gate did not need to leave 8788
Ezr 2:42 The **g** of the temple: 8788
2:70 the **g** and the temple servants settled 8788
7: 7 Levites, singers, **g** and temple servants, 8788
7:24 on any of the priests, Levites, singers, **g**, 10777
10:24 From the **g**: Shallum, Telem and Uri. 8788
Ne 7: 1 the **g** and the singers and 8788
7: 3 While **the g** are still on duty, 2156[S]
7:45 The **g**: the descendants of Shallum, 8788
7:73 The priests, the Levites, the **g**, 8788
10:28 priests, Levites, **g**, singers, 8788
10:39 the **g** and the singers stay. 8788
11:19 The **g**: Akkub, Talmon 8788
12:25 Talmon and Akkub were **g** who guarded 8788
12:45 as did also the singers and **g**, 8788
12:47 the daily portions for the singers and **g**. 8788
13: 5 singers and **g**, as well as the contributions 8788

GATEPOST (1) [GATE, POST]

Eze 46: 2 of the gateway and stand by the **g**. 4647+9133

GATEPOSTS (1) [GATE, POST]

Eze 45:19 and on the **g** *of* the inner court. 4647+9133

GATES (111) [GATE]

Ge 24:60 your offspring possess the **g** *of* their enemies 9133
Ex 20:10 nor the alien within your **g**. 9133
Dt 3: 5 with high walls and with **g** and bars, 1946
5:14 nor the alien within your **g**, 9133
6: 9 of your houses and on your **g**. 9133
11:20 of your houses and on your **g**, 9133
20:11 If they accept and open their **g**, NIH
33:25 **bolts of** your **g** will be iron and bronze, 4981
Jos 6:26 the cost of his youngest will he set up its **g**." 1946
Jdg 5: 8 war came to the **city g**, 9133
5:11 of the LORD went down to the **city g**. 9133
1Sa 17:52 the entrance of Gath and to the **g** *of* Ekron. 9133
23: 7 by entering a town with **g** and bars." 1946
2Sa 18:24 between the inner and outer **g**, 9133
1Ki 16:34 and he set up its **g** at the cost 1946
2Ki 15:16 because they refused to open their **g**. NIH
23: 8 He broke down the shrines at the **g**— 9133
1Ch 9:23 in charge of guarding the **g** of the house of 9133
2Ch 8: 5 with walls and with **g** and bars, 1946
8:14 by divisions for the **various g**, 2256+9133+9133
14: 7 with towers, **g** and bars. 1946
23:19 He also stationed doorkeepers at the **g** *of* 9133
31: 2 to give thanks and to sing praises at the **g** 9133
Ne 1: 3 and its **g** have been burned with fire." 9133
2: 3 and its **g** have been destroyed by fire?" 9133
2: 8 to make beams for the **g** *of* the citadel by 9133
2:13 and its **g**, which had been destroyed by fire. 9133
2:17 and its **g** have been burned with fire. 9133
6: 1 to that time I had not set the doors in the **g** 9133
7: 3 "The **g** *of* Jerusalem are not to be opened 9133
11:19 who kept watch at the **g**—172 men. 9133
12:25 the storerooms at the **g**. 9133
12:30 they purified the people, the **g** and the wall. 9133
13:19 on the **g** *of* Jerusalem before the Sabbath, 9133
13:19 I stationed some of my own men at the **g** so 9133
13:22 the **g** in order to keep the Sabbath day holy. 9133
Job 17:16 Will it go down to the **g** *of* death? 964
38:17 Have the **g** *of* death been shown to you? 9133
38:17 Have you seen the **g** *of* the shadow 9133
Ps 9:13 Have mercy and lift me up from the **g** 9133
9:14 that I may declare your praises in the **g** *of* 9133
24: 7 up your heads, O you **g**; 9133
24: 9 Lift up your heads, O you **g**; 9133
87: 2 the **g** *of* Zion more than all the dwellings 9133
100: 4 Enter his **g** with thanksgiving 9133
107:16 for he breaks down **g** *of* bronze and cuts 1946
107:18 They loathed all food and drew near the **g** 9133
118:19 Open for me the **g** *of* righteousness; 9133
122: 2 Our feet are standing in your **g**, 9133
147:13 the bars of your **g** and blesses your people 9133
Pr 8: 3 beside the **g** leading into the city, at 9133
14:19 and the wicked at the **g** *of* the righteous. 9133
18:19 disputes are like the **barred g** *of* a citadel. 1378
Isa 3:26 The **g** *of* Zion will lament and mourn; 7339
13: 2 beckon to them to enter the **g** *of* the nobles. 7339
22: 7 and horsemen are posted at the **city g**; 9133
26: 2 the **g** that the righteous nation may enter, 9133
38:10 of my life must I go through the **g** *of* death 9133
45: 1 to open doors before him so that **g** will not 9133
45: 2 down **g** *of* bronze and cut through bars 1946
54:12 your **g** of sparkling jewels, 9133
60:11 Your **g** will always stand open, 9133
60:18 and your **g** Praise. 9133
62:10 Pass through, pass through the **g**! 9133
Jer 1:15 up their thrones in the entrance of the **g** 9133
7: 2 through these **g** to worship the LORD. 9133
15: 7 a winnowing fork at the **city g** *of* the land. 9133
17:19 stand also at all the other **g** *of* Jerusalem. 9133
17:20 in Jerusalem who come through these **g**. 9133
17:21 on the Sabbath day or bring it through the **g** 9133
17:24 and bring no load through the **g** *of* this city 9133
17:25 on David's throne will come through the **g** 9133
17:27 as you come through the **g** *of* Jerusalem on 9133
17:27 an unquenchable fire in the **g** *of* Jerusalem 9133
22: 2 and your people who come through these **g**. 9133
22: 4 on David's throne will come through the **g** 9133
22:19 and thrown outside the **g** *of* Jerusalem." 9133
49:31 "a nation that has neither **g** nor bars; 1946
51:30 the **bars of** her **g** are broken. 1378
51:58 be leveled and her high **g** set on fire; 9133
La 2: 9 Her **g** have sunk into the ground; 9133
4:12 and foes could enter the **g** *of* Jerusalem. 9133
Eze 21:15 the sword for slaughter at all their **g**. 9133
21:22 to set battering rams against the **g**, 9133
26:10 wagons and chariots when he enters your **g** 9133
38:11 of them living without walls and without **g** 1946
44:11 of the **g** *of* the temple and serving in it; 9133
44:17 " 'When they enter the **g** *of* the inner court, 9133
44:17 at the **g** *of* the inner court or inside 9133
48:31 the **g** *of* the city will be named after 9133
48:31 The three **g** on the north side will be 9133
48:32 which is 4,500 cubits long, will be three **g**: 9133
48:33 cubits, will be three **g**: 9133
48:34 which is 4,500 cubits long, will be three **g**: 9133
Hos 11: 6 will destroy the **bars of** their **g** and put 964
Ob 1:11 and foreigners entered his **g** and cast lots 9133
1:13 not march through the **g** *of* my people in 9133
Na 2: 6 The river **g** are thrown open and 9133
3:13 The **g** *of* your land are wide open 9133
Mt 16:18 and the **g** of Hades will not overcome it. *4783*
Ac 9:24 on the **city g** in order to kill him. *4783*
14:13 the city **g** because he and the crowd wanted *4784*
21:30 and immediately the **g** were shut. *2598*
Rev 21:12 It had a great, high wall with twelve **g**, *4784*
21:12 and with twelve angels at the **g**. *4784*

Rev 21:12 On the **g** were written the names of the twelve tribes of Israel. *NIG*
21:13 There were three **g** on the east, *4784*
21:15 its **g** and its walls. *4784*
21:21 The twelve **g** were twelve pearls, *4784*
21:25 On no day will its **g** ever be shut, *4784*
22:14 to the tree of life and may go through the **g** *4784*

GATEWAY (35) [GATE, WAY]

Ge 19: 1 and Lot was sitting in the **g** *of* the city. 9133
1Sa 9:18 Saul approached Samuel in the **g** 9133
2Sa 3:27 Joab took him aside into the **g**, 9133
18:24 the watchman went up to the roof of the **g** 9133
18:33 up to the room over the **g** and wept. 9133
19: 8 the king got up and took his seat in the **g**. 9133
19: 8 "The king is sitting in the **g**," 9133
2Ki 7:17 and the people trampled him in the **g**, 9133
7:20 for the people trampled him in the **g**, 9133
Eze 27: 3 Say to Tyre, situated at the **g** *to* the sea, 4427
40: 3 the **g** with a linen cord and a measuring rod 9133
40: 8 Then he measured the portico of the **g**; 9133
40: 9 The portico of the **g** faced the temple. 9133
40:11 the width of the entrance to the **g**; 9133
40:13 Then he measured the **g** from the top of 9133
40:14 around the inside of the **g**— 9133
40:15 The distance from the entrance of the **g** to 9133
40:16 inside the **g** were surmounted 9133
40:19 from the inside of the lower **g** to the outside 9133
40:21 as those of the first **g**. 9133
40:25 **The g** and its portico had narrow openings all around, 2257S
40:29 **The g** and its portico had openings all 2257S
40:32 and he measured the **g**; 9133
40:33 **The g** and its portico had openings all 2257S
40:39 In the portico of the **g** were two tables 9133
40:40 By the outside wall of the portico of the **g**, 9133
40:40 the entrance to the north **g** were two tables, 9133
40:41 on one side of the **g** and four on the other— 9133
44: 3 the only one who may sit inside **the g** to eat 2257S
44: 3 He is to enter by way of the portico of the **g** 9133
46: 2 through the portico of the **g** and stand by 9133
46: 2 He is to worship at the threshold of the **g** 9133
46: 3 of the LORD at the entrance to that **g**. 9133
46: 8 he is to go in through the portico of the **g**, 9133
Mt 26:71 Then he went out to the **g**, *4784*

GATEWAYS (6) [GATE, WAY]

1Ch 22: 3 to make nails for the doors of the **g** and for 9133
Pr 1:21 in the **g** of the city she makes her speech: 7339+9133
La 1: 4 All her **g** are desolate, her priests groan, 9133
Eze 40:18 of the **g** and was as wide as they were long; 9133
40:30 (The porticoes of the **g** around NIH
40:38 by the portico in each of the inner **g**, 9133

GATH (36) [GATH HEPHER, GATH RIMMON, MORESHETH GATH]

Jos 11:22 **G** and Ashdod did any survive. 1781
13: 3 Ashdod, Ashkelon, **G** and Ekron— 1785
1Sa 5: 8 the ark of the god of Israel moved to **G**." 1781
6:17 Gaza, Ashkelon, **G** and Ekron. 1781
7:14 to **G** that the Philistines had captured 1781
17: 4 Goliath, who was from **G**, 1781
17:23 Goliath, the Philistine champion from **G**, 1781
17:52 the entrance of **G** and to the gates of Ekron. 1781
17:52 along the Shaaraim road to **G** and Ekron. 1781
21:10 from Saul and went to Achish king of **G**. 1781
21:12 of Achish king of **G**. 1781
22: 1 David left **G** and escaped to the cave 9004S
27: 2 over to Achish son of Maoch king of **G**. 1781
27: 3 and his men settled in **G** with Achish. 1781
27: 4 Saul was told that David had fled to **G**, 1781
27:11 a man or woman alive to be brought to **G**, 1781
2Sa 1:20 "Tell it not in **G**, proclaim it not 1781
15:18 from **G** marched before the king. 1781
21:20 which took place at **G**, 1781
21:22 These four were descendants of Rapha in **G**, 1781
1Ki 2:39 king of **G**, and Shimei was told, 1781
2:39 "Your slaves are in **G**." 1781
2:40 to Achish at **G** in search of his slaves. 1781
2:40 and brought the slaves back from **G**. 1781
2:41 that Shimei had gone from Jerusalem to **G** 1781
2Ki 12:17 went up and attacked **G** and captured it. 1781
1Ch 7:21 by the native-born men of **G**, 1781
8:13 and who drove out the inhabitants of **G**. 1781
18: 1 and he took **G** and its surrounding villages 1781
20: 6 which took place at **G**, 1781
20: 8 These were descendants of Rapha in **G**, 1781
2Ch 11: 8 **G**, Mareshah, Ziph, 1781
26: 6 and broke down the walls of **G**, 1781
Ps 56: T When the Philistines had seized him in **G**. 1781
Am 6: 2 and then go down to **G** *in* Philistia. 1781
Mic 1:10 Tell it not in **G**; weep not at all. 1781

GATH HEPHER (2) [GATH, HEPHER]

Jos 19:13 Then it continued eastward to **G** 1783
2Ki 14:25 Jonah son of Amittai, the prophet from **G**. 1783

GATH RIMMON (4) [GATH, RIMMON]

Jos 19:45 Jehud, Bene Berak, **G**, 1784
21:24 Aijalon and **G**, together with their 1784
21:25 Taanach and **G**, together with their 1784
1Ch 6:69 Aijalon and **G**, together with their 1784

GATHER (118) [GATHERED, GATHERING, GATHERS, INGATHERING]

Ge 31:46 He said to his relatives, "**G** some stones." 4377
49: 1 **G around** so I can tell you what will happen 665
Ex 5: 7 let them go and **g** their own straw. 8006
5:12 over Egypt to **g** stubble to use for straw. 8006
16: 4 to go out each day and **g** enough for 4377
16: 5 and that is to be twice as much as *they* **g** on 4377
16:16 'Each one *is to* **g** as much as he needs. 4377
16:26 Six days *you are to* **g** it, 4377
16:27 on the seventh day to **g** it, 4377
23:16 when you **g in** your crops from the field. 665
Lev 8: 3 and **g** the entire assembly at the entrance to 7735
19: 9 not reap to the very edges of your field or **g** 4377
23:22 not reap to the very edges of your field or **g** 4377
25: 3 prune your vineyards and **g** their crops. 665
Nu 10: 7 *To* **g** the assembly, blow the trumpets, 7735
19: 9 "A man who is clean *shall* **g up** the ashes 665
20: 8 **g** the assembly **together**. 7735
21:16 "**G** the people **together** 665
Dt 11:14 so that *you may* **g in** your grain, 665
13:16 **G** all the plunder of the town into 7695
28:39 not drink the wine or **g** *the* **grapes**, 112
30: 3 on you and **g** you again from all the nations 7695
30: 4 the LORD your God *will* **g** you 7695
Ru 2: 7 'Please let me glean and **g** among 665
2Ki 4:39 the fields to **g** herbs and found a wild vine. 4377
22:20 Therefore I *will* **g** you to your fathers, 665
1Ch 16:35 **g** us and deliver us from the nations, 7695
2Ch 34:28 Now I *will* **g** you to your fathers, 665
Ne 1: 9 *I will* **g** them from there and bring them 7695
Est 4:16 **g together** all the Jews who are in Susa, 4043
Job 24: 6 *They* **g** fodder in the fields and glean in 7917
39:12 and **g** it *to* your threshing floor? 665
Ps 2: 2 the rulers **g** together against the LORD 3570
7: 7 *Let* the assembled peoples **g around** you. 6015
50: 5 "**G** to me my consecrated ones, 665
104:28 When you give it to them, *they* **g** it **up**; 4377
106:47 and **g** us from the nations, 7695
142: 7 the righteous *will* **g about** me because 4193
Ecc 3: 5 time to scatter stones and a time *to* **g** them, 4043
SS 6: 2 to browse in the gardens and to **g** lilies. 4377
Isa 10:14 as men **g** abandoned eggs, 665
11:12 He will raise a banner for the nations and **g** 665
34:15 there also the falcons *will* **g**, 7695
34:16 and his Spirit *will* **g** them **together**. 7695
43: 5 from the east and **g** you from the west. 7695
43: 9 All the nations **g** together and 7695
45:20 "**G together** and come; 7695
49: 5 and **g** Israel to himself, for I am honored in 665
49:18 all your sons **g** and come to you. 7695
56: 8 *"I will* **g** still others to them 7695
62: 9 and *those who* **g** the grapes will drink it in 7695
66:18 to come and **g** all nations and tongues, 7695
Jer 3:17 and all nations *will* **g** in Jerusalem 7748
4: 5 Cry aloud and say: '**G together!** 665
7:18 The children **g** wood, 4377
8:14 "Why are we sitting here? **G together!** 665
9:22 with no *one to* **g** them.' " 665
10:17 **G up** your belongings to leave the land, 665
12: 9 Go and **g** all the wild beasts; 665
21: 4 And *I will* **g** them inside this city. 665
23: 3 *"I* myself *will* **g** the remnant 7695
29:14 *I will* **g** you from all the nations 7695
31: 8 from the land of the north and **g** them from 7695
31:10 'He who scattered Israel *will* **g** them 7695
32:37 I *will* surely **g** them from all the lands 7695
49: 5 and no *one will* **g** the fugitives. 7695
Eze 11:17 *I will* **g** you from the nations 7695
16:37 therefore I *am going to* **g** all your lovers, 7695
16:37 *I will* **g** them against you from all around 7695
20:34 I will bring you from the nations and **g** you 7695
20:41 the nations and **g** you from the countries 7695
22:19 I *will* **g** you into Jerusalem. 7695
22:20 As men **g** silver, copper, iron, 7697
22:20 so *will I* **g** you in my anger and my wrath 7695
22:21 *I will* **g** you and I will blow on you 4043
28:25 When I **g** the people of Israel from 7695
29:13 of forty years *I will* **g** the Egyptians from 7695
34:13 the nations and **g** them from the countries, 7695
36:24 *I will* **g** you from all the countries 7695
37:21 *I will* **g** them from all around 7695
39:10 not *need to* **g** wood from the fields or cut it 5951
39:28 *I will* **g** them to their own land, 4043
Hos 7:14 *They* **g together** for grain and new wine 1591
8:10 *I will* now **g** them **together**. 7695
9: 6 Egypt *will* **g** them, 7695
Joel 2:16 **G** the people, consecrate the assembly; 665
2:16 bring together the elders, **g** the children, 665
3: 2 *I will* **g** all nations and bring them down 7695
Mic 2:12 *"I will* **surely g** all of you, O Jacob; 665+665
4: 6 declares the LORD, *"I will* **g** the lame; 665
Na 3:18 on the mountains with no *one to* **g** them. 7695
Hab 1: 9 like a desert wind and **g** prisoners like sand. 665
Zep 2: 1 **G together**, gather together, 8006
2: 1 Gather together, **g together**, 8006
3: 8 to **g** the kingdoms and 7695
3:19 and **g** those who have been scattered. 7695
3:20 At that time I *will* **g** you; 7695
Zec 10: 8 I will signal for them and **g** them **in**. 7695
10:10 from Egypt and **g** them from Assyria. 7695
14: 2 *I will* **g** all the nations to Jerusalem 665
Mt 12:30 and he who *does* not **g** with me scatters. *5251*
13:30 then **g** the wheat and bring it *5251*
23:37 I have longed to **g** your children **together**, *2190*
24:28 there the vultures *will* **g**. *5251*
24:31 *they will* **g** his elect from the four winds, *2190*
25:26 that I harvest where I have not sown and **g** *5251*
Mk 13:27 And he will send his angels and **g** his elect *2190*
Lk 3:17 to clear his threshing floor and *to* **g** *5251*
11:23 and he who *does* not **g** with me, scatters. *5251*
13:34 I have longed to **g** your children **together**, *2190*
17:37 there the vultures *will* **g**." *2190*
Jn 6:12 "**G** the pieces that are left over. *5251*
Ac 4:26 the rulers **g** together against the Lord and *5251*
2Ti 4: 3 *they will* **g around** them a great number *2197*
Rev 14:18 "Take your sharp sickle and **g** the clusters *5582*
16:14 *to* **g** them for the battle on the great day *5251*
19:17 **g together** for the great supper of God, *5251*
20: 8 Gog and Magog—*to* **g** them for battle. *5251*

GATHERED (136) [GATHER]

Ge 1: 9 the water under the sky **be g** to one place, 7748
1:10 and the **g** waters he called "seas." 5224
25: 8 and *he* **was g** to his people. 665
25:17 and *he* **was g** to his people. 665
29: 3 When all the flocks **were g** there, 665
29: 7 it is not time for the flocks *to* **be g**. 665
29: 8 "until all the flocks **are g** and 665
35:29 and died and **was g** to his people, 665
37: 7 while your sheaves **g around** mine 6015
49:29 "I *am about to* **be g** to my people. 665
49:33 breathed his last and **was g** to his people. 665
Ex 16:17 *some* **g** much, some little. 4377
16:18 he *who* **g much** did not have too much, 8049
16:18 and he *who* **g little** did not have too little. 5070
16:18 Each one **g** as much as he needed. 4377
16:21 Each morning everyone **g** as much 4377
16:22 On the sixth day, *they* **g** twice as much— 4377
32: 1 they **g** around Aaron and said, "Come, 7735
Lev 8: 4 the assembly **g** at the entrance to the Tent 7735
23:39 after you *have* **g** the crops of the land, 665
Nu 11:32 the people went out and **g** quail. 665
11:32 No one **g** less than ten homers. 665
14: 5 of the whole Israelite assembly **g** there. 7736
16:19 When Korah *had* **g** all his followers 7735
16:42 But when the assembly **g** in opposition 7735
20: 2 people **g** in opposition to Moses and Aaron. 7735
20:10 **g** the assembly **together** 7735
20:24 "Aaron *will* **be g** to his people. 665
20:26 for Aaron *will* **be g** to his people; 665
27:13 you too *will* **be g** to your people, 665
31: 2 After that, *you will* **be g** to your people." 665
Dt 16:13 for seven days after you *have* **g** the produce 665
32:50 you will die and **be g** to your people, 665
32:50 on Mount Hor and **was g** to his people. 665
Jos 18: 1 The whole assembly of the Israelites **g** 7735
22:12 the whole assembly of Israel **g** at Shiloh 7735
Jdg 2:10 After that whole generation *had* **been g** 665
4:13 Sisera **g together** his nine hundred iron chariots 2410
9: 6 the citizens of Shechem and Beth Millo **g** 665
9:27 and **g** the grapes and trodden them, 1305
11: 3 where a group of adventurers **g** around him 4377
Ru 2:17 Then she threshed the barley *she had* **g**, 4377
2:18 her mother-in-law saw how much *she had* **g**. 4377
1Sa 8: 4 of Israel **g together** and came to Samuel 7695
17: 1 Now the Philistines **g** their forces for war 665
17:47 All those **g** here will know that it is not 7736
22: 2 or in debt or discontented **g** around him, 7695
28: 1 In those days the Philistines **g** their forces 7695
28: 4 while Saul **g** all the Israelites and set 7695
29: 1 The Philistines **g** all their forces at Aphek, 7695
2Sa 10:17 When David was told of this, *he* **g** all Israel, 665
17:11 **be g** to you, with you yourself leading 665+665
20:14 *who* **g together** and followed him. 7735
21:13 and exposed *were* **g up**. 665
23: 6 *which* **are** not **g** with the hand. 4374
23: 9 when they taunted the Philistines **g** 665
1Ki 8: 5 and the entire assembly of Israel that *had* **g** 3585
11:24 *He* **g** men around him and became 7695
2Ki 4:39 *He* **g** some of its gourds and filled the fold 4377
1Ch 11:13 when the Philistines **g** there for battle. 665
19:17 *he* **g** all Israel and crossed the Jordan; 665
23: 2 *He* also **g together** all the leaders of Israel, 665
2Ch 5: 6 and the entire assembly of Israel that *had* **g** 3585
13: 7 Some worthless scoundrels **g** around him 7695
23: 2 throughout Judah and **g** the Levites and 7695
28:24 Ahaz **g together** the furnishings from 665
29:20 **g** the city officials **together** 665
Ezr 7:28 and **g** leading men from Israel to go up 7695
9: 4 the words of the God of Israel **g** around me 665
10: 1 and children—**g** around him. 7695
10: 9 of Judah and Benjamin *had* **g** *in* Jerusalem. 7695
Ne 8:13 **g** around Ezra the scribe to give attention to 665
9: 1 the Israelites **g together**, 665
Job 5:26 like sheaves **g** in season. 6590
24:24 they are brought low and **g up** 7890
30: 4 In the brush *they* **g** salt herbs, 7786
Ps 35:15 But when I stumbled, *they* **g** in glee; 665
35:15 attackers **g** against me when I was unaware. 665
107: 3 those *he* **g** from the lands, 7695
Pr 27:25 and the grass from the hills **is g in**, 665
30: 4 Who *has* **g up** the wind in the hollow 665
SS 5: 1 *I have* **g** my myrrh with my spice. 768
Isa 10:14 so I **g** all the countries; 665
27:12 O Israelites, *will* **be g up** one by one. 4377
56: 8 to them besides *those already* **g**." 7695
60: 7 All Kedar's flocks *will* **be g** to you, 7695
Jer 6:11 the street and on the young men **g** together; 6051
8: 2 *They will* not **be g up** or buried, 665
25:33 not be mourned or **g up** or buried, 665

Jer 40:15 cause all the Jews who are g around you to 7695
Eze 29: 5 on the open field and not be g or picked up. 665
38: 7 you and all the hordes g about you, 7735
38: 8 whose people were g from many nations to 7695
38:12 against the resettled ruins and the people g 665
38:13 Have you g your hordes to loot, 7735
39:27 from the nations and have g them from 7695
Hos 10:10 nations will be g against them to put them 665
Mic 1: 7 Since she g her gifts from the wages 7695
4:11 But now many nations are g against you. 665
Zec 12: 3 all the nations of the earth are g against her, 665
Mt 13: 2 Such large crowds g around him that he got 5251
16: 9 and how many basketfuls you g? 3284
16:10 and how many basketfuls you g? 3284
22:10 and g all the people they could find, 5251
22:41 While the Pharisees were g together, 5251
25:32 All the nations will be g before him, 5251
27:17 So when the crowd had g, Pilate asked 5251
27:27 the Praetorium and g the whole company 5251
Mk 1:33 The whole town g at the door, 1639+2190
2: 2 So many g that there was no room left, 5251
3:20 Jesus entered a house, and again a crowd g, 5302
4: 1 The crowd that g around him was so large 5251
5:21 a large crowd g around him while he was 5251
6:30 The apostles g around Jesus and reported 5251
7: 1 of the law who had come from Jerusalem g 5251
8: 1 During those days another large crowd g. 1639
Lk 12: 1 when a crowd of many thousands had g, 2190
23:48 When all the people who had g 5219
Jn 6:13 So they g them and filled twelve baskets 5251
8: 2 where all the people g around him, 2262
10:24 The Jews g around him, saying, 3240
Ac 5:16 Crowds g also from the towns 5302
6: 2 g all the disciples together 4673
12:12 many people had g and were praying. 5255
13:44 the next Sabbath almost the whole city g 5251
14:20 But after the disciples had g around him, 3240
14:27 they g the church together and reported all 5251
15:30 where they g the church together 5251
16:13 to speak to the women who had g there. 5302
28: 3 Paul g a pile of brushwood and, 5370
2Co 8:15 "He who g much did not have too much, NIG
8:15 and he who g little did not have too little." NIG
2Th 2: 1 of our Lord Jesus Christ and our being g to 2191
Rev 14:19 g its grapes and threw them into 5582
16:16 Then they g the kings together to the place 5251
19:19 and their armies g together to make war 5251

GATHERING (12) [GATHER]

Nu 11: 8 The people went around g it, 4377
15:32 a man was found g wood on the Sabbath 8006
15:33 Those who found him g wood brought him 8006
1Ki 17:10 a widow was there g sticks. 8006
17:12 I am g a few sticks to take home and make 8006
Ecc 2:26 the sinner he gives the task of g and storing 665
Jer 6: 9 over the branches again, like one g grapes." 1305
Mt 3:12 g his wheat into the barn and burning up 5251
25:24 harvesting where you have not sown and g 5251
Lk 8: 4 While a large crowd was g 5290
15: 1 and "sinners" were all g around to hear him 1581
Ac 10:27 Peter went inside and found a large g 5302

GATHERS (18) [GATHER]

Nu 19:10 The man who g up the ashes of 665
Ru 2:15 "Even if she g among the sheaves, 4377
Ps 33: 7 He g the waters of the sea into jars; 4043
41: 6 he speaks falsely, while his heart g slander; 7695
129: 7 nor the one who g fill his arms. 6682
147: 2 he g the exiles of Israel. 4043
Pr 6: 8 in summer and g its food at harvest. 112
10: 5 He who g crops in summer is a wise son, 112
13:11 but he who g money little by little 7695
Isa 17: 5 a reaper g the standing grain and harvests 665
40:11 He g the lambs in his arms 7695
56: 8 he who g the exiles of Israel: 7695
Mic 4:12 not understand his plan, he who g them 7695
7: 1 like one who g summer fruit at the gleaning 668
Hab 1:15 he g them up in his dragnet; 665
2: 5 he g to himself all the nations 665
Mt 23:37 as a hen g her chicks under her wings, 2190
Lk 13:34 as a hen g her chicks under her wings, NIG

GAUDY (1)

Eze 16:16 of your garments to make g high places, 3229

GAUNT (3) [GAUNTNESS]

Ge 41: 3 seven other cows, ugly and g, 1414+1987
41: 4 ugly and g ate up the seven sleek, fat 1414+1987
Ps 109:24 my body is thin and g. 4946+9043

GAUNTNESS (1) [GAUNT]

Job 16: 8 my g rises up and testifies against me. 3951

GAVE (659) [GIVE]

Ge 2:20 So the man g names to all the livestock, 7924
3: 6 She also g some to her husband, 5989
3:12 she g me some fruit from the tree, 5989
4: 1 she became pregnant and g birth to Cain. 3528
4: 2 Later she g birth to his brother Abel. 3528
4:17 she became pregnant and g birth to Enoch. 3528
4:20 Adah g birth to Jabal; 3528
4:25 she g birth to a son and named him Seth, 3528
9: 3 Just as I g you the green plants, 5989
12:20 Pharaoh g orders about Abram to his men, 7422
14:20 Then Abram g him a tenth of everything. 5989
16: 3 and g her to her husband to be his wife. 5989
16:13 She g this name to the LORD who spoke 7924
16:15 and Abram g the name Ishmael to 7924
18: 7 tender calf and g it to a servant, 5989
20:14 and female slaves and g them to Abraham, 5989
21: 3 Abraham g the name Isaac to 7924
21:14 and a skin of water and g them to Hagar. 5989
21:19 and g the boy a drink. 9197
21:27 and cattle and g them to Abimelech, 5989
24:18 the jar to her hands and g him a drink. 9197
24:53 of clothing and g them to Rebekah; 5989
24:53 he also g costly gifts to her brother and 5989
25: 6 he g gifts to the sons of his concubines 5989
25:26 when Rebekah g birth to them. 3528
25:34 Then Jacob g Esau some bread 5989
26:11 So Abimelech g orders to all the people: 7422
26:18 he g them the same names his father had 7924
27:20 "The LORD your God g me success," 7936
28: 4 the land God g to Abraham." 5989
29:22 the people of the place and g a feast. 6913
29:23 he took his daughter Leah and g her 995
29:24 And Laban g his servant girl Zilpah 5989
29:28 and then Laban g him his daughter Rachel 5989
29:29 Laban g his servant girl Bilhah 5989
29:32 Leah became pregnant and g birth to a son. 3528
29:33 and when she g birth to a son she said, 3528
29:33 he g me this one too." 5989
29:34 and when she g birth to a son she said, 3528
29:35 and when she g birth to a son she said, 3528
30: 4 So she g him her servant Bilhah as a wife. 5989
30: 9 she took her maidservant Zilpah and g her 5989
30:21 Some time later she g birth to a daughter 3528
30:23 She became pregnant and g birth to a son 3528
30:25 After Rachel g birth to Joseph, 3528
31: 8 all the flocks g birth to speckled young; 3528
35: 4 So they g Jacob all the foreign gods 5989
35:12 The land I g to Abraham and Isaac I 5989
38: 3 she became pregnant and g birth to a son, 3528
38: 4 and g birth to a son and named him Onan. 3528
38: 5 She g birth to still another son 3528
38: 5 It was at Kezib that she g birth to him. 3528
38:18 So he g them to her and slept with her, 5989
39: 3 with him and that the LORD g him success 7503
39:23 and g him success in whatever he did. 7503
40:20 and he g a feast for all his officials, 6913
41:45 Pharaoh g Joseph the name Zaphenath-Paneah 7924
41:45 and g him Asenath daughter of Potiphera, 5989
42:25 Joseph g orders to fill their bags with grain, 7422
43:24 g them water to wash their feet 5989
44: 1 Now Joseph g these instructions to 7422
45:21 Joseph g them carts, 5989
45:21 he also g them provisions for their journey. 5989
45:22 To each of them he g new clothing, 5989
45:22 but to Benjamin he g three hundred shekels 5989
47:11 and g them property in the best part of 5989
47:17 and he g them food in exchange 5989
47:22 from the allotment Pharaoh g them. 5989
49:29 g them these instructions: 7422
Ex 1:21 he g them families of their own. 6913
1:22 Pharaoh g this order to all his people: 7422
2: 2 she became pregnant and g birth to a son. 3528
2:21 who g his daughter Zipporah to Moses in marriage. 5989
2:22 Zipporah g birth to a son, 3528
4:11 "Who g man his mouth? 8492
5: 6 That same day Pharaoh g this order to 7422
12:36 they g them what they asked for; 8626
16:32 so they can see the bread I g you to eat in 430
31:18 he g him the two tablets of the Testimony, 5989
32:24 Then they g me the gold, 5989
34:32 g them all the commands the LORD 7422
36: 6 Then Moses g an order 7422
Lev 7:38 which the LORD g Moses on Mount Sinai 7422
27:34 the LORD g Moses on Mount Sinai for 7422
Nu 3:51 Moses g the redemption money to Aaron 5989
7: 6 and oxen and g them to the Levites. 5989
7: 7 He g two carts and four oxen to 5989
7: 8 and he g four carts and eight oxen to 5989
13:16 g Hoshea son of Nun the name 7924
13:27 g Moses this account: 6218
15:22 of these commands the LORD g Moses— 1819
15:23 the LORD g them and continuing through 7422
17: 6 and their leaders g him twelve staffs, 5989
21: 3 and g the Canaanites over 5989
22:18 if Balak g me his palace filled with silver 5989
22:40 and g some to Balaam and 8938
24:13 if Balak g me his palace filled with silver 5989
30:16 the regulations the LORD g Moses 7422
31:21 of the law that the LORD g Moses: 7422
31:41 Moses g the tribute to Eleazar the priest as 5989
31:47 and g them to the Levites, 5989
32:28 Then Moses g orders about them to Eleazar 7422
32:33 Then Moses g to the Gadites, 5989
32:38 They g names to the cities they rebuilt. 7924
32:40 So Moses g Gilead to the Makirites, 5989
36: 5 LORD's command Moses g this order 7422
36:13 the LORD g through Moses to the Israelites 7422
Dt 2:12 as Israel did in the land the LORD g them 5989
2:36 The LORD our God g us all of them. 5989
3: 3 also g into our hands Og king of Bashan 5989
3:12 I g the Reubenites and the Gadites 5989
3:13 I g to the half tribe of Manasseh. 5989
3:15 And I g Gilead to Makir. 5989
3:16 and the Gadites I g the territory extending 5989
4:45 decrees and laws Moses g them 1819
5:22 on two stone tablets and g them to me. 5989
8:16 g you manna to eat 430
9:10 The LORD g me two stone tablets inscribed 5989
9:11 the LORD g me the two stone tablets, 5989
10: 4 And the LORD g them to me. 5989
22:16 g my daughter in marriage 851+4200+5989
26: 9 and g us this land, a land flowing with milk 5989
28:45 the commands and decrees he g you. 7422
29: 8 and g it as an inheritance to the Reubenites, 5989
31: 9 So Moses wrote down this law and g it to 5989
31:23 The LORD g this command to Joshua son 7422
31:25 he g this command to the Levites 7422
32: 8 g the nations their inheritance, 5706
32:18 you forgot the God who g you birth. 2655
33: 4 the law that Moses g us, 7422
Jos 1: 7 the law my servant Moses g you; 7422
1:13 the servant of the LORD g you: 7422
1:14 that Moses g you east of the Jordan, 5989
1:15 the LORD g you east of the Jordan toward 5989
6:20 when the people g a loud shout, 8131+9558
8:33 when he g instructions to bless the people NIH
10:12 the LORD g the Amorites over to Israel, 5989
10:27 At sunset Joshua g the order 7422
10:30 The LORD also g that city and its king 5989
11: 8 the LORD g them into the hand of Israel. 5989
11:23 and he g it as an inheritance to Israel 5989
12: 6 the LORD g their land to the Reubenites, 5989
12: 7 toward Seir (their lands Joshua g as 5989
13:14 But to the tribe of Levi he g no inheritance, 5989
14:13 and g him Hebron as his inheritance. 5989
15:13 Joshua g to Caleb son of Jephunneh 5989
15:17 Caleb g his daughter Acsah to him in marriage. 851+4200+5989
15:19 So Caleb g her the upper and lower springs. 5989
17: 4 So Joshua g them an inheritance along with 5989
18: 7 the servant of the LORD g it to them." 5989
19:49 the Israelites g Joshua son of Nun 5989
19:50 They g him the town he asked for— 5989
21: 3 the Israelites g the Levites 5989
21:11 They g them Kiriath Arba (that is, 5989
21:13 the priest they g Hebron (a city of refuge 5989
21:17 the tribe of Benjamin they g them Gibeon, NIH
21:43 So the LORD g Israel all 5989
21:44 The LORD g them rest on every side, 5663
22: 3 the mission the LORD your God g you. 5184
22: 4 that Moses the servant of the LORD g you 5989
22: 5 the servant of the LORD g you: 7422
22: 7 the other half of the tribe Joshua g land on 5989
22:34 g the altar this name: A Witness Between 7924
23:14 not one of all the good promises the LORD your God g you has failed. 1819
24: 3 and g him many descendants. 8049
24: 3 I g him Isaac, 5989
24: 4 and to Isaac I g Jacob and Esau. 5989
24: 8 but I g them into your hands. 5989
24:11 but I g them into your hands. 5989
24:13 So I g you a land on which you did not toil 5989
Jdg 1: 4 the LORD g the Canaanites and Perizzites 5989
1:13 Caleb g his daughter Acsah to him in marriage. 851+4200+5989
1:15 Caleb g her the upper and lower springs. 5989
3: 6 and g their own daughters to their sons, 5989
3:10 The LORD g Cushan-Rishathaim king 5989
3:12 the LORD g Eglon king of Moab power 2616
3:15 and he g them a deliverer— 7756
4:19 She opened a skin of milk, g him a drink, 9197
5:25 He asked for water, and she g him milk; 5989
6: 1 for seven years he g them into the hands of 5989
6: 9 from before you and g you their land. 5989
8: 3 God g Oreb and Zeeb, 5989
9: 4 They g him seventy shekels of silver from 5989
11:21 g Sihon and all his men into Israel's hands, 5989
11:32 and the LORD g them into his hands. 5989
12: 3 the LORD g me the victory over them. 928+3338+5989
12: 9 g his daughters away in marriage 8938
13:24 The woman g birth to a boy 3528
14: 9 he g them some, and they too ate it. 5989
14:19 of their belongings and g their clothes 5989
15: 2 he said, "that I g her to your friend. 5989
17: 4 of silver and g them to a silversmith, 5989
Ru 1:12 if I had a husband tonight and then g birth 3528
2:15 Boaz g orders to his men, 7422
2:18 also brought out and g her what she had left 5989
3:17 "He g me these six measures of barley, 5989
4: 7 one party took off his sandal and g it to 5989
4:13 and she g birth to a son. 3528
1Sa 1: 5 But to Hannah he g a double portion 5989
1:20 of time Hannah conceived and g birth to 3528
2:20 the place of the one she prayed for and g to 8626
2:21 she conceived and g birth to three sons 3528
2:28 I also g your father's house all 5989
4:19 she went into labor and g birth, 3528
9:23 "Bring the piece of meat I g you, 5989
13:13 the command the LORD your God g you; 7422
15:24 I was afraid of the people and so I g in 928+7754+9048
18: 4 the robe he was wearing and g it to David, 5989
18: 5 g him a high rank in the army. 6584+8492
18:13 and g him command over a thousand men, 8492
18:27 Saul g him his daughter Michal in marriage. 851+4200+5989
20:40 Jonathan g his weapons to the boy and said, 5989
21: 6 So the priest g him the consecrated bread, 5989
22:10 he also g him provisions and the sword 5989
24:22 So David g his oath to Saul. 8678
25: 9 they g Nabal this message 1819

1Sa 27: 6 So on that day Achish g him Ziklag, 5989
30:11 *They* g him water to drink and food 5989
2Sa 3:15 So Ish-Bosheth g **orders** 8938
4:10 That was the reward I g him for his news! 5989
4:12 So David g *an* **order** to his men, 7422
6:19 Then *he* g a loaf of bread, 2745
8: 6 The LORD g David **victory** wherever he went. 3828
8:14 The LORD g David **victory** wherever he went. 3828
12: 8 *I* g your master's house to you, 5989
12: 8 *I* g you the house of Israel and Judah. 5989
12:24 *She* g **birth** *to* a son, 3528
13:25 but g him *his* **blessing.** 1385
14:16 and my son from the inheritance God g us.' NIH
16:23 the **advice** Ahithophel g was like 3619+6783
19:28 g your servant **a place** among those 8883
19:39 and g him *his* **blessing,** 1385
1Ki 1: 7 and *they* g him *their* **support.** 339+6468
2: 1 *he* g **a charge** *to* Solomon his son. 7422
2:25 So King Solomon g **orders** to Benaiah son 8938
2:43 and obey the command *I* g you?" 7422
2:46 Then the king g **the order** *to* Benaiah son 7422
3:15 Then *he* g a feast for all his court. 6913
3:25 He then g **an order:** 606
3:27 Then the king g *his* **ruling:** 6699
4:29 God g Solomon wisdom 5989
5:11 Solomon g Hiram twenty thousand cors 5989
5:12 The LORD g Solomon wisdom, 5989
6:12 I will fulfill through you the promise *I* g 1819
8:34 and bring them back to the land *you* g 5989
8:36 on the land *you* g your people for 5989
8:40 in the land *you* g our fathers. 5989
8:48 toward the land *you* g their fathers, toward 5989
8:56 of all the good promises *he* g 1819
8:58 decrees and regulations *he* g our fathers. 7422
9:11 King Solomon g twenty towns in Galilee 5989
9:16 then g it as a wedding gift to his daughter, 5989
10:10 And *she* g the king 120 talents of gold, 5989
10:10 the queen of Sheba g to King Solomon. 5989
10:13 King Solomon g the queen all she desired 5989
11:18 *who* g Hadad a house and land 5989
11:19 g him a sister of his own wife, Queen Tahpenes, **in marriage.** 851+5989
12: 8 rejected the **advice** the elders g him 3619+6783
13: 3 That same day the man of God g a sign: 5989
13:21 the command the LORD your God g you. 7422
14: 8 from the house of David and g it to you, 5989
14:15 from this good land that *he* g 5989
15: 4 for David's sake the LORD his God g him 5989
17:23 *He* g him to his mother and said, "Look, 5989
19:21 to cook the meat and g it to the people, 5989
2Ki 4:17 about that same time *she* g **birth** *to* a son, 3528
5:23 *He* g them to two of his servants, 5989
11:10 Then he g the commanders the spears 5989
12:11 *they* g the money to the men appointed 5989
12:15 an accounting from those to whom *they* g 5989
15:19 and Menahem g him a thousand talents 5989
16:15 King Ahaz then g *these* **orders** *to* Uriah 7422
17:20 he afflicted them and g them into the hands 5989
17:27 Then the king of Assyria g *this* **order:** 7422
17:34 that the LORD g the descendants of Jacob, 7422
18:15 So Hezekiah g him all the silver 5989
18:16 and g it to the king of Assyria. 5989
21: 8 from the land *I* g their forefathers, 5989
21: 8 that my servant Moses g them." 7422
22: 8 He g it to Shaphan, who read it. 5989
22:12 He g *these* **orders** *to* Hilkiah the priest, 7422
23:21 The king g *this* **order** *to* all the people: 7422
25:28 and g him a seat of honor higher than those 5989
25:30 the king g Jehoiachin a regular allowance 5989
1Ch 2:35 g his daughter **in marriage** 851+4200+5989
2:49 *She* also g **birth** *to* Shaaph the father 3528
4: 9 saying, "*I* g **birth** to him in pain." 3528
4:17 One of Mered's wives g **birth** *to* Miriam, 2225
4:18 (His Judean wife g **birth** *to* Jered the father 3528
6:64 So the Israelites g the Levites these towns 5989
6:70 the tribe of Manasseh the Israelites g Aner NIH
7:14 *She* g **birth** *to* Makir the father of Gilead. 3528
7:16 Makir's wife Maacah g **birth** *to* a son 3528
7:18 His sister Hammoleketh g **birth** *to* Ishhod, 3528
7:23 she became pregnant and g **birth** *to* a son. 3528
11:10 g his kingship **strong support** 2616+6640
14:12 and David g **orders** to burn them in the fire. 606
16: 3 Then *he* g a loaf of bread, 2745
18: 6 The LORD g David **victory** everywhere he went. 3828
18:13 The LORD g David **victory** everywhere he went. 3828
22: 2 So David g **orders** to assemble 606
22:13 that the LORD g Moses for Israel. 7422
25: 5 God g Heman fourteen sons 5989
28:11 Then David g his son Solomon the plans 5989
28:12 He g him the plans of all that NIH
28:13 He g him instructions for the divisions of NIH
28:18 He also g him the plan for the chariot, NIH
28:19 *he* g me **understanding** *in* all the details 8505
29: 6 in charge of the king's work g **willingly.** 5605
29: 7 *They* g toward the work on the temple 5989
29: 8 Any who had precious stones g them to 5989
2Ch 2: 1 Solomon g **orders** to build a temple for 606
6:25 to the land *you* g to them and their fathers. 5989
6:27 on the land *you* g your people for 5989
6:31 in the land *you* g our fathers. 5989
6:38 toward the land *you* g their fathers, toward 5989
7: 3 they worshiped and g **thanks** to the LORD, 3344
7: 6 and which were used when he g **thanks,** 2146
2Ch 9: 9 Then *she* g the king 120 talents of gold, 5989
9: 9 the queen of Sheba g to King Solomon. 5989
9:12 Solomon g the queen of Sheba all she 5989
9:12 he g her more than she had brought to him. NIH
10: 8 rejected the **advice** the elders g him 3619+6783
11:23 *He* g them abundant provisions 5989
14: 6 for the LORD g him **rest.** 5663
15:15 So the LORD g them **rest** on every side. 5663
19: 9 *He* g them *these* **orders:** 7422
20:11 the possession *you* g us **as an inheritance.** 3769
23: 9 Then he g the commanders of units of 5989
24:12 The king and Jehoiada g it to 5989
26: 5 God g him **success.** 7503
28: 9 *he* g them into your hand. 5989
28:14 the soldiers g **up** the prisoners and plunder 6440
28:20 but *he* g him **trouble** instead of help. 7674
29:27 Hezekiah g **the order** to sacrifice 606
31: 5 the Israelites **generously** g the firstfruits 8049
31:11 Hezekiah g **orders** to prepare storerooms in 606
32:24 who answered him and g him 5989
34: 9 and g him the money that had been brought 5989
34:11 also g money to the carpenters and builders 5989
34:15 He g it to Shaphan. 5989
34:20 He g *these* **orders** *to* Hilkiah, 7422
35: 8 the administrators of God's temple, g 5989
Ezr 2:68 the families g **freewill offerings** toward 5605
2:69 to their ability *they* g to the treasury 5989
3: 7 *they* g money to the masons and carpenters, 5989
3: 7 and g food and drink and oil to the people NIH
3:11 all the people g a great **shout** of praise 8131+9558
5:11 This is the answer *they* g us: 10754
5:14 "Then King Cyrus g *them* to them 10314
8:36 *who* then g **assistance** *to* the people and *to* 5951
9:11 *you* g through your servants the prophets 7422
10:19 g their hands **in pledge** to put away 5989
Ne 1: 7 and laws *you* g your servant Moses. 7422
1: 8 the instruction *you* g your servant Moses, 7422
2: 1 I took the wine and g it to the king. 5989
2: 9 of Trans-Euphrates and g them 5989
6: 4 and each time *I* g them the same answer. 8740
7:70 The governor g to the treasury 1,000 5989
7:71 the heads of the families g to the treasury 5989
9:13 *You* g them regulations and laws 5989
9:14 and g them commands, 7422
9:15 In their hunger *you* g them bread 5989
9:20 *You* g your good Spirit to instruct them. 5989
9:20 and *you* g them water for their thirst. 5989
9:22 "*You* g them kingdoms and nations, 5989
9:27 in your great compassion *you* g them deliverers, 5989
9:34 or the **warnings** *you* g them. 6343+6386
9:35 in the spacious and fertile land *you* g them, 5989
9:36 slaves in the land *you* g our forefathers 5989
12:40 The two **choirs that** g **thanks** 9343
13: 9 *I* g **orders** to purify the rooms, 606
Est 1: 3 of his reign *he* g a banquet for all his nobles 6913
1: 5 the king g a banquet, lasting seven days, 6913
1: 9 Queen Vashti also g a banquet for 6913
2:18 And the king g a great banquet, 6913
3:10 and g it to Haman son of Hammedatha, 5989
4: 8 *He* also g him a copy of the text of the edict 5989
5:12 the king to the banquet *she* g. 6913
8: 1 That same day King Xerxes g Queen Esther 5989
Job 1:21 The LORD g and and the LORD has taken 5989
8: 4 *he* g them **over** to the penalty of their sin. 8938
10:12 You g me life and showed me kindness, NIH
22: 7 *You* g no water *to* the weary 9197
32:12 g you *my* **full attention.** 1067
38:36 the heart with wisdom or g understanding 5989
39: 6 *I* g him the wasteland as his home, 8492
42:10 and g him twice as much as he had before. 3578
42:11 and each one g him a piece of silver and 5989
Ps 21: 4 and *you* g it to him— 5989
21: 5 the victories you g, his glory is great; NIH
40: 2 on a rock and g **me a firm** place to stand. 3922
44:11 *You* g us **up** to be devoured like sheep 5989
68: 9 *You* g abundant showers, O God; 5678
69:21 They put gall in my food and g me vinegar 9197
74:14 the heads of Leviathan and g him as food to 5989
78:15 the desert and g them **water** as abundant as 9197
78:23 Yet *he* g *a* **command** *to* the skies above 7422
78:24 *he* g them the grain of heaven. 5989
78:46 He g their crops to the grasshopper, 5989
78:48 *He* g **over** their cattle to the hail, 6037
78:50 not spare them from death but g them **over** 6037
78:62 *He* g his people **over** to the sword; 6037
81:12 So *I* g them **over** to their stubborn hearts 8938
99: 7 and the decrees *he* g them. 5989
105:44 *he* g them the lands of the nations, 5989
106: 7 *they* g no **thought** *to* your miracles; 8505
106:14 g **in** *to their* **craving;** 203+9294
106:15 So *he* g them what they asked for, 5989
135:12 and *he* g their land as an inheritance, 5989
136:21 and g their land as an inheritance, 5989
148: 6 *he* g a decree that will never pass away. 5989
Pr 1:24 when I called and no *one* g **heed** 7992
8:29 when he g the sea its boundary so 8492
23:22 Listen to your father, who g you **life,** 3528
23:25 may *she who* g you **birth** rejoice! 3528
Ecc 12: 7 and the spirit returns to God who g it. 5989
SS 8: 5 there she who was in labor g you **birth.** 3528
Isa 8: 3 and she conceived and g **birth** *to* a son. 3528
22:16 who g you **permission** to cut out a grave 4200
26:18 we writhed in pain, but *we* g **birth** *to* wind. 3528
41:27 *I* g to Jerusalem a messenger 5989
47: 6 *I* g them into your hand, 5989
51: 2 your father, and to Sarah, *who* g you **birth.** 2655
Isa 63: 5 I was appalled that no *one* g **support;** 6164
Jer 2:27 and to stone, 'You g me **birth.'** 3528
3: 8 *I* g faithless Israel her certificate of divorce 5989
3:18 g your forefathers *as an* **inheritance.** 5706
7: 7 in the land *I* g your forefathers for ever 5989
7:14 the place *I* g to you and your fathers. 5989
7:23 but *I* g them this **command:** 7422
12:14 the inheritance *I* g my people Israel, 5706
15:10 Alas, my mother, that *you* g me **birth,** 3528
16:15 to the land *I* g their forefathers. 5989
17: 4 the inheritance *I* g you. 5989
22:26 and the mother who g you **birth** 3528
23:39 with the city *I* g to you and your fathers. 5989
24:10 until they are destroyed from the land *I* g 5989
25: 5 and you can stay in the land the LORD g 5989
27:12 *I* g **the** same **message** to Zedekiah king of Judah. 465+1819+1821+2021+2021+3972
30: 3 to the land *I* g their forefathers to possess,' 5989
32:12 and *I* g this deed to Baruch son of Neriah, 5989
32:13 g Baruch *these* **instructions:** 7422
32:22 *You* g them this land you had sworn 5989
35: 6 son of Recab g us *this* **command:** 7422
35:16 the command their forefather g them, 7422
36:32 and g it to the scribe Baruch son of Neriah, 5989
37:21 King Zedekiah then g **orders** *for* Jeremiah 7422
39:10 at that time *he* g them vineyards and fields. 5989
40: 5 Then the commander g him provisions and 5989
50:12 *she who* g you **birth** will be disgraced. 3528
51:59 This is the message Jeremiah g *to* 7422
52:32 and g him a seat of honor higher than those 5989
52:34 by day the king of Babylon g Jehoiachin 5989
La 2:14 The oracles *they* g you were false 2600
Eze 3: 2 g me the scroll **to eat.** 430
16: 8 g you *my* **solemn oath** 8678
16:17 You also took the fine jewelry *I* g you, 5989
16:19 olive oil and honey *I* g you **to eat—** 430
16:27 *I* g you **over** to the greed of your enemies, 5989
16:36 because *you* g them your children's blood, 5989
20:11 *I* g them my decrees and made known 5989
20:12 Also *I* g them my Sabbaths as a sign 5989
20:25 I also g them **over** *to* statutes that were 5989
23: 4 They were mine and g **birth** *to* sons 3528
23: 7 *She* g herself as a prostitute to all the elite 5989
28:25 which *I* g to my servant Jacob. 5989
31: 6 of the field g **birth** under its branches; 3528
36:28 in the land *I* g your forefathers; 5989
37:25 in the land *I* g to my servant Jacob, 5989
Da 1: 7 The chief official g them new names: 8492
1:16 to drink and g them vegetables instead. 5989
1:17 To these four young men God g knowledge 5989
5: 1 King Belshazzar g a great banquet for 10522
5: 2 *he* g **orders** to bring in the gold 10042
5: 6 and his legs g **way.** 10742
5:18 the Most High God g your father Nebuchadnezzar sovereignty 10314
5:19 Because of the high position *he* g him, 10314
6:16 So the king g **the order,** 10042
6:23 and g **orders** to lift Daniel out of the den. 10042
7:16 and g me the interpretation of these things: 10313
7:23 "*He* g me this **explanation:** 10042
9:10 the laws *he* g us through his servants 5989
10:18 like a man touched me and g **me strength.** 2616
Hos 1: 6 Gomer conceived again and g **birth** *to* 3528
2: 8 the *one who* g her the grain, the new wine 5989
12:10 g them **many** visions and told parables 8049
13:11 So in my anger *I* g you a king, 5989
Am 4: 6 "I g you empty stomachs in every city 5989
Hag 1:13 g this message of the LORD to the people: 606
Zec 3: 6 of the LORD g *this* **charge** to Joshua: 6386
Mal 2: 5 covenant of life and peace, and *I* g them to 5989
4: 4 and laws *I* g him at Horeb for all Israel. 7422
Mt 1:25 with her until *she* g **birth** *to* a son. *5503*
1:25 And *he* g him the name Jesus. *2813*
2:16 and he g **orders** to kill all the boys *690*
8:18 *he* g **orders** to cross to the other side of *3027*
10: 1 to him and g them authority *1443*
14:19 *he* g **thanks** and broke the loaves. *2328*
14:19 Then *he* g them to the disciples, *1443*
14:19 and the disciples g them to the people. *NIG*
15:36 he broke them and g them to the disciples, *1443*
20:14 the same as I g you. *NIG*
21:23 "And who g you this authority?" *1443*
25:15 To one *he* g five talents of money, *1443*
25:35 For I was hungry and *you* g me something *1443*
25:35 g me something **to drink,** *4540*
25:42 I was hungry and *you* g me nothing to eat, *1443*
25:42 g me nothing **to drink,** *4540*
26:26 Jesus took bread, g **thanks** and broke it, *2328*
26:26 and g it to his disciples, saying, *1443*
26:27 g **thanks** and offered it to them, saying, *2373*
27:12 *he* g **no answer.** *646*
27:50 *he* g **up** his spirit. *918*
28:12 *they* g the soldiers a large sum of money, *1443*
Mk 2:26 And *he* also g some to his companions." *1443*
3:12 But *he* g them strict **orders** not *2203*
3:16 Simon (to whom *he* g the name Peter); *2202*
3:17 (to them *he* g the name Boanerges, *2202*
5:13 *He* g them **permission,** *2205*
5:43 *He* g strict **orders** not to let anyone know *1403*
6: 7 and g them authority over evil spirits. *1443*
6:21 On his birthday Herod g a banquet *4472*
6:28 and she g it to her mother. *1443*
6:41 *he* g **thanks** and broke the loaves. *2328*
6:41 Then *he* g them to his disciples to set before *1443*
8: 6 he broke them and g them to his disciples *1443*
8: 7 *he* g **thanks for** them also and told *2328*
9: 9 Jesus g them **orders** not to tell *1403*

Mk 11:28 "And who g you authority to do this?" 1443
12:44 They all g out of their wealth; 965
14:22 Jesus took bread, g thanks and broke it, 2328
14:22 and g it to his disciples, saying, "Take it; 1443
14:23 the cup, g thanks and offered it to them, 2373
14:57 g this false testimony 6018
14:61 But Jesus remained silent and g no answer. 646
15:45 he g the body to Joseph. 1563
Lk 1:57 she g birth to a son. 1164
2: 7 and she g birth to her firstborn, 5503
2:38 she g thanks to God and spoke about 469
4:20 g it back to the attendant and sat down. 625
5:26 Everyone was amazed and g praise to God. 1519
6: 4 And he also g some to his companions." 1443
7:15 and Jesus g him back to his mother. 1443
7:21 and g sight to many who were blind. 5919
8:32 and he g them permission. 2205
9: 1 he g them power and authority 1443
9:16 he g thanks and broke them. 2328
9:16 Then he g them to the disciples to set before 1443
9:42 healed the boy and g him back to his father. 625
10:35 and g them to the innkeeper. 1443
11:27 "Blessed is the mother who g you birth 1002
15:16 but no one g him anything. 1443
15:29 Yet you never g me even a young goat 1443
19:13 of his servants and g them ten minas. 1443
20: 2 "Who g you this authority?" 1443
21: 4 All these people g their gifts out 965+1650
22:17 After taking the cup, he g thanks and said, 2373
22:19 And he took bread, g thanks and broke it, 2373
22:19 gave thanks and broke it, and g it to them, 1443
23: 9 but Jesus g him no answer. 646
24:30 he took bread, g thanks, 2328
24:42 They g him a piece of broiled fish, 2113
Jn 1:12 he g the right to become children of God— 1443
1:32 Then John g this testimony: 3455
3:16 the world that he g his one and only Son, 1443
4:12 who g us the well and drank 1443
5:19 Jesus g them this answer: 646
5:35 John was a lamp that burned and g light, 5743
6:11 Jesus then took the loaves, g thanks, 2373
6:31 'He g them bread from heaven to eat.' " 1443
7:22 because Moses g you circumcision 1443
13:26 he g it to Judas Iscariot, son of Simon. 1443
17: 4 on earth by completing the work you g me 1443
17: 6 to those whom you g me out of the world. 1443
17: 6 you g them to me and they have obeyed 1443
17: 8 For I g them the words you gave me 1443
17: 8 For I gave them the words you g me 1443
17:11 power of your name—the name you g me— 1443
17:12 and kept them safe by that name you g me. 1443
17:22 I have given them the glory that you g me, 1443
18: 9 "I have not lost one of those you g me." 1443
19: 9 he asked Jesus, but Jesus g him no answer. 1443
19:30 he bowed his head and g up his spirit. 4140
21:13 Jesus came, took the bread and g it to them, 1443
Ac 1: 3 to these men and g many convincing proofs NIG
1: 4 he g them this command: 4133
2:45 they g to anyone as he had need. 1374
3: 5 So the man g them his attention, AIT
5:28 "We g you strict orders not to teach 4132+4133
7: 5 He g him no inheritance here, 1443
7: 8 Then he g Abraham the covenant 1443
7:10 He g Joseph wisdom and enabled him 1443
7:42 But God turned away and g them over to 4140
8:10 g him their attention and exclaimed, AIT
8:38 And he g orders to stop the chariot. 3027
10: 2 g generously to those in need 1797+4472
11:17 if God g them the same gift as he gave us, 1443
11:17 if God gave them the same gift as he g us, NIG
13:19 and g their land to his people as their inheritance. 2883
13:20 God g them judges until the time of Samuel 1443
13:21 and he g them Saul son of Kish, 1443
19:16 g them such a beating that they ran out 2710
21:14 we g up and said, "The Lord's will be done 2483
27:15 so we g way to it and were driven along. 2113
27:20 we finally g up all hope of being saved. 4311
27:35 and g thanks to God in front of them all. 2373
Ro 1:21 glorified him as God nor g thanks to him, 2373
1:24 Therefore God g them over in 4140
1:26 of this, God g them over to shameful lusts. 4140
1:28 he g them over to a depraved mind, 4140
4:20 in his faith and g glory to God, 1443
8:32 but g him up for us all— 4140
11: 8 "God g them a spirit of stupor, 1443
15:15 because of the grace God g me 1443
1Co 3: 2 I g you milk, not solid food, 4540
2Co 5:18 and g us the ministry of reconciliation: 1443
8: 3 that they g as much as they were able, NIG
8: 5 but they g themselves first to the Lord and 1443
10: 8 the authority the Lord g us for building you 1443
13: 2 already g you a warning 4625
13:10 the Lord g me for building you up, 1443
Gal 1: 4 who g himself for our sins to rescue us 1443
2: 9 g me and Barnabas the right hand 1443
2:20 who loved me and g himself for me. 4140
3:18 but God in his grace g it to Abraham 5919
Eph 4: 8 he led captives in his train and g gifts 1443
4:11 It was he who g some to be apostles, 1443
5: 2 as Christ loved us and g himself up for us 4140
5:25 as Christ loved the church and g himself up 4140
Php 2: 9 the highest place and g him the name that is 5919
3:17 according to the pattern we g you. 2400
Col 1:25 the commission God g me to present to you 1443
1Th 1: 9 what kind of reception you g us. 2400+4639
4: 2 For you know what instructions we g you 1443
2Th 2:16 by his grace g us eternal encouragement 1443
3:10 we were with you, we g you this rule: 4133
1Ti 2: 6 who g himself as a ransom for all men— 1443
2Ti 4:17 Lord stood at my side and g me strength, 1904
Tit 2:14 who g himself for us to redeem us 1443
Heb 7: 2 and Abraham g him a tenth of everything. 3532
7: 4 Even the patriarch Abraham g him a tenth 1443
11:22 and g instructions about his bones. 1948
Jas 2:25 for what she did when she g lodging to 5685
5:18 Again he prayed, and the heavens g rain, 1443
2Pe 3:15 with the wisdom that God g him. 1443
1Jn 3:24 We know it by the Spirit he g us. 1443
3Jn 1: 3 It g me great joy to have some of the AIT
Jude 1: 7 g themselves up to sexual immorality 1745
Rev 1: 1 which God g him 1443
10: 3 and he g a loud shout like the roar of 3189+5889
11:13 and the survivors were terrified and g glory 1443
12: 5 She g birth to a son, a male child, 5503
13: 2 The dragon g the beast his power 1443
15: 7 Then one of the four living creatures g to 1443
16:19 and g her the cup filled with the wine of 1443
18: 7 glory and luxury she g herself. 1519
20:13 The sea g up the dead that were in it, 1443
20:13 and Hades g up the dead that were in them, 1443

GAVE (Anglicized) See also DELIVERED

GAY (KJV) See FINE

GAZA (23)

Ge 10:19 from Sidon toward Gerar as far as G, 6445
Dt 2:23 Avvites who lived in villages as far as G, 6445
Jos 10:41 to G and from the whole region of Goshen 6445
11:22 in G, Gath and Ashdod did any survive. 6445
13: 3 of the five Philistine rulers in G, 6484
15:47 and G, its settlements and villages, 6445
Jdg 1:18 The men of Judah also took G, 6445
6: 4 the crops all the way to G and did not spare 6445
16: 1 One day Samson went to G, 6445
16: 2 people of G were told, "Samson is here!" 6484
16:21 and took him down to G. 6445
1Sa 6:17 one each for Ashdod, G, Ashkelon, 6445
1Ki 4:24 from Tiphsah to G, 6445
2Ki 18: 8 as far as G and its territory. 6445
Jer 25:20 G, Ekron, and the people left at Ashdod); 6445
47: 1 the Philistines before Pharaoh attacked G: 6445
47: 5 G will shave her head in mourning; 6445
Am 1: 6 "For three sins of G, even for four, 6445
1: 7 of G that will consume her fortresses. 6445
Zep 2: 4 G will be abandoned and Ashkelon left 6445
Zec 9: 5 G will writhe in agony, and Ekron too, 6445
9: 5 G will lose her king and Ashkelon will 6445
Ac 8:26 that goes down from Jerusalem to G." 1124

GAZATHITES (KJV) See GAZA

GAZE (11) [GAZING]

2Ki 8:11 He stared at him with a fixed g 906+2256+6641+7156+8492
Job 35: 5 g at the clouds so high above you. 8800
36:25 men g on it from afar. 5564
Ps 27: 4 to g upon the beauty of the LORD 2600
68:16 Why g in envy, O rugged mountains, 8353
Pr 4:25 fix your g directly before you. 6757
23:31 Do not g at wine when it is red, 8011
SS 6:13 come back, that we may g on you! 2600
6:13 Why would you g on the Shulammite as 2600
Hab 2:15 so that he can g on their naked bodies. 5564
Rev 11: 9 language and nation will g on their bodies 1063

GAZELLE (12) [GAZELLES]

Dt 12:15 as if it were g or deer, 7383
12:22 Eat them as you would g or deer. 7383
14: 5 the g, the roe deer, the wild goat, the ibex, 7383
15:22 as if it were g or deer. 7383
2Sa 2:18 Asahel was as fleet-footed as a wild g. 7383
Pr 6: 5 like a g from the hand of the hunter, 7383
SS 2: 9 My lover is like a g or a young stag. 7383
2:17 a g or like a young stag on the rugged hills. 7383
4: 5 like twin fawns of a g that browse among 7386
7: 3 like two fawns, twins of a g. 7386
8:14 and be like a g or like a young stag on 7383
Isa 13:14 Like a hunted g, 7383

GAZELLES (4) [GAZELLE]

1Ki 4:23 g, roebucks and choice fowl. 7383
1Ch 12: 8 they were as swift as g in the mountains. 7373
SS 2: 7 I charge you by the g and by the does of 7374
3: 5 I charge you by the g and by the does of 7374

GAZER (KJV) See GEZER

GAZEZ (2)

1Ch 2:46 the mother of Haran, Moza and G. 1606
2:46 Haran was the father of G. 1606

GAZING (3) [GAZE]

SS 2: 9 g through the windows, 8708
Da 10: 8 So I was left alone, g at this great vision; 8011
2Co 3:13 over his face to keep the Israelites from g 867

GAZINGSTOCK (KJV) See PUBLICLY EXPOSED, SPECTACLE

GAZITES (KJV) See GAZA

GAZZAM (2)

Ezr 2:48 Rezin, Nekoda, G, 1613
Ne 7:51 G, Uzza, Paseah, 1613

GE HARASHIM (1)

1Ch 4:14 father of Joab, the father of G. 1629

GEBA (15)

Jos 18:24 Kephar Ammoni, Ophni and G— 1494
21:17 of Benjamin they gave them Gibeon, G, 1494
1Sa 13: 3 the Philistine outpost at G, 1494
14: 5 the other to the south toward G. 1494
1Ki 15:22 With them King Asa built up G 1494
2Ki 23: 8 from G to Beersheba, 1494
1Ch 6:60 G, Alemeth and Anathoth, 1494
8: 6 of those living in G and were deported 1494
2Ch 16: 6 With them he built up G and Mizpah. 1494
Ezr 2:26 of Ramah and G 621 1494
Ne 7:30 of Ramah and G 621 1494
11:31 the Benjamites from G lived in Micmash, 1494
12:29 and from the area of G and Azmaveth, 1494
Isa 10:29 and say, "We will camp overnight at G." 1494
Zec 14:10 The whole land, from G to Rimmon, 1494

GEBAL (3) [GEBALITES]

1Ki 5:18 the men of G cut and prepared the timber 1490
Ps 83: 7 G, Ammon and Amalek, Philistia, with 1489
Eze 27: 9 Veteran craftsmen of G were on board 1488

GEBALITES (1) [GEBAL]

Jos 13: 5 the area of the G; 1490

GEBER (1) [BEN-GEBER, EZION GEBER]

1Ki 4:19 G son of Uri—in Gilead 1506

GEBIM (1)

Isa 10:31 the people of G take cover. 1481

GECKO (1)

Lev 11:30 the g, the monitor lizard, the wall lizard, 652

GEDALIAH (31) [GEDALIAH'S]

2Ki 25:22 of Babylon appointed G son of Ahikam, 1546
25:23 that the king of Babylon had appointed G 1546
25:23 they came to G at Mizpah— 1546
25:24 G took an oath to reassure them 1546
25:25 came with ten men and assassinated G and 1546
1Ch 25: 3 As for Jeduthun, from his sons: G, Zeri, 1546
25: 9 the second to G, he and his relatives and 1546
Ezr 10:18 Maaseiah, Eliezer, Jarib and G. 1545
Jer 38: 1 G son of Pashhur, 1546
39:14 They turned him over to G son of Ahikam, 1546
40: 5 "Go back to G son of Ahikam, 1545
40: 6 to G son of Ahikam at Mizpah and stayed 1545
40: 7 of Babylon had appointed G son of Ahikam 1546
40: 8 they came to G at Mizpah— 1545
40: 9 G son of Ahikam, the son of Shaphan, 1546
40:11 and had appointed G son of Ahikam, 1546
40:12 to G at Mizpah, 1546
40:13 in the open country came to G at Mizpah 1546
40:14 But G son of Ahikam did not believe them. 1546
40:15 of Kareah said privately to G in Mizpah, 1546
40:16 But G son of Ahikam said to Johanan son 1546
41: 1 came with ten men to G son of Ahikam 1546
41: 2 with him got up and struck down G son 1546
41: 3 also killed all the Jews who were with G 1546
41: 6 he said, "Come to G son of Ahikam." 1546
41: 9 of the men he had killed along with G was 1546
41:10 of the imperial guard had appointed G son 1546
41:16 after he had assassinated G son of Ahikam: 1545
41:18 of Nethaniah had killed G son of Ahikam, 1546
43: 6 of the imperial guard had left with G son 1546
Zep 1: 1 the son of G, the son of Amariah, 1545

GEDALIAH'S (1) [GEDALIAH]

Jer 41: 4 The day after G assassination, 1546

GEDEON (KJV) See GIDEON

GEDER (1) [GEDERITE]

Jos 12:13 the king of Debir one the king of G one 1554

GEDERAH (2) [GEDERATHITE]

Jos 15:36 Adithaim and G (or Gederothaim)— 1557
1Ch 4:23 the potters who lived at Netaim and G; 1557

GEDERATHITE (1) [GEDERAH]

1Ch 12: 4 Jahaziel, Johanan, Jozabad the G, 1561

GEDERITE (1) [GEDER]

1Ch 27:28 Baal-Hanan the G was in charge of 1559

GEDEROTH (2)

Jos 15:41 **G**, Beth Dagon, Naamah and Makkedah— 1558
2Ch 28:18 Aijalon and **G**, as well as Soco, 1558

GEDEROTHAIM (1)

Jos 15:36 Adithaim and Gederah (or **G**)— 1562

GEDI See EN GEDI

GEDOR (7)

Jos 15:58 Halhul, Beth Zur, **G**, 1530
1Ch 4: 4 Penuel was the father of **G**, 1529
4:18 to Jered the father of **G**, 1529
4:39 the outskirts of **G** to the east of the valley 1530
8:31 **G**, Ahio, Zeker 1529
9:37 **G**, Ahio, Zechariah and Mikloth. 1529
12: 7 and Zebadiah the sons of Jeroham from **G**. 1530

GEHAZI (20)

2Ki 4:12 He said to his servant **G**, 1634
4:14 **G** said, "Well, she has no son 1634
4:25 the man of God said to his servant **G**, 1634
4:27 **G** came over to push her away, 1634
4:29 Elisha said to **G**, 1634
4:31 **G** went on ahead and laid the staff on 1634
4:31 **G** went back to meet Elisha and told him, NIH
4:36 Elisha summoned **G** and said, 1634
5:20 **G**, the servant of Elisha the man 1634
5:21 So **G** hurried after Naaman. 1634
5:22 "Everything is all right," **G** answered. NIH
5:23 He urged **G** to accept them, 2257[S]
5:23 and they carried them ahead of **G**. 2257[S]
5:24 When **G** came to the hill, NIH
5:25 "Where have you been, **G**?" 1634
5:25 "Your servant didn't go anywhere," **G** answered. NIH
5:27 Then **G** went from Elisha's presence NIH
8: 4 The king was talking to **G**, 1634
8: 5 Just as **G** was telling the king 2085[S]
8: 5 **G** said, "This is the woman, 1634

GELILOTH (3)

Jos 18:17 went to En Shemesh, continued to **G**, 1667
22:10 to **G** *near* the Jordan in the land of Canaan, 1667
22:11 the altar on the border of Canaan at **G** *near* 1667

GEM (1) [GEMS]

Ex 28:11 the two stones the way a **g** cutter engraves 74

GEMALLI (1)

Nu 13:12 from the tribe of Dan, Ammiel son of **G**; 1696

GEMARIAH (5)

Jer 29: 3 to Elasah son of Shaphan and to **G** son 1701
36:10 From the room of **G** son of Shaphan 1702
36:11 When Micaiah son of **G**, 1702
36:12 Elnathan son of Acbor, **G** son of Shaphan, 1702
36:25 and **G** urged the king not to burn the scroll, 1702

GEMS (4) [GEM]

Ex 25: 7 and onyx stones and *other* **g** to be mounted 74
35: 9 and onyx stones and other **g** to be mounted 74
35:27 and other **g** to be mounted on the ephod 74
La 4: 1 The sacred **g** are scattered at the head 74

GENDER (KJV) See MATE, PRODUCE

GENEALOGICAL (11) [GENEALOGY]

1Ch 4:33 And they **kept a g record.** 3509
5: 1 not **be listed in the g record** 3509
5: 7 listed according to their **g records:** 9352
5:17 **were entered in the g records** 3509
7: 7 Their **g record listed** 22,034 fighting men. 3509
7: 9 Their **g record** listed the heads of families 9352
26:31 according to the **g records** of their families. 9352
2Ch 31:16 whose **names** *were* **in the g records**— 3509
31:17 **enrolled** by their families **in the g records** 3509
31:18 whole community **listed in** *these* **g records.** 3509
Ne 7: 5 the **g** record of those who had been the first 3510

GENEALOGIES (5) [GENEALOGY]

1Ch 9: 1 All Israel **was listed in the g** 3509
2Ch 12:15 and of Iddo the seer *that* **deal with g?** 3509
31:19 **were recorded in the g** *of* the Levites. 3509
1Ti 1: 4 devote themselves *to* myths and endless **g**. *1157*
Tit 3: 9 avoid foolish controversies and **g** and *1157*

GENEALOGY (10) [GENEALOGICAL, GENEALOGIES]

1Ch 7: 2 in their **g** numbered 22,600. 9352
7: 4 According to their family **g**, 9352
7: 5 *as* **listed in** their **g**, were 87,000 in all. 3509
7:40 *as* **listed in** their **g**, was 26,000. 3509
8:28 chiefs as **listed** in their **g**, 9352
9: 9 as **listed** in their **g**, numbered 956. 9352
9:22 They **were registered** by **g** in their villages. 3509
9:34 chiefs as **listed** in their **g**, 9352
Mt 1: 1 *of* the **g** of Jesus Christ the son of David, *1161*
Heb 7: 3 Without father or mother, **without g**, *37*

GENERAL (KJV) See COMMANDER

GENERALS (2)

Rev 6:15 the kings of the earth, the princes, the **g**, *5941*
19:18 so that you may eat the flesh of kings, **g**, *5941*

GENERATION (84) [GENERATIONS]

Ge 7: 1 I have found you righteous in this **g**. 1887
15:16 In the fourth **g** your descendants will come back here, 1887
50:23 and saw the **third g** of Ephraim's children. 9000
Ex 1: 6 and all his brothers and all that **g** died, 1887
3:15 by which I am to be remembered *from* **g** 1887
3:15 to be remembered from generation to **g**. 1887
17:16 be at war against the Amalekites from **g** 1887
17:16 the Amalekites from generation to **g**." 1887
20: 5 of the fathers to the third and **fourth g** 8067
34: 7 of the fathers to the third and **fourth g**." 8067
Nu 14:18 of the fathers to the third and **fourth g**.' 8067
32:13 the whole **g** *of* those who had done evil 1887
Dt 1:35 "Not a man of this evil **g** shall see 1887
2:14 that entire **g** *of* fighting men had perished 1887
5: 9 of the fathers to the third and **fourth g** 8067
23: 2 even down to the tenth **g**. 1887
23: 3 even down to the tenth **g**. 1887
23: 8 The third **g** of children born 1887
32: 5 but a warped and crooked **g**. 1887
32:20 for they are a perverse **g**, 1887
Jdg 2:10 After that whole **g** had been gathered 1887
2:10 another **g** grew up, who knew neither 1887
2Ki 10:30 on the throne of Israel to the **fourth g**." 8055
15:12 on the throne of Israel to the **fourth g**." 8055
Est 9:28 and observed in every **g** by every family, 1887
Job 42:16 and their children to the fourth **g**. 1887
Ps 24: 6 Such is the **g** *of* those who seek him, 1887
48:13 that you may tell of them to the next **g**. 1887
49:19 he will join the **g** *of* his fathers, 1887
71:18 till I declare your power to the next **g**, 1887
78: 4 the next **g** the praiseworthy deeds of 1887
78: 6 so the next **g** would know them, 1887
78: 8 a stubborn and rebellious **g**, 1887
79:13 **g** to generation we will recount your praise. 1887
79:13 generation to **g** we will recount your praise. 1887
95:10 For forty years I was angry with that **g**; 1887
102:18 Let this be written for a future **g**, 1887
109:13 their names blotted out from the next **g**. 1887
112: 2 the **g** *of* the upright will be blessed. 1887
145: 4 *One* **g** will commend your works 1887
Isa 34:10 From **g** to generation it will lie desolate; 1887
34:10 From generation to **g** it will lie desolate; 1887
34:17 and dwell there from **g** to generation. 1887
34:17 and dwell there from generation to **g**. 1887
Jer 2:31 of this **g**, consider the word of the LORD: 1887
7:29 and abandoned this **g** *that* is 1887
50:39 or lived in from **g** to generation. 1887
50:39 or lived in from generation to **g**. 1887
La 5:19 your throne endures from **g** to generation. 1887
5:19 your throne endures from generation to **g**. 1887
Da 4: 3 his dominion endures from **g** to generation. 10183
4: 3 his dominion endures from generation to **g**. 10183
4:34 his kingdom endures from **g** to generation. 10183
4:34 his kingdom endures from generation to **g**. 10183
Joel 1: 3 and their children to the next **g**. 1887
Mt 11:16 "To what can I compare this **g**? *1155*
12:39 "A wicked and adulterous **g** asks for *1155*
12:41 at the judgment with this **g** and condemn it; *1155*
12:42 at the judgment with this **g** and condemn it; *1155*
12:45 That is how it will be *with* this wicked **g**." *1155*
16: 4 A wicked and adulterous **g** looks for *1155*
17:17 "O unbelieving and perverse **g**," *1155*
23:36 all this will come upon this **g**. *1155*
24:34 this **g** will certainly not pass away *1155*
Mk 8:12 "Why does this **g** ask for a miraculous sign? *1155*
8:38 in this adulterous and sinful **g**, *1155*
9:19 "O unbelieving **g**," Jesus replied, *1155*
13:30 this **g** will certainly not pass away *1155*
Lk 1:50 who fear him, from **g** to generation. *1155*
1:50 who fear him, from generation to **g**. *1155*
7:31 then, can I compare the people *of* this **g**? *1155*
9:41 "O unbelieving and perverse **g**," *1155*
11:29 Jesus said, "This is a wicked **g**. *1155*
11:30 so also will the Son of Man be *to* this **g**. *1155*
11:31 with the men *of* this **g** and condemn them; *1155*
11:32 at the judgment with this **g** and condemn it; *1155*
11:50 Therefore this **g** will be held responsible *1155*
11:51 this **g** will be held responsible for it all. *1155*
17:25 and be rejected by this **g**. *1155*
21:32 this **g** will certainly not pass away *1155*
Ac 2:40 "Save yourselves from this corrupt **g**." *1155*
13:36 *in* his own **g**, he fell asleep; *1155*
Php 2:15 without fault in a crooked and depraved **g**, *1155*
Heb 3:10 That is why I was angry *with* that **g**, *1155*

GENERATIONS (80) [GENERATION]

Ge 9:12 a covenant for all **g** to come: 1887
17: 7 after you for the **g to come**. 1887
17: 9 after you for the **g to come**. 1887
17:12 For the **g to come** every male 1887
Ex 12:14 for the **g to come** you shall celebrate it as 1887
12:17 as a lasting ordinance for the **g to come**. 1887
12:42 to honor the LORD for the **g to come**. 1887
16:32 of manna and keep it for the **g to come**, 1887
16:33 the LORD to be kept for the **g to come**." 1887
20: 6 to a thousand [**g**] of those who love me NIH
27:21 among the Israelites for the **g to come**. 1887
29:42 "For the **g to come** this burnt offering is to 1887
30: 8 before the LORD for the **g to come**. 1887
30:10 the atoning sin offering for the **g to come**. 1887
30:21 and his descendants for the **g to come**." 1887
30:31 for the **g to come**. 1887
31:13 between me and you for the **g to come**, 1887
31:16 for the **g to come** as a lasting covenant. 1887
40:15 that will continue for all **g to come**." 1887
Lev 3:17 a lasting ordinance for the **g to come**, 1887
6:18 to the LORD by fire for the **g to come**. 1887
7:36 as their regular share for the **g to come**. 1887
10: 9 a lasting ordinance for the **g to come**. 1887
17: 7 for them and for the **g to come**.' 1887
21:17 'For the **g to come** none 1887
22: 3 "Say to them: 'For the **g to come**, 1887
23:14 to be a lasting ordinance for the **g to come**, 1887
23:21 to be a lasting ordinance for the **g to come**, 1887
23:31 to be a lasting ordinance for the **g to come**, 1887
23:41 to be a lasting ordinance for the **g to come**; 1887
24: 3 to be a lasting ordinance for the **g to come**. 1887
Nu 10: 8 for you and the **g to come**. 1887
15:14 For the **g to come**, 1887
15:15 this is a lasting ordinance for the **g to come**. 1887
15:21 the **g to come** you are to give this offering 1887
15:23 and continuing through the **g to come**— 1887
15:38 the **g to come** you are to make tassels on 1887
18:23 a lasting ordinance for the **g to come**. 1887
35:29 for you throughout the **g to come**, 1887
Dt 5:10 to a thousand [**g**] of those who love me NIH
7: 9 to a thousand **g** of those who love him 1887
29:22 Your children who follow you in later **g** 1887
32: 7 consider the **g long past.** 1887+1887+2256+9102
Jos 22:27 be a witness between us and you and the **g** 1887
1Ch 16:15 the word he commanded, for a thousand **g**, 1887
Job 8: 8 "Ask the former **g** and find out 1887
Ps 22:30 future **g** will be told about the Lord. 1887
33:11 the purposes of his heart through **all g**. 1887+1887+2256
45:17 I will perpetuate your memory through **all g**; 1887+1887+2256
49:11 their dwellings for **endless g**, 1887+1887+2256
61: 6 his years for **many g**. 1887+1887+2256
72: 5 as long as the moon, **through all g**. 1887+1887
85: 5 Will you prolong your anger through **all g**? 1887+1887+2256
89: 1 my mouth I will make your faithfulness known through **all g**. 1887+1887+2256
89: 4 and make your throne firm through **all g**.' " 1887+1887+2256
90: 1 you have been our dwelling place throughout **all g**. 1887+1887+2256
100: 5 his faithfulness continues through **all g**. 1887+1887+2256
102:12 your renown endures through **all g**. 1887+1887+2256
102:24 your years go on through **all g**. 1887+1887
105: 8 the word he commanded, for a thousand **g**, 1887
106:31 as righteousness for endless **g to come**. 1887+1887+2256
119:90 Your faithfulness continues through **all g**; 1887+1887+2256
135:13 your renown, O LORD, through **all g**. 1887+1887+2256
145:13 and your dominion endures through **all g**. 1887+1887+2256
146:10 your God, O Zion, for **all g**. 1887+1887+2256
Pr 27:24 a crown is not secure for **all g**. 1887+1887+2256
Ecc 1: 4 **G** come and generations go, 1887
1: 4 Generations come and **g** go, 1887
Isa 13:20 be inhabited or lived in through **all g**; 1887+1887+2256
41: 4 calling forth the **g** from the beginning? 1887
51: 8 my salvation through **all g**." 1887+1887
51: 9 awake, as in days gone by, as in **g** of old. 1887
60:15 the everlasting pride and the joy of **all g**. 1887+1887+2256
61: 4 that have been devastated for **g**. 1887+1887+2256
Joel 3:20 and Jerusalem through **all g**. 1887+1887+2256
Mt 1:17 Thus there were fourteen **g** in all *1155*
Lk 1:48 From now on all **g** will call me blessed, *1155*
Eph 3: 5 not made known to men *in* other **g** as it has *1155*
3:21 and in Christ Jesus throughout all **g**, *1155*
Col 1:26 that has been kept hidden for ages and **g**, *1155*

GENEROSITY (3) [GENEROUS]

2Co 8: 2 their extreme poverty welled up in rich **g**. *605*
9:11 and through us **your g** will result in thanksgiving to God. *4015*[S]
9:13 and *for* your **g** in sharing with them and *605*

GENEROUS (9) [GENEROSITY, GENEROUSLY]

Ps 37:26 *They are* always **g** and lend freely; 2858
112: 5 to him *who is* **g** and lends freely, 2858
Pr 11:25 A **g** man will prosper; 1388
22: 9 A **g man** will himself be blessed, 3202+6524
Mt 20:15 Or are you envious because I am **g**?' *19*
2Co 9: 5 for the **g gift** you had promised. *2330*
9: 5 Then it will be ready as a **g gift**, *2330*
9:11 so that you can be **g** on every occasion, *605*
1Ti 6:18 and to be **g** and willing to share. *2331*

GENEROUSLY (10) [GENEROUS]

Dt 15:10 **Give g** to him and do so without 5989+5989
1Ch 29:14 that we should be able to **give** as **g** as this? 5605
2Ch 31: 5 the Israelites **g gave** the firstfruits 8049
Ps 37:21 but the righteous give **g;** 2858
Ac 10: 2 he gave **g** to those in need and prayed *4498*
Ro 12: 8 to the needs of others, let him give **g;** *605+1877*
2Co 9: 6 sows **g** will also reap generously. *2093+2330*
9: 6 sows generously will also reap **g.** *2093+2330*
Tit 3: 6 he poured out on us **g** through Jesus Christ *4455*
Jas 1: 5 who gives **g** to all without finding fault, *607*

GENITALS (1)

Eze 23:20 whose **g** were like those of donkeys 1414

GENNESARET (3)

Mt 14:34 they landed at **G.** *1166*
Mk 6:53 they landed at **G** and anchored there. *1166*
Lk 5: 1 as Jesus was standing by the Lake *of* **G,** *1166*

GENTILE (11) [GENTILES]

Ezr 6:21 the unclean practices of their **G** neighbors 1580
Ne 5: 9 to avoid the reproach of our **G** enemies? 1580
Ac 10:28 for a Jew to associate with a **G** or visit him. *260*
15:23 To the **G** believers in Antioch, *1620+1666*
21:25 As for the **G** believers, *1620*
Ro 1:16 first for the Jew, then *for* the **G.** *1818*
2: 9 first for the Jew, then for the **G;** *1818*
2:10 first for the Jew, then for the **G.** *1818*
10:12 there is no difference between Jew and **G**— *1818*
Gal 2:14 yet you live **like a G** and not like a Jew. *1619*
2:15 Jews by birth and not **'G** sinners' *1620*

GENTILES (93) [GENTILE]

Ne 5: 8 we have bought back our Jewish brothers who were sold to the **G.** 1580
Isa 9: 1 in the future he will honor Galilee of the **G,** 1580
42: 6 for the people and a light for the **G,** 1580
49: 6 I will also make you a light for the **G,** 1580
49:22 "See, I will beckon to the **G,** 1580
Mt 4:15 along the Jordan, Galilee *of* the **G**— *1620*
10: 5 "Do not go among the **G** or enter any town *1620*
10:18 as witnesses to them and *to* the **G.** *1620*
20:19 over *to* the **G** to be mocked and flogged *1620*
20:25 "You know that the rulers of the **G** lord it *1620*
Mk 10:33 to death and will hand him over *to* the **G,** *1620*
10:42 as rulers *of* the **G** lord it over them, *1620*
Lk 2:32 a light for revelation *to* the **G** and for glory *1620*
18:32 He will be handed over *to* the **G.** *1620*
21:24 be trampled on by the **G** until the times of *1620*
21:24 until the times *of* the **G** are fulfilled. *1620*
22:25 "The kings *of* the **G** lord it over them; *1620*
Ac 4:27 and Pontius Pilate met together with the **G** *1620*
9:15 the **G** and their kings and before the people *1620*
10:45 Spirit had been poured out even on the **G.** *1620*
11: 1 the **G** also had received the word of God. *1620*
11:18 even the **G** repentance unto life." *1620*
13:16 of Israel and you **G** who worship God, *NIG*
13:26 and *you* **God-fearing G,** *2536+3836+5828*
13:46 we now turn to the **G.** *1620*
13:47 " 'I have made you a light *for* the **G,** *1620*
13:48 When the **G** heard this, *1620*
14: 1 a great number *of* Jews and **G** believed. *1818*
14: 2 up the **G** and poisoned their minds against *1620*
14: 5 There was a plot afoot *among* the **G** *1620*
14:27 opened the door of faith *to* the **G.** *1620*
15: 3 they told how the **G** had been converted. *1620*
15: 5 **"The G** must be circumcised and required *899S*
15: 7 the **G** might hear from my lips the message *1620*
15:12 and wonders God had done among the **G** *1620*
15:14 by taking from the **G** a people for himself. *1620*
15:17 and all the **G** who bear my name, *1620*
15:19 for the **G** who are turning to God. *1620*
18: 6 From now on I will go to the **G."** *1620*
21:11 and will hand him over to the **G.'** " *1620*
21:19 in detail what God had done among the **G** *1620*
21:21 among the **G** to turn away from Moses, *1620*
22:21 I will send you far away to the **G.'** " *1620*
26:17 from your own people and from the **G.** *1620*
26:20 and *to* the **G** also, *1620*
26:23 to his own people and *to* the **G."** *1620*
28:28 that God's salvation has been sent *to* the **G,** *1620*
Ro 1: 5 from among all the **G** to the obedience *1620*
1:13 just as I have had among the other **G.** *1620*
2:14 (Indeed, when **G,** who do not have the law, *1620*
2:24 "God's name is blasphemed among the **G** *1620*
3: 9 the charge that Jews and **G** alike are all *1818*
3:29 Is he not the God *of* **G** too? *1620*
3:29 of Gentiles too? Yes, *of* **G** too, *1620*
9:24 only from the Jews but also from the **G?** *1620*
9:30 the **G,** who did not pursue righteousness *1620*
11:11 *to* the **G** to make Israel envious. *1620*
11:12 and their loss means riches *for* the **G,** *1620*
11:13 I am talking to you **G.** *1620*
11:13 Inasmuch as I am the apostle *to* the **G,** *1620*
11:25 until the full number *of* the **G** has come in. *1620*
15: 9 that the **G** may glorify God for his mercy, *1620*
15: 9 "Therefore I will praise you among the **G;** *1620*
15:10 it says, "Rejoice, *O* **G,** with his people." *1620*
15:11 And again, "Praise the Lord, all you **G,** *1620*
15:12 the **G** will hope in him." *1620*
15:16 the **G** with the priestly duty of proclaiming *1620*
15:16 the **G** might become an offering acceptable *1620*
15:18 through me in leading the **G** to obey God *1620*
Ro 15:27 For if the **G** have shared in the Jews' *1620*
16: 4 the churches *of* the **G** are grateful to them. *1620*
1Co 1:23 to Jews and foolishness *to* **G,** *1620*
2Co 11:26 my own countrymen, in danger from **G;** *1620*
Gal 1:16 so that I might preach him among the **G,** *1620*
2: 2 the gospel that I preach among the **G.** *1620*
2: 7 the task of preaching the gospel *to* the **G,** *213*
2: 8 in my ministry as an apostle to the **G.** *1620*
2: 9 They agreed that we should go to the **G,** *1620*
2:12 he used to eat with the **G.** *1620*
2:12 from the **G** because he was afraid *NIG*
2:14 that you force **G** to follow Jewish customs? *1620*
3: 8 the **G** by faith, and announced the gospel *1620*
3:14 blessing given to Abraham might come to the **G** through Christ Jesus, *1620*
Eph 2:11 remember that formerly you who are **G** *1620*
3: 1 of Christ Jesus for the sake of you **G**— *1620*
3: 6 through the gospel the **G** are heirs together *1620*
3: 8 *to* the **G** the unsearchable riches of Christ, *1620*
4:17 that you must no longer live as the **G** do, *1620*
Col 1:27 the **G** the glorious riches of this mystery, *1620*
1Th 2:16 from speaking *to* the **G** so that they may *1620*
1Ti 2: 7 and a teacher of the true faith *to* the **G.** *1620*
2Ti 4:17 and all the **G** might hear it. *1620*
Rev 11: 2 because it has been given *to* the **G.** *1620*

GENTLE (18) [GENTLENESS, GENTLY]

Dt 28:54 Even the most **g** and sensitive man 8205
28:56 most **g** and sensitive woman among you— 8205
28:56 and **g** that she would not venture to touch 8204
2Sa 18: 5 "Be **g** with the young man Absalom 351
1Ki 19:12 And after the fire came a **g** whisper. 1987
Job 41: 3 Will he speak to you with **g** words? 8205
Pr 15: 1 A **g** answer turns away wrath, 8205
25:15 and a **g** tongue can break a bone. 8205
Jer 11:19 like a **g** lamb led to the slaughter; 476
Zec 9: 9 **g** and riding on a donkey, on a colt, 6714
Mt 11:29 for I am **g** and humble in heart, *4558*
21: 5 **g** and riding on a donkey, on a colt, *4558*
Ac 27:13 **g** south wind *began to* **blow,** *5710*
1Co 4:21 or in love and with a **g** spirit? *4559*
Eph 4: 2 Be completely humble and **g;** *4559*
1Th 2: 7 but we were **g** among you, *2473*
1Ti 3: 3 not violent but **g,** not quarrelsome, *2117*
1Pe 3: 4 the unfading beauty *of* a **g** and quiet spirit, *4558*

GENTLENESS (6) [GENTLE]

2Co 10: 1 By the meekness and **g** of Christ, *2117*
Gal 5:23 **g** and self-control. Against such things *4559*
Php 4: 5 Let your **g** be evident to all. *2117*
Col 3:12 kindness, humility, **g** and patience. *4559*
1Ti 6:11 godliness, faith, love, endurance and **g.** *4557*
1Pe 3:15 But do this with **g** and respect, *4559*

GENTLY (8) [GENTLE]

Job 15:11 words spoken **g** to you? 351+4200
29:22 my words **fell g** on their ears. 5752
SS 7: 9 **flowing g** *over* lips and teeth. 1803
Isa 8: 6 the **g** flowing waters of Shiloah 351+4200
40:11 *he* **g leads** those that have young. 5633
Gal 6: 1 you who are spiritual should restore him **g.** *1877+4460+4559*
2Ti 2:25 who oppose him he must **g** instruct, *1877+4559*
Heb 5: 2 *to* **deal g** with those who are ignorant *3584*

GENUBATH (2)

1Ki 11:20 of Tahpenes bore him a son named **G,** 1707
11:20 There **G** lived with Pharaoh's own children. 1707

GENUINE (3)

2Co 6: 8 **g,** yet regarded as impostors; *239*
Php 2:20 who takes a **g** interest in your welfare. *1189*
1Pe 1: 7 may be **proved g** and may result in praise, *1510*

GERA (9)

Ge 46:21 Bela, Beker, Ashbel, **G,** Naaman, Ehi, 1733
Jdg 3:15 the son of **G** the Benjamite. 1733
2Sa 16: 5 His name was Shimei son of **G,** 1733
19:16 Shimei son of **G,** 1733
19:18 When Shimei son of **G** crossed the Jordan, 1733
1Ki 2: 8 you have with you Shimei son of **G,** 1733
1Ch 8: 3 The sons of Bela were: Addar, **G,** Abihud, 1733
8: 5 **G,** Shephuphan and Huram. 1733
8: 7 and **G,** who deported them and who was 1733

GERAHS (5)

Ex 30:13 sanctuary shekel, which weighs twenty **g.** 1743
Lev 27:25 sanctuary shekel, twenty **g** to the shekel. 1743
Nu 3:47 sanctuary shekel, which weighs twenty **g.** 1743
18:16 sanctuary shekel, which weighs twenty **g.** 1743
Eze 45:12 The shekel is to consist of twenty **g.** 1743

GERAR (10)

Ge 10:19 of Canaan reached from Sidon toward **G** 1761
20: 1 For a while he stayed in **G,** 1761
20: 2 Then Abimelech king of **G** sent for Sarah 1761
26: 1 to Abimelech king of the Philistines in **G.** 1761
26: 6 So Isaac stayed in **G.** 1761
26:17 in the Valley of **G** and settled there. 1761
26:20 of **G** quarreled with Isaac's herdsmen 1761
26:26 Abimelech had come to him from **G,** 1761
2Ch 14:13 Asa and his army pursued them as far as **G.** 1761
2Ch 14:14 They destroyed all the villages around **G,** 1761

GERASENES (3)

Mk 5: 1 across the lake to the region *of* the **G.** *1170*
Lk 8:26 They sailed to the region *of* the **G,** *1170*
8:37 *of* the **G** asked Jesus to leave them, *1170*

GERIZIM (4)

Dt 11:29 to proclaim on Mount **G** the blessings, 1748
27:12 these tribes shall stand on Mount **G** to bless 1748
Jos 8:33 of the people stood in front of Mount **G** 1748
Jdg 9: 7 the top of Mount **G** and shouted to them, 1748

GERSHOM (7)

Ex 2:22 and Moses named him **G,** saying, 1768
18: 3 One son was named **G,** for Moses said, 1768
Jdg 18:30 and Jonathan son of **G,** the son of Moses, 1768
1Ch 23:15 The sons of Moses: **G** and Eliezer. 1768
23:16 descendants of **G:** Shubael was the first. 1768
26:24 a descendant of **G** son of Moses, 1768
Ezr 8: 2 of the descendants of Phinehas, **G;** 1768

GERSHON (15) [GERSHONITE, GERSHONITES]

Ge 46:11 The sons of Levi: **G,** Kohath and Merari. 1767
Ex 6:16 **G,** Kohath and Merari. 1767
6:17 The sons of **G,** by clans, 1767
Nu 3:17 **G,** Kohath and Merari. 1767
3:21 To **G** belonged the clans of the Libnites 1767
26:57 through **G,** the Gershonite clan; 1767
Jos 21: 6 of **G** were allotted thirteen towns from 1767
1Ch 6: 1 The sons of Levi: **G,** Kohath and Merari. 1767
6:16 The sons of Levi: **G,** Kohath and Merari. 1768
6:17 These are the names of the sons of **G:** 1768
6:20 Of **G:** Libni his son, 1768
6:43 the son of **G,** the son of Levi; 1768
6:62 The descendants of **G,** clan by clan, 1768
15: 7 from the descendants of **G,** Joel the leader 1768
23: 6 **G,** Kohath and Merari. 1767

GERSHONITE (10) [GERSHON]

Nu 3:18 These were the names of the **G** clans: 1201+1767
3:21 these were the **G** clans. 1769
3:23 The **G** clans were to camp on the west, 1769
4:24 the **G** clans as they work and carry burdens: 1769
4:28 of the **G** clans at the Tent of Meeting. 1201+1769
4:41 the total of those in the **G** clans 1201+1767
26:57 through Gershon, the **G** clan; 1769
Jos 21:33 All the towns of the **G** clans were thirteen, 1769
1Ch 26:21 of families belonging to Ladan the **G,** 1769
29: 8 the LORD in the custody of Jehiel the **G.** 1769

GERSHONITES (12) [GERSHON]

Nu 3:24 of the families of the **G** was Eliasaph son 1769
3:25 the **G** were responsible for the care of 1201+1767
4:22 of the **G** by their families and clans. 1201+1767
4:26 The **G** are to do all that needs to be done NIH
4:38 The **G** were counted by their clans 1201+1767
7: 7 gave two carts and four oxen to the **G,** 1201+1767
10:17 the **G** and Merarites, who carried it, 1201+1767
Jos 21:27 The Levite clans of the **G** were given: 1201+1767
1Ch 6:71 The **G** received the following: 1201+1768
23: 7 Belonging to the **G:** Ladan and Shimei. 1769
26:21 who were **G** through Ladan 1201+1769
2Ch 29:12 the **G,** Joah son of Zimmah and Eden son 1769

GERUTH KIMHAM (1) [KIMHAM]

Jer 41:17 at **G** near Bethlehem on their way 1745

GESHAN (1)

1Ch 2:47 The sons of Jahdai: Regem, Jotham, **G,** 1642

GESHEM (4)

Ne 2:19 Tobiah the Ammonite official and **G** 1774
6: 1 **G** the Arab and the rest of our enemies 1774
6: 2 Sanballat and **G** sent me this message: 1774
6: 6 and **G** says it is true— 1776

GESHUR (11) [GESHURITES]

Jos 12: 5 the border of the **people of G** and Maacah, 1771
13:11 of the **people of G** and Maacah, all 1771
13:13 not drive out the **people of G** and Maacah, 1771
2Sa 3: 3 of Maacah daughter of Talmai king of **G;** 1770
13:37 the king of **G.** 1770
13:38 After Absalom fled and went to **G,** 1770
14:23 to **G** and brought Absalom back 1770
14:32 "Why have I come from **G?** 1770
15: 8 While your servant was living at **G** 1770
1Ch 2:23 (But **G** and Aram captured Havvoth Jair, 1770
3: 2 of Maacah daughter of Talmai king of **G;** 1770

GESHURITES (3) [GESHUR]

Dt 3:14 as the border of the **G** and the Maacathites; 1771
Jos 13: 2 all the regions of the Philistines and **G:** 1771
1Sa 27: 8 and his men went up and raided the **G,** 1771

GET (312) [GETS, GETTING, GOT, ILL-GOTTEN]

Ge 18: 5 *Let me* **g** you something to eat, 4374

Ge 18: 6 "**g** three seahs of fine flour and knead it NIH
19: 9 "**G out** *of* our way," they replied. 5602
19:12 **G** them **out** of here, 3655
19:14 He said, "Hurry and **g out** of this place, 3655
19:32 *Let's* **g** our father *to* **drink** wine 9197
19:34 *Let's* **g** him **to drink** wine again tonight, 9197
21:10 "**G rid of** that slave woman and her son, 1763
24: 3 that *you will* not **g** a wife for my son from 4374
24: 4 to my country and my own relatives and **g** 4374
24: 7 so that *you can* **g** a wife for my son 4374
24:37 not **g** a wife for my son from the daughters 4374
24:38 and **g** a wife for my son.' 4374
24:40 so that *you can* **g** a wife for my son 4374
24:48 on the right road to **g** the granddaughter 4374
27: 3 Now then, **g** your weapons— 5951
27:13 Just do what I say; go and **g** them for me." 4374
29:20 So Jacob served seven years to **g** Rachel, 928
34: 4 "**G** me this girl as my wife." 4374
35: 2 "**G rid of** the foreign gods you have 6073
38:20 the Adullamite in order to **g** his pledge **back** 4374
40:14 to Pharaoh and **g** me **out** of this prison. 3655
42:16 of your number *to* **g** your brother; 4374
42:27 of them opened his sack to **g** feed 5989
45:19 and **g** your father and come. 5951
46:28 of him to Joseph to **g directions** to Goshen. 3723
Ex 2: 5 the reeds and sent her slave girl *to* **g** it. 4374
2: 7 and **g** one of the Hebrew women to nurse 7924
5: 4 **G back** to your work!" 2143
5:11 **g** your own straw wherever you can find it, 4374
5:18 Now **g** to work. 2143
7:24 along the Nile *to* **g drinking** water, AIT
8:20 "**G up early** in the morning 8899
9:13 "**G up early** in the morning, 8899
10:26 and until we **g** there we will 995
10:28 Pharaoh said to Moses, "**G** out of my sight! 2143
14:25 *"Let's* **g away** from the Israelites! 5674
16:24 and it did not stink or **g** maggots in it. 2118
23:11 the poor among your people *may* **g food** 430
32:25 that Aaron *had let* them **g out of control** 7277
Nu 11:13 Where *can I* **g** meat for all these people? 5989
16:10 but now *you are* **trying to g** the priesthood 1335
16:45 "**G away** from this assembly so I can put 8250
17: 2 the Israelites and **g** twelve staffs from them, 4374
20:25 **G** Aaron and his son Eleazar and take them 4374
22:23 Balaam beat her to **g** her **back on** the road. 5742
Dt 2:13 "Now **g up** and cross the Zered Valley." 7756
6: 7 when you lie down and when you **g up.** 7756
11:19 when you lie down and when you **g up.** 7756
17:16 make the people return to Egypt to **g more** 8049
22: 4 Help him **g it to its feet.** 7756+7756
24:10 into his house to **g** what he is offering as 6292
24:19 do not go back to **g** it. 4374
30:12 into heaven *to* **g** it and proclaim it to us 4374
30:13 the sea *to* **g** it and proclaim it to us 4374
Jos 1: 2 **g ready** to cross the Jordan River into 7756
1:11 '**G** your supplies **ready.** 3922
18: 7 however, do not **g** a portion among you, 4200
22:26 *'Let us* **g ready** and build an altar— 6913
Jdg 1:24 "Show us **how to g into** the city 4427
7: 9 "**G up,** go down against the camp, 7756
7:15 to the camp of Israel and called out, "**G up!** 7756
7:17 When I **g** to the edge of the camp, 995
9:29 Then *I would* **g rid of** him. 6073
11: 2 *"You are* not *going to* **g** *any* **inheritance** 5706
11: 5 of Gilead went to **g** Jephthah from the land 4374
14: 2 now **g** her for me as my wife." 4374
14: 3 the uncircumcised Philistines to **g** a wife?" 4374
14: 3 Samson said to his father, "**G** her for me. 4374
15: 3 **have a right to g even** 5927
15: 7 I won't stop until *I* **g** *my* **revenge** on you." 5933
16:28 *let me with* one blow **g revenge** on the
Philistines for my two eyes." 5933+5934
16:31 family went down *to* **g** him. 5951
18:10 When you **g there,** 995
19: 9 **Early** tomorrow **morning** *you can* **g up** 8899
19:28 He said to her, "**G up;** let's go." 7756
20:10 to **g** provisions for the army. 4374
21:22 *we did* not **g** wives for them during the war, 4374
Ru 2: 9 go and **g a drink** from the water jars 9272
1Sa 1:14 **G rid of** your wine." 6073
6: 7 "Now then, **g** a new cart ready, 4374
9:26 on the roof, "**G ready,** and I will send you 7756
18: 8 What more can he **g** but the kingdom?" 4200
19:17 "He said to me, '**Let me g away.** 8938
20:29 **let** *me* **g away** to see my brothers.' 4880
23:26 hurrying to **g away** from Saul. 2143
24:19 *does he* **let** him **g away** unharmed?
928+2006+8938
26:11 Now **g** the spear and water jug that are 4374
26:22 of your young men come over and **g** it. 4374
29:10 Now **g up early,** 8899
2Sa 2:14 the young men **g up** and fight hand to hand 7756
4: 6 of the house as if *to* **g** some wheat, 4374
5: 6 *"You will* not **g in** here; 995
5: 6 They thought, "David cannot **g in** here." 995
11: 4 Then David sent messengers *to* **g** her. 4374
11:20 'Why *did you* **g so close** to the city 5602
11:21 Why *did you* **g so close** to the wall?' 5602
12:17 beside him to **g** him **up** from the ground, 7756
12:21 *you* **g up** and eat!" 7756
13:13 Where *could I* **g rid of** my disgrace? 2143
13:15 Amnon said to her, "**G up** and get out!" 7756
13:15 Amnon said to her, "Get up and **g out!"** 2143
13:17 "**G** this woman **out of here** and
2021+2025+2575+8938
14: 7 then *we will* **g rid of** the heir as well.' 9012
15: 2 He *would* **g up early** and stand by the side 8899
2Sa 16: 7 As he cursed, Shimei said, "**G out,** get out, 3655
16: 7 As he cursed, Shimei said, "Get out, **g out,** 3655
20:18 '**G** *your* **answer** at Abel,' and that settled it.
8626+8626
23:15 that someone *would* **g** me **a drink** *of* water 9197
1Ki 12:18 managed to **g** into his chariot and escape 6590
17:11 As she was going to **g** it, he called, 4374
18:23 **G** two bulls for us. 5989
18:40 Don't **let** anyone **g away!"** 4880
19: 5 "**G up** and eat." 7756
19: 7 "**G up** and eat, 7756
19:15 *you* **g there,** anoint Hazael king over Aram. 995
20:33 "Go and **g** him," the king said. 4374
21: 7 **G up** and eat! 7756
21: 7 I'll **g** you the vineyard of Naboth 5989
21:15 "**G up** and take possession of the vineyard 7756
22:34 around and **g** me **out** of the fighting. 3655
2Ki 4:41 Elisha said, "**G** some flour." 4374
5:20 after him and **g** something from him." 4374
6: 2 where each of *us can* **g** a pole; 4374
6:27 where *can I* **g help for** you? 3828
7:12 and then we will take them alive and **g** into 995
9: 2 When *you* **g** there, 995
9: 2 **g** him **away** from his companions 7756
9:17 "**G** a horseman," Joram ordered. 4374
13:15 Elisha said, "**G** a bow and some arrows," 4374
22: 4 the high priest and **have** *him* **g ready** 9462
1Ch 11: 5 *"You will* not **g in** here." 995
11:17 that someone *would* **g** me **a drink** *of* water 9197
2Ch 10:18 managed to **g** into his chariot and escape 6590
18:33 around and **g** me **out** of the fighting. 3655
Ne 2: 6 and when *will you* **g back?"** 8740
2:14 for my mount to **g through;** 6296
5: 2 to eat and stay alive, *we must* **g** grain." 4374
5: 3 our vineyards and our homes *to* **g** grain 4374
6: 7 Now this report *will* **g back to** the king; 9048
6: 9 "Their hands *will g* too **weak** for the work, AIT
Est 6:10 "**G** the robe and the horse and do just 4374
9:16 to protect themselves and **g relief** 5663
Job 7: 4 'How long before *I* **g up?'** 7756
15:31 for he *will* **g** nothing in return. 2118
19: 7 *I* **g** no **response;** 6699
19:22 *Will you* never **g enough** of my flesh? 8425
33:27 but I *did* not **g what I deserved.** 8750
36: 3 *I* **g** my knowledge from afar; 5951
Ps 39: 6 not knowing who *will* **g** it. 665
41: 8 *he will* never **g up** *from* the place 7756
Pr 1: 5 and *let* the discerning **g** guidance— 7864
1:13 *we will* **g** all sorts of valuable things 5162
1:19 it takes away the lives of **those who g** it. 1251
4: 5 **G** wisdom, get understanding; 7864
4: 5 Get wisdom, **g** understanding; 7864
4: 7 Wisdom is supreme; therefore **g** wisdom. 7864
4: 7 it cost all you have, **g** understanding. 7864
6: 9 When *will you* **g up** from your sleep? 7756
16:16 How much better *to* **g** wisdom than gold, 7864
17:16 since he has no desire to **g** wisdom? 7864
22:25 and **g** yourself ensnared. 4374
23: 4 Do not wear yourself out to *g* **rich;** AIT
23:23 **g** wisdom, discipline and understanding. NIH
24:27 and **g** your fields **ready;** 6963
28:20 one eager to **g rich** will not go unpunished. 6947
28:22 A stingy man is eager to **g** rich NIH
Ecc 2:22 a man **g** for all the toil and anxious striving 2093
8:14 righteous men who **g** what 5595
8:14 and wicked men who **g** what 5595
SS 3: 2 *I will* **g up** now and go about the city, 7756
Isa 1:24 "Ah, *I will* **g relief** from my foes 5714
21: 5 **G up,** *you* officers, oil the shields! 7756
30:11 Leave this way, **g off** this path, 5742
35: 9 nor *will* any ferocious beast **g up** *on* it; 6590
56:12 "Come," each one cries, *"let me* **g** wine! 4374
Jer 1:17 "**G** yourself **ready!** 273+5516
8: 4 " 'When men fall down, *do they* not **g up?** 7756
13: 6 "Go now to Perath and **g** the belt I told you 4374
25:27 Drink, **g drunk** and vomit, 8910
28:13 but in its place *you will* **g** a yoke of iron. 6913
35: 3 So *I went to* **g** Jaazaniah son of Jeremiah, 4374
36:21 The king sent Jehudi to **g** the scroll, 4374
37:12 **g** *his* **share of** *the* **property** 2745
46:11 "Go up to Gilead and **g** balm, 4374
46:14 'Take your positions and **g ready,** 3922
46:16 They will say, '**G up,** 7756
51: 8 **G** balm for her pain; 4374
51:61 "When you **g** *to* Babylon, 995
La 3:44 a cloud so that no prayer *can* **g through.** 6296
5: 6 to Egypt and Assyria to **g enough** bread. 8425
5: 9 *We* **g** our bread at the risk of our lives 995
Eze 3:22 "**G up** and go out to the plain, 7756
7:14 the trumpet and **g** everything **ready,** 3922
7:26 *They will* **try to g** a vision from 1335
17:15 by sending his envoys to Egypt to **g** horses 5989
18:31 and **g** a new heart and a new spirit. 6913
20: 7 And I said to them, "Each of you, **g rid of** 8959
20: 8 they *did* not **g rid of** the vile images 8959
38: 7 " '**G ready;** be prepared, 3922
Da 7: 5 '**G up** and eat your fill of flesh!' 10624
Hos 12:12 Israel served **to g** a wife, 928
Am 2:15 the fleet-footed soldier *will* not **g away,** 4880
4: 8 for water but *did* not **g enough** to drink, 8425
7:12 Amaziah said to Amos, "**G out,** you seer! 2143
9: 1 Not one *will* **g away,** none will escape. 5674+5674
Jnh 1: 6 **G up** and call on your god! 7756
Mic 2:10 **G up,** go away! 7756
Zep 2:10 This is what they will **g** in return 4200
Mt 2:13 "**G up,**" he said, "take the child *1586*
2:20 "**G up,** take the child and his mother and go *1586*
Mt 5:26 *you will* not **g out** until you have paid *2002*
5:46 what reward *will you* **g?** *2400*
9: 5 or to say, '**G up** and walk'? *1586*
9: 6 Then he said to the paralytic, "**G up,** *1586*
13:54 "Where did this man **g** this wisdom *NIG*
13:56 then did this man **g** all these things?" *NIG*
14:22 Immediately Jesus made the disciples **g** *1832*
15:33 "Where could we **g** enough bread *NIG*
16:23 and said to Peter, "**G** behind me, Satan! *5632*
17: 7 "**G up,**" he said. *1586*
19:16 what good thing must I do to **g** eternal life?" *2400*
22:12 'how *did you* **g in** here *1656*
24:18 in the field go back *to* **g** his cloak. *149*
24:32 As soon as its twigs **g** tender *1181*
Mk 2: 4 not **g** him to Jesus because of the crowd, *4712*
2: 9 or to say, '**G up,** take your mat and walk'? *1586*
2:11 **g up,** take your mat and go home." *1586*
5:41 "Little girl, I say to you, **g up!").** *1586*
6: 2 "Where did this man **g** these things?" *NIG*
6:31 to a quiet place and **g** some **rest."** *399*
6:45 Immediately Jesus made his disciples **g** *1832*
8: 4 this remote place can anyone **g** enough bread *NIG*
8:33 "**G** behind me, Satan!" *5632*
13:16 in the field go back *to* **g** his cloak. *149*
13:28 As soon as its twigs **g** tender *1181*
15:24 they cast lots to see what each *would* **g.** *149*
16:18 and *they will* **g** well." *2400*
Lk 5:23 or to say, '**G up** and walk'? *1586*
5:24 **g up,** take your mat and go home." *1586*
6: 8 "**G up** and stand in front of everyone." *1586*
6:35 without **expecting to g** anything **back.** *594*
7:14 He said, "Young man, I say to you, **g up!"** *1586*
8:19 but they were not able *to* **g near** him *5344*
8:54 by the hand and said, "My child, **g up!"** *1586*
9:52 into a Samaritan village to **g** things **ready** *2286*
11: 7 I can't **g up** and give you anything.' *482*
11: 8 though he will not **g up** and give him *482*
11: 8 because of the man's boldness he will **g up** *1586*
12:20 Then who *will* **g** what you have prepared *1639*
12:45 and *to* eat and drink and **g drunk.** *3499*
12:47 and *does* not **g ready** or does *2286*
12:59 *you will* not **g out** until you have paid *2002*
14:24 of those men who were invited *will* **g a taste** *1174*
17: 8 **g** *yourself* **ready** and wait on me *4322*
17:31 should go down *to* **g** them. *149*
18: 8 I tell you, *he will* see that they **g** justice, *4472*
18:12 a week and give a tenth of all *I* **g.'** *3227*
21:21 *let* those in the city **g out,** *1774*
22: 2 for some way *to* **g rid of** Jesus, *359*
22:46 "**G up** and pray so that you will not fall *482*
Jn 2:16 "**G** these **out** of here! *149*
4:11 Where *can you* **g** this living water? *2400*
4:15 give me this water so that *I* won't *g* **thirsty** *1498*
5: 6 he asked him, "Do you want *to* **g** well?" *1181*
5: 7 While I *am trying to* **g in,** *2262*
5: 8 Then Jesus said to him, "**G up!** *1586*
6:25 "Rabbi, when *did you* **g** here?" *1181*
7:15 "How *did* this man **g** such **learning** *1207+3857*
11:12 "Lord, if he sleeps, *he will* **g better."** *5392*
19:24 "Let's decide by lot who will **g** it." *NIG*
20:15 and I *will* **g** him." *149*
Ac 3: 5 expecting *to* **g** something from them. *3284*
9: 6 "Now **g up** and go into the city, *482*
9:34 **G up** and take care of your mat." *482*
9:40 he said, "Tabitha, **g up."** *482*
10:13 Then a voice told him, "**G up,** Peter. *482*
10:20 So **g up** and go downstairs. *482*
10:26 But Peter **made** him **g up.** *1586*
11: 7 I heard a voice telling me, '**G up,** Peter. *482*
12: 7 "Quick, **g up!"** *482*
16:37 now *do they want to* **g rid of** us quietly? *1675*
21:34 not **g at the truth** because of the uproar, *855+1182*
22:10 " '**G up,**' the Lord said, *482*
22:16 **G up,** be baptized and wash your sins away, *482*
23:23 "**G ready** a detachment *2286*
23:35 when your accusers **g here."** *4134*
26:16 'Now **g up** and stand on your feet. *482*
27:43 *to* jump overboard first and **g** to land. *1996*
27:44 The rest were to **g** there on planks or *NIG*
1Co 5: 7 **G rid of** the old yeast that you may be *1705*
7:36 *They should* **g married.** *1138*
9:13 in the temple **g** *their* **food** from the temple, *2266*
9:24 Run in such a way as to **g the prize.** *2898*
9:25 They do it to **g** a crown that will not last; *3284*
9:25 we do it to **g** a crown that will last forever. *NIG*
14: 8 who *will* **g ready** for battle? *4186*
2Co 10:14 for *we did* **g** as far as you with the gospel *5777*
Gal 1:18 I went up to Jerusalem *to* **g acquainted
with** Peter *2707*
4:30 "**G rid of** the slave woman and her son, *1675*
Eph 4:31 **G rid of** all bitterness, rage and anger, *149*
5:18 *Do* not **g drunk** on wine, *3499*
1Th 5: 7 and those who **g drunk,** get drunk at night. *3499*
5: 7 and those who get drunk, **g drunk** at night. *3501*
1Ti 5:13 **g into the habit of being** idle *3443*
6: 9 *to* **g rich** fall into temptation and a trap and *4456*
2Ti 3: 9 But *they will* not **g very far** *2093+4498+4621*
4:11 **G** Mark and bring him with you, *377*
4:21 Do your best *to* **g here** before winter. *2262*
Jas 1:21 **g rid of** all moral filth and the evil that is *700*
4: 2 You want something but don't **g** it. *2400*
4: 3 that you may spend what you **g** *NIG*

GETHER (2)

Ge 10:23 Uz, Hul, **G** and Meshech. 1788
1Ch 1:17 Uz, Hul, **G** and Meshech. 1788

GETHSEMANE (2)

Mt 26:36 with his disciples to a place called G, *1149*
Mk 14:32 They went to a place called G, *1149*

GETS (18) [GET]

Ex 21:19 if the other **g up** and walks around outside 7756
21:21 to be punished if the slave **g up** after a day 6641
2Sa 15: 4 **see that** he **g justice."** 7405
Pr 13: 4 The sluggard craves and *g* **nothing,** AIT
19: 8 *He who* **g** wisdom loves his own soul; 7864
21:10 his neighbor **g** no **mercy** from him. 2858
21:11 a wise man is instructed, *he* **g** knowledge. 4374
29:26 it is from the LORD that man **g** justice. NIH
31:15 *She* **g up** while it is still dark; 7756
Isa 44:12 *He g* **hungry** and loses his strength; AIT
Mt 28:14 If this report **g** to the governor, *NIG*
Mk 4:27 Night and day, whether he sleeps or **g up,** *1586*
Lk 13:25 the owner of the house **g up** and closes *1586*
18: 5 **see that** she **g justice,** *1688*
Ac 23:15 We are ready to kill him before he **g here."** *1581*
1Co 9:24 but only one **g** the prize? *3284*
11:21 One remains hungry, another **g drunk.** *3501*
2Ti 2: 4 No one serving as a soldier *g* **involved in** *AIT*

GETTING (13) [GET]

Jdg 3:13 *G* the Ammonites and Amalekites *to* **join** AIT
1Sa 1:14 "How long *will you* **keep on g drunk?** 8910
1Ki 16: 9 **g drunk** in the home of Arza, 8893+9272
20:16 with him were in their tents **g drunk.** 8893+9272
Jnh 1:11 The sea *was g* **rougher and rougher.** AIT
Mt 14:15 and *it's* already **g** late. *4216*
27:24 Pilate saw that *he* **was g nowhere,** *4029+6067*
Mk 5:18 *As* Jesus *was* **g** into the boat, *1832*
5:26 yet instead of **g better** she grew worse. *6067*
Lk 23:41 for *we are* **g** what our deeds deserve. *655*
Jn 12:19 "See, *this is* **g** us **nowhere.** *4024+4029+6067*
1Co 7:36 and if she is **g along in years** *5644*
3Jn 1: 2 even as your soul is **g along well.** *2338*

GEUEL (1)

Nu 13:15 from the tribe of Gad, G son of Maki. 1451

GEZER (14)

Jos 10:33 of G had come up to help Lachish, 1618
12:12 the king of Eglon one the king of G one 1618
16: 3 of Lower Beth Horon and on to G, 1618
16:10 not dislodge the Canaanites living in G; 1618
21:21 for one accused of murder) and G, 1618
Jdg 1:29 the Canaanites living in G, 1618
2Sa 5:25 the way from Gibeon to G. 1618
1Ki 9:15 and Hazor, Megiddo and G. 1618
9:16 of Egypt had attacked and captured G. 1618
9:17 And Solomon rebuilt G.) 1618
1Ch 6:67 (a city of refuge), and G, 1618
7:28 G and its villages to the west. 1618
14:16 all the way from Gibeon to G. 1618
20: 4 war broke out with the Philistines, at G. 1618

GEZRITES (KJV) See GIRZITES

GHOST (4) [GHOSTLIKE]

Mt 14:26 "It's a **g,"** they said, and cried out in fear. *5753*
Mk 6:49 they thought he was a **g.** *5753*
Lk 24:37 thinking they saw a **g.** *4460*
24:39 a **g** does not have flesh and bones, *4460*

[GIVE UP THE] GHOST (KJV) See BREATHED HIS LAST, DIE, DIED, DYING GASP, GAVE UP HIS SPIRIT, PERISHED

[HOLY] GHOST (KJV) See [HOLY] SPIRIT

GHOSTLIKE (1) [GHOST]

Isa 29: 4 Your voice will come **g** from the earth; 200+3869

GIAH (1)

2Sa 2:24 near G on the way to the wasteland 1632

GIANT (KJV) See RAPHA, REPHAITES, WARRIOR

GIBBAR (1)

Ezr 2:20 of G 95 1507

GIBBETHON (5)

Jos 19:44 Eltekeh, G, Baalath, 1510
21:23 the tribe of Dan they received Eltekeh, G, 1510
1Ki 15:27 and he struck him down at G, 1510
16:15 The army was encamped near G, 1510
16:17 with him withdrew from G and laid siege 1510

GIBEA (1) [GIBEATHITE]

1Ch 2:49 to Sheva the father of Macbenah and G. 1495

GIBEAH (48)

Jos 15:57 Kain, G and Timnah— 1497
18:28 (that is, Jerusalem), G and Kiriath— 1497
24:33 of Aaron died and was buried at G, 1497
Jdg 19:12 We will go on to G." 1497
19:13 to reach G or Ramah and spend the night 1497
19:14 the sun set as they neared G in Benjamin. 1497
19:16 who was living in G (the men of 1497
20: 4 and my concubine came to G in Benjamin 1497
20: 5 the night the men of G came after me 1497
20: 9 But now this is what we'll do to G: 1497
20:10 when the army arrives at G *in* Benjamin, 1497
20:13 Now surrender those wicked men of G so 1497
20:14 From their towns they came together at G 1497
20:15 from those living in G. 1497
20:19 up and pitched camp near G. 1497
20:20 up battle positions against them at G. 1497
20:21 The Benjamites came out of G and cut 1497
20:25 when the Benjamites came out from G 1497
20:29 Then Israel set an ambush around G. 1497
20:30 against G as they had done before. 1497
20:31 to Bethel and the other to G. 1497
20:33 of its place on the west of G. 1497
20:34 a frontal attack on G. 1497
20:36 on the ambush they had set near G. 1497
20:37 in ambush made a sudden dash into G, 1497
20:43 and easily overran them in the vicinity of G 1497
1Sa 10: 5 "After that you will go to G *of* God, 1497
10:10 When they arrived at G, 1497
10:26 Saul also went to his home in G, 1497
11: 4 When the messengers came to G *of* Saul 1497
13: 2 and a thousand were with Jonathan at G 1497
13:15 Then Samuel left Gilgal and went up to G 1497
13:16 with them were staying in G *in* Benjamin, 1497
14: 2 the outskirts of G under a pomegranate tree 1497
14:16 Saul's lookouts at G *in* Benjamin saw 1497
15:34 but Saul went up to his home in G *of* Saul. 1497
22: 6 under the tamarisk tree on the hill at G, 1497
23:19 The Ziphites went up to Saul at G and said, 1497
26: 1 The Ziphites went to Saul at G and said, 1497
2Sa 21: 6 and exposed before the LORD at G 1497
23:29 Ithai son of Ribai from G *in* Benjamin, 1497
1Ch 11:31 Ithai son of Ribai from G *in* Benjamin, 1497
2Ch 13: 2 a daughter of Uriel of G. 1497
Isa 10:29 Ramah trembles; G *of* Saul flees. 1497
Hos 5: 8 "Sound the trumpet in G, 1497
9: 9 as in the days of G. 1497
10: 9 "Since the days of G, you have sinned, 1497
10: 9 Did not war overtake the evildoers in G? 1497

GIBEATH HAARALOTH (1)

Jos 5: 3 the Israelites at G. 1502

GIBEATHITE (1) [GIBEA]

1Ch 12: 3 and Joash the sons of Shemaah the G; 1503

GIBEON (40) [GIBEONITE, GIBEONITES]

Jos 9: 3 of G heard what Joshua had done to Jericho 1500
9:17 G, Kephirah, Beeroth and Kiriath Jearim. 1500
10: 1 of G had made a treaty of peace with Israel 1500
10: 2 because G was an important city, 1500
10: 4 "Come up and help me attack G," he said, 1500
10: 5 up positions against G and attacked it. 1500
10:10 who defeated them in a great victory at G. 1500
10:12 "O sun, stand still over G, O moon, 1500
10:41 and from the whole region of Goshen to G. 1500
11:19 Except for the Hivites living in G, 1500
18:25 G, Ramah, Beeroth, 1500
21:17 the tribe of Benjamin they gave them G, 1500
2Sa 2:12 left Mahanaim and went to G. 1500
2:13 and met them at the pool of G. 1500
2:16 in G was called Helkath Hazzurim. 1500
2:24 on the way to the wasteland of G. 1500
3:30 killed their brother Asahel in the battle at G. 1500
5:25 the Philistines all the way from G to Gezer. 1500
20: 8 While they were at the great rock in G, 1500
1Ki 3: 4 The king went to G to offer sacrifices, 1500
3: 5 At G the LORD appeared to Solomon 1500
9: 2 as he had appeared to him at G. 1500
1Ch 6:60 the tribe of Benjamin they were given G, 1500
8:29 Jeiel the father of G lived in Gibeon. 1500
8:29 Jeiel the father of Gibeon lived in G. 1500
9:35 Jeiel the father of G lived in Gibeon. 1500
9:35 Jeiel the father of Gibeon lived in G. 1500
14:16 all the way from G to Gezer. 1500
16:39 of the LORD at the high place in G 1500
21:29 at that time on the high place at G. 1500
2Ch 1: 3 to the high place at G, 1500
1: 5 in G in front of the tabernacle of NIH
1:13 to Jerusalem from the high place at G, 1500
Ne 3: 7 repairs were made by men from G 1500
3: 7 Melatiah **of** G and Jadon of Meronoth— 1498
7:25 of G 95 1500
Isa 28:21 he will rouse himself as in the Valley of G 1500
Jer 28: 1 who was from G, said to me in the house 1500
41:12 up with him near the great pool in G. 1500
41:16 and court officials he had brought from G. 1500

GIBEONITE (1) [GIBEON]

1Ch 12: 4 and Ishmaiah the G, a mighty man among 1498

GIBEONITES (10) [GIBEON]

Jos 9:16 after they made the treaty with **the** G, 2157^S
9:22 Then Joshua summoned **the** G and said, 2157^S
9:27 That day he made **the** G woodcutters 4392^S
10: 6 The G then sent word to Joshua in 408+1500
2Sa 21: 1 it is because he put the G to death." 1498
21: 2 The king summoned the G and spoke 1498
21: 2 (Now the G were not a part of Israel 1498
21: 3 David asked the G, 1498
21: 4 The G answered him, 1498
21: 9 He handed them over to the G, 1498

GIBLITES (KJV) See GEBALITES

GIDDALTI (2)

1Ch 25: 4 Hanani, Eliathah, G and Romamti-Ezer; 1547
25:29 the twenty-second to G, 1547

GIDDEL (4)

Ezr 2:47 G, Gahar, Reaiah, 1543
2:56 Jaala, Darkon, G, 1543
Ne 7:49 Hanan, G, Gahar, 1543
7:58 Jaala, Darkon, G, 1543

GIDEON (47) [GIDEON'S, JERUB-BAAL]

Jdg 6:11 where his son G was threshing wheat in 1549
6:12 the angel of the LORD appeared to G, 2257^S
6:13 G replied, "if the LORD is with us, 1549
6:15 G asked, "how can I save Israel? NIH
6:17 G replied, "If now I have found favor NIH
6:19 G went in, prepared a young goat, 1549
6:20 And G did so. NIH
6:22 G realized that it was the angel of the LORD, 1549
6:24 So G built an altar to the LORD there 1549
6:27 So G took ten of his servants and did as 1549
6:29 they were told, **"**G son of Joash did it." 1549
6:32 So that day they called G "Jerub-Baal," 2257^S
6:34 the Spirit of the LORD came upon G, 1549
6:36 G said to God, "If you will save Israel 1549
6:38 G rose early the next day; NIH
6:39 G said to God, "Do not be angry with me. 1549
7: 1 G) and all his men camped at the spring 1549
7: 2 The LORD said to G, 1549
7: 4 But the LORD said to G, 1549
7: 5 So G took the men down to the water. 1549
7: 7 The LORD said to G, 1549
7: 8 So G sent the rest of the Israelites NIH
7: 9 During that night the LORD said to G, 2257^S
7:13 G arrived just as a man was telling 1549
7:14 be nothing other than the sword of G son 1549
7:15 When G heard the dream 1549
7:18 'For the LORD and for G.'" 1549
7:19 G and the hundred men with him reached 1549
7:20 "A sword for the LORD and for G!" 1549
7:24 G sent messengers throughout 1549
7:25 the heads of Oreb and Zeeb to G, 1549
8: 1 Now the Ephraimites asked G, 2257^S
8: 4 G and his three hundred men, 1549
8: 7 Then G replied, "Just for that, 1549
8:11 G went up by the route of the nomads east 1549
8:13 G son of Joash then returned from 1549
8:15 G came and said to the men of Succoth, NIH
8:19 G replied, "Those were my brothers, NIH
8:21 So G stepped forward and killed them, 1549
8:22 The Israelites said to G, "Rule over us— 1549
8:23 But G told them, "I will not rule over you, 1549
8:27 G made the gold into an ephod, 1549
8:27 and it became a snare to G and his family. 1549
8:32 G son of Joash died at a good old age 1549
8:33 No sooner had G died than 1549
8:35 G) for all the good things he had done 1549
Heb 11:32 I do not have time to tell about G, Barak, *1146*

GIDEON'S (1) [GIDEON]

Jdg 8:28 not raise its head again. During G lifetime, 1549

GIDEONI (5)

Nu 1:11 from Benjamin, Abidan son of G; 1551
2:22 the people of Benjamin is Abidan son of G. 1551
7:60 On the ninth day Abidan son of G, 1551
7:65 This was the offering of Abidan son of G. 1551
10:24 and Abidan son of G was over the division 1551

GIDOM (1)

Jdg 20:45 after the Benjamites as far as G and struck 1550

GIER (KJV) See OSPREY

GIFT (83) [GIFTED, GIFTS]

Ge 30:20 "God has presented me with a precious **g.** 2273
32:13 from what he had with him he selected a **g** 4966
32:18 They are a **g** sent to my lord Esau, 4966
33:10 accept this **g** from me. 4966
34:12 and the **g** I am to bring as great as you like, 5508
43:11 and take them down to the man as a **g—** 4966
Lev 22:18 a **g** for a burnt offering to the LORD, 7933
Nu 18: 6 from among the Israelites as a **g** to you, 5510
18: 7 the service of the priesthood as a **g.** 5510
31:52 that Moses and Eleazar presented as a **g** to 9556
Dt 16:17 Each of you must bring a **g** in proportion to 5510
1Sa 9: 7 We have no **g** to take to the man of God. 9593
25:27 And let this **g,** which you servant has 1388
2Sa 11: 8 and a **g** *from* the king was sent after him. 5368
1Ki 9:16 then gave it as a **wedding g** to his daughter, 8933
10:25 everyone who came brought a **g—** 4966
13: 7 and I will give you a **g."** 5522

1Ki 15:19 I am sending you a **g** *of* silver and gold. 8816
2Ki 5:15 Please accept now a **g** from your servant." 1388
8: 8 "Take a **g** with you and go to meet the man 4966
8: 9 a **g** forty camel-loads of all the finest wares 4966
16: 8 and sent it as a **g** to the king of Assyria. 8816
20:12 of Babylon sent Hezekiah letters and a **g**, 4966
2Ch 9:24 everyone who came brought a **g**— 4966
Ps 45:12 The Daughter of Tyre will come with a **g**, 4966
Pr 18:16 A **g** opens the way for the giver 5508
21:14 A **g** given in secret soothes anger, 5508
Ecc 3:13 in all his toil—this is the **g** *of* God. 5522
5:19 be happy in his work—this is a **g** *of* God. 5522
Isa 39: 1 of Babylon sent Hezekiah letters and a **g**, 4966
Eze 45:13 " 'This is the **special g** you are to offer: 9556
45:16 of the land will participate in this **special g** 9556
46:16 If the prince makes a **g** from his inheritance 5510
46:17 he makes a **g** from his inheritance to one 5510
48: 8 **portion** you are to present **as a special g**. 9556
48:12 a **special g** to them from the sacred portion 9557
48:20 **As a special g** *you will* **set aside** 8123
Mt 5:23 if you are offering your **g** at the altar *1565*
5:24 leave your **g** there in front of the altar. *1565*
5:24 then come and offer your **g**. *1565*
8: 4 and offer the **g** Moses commanded, *1565*
15: 5 from me is a **g** devoted to God,' *NIG*
23:18 but if anyone swears by the **g** on it, *1565*
23:19 **g**, or the altar that makes the gift sacred? *1565*
23:19 gift, or the altar that makes the **g** sacred? *1565*
Mk 7:11 Corban' (that is, a **g devoted to God**), *1565*
Jn 4:10 the **g** of God and who it is that asks you for *1561*
Ac 1: 4 but wait for the **g** my Father promised, *NIG*
2:38 you will receive the **g** of the Holy Spirit. *1561*
8:20 because you thought you could buy the **g** *1561*
10:45 with Peter were astonished that the **g** of *1561*
11:17 if God gave them the same **g** as he gave us, *1561*
11:30 sending their **g** to the elders by Barnabas *NIG*
Ro 1:11 so that I may impart to you some spiritual **g** *5922*
4: 4 his wages are not credited to him as a **g**, *5921*
5:15 But the **g** is not like the trespass. *5922*
5:15 how much more did God's grace and the **g** *1561*
5:16 the **g** of God is not like the result of *1564*
5:16 but the **g** followed many trespasses *5922*
5:17 of grace and *of* the **g** of righteousness reign *1561*
6:23 but the **g** of God is eternal life *5922*
12: 6 If a man's **g** is prophesying, *NIG*
1Co 1: 7 Therefore you do not lack any **spiritual g** *5922*
7: 7 But each man has his own **g** from God; *5922*
7: 7 one has this **g**, another has that. *NIG*
13: 2 If I have the **g of prophecy** *4735*
14: 1 especially the **g** of prophecy. *NIG*
16: 3 and send them with your **g** to Jerusalem. *5921*
2Co 8:12 **g** is acceptable according to what one has, *NIG*
8:20 of the way we administer this liberal **g**. *NIG*
9: 5 for the **generous g** you had promised. *2330*
9: 5 Then it will be ready as a **generous g**, *2330*
9:15 Thanks be to God for his indescribable **g**! *1561*
Eph 2: 8 not from yourselves, it is the **g** of God— *1565*
3: 7 by the **g** of God's grace given me through *1561*
Php 4:17 Not that I am looking for a **g**, *1517*
1Ti 4:14 Do not neglect your **g**, *5922*
2Ti 1: 6 to fan into flame the **g** of God, *5922*
Heb 6: 4 who have tasted the heavenly **g**, *1561*
Jas 1:17 Every good and perfect **g** is from above, *1564*
1Pe 3: 7 as heirs with you *of* the **gracious g** of life, *5921*
4:10 Each one should use whatever **g** he has received *5922*
Rev 22:17 let him take the **free g** of the water of life. *1562*

GIFTED (1) [GIFT]

1Co 14:37 a prophet or spiritually **g**, *NIG*

GIFTS (87) [GIFT]

Ge 24:53 he also gave **costly g** to her brother and 4458
25: 6 he gave **g** to the sons of his concubines 5510
32:20 with these **g** I am sending on ahead; 4966
32:21 So Jacob's **g** went on ahead of him, 4966
43:15 the men took the **g** and double the amount 4966
43:25 They prepared their **g** for Joseph's arrival 4966
43:26 the **g** they had brought into the house, 4966
Ex 28:38 in the **sacred g** the Israelites consecrate, 7731
28:38 whatever their **g** may be. 5510
Lev 23:38 to your **g** and whatever you have vowed 5510
Nu 5:10 Each man's **sacred g** are his own, 7731
7: 3 They brought as their **g** before 7933
8:19 as **g** to Aaron and his sons to do the work at 5989
18: 9 the **g** they bring me as most holy offerings, 7933
18:11 from the **g** of all the wave offerings of 5508
Dt 12: 6 your tithes and **special g**, 3338+9556
12:11 your tithes and **special g**, 3338+9556
12:17 or your freewill offerings or **special g**. 3338+9556
33:15 the **choicest g** *of* the ancient mountains and 8031
33:16 with the best **g** of the earth and its fullness NIH
1Sa 10:27 They despised him and brought him no **g**. 4966
2Ki 12:18 **g** he himself had **dedicated** 7731
2Ch 17: 5 and all Judah brought **g** to Jehoshaphat, 4966
17:11 Some Philistines brought Jehoshaphat **g** 4966
21: 3 Their father had given them many **g** 5510
31:12 tithes and **dedicated g**. 7731
31:14 the LORD and also the **consecrated g**. 7731+7731
32:23 and **valuable g** for Hezekiah king 4458
Ezr 1: 6 and with **valuable g**, 4458
Est 2:18 throughout the provinces and distributed **g** 5368
9:22 of food to one another and **g** to the poor. 5510
Ps 68:18 you received **g** from men, 5510
68:29 at Jerusalem kings will bring you **g**. 8856
Ps 72:10 of Sheba and Seba will present him **g**. 868
76:11 the neighboring lands bring **g** to the One to 8856
112: 9 He has scattered abroad *his* **g** to the poor, 5989
Pr 19: 6 the friend of a man who gives **g**. 5508
22:16 to increase his wealth and *he who* **gives g** to 5989
25:14 who boasts of **g he does not give.** 5522+9214
Isa 1:23 they all love bribes and chase after **g**. 8988
18: 7 At that time **g** will be brought to 8856
18: 7 the **g** will be brought to Mount Zion, NIH
Eze 16:33 but you give **g** to all your lovers, 5621
20:26 I let them become defiled through their **g**— 5510
20:31 When you offer your **g**— 5510
20:39 with your **g** and idols. 5510
20:40 and your choice **g**, 5368
44:30 and of all your **special g** will belong to 9556
Da 2: 6 from me **g** and rewards and great honor. 10448
2:48 in a high position and lavished many **g** 10448
5:17 "You may keep your **g** for yourself 10448
11:38 with precious stones and **costly g**. 2776
Mic 1: 7 all her **temple g** will be burned with fire; 924
1: 7 Since she gathered her **g** from the wages NIH
1:14 Therefore you will give **parting g** 8933
7: 3 the ruler demands **g**, NIH
Mt 2:11 with **g** of gold and of incense and of myrrh. *1565*
7:11 know how to give good **g** to your children, *1517*
7:11 your Father in heaven give good **g** *NIG*
Lk 11:13 know how to give good **g** to your children, *1517*
21: 1 Jesus saw the rich putting their **g** into *1565*
21: 4 All these people gave their **g** out *1565*
21: 5 and *with* **g dedicated to God.** *356*
Ac 10: 4 "Your prayers and **g to the poor** have come *1797*
10:31 and remembered your **g to the poor.** *1797*
24:17 to bring my people **g for the poor** and *1797*
Ro 11:29 for God's **g** and his call are irrevocable. *5922*
12: 6 We have different **g**, according to the grace *5922*
1Co 12: 1 Now about spiritual **g**, brothers, *NIG*
12: 4 There are different kinds *of* **g**, *5922*
12: 9 to another **g** of healing by that one Spirit, *5922*
12:28 also those having **g** of healing, *5922*
12:28 **those with g of administration,** *3236*
12:30 Do all have **g** of healing? *5922*
12:31 But eagerly desire the greater **g**. *5922*
14: 1 way of love and eagerly desire spiritual **g**, *NIG*
14:12 Since you are eager to have spiritual **g**, *NIG*
14:12 try to excel in **g** that build up the church. *NIG*
2Co 9: 9 "He has scattered abroad his **g** to the poor; *1443*
Eph 4: 8 he led captives in his train and gave **g** *1517*
Php 4:18 received from Epaphroditus the **g** you sent. *NIG*
Heb 2: 4 and **g** of the Holy Spirit **distributed** *3536*
5: 1 to offer **g** and sacrifices for sins. *1565*
8: 3 to offer both **g** and sacrifices, *1565*
8: 4 the **g** prescribed by the law. *1565*
9: 9 that the **g** and sacrifices being offered were *1565*
Rev 11:10 and will celebrate by sending each other **g**, *1565*

GIGANTIC (1)

Rev 9: 2 from it like the smoke *from* a **g** furnace. *3489*

GIHON (6)

Ge 2:13 The name of the second river is the **G**; 1633
1Ki 1:33 on my own mule and take him down to **G**. 1633
1:38 and escorted him to **G**. 1633
1:45 the prophet have anointed him king at **G**. 1633
2Ch 32:30 the **G** spring and channeled the water down 1633
33:14 west of the **G** spring in the valley, 1633

GILALAI (1)

Ne 12:36 Shemaiah, Azarel, Milalai, **G**, Maai, 1675

GILBOA (8)

1Sa 28: 4 the Israelites and set up camp at **G**. 1648
31: 1 and many fell slain on Mount **G**. 1648
31: 8 and his three sons fallen on Mount **G**. 1648
2Sa 1: 6 "I happened to be on Mount **G**," 1648
1:21 "O mountains of **G**, 1648
21:12 after they struck Saul down on **G**.) 1648
1Ch 10: 1 and many fell slain on Mount **G**. 1648
10: 8 and his sons fallen on Mount **G**. 1648

GILEAD (97) [GILEAD'S, GILEADITE, GILEADITES, JABESH GILEAD, RAMOTH GILEAD]

Ge 31:21 he headed for the hill country of **G**. 1680
31:23 up with him in the hill country of **G**. 1680
31:25 of **G** when Laban overtook him, 1680
37:25 a caravan of Ishmaelites coming from **G**. 1680
Nu 26:29 Makirite clan (Makir was the father of **G**); 1680
26:29 through **G**, the Gileadite clan. 1680
26:30 These were the descendants of **G**: 1680
27: 1 the son of **G**, the son of Makir, 1680
32: 1 that the lands of Jazer and **G** were suitable 1680
32:26 in the cities of **G**. 1680
32:29 give them the land of **G** as their possession. 1680
32:39 of Makir son of Manasseh went to **G**, 1680
32:40 So Moses gave **G** to the Makirites, 1680
36: 1 The family heads of the clan of **G** son 1201+1680
Dt 2:36 even as far as **G**, 1680
3:10 the plateau, and all **G**, and all Bashan as far 1680
3:12 including half the hill country of **G**, 1680
3:13 The rest of **G** and also all of Bashan, 1680
3:15 And I gave **G** to Makir. 1680
3:16 the territory extending from **G** down to 1680
4:43 Ramoth in **G**, for the Gadites; 1680
Dt 34: 1 from **G** to Dan, 1680
Jos 12: 2 This included half of **G**. 1680
12: 5 and half of **G** to the border of Sihon king 1680
13:11 also included **G**, the territory of the people 1680
13:25 of **G** and half the Ammonite country as far 1680
13:31 half of **G**, and Ashtaroth and Edrei 1680
17: 1 who had received **G** and Bashan because 1680
17: 3 Zelophehad son of Hepher, the son of **G**, 1680
17: 5 of land besides **G** and Bashan east of 1680
17: 6 The land of **G** belonged to the rest of 1680
20: 8 Ramoth in **G** in the tribe of Gad, 1680
21:38 in **G** (a city of refuge for one accused 1680
22: 9 at Shiloh in Canaan to return to **G**, 824+1680
22:13 the priest, to the land of **G**— 1680
22:15 When they went to **G**— 824+1680
22:32 with the Reubenites and Gadites in **G** 824+1680
Jdg 5:17 **G** stayed beyond the Jordan. 1680
7: 3 and leave Mount **G**.' " 1680
10: 3 He was followed by Jair **of G**, 1682
10: 4 They controlled thirty towns in **G**, 824+1680
10: 8 on the east side of the Jordan in **G**, 1680
10:17 to arms and camped in **G**, 1680
10:18 of the people of **G** said to each other, 1680
10:18 be the head of all those living in **G**." 1680
11: 1 His father was **G**; 1680
11: 5 the elders of **G** went to get Jephthah from 1680
11: 8 The elders of **G** said to him, "Nevertheless, 1680
11: 8 you will be our head over all who live in **G**. 1680
11:10 The elders of **G** replied, 1680
11:11 So Jephthah went with the elders of **G**, 1680
11:29 He crossed **G** and Manasseh, 1680
11:29 passed through Mizpah of **G**, 1680
12: 4 Jephthah then called together the men of **G** 1680
12: 5 the men of **G** asked him, 1680
12: 7 and was buried in a town in **G**. 1680
20: 1 of **G** came out as one man and assembled 1680
1Sa 13: 7 the Jordan to the land of Gad and **G**. 1680
2Sa 2: 9 He made him king over **G**, 1680
17:26 and Absalom camped in the land of **G**. 1680
24: 6 to **G** and the region of Tahtim Hodshi, 1680
1Ki 2: 7 the sons of Barzillai of **G** and let them be 1682
4:13 of Jair son of Manasseh in **G** were his, 1680
4:19 in **G** (the country of Sihon king of 824+1680
17: 1 Now Elijah the Tishbite, from Tishbe in **G**, 1680
2Ki 10:33 the Jordan in all the land of **G** (the region 1680
10:33 from Aroer by the Arnon Gorge through **G** 1680
15:25 Taking fifty men **of G** with him, 1201+1682
15:29 He took **G** and Galilee, 1680
1Ch 2:21 Makir the father of **G** (he had married her 1680
2:22 controlled twenty-three towns in **G**. 824+1680
2:23 of Makir the father of **G**. 1680
5: 9 their livestock had increased in **G**. 824+1680
5:10 throughout the entire region east of **G**. 1680
5:14 the son of **G**, the son of Michael, 1680
5:16 The Gadites lived in **G**, 1680
6:80 of Gad they received Ramoth in **G**, 1680
7:14 She gave birth to Makir the father of **G**. 1680
7:17 These were the sons of **G** son of Makir, 1680
26:31 the Hebronites were found at Jazer in **G**. 1680
27:21 over the half-tribe of Manasseh in **G**: 1680
Ps 60: 7 **G** is mine, and Manasseh is mine; 1680
108: 8 **G** is mine, Manasseh is mine; 1680
SS 4: 1 a flock of goats descending from Mount **G**. 1680
6: 5 like a flock of goats descending from **G**. 1680
Jer 8:22 Is there no balm in **G**? 1680
22: 6 "Though you are like **G** to me, 1680
46:11 "Go up to **G** and get balm, 1680
50:19 be satisfied on the hills of Ephraim and **G**. 1680
Eze 47:18 along the Jordan between **G** and the land 1680
Hos 6: 8 **G** is a city of wicked men, 1680
12:11 Is **G** wicked? 1680
Am 1: 3 Because she threshed **G** 1680
1:13 of **G** in order to extend his borders, 1680
Ob 1:19 and Benjamin will possess **G**. 1680
Mic 7:14 in Bashan and **G** as in days long ago. 1680
Zec 10:10 I will bring them to **G** and Lebanon, 824+1680

GILEAD'S (1) [GILEAD]

Jdg 11: 2 **G** wife also bore him sons, 1680

GILEADITE (8) [GILEAD]

Nu 26:29 through Gilead, the **G** clan. 1682
Jdg 11: 1 Jephthah the **G** was a mighty warrior. 1682
11:40 the daughter of Jephthah the **G**. 1682
12: 7 Then Jephthah the **G** died, 1682
2Sa 17:27 and Barzillai the **G** from Rogelim 1682
19:31 the **G** also came down from Rogelim 1682
Ezr 2:61 a daughter of Barzillai the **G** and was called 1682
Ne 7:63 a daughter of Barzillai the **G** and was called 1682

GILEADITES (4) [GILEAD]

Jos 17: 1 Makir was the ancestor of the **G**, 1680
Jdg 12: 4 The **G** struck them down because 408+1680
12: 4 "You **G** are renegades from Ephraim 1680
12: 5 The **G** captured the fords of 1680

GILGAL (39) [BETH GILGAL]

Dt 11:30 in the Arabah in the vicinity of **G**. 1652
Jos 4:19 up from the Jordan and camped at **G** on 1652
4:20 at **G** the twelve stones they had taken out of 1652
5: 9 So the place has been called **G** to this day. 1652
5:10 while camped at **G** on the plains of Jericho, 1652
9: 6 the camp at **G** and said to him and the men 1652
10: 6 then sent word to Joshua in the camp at **G**: 1652

Jos 10: 7 marched up from G with his entire army, 1652
10: 9 After an all-night march from G, 1652
10:15 with all Israel to the camp at G. 1652
10:43 with all Israel to the camp at G. 1652
12:23 the king of Goyim in G one 1652
14: 6 the men of Judah approached Joshua at G, 1652
15: 7 the Valley of Achor and turned north to G, 1652
Jdg 2: 1 The angel of the LORD went up from G 1652
3:19 At the idols near G he himself turned back 1652
1Sa 7:16 on a circuit from Bethel to G to Mizpah, 1652
10: 8 "Go down ahead of me to G. 1652
11:14 to G and there reaffirm the kingship." 1652
11:15 the people went to G and confirmed Saul 1652
13: 4 people were summoned to join Saul at G. 1652
13: 7 Saul remained at G, 1652
13: 8 but Samuel did not come to G, 1652
13:12 down against me at G, 1652
13:15 Then Samuel left G and went up to Gibeah 1652
15:12 and has turned and gone on down to G." 1652
15:21 to the LORD your God at G." 1652
15:33 to death before the LORD at G. 1652
2Sa 19:15 of Judah had come to G to go out and meet 1652
19:40 When the king crossed over to G, 1652
2Ki 2: 1 and Elisha were on their way from G. 1652
4:38 Elisha returned to G and there was a famine 1652
Hos 4:15 "Do not go to G; 1652
9:15 "Because of all their wickedness in G, 1652
12:11 Do they sacrifice bulls in G? 1652
Am 4: 4 go to G and sin yet more. 1652
5: 5 do not go to G, 1652
5: 5 For G will surely go into exile, 1652
Mic 6: 5 from Shittim to G, 1652

GILOH (2)

Jos 15:51 Goshen, Holon and G—eleven towns 1656
2Sa 15:12 David's counselor, to come from G, 1656

GILONITE (2)

2Sa 15:12 he also sent for Ahithophel the G, 1639
23:34 Eliam son of Ahithophel the G, 1639

GIMZO (1)

2Ch 28:18 as well as Soco, Timnah and G, 1693

GIN (KJV) See TRAP

GINATH (2)

1Ki 16:21 half supported Tibni son of G for king, 1640
16:22 of Tibni son of G. 1640

GINNETHON (2) [GINNETHON'S]

Ne 10: 6 Daniel, G, Baruch, 1715
12: 4 Iddo, G, Abijah, 1715

GINNETHON'S (1) [GINNETHON]

Ne 12:16 of Iddo's, Zechariah; of G, Meshullam; 1715

GIRD (1)

Ps 45: 3 G your sword upon your side, 2520

GIRDED (KJV) See ARMED, CLOAK TUCKED INTO BELT, CLOTHED, DRESSED, FASTENED, PUT ON, STRENGTHENED, TIED, WEARING, WRAPPED

GIRGASHITES (7)

Ge 10:16 Jebusites, Amorites, G, 1739
15:21 Amorites, Canaanites, G and Jebusites." 1739
Dt 7: 1 the Hittites, G, Amorites, Canaanites, 1739
Jos 3:10 Perizzites, G, Amorites and Jebusites. 1739
24:11 Perizzites, Canaanites, Hittites, G, 1739
1Ch 1:14 Jebusites, Amorites, G, 1739
Ne 9: 8 Amorites, Perizzites, Jebusites and G. 1739

GIRGASITE (KJV) See GIRGASHITES

GIRL (57) [GIRL'S, GIRLS]

Ge 24:14 May it be that when I say to a g, 5855
24:16 The g was very beautiful, a virgin; 5855
24:28 The g ran and told her mother's household 5855
24:55 "Let the g remain with us ten days or so; 5855
24:57 "Let's call the g and ask her about it." 5855
29:24 And Laban gave his **servant g** Zilpah 9148
29:29 Laban gave his **servant g** Bilhah 9148
34: 3 he loved the g and spoke tenderly to her. 5855
34: 4 "Get me this g as my wife." 3530
34:12 Only give me the g as my wife." 5855
Ex 1:16 but if it is a g, let her live." 1426
1:22 but let every g live." 1426
2: 5 the reeds and sent her **slave g** to get it. 563
2: 8 And the g went and got the baby's mother. 6625
11: 5 to the firstborn son of the **slave g,** 9148
Lev 12: 7 the woman who gives birth to a boy or a g. 5922
19:20 with a woman who is a **slave g** promised 9148
Nu 31:18 every g who has never slept with a man 851+3251
Dt 22:24 the g because she was in a town and did 5855
22:25 a g pledged to be married and rapes her, 5855
22:26 Do nothing to the g; 5855
22:27 for the man found **the g** out in the country, 2023[S]
22:27 and though the betrothed g screamed, 5855
22:29 He must marry the g, NIH
Jdg 5:30 a g or two for each man, 8167
9:18 the son of his **slave g,** 563
1Sa 30:19 young or old, boy or g, 1426
2Sa 17:17 A **servant g** was to go and inform them, 9148
1Ki 1: 3 for a beautiful g and found Abishag, 5855
1: 4 The g was very beautiful; 5855
2Ki 5: 2 and had taken captive a young g 5855
5: 4 to his master and told him what the g 5855
Est 2: 4 the g who pleases the king be queen instead 5855
2: 7 This **g,** who was also known as Esther, 5855
2: 9 The g pleased him and won his favor. 5855
2:15 for Esther (**the g** Mordecai had adopted, 889[S]
Job 31: 1 with my eyes not to look lustfully at a **g.** 1435
Am 2: 7 the same g and so profane my holy name. 5855
Mt 9:24 The g is not dead but asleep." *3166*
9:25 he went in and took the g by the hand, *3166*
14:11 in on a platter and given *to* the g, *3166*
26:69 and a **servant g** came to him. *4087*
26:71 where **another** *g* saw him and said to *AIT*
Mk 5:41 (which means, **"Little g,** I say to you, *3166*
5:42 Immediately the g stood up and walked *3166*
6:22 The king said *to* the g, *3166*
6:25 At once the g hurried in to the king with *NIG*
6:28 He presented it *to* the g, *3166*
14:69 When the **servant** g saw him there, *4087*
Lk 8:42 a g of about twelve, was dying. *NIG*
22:56 A **servant g** saw him seated there in *4087*
Jn 18:16 to the **g on duty** there and brought Peter in. *2601*
18:17 the g at the door asked Peter. *4087*
Ac 12:13 a **servant g** named Rhoda came to answer *4087*
16:16 we were met by a **slave g** who had a spirit *4087*
16:17 **This** *g* followed Paul and the rest of us, *AIT*
16:19 When the owners *of* **the slave g** realized *899*[S]

GIRL'S (11) [GIRL]

Dt 22:15 the g father and mother shall bring proof 5855
22:16 The g father will say to the elders, 5855
22:19 of silver and give them to the g father, 5855
22:20 and no proof of the g virginity can 4200+5855
22:29 he shall pay the g father fifty shekels 5855
Jdg 19: 4 His father-in-law, the g father, 5855
19: 5 but the g father said to his son-in-law, 5855
19: 6 Afterward the g father said, 5855
19: 8 when he rose to go, the g father said, 5855
19: 9 his father-in-law, the g father, said, 5855
Est 2:12 a g turn came to go in to King Xerxes, 5855

GIRLS (24) [GIRL]

Ge 20:17 his wife and his **slave g** 563
Ex 2:18 When *the g* **returned** to Reuel their father, AIT
Jdg 11:38 She and the g went into the hills and wept 8292
21:21 When the g *of* Shiloh come out to join in 1426
21:21 of you seize a wife from the g *of* Shiloh 1426
21:23 While the *g were* **dancing,** AIT
Ru 2: 8 Stay here with my **servant g.** 5855
2: 9 and follow along after **the g.** 2177[S]
2:13 the standing of one of your **servant g."** 9148
2:22 my daughter, to go with his g, 5855
2:23 to the **servant g** *of* Boaz to glean until 5855
3: 2 with whose **servant g** you have been, 5855
1Sa 9:11 they met *some* g coming out to draw water, 5855
2Sa 6:20 in the sight of the **slave g** *of* his servants 563
6:22 But by these **slave g** you spoke of, 563
Est 2: 3 all these beautiful g into the harem 1435+5855
2: 8 many g were brought to the citadel of Susa 5855
Job 41: 5 a bird or put him on a leash for your **g?** 5855
Pr 27:27 and to nourish your **servant g.** 5855
31:15 and portions for her **servant g.** 5855
Joel 3: 3 they sold g for wine that they might drink. 3530
Na 2: 7 Its **slave g** moan like doves and beat 563
Zec 8: 5 be filled with boys and g playing there." 3530
Mk 14:66 the **servant** g of the high priest came by. *4087*

GIRZITES (1)

1Sa 27: 8 the G and the Amalekites. 1747

GISHPA (1)

Ne 11:21 and Ziha and G were in charge of them. 1778

GITTAH-HEPHER (KJV) See GATH HEPHER

GITTAIM (2)

2Sa 4: 3 of Beeroth fled to G and have lived there 1786
Ne 11:33 in Hazor, Ramah and G, 1786

GITTITE (8) [GITTITES]

2Sa 6:10 to the house of Obed-Edom the G. 1785
6:11 of Obed-Edom the G for three months, 1785
15:19 The king said to Ittai the G, 1785
15:22 So Ittai the G marched on with all his men 1785
18: 2 and a third under Ittai the G. 1785
21:19 the Bethlehemite killed Goliath the G, 1785
1Ch 13:13 to the house of Obed-Edom the G. 1785
20: 5 the brother of Goliath the G, 1785

GITTITES (1) [GITTITE]

2Sa 15:18 six hundred G who had accompanied him 1785

GITTITH (3)

Ps 8: T According to **g.** A Psalm of David. 1787
81: T According to **g.** Of Asaph. 1787
84: T According to **g.** Of the sons of Korah. 1787

GIVE (908) [GAVE, GIVEN, GIVER, GIVES, GIVING, LIFE-GIVING]

Ge 1:15 in the expanse of the sky to **g light** on 239
1:17 in the expanse of the sky to **g light** on 239
1:29 *"I* g you every seed-bearing plant on 5989
1:30 I g every green plant for food." NIH
3:16 with pain *you will* **g birth** *to* children. 3528
9: 3 I now g you everything. NIH
12: 7 "To your offspring *I will* g this land." 5989
13:15 All the land that you see *I will* g to you 5989
14:21 **"G** me the people and keep the goods 5989
15: 2 what *can you* g me since I remain childless 5989
15: 7 to g you this land to take possession of it." 5989
15:18 "To your descendants *I* g this land, 5989
17: 8 *I will* g as an everlasting possession 5989
17:16 I will bless her and *will* surely g you a son 5989
23:11 "Listen to me; *I* g you the field, 5989
23:11 and *I* g you the cave that is in it. 5989
23:11 *I* g it to you in the presence of my people. 5989
24: 7 'To your offspring *I will* g this land'— 5989
24:12 **g** me **success** today, 7936
24:17 "Please **g** me a little water from your jar." 1686
24:41 from my oath even if *they* refuse *to* g her 5989
24:45 and I said to her, 'Please **g** me **a drink.'** 9197
25:24 When the time came for her to **g birth,** 3528
26: 3 your descendants *I will* g all these lands 5989
26: 4 in the sky and *will* g them all these lands, 5989
27: 4 that I *may* g you my **blessing** before I die." 1385
27: 7 so that *I may* g you *my* **blessing** in 1385
27:10 so that *he may* g you *his* **blessing** 1385
27:19 so that you *may* g me your **blessing."** 1385
27:25 so that I *may* g you my **blessing."** 1385
27:28 *May* God g you of heaven's dew and 5989
27:31 so that you *may* g me your **blessing."** 1385
28: 4 *May he* g you and your descendants 5989
28:13 *I will* g you and your descendants 5989
28:20 and *will* g me food to eat and clothes 5989
28:22 and of all that *you* g me I will give you 5989
28:22 that you give me *I will* g you **a tenth."** 6923+6923
29:19 *that* I g her to you than to some other man. 5989
29:21 Then Jacob said to Laban, **"G** me my wife. 2035
29:26 **g** the younger daughter **in marriage** 5989
29:27 then *we will* g you the younger one also, 5989
30: 1 So she said to Jacob, **"G** me children, 2035
30:14 Please **g** me some of your son's mandrakes. 5989
30:26 **G** me my wives and children, 5989
30:31 "What *shall I* g you?" 5989
30:31 "Don't **g** me anything," Jacob replied. 5989
34: 8 Please **g** her to him as his wife. 5989
34: 9 **g** us your daughters and take our daughters 5989
34:11 and *I will* g you whatever you ask. 5989
34:12 Only **g** me the girl as my wife." 5989
34:14 we can't g our sister to a man who is 5989
34:15 *We will* g *our* **consent** to you 252
34:16 Then *we will* g you our daughters 5989
34:23 So *let us* g *our* **consent** to them, 252
35:12 to Abraham and Isaac *I* also g to you, 5989
35:12 and *I will* g this land to your descendants 5989
35:16 *to* **g birth** and had great difficulty. 3528
38:16 what *will you* g me to sleep with you?" 5989
38:17 *"Will you* g me something *as* a pledge 5989
38:18 He said, "What pledge *should I* g you?" 5989
38:26 since *I* wouldn't g her to my son Shelah." 5989
38:27 When the time came for her *to* **g birth,** 3528
41:16 God *will* g Pharaoh *the* **answer** he desires." 6699
42:22 Now *we must* **g an accounting** 2011
42:25 and to g them provisions for their journey. 5989
42:34 Then *I will* g your brother **back** to you, 5989
45:18 *I will* g you the best of the land of Egypt 5989
47:15 to Joseph and said, **"G** us food. 2035
47:19 **G** us seed so that we may live and not die, 5989
47:24 **g** a fifth of it to Pharaoh. 5989
48: 4 and *I will* g this land as 5989
48:22 I g the ridge of land I took from 5989
Ex 1:19 and **g birth** before the midwives arrive." 3528
5:10 'I *will* not g you any more straw. 5989
6: 4 with them to g them the land of Canaan, 5989
6: 8 to the land I swore with uplifted hand to g 5989
6: 8 *I will* g it to you as a possession. 5989
9:19 **G an order** now to bring your livestock 8938
12:25 the LORD *will* g you as he promised, 5989
13: 5 land he swore to your forefathers to g you, 5989
13:12 *to* **g over** to the LORD the first offspring 6296
13:21 by night in a pillar of fire to **g** them **light,** 239
17: 2 **"G** us water to drink." 5989
18:19 now to me and *I will* g you *some* **advice,** 3619
20:16 *"You shall* not g false testimony 6699
22:17 If her father absolutely refuses to g her 5989
22:29 *"You must* g me the firstborn of your sons. 5989
22:30 but g them to me on the eighth day. 5989
23: 2 When *you* **g testimony** in a lawsuit, 6699
23:26 *I will* g you *a* **full** life span. 4848
24:12 and *I will* g you the tablets of stone, 5989
25: 2 each man whose heart **prompts** him **to g.** 5605
25:16 which *I will* g you. 5989
25:21 which *I will* g you. 5989

Ex 25:22 with you and g you all my commands for 1819
28: 2 to g him dignity and honor. NIH
28:40 to g them dignity and honor. NIH
30:13 over to those already counted *is to* g 5989
30:14 *are to* g an offering to the LORD. 5989
30:15 not *to* g **more** than a half shekel and 8049
30:15 a half shekel and the poor *are* not *to* g **less** 5070
32:13 *I will* g your descendants all this land I promised them, 5989
33: 1 saying, *'I will* g it to your descendants.' 5989
33:14 and *I will* g you **rest."** 5663
Lev 5:16 add a fifth of the value to that and g it all to 5989
6: 5 the value to it and g it all to the owner on 5989
6: 9 **"G** Aaron and his sons *this* **command:** 7422
7:32 *You are to* g the right thigh 5989
7:36 that the Israelites g this to them 5989
15:14 to the Tent of Meeting and g them to 5989
18:21 not g any of your children to be sacrificed 5989
20:24 I *will* g it to you as an inheritance, 5989
23:10 *to* g you and you reap its harvest, 5989
23:38 and all the freewill offerings *you* g to 5989
25: 2 you enter the land I *am going to* g you, 5989
25:38 of Egypt to g you the land of Canaan and to 5989
Nu 3: 9 G the Levites to Aaron and his sons; 5989
3:48 G the money for the redemption of 5989
5: 7 and g it all to the person he has wronged. 5989
6:26 toward you and g you peace." ' 8492
7: 5 G them to the Levites 5989
7: 9 But Moses *did* not g any to the Kohathites, 5989
10:29 *'I will* g it to you.' 5989
11:12 *Did* I g them **birth?** 3528
11:13 **'G** us meat to eat!' 5989
11:18 Now the LORD *will* g you meat, 5989
11:21 *'I will* g them meat to eat for 5989
14: 8 and *will* g it to us. 5989
15:21 *to* g this offering to the LORD from 5989
18: 8 the holy offerings the Israelites g me I give NIH
18: 8 the Israelites give me *I* g to you 5989
18:11 *I* g this to you and your sons 5989
18:12 *"I* g you all the finest olive oil and all 5989
18:12 and all the finest new wine and grain *they* g 5989
18:19 to the LORD *I* g to you and your sons 5989
18:21 *"I* g to the Levites all the tithes in Israel 5989
18:24 *I* g to the Levites as their inheritance 5989
18:26 the tithe *I* g you as your inheritance, 5989
18:28 From these tithes *you must* g 5989
19: 3 G it to Eleazar the priest; 5989
20:12 into the land *I* g them." 5989
20:24 He will not enter the land *I* g the Israelites, 5989
21:16 and *I will* g them water." 5989
23: 5 "Go back to Balak and g him this **message."** 1819
23:16 "Go back to Balak and g him this **message."** 1819
26:54 To a larger group g a **larger** inheritance, 8049
27: 4 G us property among our father's relatives." 5989
27: 7 *You* **must certainly** g them property 5989+5989
27: 9 g his inheritance to his brothers. 5989
27:10 g his inheritance to his father's brothers. 5989
27:11 g his inheritance to the nearest relative 5989
27:20 G him some of your authority so 5989
28: 2 **"G** *this* **command** *to* the Israelites and say 7422
31:29 from their half share and g it to Eleazar 5989
31:30 G them to the Levites, 5989
32:29 g them the land of Gilead 5989
33:54 To a larger group g a **larger** inheritance, 8049
33:55 *They will* g you **trouble** in the land 7675
35: 2 the Israelites *to* g the Levites towns to live 5989
35: 2 And g them pasturelands around the towns. 5989
35: 4 around the towns that *you* g 5989
35: 6 the towns *you* g the Levites will be cities 5989
35: 6 In addition, g them forty-two other towns. 5989
35: 7 In all *you must* g 5989
35: 8 The towns *you* g the Levites from the land 5989
35:13 These six towns *you* g will be your cities 5989
35:14 G three on this side of the Jordan and three 5989
36: 2 the LORD commanded my lord to g 5989
36: 2 he ordered you to g the inheritance 5989
Dt 1: 8 the land that the LORD swore *he would* g 5989
1:35 the good land I swore to g your forefathers, 5989
1:36 and *I will* g him and his descendants 5989
1:39 *I will* g it to them and they will take 5989
2: 4 G the people *these* **orders:** 7422
2: 5 for *I will* not g you any of their land, 5989
2: 9 for *I will* not g you any part of their land. 5989
2:19 not g you possession *of* any land belonging 5989
2:30 and his heart obstinate in order to g him 5989
4: 8 of the LORD your God that I g you. 7422
4:38 to bring you into their land to g it to you 5989
5:20 *"You shall* not g false testimony 6699
5:31 so that *I may* g you all the commands, 1819
6: 2 and commands that I g you, 7422
6: 6 that I g you today are to be 7422
6:10 to Abraham, Isaac and Jacob, to g you— 5989
6:23 and g us the land that he promised on oath 5989
7: 3 *Do* not g your daughters to their sons 5989
7:11 decrees and laws I g you today. 7422
7:13 that he swore to your forefathers to g you. 5989
7:24 *He will* g their kings into your hand, 5989
10:11 that I swore to their fathers to g them." 5989
11: 9 the LORD swore to your forefathers to g 5989
11:21 the LORD swore to g your forefathers, 5989
12: 6 to g and your freewill offerings, NIH
12:10 and *he will* g you **rest** 5663
12:17 or whatever you have vowed to g, NIH
12:26 and whatever you have vowed to g, NIH
14:21 *You may* g it to an alien living in any 5989
15: 9 and g him nothing. 5989
15:10 G **generously** to him and do so 5989+5989
Dt 15:14 G to him as the LORD your God has blessed 5989
15:15 That is why I g you this command today. 7422
17: 9 of them and *they will* g you the verdict. 5583
17:10 according to the decisions *they* g you at 5583
17:11 and the decisions *they* g you. 606
18: 4 *to* g them the firstfruits of your grain, 5989
20: 3 be terrified or g **way to panic** before them. 6907
20: 4 against your enemies to g you **victory."** 3828
21:16 g **the rights of the firstborn** 1144
22: 2 Then g it **back** to him. 8740
22:19 a hundred shekels of silver and g them to 5989
25: 3 g him more than forty **lashes.** 5782
26: 3 to our forefathers to g us." 5989
26:12 *you shall* g it to the Levite, the alien, 5989
27: 1 all these commands that I g you today. 7422
27:10 and decrees that I g you today." 7422
28: 1 follow all his commands I g you today, 7422
28:11 to your forefathers to g you. 5989
28:13 the LORD your God that I g you this day 7422
28:14 from any of the commands I g you today, 7422
28:55 and he *will* not g to one of them any of 5989
28:65 the LORD *will* g you an anxious mind, 5989
30:20 and he *will* g you many years in 3782
30:20 in the land he swore to g to your fathers, 5989
31: 7 to their forefathers to g them, 5989
32:38 *Let them* g you **shelter!** 2118+6261
34: 4 *'I will* g it to your descendants.' 5989
Jos 1: 2 into the land I *am about to* g to them— 5989
1: 3 *I will* g you every place 5989
1: 6 to their forefathers to g them. 5989
2:12 G me a sure sign 5989
5: 6 to g us, a land flowing with milk 5989
6: 5 *have* all the people g a loud **shout;** 8131+9558
6:10 *"Do* not g **a war cry,** 8131
7:19 g glory to the LORD, the God of Israel, 8492
7:19 the God of Israel, and g him the praise. 5989
8: 7 The LORD your God *will* g it 5989
9:24 to g you the whole land and 5989
14:12 Now g me this hill country that 5989
15:16 *"I will* g my daughter Acsah **in marriage** 851+4200+5989
15:19 g me also springs of water." 5989
17: 4 to g us an inheritance among our brothers." 5989
20: 4 into their city and g him a place to live 5989
21: 2 through Moses that you g us towns to live 5989
21:43 the land he had sworn to g their forefathers, 5989
Jdg 1:12 *"I will* g my daughter Acsah **in marriage** 851+4200+5989
1:15 g me also springs of water." 5989
2: 1 and led you into the land that I swore to g NIH
2:19 *They* refused *to* g **up** their evil practices 5877
4: 7 to the Kishon River and g him 5989
4:19 "Please g me some water." 9197
6:17 g me a sign that it is really you talking 6913
7: 7 and g the Midianites into your hands. 5989
7: 9 because *I am going to* g it into your hands. 5989
8: 5 **"G** my troops some bread; 5989
8: 6 Why *should we* g bread to your troops?" 5989
8:15 Why *should we* g bread to your exhausted 5989
8:24 of you g me an earring from your share of 5989
8:25 *"We'll be* **glad to** g them." 5989+5989
9: 9 *'Should I* g **up** my oil, 2532
9:11 fig tree replied, *'Should I* g **up** my fruit, 2532
9:13 vine answered, *'Should I* g **up** my wine, 2532
11:13 Now g it **back** peaceably." 8740
11:17 *'G us permission to* **go** AIT
11:30 If *you* g the Ammonites into my hands 5989+5989
11:37 **"G** me two months to roam the hills 8332
13: 5 you will conceive and g **birth** *to* a son. 3528
13: 7 'You will conceive and g **birth** *to* a son. 3528
14:12 "If *you can* g me *the* **answer** within 5583+5583
14:12 *I will* g you thirty linen garments 5989
14:13 you *must* g me thirty linen garments 5989
14:14 For three days they could not g the answer. 5583
16: 5 of us *will* g you eleven hundred shekels 5989
17: 3 *I will* g it **back** to you." 8740
17:10 and I'll g you ten shekels of silver a year, 5989
20: 7 speak up and g your verdict." 2035
20:10 it *can* g them what they deserve 6913
20:28 tomorrow *I will* g them into your hands." 5989
21: 1 g his daughter **in marriage** 851+4200+5989
21: 7 oath by the LORD not *to* g them any of our daughters **in marriage?"** 851+4200+5989
21:18 We can't g them our daughters as wives, 5989
21:22 you *did* not g your daughters to them.' " 5989
1Sa 1: 4 *he would* g portions of the meat 5989
1:11 and not forget your servant but g her a son, 5989
1:11 then *I will* g him to the LORD for all 5989
1:28 So now I g him to the LORD. 8626
2:10 *"He will* g strength to his king and exalt 5989
2:15 **"G** the priest some meat to roast; 5989
2:20 the LORD g you children by this woman 8492
8: 6 when they said, **"G** us a king to lead us," 5989
8:14 and vineyards and olive groves and g them 5989
8:15 and of your vintage and g it to his officials 5989
8:22 "Listen to them and g them a **king."** 4887+4889
9: 7 "If we go, what *can we* g the man? 995
9: 8 *I will* g it to the man of God so 5989
9:27 so that *I may* g you a message from God." 9048
11: 3 **"G** us seven days 8332
14:37 *Will you* g them into Israel's hand?" 5989
14:41 the God of Israel, **"G** me the right answer." 2035
17:10 G me a man and let us fight each other." 5989
17:25 The king *will* g great **wealth** *to* 6947+6948
17:25 g him his daughter **in marriage** 5989
17:44 "and *I'll* g your flesh to the birds of 5989
17:46 Today *I will* g the carcasses of 5989
1Sa 17:47 and *he will* g all of you into our hands." 5989
18:17 g her to you **in marriage;** 851+4200+5989
18:21 *"I will* g her to him," he thought, 5989
21: 3 G me five loaves of bread, 928+3338+5989
21: 9 "There is none like it; g it to me." 5989
22: 7 of Jesse g all of you fields and vineyards? 5989
23: 4 *to* g the Philistines into your hand." 5989
23:14 but God *did* not g David into his hands. 5989
24: 4 'I *will* g your enemy into your hands 5989
25: 8 Please g your servants 5989
25:11 and g it to men coming 5989
25:14 g our master his **greetings,** 1385
27: 1 Then Saul *will* g **up** searching 3286
28:22 and *let me* g you some food 8492
2Sa 2:23 But Asahel refused to g **up** *the* **pursuit;** 6073
3:14 demanding, **"G** me my wife Michal, 5989
7:11 also g you **rest** from all your enemies. 5663
12:11 and g them to one who is close to you, 5989
13: 5 g me something **to eat.** 1356
16: 3 *will* g me **back** my grandfather's kingdom.' 8740
16:20 **"G** us your advice. 2035
17: 6 If not, g us your **opinion."** 1819
18: 3 now for you to g us **support** from the city." 6468
18:11 Then I would have had to g you ten shekels 5989
21: 6 So the king said, "I *will* g them to you." 5989
22:36 *You* g me your shield of victory; 5989
1Ki 2:17 *to* g me Abishag the Shunammite 5989
3: 5 "Ask for whatever you want *me to* g you." 5989
3: 9 So g your servant a discerning heart 5989
3:12 *I will* g you a wise and discerning heart, 5989
3:13 *I will* g you what you have 5989
3:14 *I will* g you a **long** life." 799
3:25 the living child in two and g half to one 5989
3:26 "Please, my lord, g her the living baby! 5989
3:27 **"G** the living baby to the first woman. 5989
5: 6 "So g **orders** that cedars of Lebanon be cut 7422
8:28 Yet g **attention** to your servant's prayer 7155
8:46 with them and g them **over** to the enemy, 5989
11:11 the kingdom away from you and g it to one 5989
11:13 but *will* g him one tribe for the sake 5989
11:31 of Solomon's hand and g you ten tribes. 5989
11:35 from his son's hands and g you ten tribes. 5989
11:36 *I will* g one tribe to his son so 5989
11:38 the one I built for David and *will* g Israel 5989
12: 7 g them a favorable **answer,** 1819+1821
12:27 **again** g their **allegiance** 4213+8740
13: 7 and *I will* g you a gift." 5989
13: 8 if *you were to* g me half your possessions, 5989
14: 5 g her such and such **an answer.** 1819
14:16 And *he will* g Israel **up** because of 5989
17:19 **"G** me your son," Elijah replied. 5989
20:10 in Samaria to g each of my men a handful." NIH
20:13 I *will* g it into your hand today, 5989
21: 2 In exchange *I will* g you a better vineyard 5989
21: 3 "The LORD forbid that I *should* g you 5989
21: 4 not g you the inheritance of my fathers." 5989
21: 6 *I will* g you another vineyard 5989
21: 6 he said, *'I will* not g you my vineyard.' " 5989
22: 6 the Lord *will* g it into the king's hand." 5989
22:12 the LORD *will* g it into the king's hand." 5989
22:15 the LORD *will* g it into the king's hand." 5989
22:27 Put this fellow in prison and g him nothing 430[S]
2Ki 4:42 **"G** it to the people to eat," Elisha said. 5989
4:43 Elisha answered, **"G** it to the people to eat. 5989
5:22 Please g them a talent of silver and two sets 5989
6:28 **'G up** your son so we may eat him today, 5989
6:29 **'G up** your son so we may eat him,' 5989
8: 6 **"G back** everything that belonged to her, 8740
10:15 "If so," said Jehu, **"g** me your hand." 5989
14: 9 **'G** your daughter to my son **in marriage.'** 851+4200+5989
18:23 *I will* g you two thousand horses— 5989
19:16 **G ear,** O LORD, and hear; 265+5742
1Ch 16: 4 to g **thanks,** and to praise the LORD, 3344
16: 8 **G thanks** to the LORD, call on his name; 3344
16:18 "To you *I will* g the land of Canaan as 5989
16:34 **G thanks** to the LORD, for he is good; 3344
16:35 that we *may* g **thanks** to your holy name, 3344
16:41 and designated by name to g **thanks** to 3344
21:23 *I will* g the oxen for the burnt offerings, 5989
21:23 *I will* g all this." 5989
22: 9 and *I will* g him **rest** from all his enemies 5663
22:12 *May* the LORD g you discretion 5989
29: 3 of my God *I now* g my personal treasures 5989
29:12 and power to exalt and g **strength** to all. 2616
29:13 Now, our God, we g you **thanks,** 3344
29:14 that we should be able to g as **generously** 5605
29:19 And g my son Solomon the wholehearted 5989
2Ch 1: 7 "Ask for whatever you want *me to* g you." 5989
1:10 G me wisdom and knowledge, 5989
1:12 And *I will* also g you wealth, 5989
2:10 *I will* g your servants, 5989
5:13 to g **praise** and thanks to the LORD. 2146
6:19 Yet g **attention** to your servant's prayer 7155
6:36 with them and g them **over** to the enemy, 5989
10: 7 g them a favorable **answer,** 1819+1821
12: 7 but *will* soon g them deliverance. 5989
15: 7 as for you, be strong and *do* not g **up,** 3338+8332
18: 5 "for God *will* g it into the king's hand." 5989
18:11 the LORD *will* g it into the king's hand." 5989
18:26 Put this fellow in prison and g him nothing 430[S]
19: 6 who is with you whenever you g a verdict. NIH
20: 7 before your people Israel and g it forever to 5989
20:17 the deliverance the LORD will g you, 6640
20:21 **"G thanks** to the LORD, 3344
25: 9 "The LORD *can* g you much more than that." 5989

2Ch 25:18 '**G** your daughter to my son **in marriage.**' 851+4200+5989
30:12 of God was on the people to g them unity 5989
31: 2 to minister, to g **thanks** and to sing praises 3344
31: 4 in Jerusalem to g the portion due the priests 5989
35:12 They set aside the burnt offerings to g them 5989
Ezr 9:12 g your daughters **in marriage** 5989
Ne 1:11 **G** your servant **success** 7503
2: 8 so *he will* g me timber to make beams for 5989
2:20 "The God of heaven *will* g us **success.** 7503
4: 4 **G** them **over** as plunder in a land 5989
5:11 **G back** to them immediately their fields, 8740
5:12 *"We will* g it **back,"** they said. 8740
6:13 and then they *would* g me a bad name 2118+4200
8:13 the scribe to g **attention** to the words of 8505
9: 6 You g **life** *to* everything, 2649
9: 8 a covenant with him to g to his descendants 5989
9:12 with a pillar of fire to g them **light** *on* 239
9:15 with uplifted hand to g them. 5989
10:30 g our daughters **in marriage** 5989
10:32 for carrying out the commands to g a third 5989
12:24 who stood opposite them to g **praise** 2146
12:31 I also assigned two large **choirs to g thanks** 9343
13:25 g your daughters **in marriage** 5989
Est 1:19 Also *let* the king g her royal position 5989
9:13 "g the Jews in Susa **permission** 5989
Job 2: 4 "A man *will* g all he has for his own life. 5989
6:22 '**G** something on my behalf, 2035
7:17 that *you* g him so much attention, 8883
9:16 I do not believe *he would* g me **a hearing.** 263+7754
10: 1 therefore *I will* g **free rein** to my complaint 6440
15:35 They conceive trouble and g **birth** *to* evil; 3528
17: 3 "**G** me, O God, the pledge you demand. 8492
20:10 his own hands *must* g **back** his wealth. 8740
20:18 What he toiled for *he must* g **back** uneaten; 8740
21: 2 let this be the consolation you g me. NIH
22: 3 What pleasure would it g the Almighty 4200
31:37 *I would* g him an account of my every step; 5583
35: 7 If you are righteous, what *do you* g to him, 5989
39: 1 when the mountain goats g **birth?** 3528
39: 2 Do you know the time they g **birth?** 3528
39:17 wisdom or g her a **share** of good sense. 2745
39:19 *"Do you* g the horse his strength 5989
Ps 4: 1 **G** me **relief** from my distress; 8143
5: 1 **G ear** *to* my words, O LORD, 263
7:17 *I will* g **thanks** *to* the LORD because 3344
13: 3 **G light** *to* my eyes, 239
17: 1 **G ear** *to* my prayer— 263
17: 6 g **ear** to me and hear my prayer. 265+5742
18:35 *You* g me your shield of victory, 5989
20: 4 *May he* g you the desire of your heart 5989
21: 1 How great is his joy in the victories you **g!** NIH
28: 7 for joy and *I will* g **thanks** *to* him in song. 3344
30:12 *I will* g you **thanks** forever. 3344
35:18 *I will* g you **thanks** in the great assembly; 3344
36: 8 *you* g them **drink** *from* your river 9197
37: 4 and *he will* g you the desires of your heart. 5989
37:21 but the righteous g generously; 5989
44: 7 but *you* g us **victory** over our enemies, 3828
45:10 Listen, O daughter, consider and g **ear:** 265+5742
46: 2 the earth g **way** and the mountains fall into 4614
49: 3 from my heart will g understanding. NIH
49: 7 No man can redeem the life of another or g 5989
60:11 **G** us aid against the enemy, 2035
71: 3 g *the* **command** to save me, 7422
75: 1 *We* g **thanks** to you, O God, we give thanks 3344
75: 1 We give thanks to you, O God, *we* g **thanks** 3344
78:20 But can he also g us food? 5989
85:12 The LORD *will* indeed g what is good, 5989
86:11 g me an **undivided** heart, 3479
86:17 **G** me a sign of your goodness, 6913
100: 4 g **thanks** to him and praise his name. 3344
104:11 *They* g **water** *to* all the beasts of the field; 9197
104:27 These all look to you to g them their food 5989
104:28 *When you* g it to them, they gather it up; 5989
105: 1 **G thanks** to the LORD, call on his name; 3344
105:11 "To you *I will* g the land of Canaan as 5989
105:39 and a fire to g **light** at night. 239
106: 1 **G thanks** to the LORD, for he is good; 3344
106:47 that we *may* g **thanks** to your holy name 3344
107: 1 **G thanks** to the LORD, for he is good; 3344
107: 8 *Let them* g **thanks** to the LORD 3344
107:15 *Let them* g **thanks** to the LORD 3344
107:21 *Let them* g **thanks** to the LORD 3344
107:31 *Let them* g **thanks** to the LORD 3344
108:12 **G** us aid against the enemy, 2035
109:24 My knees g **way** from fasting; 4173
118: 1 **G thanks** to the LORD, for he is good; 3344
118:19 I will enter and g **thanks** *to* the LORD. 3344
118:21 *I will* g you **thanks,** for you answered me; 3344
118:28 You are my God, and *I will* g you **thanks;** 3344
118:29 **G thanks** to the LORD, for he is good; 3344
119:34 **G** me **understanding,** 1067
119:62 to g you **thanks** for your righteous laws. 3344
119:73 g me **understanding** to learn your commands. 1067
119:125 g me **discernment** that I may understand your statutes. 1067
119:144 g me **understanding** that I may live. 1067
119:169 g me **understanding** according 1067
136: 1 **G thanks** to the LORD, for he is good. 3344
136: 2 **G thanks** to the God of gods. 3344
136: 3 **G thanks** to the Lord of lords: 3344
136:26 **G thanks** to the God of heaven. 3344
141: 8 *do* not g me **over to death.** 6867
145:15 you g them their food at the proper time. 5989

Pr 1:10 if sinners entice you, *do* not g **in** *to* them. 995
3:28 *I'll* g it tomorrow"— 5989
4: 2 *I* g you sound learning, 5989
5: 9 lest *you* g your best strength to others 5989
14: 8 The wisdom of the prudent is *to* g **thought** 1067
21:26 but the righteous g without sparing. 5989
22:21 so that *you can* g sound answers 8740
23:26 g me your heart and let your eyes keep 5989
25:14 who boasts of **gifts he does not g.** 5522+9214
25:21 g him food **to eat;** 430
25:21 g him water **to drink.** 9197
27:23 g careful attention to your herds; 8883
29:17 and *he will* g you **peace;** 5663
30: 8 g me neither poverty nor riches, 5989
30: 8 but g me only my daily bread. 3271
30:15 "The leech has two daughters. '**G!** Give! 2035
30:15 "The leech has two daughters. 'Give! **G!**' 2035
31: 6 **G** beer to those who are perishing, 5989
31:31 **G** her the reward she has earned, 5989
Ecc 3: 6 a time to search and a time to g **up,** 6
10: 1 As dead flies g perfume **a bad smell,** 944+5580
11: 2 **G** portions to seven, yes to eight, 5989
11: 9 and *let* your heart g you **joy** in the days 3512
SS 7:12 there *I will* g you my love. 5989
8: 2 g you spiced wine to **drink,** 9197
8: 7 If one *were to* g all the wealth of his house 5989
8:12 But my own vineyard is mine to **g;** 4200+7156
Isa 7:14 Therefore the Lord himself *will* g you 5989
7:14 be with child and *will* g **birth** *to* a son, 3528
7:22 of the abundance of the milk *they* **g,** 6913
11: 4 with justice *he will* g **decisions** for the poor 3519
12: 4 "**G thanks** to the LORD, call on his name; 3344
13:10 and the moon *will* not g its light. 5585
16: 3 "**G** us counsel, render a decision. 995
19:11 of Pharaoh g **senseless** advice. 1279
22:25 peg driven into the firm place *will* g **way;** 4631
24:15 in the east g **glory** *to* the LORD; 3877
26:17 to g **birth** writhes and cries out in her pain, 3528
26:19 the earth *will* g **birth** *to* her dead. 5877
29:11 And if *you* g the scroll to someone who can 5989
29:12 if you g the scroll to someone who cannot 5989
30:10 "**G** us no *more* **visions** 2600
33:11 You conceive chaff, *you* g **birth** *to* straw; 3528
34: 2 *he will* g them **over** to slaughter. 5989
35: 3 steady the knees *that* g **way;** 4173
36: 8 *I will* g you two thousand horses— 5989
37:17 **G ear,** O LORD, and hear; 265+5742
41:28 **one** among them **to** g **counsel,** 3446
41:28 no *one to* g answer when I ask them. 8740
42: 8 not g my glory to another or my praise 5989
42:12 *Let them* g glory to the LORD 8492
43: 3 *I* g Egypt for your ransom, 5989
43: 4 *I will* g men in exchange for you, 5989
43: 6 I will say to the north, '**G** them **up!**' 5989
43:20 to g **drink** *to* my people, my chosen, 9197
45: 3 *I will* g you the treasures of darkness, 5989
45:11 g me **orders** about the work of my hands? 7422
49:20 g us **more space** to live in.' 5602
53:12 Therefore *I will* g him a **portion** among 2745
55: 3 **G ear** and come to me; 265+5742
56: 5 to them *I will* g within my temple 5989
56: 5 *I will* g them an everlasting name 5989
56: 7 and g them **joy** in my house of prayer. 8523
59: 4 they conceive trouble and g **birth** *to* evil. 3528
62: 6 g yourselves no rest, 4200
62: 7 and g him no rest 5989
62: 8 "Never again *will I* g your grain as food 5989
65:15 but to his servants *he will* g another name. 7924
66: 9 the moment of birth and not g **delivery?"** 3528
Jer 3:15 Then *I will* g you shepherds 5989
3:19 like sons and g you a desirable land, 5989
6:10 To whom can I speak and g **warning?** 6386
7:22 *I did* not *just* g them **commands** 7422
8:10 Therefore *I will* g their wives 5989
11: 5 to g them a land flowing with milk 5989
12: 7 *I will* g the one I love into the hands 5989
13:16 **G** glory to the LORD your God 5989
14:13 *I will* g you lasting peace in this place.' " 5989
15:13 Your wealth and your treasures *I will* g 5989
16: 7 nor *will anyone* g them **a drink** 3926+9197
17: 3 and all your treasures *I will* g **away** 5989
18: 2 and there *I will* g you my message." 9048
18:21 So g their children **over** to famine; 5989
19: 7 and *I will* g their carcasses as food to 5989
20:13 **G praise** *to* the LORD! 2146
24: 7 *I will* g them a heart to know me, 5989
27: 4 **G** them a **message** for their masters and say, 7422
27: 5 and *I* g it to anyone I please. 5989
28:14 *I will* even g him control over 5989
29: 6 g your daughters **in marriage,** 408+4200+5989
29:11 plans to g you hope and a future. 5989
31: 2 I will come to g **rest** *to* Israel." 8089
31:13 *I will* g them **comfort** and joy instead 5714
32:22 to g their forefathers, 5989
32:39 *I will* g them singleness of heart 5989
32:42 on this people, so I *will* g them all 995
33:11 saying, "**G thanks** *to* the LORD Almighty, 3344
34:22 I *am going to* g **the order,** 7422
35: 2 g them wine **to drink."** 9197
38:15 "If *I* g you **an answer,** will you not kill me? 5583
38:15 Even if *I did* g you **counsel,** 3619
La 2:18 g yourself no relief, your eyes no rest. 5989
Eze 2: 8 open your mouth and eat what I g you." 5989
3:17 the word I speak and g them **warning** 2302
11:17 and *I will* g you **back** the land 5989
11:19 *I will* g them an undivided heart and put 5989
11:19 from them their heart of stone and g them 5989

Eze 16:33 but you g gifts to all your lovers, 5989
16:34 for you g payment and none is given 5989
16:61 *I will* g them to you as daughters, 5989
20:28 to g them and they saw any high hill 5989
20:42 the land I had sworn with uplifted hand to **g** 5989
21:22 to g *the* **command** to slaughter, 7023+7337
21:27 to him *I will* g it.' 5989
23: 8 *She did* not g **up** the prostitution she began 6440
23:46 Bring a mob against them and g them **over** 5989
25: 4 therefore I *am going to* g you to the people 5989
25: 7 and g you as plunder to the nations. 5989
25:10 *I will* g Moab along with the Ammonites 5989
29: 5 *I will* g you as food to the beasts of 5989
29:19 *to* g Egypt to Nebuchadnezzar king 5989
32: 7 and the moon *will* not g its **light.** 239+240
33: 7 the word I speak and g them **warning** 2302
33:15 follows the **decrees** *that* g life, AIT
33:27 the country *I will* g to the wild animals to 5989
35: 6 *I will* g you **over** to bloodshed 6913
36:26 *I will* g you a new heart and put 5989
36:26 from you your heart of stone and g you 5989
39: 4 *I will* g you as food to all kinds 5989
39:11 " 'On that day *I will* g Gog a burial place 5989
43:19 *You are to* g a young bull as a sin offering 5989
44: 5 and g attention *to* everything I tell you 8492
44: 5 **G** attention to the entrance of the temple 8492
44:28 *You are to* g them no possession in Israel; 5989
44:30 *You are to* g them the first portion 5989
45: 6 *to* g the city as its property an area 5,000 6073
45: 9 **G up** your violence and oppression 5989
46: 7 the lambs as much as he **wants to g,** 3338+5952
46:18 g his sons their **inheritance** 5706
47:14 Because I swore with uplifted hand to g it 5989
47:23 there *you are to* g him his inheritance," 5989
Da 1:12 **G** us nothing but vegetables to eat 5989
3:28 *to* g **up** their lives rather than serve 10314
5:16 you are able to g **interpretations** 10599+10600
5:17 and g your rewards to someone else. 10314
9:18 **G ear,** O God, and hear; 265+5742
9:22 to g you **insight** and understanding. 8505
11:17 g him a daughter **in marriage** 851+2021+5989
Hos 2: 5 *who* g me my food and my water, 5989
2:15 There *I will* g her **back** her vineyards, 5989
4:10 the LORD to g *themselves* 9068
5: 7 *they* g **birth** *to* illegitimate children. 3528
9:14 **G** them, O LORD— 5989
9:14 what *will you* g them? 5989
9:14 **G** them wombs that miscarry and breasts 5989
11: 8 "How *can I* g you **up,** Ephraim? 5989
13:10 '**G** me a king and princes'? 5989
Am 2:10 to g you the land of the Amorites. 3769
5:11 on the poor and **force** him to g you grain. 4374
9: 9 "For I *will* g *the* **command,** 7422
Jnh 3: 2 and proclaim to it the message I g you." 1819
3: 8 *Let* them g **up** their evil ways 4946+8740
4: 6 and made it grow up over Jonah to g shade 2118
Mic 1:14 Therefore *you will* g parting gifts 5989
4:13 for *I will* g you horns of iron; 8492
4:13 *I will* g you hoofs of bronze 8492
6:14 what you save *I will* g to the sword. 5989
6:16 Therefore I *will* g you **over** to ruin 5989
Na 2:10 Hearts melt, knees g **way,** bodies tremble, 7211
Hab 2: 1 what **answer** *I am to* g to this complaint. 8740
2:19 *Can* it g **guidance?** 3723
Zep 3:19 *I will* g them praise and honor 8492
3:20 *I will* g you honor and praise among all 5989
Hag 1: 5 "**G careful thought** to your ways. 4222+8492
1: 7 "**G careful thought** to your ways. 4222+8492
2:15 " 'Now g **careful thought** to this 4222+8492
2:18 g **careful thought** to the day when 4222+8492
2:18 **G careful thought:** 4222+8492
Zec 3: 7 of my courts, and *I will* g you a place 5989
8:12 g all these things **as an inheritance** 5706
10: 2 *they* g **comfort** in vain. 5714
11:12 "If you think it best, g me my pay; 2035
Mal 1:14 in his flock and **vows to** g it, 5623
Mt 1:21 *She will* g **birth to** a son, *5503*
1:21 and *you are to* g him the name Jesus, *2813*
1:23 be with child and *will* g **birth to** a son, *5503*
4: 9 "All this *I will* g you," he said, *1443*
5:31 'Anyone who divorces his wife *must* g her *1443*
5:42 **G** to the one who asks you, *1443*
6: 2 "So when *you* g **to the needy,** *1797+4472*
6: 3 But *when you* g **to the needy,** *1797+4472*
6:11 **G** us today our daily bread. *1443*
7: 6 *"Do* not g dogs what is sacred; *1443*
7: 9 if his son asks for bread, *will* g him a stone? *2113*
7:10 if he asks for a fish, *will* g him a snake? *2113*
7:11 know how *to* g good gifts to your children, *1443*
7:11 will your Father in heaven g good gifts *1443*
10: 8 Freely you have received, freely **g.** *1443*
10:12 As you enter the home, g it *your* **greeting.** *832*
11:28 weary and burdened, and I *will* g you **rest.** *399*
12:36 g **account** on the day of judgment **for** *625*
14: 7 with an oath to g her whatever she asked. *1443*
14: 8 "**G** me here on a platter the head of John *1443*
14:16 You g them something to eat." *1443*
16:19 *I will* g you the keys of the kingdom *1443*
16:26 what *can* a man g in exchange for his soul? *1443*
17:27 and g it to them for my tax and yours." *1443*
19: 7 "did Moses command that a man g his wife *1443*
19:18 do not steal, *do* not g **false testimony,** *6018*
19:21 go, sell your possessions and g to the poor, *1443*
20:14 to g the man who was hired last the same *1443*
20:28 and *to* g his life as a ransom for many." *1443*
21:41 g him *his* **share of** the crop *625*
22:21 "**G** to Caesar what is Caesar's, *625*

Mt 23:23 You g a tenth of your spices— 620
24:29 and the moon will not g its light; 1443
24:45 in his household to g them their food at 1443
25: 8 'G us some of your oil; 1443
25:28 and g it to the one who has the ten talents. 1443
25:37 g you something to drink? 4540
26:15 to g me if I hand him over to you?" 1443
27:64 So g the order for the tomb to 3027
Mk 5:43 and told them to g her something to eat. 1443
6:22 and I'll g it to you." 1443
6:23 "Whatever you ask I will g you, 1443
6:25 "I want you to g me right now the head 1443
6:37 "You g them something to eat." 1443
6:37 to go and spend that much on bread and g it 1443
7: 3 g their hands a ceremonial washing, AIT
8:37 what can a man g in exchange for his soul? 1443
10:19 do not g false testimony, do not defraud, 6018
10:21 sell everything you have and g to the poor, 1443
10:45 and to g his life as a ransom for many." 1443
12: 9 He will come and kill those tenants and g 1443
12:17 "G to Caesar what is Caesar's and 625
13:24 and the moon will not g its light; 1443
14:11 to hear this and promised to g him money. 1443
Lk 1:13 and you are to g him the name John. 2813
1:31 You will be with child and g birth to a son, 5503
1:31 and you are to g him the name Jesus. 2813
1:32 The Lord God will g him the throne 1443
1:77 to g his people the knowledge of salvation 1443
4: 6 "I will g you all their authority 1443
4: 6 and I can g it to anyone I want to. 1443
6:30 G to everyone who asks you, 1443
6:38 G, and it will be given to you. 1443
7:44 You did not g me any water for my feet, 1443
7:45 You did not g me a kiss, but this woman, 1443
8:55 Jesus told them to g her something to eat. 1443
9:13 He replied, "You g them something to eat." 1443
10: 7 eating and drinking whatever they g you, 3836
11: 3 G us each day our daily bread. 1443
11: 7 I can't get up and g you anything.' 1443
11: 8 though he will not get up and g him 1443
11: 8 up and g him as much as he needs. 1443
11:11 asks for a fish, will g him a snake instead? 2113
11:12 if he asks for an egg, will g him a scorpion? 2113
11:13 know how to g good gifts to your children, 1443
11:13 will your Father in heaven g the Holy Spirit 1443
11:41 g what is inside [the dish] to the poor, 1443+1797
11:42 g God a tenth of you mint, rue and 620
12:32 for your Father has been pleased to g you 1443
12:33 Sell your possessions and g to the poor. 1443+1797
12:42 to g them their food allowance at 1443+3836
13:15 from the stall and lead it out to g it water? 4540
14: 9 'G this man your seat.' 1443
14:12 "When you g a luncheon or dinner, 4472
14:13 But when you g a banquet, invite the poor, 4472
14:33 not g up everything he has cannot 698
15:12 'Father, g me my share of the estate.' 1443
16: 2 G an account of your management, 625
16:12 who will g you property of your own? 1443
17:18 and g praise to God except this foreigner?" 1443
18: 1 that they should always pray and not g up. 1591
18:12 I fast twice a week and g a tenth of 620
18:20 do not steal, do not g false testimony, 6018
18:22 Sell everything you have and g to the poor, 1344
19: 8 Here and now I g half of my possessions to 1443
19:24 'Take his mina away from him and g it to 1443
20:10 to the tenants so they would g him some of 1443
20:16 He will come and kill those tenants and g 1443
20:25 "Then g to Caesar what is Caesar's, 625
21:15 For I will g you words and wisdom 1443
22: 5 and agreed to g him money. 1443
24:30 broke it and began to g it to them. 2113
Jn 1:22 G us an answer to take back NIG
4: 7 Jesus said to her, "Will you g me a drink?" 1443
4:14 the water I g him will never thirst. 1443
4:14 the water I g him will become in him 1443
4:15 g me this water so that I won't get thirsty 1443
5:21 Son gives life to whom he is pleased to g it. NIG
6:27 which the Son of Man will g you. 1443
6:30 "What miraculous sign then will you g 4472
6:34 they said, "from now on g us this bread." 1443
6:51 which I will g for the life of the world." 1443
6:52 "How can this man g us his flesh to eat?" 1443
9:24 "G glory to God," they said. 1443
10:28 I g them eternal life, and they shall never perish; 1443
11:22 now God will g you whatever you ask." 1443
13:26 "It is the one to whom I will g this piece 1443
13:29 or to g something to the poor. 1443
13:34 new command I g you: Love one another. 1443
14:16 and he will g you another Counselor to be 1443
14:27 Peace I leave with you; my peace I g you. 1443
14:27 I do not g to you as the world gives. 1443
15:16 the Father will g you whatever you ask 1443
16:23 my Father will g you whatever you ask 1443
17: 2 over all people that he might g eternal life 1443
18:40 G us Barabbas!" NIG
Ac 3: 6 but what I have I g you. 1443
5:31 that he might g repentance and forgiveness 1443
6: 4 and will g our attention to prayer and 4674
8:19 "G me also this ability so that everyone 1443
12:23 because Herod did not g praise to God, 1443
13:34 " 'I will g you the holy and sure blessings 1443
20:32 which can build you up and g you 1443
20:35 'It is more blessed to g than to receive.' " 1443
21:26 to the temple to g notice of the date when 1334
23:21 Don't g in to them, 4275
Ac 24:23 under guard but to g him some freedom 2400
Ro 2: 6 God "will g to each person according 625
2: 7 he will g eternal life. NIG
8:11 also g life to your mortal bodies 2443
8:32 along with him, graciously g us all things? 5919
12: 8 to the needs of others, let him g generously; NIG
12:20 g him something to drink. 4540
13: 6 who g their full time to governing. 4674
13: 7 G everyone what you owe him: 625
14:12 of us will g an account of himself to God. 1443
15: 5 and encouragement g you a spirit of unity 1443
16: 2 to g her any help she may need from you, 4225
1Co 7:10 To the married I g this command (not I, 4133
7:25 I have no command from the Lord, but I g 1443
10:16 cup of thanksgiving for which we g thanks 2328
11:34 when I come I will g further directions. 1411
13: 3 g all I possess to the poor 6039
15:58 g yourselves fully to the work of the Lord, 4355
16: 3 I will g letters of introduction to the men NIG
2Co 1:11 many will g thanks on our behalf for 2373
4: 6 made his light shine in our hearts to g us NIG
8:10 Last year you were the first not only to g 4472
9: 2 in Achaia were ready to g; NIG
9: 7 Each man should g what he has decided NIG
9: 7 in his heart to g, NIG
Gal 2: 5 We did not g in to them for a moment, 1634+3836+5717
3: 5 Does God g you his Spirit and work 2220
6: 9 a harvest if we do not g up. 1725
Eph 1:17 may g you the Spirit of wisdom 1443
4:27 and do not g the devil a foothold. 1443
Php 2:30 up for the help you could not g me. 5729
Col 4:15 G my greetings to the brothers at Laodicea 832
1Th 5:18 g thanks in all circumstances, 2373
2Th 1: 7 and g relief to you who are troubled, NIG
3:16 of peace himself g you peace at all times 1443
1Ti 1:18 I g you this instruction in keeping with 4192
4:15 g yourself wholly to them, 3509
5: 3 G proper recognition to those widows 5506
5: 7 G the people these instructions, 4133
5:14 to g the enemy no opportunity for slander. 1443
2Ti 1: 7 For God did not g us a spirit of timidity, 1443
2: 7 the Lord will g you insight into all this. 1443
4: 1 I g you this charge: 1371
Heb 4:13 of him to whom we must g account. NIG
6:14 g you many descendants." 4437+4437
10:25 Let us not g up meeting together, 1593
13:17 over you as men who must g an account. 625
Jas 1:18 He chose to g us birth through the word 652
1Pe 3: 6 if you do what is right and do not g way 4766
3:15 to g an answer to everyone who asks you NIG
3:15 to g the reason for the hope that you have. NIG
4: 5 to g account to him who is ready to judge 625
1Jn 5:16 he should pray and God will g him life. 1443
Rev 2: 7 I will g the right to eat from the tree 1443
2:10 and I will g you the crown of life. 1443
2:17 I will g some of the hidden manna. 1443
2:17 I will also g him a white stone with 1443
2:26 I will g authority over the nations— 1443
2:28 I will also g him the morning star. 1443
3:21 I will g the right to sit with me 1443
4: 9 Whenever the living creatures g glory, 1443
10: 9 and asked him to g me the little scroll. 1443
11: 3 And I will g power to my two witnesses, 1443
11:17 "We g thanks to you, Lord God Almighty, 2373
12: 2 in pain as she was about to g birth. 5503+6048
12: 4 of the woman who was about to g birth, 5503
13:15 to g breath to the image of the first beast, 1443
14: 7 "Fear God and g him glory, 1443
17:13 and will g their power and authority to 1443
17:17 to accomplish his purpose by agreeing to g 1443
18: 6 G back to her as she has given; 625
18: 7 G her as much torture and grief as the glory 1443
19: 7 and be glad and g him glory! 1443
21: 6 To him who is thirsty I will g to drink 1443
22: 5 for the Lord God will g them light. 5894
22:12 and I will g to everyone according 625
22:16 have sent my angel to g you this testimony 3455

GIVE, GIVEN (Anglicized) See also DELIVERED, TURN

GIVEN (472) [GIVE]

Ge 9: 2 they are g into your hands. 5989
15: 3 Abram said, "You have g me no children; 5989
24:19 After she had g him a drink, she said, 9197
24:35 He has g him sheep and cattle, 5989
24:36 and he has g him everything he owns. 5989
26:18 the same names his father had g them. 7924
26:22 "Now the LORD has g us room 8143
27:41 because of the blessing his father had g him. 1385
28: 4 and your descendants the blessing g AIT
30: 6 he has listened to my plea and g me a son." 5989
31: 9 and has g them to me. 5989
33: 5 children God has graciously g your servant. 2858
38:14 she had not been g to him as his wife. 5989
38:30 came out and he was g the name Zerah. 7924
40:16 g a favorable interpretation, 7354
41:32 the dream was g to Pharaoh in two forms is 9101
43:23 has g you treasure in your sacks; 5989
46:18 whom Laban had g to his daughter Leah— 5989
46:25 whom Laban had g to his daughter Rachel— 5989
48: 9 "They are the sons God has g me here," 5989
Ex 4:21 the wonders I have g you the power to do. 8492
5:16 Your servants are g no straw, 5989
Ex 5:18 You will not be g any straw, 5989
16:15 "It is the bread the LORD has g you to eat. 5989
16:29 Bear in mind that the LORD has g you 5989
28: 3 the skilled men to whom I have g wisdom 4848
31: 6 Also I have g skill to all the craftsmen 5989
34:32 the LORD had g him on Mount Sinai. 1819
35:34 And he has g both him and Oholiab son 5989
36: 1 to whom the LORD has g skill and ability 5989
36: 2 to whom the LORD had g ability 5989
Lev 6:17 I have g it as their share of the offerings 5989
7:34 the thigh that is presented and have g them 5989
10:11 the LORD has g them through Moses." 1819
10:14 they have been g to you and your children 5989
10:17 it was g to you to take away the guilt of 5989
17:11 and I have g it to you to make atonement 5989
19:20 not been ransomed or g her freedom, 5989
26:25 and you will be g into enemy hands. 5989
27: 9 an animal g to the LORD becomes holy. 5989
Nu 1:17 Aaron took these men whose names had been g, 5918
3: 9 Israelites who are to be g wholly to him. 5989+5989
5: 8 to the LORD and must be g to the priest, NIH
8:16 Israelites who are to be g wholly to me. 5989+5989
8:19 I have g the Levites as gifts to Aaron 5989
16:14 a land flowing with milk and honey or g us 5989
18:29 and holiest part of everything g to you.' 5510
21:29 He has g up his sons as fugitives 5989
27:12 the Abarim range and see the land I have g 5989
32: 5 "let this land be g to your servants 5989
32: 7 over into the land the LORD has g them? 5989
32: 9 the land the LORD had g them. 5989
33:53 for I have g you the land to possess. 5989
34:13 that it be g to the nine and a half tribes, 5989
35: 8 the land the Israelites possess are to be g 5989
Dt 1: 8 See, I have g you this land. 5989
1:21 the LORD your God has g you the land. 5989
2: 5 I have g Esau the hill country of Seir 5989
2: 9 I have g Ar to the descendants of Lot as 5989
2:19 I have g it as a possession to 5989
2:24 I have g into your hand Sihon the Amorite, 5989
3:18 "The LORD your God has g you this land 5989
3:19 in the towns I have g you, 5989
3:20 to the possession I have g you." 5989
6:17 the stipulations and decrees he has g you. 7422
8:10 for the good land he has g you. 5989
9:23 of the land I have g you." 5989
12: 1 has g you to possess— 5989
12:21 the herds and flocks the LORD has g you, 5989
16:10 blessings the LORD your God has g 1385
22:19 because this man has g an Israelite virgin 3655
26:10 O LORD, have g me." 5989
26:11 the good things the LORD your God has g 5989
26:13 the sacred portion and have g it to 5989
26:15 and the land you have g us as you promised 5989
28:31 Your sheep will be g to your enemies, 5989
28:32 and daughters will be g to another nation, 5989
28:53 the LORD your God has g you. 5989
29: 4 to this day the LORD has not g you a mind 5989
29:26 gods he had not g them. 2745
32:30 unless the LORD had g them up? 6037
Jos 2: 9 the LORD has g this land to you and that 5989
2:24 "The LORD has surely g the whole land 5989
6:16 For the LORD has g you the city! 5989
9:19 "We have g them our oath by the LORD, 8678
10: 8 I have g them into your hand. 5989
10:19 for the LORD your God has g them 5989
13: 8 the inheritance that Moses had g them east 5989
13:15 This is what Moses had g to the tribe 5989
13:24 This is what Moses had g to the tribe 5989
13:29 This is what Moses had g to the half-tribe 5989
13:32 This is the inheritance Moses had g 5706
13:33 Moses had g no inheritance; 5989
15:19 Since you have g me land in the Negev, 5989
17:14 "Why have you g us only one allotment 5989
18: 3 the God of your fathers, has g you? 5989
21:12 around the city they had g to Caleb son 5989
21:21 of Ephraim they were g Shechem (a city 5989
21:26 and their pasturelands were g to the rest of NIH
21:27 The Levite clans of the Gershonites were g: 4200
21:34 (the rest of the Levites) were g: 4200
22: 4 LORD your God has g your brothers rest 5663
22: 7 the half-tribe of Manasseh Moses had g land 5989
23: 1 and the LORD had g Israel rest 5663
23:13 which the LORD your God has g you. 5989
23:15 from this good land he has g you. 5989
23:16 from the good land he has g you." 5989
Jdg 1: 2 I have g the land into their hands." 5989
1:15 Since you have g me land in the Negev, 5989
1:20 Hebron was g to Caleb, 5989
3: 4 which he had g their forefathers 7422
3:28 "for the LORD has g Moab, your enemy, 5989
4:14 the LORD has g Sisera into your hands. 5989
7:14 God has g the Midianites and 5989
7:15 The LORD has g the Midianite camp 5989
8: 7 the LORD has g Zebah and Zalmunna 5989
11:24 whatever the LORD our God has g us, 3769
11:36 "you have g your word to the LORD. 906+7023+7198
14:11 he was g thirty companions. 4374
14:16 You've g my people a riddle, 2554
14:20 And Samson's wife was g to 2118
15: 6 because his wife was g to his friend." 5989
15:18 "You have g your servant this great victory. 5989
20:36 men of Israel had g way before Benjamin, 5989
21:14 at that time and were g the women 5989

Ru 2:13 *"You have* g me **comfort** 5714
4:15 *has* g him **birth."** 3528
1Sa 1:28 For his whole life he *will* **be g over** to 8626
4:20 *you have* **g birth** *to* a son." 3528
14:10 that the LORD *has* g them into our hands." 5989
14:12 the LORD *has* g them into the hand 5989
15:28 of Israel from you today and *has* g it to one 5989
18:19 Saul's daughter, *to be* g to David, 5989
18:19 she **was g in marriage** to Adriel of Meholah. 851+4200+5989
25:27 **be** g to the men who follow you. 5989
25:44 But Saul *had* g his daughter Michal, 5989
28:17 the kingdom out of your hands and g it 5989
30:23 not do that with what the LORD *has* g us. 5989
2Sa 7:1 in his palace and the LORD *had* **g** him **rest** 5663
9:9 *I have* g your master's grandson everything 5989
12:8 *I would have* **g** you **even more.** 2179+2179+2256+3578+3869+3869
13:28 *Have* not I g you *this* **order?** 7422
17:6 "Ahithophel *has* g this advice. 1819
17:7 **advice** Ahithophel *has* g 3619+6783
21:6 *let* seven of his male descendants **be g** 5989
1Ki 2:21 Shunammite **be g in marriage** 851+4200+5989
3:6 to him and *have* g him a son to sit 5989
3:28 all Israel heard the verdict the king *had* **g,** 9149[S]
5:4 But now the LORD my God *has* **g** me **rest** 5663
5:7 for *he has* g David a wise son to rule 5989
8:56 who *has* g rest to his people Israel just 5989
9:6 the commands and decrees *I have* g you 5989
9:7 from the land *I have* g them 5989
9:12 to see the towns that Solomon *had* g him, 5989
9:13 of towns are these *you have* g me, 5989
10:13 besides what *he had* g her out 5989
12:13 Rejecting the **advice** g him by the elders, 3619+6783
13:5 according to the sign g *by* the man of God 5989
13:26 The LORD *has* **g** him **over** to the lion, 5989
15:29 of the LORD g through his servant Ahijah 1819
18:26 they took the bull g them and prepared it. 5989
20:27 also mustered and **g provisions,** 3920
2Ki 5:1 through him the LORD *had* g victory 5989
5:17 **be** g as much earth as a pair 5989
15:20 to contribute fifty shekels of silver to *be* g 5989
17:15 and the **warnings** *he had* g them. 6343+6386
18:6 the commands the LORD *had* g Moses. 7422
18:30 this city *will* not **be** g into the hand of 5989
22:10 "Hilkiah the priest *has* g me a book." 5989
1Ch 5:1 as firstborn **were** g to the sons of Joseph son 5989
6:55 They *were* g Hebron in Judah 5989
6:56 the city *were* g to Caleb son of Jephunneh. 5989
6:57 So the descendants of Aaron *were* g Hebron 5989
6:60 the tribe of Benjamin they were g Gibeon, NIH
6:66 Some of the Kohathite clans *were* g 2118
6:67 of Ephraim they *were* g Shechem (a city 5989
16:40 which *he had* g Israel. 7422
25:5 They were g him through the promises NIH
28:5 and the LORD *has* g me many— 5989
29:9 for *they had* **g freely** and wholeheartedly to 5605
29:14 and *we have* g you only what comes 5989
29:17 All these things *have* I **g willingly** and 5605
29:17 **willingly** your people who are here *have* **g** 5605
2Ch 1:12 wisdom and knowledge *will* **be g** you. 5989
2:12 *He has* g King David a wise son, 5989
2:14 of engraving and can execute any design **g** 5989
7:19 the decrees and commands *I have* g you 5989
7:20 which *I have* g them, 5989
8:2 the villages that Hiram *had* g him, 5989
13:5 *has* g the kingship of Israel to David 5989
14:7 and *he has* **g** us **rest** on every side." 5663
18:14 "for *they will* **be g** into your hand." 5989
20:27 **g** them **cause to rejoice** 8523
20:30 for his God *had* **g** him **rest** on every side. 5663
21:3 Their father *had* g them many gifts of silver 5989
21:3 but *he had* g the kingdom to Jehoram 5989
28:5 *He* **was** also g into the hands of the king 5989
31:14 was in charge of the **freewill offerings** *g* AIT
32:29 for God *had* g him very great riches. 5989
33:8 decrees and ordinances **g** through Moses." NIH
34:14 the LORD that had been **g** through Moses. NIH
34:18 "Hilkiah the priest *has* **g** me a book." 5989
36:23 of heaven, *has* **g** me all the kingdoms of 5989
Ezr 1:2 of heaven, *has* **g** me all the kingdoms of 5989
6:9 must be **g** them daily without fail, 10314
7:6 which the LORD, the God of Israel, *had* **g.** 5989
7:11 of the letter King Artaxerxes *had* **g** to Ezra 5989
7:15 that the king and his advisers *have* **freely g** 10461
9:9 and repair its ruins, and he *has* **g** us a wall 5989
9:13 and *have* **g** us a remnant like this. 5989
Ne 7:72 The total **g** *by* the rest of the people 5989
10:29 of God **g** through Moses the servant of God 5989
12:43 because God *had* **g** them great **joy.** 8523+8525
13:10 to the Levites *had* not **been g** to them, 5989
Est 2:3 and *let* beauty treatments *be g* to them. 5989
2:13 Anything she wanted **was g** her to take 5989
5:3 up to half the kingdom, *it will* **be g** you." 5989
5:6 *It will* **be g** you. 5989
7:2 *It will* **be g** you. 5989
8:7 *I have* **g** his estate to Esther, 5989
9:12 *It will* **be g** you. 5989
Job 3:20 "Why *is* light **g** to those in misery, 5989
3:23 Why is life **g** to a man whose way is hidden NIH
15:19 the land **was g** when no alien passed 5989
38:12 *"Have* you ever **g orders** *to* the morning, 7422
Ps 60:3 *you have* **g** us wine that makes us stagger. 9197
61:5 *you have* **g** me the heritage 5989
63:10 *be* **g over** to the sword and 3338+5599+6584
72:15 *May* gold from Sheba *be* **g** him. 5989
Ps 74:9 *We* **are g** no miraculous signs; 8011
78:29 for *he had* **g** them what they craved. 995
79:2 *They have* **g** the dead bodies 5989
94:17 Unless the LORD had **g** me help, NIH
105:42 For he remembered his holy promise **g to** 907
115:16 but the earth *he has* **g** to man. 5989
118:18 but *he has* not **g** me **over** to death. 5989
119:49 for *you have* **g** me **hope.** 3498
122:4 of the LORD according to the statute **g to** 4200
Pr 8:24 When there were no oceans, *I* **was g birth,** 2655
8:25 before the hills, *I* **was g birth,** 2655
21:14 A gift **g** in secret soothes anger, NIH
23:2 to your throat if you are **g to gluttony.** 1251+5883
Ecc 5:18 the few days of life God *has* **g** him— 5989
8:15 the days of the life God *has* **g** him under 5989
9:9 of this meaningless life that God *has* **g** you 5989
12:11 firmly embedded nails—**g** by one Shepherd. 5989
Isa 1:4 children **g to corruption!** 8845
8:18 and the children the LORD *has* **g** me. 5989
9:6 For to us a child is born, to us a son **is g,** 5989
14:32 What **answer** *shall* **be g** *to* the envoys of 6699
23:4 "I have neither been in labor nor **g birth;** 3528
23:11 *He has* **g an order** concerning Phoenicia 7422
26:18 *we have* not **g birth** *to* people of the world. 5877
34:16 For it is his mouth that *has* **g** *the* **order,** 7422
35:2 The glory of Lebanon *will* **be g** to it, 5989
36:15 this city *will* not **be g** into the hand of 5989
50:4 The Sovereign LORD *has* **g** me 5989
63:14 they *were* **g rest** *by* the Spirit of 5663
Jer 4:31 my life is **g over** to murderers." 4200
8:13 What *I have* **g** them will be taken 5989
8:14 **g** us poisoned water **to drink,** 9197
21:10 *It will* **be g** into the hands of the king 5989
32:16 "After I *had* **g** the deed of purchase 5989
35:15 the land *I have* **g** to you and your fathers." 5989
37:21 the courtyard of the guard and **g** bread from 5989
38:16 who *has* **g** us breath, 6913
39:11 of Babylon *had* **g** *these* **orders** 7422
La 4:11 LORD *has* **g full vent** *to* his wrath; 3983
Eze 11:15 this land **was g** to us as our possession.' 5989
11:24 to the exiles in Babylonia in the vision **g by** 928
15:6 As *I have* **g** the wood of the vine among 5989
16:14 splendor *I had* **g** you made your beauty perfect, 8492
16:34 for you give payment and none **is g** to you. 5989
17:18 **g** his hand **in pledge** 5989
20:15 not bring them into the land *I had* **g** them— 5989
29:20 *I have* **g** him Egypt as a reward 5989
33:24 the land *has* **been g** to us as our possession.' 5989
35:12 and *have been* **g over** to us to devour." 5989
46:5 The grain offering **g** with the ram is to be NIH
Da 2:23 *You have* **g** me wisdom and power, 10314
2:37 of heaven *has* **g** you dominion and power 10314
4:16 that of a man and *let* him **be g** the mind of 10314
5:21 from people and **g** the mind of an animal; 10702
5:28 and **g** to the Medes and Persians." 10314
7:4 and the heart of a man **was g** to it. 10314
7:6 and it **was g** authority to **rule.** 10314
7:14 He **was g** authority, glory 10314
8:12 and the daily sacrifice **were g over** to it. 5989
8:26 and mornings that *has* **been g** you is true, 606
9:2 of the LORD **g** to Jeremiah the prophet, 2118
9:23 as you began to pray, an answer *was* **g,** 3655
10:1 a revelation **was g** to Daniel 1655
10:19 my lord, since *you have* **g** me **strength."** 2616
11:4 be uprooted and **g** to others. 4200
11:21 a contemptible person who *has* not *been* **g** 5989
Hos 6:10 There Ephraim is **g to** prostitution 4200
8:13 They offer sacrifices **g** *to* me and they eat 2037
Joel 2:23 for *he has* **g** you the autumn rains 5989
Am 6:11 For the LORD *has* **g the command,** 7422
9:15 be uprooted from the land *I have* **g** them," 5989
Na 1:14 The LORD *has* **g a command** 7422
Zec 6:8 the north country *have* **g** my Spirit **rest** in 5663
6:14 The crown will be **g** to Heldai, Tobijah, 4200
13:6 'The **wounds** *I* **was g** at the house 5782
Mt 6:33 all these things *will be* **g** to you as well. *4707*
7:7 "Ask and *it will be* **g** to you; *1443*
9:8 who *had* **g** such authority to men. *1443*
10:19 At that time you *will be* **g** what to say, *1443*
12:39 *be* **g** it except the sign of the prophet Jonah. *1443*
13:11 the kingdom of heaven *has been* **g** to you, *1443*
13:12 Whoever has *will be* **g** more, *1443*
14:11 His head was brought in on a platter and **g** *1443*
15:36 and *when he had* **g thanks,** *2373*
16:4 but none *will be* **g** it except the sign *1443*
19:11 but only those to whom *it has* **been g.** *1443*
21:43 and **g** to a people who will produce its fruit. *1443*
22:30 nor *be* **g in marriage;** *1139*
25:29 For everyone who has *will be* **g** more, *1443*
26:9 a high price and the money **g** to the poor." *1443*
27:58 and Pilate ordered that *it be* **g** to him. *625*
28:18 in heaven and on earth *has been* **g** to me. *1443*
Mk 4:11 of the kingdom of God *has been* **g** to you. *1443*
4:25 Whoever has *will be* **g** more; *1443*
6:2 "What's this wisdom that *has been* **g** him, *1443*
6:17 For Herod himself *had* **g orders** *690*
8:6 the seven loaves and **g thanks,** *2373*
8:12 I tell you the truth, no sign *will be* **g** to it." *1443*
12:25 nor *be* **g in marriage;** *1139*
12:28 **g** them a good **answer,** *646*
13:11 Just say whatever *is* **g** you at the time, *1443*
14:5 a year's wages and the money **g** to *1443*
Lk 2:21 Jesus, the name the angel *had* **g** him *2813*
4:6 for *it has been* **g** to me, *4140*
6:38 Give, and *it will be* **g** to you. *1443*
8:10 the kingdom of God *has been* **g** to you, *1443*
Lk 8:18 Whoever has *will be* **g** more; *1443*
10:19 *I have* **g** you authority to trample *1443*
11:9 Ask and *it will be* **g** to you; *1443*
11:29 none *will be* **g** it except the sign of Jonah. *1443*
12:31 and these things *will be* **g** to you as well. *4707*
12:48 From everyone who *has been* **g** much, *1443*
17:27 marrying and *being* **g in marriage** up to *1139*
19:15 the servants to whom *he had* **g** the money, *1443*
19:26 to everyone who has, more *will be* **g,** *1443*
20:34 of this age marry and *are* **g in marriage.** *1140*
20:35 nor *be* **g in marriage,** *1139*
22:19 saying, "This is my body **g** for you; *1443*
Jn 1:17 For the law *was* **g** through Moses; *1443*
3:27 "A man can receive only what *is* **g** him *1443*
4:5 of ground Jacob *had* **g** to his son Joseph. *1443*
4:10 and *he* would *have* **g** you living water." *1443*
5:27 And *he has* **g** him authority to judge *1443*
5:36 For the very work that the Father *has* **g** me *1443*
6:23 the bread *after* the Lord *had* **g thanks.** *2373*
6:32 it is not Moses who *has* **g** you the bread *1443*
6:39 that I shall lose none of all that *he has* **g** me, *1443*
7:19 *Has* not Moses **g** you the law? *1443*
7:39 Up to that time the Spirit had not been **g,** *NIG*
10:29 My Father, who *has* **g** them to me, *1443*
11:57 the chief priests and Pharisees *had* **g** orders *1443*
12:2 Here a dinner *was* **g** in Jesus' honor. *4472*
12:5 and the money **g** to the poor? *1443*
12:18 that he *had* **g** this miraculous sign, *4472*
15:7 ask whatever you wish, and *it will be* **g** you. *1181*
17:2 to all those *you have* **g** him. *1443*
17:7 that everything *you have* **g** me comes *1443*
17:9 but for those *you have* **g** me, *1443*
17:14 I *have* **g** them your word and *1443*
17:22 I *have* **g** them the glory that you gave me, *1443*
17:24 I want those *you have* **g** me to be with me *1443*
17:24 the glory *you have* **g** me *1443*
18:11 not drink the cup the Father *has* **g** me?" *1443*
19:11 over me if it were not **g** to you from above. *1443*
19:35 The man who saw it *has* **g testimony,** *3455*
Ac 3:16 that *has* **g** this complete healing to him, *1443*
4:12 under heaven **g** to men by which we must *1443*
5:32 whom God *has* **g** to those who obey him." *1443*
8:18 When Simon saw that the Spirit *was* **g** at *1443*
17:31 *He has* **g proof** of this to all men *4218+4411*
20:24 the task the Lord Jesus *has* **g** me— *3284*
27:24 and God *has* **graciously g** you the lives *5919*
Ro 5:5 the Holy Spirit, whom *he has* **g** us. *1443*
5:13 for before the law was **g,** *NIG*
11:35 "Who *has* ever **g** to God, *4594*
12:3 the grace **g** me I say to every one of you: *1443*
12:3 with the measure of faith God *has* **g** you. *3532*
12:6 according to the grace **g** us. *1443*
1Co 1:4 because of his grace **g** you in Christ Jesus. *1443*
2:12 may understand what God *has* **freely g** us. *5919*
3:10 By the grace God *has* **g** me, *1443*
4:2 **have been g a trust** must prove faithful. *3874*
11:15 For long hair *is* **g** to her as a covering. *1443*
11:24 and *when he had* **g thanks,** he broke it *2373*
12:7 of the Spirit *is* **g** for the common good. *1443*
12:8 To one *there is* **g** through the Spirit *1443*
12:13 **g** the one Spirit **to drink.** *4540*
12:24 of the body and *has* **g** greater honor to *1443*
2Co 4:11 we who are alive *are* always *being* **g over** *4140*
5:5 for this very purpose and *has* **g** us the Spirit *1443*
7:7 but also by the comfort you *had* **g** *him.* *4151*
8:1 that God *has* **g** the Macedonian churches. *1443*
9:5 not as **one grudgingly g.** *4432*
9:14 of the surpassing grace God has **g** you. *NIG*
12:7 *there was* **g** me a thorn in my flesh, *1443*
Gal 2:9 when they recognized the grace **g** to me. *1443*
3:14 He redeemed us in order that the blessing **g** *NIG*
3:21 if a law *had been* **g** that could impart life, *1443*
3:22 being **g** through faith in Jesus Christ, *NIG*
3:22 *might be* **g** to those who believe. *1443*
4:15 and **g** them to me. *1443*
Eph 1:6 which *he has* **freely g** us in *5923*
1:21 and every **title** *that can be* **g,** *3950+3951*
3:2 of God's grace that *was* **g** to me for you, *1443*
3:7 of God's grace **g** me through the working *1443*
3:8 this grace *was* **g** me: *1443*
4:7 But to each one of us grace *has been* **g** *1443*
4:19 they *have* **g** themselves **over** to sensuality *4140*
6:19 words *may be* **g** me so *1443*
Php 1:19 that through your prayers and the **help g** by *2221*
Col 2:10 *you have been* **g fullness** in Christ, *1639+4444*
1Th 1:6 the joy *g by* the **Holy Spirit.** *AIT*
1Ti 1:12 Jesus our Lord, who *has* **g** me **strength,** *1904*
2:6 the testimony **g** in its proper time. *NIG*
3:3 not **g to drunkenness,** not violent *4232*
4:14 which *was* **g** you through *1443*
2Ti 1:9 This grace *was* **g** us in Christ Jesus before *1443*
Tit 1:7 not quick-tempered, not **g to drunkenness,** *4232*
Phm 1:7 Your love **has g** *me* great joy *2400*
Heb 2:13 and the children God *has* **g** me." *1443*
4:8 For if Joshua *had* **g** them **rest,** *2924*
7:11 the basis of it the **law was g** to the people), *3793*
Jas 1:5 and *it will be* **g** to him. *1443*
1Pe 1:3 In his great mercy he *has* **g** us **new birth** *335*
1:13 set your hope fully on the grace to be **g** you *5770*
2Pe 1:3 His divine power *has* **g** us everything we need for life and godliness *1563*
1:4 Through these *he has* **g** us his very great *1563*
3:2 and the command **g** by our Lord and Savior *NIG*
1Jn 4:13 because *he has* **g** us of his Spirit. *1443*
4:21 And he *has* **g** *us* this command: *608+2400*
5:9 which *he has* **g** about his Son. *3455*[S]
5:10 the testimony God *has* **g** about his Son. *3455*[S]

1Jn 5:11 God *has* g us eternal life, *1443*
5:20 and *has* g us understanding, *1443*
2Jn 1: 4 *It has g me* great **joy** to find some *AIT*
Rev 2:21 *I have* g her time to repent *1443*
6: 2 Its rider held a bow, and he *was* g a crown, *1443*
6: 4 Its rider *was* g power to take peace from *1443*
6: 4 To him *was* g a large sword. *1443*
6: 8 They *were* g power over a fourth of *1443*
6:11 Then each of them *was* g a white robe, *1443*
7: 2 to the four angels who *had been* g power *1443*
8: 2 and to them *were* g seven trumpets. *1443*
8: 3 He *was* g much incense to offer, *1443*
9: 1 star *was* g the key to the shaft of the Abyss. *1443*
9: 3 down upon the earth and *were* g power like *1443*
9: 5 They *were* not g power to kill them, *1443*
11: 1 I *was* g a reed like a measuring rod *1443*
11: 2 because *it has been* g to the Gentiles. *1443*
12:13 he pursued the woman who *had* g **birth to** *5503*
12:14 The woman *was* g the two wings of *1443*
13: 4 the dragon because *he had* g authority to *1443*
13: 5 The beast *was* g a mouth to utter proud *1443*
13: 7 He *was* g power to make war against *1443*
13: 7 And he *was* g authority over every tribe, *1443*
13:14 the signs he *was* g power to do on behalf of *1443*
13:15 He *was* g power to give breath to the image *1443*
15: 2 They held harps g them by God *NIG*
16: 6 and *you have* g them blood to drink *1443*
16: 8 sun *was* g power to scorch people with fire. *1443*
18: 6 Give back to her as she *has* **g;** *625*
19: 8 bright and clean, *was* g her to wear." *1443*
20: 4 on which were seated *those* who *had been* g authority to judge. *1443*

GIVER (2) [GIVE]

Pr 18:16 for the g and ushers him into the presence 132S
2Co 9: 7 for God loves a cheerful **g.** *1522*

GIVES (139) [GIVE]

Ex 4:11 Who g him sight or makes him blind? NIH
13:11 the land of the Canaanites and g it to you, 5989
16: 8 that it was the LORD when *he* g you meat 5989
16:29 that is why on the sixth day he g you bread 5989
21: 4 If his master g him a wife 5989
21:22 and she g **birth prematurely** 3529+3655
22: 7 "If a man g his neighbor silver or goods 5989
22:10 "If a man g a donkey, an ox, 5989
Lev 12: 2 and g **birth** *to* a son will be ceremonially 3528
12: 5 If *she* g **birth** *to* a daughter, for two weeks 3528
12: 7 regulations for the *woman who* g **birth** to 3528
20: 2 or any alien living in Israel who g any 5989
20: 4 that man g one of his children to Molech 5989
Nu 5:10 but what he g to the priest will belong to 5989
10:32 whatever good things the LORD g us." 3512
22: 8 the answer the LORD g me." 1819
Dt 3:20 until the LORD g **rest** to your brothers 5663
4:40 the LORD your God g you for all time. 5989
7:16 the peoples the LORD your God g **over** 5989
8:18 for it is he who g you the ability 5989
12:15 to the blessing the LORD your God g you. 5989
16: 5 in any town the LORD your God g you 5989
17: 2 the LORD g you is found doing evil in 5989
19: 8 g you the whole land he promised them, 5989
20:14 the plunder the LORD your God g you 5989
22:14 and slanders her and g her a bad name, 3655
24: 1 g it to her and sends her from his house, 5989
24: 3 g it to her and sends her from his house, 5989
25:19 the LORD your God g you **rest** from all 5663
Jos 1:15 until the LORD g them **rest,** 5663
2:14 and faithfully when the LORD g us 5989
Jdg 11: 9 the Ammonites and the LORD g them 5989
11:24 not take what your god Chemosh g you? 3769
21:18 be *anyone who* g a wife to a Benjamite.' 5989
Ru 4:12 the LORD g you by this young woman, 5989
2Sa 22:51 *He* g his king **great** victories; 1540
24:23 O king, Araunah g all this to the king." 5989
1Ki 17:14 not run dry until the day the LORD g rain 5989
Ezr 9: 8 and so our God g **light** *to* our eyes and 239
Est 5:13 But all this g me no **satisfaction** as long 8750
Job 8:15 He leans on his web, but *it* g **way;** 4202+6641
32: 8 *that* g him **understanding.** 1067
33: 4 the breath of the Almighty g **me life.** 2649
35:10 *who* g songs in the night, 5989
36: 6 He does not keep the wicked alive but g 5989
38:29 Who g **birth** *to* the frost from the heavens 3528
Ps 7:14 with evil and conceives trouble g **birth** 3528
18:50 *He* g his king **great** victories; 1540
29:11 The LORD g strength to his people; 5989
68:35 the God of Israel g power and strength 5989
82: 1 *he* g **judgment** among the "gods": 9149
119:130 The unfolding of your words g **light;** 239
119:130 *it* g **understanding** *to* the simple. 1067
136:25 and *who* g food to every creature. 5989
144:10 to the *One who* g victory to kings, 5989
146: 7 of the oppressed and g food to the hungry. 5989
146: 8 the LORD g **sight** *to* the blind, 7219
Pr 2: 6 For the LORD g wisdom, 5989
3:34 He mocks proud mockers but g grace to 5989
5: 6 *She* g no **thought** *to* the way of life; 7143
11:24 *One man* g **freely,** yet gains even more; 7061
12:17 A truthful witness g honest testimony, 7032
14:15 but a prudent man g **thought** to his steps. 1067
14:30 A heart at peace g life to the body, NIH
15:30 and good news g **health** *to* the bones. 2014
16:20 *Whoever* g **heed** to instruction prospers, 8505
17: 8 A bribe is a charm to the **one who** g it; 1251
Pr 19: 6 everyone is the friend of a **man** *who g* gifts. AIT
19:11 A man's wisdom g him **patience;** 678+799
21:29 but an upright man g **thought** *to* his ways. 1067
22:16 to increase his wealth and *he who* g **gifts** to 5989
25:18 the man *who* g false testimony 6699
25:26 a polluted well is a righteous man *who* g **way** to the wicked. 4572
28:27 *He who* g to the poor will lack nothing, 5989
29: 4 By justice a king g a country **stability,** 6641
29:11 A fool g full **vent** to his anger, 3655
29:13 The LORD g **sight** *to* the eyes of both. 239
Ecc 2:26 God g wisdom, knowledge and happiness, 5989
2:26 but to the sinner *he* g the task of gathering 5989
5:19 God g any man wealth and possessions, 5989
6: 2 God g a man wealth, 5989
Isa 14: 3 the LORD g you **relief** from suffering 5663
21: 9 And *he* g **back** *the* **answer:** 6699
30:20 the Lord g you the bread of adversity and 5989
40:29 *He* g strength to the weary and increases 5989
42: 5 *who* g breath to its people, 5989
66: 7 "Before she goes into labor, *she* g **birth;** 3528
66: 8 in labor than *she* g **birth** *to* her children. 3528
Jer 5:24 who g autumn and spring rains in season, 5989
La 4: 4 but no *one* g it to them. 7298
Eze 18: 7 He does not commit robbery but g his food 5989
18:16 He does not commit robbery but g his food 5989
33:15 if he g **back** what he took in pledge for 8740
Da 2:21 *He* g wisdom to the wise and knowledge to 10314
4:17 and g them to anyone he wishes and sets 10498
4:25 of men and g them to anyone he wishes. 10498
4:32 of men and g them to anyone he wishes." 10498
Mic 5: 3 the time when she who is in labor g **birth** 3528
Hab 2:15 "Woe to *him who* g **drink** *to* his neighbors, 9197
Zec 10: 1 *He* g showers of rain to men, 5989
Mt 5:15 and *it* g **light** to everyone in the house. *3290*
10:42 g even a cup of cold **water to** *4540*
26:73 for your accent g you **away."** *1316+4472*
Mk 1:27 *He* even g **orders** to evil spirits *2199*
9:41 anyone who g you **a cup** of water *4539+4540*
Lk 4:36 With authority and power *he* g **orders** *2199*
Jn 1: 9 that g **light** to every man was coming into *5894*
3: 6 Flesh g **birth to** flesh, *1164*
3: 6 but the Spirit g **birth to** spirit. *1164*
3:34 for God g the Spirit without limit. *1443*
5:21 the Father raises the dead and g them **life,** *2443*
5:21 so the Son g **life** to whom he is pleased *2443*
6:32 but it is my Father who g you *1443*
6:33 down from heaven and g life to the world." *1443*
6:37 All that the Father g me will come to me, *1443*
6:63 Spirit g **life;** the flesh counts for *1639+2443*
14:27 I do not give to you as the world **g.** *1443*
Ac 17:25 *because he* himself g all men life *1443*
Ro 4:17 the God who g **life** to the dead *2443*
14: 6 eats to the Lord, for *he* g **thanks** to God; *2373*
14: 6 does so to the Lord and g **thanks** to God. *2373*
15: 5 *g* **endurance** and **encouragement** *AIT*
1Co 12:11 and *he* g them to each one, *1349*
15:38 But God g it a body as he has determined, *1443*
15:38 and to each kind of seed he g its own body. *NIG*
15:57 He g us the victory through our Lord *1443*
2Co 3: 6 for the letter kills, but the Spirit g **life.** *2443*
Php 4:13 through him who g me **strength.** *1904*
1Th 4: 8 God, who g you his Holy Spirit. *1443*
1Ti 6:13 God, who g **life to** everything, *2441*
Jas 1: 5 God, who g generously to all *1443*
1:15 desire has conceived, *it* g **birth to** sin; *5503*
1:15 when *it is* full-grown, g **birth to** death. *652*
1:25 that *g* **freedom,** and continues to do this, *AIT*
2:12 to be judged by the law that *g* **freedom,** *AIT*
4: 6 But *he* g us more grace. *1443*
4: 6 opposes the proud but g grace to the humble. *1443*
1Pe 5: 5 opposes the proud but g grace to the humble. *1443*
Rev 21:23 for the glory of God g it **light,** *5894*

GIVING (117) [GIVE]

Ge 13:17 for *I am* g it to you." 5989
20:16 *"I am* g your brother a thousand shekels 5989
30:18 for g my maidservant to my husband." 5989
38:28 As she *was* g **birth,** 3528
41:12 g each man *the* **interpretation** 7354
49:28 g each the **blessing** appropriate to him. 1385+1388
49:33 When Jacob had finished g **instructions** 7422
Ex 20:12 in the land the LORD your God *is* g you. 5989
Lev 14:34 which I *am* g you as your possession, 5989
20: 3 for *by* g his children to Molech, 5989
27: 2 to the LORD by g equivalent values, NIH
Nu 13: 2 which I *am* g to the Israelites. 5989
15: 2 you enter the land I *am* g you as a home 5989
18: 7 *I am* g you the service of the priesthood as 5989
Dt 1:20 which the LORD our God *is* g us. 5989
1:25 that the LORD our God *is* g us." 5989
2:29 into the land the LORD our God *is* g us." 5989
3:20 that the LORD your God *is* g them, 5989
4: 1 the God of your fathers, *is* g you. 5989
4:21 the LORD your God *is* g you 5989
4:40 which I *am* g you today, 7422
5:16 in the land the LORD your God *is* g you. 5989
5:31 in the land I *am* g them to possess." 5989
8: 1 to follow every command I *am* g you today, 7422
8:11 and his decrees that I *am* g you this day. 7422
9: 6 LORD your God *is* g you this good land 5989
10:13 that I *am* g you today for your own good? 7422
10:18 g him food and clothing. 5989
11: 8 the commands I *am* g you today, 7422
11:13 the commands I *am* g you today— 7422
11:17 from the good land the LORD *is* g you. 5989
Dt 11:22 observe all these commands I *am* g you 7422
11:27 the LORD your God that I *am* g you today; 7422
11:31 of the land the LORD your God *is* g you. 5989
12: 9 the LORD your God *is* g you. 5989
12:10 g you **as an inheritance,** 5706
12:28 to obey all these regulations I *am* g you, 7422
13:12 the towns the LORD your God *is* g you 5989
13:18 commands that I *am* g you today 7422
15: 4 in the land the LORD your God *is* g you 5989
15: 5 follow all these commands I *am* g you today 7422
15: 7 that the LORD your God *is* g you, 5989
16:10 *by* g a freewill offering in proportion to 5989
16:18 the LORD your God *is* g you, 5989
16:20 the land the LORD your God *is* g you. 5989
17:14 the land the LORD your God *is* g you 5989
18: 9 the land the LORD your God *is* g you, 5989
19: 1 the nations whose land he *is* g you, 5989
19: 2 the LORD your God *is* g you to possess. 5989
19: 3 g you **as an inheritance,** 5706
19:10 which the LORD your God *is* g you 5989
19:14 the LORD your God *is* g you to possess. 5989
19:18 g false **testimony** against his brother, 6699
20:16 the nations the LORD your God *is* g you 5989
21: 1 the LORD your God *is* g you to possess, 5989
21:17 as the firstborn by g him a double share 5989
21:23 the land the LORD your God *is* g you as 5989
24: 4 the land the LORD your God *is* g you as 5989
25:15 in the land the LORD your God *is* g you. 5989
25:19 in the land he *is* g you to possess as 5989
26: 1 the land the LORD your God *is* g you as 5989
26: 2 of the land the LORD your God *is* g you 5989
27: 2 the land the LORD your God *is* g you, 5989
27: 3 the land the LORD your God *is* g you, 5989
28: 8 in the land *he is* g you. 5989
28:15 and decrees I *am* g you today, 7422
28:52 the land the LORD your God *is* g you. 5989
30: 8 follow all his commands I *am* g you today. 7422
32:49 the land I *am* g the Israelites 5989
32:52 the land I *am* g to the people of Israel." 5989
Jos 1:11 of the land the LORD your God *is* g you 5989
1:13 'The LORD your God *is* g you **rest** 5663
1:15 that the LORD your God *is* g them. 5989
3: 3 g **orders** *to* the people: 7422
Jdg 2:23 he did not drive them out at once *by* g them 5989
1Sa 22:13 g him bread and a sword and inquiring 5989
2Sa 11:19 "When you have finished g 1819
18: 5 And all the troops heard the king g **orders** 7422
24:12 I am g you three options. 5747
1Ch 21:10 I *am* g you three options. 5742
Ezr 9: 8 and g us a firm place in his sanctuary, 5989
Ne 4:10 "The strength of the laborers *is* g **out,** 4173
8: 8 making it clear and g the meaning so that 8492
Est 2:22 g **credit** to Mordecai. 928+9005
3: 1 and g him a seat of honor higher than that 8492
9:19 a day for g presents to each other. 5447
9:22 of feasting and joy and g presents of food 5447
Ps 19: 8 g **joy** *to* the heart. 8523
19: 8 g **light** *to* the eyes. 239
100: T A psalm. For g **thanks.** 9343
106: 5 and join your inheritance in g **praise.** 2146
111: 6 g them the lands of other nations. 5989
Pr 1: 4 for g prudence to the simple, knowledge 5989
15:23 A man finds joy in g **an apt reply—** 5101+7023
26: 8 a stone in a sling is the g *of* honor to a fool. 5989
Eze 3: 3 eat this scroll I *am* g you 5989
11: 2 and g wicked **advice** in this city. 3619+6783
16:54 of all you have done in g them **comfort.** 5714
Da 4:21 *g* **shelter** to the beasts of the field, AIT
6:10 g **thanks** to his God, 10312
9:13 by turning from our sins and g **attention** 8505
Mt 6: 4 so that your g may be in secret. *1797*
24:38 marrying and g **in marriage,** *1139*
Jn 16:21 A woman g **birth to a child** has pain *5503*
Ac 1: 2 *after* g **instructions** through the Holy Spirit *1948*
8: 1 Saul was there, g **approval** to his death. *5306*
14:17 He has shown kindness *by* g you rain *1443*
15: 8 that he accepted them *by* g the Holy Spirit *1443*
22:20 I stood there g my **approval** and guarding *5306*
1Co 14:17 You *may be* g **thanks** well enough, *2373*
2Co 5:12 *are* g you an opportunity to take pride in us, *1443*
8: 7 see that you also excel in this grace of **g.** *NIG*
Eph 1:16 I have not stopped g **thanks** for you, *2373*
5:20 always g **thanks** to God the Father *2373*
Php 4:15 with me in the matter *of* g and receiving, *1521*
Col 1:12 g **thanks** to the Father, *2373*
3:17 g **thanks** to God the Father through him. *2373*

GIZONITE (1)

1Ch 11:34 the sons of Hashem the **G,** 1604

GLAD (77) [GLADDENS, GLADLY, GLADNESS]

Ex 4:14 and his heart *will be* g when he sees you. 8523
Jos 22:33 They *were* g to hear the report 928+3512+6524
Jdg 8:25 answered, *"We'll be* **g to give** them." 5989+5989
18:20 Then the priest *was* **g.** 3512+4213
1Sa 19: 5 and you saw it and *were* **g.** 8523
2Sa 1:20 lest the daughters of the Philistines *be* **g,** 8523
1Ki 8:66 joyful and g *in* heart for all the good things 3202
1Ch 16:31 Let the heavens rejoice, *let* the earth *be* **g;** 1635
2Ch 7:10 joyful and g *in* heart for the good things 3202
Ps 5:11 But *let* all who take refuge in you *be* **g;** 8523
9: 2 *I will be* g and rejoice in you; 8523
14: 7 let Jacob rejoice and Israel *be* **g!** 8523
16: 9 Therefore my heart *is* g 8523

Ps 21: 6 and made him g with the joy 2525
31: 7 I will be g and rejoice in your love, 1635
32:11 Rejoice in the LORD and be g, 1635
40:16 But may all who seek you rejoice and be g 8523
45: 8 the music of the strings makes you g. 8523
46: 4 There is a river whose streams make g 8523
48:11 of Judah are g because of your judgments. 1635
53: 6 let Jacob rejoice and Israel be g! 8523
58:10 be g when they are avenged, 8523
67: 4 May the nations be g and sing for joy, 8523
68: 3 the righteous be g and rejoice before God; 8523
69:32 The poor will see and be g— 8523
70: 4 But may all who seek you rejoice and be g 8523
90:14 we may sing for joy and be g all our days. 8523
90:15 Make us g for as many days 8523
92: 4 you make me g by your deeds, O LORD; 8523
96:11 Let the heavens rejoice, let the earth be g; 1635
97: 1 The LORD reigns, let the earth be g; 8523
97: 8 and rejoices and the villages of Judah are g 1635
105:38 Egypt was g when they left, 8523
107:30 They were g when it grew calm, 8523
118:24 let us rejoice and be g in it. 8523
149: 2 let the people of Zion be g in their King. 1635
Pr 23:15 then my heart will be g; 8523
23:25 May your father and mother be g; 8523
29: 6 but a righteous one can sing and be g. 8523
Ecc 8:15 the sun than to eat and drink and be g. 8523
Isa 25: 9 let us rejoice and be g in his salvation." 8523
35: 1 desert and the parched land will be g; 8464
65:18 But be g and rejoice forever 8464
66:10 "Rejoice with Jerusalem and be g for her, 1635
Jer 20:15 who made him very g, saying, 8523+8523
31:13 Then maidens will dance and be g, 8523
41:13 with him, they were g. 8523
50:11 "Because you rejoice and are g, 6600
La 4:21 Rejoice and be g, O Daughter of Edom, 8523
Joel 2:21 Be not afraid, O land; be g and rejoice. 1635
2:23 Be g, O people of Zion, 1635
Hab 1:15 and so he rejoices and is g. 1635
Zep 3:14 Be g and rejoice with all your heart, 8523
Zec 2:10 "Shout and be g, O Daughter of Zion. 8523
8:19 and g occasions and happy festivals 8525
10: 7 and their hearts will be g as with wine. 8523
Mt 5:12 Rejoice and be g, because great is your 22
Lk 15:32 But we had to celebrate and be g, 5897
Jn 4:36 the sower and the reaper may be g together. 5897
8:56 he saw it and was g." 5897
11:15 and for your sake I am g I was not there, 5897
14:28 you would be g that I am going to 5897
Ac 2:26 my heart is g and my tongue rejoices; 2370
2:46 and ate together with g and sincere hearts, 21
11:23 he was g and encouraged them all 5897
13:48 they were g and honored the word of 5897
15: 3 This news made all the brothers very g. 5915
15:31 and were g for its encouraging message. 5897
1Co 16:17 I was g when Stephanas, 5897
2Co 2: 2 who is left to make me g but you 2370
7:16 I am g I can have complete confidence 5897
13: 9 We are g whenever we are weak 5897
Gal 4:27 For it is written: "Be g, O barren woman, 2370
Php 2:17 I am g and rejoice with all of you. 5897
2:18 you too should be g and rejoice with me. 5897
2:28 that when you see him again you may be g 5897
Rev 19: 7 and be g and give him glory! 22

GLADDENS (1) [GLAD]

Ps 104:15 wine that g the heart of man, 8523

GLADLY (11) [GLAD]

Dt 28:47 and g in the time of prosperity, 928+3206+4222
Jdg 19: 3 he g welcomed him. 8523
2Ch 24:10 the people brought their contributions g, 8523
Isa 39: 2 Hezekiah received the envoys g 6584+8523
64: 5 to the help of those who g do right, 8464
Jer 3:19 " 'How g would I treat you like sons 375
Lk 19: 6 he came down at once and welcomed him g. 5897
Ac 24:10 so I g make my defense. 2315
2Co 11:19 You g put up with fools since you are 2452
12: 9 Therefore I will boast all the more g 2452
12:15 So I will very g spend for you everything 2452

GLADNESS (23) [GLAD]

2Ch 29:30 sang praises with g and bowed their heads 8525
Est 8:16 a time of happiness and joy, g and honor. 8607
8:17 there was joy and g among the Jews, 8607
Job 3:22 who are filled with g and rejoice 448+1637+8524
Ps 35:27 in my vindication shout for joy and g; 8523
45:15 They are led in with joy and g; 1637
51: 8 Let me hear joy and g; 8525
65:12 the hills are clothed with g. 1637
100: 2 Worship the LORD with g; 8525
Ecc 5:20 God keeps him occupied with g of heart. 8525
9: 7 Go, eat your food with g, 8525
Isa 16:10 and g are taken away from the orchards; 1637
35:10 G and joy will overtake them, 8607
51: 3 Joy and g will be found in her, 8525
51:11 G and joy will overtake them, 8607
61: 3 the oil of g instead of mourning, 8607
Jer 7:34 to the sounds of joy and g and to the voices 8525
16: 9 to the sounds of joy and g and to the voices 8525
25:10 from them the sounds of joy and g, 8525
31:13 I will turn their mourning into g; 8607
33:11 the sounds of joy and g, the voices of bride 8525
48:33 and g are gone from the orchards and fields 1637
Joel 1:16 joy and g from the house of our God? 1637

GLANCE (2) [GLANCES, GLANCING]

Pr 23: 5 Cast but a g at riches, and they are gone, 6524
SS 4: 9 you have stolen my heart with one g NIH

GLANCES (1) [GLANCE]

Pr 30:13 whose g are so disdainful; 6757

GLANCING (1) [GLANCE]

Ex 2:12 G this way and that and seeing no one, 7155

GLASS (4)

Rev 4: 6 was what looked like a sea of g, 5612
15: 2 like a sea of g mixed with fire and, 5612
21:18 and the city of pure gold, as pure as g. 5613
21:21 of pure gold, like transparent g. 5613

GLASSES (KJV) See MIRROR

GLAZE (1)

Pr 26:23 of g over earthenware are fervent lips with 6213

GLEAM (2) [GLEAMED, GLEAMING]

Pr 4:18 The path of the righteous is like the first g 240
Da 10: 6 and legs like the g of burnished bronze, 6524

GLEAMED (2) [GLEAM]

Eze 1: 7 their feet were like those of a calf and g 5913
Lk 24: 4 two men in clothes that g like lightning 848

GLEAMING (1) [GLEAM]

Job 20:25 the g point out of his liver. 1398

GLEAN (8) [GLEANED, GLEANING, GLEANINGS, GLEANS]

Ru 2: 3 So she went out and began to g in the fields 4377
2: 7 'Please let me g and gather among 4377
2: 8 and g in another field and don't go away 4377
2:15 As she got up to g, 4377
2:19 "Where did you g today? 4377
2:23 to the servant girls of Boaz to g until 4377
Job 24: 6 They gather fodder in the fields and g in 4380
Jer 6: 9 g the remnant of Israel as thoroughly 6618+6618

GLEANED (1) [GLEAN]

Ru 2:17 So Ruth g in the field until evening. 4377

GLEANING (1) [GLEAN]

Mic 7: 1 like one who gathers summer fruit at the g 6622

GLEANINGS (5) [GLEAN]

Lev 19: 9 the very edges of your field or gather the g 4378
23:22 the very edges of your field or gather the g 4378
Jdg 8: 2 g of Ephraim's grapes are better than 6622
Isa 17: 6 Yet some g will remain, 6622
24:13 or as when g are left after the grape harvest. 6622

GLEANS (1) [GLEAN]

Isa 17: 5 as when a man g heads of grain in the 4377

GLEE (2)

Ps 35:15 But when I stumbled, they gathered in g; 8523
Eze 36: 5 and against all Edom, for with g and 8525

GLIDE (1) [GLIDED, GLIDING]

Dt 32:24 the venom of vipers that g in the dust. 2323

GLIDED (1) [GLIDE]

Job 4:15 A spirit g past my face, 2736

GLIDING (2) [GLIDE]

Job 26:13 his hand pierced the g serpent. 1371
Isa 27: 1 Leviathan the g serpent, 1371

GLIMPSE (2)

Job 9:25 they fly away without a g of joy. 8011
23: 9 he turns to the south, I catch no g of him. 8011

GLINT (1)

Hab 3:11 and moon stood still in the heavens at the g 240

GLISTENING (1)

Job 41:32 Behind him he leaves a g wake; 239

GLITTERING (3)

Na 3: 3 flashing swords and g spears! 1398
Rev 17: 4 and was g with gold, 5998
18:16 purple and scarlet, and g with gold, 5998

GLOAT (12) [GLOATED, GLOATING, GLOATS]

Ps 22:17 people stare and g over me. 8011
30: 1 of the depths and did not let my enemies g 8523
35:19 not those g over me who are my enemies 8523
35:24 do not let them g over me. 8523
35:26 May all who g over my distress be put 8524
38:16 not let them g or exalt themselves over me 8523
59:10 God will go before me and will let me g 8011
Pr 24:17 Do not g when your enemy falls; 8523
La 2:17 he has let the enemy g over you, 8523
Mic 4:11 let our eyes g over Zion!" 2600
7: 8 Do not g over me, my enemy! 8523
Rev 11:10 The inhabitants of the earth will g 5897

GLOATED (1) [GLOAT]

Job 31:29 or g over the trouble that came to him— 6424

GLOATING (1) [GLOAT]

Hab 3:14 g as though about to devour 6617

GLOATS (1) [GLOAT]

Pr 17: 5 whoever g over disaster will 8523

GLOOM (13) [GLOOMY]

Job 10:21 to the land of g and deep shadow, 3125
Ps 107:10 Some sat in darkness and the deepest g, 7516
107:14 the deepest g and broke away their chains. 7516
Isa 8:22 and darkness and fearful g, 5066
9: 1 there will be no more g for those who were 4599
24:11 all joy turns to g, 6845
29:18 and out of g and darkness the eyes of 694
Jer 13:16 to thick darkness and change it to deep g. 6906
Eze 31:15 clothed Lebanon with g, 7722
Joel 2: 2 a day of darkness and g, 696
Zep 1:15 a day of darkness and g, 696
Heb 12:18 to darkness, g and storm; 2432
Jas 4: 9 to mourning and your joy to g. 2993

GLOOMY (1) [GLOOM]

2Pe 2: 4 into g dungeons to be held for judgment; 2432

GLORIES (1) [GLORY]

1Pe 1:11 of Christ and the g that would follow. 1518

GLORIFIED (17) [GLORY]

Isa 66: 5 have said, 'Let the LORD be g, 3877
Eze 39:13 and the day I am g will be a memorable day 3877
Da 4:34 I honored and g him who lives forever. 10198
Jn 7:39 since Jesus had not yet been g. 1519
11: 4 for God's glory so that God's Son may be g 1519
12:16 Only after Jesus was g did they realize 1519
12:23 for the Son of Man to be g. 1519
12:28 a voice came from heaven, "I have g it, 1519
13:31 the Son of Man g and God is glorified 1519
13:31 the Son of Man glorified and God is g 1519
13:32 If God is g in him, 1519
Ac 3:13 has g his servant Jesus. 1519
Ro 1:21 they neither g him as God nor gave thanks 1519
8:30 those he justified, he also g. 1519
2Th 1:10 be g in his holy people and to be marveled 1901
1:12 so that the name of our Lord Jesus may be g 1901
1Pe 1:21 raised him from the dead and g him, 1443+1518

GLORIFIES (2) [GLORY]

Lk 1:46 And Mary said: "My soul g the Lord 3486
Jn 8:54 your God, is the one who g me. 1519

GLORIFY (19) [GLORY]

Ps 34: 3 G the LORD with me; 1540
63: 3 my lips will g you. 8655
69:30 I will praise God's name in song and g him 1540
86:12 I will g your name forever. 3877
Isa 60:13 and I will g the place of my feet. 3877
Da 4:37 praise and exalt and g the King of heaven, 10198
Jn 8:54 Jesus replied, "If I g myself, my glory 1519
12:28 Father, g your name!" 1519
12:28 "I have glorified it, and will g it again." 1519
13:32 God will g the Son in himself, 1519
13:32 and will g him at once. 1519
17: 1 G your Son, that your Son may glorify you. 1519
17: 1 Glorify your Son, that your Son may g you. 1519
17: 5 g me in your presence with the glory I had 1519
21:19 of death by which Peter would g God. 1519
Ro 15: 6 so that with one heart and mouth you may g 1519
15: 9 that the Gentiles may g God for his mercy, 1519
1Pe 2:12 they may see your good deeds and g God on 1519
Rev 16: 9 but they refused to repent and g him. 1443+1518

GLORIFYING (1) [GLORY]

Lk 2:20 g and praising God for all the things 1519

GLORIOUS (50) [GLORY]

Dt 28:58 do not revere this g and awesome name— 3877
33:29 and helper and your g sword. 1452
1Ch 29:13 and praise your g name. 9514
Ne 9: 5 "Blessed be your g name, 3883
Ps 16: 3 the g ones in whom is all my delight. 129
45:13 All g is the princess within [her chamber]; 3884
66: 2 make his praise g! 3883
72:19 Praise be to his g name forever; 3883
87: 3 G things are said of you, O city of God: 3877
111: 3 G and majestic are his deeds, 2086
145: 5 of the g splendor of your majesty, 3883

Ps 145:12 of your mighty acts and the **g** splendor 3883
Isa 3: 8 defying his **g** presence. 3883
4: 2 of the LORD will be beautiful and **g**, 3883
11:10 and his place of rest will be **g**. 3883
12: 5 for he has done **g things;** 1455
28: 1 to the fading flower, his **g** beauty, 9514
28: 4 That fading flower, his **g** beauty, 9514
28: 5 the LORD Almighty will be a **g** crown, 9514
42:21 to make his law great and **g**. 158
60: 7 and I will adorn my **g** temple. 9514
63:12 who sent his **g** arm of power to be 9514
63:14 to make for yourself a **g** name. 9514
63:15 and see from your lofty throne, holy and **g**. 9514
64:11 Our holy and **g** temple, 9514
Jer 13:18 your **g** crowns will fall from your heads." 9514
14:21 do not dishonor your **g** throne. 3883
17:12 A **g** throne, exalted from the beginning, 3883
48:17 how broken the **g** staff!' 9514
Mt 19:28 when the Son of Man sits on his **g** throne, *1518*
Lk 9:31 appeared in **g splendor**, *1518*
Ac 2:20 before the coming of the great and **g** day of *2212*
Ro 8:21 to decay and brought into the **g** freedom of *1518*
2Co 3: 8 ministry of the Spirit be even more **g**? *1518+1877*
3: 9 If the ministry that condemns men is **g**, *1518*
3: 9 how much more **g** is the ministry that *1518*
3:10 For what *was* **g** has no glory now *1519*
Eph 1: 6 to the praise *of* his **g** grace, *1518*
1:17 of our Lord Jesus Christ, the **g** Father, *1518*
1:18 the riches *of* his **g** inheritance in the saints, *1518*
3:16 of his **g** riches he may strengthen you *1518*
Php 3:21 so that they will be like his **g** body. *1518*
4:19 according to his **g** riches in Christ Jesus. *1518*
Col 1:11 with all power according to his **g** might so *1518*
1:27 the Gentiles the **g** riches of this mystery, *1518*
1Ti 1:11 to the **g** gospel of the blessed God, *1518*
Tit 2:13 the **g** appearing of our great God *1518*
Jas 2: 1 as believers *in* our **g** Lord Jesus Christ, *1518*
1Pe 1: 8 with an inexpressible and **g** joy, *1519*
Jude 1:24 and to present you before his **g presence** *1518*

GLORIOUSLY (1) [GLORY]

Isa 24:23 and before its elders, **g**. 3883

GLORY (295) [GLORIES, GLORIFIED, GLORIFIES, GLORIFY, GLORIFYING, GLORIOUS, GLORIOUSLY]

Ex 14: 4 *I will* **gain g for myself** through Pharaoh 3877
14:17 And *I will* **gain g** through Pharaoh 3877
14:18 the LORD when I **gain g** through Pharaoh, 3877
15:11 majestic in holiness, awesome in **g**, 9335
16: 7 the morning you will see the **g** *of* the LORD 3883
16:10 the **g** *of* the LORD appearing in the cloud. 3883
24:16 **g** *of* the LORD settled on Mount Sinai. 3883
24:17 the Israelites the **g** *of* the LORD looked 3883
29:43 and the place will be consecrated by my **g**. 3883
33:18 Then Moses said, "Now show me your **g**." 3883
33:22 When my **g** passes by, 3883
40:34 the **g** *of* the LORD filled the tabernacle. 3883
40:35 the **g** *of* the LORD filled the tabernacle. 3883
Lev 9: 6 the **g** *of* the LORD may appear to you." 3883
9:23 **g** *of* the LORD appeared to all the people. 3883
Nu 14:10 the **g** *of* the LORD appeared at the Tent 3883
14:21 as I live and as surely as the **g** *of* the LORD 3883
14:22 not one of the men who saw my **g** and 3883
16:19 the **g** *of* the LORD appeared to 3883
16:42 the cloud covered it and the **g** *of* the LORD 3883
20: 6 and the **g** *of* the LORD appeared to them. 3883
Dt 5:24 "The LORD our God has shown us his **g** 3883
Jos 7:19 give **g** to the LORD, the God of Israel, 3883
1Sa 4:21 saying, "The **g** has departed from Israel"— 3883
4:22 She said, "The **g** has departed from Israel, 3883
15:29 He who is the **G** *of* Israel does not lie 5905
2Sa 1:19 "Your **g**, O Israel, lies slain 7382
1Ki 8:11 for the **g** *of* the LORD filled his temple. 3883
2Ki 14:10 **G** in your victory, but stay at home! 3877
1Ch 16:10 **G** in his holy name; 2146
16:24 Declare his **g** among the nations, 3883
16:28 ascribe to the LORD **g** and strength, 3883
16:29 ascribe to the LORD the **g** *due* his name. 3883
16:35 that we *may* **g** in your praise." 8655
29:11 and the **g** and the majesty and the splendor, 9514
2Ch 5:14 **g** *of* the LORD filled the temple of God. 3883
7: 1 and the **g** *of* the LORD filled the temple. 3883
7: 2 of the LORD because the **g** *of* the LORD 3883
7: 3 and the **g** *of* the LORD above the temple, 3883
Est 1: 4 of his kingdom and the splendor and **g** 9514
Job 29:20 My **g** will remain fresh in me, 3883
40:10 Then adorn yourself with **g** and splendor, 1454
Ps 3: 3 you bestow **g** *on* me and lift up my head. 3883
4: 2 O men, will you turn my **g** into shame? 3883
8: 1 You have set your **g** above the heavens. 2086
8: 5 and crowned him with **g** and honor. 3883
19: 1 The heavens declare the **g** *of* God; 3883
21: 5 the victories you gave, his **g** is great; 3883
24: 7 that the King of **g** may come in. 3883
24: 8 Who is this King of **g**? 3883
24: 9 that the King of **g** may come in. 3883
24:10 Who is he, this King of **g**? 3883
24:10 LORD Almighty—he is the King of **g**. 3883
26: 8 O LORD, the place where your **g** dwells. 3883
29: 1 ascribe to the LORD **g** and strength. 3883
29: 2 Ascribe to the LORD the **g** *due* his name; 3883
29: 3 the God of **g** thunders, 3883
29: 9 And in his temple all cry, "**G**!" 3883
57: 5 let your **g** be over all the earth. 3883
Ps 57:11 let your **g** be over all the earth. 3883
63: 2 and beheld your power and your **g**. 3883
66: 2 Sing the **g** *of* his name; 3883
72:19 may the whole earth be filled with his **g**. 3883
73:24 and afterward you will take me into **g**. 3883
79: 9 O God our Savior, for the **g** *of* your name; 3883
85: 9 that his **g** may dwell in our land. 3883
86: 9 *they will* **bring g** to your name. 3877
89:17 For you are their **g** and strength, 9514
96: 3 Declare his **g** among the nations, 3883
96: 6 strength and **g** are in his sanctuary. 9514
96: 7 ascribe to the LORD **g** and strength. 3883
96: 8 Ascribe to the LORD the **g** *due* his name; 3883
97: 6 and all the peoples see his **g**. 3883
102:15 all the kings of the earth will revere your **g**. 3883
102:16 and appear in his **g**. 3883
104:31 May the **g** *of* the LORD endure forever; 3883
105: 3 **G** in his holy name; 2146
106:20 They exchanged their **G** for an image of 3883
106:47 to your holy name and **g** in your praise. 8655
108: 5 and let your **g** be over all the earth. 3883
113: 4 his **g** above the heavens. 3883
115: 1 not to us but to your name be the **g**, 3883
138: 5 for the **g** *of* the LORD is great. 3883
145:11 They will tell of the **g** *of* your kingdom 3883
149: 9 This is the **g** of all his saints. 2077
Pr 14:28 A large population is a king's **g**, 2079
19:11 it is to his **g** to overlook an offense. 9514
20:29 The **g** *of* young men is their strength, 9514
25: 2 It is the **g** *of* God to conceal a matter; 3883
25: 2 to search out a matter is the **g** *of* kings. 3883
Isa 4: 2 be the pride and **g** of the survivors in Israel. 9514
4: 5 over all the **g** will be a canopy. 3883
6: 3 the whole earth is full of his **g**." 3883
13:19 the **g** *of* the Babylonians' pride, 9514
17: 3 the remnant of Aram will be like the **g** *of* 3883
17: 4 "In that day the **g** of Jacob will fade; 3883
22:24 All the **g** *of* his family will hang on him: 3883
23: 9 to bring low the pride of all **g** and 7382
24:15 Therefore in the east **give g** *to* the LORD; 3877
24:16 "**G** to the Righteous One." 7382
26:15 **gained g for yourself;** 3877
35: 2 The **g** *of* Lebanon will be given to it, 3883
35: 2 they will see the **g** *of* the LORD, 3883
40: 5 And the **g** *of* the LORD will be revealed, 3883
40: 6 all their **g** is like the flowers of the field. 2876
41:16 the LORD and **g** in the Holy One of Israel. 2146
42: 8 I will not give my **g** to another or my praise 3883
42:12 Let them give **g** to the LORD 3883
43: 7 whom I created for my **g**, 3883
44:13 of man in all his **g**, 9514
44:23 *he* **displays** *his* **g** in Israel. 6995
48:11 I will not yield my **g** to another. 3883
58: 8 **g** *of* the LORD will be your rear guard. 3883
59:19 they will revere his **g**. 3883
60: 1 and the **g** *of* the LORD rises upon you. 3883
60: 2 upon you and his **g** appears over you. 3883
60:13 "The **g** *of* Lebanon will come to you, 3883
60:19 and your God will be your **g**. 9514
62: 2 and all kings your **g**; 3883
66:18 and they will come and see my **g**. 3883
66:19 not heard of my fame or seen my **g**. 3883
66:19 They will proclaim my **g** among 3883
Jer 2:11 But my people have exchanged their **G** 3883
4: 2 be blessed by him and in him *they will* **g**." 2146
13:16 Give **g** to the LORD your God 3883
48:18 from your **g** and sit on the parched ground, 3883
Eze 1:28 the appearance of the likeness of the **g** *of* the LORD. 3883
3:12 May the **g** *of* the LORD be praised 3883
3:23 the **g** *of* the LORD was standing there, 3883
3:23 like the **g** I had seen by the Kebar River, 3883
8: 4 And there before me was the **g** *of* the God 3883
9: 3 Now the **g** *of* the God of Israel went up 3883
10: 4 Then the **g** *of* the LORD rose from above 3883
10: 4 the court was full of the radiance of the **g** 3883
10:18 Then the **g** *of* the LORD departed from 3883
10:19 the **g** *of* the God of Israel was above them. 3883
11:22 the **g** *of* the God of Israel was above them. 3883
11:23 The **g** *of* the LORD went up from within 3883
24:25 their joy and **g**, the delight of their eyes, 9514
25: 9 the **g** *of* that land. 7382
28:22 O Sidon, and *I will* **gain g** within you. 3877
39:21 "I will display my **g** among the nations, 3883
43: 2 the **g** *of* the God of Israel coming from 3883
43: 2 and the land was radiant with his **g**. 3883
43: 4 The **g** *of* the LORD entered the temple 3883
43: 5 and the **g** *of* the LORD filled the temple. 3883
44: 4 the **g** *of* the LORD filling the temple of 3883
Da 2:37 and power and might and **g**; 10331
4:30 by my mighty power and for the **g** 10331
4:36 and splendor were returned to me for the **g** 10331
5:18 and greatness and **g** and splendor. 10331
5:20 from his royal throne and stripped of his **g**. 10331
7:14 **g** and sovereign power; 10331
Hos 4: 7 they exchanged their **G** for something 3883
9:11 Ephraim's **g** will fly away like a bird— 3883
Mic 1:15 the **g** *of* Israel will come to Adullam. 3883
Hab 2:14 with the knowledge of the **g** *of* the LORD, 3883
2:16 You will be filled with shame instead of **g**. 3883
2:16 and disgrace will cover your **g**. 3883
3: 3 His **g** covered the heavens 2086
Hag 2: 3 saw this house in its former **g**? 3883
2: 7 and I will fill this house with **g**,' 3883
2: 9 'The **g** *of* this present house will 3883
2: 9 be greater than the **g** of the former house,' NIH
Zec 2: 5 'and I will be its **g** within.' 3883
Mt 16:27 of Man is going to come in his Father's **g** *1518*
24:30 clouds of the sky, with power and great **g**. *1518*
25:31 "When the Son of Man comes in his **g**, *1518*
25:31 he will sit on his throne in heavenly **g**. *1518*
Mk 8:38 of him when he comes in his Father's **g** *1518*
10:37 and the other at your left in your **g**." *1518*
13:26 in clouds with great power and **g**. *1518*
Lk 2: 9 and the **g** of the Lord shone around them, *1518*
2:14 "**G** to God in the highest, *1518*
2:32 for revelation to the Gentiles and for **g** *1518*
9:26 be ashamed of him when he comes in his **g** *1518*
9:26 when he comes in his glory and in the **g** of *NIG*
9:32 they saw his **g** and the two men standing *1518*
19:38 "Peace in heaven and **g** in the highest!" *1518*
21:27 in a cloud with power and great **g**. *1518*
24:26 to suffer these things and then enter his **g**?" *1518*
Jn 1:14 We have seen his **g**, *1518*
1:14 the **g** of the One and Only, *1518*
2:11 He thus revealed his **g**, *1518*
8:50 I am not seeking **g** for myself; *1518*
8:54 "If I glorify myself, my **g** means nothing. *1518*
9:24 "Give **g** to God," they said. *1518*
11: 4 it is for God's **g** so that God's Son may *1518*
11:40 you would see the **g** of God?" *1518*
12:41 Isaiah said this because he saw Jesus' **g** *1518*
14:13 so that the Son *may* **bring g to** the Father. *1519*
15: 8 This *is to* my Father's **g**, *1519*
16:14 He *will* **bring g to** me by taking *1519*
17: 4 I *have* **brought** you **g** on earth *1519*
17: 5 in your presence *with* the **g** I had with you *1518*
17:10 And **g** *has* **come to** *me* through them. *1519*
17:22 I have given them the **g** that you gave me, *1518*
17:24 to see my **g**, the glory you have given me *1518*
17:24 **the g** you have given me *4005S*
Ac 7: 2 God *of* **g** appeared to our father Abraham *1518*
7:55 looked up to heaven and saw the **g** of God, *1518*
Ro 1:23 the **g** of the immortal God for images made *1518*
2: 7 by persistence in doing good seek **g**, *1518*
2:10 but **g**, honor and peace *1518*
3: 7 and so increases his **g**, *1518*
3:23 for all have sinned and fall short *of* the **g** *1518*
4:20 in his faith and gave **g** to God, *1518*
5: 2 we rejoice in the hope *of* the **g** of God. *1518*
6: 4 from the dead through the **g** of the Father, *1518*
8:17 in order that *we may* also **share in** his **g**. *5280*
8:18 not worth comparing with the **g** that will *1518*
9: 4 theirs the divine **g**, the covenants, *1518*
9:23 *of* his **g** known to the objects of his mercy, *1518*
9:23 whom he prepared in advance for **g**— *1518*
11:36 To him be the **g** forever! *1518*
15:17 *I* **g** in Christ Jesus **in** my service to *2400+3018*
16:27 be **g** forever through Jesus Christ! *1518*
1Co 2: 7 and that God destined for our **g** *1518*
2: 8 not have crucified the Lord *of* **g**. *1518*
10:31 do it all for the **g** of God. *1518*
11: 7 since he is the image and **g** of God; *1518*
11: 7 but the woman is the **g** of man. *1518*
11:15 if a woman has long hair, it is her **g**? *1518*
15:31 *I* **g over** you in Christ Jesus our Lord. *2400+3018*
15:43 it is sown in dishonor, it is raised in **g**; *1518*
2Co 1:20 the "Amen" is spoken by us to the **g** *1518*
3: 7 came with **g**, so that the Israelites could *1518*
3: 7 at the face of Moses because of its **g**, *1518*
3:10 For what was glorious *has* no **g** *now* *1519*
3:10 now in comparison with the surpassing **g**. *1518*
3:11 And if what was fading away came with **g**, *1518*
3:11 much greater is the **g** of that which lasts! *1518*
3:18 with unveiled faces all reflect the Lord's **g**, *1518*
3:18 **with ever-increasing g**, *608+1518+1518+1650*
4: 4 the light of the gospel *of* the **g** of Christ, *1518*
4: 6 the light of the knowledge *of* the **g** of God *1518*
4:15 to overflow to the **g** of God. *1518*
4:17 an eternal **g** that far outweighs them all. *1518*
6: 8 **g** and dishonor, bad report and good report; *1518*
Gal 1: 5 to whom be **g** for ever and ever. Amen. *1518*
Eph 1:12 might be for the praise *of* his **g**. *1518*
1:14 to the praise *of* his **g**. *1518*
3:13 my sufferings for you, which are your **g**. *1518*
3:21 be **g** in the church and in Christ Jesus *1518*
Php 1:11 to the **g** and praise of God. *1518*
2:11 to the **g** of God the Father. *1518*
3: 3 who **g** in Christ Jesus, *3016*
3:19 and their **g** is in their shame. *1518*
4:20 To our God and Father be **g** for ever *1518*
Col 1:27 which is Christ in you, the hope *of* **g**. *1518*
3: 4 then you also will appear with him in **g**. *1518*
1Th 2:12 who calls you into his kingdom and **g**. *1518*
2:19 or the crown in which we will **g** in *3018*
2:20 Indeed, you are our **g** and joy. *1518*
2Th 2:14 *in* the **g** of our Lord Jesus Christ. *1518*
1Ti 1:17 be honor and **g** for ever and ever. *1518*
3:16 believed on in the world, was taken up in **g**. *1518*
2Ti 2:10 that is in Christ Jesus, with eternal **g**. *1518*
4:18 To him be **g** for ever and ever. *1518*
Heb 1: 3 of God's **g** and the exact representation *1518*
2: 7 you crowned him *with* **g** and honor *1518*
2: 9 now crowned *with* **g** and honor *1518*
2:10 In bringing many sons to **g**, *1518*
5: 5 Christ also *did* not **take** upon himself the **g** *1519*
9: 5 Above the ark were the cherubim *of* the **G**, *1518*
13:21 to whom be **g** for ever and ever. *1518*
1Pe 1: 7 **g** and honor when Jesus Christ is revealed. *1518*
1:24 all their **g** is like the flowers of the field; *1518*
4:11 be the **g** and the power for ever and ever. *1518*
4:13 be overjoyed when his **g** is revealed. *1518*
4:14 for the Spirit *of* **g** and of God rests on you. *1518*
5: 1 and one who also will share *in* the **g** to *1518*

1Pe 5: 4 the crown *of* g that will never fade away. 1518
5:10 who called you to his eternal g in Christ, 1518
2Pe 1: 3 of him who called us *by* his own g 1518
1:17 For he received honor and g from God 1518
1:17 the voice came to him from the Majestic G, 1518
3:18 To him be g both now and forever! 1518
Jude 1:25 to the only God our Savior be g, 1518
Rev 1: 6 to him be g and power for ever and ever! 1518
4: 9 Whenever the living creatures give g, 1518
4:11 to receive g and honor and power, 1518
5:12 and wisdom and strength and honor and g 1518
5:13 and to the Lamb be praise and honor and g 1518
7:12 and g and wisdom and thanks and honor 1518
11:13 and the survivors were terrified and gave g 1518
14: 7 "Fear God and give him g, 1518
15: 4 O Lord, and **bring** g **to** your name? 1519
15: 8 from the g of God and from his power, 1518
18: 7 g and luxury *she* **gave** herself. 1519
19: 1 and g and power belong to our God, 1518
19: 7 Let us rejoice and be glad and give him g! 1518
21:11 *It* **shone with** the g of God, 1518+2400
21:23 for the g of God gives it light, 1518
21:26 The g and honor of the nations will 1518

GLOW (1) [GLOWING, GLOWS]
Isa 4: 5 of smoke by day and a g *of* flaming fire 5586

GLOWING (5) [GLOW]
Ps 102: 3 my bones burn like g **embers.** 4611
Eze 1: 4 The center of the fire looked like g **metal,** 3133
1:27 up he looked like g **metal,** as if full of fire, 3133
8: 2 as bright as g **metal.** 3133
Rev 1:15 His feet were like bronze g in a furnace, 4792

GLOWS (1) [GLOW]
Eze 24:11 and its copper g so its impurities may 3081

GLUTTED (1) [GLUTTON]
Eze 39:19 till you are g and drink blood 8429

GLUTTON (2) [GLUTTED, GLUTTONS, GLUTTONY]
Mt 11:19 and they say, 'Here is a g and a drunkard, 5741
Lk 7:34 and you say, 'Here is a g and a drunkard, 5741

GLUTTONS (3) [GLUTTON]
Pr 23:21 for drunkards and g become poor, 2361
28: 7 but a companion of g disgraces his father. 2361
Tit 1:12 Cretans are always liars, evil brutes, lazy g. 1143

GLUTTONY (1) [GLUTTON]
Pr 23: 2 put a knife to your throat if you are **given to** g. 1251+5883

GNASH (3) [GNASHED, GNASHES, GNASHING]
Ps 37:12 the righteous and g their teeth at them; 3080
112:10 *he will* g his teeth and waste away; 3080
La 2:16 they scoff and g their teeth and say, 3080

GNASHED (2) [GNASH]
Ps 35:16 *they* g their teeth at me. 3080
Ac 7:54 they were furious and g their teeth at him. 1107

GNASHES (2) [GNASH]
Job 16: 9 and tears me in his anger and g his teeth 3080
Mk 9:18 g his teeth and becomes rigid. 5563

GNASHING (7) [GNASH]
Mt 8:12 there will be weeping and g of teeth." 1106
13:42 where there will be weeping and g of teeth. 1106
13:50 where there will be weeping and g of teeth. 1106
22:13 where there will be weeping and g of teeth. 1106
24:51 where there will be weeping and g of teeth. 1106
25:30 there will be weeping and g of teeth.' 1106
Lk 13:28 will be weeping there, and g of teeth, 1106

GNAT (1) [GNATS]
Mt 23:24 You strain out a g but swallow a camel. 3270

GNATS (6) [GNAT]
Ex 8:16 the land of Egypt the dust will become **g."** 4031
8:17 g came upon men and animals. 4038
8:17 throughout the land of Egypt became **g.** 4031
8:18 But when the magicians tried to produce g 4031
8:18 And the g were on men and animals. 4038
Ps 105:31 and g throughout their country. 4031

GNAWED (1) [GNAWING]
Rev 16:10 *Men* g their tongues in agony 3460

GNAWING (1) [GNAWED]
Job 30:17 my g **pains** never rest. 6908

GO (1413) [GOES, GOING, GONE, WENT]
Ge 4: 8 *"Let's* **g out** *to* the field." 2143
7: 1 LORD then said to Noah, "G into the ark, 995
11: 7 *let us* **g down** and confuse their language 3718
11:31 from Ur of the Chaldeans to g to Canaan. 2143
12: 1 and your father's household and g to NIH
12:19 Take her and g!" 2143
13: 9 If you g to the left, I'll go to the right; NIH
13: 9 If you go to the left, *I'll* **g to the right;** 3554
13: 9 if you g to the right, I'll go to the left." NIH
13: 9 if you go to the right, *I'll* **g to the left."** 8521
13:17 G, walk through the length and breadth of 7756
15:15 *will* g to your fathers in peace and 995
16: 2 **G, sleep with** my maidservant; 448+995
16: 9 "**G back** to your mistress and submit 8740
18: 5 be refreshed and then **g on** *your* **way—** 6296
18:21 that *I will* **g down** and see 3718
19: 2 then g on your way early in the morning." 2143
19: 3 But he insisted so strongly that *they did* g 6073
19:34 and *you* **g in** and lie with him 995
20:13 Everywhere *we* g, say of me, 995
22: 2 and g to the region of Moriah. 2143
22: 5 with the donkey while I and the boy g 2143
24: 4 but *will* g to my country 2143
24:11 the time the women **g out** to draw water. 3655
24:38 but g to my father's family and 2143
24:41 Then, when *you* g to my clan, 995
24:51 Here is Rebekah; take her and g, 2143
24:55 then *you may* g." 2143
24:56 on my way so *I may* g to my master." 2143
24:58 *"Will you* g with this man?" 2143
24:58 *"I will* g," she said. 2143
25:18 *as* you g toward Asshur. 995
26: 2 *"Do* not **g down** to Egypt; 3718
27: 3 and **g out** *to* the open country 3655
27: 9 **G out** to the flock 2143
27:13 Just do what I say; g and get them for me." 2143
28: 2 G at once to Paddan Aram, 2143
28:15 and will watch over you wherever *you* g, 2143
30:25 so *I can* **g back** to my own homeland. 2143
30:31 *I will* **g on** tending your flocks 8740
30:32 *Let me* g through all your flocks today 6296
31: 3 "**G back** to the land of your fathers and 8740
31:13 at once and **g back** to your native land.' " 8740
31:18 to g to his father Isaac in the land 995
31:52 that I *will* not **g past** this heap to your side 6296
31:52 to harm you and that you *will* not **g past** 6296
32: 9 '**G back** to your country and your relatives, 8740
32:16 and said to his servants, "G ahead of me, 6296
32:26 man said, "**Let** me g, for it is daybreak." 8938
32:26 not **let** you g unless you bless me." 8938
33:14 So *let* my lord **g on** ahead of his servant, 6296
34:17 we'll take our sister and g." 2143
35: 1 "G up to Bethel and settle there, 7756
35: 3 Then come, *let us* **g up** *to* Bethel, 6590
37:14 "G and see if all is well with your brothers 2143
37:17 "I heard them say, *'Let's* g to Dothan.' " 2143
37:35 "in mourning *will I* **g down** to the grave 3718
39:10 he refused to **g to bed with** her or 725+8886
41:55 "G to Joseph and do what he tells you." 2143
42: 2 **G down** there and buy some for us, 3718
42:19 while the rest of you g and take grain back 2143
42:33 for your starving households and g. 2143
42:38 "My son *will* not **g down** there with you; 3718
43: 2 "**G back** and buy us a little more food." 8740
43: 4 *we will* **g down** and buy food for you. 3718
43: 5 you will not send him, *we will* not **g down,** 3718
43: 8 along with me and *we will* g at once, 2143
43:13 Take your brother also and **g back** to 8740
44: 4 "G after those men at once, 8103
44:17 **g back** to your father in peace." 6590
44:25 '**G back** and buy a little more food.' 8740
44:26 But we said, 'We cannot **g down.** 3718
44:26 youngest brother is with us *will we* g. 3718
44:30 when I **g back** to your servant my father and 995
44:34 How *can I* **g back** to my father if the boy is 6590
45:28 *I will* g and see him before I die." 2143
46: 3 "Do not be afraid *to* **g down** to Egypt, 3718
46: 4 I *will* **g down** to Egypt with you, 3718
46:31 *"I will* **g up** and speak to Pharaoh 6590
50: 5 Now *let me* **g up** and bury my father; 6590
50: 6 Pharaoh said, "**G up** and bury your father, 6590
Ex 2: 7 *"Shall I* g and get one of the Hebrew 2143
2: 8 "Yes, g," she answered. 2143
3: 3 *"I will* **g over** and see this strange sight— 6073
3:10 So now, g. I am sending you to Pharaoh 2143
3:11 that *I should* g to Pharaoh and bring 2143
3:13 "Suppose I g to the Israelites and say 995
3:16 "G, assemble the elders of Israel and say 2143
3:18 and the elders *are to* g to the king of Egypt 995
3:19 the king of Egypt will not let you g unless 2143
3:20 After that, *he will* **let** you g. 8938
3:21 you leave *you will* not g empty-handed. 2143
4:12 Now g; I will help you speak 2143
4:18 *"Let me* g back to my own people in Egypt 2143
4:18 Jethro said, "G, and I wish you well." 2143
4:19 "G back to Egypt, 2143
4:21 so that *he will* not **let** the people g. 8938
4:23 "**Let** my son g, so he may worship me." 8938
4:23 But you refused to **let** him g; 8938
4:27 "G into the desert to meet Moses." 2143
5: 1 '**Let** my people g, 8938
5: 2 that I should obey him and **let** Israel g? 8938
5: 2 and *I will* not **let** Israel g." 8938
5: 7 *let* them g and gather their own straw. 2143
5: 8 *'Let us* g and sacrifice to our God.' 2143
5:11 G and get your own straw wherever you can find it, 2143
5:17 *'Let us* g and sacrifice to the LORD.' 2143
Ex 6: 1 of my mighty hand *he will* **let** them g; 8938
6:11 "G, tell Pharaoh king of Egypt to let 995
6:11 *to* **let** the Israelites g out of his country." 8938
7: 2 to tell Pharaoh *to* **let** the Israelites g out 8938
7:14 he refuses to **let** the people g. 8938
7:15 G to Pharaoh in the morning as he goes out 2143
7:16 **Let** my people g, 8938
8: 1 "G to Pharaoh and say to him, 995
8: 1 **Let** my people g, 8938
8: 2 If you refuse to **let** them g, 8938
8: 4 The frogs *will* **g up** on you 6590
8: 8 and *I will* **let** your people g 8938
8:20 **Let** my people g, 8938
8:21 If you *do* not **let** my people g, 8938
8:25 "G, sacrifice to your God here in the land." 2143
8:28 "I *will* **let** you g to offer sacrifices to 8938
8:28 but you must not g very far. 2143
8:29 not **letting** the people g to offer sacrifices 8938
8:32 and *would* not **let** the people g. 8938
9: 1 "G to Pharaoh and say to him, 995
9: 1 "**Let** my people g, 8938
9: 2 If you refuse to **let** them g and continue 8938
9: 7 and *he would* not **let** the people g. 8938
9:13 **Let** my people g, 8938
9:17 and *will* not **let** them g. 8938
9:28 *I will* **let** you g; 8938
9:35 and *he would* not **let** the Israelites g, 8938
10: 1 the LORD said to Moses, "G to Pharaoh, 995
10: 3 **Let** my people g, 8938
10: 4 If you refuse to **let** them g, 8938
10: 7 **Let** the people g, 8938
10: 8 "G, worship the LORD your God," 2143
10: 9 *"We will* g with our young and old, 2143
10:10 if *I* **let** you g, 8938
10:11 *Have* only the men g; 2143
10:20 and *he would* not **let** the Israelites g. 8938
10:24 Pharaoh summoned Moses and said, "G, 2143
10:24 your women and children *may* g with you; 2143
10:26 Our livestock too *must* g with us; 2143
10:27 and he was not willing to **let** them g. 8938
11: 1 After that, *he will* **let** you g from here, 8938
11: 4 'About midnight I *will* g 3655
11: 8 bowing down before me and saying, 'G, 3655
11:10 not **let** the Israelites g out of his country. 8938
12:21 "**G at once** and select the animals 5432
12:22 of you *shall* **g out** the door of his house 3655
12:31 G, worship the LORD 2143
12:32 as you have said, and g. 2143
13:15 Pharaoh stubbornly refused to **let** us g, 8938
13:17 When Pharaoh **let** the people g, 8938
14: 5 *We have* **let** the Israelites g 8938
14:16 so that the Israelites *can* g through the sea 995
14:17 of the Egyptians so that *they will* **g in** 995
16: 4 *to* **g out** each day and gather enough for 3655
16:29 no one *is to* **g out."** 3655
17: 5 with which you struck the Nile, and g. 2143
17: 9 "Choose some of our men and **g out** 3655
18:23 and all these people *will* g home satisfied." 995
19:10 "G to the people and consecrate them today 2143
19:12 that you *do* not **g up** the mountain or touch 6590
19:13 a long blast *may* they **g up** to the mountain." 6590
19:21 "**G down** and warn the people so they do 3718
19:24 "G down and bring Aaron up with you. 2143
20:26 And *do* not **g up** to my altar on steps, 6590
21: 2 But in the seventh year, *he shall* g free, 3655
21: 3 If he comes alone, *he is to* **g free** alone; 3655
21: 3 she *is to* g with him. 3655
21: 4 and only the man *shall* **g free.** 3655
21: 5 and children and *do* not *want to* g free,' 3655
21: 7 *she is* not *to* **g free** as menservants do. 3655
21:11 *she is to* **g free,** 3655
21:26 *he must* **let** the servant g free 8938
21:27 *he must* **let** the servant g free 8938
23:23 My angel *will* g ahead of you 2143
24:14 and anyone involved in a dispute *can* g 5602
26:19 make forty silver bases to g under them— NIH
32: 1 make us gods who *will* g before us. 2143
32: 7 Then the LORD said to Moses, "G down, 2143
32:23 'Make us gods who *will* g before us. 2143
32:27 **G back** and forth through the camp 8740
32:30 But now *I will* **g up** to the LORD; 6590
32:34 Now g, lead the people to the place I spoke 2143
32:34 and my angel *will* g before you. 2143
33: 1 and **g up** to the land I promised on oath 6590
33: 3 G up to the land flowing with milk NIH
33: 3 But *I will* not g with you, 6590
33: 5 *I were to* g with you even for a moment, 6590
33: 7 Anyone inquiring of the LORD *would* g 3655
33:14 "My Presence *will* g with you, 2143
33:15 "If your Presence *does* not g with us, 2143
33:16 and with your people unless you g with us? 2143
34: 9 he said, "then *let* the Lord g with us. 2143
34:24 when you **g up** three times each year 6590
36:24 made forty silver bases to g under them— NIH
Lev 6:12 must be kept burning; *it must* not **g out.** 3882
6:13 continuously; *it must* not **g out.** 3882
10: 9 or other fermented drink whenever you g 995
12: 4 She must not touch anything sacred or g to 995
13:16 *he must* g to the priest. 995
14: 3 *to* g outside the camp and examine him. 3655
14:35 the owner of the house *must* g and tell 995
14:36 the priest *is to* **g in** and inspect the house. 995
14:38 the priest *shall* **g out** the doorway of 3655
14:44 the priest *is to* g and examine it and, if 995
16:23 *to* g into the Tent of Meeting and take off 995
19:10 **g over** your vineyard **a second time** 6618
19:16 " *'Do* not **g about** spreading slander 2143

Lev 21:23 not **g** near the curtain or approach the altar, 995
25:27 *he can* then **g back** to his own property. 8740
25:28 and *he can* then **g back** to his property. 8740
25:41 and *he will* **g back** to his own clan and to 8740
Nu 4: 5 *to* **g in** and take down the shielding curtain 995
4:19 and his sons *are to* **g into** the sanctuary 995
4:20 But the Kohathites *must* not **g in** to look at 995
5:27 water that brings a curse, it *will* **g** into her 995
6: 6 to the LORD *he must* not **g** near 995
8:19 when they **g near** the sanctuary." 5602
10: 9 When *you* **g into** battle in your own land 995
10:30 He answered, "No, *I will* not **g;** 2143
11:26 but *did* not **g out** to the Tent. 3655
13:17 **"G up** through the Negev and on into 6590
13:30 *"We* **should g up** and take possession 6590+6590
14: 3 Wouldn't it be better for us *to* **g back** 8740
14: 4 "We should choose a leader and **g back** 8740
14:14 that you **g** before them in a pillar of cloud 2143
14:40 *"We will* **g up** to the place 6590
14:42 *Do* not **g up,** because the LORD is not with 6590
16:30 and *they* **g down** alive into the grave, 3718
18: 3 but *they must* not **g near** the furnishings of 7928
18:22 From now on the Israelites *must* not **g near** 7928
20:17 not **g** through any field or vineyard, 6296
20:19 *"We will* **g** along the main road, 6590
20:21 to let them **g** through their territory, 6296
21: 4 to **g around** Edom. 6015
22:12 God said to Balaam, *"Do* not **g** with them. 2143
22:13 **"G back** to your own country, 2143
22:13 LORD has refused to let me **g** with you." 2143
22:18 not do anything great or small to **g beyond** 6296
22:20 **g** with them, but do only what I tell you." 2143
22:34 Now if you are displeased, *I will* **g back."** 8740
22:35 **"G** with the men, 2143
23: 3 beside your offering while *I* **g aside.** 2143
23: 5 **"G back** to Balak 8740
23:16 **"G back** to Balak 8740
24:11 Now leave at once and **g** home! NIH
24:13 *to* **g beyond** the command of the LORD— 6296
27:12 **"G up** this mountain in the Abarim range 6590
27:17 *to* **g out** and come in before them, 3655
27:21 of the Israelites *will* **g out,** 3655
31: 3 *to* **g** to war against the Midianites and 2118
32: 6 *"Shall* your countrymen **g** to war 995
32:17 But we are ready to arm ourselves and **g** NIH
32:21 if all of you *will* **g** armed **over** the Jordan 6296
34: 4 on to Zin and **g** south of Kadesh Barnea. 2118
34: 4 Then *it will* **g** *to* Hazar Addar and over 3655
34: 8 Then the boundary *will* **g** to Zedad, 2118
34:11 The boundary *will* **g down** from Shepham 3718
34:12 the boundary *will* **g down** along the Jordan 3718
35:32 a city of refuge and so *allow* him *to* **g back** 8740
Dt 1: 2 to **g** from Horeb to Kadesh Barnea by NIH
1: 7 **g** to all the neighboring peoples in 995
1: 8 **G in** and take possession of the land that 995
1:21 **G up** and take possession of it as 6590
1:26 But you were unwilling to **g up;** 6590
1:28 Where *can* we **g?** 6590
1:33 and to show you the way *you should* **g.** 2143
1:41 We *will* **g up** and fight, 6590
1:41 to **g up** into the hill country. 6590
1:42 "Tell them, *'Do* not **g up** and fight, 6590
3:20 each of you *may* **g back** to 8740
3:25 *Let me* **g over** and see the good land 6296
3:27 **G up** *to* the top of Pisgah and look west 6590
4: 1 and *may* **g in** and take possession of 995
4:40 so that *it may* **g well** with you 3512
5: 5 of the fire and *did* not **g up** the mountain.) 6590
5:16 that *it may* **g well** with you in the land 3512
5:27 **G near** and listen to all that 7928
5:29 so that *it might* **g well** with them 3512
5:30 **"G,** tell them to return to their tents. 2143
6: 3 be careful to obey so that *it may* **g well** 3512
6:18 so that *it may* **g well** with you 3512
6:18 with you and *you may* **g in** and take over 995
8:16 that in the end *it might* **g well** *with* you. 3512
9: 1 to **g in** and dispossess nations greater 995
9:12 **"G down** from here at once, 3718
9:23 **"G up** and take possession of the land 6590
10:11 **"G,"** the LORD said to me, 7756
11: 8 the strength to **g in** and take over the land 995
11:25 of you on the whole land, wherever *you* **g.** 2005
12: 5 To that place *you must* **g;** 995
12:25 so that *it may* **g well** with you 3512
12:26 and **g** to the place the LORD will choose. 995
12:28 so that *it may* always **g well** with you 3512
13: 6 *"Let us* **g** and worship other gods" (gods 2143
13:13 of their town astray, saying, *"Let us* **g** 2143
14:25 the silver with you and **g** to the place 2143
15:12 the seventh year *you must* **let** him **g** free. 8938
17: 9 **G** to the priests, who are Levites, 995
17:16 *"You are* not to **g back** that way again." 8740
19: 5 a man *may* **g** into the forest 995
19:13 so that *it may* **g well** with you. 3201
20: 1 When *you* **g** to war against your enemies 3655
20: 2 When you *are about to* **g** into battle, 7928
20: 5 *Let him* **g** home, or he may die 2143+2256+8740
20: 6 *Let him* **g** home, or he may die 2143+2256+8740
20: 7 *Let him* **g** home, or he may die 2143+2256+8740
20: 8 *Let him* **g** home so that his brothers will not become disheartened too." 2143+2256+8740
21: 2 and judges *shall* **g** out and measure 3655
21:10 When *you* **g** to war against your enemies 3655
21:13 then *you may* **g** to her and be her husband 995
21:14 **let** her **g** wherever she wishes. 8938
22: 7 **be sure to let** the mother **g,** 8938+8938
22: 7 so that *it may* **g well** with you 3512

Dt 23:10 *he is to* **g** outside the camp and stay there. 3655
23:12 a place outside the camp where *you can* **g** 3655
24:10 *do* not **g** into his house 995
24:12 *do* not **g to sleep** with his pledge 8886
24:19 *do* not **g back** to get it. 8740
24:20 not **g over the branches a second time** 339+6994
24:21 *do* not **g over the vines again.** 339+6618
25: 7 she *shall* **g** to the elders at the town gate 6590
25: 9 his brother's widow *shall* **g up** to him in 5602
26: 2 Then **g** to the place the LORD your God 2143
28: 6 in and blessed when you **g out.** 3655
28:19 in and cursed when you **g out.** 3655
28:41 because *they will* **g** into captivity. 2143
29:18 from the LORD our God to **g** and worship 2143
31: 7 for you *must* **g** with this people into 995
32:49 **"G up** into the Abarim Range 6590
Jos 1: 7 you may be successful wherever *you* **g.** 2143
1: 9 be with you wherever *you* **g."** 2143
1:11 **"G** through the camp and tell the people, 6296
1:11 the Jordan here to **g in** and take possession 995
1:15 *you may* **g back** and occupy your own land, 8740
1:16 and wherever you send us *we will* **g.** 2143
2: 1 **"G,** look over the land," he said, 2143
2: 5 **G** after them quickly. 8103
2:16 **"G** to the hills so the pursuers will 2143
2:16 and then **g** on your way." 2143
3: 4 Then you will know which way *to* **g,** 2143
3: 4 and the ark; *do* not **g near** it." 7928
3: 8 **g** and stand in the river.' " NIH
3:11 of the Lord of all the earth *will* **g** into 6296
4: 5 **"G over** before the ark of the LORD 6296
6: 5 and the people *will* **g up,** 6590
6:19 the LORD and *must* **g into** his treasury." 995
6:22 **"G into** the prostitute's house 995
7: 2 **"G up** and spy out the region." 6590
7: 3 the people *will have to* **g up** *against* Ai. 6590
7:13 **"G,** consecrate the people. 7756
8: 1 and **g up** and attack Ai. 7756
8: 4 Don't **g** very **far** from it. 8178
8:17 in Ai or Bethel who *did* not **g** after Israel. 3655
9:11 **g** and meet them and say to them, 2143
14:11 I'm just as vigorous to **g out** to battle now 3655
17:15 **g up** into the forest and clear land 6590
18: 8 **"G** and make a survey of the land and write 2143
20: 6 Then he may **g** back to his own home in 995
22:12 of Israel gathered at Shiloh to **g** to war 6590
23:14 "Now I *am about to* **g** the way of all 2143
23:16 and **g** and serve other gods and bow down 2143
Jdg 1: 1 be the first *to* **g up** and fight for us against 6590
1: 2 The LORD answered, "Judah *is to* **g;** 6590
1: 3 We in turn *will* **g** with you into yours." 2143
4: 6 **'G,** take with you ten thousand men 2143
4: 8 Barak said to her, "If *you* **g** with me, 2143
4: 8 "If you go with me, *I will* **g;** 2143
4: 8 but if *you* don't **g** with me, I won't go." 2143
4: 8 but if you don't go with me, *I* won't **g."** 2143
4: 9 **"Very well,"** Deborah said, *"I will* **g** 2143+2143
4:14 Then Deborah said to Barak, **"G!** 7756
5:22 galloping, galloping **g** his mighty steeds. NIH
6:14 **"G** in the strength you have 2143
6:18 Please *do* not **g away** until I come back 4631
7: 4 If I say, 'This one *shall* **g** with you,' 2143
7: 4 'This one shall go with you,' he *shall* **g;** 2143
7: 4 'This one *shall* not **g** with you,' 2143
7: 4 not go with you,' he *shall* not **g."** 2143
7: 7 *Let* all the other men **g,** 2143
7: 9 "Get up, **g down** against the camp, 3718
7:10 **g down** to the camp with your servant Purah 3718
9:38 **G out** and fight them!" 3655
10:14 **G** and cry out to the gods you have chosen. 2143
11:17 *to* **g** through your country,' 6296
11:38 *"You may* **g,"** he said. 2143
11:38 And *he* **let** her **g** for two months. 8938
11:40 the young women of Israel **g** *out* 2143
12: 1 "Why *did* you **g** to fight the Ammonites 6296
12: 1 the Ammonites without calling us to **g** 2143
14: 3 *Must* you **g** to the uncircumcised 2143
15: 1 But her father would not let him **g in.** 995
16:20 *"I'll* **g out** as before 3655
18: 2 They told them, **"G,** explore the land." 2143
18: 6 The priest answered them, **"G** in peace. 2143
18: 9 Don't hesitate to **g** there and take it over. 2143
19: 5 then *you can* **g."** 2143
19: 7 And when the man got up to **g,** 2143
19: 8 when he rose to **g,** the girl's father said, 2143
19:12 *We* won't **g** into an alien city, 6073
19:12 *We will* **g on** to Gibeah." 6296
19:25 and at dawn *they* **let** her **g.** 8938
19:28 He said to her, "Get up; *let's* **g."** 2143
20: 8 saying, "None of *us will* **g** home. 2143
20: 9 We'll **g** up against it as the lot directs. NIH
20:18 "Who of us *shall* **g** first to fight against 6590
20:18 The LORD replied, "Judah shall **g** first." NIH
20:23 "Shall we **g up** again to battle against 5602
20:23 **"G up** against them." 6590
20:28 "Shall we **g up** again to battle 3655
20:28 The LORD responded, **"G,** 6590
21:10 with instructions *to* **g** *to* Jabesh Gilead 2143
21:20 **"G** and hide in the vineyards 2143
21:21 from the girls of Shiloh and **g** *to* the land 2143
Ru 1: 8 **"G** back, each of *you,* 2143
1:10 *"We will* **g back** with you to your people." 8740
1:15 **G back** with her." 8740
1:16 Where *you* **g** I will go, 2143
1:16 Where you go *I will* **g,** 2143
1:18 that Ruth was determined to **g** with her, 2143
2: 2 *"Let me* **g** *to* the fields and pick up 2143

Ru 2: 2 Naomi said to her, **"G ahead,** my daughter. 2143
2: 8 Don't **g** and glean in another field 2143
2: 8 in another field and don't **g away** from here. 6296
2: 9 **g** and get a drink from the water jars 2143
2:22 my daughter, *to* **g** with his girls, 3655
3: 3 Then **g down** to the threshing floor, 3718
3: 4 Then **g** and uncover his feet and lie down. 995
3:16 Naomi asked, **"How did it g,** my daughter?" 905+4769
3:17 of barley, saying, 'Don't **g back** 995
1Sa 1:17 Eli answered, **"G** in peace, 2143
1:22 Hannah *did* not **g.** 6590
2:20 Then *they would* **g** home. 2143
2:28 to **g up** to my altar, to burn incense, 6590
3: 5 **g back** and lie down." 8740
3: 6 **g back** and lie down." 8740
3: 9 So Eli told Samuel, **"G** and lie down, 2143
4: 3 so that *it may* **g** with us and save us from 995
5:11 *let* it **g back** to its own place, 8740
6: 6 so *they could* **g on** *their* **way?** 2143
6:20 To whom *will* the ark **g up** from here?" 6590
6:20 *to* **g out** before us and fight our battles." 3655
8:22 "Everyone **g back** to his town." 2143
9: 3 of the servants with you and **g** and look for 2143
9: 5 with him, "Come, *let's* **g back,** 8740
9: 6 *Let's* **g** there now. 2143
9: 7 Saul said to his servant, "If *we* **g,** 2143
9: 9 "Come, *let us* **g** to the seer," 2143
9:10 "Come, *let's* **g."** 2143
9:13 those who are invited will eat. **G up** now; 6590
9:19 **"G up** ahead of me *to* the high place, 6590
9:19 and in the morning *I will* **let** you **g** 8938
9:27 "Tell the servant *to* **g on** ahead of us"— 6296
10: 3 "Then *you will* **g** on from there 2736
10: 5 "After that *you will* **g** to Gibeah of God, 995
10: 8 **"G down** ahead of me *to* Gilgal. 3718
11:14 *let us* **g** to Gilgal and there reaffirm 2143
14: 1 *let's* **g over** to the Philistine outpost on 6296
14: 6 *let's* **g over** to the outpost 6296
14: 7 **"G ahead;** I am with you heart and soul." 5742
14: 9 we will stay where we are and not **g up** 6590
14:34 **"G out** among the men and tell them, 7046
14:36 *"Let us* **g down** after the Philistines 3718
14:37 *"Shall I* **g down** after the Philistines? 3718
15: 3 Now **g,** attack the Amalekites 2143
15: 6 Then he said to the Kenites, **"G** away, 2143
15:18 And he sent you on a mission, saying, **'G** 2143
15:26 *"I will* not **g back** with you. 8740
15:35 he did not **g** to see Saul again, NIH
16: 2 But Samuel said, "How *can I* **g?** 2143
17:32 your servant *will* **g** and fight him." 2143
17:33 not able to **g out** against this Philistine 2143
17:37 Saul said to David, **"G,** 2143
17:39 "I cannot **g** in these," he said to Saul, 2143
18:30 continued *to* **g out** to battle, 3655
19: 2 **g** into hiding and stay there. 3782
19: 3 I *will* **g out** and stand with my father in 3655
20: 5 but **let** me **g** and hide in the field until 8938
20:11 Jonathan said, *"Let's* **g out** *into* the field." 3655
20:19 **g** to the place where you hid 995
20:21 Then I will send a boy and say, **'G,** 2143
20:22 then *you must* **g,** 2143
20:28 for permission to **g** to Bethlehem. NIH
20:29 He said, **'Let** me **g,** 8938
20:38 Then he shouted, "Hurry! **G quickly!** 2590
20:40 **"G,** carry them back to town." 2143
20:42 Jonathan said to David, **"G** in peace, 2143
22: 5 **G** into the land of Judah." 2143
23: 2 *"Shall I* **g** and attack these Philistines?" 2143
23: 2 The LORD answered him, **"G,** 2143
23: 3 if *we* **g** *to* Keilah against the Philistine 2143
23: 4 **"G down** *to* Keilah, 3718
23: 8 to **g down** *to* Keilah to besiege David 3718
23:13 *he did* not **g** there. 3655
23:22 **G** and make further preparation. 2143
23:23 Then *I will* **g** with you; 2143
25: 5 **"G** up to Nabal at Carmel and greet him 995
25:19 Then she told her servants, **"G on** ahead; 6296
25:35 **"G** home in peace. 6590
26: 6 "Who *will* **g down** into the camp with me 3718
26: 6 "I'll **g** with you," said Abishai. 3718
26:10 or *he will* **g** into battle and perish. 3718
26:11 that are near his head, and *let's* **g."** 2143
26:19 **'G,** serve other gods.' 2143
27:10 "Where *did you* **g raiding** today?" 7320
28: 7 so *I may* **g** and inquire of her." 2143
28:22 so you may eat and have the strength *to* **g** 2143
29: 4 *He must* not **g** with us into battle, 3718
29: 7 Turn back and **g** in peace; 2143
29: 8 Why can't *I* **g** and fight against 995
29: 9 *'He must* not **g up** with us into battle.' 6590
29:11 to **g** back to the land of the Philistines, 2143
30:22 "Because *they did* not **g out** with us, 2143
30:22 and children and **g."** 2143
2Sa 1:15 David called one of his men and said, **"G,** 5602
2: 1 *"Shall I* **g up** to one of the towns 6590
2: 1 The LORD said, **"G up."** 6590
2: 1 David asked, "Where *shall I* **g?"** 6590
3:16 Then Abner said to him, **"G** back home!" 2143
3:21 *"Let me* **g** at once and assemble all Israel 2143
3:24 Why *did you* **let** him **g?** 8938
5:19 *"Shall I* **g** and attack the Philistines? 6590
5:19 The LORD answered him, **"G,** 6590
5:23 and he answered, *"Do* not **g straight up,** 6590
7: 3 you have in mind, **g ahead** and do it, 2143
7: 5 **"G** and tell my servant David, 'This is what 2143
11: 1 at the time when kings **g off to war,** 3655

2Sa 11: 8 **"G down** to your house 3718
11: 9 and *did* not **g down** to his house. 3718
11:10 David was told, "Uriah *did* not g home," 3718
11:10 Why didn't *you* g home?" 3718
11:11 *How could* **I** g to my house to eat and drink 995
11:13 *he did* not g home. 3718
12:23 I *will* g to him, but he will not return to me. 2143
13: 5 **"G** to bed and pretend to be ill," 8886
13: 7 **"G** *to* the house of your brother Amnon 2143
13:25 "All of us *should* not **g;** 2143
13:25 Absalom urged him, he still refused to **g,** 2143
13:26 "Why *should he* g with you?" 2143
13:39 spirit of the king longed to g to Absalom, 3655
14: 3 Then g to the king and speak these words 995
14: 8 The king said to the woman, **"G** home, 2143
14:21 **G,** bring back the young man Absalom." 2143
14:24 the king said, *"He must* g to his own house; 6015
14:30 **G** and set it on fire." 2143
14:31 Then Joab *did* g to Absalom's house 995
15: 7 *"Let me* g to Hebron and fulfill 2143
15: 9 The king said to him, **"G** in peace." 2143
15:19 **G back** and stay with King Absalom. 8740
15:20 **G back,** and take your countrymen. 8740
15:22 David said to Ittai, **"G ahead,** march on." 2143
15:27 **G back** *to* the city in peace, 8740
15:33 David said to him, "If *you* g with me, 6296
16: 9 *Let me* **g over** and cut off his head." 6296
16:17 Why didn't *you* g with your friend?" 2143
17:17 A servant girl *was to* g and inform them, 2143
17:17 and they *were to* g and tell King David, 2143
18: 3 But the men said, *"You must* not **g out;** 3655
18:21 Then Joab said to a Cushite, **"G,** 2143
18:22 "My son, why *do* you *want to* **g?** 8132
19: 7 Now g out and encourage your men. 7756
19: 7 by the LORD that if you don't **g out,** 3655
19:15 to **g out** and meet the king and bring him 2143
19:25 "Why didn't *you* g with me, 2143
19:26 so *I can* g with the king.' 2143
19:34 *I should* **g up** *to* Jerusalem with the king? 6590
21:17 "Never again *will you* **g out** with us 3655
24: 1 **"G** and take a census of Israel and Judah." 2143
24: 2 **"G** throughout the tribes of Israel from Dan 8763
24:12 **"G** and tell David, 'This is what 2143
24:18 **"G up** and build an altar to the LORD on 6590
1Ki 1:13 **G in** to King David and say to 995+2143+2256
1:35 Then *you are to* **g up** with him, 6590
1:53 and Solomon said, **"G** to your home." 2143
2: 2 "I *am about to* g the way of all the earth," 2143
2: 3 in all you do and wherever *you* **g,** 7155
2: 6 *do* not **let** his gray head **g down** 3718
2:26 **"G back** to your fields in Anathoth. 2143
2:29 **"G,** strike him down!" 2143
2:36 but *do* not g anywhere else. 3655
2:42 'On the day you leave *to* g anywhere else, 2143
7:38 one basin to g on each of the ten stands. NIH
8:44 your people g to war against their enemies, 3655
9: 6 and decrees I have given you and **g off** 2143
11:21 Then Hadad said to Pharaoh, **"Let me g,** 8938
11:22 to **g back** to your own country?" 2143
11:22 Hadad replied, "but **do let me g!"** 8938+8938
12: 5 **"G away** for three days and then come back 2143
12:24 *Do* not **g up** to fight against your brothers, 6590
12:24 **G** home, every one of you, 8740
12:27 If these people **g up** to offer sacrifices at 6590
12:28 "It is too much for you *to* **g up** 6590
13: 8 *I would* not g with you, 995
13:12 "Which way *did he* **g?"** 2143
13:16 "I cannot turn back and g with you, 995
14: 2 **"G,** disguise yourself, 7756
14: 2 Then g *to* Shiloh. 2143
14: 3 cakes and a jar of honey, and g to him. 995
14: 7 **G,** tell Jeroboam that this is what 2143
14:12 "As for you, **g back** home. 2143
17: 9 **"G** at once to Zarephath of Sidon 2143
17:13 **G home** and do as you have said. 995
18: 1 **"G** and present yourself to Ahab, 2143
18: 5 **"G** through the land to all the springs 2143
18: 8 **"G** tell your master, 'Elijah is here.' " 2143
18:11 now you tell me *to* g to my master and say, 2143
18:12 *I* g and tell Ahab and he doesn't find you, 995
18:14 now you tell me *to* g to my master and say, 2143
18:41 And Elijah said to Ahab, **"G,** eat and drink, 6590
18:43 **"G** and look toward the sea," 6590
18:43 Seven times Elijah said, **"G back."** 8740
18:44 So Elijah said, **"G** and tell Ahab, 6590
18:44 'Hitch up your chariot and **g down** before 3718
19:11 **"G out** and stand on the mountain in 3655
19:15 **"G** back the way you came, 2143
19:15 and g to the Desert of Damascus. NIH
19:20 **"G** back," Elijah replied. 2143
20:31 *Let us* g to the king of Israel 3655
20:33 **"G** and get him," the king said. 995
20:34 he made a treaty with him, and **let** him **g.** 8938
21:18 **"G** down to meet Ahab king of Israel, 7756
22: 4 *"Will you* g with me to fight 2143
22: 6 *"Shall I* g to war against Ramoth Gilead, 2143
22: 6 **"G,"** they answered, "for 6590
22:15 *shall we* g to war against Ramoth Gilead, 2143
22:17 *Let* each one g home in peace.' " 8740
22:22 " *'I will* **g out** and be a lying spirit in 3655
22:22 **'G** and do it.' 3655
22:24 the spirit from the LORD g when he went 6296
22:25 "You will find out on the day *you* g to hide 995
22:48 of trading ships to g to Ophir for gold, 2143
2Ki 1: 2 **"G** and consult Baal-Zebub, 2143
1: 3 **"G up** and meet the messengers of the king 6590
1: 6 **'G** back to the king who sent you 2143

2Ki 1:15 **"G down** with him; 3718
2:16 *Let them* g and look for your master. 2143
2:18 "Didn't I tell you not *to* **g?"** 2143
2:23 **"G on up,** *you* baldhead!" 6590
2:23 **"G on up,** *you* baldhead!" 6590
3: 7 *Will you* g with me to fight 2143
3: 7 *"I will* g with you," he replied. 6590
3:13 **G** to the prophets of your father and 2143
4: 3 **"G** around and ask all your neighbors 2143
4: 4 Then g *inside* and shut the door 995
4: 7 **"G,** sell the oil and pay your debts. 2143
4:22 g to the man of God **quickly** 8132
4:23 "Why g to him today?" 2143
5: 5 **"By all means, g,"** 995+2143
5:10 Elisha sent a messenger to say to him, **"G,** 2143
5:19 **"G** in peace," Elisha said. 2143
5:25 "Your servant didn't g anywhere," 2143
6: 2 *Let us* g to the Jordan, 2143
6: 2 And he said, **"G."** 2143
6:13 **"G,** find out where he is," the king ordered, 2143
6:22 that they may eat and drink and then **g back** 2143
7: 4 If we say, *'We'll* **g into** the city'— 995
7: 4 So *let's* **g over** to the camp of the Arameans 2143
7: 9 *Let's* **g at once** and report this to 995+2143+2256
7:14 **"G** and find out what has happened." 2143
8: 1 **"G away** with your family and stay for a 2143
8: 8 with you and g to meet the man of God. 2143
8:10 Elisha answered, **"G** and say to him, 2143
9: 1 of oil with you and g *to* Ramoth Gilead. 2143
9: 2 **G** *to* him, get him away 995
9:15 the city to g and tell the news in Jezreel." 2143
10:25 **"G in** and kill them; let no one escape." 995
11: 7 *that* normally **g off** Sabbath **duty** are all 3655
17:27 **"Have** one of the priests you took captive
from Samaria g back to live there 2143
19:27 where you stay and when you come and g 3655
20: 5 **"G back** and tell Hezekiah, the leader 8740
20: 5 On the third day from now *you will* **g up** 6590
20: 8 and that *I will* **g up** *to* the temple of 6590
20: 9 *Shall* the shadow **g forward** ten steps, 2143
20: 9 or *shall it* **g back** ten steps?" 8740
20:10 for the shadow to **g forward** ten steps," 5742
20:10 "Rather, *have* it **g back** ten steps." 345+8740
20:11 **made** the shadow **g back** the ten steps 8740
22: 4 **"G up** to Hilkiah the high priest 6590
22:13 **"G** and inquire of the LORD for me and 2143
25:24 and *it will* **g well** with you." 3512
1Ch 7:11 fighting men **ready to g out** to war. 3655+7372
14:10 *"Shall I* g and attack the Philistines? 6590
14:10 The LORD answered him, **"G,** 6590
14:14 *"Do* not **g straight up,** 6590
17: 4 **"G** and tell my servant David, 'This is what 2143
17:11 When your days are over and you g to be 2143
20: 1 at the time when kings **g off** to war, 3655
21: 2 **"G** and count the Israelites from Beersheba 2143
21:10 **"G** and tell David, 'This is what 2143
21:18 *to* **g up** and build an altar to the LORD on 6590
21:30 But David could not g before it to inquire 2143
2Ch 6:34 your people g to war against their enemies, 3655
7:19 and commands I have given you and **g off** 2143
11: 4 *Do* not **g up** to fight against your brothers. 6590
11: 4 **G** home, every one of you, 8740
18: 3 *"Will you* g with me against Ramoth Gilead 2143
18: 5 *"Shall we* g to war against Ramoth Gilead, 2143
18: 5 **"G,"** they answered, "for God will give it 6590
18:14 *shall we* g to war against Ramoth Gilead, 2143
18:16 *Let* each one g home in peace.' " 8740
18:21 " *'I will* g and be a lying spirit in 3655
18:21 **'G** and do it.' 3655
18:23 the spirit from the LORD g when he went 6296
18:24 "You will find out on the day *you* g to hide 995
20:17 **G out** to face them tomorrow, 3655
24: 5 **"G** to the towns of Judah and collect 3655
25: 8 if you g and fight courageously in battle, 995
26:11 **ready to g out** by divisions according 3655+7372
34:21 **"G** and inquire of the LORD for me and 2143
36:23 and *let him* **g up.' "** 6590
Ezr 1: 3 may his God be with him, and *let him* **g up** 6590
1: 5 to **g up** and build the house of the LORD 6590
4: 4 and make them afraid to *g on* **building.** AIT
5: 5 not stopped until a report *could* g to Darius 10207
5:15 'Take these articles and g and deposit them 10016
7:13 who wish to g to Jerusalem with you, 10207
7:13 to go to Jerusalem with you, *may* **g.** 10207
7:28 from Israel to **g up** with me. 6590
8:31 from the Ahava Canal to g *to* Jerusalem. 2143
Ne 6: 3 on a great project and cannot **g down.** 3718
6: 3 the work stop while I leave it and **g down** 3718
6:11 like me g into the temple to save his life? 995
6:11 *I will* not **g!"** 995
8:10 **"G** and enjoy choice food and sweet drinks, 2143
8:15 **"G out** *into* the hill country 3655
9:15 you told them to **g in** and take possession 995
12:31 **had** the leaders of Judah **g up** 6590
13:22 and g and guard the gates in order to keep 995
Est 2:12 a girl's turn came to **g in** to King Xerxes, 995
2:13 And this is how she *would* g to the king: 995
2:14 In the evening she *would* g there and in 995
2:15 the daughter of his uncle Abihail) to g to 995
4: 8 to urge her to g into the king's presence 995
4:11 since I was called to g to the king." 995
4:16 **"G,** gather together all the Jews who are 2143
4:16 When this is done, *I will* g to the king, 995
5:14 Then g with the king to the dinner and 995
6:10 **"G at once,"** the king commanded Haman. 4554
Job 2:11 by agreement to g and sympathize with him 995
6:18 *they* **g up** into the wasteland and perish. 6590

Job 10:14 **let** my offense **g unpunished.** 5927
10:21 before *I* g to the place of no return, 2143
11: 2 *Are* all these words *to* **g unanswered?** 4202+6699
16: 6 and if I refrain, *it does* not g away. 2143
16:22 "Only a few years will pass before *I* g *on* 2143
17:16 *Will it* **g down** *to* the gates of death? 3718
20:13 *to let* it g and keeps it in his mouth, 6440
21:13 in prosperity and **g down** *to* the grave 5737
23: 3 if only *I could* g to his dwelling! 995
23: 8 "But if *I* g *to* the east, he is not there; 2143
23: 8 if I g to the west, I do not find him. NIH
24: 5 poor **g about** their labor of foraging food; 3655
24:10 Lacking clothes, *they* **g about** naked; 2143
24:10 they carry the sheaves, but still g hungry. NIH
27: 6 and never **let** g *of* it; 8332
30:28 *I* **g about** blackened, but not by the sun; 2143
31:34 that I kept silent and *would* not g outside 3655
39: 5 "Who **let** the wild donkey g free? 8938
42: 8 now take seven bulls and seven rams and g 2143
Ps 22:29 all *who* **g down** *to* the dust will kneel 3718
26: 6 and **g about** your altar, O LORD, 6015
32: 8 and teach you in the way *you should* **g;** 2143
38: 6 all day long *I* **g about** mourning. 2143
42: 2 When *can I* g and meet with God? 995
42: 4 how *I used to* g with the multitude, 6296
42: 9 Why *must I* **g about** mourning, 2143
43: 2 Why *must I* **g about** mourning, 2143
43: 4 Then *will I* g to the altar of God, to God, 995
44: 9 *you* no *longer* **g out** with our armies. 3655
48:12 Walk about Zion, **g around** her, 5938
55:15 *let them* **g down** alive *to* the grave, 3718
58: 3 Even from birth the wicked **g astray;** 2319
59:10 God *will* **g before** me and will let me gloat 7709
60:10 and no longer **g out** with our armies? 3655
63: 9 *they will* **g down** to the depths of the earth. 995
68:21 hairy crowns of *those who* **g on** in their sins. 2143
71: 3 to which I *can* always **g;** 995
84: 7 *They* g from strength to strength, 2143
88: 4 I am counted among *those who* **g down** *to* 3718
89:14 love and faithfulness g before you. 7709
95:10 "They are a people whose hearts **g astray,** 9494
102:24 your years g on through all generations. NIH
104:19 and the sun knows when to **g down.** 4427
104:26 There the ships **g to and fro,** 2143
108:11 and no longer **g out** with our armies? 3655
115:17 those *who* **g down** *to* silence; 3718
122: 1 *"Let us* g *to* the house of the LORD." 2143
122: 4 That is where the tribes **g up,** 6590
132: 3 not enter my house or g to my bed— 6590
132: 7 *"Let us* g to his dwelling place; 995
139: 7 Where *can I* g from your Spirit? 2143
139: 8 If *I* **g up** *to* the heavens, you are there; 6158
143: 7 or I will be like *those who* **g down** *to* the pit. 3718
143: 8 Show me the way *I should* **g,** 2143
Pr 1:12 and whole, like *those who* **g down** *to* the pit; 3718
1:15 *do* not g along with them, 928+2006+2143
1:19 all *who* **g after ill-gotten gain;** 1298+1299
2:19 None *who* g *to* her return or attain the paths 995
3:23 Then *you will* g *on* your way in safety, 2143
4:13 Hold on to instruction, *do* not **let it g;** 8332
4:15 turn from it and **g** *on your* **way.** 6296
5: 5 Her feet **g down** *to* death; 3718
5: 8 *do* not **g near** the door of her house, 7928
6: 3 **G** and humble yourself; 2143
6: 6 **G** to the ant, *you* sluggard; 2143
6:29 no one who touches her *will* **g unpunished.** 5927
9:15 who **g straight** *on* their way. 3837
10: 3 **let** the righteous **g hungry** 8279
11:21 The wicked *will* not **g unpunished,** 5927
11:21 but those who are righteous *will* **g free.** 4880
14:22 *Do* not those who plot evil **g astray?** 9494
16: 5 Be sure of this: *They will* not **g unpunished.** 5927
17: 5 over disaster *will* not **g unpunished.** 5927
18: 8 they **g down** *to* a man's inmost parts. 3718
19: 5 A false witness *will* not **g unpunished,** 5927
19: 5 and he who pours out lies *will* not **g free,** 4880
19: 9 A false witness *will* not **g unpunished,** 5927
22: 6 a child **in the way** he **should g,** 2006+6584+7023
23:30 who g to sample bowls of mixed wine. 995
24:25 But *it will* **g well** with those who convict 5838
26:22 they **g down** *to* a man's inmost parts. 3718
27:10 and *do* not g *to* your brother's house 995
28:12 wicked rise to power, men **g into hiding.** 2924
28:20 one eager to get rich *will* not **g unpunished.** 5927
28:28 wicked rise to power, people **g into hiding;** 6259
31:18 and her lamp *does* not **g out** at night. 3882
Ecc 1: 4 Generations come and generations **g,** 995
3:20 All **g** to the same place; 2143
5: 1 Guard your steps when *you* g to the house 2143
5: 1 **G near** to listen rather than to offer 7928
6: 6 *Do* not all g to the same place? 2143
7: 2 It is better to g to a house of mourning than 2143
7: 2 to go to a house of mourning than *to* g to 2143
7:18 It is good to grasp the one and not **let g** of
the other. 906+3338+5663
8:10 those who used to come and g from 2143
8:12 I know that *it will* g better 2118
8:13 *it will* not g well with them, 2118
9: 7 **G,** eat your food with gladness, 2143
10: 7 while princes g on foot like slaves. 2143
12: 5 to his eternal home and mourners **g about** 6015
SS 3: 2 I will get up now and **g about** the city, 6015
3: 4 I held him and *would* not **let** him **g** 8332
4: 6 *I will* g to the mountain of myrrh and to 2143
7: 9 *May* the wine g straight to my lover, 2143
7:11 my lover, *let us* g *to* the countryside, 3655
7:12 *Let us* **g early** to the vineyards to see if 8899

Isa 2: 3 let us g up to the mountain of the LORD 6590
2: 3 The law will g out from Zion, 3655
2:10 G into the rocks, hide in the ground 995
5:13 Therefore my people will g into exile 1655
6: 8 And who will g for us?" 2143
6: 9 He said, "G and tell this people: 2143
7: 3 Then the LORD said to Isaiah, "G out, 3655
7:24 Men will g there with bow and arrow, 995
7:25 you will no longer g there for fear of 995
10:29 They g over the pass, and say, 6296
13: 7 Because of this, all hands will g limp, 8332
14:17 and would not let his captives g home?" 7337
15: 5 They g up the way to Luhith, 6590
15: 5 weeping as they g; NIH
18: 2 G, swift messengers, to a people tall 2143
19:23 The Assyrians will g to Egypt and 995
21: 6 This is what the Lord says to me: "G, 2143
22:15 "G, say to this steward, to Shebna, 995+2143
23:18 Her profits will g to those who live before 2118
26:10 a land of uprightness they g on doing evil AIT
26:20 G, my people, enter your rooms and shut 2143
28:13 so that they will g and fall backward, 2143
28:28 so one does not g on threshing it forever. 1889+1889
29: 1 let your cycle of festivals g on. 5938
29:15 Woe to those who g to great depths 6676
30: 2 who g down to Egypt 2143
30: 8 G now, write it on a tablet for them, 995
30:29 your hearts will rejoice as when people g up 2143
31: 1 Woe to those who g down to Egypt for help, 3718
35: 8 wicked fools will not g about on it. 9494
37:28 where you stay and when you come and g 3655
38: 5 "G and tell Hezekiah, 'This is what 2143
38: 8 make the shadow cast by the sun g 8740
38:10 "In the prime of my life must I g through 2143
38:18 those who g down to the pit cannot hope 3718
38:22 "What will be the sign that I will g up to 6590
40: 9 g up on a high mountain. 6590
42:10 you who g down to the sea, 3718
45: 2 I will g before you and will level 2143
45:16 they will g off into disgrace together. 2143
46: 2 they themselves g off into captivity. 2143
47: 1 "G down, sit in the dust, 3718
47: 5 "Sit in silence, g into darkness, 995
48:17 who directs you in the way you should g. 2143
50:11 g, walk in the light of your fires and of AIT
51: 4 The law will g out from me; 3655
52:11 Depart, depart, g out from there! 3655
52:12 you will not leave in haste or g in flight; 2143
52:12 for the LORD will g before you, 2143
55:12 You will g out in joy and be led forth 3655
58: 8 then your righteousness will g before you, 2143
63:14 like cattle that g down to the plain, 3718
65:13 but you will g hungry; AIT
65:13 but you will g thirsty; AIT
66:17 and purify themselves to g into the gardens, NIH
66:24 "And they will g out and look upon 3655
Jer 1: 7 You must g to everyone I send you to 2143
2: 2 "G and proclaim in the hearing 2143
2:18 Now why g to Egypt to drink water from 2006
2:18 And why g to Assyria to drink water from 2006
2:25 and I must g after them.' 2143
2:36 Why do you g about so much, 261
3:12 G, proclaim this message toward the north: 2143
4: 1 of my sight and no longer g astray, 5653
4: 6 Raise the signal to g to Zion! NIH
4:29 Some g into the thickets; 995
5: 1 "G up and down the streets of Jerusalem, 8763
5: 5 I will g to the leaders and speak to them; 2143
5:10 "G through her vineyards and ravage them, 6590
6:25 Do not g out to the fields or walk on 3655
7:12 " 'G now to the place in Shiloh 2143
7:21 G ahead, add your burnt offerings AIT
7:23 that it may g well with you. 3512
9: 2 so that I might leave my people and g away 2143
9: 3 They g from one sin to another; 3655
11:12 of Jerusalem will g and cry out to the gods 2143
12: 9 G and gather all the wild beasts; 2143
13: 1 "G and buy a linen belt and put it 2143
13: 4 and g now to Perath and hide it there in 2143
13: 6 "G now to Perath and get the belt I told you 2143
13:10 the stubbornness of their hearts and g 2143
14: 3 they g to the cisterns but find no water. 995
14:18 If I g into the country, 3655
14:18 if I g into the city, 995
15: 1 my heart would not g out to this people. NIH
15: 1 them away from my presence! Let them g! 3655
15: 2 And if they ask you, 'Where shall we g?' 3655
16: 5 do not g to mourn or show sympathy, 2143
17:19 "G and stand at the gate of the people, 2143
17:19 through which the kings of Judah g in 995
18: 2 "G down to the potter's house, 3718
19: 1 "G and buy a clay jar from a potter. 2143
19: 2 and g out to the Valley of Ben Hinnom, 3655
19:10 while those who g with you are watching, 2143
20: 6 in your house will g into exile to Babylon. 2143
22: 1 "G down to the palace of the king of Judah 3718
22:20 "G up to Lebanon and cry out, 6590
22:22 and your allies will g into exile. 2143
25:16 and g mad because of the sword I will send 2147
25:29 and will you indeed g unpunished? 5927+5927
25:29 You will not g unpunished, 5927
28:13 "G and tell Hananiah, 'This is what 2143
29:16 your countrymen who did not g with you 3655
30:11 let you g entirely unpunished.' 5927+5927
30:16 all your enemies will g into exile. 2143
31: 4 up your tambourines and g out to dance 3655
Jer 31: 6 'Come, let us g up to Zion, 6590
34: 2 G to Zedekiah king of Judah and tell him, 2143
34: 3 And you will g to Babylon. 995
34:14 you must let him g free.' 8938
34:16 and female slaves you had set free to g NIH
35: 2 "G to the Recabite family and invite them 2143
35:11 we must g to Jerusalem to escape 995
35:13 G and tell the men of Judah and the people 2143
36: 5 I cannot g to the LORD's temple. 995
36: 6 So you g to the house of the LORD on 995
36:19 "You and Jeremiah, g and hide. 2143
37: 4 Now Jeremiah was free to come and g 3655
37: 7 will g back to its own land, to Egypt. 8740
37:12 the city to g to the territory of Benjamin 2143
38:20 Then it will g well with you, 3512
39:16 "G and tell Ebed-Melech the Cushite, 2143
40: 4 g wherever you please." 2143
40: 5 However, before Jeremiah turned to g, 8740
40: 5 "G back to Gedaliah son of Ahikam, 8740
40: 5 or g anywhere else you please." 2143
40: 5 and a present and let him g. 8938
40: 9 and it will g well with you. 3512
40:15 "Let me g and kill Ishmael son 2143
42: 3 your God will tell us where we should g 2143
42: 6 so that it will g well with us, 3512
42:14 'No, we will g and live in Egypt, 995
42:15 to g to Egypt and you do go to settle there, 995
42:15 to go to Egypt and you do g to settle there, 995
42:17 to g to Egypt to settle there will die by 995
42:18 be poured out on you when you g 995
42:19 'Do not g to Egypt.' 995
42:22 in the place where you want to g to settle." 995
43: 2 'You must not g to Egypt to settle there.' 995
44:12 of Judah who were determined to g 995
44:25 "G ahead then, do what you promised! AIT
45: 5 but wherever you g I will let you escape 2143
46:11 "G up to Gilead and get balm, 6590
46:16 let us g back to our own people 8740
46:28 not let you g entirely unpunished." 5927+5927
48: 5 They g up the way to Luhith, 6590
48: 5 weeping bitterly as they g; NIH
48: 7 and Chemosh will g into exile, 3655
48:15 her finest young men will g down in 3718
49: 3 for Molech will g into exile, 2143
49:12 why should you g unpunished? 5927+5927
49:12 You will not g unpunished, 5927
49:36 be a nation where Elam's exiles do not g. 995
50: 4 the people of Judah together will g in tears 995
50:27 let them g down to the slaughter! 3718
50:33 refusing to let them g. 8938
50:38 idols that will g mad with terror. 2147
51: 9 let us leave her and each g to his own land, 2143
La 4:15 "G away! You are unclean!" 6073
Eze 1:12 Wherever the spirit would g, 2143
1:12 the spirit would go, they would g, 2143
1:17 they would g in any one of 2143
1:20 Wherever the spirit would g, 2143
1:20 they would g, and the wheels would rise 2143
3: 1 then g and speak to the house of Israel." 2143
3: 4 of man, g now to the house of Israel 995+2143
3:11 G now to your countrymen in exile 995+2143
3:22 "Get up and g out to the plain, 3655
3:24 "G, shut yourself inside your house. 995
3:25 you will be bound so that you cannot g out 3655
7:14 no one will g into battle, 2143
7:17 Every hand will g limp, 8332
8: 9 "G in and see the wicked 995
9: 4 "G throughout the city of Jerusalem 6296
9: 7 and fill the courts with the slain. G!" 3655
10: 2 "G in among the wheels beneath 995
10:11 they would g in any one of the four 2143
12: 3 and g from where you are to another place. 1655
12: 4 g out like those who go into exile. 3655
12: 4 go out like those who g into exile. 4604
12:11 They will g into exile as captives. 2143
12:12 be dug in the wall for him to g through. 3655
12:16 where they g they may acknowledge all
their detestable practices. 995
12:22 'The days g by and every vision comes 799
20:29 What is this high place you g to?' " 995
20:39 G and serve your idols, every one of you! 2143
21: 7 and every hand g limp; 8332
24: 6 whose deposit will not g away! 3655
26:20 down with those who g down to the pit, 3718
26:20 with those who g down to the pit, 3718
30: 9 that day messengers will g out from me 3655
30:17 the cities themselves will g into captivity. 2143
30:18 and her villages will g into captivity. 2143
31:14 with those who g down to the pit. 3718
31:16 down to the grave with those who g down to 3718
32:18 with those who g down to the pit. 3718
32:19 G down and be laid among 3718
32:24 with those who g down to the pit. 3718
32:25 with those who g down to the pit; 3718
32:29 with those who g down to the pit. 3718
32:30 bear their shame with those who g down 3718
35: 7 and cut off from it all who come and g. 8740
38: 9 and the many nations with you will g up, 6590
39: 9 of Israel will g out and use the weapons 3655
39:14 Some will g throughout the land and, 6296
39:15 As they g through the land and one 6296
42:14 to g into the outer court until they leave 3655
42:14 to put on other clothes before they g near 7928
44: 3 of the gateway and g out the same way." 3655
44:19 When they g out into the outer court where 3655
46: 2 of the gateway and then g out, 3655
46: 8 to g in through the portico of the gateway, 995
Eze 46: 9 by the north gate to worship is to g out 3655
46: 9 the south gate is to g out the north gate. 3655
46: 9 but each is to g out the opposite gate. 3655
46:10 going in when they g in and going out 995
46:10 in and going out when they g out. 3655
46:12 Then he shall g out, 3655
48:11 and did not g astray as the Levites did 9494
Da 10:20 when I g, the prince of Greece will come; 3655
11: 4 It will not g to his descendants, NIH
11: 6 the king of the South will g to the king of 995
12: 4 Many will g here and there 8763
12: 9 He replied, "G your way, Daniel, 2143
12:13 "As for you, g your way till the end. 2143
Hos 1: 2 the LORD said to him, "G, take to yourself 2143
2: 5 She said, 'I will g after my lovers, 2143
2: 7 'I will g back to my husband as at first, 2143
3: 1 The LORD said to me, "G, show your love 2143
4:15 "Do not g to Gilgal; 995
4:15 do not g up to Beth Aven. 6590
5: 6 When they g with their flocks and herds 2143
5:14 I will tear them to pieces and g away; 2143
5:15 Then I will g back to my place 2143
7:12 they g, I will throw my net over them; 2143
Joel 2:20 its stench will g up; its smell will rise." 6590
Am 1: 5 The people of Aram will g into exile 1655
1:15 Her king will g into exile, 2143
2: 2 Moab will g down in great tumult 4637
4: 3 You will each g straight out 3655
4: 4 "G to Bethel and sin; 995
4: 4 g to Gilgal and sin yet more. NIH
5: 5 do not g to Gilgal, 995
5: 5 For Gilgal will surely g into exile, 1655+1655
6: 2 G to Calneh and look at it; 6296
6: 2 g from there to great Hamath, 2143
6: 2 and then g down to Gath in Philistia. 3718
6: 7 be among the first to g into exile; 1655+1655
7:11 and Israel will surely g into exile, 1655+1655
7:12 G back to the land of Judah. 1368
7:15 'G, prophesy to my people Israel.' 2143
7:17 Israel will certainly g into exile, 1655+1655
8: 9 "I will make the sun g down 995
Ob 1: 1 and let us g against her for battle"— 7756
1:21 Deliverers will g up on Mount Zion 6590
Jnh 1: 2 "G to the great city of Nineveh and preach 2143
3: 2 "G to the great city of Nineveh 2143
Mic 1: 8 I will g about barefoot and naked. 2143
1:16 g from you into exile. 1655
2:10 Get up, g away! 2143
2:13 One who breaks open the way will g up 6590
2:13 they will break through the gate and g out. 3655
3: 6 and the day will g dark for them. 7722
4: 2 let us g up to the mountain of the LORD, 6590
4: 2 The law will g out from Zion, 3655
4:10 You will g to Babylon; 995
Na 3:11 you will g into hiding and seek refuge 2118
Hab 1:11 they sweep past like the wind and g on— 6296
2: 6 How long must this g on?' NIH
3:19 he enables me to g on the heights. 2005
Zep 1:10 "a cry will g up from the Fish Gate, NIH
Hag 1: 8 G up into the mountains and bring 6590
Zec 1:10 the LORD has sent to g throughout 2143
6: 7 they were straining to g throughout 2143+2143
6: 7 he said, "G throughout the earth!" 2143+2143
6:10 G the same day to the house of Josiah son 995
7:14 behind them that no one could come or g. 6296
8:10 No one could g about his business safely 995+2256+3655
8:21 and the inhabitants of one city will g 2143
8:21 'Let us g at once to entreat the LORD 2143+2143
8:23 'Let us g with you, 2143
11: 5 buyers slaughter them and g unpunished. AIT
14: 2 Half of the city will g into exile, 3655
14: 3 Then the LORD will g out and fight 3655
14:16 that have attacked Jerusalem will g up 6590
14:17 not g up to Jerusalem to worship the King, 6590
14:18 If the Egyptian people do not g up 6590
14:18 on the nations that do not g up to celebrate 6590
14:19 the nations that do not g up to celebrate 6590
Mal 4: 2 And you will g out and leap 3655
Mt 2: 8 "G and make a careful search for the child. 4513
2: 8 so that I too may g and worship him." 2262
2:12 in a dream not to g back to Herod, 366
2:20 and his mother and g to the land of Israel, 4513
2:22 he was afraid to g there. 599
5:24 First g and be reconciled to your brother; 5632
5:30 of your body than for your whole body to g 599
5:41 If someone forces you to g one mile, NIG
5:41 g with him two miles. 5632
6: 6 But when you pray, g into your room, 1656
8: 4 But g, show yourself to the priest and offer 5632
8: 7 Jesus said to him, "I will g and heal him." 2262
8: 9 I tell this one, 'G,' and he goes; 4513
8:13 Then Jesus said to the centurion, "G! 5632
8:19 I will follow you wherever you g." 599
8:21 "Lord, first let me g and bury my father." 599
8:32 He said to them, "G!" 5632
9: 6 "Get up, take your mat and g home." 5632
9:13 But g and learn what this means: 4513
9:24 he said, "G away. The girl is not dead 432
10: 5 not g among the Gentiles or enter any town 599
10: 6 G rather to the lost sheep of Israel. 4513
10: 7 As you g, preach this message: 4513
11: 4 "G back and report to John what you hear 4513
11: 7 "What did you g out into the desert to see? 2002
11: 8 If not, what did you g out to see? 2002
11: 9 Then what did you g out to see? 2002
11:23 No, you will g down to the depths. 2849

Mt 12:45 and *they* g in and live there. *1656*
13:28 'Do you want us *to* g and pull them up?' *599*
14:15 so they can g to the villages *599*
14:16 Jesus replied, "They do not need *to* g away. *599*
14:22 and g on ahead of him to the other side, *4575*
16:21 to his disciples that he must g to Jerusalem *599*
17:27 g to the lake and throw out your line. *4513*
18:12 not leave the ninety-nine on the hills and g *4513*
18:15 g and show him his fault, *5632*
18:27 canceled the debt and let him g. *668*
19:21 "If you want to be perfect, g, *5632*
19:24 it is easier for a camel *to* g through the eye *1451*
20: 4 'You also g and work in my vineyard, *5632*
20: 7 'You also g and work in my vineyard.' *5632*
20:14 Take your pay and g. *5632*
21: 2 "G to the village ahead of you, *4513*
21:21 but also you can say to this mountain, 'G, *149*
21:28 'Son, g and work today in the vineyard.' *5632*
21:30 He answered, 'I will, sir,' but *he did* not g. *599*
22: 9 G to the street corners and invite to *4513*
24:17 *Let* no one on the roof of his house g down *2849*
24:18 in the field g back to get his cloak. *2188*
24:26 out in the desert,' *do* not g out; *2002*
25: 9 g to those who sell oil and buy some *4513*
25:39 or in prison and g to visit you?' *2262*
25:46 they *will* g away to eternal punishment, *599*
26:18 "G into the city to a certain man *5632*
26:24 The Son of Man *will* g just as it is written *5632*
26:32 *I will* g ahead of you into Galilee." *4575*
26:36 "Sit here while I g over there and pray." *599*
26:46 Rise, *let us* g! Here comes my betrayer!" *72*
27:65 "G, make the tomb as secure *5632*
28: 7 Then g quickly and tell his disciples: *4513*
28:10 G and tell my brothers to go to Galilee; *5632*
28:10 Go and tell my brothers to g to Galilee; *599*
28:16 where Jesus had told them to g. *NIG*
28:19 g and make disciples of all nations, *4513*
Mk 1:38 Jesus replied, *"Let us* g somewhere else— *72*
1:44 But g, show yourself to the priest and offer *5632*
2:11 get up, take your mat and g home." *5632*
4:35 *"Let us* g over to the other side." *1451*
5:12 allow *us to* g into them." *1656*
5:18 begged to g with him. *1639*
5:19 "G home to your family and tell them *5632*
5:34 G in peace and be freed *5632*
6:36 Send the people away so they can g to *599*
6:37 Are we to g and spend that much on bread *599*
6:38 he asked. "G and see." *5632*
6:45 and g on ahead of him to Bethsaida, *4575*
7: 8 *You have* let g of the commands of God *918*
7:19 For *it* doesn't g into his heart but *1660*
7:29 he told her, "For such a reply, *you may* g; *5632*
8:26 saying, "Don't g into the village." *1656*
9:43 with two hands *to* g into hell, *599*
10:21 "G, sell everything you have and give to *5632*
10:25 It is easier for a camel *to* g through the eye *1451*
10:52 "G," said Jesus, "your faith has healed you. *5632*
11: 2 "G to the village ahead of you, *5632*
11: 6 and the *people* let them g. *918*
11:23 if anyone says to this mountain, 'G, *149*
13:15 *Let* no one on the roof of his house g down *2849*
13:16 in the field g back to get his cloak. *2188*
14:12 *to* g and make preparations for you to eat *599*
14:13 telling them, "G into the city, *5632*
14:21 The Son of Man *will* g just as it is written *5632*
14:28 *I will* g ahead of you into Galilee." *4575*
14:42 Rise! *Let us* g! Here comes my betrayer!" *72*
16: 1 so that they might g to anoint Jesus' body. *2262*
16: 7 But g, tell his disciples and Peter, *5632*
16:15 "G into all the world and preach *4513*
Lk 1: 9 to g into the temple of the Lord *1656*
1:17 And he *will* g on before the Lord, *4601*
1:76 for *you will* g on before the Lord *4638*
2:15 *"Let's* g to Bethlehem and see this thing *1451*
5: 8 "G away from me, Lord; *2002*
5:14 "Don't tell anyone, but g, *599*
5:24 get up, take your mat and g home." *4513*
5:33 *g on* eating and drinking." *AIT*
6:25 for *you will* g hungry. *4277*
7: 8 I tell this one, 'G,' and he goes; *4513*
7:22 "G back and report to John *4513*
7:24 "What *did you* g out into the desert to see? *2002*
7:25 If not, what *did you* g out to see? *2002*
7:26 But what *did you* g out to see? *2002*
7:50 "Your faith has saved you; g in peace." *4513*
8:14 but *as they* g on their way they are choked *4513*
8:22 *"Let's* g over to the other side of the lake." *1451*
8:31 not to order them *to* g into the Abyss. *599*
8:32 to let them g into them, *1656*
8:38 the demons had gone out begged *to* g *1639*
8:47 seeing that *she could* not g unnoticed, *3291*
8:48 your faith has healed you. G in peace." *4513*
8:51 not let anyone g in with him except Peter, *1656*
9:12 so *they can* g to the surrounding villages *4513*
9:13 we g and buy food for all this crowd." *4513*
9:57 "I will follow you wherever *you* g." *599*
9:59 "Lord, first let me g and bury my father." *599*
9:60 you g and proclaim the kingdom of God." *599*
9:61 but first let me g back and say good-by *NIG*
10: 1 and place where he was about to g. *2262*
10: 3 G! I am sending you out like lambs *5632*
10:10 g into its streets and say, *2002*
10:15 No, *you will* g down to the depths. *2849*
10:37 Jesus told him, "G and do likewise." *4513*
11:26 and they g in and live there. *1656*
13:31 "Leave this place and g somewhere else. *4513*
13:32 He replied, "G tell that fox, *4513*
Lk 14:18 and *I* must g and see it. *2002*
14:21 'G out quickly into the streets and alleys *2002*
14:23 'G out to the roads and country lanes *2002*
14:31 Or suppose a king is about *to* g to war *4483+5202*
15: 4 the open country and g after the lost sheep *4513*
15:18 and g back to my father and say to him: *4513*
15:28 and refused *to* g in. *1656*
16:26 so that those who want *to* g from here *1329*
17:14 When he saw them, he said, "G, *4513*
17:19 Then he said to him, "Rise and g; *4513*
17:23 *Do* not g running off after them. *599+1503+3593*
17:31 *should* g down to get them. *2849*
17:31 in the field *should* g back for anything. *2188*
18:25 it is easier for a camel *to* g through the eye *1656*
19:30 "G to the village ahead of you, *5632*
22: 8 "G and make preparations for us to eat *4513*
22:22 of Man *will* g as it has been decreed, *4513*
22:33 I am ready *to* g with you to prison and *4513*
Jn 4: 4 Now he had *to* g through Samaria. *1451*
4:16 "G, call your husband and come back." *5632*
4:50 Jesus replied, *"You may* g. *4513*
6: 9 how far will they g among *1639+4047+5515*
6:35 He who comes to me *will* never g hungry, *4277*
6:68 "Lord, to whom *shall we* g? *599*
7: 3 "You ought to leave here and g to Judea, *5632*
7: 8 You g to the Feast. *326*
7:14 the Feast *did* Jesus g up to the temple courts *326*
7:33 and then *I* g to the one who sent me. *5632*
7:35 "Where does this man intend *to* g *4513*
7:35 Will *he* g where our people live scattered *4513*
8: 9 those who heard *began to* g away one at *2002*
8:11 "G now and leave your life of sin." *4513*
8:21 Where I g, you cannot come." *5632*
8:22 Is that why he says, 'Where I g, *5632*
9: 7 "G," he told him, "wash in the Pool *5632*
9:11 He told me *to* g to Siloam and wash. *5632*
10: 9 He will come in and g out, *2002*
11: 7 *"Let us* g back to Judea." *72*
11:15 But *let us* g to him." *72*
11:16 *"Let us* also g, that we may die with him." *72*
11:44 "Take off the grave clothes and let him g." *5632*
11:48 If *we* let him g on like this, *918*
13: 1 to leave this world and g to the Father. *NIG*
14: 3 And if *I* g and prepare a place for you, *4513*
15:16 and appointed you to g and bear fruit— *5632*
16: 1 so that *you will* not g astray. *4997*
16: 7 Unless *I* g away, the Counselor will *599*
16: 7 but if *I* g, I will send him to you. *4513*
18: 8 then let these men g." *5632*
19:12 "If *you* let this man g, *668*
20: 5 of linen lying there but *did* not g in. *1656*
20:17 G instead to my brothers and tell them, *4513*
21: 3 and they said, "We'll g with you." *2262*
21:18 and lead you where you do not want to g." *NIG*
Ac 1:11 in the same way you have seen him g *4513*
1:25 which Judas left *to* g where he belongs." *4513*
3:13 though he had decided *to* let him g. *668*
4:21 After further threats they let them g. *668*
5:20 "G, stand in the temple courts," he said, *4513*
5:38 Let them g! *918*
5:40 and let them g. *668*
7: 3 'and g to the land I will show you.' *1306*
7:40 'Make us gods who *will* g before us. *4638*
8:26 "G south to the road— *4513*
8:29 "G to that chariot and stay near it." *4665*
9: 6 "Now get up and g into the city, *1656*
9:11 "G to the house of Judas on Straight Street *4513*
9:15 But the Lord said to Ananias, "G! *4513*
10:20 So get up and g downstairs. *2849*
10:20 Do not hesitate *to* g with them, *4513*
14:16 he let all nations g their own way. *4513*
14:22 "We must g through many hardships *1328*
15: 2 *to* g up to Jerusalem to see the apostles *326*
15:36 "Let us g back and visit the brothers in all *2188*
16:36 Now you can leave. G in peace." *4513*
17: 9 and the others post bond and let them g. *668*
18: 6 From now on *I will* g to the Gentiles." *4513*
18:27 When Apollos wanted *to* g to Achaia, *1451*
19:21 Paul decided *to* g to Jerusalem, *4513*
20: 3 he decided *to* g back through Macedonia. *5715*
21: 4 the Spirit they urged Paul not *to* g on *2094*
21:12 with Paul not *to* g up to Jerusalem. *326*
22:10 the Lord said, 'and g into Damascus. *4513*
22:21 "Then the Lord said to me, 'G; *4513*
23:10 to g down and take him away from them *2849*
23:23 and two hundred spearmen to g to Caesarea *4513*
23:32 The next day they let the cavalry g on *599*
25: 9 "Are you willing to g up to Jerusalem *326*
25:12 To Caesar *you will* g!" *4513*
25:20 if he would be willing *to* g to Jerusalem *4513*
27: 3 *to* g to his friends so they might provide *4513*
28:26 " 'G to this people and say, "You will *4513*
Ro 6: 1 *Shall we* g on sinning so that grace can *2152*
15:24 I plan to do so when *I* g to Spain. *4513*
15:28 *I will* g to Spain and visit you on *599*
1Co 4: 6 "Do not g beyond what is written." *NIG*
4:11 To this very hour *we* g hungry and thirsty, *4277*
10:27 to a meal and you want *to* g, *4513*
16: 4 If it seems advisable for me *to* g also, *4513*
16: 5 After *I* g through Macedonia, *1451*
16: 6 on my journey, wherever *I* g. *4513*
16:12 I strongly urged him to g to you with *2262*
16:12 He was quite unwilling to g now, *2262*
16:12 but *he will* g when he has the opportunity. *2262*
2Co 9:14 their hearts *will* g out to you, *2160*
10:15 Neither do we g beyond our limits *NIG*
12: 1 I must *g on* boasting. *AIT*
2Co 12: 1 *I will* g on to visions and revelations *2262*
12:18 to g to you and I sent our brother with him. *NIG*
Gal 1:17 nor *did I* g up to Jerusalem *456*
2: 9 that we should g to the Gentiles, *NIG*
5:12 I wish they would g the whole way *NIG*
Eph 4:26 the sun g down while you are still angry, *2115*
6: 3 "that *it may* g well with you and *1181*
Php 1:22 If I am *to g on* living in the body, *AIT*
2:23 as soon as I see how things g with me. *4309*
2Ti 3:13 and impostors *will* g from bad to worse, *4621*
Heb 4: 6 the gospel preached to them *did* not g in, *1656*
6: 1 about Christ and g on to maturity, *5770*
11: 8 *to* g to a place he would later receive *2002*
13:13 *Let us,* then, g to him outside the camp, *2002*
Jas 2:16 "G, I wish you well; *1645+1877+5632*
3: 4 the pilot wants *to* g. *2316*
4:13 or tomorrow *we will* g to this or that city, *4513*
1Jn 3: 9 he cannot *g on* sinning, *AIT*
3Jn 1: 2 and that all *may* g well with you, *2338*
Rev 10: 8 "G, take the scroll that lies open in *5632*
11: 1 "G and measure the temple of God and *1586*
13:10 If anyone is to g into captivity, *NIG*
13:10 into captivity *he will* g. *5632*
16: 1 the temple saying to the seven angels, "G, *5632*
16:14 they g out to the kings of the whole world, *1744*
16:15 not g naked and be shamefully exposed." *4344*
17: 8 and will come up out of the Abyss and g *5632*
20: 8 and *will* g out to deceive the nations in *2002*
22:14 *may* g through the gates into the city. *1656*

GO (Anglicized) See also GET AWAY

GOAD (KJV) See OXGOAD

GOADS (3)

1Sa 13:21 and axes and for repointing g. 1995
Ecc 12:11 The words of the wise are like g, 1996
Ac 26:14 It is hard for you to kick against the g.' *3034*

GOAH (1)

Jer 31:39 to the hill of Gareb and then turn to G. 1717

GOAL (6)

Lk 13:32 and on the third day *I will* reach *my* g.' *5457*
2Co 5: 9 So *we* make it *our* g to please him, *5818*
Gal 3: 3 *are you* now *trying to* attain *your* g *2200*
Php 3:14 I press on toward the g to win the prize *5024*
1Ti 1: 5 The g of this command is love, *5465*
1Pe 1: 9 for you are receiving the g of your faith, *5465*

GOAT (86) [GOAT'S, GOATS, GOATS', GOATSKINS, HE-GOAT, SCAPEGOAT]

Ge 15: 9 a g and a ram, each three years old, 6436
30:32 and every spotted or speckled g. 6436
30:33 Any g in my possession that is not speckled 6436
37:31 slaughtered a g and dipped the robe in 6436+8538
38:17 "I'll send you a young g from my flock," 1531+6436
38:20 Judah sent the young g by his friend 1531+6436
38:23 After all, I did send her this young g, 1531
Ex 23:19 not cook a young g in its mother's milk. 1531
25: 4 and fine linen; g hair; 6436
26: 7 of g hair for the tent over the tabernacle— 6436
34:26 not cook a young g in its mother's milk." 1531
35: 6 and fine linen; g hair; 6436
35:23 or fine linen, or g hair, ram skins dyed red 6436
35:26 and had the skill spun the g hair. 6436
36:14 of g hair for the tent over the tabernacle— 6436
Lev 3:12 " 'If his offering is a g, 6436
4:23 as his offering a male g without defect. 6436+8538
4:28 for the sin he committed a female g 6436+8544
5: 6 to the LORD a female lamb or g from 6436+8544
9: 3 'Take a male g for a sin offering, 6436+8538
9:15 He took the g for the people's sin offering 8538
10:16 about the g *of* the sin offering and found 8538
10:18 you should have eaten the g in 2023S
16: 9 Aaron shall bring the g whose lot falls to 8538
16:10 the g chosen by lot as the scapegoat shall 8538
16:15 then slaughter the g *for* the sin offering for 8538
16:20 he shall bring forward the live g. 8538
16:21 the head of the live g and confess over it all 8538
16:21 He shall send the g away into the desert in NIH
16:22 The g will carry on itself all their sins to 8538
16:26 the man who releases the g as a scapegoat 8538
16:27 The bull and the g *for* the sin offerings, 8538
17: 3 a lamb or a g in the camp or outside of it 6436
17: 7 of their sacrifices to the g idols 8539
22:27 a lamb or a g is born, 6436
23:19 sacrifice one male g for a sin offering 6436+8538
Nu 7:16 one male g for a sin offering; 6436+8538
7:22 one male g for a sin offering; 6436+8538
7:28 one male g for a sin offering; 6436+8538
7:34 one male g for a sin offering; 6436+8538
7:40 one male g for a sin offering; 6436+8538
7:46 one male g for a sin offering; 6436+8538
7:52 one male g for a sin offering; 6436+8538
7:58 one male g for a sin offering; 6436+8538
7:64 one male g for a sin offering; 6436+8538
7:70 one male g for a sin offering; 6436+8538
7:76 one male g for a sin offering; 6436+8538
7:82 one male g for a sin offering; 6436+8538
15:11 Each bull or ram, each lamb or young g, 6436
15:24 and a male g for a sin offering. 6436+8538

Nu 15:27 a year-old female **g** for a sin offering. 6436
18:17 a sheep or a **g**; they are holy. 6436
28:15 one **male g** is to be presented to 6436+8538
28:22 Include one **male g** as a sin offering 8538
28:30 Include one **male g** to make atonement 6436+8538
29: 5 Include one **male g** as a sin offering 6436+8538
29:11 Include one **male g** as a sin offering, 6436+8538
29:16 Include one **male g** as a sin offering, 6436+8538
29:19 Include one **male g** as a sin offering, 6436+8538
29:22 Include one **male g** as a sin offering, 8538
29:25 Include one **male g** as a sin offering, 6436+8538
29:28 Include one **male g** as a sin offering, 8538
29:31 Include one **male g** as a sin offering, 8538
29:34 Include one **male g** as a sin offering, 8538
29:38 Include one **male g** as a sin offering, 8538
31:20 **g hair** or wood." 6436
Dt 14: 4 the ox, the sheep, the **g**, 6436+8445
14: 5 the gazelle, the roe deer, the **wild g**, 735
14:21 Do not cook a **young g** in its mother's milk. 1531
Jdg 6:19 Gideon went in, prepared a **young g**, 1531+6436
13:15 until we prepare a **young g** for you." 1531+6436
13:19 Then Manoah took a **young g**, 1531+6436
14: 6 as he might have torn a **young g**. 1531
15: 1 a **young g** and went to visit his wife. 1531+6436
1Sa 16:20 a **young g** and sent them with his son 1531+6436
2Ch 11:15 and for the **g** and calf **idols** he had made. 8539
Isa 11: 6 the leopard will lie down with the **g**, 1531
Eze 43:22 a **male g** without defect for a sin offering, 6436+8538
43:25 to provide a **male g** daily for a sin offering; 8538
45:23 and a **male g** for a sin offering. 6436+8538
Da 8: 5 suddenly a **g** with a prominent horn 6436+7618
8: 7 the **g** knocked him to the ground NIH
8: 8 The **g** became very great, 6436+7618
8:21 The shaggy **g** is the king of Greece, 7618
Lk 15:29 Yet you never gave me even a **young g** *2253*
Rev 6:12 like sackcloth made of **g** hair, *NIG*

GOAT'S (3) [GOAT]

Lev 4:24 on the **g** head and slaughter it at the place 8538
16:18 of the bull's blood and some of the **g** blood 8538
16:21 and put them on the **g** head. 8538

GOATH (KJV) See GOAH

GOATS (79) [GOAT]

Ge 27: 9 and bring me two choice **young g**, 1531+6436
30:35 That same day he removed all the **male g** 9411
30:35 and all the speckled or spotted female **g** 6436
31:10 up and saw that the **male g** mating with 6966
31:12 'Look up and see that all the **male g** mating 6966
31:38 Your sheep and **g** have not miscarried, 6436
32: 5 I have cattle and donkeys, **sheep and g**, 7366
32:14 two hundred female **g** 6436
32:14 and twenty **male g**, 9411
47:17 their **sheep and g**, their cattle and 5238+7366
Ex 9: 3 and on your cattle and **sheep and g**. 7366
12: 5 you may take them from the sheep or the **g**. 6436
20:24 your **sheep and g** and your cattle. 7366
Lev 1:10 from either the sheep or the **g**, 6436
7:23 not eat any of the fat of cattle, sheep or **g**. 6436
16: 5 to take two **male g** for a sin offering 6436+8538
16: 7 to take the two **g** and present them before 8538
16: 8 He is to cast lots for the two **g**— 8538
22:19 sheep or **g** in order that it may be accepted 6436
Nu 7:17 five **male g** and five male lambs a year old, 6966
7:23 five **male g** and five male lambs a year old, 6966
7:29 five **male g** and five male lambs a year old, 6966
7:35 five **male g** and five male lambs a year old, 6966
7:41 five **male g** and five male lambs a year old, 6966
7:47 five **male g** and five male lambs a year old, 6966
7:53 five **male g** and five male lambs a year old, 6966
7:59 five **male g** and five male lambs a year old, 6966
7:65 five **male g** and five male lambs a year old, 6966
7:71 five **male g** and five male lambs a year old, 6966
7:77 five **male g** and five male lambs a year old, 6966
7:83 five **male g** and five male lambs a year old, 6966
7:87 Twelve **male g** were used for 6436+8538
7:88 sixty **male g** and sixty male lambs 6966
31:28 persons, cattle, donkeys, **sheep or g**. 7366
31:30 cattle, donkeys, **sheep, g or** other animals. 7366
Dt 32:14 and flock and with fattened lambs and **g**, 6966
1Sa 10: 3 One will be carrying three **young g**, 1531
24: 2 and his men near the Crags of the **Wild G**. 3604
25: 2 a thousand **g** and three thousand sheep, 6436
1Ki 4:23 and a hundred **sheep and g**, 7366
8:63 hundred and twenty thousand **sheep and g**. 7366
20:27 like two small flocks of **g**, 6436
2Ch 7: 5 hundred and twenty thousand **sheep and g**. 7366
14:15 and carried off droves of **sheep and g** 7366
15:11 of cattle and seven thousand **sheep and g** 7366
17:11 and seven thousand seven hundred **g**. 9411
29:21 seven male lambs and seven **male g** 6436+7618
29:23 The **g** *for* the sin offering were brought 8538
29:24 The priests then slaughtered **the g** 4392[S]
29:33 and three thousand **sheep and g**. 7366
30:24 and seven thousand **sheep and g** for 7366
30:24 and ten thousand **sheep and g**. 7366
35: 7 total of thirty thousand sheep and **g** 1201+6436
Ezr 6:17 a sin offering for all Israel, twelve **male g**, 10535+10615
8:35 as a sin offering, twelve **male g**. 7618
Job 39: 1 when the mountain **g** give birth? 3604
Ps 50: 9 from your stall or of **g** from your pens, 6966
50:13 the flesh of bulls or drink the blood of **g**? 6966
Ps 66:15 I will offer bulls and **g**. 6966
104:18 The high mountains belong to the **wild g**; 3604
Pr 27:26 and the **g** with the price of a field. 6966
SS 1: 8 of the sheep and graze your **young g** by 1537
4: 1 Your hair is like a flock of **g** descending 6436
6: 5 like a flock of **g** descending from Gilead. 6436
Isa 1:11 in the blood of bulls and lambs and **g**. 6966
7:21 a young cow and two **g**. 7366
13:21 and there the **wild g** will leap about. 8538
34: 6 the blood of lambs and **g**, 6966
34:14 and **wild g** will bleat to each other; 8538
Jer 50: 8 and be like the **g** that lead the flock. 6966
51:40 like rams and **g**. 6966
Eze 27:21 with you in lambs, rams and **g**. 6966
34:17 and between rams and **g**. 6966
39:18 if they were rams and lambs, **g** and bulls— 6966
Mt 25:32 a shepherd separates the sheep from the **g**. *2253*
25:33 He will put the sheep on his right and the **g** *2252*
Heb 9:12 by means of the blood *of* **g** and calves; *5543*
9:13 The blood *of* **g** and bulls and the ashes of *5543*
10: 4 the blood of bulls and **g** to take away sins. *5543*

GOATS' (3) [GOAT]

1Sa 19:13 a garment and putting some **g' hair** at 3889+6436
19:16 and at the head was some **g' hair.** 3889+6436
Pr 27:27 You will have plenty of **g'** milk to feed you 6436

GOATSKINS (2) [GOAT, SKIN]

Ge 27:16 the smooth part of his neck with the **g**. 1531+6425+6436
Heb 11:37 They went about in sheepskins and **g**, *128+1293*

GOB (2)

2Sa 21:18 with the Philistines, at **G**. 1570
21:19 In another battle with the Philistines at **G**, 1570

GOBLET (3) [GOBLETS]

SS 7: 2 a rounded **g** that never lacks blended wine. 110
Isa 51:17 its dregs the **g** that makes men stagger. 3926+7694
51:22 from that cup, the **g** *of* my wrath, 3926+7694

GOBLETS (6) [GOBLET]

1Ki 10:21 All King Solomon's **g** were gold, 3998+5482
2Ch 9:20 All King Solomon's **g** were gold, 3998+5482
Est 1: 7 Wine was served in **g** *of* gold, 3998
Da 5: 2 to bring in the gold and silver **g** 10398
5: 3 in the gold **g** that had been taken from 10398
5:23 You had the **g** from his temple brought 10398

GOD (3969) [GOD'S, GOD-BREATHED, GOD-FEARING, GOD-HATERS, GODDESS, GODLESS, GODLESSNESS, GODLINESS, GODLY, GODS]

Ge 1: 1 In the beginning **G** created the heavens and 466
1: 2 Spirit of **G** was hovering over the waters. 466
1: 3 And **G** said, "Let there be light," 466
1: 4 **G** saw that the light was good, 466
1: 5 **G** called the light "day," 466
1: 6 And **G** said, "Let there be an expanse 466
1: 7 So **G** made the expanse and separated 466
1: 8 **G** called the expanse "sky." 466
1: 9 And **G** said, "Let the water under the sky 466
1:10 **G** called the dry ground "land," 466
1:10 And **G** saw that it was good. 466
1:11 **G** said, "Let the land produce vegetation: 466
1:12 And **G** saw that it was good. 466
1:14 And **G** said, "Let there be lights in 466
1:16 **G** made two great lights— 466
1:17 **G** set them in the expanse of the sky 466
1:18 And **G** saw that it was good. 466
1:20 And **G** said, "Let the water teem 466
1:21 So **G** created the great creatures of the sea 466
1:21 And **G** saw that it was good. 466
1:22 **G** blessed them and said, 466
1:24 And **G** said, "Let the land produce 466
1:25 **G** made the wild animals according 466
1:25 And **G** saw that it was good. 466
1:26 Then **G** said, "Let us make man 466
1:27 So **G** created man in his own image, 466
1:27 in the image of **G** he created him; 466
1:28 **G** blessed them and said to them, 466
1:29 **G** said, "I give you every seed-bearing plant 466
1:31 **G** saw all that he had made, 466
2: 2 By the seventh day **G** had finished 466
2: 3 And **G** blessed the seventh day 466
2: 4 When the LORD **G** made the earth and 466
2: 5 the LORD **G** had not sent rain on the earth 466
2: 7 the LORD **G** formed the man from 466
2: 8 LORD **G** had planted a garden in the east, 466
2: 9 And the LORD **G** made all kinds 466
2:15 The LORD **G** took the man and put him in 466
2:16 And the LORD **G** commanded the man, 466
2:18 The LORD **G** said, "It is not good for the man 466
2:19 Now the LORD **G** had formed out of 466
2:21 the LORD **G** caused the man to fall into 466
2:22 Then the LORD **G** made a woman from 466
3: 1 the wild animals the LORD **G** had made. 466
3: 1 He said to the woman, "Did **G** really say, 466
3: 3 but **G** did say, 'You must not eat 466
3: 5 "For **G** knows that when you eat 466
3: 5 and you will be like **G**, 466
3: 8 of the LORD **G** as he was walking in 466
Ge 3: 8 and they hid from the LORD **G** among 466
3: 9 But the LORD **G** called to the man, 466
3:13 Then the LORD **G** said to the woman, 466
3:14 So the LORD **G** said to the serpent, 466
3:21 The LORD **G** made garments of skin 466
3:22 And the LORD **G** said, 466
3:23 So the LORD **G** banished him from 466
4:25 **"G** has granted me another child in place 466
5: 1 When **G** created man, 466
5: 1 he made him in the likeness of **G**. 466
5:22 with **G** 300 years and had other sons 466
5:24 Enoch walked with **G**; then he was no more, 466
5:24 he was no more, because **G** took him away. 466
6: 2 the sons of **G** saw that the daughters 466
6: 4 the sons of **G** went to the daughters of men 466
6: 9 and he walked with **G**. 466
6:12 **G** saw how corrupt the earth had become, 466
6:13 So **G** said to Noah, 466
6:22 as **G** commanded him. 466
7: 9 as **G** had commanded Noah. 466
7:16 as **G** had commanded Noah. 466
8: 1 But **G** remembered Noah and all 466
8:15 Then **G** said to Noah, 466
9: 1 Then **G** blessed Noah and his sons, 466
9: 6 for in the image of **G** has God made man. 466
9: 6 for in the image of God has **G** made man. NIH
9: 8 **G** said to Noah and to his sons with him: 466
9:12 And **G** said, "This is the sign of 466
9:16 the everlasting covenant between **G** 466
9:17 So **G** said to Noah, 466
9:26 "Blessed be the LORD, the **G** *of* Shem! 466
9:27 May **G** extend the territory of Japheth; 466
14:18 He was priest of **G** Most High, 446
14:19 "Blessed be Abram by **G** Most High, 446
14:20 And blessed be **G** Most High, 446
14:22 **G** Most High, Creator of heaven and earth, 446
16:13 "You are the **G** who sees me," for she said, 446
17: 1 "I am **G** Almighty; walk before me 446
17: 3 Abram fell facedown, and **G** said to him, 466
17: 7 be your **G** and the God of your descendants 466
17: 7 be your God and the **G** of your descendants NIH
17: 8 and I will be their **G**." 466
17: 9 Then **G** said to Abraham, "As for you, 466
17:15 **G** also said to Abraham, 466
17:18 And Abraham said to **G**, 466
17:19 Then **G** said, "Yes, 466
17:22 **G** went up from him. 466
17:23 and circumcised them, as **G** told him. 466
19:29 So when **G** destroyed the cities of the plain, 466
20: 3 But **G** came to Abimelech in a dream 466
20: 6 Then **G** said to him in the dream, "Yes, 466
20:11 'There is surely no fear of **G** in this place, 466
20:13 And when **G** had me wander 466
20:17 Then Abraham prayed to **G**, 466
20:17 and **G** healed Abimelech, 466
21: 2 at the very time **G** had promised him. 466
21: 4 as **G** commanded him. 466
21: 6 Sarah said, **"G** has brought me laughter, 466
21:12 But **G** said to him, 466
21:17 **G** heard the boy crying, 466
21:17 the angel of **G** called to Hagar from heaven 466
21:17 **G** has heard the boy crying as he lies there. 466
21:19 Then **G** opened her eyes and she saw a well 466
21:20 **G** was with the boy as he grew up. 466
21:22 **"G** is with you in everything you do. 466
21:23 before **G** that you will not deal falsely 466
21:33 the name of the LORD, the Eternal **G**. 446
22: 1 Some time later **G** tested Abraham. 466
22: 2 Then **G** said, "Take your son, NIH
22: 3 for the place **G** had told him about. 466
22: 8 **"G** himself will provide the lamb for 466
22: 9 the place **G** had told him about, 466
22:12 Now I know that you fear **G**, 466
24: 3 the **G** *of* heaven and the God of earth, 466
24: 3 the God of heaven and the **G** *of* earth, 466
24: 7 "The LORD, the **G** *of* heaven, 466
24:12 "O LORD, **G** *of* my master Abraham, 466
24:27 the **G** *of* my master Abraham, 466
24:42 'O LORD, **G** *of* my master Abraham, 466
24:48 the **G** *of* my master Abraham, 466
25:11 **G** blessed his son Isaac, 466
26:24 "I am the **G** *of* your father Abraham. 466
27:20 "The LORD your **G** gave me success," 466
27:28 May **G** give you of heaven's dew and 466
28: 3 May **G** Almighty bless you 446
28: 4 the land **G** gave to Abraham." 466
28:12 of **G** were ascending and descending on it. 466
28:13 the **G** *of* your father Abraham and the God 466
28:13 of your father Abraham and the **G** *of* Isaac. 466
28:17 This is none other than the house of **G**; 466
28:20 "If **G** will be with me and will watch 466
28:21 then the LORD will be my **G** 466
30: 2 "Am I in the place of **G**, 466
30: 6 Then Rachel said, **"G** has vindicated me; 466
30:17 **G** listened to Leah, and she became pregnant 466
30:18 **"G** has rewarded me 466
30:20 **"G** has presented me with a precious gift. 466
30:22 Then **G** remembered Rachel; 466
30:23 **"G** has taken away my disgrace." 466
31: 5 but the **G** *of* my father has been with me. 466
31: 7 **G** has not allowed him to harm me. 466
31: 9 **G** has taken away your father's livestock 466
31:11 The angel of **G** said to me in the dream, 466
31:13 I am the **G** *of* Bethel, 446
31:16 that **G** took away from our father belongs 466
31:16 So do whatever **G** has told you." 466
31:24 Then **G** came to Laban the Aramean in 466

Ge 31:29 last night the **G** *of* your father said to me, 466
31:42 If the **G** *of* my father, the God of Abraham 466
31:42 the **G** *of* Abraham and the Fear of Isaac, 466
31:42 But **G** has seen my hardship and the toil 466
31:50 remember that **G** is a witness between you 466
31:53 the **G** *of* Abraham and the God of Nahor, 466
31:53 the God of Abraham and the **G** *of* Nahor, 466
31:53 the **G** *of* their father, judge between us." 466
32: 1 and the angels of **G** met him. 466
32: 2 he said, "This is the camp of **G**!" 466
32: 9 Jacob prayed, "O **G** *of* my father Abraham, 466
32: 9 **G** *of* my father Isaac, O LORD, 466
32:28 with **G** and with men and have overcome." 466
32:30 saying, "It is because I saw **G** face to face, 466
33: 5 the children **G** has graciously given your servant." 466
33:10 to see your face is like seeing the face of **G**, 466
33:11 for **G** has been gracious to me 466
35: 1 Then **G** said to Jacob, 466
35: 1 and build an altar there to **G**, 446
35: 3 where I will build an altar to **G**, 446
35: 5 of **G** fell upon the towns all around them so 466
35: 7 that **G** revealed himself to him 466
35: 9 **G** appeared to him again and blessed him. 466
35:10 **G** said to him, "Your name is Jacob, 466
35:11 And **G** said to him, "I am God Almighty; 466
35:11 And God said to him, "I am **G** Almighty; 446
35:13 Then **G** went up from him at the place 466
35:14 at the place where **G** had talked with him, NIH
35:15 Jacob called the place where **G** had talked 466
39: 9 a wicked thing and sin against **G**?" 466
40: 8 "Do not interpretations belong to **G**? 466
41:16 "but **G** will give Pharaoh the answer 466
41:25 **G** has revealed to Pharaoh what he is about 466
41:28 **G** has shown Pharaoh what he is about 466
41:32 the matter has been firmly decided by **G**, 466
41:32 and **G** will do it soon. 466
41:38 one in whom is the spirit of **G**?" 466
41:39 "Since **G** has made all this known to you, 466
41:51 **G** has made me forget all my trouble 466
41:52 because **G** has made me fruitful in the land 466
42:18 "Do this and you will live, for I fear **G**: 466
42:28 "What is this that **G** has done to us?" 466
43:14 And may **G** Almighty grant you mercy 446
43:23 Your **G**, the God of your father, 466
43:23 Your God, the **G** *of* your father, 466
43:29 he said, "**G** be gracious to you, my son." 466
44:16 **G** has uncovered your servants' guilt. 466
45: 5 because it was to save lives that **G** sent me 466
45: 7 But **G** sent me ahead of you to preserve 466
45: 8 it was not you who sent me here, but **G**. 466
45: 9 **G** has made me lord of all Egypt. 466
46: 1 he offered sacrifices to the **G** *of* his father 466
46: 2 And **G** spoke to Israel in a vision at night 466
46: 3 "I am **G**, the God of your father," he said. 446
46: 3 "I am God, the **G** *of* your father," he said. 466
48: 3 "**G** Almighty appeared to me at Luz in 446
48: 9 "They are the sons **G** has given me here," 466
48:11 and now **G** has allowed me to see your 466
48:15 the **G** before whom my fathers Abraham 466
48:15 **G** who has been my shepherd all my life 466
48:20 'May **G** make you like Ephraim 466
48:21 but **G** will be with you and take you back 466
49:25 because of your father's **G**, 446
50:17 of the servants of the **G** *of* your father." 466
50:19 Am I in the place of **G**? 466
50:20 to harm me, but **G** intended it for good 466
50:24 But **G** will surely come to your aid 466
50:25 "**G** will surely come to your aid, 466
Ex 1:17 feared **G** and did not do what the king 466
1:20 So **G** was kind to the midwives and 466
1:21 And because the midwives feared **G**, 466
2:23 because of their slavery went up to **G**. 466
2:24 **G** heard their groaning 466
2:25 So **G** looked on the Israelites 466
3: 1 came to Horeb, the mountain of **G**. 466
3: 4 **G** called to him from within the bush, 466
3: 5 "Do not come any closer," **G** said. NIH
3: 6 Then he said, "I am the **G** *of* your father, 466
3: 6 the **G** *of* Abraham, 466
3: 6 the **G** *of* Isaac and the God of Jacob." 466
3: 6 the God of Isaac and the **G** *of* Jacob." 466
3: 6 because he was afraid to look at **G**. 466
3:11 But Moses said to **G**, "Who am I, 466
3:12 And **G** said, "I will be with you. NIH
3:12 you will worship **G** on this mountain." 466
3:13 Moses said to **G**, "Suppose I go 466
3:13 'The **G** *of* your fathers has sent me to you,' 466
3:14 **G** said to Moses, "Say to the Israelites, 466
3:15 **G** also said to Moses, "Say to the Israelites, 466
3:15 'The LORD, the **G** *of* your fathers— 466
3:15 the **G** *of* Abraham, the God of Isaac and 466
3:15 the **G** *of* Isaac and the God of Jacob— 466
3:15 the God of Isaac and the **G** *of* Jacob— 466
3:16 'The LORD, the **G** *of* your fathers— 466
3:16 the **G** *of* Abraham, Isaac and Jacob— 466
3:18 the **G** *of* the Hebrews, has met with us. 466
3:18 to offer sacrifices to the LORD our **G**.' 466
4: 5 the **G** *of* their fathers— 466
4: 5 the **G** *of* Abraham, the God of Isaac and 466
4: 5 the **G** *of* Isaac and the God of Jacob— 466
4: 5 the God of Isaac and the **G** *of* Jacob— 466
4:16 if he were your mouth and as if you were **G** 466
4:20 And he took the staff of **G** in his hand. 466
4:27 So he met Moses at the mountain of **G** 466
5: 1 "This is what the LORD, the **G** *of* Israel, 466
5: 3 "The **G** *of* the Hebrews has met with us. 466

Ex 5: 3 to offer sacrifices to the LORD our **G**, 466
5: 8 'Let us go and sacrifice to our **G**.' 466
6: 2 **G** also said to Moses, "I am the LORD. 466
6: 3 to Isaac and to Jacob as **G** Almighty, 446
6: 7 and I will be your **G**. 466
6: 7 that I am the LORD your **G**, 466
7: 1 "See, I have made you like **G** to Pharaoh, 466
7:16 'The LORD, the **G** *of* the Hebrews, 466
8:10 like the LORD our **G**. 466
8:19 "This is the finger of **G**." 466
8:25 "Go, sacrifice to your **G** here in the land." 466
8:26 the LORD our **G** would be detestable to 466
8:27 to offer sacrifices to the LORD our **G**, 466
8:28 to offer sacrifices to the LORD your **G** in 466
9: 1 the **G** *of* the Hebrews, says: 466
9:13 the **G** *of* the Hebrews, says: 466
9:30 not fear the LORD **G**." 466
10: 3 the **G** *of* the Hebrews, says: 466
10: 7 that they may worship the LORD their **G**. 466
10: 8 "Go, worship the LORD your **G**," he said. 466
10:16 against the LORD your **G** and against you. 466
10:17 and pray to the LORD your **G** 466
10:25 to present to the LORD our **G**. 466
10:26 of them in worshiping the LORD our **G**, 466
13:17 **G** did not lead them on the road through 466
13:17 For **G** said, "If they face war, 466
13:18 So **G** led the people around by 466
13:19 "**G** will surely come to your aid, 466
14:19 Then the angel of **G**, 466
15: 2 He is my **G**, and I will praise him, 446
15: 2 and I will praise him, my father's **G**, 466
15:26 of the LORD your **G** and do what is right 466
16:12 that I am the LORD your **G**.' " 466
17: 9 of the hill with the staff of **G** in my hands." 466
18: 1 heard of everything **G** had done for Moses 466
18: 4 for he said, "My father's **G** was my helper; 466
18: 5 near the mountain of **G**. 466
18:12 a burnt offering and other sacrifices to **G**, 466
18:12 in the presence of **G**. 466
18:19 and may **G** be with you. 466
18:19 before **G** and bring their disputes to him. 466
18:21 men who fear **G**, trustworthy 466
18:23 If you do this and **G** so commands, 466
19: 3 Then Moses went up to **G**, 466
19:17 the people out of the camp to meet with **G**, 466
19:19 and the voice of **G** answered him. 466
20: 1 And **G** spoke all these words: 466
20: 2 "I am the LORD your **G**, who brought you 466
20: 5 for I, the LORD your **G**, am a jealous God, 466
20: 5 I, the LORD your God, am a jealous **G**, 446
20: 7 not misuse the name of the LORD your **G**, 466
20:10 a Sabbath to the LORD your **G**. 466
20:12 the land the LORD your **G** is giving you. 466
20:19 do not have **G** speak to us or we will die." 466
20:20 **G** has come to test you, 466
20:20 the fear of **G** will be with you to keep you 2257S
20:21 the thick darkness where **G** was. 466
21:13 but **G** lets it happen, 466
22:20 "Whoever sacrifices to any **g** other than 466
22:28 "Do not blaspheme **G** or curse the ruler 466
23:19 to the house of the LORD your **G**. 466
23:25 Worship the LORD your **G**, 466
24:10 and saw the **G** *of* Israel. 466
24:11 But **G** did not raise his hand NIH
24:11 they saw **G**, and they ate and drank. 466
24:13 and Moses went up on the mountain of **G**. 466
29:45 among the Israelites and be their **G**. 466
29:46 that I am the LORD their **G**, 466
29:46 I am the LORD their **G**. 466
31: 3 and I have filled him with the Spirit of **G**, 466
31:18 of stone inscribed by the finger of **G**. 466
32:11 the favor of the LORD his **G**. 466
32:16 The tablets were the work of **G**; 466
32:16 the writing was the writing of **G**, 466
32:27 "This is what the LORD, the **G** *of* Israel, 466
34: 6 the compassionate and gracious **G**, 446
34:14 Do not worship any other **g**, 446
34:14 whose name is Jealous, is a jealous **G**. 446
34:23 the Sovereign LORD, the **G** *of* Israel. 466
34:24 to appear before the LORD your **G**. 466
34:26 to the house of the LORD your **G**. 466
35:31 and he has filled him with the Spirit of **G**, 466
Lev 2:13 of your **G** out of your grain offerings; 466
4:22 of the commands of the LORD his **G**, 466
11:44 I am the LORD your **G**; 466
11:45 brought you up out of Egypt to be your **G**; 466
18: 2 'I am the LORD your **G**. 466
18: 4 I am the LORD your **G**. 466
18:21 you must not profane the name of your **G**. 466
18:30 I am the LORD your **G**.' " 466
19: 2 'Be holy because I, the LORD your **G**, 466
19: 3 I am the LORD your **G**. 466
19: 4 I am the LORD your **G**. 466
19:10 I am the LORD your **G**. 466
19:12 and so profane the name of your **G**. 466
19:14 but fear your **G**. 466
19:25 I am the LORD your **G**. 466
19:31 I am the LORD your **G**. 466
19:32 for the elderly and revere your **G**. 466
19:34 I am the LORD your **G**. 466
19:36 I am the LORD your **G**, 466
20: 7 because I am the LORD your **G**. 466
20:24 I am the LORD your **G**, 466
21: 6 to their **G** and must not profane the name 466
21: 6 and must not profane the name of their **G**. 466
21: 6 the food of their **G**, they are to be holy. 466
21: 7 because priests are holy to their **G**. 466

Lev 21: 8 because they offer up the food of your **G**. 466
21:12 the sanctuary of his **G** or desecrate it, 466
21:12 by the anointing oil of his **G**. 466
21:17 near to offer the food of his **G**. 466
21:21 not come near to offer the food of his **G**. 466
21:22 He may eat the most holy food of his **G**, 466
22:25 and offer them as the food of your **G**. 466
22:33 of Egypt to be your **G**. 466
23:14 very day you bring this offering to your **G**. 466
23:22 I am the LORD your **G**.' " 466
23:28 for you before the LORD your **G**. 466
23:40 before the LORD your **G** for seven days. 466
23:43 I am the LORD your **G**.' " 466
24:15 'If anyone curses his **G**, 466
24:22 I am the LORD your **G**.' " 466
25:17 but fear your **G**. 466
25:17 I am the LORD your **G**. 466
25:36 but fear your **G**, 466
25:38 I am the LORD your **G**, 466
25:38 to give you the land of Canaan and to be your **G**. 466
25:43 but fear your **G**. 466
25:55 I am the LORD your **G**. 466
26: 1 I am the LORD your **G**. 466
26:12 I will walk among you and be your **G**, 466
26:13 I am the LORD your **G**, 466
26:44 I am the LORD their **G**. 466
26:45 in the sight of the nations to be their **G**. 466
Nu 6: 7 of his separation to **G** is on his head. 466
10: 9 be remembered by the LORD your **G** 466
10:10 be a memorial for you before your **G**. 466
10:10 I am the LORD your **G**." 466
12:13 So Moses cried out to the LORD, "O **G**, 446
15:40 and will be consecrated to your **G**. 466
15:41 I am the LORD your **G**, 466
15:41 of Egypt to be your **G**. 466
15:41 I am the LORD your **G**.' " 466
16: 9 that the **G** *of* Israel has separated you from 466
16:22 "O **G**, God of the spirits of all mankind, 446
16:22 "O God, **G** *of* the spirits of all mankind, 466
21: 5 they spoke against **G** and against Moses, 466
22: 9 **G** came to Balaam and asked, 466
22:10 Balaam said to **G**, "Balak son of Zippor, 466
22:12 **G** said to Balaam, "Do not go with them. 466
22:18 beyond the command of the LORD my **G**. 466
22:20 That night **G** came to Balaam and said, 466
22:22 But **G** was very angry when he went, 466
22:38 I must speak only what **G** puts 466
23: 4 **G** met with him, and Balaam said, 466
23: 8 can I curse those whom **G** has not cursed? 446
23:19 **G** is not a man, that he should lie, 446
23:21 The LORD their **G** is with them; 466
23:22 **G** brought them out of Egypt; 446
23:23 'See what **G** has done!' 446
23:27 Perhaps it will please **G** 466
24: 2 the Spirit of **G** came upon him 466
24: 4 of one who hears the words of **G**, who sees 446
24: 8 "**G** brought them out of Egypt; 446
24:16 the words of **G**, who has knowledge from 446
24:23 "Ah, who can live when **G** does this? 446
25:13 the honor of his **G** and made atonement for 466
27:16 the **G** *of* the spirits of all mankind, 466
Dt 1: 6 The LORD our **G** said to us at Horeb, 466
1:10 LORD your **G** has increased your numbers 466
1:11 May the LORD, the **G** *of* your fathers, 466
1:17 for judgment belongs to **G**. 466
1:19 Then, as the LORD our **G** commanded us, 466
1:20 which the LORD our **G** is giving us. 466
1:21 the LORD your **G** has given you the land. 466
1:21 the **G** *of* your fathers, told you. 466
1:25 that the LORD our **G** is giving us." 466
1:26 the command of the LORD your **G**. 466
1:30 The LORD your **G**, who is going before you, 466
1:31 how the LORD your **G** carried you, 466
1:32 you did not trust in the LORD your **G**, 466
1:41 as the LORD our **G** commanded us." 466
2: 7 The LORD your **G** has blessed you in all 466
2: 7 the LORD your **G** has been with you, 466
2:29 the land the LORD our **G** is giving us." 466
2:30 LORD your **G** had made his spirit stubborn 466
2:33 the LORD our **G** delivered him over to us 466
2:36 The LORD our **G** gave us all of them. 466
2:37 with the command of the LORD our **G**, 466
3: 3 So the LORD our **G** also gave 466
3:18 "The LORD your **G** has given you this land 466
3:20 that the LORD your **G** is giving them, 466
3:21 that the LORD your **G** has done 466
3:22 the LORD your **G** himself will fight 466
3:24 For what **g** is there in heaven or 446
4: 1 the **G** *of* your fathers, is giving you. 466
4: 2 of the LORD your **G** that I give you. 466
4: 3 The LORD your **G** destroyed from 466
4: 4 to the LORD your **G** are still alive today. 466
4: 5 as the LORD my **G** commanded me, 466
4: 7 near them the way the LORD our **G** is 466
4:10 before the LORD your **G** at Horeb, 466
4:19 the LORD your **G** has apportioned to all 466
4:21 the LORD your **G** is giving you 466
4:23 the LORD your **G** that he made with you; 466
4:23 the LORD your **G** has forbidden. 466
4:24 For the LORD your **G** is a consuming fire, 466
4:24 a consuming fire, a jealous **G**. 446
4:25 doing evil in the eyes of the LORD your **G** 466
4:29 if from there you seek the LORD your **G**, 466
4:30 to the LORD your **G** and obey him. 466
4:31 For the LORD your **G** is a merciful God; 466
4:31 For the LORD your God is a merciful **G**; 446

Dt 4:32 from the day G created man on the earth; 466
4:33 the voice of G speaking out of fire, 466
4:34 Has any g ever tried to take 466
4:34 the things the LORD your G did for you 466
4:35 that you might know that the LORD is G; 466
4:39 that the LORD is G in heaven above and 466
4:40 the LORD your G gives you for all time. 466
5: 2 The LORD our G made a covenant 466
5: 6 "I am the LORD your G, who brought you 466
5: 9 for I, the LORD your G, am a jealous God, 466
5: 9 I, the LORD your God, am a jealous G, 446
5:11 not misuse the name of the LORD your G, 466
5:12 as the LORD your G has commanded you. 466
5:14 a Sabbath to the LORD your G. 466
5:15 that the LORD your G brought you out 466
5:15 the LORD your G has commanded you 466
5:16 as the LORD your G has commanded you, 466
5:16 the land the LORD your G is giving you. 466
5:24 "The LORD our G has shown us his glory 466
5:24 a man can live even if G speaks with him. 466
5:25 the voice of the LORD our G any longer. 466
5:26 the voice of the living G speaking out 466
5:27 and listen to all that the LORD our G says. 466
5:27 the LORD our G tells you. 466
5:32 the LORD your G has commanded you; 466
5:33 the LORD your G has commanded you, 466
6: 1 and laws the LORD your G directed me 466
6: 2 after them may fear the LORD your G 466
6: 3 just as the LORD, the G *of* your fathers, 466
6: 4 The LORD our G, the LORD is one. 466
6: 5 Love the LORD your G with all your heart 466
6:10 When the LORD your G brings you into 466
6:13 Fear the LORD your G, 466
6:15 for the LORD your G, who is among you, 466
6:15 is a jealous G and his anger will burn 446
6:16 Do not test the LORD your G as you did 466
6:17 of the LORD your G and the stipulations 466
6:20 the LORD our G has commanded you?" 466
6:24 and to fear the LORD our G, 466
6:25 before the LORD our G, 466
7: 1 When the LORD your G brings you into 466
7: 2 the LORD your G has delivered them over 466
7: 6 a people holy to the LORD your G. 466
7: 6 The LORD your G has chosen you out 466
7: 9 Know therefore that the LORD your G is God; 466
7: 9 therefore that the LORD your God is G; 466
7: 9 he is the faithful G, keeping his covenant 446
7:12 the LORD your G will keep his covenant 466
7:16 the peoples the LORD your G gives over 466
7:18 the LORD your G did to Pharaoh and 466
7:19 the LORD your G brought you out. 466
7:19 The LORD your G will do the same to all 466
7:20 the LORD your G will send the hornet 466
7:21 for the LORD your G, who is among you, 466
7:21 is a great and awesome G. 446
7:22 The LORD your G will drive out those nations 466
7:23 the LORD your G will deliver them over 466
7:25 for it is detestable to the LORD your G. 466
8: 2 how the LORD your G led you all the way 466
8: 5 so the LORD your G disciplines you. 466
8: 6 the commands of the LORD your G, 466
8: 7 For the LORD your G is bringing you into 466
8:10 praise the LORD your G for 466
8:11 that you do not forget the LORD your G, 466
8:14 and you will forget the LORD your G, 466
8:18 But remember the LORD your G, 466
8:19 the LORD your G and follow other gods 466
8:20 for not obeying the LORD your G. 466
9: 3 that the LORD your G is the one who goes 466
9: 4 the LORD your G has driven them out 466
9: 5 the LORD your G will drive them out 466
9: 6 LORD your G is giving you this good land 466
9: 7 the LORD your G to anger in the desert. 466
9:10 stone tablets inscribed by the finger of G. 466
9:16 against the LORD your G; 466
9:23 the command of the LORD your G. 466
10: 9 as the LORD your G told them.) 466
10:12 the LORD your G ask of you but to fear 466
10:12 of you but to fear the LORD your G, 466
10:12 the LORD your G with all your heart and 466
10:14 To the LORD your G belong the heavens, 466
10:17 For the LORD your G is God of gods 466
10:17 For the LORD your God is G *of* gods 466
10:17 the great G, mighty and awesome, 446
10:20 Fear the LORD your G and serve him. 466
10:21 He is your praise; he is your G, 466
10:22 and now the LORD your G has made you 466
11: 1 Love the LORD your G and keep his 466
11: 2 the discipline of the LORD your G: 466
11:12 It is a land the LORD your G cares for; 466
11:12 of the LORD your G are continually on it 466
11:13 to love the LORD your G and to serve him 466
11:22 to love the LORD your G, to walk in all 466
11:25 The LORD your G, as he promised you, 466
11:27 the commands of the LORD your G 466
11:28 the LORD your G and turn from the way 466
11:29 When the LORD your G has brought you 466
11:31 the land the LORD your G is giving you. 466
12: 1 the LORD, the G *of* your fathers, 466
12: 4 You must not worship the LORD your G 466
12: 5 the place the LORD your G will choose 466
12: 7 in the presence of the LORD your G, 466
12: 7 the LORD your G has blessed you. 466
12: 9 the LORD your G is giving you. 466
12:10 the land the LORD your G is giving you 466

Dt 12:11 the place the LORD your G will choose as 466
12:12 there rejoice before the LORD your G, 466
12:15 the blessing the LORD your G gives you. 466
12:18 in the presence of the LORD your G at 466
12:18 the place the LORD your G will choose— 466
12:18 to rejoice before the LORD your G 466
12:20 LORD your G has enlarged your territory 466
12:21 where the LORD your G chooses 466
12:27 on the altar of the LORD your G, 466
12:27 beside the altar of the LORD your G, 466
12:28 and right in the eyes of the LORD your G. 466
12:29 The LORD your G will cut off before you 466
12:31 You must not worship the LORD your G 466
13: 3 The LORD your G is testing you 466
13: 4 It is the LORD your G you must follow, 466
13: 5 the LORD your G, who brought you out 466
13: 5 the LORD your G commanded you 466
13:10 to turn you away from the LORD your G, 466
13:12 the towns the LORD your G is giving you 466
13:16 whole burnt offering to the LORD your G. 466
13:18 because you obey the LORD your G, 466
14: 1 You are the children of the LORD your G. 466
14: 2 a people holy to the LORD your G. 466
14:21 a people holy to the LORD your G. 466
14:23 in the presence of the LORD your G at 466
14:23 to revere the LORD your G always. 466
14:24 blessed by the LORD your G 466
14:25 the place the LORD your G will choose. 466
14:26 in the presence of the LORD your G 466
14:29 so that the LORD your G may bless you 466
15: 4 the LORD your G is giving you to possess 466
15: 5 if only you fully obey the LORD your G 466
15: 6 For the LORD your G will bless you 466
15: 7 that the LORD your G is giving you, 466
15:10 of this the LORD your G will bless you 466
15:14 as the LORD your G has blessed you. 466
15:15 and the LORD your G redeemed you. 466
15:18 And the LORD your G will bless you 466
15:19 for the LORD your G every firstborn male 466
15:20 in the presence of the LORD your G at 466
15:21 not sacrifice it to the LORD your G. 466
16: 1 the Passover of the LORD your G, 466
16: 2 as the Passover to the LORD your G 466
16: 5 in any town the LORD your G gives you 466
16: 7 at the place the LORD your G will choose. 466
16: 8 to the LORD your G and do no work. 466
16:10 of Weeks to the LORD your G by giving 466
16:10 the LORD your G has given you. 466
16:11 And rejoice before the LORD your G at 466
16:15 the Feast to the LORD your G at the place 466
16:15 For the LORD your G will bless you 466
16:16 must appear before the LORD your G at 466
16:17 the LORD your G has blessed you. 466
16:18 the LORD your G is giving you, 466
16:20 the land the LORD your G is giving you. 466
16:21 the altar you build to the LORD your G, 466
16:22 for these the LORD your G hates. 466
17: 1 not sacrifice to the LORD your G an ox or 466
17: 2 the eyes of the LORD your G in violation 466
17: 8 the place the LORD your G will choose. 466
17:12 to the LORD your G must be put to death. 466
17:14 the land the LORD your G is giving you 466
17:15 the king the LORD your G chooses. 466
17:19 the LORD his G and follow carefully all 466
18: 5 for the LORD your G has chosen them 466
18: 7 minister in the name of the LORD his G 466
18: 9 the land the LORD your G is giving you, 466
18:12 LORD your G will drive out those nations 466
18:13 be blameless before the LORD your G. 466
18:14 the LORD your G has not permitted you 466
18:15 The LORD your G will raise up for you 466
18:16 the LORD your G at Horeb on the day of 466
18:16 not hear the voice of the LORD our G 466
19: 1 When the LORD your G has destroyed 466
19: 2 the land the LORD your G is giving you 466
19: 3 the land the LORD your G is giving you 466
19: 8 the LORD your G enlarges your territory, 466
19: 9 the LORD your G and to walk always 466
19:10 which the LORD your G is giving you 466
19:14 the land the LORD your G is giving you 466
20: 1 because the LORD your G, 466
20: 4 For the LORD your G is the one who goes 466
20:13 LORD your G delivers it into your hand, 466
20:14 the plunder the LORD your G gives you 466
20:16 the LORD your G is giving you as 466
20:17 as the LORD your G has commanded you. 466
20:18 you will sin against the LORD your G. 466
21: 1 the land the LORD your G is giving you 466
21: 5 for the LORD your G has chosen them 466
21:10 and the LORD your G delivers them 466
21:23 the land the LORD your G is giving you 466
22: 5 LORD your G detests anyone who does this. 466
23: 5 the LORD your G would not listen 466
23: 5 because the LORD your G loves you. 466
23:14 For the LORD your G moves about 466
23:18 of the LORD your G to pay any vow, 466
23:18 the LORD your G detests them both. 466
23:20 so that the LORD your G may bless you 466
23:21 If you make a vow to the LORD your G, 466
23:21 the LORD your G will certainly demand it 466
23:23 the LORD your G with your own mouth. 466
24: 4 the land the LORD your G is giving you 466
24: 9 Remember what the LORD your G did 466
24:13 in the sight of the LORD your G. 466
24:18 and the LORD your G redeemed you 466
24:19 so that the LORD your G may bless you 466
25:15 the land the LORD your G is giving you. 466

Dt 25:16 LORD your G detests anyone who does these things, 466
25:18 they had no fear of G. 466
25:19 the LORD your G gives you rest from all 466
26: 1 the land the LORD your G is giving you 466
26: 2 the land the LORD your G is giving you 466
26: 2 the place the LORD your G will choose as 466
26: 3 to the LORD your G that I have come to 466
26: 4 in front of the altar of the LORD your G. 466
26: 5 before the LORD your G: 466
26: 7 the LORD, the G *of* our fathers, 466
26:10 Place the basket before the LORD your G 466
26:11 the LORD your G has given to you 466
26:13 Then say to the LORD your G: 466
26:14 I have obeyed the LORD my G; 466
26:16 LORD your G commands you this day 466
26:17 that the LORD is your G and 466
26:19 be a people holy to the LORD your G, 466
27: 2 the land the LORD your G is giving you, 466
27: 3 the land the LORD your G is giving you, 466
27: 3 just as the LORD, the G *of* your fathers, 466
27: 5 Build there an altar to the LORD your G, 466
27: 6 of the LORD your G with fieldstones 466
27: 6 on it to the LORD your G. 466
27: 7 in the presence of the LORD your G. 466
27: 9 the people of the LORD your G. 466
27:10 Obey the LORD your G and follow his 466
28: 1 If you fully obey the LORD your G 466
28: 1 the LORD your G will set you high 466
28: 2 if you obey the LORD your G: 466
28: 8 The LORD your G will bless you in 466
28: 9 the LORD your G and walk in his ways. 466
28:13 the LORD your G that I give you this day 466
28:15 if you do not obey the LORD your G 466
28:45 not obey the LORD your G and observe 466
28:47 the LORD your G joyfully and gladly in 466
28:52 the land the LORD your G is giving you. 466
28:53 the LORD your G has given you. 466
28:58 the LORD your G— 466
28:62 not obey the LORD your G. 466
29: 6 that I am the LORD your G. 466
29:10 in the presence of the LORD your G— 466
29:12 into a covenant with the LORD your G, 466
29:13 that he may be your G as he promised you 466
29:15 the presence of the LORD our G but also 466
29:18 from the LORD our G to go and worship 466
29:25 the G *of* their fathers, 466
29:29 secret things belong to the LORD our G, 466
30: 1 the LORD your G disperses you among 466
30: 2 to the LORD your G and obey him 466
30: 3 LORD your G will restore your fortunes 466
30: 4 the LORD your G will gather you 466
30: 6 The LORD your G will circumcise your hearts 466
30: 7 The LORD your G will put all these curses 466
30: 9 LORD your G will make you most prosperous 466
30:10 the LORD your G and keep his commands 466
30:10 the LORD your G with all your heart and 466
30:16 the LORD your G, to walk in his ways, 466
30:16 and the LORD your G will bless you in 466
30:20 and that you may love the LORD your G, 466
31: 3 The LORD your G himself will cross over 466
31: 6 for the LORD your G goes with you; 466
31:11 to appear before the LORD your G at 466
31:12 the LORD your G and follow carefully all 466
31:13 and learn to fear the LORD your G as long 466
31:17 upon us because our G is not with us?' 466
31:26 of the covenant of the LORD your G. 466
32: 3 Oh, praise the greatness of our G! 466
32: 4 A faithful G who does no wrong, 446
32:12 no foreign g was with him. 446
32:15 He abandoned the G who made him 468
32:17 They sacrificed to demons, which are not G 468
32:18 you forgot the G who gave you birth. 446
32:21 They made me jealous by what is no g 446
32:39 There is no g besides me. 466
33: 1 the man of G pronounced on the Israelites 466
33:26 "There is no one like the G *of* Jeshurun, 446
33:27 The eternal G is your refuge, 466

Jos 1: 9 be discouraged, for the LORD your G will 466
1:11 the land the LORD your G is giving you 466
1:13 'The LORD your G is giving you rest 466
1:15 that the LORD your G is giving them. 466
1:17 Only may the LORD your G be with you 466
2:11 the LORD your G is God in heaven above 466
2:11 the LORD your God is G in heaven above 466
3: 3 of the covenant of the LORD your G, 466
3: 9 to the words of the LORD your G. 466
3:10 how you will know that the living G is 446
4: 5 over before the ark of the LORD your G 466
4:23 For the LORD your G dried up the Jordan 466
4:23 The LORD your G did to the Jordan 466
4:24 the LORD your G." 466
7:13 for this is what the LORD, the G *of* Israel, 466
7:19 give glory to the LORD, the G *of* Israel, 466
7:20 the LORD, the G *of* Israel. 466
8: 7 The LORD your G will give it 466
8:30 the LORD, the G *of* Israel, 466
9: 9 because of the fame of the LORD your G. 466
9:18 the LORD, the G *of* Israel. 466
9:19 the LORD, the G *of* Israel, 466
9:23 and water carriers for the house of my G." 466
9:24 the LORD your G had commanded his servant Moses 466
10:19 for the LORD your G has given them 466
10:40 just as the LORD, the G *of* Israel, 466
10:42 because the LORD, the G *of* Israel, 466

Jos	13:14	made by fire to the LORD, the **G** *of* Israel,	466
	13:33	the LORD, the **G** *of* Israel, is their inheritance	466
	14: 6	the man of **G** at Kadesh Barnea about you	466
	14: 8	followed the LORD my **G** wholeheartedly.	466
	14: 9	the LORD my **G** wholeheartedly.'	466
	14:14	the LORD, the **G** *of* Israel, wholeheartedly.	466
	18: 3	the **G** *of* your fathers, has given you?	466
	18: 6	in the presence of the LORD our **G**.	466
	22: 3	the mission the LORD your **G** gave you.	466
	22: 4	LORD your **G** has given your brothers rest	466
	22: 5	to love the LORD your **G**,	466
	22:16	'How could you break faith with the **G**	466
	22:19	other than the altar of the LORD our **G**.	466
	22:22	"The Mighty One, **G**, the LORD!	466
	22:22	The Mighty One, **G**, the LORD!	466
	22:24	the LORD, the **G** *of* Israel?	466
	22:29	the altar of the LORD our **G** that stands	466
	22:33	to hear the report and praised **G**.	466
	22:34	A Witness Between Us that the LORD is **G**.	466
	23: 3	the LORD your **G** has done	466
	23: 3	the LORD your **G** who fought for you.	466
	23: 5	The LORD your **G** himself will drive them out of your way.	466
	23: 5	as the LORD your **G** promised you.	466
	23: 8	you are to hold fast to the LORD your **G**,	466
	23:10	because the LORD your **G** fights for you,	466
	23:11	be very careful to love the LORD your **G**.	466
	23:13	the LORD your **G** will no longer drive out these nations	466
	23:13	which the LORD your **G** has given you.	466
	23:14	the LORD your **G** gave you has failed,	466
	23:15	of the LORD your **G** has come true,	466
	23:16	the covenant of the LORD your **G**,	466
	24: 1	and they presented themselves before **G**.	466
	24: 2	"This is what the LORD, the **G** *of* Israel,	466
	24:17	the LORD our **G** himself who brought us	466
	24:18	because he is our **G**."	466
	24:19	He is a holy **G**; he is a jealous God.	466
	24:19	He is a holy God; he is a jealous **G**.	446
	24:23	the LORD, the **G** *of* Israel."	466
	24:24	the LORD our **G** and obey him."	466
	24:26	in the Book of the Law of **G**.	466
	24:27	against you if you are untrue to your **G**."	466
Jdg	1: 7	Now **G** has paid me back for what I did	466
	2:12	the **G** *of* their fathers,	466
	3: 7	they forgot the LORD their **G** and served	466
	3:20	"I have a message from **G** for you."	466
	4: 6	the **G** *of* Israel, commands you:	466
	4:23	On that day **G** subdued Jabin,	466
	5: 3	I will make music to the LORD, the **G**	466
	5: 5	before the LORD, the **G** *of* Israel.	466
	6: 8	"This is what the LORD, the **G** *of* Israel,	466
	6:10	I said to you, 'I am the LORD your **G**;	466
	6:20	The angel of **G** said to him,	466
	6:26	a proper kind of altar to the LORD your **G**	466
	6:31	If Baal really is a **g**,	466
	6:36	Gideon said to **G**, "If you will save Israel	466
	6:39	Then Gideon said to **G**,	466
	6:40	That night **G** did so.	466
	7:14	**G** has given the Midianites and	466
	7:15	and its interpretation, he worshiped **G**.	NIH
	8: 3	**G** gave Oreb and Zeeb,	466
	8:33	They set up Baal-Berith as their **g**	466
	8:34	and did not remember the LORD their **G**,	466
	9: 7	so that **G** may listen to you.	466
	9:23	**G** sent an evil spirit between Abimelech	466
	9:24	**G** did this in order that the crime	NIH
	9:27	they held a festival in the temple of their **g**.	466
	9:56	Thus **G** repaid the wickedness	466
	9:57	**G** also made the men of Shechem pay	466
	10:10	forsaking our **G** and serving the Baals."	466
	11:21	"Then the LORD, the **G** *of* Israel,	466
	11:23	"Now since the LORD, the **G** *of* Israel,	466
	11:24	not take what your **g** Chemosh gives you?	466
	11:24	whatever the LORD our **G** has given us,	466
	13: 5	set apart to **G** from birth,	466
	13: 6	"A man of **G** came to me.	466
	13: 6	He looked like an angel of **G**,	466
	13: 7	be a Nazirite of **G** from birth until the day	466
	13: 8	let the man of **G** you sent to us come again	466
	13: 9	**G** heard Manoah, and the angel	466
	13: 9	the angel of **G** came again to the woman	466
	13:22	"We have seen **G**!"	466
	15:19	**G** opened up the hollow place in Lehi,	466
	16:17	a Nazirite set apart to **G** since birth.	466
	16:23	to offer a great sacrifice to Dagon their **g**	466
	16:23	"Our **g** has delivered Samson, our enemy,	466
	16:24	the people saw him, they praised their **g**,	466
	16:24	"Our **g** has delivered our enemy	466
	16:28	O **G**, please strengthen me just once more,	466
	18: 5	of **G** to learn whether our journey will	466
	18:10	and a spacious land that **G** has put	466
	18:31	all the time the house of **G** was in Shiloh.	466
	20: 2	in the assembly of the people of **G**,	466
	20:18	up to Bethel and inquired of **G**.	466
	20:27	the ark of the covenant of **G** was there,	466
	21: 2	where they sat before **G** until evening,	466
	21: 3	"O LORD, the **G** *of* Israel," they cried,	466
Ru	1:16	be my people and your **G** my God.	466
	1:16	be my people and your God my **G**.	466
	2:12	rewarded by the LORD, the **G** *of* Israel,	466
1Sa	1:17	and may the **G** *of* Israel grant you	466
	2: 2	there is no Rock like our **G**.	466
	2: 3	for the LORD is a **G** who knows,	446
	2:25	**G** may mediate for him;	466
	2:27	a man of **G** came to Eli and said to him,	466
	2:30	"Therefore the LORD, the **G** *of* Israel,	466
1Sa	3: 3	The lamp of **G** had not yet gone out,	466
	3: 3	where the ark of **G** was.	466
	3:17	May **G** deal with you,	466
	4: 4	with the ark of the covenant of **G**.	466
	4: 7	"A **g** has come into the camp," they said.	466
	4:11	The ark of **G** was captured,	466
	4:13	because his heart feared for the ark of **G**.	466
	4:17	and the ark of **G** has been captured."	466
	4:18	When he mentioned the ark of **G**,	466
	4:19	that the ark of **G** had been captured and	466
	4:21	because of the capture of the ark of **G** and	466
	4:22	for the ark of **G** has been captured."	466
	5: 1	the Philistines had captured the ark of **G**,	466
	5: 7	the **g** *of* Israel must not stay here with us,	466
	5: 7	upon us and upon Dagon our **g**."	466
	5: 8	"What shall we do with the ark of the **g**	466
	5: 8	the ark of the **g** *of* Israel moved to Gath."	466
	5: 8	So they moved the ark of the **G** *of* Israel.	466
	5:10	So they sent the ark of **G** to Ekron.	466
	5:10	As the ark of **G** was entering Ekron,	466
	5:10	of the **g** *of* Israel around to us to kill us	466
	5:11	"Send the ark of the **g** *of* Israel away;	466
	6: 3	"If you return the ark of the **g** *of* Israel,	466
	6: 5	and pay honor to Israel's **g**.	466
	6:19	But **G** struck down some of the men	NIH
	6:20	the presence of the LORD, this holy **G**?	466
	7: 8	not stop crying out to the LORD our **G**	466
	9: 6	"Look, in this town there is a man of **G**;	466
	9: 7	We have no gift to take to the man of **G**.	466
	9: 8	of **G** so that he will tell us what way	466
	9: 9	if a man went to inquire of **G**,	466
	9:10	for the town where the man of **G** was.	466
	9:27	so that I may give you a message from **G**."	466
	10: 3	up to **G** at Bethel will meet you there.	466
	10: 5	"After that you will go to Gibeah of **G**,	466
	10: 7	your hand finds to do, for **G** is with you.	466
	10: 9	**G** changed Saul's heart,	466
	10:10	the Spirit of **G** came upon him in power,	466
	10:18	"This is what the LORD, the **G** *of* Israel,	466
	10:19	But you have now rejected your **G**,	466
	10:26	by valiant men whose hearts **G** had touched.	466
	11: 6	the Spirit of **G** came upon him in power,	466
	12: 9	"But they forgot the LORD their **G**;	466
	12:12	though the LORD your **G** was your king.	466
	12:14	over you follow the LORD your **G**—	466
	12:19	to the LORD your **G** for your servants so	466
	13:13	the command the LORD your **G** gave you;	466
	14:15	It was a panic sent by **G**.	466
	14:18	Saul said to Ahijah, "Bring the ark of **G**."	466
	14:36	the priest said, "Let us inquire of **G** here."	466
	14:37	So Saul asked **G**,	466
	14:37	But **G** did not answer him that day.	NIH
	14:41	Saul prayed to the LORD, the **G** *of* Israel,	466
	14:44	Saul said, "May **G** deal with me,	466
	15:15	to sacrifice to the LORD your **G**,	466
	15:21	the best of what was **devoted to G**,	3051
	15:21	to sacrifice them to the LORD your **G**	466
	15:30	so that I may worship the LORD your **G**."	466
	16:15	an evil spirit from **G** is tormenting you.	466
	16:16	the evil spirit from **G** comes upon you,	466
	16:23	the spirit from **G** came upon Saul,	466
	17:26	the armies of the living **G**?"	466
	17:36	he has defied the armies of the living **G**.	466
	17:45	the **G** *of* the armies of Israel,	466
	17:46	the whole world will know that there is a **G**	466
	18:10	an evil spirit from **G** came forcefully	466
	19:20	the Spirit of **G** came upon Saul's men	466
	19:23	But the Spirit of **G** came even upon him,	466
	20:12	"By the LORD, the **G** *of* Israel,	466
	22: 3	with you until I learn what **G** will do	466
	22:13	and a sword and inquiring of **G** for him,	466
	22:15	Was that day the first time I inquired of **G**	466
	23: 7	and he said, "**G** has handed him over to me,	466
	23:10	David said, "O LORD, **G** *of* Israel,	466
	23:11	O LORD, **G** *of* Israel, tell your servant."	466
	23:14	but **G** did not give David into his hands.	466
	23:16	and helped him find strength in **G**.	466
	25:22	May **G** deal with David,	466
	25:29	of the living by the LORD your **G**.	466
	25:32	"Praise be to the LORD, the **G** *of* Israel,	466
	25:34	as surely as the LORD, the **G** *of* Israel,	466
	26: 8	"Today **G** has delivered your enemy	466
	28:15	and **G** has turned away from me.	466
	29: 9	as pleasing in my eyes as an angel of **G**;	466
	30: 6	David found strength in the LORD his **G**.	466
	30:15	to me before **G** that you will not kill me	466
2Sa	2:27	Joab answered, "As surely as **G** lives,	466
	3: 9	May **G** deal with Abner,	466
	3:35	saying, "May **G** deal with me,	466
	5:10	the LORD **G** Almighty was with him.	466
	6: 2	to bring up from there the ark of **G**,	466
	6: 3	the ark of **G** on a new cart and brought it	466
	6: 4	with the ark of **G** on it,	466
	6: 6	and took hold of the ark of **G**,	466
	6: 7	therefore **G** struck him down	466
	6: 7	down and he died there beside the ark of **G**.	466
	6:12	because of the ark of **G**."	466
	6:12	and brought up the ark of **G** from the house	466
	7: 2	while the ark of **G** remains in a tent."	466
	7:22	and there is no **G** but you,	466
	7:23	the one nation on earth that **G** went out	466
	7:24	and you, O LORD, have become their **G**.	466
	7:25	And now, LORD **G**, keep forever the promise	466
	7:26	'The LORD Almighty is **G** over Israel!'	466
	7:27	"O LORD Almighty, **G** *of* Israel,	466
	7:28	O Sovereign LORD, you are **G**!	466
	10:12	for our people and the cities of our **G**.	466
2Sa	12: 7	This is what the LORD, the **G** *of* Israel,	466
	12:16	David pleaded with **G** for the child.	466
	14:11	"Then let the king invoke the LORD his **G**	466
	14:13	a thing like this against the people of **G**?	466
	14:14	But **G** does not take away life;	466
	14:16	from the inheritance **G** gave us.'	466
	14:17	an angel of **G** in discerning good and evil.	466
	14:17	May the LORD your **G** be with you.' "	466
	14:20	like that of an angel of **G**—	466
	15:24	the ark of the covenant of **G**.	466
	15:24	They set down the ark of **G**,	466
	15:25	"Take the ark of **G** back into the city.	466
	15:29	of **G** back to Jerusalem and stayed there.	466
	15:32	where people used to worship **G**,	466
	16:23	like that of one who inquires of **G**.	466
	18:28	"Praise be to the LORD your **G**!	466
	19:13	May **G** deal with me, be it ever so severely,	466
	19:27	My lord the king is like an angel of **G**;	466
	21:14	**G** answered prayer in behalf of the land.	466
	22: 3	my **G** is my rock, in whom I take refuge,	466
	22: 7	I called out to my **G**.	466
	22:22	I have not done evil by turning from my **G**.	466
	22:30	with my **G** I can scale a wall.	466
	22:31	"As for **G**, his way is perfect;	446
	22:32	For who is **G** besides the LORD?	446
	22:32	And who is the Rock except our **G**?	466
	22:33	It is **G** who arms me with strength	446
	22:47	Exalted be **G**, the Rock, my Savior!	466
	22:48	He is the **G** who avenges me,	446
	23: 1	the man anointed by the **G** *of* Jacob,	466
	23: 3	The **G** *of* Israel spoke,	466
	23: 3	when he rules in the fear of **G**,	466
	23: 5	"Is not my house right with **G**?	446
	24: 3	the LORD your **G** multiply the troops	466
	24:23	"May the LORD your **G** accept you."	466
	24:24	to the LORD my **G** burnt offerings	466
1Ki	1:17	to me your servant by the LORD your **G**:	466
	1:30	the LORD, the **G** *of* Israel:	466
	1:36	the **G** *of* my lord the king, so declare it.	466
	1:47	'May your **G** make Solomon's name more famous than yours	466
	1:48	'Praise be to the LORD, the **G** *of* Israel,	466
	2: 3	observe what the LORD your **G** requires:	466
	2:23	"May **G** deal with me,	466
	3: 5	during the night in a dream, and **G** said,	466
	3: 7	"Now, O LORD my **G**,	466
	3:11	So **G** said to him,	466
	3:28	he had wisdom from **G** to administer justice	466
	4:29	**G** gave Solomon wisdom	466
	5: 3	a temple for the Name of the LORD his **G**	466
	5: 4	now the LORD my **G** has given me rest	466
	5: 5	a temple for the Name of the LORD my **G**,	466
	8:15	"Praise be to the LORD, the **G** *of* Israel,	466
	8:17	the LORD, the **G** *of* Israel,	466
	8:20	the Name of the LORD, the **G** *of* Israel.	466
	8:23	"O LORD, **G** *of* Israel,	466
	8:23	of Israel, there is no **G** like you in heaven	466
	8:25	"Now LORD, **G** *of* Israel,	466
	8:26	And now, O **G** *of* Israel,	466
	8:27	"But will **G** really dwell on earth?	466
	8:28	O LORD my **G**.	466
	8:57	the LORD our **G** be with us as he was	466
	8:59	be near to the LORD our **G** day and night,	466
	8:60	of the earth may know that the LORD is **G**	466
	8:61	be fully committed to the LORD our **G**,	466
	8:65	They celebrated it before the LORD our **G**	466
	9: 9	they have forsaken the LORD their **G**,	466
	10: 9	Praise be to the LORD your **G**,	466
	10:24	to hear the wisdom **G** had put in his heart.	466
	11: 4	not fully devoted to the LORD his **G**,	466
	11: 5	the **detestable g** *of* the Ammonites.	9199
	11: 7	a high place for Chemosh the **detestable g**	9199
	11: 7	the **detestable g** *of* the Ammonites.	9199
	11: 9	the LORD, the **G** *of* Israel,	466
	11:23	And **G** raised up against Solomon	466
	11:31	for this is what the LORD, the **G** *of* Israel,	466
	11:33	Chemosh the **g** *of* the Moabites,	466
	11:33	and Molech the **g** *of* the Ammonites,	466
	12:22	of **G** came to Shemaiah the man of God:	466
	12:22	of God came to Shemaiah the man of **G**:	466
	13: 1	of the LORD a man of **G** came from Judah	466
	13: 3	That same day the man of **G** gave a sign:	NIH
	13: 4	of **G** cried out against the altar at Bethel,	466
	13: 5	the sign given by the man of **G** by the word	466
	13: 6	Then the king said to the man of **G**,	466
	13: 6	with the LORD your **G** and pray for me	466
	13: 6	the man of **G** interceded with the LORD,	466
	13: 7	The king said to the man of **G**,	466
	13: 8	But the man of **G** answered the king,	466
	13:11	that the man of **G** had done there that day.	466
	13:12	the man of **G** from Judah had taken.	466
	13:14	and rode after the man of **G**.	466
	13:14	the man of **G** who came from Judah?"	466
	13:16	The man of **G** said,	NIH
	13:19	So the man of **G** returned with him and ate	NIH
	13:21	to the man of **G** who had come from Judah,	466
	13:21	the command the LORD your **G** gave you.	466
	13:23	When the man of **G** had finished eating	NIH
	13:26	"It is the man of **G** who defied the word of	466
	13:29	up the body of the man of **G**,	466
	13:31	in the grave where the man of **G** is buried;	466
	14: 7	the LORD, the **G** *of* Israel, says:	466
	14:13	the **G** *of* Israel, has found anything good.	466
	15: 3	not fully devoted to the LORD his **G**,	466
	15: 4	the LORD his **G** gave him a lamp	466
	15:30	provoked the LORD, the **G** *of* Israel, to anger	466
	16:13	provoked the LORD, the **G** *of* Israel, to anger	466

1Ki 16:26 the LORD, the G of Israel, to anger 466
16:33 the LORD, the G of Israel, to anger 466
17: 1 "As the LORD, the G of Israel, lives, 466
17:12 "As surely as the LORD your G lives," 466
17:14 this is what the LORD, the G of Israel, 466
17:18 "What do you have against me, man of G? 466
17:20 "O LORD my G, 466
17:21 "O LORD my G, 466
17:24 "Now I know that you are a man of G and 466
18:10 As surely as the LORD your G lives, 466
18:21 If the LORD is G, follow him; 466
18:21 but if Baal is G, follow him." NIH
18:24 Then you call on the name of your g, 466
18:24 The g who answers by fire—he is God." 466
18:24 The god who answers by fire—he is G." 466
18:25 Call on the name of your g, 466
18:27 "Surely he is a g! 466
18:36 "O LORD, G of Abraham, 466
18:36 be known today that you are G in Israel and 466
18:37 that you, O LORD, are G, and 466
18:39 "The LORD—he is G! 466
18:39 The LORD—he is G!" 466
19: 8 he reached Horeb, the mountain of G. 466
19:10 for the LORD G Almighty. 466
19:14 for the LORD G Almighty. 466
20:28 of G came up and told the king of Israel, 466
20:28 a g of the hills and not a god of the valleys, 466
20:28 a god of the hills and not a g of the valleys, 466
21:10 that he has cursed both G and the king. 466
21:13 "Naboth has cursed both G and the king." 466
22:53 the G of Israel, to anger, 466
2Ki 1: 2 consult Baal-Zebub, the g of Ekron, 466
1: 3 'Is it because there is no G in Israel 466
1: 3 to consult Baal-Zebub, the g of Ekron?' 466
1: 6 Is it because there is no G in Israel 466
1: 6 to consult Baal-Zebub, the g of Ekron? 466
1: 9 "Man of G, the king says, 'Come down!' " 466
1:10 "If I am a man of G, 466
1:11 The captain said to him, "Man of G, 466
1:12 "If I am a man of G," Elijah replied, 466
1:12 of G fell from heaven and consumed him 466
1:13 "Man of G," he begged, 466
1:16 Is it because there is no G in Israel for you 466
1:16 to consult Baal-Zebub, the g of Ekron? 466
2:14 Where now the LORD, the G of Elijah?" 466
4: 7 She went and told the man of G, 466
4: 9 comes our way a holy man of G. 466
4:16 "Don't mislead your servant, O man of G!" 466
4:21 and laid him on the bed of the man of G, 466
4:22 to the man of G quickly and return." 466
4:25 So she set out and came to the man of G 466
4:25 the man of G said to his servant Gehazi, 466
4:27 she reached the man of G at the mountain, 466
4:27 but the man of G said, "Leave her alone! 466
4:40 "O man of G, there is death in the pot!" 466
4:42 of G twenty loaves of barley bread baked 466
5: 7 he tore his robes and said, "Am I G? 466
5: 8 When Elisha the man of G heard that 466
5:11 and call on the name of the LORD his G, 466
5:14 as the man of G had told him, 466
5:15 went back to the man of G. 466
5:15 that there is no G in all the world except 466
5:17 and sacrifices to any other g but 466
5:20 the servant of Elisha the man of G, 466
6: 6 The man of G asked, "Where did it fall?" 466
6: 9 of G sent word to the king of Israel: 466
6:10 on the place indicated by the man of G. 466
6:15 of the man of G got up and went out early 466
6:31 He said, "May G deal with me, 466
7: 2 the king was leaning said to the man of G, 466
7:17 just as the man of G had foretold when 466
7:18 It happened as the man of G had said to 466
7:19 The officer had said to the man of G, 466
7:19 The man of G had replied, NIH
8: 2 to do as the man of G said. 466
8: 4 the servant of the man of G, and had said, 466
8: 7 "The man of G has come all the way 466
8: 8 with you and go to meet the man of G. 466
8:11 Then the man of G began to weep. 466
9: 6 "This is what the LORD, the G of Israel, 466
10:31 the LORD, the G of Israel, with all his heart. 466
13:19 of G was angry with him and said, 466
14:25 the LORD, the G of Israel, 466
16: 2 in the eyes of the LORD his G. 466
17: 7 against the LORD their G, 466
17: 9 the LORD their G that were not right. 466
17:14 who did not trust in the LORD their G. 466
17:16 the commands of the LORD their G 466
17:19 the commands of the LORD their G. 466
17:26 of Samaria do not know what the g of 466
17:27 the people what the g of the land requires." 466
17:39 Rather, worship the LORD your G; 466
18: 5 trusted in the LORD, the G of Israel. 466
18:12 not obeyed the LORD their G, 466
18:22 "We are depending on the LORD our G"— 466
18:33 the g of any nation ever delivered his land 466
19: 4 the LORD your G will hear all the words 466
19: 4 has sent to ridicule the living G, 466
19: 4 for the words the LORD your G has heard. 466
19:10 Do not let the g you depend on deceive you 466
19:15 "O LORD, G of Israel, 466
19:15 you alone are G over all the kingdoms of 466
19:16 to insult the living G. 466
19:19 Now, O LORD our G, 466
19:19 that you alone, O LORD, are G." 466
19:20 "This is what the LORD, the G of Israel, 466
19:37 in the temple of his g Nisroch, 466

2Ki 20: 5 the LORD, the G of your father David, says: 466
21:12 the LORD, the G of Israel, says: 466
21:22 the LORD, the G of his fathers, 466
22:15 "This is what the LORD, the G of Israel, 466
22:18 'This is what the LORD, the G of Israel, 466
23:13 for Chemosh the vile g of Moab, 9199
23:13 the detestable g of the people of Ammon. 9359
23:16 by the man of G who foretold these things. 466
23:17 of the man of G who came from Judah 466
23:21 the Passover to the LORD your G, 466
1Ch 4:10 Jabez cried out to the G of Israel, "Oh, 466
4:10 And G granted his request. 466
5:20 and G handed the Hagrites 466
5:25 But they were unfaithful to the G 466
5:25 whom G had destroyed before them. 466
5:26 So the G of Israel stirred up the spirit 466
6:48 the tabernacle, the house of G. 466
6:49 the servant of G had commanded. 466
9:11 the official in charge of the house of G; 466
9:13 for ministering in the house of G. 466
9:26 the rooms and treasuries in the house of G. 466
9:27 the night stationed around the house of G, 466
11: 2 And the LORD your G said to you, 466
11:19 "G forbid that I should do this!" 466
12:17 the G of our fathers see it and judge you." 466
12:18 for your G will help you." 466
12:22 like the army of G. 466
13: 2 and if it is the will of the LORD our G, 466
13: 3 Let us bring the ark of our G back to us, 466
13: 5 to bring the ark of G from Kiriath Jearim. 466
13: 6 the ark of G the LORD, who is enthroned 466
13: 7 of G from Abinadab's house on a new cart, 466
13: 8 with all their might before G, 466
13:10 So he died there before G. 466
13:12 David was afraid of G that day and asked, 466
13:12 "How can I ever bring the ark of G to me?" 466
13:14 The ark of G remained with the family 466
14:10 so David inquired of G: 466
14:11 G has broken out against my enemies 466
14:14 so David inquired of G again, 466
14:14 and G answered him, 466
14:15 because that will mean G has gone out 466
14:16 So David did as G commanded him, 466
15: 1 a place for the ark of G and pitched a tent 466
15: 2 but the Levites may carry the ark of G, 466
15:12 and bring up the ark of the LORD, the G 466
15:13 that the LORD our G broke out in anger 466
15:14 the ark of the LORD, the G of Israel. 466
15:15 And the Levites carried the ark of G with 466
15:24 to blow trumpets before the ark of G. 466
15:26 Because G had helped the Levites 466
16: 1 They brought the ark of G and set it inside 466
16: 1 and fellowship offerings before G. 466
16: 4 and to praise the LORD, the G of Israel: 466
16: 6 before the ark of the covenant of G. 466
16:14 He is the LORD our G; 466
16:35 Cry out, "Save us, O G our Savior; 466
16:36 Praise be to the LORD, the G of Israel, 466
17: 2 do it, for G is with you." 466
17: 3 That night the word of G came to Nathan, 466
17:16 "Who am I, O LORD G, 466
17:17 if this were not enough in your sight, O G, 466
17:17 the most exalted of men, O LORD G. 466
17:20 O LORD, and there is no G but you, 466
17:21 the one nation on earth whose G went out 466
17:22 and you, O LORD, have become their G. 466
17:24 'The LORD Almighty, the G over Israel, 466
17:24 the God over Israel, is Israel's G!' 466
17:25 my G, have revealed to your servant 466
17:26 O LORD, you are G! 466
19:13 for our people and the cities of our G. 466
21: 7 also evil in the sight of G; 466
21: 8 Then David said to G, "I have sinned 466
21:15 And G sent an angel to destroy Jerusalem. 466
21:17 David said to G, "Was it not I who ordered 466
21:17 O LORD my G, let your hand fall upon me 466
21:30 not go before it to inquire of G, 466
22: 1 "The house of the LORD G is to be here, 466
22: 2 for building the house of G. 466
22: 6 a house for the LORD, the G of Israel. 466
22: 7 a house for the Name of the LORD my G. 466
22:11 and build the house of the LORD your G, 466
22:12 the law of the LORD your G. 466
22:18 "Is not the LORD your G with you? 466
22:19 and soul to seeking the LORD your G. 466
22:19 to build the sanctuary of the LORD G, 466
22:19 and the sacred articles belonging to G into 466
23:14 of G were counted as part of the tribe 466
23:25 "Since the LORD, the G of Israel, 466
23:28 of other duties at the house of G. 466
24: 5 of the sanctuary and officials of G among 466
24:19 the G of Israel, had commanded him. 466
25: 5 through the promises of G to exalt him. 466
25: 5 G gave Heman fourteen sons 466
25: 6 for the ministry at the house of G. 466
26: 5 (For G had blessed Obed-Edom.) 466
26:20 in charge of the treasuries of the house of G 466
26:32 for every matter pertaining to G and for 466
28: 2 for the footstool of our G, 466
28: 3 But G said to me, 466
28: 4 "Yet the LORD, the G of Israel, 466
28: 8 and in the hearing of our G: 466
28: 8 the commands of the LORD your G, 466
28: 9 acknowledge the G of your father, 466
28:12 for the treasuries of the temple of G and for 466
28:20 for the LORD G, my God, is with you. 466
28:20 for the LORD God, my G, is with you. 466

1Ch 28:21 for all the work on the temple of G, 466
29: 1 the one whom G has chosen, 466
29: 1 not for man but for the LORD G. 466
29: 2 for the temple of my G— 466
29: 3 of my G I now give my personal treasures 466
29: 3 and silver for the temple of my G, over and 466
29: 7 on the temple of G five thousand talents 466
29:10 O LORD, G of our father Israel, 466
29:13 Now, our G, we give you thanks, 466
29:16 O LORD our G, as for all this abundance 466
29:17 I know, my G, that you test the heart 466
29:18 O LORD, G of our fathers Abraham, 466
29:20 "Praise the LORD your G." 466
29:20 praised the LORD, the G of their fathers; 466
2Ch 1: 1 for the LORD his G was with him 466
1: 4 Now David had brought up the ark of G 466
1: 7 That night G appeared to Solomon and said 466
1: 8 Solomon answered G, 466
1: 9 Now, LORD G, let your promise 466
1:11 G said to Solomon, 466
2: 4 a temple for the Name of the LORD my G 466
2: 4 the appointed feasts of the LORD our G. 466
2: 5 our G is greater than all other gods. 466
2:12 "Praise be to the LORD, the G of Israel, 466
3: 3 the temple of G was sixty cubits long 466
4:11 for King Solomon in the temple of G: 466
5:14 glory of the LORD filled the temple of G. 466
6: 4 "Praise be to the LORD, the G of Israel, 466
6: 7 for the Name of the LORD, the G of Israel. 466
6:10 for the Name of the LORD, the G of Israel. 466
6:14 He said: "O LORD, G of Israel, 466
6:14 of Israel, there is no G like you in heaven 466
6:16 "Now LORD, G of Israel, 466
6:17 And now, O LORD, G of Israel, 466
6:18 will G really dwell on earth with men? 466
6:19 O LORD my G. 466
6:40 "Now, my G, may your eyes be open 466
6:41 "Now arise, O LORD G, 466
6:41 May your priests, O LORD G, 466
6:42 O LORD G, do not reject your anointed one. 466
7: 5 the people dedicated the temple of G. 466
7:22 forsaken the LORD, the G of their fathers, 466
8:14 the man of G had ordered. 466
9: 8 Praise be to the LORD your G, 466
9: 8 as king to rule for the LORD your G. 466
9: 8 the love of your G for Israel and his desire 466
9:23 to hear the wisdom G had put in his heart. 466
10:15 for this turn of events was from G, 466
11: 2 to Shemaiah the man of G: 466
11:16 the LORD, the G of Israel, 466
11:16 the LORD, the G of their fathers. 466
13: 5 the LORD, the G of Israel, 466
13:10 "As for us, the LORD is our G, 466
13:11 the requirements of the LORD our G. 466
13:12 G is with us; he is our leader. 466
13:12 the LORD, the G of your fathers, 466
13:15 G routed Jeroboam and all Israel 466
13:16 and G delivered them into their hands. 466
13:18 relied on the LORD, the G of their fathers. 466
14: 2 and right in the eyes of the LORD his G. 466
14: 4 to seek the LORD, the G of their fathers, 466
14: 7 we have sought the LORD our G; 466
14:11 Asa called to the LORD his G and said, 466
14:11 Help us, O LORD our G, 466
14:11 O LORD, you are our G; 466
15: 1 The Spirit of G came upon Azariah son 466
15: 3 a long time Israel was without the true G, 466
15: 4 the LORD, the G of Israel, and sought him, 466
15: 6 because G was troubling them 466
15: 9 when they saw that the LORD his G was 466
15:12 seek the LORD, the G of their fathers, 466
15:13 the G of Israel, were to be put to death, 466
15:15 They sought G eagerly, 2084[S]
15:18 into the temple of G the silver and gold and 466
16: 7 of Aram and not on the LORD your G, 466
17: 4 but sought the G of his father 466
18: 5 "for G will give it into the king's hand." 466
18:13 I can tell him only what my G says." 466
18:31 G drew them away from him, 466
19: 3 and have set your heart on seeking G." 466
19: 4 the G of their fathers. 466
19: 7 with the LORD our G there is no injustice 466
20: 6 "O LORD, G of our fathers, 466
20: 6 are you not the G who is in heaven? 466
20: 7 O our G, did you not drive out 466
20:12 O our G, will you not judge them? 466
20:19 the G of Israel, with very loud voice. 466
20:20 the LORD your G and you will be upheld; 466
20:29 The fear of G came upon all the kingdoms 466
20:30 for his G had given him rest on every side. 466
20:33 not set their hearts on the G 466
21:10 forsaken the LORD, the G of his fathers. 466
21:12 the LORD, the G of your father David, says: 466
22: 7 G brought about Ahaziah's downfall. 466
22:12 with them at the temple of G for six years 466
23: 3 with the king at the temple of G. 466
23: 9 and that were in the temple of G. 466
24: 5 to repair the temple of your G. 466
24: 7 of G and had used even its sacred objects 466
24: 9 that Moses the servant of G had required 466
24:13 They rebuilt the temple of G according 466
24:16 of the good he had done in Israel for G 466
24:18 the LORD, the G of their fathers, 466
24:20 of G came upon Zechariah son of Jehoiada 466
24:20 "This is what G says: 466
24:24 forsaken the LORD, the G of their fathers, 466
24:27 of G are written in the annotations on 466

2Ch 25: 7 But a man of G came to him and said, 466
25: 8 G will overthrow you before the enemy, 466
25: 8 G has the power to help or to overthrow." 466
25: 9 Amaziah asked the man of G, 466
25: 9 The man of G replied, 466
25:16 that G has determined to destroy you, 466
25:20 for G so worked that he might hand them 466
25:24 and all the articles found in the temple of G 466
26: 5 He sought G during the days of Zechariah, 466
26: 5 who instructed him in the fear of G. 466
26: 5 G gave him success. 466
26: 7 G helped him against the Philistines and 466
26:16 He was unfaithful to the LORD his G, 466
26:18 you will not be honored by the LORD G." 466
27: 6 before the LORD his G. 466
28: 5 Therefore the LORD his G handed him 466
28: 6 the LORD, the G of their fathers. 466
28: 9 the LORD, the G of your fathers, 466
28:10 of sins against the LORD your G? 466
28:24 from the temple of G and took them away. 466
28:25 the LORD, the G of his fathers, to anger. 466
29: 5 the LORD, the G of your fathers. 466
29: 6 of the LORD our G and forsook him. 466
29: 7 at the sanctuary to the G of Israel. 466
29:10 the LORD, the G of Israel, 466
29:36 at what G had brought about for his people, 466
30: 1 Passover to the LORD, the G of Israel. 466
30: 5 Passover to the LORD, the G of Israel. 466
30: 6 return to the LORD, the G of Abraham, 466
30: 7 the LORD, the G of their fathers, 466
30: 8 Serve the LORD your G, 466
30: 9 for the LORD your G is gracious 466
30:12 of G was on the people to give them unity 466
30:16 in the Law of Moses the man of G. 466
30:19 who sets his heart on seeking G— 466
30:19 the LORD, the G of his fathers— 466
30:22 praised the LORD, the G of their fathers. 466
30:27 and G heard them, NIH
31: 6 to the LORD their G, 466
31:13 the official in charge of the temple of G. 466
31:14 of the freewill offerings given to G, 466
31:20 and faithful before the LORD his G. 466
31:21 he sought his G 466
32: 8 with us is the LORD our G to help us and 466
32:11 'The LORD our G will save us from 466
32:14 then can your g deliver you from my hand? 466
32:15 for no g of any nation 468
32:15 How much less will your g deliver you 466
32:16 against the LORD G and 466
32:17 G of Israel, and saying this against him: 466
32:17 from my hand, so the g of Hezekiah will 466
32:19 about the G of Jerusalem as they did about 466
32:21 And when he went into the temple of his g, 466
32:29 for G had given him very great riches. 466
32:31 G left him to test him and 466
33: 7 of which G had said to David and 466
33:12 the favor of the LORD his G 466
33:12 and humbled himself greatly before the G 466
33:13 Then Manasseh knew that the LORD is G. 466
33:16 to serve the LORD, the G of Israel. 466
33:17 but only to the LORD their G. 466
33:18 including his prayer to his G and the words 466
33:18 the LORD, the G of Israel, 466
33:19 how G was moved by his entreaty, as well NIH
34: 3 he began to seek the G of his father David. 466
34: 8 to repair the temple of the LORD his G. 466
34: 9 that had been brought into the temple of G, 466
34:23 "This is what the LORD, the G of Israel, 466
34:26 'This is what the LORD, the G of Israel, 466
34:27 before G when you heard what he spoke 466
34:32 in accordance with the covenant of G, 466
34:32 covenant of God, the G of their fathers. 466
34:33 in Israel serve the LORD their G. 466
34:33 the LORD, the G of their fathers. 466
35: 3 the LORD your G and his people Israel. 466
35:21 G has told me to hurry; 466
35:21 so stop opposing G, who is with me, 466
36: 5 He did evil in the eyes of the LORD his G. 466
36:12 He did evil in the eyes of the LORD his G 466
36:13 not turn to the LORD, the G of Israel 466
36:15 The LORD, the G of their fathers, 466
36:17 G handed all of them over NIH
36:18 the articles from the temple of G, 466
36:23 " 'The LORD, the G of heaven, 466
36:23 may the LORD his G be with him, 466
Ezr 1: 2 " 'The LORD, the G of heaven, 466
1: 3 may his G be with him, 466
1: 3 and build the temple of the LORD, the G 466
1: 3 the G who is in Jerusalem. 466
1: 4 with freewill offerings for the temple of G 466
1: 5 everyone whose heart G had moved— 466
1: 7 and had placed in the temple of his g. 466
2:68 the rebuilding of the house of G on its site. 466
3: 2 the G of Israel to sacrifice burnt offerings 466
3: 2 in the Law of Moses the man of G. 466
3: 8 after their arrival at the house of G 466
3: 9 on the house of G. 466
4: 1 temple for the LORD, the G of Israel, 466
4: 2 we seek your G and have been sacrificing 466
4: 3 with us in building a temple to our G. 466
4: 3 the G of Israel, as King Cyrus, 466
4:24 of G in Jerusalem came to a standstill until 10033
5: 1 and Jerusalem in the name of the G 10033
5: 2 to rebuild the house of G in Jerusalem. 10033
5: 2 And the prophets of G were with them, 10033
5: 5 of their G was watching over the elders of 10033
5: 8 to the temple of the great G. 10033

Ezr 5:11 the servants of the G of heaven and earth, 10033
5:12 our fathers angered the G of heaven, 10033
5:13 a decree to rebuild this house of G. 10033
5:14 and silver articles of the house of G, 10033
5:15 And rebuild the house of G on its site. 10033
5:16 and laid the foundations of the house of G 10033
5:17 to rebuild this house of G in Jerusalem. 10033
6: 3 concerning the temple of G in Jerusalem: 10033
6: 5 gold and silver articles of the house of G, 10033
6: 5 they are to be deposited in the house of G. 10033
6: 7 with the work on this temple of G. 10033
6: 7 the Jewish elders rebuild this house of G 10033
6: 8 in the construction of this house of G: 10033
6: 9 to the G of heaven, and wheat, salt, wine 10033
6:10 to the G of heaven and pray for 10033
6:12 May G, who has caused his Name 10033
6:14 of the G of Israel and the decrees of Cyrus, 10033
6:16 celebrated the dedication of the house of G 10033
6:17 of G they offered a hundred bulls, 10033
6:18 in their groups for the service of G 10033
6:21 seek the LORD, the G of Israel. 466
6:22 in the work on the house of G, 466
6:22 house of God, the G of Israel. 466
7: 6 which the LORD, the G of Israel, 466
7: 6 the hand of the LORD his G was on him. 466
7: 9 for the gracious hand of his G was on him. 466
7:12 a teacher of the Law of the G of heaven: 10033
7:14 with regard to the Law of your G, 10033
7:15 and his advisers have freely given to the G 10033
7:16 for the temple of their G in Jerusalem. 10033
7:17 of the temple of your G in Jerusalem. 10033
7:18 in accordance with the will of your G. 10033
7:19 the G of Jerusalem all the articles entrusted 10033
7:19 to you for worship in the temple of your G. 10033
7:20 of your G that you may have occasion 10033
7:21 a teacher of the Law of the G of heaven, 10033
7:23 Whatever the G of heaven has prescribed, 10033
7:23 with diligence for the temple of the G 10033
7:24 or other workers at this house of G. 10033
7:25 in accordance with the wisdom of your G, 10033
7:25 all who know the laws of your G. 10033
7:26 Whoever does not obey the law of your G 10033
7:27 Praise be to the LORD, the G of our fathers, 466
7:28 the hand of the LORD my G was on me, 466
8:17 to us for the house of our G. 466
8:18 the gracious hand of our G was on us, 466
8:21 before our G and ask him for a safe journey 466
8:22 of our G is on everyone who looks to him, 466
8:23 we fasted and petitioned our G about this, 466
8:25 for the house of our G. 466
8:28 offering to the LORD, the G of your fathers. 466
8:30 to the house of our G in Jerusalem. 466
8:31 The hand of our G was on us, 466
8:33 On the fourth day, in the house of our G, 466
8:35 burnt offerings to the G of Israel: 466
8:36 to the people and to the house of G. 466
9: 4 the G of Israel gathered around me because 466
9: 5 my hands spread out to the LORD my G 466
9: 6 "O my G, I am too ashamed and disgraced 466
9: 6 to lift up my face to you, my G, 466
9: 8 the LORD our G has been gracious 466
9: 8 and so our G gives light to our eyes and 466
9: 9 our G has not deserted us in our bondage. 466
9: 9 the house of our G and repair its ruins, 466
9:10 now, O our G, what can we say after this? 466
9:13 and our great guilt, and yet, our G, 466
9:15 O LORD, G of Israel, you are righteous! 466
10: 1 down before the house of G, a large crowd 466
10: 2 to our G by marrying foreign women from 466
10: 3 before our G to send away all these women 466
10: 3 of those who fear the commands of our G. 466
10: 6 before the house of G and went to the room 466
10: 9 in the square before the house of G, 466
10:11 the G of your fathers, and do his will. 466
10:14 of our G in this matter is turned away 466
Ne 1: 4 and prayed before the G of heaven. 466
1: 5 Then I said: "O LORD, G of heaven, 466
1: 5 God of heaven, the great and awesome G, 446
2: 4 Then I prayed to the G of heaven, 466
2: 8 the gracious hand of my G was upon me, 466
2:12 I had not told anyone what my G had put 466
2:18 about the gracious hand of my G upon me 466
2:20 "The G of heaven will give us success. 466
4: 4 Hear us, O our G, for we are despised. 466
4: 9 to our G and posted a guard day and night 466
4:15 of their plot and that G had frustrated it, 466
4:20 Our G will fight for us!" 466
5: 9 in the fear of our G to avoid the reproach 466
5:13 "In this way may G shake out of his house 466
5:15 of reverence for G I did not act like that. 466
5:19 Remember me with favor, O my G, 466
6:10 He said, "Let us meet in the house of G, 466
6:12 I realized that G had not sent him, 466
6:14 Remember Tobiah and Sanballat, O my G, 466
6:16 with the help of our G. 466
7: 2 and feared G more than most men do. 466
7: 5 So my G put it into my heart to assemble 466
8: 6 Ezra praised the LORD, the great G; 466
8: 8 They read from the Book of the Law of G, 466
8: 9 "This day is sacred to the LORD your G. 466
8:16 of G and in the square by the Water Gate 466
8:18 Ezra read from the Book of the Law of G. 466
9: 3 the Law of the LORD their G for a quarter 466
9: 3 and in worshiping the LORD their G. 466
9: 4 with loud voices to the LORD their G. 466
9: 5 "Stand up and praise the LORD your G, 466
9: 7 "You are the LORD G, 466

Ne 9:17 But you are a forgiving G, 468
9:18 'This is your g, who brought you up out of 466
9:31 for you are a gracious and merciful G. 446
9:32 "Now therefore, O our G, the great, 466
9:32 the great, mighty and awesome G, 446
10:28 of the Law of G, together with their wives 466
10:29 and an oath to follow the Law of G given 466
10:29 the servant of G and to obey carefully all 466
10:32 for the service of the house of our G: 466
10:33 and for all the duties of the house of our G. 466
10:34 to the house of our G at set times each year 466
10:34 to burn on the altar of the LORD our G, 466
10:36 and of our flocks to the house of our G, 466
10:37 to the storerooms of the house of our G, 466
10:38 of the tithes up to the house of our G, 466
10:39 "We will not neglect the house of our G." 466
11:11 supervisor in the house of G, 466
11:16 of the outside work of the house of G; 466
11:22 for the service of the house of G. 466
12:24 as prescribed by David the man of G. 466
12:36 by] David the man of G. 466
12:40 then took their places in the house of G; 466
12:43 because G had given them great joy. 466
12:45 They performed the service of their G and 466
12:46 the songs of praise and thanksgiving to G. 466
13: 1 be admitted into the assembly of G, 466
13: 2 (Our G, however, turned the curse into 466
13: 4 of the storerooms of the house of our G. 466
13: 7 a room in the courts of the house of G. 466
13: 9 into them the equipment of the house of G, 466
13:11 "Why is the house of G neglected?" 466
13:14 Remember me for this, O my G, 466
13:14 so faithfully done for the house of my G 466
13:18 that our G brought all this calamity upon us 466
13:22 Remember me for this also, O my G, 466
13:26 He was loved by his G, 466
13:26 and G made him king over all Israel, 466
13:27 to our G by marrying foreign women?" 466
13:29 Remember them, O my G, 466
13:31 Remember me with favor, O my G. 466
Job 1: 1 he feared G and shunned evil. 466
1: 5 and cursed G in their hearts." 466
1: 8 a man who fears G and shuns evil." 466
1: 9 "Does Job fear G for nothing?" 466
1:16 "The fire of G fell from the sky and burned 466
1:22 not sin by charging G with wrongdoing. 466
2: 3 a man who fears G and shuns evil. 466
2: 9 Curse G and die!" 466
2:10 Shall we accept good from G, 466
3: 4 may G above not care about it; 468
3:23 whom G has hedged in? 468
4: 9 At the breath of G they are destroyed; 468
4:17 'Can a mortal be more righteous than G? 468
4:18 If G places no trust in his servants, NIH
5: 8 "But if it were I, I would appeal to G; 446
5:17 "Blessed is the man whom G corrects; 468
6: 8 that G would grant what I hope for, 468
6: 9 that G would be willing to crush me, 468
7: 7 O G, that my life is but a breath; NIH
8: 3 Does G pervert justice? 446
8: 5 But if you will look to G and plead with 446
8:13 Such is the destiny of all who forget G; 446
8:20 "Surely G does not reject a blameless man 446
9: 2 how can a mortal be righteous before G? 446
9:13 G does not restrain his anger; 468
10: 2 I will say to G: Do not condemn me, 468
11: 4 You say to G, 'My beliefs are flawless NIH
11: 5 Oh, how I wish that G would speak, 468
11: 6 G has even forgotten some of your sin. 468
11: 7 "Can you fathom the mysteries of G? 468
12: 4 though I called upon G and he answered— 468
12: 6 and those who provoke G are secure— 446
12: 6 those who carry their g in their hands. 468
12:13 "To G belong wisdom and power; 2257S
13: 3 the Almighty and to argue my case with G. 446
13: 8 Will you argue the case for G? 446
13:20 "Only grant me these two things, O G, 446
15: 4 and hinder devotion to G. 446
15:13 so that you vent your rage against G 446
15:15 If G places no trust in his holy ones, NIH
15:25 at G and vaunts himself against 446
16: 7 Surely, O G, you have worn me out; NIH
16: 9 G assails me and tears me in his anger NIH
16:11 G has turned me over to evil men 446
16:20 as my eyes pour out tears to G; 468
16:21 of a man he pleads with G as a man pleads 468
17: 3 "Give me, O G, the pledge you demand. NIH
17: 6 "G has made me a byword to everyone, NIH
18:21 such is the place of one who knows not G." 446
19: 6 that G has wronged me and drawn his net 468
19:21 have pity, for the hand of G has struck me. 468
19:22 Why do you pursue me as G does? 446
19:26 yet in my flesh I will see G; 468
20:15 G will make his stomach vomit them up. 446
20:23 G will vent his burning anger against him NIH
20:29 Such is the fate G allots the wicked, 466
20:29 the heritage appointed for them by G." 446
21: 9 the rod of G is not upon them. 468
21:14 Yet they say to G, 'Leave us alone! 446
21:17 the fate G allots in his anger? NIH
21:19 'G stores up a man's punishment 468
21:22 "Can anyone teach knowledge to G, 446
22: 2 "Can a man be of benefit to G? 446
22:12 "Is not G in the heights of heaven? 468
22:13 Yet you say, 'What does G know? 446
22:17 They said to G, 'Leave us alone! 446
22:21 "Submit to G and be at peace with him; 2257S

Job	22:26	and will lift up your face to G.	468
	23:16	G has made my heart faint;	446
	24:12	But G charges no one with wrongdoing.	468
	24:22	But G drags away the mighty by his power;	NIH
	25: 2	"Dominion and awe belong to G;	2257S
	25: 4	then can a man be righteous before G?	446
	26: 6	Death is naked before G;	2257S
	27: 2	"As surely as G lives,	446
	27: 3	the breath of G in my nostrils,	468
	27: 8	when G takes away his life?	468
	27: 9	Does G listen to his cry	446
	27:10	Will he call upon G at all times?	468
	27:11	"I will teach you about the power of G;	446
	27:13	"Here is the fate G allots to the wicked,	446
	28:23	G understands the way to it	466
	29: 2	for the days when G watched over me,	468
	30:11	G has unstrung my bow and afflicted me,	NIH
	30:18	In his great power [G] becomes	NIH
	30:20	"I cry out to you, O G,	NIH
	31: 2	For what is man's lot from G above,	468
	31: 6	let G weigh me in honest scales	468
	31:14	what will I do when G confronts me?	446
	31:23	For I dreaded destruction from G,	446
	31:28	I would have been unfaithful to G on high.	446
	32: 2	for justifying himself rather than G.	466
	32:13	let G refute him, not man.'	446
	33: 4	The Spirit of G has made me;	446
	33: 6	I am just like you before G;	446
	33:10	Yet G has found fault with me;	NIH
	33:12	for G is greater than man.	468
	33:14	For G does speak—	446
	33:26	He prays to G and finds favor with him,	468
	33:26	he is restored by G to his righteous state.	NIH
	33:29	"G does all these things to a man—	446
	34: 5	'I am innocent, but G denies me justice.	446
	34: 9	a man nothing when he tries to please G.'	466
	34:10	Far be it from G to do evil,	446
	34:12	It is unthinkable that G would do wrong,	446
	34:23	G has no need to examine men further,	446
	34:31	"Suppose a man says to G,	446
	34:33	Should G then reward you on your terms,	NIH
	34:37	and multiplies his words against G."	446
	35: 2	You say, 'I will be cleared by G.'	446
	35:10	But no one says, 'Where is G my Maker,	468
	35:13	G does not listen to their empty plea;	446
	36: 5	"G is mighty, but does not despise men;	446
	36:22	"G is exalted in his power.	446
	36:26	How great is G—beyond our understanding!	446
	37:10	The breath of G produces ice,	446
	37:15	Do you know how G controls the clouds	468
	37:22	G comes in awesome majesty.	468
	38:41	for the raven when its young cry out to G	446
	39:17	for G did not endow her with wisdom	468
	40: 2	Let him who accuses G answer him!"	468
	40:19	He ranks first among the works of G,	446
Ps	3: 2	"G will not deliver him."	466
	3: 7	Deliver me, O my G!	466
	4: 1	O my righteous G.	466
	5: 2	my King and my G, for to you I pray.	466
	5: 4	You are not a G who takes pleasure in evil;	446
	5:10	Declare them guilty, O G!	466
	7: 1	O LORD my G, I take refuge in you;	466
	7: 3	O LORD my G, if I have done this	466
	7: 6	Awake, my G; decree justice.	446
	7: 9	O righteous G, who searches minds	466
	7:10	My shield is G Most High,	466
	7:11	G is a righteous judge,	466
	7:11	a G who expresses his wrath every day.	446
	9:17	all the nations that forget G.	466
	10: 4	in all his thoughts there is no room for G.	466
	10:11	He says to himself, "G has forgotten;	446
	10:12	Lift up your hand, O G.	446
	10:13	Why does the wicked man revile G?	466
	10:14	But you, O G, do see trouble and grief;	NIH
	13: 3	Look on me and answer, O LORD my G.	466
	14: 1	The fool says in his heart, "There is no G."	466
	14: 2	any who seek G.	466
	14: 5	for G is present in the company of	466
	16: 1	Keep me safe, O G,	446
	17: 6	I call on you, O G, for you will answer me;	446
	18: 2	my G is my rock, in whom I take refuge.	446
	18: 6	I cried to my G for help.	466
	18:21	I have not done evil by turning from my G.	466
	18:28	my G turns my darkness into light.	466
	18:29	with my G I can scale a wall.	466
	18:30	As for G, his way is perfect;	446
	18:31	For who is G besides the LORD?	468
	18:31	And who is the Rock except our G?	466
	18:32	It is G who arms me with strength	446
	18:46	Exalted be G my Savior!	466
	18:47	He is the G who avenges me,	446
	19: 1	The heavens declare the glory of G;	446
	20: 1	the name of the G of Jacob protect you.	466
	20: 5	up our banners in the name of our G.	466
	20: 7	we trust in the name of the LORD our G.	466
	22: 1	My G, my God, why have you forsaken me?	446
	22: 1	my G, why have you forsaken me?	446
	22: 2	O my G, I cry out by day,	466
	22:10	from my mother's womb you have been my G.	446
	24: 5	and vindication from G his Savior.	466
	24: 6	who seek your face, O G of Jacob.	466
	25: 2	in you I trust, O my G.	466
	25: 5	for you are G my Savior,	466
	25:22	Redeem Israel, O G, from all their troubles!	466
	27: 9	O G my Savior.	466
	29: 3	the G of glory thunders,	446
Ps	30: 2	O LORD my G, I called to you for help	466
	30:12	O LORD my G, I will give you thanks	466
	31: 5	redeem me, O LORD, the G of truth.	446
	31:14	I say, "You are my G."	466
	33:12	the nation whose G is the LORD,	466
	35:23	Contend for me, my G and Lord.	466
	35:24	O LORD my G; do not let them gloat	466
	36: 1	There is no fear of G before his eyes.	466
	37:31	The law of his G is in his heart;	466
	38:15	you will answer, O Lord my G.	466
	38:21	be not far from me, O my G.	466
	40: 3	a hymn of praise to our G.	466
	40: 5	Many, O LORD my G, are the wonders	466
	40: 8	I desire to do your will, O my G;	466
	40:17	O my G, do not delay.	466
	41:13	Praise be to the LORD, the G of Israel,	466
	42: 1	so my soul pants for you, O G.	466
	42: 2	My soul thirsts for G, for the living God.	466
	42: 2	My soul thirsts for God, for the living G.	446
	42: 2	When can I go and meet with G?	466
	42: 3	"Where is your G?"	466
	42: 4	leading the procession to the house of G,	466
	42: 5	Put your hope in G,	466
	42: 6	my G. My soul is downcast within me;	466
	42: 8	a prayer to the G of my life.	446
	42: 9	I say to G my Rock,	446
	42:10	"Where is your G?"	466
	42:11	Put your hope in G,	466
	42:11	my Savior and my G.	466
	43: 1	O G, and plead my cause against	466
	43: 2	You are G my stronghold.	466
	43: 4	Then will I go to the altar of G, to God,	466
	43: 4	Then will I go to the altar of God, to G,	446
	43: 4	I will praise you with the harp, O G,	466
	43: 4	with the harp, O God, my G.	466
	43: 5	Put your hope in G,	466
	43: 5	my Savior and my G.	466
	44: 1	We have heard with our ears, O G;	466
	44: 4	You are my King and my G,	466
	44: 8	In G we make our boast all day long,	466
	44:20	the name of our G or spread out our hands	466
	44:20	or spread out our hands to a foreign g,	446
	44:21	would not G have discovered it,	466
	45: 2	since G has blessed you forever.	466
	45: 6	O G, will last for ever and ever;	466
	45: 7	therefore G, your God,	466
	45: 7	therefore God, your G,	466
	46: 1	G is our refuge and strength,	466
	46: 4	whose streams make glad the city of G,	466
	46: 5	G is within her, she will not fall;	466
	46: 5	G will help her at break of day.	466
	46: 7	the G of Jacob is our fortress.	466
	46:10	"Be still, and know that I am G;	466
	46:11	the G of Jacob is our fortress.	466
	47: 1	shout to G with cries of joy.	466
	47: 5	G has ascended amid shouts of joy,	466
	47: 6	Sing praises to G, sing praises;	466
	47: 7	For G is the King of all the earth;	466
	47: 8	G reigns over the nations;	466
	47: 8	G is seated on his holy throne.	466
	47: 9	the nations assemble as the people of the G	466
	47: 9	for the kings of the earth belong to G;	466
	48: 1	in the city of our G, his holy mountain.	466
	48: 3	G is in her citadels;	466
	48: 8	in the city of our G:	466
	48: 8	G makes her secure forever.	466
	48: 9	O G, we meditate on your unfailing love.	466
	48:10	Like your name, O G,	466
	48:14	For this G is our God for ever and ever;	466
	48:14	For this God is our G for ever and ever;	466
	49: 7	of another or give to G a ransom for him—	466
	49:15	But G will redeem my life from the grave;	466
	50: 1	The Mighty One, G, the LORD,	446
	50: 2	perfect in beauty, G shines forth.	466
	50: 3	Our G comes and will not be silent;	466
	50: 6	for G himself is judge.	466
	50: 7	I am G, your God.	466
	50: 7	I am God, your G.	466
	50:14	Sacrifice thank offerings to G,	466
	50:16	But to the wicked, G says:	466
	50:22	"Consider this, you who forget G,	468
	50:23	so that I may show him the salvation of G."	466
	51: 1	Have mercy on me, O G,	466
	51:10	Create in me a pure heart, O G,	466
	51:14	Save me from bloodguilt, O G,	466
	51:14	O God, the G who saves me,	466
	51:17	The sacrifices of G are a broken spirit;	466
	51:17	a broken and contrite heart, O G,	466
	52: 1	you who are a disgrace in the eyes of G?	446
	52: 5	G will bring you down to everlasting ruin:	446
	52: 7	not make G his stronghold but trusted	466
	52: 8	an olive tree flourishing in the house of G;	466
	53: 1	The fool says in his heart, "There is no G."	466
	53: 2	G looks down from heaven on the sons	466
	53: 2	any who seek G.	466
	53: 4	and who do not call on G?	466
	53: 5	G scattered the bones of those who attacked	466
	53: 5	to shame, for G despised them.	466
	53: 6	When G restores the fortunes of his people,	466
	54: 1	Save me, O G, by your name;	466
	54: 2	Hear my prayer, O G;	466
	54: 3	men without regard for G.	466
	54: 4	Surely G is my help;	466
	55: 1	Listen to my prayer, O G,	466
	55:14	with the throng at the house of G.	466
	55:16	But I call to G, and the LORD saves me.	466
	55:19	G, who is enthroned forever,	446
Ps	55:19	and have no fear of G.	466
	55:23	O G, will bring down the wicked into	466
	56: 1	Be merciful to me, O G,	466
	56: 4	In G, whose word I praise, in God I trust;	466
	56: 4	In God, whose word I praise, in G I trust;	466
	56: 7	in your anger, O G,	466
	56: 9	By this I will know that G is for me.	466
	56:10	In G, whose word I praise, in the LORD,	466
	56:11	in G I trust; I will not be afraid.	466
	56:12	I am under vows to you, O G;	466
	56:13	that I may walk before G in the light of life.	466
	57: 1	Have mercy on me, O G,	466
	57: 2	I cry out to G Most High, to God,	466
	57: 2	I cry out to God Most High, to G,	446
	57: 3	G sends his love and his faithfulness.	466
	57: 5	Be exalted, O G, above the heavens;	466
	57: 7	O G, my heart is steadfast;	466
	57:11	Be exalted, O G, above the heavens;	466
	58: 6	Break the teeth in their mouths, O G;	466
	58:11	surely there is a G who judges the earth."	466
	59: 1	Deliver me from my enemies, O G;	466
	59: 5	O LORD G Almighty, the God of Israel,	466
	59: 5	O LORD God Almighty, the G of Israel,	466
	59: 9	O my Strength, I watch for you; you, O G,	466
	59:10	my loving G. God will go	466
	59:10	G will go before me and will let me gloat	466
	59:13	of the earth that G rules over Jacob.	466
	59:17	you, O G, are my fortress, my loving God.	466
	59:17	you, O God, are my fortress, my loving G.	466
	60: 1	You have rejected us, O G,	466
	60: 6	G has spoken from his sanctuary:	466
	60:10	Is it not you, O G,	466
	60:12	With G we will gain the victory,	466
	61: 1	Hear my cry, O G; listen to my prayer.	466
	61: 5	For you have heard my vows, O G;	466
	62: 1	My soul finds rest in G alone;	466
	62: 5	in G alone; my hope comes from him.	466
	62: 7	My salvation and my honor depend on G;	466
	62: 8	for G is our refuge.	466
	62:11	One thing G has spoken,	466
	62:11	that you, O G, are strong,	466
	63: 1	O G, you are my God, earnestly I seek you;	466
	63: 1	O God, you are my G, earnestly I seek you;	446
	63:11	But the king will rejoice in G;	466
	64: 1	Hear me, O G, as I voice my complaint;	466
	64: 7	But G will shoot them with arrows;	466
	64: 9	of G and ponder what he has done.	466
	65: 1	Praise awaits you, O G, in Zion;	466
	65: 5	O G our Savior,	466
	65: 9	The streams of G are filled with water	466
	66: 1	Shout with joy to G, all the earth!	466
	66: 3	Say to G, "How awesome are your deeds!	466
	66: 5	Come and see what G has done,	466
	66: 8	Praise our G, O peoples, let the sound	466
	66:10	For you, O G, tested us;	466
	66:16	all you who fear G;	466
	66:19	but G has surely listened	466
	66:20	Praise be to G,	466
	67: 1	May G be gracious to us and bless us	466
	67: 3	May the peoples praise you, O G;	466
	67: 5	O G; may all the peoples praise you.	466
	67: 6	Then the land will yield its harvest, and G,	466
	67: 6	land will yield its harvest, and God, our G,	466
	67: 7	G will bless us,	466
	68: 1	May G arise, may his enemies be scattered;	466
	68: 2	may the wicked perish before G.	466
	68: 3	the righteous be glad and rejoice before G;	466
	68: 4	Sing to G, sing praise to his name,	466
	68: 5	is G in his holy dwelling.	466
	68: 6	G sets the lonely in families,	466
	68: 7	you went out before your people, O G,	466
	68: 8	the heavens poured down rain, before G,	466
	68: 8	before God, the One of Sinai, before G,	466
	68: 8	before God, the G of Israel.	466
	68: 9	You gave abundant showers, O G;	466
	68:10	O G, you provided for the poor.	466
	68:16	at the mountain where G chooses to reign,	466
	68:17	of G are tens of thousands and thousands	466
	68:18	that you, O LORD G, might dwell there.	466
	68:19	Praise be to the Lord, to G our Savior,	446
	68:20	Our G is a God who saves;	446
	68:20	Our God is a G who saves;	446
	68:21	G will crush the heads of his enemies,	466
	68:24	Your procession has come into view, O G,	466
	68:24	the procession of my G and King into	446
	68:26	Praise G in the great congregation;	466
	68:28	Summon your power, O G;	466
	68:28	show us your strength, O G,	466
	68:31	Cush will submit herself to G.	466
	68:32	Sing to G, O kingdoms of the earth,	466
	68:34	Proclaim the power of G,	466
	68:35	You are awesome, O G, in your sanctuary;	466
	68:35	the G of Israel gives power and strength	446
	68:35	Praise be to G!	466
	69: 1	O G, for the waters have come up	466
	69: 3	My eyes fail, looking for my G.	466
	69: 5	You know my folly, O G;	466
	69: 6	not be put to shame because of me, O G	466
	69:13	in your great love, O G,	466
	69:29	may your salvation, O G, protect me.	466
	69:32	you who seek G, may your hearts live!	466
	69:35	for G will save Zion and rebuild the cities	466
	70: 1	Hasten, O G, to save me;	466
	70: 4	"Let G be exalted!"	466
	70: 5	come quickly to me, O G.	466
	71: 4	Deliver me, O my G,	466
	71:11	They say, "G has forsaken him;	466

Ps 71:12 Be not far from me, O **G**; 466
71:12 come quickly, O my **G**, to help me. 466
71:17 Since my youth, O **G**, you have taught me, 466
71:18 do not forsake me, O **G**, 466
71:19 O **G**, you who have done great things. 466
71:19 Who, O **G**, is like you? 466
71:22 the harp for your faithfulness, O my **G**; 466
72:1 Endow the king with your justice, O **G**, 466
72:18 Praise be to the LORD **G**, 466
72:18 the **G** *of* Israel, 466
73:1 Surely **G** is good to Israel, 466
73:11 They say, "How can **G** know? 446
73:17 till I entered the sanctuary of **G**; 446
73:26 but **G** is the strength of my heart 466
73:28 But as for me, it is good to be near **G**. 466
74:1 Why have you rejected us forever, O **G**? 466
74:8 where **G** was worshiped in the land. 446
74:10 How long will the enemy mock you, O **G**? 466
74:12 But you, O **G**, are my king from of old; 466
74:22 Rise up, O **G**, and defend your cause; 466
75:1 We give thanks to you, O **G**, 466
75:7 But it is **G** who judges: 466
75:9 I will sing praise to the **G** *of* Jacob. 466
76:1 In Judah **G** is known; 466
76:6 At your rebuke, O **G** *of* Jacob, 466
76:9 O **G**, rose up to judge, 466
76:11 to the LORD your **G** and fulfill them; 466
77:1 I cried out to **G** for help; 466
77:1 I cried out to **G** to hear me. 466
77:3 I remembered you, O **G**, and I groaned; 466
77:9 Has **G** forgotten to be merciful? 446
77:13 Your ways, O **G**, are holy. 466
77:13 What **g** is so great as our God? 446
77:13 What god is so great as our **G**? 466
77:14 You are the **G** who performs miracles; 446
77:16 O **G**, the waters saw you and writhed; 466
78:7 Then they would put their trust in **G** 466
78:8 whose hearts were not loyal to **G**, 446
78:18 They willfully put **G** to the test 446
78:19 They spoke against **G**, saying, 466
78:19 saying, "Can **G** spread a table in the desert? 446
78:22 not believe in **G** or trust in his deliverance. 466
78:34 Whenever **G** slew them, 446
78:35 They remembered that **G** was their Rock, 466
78:35 that **G** Most High was their Redeemer. 446
78:41 Again and again they put **G** to the test; 446
78:56 But they put **G** to the test and rebelled 446
78:59 When **G** heard them, he was very angry; 466
79:1 O **G**, the nations have invaded your inheritance; 466
79:9 Help us, O **G** our Savior, 466
79:10 "Where is their **G**?" 466
80:3 Restore us, O **G**; make your face shine upon us, 466
80:4 O LORD **G** Almighty, 466
80:7 Restore us, O **G** Almighty; 466
80:14 Return to us, O **G** Almighty! 466
80:19 Restore us, O LORD **G** Almighty; 466
81:1 Sing for joy to **G** our strength; 466
81:1 shout aloud to the **G** *of* Jacob! 466
81:4 an ordinance of the **G** *of* Jacob. 466
81:9 You shall have no foreign **g** among you; 446
81:9 you shall not bow down to an alien **g**. 446
81:10 I am the LORD your **G**, 466
82:1 **G** presides in the great assembly; 466
82:8 Rise up, O **G**, judge the earth, 466
83:1 O **G**, do not keep silent; 466
83:1 be not quiet, O **G**, be not still. 446
83:12 of the pasturelands of **G**." 466
83:13 Make them like tumbleweed, O my **G**, 466
84:2 and my flesh cry out for the living **G**. 446
84:3 O LORD Almighty, my King and my **G**. 466
84:7 till each appears before **G** in Zion. 466
84:8 Hear my prayer, O LORD **G** Almighty; 466
84:8 listen to me, O **G** *of* Jacob. 466
84:9 upon our shield, O **G**; 466
84:10 in the house of my **G** than dwell in the tents 466
84:11 For the LORD **G** is a sun and shield; 466
85:4 Restore us again, O **G** our Savior, 466
85:8 I will listen to what **G** the LORD will say; 446
86:2 You are my **G**; 466
86:10 you alone are **G**. 466
86:12 I will praise you, O Lord my **G**, 466
86:14 The arrogant are attacking me, O **G**; 466
86:15 are a compassionate and gracious **G**, 446
87:3 O city of **G**: 466
88:1 O LORD, the **G** who saves me, 466
89:7 of the holy ones **G** is greatly feared; 446
89:8 O LORD **G** Almighty, who is like you? 466
89:26 my **G**, the Rock my Savior.' 446
90:T A prayer of Moses the man of **G**. 466
90:2 from everlasting to everlasting you are **G**. 446
90:17 the favor of the Lord our **G** rest upon us; 466
91:2 "He is my refuge and my fortress, my **G**, 466
92:13 they will flourish in the courts of our **G**. 466
94:1 O LORD, the **G** *who* avenges, 446
94:1 the God who avenges, O **G** *who* avenges, 446
94:7 the **G** *of* Jacob pays no heed." 466
94:22 and my **G** the rock in whom I take refuge. 466
94:23 the LORD our **G** will destroy them. 466
95:3 For the LORD is the great **G**, 446
95:7 for he is our **G** and we are the people 466
98:3 of the earth have seen the salvation of our **G**. 466
99:5 Exalt the LORD our **G** and worship 466
99:8 O LORD our **G**, you answered them; 466
99:8 you were to Israel a forgiving **G**, 446
99:9 Exalt the LORD our **G** and worship 466
Ps 99:9 for the LORD our **G** is holy. 466
100:3 Know that the LORD is **G**. 466
102:24 So I said: "Do not take me away, O my **G**, 446
104:1 O LORD my **G**, you are very great; 466
104:21 for their prey and seek their food from **G**. 446
104:33 I will sing praise to my **G** as long as I live. 466
105:7 He is the LORD our **G**; 466
106:14 in the wasteland they put **G** to the test. 446
106:21 They forgot the **G** who saved them, 446
106:33 for they rebelled against the Spirit of **G**, 2257[S]
106:47 Save us, O LORD our **G**, 466
106:48 Praise be to the LORD, the **G** *of* Israel, 466
107:11 the words of **G** and despised the counsel of 446
108:1 My heart is steadfast, O **G**; 466
108:5 Be exalted, O **G**, above the heavens, 466
108:7 **G** has spoken from his sanctuary: 466
108:11 Is it not you, O **G**, 466
108:13 With **G** we will gain the victory, 466
109:1 O **G**, whom I praise, do not remain silent, 466
109:26 Help me, O LORD my **G**; 466
113:5 Who is like the LORD our **G**, 466
114:7 at the presence of the **G** *of* Jacob, 468
115:2 "Where is their **G**?" 466
115:3 Our **G** is in heaven; 466
116:5 our **G** is full of compassion. 466
118:27 The LORD is **G**, 446
118:28 You are my **G**, and I will give you thanks; 446
118:28 you are my **G**, and I will exalt you. 466
119:115 that I may keep the commands of my **G**! 466
122:9 the sake of the house of the LORD our **G**, 466
123:2 so our eyes look to the LORD our **G**, 466
135:2 in the courts of the house of our **G**. 466
136:2 Give thanks to the **G** *of* gods. 466
136:26 Give thanks to the **G** *of* heaven. 446
139:17 to me are your thoughts, O **G**! 446
139:19 If only you would slay the wicked, O **G**! 468
139:23 Search me, O **G**, and know my heart; 446
140:6 I say to you, "You are my **G**." 446
143:10 for you are my **G**; 466
144:2 He is my loving **G** and my fortress, NIH
144:9 I will sing a new song to you, O **G**; 466
144:15 the people whose **G** is the LORD. 466
145:1 I will exalt you, my **G** the King; 466
146:2 I will sing praise to my **G** as long as I live. 466
146:5 Blessed is he whose help is the **G** *of* Jacob, 446
146:5 whose hope is in the LORD his **G**, 466
146:10 The LORD reigns forever, your **G**, 466
147:1 How good it is to sing praises to our **G**, 466
147:7 make music to our **G** on the harp. 466
147:12 praise your **G**, O Zion, 466
149:6 May the praise of **G** be in their mouths and 446
150:1 Praise **G** in his sanctuary; 446
Pr 2:5 the LORD and find the knowledge of **G**. 466
2:17 the covenant she made before **G**. 466
3:4 and a good name in the sight of **G** and man. 466
14:31 but whoever is kind to the needy honors **G**. 2257[S]
25:2 It is the glory of **G** to conceal a matter; 466
30:5 "Every word of **G** is flawless; 468
30:9 and so dishonor the name of my **G**. 466
Ecc 1:13 What a heavy burden **G** has laid on men! 466
2:24 This too, I see, is from the hand of **G**, 466
2:26 **G** gives wisdom, knowledge and happiness, NIH
2:26 to hand it over to the one who pleases **G**. 466
3:10 I have seen the burden **G** has laid on men. 466
3:11 yet they cannot fathom what **G** has done 466
3:13 this is the gift of **G**. 466
3:14 that everything **G** does will endure forever; 466
3:14 **G** does it so that men will revere him. 466
3:15 and **G** will call the past to account. 466
3:17 "**G** will bring to judgment both 466
3:18 **G** tests them so that they may see 466
5:1 when you go to the house of **G**. 466
5:2 in your heart to utter anything before **G**. 466
5:2 **G** is in heaven and you are on earth, 466
5:4 When you make a vow to **G**, 466
5:6 Why should **G** be angry at what you say 466
5:7 Therefore stand in awe of **G**. 466
5:18 the few days of life **G** has given him— 466
5:19 **G** gives any man wealth and possessions, 466
5:19 this is a gift of **G**. 466
5:20 because **G** keeps him occupied 466
6:2 **G** gives a man wealth, 466
6:2 but **G** does not enable him to enjoy them, 466
7:13 Consider what **G** has done: 466
7:14 **G** has made the one as well as the other. 466
7:18 man who fears **G** will avoid all [extremes]. 466
7:26 The man who pleases **G** will escape her, 466
7:29 **G** made mankind upright, 466
8:2 I say, because you took an oath before **G**. 466
8:12 who are reverent before **G**. 2257[S]
8:13 Yet because the wicked do not fear **G**, 466
8:15 the days of the life **G** has given him under 466
8:17 then I saw all that **G** has done. 466
9:7 for it is now that **G** favors what you do. 466
9:9 that **G** has given you under the sun— NIH
11:5 so you cannot understand the work of **G**, 466
11:9 that for all these things **G** will bring you 466
12:7 and the spirit returns to **G** who gave it. 466
12:13 Fear **G** and keep his commandments, 466
12:14 For **G** will bring every deed into judgment, 466
Isa 1:10 listen to the law of our **G**, 466
2:3 to the house of the **G** *of* Jacob. 466
5:16 and the holy **G** will show himself holy 446
5:19 "Let **G** hurry, let him hasten his work NIH
7:11 "Ask the LORD your **G** for a sign, 466
7:13 Will you try the patience of my **G** also? 466
8:10 but it will not stand, for **G** is with us. 446
Isa 8:19 should not a people inquire of their **G**? 466
8:21 will curse their king and their **G**. 466
9:6 Mighty **G**, Everlasting Father, 446
10:21 of Jacob will return to the Mighty **G**. 446
12:2 Surely **G** is my salvation; 446
13:19 will be overthrown by **G** like Sodom 466
14:13 I will raise my throne above the stars of **G**; 446
17:6 declares the LORD, the **G** *of* Israel. 466
17:10 You have forgotten **G** your Savior; 466
21:10 from the **G** *of* Israel. 466
21:17 The LORD, the **G** *of* Israel, has spoken. 466
24:15 the **G** *of* Israel, in the islands of the sea. 466
25:1 O LORD, you are my **G**; 466
25:9 "Surely this is our **G**; 466
25:11 **G** will bring down their pride despite NIH
26:1 **G** makes salvation its walls and ramparts. NIH
26:13 our **G**, other lords besides you have ruled 466
28:11 and strange tongues **G** will speak NIH
28:26 His **G** instructs him and teaches him 466
29:23 and will stand in awe of the **G** *of* Israel. 466
30:18 For the LORD is a **G** *of* justice. 466
31:3 But the Egyptians are men and not **G**; 446
34:11 **G** will stretch out over Edom NIH
35:2 the splendor of our **G**. 466
35:4 your **G** will come, he will come 466
36:7 "We are depending on the LORD our **G**"— 466
36:18 the **g** *of* any nation ever delivered his land 466
37:4 that the LORD your **G** will hear the words 466
37:4 has sent to ridicule the living **G**, 466
37:4 for the words the LORD your **G** has heard. 466
37:10 Do not let the **g** you depend on deceive you 466
37:16 **G** *of* Israel, enthroned between 466
37:16 you alone are **G** over all the kingdoms of 466
37:17 to insult the living **G**. 466
37:20 Now, O LORD our **G**, 466
37:20 that you alone, O LORD, are **G**." NIH
37:21 "This is what the LORD, the **G** *of* Israel, 466
37:38 in the temple of his **g** Nisroch, 466
38:5 the **G** *of* your father David, says: 466
40:1 Comfort, comfort my people, says your **G**. 466
40:3 in the wilderness a highway for our **G**. 466
40:8 but the word of our **G** stands forever." 466
40:9 say to the towns of Judah, "Here is your **G**!" 466
40:18 To whom, then, will you compare **G**? 446
40:27 my cause is disregarded by my **G**"? 466
40:28 The LORD is the everlasting **G**, 466
41:10 do not be dismayed, for I am your **G**. 466
41:13 For I am the LORD, your **G**, 466
41:17 I, the **G** *of* Israel, will not forsake them. 466
42:5 This is what **G** the LORD says— 446
43:3 For I am the LORD, your **G**, 466
43:10 Before me no **g** was formed, 446
43:12 I, and not some foreign **g** among you. NIH
43:12 declares the LORD, "that I am **G**. 446
44:6 apart from me there is no **G**. 466
44:8 Is there any **G** besides me? 468
44:10 Who shapes a **g** and casts an idol, 446
44:15 But he also fashions a **g** and worships it; 446
44:17 From the rest he makes a **g**, his idol; 446
44:17 "Save me; you are my **g**." 446
45:3 I am the LORD, the **G** *of* Israel, 466
45:5 apart from me there is no **G**. 466
45:14 saying, 'Surely **G** is with you, 446
45:14 there is no other **g**.' " 466
45:15 Truly you are a **G** who hides himself, 446
45:15 O **G** and Savior *of* Israel. 466
45:18 he who created the heavens, he is **G**; 466
45:21 And there is no **G** apart from me, 466
45:21 a righteous **G** and a Savior; 446
45:22 for I am **G**, and there is no other. 446
46:6 they hire a goldsmith to make it into a **g**, 446
46:9 I am **G**, and there is no other; 446
46:9 I am **G**, and there is none like me. 466
48:1 of the LORD and invoke the **G** *of* Israel— 466
48:2 the holy city and rely on the **G** *of* Israel— 466
48:5 and **metal g** ordained them.' 5822
48:17 "I am the LORD your **G**, 466
49:4 and my reward is with my **G**." 466
49:5 and my **G** has been my strength— 466
50:10 the name of the LORD and rely on his **G**. 466
51:15 For I am the LORD your **G**, 466
51:20 of the LORD and the rebuke of your **G**. 466
51:22 your **G**, who defends his people: 466
52:7 who say to Zion, "Your **G** reigns!" 466
52:10 of the earth will see the salvation of our **G**. 466
52:12 the **G** *of* Israel will be your rear guard. 466
53:4 yet we considered him stricken by **G**, 466
54:5 he is called the **G** *of* all the earth. 466
54:6 only to be rejected," says your **G**. 466
55:5 because of the LORD your **G**, 466
55:7 and to our **G**, for he will freely pardon. 466
57:21 "There is no peace," says my **G**, 466
58:2 not forsaken the commands of its **G**. 466
58:2 and seem eager for **G** to come near them. 466
59:2 But your iniquities have separated you from your **G**; 466
59:13 turning our backs on our **G**, 466
60:9 to the honor of the LORD your **G**, 466
60:19 and your **G** will be your glory. 466
61:2 and the day of vengeance of our **G**, 466
61:6 you will be named ministers of our **G**. 466
61:10 my soul rejoices in my **G**. 466
62:3 a royal diadem in the hand of your **G**. 466
62:5 so will your **G** rejoice over you. 466
64:4 no eye has seen any **G** besides you, 466
65:16 a blessing in the land will do so by the **G** 466
65:16 in the land will swear by the **G** *of* truth. 466

Isa 66: 9 says your **G**. 466
Jer 2:17 the LORD your **G** when he led you in 466
2:19 when you forsake the LORD your **G** 466
3:13 against the LORD your **G**, 466
3:21 and have forgotten the LORD their **G**. 466
3:22 for you are the LORD our **G**. 466
3:23 the LORD our **G** is the salvation of Israel. 466
3:25 We have sinned against the LORD our **G**, 466
3:25 not obeyed the LORD our **G**." 466
5: 4 the requirements of their **G**. 466
5: 5 the requirements of their **G**." 466
5:14 the LORD **G** Almighty says: 466
5:19 'Why has the LORD our **G** done all this 466
5:24 'Let us fear the LORD our **G**, 466
7: 3 the LORD Almighty, the **G** *of* Israel, says: 466
7:21 the LORD Almighty, the **G** *of* Israel, says: 466
7:23 I will be your **G** and you will be my people. 466
7:28 not obeyed the LORD its **G** or responded 466
8:14 the LORD our **G** has doomed us to perish 466
9:15 the LORD Almighty, the **G** *of* Israel, says: 466
10:10 But the LORD is the true **G**; 466
10:10 he is the living **G**, the eternal King. 466
10:12 But **G** made the earth by his power; NIH
11: 3 the LORD, the **G** *of* Israel, says: 466
11: 4 and I will be your **G**. 466
11:13 to burn incense to that **shameful g** Baal are 1425
13:12 'This is what the LORD, the **G** *of* Israel, 466
13:16 to the LORD your **G** before he brings 466
14:22 No, it is you, O LORD our **G**. 466
15:16 O LORD **G** Almighty. 466
16: 9 the LORD Almighty, the **G** *of* Israel, says: 466
16:10 against the LORD our **G**?' 466
19: 3 the **G** *of* Israel, says: Listen! 466
19:15 the **G** *of* Israel, says: 'Listen! 466
21: 4 the LORD, the **G** *of* Israel, says: 466
22: 9 of the LORD their **G** and have worshiped 466
23: 2 the LORD, the **G** *of* Israel, says to 466
23:23 "Am I only a **G** nearby," 466
23:23 "and not a **G** far away? 466
23:36 so you distort the words of the living **G**, 466
23:36 the LORD Almighty, our **G**. 466
24: 5 the LORD, the **G** *of* Israel, says: 466
24: 7 and I will be their **G**, 466
25:15 This is what the LORD, the **G** *of* Israel, 466
25:27 the LORD Almighty, the **G** *of* Israel, says: 466
26:13 and obey the LORD your **G**. 466
26:16 to us in the name of the LORD our **G**." 466
27: 4 the LORD Almighty, the **G** *of* Israel, says: 466
27:21 the **G** *of* Israel, says about the things 466
28: 2 the LORD Almighty, the **G** *of* Israel, says: 466
28:14 the LORD Almighty, the **G** *of* Israel, says: 466
29: 4 the **G** *of* Israel, says to all those I carried 466
29: 8 the LORD Almighty, the **G** *of* Israel, says: 466
29:21 the **G** *of* Israel, says about Ahab son 466
29:25 the LORD Almighty, the **G** *of* Israel, says: 466
30: 2 the LORD, the **G** *of* Israel, says: 466
30: 9 the LORD their **G** and David their king, 466
30:22 and I will be your **G**.' " 466
31: 1 "I will be the **G** of all the clans of Israel, 466
31: 6 let us go up to Zion, to the LORD our **G**.' " 466
31:18 because you are the LORD my **G**. 466
31:23 the LORD Almighty, the **G** *of* Israel, says: 466
31:33 I will be their **G**, 466
32:14 the LORD Almighty, the **G** *of* Israel, says: 466
32:15 the LORD Almighty, the **G** *of* Israel, says: 466
32:18 O great and powerful **G**, 446
32:27 the **G** *of* all mankind. 466
32:36 the LORD, the **G** *of* Israel, says: 466
32:38 and I will be their **G**. 466
33: 4 this is what the LORD, the **G** *of* Israel, 466
34: 2 the LORD, the **G** *of* Israel, says: 466
34:13 the LORD, the **G** *of* Israel, says: 466
35: 4 of Hanan son of Igdaliah the man of **G**. 466
35:13 the LORD, the **G** *of* Israel, says: 466
35:17 this is what the LORD **G** Almighty, 466
35:17 the **G** *of* Israel, says: 'Listen! 466
35:18 the LORD Almighty, the **G** *of* Israel, says: 466
35:19 the LORD Almighty, the **G** *of* Israel, says: 466
37: 3 "Please pray to the LORD our **G** for us." 466
37: 7 the LORD, the **G** *of* Israel, says: 466
38:17 "This is what the LORD **G** Almighty, 466
38:17 the LORD Almighty, the **G** *of* Israel, says: 466
39:16 the LORD Almighty, the **G** *of* Israel, says: 466
40: 2 "The LORD your **G** decreed this disaster 466
42: 2 the LORD your **G** for this entire remnant. 466
42: 3 Pray that the LORD your **G** will tell us 466
42: 4 "I will certainly pray to the LORD your **G** 466
42: 5 the LORD your **G** sends you to tell us. 466
42: 6 we will obey the LORD our **G**, 466
42: 6 for we will obey the LORD our **G**." 466
42: 9 "This is what the LORD, the **G** *of* Israel, 466
42:13 and so disobey the LORD your **G**, 466
42:15 the LORD Almighty, the **G** *of* Israel, says: 466
42:18 the LORD Almighty, the **G** *of* Israel, says: 466
42:20 when you sent me to the LORD your **G** 466
42:20 'Pray to the LORD our **G** for us; 466
42:21 the LORD your **G** in all he sent me 466
43: 1 the words of the LORD their **G**— 466
43: 2 The LORD our **G** has not sent you to say, 466
43:10 the LORD Almighty, the **G** *of* Israel, says: 466
44: 2 the LORD Almighty, the **G** *of* Israel, says: 466
44: 7 "Now this is what the LORD **G** Almighty, 466
44: 7 the LORD Almighty, the **G** *of* Israel, says: 466
44:11 the LORD Almighty, the **G** *of* Israel, says: 466
44:25 the LORD Almighty, the **G** *of* Israel, says: 466
45: 2 the **G** *of* Israel, says to you, Baruch: 466
46:25 the LORD Almighty, the **G** *of* Israel, says: 466
Jer 46:25 to bring punishment on Amon **g** of Thebes, NIH
48: 1 the LORD Almighty, the **G** *of* Israel, says: 466
50: 4 in tears to seek the LORD their **G**. 466
50:18 the LORD Almighty, the **G** *of* Israel, says: 466
50:28 the LORD our **G** has taken vengeance, 466
50:40 As **G** overthrew Sodom and Gomorrah 466
51: 5 not been forsaken by their **G**, 466
51:10 in Zion what the LORD our **G** has done.' 466
51:33 the LORD Almighty, the **G** *of* Israel, says: 466
51:56 For the LORD is a **G** *of* retribution; 446
La 3:41 up our hearts and our hands to **G** in heaven, 446
Eze 1: 1 and I saw visions of **G**. 466
8: 3 and heaven and in visions of **G** he took me 466
8: 4 And there before me was the glory of the **G** 466
9: 3 Now the glory of the **G** *of* Israel went up 466
10: 5 the voice of **G** Almighty when he speaks. 446
10:19 glory of the **G** *of* Israel was above them. 466
10:20 the **G** *of* Israel by the Kebar River, 466
11:20 and I will be their **G**. 466
11:22 glory of the **G** *of* Israel was above them. 466
11:24 in the vision given by the Spirit of **G**. 466
14:11 and I will be their **G**, 466
20: 5 "I am the LORD your **G**." 466
20: 7 I am the LORD your **G**." 466
20:19 I am the LORD your **G**; 466
20:20 that I am the LORD your **G**." 466
28: 2 the pride of your heart you say, "I am a **g**; 446
28: 2 the throne of a **g** in the heart of the seas." 466
28: 2 But you are a man and not a **g**, 446
28: 2 though you think you are as wise as a **g**. 466
28: 6 you think you are wise, as wise as a **g**, 466
28: 9 Will you then say, "I am a **g**," 466
28: 9 You will be but a man, not a **g**, 446
28:13 You were in Eden, the garden of **G**; 466
28:14 You were on the holy mount of **G**; 466
28:16 in disgrace from the mount of **G**, 466
28:26 that I am the LORD their **G**.' " 466
31: 8 cedars in the garden of **G** could not rival it, 466
31: 8 in the garden of **G** could match its beauty. 466
31: 9 of all the trees of Eden in the garden of **G**. 466
34:24 I the LORD will be their **G**, 466
34:30 they will know that I, the LORD their **G**, 466
34:31 are people, and I am your **G**, 466
36:28 and I will be your **G**. 466
37:23 and I will be their **G**. 466
37:27 I will be their **G**, 466
39:22 that I am the LORD their **G**. 466
39:28 that I am the LORD their **G**, 466
40: 2 In visions of **G** he took me to the land 466
43: 2 the glory of the **G** *of* Israel coming from 466
44: 2 the **G** *of* Israel, has entered through it. 466
Da 1: 2 of the articles from the temple of **G**. 466
1: 2 the temple of his **g** in Babylonia and put in 466
1: 2 and put in the treasure house of his **g**. 466
1: 9 Now **G** had caused the official 466
1:17 To these four young men **G** gave knowledge 466
2:18 the **G** *of* heaven concerning this mystery, 10033
2:19 Then Daniel praised the **G** *of* heaven 10033
2:20 be to the name of **G** for ever and ever; 10033
2:23 I thank and praise you, O **G** *of* my fathers: 10033
2:28 a **G** in heaven who reveals mysteries. 10033
2:37 The **G** *of* heaven has given you dominion 10033
2:44 the **G** *of* heaven will set up a kingdom 10033
2:45 "The great **G** has shown 10033
2:47 "Surely your **G** is the God of gods and 10033
2:47 the **G** *of* gods and the Lord of kings and 10033
3:15 Then what **g** will be able to rescue you 10033
3:17 the **G** we serve is able to save us from it, 10033
3:26 servants of the Most High **G**, come out! 10033
3:28 "Praise be to the **G** of Shadrach, 10033
3:28 or worship any **g** except their own God. 10033
3:28 or worship any god except their own **G**. 10033
3:29 or language who say anything against the **G** 10033
3:29 for no other **g** can save in this way." 10033
4: 2 the Most High **G** has performed for me. 10033
4: 8 after the name of my **g**, 10033
5: 3 that had been taken from the temple of **G** 10033
5:18 the Most High **G** gave your father
Nebuchadnezzar sovereignty 10033
5:21 that the Most High **G** is sovereign over 10033
5:23 But you did not honor the **G** who holds 10033
5:26 **G** has numbered the days of your reign 10033
6: 5 to do with the law of his **G**." 10033
6: 7 to any **g** or man during the next thirty days, 10033
6:10 giving thanks to his **G**, 10033
6:11 and found Daniel praying and asking **G** 10033
6:12 to any **g** or man except to you, 10033
6:16 The king said to Daniel, "May your **G**, 10033
6:20 servant of the living **G**, has your God, 10033
6:20 has your **G**, whom you serve continually, 10033
6:22 My **G** sent his angel, 10033
6:23 because he had trusted in his **G**. 10033
6:26 and reverence the **G** of Daniel. 10033
6:26 he is the living **G** and he endures forever; 10033
9: 3 the Lord **G** and pleaded with him in prayer 466
9: 4 to the LORD my **G** and confessed: 466
9: 4 "O Lord, the great and awesome **G**, 446
9: 9 The Lord our **G** is merciful and forgiving, 466
9:10 we have not obeyed the LORD our **G** 466
9:11 the law of Moses, the servant of **G**, 466
9:13 the LORD our **G** by turning from our sins 466
9:14 for the LORD our **G** is righteous 466
9:15 "Now, O Lord our **G**, 466
9:17 "Now, our **G**, hear the prayers and petitions 466
9:18 Give ear, O **G**, and hear; 466
9:19 For your sake, O my **G**, do not delay, 466
9:20 to the LORD my **G** for his holy hill— 466
Da 10:12 and to humble yourself before your **G**, 466
11:32 who know their **G** will firmly resist him. 466
11:36 and magnify himself above every **g** 446
11:36 against the **G** *of* gods. 446
11:37 nor will he regard any **g**, 468
11:38 he will honor a **g** *of* fortresses; 468
11:38 a **g** unknown to his fathers he will honor 468
11:39 with the help of a foreign **g** 468
Hos 1: 7 but by the LORD their **G**." 466
1: 9 and I am not your **G**. NIH
1:10 they will be called 'sons of the living **G**.' 446
2:23 and they will say, 'You are my **G**.' " 466
3: 5 the LORD their **G** and David their king. 466
4: 1 no acknowledgment of **G** in the land. 466
4: 6 you have ignored the law of your **G**, 466
4:12 they are unfaithful to their **G**. 466
5: 4 not permit them to return to their **G**. 466
6: 6 of **G** rather than burnt offerings. 466
7:10 not return to the LORD his **G** or search 466
8: 2 Israel cries out to me, 'O our **G**, 466
8: 6 a craftsman has made it; it is not **G**. 466
9: 1 For you have been unfaithful to your **G**; 466
9: 8 The prophet, along with my **G**, 466
9: 8 and hostility in the house of his **G**. 466
9: 9 **G** will remember their wickedness NIH
9:17 My **G** will reject them because they have 466
11: 9 For I am **G**, and not man— 446
11:12 And Judah is unruly against **G**, 446
12: 3 as a man he struggled with **G**. 466
12: 5 the LORD **G** Almighty, 466
12: 6 But you must return to your **G**; 466
12: 6 and wait for your **G** always. 466
12: 9 "I am the LORD your **G**, 466
13: 4 "But I am the LORD your **G**, 466
13: 4 You shall acknowledge no **G** but me, 466
13:16 because they have rebelled against their **G**. 466
14: 1 Return, O Israel, to the LORD your **G**. 466
Joel 1:13 you who minister before my **G**; 466
1:13 from the house of your **G**. 466
1:14 to the house of the LORD your **G**, 466
1:16 joy and gladness from the house of our **G**? 466
2:13 Return to the LORD your **G**, 466
2:14 and drink offerings for the LORD your **G**. 466
2:17 'Where is their **G**?' " 466
2:23 rejoice in the LORD your **G**, 466
2:26 the name of the LORD your **G**, 466
2:27 that I am the LORD your **G**, 466
3:17 you will know that I, the LORD your **G**, 466
Am 2: 8 the house of their **g** they drink wine taken 466
3:13 declares the Lord, the LORD **G** Almighty. 466
4:12 prepare to meet your **G**, O Israel." 466
4:13 the LORD **G** Almighty is his name. 466
5:14 the LORD **G** Almighty will be with you, 466
5:15 the LORD **G** Almighty will have mercy 466
5:16 the LORD **G** Almighty, says: 466
5:26 the pedestal of your idols, the star of your **g** 466
5:27 whose name is **G** Almighty. 466
6: 8 the LORD **G** Almighty declares: 466
6:14 For the LORD **G** Almighty declares, 466
8:14 or say, 'As surely as your **g** lives, O Dan,' 466
8:14 'As surely as the **g** *of* Beersheba lives'— 2006
9:15 says the LORD your **G**. 466
Jnh 1: 5 and each cried out to his own **g**. 466
1: 6 Get up and call on your **g**! 466
1: 9 I worship the LORD, the **G** *of* heaven, 466
2: 1 the fish Jonah prayed to the LORD his **G**. 466
2: 6 O LORD my **G**. 466
3: 5 The Ninevites believed **G**. 466
3: 8 Let everyone call urgently on **G**. 466
3: 9 **G** may yet relent and with compassion turn 466
3:10 When **G** saw what they did and 466
4: 2 a gracious and compassionate **G**, 446
4: 2 a **G** who relents from sending calamity. NIH
4: 6 Then the LORD **G** provided a vine 466
4: 7 at dawn the next day **G** provided a worm, 466
4: 8 **G** provided a scorching east wind, 466
4: 9 But **G** said to Jonah, 466
Mic 3: 7 because there is no answer from **G**." 466
4: 2 to the house of the **G** *of* Jacob. 466
4: 5 in the name of the LORD our **G** for ever 466
5: 4 of the name of the LORD his **G**. 466
6: 6 and bow down before the exalted **G**? 466
6: 8 and to walk humbly with your **G**. 466
7: 4 the day **G** visits you. NIH
7: 7 I wait for **G** my Savior; 466
7: 7 my **G** will hear me. 466
7:10 "Where is the LORD your **G**?" 466
7:17 the LORD our **G** and will be afraid of you. 466
7:18 Who is a **G** like you, 446
Na 1: 2 The LORD is a jealous and avenging **G**; 446
Hab 1:11 guilty men, whose own strength is their **g**." 468
1:12 My **G**, my Holy One, we will not die. 466
3: 3 **G** came from Teman, 468
3:18 I will be joyful in **G** my Savior. 466
Zep 2: 7 The LORD their **G** will care for them; 466
2: 9 the **G** *of* Israel, "surely Moab will become 466
3: 2 she does not draw near to her **G**. 466
3:17 The LORD your **G** is with you, 466
Hag 1:12 of the LORD their **G** and the message of 466
1:12 because the LORD their **G** had sent him. 466
1:14 the house of the LORD Almighty, their **G**, 466
Zec 4: 7 the capstone to shouts of '**G** bless it! NIH
4: 7 **G** bless it!' " NIH
6:15 if you diligently obey the LORD your **G**." 466
8: 8 be faithful and righteous to them as their **G**. 466
8:23 we have heard that **G** is with you.' " 466
9: 7 Those who are left will belong to our **G** 466

Zec 9:16 The LORD their G will save them on 466
10: 6 the LORD their G and I will answer them. 466
11: 4 This is what the LORD my G says: 466
12: 5 because the LORD Almighty is their G.' 466
12: 8 and the house of David will be like G, 466
13: 9 and they will say, 'The LORD is our G.' " 466
14: 5 Then the LORD my G will come, 466
Mal 1: 9 "Now implore G to be gracious to us. 446
2:10 Did not one G create us? 446
2:11 by marrying the daughter of a foreign g. 446
2:16 says the LORD G of Israel, 466
2:17 with them" or "Where is the G of justice?" 466
3: 8 "Will a man rob G? 466
3:14 "You have said, 'It is futile to serve G. 466
3:15 and even those who challenge G escape.' " 466
3:18 between those who serve G 466
Mt 1:23 Immanuel"—which means, "G with us." 2536
3: 9 of these stones G can raise up children 2536
3:16 and he saw the Spirit of G descending like 2536
4: 3 "If you are the Son of G, 2536
4: 4 that comes from the mouth of G.' " 2536
4: 6 "If you are the Son of G," he said, 2536
4: 7 'Do not put the Lord your G to the test.' " 2536
4:10 'Worship the Lord your G, 2536
5: 8 for they will see G. 2536
5: 9 for they will be called sons of G. 2536
6:24 You cannot serve both G and Money. 2536
6:30 that is how G clothes the grass of the field, 2536
8:29 "What do you want with us, Son of G?" 2536
9: 8 and they praised G, 2536
12: 4 He entered the house of G, 2536
12:28 if I drive out demons by the Spirit of G, 2536
12:28 then the kingdom of G has come upon you. 2536
14:33 saying, "Truly you are the Son of G." 2536
15: 3 "And why do you break the command of G 2536
15: 4 For G said, 'Honor your father and mother' 2536
15: 5 from me is a gift devoted to G,' NIG
15: 6 Thus you nullify the word of G for 2536
15:31 And they praised the G of Israel. 2536
16:16 the Son of the living G." 2536
16:23 you do not have in mind the things of G, 2536
19: 6 Therefore what G has joined together, 2536
19:24 for a rich man to enter the kingdom of G." 2536
19:26 but with G all things are possible." 2536
21:31 the kingdom of G ahead of you. 2536
21:43 that the kingdom of G will be taken away 2536
22:16 the way of G in accordance with the truth. 2536
22:21 and to G what is God's." 2536
22:29 not know the Scriptures or the power of G. 2536
22:31 have you not read what G said to you, 2536
22:32 'I am the G of Abraham, 2536
22:32 the G of Isaac, and the God of Jacob'? 2536
22:32 the God of Isaac, and the G of Jacob'? 2536
22:32 not the G of the dead but of the living." 2536
22:37 " 'Love the Lord your G with all your heart 2536
26:61 to destroy the temple of G and rebuild it 2536
26:63 "I charge you under oath by the living G: 2536
26:63 Tell us if you are the Christ, the Son of G." 2536
27:40 if you are the Son of G!" 2536
27:43 He trusts in G. 2536
27:43 Let G rescue him now if he wants him, NIG
27:43 for he said, 'I am the Son of G.' " 2536
27:46 which means, "My G, my God, why 2536
27:46 which means, "My God, my G, why 2536
27:54 "Surely he was the Son of G!" 2536
Mk 1: 1 Jesus Christ, the Son of G. 2536
1:14 proclaiming the good news of G. 2536
1:15 "The kingdom of G is near. 2536
1:24 I know who you are—the Holy One of G!" 2536
2: 7 Who can forgive sins but G alone?" 2536
2:12 This amazed everyone and they praised G, 2536
2:26 of G and ate the consecrated bread, 2536
3:11 "You are the Son of G." 2536
4:11 the kingdom of G has been given to you. 2536
4:26 "This is what the kingdom of G is like. 2536
4:30 "What shall we say the kingdom of G is 2536
5: 7 Jesus, Son of the Most High G? 2536
5: 7 Swear to G that you won't torture me!" 2536
7: 8 of the commands of G and are holding on 2536
7: 9 of setting aside the commands of G 2536
7:11 Corban' (that is, a gift devoted to G), 1565
7:13 the word of G by your tradition 2536
8:33 "You do not have in mind the things of G, 2536
9: 1 before they see the kingdom of G come 2536
9:47 of G with one eye than to have two eyes 2536
10: 6 of creation G 'made them male NIG
10: 9 Therefore what G has joined together, 2536
10:14 the kingdom of G belongs to such as these. 2536
10:15 of G like a little child will never enter it." 2536
10:18 "No one is good—except G alone. 2536
10:23 for the rich to enter the kingdom of G!" 2536
10:24 how hard it is to enter the kingdom of G! 2536
10:25 for a rich man to enter the kingdom of G." 2536
10:27 man this is impossible, but not with G; 2536
10:27 all things are possible with G." 2536
11:22 "Have faith in G," Jesus answered. 2536
12:14 the way of G in accordance with the truth. 2536
12:17 and to G what is God's." 2536
12:24 the Scriptures or the power of G? 2536
12:26 how G said to him, 2536
12:26 'I am the G of Abraham, the God of Isaac, 2536
12:26 'I am the God of Abraham, the G of Isaac, 2536
12:26 the God of Isaac, and the G of Jacob'? 2536
12:27 He is not the G of the dead, 2536
12:29 'Hear, O Israel, the Lord our G, 2536
12:30 Love the Lord your G with all your heart 2536
12:32 in saying that G is one and there is no other NIG
Mk 12:34 "You are not far from the kingdom of G." 2536
13:19 when G created the world, until now— 2536
14:25 when I drink it anew in the kingdom of G." 2536
15:34 which means, "My G, my God, why 2536
15:34 which means, "My God, my G, why 2536
15:39 "Surely this man was the Son of G!" 2536
15:43 waiting for the kingdom of G, 2536
16:19 and he sat at the right hand of G. 2536
Lk 1: 6 of them were upright in the sight of G, 2536
1: 8 and he was serving as priest before G, 2536
1:16 bring back to the Lord their G. 2536
1:19 I stand in the presence of G, 2536
1:26 G sent the angel Gabriel to Nazareth, 2536
1:30 Mary, you have found favor with G. 2536
1:32 The Lord G will give him the throne 2536
1:35 to be born will be called the Son of G. 2536
1:37 For nothing is impossible with G." 2536
1:47 and my spirit rejoices in G my Savior, 2536
1:64 and he began to speak, praising G. 2536
1:68 "Praise be to the Lord, the G of Israel, 2536
1:78 because of the tender mercy of our G, 2536
2:13 praising G and saying, 2536
2:14 "Glory to G in the highest, 2536
2:20 glorifying and praising G for all 2536
2:28 in his arms and praised G, saying: 2536
2:38 she gave thanks to G and spoke about 2536
2:40 and the grace of G was upon him. 2536
2:52 and in favor with G and men. 2536
3: 2 word of G came to John son of Zechariah in 2536
3: 8 of these stones G can raise up children 2536
3:38 the son of Adam, the son of G. 2536
4: 3 "If you are the Son of G, 2536
4: 8 the Lord your G and serve him only.' " 2536
4: 9 "If you are the Son of G," he said, 2536
4:12 'Do not put the Lord your G to the test.' " 2536
4:34 I know who you are—the Holy One of G!" 2536
4:41 shouting, "You are the Son of G!" 2536
4:43 the kingdom of G to the other towns also, 2536
5: 1 around him and listening to the word of G, 2536
5:21 Who can forgive sins but G alone?" 2536
5:25 on and went home praising G. 2536
5:26 and gave praise to G. 2536
6: 4 He entered the house of G, 2536
6:12 and spent the night praying to G. 2536
6:20 for yours is the kingdom of G. 2536
7:16 with awe and praised G. 2536
7:16 "G has come to help his people." 2536
7:28 in the kingdom of G is greater than he." 2536
8: 1 the good news of the kingdom of G. 2536
8:10 the kingdom of G has been given to you, 2536
8:11 The seed is the word of G. 2536
8:28 Jesus, Son of the Most High G? 2536
8:39 and tell how much G has done for you." 2536
9: 2 to preach the kingdom of G and to heal 2536
9:11 to them about the kingdom of G, 2536
9:20 Peter answered, "The Christ of G." 2536
9:27 before they see the kingdom of G." 2536
9:43 they were all amazed at the greatness of G. 2536
9:60 you go and proclaim the kingdom of G." 2536
9:62 for service in the kingdom of G." 2536
10: 9 'The kingdom of G is near you.' 2536
10:11 be sure of this: The kingdom of G is near.' 2536
10:27 " 'Love the Lord your G with all your heart 2536
11:20 if I drive out demons by the finger of G, 2536
11:20 then the kingdom of G has come to you. 2536
11:28 the word of G and obey it." 2536
11:42 you give G a tenth of your mint, rue and 620
11:42 but you neglect justice and the love of G. 2536
11:49 Because of this, G in his wisdom said, 2536
12: 6 Yet not one of them is forgotten by G. 2536
12: 8 before the angels of G. 2536
12: 9 be disowned before the angels of G. 2536
12:20 "But G said to him, 'You fool! 2536
12:21 for himself but is not rich toward G." 2536
12:24 yet G feeds them. And how much more 2536
12:28 that is how G clothes the grass of the field, 2536
13:13 she straightened up and praised G. 2536
13:18 "What is the kingdom of G like? 2536
13:20 compare the kingdom of G to? 2536
13:28 and all the prophets in the kingdom of G, 2536
13:29 at the feast in the kingdom of G. 2536
14:15 at the feast in the kingdom of G." 2536
15:10 of G over one sinner who repents." 2536
16:13 You cannot serve both G and Money." 2536
16:15 but G knows your hearts. 2536
16:16 of the kingdom of G is being preached, 2536
17:15 came back, praising G in a loud voice. 2536
17:18 to G except this foreigner?" 2536
17:20 when the kingdom of G would come, 2536
17:20 "The kingdom of G does not come 2536
17:21 because the kingdom of G is within you." 2536
18: 2 a judge who neither feared G nor cared 2536
18: 4 though I don't fear G or care about men, 2536
18: 7 And will not G bring about justice 2536
18:11 'G, I thank you that I am not like other men 2536
18:13 'G, have mercy on me, a sinner.' 2536
18:14 went home justified before G. 1467
18:16 the kingdom of G belongs to such as these. 2536
18:17 of G like a little child will never enter it." 2536
18:19 "No one is good—except G alone. 2536
18:24 for the rich to enter the kingdom of G! 2536
18:25 for a rich man to enter the kingdom of G." 2536
18:27 with men is possible with G." 2536
18:29 for the sake of the kingdom of G 2536
18:43 and followed Jesus, praising G. 2536
18:43 all the people saw it, they also praised G. 2536
19:11 that the kingdom of G was going to appear 2536
Lk 19:37 of disciples began joyfully to praise G 2536
20:21 but teach the way of G in accordance with 2536
20:25 and to G what is God's." 2536
20:37 for he calls the Lord 'the G of Abraham, 2536
20:37 and the G of Isaac, and the God of Jacob.' 2536
20:37 and the God of Isaac, and the G of Jacob.' 2536
20:38 He is not the G of the dead, 2536
21: 5 and with gifts dedicated to G. 356
21:31 you know that the kingdom of G is near. 2536
22:16 in the kingdom of G." 2536
22:18 of the vine until the kingdom of G comes." 2536
22:69 be seated at the right hand of the mighty G." 2536
22:70 "Are you then the Son of G?" 2536
23:35 if he is the Christ of G, 2536
23:40 "Don't you fear G," he said, 2536
23:47 seeing what had happened, praised G 2536
23:51 and he was waiting for the kingdom of G. 2536
24:19 powerful in word and deed before G and all 2536
24:53 continually at the temple, praising G. 2536
Jn 1: 1 and the Word was with G, 2536
1: 1 and the Word was G. 2536
1: 2 He was with G in the beginning. 2536
1: 6 There came a man who was sent from G; 2536
1:12 he gave the right to become children of G— 2536
1:13 or a husband's will, but born of G. 2536
1:18 No one has ever seen G, 2536
1:18 but G the One and Only, 2536
1:29 "Look, the Lamb of G, 2536
1:34 and I testify that this is the Son of G." 2536
1:36 he said, "Look, the Lamb of G!" 2536
1:49 "Rabbi, you are the Son of G; 2536
1:51 of G ascending and descending on the Son 2536
3: 2 a teacher who has come from G. 2536
3: 2 if G were not with him." 2536
3: 3 the kingdom of G unless he is born again." 2536
3: 5 the kingdom of G unless he is born 2536
3:16 "For G so loved the world 2536
3:17 For G did not send his Son into the world 2536
3:21 that what he has done has been done
through G." 2536
3:33 has certified that G is truthful. 2536
3:34 the one whom G has sent speaks the words 2536
3:34 speaks the words of G, 2536
3:34 for G gives the Spirit without limit. NIG
4:10 the gift of G and who it is that asks you for 2536
4:24 G is spirit, and his worshipers must
worship in spirit and in truth." 2536
5:18 but he was even calling G his own Father, 2536
5:18 making himself equal with G. 2536
5:25 the Son of G and those who hear will live. 2536
5:42 I know that you do not have the love of G 2536
5:44 the praise that comes from the only G? 2536
6:27 On him G the Father has placed his seal 2536
6:28 to do the works G requires?" 2536
6:29 Jesus answered, "The work of G is this: 2536
6:33 For the bread of G is he who comes down 2536
6:45 'They will all be taught by G.' 2536
6:46 the Father except the one who is from G; 2536
6:69 and know that you are the Holy One of G." 2536
7:17 from G or whether I speak on my own. 2536
8:40 the truth that I heard from G. 2536
8:41 "The only Father we have is G himself." 2536
8:42 Jesus said to them, "If G were your Father, 2536
8:42 for I came from G and now am here. 2536
8:47 He who belongs to G hears what God says. 2536
8:47 He who belongs to God hears what G says. 2536
8:47 not hear is that you do not belong to G." 2536
8:54 My Father, whom you claim as your G, 2536
9: 3 so that the work of G might be displayed 2536
9:16 "This man is not from G, 2536
9:24 "Give glory to G," they said. 2536
9:29 We know that G spoke to Moses, 2536
9:31 We know that G does not listen to sinners. 2536
9:33 If this man were not from G, 2536
10:33 because you, a mere man, claim to be G." 2536
10:35 to whom the word of G came— 2536
11:22 now G will give you whatever you ask." 2536
11:27 you are the Christ, the Son of G, 2536
11:40 you would see the glory of G?" 2536
11:52 but also for the scattered children of G, 2536
12:43 from men more than praise from G. 2536
13: 3 that he had come from G and was returning 2536
13: 3 from God and was returning to G; 2536
13:31 the Son of Man glorified and G is glorified 2536
13:32 If G is glorified in him, 2536
13:32 G will glorify the Son in himself, 2536
14: 1 Trust in G; trust also in me. 2536
16: 2 will think he is offering a service to G. 2536
16:27 and have believed that I came from G. 2536
16:30 that you came from G." 2536
17: 3 that they may know you, the only true G, 2536
19: 7 because he claimed to be the Son of G." 2536
20:17 to my G and your God.' " 2536
20:17 to my God and your G.' " 2536
20:28 Thomas said to him, "My Lord and my G!" 2536
20:31 that Jesus is the Christ, the Son of G, 2536
21:19 of death by which Peter would glorify G. 2536
Ac 1: 3 and spoke about the kingdom of G. 2536
2:11 we hear them declaring the wonders of G 2536
2:17 G says, I will pour out my Spirit 2536
2:22 a man accredited by G to you by miracles, 2536
2:22 which G did among you through him, 2536
2:24 But G raised him from the dead, 2536
2:30 and knew that G had promised him on oath 2536
2:32 G has raised this Jesus to life, 2536
2:33 Exalted to the right hand of G, 2536
2:36 G has made this Jesus, 2536

Ac 2:39 for all whom the Lord our G will call." 2536
2:47 praising G and enjoying the favor of all 2536
3: 8 walking and jumping, and praising G. 2536
3: 9 When all the people saw him walking and praising G, 2536
3:13 The G of Abraham, Isaac and Jacob, 2536
3:13 Isaac and Jacob, the G of our fathers, 2536
3:15 but G raised him from the dead. 2536
3:18 how G fulfilled what he had foretold 2536
3:19 Repent, then, and turn to G, NIG
3:21 the time comes for G to restore everything, 2536
3:22 'The Lord your G will raise up for you 2536
3:25 of the prophets and of the covenant G made 2536
3:26 When G raised up his servant, 2536
4:10 whom you crucified but whom G raised 2536
4:19 in God's sight to obey you rather than G. 2536
4:21 because all the people were praising G 2536
4:24 raised their voices together in prayer to G. 2536
4:31 and spoke the word *of* G boldly. 2536
5: 4 You have not lied to men but *to* G." 2536
5:29 "We must obey G rather than men! 2536
5:30 The G of our fathers raised Jesus from 2536
5:31 G exalted him to his own right hand 2536
5:32 the Holy Spirit, whom G has given 2536
5:39 But if it is from G, you will not be able to 2536
5:39 you will only find yourselves **fighting against G."** 2534
6: 2 of the word *of* G in order to wait on tables. 2536
6: 7 So the word *of* G spread. 2536
6:11 blasphemy against Moses and against G." 2536
7: 2 The G of glory appeared 2536
7: 3 and your people,' G said, 'and go to NIG
7: 4 G sent him to this land where you are NIG
7: 5 But G promised him that he NIG
7: 6 G spoke to him in this way: 2536
7: 7 G said, 'and afterward they will come out 2536
7: 9 But G was with him 2536
7:17 for G to fulfill his promise to Abraham, 2536
7:25 that G was using him to rescue them, 2536
7:32 'I am the G of your fathers, 2536
7:32 the G of Abraham, Isaac and Jacob.' 2536
7:35 to be their ruler and deliverer *by* G himself, 2536
7:37 'G will send you a prophet like me 2536
7:42 But G turned away and gave them over to 2536
7:43 of Molech and the star *of* your g Rephan, 2536
7:44 It had been made as G directed Moses, NIG
7:45 from the nations G drove out before them. 2536
7:46 a dwelling place *for* the G of Jacob. 2536
7:55 up to heaven and saw the glory *of* G, 2536
7:55 and Jesus standing at the right hand *of* G. 2536
7:56 Son of Man standing at the right hand *of* G. 2536
8:12 the good news of the kingdom *of* G and 2536
8:14 that Samaria had accepted the word *of* G, 2536
8:20 could buy the gift *of* G with money! 2536
8:21 because your heart is not right before G. 2536
9:20 the synagogues that Jesus is the Son *of* G. 2536
10: 2 to those in need and prayed to G regularly. 2536
10: 3 He distinctly saw an angel *of* G, 2536
10: 4 up as a memorial offering before G. 2536
10:15 that G has made clean." 2536
10:28 But G has shown me that I should 2536
10:31 G has heard your prayer 2536
10:33 in the presence *of* G to listen to everything 2536
10:34 "I now realize how true it is that G does 2536
10:36 the message G sent to the people of Israel, NIG
10:38 how G anointed Jesus of Nazareth with 2536
10:38 because G was with him. 2536
10:40 but G raised him from the dead on 2536
10:41 by witnesses whom G had already chosen— 2536
10:42 the one whom G appointed as judge of 2536
10:46 in tongues and praising G. 2536
11: 1 also had received the word *of* G. 2536
11: 9 that G has made clean.' 2536
11:17 if G gave them the same gift as he gave us, 2536
11:17 who was I to think that I could oppose G?" 2536
11:18 and praised G, saying, "So 2536
11:18 G has granted even the Gentiles 2536
11:23 and saw the evidence of the grace *of* G, 2536
12: 5 but the church was earnestly praying to G 2536
12:22 They shouted, "This is the voice *of* a g, 2536
12:23 because Herod did not give praise *to* G, 2536
12:24 But the word *of* G continued to increase 2536
13: 5 the word *of* G in the Jewish synagogues. 2536
13: 7 because he wanted to hear the word *of* G. 2536
13:16 of Israel and you Gentiles who worship G, 2536
13:17 G of the people of Israel chose our fathers; 2536
13:20 G gave them judges until the time NIG
13:23 "From this man's descendants G has brought to Israel the Savior Jesus, 2536
13:30 But G raised him from the dead, 2536
13:32 What G promised our fathers NIG
13:34 The fact that G raised him from the dead, NIG
13:37 the one whom G raised from the dead did 2536
13:43 to continue in the grace *of* G. 2536
13:46 to speak the word *of* G to you first. 2536
14:15 from these worthless things to the living G, 2536
14:22 to enter the kingdom *of* G," 2536
14:26 *of* G for the work they had now completed. 2536
14:27 that G had done through them and 2536
15: 4 they reported everything G had done 2536
15: 7 you know that some time ago G made 2536
15: 8 G, who knows the heart, 2536
15:10 why do you try to test G by putting on 2536
15:12 and wonders G had done among 2536
15:14 to us how G at first showed his concern 2536
15:19 for the Gentiles who are turning to G. 2536
16:10 concluding that G had called us to preach 2536

Ac 16:14 who was a worshiper of G. 2536
16:17 servants *of* the Most High G, 2536
16:25 and singing hymns to G, 2536
16:34 because he had come to believe *in* G— 2536
17:13 that Paul was preaching the word *of* G 2536
17:23 this inscription: TO AN UNKNOWN G. 2536
17:24 "The G who made the world 2536
17:27 G did this so that men would seek him NIG
17:30 In the past G overlooked such ignorance, 2536
18: 7 Titius Justus, a worshiper of G. 2536
18:11 teaching them the word *of* G. 2536
18:13 to worship G in ways contrary to the law." 2536
18:26 to him the way *of* G more adequately. 2536
19: 8 about the kingdom *of* G. 2536
19:11 G did extraordinary miracles through Paul, 2536
20:21 that they must turn to G in repentance 2536
20:27 to proclaim to you the whole will *of* G. 2536
20:28 Be shepherds of the church *of* G, 2536
20:32 "Now I commit you *to* G and to the word 2536
21:19 and reported in detail what G had done 2536
21:20 When they heard this, they praised G. 2536
22: 3 of our fathers and was just as zealous *for* G 2536
22:14 'The G of our fathers has chosen you 2536
23: 1 *to* G in all good conscience to this day." 2536
23: 3 Then Paul said to him, "G will strike you, 2536
24:14 I admit that I worship the G of our fathers 2536
24:15 I have the same hope in G as these men, 2536
24:16 to keep my conscience clear before G 2536
26: 6 in what G has promised our fathers 2536
26: 7 as they earnestly serve G day and night. NIG
26: 8 of you consider it incredible that G raises 2536
26:18 and from the power of Satan to G, 2536
26:20 and turn to G and prove their repentance 2536
26:29 I pray G that not only you 2536
27:23 the G whose I am and whom I serve stood 2536
27:24 and G has graciously given you the lives 2536
27:25 for I have faith *in* G that it will happen just 2536
27:35 and gave thanks *to* G in front of them all. 2536
28: 6 and said he was a g. 2536
28:15 At the sight of these men Paul thanked G 2536
28:23 and declared to them the kingdom *of* G 2536
28:31 the kingdom *of* G and taught about 2536
Ro 1: 1 an apostle and set apart for the gospel *of* G 2536
1: 4 to be the Son *of* G by his resurrection from 2536
1: 7 in Rome who are loved *by* G and called to 2536
1: 7 Grace and peace to you from G our Father 2536
1: 8 I thank my G through Jesus Christ for all 2536
1: 9 G, whom I serve with my whole heart 2536
1:16 the power *of* G for the salvation 2536
1:17 *from* G is revealed, a righteousness that is 2536
1:18 wrath *of* G is being revealed from heaven 2536
1:19 since what may be known *about* G is plain 2536
1:19 because G has made it plain to them. 2536
1:21 For although they knew G, 2536
1:21 they neither glorified him as G 2536
1:23 and exchanged the glory *of* the immortal G 2536
1:24 Therefore G gave them over in 2536
1:25 They exchanged the truth *of* G for a lie, 2536
1:26 of this, G gave them over to shameful lusts. 2536
1:28 to retain the knowledge of G, 2536
2: 6 G "will give to each person according 4005S
2:11 For G does not show favoritism. 2536
2:16 on the day when G will judge men's secrets 2536
2:17 and brag about your relationship to G; 2536
2:23 do you dishonor G by breaking the law? 2536
2:29 not from men, but from G. 2536
3: 2 with the very words *of* G. 2536
3: 4 Let G be true, and every man a liar. 2536
3: 5 G is unjust in bringing his wrath on us? 2536
3: 6 how could G judge the world? 2536
3:11 no one who seeks G. 2536
3:18 "There is no fear *of* G before their eyes." 2536
3:19 the whole world held accountable *to* G. 2536
3:21 But now a righteousness *from* G, 2536
3:22 *from* G comes through faith in Jesus Christ 2536
3:23 sinned and fall short of the glory *of* G, 2536
3:25 G presented him as a sacrifice 2536
3:29 Is G the God of Jews only? NIG
3:29 Is God the G of Jews only? 2536
3:29 Is he not the G of Gentiles too? NIG
3:30 since there is only one G, 2536
4: 2 but not before G. 2536
4: 3 "Abraham believed G, and it was credited 2536
4: 5 but trusts G who justifies the wicked, NIG
4: 6 to whom G credits righteousness apart 2536
4:17 He is our father in the sight of G, NIG
4:17 the G who gives life to the dead 2536
4:20 regarding the promise *of* G, 2536
4:20 in his faith and gave glory *to* G, 2536
4:21 being fully persuaded that G had power NIG
4:24 to whom G will credit righteousness— NIG
5: 1 with G through our Lord Jesus Christ, 2536
5: 2 we rejoice in the hope of the glory *of* G. 2536
5: 5 because G has poured out his love 2536
5: 8 G demonstrates his own love for us in this: 2536
5:11 in G through our Lord Jesus Christ, 2536
5:16 the gift of G is not like the result of NIG
6:10 but the life he lives, he lives *to* G. 2536
6:11 count yourselves dead to sin but alive *to* G 2536
6:13 but rather offer yourselves *to* G, 2536
6:17 But thanks be *to* G that, 2536
6:22 from sin and have become slaves *to* G, 2536
6:23 but the gift *of* G is eternal life 2536
7: 4 in order that we might bear fruit *to* G. 2536
7:25 Thanks be *to* G— 2536
8: 3 G did by sending his own Son in 2536
8: 7 the sinful mind is hostile to G. 2536

Ro 8: 8 by the sinful nature cannot please G. 2536
8: 9 if the Spirit *of* G lives in you. 2536
8:14 by the Spirit *of* G are sons of God. 2536
8:14 by the Spirit of God are sons *of* G. 2536
8:17 heirs *of* G and co-heirs with Christ, 2536
8:19 in eager expectation for the sons *of* G to 2536
8:21 the glorious freedom of the children *of* G. 2536
8:28 And we know that in all things G works for NIG
8:29 For those G foreknew he also predestined NIG
8:31 If G is for us, who can be against us? 2536
8:33 against those whom G has chosen? 2536
8:33 It is G who justifies. 2536
8:34 the right hand *of* G and is also interceding 2536
8:39 be able to separate us from the love *of* G 2536
9: 5 who is G over all, forever praised! 2536
9:14 Is G unjust? Not at all! 2536
9:18 Therefore G has mercy on whom he wants NIG
9:19 "Then why does G still blame us? NIG
9:20 who are you, O man, to talk back *to* G? 2536
9:22 What if G, choosing to show his wrath 2536
9:26 they will be called 'sons *of* the living G.' " 2536
10: 1 to G for the Israelites is that they may 2536
10: 2 about them that they are zealous *for* G, 2536
10: 3 *from* G and sought to establish their own, 2536
10: 9 and believe in your heart that G raised him 2536
11: 1 I ask then: Did G reject his people? 2536
11: 2 G did not reject his people, 2536
11: 2 how he appealed *to* G against Israel: 2536
11: 8 "G gave them a spirit of stupor, 2536
11:21 For if G did not spare the natural branches, 2536
11:22 therefore the kindness and sternness *of* G: 2536
11:23 for G is able to graft them in again. 2536
11:30 *to* G have now received mercy as a result 2536
11:32 For G has bound all men over 2536
11:33 of the wisdom and knowledge *of* G! 2536
11:35 "Who has ever given *to* G, 899S
11:35 that G should repay him?" NIG
12: 1 holy and pleasing *to* G— 2536
12: 3 with the measure of faith G has given you. 2536
13: 1 that which G has established. 2536
13: 1 that exist have been established by G. 2536
13: 2 against what G has instituted, 2536
14: 3 for G has accepted him. 2536
14: 6 eats to the Lord, for he gives thanks *to* G; 2536
14: 6 does so to the Lord and gives thanks *to* G. 2536
14:11 every tongue will confess *to* G.' " 2536
14:12 of us will give an account of himself *to* G. 2536
14:17 *of* G is not a matter of eating and drinking, 2536
14:18 in this way is pleasing *to* G and approved 2536
14:20 Do not destroy the work *of* G for the sake 2536
14:22 between yourself and G. 2536
15: 5 May the G who gives endurance 2536
15: 6 the G and Father of our Lord Jesus Christ. 2536
15: 7 in order to bring praise to G. 2536
15: 9 the Gentiles may glorify G for his mercy, 2536
15:13 May the G of hope fill you with all joy 2536
15:15 because of the grace G gave me 2536
15:16 of proclaiming the gospel *of* G, 2536
15:16 an offering acceptable to G, NIG
15:17 I glory in Christ Jesus in my service to G. 2536
15:18 the Gentiles to obey G by what I have said NIG
15:30 to join me in my struggle by praying to G 2536
15:33 The G of peace be with you all. Amen. 2536
16:20 The G of peace will soon crush Satan 2536
16:26 by the command *of* the eternal G, 2536
16:27 *to* the only wise G be glory forever 2536
1Co 1: 1 an apostle of Christ Jesus by the will *of* G, 2536
1: 2 church *of* G in Corinth, to those sanctified 2536
1: 3 Grace and peace to you from G our Father 2536
1: 4 I always thank G for you because 2536
1: 9 G, who has called you into fellowship 2536
1:18 who are being saved it is the power *of* G. 2536
1:20 Has not G made foolish the wisdom of 2536
1:21 For since in the wisdom *of* G the world 2536
1:21 G was pleased through the foolishness 2536
1:24 but to those whom G has called, NIG
1:24 the power *of* G and the wisdom of God. 2536
1:24 the power of God and the wisdom *of* G. 2536
1:25 the foolishness *of* G is wiser than man's wisdom, 2536
1:25 the weakness *of* G is stronger than man's strength. 2536
1:27 But G chose the foolish things of the world 2536
1:27 G chose the weak things of the world 2536
1:30 who has become for us wisdom from G— 2536
2: 1 to you the testimony *about* G. 2536
2: 7 that has been hidden and that G destined 2536
2: 9 no mind has conceived what G has prepared 2536
2:10 but G has revealed it to us by his Spirit. 2536
2:10 even the deep things *of* G. 2536
2:11 the thoughts *of* G except the Spirit of God. 2536
2:11 the thoughts of God except the Spirit *of* G. 2536
2:12 of the world but the Spirit who is from G, 2536
2:12 we may understand what G has freely given us. 2536
2:14 the things that come from the Spirit *of* G, 2536
3: 6 Apollos watered it, but G made it grow. 2536
3: 7 but only G, who makes things grow. 2536
3:10 By the grace G has given me, 2536
3:17 destroys God's temple, G will destroy him; 2536
3:23 and you are of Christ, and Christ is *of* G. 2536
4: 1 with the secret things *of* G. 2536
4: 5 time each will receive his praise from G. 2536
4: 9 to me that G has put us apostles on display 2536
4:20 *of* G is not a matter of talk but of power. 2536
5:13 G will judge those outside. 2536
6: 9 not inherit the kingdom *of* G? 2536

1Co	6:10	will inherit the kingdom *of* **G**.	*2536*
	6:11	and by the Spirit *of* our **G**.	*2536*
	6:13	but **G** will destroy them both.	*2536*
	6:14	By his power **G** raised the Lord from	*2536*
	6:19	whom you have received from **G**?	*2536*
	6:20	Therefore honor **G** with your body.	*2536*
	7:7	But each man has his own gift from **G**;	*2536*
	7:15	**G** has called us to live in peace.	*2536*
	7:17	to him and to which **G** has called him.	*2536*
	7:20	in when **G** called him.	*NIG*
	7:24	Brothers, each man, as responsible to **G**,	*2536*
	7:24	in the situation **G** called him to.	*NIG*
	7:40	and I think that I too have the Spirit *of* **G**.	*2536*
	8:3	the man who loves **G** is known by God.	*2536*
	8:3	the man who loves God is known by **G**.	*899*[S]
	8:4	in the world and that there is no **G** but one.	*2536*
	8:6	yet for us there is but one **G**, the Father,	*2536*
	8:8	But food does not bring us near *to* **G**;	*2536*
	9:9	Is it about oxen that **G** is concerned?	*2536*
	10:5	**G** was not pleased with most of them;	*2536*
	10:13	And **G** is faithful;	*2536*
	10:20	to demons, not *to* **G**, and I do not want you	*2536*
	10:30	because of something I thank **G** for?	*NIG*
	10:31	do it all for the glory *of* **G**.	*2536*
	10:32	whether Jews, Greeks or the church *of* **G**—	*2536*
	11:3	and the head of Christ is **G**.	*2536*
	11:7	since he is the image and glory *of* **G**;	*2536*
	11:12	But everything comes from **G**.	*2536*
	11:13	to pray *to* **G** with her head uncovered?	*2536*
	11:16	nor do the churches *of* **G**.	*2536*
	11:22	Or do you despise the church *of* **G**	*2536*
	12:3	by the Spirit *of* **G** says,	*2536*
	12:6	the same **G** works all of them in all men.	*2536*
	12:18	in fact **G** has arranged the parts in the body,	*2536*
	12:24	But **G** has combined the members of	*2536*
	12:28	And in the church **G** has appointed first	*2536*
	14:2	a tongue does not speak to men but *to* **G**.	*2536*
	14:16	If you are praising **G** with your spirit,	*NIG*
	14:18	I thank **G** that I speak in tongues more than	*2536*
	14:25	So he will fall down and worship **G**,	*2536*
	14:25	exclaiming, "**G** is really among you!"	*2536*
	14:28	in the church and speak *to* himself and **G**.	*2536*
	14:33	For **G** is not a God of disorder but of peace.	*2536*
	14:33	For God is not a **G** of disorder but of peace.	*NIG*
	14:36	Did the word *of* **G** originate with you?	*2536*
	15:9	because I persecuted the church *of* **G**.	*2536*
	15:10	But by the grace *of* **G** I am what I am,	*2536*
	15:10	not I, but the grace *of* **G** that was with me.	*2536*
	15:15	then found to be false witnesses about **G**,	*2536*
	15:15	about **G** that he raised Christ from the dead.	*2536*
	15:24	when he hands over the kingdom *to* **G**	*2536*
	15:27	that this does not include **G** himself,	*NIG*
	15:28	so that **G** may be all in all.	*2536*
	15:34	for there are some who are ignorant *of* **G**—	*2536*
	15:38	But **G** gives it a body as he has determined,	*2536*
	15:50	cannot inherit the kingdom *of* **G**,	*2536*
	15:57	But thanks be *to* **G**!	*2536*
2Co	1:1	an apostle of Christ Jesus by the will *of* **G**,	*2536*
	1:1	To the church *of* **G** in Corinth,	*2536*
	1:2	Grace and peace to you from **G** our Father	*2536*
	1:3	the **G** and Father of our Lord Jesus Christ,	*2536*
	1:3	of compassion and the **G** of all comfort,	*2536*
	1:4	with the comfort we ourselves have received from **G**.	*2536*
	1:9	not rely on ourselves but on **G**,	*2536*
	1:12	the holiness and sincerity that are *from* **G**.	*2536*
	1:18	But as surely as **G** is faithful,	*2536*
	1:19	For the Son *of* **G**, Jesus Christ,	*2536*
	1:20	no matter how many promises **G** has made,	*2536*
	1:20	by us to the glory *of* **G**.	*2536*
	1:21	Now it is **G** who makes both us and you	*2536*
	1:23	I call **G** as my witness that it was in order	*2536*
	2:14	But thanks be *to* **G**,	*2536*
	2:15	For we are *to* **G** the aroma of Christ	*2536*
	2:17	we do not peddle the word *of* **G** for profit.	*2536*
	2:17	in Christ we speak before **G** with sincerity,	*2536*
	2:17	like men sent from **G**.	*2536*
	3:3	with ink but with the Spirit *of* the living **G**,	*2536*
	3:4	as this is ours through Christ before **G**.	*2536*
	3:5	but our competence comes from **G**.	*2536*
	4:2	nor do we distort the word *of* **G**.	*2536*
	4:2	every man's conscience in the sight *of* **G**.	*2536*
	4:4	The **g** of this age has blinded the minds	*2536*
	4:4	Christ, who is the image *of* **G**.	*2536*
	4:6	For **G**, who said, "Let light shine out	*2536*
	4:6	the knowledge of the glory *of* **G** in the face	*2536*
	4:7	that this all-surpassing power is *from* **G** and	*2536*
	4:15	to overflow to the glory *of* **G**.	*2536*
	5:1	we have a building from **G**,	*2536*
	5:5	Now it is **G** who has made us	*2536*
	5:11	What we are is plain *to* **G**,	*2536*
	5:13	out of our mind, it is *for the sake of* **G**;	*2536*
	5:18	All this is from **G**, who reconciled us	*2536*
	5:19	that **G** was reconciling the world to himself	*2536*
	5:20	**G** were making his appeal through us.	*2536*
	5:20	Be reconciled *to* **G**.	*2536*
	5:21	**G** made him who had no sin to be sin	*NIG*
	5:21	we might become the righteousness *of* **G**.	*2536*
	6:4	*of* **G** we commend ourselves in every way:	*2536*
	6:7	in truthful speech and in the power *of* **G**;	*2536*
	6:16	between the temple *of* **G** and idols?	*2536*
	6:16	For we are the temple *of* the living **G**.	*2536*
	6:16	As **G** has said: "I will live with them	*2536*
	6:16	and I will be their **G**,	*2536*
	7:1	perfecting holiness out of reverence *for* **G**.	*2536*
	7:6	But **G**, who comforts the downcast,	*2536*
	7:9	For you became sorrowful as **G** intended	*2536*
2Co	7:12	that before **G** you could see for yourselves	*2536*
	8:1	that **G** has given the Macedonian churches.	*2536*
	8:16	I thank **G**, who put into the heart of Titus	*2536*
	9:7	for **G** loves a cheerful giver.	*2536*
	9:8	**G** is able to make all grace abound to you,	*2536*
	9:11	generosity will result in thanksgiving *to* **G**.	*2536*
	9:12	in many expressions of thanks *to* **G**.	*2536*
	9:13	men will praise **G** for the obedience	*2536*
	9:14	of the surpassing grace **G** has given you.	*2536*
	9:15	Thanks be *to* **G** for his indescribable gift!	*2536*
	10:5	sets itself up against the knowledge *of* **G**,	*2536*
	10:13	to the field **G** has assigned to us,	*2536*
	11:7	by preaching the gospel *of* **G** to you free	*2536*
	11:11	**G** knows I do!	*2536*
	11:31	The **G** and Father of the Lord Jesus,	*2536*
	12:2	I do not know—**G** knows.	*2536*
	12:3	the body I do not know, but **G** knows—	*2536*
	12:19	We have been speaking in the sight *of* **G**	*2536*
	12:21	when I come again my **G** will humble me	*2536*
	13:7	to **G** that you will not do anything wrong.	*2536*
	13:11	the **G** of love and peace will be with you.	*2536*
	13:14	and the love *of* **G**,	*2536*
Gal	1:1	but by Jesus Christ and **G** the Father,	*2536*
	1:3	Grace and peace to you from **G** our Father	*2536*
	1:4	according to the will *of* our **G** and Father,	*2536*
	1:10	to win the approval of men, or of **G**?	*2536*
	1:13	how intensely I persecuted the church *of* **G**	*2536*
	1:15	But when **G**, who set me apart from birth	*2536*
	1:20	I assure you before **G** that what I	*2536*
	1:24	And they praised **G** because of me.	*2536*
	2:6	**G** does not judge by external appearance—	*2536*
	2:8	For **G, who** was at work in the ministry	*3836*[S]
	2:19	to the law so that I might live *for* **G**.	*2536*
	2:20	I live by faith in the Son *of* **G**,	*2536*
	2:21	I do not set aside the grace *of* **G**,	*2536*
	3:5	Does **G** give you his Spirit and work	*3836*[S]
	3:6	Consider Abraham: "He believed **G**,	*2536*
	3:8	The Scripture foresaw that **G** would justify	*2536*
	3:11	Clearly no one is justified before **G** by	*2536*
	3:17	the covenant previously established by **G**	*2536*
	3:18	but **G** in his grace gave it to Abraham	*2536*
	3:20	but **G** is one.	*2536*
	3:21	therefore, opposed to the promises *of* **G**?	*2536*
	3:26	You are all sons *of* **G** through faith	*2536*
	4:4	the time had fully come, **G** sent his Son,	*2536*
	4:6	**G** sent the Spirit of his Son into our hearts,	*2536*
	4:7	you are a son, **G** has made you also an heir.	*2536*
	4:8	Formerly, when you did not know **G**,	*2536*
	4:9	But now that you know **G**—	*2536*
	4:9	or rather are known by **G**—	*2536*
	4:14	as if I were an angel *of* **G**,	*2536*
	5:21	like this will not inherit the kingdom *of* **G**.	*2536*
	6:7	Do not be deceived: **G** cannot be mocked.	*2536*
	6:16	even to the Israel *of* **G**.	*2536*
Eph	1:1	an apostle of Christ Jesus by the will *of* **G**,	*2536*
	1:2	Grace and peace to you from **G** our Father	*2536*
	1:3	the **G** and Father of our Lord Jesus Christ,	*2536*
	1:17	that the **G** of our Lord Jesus Christ,	*2536*
	1:22	And **G** placed all things under his feet	*NIG*
	2:4	But because of his great love for us, **G**,	*2536*
	2:6	And **G** raised us up with Christ	*NIG*
	2:8	this not from yourselves, it is the gift *of* **G**—	*2536*
	2:10	which **G** prepared in advance for us to do.	*2536*
	2:12	without hope and **without G** in the world.	*117*
	2:16	to reconcile both of them *to* **G** through	*2536*
	2:22	a dwelling in which **G** lives by his Spirit.	*2536*
	3:9	which for ages past was kept hidden in **G**,	*2536*
	3:10	*of* **G** should be made known to the rulers	*2536*
	3:12	in him we may approach **G** with freedom	*NIG*
	3:19	to the measure of all the fullness *of* **G**.	*2536*
	4:6	one **G** and Father of all,	*2536*
	4:13	and in the knowledge of the Son *of* **G**	*2536*
	4:18	and separated from the life *of* **G** because of	*2536*
	4:24	like **G** in true righteousness and holiness.	*2536*
	4:30	And do not grieve the Holy Spirit *of* **G**,	*2536*
	4:32	just as in Christ **G** forgave you.	*2536*
	5:1	Be imitators *of* **G**, therefore,	*2536*
	5:2	as a fragrant offering and sacrifice *to* **G**.	*2536*
	5:5	in the kingdom of Christ and *of* **G**.	*2536*
	5:20	always giving thanks *to* **G** the Father	*2536*
	6:6	doing the will *of* **G** from your heart.	*2536*
	6:11	*of* **G** so that you can take your stand	*2536*
	6:13	Therefore put on the full armor *of* **G**,	*2536*
	6:17	which is the word *of* **G**.	*2536*
	6:23	and love with faith from **G** the Father and	*2536*
Php	1:2	Grace and peace to you from **G** our Father	*2536*
	1:3	I thank my **G** every time I remember you.	*2536*
	1:8	**G** can testify how I long for all of you with	*2536*
	1:11	to the glory and praise *of* **G**.	*2536*
	1:14	to speak the word *of* **G** more courageously	*2536*
	1:28	that you will be saved—and that by **G**.	*2536*
	2:6	Who, being in very nature **G**,	*2536*
	2:6	did not consider equality *with* **G** something	*2536*
	2:9	Therefore **G** exalted him to the highest	*2536*
	2:11	to the glory *of* **G** the Father.	*2536*
	2:13	for it is **G** who works in you to will and	*2536*
	2:15	children *of* **G** without fault in a crooked	*2536*
	2:27	But **G** had mercy on him,	*2536*
	3:3	we who worship by the Spirit *of* **G**,	*2536*
	3:9	the righteousness that comes from **G** and is	*2536*
	3:14	for which **G** has called me heavenward	*2536*
	3:15	that too **G** will make clear to you.	*2536*
	3:19	their **g** is their stomach,	*2536*
	4:6	present your requests to **G**.	*2536*
	4:7	And the peace *of* **G**,	*2536*
	4:9	And the **G** of peace will be with you.	*2536*
	4:18	an acceptable sacrifice, pleasing *to* **G**.	*2536*
Php	4:19	And my **G** will meet all your needs	*2536*
	4:20	*To* our **G** and Father be glory for ever	*2536*
Col	1:1	an apostle of Christ Jesus by the will *of* **G**,	*2536*
	1:2	Grace and peace to you from **G** our Father.	*2536*
	1:3	We always thank **G**, the Father of our Lord	*2536*
	1:9	not stopped praying for you and asking **G**	*NIG*
	1:10	growing in the knowledge *of* **G**,	*2536*
	1:15	He is the image *of* the invisible **G**,	*2536*
	1:19	For **G** was pleased to have all his fullness	*NIG*
	1:21	from **G** and were enemies in your minds	*NIG*
	1:25	by the commission **G** gave me to present	*2536*
	1:25	to you the word *of* **G** in its fullness—	*2536*
	1:27	To them **G** has chosen to make known	*2536*
	2:2	that they may know the mystery *of* **G**,	*2536*
	2:12	through your faith in the power *of* **G**,	*2536*
	2:13	**G** made you alive with Christ.	*NIG*
	2:19	grows as **G** causes it to grow.	*2536*
	3:1	Christ is seated at the right hand *of* **G**.	*2536*
	3:3	your life is now hidden with Christ in **G**.	*2536*
	3:6	of these, the wrath *of* **G** is coming.	*2536*
	3:16	with gratitude in your hearts *to* **G**.	*2536*
	3:17	giving thanks *to* **G** the Father through him.	*2536*
	4:3	that **G** may open a door for our message,	*2536*
	4:11	fellow workers for the kingdom *of* **G**,	*2536*
	4:12	you may stand firm in all the will *of* **G**,	*2536*
1Th	1:1	in **G** the Father and the Lord Jesus Christ:	*2536*
	1:2	We always thank **G** for all of you,	*2536*
	1:3	We continually remember before our **G**	*2536*
	1:4	For we know, brothers loved by **G**,	*2536*
	1:8	in **G** has become known everywhere.	*2536*
	1:9	They tell how you turned to **G** from idols	*2536*
	1:9	from idols to serve the living and true **G**,	*2536*
	2:2	of our **G** we dared to tell you his gospel	*2536*
	2:4	as men approved by **G** to be entrusted with	*2536*
	2:4	We are not trying to please men but **G**,	*2536*
	2:5	**G** is our witness.	*2536*
	2:8	to share with you not only the gospel *of* **G**	*2536*
	2:9	while we preached the gospel *of* **G** to you.	*2536*
	2:10	You are witnesses, and so is **G**,	*2536*
	2:12	and urging you to live lives worthy *of* **G**,	*2536*
	2:13	And we also thank **G** continually because,	*2536*
	2:13	when you received the word *of* **G**,	*2536*
	2:13	but as it actually is, the word *of* **G**,	*2536*
	2:15	They displease **G** and are hostile to all men	*2536*
	2:16	The wrath *of* **G** has come upon them	*2536*
	3:9	How can we thank **G** enough for you	*2536*
	3:9	in the presence *of* our **G** because of you?	*2536*
	3:11	Now may our **G** and Father himself	*2536*
	3:13	in the presence *of* our **G** and Father	*2536*
	4:1	how to live in order to please **G**,	*2536*
	4:5	who do not know **G**;	*2536*
	4:7	For **G** did not call us to be impure,	*2536*
	4:8	not reject man but **G**,	*2536*
	4:9	for you yourselves have been **taught by G**	*2531*
	4:14	and so we believe that **G** will bring	*2536*
	4:16	and with the trumpet call *of* **G**,	*2536*
	5:9	For **G** did not appoint us to suffer wrath but	*2536*
	5:23	May **G** himself, the God of peace,	*NIG*
	5:23	May God himself, the **G** of peace,	*2536*
2Th	1:1	in **G** our Father and the Lord Jesus Christ:	*2536*
	1:2	Grace and peace to you from **G** the Father	*2536*
	1:3	We ought always to thank **G** for you,	*2536*
	1:5	be counted worthy of the kingdom *of* **G**,	*2536*
	1:6	**G** is just: He will pay back trouble to those	*2536*
	1:8	He will punish those who do not know **G**	*2536*
	1:11	our **G** may count you worthy of his calling,	*2536*
	1:12	according to the grace *of* our **G** and	*2536*
	2:4	that is called **G** or is worshiped,	*2536*
	2:4	proclaiming himself to be **G**.	*2536*
	2:11	For this reason **G** sends them	*2536*
	2:13	But we ought always to thank **G** for you,	*2536*
	2:13	because from the beginning **G** chose you to	*2536*
	2:16	and **G** our Father, who loved us	*2536*
1Ti	1:1	by the command *of* **G** our Savior and	*2536*
	1:2	Grace, mercy and peace from **G** the Father	*2536*
	1:11	to the glorious gospel *of* the blessed **G**,	*2536*
	1:17	immortal, invisible, the only **G**,	*2536*
	2:3	This is good, and pleases **G** our Savior,	*2536*
	2:5	For there is one **G** and one mediator	*2536*
	2:5	and one mediator between **G** and men,	*2536*
	2:10	for women who profess to **worship G**.	*2537*
	3:15	which is the church *of* the living **G**,	*2536*
	4:3	which **G** created to be received	*2536*
	4:4	For everything **G** created is good,	*2536*
	4:5	because it is consecrated by the word *of* **G**	*2536*
	4:10	that we have put our hope in the living **G**,	*2536*
	5:4	for this is pleasing to **G**.	*2536*
	5:5	in need and left all alone puts her hope in **G**	*2536*
	5:5	to pray and *to* **ask G** for help.	*4666*
	5:21	*of* **G** and Christ Jesus and the elect angels,	*2536*
	6:11	But you, man *of* **G**, flee from all this,	*2536*
	6:13	In the sight *of* **G**, who gives life	*2536*
	6:15	which **G** will bring about in his own time—	*NIG*
	6:15	**G**, the blessed and only Ruler,	*NIG*
	6:17	but to put their hope in **G**,	*2536*
2Ti	1:1	an apostle of Christ Jesus by the will *of* **G**,	*2536*
	1:2	Grace, mercy and peace from **G** the Father	*2536*
	1:3	I thank **G**, whom I serve,	*2536*
	1:6	to fan into flame the gift *of* **G**,	*2536*
	1:7	For **G** did not give us a spirit of timidity,	*2536*
	1:8	by the power *of* **G**,	*2536*
	2:14	before **G** against quarreling about words;	*2536*
	2:15	to present yourself *to* **G** as one approved,	*2536*
	2:25	**G** will grant them repentance leading them	*2536*
	3:4	lovers of pleasure rather than **lovers of G**—	*5806*
	3:17	the man *of* **G** may be thoroughly equipped	*2536*
	4:1	In the presence of **G** and of Christ Jesus,	*2536*

Tit 1: 1 servant *of* G and an apostle of Jesus Christ 2536
1: 2 which G, who does not lie, 2536
1: 3 to me by the command *of* G our Savior, 2536
1: 4 Grace and peace from G the Father 2536
1:16 They claim to know G, 2536
2: 5 so that no one will malign the word *of* G. 2536
2:10 the teaching *about* G our Savior attractive. 2536
2:11 *of* G that brings salvation has appeared 2536
2:13 the glorious appearing *of* our great G 2536
3: 4 and love *of* G our Savior appeared, 2536
3: 8 *in* G may be careful to devote themselves 2536
Phm 1: 3 Grace to you and peace from G our Father 2536
1: 4 I always thank my G as I remember you 2536
Heb 1: 1 the past G spoke to our forefathers through 2536
1: 5 For to which of the angels did G ever say, NIG
1: 6 when G brings his firstborn into the world, NIG
1: 8 about the Son he says, "Your throne, O G, 2536
1: 9 therefore G, your God, has set you above 2536
1: 9 therefore God, your G, has set you above 2536
1:13 To which of the angels did G ever say, NIG
2: 4 G also testified to it by signs, 2536
2: 8 G left nothing that is not subject to him. NIG
2: 9 that by the grace *of* G he might taste death 2536
2:10 it was fitting **that G,** 899S
2:13 and the children G has given me." 2536
2:17 and faithful high priest in service to G, 2536
3: 4 but G is the builder of everything. 2536
3:12 that turns away from the living G. 2536
3:18 And to whom did G swear NIG
4: 3 enter that rest, just as G has said, NIG
4: 4 "And on the seventh day G rested 2536
4: 7 Therefore G again set a certain day, NIG
4: 8 G would not have spoken later NIG
4: 9 then, a Sabbath-rest for the people *of* G; 2536
4:10 just as G did from his. 2536
4:12 For the word *of* G is living and active. 2536
4:14 Jesus the Son *of* G, 2536
5: 1 to represent them in matters related to G, 2536
5: 4 he must be called by G, just as Aaron was. 2536
5: 5 But G said to him, "You are my Son; 3836S
5:10 and was designated by G to be high priest 2536
6: 1 and of faith in G, 2536
6: 3 And G permitting, we will do so. 2536
6: 5 *of* G and the powers of the coming age, 2536
6: 6 *of* G all over again and subjecting him 2536
6: 7 receives the blessing of G. 2536
6:10 G is not unjust; he will not forget 2536
6:13 When G made his promise to Abraham, 2536
6:17 Because G wanted to make 2536
6:18 G did this so that, NIG
6:18 in which it is impossible for G to lie, 2536
7: 1 king of Salem and priest *of* G Most High. 2536
7: 3 the Son *of* G he remains a priest forever. 2536
7:19 by which we draw near *to* G. 2536
7:21 a priest with an oath when G said to him: NIG
7:25 to save completely those who come to G 2536
8: 8 But G found fault with the people and said: NIG
8:10 I will be their G, and they will be my 2536
9:14 *to* G, cleanse our consciences from acts 2536
9:14 so that we may serve the living G! 2536
9:20 which G has commanded you to keep." 2536
10: 7 I have come to do your will, O G.' " 2536
10:12 he sat down at the right hand *of* G. 2536
10:21 we have a great priest over the house *of* G, 2536
10:22 to G with a sincere heart in full assurance NIG
10:27 that will consume the enemies of G. NIG
10:29 trampled the Son *of* G under foot, 2536
10:31 to fall into the hands *of* the living G. 2536
10:36 so that when you have done the will *of* G, 2536
11: 4 By faith Abel offered G a better sacrifice 2536
11: 4 when G spoke well of his offerings. 2536
11: 5 because G had taken him away. 2536
11: 5 he was commended as one who pleased G. 2536
11: 6 without faith it is impossible to please G, NIG
11:10 whose architect and builder is G. 2536
11:16 G is not ashamed to be called their God, 2536
11:16 God is not ashamed to be called their G, 2536
11:17 By faith Abraham, when G tested him, NIG
11:18 even though G had said to him, NIG
11:19 Abraham reasoned that G could raise 2536
11:25 with the people *of* G rather than to enjoy 2536
11:40 G had planned something better for us so 2536
12: 2 down at the right hand of the throne *of* G. 2536
12: 7 G is treating you as sons. 2536
12:10 but G disciplines us for our good, 3836S
12:15 the grace *of* G and that no bitter root grows 2536
12:22 heavenly Jerusalem, the city *of* the living G. 2536
12:23 You have come to G, the judge of all men, 2536
12:28 so worship G acceptably with reverence 2536
12:29 for our "G is a consuming fire." 2536
13: 4 for G will judge the adulterer and all 2536
13: 5 G has said, "Never will I leave you; 899S
13: 7 who spoke the word *of* G to you. 2536
13:15 let us continually offer *to* G a sacrifice 2536
13:16 for with such sacrifices G is pleased. 2536
13:20 May the G of peace, 2536
Jas 1: 1 servant *of* G and of the Lord Jesus Christ, 2536
1: 5 he should ask G, 2536
1:12 that G has promised to those who love him. NIG
1:13 no one should say, "G is tempting me." 2536
1:13 For G cannot be tempted by evil, 2536
1:20 about the righteous life that G desires. 2536
1:27 Religion that G our Father accepts as pure 2536
2: 5 Has not G chosen those who are poor in 2536
2:19 You believe that there is one G. 2536
2:23 "Abraham believed G, and it was credited 2536
4: 2 You do not have, because you do not ask G. NIG
Jas 4: 4 with the world is hatred *toward* G? 2536
4: 4 of the world becomes an enemy *of* G. 2536
4: 6 "G opposes the proud but gives grace to 2536
4: 7 Submit yourselves, then, *to* G. 2536
4: 8 near *to* G and he will come near to you. 2536
1Pe 1: 2 to the foreknowledge *of* G the Father, 2536
1: 3 the G and Father of our Lord Jesus Christ! 2536
1:21 Through him you believe in G, 2536
1:21 and so your faith and hope are in G. 2536
1:23 through the living and enduring word *of* G. 2536
2: 4 but chosen by G and precious to him— 2536
2: 5 offering spiritual sacrifices acceptable *to* G 2536
2: 9 a holy nation, a people belonging to G, NIG
2:10 but now you are the people *of* G; 2536
2:12 and glorify G on the day he visits us. 2536
2:16 live as servants *of* G. 2536
2:17 Love the brotherhood of believers, fear G, 2536
2:19 because he is conscious *of* G. 2536
2:20 this is commendable before G. 2536
3: 5 of the past who put their hope in G used 2536
3:18 to bring you *to* G. 2536
3:20 when G waited patiently in the days 2536
3:21 the pledge of a good conscience toward G. 2536
4: 2 but rather for the will *of* G. 2536
4: 6 live according to G in regard to the spirit. 2536
4:11 as one speaking the very words *of* G. 2536
4:11 with the strength G provides, 2536
4:11 so that in all things G may be praised 2536
4:14 the Spirit of glory and *of* G rests on you. 2536
4:16 but praise G that you bear that name. 2536
4:17 to begin with the family *of* G; 2536
4:17 not obey the gospel *of* G? 2536
5: 2 you are willing, as G wants you to be; 2536
5: 5 "G opposes the proud but gives grace to 2536
5:10 And the G of all grace, 2536
5:12 that this is the true grace *of* G. 2536
2Pe 1: 1 through the righteousness *of* our G 2536
1: 2 the knowledge *of* G and of Jesus our Lord. 2536
1:17 For he received honor and glory from G 2536
1:21 but men spoke from G as they were carried 2536
2: 4 if G did not spare angels when they sinned, 2536
3:12 to the day *of* G and speed its coming. 2536
3:15 with the wisdom that G gave him. NIG
1Jn 1: 5 G is light; in him there is no darkness at all. 2536
2:14 and the word *of* G lives in you, 2536
2:17 man who does the will *of* G lives forever. 2536
3: 1 that we should be called children *of* G! 2536
3: 2 Dear friends, now we are children *of* G, 2536
3: 8 The reason the Son *of* G appeared was 2536
3: 9 No one who is born of G will continue 2536
3: 9 because he has been born of G. 2536
3:10 the children *of* G are and who the children 2536
3:10 not do what is right is not a child of G; 2536
3:17 how can the love *of* G be in him? 2536
3:20 For G is greater than our hearts, 2536
3:21 we have confidence before G 2536
4: 1 the spirits to see whether they are from G, 2536
4: 2 how you can recognize the Spirit *of* G: 2536
4: 2 Jesus Christ has come in the flesh is from G 2536
4: 3 not acknowledge Jesus is not from G. 2536
4: 4 are from G and have overcome them, 2536
4: 6 We are from G, and whoever knows God 2536
4: 6 and whoever knows G listens to us; 2536
4: 6 whoever is not from G does not listen to us. 2536
4: 7 for love comes from G. 2536
4: 7 Everyone who loves has been born of G 2536
4: 7 has been born of God and knows G. 2536
4: 8 Whoever does not love does not know G, 2536
4: 8 because G is love. 2536
4: 9 This is how G showed his love among us: 2536
4:10 This is love: not that we loved G, 2536
4:11 Dear friends, since G so loved us, 2536
4:12 No one has ever seen G; 2536
4:12 G lives in us and his love is made complete 2536
4:15 that Jesus is the Son *of* G, 2536
4:15 G lives in him and he in God. 2536
4:15 God lives in him and he in G. 2536
4:16 we know and rely on the love G has for us. 2536
4:16 G is love. 2536
4:16 Whoever lives in love lives in G, 2536
4:16 and G in him. 2536
4:20 If anyone says, "I love G," 2536
4:20 cannot love G, whom he has not seen. 2536
4:21 Whoever loves G must also love 2536
5: 1 that Jesus is the Christ is born of G, 2536
5: 2 that we love the children *of* G: 2536
5: 2 by loving G and carrying out his 2536
5: 3 This is love *for* G: to obey his commands. 2536
5: 4 everyone born of G overcomes the world. 2536
5: 5 that Jesus is the Son *of* G. 2536
5: 9 because it is the testimony *of* G, 2536
5:10 *of* G has this testimony in his heart. 2536
5:10 not believe G has made him out to be a liar, 2536
5:10 the testimony G has given about his Son. 2536
5:11 G has given us eternal life, 2536
5:12 not have the Son *of* G does not have life. 2536
5:13 of the Son *of* G so that you may know 2536
5:14 the confidence we have in approaching G: 899S
5:16 he should pray and G will give him life. NIG
5:18 anyone born of G does not continue to sin; 2536
5:18 the one who was born of G keeps him safe, 2536
5:19 We know that we are children of G, 2536
5:20 We know also that the Son *of* G has come 2536
5:20 He is the true G and eternal life. 2536
2Jn 1: 3 from G the Father and from Jesus Christ, 2536
1: 9 in the teaching of Christ does not have G; 2536
3Jn 1: 6 on their way in a manner worthy **of G.** 2536
3Jn 1:11 Anyone who does what is good is from G. 2536
1:11 Anyone who does what is evil has not seen G. 2536
Jude 1: 1 by G the Father and kept by Jesus Christ: 2536
1: 4 *of* our G into a license for immorality 2536
1:25 *to* the only G our Savior be glory, 2536
Rev 1: 1 revelation of Jesus Christ, which G gave 2536
1: 2 that is, the word *of* G and the testimony 2536
1: 6 to be a kingdom and priests to serve his G 2536
1: 8 says the Lord G, "who is, and who was, 2536
1: 9 the word *of* G and the testimony of Jesus. 2536
2: 7 which is in the paradise *of* G. 2536
2:18 These are the words of the Son *of* G, 2536
3: 1 the seven spirits *of* G and the seven stars. 2536
3: 2 your deeds complete in the sight *of* my G. 2536
3:12 a pillar in the temple *of* my G. 2536
3:12 the name *of* my G and the name of the city 2536
3:12 and the name of the city *of* my G, 2536
3:12 down out of heaven from my G; 2536
4: 5 These are the seven spirits *of* G. 2536
4: 8 "Holy, holy, holy is the Lord G Almighty, 2536
4:11 "You are worthy, our Lord and G, 2536
5: 6 which are the seven spirits *of* G sent out 2536
5: 9 with your blood you purchased men *for* G 2536
5:10 to be a kingdom and priests to serve our G, 2536
6: 9 because of the word *of* G and 2536
7: 2 having the seal *of* the living G. 2536
7: 3 on the foreheads of the servants *of* our G." 2536
7:10 "Salvation *belongs to* our G, 2536
7:11 before the throne and worshiped G, 2536
7:12 and strength be *to* our G for ever and ever. 2536
7:15 before the throne *of* G and serve him day 2536
7:17 And G will wipe away every tear 2536
8: 2 I saw the seven angels who stand before G, 2536
8: 4 went up before G from the angel's hand. 2536
9: 4 not have the seal *of* G on their foreheads. 2536
9:13 of the golden altar that is before G. 2536
10: 7 the mystery *of* G will be accomplished, 2536
11: 1 and measure the temple *of* G and the altar, 2536
11:11 a breath of life from G entered them, 2536
11:13 and gave glory *to* the G of heaven. 2536
11:16 who were seated on their thrones before G, 2536
11:16 fell on their faces and worshiped G, 2536
11:17 "We give thanks to you, Lord G Almighty, 2536
12: 5 And her child was snatched up to G and 2536
12: 6 the desert to a place prepared for her by G, 2536
12:10 and the power and the kingdom *of* our G, 2536
12:10 who accuses them before our G day 2536
13: 6 He opened his mouth to blaspheme G, 2536
14: 4 among men and offered as firstfruits *to* G 2536
14: 7 "Fear G and give him glory, 2536
15: 2 They held harps given them by G 2536
15: 3 the servant *of* G and the song of the Lamb: 2536
15: 3 and marvelous are your deeds, Lord G Almighty. 2536
15: 7 golden bowls filled with the wrath *of* G, 2536
15: 8 from the glory *of* G and from his power, 2536
16: 7 "Yes, Lord G Almighty, 2536
16: 9 and they cursed the name *of* G, 2536
16:11 the G of heaven because of their pains 2536
16:14 the battle on the great day *of* G Almighty. 2536
16:19 G remembered Babylon the Great 2536
16:21 And they cursed G on account of 2536
17:17 For G has put it into their hearts 2536
18: 5 and G has remembered her crimes. 2536
18: 8 for mighty is the Lord G who judges her. 2536
18:20 G has judged her for the way she treated 2536
19: 1 and glory and power *belong to* our G, 2536
19: 4 fell down and worshiped G, 2536
19: 5 "Praise our G, all you his servants, 2536
19: 6 For our Lord G Almighty reigns. 2536
19: 9 he added, "These are the true words *of* G." 2536
19:10 to the testimony of Jesus. Worship G! 2536
19:13 and his name is the Word *of* G. 2536
19:15 of the fury of the wrath *of* G Almighty. 2536
19:17 gather together for the great supper *of* G, 2536
20: 4 for Jesus and because of the word *of* G. 2536
20: 6 be priests *of* G and of Christ and will reign 2536
21: 2 coming down out of heaven from G, 2536
21: 3 "Now the dwelling *of* G is with men, 2536
21: 3 and G himself will be with them and 2536
21: 3 be with them and be their G. 2536
21: 7 and I will be his G and he will be my son. 2536
21:10 coming down out of heaven from G. 2536
21:11 It shone with the glory *of* G, 2536
21:22 because the Lord G Almighty and 2536
21:23 for the glory *of* G gives it light, 2536
22: 1 from the throne *of* G and of the Lamb 2536
22: 3 The throne *of* G and of the Lamb will be in 2536
22: 5 for the Lord G will give them light. 2536
22: 6 the G of the spirits of the prophets, 2536
22: 9 keeps the words of this book. Worship G!" 2536
22:18 G will add to him the plagues described 2536
22:19 G will take away from him his share in 2536

GOD'S (207) [GOD]

Ge 6:11 Now the earth was corrupt in G sight 466
28:22 up as a pillar will be G house, 466
Ex 18:15 the people come to me to seek G will. 466
18:16 and inform them of G decrees and laws." 466
Dt 21:23 on a tree is under G curse. 466
1Sa 5:11 G hand was very heavy upon it. 466
14:45 for he did this today with G help." 466
2Sa 9: 3 of Saul to whom I can show G kindness?" 466
1Ch 5:22 because the battle was G. 466+4946
2Ch 1: 3 for G Tent of Meeting was there, 466

2Ch 4:19 the furnishings that were in G temple: 466
5: 1 in the treasuries of G temple. 466
20:15 For the battle is not yours, but G. 466+4200
24:18 G anger came upon Judah and Jerusalem. NIH
31:21 the service of G temple and in obedience to 466
32:12 Hezekiah himself remove **this g** high places 2257S
33: 7 and put it in G temple, 466
35: 8 the administrators of G temple, 466
35:22 at G command but went to fight him on 466
36:13 who had made him take an oath in G name. 466
36:16 But they mocked G messengers, 466
36:19 They set fire to G temple and broke down 466
Ne 13:25 I made them take an oath in G name 466
Job 6: 4 G terrors are marshaled against me. 468
9:34 someone to remove G rod from me, 2257S
13: 7 Will you speak wickedly on G behalf? 446
15: 8 Do you listen in on G council? 468
15:11 Are G consolations not enough for you, 446
15:30 the breath of G mouth will carry him away. 2257S
20:28 rushing waters on the day of G wrath. 2257S
29: 4 G intimate friendship blessed my house, 468
33:26 he sees G face and shouts for joy; 2257S
36: 2 that there is more to be said in G behalf. 468
37: 5 G voice thunders in marvelous ways; 446
37:14 stop and consider G wonders. 446
38:33 Can you set up [G] dominion over 2257S
40: 9 Do you have an arm like G, 446
Ps 52: 8 I trust in G unfailing love for ever and ever. 466
61: 7 be enthroned in G presence forever; 466
63:11 all who swear by G **name** will praise him, 2257S
69:30 I will praise G name in song 466
78:10 they did not keep G covenant and refused 466
78:31 G anger rose against them; 466
114: 2 Judah became G sanctuary, 2257S
Ecc 9: 1 the wise and what they do are in G hands, 466
Mt 5:34 either by heaven, for it is G throne; 2536
22:21 and to God what is G." 2536
23:22 by G throne and by the one who sits on it. 2536
Mk 3:35 Whoever does G will is my brother 2536
12:17 and to God what *is* G." 2536
Lk 3: 6 And all mankind will see G salvation.' " 2536
7:29 acknowledged that G way was right, 2536
7:30 the law rejected G purpose for themselves, 2536
8:21 and brothers are those who hear G word 2536
16:15 among men is detestable in G sight. 2536
19:44 not recognize the time of G coming NIG
20:25 and to God what *is* G." 2536
20:36 They are G children, 2536
Jn 3:18 in the name *of* G one and only Son. 2536
3:36 for G wrath remains on him." 2536
7:17 If anyone chooses to do G will, 899S
10:36 blasphemy because I said, 'I am G Son'? 2536
11: 4 it is for G glory so that God's Son may 2536
11: 4 so that G Son may be glorified through it." 2536
Ac 2:23 by G set purpose and foreknowledge, 2536
4:19 for yourselves whether it is right in G sight 2536
6: 8 Stephen, a man full of G grace and power, NIG
7:46 who enjoyed G favor and asked 2536
13:36 "For when David had served G purpose 2536
17:29 "Therefore since we are G offspring, 2536
18:21 "I will come back if it is G will." 2536
20:24 task of testifying to the gospel *of* G grace. 2536
23: 4 "You dare to insult G high priest?" 2536
26:22 But I have had G help to this very day, 2536
28:28 to know that G salvation has been sent to 2536
Ro 1:10 by G will the way may be opened for me 2536
1:20 of the world G invisible qualities— 899S
1:32 Although they know G righteous decree 2536
2: 2 Now we know that G judgment 2536
2: 3 do you think you will escape G judgment? 2536
2: 4 not realizing that G kindness leads you 2536
2: 5 against yourself for the day of G wrath, 2536
2:13 it is not those who hear the law who are
righteous **in G sight,** 2536+3836+4123
2:24 "G name is blasphemed among 2536
3: 3 of faith nullify G faithfulness? 2536
3: 5 But if our unrighteousness brings out G
righteousness more clearly, 2536
3: 7 "If my falsehood enhances G truthfulness 2536
5: 9 be saved from G wrath through him! NIG
5:10 For if, when we were G enemies, NIG
5:15 how much more did G grace and the gift 2536
5:17 much more will those who receive G
abundant provision of grace NIG
7:22 For in my inner being I delight in G law; 2536
7:25 I myself in my mind am a slave *to* G law, 2536
8: 7 It does not submit *to* G law, 2536
8:16 with our spirit that we are G children. 2536
8:27 for the saints in accordance with G will. 2536
9: 6 It is not as though G word had failed. 2536
9: 8 not the natural children who are G children, 2536
9:11 that G purpose in election might stand: 2536
9:16 man's desire or effort, but on G mercy. 2536
10: 3 they did not submit to G righteousness. 2536
11: 4 And what was G answer to him? 5977
11:29 for G gifts and his call are irrevocable. 2536
11:31 now receive mercy as a result of G mercy NIG
12: 1 I urge you, brothers, in view of G mercy, 2536
12: 2 to test and approve what G will is— 2536
12:13 Share with **G people** who are in need. 41
12:19 my friends, but leave room *for* G wrath, 3836S
13: 4 For he is G servant to do you good. 2536
13: 4 He is G servant, an agent of wrath 2536
13: 6 for the authorities are G servants, 2536
14:10 we will all stand before G judgment seat. 2536
15: 8 a servant of the Jews on behalf of G truth, 2536
15:32 that by G will I may come to you with joy 2536

1Co 2: 5 not rest on man's wisdom, but on G power. 2536
2: 7 No, we speak *of* G secret wisdom, 2536
3: 9 For we are G fellow workers; 2536
3: 9 you are G field, God's building. 2536
3: 9 you are God's field, G building. 2536
3:16 that you yourselves are G temple and 2536
3:16 and that G Spirit lives in you? 2536
3:17 If anyone destroys G temple, 2536
3:17 G temple is sacred, and you are that temple. 2536
3:19 the wisdom of this world is foolishness **in
G sight.** 2536+4123
7:19 Keeping G commands is what counts. 2536
9:21 (though I am not free from G law 2536
11:19 to show which of you have G approval. NIG
16: 1 Now about the collection for **G people:** 41
2Co 1:12 but according to G grace. 2536
4: 1 through G mercy we have this ministry, NIG
6: 1 As G fellow workers we urge you not NIG
6: 1 not to receive G grace in vain. 2536
6: 2 I tell you, now is the time of G favor, NIG
8: 5 and then to us in keeping with G will. 2536
9:12 not only supplying the needs *of* **G people** 41
13: 4 yet he lives by G power. 2536
13: 4 yet by G power we will live with him 2536
Eph 1: 7 in accordance with the riches of G grace 899S
1:14 of those who are G possession— NIG
2:10 For we are G workmanship, 899S
2:19 but fellow citizens with **G people** 41
2:19 and members of G household, 2536
3: 2 of G grace that was given to me for you, 2536
3: 5 the Spirit to G holy apostles and prophets. 899S
3: 7 *of* G grace given me through the working 2536
3: 8 I am less than the least *of* all **G people,** 41
4:12 to prepare **G people** for works of service, 41
5: 3 these are improper *for* **G holy people.** 41
5: 6 for because of such things G wrath comes 2536
Php 1: 7 all of you share in G grace with me. NIG
Col 1: 6 and understood G grace in all its truth. 2536
3:12 Therefore, as G chosen people, 2536
1Th 2:14 became imitators *of* G churches in Judea, 2536
3: 2 who is our brother and G fellow worker 2536
4: 3 It is G will that you should be sanctified: 2536
5:18 for this is G will for you in Christ Jesus. 2536
2Th 1: 4 among G churches we boast 2536
1: 5 that G judgment is right, 2536
2: 4 so that he sets himself up in G temple, 2536
3: 5 May the Lord direct your hearts into G love 2536
1Ti 1: 4 These promote controversies rather than G
work— 2536
3: 5 how can he take care of G church?) 2536
3:15 to conduct themselves in G household, 2536
6: 1 so that G name and our teaching may not 2536
2Ti 2: 9 But G word is not chained. 2536
2:19 G solid foundation stands firm, 2536
Tit 1: 1 of Jesus Christ for the faith *of* G elect and 2536
1: 7 Since an overseer is entrusted with G work, 2536
Heb 1: 3 of G glory and the exact representation NIG
1: 6 he says, "Let all G angels worship him." 2536
3: 2 just as Moses was faithful in all G house. 899S
3: 5 as a servant in all G house, 899S
3: 6 But Christ is faithful as a son over G house. 899S
4:10 for anyone who enters G rest also rests 899S
4:13 from G sight Everything is uncovered 899S
5:12 the elementary truths of G word all 2536
9:24 now to appear for us in G presence. 2536
11: 3 the universe was formed at G command, 2536
13:24 Greet all your leaders and all **G people.** 41
Jas 2:23 and he was called G friend. 2536
3: 9 who have been made in G likeness. 2536
1Pe 1: 1 an apostle of Jesus Christ, To G elect, NIG
1: 5 through faith are shielded by G power until 2536
2:15 For it is G will that by doing good 2536
3: 4 which is of great worth in G sight. 2536
3:17 It is better, if it is G will, to suffer for 2536
3:22 into heaven and is at G right hand— 2536
4:10 faithfully administering G grace 2536
4:19 to G will should commit themselves 2536
5: 2 of G flock that is under your care, serving 2536
5: 6 therefore, under G mighty hand, 2536
2Pe 3: 5 by G word the heavens existed and 2536
1Jn 2: 5 G love is truly made complete in him. 2536
3: 9 because G seed remains in him; 899S
5: 9 but G testimony is greater because it is 2536
Jude 1:21 Keep yourselves in G love as you wait for 2536
Rev 3:14 faithful witness, the ruler *of* G creation. 2536
11:19 Then G temple in heaven was opened, 2536
12:17 those who obey G commandments 2536
14:10 too, will drink of the wine *of* G fury, 2536
14:12 of the saints who obey G commandments 2536
14:19 into the great winepress of G wrath. 2536
15: 1 because with them G wrath is completed. 2536
16: 1 the seven bowls *of* G wrath on the earth." 2536
17:17 until G words are fulfilled. 2536
20: 9 and surrounded the camp *of* **G people,** 41
22:21 The grace of the Lord Jesus be with **G
people.** 41

GOD-BREATHED (1) [GOD, BREATH]

2Ti 3:16 All Scripture is G and is useful 2535

GOD-FEARING (8) [GOD, FEAR]

Ecc 8:12 I know that it will go better with G *men,* 466+2021+3710
Ac 2: 5 in Jerusalem G Jews from every nation 2327
10: 2 his family were devout and G; 2536+3836+5828
10:22 He is a righteous and G man, 2536+3836+5828
13:26 "Brothers, children of Abraham, and *you* **G
Gentiles,** 2536+3836+5828
13:50 the G women of high standing and 4936
17: 4 as did a large number *of* G Greeks and not 4936
17:17 *with* the Jews and the **G Greeks,** 4936

GOD-HATERS (1) [GOD, HATE]

Ro 1:30 G, insolent, arrogant and boastful; 2539

GOD-WARD (KJV) See BEFORE GOD, IN GOD

GODDESS (6) [GOD]

1Ki 11: 5 followed Ashtoreth the g *of* the Sidonians, 466
11:33 worshiped Ashtoreth the g *of* the Sidonians, 466
2Ki 23:13 of Israel had built for Ashtoreth the **vile g** 9199
Ac 19:27 that the temple *of* the great g Artemis will 2516
19:27 and the g herself, who is worshiped NIG
19:37 nor blasphemed our g. 2536

GODHEAD (KJV) See DEITY, DIVINE BEING, DIVINE NATURE

GODLESS (16) [GOD]

Job 8:13 so perishes the hope of the g. 2868
13:16 for no g *man* would dare come before him! 2868
15:34 For the company of the g will be barren, 2868
20: 5 the joy of the g lasts but a moment. 2868
27: 8 For what hope has the g when he is cut off, 2868
34:30 to keep a g man from ruling, 2868
36:13 "The g *in* heart harbor resentment; 2868
Pr 11: 9 With his mouth the g destroys his neighbor, 2868
Isa 10: 6 I send him against a g nation, 2868
33:14 trembling grips the g: 2868
Jer 23:11 "Both prophet and priest *are* g; 2866
1Ti 4: 7 to do with g myths and old wives' tales; 1013
6:20 from g chatter and the opposing ideas 1013
2Ti 2:16 Avoid g chatter, because those who indulge 1013
Heb 12:16 or *is* g like Esau, who for a single meal 1013
Jude 1: 4 They are g *men,* who change the grace of 815

GODLESSNESS (2) [GOD]

Ro 1:18 the g and wickedness of men who suppress 813
11:26 he will turn g away from Jacob. 813

GODLINESS (12) [GOD]

Ac 3:12 or g we had made this man walk? 2354
1Ti 2: 2 and quiet lives in all g and holiness. 2354
3:16 the mystery of g is great: 2354
4: 8 but g has value for all things, 2354
6: 5 of the truth and who think that g is a means 2354
6: 6 But g with contentment is great gain. 2354
6:11 g, faith, love, endurance and gentleness. 2354
2Ti 3: 5 having a form *of* g but denying its power. 2354
Tit 1: 1 the knowledge of the truth that leads to g— 2354
2Pe 1: 3 for life and g through our knowledge 2354
1: 6 and to perseverance, g; 2354
1: 7 and to g, brotherly kindness; 2354

GODLY (16) [GOD]

Ps 4: 3 the LORD has set apart the g for himself; 2883
12: 1 Help, LORD, for the g are no more; 2883
32: 6 Therefore let everyone *who* is g pray to you 2883
Mic 7: 2 The g have been swept from the land; 2883
Mal 2:15 Because he was seeking g offspring. 466
Jn 9:31 He listens to the **g man** who does his will. 2538
Ac 8: 2 G men buried Stephen and mourned deeply 2327
2Co 7:10 G sorrow brings repentance that leads 2536+2848
7:11 See what this g sorrow has produced 2536+2848
11: 2 I am jealous for you with a g jealousy. 2536
1Ti 4: 7 rather, train yourself to be g. 2354
6: 3 of our Lord Jesus Christ and to g teaching, 2354
2Ti 3:12 a **g life** in Christ Jesus will be persecuted, 2357
Tit 2:12 upright and g *lives* in this present age, 2357
2Pe 2: 9 how to rescue g *men* from trials and to hold 2356
3:11 You ought to live holy and g *lives* 2354

GODS (271) [GOD]

Ge 31:19 Rachel stole her father's **household g.** 9572
31:30 But why did you steal my **g?"** 466
31:32 But if you find anyone who has your **g,** 466
31:32 not know that Rachel had stolen **the g.** 4392S
31:34 Now Rachel had taken the **household g** 9572
31:35 but could not find the **household g.** 9572
35: 2 of the foreign g you have with you, 466
35: 4 the foreign g they had and the rings 466
Ex 12:12 I will bring judgment on all the g *of* Egypt. 466
15:11 "Who among the g is like you, O LORD? 446
18:11 that the LORD is greater than all other g, 466
20: 3 "You shall have no other g before me. 466
20:23 Do not make any g to be alongside me; NIH
20:23 not make for yourselves g *of* silver or gods 466
20:23 not make for yourselves gods of silver or g 466
23:13 Do not invoke the names of other g; 466
23:24 down before their g or worship them 466
23:32 a covenant with them or with their g. 466
23:33 of their g will certainly be a snare to you." 466
32: 1 "Come, make us g who will go before us. 466
32: 4 Then they said, "These are your g, O Israel, 466

Ex 32: 8 'These are your g, O Israel, 466
32:23 'Make us g who will go before us. 466
32:31 They have made themselves g *of* gold. 466
34:15 when they prostitute themselves to their g 466
34:16 to their g, they will lead your sons to do 466
Lev 19: 4 not turn to idols or make g *of* cast metal 466
Nu 25: 2 to the sacrifices to their g. 466
25: 2 and bowed down before these g. 466
33: 4 LORD had brought judgment on their g. 466
Dt 4: 7 as to have their g near them the way 466
4:28 There you will worship man-made g 466
5: 7 "You shall have no other g before me. 466
6:14 Do not follow other g, 466
6:14 the g *of* the peoples around you; 466
7: 4 from following me to serve other g, 466
7:16 on them with pity and do not serve their g, 466
7:25 images of their g you are to burn in the fire. 466
8:19 the LORD your God and follow other g 466
10:17 the LORD your God is God of g and Lord 466
11:16 to turn away and worship other g and bow 466
11:28 by following other g, 466
12: 2 you are dispossessing worship their g. 466
12: 3 of their g and wipe out their names 466
12:30 to be ensnared by inquiring about their g, 466
12:30 "How do these nations serve their g? 466
12:31 because in worshiping their g, 466
12:31 in the fire as sacrifices to their g. 466
13: 2 "Let us follow other g" (gods you have 466
13: 2 "Let us follow other gods" (g you have 4392S
13: 6 and worship other g" (gods that neither you 466
13: 6 and worship other gods" (g that neither you NIH
13: 7 g *of* the peoples around you, 466
13:13 and worship other g" (gods you have 466
13:13 and worship other gods" (g you have 889S
17: 3 to my command has worshiped other g, 466
18:20 prophet who speaks in the name of other g, 466
20:18 in worshiping their g, 466
28:14 following other g and serving them. 466
28:36 There you will worship other g, 466
28:36 g of wood and stone. NIH
28:64 There you will worship other g— 466
28:64 g of wood and stone, NIH
29:18 to go and worship the g *of* those nations; 466
29:26 and worshiped other g and bowed down 466
29:26 g they did not know, 466
29:26 g he had not given them. NIH
30:17 to bow down to other g and worship them, 466
31:16 the foreign g *of* the land they are entering. 466
31:18 in turning to other g. 466
31:20 they will turn to other g and worship them, 466
32:16 They made him jealous with their foreign g NIH
32:17 g they had not known, 466
32:17 g that recently appeared, NIH
32:17 g your fathers did not fear. 4392S
32:37 He will say: "Now where are their g, 466
32:38 the g who ate the fat of their sacrifices NIH
Jos 23: 7 do not invoke the names of their g or swear 466
23:16 and serve other g and bow down to them, 466
24: 2 beyond the River and worshiped other g. 466
24:14 the g your forefathers worshiped beyond 466
24:15 whether the g your forefathers served 466
24:15 or the g *of* the Amorites, 466
24:16 to forsake the LORD to serve other g! 466
24:20 the LORD and serve foreign g, 466
24:23 "throw away the foreign g that are 466
Jdg 2: 3 be [thorns] in your sides and their g will be 466
2:12 They followed and worshiped various g of 466
2:17 but prostituted themselves to other g 466
2:19 following other g and serving 466
3: 6 and served their g. 466
5: 8 When they chose new g, 466
6:10 do not worship the g *of* the Amorites, 466
9: 9 by which both g and men are honored, 466
9:13 which cheers both g and men, 466
10: 6 and the g *of* Aram, the gods of Sidon, 466
10: 6 and the gods of Aram, the g *of* Sidon, 466
10: 6 the gods of Sidon, the g *of* Moab, 466
10: 6 the g *of* the Ammonites and the gods of 466
10: 6 the Ammonites and the g *of* the Philistines. 466
10:13 you have forsaken me and served other g, 466
10:14 Go and cry out to the g you have chosen. 466
10:16 of the foreign g among them and served 466
18:14 other **household** g, a carved image and 9572
18:17 the other **household** g and the cast idol 9572
18:18 the other **household** g and the cast idol, 9572
18:20 the other **household** g and the carved image 9572
18:24 He replied, "You took the g I made, 466
Ru 1:15 to her people and her g. 466
1Sa 4: 8 from the hand of these mighty g? 466
4: 8 They are the g who struck the Egyptians 466
6: 5 from you and your g and your land. 466
7: 3 then rid yourselves of the foreign g and 466
8: 8 forsaking me and serving other g, 466
17:43 And the Philistine cursed David by his g. 466
26:19 and have said, 'Go, serve other g.' 466
2Sa 7:23 by driving out nations and their g from 466
1Ki 9: 6 to serve other g and worship them, 466
9: 9 and have embraced other g, 466
11: 2 surely turn your hearts after their g." 466
11: 4 his wives turned his heart after other g, 466
11: 8 and offered sacrifices to their g. 466
11:10 to follow other g, 466
12:28 Here are your g, O Israel, 466
14: 9 You have made for yourself other g, 466
19: 2 "May the g deal with me, 466
20:10 "May the g deal with me, 466
20:23 "Their g are gods of the hills. 466
1Ki 20:23 "Their gods are g *of* the hills. 466
2Ki 17: 7 They worshiped other g 466
17:29 each national group made its own g in 466
17:31 and Anammelech, the g *of* Sepharvaim. 466
17:33 also served their own g in accordance with 466
17:35 "Do not worship any other g or bow down 466
17:37 Do not worship other g. 466
17:38 and do not worship other g. 466
18:34 Where are the g *of* Hamath and Arpad? 466
18:34 are the g *of* Sepharvaim, Hena and Ivvah? 466
18:35 of all the g *of* these countries has been able 466
19:12 the g *of* the nations that were destroyed 466
19:12 the g of Gozan, Haran, NIH
19:18 They have thrown their g into the fire 466
19:18 they were not g but only wood and stone, 466
22:17 to other g and provoked me to anger by all 466
23:24 the mediums and spiritists, the **household** g, 9572
1Ch 5:25 and prostituted themselves to the g *of* 466
10:10 They put his armor in the temple of their g 466
14:12 The Philistines had abandoned their g there, 466
16:25 he is to be feared above all g. 466
16:26 For all the g *of* the nations are idols, 466
2Ch 2: 5 because our God is greater than all other g. 466
7:19 to serve other g and worship them, 466
7:22 and have embraced other g, 466
13: 8 that Jeroboam made to be your g. 466
13: 9 a priest of what are not g. 466
25:14 he brought back the g *of* the people of Seir. 466
25:14 He set them up as his own g, 466
25:15 "Why do you consult this people's g, 466
25:20 because they sought the g *of* Edom. 466
28:23 He offered sacrifices to the g *of* Damascus, 466
28:23 g *of* the kings of Aram have helped them, 466
28:25 to burn sacrifices to other g and provoked 466
32:13 Were the g *of* those nations ever able 466
32:14 Who of all the g *of* these nations 466
32:17 the g *of* the peoples of the other lands did 466
32:19 as they did about the g *of* the other peoples 466
33:15 the foreign g and removed the image from 466
34:25 to other g and provoked me to anger by all 466
Ps 4: 2 and seek **false** g? 3942
16: 4 of those will increase who run after **other** g. 337
40: 4 to those who turn aside to **false** g. 3942
82: 1 he gives judgment among the "g": 466
82: 6 "I said, 'You are "g"; 466
86: 8 Among the g there is none like you, 466
95: 3 the great King above all g. 466
96: 4 he is to be feared above all g. 466
96: 5 For all the g *of* the nations are idols, 466
97: 7 worship him, all you g! 466
97: 9 you are exalted far above all g. 466
106:28 and ate sacrifices offered to lifeless g; NIH
135: 5 that our Lord is greater than all g. 466
136: 2 Give thanks to the God of g. 466
138: 1 before the "g" I will sing your praise. 466
Isa 21: 9 All the images of its g lie shattered on 466
36:19 Where are the g *of* Hamath and Arpad? 466
36:19 Where are the g *of* Sepharvaim? 466
36:20 of all the g *of* these countries has been able 466
37:12 the g *of* the nations that were destroyed 466
37:12 the g of Gozan, Haran, NIH
37:19 They have thrown their g into the fire 466
37:19 they were not g but only wood and stone, 466
41:23 so we may know that you are g. 466
42:17 who say to images, 'You are our g,' 466
45:20 who pray to g that cannot save. 446
Jer 1:16 in burning incense to other g and 466
2:11 Has a nation ever changed its g? 466
2:11 (Yet they are not g at all.) 466
2:25 I love foreign g, and I must go after them.' NIH
2:28 then are the g you made for yourselves? 466
2:28 For you have as many g as you have towns, 466
3:13 you have scattered your favors to foreign g NIH
3:24 From our youth **shameful** g have consumed 1425
5: 7 and sworn by g that are not gods. NIH
5: 7 and sworn by gods that are not g. 466
5:19 and served foreign g in your own land, 466
7: 6 not follow other g to your own harm, 466
7: 9 and follow other g you have not known, 466
7:18 They pour out drink offerings to other g 466
10:11 "Tell them this: 'These g, who did not 10033
11:10 They have followed other g to serve them. 466
11:12 of Jerusalem will go and cry out to the g 466
11:13 You have as many g as you have towns, 466
13:10 of their hearts and go after other g to serve 466
13:25 and trusted in **false** g. 9214
16:11 'and followed other g and served 466
16:13 there you will serve other g day and night, 466
16:19 but **false** g, worthless idols 9214
16:20 Do men make their own g? 466
16:20 Yes, but they are not g!" 466
19: 4 and made this a place of foreign g; NIH
19: 4 in it to g that neither they nor their fathers 466
19:13 and poured out drink offerings to other g.' " 466
22: 9 and have worshiped and served other g.' " 466
25: 6 Do not follow other g to serve 466
32:29 by pouring out drink offerings to other g. 466
35:15 do not follow other g to serve them. 466
43:12 He will set fire to the temples of the g 466
43:12 and take **their** g captive. 4392S
43:13 and will burn down the temples of the g 466
44: 3 and by worshiping other g that neither they 466
44: 5 or stop burning incense to other g. 466
44: 8 burning incense to other g in Egypt, 466
44:15 to other g, along with all 466
46:25 on Egypt and her g and her kings, 466
48:35 the high places and burn incense to their g," 466
Da 2:11 can reveal it to the king except the g, 10033
2:47 of g and the Lord of kings and a revealer 10033
3:12 They neither serve your g nor worship 10033
3:14 that you do not serve my g or worship 10033
3:18 that we will not serve your g or worship 10033
3:25 and the fourth looks like a son of the g." 10033
4: 8 and the spirit of the holy g is in him.) 10033
4: 9 I know that the spirit of the holy g is 10033
4:18 because the spirit of the holy g is in you." 10033
5: 4 they praised the g *of* gold and silver, 10033
5:11 the spirit of the holy g in him. 10033
5:11 and wisdom like that of the g. 10033
5:14 I have heard that the spirit of the g is in you 10033
5:23 You praised the g *of* silver and gold, 10033
11: 8 He will also seize their g, 466
11:36 against the God of g. 446
11:37 the g *of* his fathers or for the one desired 466
Hos 3: 1 to other g and love the sacred raisin cakes." 466
14: 3 We will never again say 'Our g' 466
Am 2: 4 they have been led astray by **false** g, 3942
2: 4 **the** g their ancestors followed, 889S
Mic 4: 5 in the name of their g; 466
Na 1:14 that are in the temple of your g. 466
Zep 1: 9 who fill the temple of their g with violence 123
2:11 when he destroys all the g *of* the land. 466
Jn 10:34 'I have said you are g'? *2536*
10:35 If he called them 'g,' *2536*
Ac 7:40 'Make us g who will go before us. *2536*
14:11 "The g have come down to us *2536*
17:18 "He seems to be advocating foreign g." *1228*
19:26 He says that man-made g are no gods at all. *3836S*
19:26 He says that man-made gods are no g at all. *2536*
28:11 the **twin** g **Castor and Pollux.** *1483*
1Co 8: 5 For even if there are so-called g, *2536*
8: 5 or on earth (as indeed there are many "g" *2536*
Gal 4: 8 to those who by nature are not g. *2536*

GOES (96) [GO]

Ge 40:14 But when *all* g **well** with you, 3512
Ex 7:15 Go to Pharaoh in the morning *as he* g **out** 3655
8:20 the morning and confront Pharaoh *as he* g 3655
12:23 the LORD g **through** the land to strike 6296
Lev 14:36 to be emptied before he g **in** to examine 995
14:46 "Anyone *who* g into the house 995
16:17 the time Aaron g **in** to make atonement in 995
22: 7 When the sun g **down**, he will be clean, 995
Nu 1:51 Anyone else who g **near** it shall be put 7929
5:12 'If a man's wife g **astray** and is unfaithful 8474
5:29 the law of jealousy when a woman g **astray** 8474
35:26 if the accused **ever** g **outside** the limits of
the city of refuge 3655+3655
Dt 9: 3 the *one who* g **across** ahead of you like 6296
16: 6 when the sun g **down,** 995
20: 4 For the LORD your God *is the one who* g 2143
31: 6 for the LORD your God g with you; 2143
31: 8 The LORD himself g before you and will 2143
Jos 2:19 If anyone g outside your house into 3655
Jdg 21:19 of the road that g from Bethel to Shechem, 6590
1Sa 6: 9 If *it* g **up** to its own territory, 6590
9:13 before he g **up** to the high place to eat. 6590
23:22 Find out where David *usually* g 2118+8079
24:13 As the old saying g, 606
25:25 his name is Fool, and folly g with him. NIH
2Ki 11: 8 Stay close to the king **wherever** he g."
928+928+995+2256+3655
2Ch 23: 7 Stay close to the king **wherever** he g."
928+928+995+2256+3655
Ne 9:37 its abundant harvest g to the kings NIH
Job 7: 9 *he who* g **down** *to* the grave does not return. 3718
9:11 when *he* g **by**, I cannot perceive him. 2736
18: 6 the lamp beside him g **out.** 1980
21:33 and a countless throng g before him. NIH
22:14 as *he* g **about** *in* the vaulted heavens.' 2143
24:18 so that no *one* g to the vineyards. 7155
41:22 dismay g before him. 1881
Ps 19: 4 Their voice g **out** into all the earth, 3655
39: 6 Man is a mere phantom *as he* g **to and fro:** 2143
41: 6 then *he* g **out** and spreads it abroad. 3655
85:13 Righteousness g before him and prepares 2143
97: 3 Fire g before him and consumes his foes 2143
104:23 Then man g **out** to his work, 3655
126: 6 *He who* g **out** weeping, 2143+2143
Pr 6:12 *who* g **about** with a corrupt mouth, 2143
11:19 but he who pursues evil g to his death. NIH
13:25 but the stomach of the wicked g **hungry.** 2893
16:18 Pride g before destruction, NIH
19:15 and the shiftless man g **hungry.** 8279
20:14 **off** *he* g and boasts about his purchase. 261
22:10 Drive out the mocker, and **out** g strife; 3655
23:31 when *it* g **down** smoothly! 2143
26:20 Without wood a fire g **out;** 3882
29: 9 If a wise man g **to court** with a fool, 9149
Ecc 1: 6 round and round *it* g, 2143
3:21 and if the spirit of the animal g **down** into
the earth?" 3718+4200+4752
8:17 No one can comprehend what g **on** under 6913
12: 5 Then man g to his eternal home 2143
Isa 15: 2 Dibon g **up** *to* its temple, 6590
16:12 *she* g to her shrine to pray, it is to no avail. 995
47:15 Each of them g **on** in his error; 6298
55:11 so is my word that g **out** from my mouth: 3655
66: 7 "Before *she* g **into labor,** she gives birth; 2655
Jer 6:29 but *the* **refining** g **on** in vain; 7671+7671
14: 2 and a cry g **up** from Jerusalem. 6590
21: 9 But whoever g **out** and surrenders to 3655
38: 2 or plague, but whoever g **over** to 3655

Eze 14: 4 before his face and then **g** to a prophet, 995
14: 7 and then **g** to a prophet to inquire of me, 995
44:27 On the day he **g** into the inner court of 995
47: 8 toward the eastern region and **g down** into 3718
Mic 5: 8 which mauls and mangles as *it* **g,** 6296
Mt 8: 9 I tell this one, 'Go,' and *he* **g;** *4513*
12:43 *it* **g through** arid places seeking rest *1451*
12:45 Then *it* **g** and takes with it *4513*
15:11 What **g into** a man's mouth does *1656*
15:17 the mouth **g** into the stomach and then out *6003*
Mk 9:43 where the fire **never g out.** *812*
Lk 7: 8 I tell this one, 'Go,' and *he* **g;** *4513*
11: 5 and *he* **g** to him at midnight and says, *4513*
11:24 *it* **g through** arid places seeking rest *1451*
11:26 Then *it* **g** and takes seven other spirits more *4513*
15: 6 and **g** home. Then he calls his friends *2262*
16:30 'but if someone from the dead **g** to them, *4513*
19:37 near the **place where the road g down** *2853*
Jn 5: 7 someone else **g down** ahead of me." *2849*
10: 4 *he* **g** on ahead of them, *4513*
15:26 Spirit of truth who **g out** from the Father, *1744*
Ac 8:26 that **g down** from Jerusalem to Gaza." *2849*
1Co 6: 6 one brother **g to law** against another— *3212*
9:25 in the games **g into** strict **training.** *1603*
11:21 each of you **g ahead** without waiting *4624*
Col 2:18 **g into great detail about** what he has *1836*
Jas 1:11 even while he **g about his business.** *4512*
1:24 and, after looking at himself, **g away** *599*
2Pe 2:22 that is washed **g** back to her wallowing in *NIG*
3: 4 everything **g on** as it has since *1373*
Rev 14: 4 They follow the Lamb wherever *he* **g.** *5632*
19: 3 The smoke from her **g up** for ever *326*

GOG (12)

1Ch 5: 4 Shemaiah his son, **G** his son, 1573
Eze 38: 2 set your face against **G,** 1573
38: 3 I am against you, O **G,** 1573
38:14 son of man, prophesy and say to **G:** 1573
38:16 In days to come, O **G,** 1573
38:18 When **G** attacks the land of Israel, 1573
38:21 a sword against **G** on all my mountains, 2257[S]
39: 1 "Son of man, prophesy against **G** and say: 1573
39: 1 I am against you, O **G,** 1573
39:11 " 'On that day I will give **G** a burial place 1573
39:11 **G** and all his hordes will be buried there. 1573
Rev 20: 8 **G** and Magog—to gather them for battle. *1223*

GOIIM (2)

Ge 14: 1 of Elam and Tidal king of **G** 1582
14: 9 Tidal king of **G,** Amraphel king of Shinar 1582

GOING (309) [GO]

Ge 6:13 "I *am g to* **put** an end to all people, AIT
6:13 surely *g to* **destroy** both them and the earth. AIT
6:17 I *am g to* **bring** floodwaters on the earth AIT
7:16 The *animals* **g in** were male and female 995
16: 8 and where *are you* **g?"** 2143
19:13 because we *are g to* **destroy** this place. AIT
32:17 and where *are you* **g,** 2143
37:13 Come, *I am g to* **send** you to them." AIT
48: 4 *g to* **make** you **fruitful** AIT
Ex 10: 8 "But just who *will be* **g?"** 2143
19: 9 "I *am g to* **come** to you in a dense cloud, AIT
34:12 in the land where you *are* **g,** 995
Lev 18:24 how the nations that I *am g to* **drive out** AIT
20:23 the nations I *am g to* **drive out** before you. AIT
23:10 the land I *am g to* **give** you AIT
25: 2 you enter the land I *am g to* **give** you, AIT
Nu 10:30 *I am* **g back** to my own land 2143
11:15 If this is how you *are g to* **treat** me, AIT
15:39 not prostitute yourselves by **g** after the lusts 9365
16:34 "The earth *is g to* **swallow** us too!" AIT
17:13 Are we all *g to* **die?"** AIT
22: 4 "This horde is **g to** lick up everything 6964
24:14 Now I *am* **g back** to my people, but come, 2143
32: 7 the Israelites from **g** over into the land 6296
Dt 1:30 LORD your God, who *is* **g** before you, 2143
3:21 **over** there where you *are* **g.** 6296
3:27 since *you are* not *g to* **cross** this Jordan. AIT
9: 4 *g to* **drive** them **out** AIT
9: 5 that you *are* **g in** to take possession 995
20: 3 "Hear, O Israel, today you are **g** into battle 7929
29:19 even though *I* persist in **g** my own way." 2143
31:16 "You *are g to* **rest** with your fathers, AIT
33:18 "Rejoice, Zebulun, in your **g out,** and you, 3655
Jos 6: 7 with the armed guard **g** ahead of the ark of 6296
8:21 and that smoke *was* **g up** *from* the city, 6590
10:10 the road **g up** *to* Beth Horon and cut them 5090
10:13 in the middle of the sky and delayed **g down** 995
10:25 to all the enemies you *are g to* **fight."** AIT
19:11 **G** west it ran to Maralah, 4200
22:33 about **g** to war against them to devastate 6590
Jdg 4: 9 because of the way you *are* **g about** this, 2143
6:23 *You are* not *g to* **die."** AIT
6:31 *g to* **plead** Baal's **cause?** AIT
7: 9 because *I am g to* **give** it into your hands. AIT
11: 2 not *g to* **get** *any* **inheritance** AIT
12: 1 *We're g to* **burn down** your house AIT
13: 3 but *you are g to* **conceive** and have a son. AIT
15: 1 He said, *"I'm* **g** to my wife's room." 995
18: 9 **Aren't** you *g to* **do something?** AIT
19:17 the old man asked, "Where *are you* **g?** 2143
19:18 and now I *am* **g** *to* the house of the LORD. 2143
20:40 and saw the smoke of the whole city **g up** 6590
Ru 1:11 Am I **g** to have any more sons, NIH
Ru 1:15 "your sister-in-law *is* **g back** to her people 8740
1Sa 9:11 As they *were* **g up** the hill to the town, 6590
9:27 they *were* **g down** to the edge of the town, 3718
10: 3 Three men **g up** to God at Bethel 6590
12: 7 *g to* **confront** you **with evidence** AIT
17:20 He reached the camp as the army *was* **g out** 3655
17:55 As Saul watched David **g out** to meet 3655
20: 2 *"You are* not *g to* **die!** AIT
23: 4 for I *am g to* **give** the Philistines AIT
23:26 Saul *was* **g** along one side of the mountain, 2143
26:14 "Aren't *you g to* **answer** me, Abner?" AIT
2Sa 11: 7 **how** the war **was g.** 4200+8934
12:11 'Out of your own household I *am g to* **bring** calamity AIT
12:13 *You are* not *g to* **die.** AIT
14:18 the answer to what I *am g to* **ask** you." AIT
15:20 I **do not know where I am g?** 889+2143+2143+6584
16:13 along the road while Shimei *was* **g** along 2143
18: 9 while the mule he was riding **kept on g.** 6296
18:14 *"I'm* not *g to* **wait** like this for you." AIT
1Ki 11:29 that time Jeroboam *was* **g out** of Jerusalem, 3655
11:31 'See, I *am g to* **tear** the kingdom out AIT
14:10 I *am g to* **bring** disaster on the house AIT
17:11 As *she* was **g** to get it, he called, 2143
18: 6 Ahab **g** in one direction and Obadiah 2143
20: 6 tomorrow *I am g to* **send** my officials AIT
21:21 'I *am g to* **bring** disaster on you. AIT
21:26 He behaved in the vilest manner by **g** 2143
22:20 and **g** to *his* **death** there?' 5877
2Ki 1: 3 that you *are* **g off** to consult Baal-Zebub, 2143
2: 3 that the LORD *is g to* **take** your master AIT
2: 5 that the LORD *is g to* **take** your master AIT
6: 9 because the Arameans are **g down** there." 5741
10:19 I am **g** to hold a great sacrifice for Baal. NIH
11: 5 the three companies *that are* **g on duty** *on* 995
11: 9 *those who were* **g on duty** *on* the Sabbath 995
11: 9 the Sabbath and *those who were* **g off duty** 3655
19: 7 I *am g to* **put** such a spirit in him that AIT
20: 1 because you *are g to* **die;** AIT
21:12 I *am g to* **bring** such disaster on Jerusalem AIT
22:16 I *am g to* **bring** disaster on this place AIT
22:20 the disaster I *am g to* **bring** on this place.' " AIT
2Ch 2: 5 "The temple I *am g to* **build** will be great, AIT
18:19 and **g** to *his* **death** there?' 5877
23: 4 you priests and Levites *who are* **g on duty** 995
23: 8 *those who were* **g on duty** *on* the Sabbath 995
23: 8 the Sabbath and *those who were* **g off duty** 3655
34:24 I *am g to* **bring** disaster on this place AIT
34:28 the disaster I *am g to* **bring** on this place AIT
Ne 3:15 as the steps **g down** from the City of David. 3718
13: 6 But while all this was **g** on, NIH
Job 1: 7 through the earth and **g back and forth** 2143
2: 2 through the earth and **g back and forth** 2143
33:24 'Spare him from **g down** *to* the pit; 3718
33:28 He redeemed my soul from **g down** to 6296
Ps 30: 3 you spared me from **g down** *into* the pit. 3718
30: 9 in my **g down** into the pit? 3718
121: 8 over your coming and **g** both now 3655
139: 3 You discern my **g out** and my lying down; 782
144:14 no **g into captivity,** 3448
Pr 7: 8 *He was* **g down** the street near her corner, 6296
7:22 All at once he followed her like an ox **g** to 995
15:24 for the wise to keep him from **g down to** 4752
22: 3 but the simple *keep* **g** and suffer for it. 6296
27:12 but the simple *keep* **g** and suffer for it. 6296
Ecc 9:10 for in the grave, where you *are* **g,** 2143
Isa 5: 5 Now I will tell you what *I am g to* **do** AIT
20: 2 he did so, **g around** stripped and barefoot. 2143
24: 1 the LORD *is g to* **lay waste** the earth AIT
37: 7 I *am g to* **put** a spirit in him so that AIT
38: 1 because you *are g to* **die;** AIT
41:22 to tell us what *is g to* **happen.** AIT
58:13 and if you honor it by not **g** your own way 6913
Jer 6:28 hardened rebels, **g about** to slander. 2143
13:13 I *am g to* **fill** with drunkenness all who AIT
19: 3 I *am g to* **bring** a disaster on this place AIT
19:15 I *am g to* **bring** on this city and the villages AIT
28:16 This very year you *are g to* **die,** AIT
32: 7 of Shallum your uncle *is g to* **come** to you AIT
34:22 *g to* **give the order,** AIT
35:17 I *am g to* **bring** on Judah and AIT
38:14 "I *am g to* **ask** you something," AIT
44:30 'I *am g to* **hand** Pharaoh Hophra king of Egypt **over** AIT
Eze 9: 8 *Are* you *g to* **destroy** the entire remnant AIT
11: 5 but I know **what is g through** your mind. 5091
12:23 I *am g to* **put an end** *to* this proverb AIT
13:11 with whitewash that *it is g to* **fall.** AIT
16:37 therefore I *am g to* **gather** all your lovers, AIT
21: 4 Because *I am g to* **cut off** the righteous AIT
25: 4 therefore I *am g to* **give** you to the people of AIT
26: 7 From the north I *am g to* **bring** AIT
28: 7 I *am g to* **bring** foreigners against you, AIT
29:19 I *am g to* **give** Egypt to Nebuchadnezzar AIT
36:22 that I *am g to* **do** these things, AIT
37:12 I *am g to* **open** your graves and bring you up from them; AIT
37:19 I *am g to* **take** the stick of Joseph— AIT
40: 4 to everything I *am g to* **show** you, AIT
44:25 not defile himself by **g** near a dead person; 995
46:10 **g in** when they go in and going out 995
46:10 going in when they go in and **g out** 3655
Da 2:29 revealer of mysteries showed you what *is g to* **happen.** AIT
8:19 "I *am g to* **tell** you what will happen later AIT
Hos 2:14 "Therefore I *am* now *g to* **allure** her; AIT
Joel 2:20 with its front columns **g** into the eastern sea NIH
3: 7 I *am g to* **rouse** them out of the places AIT
Hab 1: 5 For *I am g to* **do** something in your days AIT
Zec 2: 2 I asked, "Where *are* you **g?"** 2143
3: 8 I *am g to* **bring** my servant, the Branch. AIT
5: 3 the curse that *is* **g out** over the whole land; 3655
6: 5 **g out** from standing in the presence of 3655
6: 6 The one with the black horses *is* **g** toward 3655
6: 8 Then he called to me, "Look, those **g** 3655
8:21 *I* myself *am* **g.'** 2143
11:16 For I *am g to* **raise up** a shepherd over AIT
12: 2 "I *am g to* **make** Jerusalem a cup AIT
12: 8 the Angel of the LORD **g** before them. NIH
Mal 3:14 and **g about** like mourners before 2143
Mt 2:13 for Herod *is* **g** to search for the child *3516*
4:21 **G on** from there, he saw two other brothers, *4581*
8:25 *We're* **g** *to* **drown!"** *AIT*
9:32 *While* they *were* **g out,** *2002*
10:23 you will not finish **g** through the cities *NIG*
12: 9 **G on** from that place, *3553*
16:27 of Man *is* **g to** come in his Father's glory *3516*
17:12 In the same way the Son of Man *is* **g to** *3516*
17:22 of Man *is* **g to** be betrayed into the hands *3516*
20: 8 the last ones hired and **g on to** the first.' *2401*
20:17 Now *as* Jesus *was* **g up** to Jerusalem, *326*
20:18 *"We are* **g up** to Jerusalem, *326*
20:22 "Can you drink the cup I *am* **g to** drink?" *3516*
20:30 and when they heard that Jesus *was* **g by,** *4135*
25: 8 our lamps *are* **g out.'** *4931*
25:14 it will be like a man **g on a journey,** *623*
26:18 *I am g to* **celebrate** the Passover *AIT*
26:39 **G** a little **farther,** *4601*
26:49 **G** at once to Jesus, Judas said, "Greetings, *4665*
26:62 *"Are you* not *g to* **answer?** *AIT*
27:32 *As they were* **g out,** *2002*
27:40 "You who *are g to* **destroy** the temple *AIT*
27:58 **G to** Pilate, he asked for Jesus' body, *4665*
28: 2 **g to** the tomb, rolled back the stone *4665*
28: 7 from the dead and *is* **g ahead** of you *4575*
Mk 2:23 One Sabbath Jesus *was* **g** through *4182*
6:31 and **g** that they did not even have a chance *5632*
7:15 a man can make him 'unclean' *by* **g into** *1660*
9:31 of Man *is g to be* **betrayed** into the hands *AIT*
10:32 and told them what *was* **g to** happen *3516*
10:33 *"We are* **g up** to Jerusalem," he said, *326*
13:34 It's like a man **g away:** *624*
14:35 **G** a little **farther,** *4601*
14:45 **G** at once to Jesus, Judas said, "Rabbi!" *2262*
14:60 *"Are you* not **g** *to* **answer?** *646*
15: 4 "Aren't *you* **g** *to* **answer?** *646*
15:29 You who *are g to* **destroy** the temple *AIT*
16: 7 *'He is* **g ahead** of you into Galilee. *4575*
Lk 1:36 Even Elizabeth your relative *is g to* **have** *AIT*
1:59 and *they were g to* **name** him *AIT*
1:66 asking, "What then *is* this child *g to* **be?"** *AIT*
6: 1 One Sabbath Jesus *was* **g through** *1388*
8:24 "Master, Master, *we're g to* **drown!"** *AIT*
9: 7 the tetrarch heard about all that **was g on.** *1181*
9:44 of Man *is* **g to** be betrayed into the hands *3516*
10:30 man *was* **g down** from Jerusalem to Jericho, *2849*
10:31 A priest happened *to be* **g down** *2849*
12:54 immediately you say, *'It's* **g to rain,'** *2262+3915*
12:55 you say, *'It's g to* **be** hot,' and it is. *AIT*
12:58 As *you are* **g** with your adversary to *5632*
13:23 *are* only a few people *g to be* **saved?"** *AIT*
13:33 I must *keep* **g** today and tomorrow and *4513*
15:26 and asked him **what was g on.** *323+4047+5515*
17:12 *As* he *was* **g into** a village, *1656*
18:31 *"We are* **g up** to Jerusalem, *326*
18:36 When he heard the crowd **g by,** *1388*
19:11 that the kingdom of God *was* **g to** appear *3516*
19:28 he went on ahead, **g up** to Jerusalem. *326*
22:21 of him who *is g to* **betray** me is with mine *AIT*
22:49 Jesus' followers saw what *was g to* **happen,** *AIT*
23:52 **G to** Pilate, he asked for Jesus' body. *4665*
24:13 of them were **g** to a village called Emmaus, *4513*
24:21 the one who *was* **g to** redeem Israel. *3516*
24:28 the village to which *they were* **g,** *4513*
24:28 Jesus acted as if *he were* **g** farther. *4513*
24:49 I *am g to* **send** you what my Father has promised; *AIT*
Jn 2:20 and you *are g to* **raise it** in three days?" *AIT*
3: 8 where it comes from or where *it is* **g.** *5632*
3:26 he is baptizing, and everyone *is* **g** to him." *2262*
5:47 how *are you g to* **believe** what I say?" *AIT*
6: 6 for he already had in mind what *he was* **g to** *3516*
7: 8 I *am* not yet **g up** to this Feast, *326*
8:14 where I came from and where *I am* **g.** *5632*
8:14 where I come from or where *I am* **g.** *5632*
8:21 "I *am* **g away,** and you will look for me, *5632*
11: 8 and yet *you are* **g back** there?" *5632*
11:11 but *I am* **g** there to wake him up." *4513*
11:31 supposing *she* was **g** to the tomb *5632*
12:11 of him many of the Jews *were* **g over** *5632*
12:33 to show the kind of death *he was* **g to** die. *3516*
12:35 "You *are g to* **have** the light just a little *AIT*
12:35 in the dark does not know where *he is* **g.** *5632*
13: 6 "Lord, *are* you *g to* **wash** my feet?" *AIT*
13:11 For he knew who *was g to* **betray** him, *AIT*
13:21 one of you *is g to* **betray** me." *AIT*
13:33 Where I *am* **g,** you cannot come. *5632*
13:36 "Lord, where *are you* **g?"** *5632*
13:36 Jesus replied, "Where *I am* **g,** *5632*
14: 2 *I am* **g** there to prepare a place for you. *4513*
14: 4 the way to the place where I *am* **g."** *5632*
14: 5 "Lord, we don't know where *you are* **g,** *5632*
14:12 because I *am* **g** to the Father. *4513*

Jn 14:28 *'I am* **g away** and I am coming back *5632*
14:28 be glad that *I am* **g** to the Father, *4513*
16: 5 "Now *I am* **g** to him who sent me, *5632*
16: 5 'Where *are you* **g?'** *5632*
16: 7 It is for your good that I *am* **g away.** *599*
16:10 because *I am* **g** to the Father, *5632*
16:17 and 'Because *I am* **g** to the Father'?" *5632*
16:28 now I am leaving the world and **g** back to *4513*
18: 4 knowing all that *was* **g to happen** to him, *2262*
18:32 of death *he was* **g to** die would be fulfilled. *3516*
21: 3 *"I'm* **g out** to fish," Simon Peter told them, *5632*
21:20 "Lord, who is *g to* **betray** you?") *AIT*
Ac 1: 6 at this time *g to* **restore** the kingdom *AIT*
1:10 up into the sky *as* he *was* **g,** *4513*
3: 1 One day Peter and John *were* **g up** to *326*
3: 2 to beg from those **g into** the temple courts. *1660*
4:16 "What *are we g to* **do with** these men?" *AIT*
8: 3 **G** from house to house, *1660*
11:12 *to* have no hesitation about **g with** them. *5302*
13:11 *You are g to* **be** blind, *AIT*
13:41 for I *am g to* **do** something in your days *AIT*
14:24 *After* **g through** Pisidia, *1451*
16:16 Once *when* we *were* **g** to the place of prayer, *4513*
17:23 as something unknown I *am g to* **proclaim** *AIT*
18:10 and no one *is g to* **attack** and harm you, *AIT*
20:13 where *we were* **g to** take Paul aboard. *3516*
20:13 *because* he was **g** there on foot. *3516*
20:22 I *am* **g** to Jerusalem, *4513*
22:26 "What *are you* **g to** do?" *3516*
25: 4 and *I* myself *am* **g** there soon. *1744*
26:12 of these journeys *I was* **g** to Damascus *4513*
27:10 that our voyage *is* **g to** be disastrous *3516*
27:30 pretending they were **g to** *3516*
1Co 16: 5 for *I will be* **g through** Macedonia. *1451*
2Co 10:14 *We are* not **g too far** in our boasting, *5657*
Php 1:30 **since** you are **g through** *2400*
1Ti 5:13 into the habit of being idle and **g about** *4320*
Heb 3:10 'Their hearts *are* always **g astray,** *4414*
5: 2 and *are* **g astray,** *4414*
11: 8 though he did not know where *he was* **g.** *2262*
Jas 2:12 as *those who are* **g to** be judged by the law *3516*
1Pe 2:25 For you were like sheep **g astray,** *4414*
3:13 Who *is g to* **harm** you if you are eager *AIT*
2Pe 2: 6 *of what is* **g to happen to** the ungodly; *3516*
1Jn 2:11 he does not know where *he is* **g,** *5632*
2:19 but their **g** showed that none *NIG*
Rev 3:10 that *is* **g to** come upon the whole world *3516*
17:11 to the seven and *is* **g** to his destruction. *5632*

GOLAN (4)

Dt 4:43 and **G** in Bashan, for the Manassites. 1584
Jos 20: 8 and **G** in Bashan in the tribe of Manasseh. 1584
21:27 of Manasseh, **G** in Bashan (a city of refuge 1584
1Ch 6:71 the half-tribe of Manasseh they received **G** 1584

GOLD (455) [GOLD-COVERED, GOLDEN, GOLDSMITH, GOLDSMITHS]

Ge 2:11 the entire land of Havilah, where there is **g.** 2298
2:12 (The **g** *of* that land is good; 2298
13: 2 in livestock and in silver and **g.** 2298
24:22 the man took out a **g** nose ring weighing 2298
24:22 and two **g** bracelets weighing ten shekels. 2298
24:35 and **g,** menservants and maidservants, 2298
24:53 the servant brought out **g** and silver jewelry 2298
41:42 in robes of fine linen and put a **g** chain 2298
44: 8 So why would we steal silver or **g** 2298
Ex 3:22 for articles of silver and **g** and for clothing, 2298
11: 2 for articles of silver and **g."** 2298
12:35 for articles of silver and **g** and for clothing. 2298
20:23 for yourselves gods of silver or gods of **g.** 2298
25: 3 **g,** silver and bronze; 2298
25:11 Overlay it with pure **g,** both inside and out, 2298
25:11 and make a **g** molding around it. 2298
25:12 Cast four **g** rings for it and fasten them 2298
25:13 of acacia wood and overlay them with **g.** 2298
25:17 "Make an atonement cover of pure **g—** 2298
25:18 of hammered **g** at the ends of the cover. 2298
25:24 with pure **g** and make a gold molding 2298
25:24 with pure gold and make a **g** molding 2298
25:25 a handbreadth wide and put a **g** molding on 2298
25:26 Make four **g** rings for the table 2298
25:28 overlay them with **g** and carry the table 2298
25:29 And make its plates and dishes of pure **g,** 2298
25:31 a lampstand of pure **g** and hammer it out, 2298
25:36 hammered out of pure **g.** 2298
25:38 and trays are to be of pure **g.** 2298
25:39 of pure **g** is to be used for the lampstand 2298
26: 6 Then make fifty **g** clasps and use them 2298
26:29 the frames with **g** and make gold rings 2298
26:29 and make **g** rings to hold the crossbars. 2298
26:29 Also overlay the crossbars with **g.** 2298
26:32 Hang it with **g** hooks on four posts 2298
26:32 with **g** and standing on four silver bases. 2298
26:37 Make **g** hooks for this curtain 2298
26:37 of acacia wood overlaid with **g.** 2298
28: 5 Have them use **g,** and blue, 2298
28: 6 "Make the ephod of **g,** and of blue, 2298
28: 8 with the ephod and made with **g,** 2298
28:11 Then mount the stones in **g** filigree settings 2298
28:13 Make **g** filigree settings 2298
28:14 and two braided chains of pure **g,** 2298
28:15 of **g,** and of blue, purple and scarlet yarn, 2298
28:20 Mount them in **g** filigree settings. 2298
28:22 breastpiece make braided chains of pure **g,** 2298
28:23 Make two **g** rings for it and fasten them 2298
Ex 28:24 the two **g** chains to the rings at the corners 2298
28:26 Make two **g** rings and attach them to 2298
28:27 Make two more **g** rings and attach them to 2298
28:33 with **g** bells between them. 2298
28:34 The **g** bells and the pomegranates are 2298
28:36 "Make a plate of pure **g** and engrave on it 2298
30: 3 and all the sides and the horns with pure **g,** 2298
30: 3 and make a **g** molding around it. 2298
30: 4 Make two **g** rings for the altar below 2298
30: 5 of acacia wood and overlay them with **g.** 2298
31: 4 to make artistic designs for work in **g,** 2298
31: 8 the pure **g** lampstand and all its accessories, NIH
32: 2 "Take off the **g** earrings that your wives, 2298
32:24 I told them, 'Whoever has any **g** jewelry, 2298
32:24 Then they gave me the **g,** NIH
32:31 They have made themselves gods of **g.** 2298
35: 5 to bring to the LORD an offering of **g,** 2298
35:22 came and brought **g** jewelry of all kinds: 2298
35:22 They all presented their **g** as 2298
35:32 to make artistic designs for work in **g,** 2298
36:13 Then they made fifty **g** clasps 2298
36:34 the frames with **g** and made gold rings 2298
36:34 and made **g** rings to hold the crossbars. 2298
36:34 They also overlaid the crossbars with **g.** 2298
36:36 for it and overlaid them with **g.** 2298
36:36 They made **g** hooks for them 2298
36:38 with **g** and made their five bases of bronze. 2298
37: 2 He overlaid it with pure **g,** 2298
37: 2 and made a **g** molding around it. 2298
37: 3 He cast four **g** rings for it 2298
37: 4 of acacia wood and overlaid them with **g.** 2298
37: 6 He made the atonement cover of pure **g—** 2298
37: 7 of hammered **g** at the ends of the cover. 2298
37:11 Then they overlaid it with pure **g** and made 2298
37:11 with pure gold and made a **g** molding 2298
37:12 a handbreadth wide and put a **g** molding on 2298
37:13 They cast four **g** rings for the table 2298
37:15 of acacia wood and were overlaid with **g.** 2298
37:16 And they made from pure **g** the articles for 2298
37:17 of pure **g** and hammered it out, base 2298
37:22 hammered out of pure **g.** 2298
37:23 as its wick trimmers and trays, of pure **g.** 2298
37:24 from one talent of pure **g.** 2298
37:26 and all the sides and the horns with pure **g,** 2298
37:26 and made a **g** molding around it. 2298
37:27 They made two **g** rings below 2298
37:28 of acacia wood and overlaid them with **g.** 2298
38:24 of the **g** *from* the wave offering used for all 2298
39: 2 They made the ephod of **g,** and of blue, 2298
39: 3 of **g** and cut strands to be worked into 2298
39: 5 with the ephod and made with **g,** 2298
39: 6 in **g** filigree settings and engraved them 2298
39: 8 of **g,** and of blue, purple and scarlet yarn, 2298
39:13 They were mounted in **g** filigree settings. 2298
39:15 For the breastpiece they made braided chains of pure **g,** 2298
39:16 They made two **g** filigree settings 2298
39:16 and two **g** rings, 2298
39:17 They fastened the two **g** chains to the rings 2298
39:19 They made two **g** rings and attached them 2298
39:20 Then they made two more **g** rings 2298
39:25 of pure **g** and attached them around 2298
39:30 out of pure **g** and engraved on it, 2298
39:37 the pure **g** lampstand with its row of lamps NIH
39:38 the **g** altar, the anointing oil, 2298
40: 5 the **g** altar of incense in front of the ark of 2298
40:26 the **g** altar in the Tent of Meeting in front 2298
Lev 8: 9 on Aaron's head and set the **g** plate, 2298
24: 4 The lamps on the pure **g** lampstand before NIH
24: 6 on the table of pure **g** before the LORD. NIH
Nu 4:11 the **g** altar they are to spread a blue cloth 2298
7:14 one **g** dish weighing ten shekels, filled 2298
7:20 one **g** dish weighing ten shekels, filled 2298
7:26 one **g** dish weighing ten shekels, filled 2298
7:32 one **g** dish weighing ten shekels, filled 2298
7:38 one **g** dish weighing ten shekels, filled 2298
7:44 one **g** dish weighing ten shekels, filled 2298
7:50 one **g** dish weighing ten shekels, filled 2298
7:56 one **g** dish weighing ten shekels, filled 2298
7:62 one **g** dish weighing ten shekels, filled 2298
7:68 one **g** dish weighing ten shekels, filled 2298
7:74 one **g** dish weighing ten shekels, filled 2298
7:80 one **g** dish weighing ten shekels, filled 2298
7:84 and twelve **g** dishes. 2298
7:86 The twelve **g** dishes filled 2298
7:86 the **g** dishes weighed a hundred 2298
8: 4 It was made of hammered **g—** 2298
22:18 gave me his palace filled with silver and **g,** 2298
24:13 gave me his palace filled with silver and **g,** 2298
31:22 **G,** silver, bronze, iron, tin, lead 2298
31:50 the **g** articles each of us acquired— 2298
31:51 the priest accepted from them the **g—** 2298
31:52 the **g** from the commanders of thousands 2298
31:54 Moses and Eleazar the priest accepted the **g** 2298
Dt 7:25 Do not covet the silver and **g** on them, 2298
8:13 and your silver and **g** increase 2298
17:17 large amounts of silver and **g.** 2298
29:17 idols of wood and stone, of silver and **g.** 2298
Jos 6:19 the silver and **g** and the articles of bronze 2298
6:24 but they put the silver and **g** and the articles 2298
7:21 and a wedge of **g** weighing fifty shekels, 2298
7:24 the **g** wedge, his sons and daughters, 2298
22: 8 with large herds of livestock, with silver, **g,** 2298
Jdg 8:24 of the Ishmaelites to wear **g** earrings.) 2298
8:26 The weight of the **g** rings he asked 2298
8:27 Gideon made **the g** into an ephod, 2257[S]
1Sa 6: 4 "Five **g** tumors and five gold rats, 2298
1Sa 6: 4 "Five gold tumors and five **g** rats, 2298
6: 8 the **g** objects you are sending back to him 2298
6:11 along with it the chest containing the **g** rats 2298
6:15 with the chest containing the **g** objects, 2298
6:17 These are the **g** tumors the Philistines sent 2298
6:18 And the number of the **g** rats was according 2298
2Sa 1:24 garments with ornaments of **g.** 2298
8: 7 the **g** shields that belonged to the officers 2298
8:10 with him articles of silver and **g** 2298
8:11 and **g** from all the nations he had subdued: 2298
12:30 its weight was a talent of **g,** 2298
21: 4 "We have no right to demand silver or **g** 2298
1Ki 6:20 He overlaid the inside with pure **g,** 2298
6:21 the inside of the temple with pure **g,** 2298
6:21 and he extended **g** chains across the front of 2298
6:21 which was overlaid with **g.** 2298
6:22 So he overlaid the whole interior with **g.** 2298
6:22 also overlaid with **g** the altar that belonged 2298
6:28 He overlaid the cherubim with **g.** 2298
6:30 and outer rooms of the temple with **g.** 2298
6:32 the cherubim and palm trees with beaten **g.** 2298
6:35 and overlaid them with **g** hammered evenly 2298
7:49 the lampstands of pure **g** (five on the right 2298
7:49 the **g** floral work and lamps and tongs; 2298
7:50 the pure **g** basins, wick trimmers, 2298
7:50 and the **g** sockets for the doors of 2298
7:51 the silver and **g** and the furnishings— 2298
9:11 the cedar and pine and **g** he wanted. 2298
9:14 Hiram had sent to the king 120 talents of **g.** 2298
9:28 to Ophir and brought back 420 talents of **g,** 2298
10: 2 large quantities of **g,** and precious stones— 2298
10:10 And she gave the king 120 talents of **g,** 2298
10:11 (Hiram's ships brought **g** from Ophir; 2298
10:14 The weight of the **g** that Solomon 2298
10:16 King Solomon made two hundred large shields of hammered **g;** 2298
10:16 six hundred bekas of **g** went 2298
10:17 of hammered **g,** with three minas of gold 2298
10:17 with three minas of **g** in each shield. 2298
10:18 with ivory and overlaid with fine **g.** 2298
10:21 All King Solomon's goblets were **g,** 2298
10:21 of the Forest of Lebanon were pure **g.** 2298
10:22 carrying **g,** silver and ivory, 2298
10:25 articles of silver and **g,** robes, 2298
14:26 the **g** shields Solomon had made. 2298
15:15 the LORD the silver and **g** and the articles 2298
15:18 then took all the silver and **g** that was left 2298
15:19 See, I am sending you a gift of silver and **g.** 2298
20: 3 'Your silver and **g** are mine, 2298
20: 5 'I sent to demand your silver and **g,** 2298
20: 7 my silver and my **g,** I did not refuse him." 2298
22:48 a fleet of trading ships to go to Ophir for **g,** 2298
2Ki 5: 5 six thousand shekels of **g** and ten sets 2298
7: 8 **g** and clothes, and went off and hid them. 2298
12:13 of **g** or silver for the temple of the LORD; 2298
12:18 the **g** found in the treasuries of the temple 2298
14:14 the **g** and silver and all the articles found in 2298
16: 8 and **g** found in the temple of the LORD 2298
18:14 of silver and thirty talents of **g.** 2298
18:16 the **g** with which he had covered the doors NIH
20:13 silver, the **g,** the spices and the fine oil— 2298
23:33 a hundred talents of silver and a talent of **g.** 2298
23:35 the silver and **g** he demanded. 2298
23:35 and **g** from the people of the land according 2298
24:13 the **g** articles that Solomon king of Israel 2298
25:15 all that were made of **pure g** or silver. 2298+2298
1Ch 18: 7 the **g** shields carried by the officers 2298
18:10 Hadoram brought all kinds of articles of **g** 2298
18:11 and **g** he had taken from all these nations: 2298
20: 2 its weight was found to be a talent of **g,** 2298
21:25 six hundred shekels of **g** for the site. 2298
22:14 a hundred thousand talents of **g,** 2298
22:16 in **g** and silver, bronze and iron— 2298
28:14 the weight of **g** for all the gold articles to 2298
28:14 the weight of gold for all the **g** articles to 2298
28:15 the weight of **g** for the gold lampstands 2298
28:15 for the **g** lampstands and their lamps, with 2298
28:16 of **g** for each table for consecrated bread; 2298
28:17 of pure **g** for the forks, sprinkling bowls 2298
28:17 the weight of **g** for each gold dish; 2298
28:17 the weight of gold for each **g** dish; NIH
28:18 and the weight of the refined **g** for the altar 2298
28:18 the cherubim of **g** that spread their wings 2298
29: 2 **g** for the gold work, silver for the silver, 2298
29: 2 gold for the **g** *work,* silver for the silver, 2298
29: 3 of **g** and silver for the temple of my God, 2298
29: 4 three thousand talents of **g** (gold of Ophir) 2298
29: 4 three thousand talents of gold (**g** *of* Ophir) 2298
29: 5 for the **g** *work* and the silver work, 2298
29: 7 and ten thousand darics of **g,** 2298
2Ch 1:15 and **g** as common in Jerusalem as stones, 2298
2: 7 a man skilled to work in **g** and silver, 2298
2:14 He is trained to work in **g** and silver, 2298
3: 4 He overlaid the inside with pure **g.** 2298
3: 5 with fine **g** and decorated it with palm tree 2298
3: 6 And the **g** he used was gold of Parvaim. 2298
3: 6 And the gold he used was **g** *of* Parvaim. 2298
3: 7 walls and doors of the temple with **g,** 2298
3: 8 inside with six hundred talents of fine **g.** 2298
3: 9 The **g** nails weighed fifty shekels. 2298
3: 9 He also overlaid the upper parts with **g.** 2298
3:10 and overlaid them with **g.** 2298
4: 7 He made ten **g** lampstands according to 2298
4: 8 also made a hundred **g** sprinkling bowls. 2298
4:20 of pure **g** with their lamps, to burn in front 2298
4:21 the **g** floral work and lamps 2298
4:21 and lamps and tongs (they were solid **g**); 2298

2Ch 4:22 the pure **g** wick trimmers, 2298
4:22 and the **g** doors of the temple: 2298
5: 1 the silver and **g** and all the furnishings— 2298
8:18 and fifty talents of **g**, 2298
9: 1 large quantities of **g**, and precious stones— 2298
9: 9 Then she gave the king 120 talents of **g**, 2298
9:10 the men of Solomon brought **g** from Ophir; 2298
9:13 The weight of the **g** 2298
9:14 the land brought **g** and silver to Solomon. 2298
9:15 King Solomon made two hundred large shields of hammered **g**; 2298
9:15 six hundred bekas of hammered **g** went 2298
9:16 of hammered **g**, with three hundred bekas 2298
9:16 with three hundred bekas of **g** 2298
9:17 with ivory and overlaid with pure **g**. 2298
9:18 and a footstool of **g** was attached to it. 2298
9:20 All King Solomon's goblets were **g**, 2298
9:20 of the Forest of Lebanon were pure **g**. 2298
9:21 carrying **g**, silver and ivory, 2298
9:24 articles of silver and **g**, and robes, 2298
12: 9 including the **g** shields Solomon had made. 2298
13:11 on the **g** lampstand every evening. 2298
15:18 into the temple of God the silver and **g** and 2298
16: 2 the silver and **g** out of the treasuries of 2298
16: 3 See, I am sending you silver and **g**. 2298
21: 3 of silver and **g** and articles of value, 2298
24:14 and also dishes and other objects of **g** 2298
25:24 the **g** and silver and all the articles found in 2298
32:27 and he made treasuries for his silver and **g** 2298
36: 3 a hundred talents of silver and a talent of **g**. 2298
Ezr 1: 4 to provide him with silver and **g**, 2298
1: 6 with articles of silver and **g**, 2298
1: 9 **g** dishes 30 silver dishes 1,000 2298
1:10 **g** bowls 30 matching silver bowls 410 2298
1:11 there were 5,400 articles of **g** and of silver. 2298
2:69 drachmas of **g**, 5,000 minas of silver 2298
5:14 of Babylon the **g** and silver articles of 10160
6: 5 **g** and silver articles of the house of God, 10160
7:15 you are to take with you the silver and **g** 10160
7:16 and **g** you may obtain from the province 10160
7:18 with the rest of the silver and **g**, 10160
8:25 the offering of silver and **g** and the articles 2298
8:26 100 talents of **g**, 2298
8:27 20 bowls of **g** valued at 1,000 2298
8:27 as precious as **g**. 2298
8:28 and **g** are a freewill offering to the LORD, 2298
8:30 and Levites received the silver and **g** 2298
8:33 and **g** and the sacred articles into the hands 2298
Ne 7:70 the treasury 1,000 drachmas of **g**, 50 bowls 2298
7:71 drachmas of **g** and 2,200 minas of silver. 2298
7:72 of **g**, 2,000 minas of silver and 67 garments 2298
Est 1: 6 There were couches of **g** and silver on 2298
1: 7 Wine was served in goblets of **g**, 2298
4:11 for the king to extend the **g** scepter to him 2298
5: 2 and held out to her the **g** scepter that was 2298
8: 4 the king extended the **g** scepter to Esther 2298
8:15 a large crown of **g** and a purple robe 2298
Job 3:15 with rulers who had **g**, 2298
22:24 your **g of Ophir** to the rocks in the ravines, 234
22:25 then the Almighty will be your **g**, 1309
23:10 I will come forth as **g**. 2298
28: 1 for silver and a place where **g** is refined. 2298
28: 6 and its dust contains **nuggets of g**. 2298
28:15 It cannot be bought with the **finest g**, 6034
28:16 It cannot be bought with the **g** *of* Ophir, 4188
28:17 Neither **g** nor crystal can compare with it, 2298
28:17 nor can it be had for jewels of **g**. 7058
28:19 it cannot be bought with pure **g**. 4188
31:24 "If I have put my trust in **g** or said 2298
31:24 in gold or said to **pure g**, 4188
42:11 a piece of silver and a **g** ring. 2298
Ps 19:10 They are more precious than **g**, 2298
19:10 than much **pure g**; 7058
21: 3 and placed a crown of **pure g** on his head. 7058
45: 9 at your right hand is the royal bride in **g** 4188
45:13 her gown is interwoven with **g**. 2298
68:13 its feathers with shining **g**." 3021
72:15 May **g** *from* Sheba be given him. 2298
105:37 laden with silver and **g**, 2298
115: 4 But their idols are silver and **g**, 2298
119:72 of pieces of silver and **g**. 2298
119:127 Because I love your commands more than **g**, 2298
119:127 more than **pure g**, 7058
135:15 The idols of the nations are silver and **g**, 2298
Pr 3:14 and yields better returns than **g**. 3021
8:10 knowledge rather than choice **g**, 3021
8:19 My fruit is better than **fine g**; 7058
11:22 Like a **g** ring in a pig's snout is 2298
16:16 How much better to get wisdom than **g**, 3021
17: 3 crucible for silver and the furnace for **g**, 2298
20:15 **G** there is, and rubies in abundance, 2298
22: 1 to be esteemed is better than silver or **g**. 2298
25:11 A word aptly spoken is like apples of **g** 2298
25:12 Like an earring of **g** or an ornament 2298
25:12 of **fine g** is a wise man's rebuke to 4188
27:21 crucible for silver and the furnace for **g**, 2298
Ecc 2: 8 I amassed silver and **g** for myself, 2298
SS 1:11 We will make you earrings of **g**, 2298
3:10 Its posts he made of silver, its base of **g**. 2298
5:11 His head is **purest g**; 4188+7058
5:14 His arms are rods of **g** set with chrysolite. 2298
5:15 of marble set on bases of **pure g**. 7058
Isa 2: 7 Their land is full of silver and **g**; 2298
2:20 and bats their idols of silver and idols of **g**, 2298
13:12 I will make man scarcer than **pure g**, 7058
13:12 more rare than the **g** *of* Ophir. 4188
13:17 not care for silver and have no delight in **g**. 2298
Isa 30:22 and your images covered with **g**; 2298
31: 7 and **g** your sinful hands have made. 2298
39: 2 the silver, the **g**, the spices, the fine oil, 2298
40:19 with **g** and fashions silver chains for it. 2298
46: 6 Some pour out **g** from their bags 2298
60: 6 bearing **g** and incense and proclaiming 2298
60: 9 with their silver and **g**, 2298
60:17 Instead of bronze I will bring you **g**, 2298
Jer 4:30 in scarlet and put on jewels of **g**? 2298
10: 4 They adorn it with silver and **g**; 2298
10: 9 from Tarshish and **g** from Uphaz. 2298
51: 7 Babylon was a **g** cup in the LORD's hand; 2298
52:19 all that were made of **pure g** or silver. 2298+2298
La 4: 1 How the **g** has lost its luster, 2298
4: 1 the fine **g** become dull! 4188
4: 2 once worth their weight in **g**, 7058
Eze 7:19 and their **g** will be an unclean thing. 2298
7:19 and **g** will not be able to save them in 2298
16:13 So you were adorned with **g** and silver; 2298
16:17 the jewelry made of my **g** and silver, 2298
27:22 of spices and precious stones, and **g**. 2298
28: 4 and amassed **g** and silver in your treasuries. 2298
28:13 and mountings were made of **g**; 2298
38:13 to carry off silver and **g**, 2298
Da 2:32 The head of the statue was made of pure **g**, 10160
2:35 the silver and the **g** were broken to pieces 10160
2:38 You are that head of **g**. 10160
2:45 the clay, the silver and the **g** to pieces. 10160
3: 1 King Nebuchadnezzar made an image of **g**, 10160
3: 5 of **g** that King Nebuchadnezzar has set up. 10160
3: 7 of **g** that King Nebuchadnezzar had set up. 10160
3:10 down and worship the image of **g**, 10160
3:12 the image of **g** you have set up." 10160
3:14 or worship the image of **g** I have set up? 10160
3:18 or worship the image of **g** you have set up." 10160
5: 2 to bring in the **g** and silver goblets 10160
5: 3 in the **g** goblets that had been taken from 10160
5: 4 they praised the gods of **g** and silver, 10160
5: 7 and have a **g** chain placed around his neck, 10160
5:16 in purple and have a **g** chain placed 10160
5:23 You praised the gods of silver and **g**, 10160
5:29 a **g** chain was placed around his neck, 10160
10: 5 a belt of the **finest g** around his waist. 233+4188
11: 8 of silver and **g** and carry them off to Egypt. 2298
11:38 to his fathers he will honor with **g** 2298
11:43 of **g** and silver and all the riches of Egypt, 2298
Hos 2: 8 who lavished on her the silver and **g**— 2298
8: 4 With their silver and **g** they make idols 2298
Joel 3: 5 For you took my silver and my **g** 2298
Na 2: 9 Plunder the **g**! 2298
Hab 2:19 It is covered with **g** and silver; 2298
Zep 1:18 Neither their silver nor their **g** will be able 2298
Hag 2: 8 'The silver is mine and the **g** is mine,' 2298
Zec 4: 2 a solid **g** lampstand with a bowl at the top 2298
4:12 the two **g** pipes that pour out golden oil?" 2298
6:10 "Take [silver and **g**] from the exiles Heldai, NIH
6:11 Take the silver and **g** and make a crown, 2298
9: 3 and **g** like the dirt of the streets. 3021
13: 9 like silver and test them like **g**. 2298
14:14 great quantities of **g** and silver 2298
Mal 3: 3 the Levites and refine them like **g** 2298
Mt 2:11 with gifts of **g** and of incense and of myrrh. *5996*
10: 9 Do not take along any **g** or silver or copper *5996*
23:16 but if anyone swears by the **g** of the temple, *5996*
23:17 Which is greater: the **g**, *5996*
23:17 or the temple that makes the **g** sacred? *5996*
Ac 3: 6 Then Peter said, "Silver or **g** I do not have, *5992*
17:29 not think that the divine being is like **g** *5996*
20:33 I have not coveted anyone's silver or **g** *5992*
1Co 3:12 on this foundation using **g**, *5996*
1Ti 2: 9 or **g** or pearls or expensive clothes, *5996*
2Ti 2:20 not only **of g** and silver, but also of wood *5991*
Heb 9: 4 This ark contained the **g** jar of manna, *5991*
Jas 2: 2 into your meeting **wearing a g ring** *5993*
5: 3 Your **g** and silver are corroded. *5996*
1Pe 1: 7 your faith—of greater worth than **g**, *5992*
1:18 as silver or **g** that you were redeemed from *5992*
3: 3 the wearing *of* **g jewelry** and fine clothes. *5992*
Rev 3:18 I counsel you to buy from me **g** refined in *5992*
4: 4 and had crowns **of g** on their heads. *5991*
9: 7 wore something like crowns of **g**, *5996*
9:20 and idols **of g**, silver, bronze, *5991*
14:14 a crown **of g** on his head and a sharp sickle *5991*
17: 4 and was glittering *with* **g**, *5992*
18:12 *of* **g**, silver, precious stones and pearls; *5996*
18:16 purple and scarlet, and glittering with **g**, *5992*
21:15 a measuring rod **of g** to measure the city, *5991*
21:18 and the city of pure **g**, as pure as glass. *5992*
21:21 The great street of the city was of pure **g**, *5992*

GOLD-COVERED (1) [GOLD, COVER]

Heb 9: 4 and the **g** ark of the covenant. *4119+4328+5992*

GOLDEN (21) [GOLD]

1Ki 7:48 in the LORD's temple: the **g** altar; 2298
7:48 the **g** table on which was the bread of 2298
12:28 the king made two **g** calves. 2298
2Ki 10:29 the worship of the **g** calves at Bethel 2298
2Ch 4:19 in God's temple: the **g** altar; 2298
13: 8 a vast army and have with you the **g** calves 2298
Job 37:22 Out of the north he comes in **g** splendor; 2298
Ecc 12: 6 or the **g** bowl is broken; 2298
Zec 4:12 the two gold pipes that pour out **g** *oil?"* 2298
Heb 9: 4 which had the **g** altar of incense and *5991*
Rev 1:12 when I turned I saw seven **g** lampstands, *5991*
1:13 and with a **g** sash around his chest. *5991*
1:20 and of the seven **g** lampstands is this: *5991*
2: 1 and walks among the seven **g** lampstands: *5991*
5: 8 a harp and they were holding **g** bowls full *5991*
8: 3 Another angel, who had a **g** censer, *5991*
8: 3 on the **g** altar before the throne. *5991*
9:13 the horns *of* the **g** altar that is before God. *5991*
15: 6 and wore **g** sashes around their chests. *5991*
15: 7 the seven angels seven **g** bowls filled with *5991*
17: 4 She held a **g** cup in her hand, *5991*

GOLDSMITH (6) [GOLD]

Isa 40:19 and a **g** overlays it with gold 7671
41: 7 The craftsman encourages the **g**, 7671
46: 6 they hire a **g** to make it into a god, 7671
Jer 10: 9 and **g** have made is then dressed in blue 7671
10:14 every **g** is shamed by his idols. 7671
51:17 every **g** is shamed by his idols. 7671

GOLDSMITHS (3) [GOLD]

Ne 3: 8 Uzziel son of Harhaiah, one of the **g**, 7671
3:31 Next to him, Malkijah, one of the **g**, 7672
3:32 above the corner and the Sheep Gate the **g** 7671

GOLGOTHA (3)

Mt 27:33 **G** (which means The Place of the Skull). *1201*
Mk 15:22 **G** (which means The Place of the Skull). *1201*
Jn 19:17 the Skull (which in Aramaic is called **G**). *1201*

GOLIATH (7)

1Sa 17: 4 A champion named **G**, who was from Gath, 1669
17: 8 **G** stood and shouted to the ranks of Israel, NIH
17:23 As he was talking with them, **G**, 1669
21: 9 "The sword of **G** the Philistine, 1669
22:10 and the sword of **G** the Philistine." 1669
2Sa 21:19 of Jaare-Oregim the Bethlehemite killed **G** 1669
1Ch 20: 5 of Jair killed Lahmi the brother of **G** 1669

GOMER (8)

Ge 10: 2 The sons of Japheth: **G**, Magog, Madai, 1699
10: 3 The sons of **G**: 1699
1Ch 1: 5 The sons of Japheth: **G**, Magog, Madai, 1699
1: 6 The sons of **G**: 1699
Eze 38: 6 also **G** with all its troops, 1699
Hos 1: 3 So he married **G** daughter of Diblaim, 1700
1: 6 **G** conceived again and gave birth to NIH
1: 8 **G** had another son. NIH

GOMORRAH (23)

Ge 10:19 **G**, Admah and Zeboiim, as far as Lasha. 6686
13:10 the LORD destroyed Sodom and **G**.) 6686
14: 2 Birsha king of **G**, Shinab king of Admah, 6686
14: 8 Then the king of Sodom, the king of **G**, 6686
14:10 and when the kings of Sodom and **G** fled, 6686
14:11 of Sodom and **G** and all their food; 6686
18:20 and **G** is so great and their sin so grievous 6686
19:24 down burning sulfur on Sodom and **G**— 6686
19:28 He looked down toward Sodom and **G**, 6686
Dt 29:23 be like the destruction of Sodom and **G**, 6686
32:32 the vine of Sodom and from the fields of **G**. 6686
Isa 1: 9 we would have been like **G**. 6686
1:10 to the law of our God, you people of **G**! 6686
13:19 be overthrown by God like Sodom and **G**. 6686
Jer 23:14 the people of Jerusalem are like **G**." 6686
49:18 As Sodom and **G** were overthrown, 6686
50:40 and **G** along with their neighboring towns," 6686
Am 4:11 of you as I overthrew Sodom and **G**. 6686
Zep 2: 9 the Ammonites like **G**— 6686
Mt 10:15 it will be more bearable *for* Sodom and **G** *1202*
Ro 9:29 we would have been like **G**." *1202*
2Pe 2: 6 if he condemned the cities *of* Sodom and **G** *1202*
Jude 1: 7 Sodom and **G** and the surrounding towns *1202*

GONE (207) [GO]

Ge 8: 3 and fifty days the water *had* **g down**, 2893
19: 4 Before *they had* **g to bed**, 8886
20: 4 Now Abimelech *had* not **g near** her, 7928
21:15 When the water in the skin *was* **g**, 3983
28: 7 and mother and *had* **g** to Paddan Aram. 2143
31:19 When Laban *had* **g** to shear his sheep, 2143
31:30 *you have* **g off** because you longed 2143+2143
35: 3 with me wherever *I have* **g**." 2143
37:12 Now his brothers *had* **g** 2143
43:10 we could have **g** and returned twice." NIH
44: 4 not **g** far **from** the city when Joseph said 3655
47:15 of the people of Egypt and Canaan *was* **g**, 9462
47:16 since your money *is* **g**." 699
47:18 the fact that since our money *is* **g** 9462
50:14 his brothers and all the *others who had* **g** 6590
Ex 3: 4 the LORD saw that *he had* **g over** to look, 6073
9:29 "When I *have* **g out** *of* the city, 3655
16:14 When the dew *was* **g**, 6590
19:14 After Moses *had* **g down** the mountain to 3718
Lev 14:48 because the mildew *is* **g**. 8324
Nu 5:19 with you and *you have* not **g astray** 8474
5:20 But if you *have* **g astray** while married 8474
13:31 But the men who *had* **g up** with him said, 6590
14: 9 Their protection *is* **g**, 6073
16: 3 "You have **g too far!** 8041
16: 7 You Levites have **g too far!"** 8041
16:33 and they perished and were **g from** 4946+9348
31:21 the soldiers who *had* **g** into battle, 995

Nu 32:13 who had done evil in his sight *was* **g.** 9462
Dt 32:36 when he sees their strength *is* g 261
34: 7 his eyes were not weak nor his strength **g.** 5674
Jos 2: 7 and as soon as the pursuers *had* **g out,** 3655
Jdg 3:24 After he *had* **g,** 3655
4:12 of Abinoam *had* **g up** *to* Mount Tabor, 6590
4:14 *Has* not the LORD g ahead of you?" 3655
9:27 After *they had* **g out** *into* the fields 3655
9:35 of Ebed *had* **g out** and was standing at 3655
18:22 When they *had* **g some distance** 8178
19:11 near Jebus and the day *was* almost **g,** 3718
20: 3 that the Israelites *had* **g up** *to* Mizpah.) 6590
Ru 1:13 the LORD's hand *has* **g out** against me!" 3655
1Sa 3: 3 The lamp of God *had* not yet **g out,** 3882
9: 7 The food in our sacks *is* **g.** 261
13:23 Now a detachment of Philistines *had* **g out** 3655
14:21 with the Philistines and *had* **g up** with them 6590
15:12 but he was told, "Saul *has* g to Carmel. 995
15:12 in his own honor and has turned and **g on** 6296
20:41 After the boy *had* **g,** 995
23: 7 Saul was told that David *had* g *to* Keilah, 995
28:20 His strength *was* **g,** 928+2118+4202
2Sa 3:22 and *he had* g in peace. 2143
3:23 king had sent him away and that *he had* g 2143
3:24 Now *he is* **g!** 2143+2143
4: 7 *They had* **g into** the house 995
5:24 the LORD *has* **g out** in front of you 3655
7: 9 I have been with you wherever *you have* **g,** 2143
12:15 After Nathan *had* g home, 2143
16: 1 When David *had* g a short distance beyond 6296
17:21 After the men *had* **g,** 2143
24: 8 After *they had* g through the entire land, 8763
1Ki 1:25 Today *he has* **g down** 3718
1:45 From there *they have* **g up** cheering, 6590
2:15 and the kingdom *has* g to my brother; 2118
2:41 When Solomon was told that Shimei *had* g 2143
11:15 *who had* **g up** to bury the dead, 6590
12: 1 the Israelites *had* g there to make him king. 995
14: 4 his sight *was* g because of his age. 7756
14:10 as one burns dung, until it *is* **all g.** 9462
21:18 where *he has* g to take possession of it. 3718
22:13 The messenger who *had* g 2143
2Ki 3:26 the king of Moab saw that the battle *had* g 2616[S]
4:13 **g to all this trouble** 3006+3010
5: 2 from Aram *had* **g out** and had taken captive 3655
9:16 and Ahaziah king of Judah *had* **g down** 3718
20:11 ten steps *it had* **g down** on the stairway 345+3718
25:11 of the populace and those who *had* **g over** to 5877
1Ch 14:15 because that will mean God *has* **g out** 3655
17: 8 I have been with you wherever *you have* **g,** 2143
2Ch 10: 1 the Israelites *had* g there to make him king. 995
18:12 The messenger who *had* g 2143
Ezr 4:12 up to us from you *have* g to Jerusalem 10085
Ne 2:16 The officials did not know where *I had* g 2143
4: 7 the repairs to Jerusalem's walls *had* **g ahead** 6590
13:10 the service *had* **g back** to their own fields. 1368
Job 7: 9 As a cloud vanishes and *is* **g,** 2143
11:16 recalling it only as waters **g by.** 6296
14:20 You overpower him once for all, and *he is* g 2143
19: 4 If it is true that *I have* **g astray,** 8706
19:10 down on every side till *I am* **g;** 2143
19:14 My kinsmen *have* **g away;** 2532
24:14 When daylight is **g,** the murderer rises up NIH
24:24 and then they are **g;** 401
27:19 when he opens his eyes, all is **g.** 401
27:21 The east wind carries him off, and *he is* **g;** 2143
29: 2 "How I long for the months **g by,** 7710
30: 2 since their vigor *had* g from them? 6
Ps 28: 1 be like *those who have* **g down** *to* the pit. 3718
38:10 even the light has **g from** my eyes. 401+907
52: T the Edomite *had* g to Saul and told him: 995
52: T "David *has* g to the house of Ahimelech." 995
54: T When the Ziphites *had* g to Saul and said, 995
71: 9 do not forsake me when my strength *is* **g.** 3983
90: 4 like a day that *has just* **g by,** 6296
103:16 the wind blows over it and it is **g,** 401
Pr 7:19 *he has* g on a long journey. 2143
10:25 the storm has swept by, the wicked are **g,** 401
23: 5 Cast but a glance at riches, and they are **g,** 401
30: 4 Who *has* **g up** *to* heaven and come down? 6590
Ecc 6:12 will happen under the sun after he is **g?** NIH
7:29 men *have* **g in search of** many schemes." 1335
SS 2:11 The winter is past; the rains are over and **g.** 2143
5: 6 but my lover had left; *he was* **g.** 6296
6: 1 *has* your lover **g,** most beautiful of women? 2143
6: 2 My lover *has* **g down** to his garden, 3718
Isa 15: 6 vegetation *is* **g** and nothing green is left. 3983
17:14 Before the morning, they are **g!** 401
18: 5 the blossom *is* g and the flower becomes 9462
20: 3 "Just as my servant Isaiah *has* **g** stripped 2143
22: 1 that you *have* all **g up** on the roofs, 6590
38: 8 the sun go back the ten steps *it has* **g down** 3718
38: 8 the ten steps *it had* **g down.** 3718
51: 9 awake, as in days **g by,** 7710
53: 6 We all, like sheep, *have* **g astray,** 9494
Jer 3: 6 She *has* **g up** on every high hill and 2143
4:23 and at the heavens, and their light was **g.** 401
5:23 they have turned aside and **g away.** 2143
9:10 of the air have fled and the animals *are* **g.** 2143
10:20 My sons *are* **g from** me and are no more; 3655
14:18 Both prophet and priest *have* g to 6086
17:11 When his life is **half** *g,* AIT
22:11 as king of Judah but *has* g from this place: 3655
29: 2 the craftsmen and the artisans *had* g 3655
37:21 until all the bread in the city *was* **g.** 9462
38:19 "I am afraid of the Jews who *have* **g over** to 5877
39: 9 along with those who *had* **g over** to him, 5877
Jer 44:14 of the remnant of Judah who *have* g to live 995
48:11 *she has* not g into exile. 2143
48:33 Joy and gladness *are* g from the orchards 665
48:36 The wealth they acquired *is* **g.** 6
48:45 for a fire *has* **g out** from Heshbon, 3655
51: 7 therefore they *have now* **g mad.** 2147
52:15 of the craftsmen and those who *had* **g over** 5877
La 1: 3 Judah *has* **g into exile.** 1655
1: 5 Her children *have* g *into* exile, 2143
1:18 My young men and maidens *have* g 2143
3:18 "My splendor *is* g and all that I had hoped 6
5:14 The elders *are* g from the city gate; 8697
5:15 Joy *is* g *from* our hearts; 8697
Eze 11:16 in the countries where *they have* **g.'** 995
13: 5 not **g up** to the breaks in the wall to repair it 6590
13:15 "The wall is g and so are those who 401
19: 5 her expectation **g,** she took another 6
23:31 *You have* g the way of your sister; 2143
27:34 and all your company *have* **g down** 5877
31:17 *had* also **g down** to the grave with it, 3718
36:21 among the nations where *they had* **g.** 995
36:22 among the nations where *you have* **g.** 995
37:11 'Our bones are dried up and our hope *is* **g;** 6
37:21 of the nations where *they have* **g.** 2143
45: 9 You have **g far enough,** O princes of Israel! 8041
46:12 he shall go out, and after he *has* **g out,** 3655
Da 2:14 *had* **g out** to put to death the wise men 10485
10:17 My strength *is* g and I can hardly breathe." 928+4202+6641
Hos 4:18 Even when their drinks *are* **g,** 6073
8: 9 For they *have* **g up** *to* Assyria like 6590
Jnh 1: 5 But Jonah *had* g below deck, 3718
Zec 1:11 *"We have* g throughout the earth and found 2143
Mal 3: 4 as in days **g by,** as in former years. 6409
Mt 2:13 *When they had* **g,** an angel of the Lord *432*
9:28 *When he had* g indoors, *2262*
Mk 1:19 *When he had* g a little **farther,** *4581*
5:30 At once Jesus realized that power *had* **g out** *2002*
7:30 and the demon **g.** *2002*
9:28 *After* Jesus *had* g indoors, *1656*
Lk 2:15 the angels had left them and g into heaven, *NIG*
8:30 because many demons *had* **g into** him. *1656*
8:35 the man from whom the demons *had* **g out,** *2002*
8:38 from whom the demons *had* **g out** begged *2002*
8:46 I know that power *has* **g out** from me." *2002*
16: 9 so that when *it is* **g,** *1722*
19: 7 *"He has* g to be the guest of a 'sinner.' " *1656*
Jn 2: 3 *When* the wine *was* **g,** *5728*
3:13 No one *has* ever g into heaven except *326*
4: 8 (His disciples *had* g into the town *599*
6:22 but that they *had* **g away** alone. *599*
7:50 who *had* g to Jesus earlier and who was one *2262*
12:19 how the whole world *has* g after him!" *599*
13:31 When *he was* **g,** Jesus said, *2002*
Ac 8:27 This man *had* g to Jerusalem to worship, *2262*
9:23 After many days *had* **g by,** *4444*
10: 7 When the angel who spoke to him *had* **g,** *599*
16:19 that their hope of making money *was* **g,** *2002*
20:25 among whom *I have* **g about** preaching *1451*
27:21 the men *had* g a long time without food, *5639*
27:33 in constant suspense and have **g** *NIG*
Ro 10:18 "Their voice *has* **g out** into all the earth, *2002*
2Co 5:17 the old *has* **g,** the new has come! *4216*
11:27 **I have** often **g without sleep;** *71+1877*
11:27 and thirst and have often **g without food;** *3763*
2Ti 4:10 has deserted me and *has* g to Thessalonica. *4513*
4:10 Crescens has g to Galatia, *NIG*
Heb 4:14 a great high priest *who has* **g through** *1451*
1Pe 3:22 who *has* g into heaven and is *4513*
1Jn 4: 1 because many false prophets *have* **g out** *2002*
2Jn 1: 7 *have* **g out** into the world. *2002*
Rev 12:12 because the devil *has* **g down** to you! *2849*
18:14 'The fruit you longed for *is* **g from** you. *599*

GONG (1)

1Co 13: 1 a resounding g or a clanging cymbal. *5910*

GOOD (601) [BETTER, BEST, GOODNESS]

Ge 1: 4 God saw that the light was **g,** 3202
1:10 And God saw that it was **g.** 3202
1:12 And God saw that it was **g.** 3202
1:18 And God saw that it was **g.** 3202
1:21 And God saw that it was **g.** 3202
1:25 And God saw that it was **g.** 3202
1:31 and it was very **g.** 3202
2: 9 trees that were pleasing to the eye and g 3202
2: 9 and the tree of the knowledge of g and evil. 3202
2:12 (The gold of that land is **g;** 3202
2:17 not eat from the tree of the knowledge of g 3202
2:18 "It is not g for the man to be alone. 3202
3: 5 like God, knowing g and evil." 3202
3: 6 fruit of the tree was g for food and pleasing 3202
3:22 like one of us, knowing g and evil. 3202
15:15 in peace and be buried at a g old age. 3202
20: 3 "You *are* **as g as dead** because of 4637
24:10 taking with him all kinds of **g things** 3206
25: 8 at a g old age, an old man and full of years; 3202
25:32 **"What** *g* is the birthright to me?" AIT
30:11 Then Leah said, "What **g fortune!"** 1513
31:24 to say anything to Jacob, either g or bad." 3202
31:29 to say anything to Jacob, either g or bad.' 3202
34:18 Their proposal seemed g *to* Hamor 3512
41: 5 Seven heads of grain, healthy and **g,** 3202
41:22 full and **g,** growing on a single stalk. 3202
41:24 of grain swallowed up the seven g heads. 3202
Ge 41:26 The seven g cows are seven years, 3202
41:26 the seven g heads of grain are seven years; 3202
41:35 of these g years that are coming and store 3202
41:37 The plan seemed g to Pharaoh and 3512
44: 4 'Why have you repaid g with evil? 3208
49:15 When he sees how g is his resting place 3202
50:20 God intended it for g to accomplish what is 3208
Ex 3: 8 into a g and spacious land, a land flowing 3202
18: 9 the **g things** the LORD had done for Israel 3208
18:17 "What you are doing is not **g.** 3202
Lev 5: 4 takes an oath to **do** anything, whether g 3512
27:10 not exchange it or substitute a g one for 3202
27:10 or a bad one for a g *one;* 3202
27:12 who will judge its quality as g or bad. 3202
27:14 the priest will judge its quality as g or bad. 3202
27:33 He must not pick out the g from the bad 3202
Nu 10:29 for the LORD has promised **g** *things* 3202
10:32 we will share with you whatever g things 3202
13:19 Is it g or bad? 3202
14: 7 through and explored is exceedingly **g.** 3202
24:13 g or bad, to go beyond the command of 3208
Dt 1:14 "What you propose to do is **g."** 3202
1:23 The idea seemed g to me; 3512
1:25 "It is a g land that the LORD our God 3202
1:35 the g land I swore to give your forefathers, 3202
1:39 your children who do not yet know g 3202
3:25 Let me go over and see the g land beyond 3202
4:21 not cross the Jordan and enter the g land 3202
4:22 over and take possession of that g land. 3202
5:28 Everything they said *was* **g.** 3512
6:11 with all kinds of **g things** you did 3206
6:18 and g in the LORD's sight, 3202
6:18 and you may go in and take over the g land 3202
8: 7 God is bringing you into a g land— 3202
8:10 for the g land he has given you. 3202
9: 6 LORD your God is giving you this g land 3202
10:13 I am giving you today for your own **g?** 3202
11:17 from the g land the LORD is giving you. 3202
12:28 be doing what is g and right in the eyes of 3202
18:17 "What they say *is* **g.** 3512
26:11 among you shall rejoice in all the g *things* 3202
Jos 9:25 to us whatever seems g and right to you." 3202
10: 2 and all its men were **g fighters.** 1475
21:45 of all the LORD's g promises to the house 3202
23:13 until you perish from this g land, 3202
23:14 and soul that not one of all the g promises 3202
23:15 But just as every g promise of 3202
23:15 from this g land he has given you. 3202
23:16 from the g land he has given you." 3202
24:20 after *he has been* g to you." 3512
Jdg 8:32 of Joash died at a g old age and was buried 3202
8:35 for all the **g things** he had done for them. 3208
9:11 'Should I give up my fruit, so g and sweet, 3202
9:16 in **g faith** when you made Abimelech king, 9459
9:19 and in **g faith** toward Jerub-Baal 9459
17:13 I know that the LORD *will be* g to me, 3512
18: 9 We have seen that the land is very **g.** 3202
Ru 2:22 "It will be g for you, my daughter, 3202
3: 7 and drinking and *was* **in g spirits,** 3512+4213
3:13 in the morning if he wants to redeem, **g;** 3202
1Sa 1:23 only *may* the LORD **make g** his word." 7756
2:24 not a g report that I hear spreading among 3202
2:32 Although g *will be* **done** *to* Israel, 3512
3:18 let him do what is g in his eyes." 3202
9:10 **"G,"** Saul said to his servant. 3202
11:10 you can do to us whatever seems g to you." 3202
12:14 follow the LORD your God—**g!** NIH
12:21 *They can* **do** you no **g,** 3603
12:23 I will teach you the way that is g and right. 3208
15: 9 everything that was **g.** 3202
19:10 night David **made g** *his* **escape.** 2256+4880+5674
24:18 You have just now told me of the g you did 3208
25: 6 **G health** to you and your household! 8934
25: 6 And **g health** to all that is yours! 8934
25:15 Yet these men were very g to us. 3202
25:21 He has paid me back evil for **g.** 3208
25:30 for my master every **g thing** he promised 3208
25:33 May you be blessed for your **g judgment** 3248
26:16 What you have done is not **g.** 3202
2Sa 3:13 **"G,"** said David. 3202
4:10 and thought he was **bringing g news,** 1413
7:28 and you have promised these **g things** 3208
10:12 The LORD will do what is g in his sight." 3202
13:22 either g or bad; he hated Amnon 3202
14:17 an angel of God in discerning g and evil. 3202
15:26 let him do to me whatever seems g to him." 3202
16:12 and repay me with g for the cursing 3208
17: 4 This plan seemed g to Absalom and to all 3837
17: 7 Ahithophel has given is not g this time. 3202
17:14 to frustrate the g advice of Ahithophel 3202
18:25 "If he is alone, he must have **g news."** 1415
18:26 "He *must be* **bringing g news,** too." 1413
18:27 "He's a g man," the king said. 3202
18:27 "He comes with g news." 3202
18:31 "My lord the king, **hear** *the* **g news!** 1413
19:35 Can I tell the difference between what is g 3202
1Ki 1:42 like you must be bringing g news." 3202
2:38 "What you say is **g.** 3202
2:42 'What you say is **g.** 3202
7:10 with large stones of **g quality,** 3701
8:56 of all the g promises he gave 3202
8:66 joyful and glad in heart for all the **g things** 3208
14:13 the God of Israel, has found anything **g.** 3202
14:15 He will uproot Israel from this g land 3202
18:24 all the people said, "What you say is **g."** 3202
20:33 **took** *this* **as a g sign** 5727
22: 8 because he never prophesies *anything* g 3202

1Ki	22:18	that he never prophesies *anything* **g**	3202
2Ki	3:19	You will cut down every **g** tree,	3202
	3:19	and ruin every **g** field with stones."	3202
	3:25	on every **g** field until it was covered.	3202
	3:25	the springs and cut down every **g** tree.	3202
	7: 9	a day of **g news** and we are keeping it	1415
	20: 3	and have done what is **g** in your eyes."	3202
	20:19	of the LORD you have spoken is **g**,"	3202
1Ch	4:40	They found rich, **g** pasture,	3202
	13: 2	"If it seems **g** to you and if it is the will of	3202
	16:34	Give thanks to the LORD, for he is **g**;	3202
	17:26	You have promised these **g things**	3208
	19:13	The LORD will do what is **g** in his sight."	3202
	28: 8	that you may possess this **g** land and pass it	3202
	29:28	He died at a **g** old age,	3202
2Ch	5:13	"He is **g**; his love endures forever."	3202
	7: 3	saying, "He is **g**; his love endures forever."	3202
	7:10	the **g things** the LORD had done for David	3208
	12:12	Indeed, there was some **g** in Judah.	3202
	14: 2	Asa did what was **g** and right in the eyes of	3202
	18: 7	because he never prophesies *anything* **g**	3208
	18:17	that he never prophesies *anything* **g**	3202
	19: 3	There is, however, some **g** in you,	3202
	24:16	because of the **g** he had done in Israel	3208
	30:18	saying, "May the LORD, who is **g**,	3202
	30:22	who showed **g** understanding of the service	3202
	31:20	doing what was **g** and right and faithful	3202
Ezr	3:11	they sang to the LORD: "He is **g**;	3202
	7:28	and who has extended his **g favor** to me	2876
	9:12	and eat the **g things** *of* the land and leave it	3206
Ne	2:18	So they began this **g work.**	3208
	5: 5	and though our sons are **as g as** theirs,	3869
	6:19	they kept reporting to me his **g deeds** and	3208
	9:13	and decrees and commands that are **g**.	3202
	9:20	You gave your **g** Spirit to instruct them.	3202
	9:25	of houses filled with all kinds of **g things,**	3206
	9:36	and the other **g things** it *produces.*	3206
Est	10: 3	because he worked for the **g** of his people	3202
Job	2:10	Shall we accept **g** from God,	3202
	21:25	never having enjoyed anything **g**.	3208
	22:18	with **g** *things,* so I stand aloof from	3202
	30:26	Yet when I hoped for **g**, evil came;	3202
	34: 4	let us learn together what is **g**.	3202
	39:17	with wisdom or give her a share of **g sense.**	1069
Ps	4: 6	"Who can show us any **g**?"	3202
	13: 6	for *he has* **been g** to me.	1694
	14: 1	there is no one who does **g**.	3202
	14: 3	there is no one who does **g**, not even one.	3202
	16: 2	apart from you I have no **g thing.**"	3208
	25: 7	for you are **g**, O LORD.	3206
	25: 8	**G** and upright is the LORD;	3202
	34: 8	Taste and see that the LORD is **g**;	3202
	34:10	those who seek the LORD lack no **g** *thing.*	3202
	34:12	and desires to see many **g** days,	3202
	34:14	Turn from evil and do **g**;	3202
	35:12	for **g** and leave my soul forlorn.	3208
	36: 3	he has ceased to be wise and to **do g.**	3512
	37: 3	Trust in the LORD and do **g**;	3202
	37:27	Turn from evil and do **g**;	3202
	38:20	Those who repay my **g** with evil	3208
	38:20	when I pursue *what* is **g**.	3202
	39: 2	not even saying *anything* **g**,	3202
	51:18	In your **g pleasure** make Zion prosper;	8356
	52: 3	You love evil rather than **g**,	3202
	52: 9	for your name is **g**.	3202
	53: 1	there is no one who does **g**.	3202
	53: 3	there is no one who does **g**, not even one.	3202
	54: 6	O LORD, for it is **g**.	3202
	65: 4	with the **g things** *of* your house,	3206
	73: 1	Surely God is **g** to Israel,	3202
	73:28	But as for me, it is **g** to be near God.	3202
	84:11	no **g** *thing* does he withhold	3202
	85:12	The LORD will indeed give what is **g**,	3202
	86: 5	You are forgiving and **g**, O Lord,	3202
	92: 1	It is **g** to praise the LORD and make music	3202
	100: 5	LORD is **g** and his love endures forever;	3202
	103: 5	with **g** *things* so that your youth is renewed	3202
	104:28	they are satisfied with **g** *things.*	3202
	106: 1	Give thanks to the LORD, for he is **g**;	3202
	107: 1	Give thanks to the LORD, for he is **g**;	3202
	107: 9	and fills the hungry with **g** *things.*	3202
	109: 5	They repay me evil for **g**,	3208
	111:10	all who follow his precepts have **g** understanding.	3202
	112: 5	**G** will come to him who is generous	3202
	116: 7	for the LORD *has been* **g** to you.	1694
	118: 1	Give thanks to the LORD, for he is **g**;	3202
	118:29	Give thanks to the LORD, for he is **g**;	3202
	119:17	**Do g** to your servant, and I will live;	1694
	119:39	for your laws are **g**.	3202
	119:65	Do **g** to your servant according	3202
	119:66	Teach me knowledge and **g** judgment,	3206
	119:68	You are **g**, and what you do is good;	3202
	119:68	You are good, and *what you* **do** is **g**;	3512
	119:71	It was **g** for me to be afflicted so	3202
	125: 4	**Do g**, O LORD, to those who are good,	3512
	125: 4	Do good, O LORD, to those *who* are **g**,	3202
	133: 1	How **g** and pleasant it is	3202
	135: 3	Praise the LORD, for the LORD is **g**;	3202
	136: 1	Give thanks to the LORD, for he is **g**.	3202
	143:10	may your **g** Spirit lead me on level ground.	3202
	145: 9	The LORD is **g** to all;	3202
	147: 1	How **g** it is to sing praises to our God,	3202
Pr	2: 9	and fair—every **g** path.	3202
	2:20	the ways of **g** *men* and keep to the paths of	3202
	3: 4	and a **g** name in the sight of God and man.	3202
	3:27	not withhold **g** from those who deserve it,	3202

Pr	11:23	The desire of the righteous ends only in **g**,	3202
	11:27	He who seeks **g** finds goodwill,	3202
	12: 2	A **g** *man* obtains favor from the LORD,	3202
	12:14	of his lips a man is filled with **g** *things* as	3202
	13: 2	the fruit of his lips a man enjoys **g** *things,*	3202
	13:15	**G** understanding wins favor,	3202
	13:22	A **g** *man* leaves an inheritance	3202
	14:14	and the **g** man rewarded for his.	3202
	14:19	down in the presence of the **g**,	3202
	14:22	But those who plan *what* is **g** find love	3202
	15: 3	keeping watch on the wicked and the **g**.	3202
	15:23	and how **g** is a timely word!	3202
	15:30	and **g** news gives health to the bones.	3202
	16:29	and leads him down a path that is not **g**.	3202
	17:13	If a man pays back evil for **g**,	3208
	17:22	A cheerful heart *is* **g** medicine,	3512
	17:26	It is not **g** to punish an innocent man,	3202
	18: 5	It is not **g** to be partial to the wicked or	3202
	18:22	a wife finds *what* is **g** and receives favor	3202
	19: 2	It is not **g** to have zeal without knowledge,	3202
	20:14	"It's **no g**, it's no good!"	8273
	20:14	"It's no good, it's **no g!**"	8273
	22: 1	**g** name is more desirable than great riches;	NIH
	24:13	Eat honey, my son, for it is **g**;	3202
	24:23	To show partiality in judging is not **g**:	3202
	25:25	is **g** news from a distant land.	3202
	25:27	It is not **g** to eat too much honey,	3202
	28:10	the blameless will receive a **g** inheritance.	3202
	28:21	To show partiality is not **g**—	3202
	31:12	She brings him **g**, not harm,	3202
Ecc	2: 1	with pleasure to find out *what* is **g**."	3202
	3:12	to be happy and do **g** while they live.	3202
	4: 9	because they have a **g** return for their work:	3202
	5:18	Then I realized that it is **g** and proper for	3202
	6:12	For who knows what is **g** for a man in life,	3202
	7: 1	A **g** name is better than fine perfume,	3202
	7: 3	because a sad face is **g** *for* the heart.	3512
	7:11	is a **g** *thing* and benefits those who see	3202
	7:14	When times are **g**, be happy;	3208
	7:18	It is **g** to grasp the one and not let go of	3202
	9: 2	the **g** and the bad,	3202
	9: 2	As it is with the **g** *man,* so with the sinner;	3202
	9:18	but one sinner destroys much **g**.	3208
	12:14	whether it is **g** or evil.	3202
Isa	5: 2	Then he looked for a crop of **g grapes,**	6694
	5: 4	When I looked for **g grapes,**	6694
	5:20	Woe to those who call evil **g** and good evil,	3202
	5:20	Woe to those who call evil good and **g** evil,	3202
	38: 3	and have done what is **g** in your eyes."	3202
	39: 8	of the LORD you have spoken is **g**,"	3202
	40: 9	You *who* **bring g tidings** *to* Zion,	1413
	40: 9	You *who* **bring g tidings** *to* Jerusalem,	1413
	41: 7	He says of the welding, "It is **g**."	3202
	41:23	**Do** *something,* whether **g**	3512
	41:27	I gave to Jerusalem a **messenger of g tidings.**	1413
	52: 7	the feet of *those who* **bring g news,**	1413
	52: 7	who proclaim peace, who bring **g** tidings,	3202
	55: 2	Listen, listen to me, and eat *what* is **g**,	3202
	61: 1	to **preach g news** *to* the poor.	1413
	63: 7	the many **g things** he has done for the house	3206
	65: 2	who walk in ways not **g**,	3202
	65: 8	'Don't destroy it, there is yet *some* **g** in it,'	1388
Jer	4:22	they know not how to **do g**,"	3512
	5:25	your sins have deprived you of **g**.	3202
	6:16	ask where the **g** way is, and walk in it,	3202
	8:15	We hoped for peace but no **g** has come,	3202
	10: 5	they can do no harm nor *can* they **do** *any* **g**.	3512
	13:23	Neither can you **do g** who are accustomed	3512
	14:19	We hoped for peace but no **g** has come,	3202
	15:11	"Surely I will deliver you for a **g** *purpose;*	3202
	16:19	worthless idols *that* **did** them no **g**.	3603
	18:10	reconsider the **g** I had intended to **do**	3208+3512
	18:20	Should **g** be repaid with evil?	3208
	21:10	to do this city harm and not **g**,	3208
	24: 2	One basket had very **g** figs,	3202
	24: 3	"The **g** ones are very good,	3202
	24: 3	"The good ones are very **g**,	3202
	24: 5	'Like these **g** figs,	3202
	24: 5	I regard as **g** the exiles from Judah,	3208
	24: 6	My eyes will watch over them for their **g**,	3208
	26:14	with me whatever you think is **g** and right.	3202
	29:32	the **g** *things* I will do for my people,	3202
	32:39	for their own **g** and the good	3202
	32:39	and the **g** of their children after them.	NIH
	32:40	I will never stop **doing g** *to* them,	3512
	32:41	I will rejoice in **doing** them **g**	3201
	33: 9	on earth that hear of all the **g things** I do	3208
	33:11	for the LORD is **g**;	3202
	38: 4	the **g** of these people but their ruin."	8934
	44:27	over them for harm, not for **g**;	3208
La	3:25	LORD is **g** to those whose hope is in him,	3202
	3:26	it is **g** to wait quietly for the salvation of	3202
	3:27	It is **g** for a man to bear the yoke	3202
	3:38	that both calamities and **g** *things* come?	3202
Eze	17: 8	in **g** soil by abundant water so	3202
	20:25	not **g** and laws they could not live by;	3202
	30:22	the **g** arm as well as the broken one,	2617
	34:14	I will tend them in a **g** pasture,	3202
	34:14	There they will lie down in **g** grazing land,	3202
	34:18	for you to feed on the **g** pasture?	3202
Da	3:15	and worship the image I made, very **g**.	NIH
Hos	8: 3	But Israel has rejected what is **g**;	3202
Am	5:14	Seek **g**, not evil, that you may live.	3202
	5:15	love **g**; maintain justice in the courts.	3202
	9: 4	upon them for evil and not for **g**."	3208
Jnh	2: 9	What I have vowed *I will* **make g.**	8966

Mic	2: 7	"*Do* not my words **do g**	3512
	3: 2	you who hate **g** and love evil;	3202
	6: 8	He has showed you, O man, what is **g**.	3202
Na	1: 7	LORD is **g**, a refuge in times of trouble.	3202
	1:15	the feet of *one who* **brings g news,**	1413
Zep	1:12	'The LORD will do nothing, either **g** or bad.'	3512
Zec	8:15	"so now I have determined to **do g** again	3512
Mal	2:17	"All who do evil are **g** in the eyes of	3202
Mt	3:10	that does not produce **g** fruit will be cut	*2819*
	4:23	preaching the **g news** of the kingdom,	*2295*
	5:13	*It is* no longer **g** for anything,	*2710*
	5:16	that they may see your **g** deeds	*2819*
	5:45	to rise on the evil and the **g**,	*19*
	6:22	If your eyes are **g**,	*604*
	7:11	know how to give **g** gifts to your children,	*19*
	7:11	will your Father in heaven give **g** gifts	*19*
	7:17	Likewise every **g** tree bears good fruit,	*19*
	7:17	Likewise every good tree bears **g** fruit,	*2819*
	7:18	A **g** tree cannot bear bad fruit,	*19*
	7:18	and a bad tree cannot bear **g** fruit.	*2819*
	7:19	not bear **g** fruit is cut down and thrown into	*2819*
	9:35	preaching the **g news** of the kingdom	*2295*
	11: 5	**the g news is preached** to the poor.	*2294*
	11:26	Yes, Father, for this was your **g pleasure.**	*2306*
	12:12	it is lawful to do **g** on the Sabbath."	*2822*
	12:33	"Make a tree **g** and its fruit will be good,	*2819*
	12:33	"Make a tree good and its fruit will be **g**,	*2819*
	12:34	how can you who are evil say anything **g?**	*19*
	12:35	The **g** man brings good things out of	*19*
	12:35	The good man brings **g** *things* out of	*19*
	12:35	of the **g** stored up in him,	*19*
	13: 8	Still other seed fell on **g** soil,	*2819*
	13:23	on **g** soil is the man who hears the word	*2819*
	13:24	of heaven is like a man who sowed **g** seed	*2819*
	13:27	'Sir, didn't you sow **g** seed in your field?	*2819*
	13:37	"The one who sowed the **g** seed is the Son	*2819*
	13:38	**g** seed stands for the sons of the kingdom.	*2819*
	13:48	Then they sat down and collected the **g** fish	*2819*
	16:26	What **g** *will it be* **for** a man if he gains the	*6067*
	17: 4	"Lord, it is **g** for us to be here.	*2819*
	19:16	what **g** *thing* must I do to get eternal life?"	*19*
	19:17	"Why do you ask me about what is **g?**"	*19*
	19:17	"There is only One who is **g**.	*19*
	22:10	people they could find, both **g** and bad,	*19*
	24:46	It will be **g** for that servant whose master	*3421*
	25:21	'Well done, **g** and faithful servant!	*19*
	25:23	'Well done, **g** and faithful servant!	*19*
Mk	1:14	proclaiming the **g news** of God.	*2295*
	1:15	Repent and believe the **g news!**"	*2295*
	3: 4	to do **g** or to do evil, to save life or to kill?"	*19*
	4: 8	Still other seed fell on **g** soil.	*2819*
	4:20	Others, like seed sown on **g** soil,	*2819*
	8:36	What **g** *is it* for a man to gain	*6067*
	9: 5	"Rabbi, it is **g** for us to be here.	*2819*
	9:50	"Salt is **g**, but if it loses its saltiness,	*2819*
	10:17	"**G** teacher," he asked,	*19*
	10:18	"Why do you call me **g?**"	*19*
	10:18	"No one is **g**—except God alone.	*19*
	12:28	that Jesus had given them a **g** answer,	*2822*
	16:15	Go into all the world and preach the **g news**	*2295*
Lk	1: 3	*it* **seemed g** also to me to write	*1506*
	1:19	**tell** you this **g news.**	*2294*
	1:53	He has filled the hungry *with* **g** *things*	*19*
	2:10	*I* **bring** you **g news** of great joy that will be	*2294*
	3: 9	that does not produce **g** fruit will be cut	*2819*
	3:18	people and **preached the g news** to them.	*2294*
	4:18	*to* **preach g news** to the poor.	*2294*
	4:43	"I must **preach the g news** of the kingdom	*2294*
	6: 9	*to* **do g** or to do evil,	*16*
	6:27	do **g** to those who hate you,	*2822*
	6:33	if *you* **do g** to those who are good to you,	*16*
	6:33	if you do good *to* those who **are g** to you,	*16*
	6:35	But love your enemies, **do g** to them,	*16*
	6:38	A **g** measure, pressed down,	*2819*
	6:43	"No **g** tree bears bad fruit,	*2819*
	6:43	nor does a bad tree bear **g** fruit.	*2819*
	6:45	The **g** man brings good things out of	*19*
	6:45	The good man brings **g** things out of	*19*
	6:45	of the **g** stored up in his heart,	*19*
	7:22	**the g news** *is* **preached** to the poor.	*2294*
	8: 1	**proclaiming the g news** of the kingdom	*2294*
	8: 8	Still other seed fell on **g** soil.	*19*
	8:15	But the seed on **g** soil stands for those with	*2819*
	8:15	for those with a noble and **g** heart,	*19*
	9:25	What **g** *is it* for a man to gain	*6067*
	9:33	"Master, it is **g** for us to be here.	*2819*
	10:21	Yes, Father, for this was your **g pleasure.**	*2306*
	11:13	know how to give **g** gifts to your children,	*19*
	11:34	When your eyes are **g**,	*604*
	12:16	of a certain rich man **produced a g crop.**	*2369*
	12:19	"You have plenty of **g** *things* laid up	*19*
	12:37	It will be **g** for those servants whose master	*3421*
	12:38	It will be **g** for those servants whose master	*3421*
	12:43	It will be **g** for that servant whom	*3421*
	14:34	"Salt is **g**, but if it loses its saltiness,	*2819*
	16:16	**the g news** of the kingdom of God *is being* **preached,**	*2294*
	16:25	in your lifetime you received your **g** *things,*	*19*
	18:18	A certain ruler asked him, "**G** teacher,	*19*
	18:19	"Why do you call me **g?**"	*19*
	18:19	"No one is **g**—except God alone.	*19*
	19:17	" 'Well done, my **g** servant!'	*19*
	23:50	a **g** and upright man,	*19*
Jn	1:46	Can anything **g** come from there?"	*19*
	5:29	those who have done **g** will rise to live,	*19*
	7:12	Some said, "He is a **g** *man.*"	*19*
	10:11	"I am the **g** shepherd.	*2819*

Jn 10:11 g shepherd lays down his life for the sheep. *2819*
10:14 "I am the g shepherd; *2819*
16:7 *It is* **for** your g that I am going away. *5237*
18:14 that *it would be* g if one man died for *5237*
Ac 5:42 **proclaiming the** g **news** that Jesus is *2294*
8:12 *as he* **preached the** g **news** of the kingdom *2294*
8:35 **told** him **the** g **news about** Jesus. *2294*
9:36 who was always doing g and helping *19*
10:33 and it was g of you to come. *2822*
10:36 **telling the** g **news** of peace *2294*
10:38 around **doing** g and healing all who were *2308*
11:20 **telling** them **the** g **news about** the Lord *2294*
11:24 He was a g man, *19*
13:32 **tell** you **the** g **news:** *2294*
14:7 where they continued *to* **preach the** g **news.** *2294*
14:15 We are **bringing** you g **news,** *2294*
14:21 *They* **preached the** g **news** in that city *2294*
15:28 *It* **seemed** g to the Holy Spirit and to us not *1506*
17:18 because Paul *was* **preaching the** g **news** *2294*
19:25 "Men, you know we receive a g **income** *2345*
19:27 our trade *will* **lose** its g **name,** *591+1650+2262*
23:1 to God *in* all g conscience to this day." *19*
Ro 2:7 by persistence in doing g seek glory, *19*
2:10 honor and peace for everyone who does g: *19*
3:8 "Let us do evil that g may result"? *19*
3:12 there is no one who does g, not even one." *5983*
4:19 the fact that his body was **as** g **as dead** *2453+3739*
5:7 g *man* someone might possibly dare to die. *19*
7:12 the commandment is holy, righteous and g. *19*
7:13 Did that which is g, then, become death to *19*
7:13 produced death in me through what was g, *19*
7:16 I agree that the law is g. *2819*
7:18 I know that nothing g lives in me, that is, *19*
7:18 For I have the desire to do what is g, *NIG*
7:19 For what I do is not the g I want to do; *19*
7:21 I want to do g, evil is right there with me. *2819*
8:28 that in all things God works for the g *19*
9:11 the twins were born or had done anything g *19*
10:15 the feet of those who bring g news!" *19*
10:16 not all the Israelites accepted the g **news.** *2295*
12:2 his g, pleasing and perfect will. *19*
12:9 Hate what is evil; cling *to* what is g. *19*
12:21 but overcome evil with g. *19*
13:4 For he is God's servant to do you g. *19*
14:16 not allow what you consider g to be spoken *19*
15:2 of us should please his neighbor for his g, *19*
16:19 but I want you to be wise about what is g, *19*
1Co 5:6 Your boasting is not g. *2819*
7:1 It is g for a man not to marry. *2819*
7:8 It is g for them to stay unmarried, as I am. *2819*
7:26 that it is g for you to remain as you are. *2819*
7:35 I am saying this for your own g, *5239*
10:24 Nobody should seek his own g, *NIG*
10:24 but the g of others. *NIG*
10:33 not seeking my own g but the good *5239*
10:33 not seeking my own good but the g *NIG*
11:17 for your meetings do more harm than g. *3202*
12:7 of the Spirit is given for the common g. *5237*
14:6 what g *will I be* **to** you, *6067*
15:33 "Bad company corrupts g character." *5982*
2Co 5:10 done while in the body, whether g or bad. *19*
6:8 bad report and g **report;** *2367*
9:8 you will abound in every g work. *19*
Gal 4:17 zealous to win you over, but for no g. *2822*
4:18 provided the purpose is g, *2819*
5:7 You were running a g race. *2822*
6:6 in the word must share all g *things* *19*
6:9 Let us not become weary in doing g, *2819*
6:10 let us do g to all people, *19*
6:12 *to* **make a** g **impression** outwardly *2349*
Eph 1:9 of his will according to his g **pleasure,** *2306*
2:10 created in Christ Jesus to do g works, *19*
6:8 for whatever g he does, *19*
Php 1:6 a g work in you will carry it on *19*
2:13 and to act according to his g **purpose.** *2306*
4:14 Yet it was g of you to share in my troubles. *2822*
Col 1:10 bearing fruit in every g work, *19*
1Th 3:6 and *has* **brought** g **news about** your faith *2294*
5:21 Test everything. Hold on to the g. *2819*
2Th 1:11 by his power he may fulfill every g purpose *20*
2:16 by his grace gave us eternal encouragement and g hope, *19*
2:17 and strengthen you in every g deed *19*
1Ti 1:5 from a pure heart and a g conscience and *19*
1:8 that the law is g if one uses it properly. *2819*
1:18 by following them you may fight the g fight, *2819*
1:19 holding on to faith and a g conscience. *19*
2:3 This is g, and pleases God our Savior, *2819*
2:10 but with g deeds, appropriate for women *19*
3:7 also have a g reputation with outsiders, *2819*
4:4 For everything God created is g, *2819*
4:6 you will be a g minister of Christ Jesus, *2819*
4:6 the truths of the faith and *of* the g teaching *2819*
5:10 and is well known for her g deeds, *2819*
5:10 *to* all kinds of g deeds. *19*
5:25 In the same way, g deeds are obvious, *2819*
6:12 Fight the g fight of the faith. *2819*
6:12 when you made your g confession in *2819*
6:13 before Pontius Pilate made the g confession, *2819*
6:18 Command them *to* **do** g, *14*
6:18 to be rich in g deeds, and to be generous *2819*
2Ti 1:14 the g deposit that was entrusted to you— *2819*
2:3 Endure hardship with us like a g soldier *2819*
2:21 the Master and prepared to do any g work. *19*
3:3 brutal, **not lovers of** the g, *920*
3:17 be thoroughly equipped for every g work. *19*
4:7 I have fought the g fight, *2819*
Tit 1:8 **one who loves what is** g, *5787*
1:16 disobedient and unfit for doing anything g. *19*
2:3 but to **teach what is** g. *2815*
2:7 an example by doing what is g. *2819*
2:14 eager to do what is g. *2819*
3:1 to be ready to do whatever is g, *19*
3:8 to devote themselves to doing what is g. *2819*
3:14 to devote themselves to doing what is g, *2819*
Phm 1:6 *of* every g *thing* we have in Christ. *19*
1:15 that you might have him back for g— *NIG*
Heb 5:14 to distinguish g from evil. *2819*
9:11 *of* the g *things* that are already here, *19*
10:1 a shadow *of* the g *things* that are coming— *19*
10:24 one another on toward love and g deeds. *2819*
11:12 so from this one man, and he as g as dead, *NIG*
12:10 but God disciplines us for our g, *5237*
13:9 It is g for our hearts to be strengthened *2819*
13:16 not forget to **do** g and to share with others, *2343*
13:21 with everything g for doing his will, *19*
Jas 1:17 Every g and perfect gift is from above, *19*
2:3 "Here's a g seat for you," *2822*
2:14 What g is it, my brothers, *4055*
2:16 about his physical needs, what g is it? *4055*
2:19 that there is one God. G! *2822+4472*
3:13 Let him show it by his g life, *2819*
3:17 submissive, full of mercy and g fruit, *19*
4:17 the g he ought to do and doesn't do it, *2819*
1Pe 2:3 now that you have tasted that the Lord is g. *5982*
2:12 Live such g lives among the pagans that, *2819*
2:12 they may see your g deeds and glorify God *2819*
2:15 that *by* **doing** g you should silence *16*
2:18 only *to* those who are g and considerate, *19*
2:20 if you suffer *for* **doing** g and you endure it, *16*
3:10 and see g days must keep his tongue *19*
3:11 He must turn from evil and do g; *19*
3:13 to harm you if you are eager to do g? *19*
3:16 against your g behavior in Christ may *19*
3:17 to suffer *for* **doing** g than for doing evil. *16*
3:21 the body but the pledge *of* a g conscience *19*
4:19 and continue to **do** g. *17*
3Jn 1:2 I pray that you *may* **enjoy** g **health** and *5617*
1:11 do not imitate what is evil but what is g. *19*
1:11 Anyone who **does what is** g is from God. *16*

GOOD-BY (8)

Ge 31:28 **kiss** my grandchildren and my daughters g. 5975
Ru 1:14 Orpah **kissed** her mother-in-law g, 5975
1Ki 19:20 **kiss** my father and mother g," 5975
Lk 9:61 but first let me go back and **say** g *698*
Ac 20:1 **said** g and set out for Macedonia. *832*
21:6 *After* **saying** g **to** each other, *571*
2Co 2:13 I **said** g to them and went on to Macedonia. *698*
13:11 Finally, brothers, g. *5897*

GOODLIER, GOODLIEST, GOODLY

(KJV) See ADORNED, BEAUTIFUL, BEST, DELIGHTFUL, FINE, FINEST, FLOURISHING, HANDSOME, HUGE, MIGHTY, PROUD, SPLENDID, WELL-BUILT, WITHOUT EQUAL

GOODMAN (KJV) See HUSBAND, LANDOWNER, OWNER

GOODNESS (20) [GOOD]

Ex 33:19 "I will cause all my g to pass in front 3206
2Ch 6:41 may your saints rejoice in your g. 3202
Ne 9:25 they reveled in your great g. 3206
9:35 enjoying your great g to them in 3206
Ps 23:6 Surely g and love will follow me all 3202
27:13 I will see the g *of* the LORD in the land of 3206
31:19 How great is your g, 3206
69:16 O LORD, out of the g *of* your love; 3202
86:17 Give me a sign of your g, 3208
109:21 out of the g *of* your love, deliver me. 3202
116:12 can I repay the LORD for all his g to me? 9326
142:7 about me because of *your* g to me. 1694
145:7 They will celebrate your abundant g 3206
Ro 15:14 that you yourselves are full *of* g, *20*
Gal 5:22 peace, patience, kindness, g, faithfulness, *20*
Eph 5:9 (for the fruit of the light consists in all g, *20*
Heb 6:5 the g of the word of God and the powers of *2819*
2Pe 1:3 *by* his own glory and g. *746*
1:5 make every effort to add to your faith g; *746*
1:5 and to g, knowledge; *746*

GOODS (26)

Ge 14:11 The four kings seized all the g *of* Sodom 8214
14:16 the g and brought back his relative Lot 8214
14:21 the people and keep the g for yourself." 8214
31:18 the g he had accumulated in Paddan Aram, 8214
31:37 that you have searched through all my g, 3998
36:6 and all the g he had acquired in Canaan, 7871
40:17 In the top basket were all kinds of **baked** g 685+4407+5126
Ex 22:7 or g for safekeeping and they are stolen 3998
Nu 31:9 flocks and g as plunder. 2657
2Ch 21:17 invaded it and carried off all the g found in 8214
Ezr 1:4 with g and livestock, 8214
1:6 with g and livestock, 8214
Ne 13:8 and threw all Tobiah's household g out of 3998
13:20 of g spent the night outside Jerusalem. 4928
Est 3:13 the month of Adar, and to plunder their g. 8965
Ps 62:10 in extortion or take pride in **stolen** g; 1610
Ecc 5:11 g increase, so do those who consume them. 3208
Jer 49:29 be carried off with all their g and camels. 3998
Eze 27:12 because of your great **wealth of** g; 2104
27:18 and great **wealth of** g, 2104
38:12 rich in livestock and g, 7871
38:13 and g and to seize much plunder?" ' 7871
Hab 2:6 to him who piles up **stolen** g 2257+4200+4202
Lk 12:18 there I will store all my grain and my g. *19*
17:31 roof of his house, with his g inside, *5007*
Ac 2:45 Selling their possessions and g, *5638*

GOODWILL (5)

Est 9:30 words of g and assurance— 8934
Pr 11:27 He who seeks good finds g, 8356
14:9 but g is found among the upright. 8356
Ac 7:10 to gain the g of Pharaoh king of Egypt; *5921*
Php 1:15 out of envy and rivalry, but others out of g. *2306*

GOPHER [WOOD] (KJV) See CYPRESS

GORE (3) [GORES, GORING]

Dt 33:17 With them *he will* g the nations, 5590
1Ki 22:11 'With these *you will* g the Arameans 5590
2Ch 18:10 'With these *you will* g the Arameans 5590

GORES (3) [GORE]

Ex 21:28 "If a bull g a man or a woman to death, 5590
21:31 also applies if the bull g a son or daughter. 5590
21:32 If the bull g a male or female slave, 5590

GORGE (22) [GORGED]

Ex 15:9 *I will* g myself *on* them. 4848
Dt 2:24 "Set out now and cross the Arnon G. 5707
2:36 From Aroer on the rim of the Arnon G, 5707
2:36 and from the town in the g, 5707
3:8 from the Arnon G as far as Mount Hermon. 5707
3:12 of Aroer by the Arnon G, 5707
3:16 the Arnon G (the middle of the gorge being 5707
3:16 the Arnon Gorge (the middle of the g being 5707
4:48 on the rim of the Arnon G to Mount Siyon 5707
Jos 12:1 from the Arnon G to Mount Hermon, 5707
12:2 from Aroer on the rim of the Arnon G— 5707
12:2 from the middle of the g— 5707
13:9 from Aroer on the rim of the Arnon G, 5707
13:9 and from the town in the middle of the g, 5707
13:16 from Aroer on the rim of the Arnon G, 5707
13:16 and from the town in the middle of the g, 5707
15:7 the Pass of Adummim south of the g. 5707
2Sa 24:5 south of the town in the g, 5707
2Ki 10:33 from Aroer by the Arnon G through Gilead 5707
2Ch 20:16 and you will find them at the end of the g 5707
Pr 23:20 or g themselves *on* meat, 2361
Eze 32:4 and all the beasts of the earth g *themselves* 8425

GORGED (1) [GORGE]

Rev 19:21 all the birds g *themselves* on their flesh. *5963*

GORGEOUS (KJV) See ELEGANT

GORING (2) [GORE]

Ex 21:29 of g and the owner has been warned but has 5591
21:36 that the bull had the habit of g, 5591

GOSHEN (15)

Ge 45:10 You shall live in the region of G and be 1777
46:28 of him to Joseph to get directions to G. 1777
46:28 When they arrived in the region of G, 1777
46:29 and went to G to meet his father Israel. 1777
46:34 be allowed to settle in the region of G, 1777
47:1 the land of Canaan and are now in G." 824+1777
47:4 please let your servants settle in G." 824+1777
47:6 Let them live in G. 824+1777
47:27 in Egypt in the region of G. 1777
50:8 their flocks and herds were left in G. 824+1777
Ex 8:22 with the land of G, where my people live; 1777
9:26 only place it did not hail was the land of G, 1777
Jos 10:41 and from the whole region of G to Gibeon. 1777
11:16 all the Negev, the whole region of G, 1777
15:51 G, Holon and Giloh— 1777

GOSPEL (96)

Mt 24:14 And this g of the kingdom will be preached *2295*
26:13 wherever this g is preached throughout *2295*
Mk 1:1 The beginning *of* the g about Jesus Christ, *2295*
8:35 for me and for the g will save it. *2295*
10:29 or children or fields for me and the g *2295*
13:10 the g must first be preached to all nations. *2295*
14:9 the g is preached throughout the world, *2295*
Lk 9:6 from village to village, **preaching the** g, *2294*
20:1 in the temple courts and **preaching the** g, *2294*
Ac 8:25 **preaching the** g in many Samaritan villages. *2294*
8:40 **preaching the** g in all the towns *2294*
15:7 from my lips the message *of* the g *2295*
16:10 that God had called us *to* **preach the** g *2294*
20:24 task of testifying to the g of God's grace. *2295*
Ro 1:1 an apostle and set apart for the g of God— *2295*

Ro 1: 2 **the g** he promised beforehand 4005[S]
1: 9 with my whole heart in **preaching** the g 2295
1:15 so eager *to* **preach the g** also to you who 2294
1:16 I am not ashamed of the **g,** 2295
1:17 For in **the g** a righteousness from God 899[S]
2:16 through Jesus Christ, as my **g** declares. 2295
11:28 As far as the **g** is concerned, 2295
15:16 with the priestly duty of **proclaiming** the **g** 2295
15:19 I have fully proclaimed the **g** of Christ. 2295
15:20 *to* **preach the g** where Christ was 2294
16:25 to him who is able to establish you by my **g** 2295
1Co 1:17 but *to* **preach the g—** 2294
4:15 in Christ Jesus I became your father through the **g.** 2295
9:12 up with anything rather than hinder the **g** 2295
9:14 the **g** should receive their living from 2295
9:14 should receive their living from the **g.** 2295
9:16 Yet when *I* **preach the g,** I cannot boast, 2294
9:16 Woe to me if *I do* not **preach the g!** 2294
9:18 that *in* **preaching the g** I may offer it free 2294
9:23 I do all this for the sake of the **g,** 2295
15: 1 to remind you of the **g** I preached to you, 2295
15: 2 By **this g** you are saved, 4005[S]
2Co 2:12 to Troas to **preach** the **g** of Christ and found 2295
4: 3 And even if our **g** is veiled, 2295
4: 4 so that they cannot see the light *of* the **g** of 2295
8:18 by all the churches for his service *to* the **g.** 2295
9:13 that accompanies your confession of the **g** 2295
10:14 for we did get as far as you with the **g** 2295
10:16 *so that we* can **preach the g** in the regions 2294
11: 4 or a different **g** from the one you accepted, 2295
11: 7 to elevate you by **preaching** the **g** 2294+2295
Gal 1: 6 of Christ and are turning to a different **g—** 2295
1: 7 which is really no **g** at all. 257[S]
1: 7 and are trying to pervert the **g** of Christ. 2295
1: 8 from heaven *should* **preach a g** other than 2294
1: 9 **preaching** to you **a g** other than what 2294
1:11 that the **g** I **preached** is not something 2294+2295
2: 2 to a revelation and set before them the **g** 2295
2: 5 the truth *of* the **g** might remain with you. 2295
2: 7 the task *of* **preaching** the **g** to the Gentiles, 2295
2:14 not acting in line with the truth *of* the **g,** 2295
3: 8 **announced the g in advance** 4603
4:13 an illness that *I* first **preached the g** to you. 2294
Eph 1:13 the **g** of your salvation. 2295
3: 6 the **g** the Gentiles are heirs together 2295
3: 7 I became a servant *of* **this g** by the gift 4005[S]
6:15 with the readiness that comes *from* the **g** 2295
6:19 the mystery *of* the **g,** 2295
Php 1: 5 because of your partnership in the **g** from 2295
1: 7 or defending and confirming the **g,** 2295
1:12 to me has really served to advance the **g.** 2295
1:16 that I am put here for the defense *of* the **g.** 2295
1:27 in a manner worthy *of* the **g** of Christ. 2295
1:27 as one man for the faith *of* the **g** 2295
2:22 with me in the work *of* the **g.** 2295
4: 3 at my side in the cause of the **g,** 2295
4:15 *with* the **g,** when I set out from Macedonia, 2295
Col 1: 5 about in the word *of* truth, the **g** 2295
1: 6 All over the world this **g** is bearing fruit NIG
1:23 not moved from the hope held out in the **g.** 2295
1:23 This is the **g** that you heard and NIG
1Th 1: 5 our **g** came to you not simply with words, 2295
2: 2 of our God we dared to tell you his **g** 2295
2: 4 by God to be entrusted with the **g.** 2295
2: 8 not only the **g** of God but our lives as well, 2295
2: 9 to anyone while we preached the **g** of God 2295
3: 2 and God's fellow worker in **spreading** the **g** 2295
2Th 1: 8 and do not obey the **g** of our Lord Jesus. 2295
2:14 He called you to this through our **g,** 2295
1Ti 1:11 to the glorious **g** of the blessed God, 2295
2Ti 1: 8 But join with me in suffering *for* the **g,** 2295
1:10 and immortality to light through the **g.** 2295
1:11 And of **this g** I was appointed a herald and 4005[S]
2: 8 descended from David. This is my **g,** 2295
Phm 1:13 while I am in chains *for* the **g.** 2295
Heb 4: 2 For we also have had **the g preached** *to* us, 2294
4: 6 those who formerly **had the g preached** 2294
1Pe 1:12 by those who *have* **preached the g** to you 2294
4: 6 For this is the reason **the g** *was* **preached** 2294
4:17 be for those who do not obey the **g** of God? 2295
Rev 14: 6 the eternal **g to proclaim** to those 2294+2295

GOSSIP (7) [GOSSIPING, GOSSIPS]

Pr 11:13 A **g** betrays a confidence, 2143+8215
16:28 and a **g** separates close friends. 8087
18: 8 The words of a **g** are like choice morsels; 8087
20:19 A **g** betrays a confidence; 2143+8215
26:20 without **g** a quarrel dies down. 8087
26:22 The words of a **g** are like choice morsels; 8087
2Co 12:20 factions, slander, **g,** arrogance and disorder. 6030

GOSSIPING (1) [GOSSIP]

3Jn 1:10 **g** maliciously **about** us. 5826

GOSSIPS (2) [GOSSIP]

Ro 1:29 and malice. They are **g,** 6031
1Ti 5:13 but also **g** and busybodies, 5827

GOT (159) [GET]

Ge 18:16 When the men **g up** to leave, 7756
19: 1 *he* **g up** to meet them and bowed down 7756
19:27 **Early** the next morning Abraham **g up** 8899
19:33 *they* **g** their father **to drink** wine 9197
19:33 of it when she lay down or when she **g up.** 7756
19:35 *they* **g** their father **to drink** wine 9197
19:35 of it when she lay down or when she **g up.** 7756
21:21 his mother **g** a wife for him from Egypt. 4374
22: 3 **Early** the next morning Abraham **g up** 8899
24:54 When *they* **g up** the next morning, he said, 7756
24:61 Then Rebekah and her maids **g ready** 7756
24:64 *She* **g down** from her camel 5877
25:34 He ate and drank, and then **g up** and left. 7756
27:14 and **g** them and brought them to his mother, 4374
32:22 That night Jacob **g up** and took his two 7756
37:31 Then *they* **g** Joseph's robe, 4374
38: 6 Judah **g** a wife for Er, his firstborn, 4374
Ex 2: 3 *she* **g** a papyrus basket for him and coated it 4374
2: 8 And the girl went and **g** the baby's mother. 7924
2:17 but Moses **g up** and came to their rescue 7756
12:30 and all the Egyptians **g up** during the night, 7756
24: 4 *He* **g up early** the next morning and built 8899
32: 6 down to eat and drink and **g up** to indulge 7756
Nu 16:25 Moses **g up** and went to Dathan 7756
22:13 The next morning Balaam **g up** and said 7756
22:21 Balaam **g up** in the morning, 7756
24:25 Then Balaam **g up** and returned home 7756
Jos 6:12 Joshua **g up early** the next morning and 8899
6:15 *they* **g up** at daybreak and marched around 8899
15:18 When *she* **g off** her donkey, 4946+6584+7563
Jdg 1:14 When *she* **g off** her donkey, 4946+6584+7563
3:26 While they waited, Ehud **g away.** 4880
6:28 when the men of the town **g up,** 8899
7: 6 All the rest **g down** on their knees to drink. 4156
10:16 Then *they* **g rid of** the foreign gods 6073
13:11 Manoah **g up** and followed his wife. 7756
16: 3 Then *he* **g up** and took hold of the doors of 7756
19: 5 On the fourth day *they* **g up early** 8899
19: 7 And when the man **g up** to go, 7756
19: 9 **g up** to leave, his father-in-law, 7756
19:27 When her master **g up** in the morning 7756
20:11 of Israel **g together** and united as one man 665
20:19 The next morning the Israelites **g up** 7756
Ru 2:15 As *she* **g up** to glean, 7756
3:14 **g up** before anyone could be recognized; 7756
1Sa 3: 6 And Samuel **g up** and went to Eli and said, 7756
3: 8 and Samuel **g up** and went to Eli and said, 7756
9:26 When Saul **g ready,** 7756
15:12 **Early** in the morning Samuel **g up** 8899
20:34 Jonathan **g up** from the table 7756
20:41 David **g up** from the south side 7756
25:23 she quickly **g off** her donkey 3718+4946+6584
25:42 Abigail quickly **g on** a donkey and, 8206
28:23 *He* **g up** from the ground and sat on 7756
28:25 That same night *they* **g up** and left. 7756
29:11 and his men **g up early** in the morning 8899
30:17 and none of them **g away,** 4880
2Sa 11: 2 One evening David **g up** from his bed 7756
12:20 Then David **g up** from the ground. 7756
13:29 Then all the king's sons **g up,** 7756
14: 6 *They* **g into a fight** *with* each other in 5897
18: 9 Absalom's head *g* **caught** in the tree. AIT
19: 8 king **g up** and took his seat in the gateway. 7756
24:11 Before David **g up** the next morning, 7756
1Ki 1: 5 **g** chariots and horses **ready,** 6913
3:20 So *she* **g up** in the middle of the night 7756
3:21 *I* **g up** to nurse my son—and he was dead! 7756
14:17 Then Jeroboam's wife **g up** and left 7756
15:12 from the land and **g rid of** all 6073
19: 8 So *he* **g up** and ate and drank, 7756
21:16 he **g up** and went down to take possession 7756
2Ki 1:15 So Elijah **g up** and went down with him to 7756
3: 2 *He* **g rid of** the sacred stone of Baal 6073
3:22 When *they* **g up early** in the morning, 8899
4:30 So *he* **g up** and followed her. 7756
4:34 Then *he* **g on** the bed and lay upon the boy, 6590
4:35 and forth in the room and then **g on** the bed 6590
5:21 *he* **g down** from the chariot to meet him. 5877
5:26 when the man **g down** from his chariot 2200
6:15 of the man of God **g up** and went out early 7756
7: 5 At dusk *they* **g up** and went to the camp of 7756
7: 7 So *they* **g up** and fled in the dusk 7756
7:12 The king **g up** in the night and said 7756
9: 6 Jehu **g up** and went into the house. 7756
9:16 he **g into** *his* **chariot** and rode to Jezreel, 8206
19:35 When *the people* **g up** the next morning— 8899
23:24 Josiah **g rid of** the mediums and spiritists, 1278
2Ch 33:15 *He* **g rid of** the foreign gods and removed 6073
Est 6:11 So Haman **g** the robe and the horse. 4374
7: 7 The king **g up** in a rage, 7756
9: 1 and the Jews **g the upper hand** 8948
9:22 when the Jews **g relief** from their enemies, 5663
Job 1:20 Job **g up** and tore his robe 7756
Isa 37:36 When *the people* **g up** the next morning— 8899
Jer 41: 2 and the ten men who were with him **g up** 7756
Eze 3:23 So *I* **g up** and went out to the plain. 7756
29:18 Yet he and his army **g** no reward from 2118+4200
Da 6:10 Three times a day he **g down** on his knees 10121
6:19 the king **g up** and hurried to the lions' den. 10624
8:27 *I* **g up** and went about the king's business. 7756
Zec 11: 8 In one month *I* **g rid of** 3948
Mt 2:14 So he **g up,** took the child and his mother 1586
2:21 So he **g up,** took the child and his mother 1586
8:15 and *she* **g up** and began to wait on him. 1586
8:23 Then he **g** into the boat 1832
8:26 Then he **g up** and rebuked the winds and 1586
9: 7 And the man **g up** and went home. 1586
9: 9 and Matthew **g up** and followed him. 482
9:19 Jesus **g up** and went with him, 1586
9:25 and *she* **g up.** 1586
13: 2 around him that he **g** into a boat and sat 1832
14:29 Then Peter **g down** out of the boat, 2849
15:39 *he* **g into** the boat and went to the vicinity 1832
22:34 the Pharisees **g together.** 5251
27:48 one of them ran and **g** a sponge. 3284
Mk 1:35 while it was still dark, Jesus **g up,** 482
2:12 *He* **g up,** took his mat and walked out 1586
2:14 and Levi **g up** and followed him. 482
4: 1 that he **g** into a boat and sat in it out on 1832
4:39 *He* **g up,** rebuked the wind and said to 1444
5: 2 *When* Jesus **g out** of the boat, 2002
6:33 from all the towns and **g there ahead of** 4601
6:54 As soon as they **g out** of the boat, 2002
8:10 he **g** into the boat with his disciples 1832
8:13 **g** back into the boat and crossed to 1832
Lk 1:39 At that time Mary **g ready** and hurried to 482
4:29 They **g up,** drove him out of the town, 482
4:39 She **g up** at once and began to wait 482
5: 3 He **g** into one of the boats, 1832
5:28 and Levi **g up,** left everything and followed 482
6: 8 So *he* **g up** and stood there. 2705
8:22 So they **g** into a boat and set out. 1832
8:24 He **g up** and rebuked the wind and 1444
8:37 So he **g** into the boat and left. 1832
14:20 "Still another said, '*I* just **g married,** 1138+1222
15:13 the younger son **g together** all he had, 5251
15:20 So he **g up** and went to his father. 482
24:12 Peter, however, **g up** and ran to the tomb. 482
24:33 They **g up** and returned at once 482
Jn 4:52 as to the time when his son **g** better, 2400
6:17 where *they* **g** into a boat and set off across 1832
6:24 they **g** into the boats and went 1832
11:29 *she* **g up** quickly and went to him. 1586
11:31 noticed how quickly she **g up** and went out, 482
13: 4 so *he* **g up** from the meal, 1586
21: 3 So they went out and **g into** the boat, 1832
Ac 1:18 (With the reward he **g** for his wickedness, NIG
5: 8 the price *you* and Ananias **g** for the land?" 625
9: 8 Saul **g up** from the ground, 1586
9:18 He **g up** and was baptized, 482
9:34 Immediately Aeneas **g up.** 482
9:40 then *he* **g down** on his knees and prayed. 5502
14:20 he **g up** and went back into the city. 482
15: 7 Peter **g up** and addressed them: 482
16:10 *we* **g ready** at once to leave for Macedonia, 2426
21:15 we **g ready** and went up to Jerusalem. 2171
25:18 *When* his accusers **g up** to speak, 2705
28:16 When *we* **g to** Rome, 1656
1Co 10: 7 down to eat and drink and **g up** to indulge 482

GOUGE (4) [GOUGED]

Nu 16:14 *Will you* **g out** the eyes of these men? 5941
1Sa 11: 2 with you only on the condition that I **g out** 5941
Mt 5:29 **g it out** and throw it away, 1975
18: 9 **g it out** and throw it away. 1975

GOUGED (1) [GOUGE]

Jdg 16:21 **g out** his eyes and took him down to Gaza. 5941

GOURD (KJV) See VINE

GOURDS (4)

1Ki 6:18 carved with **g** and open flowers. 7225
7:24 Below the rim, **g** encircled it— 7225
7:24 The **g** were cast in two rows in one piece 7225
2Ki 4:39 of its **g** and filled the fold of his cloak. 7226

GOVERN (17) [GOVERNED, GOVERNING, GOVERNMENT, GOVERNOR, GOVERNOR'S, GOVERNORS, GOVERNS]

Ge 1:16 the greater light to **g** the day and the lesser 4939
1:16 to govern the day and the lesser light to **g** 4939
1:18 to **g** the day and the night, 5440
1Sa 9:17 he *will* **g** my people." 6806
1Ki 3: 9 a discerning heart to **g** your people and 9149
3: 9 For who is able to **g** this great people 9149
2Ch 1:10 for who *is able to* **g** this great people 9149
1:11 for wisdom and knowledge *to* **g** my people 9149
Job 34:17 Can he who hates justice **g?** 2502
Ps 9: 8 *he will* **g** the peoples with justice. 1906
136: 8 the sun to **g** the day, 4939
136: 9 the moon and stars to **g** the night; 4939
Pr 8:16 by me princes **g,** 8606
Isa 3: 4 mere children *will* **g** them. 5440
Ob 1:21 on Mount Zion to **g** the mountains of Esau. 9149
Zec 3: 7 then you *will* **g** my house and have charge 1906
Ro 12: 8 if it is leadership, let him **g** diligently; NIG

GOVERNED (3) [GOVERN]

Jdg 9:22 After Abimelech *had* **g** Israel three years, 8606
2Ki 15: 5 of the palace and **g** the people of the land. 9149
2Ch 26:21 of the palace and **g** the people of the land. 9149

GOVERNING (2) [GOVERN]

Ro 13: 1 *to* the **g** authorities, 5660
13: 6 who give their full time to **g.** 899+4047[S]

GOVERNMENT (4) [GOVERN]

1Ki 9:22 his **g officials,** his officers, his captains, 6269
Isa 9: 6 and the **g** will be on his shoulders. 5385
9: 7 the increase of his **g** and peace there will 5385
Da 6: 4 against Daniel in his conduct of **g affairs,** 10424

GOVERNMENTS (KJV) See ADMINISTRATION

GOVERNOR (50) [GOVERN]

Ge 42: 6 Now Joseph was the **g** of the land, 8954
Jdg 9:30 the **g** *of* the city heard what Gaal son 8569
1Ki 4:19 He was the only **g** over the district. 5907
2Ki 10: 5 So the palace administrator, the city **g**, 889+6584[S]
23: 8 to the Gate of Joshua, the city **g**, 8569
25:23 king of Babylon **appointed** Gedaliah **as g**, 7212
Ezr 2:63 The **g** ordered them not to eat any of 9579
5: 3 Tattenai, **g** *of* Trans-Euphrates, 10580
5: 6 Tattenai, **g** *of* Trans-Euphrates, 10580
5:14 whom he had appointed **g**, 10580
6: 6 Now then, Tattenai, **g** *of* Trans-Euphrates, 10580
6: 7 Let the **g** *of* the Jews and 10580
6:13 Tattenai, **g** *of* Trans-Euphrates, 10580
Ne 3: 7 the authority of the **g** *of* Trans-Euphrates. 7068
5:14 when I was appointed to be their **g** in 7068
5:14 the food allotted to the **g**. 7068
5:18 the food allotted to the **g**, 7068
7:65 The **g**, therefore, ordered them not 9579
7:70 The **g** gave to the treasury 1,000 9579
8: 9 Then Nehemiah the **g**, 9579
10: 1 Nehemiah the **g**, the son of Hacaliah. 9579
12:26 in the days of Nehemiah the **g** and of Ezra 7068
Isa 60:17 I will make peace your **g** 7213
Jer 40: 7 **appointed** Gedaliah son of Ahikam **as g** 7212
40:11 **appointed** Gedaliah son of Ahikam, the son of Shaphan, **as g** 7212
41: 2 the king of Babylon *had* **appointed as g** 7212
41:18 the king of Babylon *had* **appointed as g** 7212
Hag 1: 1 **g** *of* Judah, and to Joshua son 7068
1:14 of Zerubbabel son of Shealtiel, **g** *of* Judah, 7068
2: 2 **g** *of* Judah, to Joshua son of Jehozadak, 7068
2:21 "Tell Zerubbabel **g** *of* Judah that 7068
Mal 1: 8 Try offering them to your **g**! 7068
Mt 27: 2 and handed him over to Pilate, the **g**. *2450*
27:11 Meanwhile Jesus stood before the **g**, *2450*
27:11 and the **g** asked him, "Are you the king *2450*
27:14 to the great amazement of the **g**. *2450*
27:21 want me to release to you?" asked the **g**. *2450*
28:14 If this report gets to the **g**, *2450*
Lk 2: 2 that took place *while* Quirinius *was* **g** *2448*
3: 1 *when* Pontius Pilate *was* **g** of Judea, *2448*
20:20 over to the power and authority *of* the **g**. *2450*
Jn 18:28 to the **palace of the** Roman **g**. *4550*
Ac 23:24 so that he may be taken safely to **G** Felix." *2450*
23:26 *To* His Excellency, **G** Felix: Greetings. *2450*
23:33 the letter *to* the **g** and handed Paul over *2450*
23:34 The **g** read the letter and asked *NIG*
24: 1 against Paul *before* the **g**. *2450*
24:10 When the **g** motioned for him to speak, *2450*
26:30 the **g** and Bernice and those sitting *2450*
2Co 11:32 In Damascus the **g** under King Aretas had *1617*

GOVERNOR'S (2) [GOVERN]

Mt 27:15 Now it was the **g** custom at the Feast *2450*
27:27 Then the **g** soldiers took Jesus into *2450*

GOVERNORS (24) [GOVERN]

1Ki 4: 7 also had twelve **district g** over all Israel, 5893
10:15 and from all the Arabian kings and the **g** *of* 7068
2Ch 9:14 Also all the kings of Arabia and the **g** *of* 7068
Ezr 8:36 and to the **g** *of* Trans-Euphrates, 7068
Ne 2: 7 to the **g** *of* Trans-Euphrates, 7068
2: 9 to the **g** *of* Trans-Euphrates and gave them 7068
5:15 But the earlier **g**—those preceding me— 7068
Est 3:12 satraps, the **g** of the various provinces and 7068
8: 9 the satraps, **g** and nobles of 7068
9: 3 the **g** and the king's administrators helped 7068
Jer 51:23 with you I shatter **g** and officials. 7068
51:28 their **g** and all their officials, 7068
51:57 her **g**, officers and warriors as well; 7068
Eze 23: 6 in blue, **g** and commanders, all 7068
23:12 **g** and commanders, warriors in full dress, 7068
23:23 all of them **g** and commanders, 7068
Da 3: 2 He then summoned the satraps, prefects, **g**, 10580
3: 3 So the satraps, prefects, **g**, advisers, 10580
3:27 **g** and royal advisers crowded around them. 10580
6: 7 advisers and **g** have all agreed that 10580
Mt 10:18 be brought before **g** and kings as witnesses *2450*
Mk 13: 9 On account of me you will stand before **g** *2450*
Lk 21:12 you will be brought before kings and **g**, *2450*
1Pe 2:14 or *to* **g**, who are sent by him *2450*

GOVERNS (1) [GOVERN]

Job 36:31 the way *he* **g** the nations and provides food 1906

GOWN (1)

Ps 45:13 her **g** is interwoven with gold. 4230

GOYIM (1)

Jos 12:23 of Dor (in Naphoth Dor) one the king of **G** 1582

GOZAN (5)

2Ki 17: 6 in **G** on the Habor River and in the towns 1579
18:11 in **G** on the Habor River and in towns of 1579
19:12 the gods of **G**, Haran, 1579
1Ch 5:26 Habor, Hara and the river of **G**, 1579
Isa 37:12 the gods of **G**, Haran, 1579

GRABBED (4)

Jdg 15:15 *he* **g** it and struck down a thousand men. 4374
2Sa 2:16 Then each man **g** his opponent by the head 2616
13:11 she took it to him to eat, *he* **g** her and said, 2616
Mt 18:28 *He* **g** him and began to choke him. *3195*

GRACE (131) [GRACIOUS, GRACIOUSLY]

Ps 45: 2 and your lips have been anointed with **g**, 2834
Pr 1: 9 They will be a garland to **g** your head and 2834
3:22 an **ornament to g** your neck. 2834
3:34 He mocks proud mockers but gives **g** to 2834
4: 9 She will set a garland of **g** on your head 2834
Isa 26:10 Though **g is shown** *to* the wicked, 2858
Jnh 2: 8 to worthless idols forfeit the **g** that could 2876
Zec 12:10 of Jerusalem a spirit of **g** and supplication. 2834
Lk 2:40 and the **g** of God was upon him. *5921*
Jn 1:14 came from the Father, full *of* **g** and truth. *5921*
1:16 of his **g** we have all received one blessing *NIG*
1:17 **g** and truth came through Jesus Christ. *5921*
Ac 4:33 and much **g** was upon them all. *5921*
6: 8 Stephen, a man full *of* God's **g** and power, *5921*
11:23 and saw the evidence of the **g** of God, *5921*
13:43 and urged them to continue in the **g** of God. *5921*
14: 3 the message *of* his **g** by enabling them *5921*
14:26 where they had been committed *to* the **g** *5921*
15:11 the **g** of our Lord Jesus that we are saved, *5921*
15:40 commended by the brothers *to* the **g** of *5921*
18:27 to those who by **g** had believed. *5921*
20:24 task of testifying to the gospel *of* God's **g**. *5921*
20:32 to God and to the word *of* his **g**, *5921*
Ro 1: 5 we received **g** and apostleship *5921*
1: 7 **G** and peace to you from God our Father *5921*
3:24 *by* his **g** through the redemption that came *5921*
4:16 that it may be by **g** and may be guaranteed *5921*
5: 2 by faith into this **g** in which we now stand. *5921*
5:15 how much more did God's **g** and the gift *5921*
5:15 the gift that came by the **g** of the one man, *5921*
5:17 *of* **g** and of the gift of righteousness reign *5921*
5:20 sin increased, **g** increased all the more, *5921*
5:21 so also **g** might reign through righteousness *5921*
6: 1 on sinning so that **g** may increase? *5921*
6:14 because you are not under law, but under **g**. *5921*
6:15 because we are not under law but under **g**? *5921*
11: 5 a remnant chosen by **g**. *5921*
11: 6 And if *by* **g**, then it is no longer by works; *5921*
11: 6 if it were, **g** would no longer be grace. *5921*
11: 6 if it were, grace would no longer be **g**. *5921*
12: 3 the **g** given me I say to every one of you: *5921*
12: 6 according to the **g** given us. *5921*
15:15 because of the **g** God gave me *5921*
16:20 The **g** of our Lord Jesus be with you. *5921*
1Co 1: 3 **G** and peace to you from God our Father *5921*
1: 4 because of his **g** given you in Christ Jesus. *5921*
3:10 By the **g** God has given me, *5921*
15:10 But *by* the **g** of God I am what I am, *5921*
15:10 and his **g** to me was not without effect. *5921*
15:10 not I, but the **g** of God that was with me. *5921*
16:23 The **g** of the Lord Jesus be with you. *5921*
2Co 1: 2 **G** and peace to you from God our Father *5921*
1:12 but according to God's **g**. *5921*
4:15 so that the **g** that is reaching more *5921*
6: 1 not to receive God's **g** in vain. *5921*
8: 1 to know about the **g** that God has given *5921*
8: 6 to completion this **act of g** on your part. *5921*
8: 7 see that you also excel in this **g** of giving. *5921*
8: 9 you know the **g** of our Lord Jesus Christ, *5921*
9: 8 God is able to make all **g** abound to you, *5921*
9:14 of the surpassing **g** God has given you. *5921*
12: 9 he said to me, "My **g** is sufficient for you, *5921*
13:14 May the **g** of the Lord Jesus Christ, *5921*
Gal 1: 3 **G** and peace to you from God our Father *5921*
1: 6 the one who called you by the **g** of Christ *5921*
1:15 from birth and called me by his **g**, *5921*
2: 9 when they recognized the **g** given to me. *5921*
2:21 I do not set aside the **g** of God, *5921*
3:18 but God **in** his **g gave** it to Abraham *5919*
5: 4 you have fallen away from **g**. *5921*
6:18 The **g** of our Lord Jesus Christ be *5921*
Eph 1: 2 **G** and peace to you from God our Father *5921*
1: 6 to the praise *of* his glorious **g**, *5921*
1: 7 in accordance with the riches *of* God's **g** *5921*
2: 5 it is *by* **g** you have been saved. *5921*
2: 7 the incomparable riches *of* his **g**, *5921*
2: 8 For it is *by* **g** you have been saved, *5921*
3: 2 *of* God's **g** that was given to me for you, *5921*
3: 7 *of* God's **g** given me through the working *5921*
3: 8 this **g** was given me: *5921*
4: 7 But to each one of us **g** has been given *5921*
6:24 **G** to all who love our Lord Jesus Christ *5921*
Php 1: 2 **G** and peace to you from God our Father *5921*
1: 7 all of you share in God's **g** with me. *5921*
4:23 The **g** of the Lord Jesus Christ be *5921*
Col 1: 2 **G** and peace to you from God our Father. *5921*
1: 6 and understood God's **g** in all its truth. *5921*
4: 6 Let your conversation be always full of **g**, *5921*
4:18 **G** be with you. *5921*
1Th 1: 1 **G** and peace to you. *5921*
5:28 The **g** of our Lord Jesus Christ be with you. *5921*
2Th 1: 2 **G** and peace to you from God the Father *5921*
1:12 the **g** of our God and the Lord Jesus Christ. *5921*
2:16 and by his **g** gave us eternal encouragement *5921*
3:18 The **g** of our Lord Jesus Christ be with you all. *5921*
1Ti 1: 2 **G**, mercy and peace from God the Father *5921*
1:14 The **g** of our Lord was poured out *5921*
6:21 **G** be with you. *5921*
2Ti 1: 2 **G**, mercy and peace from God the Father *5921*
1: 9 but because of his own purpose and **g**. *5921*
1: 9 This **g** was given us in Christ Jesus before *NIG*
2: 1 be strong in the **g** that is in Christ Jesus. *5921*
4:22 **G** be with you. *5921*
Tit 1: 4 **G** and peace from God the Father *5921*
2:11 For the **g** of God *5921*
3: 7 having been justified *by* his **g**, *5921*
3:15 **G** be with you all. *5921*
Phm 1: 3 **G** to you and peace from God our Father *5921*
1:25 The **g** of the Lord Jesus Christ be *5921*
Heb 2: 9 so that *by* the **g** of God he might taste death *5921*
4:16 Let us then approach the throne *of* **g** *5921*
4:16 and find **g** to help us in our time of need. *5921*
10:29 and who has insulted the Spirit *of* **g**? *5921*
12:15 the **g** of God and that no bitter root grows *5921*
13: 9 for our hearts to be strengthened *by* **g**, *5921*
13:25 **G** be with you all. *5921*
Jas 4: 6 But he gives us more **g**. *5921*
4: 6 "God opposes the proud but gives **g** to the humble." *5921*
1Pe 1: 2 **G** and peace be yours in abundance. *5921*
1:10 who spoke of the **g** that was to come *5921*
1:13 set your hope fully on the **g** to be given you *5921*
4:10 faithfully administering God's **g** *5921*
5: 5 "God opposes the proud but gives **g** to the humble." *5921*
5:10 And the God *of* all **g**, who called you *5921*
5:12 and testifying that this is the true **g** of God. *5921*
2Pe 1: 2 **G** and peace be yours in abundance through *5921*
3:18 in the **g** and knowledge of our Lord *5921*
2Jn 1: 3 **G**, mercy and peace from God the Father *5921*
Jude 1: 4 who change the **g** of our God into a license *5921*
Rev 1: 4 **G** and peace to you from him who is, *5921*
22:21 **g** of the Lord Jesus be with God's people. *5921*

GRACEFUL (3)

Job 41:12 his strength and his **g** form. 2665
Pr 5:19 A loving doe, a **g** deer— 2834
SS 7: 1 Your **g** legs are like jewels, 2788

GRACIOUS (42) [GRACE]

Ge 21: 1 the LORD *was* **g** *to* Sarah as he had said, 7212
33:11 for God *has been* **g** *to* me 2858
43:29 And he said, "God *be* **g** *to* you, my son." 2858
Ex 34: 6 the LORD, the compassionate and **g** God, 2843
Nu 6:25 upon you and *be* **g** *to* you; 2858
1Sa 2:21 And the LORD *was* **g** *to* Hannah; 7212
2Sa 1:23 in life they were loved and **g**, 5833
12:22 The LORD *may be* **g** *to* me and let 2858
2Ki 13:23 But the LORD *was* **g** *to* them 2858
2Ch 30: 9 LORD your God is **g** and compassionate. 2843
Ezr 7: 9 for the **g** hand of his God was on him. 3202
8:18 Because the **g** hand of our God was on us, 3202
8:22 "The **g** hand of our God is on everyone 3208
9: 8 the LORD our God has been **g** 9382
Ne 2: 8 And because the **g** hand of my God was 3202
2:18 also told them about the **g** hand of my God 3202
9:17 a forgiving God, **g** and compassionate, 2843
9:31 for you are a **g** and merciful God. 2843
Job 33:24 *to be* **g** *to* him and say, 'Spare him 2858
Ps 25:16 Turn to me and *be* **g** *to* me, 2858
67: 1 *May* God *be* **g** *to* us and bless us 2858
86:15 O Lord, are a compassionate and **g** God, 2843
103: 8 The LORD is compassionate and **g**, 2843
111: 4 the LORD is **g** and compassionate. 2843
112: 4 **g** and compassionate and righteous man. 2843
116: 5 The LORD is **g** and righteous; 2843
119:29 *be* **g** *to* me through your law. 2858
119:58 *be* **g** *to* me according to your promise. 2858
145: 8 The LORD is **g** and compassionate, 2843
Pr 22:11 and whose speech is **g** will have the king 2834
Ecc 10:12 Words from a wise man's mouth are **g**, 2834
Isa 30:18 Yet the LORD longs to *be* **g** *to* you; 2858
30:19 *How* **g** *he will be* when you cry for help! 2858+2858
33: 2 O LORD, *be* **g** *to* us; we long for you. 2858
Jer 29:10 I will come to you and fulfill my **g** promise 3202
33:14 'when I will fulfill the **g** promise I made to 3202
Joel 2:13 for he is **g** and compassionate, 2843
Jnh 4: 2 that you are a **g** and compassionate God, 2843
Mal 1: 9 "Now implore God *to be* **g** *to* us. 2858
Lk 4:22 and were amazed at the **g** words that came *5921*
2Co 1:11 on our behalf for the **g favor granted** us *5922*
1Pe 3: 7 and as heirs with you *of* the **g gift** of life, *5921*

GRACIOUSLY (4) [GRACE]

Ge 33: 5 the children God *has* **g given** your servant." 2858
Hos 14: 2 "Forgive all our sins and receive us **g**, 3202
Ac 27:24 and God *has* **g given** you the lives *5919*
Ro 8:32 along with him, **g give** us all things? *5919*

GRAFF, GRAFFED (KJV) See GRAFTED

GRAFT (1) [GRAFTED]

Ro 11:23 for God is able *to* **g** them **in** again. *1596*

GRAFTED (5) [GRAFT]

Ro 11:17 *have been* **g in among** the others and *1596*
11:19 were broken off so that I *could be* **g in**." *1596*
11:23 *they will be* **g in**, for God is able to graft *1596*
11:24 to nature *were* **g** into a cultivated olive tree, *1596*
11:24 *be* **g into** their own olive tree! *1596*

GRAIN (265) [GRAINS, GRANARIES]

Ge 27:28 an abundance of **g** and new wine. 1841
27:37 I have sustained him with **g** and new wine. 1841
37: 7 We were binding **sheaves of g** out in 524
41: 5 Seven **heads of g,** healthy and good, 8672
41: 6 seven other **heads of g** sprouted— 8672
41: 7 The thin **heads of g** swallowed up 8672
41:22 "In my dreams I also saw seven **heads of g,** 8672
41:24 The thin **heads of g** swallowed up 8672
41:26 the seven good **heads of g** are seven years; 8672
41:27 the seven worthless **heads of g** scorched by 8672
41:35 that are coming and store up the **g** under 1339
41:49 Joseph stored up huge quantities of **g,** 1339
41:56 Joseph opened the storehouses and **sold g** 8690
41:57 the countries came to Egypt to **buy g** 8690
42: 1 Jacob learned that there was **g** in Egypt, 8692
42: 2 "I have heard that there is **g** in Egypt. 8692
42: 3 of Joseph's brothers went down to buy **g** 1339
42: 5 among those who went to **buy g,** 8690
42: 6 the *one who* **sold g** to all its people. 8690
42:19 while the rest of you go and take **g** back 8692
42:25 Joseph gave orders to fill their bags with **g,** 1339
42:26 they loaded their **g** on their donkeys 8692
43: 2 the **g** they had brought from Egypt, 8692
44: 2 along with the silver for his **g."** 8692
45:23 and ten female donkeys loaded with **g** 1339
47:14 in payment for the **g** they were buying, 8692
Ex 22: 6 so that it burns **shocks of g** or standing grain 1538
22: 6 that it burns shocks of grain or **standing g** 7850
29:41 the same **g offering** and its drink offering 4966
30: 9 or any burnt offering or **g offering,** 4966
40:29 on it burnt offerings and **g offerings,** 4966
Lev 2: 1 " 'When someone brings a **g offering** to 4966
2: 3 The rest of the **g offering** belongs to Aaron 4966
2: 4 " 'If you bring a **g offering** baked in 4966
2: 5 If your **g offering** is prepared on a griddle, 4966
2: 6 it is a **g offering.** 4966
2: 7 If your **g offering** is cooked in a pan, 4966
2: 8 Bring the **g offering** made of these things 4966
2: 9 from the **g offering** and burn it on the altar 4966
2:10 The rest of the **g offering** belongs to Aaron 4966
2:11 " 'Every **g offering** you bring to 4966
2:13 Season all your **g offerings** with salt. 4966
2:13 of your God out of your **g offerings;** 4966
2:14 " 'If you bring a **g offering** *of* firstfruits to 4966
2:14 offer crushed heads of **new g** roasted in 4152
2:15 Put oil and incense on it; it is a **g offering.** 4966
2:16 the memorial portion of the **crushed g** and 1762
5:13 as in the case of the **g offering.'** " 4966
6:14 the regulations for the **g offering:** 4966
6:15 with all the incense on the **g offering,** 4966
6:20 of fine flour as a regular **g offering,** 4966
6:21 and present the **g offering** broken in pieces 4966
6:23 Every **g offering** *of* a priest shall 4966
7: 9 Every **g offering** baked in an oven 4966
7:10 and every **g offering,** 4966
7:37 the **g offering,** the sin offering, 4966
9: 4 together with a **g offering** mixed with oil. 4966
9:17 He also brought the **g offering,** 4966
10:12 "Take the **g offering** left over from 4966
14:10 with oil for a **g offering,** 4966
14:20 together with the **g offering,** 4966
14:21 with oil for a **g offering,** 4966
14:31 together with the **g offering.** 4966
23:10 **sheaf of** the first **g** you harvest. 6684
23:13 together with its **g offering** *of* two-tenths 4966
23:14 or roasted or **new g,** 4152
23:16 and then present an **offering of** new **g** to 4966
23:18 together with their **g offerings** 4966
23:37 the burnt offerings and **g offerings,** 4966
27:30 whether **g** *from* the soil or fruit from 2446
Nu 4:16 the regular **g offering** and 4966
5:15 because it is a **g offering** *for* jealousy, 4966
5:18 the **g offering** *for* jealousy, 4966
5:25 from her hands the **g offering** *for* jealousy, 4966
5:26 then to take a handful of the **g offering** as 4966
6:15 with their **g offerings** and drink offerings, 4966
6:17 with its **g offering** and drink offering. 4966
7:13 fine flour mixed with oil as a **g offering;** 4966
7:19 fine flour mixed with oil as a **g offering;** 4966
7:25 fine flour mixed with oil as a **g offering;** 4966
7:31 fine flour mixed with oil as a **g offering;** 4966
7:37 fine flour mixed with oil as a **g offering;** 4966
7:43 fine flour mixed with oil as a **g offering;** 4966
7:49 fine flour mixed with oil as a **g offering;** 4966
7:55 fine flour mixed with oil as a **g offering;** 4966
7:61 fine flour mixed with oil as a **g offering;** 4966
7:67 fine flour mixed with oil as a **g offering;** 4966
7:73 fine flour mixed with oil as a **g offering;** 4966
7:79 fine flour mixed with oil as a **g offering;** 4966
7:87 together with their **g offering.** 4966
8: 8 with its **g offering** *of* fine flour mixed 4966
15: 4 to the LORD a **g offering** *of* a tenth of 4966
15: 6 a ram prepare a **g offering** *of* two-tenths of 4966
15: 9 with the bull a **g offering** *of* three-tenths 4966
15:24 along with its prescribed **g offering** 4966
18: 9 whether **g** or sin or guilt offerings, 4966
18:12 and **g** they give the LORD as the firstfruits 1841
18:27 to you as **g** from the threshing floor or juice 1841
20: 5 It has no **g** or figs, 2446
28: 5 with a **g offering** of a tenth of an ephah 4966
28: 8 along with the same kind of **g offering** 4966
28: 9 and a **g offering** of two-tenths of an ephah 4966
28:12 be a **g offering** of three-tenths of an ephah 4966
28:12 with the ram, a **g offering** of two-tenths of 4966
28:13 a **g offering** of a tenth of an ephah 4966
Nu 28:20 a **g offering** of three-tenths of an ephah 4966
28:26 to the LORD an **offering of** new **g** during 4966
28:28 be a **g offering** of three-tenths of an ephah 4966
28:31 and its **g offering.** 4966
29: 3 the bull prepare a **g offering** of three-tenths 4966
29: 6 with their **g offerings** and drink offerings 4966
29: 9 the bull prepare a **g offering** of three-tenths 4966
29:11 with its **g offering,** and their drink offerings 4966
29:14 of the thirteen bulls prepare a **g offering** 4966
29:16 with its **g offering** and drink offering. 4966
29:18 prepare their **g offerings** and drink offerings 4966
29:19 with its **g offering,** and their drink offerings 4966
29:21 prepare their **g offerings** and drink offerings 4966
29:22 with its **g offering** and drink offering. 4966
29:24 prepare their **g offerings** and drink offerings 4966
29:25 with its **g offering** and drink offering. 4966
29:27 prepare their **g offerings** and drink offerings 4966
29:28 with its **g offering** and drink offering. 4966
29:30 prepare their **g offerings** and drink offerings 4966
29:31 with its **g offering** and drink offering. 4966
29:33 prepare their **g offerings** and drink offerings 4966
29:34 with its **g offering** and drink offering. 4966
29:37 prepare their **g offerings** and drink offerings 4966
29:38 with its **g offering** and drink offering. 4966
29:39 your burnt offerings, **g offerings,** 4966
Dt 7:13 your **g,** new wine and oil— 1841
11:14 so that you may gather in your **g,** 1841
12:17 the tithe of your **g** and new wine and oil, 1841
14:23 Eat the tithe of your **g,** new wine and oil, 1841
16: 9 to put the sickle to the **standing g.** 7850
18: 4 to give them the firstfruits of your **g,** 1841
23:25 you must not put a sickle to his **standing g.** 7850
25: 4 an ox while it *is* **treading out** *the* **g.** 1889
28:51 They will leave you no **g,** new wine or oil, 1841
33:28 Jacob's spring is secure in a land of **g** 1841
Jos 5:11 unleavened bread and **roasted g.** 7828
22:23 to offer burnt offerings and **g offerings,** 4966
22:29 **g offerings** and sacrifices, 4966
Jdg 13:19 together with the **g offering,** 4966
13:23 and **g offering** from our hands, 4966
15: 5 and let the foxes loose in the **standing g** *of* 7850
15: 5 He burned up the shocks and **standing g,** 7850
Ru 2: 2 and pick up the **leftover g** behind anyone 8672
2:14 he offered her *some* **roasted g.** 7833
2:21 until they finish **harvesting** all my **g.'** " 7907
3: 7 to lie down at the far end of the **g pile.** 6894
1Sa 8:15 of your **g** and of your vintage and give it 2446
17:17 of **roasted g** and these ten loaves of bread 7833
25:18 five dressed sheep, five seahs of **roasted g,** 7833
2Sa 1:21 nor fields that yield offerings [of **g**]. NIH
17:19 over the opening of the well and scattered **g** 8195
17:28 flour and **roasted g,** beans and lentils, 7833
1Ki 8:64 **g offerings** and the fat of 4966
8:64 the **g offerings** and the fat of 4966
2Ki 4:42 of barley bread baked from the **first ripe g,** 1137
4:42 along with *some* **heads of new g.** 4152
16:13 up his burnt offering and **g offering,** 4966
16:15 and the evening **g offering,** 4966
16:15 and his **g offering,** 4966
16:15 their **g offering** and their drink offering. 4966
18:32 a land of **g** and new wine, 1841
1Ch 21:23 and the wheat for the **g offering.** 4966
23:29 the flour for the **g offerings,** 4966
2Ch 7: 7 the **g offerings** and the fat portions. 4966
31: 5 the firstfruits of their **g,** 1841
32:28 to store the harvest of **g,** new wine and oil; 1841
Ezr 7:17 with their **g offerings** and drink offerings, 10432
Ne 5: 2 for us to eat and stay alive, we must get **g."** 1841
5: 3 and our homes to get **g** during the famine." 1841
5:10 also lending the people money and **g.** 1841
5:11 the hundredth part of the money, **g,** 1841
10:31 or **g** to sell on the Sabbath, 8692
10:33 the regular **g offerings** and burnt offerings; 4966
10:37 of our [**g**] offerings, NIH
10:39 are to bring their contributions of **g,** 1841
13: 5 to store the **g offerings** and incense 4966
13: 5 and also the tithes of **g,** 1841
13: 9 with the **g offerings** and the incense 4966
13:12 All Judah brought the tithes of **g,** 1841
13:15 on the Sabbath and bringing in **g** 6894
Job 24:24 they are cut off like heads of **g.** 8672
31:10 *may* my wife **grind** another man's **g,** 3221
39:12 Can you trust him to bring in your **g** 2446
Ps 4: 7 when their **g** and new wine abound. 1841
65: 9 with water to provide the people with **g,** 1841
65:13 and the valleys are mantled with **g;** 1339
72:16 Let **g** abound throughout the land; 1339
78:24 he gave them the **g** *of* heaven. 1841
Pr 11:26 People curse the man who hoards **g,** 1339
27:22 grinding him like **g** with a pestle, 8195
Isa 5:10 a homer of seed only an ephah of **g."** NIH
17: 5 a reaper gathers the **standing g** and harvests 7850
17: 5 the standing grain and harvests the **g** 8672
17: 5 when a man gleans **heads of g** in the Valley 8672
19:21 with sacrifices and **g offerings;** 4966
23: 3 the great waters came the **g** *of* the Shihor; 2446
28:28 **G** must be ground to make bread; NIH
36:17 a land of **g** and new wine, 1841
43:23 I have not burdened you with **g offerings** 4966
57: 6 and offered **g offerings.** 4966
62: 8 "Never again will I give your **g** as food 1841
66: 3 whoever makes a **g offering** is 4966
66:20 as the Israelites bring their **g offerings,** 4966
Jer 9:22 like **cut g** behind the reaper, 6658
14:12 and **g offerings,** I will not accept them. 4966
17:26 **g offerings,** incense and thank offerings to 4966
23:28 For what has straw to do with **g?"** 1339
Jer 31:12 the **g,** the new wine and the oil, 1841
33:18 to burn **g offerings** and to present 4966
41: 5 bringing **g offerings** and incense with them 4966
50:11 a heifer **threshing g** and neigh like stallions, 1889
50:26 pile her up like **heaps of g.** 6894
Eze 36:29 I will call for the **g** and make it plentiful 1841
42:13 the **g offerings,** the sin offerings and 4966
44:29 They will eat the **g offerings,** 4966
45:15 These will be used for the **g offerings,** 4966
45:17 **g offerings** and drink offerings at 4966
45:17 the sin offerings, **g offerings,** 4966
45:24 as a **g offering** an ephah for each bull and 4966
45:25 burnt offerings, **g offerings** and oil. 4966
46: 5 The **g offering** given with the ram is to be 4966
46: 5 and the **g offering** with the lambs is to be 4966
46: 7 He is to provide as a **g offering** one ephah 4966
46:11 the **g offering** is to be an ephah with a bull, 4966
46:14 with it morning by morning a **g offering,** 4966
46:14 The presenting of this **g offering** to 4966
46:15 So the lamb and the **g offering** and 4966
46:20 the sin offering and bake the **g offering,** 4966
Hos 2: 8 the **g,** the new wine and oil, who lavished 1841
2: 9 "Therefore I will take away my **g** 1841
2:22 and the earth will respond to the **g,** 1841
7:14 for **g** and new wine but turn away from me. 1841
8: 7 Were it to yield **g,** foreigners would NIH
14: 7 He will flourish like the **g.** 1841
Joel 1: 9 **G offerings** and drink offerings are cut off 4966
1:10 the **g** is destroyed, the new wine is dried up 1841
1:13 for the **g offerings** and drink offerings 4966
1:17 for the **g** has dried up. 1841
2:14 **g offerings** and drink offerings for 4966
2:19 "I am sending you **g,** new wine and oil, 1841
2:24 The threshing floors will be filled with **g;** 1339
Am 2:13 as a cart crushes when loaded with **g.** 6658
5:11 on the poor and force him to give you **g.** 1339
5:22 and **g offerings,** I will not accept them. 4966
8: 5 be over that we may sell **g,** and the Sabbath 8692
9: 9 among all the nations as **g** is shaken in NIH
Hag 1:11 on the **g,** the new wine, 1841
Zec 9:17 **G** will make the young men thrive, 1841
Mt 12: 1 to pick some **heads of g** and eat them. *5092*
Mk 2:23 they began to pick some **heads of g.** *5092*
4: 7 so that they did not bear **g.** *2843*
4:28 All by itself the soil **produces g—** *2844*
4:29 As soon as the **g** is ripe, *2843*
Lk 6: 1 his disciples began to pick some **heads of g,** *5092*
12:18 there I will store all my **g** and my goods. *4992*
17:35 Two women will be **grinding g** together; *241*
Ac 7:12 When Jacob heard that there was **g** *4989*
27:38 they lightened the ship by throwing the **g** *4992*
1Co 9: 9 an ox *while it is* **treading out the g."** *262*
1Ti 5:18 the ox *while it is* **treading out the g,"** *262*

GRAINFIELD (1) [FIELD]

Dt 23:25 If you enter your neighbor's **g,** 7850

GRAINFIELDS (3) [FIELD]

Mt 12: 1 At that time Jesus went through the **g** on *5077*
Mk 2:23 through the **g,** and as his disciples walked *5077*
Lk 6: 1 through the **g,** and his disciples began *5077*

GRAIN, GRAINS (Anglicized) See also KERNEL, KERNELS

GRAINS (3) [GRAIN]

Job 29:18 my days as numerous as the **g of sand.** 2567
Ps 139:18 they would outnumber the **g of sand.** 2567
Isa 48:19 your children like its **numberless g;** 5054

GRANARIES (3) [GRAIN]

Ex 22:29 "Do not hold back offerings from your **g** 4852
Jer 50:26 Break open her **g;** pile her up like heaps 4393
Joel 1:17 the **g** have been broken down, 4923

GRANDCHILDREN (7) [CHILD]

Ge 31:28 You didn't even let me kiss my **g** 1201
31:55 Early the next morning Laban kissed his **g** 1201
45:10 you, your children and **g,** 1201+1201
Ex 10: 2 that you may tell your children and **g** 1201+1201
Dt 4:25 After you have had children and **g** 1201+1201
2Ki 17:41 To this day their children and **g** 1201+1201
1Ti 5: 4 But if a widow has children or **g,** *1681*

GRANDDAUGHTER (5) [DAUGHTER]

Ge 24:48 get the **g** *of* my master's brother for his son. 1426
36: 2 and Oholibamah daughter of Anah and **g** 1426
36:14 and **g** *of* Zibeon, whom she bore to Esau: 1426
2Ki 8:26 Athaliah, a **g** *of* Omri king of Israel. 1426
2Ch 22: 2 Athaliah, a **g** *of* Omri. 1426

GRANDDAUGHTERS (1) [DAUGHTER]

Ge 46: 7 grandsons and his daughters and **g—** 1201+1426

GRANDFATHER (1) [FATHER]

2Sa 9: 7 the land that belonged to your **g** Saul, 3

GRANDFATHER'S (2) [FATHER]

2Sa 16: 3 of Israel will give me back my **g** kingdom.' 3
19:28 All my **g** descendants deserved nothing 3

GRANDMOTHER (3) [MOTHER]
1Ki 15:13 He even deposed his **g** Maacah 562
2Ch 15:16 King Asa also deposed his **g** Maacah 562
2Ti 1: 5 in your **g** Lois and in your mother Eunice *3439*

GRANDMOTHER'S (1) [MOTHER]
1Ki 15:10 His **g** name was Maacah daughter 562

GRANDPARENTS (1) [PARENTS]
1Ti 5: 4 and so repaying their **parents and g,** *4591*

GRANDSON (9) [SON]
Ge 11:31 his **g** Lot son of Haran, 1201+1201
29: 5 "Do you know Laban, Nahor's **g?"** 1201
Jdg 8:22 you, your son and your **g—** 1201+1201
2Sa 9: 9 "I have given your master's **g** everything 1201
9:10 that your master's **g** may be provided for. 1201
9:10 And Mephibosheth, **g** *of* your master, 1201
16: 3 "Where is your master's **g?"** 1201
19:24 Mephibosheth, Saul's **g,** 1201
Jer 27: 7 his **g** until the time for his land comes; 1201+1201

GRANDSONS (7) [SON]
Ge 36:12 These were **g** *of* Esau's wife Adah. 1201
36:13 These were **g** *of* Esau's wife Basemath. 1201
36:16 they were **g** *of* Adah. 1201
36:17 they were **g** *of* Esau's wife Basemath. 1201
46: 7 took with him to Egypt his sons and **g** 1201+1201
Jdg 12:14 He had forty sons and thirty **g,** 1201+1201
1Ch 8:40 had many sons and **g—**150 in all. 1201+1201

GRANT (35) [GRANTED, GRANTING, GRANTS]
Ge 19:21 "Very well, *I will* **g** this request too; 5951+7156
24:42 please **g success** *to* the journey 7503
43:14 And *may* God Almighty **g** you mercy before 5989
Ex 21: 9 *he must* **g** her the rights of a daughter. 6913
Lev 26: 6 " '*I will* **g** peace in the land, 5989
Dt 28: 7 The LORD *will* **g** that the enemies 5989
28:11 The LORD *will* **g** you **abundant** prosperity 3855
Jdg 11:37 But **g** me this one request," she said. 6913
Ru 1: 9 the LORD **g** that each of you will find rest 5989
1Sa 1:17 of Israel **g** you what you have asked 5989
2Sa 23: 5 and **g** me my every desire? NIH
1Ki 5: 9 *to* **g** my wish by providing food 6913
1Ch 22: 9 and *I will* **g** Israel peace and quiet 5989
Est 5: 8 and if it pleases the king to **g** my petition 5989
7: 3 **g** me my life—this is my petition. 5989
Job 6: 8 that God *would* **g** what I hope for, 5989
13:20 "Only **g** me these two things, O God, 6913
Ps 20: 2 the sanctuary and **g** you **support** from Zion. 6184
20: 5 *May* the LORD **g** all your requests. 4848
51:12 of your salvation and **g** me a willing spirit, NIH
85: 7 O LORD, and **g** us your salvation. 5989
86:16 **g** your strength to your servant and save 5989
94:13 you **g** him **relief** from days of trouble, 9200
118:25 O LORD, save us; O LORD, **g** us **success.** 7503
140: 8 not **g** the wicked their desires, O LORD; 5989
Isa 46:13 *I will* **g** salvation to Zion, 5989
Hag 2: 9 'And in this place *I will* **g** peace,' 5989
Mt 20:21 "**G** that one of these two sons *3306*
20:23 to sit at my right or left is not for me *to* **g.** *1443*
Mk 10:40 to sit at my right or left is not for me *to* **g.** *1443*
Lk 18: 3 '**G** me **justice** against my adversary.' *AIT*
23:24 So Pilate decided *to* **g** their demand. *1181*
Ac 24:27 Felix wanted *to* **g** a favor to the Jews, *2960*
2Ti 1:18 the Lord **g** that he will find mercy from *1443*
2:25 God *will* **g** them repentance leading them *1443*

GRANTED (31) [GRANT]
Ge 4:25 "God *has* **g** me another child in place 8883
24:56 the LORD *has* **g success** *to* my journey. 7503
39:21 he showed him kindness and **g** him favor in 5989
Jos 1:13 and *has* **g** you this land.' 5989
14: 3 Moses *had* **g** the two-and-a-half tribes their inheritance east of the Jordan 5989
14: 3 not **g** the Levites an inheritance among 5989
1Sa 1:27 the LORD *has* **g** me what I asked of him. 5989
25:35 I have heard your words and **g** your **request."** 5951+7156
2Sa 14:22 the king *has* **g** his servant's request." 6913
1Ch 4:10 And God **g** his request. 995
22:18 And *has he* not **g** you **rest** on every side? 5663
23:25 *has* **g rest** to his people and has come 5663
Ezr 7: 6 The king *had* **g** him everything he asked, 5989
9: 9 He *has* **g** us new life to rebuild the house 5989
Ne 2: 8 the king **g** my **requests.** 5989
Est 5: 6 Even up to half the kingdom, *it will* **be g."** 6913
7: 2 Even up to half the kingdom, *it will* **be g."** 6913
8:11 The king's edict **g** the Jews in every city 5989
9:12 *It will* also **be g."** 6913
Job 42:15 and their father **g** them an inheritance along 5989
Ps 21: 2 *You have* **g** him the desire of his heart 5989
21: 6 Surely *you have* **g** him eternal blessings 8883
Pr 10:24 what the righteous desire *will be* **g.** 5989
Mt 14: 9 he ordered that her request *be* **g** *1443*
15:28 Your request *is* **g."** *1181*
Jn 5:26 so *he has* **g** the Son to have life in himself. *1443*
17: 2 For *you* **g** him authority over all people *1443*
Ac 11:18 God *has* **g** even the Gentiles repentance *1443*
Ro 11:20 **G.** But they were broken off *2822*
2Co 1:11 on our behalf for the **gracious favor g** us *5922*
Php 1:29 For *it has been* **g** to you on behalf *5919*

GRANTING (1) [GRANT]
Ne 1:11 *by* **g** him favor in the presence 5989

GRANTS (2) [GRANT]
Ps 127: 2 for *he* **g** sleep to those he loves. 5989
147:14 He **g** peace *to* your borders 8492

GRAPE (10) [GRAPES, GRAPEVINE, GRAPEVINES]
Lev 26: 5 Your threshing will continue until **g harvest** 1292
26: 5 the **g harvest** will continue until planting, 1292
Nu 6: 3 not drink **g** juice or eat grapes or raisins. 6694
Dt 32:14 You drank the foaming blood of the **g.** 6694
Jdg 8: 2 the **full g harvest** *of* Abiezer? 1292
Isa 18: 5 and the flower becomes a ripening **g,** 1235
24:13 when gleanings are left after the **g harvest.** 1292
32:10 the **g harvest** will fail, 1292
Jer 49: 9 If **g pickers** came to you, 1305
Ob 1: 5 If **g pickers** came to you, 1305

GRAPES (43) [GRAPE]
Ge 40:10 and its clusters ripened into **g.** 6694
40:11 and I took the **g,** 6694
49:11 his robes in the blood of **g.** 6694
Lev 19:10 or pick up the **g that have fallen.** 7261
25: 5 or harvest the **g** *of* your untended vines. 6694
Nu 6: 3 He must not drink grape juice or eat **g or raisins.** 2256+3313+4300+6694
13:20 (It was the season for the first ripe **g.)** 6694
13:23 a branch bearing a single cluster of **g.** 6694
13:24 the **cluster of g** the Israelites cut off there. 864
Dt 23:24 you may eat all the **g** you want, 6694
24:21 When *you* **harvest** *the* **g** *in* your vineyard, 1305
28:39 not drink the wine or **gather** *the* **g,** 112
32:32 Their **g** are *filled with* poison, 6694
Jdg 8: 2 **gleanings of** Ephraim's **g** 6622
9:27 and gathered the **g** and trodden them, 4142
Ne 13:15 **g,** figs and all other kinds of loads. 6694
Job 15:33 be like a vine stripped of its **unripe g,** 1235
Ps 80:12 so that all who pass by pick its **g?** NIH
Isa 5: 2 Then he looked for a crop of **good g,** 6694
5: 4 When I looked for **good g,** 6694
62: 9 and those who gather **the g** will drink it in 2257[S]
65: 8 when juice is still found in a **cluster of g** 864
Jer 6: 9 the branches again, like *one* **gathering g."** 1305
8:13 There will be no **g** on the vine. 6694
25:30 He will shout like those who tread the **g,** NIH
31:29 'The fathers have eaten **sour g,** 1235
31:30 whoever eats **sour g—**his own teeth will be 1235
48:32 on your ripened fruit and **g.** 1292
49: 9 would they not leave a **few g?** 6622
Eze 18: 2 " 'The fathers eat **sour g,** 1235
Hos 9:10 it was like finding **g** in the desert; 6694
Joel 3:13 Come, **trample the g,** 8097
Am 9:13 and the planter by the one treading **g.** 6694
Ob 1: 5 would they not leave a **few g?** 6622
Mic 6:15 you will crush **g** but not drink the wine. 9408
7: 1 there is no **cluster of g** to eat, 864
Hab 3:17 the fig tree does not bud and there are no **g** 3292
Mt 7:16 Do people pick **g** from thornbushes, *5091*
Lk 6:44 or **g** from briers. *5091*
1Co 9: 7 a vineyard and does not eat of its **g?** *2843*
Rev 14:18 the **clusters of g** from the earth's vine, *1084*
14:18 because its **g** are ripe." *5091*
14:19 gathered its **g** and threw them into *306*

GRAPEVINE (3) [GRAPE, VINE]
Nu 6: 4 Nazirite, he must not eat anything that comes from the **g,** 1728+3516
Jdg 13:14 She must not eat anything that comes from the **g,** 1728+3516
Jas 3:12 can a fig tree bear olives, or a **g** bear figs? *306*

GRAPEVINES (1) [GRAPE, VINE]
Nu 20: 5 It has no grain or figs, **g** or pomegranates. 1728

GRASP (9) [GRASPED, GRASPING, GRASPS]
2Ki 14: 5 After the kingdom was firmly in his **g,** 3338
Ps 71: 4 from the **g** *of* evil and cruel men. 4090
Ecc 7:18 It is good *to* **g** the one and not let go of 296
Jer 15:21 the wicked and redeem you from the **g** *of* 4090
34: 3 You will not escape from his **g** but will 3338
Lk 9:45 so that *they did* not **g** it, *150*
Jn 10:39 but he escaped their **g.** *5931*
1Co 14:11 If then *I do* not **g the meaning** 1539+3836+3857
Eph 3:18 *to* **g** how wide and long and high *2898*

GRASPED (6) [GRASP]
Ge 19:16 the men **g** his hand and the hands 2616
Eze 21:11 to *be* **g** with the hand; 9530
21:15 *it* is **g** for slaughter. 6487
29: 7 When they **g** you with their hands, 9530
Hos 12: 3 In the womb *he* **g** his brother's **heel;** 6810
Php 2: 6 with God **something to be g,** *772*

GRASPING (3) [GRASP]
Ge 25:26 with his hand **g** Esau's heel; 296
Jdg 7:20 **G** the torches in their left hands 2616
Pr 27:16 or **g** oil *with* the hand. 7924

GRASPS (2) [GRASP]
Dt 32:41 and my hand **g** it in judgment, 296
Pr 31:19 In her hand she holds the distaff and **g** 9461

GRASS (53)
Nu 22: 4 as an ox licks up the **g** *of* the field." 3764
Dt 11:15 I will provide **g** in the fields for your cattle, 6912
32: 2 like showers on **new g,** 2013
2Sa 23: 4 after rain that brings the **g** from the earth.' 2013
1Ki 18: 5 Maybe we can find *some* **g** to keep 2945
2Ki 19:26 like **g** *sprouting on* the roof, 2945
Job 5:25 your descendants like the **g** *of* the earth. 6912
6: 5 Does a wild donkey bray when it has **g,** 2013
8:12 they wither more quickly than **g.** 2945
38:27 and make it sprout with **g?** 2013+4604
40:15 with you and which feeds on **g** like an ox. 2945
Ps 37: 2 for like the **g** they will soon wither, 2945
72:16 let it thrive like the **g** *of* the field. 6912
90: 5 they are like the new **g** of the morning— 2945
92: 7 that though the wicked spring up like **g** 6912
102: 4 My heart is blighted and withered like **g;** 6912
102:11 I wither away like **g.** 6912
103:15 As for man, his days are like **g,** 2945
104:14 He makes **g** grow for the cattle, 2945
106:20 for an image of a bull, which eats **g.** 6912
129: 6 May they be like **g** *on* the roof, 2945
147: 8 the earth with rain and makes **g** grow on 2945
Pr 19:12 but his favor is like dew on the **g.** 6912
27:25 and new growth appears and the **g** *from* 6912
Isa 5:24 and as **dry g** sinks down in the flames, 3143
15: 6 up and the **g** is withered; 2945
35: 7 **g** and reeds and papyrus will grow. 2945
37:27 like **g** *sprouting on* the roof, 2945
40: 6 "All men are like **g,** 2945
40: 7 The **g** withers and the flowers fall, 2945
40: 7 Surely the people are **g.** 2945
40: 8 The **g** withers and the flowers fall, 2945
44: 4 They will spring up like **g** in a meadow, 2945
51:12 the sons of men, who are but **g,** 2945
66:14 and you will flourish like **g;** 2013
Jer 12: 4 and the **g** *in* every field be withered? 6912
14: 5 because there is no **g.** 2013
Da 4:15 remain in the ground, in the **g** of the field. 10187
4:23 in the **g** of the field, 10187
4:25 you will eat **g** like cattle and be drenched 10572
4:32 you will eat **g** like cattle. 10572
4:33 He was driven away from people and ate **g** 10572
5:21 with the wild donkeys and ate **g** like cattle; 10572
Mic 5: 7 like showers on the **g,** 6912
Mt 6:30 If that is how God clothes the **g** of the field, *5965*
14:19 he directed the people to sit down on the **g.** *5965*
Mk 6:39 down in groups on the green **g.** *5965*
Lk 12:28 If that is how God clothes the **g** of the field, *5965*
Jn 6:10 There was plenty *of* **g** in that place, *5965*
1Pe 1:24 For, "All men are like **g,** *5965*
1:24 the **g** withers and the flowers fall, *5965*
Rev 8: 7 and all the green **g** was burned up. *5965*
9: 4 not to harm the **g** of the earth or any plant *5965*

GRASSHOPPER (3) [GRASSHOPPERS]
Lev 11:22 of locust, katydid, cricket or **g.** 2506
Ps 78:46 He gave their crops to the **g,** 2885
Ecc 12: 5 and the **g** drags himself along 2506

GRASSHOPPERS (7) [GRASSHOPPER]
Nu 13:33 We seemed like **g** in our own eyes, 2506
1Ki 8:37 or blight or mildew, locusts or **g,** 2885
2Ch 6:28 or blight or mildew, locusts or **g,** 2885
Ps 105:34 and the locusts came, **g** without number; 3540
Isa 40:22 and its people are like **g.** 2506
Na 3:15 the sword will cut you down and, like **g,** 3540
3:15 Multiply like **g,** multiply like locusts! 3540

GRASSLANDS (1) [LAND]
Ps 65:12 The **g** *of* the desert overflow; 5661

GRATEFUL (1) [GRATIFY, GRATIFYING, GRATITUDE]
Ro 16: 4 the churches of the Gentiles *are* **g** to them. *2373*

GRATIFY (2) [GRATEFUL]
Ro 13:14 and do not think about how to **g** the desires *NIG*
Gal 5:16 not **g** the desires of the sinful nature. *5464*

GRATIFYING (1) [GRATEFUL]
Eph 2: 3 **g** the cravings of our sinful nature *NIG*

GRATING (6)
Ex 27: 4 Make a **g** for it, a bronze network, 4803
35:16 altar of burnt offering with its bronze **g,** 4803
38: 4 They made a **g** for the altar, 4803
38: 5 for the four corners of the bronze **g.** 4803
38:30 with its bronze **g** and all its utensils, 4803
39:39 the bronze altar with its bronze **g,** its poles 4803

GRATITUDE (2) [GRATEFUL]
Ac 24: 3 we acknowledge this with profound **g.** *2374*

Col 3:16 and spiritual songs with g in your hearts *5921*

GRAVE (84) [GRAVES]

Ge 37:35 "in mourning will I go down to the g 8619
42:38 you will bring my gray head down to the g 8619
44:29 you will bring my gray head down to the g 8619
44:31 the gray head of our father down to the g 8619
Nu 16:30 and they go down alive into the g, 8619
16:33 They went down alive into the g, 8619
19:16 anyone who touches a human bone or a g, 7700
19:18 or a g or someone who has been killed 7700
Dt 34:6 but to this day no one knows where his g is. 7690
1Sa 2:6 he brings down to the g and raises up. 8619
2Sa 22:6 The cords of the g coiled around me; 8619
1Ki 2:6 not let his gray head go down to the g 8619
2:9 Bring his gray head down to the g 8619
13:31 in the g where the man of God is buried; 7700
2Ki 21:26 He was buried in his g in the garden 7690
Job 3:22 and rejoice when they reach the g? 7700
5:26 You will come to the g in full vigor, 7700
7:9 he who goes down to the g does not return. 8619
10:19 from the womb to the g! 7700
11:8 They are deeper than the **depths of the g**— 8619
14:13 "If only you would hide me in the g 8619
17:1 my days are cut short, the g awaits me. 7700
17:13 If the only home I hope for is the g, 8619
21:13 in prosperity and go down to the g 8619
21:32 He is carried to the g, 7700
24:19 g snatches away those who have sinned. 8619
40:13 shroud their faces in the g. 3243
Ps 5:9 Their throat is an open g; 7700
6:5 Who praises you from the g? 8619
9:17 The wicked return to the g, 8619
16:10 because you will not abandon me to the g, 8619
18:5 The cords of the g coiled around me; 8619
30:3 O LORD, you brought me up from the g; 8619
31:17 be put to shame and lie silent in the g. 8619
49:14 Like sheep they are destined for the g, 8619
49:14 their forms will decay in the g, 8619
49:15 But God will redeem my life from the g; 8619
55:15 let them go down alive to the g, 8619
86:13 from the depths of the g. 8619
88:3 of trouble and my life draws near the g. 8619
88:5 like the slain who lie in the g, 7700
88:11 Is your love declared in the g, 7700
89:48 or save himself from the power of the g? 8619
107:20 he rescued them from the g. 8827
116:3 the anguish of the g came upon me; 8619
141:7 at the mouth of the g." 8619
Pr 1:12 let's swallow them alive, like the g, 8619
5:5 her steps lead straight to the g. 8619
7:27 Her house is a highway to the g, 8619
9:18 that her guests are in the depths of the g. 8619
15:24 to keep him from going down to the g. 8619
30:16 the g, the barren womb, 8619
Ecc 9:10 do it with all your might, for in the g, 8619
SS 8:6 its jealousy unyielding as the g. 8619
Isa 5:14 Therefore the g enlarges its appetite 8619
14:9 The g below is all astir to meet you 8619
14:11 to the g, along with the noise of your harps; 8619
14:15 But you are brought down to the g, 8619
22:16 and who gave you permission to cut out a g 7700
22:16 hewing your g on the height 7700
28:15 with the g we have made an agreement. 8619
28:18 your agreement with the g will not stand. 8619
38:18 For the g cannot praise you, 8619
53:9 He was assigned a g with the wicked, 7700
57:9 you descended to the g *itself!* 8619
Jer 5:16 Their quivers are like an open g; 7700
20:17 with my mother as my g, 7700
Eze 31:15 down to the g I covered the deep springs 8619
31:16 to the g with those who go down to the pit. 8619
31:17 had also gone down to the g with it, 8619
32:21 the g the mighty leaders will say of Egypt 8619
32:23 of the pit and her army lies around her g. 7690
32:24 with all her hordes around her g. 7690
32:25 with all her hordes around her g. 7700
32:27 who went down to the g with their weapons 8619
Hos 13:14 from the power of the g; 8619
13:14 Where, O g, is your destruction? 8619
Am 9:2 they dig down to the **depths of the g**, 8619
Jnh 2:2 From the depths of the g I called for help, 8619
Na 1:14 I will prepare your g, for you are vile." 7700
Hab 2:5 as the g and like death is never satisfied, 8619
Jn 11:44 "Take off the g clothes and let him go." *NIG*
Ac 2:27 because you will not abandon me to the g, *87*
2:31 that he was not abandoned to the g, *87*

GRAVECLOTHES (KJV) See STRIPS OF LINEN

GRAVED, GRAVEN (KJV) See CARVED, ENGRAVED, IDOL, INSCRIBED

GRAVEDIGGERS (1) [DIG]

Eze 39:15 a marker beside it until the g have buried it 7699

GRAVEL (2)

Pr 20:17 but he ends up with a mouth full of g. 2953
La 3:16 He has broken my teeth with g; 2953

GRAVES (14) [GRAVE]

Ex 14:11 "Was it because there were no g in Egypt 7700
2Ki 23:6 to powder and scattered the dust over the g 7700
2Ch 34:4 the g of those who had sacrificed to them. 7700
Isa 65:4 who sit among the g and spend their nights 7700
Jer 8:1 of Jerusalem will be removed from their g. 7700
Eze 32:22 she is surrounded by the g *of* all her slain, 7700
32:23 Their g are in the depths of the pit 7700
32:26 with all their hordes around their g. 7700
37:12 I am going to open your g and bring you up 7700
37:13 I open your g and bring you up from them. 7700
Mt 23:29 for the prophets and decorate the g of *3646*
Lk 11:44 because you are like unmarked g, *3646*
Jn 5:28 all who are in their g will hear his voice *3646*
Ro 3:13 "Their throats are open g; *5439*

GRAVITY (KJV) See PROPER RESPECT, SERIOUSNESS

GRAY (11)

Ge 42:38 you will bring my g **head** down to the grave 8484
44:29 you will bring my g **head** down to the grave 8484
44:31 the g **head** *of* our father down to the grave 8484
1Sa 12:2 As for me, I am old and g, 8482
1Ki 2:6 not let his g **head** go down to the grave 8484
2:9 Bring his g **head** down to the grave 8484
Ps 71:18 Even when I am old and g, 8484
Pr 16:31 G **hair** is a crown of splendor; 8484
20:29 g **hair** the splendor of the old. 8484
Isa 46:4 Even to your old age and g **hairs** I am he, 8484
Hos 7:9 His **hair** is sprinkled with g, 8484

GRAY-HAIRED (2) [HAIR]

Dt 32:25 women will perish, infants and g men. 8484
Job 15:10 The g and the aged are on our side, 8482

GRAYHEADED (KJV) See GRAY, GRAY-HAIRED

GRAZE (9) [GRAZED, GRAZES, GRAZING]

Ge 37:12 to g their father's flocks near Shechem, 8286
Ex 22:5 or vineyard and lets them stray and *they* g 1278
34:3 not even the flocks and herds *may* g in front 8286
SS 1:7 where *you* g *your* **flock** and 8286
1:8 of the sheep and g your young goats by 8286
Isa 5:17 Then sheep *will* g as in their own pasture; 8286
27:10 there the calves g, there they lie down; 8286
30:23 In that day your cattle *will* g 8286
Jer 50:19 to his own pasture and *he will* g *on* Carmel 8286

GRAZED (2) [GRAZE]

Ge 41:2 sleek and fat, and *they* g among the reeds. 8286
41:18 fat and sleek, and *they* g among the reeds. 8286

GRAZES (1) [GRAZE]

Ex 22:5 a man g his livestock *in* a field or vineyard 1278

GRAZING (7) [GRAZE]

Ge 36:24 the hot springs in the desert while he *was* g 8286
37:13 your brothers *are* g **the flocks** 8286
37:16 where they *are* g *their* **flocks?"** 8286
1Ch 27:29 the Sharonite was in charge of the herds g 8286
Job 1:14 and the donkeys *were* g nearby, 8286
Eze 34:14 of Israel will be their g **land.** 5659
34:14 There they will lie down in good g **land,** 5659

GREASE (KJV) See CALLOUS

GREAT (702) [GREATER, GREATEST, GREATLY, GREATNESS]

Ge 1:16 God made two g lights— 1524
1:21 The g creatures of the sea and every living 1524
6:5 The LORD saw how g man's wickedness 8041
7:11 the springs of the g deep burst forth, 8041
10:12 Nineveh and Calah; that is the g city. 1524
12:2 into a g nation and I will bless you; 1524
12:2 *I will* **make** your name g, 1540
12:6 the site of the g **tree** *of* Moreh at Shechem. 471
13:6 for their possessions were **so g** 8041
13:18 and went to live near the g **trees** *of* Mamre 471
14:13 near the g **trees** *of* Mamre the Amorite, 471
15:1 I am your shield, your very g reward." 2221
15:14 and afterward they will come out with g possessions. 1524
15:18 from the river of Egypt to the g river, 1524
17:20 and I will make him into a g nation. 1524
18:1 the g **trees** *of* Mamre while he was sitting 471
18:18 surely become a g and powerful nation, 1524
18:20 against Sodom and Gomorrah *is* so g 8045
19:13 to the LORD against its people *is* so g 1540
19:19 and you *have* shown g kindness to me 1540
20:9 that you have brought *such* g guilt upon me 1524
21:8 on the day Isaac was weaned Abraham held a g feast. 1524
21:18 for I will make him into a g nation." 1524
30:8 "I have had a g struggle with my sister, 466
32:7 In g fear and distress Jacob divided 4394
34:12 **Make** the price for the bride and the gift I am to bring **as g as you like,** 4394+8049
35:16 to give birth and *had* g **difficulty.** 7996
35:17 And as she *was* **having g difficulty** 7996
36:7 Their possessions were too g for them 8041
41:29 Seven years of g abundance are coming 1524
45:7 and to save your lives by a g deliverance. 1524
46:3 for I will make you into a g nation there. 1524
48:19 and he too *will become* g. 1540
Ex 10:14 area of the country *in* g **numbers.** 3878+4394
14:31 the g power the LORD displayed against 1524
32:10 Then I will make you into a g nation." 1524
32:11 of Egypt with g power and a mighty hand? 1524
32:21 that you led them into *such* g sin?" 1524
32:30 "You have committed a g sin. 1524
32:31 what a g sin these people have committed! 1524
Lev 11:17 the little owl, the cormorant, the g **owl,** 3568
11:29 the weasel, the rat, any kind of g **lizard,** 7370
19:15 to the poor or favoritism to the g, 1524
Nu 13:32 All the people we saw there are of g **size.** 4500
14:19 In accordance with your g love, 1542
22:18 not do *anything* g or small to go beyond 1524
34:6 be the coast of the G Sea. 1524
34:7 run a line from the G Sea to Mount Hor 1524
Dt 1:7 as far as the g river, the Euphrates. 1524
1:17 hear both small and g alike. 1524
3:5 there were also a g many unwalled villages. 4394
4:6 "Surely this g nation is a wise 1524
4:7 so g as to have their gods near them 1524
4:8 so g as to have such righteous decrees 1524
4:32 Has anything so g as this ever happened, 1524
4:34 or by g and awesome deeds, 1524
4:36 On earth he showed you his g fire, 1524
4:37 of Egypt by his Presence and his g strength, 1524
5:25 This g fire will consume us, 1524
6:22 and wonders—g and terrible— 1524
7:19 You saw with your own eyes the g trials, 1524
7:21 is a g and awesome God. 1524
7:23 into g confusion until they are destroyed. 1524
9:26 by your g **power** and brought out of Egypt 1542
9:29 that you brought out by your g power 1524
10:17 the g God, mighty and awesome, 1524
10:21 who performed for you those g 1524
11:7 that saw all these g things 1524
11:30 near the g **trees** *of* Moreh, 471
14:16 the little owl, the g **owl,** the white owl, 3568
17:16 *must* not **acquire** g **numbers** *of* horses for 8049
18:16 nor see this g fire anymore, 1524
19:6 overtake him if the distance *is too* g, 8049
26:5 and lived there and became a g nation, 1524
26:8 with g terror and with miraculous signs 1524
29:3 With your own eyes you saw those g trials, 1524
29:3 those miraculous signs and g wonders. 1524
29:28 and in g wrath the LORD uprooted them 1524
Jos 1:4 and from the g river, the Euphrates— 1524
1:4 to the G Sea on the west 1524
2:9 to you and that a g **fear** *of* you has fallen 399
3:16 It piled up in a heap a g distance away, 4394
7:9 then will you do for your own g name?" 1524
9:1 of the G Sea as far as Lebanon (the kings of 1524
10:10 who defeated them in a g victory 1524
15:12 the coastline of the G Sea. 1524
15:47 of Egypt and the coastline of the G Sea. 1524
17:1 because the Makirites were g **soldiers.** 408+4878
22:8 to your homes with your g wealth— 8041
22:8 and a g **quantity** *of* clothing— 2221+4394
23:4 the Jordan and the G Sea in the west. 1524
23:9 "The LORD has driven out before you g 1524
24:17 performed those g signs before our eyes. 1524
Jdg 2:7 the g things the LORD had done for Israel. 1524
2:15 They were in g distress. 4394
4:11 by the g **tree** in Zaanannim near Kedesh. 471
9:6 and Beth Millo gathered beside the g **tree** 471
10:9 and Israel was in g distress. 4394
12:2 in a g struggle with the Ammonites, 4394
15:18 "You have given your servant this g victory. 1524
16:5 the secret of his g strength and 1524
16:6 of your g strength and how you can be tied 1524
16:15 the secret of your g strength." 1524
16:23 to offer a g sacrifice to Dagon their god and 1524
20:38 up a g cloud of smoke from the city, 8049
1Sa 1:16 of my g anguish and grief." 8044
2:17 This sin of the young men was very g in 1524
4:5 all Israel raised such a g shout that 1524
4:10 The slaughter was very g; 1524
5:9 throwing it into a g panic. 1524+4394
6:9 then the LORD has brought this g disaster 1524
10:3 on from there until you reach the g **tree** 471
11:15 and all the Israelites held a g celebration. 4394
12:16 and see this g thing the LORD is about 1524
12:22 For the sake of his g name the LORD will 1524
12:24 consider what g **things** *he has* **done** 1540
14:45 about this g deliverance in Israel? 1524
17:24 they all ran from him in g fear. 4394
17:25 The king will give g wealth to 1524
18:14 In everything he did he **had g success,** 8505
19:5 The LORD won a g victory for all Israel, 1524
19:22 for Ramah and went to the g cistern 1524
20:2 my father doesn't do anything, g or small, 1524
26:25 *you will* **do g things** and surely triumph." 6913+6913
28:15 "I am in g distress," Saul said. 4394
30:16 of the g **amount** of plunder they had taken 1524
2Sa 3:22 from a raid and brought with them a g **deal** 8041
3:38 and a g *man* has fallen in Israel this day? 1524
7:9 Now I will make your name g, 1524
7:21 you have done this g **thing** 1525
7:22 "How g *you are,* O Sovereign LORD! 1540
7:23 and to perform g and awesome wonders 1525

2Sa 7:26 so that your name *will be* g forever. 1540
8:8 David took a g **quantity** of bronze. 2221+4394
12:30 He took a g **quantity** *of* plunder from 2221+4394
18:7 and the casualties that day were **g—** 1524
18:29 "I saw g confusion just as Joab was about 1524
20:8 While they were at the g rock in Gibeon, 1524
22:36 you stoop down *to* **make** me **g.** 8049
22:51 *He* **gives** his king g victories; 1540
23:10 The LORD brought about a g victory 1524
23:12 and the LORD brought about a g victory. 1524
23:20 who performed g exploits. 8041
24:14 for his mercy is g; 8041
1Ki 1:19 He has sacrificed g **numbers** of cattle, 8044
1:25 down and sacrificed g **numbers** of cattle, 8044
3:6 "You have shown g kindness 1524
3:6 You have continued this g kindness to him 1524
3:8 the people you have chosen, a g people, 8041
3:9 For who is able to govern this g people 3878
4:29 gave Solomon wisdom and very g insight, 2221
5:7 a wise son to rule over this g nation." 8041
7:9 from the outside to the g courtyard and 1524
7:12 The g courtyard was surrounded by a wall 1524
8:42 of your g name and your mighty hand 1524
10:2 at Jerusalem with a very g caravan— 3878
10:11 and from there they brought g *cargoes* 2221+4394
10:18 the king made a g throne inlaid with ivory 1524
19:11 Then a g and powerful wind tore 1524
22:31 "Do not fight with anyone, small or g, 1524
2Ki 3:27 The fury against Israel was g; 1524
5:1 He was a g man in the sight of his master 1524
5:13 prophet had told you to do some g thing, 1524
6:23 So he prepared a g feast for them, 1524
6:25 There was a g famine in the city; 1524
7:6 of chariots and horses and a g army, 1524
8:4 about all the g *things* Elisha has done." 1524
10:19 I am going to hold a g sacrifice for Baal. 1524
17:21 and caused them to commit a g sin. 1524
18:19 " 'This is what the g king, 1524
18:28 "Hear the word of the g king, 1524
22:13 G is the LORD's anger that burns 1524
1Ch 10:12 under the g **tree** in Jabesh, 461
11:14 and the LORD brought about a g victory. 1524
11:22 who performed g exploits. 8041
12:22 until he had a g army, 1524
16:25 g is the LORD and most worthy of praise; 1524
17:19 you have done this g **thing** 1525
17:19 and made known all these g *promises.* 1525
17:21 and to perform g and awesome wonders 1525
17:24 and that your name *will be* g forever. 1540
18:8 David took a g quantity of bronze, 4394
20:2 He took a g **quantity** *of* plunder from 2221+4394
21:13 for his mercy is very **g;** 8041
22:5 of g magnificence and fame and splendor 1540
22:14 "I have **taken g pains** to provide for 928+6715
22:14 bronze and iron too g to be weighed, 4200+8044
29:1 The task is g, because this palatial 1524
29:22 with g joy in the presence of the LORD 1524
2Ch 1:1 and **made** him exceedingly **g.** 1540
1:8 "You have shown g kindness 1524
1:10 for who is able to govern this g people 1524
2:5 "The temple I am going to build will be **g,** 1524
2:13 Huram-Abi, a man of g **skill,** 1069+2682+3359
6:32 from a distant land because of your g name 1524
6:42 Remember the g **love** *promised* 2876
9:1 Arriving with a very g caravan— 3878
9:17 the king made a g throne inlaid with ivory 1524
14:13 a g number of Cushites fell that they could NIH
15:5 of the lands were in g turmoil. 8041
15:13 were to be put to death, whether small or **g,** 1524
16:8 a mighty army with g **numbers** 2221+4394
17:5 so that he had g wealth and honor. 4200+8044
18:1 Jehoshaphat had g wealth and honor, 4200+8044
18:30 "Do not fight with anyone, small or g, 1524
20:25 a g **amount** of equipment and clothing 4200+8044
21:19 and he died in g pain. 8273
24:11 and collected a g **amount** of money. 4200+8044
25:10 Judah and left for home in a g **rage.** 678+3034
25:13 and carried off g **quantities** of plunder. 8041
28:8 They also took a g **deal** of plunder, 8041
28:13 For our guilt is already **g,** 8041
30:21 for seven days with g rejoicing, 1524
30:24 A g **number** of priests consecrated themselves. 4200+8044
30:26 There was g joy in Jerusalem, 1524
31:5 They brought a g **amount,** 4200+8044
31:10 and this g **amount** is left over." 2162
32:27 Hezekiah had very g riches and honor, 2221
32:29 and acquired g **numbers** of flocks and herds, 4200+8044
32:29 for God had given him very g riches. 8041
34:21 G is the LORD's anger that is poured out 1524
Ezr 3:11 And all the people gave a g shout of praise 1524
4:10 the g and honorable Ashurbanipal deported 10647
5:8 to the temple of the g God. 10647
5:11 that a g king of Israel built and finished. 10647
8:22 his g anger is against all who forsake him." 6437
9:7 until now, our guilt has been **g.** 1524
9:13 a result of our evil deeds and our g guilt, 1524
Ne 1:3 the province are in g trouble and disgrace. 1524
1:5 God of heaven, the g and awesome God, 1524
1:10 by your g strength and your mighty hand. 1524
3:27 the g projecting tower to the wall of Ophel. 1524
4:14 Remember the Lord, who is g and awesome, 1524
5:1 the men and their wives raised a g outcry 1524
6:3 on a g project and cannot go down. 1524
8:6 Ezra praised the LORD, the g God; 1524
8:12 of food and to celebrate with g joy, 1524
Ne 8:17 And their joy was very **g.** 1524
9:19 "Because of your g compassion you did 8041
9:25 they reveled in your g goodness. 1524
9:27 in your g compassion you gave them deliverers, 8041
9:31 But in your g mercy you did not put an end 8041
9:32 "Now therefore, O our God, the **g,** 1524
9:35 enjoying your g goodness to them in 8041
9:37 We are in g distress. 1524
12:43 And on that day they offered g sacrifices, 1524
12:43 because God had given them g joy. 1524
13:22 to me according to your g love. 8044
Est 2:18 And the king gave a g banquet, 1524
4:3 there was g mourning among the Jews, 1524
4:4 she was in g distress. 4394
Job 2:13 they saw how g his suffering *was.* 1540+4394
3:19 The small and the g are there, 1524
4:10 yet the teeth of the g **lions** are broken. 4097
12:23 *He* **makes** nations **g,** and destroys them; 8434
21:28 You say, 'Where now is the g **man's** house, 5618
22:5 Is not your wickedness **g?** 8041
23:6 Would he oppose me with g power? 8044
26:3 what g insight you have displayed! 4200+8044
30:18 In his g power [God] becomes like clothing 8044
31:25 if I have rejoiced over my g wealth, 8044
36:26 *How* g is God—beyond our understanding! 8438
37:5 he does g *things* beyond our understanding. 1524
37:23 in his justice and g righteousness, 8044
39:11 Will you rely on him for his g strength? 8041
Ps 5:7 But I, by your g mercy, 8044
17:7 Show the wonder of your g **love,** 2876
17:12 like a g **lion** crouching in cover. 4097
18:14 g bolts of lightning and routed them. 8041
18:35 you stoop down *to* **make** me **g.** 8049
18:50 *He* **gives** his king g victories; 1540
19:11 in keeping them there is g reward. 8041
19:13 innocent of g transgression. 8041
21:1 How g is his joy in the victories you give! 4394
21:5 the victories you gave, his glory is **g;** 1524
22:25 the theme of my praise in the g assembly; 8041
25:6 O LORD, your g **mercy** and love, 8171
25:11 forgive my iniquity, though it is **g.** 8041
26:12 in the g **assembly** I will praise the LORD. 5220
31:19 How g is your goodness, 8041
33:16 no warrior escapes by his g strength. 8044
33:17 despite *all* its g strength it cannot save. 8044
35:18 I will give you thanks in the g assembly; 8041
36:6 your justice like the g deep. 8041
37:11 the land and enjoy g peace. 8044
40:9 I proclaim righteousness in the g assembly; 8041
40:10 and your truth from the g assembly. 8041
47:2 the g King over all the earth! 1524
48:1 G is the LORD, and most worthy of praise, 1524
48:2 the city of the G King. 8041
49:6 in their wealth and boast of their g riches? 8044
51:1 g compassion blot out my transgressions. 8044
52:7 but trusted in his g wealth and grew strong 8044
57:10 For g is your love, reaching to the heavens; 1524
66:3 *So* g is your power 8044
68:11 and g was the company 8041
68:26 Praise God in the g **congregation;** 5220
68:27 there the g **throng** *of* Judah's princes, 8086
69:13 in your g love, O God, 8041
69:16 in your g mercy turn to me. 8044
71:19 O God, you who have done g *things.* 1524
76:1 his name is g in Israel. 1524
77:13 What god is *so* g as our God? 1524
82:1 God presides in the g assembly; 446
86:10 For you are g and do marvelous deeds; 1524
86:13 For g is your love toward me; 1524
89:1 I will sing of the LORD's g **love** forever; 2876
89:49 where is your former g **love,** 2876
90:11 For your wrath is as g as the fear NIH
91:13 you will trample the g **lion** and 4097
92:5 How g *are* your works, O LORD, 1540
93:4 Mightier than the thunder of the g waters, 8041
94:19 When anxiety was g within me, 8044
95:3 For the LORD is the g God, 1524
95:3 the g King above all gods. 1524
96:4 g is the LORD and most worthy of praise; 1524
99:2 G is the LORD in Zion; 1524
99:3 Let them praise your g 1524
102:10 because of your g **wrath,** 2256+2405+7912
103:11 *so* g *is* his love for those who fear him; 1504
104:1 O LORD my God, *you are* very g; 1540
106:21 who had done g *things* in Egypt, 1524
106:45 and out of his g love he relented. 8044
107:43 and consider the g **love** *of* the LORD. 2876
108:4 For g is your love, higher than the heavens; 1524
109:30 in the g *throng* I will praise him. 8041
111:2 G are the works of the LORD; 1524
112:1 who finds g delight in his commands. 4394
115:13 who fear the LORD—small and g alike. 1524
116:6 *when I was* **in g need,** he saved me. 1937
117:2 For g *is* his love toward us, 1504
119:14 as one rejoices in g riches. 3972
119:156 Your compassion is g, O LORD; 8041
119:162 in your promise like one who finds g spoil. 8041
119:165 G peace have they who love your law, 8041
126:2 "The LORD has done g *things* for them." 1540
126:3 The LORD has done g *things* for us, 1540
131:1 I do not concern myself with g *matters* 1524
135:5 I know that the LORD is g, 1524
136:4 to him who alone does g wonders, 1524
136:7 who made the g lights— 1524
136:17 who struck down g kings, 1524
138:5 for the glory of the LORD is **g.** 1524
Ps 145:3 G is the LORD and most worthy of praise; 1524
145:6 and I will proclaim your g **deeds.** 1525
147:5 G is our Lord and mighty in power; 1524
148:7 you g **sea creatures** and all ocean depths, 9490
Pr 5:23 led astray by his own g folly. 8044
6:35 he will refuse the bribe, however g it is. 8049
13:7 to be poor, yet has g wealth. 8041
14:29 A patient man has g understanding, 8041
15:6 house of the righteous contains g treasure, 8041
15:16 of the LORD than g wealth with turmoil. 8041
18:16 and ushers him into the presence of the **g.** 1524
21:14 in the cloak pacifies g wrath. 6434
22:1 good name is more desirable than g riches; 8041
23:24 father of a righteous man *has* **g joy;** 1635+1635
24:5 A wise man has g **power,** 6437
25:6 and do not claim a place among g *men;* 1524
28:12 the righteous triumph, there is g elation; 8041
Ecc 2:4 *I* **undertook** g projects: 1540
2:21 This too is meaningless and a g misfortune. 8041
5:17 with g frustration, affliction and anger. 2221
10:4 calmness can lay g errors to rest. 1524
Isa 5:9 "Surely the g houses will become desolate, 8041
9:2 in darkness have seen a g light; 1524
10:33 will lop off the boughs with g **power.** 5124
12:6 for g is the Holy One of Israel among you." 1524
13:4 like that of a g multitude! 8041
17:12 they roar like the roaring of g waters! 3888
23:3 the g waters came the grain of the Shihor; 8041
27:1 his fierce, g and powerful sword, 1524
27:13 And in that day a g trumpet will sound. 1524
29:6 with thunder and earthquake and g noise, 1524
29:15 Woe to those *who* **go to g depths** 6676
30:25 In the day of g slaughter, 8041
31:1 and in the g strength of their horsemen, 4394
31:4 "As a lion growls, a g **lion** over his prey— 4097
32:2 and the shadow of a g rock in a thirsty land. 3878
34:6 a sacrifice in Bozrah and a g slaughter 1524
34:7 the bull calves and the g bulls. 52
34:11 the g **owl** and the raven will nest there. 3568
36:4 "Tell Hezekiah, " 'This is what the g king, 1524
36:13 "Hear the words of the g king, 1524
40:26 of his g power and mighty strength, 8044
42:21 of his righteousness *to* **make** *his* law g 1540
51:10 the waters of the g deep, 8041
53:12 a portion among the **g,** 8041
54:13 and g will be your children's peace. 8041
Jer 2:12 O heavens, and shudder with g horror," 4394
2:31 a desert to Israel or a land of g **darkness?** 4420
5:6 for their rebellion *is* g 8045
6:22 a g nation is being stirred up from the ends 1524
9:19 How g is our shame! 4394
10:6 No one is like you, O LORD; you are **g,** 1524
10:22 a g commotion from the land of the north! 1524
13:9 of Judah and the g pride of Jerusalem. 8041
14:7 For our backsliding *is* **g;** 8045
16:10 the LORD decreed such a g disaster 1524
21:5 in anger and fury and g wrath. 1524
22:8 done such a thing to this g city?' 1524
22:14 a g palace with spacious upper rooms.' 4500
25:14 be enslaved by many nations and g kings; 1524
27:5 With my g power and outstretched arm 1524
27:7 and g kings will subjugate him. 1524
28:8 against many countries and g kingdoms, 1524
30:14 your guilt is *so* g and your sins so many. 8044
30:15 Because of your g guilt I have done 8044
31:8 a g throng will return. 1524
31:15 mourning and g weeping, 9476
31:20 ***I*** **have g compassion** *for* him," 8163+8163
32:17 the heavens and the earth by your g power 1524
32:18 O g and powerful God, 1524
32:19 g are your purposes 1524
32:21 and an outstretched arm and with g terror. 1524
32:37 in my furious anger and g wrath; 1524
32:42 As I have brought all this g calamity 1524
33:3 to me and I will answer you and tell you g 1524
36:7 against this people by the LORD are **g."** 1524
41:12 They caught up with him near the g pool 8041
44:2 the g disaster I brought on Jerusalem and 3972
44:7 Why bring *such* g disaster on yourselves 1524
44:26 'I swear by my g name,' says the LORD, 1524
45:5 Should you then seek g *things* for yourself? 1524
48:3 cries of g havoc and destruction. 1524
50:9 against Babylon an alliance of g nations 1524
50:22 the noise of g destruction! 1524
50:41 a g nation and many kings are being stirred 1524
51:54 the sound of g destruction from the land of 1524
51:55 Waves [of enemies] will rage like g waters; 8041
La 1:1 who once was g among the nations! 8041
3:22 Because of the LORD's g **love** we are 2876
3:23 new every morning; g is your faithfulness. 8041
3:32 so g is his unfailing love. 8044
Eze 9:9 of Israel and Judah is exceedingly **g;** 1524
14:4 in keeping with his g idolatry. 8044
17:3 A g eagle with powerful wings, 1524
17:7 " 'But there was another g eagle 1524
17:17 with his mighty army and g horde will be 8041
21:14 a sword for g slaughter, 1524
25:17 I will carry out g vengeance on them 1524
26:7 with horsemen and a g army. 8041
27:12 because of your g wealth of goods; 3972+8044
27:18 of your many products and g wealth 3972+8044
27:33 with your g wealth and your wares 8044
28:5 By your g skill in trading 8044
29:3 you g monster lying among your streams. 1524
31:6 all the g nations lived in its shade. 8041
32:3 a g throng of people I will cast my net 8041
36:23 I will show the holiness of my g name, 1524

Eze 37: 2 a g many bones on the floor of the valley, 4394
38: 4 and a g horde with large and small shields, 8041
38:15 all of them riding on horses, a g horde, 1524
38:19 at that time there shall be a g earthquake in 1524
39:17 the g sacrifice on the mountains of Israel. 1524
47: 7 I saw a g number of trees on each side of 4394
47:10 like the fish of the G Sea. 1524
47:15 the north side it will run from the G Sea by 1524
47:19 along the Wadi [of Egypt] to the G Sea. 1524
47:20 the G Sea will be the boundary to 1524
48:28 along the Wadi [of Egypt] to the G Sea. 1524
Da 2: 6 from me gifts and rewards and g honor. 10678
2:10 No king, however g and mighty, 10647
2:45 "The g God has shown the king 10647
4: 3 How g are his signs, 10647
4:22 *You have become* g and strong; 10648
4:30 "Is not this the g Babylon I have built as 10647
5: 1 a g banquet for a thousand of his nobles 10647
7: 2 winds of heaven churning up the g sea. 10647
7: 3 Four g beasts, each different from 10647
7:17 'The four g beasts are four kingdoms 10647
8: 4 He did as he pleased and *became* g. 1540
8: 6 the canal and charged at him in g rage. 3946
8: 8 The goat *became* very g, 1540
8:11 *It* set *itself* up to be as g as the Prince 1540
9: 4 "O Lord, the g and awesome God, 1524
9:12 by bringing upon us g disaster. 1524
9:18 but because of your g mercy. 8041
10: 1 and it concerned a g war. 1524
10: 4 as I was standing on the bank of the g river, 1524
10: 8 So I was left alone, gazing at this g vision; 1524
11: 3 with g power and do as he pleases. 8041
11: 5 will rule his own kingdom with g power. 8041
11:10 for war and assemble a g army, 8041
11:28 to his own country with g wealth, 1524
11:40 with chariots and cavalry and a g fleet 8041
11:44 in a g rage to destroy and annihilate many. 1524
12: 1 the g prince who protects your people, 1524
Hos 1:11 for g will be the day of Jezreel. 1524
5:13 and sent to the g king for help. 3714
5:14 like a g lion to Judah. 4097
9: 7 so many and your hostility so g, 8041
10: 6 to Assyria as tribute for the g king. 3714
10:15 Bethel, because your wickedness is g. 8288+8288
Joel 1: 4 the g locusts have eaten; 746
1: 4 what the g locusts have left 746
2:11 The day of the LORD is g; it is dreadful. 1524
2:20 Surely he has done g *things.* 1540
2:21 Surely the LORD has done g *things.* 1540
2:25 the g locust and the young locust, 746
2:25 my g army that I sent among you, 1524
2:31 before the coming of the g and dreadful day 1524
3:13 so g is their wickedness!" 8041
Am 2: 2 in g tumult amid war cries and the blast 8623
3: 9 the g unrest within her and the oppression 8041
5:12 and how g your sins. 6786
6: 2 go from there to g Hamath, 8041
6:11 the g house into pieces and the small house 1524
7: 4 up the g deep and devoured the land. 8041
Jnh 1: 2 the g city of Nineveh and preach against it, 1524
1: 4 Then the LORD sent a g wind on the sea, 1524
1:12 that this g storm has come upon you." 1524
1:17 LORD provided a g fish to swallow Jonah, 1524
3: 2 "Go to the g city of Nineveh and proclaim 1524
4:11 not be concerned about that g city?" 1524
Na 1: 3 LORD is slow to anger and g *in* power; 1524
3:10 and all her g *men* were put in chains. 1524
Hab 3:15 churning the g waters. 8041
Zep 1:14 "The g day of the LORD is near— 1524
3:17 *He will* take g delight in you, 928+8464+8525
Zec 2: 4 a city without walls because of the g number of men and livestock 8044
12:11 the weeping in Jerusalem *will be* g, 1540
14: 4 forming a g valley, 1524+4394
14:13 be *stricken* by the LORD *with* g panic. 8041
14:14 g quantities *of* gold and silver 4200+4394+8044
Mal 1: 5 'G *is* the LORD— 1540
1:11 My name will be g among the nations, 1524
1:11 my name will be g among the nations," 1524
1:14 For I am a g king," 1524
4: 5 before that g and dreadful day of 1524
Mt 2:18 weeping and g mourning, *4498*
4:16 in darkness have seen a g light; *3489*
5:12 because g is your reward in heaven, *4498*
5:19 be called g in the kingdom of heaven. *3489*
5:35 for it is the city *of* the G King. *3489*
6:23 how g is that darkness! *4531*
7:27 beat against that house, and it fell with a g crash." *899+1639+3489+3836+4774*
8:10 not found anyone in Israel with such g faith. *5537*
13:46 When he found one *of* g value, *4501*
15:28 Jesus answered, "Woman, you have g faith! *3489*
15:30 G crowds came to him, bringing the lame, *4498*
19:22 he went away sad, because he had g wealth. *4498*
20:26 to become g among you must *3489*
24:21 For then there will be g distress, *3489*
24:24 and perform g signs and miracles *3489*
24:30 with power and g glory. *4498*
27:14 to the g amazement of the governor. *3336*
27:19 a g deal today in a dream because of him." *4498*
Mk 5:26 She had suffered a g deal under the care *4498*
10:22 because he had g wealth. *4498*
10:43 to become g among you must *3489*
13: 2 "Do you see all these g buildings?" *3489*
13:26 of Man coming in clouds with g power *4498*
Lk 1:15 for he will be g in the sight of the Lord. *3489*
1:32 He will be g and will be called the Son of *3489*
Lk 1:49 Mighty One has done g *things* for me— *3489*
1:58 that the Lord *had* shown her g mercy, *3486*
2:10 I bring you good news of g joy that will be *3489*
2:13 a g company of the heavenly host appeared *4436*
5:29 Then Levi held a g banquet for Jesus *3489*
6:17 a g number of people from all over Judea, *4498*
6:23 because g is your reward in heaven. *4498*
6:35 Then your reward will be g, *4498*
7: 9 not found such g faith even in Israel." *5537*
7:16 "A g prophet has appeared among us," *3489*
8:23 and they were in g danger. *NIG*
14:16 "A certain man was preparing a g banquet *3489*
16:26 and you a g chasm has been fixed, *3489*
18:23 because he was a man of g wealth. *5379*
21:11 There will be g earthquakes, *3489*
21:11 and fearful events and g signs from heaven. *3489*
21:23 There will be g distress in the land *3489*
21:27 in a cloud with power and g glory. *4498*
24:52 and returned to Jerusalem with g joy. *3489*
Jn 5: 3 a g number of disabled people used to lie— *4436*
6: 2 and a g crowd of people followed him *4498*
6: 5 up and saw a g crowd coming toward him, *4498*
10:32 "I have shown you many g miracles from *2819*
12:12 The next day the g crowd that had come for *4498*
Ac 2:20 before the coming of the g and glorious day *3489*
4:29 to speak your word with g boldness. *4246*
4:33 *With* g power the apostles continued *3489*
5: 5 g fear seized all who heard what had *3489*
5:11 G fear seized the whole church *3489*
6: 8 did g wonders and miraculous signs among *3489*
7:11 bringing g suffering, and our fathers could *3489*
8: 1 that day a g persecution broke out against *3489*
8: 8 So there was g joy in that city. *4498*
8: 9 He boasted that he was someone g, *3489*
8:10 the divine power known as the G Power." *3489*
8:13 by the g signs and miracles he saw. *3489*
11:21 a g number of people believed and turned *4498*
11:24 and a g number *of* people were brought to *2653*
11:26 the church and taught g numbers *of* people. *2653*
14: 1 a g number of Jews and Gentiles believed. *4498*
16:16 She earned a g deal of money *4498*
17:11 with g eagerness and examined *4246*
18:25 and he spoke with g fervor and *2417+3836+4460*
18:27 he was a g help to those who *4498*
19:23 there arose a g disturbance *3900+4024+5431*
19:27 the g goddess Artemis will be discredited, *3489*
19:28 "G is Artemis of the Ephesians!" *3489*
19:34 "G is Artemis of the Ephesians!" *3489*
19:35 the guardian of the temple *of* the g Artemis *3489*
20:19 Lord with g humility and with tears, *4246+5425*
21:35 of the mob was so g he had to be carried by *NIG*
23: 9 There was a g uproar, *3489*
25:23 Agrippa and Bernice came with g pomp *4498*
26:22 and testify *to* small and g alike. *3489*
26:24 "Your g learning is driving you insane." *4498*
27:10 to be disastrous and bring g loss to ship *4498*
Ro 9: 2 I have g sorrow and unceasing anguish *3489*
9:22 with g patience the objects of his wrath— *4498*
16: 2 for she has been a g help to many people, *NIG*
1Co 16: 9 g door for effective work has opened to me, *3489*
2Co 1: 8 We were under g pressure, *2848+5651*
2: 4 of g distress and anguish of heart and *4498*
6: 4 in every way: in g endurance; *4498*
7: 4 I have g confidence in you; *4498*
7: 4 I take g pride in you. *4498*
8:22 even more so *because of* his g confidence *4498*
12: 7 *of* these surpassingly g revelations, *5651*
12:12 were done among you with g perseverance. *4246*
Eph 1:19 and his incomparably g power *3490*
2: 4 But because of his g love for us, God, *4498*
Php 2:29 Welcome him in the Lord with g joy, *4246*
Col 1:11 so that you may have g endurance *4246+5705*
2:18 goes into g detail about what he has seen, *1836*
1Ti 3:13 an excellent standing and g assurance *4498*
3:16 the mystery of godliness is g: *3489*
6: 6 But godliness with contentment is g gain. *3489*
2Ti 4: 2 g patience and careful instruction. *3429+4246*
4: 3 they will gather around them a g number *NIG*
4:14 the metalworker did me a g deal of harm. *4498*
Tit 2:13 the glorious appearing *of* our g God *3489*
Phm 1: 7 Your love has given me g joy *4498*
Heb 2: 3 if we ignore such a g salvation? *5496*
4:14 since we have a g high priest who has gone *3489*
7: 4 Just think how g he was: *4383*
10:21 we have a g priest over the house of God, *3489*
10:32 when you stood your ground in a g contest *4498*
12: 1 since we are surrounded by such a g cloud *5537*
13:20 that g Shepherd of the sheep, *3489*
Jas 3: 5 but it makes g boasts. *3489*
3: 5 Consider what a g forest is set on fire by *2462*
1Pe 1: 3 In his g mercy he has given us new birth *4498*
3: 4 which is of g worth in God's sight. *4500*
2Pe 1: 4 Through these he has given us his very g *3492*
1Jn 3: 1 How g is the love the Father has lavished *4534*
2Jn 1: 4 It has given me g joy to find some *3336*
3Jn 1: 3 It gave me g joy to have some of *3336*
Jude 1: 6 for judgment on the g Day. *3489*
1:24 without fault and with g joy— *21*
Rev 6:12 There was a g earthquake. *3489*
6:17 For the g day of their wrath has come, *3489*
7: 9 and there before me was a g multitude *4498*
7:14 who have come of the g tribulation; *3489*
8:10 and a g star, blazing like a torch, fell *3489*
9:14 who are bound at the g river Euphrates." *3489*
11: 8 in the street *of* the g city, *3489*
11:17 because you have taken your g power *3489*
11:18 reverence your name, both small and g— *3489*
Rev 11:19 an earthquake and a g hailstorm. *3489*
12: 1 A g and wondrous sign appeared in heaven: *3489*
12: 9 The g dragon was hurled down— *3489*
12:14 the two wings *of* a g eagle, *3489*
13: 2 and his throne and g authority. *3489*
13:13 And he performed g and miraculous signs, *3489*
13:16 He also forced everyone, small and g, *3489*
14: 8 Fallen is Babylon the G, *3489*
14:19 into the g winepress of God's wrath. *3489*
15: 1 in heaven another g and marvelous sign: *3489*
15: 3 "G and marvelous are your deeds, *3489*
16:12 on the g river Euphrates, *3489*
16:14 to gather them for the battle *on* the g day *3489*
16:19 The g city split into three parts, *3489*
16:19 the G and gave her the cup filled with *3489*
17: 1 the punishment *of* the g prostitute, *3489*
17: 5 MYSTERY BABYLON THE G *3489*
17:18 The woman you saw is the g city that rules *3489*
18: 1 He had g authority, *3489*
18: 2 Fallen is Babylon the G! *3489*
18:10 Woe, O g city, O Babylon, city of power! *3489*
18:16 Woe, O g city, dressed in fine linen, *3489*
18:17 In one hour such g wealth has been brought *5537*
18:18 'Was there ever a city like this g city?' *3489*
18:19 O g city, where all who had ships on *3489*
18:21 the g city of Babylon will be thrown down, *3489*
18:23 Your merchants were the world's g *men.* *3491*
19: 1 *of* a g multitude in heaven shouting: *4498*
19: 2 the g prostitute who corrupted the earth *3489*
19: 5 you who fear him, both small and g!" *3489*
19: 6 I heard what sounded like a g multitude, *4498*
19:17 gather together for the g supper of God, *3489*
19:18 free and slave, small and g." *3489*
20: 1 and holding in his hand a g chain. *3489*
20:11 a g white throne and him who was seated *3489*
20:12 And I saw the dead, g and small, *3489*
21:10 in the Spirit to a mountain g and high, *3489*
21:12 It had a g, high wall with twelve gates, *3489*
21:21 The g street of the city was of pure gold, *4423*
22: 2 down the middle *of* the g street of the city. *4423*

GREATER (80) [GREAT]

Ge 1:16 the g light to govern the day and 1524
39: 9 No one is g in this house than I am. 1524
41:40 to the throne *will I be* g than you." 1540
48:19 his younger brother *will be* g than he, 1540
49:26 Your father's blessings *are* g than 1504
Ex 18:11 that the LORD is g than all other gods, 1524
Nu 14:12 into a nation g and stronger than they." 1524
24: 7 "Their king *will be* g than Agag; 8123
Dt 4:38 before you nations g and stronger than you 1524
9: 1 the Jordan to go in and dispossess nations g 1524
20: 1 and chariots and an army g than yours, 8041
Ru 3:10 "This kindness *is* g than 3512
1Sa 14:30 of the Philistines *have been* even g?" 8049
2Sa 13:16 a g wrong than what you have already done 1524
19:43 g claim on David than you have. 4946
23:19 Was he not held in g honor than the Three? 3954
23:23 He was held in g honor than any of 4946
1Ki 1:37 make his throne *even* g than 1540
1:47 and his throne g than yours!' 1540
4:30 Solomon's wisdom *was* g than the wisdom 8049
4:30 and g than all the wisdom of Egypt. NIH
10:23 King Solomon *was* g in riches 1540
1Ch 11:25 He was held in g honor than any of 4946
2Ch 2: 5 because our God is g than all other gods. 1524
9:22 King Solomon *was* g in riches 1540
32: 7 there is a g power with us than with him. 8041
Job 33:12 for God *is* g than man. 8049
Ps 4: 7 You have filled my heart with g joy than 4946
135: 5 that our Lord is g than all gods. 4946
Ecc 2: 9 *I became* g by far than anyone 1540
La 4: 6 The punishment of my people *is* g than 1540
Da 2:30 I have g wisdom than other living men, 10427
4:36 became even g than before. 10323+10339+10650
Hag 2: 9 be g than the glory of the former house,' 1524
Zec 12: 7 not *be* g than that of Judah. 1540
Mt 11:11 not risen anyone g than John the Baptist; *3505*
11:11 in the kingdom of heaven is g than he. *3505*
12: 6 I tell you that one g than the temple is here. *3505*
12:41 and now *one* g *than* Jonah is here. *4498*
12:42 and now *one* g *than* Solomon is here. *4498*
23:17 You blind fools! Which is g: *3505*
23:19 You blind men! Which is g: *3505*
Mk 12:31 There is no commandment g than these." *3505*
Lk 7:28 of women there is no one g than John; *3505*
7:28 in the kingdom of God is g than he." *3505*
11:31 and now *one* g *than* Solomon is here. *4498*
11:32 and now *one* g *than* Jonah is here. *4498*
22:27 For who is g, the one who is at the table or *3505*
Jn 1:50 You shall see g *things* than that." *3505*
3:30 He must become g; I must become less. *889*
4:12 Are you g than our father Jacob, *3505*
5:20 he will show him even g things than these. *3505*
8:53 Are you g than our father Abraham? *3505*
10:29 who has given them to me, is g than all; *3505*
13:16 no servant is g than his master, *3505*
13:16 a messenger g than the one who sent him. *3505*
14:12 He will do even g things than these, *3505*
14:28 for the Father is g than I. *3505*
15:13 G love has no one than this, that he lay *3505*
15:20 'No servant is g than his master.' *3505*
19:11 over to you is guilty of a g sin." *3505*
Ro 11:12 how much g riches will their fullness bring! *3437*
1Co 12:24 the body and has given g honor to the parts *4358*
12:31 But eagerly desire the g gifts. *3505*

1Co 14: 5 He who prophesies is **g** than one who speaks in tongues, *3505*
2Co 3:11 **how** much **g** is the glory of that which lasts! *3437*
7: 7 so that my joy was **g than ever.** *3437*
7:15 for you is all the **g** when he remembers *4359*
Heb 3: 3 found worthy of **g** honor than Moses, *4498*
3: 3 as the builder of a house has **g** honor *than* *4498*
6:13 there was no one **g** for him to swear by, *3505*
6:16 Men swear by *someone* **g than** themselves, *3505+3836*
7: 7 the lesser person is blessed by the **g**. *3202*
9:11 through the **g** and more perfect tabernacle *3505*
11:26 as *of* **g** value **than** the treasures of Egypt, *3505*
1Pe 1: 7 your faith—of **g worth** *than* gold, *4501*
1Jn 3:20 For God is **g than** our hearts, *3505*
4: 4 because the one who is in you is **g** than *3505*
5: 9 but God's testimony is **g** because it is *3505*
3Jn 1: 4 I have no **g** joy **than** to hear *3504*

GREATER SIDON (2) [SIDON]

Jos 11: 8 and pursued them all the way to **S**, 7478
19:28 Hammon and Kanah, as far as **S**. 7478

GREATEST (31) [GREAT]

Jos 14:15 who was the **g** man among the Anakites.) 1524
2Sa 7: 9 like the names of the **g** *men* of the earth. 1524
2Ki 23: 2 all the people from the least to the **g**. 1524
25:26 all the people from the least to the **g**, 1524
1Ch 12:14 and the **g** for a thousand. 1524
17: 8 like the names of the **g** *men* of the earth. 1524
2Ch 34:30 all the people from the least to the **g**. 1524
Est 1: 5 for all the people from the least to the **g**, 1524
1:20 from the least to the **g**." 1524
Job 1: 3 the **g** man among all the people of the East. 1524
Jer 6:13 "From the least to the **g**, 1524
8:10 From the least to the **g**, 1524
31:34 from the least of them to the **g**," 1524
42: 1 from the least to the **g** approached 1524
42: 8 and all the people from the least to the **g**. 1524
44:12 From the least to the **g**, 1524
Jnh 3: 5 from the **g** to the least, put on sackcloth. 1524
Mt 18: 1 "Who is the **g** in the kingdom of heaven?" *3505*
18: 4 like this child is the **g** in the kingdom *3505*
22:36 which is the **g** commandment in the Law?" *3489*
22:38 This is the first and **g** commandment. *3489*
23:11 The **g** among you will be your servant. *3505*
Mk 9:34 they had argued about who was the **g**. *3505*
Lk 9:46 as to which of them would be the **g**. *3505*
9:48 he who is least among you all—he is the **g**." *3489*
22:24 as to which of them was considered to be **g**. *3505*
22:26 **g** among you should be like the youngest, *3505*
Jn 7:37 On the last and **g** day of the Feast, *3489*
1Co 13:13 But the **g** of these is love. *3505*
Heb 8:11 from the least of them to the **g**. *3489*
1Pe 1:10 **searched intently and with the g care,** *1699+2001+2779*

GREATLY (73) [GREAT]

Ge 3:16 *"I will* **g increase** your pains 8049+8049
7:18 The waters rose and increased **g** on 4394
7:19 They rose **g** on the earth, 4394+4394
13:13 of Sodom were wicked and were sinning **g** 4394
17: 2 will **g** increase your numbers." 928+4394+4394
17:20 and will **g** increase his numbers. 928+4394+4394
21:11 The matter distressed Abraham **g** 4394
30:30 before I came has increased **g**, 4200+8044
47:27 and were fruitful and increased **g** 4394
48:16 may they increase **g** upon the earth." 4200+8044
Ex 1: 7 the Israelites were fruitful and multiplied **g** 8049
Dt 6: 3 that you may increase **g** in a land flowing 4394
1Sa 19: 4 and what he has done has benefited you **g**. 4394
26:21 I have acted like a fool and have erred **g**." 2221+4394
28:21 to Saul and saw that he was **g** shaken, 4394
30: 6 David was **g** distressed because 4394
2Sa 10: 5 for they were **g** humiliated. 4394
24:10 "I have sinned **g** in what I have done. 4394
1Ki 1:40 playing flutes and rejoicing **g**, 1524
5: 7 he was **g** pleased and said, 4394
1Ch 4:38 Their families increased **g**, 4200+8044
19: 5 for they were **g** humiliated. 4394
21: 8 "I have sinned **g** by doing this. 4394
29: 9 David the king also rejoiced **g**. 1524
2Ch 26:15 he was **g** helped until he became powerful. 7098
33:12 the LORD his God and humbled himself **g** 4394
Ezr 10: 9 **g distressed** by the occasion and because of 8283
10:13 because *we have* sinned **g** in this thing. 8049
Ne 4: 1 he became angry and was **g** incensed. 2221
13: 8 I was **g** displeased and threw all Tobiah's 4394
Job 20: 2 to answer because I am **g disturbed.** 2591
Ps 47: 9 he is **g** exalted. 4394
89: 7 of the holy ones God is **g** feared; 8041
107:38 and their numbers **g** increased, 4394
109:30 With my mouth I will **g** extol the LORD; 4394
116:10 therefore I said, "I am **g** afflicted." 4394
119:167 I obey your statutes, for I love them **g**. 4394
129: 1 They have **g** oppressed me from my youth 8041
129: 2 they have **g** oppressed me from my youth, 8041
Ecc 9:13 example of wisdom that **g** impressed me: 1524
Isa 31: 6 to him *you have so* **g** revolted against, 6676
35: 2 *it will* **rejoice g** and shout for joy 677+1635+1638
61:10 *I* **delight g** in the LORD; 8464+8464
66:10 **rejoice g** with her, 5375+8464
Jer 3:16 **numbers** *have* **increased g** in 2256+7238+8049
14:10 "They **g** love to wander; 4027
50:12 your mother will be **g** ashamed; 4394
La 1: 8 Jerusalem *has* **sinned g** and 2627+2628
Da 4: 1 *May* you prosper **g**! 10677
4:19 (also called Belteshazzar) *was* **g perplexed** 10724
6:14 he was **g** distressed; 10678
6:25 *"May* you prosper **g**! 10677
11:39 *will* **g** honor those who acknowledge him. 8049
Jnh 1:16 At this the men **g** feared the LORD, 1524
4: 1 Jonah was **g** displeased and became angry. 1524
Zec 9: 9 Rejoice **g**, O Daughter of Zion! 4394
Mt 17:15 "He has seizures and is suffering **g**. *2809*
18:31 they were **g** distressed and went *5379*
19:25 they were **g** astonished and asked, *5379*
Mk 6:20 When Herod heard John, he was **g** puzzled; *4498*
6:26 The king was **g distressed,** *4337*
Lk 1:29 Mary *was* **g troubled** at his words *1410*
23: 8 When Herod saw Jesus, he was **g** pleased, *3336*
Ac 4: 2 *They were* **g disturbed** because *1387*
7:17 number of our people in Egypt **g increased.** *889+2779+4437*
17:16 he *was* **g distressed** to see that *4236*
20:12 and were **g** comforted. *3585+4024*
2Co 7: 4 *I am* **g encouraged;** *4155+4444*
10:15 of activity among you will **g** expand, *1650+4353*
Php 4:10 I rejoice **g** in the Lord that at all you *3487*
Heb 6:18 the hope offered to us may be **g** encouraged. *2708*
1Pe 1: 6 In this *you* **g rejoice,** though now *22*
Rev 17: 6 When I saw her, I was **g** astonished. *3489*

GREATNESS (16) [GREAT]

Ex 15: 7 In the **g** *of* your majesty you threw 8044
Dt 3:24 to show to your servant your **g** 1542
32: 3 Oh, praise the **g** of our God! 1542
1Ch 29:11 is the **g** and the power and the glory and 1525
2Ch 9: 6 half the **g** *of* your wisdom was told me; 5270
Est 10: 2 with a full account of the **g** *of* Mordecai 1525
Ps 145: 3 his **g** no one can fathom. 1525
150: 2 praise him for his surpassing **g**. 1542
Isa 63: 1 striding forward in the **g** *of* his strength? 8044
Eze 38:23 And so *I will* **show** *my* **g** and my holiness, 1540
Da 4:22 your **g** has grown until it reaches the sky, 10650
5:18 and **g** and glory and splendor. 10650
7:27 power and **g** of the kingdoms under 10650
Mic 5: 4 *his* **g** will reach to the ends of the earth. 1540
Lk 9:43 And they were all amazed at the **g** of God. *3484*
Php 3: 8 a loss compared to the **surpassing g** *5660*

GREAVES (1)

1Sa 17: 6 on his legs he wore bronze **g**, 5196

GRECIA, GRECIANS (KJV) See GREEK

GRECIAN (2) [GREECE]

Ac 6: 1 the **G Jews** among them complained against *1821*
9:29 He talked and debated with the **G Jews,** *1821*

GREECE (7) [GRECIAN, GREEK, GREEKS]

Isa 66:19 to Tubal and **G**, and to the distant islands 3430
Eze 27:13 " '**G**, Tubal and Meshech traded with you; 3430
Da 8:21 The shaggy goat is the king of **G**, 3430
10:20 and when I go, the prince of **G** will come; 3430
11: 2 up everyone against the kingdom of **G**. 3430
Zec 9:13 O **G**, and make you like a warrior's sword. 3430
Ac 20: 2 and finally arrived in **G**, *1817*

GREED (12) [GREEDY]

Isa 57:17 I was enraged by his sinful **g**; 1299
Eze 16:27 I gave you over to the **g** *of* your enemies, 5883
Mt 23:25 but inside they are full of **g** *771*
Mk 7:22 **g**, malice, deceit, lewdness, *4432*
Lk 11:39 but inside you are full of **g** and wickedness. *771*
12:15 Be on your guard against all kinds *of* **g**; *4432*
Ro 1:29 with every kind of wickedness, evil, **g** *4432*
Eph 5: 3 or of any kind of impurity, or of **g**, *4432*
Col 3: 5 lust, evil desires and **g**, which is idolatry. *4432*
1Th 2: 5 nor did we put on a mask to cover up **g**— *4432*
2Pe 2: 3 In their **g** these teachers will exploit you *4432*
2:14 they are experts *in* **g**—an accursed brood! *4432*

GREEDY (13) [GREED]

Ps 10: 3 he blesses the **g** and reviles the LORD. 1298
Pr 15:27 A **g** *man* brings trouble to his family, 1298+1299
28:25 A **g man** stirs up dissension, 5883+8146
29: 4 but **one** *who is* **g** *for* bribes tears it down. AIT
Jer 6:13 all *are* **g** *for* gain; 1298
8:10 all *are* **g** *for* gain; 1298
Eze 33:31 but their hearts *are* **g** *for* unjust gain. 339+2143
Hab 2: 5 Because he *is* as **g** as the grave and 8143
1Co 5:10 or the **g** and swindlers, or idolaters. *4431*
5:11 a brother but is sexually immoral or **g**, *4431*
6:10 nor the **g** nor drunkards nor slanderers *4431*
Eph 5: 5 No immoral, impure or **g person**— *4431*
1Pe 5: 2 not **g for money,** but eager to serve; *154*

GREEK (11) [GREECE]

Mk 7:26 The woman was a **G**, *1820*
Jn 19:20 in Aramaic, Latin and **G**. *1822*
Ac 16: 1 but whose father was a **G**. *1818*
16: 3 for they all knew that his father was a **G**. *1818*
17:12 also a number of prominent **G** women *1820*
17:12 prominent Greek women and many **G** men. *NIG*
21:37 "Do you speak **G**?" *1822*
Gal 2: 3 even though he was a **G**. *1818*
3:28 There is neither Jew nor **G**, slave nor free, *1818*
Col 3:11 Here there is no **G** or Jew, *1818*
Rev 9:11 in Hebrew is Abaddon, and in **G**, Apollyon. *1819*

GREEKS (18) [GREECE]

Eze 27:19 and **G** from Uzal bought your merchandise; 3430
Joel 3: 6 of Judah and Jerusalem to the **G**, 1201+3436
Jn 7:35 scattered among the **G**, and teach *1818*
7:35 and teach the **G**? *1818*
12:20 Now there were some **G** among those *1818*
Ac 11:20 went to Antioch and began to speak to **G** *1821*
17: 4 a large number *of* God-fearing **G** and not *1818*
17:17 *with* the Jews and the **God-fearing G,** *4936*
18: 4 trying to persuade Jews and **G**. *1818*
19:10 the Jews and **G** who lived in the province *1818*
19:17 *to* the Jews and **G** living in Ephesus, *1818*
20:21 both Jews and **G** that they must turn to God *1818*
21:28 he has brought **G** into the temple area *1818*
Ro 1:14 I am obligated both *to* **G** and non-Greeks, *1818*
1Co 1:22 Jews demand miraculous signs and **G** look *1818*
1:24 whom God has called, both Jews and **G**, *1818*
10:32 whether Jews, **G** or the church of God— *1818*
12:13 whether Jews or **G**, slave or free— *1818*

GREEN (22) [GREENISH]

Ge 1:30 I give every **g** plant for food." 3764
9: 3 Just as I gave you the **g** plants, 3764
Ex 10:15 Nothing **g** remained on tree or plant in all 3764
2Ki 19:26 like tender **g** shoots, 2013
Job 39: 8 for his pasture and searches for any **g thing.** 3728
Ps 23: 2 He makes me lie down in **g** pastures, 2013
37: 2 like **g** plants they will soon die away. 2013
37:35 and ruthless man flourishing like a **g tree** 8316
58: 9 whether they be **g** or dry— 2645
92:14 they will stay fresh and **g**, 8316
105:35 they ate up every **g thing** in their land, 6912
Pr 11:28 but the righteous will thrive like a **g leaf.** 6591
Isa 15: 6 the vegetation is gone and nothing **g** is left. 3764
37:27 like tender **g** shoots, 2013
Jer 17: 8 its leaves are always **g**. 8316
Eze 17:24 up the **g** tree and make the dry tree flourish. 4300
20:47 and it will consume all your trees, both **g** 4300
Hos 14: 8 I am like a **g** pine tree; 8316
Joel 2:22 for the open pastures *are becoming* **g**. 2012
Mk 6:39 down in groups on the **g** grass. *5952*
Lk 23:31 if men do these things when the tree is **g**, *5619*
Rev 8: 7 and all the **g** grass was burned up. *5952*

GREENISH (2) [GREEN]

Lev 13:49 or any leather article, is **g** or reddish, 3768
14:37 and if it has **g** or reddish depressions 3768

GREET (39) [GREETED, GREETING, GREETINGS, GREETS]

1Sa 10: 4 *They will* **g** you and offer you two loaves 4200+8626+8934
13:10 and Saul went out to **g** him. 1385+7925
25: 5 to Nabal at Carmel and **g** him 4200+8626+8934
2Sa 8:10 to **g** him and congratulate him 4200+8626+8934
2Ki 4:29 If you meet anyone, *do* not **g** him, 1385
10:13 and we have come down to **g** the families 8934
1Ch 18:10 to **g** him and congratulate him 4200+8626+8934
Isa 14: 9 the spirits of the departed to **g** you— NIH
Mt 5:47 And if *you* **g** only your brothers, *832*
Mk 9:15 with wonder and ran *to* **g** him. *832*
Lk 10: 4 and *do* not **g** anyone on the road. *832*
Ro 16: 3 **G** Priscilla and Aquila, *832*
16: 5 **G** also the church that meets at their house. *NIG*
16: 5 **G** my dear friend Epenetus, *832*
16: 6 **G** Mary, who worked very hard for you. *832*
16: 7 **G** Andronicus and Junias, *832*
16: 8 **G** Ampliatus, whom I love in the Lord. *832*
16: 9 **G** Urbanus, our fellow worker in Christ, *832*
16:10 **G** Apelles, tested and approved in Christ. *832*
16:10 **G** those who belong to the household *832*
16:11 **G** Herodion, my relative. *832*
16:11 **G** those in the household of Narcissus *832*
16:12 **G** Tryphena and Tryphosa, *832*
16:12 **G** my dear friend Persis, *832*
16:13 **G** Rufus, chosen in the Lord, *832*
16:14 **G** Asyncritus, Phlegon, Hermes, Patrobas, *832*
16:15 **G** Philologus, Julia, Nereus and his sister, *832*
16:16 **G** one another with a holy kiss. *832*
16:22 **g** you in the Lord. *832*
1Co 16:19 Aquila and Priscilla **g** you warmly in the Lord, *832*
16:20 **G** one another with a holy kiss. *832*
2Co 13:12 **G** one another with a holy kiss. *832*
Php 4:21 **G** all the saints in Christ Jesus. *832*
1Th 5:26 **G** all the brothers with a holy kiss. *832*
2Ti 4:19 **G** Priscilla and Aquila and the household *832*
Tit 3:15 **G** those who love us in the faith. *832*
Heb 13:24 **G** all your leaders and all God's people. *832*
1Pe 5:14 **G** one another with a kiss of love. *832*
3Jn 1:14 **G** the friends there by name. *832*

GREETED (13) [GREET]

Ex 18: 7 *They* **g** each other and then 4200+8626+8934
Jdg 18:15 at Micah's place and **g** him. 4200+8626+8934
Ru 2: 4 then Boaz arrived from Bethlehem and **g** 606
1Sa 17:22 battle lines and **g** his brothers. 4200+8626+8934
30:21 his men approached, *he* **g** them. 4200+8626+8934

2Ki 10:15 Jehu **g** him and said, 1385
Mt 23: 7 they love to be **g** in the marketplaces and *833*
Mk 12:38 to walk around in flowing robes and be **g** in *833*
Lk 1:40 where she entered Zechariah's home and **g** Elizabeth. *832*
20:46 and love to be **g** in the marketplaces *833*
Ac 18:22 at Caesarea, he went up and **g** the church *832*
21: 7 where *we* **g** the brothers and stayed *832*
21:19 Paul **g** them and reported in detail *832*

GREETING (7) [GREET]

Mt 10:12 As you enter the home, **give** it *your* **g.** *832*
Lk 1:29 and wondered what kind of **g** this might be. *833*
1:41 When Elizabeth heard Mary's **g,** *833*
1:44 as the sound *of* your **g** reached my ears, *833*
1Co 16:21 I, Paul, write this **g** in my own hand. *833*
Col 4:18 I, Paul, write this **g** in my own hand. *833*
2Th 3:17 I, Paul, write this **g** in my own hand, *833*

GREETINGS (31) [GREET]

1Sa 25:14 *to* **give** our master his **g,** 1385
Ezr 4:17 and elsewhere in Trans-Euphrates: **G.** 10720
5: 7 To King Darius: **Cordial g.** 10002+10002+10353+10720
7:12 of the Law of the God of heaven: **G.** 10147
Mt 26:49 Going at once to Jesus, Judas said, **"G,** *5897*
28: 9 Suddenly Jesus met them. **"G,"** he said. *5897*
Lk 1:28 The angel went to her and said, **"G,** *5897*
11:43 the synagogues and **g** in the marketplaces. *833*
Ac 15:23 in Antioch, Syria and Cilicia: **G.** *5897*
23:26 To His Excellency, Governor Felix: **G.** *5897*
Ro 16:16 All the churches of Christ **send g.** *832*
16:21 Timothy, my fellow worker, **sends** *his* **g** to *832*
16:23 **sends** you *his* **g.** *832*
16:23 and our brother Quartus **send** you *their* **g.** *832*
1Co 16:19 churches in the province of Asia **send** you **g.** *832*
16:20 All the brothers here **send** you **g.** *832*
2Co 13:13 All the saints **send** *their* **g.** *832*
Php 4:21 The brothers who are with me **send g.** *832*
4:22 All the saints **send** you **g,** *832*
Col 4:10 My fellow prisoner Aristarchus **sends** you *his* **g,** *832*
4:11 Jesus, who is called Justus, also sends **g.** *NIG*
4:12 and a servant of Christ Jesus, **sends g.** *832*
4:14 the doctor, and Demas **send g.** *832*
4:15 **Give** my **g to** the brothers at Laodicea, and *832*
Tit 3:15 Everyone with me **sends** you **g.** *832*
Phm 1:23 in Christ Jesus, **sends** you **g.** *832*
Heb 13:24 Those from Italy **send** you *their* **g.** *832*
Jas 1: 1 among the nations: **G.** *5897*
1Pe 5:13 **sends** you *her* **g,** and so does my son Mark. *832*
2Jn 1:13 children of your chosen sister **send** *their* **g.** *832*
3Jn 1:14 The friends here **send** *their* **g.** *832*

GREETS (2) [GREET]

2Ki 4:29 do not greet him, and if anyone **g** you, 1385
2Ti 4:21 Eubulus **g** you, and so do Pudens, Linus, *832*

GREW (72) [GROW]

Ge 10: 8 who **g** to be a mighty warrior on the earth. 2725
21: 8 The child **g** and was weaned, 1540
21:20 God was with the boy as *he* **g up.** 1540
25:27 The boys **g up,** and Esau became 1540
30:43 the man *g* exceedingly **prosperous** AIT
Ex 2:10 When the child **g older,** 1540
16:21 and when the sun **g hot,** it melted away. AIT
17:12 When Moses' hands **g** tired, NIH
19:19 **g louder and louder.** 2143+2256+2618+4394
Nu 21: 4 But the people *g* **impatient** on the way; AIT
Dt 32:15 Jeshurun **g fat** and kicked; 9042
Jos 17:13 However, when the Israelites *g* **stronger,** AIT
Jdg 2:10 another generation **g up,** who knew neither 7756
4:24 **g stronger and stronger** 2143+2256+7997
13:24 He **g** and the LORD blessed him, 1540
Ru 1:13 would you wait until *they* **g up?** 1540
1Sa 2:21 the boy Samuel **g up** in the presence of 1540
3:19 The LORD was with Samuel as he **g up,** 1540
8: 1 When Samuel **g old,** he appointed his sons 2416
31: 3 The fighting *g* **fierce** around Saul, AIT
2Sa 3: 1 David **g stronger and stronger** 2143+2256+2618
3: 1 while the house of Saul **g weaker and weaker.** 1924+2143+2256
12: 3 and *it* **g up** with him and his children. 1540
23:10 the Philistines till his hand *g* **tired** and froze AIT
1Ki 11: 4 As Solomon **g old,** his wives turned his 2420
17:17 He **g worse and worse,** 2118+2617+2716+4394
18:45 Meanwhile, the sky *g* **black** *with* clouds, AIT
2Ki 4:18 The child **g,** and one day he went out 1540
4:34 the boy's body *g* **warm.** AIT
1Ch 1:10 who **g** to be a mighty warrior on earth. 2725
10: 3 The fighting **g fierce** around Saul, 3877
2Ch 13:21 But Abijah **g in strength.** 2616
27: 6 Jotham *g* **powerful** because he walked AIT
Ps 39: 3 My heart *g* **hot** within me, AIT
52: 7 but trusted in his great wealth and *g* **strong** AIT
77: 3 I mused, and my spirit *g* **faint.** AIT
106:16 In the camp *they g* **envious** of Moses and AIT
107:30 They were glad when *it g* **calm,** AIT
Isa 38:14 My eyes *g* **weak** as I looked to the heavens. AIT
53: 2 *He* **g up** before him like a tender shoot, 6590
Eze 16: 7 *You* **g up** and developed and became 8049
16: 7 Your breasts were formed and your hair **g,** 7541
17:10 wither away in the plot where it **g?"** 7542
31: 5 and its branches *g* **long,** AIT
Da 4:11 The tree **g large** and strong 10648
4:20 tree you saw, which **g large** and strong, 10648
4:33 until his hair **g** like the feathers of an eagle 10648
5: 9 and his face **g** more pale. 10731
8: 3 the other but **g up** later. 6590
8: 8 and in its place four prominent horns **g up** 6590
8: 9 but **g** *in* power to the south and to the east 1540
8:10 *It* **g** until it reached the host of 1540
Jnh 1:13 for the sea **g even wilder** than before. 2143+2256+6192
1:15 and the raging sea *g* **calm.** AIT
4: 8 on Jonah's head so that *he g* **faint.** AIT
Zec 11: 8 and I **g weary** of them 7918
Mt 13: 7 which **g up** and choked the plants, *326*
Mk 4: 7 which **g up** and choked the plants, *326*
4: 8 It came up, **g** and produced a crop, *889*
5:26 yet instead of getting better *she* **g** worse. *1650+2262+3836*
Lk 1:80 the child **g** and became strong in spirit; *889*
2:40 And the child **g** and became strong; *889*
2:52 And Jesus **g** in wisdom and stature, *4621*
8: 7 which **g up with** it and choked the plants. *5243*
13:19 *It* **g** and became a tree, *889*
Jn 6:18 and the waters **g rough.** *1444*
Ac 4: 4 number of men **g** to about five thousand. *1181*
9:22 Saul *g* more and more **powerful** *AIT*
9:31 by the Holy Spirit, *it* **g in numbers,** *4437*
16: 5 in the faith and **g** daily in numbers. *4355*
19:20 of the Lord spread widely and **g** in power. *2710*
Rev 18: 3 and the merchants of the earth **g rich** *4456*

GREY, GREYHEADED (KJV, Anglicized) See GRAY

GREYHOUND (KJV) See ROOSTER

GRIDDLE (3)

Lev 2: 5 If your grain offering is prepared on a **g,** 4679
6:21 Prepare it with oil on a **g;** 4679
7: 9 or on a **g** belongs to the priest who offers it, 4679

GRIEF (33) [GRIEFS, GRIEVANCE, GRIEVANCES, GRIEVE, GRIEVED, GRIEVES, GRIEVING, GRIEVOUS]

Ge 26:35 a **source of g** to Isaac and Rebekah. 5289+8120
34: 7 They *were* **filled with g** and fury, 6772
38:12 When Judah *had* **recovered from** *his* **g,** 5714
1Sa 1:16 of my great anguish and **g."** 4088
Est 6:12 with his head covered in **g,** 63
Job 17: 7 My eyes have grown dim with **g;** 4089
Ps 10:14 But you, O God, do see trouble and **g;** 4088
31: 9 my soul and my body with **g.** NIH
35:14 I bowed my head *in* **g** as though weeping 7722
88: 9 my eyes are dim with **g.** 6713
Pr 10: 1 but a foolish son **g** *to* his mother. 9342
10:10 He who winks maliciously causes **g,** 6780
14:13 and joy may end in **g.** 9342
17:21 To have a fool for a son brings **g;** 9342
17:25 A foolish son brings **g** to his father 4088
29:21 he will bring **g** in the end. 4959
Ecc 1:18 the more knowledge, the more **g.** 4799
2:23 All his days his work is pain and **g;** 4088
La 1: 5 The LORD *has* **brought** her **g** because 3324
3:32 Though *he* **brings g,** 3324
3:33 not willingly bring affliction or **g** *to* 3324
3:51 What I see **brings g** to my soul because 6618
Eze 13:22 when I *had* **brought** them no **g,** 3872
21: 6 before them with broken heart and **bitter g.** 5320
Mic 4: 6 the exiles and those *I have* **brought to g.** 8317
Mt 17:23 And the disciples *were* **filled with g.** *3382+5379*
Jn 16: 6 you are filled with **g.** *3383*
16:20 You will grieve, but your **g** will turn to joy. *3383*
16:22 **is** *your* **time of g,** *2400+3383*
1Co 5: 2 Shouldn't *you* rather *have been* **filled with g** *4291*
2Co 2: 5 If anyone *has* **caused g,** *3382*
1Pe 1: 6 a little while you may have had *to* **suffer g** *3382*
Rev 18: 7 Give her as much torture and **g** as the glory *4292*

GRIEFS (1) [GRIEF]

1Ti 6:10 and pierced themselves with many **g.** *3850*

GRIEVANCE (2) [GRIEF]

Job 31:13 and maidservants when they had a **g** 8190
Ac 19:38 and his fellow craftsmen have a **g** *3364*

GRIEVANCES (1) [GRIEF]

Col 3:13 and forgive whatever **g** you may have *3664*

GRIEVE (18) [GRIEF]

1Sa 2:33 with tears and to **g** your heart, 117
2Sa 1:26 I **g** for you, Jonathan my brother; 7639
Ne 8:10 *Do* not **g,** for the joy of the LORD 6772
8:11 for this is a sacred day. *Do* not **g."** 6772
Isa 16: 7 Lament and **g** for the men of Kir Hareseth. 5778
61: 3 and provide for *those who* **g** *in* Zion— 63
La 1: 4 her maidens **g,** and she is in bitter anguish. 3324
Eze 7:12 Let not the buyer rejoice nor the seller **g,** 61
9: 4 on the foreheads of those who **g** and lament 634
Joel 1:11 **g** for the wheat and the barley, NIH
Am 6: 6 but *you do* not **g** over the ruin of Joseph. 2703
Zec 12:10 and **g bitterly** for him as one grieves for 5352
Jn 16:20 You *will* **g,** but your grief will turn to joy. *3382*
2Co 2: 2 For if I **g** you, who is left to make me glad *3382*
2: 4 not to **g** *you* but to let you know the depth *3382*
Eph 4:30 And *do* not **g** the Holy Spirit of God, *3382*
1Th 4:13 or *to* **g** like the rest of men, *3382*
Jas 4: 9 **G,** mourn and wail. *5415*

GRIEVED (22) [GRIEF]

Ge 6: 6 The LORD **was g** that he had made man on 5714
6: 7 for *I* **am g** that I have made them." 5714
Dt 34: 8 The Israelites **g** *for* Moses in the plains 1134
Jdg 21: 6 Now the Israelites **g** for their brothers, 5714
21:15 The people **g** for Benjamin, 5714
1Sa 15:11 *"I* **am g** that I have made Saul king, 5714
15:35 the LORD **was g** that he had made Saul king 5714
20: 3 must not know this or *he will* **be g.'** 6772
20:34 the month he did not eat, because *he* **was g** 6772
2Sa 24:16 the LORD **was g** because of the calamity 5714
1Ch 21:15 and **was g** because of the calamity and said 5714
Job 30:25 *Has* not my soul **g** for the poor? 6327
Ps 73:21 my heart **was g** and my spirit embittered, 2806
78:40 in the desert and **g** him in the wasteland! 6772
Isa 63:10 Yet they rebelled and **g** his Holy Spirit. 6772
Jer 42:10 for *I am* **g** over the disaster I have inflicted 5714
Eze 6: 9 *I have* **been g** *by* their adulterous hearts, 8689
Ac 20:38 What **g** them most was his statement *3849*
2Co 2: 2 to make me glad but you whom I *have* **g?** *3382*
2: 5 so much **g** me as he has grieved all of you, *3382*
2: 5 so much grieved me as he has **g** all of you, *NIG*
12:21 *be* **g over** many who have sinned earlier *4291*

GRIEVES (1) [GRIEF]

Zec 12:10 and grieve bitterly for him as *one* **g** for 5352

GRIEVING (3) [GRIEF]

2Sa 14: 2 like a woman *who has spent* many days **g** 61
19: 2 "The king *is* **g** for his son." 6772
Joel 1: 8 in sackcloth **g** for the husband of her youth. NIH

GRIEVOUS (7) [GRIEF]

Ge 18:20 and Gomorrah is so great and their sin so **g** 3877
Ecc 2:17 the work that is done under the sun was **g** 8273
5:13 I have seen a **g** evil under the sun: 2703
5:16 This too *is* a **g** evil: 2703
6: 2 This is meaningless, a **g** evil. 8273
Jer 14:17 has suffered a **g** wound, a crushing blow. 1524
15:18 Why is my pain unending and my wound **g** 631

GRIND (5) [GRINDERS, GRINDING]

Ex 30:36 **G** some of it to powder and place it in front 8835
Job 31:10 *may* my wife **g** another man's **grain,** 3221
Pr 27:22 Though *you* **g** a fool in a mortar, 4197
Isa 28:28 his horses *do* not **g** it 1990
47: 2 Take millstones and **g** flour; 3221

GRINDERS (1) [GRIND]

Ecc 12: 3 when the **g** cease because they are few, 3223

GRINDING (6) [GRIND]

Jdg 16:21 they set him to **g** in the prison. 3221
Pr 27:22 **g** him like grain with a pestle, NIH
Ecc 12: 4 and the sound of **g** fades; 3222
Isa 3:15 by crushing my people and **g** the faces of 3221
Mt 24:41 Two *women will be* **g** with a hand mill; *241*
Lk 17:35 Two women will be **g grain** together; *241*

GRIP (4) [GRIPPED, GRIPS]

Ex 15:14 anguish *will* **g** the people of Philistia. 296
Job 30:16 my life ebbs away; days of suffering **g** me. 296
Isa 13: 8 pain and anguish *will* **g** them; 296
Jer 13:21 *Will* not pain **g** you like that of a woman 296

GRIPPED (4) [GRIP]

Jer 6:24 Anguish *has* **g** us, 2616
49:24 she has turned to flee and panic *has* **g** her; 2616
50:43 Anguish *has* **g** him, 2616
Lk 1:12 he was startled and *was* **g with fear.** *2158+5832*

GRIPS (3) [GRIP]

Ps 119:53 Indignation **g** me because of the wicked, 296
Isa 33:14 trembling **g** the godless: 296
Jer 8:21 I mourn, and horror **g** me. 2616

GRISLED (KJV) See SPOTTED, DAPPLED

GROAN (19) [GROANED, GROANING, GROANS]

Ps 38: 8 *I* **g** in anguish of heart. 8613
Pr 5:11 At the end of your life *you will* **g,** 5637
29: 2 when the wicked rule, the people **g.** 634
Isa 19: 8 The fishermen *will* **g** and lament, 627
24: 7 all the merrymakers **g.** 634
Jer 4:31 a **g** as of one bearing her first child— 7650
22:23 *you will* **g** when pangs come upon you, 634
51:52 throughout her land the wounded *will* **g.** 650
La 1: 4 All her gateways are desolate, her priests **g,** 634
1:11 All her people **g** as they search for bread; 634
Eze 21: 6 "Therefore **g,** son of man! 634
21: 6 **G** before them with broken heart 634

Eze 24:17 G quietly; do not mourn for the dead. 650
24:23 of your sins and g among yourselves. 5637
26:15 the sound of your fall, when the wounded g 650
30:24 and *he will* g before him like 5543+5544
Ro 8:23 g inwardly as we wait eagerly for *5100*
2Co 5: 2 Meanwhile *we* g, longing to be clothed *5100*
5: 4 *we* g and are burdened, *5100*

GROANED (3) [GROAN]

Ex 2:23 The Israelites g in their slavery 634
Jdg 2:18 as they g under those who oppressed 5544
Ps 77: 3 I remembered you, O God, and *I* g; 2159

GROANING (15) [GROAN]

Ex 2:24 God heard their g 5544
6: 5 I have heard the g *of* the Israelites, 5544
Job 23: 2 his hand is heavy in spite of my g. 635
Ps 6: 6 I am worn out from g; 635
12: 5 of the oppression of the weak and the g *of* 651
22: 1 so far from the words of my g? 8614
31:10 by anguish and my years by g; 635
32: 3 through my g all day long. 8614
102: 5 Because of my loud g I am reduced to skin 635
Isa 21: 2 I will bring to an end all the g she caused. 635
Jer 45: 3 I am worn out with g and find no rest.' " 635
La 1:21 "People have heard my g, 634
Eze 21: 7 And when they ask you, 'Why *are* you g?' 634
Ac 7:34 I have heard their g and have come down *5099*
Ro 8:22 that the whole creation *has been* g as in *5367*

GROANS (7) [GROAN]

Job 3:24 my g pour out like water. 8614
24:12 *The* g *of* the dying *rise* from the city, 5543
Ps 79:11 the g *of* the prisoners come before you; 651
102:20 to hear the g *of* the prisoners 651
La 1: 8 *she* herself g and turns away. 634
1:22 My g are many and my heart is faint." 635
Ro 8:26 the Spirit himself intercedes for us *with* g *5099*

GROPE (5) [GROPED]

Dt 28:29 At midday *you will* g **about** like 5491
Job 5:14 at noon *they* g as in the night. 5491
12:25 *They* g *in* darkness with no light; 5491
Isa 59:10 Like the blind *we* g **along** the wall, 1779
La 4:14 Now *they* g through the streets 5675

GROPED (1) [GROPE]

Ac 13:11 and he **g about,** *4310*

GROSS (KJV) See THICK, CALLOUSED

GROUND (308) [AGROUND, GROUNDS]

Ge 1: 9 and let **dry** g appear." 3317
1:10 God called the **dry** g "land," 3317
1:24 livestock, creatures that move along the g, NIH
1:25 and all the creatures that move along the g 141
1:26 over all the creatures that move along the g. 824
1:28 that moves on the g." 824
1:30 and all the creatures that move on the g— 824
2: 5 and there was no man to work the g, 141
2: 6 and watered the whole surface of the g— 141
2: 7 the man from the dust of the g and breathed 141
2: 9 of trees grow out of the g— 141
2:19 the LORD God had formed out of the g all 141
3:17 "Cursed is the g because of you; 141
3:19 to the g, since from it you were taken; 141
3:23 from the Garden of Eden to work the g 141
4:10 brother's blood cries out to me from the g. 141
4:11 under a curse and driven from the g, 141
4:12 When you work the g, 141
5:29 by the g the LORD has cursed." 141
6: 7 **creatures that move along the g,** 8254
6:20 that moves along the g will come to you to 141
7: 8 and of all creatures that move along the g, 141
7:14 that moves along the g according to its kind 824
7:23 and the creatures that move along the g and NIH
8: 8 from the surface of the g. 141
8:13 and saw that the surface of the g was dry. 141
8:17 all the creatures that move along the g— 824
8:19 the creatures that move along the g and all NIH
8:21 "Never again will I curse the g because 141
9: 2 the g, and upon all the fish of the sea; 141
18: 2 to meet them and bowed low to the g. 824
19: 1 and bowed down with his face to the g. 824
24:52 he bowed down to the g before the LORD. 824
33: 3 and bowed down to the g seven times 824
33:19 the plot of g where he pitched his tent. 8441
37:10 and bow down to the g before you?" 824
38: 9 his semen on the g to keep from producing 824
42: 6 down to him with their faces to the g. 824
43:26 and they bowed down before him to the g. 824
44:11 of them quickly lowered his sack to the g 824
44:14 they threw themselves to the g before him. 824
47:23 here is seed for you so you can plant the g. 141
48:12 and bowed down with his face to the g. 824
Ex 3: 5 the place where you are standing is holy g." 141
4: 3 The LORD said, "Throw it on the g." 824
4: 3 Moses threw it on the g and it became 824
4: 9 from the Nile and pour it on the **dry** g. 3317
4: 9 from the river will become blood on the g." 3318
8:16 and strike the dust of the g,' 824
8:17 with the staff and struck the dust of the g, 824
Ex 8:21 and even the g where they are. 141
9:23 and lightning flashed down to the g. 824
10: 5 the face of the g so that it cannot be seen. 824
10:15 They covered all the g until it was black. 824
14:16 Israelites went through the sea on **dry** g. 3317
14:22 the Israelites went through the sea on **dry** g, 3317
14:29 the Israelites went through the sea on **dry** g, 3317
15:19 Israelites walked through the sea on **dry** g. 3317
16:14 thin flakes like frost on the g appeared on 824
16:25 You will not find any of it on the g today. 8441
32:20 then *he* g it to powder, 3221
34: 8 to the g at once and worshiped. 824
Lev 5: 2 **creatures that move along the g—** 9238
11:21 that have jointed legs for hopping on the g. 824
11:29 " 'Of the animals that move about on the g, 824
11:31 Of all those that move along the g, NIH
11:41 that moves about on the g is detestable; 824
11:42 on the g, whether it moves on its belly 824
11:44 by any creature that moves about on the g. 824
11:46 that moves about on the g. 824
16:12 of **finely** g fragrant incense and take them 1987
20:25 or bird or anything that moves along the g— 141
26: 4 and the g will yield its crops and the trees 824
26:19 like iron and the g *beneath* you like bronze. 824
Nu 11: 8 g it in a handmill or crushed it in a mortar. 3221
11:31 the camp to about three feet above the g, 824
15:20 Present a cake from the first of your **g meal** 6881
15:21 the LORD from the first of your **g meal.** 6881
16:31 the g under them split apart 141
Dt 4:18 along the g or any fish in the waters below. 141
9:21 and g it **to powder** as fine as dust 3221+3512
11:17 not rain and the g will yield no produce, 141
12:16 pour it out on the g like water. 824
12:24 pour it out on the g like water. 824
15:23 pour it out on the g like water. 824
22: 6 either in a tree or on the g, 824
28:11 of your livestock and the crops of your g— 141
28:23 the g beneath you iron. 824
28:56 that she would not venture to touch the g 824
Jos 3:17 of the LORD stood firm on **dry** g in 3000
3:17 completed the crossing on **dry** g. 3000
4:18 on the **dry** g than the waters of 3000
4:22 'Israel crossed the Jordan on **dry** g.' 3317
5:14 Joshua fell facedown to the g in reverence, 824
7: 6 and fell facedown to the g before the ark of 824
7:21 They are hidden in the g inside my tent, 824
Jdg 4:21 the peg through his temple into the g, 824
6:37 on the fleece and all the g is dry, 824
6:39 the fleece dry and the g covered with dew." 824
6:40 all the g was covered with dew. 824
13:20 and his wife fell with their faces to the g. 824
Ru 2:10 she bowed down with her face to the g. 824
1Sa 3:19 and he let none of his words fall to the g. 824
4: 5 a great shout that the g shook. 824
5: 3 fallen on his face on the g before the ark of 824
5: 4 fallen on his face on the g before the ark of 824
8:12 others to plow his g and reap his harvest, 3045
14:15 and the g shook. 824
14:25 and there was honey on the g. 8441
14:32 they butchered them on the g and ate them, 824
14:45 not a hair of his head will fall to the g, 824
17:49 and he fell facedown on the g. 824
20:41 three times, with his face to the g. 824
24: 8 prostrated himself with his face to the g. 824
25:23 down before David with her face to the g. 824
25:41 She bowed down with her face to the g 824
26: 7 with his spear stuck in the g near his head. 824
26: 8 Now let me pin him to the g with one thrust 824
26:20 the g far from the presence of the LORD. 824
28:13 "I see a spirit coming up out of the g." 824
28:14 prostrated himself with his face to the g. 824
28:20 Immediately Saul fell full length on the g, 824
28:23 He got up from the g and sat on the couch. 824
2Sa 1: 2 he fell to the g to pay him honor. 824
8: 2 down on the g and measured them off with 824
12:16 and spent the nights lying on the g. 824
12:17 beside him to get him up from the g, 824
12:20 Then David got up from the g. 824
13:31 tore his clothes and lay down on the g; 824
14: 4 with her face to the g to pay him honor, 824
14:11 of your son's head will fall to the g." 824
14:14 Like water spilled on the g, 824
14:22 with his face to the g to pay him honor, 824
14:33 down with his face to the g before the king. 824
17:12 on him as dew settles on the g. 141
18:11 strike him to the g right there? 824
18:28 down before the king with his face to the g 824
20:10 and his intestines spilled out on the g. 824
23:10 but he **stood** *his* g and struck down 7756
24:20 down before the king with his face to the g. 824
1Ki 1:23 the king and bowed with his face to the g. 824
1:31 bowed low with her face to the g and, 824
1:40 so that the g shook with the sound. 824
1:52 not a hair of his head will fall to the g; 824
18: 7 **bowed down to the g,** 5877+6584+7156
18:42 to the g and put his face between his knees. 824
2Ki 2: 8 and the two of them crossed over on **dry** g. 3000
2:15 to meet him and bowed to the g before him. 824
4:37 fell at his feet and bowed to the g. 824
8:12 **dash** their little children **to the g,** 8187
9:10 dogs will devour her on the **plot of g** 2750
9:21 the **plot of g** *that had belonged to* Naboth 2754
9:26 make you pay for it on this **plot of g,** 2754
9:36 On the **plot of g** at Jezreel dogs will devour 2750
9:37 be like refuse on the g in the plot at Jezreel, 8441
13:18 Elisha told him, "Strike the g." 824
13:19 "You should have struck the g five NIH
2Ki 23: 6 *He* g it to powder and scattered the dust 1990
23:15 the high place and g it to powder, 1990
1Ch 21:21 down before David with his face to the g. 824
2Ch 2:10 twenty thousand cors of g wheat, 4804
7: 3 the g, and they worshiped and gave thanks 824
20:18 Jehoshaphat bowed with his face to the g, 824
20:24 they saw only dead bodies lying on the g; 824
Ne 8: 6 the LORD with their faces to the g. 824
9:11 so that they passed through it on **dry** g, 3317
10:37 to the priests, the first of our **g meal,** 6881
Job 1:20 Then he fell to the g in worship 824
2:13 on the g with him for seven days 824
3:16 not hidden in the g like a stillborn child, NIH
5: 6 nor does trouble sprout from the g. 141
14: 8 in the g and its stump die in the soil, 824
16:13 and spills my gall on the g. 824
18:10 A noose is hidden for him on the g; 824
30: 6 among the rocks and in holes in the g. 6760
39:14 on the g and lets them warm in the sand, 824
39:24 In frenzied excitement he eats up the g; 824
Ps 7: 5 to the g and make me sleep in the dust. 824
17:11 with eyes alert, to throw me to the g. 824
26:12 My feet stand on **level** g; 4793
44:25 our bodies cling to the g. 824
73:18 Surely you place them on **slippery** *g;* AIT
74: 7 They burned your sanctuary to the g; 824
80: 9 *You* **cleared** *the* g for it, 7155
83:10 at Endor and became like refuse on the g. 141
89:44 to his splendor and cast his throne to the g. 824
107:33 flowing springs into **thirsty** g, 7536
107:35 and the parched g into flowing springs; 824
143: 3 he crushes me to the g; 824
143:10 may your good Spirit lead me on level g. 824
146: 4 their spirit departs, they return to the g; 141
147: 6 the humble but casts the wicked to the g. 824
Pr 24:31 the g was covered with weeds, 7156
Ecc 12: 7 and the dust returns to the g it came from, 824
Isa 2:10 hide in the g from dread of the LORD and 6760
2:19 to holes in the g from dread of the LORD 6760
3:26 destitute, she will sit on the g. 824
21: 9 of its gods lie shattered on the g!' " 824
25:12 he will bring them down to the g, 824
26: 5 he levels it to the g and casts it down to 824
28: 2 he will throw it forcefully to the g. 824
28:28 Grain *must* **be g** to make bread; 1990
29: 4 Brought low, you will speak from the g; 824
30:23 for the seed you sow in the g, 141
35: 7 the **thirsty** g bubbling springs. 7536
40: 4 the **rough** g shall become level, 6815
40:24 no sooner do they take root in the g, 824
41:18 and the parched g into springs. 824
44: 3 and streams on the **dry** g; 3317
45: 9 a potsherd among the potsherds on the g. 141
47: 1 sit on the g without a throne, 824
49:23 down before you with their faces to the g; 824
51:23 And you made your back like the g, 824
53: 2 and like a root out of dry g. 824
63: 6 and poured their blood on the g." 824
Jer 4: 3 up your **unplowed** g and do not sow 5776
7:20 of the field and on the fruit of the g, 141
8: 2 but will be like refuse lying on the g. 141
14: 4 The g is cracked because there is no rain in 141
16: 4 but will be like refuse lying on the g. 141
25:33 but will be like refuse lying on the g. 141
46:21 *they will* not **stand** *their* g, 6641
48:18 from your glory and sit on the **parched** g, 7533
La 2: 2 and its princes down to the g in dishonor. 824
2: 9 Her gates have sunk into the g; 824
2:10 the Daughter of Zion sit on the g in silence; 824
2:10 Jerusalem have bowed their heads to the g. 824
2:11 on the g because my people are destroyed, 824
Eze 1:15 I saw a wheel on the g beside each creature 824
1:19 when the living creatures rose from the g, 824
1:21 and when the creatures rose from the g, 824
10:16 spread their wings to rise from the g, 824
10:19 and rose from the g, 824
13:14 with whitewash and will level it to the g so 824
19:12 it was uprooted in fury and thrown to the g. 824
24: 7 she did not pour it on the g, 824
26:11 and your strong pillars will fall to the g. 824
26:16 Clothed with terror, they will sit on the g, 824
28:18 the g in the sight of all who were watching. 824
34:27 and the g will yield its crops; 824
38:20 every creature that moves along the g, 141
38:20 and every wall will fall to the g. 824
39:14 others will bury those that remain on the g. 824
43:14 From the gutter on the g up to 824
44:30 of your **g meal** so that a blessing may rest 6881
Da 4:15 remain in the g, in the grass of the field. 10075
4:23 while its roots remain in the g. 10075
7: 4 the g so that it stood on two feet like a man, 10075
8: 5 the whole earth without touching the g. 824
8: 7 the goat knocked him to the g and trampled 824
8:12 and truth was thrown to the g. 824
8:18 I was in a deep sleep, with my face to the g. 824
10: 9 I fell into a deep sleep, my face to the g. 824
10:15 I bowed with my face toward the g 824
Hos 2:18 and the creatures that move along the g. 141
10:11 and Jacob *must* **break up the g.** 8440
10:12 and break up your **unplowed** g; 5776
10:14 when mothers **were dashed to the g** 8187
13:16 little ones *will* **be dashed to the g,** 8187
Joel 1:10 The fields are ruined, the g is dried up; 141
Am 2: 7 of the g and deny justice to the oppressed. 824
2:15 The archer *will* not **stand** *his* g, 6641
3: 5 a trap on the g where no snare has been set? 824
3:14 of the altar will be cut off and fall to the g. 824

Am 5: 7 and cast righteousness to the **g** 824
9: 9 and not a pebble will reach the **g.** 824
Ob 1: 3 'Who can bring me down to the **g?'** 824
Mic 7:17 like creatures that crawl on the **g.** 824
Hag 1:11 the oil and whatever the **g** produces, 141
Zec 4: 7 Zerubbabel you will become **level g.** 4793
8:12 the **g** will produce its crops, 824
Mt 10:29 to the **g** apart from the will of your Father. *1178*
15:35 He told the crowd to sit down on the **g.** *1178*
17: 6 they fell facedown to the **g,** terrified. *NIG*
25:18 a hole in the **g** and hid his master's money. *1178*
25:25 and went out and hid your talent in the **g.** *1178*
26:39 **fell** with his face **to the g** *4406*
Mk 4:26 A man scatters seed on the **g.** *1178*
4:31 the smallest seed you plant in the **g.** *1178*
8: 6 He told the crowd to sit down on the **g.** *1178*
9:18 *it* **throws** him **to the g.** *4838*
9:20 He fell to the **g** and rolled around, *1178*
14:35 he fell to the **g** and prayed that if possible *1178*
Lk 5:12 with his face to the **g** and begged him, *NIG*
6:49 a man who built a house on the **g** without *1178*
9:42 the demon **threw** him **to the g** *4838*
12:16 "The **g** of a certain rich man produced *6001*
19:44 *They will* **dash** you **to the g,** *1610*
22:44 like drops of blood falling to the **g.** *1178*
24: 5 down with their faces to the **g,** *1178*
Jn 4: 5 near the **plot of g** Jacob had given *6005*
8: 6 and started to write on the **g** with his finger. *1178*
8: 8 Again he stooped down and wrote on the **g.** *1178*
9: 6 Having said this, he spit **on the g,** *5912*
12:24 a kernel of wheat falls to the **g** and dies, *1178*
18: 6 "I am he," they drew back and fell **to the g.** *5912*
Ac 7: 5 not even a **foot of g.** *1037+4546*
7:33 the place where you are standing is holy **g.** *1178*
9: 4 to the **g** and heard a voice say to him, *1178*
9: 8 Saul got up from the **g,** *1178*
13:28 Though they found no **proper g** for *162*
20: 9 he fell **to the g** from the third story *3004*
22: 7 I fell to the **g** and heard a voice say to me, *1611*
26:14 We all fell to the **g,** and I heard a voice *1178*
2Co 11:12 to cut the **g** from under those who want *929*
Eph 6:13 you may be able *to* **stand your g,** *468*
Heb 10:32 when *you* **stood** *your* **g** in a great contest *5702*
11:38 and in caves and holes in the **g.** *1178*

GROUNDS (5) [GROUND]

2Ki 11:16 where the horses enter the **palace g,** 1074+4889
2Ch 23:15 of the Horse Gate on the **palace g,** 1074+4889
Da 6: 4 and the satraps tried to find **g for charges** 10544
Lk 23:22 in him no **g for the death penalty.** *165+2505*
Jn 8:59 slipping away from the **temple g.** *2639*

GROUP (25) [GROUPS, REGROUPED]

Ge 32: 8 "If Esau comes and attacks one **g,** 4722
32: 8 the **g** that is left may escape." 4722
48:19 and his descendants will become a **g** 4850
Nu 16: 3 *They* **came as a g** to oppose Moses 7735
26:54 To a **larger** *g* give a larger inheritance, AIT
26:54 and to a **smaller** *g* a smaller one; AIT
26:55 What each **g** inherits will be according to NIH
33:54 To a **larger** *g* give a larger inheritance, AIT
33:54 and to a **smaller** *g* a smaller one. AIT
Jdg 11: 3 a **g** of adventurers gathered around him 408
1Sa 19:20 they saw a **g** *of* prophets prophesying, 4272
2Sa 2:13 **One g** sat down on one side of the pool 465S
2:13 down on one side of the pool and **one g** on 465S
2:25 a **g** and took their stand on top of a hill. 99
2Ki 17:29 **each national g** made its own gods 1580+1580
2Ch 35: 5 "Stand in the holy place with a **g** of Levites 3+1074+2755
Da 6: 6 the satraps **went as a g** to the king and said: 10656
6:11 Then these men **went as a g** 10656
6:15 the men **went as a g** to the king and said 10656
Jn 8: 3 They made her stand **before the g** *1877+3545*
Ac 1:15 among the believers (a **g** numbering about *4063*
6: 5 This proposal pleased the whole **g.** *4436*
17:18 A *g* of Epicurean and Stoic philosophers *AIT*
Gal 2:12 who belonged to **the** circumcision *g.* *AIT*
Tit 1:10 especially those of **the** circumcision *g.* *AIT*

GROUPS (8) [GROUP]

Ge 32: 7 the people who were with him into two **g,** 4722
32:10 but now I have become two **g.** 4722
Nu 26:56 by lot among the larger and smaller **g."** NIH
1Ch 23: 6 the Levites into **g** corresponding to the sons 4713
Ezr 6:18 the Levites in their **g** for the service of God 10412
Mk 6:39 sit down in **g** on the green grass. *5235+5235*
6:40 sat down in **g** of hundreds and fifties. *4555+4555*
Lk 9:14 sit down in **g** of about fifty each." *3112*

GROVE (5) [GROVES]

Ex 23:11 with your vineyard and your **olive g.** 2339
SS 6:11 the **g** *of* nut trees to look at the new growth 1708
Jn 18: 1 On the other side there was an olive **g,** *3057*
18: 3 So Judas came **to the g,** *1695S*
18:26 "Didn't I see you with him in the olive **g?"** *3057*

GROVES (8) [GROVE]

Dt 6:11 vineyards and **olive g** you did not plant— 2339
Jos 24:13 from vineyards and **olive g** that you did 2339
Jdg 15: 5 together with the vineyards and **olive g.** 2339
1Sa 8:14 and vineyards and **olive g** and give them 2339
2Ki 5:26 or to accept clothes, **olive g,** vineyards, 2339
Ne 5:11 vineyards, **olive g** and houses, 2339
Ne 9:25 **olive g** and fruit trees in abundance. 2339
Ecc 2: 6 to water **g** *of* flourishing trees. 3623

GROW (72) [FULL-GROWN, GREW, GROWERS, GROWING, GROWN, GROWS, GROWTH, OVERGROWN]

Ge 2: 9 the LORD God **made** all kinds of trees **g** 7541
26:13 *to* **g** until he became very wealthy. 2143
27:40 But when *you* *g* **restless,** AIT
Nu 6: 5 *he must let* the hair of his head **g long.** 1540
24:18 will be conquered, but Israel *will* **g** strong. 6913
Dt 8:13 and when your herds and flocks **g large** 8049
Jdg 16:22 But the hair on his head began to **g** again 7541
1Sa 2:26 the boy Samuel **continued to g** in stature 2143
Ezr 4:22 Why *let* this threat **g,** 10677
Job 8:11 *Can* papyrus **g tall** where there is no marsh? 1448
8:19 and from the soil other plants **g.** 7541
14: 8 Its roots *may* **g old** in the ground 2416
17: 9 *those with* clean hands *will* **g stronger.** 601+3578
31:16 or *let* the eyes of the widow **g weary,** 3983
39: 4 Their young thrive and **g strong** in 2730
Ps 6: 7 My eyes *g* **weak** with sorrow; AIT
31: 9 my eyes *g* **weak** with sorrow, AIT
31:10 and my bones *g* **weak.** AIT
34:10 The lions *may* *g* **weak** and hungry, AIT
92:12 *they will* **g** like a cedar of Lebanon; 8436
104:14 *He* **makes** grass **g** for the cattle, 7541
129: 6 which withers before *it can* **g;** 8990
132:17 "Here *I will* **make** a horn **g** for David 7541
147: 8 the earth with rain and **makes** grass **g** *on* 7541
Pr 13:11 gathers money little by little **makes** it **g.** 8049
20:13 Do not love sleep or *you will* **g poor;** 3769
Ecc 12: 2 the light and the moon and the stars *g* **dark,** AIT
12: 3 those looking through the windows *g* **dim;** AIT
12: 4 but all their songs *g* **faint;** AIT
Isa 5: 6 and briers and thorns *will* **g** there. 6590
17:11 *you* **make** them **g,** 8451
29:22 no longer *will* their faces **g pale.** 2578
35: 7 grass and reeds and papyrus will **g.** NIH
40:28 *He will* not *g* **tired** or weary, AIT
40:30 Even youths *g* **tired** and weary, AIT
40:31 they will run and not *g* **weary,** AIT
44:14 *He* **let** it **g** among the trees of the forest, 599
44:14 or planted a pine, and the rain **made** it **g.** 1540
45: 8 *let* righteousness **g** with it; 7541
55:13 of the thornbush *will* **g** the pine tree, 6590
55:13 and instead of briers the myrtle *will* **g.** 6590
57:16 spirit of man *would* **g faint** before me— AIT
61:11 up and a garden **causes** seeds to **g,** 7541
Jer 4:28 and the heavens above *g* **dark,** AIT
6: 4 and the shadows of evening **g long.** 5742
12: 2 *they* **g** and bear fruit. 2143
15: 9 of seven *will* **g faint** and breathe her last. AIT
La 3: 4 **made** my skin and my flesh **g old** 1162
5:17 because of these things our eyes *g* **dim** AIT
Eze 16: 7 I made you **g** like a plant of the field. 8047
17:24 **make** the low tree **g tall.** 1467
29:21 that day *I will* **make** a horn **g** for the house 7541
31: 4 deep springs **made** it **g tall;** 8123
44:20 or **let** their hair **g** long, 8938
47:12 of all kinds *will* **g** on both banks of 6590
Hos 10: 8 Thorns and thistles *will* **g up** 6590
14: 6 his young shoots *will* **g.** 2143
Jnh 4: 6 and **made** it **g up** over Jonah to give shade 6590
4:10 though you did not tend it or **make** it **g.** 1540
Zec 8:12 "The seed will **g well,** 8934
Mt 6:28 See how the lilies of the field **g.** *889*
13:30 Let both **g together** until the harvest. *5277*
24:12 the love of most *will* **g cold,** *6038*
Lk 12:27 "Consider how the lilies **g.** *889*
1Co 3: 6 Apollos watered it, but God **made** *it* **g.** *889*
3: 7 but only God, who **makes** things **g.** *889*
2Co 10:15 *as* your faith *continues to* **g,** *889*
Eph 4:15 in all things **g up** into him who is the Head, *889*
Col 2:19 grows as God causes it to **g.** *890*
Heb 12: 3 that *you will* not **g weary** and lose heart. *2827*
1Pe 2: 2 so that by it *you may* **g up** in your salvation, *889*
2Pe 3:18 But **g** in the grace and knowledge *889*

GROWERS (1) [GROW]

Joel 1:11 Despair, you farmers, wail, you vine **g;** 4144

GROWING (13) [GROW]

Ge 41: 5 healthy and good, *were* **g** on a single stalk. 6590
41:22 full and good, **g** on a single stalk. 6590
Ex 9:22 and on everything **g** in the fields of Egypt." 6912
9:25 it beat down everything **g** *in* the fields 6912
10: 5 including every tree that *is* **g** 7541
10:12 over the land and devour everything **g** *in* 6912
10:15 everything **g** *in* the fields and the fruit on 6912
Dt 29:23 nothing sprouting, no vegetation **g** on it. 6590
Job 8:12 While still **g** and uncut, 4
21: 7 **g old** and increasing in power? 6980
Col 1: 6 the world this gospel is bearing fruit and **g,** *889*
1:10 **g** in the knowledge of God, *889*
2Th 1: 3 because your faith *is* **g more and more,** *5647*

GROWL (5) [GROWLED, GROWLS]

Job 4:10 The lions may roar and **g,** 7754
Isa 5:29 *they* **g** as they seize their prey 5637
59:11 We all **g** like bears; 2159
Jer 51:38 *they* **g** like lion cubs. 5849
Am 3: 4 *Does* he **g** in his den when 5989+7754

GROWLED (1) [GROWL]

Jer 2:15 Lions have roared; *they have* **g** at him. 5989+7754

GROWLS (1) [GROWL]

Isa 31: 4 "As a lion **g,** a great lion over his prey— 2047

GROWN (21) [GROW]

Ge 38:14 she saw that, *though* Shelah *had* now **g up,** 1540
41:48 the **food** *g in* the fields surrounding it. AIT
Ex 2:11 One day, after Moses *had* **g up,** 1540
Lev 13:37 and black hair *has* **g** in it, 7541
Jdg 11: 2 and when they *were* **g up,** 1540
2Sa 10: 5 "Stay at Jericho till your beards *have* **g,** 7541
1Ki 12: 8 and consulted the young men who *had* **g up** 1540
12:10 The young men who *had* **g up** 1540
1Ch 19: 5 "Stay at Jericho till your beards *have* **g,** 7541
2Ch 10: 8 and consulted the young men who *had* **g up** 1540
10:10 The young men who *had* **g up** 1540
Job 17: 7 My eyes *have* **g dim** with grief; 3908
Ecc 1:16 I *have* **g** and increased in wisdom more 1540
SS 8: 8 and her breasts are not yet **g.** NIH
Isa 10:27 the yoke will be broken because you have **g** NIH
Jer 5:28 and *have* *g* **fat** and sleek. AIT
Eze 7:11 Violence *has* **g** into a rod 7756
28: 5 of your wealth your heart *has* *g* **proud.** AIT
Da 4:22 your greatness *has* **g** until it reaches the sky, 10648
Heb 11:24 By faith Moses, *when he had* **g up,** *1181+3489*
Rev 2: 3 and *have* not **g weary.** *3159*

GROWS (23) [GROW]

Ge 38:11 until my son Shelah **g up."** 1540
Lev 25: 5 Do not reap **what g of itself** or harvest 6206
25:11 and do not reap **what g of itself** or harvest 6206
1Ki 4:33 of Lebanon to the hyssop that **g out** 3655
2Ki 19:26 scorched before *it* **g up.** 7756
19:29 "This year you will eat **what g by itself,** 6206
Job 30:30 My skin **g black** and peels; 8837
Ps 49:16 not be overawed when a man *g* **rich,** when AIT
61: 2 I call as my heart *g* **faint;** AIT
142: 3 When my spirit *g* **faint** within me, AIT
143: 4 So my spirit *g* **faint** within me; AIT
Pr 13:20 He who walks with the wise *g* **wise,** AIT
Isa 5:27 Not one of them **g** tired or stumbles, NIH
37:27 scorched before *it* **g up.** 7756
37:30 "This year you will eat **what g by itself,** 6206
44:12 he drinks no water and *g* **faint.** AIT
Na 2:10 bodies tremble, every face **g pale.** 6999+7695
Mt 13:32 when *it* **g,** it is the largest of garden plants *889*
Mk 4:27 the seed sprouts and **g,** *3602*
4:32 *it* **g** and becomes the largest of all *326*
Eph 4:16 **g** and builds itself up in love, *890+4472*
Col 2:19 **g** as God causes it to grow. *889*
Heb 12:15 and that no bitter root **g** up to cause trouble *5886*

GROWTH (3) [GROW, UNDERGROWTH]

Pr 27:25 the hay is removed and **new g** appears and 2013
SS 6:11 to the grove of nut trees to look at the **new g** 4
Eze 17: 9 All its new **g** will wither. 7542

GRUDGE (4) [GRUDGING, GRUDGINGLY]

Ge 27:41 Esau **held a g against** Jacob because of 8475
50:15 "What if Joseph **holds a g against** us 8475
Lev 19:18 " 'Do not seek revenge or **bear a g against** 5757
Mk 6:19 So Herodias **nursed a g against** John *1923*

GRUDGING (1) [GRUDGE]

Dt 15:10 to him and do so without a **g** heart; 8317

GRUDGINGLY (1) [GRUDGE]

2Co 9: 5 not as **one g given.** *4432*

GRUMBLE (8) [GRUMBLED, GRUMBLERS, GRUMBLING]

Ex 16: 7 that *you should* **g** against us?" 4296
Nu 14:27 "How long *will* this wicked community **g** 4296
14:36 **made** the whole community **g** 4296
16:11 Who is Aaron that *you should* **g** 4296
Mt 20:11 *they began to* **g** against the landowner. *1197*
Jn 6:41 At this the Jews *began to* **g** about him *1197*
1Co 10:10 And *do* not **g,** as some of them did— *1197*
Jas 5: 9 Don't **g** against each other, brothers, *5100*

GRUMBLED (9) [GRUMBLE]

Ex 15:24 So the people **g** against Moses, saying, 4296
16: 2 the whole community **g** against Moses 4296
17: 3 and they **g** against Moses. 4296
Nu 14: 2 the Israelites **g** against Moses and Aaron, 4296
14:29 in the census and who *has* **g** against me. 4296
16:41 the whole Israelite community **g** 4296
Dt 1:27 *You* **g** in your tents and said, 8087
Jos 9:18 The whole assembly **g** against the leaders, 4296
Ps 106:25 *They* **g** in their tents and did not obey 8087

GRUMBLERS (1) [GRUMBLE]

Jude 1:16 These men are **g** and faultfinders; *1199*

GRUMBLING (11) [GRUMBLE]

Ex 16: 7 because he has heard your **g** against him. 9442
16: 8 he has heard your **g** against him. 4296+9442

Ex 16: 8 You are not g against us, 9442
16: 9 for he has heard your g.' " 9442
16:12 "I have heard the g *of* the Israelites. 9442
Nu 14:27 the complaints of these g Israelites. 4296
17: 5 I will rid myself of this **constant** g 4296+9442
17:10 This will put an end to their g against me, 9442
Jn 6:43 "Stop g among yourselves," *1197*
6:61 Aware that his disciples *were* g about this, *1197*
1Pe 4: 9 Offer hospitality to one another without g. *1198*

GUARANTEE (2) [GUARANTEED, GUARANTEEING]

Ge 43: 9 *I* myself *will* g his **safety;** 6842
Heb 7:22 Jesus has become the g of a better covenant. *1583*

GUARANTEED (2) [GUARANTEE]

Ge 44:32 Your servant g the boy's **safety** 6842
Ro 4:16 and may be g to all Abraham's offspring— *1010*

GUARANTEEING (3) [GUARANTEE]

2Co 1:22 as a deposit, g what is to come. *NIG*
5: 5 the Spirit as a **deposit,** g what is to come. *775*
Eph 1:14 who is a **deposit** g our inheritance *775*

GUARD (126) [BODYGUARD, GUARDED, GUARDIAN, GUARDIANS, GUARDING, GUARDROOM, GUARDS, SAFEGUARD]

Ge 3:24 and forth to g the way to the tree of life. 9068
37:36 of Pharaoh's officials, the captain of the g. 3184
39: 1 of Pharaoh's officials, the captain of the g, 3184
40: 3 in the house of the captain of the g, 3184
40: 4 The captain of the g assigned them 3184
41:10 in the house of the captain of the g. 3184
41:12 a servant of the captain of the g. 3184
Ex 23:20 to g you along the way and to bring you to 9068
Nu 10:25 Finally, as the **rear** g for all the units, 665
Jos 6: 7 with the **armed** g going ahead of the ark of 2741
6: 9 The **armed** g marched ahead of 2741
6: 9 and the **rear** g followed the ark. 665
6:13 the **rear** g followed the ark of the LORD, 665
10:18 and post some men there to g it. 9068
Jdg 7:19 just after they had changed the g. 9068
1Sa 2: 9 *He will* g the feet of his saints, 9068
7: 1 and consecrated Eleazar his son to g the ark 9068
19: 2 *Be* **on** *your* g tomorrow morning; 9068
26:15 Why didn't *you* g your lord the king? 9068
26:16 because *you did* not g your master, 9068
2Sa 16: 6 and the **special** g were on David's right 1475
20: 3 the palace and put them in a house **under** g. 5466
20:10 Amasa *was* not **on** *his* g against the dagger 9068
1Ki 1: 8 Shimei and Rei and David's **special** g did 1475
1:10 or the **special** g or his brother Solomon. 1475
14:27 to the commanders of the g on duty at 8132
20:39 to me with a captive and said, 'G this man. 9068
2Ki 6:10 so that *he was* **on** *his* g in such places. 9068
11: 6 and a third at the gate behind the g, 8132
11: 7 *to* g the temple for the king. 5466+9068
25: 8 commander of the **imperial** g, 3184
25:10 under the commander of the **imperial** g, 3184
25:11 the commander of the g carried into exile 3184
25:15 of the **imperial** g took away the censers 3184
25:18 commander of the g took as prisoners 3184
1Ch 9:27 because they had to g it; 5466
26:16 G was alongside of guard: 5464
26:16 Guard was alongside of g: 5464
2Ch 12:10 to the commanders of the g on duty at 8132
23: 6 *to* g what the LORD has assigned 9068
Ezr 8:29 G them carefully until you weigh them out 9193
Ne 3:25 the upper palace near the court of the g. 4766
3:29 the g *at* the East Gate, made repairs. 9068
4: 9 to our God and posted a g day and night 5464
12:39 At the Gate of the G they stopped. 4766
13:22 to purify themselves and go and g the gates 9068
Job 7:12 that you put me **under** g? 5464+6584
Ps 25:20 G my life and rescue me; 9068
86: 2 G my life, for I am devoted to you. 9068
91:11 concerning you to g you in all your ways; 9068
127: 1 the watchmen **stand** g in vain. 9193
141: 3 Set a g over my mouth, O LORD; 9072
Pr 2:11 and understanding *will* g you. 5915
4:13 g it **well,** for it is your life. 5915
4:23 Above all else, g your heart, 5915
7: 2 g my teachings as the apple of your eye. NIH
Ecc 5: 1 G your steps when you go to the house 9068
Isa 27: 3 *I* g it day and night so that no one may harm 5915
52:12 the God of Israel will be your **rear** g. 665
58: 8 glory of the LORD *will be* your **rear** g. 665
Jer 32: 2 in the courtyard of the g in the royal palace 4766
32: 8 to me in the courtyard of the g and said, 4766
32:12 the Jews sitting in the courtyard of the g. 4766
33: 1 confined in the courtyard of the g, 4766
37:13 the captain of the g, 7215
37:21 the courtyard of the g and given bread from 4766
37:21 in the courtyard of the g. 4766
38: 6 which was in the courtyard of the g. 4766
38:13 in the courtyard of the g. 4766
38:28 the g until the day Jerusalem was captured. 4766
39: 9 the **imperial** g carried into exile to Babylon 3184
39:10 the g left behind in the land of Judah some 3184
39:11 commander of the **imperial** g: 3184
39:13 So Nebuzaradan the commander of the g, 3184
39:14 taken out of the courtyard of the g. 4766
39:15 the g, the word of the LORD came to him: 4766
Jer 40: 1 the **imperial** g had released him at Ramah. 3184
40: 2 the commander of the g found Jeremiah, 3184
41:10 the **imperial** g had appointed Gedaliah son 3184
43: 6 the **imperial** g had left with Gedaliah son 3184
51:12 Reinforce the g, station the watchmen, 5464
52:12 commander of the **imperial** g, 3184
52:14 of the **imperial** g broke down all the walls 3184
52:15 of the g carried into exile some of 3184
52:19 of the **imperial** g took away the basins, 3184
52:24 of the g took as prisoners Seraiah 3184
52:30 the commander of the **imperial** g. 3184
Da 1:11 the g whom the chief official had appointed 4915
1:16 So the g took away their choice food and 4915
2:14 Arioch, the commander of the king's g, 10295
Na 2: 1 G the fortress, watch the road, 5915
Mal 2:15 So g **yourself** in your spirit, 9068
2:16 So g **yourself** in your spirit, 9068
Mt 10:17 *"Be* **on** *your* g against men; *4668*
16: 6 *"Be* **on** *your* g against the yeast of *4668*
16:11 But *be* **on** *your* g against the yeast of *4668*
16:12 not telling them *to* g against the yeast used *4668*
27:65 "Take a g," Pilate answered. *3184*
27:66 a seal on the stone and posting the g. *3184*
Mk 13: 9 "You *must be* **on** *your* g. *1063*
13:23 So *be* **on your** g; *1063*
13:33 *Be* **on** g! Be alert! *70*
14:44 arrest him and lead him away **under** g." *857*
Lk 4:10 concerning you *to* g you **carefully;** *1428+3836*
8:29 and foot and **kept under** g, *5875*
12: 1 *"Be* **on** your g against the yeast of *4668*
12:15 *Be* **on** *your* g against all kinds of greed; *5875*
22: 4 and the **officers of the temple** g *5130*
22:52 and the **officers of** the temple g, *5130*
Ac 4: 1 of the temple g and the Sadducees came up *NIG*
5:24 the captain *of* the **temple** g and *2639*
12: 6 and sentries stood g at the entrance. *5871*
16:23 jailer was commanded *to* g them carefully. *5498*
20:31 So *be* **on** *your* g! *1213*
23:35 Paul *be* **kept under** g in Herod's palace. *5875*
24:23 the centurion *to* **keep** Paul **under** g but *5498*
28:16 with a soldier *to* g him. *5875*
1Co 16:13 *Be* **on** *your* g; stand firm in the faith; *1213*
Php 1:13 the whole **palace** g and to everyone else *4550*
4: 7 *will* g your hearts and your minds *5864*
1Ti 6:20 g what has been entrusted to your care. *5875*
2Ti 1:12 that he is able *to* g what I have entrusted *5875*
1:14 G the good deposit that was entrusted *5875*
1:14 g it with the help of the Holy Spirit *NIG*
4:15 You too *should be* **on** *your* g **against** him, *5875*
2Pe 3:17 *be* **on** *your* g so that you may not *5875*

GUARDED (8) [GUARD]

Dt 32:10 *he* g him as the apple of his eye, 5915
33: 9 over your word and g your covenant. 5915
2Ki 12: 9 The priests *who* g the entrance put into 9068
Ne 12:25 and Akkub were gatekeepers *who* g 5464+9068
Est 2:21 of the king's officers *who* g the doorway, 9068
6: 2 of the king's officers *who* g the doorway, 9068
Ac 12: 4 be g by four squads of four soldiers each. *5875*
2Co 11:32 of the Damascenes g in order to arrest me. *5864*

GUARDIAN (3) [GUARD]

Eze 28:14 You were anointed as a g cherub, 6114
28:16 O g cherub, from among the fiery stones. 6114
Ac 19:35 the city of Ephesus is the **g of the temple** *3753*

GUARDIANS (4) [GUARD]

2Ki 10: 1 and to the **g of** Ahab's **children.** 587
10: 5 the elders and the g sent this message 587
1Co 4:15 though you have ten thousand g in Christ, *4080*
Gal 4: 2 He is subject to g and trustees until *2208*

GUARDING (9) [GUARD]

2Ki 11: 5 a third of you g the royal palace, 5466+9068
11: 6 *who* take turns g the temple— 5466+9068
1Ch 9:19 (the Korahites) were responsible for g 9068
9:19 as their fathers had been responsible for g 9068
9:23 of g the gates of the house of the LORD— 5466
Jer 4:17 They surround her like *men* g a field, 9068
Mt 27:54 and those with him who *were* g Jesus saw *5498*
Lk 22:63 The men who *were* g Jesus began mocking *5309*
Ac 22:20 I stood there giving my approval and g *5875*

GUARDROOM (2) [GUARD]

1Ki 14:28 afterward they returned them to the g. 8132+9288
2Ch 12:11 afterward they returned them to the g. 8132+9288

GUARDS (40) [GUARD]

1Sa 22:17 Then the king ordered the g at his side: 8132
1Ki 14:28 the g bore the shields, 8132
2Ki 10:25 he ordered the g and officers: 8132
10:25 The g and officers threw the bodies out and 8132
11: 4 the Carites and the g and had them brought 8132
11:11 The g, each with his weapon in his hand, 8132
11:13 the noise made by the g and the people, 8132
11:18 Then Jehoiada the priest posted g at 7213
11:19 the g and all the people of the land, 8132
11:19 entering by way of the gate of the g. 8132
2Ch 12:11 the g went with him, bearing the shields, 8132
Ne 4:22 as g by night and workmen by day." 5464
4:23 nor the g with me took off our clothes; 408+5464
7: 3 Also appoint residents of Jerusalem as g, 5466
Ps 97:10 for *he* g the lives of his faithful ones 9068
Pr 2: 8 for he g the course of the just and protects 5915
13: 3 *He who* g his lips guards his life, 5915
13: 3 He who guards his lips g his life, 9068
13: 6 Righteousness g the man of integrity, 5915
16:17 *he who* g his way guards his life. 5915
16:17 he who guards his way g his life. 9068
19:16 He who obeys instructions g his life, 9068
21:23 *He who* g his mouth and his tongue 9068
22: 5 but *he who* g his soul stays far from them. 9068
24:12 Does not he *who* g your life know it? 5915
Eze 9: 1 "Bring the g *of* the city here, 7213
40: 7 The **alcoves for the** g were one rod long 9288
Na 3:17 Your g are like locusts, 4964
Mt 26:58 and sat down with the g to see the outcome. *5677*
28: 4 The g were so afraid of him that they shook *5498*
28:11 *of* the g went into the city and reported to *3184*
Mk 14:54 There he sat with the g and warmed himself *5677*
14:65 And the g took him and beat him. *5677*
Lk 11:21 a strong man, fully armed, g his own house, *5875*
Jn 7:32 the Pharisees sent **temple** g to arrest him. *5677*
7:45 the **temple** g went back to the chief priests *5677*
7:46 the way this man does," the g declared. *5677*
Ac 5:23 with the g standing at the doors; *5874*
12:10 They passed the first and second g *5871*
12:19 the g and ordered that they be executed. *5874*

GUDGODAH (1)

Dt 10: 7 From there they traveled to G and on 1516

GUEST (8) [GUESTS]

Lev 22:10 the g *of* a priest or his hired worker eat it. 9369
Jdg 19:23 Since this man *is* my g, 448+995+1074
Est 1: 8 the king's command each g was allowed NIH
Mk 14:14 Where is my g **room,** *2906*
Lk 19: 7 "He has gone *to be* the g of a 'sinner.' " *2907*
22:11 Where is the g **room,** *2906*
Ac 10:32 He **is a** g in the home of Simon the tanner, *3826*
Phm 1:22 Prepare a g **room** for me, *3825*

GUESTCHAMBER (KJV) See GUEST ROOM

GUESTS (20) [GUEST]

1Sa 9:24 from the time I said, 'I have invited g.' " 6639
2Sa 15:11 *They had* **been invited as** g 7924
1Ki 1:41 and all the g who were with him heard it 7924
1:49 all Adonijah's g rose in alarm 7924
Job 19:15 My g and my maidservants count me 1074+1591
Pr 9:18 that her g are in the depths of the grave. 7924
Mt 9:15 the g of the bridegroom mourn while he is *5626*
14: 9 but because of his oaths and his **dinner** g, *5263*
22:10 and the wedding hall was filled *with* g. *367*
22:11 "But when the king came in to see the g, *367*
Mk 2:19 the g of the bridegroom fast while he is *5626*
6:22 she pleased Herod and his **dinner** g. *5263*
6:26 but because of his oaths and his **dinner** g, *367*
Lk 5:34 the g of the bridegroom fast while he is *5626*
7:49 The other g began to say *5263*
14: 7 how the g picked the places of honor at *2813*
14:10 in the presence of all your **fellow** g. *5263*
14:16 a great banquet and invited many g. *NIG*
Jn 2:10 after the g have had too much to drink; *NIG*
Ac 10:23 the men into the house *to* **be** his g. *3826*

GUIDANCE (7) [GUIDE]

2Ki 16:15 I will use the bronze altar for **seeking** g." 1329
1Ch 10:13 and even consulted a medium for g, 2011
Pr 1: 5 and let the discerning get g— 9374
11:14 For lack of g a nation falls, 9374
20:18 if you wage war, obtain g. 9374
24: 6 for waging war you need g, 9374
Hab 2:19 *Can* it **give** g? It is covered with gold 3723

GUIDE (22) [GUIDANCE, GUIDED, GUIDEPOSTS, GUIDES, GUIDING]

Ex 13:21 a pillar of cloud to g them *on* their way and 5697
15:13 In your strength *you will* g them 5633
Ne 9:19 the pillar of cloud did not cease to g them 5697
Ps 25: 5 g me in your truth and teach me, 2005
31: 3 for the sake of your name lead and g me. 5633
43: 3 your light and your truth, *let* them g me; 5697
48:14 he *will be* our g even to the end. 5627
67: 4 the peoples justly and g the nations of 5697
73:24 *You* g me with your counsel, 5697
139:10 even there your hand *will* g me, 5697
Pr 4:11 *I* g you in the way of wisdom and lead you 3723
6:22 When you walk, *they will* g you; 5697
Isa 9:16 *Those who* g this people mislead them, 886
42:16 along unfamiliar paths *I will* g them; 2005
49:10 on them *will* g them and lead them 5627
51:18 the sons she bore there was none *to* g her; 5633
57:18 *I will* g him and restore comfort to him, 5697
58:11 The LORD *will* g you always; 5697
Lk 1:79 *to* g our feet into the path of peace." *2985*
Jn 16:13 comes, *he will* g you into all truth. *3842*
Ac 1:16 as g for those who arrested Jesus— *3843*
Ro 2:19 if you are convinced that you are a g for *3843*

GUIDED (6) [GUIDE]

Job 31:18 and from my birth *I* g the widow— 5697
Ps 78:14 *He* g them with the cloud by day and 5697
78:53 *He* g them safely, so they were unafraid; 5697

Ps 107:30 and *he* **g** them to their desired haven. 5697
Isa 9:16 and *those who* **are g** are led astray. 886
63:14 This is how *you* **g** your people to make 5627

GUIDEPOSTS (1) [GUIDE]
Jer 31:21 "Set up road signs; put up **g**. 9477

GUIDES (8) [GUIDE]
Ps 23:3 *He* **g** me in paths of righteousness 5697
25:9 *He* **g** the humble in what is right 2005
Pr 11:3 The integrity of the upright **g** them, 5697
16:23 A wise man's heart **g** his mouth, 8505
Isa 3:12 O my people, your **g** lead you astray; 886
Mt 15:14 Leave them; they are blind **g.** *3843*
23:16 "Woe to you, blind **g!** *3843*
23:24 *You* blind **g!** You strain out a gnat *3843*

GUIDING (4) [GUIDE]
2Sa 6:3 sons of Abinadab, *were* **g** the new cart 5627
1Ch 13:7 with Uzzah and Ahio **g** it. 5627
Ecc 2:3 my mind *still* **g** me with wisdom. 5627
Jn 18:3 **g** a detachment of soldiers *3284*

GUILE (KJV) See FALSE, TRICKERY, DECEIT

GUILT (105) [BLOODGUILT, GUILTLESS, GUILTY]
Ge 20:9 that you have brought such great **g** 2631
26:10 and you would have brought **g** upon us." 871
44:16 God has uncovered your servants' **g.** 6411
Ex 28:38 and he will bear the **g** *involved in* 6411
28:43 so that they will not incur **g** and die. 6411
Lev 4:3 bringing **g** *on* the people, 873
5:15 It is a **g offering.** 871
5:16 for him with the ram as a **g offering,** 871
5:18 to bring to the priest as a **g offering** a ram 871
5:19 It is a **g offering;** 871
6:5 on the day he presents his **g offering.** 873
6:6 that is, to the LORD, his **g offering,** 871
6:17 Like the sin offering and the **g offering,** 871
7:1 for the **g offering,** which is most holy: 871
7:2 The **g offering** is to be slaughtered in 871
7:5 It is a **g offering.** 871
7:7 to both the sin offering and the **g offering:** 871
7:37 the sin offering, the **g offering,** 871
10:17 it was given to you to take away the **g** *of* 6411
14:12 the male lambs and offer it as a **g offering,** 871
14:13 the **g offering** belongs to the priest; 871
14:14 to take some of the blood of the **g offering** 871
14:17 on top of the blood of the **g offering.** 871
14:21 he must take one male lamb as a **g offering** 871
14:24 to take the lamb for the **g offering,** 871
14:25 the lamb for the **g offering** and take some 871
14:28 the blood of the **g offering—** 871
19:17 so you will not share in his **g.** 2628
19:21 of Meeting for a **g offering** to the LORD. 871
19:22 With the ram of the **g offering** the priest is 871
22:16 so bring upon them **g** requiring payment. 6411
Nu 5:15 a reminder offering to draw attention to **g.** 6411
5:28 she *will* **be cleared of g** and will be able 5927
6:12 a year-old male lamb as a **g offering.** 871
15:31 his **g** remains on him.' " 6411
18:9 whether grain or sin or **g offerings,** 871
30:15 then he is responsible for her **g.**" 6411
Dt 19:13 **g of shedding** innocent **blood,** 1947
21:9 **g of shedding** innocent **blood,** 1947
22:8 not bring the **g of bloodshed** on your house 1947
1Sa 3:14 'The **g** *of* Eli's house will never be atoned 6411
6:3 but by all means send a **g offering** to him. 871
6:4 "What **g offering** should we send to him?" 871
6:8 sending back to him as a **g offering.** 871
6:17 the Philistines sent as a **g offering** to 871
2Sa 14:9 let the king and his throne be **without g.**" 5929
24:10 I beg you, take away the **g** *of* your servant. 6411
1Ki 2:31 **g of** the innocent **blood** that Joab 1947
2:33 May the **g of** their **blood** rest on the head 1947
2Ki 12:16 from the **g offerings** and sin offerings was 871
1Ch 21:3 Why should he bring **g** on Israel?" 873
21:8 I beg you, take away the **g** *of* your servant. 6411
2Ch 24:18 Because of their **g,** God's anger came upon 873
28:13 Do you intend to add to our sin and **g?** 873
28:13 For our **g** is already great, 873
33:23 Amon increased his **g.** 873
Ezr 9:6 and our **g** has reached to the heavens. 873
9:7 until now, our **g** has been great. 873
9:13 a result of our evil deeds and our great **g,** 873
9:15 Here we are before you in our **g,** 873
10:10 married foreign women, adding to Israel's **g.** 873
10:19 for their **g** they each presented a ram from 873
10:19 a ram from the flock as a **g offering.)** 871
Ne 4:5 not cover up their **g** or blot out their sins 6411
Job 20:27 The heavens will expose his **g;** 6411
31:33 by hiding my **g** in my heart 6411
33:9 I am clean and free from **g.** 6411
Ps 7:3 if I have done this and there is **g** 6404
32:5 and you forgave the **g** *of* my sin. 6411
38:4 My **g** has overwhelmed me like 6411
69:5 my **g** is not hidden from you. 873
Pr 28:17 A man tormented by the **g of murder** will be a fugitive till death; 1947+5883
Isa 1:4 Ah, sinful nation, a people loaded with **g,** 6411
6:7 your **g** is taken away 6411
24:6 its people *must* **bear** *their* **g.** 870
24:20 so heavy upon it is the **g** of its **rebellion** 7322
27:9 By this, then, will Jacob's **g** be atoned for, 6411
53:10 the LORD makes his life a **g offering,** 871
59:3 stained with blood, your fingers with **g.** 6411
Jer 2:22 the stain of your **g** is still before me," 6411
3:13 Only acknowledge your **g—** 6411
14:20 we acknowledge our wickedness and the **g** 6411
25:12 the land of the Babylonians, for their **g,**" 6411
26:15 the **g of** innocent **blood** on yourselves and 1947
30:14 your **g** is so great and your sins so many. 6411
30:15 Because of your great **g** and many sins 6411
50:20 "search will be made for Israel's **g,** 6411
51:5 though their land is full of **g** before 871
Eze 14:10 They will bear their **g—** 6411
18:19 the son not share the **g** *of* his father?' 6411
18:20 The son will not share the **g** *of* the father, 6411
18:20 nor will the father share the **g** *of* the son. 6411
21:23 but he will remind them of their **g** 6411
21:24 to mind your **g** by your open rebellion, 6411
40:39 and **g offerings** were slaughtered. 871
42:13 the sin offerings and the **g offerings—** 871
44:29 the sin offerings and the **g offerings;** 871
46:20 where the priests will cook the **g offering** 871
Hos 5:15 to my place until *they* **admit** *their* **g.** 870
10:2 and now *they must* **bear** *their* **g.** 870
12:14 the **g of** his **bloodshed** and will repay him 1947
13:12 The **g** *of* Ephraim is stored up, 6411
13:16 The people of Samaria *must* **bear** *their* **g,** 870
Jn 9:41 that you claim you can see, your **g** remains. *281*
16:8 *he will* **convict** the world **of g** *1794*

GUILTLESS (4) [GUILT]
Ex 20:7 not **hold** anyone **g** who misuses his name. 5927
Dt 5:11 not **hold** anyone **g** who misuses his name. 5927
1Sa 26:9 on the LORD's anointed and *be* **g?** 5927
Job 34:6 considered a liar; although I am **g,** 1172+7322

GUILTY (83) [GUILT]
Ge 38:24 "Your daughter-in-law Tamar *is* **g of prostitution,** 2388
Ex 22:2 the defender is not **g of bloodshed;** 1947
22:3 he is **g of bloodshed.** 1947
22:9 the judges **declare g** must pay back double 8399
23:7 for I will not acquit the **g.** 8401
34:7 not **leave the g unpunished;** 5927+5927
Lev 4:13 unaware of the matter, *they are* **g.** 870
4:22 commands of the LORD his God, *he is* **g.** 870
4:27 in any of the LORD's commands, *he is* **g.** 870
5:2 he has become unclean and *is* **g.** 870
5:3 when he learns of it *he will be* **g.** 870
5:4 when he learns of it *he will be* **g.** 870
5:5 " 'When *anyone is* **g** in any of these ways, 870
5:17 *he is* **g** and will be held responsible 870
5:19 *he has been* **g of wrongdoing** against 870+870
6:4 when he thus sins and *becomes* **g,** 870
6:7 of these things he did that made him **g.**" 873
17:4 be considered **g of bloodshed;** 1947
22:9 not **become g** and die for treating them with contempt. 2628+5951+6584
Nu 5:6 to the LORD, that person *is* **g** 870
14:18 not **leave the g unpunished;** 5927+5927
18:32 of it *you will* not *be* **g** in this matter; 2628+5951
35:27 the accused without being **g of murder.** 1947
Dt 15:9 and you will be found **g of sin.** 2628
19:10 and so that you will not be **g of bloodshed.** 1947
21:8 not hold your people **g of** *the* **blood** *of* 1947
21:22 a man **g** *of* a capital offense is put to death 2628
23:21 demand it of you and you will be **g of sin.** 2628
23:22 from making a vow, you will not be **g.** 2628
24:15 and you will be **g of sin.** 2628
25:1 the innocent and condemning the **g.** 8401
25:2 If the **g** *man* deserves to be beaten, 8401
1Sa 20:8 If I am **g,** then kill me yourself! 6411
24:11 I am not **g** *of* wrongdoing or rebellion. 928+3338
26:18 and what wrong am I **g** *of?* 928+3338
2Sa 14:32 and if I am **g** of anything, 6411
19:19 "May my lord not hold me **g.** 6411
1Ki 8:32 condemning the **g** and bringing down 8401
8:32 **Declare** the innocent **not g,** 7405
2Ch 6:23 repaying the **g** by bringing down 8401
6:23 **Declare** the innocent **not g** 7405
20:35 who *was* **g of wickedness.** 8399
28:10 aren't you also **g of sins** against the LORD 873
28:13 "or we will be **g** *before* the LORD. 873
Job 9:20 *it would* **pronounce** me **g.** 6835
9:29 Since I *am already found* **g,** 8399
10:7 though you know that *I am* not **g** and 8399
10:15 If *I am* **g—**woe to me! 8399
34:31 *'I am* **g** but will offend no more. 5951
Ps 5:10 **Declare** them **g,** O God! 870
109:7 When he is tried, let him be found **g,** 8401
Pr 17:15 Acquitting the **g** and condemning the innocent— 8401
21:8 The way of the **g** is devious, 2261
24:24 to the **g,** "You are innocent"— 8401
24:25 with those who convict the **g,** NIH
Isa 5:23 who acquit the **g** for a bribe, 8401
29:21 who with a word **make** a man **out to be g,** 2627
Jer 2:3 all who devoured her *were* **held g,** 870
50:7 their enemies said, *'We are* not **g,** 870
Eze 14:10 be as **g** as the one who consults him. 6411
18:24 the **unfaithfulness** *he is* **g of** 5085+5086
22:4 *you have become* **g** because of 870
25:12 and *became* **very g** by doing so, 870+870
Hos 1:2 the land *is* **g of the vilest adultery** 2388+2388
4:15 O Israel, *let* not Judah *become* **g.** 870
13:1 But *he became* **g** of Baal worship and died. 870
Na 1:3 not **leave the g unpunished.** 5927+5927
Hab 1:11 **g** *men,* whose own strength is their god." 870
Mk 3:29 he is **g** of an eternal sin." *1944*
Lk 13:4 do you think they were more **g** than all *4050*
Jn 8:46 *Can* any of you **prove** me **g** of sin? *1794*
9:41 *you* would not **be g of sin;** *281+2400*
15:22 *they would* not **be g of sin.** *281+2400*
15:24 *they would* not **be g of sin.** *281+2400*
19:11 **g of** a greater **sin.**" *281+2400*
Ac 5:28 and are determined *to* **make** us **g of** *2042+2093*
22:25 **hasn't** even **been found g?"** *185*
25:11 *I am* **g** of doing anything deserving death, *92*
28:18 not **g of** any **crime** deserving death. *162*
1Co 11:27 be **g of sinning against** the body and blood *1944*
Heb 10:2 would no longer have **felt g** for their sins. *5287*
10:22 to cleanse us from a **g conscience** *4505+5287*
Jas 2:10 at just one point is **g** of breaking all of it. *1944*

GULF (1)
Isa 11:15 The LORD will dry up the **g** *of* the Egyptian 4383

GULL (2)
Lev 11:16 the screech owl, the **g,** any kind of hawk, 8830
Dt 14:15 the screech owl, the **g,** any kind of hawk, 8830

GULPS (1)
Pr 19:28 and the mouth of the wicked **g down** evil. 1180

GUM (1)
Ex 30:34 **g resin,** onycha and galbanum— 5753

GUNI (4) [GUNITE]
Ge 46:24 Jahziel, **G,** Jezer and Shillem. 1586
Nu 26:48 through **G,** the Gunite clan; 1586
1Ch 5:15 Ahi son of Abdiel, the son of **G,** 1586
7:13 Jahziel, **G,** Jezer and Shillem— 1586

GUNITE (1) [GUNI]
Nu 26:48 through Guni, the **G** clan; 1587

GUR (1) [GUR BAAL]
2Ki 9:27 in his chariot on the way up to **G** 1595

GUR BAAL (1) [BAAL, GUR]
2Ch 26:7 the Arabs who lived in **G** and against 1597

GUSH (1) [GUSHED, GUSHES]
Isa 35:6 Water *will* **g forth** in the wilderness 1324

GUSHED (4) [GUSH]
Nu 20:11 Water **g out,** and the community 3655+8041
Ps 78:20 When he struck the rock, water **g out,** 2307
105:41 He opened the rock, and water **g out;** 2307
Isa 48:21 he split the rock and water **g out.** 2307

GUSHES (2) [GUSH]
Pr 15:2 but the mouth of the fool **g** folly. 5580
15:28 but the mouth of the wicked **g** evil. 5580

GUTTER (3)
Eze 43:13 Its **g** is a cubit deep and a cubit wide, 2668
43:14 From the **g** *on* the ground up to 2668
43:17 of half a cubit and a **g** of a cubit all around. 2668

H

HA (1) [AHA]
Lk 4:34 **"H!** What do you want with us, *1568*

HAAHASHTARI (1)
1Ch 4:6 Hepher, Temeni and **H.** 2028

HAARALOTH See GIBEATH HAARALOTH

HABAIAH (KJV) See HOBAIAH

HABAKKUK (2)
Hab 1:1 The oracle that **H** the prophet received. 2487
3:1 A prayer of **H** the prophet. On shigionoth. 2487

HABAZZINIAH (1)
Jer 35:3 son of **H,** and his brothers and all his sons— 2484

HABERGEONS (KJV) See COAT OF ARMOR, ARMOR

HABIT (5)

Ex 21:29 bull has **had the h** of goring 4946+8997+9453
21:36 if it was known that the bull **had the h** 4946+8997+9453
Nu 22:30 *Have I* **been in the h of** this to you? 6122+6122
1Ti 5:13 *they* **get into the h of being** idle *3443*
Heb 10:25 as some are **in the h of** doing, *1621*

HABITAT (1) [INHABIT]

Job 39: 6 the salt flats as his **h.** 5438

HABITATION (KJV) See ABODE, ANCESTRY, DWELLING, FOUNDATION, HAUNT, HEAVENS, HOME, HOMELAND, HOUSE, LIVE, NEST, PASTURES, PLACE, PROPERTY, REFUGE, SETTLE, SETTLEMENT, THRONE

HABOR (3)

2Ki 17: 6 in Gozan on the **H** River and in the towns of 2466
18:11 on the **H** River and in towns of the Medes. 2466
1Ch 5:26 He took them to Halah, **H,** 2466

HACALIAH (2)

Ne 1: 1 The words of Nehemiah son of **H:** 2678
10: 1 Nehemiah the governor, the son of **H.** 2678

HACHALIAH (KJV) See HACALIAH

HACHILAH (KJV) See HAKILAH

HACHMONI (KJV) See HACMONI

HACHMONITE (KJV) See HACMONITE

HACK (1)

Eze 16:40 who will stone you and **h** you **to pieces** 1438

HACMONI (1) [HACMONITE]

1Ch 27:32 Jehiel son of **H** took care of the king's sons. 2685

HACMONITE (1) [HACMONI]

1Ch 11:11 a **H,** was chief of the officers; 1201+2685

HAD (530 of 2791) [HAVE] See Index of Articles Etc. for an Exhaustive Listing (See Introduction, page x)

Ge 4:22 Zillah also **h a son,** Tubal-Cain, 3528
4:26 Seth also **h** a son, and he named him Enosh. 3528
5: 3 *he* **h a son** in his own likeness, 3528
5: 4 Adam lived 800 years and **h** other sons 3528
5: 7 Seth lived 807 years and **h** other sons 3528
5:10 Enosh lived 815 years and **h** other sons 3528
5:13 Kenan lived 840 years and **h** other sons 3528
5:16 Mahalalel lived 830 years and **h** other sons 3528
5:19 Jared lived 800 years and **h** other sons 3528
5:22 with God 300 years and **h** other sons 3528
5:26 and **h** other sons and daughters. 3528
5:28 Lamech had lived 182 years, *he* **h** a son. 3528
5:30 Lamech lived 595 years and **h** other sons 3528
6: 4 to the daughters of men and **h children** 3528
6:10 Noah **h** three sons: Shem, Ham and Japheth. 3528
10: 1 who themselves **h** sons after the flood. 3528
11: 1 Now the whole world **h** one language and 2118
11:11 Shem lived 500 years and **h** other sons 3528
11:13 Arphaxad lived 403 years and **h** other sons 3528
11:15 Shelah lived 403 years and **h** other sons 3528
11:17 Eber lived 430 years and **h** other sons 3528
11:19 Peleg lived 209 years and **h** other sons 3528
11:21 Reu lived 207 years and **h** other sons 3528
11:23 Serug lived 200 years and **h** other sons 3528
11:25 Nahor lived 119 years and **h** other sons 3528
11:30 Now Sarai was barren; she **h** no children. 4200
12:20 with his wife and everything he **h.** 4200
13: 1 with his wife and everything he **h,** 4200
13: 5 also **h** flocks and herds and tents. 2118+4200
16: 1 But she **h** an Egyptian maidservant 4200
19:37 The older daughter **h** a son, 3528
19:38 The younger daughter also **h** a son, 3528
20:13 And when God **h** me **wander** 9494
22:24 whose name was Reumah, also **h sons:** 3528
24: 2 the one in charge of all that he **h,** 4200
24:11 **h** the camels **kneel down** 1384
24:29 Now Rebekah **h** a brother named Laban, 4200
25:28 Isaac, who **h** a taste for wild game, 928
26:14 He **h** so many flocks and herds and servants 4200
27:15 which she **h** in the house, 907
28:12 *He* **h a dream** in which he saw 2731
29:16 Now Laban **h** two daughters; 4200
30: 8 **h** a great **struggle** with my sister, 5887+7349
30:30 The little you **h** before I came 2118+4200
31: 2 toward him was not what *it* **h been.** 8997+9453
31:10 "In breeding season *I once* **h** a dream 8011[S]
31:21 So he fled with all he **h,** 4200
32:10 I **h** only my staff 928
32:13 what he **h** *with* him he selected a gift 928+3338
35: 4 the foreign gods they **h** and the rings 928+3338
35:22 Jacob **h** twelve sons: 2118
36:12 also **h** a concubine named Timna, 2118+4200
37: 5 Joseph **h a dream,** 2706+2731
37: 6 to them, "Listen to this **dream** *I* **h:** 2706+2731
37: 9 Then *he* **h** another **dream,** 2706+2731
37: 9 "Listen," he said, "*I* **h** another **dream,** 2706+2731
37:10 "What is this **dream** *you* **h?** 2706+2731
39: 5 The blessing of the LORD was on everything Potiphar **h,** 3780+4200
39: 6 So he left in Joseph's care everything he **h;** 4200
40: 5 **h a dream** the same night, 2706+2731
40: 5 and each dream **h** a meaning of its own. 3869
40: 8 "*We both* **h dreams,**" they answered, 2706+2731
40:16 he said to Joseph, "I too **h** a dream: NIH
41: 1 Pharaoh **h a dream:** 2731
41: 5 He fell asleep again and **h** a second **dream:** 2731
41:11 Each of us **h a dream** the same night, 2706+2731
41:11 and each dream **h** a meaning of its own. 3869
41:15 Pharaoh said to Joseph, "*I* **h a dream,** 2706+2731
41:43 *He* **h** him **ride** in a chariot 8206
43: 6 by telling the man you **h** another brother?" 4200
47:22 from Pharaoh and **h food enough** *from* 430
Ex 2:16 Now a priest of Midian **h** seven daughters, 4200
5:13 just as when you **h** straw." 2118
9:28 for we *have* **h** enough thunder and hail. 2118
10:23 all the Israelites **h** light in the places 2118+4200
14: 6 So *he* **h** his chariot **made ready** 673
14:25 so that they **h** difficulty driving. 928
21:29 bull has **h the habit** of goring 4946+8997+9453
21:36 if it was known that the bull **h the habit** 4946+8997+9453
35:23 Everyone who **h** blue, purple or 907+5162
35:24 and everyone who **h** acacia wood 907+5162
35:26 And all the women who were willing and **h** 928
36: 7 what *they already* **h** was more than enough 2118
37: 9 The cherubim **h** their wings spread upward, 2118
38: 9 and **h** curtains of finely twisted linen, 4200
38:11 a hundred cubits long and **h** twenty posts 4200
38:12 and **h** curtains, with ten posts and ten bases, 4200
Lev 23:43 that *I* **h** the Israelites **live** in booths 3782
Nu 3: 4 They **h** no sons; 2118+4200
5:18 the priest *has* **h** the woman **stand** before 6641
11: 4 "If only we **h** meat **to eat!** 430
11:18 "If only we **h** meat **to eat!** 430
11:24 of their elders and **h** them **stand** around 6641
12:10 toward her and saw that *she* **h leprosy;** 7665
22:29 If I **h** a sword in my hand, 3780
26:33 (Zelophehad son of Hepher **h** no sons; 2118+4200
26:33 he **h** only daughters, NIH
27: 4 from his clan because he **h** no son? 4200
27:11 If his father **h** no brothers, 4200
27:22 and **h** him **stand** before Eleazar the priest 6641
32: 1 who **h** very large herds and flocks, 2118+4200
Dt 4:25 After *you have* **h** children 3528
Jos 5: 1 they no longer **h** the courage to face 928+2118
5: 5 during the journey from Egypt **h** not. 4576[S]
7:16 next morning Joshua **h** Israel **come forward** 7928
7:17 **h** the clan of the Zerahites **come forward** 7928
7:18 **h** his family **come forward** 7928
7:24 his tent and all that he **h,** 4200
8:13 **h** the soldiers **take up** *their* **positions—** 8492
8:20 they **h** no **chance** to escape 928+2118+3338
11:10 (Hazor **h been** the head 4200+7156
11:23 Then the land **h rest** from war. 9200
14:15 Then the land **h rest** from war. 9200
17: 3 **h** no sons but only daughters, 2118+4200
17: 8 (Manasseh **h** the land of Tappuah, 2118+4200
17:11 Manasseh also **h** Beth Shan, 2118+4200
18:21 clan by clan, **h** the following cities: 2118+4200
19:47 **h difficulty taking possession of** 3655+4946
21:42 these towns **h** pasturelands surrounding it; 2118
Jdg 1:19 because they **h** iron chariots. 4200
2:18 for the LORD **h compassion** *on* them 5714
3: 2 **h** previous battle **experience):** 3359
3:11 So the land **h peace** for forty years, 9200
3:30 and the land **h peace** for eighty years. 9200
4: 3 Because he **h** nine hundred iron chariots 4200
5:31 Then the land **h peace** forty years. 9200
7:13 "*I* **h a dream,**" he was saying. 2706+2731
8: 8 but they answered as the men of Succoth **h.** 6699[S]
8:30 He **h** seventy sons of his own, 2118+4200
8:30 for he **h** many wives. 2118+4200
10: 4 He **h** thirty sons, who rode thirty donkeys. 2118+4200
11:34 for her he **h** neither son nor daughter. 4200
12: 9 He **h** thirty sons and thirty daughters. 2118+4200
12:14 He **h** forty sons and thirty grandsons, 2118+4200
13: 2 **h** a wife who was sterile 2118
17: 5 Now this man Micah **h** a shrine, 4200
17: 6 In those days Israel **h** no king; 928
18: 1 In those days Israel **h** no king. 928
18: 7 from the Sidonians and **h** no relationship 4200
18:28 and **h** no relationship with anyone else. 4200
19: 1 In those days Israel **h** no king. 928
21:25 In those days Israel **h** no king; 928
Ru 1:12 if *I* **h** a husband tonight and then 2118+4200
2: 1 Naomi **h** a relative on her husband's side, 4200
2:14 and **h some left over.** 3855
2:18 and gave her what *she* **h left over** 3855
1Sa 1: 2 He **h** two wives; 4200
1: 2 Peninnah **h** children, but Hannah had none. 2118+4200
1Sa 1: 2 Peninnah had children, but Hannah **h** none. 4200
2:12 *they* **h no regard for** the LORD. 3359
9: 2 He **h** a son named Saul, 2118+4200
13: 3 Then Saul **h** the trumpet **blown** throughout 9546
13:22 and Jonathan **h** a sword or spear in his hand; 5162
13:22 Saul and his son Jonathan **h** them. 4200+5162
16: 8 Then Jesse called Abinadab and **h** him **pass** 6296
16: 9 Jesse then **h** Shammah **pass by,** 6296
16:10 **h** seven of his sons **pass** 6296
16:12 So he sent and **h** him **brought in.** 995
17:12 Jesse **h** eight sons, 4200
18:14 In everything he did he **h great success,** 8505
20: 9 "If *I* **h the least inkling** 3359+3359
20:17 And Jonathan **h** David **reaffirm** his oath out 3578
25: 2 He **h** a thousand goats 4200
28:24 The woman **h** a fattened calf at the house, 4200
30: 4 until they **h** no strength left to weep. 928
2Sa 3: 7 Now Saul had **h** a concubine named Rizpah 4200
3:37 that the king **h** no **part in** the murder 2118+4946
4: 2 Saul's son **h** two men who were leaders 2118
4: 4 (Jonathan son of Saul **h** a son who was lame 4200
6:23 Michal daughter of Saul **h** no children 2118+4200
9: 5 King David **h** him **brought** from Lo Debar, 2256+4374+8938
9:10 Ziba **h** fifteen sons and twenty servants.) 4200
9:12 Mephibosheth **h** a young son named Mica, 4200
10:16 Hadadezer **h** Arameans **brought** from 3655
11:27 David **h** her **brought** to his house, 665
12: 2 The rich man **h** a very large number 2118+4200
12: 3 poor man **h** nothing except one little ewe lamb he had bought. 4200
12: 6 because he did such a thing and **h** no **pity.**" 2798
13: 3 Now Amnon **h** a friend named Jonadab son 4200
14: 2 **h** a wise woman **brought** from there. 4374
14: 6 I your servant **h** two sons. 4200
17:18 He **h** a well in his courtyard, 4200
18:11 Then I would have **h to** give you 6584
1Ki 1: 4 the king **h** no **intimate relations with** 3359
2:19 *He* **h** a throne **brought** for the king's mother, 8492
3:17 *I* **h a baby** while she was there with me. 3528
3:18 this woman also **h a baby.** 3528
3:28 because they saw that he **h** wisdom 928+7931
4: 7 Solomon also **h** twelve district governors 4200
4: 7 Each one **h to** provide supplies 2118+6584
4:24 and **h** peace on all sides. 2118+4200
4:26 Solomon **h** four thousand stalls 2118+4200
5:15 Solomon **h** seventy thousand carriers 2118+4200
7:28 They **h** side panels attached to uprights. 4200
7:30 Each stand **h** four bronze wheels 4200
7:30 and each **h** a basin resting on four supports, 4200
8:17 "My father David **h** *it* in his heart to build 2118
9: 1 and **h** achieved all he had desired to do, NIH
10: 2 with him about all that *she* **h** on her mind. 2118
10:19 The throne **h** six steps, 4200
10:19 and its back **h** a rounded top. NIH
10:22 The king **h** a fleet of trading ships at sea 4200
10:26 he **h** fourteen hundred chariots 2118+4200
11: 3 **h** seven hundred wives of royal birth 2118+4200
20:33 Ahab **h** him **come up** into his chariot. 6590
2Ki 1:17 Because Ahaziah **h** no son, 2118+4200
3: 9 army **h** no more water for themselves 2118+4200
4:44 and they ate and **h** *some* **left over,** 3855
5: 1 He was a valiant soldier, but *he* **h leprosy.** 7665
7: 8 The *men who* **h leprosy** reached the edge of 7665
10:16 Then *he* **h** him **ride along** in his chariot. 8206
11: 4 and the guards and **h** them **brought** to him 995
13:23 and **h compassion** and showed concern 8163
15: 5 the king's son **h charge of** the palace 6584
23:16 *he* **h** the bones **removed** from 2256+4374+8938
1Ch 2:18 of Hezron **h children** by his wife Azubah 3528
2:26 Jerahmeel **h** another wife, 2118+4200
2:34 Sheshan **h** no sons—only daughters. 2118+4200
2:34 He **h** an Egyptian servant named Jarha. 4200
4: 5 the father of Tekoa **h** two wives, 2118+4200
4:27 Shimei **h** sixteen sons and six daughters, 4200
7: 4 they **h** 36,000 men ready for battle, 6584
7: 4 for *they* **h many** wives and children. 8049
7:15 who **h** only daughters. 2118+4200
8: 9 By his wife Hodesh *he* **h** Jobab, Zibia, 3528
8:11 By Hushim *he* **h** Abitub and Elpaal. 3528
8:38 Azel **h** six sons, and these were their names: 4200
8:40 *They* **h many** sons and grandsons— 8049
9:27 because they **h to** guard it; 6584
9:27 and they **h charge of** the key 6584
9:44 Azel **h** six sons, and these were their names: 4200
13:14 and everything he **h.** 4200
19:16 and **h** Arameans **brought** from beyond 3655
22: 7 "My son, I **h** *it* in my heart to build a house 2118
23:17 Eliezer **h** no other sons, 2118+4200
23:22 he **h** only daughters. NIH
24: 2 and they **h** no sons; 2118+4200
24:28 From Mahli: Eleazar, who **h** no sons. 2118+4200
26: 2 Meshelemiah **h** sons: Zechariah 4200
26: 4 Obed-Edom also **h** sons: 4200
26: 6 His son Shemaiah also **h** sons, 3528
26: 9 Meshelemiah **h** sons and relatives, 4200
26:10 Hosah the Merarite **h** sons: 4200
26:12 **h** duties for ministering in the temple of 4200
29: 8 Any who **h** precious stones gave them 907+5162
29:25 as no king over Israel ever **h** before. 2118+6584
2Ch 1:12 such as no king who was before you *ever* **h** 2118
1:14 he **h** fourteen hundred chariots 2118+4200
6: 7 "My father David **h** *it* in his heart to build 2118
7:11 and had succeeded in carrying out all he **h** 995
9: 1 with him about all *she* **h** on her mind. 2118
9:18 The throne **h** six steps, 4200

2Ch 9:21 The king **h** a fleet of trading ships manned 4200
9:25 Solomon **h** four thousand stalls for horses 2118+4200
11:21 *he* **h** eighteen wives and sixty concubines, 5951
13:21 fourteen wives and **h** twenty-two sons 3528
14: 8 Asa **h** an army 2118+4200
17: 5 so that he **h** great wealth and honor. 2118+4200
17:13 **h** large supplies in the towns of Judah. 2118+4200
18: 1 Jehoshaphat **h** great wealth and honor, 2118+4200
24: 3 and *he* **h** sons and daughters. 3528
26:10 he **h** much livestock in the foothills 2118+4200
26:11 Uzziah **h** a well-trained army, 2118+4200
26:20 they saw that he **h leprosy** on his forehead, 7665
26:21 King Uzziah **h leprosy** until 7665
26:21 Jotham his son **h charge of** the palace 6584
26:23 for people said, "He **h leprosy."** 7665
30:17 the Levites **h to** kill the Passover lambs 6584
31:10 we *have* **h enough** to eat and plenty to spare 8425
32:27 Hezekiah **h** very great riches and honor, 2118+4200
34:13 **h charge of** the laborers and supervised all 6584
34:32 **h** everyone in Jerusalem and Benjamin **pledge** 6641
34:33 **h** all who were present in Israel **serve** 6641
35:24 in the other chariot he **h** and brought him 4200
36:15 because *he* **h pity** on his people and 2798
Ezr 1: 8 of Persia **h** them **brought** by Mithredath 3655
2:65 also **h** 200 men and women singers. 4200
2:66 They **h** 736 horses, 245 mules, NIH
4:20 Jerusalem *has* **h** powerful kings ruling over 10201+10542
10:44 some of them **h** children by these wives. 8492
Ne 7:67 also **h** 245 men and women singers. 4200
7:73 and the Israelites **h** settled in their towns, NIH
11:16 who **h charge of** the outside work of 6584
12:31 **h** the leaders of Judah **go up** 6590
Est 1:14 *who* **h special access to** the king 7156+8011
2: 7 up because she **h** neither father nor mother. 4200
2: 8 *who* **h charge of** the harem. 9068
Job 1: 2 He **h** seven sons and three daughters, 3528
3:15 with rulers who **h** gold, 4200
28:17 nor can it be **h for** jewels of gold. 9455
31:31 'Who *has* not **h** *his* **fill** of Job's meat?'— 8425
31:35 that I **h** someone to hear me! 4200
32: 5 the three men **h** nothing more to say, 928+7023
34:27 and **h** no **regard for** any of his ways. 8505
42:10 and gave him twice as much as he **h** before. 4200
42:12 He **h** fourteen thousand sheep, 2118+4200
42:13 also **h** seven sons and three daughters. 2118+4200
Ps 55: 6 I said, "Oh, that I **h** the wings of a dove! 4200
78:29 They ate till *they* **h** more than **enough,** 8425
78:63 and their maidens **h** no **wedding songs;** 2146
Ecc 2: 7 and **h** other slaves who were born 2118+4200
4: 8 he **h** neither son nor brother. 4200
SS 8:11 Solomon **h** a vineyard in Baal Hamon; 2118+4200
Isa 5: 1 My loved one **h** a vineyard on 2118+4200
53: 2 He **h** no beauty or majesty to attract us 4200
Jer 20: 2 **h** Jeremiah the prophet **beaten** 5782
23:25 They say, '*I* **h a dream!** 2731
23:25 *I* **h a dream!'** 2731
26:23 *who* **h** him **struck down** with a sword 5782
32:10 and sealed the deed, **h** it **witnessed,** 6332+6386
35: 9 built houses to live in or **h** vineyards, 2118+4200
37:15 and **h** him **beaten** and imprisoned in 5782
44:17 At that time *we* **h plenty** *of* food 8425
44:18 *we have* **h nothing** and have been 2893+3972
52:27 the king **h** them **executed.** 2256+4637+5782
La 5: 4 our wood *can be* **h** only at a price. 995[S]
Eze 1: 6 each of them **h** four faces and four wings. 4200
1: 8 Under their wings on their four sides they **h** NIH
1: 8 All four of them **h** faces and wings, 4200
1:10 Each of the four **h** the face of a man, 4200
1:10 on the right side each **h** the face of a lion, 4200
1:10 each also **h** the face of an eagle. 4200
1:11 each **h** two wings, 4200
1:23 and each **h** two wings covering its body. 4200
10:14 Each of the cherubim **h** four faces: 4200
10:21 Each **h** four faces and four wings, 4200
10:22 Their faces **h** the same appearance NIH
16: 5 with pity or **h compassion** *enough* to do any 2798
22:24 that *has* **h** no **rain** or showers in the day 4763
36:21 *I* **h concern** for my holy name, 2798
40:10 the three **h** the same measurements, 4200
40:10 on each side **h** the same measurements. 4200
40:21 and its portico **h** the same measurements 2118
40:24 and they **h** the same measurements as NIH
40:25 and its portico **h** narrow openings all 4200
40:26 it **h** palm tree decorations on the faces of 4200
40:27 The inner court also **h** a gate facing south, 4200
40:28 it **h** the same measurements as the others. NIH
40:29 and its portico **h** the same measurements as NIH
40:29 and its portico **h** openings all around. NIH
40:32 it **h** the same measurements as the others. NIH
40:33 and its portico **h** the same measurements as NIH
40:33 and its portico **h** openings all around. 4200
40:35 It **h** the same measurements as the others, NIH
40:36 and it **h** openings all around. 4200
41: 8 that the temple **h** a raised base all around it, 4200
41:18 Each cherub **h** two faces: 4200
41:21 outer sanctuary **h** a rectangular doorframe, NIH
41:23 and the Most Holy Place **h** double doors. 4200
41:24 Each door **h** two leaves— 4200
41:26 of the temple also **h** overhangs. NIH
42: 6 The rooms on the third floor **h** no pillars, 4200
42: 6 as the courts **h;** NIH
42:11 they **h** the same length and width, NIH
42:20 It **h** a wall around it, 4200

Da 2: 1 Nebuchadnezzar **h dreams;** 2706+2731
2: 3 "*I have* **h a dream** that troubles me 2706+2731
4: 5 *I* **h** a dream that made me afraid. 10255
4:18 King Nebuchadnezzar, **h.** 10255[S]
7: 1 Daniel **h** a dream, 10255[S]
7: 4 and it **h** the wings of an eagle. 10378
7: 6 And on its back it **h** four wings like those 10378
7: 6 This beast **h** four heads, 10378
7: 7 It **h** large iron teeth; 10378
7: 7 and it **h** ten horns. 10378
7: 8 This horn **h** eyes like the eyes of a man 10089
7:20 the others and that **h** eyes and a mouth 10378
8: 1 I, Daniel, **h** a vision, 8011[S]
10: 8 I **h** no strength left, 928
Hos 1: 8 Gomer **h** another son. 3528
10: 3 if we **h** a king, what could he do for us?" NIH
Am 4: 7 One field **h rain;** 4763
4: 7 another **h** none and dried up. 4763[S]
Zec 1: 8 During the night *I* **h a vision—** 8011
5: 9 They **h** wings like those of a stork, 4200
6: 2 The first chariot **h** red horses, 928
Mt 1:19 *he* **h in mind** to divorce her quietly. *1089*
7:29 because he taught as **one who h** authority, *2400*
8:33 including **what h happened to** *3836*
9:33 **man who h been mute** spoke. *3273*
9:36 *he* **h compassion** on them, *5072*
13: 6 and they withered because they **h** no root. *2400*
13:44 in his joy went and sold all *he* **h** and bought *2400*
13:46 and sold everything *he* **h** and bought it. *2400*
14:14 *he* **h compassion** on them *5072*
18:25 and all that *he* **h** be sold to repay the debt. *2400*
18:33 Shouldn't you *have* **h mercy on** *1796*
18:33 on your fellow servant just as I **h** on you?' *1796[S]*
19:22 because *he* **h** great wealth. *1639+2400*
20:34 Jesus **h compassion** on them *5072*
21:28 There was a man who **h** two sons. *2400*
22:25 and *since he* **h** no children, *2400*
27:16 At that time *they* **h** a notorious prisoner, *2400*
27:26 But he **h** Jesus **flogged,** *5849*
Mk 1:22 he taught them as *one who* **h** authority, *2400*
1:34 Jesus healed many *who* **h** various diseases. *2400*
4: 6 and they withered because they **h** no root. *2400*
5:19 and how *he has* **h mercy on** you." *1796*
5:26 many doctors and had spent all she **h,** *3836+4123[S]*
6:34 *he* **h compassion** on them, *5072*
8: 1 Since *they* **h** nothing to eat, *2400*
8: 7 *They* **h** a few small fish as well; *2400*
8:14 for one loaf *they* **h** with them in the boat. *2400*
10:22 because *he* **h** great wealth. *1639+2400*
12: 6 "*He* **h** one left to send, a son, *2400*
12:44 out of her poverty, put in everything—all she **h** to live on." *2400*
15:15 He **h** Jesus **flogged,** *5849*
Lk 1: 7 But they **h** no children, *1639*
2:49 "Didn't you know I **h** to be in my Father's house?" *1256*
4:32 his message **h authority.** *1639+1877+2026*
4:40 to Jesus all who **h** various kinds of sickness, *2400*
5:17 who **h** come from every village of Galilee *1639*
7:42 of them **h** the money to pay him back, *2400*
8: 6 plants withered because they **h** no moisture. *2400*
10:37 "The one who **h** mercy on him." *4472*
10:39 She **h** a sister called Mary, *1639*
11:14 **man who h been mute** spoke, *3273*
13: 6 "A man **h** a fig tree, planted in his vineyard, *2400*
14: 6 And *they* **h** nothing to say. *2710*
15:11 "There was a man who **h** two sons. *2400*
15:32 But *we* **h** to celebrate and be glad, *1256*
17: 7 of you **h** a servant plowing or looking after *2400*
17:12 ten men who **h leprosy** met him. *3320*
18:28 "We have left **all** *we* **h** to follow you!" *2625+3836*
21: 4 of her poverty put in all *she* **h** to live on." *2400*
22: 7 the Passover lamb **h** to be sacrificed. *1256*
23:51 who **h** not consented to their decision *1639*
23:55 The women who **h** come with Jesus *1639*
Jn 2:10 after the guests *have* **h too much to drink;** *3499*
4: 4 Now he **h** to go through Samaria. *1256*
4:18 The fact is, *you have* **h** five husbands, *2400*
5: 5 One who was there **h** been an invalid *2400*
5: 6 and learned that *he* **h** been in this condition *2400*
6:12 When *they had* all **h enough** to eat, *1855*
9:13 to the Pharisees the man who **h been** blind. *4537*
12:29 and heard it said *it* **h** thundered; *1181*
13:10 "A person who *has* **h a bath** needs only *3374*
13:29 Since Judas **h charge of** the money, *2400*
17: 5 in your presence with the glory *I* **h** *2400*
18:10 Then Simon Peter, *who* **h** a sword, *2400*
18:16 but Peter **h to wait** outside at the door. *2705*
18:40 **h taken part in a rebellion.** *1639+3334*
19:19 Pilate **h a notice prepared** and *1211+5518*
20: 9 not understand from Scripture that Jesus **h** to rise from the dead.) *1256*
21: 7 (for *he* **h** taken it off) and jumped into *1639*
Ac 1:16 the Scripture **h** to be fulfilled which *1256*
2:13 "*They have* **h too much** wine." *1639+3551*
2:44 the believers were together and **h** everything *2400*
2:45 they gave to anyone as he **h** need. *2400*
4:32 but they shared everything **they h.** *899+1639*
4:35 was distributed to anyone as he **h** need. *323+2400*
7: 5 *though* at that time Abraham **h** no child. *1639*
7:29 he settled as a foreigner and **h** two sons. *1164*
7:30 **"After** forty years **h passed,** *4444*
7:44 "Our forefathers **h** the tabernacle of *1639*
11: 4 to them precisely **as it h happened:** *2759*
12: 9 but *he* **h** no **idea** that what *3857*
12:12 many people **h** gathered and were praying. *1639*
13:46 "We **h** to speak the word of God *338+1639*

Ac 14: 9 saw that *he* **h** faith to be healed *2400*
15: 3 how the Gentiles **h been converted.** *2189+3836*
15:39 *They* **h** such a sharp disagreement that they parted company. *1181*
16: 9 the night Paul **h a vision** of a man *3969+3972*
16:16 we were met by a slave girl who **h** a spirit *2400*
17: 3 the Christ **h** to suffer and rise from the dead. *1256*
18:16 So *he* **h** them **ejected from** the court. *590*
19:12 and aprons **that h touched** him *608+3836+5999*
19:16 the man who **h** the evil spirit jumped *1639+1877*
21: 9 He **h** four unmarried daughters who prophesied. *1639*
21:35 the mob was so great he **h to be** carried by *5201*
25:16 and *has* **h** an opportunity to defend himself *3284*
25:19 *they* **h** some points of dispute with him *2400*
26:22 But *I have* **h** God's help to this very day, *5593*
28:19 not that I **h** any charge to bring *2400*
Ro 1:13 just as I have **h** among the other Gentiles. *NIG*
4: 2 *he* **h** something to boast about— *2400*
4:21 fully persuaded that God **h power** *1543+1639*
9:10 but Rebekah's children **h** one and the same father, *2400*
1Co 7:29 as if *they* **h** none; *2400*
2Co 2:13 *I* still **h** no peace of mind, *2400*
5:21 God made him who **h** no sin to be sin *1182*
7: 5 this body of ours **h** no rest, *2400*
Gal 4:22 For it is written that Abraham **h** two sons, *2400*
Php 2:27 But God **h mercy on** him, *1796*
4:10 but you **h no opportunity** to show it. *177*
Heb 2:17 For this reason *he* **h** to be made *4053*
4: 2 *we* also *have* **h** the gospel preached to us, *1639*
4: 6 those who formerly **h the gospel preached** *2294*
7: 6 from Abraham and blessed him **who h** *2400*
9: 1 the first covenant **h** regulations for worship *2400*
9: 4 **which h** the golden altar of incense and *2400*
9:26 Then Christ *would have* **h** *1256*
10:34 that you yourselves **h** better *2400*
11:15 *they* would *have* **h** opportunity to return. *2400*
11:39 none of them received **what h been promised.** *2039+3836*
12: 9 *we have* all **h** human fathers who disciplined us *2400*
1Pe 1: 6 while you may *have* **h** to suffer grief *1256+1639*
1Jn 2: 7 which *you have* **h** since the beginning. *2400*
2Jn 1: 5 a new command but one *we have* **h** from *2400*
Jude 1: 3 I felt I **h** to write and urge you to contend *340*
Rev 4: 7 the third **h** a face like a man, *2400*
4: 8 Each of the four living creatures **h** six wings *2400*
5: 6 *He* **h** seven horns and seven eyes, *2400*
5: 8 Each one **h** a harp *2400*
8: 3 Another angel, **who h** a golden censer, *2400*
8: 6 Then the seven angels who **h** *2400*
9: 9 *They* **h** breastplates like breastplates of iron, *2400*
9:10 *They* **h** tails and stings like scorpions, *2400*
9:11 *They* **h** as king over them the angel of *2400*
9:14 It said to the sixth angel who **h** the trumpet, *2400*
13: 1 *He* **h** ten horns and seven heads, *2400*
13: 2 but **h** feet like those of a bear and a mouth *899*
13: 3 the beast seemed *to have* **h** a fatal **wound,** *5377*
13:11 *He* **h** two horns like a lamb, *2400*
13:17 so that no one could buy or sell unless he **h** *2400*
14: 1 144,000 who **h** his name and his Father's *2400*
14: 6 and *he* **h** the eternal gospel to proclaim *2400*
14:17 and he too **h** a sharp sickle. *2400*
14:18 Still another angel, *who* **h** charge of the fire, *2400*
14:18 a loud voice *to* him who **h** the sharp sickle, *2400*
16: 2 on the people who **h** the mark of the beast *2400*
16: 9 who **h** control over these plagues, *2400*
16:11 they refused to repent of what they **h done.** *2240*
17: 1 One of the seven angels who **h** the seven *2400*
17: 3 with blasphemous names and **h** seven heads *2400*
18: 1 *He* **h** great authority, *2400*
18:19 where all who **h** ships on the sea *2400*
21: 9 the seven angels who **h** the seven bowls full *2400*
21:12 *It* **h** a great, high wall with twelve gates, *2400*
21:14 The wall of the city **h** twelve foundations, *2400*
21:15 with me **h** a measuring rod of gold *2400*

HADAD (17) [BEN-HADAD, HADAD RIMMON]

Ge 25:15 **H,** Tema, Jetur, Naphish and Kedemah. 2524
36:35 When Husham died, **H** son of Bedad, 2060
36:36 When **H** died, Samlah from Masrekah 2060
36:39 **H** succeeded him as king. 2060
1Ki 11:14 **H** the Edomite, from the royal line of Edom. 2060
11:17 But **H,** still only a boy, 119
11:18 who gave **H** a house and land 2257[S]
11:19 so pleased with **H** that he gave him a sister 2060
11:21 **H** heard that David rested with his fathers 2060
11:21 Then **H** said to Pharaoh, "Let me go, 2060
11:22 "Nothing," **H** replied, "but do let me go!" NIH
11:25 adding to the trouble caused by **H.** 2060
1Ch 1:30 Mishma, Dumah, Massa, **H,** Tema, 2524
1:46 When Husham died, **H** son of Bedad, 2060
1:47 When **H** died, Samlah from Masrekah 2060
1:50 Baal-Hanan died, **H** succeeded him as king. 2060
1:51 **H** also died. 2060

HADAD RIMMON (1) [HADAD, RIMMON]

Zec 12:11 like the weeping of **H** in the plain 2062

HADADEZER (17) [HADADEZER'S]

2Sa 8: 3 Moreover, David fought **H** son of Rehob, 2061
8: 5 of Damascus came to help **H** king of Zobah, 2061

2Sa 8: 7 to the officers of **H** and brought them 2061
8: 8 towns that belonged to **H,** 2061
8: 9 the entire army of **H,** 2061
8:10 on his victory in battle over **H,** 2061
8:12 also dedicated the plunder taken from **H** son 2061
10:16 **H** had Arameans brought from beyond 2061
10:19 of **H** saw that they had been defeated 2061
1Ki 11:23 **H** king of Zobah. 2061
1Ch 18: 3 Moreover, David fought **H** king of Zobah, 2061
18: 5 of Damascus came to help **H** king of Zobah, 2061
18: 7 the gold shields carried by the officers of **H** 2061
18: 8 towns that belonged to **H,** 2061
18: 9 the entire army of **H** king of Zobah, 2061
18:10 on his victory in battle over **H,** 2061
19:19 of **H** saw that they had been defeated 2061

HADADEZER'S (2) [HADADEZER]

2Sa 10:16 the commander of **H** army leading them. 2061
1Ch 19:16 the commander of **H** army leading them. 2061

HADASHAH (1)

Jos 15:37 Zenan, **H,** Migdal Gad, 2546

HADASSAH (1)

Est 2: 7 Mordecai had a cousin named **H,** 2073

HADATTAH See HAZOR HADATTAH

HADDAH See EN HADDAH

HADES (5)

Mt 16:18 and the gates *of* **H** will not overcome it. *87*
Rev 1:18 And I hold the keys *of* death and **H.** *87*
6: 8 and **H** was following close behind him. *87*
20:13 and death and **H** gave up the dead that were *87*
20:14 Then death and **H** were thrown into the lake *87*

HADID (3)

Ezr 2:33 of Lod, **H** and Ono 725 2531
Ne 7:37 of Lod, **H** and Ono 721 2531
11:34 in **H,** Zeboim and Neballat, 2531

HADLAI (1)

2Ch 28:12 and Amasa son of **H**— 2536

HADORAM (4)

Ge 10:27 **H,** Uzal, Diklah, 2066
1Ch 1:21 **H,** Uzal, Diklah, 2066
18:10 sent his son **H** to King David to greet him 2067
18:10 **H** brought all kinds of articles of gold NIH

HADRACH (1)

Zec 9: 1 of the LORD is against the land of **H** 2541

HAELEPH (1)

Jos 18:28 **H,** the Jebusite city (that is, Jerusalem), 2030

HAFT (KJV) See HANDLE

HAGAB (1)

Ezr 2:46 **H,** Shalmai, Hanan, 2507

HAGABA (1)

Ne 7:48 Lebana, **H,** Shalmai, 2509

HAGABAH (1)

Ezr 2:45 Lebanah, **H,** Akkub, 2509

HAGAR (15)

Ge 16: 1 she had an Egyptian maidservant named **H;** 2057
16: 3 Sarai his wife took her Egyptian maidservant **H** 2057
16: 4 He slept with **H,** and she conceived. 2057
16: 6 Sarai mistreated **H;** so she fled from her. 2023[S]
16: 7 of the LORD found **H** near a spring in 2023[S]
16: 8 And he said, "**H,** servant of Sarai, 2057
16:15 So **H** bore Abram a son, 2057
16:16 when **H** bore him Ishmael. 2057
21: 9 the son whom **H** the Egyptian had borne 2057
21:14 and a skin of water and gave them to **H.** 2057
21:17 the angel of God called to **H** from heaven 2057
21:17 "What is the matter, **H?** 2057
25:12 whom Sarah's maidservant, **H** the Egyptian, 2057
Gal 4:24 children who are to be slaves: This is **H.** *29*
4:25 Now **H** stands for Mount Sinai in Arabia *29*

HAGARENES (KJV) See HAGAR

HAGARITES, HAGERITE (KJV) See HAGRITE

HAGGAI (11)

Ezr 5: 1 **H** the prophet and Zechariah the prophet, 10247
6:14 and prosper under the preaching of **H** 10247
Hag 1: 1 of the LORD came through the prophet **H** 2516
1: 3 of the LORD came through the prophet **H:** 2516
1:12 and the message of the prophet **H,** 2516
1:13 Then **H,** the LORD's messenger, 2516
2: 1 of the LORD came through the prophet **H:** 2516
2:10 word of the LORD came to the prophet **H:** 2516
2:13 Then **H** said, "If a person defiled by contact 2516
2:14 Then **H** said, " 'So it is with this people 2516
2:20 to **H** a second time on the twenty-fourth day 2516

HAGGAN See BETH HAGGAN

HAGGARD (2)

2Sa 13: 4 look so **h** morning after morning? 1924
Job 30: 3 **H** from want and hunger, 1678

HAGGEDOLIM (1)

Ne 11:14 Their chief officer was Zabdiel son of **H.** 2045

HAGGERI (KJV) See HAGRI

HAGGI (2) [HAGGITE]

Ge 46:16 The sons of Gad: Zephon, **H,** Shuni, Ezbon, 2515
Nu 26:15 through **H,** the Haggite clan; 2515

HAGGIAH (1)

1Ch 6:30 **H** his son and Asaiah his son. 2517

HAGGIDGAD See HOR HAGGIDGAD

HAGGITE (1) [HAGGI]

Nu 26:15 through Haggi, the **H** clan; 2515

HAGGITES (KJV) See HAGGI

HAGGITH (5)

2Sa 3: 4 Adonijah the son of **H;** 2518
1Ki 1: 5 Now Adonijah, whose mother was **H,** 2518
1:11 Adonijah, the son of **H,** has become king 2518
2:13 Now Adonijah, the son of **H,** 2518
1Ch 3: 2 the fourth, Adonijah the son of **H;** 2518

HAGGOYIM See HAROSHETH HAGGOYIM

HAGRI (2) [HAGRITE, HAGRITES]

2Sa 23:36 son of Nathan from Zobah, the son of **H,** 2058
1Ch 11:38 the brother of Nathan, Mibhar son of **H,** 2058

HAGRITE (1) [HAGRI]

1Ch 27:31 Jaziz the **H** was in charge of the flocks. 2058

HAGRITES (6) [HAGRI]

1Ch 5:10 the **H,** who were defeated at their hands; 2058
5:10 of **the H** throughout the entire region east 2157[S]
5:19 They waged war against the **H,** Jetur, 2058
5:20 and God handed the **H** and all their allies 2058
5:21 They seized the livestock of **the H**— 2157[S]
Ps 83: 6 and the Ishmaelites, of Moab and the **H,** 2058

HAHIROTH See PI HAHIROTH

HAI (KJV) See AI

HAIL (29) [HAILSTONES, HAILSTORM]

Ex 9:19 the **h** will fall on every man and animal 1352
9:22 the sky so that **h** will fall all over Egypt— 1352
9:23 the LORD sent thunder and **h,** 1352
9:23 the LORD rained **h** on the land of Egypt; 1352
9:24 **h** fell and lightning flashed back and forth. 1352
9:25 Throughout Egypt **h** struck everything in 1352
9:26 The only place it did not **h** was the land 1352
9:28 for we have had enough thunder and **h.** 1352
9:29 and there will be no more **h,** 1352
9:33 the thunder and **h** stopped, 1352
9:34 that the rain and **h** and thunder had stopped, 1352
10: 5 the **h,** including every tree that is growing 1352
10:12 everything left by the **h.**" 1352
10:15 They devoured all that was left after the **h**— 1352
Job 38:22 the snow or seen the storehouses of the **h,** 1352
Ps 78:47 with **h** and their sycamore-figs with sleet. 1352
78:48 He gave over their cattle to the **h,** 1352
105:32 He turned their rain into **h,** 1352
147:17 He hurls down his **h** like pebbles. 7943
148: 8 and **h,** snow and clouds, stormy winds 1352
Isa 28:17 **h** will sweep away your refuge, the lie, 1352
30:30 with cloudburst, thunderstorm and **h.** 74+1352
32:19 Though **h** flattens the forest and 1351
Hag 2:17 mildew and **h,** yet you did not turn to me,' 1352
Mt 27:29 "**H,** king of the Jews!" *5897*
Mk 15:18 And they began to call out to him, "**H,** *5897*
Jn 19: 3 saying, "**H,** king of the Jews!" *5897*
Rev 8: 7 and there came **h** and fire mixed with blood, *5898*
16:21 on account of the plague *of* **h,** *5898*

HAILSTONES (7) [HAIL]

Jos 10:11 the LORD hurled large **h** down on them 74
10:11 more of them died from the **h** than were 74+1352
Ps 18:12 with **h** and bolts of lightning. 1352
Eze 13:11 and I will send **h** hurtling down, 74+453
13:13 in my anger **h** and torrents of rain will fall 74+453
38:22 down torrents of rain, **h** and burning sulfur 74+453
Rev 16:21 From the sky huge **h** of about *5898*

HAILSTORM (3) [HAIL]

Ex 9:18 the worst **h** that has ever fallen on Egypt, 1352
Isa 28: 2 Like a **h** and a destructive wind, 1352+2443
Rev 11:19 an earthquake and a great **h.** *5898*

HAIR (95) [GRAY-HAIRED, HAIRS, HAIRY]

Ex 25: 4 and fine linen; **goat h;** 6436
26: 7 of **goat h** for the tent over the tabernacle— 6436
35: 6 and fine linen; **goat h;** 6436
35:23 or fine linen, or **goat h,** ram skins dyed red 6436
35:26 and had the skill spun the **goat h.** 6436
36:14 of **goat h** for the tent over the tabernacle— 6436
Lev 10: 6 "Do not let your **h** become unkempt, 8031
13: 3 and if the **h** in the sore has turned white and 8552
13: 4 be more than skin deep and the **h** *in* it has 8552
13:10 in the skin that has turned the **h** white and 8552
13:20 to be more than skin deep and the **h** 8552
13:21 there is no white **h** in it and it is 8552
13:25 and if the **h** in it has turned white, 8552
13:26 and there is no white **h** in the spot and 8552
13:30 to be more than skin deep and the **h** 8552
13:31 and there is no black **h** in it, 8552
13:32 and there is no yellow **h** in it and it does 8552
13:36 priest does not need to look for yellow **h;** 8552
13:37 and black **h** has grown in it, 8552
13:40 When a man *has* **lost** his **h** and is bald, 5307+8031
13:41 If *he has* **lost** his **h** from the front 5307+8031
13:45 let his **h** be unkempt, 8031
14: 8 shave off all his **h** and bathe with water; 8552
14: 9 the seventh day he must shave off all his **h;** 8552
14: 9 his eyebrows and the rest of his **h.** 8552
19:27 " *'Do* not **cut** the **h** at the sides of your head 5938
21:10 must not let his **h** become unkempt 8031
Nu 5:18 he shall loosen her **h** and place in her hands 8031
6: 5 must let the **h** *of* his head grow long. 7279+8552
6: 9 thus defiling the **h** he has dedicated, 8031
6:18 the Nazirite must shave off the **h** 8031
6:18 to take the **h** and put it in the fire that is 8552
6:19 " 'After the Nazirite has shaved off the **h** NIH
31:20 made of leather, **goat h** or wood." 6436
Jdg 16:19 a man to shave off the seven braids of his **h,** 8031
16:22 But the **h** *on* his head began to grow again 8552
20:16 each of whom could sling a stone at a **h** and 8553
1Sa 14:45 not a **h** of his head will fall to the ground, 8553
17:35 When it turned on me, I seized it by its **h,** 2417
19:13 putting some **goats' h** at the head. 3889+6436
19:16 and at the head was some **goats' h.** 3889+6436
2Sa 14:11 "not one **h** of your son's **head** 8553
14:26 Whenever he **cut** *the* **h** *of* his head— 1662
14:26 he used to **cut** *his* **h** from time to time 1662
1Ki 1:52 not a **h of** his **head** will fall to the ground; 8553
2Ki 1: 8 with a **garment of h** and with a leather belt 8552
9:30 arranged her **h** and looked out of a window. 8031
Ezr 9: 3 pulled **h** from my head and beard and sat 8552
Ne 13:25 of the men and **pulled out** their **h.** 5307
Job 4:15 and the **h** *on* my body stood on end. 8553
41:32 one would think the deep had **white h.** 8484
Pr 16:31 **Gray h** is a crown of splendor; 8484
20:29 **gray h** the splendor of the old. 8484
SS 4: 1 Your **h** is like a flock of goats descending 8552
5: 2 my **h** with the dampness of the night." 7767
5:11 his **h** is wavy and black as a raven. 7767
6: 5 Your **h** is like a flock of goats descending 8552
7: 5 Your **h** is like royal tapestry; 1929+8031
Isa 3:24 instead of **well-dressed h,** baldness; 5126+5250
7:20 to shave your head and the **h** *of* your legs, 8552
22:12 to **tear out** your **h** and put on sackcloth. 7947
Jer 7:29 Cut off your **h** and throw it away; 5694
Eze 5: 1 take a set of scales and divide up **the h.** 4392[S]
5: 2 burn a third of the **h** with fire inside the city. NIH
5: 3 a few strands of **h** and tuck them away in NIH
8: 3 a hand and took me by the **h** *of* my head. 7492
16: 7 Your breasts were formed and your **h** grew, 8552
44:20 or let their **h** grow **long,** 7279
44:20 **keep** *the* **h** of their heads **trimmed.** 4080+4080
Da 3:27 nor was a **h** *of* their heads singed; 10687
4:33 with the dew of heaven until his **h** grew like 10687
7: 9 the **h** *of* his head was white like wool. 10687
Hos 7: 9 **h** is sprinkled with **gray,** 8484
Zec 13: 4 not put on a prophet's garment of **h** in order 8552
Mt 3: 4 John's clothes were made of camel's **h,** *2582*
5:36 you cannot make even one **h** white or black. *2582*
Mk 1: 6 John wore clothing *made of* camel's **h,** *2582*
Lk 7:38 Then she wiped them *with* her **h,** *2582*
7:44 with her tears and wiped them *with* her **h.** *2582*
21:18 But not a **h** of your head will perish. *2582*
Jn 11: 2 on the Lord and wiped his feet *with* her **h.** *2582*
12: 3 on Jesus' feet and wiped his feet *with* her **h.** *2582*
Ac 18:18 he had his **h** cut off at Cenchrea because of *3051*
27:34 of you will lose a single **h** from his head." *2582*
1Co 11: 6 she should have her **h** cut off; *NIG*
11: 6 a woman *to have her* **h cut** or shaved off, *3025*
11:14 that if a man **has long h,** it is a disgrace to *3150*
11:15 that if a woman **has long h,** it is her glory? *3150*
11:15 For **long h** is given to her as a covering. *3151*
1Ti 2: 9 not with **braided h** or gold or pearls *4427*

1Pe 3: 3 such as braided **h** and the wearing 2582
Rev 1:14 His head and **h** were white like wool, 2582
6:12 like sackcloth **made of** goat **h,** 5570
9: 8 **Their h** was like women's hair, 2400+2582
9: 8 Their hair was like women's **h,** *NIG*

HAIRS (5) [HAIR]

Ps 40:12 They are more than the **h** *of* my head, 8553
69: 4 outnumber the **h** of my head; 8553
Isa 46: 4 Even to your old age and **gray h** I am he, 8484
Mt 10:30 the very **h** of your head are all numbered. *2582*
Lk 12: 7 the very **h** of your head are all numbered. *2582*

HAIRY (4) [HAIR]

Ge 25:25 and his whole body was like a **h** garment; 8552
27:11 "But my brother Esau is a **h** man, 8537
27:23 for his hands were **h** like those of his 8537
Ps 68:21 **h** crowns of those who go on in their sins. 8552

HAKILAH (3)

1Sa 23:19 on the hill of **H,** south of Jeshimon? 2677
26: 1 "Is not David hiding on the hill of **H,** 2677
26: 3 the road on the hill of **H** facing Jeshimon, 2677

HAKKATAN (1)

Ezr 8:12 Johanan son of **H,** and with him 110 men; 2214

HAKKEREM See BETH HAKKEREM

HAKKORE See EN HAKKORE

HAKKOZ (5)

1Ch 24:10 the seventh to **H,** the eighth to Abijah, 2212
Ezr 2:61 **H** and Barzillai (a man who had married 2212
Ne 3: 4 Meremoth son of Uriah, the son of **H,** 2212
3:21 the son of **H,** repaired another section, 2212
7:63 the descendants of Hobaiah, **H** and Barzillai 2212

HAKUPHA (2)

Ezr 2:51 Bakbuk, **H,** Harhur, 2979
Ne 7:53 Bakbuk, **H,** Harhur, 2979

HALAH (3)

2Ki 17: 6 He settled them in **H,** 2712
18:11 to Assyria and settled them in **H,** 2712
1Ch 5:26 He took them to **H,** Habor, 2712

HALAK (2)

Jos 11:17 from Mount **H,** which rises toward Seir, 2748
12: 7 in the Valley of Lebanon to Mount **H,** 2748

HALE (KJV) See DRAG OFF

HALF (114) [HALF-DISTRICT, HALF-TRIBE, HALFWAY, HALVES, TWO-AND-A-HALF]

Ge 15:10 the birds, however, *he did* not **cut in h.** 1439
Ex 24: 6 Moses took **h** *of* the blood and put it 2942
24: 6 and the other **h** he sprinkled on the altar. 2942
25:10 two and a **h** cubits long, 2942
25:10 a cubit and a **h** wide, 2942
25:10 and a cubit and a **h** high. 2942
25:17 a **h** cubits long and a cubit and a half wide. 2942
25:17 a half cubits long and a cubit and a **h** wide. 2942
25:23 a cubit wide and a cubit and a **h** high. 2942
26:12 the **h** curtain that is left over is to hang 2942
26:16 be ten cubits long and a cubit and a **h** wide, 2942
30:13 to give a **h** shekel, according to 4734
30:13 This **h** shekel is an offering to the LORD. 4734
30:15 a **h** shekel and the poor are not to give less 4734
30:23 **h as much** (that is, 250 shekels) 4734
36:21 and a cubit and a **h** wide, 2942
37: 1 two and a **h** cubits long, 2942
37: 1 a cubit and a **h** wide, 2942
37: 1 and a cubit and a **h** high. 2942
37: 6 a **h** cubits long and a cubit and a half wide. 2942
37: 6 a half cubits long and a cubit and a **h** wide. 2942
37:10 a cubit wide, and a cubit and a **h** high. 2942
38:26 one beka per person, that is, **h** a shekel, 4734
Lev 6:20 of fine flour as a regular grain offering, **h** 4734
6:20 of it in the morning and **h** in the evening. 4734
Nu 12:12 with its flesh **h** eaten away." 2942
15: 9 of an ephah of fine flour mixed with **h** a hin 2942
15:10 bring **h** a hin of wine as a drink offering. 2942
28:14 to be a drink offering of **h** a hin of wine; 2942
31:29 from their **h share** and give it to Eleazar 4734
31:30 From the Israelites' **h,** 4734
31:36 The **h** share of those who fought in 4733
31:42 The **h** *belonging to* the Israelites, 4734
31:43 the community's **h**—was 337,500 sheep, 4733
31:47 From the Israelites' **h,** Moses selected 4734
34:13 that it be given to the nine and a **h** tribes, 2942
34:15 a **h** tribes have received their inheritance on 2942
Dt 3:12 including **h** the hill country of Gilead, 2942
3:13 I gave to the **h** tribe of Manasseh. 2942
Jos 8:33 **H** *of* the people stood in front 2942
8:33 of Mount Gerizim and **h** *of* them in front 2942
12: 2 This included **h** *of* Gilead. 2942
12: 5 and **h** *of* Gilead to the border of Sihon king 2942
13: 7 an inheritance among the nine tribes and **h** 2942
Jos 13: 8 **The other h of Manasseh,** 2257S
13:25 of Gilead and **h** the Ammonite country 2942
13:29 to **h** the family of the descendants 2942
13:31 **h** *of* Gilead, and Ashtaroth and Edrei 2942
13:31 for **h** *of* the sons of Makir, clan by clan. 2942
21: 5 Dan and **h** *of* Manasseh. 2942
21:25 From **h** the tribe of Manasseh 4734
22: 7 the other **h** *of* the tribe Joshua gave land on 2942
Jdg 3:16 sword **about a foot and a h** long, 1688
1Sa 14:14 in an area of about **h** an acre. 2942
2Sa 10: 4 shaved off **h** *of* each man's beard, 2942
18: 3 Even if **h** *of* us die, they won't care; 2942
19:40 of Judah and **h** the troops of Israel had taken 2942
1Ki 3:25 the living child in two and give **h** to one 2942
3:25 and give half to one and **h** to the other." 2942
7:31 it measured a cubit and a **h.** 2942
7:32 of each wheel was a cubit and a **h.** 2942
7:35 of the stand there was a circular band **h** 2942
10: 7 Indeed, not even **h** was told me; 2942
13: 8 if you were to give me **h** your possessions, 2942
16: 9 who had command of **h** his chariots, 4734
16:21 **h** supported Tibni son of Ginath for king, 2942
16:21 and the other **h** supported Omri. 2942
2Ki 25:17 pillar was **four and a h feet** high 564+8993
1Ch 2:52 Haroeh, **h** the Manahathites, 2942
2:54 Atroth Beth Joab, **h** the Manahathites, 2942
6:61 from the clans of **h** the tribe of Manasseh. 4734
6:70 And from **h** the tribe of Manasseh 4734
11:23 **seven and a h feet** tall. 564+928+2021+2822
12:31 men of **h** the tribe of Manasseh, designated 2942
27:20 over **h** the tribe of Manasseh: 2942
2Ch 9: 6 not even **h** the greatness of your wisdom 2942
Ne 3:17 Hashabiah, ruler of **h** the district of Keilah, 2942
4: 6 the wall till all of it reached **h** its height, 2942
4:16 **h** *of* my men did the work, 2942
4:16 the other **h** were equipped with spears, 2942
4:21 the work with **h** the men holding spears, 2942
12:32 and **h** the leaders of Judah followed them, 2942
12:38 together with **h** the people— 2942
12:40 so did I, together with **h** the officials, 2942
13:24 **H** *of* their children spoke the language 2942
Est 5: 3 up to **h** the kingdom, it will be given you." 2942
5: 6 up to **h** the kingdom, it will be granted." 2942
7: 2 up to **h** the kingdom, it will be granted." 2942
Ps 55:23 not **live out h** their days. 2936
Isa 44:16 **H** *of* the wood he burns in the fire; 2942
44:19 **"H** *of* it I used for fuel; 2942
Jer 17:11 When his life is **h** *gone,* 2942
Eze 16:51 Samaria did not commit **h** the sins you did. 2942
40:42 each a cubit and a **h** long, 2942
40:42 a cubit and a **h** wide and a cubit high. 2942
43:17 with a rim of **h** a cubit and a gutter of 2942
Da 7:25 for a time, times and **h** a time. 10584
12: 7 "It will be for a time, times and **h** a time. 2942
Zec 14: 2 **H** *of* the city will go into exile, 2942
14: 4 with **h** *of* the mountain moving north 2942
14: 4 and **h** moving south. 2942
14: 8 **h** to the eastern sea and half to 2942
14: 8 to the eastern sea and **h** to the western sea, 2942
Mk 6:23 up to **h** my kingdom." *2468*
Lk 4:25 sky was shut for three and a **h** years *1971+3604*
10:30 leaving him **h dead.** *2467*
19: 8 Here and now I give **h** of my possessions to *2468*
Jn 6:19 they rowed **three or three and a h miles,** *1633+2445+4297+5084+5558*
Ac 18:11 So Paul stayed *for* a year and **a h,** *1971+3604*
Jas 5:17 on the land *for* three and a **h** years. *1971+3604*
Rev 8: 1 silence in heaven for about **h an hour.** *2469*
11: 9 and a **h** days men from every people, *2468*
11:11 after the three and a **h** days a breath of life *2468*
12:14 for a time, times and **h** a time, *2468*

HALF-DISTRICT (4) [HALF, DISTRICT]

Ne 3: 9 ruler of a **h** *of* Jerusalem, 2942+7135
3:12 ruler of a **h** *of* Jerusalem, 2942+7135
3:16 ruler of a **h** *of* Beth Zur, 2942+7135
3:18 ruler of the other **h** *of* Keilah. 2942+7135

HALF-TRIBE (24) [HALF, TRIBE]

Nu 32:33 the Reubenites and the **h** *of* Manasseh 2942+8657
34:14 tribe of Gad and the **h** *of* Manasseh 2942+4751
Dt 29: 8 the Gadites and the **h** *of* Manasseh. 2942+8657
Jos 1:12 the Gadites and the **h** *of* Manasseh, 2942+8657
4:12 and the **h** *of* Manasseh crossed over, 2942+8657
12: 6 **h** *of* Manasseh to be their possession. 2942+8657
13:29 This is what Moses had given to the **h** 2942+8657
18: 7 Reuben and the **h** *of* Manasseh 2942+8657
21: 6 and the **h** *of* Manasseh in Bashan. 2942+4751
21:27 from the **h** *of* Manasseh, 2942+4751
22: 1 the Gadites and the **h** *of* Manasseh 2942+4751
22: 7 **h** *of* Manasseh Moses had given land 2942+8657
22: 9 the **h** *of* Manasseh left the Israelites 2942+8657
22:10 Gadites and the **h** *of* Manasseh built 2942+8657
22:13 Reuben, Gad and the **h** *of* Manasseh. 2942+8657
22:15 Reuben, Gad and the **h** *of* Manasseh— 2942+8657
22:21 and the **h** *of* Manasseh replied to 2942+8657
1Ch 5:18 the **h** *of* Manasseh had 44,760 men 2942+8657
5:23 of the **h** *of* Manasseh were numerous; 2942+8657
5:26 the Gadites and the **h** *of* Manasseh 2942+8657
6:71 **h** *of* Manasseh they received Golan 2942+4751
12:37 Gad and the **h** *of* Manasseh, 2942+8657
26:32 the Gadites and the **h** *of* Manasseh 2942+8657
27:21 over the **h** *of* Manasseh in Gilead: 2942

HALFWAY (3) [HALF]

Ex 27: 5 under the ledge of the altar so that it is **h** up 2942
38: 4 to be under its ledge, **h** up the altar. 2942
Jn 7:14 Not until **h through** the Feast did Jesus go *3548*

HALHUL (1)

Jos 15:58 **H,** Beth Zur, Gedor, 2713

HALI (1)

Jos 19:25 Their territory included: Helkath, **H,** Beten, 2718

HALL (19)

1Sa 9:22 and his servant into the **h** and seated them at 4384
1Ki 6: 3 the **main h** *of* the temple extended the width 2121
6: 5 of the **main h** and inner sanctuary he built 2121
6:17 The **main h** in front of this room 2121
6:33 olive wood for the entrance to the **main h.** 2121
7: 7 He built the throne **h,** the Hall of Justice, 395
7: 7 He built the throne hall, the **H** *of* Justice, 395
7: 8 a palace like this **h** for Pharaoh's daughter, 395
7:50 for the doors of the **main h** of the temple. 2121
2Ch 3: 5 the main **h** with pine and covered it 1074
3:13 They stood on their feet, facing the **main h.** 1074
4:22 and the doors of the **main h.** 2121
Est 5: 1 in front of the king's **h.** 1074
5: 1 on his royal throne in the **h,** 1074
7: 8 from the palace garden to the banquet **h,** 1074
SS 2: 4 He has taken me to the **banquet h,** 1074+3516
Da 5:10 came into the banquet **h.** 10103
Mt 22:10 and the **wedding h** was filled with guests. *1141*
Ac 19: 9 and had discussions daily in the **lecture h** *5391*

HALLELUJAH (4)

Rev 19: 1 in heaven shouting: **"H!** *252*
19: 3 And again they shouted: **"H!** *252*
19: 4 And they cried: "Amen, **H!"** *252*
19: 6 of thunder, shouting: **"H!** *252*

HALLOHESH (2)

Ne 3:12 Shallum son of **H,** 2135
10:24 **H,** Pilha, Shobek, 2135

HALLOW, HALLOWED (KJV) See CONSECRATE, CONSECRATED, HOLY, SACRED, SET APART

HALLOWED (2) [HOLY]

Mt 6: 9 " 'Our Father in heaven, **h** *be* your name, *39*
Lk 11: 2 " 'Father, **h** *be* your name, *39*

HALOHESH (KJV) See HALLOHESH

HALT (4) [HALTED]

2Sa 2:28 and all the men **came to a h;** 6641
20:12 that all the troops **came to a h** there. 6641
Job 38:11 here is where your proud waves **h'?** 8883
Isa 10:32 This day they *will* **h** at Nob; 6641

HALTED (2) [HALT]

2Sa 15:17 and *they* **h** *at* a place some distance away. 6641
18:16 stopped pursuing Israel, for Joab **h** them. 3104

HALTER (1)

Pr 26: 3 A whip for the horse, a **h** for the donkey, 5496

HALVES (3) [HALF]

Ge 15:10 and arranged the **h** opposite each other; 1440
SS 4: 3 Your temples behind your veil are like the **h** 7115
6: 7 Your temples behind your veil are like the **h** 7115

HAM (16) [HAMITES]

Ge 5:32 the father of Shem, **H** and Japheth. 2769
6:10 Noah had three sons: Shem, **H** and Japheth. 2769
7:13 and his sons, Shem, **H** and Japheth, together 2769
9:18 of the ark were Shem, **H** and Japheth. 2769
9:18 (**H** was the father of Canaan.) 2769
9:22 **H,** the father of Canaan, 2769
10: 1 This is the account of Shem, **H** and Japheth, 2769
10: 6 sons of **H:** Cush, Mizraim, Put and Canaan. 2769
10:20 the sons of **H** by their clans and languages, 2769
14: 5 the Zuzites in **H,** the Emites in Shaveh 2154
1Ch 1: 4 The sons of Noah: Shem, **H** and Japheth. 2769
1: 8 sons of **H:** Cush, Mizraim, Put and Canaan. 2769
Ps 78:51 the firstfruits of manhood in the tents of **H.** 2769
105:23 Jacob lived as an alien in the land of **H.** 2769
105:27 his wonders in the land of **H.** 2769
106:22 of **H** and awesome deeds by the Red Sea. 2769

HAMAN (44) [HAMAN'S]

Est 3: 1 King Xerxes honored **H** son 2172
3: 2 knelt down and paid honor to **H,** 2172
3: 4 Therefore they told **H** about it 2172
3: 5 When **H** saw that Mordecai would not kneel 2172
3: 6 Instead **H** looked for a way to destroy 2172
3: 7 the presence of **H** to select a day and month. 2172
3: 8 Then **H** said to King Xerxes, 2172
3:10 and gave it to **H** son of Hammedatha, 2172

Est 3:11 "Keep the money," the king said to **H,** 2172
3:15 The king and **H** sat down to drink, 2172
4: 7 the exact amount of money **H** had promised 2172
5: 4 "let the king, together with **H,** 2172
5: 5 "Bring **H** at once," the king said, 2172
5: 5 So the king and **H** went to the banquet 2172
5: 8 let the king and **H** come tomorrow to 2172
5: 9 **H** went out that day happy and 2172
5:10 **H** restrained himself and went home. 2172
5:11 **H** boasted to them about his vast wealth, 2172
5:12 "And that's not all," **H** added. 2172
5:14 This suggestion delighted **H,** 2172
6: 4 Now **H** had just entered the outer court of 2172
6: 5 "**H** is standing in the court." 2172
6: 6 When **H** entered, the king asked him, 2172
6: 6 Now **H** thought to himself, 2172
6:10 "Go at once," the king commanded **H.** 2172
6:11 So **H** got the robe and the horse. 2172
6:12 But **H** rushed home, 2172
6:14 and hurried **H** away to the banquet 2172
7: 1 king and **H** went to dine with Queen Esther, 2172
7: 6 "The adversary and enemy is this vile **H.**" 2172
7: 6 **H** was terrified before the king and queen. 2172
7: 7 But **H,** realizing that the king had already 2172
7: 8 **H** was falling on the couch where Esther 2172
7:10 So they hanged **H** on the gallows he had 2172
8: 1 gave Queen Esther the estate of **H,** 2172
8: 2 which he had reclaimed from **H,** 2172
8: 3 an end to the evil plan of **H** the Agagite, 2172
8: 5 the dispatches that **H** son of Hammedatha, 2172
8: 7 "Because **H** attacked the Jews, 2172
9:10 the ten sons of **H** son of Hammedatha, 2172
9:12 and the ten sons of **H** in the citadel of Susa. 2172
9:14 and they hanged the ten sons of **H.** 2172
9:24 For **H** son of Hammedatha, the Agagite, 2172
9:25 that the evil scheme **H** had devised against 2257[S]

HAMAN'S (5) [HAMAN]

Est 3:12 the language of each people all **H** orders to 2172
7: 8 they covered **H** face. 2172
7: 9 "A gallows seventy-five feet high stands by **H** house. 2172
8: 2 And Esther appointed him over **H** estate. 2172
9:13 and let **H** ten sons be hanged on gallows." 2172

HAMATH (24) [HAMATH ZOBAH, HAMATHITES, LEBO HAMATH]

2Sa 8: 9 king of **H** heard that David had defeated 2828
2Ki 14:28 for Israel both Damascus and **H,** 2828
17:24 **H** and Sepharvaim and settled them in 2828
17:30 and the men from **H** made Ashima; 2828
18:34 Where are the gods of **H** and Arpad? 2828
19:13 Where is the king of **H,** the king of Arpad, 2828
23:33 land of **H** so that he might not reign in Jerusalem, 2828
25:21 There at Riblah, in the land of **H,** 2828
1Ch 18: 3 king of Zobah, as far as **H,** 2828
18: 9 king of **H** heard that David had defeated 2828
2Ch 8: 4 and all the store cities he had built in **H.** 2828
Isa 10: 9 Is not **H** like Arpad, 2828
11:11 from **H** and from the islands of the sea. 2828
36:19 Where are the gods of **H** and Arpad? 2828
37:13 Where is the king of **H,** the king of Arpad, 2828
Jer 39: 5 of Babylon at Riblah in the land of **H,** 2828
49:23 "**H** and Arpad are dismayed, 2828
52: 9 of Babylon at Riblah in the land of **H,** 2828
52:27 There at Riblah, in the land of **H,** 2828
Eze 47:16 on the border between Damascus and **H),** 2828
47:17 with the border of **H** to the north. 2828
48: 1 of Damascus next to **H** will be part 2828
Am 6: 2 go from there to great **H,** 2828
Zec 9: 2 and upon **H** too, which borders on it, 2828

HAMATH ZOBAH (1) [HAMATH, ZOBAH]

2Ch 8: 3 then went to **H** and captured it. 2832

HAMATHITES (2) [HAMATH]

Ge 10:18 Arvadites, Zemarites and **H.** 2833
1Ch 1:16 Arvadites, Zemarites and **H.** 2833

HAMITES (2) [HAM]

1Ch 4:40 Some **H** had lived there formerly. 2769
4:41 They attacked the **H** in their dwellings and NIH

HAMMAHLEKOTH See SELA HAMMAHLEKOTH

HAMMATH (2)

Jos 19:35 The fortified cities were Ziddim, Zer, **H,** 2829
1Ch 2:55 These are the Kenites who came from **H,** 2830

HAMMEDATHA (5)

Est 3: 1 King Xerxes honored Haman son of **H,** 2158
3:10 and gave it to Haman son of **H,** 2158
8: 5 the dispatches that Haman son of **H,** 2158
9:10 the ten sons of Haman son of **H,** 2158
9:24 For Haman son of **H,** the Agagite, 2158

HAMMELECH (KJV) See THE KING

HAMMER (9) [HAMMERED, HAMMERS]

Ex 25:31 a lampstand of pure gold and **h** it **out,** 5251+6913
Nu 16:38 **H** the censers *into* sheets to overlay 6913+8393
Jdg 4:21 a tent peg and a **h** and went quietly to him 5216
5:26 her right hand for the workman's **h.** 2153
1Ki 6: 7 at the quarry were used, and no **h,** chisel 5216
Isa 41: 7 the **h** spurs on him who strikes the anvil. 7079
Jer 10: 4 they fasten it with **h** and nails so it will 5216
23:29 "and like a **h** that breaks a rock in pieces? 7079
50:23 and shattered is the **h** *of* the whole earth! 7079

HAMMERED (17) [HAMMER]

Ex 25:18 And make two cherubim out of **h** gold at 5251
25:36 **h** out of pure gold. 5251
37: 7 Then he made two cherubim out of **h** gold 5251
37:17 of pure gold and **h** it **out,** base and shaft; 5251
37:22 **h out** *of* pure gold. 5251
39: 3 *They* **h out** thin sheets of gold 8392
Nu 8: 4 It was made of **h** gold— 5251
10: 2 "Make two trumpets of **h** silver, 5251
16:39 and *he had* them **h out** to overlay the altar, 8392
1Ki 6:35 and overlaid them with gold **h evenly** over 3837
7:29 the lions and bulls were wreaths of **h** work. 4618
10:16 King Solomon made two hundred large shields of **h** gold; 8822
10:17 of **h** gold, with three minas of gold 8822
2Ch 9:15 King Solomon made two hundred large shields of **h** gold; 8822
9:15 six hundred bekas of **h** gold went 8822
9:16 of **h** gold, with three hundred bekas of gold 8822
Jer 10: 9 **H** silver is brought from Tarshish and gold 8392

HAMMERS (1) [HAMMER]

Isa 44:12 he shapes an idol with **h,** 5216

HAMMOLEKETH (1)

1Ch 7:18 His sister **H** gave birth to Ishhod, 2168

HAMMON (2)

Jos 19:28 It went to Abdon, Rehob, **H** and Kanah, 2785
1Ch 6:76 in Galilee, **H** and Kiriathaim, together 2785

HAMMOTH DOR (1) [DOR]

Jos 21:32 **H** and Kartan, together 2831

HAMMUEL (1)

1Ch 4:26 The descendants of Mishma: **H** his son, 2781

HAMON See BAAL HAMON, HAMON GOG

HAMON GOG (2) [BAAL HAMON]

Eze 39:11 So it will be called the Valley of **H.** 2163
39:15 in the Valley of **H.** 2163

HAMONAH (1)

Eze 39:16 (Also a town called **H** will be there.) 2164

HAMOR (13)

Ge 33:19 he bought from the sons of **H,** 2791
34: 2 When Shechem son of **H** the Hivite, 2791
34: 4 And Shechem said to his father **H,** 2791
34: 6 Then Shechem's father **H** went out to talk 2791
34: 8 But **H** said to them, 2791
34:13 as they spoke to Shechem and his father **H.** 2791
34:18 Their proposal seemed good to **H** 2791
34:20 So **H** and his son Shechem went to the gate 2791
34:24 of the city gate agreed with **H** 2791
34:26 put **H** and his son Shechem to the sword 2791
Jos 24:32 of silver from the sons of **H,** 2791
Jdg 9:28 Serve the men of **H,** Shechem's father! 2791
Ac 7:16 the sons *of* **H** at Shechem for a certain sum *1846*

HAMPERED (1)

Pr 4:12 When you walk, your steps *will* not be **h;** 7674

HAMSTRING (1) [HAMSTRUNG]

Jos 11: 6 *to* **h** their horses and burn their chariots." 6828

HAMSTRUNG (4) [HAMSTRING]

Ge 49: 6 in their anger and **h** oxen as they pleased. 6828
Jos 11: 9 *He* **h** their horses and burned their chariots. 6828
2Sa 8: 4 He **h** all but a hundred of the chariot horses. 6828
1Ch 18: 4 He **h** all but a hundred of the chariot horses. 6828

HAMUEL (KJV) See HAMMUEL

HAMUL (3) [HAMULITE]

Ge 46:12 The sons of Perez: Hezron and **H.** 2783
Nu 26:21 through **H,** the Hamulite clan. 2783
1Ch 2: 5 The sons of Perez: Hezron and **H.** 2783

HAMULITE (1) [HAMUL]

Nu 26:21 through Hamul, the **H** clan. 2784

HAMUTAL (3)

2Ki 23:31 His mother's name was **H** daughter 2782
24:18 His mother's name was **H** daughter 2782
Jer 52: 1 His mother's name was **H** daughter 2782

HANAMEL (4)

Jer 32: 7 **H** son of Shallum your uncle is going 2856
32: 8 my cousin **H** came to me in the courtyard of 2856
32: 9 the field at Anathoth from my cousin **H** 2856
32:12 in the presence of my cousin **H** and of 2856

HANAN (12) [BAAL-HANAN, BEN-HANAN]

1Ch 8:23 Abdon, Zicri, **H,** 2860
8:38 Bokeru, Ishmael, Sheariah, Obadiah and **H.** 2860
9:44 Bokeru, Ishmael, Sheariah, Obadiah and **H.** 2860
11:43 **H** son of Maacah, Joshaphat the Mithnite, 2860
Ezr 2:46 Hagab, Shalmai, **H,** 2860
Ne 7:49 **H,** Giddel, Gahar, 2860
8: 7 Kelita, Azariah, Jozabad, **H** and Pelaiah— 2860
10:10 Shebaniah, Hodiah, Kelita, Pelaiah, **H,** 2860
10:22 Pelatiah, **H,** Anaiah, 2860
10:26 Ahiah, **H,** Anan, 2860
13:13 in charge of the storerooms and made **H** son 2860
Jer 35: 4 the room of the sons of **H** son of Igdaliah 2860

HANANEL (4)

Ne 3: 1 and as far as the Tower of **H.** 2861
12:39 of **H** and the Tower of the Hundred, 2861
Jer 31:38 be rebuilt for me from the Tower of **H** to 2861
Zec 14:10 the Tower of **H** to the royal winepresses. 2861

HANANI (11)

1Ki 16: 1 word of the LORD came to Jehu son of **H** 2862
16: 7 the prophet Jehu son of **H** to Baasha 2862
1Ch 25: 4 Hananiah, **H,** Eliathah, 2862
25:25 the eighteenth to **H,** 2862
2Ch 16: 7 At that time **H** the seer came to Asa king 2862
19: 2 Jehu the seer, the son of **H,** went out 2862
20:34 are written in the annals of Jehu son of **H,** 2862
Ezr 10:20 of Immer: **H** and Zebadiah. 2862
Ne 1: 2 **H,** one of my brothers, came from Judah 2862
7: 2 I put in charge of Jerusalem my brother **H,** 2862
12:36 Gilalai, Maai, Nethanel, Judah and **H—** 2862

HANANIAH (28)

1Ch 3:19 The sons of Zerubbabel: Meshullam and **H.** 2863
3:21 The descendants of **H:** 2863
8:24 **H,** Elam, Anthothijah, 2863
25: 4 **H,** Hanani, Eliathah, Giddalti 2863
25:23 the sixteenth to **H,** his sons and relatives, 2864
2Ch 26:11 the officer under the direction of **H,** 2864
Ezr 10:28 Jehohanan, **H,** Zabbai and Athlai. 2863
Ne 3: 8 and **H,** one of the perfume-makers, 2863
3:30 Next to him, **H** son of Shelemiah, 2863
7: 2 along with **H** the commander of the citadel, 2863
10:23 Hoshea, **H,** Hasshub, 2863
12:12 Meraiah; of Jeremiah's, **H;** 2863
12:41 Zechariah and **H** with their trumpets— 2863
Jer 28: 1 the prophet **H** son of Azzur, 2863
28: 5 replied to the prophet **H** before the priests 2863
28:10 the prophet **H** took the yoke off the neck of 2863
28:12 after the prophet **H** had broken the yoke off 2863
28:13 and tell **H,** 'This is what the LORD says: 2863
28:15 the prophet Jeremiah said to **H** the prophet, 2863
28:15 to Hananiah the prophet, "Listen, **H!** 2863
28:17 **H** the prophet died. 2863
36:12 of Shaphan, Zedekiah son of **H,** 2864
37:13 the son of **H,** arrested him and said, 2863
Da 1: 6 Daniel, **H,** Mishael and Azariah. 2863
1: 7 the name Belteshazzar; to **H,** Shadrach; 2863
1:11 **H,** Mishael and Azariah, 2863
1:19 and he found none equal to Daniel, **H,** 2863
2:17 and explained the matter to his friends **H,** 10275

HAND (847) [HANDBREADTH, HANDED, HANDFUL, HANDFULS, HANDING, HANDS, LEFT-HANDED, OPENHANDED, RIGHT-HANDED]

Ge 3:22 to reach out his **h** and take also from the tree 3338
4:11 to receive your brother's blood from your **h.** 3338
8: 9 He reached out his **h** and took the dove 3338
14:20 who delivered your enemies into your **h.**" 3338
14:22 "I have raised my **h** to the LORD, 3338
16:12 his **h** will be against everyone 3338
16:12 be against everyone and everyone's **h** 3338
19:16 the men grasped his **h** and the hands 3338
21:18 Lift the boy up and take him by the **h,** 3338
21:30 from my **h** as a witness that I dug this well." 3338
22:10 Then he reached out his **h** and took 3338
22:12 "Do not lay a **h** on the boy," he said. 3338
24: 2 "Put your **h** under my thigh. 3338
24: 9 So the servant put his **h** under the thigh 3338
25:26 with his **h** grasping Esau's heel; 3338
32:11 I pray, from the **h** *of* my brother Esau, 3338
37:22 but don't lay a **h** on him." 3338
38:18 and the staff in your **h,**" she answered. 3338
38:28 one of them put out his **h;** 3338
38:29 But when he drew back his **h,** 3338
39:12 But he left his cloak in her **h** and ran out of 3338
39:13 in her **h** and had run out of the house, 3338
40:11 Pharaoh's cup was in my **h,** 3338

Ge 40:11 into Pharaoh's cup and put the cup in his **h.** 4090
40:13 and you will put Pharaoh's cup in his **h,** 3338
40:21 he once again put the cup into Pharaoh's **h,** 4090
41:44 without your word no one will lift **h** or foot 3338
46:4 And Joseph's own **h** will close your eyes." 3338
47:29 put your **h** under my thigh and promise 3338
48:13 Ephraim on his right toward Israel's left **h** NIH
48:13 on his left toward Israel's right **h,** NIH
48:14 But Israel reached out his right **h** and put it NIH
48:14 he put his left **h** on Manasseh's head, NIH
48:17 Joseph saw his father placing his right **h** 3338
48:17 so he took hold of his father's **h** to move it 3338
48:18 put your right **h** on his head." NIH
49:8 your **h** will be on the neck of your enemies; 3338
49:24 of the **h** *of* the Mighty One of Jacob, 3338
Ex 3:8 to rescue them from the **h** *of* the Egyptians 3338
3:19 unless a mighty **h** compels him. 3338
3:20 So I will stretch out my **h** and strike 3338
4:2 "What is that in your **h?"** 3338
4:4 "Reach out your **h** and take it by the tail." 3338
4:4 and it turned back into a staff in his **h.** 4090
4:6 "Put your **h** inside your cloak." 3338
4:6 So Moses put his **h** into his cloak, 3338
4:7 So Moses put his **h** back into his cloak, 3338
4:17 But take this staff in your **h** 3338
4:20 And he took the staff of God in his **h.** 3338
5:21 and have put a sword in their **h** to kill us." 3338
6:1 Because of my mighty **h** he will let them go; 3338
6:1 of my mighty **h** he will drive them out 3338
6:8 to the land I swore with uplifted **h** to give 3338
7:4 Then I will lay my **h** on Egypt and 3338
7:5 when I stretch out my **h** against Egypt 3338
7:15 in your **h** the staff that was changed into 3338
7:17 in my **h** I will strike the water of the Nile, 3338
7:19 'Take your staff and stretch out your **h** over 3338
8:5 'Stretch out your **h** with your staff over 3338
8:6 So Aaron stretched out his **h** over the waters 3338
8:17 and when Aaron stretched out his **h** with 3338
9:3 the **h** *of* the LORD will bring 3338
9:15 For by now I could have stretched out my **h** 3338
9:22 "Stretch out your **h** toward the sky so 3338
10:12 "Stretch out your **h** over Egypt so 3338
10:21 "Stretch out your **h** toward the sky so 3338
10:22 Moses stretched out his **h** toward the sky, 3338
11:5 who is at her **h mill,** 8160
12:11 on your feet and your staff in your **h.** 3338
13:3 out of it with a mighty **h.** 3338
13:9 for you like a sign on your **h** and a reminder 3338
13:9 brought you out of Egypt with his mighty **h.** 3338
13:14 'With a mighty **h** the LORD brought us out 3338
13:16 like a sign on your **h** and a symbol on your 3338
13:16 out of Egypt with his mighty **h."** 3338
14:16 and stretch out your **h** over the sea to divide 3338
14:21 Then Moses stretched out his **h** over the sea, 3338
14:26 "Stretch out your **h** over the sea so that 3338
14:27 Moses stretched out his **h** over the sea, 3338
15:6 "Your right **h,** O LORD, NIH
15:6 Your right **h,** O LORD, NIH
15:9 and my **h** will destroy them.' 3338
15:12 You stretched out your right **h** and NIH
15:20 Aaron's sister, took a tambourine in her **h,** 3338
16:3 "If only we had died by the LORD's **h** 3338
17:5 in your **h** the staff with which you struck 3338
18:9 for Israel in rescuing them from the **h** *of* 3338
18:10 from the **h** *of* the Egyptians and of Pharaoh, 3338
18:10 and who rescued the people from the **h** *of* 3338
19:13 not a **h** is to be laid on him. 3338
21:24 tooth for tooth, **h** for hand, foot for foot, 3338
21:24 tooth for tooth, hand for **h,** foot for foot, 3338
23:31 *I will* **h over to** you the people 928+3338+5989
24:11 not raise his **h** against these leaders of 3338
32:11 of Egypt with great power and a mighty **h?** 3338
33:22 a cleft in the rock and cover you with my **h** 4090
33:23 Then I will remove my **h** and you will see 4090
Lev 1:4 He is to lay his **h** on the head of the burnt 3338
3:2 He is to lay his **h** on the head of his offering 3338
3:8 He is to lay his **h** on the head of his offering 3338
3:13 He is to lay his **h** on its head and slaughter it 3338
4:4 He is to lay his **h** on its head and slaughter it 3338
4:24 He is to lay his **h** on the goat's head 3338
4:29 to lay his **h** on the head of the sin offering 3338
4:33 He is to lay his **h** on its head and slaughter it 3338
8:23 the thumb of his right **h** and on the big toe 3338
14:14 the thumb of his right **h** and on the big toe 3338
14:15 **palm of** his own left **h,** 4090
14:17 the thumb of his right **h** and on the big toe 3338
14:25 the thumb of his right **h** and on the big toe 3338
14:26 **palm of** his own left **h,** 4090
14:28 be cleansed, on the thumb of his right **h** and 3338
21:19 no man with a crippled foot or **h,** 3338
22:25 from the **h** *of* a foreigner and offer them as 3338
Nu 14:30 with uplifted **h** to make your home, 3338
22:23 in the road with a drawn sword in his **h,** 3338
22:29 If I had a sword in my **h,** 3338
25:7 took a spear in his **h** 3338
27:18 and lay your **h** on him. 3338
35:17 if anyone has a stone in his **h** that could kill, 3338
35:18 in his **h** that could kill, and he hits someone 3338
Dt 2:15 The LORD's **h** was against them 3338
2:24 I have given into your **h** Sihon the Amorite, 3338
3:24 your greatness and your strong **h.** 3338
4:34 by a mighty **h** and an outstretched arm, 3338
5:15 with a mighty **h** and an outstretched arm. 3338
6:21 out of Egypt with a mighty **h.** 3338
7:8 a mighty **h** and redeemed you from the land 3338
7:19 the mighty **h** and outstretched arm, 3338
7:24 He will give their kings into your **h,** 3338
Dt 9:26 and brought out of Egypt with a mighty **h.** 3338
11:2 his majesty, his mighty **h,** 3338
12:7 in everything you have put your **h** to, 3338
12:18 in everything you put your **h** to. 3338
13:9 Your **h** must be the first in putting him 3338
15:10 and in everything you put your **h** to. 3338
15:18 as much as that of a **hired h.** 8502
19:12 **h** him **over** *to* the avenger of blood to die. 928+3338+5989
19:21 tooth for tooth, **h** for hand, foot for foot. 3338
19:21 tooth for tooth, hand for **h,** foot for foot. 3338
20:13 LORD your God delivers it into your **h,** 3338
23:15 *do* not **h** him **over** to his master. 6037
23:20 in everything you put your **h** to in 3338
25:12 you shall cut off her **h.** Show her no pity. 4090
26:8 with a mighty **h** and an outstretched arm, 3338
28:8 and on everything you put your **h** to. 3338
28:20 and rebuke in everything you put your **h** to, 3338
28:32 powerless to lift a **h.** 3338
32:27 'Our **h** has triumphed; 3338
32:39 and no one can deliver out of my **h.** 3338
32:40 I lift my **h** to heaven and declare: 3338
32:41 and my **h** grasps it in judgment, 3338
33:3 all the holy ones are in your **h.** 3338
Jos 2:19 his blood will be on our head if a **h** is laid 3338
4:24 that the **h** *of* the LORD is powerful and so 3338
5:13 in front of him with a drawn sword in his **h.** 3338
8:7 The LORD your God will give it into your **h.** 3338
8:18 toward Ai the javelin that is in your **h,** 3338
8:18 for into your **h** I will deliver the city." 3338
8:26 not draw back the **h** that held out his javelin 3338
10:8 I have given them into your **h.** 3338
10:19 for the LORD your God has given them into your **h."** 3338
10:30 that city and its king into Israel's **h.** 3338
11:6 **h** all of them **over** to Israel, slain. 5989
11:8 the LORD gave them into the **h** *of* Israel. 3338
22:31 the Israelites from the LORD's **h."** 3338
24:10 and I delivered you out of his **h.** 3338
Jdg 2:15 the **h** *of* the LORD was against them 3338
3:21 Ehud reached with his left **h,** 3338
4:9 for the LORD *will* **h** Sisera **over** *to* a woman." 928+3338+4835
4:24 And the **h** *of* the Israelites grew stronger 3338
5:26 Her **h** reached for the tent peg, 3338
5:26 her right **h** for the workman's hammer. NIH
6:9 from the power of Egypt and from the **h** 3338
6:13 and put us into the **h** *of* Midian." 4090
6:14 and save Israel out of Midian's **h.** 4090
6:21 With the tip of the staff that was in his **h,** 3338
6:36 by my **h** as you have promised— 3338
6:37 that you will save Israel by my **h,** 3338
8:7 and Zalmunna into my **h,** 3338
8:22 you have saved us out of the **h** *of* Midian." 3338
9:17 risked his life to rescue you from the **h** 3338
9:33 do whatever your **h** finds to do." 3338
15:12 to tie you up and **h** you **over** 928+3338+5989
15:13 only tie you up and **h** you **over** 928+3338+5989
16:26 Samson said to the servant who held his **h,** 3338
16:29 his right **h** on the one and his left hand on NIH
16:29 his right hand on the one and his left **h** on NIH
Ru 1:13 the LORD's **h** has gone out against me!" 3338
1Sa 2:13 with a three-pronged fork in his **h.** 3338
2:16 "No, **h** it **over** now; 5989
4:3 and save us from the **h** *of* our enemies." 4090
4:8 from the **h** *of* these mighty gods? 3338
5:6 The LORD's **h** was heavy upon the people 3338
5:7 because his **h** is heavy upon us and 3338
5:9 the LORD's **h** was against that city, 3338
5:11 God's **h** was very heavy upon it. 3338
6:3 and you will know why his **h** has 3338
6:5 Perhaps he will lift his **h** from you 3338
6:9 not his **h** that struck us and that it happened 3338
7:3 and he will deliver you out of the **h** *of* 3338
7:8 that he may rescue us from the **h** *of* 3338
7:13 **h** *of* the LORD was against the Philistines. 3338
9:16 he will deliver my people from the **h** *of* 3338
10:7 do whatever your **h** finds to do, 3338
12:3 From whose **h** have I accepted a bribe 3338
12:4 not taken anything from anyone's **h."** 3338
12:5 that you have not found anything in my **h."** 3338
12:9 so he sold them into the **h** *of* Sisera, 3338
12:15 his **h** will be against you, 3338
13:22 and Jonathan had a sword or spear in his **h;** 3338
14:12 the LORD has given them into the **h** 3338
14:19 to the priest, "Withdraw your **h."** 3338
14:26 yet no one put his **h** to his mouth, 3338
14:27 the staff that was in his **h** and dipped it into 3338
14:27 He raised his **h** to his mouth, 3338
14:37 Will you give them into Israel's **h?"** 3338
17:37 of the bear will deliver me from the **h** 3338
17:40 Then he took his staff in his **h,** 3338
17:40 with his sling in his **h,** 3338
17:46 This day the LORD *will* **h** you **over** to me, 928+3338+6037
17:50 without a sword in his **h** he struck down 3338
18:10 Saul had a spear in his **h** 3338
18:17 "I will not raise a **h** against him. 3338
18:21 and so that the **h** *of* the Philistines may be 3338
19:9 in his house with his spear in his **h.** 3338
20:8 Why **h** me **over** to your father?" 995
21:3 then, what *do* you **have on h?** 3338+3780+9393
21:4 **have** any ordinary bread **on h;** 448+3338+9393
22:6 And Saul, spear in **h,** 3338
22:17 not willing to raise a **h** to strike the priests 3338
23:4 to give the Philistines into your **h."** 3338
23:17 "My father Saul will not lay a **h** on you. 3338
1Sa 24:6 or lift my **h** against him; 3338
24:10 'I will not lift my **h** against my master, 3338
24:11 look at this piece of your robe in my **h!** 3338
24:12 but my **h** will not touch you. 3338
24:13 so my **h** will not touch you. 3338
24:15 by delivering me from your **h."** 3338
25:35 from her **h** what she had brought him 3338
26:9 Who can lay a **h** on the LORD's anointed 3338
26:11 But the LORD forbid that I should lay a **h** 3338
26:23 not lay a **h** on the LORD's anointed. 3338
27:1 of these days I will be destroyed by the **h** 3338
27:1 and I will slip out of his **h."** 3338
28:19 The LORD *will* **h over** both Israel 928+3338+5989
28:19 The LORD *will* also **h over** the army of Israel 928+3338+5989
30:15 or **h** me **over** *to* my master, 928+3338+6037
2Sa 1:14 "Why were you not afraid to lift your **h** 3338
2:14 the young men get up and **fight h to hand** 8471
2:14 the young men get up and **fight hand to h** 8471
3:18 the **h** *of* the Philistines and from the hand 3338
3:18 the hand of the Philistines and from the **h** 3338
4:11 now demand his blood from your **h** and rid 3338
5:19 *Will you* **h** them **over** *to* me?" 928+3338+5989
5:19 **surely h** the Philistines **over** *to* you." 928+3338+5989+5989
12:7 and I delivered you from the **h** *of* Saul. 3338
13:5 and then eat it from her **h.'** " 3338
13:6 so I may eat from her **h."** 3338
13:10 into my bedroom so I may eat from your **h."** 3338
13:19 She put her **h** on her head and went away, 3338
14:7 **'H over** the one who struck his brother 5989
14:16 the **h** *of* the man who is trying to cut off 4090
14:19 "Isn't the **h** *of* Joab with you in all this?" 3338
15:5 Absalom would reach out his **h,** 3338
18:12 I would not lift my **h** against the king's son. 3338
18:14 So he took three javelins in his **h** 4090
18:19 the LORD has delivered him from the **h** 3338
19:9 "The king delivered us from the **h** 4090
19:9 he is the one who rescued us from the **h** *of* 4090
20:9 by the beard with his right **h** to kiss him. 3338
20:10 on his guard against the dagger in Joab's **h,** 3338
20:21 has lifted up his **h** against the king, 3338
20:21 **H over** this one man, 5989
21:20 with six fingers on each **h** and six toes 3338
22:1 when the LORD delivered him from the **h** 4090
22:1 the hand of all his enemies and from the **h** 4090
23:6 which are not gathered with the **h.** 3338
23:10 the Philistines till his **h** grew tired and froze 3338
23:21 Although the Egyptian had a spear in his **h,** 3338
23:21 He snatched the spear from the Egyptian's **h** 3338
24:16 When the angel stretched out his **h** 3338
24:16 Withdraw your **h."** 3338
24:17 Let your **h** fall upon me and my family." 3338
1Ki 2:19 and she sat down at his right **h.** NIH
8:15 with his own **h** has fulfilled what he promised 3338
8:24 and with your **h** you have fulfilled it— 3338
8:42 of your great name and your mighty **h** 3338
11:12 I will tear it out of the **h** *of* your son. 3338
11:31 of Solomon's **h** and give you ten tribes. 3338
11:34 the whole kingdom out of Solomon's **h;** 3338
13:4 he stretched out his **h** from the altar 3338
13:4 But the **h** he stretched out toward 3338
13:6 and pray for me that my **h** may be restored." 3338
13:6 and the king's **h** was restored and became 3338
18:44 "A cloud as small as a man's **h** is rising 4090
20:13 I will give it into your **h** today, 3338
22:6 "for the Lord will give it into the king's **h."** 3338
22:12 the LORD will give it into the king's **h."** 3338
22:15 the LORD will give it into the king's **h."** 3338
2Ki 3:10 to **h** us **over** *to* Moab?" 928+3338+5989
3:13 to **h** us **over** *to* Moab." 928+3338+5989
3:15 the **h** *of* the LORD came upon Elisha 3338
3:18 *he will* also **h** Moab **over** *to* you. 928+3338+5989
4:29 take my staff in your **h** and run. 3338
5:11 wave his **h** over the spot and cure me 3338
6:7 Then the man reached out his **h** and took it. 3338
10:15 "If so," said Jehu, "give me your **h."** 3338
11:8 each man with his weapon in his **h.** 3338
11:11 The guards, each with his weapon in his **h,** 3338
12:7 but **h** it **over** for repairing the temple." 5989
14:27 he saved them by the **h** *of* Jeroboam son 3338
16:7 of the **h** *of* the king of Aram and of the king 4090
17:39 it is he who will deliver you from the **h** 3338
18:21 a man's **h** and wounds him if he leans on it! 4090
18:29 He cannot deliver you from my **h.** 3338
18:30 be given into the **h** *of* the king of Assyria.' 3338
18:33 from the **h** *of* the king of Assyria? 3338
18:34 Have they rescued Samaria from my **h?** 3338
18:35 the LORD deliver Jerusalem from my **h?"** 3338
19:19 O LORD our God, deliver us from his **h,** 3338
20:6 and this city from the **h** *of* the king 4090
21:14 my inheritance and **h** them **over** 928+3338+5989
1Ch 4:10 Let your **h** be with me, 3338
6:15 into exile by the **h** *of* Nebuchadnezzar. 3338
6:39 who served at his right **h:** NIH
6:44 the Merarites, at his left **h:** NIH
11:23 a spear like a weaver's rod in his **h,** 3338
11:23 He snatched the spear from the Egyptian's **h** 3338
13:9 Uzzah reached out his **h** to steady the ark, 3338
13:10 down because he had put his **h** on the ark. 3338
14:10 *Will you* **h** them **over** *to* me?" 928+3338+5989
14:10 "Go, *I will* **h** them **over** *to* you." 928+3338+5989
14:11 against my enemies by my **h."** 3338
20:6 with six fingers on each **h** and six toes NIH
21:15 Withdraw your **h."** 3338
21:16 with a drawn sword in his **h** extended 3338

1Ch 21:17 let your **h** fall upon me and my family, 3338
28:19 "I have in writing from the **h** *of* the LORD 3338
29:14 and we have given you only what comes from your **h.** 3338
29:16 it comes from your **h,** 3338
2Ch 6:15 and with your **h** you have fulfilled it— 3338
6:32 of your great name and your mighty **h** 3338
16: 7 the king of Aram has escaped from your **h.** 3338
16: 8 he delivered them into your **h.** 3338
18: 5 "for God will give it into the king's **h."** 3338
18:11 the LORD will give it into the king's **h."** 3338
18:14 "for they will be given into your **h."** 3338
20: 6 Power and might are in your **h,** 3338
23: 7 each man with his weapons in his **h.** 3338
23:10 each with his weapon in his **h,** 3338
25:15 not save their own people from your **h?"** 3338
25:20 that he *might* **h** them **over** to 928+3338+5989
26:19 a censer in his **h** ready to burn incense, 3338
28: 9 he gave them into your **h.** 3338
30: 6 who have escaped from the **h** *of* the kings 4090
30:12 in Judah the **h** *of* God was on the people 3338
32:11 from the **h** *of* the king of Assyria,' 4090
32:13 to deliver their land from my **h?** 3338
32:14 then can your god deliver you from my **h?** 3338
32:15 to deliver his people from my **h** or the hand 3338
32:15 to deliver his people from my hand or the **h** 3338
32:15 will your god deliver you from my **h!"** 3338
32:17 not rescue their people from my **h,** 3338
32:17 not rescue his people from my **h."** 3338
32:22 from the **h** *of* Sennacherib king of Assyria 3338
32:22 of Assyria and from the **h** *of* all others. 3338
Ezr 6:12 or people who lifts a **h** to change this decree 10311
7: 6 the **h** *of* the LORD his God was on him. 3338
7: 9 for the gracious **h** *of* his God was on him. 3338
7:14 the Law of your God, which is in your **h.** 10311
7:28 the **h** *of* the LORD my God was on me, 3338
8:18 the gracious **h** *of* our God was on us, 3338
8:22 "The gracious **h** *of* our God is 3338
8:31 The **h** *of* our God was on us, 3338
9: 7 and humiliation at the **h** *of* foreign kings, 3338
Ne 1:10 by your great strength and your mighty **h.** 3338
2: 8 And because the gracious **h** *of* my God was 3338
2:18 about the gracious **h** *of* my God upon me 3338
4:17 with one **h** and held a weapon in the other, 3338
6: 5 and in his **h** was an unsealed letter 3338
9:15 of the land you had sworn with uplifted **h** 3338
9:27 who rescued them from the **h** 3338
9:28 to the **h** *of* their enemies so that they ruled 3338
Est 5: 2 to her the gold scepter that was in his **h.** 3338
9: 1 and the Jews **got the upper h** 8948
Job 1:11 But stretch out your **h** and strike everything 3338
2: 5 But stretch out your **h** and strike his flesh 3338
6: 9 to let loose his **h** and cut me off! 3338
6:23 deliver me from the **h** *of* the enemy, 3338
9:33 to lay his **h** upon us both, 3338
10: 7 that no one can rescue me from your **h?** 3338
11:14 if you put away the sin that is in your **h** 3338
12: 9 Which of all these does not know that the **h** 3338
12:10 In his **h** is the life of every creature and 3338
13:21 Withdraw your **h** far from me, 4090
15:23 he knows the day of darkness is at **h.** 3338
19:21 have pity, for the **h** *of* God has struck me. 3338
21: 5 clap your **h** over your mouth. 3338
23: 2 his **h** is heavy in spite of my groaning. 3338
26:13 his **h** pierced the gliding serpent. 3338
28: 9 Man's **h** assaults the flinty rock 3338
29:20 the bow ever new in my **h.'** 3338
30:21 with the might of your **h** you attack me. 3338
30:24 a **h** on a broken man when he cries for help 3338
31:21 if I have raised my **h** against the fatherless, 3338
31:27 and my **h** offered them a kiss of homage, 3338
33: 7 nor should my **h** be heavy upon you. 437
34:20 the mighty are removed without human **h.** 3338
35: 7 or what does he receive from your **h?** 3338
40: 4 I put my **h** over my mouth. 3338
40:14 to you that your own right **h** can save you. NIH
41: 8 If you lay a **h** on him, 4090
Ps 10:12 Lift up your **h,** O God. 3338
10:14 you consider it to take it in **h.** 3338
16: 8 he is at my right **h,** I will not be shaken. NIH
16:11 with eternal pleasures at your right **h.** NIH
17: 7 by your right **h** those who take refuge NIH
17:14 by your **h** save me from such men, 3338
18: T when the LORD delivered him from the **h** 4090
18: T the hand of all his enemies and from the **h** 3338
18:35 and your right **h** sustains me; NIH
20: 6 with the saving power of his right **h.** NIH
21: 8 Your **h** will lay hold on all your enemies; 3338
21: 8 your right **h** will seize your foes. NIH
32: 4 day and night your **h** was heavy upon me; 3338
36:11 nor the **h** *of* the wicked drive me away. 3338
37:24 for the LORD upholds him with his **h.** 3338
38: 2 and your **h** has come down upon me. 3338
39:10 I am overcome by the blow of your **h.** 3338
44: 2 With your **h** you drove out the nations 3338
44: 3 it was your right **h,** your arm, NIH
45: 4 let your right **h** display awesome deeds. NIH
45: 9 at your right **h** is the royal bride in gold NIH
48:10 your right **h** is filled with righteousness. NIH
60: 5 Save us and help us with your right **h,** NIH
63: 8 your right **h** upholds me. NIH
71: 4 O my God, from the **h** *of* the wicked, 3338
73:23 you hold me by my right **h.** 3338
74:11 Why do you hold back your **h,** 3338
74:11 Why do you hold back your hand, your right **h?** NIH
74:19 *Do* not **h over** the life of your dove 5989
Ps 75: 8 In the **h** *of* the LORD is a cup full 3338
77:10 the years of the right **h** of the Most High." NIH
77:20 like a flock by the **h** *of* Moses and Aaron. 3338
78:54 to the hill country his right **h** had taken. NIH
80:15 the root your right **h** has planted, NIH
80:17 Let your **h** rest on the man 3338
80:17 on the man at your right **h,** NIH
81:14 and turn my **h** against their foes! 3338
82: 4 deliver them from the **h** *of* the wicked. 3338
89:13 your **h** is strong, your right hand exalted. 3338
89:13 your hand is strong, your right **h** exalted. NIH
89:21 My **h** will sustain him; 3338
89:25 I will set his **h** over the sea, 3338
89:25 his right **h** over the rivers. NIH
89:42 You have exalted the right **h** of his foes; NIH
91: 7 ten thousand at your right **h,** NIH
95: 4 In his **h** are the depths of the earth, 3338
97:10 and delivers them from the **h** *of* the wicked. 3338
98: 1 right **h** and his holy arm have worked salvation for him. NIH
104:28 when you open your **h,** 3338
106:10 He saved them from the **h** *of* the foe; 3338
106:10 from the **h** *of* the enemy he redeemed them. 3338
106:26 So he swore to them with uplifted **h** 3338
107: 2 those he redeemed from the **h** *of* the foe, 3338
108: 6 Save us and help us with your right **h,** NIH
109: 6 let an accuser stand at his right **h.** NIH
109:27 Let them know that it is your **h,** that you, 3338
109:31 he stands at the right **h** of the needy one, NIH
110: 1 "Sit at my right **h** until I make your enemies NIH
110: 5 The Lord is at your right **h;** NIH
118:15 LORD's right **h** has done mighty things! NIH
118:16 The LORD's right **h** is lifted high; NIH
118:16 the LORD's right **h** has done mighty things!" NIH
118:27 **With** boughs **in h,** 928
119:173 May your **h** be ready to help me, 3338
121: 5 the LORD is your shade at your right **h;** 3338
123: 2 of slaves look to the **h** *of* their master, 3338
123: 2 eyes of a maid look to the **h** *of* her mistress, 3338
136:12 with a mighty **h** and outstretched arm; 3338
137: 5 may my right **h** forget [its skill]. NIH
138: 7 you stretch out your **h** against the anger 3338
138: 7 with your right **h** you save me. NIH
139: 5 you have laid your **h** upon me. 4090
139:10 even there your **h** will guide me, 3338
139:10 your right **h** will hold me fast. NIH
144: 7 Reach down your **h** from on high; 3338
145:16 You open your **h** and satisfy the desires 3338
Pr 1:24 when I stretched out my **h,** 3338
3:16 Long life is in her right **h;** NIH
3:16 in her left **h** are riches and honor. NIH
6: 5 like a gazelle from the **h** of the hunter, 3338
17:16 Of what use is money in the **h** *of* a fool, 3338
19:24 The sluggard buries his **h** in the dish; 3338
21: 1 The king's heart is in the **h** *of* the LORD; 3338
26: 6 the sending of a message by the **h** *of* a fool. 3338
26: 9 a thornbush in a drunkard's **h** is a proverb in 3338
26:15 The sluggard buries his **h** in the dish; 3338
27:16 the wind or grasping oil with the **h.** 3545
30:28 a lizard can be caught with the **h,** 3338
30:32 clap your **h** over your mouth! 3338
31:19 In her **h** she holds the distaff and grasps 3338
Ecc 2:24 This too, I see, is from the **h** *of* God, 3338
2:26 to **h** it **over** to the one who pleases God. 5989
5:15 from his labor that he can carry in his **h.** 3338
9:10 Whatever your **h** finds to do, 3338
SS 5: 4 My lover thrust his **h** through the 3338
Isa 1:25 I will turn my **h** against you; 3338
5:25 his **h** is raised and he strikes them down. 3338
5:25 his **h** is still upraised. 3338
6: 6 to me with a live coal in his **h,** 3338
8:11 The LORD spoke to me with his strong **h** 3338
9:12 his **h** is still upraised. 3338
9:17 his **h** is still upraised. 3338
9:21 his **h** is still upraised. 3338
10: 4 his **h** is still upraised. 3338
10: 5 in whose **h** is the club of my wrath! 3338
10:10 As my **h** seized the kingdoms of the idols, 3338
10:13 " 'By the strength of my **h** I have done this, 3338
10:14 my **h** reached for the wealth of the nations; 3338
11: 8 young child put his **h** into the viper's nest. 3338
11:11 the Lord will reach out his **h** a second time 3338
11:15 with a scorching wind he will sweep his **h** 3338
13:22 Her time *is* **at h,** 995+4200+7940
14:26 this is the **h** stretched out over all nations. 3338
14:27 His **h** is stretched out, 3338
19: 4 *I will* **h** the Egyptians **over** to the power 6127
19:16 They will shudder with fear at the uplifted **h** 3338
22:21 and **h** your authority **over** 928+3338+5989
23:11 The LORD has stretched out his **h** over 3338
25:10 The **h** *of* the LORD will rest 3338
26:11 O LORD, your **h** is lifted high, 3338
28: 4 as someone sees it and takes it in his **h,** 4090
31: 3 When the LORD stretches out his **h,** 3338
33:15 and keeps his **h** from accepting bribes, 4090
34:17 his **h** distributes them by measure. 3338
36: 6 a man's **h** and wounds him if he leans on it! 4090
36:15 be given into the **h** *of* the king of Assyria.' 3338
36:18 from the **h** *of* the king of Assyria? 3338
36:19 Have they rescued Samaria from my **h?** 3338
36:20 the LORD deliver Jerusalem from my **h?"** 3338
37:20 O LORD our God, deliver us from his **h,** 3338
38: 6 and this city from the **h** *of* the king 4090
40: 2 from the LORD's **h** double for all her sins. 3338
40:12 the waters in the **hollow of** his **h,** 9123
40:12 or with the **breadth of** his **h** marked off 2455
41:10 I will uphold you with my righteous right **h.** NIH
Isa 41:13 of your right **h** and says to you, Do not fear; NIH
41:20 that the **h** *of* the LORD has done this, 3338
42: 6 I will take hold of your **h.** 3338
43:13 No one can deliver out of my **h.** 3338
44: 5 still another will write on his **h,** 3338
44:20 "Is not this thing in my right **h** a lie?" NIH
45: 1 whose right **h** I take hold of NIH
47: 6 I gave them into your **h,** 3338
48:13 My own **h** laid the foundations of the earth, 3338
48:13 and my right **h** spread out the heavens; NIH
49: 2 in the shadow of his **h** he hid me; 3338
49: 4 Yet what is due me is **in** the LORD's **h,** 907
50:11 This is what you shall receive from my **h:** 3338
51:16 and covered you with the shadow of my **h—** 3338
51:17 the **h** *of* the LORD the cup of his wrath, 3338
51:18 to take her by the **h.** 3338
51:22 of your **h** the cup that made you stagger; 3338
53:10 the will of the LORD will prosper in his **h.** 3338
56: 1 for my salvation is close **at h** 995
56: 2 and keeps his **h** from doing any evil." 3338
62: 3 be a crown of splendor in the LORD's **h,** 3338
62: 3 a royal diadem in the **h** *of* your God. 4090
62: 8 The LORD has sworn by his right **h** and NIH
63:12 of power to be at Moses' right **h,** NIH
64: 8 we are all the work of your **h.** 3338
66: 2 Has not my **h** made all these things, 3338
66:14 the **h** *of* the LORD will be made known 3338
Jer 1: 9 Then the LORD reached out his **h** 3338
6: 9 pass your **h** over the branches again, 3338
6:12 when I stretch out my **h** 3338
15:17 I sat alone because your **h** was on me 3338
18: 6 "Like clay in the **h** *of* the potter, 3338
18: 6 so are you in my **h,** O house of Israel. 3338
18:21 **h** them **over** to the power of the sword. 5599
20: 4 *I will* **h** all Judah **over** *to* the king 928+3338+5989
20: 5 *I will* **h over** *to* their enemies all 928+3338+5989
21: 5 an outstretched **h** and a mighty arm in anger 3338
21: 7 *I will* **h over** Zedekiah king of Judah, 928+3338+5989
21:12 rescue from the **h** *of* his oppressor 3338
22: 3 Rescue from the **h** *of* his oppressor 3338
22:24 were a signet ring on my right **h,** 3338
22:25 *I will* **h** you **over** 928+3338+5989
25:15 from my **h** this cup filled with the wine 3338
25:17 the cup from the LORD's **h** and made all 3338
25:28 if they refuse to take the cup from your **h** 3338
27: 6 **h** all your countries **over** 928+3338+5989
27: 8 until I destroy it by his **h.** 3338
29:21 "*I will* **h** them **over** 928+3338+5989
31:11 from the **h** *of* those stronger than they. 3338
31:32 when I took them by the **h** to lead them out 3338
32: 3 *to* **h** this city **over** *to* the king of Babylon, 928+3338+5989
32:21 by a mighty **h** and an outstretched arm and 3338
32:28 *to* **h** this city **over** *to* the Babylonians 928+3338+5989
33:13 under the **h** *of* the one who counts them,' 3338
34: 2 *to* **h** this city **over** *to* the king of Babylon, 928+3338+5989
34:20 *I will* **h over** 928+3338+5989
34:21 **h** Zedekiah king of Judah and his officials **over** 928+3338+5989
36:14 to them with the scroll in his **h.** 3338
38:16 I will neither kill you nor **h** you **over** 928+3338+5989
38:19 for the Babylonians *may* **h** me **over** *to* them 928+3338+5989
38:20 *"They will* not **h** you **over,"** 5989
43: 3 against us to **h** us **over** *to* the Babylonians, 928+3338+5989
44:30 **h** Pharaoh Hophra king of Egypt **over** 928+3338+5989
46:26 *I will* **h** them **over** to those 928+3338+5989
48:16 "The fall of Moab *is* **at h;** 995+7940
48:37 every **h** is slashed 3338
51: 7 Babylon was a gold cup in the LORD's **h;** 3338
51:25 "I will stretch out my **h** against you, 3338
La 2: 3 He has withdrawn his right **h** at NIH
2: 4 his right **h** is ready. NIH
2: 8 and did not withhold his **h** from destroying. 3338
3: 3 he has turned his **h** against me again 3338
4: 6 in a moment without a **h** turned to help her. 3338
Eze 1: 3 There the **h** *of* the LORD was upon him. 3338
2: 9 I looked, and I saw a **h** stretched out to me. 3338
3:14 with the strong **h** *of* the LORD upon me. 3338
3:22 The **h** *of* the LORD was upon me there, 3338
6:14 And I will stretch out my **h** against them 3338
7:17 Every **h** will go limp, 3338
7:21 *I will* **h** it all **over** as plunder 928+3338+5989
8: 1 the **h** *of* the Sovereign LORD came 3338
8: 3 like a **h** and took me by the hair of my head. 3338
8:11 Each had a censer in his **h,** 3338
9: 1 each with a weapon in his **h."** 3338
9: 2 each with a deadly weapon in his **h.** 3338
10: 7 of the cherubim reached out his **h** to the fire 3338
11: 9 and **h** you **over** *to* foreigners 928+3338+5989
13: 9 My **h** will be against 3338
14: 9 and I will stretch out my **h** against him 3338
14:13 by being unfaithful and I stretch out my **h** 3338
16:27 So I stretched out my **h** against you 3338
16:39 *I will* **h** you **over** *to* your lovers, 928+3338+5989
17:18 Because he had given his **h** in pledge and 3338
18: 8 He withholds his **h** from doing wrong 3338
18:17 He withholds his **h** from sin 3338
20: 5 I swore with uplifted **h** to the descendants 3338
20: 5 With uplifted **h** I said to them, 3338
20:15 with uplifted **h** I swore to them in the desert 3338

Eze 20:22 But I withheld my **h**, 3338
20:23 with uplifted **h** I swore to them in the desert 3338
20:33 with a mighty **h** and an outstretched arm 3338
20:34 with a mighty **h** and an outstretched arm 3338
20:42 the land I had sworn with uplifted **h** to give 3338
21: 7 Every heart will melt and every **h** go limp; 3338
21:11 to be grasped with the **h;** 4090
21:11 made ready for the **h** *of* the slayer. 3338
21:22 Into his right **h** will come the lot NIH
21:31 *I will* **h** you **over** *to* brutal men, 928+3338+5989
23:28 *about to* **h** you **over** *to* those you hate, 928+3338+5989
23:31 so I will put her cup into your **h.** 3338
25: 7 therefore I will stretch out my **h** against you 3338
25:13 I will stretch out my **h** against Edom 3338
25:14 I will take vengeance on Edom by the **h** 3338
25:16 to stretch out my **h** against the Philistines, 3338
30:10 of Egypt by the **h** *of* Nebuchadnezzar king 3338
30:12 the **h** *of* foreigners I will lay waste the land 3338
30:22 and make the sword fall from his **h.** 3338
30:24 of Babylon and put my sword in his **h,** 3338
30:25 when I put my sword into the **h** *of* the king 3338
33:22 the **h** *of* the LORD was upon me, 3338
35: 3 and I will stretch out my **h** against you 3338
36: 7 I swear with uplifted **h** that the nations 3338
37: 1 The **h** *of* the LORD was upon me, 3338
37:17 so that they will become one in your **h.** 3338
37:19 which is in Ephraim's **h—** 3338
37:19 and they will become one in my **h.'** 3338
38:12 and turn my **h** against the resettled ruins and 3338
39: 3 strike the bow from your left **h** 3338
39: 3 make your arrows drop from your right **h.** 3338
39:21 the punishment I inflict and the **h** I lay 3338
40: 1 on that very day the **h** *of* the LORD was 3338
40: 3 a linen cord and a measuring rod in his **h.** 3338
40: 5 in the man's **h** was six long cubits, 3338
44:12 therefore I have sworn with uplifted **h** 3338
47: 3 with a measuring line in his **h,** 3338
47:14 with uplifted **h** to give it to your forefathers, 3338
Da 1: 2 Jehoiakim king of Judah into his **h,** 3338
3:15 be able to rescue you from my **h?"** 10311
3:17 and he will rescue us from your **h,** O king. 10311
4:35 No one can hold back his **h** or say to him: 10311
5: 5 the fingers of a human **h** appeared 10311
5: 5 The king watched the **h** as it wrote. 10311+10589
5:23 the God who holds in his **h** your life 10311
5:24 Therefore he sent the **h** that wrote 10311+10589
9:15 with a mighty **h** and who made for yourself 3338
10:10 A **h** touched me and set me trembling 3338
11:41 of Ammon will be delivered from his **h.** 3338
12: 7 lifted his right **h** and his left hand NIH
12: 7 lifted his right hand and his left **h** NIH
Hos 9: 7 the days of reckoning *are* **at h.** 995
11: 8 How *can I* **h** you **over,** Israel? 4481
Joel 2: 1 It is **close at h—** 7940
Am 1: 8 I will turn my **h** against Ekron, 3338
5:19 though he entered his house and rested his **h** 3338
7: 7 with a plumb line in his **h.** 3338
9: 2 from there my **h** will take them. 3338
Ob 1:14 nor **h over** their survivors in the day 6037
Jnh 4:11 people who cannot tell their right **h** from their left, NIH
Mic 4:10 the LORD will redeem you out of the **h** 4090
5: 9 Your **h** will be lifted up in triumph 3338
Hab 2:16 from the LORD's right **h** is coming around NIH
3: 4 rays flashed from his **h,** 3338
Zep 1: 4 "I will stretch out my **h** against Judah and 3338
2:13 He will stretch out his **h** against the north 3338
Zec 2: 1 a man with a measuring line in his **h!** 3338
2: 9 I will surely raise my **h** against them so 3338
4:10 the plumb line in the **h** *of* Zerubbabel. 3338
8: 4 each with cane in **h** because of his age. 3338
11: 6 "I *will* **h** everyone **over** *to* his neighbor 928+3338+5162
13: 7 and I will turn my **h** against the little ones. 3338
14:13 Each man will seize the **h** *of* another, 3338
Mt 3:12 His winnowing fork is in his **h,** *5931*
5:25 or he *may* **h** you **over** to the judge, *4140*
5:25 and the judge may **h** you over to the officer, *NIG*
5:30 And if your right **h** causes you to sin, *5931*
6: 3 do not let your **left h** know what your right hand is doing, *754*
6: 3 do not let your left hand know what your **right h** is doing, *1288*
8: 3 Jesus reached out his **h** and touched *5931*
8:15 He touched her **h** and the fever left her, *5931*
9:18 But come and put your **h** on her, *5931*
9:25 he went in and took the girl *by* the **h,** *5931*
10:17 *they will* **h** you **over** to the local councils *4140*
12:10 and a man with a shriveled **h** was there. *5931*
12:13 he said to the man, "Stretch out your **h."** *5931*
14:31 Immediately Jesus reached out his **h** *5931*
18: 8 If your **h** or your foot causes you to sin, *5931*
22:13 'Tie him **h** and foot, and throw him outside, *5931*
22:44 "Sit at my **right h** until I put your enemies *1288*
24:41 be grinding with a **h mill;** *3685*
26:15 to give me if I **h** him **over** to you?" *4140*
26:16 for an opportunity to **h** him **over.** *4140*
26:23 "The one who has dipped his **h** into *5931*
26:64 sitting at the **right h** of the Mighty One *1288*
27:29 They put a staff in his **right h** and knelt *1288*
Mk 1:31 took her **h** and helped her up. *5931*
1:41 Jesus reached out his **h** and touched *5931*
3: 1 and a man with a shriveled **h** was there. *5931*
3: 3 Jesus said to the man with the shriveled **h,** *5931*
3: 5 said to the man, "Stretch out your **h."** *5931*
3: 5 and his **h** was completely restored. *5931*
Mk 5: 4 he had often *been* **chained h** and foot, *268+1313*
5:41 He took her *by* the **h** and said to her, *5931*
7:32 they begged him to place his **h** on the man. *5931*
8:23 the blind man by the **h** and led him outside *5931*
9:27 But Jesus took him by the **h** and lifted him *5931*
9:43 If your **h** causes you to sin, cut it off. *5931*
10:33 and *will* **h** him **over** to the Gentiles, *4140*
12:36 "Sit at my **right h** until I put your enemies *1288*
14:11 for an opportunity *to* **h** him **over.** *4140*
14:62 sitting at the **right h** of the Mighty One *1288*
16:19 into heaven and he sat at the **right h** of God. *1288*
Lk 1:66 For the Lord's **h** was with him. *5931*
1:71 salvation from our enemies and from the **h** *5931*
1:74 to rescue us from the **h** of our enemies, *5931*
3:17 in his **h** to clear his threshing floor and *5931*
5:13 Jesus reached out his **h** and touched *5931*
6: 6 man was there whose right **h** was shriveled. *5931*
6: 8 and said to the man with the shriveled **h,** *5931*
6:10 "Stretch out your **h."** *5931*
6:10 and his **h** was completely restored. *5931*
8:29 though *he was* **chained h** and foot and *268+1297*
8:54 But he took her *by* the **h** and said, *5931*
9:62 "No one who puts his **h** to the plow *5931*
20:20 so that *they might* **h** him **over** to the power *4140*
20:42 "Sit at my **right h** *1288*
22: 6 for an opportunity *to* **h** Jesus **over** to them *4140*
22:21 the **h** of him who is going to betray me is *5931*
22:53 and you did not lay a **h** on me. *5931*
22:69 be seated at the **right h** of the mighty God." *1288*
Jn 7:30 but no one laid a **h** on him, *5931*
7:44 but no one laid a **h** on him. *5931*
10:12 The **hired h** is not the shepherd who owns *3638*
10:13 because he is a **hired h** and cares nothing *3638*
10:28 no one can snatch them out of my **h.** *5931*
10:29 no one can snatch them out of my Father's **h** *5931*
20:25 and put my **h** into his side, *5931*
20:27 Reach out your **h** and put it into my side. *5931*
Ac 2:25 he is at my **right h,** I will not be shaken. *1288*
2:33 Exalted *to* the **right h** of God, *1288*
2:34 "Sit at my **right h** *1288*
3: 7 Taking him by the right **h,** *5931*
4:30 Stretch out your **h** to heal *5931*
5:31 *to* his own **right h** as Prince and Savior *1288*
7:50 Has not my **h** made all these things?' *5931*
7:55 and Jesus standing at the **right h** of God. *1288*
7:56 and the Son of Man standing at the **right h** *1288*
9: 8 So they led him **by the h** into Damascus. *5932*
9:41 He took her by the **h** and helped her *5931*
11:21 The Lord's **h** was with them, *5931*
12:17 Peter motioned *with* his **h** for them to *5931*
13:11 Now the **h** of the Lord is against you. *5931*
13:11 **someone to lead** him **by the h.** *5933*
13:16 Paul motioned *with* his **h** and said: *5931*
21:11 *will* **h** him **over to** the Gentiles.' *1650+4140+5931*
22:11 My companions **led** me **by the h** *5932*
23:19 took the young man by the **h,** *5931*
25:11 no one has the right *to* **h** me **over** to them. *5919*
25:16 not the Roman custom *to* **h over** any man *5919*
26: 1 with his **h** and began his defense: *5931*
28: 3 fastened itself on his **h.** *5931*
28: 4 the snake hanging from his **h,** they said *5931*
Ro 8:34 at the **right h** of God and is also interceding *1288*
1Co 5: 5 **h** this man **over** to Satan, *4140*
12:15 the foot should say, "Because I am not a **h,** *5931*
12:21 The eye cannot say *to* the **h,** *5931*
16:21 I, Paul, write this greeting *in* my own **h.** *5931*
2Co 6: 7 weapons of righteousness *in* the **right h** and *1288*
Gal 2: 9 and Barnabas the **right h** of fellowship *1288*
6:11 as I write to you *with* my own **h!** *5931*
Eph 1:20 from the dead and seated him at his **right h** *1288*
Col 3: 1 where Christ is seated at the **right h** of God. *1288*
4:18 I, Paul, write this greeting *in* my own **h.** *5931*
2Th 3:17 I, Paul, write this greeting *in* my own **h,** *5931*
Phm 1:19 I, Paul, am writing this *with* my own **h.** *5931*
Heb 1: 3 he sat down at the **right h** of the Majesty *1288*
1:13 "Sit at my **right h** until I make your enemies a footstool *1288*
8: 1 a high priest, who sat down at the **right h** of *1288*
8: 9 when I took them *by* the **h** to lead them out *5931*
10:12 he sat down at the **right h** of God. *1288*
12: 2 sat down at the **right h** of the throne of God. *1288*
1Pe 3:22 into heaven and is at God's **right h—** *1288*
5: 6 therefore, under God's mighty **h,** *5931*
Rev 1:16 In his right **h** he held seven stars, *5931*
1:17 Then he placed his **right h** on me and said: *1288*
1:20 the seven stars that you saw in my **right h** *1288*
2: 1 the seven stars in his **right h** and walks *1288*
5: 1 Then I saw in the **right h** of him who sat on *1288*
5: 7 the scroll from the **right h** of him who sat *1288*
6: 5 a pair of scales in his **h.** *5931*
8: 4 went up before God from the angel's **h.** *5931*
10: 2 which lay open in his **h.** *5931*
10: 5 and on the land raised his right **h** to heaven. *5931*
10: 8 the **h** of the angel who is standing on the sea *5931*
10:10 the little scroll from the angel's **h** and ate it. *5931*
13:16 a mark on his right **h** or on his forehead, *5931*
14: 9 his mark on the forehead or on the **h,** *5931*
14:14 on his head and a sharp sickle in his **h.** *5931*
17: 4 She held a golden cup in her **h,** *5931*
20: 1 the key to the Abyss and holding in his **h** *5931*

HANDBREADTH (8) [HAND]

Ex 25:25 a **h** *wide* and put a gold molding on the rim. 3256
37:12 a **h** wide and put a gold molding on the rim. 3256
1Ki 7:26 It was a **h** in thickness, 3255
2Ch 4: 5 It was a **h** in thickness, 3255
Ps 39: 5 You have made my days a mere **h;** 3257
Eze 40: 5 each of which was a cubit and a **h.** 3256
40:43 And double-pronged hooks, each a **h** long, 3256
43:13 that cubit being a cubit and a **h:** 3256

HAND, HANDED (Anglicized) See also TURN, TURNED

HANDCRAFTED (Anglicized) See CRAFTED

HANDED (77) [HAND]

Ge 27:17 Then *she* **h** to her son Jacob the tasty food 928+3338+5989
Ex 32: 4 He took what they **h** him and made it into 3338
Lev 9:12 His sons **h** him the blood, 5162
9:13 *They* **h** him the burnt offering piece 5162
9:18 His sons **h** him the blood, 5162
Nu 21:34 for *I have* **h** him **over** *to* you, 928+3338+5989
Dt 3: 2 for *I have* **h** him **over** *to* you 928+3338+5989
Jos 10:32 LORD **h** Lachish **over** *to* Israel, 928+3338+5989
21:44 **h** all their enemies **over** 928+3338+5989
Jdg 2:14 the LORD **h** them **over** *to* raiders 928+3338+5989
1Sa 23: 7 said, "God *has* **h** him **over** *to* me, 928+3338+5796
30:23 and **h over** to us the forces that 928+3338+5989
2Sa 3: 8 *I* haven't **h** you **over** *to* David. 928+3338+5162
16: 8 LORD *has* **h** the kingdom **over** 928+3338+5989
21: 9 **h** them **over** *to* the Gibeonites, 928+3338+5989
2Ki 19:10 'Jerusalem *will* not **be h over** *to* the king of Assyria.' 928+3338+5989
1Ch 5:20 God **h** the Hagrites and all their allies **over** 928+3338+5989
22:18 **h** the inhabitants of the land **over** 928+3338+5989
2Ch 28: 5 the LORD his God **h** him **over** *to* the king of Aram. 928+3338+5989
30:16 The priests sprinkled the blood **h** to them by 3338
35:11 priests sprinkled the blood **h** *to* them, 3338+4946
36:17 God **h** all of them **over** 928+3338+5989
Ezr 5:12 *he* **h** them **over** *to* Nebuchadnezzar 10089+10311+10314
Ne 9:24 **h** the Canaanites **over** *to* them, 928+3338+5989
9:27 *you* **h** them **over** *to* their enemies 928+3338+5989
9:30 so *you* **h** them **over** *to* 928+3338+5989
Ps 31: 8 *You have* not **h** me **over** *to* the enemy 928+3338+6037
106:41 *He* **h** them **over** *to* the nations, 928+3338+5989
Isa 37:10 'Jerusalem *will* not **be h over** *to* the king of Assyria.' 928+3338+5989
42:24 Who **h** Jacob **over** to become loot, 5989
Jer 26:24 he *was* not **h over** *to* the people 928+3338+5989
32: 4 but *will* **certainly be h over** *to* the king of Babylon, 928+3338+5989+5989
32:24 the city *will* **be h over** *to* the Babylonians, 928+3338+5989
32:25 the city *will* **be h over** *to* the Babylonians, 928+3338+5989
32:36 *it will* **be h over** *to* the king 928+3338+5989
32:43 for *it has* **been h over** *to* the Babylonians.' 928+3338+5989
34: 3 surely be captured and **h over** 928+3338+5989
37:17 *"you will* **be h over** *to* the king 928+3338+5989
38: 3 'This city *will* **certainly be h over** *to* the army 928+3338+5989+5989
38:18 this city *will* **be h over** *to* the Babylonians 928+3338+5989
39:17 *you will* not **be h over** *to* those you fear. 928+3338+5989
44:30 **h** Zedekiah king of Judah **over** 928+3338+5989
46:24 **h over** *to* the people of the north." 928+3338+5989
La 1:14 *He has* **h** me **over** *to* those 928+3338+5989
2: 7 *He has* **h over** *to* the enemy the 928+3338+6037
Eze 23: 9 *I* **h** her **over** *to* her lovers, 928+3338+5989
31:11 *I* **h** it **over** to the ruler of the nations, 5989
39:23 **h** them **over** *to* their enemies, 928+3338+5989
Da 7:25 The saints *will* **be h over** *to* him for a time, 10089+10311+10314
7:27 under the whole heaven *will* **be h over** to 10314
11: 6 In those days she *will* **be h over,** 5989
Mt 24: 9 *be* **h over** to be persecuted and put to death, *4140*
26: 2 of Man *will be* **h over** to be crucified." *4140*
27: 2 led him away and **h** him **over** to Pilate, *4140*
27:18 of envy that *they had* **h** Jesus **over** to him. *4140*
27:26 and **h** him **over** to be crucified. *4140*
Mk 7:13 by your tradition that *you have* **h down.** *4140*
13: 9 *be* **h over** to the local councils and flogged *4140*
15: 1 led him away and **h** him **over** to Pilate. *4140*
15:10 the chief priests *had* **h** Jesus **over** to him. *4140*
15:15 and **h** him **over** to be crucified. *4140*
Lk 1: 2 as *they were* **h down** to us by those who *4140*
4:17 The scroll of the prophet Isaiah *was* **h** *2113*
18:32 *He will be* **h over** to the Gentiles. *4140*
24:20 The chief priests and our rulers **h** him **over** *4140*
Jn 18:30 *"we* would not *have* **h** him **over** to you." *4140*
18:35 and your chief priests who **h** you **over** *4140*
19:11 the one who **h** me **over** to you is guilty of *4140*
19:16 Finally Pilate **h** him **over** to them to *4140*
Ac 2:23 This man *was* **h over** to you *1692*
3:13 You **h** him **over** to be killed, *4140*
6:14 and change the customs Moses **h down** *4140*
23:33 the letter to the governor and **h** Paul **over** *4225*
27: 1 Paul and some other prisoners *were* **h over** *4140*
28:17 *I was* arrested in Jerusalem and **h over** to *4140*
1Ti 1:20 whom *I have* **h over** to Satan to be taught *4140*
1Pe 1:18 **h down** to you **from** your **forefathers,** *4261*

HANDFUL (8) [HAND]
Lev 2: 2 The priest *shall* **take a h** of the fine flour 4850+7858+7859
5:12 who *shall* **take a h** of it as 4850+7858+7859
6:15 The priest is to take a **h** of fine flour and oil, 7859
9:17 **took a h** of it and burned it on the altar 4090+4848
Nu 5:26 then *to* **take a h** of the grain offering as 7858
1Ki 17:12 a **h** *of* flour in a jar and a little oil in 4090+4850
20:10 in Samaria to give each of my men a **h**." 9123
Ecc 4: 6 Better *one* **h** with tranquillity 4090+4850

HANDFULS (4) [HAND]
Ex 9: 8 "Take **h** *of* soot from a furnace 2908+4850
Lev 16:12 and **two h** *of* finely ground fragrant incense 2908+4850
Ecc 4: 6 with tranquillity than *two* **h** with toil 2908+4850
Eze 13:19 for a *few* **h** *of* barley and scraps of bread. 9123

HANDING (3) [HAND]
1Sa 23:20 for **h** him **over** *to* the king." 928+3338+6037
1Ki 18: 9 *are* **h** your servant **over** *to* Ahab 928+3338+5989
Ac 12: 4 **h** him **over** to be guarded by four squads *4140*

HANDIWORK (1)
Isa 19:25 Assyria my **h**, and Israel my inheritance." 3338+5126

HANDKERCHIEFS (1)
Ac 19:12 so that even **h** and aprons *5051*

HANDLE (10) [HANDLED, HANDLES, HANDLING]
Ex 18:18 you cannot **h** it alone. 6913
Jdg 3:22 Even the **h** sank in after the blade, 5896
2Sa 24: 9 able-bodied men *who could* **h** a sword, 8990
1Ch 5:18 able-bodied men *who could* **h** shield 5951
8:40 of Ulam were brave warriors *who could* **h** 2005
12: 8 ready for battle and *able to* **h** the shield 6885
21: 5 men *who could* **h** a sword, 8990
2Ch 25: 5 *able to* **h** the spear and shield. 296
Eze 27:29 All *who* **h** the oars will abandon their ships; 9530
Col 2:21 "*Do* not **h**! Do not taste! Do not touch!"? *721*

HANDLED (1) [HANDLE]
Jer 8: 8 the lying pen of the scribes *has* **h** it falsely? 6913

HANDLES (3) [HANDLE]
1Ki 7:34 Each stand had four **h**, one on each corner, 4190
SS 5: 5 on the **h** *of* the lock. 4090
2Ti 2:15 be ashamed and *who* **correctly h** the word *3982*

HANDLING (1) [HANDLE]
Lk 16:11 not been trustworthy in **h** worldly wealth, *NIG*

HANDMAID (KJV) See MAIDSERVANT, SERVANT

HANDMILL (1) [MILL]
Nu 11: 8 ground it in a **h** or crushed it in a mortar. 8160

HANDS (527) [HAND]
Ge 5:29 the labor and painful toil of our **h** caused by 3338
9: 2 they are given into your **h**. 3338
16: 6 "Your servant is in your **h**," Abram said. 3338
19:16 the **h** *of* his wife and of his two daughters 3338
20: 5 with a clear conscience and clean **h**." 4090
24:18 the jar to her **h** and gave him a drink. 3338
27:16 She also covered his **h** and the smooth part 3338
27:22 but the **h** are the hands of Esau." 3338
27:22 but the hands are the **h** *of* Esau." 3338
27:23 for his **h** were hairy like those 3338
31:42 and the toil of my **h**, 4090
37:21 he tried to rescue him from their **h**. 3338
37:27 to the Ishmaelites and not lay our **h** on him; 3338
Ex 9:29 I will spread out my **h** in prayer to 4090
9:33 He spread out his **h** toward the LORD; 4090
14:30 That day the LORD saved Israel from the **h** 3338
15:17 the sanctuary, O Lord, your **h** established. 3338
17: 9 of the hill with the staff of God in my **h**." 3338
17:11 As long as Moses held up his **h**, 3338
17:11 but whenever he lowered his **h**, 3338
17:12 When Moses' **h** grew tired, 3338
17:12 Aaron and Hur held his **h** up— 3338
17:12 so that his **h** remained steady till sunset. 3338
17:16 **h** were lifted up to the throne of the LORD. 3338
22: 8 to determine whether he has laid his **h** on 3338
22:11 the LORD that the neighbor did not lay **h** 3338
29:10 and his sons shall lay their **h** on its head. 3338
29:15 and his sons shall lay their **h** on its head. 3338
29:19 and his sons shall lay their **h** on its head. 3338
29:20 on the thumbs of their right **h**, 3338
29:24 the **h** *of* Aaron and his sons and wave them 4090
29:25 Then take them from their **h** and burn them 3338
30:19 to wash their **h** and feet with water from it. 3338
30:21 they shall wash their **h** and feet so 3338
32:15 the two tablets of the Testimony in his **h**. 3338
32:19 and he threw the tablets out of his **h**, 3338
34: 4 and he carried the two stone tablets in his **h**. 3338
34:29 the two tablets of the Testimony in his **h**, 3338
Ex 35:25 with her **h** and brought what she had spun— 3338
40:31 and his sons used it to wash their **h** and feet. 3338
Lev 4:15 to lay their **h** on the bull's head before 3338
7:30 With his own **h** he is to bring 3338
8:14 Aaron and his sons laid their **h** on its head. 3338
8:18 Aaron and his sons laid their **h** on its head. 3338
8:22 Aaron and his sons laid their **h** on its head. 3338
8:24 on the thumbs of their right **h** and on 3338
8:27 He put all these in the **h** *of* Aaron 4090
8:28 from their **h** and burned them on the altar 4090
9:22 Then Aaron lifted his **h** toward the people 3338
15:11 a discharge touches without rinsing his **h** 3338
16:21 to lay both **h** on the head of the live goat 3338
24:14 All those who heard him are to lay their **h** 3338
26:25 and you will be given into enemy **h**. 3338
Nu 5:18 he shall loosen her hair and place in her **h** 4090
5:25 from her **h** the grain offering for jealousy, 3338
6:19 in his **h** a boiled shoulder of the ram, 4090
8:10 and the Israelites are to lay their **h** on them. 3338
8:12 Levites lay their **h** on the heads of the bulls, 3338
21: 2 "If you will deliver these people into our **h**, 3338
24:10 He struck his **h** together and said to him, 4090
27:23 he laid his **h** on him and commissioned him, 3338
Dt 1:27 into the **h** *of* the Amorites to destroy us. 3338
2: 7 blessed you in all the work of your **h**. 3338
2:30 in order to give him into your **h**, 3338
3: 3 also gave into our **h** Og king of Bashan 3338
6: 8 on your **h** and bind them on your foreheads. 3338
8:17 of my **h** have produced this wealth for me." 3338
9:15 two tablets of the covenant were in my **h**. 3338
9:17 the two tablets and threw them out of my **h**, 3338
10: 3 the mountain with the two tablets in my **h**. 3338
11:18 on your **h** and bind them on your foreheads. 3338
13: 9 and then the **h** *of* all the people. 3338
13:17 in your **h**, so that the LORD will turn 3338
14:29 in all the work of your **h**. 3338
16:15 and in all the work of your **h**, 3338
17: 7 The **h** *of* the witnesses must be the first 3338
17: 7 and then the **h** *of* all the people. 3338
21: 6 the town nearest the body shall wash their **h** 3338
21: 7 "Our **h** did not shed this blood, 3338
21:10 into your **h** and you take captives, 3338
23:25 you may pick kernels with your **h**, 3338
24:19 bless you in all the work of your **h**. 3338
26: 4 The priest shall take the basket from your **h** 3338
27:15 the work of the craftsman's **h**— 3338
28:12 and to bless all the work of your **h**. 3338
30: 9 of your **h** and in the fruit of your womb, 3338
31:29 to anger by what your **h** have made." 3338
33: 7 With his own **h** he defends his cause. 3338
33:11 and be pleased with the work of his **h**. 3338
34: 9 because Moses had laid his **h** of him. 3338
Jos 2:24 surely given the whole land into our **h**; 3338
6: 2 "See, I have delivered Jericho into your **h**, 3338
7: 7 across the Jordan to deliver us into the **h** *of* 3338
8: 1 I have delivered into your **h** the king of Ai, 3338
9:25 We are now in your **h**. 3338
24: 8 but I gave them into your **h**. 3338
24:11 but I gave them into your **h**. 3338
Jdg 1: 2 I have given the land into their **h**." 3338
1: 4 and Perizzites into their **h** and they struck 3338
2:16 who saved them out of the **h** 3338
2:18 with the judge and saved them out of the **h** 3338
2:23 at once by giving them into the **h** *of* Joshua. 3338
3: 8 against Israel so that he sold them into the **h** 3338
3:10 king of Aram into the **h** *of* Othniel, 3338
3:28 given Moab, your enemy, into your **h**." 3338
4: 2 the LORD sold them into the **h** *of* Jabin, 3338
4: 7 and give him into your **h**.' " 3338
4:14 the LORD has given Sisera into your **h**. 3338
6: 1 and for seven years he gave them into the **h** 3338
7: 2 for me to deliver Midian into their **h**. 3338
7: 6 Three hundred men lapped with their **h** 3338
7: 7 and give the Midianites into your **h**. 3338
7: 9 because I am going to give it into your **h**. 3338
7:14 and the whole camp into his **h**." 3338
7:15 the Midianite camp into your **h**." 3338
7:16 he placed trumpets and empty jars in the **h** 3338
7:19 and broke the jars that were in their **h**. 3338
7:20 the torches in their left **h** and holding 3338
7:20 in their right **h** the trumpets they were 3338
8: 3 the Midianite leaders, into your **h**. 3338
8: 6 "Do you already have the **h** *of* Zebah 4090
8:15 'Do you already have the **h** *of* Zebah 4090
8:34 the **h** *of* all their enemies on every side. 3338
10: 7 the **h** *of* the Philistines and the Ammonites, 3338
10:12 did I not save you from their **h**? 3338
11:21 gave Sihon and all his men into Israel's **h**, 3338
11:30 "If you give the Ammonites into my **h**, 3338
11:32 and the LORD gave them into his **h**. 3338
12: 2 you didn't save me out of their **h**. 3338
12: 3 I took my life in my **h** and crossed over 4090
13: 1 so the LORD delivered them into the **h** *of* 3338
13: 5 of Israel from the **h** *of* the Philistines." 3338
13:23 and grain offering from our **h**, 3338
14: 6 so that he tore the lion apart with his bare **h** 3338
14: 9 which he scooped out with his **h** and ate 4090
15:14 and the bindings dropped from his **h**. 3338
15:18 Must I now die of thirst and fall into the **h** 3338
16:18 with the silver in their **h**. 3338
16:23 delivered Samson, our enemy, into our **h**." 3338
16:24 into our **h**, the one who laid waste our land 3338
18:10 that God has put into your **h**, 3338
19:27 with her **h** on the threshold. 3338
20:28 for tomorrow I will give them into your **h**." 3338
1Sa 5: 4 His head and **h** had been broken off 3338+4090
12: 9 and into the **h** *of* the Philistines 3338
1Sa 12:10 now deliver us from the **h** *of* our enemies, 3338
12:11 from the **h** *of* your enemies on every side, 3338
14:10 that the LORD has given them into our **h**." 3338
14:13 Jonathan climbed up, using his **h** and feet, 3338
14:48 the **h** *of* those who had plundered them. 3338
17:47 and he will give all of you into our **h**." 3338
18:25 Saul's plan was to have David fall by the **h** 3338
19: 5 He took his life in his **h** when he killed 4090
21:13 he was in their **h** he acted like a madman, 3338
23:14 but God did not give David into his **h**. 3338
24: 4 'I will give your enemy into your **h** for you 3338
24:10 how the LORD delivered you into my **h** in 3338
24:18 the LORD delivered me into your **h**, 3338
24:20 of Israel will be established in your **h**. 3338
25:26 from avenging yourself with your own **h**, 3338
25:33 and from avenging myself with my own **h**. 3338
26: 8 God has delivered your enemy into your **h**. 3338
26:23 The LORD delivered you into my **h** today, 3338
28:17 the kingdom out of your **h** and given it 3338
28:21 in my **h** and did what you told me to do. 4090
2Sa 3:34 Your **h** were not bound, 3338
4:12 They cut off their **h** and feet and hung 3338
16:21 and the **h** *of* everyone with you will 3338
18:12 into my **h**, I would not lift my hand against 4090
18:28 the men who lifted their **h** against my lord 3338
21:22 and they fell at the **h** *of* David and his men. 3338
22:21 the cleanness of my **h** he has rewarded me. 3338
22:35 He trains my **h** for battle; 3338
24:14 Let us fall into the **h** *of* the LORD, 3338
24:14 but do not let me fall into the **h** *of* men." 3338
1Ki 2:46 now firmly established in Solomon's **h**. 3338
8:22 spread out his **h** toward heaven 4090
8:38 spreading out his **h** toward this temple— 4090
8:54 with his **h** spread out toward heaven. 4090
11:35 from his son's **h** and give you ten tribes. 3338
20:28 I will deliver this vast army into your **h**, 3338
2Ki 3:11 He used to pour water on the **h** *of* Elijah." 3338
4:34 mouth to mouth, eyes to eyes, **h** to hands. 4090
4:34 mouth to mouth, eyes to eyes, hands to **h**. 4090
9:35 her skull, her feet and her **h**. 3338+4090
10:24 of the men I am placing in your **h** escape, 3338
11:12 and the people clapped their **h** and shouted, 4090
13:16 "Take the bow in your **h**," 3338
13:16 Elisha put his **h** on the king's hands. 3338
13:16 Elisha put his hands on the king's **h**. 3338
17:20 he afflicted them and gave them into the **h** 3338
19:18 wood and stone, fashioned by men's **h**. 3338
22:17 to anger by all the idols their **h** have made, 3338
1Ch 5:10 who were defeated at their **h**; 3338
12:17 to my enemies when my **h** are free 4090
20: 8 and they fell at the **h** *of* David and his men. 3338
21:13 Let me fall into the **h** *of* the LORD, 3338
21:13 but do not let me fall into the **h** *of* men." 3338
29:12 In your **h** are strength and power to exalt 3338
2Ch 6: 4 with his **h** has fulfilled what he promised 3338
6:12 of Israel and spread out his **h**. 4090
6:13 and spread out his **h** toward heaven. 4090
6:29 and pains, and spreading out his **h** 4090
13: 8 which is in the **h** *of* David's descendants. 3338
13:16 and God delivered them into their **h**. 3338
23:18 of the temple of the LORD in the **h** *of* 3338
24:24 the LORD delivered into their **h** 3338
28: 5 also given into the **h** *of* the king of Israel, 3338
29:23 and they laid their **h** on them. 3338
32:19 the work of men's **h**. 3338
34:25 to anger by all that their **h** have made, 3338
Ezr 8:33 and gold and the sacred articles into the **h** 3338
9: 5 and fell on my knees with my **h** spread out 4090
10: 4 Rise up; this matter is **in** your **h**. 6584
10:19 (They all gave their **h** in pledge 3338
Ne 6: 9 "Their **h** will get too weak for the work, 3338
6: 9 [But I prayed,] "Now strengthen my **h**." 3338
8: 6 all the people lifted their **h** and responded, 3338
13:21 If you do this again, I will lay **h** on you." 3338
Est 9:10 But they did not lay their **h** on the plunder. 3338
9:15 but they did not lay their **h** on the plunder. 3338
9:16 but did not lay their **h** on the plunder. 3338
Job 1:10 You have blessed the work of his **h**, 3338
1:12 then, everything he has is in your **h**, 3338
2: 6 "Very well, then, he is in your **h**; 3338
4: 3 how you have strengthened feeble **h**. 3338
5:12 so that their **h** achieve no success. 3338
5:18 he injures, but his **h** also heal. 3338
8:20 a blameless man or strengthen the **h** 3338
9:24 When a land falls into the **h** *of* the wicked, 3338
9:30 with soap and my **h** with washing soda, 4090
10: 3 to spurn the work of your **h**, 4090
10: 8 "Your **h** shaped me and made me. 3338
11:13 to him and stretch out your **h** to him, 4090
12: 6 those who carry their god in their **h**. 3338
13:14 in jeopardy and take my life in my **h**? 4090
14:15 for the creature your **h** have made. 3338
16:17 yet my **h** have been free of violence 4090
17: 9 and those with clean **h** will grow stronger. 3338
20:10 his own **h** must give back his wealth. 3338
21:16 But their prosperity is not in their own **h**, 3338
22:30 through the cleanness of your **h**." 4090
27:23 It claps its **h** in derision and hisses him out 4090
29: 9 and covered their mouths with their **h**; 4090
30: 2 Of what use was the strength of their **h** 3338
31: 7 or if my **h** have been defiled, 4090
31:25 the fortune my **h** had gained, 3338
34:19 for they are all the work of his **h**? 3338
34:37 **scornfully** *he* **claps** *his* **h** among us 6215
36:32 He fills his **h** with lightning 4090
Ps 7: 3 if I have done this and there is guilt on my **h** 4090
8: 6 made him ruler over the works of your **h**; 3338

Ps 9:16 wicked are ensnared by the work of their **h.** 4090
18:20 the cleanness of my **h** he has rewarded me. 3338
18:24 to the cleanness of my **h** in his sight. 3338
18:34 He trains my **h** for battle; 3338
19: 1 the skies proclaim the work of his **h.** 3338
22:16 they have pierced my **h** and my feet. 3338
24: 4 He who has clean **h** and a pure heart, 4090
26: 6 I wash my **h** in innocence, 4090
26:10 in whose **h** are wicked schemes, 3338
26:10 whose right **h** are full of bribes. NIH
28: 2 I lift up my **h** toward your Most Holy Place. 3338
28: 4 for what their **h** have done and bring back 3338
28: 5 of the LORD and what his **h** have done, 3338
31: 5 Into your **h** I commit my spirit; 3338
31:15 My times are in your **h;** 3338
44:20 the name of our God or spread out our **h** to 4090
47: 1 Clap your **h,** all you nations; 4090
58: 2 and your **h** mete out violence on the earth. 3338
63: 4 and in your name I will lift up my **h.** 4090
73:13 in vain have I washed my **h** in innocence. 4090
76: 5 not one of the warriors can lift his **h.** 3338
77: 2 at night I stretched out untiring **h** 3338
78:61 his splendor into the **h** *of* the enemy. 3338
78:72 with skillful **h** he led them. 4090
81: 6 their **h** were set free from the basket. 4090
88: 9 I spread out my **h** to you. 4090
90:17 establish the work of our **h** for us— 3338
90:17 yes, establish the work of our **h.** 3338
91:12 they will lift you up in their **h,** 4090
92: 4 I sing for joy at the works of your **h.** 3338
95: 5 and his **h** formed the dry land. 3338
98: 8 Let the rivers clap their **h,** 4090
102:25 and the heavens are the work of your **h.** 3338
111: 7 The works of his **h** are faithful and just; 3338
115: 4 made by the **h** *of* men. 3338
115: 7 they have **h,** but cannot feel, feet, 3338
119:48 I lift up my **h** to your commands, 4090
119:73 Your **h** made me and formed me; 3338
119:109 Though I constantly take my life in my **h,** 4090
125: 3 the righteous might use their **h** to do evil. 3338
127: 4 in the **h** *of* a warrior are sons born 3338
129: 7 with it the reaper cannot fill his **h,** 4090
134: 2 Lift up your **h** in the sanctuary and praise 3338
135:15 made by the **h** *of* men. 3338
138: 8 do not abandon the works of your **h.** 3338
140: 4 O LORD, from the **h** *of* the wicked; 3338
141: 2 up of my **h** be like the evening sacrifice. 4090
143: 5 and consider what your **h** have done. 3338
143: 6 I spread out my **h** to you; 3338
144: 1 who trains my **h** for war, 3338
144: 7 the mighty waters, from the **h** *of* foreigners 3338
144: 8 whose right **h** are deceitful. NIH
144:11 the **h** *of* foreigners whose mouths are full 3338
144:11 whose right **h** are deceitful. NIH
149: 6 and a double-edged sword in their **h,** 3338
Pr 6: 1 if you have struck **h** in pledge for another, 4090
6: 3 you have fallen into your neighbor's **h:** 4090
6:10 a little folding of the **h** to rest— 3338
6:17 a lying tongue, **h** that shed innocent blood, 3338
10: 4 Lazy **h** make a man poor, 4090
10: 4 but diligent **h** bring wealth. 3338
11:15 to **strike h in pledge** is safe. 9364
12:14 as surely as the work of his **h** rewards him. 3338
12:24 Diligent **h** will rule, 3338
14: 1 but with her own **h** the foolish one tears 3338
17:18 in judgment strikes **h** in pledge and puts 4090
21:25 because his **h** refuse to work. 3338
22:26 not be a man who strikes **h** in pledge or puts 4090
24:33 a little folding of the **h** to rest— 3338
30: 4 up the wind in the **hollow of his h?** 2908
31:13 and flax and works with eager **h.** 4090
31:20 to the poor and extends her **h** to the needy. 3338
Ecc 2:11 Yet when I surveyed all that my **h** had done 3338
4: 5 The fool folds his **h** and ruins himself. 3338
5: 6 and destroy the work of your **h?** 3338
7:26 a trap and whose **h** are chains. 3338
9: 1 the wise and what they do are in God's **h,** 3338
10:18 if his **h** are idle, the house leaks. 3338
11: 6 and at evening let not your **h** be idle, 3338
SS 5: 5 and my **h** dripped with myrrh, 3338
7: 1 the work of a craftsman's **h.** 3338
Isa 1:15 When you spread out your **h** in prayer, 4090
1:15 Your **h** are full of blood; 3338
2: 6 the Philistines and **clasp h** with pagans. 8562
2: 8 they bow down to the work of their **h,** 3338
3:11 be paid back for what their **h** have done. 3338
5:12 no respect for the work of his **h.** 3338
11:14 They will lay **h** on Edom and Moab, 3338
13: 7 Because of this, all **h** will go limp, 3338
17: 8 the altars, the work of their **h,** 3338
25:11 They will spread out their **h** in it, 3338
25:11 as a swimmer spreads out his **h** to swim. NIH
25:11 despite the cleverness of their **h.** 3338
29:23 their children, the work of my **h,** 3338
31: 7 of silver and gold your sinful **h** have made. 3338
35: 3 Strengthen the feeble **h,** 3338
37:19 wood and stone, fashioned by human **h.** 3338
41: 2 *He* **h** nations **over** *to* him and subdues kings 5989
45: 9 Does your work say, 'He has no **h'?** 3338
45:11 or give me orders about the work of my **h?** 3338
45:12 My own **h** stretched out the heavens; 3338
49:16 I have engraved you on the **palms of** my **h;** 4090
51:23 I will put it into the **h** *of* your tormentors, 3338
55:12 and all the trees of the field will clap their **h.** 4090
59: 3 For your **h** are stained with blood, 4090
59: 6 and acts of violence are in their **h.** 4090
60:21 shoot I have planted, the work of my **h,** 3338
Isa 65: 2 All day long I have held out my **h** to 3338
65:22 will long enjoy the works of their **h.** 3338
Jer 1:16 and in worshiping what their **h** have made. 3338
2:37 You will also leave that place with your **h** 3338
4:31 stretching out her **h** and saying, "Alas! 4090
6:24 and our **h** hang limp. 3338
11:21 of the LORD or you will die by our **h'—** 3338
12: 7 the one I love into the **h** *of* her enemies. 4090
15: 6 So I will lay **h** on you and destroy you; 3338
15:21 the **h** *of* the wicked and redeem you from 3338
18: 4 from the clay was marred in his **h;** 3338
19: 7 at the **h** *of* those who seek their lives, 3338
20:13 He rescues the life of the needy from the **h** 3338
21: 4 the weapons of war that are in your **h,** 3338
21:10 be given into the **h** *of* the king of Babylon, 3338
23:14 They strengthen the **h** *of* evildoers, 3338
25: 6 to anger with what your **h** have made. 3338
25: 7 with what your **h** have made, 3338
25:14 to their deeds and the work of their **h."** 3338
26:14 As for me, I am in your **h;** 3338
30: 6 with his **h** on his stomach like a woman 3338
32: 4 the **h** *of* the Babylonians but will certainly 3338
32:30 with what their **h** have made, 3338
38: 5 "He is in your **h,"** King Zedekiah answered. 3338
38:18 you yourself will not escape from their **h.' "** 3338
38:23 from their **h** but will be captured by the king 3338
42:11 and deliver you from his **h.** 3338
44: 8 to anger with what your **h** have made, 3338
47: 3 their **h** will hang limp. 3338
50:43 and his **h** hang limp. 3338
La 1: 7 When her people fell into enemy **h,** 3338
1:10 The enemy laid **h** on all her treasures; 3338
1:14 by his **h** they were woven together. 3338
1:17 Zion stretches out her **h,** 3338
2:15 All who pass your way clap their **h** at you; 4090
2:19 Lift up your **h** to him for the lives 4090
3:41 up our hearts and our **h** to God in heaven, 4090
3:64 O LORD, for what their **h** have done. 3338
4: 2 the work of a potter's **h!** 3338
4:10 With their own **h** compassionate women have cooked their own children, 3338
5: 8 and there is none to free us from their **h.** 3338
5:12 Princes have been hung up by their **h;** 3338
Eze 1: 8 on their four sides they had the **h** *of* a man. 3338
6:11 Strike your **h** together and stamp your feet 4090
7:27 the **h** *of* the people of the land will tremble. 3338
10: 2 Fill your **h** with burning coals from among 2908
10: 7 He took up some of it and put it into the **h** 2908
10: 8 be seen what looked like the **h** *of* a man.) 3338
10:12 their backs, their **h** and their wings, 3338
10:21 what looked like the **h** *of* a man. 3338
12: 7 through the wall with my **h.** 3338
13:21 and save my people from your **h,** 3338
13:23 I will save my people from your **h.** 3338
21:14 and strike your **h together.** 448+4090+4090
21:17 I too will strike my **h together,** 448+4090+4090
22:13 " 'I will surely strike my **h** together at 4090
22:14 or your **h** be strong in the day I deal 3338
23:37 and blood is on their **h.** 3338
23:45 they are adulterous and blood is on their **h.** 3338
25: 6 Because you have clapped your **h** 3338
28: 9 not a god, in the **h** *of* those who slay you. 3338
28:10 of the uncircumcised at the **h** *of* foreigners. 3338
29: 7 When they grasped you with their **h,** 4090
34:27 of their yoke and rescue them from the **h** 3338
48:14 of the land and *must* not **pass into other h,** 6296
Da 2:34 a rock was cut out, but not by human **h.** 10311
2:38 in your **h** he has placed mankind and 10311
2:45 but not by human **h—** 10311
10:10 set me trembling on my **h** and knees. 3338+4090
Hos 2:10 no one will take her out of my **h.** 3338
7: 5 and he joins **h** with the mockers. 3338
14: 3 to what our own **h** have made, 3338
Mic 5:13 down to the work of your **h.** 3338
7: 3 *Both* **h** are skilled in doing evil; 4090
7:16 They will lay their **h** on their mouths 3338
Na 3:19 the news about you claps his **h** at your fall, 4090
Zep 3:16 do not let your **h** hang limp. 3338
Hag 1:11 and on the labor of your **h."** 4090
2:17 I struck all the work of your **h** with blight, 3338
Zec 4: 9 "The **h** *of* Zerubbabel have laid the 3338
4: 9 his **h** will also complete it. 3338
8: 9 let your **h** be strong so that the temple may 3338
8:13 Do not be afraid, but let your **h** be strong." 3338
11: 6 and I will not rescue them from their **h."** 3338
Mal 1: 9 With such offerings from your **h,** 3338
1:10 "and I will accept no offering from your **h.** 3338
1:13 should I accept them from your **h?"** 3338
2:13 or accepts them with pleasure from your **h.** 3338
Mt 4: 6 and they will lift you up in their **h,** *5931*
15: 2 They don't wash their **h** before they eat!" *5931*
15:20 but eating *with* unwashed **h** does *5931*
16:21 and suffer many things **at the h of** *608*
17:12 the Son of Man is going to suffer **at their h."** *899+5679*
17:22 "The Son of Man is going to be betrayed into the **h** *5931*
18: 8 or crippled than to have two **h** or two feet *5931*
19:13 to place his **h** on them and pray for them. *5931*
19:15 When he had placed his **h** on them, *5931*
26:45 and the Son of Man is betrayed into the **h** *5931*
27:24 he took water and washed his **h** in front of *5931*
Mk 5:23 Please come and put your **h** on her so *5931*
6: 5 except lay his **h** on a few sick people *5931*
7: 2 saw some of his disciples eating food *with* **h** *5931*
7: 3 the Jews do not eat unless they give their **h** *5931*
7: 5 of eating their food *with* 'unclean' **h?"** *5931*
Mk 8:23 on the man's eyes and put his **h** on him, *5931*
8:25 Jesus put his **h** on the man's eyes. *5931*
9:31 is going to be betrayed into the **h** of men. *5931*
9:43 for you to enter life maimed than with two **h** *5931*
10:16 put his **h** on them and blessed them. *5931*
14:41 the Son of Man is betrayed into the **h** of sinners. *5931*
16:18 they will pick up snakes with their **h;** *5931*
16:18 they will place their **h** on sick people, *5931*
Lk 4:11 they will lift you up in their **h,** *5931*
4:40 and laying his **h** on each one, *5931*
6: 1 rub them *in* their **h** and eat the kernels. *5931*
9:44 of Man is going to be betrayed into the **h** *5931*
10:30 when *he* **fell into the h of** robbers. *4346*
10:36 to the man who fell into the **h** of robbers?" *NIG*
13:13 Then he put his **h** on her, *5931*
21:12 they will lay **h** on you and persecute you. *5931*
23:46 "Father, into your **h** I commit my spirit." *5931*
24: 7 be delivered into the **h** of sinful men, *5931*
24:39 Look at my **h** and my feet. *5931*
24:40 he showed them his **h** and feet. *5931*
24:50 he lifted up his **h** and blessed them. *5931*
Jn 3:35 the Son and has placed everything in his **h.** *5931*
11:44 his **h** and feet wrapped with strips of linen, *5931*
13: 9 "not just my feet but my **h** and my head *5931*
20:20 he showed them his **h** and side. *5931*
20:25 the nail marks in his **h** and put my finger *5931*
20:27 "Put your finger here; see my **h.** *5931*
21:18 you are old you will stretch out your **h,** *5931*
Ac 6: 6 who prayed and laid their **h** on them. *5931*
7:41 in honor of what their **h** had made. *5931*
8:17 Then Peter and John placed their **h** on them, *5931*
8:18 at the laying on *of* the apostles' **h,** *5931*
8:19 on whom I lay my **h** may receive *5931*
9:12 a man named Ananias come and place his **h** *5931*
9:17 Placing his **h** on Saul, he said, *5931*
13: 3 they placed their **h** on them *5931*
17:24 and does not live in temples **built by h.** *5935*
17:25 And he is not served by human **h,** *5931*
19: 6 When Paul placed his **h** on them, *5931*
20:34 You yourselves know that these **h** *5931*
21:11 tied his own **h** and feet with it and said, *5931*
27:19 ship's tackle overboard **with** *their* **own h.** *901*
28: 8 placed his **h** on him and healed him. *5931*
Ro 10:21 "All day long I have held out my **h** to *5931*
1Co 4:12 We work hard *with* our own **h.** *5931*
15:24 when *he* **h over** the kingdom to God *4140*
2Co 5: 1 house in heaven, **not built by human h.** *942*
11:33 in the wall and slipped through his **h.** *5931*
Eph 2:11 **done** in the body **by the h** of men)— *5935*
4:28 doing something useful *with* his own **h,** *5931*
Col 2:11 **not** with a circumcision **done by the h of men** *942*
1Th 4:11 and to work *with* your **h,** *5931*
1Ti 2: 8 I want men everywhere to lift up holy **h** *5931*
4:14 when the body of elders laid their **h** on you. *5931*
5:22 Do not be hasty in the laying on *of* **h,** *5931*
2Ti 1: 6 in you through the laying on *of* my **h.** *5931*
Heb 1:10 and the heavens are the work *of* your **h.** *5931*
6: 2 about baptisms, the laying on *of* **h,** *5931*
10:31 It is a dreadful thing to fall into the **h** of *5931*
Jas 4: 8 Wash your **h,** you sinners, *5931*
1Jn 1: 1 at and our **h** have touched— *5931*
Rev 7: 9 and were holding palm branches in their **h.** *5931*
9:20 not repent of the work *of* their **h;** *5931*
20: 4 on their foreheads or their **h.** *5931*

HANDSOME (11) [HANDSOMELY]

Ge 39: 6 Now Joseph was well-built and **h,** 3637+5260
1Sa 16:12 with a fine appearance and **h** features. 3202
17:42 ruddy and **h,** and he despised him. 3637+5260
2Sa 14:25 so highly praised for his **h appearance** 3637
1Ki 1: 6 He was also very **h** and was born next 3202+9307
SS 1:16 How **h** you are, my lover! 3637
Eze 23: 6 all of them **h** young men, 2774
23:12 mounted horsemen, all **h** young men 2774
23:23 the Assyrians with them, **h** young men, all 2774
Da 1: 4 **h,** showing aptitude for every kind 3202+5260
Zec 11:13 the **h** price at which they priced me! 159

HANDSOMELY (2) [HANDSOME]

Nu 22:17 because *I will* **reward** you **h** 3877+3877+4394
24:11 I said *I would* **reward** you **h,** 3877+3877

HANDSTAVES (KJV) See WAR CLUB

HANDWRITTEN (KJV) See WRITTEN

HANDYWORK (KJV) See WORK OF HIS HANDS

HANES (1)

Isa 30: 4 in Zoan and their envoys have arrived in **H,** 2865

HANG (16) [HANGED, HANGING, HANGINGS, HANGS, HUNG, OVERHANG, OVERHANGING, OVERHANGS]

Ge 40:19 will lift off your head and **h** you on a tree. 9434
Ex 26:12 that is left over *is to* **h down** at the rear of 6243
26:13 what is left *will* **h** over the sides of 6243

Ex 26:32 H it with gold hooks on four posts 5989
26:33 H the curtain from the clasps and place 5989
Est 7: 9 The king said, "H him on it!" 9434
Job 37:16 Do you know how the clouds h poised, 5146
Pr 26: 7 a lame man's legs that h limp is a proverb 1927
SS 4: 4 on it h a thousand shields, 9434
Isa 22:24 All the glory of his family will h on him: 9434
Jer 6:24 and our hands h limp. 8332
47: 3 their hands will h limp. 8342
50:43 and his hands h limp. 8332
Eze 15: 3 Do they make pegs from it to h things on? 9434
Zep 3:16 do not let your hands h limp. 8332
Mt 22:40 All the Law and the Prophets h 3203

HANGED (11) [HANG]

Ge 40:22 but he h the chief baker, 9434
41:13 and the other man was h." 9434
2Sa 17:23 in order and then h himself. 2871
Est 2:23 the two officials were h on a gallows. 9434
5:14 the king in the morning to have Mordecai h 9434
7:10 So they h Haman on the gallows he had 9434
8: 7 and they have h him on the gallows. 9434
9:13 let Haman's ten sons be h on gallows." 9434
9:14 and they h the ten sons of Haman. 9434
9:25 he and his sons should be h on the gallows. 9434
Mt 27: 5 Then he went away and h himself. 551

HANGING (10) [HANG]

Jos 10:26 they were left h on the trees until evening. 9434
1Sa 25:17 because disaster is h over our master 3983
2Sa 18: 9 He was left h in midair, 5989
18:10 "I just saw Absalom h in an oak tree." 9434
Est 6: 4 to speak to the king about h Mordecai on 9434
Isa 22:25 and the load h on it will be cut down." 6584
Ac 5:30 whom you had killed by h him on a tree. 3203
10:39 They killed him by h him on a tree, 3203
28: 4 the islanders saw the snake h from his hand, 3203
2Pe 2: 3 Their condemnation has long been h NIG

HANGINGS (1) [HANG]

Est 1: 6 h of white and blue linen, 4158

HANGS (1) [HANG]

Isa 33:23 Your rigging h loose: 5759

HANIEL (KJV) See HANNIEL

HANNAH (14)

1Sa 1: 2 one was called H and the other Peninnah. 2839
1: 2 Peninnah had children, but H had none. 2839
1: 5 But to H he gave a double portion 2839
1: 7 Whenever H went up to the house of 2023S
1: 8 Elkanah her husband would say to her, "H, 2839
1: 9 eating and drinking in Shiloh, H stood up. 2839
1:10 bitterness of soul H wept much and prayed 2085S
1:13 H was praying in her heart, 2839
1:15 "Not so, my lord," H replied, 2839
1:19 Elkanah lay with H his wife, 2839
1:20 H conceived and gave birth to a son. 2839
1:22 H did not go. 2839
2: 1 Then H prayed and said: 2839
2:21 And the LORD was gracious to H; 2839

HANNATHON (1)

Jos 19:14 the boundary went around on the north to H 2872

HANNIEL (2)

Nu 34:23 H son of Ephod, the leader from the tribe 2848
1Ch 7:39 The sons of Ulla: Arah, H and Rizia. 2848

HANOCH (6) [HANOCHITE]

Ge 25: 4 The sons of Midian were Ephah, Epher, H, 2840
46: 9 H, Pallu, Hezron and Carmi. 2840
Ex 6:14 of Reuben the firstborn son of Israel were H 2840
Nu 26: 5 through H, the Hanochite clan; 2840
1Ch 1:33 Ephah, Epher, H, Abida and Eldaah. 2840
5: 3 H, Pallu, Hezron and Carmi. 2840

HANOCHITE (1) [HANOCH]

Nu 26: 5 through Hanoch, the H clan; 2854

HANUN (13)

2Sa 10: 1 and his son H succeeded him as king. 2842
10: 2 "I will show kindness to H son of Nahash, 2842
10: 2 a delegation to express his sympathy to H NIH
10: 3 the Ammonite nobles said to H their lord, 2842
10: 4 So H seized David's men, 2842
1Ch 19: 2 "I will show kindness to H son of Nahash, 2842
19: 2 a delegation to express his sympathy to H 2257S
19: 2 When David's men came to H in the land of 2842
19: 3 the Ammonite nobles said to H, 2842
19: 4 So H seized David's men, shaved them, 2842
19: 6 H and the Ammonites sent 2842
Ne 3:13 The Valley Gate was repaired by H and 2842
3:30 Hananiah son of Shelemiah, and H, 2842

HAP (KJV) See AS IT TURNED OUT

HAPHARAIM (1)

Jos 19:19 H, Shion, Anaharath, 2921

HAPLY (KJV) See BETTER, FIND, PERHAPS

HAPPEN (57) [HAPPENED, HAPPENING, HAPPENS]

Ge 49: 1 so I can tell you what will h to you in days 7925
Ex 2: 4 at a distance to see what would h to him. 6913
21:13 but God lets it h, 628+3338+4200
1Ki 14: 3 He will tell you what will h to the boy." 2118
2Ki 7: 2 floodgates of the heavens, could this h?" 2118
7:19 floodgates of the heavens, could this h?" 2118
Ecc 3:22 For who can bring him to see what will h 2118
6:12 Who can tell him what will h under the sun 2118
9:11 but time and chance h to them all. 7936
10:14 who can tell him what will h after him? 2118
Isa 7: 7 " 'It will not take place, it will not h, 2118
23:15 it will h to Tyre as in the song of 2118
41:22 in [your idols] to tell us what is going to h. 7936
47: 7 or reflect on what might h. 344
Jer 6:18 observe, O witnesses, what will h to them. NIH
La 3:37 and have it h if the Lord has not decreed it? 2118
Eze 16:16 Such things should not h, 995
20:32 But what you have in mind will never h. 2118
38:18 This is what will h in that day: 2118
Da 2:28 He has shown King Nebuchadnezzar what will h in days to come. 10201
2:29 mysteries showed you what is going to h. 10201
8:19 "I am going to tell you what will h later in 2118
10:14 to you what will h to your people in 7936
Hos 10:15 Thus will it h to you, O Bethel, 6913
Am 7: 3 "This will not h," the LORD said. 2118
7: 6 "This will not h either," 2118
Jnh 4: 5 in its shade and waited to see what would h 2118
Zec 6:15 This will h if you diligently obey 2118
Mt 16:22 "This shall never h to you!" 1639
24: 3 "Tell us," they said, "when will this h, 1639
24: 6 Such things must h, 1181
24:39 and they knew nothing about what would h NIG
26:54 the Scriptures be fulfilled that say it must h 1181
Mk 10:32 and told them what was going to h to him. 5201
11:23 but believes that what he says will h, 1181
13: 4 when will these things h? 1639
13: 7 Such things must h, but the end is still 1181
Lk 21: 7 they asked, "when will these things h? 1639
21: 9 These things must h first, 1181
21:36 be able to escape all that is about to h, 1181
22:49 Jesus' followers saw what was going to h, 1639
23:31 what will h when it is dry?" 1181
Jn 5:14 Stop sinning or something worse may h 1181
13:19 it does h you will believe that I am He. 1181
14:29 so that when it does h you will believe. 1181
18: 4 knowing all that was going to h to him, 2262
Ac 4:28 and will had decided beforehand should h. 1181
8:24 so that nothing you have said may h to me." 2088
13:40 what the prophets have said does not h to 2088
20:22 not knowing what will h to me there. 5267
26:22 the prophets and Moses said would h— 1181
27:25 for I have faith in God that it will h just 1639
28: 6 a long time and seeing nothing unusual h 1181
Ro 9:26 "It will h that in the very place 1639
2Th 1: 7 This will h when the Lord Jesus is revealed NIG
Jas 4:14 not even know what will h tomorrow. 3836+4481
2Pe 2: 6 of what is going to h to the ungodly; 3516

HAPPENED (109) [HAPPEN]

Ge 20: 8 and when he told them all that had h, 465+1821+2021+2021
34: 7 the fields as soon as they heard what had h. NIH
42:29 they told him all that had h to them. 7936
Ex 32: 1 we don't know what has h to him." 2118
32:23 we don't know what has h to him.' 2118
Lev 10:19 but such things as this have h to me. 7925
Nu 31:16 from the LORD in what h at Peor, 1821
Dt 4:30 in distress and all these things have h 5162
4:32 Has anything so great as this ever h, 2118
Jos 2:23 and told him everything that had h to them. 5162
Jdg 6:13 why has all this h to us? 5162
6:38 And that is what h. 2118
20: 3 "Tell us how this awful thing h." 2118
21: 3 they cried, "why has this h to Israel? 2118
1Sa 4: 7 Nothing like this has h before. 2118
4:13 man entered the town and told what had h, NIH
4:16 Eli asked, "What h, my son?" 2118
6: 9 not his hand that struck us and that it h to us 2118
10:11 "What is this that has h to the son of Kish? 2118
20:26 "Something must have h to David 5247
2Sa 1: 4 "What h?" David asked. 2118
1: 6 "I h to be on Mount Gilboa," 7925+7936
13:35 it has h just as your servant said." 2118
18: 9 Now Absalom h to meet David's men. 7925
20: 1 a Benjamite, h to be there. 7925
2Ki 7:13 So let us send them to find out what h." NIH
7:14 "Go and find out what has h." NIH
7:18 It h as the man of God had said to 2118
7:20 And that is exactly what h to him, 2118
9:27 Ahaziah king of Judah saw what had h, NIH
18:12 This h because they had not obeyed NIH
24: 3 Surely these things h to Judah according to 2118
24:20 anger that all this h to Jerusalem and Judah, 2118
Ezr 9:13 "What has h to us is a result 995
Ne 9:33 In all that has h to us, you have been just; 995
Est 1: 1 This is what h during the time of Xerxes, 2118
4: 7 Mordecai told him everything that had h 7936
6:13 and all his friends everything that had h 7936
9:17 This h on the thirteenth day of the month NIH
9:26 of what they had seen and what had h 5595
Job 3:25 what I dreaded has h to me. 995
Ps 44:17 All this h to us, 995
Isa 20: 6 'See what has h to those we relied on, 3907
44: 7 and lay out before me what has h 2023S
48: 5 before they h I announced them to you so 995
Jer 5:30 "A horrible and shocking thing has h in 2118
13:22 "Why has this h to me?"— 7925
32:24 What you said has h, as you now see. 2118
40: 3 All this h because you people sinned against 2118
48:19 ask them, 'What has h?' 2118
52: 3 that all this h to Jerusalem and Judah, 2118
La 4:13 But it h because of the sins of her prophets NIH
5: 1 Remember, O LORD, what has h to us; 2118
Eze 16:19 That is what h, declares the Sovereign 2118
Da 4:28 All this h to King Nebuchadnezzar. 10413
12: 1 be a time of distress such as has not h from 2118
Joel 1: 2 Has anything like this ever h in your days or 2118
Mt 8:33 including what had h to the 3836
14:13 When Jesus heard what had h, NIG
18:31 When the other servants saw what had h, 1181
18:31 and told their master everything that had h. 1181
22:26 The same thing h to the second and third NIG
24:34 not pass away until all these things have h. 1181
27:54 the earthquake and all that had h, 1181
28:11 to the chief priests everything that had h. 1181
Mk 5:14 the people went out to see what had h. 1181+1639
5:16 told the people what had h to 1181
5:33 the woman, knowing what had h to her, 1181
13:30 not pass away until all these things have h. 1181
Lk 2:15 to Bethlehem and see this thing that has h, 1181
8:34 those tending the pigs saw what had h, 1181
8:35 and the people went out to see what had h. 1181
8:56 not to tell anyone what had h. 1181
10:31 A priest h to be going down the same road, 2848+5175
21:32 not pass away until all these things have h. 1181
23:47 The centurion, seeing what had h, 1181
24:12 wondering to himself what had h. 1181
24:14 with each other about everything that had h. 5201
24:18 and do not know the things that have h there 1181
24:35 Then the two told what had h on the way, NIG
Jn 1:28 This all h at Bethany on the other side of 1181
9: 3 "but this h so that the work of God might NIG
18: 9 This h so that the words he had spoken NIG
18:32 This h so that the words Jesus had spoken NIG
19:24 This h that the scripture might be NIG
19:36 These things h so that the scripture would 1181
21: 1 It h this way: NIG
Ac 3:10 with wonder and amazement at what had h 5201
4:21 people were praising God for what had h. 1181
5: 5 great fear seized all who heard what had h. NIG
5: 7 not knowing what had h. 1181
7:40 we don't know what has h to him!' 1181
10: 8 He told them everything that had h NIG
10:16 This h three times, 1181
10:37 You know what has h throughout Judea, 1181
11: 4 to them precisely as it had h: 2759
11:10 This h three times, 1181
11:28 (This h during the reign of Claudius.) 1181
12: 3 This h during the Feast of Unleavened 1639
13:12 When the proconsul saw what had h, 1181
17:17 by day with those who h to be there. 4193
19:21 After all this had h, Paul decided to go 4444
28: 9 When this had h, the rest of the sick 1181
1Co 10:11 These things h to them as examples 5201
2Co 1: 9 But this h that we might not rely 2671
Gal 4:15 What has h to all your joy? NIG
Php 1:12 what has h to me has really served to 2848+3836
1:19 what has h to me will turn out for my 609
2Ti 3:11 what kinds of things h to me in Antioch, 1181

HAPPENING (10) [HAPPEN]

Ge 25:22 and she said, "Why is this h to me?" NIH
1Sa 5: 7 When the men of Ashdod saw what was h, 4027S
Ne 6: 8 "Nothing like what you are saying is h; 2118
Est 2:11 to find out how Esther was and what was h 6913
Mk 13:29 Even so, when you see these things h, 1181
Lk 18:36 he asked what was h. 4047S
21:31 Even so, when you see these things h, 1181
Ac 12: 9 that what the angel was doing was really h; 1181
Col 4: 9 They will tell you everything that is h here. NIG
1Pe 4:12 as though something strange were h to you. 5201

HAPPENS (17) [HAPPEN]

Ex 22: 3 but if it h after sunrise, NIH
Nu 16:29 and experience only what usually h 7213
Dt 22:23 a man h to meet in a town a virgin pledged AIT
22:25 a man h to meet a girl pledged to be married AIT
22:28 a man h to meet a virgin who is not pledged AIT
Ru 3:18 my daughter, until you find out what h. 5877
1Sa 2:34 " 'And what h to your two sons, 995
2Sa 14:20 he knows everything that h in the land." NIH
Ecc 9: 3 the evil in everything that h under the sun: 6913
9: 6 a part in anything that h under the sun. 6913
Isa 48:16 at the time it h, I am there." 2118
Jer 12: 4 "He will not see what h to us." 344
Eze 24:24 When this h, you will know that I am 995

Lk 1:20 and not able to speak until the day this **h**, *1181*
Jn 13:19 "I am telling you now before it **h**, *1181*
14:29 I have told you now before *it* **h**, *1181*
Php 1:27 **Whatever h**, conduct yourselves in a *3668*

HAPPIER (3) [HAPPY]
Ecc 4:2 who had already died, are **h** than the living, NIH
Mt 18:13 *he is* **h** about that one sheep than *3437+5897*
1Co 7:40 she is **h** if she stays as she is— *3421*

HAPPINESS (6) [HAPPY]
Dt 24:5 to be free to stay at home and **bring h** *to* 8523
Est 8:16 For the Jews it was a **time of h** and joy, 245
Job 7:7 my eyes will never see **h** again. 3202
Ecc 2:26 God gives wisdom, knowledge and **h**, 8525
Mt 25:21 Come and share your master's **h!'** *5915*
25:23 Come and share your master's **h!'** *5915*

HAPPIZZEZ (1)
1Ch 24:15 the eighteenth to **H**, 2204

HAPPY (24) [HAPPIER, HAPPINESS]
Ge 30:13 Then Leah said, "How **h** I am! 891
30:13 The women *will* **call** me **h.**" 887
1Ki 4:20 they ate, they drank and they were **h.** 8524
10:8 **How h** your men must be! 897
10:8 **How h** your officials, 897
2Ch 9:7 **How h** your men must be! 897
9:7 **How h** your officials, 897
Est 5:9 Haman went out that day **h** and 8524
5:14 go with the king to the dinner and be **h.**" 8524
Ps 10:6 I'll always be **h** and never have trouble." 890
68:3 *may they be* **h** and joyful. 8464
113:9 in her home as a **h** mother of children. 8524
137:8 **h** is he who repays you for what you have 897
Pr 15:13 A **h** heart makes the face cheerful, 8524
Ecc 3:12 to *be* **h** and do good while they live. 8523
5:19 to accept his lot and *be* **h** in his work— 8523
7:14 When times are good, be **h;** 3202
11:9 *Be* **h**, young man, while you are young, 8523
Jnh 4:6 and Jonah *was* very **h** about the vine. 8523+8525
Zec 8:19 and glad occasions and **h** festivals 3202
1Co 7:30 those who *are* **h**, as if they were not; *5897*
2Co 7:9 yet now *I am* **h**, not because you were *5897*
7:13 delighted to see how **h** Titus was, *5915*
Jas 5:13 *Is* anyone **h?** Let him sing songs of praise. *2313*

HARA (1)
1Ch 5:26 Habor, **H** and the river of Gozan, 2217

HARADAH (2)
Nu 33:24 They left Mount Shepher and camped at **H.** 3011
33:25 They left **H** and camped at Makheloth. 3011

HARAM See BETH HARAM

HARAN (21) [BETH HARAN]
Ge 11:26 the father of Abram, Nahor and **H.** 2237
11:27 the father of Abram, Nahor and **H.** 2237
11:27 And **H** became the father of Lot. 2237
11:28 **H** died in Ur of the Chaldeans, 2237
11:29 she was the daughter of **H**, 2237
11:31 his grandson Lot son of **H**, 2237
11:31 But when they came to **H**, they settled there. 3059
11:32 Terah lived 205 years, and he died in **H.** 3059
12:4 when he set out from **H.** 3059
12:5 and the people they had acquired in **H**, 3059
27:43 Flee at once to my brother Laban in **H.** 3059
28:10 Jacob left Beersheba and set out for **H.** 3059
29:4 "We're from **H**," they replied. 3059
2Ki 19:12 the gods of Gozan, **H**, 3059
1Ch 2:46 Ephah was the mother of **H**, 3060
2:46 **H** was the father of Gazez. 3060
23:9 Shelomoth, Haziel and **H**—three in all. 2237
Isa 37:12 the gods of Gozan, **H**, 3059
Eze 27:23 " '**H**, Canneh and Eden and merchants 3059
Ac 7:2 before he lived in **H.** *5924*
7:4 the land of the Chaldeans and settled in **H.** *5924*

HARARITE (5)
2Sa 23:11 to him was Shammah son of Agee the **H.** 2240
23:33 son of Shammah the **H**, 2240
23:33 Ahiam son of Sharar the **H**, 2240
1Ch 11:34 Jonathan son of Shagee the **H**, 2240
11:35 Ahiam son of Sacar the **H**, 2240

HARASHIM See GE HARASHIM

HARASS (2) [HARASSED]
Dt 2:9 not **h** the Moabites or provoke them to war, 7444
2:19 *do* not **h** them or provoke them to war, 7444

HARASSED (2) [HARASS]
Mt 9:36 because they were **h** and helpless, *5035*
2Co 7:5 but *we were* **h** at every turn— *2567*

HARBONA (2)
Est 1:10 Mehuman, Biztha, **H**, Bigtha, Abagtha, 3002
7:9 Then **H**, one of the eunuchs attending 3003

HARBOR (10) [HARBORED, HARBORS]
Dt 15:9 Be careful not *to* **h** this wicked thought: 2118+4222+6640
Job 36:13 "The godless in heart **h** resentment; 8492
Ps 28:3 with their neighbors but **h** malice **in** 928
103:9 nor *will he* **h** *his* **anger** forever; 5757
Isa 23:1 and left without house or **h.** 995
23:10 for you no longer have a **h.** 4651
Jer 4:14 How long *will you* **h** wicked thoughts? 928+4328+7931
Ac 27:12 Since the **h** was unsuitable to winter in, *3348*
27:12 This was a **h** in Crete, *3348*
Jas 3:14 if *you* **h** bitter envy and selfish ambition *2400*

HARBORED (1) [HARBOR]
Eze 35:5 " 'Because you **h** an ancient hostility 2118+4200

HARBORS (1) [HARBOR]
Pr 26:24 but in his heart *he* **h** deceit. 8883

HARD (65) [HARDEN, HARDENED, HARDENING, HARDENS, HARDER, HARDEST, HARDSHIP, HARDSHIPS]
Ge 18:14 *Is* anything too **h** for the LORD? 7098
33:13 If they *are* **driven h** just one day, 1985
Ex 1:14 They made their lives bitter with **h** labor 7997
1:14 in all their **h** labor the Egyptians used them NIH
2:11 and watched them at their **h labor.** 6026
7:13 Yet Pharaoh's heart *became* **h** and he would 2616
7:22 and Pharaoh's heart *became* **h;** 2616
8:19 But Pharaoh's heart *was* **h** and he would 2616
9:35 So Pharaoh's heart *was* **h** and he would 2616
Dt 1:17 Bring me any case too **h** for you, 7996
8:15 He brought you water out of **h** rock. 2734
26:6 made us suffer, putting us to **h** labor. 7997
1Sa 13:6 and that their army *was* **h pressed,** 5601
31:2 The Philistines **pressed h after** Saul 1815
1Ki 10:1 she came to test him with **h questions.** 2648
10:3 nothing was too **h** for the king to explain 6623
1Ch 10:2 The Philistines **pressed h** after Saul 1815
2Ch 9:1 to Jerusalem to test him with **h questions.** 2648
9:2 nothing *was* too **h** for him to explain to her. 6623
32:5 Then *he* **worked h** repairing all 2616
Job 7:1 "Does not man have **h service** on earth? 7372
14:14 of my **h service** I will wait for my renewal 7372
37:18 **h** as a mirror of cast bronze? 2617
38:30 *when* the waters **become h** as stone, 2461
38:38 when the dust *becomes* **h** 2021+3668+4200+4607
41:24 His chest *is* **h** as rock, 3668
41:24 **h** as a lower millstone. 3668
Ps 114:8 the **h rock** into springs of water 2734
Pr 13:15 but the way of the unfaithful is **h.** 419
14:23 All **h work** brings a profit, 6776
Ecc 8:1 a man's face and changes its **h** appearance. 6437
Isa 40:2 that her **h service** has been completed, 7372
Jer 32:17 Nothing *is* too **h** for you. 7098
32:27 *Is* anything too **h** for me? 7098
Eze 29:18 of Babylon drove his army in a **h** campaign 1524
Zec 7:12 They made their hearts **as h as flint** 9032
Mt 19:8 because your **hearts** were **h.** *5016*
19:23 it is **h** for a rich man to enter the kingdom *1552*
25:24 he said, 'I knew that you are a **h** man, *5017*
Mk 10:5 "It was because your **hearts** were **h** *5016*
10:23 How **h** it is for the rich to enter the kingdom *1552*
10:24 how **h** it is to enter the kingdom of God! *1551*
Lk 5:5 we've **worked h** all night *3159*
12:58 **try h** to be reconciled to him on the way, *1443+2238*
18:24 How **h** it is for the rich to enter the kingdom *1552*
19:21 because you are a **h** man. *893*
19:22 You knew, did you, that I am a **h** man, *893*
Jn 4:38 Others *have done* the **h work,** *3159*
6:60 "This is a **h** teaching. *5017*
Ac 20:35 that by this kind of **h work** we must help *3159*
26:14 It is **h** for you to kick against the goads.' *5017*
Ro 16:6 Greet Mary, who worked **very h** for you. *4498*
16:12 those women who **work h** in the Lord. *3159*
16:12 another woman who *has* **worked** very **h** in *3159*
1Co 4:12 *We* **work h** with our own hands. *2237+3159*
2Co 4:8 We are **h pressed** on every side, *2567*
6:5 in **h work,** sleepless nights and hunger; *3160*
8:13 be relieved while you are **h pressed,** *2568*
Col 4:13 he *is* working **h** for you and for those *2400+4498*
1Th 5:12 to respect those who **work h** among you, *3159*
2Ti 1:17 he searched **h** for me until he found me. *5081*
Heb 5:11 but *it is* **h to explain** because you are slow *1549*
1Pe 4:18 And, "If it is **h** for the righteous to be saved, *3660*
2Pe 3:16 some things that are **h to understand,** *1554*
Rev 2:2 your **h work** and your perseverance. *3160*

HARDEN (11) [HARD]
Ex 4:21 But I *will* **h** his heart so that he will not let 2616
7:3 But I *will* **h** Pharaoh's heart, 7996
14:4 And *I will* **h** Pharaoh's heart, 2616
14:17 I *will* **h** the hearts of the Egyptians so 2616
1Sa 6:6 Why *do you* **h** your hearts as the Egyptians 3877
Ps 95:8 *do* not **h** your hearts as you did at Meribah, 7996
Isa 63:17 from your ways and **h** our hearts so we do 7998
Ro 9:18 and he hardens whom he wants to **h.** *NIG*
Heb 3:8 not **h** your hearts as you did in the rebellion, *5020*
3:15 if you hear his voice, *do* not **h** your hearts *5020*
4:7 if you hear his voice, *do* not **h** your hearts." *5020*

HARDENED (19) [HARD]
Ex 8:15 *he* **h** his heart and would not listen to Moses 3877
8:32 also Pharaoh **h** his heart and would not let 3877
9:12 the LORD **h** Pharaoh's heart and he would 2616
9:34 He and his officials **h** their hearts. 3877
10:1 for I *have* **h** his heart and the hearts 3877
10:20 But the LORD **h** Pharaoh's heart, 2616
10:27 But the LORD **h** Pharaoh's heart, 2616
11:10 but the LORD **h** Pharaoh's heart, 2616
14:8 The LORD **h** the heart of Pharaoh king 2616
Jos 11:20 the LORD himself *who* **h** their hearts 2616
2Ch 36:13 He became stiff-necked and **h** his heart 599
Jer 6:28 They are all **h rebels,** 6073+6253
Eze 3:7 house of Israel is **h** and obstinate. 2617+5195
3:8 I will make you as unyielding and **h** 2617+5195
Da 5:20 his heart became arrogant and **h** with pride, 10772
Mk 6:52 their hearts were **h.** *4800*
8:17 *Are* your hearts **h?** *2400+4800*
Ro 11:7 The others *were* **h**, *4800*
Heb 3:13 none of you *may be* **h** by sin's deceitfulness. *5020*

HARDENING (2) [HARD]
Ro 11:25 Israel has experienced a **h** in part until *4801*
Eph 4:18 of the ignorance that is in them due to the **h** *4801*

HARDENS (2) [HARD]
Pr 28:14 but *he who* **h** his heart falls into trouble. 7996
Ro 9:18 and *he* **h** whom he wants to harden. *5020*

HARDER (6) [HARD]
Ex 5:9 *Make* the work **h** for the men so 3877
Jer 5:3 *They* **made** their faces **h** than stone 2616
Eze 3:9 like the hardest stone, **h** than flint. 2617
Jn 5:18 For this reason the Jews tried **all the h** *3437*
1Co 15:10 No, I worked **h than** all of them— *4358*
2Co 11:23 I have worked **much h**, *4359*

HARDEST (1) [HARD]
Eze 3:9 I will make your forehead like the **h stone,** 9032

HARDHEARTED (1) [HEART]
Dt 15:7 *do* not *be* **h** or tightfisted toward your poor brother. 599+906+4222

HARDLY (8)
Ge 48:10 and he could **h** see. 4202
Job 2:12 they could **h** recognize him; 4202
Da 10:17 My strength is gone and I **can h breathe.**" 4202+5972+8636
Mt 13:15 they **h** hear with their ears. *977*
Mk 7:32 a man who was deaf and **could h talk,** *3652*
Lk 11:46 down with burdens *they can* **h** carry, *1546*
Ac 27:16 we were **h** able to make the lifeboat secure. *3660*
28:27 they **h** hear with their ears, *977*

HARDSHIP (12) [HARD]
Ge 31:42 But God has seen my **h** and the toil 6715
Dt 15:18 not consider it a **h** to set your servant free, 7996
Ne 9:32 not let all this **h** seem trifling in your eyes— 9430
9:32 the **h** that has come upon us, NIH
Job 5:6 For **h** does not spring from the soil, 224
Isa 30:6 Through a land of **h** and distress, 7650
La 3:5 and surrounded me with bitterness and **h.** 9430
Ro 8:35 or **h** or persecution or famine or nakedness *5103*
1Th 2:9 you remember, brothers, our toil and **h;** *3677*
2Ti 2:3 Endure **h** with us **like** a good soldier *6055*
4:5 keep your head in all situations, **endure h,** *2802*
Heb 12:7 Endure **h** as discipline; *NIG*

HARDSHIPS (11) [HARD]
Ex 18:8 about all the **h** they had met along the way 9430
Nu 11:1 Now the people complained about their **h** in 8273
20:14 You know about all the **h** that have come 9430
1Ki 2:26 **shared** all my father's **h.**" 889+928+6700+6700
Ps 132:1 remember David and all *the* **h** he **endured.** 6700
Ac 14:22 "We must go through many **h** to enter *2568*
20:23 that prison and **h** are facing me. *2568*
2Co 1:8 the **h** we suffered in the province of Asia. *2568*
6:4 in troubles, **h** and distresses; *340*
12:10 I delight in weaknesses, in insults, in **h**, *340*
Rev 2:3 You have persevered and *have* **endured h** *1002*

HARDWORKING (1) [WORK]
2Ti 2:6 The **h** farmer should be the first to receive *3159*

HARE (KJV) See RABBIT

HAREM (8)
Est 2:3 bring all these beautiful girls into the **h** 851+1074
2:8 who had charge of the **h.** 851
2:9 her maids into the best place in the **h.** 851+1074
2:11 near the courtyard of the **h** to find out 851+1074
2:13 with her from the **h** to the king's palace. 851+1074
2:14 morning return to another part of the **h** 851+1074
2:15 king's eunuch who was in charge of the **h**, 851
Ecc 2:8 and a **h** as well— 2256+8721+8721

HAREPH (1)
1Ch 2:51 and **H** the father of Beth Gader. 3073

HARESETH See KIR HARESETH

HARETH (KJV) See HERETH

HARHAIAH (1)

Ne 3: 8 Uzziel son of **H,** one of the goldsmiths, 3015

HARHAS (1)

2Ki 22:14 the son of **H,** keeper of the wardrobe. 3030

HARHUR (2)

Ezr 2:51 Bakbuk, Hakupha, **H,** 3028
Ne 7:53 Bakbuk, Hakupha, **H,** 3028

HARIM (10) [HARIM'S]

1Ch 24: 8 the third to **H,** the fourth to Seorim, 3053
Ezr 2:32 of **H** 320 3053
2:39 of **H** 1,017 3053
10:21 From the descendants of **H:** 3053
10:31 From the descendants of **H:** 3053
Ne 3:11 Malkijah son of **H** and Hasshub son 3053
7:35 of **H** 320 3053
7:42 of **H** 1,017 3053
10: 5 **H,** Meremoth, Obadiah, 3053
10:27 Malluch, **H** and Baanah. 3053

HARIM'S (1) [HARIM]

Ne 12:15 of **H,** Adna; of Meremoth's, Helkai; 3053

HARIPH (2)

Ne 7:24 of **H** 112 3040
10:19 **H,** Anathoth, Nebai, 3040

HARLOT (KJV) See also PROSTITUTE

HARLOT (2) [HARLOTS]

Isa 1:21 See how the faithful city has become a **h!** 2390
Na 3: 4 all because of the wanton lust of a **h,** 2390

HARLOTS (1) [HARLOT]

Hos 4:14 because the men themselves consort with **h** 2390

HARM (73) [HARMED, HARMFUL, HARMING, HARMLESS, HARMS]

Ge 26:29 that you will do us no **h,** 8288
31: 7 However, God has not allowed him to **h** me. 8317
31:29 I have the power to **h** you; 6913+8273
31:52 not go past this heap to your side to **h** you NIH
31:52 past this heap and pillar to my side to **h** me. 8288
42: 4 he was afraid that **h** might come to him. 656
42:38 If **h** comes to him on the journey 656
44:29 from me too and **h** comes to him, 656
48:16 the Angel who has delivered me from all **h** 8273
50:20 You intended to **h** me, 8288
Nu 5:19 that brings a curse **not h** *you.* 4946+5927
35:23 and he did not intend to **h** him, 8288
Jdg 15: 3 I *will* really **h** them." 6913+8288
1Sa 20: 7 be sure that he is determined to **h** me. 8288
20: 9 that my father was determined to **h** you, 8288
20:13 But if my father is inclined to **h** you, 8288
25:26 and all who intend to **h** my master be 8288
26:21 *I will* not *try to* **h** you again. 8317
2Sa 18:32 the king and all who rise up to **h** you be like 8288
20: 6 Sheba son of Bicri *will* **do** us more **h** than Absalom did. 8317
2Ki 8:12 "Because I know the **h** you will do to 8288
1Ch 4:10 and keep me from **h** so that I will be free 8288
16:22 *do* my prophets no **h."** 8317
Ne 6: 2 But they were scheming to **h** me; 6913+8288
Job 5:19 in seven no **h** will befall you. 8273
Ps 38:12 those who would **h** me talk of my ruin; 8288
56: 5 they are always plotting to **h** me. 8273
71:13 to **h** me be covered with scorn and disgrace. 8288
71:24 for those who wanted to **h** me have been put 8288
91:10 then no **h** will befall you, 8288
105:15 **do** my prophets no **h."** 8317
121: 6 the sun *will* not **h** you by day, 5782
121: 7 The LORD will keep you from all **h—** 8273
Pr 1:33 and be at ease, without fear of **h."** 8288
3:29 Do not plot **h** against your neighbor, 8288
3:30 when he has done you no **h.** 8288
12:21 No **h** befalls the righteous, 224
13:20 but a companion of fools **suffers h.** 8317
31:12 She brings him good, not **h,** 8273
Ecc 5:13 wealth hoarded to the **h** *of* its owner, 8288
8: 5 to no **h,** and the wise heart will know 1821+8273
Isa 11: 9 *They will* neither **h** nor destroy 8317
27: 3 and night so that no *one may* **h** it. 7212
65:25 *They will* neither **h** nor destroy 8317
Jer 5:12 No **h** will come to us; 8288
7: 6 you do not follow other gods to your own **h,** 8273
10: 5 *they can* **do** no **h** nor can they do any good." 8317
21:10 I have determined to do this city **h** and 8288
23:17 'No **h** will come to you.' 8288
25: 6 Then *I will* not **h** you." 8317
25: 7 and you have brought **h** to yourselves." 8273
29:11 "plans to prosper you and not to **h** you, 8288
39:12 don't **h** him but do for him whatever 6913+8273
44:17 of food and were well off and suffered no **h.** 8288
Jer 44:27 For I am watching over them for **h,** 8288
44:29 'so that you will know that my threats of **h** 8288
Zep 3:15 never again will you fear any **h.** 8273
Lk 10:19 nothing *will* **h** you. *92*
Ac 9:13 about this man and all the **h** he has done *2805*
16:28 But Paul shouted, "Don't **h** yourself! *2805+4556*
18:10 and no one is going to attack and **h** you, *2808*
Ro 13:10 Love does no **h** to its neighbor. *2805*
1Co 11:17 for your meetings do more **h** than good. *2482*
2Ti 4:14 the metalworker did me a great deal of **h.** *2805*
1Pe 3:13 Who *is going to* **h** you if you are eager *2808*
2Pe 2:13 *with* **h** for the harm they have done. *94*
2:13 with harm for the **h** *they have* **done.** *92*
1Jn 5:18 and the evil one cannot **h** him. *721*
Rev 7: 2 power *to* **h** the land and the sea: *92*
7: 3 **"Do** not **h** the land or the sea or the trees *92*
9: 4 not *to* **h** the grass of the earth or any plant *92*
11: 5 If anyone tries *to* **h** them, *92*
11: 5 how anyone who wants *to* **h** them must die. *92*

HARMED (3) [HARM]

Ru 2:22 in someone else's field you *might be* **h."** 7003
Da 3:27 saw that the fire *had* not **h** their bodies, 10715
2Co 7: 9 and so *were* not **h** in any way by us. *2423*

HARMFUL (3) [HARM]

2Ki 4:41 And there was nothing **h** in the pot. 8273
Ps 52: 4 You love every **h** word, 1184
1Ti 6: 9 a trap and into many foolish and **h** desires *1054*

HARMING (3) [HARM]

1Sa 24: 9 'David is bent on **h** you'? 8288
25:34 lives, who has kept me from **h** you, 8317
Jer 7:19 Are they not rather **h** themselves, NIH

HARMLESS (2) [HARM]

Lev 13:39 a **h rash** that has broken out on the skin; 993
Pr 1:11 let's waylay some **h soul;** 2855+5929

HARMON (1)

Am 4: 3 and you will be cast out toward **H,"** 2236

HARMONY (4)

Zec 6:13 And there will be **h** between the two.' 6783+8934
Ro 12:16 **Live in h** with one another. *899+3836+5858*
2Co 6:15 What **h** is there between Christ and Belial? *5245*
1Pe 3: 8 all of you, **live in h with** one another; *3939*

HARMS (1) [HARM]

Pr 8:36 But whoever fails to find me **h** himself; 2803

HARNEPHER (1)

1Ch 7:36 The sons of Zophah: Suah, **H,** Shual, Beri, 3062

HARNESS (4) [HARNESSED]

Job 39:10 Can you hold him to the furrow with a **h?** 6310
Ps 50:19 for evil and **h** your tongue *to* deceit. 7537
Jer 46: 4 **H** the horses, mount the steeds! 673
Mic 1:13 **h** the team to the chariot. 8412

HARNESSED (1) [HARNESS]

SS 1: 9 a mare **h to** one of the chariots of Pharaoh. 928

HAROD (1) [HARODITE]

Jdg 7: 1 and all his men camped at the spring of **H.** 3008

HARODITE (2) [HAROD]

2Sa 23:25 Shammah the **H,** Elika the Harodite, 3012
23:25 Shammah the Harodite, Elika the **H,** 3012

HAROEH (1)

1Ch 2:52 **H,** half the Manahathites, 2218

HARORITE (1)

1Ch 11:27 Shammoth the **H,** Helez the Pelonite, 2229

HAROSHETH HAGGOYIM (3)

Jdg 4: 2 who lived in **H.** 3099
4:13 from **H** to the Kishon River. 3099
4:16 and army as far as **H.** 3099

HARP (32) [HARPIST, HARPISTS, HARPS]

Ge 4:21 the father of all who play the **h** and flute. 4036
1Sa 16:16 to search for someone who can play the **h.** 4036
16:18 who knows how *to* **play the h.** 5594
16:23 David would take his **h** and play. 4036
18:10 while David *was* **playing the h,** 928+3338+5594
19: 9 While David *was* **playing the h,** 928+3338+5594
1Ch 25: 3 the **h** in thanking and praising the LORD. 4036
Job 21:12 to the music of tambourine and **h;** 4036
30:31 My **h** is tuned to mourning, 4036
Ps 33: 2 Praise the LORD with the **h;** 4036
43: 4 I will praise you with the **h,** O God, 4036
49: 4 with the **h** I will expound my riddle: 4036
57: 8 Awake, **h** and lyre! 4036
71:22 with the **h** for your faithfulness, O my God; 5575
81: 2 play the melodious **h** and lyre. 4036
Ps 92: 3 and the melody of the **h.** 4036
98: 5 make music to the LORD with the **h,** 4036
98: 5 with the **h** and the sound of singing, 4036
108: 2 Awake, **h** and lyre! I will awaken the dawn. 4036
147: 7 make music to our God on the **h.** 4036
149: 3 to him with tambourine and **h.** 4036
150: 3 praise him with the **h** and lyre, 4036
Isa 16:11 My heart laments for Moab like a **h,** 4036
23:16 "Take up a **h,** walk through 4036
23:16 **play the h** well, sing many a song, 5594
24: 8 the joyful **h** is silent. 4036
Da 3: 5 zither, lyre, **h,** pipes and all kinds of music, 10590
3: 7 flute, zither, lyre, **h** and all kinds of music, 10590
3:10 the sound of the horn, flute, zither, lyre, **h,** 10590
3:15 zither, lyre, **h,** pipes and all kinds of music, 10590
1Co 14: 7 such as the flute or **h,** *3067*
Rev 5: 8 a **h** and they were holding golden bowls full *3067*

HARPIST (2) [HARP]

2Ki 3:15 But now bring me a **h."** 5594
3:15 While the **h** was playing, 5594

HARPISTS (2) [HARP]

Rev 14: 2 like that *of* **h** playing their harps. *3069*
18:22 The music *of* **h** and musicians, *3069*

HARPOONS (1)

Job 41: 7 Can you fill his hide with **h** or his head 8496

HARPS (25) [HARP]

Ge 31:27 to the music of tambourines and **h?** 4036
1Sa 10: 5 flutes and **h** being played before them, 4036
2Sa 6: 5 with songs and with **h,** lyres, tambourines, 4036
1Ki 10:12 and to make **h** and lyres for the musicians. 4036
1Ch 13: 8 with songs and with **h,** lyres, tambourines, 4036
15:16 lyres, **h** and cymbals. 4036
15:21 Jeiel and Azaziah were to play the **h,** 4036
15:28 and the playing of lyres and **h.** 4036
16: 5 They were to play the lyres and **h,** 4036
25: 1 accompanied by **h,** lyres and cymbals. 4036
25: 6 with cymbals, lyres and **h,** 4036
2Ch 5:12 in fine linen and playing cymbals, **h** 4036
9:11 and to make **h** and lyres for the musicians. 4036
20:28 to the temple of the LORD with **h** and lutes 5575
29:25 **h** and lyres in the way prescribed by David 4036
Ne 12:27 and with the music of cymbals, **h** and lyres. 4036
Ps 137: 2 There on the poplars we hung our **h,** 4036
Isa 5:12 They have **h** and lyres at their banquets, 4036
14:11 along with the noise of your **h;** 5575
30:32 be to the music of tambourines and **h,** 4036
Eze 26:13 the music of your **h** will be heard no more. 4036
Am 5:23 I will not listen to the music of your **h.** 5575
6: 5 You strum away on your **h** like David 5575
Rev 14: 2 like that of harpists playing their **h.** *3067*
15: 2 They held **h** given them by God *3067*

HARROW (KJV) See TILL

HARROWING (1)

Isa 28:24 Does he keep on breaking up and **h** the soil? 8440

HARSH (13) [HARSHLY]

Dt 28:59 **h** and prolonged disasters, 1524
1Ki 12: 4 the **h** labor and the heavy yoke he put on us, 7997
2Ch 10: 4 the **h** labor and the heavy yoke he put on us, 7997
Pr 15: 1 but a **h** word stirs up anger. 6776
Isa 66: 4 so I also will choose **h treatment** *for* them 9500
La 1: 3 After affliction and **h** labor, 8044
Da 2:15 "Why did the king issue *such a* **h** decree?" 10280
Mal 3:13 "You have said **h** things against me," 2616
2Co 13:10 not have to be **h** in my use of authority— *705*
Col 2:23 their false humility and their **h treatment** of *910*
3:19 love your wives and *do* not **be h** with them. *4393*
1Pe 2:18 but also *to* those who *are* **h.** *5021*
Jude 1:15 the **h** *words* ungodly sinners have spoken *5017*

HARSHA (2) [TEL HARSHA]

Ezr 2:52 Bazluth, Mehida, **H,** 3095
Ne 7:54 Bazluth, Mehida, **H,** 3095

HARSHLY (13) [HARSH]

Ge 42: 7 to be a stranger and spoke **h** to them. 7997
42:30 over the land spoke **h** to us and treated us as 7997
Ex 10: 2 and grandchildren how *I* **dealt h** with 6618
1Sa 6: 6 When *he* **treated** them **h,** 6618
20:10 if your father answers you **h?"** 7997
2Sa 19:43 men of Judah responded even more **h** than 7996
1Ki 12:13 The king answered the people **h.** 7997
2Ch 10:13 The king answered them **h.** 7997
Job 39:16 *She* **treats** her young **h,** 7996
Pr 18:23 but a rich man answers **h.** 6434
Eze 34: 4 You have ruled them **h** and brutally. 928+2622
Mk 14: 5 And *they* **rebuked** her **h.** *1839*
1Ti 5: 1 *Do* not **rebuke** an older man **h,** *2159*

HART (KJV) See DEER, STAG

HARUM (1)

1Ch 4: 8 and of the clans of Aharhel son of **H.** 2227

HARUMAPH (1)

Ne 3:10 of H made repairs opposite his house, 3018

HARUPHITE (1)

1Ch 12: 5 Bealiah, Shemariah and Shephatiah the H; 3020

HARUZ (1)

2Ki 21:19 His mother's name was Meshullemeth daughter of H; 3027

HARVEST (96) [HARVESTED, HARVESTERS, HARVESTING, HARVESTS]

Ge 8:22 long as the earth endures, seedtime and h, 7907
30:14 During wheat h, Reuben went out into 7907
41:34 of the h of Egypt during the seven years NIH
Ex 23:10 to sow your fields and h the crops, 665
23:16 Feast of H with the firstfruits of the crops 7907
34:21 the plowing season and h you must rest. 7907
34:22 Feast of Weeks with the firstfruits of the wheat h, 7907
Lev 19: 9 " 'When you reap the h of your land, 7907
19: 9 or gather the gleanings of your h. 7907
19:25 In this way your h will be increased. 9311
23:10 to give you and you reap its h, 7907
23:10 to the priest a sheaf of the first grain you h. 7907
23:22 " 'When you reap the h of your land, 7907
23:22 or gather the gleanings of your h. 7907
25: 5 not reap what grows of itself or h the grapes 1305
25:11 and do not reap what grows of itself or h 1305
25:20 if we do not plant or h our crops?" 665
25:22 and will continue to eat from it until the h 9311
26: 5 Your threshing will continue until grape h 1292
26: 5 and the grape h will continue until planting, 1292
26:10 still be eating last year's h when you 3823+3824
Nu 18:12 the LORD as the firstfruits of their h. 8040
Dt 16:15 in all your h and in all the work 9311
24:21 When you h the grapes in your vineyard, 1305
28:38 in the field but you will h little, 665
Jos 3:15 the Jordan is at flood stage all during h. 7907
Jdg 8: 2 the full grape h of Abiezer? 1292
15: 1 Later on, at the time of wheat h, 7907
Ru 1:22 in Bethlehem as the barley h was beginning. 7907
1Sa 8:12 others to plow his ground and reap his h, 7907
12:17 Is it not wheat h now? 7907
2Sa 21: 9 to death during the first days of the h, 7907
21: 9 just as the barley h was beginning. 7907
21:10 the beginning of the h till the rain poured 7907
23:13 During h time, three of the thirty chief 7907
2Ch 32:28 also made buildings to store the h of grain, 9311
Ne 9:37 its abundant h goes to the kings 9311
Job 5: 5 The hungry consume his h, 7907
31:12 it would have uprooted my h. 9311
Ps 67: 6 Then the land will yield its h, and God, 3292
85:12 and our land will yield its h. 3292
107:37 that yielded a fruitful h; 9311
Pr 6: 8 in summer and gathers its food at h. 7907
10: 5 he who sleeps during h is a disgraceful son. 7907
14: 4 the strength of an ox comes an abundant h. 9311
18:20 with the h from his lips he is satisfied. 9311
20: 4 so at h time he looks but finds nothing. 7907
25:13 Like the coolness of snow at h time is 7907
26: 1 Like snow in summer or rain in h, 7907
Isa 9: 3 before you as people rejoice at the h, 7907
17:11 yet the h will be as nothing in the day 7907
18: 4 like a cloud of dew in the heat of h." 7907
18: 5 For, before the h, when the blossom is gone 7907
23: 3 the h of the Nile was the revenue of Tyre, 7907
24:13 as when gleanings are left after the grape h. 1292
28: 4 will be like a fig ripe before h— 7811
32:10 the grape h will fail, 1292
32:10 and the h of fruit will not come. 668
62: 9 but those who h it will eat it and praise 665
Jer 2: 3 the firstfruits of his h; 9311
5:24 who assures us of the regular weeks of h.' 7907
8:13 " 'I will take away their h, 658
8:20 "The h is past, the summer has ended, 7907
12:13 So bear the shame of your h because of 9311
40:10 but you are to h the wine, 665
50:16 and the reaper with his sickle at h. 7907
51:33 the time to h her will soon come." 7907
Hos 6:11 "Also for you, Judah, a h is appointed. 7907
Joel 1:11 because the h of the field is destroyed. 7907
3:13 Swing the sickle, for the h is ripe. 7907
Am 4: 7 when the h was still three months away. 7907
Mic 6:15 You will plant but not h; 7917
Mt 9:37 "The h is plentiful but the workers are few. 2546
9:38 Ask the Lord of the h, therefore, 2546
9:38 to send out workers into his h field." 2546
13:30 Let both grow together until the h. 2546
13:39 The h is the end of the age, 2546
21:34 When the h time approached, 2843
21:41 his share of the crop at h time." NIG
25:26 that I h where I have not sown and gather 2545
Mk 4:29 because the h has come." 2546
12: 2 At h time he sent a servant to the tenants NIG
Lk 10: 2 He told them, "The h is plentiful, 2546
10: 2 Ask the Lord of the h, therefore, 2546
10: 2 to send out workers into his h field. 2546
20:10 At h time he sent a servant to the tenants NIG
Jn 4:35 'Four months more and then the h'? 2546
4:35 They are ripe for h. 2546
Ro 1:13 in order that I might have a h among you, 2843
1Co 9:10 to do so in the hope of sharing in the h. NIG
9:11 is it too much if we reap a material h 2545
2Co 9:10 of seed and will enlarge the h 1163
Gal 6: 9 at the proper time we will reap a h if we do 2545
Heb 12:11 it produces a h of righteousness and peace 2843
Jas 3:18 Peacemakers who sow in peace raise a h 2843
Rev 14:15 for the h of the earth is ripe." 2546

HARVESTED (5) [HARVEST]

Isa 33: 4 O nations, is h as by young locusts; 665
Jer 40:12 And they h an abundance of wine 665
Am 7: 1 after the king's share had been h and just as 1600
Hag 1: 6 You have planted much, but have h little. 995
Rev 14:16 and the earth was h. 2545

HARVESTERS (8) [HARVEST]

Ru 2: 3 to glean in the fields behind the h. 7917
2: 4 from Bethlehem and greeted the h, 7917
2: 5 Boaz asked the foreman of his h, 7917
2: 7 among the sheaves behind the h.' 7917
2:14 When she sat down with the h, 7917
Mt 13:30 At that time I will tell the h: 2547
13:39 and the h are angels. 2547
Jas 5: 4 The cries of the h have reached the ears of 2545

HARVESTING (6) [HARVEST]

Lev 25:15 of the number of years left for h crops. 9311
Dt 24:19 When you are h in your field 7907+7917
Ru 2: 9 Watch the field where the men are h, 7917
2:21 until they finish h all my grain.' " 7907
1Sa 6:13 of Beth Shemesh were h their wheat 7907+7917
Mt 25:24 h where you have not sown and gathering 2545

HARVESTS (6) [HARVEST]

Dt 32:22 It will devour the earth and its h 3292
Ru 2:23 until the barley and wheat h were finished. 7907
Isa 16: 9 and over your h have been stilled. 7907
17: 5 a reaper gathers the standing grain and h 7917
Jer 5:17 They will devour your h and food, 7907
Jn 4:36 even now he h the crop for eternal life, 5251

HAS (266 of 2407) [HAVE] See Index of Articles Etc. for an Exhaustive Listing (See Introduction, page x)

Ge 31:32 But if you find anyone who h your gods, 6640
38:23 Then Judah said, "Let her keep what she h, 4200
Ex 21: 3 but if he h a wife when he comes, 1251
21: 8 He h no right to sell her to foreigners, 5440
21:16 still h him when he is caught must be 928+3338
22: 3 but if he h nothing, he must be sold 4200
22:19 h sexual relations with an animal 6640+8886
32:24 I told them, 'Whoever h any gold jewelry, 4200
Lev 11:34 but h water on it from such a pot is unclean, 995
13: 2 "When anyone h a swelling or a rash or 2118
13: 9 anyone h an infectious skin disease, 928+2118
13:18 "When someone h a boil on his skin 928+2118
13:24 "When someone h a burn on his skin and 2118
13:29 If a man or woman h a sore on the head 928+2118
13:38 a man or woman h white spots on the skin, 2118
13:42 if he h a reddish-white sore on his bald head 2118
13:46 as he h the infection he remains unclean. 928
13:52 that h the contamination in it, because 2118
13:57 and whatever h the mildew must be burned 928
14:32 for anyone who h an infectious skin disease 928
15: 2 'When any man h a bodily discharge, 2118
15:16 " 'When a man h an emission of semen, 3655
15:17 Any clothing or leather that h semen 2118
15:19 a woman h her regular flow of blood, 2118
15:25 a woman h a discharge of blood 2307+2308
20:15 h sexual relations with an animal, 5989+8888
20:18 h sexual relations with her, 906+1655+6872
21: 3 on him since she h no husband— 2118+4200
21:17 who h a defect may come near to offer 928+2118
21:18 No man who h any defect may come near: 928
21:20 or who h any eye defect, 928
21:20 or who h festering or running sores NIH
21:21 the priest who h any defect is to come near 928
21:21 He h a defect; 928
22: 4 h an infectious skin disease or 7665
22: 4 or by anyone who h an emission of semen, 3655
22:13 widow or is divorced, yet h no children, 4200
25:26 a man h no one to redeem it for him 2118+4200
Nu 5: 2 anyone who h an infectious skin disease 7665
5: 8 But if that person h no close relative 4200
14:24 my servant Caleb h a different spirit 2118+6640
24:16 h knowledge from the Most High, 1981+3359
27: 9 If he h no daughter, 4200
27:10 If he h no brothers, 4200
35:17 anyone h a stone in his hand that could kill, 928
35:18 Or if anyone h a wooden object in his hand 928
Dt 14: 9 you may eat any that h fins and scales. 4200
15:21 If an animal h a defect, is lame or blind, 928+2118
15:21 is lame or blind, or h any serious flaw, NIH
17: 1 an ox or a sheep that h any defect or flaw 2118
21:15 If a man h two wives, 2118+4200
21:17 giving him a double share of all he h. 4200+5162
21:18 If a man h a stubborn and rebellious 2118+4200
26:19 He h declared that he will set you in praise, NIH
27:21 h sexual relations with any animal." 6640+8886
28:55 It will be all he h left because of 4200
Jdg 18:14 that one of these houses h an ephod, 928+3780
Ru 4: 4 For no one h the right to do it 1457[S]
4:17 women living there said, "Naomi h a son." 3528
1Sa 2: 8 with princes and h them inherit a throne 5706
2Sa 6:12 of Obed-Edom and everything he h, 4200
14:30 and he h barley there. 4200
15: 4 Then everyone who h a complaint 2118+4200
17: 5 so we can hear what he h to say." 928
2Ki 4: 2 "Your servant h nothing there at all," 4200
4:14 she h no son and her husband is old." 4200
2Ch 25: 8 God h the power to help or to overthrow." 928+3780
Job 1:10 and his household and everything he h? 4200
1:11 and strike everything he h, 4200
1:12 then, everything he h is in your hands, 4200
2: 4 "A man will give all he h for his own life. 4200
11: 6 for true wisdom h two sides. 4200
18:17 he h no name in the land. 4200
18:19 He h no offspring or descendants 4200
20:23 When he h filled his belly, 2118
38:37 Who h the wisdom to count the clouds? 928
41:11 Who h a claim against me that I must pay? 7709
41:26 The sword that reaches him h no effect, 7756
42: 8 what is right, as my servant Job h." NIH
Ps 41: 1 Blessed is he who h regard for the weak; 8505
49:20 A man who h riches without understanding 928
73:25 And earth h nothing I desire besides you. 928
103:13 As a father h compassion on his children, 8163
103:13 the LORD h compassion on those who fear 8163
109:11 May a creditor seize all he h; 4200
147: 5 his understanding h no limit. 4200
Pr 6: 7 It h no commander, no overseer or ruler, 4200
14:26 the LORD h a secure fortress, 928
18:21 The tongue h the power of life and death, 928
21:20 but a foolish man devours all he h. 5647[S]
23:24 he who h a wise son delights in him. 3528
23:29 Who h woe? 4200
23:29 Who h sorrow? 4200
23:29 Who h strife? 4200
23:29 Who h complaints? 4200
23:29 Who h needless bruises? 4200
23:29 Who h bloodshot eyes? 4200
24:20 for the evil man h no future hope, 2118+4200
30:15 "The leech h two daughters. 'Give!' 4200
31:11 Her husband h full confidence in her 1053+4213
Ecc 1: 8 The eye never h enough of seeing, 8425
1:16 in wisdom more than anyone who h ruled 2118
5:10 Whoever loves money never h money enough; 8425
5:14 when he h a son there is nothing left for him 3528
6: 5 it h more rest than does that man— 4200
6: 8 What advantage h a wise man over a fool? 4200
9: 4 Anyone who is among the living h hope— 3780
SS 4: 2 Each h its twin; not one of them is alone. 9298
6: 6 Each h its twin, not one of them is alone. 9298
Isa 2:12 The LORD Almighty h a day in store 4200
10: 7 this is not what he h in mind; 3108+4222
22: 5 h a day of tumult and trampling and terror 4200
28: 2 the Lord h one who is powerful and strong. 4200
34: 6 For the LORD h a sacrifice in Bozrah and 4200
34: 8 For the LORD h a day of vengeance, 4200
45: 9 Does your work say, 'He h no hands'? 4200
49:10 He who h compassion on them 8163
50:10 who h no light, 4200
54: 1 of her who h a husband," 1249
54:10 says the LORD, who h compassion on you. 8163
Jer 6:25 for the enemy h a sword, 4200
17: 8 It h no worries in a year of drought 1793
23:28 the prophet who h a dream tell his dream, 907
23:28 the one who h my word speak it faithfully. 907
23:28 what h straw to do with grain?" 4200
49: 1 "H Israel no sons? 4200
49: 1 H she no heirs? 4200
49:31 "a nation that h neither gates nor bars; 4200
50:25 the Sovereign LORD Almighty h work to do 4200
Eze 9: 6 but do not touch anyone who h the mark. 6584
18:10 "Suppose he h a violent son, 3528
18:14 "But suppose this son h a son who sees all 3528
33:13 none of the righteous things he h done will NIH
Hos 4: 1 because the LORD h a charge to bring 4200
8: 7 stalk h no head; it will produce no flour. 4200
12: 2 The LORD h a charge to bring 4200
Joel 1: 6 it h the teeth of a lion, the fangs of a lioness. 4200
Am 3: 4 a lion roar in the thicket when he h no prey? 4200
Jnh 4:11 But Nineveh h more than a hundred 928+3780
Mic 6: 2 For the LORD h a case against his people; 4200
Zec 2: 8 "After he h honored me and has sent me NIH
Mal 1:14 the cheat who h an acceptable male 3780
Mt 5:23 that your brother h something against you, 2400
8:20 the Son of Man h no place to lay his head." 2400
9: 6 Son of Man h authority on earth to forgive sins...." 2400
11:15 He who h ears, let him hear. 2400
11:18 and they say, 'He h a demon.' 2400
12:11 of you h a sheep and it falls into a pit on 2400
13: 9 He who h ears, let him hear." 2400
13:12 Whoever h will be given more, 2400
13:12 even what he h will be taken from him. 2400
13:21 he h no root, he lasts only a short time. 2400
13:43 He who h ears, let him hear. 2400
16:27 according to what he h done. 4552
25:28 and give it to the one who h the ten talents. 2400
25:29 For everyone who h will be given more, 2400
25:29 even what he h will be taken from him. 2400
Mk 2:10 Son of Man h authority on earth to forgive sins...." 2400
3:26 he cannot stand; his end h come. 2400
3:30 "He h an evil spirit." 2400
4: 9 Then Jesus said, "He who h ears to hear, 2400
4:23 If anyone h ears to hear, let him hear." 2400

Mk 4:25 Whoever **h** will be given more; 2400
4:25 even what *he* **h** will be taken from him." 2400
Lk 1:61 among your relatives who **h** that name." *2813*
3:11 should share with him who **h** none, 2400
3:11 the one who **h** food should do the same." 2400
5:24 Son of Man **h** authority on earth to forgive sins…." 2400
7:33 and you say, *'He* **h** a demon.' 2400
8:8 "He who **h** ears to hear, let him hear." 2400
8:18 Whoever **h** will be given more; 2400
8:18 what he thinks *he* **h** will be taken from him. 2400
9:58 the Son of Man **h** no place to lay his head." 2400
11:5 "Suppose one of you **h** a friend, 2400
12:5 **h** power to throw you into hell. 2400
14:28 to see if *he* **h enough** money to *1650*+2400
14:33 who does not give up everything he **h** cannot be my disciple. *3836*+*5639*
14:35 "He who **h** ears to hear, let him hear." 2400
15:4 "Suppose one of you **h** a hundred sheep 2400
15:8 a woman **h** ten silver coins and loses one. 2400
15:27 'Your brother **h come,'** he replied, 2457
15:27 the fattened calf because *he* **h** him **back** safe *655*
19:24 and give it *to* the one who **h** ten minas.' 2400
19:25 " 'Sir,' they said, *'he already* **h** ten!' 2400
19:26 'I tell you that to everyone who **h,** 2400
19:26 but as for the one who **h** nothing, 2400
19:26 even what *he* **h** will be taken away. 2400
Jn 3:36 Whoever believes in the Son **h** eternal life, 2400
4:44 a prophet **h** no honor in his own country.) 2400
5:24 and believes him who sent me **h** eternal life 2400
5:26 For as the Father **h** life in himself, 2400
6:47 he who believes **h** everlasting life. 2400
6:54 and drinks my blood **h** eternal life, 2400
11:10 he stumbles, for he **h** no light." *1639*
14:21 Whoever **h** my commands and obeys them, 2400
14:30 *He* **h** no **hold** on me, 2400
15:13 Greater love **h** no one than this, 2400
16:21 **h** pain because her time has come; 2400
Ac 23:17 *he* **h** something to tell him." 2400
23:18 to you *because he* **h** something to tell you." 2400
Ro 6:9 death no longer **h mastery over** him. *3259*
8:24 Who hopes for what *he already* **h?** *1063*[S]
9:18 Therefore God **h mercy on** whom he wants *1796*
12:4 of *us* **h** one body with many members, 2400
1Co 5:1 A man **h** his father's wife. 2400
6:1 *If* any of you **h** a dispute with another, 2400
7:7 But each man **h** his own gift from God; 2400
7:7 one **h** this gift, another has that. *NIG*
7:7 one has this gift, another **h** that. *NIG*
7:12 If any brother **h** a wife who is not a believer 2400
7:13 a woman **h** a husband who is not a believer 2400
7:37 who is under no compulsion but **h** control 2400
11:14 that if a man **h long hair,** *3150*
11:15 but that if a woman **h long hair,** *3150*
14:26 you come together, everyone **h** a hymn, 2400
16:10 see to it that *he* **h** nothing to fear while he is *1181*
16:12 but he will go when *he* **h the opportunity.** *2320*
2Co 8:12 gift is acceptable according to what *one* **h,** 2400
Gal 4:27 of the desolate woman than *of* her who **h** 2400
Eph 5:5 **h** any inheritance in the kingdom of Christ 2400
Php 1:12 that **what h happened to** me has really served *2848*+*3836*
1:12 to me **h** really **served** to advance the gospel. *2262*
1Ti 4:8 but godliness **h** value for all things, *1639*
5:4 But if a widow **h** children or grandchildren, 2400
5:16 If any woman who is a believer **h** widows 2400
6:20 **what h been entrusted to** *your* **care.** *4146*
2Ti 4:10 Crescens **h** gone to Galatia, *NIG*
Phm 1:7 Your love **h given** *me* great joy 2400
Heb 3:3 the builder of a house **h** greater honor than 2400
3:12 brothers, that none of you **h** a sinful, *1639*
3:15 **As h just been said:** *1877*+*3306*+*3836*
5:3 This is why *he* **h** to offer sacrifices *4053*
6:12 inherit **what h been promised.** *2039*+*3836*
7:24 *he* **h** a permanent priesthood. 2400
10:36 you will receive what he **h promised.** *2039*
Jas 2:14 a man claims to have faith but **h** no deeds? 2400
2Pe 3:4 on **as it h** since the beginning of creation." *4048*
1Jn 2:16 **what he h and does—** *1050*
2:23 No one who denies the Son **h** the Father; 2400
2:23 whoever acknowledges the Son **h** 2400
3:3 Everyone who **h** this hope 2400
3:15 that no murderer **h** eternal life in him. 2400
3:17 If anyone **h** material possessions 2400
3:17 brother in need but **h no pity** *3091*+*3836*+*5073*
4:16 we know and rely on the love God **h** for us. 2400
4:18 because fear **h** to do with punishment. 2400
5:10 the Son of God **h** this testimony in his heart. 2400
5:12 He who **h** the Son has life; 2400
5:12 He who has the Son **h** life; 2400
5:20 We know also that the Son of God **h come** 2457
2Jn 1:9 the teaching **h** both the Father and the Son. 2400
Rev 2:7 He who **h** an ear, let him hear 2400
2:11 He who **h** an ear, let him hear 2400
2:12 These are the words of him who **h** the sharp, 2400
2:17 He who **h** an ear, let him hear 2400
2:29 He who **h** an ear, let him hear 2400
3:6 He who **h** an ear, let him hear 2400
3:13 He who **h** an ear, let him hear 2400
3:22 He who **h** an ear, let him hear 2400
13:9 He who **h** an ear, let him hear. 2400
13:18 *If* anyone **h** insight, 2400
17:7 which **h** the seven heads and ten horns. 2400
19:12 *He* **h** a name written on him 2400
19:16 and on his thigh *he* **h** this name written: 2400
20:6 The second death **h** no power over them, 2400
22:12 to everyone according to what he **h** done. *1639*

HASADIAH (1)

1Ch 3:20 Ohel, Berekiah, **H** and Jushab-Hesed. 2878

HASENUAH (KJV) See HASSENUAH

HASHABIAH (15)

1Ch 6:45 the son of **H,** 3116
9:14 the son of Azrikam, the son of **H,** 3116
25:3 Zeri, Jeshaiah, Shimei, **H** and Mattithiah, 3117
25:19 the twelfth to **H,** his sons and relatives, 12 3116
26:30 From the Hebronites: **H** and his relatives— 3117
27:17 **H** son of Kemuel; 3116
2Ch 35:9 his brothers, and **H,** Jeiel and Jozabad, 3117
Ezr 8:19 and **H,** together with Jeshaiah from 3116
8:24 **H** and ten of their brothers, 3116
Ne 3:17 **H,** ruler of half the district of Keilah, 3116
10:11 Mica, Rehob, **H,** 3116
11:15 the son of Azrikam, the son of **H,** 3116
11:22 the son of **H,** the son of Mattaniah, 3116
12:21 of Hilkiah's, **H;** of Jedaiah's, Nethanel. 3116
12:24 And the leaders of the Levites were **H,** 3116

HASHABNAH (1)

Ne 10:25 Rehum, **H,** Maaseiah, 3118

HASHABNEIAH (2)

Ne 3:10 Hattush son of **H** made repairs next to him. 3119
9:5 Jeshua, Kadmiel, Bani, **H,** Sherebiah, 3119

HASHBADDANAH (1)

Ne 8:4 Hashum, **H,** Zechariah and Meshullam. 3111

HASHEM (1)

1Ch 11:34 the sons of **H** the Gizonite, 2244

HASHMONAH (2)

Nu 33:29 They left Mithcah and camped at **H.** 3135
33:30 They left **H** and camped at Moseroth. 3135

HASHUB (KJV) See HASSHUB

HASHUBAH (1)

1Ch 3:20 There were also five others: **H,** Ohel, 3112

HASHUM (5)

Ezr 2:19 of **H** 223 3130
10:33 From the descendants of **H:** 3130
Ne 7:22 of **H** 328 3130
8:4 Mishael, Malkijah, **H,** Hashbaddanah, 3130
10:18 Hodiah, **H,** Bezai, 3130

HASHUPHA (KJV) See HASUPHA

HASN'T (7) [HAVE, NOT]

Ge 38:21 "There **h** been any shrine prostitute here," 4202
38:22 'There **h** been any shrine prostitute here.' " 4202
Nu 12:2 "**H** he also spoken through us?" 4202
1Sa 20:27 "Why **h** the son of Jesse come to the meal, 4202
2Sa 10:3 **H** David sent them to you to explore the city 4202
Ac 9:21 *h he* **come** here to take them as prisoners *AIT*
22:25 **h** even **been found guilty?"** *185*

HASRAH (1)

2Ch 34:22 the son of **H,** keeper of the wardrobe. 2897

HASSENAAH (1)

Ne 3:3 The Fish Gate was rebuilt by the sons of **H.** 2189

HASSENUAH (2)

1Ch 9:7 the son of Hodaviah, the son of **H;** 2190
Ne 11:9 of **H** was over the Second District of 2190

HASSHUB (5)

1Ch 9:14 Shemaiah son of **H,** the son of Azrikam, 3121
Ne 3:11 Malkijah son of Harim and **H** son 3121
3:23 and **H** made repairs in front of their house; 3121
10:23 Hoshea, Hananiah, **H,** 3121
11:15 Shemaiah son of **H,** the son of Azrikam, 3121

HASSOPHERETH (1)

Ezr 2:55 the descendants of Sotai, **H,** Peruda, 2191

HASTE (7) [HASTEN, HASTILY, HASTY]

Ex 12:11 Eat it in **h;** it is the LORD's Passover. 2906
Dt 16:3 because you left Egypt in **h—** 2906
Ps 68:12 "Kings and armies **flee in h;** 5610+5610
Pr 21:5 to profit as surely as **h** leads to poverty. 237
29:20 Do you see a man *who* speaks **in h?** 237
Isa 52:12 But you will not leave in **h** or go in flight; 2906
Jer 46:5 *They* **flee in h** without looking back, 4960+5674

HASTEN (5) [HASTE]

Ps 70:1 **H,** O God, to save me; NIH
119:60 *I will* **h** and not delay 2590
Isa 5:19 *let him* **h** his work so we may see it. 2590
49:17 Your sons **h** back, 4554
55:5 nations that do not know you *will* **h** to you, 8132

HASTEN (KJV) See also HURRIED, HURRY, RUN, SWIFTLY

HASTILY (1) [HASTE]

Pr 25:8 do not bring **h** to court, 4554

HASTY (3) [HASTE]

Pr 19:2 nor *to be* **h** and miss the way. 237+928+8079
Ecc 5:2 *do not be* **h** in your heart to utter anything 4554
1Ti 5:22 Do not be **h** in the laying on of hands, *5441*

HASUPHA (2)

Ezr 2:43 the descendants of Ziha, **H,** Tabbaoth, 3102
Ne 7:46 the descendants of Ziha, **H,** Tabbaoth, 3102

HATACH (KJV) See HATHACH

HATCH (2) [HATCHED, HATCHES]

Isa 34:15 *she will* **h** them, and care for her young 1324
59:5 *They* **h** the eggs of vipers and spin 1324

HATCHED (1) [HATCH]

Isa 59:5 and when one is broken, an adder **is h.** 1324

HATCHES (1) [HATCH]

Jer 17:11 Like a partridge *that* **h eggs** it did not lay is 1842

HATCHETS (1) [HATCHET]

Ps 74:6 the carved paneling with their axes and **h.** 3965

HATE (80) [GOD-HATERS, HATED, HATES, HATING, HATRED]

Ex 18:21 trustworthy men *who* **h** dishonest gain— 8533
20:5 and fourth generation of *those who* **h** me, 8533
Lev 19:17 " *'Do* not **h** your brother in your heart. 8533
26:17 *those who* **h** you will rule over you, 8533
Dt 5:9 and fourth generation of *those who* **h** me, 8533
7:10 But *those who* **h** him he will repay 8533
7:10 to repay to their face *those who* **h** him. 8533
7:15 but he will inflict them on all *who* **h** you. 8533
30:7 on your enemies who **h** and persecute you. 8533
32:41 and repay *those who* **h** me. 8533
Jdg 11:7 "Didn't you **h** me and drive me 8533
14:16 on him, sobbing, *"You* **h** me! 8533
2Sa 19:6 You love *those who* **h** you 8533
19:6 and **h** those who love you. 8533
1Ki 22:8 but I **h** him because he never prophesies 8533
2Ch 18:7 but I **h** him because he never prophesies 8533
19:2 and love *those who* **h** the LORD? 8533
Ps 5:5 *you* **h** all who do wrong. 8533
25:19 and how fiercely *they* **h** me! 8533+8534
31:6 *I* **h** those who cling to worthless idols; 8533
35:19 let not *those who* **h** me 8533
36:2 to detect or **h** his sin. 8533
38:19 *those who* **h** me without reason 8533
45:7 You love righteousness and **h** wickedness; 8533
50:17 You **h** my instruction and cast my words 8533
69:4 *Those who* **h** me without reason outnumber 8533
69:14 deliver me from *those who* **h** me, 8533
81:15 *Those who* **h** the LORD would cringe 8533
97:10 Let those who love the LORD **h** evil, 8533
101:3 The deeds of faithless men *I* **h;** 8533
105:25 whose hearts he turned to **h** his people, 8533
119:104 therefore *I* **h** every wrong path. 8533
119:113 *I* **h** double-minded men, 8533
119:128 *I* **h** every wrong path. 8533
119:163 *I* **h** and abhor falsehood 8533
120:6 among *those who* **h** peace. 8533
129:5 all *who* **h** Zion be turned back in shame. 8533
139:21 *Do I* not **h** those who hate you, O LORD, 8533
139:21 Do I not hate *those who* **h** you, O LORD, 8533
Pr 1:22 in mockery and fools **h** knowledge? 8533
8:13 To fear the LORD is *to* **h** evil; 8533
8:13 *I* **h** pride and arrogance, 8533
8:36 all *who* **h** me love death." 8533
9:8 Do not rebuke a mocker *or he will* **h** you; 8533
13:5 The righteous **h** what is false, 8533
25:17 too much of you, and *he will* **h** you. 8533
29:10 Bloodthirsty men **h** a man of integrity 8533
Ecc 3:8 a time to love and a time to **h,** 8533
9:1 no man knows whether love or **h** awaits him 8534
9:6 their **h** and their jealousy have long since 8534
Isa 61:8 I **h** robbery and iniquity. 8533
66:5 "Your brothers *who* **h** you, 8533
Jer 12:8 She roars at me; therefore *I* **h** her. 8533
44:4 'Do not do this detestable thing that *I* **h!'** 8533
Eze 23:28 I am about to hand you over to those *you* **h,** 8533
35:6 Since *you did* not **h** bloodshed, 8533
Am 5:10 *you* **h** the one who reproves in court 8533
5:15 **H** evil, love good; 8533
5:21 *"I* **h,** I despise your religious feasts; 8533
Mic 3:2 *you who* **h** good and love evil; 8533
Zec 8:17 *I* **h** all this," declares the LORD. 8533
Mal 2:16 *"I* **h** divorce," says the LORD God 8533
2:16 "and I **h** a man's covering himself NIH
Mt 5:43 'Love your neighbor and **h** your enemy.' *3631*

Mt 6:24 Either *he will* **h** the one and love the other, *3631*
10:22 All men *will* **h** *you* because of me, *1639+3631*
24:10 the faith and will betray and **h** each other, *3631*
Mk 13:13 All men *will* **h** *you* because of me, *1639+3631*
Lk 1:71 and from the hand of all who **h** us— *3631*
6:22 Blessed are you when men **h** you, *3631*
6:27 do good *to* those who **h** you, *3631*
14:26 to me and *does* not **h** his father and mother, *3631*
16:13 Either *he will* **h** the one and love the other, *3631*
21:17 All men *will* **h** *you* because of me. *1639+3631*
Jn 7:7 The world cannot **h** you, *3631*
Ro 7:15 I do not do, but what *I* **h** I do. *3631*
12:9 **H** what is evil; cling to what is good. *696*
Rev 2:6 *You* **h** the practices of the Nicolaitans, *3631*
2:6 of the Nicolaitans, which I also **h.** *3631*
17:16 The beast and the ten horns you saw *will* **h** *3631*

HATED (29) [HATE]

Ge 37:4 *they* **h** him and could not speak a kind word 8533
37:5 *they* **h** him all the more. 8533
37:8 And *they* **h** him all the more because 8533
Dt 9:28 and because he **h** them, 8534
Jdg 15:2 "I was so sure *you* **thoroughly h** her," 8533+8533
2Sa 13:15 Then Amnon **h** her *with* intense hatred. 8533
13:15 In fact, *he* **h** her more than he had loved her. 8533
13:22 he **h** Amnon because he had disgraced his sister Tamar. 8533
Est 9:1 the upper hand over *those who* **h** them. 8533
9:5 did what they pleased to *those who* **h** them. 8533
Pr 1:29 Since *they* **h** knowledge and did not choose 8533
5:12 You will say, "How *I* **h** discipline! 8533
14:17 and a crafty man **is h.** 8533
Ecc 2:17 So *I* **h** life, because the work that is done 8533
2:18 I **h** all the things I had toiled for under 8533
Isa 60:15 "Although you have been forsaken and **h,** 8533
Eze 16:37 those you loved as well as those *you* **h.** 8533
Hos 9:15 wickedness in Gilgal, *I* **h** them there. 8533
Mal 1:3 but Esau *I have* **h,** 8533
Mt 24:9 you will be **h** by all nations because of me. *3631*
Lk 19:14 "But his subjects **h** him and sent *3631*
Jn 15:18 keep in mind that *it* **h** me first. *3631*
15:24 and yet *they have* **h** both me and my Father. *3631*
15:25 '*They* **h** me without reason.' *3631*
17:14 and the world *has* **h** them, *3631*
Ro 9:13 "Jacob I loved, but Esau *I* **h."** *3631*
Eph 5:29 After all, no one ever **h** his own body, *3631*
Tit 3:3 being **h** and hating one another. *5144*
Heb 1:9 You have loved righteousness and **h** wickedness; *3631*

HATEFUL (KJV) See DESTESTABLE, HATE, HATED

HATES (27) [HATE]

Ex 23:5 the donkey of *someone who* **h** you fallen 8533
Dt 1:27 "The LORD **h** us; so he brought us out 8534
12:31 kinds of detestable things the LORD **h.** 8533
16:22 for these the LORD your God **h.** 8533
19:11 But if a man **h** his neighbor and lies in wait 8533
Job 34:17 *Can he* **h** justice govern? 8533
Ps 11:5 and those who love violence his soul **h.** 8533
Pr 6:16 There are six things the LORD **h,** 8533
12:1 but *he who* **h** correction is stupid. 8533
13:24 He who spares the rod **h** his son, 8533
15:10 *he who* **h** correction will die. 8533
15:27 but *he who* **h** bribes will live. 8533
26:28 A lying tongue **h** those it hurts, 8533
28:16 but *he who* **h** ill-gotten gain will enjoy 8533
Isa 1:14 and your appointed feasts my soul **h.** 8533
Jn 3:20 Everyone who does evil **h** the light, *3631*
7:7 but *it* **h** me because I testify *3631*
12:25 while the man who **h** his life in this world *3631*
15:18 "If the world **h** you, keep in mind that *3631*
15:19 That is why the world **h** you. *3631*
15:23 He who **h** me hates my Father as well. *3631*
15:23 He who hates me **h** my Father as well. *3631*
1Jn 2:9 but **h** his brother is still in the darkness. *3631*
2:11 But whoever **h** his brother is in the darkness *3631*
3:13 my brothers, if the world **h** you. *3631*
3:15 Anyone who **h** his brother is a murderer, *3631*
4:20 "I love God," yet **h** his brother, he is a liar. *3631*

HATHACH (3)

Est 4:5 Then Esther summoned **H,** 2251
4:6 So **H** went out to Mordecai in 2251
4:9 **H** went back and reported 2251

HATHATH (1)

1Ch 4:13 The sons of Othniel: **H** and Meonothai. 3171

HATING (2) [HATE]

Tit 3:3 being hated and **h** one another. *3631*
Jude 1:23 **h** even the clothing stained *3631*

HATIPHA (2)

Ezr 2:54 Neziah and **H** 2640
Ne 7:56 Neziah and **H** 2640

HATITA (2)

Ezr 2:42 of Shallum, Ater, Talmon, Akkub, **H** 2638
Ne 7:45 of Shallum, Ater, Talmon, Akkub, **H** 2638

HATRED (11) [HATE]

2Sa 13:15 Then Amnon hated her with intense **h.** 8534
Ps 109:3 With words of **h** they surround me; 8534
109:5 and **h** for my friendship. 8534
139:22 *I* **have** nothing but **h** *for* them; 8533+8534
Pr 10:12 **H** stirs up dissension, 8534
10:18 He who conceals his **h** has lying lips, 8534
15:17 a fattened calf with **h.** 8534
Eze 23:29 They will deal with you in **h** 8534
35:11 and jealousy you showed in your **h** of them 8534
Gal 5:20 **h,** discord, jealousy, fits of rage, *2397*
Jas 4:4 that friendship with the world is **h** *2397*

HATTAAVAH See KIBROTH HATTAAVAH

HATTICON See HAZER HATTICON

HATTIL (2)

Ezr 2:57 **H,** Pokereth-Hazzebaim 2639
Ne 7:59 **H,** Pokereth-Hazzebaim 2639

HATTUSH (5)

1Ch 3:22 **H,** Igal, Bariah, Neariah and Shaphat— 2637
Ezr 8:2 of the descendants of David, **H** 2637
Ne 3:10 and **H** son of Hashabneiah made repairs 2637
10:4 **H,** Shebaniah, Malluch, 2637
12:2 Amariah, Malluch, **H,** 2637

HAUGHTINESS (1) [HAUGHTY]

Jer 48:29 and arrogance and the **h** *of* her heart. 8124

HAUGHTY (15) [HAUGHTINESS]

2Sa 22:28 your eyes are on the **h** to bring them low. 8123
Job 41:34 He looks down on all *that* are **h;** 1469
Ps 10:5 he is **h** and your laws are far from him; 5294
18:27 but bring low *those* whose eyes *are* **h.** 8123
101:5 whoever has **h** eyes and a proud heart, 1468
131:1 O LORD, my eyes are not **h;** 8123
Pr 6:17 **h** eyes, a lying tongue, hands 8123
16:18 a **h** spirit before a fall. 1470
21:4 **H** eyes and a proud heart, 8124
30:13 so **h,** whose glances are so disdainful; 8123
Isa 3:16 "The women of Zion *are* **h,** 1467
10:12 the willful pride of his heart and the **h** look 8124
13:11 I will put an end to the arrogance of the **h** 2294
Eze 16:50 *They were* **h** and did detestable things 1467
Zep 3:11 Never again *will you be* **h** on my holy hill. 1467

HAUL (3)

1Ki 5:9 My men *will* **h** them **down** from Lebanon 3718
Eze 32:3 and *they will* **h** you **up** in my net. 6590
Jn 21:6 they were unable *to* **h** the net **in** because of *1816*

HAUNT (8) [HAUNTS]

Ps 44:19 and made us a **h** *for* jackals and covered us 5226
Isa 34:13 She will become a **h** *for* jackals, 5659
Jer 9:11 Jerusalem a heaps of ruins, a **h** *of* jackals; 5061
10:22 towns of Judah desolate, a **h** *of* jackals. 5061
49:33 "Hazor will become a **h** *of* jackals, 5061
51:37 a **h** *of* jackals, an object of horror 5061
Rev 18:2 She has become a home for demons and a **h** *5871*
18:2 a **h** for every unclean and detestable bird. *5871*

HAUNTS (3) [HAUNT]

Ps 74:20 because **h** *of* violence fill the dark places of 5661
SS 4:8 from the lions' dens and the **mountain h** *of* 2215
Isa 35:7 In the **h** where jackals once lay, 5659

HAURAN (2)

Eze 47:16 which is on the border of **H.** 2588
47:18 the boundary will run between **H** 2588

HAVE (827 of 4313) [HAD, HASN'T, HAVE, HAVEN'T, HAVING] See Index of Articles Etc. for an Exhaustive Listing (See Introduction page x)

Ge 13:8 not **h** any quarreling between you and me, 2118
14:24 *Let* them **h** their share." 4374
16:11 "You are now with child and *you will* **h** 3528
18:10 and Sarah your wife will **h** a son." 4200
18:12 *will* I *now* **h** this pleasure?" 2118+4200
18:13 '*Will I* really **h a child,** 3528
18:14 and Sarah will **h** a son." 4200
19:5 to us so that *we can* **h sex with** them." 3359
19:8 I **h** two daughters who have never slept with 4200
19:12 "Do you **h** anyone else here— 4200
20:17 so *they could* **h children** again, 3528
24:14 that *I may* **h a drink,'** and she says, 'Drink, 9272
24:25 "We **h** plenty of straw and fodder, 6640
24:33 **what I h to say."** 1821
25:30 "Quick, **let** me **h** some of that red stew! 4358
26:10 the men **might well h** slept with your wife, 3869+5071
27:38 "Do you **h** only one blessing, my father? 4200
31:14 "*Do* we still **h** any share in the inheritance 4200
31:29 I **h** the power to harm you; 3780+4200
32:5 I **h** cattle and donkeys, sheep and 2118+4200
33:9 Esau said, "I *already* **h** plenty, 3780+4200
33:9 Keep what you **h** for yourself." 4200
33:11 to me and I **h** all I need." 3780+4200
35:17 "Don't be afraid, for you **h** another son." 4200
43:7 '*Do* you **h** another brother?' 3780+4200
44:9 If any of your servants is found to **h** it, 907
44:10 to **h** it will become my slave; 907
44:16 the one who was found to **h** the cup." 928+3338
44:17 to **h** the cup will become my slave. 928+3338
44:19 '*Do* you **h** a father or a brother?' 3780+4200
44:20 we answered, 'We **h** an aged father, 3780+4200
45:1 **"H** everyone **leave** my presence!" 3655
45:10 your flocks and herds, and all you **h.** 4200
47:4 and your servants' flocks **h** no pasture. 4200
Ex 9:19 and everything you **h** in the field to a place 4200
10:5 They will devour what little you **h** left after 4200
10:25 "You must allow us to **h** sacrifices 928+3338
12:39 and *did* not **h time** to prepare food 3523+4538
16:16 for each person you **h** in your tent.'" 889+4200
16:18 he who gathered much *did* not **h too much,** 6369
16:18 he who gathered little *did* not **h too little.** 2893
18:16 Whenever they **h** a dispute, 2118+4200
20:3 You *shall* **h** no other gods before me. 2118+4200
23:7 **H nothing to do** with a false charge and do 8178
25:20 *to* **h** their wings spread upward, 2118
27:9 be a hundred cubits long and is to **h** curtains 4200
28:1 **"H** Aaron your brother **brought** to you 278
28:7 *to* **h** two shoulder pieces attached to 2118+4200
33:19 *I will* **h mercy** *on* whom I will have mercy, 2858
33:19 I will have mercy on whom *I will* **h mercy,** 2858
33:19 and *I will* **h compassion** 8163
33:19 on whom *I will* **h compassion.** 8163
35:5 From what you **h,** 907
Lev 7:33 fat of the fellowship offering *shall* **h** 2118+4200
11:9 you may eat any that **h** fins and scales. 4200
11:10 or streams that do not **h** fins and scales— 4200
11:12 the water that does not **h** fins and scales is 4200
11:21 those that **h** jointed legs for hopping on 4200
11:23 that **h** four legs you are to detest. 4200
14:41 **h** all the inside walls of the house **scraped** 7909
18:6 close relative to **h sexual relations.** 1655+6872
18:7 *do* not **h relations with** her. 1655+6872
18:8 " '*Do* not **h sexual relations with** 1655+6872
18:9 " '*Do* not **h sexual relations with** 1655+6872
18:10 " '*Do* not **h sexual relations with** 1655+6872
18:11 " '*Do* not **h sexual relations with** 1655+6872
18:12 " '*Do* not **h sexual relations with** 1655+6872
18:13 " '*Do* not **h sexual relations with** 1655+6872
18:14 " '*Do* not **dishonor** your father's brother **by approaching his wife to h sexual relations;** 1655+6872
18:15 " '*Do* not **h sexual relations with** 1655+6872
18:15 *do* not **h relations with** her. 1655+6872
18:16 " '*Do* not **h sexual relations with** 1655+6872
18:17 " '*Do* not **h sexual relations with** 1655+6872
18:17 *Do* not **h sexual relations with** 1655+6872
18:18 as a rival wife and **h sexual relations** 1655+6872
18:19 a woman to **h sexual relations** during 1655+6872
18:20 *Do* not **h sexual relations** 2446+4200+5989+8888
18:23 not **h sexual relations** with an animal 5989+8888
18:23 to an animal to **h sexual relations** *with* it; 8061
19:10 **grapes that h fallen.** 7261
19:30 and **h reverence for** my sanctuary. 3707
20:16 to **h sexual relations with** 8061
20:17 and *they* **h sexual relations,** 906+6872+8011
20:19 " '*Do* not **h sexual relations with** 1655+6872
22:25 because they are deformed and **h** defects.' " 928
23:24 the seventh month you *are to* **h** a day 2118+4200
24:22 *are to* **h** the same law for the alien and 2118+4200
25:4 seventh year the land *is to* **h** a sabbath 2118+4200
25:5 The land *is to* **h** a year of rest. 2118+4200
25:9 Then **h** the trumpet **sounded** everywhere on 6296
25:32 " 'The Levites always **h** the right 2118+4200
26:2 " 'Observe my Sabbaths and **h reverence** 3707
26:35 the land *will* **h** *the* **rest** it did not have 8697
26:35 not **h** during the sabbaths you lived in it. 8697[S]
Nu 5:16 " 'The priest shall bring her and **h** her **stand** 6641
5:24 *He shall* **h** the woman **drink** the bitter water 9197
5:26 *he is to* **h** the woman **drink** the water. 9197
5:28 **be able to h children.** 2445+2446
5:30 *to* **h** her **stand** before the LORD and is 6641
8:7 then **h** *them* **shave** their whole bodies 6296+9509
8:13 **H** the Levites **stand** in front of Aaron 6641
9:14 You *must* **h** the same regulations for 2118+4200
11:16 **H** them **come** to the Tent of Meeting, 4374
11:22 *Would* they **h enough** if flocks 5162
11:22 *Would* they **h enough** if all the fish in 5162
15:39 You *will* **h** these tassels to look at and 2118+4200
16:5 **h** that person **come near** 7928
18:9 *to* **h** the part of the most holy offerings 2118+4200
18:20 "*You will* **h** no **inheritance** in their land, 5706
18:20 nor *will* you **h** any share among them; 2118+4200
18:24 '*They will* **h** no **inheritance** among 5706+5709
23:22 they **h** the strength of a wild ox. 4200
24:7 their seed will **h** abundant water. 928
24:8 they **h** the strength of a wild ox. 4200
25:13 and his descendants *will* **h** a covenant 2118+4200
27:19 **H** him **stand** before Eleazar the priest and 6641
32:4 and your servants **h** livestock. 4200
35:3 Then they *will* **h** towns to live in 2118+4200
35:5 They *will* **h** this area as pastureland 2118+4200
Dt 3:19 (I know you **h** much livestock) may stay 4200
4:7 as to **h** their gods near them the way 4200
4:8 as to **h** such righteous decrees and laws 4200
4:33 as you **h,** and lived? 9048[S]
5:7 You *shall* **h** no other gods before me. 2118+4200
5:26 as we **h,** and survived? NIH
8:13 and all you **h** is multiplied, 4200

Dt 10: 9 the Levites **h** no share or inheritance 2118+4200
11: 8 so that *you may* **h** *the* **strength** *to* go in 2616
12:12 who **h** no allotment or inheritance 4200
12:26 and whatever you **h** vowed to give, 2118+4200
13:17 he will show you mercy, **h compassion** 8163
14:10 that does not **h** fins and scales you may 4200
14:27 for they **h** no allotment or inheritance 4200
14:29 so that the Levites (who **h** no allotment 4200
18: 1 *to* **h** no allotment or inheritance with 2118+4200
18: 2 They *shall* **h** no inheritance 2118+4200
22: 7 with you and *you may* **h** *a* **long** life. 799
23:13 equipment **h** something to dig with, 2118+4200
25: 1 When men **h** a dispute, 1068+2118
25: 2 down and **h** him **flogged** in his presence 5782
25:13 not **h** two differing weights in your bag— 2118+4200
25:14 *Do* not **h** two differing measures 2118+4200
25:15 You *must* **h** accurate and honest weights 2118+4200
28:33 and *you will* **h** nothing 2118
28:40 You *will* **h** olive trees 2118+4200
28:41 *You will* **h** sons and daughters but you will 3528
28:54 among you *will* **h no compassion** 6524+8317
30: 3 and **h compassion** *on* you 8163
32:36 and **h compassion** on his servants 5714
33: 9 *'I* **h** no **regard for** them.' 8011
Jos 17:16 in the plain **h** iron chariots, 928
17:17 You *will* **h** not only one allotment 2118+4200
17:18 though the Canaanites **h** iron chariots and 4200
22:24 'What do you **h to do with** the LORD, 4200
22:25 You **h** no share in the LORD.' 4200
22:27 'You **h** no share in the LORD.' 4200
23: 8 as *you* **h** until now. 6913[S]
Jdg 3:19 "I **h** a secret message for you, O king." 4200
3:20 "I **h** a message from God for you." 4200
7: 2 "You **h** too many men for me 907
8:24 And he said, *"I do* **h** *one* **request,** 8626+8629
11:12 "What do you **h** against us 4200
13: 3 but you are going to conceive and **h** a son. 3528
15: 3 "This time *I* **h a right to get even** 5927
18:24 What else do I **h?** 4200
19:19 We **h** both straw and fodder for our donkeys 3780
19:22 to your house so *we can* **h sex with** him." 3359
21:17 The Benjamite survivors must **h** heirs," 4200
Ru 1:11 Am I going to **h** any more sons, 928+5055
1:12 I am too old *to* **h** another husband. 2118+4200
2:13 though I *do* not **h** the standing of one 2118
2:14 **H** some bread and dip it in 430[S]
4:11 *May you* **h** standing in Ephrathah and 6913
1Sa 9: 7 We **h** no gift to take to the man of God. NIH
9: 7 What do we **h?"** 907
9: 8 I **h** a quarter of a shekel of silver. 928+3338+5162
9:12 for the people **h** a sacrifice at the high place. 4200
18:25 Saul's plan was to **h** David **fall** by 5877
21: 3 then, what *do* you **h on hand?** 3338+3780+9393
21: 4 **h** any ordinary bread **on hand;** 448+3338+9393
21: 8 you **h** a spear or a sword here? 3338+3780+9393
25:31 my master *will* not **h** on his conscience 2118+4200
28:22 so you may eat and **h** the strength to go 928+2118
2Sa 1:21 may you **h** neither dew nor rain, 6584
7:10 plant them so that *they can* **h a home** 8905+9393
16:10 "What do you and I **h in common,** 4200
18:18 "I **h** no son to carry on the memory 4200
18:22 You don't **h** any news that will bring you 4200
18:25 "If he is alone, he must **h** good news." 928+7023
19:22 "What do you and I **h in common,** 4200
19:26 *'I will* **h** my donkey **saddled** and will ride 2502
19:28 So what right do I **h** 3780+4200
19:43 "We **h** ten shares in the king; 4200
19:43 **h** a greater **claim on** David than 928
19:43 a greater claim on David than you **h.** NIH
20: 1 "We **h** no share in David, 4200
21: 4 "We **h** no **right** to demand silver or gold 4200
21: 4 nor do we **h the right** to put anyone in Israel 4200
1Ki 2: 4 you *will* never **fail to h** a man on 4162+4200
2:14 he added, "I **h** something to say to you." 4200
2:16 **h** one **request to make** 8626+8629
2:20 **h** one small **request to make** 8626+8629
3:13 so that in your lifetime you *will* **h** no equal 2118
3:26 "Neither I nor you *shall* **h** *him.* 2118+4200
5: 6 that we **h** no one so skilled in felling timber 928
8:18 you did well *to* **h** this in your heart. 2118
8:25 'You *shall* never **fail to h** a man to sit 4162+4200
9: 5 *'You shall* never **fail to h** a man on 4162+4200
11:32 he *will* **h** one tribe. 2118+4200
11:36 that David my servant *may* always **h** a lamp 2118+4200
12:16 "What share do we **h** in David, 4200
13: 7 with me and **h something to eat,** 6184
17:12 she replied, "I don't **h** any bread— 3780+4200
17:13 for me from what you **h** and bring it to me, NIH
17:18 "What do you **h** against me, man of God? 4200
18:18 "But you and your father's family **h.** NIH
20: 4 I and all I **h** are yours." 4200
21: 2 **"Let me h** your vineyard to use for 5989
21:10 and **h** *them* **testify** that he has cursed 6386
22:17 'These people **h** no master. 4200
2Ki 1:13 please **h respect for** my life and 928+3700+6524
1:14 But now **h respect for** my life!" 928+3700+6524
1:16 Because you **h** done this, NIH
2:16 "we your servants **h** fifty able men. 907+3780
3:13 "What do we **h to do with** each 2256+4200+4200
3:14 if I *did* not **h respect for** the presence 5951
3:23 "Those kings **must h fought** 2991+2991
4: 2 Tell me, what do you **h** in your house? 3780+4200
4:13 "I **h a home** among my own people." 3782
2Ki 4:43 'They will eat and **h** *some* **left over.'** " 3855
9: 5 "I **h** a message for you, commander," 4200
9:18 "What do you **h to do with** peace?" 4200
9:19 "What do you **h to do with** peace? 4200
10: 2 with you and you **h** chariots and horses, 907
17:27 **"H** one of the priests you took captive from Samaria **go** back to live there 2143
19: 7 and there *I will* **h** him **cut down** with 5877
21:15 in my eyes and **h** provoked me to anger 2118
22: 4 the high priest and **h** *him* **get ready** 9462
1Ch 4:27 but his brothers did not **h** many children; 4200
17: 9 plant them so that *they can* **h a home** 8905+9393
21:22 *"Let* me **h** the site of your threshing floor 5989
22: 9 But you *will* **h** a son who will be a man 3528
22:11 and *may you* **h success** and build the house 7503
22:13 Then *you will* **h success** if you are careful 7503
22:15 You **h** many workmen: 6640
23:11 but Jeush and Beriah *did* not **h many** sons; 8049
2Ch 1:12 and none after you *will* **h."** 2118
6: 8 you did well *to* **h** this in your heart. 2118
6:16 You *shall* never **fail to h** a man to sit 4162+4200
7:18 You *shall* never **fail to h** a man to rule 4162+4200
10:16 "What share do we **h** in David, 4200
18:16 'These people **h** no master. 4200
20:12 For we **h** no power to face this vast army 928
20:20 **H faith** in the LORD your God 586
20:20 **h faith** in his prophets and you will 586
Ezr 4: 3 "You **h** no **part** with us in building a temple 4200
7:20 of your God that you *may* **h occasion** 10484
7:24 that you **h** no authority to impose taxes, NIH
Ne 2: 7 *may* I **h** letters to the governors 4200+5989
2: 8 And may I **h** a letter to Asaph, NIH
Est 9:21 to **h** them celebrate annually the fourteenth 7756
Job 1: 5 Job would send and **h** them **purified.** 7727
3:26 *I* **h** no **peace,** no quietness; 8922
3:26 *I* **h** no **rest,** but only turmoil." 5663
5:16 So the poor **h** hope, and injustice 2118+4200
6: 8 "Oh, that I *might* **h** my request, 995
6:10 Then I *would* still **h** this consolation— 2118
6:13 Do I **h** any power to help myself, 928
6:14 "A despairing man should **h** the devotion 4200
7: 1 "Does not man **h** hard service on earth? 4200
9:21 I am blameless, *I* **h** no **concern for** myself; 3359
10: 4 Do you **h** eyes of flesh? 4200
10:20 from me so *I can* **h** a moment's **joy** 1158
12: 3 But I **h** a mind as well as you; 4200
12: 5 at ease **h** contempt for misfortune as the fate 6953
15: 3 with speeches that **h** no **value?** 3603
15: 9 What **insights** *do you* **h** that we do not 1067
15: 9 that we do not **h?** 6640
19:21 **"H pity** *on* me, my friends, have pity, 2858
19:21 "Have pity on me, my friends, **h pity,** 2858
20:20 *he will* **h** no respite from his craving; 3359
21:14 *We* **h** no **desire** to know your ways. 2911
24:22 *they* **h** no **assurance** of life. 586
27:14 his offspring *will* never **h enough** to eat. 8425
32:17 I too *will* **h** my **say;** 2750+6699
33:32 If you **h** anything to say, answer me; 3780
37:24 for *does he* not **h regard for** all the wise 8011
38:28 *Does* the rain **h** a father? 3780+4200
40: 5 I spoke once, but *I* **h** no **answer—** 6699
40: 9 Do you **h** an arm like God's, 4200
Ps 9:13 **H mercy** and lift me up from the gates 2858
10: 6 I'll always be happy and never **h** trouble." 928
16: 6 surely I **h** a delightful inheritance. 6584
17:14 their sons **h plenty,** 8425
32: 9 *which* **h** no **understanding** but must 1067
37:16 the little that the righteous **h** than the wealth 4200
38: 3 my bones **h** no soundness because 928
41: 4 I said, "O LORD, **h mercy** *on* me; 2858
41:10 But you, O LORD, **h mercy** *on* me; 2858
50:16 **"What right h you** to recite my laws 3870+4200+4537
51: 1 **H mercy** *on* me, O God, 2858
57: 1 **H mercy** *on* me, O God, have mercy on me, 2858
57: 1 Have mercy on me, O God, **h mercy** *on* me, 2858
73: 4 They **h** no struggles; 4200
73:11 Does the Most High **h** knowledge?" 928+3780
73:25 Whom **h** I in heaven but you? 4200
74:20 **H regard** for your covenant, 4200+5564
81: 9 You *shall* **h** no foreign god among you; 2118
84: 3 where *she may* **h** her young— 8883
86: 3 **H mercy** *on* me, O Lord, 2858
86:16 Turn to me and **h mercy** *on* me; 2858
90:10 or eighty, if we **h** the strength; 928
90:13 **H compassion** on your servants. 5714
101: 4 **h** nothing **to do with** 3359
102:13 You will arise and **h compassion** *on* Zion, 8163
111:10 all who follow his precepts **h** good understanding. 4200
112: 7 *He will* **h** no **fear** of bad news; 3707
112: 8 His heart is secure, *he will* **h** no **fear;** 3707
115: 5 They **h** mouths, but cannot speak, eyes, 4200
115: 6 they **h** ears, but cannot hear, noses, 4200
115: 7 they **h** hands, but cannot feel, feet, NIH
119:99 *I* **h** more **insight** than all my teachers, 8505
119:100 *I* **h** more **understanding** than the elders, 1067
119:117 *I will* always **h regard** for your decrees. 9120
119:132 Turn to me and **h mercy** *on* me, 2858
119:165 Great peace **h** they who love your law, 4200
123: 3 **H mercy** *on* us, O LORD, have mercy on us, 2858
123: 3 O LORD, **h mercy** *on* us, 2858
135:14 and **h compassion** on his servants. 5714
135:16 They **h** mouths, but cannot speak, eyes, 4200
135:17 they **h** ears, but cannot hear, 4200
139:22 *I* **h** nothing but **hatred** *for* them; 8533+8534
142: 4 I **h no** refuge; no one cares for my life. 6+4946
Pr 3:28 when you *now* **h** it with you. 3780
4: 7 Though it cost all you **h,** get understanding. 7871
7:14 "I **h** fellowship offerings at home; 6584
8: 9 they are faultless to *those who* **h** knowledge. 5162
8:14 I **h** understanding and power. 4200
12: 9 a nobody and yet **h** a servant than pretend to 4200
12: 9 to be somebody and **h no** food. 2894
12:11 who works his land *will* **h abundant** food, 8425
12:21 but the wicked **h** *their* **fill** *of* trouble. 4848
14:32 but even in death the righteous **h a refuge.** 2879
16:22 a fountain of life to **those who h** it, 1251
17:21 *To* **h** a fool *for a* **son** brings grief; 3528
20:13 stay awake and *you will* **h** food **to spare.** 8425
22: 2 Rich and poor **h** *this* **in common:** 7008
22:18 **h** all of them **ready** 3922
28:19 who works his land *will* **h abundant** food, 8425
28:19 one who chases fantasies *will* **h** *his* **fill** 8425
29: 7 but the wicked **h** no *such* **concern.** 1067+1981
29:13 and the oppressor **h** *this* **in common:** 7008
30: 2 I do not **h** a man's understanding. 4200
30: 3 nor **h** *I* **knowledge** *of* the Holy One. 1981+3359
30: 9 *I may* **h too much** and disown you and say, 8425
30:27 locusts **h** no king, yet they advance together 4200
Ecc 2:19 Yet *he will* **h control** over all the work 8948
3:19 All **h** the same breath; 4200
4: 1 and they **h** no comforter; 4200
4: 1 and they **h** no comforter. 4200
4: 9 they **h** a good return for their work: 3780+4200
6: 3 A man *may* **h** a hundred **children** 3528
9: 5 they **h** no further reward, 4200
9: 6 never again will they **h** a part in anything 4200
SS 8: 8 We **h** a young sister, 4200
Isa 1:11 *"I* **h more than enough** *of* burnt offerings, 8425
1:11 *I* **h** no **pleasure** *in* the blood of bulls 2911
3: 6 and say, "You **h** a cloak, you be our leader; 4200
3: 7 in that day he will cry out, *"I* **h** no remedy. 2118
3: 7 I **h** no food or clothing in my house; NIH
5:12 *They* **h** harps and lyres at their banquets, 2118
5:12 but *they* **h** no **regard for** the deeds of 5564
8:20 they **h** no light of dawn. 4200
10:13 because *I* **h understanding.** 1067
13:17 not care for silver and **h** no **delight** in gold. 2911
13:18 *they will* **h** no **mercy** *on* infants 8163
14: 1 The LORD *will* **h compassion** *on* Jacob; 8163
17: 8 and *they will* **h** no **regard for** 8011
22:11 or **h regard for** 8011
26: 1 We **h** a strong city; 4200
29:20 all *who* **h an eye** *for* evil will be cut down 9193
30: 4 Though they **h** officials in Zoan 2118
30:15 but *you* **would h** none of it. 14
32: 9 hear **what I h to say!** 614
37: 7 and there *I will* **h** him **cut down** with 5877
40:11 he gently leads *those that* **h young.** 6402
43: 8 Lead out those who **h** eyes but are blind, 3780
43: 8 who **h** ears but are deaf. 4200
49:15 the baby at her breast and **h** no **compassion** 8163
52: 5 "And now what do I **h** here?" 4200
54: 8 with everlasting kindness *I will* **h compassion** *on* you," 8163
55: 1 you who **h** no money, come, buy and eat! 4200
55: 7 and *he will* **h mercy** *on* him, 8163
56:11 *they* never **h** enough. 3359
Jer 2:19 the LORD your God and **h** no awe of me," 448
2:28 For you **h** as many gods as you have towns, 2118
2:28 For you have as many gods as you **h** towns, NIH
3: 3 you **h** the brazen look of a prostitute; 2118+4200
4:10 'You *will* **h** peace,' 2118+4200
4:19 I **h** heard the battle cry. NIH
4:22 they **h** no **understanding.** 1067
5:21 who **h** eyes but do not see, 4200
5:21 who **h** ears but do not hear: 4200
5:23 But these people **h** stubborn 2118+4200
5:28 Their evil deeds **h no limit;** 6296
6:15 **h** no **shame at all;** 1017+1017
8: 8 for we **h** the law of the LORD," 907
8: 9 what kind of wisdom do they **h?** 4200
8:12 No, *they* **h** no **shame at all;** 1017+1017
11:13 You **h** as many gods as you have towns, 2118
11:13 You have as many gods as you **h** towns, NIH
12:15 I will again **h compassion** 8163
15: 5 "Who *will* **h pity** on you, O Jerusalem? 2798
16: 2 and **h** sons or daughters in this place." 2118+4200
22:15 a king *to* **h more and more** cedar? 3013
22:15 *Did* not your father **h food** and drink? 430
22:19 *He will* **h** *the* **burial** *of* a donkey— 7690+7699
23:17 You *will* **h** peace.' 2118+4200
25:35 The shepherds *will* **h nowhere** to flee, 6+4946
27:18 If they are prophets and **h** the word of 907+3780
29: 6 Marry and **h** sons and daughters; 3528
29: 6 so that *they* too *may* **h** sons and daughters. 3528
29: 8 **dreams** you **encourage** them **to h.** 2706+2731
29:11 For I know the **plans** I **h** for you," 3108+4742
29:32 *will* **h** no one left among this people, 2118+4200
30:10 Jacob will again **h peace** and security, 9200
30:18 and **h compassion** *on* his dwellings; 8163
31:20 *I* **h great compassion** *for* him," 8163+8163
32:25 **h the transaction witnessed.' "** 6332+6386
33:17 'David *will* never **fail to h** a man to sit 4162+4200
33:18 *ever* **fail to h** a man to stand 4162+4200
33:21 David *will* no longer **h** a descendant 2118+4200
33:26 and **h compassion** *on* them.' " 8163
35: 7 you *must* never **h** any of these things, 2118+4200
35:19 Recab *will* never **fail to h** a man 4162+4200
36:30 *He will* **h** no one to sit on the throne 2118+4200
41: 8 We **h** wheat and barley, oil and honey, 3780+4200
42:12 so that *he will* **h compassion** *on* you 8163
46:27 Jacob will again **h peace** and security, 9200

Eze 12: 2 They **h** eyes to see but do not see and ears 4200
12:22 what is this proverb you **h** in the land 4200
20:32 But what you **h** in mind will never happen. 6590
24:14 *I will* not **h pity,** nor will I relent. 2571
24:19 tell us what these things **h to do with** us? 4200
28:24 people of Israel **h** malicious neighbors who are painful briers 2118+4200
34:15 and **h** them **lie down,** 8069
37:24 and they *will* all **h** one shepherd. 2118+4200
39:25 from captivity and *will* **h compassion** *on* all 8163
40:45 priests *who* **h charge of** the temple, 5466+9068
40:46 priests *who* **h charge of** the altar. 5466+9068
45: 7 " 'The prince will **h** the land bordering 4200
47:22 among you and who **h** children. 3528
Da 1:10 The king would then **h** my head because 4200
2:30 I **h** greater wisdom than other living men, 10029+10089
2:41 *it will* **h** some of the strength of iron in it, 10201
5:11 to **h** insight and intelligence and wisdom 10089
5:12 was found to **h** a keen mind and knowledge 10089
5:14 of the gods is in you and that you **h** insight, 10089
8:22 but will not **h** the same power. 928
9:26 be cut off and will **h** nothing. 4200
11:16 and will **h** the power to destroy it. 928+3338
Hos 4:10 "They will eat but not **h enough;** 8425
10: 3 "We **h** no king because we did not revere 4200
13:14 "I *will* **h no** compassion, 4946+6259+6524
14: 8 what more **h** I **to do with** idols? 4200
Joel 1:18 herds mill about because they **h** no pasture; 4200
2:14 He may turn and **h pity** and leave behind 5714
2:26 *You will* **h plenty to eat,** 430+430
Am 5: 3 **h** only a hundred **left;** 8636
5: 3 a hundred strong *will* **h** only ten **left."** 8636
5: 6 and Bethel *will* **h** no one to quench it. 4200
5:15 the LORD God Almighty *will* **h mercy** *on* 2858
5:22 *I will* **h** no **regard for** them. 5564
Jnh 4: 4 **"H** you **any right** to be angry?" 3512
4: 9 *"Do* you **h a right** to be angry about 3512
Mic 2: 5 Therefore you *will* **h** no one in 2118+4200
4: 9 **h** you no king? 928
6: 1 hear what you **h to say.** 7754
7:19 You will again **h compassion** *on* us; 8163
Na 1:14 *"You will* **h** no **descendants** 2445
Hab 1:14 like sea creatures that **h** no ruler. 928
Zep 1: 3 The wicked will **h** only heaps of rubble 907
Hag 1: 6 You eat, but never **h enough.** 8425
1: 6 You drink, but never **h** *your* **fill.** 8910
Zec 3: 7 and **h charge of** my courts, 9068
10: 6 I will restore them because *I* **h compassion** 8163
11: 6 For *I will* no longer **h pity** on the people 2798
14:17 LORD Almighty, they *will* **h** no rain. 2118+6584
14:18 they *will* **h** no rain. 6584
Mal 2:10 **H** we not all one Father? 4200
3: 3 LORD *will* **h** men who will bring 2118+4200
3:10 that you will not **h** room enough for it. 4200
Mt 3: 9 *'We* **h** Abraham as our father.' 2400
6: 1 *you will* **h** no reward from your Father 2400
8:20 "Foxes **h** holes and birds of 2400
8:20 and birds of the air **h** nests, *NIG*
9:27 **"H mercy on** us, Son of David!" *1796*
10: 8 raise the dead, cleanse **those who h leprosy,** *3320*
11: 5 *those* **who h leprosy** are cured, *3320*
13: 5 where *it did* not **h** much soil. *2400*
13:12 and *he will* **h an abundance.** *4355*
13:12 Whoever *does* not **h,** *2400*
14: 4 "It is not lawful for you *to* **h** her." *2400*
14:17 *"We* **h** here only five loaves of bread *2400*
15:22 "Lord, Son of David, **h mercy on** me! *1796*
15:32 *"I* **h compassion** for these people; *5072*
15:32 with me three days and **h** nothing to eat. *2400*
15:34 "How many loaves *do you* **h?"** *2400*
16:23 *you do* not **h in mind** the things of God, *5858*
17: 9 "Don't tell anyone what **you h seen,** *3969*
17:15 "Lord, **h mercy** on my son," he said. *1796*
17:20 if *you* **h** faith as small as a mustard seed, *2400*
18: 8 or crippled than *to* **h** two hands or two feet *2400*
18: 9 to enter life with one eye than *to* **h** two eyes *2400*
19:21 and *you will* **h** treasure in heaven. *2400*
20:15 Don't I **h the right** to do what I want *2003*
20:30 "Lord, Son of David, **h mercy on** us!" *1796*
20:31 "Lord, Son of David, **h mercy on** us!" *1796*
21:21 if *you* **h** faith and do not doubt, *2400*
22:24 the widow and **h children** for him. *482+5065*
23: 8 for you **h** only one Master *1639*
23: 9 for you **h** one Father, and he is in heaven. *1639*
23:10 for you **h** one Teacher, the Christ. *1639*
23:23 But *you* **h neglected** *918*
25:29 and *he will* **h an abundance.** *4355*
25:29 Whoever *does* not **h,** *2400*
26:11 The poor *you will* always **h** with you, *2400*
26:11 but *you will* not always **h** me. *2400*
26:35 Peter declared, "Even if I **h** to die with you, *1256*
Mk 2:19 so long as *they* **h** him with them. *2400*
3:15 and *to* **h** authority to drive out demons. *2400*
4: 5 where *it did* not **h** much soil. *2400*
4:17 *they* **h** no root, they last only a short time. *2400*
4:25 whoever *does* not **h,** *2400*
4:40 *Do you* still **h** no faith?" *2400*
6:18 for you *to* **h** your brother's wife." *2400*
6:31 and going that they did not even **h a chance** *2320*
6:38 "How many loaves *do you* **h?"** *2400*
6:39 **h** all the people **sit down** *369*
8: 2 *"I* **h compassion** for these people; *5072*
8: 2 with me three days and **h** nothing to eat. *2400*
8: 5 "How many loaves *do you* **h?"** *2400*
8:16 "It is because *we* **h** no bread." *2400*
8:18 Do you **h** eyes but fail to see, *2400*
Mk 8:33 *"You do* not **h in mind** the things of God, *5858*
9:45 to enter life crippled than *to* **h** two feet and *2400*
9:47 of God with one eye than *to* **h** two eyes and *2400*
9:50 **H** salt in yourselves, *2400*
10:21 sell everything *you* **h** and give to the poor, *2400*
10:21 and *you will* **h** treasure in heaven. *2400*
10:47 "Jesus, Son of David, **h mercy on** me!" *1796*
10:48 "Son of David, **h mercy on** me!" *1796*
11:22 **"H** faith in God," Jesus answered. *2400*
12:19 widow and **h children** for his brother. *1985+5065*
14: 7 The poor *you* will always **h** with you, *2400*
14: 7 But *you will* not always **h** me. *2400*
14:31 "Even if I **h** to die with you, *1256*
Lk 1:36 Even Elizabeth your relative *is going to* **h** *5197*
1:57 for Elizabeth *to* **h** *her* **baby,** *5503*
3: 8 *'We* **h** Abraham as our father.' *2400*
6:31 Do to others as you would **h** them **do** to you *4472*
7:22 *those who* **h leprosy** are cured, *3320*
7:36 of the Pharisees invited Jesus to **h dinner** *2266*
7:40 "Simon, *I* **h** something to tell you." *2400*
8:13 but they **h** no root. *2400*
8:18 whoever *does* not **h,** *2400*
9:13 "We **h** only five loaves of bread *1639*
9:58 "Foxes **h** holes and birds of *2400*
9:58 and birds of the air **h** nests, *NIG*
11: 6 and *I* **h** nothing to set before him.' *2400*
12:17 *I* **h** no place to store my crops.' *2400*
12:19 "You **h** plenty of good things laid up *2400*
12:24 they **h** no storeroom or barn; *1639*
12:37 **h** them **recline at the table** *369*
12:50 But *I* **h** a baptism to undergo, *2400*
15:17 of my father's hired men **h** food **to spare,** *4355*
15:23 Let's **h a feast** and celebrate. *2266*
15:31 and everything **I h** is yours. *1847+3836*
16:24 **h pity** on me and send Lazarus to dip the tip *1796*
16:28 for *I* **h** five brothers. *2400*
16:29 *'They* **h** Moses and the Prophets; *2400*
17: 6 "If *you* **h** faith as small as a mustard seed, *2400*
17:13 "Jesus, Master, **h pity** on us!" *1796*
18:22 Sell everything *you* **h** and give to the poor, *2400*
18:22 and *you will* **h** treasure in heaven. *2400*
18:38 "Jesus, Son of David, **h mercy on** me!" *1796*
18:39 "Son of David, **h mercy on** me!" *1796*
19:20 *I* **h kept** it laid away in a piece of cloth. *2400*
20:28 must marry the widow and **h children** for his brother. *1985+5065*
22:36 "But now *if you* **h** a purse, take it, *2400+3836*
22:36 and *if you* don't **h** a sword, *2400+3836*
24:26 not the Christ **h** to suffer these things and *1256*
24:39 a ghost *does* not **h** flesh and bones, *2400*
24:39 as you see I **h."** *2400*
24:41 *"Do you* **h** anything here to eat?" *2400*
Jn 2: 3 *"They* **h** no more wine." *2400*
3:15 in him *may* **h** eternal life. *2400*
3:16 in him shall not perish but **h** eternal life. *2400*
4:11 *"you* **h** nothing to draw with and *2400*
4:17 *"I* **h** no husband," she replied. *2400*
4:17 when you say *you* **h** no husband. *2400*
4:18 the man *you* now **h** is not your husband. *2400*
4:32 "I **h** food to eat that you know nothing about *2400*
5: 7 *"I* **h** no one to help me into the pool when *2400*
5:26 he has granted the Son *to* **h** life in himself. *2400*
5:36 "I **h** testimony weightier than that of John. *2400*
5:40 yet you refuse to come to me to **h** life. *2400*
5:42 I know that *you do* not **h** the love of God *2400*
6: 7 not buy enough bread for each one *to* **h** *3284*
6:10 Jesus said, **"H** the people sit down." *4472*
6:40 and believes in him *shall* **h** eternal life, *2400*
6:53 *you* **h** no life in you. *2400*
6:68 *You* **h** the words of eternal life. *2400*
8: 6 in order to **h** a basis for accusing him. *2400*
8:12 but *will* **h** the light of life." *2400*
8:26 *"I* **h** much to say in judgment of you. *2400*
8:41 "The only Father *we* **h** is God himself." *2400*
10:10 I have come that *they may* **h** life, *2400*
10:10 and **h** it to the full. *2400*
10:16 *I* **h** other sheep that are not *2400*
10:18 *I* **h** authority to lay it down and authority *2400*
12: 8 *You will* always **h** the poor among you, *2400*
12: 8 but *you will* not always **h** me." *2400*
12:35 "You *are going to* **h** the light just a little *1639*
12:35 Walk while *you* **h** the light, *2400*
12:36 Put your trust in the light while *you* **h** it, *2400*
13: 8 *you* **h** no part with me." *2400*
15:22 however, *they* **h** no excuse for their sin. *2400*
16:12 *"I* **h** much more to say to you, *2400*
16:33 so that in me *you may* **h** peace. *2400*
16:33 In this world *you will* **h** trouble. *2400*
17:10 All **I h** is yours, and all you have is *1847+3836*
17:10 I have is yours, and all **you h** is mine. *3836+5050*
17:13 that *they may* **h** the full measure of my joy *2400*
18:31 "But we **h** no **right** to execute anyone," *2003*
19: 7 The Jews insisted, "We **h** a law, *2400*
19:10 "Don't you realize *I* **h** power either *2400*
19:11 *"You would* **h** no power over me if it were *2400*
19:15 *"We* **h** no king but Caesar," *2400*
20:31 by believing *you may* **h** life in his name. *2400*
21:25 even the whole world *would* not **h room for** *6003*
Ac 3: 6 Then Peter said, "Silver or gold I *do* not **h,** *5639*
3: 6 but what *I* **h** I give you. *2400*
8:21 You **h** no part or share in this ministry, *1639*
10:22 that he could hear what **you h** to say." *4123+5148*
13:15 if you **h** a message of encouragement for *1639*
17:28 in him *we* live and move and **h** *our* **being.'** *1639*
18:10 because I **h** many people in this city." *1639*
19:38 and his fellow craftsmen **h** a grievance *2400*
21:23 There are four men with us *who* **h made** *2400*
Ac 24:15 and *I* **h** the same hope in God as these men, *2400*
24:19 and bring charges if *they* **h** anything *2400*
25: 3 to **h** Paul **transferred** to Jerusalem, *3569*
25:26 But *I* **h** nothing definite to write *2400*
25:26 of this investigation *I may* **h** something *2400*
Ro 1:13 in order that *I might* **h** a harvest among you, *2400*
2: 1 You, therefore, **h** no excuse, *1639*
2:14 when Gentiles, who *do* not **h** the law, *2400*
2:14 *even though they do* not **h** the law, *2400*
2:20 *because you* **h** in the law the embodiment *2400*
3: 3 What if some *did* **not h faith?** *601*
3:26 one who justifies those who **h faith** *1666+4411*
5: 1 *we* **h** peace with God through our Lord *2400*
5: 2 through whom *we* **h** *gained* access by faith *2400*
7:18 For I **h** the desire to do what is good, *4154*
8: 5 with the Spirit **h** their minds set on what *NIG*
8: 9 if anyone *does* not **h** the Spirit of Christ, *2400*
8:12 brothers, *we* **h an obligation—** *1639+4050*
8:23 **who h** the firstfruits of the Spirit, *2400*
8:25 But if we hope for what *we do* not yet **h,** *1063*[S]
9: 2 I **h** great sorrow and unceasing anguish *1639*
9: 9 and Sarah *will* **h** a son." *1639*
9:15 *"I will* **h mercy on** whom I have mercy, *1796*
9:18 on whom he wants to **h** mercy, *NIG*
9:21 *Does* not the potter **h** the right to make out *2400*
11:32 to disobedience so that *he may* **h mercy on** *1796*
12: 4 and these members *do* not all **h** *2400*
12: 6 *We* **h** different gifts, *2400*
15: 4 of the Scriptures *we might* **h** hope. *2400*
15:23 and *since I* **h** *been* longing for many years *2400*
1Co 2:16 But we **h** the mind of Christ. *2400*
4: 2 **h been given a trust** must prove faithful. *3874*
4: 7 What *do you* **h** that you did not receive? *2400*
4: 8 Already *you* **h all you want!** *1639+3170*
4:15 Even though *you* **h** ten thousand guardians *2400*
4:15 you do not **h** many fathers, *NIG*
5:10 that case *you would* **h** to leave this world. *4053*
6: 4 if *you* **h** disputes about such matters, *2400*
6: 7 The very fact that *you* **h** lawsuits *2400*
6:19 whom *you* **h** received from God? *2400*
7: 2 each man *should* **h** his own wife, *2400*
7:25 *I* **h** no command from the Lord, *2400*
7:29 From now on those who **h** wives should live *2400*
7:40 and I think that I too **h** the Spirit of God. *2400*
8:10 weak conscience sees you who **h** this knowledge eating *2400*
9: 4 Don't *we* **h** the right to food and drink? *2400*
9: 5 Don't *we* **h** the right to take a believing wife *2400*
9:12 If others **h** this right of support from you, *3576*
9:12 shouldn't we **h** it all the more? *NIG*
9:17 If I preach voluntarily, *I* **h** a reward; *2400*
10:21 you cannot **h a part** in both the Lord's table *3576*
11:10 the woman ought *to* **h** a sign of authority *2400*
11:16 we **h** no other practice— *2400*
11:17 In the following directives *I* **h** no **praise** *2046*
11:19 No doubt **there h** to be differences *1256*
11:22 Don't *you* **h** homes to eat and drink in? *2400*
11:22 of God and humiliate those who **h** nothing? *2400*
12:25 but that its parts *should* **h** equal **concern** *3534*
12:30 Do all **h** gifts of healing? *2400*
13: 1 but **h** not love, *2400*
13: 2 If *I* **h** the gift of prophecy *2400*
13: 2 and if *I* **h** a faith that can move mountains, *2400*
13: 2 but **h** not love, I am nothing. *2400*
13: 3 but **h** not love, I gain nothing. *2400*
14: 5 but I would rather **h** *you* **prophesy.** *4736*
15:19 If only for this life *we* **h hope** in Christ, *1639+1827*
2Co 3:12 *since we* **h** such a hope, we are very bold. *2400*
4: 1 through God's mercy we **h** this ministry, *2400*
4: 7 But *we* **h** this treasure in jars of clay to show *2400*
5: 1 *we* **h** a building from God, *2400*
7: 1 *Since we* **h** these promises, dear friends, *2400*
7: 3 before that *you* **h such a place** in our hearts *1639*
8:10 to give but also *to* **h** the **desire** to do so. *2527*
8:12 not according to what *he does* not **h.** *2400*
8:15 He who gathered much *did* not **h too much,** *4429*
8:15 who gathered little *did* not **h too little."** *1782*
11:27 **h** often **gone without sleep;** *71+1877*
12:14 children **should** not **h** to save up *4053*
12:15 **everything I h** and **expend** *1682*
13: 7 even though we *may* seem **to h failed.** *99+1639*
Gal 2: 4 to spy on the freedom *we* **h** in Christ Jesus *2400*
3: 9 So those who **h faith** are blessed along *1666+4411*
4:15 I can testify that, if you **could h done so,** *1543*
4:27 you who **h** no **labor pains;** *6048*
6:10 Therefore, as *we* **h** opportunity, *2400*
Eph 1: 7 In him *we* **h** redemption through his blood, *2400*
2:18 through him *we* both **h** access to the Father *2400*
4:28 that *he may* **h** something to share with those *2400*
Php 1: 7 since I **h** you in my heart; *2400*
2:20 *I* **h** no one else like him, *2400*
2:28 be glad and I *may* **h** less anxiety. *1639*
3: 4 I myself **h** reasons for such confidence. *2400*
4:18 I am amply supplied, now that I **h received** *1312*
Col 1: 4 in Christ Jesus and of the love *you* **h** for all *2400*
1:14 in whom *we* **h** redemption, *2400*
1:18 in everything he *might* **h** the supremacy. *1181*
2:23 regulations indeed **h** an appearance *1639+2400*
3:13 and forgive whatever grievances *you may* **h** *2400*
4: 1 because you know that you also **h** a Master *2400*
1Th 3: 6 that *you* always **h** pleasant memories of us *2400*
3: 9 for all the **joy** *we* **h** in the presence *5897+5915*
4:13 who **h** no hope. *2400*
2Th 3: 9 because *we do* not **h** the right to such help, *2400*
1Ti 2:12 a woman to teach or *to* **h authority over** *883*
3: 7 also **h** a good reputation with outsiders, *2400*

1Ti 5:14 *to* **h children,** to manage their homes and 5449
6:2 Those who **h** believing masters are not 2400
6:8 But *if we* **h** food and clothing, 2400
2Ti 2:23 **Don't h anything to do with** foolish and 4148
3:5 **H nothing to do with** them. 706
Tit 2:8 be ashamed *because they* **h** nothing bad 2400
3:13 **h everything** they **need.** 3309+3594
Phm 1:15 a little while was that *you might* **h** him **back** 600
Heb 2:14 Since the children **h** flesh and blood, 3125
4:14 *since we* **h** a great high priest who has gone 2400
4:15 For *we do* not **h** a high priest who is unable 2400
4:15 but we **h** one who has been tempted NIG
5:14 who by constant use **h** trained themselves 2400
6:19 *We* **h** this hope as an anchor for the soul, 2400
8:1 *We do* **h** such a high priest, 2400
8:3 for this one also *to* **h** something to offer. 2400
10:2 would no longer **h** felt guilty for their sins. 2400
10:7 *I* **h come** to do your will, O God.'" 2457
10:9 "Here I am, *I* **h come** to do your will." 2457
10:19 *since we* **h** confidence to enter 2400
10:21 we **h** a great priest over the house of God, NIG
11:32 I *do* **not h** time to tell about Gideon, Barak, 2142
13:5 of money and be content *with* what *you* **h,** 4205
13:10 *We* **h** an altar from which those who 2400
13:10 at the tabernacle **h** no right to eat. 2400
13:14 For here *we do* not **h** an enduring city, 2400
13:18 We are sure that *we* **h** a clear conscience 2400
Jas 2:14 if a man claims *to* **h** faith but has no deeds? 2400
2:18 But someone will say, "You **h** faith; 2400
2:18 "You have faith; I **h** deeds." 2400
4:2 but you cannot **h** what you want. 2209
4:2 *You do* not **h,** because you do not ask God. 2400
5:2 and **moths h eaten** your clothes. 1181+4963
1Pe 3:15 the reason for the hope that **you h.** 1877+5148
2Pe 1:9 But *if* anyone *does* not **h** them, 4205
1:12 in the truth *you* **now h.** 4205
1:19 And *we* **h** the word of the prophets 2400
1Jn 1:3 so that you also *may* **h** fellowship with us. 2400
1:6 If we claim *to* **h** fellowship with him 2400
1:7 *we* **h** fellowship with one another, 2400
2:1 *we* **h** one who speaks to the Father 2400
2:20 But you **h** an anointing from the Holy One, 2400
3:21 *we* **h** confidence before God 2400
4:17 among us so that *we will* **h** confidence on 2400
5:12 not **h** the Son of God does not have life. 2400
5:12 not have the Son of God *does* not **h** life. 2400
5:13 that you may know that *you* **h** eternal life. 2400
5:14 the confidence *we* **h** in approaching God: 2400
5:15 we know that *we* **h** what we asked of him. 2400
2Jn 1:9 in the teaching of Christ *does* not **h** God; 2400
1:12 I **h** much to write to you, 2400
3Jn 1:4 *I* **h** no greater joy than to hear 2400
1:9 *will* **h** nothing *to do with* us. 2110
1:13 *I* **h** much to write you, 2400
Jude 1:19 and *do* not **h** the Spirit. 2400
Rev 2:6 But *you* **h** this in your favor: 2400
2:14 Nevertheless, *I* **h** a few things against you: 2400
2:14 *You* **h** people there who hold to the teaching 2400
2:15 also **h** those who hold to the teaching of 2400
2:20 Nevertheless, *I* **h** this against you: 2400
2:25 Only hold on to what *you* **h** until I come. 2400
3:1 *you* **h** a reputation of being alive, 2400
3:4 Yet *you* **h** a few people in Sardis who have 2400
3:8 I know that *you* **h** little strength, 2400
3:11 Hold on to what *you* **h,** 2400
9:4 but only those people who *did* not **h** the seal 2400
11:6 These men **h** power to shut up the sky so 2400
11:6 and *they* **h** power to turn the waters 2400
17:13 They **h** one purpose 2400
20:6 Blessed and holy are those who **h** part in 2400
22:14 that they *may* **h** the right to the tree of life 1639

HAVEN (2)
Ge 49:13 by the seashore and become a **h** *for* ships; 2572
Ps 107:30 and he guided them to their desired **h.** 4685

HAVEN'T (19) [HAVE, NOT]
Ge 27:36 **"H** you reserved any blessing for me?" 4202
Nu 16:14 you **h** brought us into a land flowing 4202
Jdg 14:16 but you **h** told me the answer." 4202
14:16 "I **h** even explained it to my father 4202
16:15 a fool of me and **h** told me the secret 4202
1Sa 21:8 I **h** brought my sword or any other weapon, 4202
2Sa 3:8 I **h** handed you over to David. 4202
11:10 **"H** you just come from a distance? 4202
1Ki 18:13 **H** you heard, my lord, 4202
1Ch 19:3 **H** his men come to you to explore 4202
2Ch 24:6 "Why **h** you required the Levites to bring in 4202
Mt 12:3 **"H** you read what David did when he 4024
12:5 Or **h** you read in the Law that on 4024
19:4 **"H** you read," he replied, 4024
Mk 12:10 **H** you read this scripture: 4028
Lk 5:5 and **h** caught **anything.** 4029
13:7 for fruit on this fig tree and **h** found any. 4024
Jn 21:5 "Friends, **h** *you* any fish?" 2400+3590
Ac 27:33 you **h** eaten **anything.** 3594

HAVENS See FAIR HAVENS

HAVILAH (7)
Ge 2:11 it winds through the entire land *of* **H,** 2564
10:7 Seba, **H,** Sabtah, Raamah and Sabteca. 2564
10:29 Ophir, **H** and Jobab. All these were sons of Joktan. 2564
Ge 25:18 His descendants settled in the area from **H** 2564
1Sa 15:7 the Amalekites all the way from **H** to Shur, 2564
1Ch 1:9 Seba, **H,** Sabta, Raamah and Sabteca. 2564
1:23 Ophir, **H** and Jobab. All these were sons of Joktan. 2564

HAVING (73) [HAVE]
Ge 16:2 "The LORD has kept me from **h children.** 3528
29:35 Then she stopped **h children.** 3528
30:2 who has kept you from *h* **children?"** AIT
30:9 Leah saw that she had stopped **h children,** 3528
31:35 I'm **h** my period." 4200
35:17 as she *was* **h great difficulty** in childbirth, 7996
Ex 12:4 **h** taken into account the number NIH
Lev 9:22 And *h* **sacrificed** the sin offering, AIT
16:17 *h* **made atonement** for himself, AIT
18:7 *'Do* not **dishonor** your father **by h sexual relations with** your mother. 1655+6872
Nu 10:2 **h** the camps **set out.** 5023
Jdg 16:19 *H* **put** him **to sleep** AIT
1Sa 24:5 for *h* **cut off** a corner of his robe. AIT
25:31 or of *h* **avenged** himself. AIT
1Ki 6:34 each **h** two leaves that turned in sockets. NIH
1Ch 23:22 Eleazar died without **h** sons: 2118+4200
29:28 **h** enjoyed long life, wealth and honor. NIH
Ne 9:1 fasting and wearing sackcloth and **h** dust NIH
Est 3:6 *h* **learned** who Mordecai's people were, AIT
Job 21:25 never *h* **enjoyed** anything good. AIT
Ps 65:6 *h* **armed yourself** with strength, AIT
Isa 22:3 *h* **fled** while the enemy was still far away. AIT
Eze 44:11 **h charge** of the gates of the temple 7213
Da 4:21 and *h* **nesting places** in its branches for AIT
Am 1:3 with **sledges** *h* iron teeth, AIT
Zec 9:9 righteous and **h salvation,** 3828
Mt 2:12 And *h* **been warned** in a dream not AIT
2:22 *H* **been warned** in a dream, AIT
4:24 the demon-possessed, those *h* **seizures,** AIT
9:10 *While* Jesus *was* **h dinner** 367
16:8 among yourselves about **h** no bread? 2400
22:24 that if a man dies without **h** children, 2400
Mk 2:15 While Jesus was **h dinner** at Levi's house, AIT
8:9 And *h* **sent** them **away,** AIT
8:17 "Why are you talking about **h** no bread? 2400
Lk 17:20 *h* **been asked** by the Pharisees when AIT
Jn 4:54 *h* **come** from Judea to Galilee. AIT
7:9 *H* **said** this, he stayed in Galilee. AIT
7:15 "How did this man get such learning without *h* **studied?"** AIT
9:6 *H* **said** this, he spit on the ground, AIT
13:1 *H* **loved** his own who were in the world, AIT
Ac 5:27 *H* **brought** the apostles, AIT
7:45 *H* **received** the tabernacle, AIT
8:22 Perhaps he will forgive you for **h** such NIG
12:20 *H* **secured the support** of Blastus, AIT
16:6 *h* **been kept** by the Holy Spirit **from** AIT
21:40 *H* **received** the commander's **permission,** AIT
Ro 5:10 how much more, *h* **been reconciled,** AIT
1Co 8:7 of it as **h** been sacrificed to an idol, NIG
9:21 *To* those **not h the law** I became like one 491
9:21 the law I became like one **not h the law** 491
9:21 so as to win those **not h the law.** 491
12:28 also those **h** gifts of healing, NIG
2Co 6:10 **h** nothing, and yet possessing everything. 2400
9:4 would be ashamed of **h** been so confident. NIG
9:8 **h** all that you need, 2400
Eph 1:11 *h* **been predestined** according to the plan AIT
1:13 *H* **believed,** you were marked in him with AIT
4:19 *H* **lost all sensitivity,** AIT
Php 2:2 **h** the same love, 2400
3:9 not **h** a righteousness of my own that comes 2400
Col 2:12 *h* **been buried with** him in baptism AIT
2:14 *h* **canceled** the written code, AIT
2:15 And *h* **disarmed** the powers and authorities, AIT
2Ti 3:5 **h** a form of godliness but denying its power. 2400
Tit 3:7 *h* **been justified** by his grace, AIT
3:7 we might become heirs **h** the hope NIG
Heb 9:12 *h* **obtained** eternal redemption. AIT
10:22 *h* our hearts **sprinkled to cleanse** AIT
10:22 and *h* our bodies **washed** with pure water. AIT
Rev 7:2 **h** the seal of the living God. 2400
9:19 **h** heads with which they inflict injury. 2400
20:1 **h** the key to the Abyss and holding 2400

HAVOC (3)
Isa 54:16 the destroyer to **work h;** 2472
Jer 48:3 cries of great **h** and destruction. 8719
Ac 9:21 "Isn't he the man who **raised h** in Jerusalem 4514

HAVOCK (KJV) See DESTROY

HAVVOTH JAIR (4) [JAIR]
Nu 32:41 and called them **H.** 2596
Dt 3:14 so that to this day Bashan is called **H.)** 2596
Jdg 10:4 which to this day are called **H.** 2596
1Ch 2:23 (But Geshur and Aram captured **H,** 2596

HAWK (3)
Lev 11:16 the screech owl, the gull, any kind of **h,** 5891
Dt 14:15 the screech owl, the gull, any kind of **h,** 5891
Job 39:26 "Does the **h** take flight by your wisdom 5891

HAY (2)
Pr 27:25 the **h** is removed and new growth appears 2945
1Co 3:12 silver, costly stones, wood, **h** or straw, 5965

HAZAEL (24)
1Ki 19:15 you get there, anoint **H** king over Aram. 2599
19:17 to death any who escape the sword of **H,** 2599
2Ki 8:8 he said to **H,** "Take a gift with you 2599
8:9 **H** went to meet Elisha, 2599
8:11 with a fixed gaze until **H** felt ashamed. NIH
8:12 "Why is my lord weeping?" asked **H.** 2599
8:13 **H** said, "How could your servant, 2599
8:14 **H** left Elisha and returned to his master. NIH
8:14 **H** replied, "He told me NIH
8:15 Then **H** succeeded him as king. 2599
8:28 against **H** king of Aram at Ramoth Gilead. 2599
8:29 on him at Ramoth in his battle with **H** king 2599
9:14 against **H** king of Aram, 2599
9:15 on him in the battle with **H** king of Aram.) 2599
10:32 **H** overpowered the Israelites 2599
12:17 About this time **H** king of Aram went up 2599
12:18 and he sent them to **H** king of Aram, 2599
13:3 of **H** king of Aram and Ben-Hadad his son. 2599
13:22 **H** king of Aram oppressed Israel throughout 2599
13:24 **H** king of Aram died, 2599
13:25 of **H** the towns he had taken in battle 2599
2Ch 22:5 of Ahab king of Israel to war against **H** king 2599
22:6 on him at Ramoth in his battle with **H** king 2599
Am 1:4 upon the house of **H** that will consume 2599

HAZAIAH (1)
Ne 11:5 the son of Col-Hozeh, the son of **H,** 2610

HAZAR ADDAR (1) [ADDAR]
Nu 34:4 Then it will go to **H** and over 2960

HAZAR ENAN (4) [ENAN]
Nu 34:9 continue to Ziphron and end at **H.** 2966
34:10 run a line from **H** to Shepham. 2966
Eze 47:17 from the sea to **H,** 2965
48:1 **H** and the northern border 2966

HAZAR GADDAH (1)
Jos 15:27 **H,** Heshmon, Beth Pelet, 2961

HAZAR SHUAL (4) [SHUAL]
Jos 15:28 **H,** Beersheba, Biziothiah, 2967
19:3 **H,** Balah, Ezem, 2967
1Ch 4:28 in Beersheba, Moladah, **H,** 2967
Ne 11:27 in **H,** in Beersheba 2967

HAZAR SUSAH (1)
Jos 19:5 Ziklag, Beth Marcaboth, **H,** 2963

HAZAR SUSIM (1)
1Ch 4:31 **H,** Beth Biri and Shaaraim. 2964

HAZARDED (KJV) See RISKED

HAZARHATTICON (KJV) See HAZER HATTICON

HAZARMAVETH (2)
Ge 10:26 the father of Almodad, Sheleph, **H,** 2975
1Ch 1:20 the father of Almodad, Sheleph, **H,** 2975

HAZAZON TAMAR (2) [EN GEDI, TAMAR]
Ge 14:7 the Amorites who were living in **H.** 2954
2Ch 20:2 It is already in **H"** (that is, En Gedi). 2954

HAZEL (KJV) See ALMOND

HAZELELPONI (KJV) See HAZZELELPONI

HAZER HATTICON (1)
Eze 47:16 as far as **H,** 2962

HAZERIM (KJV) See VILLAGE

HAZEROTH (5)
Nu 11:35 the people traveled to **H** and stayed there. 2972
12:16 the people left **H** and encamped in 2972
33:17 and camped at **H.** 2972
33:18 They left **H** and camped at Rithmah. 2972
Dt 1:1 Laban, **H** and Dizahab. 2972

HAZIEL (1)
1Ch 23:9 Shelomoth, **H** and Haran—three in all. 2609

HAZO (1)
Ge 22:22 Kesed, **H,** Pildash, Jidlaph and Bethuel." 2605

HAZOR (18) [BAAL HAZOR, EN HAZOR, HAZOR HADATTAH, KERIOTH HEZRON]
Jos 11:1 When Jabin king of **H** heard of this, 2937
11:10 that time Joshua turned back and captured **H** 2937

Jos 11:10 **H** had been the head of all these kingdoms.) 2937
11:11 and he burned up **H** itself. 2937
11:13 except **H,** which Joshua burned. 2937
12:19 the king of Madon one the king of **H** one 2937
15:23 Kedesh, **H,** Ithnan, 2937
15:25 Kerioth Hezron (that is, **H**), 2937
19:36 Adamah, Ramah, **H,** 2937
Jdg 4: 2 a king of Canaan, who reigned in **H.** 2937
4:17 of **H** and the clan of Heber the Kenite. 2937
1Sa 12: 9 the commander of the army of **H,** 2937
1Ki 9:15 the wall of Jerusalem, and **H,** 2937
2Ki 15:29 Abel Beth Maacah, Janoah, Kedesh and **H.** 2937
Ne 11:33 in **H,** Ramah and Gittaim, 2937
Jer 49:28 Concerning Kedar and the kingdoms of **H,** 2937
49:30 Stay in deep caves, you who live in **H,**" 2937
49:33 "**H** will become a haunt of jackals, 2937

HAZOR HADATTAH (1) [HAZOR]

Jos 15:25 **H,** Kerioth Hezron 2939

HAZZELELPONI (1)

1Ch 4: 3 Their sister was named **H.** 2209

HAZZOBEBAH (1)

1Ch 4: 8 who was the father of Anub and **H** and of 2206

HAZZURIM See HELKATH HAZZURIM

HE (9660) [HE'S, HIM, HIS] See Index of Articles Etc.

HE'S (12) [BE, HE]

Ge 27:36 and now *h* **taken** my blessing!" AIT
Jdg 13:10 to tell her husband, "**H** here! NIH
1Sa 9:12 "**H** ahead of you. NIH
2Sa 18:27 "**H** a good man," the king said. 2296
Mt 27:42 **H** the King of Israel! *1639*
27:47 they said, "**H** calling Elijah." *4047*
Mk 2: 7 like that? *H* **blaspheming!** *AIT*
9:26 like a corpse that many said, "*H* **dead.**" *AIT*
10:49 *H* **calling** you." *AIT*
15:35 they said, "Listen, *h* **calling** Elijah." *AIT*
Ac 20:10 be alarmed," he said. "**H** alive!" *899+1639+6034*
22:22 **H** not fit to live!" *899*

HE-GOAT (1) [GOAT]

Pr 30:31 a **h,** and a king with his army around him. 9411

HEAD (335) [AHEAD, FIGUREHEAD, HEADED, HEADING, HEADS, HOTHEADED]

Ge 3:15 he will crush your **h,** and you will strike his 8031
28:11 he put it **under** his **h** and lay down to sleep. 5265
28:18 the stone he had placed **under** his **h** 5265
40:13 up your **h** and restore you to your position, 8031
40:16 On my **h** were three baskets of bread. 8031
40:17 of the basket on my **h.**" 8031
40:19 three days Pharaoh will lift off your **h** 8031
42:38 you will bring my **gray h** down to the grave 8484
44:29 you will bring my **gray h** down to the grave 8484
44:31 the **gray h** *of* our father down to the grave 8484
48:14 and put it on Ephraim's **h,** 8031
48:14 he put his left hand on Manasseh's **h,** 8031
48:17 on Ephraim's **h** he was displeased; 8031
48:17 from Ephraim's **h** to Manasseh's head. 8031
48:17 from Ephraim's head to Manasseh's **h.** 8031
48:18 put your right hand on his **h.**" 8031
49:26 Let all these rest on the **h** *of* Joseph, 8031
Ex 12: 9 **h,** legs and inner parts. 8031
22: 1 he must pay back five *h of* **cattle** for AIT
28:32 with an opening for the **h** in its center. 8031
29: 6 on his **h** and attach the sacred diadem to 8031
29: 7 and anoint him by pouring it on his **h.** 8031
29:10 and his sons shall lay their hands on its **h.** 8031
29:15 and his sons shall lay their hands on its **h.** 8031
29:17 with the **h** and the other pieces. 8031
29:19 and his sons shall lay their hands on its **h.** 8031
Lev 1: 4 He is to lay his hand on the **h** *of* 8031
1: 8 including the **h** and the fat, 8031
1:12 including the **h** and the fat, 8031
1:15 wring off the **h** and burn it on the altar; 8031
3: 2 on the **h** *of* his offering and slaughter it at 8031
3: 8 the **h** *of* his offering and slaughter it in front 8031
3:13 on its **h** and slaughter it in front of the Tent 8031
4: 4 on its **h** and slaughter it before the LORD. 8031
4:11 as well as the **h** and legs, 8031
4:15 to lay their hands on the bull's **h** before 8031
4:24 on the goat's **h** and slaughter it at the place 8031
4:29 on the **h** *of* the sin offering and slaughter it 8031
4:33 on its **h** and slaughter it for a sin offering at 8031
5: 8 He is to wring its **h** from its neck, 8031
8: 9 Then he placed the turban on Aaron's **h** 8031
8:12 of the anointing oil on Aaron's **h** 8031
8:14 Aaron and his sons laid their hands on its **h.** 8031
8:18 Aaron and his sons laid their hands on its **h.** 8031
8:20 He cut the ram into pieces and burned the **h,** 8031
8:22 Aaron and his sons laid their hands on its **h.** 8031
9:13 including the **h,** and he burned them on 8031
13:12 the skin of the infected person from **h** 8031
13:29 or woman has a sore on the **h** or on the chin, 8031
13:30 an infectious disease of the **h** or chin. 8031
Lev 13:42 if he has a reddish-white sore on his **bald h** 7949
13:42 an infectious disease breaking out on his **h** 7949
13:43 on his **h** or forehead is reddish-white like 7949
13:44 because of the sore on his **h.** 8031
14: 9 he must shave his **h,** his beard, 8031
14:18 in his palm the priest shall put on the **h** *of* 8031
14:29 in his palm the priest shall put on the **h** *of* 8031
16:21 the **h** *of* the live goat and confess over it all 8031
16:21 and put them on the goat's **h.** 8031
19:27 " 'Do not cut the hair at the sides of your **h** 8031
20: 9 and his blood will be on his own **h.** NIH
21:10 on his **h** and who has been ordained to wear 8031
24:14 to lay their hands on his **h,** 8031
Nu 1: 4 each the **h** of his family, is to help you. 8031
6: 5 of separation no razor may be used on his **h.** 8031
6: 5 he must let the hair of his **h** grow long. 8031
6: 7 symbol of his separation to God is on his **h.** 8031
6: 9 he must shave his **h** on the day 8031
6:11 That same day he is to consecrate his **h.** 8031
17: 3 be one staff for the **h** *of* each ancestral tribe. 8031
Dt 19: 5 the **h** may fly off and hit his neighbor 1366
21:12 into your home and have her shave her **h,** 8031
28:13 The LORD will make you the **h,** 8031
28:23 The sky over your **h** will be bronze, 8031
28:35 the soles of your feet to the **top of** your **h.** 7721
28:44 He will be the **h,** but you will be the tail. 8031
33:16 Let all these rest on the **h** *of* Joseph, 8031
33:20 tearing at arm or **h.** 7721
Jos 2:19 his blood will be on his own **h;** 8031
2:19 his blood will be on our **h** if a hand is laid 8031
11:10 the **h** *of* all these kingdoms.) 8031
22:14 each the **h** *of* a family division among 8031
Jdg 5:26 She struck Sisera, she crushed his **h,** 8031
8:28 the Israelites and did not raise its **h** again. 8031
9:53 on his **h** and cracked his skull. 8031
10:18 be the **h** of all those living in Gilead." 8031
11: 8 and you will be our **h** over all who live 8031
11: 9 will I really be your **h?**" 8031
11:11 and the people made him **h** and commander 8031
12: 1 to burn down your house over your **h.**" NIH
13: 5 No razor may be used on his **h,** 8031
16:13 "If you weave the seven braids of my **h** into 8031
16:13 Delilah took the seven braids of his **h,** 8031
16:17 "No razor has ever been used on my **h,**" 8031
16:17 If my **h** were shaved, NIH
16:22 But the hair on his **h** began to grow again 8031
1Sa 1:11 and no razor will ever be used on his **h.**" 8031
4:12 his clothes torn and dust on his **h.** 8031
5: 4 His **h** and hands had been broken off 8031
9: 2 a **h** taller than any of the others.
2025+2256+4946+5087+8900
9:22 at the **h** *of* those who were invited— 8031
10: 1 and poured it on Saul's **h** and kissed him, 8031
10:23 among the people he was a **h** taller than any
of the others. 2025+2256+4946+5087+8900
14:45 not a hair of his **h** will fall to the ground, 8031
15:17 not become the **h** *of* the tribes of Israel? 8031
17: 5 He had a bronze helmet on his **h** and wore 8031
17:38 on him and a bronze helmet on his **h.** 8031
17:46 and I'll strike you down and cut off your **h.** 8031
17:51 he cut off his **h** with the sword. 8031
17:54 David took the Philistine's **h** and brought it 8031
17:57 with David still holding the Philistine's **h.** 8031
19:13 and putting some goats' hair at the **h.** 5265
19:16 and at the **h** was some goats' hair. 5265
21: 7 the Edomite, Saul's **h** shepherd. 52
25:39 wrongdoing down on his own **h.**" 8031
26: 7 in the ground **near** his **h.** 5265
26:11 the spear and water jug that are **near** his **h,** 5265
26:12 the spear and water jug **near** Saul's **h,** 5265
26:16 and water jug that were **near** his **h?**" 5265
31: 9 They cut off his **h** 8031
2Sa 1: 2 with his clothes torn and with dust on his **h.** 8031
1:10 And I took the crown that was on his **h** and 8031
1:16 "Your blood be on your own **h.** 8031
2:16 by the **h** and thrust his dagger 8031
3: 8 "Am I a dog's **h**—on Judah's side? 8031
3:29 May his blood fall upon the **h** *of* Joab and 8031
4: 7 they cut off his **h.** 8031
4: 8 They brought the **h** *of* Ish-Bosheth to David 8031
4: 8 "Here is the **h** *of* Ish-Bosheth son of Saul, 8031
4:12 But they took the **h** *of* Ish-Bosheth 8031
12:30 the crown from the **h** *of* their king— 8031
12:30 and it was placed on David's **h.** 8031
13:19 Tamar put ashes on her **h** and tore 8031
13:19 She put her hand on her **h** and went away, 8031
14:11 **hair of** your son's **h** 8553
14:25 From the **top of** his **h** to the sole 7721
14:26 Whenever he cut the hair of his **h—** 8031
15:30 his **h** was covered and he was barefoot. 8031
15:32 his robe torn and dust on his **h.** 8031
16: 9 Let me go over and cut off his **h.**" 8031
18: 9 Absalom's **h** got caught in the tree. 8031
20:21 "His **h** will be thrown to you from 8031
20:22 and they cut off the **h** *of* Sheba son of Bicri 8031
22:44 you have preserved me as the **h** *of* nations. 8031
1Ki 1:52 not a **hair of** his **h** will fall to the ground; 8553
2: 6 not let his **gray h** go down to the grave 8484
2: 9 Bring his **gray h** down to the grave 8484
2:33 the guilt of their blood rest on the **h** *of* Joab 8031
2:37 your blood will be on your own **h.**" 8031
4:23 ten *h of* stall-fed **cattle,** AIT
8:32 down on his own **h** what he has done. 8031
19: 6 there **by** his **h** was a cake of bread baked 5265
2Ki 4:19 "My **h!** My head!" he said to his father. 8031
4:19 "My head! My **h!**" he said to his father. 8031
6:25 that a donkey's **h** sold for eighty shekels 8031
2Ki 6:31 if the **h** *of* Elisha son of Shaphat remains 8031
6:32 sending someone to cut off my **h?** 8031
9: 3 Then take the flask and pour the oil on his **h** 8031
9: 6 Then the prophet poured the oil on Jehu's **h** 8031
19:21 The Daughter of Jerusalem tosses her **h** 8031
1Ch 5:15 the son of Guni, was **h** of their family. 8031
10: 9 They stripped him and took his **h** 8031
10:10 the temple of their gods and hung up his **h** 1653
15:22 the **h** Levite was in charge of the singing; 8569
20: 2 the crown from the **h** *of* their king— 8031
20: 2 and it was placed on David's **h.** 8031
29:11 you are exalted as **h** over all. 8031
2Ch 6:23 down on his own **h** what he has done. 8031
7: 5 of twenty-two thousand *h of* **cattle** and AIT
15:11 to the LORD seven hundred *h of* **cattle** AIT
20:21 as they went out **at the h of** the army, 4200+7156
35: 9 and five hundred *h of* **cattle** for AIT
Ezr 9: 3 pulled hair from my **h** and beard and sat 8031
Ne 6: 8 you are just making it up out of your **h.**" 4213
Est 2:17 on her **h** and made her queen instead 8031
6: 8 one with a royal crest placed on its **h.** 8031
6:12 with his **h** covered in grief, 8031
9:25 the Jews should come back onto his own **h,** 8031
Job 1:20 up and tore his robe and shaved his **h.** 8031
2: 7 the soles of his feet to the **top of** his **h.** 7721
10:15 Even if I am innocent, I cannot lift my **h,** 8031
10:16 If I **hold** my **h high,** 1448
16: 4 against you and shake my **h** at you. 8031
19: 9 and removed the crown from my **h.** 8031
20: 6 to the heavens and his **h** touches the clouds, 8031
29: 3 when his lamp shone upon my **h** and 8031
41: 7 Can you fill his hide with harpoons or his **h** 8031
Ps 3: 3 you bestow glory on me and lift up my **h.** 8031
7:16 his violence comes down on his own **h.** 7721
18:43 you have made me the **h** *of* nations; 8031
21: 3 and placed a crown of pure gold on his **h.** 8031
23: 5 You anoint my **h** with oil; 8031
27: 6 Then my **h** will be exalted above 8031
35:14 *I* **bowed** *my* **h** in grief as though weeping 8820
40:12 They are more than the hairs of my **h,** 8031
69: 4 outnumber the hairs of my **h;** 8031
110: 7 therefore he will lift up his **h.** 8031
132:18 but the crown on his **h** will be resplendent." NIH
133: 2 It is like precious oil poured on the **h,** 8031
140: 7 who shields my **h** in the day of battle— 8031
141: 5 let him rebuke me—it is oil on my **h.** 8031
141: 5 My **h** will not refuse it. 8031
Pr 1: 9 They will be a garland to grace your **h** and 8031
1:21 at the **h** *of* the noisy streets she cries out, in 8031
4: 9 She will set a garland of grace on your **h** 8031
10: 6 Blessings crown the **h** *of* the righteous, 8031
25:22 you will heap burning coals on his **h,** 8031
Ecc 2:14 The wise man has eyes in his **h,** 8031
9: 8 and always anoint your **h** with oil. 8031
SS 2: 6 His left arm is under my **h,** 8031
5: 2 My **h** is drenched with dew, 8031
5:11 His **h** is purest gold; 8031
7: 5 Your **h** crowns you like Mount Carmel. 8031
8: 3 under my **h** and his right arm embraces me. 8031
Isa 1: 5 Your whole **h** is injured, 8031
1: 6 to the *top of* your **h** there is no soundness— 8031
7: 8 for the **h** *of* Aram is Damascus, 8031
7: 8 and the **h** *of* Damascus is only Rezin. 8031
7: 9 The **h** *of* Ephraim is Samaria, 8031
7: 9 the **h** *of* Samaria is only Remaliah's son. 8031
7:20 to shave your **h** and the hair of your legs, 8031
9:14 both **h** and tail, both palm branch and reed 8031
9:15 the elders and prominent men are the **h,** 8031
15: 2 Every **h** is shaved and every beard cut off. 8031
19:15 **h** or tail, palm branch or reed. 8031
28: 1 set on the **h** *of* a fertile valley— 8031
28: 4 set on the **h** *of* a fertile valley, 8031
37:22 The Daughter of Jerusalem tosses her **h** 8031
51:20 they lie at the **h** *of* every street, 8031
58: 5 Is it only for bowing one's **h** like a reed and 8031
59:17 and the helmet of salvation on his **h;** 8031
61:10 as a bridegroom **adorns** his **h** like a priest, 6996
Jer 2:16 have shaved the **crown of** your **h.** 7721
2:37 that place with your hands on your **h,** for 8031
9: 1 that my **h** were a spring of water 8031
16: 6 and no one will cut himself or **shave** *his* **h** 7942
47: 5 **shave** *her* **h in mourning;** 995+7947
48:27 **shake** *your* **h in scorn** 5653
48:37 Every **h** is shaved and every beard cut off; 8031
La 2:19 from hunger at the **h** *of* every street. 8031
3:54 the waters closed over my **h,** 8031
4: 1 The sacred gems are scattered at the **h** 8031
5:16 The crown has fallen from our **h.** 8031
Eze 5: 1 as a barber's razor to shave your **h** 8031
8: 3 like a hand and took me by the hair of my **h.** 8031
10:11 in whatever direction the **h** faced, 8031
16:12 and a beautiful crown on your **h.** 8031
16:25 At the **h** *of* every street you built 8031
16:31 When you built your mounds at the **h** 8031
16:43 down on your **h** what you have done, 8031
17:19 as I live, I will bring down on his **h** my oath 8031
18:13 to death and his blood will be on his own **h.** NIH
29:18 every **h** was rubbed bare 8031
33: 4 his blood will be on his own **h.** 8031
33: 5 his blood will be on his own **h.** NIH
Da 1:10 The king would then have my **h** because 8031
2:32 The **h** *of* the statue was made of pure gold, 10646
2:38 You are that **h** of gold. 10646
7: 9 the hair of his **h** was white like wool. 10646
7:20 on its **h** and about the other horn that came 10646
Hos 8: 7 The stalk has no **h;** it will produce no flour. 7542
Joel 2:11 The LORD thunders at the **h** *of* his army; 7156

Ob 1:15 your deeds will return upon your own **h.** 8031
Jnh 2: 5 seaweed was wrapped around my **h.** 8031
4: 6 up over Jonah to give shade for his **h** 8031
4: 8 and the sun blazed on Jonah's **h** so 8031
Mic 2:13 the LORD at their **h."** 8031
Na 3:10 Her infants were dashed to pieces at the **h** 8031
Hab 3:13 you stripped him from **h** to foot. 7418
3:14 With his own spear you pierced his **h** 8031
Zec 1:21 so that no one could raise his **h,** 8031
3: 5 Then I said, "Put a clean turban on his **h."** 8031
3: 5 a clean turban on his **h** and clothed him, 8031
6:11 and set it on the **h** *of* the high priest, 8031
Mt 5:36 And do not swear by your **h,** *3051*
6:17 put oil on your **h** and wash your face, *3051*
8:20 the Son of Man has no place to lay his **h."** *3051*
10:25 **h of the house** has been called Beelzebub, *3867*
10:30 the very hairs *of* your **h** are all numbered. *3051*
14: 8 "Give me here on a platter the **h** of John *3051*
14:11 His **h** was brought in on a platter and given *3051*
26: 7 on his **h** as he was reclining at the table. *3051*
27:29 a crown of thorns and set it on his **h.** *3051*
27:30 and struck him on the **h** again and again. *3051*
27:37 Above his **h** they placed the written charge *3051*
Mk 4:28 first the stalk, then the **h,** *5092*
4:28 then the head, then the full kernel in the **h.** *5092*
6:24 "The **h** of John the Baptist," she answered. *3051*
6:25 now the **h** of John the Baptist on a platter." *3051*
6:27 with orders to bring John's **h.** *3051*
6:28 and brought back his **h** on a platter. *3051*
12: 4 **struck** this man **on the h** *3052*
14: 3 the jar and poured the perfume on his **h.** *3051*
15:19 Again and again they struck him on the **h** *3051*
Lk 7:46 You did not put oil on my **h,** *3051*
9:58 the Son of Man has no place to lay his **h."** *3051*
12: 7 the very hairs *of* your **h** are all numbered. *3051*
21:18 But not a hair of your **h** will perish. *3051*
Jn 13: 9 "not just my feet but my hands and my **h** *3051*
19: 2 a crown of thorns and put it *on* his **h.** *3051*
19:30 he bowed his **h** and gave up his spirit. *3051*
20: 7 that had been around Jesus' **h.** *3051*
20:12 one at the **h** and the other at the foot. *3051*
Ac 27:15 by the storm and could not **h into** the wind; *535*
27:34 of you will lose a single hair from his **h."** *3051*
Ro 12:20 you will heap burning coals on his **h."** *3051*
1Co 11: 3 to realize that the **h** of every man is Christ, *3051*
11: 3 and the **h** of the woman is man, *3051*
11: 3 and the **h** of Christ is God. *3051*
11: 4 with his **h** covered dishonors his head. *3051*
11: 4 with his head covered dishonors his **h.** *3051*
11: 5 *with* her **h** uncovered dishonors her head— *3051*
11: 5 with her head uncovered dishonors her **h—** *3051*
11: 5 it is just as though her **h** were shaved. *NIG*
11: 6 If a woman does not cover her **h,** *NIG*
11: 6 she should cover her **h.** *NIG*
11: 7 A man ought not to cover his **h,** *3051*
11:10 to have a sign of authority on her **h.** *3051*
11:13 to pray to God with her **h** uncovered? *NIG*
12:21 And the **h** cannot say to the feet, *3051*
Eph 1:10 **bring** all things in heaven and on earth
together under one h, *368*
1:22 and appointed him to be **h** over everything *3051*
4:15 in all things grow up into him who is the **H,** *3051*
5:23 the husband is the **h** of the wife as Christ is *3051*
5:23 of the wife as Christ is the **h** of the church, *3051*
Col 1:18 And he is the **h** of the body, the church; *3051*
2:10 the **h** over every power and authority. *3051*
2:19 He has lost connection with the **H,** *3051*
2Ti 4: 5 But you, **keep** *your* **h** in all situations, *3768*
Rev 1:14 His **h** and hair were white like wool, *3051*
10: 1 with a rainbow above his **h;** *3051*
12: 1 and a crown of twelve stars on her **h.** *3051*
13: 1 and on each **h** a blasphemous name. *3051*
14:14 a son of man" with a crown of gold on his **h** *3051*
19:12 and on his **h** are many crowns. *3051*

HEADBAND (2) [HEADBANDS]

1Ki 20:38 He disguised himself with his **h** down 710
20:41 Then the prophet quickly removed the **h** 710

HEADBANDS (5) [HEADBAND]

Ex 28:40 Make tunics, sashes and **h** for Aaron's sons, 4457
29: 9 and put **h** on them. Then tie sashes on 4457
39:28 the linen **h** and the undergarments 4457+6996
Lev 8:13 tied sashes around them and put **h** on them, 4457
Isa 3:18 the bangles and **h** and crescent necklaces, 8667

HEADDRESSES (1)

Isa 3:20 the **h** and ankle chains and sashes, 6996

HEADED (6) [HEAD]

Ge 31:21 he **h for** the hill country of Gilead. 7156+8492
Ex 9:31 the barley had **h** and the flax was in bloom. 26
Jos 15: 9 the hilltop the boundary **h** toward the spring 9305
18:12 of Jericho and **h** west into the hill country, 6590
Jer 39: 4 and **h** toward the Arabah. 3655
Jnh 1: 3 But Jonah ran away from the LORD and **h** NIH

HEADING (2) [HEAD]

Lk 9:53 because he was **h** for Jerusalem. *4513*
Jn 6:21 the shore where *they were* **h.** *5632*

HEADLONG (4)

2Ki 7:15 in their **h flight.** 2905
Job 27:22 *as he* **flees h** from its power. 1368+1368
Hab 1: 8 Their cavalry **gallops h;** 7055
Ac 1:18 there *he* **fell h,** his body burst open *1181+4568*

HEADS (177) [HEAD]

Ge 40:20 He lifted up the **h** *of* the chief cupbearer 8031
41: 5 Seven **h of grain,** healthy and good, 8672
41: 6 seven other **h of grain** sprouted— 8672
41: 7 The thin **h of grain** swallowed up 8672
41: 7 up the seven healthy, full **h.** 8672
41:22 "In my dreams I also saw seven **h of grain,** 8672
41:23 After them, seven other **h** sprouted— 8672
41:24 The thin **h of grain** swallowed up 8672
41:24 of grain swallowed up the seven good **h.** 8672
41:26 the seven good **h of grain** are seven years; 8672
41:27 the seven worthless **h of grain** scorched by 8672
Ex 6:14 These were the **h** *of* their families: 8031
6:25 These were the **h** *of* the Levite families, 8031
Lev 2:14 offer crushed **h** *of* new grain roasted in 26
20:11 their blood will be on their own **h.** NIH
20:12 their blood will be on their own **h.** NIH
20:13 their blood will be on their own **h.** NIH
20:16 their blood will be on their own **h.** NIH
20:27 their blood will be on their own **h.'"** NIH
21: 5 not shave their **h** or shave off the edges 8031
26:13 and enabled you to walk **with h held high.** 7758
Nu 1:16 They were the **h** *of* the clans of Israel. 8031
7: 2 the **h** *of* families who were the tribal leaders 8031
8:12 Levites lay their hands on the **h** *of* the bulls, 8031
10: 4 the **h** *of* the clans of Israel— 8031
30: 1 Moses said to the **h** *of* the tribes of Israel: 8031
31:26 and Eleazar the priest and the family **h** *of* 8031
32:28 and Joshua son of Nun and to the family **h** 8031
36: 1 The family **h** of the clan of Gilead son 8031
36: 1 the **h** of the Israelite families. 8031
Dt 14: 1 shave the **front of** your **h** for the dead, 1068+6524
32:42 the **h** *of* the enemy leaders." 8031
33:21 When the **h** *of* the people assembled, 8031
Jos 7: 6 and sprinkled dust on their **h.** 8031
14: 1 the **h** *of* the tribal clans of Israel allotted 8031
19:51 the **h** *of* the tribal clans of Israel assigned 8031
21: 1 Now the family **h** *of* the Levites 8031
21: 1 the **h** *of* the other tribal families of Israel 8031
22:21 the half-tribe of Manasseh replied to the **h** 8031
22:30 the **h** *of* the clans of the Israelites— 8031
Jdg 7:25 and brought the **h** *of* Oreb and Zeeb to 8031
1Sa 29: 4 by taking the **h** *of* our own men? 8031
2Sa 15:30 All the people with him covered their **h** too 8031
1Ki 8: 1 all the **h** *of* the tribes and the chiefs of 8031
20:31 around our waists and ropes around our **h.** 8031
20:32 and ropes around their **h,** they went to 8031
2Ki 4:42 along with *some* **h of new grain.** 4152
10: 6 the **h** *of* your master's sons and come to me 8031
10: 7 They put their **h** in baskets and sent them 8031
10: 8 "They have brought the **h** *of* the princes." 8031
1Ch 5:24 These were the **h** *of* their families: 8031
5:24 famous men, and **h** of their families. 8031
7: 2 **h** of their families. 8031
7: 7 Jerimoth and Iri, **h** *of* families—five in all. 8031
7: 9 Their genealogical record listed the **h** 8031
7:11 All these sons of Jediael were **h** *of* families. 8031
7:40 **h** *of* families, choice men, 8031
8: 6 who were **h** *of* families of those living 8031
8:10 These were his sons, **h** *of* families. 8031
8:13 who were **h** *of* families of those living 8031
8:28 All these were **h** *of* families, 8031
9: 9 All these men were **h** of their families. 8031
9:13 The priests, who were **h** of families, 8031
9:33 **h** of Levite families, 8031
9:34 All these were **h** of Levite families, 8031
12:19 "It will cost us our **h** if he deserts 8031
15:12 "You are the **h** of the Levitical families; 8031
23: 9 These were the **h** *of* the families of Ladan. 8031
23:24 the **h** *of* families as they were registered 8031
24: 4 sixteen **h** of families 8031
24: 4 from Eleazar's descendants and eight **h** NIH
24: 6 and the **h** *of* families of the priests and of 8031
24:31 and the **h** *of* families of the priests and of 8031
26:21 and who were **h** *of* families belonging 8031
26:26 the **h** *of* families who were the commanders 8031
26:32 who were able men and **h** *of* families, 8031
27: 1 **h** *of* families, commanders of thousands 8031
2Ch 1: 2 the leaders in Israel, the **h** *of* families— 8031
5: 2 all the **h** *of* the tribes and the chiefs of 8031
19: 8 and **h** of Israelite families to administer 8031
23: 2 the Levites and the **h** of Israelite families 8031
29:30 and **bowed** *their* **h** and worshiped. 7702
Ezr 1: 5 Then the family **h** of Judah and Benjamin, 8031
2:68 the **h** *of* the families gave freewill offerings 8031
3:12 the older priests and Levites and family **h,** 8031
4: 2 to Zerubbabel and to the **h** *of* the families 8031
4: 3 of the **h** *of* the families of Israel answered, 8031
8: 1 These are the family **h** and those registered 8031
8:29 and the Levites and the family **h** of Israel." 8569
9: 6 because our sins are higher than our **h** 8031
10:16 the priest selected men who were family **h,** 8031
Ne 4: 4 Turn their insults back on their own **h.** 8031
7:70 Some of the **h** *of* the families contributed to 8031
7:71 the **h** *of* the families gave to the treasury for 8031
8:13 the **h** of all the families, 8031
9: 1 and having dust on their **h.** NIH
11:13 who were **h** of families— 8031
11:16 two of the **h** *of* the Levites, 8031
12:12 these were the **h** *of* the priestly families: 8031
12:22 The family **h** of the Levites in the days 8031
12:23 The family **h** among the descendants 8031
Job 2:12 and sprinkled dust on their **h.** 8031
24:24 they are cut off like **h** *of* grain. 8031
Ps 22: 7 they hurl insults, shaking their **h:** 8031
24: 7 Lift up your **h,** O you gates; 8031
24: 9 Lift up your **h,** O you gates; 8031
44:14 the peoples shake their **h** at us. 8031
64: 8 *will* **shake** *their* **h in scorn.** 5653
66:12 You let men ride over our **h;** 8031
68:21 Surely God will crush the **h** *of* his enemies, 8031
74:13 broke the **h** *of* the monster in the waters. 8031
74:14 you who crushed the **h** *of* Leviathan and 8031
83: 2 how your foes rear their **h.** 8031
109:25 when they see me, they shake their **h.** 8031
140: 9 the **h** *of* those who surround me be covered 8031
Isa 3:17 Therefore the Lord will bring sores on the **h** 7721
17: 5 when a man gleans **h of grain** in the Valley 8672
29:10 he has covered your **h** (the seers). 8031
35:10 everlasting joy will crown their **h.** 8031
51:11 everlasting joy will crown their **h.** 8031
Jer 13:18 your glorious crowns will fall from your **h."** 5265
14: 3 dismayed and despairing, they cover their **h.** 8031
14: 4 the farmers are dismayed and cover their **h.** 8031
18:16 by will be appalled and will shake their **h.** 8031
23:19 a whirlwind swirling down on the **h** *of* 8031
30:23 a driving wind swirling down on the **h** *of* 8031
La 2:10 they have sprinkled dust on their **h** and put 8031
2:10 of Jerusalem have bowed their **h** to 8031
2:15 they scoff and shake their **h** at the Daughter 8031
Eze 1:22 Spread out above the **h** *of* 8031
1:25 above the expanse over their **h** as they stood 8031
1:26 over their **h** was what looked like a throne 8031
7:18 be covered with shame and their **h** will 8031
9:10 down on their own **h** what they have done." 8031
10: 1 above the expanse that was over the **h** *of* 8031
11:21 down on their own **h** what they have done, 8031
13:18 and make veils of various lengths for their **h** 8031
22:31 down on their own **h** all they have done, 8031
23:15 and flowing turbans on their **h;** 8031
23:42 and beautiful crowns on their **h.** 8031
24:23 on your **h** and your sandals on your feet. 8031
27:30 they will sprinkle dust on their **h** and roll 8031
27:31 *They will* **shave** *their* **h** because of you 7942+7947
32:27 whose swords were placed under their **h?** 8031
44:18 They are to wear linen turbans on their **h** 8031
44:20 not shave their **h** or let their hair grow long, 8031
44:20 they are to keep the hair of their **h** trimmed. 8031
Da 3:27 nor was a hair of their **h** singed; 10646
7: 6 This beast had four **h,** 10646
Joel 3: 4 return on your own **h** what you have done. 8031
3: 7 return on your own **h** what you have done. 8031
Am 2: 7 They trample on the **h** *of* the poor as upon 8031
8:10 of you wear sackcloth and shave your **h.** 8031
9: 1 Bring them down on the **h** *of* all the people; 8031
Mic 1:16 **Shave** *your* **h** in mourning for the children
1605+7942
Mt 12: 1 to pick some **h of grain** and eat them. *5092*
13:26 When the wheat sprouted and formed **h,** *2843*
27:39 by hurled insults at him, shaking their **h** *3051*
Mk 2:23 they began to pick some **h of grain.** *5092*
15:29 shaking their **h** and saying, "So! *3051*
Lk 6: 1 his disciples began to pick some **h of grain,** *5092*
21:28 stand up and lift up your **h,** *3051*
Ac 18: 6 "Your blood be on your own **h!** *3051*
21:24 so that they can have their **h** shaved. *3051*
Rev 4: 4 in white and had crowns of gold on their **h.** *3051*
9: 7 On their **h** they wore something like crowns *3051*
9:17 The **h** of the horses resembled the heads *3051*
9:17 the horses resembled the **h** of lions, *3051*
9:19 having **h** with which they inflict injury. *3051*
12: 3 an enormous red dragon with seven **h** *3051*
12: 3 and ten horns and seven crowns on his **h.** *3051*
13: 1 He had ten horns and seven **h,** *3051*
13: 3 of the **h** of the beast seemed to have had *3051*
17: 3 with blasphemous names and had seven **h** *3051*
17: 7 which has the seven **h** and ten horns. *3051*
17: 9 The seven **h** are seven hills on which *3051*
18:19 They will throw dust on their **h,** *3051*

HEADSTONE (KJV) See CAPSTONE

HEADWATERS (1) [WATER]

Ge 2:10 from there it was separated into four **h.** 8031

HEADWAY (1)

Ac 27: 7 *We* **made slow h** for many days *1095*

HEADY (KJV) See RASH

HEAL (44) [HEALED, HEALING, HEALS]

Nu 12:13 "O God, please **h** her!" 8324
Dt 32:39 I have wounded and I *will* **h,** 8324
2Ki 20: 5 I *will* **h** you. 8324
20: 8 the LORD *will* **h** me and that I will go up 8324
2Ch 7:14 and *will* **h** their land. 8324
Job 5:18 he injures, but his hands also **h.** 8324
Ps 6: 2 O LORD, **h** me, for my bones are in agony. 8324
41: 4 **h** me, for I have sinned against you." 8324
Ecc 3: 3 a time to kill and a time to **h,** 8324
Isa 19:22 he will strike them and **h** them. 8324
19:22 he will respond to their pleas and **h** them. 8324
57:18 I have seen his ways, but *I will* **h** him; 8324
57:19 "And *I will* **h** them." 8324
Jer 17:14 **H** me, O LORD, and I will be healed; 8324
30:17 to health and **h** your wounds,' 8324

Jer 33: 6 *I will* **h** my people 8324
La 2:13 Who *can* **h** you? 8324
Hos 5:13 not able *to* **h** your sores. 1564
6: 1 He has torn us to pieces but *he will* **h** us; 8324
7: 1 whenever I *would* **h** Israel, 8324
14: 4 "*I will* **h** their waywardness 8324
Na 3:19 Nothing can **h** your wound; 3911
Zec 11:16 or **h** the injured, or feed the healthy, 8324
Mt 8: 7 Jesus said to him, "I *will* go and **h** him." 2543
10: 1 and *to* **h** every disease and sickness. 2543
10: 8 **H** the sick, raise the dead, 2543
12:10 "Is it lawful *to* **h** on the Sabbath?" 2543
13:15 and turn, and *I would* **h** them.' 2615
17:16 but they could not **h** him." 2543
Mk 3: 2 to see if *he would* **h** him on the Sabbath. 2543
6: 5 on a few sick people and **h** them. 2543
Lk 4:23 'Physician, **h** yourself! 2543
5:17 the Lord was present for him *to* **h** the sick. 2615
6: 7 to see if *he would* **h** on the Sabbath. 2543
7: 3 asking him to come and **h** his servant. 1407
8:43 but no one could **h** her. 2543
9: 2 to preach the kingdom of God and *to* **h** 2615
10: 9 **H** the sick who are there and tell them, 2543
13:32 and **h people** today and tomorrow, 699+2617
14: 3 "Is it lawful *to* **h** on the Sabbath or not?" 2543
Jn 4:47 and begged him *to* come and **h** his son, 2615
12:40 nor turn—and *I would* **h** them." 2615
Ac 4:30 to **h** and perform miraculous signs 2617
28:27 and turn, and *I would* **h** them.' 2615

HEALED (73) [HEAL]

Ge 20:17 and God **h** Abimelech, 8324
Ex 21:19 **see that** *he* **is completely h.** 8324+8324
Lev 13:37 the itch *is* **h.** 8324
14: 3 If the person *has* **been h** 8324
Jos 5: 8 where they were in camp until they *were* **h.** 2649
1Sa 6: 3 Then *you will* **be h,** 8324
2Ki 2:21 '*I have* **h** this water. 8324
2Ch 30:20 the LORD heard Hezekiah and **h** the people. 8324
Ps 30: 2 I called to you for help and *you* **h** me. 8324
107:20 He sent forth his word and **h** them; 8324
Isa 6:10 and turn and *be* **h."** 8324
53: 5 and by his wounds we **are h.** 8324
Jer 14:19 so that we cannot **be h?** 5340
17:14 Heal me, O LORD, and *I will* **be h;** 8324
51: 8 Get balm for her pain; perhaps *she can* **be h.** 8324
51: 9 " '*We would have* **h** Babylon, 8324
51: 9 but *she* cannot **be h;** 8324
Eze 34: 4 You have not strengthened the weak or **h** 8324
Hos 11: 3 they did not realize *it was I who* **h** them. 8324
Mt 4:24 and the paralyzed, and *he* **h** them. 2543
8: 8 and my servant *will be* **h.** 2615
8:13 And his servant *was* **h** at that very hour. 2615
8:16 the spirits with a word and **h** all the sick. 2543
9:21 "If I only touch his cloak, *I will be* **h."** 5392
9:22 daughter," he said, "your faith *has* **h** you." 5392
9:22 And the woman *was* **h** from that moment. 5392
12:15 Many followed him, and *he* **h** all their sick, 2543
12:22 Jesus **h** him, so that he could both talk and 2543
14:14 he had compassion on them and **h** their sick. 2543
14:36 and all who touched him *were* **h.** 1407
15:28 her daughter *was* **h** from that very hour. 2615
15:30 laid them at his feet; and *he* **h** them. 2543
17:18 and he *was* **h** from that moment. 2543
19: 2 crowds followed him, and *he* **h** them there. 2543
21:14 at the temple, and *he* **h** them. 2543
Mk 1:34 and Jesus **h** many who had various diseases. 2543
3:10 For *he had* **h** many, 2543
5:23 on her so that *she will be* **h** and live." 5392
5:28 "If I just touch his clothes, *I will be* **h."** 5392
5:34 "Daughter, your faith *has* **h** you. 5392
6:13 many sick people with oil and **h** them. 2543
6:56 and all who touched him *were* **h.** 5392
10:52 "Go," said Jesus, "your faith *has* **h** you." 5392
Lk 4:40 laying his hands on each one, he **h** them. 2543
5:15 to hear him and *to be* **h** of their sicknesses. 2543
6:18 to hear him and *to be* **h** of their diseases. 2615
7: 7 say the word, and my servant *will be* **h.** 2615
8:47 and how *she had been* instantly **h.** 2615
8:48 "Daughter, your faith *has* **h** you. 5392
8:50 just believe, and *she will be* **h."** 5392
9:11 and **h** those who needed healing. 2615
9:42 **h** the boy and gave him back to his father. 2615
13:14 because Jesus *had* **h** on the Sabbath, 2543
13:14 So come and *be* **h** on those days, 2543
14: 4 *he* **h** him and sent him away. 2615
17:15 One of them, when he saw *he was* **h,** 2615
18:42 your faith *has* **h** you." 5392
22:51 And *he* touched the man's ear and **h** him. 2615
Jn 5:10 so the Jews said *to* the man who *had been* **h,** 2543
5:13 The man who *was* **h** had no idea who it was, 2615
Ac 4: 9 to a cripple and are asked how he *was* **h,** 5392
4:10 that this man stands before you **h.** 5618
4:14 the man who *had been* **h** standing there 2543
4:22 For the man who was miraculously **h** was 2617
5:16 and all of them *were* **h.** 2543
8: 7 and many paralytics and cripples *were* **h.** 2543
14: 9 saw that he had faith *to be* **h** 3836+5392
28: 8 placed his hands on him and **h** him. 2615
Heb 12:13 the lame may not be disabled, but rather **h.** 2615
Jas 5:16 pray for each other so that **you may be h.** 2615
1Pe 2:24 by his wounds *you have been* **h.** 2615
Rev 13: 3 but the fatal wound *had been* **h.** 2543
13:12 whose fatal wound *had been* **h.** 2543

HEALING (28) [HEAL]

2Ch 28:15 food and drink, and **h balm.** 6057
Pr 12:18 but the tongue of the wise brings **h.** 5340
13:17 but a trustworthy envoy brings **h.** 5340
15: 4 The tongue that brings **h** is a tree of life, 5340
16:24 sweet to the soul and **h** to the bones. 5340
Isa 58: 8 and your **h** will quickly appear; 776
Jer 8:15 for a time of **h** but there was only terror. 5340
8:22 Why then is there no **h for** the **wound** 776
14:19 for a time of **h** but there is only terror. 5340
30:12 your injury **beyond h.** 2703
30:13 no remedy for your sore, no **h** for you. 9499
33: 6 I will bring health and **h** to it; 5340
46:11 there is no **h** for you. 9499
Eze 30:21 not been bound up for **h** or put in 5989+8337
47:12 for food and their leaves for **h."** 9559
Mal 4: 2 the sun of righteousness will rise with **h** 5340
Mt 4:23 and **h** every disease and sickness among 2543
9:35 of the kingdom and **h** every disease 2543
Lk 6:19 power was coming from him and **h** them all. 2615
9: 6 the gospel and **h** people everywhere. 2543
9:11 and healed those who needed **h.** 2542
Jn 7:23 for **h** the whole man on the Sabbath? 4472+5618
Ac 3:16 through him that has given this **complete h** 3907
10:38 and **h** all who were under the power of 2615
1Co 12: 9 to another gifts *of* **h** by that one Spirit, 2611
12:28 also those having gifts *of* **h,** 2611
12:30 Do all have gifts *of* **h?** 2611
Rev 22: 2 And the leaves of the tree are for the **h** of 2542

HEALS (6) [HEAL]

Ex 15:26 for I am the LORD, *who* **h** you." 8324
Lev 13:18 a boil on his skin and *it* **h,** 8324
Ps 103: 3 and **h** all your diseases, 8324
147: 3 He **h** the brokenhearted and binds 8324
Isa 30:26 of his people and **h** the wounds he inflicted. 8324
Ac 9:34 Peter said to him, "Jesus Christ **h** you. 2615

HEALTH (11) [HEALTHIER, HEALTHY]

1Sa 25: 6 **Good h** to you and your household! 8934
25: 6 And **good h** to all that is yours! 8934
Ps 38: 3 of your wrath there is no **h** in my body; 5507
38: 7 there is no **h** in my body. 5507
Pr 3: 8 This will bring **h** to your body 8326
4:22 to those who find them and **h** to 5340
15:30 and good news **gives h** *to* the bones. 2014
Isa 38:16 *You* **restored** me to **h** and let me live. 2730
Jer 30:17 to **h** and heal your wounds,' 776
33: 6 I will bring **h** and healing to it; 776
3Jn 1: 2 I pray that you *may* **enjoy good h** and 5617

HEALTHIER (1) [HEALTH]

Da 1:15 At the end of the ten days they looked **h** 3202

HEALTHY (7) [HEALTH]

Ge 41: 5 Seven heads of grain, **h** and good, 1374
41: 7 of grain swallowed up the seven **h,** 1374
Ps 73: 4 their bodies are **h** and strong. 1374
Zec 11:16 or heal the injured, or feed the **h,** 5893
Mt 9:12 "It is not the **h** who need a doctor, 2710
Mk 2:17 "It is not the **h** who need a doctor, 2710
Lk 5:31 "It is not the **h** who need a doctor, 5617

HEAP (29) [HEAPED, HEAPING, HEAPS]

Ge 31:46 So they took stones and piled them in a **h,** 1643
31:46 and they ate there by the **h.** 1643
31:48 "This **h** is a witness between you 1643
31:51 Laban also said to Jacob, "Here is this **h,** 1643
31:52 This **h** is a witness, 1643
31:52 not go past this **h** to your side to harm you 1643
31:52 past this **h** and pillar to my side to harm me. 1643
Lev 4:12 and burn it in a wood fire on the ash **h.** 9162
Dt 32:23 "*I will* **h** calamities upon them 3578
Jos 3:13 be cut off and stand up in a **h."** 5603
3:16 It piled up in a **h** a great distance away, 5603
8:28 and made it a permanent **h of ruins,** 9424
1Sa 2: 8 the dust and lifts the needy from the **ash h;** 883
2Sa 18:17 in the forest and piled up a large **h** *of* rocks 1643
Ps 113: 7 the dust and lifts the needy from the **ash h;** 883
Pr 25:22 you *will* **h** burning coals on his head, 3149
Isa 3: 6 take charge of this **h of ruins!"** 4843
17: 1 be a city but will become a **h** *of* ruins. 5075
25: 2 You have made the city a **h of rubble,** 1643
Jer 9:11 "I will make Jerusalem a **h of ruins,** 1643
26:18 Jerusalem will become a **h of rubble,** 6505
51:37 Babylon will be a **h of ruins,** 1643
Eze 24:10 So **h** *on* the wood and kindle the fire. 8049
Mic 1: 6 I will make Samaria a **h of rubble,** 6505
3:12 Jerusalem will become a **h of rubble,** 6505
Hag 2:16 anyone came to a **h** *of* twenty measures, 6894
Ro 12:20 *you will* **h** burning coals on his head." 5397
1Th 2:16 **h up** their sins **to the limit.** 405
1Pe 4: 4 and *they* **h abuse on** you. 1059

HEAP (Anglicized) See also PILE

HEAPED (6) [HEAP]

Jos 7:26 Over Achan *they* **h up** a large pile of rocks, 7756
2Ki 19:23 By your messengers *you have* **h insults on** 3070
Isa 37:24 By your messengers *you have* **h insults on** 3070
Zec 9: 3 *she has* **h up** silver like dust, 7392
Mt 27:44 with him also **h insults on** him. 3943
Mk 15:32 Those crucified with him also **h insults on** 3943

HEAPING (2) [HEAP]

Ps 110: 6 **h up** the dead and crushing the rulers of 4848
Isa 30: 1 but not by my Spirit, **h** sin upon sin; 3578

HEAPS (10) [HEAP]

Ex 8:14 They were piled into **h,** 2818+2818
2Ch 31: 6 and they piled them **in h.** 6894+6894
31: 8 and his officials came and saw the **h,** 6894
31: 9 the priests and Levites about the **h;** 6894
Ne 4: 2 the stones back to life from those **h** 6894
Job 27:16 Though *he* **h up** silver like dust and clothes 7392
Ps 39: 6 *he* **h up wealth,** not knowing who will get it 7392
Jer 50:26 pile her up like **h of grain.** 6894
La 4: 5 Those nurtured in purple now lie on **ash h.** 883
Zep 1: 3 The wicked will have only **h of rubble** 4843

HEAR (379) [HEARD, HEARERS, HEARING, HEARS, OVERHEARD]

Ge 4:23 wives of Lamech, **h** my words. 263
41:15 *when you* **h** a dream you can interpret it." 9048
Ex 15:14 The nations *will* **h** and tremble; 9048
18: 9 Jethro was delighted to **h** about all NIH
19: 9 the people *will* **h** me speaking with you 9048
22:23 *I will* **certainly h** their cry. 9048+9048
22:27 When he cries out to me, *I will* **h,** 9048
32:18 it is the sound of singing that I **h."** 9048
Nu 14:13 "Then the Egyptians *will* **h** *about* it! 9048
23:18 **h** me, son of Zippor. 263
Dt 1:16 **H** the disputes between your brothers 9048
1:17 **h** both small and great alike. 9048
1:17 and *I will* **h** it. 9048
2:25 *They will* **h** reports of you and will tremble 9048
4: 1 **H** now, O Israel, the decrees and laws I am 9048
4: 6 who *will* **h** *about* all these decrees 9048
4:10 the people before me *to* **h** my words so 9048
4:28 which cannot see or **h** or eat or smell. 9048
4:36 From heaven *he* **made** you **h** his voice 9048
5: 1 Moses summoned all Israel and said: **H,** 9048
5:25 and we will die if we **h** the voice of 9048
6: 3 **H,** O Israel, and be careful to obey so 9048
6: 4 **H,** O Israel: The LORD our God, 9048
9: 1 **H,** O Israel. You are now about to cross 9048
13:11 Then all Israel *will* **h** and be afraid, 9048
13:12 If *you* **h** it said about one of the towns 9048
17:13 All the people *will* **h** and be afraid, 9048
18:16 not **h** the voice of the LORD our God 9048
19:20 of the people *will* **h** of this and be afraid, 9048
20: 3 He shall say: **"H,** O Israel, 9048
21:21 All Israel *will* **h** of it and be afraid. 9048
29: 4 or eyes that see or ears that **h.** 9048
31:13 *must* **h** it and learn to fear 9048
32: 1 **h,** O earth, the words of my mouth. 9048
33: 7 **"H,** O LORD, the cry of Judah; 9048
Jos 6: 5 When you **h** them sound a long blast on 9048
7: 9 and the other people of the country *will* **h** 9048
22:33 to **h** the report and praised God. NIH
Jdg 5: 3 **"H** this, *you* kings! 9048
5:16 Why did you stay among the campfires to **h** 9048
14:13 "*Let's* **h** it." 9048
1Sa 2:23 I **h** from all the people 9048
2:24 not a good report that I **h** spreading among 9048
13: 3 "*Let* the Hebrews **h!"** 9048
15:14 What is this lowing of cattle that I **h?"** 9048
16: 2 Saul *will* **h** *about* it and kill me." 9048
25: 7 " 'Now *I* **h** that it is sheep-shearing time. 9048
25:24 **h** what your servant has to say. 9048
2Sa 5:24 As soon as you **h** the sound of marching in 9048
15: 3 no representative of the king *to* **h** you." 9048
15:10 soon as you **h** the sound of the trumpets, 9048
15:35 Tell them anything *you* **h** in the king's 9048
15:36 Send them to me with anything *you* **h."** 9048
16:21 Then all Israel *will* **h** that you have made 9048
17: 5 so *we can* **h** what he has to say." 9048
18:31 "My lord the king, **h** *the* **good news!** 1413
19:35 *Can I* still **h** the voices of men 9048
22:45 as soon as they **h** me, they obey me. 9048
1Ki 1:45 That's the noise *you* **h.** 9048
8:28 **H** the cry and the prayer 9048
8:29 so that you *will* **h** the prayer your servant 9048
8:30 **H** the supplication of your servant and 9048
8:30 **H** from heaven, your dwelling place, 9048
8:30 your dwelling place, and when *you* **h,** 9048
8:32 then **h** from heaven and act. 9048
8:34 then **h** from heaven and forgive the sin 9048
8:36 then **h** from heaven and forgive the sin 9048
8:39 then **h** from heaven, your dwelling place. 9048
8:42 for *men will* **h** *of* your great name 9048
8:43 then **h** from heaven, your dwelling place, 9048
8:45 **h** from heaven their prayer and their plea, 9048
8:49 **h** their prayer and their plea, 9048
10: 8 before you and **h** your wisdom! 9048
10:24 with Solomon to **h** the wisdom God had put 9048
22:19 "Therefore **h** the word of the LORD: 9048
2Ki 7: 1 Elisha said, **"H** the word of the LORD. 9048
7: 6 **caused** the Arameans **to h** the sound of 9048
18:28 **"H** the word of the great king, 9048
19: 4 the LORD your God *will* **h** all the words 9048
19:16 Give ear, O LORD, and **h;** 9048
20:16 **"H** the word of the LORD: 9048
1Ch 14:15 As soon as you **h** the sound of marching in 9048
2Ch 6:19 **H** the cry and the prayer that your servant 9048
6:20 *May* you **h** the prayer your servant prays 9048

2Ch 6:21 **H** the supplications of your servant and 9048
6:21 **H** from heaven, your dwelling place; 9048
6:21 and when *you* **h**, forgive. 9048
6:23 then **h** from heaven and act. 9048
6:25 then **h** from heaven and forgive the sin 9048
6:27 then **h** from heaven and forgive the sin 9048
6:30 then **h** from heaven, your dwelling place. 9048
6:33 then **h** from heaven, your dwelling place, 9048
6:35 **h** from heaven their prayer and their plea, 9048
6:39 **h** their prayer and their pleas, 9048
7:14 then *will* I **h** from heaven 9048
9:7 before you and **h** your wisdom! 9048
9:23 with Solomon to **h** the wisdom God had put 9048
18:18 "Therefore **h** the word of the LORD: 9048
20:9 and *you will* **h** us and save us.' 9048
Ne 1:6 to **h** the prayer your servant is praying 9048
4:4 **H** us, O our God, for we are despised. 9048
4:20 Wherever *you* **h** the sound of the trumpet, 9048
13:27 *Must we* **h** now that you too are doing 9048
Job 3:18 *they* no longer **h** the slave driver's shout. 9048
5:27 So **h** it and apply it to yourself." 9048
13:6 **H** now my argument; 9048
20:3 *I* **h** a rebuke that dishonors me, 9048
22:27 You will pray to him, and *he will* **h** you, 9048
26:14 how faint the whisper *we* **h** of him! 9048
31:35 that I had *someone to* **h** me! 9048
34:2 "**H** my words, you wise men; 9048
34:16 "If you have understanding, **h** this; 9048
34:34 wise men *who* **h** me say to me, 9048
39:7 *he does* not **h** a driver's shout. 9048
Ps 4:1 be merciful to me and **h** my prayer. 9048
4:3 the LORD *will* **h** when I call to him. 9048
5:3 In the morning, O LORD, *you* **h** my voice; 9048
10:17 *You* **h**, O LORD, the desire of the afflicted; 9048
17:1 **H**, O LORD, my righteous plea; 9048
17:6 give ear to me and **h** my prayer. 9048
18:44 As soon as they **h** me, they obey me; 9051
27:7 **H** my voice when I call, O LORD; 9048
28:2 **H** my cry for mercy as I call to you for help, 9048
30:10 **H**, O LORD, and be merciful to me; 9048
31:13 For *I* **h** the slander of many; 9048
34:2 *let* the afflicted **h** and rejoice. 9048
38:13 I am like a deaf man, *who* cannot **h**, 9048
38:14 I have become like a man who *does* not **h**, 9048
39:12 "**H** my prayer, O LORD, listen to my cry 9048
49:1 **H** this, all you peoples; 9048
50:7 "**H**, O my people, and I will speak, O Israel, 9048
51:8 **Let** me **h** joy and gladness; 9048
54:2 **H** my prayer, O God; 9048
55:2 **h** me and answer me. 7992
55:19 *will* **h** them and afflict them— 9048
59:7 and they say, "Who *can* **h** us?" 9048
61:1 **H** my cry, O God; listen to my prayer. 9048
64:1 **H** me, O God, as I voice my complaint; 9048
65:2 O you *who* **h** prayer, 9048
77:1 I cried out to God *to* **h** me. 263
78:1 O my people, **h** my teaching; 263
80:1 **H** us, O Shepherd of Israel, 263
81:8 "**H**, O my people, and I will warn you— 9048
84:8 **H** my prayer, O LORD God Almighty; 9048
86:1 **H**, O LORD, and answer me, 265+5742
86:6 **H** my prayer, O LORD; 263
94:9 *Does he* who implanted the ear not **h**? 9048
95:7 Today, if *you* **h** his voice, 9048
102:1 **H** my prayer, O LORD; 9048
102:20 to **h** the groans of the prisoners 9048
115:6 but cannot **h**, noses, but they cannot smell; 9048
119:149 **H** my voice in accordance with your love; 9048
130:2 O Lord, **h** my voice. 9048
135:17 but cannot **h**, nor is there breath 263
138:4 when *they* **h** the words of your mouth. 9048
140:6 **H**, O LORD, my cry for mercy. 263
141:1 **H** my voice when I call to you. 263
143:1 O LORD, **h** my prayer, 9048
Pr 20:12 Ears *that* **h** and eyes that see— 9048
Ecc 7:21 or *you may* **h** your servant cursing you— 9048
SS 2:14 show me your face, **let** me **h** your voice; 9048
8:13 **let** me **h** your voice! 9048
Isa 1:2 **H**, O heavens! 9048
1:10 **H** the word of the LORD, 9048
6:10 **h** with their ears, 9048
7:13 Isaiah said, "**H** now, you house of David! 9048
18:3 and when a trumpet sounds, *you will* **h** it. 9048
21:3 I am staggered by *what* I **h**, 9048
24:16 From the ends of the earth *we* **h** singing: 9048
28:14 Therefore **h** the word of the LORD, 9048
28:23 Listen and **h** my voice; 9048
28:23 pay attention and **h** what I say. 9048
29:18 In that day the deaf *will* **h** the words of 9048
30:21 your ears *will* **h** a voice behind you, 9048
30:30 The LORD *will* **cause** men **to h** his majestic voice 9048
32:3 and the ears of *those who* **h** will listen. 9048
32:9 **h** what I have to say! 263
33:13 You who are far away, **h** what I have done; 9048
34:1 *Let* the earth **h**, and all that is in it, 9048
36:13 "**H** the words of the great king, 9048
37:4 that the LORD your God *will* **h** the words 9048
37:17 Give ear, O LORD, and **h**; 9048
39:5 "**H** the word of the LORD Almighty: 9048
42:18 "**H**, *you* deaf; look, you blind, and see! 9048
42:20 your ears are open, but *you* **h** nothing." 9048
43:9 so that *others may* **h** and say, "It is true." 9048
49:1 **h** this, *you* distant nations: 7992
51:4 "Listen to me, my people; **h** me, my nation: 263
51:7 "**H** me, you who know what is right, 9048
51:21 Therefore **h** this, *you* afflicted one, 9048
Isa 55:3 **h** me, that your soul may live. 9048
59:1 nor his ear too dull *to* **h**. 9048
59:2 so that *he will* not **h**. 9048
65:24 while they are still speaking I *will* **h**. 9048
66:5 **H** the word of the LORD, 9048
66:6 **H** that uproar from the city, 7754
66:6 **h** that noise from the temple! NIH
Jer 2:4 **H** the word of the LORD, 9048
4:21 the battle standard and **h** the sound of 9048
4:31 *I* **h** a cry as of a woman in labor, 9048
5:21 **H** this, *you* foolish and senseless people, 9048
5:21 who have ears but *do* not **h**: 9048
6:10 Their ears are closed so they cannot **h**. 7992
6:18 Therefore **h**, O nations; 9048
6:19 **H**, O earth: I am bringing disaster on 9048
7:2 " '**H** the word of the LORD, 9048
9:20 Now, O women, **h** the word of the LORD; 9048
10:1 **H** what the LORD says to you, 9048
13:15 **H** and pay attention, do not be arrogant, 9048
17:20 Say to them, '**H** the word of the LORD, 9048
18:19 **h** what my accusers are saying! 9048
19:3 '**H** the word of the LORD, 9048
20:10 *I* **h** many whispering, 9048
20:16 *May he* **h** wailing in the morning, 9048
21:11 '**H** the word of the LORD; 9048
22:2 '**H** the word of the LORD, O king 9048
22:29 land, land, **h** the word of the LORD! 9048
23:18 of the LORD to see or *to* **h** his word? 9048
25:36 **H** the cry of the shepherds, 7754
29:20 Therefore, **h** the word of the LORD, 9048
31:10 "**H** the word of the LORD, O nations; 9048
33:9 and honor before all nations on earth that **h** 9048
34:4 " 'Yet **h** the promise of the LORD, 9048
36:3 of Judah **h** *about* every disaster I plan 9048
38:25 If the officials **h** that I talked with you, 9048
42:2 "Please **h** our petition and pray 4200+5877+7156
42:14 where we will not see war or **h** the trumpet 9048
42:15 then **h** the word of the LORD, 9048
44:24 "**H** the word of the LORD, 9048
44:26 But **h** the word of the LORD, 9048
46:12 The nations *will* **h** *of* your shame; 9048
49:20 **h** what the LORD has planned 9048
50:45 **h** what the LORD has planned 9048
Eze 3:17 so **h** the word I speak 9048
6:3 **h** the word of the Sovereign LORD. 9048
12:2 but do not see and ears to **h** but do not hear, 9048
12:2 but do not see and ears to hear but *do* not **h**, 9048
13:2 '**H** the word of the LORD! 9048
16:35 you prostitute, **h** the word of the LORD! 9048
18:25 **H**, O house of Israel: Is my way unjust? 9048
20:47 '**H** the word of the LORD. 9048
25:3 '**H** the word of the Sovereign LORD. 9048
33:7 so **h** the word I speak 9048
33:30 'Come and **h** the message that has come 9048
33:32 for *they* **h** your words but do not put them 9048
34:7 you shepherds, **h** the word of the LORD: 9048
34:9 O shepherds, **h** the word of the LORD: 9048
36:1 **h** the word of the LORD. 9048
36:4 **h** the word of the Sovereign LORD: 9048
36:15 No longer *will* **I make** you **h** the taunts of 9048
37:4 'Dry bones, **h** the word of the LORD! 9048
40:4 look with your eyes and **h** with your ears 9048
Da 3:5 As soon as *you* **h** the sound of the horn, 10725
3:15 Now when *you* **h** the sound of the horn, 10725
5:23 which cannot see or **h** or understand. 10725
9:17 **h** the prayers and petitions of your servant. 9048
9:18 Give ear, O God, and **h**; 9048
9:19 O Lord, **h** and act! 7992
Hos 4:1 **H** the word of the LORD, you Israelites, 9048
5:1 "**H** this, *you* priests! 9048
7:12 When I **h** them flocking together, 9051
Joel 1:2 **H** this, you elders; 9048
Am 3:1 **H** this word the LORD has spoken 9048
3:13 "**H** this and testify against the house 9048
4:1 **H** this word, you cows of Bashan 9048
5:1 **H** this word, O house of Israel, 9048
7:16 Now then, **h** the word of the LORD. 9048
8:4 **H** this, you who trample the needy 9048
Mic 1:2 **H**, O peoples, all of you, listen, 9048
3:9 **H** this, you leaders of the house of Jacob, 9048
6:1 *let* the hills **h** what you have to say. 9048
6:2 **H**, O mountains, the LORD's accusation; 9048
7:7 my God *will* **h** me. 9048
Zec 8:9 *"You* who now **h** these words spoken by 9048
Mt 11:4 "Go back and report to John what *you* **h** *201*
11:5 the deaf **h**, the dead are raised, *201*
11:15 He who has ears, *let him* **h**. *201*
12:19 no one *will* **h** his voice in the streets. *201*
13:9 He who has ears, *let him* **h**." *201*
13:13 though hearing, *they do* not **h** or understand. *201*
13:15 *they* hardly **h** with their ears, *201*
13:15 might see with their eyes, **h** with their ears, *201*
13:16 and your ears because *they* **h**. *201*
13:17 and *to* **h** what you hear but did not hear it. *201*
13:17 and to hear what *you* **h** but did not hear it. *201*
13:17 and to hear what you hear but *did* not **h** it. *201*
13:43 He who has ears, *let him* **h**. *201*
21:16 *"Do you* **h** what these children are saying?" *201*
24:6 *You* will **h** of wars and rumors of wars, *201*
27:13 Then Pilate asked him, "Don't *you* **h** *201*
Mk 4:9 Then Jesus said, "He who has ears *to* **h**, *201*
4:9 "He who has ears to hear, *let him* **h**." *201*
4:15 As soon as *they* **h** it, *201*
4:16 **h** the word and at once receive it with joy. *201*
4:18 like seed sown among thorns, **h** the word; *201+1639+4047*
4:20 **h** the word, accept it, and produce a *201+4015*
Mk 4:23 If anyone has ears *to* **h**, let him hear." *201*
4:23 If anyone has ears to hear, *let him* **h**." *201*
4:24 "Consider carefully what *you* **h**," *201*
7:37 even makes the deaf **h** and the mute speak." *201*
8:18 and ears but fail to **h**? *201*
12:29 '**H**, O Israel, the Lord our God, *201*
13:7 When *you* **h** of wars and rumors of wars, *201*
14:11 They were delighted *to* **h** this and promised *201*
15:44 to **h** that he was already dead. *NIG*
Lk 5:15 so that crowds of people came *to* **h** him and *201*
6:18 *to* **h** him and to be healed of their diseases. *201*
6:27 "But I tell you who **h** me: *201*
7:22 the deaf **h**, the dead are raised, *201*
8:8 "He who has ears *to* **h**, let him hear." *201*
8:8 "He who has ears to hear, *let him* **h**." *201*
8:12 Those along the path are the ones who **h**, *201*
8:13 the word with joy when *they* **h** it, *201*
8:14 among thorns stands for those who **h**, *201*
8:15 *who* **h** the word, retain it, *201*
8:21 and brothers are those who **h** God's word *201*
9:9 Who, then, is this *I* **h** such things about?" *201*
10:24 and *to* **h** what you hear but did not hear it." *201*
10:24 and to hear what *you* **h** but did not hear it." *201*
10:24 and to hear what you hear but *did* not **h** it." *201*
11:28 "Blessed rather are those who **h** the word *201*
14:35 "He who has ears *to* **h**, let him hear." *201*
14:35 "He who has ears to hear, *let him* **h**." *201*
15:1 were all gathering around *to* **h** him. *201*
16:2 'What is this *I* **h** about you? *201*
21:9 When *you* **h** of wars and revolutions, *201*
21:38 in the morning *to* **h** him at the temple. *201*
Jn 3:8 *You* **h** its sound, but you cannot tell where *201*
5:25 the dead *will* **h** the voice of the Son of God *201*
5:25 of the Son of God and those who **h** will live. *201*
5:28 in their graves *will* **h** his voice *201*
5:30 I judge only as *I* **h**, *201*
8:43 Because you are unable *to* **h** what I say. *201*
8:47 not **h** is that you do not belong to God." *201*
9:27 Why do you want *to* **h** it again? *201*
11:42 I knew that *you* always **h** me, *201*
14:24 These words *you* **h** are not my own; *201*
Ac 2:11 *we* **h** them declaring the wonders of God *201*
2:33 and has poured out what you now see and **h**. *201*
10:22 *so that he could* **h** what you have to say." *201*
13:7 and Saul because he wanted *to* **h** the word *201*
13:44 the whole city gathered *to* **h** the word of *201*
15:7 that the Gentiles *might* **h** from my lips *201*
17:32 *"We want to* **h** you again on this subject." *201*
19:26 and **h** how this fellow Paul has convinced *201*
21:22 *They will* certainly **h** that you have come, *201*
22:14 to see the Righteous One and *to* **h** words *201*
23:35 *"I will* **h** your **case** when your accusers *1358*
24:4 that you be kind enough *to* **h** us briefly. *201*
25:22 "I would like *to* **h** this man myself." *201*
25:22 He replied, "Tomorrow *you will* **h** him." *201*
28:22 But we want *to* **h** what your views are, *201*
28:27 *they* hardly **h** with their ears, *201*
28:27 **h** with their ears, *201*
Ro 2:13 not those who **h** the law who are righteous *212*
10:14 how *can they* **h** without someone preaching *201*
10:18 But I ask: *Did they* not **h**? *201*
11:8 not see and ears so that *they could* not **h**, *201*
1Co 11:18 *I* **h** that when you come together as *201*
Php 1:27 whether I come and see you or only **h** *201*
1:30 and now **h** that I still have. *201*
2Th 3:11 *We* **h** that some among you are idle. *201*
2Ti 4:3 to say **what** their itching **ears want to h**. *NIG*
4:17 and all the Gentiles *might* **h** it. *201*
Phm 1:5 *because* I **h** about your faith in *201*
Heb 3:7 "Today, if *you* **h** his voice, *201*
3:15 "Today, if *you* **h** his voice, *201*
4:7 "Today, if *you* **h** his voice, *201*
3Jn 1:4 to **h** that my children are walking in *201*
Rev 1:3 blessed are those who **h** it and take to heart *201*
2:7 *let him* **h** what the Spirit says to the churches *201*
2:11 *let him* **h** what the Spirit says to the churches *201*
2:17 *let him* **h** what the Spirit says to the churches *201*
2:29 *let him* **h** what the Spirit says to the churches *201*
3:6 *let him* **h** what the Spirit says to the churches *201*
3:13 *let him* **h** what the Spirit says to the churches *201*
3:22 *let him* **h** what the Spirit says to the churches *201*
9:20 idols that cannot see or **h** or walk. *201*
13:9 He who has an ear, *let him* **h**. *201*

HEARD (577) [HEAR]

Ge 3:8 and his wife **h** the sound of the LORD God 9048
3:10 He answered, *"I* **h** you in the garden, 9048
14:14 When Abram **h** that his relative had been taken captive, 9048
16:11 for the LORD *has* **h** of your misery. 9048
17:20 And as for Ishmael, *I have* **h** you: 9048
21:17 God **h** the boy crying, 9048
21:17 God *has* **h** the boy crying as he lies there. 9048
21:26 and I **h** *about* it only today." 9048
24:30 *had* **h** Rebekah tell what the man said 9048
24:52 When Abraham's servant **h** what they said, 9048
27:34 When Esau **h** his father's words, 9048
29:13 As soon as Laban **h** the news about Jacob, 9048
29:33 "Because the LORD **h** that I am not loved, 9048
31:1 Jacob **h** that Laban's sons were saying, 9048
34:5 When Jacob **h** that his daughter Dinah had been defiled, 9048
34:7 as soon as they **h** what had happened. 9048
35:22 and Israel **h** *of* it. 9048
37:17 *"I* **h** them say, 'Let's go to Dothan.' " 9048
37:21 When Reuben **h** this, he tried to rescue him 9048

Ge 39:15 When he **h** me scream for help, 9048
39:19 When his master **h** the story his wife told 9048
41:15 But I *have* **h** it said of you *that* 9048
42: 2 *"I have* **h** that there is grain in Egypt. 9048
43:25 *they had* **h** that they were to eat there. 9048
45: 2 he wept so loudly that the Egyptians **h** him, 9048
45: 2 and Pharaoh's household **h** *about* it. 9048
Ex 2:15 When Pharaoh **h** *of* this, 9048
2:24 God **h** their groaning 9048
3: 7 *I have* **h** them crying out because 9048
4:31 when *they* **h** that the LORD was concerned 9048
6: 5 I *have* **h** the groaning of the Israelites, 9048
16: 7 he *has* **h** your grumbling against him. 9048
16: 8 he *has* **h** your grumbling against him. 9048
16: 9 for *he has* **h** your grumbling.' " 9048
16:12 *"I have* **h** the grumbling of the Israelites. 9048
18: 1 **h** *of* everything God had done for Moses 9048
20:18 the thunder and lightning and **h** the trumpet 7754
23:13 *do* not *let them* **be h** on your lips. 9048
28:35 of the bells *will* **be h** when he enters 9048
32:17 Joshua **h** the noise of the people shouting, 9048
33: 4 When the people **h** these distressing words, 9048
Lev 10:20 When Moses **h** this, he was satisfied. 9048
24:14 All those *who* **h** him are to lay their hands 9048
Nu 7:89 *he* **h** the voice speaking to him from 9048
11: 1 and when he **h** them his anger was aroused. 9048
11:10 Moses **h** the people of every family wailing, 9048
11:18 The LORD **h** you when you wailed, 265
12: 2 And the LORD **h** this. 9048
14:14 *They have already* **h** that you, O LORD, 9048
14:15 the nations who *have* **h** this report 9048
14:27 *I have* **h** the complaints of these grumbling 9048
14:28 do to you the very things I **h** you say: 265+928
16: 4 When Moses **h** this, he fell facedown. 9048
20:16 *he* **h** our cry and sent an angel 9048
21: 1 **h** that Israel was coming along the road 9048
22:36 When Balak **h** that Balaam was coming, 9048
33:40 **h** that the Israelites were coming. 9048
Dt 1:34 When the LORD **h** what you said, 9048
4:12 You **h** the sound of words but saw no form; 9048
4:32 or *has* anything like it *ever* **been h of?** 9048
4:33 *Has* any other people **h** the voice 9048
4:36 and *you* **h** his words from out of the fire. 9048
5:23 When you **h** the voice out of the darkness, 9048
5:24 and *we have* **h** his voice from the fire. 9048
5:26 For what mortal man *has* ever **h** the voice of 9048
5:28 The LORD **h** you when you spoke to me 9048
5:28 *"I have* **h** what this people said to you. 9048
5:28 You know about them and *have* **h** it said: 9048
26: 7 the LORD **h** our voice and saw our misery, 9048
Jos 2:10 *We have* **h** how the LORD dried up 9048
2:11 When *we* **h** of it, our hearts melted 9048
5: 1 along the coast **h** how the LORD had dried 9048
9: 1 when all the kings west of the Jordan **h** 9048
9: 3 people of Gibeon **h** what Joshua had done 9048
9: 9 For *we have* **h** reports of him: 9048
9:16 the Israelites **h** that they were neighbors, 9048
10: 1 of Jerusalem **h** that Joshua had taken Ai 9048
11: 1 When Jabin king of Hazor **h** of this, 9048
14:12 *You* yourself **h** then that 9048
22:11 And *when* the Israelites **h** that they had built 9048
22:30 **h** what Reuben, Gad and Manasseh had 9048
24:27 It *has* **h** all the words the LORD has said 9048
Jdg 7:15 When Gideon **h** the dream 9048
9:30 of the city **h** what Gaal son of Ebed said, 9048
9:47 Abimelech **h** that they had assembled there, 5583
13: 9 God **h** Manoah, and the angel 7754+9048
17: 2 about which I **h** you utter a curse— 265+606+928
20: 3 (The Benjamites **h** that the Israelites 9048
Ru 1: 6 When *she* **h** in Moab that 9048
1Sa 1:13 but her voice **was** not **h.** 9048
2:22 **h** *about* everything his sons were doing 9048
4:14 Eli **h** the outcry and asked, 9048
4:19 When *she* **h** the news that the ark 9048
7: 7 the Philistines **h** that Israel had assembled 9048
7: 7 And when the Israelites **h** *of* it, 9048
8:21 When Samuel **h** all that the people said, 9048
11: 6 When Saul **h** their words, 9048
13: 3 and the Philistines **h** *about* it. 9048
13: 4 So all Israel **h** the news: 9048
14:22 of Ephraim **h** that the Philistines were on 9048
14:27 not **h** that his father had bound the people 9048
17:23 shouted his usual defiance, and David **h** it. 9048
17:28 **h** him speaking with the men, 9048
22: 1 and his father's household **h** *about* it, 9048
22: 6 Now Saul **h** that David and his men 9048
23:10 your servant *has* **h definitely** 9048+9048
23:11 as your servant *has* **h?** 9048
23:25 When Saul **h** this, 9048
25: 4 *he* **h** that Nabal was shearing sheep. 9048
25:35 *I have* **h** your words 9048
25:39 When David **h** that Nabal was dead, he said, 9048
31:11 When the people of Jabesh Gilead **h** of what 9048
2Sa 3:28 Later, when David **h** *about* this, he said, 9048
4: 1 of Saul **h** that Abner had died in Hebron, 9048
5:17 When the Philistines **h** that David 9048
5:17 but David **h** *about* it and went down to 9048
7:22 as *we have* **h** with our own ears. 9048
8: 9 of Hamath **h** that David had defeated 9048
11:26 Uriah's wife **h** that her husband was dead, 9048
13:21 When King David **h** all this, he was furious. 9048
18: 5 And all the troops **h** the king giving orders 9048
19: 2 because on that day the troops **h** it said, 9048
22: 7 From his temple *he* **h** my voice; 9048
1Ki 1:11 *"Have you* not **h** that Adonijah, 9048
1:41 and all the guests who were with him **h** it 9048
3:28 all Israel **h** the verdict the king had given, 9048
1Ki 4:34 who *had* **h** *of* his wisdom. 9048
5: 1 When Hiram king of Tyre **h** 9048
5: 7 When Hiram **h** Solomon's message, 9048
6: 7 chisel or any other iron tool **was h** at 9048
9: 3 *I have* **h** the prayer and plea you have made 9048
10: 1 When the queen of Sheba **h** *about* the fame 9048
10: 6 "The report *I* **h** in my own country 9048
10: 7 you have far exceeded the report *I* **h.** 9048
11:21 Hadad **h** that David rested with his fathers 9048
12: 2 of Nebat **h** this (he was still in Egypt, 9048
12:20 the Israelites **h** that Jeroboam had returned, 9048
13: 4 When King Jeroboam **h** what the man 9048
13:26 from his journey **h** *of* it, 9048
14: 6 when Ahijah **h** the sound of her footsteps at 9048
15:21 When Baasha **h** this, 9048
16:16 in the camp **h** that Zimri had plotted against 9048
17:22 The LORD **h** Elijah's cry, 9048
18:13 Haven't you **h,** my lord, 5583
19:13 When Elijah **h** it, 9048
20:12 Ben-Hadad **h** this message while he and 9048
20:31 *we have* **h** that the kings of the house 9048
21:15 as Jezebel **h** that Naboth had been stoned 9048
21:16 When Ahab **h** that Naboth was dead, 9048
21:27 When Ahab **h** these words, 9048
2Ki 3:21 the Moabites *had* **h** that the kings had come 9048
5: 8 When Elisha the man of God **h** that the king 9048
6:30 When the king **h** the woman's words, 9048
9:30 When Jezebel **h** *about* it, 9048
11:13 When Athaliah **h** the noise made by 9048
19: 1 When King Hezekiah **h** this, 9048
19: 4 for the words the LORD your God *has* **h.** 9048
19: 6 Do not be afraid of what *you have* **h—** 9048
19: 8 When the field commander **h** that the king 9048
19:11 Surely you *have* **h** what the kings 9048
19:20 *I have* **h** your prayer 9048
19:25 " *'Have you* not **h?** 9048
20: 5 *I have* **h** your prayer and seen your tears; 9048
20:12 because *he had* **h** *of* Hezekiah's illness. 9048
22:11 When the king **h** the words of the Book of 9048
22:18 says concerning the words *you* **h:** 9048
22:19 the LORD when you **h** what I have spoken 9048
22:19 I *have* **h** you, declares the LORD. 9048
25:23 When all the army officers and their men **h** 9048
1Ch 10:11 When all the inhabitants of Jabesh Gilead **h** 9048
14: 8 When the Philistines **h** 9048
14: 8 but David **h** *about* it and went out 9048
17:20 as *we have* **h** with our own ears. 9048
18: 9 of Hamath **h** that David had defeated 9048
2Ch 7:12 *"I have* **h** your prayer 9048
9: 1 the queen of Sheba **h** *of* Solomon's fame, 9048
9: 5 "The report *I* **h** in my own country 9048
9: 6 you have far exceeded the report *I* **h.** 9048
10: 2 When Jeroboam son of Nebat **h** this 9048
15: 8 When Asa **h** these words and the prophecy 9048
16: 5 When Baasha **h** this, 9048
20:29 the kingdoms of the countries when they **h** 9048
23:12 When Athaliah **h** the noise of 9048
30:20 LORD **h** Hezekiah and healed the people. 9048
30:27 and God **h** them, for their prayer 7754+9048
34:19 When the king **h** the words of the Law, 9048
34:26 says concerning the words *you* **h:** 9048
34:27 before God when you **h** what he spoke 9048
34:27 I *have* **h** you, declares the LORD. 9048
Ezr 3:13 And the sound **was h** far away. 9048
4: 1 When the enemies of Judah and Benjamin **h** 9048
9: 3 When I **h** this, I tore my tunic and cloak, 9048
Ne 1: 4 When I **h** these things, I sat down and wept. 9048
2:10 the Ammonite official **h** *about* this, 9048
2:19 and Geshem the Arab **h** *about* it, 9048
4: 1 When Sanballat **h** that we were rebuilding 9048
4: 7 the Ammonites and the men of Ashdod **h** 9048
4:15 When our enemies **h** that we were aware 9048
5: 6 When *I* **h** their outcry and these charges, 9048
6:16 When all our enemies **h** *about* this, 9048
9: 9 *you* **h** their cry at the Red Sea. 9048
9:27 From heaven you **h** them, 9048
9:28 you **h** from heaven, 9048
12:43 **sound** of rejoicing in Jerusalem *could* **be h** 9048
13: 3 When the people **h** this law, 9048
Est 1:18 of the nobility who *have* **h** *about* 9048
Job 2:11 **h** *about* all the troubles that had come 9048
3: 7 *may* no shout of joy **be h** in it. 995[S]
4:16 and *I* **h** a hushed voice: 9048
13: 1 my ears *have* **h** and understood it. 9048
16: 2 *"I have* **h** many things like these; 9048
29:11 Whoever **h** me spoke well of me, 9048
33: 8 *I* **h** the very words— 9048
34:28 so that *he* **h** the cry of the needy. 9048
42: 5 My ears *had* **h** *of* you but 9048+9051
Ps 6: 8 for the LORD *has* **h** my weeping. 9048
6: 9 The LORD *has* **h** my cry for mercy; 9048
18: 6 From his temple *he* **h** my voice; 9048
19: 3 or language where their voice **is** not **h.** 9048
28: 6 for *he has* **h** my cry for mercy. 9048
31:22 Yet *you* **h** my cry for mercy when I called 9048
34: 6 and the LORD **h** him; 9048
40: 1 he turned to me and **h** my cry. 9048
44: 1 *We have* **h** with our ears, O God; 9048
48: 8 As *we have* **h,** so have we seen in the city of 9048
61: 5 For you *have* **h** my vows, O God; 9048
62:11 two things *have I* **h:** 9048
66: 8 **let** the sound of his praise **be h;** 9048
66:19 but God has surely listened and **h** my voice 7992
77:18 Your thunder **was h** in the whirlwind, 7754
78: 3 what *we have* **h** and known, 9048
78:21 *When* the LORD **h** them, 9048
78:59 *When* God **h** them, he was very angry; 9048
Ps 81: 5 *we* **h** a language we did not understand. 9048
92:11 my ears *have* **h** the rout of my wicked foes. 9048
106:44 of their distress when he **h** their cry; 9048
116: 1 I love the LORD, for *he* **h** my voice; 9048
116: 1 he **h** my cry for mercy. NIH
132: 6 *We* **h** it in Ephrathah, 9048
Ecc 12:13 Now all *has* **been h;** 9048
SS 2:12 the cooing of doves **is h** in our land. 9048
Isa 5: 7 for righteousness, but **h** cries of distress. 2180
6: 8 Then *I* **h** the voice of the Lord saying, 9048
15: 4 their voices **are h** all the way to Jahaz. 9048
16: 6 *We have* **h** *of* Moab's pride— 9048
21:10 I tell you what *I have* **h** from 9048
37: 1 When King Hezekiah **h** this, 9048
37: 4 for the words the LORD your God *has* **h.** 9048
37: 6 Do not be afraid of what *you have* **h—** 9048
37: 8 When the field commander **h** that the king 9048
37: 9 When *he* **h** it, he sent messengers 9048
37:11 Surely you *have* **h** what the kings 9048
37:26 *"Have you* not **h?** 9048
38: 5 *I have* **h** your prayer and seen your tears; 9048
39: 1 because *he had* **h** *of* his illness and recovery. 9048
40:21 *Have you* not **h?** 9048
40:28 *Have you* not **h?** 9048
41:26 no *one* **h** any words from you. 9048
48: 6 *You have* **h** these things; look at them all. 9048
48: 7 *you have* not **h** *of* them before today. 9048
48: 8 *You have* neither **h** nor understood; 9048
52:15 they will see, and what *they have* not **h,** 9048
58: 4 and **expect** your voice **to be h** on high. 9048
60:18 No longer *will* violence **be h** in your land, 9048
64: 4 Since ancient times no *one has* **h,** 9048
65:19 and of crying *will* **be h** in it no more. 9048
66: 8 Who *has ever* **h** *of* such a thing? 9048
66:19 and to the distant islands that *have* not **h** 9048
Jer 3:21 A cry **is h** on the barren heights, 9048
4:19 For I *have* **h** the sound of the trumpet; 9048
4:19 I have **h** the battle cry. NIH
6:24 *We have* **h** reports about them, 9048
8:16 The snorting of the enemy's horses **is h** 9048
9:10 and the lowing of cattle *is* not **h.** 9048
9:19 The sound of wailing **is h** from Zion: 9048
18:13 Who *has ever* **h** anything like this? 9048
18:22 *Let* a cry **be h** from their houses 9048
20: 1 **h** Jeremiah prophesying these things, 9048
22:20 **let** your voice **be h** in Bashan, 5989
23:18 Who has listened and **h** his word? 9048
23:25 *"I have* **h** what the prophets say 9048
26: 7 the people **h** Jeremiah speak these words in 9048
26:10 the officials of Judah **h** *about* these things, 9048
26:11 *You have* **h** it with your own ears!" 9048
26:12 and this city all the things *you have* **h.** 9048
26:21 and all his officers and officials **h** his words, 9048
26:21 But Uriah **h** of it and fled in fear to Egypt. 9048
30: 5 " 'Cries of fear *are* **h—**terror, not peace. 9048
31: 7 **Make** your praises **h,** and say, 'O LORD, 9048
31:15 "A voice **is h** in Ramah, 9048
31:18 *"I have* **surely h** Ephraim's moaning: 9048+9048
33:10 *there will* **be h** once more 9048
36:11 **h** all the words of the LORD from 9048
36:13 Micaiah told them everything *he had* **h** Baruch read 9048
36:16 When they **h** all these words, 9048
36:24 all his attendants who **h** all these words showed no fear, 9048
37: 5 Babylonians who were besieging Jerusalem **h** the report 9048
38: 1 of Malkijah **h** what Jeremiah was telling all 9048
38: 7 **h** that they had put Jeremiah into the cistern. 9048
38:27 no *one had* **h** his conversation with the king. 9048
40: 7 in the open country **h** that the king 9048
40:11 and all the other countries **h** that the king 9048
41:11 the army officers who were with him **h** 9048
42: 4 *"I have* **h** you," replied Jeremiah 9048
48: 5 cries over the destruction *are* **h.** 9048
48:29 *"We have* **h** *of* Moab's pride— 9048
49:14 *I have* **h** a message from the LORD: 9048
49:23 for *they have* **h** bad news. 9048
50:43 king of Babylon *has* **h** reports about them, 9048
51:46 or be afraid when rumors **are h** in the land; 9048
La 1:21 *"People have* **h** my groaning, 9048
1:21 All my enemies *have* **h** *of* my distress; 9048
3:56 *You* **h** my plea: 9048
3:61 O LORD, *you have* **h** their insults, 9048
Eze 1:24 *I* **h** the sound of their wings, 9048
1:28 and *I* **h** the voice of one speaking. 9048
2: 2 and *I* **h** him speaking to me. 9048
3:12 *I* **h** behind me a loud rumbling sound— 9048
9: 1 Then I **h** him call out in a loud voice, 265+928
10: 5 of the cherubim *could* **be h** as far away as 9048
10:13 I **h** the wheels being called 265+928
19: 4 The nations **h** about him, 9048
19: 9 his roar **was h** no longer on the mountains 9048
26:13 the music of your harps *will* **be h** no more. 9048
33: 5 Since *he* **h** the sound of the trumpet but did 9048
35:12 that I the LORD *have* **h** all the contemptible 9048
35:13 without restraint, and I **h** it. 9048
43: 6 *I* **h** someone speaking to me from inside 9048
Da 3: 7 as soon as they **h** the sound of the horn, 10725
5:14 *I have* **h** that the spirit of the gods is in you 10725
5:16 Now I *have* **h** that you are able 10725
6:14 When the king **h** this, 10725
8:13 Then *I* **h** a holy one speaking, 9048
8:16 *I* **h** a man's voice from the Ulai calling, 9048
10: 9 Then *I* **h** him speaking, 9048
10:12 your words **were h,** and I have come 9048
12: 7 *I* **h** him swear by him who lives forever, 9048

Da 12: 8 I **h,** but I did not understand. 9048
Ob 1: 1 *We have* **h** a message from the LORD: 9048
Na 2:13 of your messengers *will* no longer **be h."** 9048
Hab 3: 2 LORD, *I have* **h** *of* your fame; 9048
3:16 *I* **h** and my heart pounded, 9048
Zep 2: 8 *"I have* **h** the insults of Moab and the taunts 9048
Zec 8:23 because *we have* **h** that God is with you.' " 9048
Mal 3:16 and the LORD listened and **h.** 9048
Mt 2: 3 *When* King Herod **h** this he was disturbed, 201
2: 9 *After* they *had* **h** the king, 201
2:18 "A voice *is* **h** in Ramah, 201
2:22 But *when he* **h** that Archelaus was reigning 201
4:12 *When* Jesus **h** that John had been put 201
5:21 *"You have* **h** that it was said to 201
5:27 *"You have* **h** that it was said, 201
5:33 *you have* **h** that it was said to 201
5:38 *"You have* **h** that it was said, 'Eye for eye, 201
5:43 *"You have* **h** that it was said, 201
6: 7 for they think *they will be* **h** because 1653
8:10 *When* Jesus **h** this, he was astonished 201
11: 2 *When* John **h** in prison what Christ was doing, 201
12:24 But *when* the Pharisees **h** this, they said, 201
14: 1 At that time Herod the tetrarch **h** the reports 201
14:13 *When* Jesus **h** what had happened, 201
15:12 *when they* **h** this?" 201
17: 6 *When* the disciples **h** this, 201
19:22 *When* the young man **h** this, 201
19:25 *When* the disciples **h** this, 201
20:24 *When* the ten **h about** this, 201
20:30 and *when they* **h** that Jesus was going by, 201
21:45 and the Pharisees **h** Jesus' parables, 201
22:22 *When they* **h** this, they were amazed. 201
22:33 When the crowds **h** this, 201
26:65 Look, now *you have* **h** the blasphemy. 201
27:47 *When* some of those standing there **h** this, 201
Mk 2: 1 the *people* **h** that he had come home. 201
3: 8 *When they* **h** all he was doing, 201
3:21 *When* his family **h about** this, 201
5:27 *When she* **h** about Jesus, 201
6: 2 and many who **h** him were amazed. 201
6:14 King Herod **h about** this, 201
6:16 But *when* Herod **h** this, he said, "John, 201
6:20 *When* Herod **h** John, he was greatly puzzled; 201
6:55 the sick on mats to wherever *they* **h** he was. 201
7:25 In fact, as soon as she **h** about him, 201
10:41 *When* the ten **h about** this, 201
10:47 *When he* **h** that it was Jesus of Nazareth, 201
11:14 And his disciples **h** him say it. 201
11:18 the law **h** this and began looking for a way 201
12:28 of the law came and **h** them debating. 201
14:58 "We **h** him say, 'I will destroy this 201
14:64 *"You have* **h** the blasphemy. 201
15:35 *When* some of those standing near **h** this, 201
15:39 **h** his cry and saw how he died, he said, NIG
16:11 *When* they **h** that Jesus was alive and 201
Lk 1:13 your prayer *has been* **h.** 1653
1:41 When Elizabeth **h** Mary's greeting, 201
1:58 Her neighbors and relatives **h** that 201
1:66 Everyone who **h** this wondered about it, 201
2:18 and all who **h** it were amazed at what 201
2:20 for all the things *they had* **h** and seen, 201
2:47 Everyone who **h** him was amazed 201
4:23 Do here in your hometown what *we have* **h** 201
4:28 synagogue were furious *when they* **h** this. 201
7: 3 The centurion **h** of Jesus 201
7: 9 *When* Jesus **h** this, he was amazed at him, 201
7:22 to John what you have seen and **h:** 201
7:29 *when they* **h** Jesus' words, 201
9: 7 the tetrarch **h about** all that was going on. 201
12: 3 What you have said in the dark *will be* **h** in 201
14:15 of those at the table with him **h** this, 201
15:25 *he* **h** music and dancing. 201
16:14 **h** all this and were sneering at Jesus. 201
18:22 *When* Jesus **h** this, he said to him, 201
18:23 *When* he **h** this, he became very sad, 201
18:26 Those who **h** this asked, 201
18:36 When *he* **h** the crowd going by, 201
20:16 *When* the *people* **h** this, they said, 201
22:71 We *have* **h** it from his own lips." 201
23: 8 From what *he had* **h** about him, 201
Jn 1:37 When the two disciples **h** him say this, 201
1:40 of the two who **h** what John had said 201
3:32 He testifies to what he has seen and **h,** 201
4: 1 The Pharisees **h** that Jesus was gaining 201
4:42 now *we have* **h** for ourselves, 201
4:47 *When* this man **h** that Jesus had arrived 201
5:37 *You have* never **h** his voice 201
7:32 The Pharisees **h** the crowd whispering such things about him. 201
8: 9 those who **h** began to go away one at a time, 201
8:26 what I *have* **h** from him I tell the world." 201
8:38 you do what *you have* **h** from your father." 201
8:40 a man who has told you the truth that *I* **h** 201
9:32 Nobody *has* ever **h** of opening the eyes of 201
9:35 Jesus **h** that they had thrown him out, 201
9:40 with him **h** him say this and asked, 201
11: 4 *When he* **h** this, Jesus said, 201
11: 6 Yet when *he* **h** that Lazarus was sick, 201
11:20 When Martha **h** that Jesus was coming, 201
11:29 When Mary **h** this, she got up quickly 201
11:41 "Father, I thank you that *you have* **h** me. 201
12:12 that had come for the Feast **h** that Jesus was 201
12:18 because *they had* **h** that he had given this 201
12:29 that was there and **h** it said it had thundered; 201
12:34 "We *have* **h** from the Law that the Christ 201
14:28 *"You* **h** me say, 'I am going away 201
Jn 18:21 Ask those who **h** me. 201
19: 8 When Pilate **h** this, 201
19:13 *When* Pilate **h** this, 201
21: 7 *As soon as* Simon Peter **h** him say, 201
Ac 1: 4 which *you have* **h** me speak about. 201
1:19 Everyone in Jerusalem **h about** this, 1181+1196
2: 6 When they **h** this **sound,** 1181+5889
2: 6 because each one **h** them speaking 201
2:37 *When* the *people* **h** this, 201
4: 4 But many who **h** the message believed, 201
4:20 about what *we have* seen and **h."** 201
4:24 *When* they **h** this, 201
5: 5 *When* Ananias **h** this, he fell down and died. 201
5: 5 great fear seized all who **h** what had happened. 201
5:11 the whole church and all who **h about** 201
5:33 *When they* **h** this, they were furious 201
6:11 *"We have* **h** Stephen speak words 201
6:14 For *we have* **h** him say that this Jesus 201
7:12 *When* Jacob **h** that there was grain in Egypt, 201
7:29 When Moses **h** this, he fled to Midian, 3364
7:31 he **h** the Lord's voice: NIG
7:34 *I have* **h** their groaning and have come 201
7:54 *When they* **h** this, they were furious 201
8: 6 When the crowds **h** Philip and saw 201
8:14 in Jerusalem **h** that Samaria had accepted 201
8:30 to the chariot and **h** the man reading Isaiah 201
9: 4 to the ground and **h** a voice say to him, 201
9: 7 *they* **h** the sound but did not see anyone. 201
9:13 *"I have* **h** many reports about this man 201
9:21 All those who **h** him were astonished 201
9:38 *when* the disciples **h** that Peter was in Lydda, 201
10:31 God *has* **h** your prayer 1653
10:44 Holy Spirit came on all who **h** the message. 201
10:46 For *they* **h** them speaking in tongues 201
11: 1 and the brothers throughout Judea **h** that 201
11: 7 Then *I* **h** a voice telling me, 'Get up, Peter. 201
11:18 *When they* **h** this, they had no further 201
13:48 *When* the Gentiles **h** this, 201
14:14 the apostles Barnabas and Paul **h** of this, 201
15:24 *We have* **h** that some went out from us 201
16:38 and *when they* **h** that Paul 201
17: 8 *When they* **h** this, 201
17:32 *When they* **h about** the resurrection of 201
18: 8 of the Corinthians *who* **h** him believed 201
18:26 *When* Priscilla and Aquila **h** him, 201
19: 2 not even **h** that there is a Holy Spirit." 201
19:10 the province of Asia **h** the word of the Lord. 201
19:28 *When they* **h** this, they were furious 201
21:12 When *we* **h** this, 201
21:20 When they **h** this, they praised God. 201
22: 2 *When they* **h** him speak to them in Aramaic, 201
22: 7 I fell to the ground and **h** a voice say to me, 201
22:15 to all men of what *you have* seen and **h.** 201
22:26 *When* the centurion **h** this, 201
23:16 *when* the son of Paul's sister **h of** this plot, 201
26:14 and *I* **h** a voice saying to me in Aramaic, 201
28:15 brothers there *had* **h** that we were coming, 201
Ro 10:14 in the one of whom *they have* not **h?** 201
10:17 the message is **h** through the word of Christ. NIG
15:21 and those who *have* not **h** will understand." 201
16:19 Everyone *has* **h about** your obedience, 919
1Co 2: 9 "No eye has seen, no ear *has* **h,** 201
2Co 6: 2 he says, "In the time of my favor *I* **h** you, 2052
12: 4 *He* **h** inexpressible things, 201
Gal 1:13 For *you have* **h of** my previous way of life 201
1:23 *They* only **h** the report: 201+1639
3: 2 or by believing **what** you **h?** 198
3: 5 or because you believe **what** you **h?** 198
Eph 1:13 also were included in Christ *when* you **h** 201
1:15 *since* I **h about** your faith in the Lord Jesus 201
3: 2 Surely *you have* **h about** the administration 201
4:21 Surely *you* **h of** him and were taught 201
Php 2:26 and is distressed because *you* **h** he was ill. 201
4: 9 Whatever you have learned or received or **h** 201
Col 1: 4 **h** of your faith in Christ Jesus and of 201
1: 5 that *you have* **already h about** in the word 4578
1: 6 among you since the day *you* **h** it 201
1: 9 since the day we **h about** you, 201
1:23 that *you* **h** and that has been proclaimed 201
1Th 2:13 which you **h** from us, 198
2Ti 1:13 What *you* **h** from me, 201
2: 2 And the things *you have* **h** me say in 201
Heb 2: 1 therefore, to what *we have* **h,** 201
2: 3 was confirmed to us by those who **h** him. 201
3:16 Who were they *who* **h** and rebelled? 201
4: 2 the message they **h** was of no value to them, 198
4: 2 those who **h** did not combine it with faith. 201
5: 7 *he was* **h** because of his reverent submission 1653
12:19 that those who **h** it begged 201
Jas 1:25 not forgetting *what he has* **h,** but doing 212+1181
5:11 *You have* **h of** Job's perseverance 201
2Pe 1:18 *We* ourselves **h** this voice that came 201
2: 8 by the lawless deeds he saw and **h)—** 198
1Jn 1: 1 which *we have* **h,** which we have seen 201
1: 3 to you what *we have* seen and **h,** 201
1: 5 the message *we have* **h** from him and 201
2: 7 the message *you have* **h.** 201
2:18 as *you have* **h** that the antichrist is coming, 201
2:24 See that what you *have* **h** from 201
3:11 the message *you have* **h** from the beginning: 201
4: 3 which *you have* **h** is coming and even 201
2Jn 1: 6 As *you have* **h** from the beginning, 201
Rev 1:10 *I* **h** behind me a loud voice like a trumpet, 201
3: 3 therefore, what *you have* received and **h;** 201
4: 1 And the voice *I had* first **h** speaking to me 201
Rev 5:11 *I* looked and **h** the voice of many angels, 201
5:13 Then *I* **h** every creature in heaven and 201
6: 1 Then *I* **h** one of the four living creatures 201
6: 3 *I* **h** the second living creature say, "Come!" 201
6: 5 *I* **h** the third living creature say, "Come!" 201
6: 6 Then *I* **h** what sounded like a voice among 201
6: 7 *I* **h** the voice of the fourth living creature 201
7: 4 *I* **h** the number of those who were sealed: 201
8:13 *I* **h** an eagle that was flying 201
9:13 and *I* **h** a voice coming from the horns of 201
9:16 *I* **h** their number. 201
10: 4 but *I* **h** a voice from heaven say, 201
10: 8 the voice that *I had* **h** from heaven spoke 201
11:12 Then *they* **h** a loud voice 201
12:10 Then *I* **h** a loud voice in heaven say: 201
14: 2 And *I* **h** a sound from heaven like the roar 201
14: 2 The sound *I* **h** was like that 201
14:13 Then *I* **h** a voice from heaven say, "Write: 201
16: 1 Then *I* **h** a loud voice from 201
16: 5 *I* **h** the angel in charge of the waters say: 201
16: 7 And *I* **h** the altar respond: 201
18: 4 Then *I* **h** another voice from heaven say: 201
18:22 *will* never *be* **h** in you again. 201
18:22 of a millstone *will* never *be* **h** in you again. 201
18:23 of bridegroom and bride *will* never *be* **h** 201
19: 1 After this *I* **h** what sounded like the roar of 201
19: 6 *I* **h** what sounded like a great multitude, 201
21: 3 *I* **h** a loud voice from the throne saying, 201
22: 8 am the one who **h** and saw these things. 201
22: 8 And when *I had* **h** and seen them, 201

HEARERS (1) [HEAR]

1Ti 4:16 you will save both yourself and your **h.** 201

HEARING (56) [HEAR]

Ge 23:10 in the **h** of all the Hittites who had come to 265
23:13 and he said to Ephron in their **h,** 265
23:16 for him the price he had named in the **h** *of* 265
Nu 11: 1 about their hardships in the **h** *of* 265
Dt 5: 1 and laws I declare in your **h** today. 265
31:11 before them in their **h.** 265
31:28 so that I can speak these words in their **h** 265
31:30 of this song from beginning to end in the **h** 265
32:44 and spoke all the words of this song in the **h** 265
Jdg 9:46 On **h** this, the citizens in the tower 9048
1Sa 4: 6 **H** the uproar, the Philistines asked, 9048
17:11 On **h** the Philistine's words, 9048
2Sa 10: 7 On **h** this, David sent Joab out with 9048
18:12 In our **h** the king commanded you 265
1Ki 1:41 *On* **h** the sound of the trumpet, Joab asked, 9048
2Ki 18:26 to us in Hebrew in the **h** *of* the people on 265
23: 2 He read in their **h** all the words of the Book 265
1Ch 19: 8 On **h** this, David sent Joab out with 9048
28: 8 and in the **h** *of* our God: 265
2Ch 34:30 He read in their **h** all the words of the Book 265
Ne 13: 1 the Book of Moses was read aloud in the **h** 265
Job 9:16 I do not believe *he would* **give** me **a h.** 263+7754
33: 8 "But you have said in my **h—** 265
Ecc 1: 8 nor the ear its fill of **h.** 9048
Isa 5: 9 LORD Almighty has declared in my **h:** 265
6: 9 " *'Be* **ever h,** but never understanding; 9048+9048
22:14 LORD Almighty has revealed this in my **h:** 265
36:11 to us in Hebrew in the **h** *of* the people on 265
49:20 yet say in your **h,** 'This place is too small 265
Jer 2: 2 "Go and proclaim in the **h** *of* Jerusalem: 265
26:15 to you to speak all these words in your **h."** 265
28: 7 listen to what I have to say in your **h** and in 265
28: 7 to say in your hearing and in the **h** *of* all 265
Da 5:10 **h** the voices of the king and his nobles, NIH
Am 8:11 but a famine of **h** the words of the LORD. 9048
Mt 9:12 *On* **h** this, Jesus said, 201
13:13 *though* **h,** they do not hear or understand. 201
13:14 *be* **ever h** but never understanding; 198+201
14:13 **H** of this, the crowds followed him on foot 201
22:34 **H** that Jesus had silenced the Sadducees, 201
Mk 2:17 *On* **h** this, Jesus said to them, 201
4:12 and **ever h** but never understanding; 201+201
6:29 *On* **h** of this, John's disciples came 201
Lk 4:21 "Today this scripture is fulfilled in your **h."** 4044
7: 1 saying this in the **h** of the people, 198
8:10 *though* **h,** they may not understand.' 201
8:50 **H** this, Jesus said to Jairus, "Don't be afraid; 201
23: 6 *On* **h** this, Pilate asked if the man was 201
Jn 6:60 *On* **h** it, many of his disciples said, 201
7:40 *On* **h** his words, some of the people said, 201
7:51 condemn anyone without first **h** him 201
Ac 5:24 On **h** this report, 201
19: 5 On **h** this, they were baptized into the name 201
28:26 *be* **ever h** but never understanding; 198+201
Ro 10:17 faith comes from **h** the message, NIG
1Co 12:17 where would the **sense of h** be? 198

HEARKEN, HEARKENED, HEARKENETH, HEARKENING (KJV)

See AGREE, ANSWER, ATTENTION, FOLLOW, HEAR, HEARD, HEED, MARK WORDS, OBEYED, OBEYING

HEARS (52) [HEAR]

Ge 21: 6 and everyone who **h** *about* this will laugh 9048
Ex 17:14 **make sure** *that* Joshua **h** it, 265+928+8492
Lev 5: 1 he does not speak up when *he* **h** 7754+9048

Nu 24: 4 the oracle of *one who* **h** the words of God, 9048
24:16 the oracle of *one who* **h** the words of God, 9048
30: 4 and her father **h** *about* her vow or pledge 9048
30: 5 if her father forbids her when he **h** *about* it, 9048
30: 7 and her husband **h** *about* it 9048
30: 8 But if her husband forbids her when he **h** 9048
30:11 and her husband **h** *about* it 9048
30:12 But if her husband nullifies them when he **h** 9048
30:14 by saying nothing to her when he **h** 9048
30:15 he nullifies them some time after he **h** 9048
Dt 29:19 a person **h** the words of this oath, 9048
1Sa 3:11 that will make the ears of everyone *who* **h** 9048
2Sa 17: 9 whoever **h** *about* it will say, 9048+9048
2Ki 19: 7 to put such a spirit in him that when *he* **h** 9048
21:12 the ears of everyone *who* **h** *of* it will tingle. 9048
Ps 34:17 righteous cry out, and the LORD **h** them; 9048
55:17 and *he* **h** my voice. 9048
69:33 The LORD **h** the needy and does 9048
97: 8 Zion **h** and rejoices and the villages 9048
145:19 *he* **h** their cry and saves them. 9048
Pr 13: 8 but a poor man **h** no threat. 9048
15:29 The LORD is far from the wicked but *he* **h** 9048
25:10 or *he who* **h** it may shame you 9048
Isa 11: 3 or decide by **what** he **h** *with* his ears; 5461
30:19 As soon as he **h**, he will answer you. 9048
37: 7 in him so that *when he* **h** a certain report, 9048
Jer 19: 3 that will make the ears of everyone *who* **h** 9048
Eze 33: 4 then if *anyone* **h** the trumpet but 7754+9048+9048
Da 3:10 that everyone who **h** the sound of the horn, 10725
Na 3:19 Everyone *who* **h** the news 9048
Mt 7:24 "Therefore everyone who **h** these words *201*
7:26 But everyone who **h** these words of mine *201*
13:19 *When* anyone **h** the message about *201*
13:20 on rocky places is the man who **h** the word *201*
13:22 that fell among the thorns is the man who **h** *201*
13:23 the man who **h** the word and understands it. *201*
Lk 6:47 and **h** my words and puts them into practice. *201*
6:49 But the one who **h** my words and does *201*
Jn 3:29 of joy when he **h** the bridegroom's voice. *NIG*
5:24 whoever **h** my word and believes him *201*
8:47 He who belongs to God **h** what God says. *201*
12:47 for the person who **h** my words but does *201*
16:13 he will speak only what *he* **h**, *201*
Ac 2: 8 of us **h** them in his own native language? *201*
1Jn 5:14 according to his will, *he* **h** us. *201*
5:15 And if we know that *he* **h** us— *201*
Rev 3:20 If anyone **h** my voice and opens the door, *201*
22:17 And let him who **h** say, "Come!" *201*
22:18 I warn everyone who **h** the words of *201*

HEART (570) [BROKENHEARTED, DISHEARTENED, DOWNHEARTED, FAINTHEARTED, HARDHEARTED, HEART'S, HEARTACHE, HEARTLESS, HEARTS, HEARTS', KINDHEARTED, SIMPLEHEARTED, STOUTHEARTED, STUBBORN-HEARTED, WHOLEHEARTED, WHOLEHEARTEDLY]

Ge 6: 5 thoughts of his **h** was only evil all the time. 4213
6: 6 and his **h** was filled with pain. 4213
8:21 the pleasing aroma and said in his **h**: 4213
8:21 though every inclination of his **h** is evil 4213
24:45 "Before I finished praying in my **h**, 4213
34: 3 His **h** was drawn to Dinah daughter 5883
34: 8 "My son Shechem has his **h** set 5883
Ex 4:14 and his **h** will be glad when he sees you. 4213
4:21 But I will harden his **h** so that he will not let 4213
7: 3 But I will harden Pharaoh's **h**, 4213
7:13 Yet Pharaoh's **h** became hard and he would 4213
7:14 "Pharaoh's **h** is unyielding; 4213
7:22 and Pharaoh's **h** became hard; 4213
7:23 and did not take even this to **h**. 4213
8:15 he hardened his **h** and would not listen 4213
8:19 But Pharaoh's **h** was hard and he would 4213
8:32 But this time also Pharaoh hardened his **h** 4213
9: 7 Yet his **h** was unyielding and he would 4213
9:12 But the LORD hardened Pharaoh's **h** 4213
9:35 So Pharaoh's **h** was hard and he would 4213
10: 1 for I have hardened his **h** and the hearts 4213
10:20 But the LORD hardened Pharaoh's **h**, 4213
10:27 But the LORD hardened Pharaoh's **h**, 4213
11:10 but the LORD hardened Pharaoh's **h**, 4213
14: 4 And I will harden Pharaoh's **h**, 4213
14: 8 the **h** *of* Pharaoh king of Egypt, 4213
15: 8 deep waters congealed in the **h** *of* the sea. 4213
25: 2 from each man whose **h** prompts him 4213
28:29 the names of the sons of Israel over his **h** on 4213
28:30 be over Aaron's **h** whenever he enters 4213
28:30 the Israelites over his **h** before the LORD. 4213
35:21 and whose **h** moved him came and brought 4213
Lev 19:17 " 'Do not hate your brother in your **h**. 4222
Dt 1:28 Our brothers have made us lose **h**. 4222
2:30 and his **h** obstinate in order to give him 4222
4: 9 or let them slip from your **h** as long 4222
4:29 if you look for him with all your **h** and 4222
4:39 Acknowledge and take to **h** this day that 4222
6: 5 Love the LORD your God with all your **h** 4222
8: 2 in order to know what was in your **h**, 4222
8: 5 in your **h** that as a man disciplines his son, 4222
8:14 then your **h** will become proud 4222
10:12 the LORD your God with all your **h** and 4222
11: 3 and the things he did in the **h** *of* Egypt, both 9348
11:13 with all your **h** and with all your soul— 4222

Dt 13: 3 with all your **h** and with all your soul. 4222
15:10 to him and do so without a grudging **h**; 4222
17:17 or his **h** will be led astray. 4222
26:16 carefully observe them with all your **h** and 4222
28:65 weary with longing, and a despairing **h**. 5883
29:18 among you today whose **h** turns away from 4222
30: 1 upon you and you take them to **h** wherever 4222
30: 2 with all your **h** and with all your soul 4222
30: 6 that you may love him with all your **h** and 4222
30:10 to the LORD your God with all your **h** and 4222
30:14 and in your **h** so you may obey it. 4222
30:17 your **h** turns away and you are not obedient, 4222
32:46 to **h** all the words I have solemnly declared 4222
Jos 22: 5 to him and to serve him with all your **h** 4222
23:14 with all your **h** and soul that not one of all 4222
Jdg 5: 9 My **h** is with Israel's princes, 4213
5:15 of Reuben there was much searching of **h**. 4213
5:16 of Reuben there was much searching of **h**. 4213
1Sa 1:13 Hannah was praying in her **h**, 4213
2: 1 "My **h** rejoices in the LORD; 4213
2:33 with tears and to grieve your **h**, 5883
2:35 who will do according to what is in my **h** 4222
4:13 because his **h** feared for the ark of God. 4213
9:19 and will tell you all that is in your **h**. 4222
10: 9 God changed Saul's **h**, 4213
12:20 but serve the LORD with all your **h**. 4222
12:24 and serve him faithfully with all your **h**; 4222
13:14 after his own **h** and appointed him leader 4222
14: 7 "Go ahead; I am with you **h and soul.**" 3869+4222
16: 7 but the LORD looks at the **h**." 4222
17:28 and how wicked your **h** is; 4222
17:32 "Let no one lose **h** on account of this 4213
21:12 words to **h** and was very much afraid 4222
25:37 his **h** failed him and he became like a stone. 4213
28: 5 he was afraid; terror filled his **h**. 4213
2Sa 3:21 you may rule over all that your **h** desires." 5883
6:16 she despised him in her **h**. 4213
13:20 Don't take this thing to **h**." 4213
14: 1 of Zeruiah knew that the king's **h** longed 4213
17:10 whose **h** is like the heart of a lion, 4213
17:10 whose heart is like the **h** *of* a lion, 4213
18:14 and plunged them into Absalom's **h** 4213
22:46 They all **lose h**; they come trembling 5570
1Ki 2: 4 before me with all their **h** and soul, 4222
2:44 "You know in your **h** all the wrong you did 4222
3: 6 to you and righteous and upright in **h**. 4222
3: 9 a discerning **h** to govern your people and 4213
3:12 I will give you a wise and discerning **h**, 4213
8:17 in his **h** to build a temple for the Name of 4222
8:18 'Because it was in your **h** to build a temple 4222
8:18 you did well to have this in your **h**. 4222
8:38 of his own **h**, and spreading out his hands 4222
8:39 since you know his **h** (for you alone know 4222
8:47 of **h** in the land where they are held captive, 4213
8:48 and if they turn back to you with all their **h** 4222
8:66 joyful and glad in **h** for all the good things 4213
9: 3 My eyes and my **h** will always be there. 4213
9: 4 before me in integrity of **h** and uprightness, 4222
10:24 to hear the wisdom God had put in his **h**. 4213
11: 4 his wives turned his **h** after other gods, 4222
11: 4 his **h** was not fully devoted to 4222
11: 4 as the **h** *of* David his father had been. 4222
11: 9 because his **h** had turned away from 4222
11:37 you will rule over all that your **h** desires; 5883
14: 8 and followed me with all his **h**, 4222
15: 3 his **h** was not fully devoted to the LORD 4222
15: 3 as the **h** *of* David his forefather had been. 4222
15:14 Asa's **h** was fully committed to the LORD 4222
2Ki 9:24 The arrow pierced his **h** and he slumped 4213
10:31 the God of Israel, with all his **h**. 4222
22:19 Because your **h** was responsive 4222
23: 3 and decrees with all his **h** and all his soul, 4213
23:25 with all his **h** and with all his soul and 4222
1Ch 15:29 she despised him in her **h**. 4213
22: 7 "My son, I had it in my **h** to build a house 4222
22:19 Now devote your **h** and soul to seeking 4222
28: 2 I had it in my **h** to build a house as a place 4222
28: 9 for the LORD searches every **h** 4222
29:17 you test the **h** and are pleased with integrity. 4222
2Ch 6: 7 in his **h** to build a temple for the Name of 4222
6: 8 'Because it was in your **h** to build a temple 4222
6: 8 you did well to have this in your **h**. 4222
6:30 since you know his **h** (for you alone know 4222
6:37 of **h** in the land where they are held captive, 4222
6:38 and if they turn back to you with all their **h** 4222
7:10 joyful and glad in **h** for the good things 4213
7:16 My eyes and my **h** will always be there. 4213
9:23 to hear the wisdom God had put in his **h**. 4213
12:14 He did evil because he had not set his **h** 4213
15:12 with all their **h** and soul. 4222
15:17 Asa's **h** was fully committed 4222
17: 6 His **h** was devoted to the ways of the LORD 4213
19: 3 of the Asherah poles and have set your **h** 4222
22: 9 who sought the LORD with all his **h**." 4222
30:19 who sets his **h** on seeking God— 4222
32:25 But Hezekiah's **h** was proud and he did 4213
32:26 Hezekiah repented of the pride of his **h**, 4213
32:31 and to know everything that was in his **h**. 4222
34:27 Because your **h** was responsive 4222
34:31 and decrees with all his **h** and all his soul, 4222
36:13 He became stiff-necked and hardened his **h** 8120
36:22 the LORD moved the **h** *of* Cyrus king 8120
Ezr 1: 1 the LORD moved the **h** *of* Cyrus king 8120
1: 5 everyone whose **h** God had moved— 8120
7:27 into the king's **h** to bring honor to the house 4213
Ne 2: 2 This can be nothing but sadness of **h**." 4213
2:12 in my **h** to do for Jerusalem. 4213

Ne 4: 6 for the people worked *with all* their **h**. 4213
7: 5 So my God put it into my **h** to assemble 4213
9: 8 You found his **h** faithful to you, 4222
Job 10:13 "But this is what you concealed in your **h**, 4222
11:13 "Yet if you devote your **h** to him 4213
15:12 Why has your **h** carried you away, 4213
17:11 and so are the desires of my **h**. 4222
19:27 How my **h** yearns within me! 4000
22:22 and lay up his words in your **h**. 4222
23:16 God has made my **h** faint; 4213
29:13 I made the widow's **h** sing. 4213
31: 7 if my **h** has been led by my eyes, 4213
31: 9 "If my **h** has been enticed by a woman, 4213
31:20 and his **h** did not bless me for warming him 2743
31:27 so that my **h** was secretly enticed 4213
31:33 by hiding my guilt in my **h** 2460
33: 3 My words come from an upright **h**; 4213
36:13 "The godless in **h** harbor resentment; 4213
37: 1 "At this my **h** pounds and leaps 4213
37:24 not have regard for all the wise in **h**?" 4213
38:36 the **h** with wisdom or gave understanding to 3219
Ps 4: 7 You have filled my **h** with greater joy than 4213
5: 9 their **h** is filled with destruction. 7931
7:10 who saves the upright in **h**. 4213
9: 1 I will praise you, O LORD, with all my **h**; 4213
10: 3 He boasts of the cravings of his **h**; 5883
11: 2 from the shadows at the upright in **h**. 4213
13: 2 and every day have sorrow in my **h**? 4222
13: 5 my **h** rejoices in your salvation. 4213
14: 1 The fool says in his **h**, "There is no God." 4213
15: 2 who speaks the truth from his **h** 4222
16: 7 even at night my **h** instructs me. 4000
16: 9 Therefore my **h** is glad 4213
17: 3 you probe my **h** and examine me at night, 4213
18:45 They all **lose h**; 5570
19: 8 giving joy to the **h**. 4213
19:14 of my mouth and the meditation of my **h** 4213
20: 4 of your **h** and make all your plans succeed. 4222
21: 2 of his **h** and have not withheld the request 4213
22:14 My **h** has turned to wax; 4213
24: 4 He who has clean hands and a pure **h**, 4222
25:17 The troubles of my **h** have multiplied; 4222
26: 2 and try me, examine my **h** and my mind; 4000
27: 3 an army besiege me, my **h** will not fear; 4213
27: 8 My **h** says of you, "Seek his face!" 4213
27:14 and **take h** and wait for the LORD. 599+4213
28: 7 my **h** trusts in him, and I am helped. 4213
28: 7 My **h** leaps for joy and I will give thanks 4213
30:12 that my **h** may sing to you and not be silent. 3883
31:24 Be strong and **take h**, 599+4222
32:11 sing, all you who are upright in **h**! 4213
33:11 purposes of his **h** through all generations. 4213
36: 1 within my **h** concerning the sinfulness of 4213
36:10 your righteousness to the upright in **h**. 4213
37: 4 and he will give you the desires of your **h**. 4213
37:31 The law of his God is in his **h**; 4213
38: 8 I groan in anguish of **h**. 4213
38:10 My **h** pounds, my strength fails me; 4213
39: 3 My **h** grew hot within me, 4213
40: 8 your law is within my **h**." 5055
40:10 I do not hide your righteousness in my **h**; 4213
40:12 and my **h** fails within me. 4213
41: 6 while his **h** gathers slander; 4213
44:21 since he knows the secrets of the **h**? 4213
45: 1 My **h** is stirred by a noble theme 4213
46: 2 and the mountains fall into the **h** *of* the sea, 4213
49: 3 from my **h** will give understanding. 4213
51:10 Create in me a pure **h**, O God, 4213
51:17 a broken and contrite **h**, O God, 4213
53: 1 The fool says in his **h**, "There is no God." 4213
55: 4 My **h** is in anguish within me; 4213
55:21 yet war is in his **h**; 4213
57: 7 My **h** is steadfast, 4213
57: 7 O God, my **h** is steadfast; 4213
58: 2 No, in your **h** you devise injustice, 4213
61: 2 I call as my **h** grows faint; 4213
62:10 do not set your **h** on them. 4213
64: 6 Surely the mind and **h** of man are cunning. 4213
64:10 let all the upright in **h** praise him! 4213
66:18 If I had cherished sin in my **h**, 4213
69:20 Scorn has broken my **h** 4213
73: 1 to those who are pure in **h**. 4222
73:13 Surely in vain have I kept my **h** pure; 4222
73:21 my **h** was grieved and my spirit embittered, 4222
73:26 My flesh and my **h** may fail, 4222
73:26 of my **h** and my portion forever. 4222
77: 6 My **h** mused and my spirit inquired: 4222
78:72 David shepherded them with integrity of **h**; 4222
84: 2 my **h** and my flesh cry out for 4213
86:11 give me an undivided **h**, 4222
86:12 O Lord my God, with all my **h**; 4222
89:50 I bear in my **h** the taunts of all the nations, 2668
90:12 that we may gain a **h** *of* wisdom. 4222
94:15 and all the upright in **h** will follow it. 4213
97:11 the righteous and joy on the upright in **h**. 4213
101: 2 I will walk in my house with blameless **h**. 4222
101: 4 Men of perverse **h** shall be far from me; 4222
101: 5 whoever has haughty eyes and a proud **h**, 4222
102: 4 My **h** is blighted and withered like grass; 4213
104:15 wine that gladdens the **h** *of* man, 4222
104:15 and bread that sustains his **h**. 4222
108: 1 My **h** is steadfast, O God; 4213
109:22 and my **h** is wounded within me. 4213
111: 1 I will extol the LORD with all my **h** 4222
112: 7 his **h** is steadfast, trusting in the LORD. 4213
112: 8 His **h** is secure, he will have no fear; 4213
119: 2 and seek him with all their **h**. 4213

Ps 119: 7 an upright **h** as I learn your righteous laws. 4222
119:10 I seek you with all my **h;** 4213
119:11 in my **h** that I might not sin against you. 4213
119:30 *I have* **set** *my* **h** *on* your laws. 8751
119:32 for you have set my **h** free. 4213
119:34 and obey it with all my **h.** 4213
119:36 Turn my **h** toward your statutes and not 4213
119:58 I have sought your face with all my **h;** 4213
119:69 I keep your precepts with all my **h.** 4213
119:80 May my **h** be blameless 4213
119:111 they are the joy of my **h.** 4213
119:112 My **h** is set on keeping your decrees to 4213
119:145 I call with all my **h;** 4213
119:161 but my **h** trembles at your word. 4213
125: 4 to those who are upright in **h.** 4213
131: 1 My **h** is not proud, O LORD, 4213
138: 1 I will praise you, O LORD, with all my **h;** 4213
139:23 Search me, O God, and know my **h;** 4222
141: 4 Let not my **h** be drawn to what is evil, 4213
143: 4 my **h** within me is dismayed. 4213
148:14 of Israel, the people **close to** his **h.** 7940
Pr 1:23 I would have poured out my **h** to you 8120
2: 2 and applying your **h** to understanding, 4213
2:10 For wisdom will enter your **h,** 4213
3: 1 but keep my commands in your **h,** 4213
3: 3 write them on the tablet of your **h.** 4213
3: 5 Trust in the LORD with all your **h** and lean 4213
4: 4 "Lay hold of my words with all your **h;** 4213
4:21 keep them within your **h;** 4222
4:23 Above all else, guard your **h,** 4213
5:12 How my **h** spurned correction! 4213
6:14 who plots evil with deceit in his **h—** 4213
6:18 a **h** that devises wicked schemes, 4213
6:21 Bind them upon your **h** forever; 4213
6:25 Do not lust in your **h** after her beauty 4222
7: 3 write them on the tablet of your **h.** 4213
7:25 Do not let your **h** turn to her ways or stray 4213
10: 8 The wise in **h** accept commands, 4213
10:20 but the **h** *of* the wicked is of little value. 4213
11:20 The LORD detests men of perverse **h** 4213
12:23 but the **h** *of* fools blurts out folly. 4213
12:25 An anxious **h** weighs a man down, 4213
13:12 Hope deferred makes the **h** sick, 4213
14:10 *Each* **h** knows its own bitterness, 4213
14:13 Even in laughter the **h** may ache, 4213
14:30 A **h** at peace gives life to the body, 4213
14:33 Wisdom reposes in the **h** *of* the discerning 4213
15:13 A happy **h** makes the face cheerful, 4213
15:14 The discerning **h** seeks knowledge, 4213
15:15 but the cheerful **h** has a continual feast. 4213
15:28 The **h** *of* the righteous weighs its answers, 4213
15:30 A cheerful look brings joy to the **h,** 4213
16: 1 To man belong the plans of the **h,** 4213
16: 5 The LORD detests all the proud of **h.** 4213
16: 9 In his **h** a man plans his course, 4213
16:21 The wise in **h** are called discerning, 4213
16:23 A wise man's **h** guides his mouth, 4213
17: 3 but the LORD tests the **h.** 4213
17:20 A man of perverse **h** does not prosper; 4213
17:22 A cheerful **h** is good medicine, 4213
18:12 Before his downfall a man's **h** is proud, 4213
18:15 **h** *of* the discerning acquires knowledge; 4213
19: 3 yet his **h** rages against the LORD. 4213
19:21 Many are the plans in a man's **h,** 4213
20: 5 The purposes of a man's **h** are deep waters, 4213
20: 9 Who can say, "I have kept my **h** pure; 4213
21: 1 The king's **h** is in the hand of the LORD; 4213
21: 2 but the LORD weighs the **h.** 4213
21: 4 Haughty eyes and a proud **h,** 4213
22:11 He who loves a pure **h** 4213
22:15 Folly is bound up in the **h** *of* a child, 4213
22:17 apply your **h** to what I teach, 4213
22:18 when you keep them in your **h** and have all 1061
23: 7 he says to you, but his **h** is not with you. 4213
23:12 Apply your **h** to instruction and your ears 4213
23:15 My son, if your **h** is wise, 4213
23:15 if your heart is wise, then my **h** will be glad; 4213
23:17 Do not let your **h** envy sinners, 4213
23:19 and keep your **h** on the right path. 4213
23:26 give me your **h** and let your eyes keep 4213
24:12 does not he who weighs the **h** perceive it? 4213
24:17 when he stumbles, do not let your **h** rejoice, 4213
24:32 I applied my **h** to what I observed 4213
25:20 is one who sings songs to a heavy **h.** 4213
26:23 are fervent lips with an evil **h.** 4213
26:24 but in his **h** he harbors deceit. 7931
26:25 for seven abominations fill his **h.** 4213
27: 9 Perfume and incense bring joy to the **h,** 4213
27:11 Be wise, my son, and bring joy to my **h;** 4213
27:19 so a man's **h** reflects the man. 4213
28:14 but he who hardens his **h** falls into trouble. 4213
Ecc 2: 1 I thought in my **h,** "Come now, 4213
2: 8 the **delights of the h** *of* man. 9503
2:10 I refused my **h** no pleasure. 4213
2:10 My **h** took delight in all my work, 4213
2:15 Then I thought in my **h,** 4213
2:15 I said in my **h,** "This too is meaningless." 4213
2:20 So my **h** began to despair 4213
3:17 I thought in my **h,** "God will bring to 4213
5: 2 do not be hasty in your **h** to utter anything 4213
5:20 God keeps him occupied with gladness of **h.** 4213
6: 2 so that he lacks nothing his **h** desires, 5883
7: 2 the living should take this to **h.** 4213
7: 3 because a sad face is good for the **h.** 4213
7: 4 **h** *of* the wise is in the house of mourning, 4213
7: 4 the **h** *of* fools is in the house of pleasure. 4213
7: 7 and a bribe corrupts the **h.** 4213
Ecc 7:22 for you know in your **h** that many times 4213
7:26 whose **h** is a trap and whose hands are 4213
8: 5 and the wise **h** will know the proper time 4213
9: 7 and drink your wine with a joyful **h,** 4213
10: 2 The **h** *of* the wise inclines to the right, 4213
10: 2 but the **h** *of* the fool to the left. 4213
11: 9 and let your **h** give you joy in the days 4213
11: 9 of your **h** and whatever your eyes see, 4213
11:10 banish anxiety from your **h** and cast off 4213
SS 3: 1 on my bed I looked for the one my **h** loves; 5883
3: 2 I will search for the one my **h** loves. 5883
3: 3 "Have you seen the one my **h** loves?" 5883
3: 4 when I found the one my **h** loves. 5883
3:11 the day his **h** rejoiced. 4213
4: 9 *You have* **stolen** my **h,** my sister, my bride; 4220
4: 9 *you have* **stolen** my **h** with one glance 4220
5: 2 I slept but my **h** was awake. 4213
5: 4 my **h** began to pound for him. 5055
5: 6 My **h** sank at his departure. 5883
8: 6 Place me like a seal over your **h,** 4213
Isa 1: 5 your whole **h** afflicted. 4222
6:10 Make the **h** *of* this people calloused; 4213
7: 4 Do not lose **h** because 4222
9: 9 who say with pride and arrogance of **h,** 4222
10:12 of Assyria for the willful pride of his **h** and 4222
13: 7 every man's **h** will melt. 4222
14:13 You said in your **h,** "I will ascend to heaven 4222
15: 5 My **h** cries out over Moab; 4213
16:11 My **h** laments for Moab like a harp, 5055
19: 3 The Egyptians *will* **lose h,** 928+1327+7931+8120
19:10 and all the wage earners will be sick at **h.** 5883
19:19 be an altar to the LORD in the **h** *of* Egypt, 9348
21: 4 My **h** falters, fear makes me tremble; 4222
40:11 in his arms and carries them close to his **h;** 2668
42:25 but they did not take it to **h.** 4213
44:20 a deluded **h** misleads him; 4213
46: 8 "Remember this, fix it in mind, take it to **h,** 4213
49:21 Then you will say in your **h,** 4222
57: 1 and no one ponders it in his **h;** 4213
57:15 the lowly and to revive the **h** *of* the contrite. 4213
60: 5 your **h** will throb and swell with joy; 4222
63: 4 For the day of vengeance was in my **h,** 4213
65:14 from anguish of **h** and wail in brokenness 4213
66:14 your **h** will rejoice and you will flourish 4213
Jer 3:10 Judah did not return to me with all her **h,** 4213
3:15 I will give you shepherds after my own **h,** 4213
4: 9 "the king and the officials will lose **h,** 4213
4:14 wash the evil from your **h** and be saved. 4213
4:18 How it pierces to the **h!"** 4213
4:19 Oh, the agony of my **h!** 4213
4:19 My **h** pounds within me, 4213
8:18 my **h** is faint within me. 4213
9: 8 but in his **h** he sets a trap for him. 7931
9:26 whole house of Israel is uncircumcised in **h.** 4213
11:20 you who judge righteously and test the **h** 4213
15: 1 my **h** would not go out to this people. 5883
16:12 the stubbornness of his evil **h** instead 4213
17: 5 and whose **h** turns away from the LORD. 4213
17: 9 The **h** is deceitful above all things and 4213
17:10 "I the LORD search the **h** and examine 4213
18:12 the stubbornness of his evil **h.' "** 4213
20: 9 his word is in my **h** like a fire, 4213
20:12 the righteous and probe the **h** and mind, 4213
22:17 and your **h** are set only on dishonest gain, 4213
23: 9 My **h** is broken within me; 4213
23:20 fully accomplishes the purposes of his **h.** 4213
24: 7 I will give them a **h** to know me, 4213
24: 7 for they will return to me with all their **h.** 4213
29:13 when you seek me with all your **h.** 4222
30:24 fully accomplishes the purposes of his **h.** 4213
31:20 Therefore my **h** yearns for him; 5055
32:39 I will give them singleness of **h** and action, 4213
32:41 in this land with all my **h** and soul. 4213
48:29 and arrogance and the haughtiness of her **h.** 4213
48:36 "So my **h** laments for Moab like a flute; 4213
48:41 of Moab's warriors will be like the **h** *of* 4213
49:16 and the pride of your **h** have deceived you, 4213
49:22 of Edom's warriors will be like the **h** *of* 4213
51:46 Do not lose **h** or be afraid 4222
La 1:20 and in my **h** I am disturbed, 4213
1:22 My groans are many and my **h** is faint." 4213
2:11 my **h** is poured out on the ground 3879
2:19 pour out your **h** like water in the presence of 4213
3:13 He pierced my **h** with arrows 4000
Eze 3:10 and take to **h** all the words I speak to you. 4222
11:19 an undivided **h** and put a new spirit in them; 4213
11:19 from them their **h** *of* stone and give them 4213
11:19 of stone and give them a **h** *of* flesh. 4213
14: 4 in his **h** and puts a wicked stumbling block 4213
14: 7 in his **h** and puts a wicked stumbling block 4213
18:31 and get a new **h** and a new spirit. 4213
21: 6 before them with broken **h** and bitter grief. 5516
21: 7 Every **h** will melt and every hand go limp; 4213
25: 6 rejoicing with all the malice of your **h** 5883
27:25 You are filled with heavy cargo in the **h** *of* 4213
27:26 to pieces in the **h** *of* the sea. 4213
27:27 on board will sink into the **h** *of* the sea on 4213
28: 2 " 'In the pride of your **h** you say, 4213
28: 2 on the throne of a god in the **h** *of* the seas." 4213
28: 5 of your wealth your **h** has grown proud. 4222
28: 8 and you will die a violent death in the **h** *of* 4213
28:17 Your **h** became proud on account 4213
36:26 I will give you a new **h** and put a new spirit 4213
36:26 I will remove from you your **h** *of* stone 4213
36:26 of stone and give you a **h** *of* flesh. 4213
44: 7 you brought foreigners uncircumcised in **h** 4213
44: 9 in **h** and flesh is to enter my sanctuary, 4213
Da 5:20 when his **h** became arrogant and hardened 10381
7: 4 and the **h** *of* a man was given to it. 10381
11:28 his **h** will be set against the holy covenant. 4222
11:30 and *he will* **lose h.** 3874
Hos 5: 4 A spirit of prostitution is in their **h;** 7931
10: 2 Their **h** is deceitful, 4213
11: 8 My **h** is changed within me; 4213
Joel 2:12 "return to me with all your **h,** 4222
2:13 Rend your **h** and not your garments. 4222
Am 7:10 a conspiracy against you in the very **h** 7931
Ob 1: 3 The pride of your **h** has deceived you, 4213
Jnh 2: 3 into the very **h** *of* the seas, 4222
Hab 3:16 I heard and my **h** pounded, 1061
Zep 3:14 Be glad and rejoice with all your **h,** 4213
Mal 2: 2 if you do not set your **h** to honor my name," 4213
2: 2 you have not set your **h** to honor me. 4213
Mt 5: 8 Blessed are the pure *in* **h,** *2840*
5:28 committed adultery with her in his **h.** *2840*
6:21 your treasure is, there your **h** will be also. *2840*
9: 2 **"Take h,** son; your sins are forgiven." *2510*
9:22 **"Take h,** daughter," he said, *2510*
11:29 for I am gentle and humble *in* **h,** *2840*
12:34 of the overflow *of* the **h** the mouth speaks. *2840*
12:40 three days and three nights in the **h** of *2840*
13:15 For this people's **h** has become calloused; *2840*
13:19 and snatches away what was sown in his **h.** *2840*
15:18 of the mouth come from the **h,** *2840*
15:19 For out of the **h** come evil thoughts, murder, *2840*
18:35 you forgive your brother from your **h."** *2840*
22:37 " 'Love the Lord your God with all your **h** *2840*
Mk 7:19 it doesn't go into his **h** but into his stomach, *2840*
11:23 and does not doubt in his **h** but believes *2840*
12:30 Love the Lord your God with all your **h** and *2840*
12:33 To love him with all your **h,** *2840*
Lk 2:19 and pondered them in her **h.** *2840*
2:51 But his mother treasured all these things in
her **h.** *2840*
6:45 of the good stored up *in* his **h,** *2840*
6:45 of the evil stored up *in* his **h.** *2840*
6:45 of the overflow *of* his **h** his mouth speaks. *2840*
7:13 *his* **h went out** to her and he said, *5072*
8:15 for those with a noble and good **h,** *2840*
10:27 " 'Love the Lord your God with all your **h** *2840*
12:29 not **set** *your* **h on** what you will eat or drink; *2426*
12:34 your treasure is, there your **h** will be also. *2840*
24:25 and how slow *of* **h** to believe all that *2840*
Jn 12:27 my **h** is troubled, and what shall I say? *6034*
16:33 But **take h!** I have overcome the world. *2510*
Ac 1:24 they prayed, "Lord, you **know** everyone's **h.** *2841*
2:26 my **h** is glad and my tongue rejoices; *2840*
2:37 they were cut to the **h** and said to Peter and *2840*
4:32 All the believers were one *in* **h** and mind. *2840*
5: 3 how is it that Satan has so filled your **h** *2840*
8:21 because your **h** is not right before God. *2840*
8:22 for having such a thought *in* your **h.** *2840*
13:22 of Jesse a man after my own **h;** *2840*
15: 8 God, who **knows the h,** *2841*
16:14 The Lord opened her **h** to respond *2840*
21:13 Why are you weeping and breaking my **h?** *2840*
28:27 For this people's **h** has become calloused; *2840*
Ro 1: 9 whom I serve with my whole **h** in preaching *4460*
2: 5 stubbornness and your unrepentant **h,** *2840*
2:29 and circumcision is circumcision *of* the **h,** *2840*
9: 2 and unceasing anguish *in my* **h.** *2840*
10: 6 "Do not say in your **h,** 'Who will ascend *2840*
10: 8 it is in your mouth and in your **h,"** that is, *2840*
10: 9 and believe in your **h** that God raised him *2840*
10:10 For it is *with* your **h** that you believe *2840*
15: 6 that with one **h** and mouth you may glorify *3924*
1Co 14:25 and the secrets *of* his **h** will be laid bare. *2840*
2Co 2: 4 and anguish *of* **h** and with many tears, *2840*
4: 1 we have this ministry, *we do* not **lose h.** *1591*
4:16 Therefore *we do* not **lose h.** *1591*
5:12 rather than in what is in the **h.** *2840*
8:16 into the **h** of Titus the same concern I have *2840*
9: 7 what he has decided *in* his **h** to give, *2840*
Eph 1:18 that the eyes *of* your **h** may be enlightened *2840*
5:19 Sing and make music *in* your **h** to the Lord, *2840*
6: 5 and with sincerity *of* **h,** *2840*
6: 6 doing the will of God from your **h.** *6034*
Php 1: 7 since I have you in my **h;** *2840*
Col 2: 2 that they may be encouraged in **h** and united *2840*
3:22 to win their favor, but with sincerity *of* **h** *2840*
3:23 Whatever you do, work at it with all your **h,** *6034*
1Ti 1: 5 from a pure **h** and a good conscience and *2840*
3: 1 anyone **sets** his **h on being** an overseer, *3977*
2Ti 2:22 who call on the Lord out of a pure **h.** *2840*
Phm 1:12 I am sending him—who is my **very h—** *5073*
1:20 refresh my **h** in Christ. *5073*
Heb 3:12 unbelieving **h** that turns away from *2840*
4:12 it judges the thoughts and attitudes *of* the **h.** *2840*
10:22 with a sincere **h** in full assurance of faith, *2840*
12: 3 so that you will not grow weary and lose **h.** *6034*
12: 5 and *do* not **lose h** when he rebukes you, *1725*
1Pe 1:22 love one another deeply, from the **h.** *2840*
1Jn 5:10 who believes in the Son of God has this
testimony in **his h.** *1571*
Rev 1: 3 and **take to h** what is written in it, *5498*
18: 7 In her **h** she boasts, 'I sit as queen; *2840*

HEART'S (4) [HEART]

2Ch 1:11 "Since this is your **h** desire and you have 4222
Jer 15:16 they were my joy and my **h** delight, 4222
Eze 24:25 the delight of their eyes, their **h** desire, 5883
Ro 10: 1 my **h** desire and prayer to God for the
Israelites is that they may be saved. *2840*

HEARTACHE (1) [HEART]
Pr 15:13 but **h** crushes the spirit. 4213+6780

HEARTH (6)
Lev 6: 9 to remain on the altar **h** throughout 4612
Isa 29: 2 she will be to me like an **altar h.** 789
30:14 from a **h** or scooping water out of a cistern." 3683
Eze 43:15 The **altar h** is four cubits high, 2219
43:15 and four horns project upward from the **h.** 789
43:16 The **altar h** is square, 789

HEARTILY (KJV) See WITH ALL HEART

HEARTLESS (2) [HEART]
La 4: 3 but my people have become **h** like ostriches 425
Ro 1:31 they are senseless, faithless, **h,** ruthless. *845*

HEARTS (207) [HEART]
Ge 42:28 Their **h** sank and they turned 4213
Ex 9:34 He and his officials hardened their **h.** 4213
10: 1 for I have hardened his heart and the **h** 4213
14:17 the **h** *of* the Egyptians so that they will go 4213
Lev 26:36 I will make their **h** so fearful in the lands 4222
26:41 when their uncircumcised **h** are humbled 4222
Nu 15:39 after the lusts of your own **h** and eyes. 4222
Dt 5:29 that their **h** would be inclined to fear me 4222
6: 6 that I give you today are to be upon your **h.** 4222
10:16 Circumcise your **h,** therefore, 4222
11:18 Fix these words of mine in your **h** 4222
28:67 because of the terror that will fill your **h** and 4222
30: 6 The LORD your God will circumcise your **h** 4222
30: 6 and the **h** *of* your descendants, 4222
Jos 2:11 our **h** melted and everyone's courage failed 4222
5: 1 their **h** melted and they no longer had 4222
7: 5 the **h** *of* the people melted and became 4222
11:20 the LORD himself who hardened their **h** 4213
14: 8 up with me made the **h** *of* the people melt 4213
24:23 among you and yield your **h** to the LORD, 4222
1Sa 6: 6 Why do you harden your **h** as the Egyptians 4222
7: 3 to the LORD with all your **h,** 4222
10:26 by valiant men whose **h** God had touched. 4213
2Sa 15: 6 and so he stole the **h** *of* the men of Israel. 4213
15:13 **h** *of* the men of Israel are with Absalom." 4213
19:14 He won over the **h** *of* all the men of Judah 4222
1Ki 8:39 (for you alone know the **h** *of* all men), 4222
8:58 May he turn our **h** to him, 4222
8:61 But your **h** must be fully committed to 4222
11: 2 because they will surely turn your **h** 4222
18:37 and that you are turning their **h** back again." 4213
1Ch 16:10 the **h** *of* those who seek the LORD rejoice. 4213
29:18 in the **h** *of* your people forever, 4222
29:18 and keep their **h** loyal to you. 4222
2Ch 6:30 (for you alone know the **h** *of* men), 4222
11:16 from every tribe of Israel who set their **h** 4222
16: 9 to strengthen those whose **h** are fully
committed to him. 4222
20:33 not set their **h** on the God of their fathers. 4222
29:31 all whose **h** were willing brought burnt
offerings. 4213
Job 1: 5 and cursed God in their **h.**" 4222
Ps 4: 4 search your **h** and be silent. 4222
7: 9 who searches minds and **h,** 4213
17:10 They close up their **callous h,** 2693
22:26 may your **h** live forever! 4222
28: 3 but harbor malice in their **h.** 4222
33:15 he who forms the **h** *of* all, 4213
33:21 In him our **h** rejoice, 4213
37:15 But their swords will pierce their own **h,** 4213
44:18 Our **h** had not turned back; 4213
45: 5 Let your sharp arrows pierce the **h** *of* 4213
62: 4 but in their **h** they curse. 7931
62: 8 pour out your **h** to him, 4222
69:32 you who seek God, may your **h** live! 4222
73: 7 From their **callous h** comes iniquity; 2693
74: 8 They said in their **h,** 4213
78: 8 whose **h** were not loyal to God, 4213
78:37 their **h** were not loyal to him, 4213
81:12 So I gave them over to their stubborn **h** 4213
84: 5 who have set their **h** on pilgrimage. 4222
95: 8 do not harden your **h** as you did at Meribah, 4222
95:10 "They are a people whose **h** go astray, 4222
105: 3 the **h** *of* those who seek the LORD rejoice. 4213
105:25 whose **h** he turned to hate his people, 4213
119:70 Their **h** are callous and unfeeling, 4213
140: 2 who devise evil plans in their **h** and stir 4213
Pr 12:20 in the **h** *of* those who plot evil, 4213
15: 7 not so the **h** *of* fools. 4213
15:11 how much more the **h** *of* men! 4213
24: 2 for their **h** plot violence, 4213
25: 3 so the **h** *of* kings are unsearchable. 4213
Ecc 3:11 He has also set eternity in the **h** *of* men; 4213
8:11 the **h** *of* the people are filled with schemes 4213
9: 3 The **h** *of* men, moreover, are full of evil 4213
9: 3 of evil and there is madness in their **h** 4213
Isa 6:10 hear with their ears, understand with their **h,** 4222
7: 2 the **h** *of* Ahaz and his people were shaken, 4222
15: 4 and their **h** are faint. 5883
19: 1 the **h** *of* the Egyptians melt within them. 4222
26: 8 and renown are the desire of our **h.** 5883
29:13 but their **h** are far from me. 4213
30:29 your **h** will rejoice as when people go up 4222
35: 4 say to those with fearful **h,** "Be strong, do 4213
51: 7 you people who have my law in your **h:** 4213
57:11 nor pondered this in your **h?** 4213
Isa 59:13 uttering lies our **h** have conceived. 4213
63:17 harden our **h** so we do not revere you? 4213
65:14 servants will sing out of the joy of their **h,** 4213
Jer 3:17 the stubbornness of their evil **h.** 4213
4: 4 circumcise your **h,** you men of Judah 4222
5:23 But these people have stubborn and
rebellious **h;** 4213
7:24 the stubborn inclinations of their evil **h.** 4213
9:14 the stubbornness of their **h;** 4213
11: 8 the stubbornness of their evil **h.** 4213
12: 2 on their lips but far from their **h.** 4000
13:10 stubbornness of their **h** and go after other 4213
17: 1 on the tablets of their **h** and on the horns of 4213
23:17 the stubbornness of their **h** they say, 4213
23:26 How long will this continue in the **h** 4213
31:33 in their minds and write it on their **h.** 4213
48:41 In that day the **h** *of* Moab's warriors will be 4213
49:22 In that day the **h** *of* Edom's warriors will be 4213
La 2:18 The **h** *of* the people cry out to the Lord. 4213
3:41 up our **h** and our hands to God in heaven, 4222
3:65 Put a veil over their **h,** 4213
5:15 Joy is gone from our **h;** 4213
5:17 Because of this our **h** are faint, 4213
Eze 6: 9 I have been grieved by their adulterous **h,** 4213
11:21 But as for those whose **h** are devoted 4213
14: 3 in their **h** and put wicked stumbling blocks 4213
14: 5 to recapture the **h** *of* the people of Israel, 4213
20:16 For their **h** were devoted to their idols. 4213
21:15 So that **h** may melt and the fallen be many, 4213
25:15 and took revenge with malice in their **h,** 5883
32: 9 I will trouble the **h** *of* many peoples 4213
33:31 but their **h** are greedy for unjust gain. 4213
36: 5 with malice in their **h** they made my land 4222
Da 11:27 The two kings, with their **h** bent on evil, 4222
Hos 7: 6 Their **h** are like an oven; 4213
7:14 to me from their **h** but wail upon their beds. 4213
Na 2:10 **H** melt, knees give way, bodies tremble, 4213
Zec 7:10 In your **h** do not think evil of each other.' 4222
7:12 They made their **h** as hard as flint 4213
10: 7 and their **h** will be glad as with wine. 4213
10: 7 their **h** will rejoice in the LORD. 4213
12: 5 the leaders of Judah will say in their **h,** 4213
Mal 4: 6 the **h** *of* the fathers to their children, and 4213
4: 6 and the **h** *of* the children to their fathers; 4213
Mt 9: 4 "Why do you entertain evil thoughts in
your **h?** *2840*
13:15 understand *with* their **h** and turn, *2840*
15: 8 but their **h** are far from me. *2840*
19: 8 because your **h** were **hard.** *5016*
Mk 2: 8 what they were thinking in **their h,** *1571*
3: 5 deeply distressed at their stubborn **h,** *2840*
6:52 their **h** were hardened. *2840*
7: 6 but their **h** are far from me. *2840*
7:21 For from within, out of men's **h,** *2840*
8:17 Are your **h** hardened? *2840*
10: 5 "It was because your **h** were **hard** *5016*
Lk 1:17 to turn the **h** of the fathers to their children *2840*
2:35 the thoughts of many **h** will be revealed. *2840*
3:15 wondering in their **h** if John might possibly *2840*
5:22 "Why are you thinking these things in
your **h?** *2840*
8:12 and takes away the word from their **h,** *2840*
16:15 but God knows your **h.** *2840*
21:34 or your **h** will be weighed down *2840*
24:32 not our **h** burning within us while he talked *2840*
Jn 5:42 not have the love of God in **your h.** *1571*
12:40 and deadened their **h,** so they can neither *2840*
12:40 nor understand *with* their **h,** nor turn— *2840*
14: 1 "Do not let your **h** be troubled. *2840*
14:27 Do not let your **h** be troubled and do not *2840*
Ac 2:46 and ate together with glad and sincere **h,** *2840*
7:39 they rejected him and in their **h** turned back *2840*
7:51 with uncircumcised **h** and ears! *2840*
11:23 to remain true to the Lord *with* all their **h.** *2840*
14:17 plenty of food and fills your **h** with joy." *2840*
15: 9 for he purified their **h** by faith. *2840*
28:27 understand *with* their **h** and turn, *2840*
Ro 1:21 and their foolish **h** were darkened. *2840*
1:24 over in the sinful desires *of* their **h** *2840*
2:15 of the law are written on their **h,** *2840*
5: 5 into our **h** by the Holy Spirit, *2840*
8:27 And he who searches our **h** knows the mind *2840*
1Co 4: 5 and will expose the motives *of* men's **h.** *2840*
10: 6 to keep us from **setting** our **h on** evil things *2122*
2Co 1: 9 in **our h** we felt the sentence of death. *1571*
1:22 and put his Spirit in our **h** as a deposit, *2840*
3: 2 written on our **h,** known and read by *2840*
3: 3 of stone but on tablets of human **h.** *2840*
3:15 when Moses is read, a veil covers their **h.** *2840*
4: 6 made his light shine in our **h** to give us *2840*
6:11 Corinthians, and opened wide our **h** to you. *2840*
6:13 open wide your **h** also. *NIG*
7: 2 Make room for us in your **h.** *NIG*
7: 3 in our **h** that we would live or die with you. *2840*
9:14 their **h** *will* **go out to** you, *2160*
Gal 4: 6 God sent the Spirit of his Son into our **h,** *2840*
Eph 3:17 Christ may dwell in your **h** through faith. *2840*
4:18 in them due to the hardening *of* their **h.** *2840*
Php 4: 7 will guard your **h** and your minds *2840*
Col 3: 1 **set** *your* **h on** things above, *2426*
3:15 Let the peace of Christ rule in your **h,** *2840*
3:16 and spiritual songs with gratitude in your **h** *2840*
4: 8 and that he may encourage your **h.** *2840*
1Th 2: 4 but God, who tests our **h.** *2840*
3:13 May he strengthen your **h** so that you will *2840*
2Th 2:17 encourage your **h** and strengthen you *2840*
3: 5 May the Lord direct your **h** into God's love *2840*
Phm 1: 7 brother, have refreshed the **h** of the saints. *5073*
Heb 3: 8 do not harden your **h** as you did in *2840*
3:10 and I said, 'Their **h** are always going astray, *2840*
3:15 if you hear his voice, do not harden your **h** *2840*
4: 7 if you hear his voice, do not harden your **h.**" *2840*
8:10 in their minds and write them on their **h.** *2840*
10:16 I will put my laws in their **h,** *2840*
10:22 having our **h** sprinkled to cleanse us from *2840*
13: 9 It is good for our **h** to be strengthened *2840*
Jas 3:14 and selfish ambition in your **h,** *2840*
4: 8 and purify your **h,** you double-minded. *2840*
1Pe 3:15 But in your **h** set apart Christ as Lord. *2840*
2Pe 1:19 and the morning star rises in your **h.** *2840*
1Jn 3:19 and how we set our **h** at rest in his presence *2840*
3:20 whenever our **h** condemn us. *2840*
3:20 For God is greater than our **h,** *2840*
3:21 Dear friends, if our **h** do not condemn us, *2840*
Rev 2:23 that I am he who searches **h** and minds, *2840*
17:17 into their **h** to accomplish his purpose *2840*

HEARTS' (1) [HEART]
Pr 13:25 The righteous eat to their **h'** content, 5883

HEARTY (KJV) See EARNEST

HEAT (32) [HEATED]
Ge 8:22 seedtime and harvest, cold and **h,** 2770
18: 1 the entrance to his tent in the **h** *of* the day. 2770
30:38 the flocks *were* **in h** and came to drink, 3501
30:41 Whenever the stronger females *were* **in h,** 3501
31:40 The **h** consumed me in the daytime and 2996
Dt 28:22 with **scorching h** and drought, 3031
1Sa 11:11 and slaughtered them until the **h** *of* the day. 2770
2Sa 4: 5 and they arrived there in the **h** *of* the day 2770
2Ki 23:26 the LORD did not turn away from the **h** 3019
Job 6:17 and in the **h** vanish from their channels. 2801
24:19 As **h** and drought snatch away 2770
Ps 19: 6 nothing is hidden from its **h.** 2780
32: 4 my strength was sapped as in the **h** 3001
58: 9 Before your pots can feel [the **h** of] NIH
Isa 4: 6 be a shelter and shade from the **h** of the day, 2996
18: 4 like shimmering **h** in the sunshine, 2770
18: 4 like a cloud of dew in the **h** *of* harvest." 2770
21:15 from the bent bow and from the **h** *of* battle. 3880
25: 4 from the storm and a shade from the **h.** 2996
25: 5 and like the **h** of the desert. 2996
25: 5 as **h** is reduced by the shadow of a cloud, 2996
49:10 the **desert h** or the sun beat upon them. 9220
Jer 2:24 **in her h** who can restrain her? 9299
17: 8 It does not fear when **h** comes; 2770
36:30 be thrown out and exposed to the **h** by day 2996
Hos 13: 5 in the land of **burning h,** 9429
Mt 20:12 of the work and the **h of the day.'** *3014*
Ac 28: 3 a viper, driven out by the **h,** *2549*
Jas 1:11 the sun rises with **scorching h** and withers *3014*
2Pe 3:12 and the elements will melt *in* the **h.** *3012*
Rev 7:16 nor any **scorching h.** *3008*
16: 9 by the intense **h** and they cursed the name *3008*

HEATED (1) [HEAT]
Da 3:19 the furnace **h** seven times hotter than usual 10015

HEATH (KJV) See BUSH

HEATHEN (1)
1Th 4: 5 not in passionate lust like the **h,** who do *1620*

HEAVE [OFFERING] (KJV) See WAVE [OFFERING]

HEAVEN (422) [HEAVEN'S, HEAVENLY, HEAVENS, HEAVENWARD]
Ge 14:19 God Most High, Creator of **h** and earth. 9028
14:22 God Most High, Creator of **h** and earth, 9028
21:17 and the angel of God called to Hagar from **h** 9028
22:11 of the LORD called out to him from **h,** 9028
22:15 of the LORD called to Abraham from **h** 9028
24: 3 the God of **h** and the God of earth, 9028
24: 7 "The LORD, the God of **h,** 9028
27:39 away from the dew of **h** above. 9028
28:12 with its top reaching to **h,** 9028
28:17 the house of God; this is the gate of **h.**" 9028
Ex 16: 4 "I will rain down bread from **h** for you. 9028
17:14 the memory of Amalek from under **h.**" 9028
20: 4 an idol in the form of anything in **h** above 9028
20:22 that I have spoken to you from **h:** 9028
Dt 2:25 and fear of you on all the nations under **h.** 9028
3:24 in **h** or on earth who can do the deeds 9028
4:19 to all the nations under **h.** 9028
4:26 I call **h** and earth as witnesses 9028
4:36 From **h** he made you hear his voice 9028
4:39 to heart this day that the LORD is God in **h** 9028
5: 8 an idol in the form of anything in **h** above 9028
7:24 you will wipe out their names from under **h.** 9028
9:14 and blot out their name from under **h.** 9028
11:11 and valleys that drinks rain from **h.** 9028
25:19 the memory of Amalek from under **h.** 9028
26:15 Look down from **h,** your holy dwelling 9028
29:20 LORD will blot out his name from under **h.** 9028
30:12 It is not up in **h,** so that you have to ask, 9028
30:12 ascend into **h** to get it and proclaim it to us 9028

Dt 30:19 This day I call **h** and earth as witnesses 9028
31:28 and call **h** and earth to testify against them. 9028
32:40 I lift my hand to **h** and declare: 9028
33:13 the precious dew from **h** above and with 9028
Jos 2:11 the LORD your God is God in **h** above and 9028
Jdg 13:20 the flame blazed up from the altar toward **h,** 9028
1Sa 2:10 He will thunder against them from **h;** 9028
5:12 and the outcry of the city went up to **h.** 9028
2Sa 22:14 The LORD thundered from **h;** 9028
1Ki 8:22 spread out his hands toward **h** 9028
8:23 like you in **h** above or on earth below— 9028
8:27 The heavens, even the **highest h,** 9028+9028
8:30 Hear from **h,** your dwelling place, 9028
8:32 then hear from **h** and act. 9028
8:34 then hear from **h** and forgive the sin 9028
8:36 from **h** and forgive the sin of your servants, 9028
8:39 then hear from **h,** your dwelling place. 9028
8:43 then hear from **h,** your dwelling place, 9028
8:45 then hear from **h** their prayer and their plea, 9028
8:49 then from **h,** your dwelling place, 9028
8:54 with his hands spread out toward **h.** 9028
22:19 on his throne with all the host of **h** standing 9028
2Ki 1:10 down from **h** and consume you 9028
1:10 Then fire fell from **h** and consumed 9028
1:12 down from **h** and consume you 9028
1:12 of God fell from **h** and consumed him 9028
1:14 from **h** and consumed the first two captains 9028
2:1 the LORD was about to take Elijah up to **h** 9028
2:11 and Elijah went up to **h** in a whirlwind. 9028
14:27 the name of Israel from under **h,** 9028
19:15 You have made **h** and earth. 9028
1Ch 21:16 the angel of the LORD standing between **h** 9028
21:26 the LORD answered him with fire from **h** 9028
29:11 for everything in **h** and earth is yours. 9028
2Ch 2:12 the God of Israel, who made **h** and earth! 9028
6:13 of Israel and spread out his hands toward **h.** 9028
6:14 there is no God like you in **h** or on earth— 9028
6:21 Hear from **h,** your dwelling place; 9028
6:23 then hear from **h** and act. 9028
6:25 then hear from **h** and forgive the sin 9028
6:27 from **h** and forgive the sin of your servants, 9028
6:30 then hear from **h,** your dwelling place. 9028
6:33 then hear from **h,** your dwelling place, 9028
6:35 then hear from **h** their prayer and their plea, 9028
6:39 then from **h,** your dwelling place, 9028
7:1 from **h** and consumed the burnt offering and 9028
7:14 from **h** and will forgive their sin 9028
18:18 on his throne with all the host of **h** standing 9028
20:6 are you not the God who is in **h?** 9028
28:9 in a rage that reaches to **h.** 9028
30:27 for their prayer reached **h,** 9028
32:20 of Amoz cried out in prayer to **h** about this. 9028
36:23 " 'The LORD, the God of **h,** 9028
Ezr 1:2 " 'The LORD, the God of **h,** 9028
5:11 the servants of the God of **h** and earth, 10723
5:12 because our fathers angered the God of **h,** 10723
6:9 the God of **h,** and wheat, salt, wine and oil, 10723
6:10 of **h** and pray for the well-being of the king 10723
7:12 a teacher of the Law of the God of **h:** 10723
7:21 a teacher of the Law of the God of **h,** 10723
7:23 Whatever the God of **h** has prescribed, 10723
7:23 for the temple of the God of **h.** 10723
Ne 1:4 and fasted and prayed before the God of **h.** 9028
1:5 Then I said: "O LORD, God of **h,** 9028
2:4 Then I prayed to the God of **h,** 9028
2:20 "The God of **h** will give us success. 9028
9:6 and the multitudes of **h** worship you. 9028
9:13 you spoke to them from **h.** 9028
9:15 In their hunger you gave them bread from **h** 9028
9:27 From **h** you heard them, 9028
9:28 you heard from **h,** 9028
Job 16:19 my witness is in **h;** my advocate is on high. 9028
22:12 "Is not God in the heights of **h?** 9028
25:2 he establishes order in the **heights of h.** 5294
37:3 the whole **h** and sends it to the ends of 9028
41:11 Everything under **h** belongs to me. 9028
Ps 2:4 The One enthroned in **h** laughs; 9028
14:2 The LORD looks down from **h** on the sons 9028
18:13 The LORD thundered from **h;** 9028
20:6 he answers him from his holy **h** with 9028
33:13 From **h** the LORD looks down 9028
53:2 God looks down from **h** on the sons of men 9028
57:3 He sends from **h** and saves me, 9028
69:34 Let **h** and earth praise him, 9028
73:9 Their mouths lay claim to **h,** 9028
73:25 Whom have I in **h** but you? 9028
75:5 Do not lift your horns against **h;** 5294
76:8 From **h** you pronounced judgment, 9028
78:24 he gave them the grain of **h.** 9028
80:14 Look down from **h** and see! 9028
85:11 and righteousness looks down from **h.** 9028
89:2 you established your faithfulness in **h** itself. 9028
102:19 from **h** he viewed the earth, 9028
103:19 The LORD has established his throne in **h,** 9028
105:40 and satisfied them with the bread of **h.** 9028
115:3 Our God is in **h;** he does whatever he 9028
115:15 the LORD, the Maker of **h** and earth. 9028
121:2 the LORD, the Maker of **h** and earth. 9028
123:1 to you whose throne is in **h.** 9028
124:8 the LORD, the Maker of **h** and earth. 9028
134:3 May the LORD, the Maker of **h** and earth, 9028
136:26 Give thanks to the God of **h.** 9028
146:6 of **h** and earth, the sea, and everything 9028
Pr 30:4 Who has gone up to **h** and come down? 9028
Ecc 1:13 by wisdom all that is done under **h.** 9028
2:3 for men to do under **h** during the few days 9028
3:1 and a season for every activity under **h:** 9028
Ecc 5:2 God is in **h** and you are on earth, 9028
Isa 13:10 The stars of **h** and their constellations will 9028
14:12 How you have fallen from **h,** 9028
14:13 You said in your heart, "I will ascend to **h;** 9028
37:16 You have made **h** and earth. 9028
55:10 the rain and the snow come down from **h,** 9028
63:15 from **h** and see from your lofty throne, 9028
66:1 "**H** is my throne, and the earth is my 9028
Jer 7:18 cakes of bread for the Queen of **H.** 9028
23:24 "Do not I fill **h** and earth?" 9028
33:25 and night and the fixed laws of **h** and earth, 9028
44:17 We will burn incense to the Queen of **H** 9028
44:18 Queen of **H** and pouring out drink offerings 9028
44:19 we burned incense to the Queen of **H** 9028
44:25 drink offerings to the Queen of **H.'** 9028
51:48 Then **h** and earth and all that is in 9028
La 2:1 down the splendor of Israel from **h** to earth; 9028
3:41 up our hearts and our hands to God in **h,** 9028
3:50 the LORD looks down from **h** and sees. 9028
Eze 8:3 The Spirit lifted me up between earth and **h** 9028
Da 2:18 from the God of **h** concerning this mystery, 10723
2:19 Then Daniel praised the God of **h** 10723
2:28 there is a God in **h** who reveals mysteries. 10723
2:37 of **h** has given you dominion and power 10723
2:44 of **h** will set up a kingdom that will never 10723
4:13 a holy one, coming down from **h.** 10723
4:15 " 'Let him be drenched with the dew of **h,** 10723
4:23 coming down from **h** and saying, 10723
4:23 Let him be drenched with the dew of **h;** 10723
4:25 and be drenched with the dew of **h.** 10723
4:26 to you when you acknowledge that **H** rules. 10723
4:31 on his lips when a voice came from **h,** 10723
4:33 of **h** until his hair grew like the feathers of 10723
4:34 Nebuchadnezzar, raised my eyes toward **h,** 10723
4:35 the powers of **h** and the peoples of the earth 10723
4:37 praise and exalt and glorify the King of **h,** 10723
5:21 his body was drenched with the dew of **h,** 10723
5:23 set yourself up against the Lord of **h.** 10723
7:2 the four winds of **h** churning up 10723
7:13 a son of man, coming with the clouds of **h.** 10723
7:27 under the whole **h** will be handed over to 10723
8:8 up toward the four winds of **h.** 9028
9:12 the whole **h** nothing has ever been done 9028
11:4 and parceled out toward the four winds of **h.** 9028
12:7 and his left hand toward **h,** 9028
Jnh 1:9 I worship the LORD, the God of **h,** 9028
Zec 2:6 I have scattered you to the four winds of **h,**" 9028
5:9 and they lifted up the basket between **h** 9028
6:5 "These are the four spirits of **h,** 9028
Mal 3:10 if I will not throw open the floodgates of **h** 9028
Mt 3:2 "Repent, for the kingdom *of* **h** is near." 4041
3:16 At that moment **h** was opened, 4041
3:17 And a voice from **h** said, "This is my Son, 4041
4:17 "Repent, for the kingdom *of* **h** is near." 4041
5:3 for theirs is the kingdom *of* **h.** 4041
5:10 for theirs is the kingdom *of* **h.** 4041
5:12 because great is your reward in **h,** 4041
5:16 and praise your Father in **h.** 4041
5:18 until **h** and earth disappear, 4041
5:19 be called least in the kingdom *of* **h,** 4041
5:19 be called great in the kingdom *of* **h—** 4041
5:20 certainly not enter the kingdom *of* **h.** 4041
5:34 either by **h,** for it is God's throne; 4041
5:45 that you may be sons of your Father in **h.** 4041
6:1 have no reward from your Father in **h.** 4041
6:9 " 'Our Father in **h,** hallowed be your name, 4041
6:10 your will be done on earth as it is in **h.** 4041
6:20 But store up for yourselves treasures in **h,** 4041
7:11 Father in **h** give good gifts to those who ask 4041
7:21 'Lord, Lord,' will enter the kingdom *of* **h,** 4041
7:21 the will of my Father who is in **h.** 4041
8:11 Isaac and Jacob in the kingdom *of* **h.** 4041
10:7 'The kingdom *of* **h** is near.' 4041
10:32 before my Father in **h.** 4041
10:33 I will disown him before my Father in **h.** 4041
11:11 in the kingdom *of* **h** is greater than he. 4041
11:12 kingdom *of* **h** has been forcefully advancing 4041
11:25 "I praise you, Father, Lord *of* **h** and earth, 4041
12:50 in **h** is my brother and sister and mother." 4041
13:11 of the kingdom *of* **h** has been given to you, 4041
13:24 *of* **h** is like a man who sowed good seed 4041
13:31 "The kingdom *of* **h** is like a mustard seed, 4041
13:33 "The kingdom *of* **h** is like yeast that 4041
13:44 "The kingdom *of* **h** is like treasure hidden 4041
13:45 the kingdom *of* **h** is like a merchant looking 4041
13:47 the kingdom *of* **h** is like a net that was let 4041
13:52 about the kingdom *of* **h** is like the owner of 4041
14:19 and the two fish and looking up to **h,** 4041
16:1 by asking him to show them a sign from **h.** 4041
16:17 to you by man, but by my Father in **h.** 4041
16:19 will give you the keys of the kingdom *of* **h;** 4041
16:19 you bind on earth will be bound in **h,** 4041
16:19 you loose on earth will be loosed in **h.**" 4041
18:1 "Who is the greatest in the kingdom *of* **h?**" 4041
18:3 you will never enter the kingdom *of* **h.** 4041
18:4 child is the greatest in the kingdom *of* **h.** 4041
18:10 that their angels in **h** always see the face 4041
18:10 the face of my Father in **h.** 4041
18:14 the same way your Father in **h** is not willing 4041
18:18 you bind on earth will be bound in **h,** 4041
18:18 you loose on earth will be loosed in **h.** 4041
18:19 it will be done for you by my Father in **h.** 4041
18:23 the kingdom *of* **h** is like a king who wanted 4041
19:12 because of the kingdom *of* **h.** 4041
19:14 the kingdom *of* **h** belongs to such as these." 4041
19:21 and you will have treasure in **h.** 4041
19:23 for a rich man to enter the kingdom *of* **h.** 4041
Mt 20:1 kingdom *of* **h** is like a landowner who went 4041
21:25 Was it from **h,** or from men?" 4041
21:25 "If we say, 'From **h,**' he will ask, 4041
22:2 kingdom *of* **h** is like a king who prepared 4041
22:30 they will be like the angels in **h.** 4041
23:9 for you have one Father, and he is **in h.** 4039
23:13 You shut the kingdom *of* **h** in men's faces. 4041
23:22 by **h** swears by God's throne and by 4041
24:35 **H** and earth will pass away, 4041
24:36 not even the angels in **h,** nor the Son, 4041
25:1 "At that time the kingdom *of* **h** will be 4041
26:64 and coming on the clouds *of* **h.**" 4041
28:2 angel of the Lord came down from **h** and, 4041
28:18 "All authority in **h** and on earth has been given to me. 4041
Mk 1:10 he saw **h** being torn open and the Spirit 4041
1:11 And a voice came from **h:** 4041
6:41 and the two fish and looking up to **h,** 4041
7:34 He looked up to **h** and with a deep sigh said 4041
8:11 they asked him for a sign from **h.** 4041
10:21 and you will have treasure in **h.** 4041
11:25 your Father in **h** may forgive you your sins. 4041
11:30 was it from **h,** or from men? 4041
11:31 "If we say, 'From **h,**' he will ask, 4041
12:25 they will be like the angels in **h.** 4041
13:31 **H** and earth will pass away, 4041
13:32 not even the angels in **h,** nor the Son, 4041
14:62 and coming on the clouds *of* **h.**" 4041
16:19 into **h** and he sat at the right hand of God. 4041
Lk 1:78 the rising sun will come to us from **h** 5737
2:15 the angels had left them and gone into **h,** 4041
3:21 And as he was praying, **h** was opened 4041
3:22 And a voice came from **h:** 4041
6:23 because great is your reward in **h.** 4041
9:16 and the two fish and looking up to **h,** 4041
9:51 for him to be taken up to **h,** NIG
9:54 to call fire down from **h** to destroy them?" 4041
10:18 "I saw Satan fall like lightning from **h.** 4041
10:20 rejoice that your names are written in **h.**" 4041
10:21 "I praise you, Father, Lord *of* **h** and earth, 4041
11:13 how much more will your Father in **h** give 4041
11:16 by asking for a sign from **h.** 4041
12:33 a treasure in **h** that will not be exhausted, 4041
15:7 rejoicing in **h** over one sinner who repents 4041
15:18 I have sinned against **h** and against you. 4041
15:21 I have sinned against **h** and against you. 4041
16:17 It is easier for **h** and earth to disappear than 4041
17:29 down from **h** and destroyed them all. 4041
18:13 He would not even look up to **h,** 4041
18:22 and you will have treasure in **h.** 4041
19:38 "Peace in **h** and glory in the highest!" 4041
20:4 was it from **h,** or from men?" 4041
20:5 "If we say, 'From **h,**' he will ask, 4041
21:11 and fearful events and great signs from **h.** 4041
21:33 **H** and earth will pass away, 4041
22:43 An angel from **h** appeared to him 4041
24:51 he left them and was taken up into **h.** 4041
Jn 1:32 down from **h** as a dove and remain on him. 4041
1:51 "I tell you the truth, you shall see **h** open, 4041
3:13 No one has ever gone into **h** except 4041
3:13 the one who came from **h—** 4041
3:27 can receive only what is given him from **h.** 4041
3:31 The one who comes from **h** is above all. 4041
6:31 'He gave them bread from **h** to eat.' " 4041
6:32 who has given you the bread from **h,** 4041
6:32 who gives you the true bread from **h.** 4041
6:33 down from **h** and gives life to the world." 4041
6:38 from **h** not to do my will but to do the will 4041
6:41 "I am the bread that came down from **h.**" 4041
6:42 can he now say, 'I came down from **h**'?" 4041
6:50 here is the bread that comes down from **h,** 4041
6:51 the living bread that came down from **h.** 4041
6:58 This is the bread that came down from **h.** 4041
12:28 Then a voice came from **h,** 4041
17:1 he looked toward **h** and prayed: 4041
Ac 1:2 until the day he was taken up to **h,** NIG
1:11 who has been taken from you into **h,** 4041
1:11 the same way you have seen him go into **h.**" 4041
2:2 the blowing of a violent wind came from **h** 4041
2:5 from every nation under **h.** 4041
2:19 in the **h** above and signs on the earth below, 4041
2:34 For David did not ascend to **h,** 4041
3:21 He must remain in **h** until the time comes 4041
4:12 under **h** given to men by which we must 4041
4:24 "you made the **h** and the earth and the sea, 4041
7:49 " '**H** is my throne, and the earth 4041
7:55 looked up to **h** and saw the glory of God, 4041
7:56 "I see **h** open and the Son of Man standing 4041
9:3 suddenly a light from **h** flashed around him. 4041
10:11 He saw **h** opened and something like 4041
10:16 immediately the sheet was taken back to **h.** 4041
11:5 like a large sheet being let down from **h** 4041
11:9 "The voice spoke from **h** a second time, 4041
11:10 and then it was all pulled up to **h** again. 4041
14:15 who made **h** and earth and sea 4041
14:17 by giving you rain **from h** and crops 4040
17:24 the Lord *of* **h** and earth and does not live 4041
19:35 and of her **image, which fell from h?** 1479
22:6 a bright light from **h** flashed around me. 4041
26:13 I saw a light **from h,** brighter than the sun, 4040
26:19 I was not disobedient *to* the vision from **h.** 4041
Ro 1:18 of God is being revealed from **h** against all 4041
10:6 'Who will ascend into **h?**' " 4041
1Co 8:5 so-called gods, whether in **h** or on earth 4041
15:47 dust of the earth, the second man from **h.** 4041
15:48 and as is the *man from* **h,** 2230
15:48 so also are those who are *of* **h.** 2230

1Co 15:49 we bear the likeness *of* the *man from* **h.** *2230*
2Co 5: 1 an eternal house in **h,** not built by human *4041*
12: 2 was caught up to the third **h.** *4041*
Gal 1: 8 even if we or an angel from **h** should preach *4041*
Eph 1:10 to bring all things in **h** and on earth together *4041*
3:15 from whom his whole family in **h** and *4041*
6: 9 both their Master and yours is in **h,** *4041*
Php 2:10 **in h** and on earth and under the earth, *2230*
3:20 But our citizenship is in **h.** *4041*
Col 1: 5 for you in **h** and that you have already heard *4041*
1:16 created: things in **h** and on earth, *4041*
1:20 whether things on earth or things in **h,** *4041*
1:23 to every creature under **h,** *4041*
4: 1 you know that you also have a Master in **h.** *4041*
1Th 1:10 to wait for his Son from **h,** whom he raised *4041*
4:16 the Lord himself will come down from **h,** *4041*
2Th 1: 7 when the Lord Jesus is revealed from **h** *4041*
Heb 1: 3 down at the right hand of the Majesty in **h.** *5734*
8: 1 of the throne of the Majesty in **h,** *4041*
8: 5 that is a copy and shadow *of* what *is in* **h.** *2230*
9:24 he entered **h** itself, *4041*
9:25 Nor did he enter **h** to offer himself again *NIG*
12:23 whose names are written in **h.** *4041*
12:25 from him who warns us from **h?** *4041*
Jas 3:15 Such "wisdom" does not come down from **h** *NIG*
3:17 But the wisdom that comes from **h** is first *NIG*
5:12 not by **h** or by earth or by anything else. *4041*
1Pe 1: 4 kept in **h** for you, *4041*
1:12 to you by the Holy Spirit sent from **h.** *4041*
3:22 into **h** and is at God's right hand— *4041*
2Pe 1:18 that came from **h** when we were with him *4041*
3:13 to a new **h** and a new earth, *4041*
Rev 3:12 which is coming down out of **h** *4041*
4: 1 before me was a door standing open in **h.** *4041*
4: 2 a throne in **h** with someone sitting on it. *4041*
5: 3 But no one in **h** or on earth or under *4041*
5:13 in **h** and on earth and under the earth and on *4041*
8: 1 silence in **h** for about half an hour. *4041*
10: 1 another mighty angel coming down from **h.** *4041*
10: 4 but I heard a voice from **h** say, *4041*
10: 5 and on the land raised his right hand to **h.** *4041*
10: 8 the voice that I had heard from **h** spoke *4041*
11:12 Then they heard a loud voice from **h** saying *4041*
11:12 And they went up to **h** in a cloud, *4041*
11:13 and gave glory to the God *of* **h.** *4041*
11:15 and there were loud voices in **h,** which said: *4041*
11:19 Then God's temple in **h** was opened, *4041*
12: 1 A great and wondrous sign appeared in **h:** *4041*
12: 3 Then another sign appeared in **h:** *4041*
12: 7 And there was war in **h.** *4041*
12: 8 and they lost their place in **h.** *4041*
12:10 Then I heard a loud voice in **h** say: *4041*
13: 6 and those who live in **h.** *4041*
13:13 to come down from **h** to earth in full view *4041*
14: 2 from **h** like the roar of rushing waters and *4041*
14:13 Then I heard a voice from **h** say, "Write: *4041*
14:17 Another angel came out of the temple in **h,** *4041*
15: 1 I saw in **h** another great and marvelous sign: *4041*
15: 5 After this I looked and in **h** the temple, *4041*
16:11 *of* **h** because of their pains and their sores, *4041*
18: 1 I saw another angel coming down from **h.** *4041*
18: 4 Then I heard another voice from **h** say: *4041*
18: 5 for her sins are piled up to **h,** *4041*
18:20 Rejoice over her, *O* **h!** *4041*
19: 1 the roar of a great multitude in **h** shouting: *4041*
19:11 I saw **h** standing open and there *4041*
19:14 The armies of **h** were following him, *4041*
20: 1 And I saw an angel coming down out of **h,** *4041*
20: 9 fire came down from **h** and devoured them. *4041*
21: 1 Then I saw a new **h** and a new earth, *4041*
21: 1 first **h** and the first earth had passed away, *4041*
21: 2 coming down out of **h** from God, *4041*
21:10 Jerusalem, coming down out of **h** from God. *4041*

HEAVEN'S (1) [HEAVEN]

Ge 27:28 give you of **h** dew and of earth's richness— 9028

HEAVENLY (36) [HEAVEN]

Dt 4:19 the moon and the stars—all the **h** array— 9028
Ps 8: 5 the **h beings** and crowned him with glory 466
11: 4 the LORD is on his **h** throne. 9028
89: 6 like the LORD among the **h beings?** 446+1201
103:21 Praise the LORD, all his **h hosts,** 7372
148: 2 all his angels, praise him, all his **h hosts.** 7372
Mt 5:48 therefore, as your **h** Father is perfect. *4039*
6:14 your **h** Father will also forgive you. *4039*
6:26 and yet your **h** Father feeds them. *4039*
6:32 your **h** Father knows that you need them. *4039*
15:13 that my **h** Father has not planted will *4039*
18:35 "This is how my **h** Father will treat each *4039*
24:29 and the **h** bodies will be shaken.' *4041*
25:31 he will sit on his throne in **h** glory. *NIG*
Mk 13:25 and the **h** bodies will be shaken.' *4041*
Lk 2:13 a great company *of* the **h** host appeared *4039*
21:26 for the **h bodies** will be shaken. *1539+3836+4041*
Jn 3:12 then will you believe if I speak of **h things?** *2230*
Ac 7:42 over to the worship *of* the **h** bodies. *4041*
1Co 15:40 also **h** bodies and there are earthly bodies; *2230*
15:40 but the splendor *of* the **h** bodies is one kind, *2230*
2Co 5: 2 longing to be clothed with our **h** dwelling, *1666+4041*
5: 4 but to be clothed with our **h** dwelling, *NIG*
Eph 1: 3 in the **h realms** with every spiritual blessing *2230*
1:20 at his right hand in the **h realms,** *2230*
2: 6 with him in the **h realms** in Christ Jesus, *2230*
3:10 to the rulers and authorities in the **h realms,** *2230*
6:12 the spiritual forces of evil in the **h realms.** *2230*
2Ti 4:18 and will bring me safely to his **h** kingdom. *2230*
Heb 3: 1 holy brothers, who share in the **h** calling, *2230*
6: 4 who have tasted the **h** gift, *2230*
9:23 the copies of the **h things** to be *1877+3836+4041*
9:23 but the **h** *things* themselves *2230*
11:16 longing for a better country—a **h** *one.* *2230*
12:22 to Mount Zion, to the **h** Jerusalem, *2230*
Jas 1:17 down from the Father of the **h** lights, *NIG*

HEAVENS (173) [HEAVEN]

Ge 1: 1 In the beginning God created the **h** and 9028
2: 1 Thus the **h** and the earth were completed 9028
2: 4 the **h** and the earth when they were created. 9028
2: 4 the LORD God made the earth and the **h**— 9028
6:17 on the earth to destroy all life under the **h,** 9028
7:11 and the floodgates of the **h** were opened. 9028
7:19 under the entire **h** were covered. 9028
8: 2 and the floodgates of the **h** had been closed, 9028
11: 4 with a tower that reaches to the **h,** 9028
15: 5 "Look up at the **h** and count the stars— 9028
19:24 from the LORD out of the **h.** 9028
49:25 who blesses you with blessings of the **h** 9028
Ex 20:11 For in six days the LORD made the **h** and 9028
31:17 for in six days the LORD made the **h** and 9028
Dt 4:11 while it blazed with fire to the very **h,** 9028
4:32 ask from one end of the **h** to the other. 9028
10:14 To the LORD your God belong the **h,** 9028
10:14 even the **highest h,** the earth and 9028+9028
11:17 and he will shut the **h** so that it will not rain 9028
11:21 as the days that the **h** are above the earth. 9028
28:12 The LORD will open the **h,** 9028
30: 4 to the most distant land under the **h,** 9028
32: 1 O **h,** and I will speak; 9028
33:26 on the **h** to help you and on the clouds 9028
33:28 where the **h** drop dew. 9028
Jdg 5: 4 the earth shook, the **h** poured, 9028
5:20 From the **h** the stars fought, 9028
2Sa 21:10 till the rain poured down from the **h** on 9028
22: 8 the foundations of the **h** shook; 9028
22:10 He parted the **h** and came down; 9028
1Ki 8:27 The **h,** even the highest heaven, 9028
8:35 "When the **h** are shut up and there is no rain 9028
2Ki 7: 2 LORD should open the floodgates of the **h,** 9028
7:19 LORD should open the floodgates of the **h,** 9028
1Ch 16:26 but the LORD made the **h.** 9028
16:31 Let the **h** rejoice, let the earth be glad; 9028
2Ch 2: 6 since the **h,** even the highest heavens, 9028
2: 6 the **highest h,** cannot contain him? 9028+9028
6:18 The **h,** even the highest heavens, 9028
6:18 The heavens, even the **highest h,** 9028+9028
6:26 "When the **h** are shut up and there is no rain 9028
7:13 I shut up the **h** so that there is no rain, 9028
Ezr 9: 6 and our guilt has reached to the **h.** 9028
Ne 9: 6 You made the **h,** even the highest heavens, 9028
9: 6 made the heavens, even the **highest h,** 9028+9028
Job 9: 8 He alone stretches out the **h** and treads on 9028
11: 8 They are higher than the **h**— 9028
14:12 till the **h** are no more, 9028
15:15 if even the **h** are not pure in his eyes, 9028
20: 6 to the **h** and his head touches the clouds, 9028
20:27 The **h** will expose his guilt; 9028
22:14 as he goes about in the vaulted **h.'** 9028
26:11 pillars of the **h** quake, aghast at his rebuke. 9028
28:24 of the earth and sees everything under the **h.** 9028
35: 5 Look up at the **h** and see; 9028
38:29 Who gives birth to the frost from the **h** 9028
38:33 Do you know the laws of the **h?** 9028
38:37 Who can tip over the water jars of the **h** 9028
Ps 8: 1 You have set your glory above the **h.** 9028
8: 3 When I consider your **h,** 9028
18: 9 He parted the **h** and came down; 9028
19: 1 The **h** declare the glory of God; 9028
19: 4 **In the h** he has pitched a tent for the sun, 2157[S]
19: 6 at one end of the **h** and makes its circuit to 9028
33: 6 the word of the LORD were the **h** made, 9028
36: 5 Your love, O LORD, reaches to the **h,** 9028
50: 4 He summons the **h** above, and the earth, 9028
50: 6 And the **h** proclaim his righteousness, 9028
57: 5 Be exalted, O God, above the **h;** 9028
57:10 For great is your love, reaching to the **h;** 9028
57:11 Be exalted, O God, above the **h;** 9028
68: 8 the **h** poured down rain, before God, 9028
78:23 above and opened the doors of the **h;** 9028
78:26 from the **h** and led forth the south wind 9028
89: 5 The **h** praise your wonders, 9028
89:11 The **h** are yours, and yours also the earth; 9028
89:29 his throne as long as the **h** endure. 9028
96: 5 but the LORD made the **h.** 9028
96:11 Let the **h** rejoice, let the earth be glad; 9028
97: 6 The **h** proclaim his righteousness, 9028
102:25 and the **h** are the work of your hands. 9028
103:11 For as high as the **h** are above the earth, 9028
104: 2 he stretches out the **h** like a tent 9028
107:26 They mounted up to the **h** and went down to 9028
108: 4 For great is your love, higher than the **h;** 9028
108: 5 Be exalted, O God, above the **h,** 9028
113: 4 his glory above the **h.** 9028
113: 6 who stoops down to look on the **h** and 9028
115:16 The **highest h** belong to the LORD, 9028+9028
119:89 it stands firm in the **h.** 9028
135: 6 pleases him, in the **h** and on the earth, 9028
136: 5 who by his understanding made the **h,** 9028
139: 8 If I go up to the **h,** you are there; 9028
144: 5 Part your **h,** O LORD, and come down; 9028
148: 1 Praise the LORD from the **h,** 9028
148: 4 you **highest h** and you waters above 9028+9028
148:13 his splendor is above the earth and the **h.** 9028
150: 1 praise him in his mighty **h.** 8385
Pr 3:19 by understanding he set the **h** in place; 9028
8:27 I was there when he set the **h** in place, 9028
25: 3 As the **h** are high and the earth is deep, 9028
Isa 1: 2 Hear, O **h!** Listen, O earth! 9028
13: 5 from the ends of the **h**— 9028
13:13 Therefore I will make the **h** tremble; 9028
24:18 The floodgates of the **h** are opened, 5294
24:21 the LORD will punish the powers in the **h** 5294
34: 4 the **h** will be dissolved and the sky rolled up 9028
34: 5 My sword has drunk its fill in the **h;** 9028
38:14 My eyes grew weak as I looked to the **h.** 5294
40:12 the breadth of his hand marked off the **h?** 9028
40:22 He stretches out the **h** like a canopy, 9028
40:26 Lift your eyes and look to the **h:** 5294
42: 5 the **h** and stretched them out, 9028
44:23 Sing for joy, O **h,** for the LORD has done 9028
44:24 who alone stretched out the **h,** 9028
45: 8 "You **h** above, rain down righteousness; 9028
45:12 My own hands stretched out the **h;** 9028
45:18 he who created the **h,** he is God; 9028
48:13 and my right hand spread out the **h;** 9028
49:13 Shout for joy, O **h;** rejoice, O earth; 9028
51: 6 Lift up your eyes to the **h,** 9028
51: 6 the **h** will vanish like smoke, 9028
51:13 the **h** and laid the foundations of the earth, 9028
51:16 I who set the **h** in place, 9028
55: 9 "As the **h** are higher than the earth, 9028
64: 1 that you would rend the **h** and come down, 9028
65:17 I will create new **h** and a new earth. 9028
66:22 "As the new **h** and the new earth 9028
Jer 2:12 Be appalled at this, O **h,** 9028
4:23 and at the **h,** and their light was gone. 9028
4:28 Therefore the earth will mourn and the **h** 9028
8: 2 and the moon and all the stars of the **h,** 9028
10:11 who did not make the **h** and the earth, 10723
10:11 from the earth and from under the **h.'** " 10723
10:12 by his wisdom and stretched out the **h** 9028
10:13 When he thunders, the waters in the **h** roar; 9028
31:37 "Only if the **h** above can be measured and 9028
32:17 the **h** and the earth by your great power 9028
49:36 from the four quarters of the **h;** 9028
51:15 by his wisdom and stretched out the **h** 9028
51:16 When he thunders, the waters in the **h** roar; 9028
La 3:66 in anger and destroy them from under the **h** 9028
Eze 1: 1 **h** were opened and I saw visions of God. 9028
32: 7 I will cover the **h** and darken their stars; 9028
32: 8 All the shining lights in the **h** I will darken 9028
Da 6:27 he performs signs and wonders in the **h** and 10723
8:10 It grew until it reached the host of the **h,** 9028
12: 3 like the brightness of the **h,** 8385
Joel 2:30 I will show wonders in the **h** and on 9028
Am 9: 2 Though they climb up to the **h,** 9028
9: 6 in the **h** and sets its foundation on the earth, 9028
Hab 3: 3 the **h** and his praise filled the earth. 9028
3:11 Sun and moon stood still in the **h** at the glint 2292
Hag 1:10 of you the **h** have withheld their dew and 9028
2: 6 a little while I will once more shake the **h** 9028
2:21 that I will shake the **h** and the earth, 9028
Zec 8:12 and the **h** will drop their dew. 9028
12: 1 The LORD, who stretches out the **h,** 9028
Mt 24:31 from one end *of* the **h** to the other. *4041*
Mk 13:27 the ends of the earth to the ends *of* the **h.** *4041*
Eph 4:10 who ascended higher than all the **h,** *4041*
Heb 1:10 and the **h** are the work of your hands. *4041*
4:14 through the **h,** Jesus the Son of God, *4041*
7:26 set apart from sinners, exalted above the **h.** *4041*
12:26 not only the earth but also the **h."** *4041*
Jas 5:18 Again he prayed, and the **h** gave rain, *4041*
2Pe 3: 5 the **h** existed and the earth was formed out *4041*
3: 7 the present **h** and earth are reserved for fire, *4041*
3:10 The **h** will disappear with a roar; *4041*
3:12 about the destruction of the **h** by fire, *4041*
Rev 10: 6 who created the **h** and all that is in them, *4041*
12:12 you **h** and you who dwell in them! *4041*
14: 7 Worship him who made the **h,** the earth, *4041*

HEAVENWARD (1) [HEAVEN]

Php 3:14 the prize for which God has called me **h** *539*

HEAVIER (6) [HEAVY]

1Ki 12:11 I *will* **make** it **even h.** 3578
12:14 I *will* **make** it **even h.** 3578
2Ch 10:11 I *will* **make** it **even h.** 3578
10:14 I *will* **make** it **even h.** 3578
Pr 27: 3 but provocation by a fool is **h** than both. 3878
Isa 28:22 or your chains *will become* **h;** 2616

HEAVILY (3) [HEAVY]

Ps 88: 7 Your wrath **lies h** upon me; 6164
Ecc 6: 1 and it **weighs h** on men: 8041
8: 6 though a man's misery **weighs h** upon him. 8041

HEAVY (48) [HEAVIER, HEAVILY]

Ex 18:18 The work is too **h** for you; 3878
Nu 11:14 the burden is too **h** for me. 3878
Dt 1: 9 **too h a burden** for me **to carry** 3523+4202+5951
25:13 in your bag—one **h,** 1524
32:15 filled with food, *he became* **h** and sleek. 6286
Jdg 20:34 *so* **h** that the Benjamites did not realize how 3877
1Sa 4:17 and the army has suffered **h** losses. 1524

1Sa 4:18 for he was an old man and **h.** 3878
5: 6 The LORD's hand *was* **h** upon the people 3877
5: 7 because his hand *is* **h** upon us and 7996
5:11 God's hand *was* very **h** *upon* it. 3877
6:19 The people mourned because of the **h** blow 1524
23: 5 He inflicted **h** losses on the Philistines 1524
2Sa 14:26 to time when it became too **h** for him— 3878
1Ki 12: 4 "Your father **put** *a* **h** yoke on us, 7996
12: 4 the harsh labor and the **h** yoke he put on us, 3878
12:10 'Your father **put** *a* **h** yoke on us, 3877
12:11 My father laid on you a **h** yoke; 3878
12:14 "My father **made** your yoke **h;** 3877
18:41 for there is the sound of a **h** rain." 2162
18:45 a **h** rain came on and Ahab rode off 1524
20:21 and inflicted **h** losses on the Arameans. 1524
2Ch 10: 4 "Your father **put** *a* **h** yoke on us, 7996
10: 4 the harsh labor and the **h** yoke he put on us, 3878
10:10 'Your father **put** *a* **h** yoke on us, 3877
10:11 My father laid on you a **h** yoke; 3878
10:14 "My father **made** your yoke **h;** 3877
13:17 and his men inflicted **h** losses on them, 8041
21:14 everything that is yours, with a **h** blow. 1524
28: 5 who inflicted **h** casualties on him. 1524
Ne 5:15 **placed a h burden** on the people 3877
5:18 the demands *were* **h** on these people. 3877
Job 23: 2 his hand *is* **h** in spite of my groaning. 3877
33: 7 nor *should* my hand *be* **h** upon you. 3877
39:11 Will you leave your **h work** to him? 3330
Ps 32: 4 day and night your hand *was* **h** upon me; 3877
38: 4 like a burden too **h** to bear. 3877+3878
144:14 our oxen *will* **draw h loads.** 6022
Pr 25:20 is one who sings songs to a **h** heart. 8273
27: 3 Stone is **h** and sand a burden, 3880
Ecc 1:13 What a **h** burden God has laid on men! 8273
Isa 24:20 *so* **h** upon it *is* the guilt of its rebellion 3877
47: 6 Even on the aged *you* **laid** a very **h** yoke. 3877
Eze 24:12 its **h** deposit has not been removed, 8041
27:25 You are filled with **h** *cargo* in the 3877+4394
Mt 23: 4 They tie up **h** loads and put them on men's *987*
26:43 sleeping, because their eyes were **h.** *976*
Mk 14:40 sleeping, because their eyes were **h.** *2852*

HEBER (10) [HEBER'S, HEBERITE]

Ge 46:17 The sons of Beriah: **H** and Malkiel. 2491
Nu 26:45 through **H,** the Heberite clan; 2491
Jdg 4:11 **H** the Kenite had left the other Kenites, 2491
4:17 the wife of **H** the Kenite, 2491
4:17 of Hazor and the clan of **H** the Kenite. 2491
5:24 the wife of **H** the Kenite, 2491
1Ch 4:18 **H** the father of Soco, 2491
7:31 The sons of Beriah: **H** and Malkiel, 2491
7:32 **H** was the father of Japhlet, 2491
8:17 Zebadiah, Meshullam, Hizki, **H,** 2491

HEBER'S (1) [HEBER]

Jdg 4:21 **H** wife, picked up a tent peg and a hammer 2491

HEBERITE (1) [HEBER]

Nu 26:45 through Heber, the **H** clan; 2499

HEBRAIC (1) [HEBREW]

Ac 6: 1 among them complained against the **H Jews** *1578*

HEBREW (25) [HEBRAIC, HEBREWS]

Ge 14:13 and reported this to Abram the **H.** 6303
39:14 "this **H** has been brought to us to make sport 6303
39:17 "That **H** slave you brought us came to me 6303
41:12 Now a young **H** was there with us, 6303
Ex 1:15 The king of Egypt said to the **H** midwives, 6303
1:16 the **H** *women* in childbirth and observe them 6303
1:19 **"H** *women* are not like Egyptian women; 6303
2: 6 "This is one of the **H** babies," she said. 6303
2: 7 of the **H** women to nurse the baby for you?" 6303
2:11 He saw an Egyptian beating a **H,** 6303
2:13 "Why are you hitting your fellow **H?"** NIH
21: 2 "If you buy a **H** servant, 6303
Dt 15:12 If a fellow **H,** a *man* or a woman, 6303
1Sa 4: 6 "What's all this shouting in the **H** camp?" 6303
2Ki 18:26 to us **in H** in the hearing of the people on 3376
18:28 the commander stood and called out **in H:** 3376
2Ch 32:18 Then they called out **in H** to the people 3376
Isa 36:11 to us **in H** in the hearing of the people on 3376
36:13 the commander stood and called out **in H,** 3376
Jer 34: 9 Everyone was to free his **H** slaves, 6303
34:14 must free any fellow **H** who has sold
himself to you. 6303
Jnh 1: 9 "I am a **H** and I worship the LORD, 6303
Php 3: 5 of the tribe of Benjamin, a **H** of Hebrews; *1578*
Rev 9:11 whose name **in H** is Abaddon, and in Greek, *1580*
16:16 to the place that **in H** is called Armageddon. *1580*

HEBREWS (18) [HEBREW]

Ge 40:15 from the land of the **H,** 6303
43:32 because Egyptians could not eat with **H,** 6303
Ex 2:13 and saw two **H** fighting. 6303
3:18 the God of the **H,** has met with us. 6303
5: 3 "The God of the **H** has met with us. 6303
7:16 say to him, 'The LORD, the God of the **H,** 6303
9: 1 'This is what the LORD, the God of the **H,** 6303
9:13 'This is what the LORD, the God of the **H,** 6303
10: 3 "This is what the LORD, the God of the **H,** 6303
1Sa 4: 9 Be men, or you will be subject to the **H,** 6303
13: 3 "Let the **H** hear!" 6303
1Sa 13: 7 *Some* **H** even crossed the Jordan to the land 6303
13:19 "Otherwise the **H** will make swords 6303
14:11 "The **H** are crawling out of the holes 6303
14:21 Those **H** who had previously been with 6303
29: 3 "What about these **H?"** 6303
2Co 11:22 Are they **H?** So am I. *1578*
Php 3: 5 of the tribe of Benjamin, a Hebrew of **H;** *1578*

HEBRON (74) [HEBRONITE, HEBRONITES, KIRIATH ARBA]

Ge 13:18 to live near the great trees of Mamre at **H,** 2496
23: 2 (that is, **H**) in the land of Canaan, 2496
23:19 of Machpelah near Mamre (which is at **H**) 2496
35:27 **H**), where Abraham and Isaac had stayed. 2496
37:14 Then he sent him off from the Valley of **H.** 2496
Ex 6:18 The sons of Kohath were Amram, Izhar, **H** 2497
Nu 3:19 Amram, Izhar, **H** and Uzziel. 2497
13:22 up through the Negev and came to **H,** 2496
13:22 (**H** had been built seven years before Zoan 2496
Jos 10: 3 of Jerusalem appealed to Hoham king of **H,** 2496
10: 5 the kings of Jerusalem, **H,** Jarmuth, 2496
10:23 the kings of Jerusalem, **H,** Jarmuth, 2496
10:36 up from Eglon to **H** and attacked it. 2496
10:39 to Libnah and its king and to **H.** 2496
11:21 from **H,** Debir and Anab, 2496
12:10 the king of Jerusalem one the king of **H** one 2496
14:13 and gave him **H** as his inheritance. 2496
14:14 So **H** has belonged to Caleb son 2496
14:15 **H** used to be called Kiriath Arba after Arba, 2496
15:13 Kiriath Arba, that is, **H.** 2496
15:14 From **H** Caleb drove out 9004S
15:54 **H**) and Zior—nine towns and their villages. 2496
20: 7 **H**) in the hill country of Judah. 2496
21:11 **H**), with its surrounding pastureland, 2496
21:13 the priest they gave **H** (a city of refuge 2496
Jdg 1:10 in **H** (formerly called Kiriath Arba) 2496
1:20 **H** was given to Caleb, 2496
16: 3 to the top of the hill that faces **H.** 2496
1Sa 30:31 and **H;** and to those in all the other places 2496
2Sa 2: 1 "To **H,**" the LORD answered. 2496
2: 3 and they settled in **H** and its towns. 2496
2: 4 to **H** and there they anointed David king NIH
2:11 of time David was king in **H** over the house 2496
2:32 and arrived at **H** by daybreak. 2496
3: 2 Sons were born to David in **H:** 2496
3: 5 These were born to David in **H.** 2496
3:19 to **H** to tell David everything that Israel and 2496
3:20 came to David at **H,** 2496
3:22 But Abner was no longer with David in **H,** 2496
3:27 Now when Abner returned to **H,** 2496
3:32 They buried Abner in **H,** 2496
4: 1 son of Saul heard that Abner had died in **H,** 2496
4: 8 of Ish-Bosheth to David at **H** and said to 2496
4:12 and hung the bodies by the pool in **H.** 2496
4:12 and buried it in Abner's tomb at **H.** 2496
5: 1 All the tribes of Israel came to David at **H** 2496
5: 3 of Israel had come to King David at **H,** 2496
5: 3 the king made a compact with them at **H** 2496
5: 5 In **H** he reigned over Judah seven years 2496
5:13 After he left **H,** David took more 2496
15: 7 to **H** and fulfill a vow I made to the LORD. 2496
15: 8 I will worship the LORD in **H.'** " 2496
15: 9 So he went to **H.** 2496
15:10 then say, 'Absalom is king in **H.'** " 2496
1Ki 2:11 in **H** and thirty-three in Jerusalem. 2496
1Ch 2:42 who was the father of **H.** 2497
2:43 The sons of **H:** 2497
3: 1 the sons of David born to him in **H:** 2496
3: 4 These six were born to David in **H,** 2496
6: 2 Amram, Izhar, **H** and Uzziel. 2497
6:18 Amram, Izhar, **H** and Uzziel. 2497
6:55 They were given **H** in Judah 2496
6:57 So the descendants of Aaron were given **H** 2496
11: 1 All Israel came together to David at **H** 2496
11: 3 of Israel had come to King David at **H,** 2496
11: 3 he made a compact with them at **H** before 2496
12:23 at **H** to turn Saul's kingdom over to him, as 2496
12:38 to **H** fully determined to make David king 2496
15: 9 from the descendants of **H,** Eliel the leader 2497
23:12 Amram, Izhar, **H** and Uzziel—four in all. 2497
23:19 The sons of **H:** 2497
24:23 The sons of **H:** 2497
29:27 seven in **H** and thirty-three in Jerusalem. 2496
2Ch 11:10 Zorah, Aijalon and **H.** These were fortified 2496

HEBRONITE (1) [HEBRON]

Nu 26:58 the Libnite clan, the **H** clan, 2498

HEBRONITES (5) [HEBRON]

Nu 3:27 Izharites, **H** and Uzzielites; 2498
1Ch 26:23 the Izharites, the **H** and the Uzzielites: 2498
26:30 From the **H:** Hashabiah 2498
26:31 As for the **H,** Jeriah was their chief 2498
26:31 among **the H** were found at Jazer in Gilead. 2157S

HEDGE (3) [HEDGED]

Job 1:10 not **put a h** around him and his household 8455
Isa 5: 5 I will take away its **h,** 5372
Mic 7: 4 the most upright worse than a **thorn h.** 5004

HEDGED (1) [HEDGE]

Job 3:23 whom God *has* **h in?** 6114

HEED (9) [HEEDED, HEEDS]

1Sa 15:22 and to **h** is better than the fat of rams. 7992
Ps 58: 5 that *will* not **h** the tune of the charmer, 9048
94: 7 the God of Jacob **pays** no **h."** 1067
94: 8 **Take h,** *you* senseless ones among 1067
107:43 *let him* **h** these things and consider 9068
Pr 1:24 when I called and no *one* **gave h** 7992
16:20 *Whoever* **gives h** to instruction prospers, 8505
Ecc 7: 5 to **h** a wise man's rebuke than to listen to 9048
Mic 6: 9 **"H** the rod and the One who appointed it. 9048

HEEDED (2) [HEED]

Ecc 9:16 and his words **are** no longer **h.** 9048
9:17 the wise *are* more *to* **be h** than the shouts of 9048

HEEDS (5) [HEED]

Pr 10:17 *He who* **h** discipline shows the way to life, 9068
13: 1 A wise son **h** his father's instruction, NIH
13:18 but *whoever* **h** correction is honored. 9068
15: 5 but *whoever* **h** correction shows prudence. 9068
15:32 *whoever* **h** correction gains understanding. 9048

HEEL (6) [HEELS]

Ge 3:15 crush your head, and you will strike his **h."** 6811
25:26 with his hand grasping Esau's **h;** 6811
Job 18: 9 A trap seizes him by the **h;** 6811
Ps 41: 9 has lifted up his **h** against me. 6811
Hos 12: 3 **grasped** his brother's **h;** 6810
Jn 13:18 'He who shares my bread has lifted up his **h** *4761*

HEELS (3) [HEEL]

Ge 49:17 that bites the horse's **h** so 6811
49:19 but he will attack them at their **h.** 6811
La 5: 5 Those who pursue us are **at** our **h;** 6584+7418

HEGAI (4)

Est 2: 3 Let them be placed under the care of **H,** 2043
2: 8 of Susa and put under the care of **H.** 2051
2: 8 to the king's palace and entrusted to **H,** 2051
2:15 she asked for nothing other than what **H,** 2051

HEIFER (15) [HEIFER'S]

Ge 15: 9 So the LORD said to him, "Bring me a **h,** 6320
Nu 19: 2 Tell the Israelites to bring you a red **h** 7239
19: 5 While he watches, the **h** is to be burned— 7239
19: 6 and throw them onto the burning **h.** 7239
19: 9 up the ashes of the **h** and put them in 7239
19:10 of the **h** must also wash his clothes, 7239
Dt 21: 3 town nearest the body shall take a **h** 1330+6320
21: 6 the **h** whose neck was broken in the valley, 6320
Jdg 14:18 "If you had not plowed with my **h,** 6320
1Sa 16: 2 "Take a **h** with you and say, 1330+6320
Jer 46:20 "Egypt is a beautiful **h,** 6320
50:11 a **h** threshing grain and neigh like stallions, 6320
Hos 4:16 Israelites are stubborn, like a stubborn **h.** 7239
10:11 Ephraim is a trained **h** that loves to thresh; 6320
Heb 9:13 and bulls and the ashes *of* a **h** sprinkled *1239*

HEIFER'S (1) [HEIFER]

Dt 21: 4 in the valley they are to break the **h** neck. 6320

HEIGHT (15) [HEIGHTS]

Nu 23: 3 Then he went off to a **barren h.** 9155
Jdg 6:26 to the LORD your God on the top of this **h.** 5057
1Sa 16: 7 not consider his appearance or his **h,** 1469+7757
1Ki 6:10 The **h** *of* each was five cubits, 7757
6:26 The **h** *of* each cherub was ten cubits. 7757
Ne 4: 6 the wall till all of it **reached** half its **h,** 6330+8003
Isa 22:16 *on* the **h** and chiseling your resting place in 5294
Eze 19:11 for its **h** and for its many branches. 1470
31:10 and because it was proud of its **h,** 1470
31:14 so well-watered are ever to reach *such* a **h;** 1470
43:13 And this is the **h** *of* the altar: 1470
Da 4:10 Its **h** was enormous. 10660
8: 8 **h** of his **power** his large horn was broken 6793
Ro 8:39 neither **h** nor depth, nor anything else *5739*
Rev 2: 5 the **h** from which you have fallen! *NIG*

HEIGHTS (40) [HEIGHT]

Nu 21:28 the citizens of Arnon's **h.** 1195
23: 9 from the **h** I view them. 1496
Dt 32:13 the **h** *of* the land and fed him with the fruit 1195
Jdg 5:18 so did Naphtali on the **h** *of* the field. 5294
2Sa 1:19 O Israel, lies slain on your **h.** 1195
1:25 Jonathan lies slain on your **h.** 1195
22:34 he enables me to stand on the **h.** 1195
2Ki 19:23 the **h** *of* the mountains, 5294
19:23 the **utmost h** *of* Lebanon. 3752
Job 22:12 "Is not God in the **h** *of* heaven? 1470
25: 2 he establishes order in the **h of heaven.** 5294
Ps 18:33 he enables me to stand on the **h.** 1195
42: 6 the **h of Hermon**—from Mount Mizar. 3056
48: 2 the **utmost h** *of* Zaphon is Mount Zion, 3752
78:69 He built his sanctuary like the **h,** 8123
148: 1 praise him in the **h above.** 5294
Pr 8: 2 On the **h** along the way, 5294+8031
Ecc 12: 5 when men are afraid of **h** and of dangers in 1469
Isa 7:11 depths or *in* the highest **h."** 2025+4200+5087
14:13 on the **utmost h** *of* the sacred mountain. 3752
31: 4 to do battle on Mount Zion and on its **h.** 1496
33:16 this is the man who will dwell **on** the **h,** 5294

Isa 37:24 the **h** *of* the mountains, 5294
37:24 the **utmost h** *of* Lebanon. 3752
37:24 I have reached its remotest **h,** 5294
41:18 I will make rivers flow on **barren h,** 9155
58:14 to ride on the **h** *of* the land and to feast on 1195
Jer 3: 2 "Look up to the **barren h** and see. 9155
3:21 A cry is heard on the **barren h,** 9155
4:11 "A scorching wind from the **barren h** in 9155
7:29 take up a lament on the **barren h,** 9155
12:12 Over all the **barren h** in the desert 9155
14: 6 on the **barren h** and pant like jackals; 9155
31:12 They will come and shout for joy on the **h** 5294
49:16 who occupy the **h** *of* the hill. 5294
Eze 17:23 On the mountain **h** *of* Israel I will plant it; 5294
34:14 and the mountain **h** *of* Israel will 5294
36: 2 The ancient **h** have become our possession. 1195
Ob 1: 3 of the rocks and make your home on the **h,** 5294
Hab 3:19 he enables me to go on the **h.** 1195

HEINOUS (KJV) See SHAMEFUL

HEIR (13) [INHERIT]
Ge 15: 3 so a servant in my household *will be* my **h."** 3769
15: 4 "This man *will* not *be* your **h,** 3769
15: 4 from your own body *will be* your **h."** 3769
2Sa 14: 7 then we will get rid of the **h** as well.' 3769
Ps 105:44 and *they* **fell h** to what others had toiled for 3769
Mt 21:38 they said to each other, 'This is the **h.** *3101*
Mk 12: 7 'This is the **h.** Come, let's kill him, *3101*
Lk 20:14 'This is the **h,'** they said. 'Let's kill him, *3101*
Ro 4:13 the promise that he would be **h** of the world, *3101*
Gal 4: 1 What I am saying is that as long as the **h** is *3101*
4: 7 you are a son, God has made you also an **h.** *3101*
Heb 1: 2 whom he appointed **h** of all things, *3101*
11: 7 and became **h** of the righteousness *3101*

HEIRS (12) [INHERIT]
Jdg 21:17 The Benjamite survivors must have **h,"** 3772
Jer 49: 1 "Has Israel no sons? Has she no **h?** 3769
Ac 3:25 And you are **h** of the prophets and of *5626*
Ro 4:14 For if those who live by law are **h,** *3101*
8:17 Now if we are children, then we are **h—** *3101*
8:17 **h** of God and co-heirs with Christ, *3101*
Gal 3:29 and **h** according to the promise. *3101*
Eph 3: 6 the Gentiles are **h together with** Israel, *5169*
Tit 3: 7 we might become **h** having the hope *3101*
Heb 6:17 of his purpose very clear *to* the **h** *3101*
11: 9 who *were* **h with** him of the same promise. *5169*
1Pe 3: 7 as **h with** you of the gracious gift of life, *5169*

HELAH (2)
1Ch 4: 5 of Tekoa had two wives, **H** and Naarah. 2690
4: 7 The sons of **H:** Zereth, Zohar, Ethnan, 2690

HELAM (2)
2Sa 10:16 they went to **H,** 2663
10:17 crossed the Jordan and went to **H.** 2663

HELBAH (1)
Jdg 1:31 or Ahlab or Aczib or **H** or Aphek or Rehob, 2695

HELBON (1)
Eze 27:18 in wine from **H** and wool from Zahar. 2696

HELD (83) [HOLD]
Ge 21: 8 on the day Isaac was weaned Abraham **h** 6913
27:41 Esau **h a grudge against** Jacob because of 8475
39:22 in charge of all those **h** in the prison, 659
40: 5 who **were** *being* **h** in prison— 673
41:36 This food should be **h in reserve** for 7214
Ex 17:11 As long as Moses **h up** his hands, 8123
17:12 Aaron and Hur **h** his hands **up—** 9461
21:19 *will* **not be h responsible** if the other gets 5927
21:28 of the bull will **not be h responsible.** 5929
Lev 5: 1 he *will be* **h responsible.** 5951+6411
5:17 he is guilty and *will be* **h responsible.** 5951+6411
7:18 of it *will be* **h responsible.** 5951+6411
17:16 he *will be* **h responsible.'** " 5951+6411
19: 8 Whoever eats it *will be* **h responsible** 5951+6411
20:17 and *will be* **h responsible.** 5951+6411
20:19 both of you *would be* **h responsible.** 5951+6411
20:20 They *will be* **h responsible;** 2628+5951
24:15 he *will be* **h responsible;** 2628+5951
26:13 and enabled you to walk **with heads h high.** 7758
Nu 28:16 the LORD's Passover is to be **h.** NIH
Dt 4: 4 but all of you who **h fast** to the LORD your 1816
Jos 8:18 So Joshua **h out** his javelin toward Ai. 5742
8:26 the hand that **h out** his javelin 5742
21:41 The towns of the Levites in the **territory** *h* AIT
Jdg 4: 5 She **h court** under the Palm of Deborah 3782
7:21 each man **h** his position around the camp, 6641
9:27 *they* **h** a festival in the temple of their god. 6913
16:26 Samson said to the servant who **h** his hand, 2616
1Sa 11:15 all the Israelites **h** a great **celebration.** 8523
2Sa 6:22 *I will* **be h in honor."** 3877
23:19 not **h in** greater **honor** than the Three? 3877
23:23 **was h in** greater **honor** than any of the 3877
1Ki 3:28 *they* **h** the king **in awe,** 3707
7:26 *It* **h** two thousand baths. 3920
8:47 in the land where *they* **are h captive,** 8647
11: 2 Solomon **h fast** to them in love. 1815
12:32 like the festival **h** in Judah, NIH

2Ki 18: 6 *He* **h fast** to the LORD and did not cease 1815
1Ch 11:25 **was h** in greater **honor** than any of the 3877
2Ch 4: 5 *It* **h** three thousand baths. 3920
6:37 in the land where *they* **are h captive,** 8647
7: 9 On the eighth day *they* **h** an assembly, 6913
Ne 4:17 with one hand and **h** a weapon in the other, 2616
Est 5: 2 and **h out** to her the gold scepter that was 3804
8:15 Susa **h a** joyous **celebration.** 7412
10: 3 **h in high esteem** by his many fellow Jews, 8354
Job 36: 8 **h fast** by cords of affliction, 4334
Ps 17: 5 My steps *have* **h** to your paths; 9461
106:46 to be pitied by all *who* **h** them **captive.** 8647
SS 3: 4 *I* **h** him and would not let him go 296
7: 5 the king **is h captive** by its tresses. 673
Isa 33:23 mast *is* not **h secure,** the sail is not spread. 2616
40:12 *Who has* **h** the dust of the earth in a basket, 3920
42:14 I have been quiet and **h myself back.** 706
65: 2 All day long *I have* **h out** my hands to 7298
Jer 2: 3 all who devoured her *were* **h guilty,** 870
Eze 31:15 *I* **h back** its streams, 4979
Mt 21:46 because the people **h** that he was a prophet. *2400*
Mk 11:32 everyone **h** that John really was a prophet.) *2400*
Lk 5:29 Then Levi **h** a great banquet for Jesus *4472*
11:50 *be* **h responsible for** the blood of all *1699*
11:51 this generation *will be* **h responsible** *1699*
Ac 3:11 *While* the beggar **h on to** Peter and John, *3195*
7:41 to it and **h a celebration** in honor *2370*
19:17 the name of the Lord Jesus *was* **h in high honor.** *3486*
25: 4 "Paul *is being* **h** at Caesarea, *5498*
25:21 When Paul made his appeal *to be* **h over** *5498*
25:21 I ordered him **h** until I could send him *5498*
27:32 the soldiers cut the ropes that **h** the lifeboat *NIG*
27:40 and at the same time untied the ropes that **h** *NIG*
Ro 3:19 whole world **h accountable** to God. *1181+5688*
10:21 "All day long *I have* **h out** my hands to *1736*
Gal 3:23 *we were* **h prisoners** by the law, *5864*
Eph 4:16 joined and **h together** by every supporting *5204*
Col 1:23 from the hope **h** out in the gospel. *NIG*
2:19 and **h together** by its ligaments and sinews, *5204*
2Ti 4:16 *May it* not *be* **h** against them. *3357*
Heb 2:15 and free those who all their lives were **h** *1944*
2Pe 2: 4 putting them into gloomy dungeons *to be* **h** *5498*
Rev 1:16 In his right hand *he* **h** seven stars, *2400*
6: 2 Its rider **h** a bow, and he was given a crown, *2400*
15: 2 *They* **h** harps given them by God *2400*
17: 4 *She* **h** a golden cup in her hand, *2400*

HELDAI (3)
1Ch 27:15 was **H** the Netophathite, 2702
Zec 6:10 "Take [silver and gold] from the exiles **H,** 2702
6:14 The crown will be given to **H,** Tobijah, 2702

HELECH (1)
Eze 27:11 Men of Arvad and **H** manned your walls 2662

HELED (2)
2Sa 23:29 **H** son of Baanah the Netophathite, 2699
1Ch 11:30 **H** son of Baanah the Netophathite, 2699

HELEK (2) [HELEKITE]
Nu 26:30 through **H,** the Helekite clan; 2751
Jos 17: 2 the clans of Abiezer, **H,** Asriel, Shechem, 2751

HELEKITE (1) [HELEK]
Nu 26:30 through Helek, the **H** clan; 2757

HELEM (1)
1Ch 7:35 The sons of his brother **H:** 2152

HELEPH (1)
Jos 19:33 from **H** and the large tree in Zaanannim, 2738

HELEZ (5)
2Sa 23:26 **H** the Paltite, Ira son of Ikkesh from Tekoa, 2742
1Ch 2:39 Azariah the father of **H,** 2742
2:39 **H** the father of Eleasah, 2742
11:27 Shammoth the Harorite, **H** the Pelonite, 2742
27:10 for the seventh month, was **H** the Pelonite, 2742

HELI (1)
Lk 3:23 so it was thought, of Joseph, the son *of* **H,** *2459*

HELIOPOLIS (1)
Eze 30:17 The young men of **H** and Bubastis will fall 225

HELKAI (1)
Ne 12:15 of Harim's, Adna; of Meremoth's, **H;** 2758

HELKATH (2) [HELKATH HAZZURIM]
Jos 19:25 Their territory included: **H,** Hali, Beten, 2762
21:31 **H** and Rehob, together 2762

HELKATH HAZZURIM (1) [HELKATH]
2Sa 2:16 in Gibeon was called **H.** 2763

HELL (14)
Mt 5:22 will be in danger of the fire of **h.** *1147*
5:29 for your whole body to be thrown into **h.** *1147*
5:30 for your whole body to go into **h.** *1147*
10:28 both soul and body in **h.** *1147*
18: 9 and be thrown into the fire *of* **h.** *1147*
23:15 you make him twice as much a son *of* **h** *1147*
23:33 will you escape being condemned to **h?** *1147*
Mk 9:43 with two hands to go into **h,** *1147*
9:45 to have two feet and be thrown into **h.** *1147*
9:47 to have two eyes and be thrown into **h,** *1147*
Lk 12: 5 has power to throw you into **h.** *1147*
16:23 In **h,** where he was in torment, *87*
Jas 3: 6 and is itself set on fire by **h.** *1147*
2Pe 2: 4 when they sinned, but **sent** them **to h,** *5434*

HELM (KJV) See RUDDER

HELMET (7) [HELMETS]
1Sa 17: 5 He had a bronze **h** on his head and wore 3916
17:38 of armor on him and a bronze **h** on his head. 7746
Ps 60: 7 Ephraim is my **h,** Judah my scepter. 5057+8031
108: 8 Ephraim is my **h,** Judah my scepter. 5057+8031
Isa 59:17 and the **h** *of* salvation on his head; 3916
Eph 6:17 Take the **h** of salvation and the sword of *4330*
1Th 5: 8 and the hope of salvation as a **h.** *4330*

HELMETS (5) [HELMET]
2Ch 26:14 Uzziah provided shields, spears, **h,** 3916
Jer 46: 4 Take your positions with **h** on! 3916
Eze 23:24 with large and small shields and with **h.** 7746
27:10 They hung their shields and **h** 3916
38: 5 all with shields and **h,** 3916

HELON (5)
Nu 1: 9 from Zebulun, Eliab son of **H;** 2735
2: 7 of the people of Zebulun is Eliab son of **H.** 2735
7:24 On the third day, Eliab son of **H,** 2735
7:29 This was the offering of Eliab son of **H.** 2735
10:16 and Eliab son of **H** was over the division of 2735

HELP (219) [HELPED, HELPER, HELPERS, HELPFUL, HELPING, HELPLESS, HELPS]
Ge 4: 1 **"With the h of** the LORD I have brought 907
39:15 When he heard me **scream for h,** he left his cloak 2256+7754+7924+8123
39:18 soon as I **screamed for h,** 2256+7754+7924+8123
Ex 1:16 **h** the Hebrew women **in childbirth** 3528
2:23 and their **cry for h** because of their slavery 8784
4:12 I *will* **h** you speak and will teach you 2118+6640
4:15 I *will* **h** both of you speak 2118+6640
23: 1 *Do* not **h** a wicked man by being 3338+6640+8883
23: 5 **be sure** *you* **h** him with it. 6441+6441
31: 6 of the tribe of Dan, to **h** him. 907
Lev 25:35 **h** him as you would an alien or 2616
Nu 1: 4 each the head of his family, *is to* **h** you. 907+2118
11:17 They will **h** you carry the burden of 907
34:18 from each tribe to **h assign** the land. 5706
Dt 22: 4 **H** him get it to its feet. 6640
22:24 in a town and *did* not **scream for h,** 7590
32:38 Let them rise up *to* **h** you! 6468
33: 7 Oh, be his **h** against his foes!" 6469
33:26 on the heavens to **h** you and on the clouds 6469
Jos 1:14 *You are to* **h** your brothers 6468
10: 4 "Come up and **h** me attack Gibeon," 6468
10: 6 **H** us, because all the Amorite kings from 6468
10:33 up to **h** Lachish, but Joshua defeated him 6468
24: 7 But *they* **cried** to the LORD **for h,** 7590
Jdg 4: 3 *they* **cried** to the LORD **for h.** 7590
5:23 because they did not come to **h** the LORD, 6476
5:23 to **h** the LORD against the mighty.' 6476
6: 6 *they* **cried out** to the LORD **for h.** 2410
10:12 *you* **cried** to me **for h,** 7590
12: 3 When I saw that you wouldn't **h,** 3828
1Sa 12: 8 *they* **cried** to the LORD **for h,** 2410
14:45 for he did this today **with God's h."** 6640
2Sa 3:12 will **h** you bring all Israel over to you. 3338+6640
8: 5 of Damascus came to **h** Hadadezer king 6468
10:19 So the Arameans were afraid to **h** . 3828
14: 4 and she said, **"H** me, O king!" 3828
15:34 then you can **h** me by frustrating 4200
22:30 **With** your **h** I can advance against a troop; 928
22:42 *They* **cried for h,** but there was no one 8775
2Ki 4: 2 Elisha replied to her, "How *can I* **h** you? 4200+6913
6:26 a woman cried to him, **"H** me, 3828
6:27 "If the LORD *does* not **h** you, 3828
6:27 where *can I* **get h for** you? 3828
14:26 there was no *one to* **h** them. 6468
23:29 went up to the Euphrates River to **h** the king 6584
1Ch 12:17 "If you have come to me in peace, to **h** me, 6468
12:18 and success to *those who* **h** you, 6468
12:18 for your God *will* **h** you." 6468
12:19 *(He and his men did* not **h** the Philistines 6468
12:22 Day after day men came to **h** David, 6468
12:33 to **h** David with undivided loyalty— 6370
18: 5 of Damascus came to **h** Hadadezer king 6468
19:19 not willing to **h** the Ammonites anymore. 3828
22:17 the leaders of Israel to **h** his son Solomon. 6468
23:28 was to **h** Aaron's descendants in the 3338+4200
24: 3 **With the h of** Zadok a descendant of 2256
28:21 in any craft will **h** you in all the work. 6640
2Ch 14:11 there is no one like you to **h** the powerless 6468
14:11 **H** us, O LORD our God, for we rely on you, 6468
16:12 even in his illness *he did* not **seek h** *from* 2011

2Ch 19: 2 *"Should you* **h** the wicked 6468
20: 4 people of Judah came together to **seek h** 1335
25: 8 God has the power to **h** or to overthrow." 6468
28:16 Ahaz sent to the king of Assyria **for h.** 6468
28:20 but he gave him trouble instead of **h.** 2616
28:21 but that did not **h** him. 6476
28:23 I will sacrifice to them so *they will* **h** me." 6468
32: 8 with us is the LORD our God to **h** us and 6468
Ezr 4: 2 "Let us **h** you build because, like you, 6640
Ne 3:12 the next section **with the h of** his daughters. 2256
6:16 this work had been done **with the h of** 907+4946
Est 7: 9 who spoke up to **h** the king." 3202
Job 6:13 Do I have any power to **h** myself, 6476
6:21 Now you too have proved to be of no **h;** NIH
19: 7 though *I* **call for h,** there is no justice. 8775
24:12 and the souls of the wounded **cry out for h.** 8775
29:12 because I rescued the poor *who* **cried for h,** 8775
30:24 a hand on a broken man when *he* **cries for h** 8780
30:28 I stand up in the assembly and **cry for h.** 8775
36:13 when he fetters them, *they do* not **cry for h.** 8775
Ps 5: 2 Listen to my **cry for h,** 7754+8776
12: 1 **H,** LORD, for the godly are no more; 3828
18: 6 *I* **cried** to my God **for h.** 8775
18:29 **With** your **h** I can advance against a troop; 928
18:41 *They* **cried for h,** but there was no one 8775
20: 2 May he send you **h** from the sanctuary 6469
22:11 for trouble is near and there is no *one to* **h.** 6468
22:19 O my Strength, come quickly to **h** me. 6476
22:24 from him but has listened to his **cry for h.** 8775
28: 2 **I call** to you **for h,** 8775
30: 2 *I* **called** to you **for h** 8775
30:10 O LORD, be my **h."** 6468
31:22 **I called** to you **for h.** 8775
33:20 he is our **h** and our shield. 6469
38:22 Come quickly to **h** me, O Lord my Savior. 6476
39:12 O LORD, listen to my **cry for h;** 8784
40:13 O LORD, come quickly to **h** me. 6476
40:17 You are my **h** and my deliverer; 6476
44:26 Rise up and **h** us; 6476
46: 1 an ever-present **h** in trouble. 6476
46: 5 God *will* **h** her at break of day. 6468
54: 4 Surely God *is* my **h;** 6468
56: 9 when *I* **call for h.** 7924
59: 4 Arise to **h** me; look on my plight! 7925
60: 5 Save us and **h** us with your right hand, 6699
60:11 for the **h** *of* man is worthless. 9591
63: 7 Because you are my **h,** 6476
69: 3 I am worn out **calling for h;** 7924
70: 1 O LORD, come quickly to **h** me. 6476
70: 5 You are my **h** and my deliverer; 6469
71:12 come quickly, O my God, to **h** me. 6476
72:12 the afflicted who have no *one to* **h.** 6468
77: 1 *I* **cried out** to God **for h;** 7590+7754
79: 9 **H** us, O God our Savior, 6468
88:13 But I **cry** to you **for h,** O LORD; 8775
94:17 Unless the LORD had given me **h,** 6476
102: 1 let my **cry for h** come to you. 8784
107:12 they stumbled, and there was no *one to* **h.** 6468
108: 6 Save us and **h** us with your right hand, 6699
108:12 for the **h** *of* man is worthless. 9591
109:26 **H** me, O LORD my God; 6468
115: 9 he is their **h** and shield. 6469
115:10 he is their **h** and shield. 6469
115:11 he is their **h** and shield. 6469
119:86 **h** me, for men persecute me without cause. 6468
119:147 I rise before dawn and **cry for h;** 8775
119:173 May your hand be ready to **h** me, 6468
121: 1 where does my **h** come from? 6469
121: 2 My **h** comes from the LORD, 6469
124: 8 Our **h** is in the name of the LORD, 6469
146: 5 Blessed is he whose **h** is the God of Jacob, 6469
Ecc 4:10 his friend *can* **h** him **up.** 7756
4:10 and has no one to **h** him **up!** 7756
Isa 10: 3 To whom will you run for **h?** 6476
20: 6 those we fled to for **h** and deliverance from 6476
30: 2 *who* **look for h** to Pharaoh's protection, 6395
30: 5 who bring neither **h** nor advantage, 6469
30: 7 *whose* **h** is utterly useless. 6468
30:19 How gracious he will be when you **cry for h!** 2410+7754
31: 1 Woe to those who go down to Egypt for **h,** 6476
31: 1 or **seek h** *from* the LORD. 2011
31: 2 against *those who* **h** evildoers. 6476
41:10 I will strengthen you and **h** you; 6468
41:13 Do not fear; I *will* **h** you. 6468
41:14 O little Israel, for *I* myself *will* **h** you," 6468
44: 2 and *who will* **h** you: 6468
49: 8 and in the day of salvation *I will* **h** you; 6468
57:13 When you **cry out for h,** 2410
58: 9 *you will* **cry for h,** and he will say: 8775
63: 5 I looked, but there was no *one to* **h,** 6468
64: 5 **come to the h of** those who gladly do right, 7003
Jer 11:12 not **h** them **at all** when disaster strikes. 3828+3828
47: 3 Fathers *will* not **turn to h** their children; 7155
47: 4 to cut off all survivors *who could* **h** Tyre 6468
50:32 and fall and no *one will* **h** her **up;** 7756
La 1: 7 there was no *one to* **h** her. 6468
3: 8 Even when I call out or **cry for h,** 8775
3:11 and mangled me and left me **without h.** 9037
4: 6 in a moment without a hand turned to **h** her. NIH
4:17 our eyes failed, looking in vain for **h;** 6476
Eze 16:49 *they did* not **h** the poor and needy. 2616+3338
17:17 and great horde *will be of* no **h** *to* him 6913
29:16 of their sin in turning to her for **h.** NIH
Da 6:11 and **asking** God **for h.** 10274
10:13 one of the chief princes, came to **h** me, 6468
11:17 his plans will not succeed or **h** him. 2118+4200
Da 11:34 *they will* **receive** a little **h,** 6468+6469
11:39 the mightiest fortresses **with the h of** 6640
11:45 and no *one will* **h** him. 6468
Hos 5:13 **sent** to the great king **for h.** 8938
Jnh 2: 2 the depths of the grave *I* **called for h,** 8775
Hab 1: 2 How long, O LORD, *must I* **call for h,** 8775
Zec 6:15 and *h to* **build** the temple of the LORD, AIT
Mt 8: 5 a centurion came to him, **asking for h.** *4151*
15: 5 **h** you might otherwise have received from *1565*
15:25 "Lord, **h** me!" she said. *1070*
25:44 sick or in prison, and *did* not **h** you?' *1354*
Mk 7:11 **h** *you might* otherwise *have* **received** *6067*
9:22 take pity on us and **h** us." *1070*
9:24 **h** me overcome my unbelief!" *1070*
14: 7 you can **h** them any time you want. *2292+4472*
Lk 4:38 and they asked Jesus **to h** her. *4309*
5: 7 in the other boat *to* come and **h** them, *5197*
7:16 "God *has* **come to h** his people." *2170*
10:40 Tell her *to* **h** me!" *5269*
11:46 not lift one finger *to* **h** them. *5845*
Jn 5: 7 "I have no one *to* **h** me into the pool when *965*
12: 6 of the money bag, *he used to* **h himself to** *1002*
Ac 2:23 and you, with the **h** of wicked men, *5931*
4:20 For we cannot **h speaking about** *3281+3590*
11:29 to provide **h** for the brothers living in Judea. *1355*
16: 9 "Come over to Macedonia and **h** us." *1070*
18:27 he *was* **a great h** to those who *5202*
20:35 that by this kind of hard work we must **h** *514*
21:28 "Men of Israel, **h** us! *1070*
26:22 But I have had God's **h** to this very day, *2135*
Ro 16: 2 to give her any **h** she may need from you, *NIG*
16: 2 for she has been a great **h** to many people, *4706*
1Co 12:28 **those able to h** others, *516*
16: 6 **h** me **on** my **journey,** *4636*
2Co 1:11 *as* you **h** us by your prayers. *5348*
8:19 and to show our eagerness **to h.** *NIG*
9: 2 For I know your eagerness **to h,** *5642*
Php 1:19 that through your prayers and the **h given** *2221*
2:30 to make up for the **h** you could not give me. *3311*
4: 3 **h** these women who have contended *5197*
1Th 2: 2 but **with the h of** our God we dared *1877*
5:14 **h** the weak, be patient with everyone. *504*
2Th 3: 9 because we do not have the right to such **h,** *NIG*
1Ti 5: 5 **pray** and to ask God **for h.** *1255*
5:16 *she should* **h** them and not let the church *2064*
5:16 church *can* **h** those widows who are really *2064*
2Ti 1:14 the **h** of the Holy Spirit who lives in us. *NIG*
Tit 3:13 *to* **h** Zenas the lawyer and Apollos **on** *their* **way** *4636*
Heb 2:18 *to* **h** those who are being tempted. *1070*
4:16 and find grace to **h** us in our time of need. *1069*
6:10 and *continue to* **h** them. *1354*
1Pe 5:12 **With the h of** Silas, *1328*
3Jn 1: 7 receiving no **h** from the pagans. *NIG*

HELPED (31) [HELP]

Jdg 9:24 *had* **h** him murder his brothers. 906+2616+3338
1Sa 7:12 saying, "Thus far *has* the LORD **h** us." 6468
23:16 to David at Horesh and **h** him **find strength** 906+2616+3338
2Ki 10:15 he did, and Jehu **h** him **up** into the chariot. 6590
1Ch 5:20 *They* **were h** *in* fighting them, 6468
12: 1 among the warriors *who* **h** him *in* battle; 6468
12:21 They **h** David against raiding bands, 6468
15:26 Because God *had* **h** the Levites 6468
2Ch 18:31 cried out, and the LORD **h** him. 6468
20:23 *they* **h** to destroy one another. 6468
26: 7 God **h** him against the Philistines and 6468
26:15 he **was** greatly **h** until he became powerful. 6468
28:23 the gods of the kings of Aram *have* **h** them, 6468
29:34 so their kinsmen the Levites **h** them until 2616
32: 3 and *they* **h** him. 6468
Est 9: 3 and the king's administrators **h** the Jews, 5951
Job 26: 2 "How *you have* **h** the powerless! 6468
26: 4 Who has **h** you utter these words? 907
Ps 28: 7 my heart trusts in him, and *I* **am h.** 6468
86:17 O LORD, *have* **h** me and comforted me. 6468
118:13 about to fall, but the LORD **h** me. 6468
Isa 31: 3 *he who* **is h** will fall; 6468
Jer 2:37 *you will* not *be* **h** by them. 7503
Mk 1:31 he went to her, took her hand and **h** her **up.** *1586*
Lk 1:54 *He has* **h** his servant Israel, *514*
Ac 3: 7 Taking him by the right hand, *he* **h** him **up,** *1586*
9:41 by the hand and **h** her **to her feet.** *482*
2Co 6: 2 and in the day of salvation *I* **h** you." *1070*
2Ti 1:18 in how many ways *he* **h** me in Ephesus. *1354*
Heb 6:10 *as you have* **h** his people and continue *1354*
Rev 12:16 the earth **h** the woman by opening its mouth *1070*

HELPER (11) [HELP]

Ge 2:18 I will make a **h** suitable for him." 6469
2:20 But for Adam no suitable **h** was found. 6469
Ex 18: 4 for he said, "My father's God was my **h;** 6469
Dt 33:29 and **h** and your glorious sword. 6469
Ne 4:22 and his **h** stay inside Jerusalem at night, 5853
Ps 10:14 you are the **h** of the fatherless. 6468
27: 9 you have been my **h.** 6476
118: 7 The LORD is with me; *he is* my **h.** 6468
Hos 13: 9 because you are against me, against your **h.** 6469
Ac 13: 5 John was with them as their **h.** *5677*
Heb 13: 6 "The Lord is my **h;** I will not be afraid. *1071*

HELPERS (2) [HELP]

Eze 30: 8 I set fire to Egypt and all her **h** are crushed. 6468
Ac 19:22 He sent two *of* his **h,** Timothy and Erastus, *1354*

HELPFUL (3) [HELP]

Ac 20:20 to preach anything that *would be* **h** to you *5237*
Eph 4:29 but only what is **h** for building others up *19*
2Ti 4:11 because he is **h** to me in my ministry. *2378*

HELPING (8) [HELP]

Jos 14:12 but, the LORD **h** me, I will drive them out 907
Jdg 21:22 'Do us a kindness by **h** them, NIH
Ezr 5: 2 prophets of God were with them, **h** them. 10514
Job 30:13 without *anyone's* **h** them. 6468
Lk 8: 3 These women *were* **h to support** them out *1354*
Ac 9:36 who was always doing good and **h the poor.** *1797+4472*
1Ti 5:10 **h** those in trouble and devoting herself *2064*
Phm 1:13 in **h** me while I am in chains for the gospel. *1354*

HELPLESS (9) [HELP]

Ps 10: 9 he lies in wait to catch the **h;** 6714
10: 9 he catches the **h** and drags them off 6714
10:12 Do not forget the **h.** 6705
69:20 and *has left me* **h;** 5683
Pr 28:15 a wicked man ruling over a **h** people. 1924
Jer 48:45 the fugitives stand **h,** for a fire has 3946+4946
Da 10: 8 my face turned deathly pale and *I was* **h.** 3946+4202+6806
10:16 my lord, and *I am* **h.** 3946+4202+6806
Mt 9:36 because they were harassed and **h,** *4849*

HELPS (8) [HELP]

Ge 49:25 *who* **h** you, because of the Almighty, 6468
Ps 37:40 The LORD **h** them and delivers them; 6468
Isa 31: 3 *he who* **h** will stumble, 6468
41: 6 each **h** the other and says to his brother, 6468
50: 7 Because the Sovereign LORD **h** me, 6468
50: 9 It is the Sovereign LORD *who* **h** me. 6468
Ro 8:26 the Spirit **h** us in our weakness. *5269*
Heb 2:16 For surely it is not angels *he* **h,** *2138*

HEM (10) [HEMMED]

Ex 28:33 and scarlet yarn around the **h** *of* the robe, 8767
28:34 to alternate around the **h** *of* the robe. 8767
39:24 and finely twisted linen around the **h** *of* 8767
39:25 of pure gold and attached them around the **h** 8767
39:26 the **h** *of* the robe to be worn for ministering, 8767
1Sa 15:27 Saul caught hold of the **h** *of* his robe, 4053
Ps 139: 5 *You* **h** me **in**—behind and before; 7443
Hab 1: 4 The wicked **h in** the righteous, 4193
Zec 8:23 of one Jew by the **h** of his **robe** and say, 4053
Lk 19:43 and encircle you and **h** you **in** on every side. *5309*

HEMAN (16) [HEMAN'S]

1Ki 4:31 wiser than **H,** Calcol and Darda, 2124
1Ch 2: 6 Zimri, Ethan, **H,** Calcol and Darda— 2124
6:33 **H,** the musician, the son of Joel, 2124
15:17 So the Levites appointed **H** son of Joel; 2124
15:19 The musicians **H,** Asaph and Ethan were 2124
16:41 With them were **H** and Jeduthun and the 2124
16:42 **H** and Jeduthun were responsible for 2124
25: 1 **H** and Jeduthun for the ministry 2124
25: 4 As for **H,** from his sons: 2124
25: 5 All these were sons of **H** the king's seer. 2124
25: 5 God gave **H** fourteen sons 2124
25: 6 Jeduthun and **H** were under the supervision 2124
2Ch 5:12 **H,** Jeduthun and their sons and relatives— 2124
29:14 the descendants of **H,** Jehiel and Shimei; 2124
35:15 Asaph, **H** and Jeduthun the king's seer. 2124
Ps 88: T A maskil of **H** the Ezrahite. 2124

HEMAN'S (1) [HEMAN]

1Ch 6:39 and **H** associate Asaph, who served 2257[S]

HEMATH (KJV) See HAMATH, HAMMATH

HEMDAN (2)

Ge 36:26 **H,** Eshban, Ithran and Keran. 2777
1Ch 1:41 **H,** Eshban, Ithran and Keran. 2777

HEMLOCK (KJV) See POISON, POISONOUS

HEMMED (1) [HEM]

Ex 14: 3 **h in** *by* the desert.' 6037

HEN (3)

Zec 6:14 and **H** son of Zephaniah as a memorial in 2835
Mt 23:37 as a **h** gathers her chicks under her wings, *3998*
Lk 13:34 as a **h** gathers her chicks under her wings, *3998*

HENA (3)

2Ki 18:34 are the gods of Sepharvaim, **H** and Ivvah? 2184
19:13 Sepharvaim, or of **H** or Ivvah?" 2184
Isa 37:13 Sepharvaim, or of **H** or Ivvah?" 2184

HENADAD (4)

Ezr 3: 9 the sons of **H** and their sons and brothers— 2836
Ne 3:18 by their countrymen under Binnui son of **H,** 2836
3:24 Binnui son of **H** repaired another section, 2836
10: 9 Binnui of the sons of **H,** Kadmiel, 2836

HENCE (KJV) See AWAY, FROM HERE, LEAVE, PLACE, SOMEWHERE ELSE

HENNA (2)

SS 1:14 a cluster of **h blossoms** from the vineyards 4110
4:13 with choice fruits, with **h** and nard, 4110

HENOCH (KJV) See ENOCH

HEPHER (9) [GATH HEPHER, HEPHERITE]

Nu 26:32 through **H,** the Hepherite clan. 2918
26:33 (Zelophehad son of **H** had no sons; 2918
27:1 The daughters of Zelophehad son of **H,** 2918
Jos 12:17 the king of Tappuah one the king of **H** one 2919
17:2 Helek, Asriel, Shechem, **H** and Shemida. 2918
17:3 Now Zelophehad son of **H,** 2918
1Ki 4:10 and all the land of **H** were his); 2919
1Ch 4:6 Naarah bore him Ahuzzam, **H,** 2918
11:36 **H** the Mekerathite, Ahijah the Pelonite, 2918

HEPHERITE (1) [HEPHER]

Nu 26:32 through Hepher, the **H** clan. 2920

HEPHZIBAH (2)

2Ki 21:1 His mother's name was **H.** 2915
Isa 62:4 But you will be called **H,** 2915

HER (1669) [SHE] See Index of Articles Etc.

HERALD (4)

Da 3:4 Then the **h** loudly proclaimed, 10370
Hab 2:2 on tablets so that a **h** may run with it. 7924
1Ti 2:7 And for this purpose I was appointed a **h** *3061*
2Ti 1:11 And of this gospel I was appointed a **h** and *3061*

HERBS (6)

Ex 12:8 along with **bitter h,** and bread made 5353
Nu 9:11 with unleavened bread and **bitter h.** 5353
2Ki 4:39 the fields to gather **h** and found a wild vine. 246
Job 30:4 In the brush they gathered **salt h,** 4865
La 3:15 He has filled me with **bitter h** and sated me 5353
Lk 11:42 rue and all other kinds of **garden h,** *3303*

HERD (21) [HERDED, HERDING, HERDS, HERDSMEN]

Ge 18:7 Then he ran to the **h** and selected a choice, 1330
32:16 care of his servants, **each h** by itself, 6373+6373
Ex 34:19 whether from **h** or flock. 8802
Lev 1:2 as your offering an animal from either the **h** 1330
1:3 the offering is a burnt offering from the **h,** 1330
3:1 and he offers an animal from the **h,** 1330
22:21 from the **h** or flock a fellowship offering to 1330
27:32 The entire tithe of the **h** and flock— 1330
Nu 15:3 from the **h** or the flock, 1330
Dt 16:2 an animal from your flock or **h** at the place 1330
32:14 with curds and milk from **h** and flock and 1330
Jdg 6:25 "Take the second bull from your father's **h,** 8802
Ps 68:30 **h** *of* bulls among the calves of the nations. 6337
Jnh 3:7 Do not let any man or beast, **h** or flock, 1330
Mt 8:30 from them a large **h** of pigs was feeding *36*
8:31 send us into the **h** of pigs." *36*
8:32 and the whole **h** rushed down the steep bank *36*
Mk 5:11 A large **h** of pigs was feeding on *36*
5:13 The **h,** about two thousand in number, *36*
Lk 8:32 A large **h** of pigs was feeding there on *36*
8:33 and the **h** rushed down the steep bank into *36*

HERDED (1) [HERD]

Isa 24:22 *They will* **be h together** like 665+669

HERDING (1) [HERD]

1Sa 25:16 around us all the time we were **h** our sheep 8286

HERDS (53) [HERD]

Ge 13:5 also had flocks and **h** and tents. 1330
26:14 He had so many flocks and **h** and 1330+5238
32:7 and the flocks and **h** and camels as well. 1330
32:16 and keep some space between the **h."** 6373
32:19 and all the others who followed the **h:** 6373
34:28 They seized their flocks and **h** and donkeys 1330
45:10 your flocks and **h,** and all you have. 1330
46:32 and **h** and everything they own.' 1330
47:1 and **h** and everything they own, 1330
50:8 and their flocks and **h** were left in Goshen. 1330
Ex 10:9 and with our flocks and **h,** 1330
10:24 only leave your flocks and **h** behind." 1330
12:32 Take your flocks and **h,** as you have said, 1330
12:38 both flocks and **h.** 1330
34:3 not even the flocks and **h** may graze in front 1330
Nu 11:22 if flocks and **h** were slaughtered for them? 1330
31:9 and children and took all the Midianite **h,** 989
32:1 who had very large **h and flocks,** 5238
32:26 our flocks and **h** will remain here in 989
Dt 7:13 of your **h** and the lambs of your flocks in 546
8:13 and when your **h** and flocks grow large 1330
12:6 and the firstborn of your **h** and flocks. 1330
12:17 or the firstborn of your **h** and flocks, 1330
12:21 the **h** and flocks the LORD has given you, 1330
14:23 and the firstborn of your **h** and flocks in 1330
15:19 of your **h** and flocks. 1330
28:4 of your **h** and the lambs of your flocks. 546
28:18 of your **h** and the lambs of your flocks. 546
28:51 nor any calves of your **h** or lambs 546
Jos 14:4 with pasturelands for their flocks and **h.** 7871
22:8 with large **h of livestock,** with silver, 5238
1Sa 30:20 He took all the flocks and **h,** 1330
2Ki 5:26 flocks, **h,** or menservants and maidservants? 1330
1Ch 27:29 the Sharonite was in charge of the **h** grazing 1330
27:29 Shaphat son of Adlai was in charge of the **h** 1330
2Ch 31:6 also brought a tithe of their **h** and flocks and 1330
32:29 and acquired great numbers of flocks and **h,** 1330
Ne 10:36 of our **h** and of our flocks to the house 1330
Job 1:10 that his **flocks and h** are spread throughout 5238
Ps 8:7 all flocks and **h,** and the beasts of the field, 546
107:38 and he did not let their **h** diminish. 989
Pr 27:23 give careful attention to your **h;** 6373
Ecc 2:7 I also owned more **h** and flocks than anyone 1330
Isa 60:6 **H** *of* camels will cover your land, 9180
65:10 the Valley of Achor a resting place for **h,** 1330
Jer 3:24 their flocks and **h,** their sons and daughters. 1330
5:17 they will devour your flocks and **h,** 1330
31:12 the young of the flocks and **h.** 1330
49:32 and their large **h** will be booty. 5238
Hos 5:6 with their flocks and **h** to seek the LORD, 1330
Joel 1:18 **h** mill about because they have no pasture; 1330+6373
Zep 2:14 **Flocks and h** will lie down there, 6373
Jn 4:12 as did also his sons and his **flocks and h?"** *2576*

HERDSMEN (6) [HERD]

Ge 13:7 quarreling arose between Abram's **h** 5238+8286
13:7 Abram's herdsmen and the **h** of Lot. 5238+8286
13:8 or between your **h** and mine, 8286
26:20 But the **h** *of* Gerar quarreled 8286
26:20 of Gerar quarreled with Isaac's **h** and said, 8286
2Ch 14:15 the camps of the **h** and carried off droves 5238

HERE (398) [HERE'S, HEREBY]

Ge 3:12 "The woman you put *h* **with** me— AIT
12:19 Now then, **h** is your wife. 2180
15:16 In the fourth generation your descendants will come back **h,** 2025+2178
19:9 they said, "This fellow came **h** as an alien, NIH
19:12 "Do you have anyone else **h—** 7024
19:12 Get them out of **h,** 2021+5226[S]
19:15 and your two daughters who *are* **h,** 5162
19:20 Look, **h** is a town near enough to run to, 2296
19:31 there is no man around **h** to lie with us 824+2021[S]
21:23 swear to me **h** before God that you will 2178
22:1 **"H** I am," he replied. 2180
22:5 "Stay **h** with the donkey while I and 7024
22:7 "The fire and wood are **h,"** Isaac said, 2180
22:11 **"H** I am," he replied. 2180
23:4 for a burial site **h** so I can bury my dead." 6640
24:31 "Why are you standing **out h?** 928+2021+2575
24:51 **H** is Rebekah; take her 2180
27:1 **"H** I am," he answered. 2180
27:26 Then his father Isaac said to him, **"Come h,** 5602
29:6 "and **h** comes his daughter Rachel with 2180
29:19 **Stay** *h* with me." AIT
29:26 "It is not our custom **h** to give 928+5226[S]
30:3 she said, **"H** is Bilhah, my maidservant. 2180
31:11 I answered, '**H** I am.' 2180
31:32 there is anything of yours *h* with me; AIT
31:37 Put it **h** in front of your relatives and mine, 3907
31:51 Laban also said to Jacob, **"H** is this heap, 2180
31:51 and **h** is this pillar I have set up 2180
37:17 "They have moved on from **h,"** 2296
37:19 **"H** comes that dreamer!" 2180
37:22 Throw him into this cistern **h** in the desert, 889
38:21 hasn't been any shrine prostitute **h,"** 928+2296
38:22 hasn't been any shrine prostitute **h.'"** 928+2296
39:14 He came in **h** to sleep with me, NIH
40:15 and even **h** I have done nothing 7024
42:15 unless your youngest brother comes **h.** 2178
42:19 let one of your brothers stay *h* **in** prison, AIT
42:28 **"H** it is in my sack." 2180
42:33 Leave one of your brothers *h* **with** me, AIT
43:7 'Bring your brother down **h'?"** NIH
43:9 not bring him back to you and set him **h** NIH
43:18 "We were brought **h** because of the silver NIH
43:20 "we came down **h** the first time to buy food. NIH
44:33 please let your servant remain **h** NIH
45:5 be angry with yourselves for selling me **h,** 2178
45:8 it was not you who sent me **h,** but God. 2178
45:13 And bring my father down **h** quickly." 2178
46:2 **"H** I am," he replied. 2180
47:4 "We have come to live **h** awhile, 824+928+2021[S]
47:23 **h** is seed for you so you can plant 2026
48:5 in Egypt before I came to you **h** will 2025+5213[S]
48:9 They are the sons God has given me **h,** 928+2296
Ex 3:4 And Moses said, **"H** I am." 2180
8:25 "Go, sacrifice to your God **h** in the land." NIH
11:1 After that, he will let you go from **h,** 2296
24:12 up to me on the mountain and stay **h,** 9004
24:14 "Wait **h** for us until we come back to 928+2296
33:15 do not send us up from **h.** 2296
Lev 10:4 and said to them, **"Come h;** 7928
Nu 5:21 **h** the priest is to put the woman 2256
11:21 **"H** I am among six hundred thousand men 889
13:27 flow with milk and honey! **H** is its fruit. 2296
14:33 children will be shepherds **h** 928+2021+4497[S]
14:35 in this desert; **h** they will die." 9004
Nu 20:4 that we and our livestock should die **h?** 9004
20:16 "Now we are **h** at Kadesh, NIH
20:18 "You may not pass through **h;** 3276[S]
22:8 "Spend the night **h,"** Balaam said to them, 7024
22:19 Now stay **h** tonight as the others did, 928+2296
22:32 I have come **h** to oppose you 2180
23:1 Balaam said, "Build me seven altars **h,** 928+2296
23:3 "Stay **h** beside your offering while I go NIH
23:15 "Stay **h** beside your offering while I meet 3907
23:29 Balaam said, "Build me seven altars **h,** 928+2296
32:6 countrymen go to war while you sit **h?** 7024
32:14 "And **h** you are, a brood of sinners, 2180
32:16 to build pens **h** for our livestock and cities 7024
32:26 our flocks and herds will remain **h** in 9004
33:1 **H** are the stages in the journey of 465
Dt 5:3 with all of us who are alive **h** today. 7024
5:31 But you stay **h** with me so 7024
9:4 "The LORD has brought me **h** NIH
9:7 the day you left Egypt until you arrived **h,** 2021+2021+2296+5226[S]
9:12 LORD told me, "Go down from **h** at once, 2296
12:8 You are not to do as we do **h** today, 7024
22:17 **h** is the proof of my daughter's virginity." 465
29:12 You are standing **h** in order to enter into NIH
29:15 who are standing **h** with us today in 7024
29:15 but also with those who are not **h** today. 7024
29:16 through the countries on the way **h.** NIH
Jos 1:11 the Jordan **h** to go in and take possession of 2296
2:2 the Israelites have come **h** tonight to spy out 2178
3:9 "Come **h** and listen to the words of 2178
10:24 **"Come h** and put your feet on the necks 7928
14:10 So **h** I am today, eighty-five years old! 2180
18:6 bring them **h** to me and I will cast lots 2178
18:8 and I will cast lots for you **h** at Shiloh in 7024
Jdg 4:20 by and asks you, 'Is anyone **h?'** 7024
8:15 **"H** are Zebah and Zalmunna, 2180
13:10 to tell her husband, "He's **h!** 2180
14:15 Did you invite us **h** to rob us?" NIH
16:2 people of Gaza were told, "Samson is **h!"** 2178
18:3 "Who brought you **h?** 2151
18:3 Why are you **h?"** 7024
19:9 Spend the night **h;** the day is nearly over. 7024
19:24 Look, **h** is my virgin daughter, NIH
Ru 2:8 in another field and don't go away from **h.** 2296
2:8 Stay **h** with my servant girls. 3907
2:14 to her, "Come **over h.** 2151
3:13 Stay **h** for the night, NIH
3:13 Lie **h** until morning." NIH
4:1 "Come over **h,** my friend, and sit down." 7024
4:2 "Sit **h,"** and they did so. 7024
4:4 of these seated **h** and in the presence of NIH
1Sa 1:16 I have been praying **h** out 2178+6330
1:23 "Stay **h** until you have weaned him; NIH
1:26 woman who stood **h** beside you praying 928+2296
3:4 Samuel answered, **"H** I am." 2180
3:5 And he ran to Eli and said, **"H** I am; 2180
3:6 **"H** I am; you called me." 2180
3:8 **"H** I am; you called me." 2180
3:16 Samuel answered, **"H** I am." 2180
5:7 "The ark of the god of Israel must not stay **h** NIH
6:20 To whom will the ark go up from **h?"** 5646[S]
9:11 and they asked them, "Is the seer **h?"** 928+2296
9:24 **"H** is what has been kept for you. 2180
9:27 "but you stay **h** awhile, NIH
10:22 "Has the man come **h** yet?" 2151
12:2 and my sons are **h** with you. 2180
12:3 **H** I stand. Testify against me 2180
12:7 stand **h,** because I am going to confront you NIH
12:13 Now **h** is the king you have chosen, 2180
14:33 "Roll a large stone over **h** at once." 3276[S]
14:34 and slaughter them **h** and eat them. 928+2296
14:36 the priest said, "Let us inquire of God **h."** 2151
14:38 Saul therefore said, "Come **h,** 2151
14:40 I and Jonathan my son will stand **over h."** 285+4200+6298
16:6 "Surely the LORD's anointed stands **h** NIH
16:16 Let our lord command his servants **h** 4200+7156
17:28 "Why have you come down **h?** 2296
17:44 "Come **h,"** he said, "and I'll give your flesh 448
17:47 All those gathered **h** will know that it is not NIH
18:17 **"H** is my older daughter Merab. 2180
20:21 bring them **h,'** then come, because, NIH
21:4 there is some consecrated bread **h—** NIH
21:8 "Don't you have a spear or a sword **h?** 7024
21:9 in the Valley of Elah, is **h;** 2180
21:9 there is no sword **h** but that one." 928+2296
21:15 that you have to bring this fellow **h** to carry NIH
23:3 **"H** in Judah we are afraid. 7024
25:41 **"H** is your maidservant, 2180
26:22 **"H** is the king's spear," David answered. 2180
30:26 **"H** is a present for you from the plunder of 2180
2Sa 1:10 and have brought them **h** to my lord." 2178
4:8 **"H** is the head of Ish-Bosheth son of Saul, 2180
5:6 "You will not get in **h;** 2178
5:6 They thought, "David cannot get in **h."** 2178
7:2 **"H** I am, living in a palace of cedar, 8011
11:12 said to him, "Stay **h** one more day, 928+2296
13:9 "Send everyone out of **h,"** Amnon 3276+6584[S]
13:10 the food **h** into my bedroom so I may eat NIH
13:17 **Get** this woman **out of h** 2021+2025+2575+8938
13:35 "See, the king's sons *are* **h;** 995
14:32 'Come **h** so I can send you to the king 2178
18:30 The king said, "Stand aside and wait **h."** 3907
19:20 but today I have come **h** as the first of 2180
19:37 But **h** is your servant Kimham. 2180
20:4 and be **h** yourself." 7024
20:16 Tell Joab to come **h** so I can speak to him." 2178

2Sa 24:22 **H** are oxen for the burnt offering, 8011
24:22 and **h** are threshing sledges and ox yokes NIH
1Ki 1:23 told the king, "Nathan the prophet is **h.**" 2180
2:30 But he answered, "No, I will die **h.**" 7024
3: 8 Your servant is **h** among the people NIH
9:15 **H** is the account of the forced labor 2296
11:22 "What have you lacked **h** that you 3276+6640^S
11:27 **H** is the account of how he rebelled against 2296
12:28 **H** are your gods, O Israel, 2180
13: 2 who now make offerings **h,** 3870+6584^S
13: 8 nor would I eat bread or drink water **h.** 928+2021+2021+2296+5226^S
17: 3 "Leave **h,** turn eastward and hide in 2296
18: 8 "Go tell your master, 'Elijah is **h.**' " 2180
18:11 to go to my master and say, 'Elijah is **h.**' 2180
18:14 to go to my master and say, 'Elijah is **h.**' 2180
18:30 **"Come h** to me." 5602
19: 9 "What are you doing **h,** Elijah?" 7024
19:13 a voice said to him, "What are you doing **h,** 7024
20:40 While your servant was busy **h** and there, 2178
22: 7 of the LORD **h** whom we can inquire of?" 7024
2Ki 2: 2 Elijah said to Elisha, "Stay **h;** 7024
2: 4 Then Elijah said to him, "Stay **h,** Elisha; 7024
2: 6 Then Elijah said to him, "Stay **h;** 7024
3:11 "Is there no prophet of the LORD **h,** 7024
3:11 "Elisha son of Shaphat is **h.** 7024
7: 3 "Why stay **h** until we die? 7024
7: 4 And if we stay **h,** we will die. 7024
7:13 be like that of all the Israelites left **h**— 928+2023^S
8: 7 of God has come all the way up **h,"** 2178
9:12 Jehu said, **"H is what** he told me: 2256+2296+2296+3869+3869
10:23 and see that no servants of the LORD are **h** 7024
19:32 not enter this city or shoot an arrow **h.** 9004
1Ch 6:33 **H** are the men who served, 465
11: 5 "You will not get in **h."** 2178
17: 1 he said to Nathan the prophet, **"H** I am, 2180
22: 1 "The house of the LORD God is to be **h,** 2296
25: 1 *H* **is** the list of the men who performed AIT
29:17 willingly your people who are **h** have given 7024
2Ch 18: 6 of the LORD **h** whom we can inquire of?" 7024
20:10 "But now **h** are men from Ammon, 2180
28:13 "You must not bring those prisoners **h,"** 2178
34:28 on this place and on those who live **h.'** " 2257^S
Ezr 4: 2 king of Assyria, who brought us **h."** 7024
9:15 **H** we are before you in our guilt, 2180
10:13 But there are many people **h** and it is NIH
Ne 13: 7 **H** I learned about the evil thing 2256
Job 27:13 **"H** is the fate God allots to the wicked, 2296
38:11 **h** is where your proud waves halt'? 7024
38:35 Do they report to you, **'H** we are'? 2180
Ps 40: 7 Then I said, **"H** I am, I have come— 2180
52: 7 **"H now** is the man who did not make 2180
132:14 **h** I will sit enthroned, for I have desired it— 7024
132:17 **"H** I will make a horn grow for David 9004
Pr 9: 4 "Let all who are simple come in **h!"** 2178
9:16 "Let all who are simple come in **h!"** 2178
25: 7 "Come up **h,"** than for him to humiliate you 2178
Ecc 1:10 It was **h** already, long ago; NIH
1:10 it was **h** before our time. NIH
12:13 **h** is the conclusion of the matter: NIH
SS 2: 8 **H** he comes, leaping across the mountains, 2296
Isa 5:26 **H** they come, swiftly and speedily! 2180
6: 8 And I said, **"H** am I. 2180
8:18 **H** am I, and the children 2180
21: 9 **h** comes a man in a chariot with a team 2296
22:16 What are you doing **h** 7024
22:16 to cut out a grave for yourself **h,** 7024
28:10 a little **h,** a little there." 9004
28:13 a little **h,** a little there— 9004
37:33 not enter this city or shoot an arrow **h.** 9004
40: 9 say to the towns of Judah, **"H** is your God!" 2180
41:27 the first to tell Zion, 'Look, **h** they are!' 2180
42: 1 **"H** is my servant, whom I uphold, 2176
47:14 **H are no** coals to warm anyone; 401
47:14 **h** is no fire to sit by. NIH
52: 5 "And now what do I have **h?"** 7024
57: 3 come **h,** you sons of a sorceress, 2178
58: 9 and he will say: **H** am I. 2180
65: 1 I said, **'H** am I, here am I.' 2180
65: 1 I said, 'Here am I, **h** am I.' 2180
Jer 2:23 swift she-camel **running h and there,** 2006+8592
8:14 "Why are we sitting **h?"** NIH
19:12 to this place and to those who live **h,** 2257^S
28: 3 king of Babylon removed from **h** and took to Babylon. 2021+2021+2296+5226^S
38:10 "Take thirty men from **h** with you 2296
43:10 over these stones I have buried **h;** NIH
48:47 **H** ends the judgment on Moab. 2178
49: 3 **rush h and there** inside the walls, 8763
51:64 The words of Jeremiah end **h.** 2178
La 4:15 "They can stay **h** no longer." NIH
Eze 7:10 "The day is **h!** 2180
8: 6 the house of Israel is doing **h,** 7024
8: 9 and detestable things they are doing **h."** 7024
8:17 the detestable things they are doing **h?** 7024
9: 1 **"Bring** the guards of the city **h,** 7928
40: 4 for that is why you have been brought **h.** 2178
Da 3:26 of the Most High God, come out! Come **h!"** NIH
4: 9 **H** is my dream; interpret it for me. NIH
12: 4 Many *will* **go h and there** 8763
Zec 3: 7 a place among these standing **h.** NIH
6:12 **'H** is the man whose name is the Branch, 2180
Mt 6:30 which is **h** today and tomorrow is thrown *NIG*
8:29 "Have you come **h** to torture us before *6045*
11:19 and they say, **'H** is a glutton and a drunkard, *2627*
12: 6 that one greater than the temple is **h.** *6045*
Mt 12:18 **"H is** my servant whom I have chosen, *2627*
12:41 and now one greater than Jonah is **h.** *6045*
12:42 and now one greater than Solomon is **h.** *6045*
12:49 he said, **"H** are my mother and my brothers. *2627*
14: 8 "Give me **h** on a platter the head of John *6045*
14:17 "We have **h** only five loaves of bread *6045*
14:18 "Bring them **h** to me," he said. *6045*
16:28 some who are standing **h** will *6045*
17: 4 "Lord, it is good for us to be **h.** *6045*
17:17 Bring the boy **h** to me." *6045*
17:20 'Move **from h** to there' and it will move. *1925*
20: 6 standing **h** all day long doing nothing?' *6045*
22:12 get in **h** without wedding clothes?' *6045*
24: 2 not one stone **h** will be left on another; *6045*
24:23 'Look, **h** is the Christ!' *6045*
24:26 or, **'H** he is, in the inner rooms,' *2627*
25:25 See, **h** is what belongs to you.' *NIG*
26:36 "Sit **h** while I go over there and pray." *899*
26:38 Stay **h** and keep watch with me." *6045*
26:46 Rise, let us go! **H** comes my betrayer!" *2627*
28: 6 He is not **h;** he has risen, just as he said. *6045*
Mk 3:34 **"H** *are* my mother and my brothers! *3972*
6: 3 Aren't his sisters **h** with us?" *6045*
9: 1 some who are standing **h** will not taste death *6045*
9: 5 "Rabbi, it is good for us to be **h.** *6045*
11: 2 Untie it and bring it **h.** *NIG*
11: 3 and will send it back **h** shortly.' " *6045*
13: 2 "Not one stone **h** will be left on another; *6045*
13:21 'Look, **h** is the Christ!' *6045*
14:32 "Sit **h** while I pray." *6045*
14:34 "Stay **h** and keep watch." *6045*
14:42 Rise! Let us go! **H** comes my betrayer!" *2627*
16: 6 He has risen! He is not **h.** *6045*
Lk 4: 9 he said, "throw yourself down **from h.** *1949*
4:23 **h** in your hometown what we have heard that you did in Capernaum.' " *6045*
7:34 **'H** *is* a glutton and a drunkard, *2627*
9:12 because we are in a remote place **h."** *6045*
9:27 some who are standing **h** will *899*
9:33 "Master, it is good for us to be **h.** *6045*
9:41 Bring your son **h."** *6045*
11:31 and now one greater than Solomon is **h.** *6045*
11:32 and now one greater than Jonah is **h.** *6045*
12:28 grass of the field, which is **h** today, *NIG*
15:17 and **h** I am starving to death! *6045*
16: 4 when I lose my job **h,** *NIG*
16:25 he is comforted **h** and you are in agony. *6045*
16:26 those who want to go **from h** to you cannot, *1925*
17:21 **'H** it is,' or 'There it is,' *6045*
17:23 'There he is!' or **'H** he is!' *6045*
19: 8 **H** and now I give half of my possessions to *NIG*
19:20 'Sir, **h** is your mina; *2627*
19:27 bring them **h** and kill them in front of me.' " *6045*
19:30 Untie it and bring it **h.** *NIG*
21: 6 for what *you* **see h,** the time will come *2555+4047*
22:38 "See, Lord, **h** are two swords." *6045*
23: 5 in Galilee and has come all the way **h."** *6045*
24: 6 He is not **h;** he has risen! *6045*
24:41 "Do you have anything **h** to eat?" *1924*
Jn 1:47 he said of him, **"H** is a true Israelite, *6045*
2:16 "Get these out **of h!** *1949*
4:15 and have to keep coming **h** to draw water." *1924*
5: 3 **H** a great number of disabled people *1877+4047*
6: 9 **"H** is a boy with five small barley loaves *6045*
6:25 "Rabbi, when did you get **h?"** *6045*
6:50 But **h** is the bread that comes down *4047*
7: 3 "You ought to leave **h** and go to Judea, *1949*
7:26 **H** *he* **is,** speaking publicly, *3972*
7:28 *I am* not **h** on my own, *2262*
8:13 The Pharisees challenged him, **"H** you are, *NIG*
8:42 for I came from God and *now am* **h.** *2457*
10:40 in the early days. **H** he stayed *1695*
11:21 Martha said to Jesus, "if you had been **h,** *6045*
11:28 "The Teacher **is h,"** she said, *4205*
11:32 "Lord, if you had been **h,** *6045*
11:42 for the benefit of the people **standing h,** *4325*
11:47 **"H** is this man performing many miraculous signs. *4022*
12: 2 **H** a dinner was given in Jesus' honor. *1695*
19: 5 Pilate said to them, **"H is** the man!" *2627*
19:14 **"H** is your king," Pilate said to the Jews. *3972*
19:18 **H** they crucified him, and *3963*
19:26 "Dear woman, **h** is your son," *3972*
19:27 **"H** is your mother." *3972*
20:27 he said to Thomas, "Put your finger **h;** *6045*
Ac 1:11 "why do you stand **h** looking into the sky? *NIG*
2:29 and his tomb is **h** to this day. *1609+1877*
7: 5 He gave him no inheritance **h,** *899+1877*
8:36 and the eunuch said, "Look, **h** is water. *NIG*
9:14 And he has come **h** with authority from *6045*
9:17 to you on the road as you were coming **h**— *NIG*
9:21 And hasn't he come **h** to take them *6045*
10:33 Now we **are** all **h** in the presence of God *4205*
16:28 "Don't harm yourself! We are all **h!"** *1924*
17: 6 over the world have now come **h,** *1924*
19:26 of people **h** in Ephesus and in practically *NIG*
19:37 You have brought these men **h,** *NIG*
23:15 We are ready to kill him before he **gets h."** *1581*
23:35 when your accusers **get h."** *4134*
24:19 *to be* **h** before you and bring charges *4205*
24:20 these **who are h** should state what crime *4047*
25:14 a man **h** whom Felix left as a prisoner. *NIG*
25:17 When they came **h** with me, *1924*
25:24 about him in Jerusalem and **h** in Caesarea, *1924*
26:22 and so I stand **h** and testify to small *NIG*
Ro 13:12 night is nearly over; the day *is* **almost h.** *1581*
16:23 hospitality I and the whole church **h** enjoy, *NIG*
1Co 16:20 All the brothers **h** send you greetings. *NIG*
2Co 8:10 And **h** is my advice about what is best *1877+4047*
Eph 4:14 and **blown h and there** by every wind *4367*
Php 1:16 knowing that *I am* **put h** for the defense of *3023*
Col 3:11 **H** there is no Greek or Jew, *3963*
4: 9 tell you everything that is happening **h.** *6045*
1Ti 1:15 **H** is a trustworthy saying *NIG*
3: 1 **H** is a trustworthy saying: *NIG*
2Ti 2:11 **H** is a trustworthy saying: *NIG*
4:21 Do your best *to* **get h** before winter. *2262*
Heb 2:13 And again he says, **"H** am I, *2627*
9:11 of the good things that are already **h,** *NIG*
10: 7 Then I said, **'H** I am— *2627*
10: 9 Then he said, **"H** I am, *2627*
13:14 For **h** we do not have an enduring city, *6045*
1Pe 1:17 your lives as strangers **h** in reverent fear. *NIG*
3Jn 1:14 The friends **h** send their greetings. *NIG*
Rev 3:20 **H** I am! I stand at the door and knock. *2627*
4: 1 to me like a trumpet said, "Come up **h,** *6045*
11:12 from heaven saying to them, "Come up **h."** *6045*

HERE'S (2) [BE, HERE]

Mt 25: 6 the cry rang out: **'H** the bridegroom! *2627*
Jas 2: 3 **"H** a good seat for you," *6045*

HEREAFTER (KJV) See AFTER, AFTERWARD, FROM NOW ON, FUTURE, LATER, LONGER, TO COME

HEREBY (2) [HERE]

Ge 41:41 *"I* **h put** you in charge of the whole land AIT
Ezr 6: 8 I **h** decree what you are to do NIH

HEREIN (KJV) See HERE, ON CONDITION, THIS, THIS WAY, THUS

HERES (2)

Jdg 1:35 also to hold out in Mount **H,** 3065
8:13 from the battle by the Pass of **H.** 3065

HERESH (1)

1Ch 9:15 **H,** Galal and Mattaniah son of Mica, 3090

HERESIES (1)

2Pe 2: 1 They will secretly introduce destructive **h,** *146*

HERETH (1)

1Sa 22: 5 So David left and went to the forest of **H.** 3101

HERETICK (KJV) See DIVISIVE PERSON

HERETOFORE (KJV) See BEFORE, EARLIER, IN THE PAST

HERITAGE (7) [INHERIT]

Job 20:29 the **h** appointed for them by God." 5709
27:13 the **h** a ruthless man receives from 5709
31: 2 his **h** *from* the Almighty on high? 5709
Ps 61: 5 the **h** *of* those who fear your name. 3772
119:111 Your statutes *are my* **h** forever; 5706
127: 3 Sons are a **h** *from* the LORD, 5709
Isa 54:17 This is the **h** *of* the servants of the LORD, 5709

HERMAS (1)

Ro 16:14 Patrobas, **H** and the brothers with them. *2254*

HERMES (2)

Ac 14:12 and Paul they called **H** because he was *2258*
Ro 16:14 Greet Asyncritus, Phlegon, **H,** Patrobas, *2258*

HERMOGENES (1)

2Ti 1:15 including Phygelus and **H.** *2259*

HERMON (14) [BAAL HERMON, SENIR, SIRION, SIYON]

Dt 3: 8 from the Arnon Gorge as far as Mount **H.** 3056
3: 9 (**H** is called Sirion by the Sidonians; 3056
4:48 to Mount Siyon (that is, **H**), 3056
Jos 11: 3 and to the Hivites below **H** in the region 3056
11:17 in the Valley of Lebanon below Mount **H.** 3056
12: 1 from the Arnon Gorge to Mount **H,** 3056
12: 5 He ruled over Mount **H,** Salecah, 3056
13: 5 to the east, from Baal Gad below Mount **H** 3056
13:11 all of Mount **H** and all Bashan as far 3056
1Ch 5:23 that is, to Senir (Mount **H**). 3056
Ps 42: 6 the **heights of H**—from Mount Mizar. 3056
89:12 Tabor and **H** sing for joy at your name. 3056
133: 3 if the dew of **H** were falling on Mount Zion. 3056
SS 4: 8 from the top of Senir, the summit of **H,** 3056

HERO (2) [HEROES]

1Sa 17:51 the Philistines saw that their **h** was dead, 1475
Isa 3: 2 the **h** and warrior, the judge and prophet, 1475

HEROD (43) [HEROD'S, HERODIANS]

Mt 2: 1 during the time *of* King **H**, *2476*
2: 3 When King **H** heard this he was disturbed, *2476*
2: 7 Then **H** called the Magi secretly *2476*
2:12 in a dream not to go back to **H**, *2476*
2:13 for **H** is going to search for the child *2476*
2:15 where he stayed until the death *of* **H**. *2476*
2:16 When **H** realized that he had been outwitted *2476*
2:19 After **H** died, an angel of the Lord appeared *2476*
2:22 in Judea in place of his father **H**, *2476*
14: 1 At that time **H** the tetrarch heard the reports *2476*
14: 3 Now **H** had arrested John and bound him *2476*
14: 5 **H** wanted to kill John, *NIG*
14: 6 of Herodias danced for them and pleased **H** *2476*
Mk 6:14 King **H** heard about this, *2476*
6:16 But when **H** heard this, he said, "John, *2476*
6:17 For **H** himself had given orders *2476*
6:18 For John had been saying *to* **H**, *2476*
6:20 because **H** feared John and protected him, *2476*
6:20 When **H** heard John, he was greatly puzzled; *NIG*
6:21 On his birthday **H** gave a banquet *2476*
6:22 she pleased **H** and his dinner guests. *2476*
8:15 for the yeast of the Pharisees and that *of* **H**." *2476*
Lk 1: 5 In the time *of* **H** king of Judea there was *2476*
3: 1 of Judea, **H** tetrarch of Galilee, *2476*
3:19 when John rebuked **H** the tetrarch because *2476*
3:20 **H** added this to them all: *2476*
9: 7 Now **H** the tetrarch heard about all *2476*
9: 9 But **H** said, "I beheaded John. *2476*
13:31 **H** wants to kill you." *2476*
23: 7 he sent him to **H**, who was also in Jerusalem *2476*
23: 8 When **H** saw Jesus, he was greatly pleased, *2476*
23:11 Then **H** and his soldiers ridiculed *2476*
23:12 That day **H** and Pilate became friends— *2476*
23:15 Neither has **H**, for he sent him back to us; *2476*
Ac 4:27 Indeed **H** and Pontius Pilate met together *2476*
12: 1 that King **H** arrested some who belonged to *2476*
12: 4 **H** intended to bring him out for public trial *NIG*
12: 6 The night before **H** was to bring him to trial, *2476*
12:19 After **H** had a thorough search made for him *2476*
12:19 Then **H** went from Judea to Caesarea *NIG*
12:21 On the appointed day **H**, *2476*
12:23 because **H** did not give praise to God, *NIG*
13: 1 Manaen (who had been brought up with **H** *2476*

HEROD'S (5) [HEROD]

Mt 14: 6 On **H** birthday the daughter *2476*
Lk 8: 3 the manager *of* **H** household; *2476*
23: 7 that Jesus was under **H** jurisdiction, *2476*
Ac 12:11 rescued me from **H** clutches and from *2476*
23:35 that Paul be kept under guard in **H** palace. *2476*

HERODIANS (3) [HEROD]

Mt 22:16 to him along with the **H**. *2477*
Mk 3: 6 to plot with the **H** how they might kill Jesus. *2477*
12:13 *of* the Pharisees and **H** to Jesus to catch him *2477*

HERODIAS (6)

Mt 14: 3 and put him in prison because of **H**, *2478*
14: 6 *of* **H** danced for them and pleased Herod *2478*
Mk 6:17 He did this because of **H**, *2478*
6:19 So **H** nursed a grudge against John *2478*
6:22 the daughter *of* **H** came in and danced, *2478*
Lk 3:19 the tetrarch because of **H**, *2478*

HERODION (1)

Ro 16:11 Greet **H**, my relative. *2479*

HEROES (3) [HERO]

Ge 6: 4 They were the **h** of old, men of renown. 1475
Ne 3:16 as the artificial pool and the House of the **H**. 1475
Isa 5:22 Woe to *those who* are **h** at drinking wine 1475

HERON (2)

Lev 11:19 any kind of **h**, the hoopoe and the bat. 649
Dt 14:18 any kind of **h**, the hoopoe and the bat. 649

HERS (4) [SHE]

Ge 3:15 and between your offspring and **h**; 2023
Job 39:16 as if they were not **h**; 2023+4200
Pr 14: 1 the foolish one tears **h** down. 5647
La 1: 7 the treasures that were **h** in days of old. 2023

HERSELF (45) [SELF, SHE] See Index of Articles Etc.

HESED (KJV) See BEN-HESED

HESHBON (38)

Nu 21:25 and occupied them, including **H** 3114
21:26 **H** was the city of Sihon king of 3114
21:27 "Come to **H** and let it be rebuilt; 3114
21:28 "Fire went out from **H**, 3114
21:30 **H** is destroyed all the way to Dibon. 3114
21:34 king of the Amorites, who reigned in **H**." 3114
32: 3 Dibon, Jazer, Nimrah, **H**, Elealeh, Sebam, 3114
32:37 And the Reubenites rebuilt **H**, 3114
Dt 1: 4 king of the Amorites, who reigned in **H**, 3114
2:24 king of **H**, and his country. 3114
2:26 to Sihon king of **H** offering peace 3114
2:30 king of **H** refused to let us pass through. 3114
3: 2 of the Amorites, who reigned in **H**." 3114
3: 6 as we had done with Sihon king of **H**, 3114
4:46 in **H** and was defeated by Moses and 3114
29: 7 of **H** and Og king of Bashan came out 3114
Jos 9:10 Sihon king of **H**, and Og king of Bashan, 3114
12: 2 of the Amorites, who reigned in **H**. 3114
12: 5 of Gilead to the border of Sihon king of **H**. 3114
13:10 of the Amorites, who ruled in **H**, 3114
13:17 to **H** and all its towns on the plateau, 3114
13:21 of the Amorites, who ruled at **H**. 3114
13:26 from **H** to Ramath Mizpah and Betonim, 3114
13:27 with the rest of the realm of Sihon king of **H** 3114
21:39 **H** and Jazer, together 3114
Jdg 11:19 who ruled in **H**, and said to him, 3114
11:26 For three hundred years Israel occupied **H**, 3114
1Ch 6:81 **H** and Jazer, together with 3114
Ne 9:22 of **H** and the country of Og king of Bashan. 3114
SS 7: 4 the pools of **H** by the gate of Bath Rabbim. 3114
Isa 15: 4 **H** and Elealeh cry out, 3114
16: 8 The fields of **H** wither, 3114
16: 9 O **H**, O Elealeh, I drench you with tears! 3114
Jer 48: 2 in **H** men will plot her downfall: 3114
48:34 "The sound of their cry rises from **H** 3114
48:45 shadow of **H** the fugitives stand helpless, 3114
48:45 for a fire has gone out from **H**, 3114
49: 3 "Wail, O **H**, for Ai is destroyed! 3114

HESHMON (1)

Jos 15:27 Hazar Gaddah, **H**, Beth Pelet, 3132

HESITATE (4) [HESITATED, HESITATION]

Jdg 18: 9 Don't **h** to go there and take it over. 6788
Job 30:10 *they do* not **h** to spit in my face. 3104
Da 9:14 The LORD **did not h** to bring the disaster 9193
Ac 10:20 *Do* not **h** to go with them, *1359*

HESITATED (3) [HESITATE]

Ge 19:16 When *he* **h**, the men grasped his hand and 4538
Ac 20:20 that *I have* not **h** to preach anything *5713*
20:27 not **h** to proclaim to you the whole will *5713*

HESITATION (1) [HESITATE]

Ac 11:12 The Spirit told me to *have* no **h** about going *1359*

HETHLON (2)

Eze 47:15 by the **H** road past Lebo Hamath to Zedad, 3158
48: 1 it will follow the **H** road to Lebo Hamath; 3158

HEW (KJV) See CHISEL

HEWER (KJV) See WOODCUTTER

HEWING (1) [HEWN]

Isa 22:16 **h** your grave on the height 2933

HEWN (2) [HEWING]

Pr 9: 1 *she has* **h out** its seven pillars. 2933
Isa 51: 1 and to the quarry from which *you* were **h**; 5941

HEZEKI (KJV) See HIZKI

HEZEKIAH (123) [HEZEKIAH'S]

2Ki 16:20 And **H** his son succeeded him as king. 2625
18: 1 **H** son of Ahaz king of Judah began to reign. 2624
18: 5 **H** trusted in the LORD, the God of Israel. NIH
18:14 So **H** king of Judah sent this message to 2624
18:14 from **H** king of Judah three hundred talents 2624
18:15 So **H** gave him all the silver that was found 2624
18:16 At this time **H** king of Judah stripped off 2624
18:17 from Lachish to King **H** at Jerusalem. 2625
18:19 The field commander said to them, "Tell **H**: 2625
18:22 high places and altars **H** removed, 2625
18:29 Do not let **H** deceive you. 2625
18:30 Do not let **H** persuade you to trust in 2625
18:31 "Do not listen to **H**. 2625
18:32 "Do not listen to **H**, 2625
18:37 of Asaph the recorder went to **H**, 2625
19: 1 When King **H** heard this, 2625
19: 3 They told him, "This is what **H** says: 2625
19: 9 So he again sent messengers to **H** 2625
19:10 "Say to **H** king of Judah: 2625
19:14 **H** received the letter from the messengers 2625
19:15 And **H** prayed to the LORD: 2625
19:20 Isaiah son of Amoz sent a message to **H**: 2625
19:29 "This will be the sign for you, O **H**: NIH
20: 1 In those days **H** became ill and was at 2625
20: 2 **H** turned his face to the wall and prayed to NIH
20: 3 And **H** wept bitterly. 2625
20: 5 "Go back and tell **H**, the leader 2625
20: 8 **H** had asked Isaiah, 2625
20:10 the shadow to go forward ten steps," said **H**. 3491
20:12 of Baladan king of Babylon sent **H** letters 2625
20:13 **H** received the messengers 2625
20:13 or in all his kingdom that **H** did not show 2625
20:14 Then Isaiah the prophet went to King **H** 2625
20:14 "From a distant land," **H** replied. 2625
20:15 everything in my palace," **H** said. 2625
20:16 Then Isaiah said to **H**, 2625
20:19 you have spoken is good," **H** replied. 2625
2Ki 20:21 **H** rested with his fathers. 2625
21: 3 the high places his father **H** had destroyed; 2625
1Ch 3:13 Ahaz his son, **H** his son, Manasseh his son, 2625
4:41 in the days of **H** king of Judah. 3491
2Ch 28:27 And **H** his son succeeded him as king. 3491
29: 1 **H** was twenty-five years old 3491
29:18 Then they went in to King **H** and reported: 2625
29:20 Early the next morning King **H** gathered 3491
29:27 **H** gave the order to sacrifice 2625
29:30 King **H** and his officials ordered the Levites 3491
29:31 Then **H** said, "You have now dedicated 3491
29:36 **H** and all the people rejoiced 3491
30: 1 **H** sent word to all Israel and Judah and 3491
30:18 But **H** prayed for them, saying, 3491
30:20 the LORD heard **H** and healed the people. 3491
30:22 **H** spoke encouragingly to all the Levites, 3491
30:24 **H** king of Judah provided a thousand bulls 2625
31: 2 **H** assigned the priests and Levites 3491
31: 8 **H** and his officials came and saw the heaps, 3491
31: 9 **H** asked the priests and Levites about 3491
31:11 **H** gave orders to prepare storerooms in 3491
31:13 of King **H** and Azariah the official in charge 3491
31:20 This is what **H** did throughout Judah, 3491
32: 1 After all that **H** had so faithfully done, NIH
32: 2 When **H** saw that Sennacherib had come 3491
32: 8 the people gained confidence from what **H** 3491
32: 9 with this message for **H** king of Judah and 3491
32:11 **H** says, 'The LORD our God will save us 3491
32:12 not **H** himself remove this god's high places 3491
32:15 not let **H** deceive you and mislead you 2625
32:16 the LORD God and against his servant **H**. 3491
32:17 so the god of **H** will not rescue his people 3491
32:20 King **H** and the prophet Isaiah son 3491
32:22 So the LORD saved **H** and the people 3491
32:23 for the LORD and valuable gifts for **H** king 3491
32:24 In those days **H** became ill and was at 3491
32:26 Then **H** repented of the pride of his heart, 3491
32:26 not come upon them during the days of **H**. 3491
32:27 **H** had very great riches and honor, 3491
32:30 It was **H** who blocked the upper outlet of 3491
32:33 **H** rested with his fathers and was buried on 3491
33: 3 the high places his father **H** had demolished; 3491
Ezr 2:16 of Ater (through **H**) 98 3490
Ne 7:21 of Ater (through **H**) 98 2624
10:17 Ater, **H**, Azzur, 2624
Pr 25: 1 copied by the men of **H** king of Judah: 2624
Isa 1: 1 Jotham, Ahaz and **H**, kings of Judah. 3491
36: 1 with a large army from Lachish to King **H** 2625
36: 4 The field commander said to them, "Tell **H**, 2625
36: 7 high places and altars **H** removed, 2625
36:14 Do not let **H** deceive you. 2625
36:15 Do not let **H** persuade you to trust in 2625
36:16 "Do not listen to **H**. 2625
36:18 "Do not let **H** mislead you when he says, 2625
36:22 Joah son of Asaph the recorder went to **H**, 2625
37: 1 When King **H** heard this, 2625
37: 3 They told him, "This is what **H** says: 2625
37: 9 he sent messengers to **H** with this word: 2625
37:10 "Say to **H** king of Judah: 2625
37:14 **H** received the letter from the messengers 2625
37:15 And **H** prayed to the LORD: 2625
37:21 Isaiah son of Amoz sent a message to **H**: 2625
37:30 "This will be the sign for you, O **H**: NIH
38: 1 In those days **H** became ill and was at 2625
38: 2 **H** turned his face to the wall and prayed to 2625
38: 3 And **H** wept bitterly. 2625
38: 5 "Go and tell **H**, 'This is what the LORD, 2625
38: 9 writing of **H** king of Judah after his illness 2625
38:22 **H** had asked, "What will be the sign 2625
39: 1 of Baladan king of Babylon sent **H** letters 2625
39: 2 **H** received the envoys gladly 2625
39: 2 or in all his kingdom that **H** did not show 2625
39: 3 Then Isaiah the prophet went to King **H** 2625
39: 3 "From a distant land," **H** replied. 2625
39: 4 everything in my palace," **H** said. 2625
39: 5 Then Isaiah said to **H**, 2625
39: 8 you have spoken is good," **H** replied. 2625
Jer 15: 4 because of what Manasseh son of **H** king 3491
26:18 in the days of **H** king of Judah. 2625
26:19 "Did **H** king of Judah or anyone else 2625
26:19 not **H** fear the LORD and seek his favor? NIH
Hos 1: 1 Jotham, Ahaz and **H**, kings of Judah, 3490
Mic 1: 1 Ahaz and **H**, kings of Judah— 3490
Zep 1: 1 the son of Amariah, the son of **H**, 2624
Mt 1: 9 Ahaz the father of **H**, *1614*
1:10 **H** the father of Manasseh, *1614*

HEZEKIAH'S (10) [HEZEKIAH]

2Ki 18: 9 In King **H** fourth year, 2625+4200
18:10 Samaria was captured in **H** sixth year, 2624+4200
18:13 In the fourteenth year of King **H** reign, 2624
19: 5 When King **H** officials came to Isaiah, 2625
20:12 because he had heard of **H** illness. 2625
20:20 As for the other events of **H** reign, 2625
2Ch 32:25 But **H** heart was proud and he did 3491
32:32 The other events of **H** reign and his acts 3491
Isa 36: 1 In the fourteenth year of King **H** reign, 2625
37: 5 When King **H** officials came to Isaiah, 2625

HEZION (1)

1Ki 15:18 the son of **H**, the king of Aram, 2611

HEZIR (2)

1Ch 24:15 the seventeenth to **H**, 2615
Ne 10:20 Magpiash, Meshullam, **H**, 2615

HEZRAI (KJV) See HEZRO

HEZRO (2)
2Sa 23:35 **H** the Carmelite, Paarai the Arbite, 2968
1Ch 11:37 **H** the Carmelite, Naarai son of Ezbai, 2968

HEZRON (20) [HEZRONITE, KIRIOTH HEZRON]
Ge 46: 9 Hanoch, Pallu, **H** and Carmi. 2969
46:12 The sons of Perez: **H** and Hamul. 2969
Ex 6:14 of Israel were Hanoch and Pallu, **H** 2969
Nu 26: 6 through **H,** the Hezronite clan; 2969
26:21 through **H,** the Hezronite clan; 2969
Jos 15: 3 Then it ran past **H** up to Addar and curved 2970
Ru 4:18 Perez was the father of **H,** 2969
4:19 **H** the father of Ram, 2969
1Ch 2: 5 The sons of Perez: **H** and Hamul. 2969
2: 9 The sons born to **H** were: 2969
2:18 of **H** had children by his wife Azubah (and 2969
2:21 **H** lay with the daughter of Makir the father 2969
2:24 After **H** died in Caleb Ephrathah, 2969
2:24 of **H** bore him Ashhur the father of Tekoa. 2969
2:25 The sons of Jerahmeel the firstborn of **H:** 2969
4: 1 Perez, **H,** Carmi, Hur and Shobal. 2969
5: 3 Hanoch, Pallu, **H** and Carmi. 2969
Mt 1: 3 Perez the father of **H,** *2272*
1: 3 **H** the father of Ram, *2272*
Lk 3:33 the son *of* **H,** the son of Perez, *2272*

HEZRONITE (2) [HEZRON]
Nu 26: 6 through Hezron, the **H** clan; through Carmi, 2971
26:21 through Hezron, the **H** clan; 2971

HID (34) [HIDE]
Ge 3: 8 and *they* **h** from the LORD God among 2461
3:10 because I was naked; so *I* **h."** 2461
Ex 2: 2 *she* **h** him for three months. 7621
2:12 the Egyptian and **h** him in the sand. 3243
3: 6 At this, Moses **h** his face, 6259
Jos 6:17 because *she* **h** the spies we sent. 2461
6:25 because *she* **h** the men Joshua had sent 2461
1Sa 13: 6 they **h** in caves and thickets, 2461
20:19 where *you* **h** when this trouble began, 6259
20:24 So David **h** in the field, 6259
1Ki 18:13 *I* **h** a hundred of the LORD's prophets 2461
20:30 And Ben-Hadad fled to the city and **h in** 995
2Ki 7: 8 gold and clothes, and went off and **h** them. 3243
7: 8 from it and **h** them also. 3243
1Ch 21:20 sons who were with him **h themselves.** 2461
2Ch 22:11 *she* **h** the child from Athaliah so she could 6259
Ps 30: 7 but *when you* **h** your face, I was dismayed. 6259
35: 7 Since *they* **h** their net for me without cause 3243
35: 8 may the net *they* **h** entangle them, 3243
Isa 49: 2 in the shadow of his hand *he* **h** me; 2461
54: 8 a surge of anger *I* **h** my face from you for 6259
57:17 I punished him, and **h** my face in anger, 6259
Jer 13: 5 So I went and **h** it at Perath, 3243
Eze 39:23 So *I* **h** my face from them and handed them 6259
39:24 and *I* **h** my face from them. 6259
Da 10: 7 that they fled and **h themselves.** 2461
Mt 13:44 When a man found it, *he* **h** it again, *3221*
25:18 in the ground and **h** his master's money. *3221*
25:25 and went out and **h** your talent in *3221*
Jn 8:59 but Jesus **h** *himself,* *3221*
12:36 Jesus left and **h** *himself* from them. *3221*
Ac 1: 9 and a cloud **h** him from their sight. *5696*
Heb 11:23 By faith Moses' parents **h** *him* *3221*
Rev 6:15 and every free man **h** in caves and among *3221*

HIDDAI (1)
2Sa 23:30 **H** from the ravines of Gaash, 2068

HIDDEKEL (KJV) See TIGRIS

HIDDEN (82) [HIDE]
Ge 4:14 and *I will be* **h** from your presence; 6259
Nu 5:13 and *this is* **h** from her husband 6623
Dt 33:19 on the **treasures h** *in* the sand." 3243+8561
Jos 2: 4 woman had taken the two men and **h** them. 7621
2: 6 up to the roof and **h** them under the stalks 3243
7:21 They *are* **h** in the ground inside my tent, 3243
7:22 **h** in his tent, with the silver underneath. 3243
10:16 the five kings had fled and **h** in the cave 2461
Jdg 16: 9 With men **h** in the room, she called to him, 741
16:12 Then, with men **h** in the room, 741
1Sa 10:22 he *has* **h himself** among the baggage." 2461
14:22 the Israelites who *had* **h** in the hill country 2461
2Sa 17: 9 now, he *is* **h** in a cave or some other place. 2461
18:13 and nothing *is* **h** from the king— 3948
1Ki 18: 4 a hundred prophets and **h** them 2461
2Ki 4:27 but the LORD *has* **h** it from me and has 6623
6:29 but *she had* **h** him." 2461
11: 3 He remained **h** with his nurse at the temple 2461
2Ch 22:12 He remained **h** with them at the temple 2461
Job 3:16 not **h** in the ground like a stillborn child, 3243
3:21 who search for it more than for **h treasure,** 4759
3:23 Why is life given to a man whose way *is* **h,** 6259
18:10 A noose *is* **h** for him on the ground; 3243
28: 7 No bird of prey knows that **h path,** 5985
28:11 and brings **h things** to light. 9502
28:21 *It is* **h** from the eyes of every living thing, 6623
33:21 and his bones, *once* **h,** now stick out. 4202+8011
40:21 **h** *among* the reeds in the marsh. 6260
Ps 9:15 their feet are caught in the net *they have* **h.** 3243
19: 6 nothing **is h** from its heat. 6259
19:12 Forgive my **h** *faults.* 6259
22:24 not **h** his face from him but has listened 6259
38: 9 my sighing **is** not **h** from you. 6259
69: 5 my guilt *is* not **h** from you. 3948
78: 2 I will utter **h things,** things from of old— 2648
119:11 *I have* **h** your word in my heart that I might 7621
139:15 My frame **was** not **h** from you 3948
140: 5 Proud men *have* **h** a snare for me; 3243
142: 3 In the path where I walk *men have* **h** a snare 3243
Pr 2: 4 for silver and search for it as for **h treasure,** 4759
27: 5 Better is open rebuke than **h** love. 6259
Ecc 12:14 into judgment, including every **h** *thing,* 6623
Isa 30:20 your teachers *will be* **h** no more; 4052
40:27 O Israel, "My way *is* **h** from the LORD; 6259
42:22 of them trapped in pits or **h away** in prisons. 2461
48: 6 of **h** *things* unknown to you. 5915
59: 2 your sins *have* **h** his face from you, 6259
64: 7 for *you have* **h** your face from us 6259
65:16 For the past troubles will be forgotten and **h** 6259
Jer 13: 7 and took it from the place where *I had* **h** it, 3243
16:17 *they* **are** not **h** from me, 6259
18:22 to capture me and *have* **h** snares for my feet. 3243
36:26 But the LORD *had* **h** them. 6259
41: 8 oil and honey, **h** in a field." 4759
Eze 28: 3 *Is* no secret **h** *from* you? 6670
Da 2:22 He reveals deep and **h** *things;* 10519
Hos 5: 3 Israel *is* not **h** from me. 3948
Ob 1: 6 his **h treasures** pillaged! 5208
Hab 3: 4 where his power was **h.** 2470
Mt 5:14 A city on a hill cannot *be* **h.** *3221*
10:26 or **h** that will not be made known. *3220*
11:25 because *you have* **h** these things from *3221*
13:35 I will utter *things* **h** since the creation of *3221*
13:44 "The kingdom of heaven is like treasure **h** *3221*
Mk 4:22 For whatever is **h** is meant to be disclosed, *3220*
Lk 8:17 there is nothing **h** that will not be disclosed, *3220*
9:45 It was **h** from them, *4152*
10:21 because *you have* **h** these things **from** *648*
11:33 **place** where it will be **h,** *3219*
12: 2 or **h** that will not be made known. *3220*
18:34 Its meaning was **h** from them, *3221*
19:42 but now *it is* **h** from your eyes. *3221*
Ro 16:25 the revelation of the mystery **h** for long ages *4967*
1Co 2: 7 that *has been* **h** and that God destined *648*
4: 5 He will bring to light what **is h** in darkness *3220*
Eph 3: 9 which for ages past *was kept* **h** in God, *648*
Col 1:26 the mystery that *has been* **kept h for** ages *648*
2: 3 in whom are **h** all the treasures of wisdom *649*
3: 3 and your life *is now* **h** with Christ in God. *3221*
1Ti 5:25 and even those that are not cannot *be* **h.** *3221*
Heb 4:13 Nothing in all creation is **h from** *905*
Rev 2:17 I will give some of the **h** manna. *3221*

HIDE (74) [HID, HIDDEN, HIDES, HIDING]
Ge 18:17 *"Shall* I **h** from Abraham what I am about 4059
47:18 *"We* cannot **h** from our lord the fact that 3948
Ex 2: 3 But when she could **h** him no longer, 7621
29:14 the bull's flesh and its **h** and its offal outside 6425
Lev 4:11 But the **h** *of* the bull and all its flesh, 6425
7: 8 a burnt offering for anyone may keep its **h** 6425
8:17 But the bull with its **h** and its flesh 6425
9:11 and the **h** he burned up outside the camp. 6425
11:32 of wood, cloth, **h** or sackcloth. 6425
Nu 19: 5 its **h,** flesh, blood and offal. 6425
Dt 7:20 among them until even the survivors who **h** 6259
31:17 *I will* **h** my face from them, 6259
31:18 And I *will* **certainly h** my face on 6259+6259
32:20 *"I will* **h** my face from them," he said, 6259
Jos 2:16 **H yourselves** there three days 2461
7:19 *do* not **h** it from me." 3948
Jdg 21:20 "Go and **h** in the vineyards 741
1Sa 3:17 *"Do* not **h** it from me. 3948
3:17 if *you* **h** from me anything he told you." 3948
20: 2 Why *would* he **h** this from me? 6259
20: 5 and **h** in the field until the evening of 6259
1Ki 17: 3 turn eastward and **h** in the Kerith Ravine, 6259
22:25 on the day you go to **h** *in* an inner room." 2461
2Ki 7:12 so they have left the camp to **h** in 2461
11: 2 in a bedroom *to* **h** him from Athaliah; 6259
2Ch 18:24 on the day you go to **h** *in* an inner room." 2461
Job 3:10 on me *to* **h** trouble from my eyes. 6259
13:20 O God, and then *I will* not **h** from you: 6259
13:24 Why *do you* **h** your face 6259
14:13 "If only *you would* **h** me in the grave 7621
34:22 no deep shadow, where evildoers *can* **h.** 6259
41: 7 Can you fill his **h** with harpoons or his head 6425
Ps 10: 1 *Why do you* **h** *yourself* in times of trouble? 6623
13: 1 How long *will you* **h** your face from me? 6259
17: 8 **h** me in the shadow of your wings 6259
27: 5 *he will* **h** me in the shelter of his tabernacle 6259
27: 9 *Do* not **h** your face from me, 6259
31:20 In the shelter of your presence *you* **h** them 6259
40:10 *I do* not **h** your righteousness in my heart; 4059
44:24 Why *do you* **h** your face 6259
51: 9 **H** your face from my sins 6259
55:12 *I could* **h** from him. 6259
64: 2 **H** me from the conspiracy of the wicked, 6259
69:17 *Do* not **h** your face from your servant; 6259
78: 4 *We will* not **h** them from their children; 3948
88:14 do you reject me and **h** your face from me? 6259
89:46 *Will you* **h yourself** forever? 6259
102: 2 *Do* not **h** your face from me when I am 6259
104:29 *When you* **h** your face, they are terrified; 6259
119:19 *do* not **h** your commands from me. 6259
139:11 "Surely the darkness *will* **h** me and 8503
143: 7 *Do* not **h** your face from me or I will be 6259
143: 9 O LORD, for *I* **h** *myself* in you. 4059
Isa 1:15 *I will* **h** my eyes from you; 6623
2:10 **h** in the ground from dread of the LORD 3243
3: 9 parade their sin like Sodom; *they do* not **h** it. 3948
16: 3 **H** the fugitives, do not betray the refugees. 6259
26:20 **h** *yourselves* for a little while 2464
29:15 to great depths to **h** their plans from 6259
50: 6 not **h** my face from mocking and spitting. 6259
53: 3 Like one from whom men **h** their faces he was despised, 5040
Jer 13: 4 now to Perath and **h** it there in a crevice in 3243
13: 6 and get the belt I told you to **h** there " 3243
23:24 *Can* anyone **h** in secret places so 6259
33: 5 *I will* **h** my face from this city because 6259
36:19 "You and Jeremiah, go and **h.** 6259
38:14 *"Do* not **h** anything from me." 3948
38:25 *do* not **h** it from us or we will kill you,' 3948
49: 8 Turn and flee, **h in** deep caves, 3782
Eze 39:29 *I will* no longer **h** my face from them, 6259
Am 9: 3 Though *they* **h themselves** on the top 2461
9: 3 Though *they* **h** from me at the bottom of 6259
Mic 3: 4 At that time *he will* **h** his face from them 6259
Rev 6:16 on us and **h** us from the face of him who sits *3221*

HIDES (18) [HIDE]
Ex 25: 5 ram skins dyed red and **h** *of* sea cows; 6425
26:14 and over that a covering of **h** *of* sea cows. 6425
35: 7 ram skins dyed red and **h** *of* sea cows; 6425
35:23 or **h** *of* sea cows brought them. 6425
36:19 and over that a covering of **h** *of* sea cows. 6425
39:34 of **h** *of* sea cows and the shielding curtain; 6425
Lev 16:27 their **h,** flesh and offal are to be burned up. 6425
Nu 4: 6 they are to cover this with **h** *of* sea cows, 6425
4: 8 that with **h** *of* sea cows and put its poles 6425
4:10 in a covering of **h** *of* sea cows and put it on 6425
4:11 to spread a blue cloth and cover that with **h** 6425
4:12 cover that with **h** *of* sea cows and put them 6425
4:14 of **h** *of* sea cows and put its poles in place. 6425
4:25 and the outer covering of **h of sea cows,** 9391
Job 20:12 in his mouth and *he* **h** it under his tongue, 3948
34:29 If *he* **h** his face, who can see him? 6259
Isa 45:15 Truly you are a God *who* **h himself,** 6259
Lk 8:16 a lamp and **h** it in a jar or puts it under *2821*

HIDING (29) [HIDE]
Jos 10:17 the five kings had been found **h** in the cave 2461
10:27 into the cave where *they had been* **h.** 2461
Jdg 9: 5 of Jerub-Baal, escaped by **h.** 2461
9:35 came out from their **h place.** 4422
1Sa 3:18 **h** nothing from him. 3948
14:11 of the holes *they were* **h** in." 2461
19: 2 go into **h** and stay there. 6260
23:19 *"Is* not David **h** among us in the strongholds 6259
23:23 the **h places** he uses and come back to me 4676
26: 1 *"Is* not David **h** on the hill of Hakilah, 6259
2Ch 22: 9 and his men captured him while he *was* **h** 2461
Job 15:18 **h** nothing received from their fathers 3948
24: 4 **force** all the poor of the land **into h.** 2461
31:33 by **h** my guilt in my heart 3243
Ps 32: 7 You are my **h place;** 6260
54: T *"Is* not David **h** among us?" 6259
64: 5 they talk about **h** their snares; 3243
Pr 28:12 the wicked rise to power, men **go into h.** 2924
28:28 the wicked rise to power, people **go into h;** 6259
SS 2:14 in the **h places** *on* the mountainside, 6260
Isa 4: 6 and a refuge and **h place** from the storm 5039
8:17 who *is* **h** his face from the house of Jacob. 6259
28:15 a lie our refuge and falsehood *our* **h place."** 6259
28:17 and water will overflow your **h place.** 6260
Jer 49:10 I will uncover his **h places,** 5041
La 3:10 Like a bear lying in wait, like a lion in **h,** 5041
Am 6:10 of the house and asks anyone still **h** there, NIH
Na 3:11 you will go into **h** and seek refuge from 6623
Hab 3:14 to devour the wretched who were in **h.** 5041

HIEL (1)
1Ki 16:34 In Ahab's time, **H** of Bethel rebuilt Jericho. 2647

HIERAPOLIS (1)
Col 4:13 for you and for those at Laodicea and **H.** *2631*

HIGGAION (1)
Ps 9:16 by the work of their hands. **H.** 2053

HIGH (380) [HIGH-GRADE, HIGHBORN, HIGHER, HIGHEST, HIGHLY]
Ge 6:15 75 feet wide and 45 feet **h.** 7757
7:17 as the waters increased they lifted the ark **h** 8123
7:19 and all the **h** mountains under 1469
14:18 He was priest of God **Most H,** 6610
14:19 saying, "Blessed be Abram by God **Most H,** 6610
14:20 And blessed be God **Most H,** 6610
14:22 God **Most H,** Creator of heaven and earth, 6610
29: 7 "Look," he said, "the sun is still **h;** 1524
Ex 25:10 and a cubit and a half **h.** 7757
25:23 a cubit wide and a cubit and a half **h.** 7757
27: 1 an altar of acacia wood, three cubits **h;** 7757
27:18 of finely twisted linen five cubits **h,** 7757
30: 2 a cubit wide, and two cubits **h—** 7757

Ex 37: 1 and a cubit and a half **h.** 7757
37:10 a cubit wide, and a cubit and a half **h.** 7757
37:25 and two cubits **h—** 7757
38: 1 of acacia wood, three cubits **h;** 7757
38:18 the curtains of the courtyard, five cubits **h,** 7757
Lev 16:32 to succeed his father as **h priest** is 3912
21:10 " 'The **h** priest, the one 1524
26:13 and enabled you to walk **with heads held h.** 7758
26:30 I will destroy your **h places,** 1195
Nu 14:40 up toward the **h** hill country. 8031
14:44 up toward the **h** hill country, 8031
24:16 who has knowledge from the **Most H,** 6610
33:52 and demolish all their **h places.** 1195
35:25 until the death of the **h** priest, 1524
35:28 of refuge until the death of the **h** priest; 1524
35:28 after the death of the **h** priest may he return 1524
35:32 before the death of the **h** priest. NIH
Dt 3: 5 All these cities were fortified with **h** walls 1469
12: 2 on the **h** mountains and on the hills and 8123
26:19 fame and honor **h** above all 6609
28: 1 the LORD your God will set you **h** 6609
28:52 until the **h** fortified walls 1469
32: 8 **Most H** gave the nations their inheritance, 6610
33:29 and you will trample down their **h places."** 1195
Jos 20: 6 until the death of the **h** priest who is serving 1524
Jdg 16:25 they *were* **in h spirits,** they shouted, 3201+4213
1Sa 2: 1 in the LORD my horn *is* **lifted h.** 8123
9:12 the people have a sacrifice at the **h place.** 1195
9:13 before he goes up to the **h place** to eat. 1195
9:14 toward them on his way up to the **h place.** 1195
9:19 "Go up ahead of me to the **h place,** 1195
9:25 After they came down from the **h place** to 1195
10: 5 of prophets coming down from the **h place** 1195
10:13 he went to the **h place.** 1195
18: 5 **gave** him **a h rank in** the army. 6584+8492
25:36 He *was* **in h spirits** and very drunk. 3201+4213
2Sa 13:28 When Amnon *is* **in h spirits** 3201+4213
22:14 the voice of the **Most H** resounded. 6610
22:17 "He reached down from **on h** and took hold 5294
23: 1 oracle of the man exalted by the **Most H,** 6583
1Ki 3: 2 were still sacrificing at the **h places,** 1195
3: 3 and burned incense on the **h places.** 1195
3: 4 for that was the most important **h place,** 1195
6: 2 twenty wide and thirty **h.** 7757
6:20 twenty wide and twenty **h.** 7757
6:23 each ten cubits **h.** 7757
7: 2 fifty wide and thirty **h,** 7757
7: 4 **windows** were **placed h** 9209
7:15 each eighteen cubits **h** and twelve cubits 7757
7:16 each capital was five cubits **h.** 7757
7:19 in the shape of lilies, four cubits **h.** NIH
7:23 from rim to rim and five cubits **h.** 7757
7:27 four wide and three **h.** 7757
11: 7 a **h place** for Chemosh the detestable god 1195
12:31 Jeroboam built shrines on **h places** 1195
12:32 at the **h places** he had made. 1195
13: 2 the **h places** who now make offerings here, 1195
13:32 and against all the shrines on the **h places** 1195
13:33 for the **h places** from all sorts of people. 1195
13:33 a priest he consecrated for the **h places.** 1195
14:23 They also set up for themselves **h places,** 1195
14:23 and Asherah poles on every **h** hill and 1469
15:14 Although he did not remove the **h places,** 1195
22:43 The **h places,** however, were not removed, 1195
2Ki 12: 3 The **h places,** however, were not removed; 1195
12:10 the royal secretary and the **h** priest came, 1524
14: 4 The **h places,** however, were not removed; 1195
15: 4 The **h places,** however, were not removed; 1195
15:35 The **h places,** however, were not removed; 1195
16: 4 and burned incense at the **h places,** 1195
17: 9 fortified city they built themselves **h places** 1195
17:10 and Asherah poles on every **h** hill and 1469
17:11 At every **h place** they burned incense, 1195
17:29 of Samaria had made at the **h places.** 1195
17:32 as priests in the shrines at the **h places.** 1195
18: 4 He removed the **h places,** 1195
18:22 isn't he the one whose **h places** 1195
21: 3 **h places** his father Hezekiah had destroyed; 1195
22: 4 the **h** priest and have him get ready 1524
22: 8 the **h** priest said to Shaphan the secretary, 1524
23: 4 The king ordered Hilkiah the **h** priest, 1524
23: 5 of Judah to burn incense on the **h places** of 1195
23: 8 of Judah and desecrated the **h places,** 1195
23: 9 of the **h places** did not serve at the altar of 1195
23:13 the **h places** that were east of Jerusalem on 1195
23:15 the **h place** made by Jeroboam son 1195
23:15 even that altar and **h place** he demolished. 1195
23:15 the **h place** and ground it to powder, 1195
23:19 and defiled all the shrines at the **h places** 1195
23:20 the priests of those **h places** on the altars 1195
25:17 Each pillar was twenty-seven feet **h.** 7757
25:17 and a half feet **h** and was decorated with 7757
1Ch 16:39 the tabernacle of the LORD at the **h place** 1195
21:29 at that time on the **h place** at Gibeon. 1195
2Ch 1: 3 the whole assembly went to the **h place** 1195
1:13 to Jerusalem from the **h place** at Gibeon, 1195
3: 4 of the building and twenty cubits **h.** 1470
4: 1 twenty cubits wide and ten cubits **h.** 7757
4: 2 from rim to rim and five cubits **h.** 7757
6:13 five cubits wide and three cubits **h,** 7757
11:15 for the **h places** and for the goat 1195
14: 3 the foreign altars and the **h places,** 1195
14: 5 He removed the **h places** and incense altars 1195
15:17 Although he did not remove the **h places** 1195
17: 6 furthermore, he removed the **h places** and 1195
20:33 The **h places,** however, were not removed, 1195
21:11 also built **h places** on the hills of Judah 1195
2Ch 28: 4 and burned incense at the **h places,** 1195
28:25 in Judah he built **h places** to burn sacrifices 1195
31: 1 They destroyed the **h places** and the altars 1195
32:12 Hezekiah himself remove this god's **h places** and altars, 1195
33: 3 rebuilt the **h places** his father Hezekiah had demolished; 1195
33:17 continued to sacrifice at the **h places,** 1195
33:19 the sites where he built **h places** and set 1195
34: 3 to purge Judah and Jerusalem of **h places,** 1195
34: 9 the **h** priest and gave him the money 1524
Ezr 6: 3 It is to be ninety feet **h** and ninety feet wide, 10660
Ne 3: 1 the **h** priest and his fellow priests went 1524
3:20 of the house of Eliashib the **h** priest. 1524
8: 4 on a **h** wooden **platform** built for 4463
13:28 the **h** priest was son-in-law to Sanballat 1524
Est 1:10 Xerxes *was* **in h spirits** from wine, 3201+4213
5: 9 that day happy and **in h spirits.** 3201+4213
5:14 "Have a gallows built, seventy-five feet **h,** 1469
7: 9 "A gallows seventy-five feet **h** stands 1469
10: 3 **held in h esteem** by his many fellow Jews, 8354
Job 5:11 The lowly he sets **on h,** 5294
10:16 If I **hold** my **head h,** 1448
16:19 my advocate is **on h.** 928+2021+5294
31: 2 his heritage from the Almighty **on h?** 4946+5294
31:28 I would have been unfaithful to God **on h.** 4946+5087
35: 5 gaze at the clouds *so* **h** above you. 1467
39:27 and **build** his nest **on h?** 8123
Ps 7: 7 Rule over them from **on h;** 2021+5294
7: 8 according to my integrity, O **Most H.** 6604
7:10 My shield is God **Most H,** 6583
7:17 to the name of the LORD **Most H.** 6610
9: 2 I will sing praise to your name, O **Most H.** 6610
18:13 the voice of the **Most H** resounded. 6610
18:16 He reached down from **on h** and took hold 5294
21: 7 the unfailing love of the **Most H** he will not 6610
27: 5 in the shelter of his tabernacle and set me **h** 8123
36: 7 Both **h** and low among men find refuge in 466
46: 4 the holy place where the **Most H** dwells. 6610
47: 2 How awesome is the LORD **Most H,** 6610
49: 2 both low and **h,** rich and poor alike: 408+1201
50:14 fulfill your vows to the **Most H,** 6610
57: 2 I cry out to God **Most H,** to God, 6610
68:18 When you ascended **on h,** 2021+4200+5294
73:11 Does the **Most H** have knowledge?" 6610
77:10 the years of the right hand of the **Most H."** 6610
78:17 rebelling in the desert against the **Most H.** 6610
78:35 that God **Most H** was their Redeemer. 6610
78:56 to the test and rebelled against the **Most H;** 6610
78:58 They angered him with their **h places;** 1195
82: 6 you are all sons of the **Most H.'** 6610
83:18 you alone are the **Most H** over all the earth. 6610
87: 5 and the **Most H** himself will establish her." 6610
91: 1 of the **Most H** will rest in the shadow of 6610
91: 9 If you make the **Most H** your dwelling— 6610
92: 1 and make music to your name, O **Most H,** 6610
93: 4 the LORD **on h** is mighty. 928+2021+5294
97: 9 O LORD, are the **Most H** over all the earth; 6610
102:19 down from his sanctuary **on h,** 5294
103:11 For as **h** as the heavens are above the earth, 1469
104:18 The **h** mountains belong to the wild goats; 1469
107:11 and despised the counsel of the **Most H.** 6610
107:25 and stirred up a tempest that **lifted h** 8123
112: 9 his horn *will be* **lifted h** in honor. 8123
113: 5 the *One who* sits enthroned *on* **h,** 1467
118:16 The LORD's right hand *is* **lifted h;** 8123
138: 6 Though the LORD *is on* **h,** 8123
144: 7 Reach down your hand from **on h;** 5294
Pr 17:19 *he who* **builds** a **h** gate invites destruction. 1467
23:34 You will be like one sleeping on the **h seas,** 3542+4213
24: 7 Wisdom *is too* **h** for a fool; 8123
25: 3 As the heavens are **h** and the earth is deep, 8124
30:19 the way of a ship on the **h seas,** 3542+4213
Ecc 10: 6 Fools are put in many **h positions,** 5294
Isa 2:14 the towering mountains and all the **h** hills, 5951
6: 1 **h** and exalted, and the train of his robe filled 8123
14:14 I will make myself like the **Most H."** 6610
15: 2 to its **h places** to weep; 1195
16: 3 Make your shadow like night—at **h noon.** 7416
16:12 When Moab appears at her **h place,** 1195
25:12 He will bring down your **h** fortified walls 5369
26: 5 He humbles those who dwell **on h,** 5294
26:11 O LORD, your hand *is* **lifted h,** 8123
30:13 this sin will become for you like a **h** wall, 8435
30:25 on every **h** mountain and every lofty hill. 1469
32:15 till the Spirit is poured upon us from **on h,** 5294
33: 5 The LORD is exalted, for he dwells **on h;** 5294
36: 7 isn't he the one whose **h places** 1195
40: 9 go up on a **h** mountain. 1469
57: 7 You have made your bed on a **h** 1469
57:15 For this is what the **h** and lofty One says— 8123
57:15 "I live in a **h** and holy place, 5294
58: 4 your voice to be heard **on h.** 928+2021+5294
Jer 2:20 on every **h** hill and under every spreading 1469
3: 6 She has gone up on every **h** hill and 1469
7:31 They have built the **h** places *of* Topheth in 1195
16: 6 "Both **h** and low will die in this land. 1524
17: 2 beside the spreading trees and on the **h** hills. 1469
17: 3 together with your **h places,** 1195
19: 5 the **h places** *of* Baal to burn their sons in 1195
25:30 " 'The LORD will roar from **on h;** 5294
32:35 They built **h places** *for* Baal in the Valley 1195
39: 3 a chief officer, Nergal-Sharezer a **h** official 8042
39:13 a **h** official and all the other officers of 8042
48:35 on the **h places** and burn incense 1195
Jer 49:16 **build** your nest as **h** as the eagle's, 1467
51: 9 *it* **rises** as **h** as the clouds.' 5951
51:58 be leveled and her **h** gates set on fire; 1469
52:21 Each of the pillars was eighteen cubits **h** 7757
52:22 on top of the one pillar was five cubits **h** 7757
La 1:13 "From **on h** he sent fire, 5294
3:35 to deny a man his rights before the **Most H,** 6610
3:38 from the mouth of the **Most H** that both calamities and good 6610
Eze 1:18 Their rims were **h** and awesome, 1470
1:26 and **h above** on the throne was a figure like that of a man. 2025+4200+4946+5087
6: 3 and I will destroy your **h places.** 1195
6: 6 be laid waste and the **h places** demolished, 1195
6:13 on every **h** hill and on all the mountaintops, 8123
16:16 of your garments to make gaudy **h places,** 1195
17:22 from its topmost shoots and plant it on a **h** 1469
19:11 It towered **h** above the thick foliage, 7757
20:28 and they saw any **h** hill or any leafy tree, 8123
20:29 What is this **h place** you go to?' " 1195
20:40 the **h** mountain of Israel, 5294
23:23 chariot officers and **men of h rank,** 7924
24: 9 I, too, *will* **pile** the wood **h.** 1540
27: 4 Your domain was on the **h seas;** 3542+4213
27:26 Your oarsmen take you out to the **h** seas. 8041
31: 3 it towered **on h,** its top above the thick 7757
31:10 Because it towered **on h,** 928+7757
31:14 are ever to tower proudly **on h,** 928+7757
34: 6 over all the mountains and on every **h** hill. 8123
40: 2 of Israel and set me on a very **h** mountain, 1469
40: 5 rod thick and one rod **h.** 7757
40:12 of each alcove was a wall one cubit **h,** NIH
40:42 a cubit and a half wide and a cubit **h.** 1470
41:22 There was a wooden altar three cubits **h** 1469
43: 7 of their kings at their **h places.** 1195
43:14 up to the lower ledge it is two cubits **h** and NIH
43:14 up to the larger ledge it is four cubits **h** and NIH
43:15 The altar hearth is four cubits **h,** NIH
Da 2:48 the king **placed** Daniel **in a h position** 10648
3: 1 ninety feet **h** and nine feet wide, 10660
3:26 servants of the **Most H** God, come out! 10546
4: 2 that the **Most H** God has performed for me. 10546
4:17 the **Most H** is sovereign over the kingdoms 10546
4:24 and this is the decree the **Most H** has issued 10546
4:25 the **Most H** is sovereign over the kingdoms 10546
4:32 the **Most H** is sovereign over the kingdoms 10546
4:34 Then I praised the **Most H;** 10546
5:18 the **Most H** God gave your father Nebuchadnezzar sovereignty 10546
5:19 Because of the **h position** he gave him, 10650
5:21 that the **Most H** God is sovereign over 10546
7:18 But the saints of the **Most H** will receive 10548
7:22 in favor of the saints of the **Most H,** 10548
7:25 against the **Most H** and oppress his saints 10546
7:27 the people of the **Most H.** 10548
Hos 7:16 They do not turn to the **Most H;** 6583
10: 8 The **h places** *of* wickedness will 1195
11: 7 Even if they call to the **Most H,** 6583
Am 4:13 and treads the **h places** *of* the earth— 1195
7: 9 "The **h places** *of* Isaac will be destroyed 1195
Mic 1: 3 he comes down and treads the **h places** *of* 1195
1: 5 What is Judah's **h place?** 1195
Hab 2: 9 by unjust gain to set his nest **on h,** 5294
3:10 the deep roared and lifted its waves *on* **h.** 8125
Hag 1: 1 to Joshua son of Jehozadak, the **h** priest: 1524
1:12 Joshua son of Jehozadak, the **h** priest, 1524
1:14 of Jehozadak, the **h** priest, and the spirit of 1524
2: 2 to Joshua son of Jehozadak, the **h** priest, 1524
2: 4 O Joshua son of Jehozadak, the **h** priest. 1524
Zec 3: 1 the **h** priest standing before the angel of 1524
3: 8 O **h** priest Joshua and your associates seated 1524
6:11 and set it on the head of the **h** priest, 1524
Mt 4: 8 to a very **h** mountain and showed him all *5734*
17: 1 led them up a **h** mountain by themselves. *5734*
20:25 and their **h officials** exercise authority *3489*
26: 3 in the palace *of* the **h priest,** *797*
26: 9 a **h** *price* and the money given to the poor." *4498*
26:51 and struck the servant *of* the **h priest,** *797*
26:57 to Caiaphas, the **h priest,** where the teachers *797*
26:58 right up to the courtyard *of* the **h priest.** *797*
26:62 Then the **h priest** stood up and said to Jesus, *797*
26:63 The **h priest** said to him, *797*
26:65 Then the **h priest** tore his clothes and said, *797*
Mk 2:26 In the days of Abiathar the **h priest,** *797*
5: 7 Jesus, Son *of* the **Most H** God? *5736*
6:21 a banquet *for* his **h officials** *3491*
9: 2 with him and led them up a **h** mountain, *5734*
10:42 and their **h officials** exercise authority *3489*
14:47 and struck the servant *of* the **h priest,** *797*
14:53 They took Jesus to the **h priest,** *797*
14:54 right into the courtyard *of* the **h priest.** *797*
14:60 Then the **h priest** stood up before them *797*
14:61 Again the **h priest** asked him, *797*
14:63 The **h priest** tore his clothes. *797*
14:66 of the servant girls *of* the **h priest** came by. *797*
Lk 1:32 and will be called the Son *of* the **Most H.** *5736*
1:35 power *of* the **Most H** will overshadow you. *5736*
1:76 will be called a prophet *of* the **Most H;** *5736*
3: 2 the **h priesthood** of Annas and Caiaphas, *797*
4: 5 a **h** place and showed him in an instant all *5734*
4:38 was suffering *from* a **h** fever, *3489*
6:35 and you will be sons *of* the **Most H,** *5736*
8:28 Jesus, Son *of* the **Most H** God? *5736*
22:50 of them struck the servant *of* the **h priest,** *797*
22:54 and took him into the house *of* the **h priest.** *797*
24:49 with power from **on h."** *5737*
Jn 11:49 Caiaphas, who was **h priest** that year, *797*

Jn 11:51 but as **h priest** that year he prophesied 797
18:10 drew it and struck the **h priest's** servant, 797
18:13 Caiaphas, the **h priest** that year. 797
18:15 this disciple was known *to* the **h priest,** 797
18:15 with Jesus into the **h priest's** courtyard, 797
18:16 who was known *to* the **h priest,** came back, 797
18:19 the **h priest** questioned Jesus 797
18:22 "Is this the way you answer the **h priest?"** 797
18:24 still bound, to Caiaphas the **h priest.** 797
18:26 One of the **h priest's** servants, 797
Ac 4: 6 Annas the **h priest** was there, 797
4: 6 and the other men of the **h priest's** family. 796
5:17 Then the **h priest** and all his associates, 797
5:21 the **h priest** and his associates arrived, 797
5:27 to be questioned by the **h priest.** 797
7: 1 Then the **h priest** asked him, 797
7:48 the **Most H** does not live in houses made 5736
8:10 all the people, both **h** and low, 3489
9: 1 He went to the **h priest** 797
13:50 the God-fearing women of **h standing** and 2363
16:17 servants *of* the **Most H** God, 5736
19:17 the name of the Lord Jesus *was* **held in h honor.** 3486
22: 5 the **h priest** and all the Council can testify. 797
23: 2 the **h priest** Ananias ordered those standing 797
23: 4 "You dare to insult God's **h priest?"** 797
23: 5 I did not realize that he was the **h priest;** 797
24: 1 the **h priest** Ananias went down to Caesarea 797
25:23 the **h ranking officers** and the leading men 5941
Eph 3:18 how wide and long and **h** and deep is 5737
4: 8 "When he ascended on **h,** 5737
Heb 2:17 a merciful and faithful **h priest** in service 797
3: 1 the apostle and **h priest** whom we confess. 797
4:14 since we have a great **h priest** who has gone 797
4:15 For we do not have a **h priest** who is unable 797
5: 1 Every **h priest** is selected from among men 797
5: 5 the glory of becoming a **h priest.** 797
5:10 and was designated by God to be **h priest** in 797
6:20 He has become a **h priest** forever, 797
7: 1 of Salem and priest of God **Most H.** 5736
7:26 Such a **h priest** meets our need— 797
7:27 Unlike the other **h priests,** 797
7:28 as **h priests** men who are weak; 797
8: 1 We do have such a **h priest,** 797
8: 3 Every **h priest** is appointed to offer 797
9: 7 only the **h priest** entered the inner room, 797
9:11 When Christ came as **h priest** of 797
9:25 the way the **h priest** enters 797
13:11 The **h priest** carries the blood of animals 797
Jas 1: 9 to take pride in his **h position.** 5737
Rev 14:20 rising **as h as** the horses' bridles for 948
21:10 in the Spirit to a mountain great and **h,** 5734
21:12 It had a great, **h** wall with twelve gates, 5734
21:16 and as wide and **h** as it is long. 5737

HIGH-GRADE (2) [HIGH]

1Ki 7: 9 of blocks of **h** stone cut to size and trimmed 3701
7:11 Above were **h** stones, cut to size, 3701

HIGHBORN (1) [BEAR, HIGH]

Ps 62: 9 the **h** are but a lie; 408+1201

HIGHER (16) [HIGH]

Dt 28:43 among you will rise above you **h** 2025+5087
28:43 above you higher and **h,** 2025+5087
2Ki 25:28 gave him a seat of honor **h than** those 4946+6584
2Ch 33:14 *he* also **made** it much **h.** 1467
Ezr 9: 6 because our sins *are* **h than** our heads 2025+4200+5087+8049
Est 3: 1 seat of honor **h than** that of all the other nobles. 4946+6584
Job 11: 8 They are **h** *than* the heavens— 1470
Ps 61: 2 lead me to the rock *that is* **h** than I. 8123
108: 4 For great is your love, **h than** the heavens; 4946+6584
Ecc 5: 8 for one official is eyed by a **h** one, 4946+6584
5: 8 **over** them both are others **h** 6584
Isa 55: 9 "As the heavens *are* **h** than the earth, 1467
55: 9 so *are* my ways **h** than your ways 1467
Jer 52:32 gave him a seat of honor **h** than those 4946+5087
Eze 31: 5 So it towered **h** than all the trees of 7757
Eph 4:10 the very one who ascended **h** than all 5645

HIGHEST (25) [HIGH]

Dt 10:14 even the **h heavens,** 9028+9028
1Ki 8:27 The heavens, even the **h heaven,** 9028+9028
2Ch 2: 6 the **h heavens,** cannot contain him? 9028+9028
6:18 The heavens, even the **h heavens,** 9028+9028
Ne 9: 6 You made the heavens, even the **h heavens,** 9028+9028
Est 1:14 to the king and were **h** in the kingdom. 8037
Job 21:22 since he judges even the **h?** 8123
22:12 And see how lofty are the **h** stars! 8031
Ps 115:16 The **h heavens** belong to the LORD, 9028+9028
137: 6 I do not consider Jerusalem my **h** joy. 6584+8031
148: 4 you **h heavens** and you waters above 9028+9028
Pr 9: 3 she calls from the **h point** *of* the city. 1726+5294
9:14 on a seat at the **h point** *of* the city, 5294
Isa 7:11 in the deepest depths or in the **h** heights." 1467
Da 5: 7 be made the **third h** ruler in the kingdom." 10761
5:16 be made the **third h** ruler in the kingdom." 10761
5:29 and he was proclaimed the **third h** ruler in 10761
Mt 4: 5 had him stand on the **h point** of the temple. 4762
21: 9 "Hosanna in the **h!"** 5736
Mk 11:10 "Hosanna in the **h!"** 5736
Lk 2:14 "Glory to God in the **h,** 5736
4: 9 had him stand on the **h point** of the temple. 4762
19:38 "Peace in heaven and glory in the **h!"** 5736
Php 2: 9 God **exalted** him **to the h place** 5671
1Th 5:13 Hold them *in* the **h regard** in love because 5655

HIGHLY (23) [HIGH]

Ex 11: 3 and Moses himself was **h regarded** in Egypt 1524+4394
15: 1 sing to the LORD, for *he is* **h exalted.** 1448+1448
15:21 "Sing to the LORD, for *he is* **h exalted.** 1448+1448
Jdg 5:30 **h embroidered** garments for my neck— 8391
1Sa 9: 6 he *is* **h respected,** 3877
22:14 captain of your bodyguard and **h respected** 3877
2Sa 14:25 In all Israel there was not a man **so h** praised 4394
1Ki 7:14 Huram *was* **h** skilled and experienced 4848
2Ki 5: 1 sight of his master and **h regarded,** 5951+7156
1Ch 14: 2 his kingdom had been **h** exalted 2025+4200+5087
29:25 The LORD **h** exalted Solomon 2025+4200+5087
2Ch 32:23 *he* **was h regarded** by all the nations. 5951
Isa 32: 5 nor the scoundrel be **h respected.** 8777
52:13 he will be raised and lifted up and **h** exalted. 4394
Da 9:23 for you are **h esteemed.** 2776
10:11 He said, "Daniel, you who are **h esteemed,** 2776
10:19 "Do not be afraid, O man **h esteemed,"** 2776
Lk 1:28 "Greetings, *you* who *are* **h favored!** 5923
7: 2 whom his master **valued h,** 1639+1952
16:15 is **h valued** among men is detestable 3836+5734
Ac 5:13 though they *were* **h regarded** by the people. 3486
22:12 and **h** respected by all the Jews living there. NIG
Ro 12: 3 *Do* not **think** of yourself more **h** than 5672

HIGHMINDED (KJV) See ARROGANT, CONCEITED

HIGHWAY (11) [HIGHWAYS]

Nu 20:17 along the king's **h** and not turn to the right 2006
21:22 along the king's **h** until we have passed 2006
Pr 7:27 Her house is a **h** *to* the grave, 2006
15:19 but the path of the upright **is a h.** 6148
16:17 The **h** *of* the upright avoids evil; 5019
Isa 11:16 a **h** for the remnant of his people that is left 5019
19:23 In that day there will be a **h** from Egypt 5019
35: 8 And a **h** will be there; 5020
40: 3 make straight in the wilderness a **h** 5019
62:10 Build up, build up the **h!** 5019
Jer 31:21 Take note of the **h,** the road that you take. 5019

HIGHWAYS (2) [HIGHWAY]

Isa 33: 8 **h** are deserted, no travelers are on the roads. 5019
49:11 and my **h** will be raised up. 5019

HILEN (1)

1Ch 6:58 **H,** Debir, 2664

HILKIAH (31) [HILKIAH'S]

2Ki 18:18 Eliakim son of **H** the palace administrator, 2760
18:26 Then Eliakim son of **H,** 2760
18:37 Eliakim son of **H** the palace administrator, 2759
22: 4 to **H** the high priest and have him get ready 2760
22: 8 **H** the high priest said to Shaphan 2760
22:10 **"H** the priest has given me a book." 2759
22:12 He gave these orders to **H** the priest, 2759
22:14 **H** the priest, Ahikam, Acbor, 2760
23: 4 The king ordered **H** the high priest, 2760
23:24 the book that **H** the priest had discovered in 2760
1Ch 6:13 Shallum the father of **H,** 2759
6:13 **H** the father of Azariah, 2759
6:45 the son of Amaziah, the son of **H,** 2759
9:11 Azariah son of **H,** the son of Meshullam, 2759
26:11 **H** the second, Tabaliah the third 2760
2Ch 34: 9 They went to **H** the high priest and gave 2760
34:14 **H** the priest found the Book of the Law of 2760
34:15 **H** said to Shaphan the secretary, 2760
34:18 **"H** the priest has given me a book." 2760
34:20 He gave these orders to **H,** 2760
34:22 **H** and those the king had sent with him 2760
35: 8 **H,** Zechariah and Jehiel, 2759
Ezr 7: 1 the son of Azariah, the son of **H,** 2759
Ne 8: 4 Shema, Anaiah, Uriah, **H** and Maaseiah; 2759
11:11 Seraiah son of **H,** 2759
12: 7 **H** and Jedaiah. These were the leaders of 2759
Isa 22:20 Eliakim son of **H.** 2760
36: 3 Eliakim son of **H** the palace administrator, 2760
36:22 Eliakim son of **H** the palace administrator, 2760
Jer 1: 1 The words of Jeremiah son of **H,** 2760
29: 3 of Shaphan and to Gemariah son of **H,** 2759

HILKIAH'S (1) [HILKIAH]

Ne 12:21 of **H,** Hashabiah; of Jedaiah's, Nethanel. 2759

HILL (157) [FOOTHILLS, HILLS, HILLSIDE, HILLTOP, HILLTOPS]

Ge 10:30 in the eastern **h country.** 2215
14: 6 and the Horites in the **h country** *of* Seir, 2215
31:21 he headed for the **h country** *of* Gilead. 2215
31:23 and caught up with him in the **h country** 2215
31:25 Jacob had pitched his tent in the **h country** 2215
31:54 He offered a sacrifice there in the **h country** 2215
36: 8 Edom) settled in the **h country** *of* Seir. 2215
36: 9 the father of the Edomites in the **h country** 2215
Ex 17: 9 of the **h** with the staff of God in my hands." 1496
17:10 Aaron and Hur went to the top of the **h.** 1496
Nu 13:17 the Negev and on into the **h country.** 2215
13:29 and Amorites live in the **h country;** 2215
14:40 up toward the high **h country.** 2215
14:44 up toward the high **h country,** 2215
14:45 in that **h country** came down 2215
Dt 1: 7 Break camp and advance into the **h country** 2215
1:19 from Horeb and went toward the **h country** 2215
1:20 "You have reached the **h country** *of* 2215
1:24 They left and went up into the **h country,** 2215
1:41 thinking it easy to go up into the **h country.** 2215
1:43 up into the **h country.** 2215
2: 1 around the **h country** *of* Seir. 2215
2: 3 around this **h country** long enough; 2215
2: 5 I have given Esau the **h country** *of* Seir 2215
3:12 including half the **h country** *of* Gilead, 2215
3:25 that fine **h country** and Lebanon." 2215
Jos 9: 1 those in the **h country,** 2215
10: 6 from the **h country** have joined forces 2215
10:40 including the **h country,** the Negev, 2215
11: 3 Perizzites and Jebusites in the **h country;** 2215
11:16 the **h country,** all the Negev, 2215
11:21 the Anakites from the **h country:** 2215
11:21 from all the **h country** *of* Judah, 2215
11:21 and from all the **h country** *of* Israel. 2215
12: 8 the **h country,** the western foothills, 2215
13:19 Zereth Shahar on the **h** *in* the valley, 2215
14:12 Now give me this **h country** that 2215
15: 8 the top of the **h** west of the Hinnom Valley 2215
15:48 In the **h country:** Shamir, Jattir, Socoh, 2215
16: 1 the desert into the **h country** *of* Bethel. 2215
17:15 if the **h country** *of* Ephraim is too small 2215
17:16 "The **h country** is not enough for us, 2215
17:18 but the forested **h country** as well. 2215
18:12 and headed west into the **h country,** 2215
18:13 down to Ataroth Addar on the **h** south 2215
18:14 From the **h** facing Beth Horon on the south 2215
18:16 down to the foot of the **h** facing the Valley 2215
19:50 Timnath Serah in the **h country** 2215
20: 7 in Galilee in the **h country** *of* Naphtali, 2215
20: 7 Shechem in the **h country** *of* Ephraim, 2215
20: 7 Hebron) in the **h country** *of* Judah. 2215
21:11 in the **h country** *of* Judah. 2215
21:21 In the **h country** *of* Ephraim 2215
24: 4 I assigned the **h country** *of* Seir to Esau, 2215
24:30 at Timnath Serah in the **h country** 2215
24:33 to his son Phinehas in the **h country** 2215
Jdg 1: 9 the Canaanites living in the **h country,** 2215
1:19 They took possession of the **h country,** 2215
1:34 the Danites to the **h country,** 2215
2: 9 at Timnath Heres in the **h country** 2215
3:27 a trumpet in the **h country** *of* Ephraim, 2215
4: 5 and Bethel in the **h country** *of* Ephraim, 2215
7: 1 of them in the valley near the **h** *of* Moreh. 1496
7:24 throughout the **h country** *of* Ephraim, 2215
10: 1 in the **h country** *of* Ephraim. 2215
12:15 in the **h country** *of* the Amalekites. 2215
16: 3 to the top of the **h** that faces Hebron. 2215
17: 1 a man named Micah from the **h country** 2215
17: 8 to Micah's house in the **h country** 2215
18: 2 The men entered the **h country** *of* Ephraim 2215
18:13 on to the **h country** *of* Ephraim and came 2215
19: 1 the **h country** *of* Ephraim took a concubine 2215
19:16 an old man from the **h country** *of* Ephraim, 2215
19:18 a remote area in the **h country** *of* Ephraim 2215
1Sa 1: 1 a Zuphite from the **h country** *of* Ephraim, 2215
7: 1 They took it to Abinadab's house on the **h** 1496
9: 4 the **h country** *of* Ephraim and through 2215
9:11 As they were going up the **h** *to* the town, 5090
13: 2 at Micmash and in the **h country** *of* Bethel, 2215
14:22 in the **h country** *of* Ephraim heard that 2215
17: 3 The Philistines occupied one **h** and 2215
22: 6 was seated under the tamarisk tree on the **h** 8229
23:19 on the **h** *of* Hakilah, south of Jeshimon? 1496
26: 1 "Is not David hiding on the **h** *of* Hakilah, 1496
26: 3 on the **h** *of* Hakilah facing Jeshimon, 1496
26:13 on top of the **h** some distance away; 2215
2Sa 2:24 they came to the **h** *of* Ammah, 1496
2:25 a group and took their stand on top of a **h.** 1496
6: 3 house of Abinadab, which was on the **h.** 1496
13:34 coming down the side of the **h.** 2215
13:34 on the side of the **h."** 2215
20:21 from the **h country** *of* Ephraim, 2215
21: 9 who killed and exposed them on a **h** before 2215
1Ki 4: 8 in the **h country** *of* Ephraim; 2215
11: 7 On a **h** east of Jerusalem, 2215
12:25 the **h country** *of* Ephraim and lived there. 2215
14:23 and Asherah poles on every high **h** and 1496
16:24 He bought the **h** *of* Samaria from Shemer 2215
16:24 of silver and built a city on the **h,** 2215
16:24 the name of the former owner of the **h.** 2215
2Ki 1: 9 who was sitting on the top of a **h,** 2215
5:22 to me from the **h country** *of* Ephraim. 2215
5:24 When Gehazi came to the **h,** 6755
17:10 and Asherah poles on every high **h** and 1496
23:13 on the south of the **H** *of* Corruption— 2215
1Ch 4:42 invaded the **h country** *of* Seir. 2215
6:67 In the **h country** *of* Ephraim 2215
2Ch 13: 4 in the **h country** *of* Ephraim, and said, 2215
19: 4 the people from Beersheba to the **h country** 2215
27: 3 on the wall at the **h of Ophel.** 6755
32:33 and was buried on the **h** *where* the tombs 5090
33:14 and encircling the **h of Ophel;** 6755
33:15 as all the altars he had built on the temple **h** 2215

Ne 3:26 on the **h of Ophel** made repairs up to 6755
8:15 into the **h country** and bring back branches 2215
11:21 temple servants lived on the **h of Ophel,** 6755
Ps 2: 6 on Zion, my holy **h."** 2215
3: 4 and he answers me from his holy **h.** 2215
15: 1 Who may live on your holy **h?** 2215
24: 3 Who may ascend the **h** *of* the LORD? 2215
78:54 to the **h country** his right hand had taken. 2215
SS 4: 6 mountain of myrrh and to the **h** of incense. 1496
Isa 10:32 at the **h** *of* Jerusalem. 1496
30:17 like a banner on a **h."** 1496
30:25 on every high mountain and every lofty **h.** 1496
40: 4 every mountain and **h** made low; 1496
49: 9 and find pasture on every **barren h.** 9155
57: 7 on a high and lofty **h;** 2215
Jer 2:20 on every high **h** and under every spreading 1496
3: 6 She has gone up on every high **h** and 2215
16:16 down on every mountain and **h** and from 1496
17:26 from the **h country** and the Negev, 2215
26:18 of rubble, the temple **h** a mound overgrown 2215
31:39 from there straight to the **h** *of* Gareb and 1496
32:44 of Judah and in the towns of the **h country,** 2215
33:13 In the towns of the **h country,** 2215
49:16 who occupy the heights of the **h.** 1496
50: 6 and **h** and forgot their own resting place. 1496
Eze 6:13 on every high **h** and on all 1496
20:28 and they saw any high **h** or any leafy tree, 1496
34: 6 over all the mountains and on every high **h.** 1496
34:26 and the places surrounding my **h.** 1496
Da 9:16 from Jerusalem, your city, your holy **h.** 2215
9:20 to the LORD my God for his holy **h**— 2215
Joel 2: 1 sound the alarm on my holy **h.** 2215
3:17 dwell in Zion, my holy **h.** 2215
Ob 1:16 Just as you drank on my holy **h,** 2215
Mic 3:12 the temple **h** a mound overgrown 2215
Zep 3:11 be haughty on my holy **h.** 2215
Mt 5:14 A city on a **h** cannot be hidden. *4001*
Lk 1:39 and hurried to a town in the **h country** *3978*
1:65 and throughout the **h country** of Judea *3978*
3: 5 every mountain and **h** made low. *1090*
4:29 and took him to the brow *of* the **h** on which *4001*
19:29 at the **h** called the Mount of Olives, *4001*
21:37 night on the **h** called the Mount of Olives, *4001*
Ac 1:12 from the **h** called the Mount of Olives, *4001*

HILLEL (2)

Jdg 12:13 After him, Abdon son of **H,** from Pirathon, 2148
12:15 Then Abdon son of **H** died, 2148

HILLS (80) [HILL]

Ge 12: 8 From there he went on toward the **h** east 2215
14:10 into them and the rest fled to the **h.** 2215
49:26 than the bounty of the age-old **h.** 1496
Dt 1:44 in those **h** came out against you; 2215
2:37 nor that around the towns in the **h.** 2215
8: 7 with springs flowing in the valleys and **h;** 2215
8: 9 and you can dig copper out of the **h.** 2215
12: 2 and on the **h** and under every spreading tree 1496
33:15 and the fruitfulness of the everlasting **h;** 1496
Jos 2:16 to the **h** so the pursuers will not find you. 2215
2:22 into the **h** and stayed there three days, 2215
2:23 They went down out of the **h,** 2215
Jdg 3:27 Israelites went down with him from the **h,** 2215
11:37 to roam the **h** and weep with my friends, 2215
11:38 She and the girls went into the **h** and wept 2215
1Sa 23:14 in the desert strongholds and in the **h** of 2215
1Ki 5:15 and eighty thousand stonecutters in the **h,** 2215
20:23 "Their gods are gods of the **h.** 2215
20:28 a god of the **h** and not a god of the valleys, 2215
22:17 on the **h** like sheep without a shepherd, 2215
2Ki 6:17 and he looked and saw the **h** full of horses 2215
2Ch 2: 2 and eighty thousand as stonecutters in the **h** 2215
2:18 to be stonecutters in the **h,** with 3,600 2215
15: 8 and from the towns he had captured in the **h** 2215
18:16 on the **h** like sheep without a shepherd, 2215
21:11 the **h** of Judah and had caused the people 2215
26:10 in the **h** and in the fertile lands, 2215
27: 4 He built towns in the Judean **h** and forts 2215
Job 15: 7 Were you brought forth before the **h?** 1496
39: 8 He ranges the **h** for his pasture and searches 2215
40:20 The **h** bring him their produce, 2215
Ps 50:10 and the cattle on a thousand **h.** 2215
65:12 the **h** are clothed with gladness. 1496
72: 3 the **h** the fruit of righteousness. 1496
72:16 on the tops of the **h** may it sway 2215
114: 4 the **h** like lambs. 1496
114: 6 that you skipped like rams, you **h,** 1496
121: 1 I lift up my eyes to the **h**— 2215
147: 8 with rain and makes grass grow on the **h.** 2215
148: 9 you mountains and all **h,** 1496
Pr 8:25 before the **h,** I was given birth, 1496
27:25 and the grass from the **h** is gathered in, 2215
SS 2: 8 bounding over the **h.** 1496
2:17 or like a young stag on the rugged **h.** 2215
Isa 2: 2 it will be raised above the **h,** 1496
2:14 the towering mountains and all the high **h,** 1496
7:25 As for all the **h** once cultivated by the hoe, 2215
17:13 driven before the wind like chaff on the **h,** 2215
40:12 the mountains on the scales and the **h** in 1496
41:15 and reduce the **h** to chaff. 1496
42:15 I will lay waste the mountains and **h** and dry 1496
54:10 mountains be shaken and the **h** be removed, 1496
55:12 the mountains and **h** will burst into song 1496
65: 7 on the mountains and defied me on the **h,** 1496
Jer 3:23 Surely the [idolatrous] commotion on the **h** 1496
4:15 proclaiming disaster from the **h** *of* Ephraim. 2215
4:24 all the **h** were swaying. 1496
13:16 your feet stumble on the darkening **h.** 2215
13:27 I have seen your detestable acts on the **h** 1496
17: 2 the spreading trees and on the high **h.** 1496
31: 5 Again you will plant vineyards on the **h** 2215
31: 6 be a day when watchmen cry out on the **h** 2215
50:19 his appetite will be satisfied on the **h** 2215
Eze 6: 3 to the mountains and **h,** to the ravines 1496
35: 8 those killed by the sword will fall on your **h** 1496
36: 4 to the mountains and **h,** to the ravines 1496
36: 6 of Israel and say to the mountains and **h,** to 1496
Hos 4:13 and burn offerings on the **h,** 1496
10: 8 and to the **h,** "Fall on us!" 1496
Joel 3:18 and the **h** will flow with milk; 1496
Am 9:13 from the mountains and flow from all the **h.** 1496
Mic 4: 1 it will be raised above the **h,** 1496
6: 1 let the **h** hear what you have to say. 1496
Na 1: 5 before him and the **h** melt away. 1496
Hab 3: 6 and the age-old **h** collapsed. 1496
Zep 1:10 and a loud crash from the **h.** 1496
Mt 18:12 the ninety-nine on the **h** and go to look for *4001*
Mk 5: 5 in the **h** he would cry out and cut himself *4001*
Lk 23:30 and *to* the **h,** "Cover us!" ' *1090*
Rev 17: 9 The seven heads are seven **h** on which *4001*

HILLSIDE (5) [HILL]

2Sa 16:13 along the **h** opposite him, 2215+7521
2Ki 23:16 he saw the tombs that were there on the **h,** 2215
Isa 5: 1 My loved one had a vineyard on a fertile **h.** 7967
Mk 5:11 of pigs was feeding on the nearby **h.** *4001*
Lk 8:32 of pigs was feeding there on the **h.** *4001*

HILLTOP (2) [HILL]

Jos 15: 9 From the **h** the boundary headed 2215+8031
Isa 13: 2 Raise a banner on a bare **h,** shout to them; 2215

HILLTOPS (3) [HILL]

Jdg 9:25 Shechem set men on the **h** to ambush 2215+8031
2Ki 16: 4 on the **h** and under every spreading tree. 1496
2Ch 28: 4 on the **h** and under every spreading tree. 1496

HIM (5427) [HE] See Index of Articles Etc.

HIMSELF (430) [HE, SELF] See Index of Articles Etc.

HIN (22)

Ex 29:40 a quarter of a **h** *of* oil from pressed olives, 2125
29:40 a quarter of a **h** *of* wine as a drink offering. 2125
30:24 and a **h** *of* olive oil. 2125
Lev 19:36 an honest ephah and an honest **h.** 2125
23:13 its drink offering of a quarter of a **h** of wine 2125
Nu 15: 4 of fine flour mixed with a quarter of a **h** 2125
15: 5 a quarter of a **h** *of* wine as a drink offering. 2125
15: 6 of fine flour mixed with a third of a **h** 2125
15: 7 a third of a **h** *of* wine as a drink offering. 2125
15: 9 of an ephah of fine flour mixed with half a **h** 2125
15:10 bring half a **h** *of* wine as a drink offering. 2125
28: 5 a quarter of a **h** *of* oil from pressed olives. 2125
28: 7 of a **h** of fermented drink with each lamb. 2125
28:14 to be a drink offering of half a **h** of wine; 2125
28:14 with the ram, a third of a **h;** 2125
28:14 and with each lamb, a quarter of a **h.** 2125
Eze 4:11 Also measure out a sixth of a **h** of water 2125
45:24 along with a **h** *of* oil for each ephah. 2125
46: 5 along with a **h** *of* oil for each ephah. 2125
46: 7 along with a **h** of oil with each ephah. 2125
46:11 along with a **h** of oil for each ephah. 2125
46:14 a sixth of an ephah with a third of a **h** of oil 2125

HIND (KJV) See DOE, MOUNTAIN GOAT

HINDER (7) [HINDERED, HINDERS, HINDRANCE]

1Sa 14: 6 Nothing can **h** the LORD *from* saving, 5109
Job 15: 4 even undermine piety and **h** devotion 1757
Mt 19:14 and *do* not **h** them, *3266*
Mk 10:14 and *do* not **h** them, *3266*
Lk 18:16 and *do* not **h** them, *3266*
1Co 9:12 put up with anything rather than **h** the gospel of Christ. *1443+1600*
1Pe 3: 7 so that nothing *will* **h** your prayers. *1601*

HINDERED (2) [HINDER]

Lk 11:52 and *you have* **h** those who were entering." *3266*
Ro 15:22 This is why *I have* often *been* **h from** *1601*

HINDERMOST (KJV) See IN THE REAR, LEAST

HINDERS (1) [HINDER]

Heb 12: 1 let us throw off everything that **h** and the sin *3839*

HINDMOST (KJV) See LAST, LAGGING BEHIND, REAR

HINDQUARTERS (2)

1Ki 7:25 and their **h** were toward the center. 294
2Ch 4: 4 and their **h** were toward the center. 294

HINDRANCE (1) [HINDER]

Ac 28:31 and **without h** he preached the kingdom *219*

HINGED (1) [HINGES]

Eze 41:24 two **h** leaves for each door. 6015

HINGES (1) [HINGED]

Pr 26:14 As a door turns on its **h,** 7494

HINNOM (3) [BEN HINNOM]

Jos 15: 8 to the top of the hill west of the **H** Valley at 2183
18:16 down the **H** Valley along the southern slope 2183
Ne 11:30 the way from Beersheba to the Valley of **H.** 2183

HINT (1)

Eph 5: 3 among you *there must* not *be* even **a h of** *3951*

HIP (5)

Ge 32:25 of Jacob's **h** so that his hip was wrenched 3751
32:25 that his **h** was wrenched as he wrestled with 3751
32:31 and he was limping because of his **h.** 3751
32:32 the tendon attached to the socket of the **h,** 3751
32:32 because the socket of Jacob's **h** was touched 3751

HIRAH (2)

Ge 38: 1 to stay with a man of Adullam named **H.** 2669
38:12 his friend **H** the Adullamite went with him. 2669

HIRAM (23) [HIRAM'S]

2Sa 5:11 **H** king of Tyre sent messengers to David, 2671
1Ki 5: 1 When **H** king of Tyre heard 2671
5: 2 Solomon sent back this message to **H:** 2671
5: 7 When **H** heard Solomon's message, 2671
5: 8 So **H** sent word to Solomon: 2671
5:10 In this way **H** kept Solomon supplied 2670
5:11 and Solomon gave **H** twenty thousand cors 2671
5:11 Solomon continued to do this for **H** year 2671
5:12 There were peaceful relations between **H** 2671
5:18 of Solomon and **H** and the men of Gebal cut 2670
9:11 in Galilee to **H** king of Tyre, 2671
9:11 because **H** had supplied him with all 2671
9:12 when **H** went from Tyre to see the towns 2671
9:14 **H** had sent to the king 120 talents of gold, 2671
9:27 And **H** sent his men— 2671
10:22 at sea along with the ships of **H.** 2671
1Ch 14: 1 **H** king of Tyre sent messengers to David, 2671
2Ch 2: 3 Solomon sent this message to **H** king 2586
2:11 **H** king of Tyre replied by letter to Solomon: 2586
2:12 And **H** added: "Praise be to the LORD, 2586
8: 2 the villages that **H** had given him, 2586
8:18 And **H** sent him ships commanded 2586
9:10 of **H** and the men of Solomon brought gold 2586

HIRAM'S (2) [HIRAM]

1Ki 10:11 (**H** ships brought gold from Ophir; 2671
2Ch 9:21 a fleet of trading ships manned by **H** men. 2586

HIRE (7) [HIRED, HIRES]

Ex 22:15 **money paid for** *the* **h** covers the loss. 8510
Jdg 9: 4 Abimelech used it *to* **h** reckless adventurers 8509
1Sa 2: 5 Those who were full **h themselves out** 8509
1Ch 19: 6 a thousand talents of silver to **h** chariots 8509
Isa 23:17 She will return to her **h as a prostitute** 924
46: 6 *they* **h** a goldsmith to make it into a god, 8509
Mt 20: 1 *to* **h** men to work in his vineyard. *3636*

HIRED (38) [HIRE]

Ge 30:16 *"I have* **h** you with my son's mandrakes." 8509+8509
Ex 12:45 a temporary resident and a **h worker** may 8502
22:15 If the animal was **h,** the money paid for 8502
Lev 19:13 hold back the wages of a **h man** overnight. 8502
22:10 the guest of a priest or his **h worker** eat it. 8502
25: 6 and maidservant, and the **h worker** 8502
25:40 as a **h worker** or a temporary resident 8502
25:50 on the rate paid to a **h man** for that number 8502
25:53 to be treated as a **man h** *from* year to year; 8502
Dt 15:18 as much as that of a **h hand.** 8502
23: 4 and *they* **h** Balaam son of Beor from Pethor 8509
24:14 not take advantage of a **h** *man* who is poor 8502
Jdg 18: 4 and said, *"He has* **h** me and I am his priest." 8509
2Sa 10: 6 **h** twenty thousand Aramean foot soldiers 8509
2Ki 7: 6 the king of Israel *has* **h** the Hittite 8509
1Ch 19: 7 *They* **h** thirty-two thousand chariots 8509
2Ch 24:12 *They* **h** masons and carpenters to restore 8509
25: 6 *He* also **h** a hundred thousand fighting men 8509
Ezr 4: 5 *They* **h** counselors to work against them 6128
Ne 6:12 because Tobiah and Sanballat *had* **h** him. 8509
6:13 He *had* **been h** to intimidate me so 8509
13: 2 but *had* **h** Balaam to call a curse down on 8509
Job 7: 1 Are not his days like those of a **h man?** 8502
7: 2 or a **h man** waiting eagerly for his wages, 8502
14: 6 till he has put in his time like a **h man.** 8502
Isa 7:20 In that day the Lord will use a razor **h** from 8502
Mt 20: 7 " 'Because no one *has* **h** us,' they answered. *3636*

Mt 20: 8 beginning with the last ones **h** and going on *NIG*
20: 9 "The workers who were **h** about *NIG*
20:10 So when those came who were **h** first, *NIG*
20:12 'These men who were **h** last worked only one hour,' *NIG*
20:14 to give the man who was **h** last the same *NIG*
Mk 1:20 Zebedee in the boat with the **h men** and *3638*
Lk 15:15 So *he* went and **h** *himself* **out to** a citizen *3140*
15:17 'How many of my father's **h men** have food *3634*
15:19 make me like one *of* your **h men.'** *3634*
Jn 10:12 The **h hand** is not the shepherd who owns *3638*
10:13 because he is a **h hand** and cares nothing for the sheep. *3638*

HIRELING (KJV) See HIRED, LABORERS, MAN, SERVANT

HIRES (1) [HIRE]
Pr 26:10 wounds at random is *he who* **h** a fool 8509

HIS (7165) [HE] See Index of Articles Etc.

HISS (2) [HISSES]
Jer 46:22 Egypt will **h** like a fleeing serpent as 7754
Eze 27:36 The merchants among the nations **h** at you; 9239

HISSES (1) [HISS]
Job 27:23 It claps its hands in derision and **h** him out 9239

HISTORIC (1) [HISTORY]
Ne 2:20 in Jerusalem or any claim or **h right** to it." 2355

HISTORY (1) [HISTORIC]
Ezr 4:19 and it was found that this city has a **long h** of revolt against kings 10317+10427+10550

HIT (7) [HITS, HITTING]
Ex 21:22 "If men who are fighting **h** 5597
Dt 19: 5 the head may fly off and **h** his neighbor 5162
1Ki 22:34 and **h** the king of Israel between the sections 5782
2Ch 18:33 and **h** the king of Israel between the sections 5782
Pr 23:35 *"They* **h** me," you will say, "but I'm not hurt! 5782
Mt 26:68 "Prophesy to us Christ. Who **h** you?" *4091*
Lk 22:64 "Prophesy! Who **h** you?" *4091*

HITCH (3) [HITCHED]
1Sa 6: 7 **H** the cows to the cart, 673
1Ki 18:44 **'H up** your chariot and go down before 673
2Ki 9:21 **"H up** my chariot," Joram ordered. 673

HITCHED (2) [HITCH]
1Sa 6:10 They took two such cows and **h** them to 673
2Ki 9:21 And when *it was* **h up,** 673

HITHER (KJV) See BACK, HERE, RIGHT

HITHERTO (KJV) See ABUNDANTLY, IN THE PAST, THIS FAR, THUS FAR, TO THIS DAY, UNTIL NOW, UP TO

HITS (4) [HIT]
Ex 21:18 "If men quarrel and one **h** the other with 5782
21:26 "If a man **h** a manservant or maidservant *in* 5782
Nu 35:18 and *he* **h** someone so that he dies, 5782
35:21 or if in hostility *he* **h** him with his fist so 5782

HITTING (1) [HIT]
Ex 2:13 "Why *are you* **h** your fellow Hebrew?" 5782

HITTITE (25) [HITTITES]
Ge 23:10 Ephron the **H** was sitting among his people 3153
25: 9 in the field of Ephron son of Zohar the **H,** 3153
26:34 he married Judith daughter of Beeri the **H,** 3153
26:34 and also Basemath daughter of Elon the **H.** 3153
27:46 with living because of these **H** women. 3147
27:46 from **H** women like these, 3147
36: 2 Adah daughter of Elon the **H,** 3153
49:29 in the cave in the field of Ephron the **H,** 3153
49:30 as a burial place from Ephron the **H,** 3153
50:13 as a burial place from Ephron the **H,** 3153
Jos 1: 4 all the **H** country— 3153
1Sa 26: 6 David then asked Ahimelech the **H** 3153
2Sa 11: 3 of Eliam and the wife of Uriah the **H?"** 3153
11: 6 "Send me Uriah the **H."** 3153
11:17 moreover, Uriah the **H** died. 3153
11:21 'Also, your servant Uriah the **H** is dead.'" 3153
11:24 your servant Uriah the **H** is dead." 3153
12: 9 the **H** with the sword and took his wife to 3153
12:10 the wife of Uriah the **H** to be your own.' 3153
23:39 and Uriah the **H.** 3153
1Ki 15: 5 except in the case of Uriah the **H.** 3153
2Ki 7: 6 of Israel has hired the **H** and Egyptian kings 3153
1Ch 11:41 Uriah the **H,** Zabad son of Ahlai, 3153
Eze 16: 3 an Amorite and your mother a **H.** 3153
16:45 Your mother was a **H** and your father 3153

HITTITES (36) [HITTITE]
Ge 10:15 Sidon his firstborn, and of the **H,** 3147
15:20 **H,** Perizzites, Rephaites, 3153
23: 3 his dead wife and spoke to the **H.** 1201+3147
23: 5 The **H** replied to Abraham, 1201+3147
23: 7 before the people of the land, the **H.** 1201+3147
23:10 in the hearing of all the **H** who 1201+3147
23:16 in the hearing of the **H:** 1201+3147
23:18 in the presence of all the **H** who 1201+3147
23:20 were deeded to Abraham by the **H** as 1201+3147
25:10 field Abraham had bought from the **H.** 1201+3147
49:32 cave in it were bought from the **H."** 1201+3147
Ex 3: 8 the home of the Canaanites, **H,** Amorites, 3153
3:17 **H,** Amorites, Perizzites, 3153
13: 5 **H,** Amorites, Hivites and Jebusites— 3153
23:23 **H,** Perizzites, Canaanites, 3153
23:28 Canaanites and **H** out of your way. 3153
33: 2 **H,** Perizzites, Hivites and Jebusites. 3153
34:11 **H,** Perizzites, Hivites and Jebusites. 3153
Nu 13:29 The Amalekites live in the Negev; the **H,** 3153
Dt 7: 1 the **H,** Girgashites, Amorites, Canaanites, 3153
20:17 the **H,** Amorites, Canaanites, Perizzites, 3153
Jos 3:10 **H,** Hivites, Perizzites, Girgashites, 3153
9: 1 as far as Lebanon (the kings of the **H,** 3153
11: 3 to the Amorites, **H,** Perizzites and Jebusites 3153
12: 8 the lands of the **H,** Amorites, Canaanites, 3153
24:11 Perizzites, Canaanites, **H,** Girgashites, 3153
Jdg 1:26 He then went to the land of the **H,** 3153
3: 5 **H,** Amorites, Perizzites, 3153
1Ki 9:20 All the people left from the Amorites, **H,** 3153
10:29 also exported them to all the kings of the **H** 3153
11: 1 Ammonites, Edomites, Sidonians and **H.** 3153
1Ch 1:13 Sidon his firstborn, and of the **H,** 3147
2Ch 1:17 also exported them to all the kings of the **H** 3153
8: 7 All the people left from the **H,** Amorites, 3153
Ezr 9: 1 like those of the Canaanites, **H,** Perizzites, 3153
Ne 9: 8 **H,** Amorites, Perizzites, 3153

HIVITE (2) [HIVITES]
Ge 34: 2 When Shechem son of Hamor the **H,** 2563
36: 2 and granddaughter of Zibeon the **H—** 2563

HIVITES (23) [HIVITE]
Ge 10:17 **H,** Arkites, Sinites, 2563
Ex 3: 8 Amorites, Perizzites, **H** and Jebusites. 2563
3:17 Amorites, Perizzites, **H** and Jebusites— 2563
13: 5 Hittites, Amorites, **H** and Jebusites— 2563
23:23 **H** and Jebusites, and I will wipe them out. 2563
23:28 the hornet ahead of you to drive the **H,** 2563
33: 2 Hittites, Perizzites, **H** and Jebusites. 2563
34:11 Hittites, Perizzites, **H** and Jebusites. 2563
Dt 7: 1 Canaanites, Perizzites, **H** and Jebusites, 2563
20:17 Canaanites, Perizzites, **H** and Jebusites— 2563
Jos 3:10 Hittites, **H,** Perizzites, Girgashites, 2563
9: 1 Canaanites, Perizzites, **H** and Jebusites)— 2563
9: 7 The men of Israel said to the **H,** 2563
11: 3 and to the **H** below Hermon in the region 2563
11:19 Except for the **H** living in Gibeon, 2563
12: 8 Canaanites, Perizzites, **H** and Jebusites): 2563
24:11 Hittites, Girgashites, **H** and Jebusites. 2563
Jdg 3: 3 and the **H** living in the Lebanon mountains 2563
3: 5 Amorites, Perizzites, **H** and Jebusites. 2563
2Sa 24: 7 and all the towns of the **H** and Canaanites. 2563
1Ki 9:20 **H** and Jebusites (these peoples were 2563
1Ch 1:15 **H,** Arkites, Sinites, 2563
2Ch 8: 7 **H** and Jebusites (these peoples were 2563

HIZKI (1)
1Ch 8:17 Zebadiah, Meshullam, **H,** Heber, 2623

HIZKIAH (1)
1Ch 3:23 Elioenai, **H** and Azrikam—three in all. 2624

HO (KJV) See COME

HOAR (KJV) See GRAY, THIN FLAKES

HOARD (1) [HOARDED, HOARDS]
Am 3:10 "who **h** plunder and loot in their fortresses." 732

HOARDED (3) [HOARD]
Ecc 5:13 wealth **h** to the harm of its owner, 9068
Isa 23:18 they will not be stored up or **h.** 2889
Jas 5: 3 *You have* **h wealth** in the last days. *2564*

HOARDS (1) [HOARD]
Pr 11:26 People curse the *man who* **h** grain, 4979

HOARY (KJV) See AGED, GRAY HAIR, WHITE HAIR

HOBAB (2)
Nu 10:29 Moses said to **H** son of Reuel the Midianite, 2463
Jdg 4:11 the descendants of **H,** 2463

HOBAH (1)
Ge 14:15 pursuing them as far as **H,** 2551

HOBAIAH (2)
Ezr 2:61 The descendants of **H,** 2469
Ne 7:63 the descendants of **H,** 2469

HOD (1)
1Ch 7:37 **H,** Shamma, Shilshah, Ithran and Beera. 2087

HODAIAH, HODEVAH (KJV) See HODAVIAH

HODAVIAH (6)
1Ch 3:24 The sons of Elioenai: **H,** Eliashib, Pelaiah, 2090
5:24 Ishi, Eliel, Azriel, Jeremiah, **H** and Jahdiel. 2089
9: 7 Sallu son of Meshullam, the son of **H,** 2089
Ezr 2:40 and Kadmiel (through the line of **H**) 74 2089
3: 9 and his sons (descendants of **H**) and 2088
Ne 7:43 (through Kadmiel through the line of **H**) 74 2088

HODESH (1)
1Ch 8: 9 By his wife **H** he had Jobab, Zibia, Mesha, 2545

HODIAH (5) [HODIAH'S]
Ne 8: 7 Shabbethai, **H,** Maaseiah, Kelita, Azariah, 2091
9: 5 Kadmiel, Bani, Hashabneiah, Sherebiah, **H,** 2091
10:10 Shebaniah, **H,** Kelita, Pelaiah, Hanan, 2091
10:13 **H,** Bani and Beninu. 2091
10:18 **H,** Hashum, Bezai, 2091

HODIAH'S (1) [HODIAH]
1Ch 4:19 The sons of **H** wife, the sister of Naham: 2091

HODIJAH (KJV) See HODIAH

HODSHI See TAHTIM HODSHI

HOE (1)
Isa 7:25 As for all the hills once cultivated by the **h,** 5053

HOGLAH (4) [BETH HOGLAH]
Nu 26:33 whose names were Mahlah, Noah, **H,** 2519
27: 1 Noah, **H,** Milcah and Tirzah. 2519
36:11 Mahlah, Tirzah, **H,** Milcah and Noah— 2519
Jos 17: 3 whose names were Mahlah, Noah, **H,** 2519

HOHAM (1)
Jos 10: 3 of Jerusalem appealed to **H** king of Hebron, 2097

HOISED (KJV) See HOISTED

HOISTED (2)
Ac 27:17 *When* the men *had* **h** it **aboard,** *149*
27:40 Then they **h** the foresail to the wind *2048*

HOLD (163) [HELD, HOLDING, HOLDS]
Ge 43: 9 **h** me personally **responsible** 1335+3338+4946
48:17 so *he* **took h** *of* his father's hand to move it 9461
Ex 4: 4 and **took h** of the snake and it turned back 2616
5: 1 so that *they may* **h** a **festival** to me in 2510
9: 2 to let them go and continue *to* **h** them **back,** 2616
12:16 On the first day **h** a sacred assembly, 2118
13: 6 the seventh day **h** a festival to the LORD. NIH
20: 7 **h** anyone **guiltless** who misuses his name. 5927
22:29 *"Do* not **h back** offerings from your granaries 336
25:27 to the rim to **h** the poles used in carrying 1074
26:29 and make gold rings to **h** the crossbars. 1074
30: 4 to **h** the poles used to carry it. 1074
36:34 and made gold rings to **h** the crossbars. 1074
37:14 to the rim to **h** the poles used in carrying 1074
37:27 to **h** the poles used to carry it. 1074
38: 5 They cast bronze rings to **h** the poles for 1074
Lev 19:13 " *'Do* not **h back** the wages of a hired man **overnight.** 1332+4328+6330
23: 7 On the first day **h** a sacred assembly 2118
23: 8 And on the seventh day **h** a sacred assembly NIH
23:27 **H** a sacred assembly and deny yourselves, 2118
23:36 and on the eighth day **h** a sacred assembly 2118
25:24 the country that you **h as a possession,** 299
25:33 that is, a house sold in any town they **h—** 299
Nu 12:11 *do* not **h** against us the sin we have 8883
28:18 On the first day **h** a sacred assembly NIH
28:25 On the seventh day **h** a sacred assembly 2118
28:26 Feast of Weeks, **h** a sacred assembly 2118
29: 1 " 'On the first day of the seventh month **h** 2118
29: 7 " 'On the tenth day of this seventh month **h** 2118
29:12 of the seventh month, **h** a sacred assembly 2118
29:35 " 'On the eighth day **h** an assembly 2118
Dt 5:11 **h** anyone **guiltless** who misuses his name. 5927
10:20 **H fast** to him and take your oaths 1815
11:22 in all his ways and to **h fast** to him— 1815
13: 4 serve him and **h fast** to him. 1815
16: 8 and on the seventh day **h** an assembly to NIH
21: 8 and *do* not **h** your people guilty of the blood 5989
21:19 his father and mother *shall* **take h** of him 9530
30:20 listen to his voice, and **h fast** to him. 1815
Jos 8:18 **"H out** toward Ai the javelin that is 5742
22: 5 to obey his commands, to **h fast** to him and 1815

Jos 23: 8 *you are to* **h fast** to the LORD your God, 1815
Jdg 1:35 the Amorites were determined also to **h out** 3782
9: 9 to **h sway** over the trees?' 5675
9:11 to **h sway** over the trees?' 5675
9:13 to **h sway** over the trees?' 5675
16: 3 up and **took h** of the doors of the city gate, 296
Ru 3:15 the shawl you are wearing and **h** it **out."** 296
1Sa 15:27 Saul **caught h** of the hem of his robe, 2616
17:51 *He* **took h** *of* the Philistine's sword 4374
2Sa 1:11 David and all the men with him **took h** 2616
6: 6 Uzzah reached out and **took h** of the ark 296
15: 5 **take h** of him and kiss him. 2616
19:19 *"May* my lord not **h** me guilty. 3108
22:17 "He reached down from on high and **took h** 4374
1Ki 1:50 went and **took h** of the horns of the altar. 2616
2:28 he fled to the tent of the LORD and **took h** 2616
8:64 before the LORD was too small *to* **h** 3920
11:30 and Ahijah **took h** of the new cloak 9530
18:32 around it large enough to **h** two seahs 1074
2Ki 2:12 Then *he* **took h** of his own clothes 2616
4:16 **h** a son in your **arms."** 2485
4:27 *she* **took h** of his feet. 2616
6:32 shut the door and **h** it **shut** *against* him. 4315
10:19 I am going to **h** a great sacrifice for Baal. 4200
15:19 to gain his support and strengthen his own **h** 3338
2Ch 7: 7 the bronze altar he had made could not **h** 3920
Job 8:15 he clings to it, but it *does* not **h.** 7756
9:28 for I know *you will* not **h** me **innocent.** 5927
10:16 If I **h** my **head high,** 1448
17: 9 the righteous *will* **h** *to* their ways, 296
36:17 judgment and justice *have* **taken h** of you. 9461
39:10 *Can you* **h** him to the furrow with 8003
Ps 18:16 He reached down from on high and **took h** 4374
21: 8 Your hand *will* **lay h** on all your enemies; 5162
73:23 *you* **h** me by my right hand. 296
74:11 Why *do you* **h back** your hand, 8740
75: 3 it is I *who* **h** its pillars **firm.** 9419
79: 8 *Do* not **h** against us the sins of the fathers; 2349
119:31 *I* **h fast** to your statutes, O LORD; 1815
139:10 your right hand *will* **h** me **fast.** 296
Pr 3:18 *those who* **lay h** *of* her will be blessed. 9461
4: 4 **"Lay h** *of* my words *with* all your heart; 9461
4:13 **H on** to instruction, do not let it go; 2616
5:22 the cords of his sin **h** *him* **fast.** 9461
7:13 *She* **took h** of him and kissed him and with 2616
20:16 **h** it **in pledge** if he does it for 2471
24:11 **h back** those staggering toward slaughter. 3104
27:13 **h** it **in pledge** if he does it for a wayward 2471
SS 7: 8 *I will* **take h** of its fruit." 296
Isa 4: 1 In that day seven women *will* **take h** 2616
22:17 LORD *is about to* **take firm h** *of* you 6487+6487
41:13 *who* **takes h** *of* your right hand and says 2616
42: 6 *I will* **take h** of your hand. 2616
43: 6 and to the south, '*Do* not **h** them **back.'** 3973
45: 1 whose right hand *I* **take h** *of* 2616
48: 9 the sake of my praise *I* **h** it **back** from you, 2641
54: 2 *do* not **h back;** 3104
56: 4 who choose what pleases me and **h fast** 2616
56: 6 without desecrating it and *who* **h fast** 2616
58: 1 "Shout it aloud, *do* not **h back.** 3104
64: 7 on your name or strives to **lay h** of you; 2616
64:12 O LORD, *will you* **h yourself back?** 706
65: 4 and whose pots **h** broth of unclean meat; NIH
Jer 2:13 broken cisterns that cannot **h** water. 3920
6:11 of wrath of the LORD, and I cannot **h** it **in.** 3920
34: 9 **h** a fellow Jew **in bondage.** 6268
34:10 and no longer **h** them **in bondage.** 6268
50:33 All their captors **h** them **fast,** 2616
Eze 3:18 *I will* **h** you **accountable** *for* his blood. 1335+3338+4946
3:20 *I will* **h** you **accountable** *for* his blood. 1335+3338+4946
17: 3 **Taking h** *of* the top of a cedar, 4374
24:14 *I will* not **h back;** 7277
30: 9 Anguish *will* **take h of** them on the day 928+2118
30:21 so as to become strong enough to **h** a sword. 9530
33: 6 *I will* **h** the watchman **accountable** *for* his blood.' 2011+3338+4946
33: 8 *I will* **h** you **accountable** *for* his blood. 1335+3338+4946
34:10 and *will* **h** them **accountable** 2011+3338+4946
37:20 **H** before their eyes the sticks 928+2118+3338
Da 4:35 No one *can* **h back** his hand or say to him: 10411
Jnh 1:14 *Do* not **h** us **accountable** *for* killing 5989+6584
Zec 8:23 and nations *will* **take firm h** *of* one Jew by 2616
Mt 11:12 and forceful men **lay h** of it. *773*
12:11 *will you* not **take h** of it and lift it out? *3195*
21:26 for *they* all **h** that John was a prophet." *2400*
Mk 11:25 if *you* **h** anything against anyone, *2400*
Lk 14: 4 So **taking h** of the man, *2138*
Jn 8:31 Jesus said, "If you **h** to my teaching, *3531*
14:30 *He* **has** no **h** on me, *2400*
20:17 Jesus said, *"Do* not **h on to** me, *721*
Ac 2:24 for death *to keep* its **h on** him. *3195*
7:60 "Lord, *do* not **h** this sin against them." *2705*
27: 7 wind *did* not **allow** us to **h** our **course,** *4661*
27:17 *they* **passed** ropes **under** the ship itself **to h** it **together.** *5690*
Ro 13: 3 For rulers **h** no **terror** for those who do right, *1639+5832*
1Co 15: 2 if *you* **h firmly** to the word I preached *2988*
Php 2:16 *as* you **h out** the word of life— *2091*
3:12 but I press on to **take h** of that *2898*
3:12 of that for which Christ Jesus **took h** of *me.* *2898*
3:13 not consider myself yet *to have* **taken h of** *2898*
Col 1:17 and in him all things **h together.** *5319*
1Th 5:13 **H** them in the highest regard in love *2451*
1Th 5:21 Test everything. **H on to** the good. *2988*
2Th 2:15 stand firm and **h to** the teachings we passed *3195*
1Ti 3: 9 They must **keep h of** the deep truths of *2400*
6:12 **Take h** of the eternal life *2138*
6:19 *they may* **take h** of the life that is truly life. *2138*
Tit 1: 9 He must **h firmly to** the trustworthy message *504*
Heb 3: 6 if *we* **h on to** our courage and the hope *2988*
3:14 to share in Christ if *we* **h** firmly till the end *2988*
4:14 *let us* **h firmly to** the faith we profess. *3195*
6:18 *to* **take h** of the hope offered to us may *3195*
10:23 *Let us* **h** unswervingly **to** the hope *2988*
2Pe 2: 9 to rescue godly men from trials and *to* **h** *5498*
Rev 1:18 And *I* **h** the keys of death and Hades. *2400*
2: 4 Yet *I* **h** this against you: *2400*
2:14 You have *people* there *who* **h to** the teaching of Balaam, *3195*
2:15 also have *those who* **h to** the teaching of *3195*
2:24 to you who *do* not **h to** her teaching *2400*
2:25 Only **h on to** what you have until I come. *3195*
3:11 **H on to** what you have, *3195*
12:17 and **h to** the testimony of Jesus. *2400*
19:10 with your brothers who **h to** the testimony *2400*

HOLDING (24) [HOLD]

Ge 50:11 "The Egyptians are **h** a solemn ceremony 4200
Jdg 7:20 in their left hands and **h** in their right hands NIH
1Sa 17:57 with David still **h** the Philistine's head. 928+3338
25:36 he was in the house **h** a banquet like that of 4200
1Ki 7:38 each **h** forty baths 3920
Ne 4:21 the work with half the men **h** spears, 2616
Job 1: 4 to take turns **h** feasts in their homes, 6913
2: 9 *"Are* you still **h on** to your integrity? 2616
Jer 20: 9 I am weary of **h** it **in;** indeed, I cannot. 3920
34: 7 of Judah that *were still* **h out—** 3855
Mk 7: 3 **h to** the tradition of the elders. *3195*
7: 8 of the commands of God and *are* **h on to** *3195*
Jn 2: 6 each **h** from twenty to thirty gallons. *6003*
8:44 not **h** to the truth, for there is no truth in him *2705*
1Co 11: 2 in everything and for **h to** the teachings, *2988*
2Th 2: 6 And now you know what *is* **h** him **back,** *2988*
1Ti 1:19 **h on to** faith and a good conscience. *2400*
4: 8 **h** promise for both the present life and *2400*
Rev 5: 8 a harp and they were **h** golden bowls full *NIG*
6: 5 Its rider *was* **h** a pair of scales in his hand. *2400*
7: 1 **h back** the four winds of the earth *3195*
7: 9 and were **h** palm branches in their hands. *NIG*
10: 2 *He was* **h** a little scroll, *2400*
20: 1 to the Abyss and **h in** his hand a great chain. *2093*

HOLDS (22) [HOLD]

Ge 50:15 "What if Joseph **h a grudge against** us 8475
Nu 5:18 he himself **h** the bitter water 928+2118+3338
Job 12:15 If *he* **h back** the waters, there is drought; 6806
18: 9 a snare **h** him **fast.** 2616
37: 4 his voice resounds, *he* **h** nothing **back.** 6810
Pr 2: 7 *He* **h** victory **in store** for the upright, 7621
3:35 but fools *he* **h up** *to* shame. 8123
10:19 but *he who* **h** his tongue is wise. 3104
11:12 but a man of understanding **h** *his* **tongue.** 3087
17:28 and discerning if *he* **h** his tongue. 357
31:19 In her hand *she* **h** the distaff and grasps 8938
Isa 41:23 tell us what the future **h,** 910
56: 2 the man *who* **h** it **fast,** 2616
Eze 23:32 for it **h** so much. 3920
Da 5:23 But you did not honor the God who **h** NIH
Am 1: 5 and the *one who* **h** the scepter in Beth Eden. 9461
1: 8 and the *one who* **h** the scepter in Ashkelon. 9461
2Th 2: 7 but the one who now **h** it **back** will continue *2988*
Heb 2:14 by his death he might destroy him who **h** *2400*
Rev 2: 1 the words of him who **h** the seven stars *3195*
3: 1 of him who **h** the seven spirits of God and *2400*
3: 7 who **h** the key of David. *2400*

HOLE (7) [HOLES]

Dt 23:13 **dig a h** and cover up your excrement. 2916
2Ki 12: 9 the priest took a chest and bored a **h** 2986
Ps 7:15 He who digs a **h** and scoops it out falls into 1014
Isa 11: 8 The infant will play near the **h** *of* the cobra, 2987
Eze 8: 7 I looked, and I saw a **h** in the wall. 2986
12:12 and a **h** will be dug in the wall for him NIH
Mt 25:18 **dug a h** in the ground *4002*

HOLES (8) [HOLE]

1Sa 14:11 crawling out of the **h** they were hiding in." 2986
Job 30: 6 among the rocks and in **h** *in* the ground. 2986
Isa 2:19 the rocks and to **h** *in* the ground from dread 4704
7:19 all the thornbushes and at all the **water h.** 5635
Hag 1: 6 only to put them in a purse *with* **h** in it." 5918
Mt 8:20 "Foxes have **h** and birds of the air have *5887*
Lk 9:58 "Foxes have **h** and birds of the air have *5887*
Heb 11:38 and in caves and **h** in the ground. *3956*

HOLIDAY (1)

Est 2:18 He proclaimed a **h** throughout the provinces 2182

HOLIEST (1) [HOLY]

Nu 18:29 as the LORD's portion the best and **h** part 5219

HOLILY (KJV) See HOLY

HOLINESS (25) [HOLY]

Ex 15:11 Who is like you—majestic in **h,** 7731
Dt 32:51 because *you did* not **uphold** my **h** among 7727
1Ch 16:29 worship the LORD in the splendor of his **h.** 7731
2Ch 20:21 for the splendor of his **h** as they went out at 7731
Ps 29: 2 worship the LORD in the splendor of his **h.** 7731
89:35 Once for all, I have sworn by my **h—** 7731
93: 5 **h** adorns your house for endless days, 7731
96: 9 Worship the LORD in the splendor of his **h;** 7731
Isa 29:23 *they will* **acknowledge** *the* **h** *of* the Holy One 7727
35: 8 it will be called the Way of **H.** 7731
Eze 36:23 *I will* **show** *the* **h** *of* my great name, 7727
38:23 And so I will show my greatness and *my* **h,** 7727
Am 4: 2 The Sovereign LORD has sworn by his **h:** 7731
Lk 1:75 in **h** and righteousness before him *4009*
Ro 1: 4 through the Spirit *of* **h** was declared with *43*
6:19 in slavery to righteousness leading to **h.** *40*
6:22 the benefit you reap leads to **h,** *40*
1Co 1:30 that is, our righteousness, **h** and redemption. *40*
2Co 1:12 in the **h** and sincerity that are from God. *605*
7: 1 perfecting **h** out of reverence for God. *43*
Eph 4:24 to be like God in true righteousness and **h.** *4009*
1Ti 2: 2 and quiet lives in all godliness and **h.** *4949*
2:15 love and **h** with propriety. *40*
Heb 12:10 that we may share in his **h.** *42*
12:14 without **h** no one will see the Lord. *4005*[S]

HOLLOW (8)

Ex 27: 8 Make the altar **h,** out of boards. 5554
38: 7 They made it **h,** *out of* boards. 5554
Jdg 15:19 Then God opened up the **h place** in Lehi, 4847
Pr 30: 4 up the wind in the **h of** his **hands?** 2908
Isa 40:12 the waters in the **h of** his **hand,** 9123
Jer 52:21 each was four fingers thick, and **h.** 5554
2Co 9: 3 in this matter *should* not **prove h,** *3033*
Col 2: 8 to it that no one takes you captive through **h** *3031*

HOLON (3)

Jos 15:51 Goshen, **H** and Giloh— 2708
21:15 **H,** Debir, 2708
Jer 48:21 Judgment has come to the plateau—to **H,** 2708

HOLPEN (KJV) See HELPED, LEND STRENGTH

HOLY (584) [HALLOWED, HOLIEST, HOLINESS]

Ge 2: 3 God blessed the seventh day and **made** it **h,** 7727
Ex 3: 5 where you are standing is **h** ground." 7731
15:13 you will guide them to your **h** dwelling. 7731
16:23 a **h** Sabbath to the LORD. 7731
19: 6 for me a kingdom of priests and a **h** nation.' 7705
19:23 the mountain and **set** it **apart as h.'** " 7727
20: 8 Remember the Sabbath day by **keeping** it **h.** 7727
20:11 blessed the Sabbath day and **made** it **h.** 7727
22:31 "You are to be my **h** people. 7731
26:33 The curtain will separate the **H Place** from 7731
26:33 Holy Place from the **Most H Place.** 7731+7731
26:34 of the Testimony in the **Most H Place.** 7731+7731
28:29 "Whenever Aaron enters the **H Place,** 7731
28:35 be heard when he enters the **H Place** 7731
28:36 as on a seal: **H** TO THE LORD. 7731
28:43 the altar to minister in the **H Place,** 7731
29:30 in the **H Place** is to wear them seven days. 7731
29:37 Then the altar will be **most h,** 7731+7731
29:37 and whatever touches it *will be* **h.** 7727
30:10 It is **most h** to the LORD." 7731+7731
30:29 so they will be **most h,** 7731+7731
30:29 and whatever touches them *will be* **h.** 7727
30:36 It shall be **most h** to you. 7731+7731
30:37 consider it **h** to the LORD. 7731
31:11 and fragrant incense for the **H Place.** 7731
31:13 I am the LORD, *who* **makes** you **h.** 7727
31:14 because it is **h** to you. 7731
31:15 a Sabbath of rest, **h** to the LORD. 7731
35: 2 but the seventh day shall be your **h** day, 7731
39:30 inscription on a seal: **H** TO THE LORD. 7731
40: 9 and it will be **h.** 7731
40:10 the altar, and it will be **most h.** 7731+7731
Lev 2: 3 it is a **most h** *part* of the offerings 7731+7731
2:10 it is a **most h** *part* of the offerings 7731+7731
5:15 in regard to any of the LORD's **h things,** 7731
5:16 to do in regard to the **h things,** 7731
6:16 it is to be eaten without yeast in a **h** place; 7705
6:17 and the guilt offering, it is **most h.** 7731+7731
6:18 Whatever touches them *will become* **h.'** " 7727
6:25 it is **most h.** 7731+7731
6:26 it is to be eaten in a **h** place, 7705
6:27 of the flesh *will become* **h,** 7727
6:27 you must wash it in a **h** place. 7705
6:29 it is **most h.** 7731+7731
6:30 to make atonement in the **H Place** must not 7731
7: 1 which is **most h:** 7731+7731
7: 6 but it must be eaten in a **h** place; 7705
7: 6 it is **most h.** 7731+7731
10: 3 " 'Among those who approach me *I will* **show myself h;** 7727
10:10 You must distinguish between the **h** and 7731
10:12 for it is **most h.** 7731+7731
10:13 Eat it in a **h** place, 7705
10:17 It is **most h;** 7731+7731
10:18 its blood was not taken into the **H Place,** 7731
11:44 consecrate yourselves and be **h,** 7705
11:44 and be holy, because I am **h.** 7705
11:45 therefore be **h,** because I am holy. 7705

Lev 11:45 therefore be holy, because I am **h.** 7705
14:13 to slaughter the lamb in the **h** place where 7731
14:13 belongs to the priest; it is **most h.** 7731+7731
16: 2 into the **Most H Place** behind the curtain 7731
16:16 for the **Most H Place** because of 7731
16:17 in to make atonement in the **Most H Place** 7731
16:20 for the **Most H Place,** 7731
16:23 on before he entered the **Most H Place,** 7731
16:24 in a **h** place and put on his regular garments. 7705
16:27 the **Most H Place** to make atonement, 7731
16:33 make atonement for the **Most H Place,** 5219+7731
19: 2 'Be **h** because I, the LORD your God, 7705
19: 2 the LORD your God, am **h.** 7705
19: 8 because he has desecrated **what** is **h** *to* 7731
19:24 In the fourth year all its fruit will be **h,** 7731
20: 3 and profaned my **h** name. 7731
20: 7 " 'Consecrate yourselves and be **h,** 7705
20: 8 I am the LORD, *who* **makes** you **h.** 7727
20:26 You are to be **h** to me because I, 7705
20:26 be holy to me because I, the LORD, am **h,** 7705
21: 6 be **h** to their God and must not profane 7705
21: 6 the food of their God, they are to be **h.** 7731
21: 7 because priests are **h** to their God. 7705
21: 8 **Regard** them **as h,** 7727
21: 8 Consider them **h,** because I the LORD 7705
21: 8 because I the LORD am **h—** 7705
21: 8 I *who* **make** you **h.** 7727
21:15 I am the LORD, *who* **makes** him **h.' "** 7727
21:22 may eat the **most h** food of his God, 7731+7731
21:22 as well as the **h** food; 7731
21:23 I am the LORD, *who* **makes** them **h.' "** 7727
22: 2 so they will not profane my **h** name. 7731
22: 9 I am the LORD, *who* **makes** them **h.** 7727
22:16 I am the LORD, *who* **makes** them **h.' "** 7727
22:32 Do not profane my **h** name. 7731
22:32 *I must* **be acknowledged as h** by 7727
22:32 I am the LORD, *who* **makes** you **h** 7727
24: 9 who are to eat it in a **h** place, 7705
24: 9 a **most h** part of their regular share of 7731+7731
25:12 For it is a jubilee and is to be **h** for you; 7731
27: 9 an animal given to the LORD becomes **h.** 7731
27:10 both it and the substitute become **h.** 7731
27:14 a man dedicates his house as **something h** 7731
27:21 it will become **h,** like a field devoted to 7731
27:23 on that day as **something h** to the LORD. 7731
27:28 so devoted is **most h** to the LORD. 7731+7731
27:30 belongs to the LORD; it is **h** to the LORD. 7731
27:32 will be **h** to the LORD. 7731
27:33 both the animal and its substitute become **h** 7731
Nu 4: 4 the care of the **most h things.** 7731+7731
4:15 the **h furnishings** and all the holy articles, 7731
4:15 the holy furnishings and all the **h** articles, 7731
4:15 not touch the **h things** or they will die. 7731
4:16 including its **h furnishings** and articles." 7731
4:19 near the **most h things,** do this for them 7731+7731
4:20 not go in to look at the **h things,** 7731
5:17 Then he shall take some **h** water in 7705
6: 5 be **h** until the period of his separation to 7705
6:20 they are **h** and belong to the priest, 7731
7: 9 to carry on their shoulders the **h things,** 7731
10:21 Kohathites set out, carrying the **h things.** 5219
16: 3 The whole community is **h,** 7705
16: 5 who belongs to him and who is **h,** 7705
16: 7 chooses will be the one who is **h.** 7705
16:37 for the censers *are* **h—** 7727
16:38 before the LORD and *have become* **h.** 7727
18: 8 the **h offerings** the Israelites give me I give 7731
18: 9 of the **most h offerings** that is kept 7731+7731
18: 9 the gifts they bring me as **most h offerings,** 7731+7731
18:10 Eat it as something **most h;** 7731+7731
18:10 You must regard it as **h.** 7731
18:17 or a goat; they are **h.** 7731
18:19 from the **h offerings** the Israelites present to 7731
18:32 not defile the **h offerings** *of* the Israelites, 7731
20:12 in me enough to **honor** me **as h** in the sight 7727
20:13 where *he* **showed himself h** among them. 7727
27:14 to **honor** me **as h** before their eyes." 7727
35:25 who was anointed with the **h** oil. 7731
Dt 5:12 "Observe the Sabbath day by **keeping** it **h,** 7727
7: 6 you are a people **h** to the LORD your God. 7705
14: 2 you are a people **h** to the LORD your God. 7705
14:21 you are a people **h** to the LORD your God. 7705
23:14 Your camp must be **h,** 7705
26:15 your **h** dwelling place, 7731
26:19 be a people **h** to the LORD your God, 7705
28: 9 LORD will establish you as his **h** people, 7705
33: 2 with myriads of **h ones** from the south, 7731
33: 3 all the **h** *ones* are in your hand. 7705
Jos 5:15 for the place where you are standing is **h."** 7731
24:19 He is a **h** God; he is a jealous God. 7705
24:26 up there under the oak near the **h place** *of* 5219
1Sa 2: 2 "There is no *one* **h** like the LORD; 7705
6:20 in the presence of the LORD, this **h** God? 7705
21: 5 The men's things are **h** even on missions 7731
21: 5 even on missions that are **not h.** 2687
1Ki 6:16 inner sanctuary, the **Most H Place.** 7731+7731
7:50 innermost room, the **Most H Place,** 7731+7731
8: 6 of the temple, the **Most H Place,** 7731+7731
8: 8 the **H Place** in front of the inner sanctuary, 7731
8: 8 but not from outside the **H** Place; NIH
8:10 the priests withdrew from the **H Place,** 7731
2Ki 4: 9 who often comes our way a **h** man of God. 7731
19:22 Against the **H** *One* of Israel! 7705
1Ch 6:49 all that was done in the **Most H Place,** 7731+7731
16:10 Glory in his **h** name; 7731
16:35 that we may give thanks to your **h** name, 7731
1Ch 23:13 to consecrate the **most h things,** 7731+7731
23:32 for the **H Place** and, 7731
29: 3 I have provided for this **h** temple: 7731
29:16 for building you a temple for your **H** Name, 7731
2Ch 3: 8 He built the **Most H Place,** 7731+7731
3:10 In the **Most H** Place he made a pair 7731+7731
4:22 the inner doors to the **Most H Place** 7731+7731
5: 7 of the temple, the **Most H Place,** 7731+7731
5: 9 but not from outside the **H** Place; NIH
5:11 priests then withdrew from the **H Place.** 7731
8:11 the ark of the LORD has entered are **h."** 7731
30:27 heaven, his **h** dwelling place. 7731
31: 6 and a tithe of the **h things** dedicated to 7731
35: 5 in the **h place** with a group of Levites 7731
35:13 and boiled the **h offerings** in pots, 7731
Ezr 9: 2 the **h** race with the peoples around them. 7731
Ne 9:14 You made known to them your **h** Sabbath 7731
10:31 from them on the Sabbath or on any **h** day. 7731
10:33 for the **h offerings;** for sin offerings 7731
11: 1 of every ten to live in Jerusalem, the **h** city, 7731
11:18 The Levites in the **h** city totaled 284. 7731
13:22 in order to **keep** the Sabbath day **h.** 7727
Job 5: 1 To which of the **h** *ones* will you turn? 7705
6:10 I had not denied the words of the **H One.** 7705
15:15 If God places no trust in his **h** *ones,* 7705
Ps 2: 6 on Zion, my **h** hill." 7731
3: 4 and he answers me from his **h** hill. 7731
5: 7 down toward your **h** temple. 7731
11: 4 The LORD is in his **h** temple; 7731
15: 1 Who may live on your **h** hill? 7731
16:10 nor will you let your **H** *One* see decay. 2883
20: 6 from his **h** heaven with the saving power 7731
22: 3 Yet you are enthroned as the **H One;** 7705
24: 3 Who may stand in his **h** place? 7731
28: 2 my hands toward your **Most H Place.** 1808+7731
30: 4 praise his **h** name. 7731
33:21 for we trust in his **h** name. 7731
43: 3 let them bring me to your **h** mountain, 7731
46: 4 the **h** *place* where the Most High dwells. 7705
47: 8 God is seated on his **h** throne. 7731
48: 1 in the city of our God, his **h** mountain. 7731
51:11 from your presence or take your **H** Spirit 7731
65: 4 of your house, of your **h** temple. 7705
68: 5 a defender of widows, is God in his **h** dwelling. 7731
71:22 O **H One** *of* Israel. 7705
77:13 Your ways, O God, are **h.** 7731
78:41 they vexed the **H One** *of* Israel. 7705
78:54 to the border of his **h** land, 7731
79: 1 they have defiled your **h** temple, 7731
87: 1 set his foundation on the **h** mountain; 7731
89: 5 in the assembly of the **h** *ones.* 7705
89: 7 of the **h** *ones* God is greatly feared; 7705
89:18 our king to the **H One** *of* Israel. 7705
97:12 and praise his **h** name. 7731
98: 1 and his **h** arm have worked salvation 7731
99: 3 and awesome name—he is **h.** 7705
99: 5 at his footstool; he is **h.** 7705
99: 9 and worship at his **h** mountain, 7731
99: 9 for the LORD our God is **h.** 7705
103: 1 all my inmost being, praise his **h** name. 7731
105: 3 Glory in his **h** name; 7731
105:42 For he remembered his **h** promise given 7731
106:47 to your **h** name and glory in your praise. 7731
110: 3 Arrayed in **h** majesty, 7731
111: 9 **h** and awesome is his name. 7705
138: 2 I will bow down toward your **h** temple 7731
145:21 Let every creature praise his **h** name 7731
Pr 9:10 knowledge of the **H One** is understanding. 7705
30: 3 nor have I knowledge of the **H One.** 7705
Ecc 8:10 and go from the **h** place and receive praise 7705
Isa 1: 4 the **H One** of Israel and turned their backs 7705
4: 3 who remain in Jerusalem, will be called **h,** 7705
5:16 and the **h** God will show himself holy 7705
5:16 and the holy God *will* **show himself h** 7727
5:19 let the plan of the **H One** *of* Israel come, 7705
5:24 spurned the word of the **H One** *of* Israel. 7705
6: 3 **"H,** holy, holy is the LORD Almighty; 7705
6: 3 "Holy, **h,** holy is the LORD Almighty; 7705
6: 3 "Holy, holy, **h** is the LORD Almighty; 7705
6:13 so the **h** seed will be the stump in the land." 7731
8:13 the one *you are to* **regard as h,** 7727
10:17 their **H One** a flame; 7705
10:20 the LORD, the **H One** *of* Israel. 7705
11: 9 nor destroy on all my **h** mountain, 7731
12: 6 for great is the **H One** *of* Israel among you." 7705
13: 3 I have commanded my **h** *ones;* 7727
17: 7 and turn their eyes to the **H One** *of* Israel. 7705
27:13 the LORD on the **h** mountain in Jerusalem. 7731
29:19 needy will rejoice in the **H One** *of* Israel. 7705
29:23 *they will* **keep** my name **h;** 7727
29:23 the holiness of the **H One** *of* Jacob, 7705
30:11 and stop confronting us with the **H One** 7705
30:12 this is what the **H One** *of* Israel says: 7705
30:15 the Sovereign LORD, the **H One** *of* Israel, 7705
30:29 as on the night you **celebrate** a **h** festival; 7727
31: 1 but do not look to the **H One** *of* Israel, 7705
37:23 Against the **H One** *of* Israel! 7705
40:25 says the **H One.** 7705
41:14 your Redeemer, the **H One** *of* Israel. 7705
41:16 the LORD and glory in the **H One** *of* Israel. 7705
41:20 that the **H One** *of* Israel has created it. 7705
43: 3 your God, the **H One** *of* Israel, your Savior; 7705
43:14 your Redeemer, the **H One** *of* Israel: 7705
43:15 I am the LORD, your **H One,** 7705
45:11 the **H One** *of* Israel, and its Maker: 7705
47: 4 is the **H One** *of* Israel. 7705
Isa 48: 2 of the **h** city and rely on the God of Israel— 7731
48:17 your Redeemer, the **H One** *of* Israel: 7705
49: 7 the Redeemer and **H One** *of* Israel— 7705
49: 7 the **H One** *of* Israel, who has chosen you." 7731
52: 1 O Jerusalem, the **h** city. 7731
52:10 The LORD will lay bare his **h** arm in 7731
54: 5 the **H One** *of* Israel is your Redeemer; 7705
55: 5 the LORD your God, the **H One** *of* Israel, 7705
56: 7 to my **h** mountain and give them joy 7731
57:13 the land and possess my **h** mountain." 7731
57:15 he who lives forever, whose name is **h:** 7705
57:15 "I live in a high and **h** *place,* 7705
58:13 and from doing as you please on my **h** day, 7731
58:13 and the LORD's **h** day honorable, 7705
60: 9 the LORD your God, the **H One** *of* Israel, 7705
60:14 Zion of the **H One** *of* Israel. 7705
62:12 They will be called the **H** People, 7731
63:10 Yet they rebelled and grieved his **H** Spirit. 7731
63:11 is he who set his **H** Spirit among them, 7731
63:15 from your lofty throne, **h** and glorious. 7731
63:18 while your people possessed your **h place,** 7731
64:11 Our **h** and glorious temple, 7731
65:11 the LORD and forget my **h** mountain, 7731
65:25 nor destroy on all my **h** mountain," 7731
66:20 to my **h** mountain in Jerusalem as 7731
Jer 2: 3 Israel was **h** to the LORD, 7731
17:22 **keep** the Sabbath day **h,** 7727
17:24 **keep** the Sabbath day **h** 7727
17:27 **keep** the Sabbath day **h** 7727
23: 9 because of the LORD and his **h** words. 7731
25:30 from his **h** dwelling and roar mightily 7731
31:40 will be **h** to the LORD. 7731
50:29 defied the LORD, the **H One** *of* Israel. 7705
51: 5 of guilt before the **H One** *of* Israel. 7705
51:51 the **h places** *of* the LORD's house." 5219
Eze 20:12 that I the LORD **made** them **h.** 7727
20:20 **Keep** my Sabbaths **h,** 7727
20:39 to me and no longer profane my **h** name 7731
20:40 For on my **h** mountain, 7731
20:40 along with all your **h** sacrifices. 7731
20:41 and *I will* **show myself h** among you in 7727
22: 8 You have despised my **h things** 7731
22:26 to my law and profane my **h things;** 7731
22:26 they do not distinguish between the **h** and 7731
28:14 You were on the **h** mount of God; 7731
28:22 on her and **show myself h** within her. 7727
28:25 *I will* **show myself h** among them in 7727
36:20 the nations they profaned my **h** name, 7731
36:21 I had concern for my **h** name, 7731
36:22 but for the sake of my **h** name, 7731
36:23 when I **show myself h** through you 7727
37:28 that I the LORD **make** Israel **h,** 7727
38:16 when I **show myself h** through you 7727
39: 7 " 'I will make known my **h** name 7731
39: 7 I will no longer let my **h** name be profaned, 7731
39: 7 that I the LORD am the **H One** in Israel. 7705
39:25 and I will be zealous for my **h** name. 7731
39:27 *I will* **show myself h** through them in 7727
41: 4 to me, "This is the **Most H Place."** 7731+7731
41:21 the front of the **Most H Place** was similar. 7731
41:23 and the **Most H Place** had double doors. 7731
42:13 LORD will eat the **most h offerings.** 7731+7731
42:13 they will put the **most h offerings—** 7731+7731
42:13 for the place is **h.** 7705
42:14 Once the priests enter the **h precincts,** 7731
42:14 for these are **h.** 7731
42:20 to separate the **h** from the common. 7731
43: 7 The house of Israel will never again defile my **h** name— 7731
43: 8 they defiled my **h** name by their detestable 7731
43:12 on top of the mountain will be **most h.** 7731+7731
44: 8 in regard to my **h things,** 7731
44:13 as priests or come near any of my **h things** 7731
44:13 holy things or my **most h offerings;** 7731+7731
44:23 the **h** and the common and show them how 7731
44:24 and *they are to* **keep** my Sabbaths **h.** 7727
45: 1 the entire area will be **h.** 7731
45: 3 the sanctuary, the **Most H Place.** 7731+7731
45: 4 a place for their houses as well as a **h place** 5219
48:12 of the land, a **most h** portion, 7731+7731
48:14 because it is **h** to the LORD. 7731
Da 4: 8 and the spirit of the **h** gods is in him.) 10620
4: 9 I know that the spirit of the **h** gods is in you 10620
4:13 a **h** *one,* coming down from heaven. 10620
4:17 the **h** *ones* declare the verdict, 10620
4:18 because the spirit of the **h** gods is in you." 10620
4:23 "You, O king, saw a messenger, a **h** *one,* 10620
5:11 the spirit of the **h** gods in him. 10620
8:13 Then I heard a **h** *one* speaking, 7705
8:13 and another **h** *one* said to him, 7705
8:24 the mighty men and the **h** people. 7705
9:16 your city, your **h** hill. 7731
9:20 to the LORD my God for his **h** hill— 7731
9:24 and your **h** city to finish transgression, 7731
9:24 prophecy and to anoint the **most h.** 7731+7731
11:28 his heart will be set against the **h** covenant. 7731
11:30 and vent his fury against the **h** covenant. 7731
11:30 to those who forsake the **h** covenant. 7731
11:45 the seas at the beautiful **h** mountain. 7731
12: 7 of the **h** people has been finally broken, 7731
Hos 11: 9 the **H One** among you. 7705
11:12 even against the faithful **H One.** 7705
Joel 1:14 **Declare** *a* **h** fast; call a sacred assembly. 7727
2: 1 sound the alarm on my **h** hill. 7731
2:15 Blow the trumpet in Zion, **declare** a **h** fast, 7727
3:17 dwell in Zion, my **h** hill. 7731
3:17 Jerusalem will be **h;** 7731

Am 2: 7 the same girl and so profane my **h** name. 7731
Ob 1:16 Just as you drank on my **h** hill, 7731
1:17 it will be **h,** and the house of Jacob 7731
Jnh 2: 4 yet I will look again toward your **h** temple.' 7731
2: 7 my prayer rose to you, to your **h** temple. 7731
Mic 1: 2 the Lord from his **h** temple. 7731
Hab 1:12 My God, my **H One,** we will not die. 7705
2:20 But the LORD is in his **h** temple; 7731
3: 3 the **H One** from Mount Paran. 7705
Zep 3:11 Never again will you be haughty on my **h** hill. 7731
Zec 2:12 the **h** land and will again choose Jerusalem. 7731
2:13 he has roused himself from his **h** dwelling." 7731
8: 3 be called the **H** Mountain." 7731
14: 5 and all the **h** *ones* with him. 7705
14:20 On that day **H TO THE LORD** will be 7731
14:21 Every pot in Jerusalem and Judah will be **h** 7731
Mt 1:18 to be with child through the **H** Spirit. 41
1:20 in her is from the **H** Spirit. 41
3:11 He will baptize you with the **H** Spirit and 41
4: 5 Then the devil took him to the **h** city 41
12:32 anyone who speaks against the **H** Spirit will not be forgiven, 41
24:15 "So when you see standing in the **h** place 41
27:52 *of* many **h people** who had died were raised 41
27:53 into the **h** city and appeared to many people. 41
28:19 the Father and of the Son and *of* the **H** Spirit, 41
Mk 1: 8 but he will baptize you with the **H** Spirit." 41
1:24 I know who you are—the **H** *One* of God!" 41
3:29 whoever blasphemes against the **H** Spirit will never be forgiven; 41
6:20 knowing him to be a righteous and **h** man. 41
8:38 in his Father's glory with the **h** angels." 41
12:36 David himself, speaking by the **H** Spirit, 41
13:11 for it is not you speaking, but the **H** Spirit. 41
Lk 1:15 and he will be filled *with* the **H** Spirit even 41
1:35 "The **H** Spirit will come upon you, 41
1:35 the **h** *one* to be born will be called the Son 41
1:41 and Elizabeth was filled *with* the **H** Spirit. 41
1:49 **h** is his name. 41
1:67 *with* the **H** Spirit and prophesied: 41
1:70 he said through his **h** prophets of long ago), 41
1:72 and to remember his **h** covenant, 41
2:25 and the **H** Spirit was upon him. 41
2:26 to him by the **H** Spirit that he would not die 41
3:16 He will baptize you with the **H** Spirit and 41
3:22 and the **H** Spirit descended on him 41
4: 1 Jesus, full *of* the **H** Spirit, 41
4:34 I know who you are—the **H** *One* of God!" 41
9:26 the glory of the Father and *of* the **h** angels. 41
10:21 full of joy through the **H** Spirit, said, 41
11:13 the **H** Spirit to those who ask him!" 41
12:10 anyone who blasphemes against the **H** Spirit will not be forgiven. 41
12:12 for the **H** Spirit will teach you at 41
Jn 1:33 he who will baptize you with the **H** Spirit.' 41
6:69 and know that you are the **H** *One* of God." 41
14:26 But the Counselor, the **H** Spirit, 41
17:11 **H** Father, protect them by the power 41
20:22 "Receive the **H** Spirit. 41
Ac 1: 2 giving instructions through the **H** Spirit 41
1: 5 you will be baptized with the **H** Spirit." 41
1: 8 when the **H** Spirit comes on you; 41
1:16 the **H** Spirit spoke long ago through 41
2: 4 All of them were filled *with* the **H** Spirit 41
2:27 nor will you let your **H** *One* see decay. 4008
2:33 from the Father the promised **H** Spirit 41
2:38 you will receive the gift *of* the **H** Spirit. 41
3:14 You disowned the **H** and Righteous *One* 41
3:21 through his **h** prophets. 41
4: 8 Peter, filled *with* the **H** Spirit, said to them: 41
4:25 You spoke by the **H** Spirit through 41
4:27 to conspire against your **h** servant Jesus, 41
4:30 through the name *of* your **h** servant Jesus." 41
4:31 And they were all filled *with* the **H** Spirit 41
5: 3 you have lied to the **H** Spirit 41
5:32 so is the **H** Spirit, whom God has given 41
6: 5 a man full of faith and *of* the **H** Spirit; 41
6:13 against this **h** place and against the law. 41
7:33 where you are standing is **h** ground. 41
7:51 You always resist the **H** Spirit! 41
7:55 But Stephen, full *of* the **H** Spirit, 41
8:15 that they might receive the **H** Spirit, 41
8:16 **H** Spirit had not yet come upon any of them NIG
8:17 and they received the **H** Spirit. 41
8:19 on whom I lay my hands may receive the **H** Spirit." 41
9:17 and be filled *with* the **H** Spirit." 41
9:31 and encouraged *by* the **H** Spirit, 41
10:22 A **h** angel told him to have you come 41
10:38 of Nazareth *with* the **H** Spirit and power, 41
10:44 the **H** Spirit came on all who heard the message. 41
10:45 *of* the **H** Spirit had been poured out even on 41
10:47 They have received the **H** Spirit just as we 41
11:15 the **H** Spirit came on them as he had come 41
11:16 but you will be baptized with the **H** Spirit.' 41
11:24 full *of* the **H** Spirit and faith, 41
13: 2 the **H** Spirit said, "Set apart for me Barnabas 41
13: 4 sent on their way by the **H** Spirit, 41
13: 9 filled *with* the **H** Spirit, 41
13:34 **h** and sure **blessings promised** to David.' 4008
13:35 " 'You will not let your **H** *One* see decay.' 4008
13:52 with joy and *with* the **H** Spirit. 41
15: 8 that he accepted them by giving the **H** Spirit 41
15:28 It seemed good *to* the **H** Spirit and to us not 41
16: 6 by the **H** Spirit from preaching the word in 41
Ac 19: 2 receive the **H** Spirit when you believed?" 41
19: 2 not even heard that there is a **H** Spirit." 41
19: 6 the **H** Spirit came on them, 41
20:23 that in every city the **H** Spirit warns me 41
20:28 the **H** Spirit has made you overseers. 41
21:11 "The **H** Spirit says, 'In this way 41
21:28 the temple area and defiled this **h** place." 41
28:25 "The **H** Spirit spoke the truth 41
Ro 1: 2 through his prophets in the **H** Scriptures 41
5: 5 his love into our hearts by the **H** Spirit, 41
7:12 So then, the law is **h,** 41
7:12 the law is holy, and the commandment is **h,** 41
9: 1 my conscience confirms it in the **H** Spirit— 41
11:16 of the dough offered as firstfruits is **h,** then 41
11:16 then the whole batch is **h;** NIG
11:16 if the root is **h,** so are the branches. 41
12: 1 living sacrifices, **h** and pleasing to God— 41
14:17 peace and joy in the **H** Spirit, 41
15:13 with hope by the power *of* the **H** Spirit. 41
15:16 sanctified by the **H** Spirit. 41
16:16 Greet one another with a **h** kiss. 41
1Co 1: 2 in Christ Jesus and called to be **h,** together 41
6:19 that your body is a temple *of* the **H** Spirit, 41
7:14 but as it is, they are **h.** 41
12: 3 "Jesus is Lord," except by the **H** Spirit. 41
16:20 Greet one another with a **h** kiss. 41
2Co 6: 6 in the **H** Spirit and in sincere love; 41
13:12 Greet one another with a **h** kiss. 41
13:14 fellowship *of* the **H** Spirit be with you all. 41
Eph 1: 4 the world to be **h** and blameless in his sight. 41
1:13 the promised **H** Spirit, 41
2:21 and rises to become a **h** temple in the Lord. 41
3: 5 the Spirit to God's **h** apostles and prophets. 41
4:30 And do not grieve the **H** Spirit of God, 41
5: 3 these are improper *for* **God's h people.** 41
5:26 to **make** her **h,** cleansing her by 39
5:27 but **h** and blameless. 41
Col 1: 2 *To* the **h** and faithful brothers in Christ 41
1:22 through death to present you **h** in his sight, 41
3:12 as God's chosen people, **h** and dearly loved, 41
1Th 1: 5 with the **H** Spirit and with deep conviction. 41
1: 6 with the joy *given by* the **H** Spirit. 41
2:10 You are witnesses, and so is God, of how **h,** 4010
3:13 **h** in the presence of our God and Father 43+1877
3:13 Lord Jesus comes with all his **h** *ones.* 41
4: 4 to control his own body in a way that is **h** 40
4: 7 but to live a **h life.** 40
4: 8 who gives you his **H** Spirit. 41
5:26 Greet all the brothers with a **h** kiss. 41
2Th 1:10 in his **h people** and to be marveled at 41
1Ti 2: 8 I want men everywhere to lift up **h** hands 4008
2Ti 1: 9 who has saved us and called us *to* a **h** life— 41
1:14 with the help *of* the **H** Spirit who lives in us. 41
2:21 an instrument for noble purposes, **made h,** 39
3:15 known the **h** Scriptures, which are able 2641
Tit 1: 8 upright, **h** and disciplined. 4008
3: 5 of rebirth and renewal *by* the **H** Spirit, 41
Heb 2: 4 **H** Spirit distributed according to his will. 41
2:11 Both the one who **makes** men **h** 39
2:11 and those who *are* **made h** are of 39
3: 1 Therefore, **h** brothers, who share in 41
3: 7 So, as the **H** Spirit says: 41
6: 4 who have shared in the **H** Spirit, 41
7:26 one who is **h,** blameless, pure, 4008
9: 2 this was called the **H Place.** 41
9: 3 a room called the **Most H Place,** 41+41
9: 8 The **H** Spirit was showing by this that 41
9: 8 the Most **H** Place had not yet been disclosed 41
9:12 but he entered the Most **H** Place once for all 41
9:25 the Most **H** Place every year with blood 41
10:10 *we have been* **made h** through the sacrifice of the body of Jesus Christ 39+1639
10:14 by one sacrifice he has made perfect forever those who *are being* **made h.** 39
10:15 The **H** Spirit also testifies to us about this. 41
10:19 the Most **H** *Place* by the blood of Jesus, 41
11: 7 *in* **h fear** built an ark to save his family. 2326
12:14 to live in peace with all men and to be **h;** 40
13:11 the blood of animals into the Most **H** *Place* 41
13:12 **make** the people **h** through his own blood. 39
1Pe 1:12 to you by the **H** Spirit sent from heaven. 41
1:15 But just as he who called you is **h,** 41
1:15 so be **h** in all you do; 41
1:16 for it is written: "Be **h,** because I am holy." 41
1:16 for it is written: "Be holy, because I am **h.**" 41
2: 5 into a spiritual house to be a **h** priesthood, 41
2: 9 a **h** nation, a people belonging to God, 41
3: 5 the **h** women of the past who put their hope 41
2Pe 1:21 as they were carried along by the **H** Spirit. 41
3: 2 by the **h** prophets and the command given 41
3:11 You ought to live **h** and godly *lives* 41
1Jn 2:20 But you have an anointing from the **H One,** 41
Jude 1:14 with thousands upon thousands of his **h ones** 41
1:20 build yourselves up *in your most* **h** faith 41
1:20 and pray in the **H** Spirit. 41
Rev 3: 7 These are the words of him who is **h** 41
4: 8 Day and night they never stop saying: "**H,** 41
4: 8 "Holy, **h,** holy is the Lord God Almighty, 41
4: 8 "Holy, holy, **h** is the Lord God Almighty, 41
6:10 "How long, Sovereign Lord, **h** and true, 41
11: 2 They will trample on the **h** city 41
14:10 in the presence *of* the **h** angels and of 41
15: 4 For you alone are **h.** 4008
16: 5 the **H** *One,* because you have so judged; 4008
20: 6 Blessed and **h** are those who have part in 41
21: 2 I saw the **H** City, the new Jerusalem, 41
21:10 and showed me the **H** City, Jerusalem, 41
Rev 22:11 and let him who *is* **h** continue to be holy." 41
22:11 and *let* him who is holy continue *to be* **h.**" 39
22:19 in the tree of life and in the **h** city, 41

HOLYDAY (KJV) See RELIGIOUS FESTIVAL

HOMAGE (3)

2Ch 24:17 the officials of Judah came and **paid h** to 2556
Job 31:27 hand **offered** them **a kiss of h,** 4200+5975+7023
Mk 15:19 Falling on their knees, *they* **paid h** to him. *4686*

HOMAM (2)

Ge 36:22 The sons of Lotan: Hori and **H.** 2123
1Ch 1:39 The sons of Lotan: Hori and **H.** 2102

HOME (186) [HOMELAND, HOMELESS, HOMES]

Ge 18:33 he left, and Abraham returned **h.** 5226
29:13 and kissed him and brought him to his **h,** 1074
31:55 Then he left and returned **h.** 5226
34: 5 so he kept quiet about it until they **came h.** 995
35:27 Jacob **came h** to his father Isaac in Mamre, 995
39:16 beside her until his master came **h.** 1074
43:26 When Joseph came **h,** 1074
Ex 3: 8 the **h** *of* the Canaanites, Hittites, Amorites, 5226
18:23 and all these people will go **h** satisfied." 5226
Lev 18: 9 **born in the same h** or elsewhere. 1074+4580
Nu 14:30 with uplifted hand to **make** your **h,** 8905
15: 2 you enter the land I am giving you as a **h** 4632
24:11 Now leave at once and go **h!** 5226
24:25 Then Balaam got up and returned **h** 5226
Dt 6: 7 when you sit at **h** and when you walk along 1074
11:19 when you sit at **h** and when you walk along 1074
20: 5 Let him go **h,** or he may die in battle 1074
20: 6 Let him go **h,** or he may die in battle 1074
20: 7 Let him go **h,** or he may die in battle 1074
20: 8 Let him go **h** so that his brothers will 1074
21:12 into your **h** and have her shave her head, 1074
22: 2 take it **h** with you and keep it 1074
24: 5 to be free to stay at **h** and bring happiness to 1074
Jos 9:12 when we packed it at **h** on the day we left 1074
20: 6 Then he may go back to his own **h** in 1074
22: 7 When Joshua sent them **h,** he blessed them, 185
Jdg 8:29 Jerub-Baal son of Joash went back **h** to live. 1074
9: 5 He went to his father's **h** in Ophrah and 1074
9:55 that Abimelech was dead, they went **h.** 5226
11:34 When Jephthah returned to his **h** in Mizpah, 1074
18:26 turned around and went back **h.** 1074
19: 9 up and be on your way **h.**" 185
19:15 no one took them into his **h** for the night. 1074
19:28 man put her on his donkey and set out for **h.** 5226
19:29 When he reached **h,** 1074
20: 8 saying, "None of us will go **h.** 185
21:24 the Israelites left that place and went **h** NIH
Ru 1: 6 to return **h** from there. NIH
1: 8 "Go back, each of you, to your mother's **h.** 1074
1: 9 that each of you will find rest in the **h** 1074
1:11 But Naomi said, "Return **h,** my daughters. NIH
1:12 Return **h,** my daughters; NIH
3: 1 should I not try to find a **h** for you, 4955
4:11 the woman who is coming into your **h** 1074
1Sa 1:19 the LORD and then went back to their **h** 1074
1:23 the woman **stayed at h** and nursed her son 3782
2:11 Then Elkanah went **h** to Ramah, 1074
2:20 Then they would go **h.** 5226
7:17 went back to Ramah, where his **h** was, 1074
10:25 each to his own **h.** 1074
10:26 Saul also went to his **h** in Gibeah, 1074
15:34 but Saul went up to his **h** *in* Gibeah of Saul. 1074
18: 6 When the men were returning **h** NIH
23:18 Then Jonathan went **h,** 1074
24:22 Then Saul returned **h,** 1074
25: 1 and they buried him at his **h** in Ramah. 1074
25:35 "Go **h** in peace. 1074
26:25 and Saul returned **h.** 5226
2Sa 3:16 Then Abner said to him, "Go back **h!**" NIH
6:20 David returned **h** to bless his household, NIH
7:10 so that *they can* **have a h** *of* their own 8905+9393
11: 4 Then she went back **h.** 1074
11:10 When David was told, "Uriah did not go **h,**" 1074
11:10 Why didn't you go **h?**" 1074
11:13 he did not go **h.** 1074
12:15 After Nathan had gone **h,** 1074
14: 8 The king said to the woman, "Go **h,** 1074
19:30 that my lord the king has arrived **h** safely." 1074
19:39 and Barzillai returned to his **h.** 5226
20:22 each returning to his **h.** 185
1Ki 1:53 and Solomon said, "Go to your **h.**" 1074
5:14 in Lebanon and two months at **h.** 1074
8:66 They blessed the king and then went **h,** 185
12:16 So the Israelites went **h.** 185
12:24 Go **h,** every one of you, 1074
12:24 the word of the LORD and **went h** again, 2143
13: 7 "Come **h** with me and have something 1074
13:15 "Come **h** with me and eat." 1074
14:12 "As for you, go back **h.** 1074
16: 9 getting drunk in the **h** *of* Arza, 1074
17:12 a few sticks *to* **take h** and make a meal 995
17:13 Go **h** and do as you have said. 995
21: 4 So Ahab went **h,** sullen and angry 1074
22:17 Let each one go **h** in peace.' " 1074
2Ki 4:13 "**I have a h** among my own people." 3782

2Ki 8:21 his army, however, fled back **h**. 185
14:10 Glory in your victory, but stay at **h**! 1074
14:12 and every man fled to his **h**. 185
1Ch 16:43 Then all the people left, each for his own **h**, 1074
16:43 and David **returned h** to bless his family. 6015
17: 9 so that *they can* **have a h** *of their own* 8905+9393
2Ch 10:16 So all the Israelites went **h**. 185
11: 4 Go **h**, every one of you, 1074
18:16 Let each one go **h** in peace.' " 1074
25:10 to him from Ephraim and sent them **h**. 5226
25:10 They were furious with Judah and left for **h** 5226
25:19 But stay at **h**! 1074
25:22 and every man fled to his **h**. 185
Ne 6:10 who was shut in at his **h**. NIH
Est 5:10 Haman restrained himself and went **h**. 1074
6:12 But Haman rushed **h**, 1074
Job 17:13 If the only **h** I hope for is the grave, 1074
39: 6 I gave him the wasteland as his **h**, 1074
Ps 84: 3 Even the sparrow has found a **h**, 1074
104:17 the stork has its **h** in the pine trees. 1074
113: 9 He settles the barren woman in her **h** as 1074
Pr 3:33 but he blesses the **h** *of* the righteous. 5659
7:11 her feet never stay at **h**; 1074
7:14 "I have fellowship offerings at **h**; NIH
7:19 My husband is not at **h**; 1074
7:20 and will not be **h** till full moon." 1074
15:31 to a life-giving rebuke *will be* **at h** among 4328
27: 8 a man who strays from his **h**. 5226
30:26 yet they make their **h** in the crags; 1074
Ecc 12: 5 to his eternal **h** and mourners go about 1074
Isa 3: 6 at his father's **h**, and say, "You have 1074
14:17 and would not let his captives go **h**?" 1074
34:13 a haunt for jackals, a **h** for owls. 2948
Jer 39:14 to take him back to his **h**. 1074
Eze 36: 8 for *they will* soon **come h**. 995
Da 4: 4 I, Nebuchadnezzar, was at **h** in my palace, 10103
6:10 he went **h** to his upstairs room where 10103
Ob 1: 3 the clefts of the rocks and make your **h** on 8699
Jnh 4: 2 is this not what I said when I was still at **h**? 141
Mic 2: 2 They defraud a man of his **h**, 1074
Zep 3:20 at that time *I will* **bring** you **h**. 995
Hag 1: 9 What you brought **h**, I blew away. 1074
Mt 1:20 not be afraid to take Mary **h** as your wife, *NIG*
1:24 and took Mary **h** as his wife. *NIG*
8: 6 at **h** paralyzed and in terrible suffering." *3864*
9: 6 "Get up, take your mat and go **h**." *3875*
9: 7 And the man got up and went **h**. *3875*
10:12 As you enter the **h**, give it your greeting. *3864*
10:13 If the **h** is deserving, let your peace rest on *3864*
10:14 the dust off your feet when you leave that **h** *3864*
26: 6 the **h** of a man known as Simon the Leper, *3864*
Mk 1:29 and John to the **h** of Simon and Andrew. *3864*
2: 1 the people heard that he had come **h**. *3875*
2:11 "I tell you, get up, take your mat and go **h**." *1650+3836+3875+5148*
5:19 "Go **h** to your family and tell them *3875*
5:38 to the **h** of the synagogue ruler, *3875*
7:30 She went **h** and found her child *899+3836+3875*
8: 3 If I send them **h** hungry, *899+1650+3875*
8:26 Jesus sent him **h**, saying, *899+1650+3875*
10:29 "no one who has left **h** or brothers or sisters *3864*
14: 3 the table in the **h** of a man known as Simon *3864*
Lk 1:23 of service was completed, he returned **h**. *3875*
1:40 where she entered Zechariah's **h** *3875*
1:56 for about three months and then returned **h**. *3875*
2:43 while his parents were returning **h**, *NIG*
4:38 the synagogue and went to the **h** of Simon. *3864*
5:24 get up, take your mat and go **h**. *1650+3836+3875*
5:25 and went **h** praising God. *899+1650+3836+3875*
8:39 "Return **h** and tell how much God has done *3875+5148*
10:38 a woman named Martha **opened** her **h to** *5685*
15: 6 and goes **h**. Then he calls his friends *3875*
15:30 with prostitutes **comes h**, *2262*
18:14 went **h** justified before God. *899+3836+3875*
18:29 "no one who has left **h** or wife or brothers *3864*
19:15 however, and returned **h**. *NIG*
23:56 Then they *went* **h** and prepared spices *5715*
Jn 7:53 Then each went to his own **h**. *3875*
9: 7 man went and washed, and came **h** seeing. *NIG*
11:20 but Mary stayed at **h**. *3875*
14:23 and we will come to him and make our **h** *3665*
16:32 each to **his own h**. *2625+3836*
19:27 this disciple took her into **his h**. *2625+3836*
Ac 8:28 and **on** *his* **way h** was sitting *5715*
10:32 He is a guest in the **h** of Simon the tanner, *3864*
16:15 she invited us to her **h**. *NIG*
18:26 **invited** him **to** *their* **h** *4689*
20:12 The people took the young man **h** alive *NIG*
21: 6 and they returned **h**. *2625+3836*
21:16 and brought us to the **h** of Mnason, *NIG*
28: 7 He welcomed us to his **h** and *NIG*
1Co 11:34 If anyone is hungry, he should eat at **h**, *3875*
14:35 they should ask their own husbands at **h**; *3875*
2Co 5: 6 that *as long as we are* **at h** in the body, *1897*
5: 8 away from the body and **at h** with the Lord. *1897*
5: 9 whether *we are* **at h** in the body or away *1897*
Tit 2: 5 to be **busy at h**, to be kind, *3877*
Phm 1: 2 and to the church that meets in your **h**: *3875*
Heb 11: 9 By faith *he* **made** *his* **h** in the promised land *4228*
2Pe 3:13 and a new earth, the **h** of righteousness. *2997*
Jude 1: 6 of authority but abandoned their own **h**— *3863*
Rev 18: 2 She has become a **h** for demons and a haunt *2999*

HOMEBORN (KJV) See BY BIRTH, NATIVE BORN

HOMELAND (7) [HOME]

Ge 30:25 so I can go back to my own **h**. 824+5226
Ru 2:11 mother and your **h** and came to live 824+4580
2Sa 15:19 You are a foreigner, an exile from your **h**. 5226
2Ki 17:23 the people of Israel were taken from their **h** 141
Ps 79: 7 devoured Jacob and destroyed his **h**. 5659
Jer 10:25 completely and destroyed his **h**. 5659
Joel 3: 6 that you might send them far from their **h**. 1473

HOMELESS (1) [HOME]

1Co 4:11 we are brutally treated, *we are* **h**. *841*

HOMER (10) [HOMERS]

Lev 27:16 fifty shekels of silver to a **h** *of* barley seed. 2818
Isa 5:10 a **h** of seed only an ephah of grain." 2818
Eze 45:11 of a **h** and the ephah a tenth of a homer; 2818
45:11 of a homer and the ephah a tenth of a **h**; 2818
45:11 the **h** is to be the standard measure for both. 2818
45:13 an ephah from each **h** *of* wheat and a sixth 2818
45:13 a sixth of an ephah from each **h** *of* barley. 2818
45:14 of ten baths or one **h**, 2818
45:14 for ten baths are equivalent to a **h**). 2818
Hos 3: 2 for fifteen shekels of silver and about a **h** 2818

HOMERS (1) [HOMER]

Nu 11:32 No one gathered less than ten **h**. 2818

HOMES (30) [HOME]

Ex 12:27 of the Israelites in Egypt and spared our **h** 1074
Nu 32:18 We will not return to our **h** 1074
Dt 32:25 in their **h** terror will reign. 2540
Jos 22: 4 to your **h** in the land that Moses the servant 185
22: 6 and they went to their **h**. 185
22: 8 "Return to your **h** with your great wealth— 185
1Sa 13: 2 The rest of the men he sent back to their **h**. 185
2Sa 6:19 And all the people went to their **h**. 1074
18:17 Meanwhile, all the Israelites fled to their **h**. 185
19: 8 Meanwhile, the Israelites had fled to their **h**. 185
2Ki 13: 5 So the Israelites lived in their own **h** 185
2Ch 7:10 he sent the people to their **h**, joyful 185
Ne 4:14 your wives and your **h**." 1074
5: 3 our vineyards and our **h** to get grain during 1074
Job 1: 4 to take turns holding feasts in their **h**, 1074
2:11 from their **h** and met together by agreement 5226
21: 9 Their **h** are safe and free from fear; 1074
36:20 to drag people away from their **h**. 9393
Ps 78:55 he settled the tribes of Israel in their **h**. 185
109:10 may they be driven from their **ruined h**. 2999
Isa 32:18 in secure **h**, in undisturbed places of rest. 5438
La 5: 2 to aliens, our **h** to foreigners. 1074
Hos 11:11 I will settle them in their **h**," 1074
Mic 2: 9 of my people from their pleasant **h**. 1074
Mk 10:30 as much in this present age (**h**, brothers, *3864*
Jn 20:10 Then the disciples went back to **their h**, *899S*
Ac 2:46 They broke bread **in their h** and ate together *2848+3875*
1Co 11:22 Don't you have **h** to eat and drink in? *3864*
1Ti 5:14 *to* **manage** *their* **h** and to give *3866*
2Ti 3: 6 the kind who worm their way into **h** *3864*

HOMETOWN (9) [TOWN]

1Sa 20: 6 to hurry to Bethlehem, his **h**, because 6551
2Sa 15:12 to come from Giloh, his **h**. 6551
17:23 and set out for his house in his **h**. 6551
Mt 13:54 Coming to his **h**, he began teaching *4258*
13:57 in his **h** and in his own house is a prophet *4258*
Mk 6: 1 Jesus left there and went to his **h**, *4258*
6: 4 Jesus said to them, "Only in his **h**, *4258*
Lk 4:23 in your **h** what we have heard that you did *4258*
4:24 "no prophet is accepted in his **h**. *4258*

HOMOSEXUAL (1)

1Co 6: 9 nor male prostitutes nor **h offenders** *780*

HONEST (19) [HONESTLY, HONESTY]

Ge 42:11 Your servants are **h** *men,* not spies." 4026
42:19 If you are **h** *men,* 4026
42:31 But we said to him, 'We are **h** *men;* 4026
42:33 how I will know whether you are **h** *men:* 4026
42:34 that you are not spies but **h** *men.* 4026
Ex 23: 7 not put an innocent or **h** *person* to death, 7404
Lev 19:36 Use **h** scales and honest weights, 7406
19:36 Use honest scales and **h** weights, 7406
19:36 an **h** ephah and an honest hin. 7406
19:36 an honest ephah and an **h** hin. 7406
Dt 25:15 You must have accurate and **h** weights 7406
1Ch 29:17 and with **h** intent. 3841
Job 6:25 How painful are **h** words! 3841
31: 6 let God weigh me in **h** scales 7406
Pr 12:17 A truthful witness gives **h** testimony, 7406
16:11 **H** scales and balances are from the LORD; 5477
16:13 Kings take pleasure in **h** lips; 7406
24:26 An **h** answer is like a kiss on the lips. 5791
Lk 20:20 they sent spies, who pretended to be **h**. *1465*

HONESTLY (1) [HONEST]

Jer 5: 1 If you can find but one person who deals **h** 5477

HONESTY (3) [HONEST]

Ge 30:33 And my **h** will testify for me in the future, 7407
2Ki 12:15 because they acted with **complete h**. 575
Isa 59:14 in the streets, **h** cannot enter. 5791

HONEY (60) [HONEYCOMB]

Ge 43:11 a little balm and a little **h**, 1831
Ex 3: 8 a land flowing with milk and **h**— 1831
3:17 a land flowing with milk and **h**.' 1831
13: 5 a land flowing with milk and **h**— 1831
16:31 and tasted like wafers made with **h**. 1831
33: 3 Go up to the land flowing with milk and **h**. 1831
Lev 2:11 to burn any yeast or **h** in an offering made 1831
20:24 a land flowing with milk and **h**." 1831
Nu 13:27 and it does flow with milk and **h**! 1831
14: 8 a land flowing with milk and **h**, 1831
16:13 of a land flowing with milk and **h** to kill us 1831
16:14 a land flowing with milk and **h** or given us 1831
Dt 6: 3 in a land flowing with milk and **h**, 1831
8: 8 pomegranates, olive oil and **h**; 1831
11: 9 a land flowing with milk and **h**. 1831
26: 9 a land flowing with milk and **h**; 1831
26:15 a land flowing with milk and **h**." 1831
27: 3 a land flowing with milk and **h**, 1831
31:20 into the land flowing with milk and **h**, 1831
32:13 He nourished him with **h** from the rock, 1831
Jos 5: 6 a land flowing with milk and **h**. 1831
Jdg 14: 8 In it was a swarm of bees and *some* **h**, 1831
14: 9 not tell them that he had taken the **h** from 1831
14:18 "What is sweeter than **h**? 1831
1Sa 14:25 and there was **h** on the ground. 1831
14:26 they saw the **h** oozing out, 1831
14:29 when I tasted a little of this **h**. 1831
14:43 "I merely tasted a little **h** with the end 1831
2Sa 17:29 **h** and curds, sheep, and cheese 1831
1Ki 14: 3 some cakes and a jar of **h**, and go to him. 1831
2Ki 18:32 a land of olive trees and **h**. 1831
2Ch 31: 5 oil and **h** and all that the fields produced. 1831
Job 20:17 the rivers flowing with **h** and cream. 1831
Ps 19:10 they are sweeter than **h**, 1831
19:10 than **h** *from* the comb. 5885
81:16 with **h** from the rock I would satisfy you." 1831
119:103 sweeter than **h** to my mouth! 1831
Pr 5: 3 For the lips of an adulteress drip **h**, 5885
24:13 Eat **h**, my son, for it is good; 1831
24:13 **h from the comb** is sweet to your taste. 5885
25:16 If you find **h**, eat just enough— 1831
25:27 It is not good to eat too much **h**, 1831
27: 7 He who is full loathes **h**, 5885
SS 4:11 milk and **h** are under your tongue. 1831
5: 1 I have eaten my honeycomb and my **h**; 1831
Isa 7:15 and **h** when he knows enough to reject 1831
7:22 in the land will eat curds and **h**. 1831
Jer 11: 5 a land flowing with milk and **h**'— 1831
32:22 a land flowing with milk and **h**. 1831
41: 8 We have wheat and barley, oil and **h**, 1831
Eze 3: 3 and it tasted as sweet as **h** in my mouth. 1831
16:13 Your food was fine flour, **h** and olive oil. 1831
16:19 olive oil and **h** I gave you to eat— 1831
20: 6 a land flowing with milk and **h**, 1831
20:15 a land flowing with milk and **h**, 1831
27:17 **h**, oil and balm for your wares. 1831
Mt 3: 4 His food was locusts and wild **h**. *3510*
Mk 1: 6 and he ate locusts and wild **h**. *3510*
Rev 10: 9 but in your mouth it will be as sweet as **h**." *3510*
10:10 It tasted as sweet as **h** in my mouth, *3510*

HONEYCOMB (4) [HONEY]

1Sa 14:27 in his hand and dipped it into the **h**. 1831+3626
Pr 16:24 Pleasant words are a **h**, 1831+7430
SS 4:11 Your lips drop **sweetness as the h**, my bride; 5885
5: 1 I have eaten my **h** and my honey; 3624

HONOR (174) [HONORABLE, HONORABLY, HONORED, HONORING, HONORS]

Ge 30:20 This time my husband *will* **treat** me **with h**, 2290
43:28 And they bowed low *to* **pay** him **h**. 2556
45:13 Tell my father about all the **h** *accorded* me 3883
49: 3 the first sign of my strength, excelling in **h**, 8420
Ex 8: 9 **leave** *to you* **the h** of setting the time 6995
12:42 the Israelites are to keep vigil **to h** 4200
20:12 "**H** your father and your mother, 3877
28: 2 to give him dignity and **h**. 9514
28:40 to give them dignity and **h**. 9514
Nu 20:12 in me enough to **h** me **as holy** in the sight of 7727
25:11 as zealous as I am for my **h** among them, NIH
25:13 because he was zealous for the **h** of his God NIH
27:14 to **h** me **as holy** before their eyes." 7727
Dt 5:16 "**H** your father and your mother, 3877
26:19 fame and **h** high above all the nations 9514
Jdg 4: 9 the **h** will not be yours, 9514
13:17 *we may* **h** you when your word comes true? 3877
1Sa 2: 8 and has them inherit a throne of **h**. 3883
2:29 Why *do you* **h** your sons more than me 3877
2:30 *Those who* **h** me I will honor, 3877
2:30 Those who honor me *I will* **h**, 3877
6: 5 and pay **h** to Israel's god. 3883
15:12 up a monument **in** his own **h** and has turned 4200
15:30 But please **h** me before the elders 3877
2Sa 1: 2 he fell to the ground *to* **pay** him **h**. 2556
6:22 *I will* **be held in h**." 3877
9: 6 he bowed down *to* **pay** him **h**. 2556
14: 4 with her face to the ground *to* **pay** him **h**, 2556
14:22 with his face to the ground *to* **pay** him **h**, 2556
23:19 *he* not **held in** greater **h** than the Three? 3877

2Sa 23:23 *He* **was held in** greater **h** than any of 3877
1Ki 3:13 have not asked for—both riches and **h**— 3883
2Ki 10:20 **"Call** an assembly **in h of** Baal." 4200+7727
25:28 and gave him a **seat of h** higher than those 4058
1Ch 11:25 *He* **was held in** greater **h** than any of 3877
29:12 Wealth and **h** come from you; 3883
29:28 having enjoyed long life, wealth and **h.** 3883
2Ch 1:11 or **h,** nor for the death of your enemies, and 3883
1:12 I will also give you wealth, riches and **h,** 3883
16:14 and they made a huge fire **in** his **h.** 4200
17:5 so that he had great wealth and **h.** 3883
18:1 Now Jehoshaphat had great wealth and **h,** 3883
21:19 His people made no fire **in** his **h,** 4200
32:27 Hezekiah had very great riches and **h,** 3883
Ezr 7:27 into the king's heart to **bring h** *to* the house 6995
Est 3:1 and giving him a **seat of h** higher than that 4058
3:2 at the king's gate knelt down and **paid h** 2556
3:2 not kneel down or **pay** him **h.** 2556
3:5 not kneel down or **pay** him **h,** 2556
6:3 "What **h** and recognition has Mordecai received 3702
6:6 be done for the man the king delights to **h?"** 3702
6:6 that the king would rather **h** than me?" 3702+6913
6:7 "For the man the king delights to **h,** 3702
6:9 robe the man the king delights to **h,** 3702
6:9 done for the man the king delights to **h!' "** 3702
6:11 done for the man the king delights to **h!"** 3702
8:16 a time of happiness and joy, gladness and **h.** 3702
Job 19:9 He has stripped me of my **h** and removed 3883
40:10 and clothe yourself in **h** and majesty. 2086
Ps 8:5 and crowned him with glory and **h.** 2077
22:23 All *you* descendants of Jacob, **h** him! 3877
45:11 **h** him, for he is your lord. 2556
50:15 I will deliver you, and *you will* **h** me." 3877
62:7 My salvation and my **h** depend on God; 3883
71:21 You will increase my **h** 1525
84:11 the LORD bestows favor and **h;** 3883
91:15 I will deliver him and **h** him. 3877
112:9 his horn will be lifted high in **h.** 3883
149:5 the saints rejoice in this **h** and sing for joy 3883
Pr 3:9 **H** the LORD with your wealth, 3877
3:16 in her left hand are riches and **h.** 3883
3:35 The wise inherit **h,** 3883
4:8 embrace her, and *she will* **h** you. 3877
8:18 With me are riches and **h,** 3883
15:33 and humility comes before **h.** 3883
18:12 but humility comes before **h.** 3883
20:3 It is to a man's **h** to avoid strife, 3883
21:21 and love finds life, prosperity and **h.** 3883
22:4 of the LORD bring wealth and **h** and life. 3883
25:27 nor is it honorable to seek one's own **h.** 3883
26:1 **h** is not fitting for a fool. 3883
26:8 a stone in a sling is the giving of **h** to a fool. 3883
29:23 but a man of lowly spirit gains **h.** 3883
Ecc 6:2 a man wealth, possessions and **h,** so 3883
10:1 so a little folly outweighs wisdom and **h.** 3883
Isa 9:1 the future *he will* **h** Galilee of the Gentiles, 3877
22:23 be a seat of **h** for the house of his father. 3883
25:3 Therefore strong peoples *will* **h** you; 3877
26:13 but your name alone *do we* **h.** 2349
29:13 with their mouth and **h** me with their lips, 3877
43:20 The wild animals **h** me, 3877
45:4 **bestow** *on* you **a title of h,** 4033
58:13 and if *you* **h** it by not going your own way 3877
60:9 to the **h** *of* the LORD your God, 9005
Jer 3:17 and all nations will gather in Jerusalem to **h** NIH
13:11 for my renown and praise and **h.** 9514
30:19 *I will* **bring** them **h,** 3877
33:9 and **h** before all nations on earth that hear 9514
34:5 As people made a **funeral fire** *in h* AIT
34:5 they will make a fire **in** your **h** and lament, 4200
52:32 and gave him a **seat of h** higher than those 4058
La 4:16 priests *are* **shown** no **h,** the elders no favor. 5951+7156
Da 2:6 from me gifts and rewards and great **h.** 10331
2:46 and **paid** him **h** and ordered that an offering 10504
4:36 my **h** and splendor were returned to me for 10199
5:23 But *you did* not **h** the God who holds 10198
11:21 not been given the **h** *of* royalty. 2086
11:38 *he will* **h** a god of fortresses; 3877
11:38 to his fathers *he will* **h** with gold and silver, 3877
11:39 will greatly **h** those who acknowledge him. 3883
Hab 1:7 to themselves and promote their own **h.** 8420
Zep 3:19 I will give them praise and **h** in every land 9005
3:20 I will give you **h** and praise among all 9005
Zec 12:7 so that the **h** *of* the house of David and 9514
Mal 1:6 If I am a father, where is the **h** *due* me? 3883
2:2 if you do not set your heart to **h** my name," 3883+5989
2:2 you have not set your heart to **h** me. NIH
Mt 13:57 in his own house is a prophet **without h."** *872*
15:4 **'H** your father and mother' *5506*
15:6 *he is* not *to* **'h** his father' with it. *5506*
15:8 " 'These people **h** me with their lips, *5506*
19:19 **h** your father and mother,' *5506*
23:6 they love the **place of h** at banquets and *4752*
Mk 6:4 in his own house is a prophet **without h."** *872*
7:6 " 'These people **h** me with their lips, *5506*
7:10 **'H** your father and your mother,' and, *5506*
10:19 do not defraud, **h** your father and mother.' " *5506*
12:39 in the synagogues and the **places of h** *4752*
Lk 14:7 guests picked the **places of h at the table,** *4752*
14:8 do not take the **place of h,** *4752*
18:20 **h** your father and mother.' " *5506*
20:46 in the synagogues and the **places of h** *4752*
Jn 4:44 that a prophet has no **h** in his own country.) *5507*
5:23 that all *may* **h** the Son just as they honor *5506*
5:23 honor the Son just as *they* **h** the Father, *5506*
5:23 He who *does* not **h** the Son does not honor *5506*
5:23 not honor the Son *does* not **h** the Father, *5506*
7:18 He who speaks on his own does so to gain **h** *1518*
7:18 for the **h** of the one who sent him is a man *1518*
8:49 "but *I* **h** my Father and you dishonor me. *5506*
12:2 Here a dinner was given *in* **Jesus'** *h.* *AIT*
12:26 My Father *will* **h** the one who serves me. *5506*
Ac 7:41 in **h** of what their hands had made. *NIG*
19:17 name of the Lord Jesus *was* **held in high h.** *3486*
Ro 2:7 **h** and immortality, he will give eternal life. *5507*
2:10 **h** and peace for everyone who does good: *5507*
12:10 **H** one another above yourselves. *5507*
13:7 if respect, then respect; if **h,** then honor. *5507*
13:7 if respect, then respect; if honor, then **h.** *5507*
1Co 6:20 Therefore **h** God with your body. *1519*
12:23 that we think are less honorable we treat with special **h.** *5507*
12:24 the body and has given greater **h** to the parts *5507*
2Co 8:19 in order to **h** the Lord himself and *1518*
8:23 of the churches and an **h** to Christ. *1518*
Eph 6:2 **"H** your father and mother"— *5506*
Php 2:29 and **h** men like him, *1952+2400*
1Ti 1:17 be **h** and glory for ever and ever. *5507*
5:17 of the church well are worthy *of* double **h,** *5507*
6:16 To him be **h** and might forever. *5507*
Heb 2:7 you crowned him *with* glory and **h** *5507*
2:9 *with* glory and **h** because he suffered death, *5507*
3:3 found worthy of greater **h** than Moses, *1518*
3:3 as the builder of a house has greater **h** than *5507*
5:4 No one takes this **h** upon himself; *5507*
1Pe 1:7 glory and **h** when Jesus Christ is revealed. *5507*
2:17 fear God, **h** the king. *5506*
2Pe 1:17 For he received **h** and glory from God *5507*
Rev 4:9 **h** and thanks to him who sits on the throne *5507*
4:11 to receive glory and **h** and power, *5507*
5:12 and wealth and wisdom and strength and **h** *5507*
5:13 the throne and to the Lamb be praise and **h** *5507*
7:12 and **h** and power and strength be to our God *5507*
13:14 *in h of* **the beast** who was wounded by *AIT*
21:26 and **h** of the nations will be brought into it. *5507*

HONORABLE (7) [HONOR]

1Ch 4:9 Jabez was more **h** than his brothers. 3877
Ezr 4:10 and **h** Ashurbanipal deported and settled in 10330
Pr 25:27 nor is it **h** to seek one's own honor. 3883
Isa 3:5 the base against the **h.** 3877
58:13 a delight and the LORD's holy day **h,** 3877
1Co 12:23 the parts that we think are **less h** we treat *872*
1Th 4:4 in a way that is holy and **h,** *5507*

HONORABLY (3) [HONOR]

Jdg 9:16 if you have acted **h** and in good faith 622+928
9:19 if then you have acted **h** and in good faith 622+928
Heb 13:18 a clear conscience and desire to live **h** *2822*

HONORED (32) [HONOR]

Ge 34:19 the most **h** of all his father's household, 3877
Ex 20:24 **cause** my name to **be h,** 2349
Lev 10:3 in the sight of all the people *I will* **be h.' "** 3877
Jdg 9:9 by which both gods and men *are* **h,** 3877
1Ch 11:21 *He* **was** doubly **h** above the Three 3877
2Ch 26:18 and you will not be **h** by the LORD God." 3883
32:33 and the people of Jerusalem **h** him 3883+6913
Est 3:1 King Xerxes **h** Haman son of Hammedatha, 1540
5:11 and all the ways the king *had* **h** him and 1540
Job 14:21 If his sons *are* **h,** he does not know it; 3877
22:8 an **h** *man,* living on it. 5951+7156
Ps 12:8 about when what is vile *is* **h** among men. 8123
45:9 of kings are among your **h** *women;* 3701
Pr 13:18 but whoever heeds correction is **h.** 3877
27:18 and he who looks after his master *will* **be h.** 3877
Isa 43:4 Since you are precious and **h** in my sight, 3877
43:23 nor **h** me *with* your sacrifices. 3877
49:5 and gather Israel to himself, for *I* **am h** in 3877
La 1:8 All *who* **h** her despise her, 3877
Da 4:34 *I* **h** and glorified him who lives forever. 10693
Hag 1:8 so that I may take pleasure in it and **be h,"** 3877
Zec 2:8 "After he has **h** me and has sent me against 3883
Mal 3:16 feared the LORD and **h** his name. 3108
Mt 6:2 to *be* **h** by men. *1519*
Lk 14:10 Then you will be **h** in the presence *1518*
Ac 5:34 who was **h** by all the people, *5508*
13:48 they were glad and **h** the word of the Lord; *1519*
28:10 They **h** us in many ways and *5506+5507*
1Co 4:10 You are **h,** we are dishonored! *1902*
12:26 if one part *is* **h,** every part rejoices with it. *1519*
2Th 3:1 of the Lord may spread rapidly and *be* **h,** *1519*
Heb 13:4 Marriage should be **h** by all, *5508*

HONORING (3) [HONOR]

2Sa 10:3 "Do you think David *is* **h** your father 3877
1Ch 17:18 to you for **h** your servant? 3883
19:3 "Do you think David *is* **h** your father 3877

HONORS (4) [HONOR]

Ps 15:4 a vile man but **h** those who fear the LORD, 3877
50:23 He who sacrifices thank offerings **h** me, 3877
Pr 14:31 but whoever is kind to the needy **h** God. 3877
Mal 1:6 son **h** his father, and a servant his master. 3877

HOOF (12) [HOOFS]

Ex 10:26 not a **h** is to be left behind. 7274
Lev 11:3 a split **h** completely divided and that chews 7274
11:4 the cud or only have a split **h,** 7274
11:4 does not have a split **h;** 7274
11:5 does not have a split **h;** 7274
11:6 does not have a split **h;** 7274
11:7 though it has a split **h** completely divided, 7274
11:26 a split **h** not completely divided or that does 7274
Dt 14:6 a split **h** divided in two and that chews 7274
14:7 a split **h** completely divided you may 7274
14:7 they do not have a split **h;** 7274
14:8 although it has a split **h,** 7274

HOOFS (8) [HOOF]

Jdg 5:22 Then thundered the horses' **h**— 6811
Ps 69:31 more than a bull with its horns and **h.** 7271
Isa 5:28 their horses' **h** seem like flint, 7274
Jer 47:3 at the sound of the **h** *of* galloping steeds, 7274
Eze 26:11 **h** *of* his horses will trample all your streets; 7274
32:13 by the foot of man or muddied by the **h** 7274
Mic 4:13 I will give you **h** *of* bronze 7274
Zec 11:16 tearing off their **h.** 7274

HOOK (4) [FISHHOOK, FISHHOOKS, HOOKS]

2Ki 19:28 I will put my **h** in your nose and my bit 2626
2Ch 33:11 took Manasseh prisoner, put a **h** in his nose, 2560
Job 41:2 or pierce his jaw with a **h?** 2560
Isa 37:29 I will put my **h** in your nose and my bit 2626

HOOKS (24) [HOOK]

Ex 26:32 Hang it with gold **h** on four posts 2260
26:37 Make gold **h** for this curtain and five posts 2260
27:10 and twenty bronze bases and with silver **h** 2260
27:11 and twenty bronze bases and with silver **h** 2260
27:17 the courtyard are to have silver bands and **h,** 2260
36:36 They made gold **h** for them 2260
36:38 and they made five posts with **h** *for* them. 2260
38:10 and with silver **h** and bands *on* the posts. 2260
38:11 with silver **h** and bands *on* the posts. 2260
38:12 with silver **h** and bands *on* the posts. 2260
38:17 The **h** and bands *on* the posts were silver, 2260
38:19 Their **h** and bands were silver, 2260
38:28 shekels to make the **h** for the posts, 2260
Isa 2:4 and their spears into **pruning h.** 4661
19:8 all who cast **h** into the Nile; 2676
Eze 19:4 They led him with **h** to the land of Egypt. 2626
19:9 With **h** they pulled him into a cage 2626
29:4 But I will put **h** in your jaws and make 2626
38:4 put **h** in your jaws and bring you out 2626
40:43 And **double-pronged h,** 9191
Joel 3:10 into swords and your **pruning h** into spears. 4661
Am 4:2 when you will be taken away with **h,** 7553
Mic 4:3 and their spears into **pruning h.** 4661
Hab 1:15 The wicked foe pulls all of them up with **h,** 2676

HOOPOE (2)

Lev 11:19 any kind of heron, the **h** and the bat. 1871
Dt 14:18 any kind of heron, the **h** and the bat. 1871

HOPE (166) [HOPED, HOPELESS, HOPES, HOPING]

Ru 1:12 Even if I thought there was still **h** for me— 9536
1Ch 29:15 on earth are like a shadow, without **h.** 5223
Ezr 10:2 But in spite of this, there is still **h** for Israel. 5223
Job 4:6 and your blameless ways your **h?** 9536
5:16 poor have **h,** and injustice shuts its mouth. 9536
6:8 that God would grant *what* I **h** *for,* 9536
6:11 strength do I have, that *I should still* **h?** 3498
6:19 the traveling merchants of Sheba **look in h.** 7747
7:6 and they come to an end without **h.** 9536
8:13 so perishes the **h** *of* the godless. 9536
11:18 You will be secure, because there is **h;** 9536
11:20 their **h** will become a dying gasp." 9536
13:15 Though he slay me, yet *will I* **h** in him; 3498
14:7 "At least there is **h** for a tree: 9536
14:19 so you destroy man's **h.** 9536
17:13 If the only home *I* **h for** is the grave, 7747
17:15 where then is my **h?** 9536
17:15 Who can see any **h** *for* me? 9536
19:10 he uproots my **h** like a tree. 9536
27:8 what **h** has the godless when he is cut off, 9536
41:9 Any **h** *of* subduing him is false; 9347
Ps 9:18 nor the **h** *of* the afflicted ever perish. 9536
25:3 No one *whose* **h** *is* **in** you will ever be put to shame, 7747
25:5 and *my* **h** *is* **in** you all day long. 7747
25:21 because *my* **h** *is* **in** you. 7747
31:24 all you who **h** in the LORD. 3498
33:17 A horse is a **vain h** for deliverance; 9214
33:18 on those *whose* **h** *is* in his unfailing love, 3498
33:20 We **wait in h** for the LORD; 2675
33:22 O LORD, even as *we* **put** *our* **h** in you. 3498
37:9 but *those who* **h in** the LORD will inherit 7747
39:7 *My* **h** is in you. 3498
42:5 **Put** *your* **h** in God, 3498
42:11 **Put** *your* **h** in God, 3498
43:5 **Put** *your* **h** in God, 3498
52:9 in your name *I will* **h,** 7747
62:5 my **h** comes from him. 9536
65:5 the **h** *of* all the ends of the earth and of 4440
69:6 May *those who* **h in** you not be disgraced 7747
71:5 For you have been my **h,** 9536
71:14 But as for me, *I will* always *have* **h;** 3498

Ps 119:43 for *I have* **put** *my* **h** in your laws. 3498
119:49 for *you have* **given** me **h.** 3498
119:74 for *I have* **put** *my* **h** in your word. 3498
119:81 but *I have* **put** *my* **h** in your word. 3498
119:114 *I have* **put** *my* **h** in your word. 3498
119:147 *I have* **put** *my* **h** in your word. 3498
130:5 my soul waits, and in his word *I* **put** *my* **h.** 3498
130:7 O Israel, **put** *your* **h** in the LORD, 3498
131:3 **put** *your* **h** in the LORD both now 3498
146:5 whose **h** is in the LORD his God, 8433
147:11 who **put** *their* **h** in his unfailing love. 3498
Pr 11:7 When a wicked man dies, his **h** perishes; 9536
11:23 but the **h** *of* the wicked only in wrath. 9536
13:12 **H** deferred makes the heart sick, 9347
19:18 Discipline your son, for in that there is **h;** 9536
23:18 There is surely a **future h** for you, 344
23:18 and your **h** will not be cut off. 9536
24:14 if you find it, there is a **future h** for you, 344
24:14 and your **h** will not be cut off. 9536
24:20 for the evil man has no **future h,** 344
26:12 There is more **h** for a fool than for him. 9536
29:20 There is more **h** for a fool than for him. 9536
Ecc 9:4 Anyone who is among the living has **h—** 1059
Isa 19:9 the weavers of fine linen will lose **h.** NIH
38:18 to the pit cannot **h** for your faithfulness. 8432
40:31 but *those who* **h** in the LORD will renew 7747
42:4 In his law the islands *will* **put** *their* **h."** 3498
49:23 those *who* **h in** me will not be disappointed. 7747
51:5 The islands will look to me and **wait in h** 3498
Jer 13:16 *You* **h** for light, but he will turn it 7747
14:8 O **H** *of* Israel, its Savior in times of distress, 5223
14:22 Therefore *our* **h** is in you, 7747
17:13 O LORD, the **h** *of* Israel, 5223
29:11 plans to give you **h** and a future. 9536
31:17 So there is **h** for your future," 9536
50:7 the LORD, the **h** *of* their fathers.' 5223
La 3:21 this I call to mind and therefore *I have* **h:** 3498
3:25 LORD is good to *those whose* **h** *is in* him, 7747
3:29 there may yet be **h.** 9536
Eze 19:5 " 'When she saw *her* **h unfulfilled,** 3498
37:11 'Our bones are dried up and our **h** is gone; 9536
Hos 2:15 will make the Valley of Achor a door of **h.** 9536
Mic 7:7 But as for me, *I* **watch in h** for the LORD, 7595
Zec 9:5 and Ekron too, for her **h** will wither. 4438
9:12 Return to your fortress, O prisoners of **h;** 9536
Mt 12:21 In his name the nations *will* **put** *their* **h."** *1827*
Ac 2:26 my body also will live in **h,** *1828*
16:19 that their **h** of making money was gone, *1828*
23:6 on trial because of my **h** in the resurrection *1828*
24:15 and I have the same **h** in God as these men, *1828*
26:6 And now it is because of my **h** *1828*
26:7 *of* this **h** that the Jews are accusing me. *1828*
27:20 we finally gave up all **h** of being saved. *1828*
28:20 because of the **h** of Israel that I am bound *1828*
Ro 4:18 Against **all h,** Abraham in hope believed *1828*
4:18 in **h** believed and so became the father *1828*
5:2 And we rejoice in the **h** of the glory of God. *1828*
5:4 perseverance, character; and character, **h.** *1828*
5:5 And **h** does not disappoint us, *1828*
8:20 by the will of the one who subjected it, in **h** *1828*
8:24 For *in* this **h** we were saved. *1828*
8:24 But **h** that is seen is no hope at all. *1828*
8:24 But hope that is seen is no **h** at all. *1828*
8:25 But if *we* **h for** what we do not yet have, *1827*
11:14 **in the h that** I may somehow arouse my *1623*
12:12 Be joyful *in* **h,** patient in affliction, *1828*
15:4 of the Scriptures we might have **h.** *1828*
15:12 the Gentiles *will* **h** in him." *1827*
15:13 the God *of* **h** fill you with all joy and peace *1828*
15:13 that you may overflow with **h** by the power *1828*
15:24 *I* **h** to visit you while passing through and *1827*
1Co 9:10 to do so in the **h** of sharing in the harvest. *1828*
9:15 And I am not writing this **in the h that** *2671*
13:13 now these three remain: faith, **h** and love. *1828*
15:19 only for this life *we* **have h** in Christ, *1639+1827*
16:7 *I* **h** to spend some time with you, *1827*
2Co 1:7 And our **h** for you is firm, *1828*
1:10 On him *we have* **set** *our* **h** *1827*
1:13 And *I* **h** that, *1827*
3:12 since we have such a **h,** we are very bold. *1828*
5:11 and *I* **h** it is also plain to your conscience. *1827*
10:15 *Our* **h** is that, as your faith continues to *1828*
11:1 **I h** you will put up with a little *4054*
Gal 5:5 the Spirit the righteousness for which we **h.** *1828*
Eph 1:12 we, who were the **first to h** in Christ, *4598*
1:18 in order that you may know the **h** *1828*
2:12 without **h** and without God in the world. *1828*
4:4 to one **h** when you were called— *1828*
Php 1:20 I eagerly expect and **h** that I will in no way *1828*
2:19 *I* **h** in the Lord Jesus to send Timothy *1827*
2:23 *I* **h,** therefore, to send him as soon as I see *1827*
Col 1:5 and love that spring from the **h** that is stored *1828*
1:23 from the **h** held out in the gospel. *1828*
1:27 which is Christ in you, the **h** of glory. *1828*
1Th 1:3 and your endurance *inspired by* **h** *1828*
2:19 For what is our **h,** our joy, *1828*
4:13 like the rest of men, who have no **h.** *1828*
5:8 and the **h** of salvation as a helmet. *1828*
2Th 2:16 gave us eternal encouragement and good **h,** *1828*
1Ti 1:1 and *of* Christ Jesus our **h,** *1828*
3:14 *Although I* **h** to come to you soon, *1827*
4:10 that *we have* **put** *our* **h** in the living God, *1827*
5:5 in need and left all alone **puts** *her* **h** in God *1827*
6:17 to be arrogant nor *to* **put** their **h** in wealth, *1827*
6:17 but to put their **h** in God, *NIG*
2Ti 2:25 **in the h that** God will grant them *3607*
Tit 1:2 a faith and knowledge resting on the **h** *1828*
Tit 2:13 while we wait for the blessed **h—** *1828*
3:7 we might become heirs having the **h** *1828*
Phm 1:22 Prepare a guest room for me, because *I* **h** to *1827*
Heb 3:6 to our courage and the **h** of which we boast. *1828*
6:11 in order to make your **h** sure. *1828*
6:18 to take hold of the **h** offered to us may *1828*
6:19 We have **this h** as an anchor for the soul, *4005*[S]
7:19 and a better **h** is introduced, *1828*
10:23 hold unswervingly to the **h** we profess, *1828*
11:1 *of what* we **h for** and certain of what we do *1827*
1Pe 1:3 into a living **h** through the resurrection *1828*
1:13 **set** *your* **h** fully on the grace to be given *1827*
1:21 and so your faith and **h** are in God. *1828*
3:5 the holy women of the past who **put** *their* **h** *1827*
3:15 to give the reason for the **h** that you have. *1828*
1Jn 3:3 Everyone who has this **h** in him purifies *1828*
2Jn 1:12 *I* **h** to visit you and talk with you face *1827*
3Jn 1:14 *I* **h** to see you soon, *1827*

HOPED (8) [HOPE]

Est 9:1 On this day the enemies of the Jews *had* **h** 8432
Job 30:26 Yet *when I* **h for** good, evil came; 7747
Jer 8:15 We **h** for peace but no good has come, 7747
14:19 We **h** for peace but no good has come, 7747
La 3:18 "My splendor is gone and *all that* I had **h** 9347
Lk 20:20 They **h** to catch Jesus in something he said *2671*
23:8 *he* **h** to see him perform some miracle. *1827*
24:21 but we *had* **h** that he was *1827*

HOPELESS (1) [HOPE]

Isa 57:10 but you would not say, '*It is* **h.**' 3286

HOPES (7) [HOPE]

2Ki 4:28 "Didn't I tell you, 'Don't **raise** my **h'?"** 8922
Ps 119:116 do not let my **h** be dashed. 8433
Pr 10:28 but the **h** *of* the wicked come to nothing. 9536
Jer 23:16 **fill** you **with false h.** 2038
Jn 5:45 on whom your **h are set.** *1827*
Ro 8:24 Who **h for** what he already has? *1827*
1Co 13:7 It always protects, always trusts, always **h,** *1827*

HOPHNI (5)

1Sa 1:3 where **H** and Phinehas, the two sons of Eli, 2909
2:34 **H** and Phinehas, will be a sign to you— 2909
4:4 And Eli's two sons, **H** and Phinehas, 2909
4:11 and Eli's two sons, **H** and Phinehas, died. 2909
4:17 your two sons, **H** and Phinehas, are dead, 2909

HOPHRA (1)

Jer 44:30 to hand Pharaoh **H** king of Egypt over 2922

HOPING (4) [HOPE]

Da 2:9 **h** the situation will change. 10168+10527
Ac 24:26 At the same time *he was* **h** *1827*
26:7 This is the promise our twelve tribes *are* **h** *1827*
27:12 **h** to reach Phoenix and winter there. *1623+4803*

HOPPING (1)

Lev 11:21 that have jointed legs for **h** on the ground. 6001

HOR (12) [HOR HAGGIDGAD]

Nu 20:22 from Kadesh and came to Mount **H.** 2216
20:23 At Mount **H,** near the border of Edom, 2216
20:25 and take them up Mount **H.** 2216
20:27 They went up Mount **H** in the sight of 2216
21:4 traveled from Mount **H** along the route 2216
33:37 They left Kadesh and camped at Mount **H,** 2216
33:38 Aaron the priest went up Mount **H,** 2216
33:39 when he died on Mount **H.** 2216
33:41 They left Mount **H** and camped 2216
34:7 run a line from the Great Sea to Mount **H** 2216
34:8 and from Mount **H** to Lebo Hamath. 2216
Dt 32:50 on Mount **H** and was gathered to his people. 2216

HOR HAGGIDGAD (2) [HOR]

Nu 33:32 and camped at **H.** 2988
33:33 They left **H** and camped 2988

HORAM (1)

Jos 10:33 **H** king of Gezer had come up 2235

HORDE (4) [HORDES]

Nu 22:4 "This **h** is going to lick up everything 7736
Eze 17:17 and great **h** will be of no help to him in war, 7736
38:4 and a great **h** with large and small shields, 7736
38:15 all of them riding on horses, a great **h,** 7736

HORDES (21) [HORDE]

Isa 29:5 the ruthless **h** like blown chaff. 2162
29:7 **h** *of* all the nations that fight against Ariel, 2162
29:8 So will it be with the **h** *of* all the nations 2162
Eze 30:10 " 'I will put an end to the **h** *of* Egypt by 2162
30:15 and cut off the **h** *of* Thebes. 2162
31:2 say to Pharaoh king of Egypt and to his **h:** 2162
31:18 " 'This is Pharaoh and all his **h,** 2162
32:12 I will cause your **h** to fall by the swords 2162
32:12 and all her **h** will be overthrown. 2162
32:16 for Egypt and all her **h** they will chant it, 2162
32:18 wail for the **h** *of* Egypt and consign to 2162
Eze 32:20 let her be dragged off with all her **h.** 2162
32:24 with all her **h** around her grave. 2162
32:25 with all her **h** around her grave. 2162
32:26 with all their **h** around their graves. 2162
32:31 be consoled for all his **h** that were killed by 2162
32:32 Pharaoh and all his **h** will be laid among 2162
38:7 you and all the **h** gathered about you, 7736
38:13 Have you gathered your **h** to loot, 7736
39:11 Gog and all his **h** will be buried there. 2162
Hab 1:9 Their **h** advance like a desert wind 4480

HOREB (17) [SINAI]

Ex 3:1 to the far side of the desert and came to **H,** 2998
17:6 before you by the rock at **H.** 2998
33:6 So the Israelites stripped off their ornaments at Mount **H.** 2998
Dt 1:2 to go from **H** to Kadesh Barnea by 2998
1:6 The LORD our God said to us at **H,** 2998
1:19 from **H** and went toward the hill country of 2998
4:10 before the LORD your God at **H,** 2998
4:15 the LORD spoke to you at **H** out of the fire. 2998
5:2 our God made a covenant with us at **H.** 2998
9:8 At **H** you aroused the LORD's wrath so 2998
18:16 of the LORD your God at **H** on the day of 2998
29:1 the covenant he had made with them at **H.** 2998
1Ki 8:9 that Moses had placed in it at **H,** 2998
19:8 and forty nights until he reached **H,** 2998
2Ch 5:10 that Moses had placed in it at **H,** 2998
Ps 106:19 At **H** they made a calf and worshiped 2998
Mal 4:4 and laws I gave him at **H** for all Israel. 2998

HOREM (1)

Jos 19:38 **H,** Beth Anath and Beth Shemesh. 3054

HORESH (4)

1Sa 23:15 While David was at **H** in the Desert of Ziph, 3092
23:16 And Saul's son Jonathan went to David at **H** 3092
23:18 but David remained at **H.** 3092
23:19 among us in the strongholds at **H,** 3092

HORI (3) [HORITE, HORITES]

Ge 36:22 The sons of Lotan: **H** and Homam. 3036
Nu 13:5 from the tribe of Simeon, Shaphat son of **H;** 3036
1Ch 1:39 The sons of Lotan: **H** and Homam. 3036

HORIMS (KJV) See HORITE, HORITES

HORITE (4) [HORI]

Ge 36:20 These were the sons of Seir the **H,** 3037
36:21 These sons of Seir in Edom were **H** chiefs. 3037
36:29 These were the **H** chiefs: 3037
36:30 These were the **H** chiefs, 3037

HORITES (4) [HORI]

Ge 14:6 and the **H** in the hill country of Seir, 3037
Dt 2:12 **H** used to live in Seir, 3037
2:12 They destroyed **the H** from before them 4392[S]
2:22 when he destroyed the **H** from before them. 3037

HORIZON (3)

Ne 1:9 if your exiled people are at the farthest **h,** 9028
Job 26:10 He marks out the **h** on the face of the waters 2976
Pr 8:27 he marked out the **h** on the face of the deep, 2553

HORMAH (9)

Nu 14:45 and beat them down all the way to **H.** 3055
21:3 so the place was named **H.** 3055
Dt 1:44 down from Seir all the way to **H.** 3055
Jos 12:14 the king of **H** one the king of Arad one 3055
15:30 Eltolad, Kesil, **H,** 3055
19:4 Eltolad, Bethul, **H,** 3055
Jdg 1:17 Therefore it was called **H.** 3055
1Sa 30:30 to those in **H,** Bor Ashan, Athach 3055
1Ch 4:30 Bethuel, **H,** Ziklag, 3055

HORN (38) [HORNED, HORNS, TWO-HORNED]

Ex 19:13 the **ram's h** sounds a long blast may they go 3413
27:2 Make a **h** at each of the four corners, 7967
38:2 They made a **h** at each of the four corners, 7967
1Sa 2:1 in the LORD my **h** is lifted high. 7967
2:10 to his king and exalt the **h** *of* his anointed." 7967
16:1 Fill your **h** with oil and be on your way; 7967
16:13 Samuel took the **h** *of* oil and anointed him 7967
2Sa 22:3 my shield and the **h** *of* my salvation. 7967
1Ki 1:39 Zadok the priest took the **h** *of* oil from 7967
Ps 18:2 He is my shield and the **h** *of* my salvation, 7967
81:3 Sound the **ram's h** at the New Moon, 8795
89:17 and by your favor you exalt our **h.** 7967
89:24 and through my name his **h** will be exalted. 7967
92:10 You have exalted my **h** like that of 7967
98:6 with trumpets and the blast of the **ram's h** 8795
112:9 his **h** will be lifted high in honor. 7967
132:17 "Here I will make a **h** grow for David 7967
148:14 He has raised up for his people a **h,** 7967
Jer 48:25 Moab's **h** is cut off; 7967
La 2:3 In fierce anger he has cut off every **h** 7967
2:17 he has exalted the **h** *of* your foes. 7967
Eze 29:21 that day I will make a **h** grow for the house 7967
Da 3:5 As soon as you hear the sound of the **h,** 10641

Da 3: 7 as soon as they heard the sound of the **h**, 10641
3:10 that everyone who hears the sound of the **h**, 10641
3:15 Now when you hear the sound of the **h**, 10641
7: 8 there before me was another **h**, a little one, 10641
7: 8 This **h** had eyes like the eyes of a man and 10641
7:11 of the boastful words the **h** was speaking. 10641
7:20 the other **h** that came up, before which three NIH
7:20 the **h** that looked more imposing than 10641
7:21 this **h** was waging war against the saints 10641
8: 5 a prominent **h** between his eyes came from 7967
8: 8 of his power his large **h** was broken off, 7967
8: 9 Out of one of them came another **h**, 7967
8:21 large **h** between his eyes is the first king. 7967
Hos 5: 8 the trumpet in Gibeah, the **h** in Ramah. 2956
Lk 1:69 He has raised up a **h** of salvation for us in *3043*

HORNED (2) [HORN]

Lev 11:16 the **h owl**, the screech owl, 1426+3613
Dt 14:15 the **h owl**, the screech owl, 1426+3613

HORNET (3)

Ex 23:28 the **h** ahead of you to drive the Hivites, 7667
Dt 7:20 the LORD your God will send the **h** 7667
Jos 24:12 I sent the **h** ahead of you, 7667

HORNS (66) [HORN]

Ge 22:13 in a thicket he saw a ram caught by its **h**. 7967
Ex 27: 2 so that the **h** and the altar are of one piece, 7967
29:12 of the bull's blood and put it on the **h** *of* 7967
30: 2 its **h** of one piece with it. 7967
30: 3 Overlay the top and all the sides and the **h** 7967
30:10 a year Aaron shall make atonement on its **h**. 7967
37:25 its **h** of one piece with it. 7967
37:26 and all the sides and the **h** with pure gold, 7967
38: 2 so that the **h** and the altar were of one piece, 7967
Lev 4: 7 the **h** *of* the altar of fragrant incense that is 7967
4:18 the blood on the **h** *of* the altar that is before 7967
4:25 on the **h** *of* the altar of burnt offering 7967
4:30 the blood with his finger and put it on the **h** 7967
4:34 on the **h** *of* the altar of burnt offering 7967
8:15 and with his finger he put it on all the **h** *of* 7967
9: 9 the blood and put it on the **h** *of* the altar; 7967
16:18 of the goat's blood and put it on all the **h** *of* 7967
Dt 33:17 his **h** are the horns of a wild ox. 7967
33:17 his horns are the **h** *of* a wild ox. 7967
Jos 6: 4 seven priests carry trumpets of **rams' h** 3413
1Ki 1:50 went and took hold of the **h** *of* the altar. 7967
1:51 and is clinging to the **h** *of* the altar. 7967
2:28 LORD and took hold of the **h** *of* the altar. 7967
22:11 Zedekiah son of Kenaanah had made iron **h** 7967
1Ch 15:28 with the sounding of **rams' h** and trumpets, 8795
2Ch 15:14 with shouting and with trumpets and **h**. 8795
18:10 Zedekiah son of Kenaanah had made iron **h**, 7967
Ps 22:21 save me from the **h** *of* the wild oxen. 7967
69:31 more than a bull *with its* **h** and hoofs. 7966
75: 4 and to the wicked, 'Do not lift up your **h**. 7967
75: 5 Do not lift your **h** against heaven; 7967
75:10 I will cut off the **h** *of* all the wicked, 7967
75:10 but the **h** *of* the righteous will be lifted up. 7967
118:27 the festal procession up to the **h** *of* the altar. 7967
Jer 17: 1 of their hearts and on the **h** *of* their altars. 7967
Eze 34:21 butting all the weak sheep with your **h** 7967
43:15 and four **h** project upward from the hearth. 7967
43:20 and put it on the four **h** *of* the altar and on 7967
Da 7: 7 from all the former beasts, and it had ten **h**. 10641
7: 8 "While I was thinking about the **h**, 10641
7: 8 and three of the first **h** were uprooted 10641
7:20 to know about the ten **h** on its head and 10641
7:24 The ten **h** are ten kings who will come 10641
8: 3 and there before me was a ram with *two* **h**, 7967
8: 3 and the **h** were long. 7967
8: 3 One of the **h** was longer than the other but NIH
8: 7 striking the ram and shattering his two **h**. 7967
8: 8 and in its place four prominent **h** grew up NIH
8:22 The four **h** that replaced the one NIH
Am 3:14 the **h** *of* the altar will be cut off and fall to 7967
Mic 4:13 for I will give you **h** *of* iron; 7967
Zec 1:18 and there before me were four **h**! 7967
1:19 "These are the **h** that scattered Judah, 7967
1:21 "These are the **h** that scattered Judah so 7967
1:21 to terrify them and throw down these **h** *of* 7967
1:21 of the nations who lifted up their **h** against 7967
Rev 5: 6 He had seven **h** and seven eyes, *3043*
9:13 the **h** of the golden altar that is before God. *3043*
12: 3 and ten **h** and seven crowns on his heads. *3043*
13: 1 He had ten **h** and seven heads, *3043*
13: 1 with ten crowns on his **h**, *3043*
13:11 He had two **h** like a lamb, *3043*
17: 3 and had seven heads and ten **h**. *3043*
17: 7 which has the seven heads and ten **h**. *3043*
17:12 "The ten **h** you saw are ten kings who have *3043*
17:16 The beast and the ten **h** you saw will hate *3043*

HORON See BETH HORON

HORONAIM (5)

2Sa 13:34 "I see men in the direction of **H**, 2589
Isa 15: 5 the road to **H** they lament their destruction. 2589
Jer 48: 3 Listen to the cries from **H**, 2589
48: 5 on the road down to **H** anguished cries over 2589
48:34 as far as **H** and Eglath Shelishiyah, 2589

HORONITE (3) [BETH HORON]

Ne 2:10 When Sanballat the **H** and Tobiah 3061
2:19 But when Sanballat the **H**, 3061
13:28 son-in-law to Sanballat the **H**. 3061

HORRIBLE (8) [HORROR]

Dt 7:15 not inflict on you the **h** diseases you knew 8273
Jer 5:30 "A **h** and shocking thing has happened in 9014
18:13 most **h thing** has been done by Virgin Israel 9137
23:14 of Jerusalem I have seen **something h**: 9136
Eze 26:21 I will bring you to a **h end** and you will 1166
27:36 you have come to a **h end** and will 1166
28:19 you have come to a **h end** and will 1166
Hos 6:10 I have seen a **h thing** in the house of Israel. 9137

HORRIFIED (2) [HORROR]

Jer 4: 9 the priests *will be* **h**, 9037
50:13 All who pass Babylon *will be* **h** and scoff 9037

HORROR (23) [HORRIBLE, HORRIFIED]

Dt 28:25 a **thing of h** to all the kingdoms on earth. 2400
28:37 You will become a **thing of h** and an object 9014
2Ch 29: 8 he has made them an object of dread and **h** 9014
30: 7 so that he made them an **object of h**, 9014
Job 18:20 men of the east are seized with **h**. 8550
Ps 55: 5 **h** has overwhelmed me. 7146
Isa 21: 4 the twilight I longed for has become a **h** 3010
Jer 2:12 O heavens, and shudder with great **h**," 2990
8:21 I mourn, and **h** grips me. 9014
25: 9 and make them an **object of h** and scorn, 9014
25:18 and an **object of h** and scorn and cursing, 9014
29:18 of the earth and an object of cursing and **h**, 9014
42:18 You will be an object of cursing and **h**, 9014
44:12 an object of cursing and **h**, 9014
48:39 an **object of h** to all those around her." 4745
49:13 an **object of h**, of reproach and of cursing; 2997
49:17 "Edom will become an **object of h**; 9014
51:37 an **object of h** and scorn, 9014
51:41 a **h** Babylon will be among the nations! 9014
Eze 5:15 a warning and an **object of h** to the nations 5457
20:26 that *I might* **fill** them **with h** 9037
27:35 with **h** and their faces are distorted 8550
32:10 and their kings will shudder with **h** because 8550

HORSE (37) [HORSE'S, HORSEBACK, HORSEMAN, HORSEMEN, HORSES, HORSES', WAR-HORSES]

Ex 15: 1 The **h** and its rider he has hurled into 6061
15:21 The **h** and its rider he has hurled into 6061
1Ki 10:29 and a **h** for a hundred and fifty. 6061
20:25 **h** for horse and chariot for chariot— 6061
20:25 horse for **h** and chariot for chariot— 6061
2Ki 14:20 He was brought back by **h** and was buried 6061
2Ch 1:17 and a **h** for a hundred and fifty. 6061
23:15 as she reached the entrance of the **H** Gate on 6061
25:28 He was brought back by **h** and was buried 6061
Ne 3:28 Above the **H** Gate, the priests made repairs, 6061
Est 6: 8 king has worn and a **h** the king has ridden, 6061
6: 9 Then let the robe and **h** be entrusted to one 6061
6: 9 on the **h** through the city streets, 6061
6:10 and the **h** and do just as you have suggested 6061
6:11 So Haman got the robe and the **h**. 6061
Job 39:18 she laughs at **h** and rider. 6061
39:19 the **h** his strength or clothe his neck with 6061
Ps 32: 9 Do not be like the **h** or the mule, 6061
33:17 A **h** is a vain hope for deliverance; 6061
76: 6 O God of Jacob, both **h** and chariot lie still. 6061
147:10 His pleasure is not in the strength of the **h**, 6061
Pr 21:31 The **h** is made ready for the day of battle, 6061
26: 3 A whip for the **h**, a halter for the donkey, 6061
Isa 63:13 Like a **h** in open country, 6061
Jer 8: 6 like a **h** charging into battle. 6061
31:40 the east as far as the corner of the **H** Gate, 6061
51:21 with you I shatter **h** and rider, 6061
Zec 1: 8 there before me was a man riding a red **h**! 6061
10: 3 and make them like a proud **h** in battle. 6061
12: 4 On that day I will strike every **h** with panic 6061
Rev 6: 2 and there before me was a white **h**! *2691*
6: 4 Then another **h** came out, a fiery red one. *2691*
6: 5 and there before me was a black **h**! *2691*
6: 8 I looked, and there before me was a pale **h**! *2691*
19:11 and there before me was a white **h**, *2691*
19:19 against the rider on the **h** and his army. *2691*
19:21 of the mouth of the rider on the **h**, *2691*

HORSE'S (1) [HORSE]

Ge 49:17 that bites the **h** heels so 6061

HORSEBACK (3) [HORSE]

1Ki 20:20 But Ben-Hadad king of Aram escaped on **h** 6061
Est 6:11 and **led** him **on h** through the city streets, 8206
Ecc 10: 7 I have seen slaves on **h**, 6061

HORSELEACH (KJV) See LEECH

HORSEMAN (4) [HORSE, MAN]

2Ki 9:17 "Get a **h**," Joram ordered. 8208
9:18 The **h** rode off to meet Jehu and said, 6061+8206
9:19 So the king sent out a second **h**. 6061+8206
Am 2:15 and the **h** will not save his life. 6061+8206

HORSEMEN (29) [HORSE, MAN]

Ge 50: 9 Chariots and **h** also went up with him. 7305
Ex 14: 9 all Pharaoh's horses and chariots, **h** 7305
14:17 through his chariots and his **h**. 7305
14:18 his chariots and his **h**." 7305
14:23 and chariots and **h** followed them into 7305
14:26 the Egyptians and their chariots and **h**." 7305
14:28 and covered the chariots and **h**— 7305
15:19 chariots and **h** went into the sea, 7305
Jos 24: 6 with chariots and **h** as far as the Red Sea. 7305
1Ki 20:20 on horseback with *some* of his **h**. 7305
2Ki 2:12 The chariots and **h** *of* Israel!" 7305
13: 7 of the army of Jehoahaz except fifty **h**, 7305
13:14 "The chariots and **h** *of* Israel!" 7305
18:24 on Egypt for chariots and **h**? 7305
2Ch 12: 3 and sixty thousand **h** and 7305
16: 8 with great numbers of chariots and **h**? 7305
Ezr 8:22 the king for soldiers and **h** to protect us 7305
Isa 22: 7 and **h** are posted at the city gates; 7305
31: 1 and in the great strength of their **h**, 7305
36: 9 on Egypt for chariots and **h**? 7305
Jer 4:29 the sound of **h** and archers every town takes 7305
Eze 23: 6 handsome young men, and mounted **h**. 7305
23:12 mounted **h**, all handsome young men. 7305
26: 7 with **h** and a great army. 7305
38: 4 your horses, your **h** fully armed, 7305
Hos 1: 7 sword or battle, or by horses and **h**, 7305
Hab 1: 8 their **h** come from afar. 7305
Zec 10: 5 they will fight and overthrow the **h**. 6061+8206
Ac 23:23 seventy **h** and two hundred spearmen to go *2689*

HORSES (123) [HORSE]

Ge 47:17 he gave them food in exchange for their **h**, 6061
Ex 9: 3 on your **h** and donkeys and camels and 6061
14: 9 all Pharaoh's **h** and chariots, 6061
14:23 and all Pharaoh's **h** and chariots 6061
15:19 When Pharaoh's **h**, chariots 6061
Dt 11: 4 Egyptian army, to its **h** and chariots, 6061
17:16 not acquire great numbers of **h** for himself 6061
20: 1 against your enemies and see **h** and chariots 6061
Jos 11: 4 with all their troops and a large number of **h** 6061
11: 6 You are to hamstring their **h** and burn 6061
11: 9 He hamstrung their **h** and burned their 6061
1Sa 8:11 make them serve with his chariots and **h**, 7304
2Sa 8: 4 but a hundred of the **chariot h**. 8207
15: 1 a chariot and **h** and with fifty men to run 6061
1Ki 1: 5 So he got chariots and **h** ready, 7304
4:26 Solomon had four thousand stalls for chariot **h**, 6061
4:26 and twelve thousand **h**. 7304
4:28 of barley and straw for the **chariot h** and 8224
4:28 for the chariot horses and the other **h**. 6061
9:19 the towns for his chariots and for his **h**— 7304
10:25 weapons and spices, and **h** and mules, 6061
10:26 Solomon accumulated chariots and **h**; 7304
10:26 and twelve thousand **h**, 7304
10:28 Solomon's **h** were imported from Egypt and 6061
18: 5 Maybe we can find some grass to keep the **h** 6061
20: 1 by thirty-two kings with their **h** 6061
20:21 the **h** and chariots and inflicted heavy losses 6061
22: 4 my **h** as your horses." 6061
22: 4 my horses as your **h**." 6061
2Ki 2:11 of fire and **h** *of* fire appeared and separated 6061
3: 7 my **h** as your horses." 6061
3: 7 my horses as your **h**." 6061
5: 9 So Naaman went with his **h** and chariots 6061
6:14 Then he sent **h** and chariots and 6061
6:15 an army with **h** and chariots had surrounded 6061
6:17 of **h** and chariots of fire all around Elisha. 6061
7: 6 to hear the sound of chariots and **h** and 6061
7: 7 and abandoned their tents and their **h** 6061
7:10 only tethered **h** and donkeys, 6061
7:13 "Have some men take five of the **h** 6061
7:14 So they selected two chariots with their **h**, 6061
9:33 and the **h** as they trampled her underfoot. 6061
10: 2 with you and you have chariots and **h**, 6061
11:16 as she reached the place where the **h** enter 6061
18:23 I will give you two thousand **h**— 6061
23:11 the **h** that the kings of Judah had dedicated 6061
1Ch 18: 4 but a hundred of the **chariot h**. 8207
2Ch 1:14 Solomon accumulated chariots and **h**; 7304
1:14 and twelve thousand **h**, 7304
1:16 Solomon's **h** were imported from Egypt and 6061
8: 6 all the cities for his chariots and for his **h**— 7304
9:24 weapons and spices, and **h** and mules. 6061
9:25 Solomon had four thousand stalls for **h** 6061
9:25 and twelve thousand **h**, 7304
9:28 Solomon's **h** were imported from Egypt and 6061
Ezr 2:66 They had 736 **h**, 245 mules, 6061
Ne 7:68 There were 736 **h**, 245 mules, NIH
Est 8:10 who rode **fast h** especially bred for 8224
8:14 The couriers, riding the royal **h**, raced out, 8224
Ps 20: 7 Some trust in chariots and some in **h**, 6061
Isa 2: 7 Their land is full of **h**; 6061
21: 7 When he sees chariots with teams of **h**, 7304
21: 9 a man in a chariot with a team of **h**. 7304
22: 6 with her charioteers and **h**; 7304
28:28 his **h** do not grind it. 7304
30:16 You said, 'No, we will flee on **h**.' 6061
30:16 You said, 'We will ride off on swift **h**.' NIH
31: 1 go down to Egypt for help, who rely on **h**, 6061
31: 3 their **h** are flesh and not spirit. 6061
36: 8 I will give you two thousand **h**— 6061
43:17 who drew out the chariots and **h**, the army 6061
66:20 on **h**, in chariots and wagons, 6061

Jer 4:13 his **h** are swifter than eagles. 6061
6:23 like the roaring sea as they ride on their **h;** 6061
8:16 The snorting of the enemy's **h** is heard 6061
12:5 how can you compete with **h?** 6061
17:25 in chariots and on **h,** accompanied by 6061
22:4 riding in chariots and on **h,** 6061
46:4 Harness the **h,** mount the steeds! 6061
46:9 Charge, O **h!** Drive furiously, 6061
50:37 A sword against her **h** and chariots and all 6061
50:42 like the roaring sea as they ride on their **h;** 6061
51:27 send up **h** like a swarm of locusts. 6061
Eze 17:15 by sending his envoys to Egypt to get **h** and 6061
23:20 and whose emission was like that of **h.** 6061
23:23 men of high rank, all mounted on **h.** 6061
26:7 king of kings, with **h** and chariots, 6061
26:10 His **h** will be so many that they will cover 6061
26:10 will tremble at the noise of the **war h,** 7304
26:11 hoofs of his **h** will trample all your streets; 6061
27:14 of Beth Togarmah exchanged **work h,** 6061
27:14 **war h** and mules for your merchandise. 7304
38:4 your **h,** your horsemen fully armed, 6061
38:15 all of them riding on **h,** a great horde, 6061
39:20 At my table you will eat your fill of **h** 6061
Hos 1:7 sword or battle, or by **h** and horsemen, 6061
Joel 2:4 They have the appearance of **h;** 6061
Am 4:10 along with your captured **h.** 6061
6:12 Do **h** run on the rocky crags? 6061
Mic 5:10 "I will destroy your **h** from among you 6061
Na 3:2 galloping **h** and jolting chariots! 6061
Hab 1:8 Their **h** are swifter than leopards, 6061
3:8 against the sea when you rode with your **h** 6061
3:15 You trampled the sea with your **h,** 6061
Hag 2:22 **h** and their riders will fall, 6061
Zec 1:8 Behind him were red, brown and white **h.** 6061
6:2 The first chariot had red **h,** 6061
6:6 The one with the black **h** is going toward 6061
6:6 the one with the white **h** toward the west, NIH
6:6 one with the dappled **h** toward the south." NIH
6:7 When the powerful **h** went out, NIH
12:4 but I will blind all the **h** *of* the nations. 6061
14:15 A similar plague will strike the **h** and mules, 6061
14:20 be inscribed on the bells of the **h,** 6061
Jas 3:3 into the mouths *of* **h** to make them obey us, *2691*
Rev 9:7 The locusts looked like **h** prepared *2691*
9:9 *of* many **h** and chariots rushing into battle. *2691*
9:17 The **h** and riders I saw in my vision looked *2691*
9:17 The heads *of* the **h** resembled the heads *2691*
9:19 The power *of* the **h** was in their mouths and *2691*
18:13 and sheep; **h** and carriages; *2691*
19:14 riding on white **h** and dressed in fine linen, *2691*
19:18 and mighty men, *of* **h** and their riders, *2691*

HORSES' (3) [HORSE]

Jdg 5:22 Then thundered the **h'** hoofs— 6061
Isa 5:28 their **h'** hoofs seem like flint, 6061
Rev 14:20 rising as high as the **h'** bridles for a distance *2691*

HOSAH (5)

Jos 19:29 turned toward **H** and came out at the sea in 2881
1Ch 16:38 Obed-Edom son of Jeduthun, and also **H,** 2880
26:10 **H** the Merarite had sons: 2880
26:11 The sons and relatives of **H** were 13 in all. 2880
26:16 on the upper road fell to Shuppim and **H.** 2880

HOSANNA (6)

Mt 21:9 **"H** to the Son of David!" *6057*
21:9 **"H** in the highest!" *6057*
21:15 **"H** to the Son of David," *6057*
Mk 11:9 and those who followed shouted, **"H!"** *6057*
11:10 **"H** in the highest!" *6057*
Jn 12:13 and went out to meet him, shouting, **"H!"** *6057*

HOSEA (5)

Hos 1:1 The word of the LORD that came to **H** son 2107
1:2 the LORD began to speak through **H,** 2107
1:4 Then the LORD said to **H,** 2257[S]
1:6 Then the LORD said to **H,** 2257[S]
Ro 9:25 As he says in **H:** "I will call them *6060*

HOSEN (KJV) See TROUSERS

HOSHAIAH (3)

Ne 12:32 **H** and half the leaders 2108
Jer 42:1 of Kareah and Jezaniah son of **H,** 2108
43:2 Azariah son of **H** and Johanan son of Kareah 2108

HOSHAMA (1)

1Ch 3:18 Shenazzar, Jekamiah, **H** and Nedabiah. 2106

HOSHEA (12) [JOSHUA]

Nu 13:8 from the tribe of Ephraim, **H** son of Nun; 2107
13:16 Moses gave **H** son of Nun the name Joshua. 2107
2Ki 15:30 Then **H** son of Elah conspired 2107
17:1 **H** son of Elah became king of Israel 2107
17:3 of Assyria came up to attack **H,** 2107
17:4 of Assyria discovered that **H** was a traitor, 2107
17:6 In the ninth year of **H,** the king of Assyria 2107
18:1 In the third year of **H** son of Elah king 2107
18:9 the seventh year of **H** son of Elah king 2107
18:10 was the ninth year of **H** king of Israel. 2107
1Ch 27:20 **H** son of Azaziah; 2107
Ne 10:23 **H,** Hananiah, Hasshub, 2107

HOSPITABLE (2) [HOSPITALITY]

1Ti 3:2 self-controlled, respectable, **h,** able to teach, *5811*
Tit 1:8 Rather he must be **h,** *5811*

HOSPITABLY (1) [HOSPITALITY]

Ac 28:7 and for three days entertained us **h.** *5819*

HOSPITALITY (5) [HOSPITABLE, HOSPITABLY]

Ro 12:13 God's people who are in need. Practice **h.** *5810*
16:23 whose **h** I and the whole church here enjoy, *3828*
1Ti 5:10 **showing h,** washing the feet of the saints, *3827*
1Pe 4:9 Offer **h** to one another without grumbling. *5811*
3Jn 1:8 We ought therefore *to* **show h to** such men *5696*

HOST (16) [HOSTS]

1Ki 22:19 the **h** *of* heaven standing around him 7372
2Ch 18:18 the **h** *of* heaven standing on his right and 7372
Ne 9:6 and all their **starry h,** 7372
Ps 33:6 their **starry h** by the breath of his mouth. 7372
Isa 34:4 all the **starry h** will fall like withered leaves 7372
40:26 He who brings out the **starry h** one by one, 7372
Da 8:10 It grew until it reached the **h** *of* the heavens, 7372
8:10 the starry **h** down to the earth and trampled 7372
8:11 up to be as great as the Prince of the **h;** 7372
8:12 the **h** [of the saints] and the daily sacrifice 7372
8:13 the surrender of the sanctuary and of the **h** 7372
Zep 1:5 down on the roofs to worship the starry **h,** 7372
Lk 2:13 *of* the heavenly **h** appeared with the angel, *5131*
14:9 the **h who invited** both of you will come *2813*
14:10 so that when your **h** comes, *2813*
14:12 Then Jesus said *to* his **h,** *2813*

HOSTAGES (2)

2Ki 14:14 also took **h** and returned to Samaria. 1201+9510
2Ch 25:24 with the palace treasures and the **h,** 1201+9510

HOSTILE (13) [HOSTILITY]

Ge 26:27 since you *were* **h** *to* me and sent me away?" 8533
Lev 26:21 " 'If you remain **h** toward me and refuse 7950
26:23 but continue to be **h** toward me, 7950
26:24 be **h** toward you and will afflict you 7950
26:27 to me but continue to be **h** toward me, 7950
26:28 then in my anger I will be **h** toward you, 7950
26:41 which made me **h** toward them so 7950
Nu 24:8 They devour **h** nations 7640
Jdg 6:31 Joash replied to the **h** crowd around him, NIH
1Ki 11:25 So Rezon ruled in Aram and *was* **h** 7762
Isa 11:13 nor Judah **h** *toward* Ephraim. 7675
Ro 8:7 the sinful mind is **h** to God. *2397*
1Th 2:15 They displease God and are **h** to all men *1885*

HOSTILITY (15) [HOSTILE]

Ge 16:12 will live **in h toward** all his brothers." 6584+7156
25:18 *they* **lived in h toward** all their brothers. 5877+6584+7156
49:23 they shot at him *with* **h.** 8475
Lev 26:40 their treachery against me and their **h** 7950
Nu 35:21 in **h** he hits him with his fist so that he dies, 368
35:22 without **h** someone suddenly shoves another 368
2Ch 21:16 against Jehoram the **h** *of* the Philistines and 8120
Job 17:2 my eyes must dwell on their **h.** 5286
Ps 78:49 his wrath, indignation and **h—** 7650
Eze 25:15 and with ancient **h** sought to destroy Judah, 368
35:5 an ancient **h** and delivered the Israelites 368
Hos 9:7 your sins are so many and your **h** so great, 5378
9:8 and **h** in the house of his God. 5378
Eph 2:14 destroyed the barrier, the dividing wall *of* **h,** *2397*
2:16 by which he put to death their **h.** *2397*

HOSTS (11) [HOST]

2Ki 17:16 They bowed down to all the starry **h,** 7372
21:3 to all the starry **h** and worshiped them. 7372
21:5 he built altars to all the starry **h.** 7372
23:4 for Baal and Asherah and all the starry **h.** 7372
23:5 to the constellations and to all the starry **h.** 7372
2Ch 33:3 to all the starry **h** and worshiped them. 7372
33:5 he built altars to all the starry **h.** 7372
Ps 103:21 Praise the LORD, all his **heavenly h,** 7372
148:2 praise him, all his **heavenly h.** 7372
Isa 45:12 I marshaled their **starry h.** 7372
Jer 19:13 the starry **h** and poured out drink offerings 7372

HOT (21) [HOTLY, HOTTER]

Ge 36:24 the Anah who discovered the **h springs** in 3553
Ex 11:8 Then Moses, **h** with anger, left Pharaoh. 3034
16:21 and when the sun *grew* **h,** it melted away. 2801
1Sa 11:9 'By the time the sun *is* **h** tomorrow, 2801
14:22 they joined the battle **in h pursuit.** 339
21:6 before the LORD and replaced by **h** bread 2770
1Ki 19:6 a cake of bread **baked over h coals,** 8363
Ne 7:3 not to be opened until the sun *is* **h.** 2801
Job 15:2 or fill his belly with the **h east wind?** 7708
Ps 39:3 My heart *grew* **h** within me, 2801
78:49 He unleashed against them his **h** anger, 3019
Pr 6:28 on **h coals** without his feet being scorched? 1624
La 5:10 Our skin *is* **h** as an oven, 4023
Eze 24:11 the empty pot on the coals till *it becomes* **h** 2801
38:18 my **h** anger will be aroused, 2779
Da 3:22 and the furnace so **h** that the flames of 10015
Hos 7:7 All of them *are* **h** as an oven; 2801
Lk 12:55 you say, 'It's going to be **h,'** and it is. *3014*
1Ti 4:2 *have been* **seared as with a h iron.** *3013*
Rev 3:15 that you are neither cold nor **h.** *2412*
3:16 you are lukewarm—neither **h** nor cold— *2412*

HOT-TEMPERED (5) [TEMPER]

Jdg 18:25 or some **h** men will attack you, 5253+5883
Pr 15:18 A **h** man stirs up dissension, 2779
19:19 A **h** *man* must pay the penalty; 1524+2779
22:24 Do not make friends with a **h** man, 678
29:22 and a **h** *one* commits many sins. 1251+2779

HOTHAM (2)

1Ch 7:32 Shomer and **H** and of their sister Shua. 2598
11:44 Shama and Jeiel the sons of **H** the Aroerite, 2598

HOTHEADED (1) [HEAD]

Pr 14:16 but a fool *is* **h** and reckless. 6297

HOTHIR (2)

1Ch 25:4 Joshbekashah, Mallothi, **H** and Mahazioth. 2110
25:28 the twenty-first to **H,** 2110

HOTLY (2) [HOT]

Ps 56:1 O God, for men **h pursue** me; 8634
57:3 rebuking *those who* **h pursue** me; 8634

HOTTER (1) [HOT]

Da 3:19 the furnace heated seven times **h** than usual 10015

HOUGH (KJV) See HAMSTRING

HOUND (1) [HOUNDED]

Job 19:28 "If you say, 'How *we will* **h** him, 8103

HOUNDED (2) [HOUND]

Ps 109:16 but **h** to death the poor and the needy and 8103
Eze 36:3 Because they ravaged and **h** you 8635

HOUR (59) [HOURS]

Ecc 9:12 no man knows when his **h** will come: 6961
Mt 6:27 Who of you by worrying can add a single **h** *4388*
8:13 And his servant was healed at that very **h.** *6052*
15:28 her daughter was healed from that very **h.** *6052*
20:3 "About the third **h** he went out *6052*
20:5 about the sixth **h** and the ninth hour and did *NIG*
20:5 about the sixth hour and the ninth **h** and did *6052*
20:6 About the eleventh **h** he went out *NIG*
20:9 the eleventh **h** came and each received *6052*
20:12 who were hired last worked only one **h,'** *6052*
24:36 "No one knows about that day or **h,** *6052*
24:44 because the Son of Man will come *at* an **h** *6052*
24:50 not expect him and at an **h** he is *6052*
25:13 because you do not know the day or the **h.** *6052*
26:40 not keep watch with me *for* one **h?"** *6052*
26:45 Look, the **h** is near, *6052*
27:45 From the sixth **h** until the ninth hour *6052*
27:45 the ninth **h** darkness came over all the land. *6052*
27:46 the ninth **h** Jesus cried out in a loud voice, *6052*
Mk 13:32 "No one knows about that day or **h,** *6052*
14:35 and prayed that if possible the **h** might pass *6052*
14:37 Could you not keep watch *for* one **h?** *6052*
14:41 The **h** has come. *6052*
15:25 It was the third **h** when they crucified him. *6052*
15:33 **At** the sixth **h** darkness came over *1181+6052*
15:33 over the whole land until the ninth **h.** *6052*
15:34 the ninth **h** Jesus cried out in a loud voice, *6052*
Lk 12:25 Who of you by worrying can add a single **h** *4388*
12:39 of the house had known *at* what **h** *6052*
12:40 because the Son of Man will come *at* an **h** *6052*
12:46 not expect him and at an **h** he is not aware *6052*
22:14 When the **h** came, Jesus and his apostles *6052*
22:53 But this is your **h—**when darkness reigns." *6052*
22:59 About an **h** later another asserted, *6052*
23:44 It was now about the sixth **h,** *6052*
23:44 over the whole land until the ninth **h,** *6052*
Jn 1:39 It was about the tenth **h.** *6052*
4:6 It was about the sixth **h.** *6052*
4:52 fever left him yesterday at the seventh **h."** *6052*
12:23 "The **h** has come for the Son of Man to *6052*
12:27 'Father, save me from this **h'?** *6052*
12:27 it was for this very reason I came to this **h.** *6052*
19:14 about the sixth **h.** *6052*
Ac 10:30 in my house praying at this **h,** *6052*
16:33 At that **h** of the night the jailer took them *6052*
Ro 13:11 The **h** has come for you to wake up *6052*
1Co 4:11 To this very **h** we go hungry and thirsty, *6052*
15:30 why do we endanger ourselves every **h?** *6052*
1Jn 2:18 Dear children, this is the last **h;** *6052*
2:18 This is how we know it is the last **h.** *6052*
Rev 3:10 the **h** of trial that is going to come upon *6052*
8:1 silence in heaven for about **half an h.** *2469*
9:15 for this very **h** and day and month *6052*
11:13 At that very **h** there was a severe earthquake *6052*
14:7 because the **h** of his judgment has come. *6052*
17:12 but who *for* one **h** will receive authority *6052*
18:10 *In* one **h** your doom has come!' *6052*
18:17 *In* one **h** such great wealth has been brought *6052*

Rev 18:19 *In* one **h** she has been brought to ruin! 6052

HOURS (3) [HOUR]

Jn 11: 9 "Are there not twelve **h** of daylight? 6052
Ac 5: 7 About three **h** later his wife came in, 6052
19:34 they all shouted in unison for about two **h**: 6052

HOUSE (971) [HOUSEHOLD, HOUSEHOLDS, HOUSES, STOREHOUSE, STOREHOUSES]

Ge 19: 2 "please turn aside to your servant's **h**. 1074
19: 3 that they did go with him and entered his **h**. 1074
19: 4 both young and old—surrounded the **h**. 1074
19:10 and pulled Lot back into the **h** and shut 1074
19:11 the men who were at the door of the **h**, 1074
24:23 in your father's **h** for us to spend the night?" 1074
24:27 to the **h** *of* my master's relatives." 1074
24:31 I have prepared the **h** and a place for 1074
24:32 So the man went to the **h**, 1074
27:15 which she had in the **h**, 1074
28: 2 to the **h** *of* your mother's father Bethuel. 1074
28:17 This is none other than the **h** *of* God; 1074
28:21 so that I return safely to my father's **h**, 1074
28:22 that I have set up as a pillar will be God's **h**, 1074
31:30 to return to your father's **h**. 1074
34:26 and took Dinah from Shechem's **h** and left. 1074
38:11 "Live as a widow in your father's **h** 1074
38:11 So Tamar went to live in her father's **h**. 1074
39: 2 he lived in the **h** *of* his Egyptian master. 1074
39: 5 both in the **h** and in the field. 1074
39: 8 not concern himself with anything in the **h**; 1074
39: 9 No one is greater in this **h** than I am. 1074
39:11 One day he went into the **h** to attend 1074
39:12 in her hand and ran out of the **h**. NIH
39:13 in her hand and had run out of the **h**, NIH
39:15 beside me and ran out of the **h**." NIH
39:18 beside me and ran out of the **h**." NIH
40: 3 in custody in the **h** *of* the captain of 1074
40: 7 in custody with him in his master's **h**, 1074
41:10 and the chief baker in the **h** *of* the captain 1074
43:16 he said to the steward of his **h**, 1074
43:16 "Take these men to my **h**, 1074
43:17 and took the men to Joseph's **h**. 1074
43:18 when they were taken to his **h**. 1074
43:19 and spoke to him at the entrance to the **h**. 1074
43:24 The steward took the men into Joseph's **h**, 1074
43:26 to him the gifts they had brought into the **h**, 1074
44: 1 to the steward of his **h**: 1074
44: 8 steal silver or gold from your master's **h**? 1074
44:14 the **h** when Judah and his brothers came in, 1074
Ex 2: 1 of the **h** *of* Levi married a Levite woman, 1074
3:22 and any woman living in her **h** for articles 1074
12:22 Not one of you shall go out the door of his **h** 1074
12:30 for there was not a **h** without someone dead. 1074
12:46 "It must be eaten inside one **h**; 1074
12:46 take none of the meat outside the **h**. 1074
19: 3 to say to the **h** *of* Jacob and what you are 1074
20:17 "You shall not covet your neighbor's **h**. 1074
22: 7 and they are stolen from the neighbor's **h**, 1074
22: 8 of the **h** must appear before the judges 1074
23:19 the best of the firstfruits of your soil to the **h** 1074
34:26 the best of the firstfruits of your soil to the **h** 1074
40:38 of all the **h** *of* Israel during all their travels. 1074
Lev 10: 6 But your relatives, all the **h** *of* Israel, 1074
14:34 I put a spreading mildew in a **h** *in* that land, 1074
14:35 the owner of the **h** must go and tell 1074
14:35 that looks like mildew in my **h**.' 1074
14:36 to order the **h** to be emptied before he goes 1074
14:36 in the **h** will be pronounced unclean. 1074
14:36 the priest is to go in and inspect the **h**. 1074
14:38 the priest shall go out the doorway of the **h** 1074
14:39 the priest shall return to inspect the **h**. NIH
14:41 the inside walls of the **h** scraped and 1074
14:42 and take new clay and plaster the **h**. 1074
14:43 the **h** after the stones have been torn out and 1074
14:43 and the **h** scraped and plastered, 1074
14:44 if the mildew has spread in the **h**, 1074
14:44 the **h** is unclean. 1074
14:46 the **h** while it is closed up will be unclean 1074
14:47 or eats in the **h** must wash his clothes. 1074
14:48 not spread after the **h** has been plastered, 1074
14:48 he shall pronounce the **h** clean, 1074
14:49 To purify the **h** he is to take two birds 1074
14:51 and sprinkle the **h** seven times. 1074
14:52 He shall purify the **h** with the bird's blood, 1074
14:53 he will make atonement for the **h**, 1074
14:55 for mildew in clothing or in a **h**, 1074
22:13 and she returns to live in her father's **h** as 1074
25:29 " 'If a man sells a **h** *in* a walled city, 1074+4632
25:30 before a full year has passed, the **h** in 1074
25:33 that is, a **h** sold in any town they hold— 1074
27:14 a man dedicates his **h** as something holy to 1074
27:15 If the man who dedicates his **h** redeems it, 1074
27:15 and the **h** will again become his. NIH
Nu 12: 7 he is faithful in all my **h**. 1074
17: 8 which represented the **h** *of* Levi, 1074
20:29 the entire **h** *of* Israel mourned 1074
30: 3 in her father's **h** makes a vow to the LORD 1074
30:16 and his young daughter still living in his **h**. 1074
Dt 5:21 not set your desire on your neighbor's **h** 1074
7:26 Do not bring a detestable thing into your **h** 1074
20: 5 "Has anyone built a new **h** and 1074
21:13 in your **h** and mourned her father 1074
22: 8 When you build a new **h**, 1074
22: 8 not bring the guilt of bloodshed on your **h** 1074
Dt 22:21 the door of her father's **h** and there the men 1074
22:21 while still in her father's **h**. 1074
23:18 of a male prostitute into the **h** *of* the LORD 1074
24: 1 gives it to her and sends her from his **h**, 1074
24: 2 after she leaves his **h** she becomes the wife 1074
24: 3 gives it to her and sends her from his **h**, 1074
24:10 not go into his **h** to get what he is offering 1074
25:14 not have two differing measures in your **h**— 1074
26:13 from my **h** the sacred portion 1074
28:30 You will build a **h**, 1074
Jos 2: 1 the **h** *of* a prostitute named Rahab 1074
2: 3 to you and entered your **h**, 1074
2:15 the **h** she lived in was part of the city wall. 1074
2:18 and all your family into your **h**. 1074
2:19 If anyone goes outside your **h** into 1074
2:19 As for anyone who is in the **h** with you, 1074
6:17 and all who are with her in her **h** shall 1074
6:22 "Go into the prostitute's **h** and bring her out 1074
6:24 into the treasury of the LORD's **h**. 1074
9:23 as woodcutters and water carriers for the **h** 1074
17:17 But Joshua said to the **h** *of* Joseph— 1074
18: 5 the south and the **h** *of* Joseph in its territory 1074
21:45 of all the LORD's good promises to the **h** 1074
Jdg 1:22 Now the **h** *of* Joseph attacked Bethel, 1074
1:35 the power of the **h** *of* Joseph increased, 1074
3:24 in the inner room of the **h**." 5249
10: 9 Benjamin and the **h** *of* Ephraim; 1074
11: 7 and drive me from my father's **h**? 1074
11:31 the door of my **h** to meet me when I return 1074
12: 1 to burn down your **h** over your head." 1074
14:19 he went up to his father's **h**. 1074
17: 4 And they were put in Micah's **h**. 1074
17: 8 to Micah's **h** in the hill country of Ephraim. 1074
17:12 became his priest and lived in his **h**. 1074
18: 2 of Ephraim and came to the **h** *of* Micah, 1074
18: 3 When they were near Micah's **h**, 1074
18:13 of Ephraim and came to Micah's **h**. 1074
18:15 So they turned in there and went to the **h** *of* 1074
18:18 into Micah's **h** and took the carved image, 1074
18:22 from Micah's **h**, the men who lived 1074
18:31 all the time the **h** *of* God was in Shiloh. 1074
19: 2 She left him and went back to her father's **h** 1074
19: 3 She took him into her father's **h**, 1074
19:18 and now I am going to the **h** *of* the LORD. 1074
19:18 No one has taken me into his **h**. 1074
19:20 "You are welcome at my **h**," NIH
19:21 he took him into his **h** and fed his donkeys. 1074
19:22 of the city surrounded the **h**. 1074
19:22 to the old man who owned the **h**, 1074
19:22 to your **h** so we can have sex with him." 1074
19:23 The owner of the **h** went outside and said 1074
19:26 At daybreak the woman went back to the **h** 1074
19:27 in the morning and opened the door of the **h** 1074
19:27 fallen in the doorway of the **h**, 1074
20: 5 after me and surrounded the **h**, 1074
20: 8 No, not one of us will return to his **h**. 1074
Ru 4:11 who together built up the **h** *of* Israel. 1074
1Sa 1: 7 Whenever Hannah went up to the **h** *of* 1074
1:24 and brought him to the **h** *of* the LORD 1074
2:27 to your father's **h** when they were in Egypt 1074
2:28 I also gave your father's **h** all 1074
2:30 'I promised that your **h** and your father's 1074
2:30 and your father's **h** would minister 1074
2:31 and the strength of your father's **h**, 1074
2:35 I will firmly establish his **h**, 1074
3:14 Therefore, I swore to the **h** *of* Eli, 1074
3:14 'The guilt of Eli's **h** will never be atoned for 1074
3:15 and then opened the doors of the **h** *of* 1074
7: 1 They took it to Abinadab's **h** on the hill 1074
7: 3 And Samuel said to the whole **h** *of* Israel, 1074
9:18 where the seer's **h** is?" 1074
9:25 with Saul on the **roof of** his **h**. 1511
18: 2 and did not let him return to his father's **h**. 1074
18:10 He was prophesying in his **h**, 1074
19: 9 as he was sitting in his **h** with his spear 1074
19:11 Saul sent men to David's **h** to watch it and 1074
20:16 So Jonathan made a covenant with the **h** 1074
21:15 Must this man come into my **h**?" 1074
25:36 the **h** holding a banquet like that of a king. 1074
28:24 The woman had a fattened calf at the **h**, 1074
2Sa 1:12 the army of the LORD and the **h** *of* Israel, 1074
2: 4 anointed David king over the **h** *of* Judah. 1074
2: 7 and the **h** *of* Judah has anointed me king 1074
2:10 The **h** *of* Judah, however, followed David. 1074
2:11 over the **h** *of* Judah was seven years 1074
3: 1 the **h** *of* Saul and the house of David lasted 1074
3: 1 the house of Saul and the **h** *of* David lasted 1074
3: 1 the **h** *of* Saul grew weaker and weaker. 1074
3: 6 During the war between the **h** *of* Saul and 1074
3: 6 the house of Saul and the **h** *of* David, 1074
3: 6 his own position in the **h** *of* Saul. 1074
3: 8 the **h** *of* your father Saul and to his family 1074
3:10 and transfer the kingdom from the **h** *of* Saul 1074
3:19 and the whole **h** *of* Benjamin wanted to do. 1074
3:29 the head of Joab and upon all his father's **h**! 1074
3:29 May Joab's **h** never be without 1074
4: 5 set out for the **h** *of* Ish-Bosheth, 1074
4: 6 They went into the inner part of the **h** as if 1074
4: 7 They had gone into the **h** while he was lying 1074
4:11 in his own **h** and on his own bed— 1074
6: 3 and brought it from the **h** *of* Abinadab, 1074
6: 5 and the whole **h** *of* Israel were celebrating 1074
6:10 he took it aside to the **h** *of* Obed-Edom 1074
6:11 The ark of the LORD remained in the **h** 1074
6:12 the ark of God from the **h** *of* Obed-Edom to 1074
6:15 and the entire **h** *of* Israel brought up the ark 1074
6:21 from his **h** when he appointed me ruler over 1074
2Sa 7: 5 Are you the one to build me a **h** to dwell in? 1074
7: 6 in a **h** from the day I brought the Israelites 1074
7: 7 "Why have you not built me a **h** of cedar?" 1074
7:11 the LORD himself will establish a **h** for you: 1074
7:13 the one who will build a **h** for my Name, 1074
7:16 Your **h** and your kingdom will endure forever before me; 1074
7:19 about the future of the **h** *of* your servant. 1074
7:25 concerning your servant and his **h**. 1074
7:26 And the **h** *of* your servant David will 1074
7:27 saying, 'I will build a **h** for you.' 1074
7:29 be pleased to bless the **h** *of* your servant, 1074
7:29 and with your blessing the **h** *of* your servant 1074
9: 1 the **h** *of* Saul to whom I can show kindness 1074
9: 3 "Is there no one still left of the **h** *of* Saul 1074
9: 4 "He is at the **h** *of* Makir son of Ammiel 1074
9: 5 from the **h** *of* Makir son of Ammiel. 1074
11: 8 "Go down to your **h** and wash your feet." 1074
11: 9 and did not go down to his **h**. 1074
11:11 How could I go to my **h** to eat and drink 1074
11:27 David had her brought to his **h**, 1074
12: 8 I gave your master's **h** to you, 1074
12: 8 I gave you the **h** *of* Israel and Judah. 1074
12:10 the sword will never depart from your **h**, 1074
12:16 He fasted and went into his **h** and spent NIH
12:20 into the **h** *of* the LORD and worshiped. 1074
12:20 Then he went to his own **h**, 1074
13: 7 "Go to the **h** *of* your brother Amnon 1074
13: 8 Tamar went to the **h** *of* her brother Amnon, 1074
13:20 in her brother Absalom's **h**, 1074
14:24 the king said, "He must go to his own **h**; 1074
14:24 to his own **h** and did not see the face of 1074
14:31 to Absalom's **h** and he said to him, 1074
16: 3 because he thinks, 'Today the **h** 1074
17:18 of them left quickly and went to the **h** *of* 1074
17:20 to the woman at the **h**, 1074
17:23 he saddled his donkey and set out for his **h** 1074
17:23 He put his **h** in order and then hanged 1074
19: 5 Joab went into the **h** to the king and said, 1074
19:20 the first of the whole **h** *of* Joseph to come 1074
20: 3 the palace and put them in a **h** under guard. 1074
21: 1 on account of Saul and his blood-stained **h**; 1074
23: 5 "Is not my **h** right with God? 1074
1Ki 2:27 had spoken at Shiloh about the **h** *of* Eli. 1074
2:31 so clear me and my father's **h** of the guilt of 1074
2:33 and his descendants, his **h** and his throne, 1074
2:36 "Build yourself a **h** in Jerusalem 1074
3:17 this woman and I live in the same **h**. 1074
3:18 there was no one in the **h** but the two of us. 1074
8:43 that this **h** I have built bears your Name. 1074
11:18 a **h** and land and provided him with food. 1074
11:28 of the whole labor force of the **h** *of* Joseph. 1074
12:16 Look after your own **h**, O David!" 1074
12:19 So Israel has been in rebellion against the **h** 1074
12:20 of Judah remained loyal to the **h** *of* David. 1074
12:21 he mustered the whole **h** *of* Judah and 1074
12:21 the **h** *of* Israel and to regain the kingdom 1074
12:23 to the whole **h** *of* Judah and Benjamin, 1074
12:26 now likely revert to the **h** *of* David. 1074
13: 2 'A son named Josiah will be born to the **h** 1074
13:18 with you to your **h** so that he may eat bread 1074
13:19 with him and ate and drank in his **h**. 1074
13:34 of the **h** *of* Jeroboam that led to its downfall 1074
14: 4 and went to Ahijah's **h** in Shiloh. 1074
14: 8 from the **h** *of* David and gave it to you, 1074
14:10 to bring disaster on the **h** *of* Jeroboam. 1074
14:10 up the **h** *of* Jeroboam as one burns dung, 1074
14:13 the only one in the **h** *of* Jeroboam in whom 1074
14:17 as she stepped over the threshold of the **h**, 1074
15:27 of the **h** *of* Issachar plotted against him, 1074
16: 3 So I am about to consume Baasha and his **h**, 1074
16: 3 and I will make your **h** like that of Jeroboam 1074
16: 7 of Hanani to Baasha and his **h**, because 1074
16: 7 and becoming like the **h** *of* Jeroboam— 1074
17:17 of the woman who owned the **h** became ill. 1074
17:23 down from the room into the **h**. 1074
20:31 that the kings of the **h** *of* Israel are merciful 1074
21:22 I will make your **h** like that of Jeroboam son 1074
21:29 but I will bring it on his **h** in the days 1074
2Ki 4: 2 Tell me, what do you have in your **h**?" 1074
4:32 When Elisha reached the **h**, 1074
5: 9 and stopped at the door of Elisha's **h**. 1074
5:24 the servants and put them away in the **h**. 1074
6:32 Now Elisha was sitting in his **h**, 1074
7:17 when the king came down to his **h**. NIH
8: 3 to the king to beg for her **h** and land. 1074
8: 5 to life came to beg the king for her **h** 1074
8:18 as the **h** *of* Ahab had done, 1074
8:27 in the ways of the **h** *of* Ahab and did evil in 1074
8:27 as the **h** *of* Ahab had done, 1074
9: 6 Jehu got up and went into the **h**. 1074
9: 7 to destroy the **h** *of* Ahab your master, 1074
9: 8 The whole **h** *of* Ahab will perish. 1074
9: 9 I will make the **h** *of* Ahab like the house 1074
9: 9 the **h** *of* Jeroboam son of Nebat and like 1074
9: 9 of Jeroboam son of Nebat and like the **h** 1074
10: 1 in Samaria seventy sons of the **h** of Ahab. NIH
10: 3 Then fight for your master's **h**." 1074
10:10 a word the LORD has spoken against the **h** 1074
10:11 in Jezreel who remained of the **h** *of* Ahab, 1074
10:30 and have done to the **h** *of* Ahab all I had 1074
13: 6 not turn away from the sins of the **h** 1074
15: 5 and he lived in a separate **h**. 1074
17:21 he tore Israel away from the **h** *of* David, 1074
19:30 of the **h** *of* Judah will take root below 1074
20: 1 Put your **h** in order, because you are going 1074
21:13 the plumb line used against the **h** *of* Ahab. 1074

1Ch 2:55 the father of the **h** *of* Recab. 1074
6:31 in the **h** *of* the LORD after the ark came 1074
6:48 of the tabernacle, the **h** *of* God. 1074
9:11 the official in charge of the **h** *of* God; 1074
9:13 responsible for ministering in the **h** *of* God. 1074
9:23 in charge of guarding the gates of the **h** *of* 1074
9:23 the **h** called the Tent. 1074
9:26 the rooms and treasuries in the **h** *of* God. 1074
9:27 the **h** *of* God, because they had to guard it; 1074
10:6 and all his **h** died together. 1074
12:29 of whom had remained loyal to Saul's **h** 1074
13:7 of God from Abinadab's **h** on a new cart, 1074
13:13 he took it aside to the **h** *of* Obed-Edom 1074
13:14 of Obed-Edom in his **h** for three months, 1074
15:25 of the LORD from the **h** *of* Obed-Edom, 1074
17:4 not the one to build me a **h** to dwell in. 1074
17:5 in a **h** from the day I brought Israel up out 1074
17:6 "Why have you not built me a **h** of cedar?" 1074
17:10 that the LORD will build a **h** for you: 1074
17:12 He is the one who will build a **h** for me, 1074
17:14 over my **h** and my kingdom forever; 1074
17:17 you have spoken about the future of the **h** 1074
17:23 concerning your servant and his **h** 1074
17:24 And the **h** *of* your servant David will 1074
17:25 to your servant that you will build a **h** 1074
17:27 Now you have been pleased to bless the **h** 1074
22:1 "The **h** *of* the LORD God is to be here, 1074
22:2 to prepare dressed stone for building the **h** 1074
22:5 and the **h** to be built for the LORD should 1074
22:6 and charged him to build a **h** for 1074
22:7 "My son, I had it in my heart to build a **h** 1074
22:8 You are not to build a **h** for my Name, 1074
22:10 the one who will build a **h** for my Name. 1074
22:11 and may you have success and build the **h** 1074
23:28 and the performance of other duties at the **h** 1074
25:6 for the ministry at the **h** *of* God. 1074
26:20 in charge of the treasuries of the **h** *of* God 1074
28:2 in my heart to build a **h** as a place of rest for 1074
28:3 'You are not to build a **h** for my Name, 1074
28:4 from the **h** *of* Judah he chose my family, 1074
28:6 the one who will build my **h** and my courts, 1074
2Ch 6:33 that this **h** I have built bears your Name. 1074
10:16 Look after your own **h**, O David!" 1074
10:19 So Israel has been in rebellion against the **h** 1074
11:1 he mustered the **h** *of* Judah and Benjamin— 1074
21:6 as the **h** *of* Ahab had done, 1074
21:7 the LORD was not willing to destroy the **h** 1074
21:13 just as the **h** *of* Ahab did. 1074
21:13 *members of* your father's **h**, 1074
22:3 He too walked in the ways of the **h** 1074
22:4 as the **h** *of* Ahab had done, 1074
22:7 the LORD had anointed to destroy the **h** 1074
22:8 executing judgment on the **h** *of* Ahab, 1074
22:9 the **h** *of* Ahaziah powerful enough to retain 1074
22:10 to destroy the whole royal family of the **h** 1074
26:21 He lived in a separate **h**— 1074
35:21 but the **h** *with which* I am at war. 1074
Ezr 1:5 and build the **h** *of* the LORD in Jerusalem. 1074
2:68 When they arrived at the **h** *of* the LORD 1074
2:68 the rebuilding of the **h** *of* God on its site. 1074
3:8 of the second year after their arrival at the **h** 1074
3:8 and older to supervise the building of the **h** 1074
3:9 in supervising those working on the **h** 1074
3:11 foundation of the **h** *of* the LORD was laid. 1074
4:24 on the **h** *of* God in Jerusalem came to 10103
5:2 of Jozadak set to work to rebuild the **h** 10103
5:13 King Cyrus issued a decree to rebuild this **h** 10103
5:14 the gold and silver articles of the **h** *of* God, 10103
5:15 And rebuild the **h** *of* God on its site.' 10103
5:16 and laid the foundations of the **h** *of* God 10103
5:17 to rebuild this **h** *of* God in Jerusalem. 10103
6:5 the gold and silver articles of the **h** *of* God, 10103
6:5 they are to be deposited in the **h** *of* God. 10103
6:7 Jews and the Jewish elders rebuild this **h** 10103
6:8 of the Jews in the construction of this **h** 10103
6:11 pulled from his **h** and **h** is to be lifted up 10103
6:11 for this crime his **h** is to be made a pile 10103
6:16 celebrated the dedication of the **h** *of* God 10103
6:17 the dedication of this **h** *of* God they offered 10103
6:22 so that he assisted them in the work on the **h** 1074
7:24 temple servants or other workers at this **h** 10103
7:27 into the king's heart to bring honor to the **h** 1074
8:17 attendants to us for the **h** *of* our God. 1074
8:25 had donated for the **h** *of* our God. 1074
8:29 of the **h** *of* the LORD in Jerusalem before 1074
8:30 be taken to the **h** *of* our God in Jerusalem. 1074
8:33 On the fourth day, in the **h** *of* our God, 1074
8:36 to the people and to the **h** *of* God. 1074
9:9 He has granted us new life to rebuild the **h** 1074
10:1 the **h** *of* God, a large crowd of Israelites— 1074
10:6 before the **h** *of* God and went to the room 1074
10:9 in the square before the **h** *of* God, 1074
Ne 1:6 including myself and my father's **h**, 1074
3:10 of Harumaph made repairs opposite his **h**, 1074
3:16 the artificial pool and the **H** *of* the Heroes. 1074
3:20 from the angle to the entrance of the **h** 1074
3:21 from the entrance of Eliashib's **h** to the end 1074
3:23 made repairs in front of their **h**; 1074
3:23 made repairs beside his **h**. 1074
3:24 from Azariah's **h** to the angle and 1074
3:28 each in front of his own **h**. 1074
3:29 of Immer made repairs opposite his **h**. 1074
3:31 as far as the **h** *of* the temple servants and 1074
5:13 "In this way may God shake out of his **h** 1074
6:10 One day I went to the **h** *of* Shemaiah son 1074
6:10 He said, "Let us meet in the **h** *of* God, 1074
8:16 the courts of the **h** *of* God and in the square 1074
Ne 10:32 of a shekel each year for the service of the **h** 1074
10:33 and for all the duties of the **h** *of* our God. 1074
10:34 to the **h** *of* our God at set times each year 1074
10:35 the **h** *of* the LORD each year the firstfruits 1074
10:36 of our herds and of our flocks to the **h** 1074
10:37 we will bring to the storerooms of the **h** 1074
10:38 a tenth of the tithes up to the **h** *of* our God, 1074
10:39 "We will not neglect the **h** *of* our God." 1074
11:11 supervisor in the **h** *of* God, 1074
11:16 who had charge of the outside work of the **h** 1074
11:22 for the service of the **h** *of* God. 1074
12:37 the wall and passed above the **h** *of* David to 1074
12:40 then took their places in the **h** *of* God; 1074
13:4 of the storerooms of the **h** *of* our God. 1074
13:7 a room in the courts of the **h** *of* God. 1074
13:9 into them the equipment of the **h** *of* God, 1074
13:11 "Why is the **h** *of* God neglected?" 1074
13:14 so faithfully done for the **h** *of* my God 1074
Est 4:13 because you are in the king's **h** you alone 1074
7:8 the queen while she is with me in the **h?"** 1074
7:9 "A gallows seventy-five feet high stands by Haman's **h.** 1074
Job 1:13 and drinking wine at the oldest brother's **h**, 1074
1:18 and drinking wine at the oldest brother's **h**, 1074
1:19 and struck the four corners of the **h**. 1074
5:3 but suddenly his **h** was cursed. 5659
7:10 He will never come to his **h** again; 1074
20:28 A flood will carry off his **h**, 1074
21:28 You say, 'Where now is the great man's **h**, 1074
27:18 The **h** he builds is like a moth's cocoon, 1074
29:4 God's intimate friendship blessed my **h**, 185
29:18 "I thought, 'I will die in my own **h**, 7860
42:11 before came and ate with him in his **h**. 1074
Ps 5:7 by your great mercy, will come into your **h**; 1074
23:6 I will dwell in the **h** *of* the LORD forever. 1074
26:8 I love the **h** where you live, O LORD, 1074
27:4 the **h** *of* the LORD all the days of my life, 1074
36:8 They feast on the abundance of your **h**; 1074
42:4 leading the procession to the **h** *of* God, 1074
45:10 Forget your people and your father's **h**. 1074
49:16 when the splendor of his **h** increases; 1074
52:T "David has gone to the **h** *of* Ahimelech." 1074
52:8 an olive tree flourishing in the **h** *of* God; 1074
55:14 as we walked with the throng at the **h** 1074
59:T to watch David's **h** in order to kill him. 1074
65:4 with the good things of your **h**, 1074
69:9 for zeal for your **h** consumes me, 1074
84:4 Blessed are those who dwell in your **h**; 1074
84:10 a doorkeeper in the **h** *of* my God than dwell 1074
92:13 planted in the **h** *of* the LORD, 1074
93:5 holiness adorns your **h** for endless days, 1074
98:3 and his faithfulness to the **h** *of* Israel; 1074
101:2 I will walk in my **h** with blameless heart. 1074
101:7 No one who practices deceit will dwell in my **h**; 1074
112:3 Wealth and riches are in his **h**, 1074
114:1 **h** *of* Jacob from a people of foreign tongue, 1074
115:9 O **h** of Israel, trust in the LORD— NIH
115:10 O **h** *of* Aaron, trust in the LORD— 1074
115:12 He will bless the **h** *of* Israel, 1074
115:12 he will bless the **h** *of* Aaron, 1074
116:19 in the courts of the **h** *of* the LORD— 1074
118:3 Let the **h** *of* Aaron say: 1074
118:26 From the **h** *of* the LORD we bless you. 1074
122:1 "Let us go to the **h** *of* the LORD." 1074
122:5 the thrones of the **h** *of* David. 1074
122:9 the sake of the **h** *of* the LORD our God, 1074
127:1 Unless the LORD builds the **h**, 1074
128:3 be like a fruitful vine within your **h**; 1074
132:3 "I will not enter my **h** or go to my bed 185+1074
134:1 the LORD who minister by night in the **h** 1074
135:2 you who minister in the **h** *of* the LORD, 1074
135:2 in the courts of the **h** *of* our God. 1074
135:19 O **h** *of* Israel, praise the LORD; 1074
135:19 O **h** *of* Aaron, praise the LORD; 1074
135:20 O **h** *of* Levi, praise the LORD; 1074
Pr 2:18 For her **h** leads down to death and her paths 1074
3:33 LORD's curse is on the **h** *of* the wicked, 1074
4:3 When I was a boy in my father's **h**, NIH
5:8 do not go near the door of her **h**, 1074
5:10 and your toil enrich another man's **h**. 1074
6:31 though it costs him all the wealth of his **h**. 1074
7:6 At the window of my **h** I looked out through 1074
7:8 walking along in the direction of her **h** 1074
7:27 Her **h** is a highway to the grave, 1074
9:1 Wisdom has built her **h**; 1074
9:14 She sits at the door of her **h**, 1074
12:7 but the **h** *of* the righteous stands firm. 1074
14:1 The wise woman builds her **h**, 1074
14:11 The **h** *of* the wicked will be destroyed, 1074
15:6 **h** *of* the righteous contains great treasure, 1074
15:25 The LORD tears down the proud man's **h** 1074
17:1 a dry crust with peace and quiet than a **h** full 1074
17:13 evil will never leave his **h**. 1074
21:9 to live on a corner of the roof than share a **h** 1074
21:12 the **h** *of* the wicked and brings the wicked 1074
21:20 the **h** *of* the wise are stores of choice food 5659
24:3 By wisdom a **h** is built, 1074
24:15 like an outlaw against a righteous man's **h**, 5659
24:27 after that, build your **h**. 1074
25:17 Seldom set foot in your neighbor's **h**— 1074
25:24 to live on a corner of the roof than share a **h** 1074
27:10 and do not go to your brother's **h** 1074
Ecc 2:7 had other slaves who were born in my **h**. 1074
5:1 Guard your steps when you go to the **h** 1074
7:2 to a **h** *of* mourning than to go to a house 1074
7:2 of mourning than to go to a **h** *of* feasting, 1074
Ecc 7:4 heart of the wise is in the **h** *of* mourning, 1074
7:4 but the heart of fools is in the **h** *of* pleasure. 1074
10:18 if his hands are idle, the **h** leaks. 1074
12:3 of the **h** tremble, and the strong men stoop, 1074
SS 1:17 The beams of our **h** are cedars; 1074
3:4 till I had brought him to my mother's **h**, 1074
8:2 and bring you to my mother's **h**— 1074
8:7 If one were to give all the wealth of his **h** 1074
Isa 2:3 to the **h** *of* the God of Jacob. 1074
2:5 Come, O **h** *of* Jacob, 1074
2:6 abandoned your people, the **h** *of* Jacob. 1074
3:7 I have no food or clothing in my **h**; 1074
5:7 of the LORD Almighty is the **h** *of* Israel, 1074
5:8 to you who add **h** to house and join field 1074
5:8 to you who add house to **h** and join field 1074
7:2 Now the **h** *of* David was told, 1074
7:13 Isaiah said, "Hear now, you **h** *of* David! 1074
7:17 on your people and on the **h** *of* your father 1074
8:17 who is hiding his face from the **h** *of* Jacob. 1074
10:20 the survivors of the **h** *of* Jacob, 1074
14:1 Aliens will join them and unite with the **h** 1074
14:2 And the **h** *of* Israel will possess the nations 1074
16:5 one from the **h** *of* David— 185
22:18 you disgrace to your master's **h!** 1074
22:21 to those who live in Jerusalem and to the **h** 1074
22:22 I will place on his shoulder the key to the **h** 1074
22:23 be a seat of honor for the **h** *of* his father. 1074
23:1 For Tyre is destroyed and left without **h** 1074
24:10 the entrance to every **h** is barred. 1074
29:22 says to the **h** *of* Jacob: 1074
31:2 He will rise up against the **h** *of* the wicked, 1074
37:31 of the **h** *of* Judah will take root below 1074
38:1 Put your **h** in order, because you are going 1074
38:12 Like a shepherd's tent my **h** has been pulled 1886
46:3 "Listen to me, O **h** *of* Jacob, 1074
46:3 all you who remain of the **h** *of* Israel, 1074
48:1 "Listen to this, O **h** *of* Jacob, 1074
56:7 and give them joy in my **h** *of* prayer. 1074
56:7 for my **h** will be called a house of prayer 1074
56:7 for my house will be called a **h** *of* prayer 1074
58:1 to my people their rebellion and to the **h** 1074
63:7 the many good things he has done for the **h** 1074
66:1 Where is the **h** you will build for me? 1074
Jer 2:4 Hear the word of the LORD, O **h** *of* Jacob, 1074
2:4 all you clans of the **h** *of* Israel. 1074
2:26 so the **h** *of* Israel is disgraced— 1074
3:18 the **h** *of* Judah will join the house of Israel, 1074
3:18 the house of Judah will join the **h** *of* Israel, 1074
3:20 O **h** *of* Israel," declares the LORD. 1074
5:11 The **h** *of* Israel and the house 1074
5:11 the **h** *of* Judah have been utterly unfaithful 1074
5:15 O **h** *of* Israel," declares the LORD, 1074
5:20 to the **h** *of* Jacob and proclaim it in Judah: 1074
7:2 "Stand at the gate of the LORD's **h** 1074
7:10 before me in this **h**, which bears my Name, 1074
7:11 Has this **h**, which bears my Name, 1074
7:14 what I did to Shiloh I will now do to the **h** 1074
7:30 up their detestable idols in the **h** 1074
9:26 even the whole **h** *of* Israel is uncircumcised 1074
10:1 what the LORD says to you, O **h** *of* Israel. 1074
11:10 Both the **h** *of* Israel and the house 1074
11:10 of Israel and the **h** *of* Judah have broken 1074
11:17 because the **h** *of* Israel and the house 1074
11:17 of Israel and the **h** *of* Judah have done evil 1074
12:7 "I will forsake my **h**, 1074
12:14 from their lands and I will uproot the **h** 1074
13:11 the whole **h** *of* Israel and the whole house 1074
13:11 of Israel and the whole **h** *of* Judah to me,' 1074
16:5 not enter a **h** *where there* is a funeral meal; 1074
16:8 "And do not enter a **h** *where there* is feasting 1074
17:26 and thank offerings to the **h** *of* the LORD. 1074
18:2 "Go down to the potter's **h**, 1074
18:3 So I went down to the potter's **h**, 1074
18:6 "O **h** *of* Israel, can I not do with you as 1074
18:6 so are you in my hand, O **h** *of* Israel. 1074
20:6 and all who live in your **h** will go into exile 1074
21:11 "Moreover, say to the royal **h** *of* Judah, 1074
21:12 O **h** *of* David, this is what the LORD says: 1074
26:2 the LORD's **h** and speak to all the people 1074
26:2 of Judah who come to worship in the **h** *of* 1074
26:6 then I will make this **h** like Shiloh 1074
26:7 these words in the **h** *of* the LORD. 1074
26:9 in the LORD's name that this **h** will be 1074
26:9 around Jeremiah in the **h** *of* the LORD. 1074
26:10 to the **h** *of* the LORD and took their places 1074
26:10 of the New Gate of the LORD's **h**. NIH
26:12 to prophesy against this **h** and this city all 1074
27:16 from the LORD's **h** will be brought back 1074
27:18 in the **h** *of* the LORD and in the palace of 1074
27:21 says about the things that are left in the **h** *of* 1074
28:1 in the **h** *of* the LORD in the presence of 1074
28:3 the LORD's **h** that Nebuchadnezzar king 1074
28:5 the people who were standing in the **h** *of* 1074
28:6 by bringing the articles of the LORD's **h** 1074
29:26 in place of Jehoiada to be in charge of the **h** 1074
31:27 the **h** *of* Israel and the house of Judah with 1074
31:27 the house of Israel and the **h** *of* Judah with 1074
31:31 the **h** *of* Israel and with the house of Judah. 1074
31:31 the house of Israel and with the **h** *of* Judah. 1074
31:33 "This is the covenant I will make with the **h** 1074
32:34 They set up their abominable idols in the **h** 1074
33:11 of those who bring thank offerings to the **h** 1074
33:14 to the **h** *of* Israel and to the house of Judah. 1074
33:14 to the house of Israel and to the **h** *of* Judah. 1074
33:17 a man to sit on the throne of the **h** *of* Israel, 1074
34:15 even made a covenant before me in the **h** 1074

Jer	35: 2	to come to one of the side rooms of the **h** *of*	1074
	35: 4	I brought them into the **h** *of* the LORD,	1074
	36: 6	So you go to the **h** *of* the LORD on a day	1074
	37:15	and had him beaten and imprisoned in the **h**	1074
	37:20	Do not send me back to the **h** *of* Jonathan	1074
	38:26	not to send me back to Jonathan's **h**	1074
	41: 5	with them to the **h** *of* the LORD.	1074
	48:13	as the **h** *of* Israel was ashamed	1074
	51:51	the holy places of the LORD's **h."**	1074
La	2: 7	a shout in the **h** *of* the LORD as on the day	1074
Eze	2: 5	for they are a rebellious **h—**	1074
	2: 6	though they are a rebellious **h.**	1074
	2: 8	Do not rebel like that rebellious **h;**	1074
	3: 1	then go and speak to the **h** *of* Israel."	1074
	3: 4	the **h** *of* Israel and speak my words to them.	1074
	3: 5	but to the **h** *of* Israel—	1074
	3: 7	the **h** *of* Israel is not willing to listen to you	1074
	3: 7	whole **h** *of* Israel is hardened and obstinate.	1074
	3: 9	though they are a rebellious **h."**	1074
	3:17	I have made you a watchman for the **h**	1074
	3:24	"Go, shut yourself inside your **h.**	1074
	3:26	though they are a rebellious **h.**	1074
	3:27	for they are a rebellious **h.**	1074
	4: 3	This will be a sign to the **h** *of* Israel.	1074
	4: 4	on your left side and put the sin of the **h**	1074
	4: 5	for 390 days you will bear the sin of the **h**	1074
	4: 6	and bear the sin of the **h** *of* Judah.	1074
	5: 4	A fire will spread from there to the whole **h**	1074
	6:11	the wicked and detestable practices of the **h**	1074
	8: 1	in my **h** and the elders of Judah were sitting	1074
	8: 6	the utterly detestable things the **h**	1074
	8:10	and all the idols of the **h** *of* Israel.	1074
	8:11	of them stood seventy elders of the **h**	1074
	8:12	of the **h** *of* Israel are doing in the darkness,	1074
	8:14	to the entrance to the north gate of the **h** *of*	1074
	8:16	then brought me into the inner court of the **h**	1074
	8:17	Is it a trivial matter for the **h** *of* Judah to do	1074
	9: 9	"The sin of the **h** *of* Israel	1074
	10:19	to the east gate of the LORD's **h,**	1074
	11: 1	up and brought me to the gate of the **h** *of*	1074
	11: 5	That is what you are saying, O **h** *of* Israel,	1074
	11:15	and the whole **h** *of* Israel—	1074
	12: 3	though they are a rebellious **h.**	1074
	12: 6	I have made you a sign to the **h** *of* Israel."	1074
	12: 9	did not that rebellious **h** *of* Israel ask you,	1074
	12:10	and the whole **h** *of* Israel who are there.'	1074
	12:25	For in your days, you rebellious **h,**	1074
	12:27	the **h** *of* Israel is saying,	1074
	13: 5	to the breaks in the wall to repair it for the **h**	1074
	13: 9	or be listed in the records of the **h** *of* Israel,	1074
	14: 6	"Therefore say to the **h** *of* Israel,	1074
	17: 2	an allegory and tell the **h** *of* Israel a parable.	1074
	17:12	"Say to this rebellious **h,**	1074
	18: 6	or look to the idols of the **h** *of* Israel.	1074
	18:15	or look to the idols of the **h** *of* Israel.	1074
	18:25	Hear, O **h** *of* Israel: Is my way unjust?	1074
	18:29	Yet the **h** *of* Israel says,	1074
	18:29	Are my ways unjust, O **h** *of* Israel?	1074
	18:30	"Therefore, O **h** *of* Israel, I will judge you,	1074
	18:31	Why will you die, O **h** *of* Israel?	1074
	20: 5	the **h** *of* Jacob and revealed myself to them	1074
	20:30	"Therefore say to the **h** *of* Israel:	1074
	20:31	let you inquire of me, O **h** *of* Israel?	1074
	20:39	" 'As for you, O **h** *of* Israel,	1074
	20:40	the land the entire **h** *of* Israel will serve me,	1074
	20:44	your corrupt practices, O **h** *of* Israel,	1074
	22:18	the **h** *of* Israel has become dross to me;	1074
	23:39	That is what they did in my **h.**	1074
	24: 3	Tell this rebellious **h** a parable and say	1074
	24:21	Say to the **h** *of* Israel, 'This is what	1074
	25: 8	'Because Moab and Seir said, "Look, the **h**	1074
	25:12	on the **h** *of* Judah and became very guilty	1074
	29: 6	" 'You have been a staff of reed for the **h**	1074
	29:21	that day I will make a horn grow for the **h**	1074
	33: 7	I have made you a watchman for the **h**	1074
	33:10	"Son of man, say to the **h** *of* Israel,	1074
	33:11	Why will you die, O **h** *of* Israel?'	1074
	33:20	Yet, O **h** *of* Israel, you say,	1074
	34:30	am with them and that they, the **h** *of* Israel,	1074
	35:15	of the **h** *of* Israel became desolate,	1074
	36:10	even the whole **h** *of* Israel.	1074
	36:21	the **h** *of* Israel profaned among the nations	1074
	36:22	"Therefore say to the **h** *of* Israel,	1074
	36:22	It is not for your sake, O **h** *of* Israel,	1074
	36:32	disgraced for your conduct, O **h** *of* Israel!	1074
	36:37	Once again I will yield to the plea of the **h**	1074
	37:11	these bones are the whole **h** *of* Israel.	1074
	37:16	and all the **h** *of* Israel associated with him.'	1074
	39:12	the **h** *of* Israel will be burying them in order	1074
	39:22	that day forward the **h** *of* Israel will know	1074
	39:29	I will pour out my Spirit on the **h** *of* Israel,	1074
	40: 4	Tell the **h** *of* Israel everything you see."	1074
	43: 7	The **h** *of* Israel will never again defile my holy name—	1074
	44: 6	Say to the rebellious **h** *of* Israel,	1074
	44: 6	of your detestable practices, O **h** *of* Israel!	1074
	44:12	in the presence of their idols and made the **h**	1074
	45: 6	it will belong to the whole **h** *of* Israel.	1074
	45: 8	the **h** *of* Israel to possess the land according	1074
	45:17	at all the appointed feasts of the **h** *of* Israel.	1074
	45:17	to make atonement for the **h** *of* Israel.	1074
Da	1: 2	in Babylonia and put in the treasure **h**	1074
	2:17	Then Daniel returned to his **h** and explained	10103
Hos	1: 4	because I will soon punish the **h** *of* Jehu for	1074
	1: 6	for I will no longer show love to the **h**	1074
	1: 7	Yet I will show love to the **h** *of* Judah;	1074
	5: 1	Listen, O royal **h!** This judgment is against	1074
Hos	6:10	I have seen a horrible thing in the **h**	1074
	8: 1	An eagle is over the **h** *of* the LORD	1074
	9: 8	and hostility in the **h** *of* his God.	1074
	9:15	I will drive them out of my **h.**	1074
	11:12	the **h** *of* Israel with deceit.	1074
Joel	1: 9	and drink offerings are cut off from the **h** *of*	1074
	1:13	and drink offerings are withheld from the **h**	1074
	1:14	the land to the **h** *of* the LORD your God,	1074
	1:16	joy and gladness from the **h** *of* our God?	1074
	3:18	of the LORD's **h** and will water the valley	1074
Am	1: 4	upon the **h** *of* Hazael that will consume	1074
	2: 8	In the **h** *of* their god they drink wine taken	1074
	3:13	and testify against the **h** *of* Jacob,"	1074
	3:15	the winter **h** along with the summer house;	1074
	3:15	the winter house along with the summer **h;**	1074
	5: 1	Hear this word, O **h** *of* Israel,	1074
	5: 4	This is what the LORD says to the **h**	1074
	5: 6	or he will sweep through the **h** *of* Joseph	1074
	5:19	though he entered his **h** and rested his hand	1074
	5:25	forty years in the desert, O **h** *of* Israel?	1074
	6: 9	If ten men are left in one **h,**	1074
	6:10	comes to carry them out of the **h**	1074
	6:11	the great **h** into pieces and the small house	1074
	6:11	the great house into pieces and the small **h**	1074
	6:14	O **h** *of* Israel, that will oppress you	1074
	7: 9	with my sword I will rise against the **h**	1074
	7:16	and stop preaching against the **h** *of* Isaac.'	1074
	9: 8	I will not totally destroy the **h** *of* Jacob,"	1074
	9: 9	and I will shake the **h** *of* Israel among all	1074
Ob	1:17	the **h** *of* Jacob will possess its inheritance.	1074
	1:18	The **h** *of* Jacob will be a fire and the house	1074
	1:18	The house of Jacob will be a fire and the **h**	1074
	1:18	the **h** *of* Esau will be stubble,	1074
	1:18	There will be no survivors from the **h**	1074
Mic	1: 5	because of the sins of the **h** *of* Israel.	1074
	2: 7	Should it be said, O **h** *of* Jacob:	1074
	3: 1	you rulers of the **h** *of* Israel.	1074
	3: 9	Hear this, you leaders of the **h** *of* Jacob,	1074
	3: 9	you rulers of the **h** *of* Israel,	1074
	4: 2	to the **h** *of* the God of Jacob.	1074
	6:10	Am I still to forget, O wicked **h,**	1074
	6:16	of Omri and all the practices of Ahab's **h,**	1074
Hab	2:10	shaming your own **h** and forfeiting your life	1074
Zep	2: 7	It will belong to the remnant of the **h**	1074
Hag	1: 2	yet come for the LORD's **h** to be built.' "	1074
	1: 4	while this **h** remains a ruin?"	1074
	1: 8	and bring down timber and build the **h,**	1074
	1: 9	"Because of my **h,** which remains a ruin,	1074
	1: 9	while each of you is busy with his own **h.**	1074
	1:14	to work on the **h** *of* the LORD Almighty,	1074
	2: 3	'Who of you is left who saw this **h**	1074
	2: 7	and I will fill this **h** with glory,'	1074
	2: 9	glory of this present **h** will be greater than	1074
	2: 9	be greater than the glory of the former **h,'**	NIH
Zec	1:16	and there my **h** will be rebuilt.	1074
	3: 7	then you will govern my **h** and have charge	1074
	5: 4	and it will enter the **h** *of* the thief and	1074
	5: 4	and the **h** *of* him who swears falsely	1074
	5: 4	It will remain in his **h** and destroy it,	1074
	5:11	the country of Babylonia to build a **h** for it.	1074
	6:10	Go the same day to the **h** *of* Josiah son	1074
	7: 3	the priests of the **h** *of* the LORD Almighty	1074
	8: 9	when the foundation was laid for the **h** *of*	1074
	9: 8	But I will defend my **h**	1074
	10: 3	for his flock, the **h** *of* Judah,	1074
	10: 6	"I will strengthen the **h** *of* Judah and save	1074
	10: 6	of Judah and save the **h** *of* Joseph.	1074
	11:13	and threw them into the **h** *of* the LORD to	1074
	12: 4	"I will keep a watchful eye over the **h**	1074
	12: 7	so that the honor of the **h** *of* David and	1074
	12: 8	and the **h** *of* David will be like God,	1074
	12:10	"And I will pour out on the **h** *of* David and	1074
	12:12	the clan of the **h** *of* David and their wives,	1074
	12:12	the clan of the **h** *of* Nathan and their wives,	1074
	12:13	the clan of the **h** *of* Levi and their wives,	1074
	13: 1	a fountain will be opened to the **h** *of* David	1074
	13: 6	'The wounds I was given at the **h**	1074
	14:20	and the cooking pots in the LORD's **h** will	1074
	14:21	in the **h** *of* the LORD Almighty.	1074
Mal	3:10	that there may be food in my **h.**	1074
Mt	2:11	On coming to the **h,** they saw the child	*3864*
	5:15	and it gives light to everyone in the **h.**	*3864*
	7:24	like a wise man who built his **h** on the rock.	*3864*
	7:25	and the winds blew and beat against that **h;**	*3864*
	7:26	like a foolish man who built his **h** on sand.	*3864*
	7:27	and the winds blew and beat against that **h,**	*3864*
	8:14	When Jesus came into Peter's **h,**	*3864*
	9:10	at Matthew's **h,** many tax collectors	*3864*
	9:23	the ruler's **h** and saw the flute players and	*3864*
	10:11	and stay **at his h** until you leave.	*1695*
	10:25	**head of the h** has been called Beelzebub,	*3867*
	12: 4	He entered the **h** of God,	*3875*
	12:29	how can anyone enter a strong man's **h**	*3864*
	12:29	Then he can rob his **h.**	*3864*
	12:44	Then it says, 'I will return to the **h** I left.'	*3875*
	12:44	When it arrives, it finds the **h** unoccupied,	*3875*
	13: 1	That same day Jesus went out of the **h**	*3864*
	13:36	Then he left the crowd and went into the **h.**	*3864*
	13:52	like the **owner of a h** who brings out	*476+3867*
	13:57	"Only in his hometown and in his own **h** is	*3864*
	17:25	When Peter came into the **h,**	*3864*
	21:13	" 'My **h** will be called a house of prayer,'	*3875*
	21:13	" 'My house will be called a **h** of prayer,'	*3875*
	23:38	Look, your **h** is left to you desolate.	*3875*
	24:17	Let no one on the **roof** of his **h** go down	*1560*
	24:17	down to take anything out of the **h.**	*3864*
	24:43	the **owner of the h** had known at what time	*3867*
Mt	24:43	and would not have let his **h** be broken into.	*3864*
	26:18	the Passover with my disciples at your **h.' "**	*NIG*
Mk	1:35	left the **h** and went off to a solitary place,	*NIG*
	2:15	While Jesus was having dinner at Levi's **h,**	*3864*
	2:26	the **h** of God and ate the consecrated bread,	*3875*
	3:20	Then Jesus entered a **h,**	*3875*
	3:25	If a **h** is divided against itself,	*3864*
	3:25	that **h** cannot stand.	*3864*
	3:27	no one can enter a strong man's **h** and	*3864*
	3:27	Then he can rob his **h.**	*3864*
	5:35	some men came from the **h** of Jairus,	*NIG*
	6: 4	in his own **h** is a prophet without honor."	*3864*
	6:10	Whenever you enter a **h,**	*3864*
	7:17	the crowd and entered the **h,**	*3875*
	7:24	He entered a **h** and did not want anyone	*3864*
	9:33	When he was in the **h,** he asked them,	*3864*
	10:10	When they were in the **h** again,	*3864*
	11:17	" 'My **h** will be called a house of prayer	*3875*
	11:17	" 'My house will be called a **h** of prayer	*3875*
	13:15	the roof *of* his **h** go down or enter the house	*3864*
	13:15	the roof of his house go down or enter the **h**	*NIG*
	13:34	He leaves his **h** and puts his servants	*3864*
	13:35	when the owner *of* the **h** will come back—	*3864*
	14:14	Say *to* the **owner of the h** he enters,	*3867*
Lk	1:33	he will reign over the **h** of Jacob forever;	*3875*
	1:69	up a horn of salvation for us in the **h**	*3875*
	2: 4	because he belonged to the **h** and line	*3875*
	2:49	I had to be in my Father's **h?"**	*3836*
	5:18	and tried to take him into the **h** to lay him	*NIG*
	5:29	Levi held a great banquet for Jesus at his **h,**	*3864*
	6: 4	He entered the **h** of God,	*3875*
	6:48	He is like a man building a **h,**	*3864*
	6:48	torrent struck that **h** but could not shake it,	*3864*
	6:49	into practice is like a man who built a **h** on	*3864*
	6:49	The moment the torrent struck that **h,**	*3864*
	7: 6	the **h** when the centurion sent friends to say	*3864*
	7:10	the men who had been sent returned to the **h**	*3875*
	7:36	to the Pharisee's **h** and reclined at the table.	*3875*
	7:37	that Jesus was eating at the Pharisee's **h,**	*3864*
	7:44	I came into your **h.**	*3864*
	8:27	not worn clothes or lived in a **h,**	*3864*
	8:41	pleading with him to come to his **h**	*3875*
	8:49	someone came from the **h** of Jairus,	*NIG*
	8:51	When he arrived at the **h** of Jairus,	*3864*
	9: 4	Whatever **h** you enter, stay there until	*3864*
	10: 5	"When you enter a **h,** first say,	*3864*
	10: 5	first say, 'Peace *to* this **h.'**	*3875*
	10: 7	Stay in that **h,** eating and drinking whatever	*3864*
	10: 7	Do not move around from **h** to house.	*3864*
	10: 7	Do not move around from house to **h.**	*3864*
	11:17	and a **h** divided against itself will fall.	*3875*
	11:21	strong man, fully armed, guards his own **h,**	*885*
	11:24	Then it says, 'I will return to the **h** I left.'	*3875*
	11:25	it finds the **h** swept clean and put in order.	*NIG*
	12:39	the **owner of the h** had known at what hour	*3867*
	12:39	he would not have let his **h** be broken into.	*3875*
	13:25	Once the **owner of the h** gets up and closes	*3867*
	13:35	Look, your **h** is left to you desolate.	*3875*
	14: 1	to eat in the **h** of a prominent Pharisee,	*3875*
	14:21	Then the **owner of the h** became angry	*3867*
	14:23	so that my **h** will be full.	*3875*
	15: 8	the **h** and search carefully until she finds it?	*3864*
	15:25	When he came near the **h,**	*3864*
	16:27	father, send Lazarus to my father's **h,**	*3875*
	17:31	that day no one who is on the roof of his **h,**	*3861*
	19: 5	I must stay at your **h** today."	*3875*
	19: 9	"Today salvation has come *to* this **h,**	*3875*
	19:46	" 'My **h** will be a house of prayer';	*3875*
	19:46	" 'My house will be a **h** of prayer';	*3875*
	22:10	Follow him to the **h** that he enters,	*3864*
	22:11	to the owner *of* the **h,** 'The Teacher asks:	*3864*
	22:54	they led him away and took him into the **h**	*3864*
Jn	2:16	How dare you turn my Father's **h** into	*3875*
	2:17	"Zeal *for* your **h** will consume me."	*3875*
	11:31	the Jews who had been with Mary in the **h,**	*3864*
	12: 3	And the **h** was filled with the fragrance of	*3864*
	14: 2	In my Father's **h** are many rooms;	*3864*
	20:26	his disciples were in the **h** again,	*NIG*
Ac	2: 2	the whole **h** where they were sitting.	*3875*
	5:42	temple courts and **from h to house,**	*2848+3875*
	5:42	temple courts and **from house to h,**	*2848+3875*
	7:20	he was cared for in his father's **h.**	*3875*
	7:42	and offerings forty years in the desert, *O* **h**	*3875*
	7:47	But it was Solomon who built the **h** for him.	*3875*
	7:49	What kind of **h** will you build for me?	*3875*
	8: 3	Going **from h to house,**	*2848+3836+3875*
	8: 3	Going **from house to h,**	*2848+3836+3875*
	9:11	the **h** of Judas on Straight Street and ask for	*3864*
	9:17	Then Ananias went to the **h** and entered it.	*3864*
	10: 6	Simon the tanner, whose **h** is by the sea."	*3864*
	10:17	where Simon's **h** was and stopped at	*3864*
	10:22	to his **h** so that he could hear what you have	*3875*
	10:23	Then Peter invited the men into the **h** to	*NIG*
	10:25	As Peter entered the **h,** Cornelius met him	*NIG*
	10:30	"Four days ago I was in my **h** praying	*3875*
	11: 3	"You went into the **h** of uncircumcised men	*NIG*
	11:11	to me from Caesarea stopped at the **h**	*3864*
	11:12	and we entered the man's **h.**	*3875*
	11:13	how he had seen an angel appear in his **h**	*3875*
	12:12	to the **h** of Mary the mother of John,	*3864*
	16:15	she said, "come and stay at my **h."**	*3875*
	16:32	to him and to all the others in his **h.**	*3864*
	16:34	The jailer brought them into his **h** and set	*3875*
	16:40	they went to Lydia's **h,**	*NIG*
	17: 5	They rushed to Jason's **h** in search of Paul	*3864*
	17: 7	**welcomed** them **into** *his* **h.**	*5685*
	18: 7	and went next door to the **h** of Titius Justus,	*3864*

Ac 19:16 a beating that they ran out of the **h** naked 3875
20:20 and **from h to house.** 2848+3875
20:20 and **from house to h.** 2848+3875
21: 8 and stayed at the **h** of Philip the evangelist, 3875
28:30 Paul stayed there in his own **rented h** 3637
Ro 16: 5 Greet also the church that meets at their **h.** 3875
1Co 16:19 and so does the church that meets at their **h.** 3875
2Co 5: 1 an eternal **h** in heaven, 3864
Col 4:15 and to Nympha and the church in her **h.** 3875
1Ti 5:13 and going about **from h to house.** 3836+3864
5:13 and going about **from house to h.** 3836+3864
2Ti 2:20 a large **h** there are articles not only of gold 3864
Heb 3: 2 just as Moses was faithful in all God's **h.** 3875
3: 3 as the builder of a **h** has greater honor than NIG
3: 3 a house has greater honor than the **h** itself. 3875
3: 4 For every **h** is built by someone, 3875
3: 5 Moses was faithful as a servant in all God's **h,** 3875
3: 6 But Christ is faithful as a son over God's **h.** 3875
3: 6 And we are his **h,** if we hold on to our 3875
8: 8 a new covenant with the **h** of Israel and with 3875
8: 8 the house of Israel and with the **h** of Judah. 3875
8:10 the covenant I will make *with* the **h** of Israel 3875
10:21 we have a great priest over the **h** of God, 3875
1Pe 2: 5 into a spiritual **h** to be a holy priesthood, 3875
2Jn 1:10 not take him into your **h** or welcome him. 3864

HOUSEHOLD (116) [HOUSE]

Ge 12: 1 your people and your father's **h** and go to 1074
12:17 and his **h** because of Abram's wife Sarai. 1074
14:14 the 318 trained men born in his **h** and went 1074
15: 3 so a servant in my **h** will be my heir." 1074
17:12 including those born in your **h** or bought 1074
17:13 in your **h** or bought with your money, 1074
17:23 and all those born in his **h** or bought 1074
17:23 every male in his **h,** and circumcised them, 1074
17:27 And every male in Abraham's **h,** 1074
17:27 including those born in his **h** or bought from 1074
18:19 so that he will direct his children and his **h** 1074
20:13 God had me wander from my father's **h,** 1074
20:18 up every womb in Abimelech's **h** because 1074
24: 2 He said to the chief servant in his **h,** 1074
24: 7 who brought me out of my father's **h** 1074
24:28 and told her mother's **h** about these things. 1074
30:30 when may I do something for my own **h?"** 1074
31:19 Rachel stole her father's **h gods.** 9572
31:34 Now Rachel had taken the **h gods** 9572
31:35 but could not find the **h gods.** 9572
31:37 have you found that belongs to your **h?** 1074
31:41 for the twenty years I was in your **h.** 1074
34:19 the most honored of all his father's **h,** 1074
34:30 I and my **h** will be destroyed." 1074
35: 2 So Jacob said to his **h** and to all who were 1074
36: 6 and daughters and all the members of his **h,** 1074
39: 4 Potiphar put him in charge of his **h,** 1074
39: 5 From the time he put him in charge of his **h** 1074
39: 5 the LORD blessed the **h** *of* the Egyptian 1074
39:11 and none of the **h** servants was inside. 1074
39:14 she called her **h** servants. 1074
41:51 all my trouble and all my father's **h."** 1074
45: 2 and Pharaoh's **h** heard about it. 1074
45: 8 lord of his entire **h** and ruler of all Egypt. 1074
45:11 and your **h** and all who belong 1074
46:31 to his brothers and to his father's **h,** 1074
46:31 'My brothers and my father's **h,** 1074
47:12 and his brothers and all his father's **h** 1074
50: 8 the members of Joseph's **h** and his brothers 1074
50: 8 and *those belonging to* his father's **h.** 1074
Ex 12: 3 a lamb for his family, one for each **h.** 1074
12: 4 If any **h** is too small for a whole lamb, 1074
12:48 the males in his **h** circumcised; NIH
23:12 and the **slave born in** your **h,** 563+1201
Lev 16: 6 to make atonement for himself and his **h.** 1074
16:11 to make atonement for himself and his **h,** 1074
16:17 his **h** and the whole community of Israel. 1074
22:11 or if a slave is born in his **h,** 1074
Nu 18:11 Everyone in your **h** who is ceremonially clean may eat it. 1074
18:13 Everyone in your **h** who is ceremonially clean may eat it. 1074
Dt 6:22 upon Egypt and Pharaoh and his whole **h.** 1074
14:26 and your **h** shall eat there in the presence of 1074
26:11 your God has given to you and your **h.** 1074
Jos 24:15 me and my **h,** we will serve the LORD." 1074
Jdg 14:15 or we will burn you and your father's **h** 1074
18:14 an ephod, other **h gods,** a carved image and 9572
18:17 the other **h gods** and the cast idol while 9572
18:18 the other **h gods** and the cast idol, 9572
18:19 as priest rather than just one man's **h?"** 1074
18:20 the other **h gods** and the carved image 9572
1Sa 22: 1 When his brothers and his father's **h** heard 1074
22:14 and highly respected in your **h?** 1074
25: 6 Good health to you and your **h!** 1074
25:17 over our master and his whole **h.** 1074
2Sa 6:11 the LORD blessed him and his entire **h.** 1074
6:12 the **h** *of* Obed-Edom and everything he has, 1074
6:20 When David returned home to bless his **h,** 1074
9: 2 there was a servant of Saul's **h** named Ziba. 1074
9:12 of Ziba's **h** were servants of Mephibosheth. 1074
12:11 of your own **h** I am going to bring calamity 1074
12:17 of his **h** stood beside him to get him up 1074
15:16 with his entire **h** following him; 1074
16: 2 donkeys are for the king's **h** to ride on, 1074
16: 8 for all the blood you shed in the **h** *of* Saul, 1074
19:17 along with Ziba, the steward of Saul's **h,** 1074
19:18 They crossed at the ford to take the king's **h** 1074
2Sa 19:41 steal the king away and bring him and his **h** 1074
1Ki 4: 7 for the king and the royal **h.** 1074
5: 9 by providing food for my royal **h."** 1074
5:11 of wheat as food for his **h,** 1074
10:21 the **h articles** *in* the Palace of the Forest 3998
2Ki 23:24 and spiritists, the **h gods,** the idols and all 9572
1Ch 13:14 and the LORD blessed his **h** and everything 1074
2Ch 9:20 the **h articles** *in* the Palace of the Forest 3998
Ne 13: 8 and threw all Tobiah's **h** goods out of 1074
Est 1:22 every man should be ruler over his own **h.** 1074
Job 1:10 not put a hedge around him and his **h** 1074
16: 7 you have devastated my entire **h.** 6337
31:31 the men of my **h** have never said, 'Who has 185
Ps 105:21 He made him master of his **h,** 1074
Pr 31:21 When it snows, she has no fear for her **h;** 1074
31:27 over the affairs of her **h** and does not eat 1074
Jer 23:34 I will punish that man and his **h.** 1074
Eze 44:30 so that a blessing may rest on your **h.** 1074
Mic 7: 6 the members of his own **h.** 1074
Mt 10:25 how much more the **members of** his **h!** 3865
10:36 enemies will be the **members of** his own **h.** 3865
12:25 or **h** divided against itself will not stand. 3864
24:45 the **servants in** his **h** to give them their food 3859
Lk 8: 3 the manager of Herod's **h;** NIG
Jn 4:53 So he and all his **h** believed. 3864
Ac 11:14 through which you and all your **h** will 3875
16:15 and the **members of her h** were baptized, 3875
16:31 and you will be saved—you and your **h."** 3875
18: 8 and his entire **h** believed in the Lord; 3875
Ro 16:10 Greet those who belong to the **h** 3836
16:11 Greet those in the **h** of Narcissus who are in NIG
1Co 1:11 some from Chloe's **h** have informed me 3836
1:16 (Yes, I also baptized the **h** of Stephanas; 3875
16:15 the **h** of Stephanas were the first converts 3864
Eph 2:19 God's people and **members of** God's **h,** 3858
Php 4:22 especially those who belong to Caesar's **h.** 3864
1Ti 3:12 must manage his children and his **h** well. 3875
3:15 to conduct themselves in God's **h,** 3875
2Ti 1:16 May the Lord show mercy *to* the **h** 3875
4:19 and Aquila and the **h** of Onesiphorus. 3875

HOUSEHOLDS (7) [HOUSE]

Ge 42:19 and take grain back for your starving **h.** 1074
42:33 and take food for your starving **h** and go. 1074
47:24 and as food for yourselves and your **h** 1074
Nu 16:32 with their **h** and all Korah's men 1074
18:31 and your **h** may eat the rest of it anywhere, 1074
Dt 11: 6 and swallowed them up with their **h,** 1074
Tit 1:11 because they are ruining whole **h** 3875

HOUSES (94) [HOUSE]

Ge 34:29 taking as plunder everything in the **h.** 1074
Ex 8: 3 the **h** *of* your officials and on your people, 1074
8: 9 that you and your **h** may be rid of the frogs, 1074
8:11 The frogs will leave you and your **h,** 1074
8:13 The frogs died in the **h,** 1074
8:21 on your people and into your **h.** 1074
8:21 The **h** *of* the Egyptians will be full of flies, 1074
8:24 into Pharaoh's palace and into the **h** 1074
10: 6 They will fill your **h** and those 1074
12: 7 the sides and tops of the doorframes of the **h** 1074
12:13 be a sign for you on the **h** where you are; 1074
12:15 the first day remove the yeast from your **h,** 1074
12:19 no yeast is to be found in your **h.** 1074
12:23 not permit the destroyer to enter your **h** 1074
12:27 who passed over the **h** *of* the Israelites 1074
Lev 25:31 But **h** *in* villages without walls 1074
25:32 to redeem their **h** *in* the Levitical towns, 1074
25:33 in the Jubilee, because the **h** *in* the towns of 1074
Dt 6: 9 Write them on the doorframes of your **h** and 1074
6:11 **h** filled with all kinds of good things 1074
8:12 when you build fine **h** and settle down, 1074
11:20 Write them on the doorframes of your **h** and 1074
19: 1 and settled in their towns and **h,** 1074
Jdg 18:14 "Do you know that one of these **h** has 1074
1Ki 20: 6 to search your palace and the **h** 1074
2Ki 25: 9 the royal palace and all the **h** *of* Jerusalem. 1074
Ne 5:11 vineyards, olive groves and **h,** 1074
7: 3 at their posts and some near their own **h."** 1074
7: 4 and the **h** had not yet been rebuilt. 1074
9:25 of **h** filled with all kinds of good things, 1074
Job 3:15 who filled their **h** with silver. 1074
4:19 much more those who live in **h** *of* clay, 1074
15:28 he will inhabit ruined towns and **h** 1074
15:28 **h** crumbling to rubble. 889S
20:19 he has seized **h** he did not build. 1074
22:18 Yet it was he who filled their **h** 1074
24:16 In the dark, men break into **h,** 1074
Ps 49:11 Their tombs will remain their **h** forever, 1074
Pr 1:13 and fill our **h** with plunder; 1074
19:14 **H** and wealth are inherited from parents, 1074
Ecc 2: 4 I built **h** for myself and planted vineyards. 1074
Isa 3:14 the plunder from the poor is in your **h.** 1074
5: 9 "Surely the great **h** will become desolate, 1074
6:11 the **h** are left deserted and the fields ruined 1074
8:14 but for both **h** *of* Israel he will be a stone 1074
13:16 their **h** will be looted 1074
13:21 jackals will fill her **h;** 1074
22:10 the buildings in Jerusalem and tore down **h** 1074
32:13 for all **h** *of* merriment and for this city 1074
65:21 They will build **h** and dwell in them; 1074
65:22 No longer will they build **h** and others live NIH
Jer 5: 7 and thronged to the **h** *of* prostitutes. 1074
5:27 their **h** are full of deceit; 1074
6:12 Their **h** will be turned over to others, 1074
Jer 9:19 We must leave our land because our **h** are 5438
17:22 of your **h** or do any work on the Sabbath, 1074
18:22 Let a cry be heard from their **h** 1074
19:13 The **h** *in* Jerusalem and those of the kings 1074
19:13 all the **h** where they burned incense on 1074
29: 5 "Build **h** and settle down; 1074
29:28 Therefore build **h** and settle down; 1074
32:15 **H,** fields and vineyards will again be bought 1074
32:29 with the **h** where the people provoked me 1074
33: 4 the **h** *in* this city and the royal palaces 1074
35: 7 Also you must never build **h,** 1074
35: 9 or built **h** to live in or had vineyards, 1074
39: 8 to the royal palace and the **h** *of* the people 1074
52:13 the royal palace and all the **h** *of* Jerusalem. 1074
Eze 7:24 of the nations to take possession of their **h;** 1074
11: 3 'Will it not soon be time to build **h?** 1074
16:41 down your **h** and inflict punishment on you 1074
23:47 and daughters and burn down their **h.** 1074
26:12 down your walls and demolish your fine **h** 1074
28:26 and will build **h** and plant vineyards; 1074
33:30 by the walls and at the doors of the **h,** 1074
45: 4 a place for their **h** as well as a holy place for 1074
48:15 for **h** and for pastureland. 4632
Da 2: 5 into pieces and your **h** turned into piles 10103
3:29 and Abednego be cut into pieces and their **h** 10103
Hos 7: 1 They practice deceit, thieves break into **h,** NIH
Joel 2: 9 They climb into the **h;** 1074
Am 3:15 the **h** *adorned with* ivory will be destroyed 1074
Mic 2: 2 They covet fields and seize them, and **h,** 1074
Zep 1:13 be plundered, their **h** demolished. 1074
1:13 They will build **h** but not live in them; 1074
2: 7 In the evening they will lie down in the **h** 1074
Hag 1: 4 to be living in your paneled **h,** 1074
Zec 14: 2 the city will be captured, the **h** ransacked, 1074
Mt 19:29 And everyone who has left **h** or brothers 3864
Mk 12:40 They devour widows' **h** and for a show 3864
Lk 16: 4 people will welcome me into their **h.'** 3875
20:47 They devour widows' **h** and for a show 3864
Ac 4:34 those who owned lands or **h** sold them, 3864
7:48 Most High does not live in **h** made by men. NIG

HOVERING (2) [HOVERS]

Ge 1: 2 and the Spirit of God *was* **h** over the waters. 8173
Isa 31: 5 Like birds **h overhead,** 6414

HOVERS (1) [HOVERING]

Dt 32:11 that stirs up its nest and **h** over its young, 8173

HOW (729) [HOWEVER, SOMEHOW]

Ge 6: 5 The LORD saw **h** great man's wickedness 3954
6:12 God saw *h* **corrupt** the earth *had become,* AIT
6:15 This is **h** you are to build it: 889
15: 8 **h** can I know that I will gain possession 928+4537
20: 9 **H** have I wronged you 4537
20:13 'This is **h** you can show your love to me: 889
27:20 **H** did you find it so quickly, my son? 2296+4537
28: 8 Esau then realized **h** displeasing 3954
28:17 **"H** awesome is this place! 4537
30:13 Then Leah said, **"H** happy I am! 928
30:26 You know **h much** work I've done for you." 889
30:29 "You know **h** I have worked for you and 889
30:29 for you and **h** your livestock has fared 889
38:29 *"So* **this is h** you have broken out!" 4537
39: 9 **H** then could I do such a wicked thing 375
39:19 saying, **"This is h** your slave treated me," 465+1821+2021+2021+3869
42:15 And **this is h** you will be tested: 928+2296
42:21 We saw *h* **distressed** he was when he AIT
42:33 **'This is h** I will know whether you are 928+2296
43: 7 *H were we to* **know** he would say, AIT
43:27 **asked** them **h they were,** 4200+8626+8934
43:27 **"H** is your aged father you told me about? 8934
44:16 **H** can we prove our innocence? 4537
44:34 **H** can I go back to my father if the boy is 375
47: 8 Pharaoh asked him, **"H** old are you?" 3869+4537
49:15 When he sees **h** good is his resting place 3954
49:15 how good is his resting place and **h** 3954
Ex 10: 2 and grandchildren **h** I dealt harshly with 889
10: 2 the Egyptians and **h** I performed my signs 889
10: 3 **'H long** will you refuse to humble yourself before me? 5503+6330
10: 7 **H long** will this man be a snare to us? 5503+6330
12:11 **This is h** you are to eat it: 3970
16:28 **"H long** will you refuse 625+2025+6330
18: 1 and **h** the LORD had brought Israel out 3954
18: 8 the way and **h** the LORD had saved them. NIH
19: 4 and **h** I carried you on eagles' wings NIH
23: 9 you yourselves know **h it feels** to 5883
32:22 "You know **h** prone these people are to evil. 3954
33:16 **H** will anyone know that you are pleased with me 686+928+4537
34:10 among will see **h** awesome is the work 3954
36: 1 and ability to **know h** to carry out all 3359
Lev 15: 3 **This is h** his discharge will bring 2296
16: 3 **"This is h** Aaron is to enter 928+2296
18:24 because **this is h** the nations that I 465+928+3972
Nu 6:23 **'This is h** you are to bless the Israelites. 3907
8: 4 **This is h** the lampstand was made: 2296
8:26 **This,** then, **is h** you are to assign 3970
9:16 **That is h** it continued to be; 4027
11:15 If **this is h** you are going to treat me, 3970
13:20 **H** is the soil? 4537
14:11 **H long** will these people treat me 625+2025+6330
14:11 **H long** will they refuse to believe in me, 625+2025+6330

Nu 14:27 **"H long** will this wicked community grumble against me? 5503+6330
16:28 **"This is h** you will know that 928+2296
23: 8 **H** can I curse those whom God has 4537
23: 8 **H** can I denounce those whom 4537
24: 5 **"H** beautiful are your tents, 4537
Dt 1:12 **But h** can I bear your problems 377
1:31 There you saw **h** the LORD your God 889
7:17 **H** can we drive them out?" 377
8: 2 Remember **h** the LORD your God led you 889
9: 7 Remember this and never forget **h** 889
11: 4 **h** he overwhelmed them with the waters of 889
11: 4 **h** the LORD brought lasting ruin on them. NIH
12:30 **"H** do these nations serve their gods? 377
15: 2 This is **h** it is to be done: 1821
18:21 **"H** can we know when a message has 377
20:15 **This is h** you are to treat all the cities that 4027
29:16 You yourselves know **h** we lived in Egypt 889
29:16 and **h** we passed through the countries on 889
31:27 For I know **h** rebellious and stiff-necked NIH
31:27 **h much more** will you rebel after I die! 677+2256+3954
32:30 **H** could one man chase a thousand, 377
Jos 2:10 We have heard **h** the LORD dried up 889
3:10 **This is h** you will know that 928+2296
5: 1 the Canaanite kings along the coast heard **h** 889
9: 7 **H** then can we make a treaty with you?" 375
9:12 But now see **h** dry and moldy it is. NIH
9:13 but see **h** cracked they are. NIH
9:24 "Your servants were clearly told **h** 889
18: 3 **H long** will you wait before you 625+2025+6330
22:16 **'H** could you break faith with the God 4537
22:16 **H** could you turn away from the LORD NIH
23: 4 Remember **h** I have allotted as NIH
Jdg 1:24 "Show us **h to get into** the city 4427
6:15 Gideon asked, **"h** can I save Israel? 928+4537
13: 8 to teach us **h** to bring up the boy who is to 4537
16: 5 and **h** we can overpower him 928+4537
16: 6 great strength and **h** you can be tied 928+4537
16:10 Come now, tell me **h** you can be tied." 928+4537
16:13 Tell me **h** you can be tied." 928+4537
16:15 Then she said to him, **"H** can you say, 375
18: 8 **"H** did you **find things?"** 4537
18:24 **H** can you ask, 'What's the matter 4537
20: 3 "Tell us **h** this awful thing happened." 377
20:34 that the Benjamites did not realize **h** 3954
21: 7 **"H** can we provide wives for those who 4537
21:16 **h** shall we provide wives for the men 4537
Ru 2:11 **h** you left your father and mother 2256
2:18 her mother-in-law saw **h much** she had gathered. 889
3:16 Naomi asked, **"H did it go,** my daughter?" 905+4769
1Sa 1:14 **"H long** will you keep on getting drunk? 5503+6330
2:14 **This is h** they treated all the Israelites 3970
2:22 to all Israel and **h** they slept with 889
6: 2 Tell us **h** we should send it back 928+4537
10:27 **"H** can this fellow save us?" 4537
14:29 See **h** my eyes brightened when I tasted 3954
14:30 **H much better** it would have been if 677+3954
16: 1 **"H long** will you mourn for Saul, 5503+6330
16: 2 But Samuel said, **"H** can I go? 375
16:18 of Bethlehem *who* **knows h** to play the harp. 3359
17:18 See **h** your brothers **are** 8934
17:25 "Do you see **h** this man keeps coming out? 3954
17:28 I know **h** conceited you are and NIH
17:28 and **h** wicked your heart is; NIH
18:15 When Saul saw **h** successful he was, 4394
20: 1 **H** have I wronged your father, 4537
21: 5 **H much more so** today!" 677+3954
23: 3 **H much more,** then, if we go to Keilah 677
24:10 your own eyes **h** the LORD has delivered 889
29: 4 **H** better could he regain his master's favor than by taking the heads of 928+4537
2Sa 1: 5 **"H** do you know that Saul 375
1:19 **H** the mighty have fallen! 375
1:25 **"H** the mighty have fallen in battle! 375
1:27 **"H** the mighty have fallen! 375
2:22 **H** could I look your brother Joab in 375
2:26 **H long** before you order your men 5503+6330
4:11 **H much more—**when wicked men have killed an innocent man 677
6: 9 **"H** can the ark of the LORD ever come 375
6:20 said, **"H** the king of Israel has distinguished 4537
7:22 **"H** great you are, O Sovereign LORD! 4027+6584
11: 7 David asked him **h** Joab **was,** 4200+8934
11: 7 **h** the soldiers **were** and how 4200+8934
11: 7 **h** the war **was going.** 4200+8934
11:11 *H could* I **go** to my house to eat and drink AIT
12:18 **H** can we tell him the child is dead? 375
16:11 **H much more,** then, this Benjamite! 677+3954
16:23 **That was h** both David 4027
19:19 Do not remember **h** your servant did wrong 889
19:34 **"H many more** years will I live, 3869+4537
20: 9 Joab said to Amasa, **"H are** you, 8934
21: 3 **H** shall I make amends so that 928+4537
24: 2 so that I may know **h many** there are." 5031
24:13 think it over and decide **h** I should answer 4537
1Ki 1:12 let me advise you **h** you can save your own 2256
2: 4 'If your descendants watch **h** they **live,** 2006
2:30 **"This is h** Joab answered me." 3907
3: 7 I am only a little child and *do* **not know h** 3359
7:28 **h** the stands were **made:** 5126
8:27 **H much less** this temple I have built! 677+3954
10: 8 **H happy** your men must be! 897
10: 8 **H happy** your officials, 897
1Ki 11:27 Here is the account of **h** he rebelled against 889
11:28 Solomon saw **h well** the young man did 3954
12: 6 **"H** would you advise me 375
12: 9 **H** should we answer these people who say NIH
14:19 his wars and **h** he ruled, 889
18:21 **"H long** will you waver 5503+6330
19: 1 and **h** he had killed all the prophets with 889
20: 7 "See **h** this man is looking for trouble! 3954
21: 7 "Is this **h** you act as king over Israel? NIH
21:29 "Have you noticed **h** Ahab 3954
22:16 **"H many** times must I make you swear to tell me nothing but the truth 3869+4537+6330
2Ki 4: 2 Elisha replied to her, **"H** can I help you? 4537
4:43 **"H** can I set this before a hundred men?" 4537
5: 7 See **h** he is trying to pick a quarrel 3954
5:13 **H much more,** then, when he tells you, 677
6:32 "Don't you see **h** this murderer 3954
8: 5 the king **h** Elisha had restored the dead 889
8:13 Hazael said, **"H** could your servant, 4537
9:22 **"H** can there be peace," Jehu replied, 4537
9:25 Remember **h** you and I were riding together 3954
10: 4 "If two kings could not resist him, **h** 375
13: 4 for he saw **h** severely the king 3954
14:26 The LORD had seen **h** bitterly everyone 4394
14:28 including **h** he recovered for Israel 889
17:28 and taught them **h** to worship the LORD. 375
18:24 **H** can you repulse one officer of the least 375
18:35 **H** then can the LORD deliver Jerusalem 3954
19:27 and when you come and go and *h* you **rage** AIT
20: 3 **h** I have walked before you faithfully and 889
20:20 all his achievements and **h** he made the pool 889
1Ch 13:12 **"H** can I ever bring the ark of God to me?" 2120
15:13 We did not inquire of him about **h** to do it in NIH
21: 2 so that I may know **h many** there are." 5031
21:12 decide **h** I should answer 4537
29:17 And now I have seen with joy **h** NIH
2Ch 6:18 **H much less** this temple I have built! 677+3954
9: 7 **H happy** your men must be! 897
9: 7 **H happy** your officials, 897
10: 6 **"H** would you advise me 375
10: 9 **H** should we answer these people who say NIH
18:15 **"H many** times must I make you swear to tell me nothing but the truth 3869+4537+6330
20:11 See *h* they *are* **repaying** us by coming AIT
20:29 when they heard **h** the LORD had fought 3954
32:14 **H** then can your god deliver you 3954
32:15 **H much less** will your god deliver you 677+3954+4202
33:19 and **h** God was moved by his entreaty, NIH
Ne 2: 6 **"H long** will your journey take, 5503+6330
9:10 for you knew **h** arrogantly the Egyptians 3954
13:24 not **know h** to speak the language of Judah. 5795
Est 2:11 of the harem to find out **h** Esther **was** 8934
2:13 And **this is h** she would go to the king: 928+2296
5:11 the ways the king had honored him and **h** 889
8: 1 for Esther had told **h** he was related to her. 4537
8: 6 For **h** can I bear to see disaster fall 379
8: 6 **H** can I bear to see the destruction 379
Job 2:13 because they saw **h** great his suffering was. 3954
4: 3 Think **h** you have instructed many, NIH
4: 3 **h** you have strengthened feeble hands. NIH
4:19 **h much more** those who live in houses 677
6:25 **H** painful are honest words! 4537
7: 4 **'H long** *before* I get up?' 5503
8: 2 **"H long** will you say such things? 625+6330
9: 2 But **h** can a mortal be righteous before God? 4537
9:14 **"H** then can I dispute with him? 3954
9:14 *H can I* **find** words to argue with him? AIT
11: 5 **Oh, h I wish** that God would speak, 4769+5989
13:23 **H many** wrongs and sins have I committed? 3869+4537
15:16 **h much less** man, who is vile and 677+3954
19: 2 **"H long** will you torment me 625+2025+6330
19:27 **H** my heart yearns within me! NIH
19:28 "If you say, **'H** we will hound him, 4537
20: 4 "Surely you know **h** it has been from of old, 2296
21:17 "Yet **h often** is the lamp of 3869+4537
21:17 **H** often does calamity come upon them, NIH
21:18 **H** often are they like straw before the wind, NIH
21:34 **h** can you console me with your nonsense? 375
22:12 And see **h** lofty are the highest stars! 3954
25: 4 **H** then can a man be righteous before God? 4537
25: 4 **H** can one born of woman be pure? 4537
25: 6 **h much less** man, who is but a maggot—677+3954
26: 2 **"H** you have helped the powerless! 4537
26: 2 **H** you have saved the arm that is feeble! NIH
26:14 **h** faint the whisper we hear of him! 4537
29: 2 **"H I long for** the months gone by, 4769+5761+5989
35: 6 If you sin, **h** does that affect him? 4537
35:14 **H much less,** then, will he listen 677+3954
36:26 *H* **great** is God—beyond our understanding! AIT
36:29 Who can understand **h** he spreads out NIH
36:29 **h** he thunders from his pavilion? NIH
36:30 See **h** he scatters his lightning about him, NIH
37:15 Do you know **h** God controls the clouds NIH
37:16 Do you know **h** the clouds hang poised, 6584
40: 4 **h** can I reply to you? 4537
Ps 3: 1 O LORD, **h** many are my foes! 4537
3: 1 **H** many rise up against me! NIH
4: 2 **H long,** O men, will you turn my glory 4537+6330
4: 2 **H** long will you love delusions NIH
6: 3 **H long,** O LORD, how long? 5503+6330
6: 3 How long, O LORD, **h** long? NIH
8: 1 **h** majestic is your name in all the earth! 4537
8: 9 **h** majestic is your name in all the earth! 4537
9:13 O LORD, see **h** my enemies persecute me! NIH
Ps 11: 1 **H** *then* can you say to me: 375
13: 1 **H long,** O LORD? 625+2025+6330
13: 1 **H long** will you hide your face from me? 625+2025+6330
13: 2 **H long** must I wrestle with my thoughts 625+2025+6330
13: 2 **H long** will my enemy triumph over me? 625+2025+6330
21: 1 **H** great is his joy in the victories you give! 4537
25:19 See **h** my enemies have increased and 3954
25:19 See how my enemies have increased and **h** NIH
31:19 **H** great is your goodness, 4537
35:17 O Lord, **h long** will you look on? 3869+4537
36: 7 **H** priceless is your unfailing love! 4537
36:12 See **h** the evildoers lie fallen— NIH
39: 4 let me know **h** fleeting is my life. 4537
42: 4 **h** I used to go with the multitude, 3954
47: 2 **H** awesome is the LORD Most High, 3954
59: 3 See **h** they lie in wait for me! 3954
62: 3 **H long** will you assault a man? 625+2025+6330
66: 3 Say to God, **"H** awesome are your deeds! 4537
66: 5 *h* **awesome** his works in man's behalf! AIT
69:19 You know **h** I am scorned, NIH
73:11 They say, **"H** can God know? 377
73:19 **H** suddenly are they destroyed, 375
74: 9 none of us knows **h long** this will be. 4537+6330
74:10 **H long** will the enemy mock you, O God? 5503+6330
74:18 Remember **h** the enemy has mocked you, 2296
74:18 **h** foolish people have reviled your name. NIH
74:22 remember **h** fools mock you all day long. NIH
78:40 **H often** they rebelled against him in 3869+4537
79: 5 **H long,** O LORD? 4537+6330
79: 5 **H** long will your jealousy burn like fire? NIH
80: 4 **h long** will your anger smolder against 5503+6330
81:14 **h quickly** would I subdue their enemies 3869+5071
82: 2 **"H long** will you defend the unjust 5503+6330
83: 2 See **h** your enemies are astir, NIH
83: 2 **h** your foes rear their heads. NIH
84: 1 **H** lovely is your dwelling place, 4537
89:46 **H long,** O LORD? Will you hide yourself forever? 4537+6330
89:46 **H** long will your wrath burn like fire? NIH
89:47 Remember **h** fleeting is my life. 4537
89:50 Lord, **h** your servant has been mocked, NIH
89:50 **h** I bear in my heart the taunts of all NIH
90:13 **H long** will it be? 5503+6330
92: 5 **H** great are your works, O LORD, 4537
92: 5 O LORD, **h** profound your thoughts! 4394
94: 3 **H long** will the wicked, O LORD, 5503+6330
94: 3 **h long** will the wicked be jubilant? 5503+6330
103:14 for he **knows h** we are formed, 3359
104:24 **H** many are your works, O LORD! 4537
116:12 **H** can I repay the LORD 4537
119: 9 **H** can a young man keep his way pure? 928+4537
119:40 **H** I long for your precepts! 2180
119:84 **H long must** your servant **wait?** 3427+3869+4537
119:97 Oh, **h** I love your law! 4537
119:103 **H** sweet are your words to my taste, 4537
119:159 See **h** I love your precepts; 3954
133: 1 **H** good and pleasant it is 4537
137: 4 **H** can we sing the songs of the LORD 375
139:17 **H** precious to me are your thoughts, O God! 4537
139:17 **H** vast is the sum of them! 4537
147: 1 **H** good it is to sing praises to our God, 3954
147: 1 **h** pleasant and fitting to praise him! 3954
Pr 1:17 **H** useless to spread a net in full view of all 3954
1:22 **"H long** will you simple ones love your simple ways? 5503+6330
1:22 **H** long will mockers delight in mockery NIH
5:12 You will say, **"H** I hated discipline! 375
5:12 **H** my heart spurned correction! NIH
6: 9 **H long** will you lie there, you sluggard? 5503+6330
11:31 **h much more** the ungodly and the sinner! 677+3954
15:11 **h much more** the hearts of men! 677+3954
15:23 and **h** good is a timely word! 4537
16:16 **H much** better to get wisdom than gold, 4537
17: 7 **h much worse** lying lips to a ruler! 677+3954
19: 7 **h much more** do his friends avoid him! 677+3954
19:10 **h much worse** for a slave to rule over princes! 677+3954
20:24 **H** then can anyone understand his own way? 4537
21:27 **h much more so** when brought 677+3954
24:10 **h** small is your strength! NIH
Ecc 4:11 But **h** can one keep warm alone? 375
4:13 but foolish king who no longer **knows h** 3359
6: 3 yet no matter **h** long he lives, 8611
6: 8 What does a poor man gain *by* **knowing h** 3359
6:11 and **h** does that profit anyone? 4537
10: 3 and shows everyone *h* **stupid** he is. AIT
11: 5 **h** the body is formed in a mother's womb, 3869
SS 1: 4 *H* **right** they are to adore you! AIT
1:15 **H** beautiful you are, my darling! 2180
1:15 Oh, **h** beautiful! 2180
1:16 **H** handsome you are, my lover! 2180
1:16 Oh, **h** charming! 677
4: 1 **H** beautiful you are, my darling! 2180
4: 1 Oh, **h** beautiful! 2180
4:10 **H** delightful is your love, my sister, 4537
4:10 **H** much more pleasing is your love than wine, 4537
5: 9 **H** is your beloved better than others, 4537
5: 9 **H** is your beloved better than others, 4537

SS 7: 1 **H** beautiful your sandaled feet, 4537
7: 6 **H** beautiful you are and how pleasing, 4537
7: 6 How beautiful you are and **h** pleasing, 377
Isa 1:21 **See h** the faithful city has become a harlot! 377
6:11 Then I said, **"For h long,** O Lord?" 5503+6330
8: 4 Before the boy **knows h** to say 'My father' 3359
14: 4 **H** the oppressor has come to an end! 375
14: 4 **H** his fury has ended! NIH
14:12 **H** you have fallen from heaven, 375
19:11 **H** can you say to Pharaoh, 375
20: 6 **H** then can we escape?' " 375
29:12 answer, *"I don't* **know h to read."** 3359+6219
30:19 ***H* gracious** *he will be* when you cry AIT
32:20 *h* **blessed** you will be, AIT
36: 9 **H** then can you repulse one officer of 375
36:20 **H** then can the LORD deliver Jerusalem 3954
37:28 and when you come and go and *h* you **rage** AIT
38: 3 **h** I have walked before you faithfully and 889
47:11 and *you will* not **know h** to conjure it away. 3359
48: 4 For I knew **h** stubborn you were; 3954
48: 8 Well do I know **h treacherous** *you are;* 953+953
48:11 **H** can I let myself be defamed? 375
52: 7 **H** beautiful on the mountains are the feet 4537
63:14 **This is h** you guided your people to make 4027
64: 5 **H** then can we be saved? NIH
Jer 1: 6 *I do* not **know h** to speak; I am only a child. 3359
2: 2 " 'I remember the devotion of your youth, **h** NIH
2:19 and realize **h** evil and bitter it is for you 3954
2:21 **H** then did you turn against me into 375
2:23 **"H** can you say, 'I am not defiled; 375
2:23 See **h** you **behaved** in the valley; 2006
2:33 **H** skilled you are at pursuing love! 4537
3: 5 **This is h** you talk, 2180
3:19 **" 'H gladly** would I treat you like sons 375
4:10 **h** completely you have deceived this people 434
4:14 **H long** will you harbor wicked thoughts? 5503+6330
4:18 **H** bitter it is! 3954
4:18 **H** it pierces to the heart!" 3954
4:21 **H long** must I see the battle standard 5503+6330
4:22 *they* **know** not **h** to do good." 3359
6:15 *they do* not even **know h** to blush. 3359
8: 8 **" 'H** can you say, "We are wise, 377
8:12 *they do* not even **know h** to blush. 3359
9:19 **'H** ruined we are! 375
9:19 **H** great is our shame! NIH
9:20 Teach your daughters **h** to wail; NIH
12: 4 **H long** will the land lie parched and 5503+6330
12: 5 **h** can you compete with horses? 375
12: 5 **h** will you manage in the thickets by 375
13:27 **H long** will you be unclean?" 339+5503+6388
15: 5 Who will stop to ask **h** you **are?** 8934
15:15 think of *h* **I suffer** reproach for your sake. AIT
16:12 See **h** each of you is following NIH
22:23 **h** you will groan when pangs come 4537
23:26 **H long** will this continue in the hearts 5503+6330
30: 7 **H** awful that day will be! 3954
31:22 **H long** will you wander, 5503+6330
32:24 "See **h** the siege ramps are built up to take NIH
36:17 "Tell us, **h** did you come to write all this? 375
38:28 **This is h** Jerusalem was taken: 889+3869
47: 2 "See **h** the waters are rising in the north; NIH
47: 5 **h long** will you cut yourselves? 5503+6330
47: 6 **'h long** till you rest? 625+2025+6330
47: 7 But **h** can it rest when the LORD 375
48:14 **"H** can you say, 'We are warriors, 375
48:17 say, **'H** broken is the mighty scepter, 377
48:17 **h** broken the glorious staff!' NIH
48:39 **"H** shattered she is! 375
48:39 **H** they wail! 375
48:39 **H** Moab turns her back in shame! NIH
50:23 **H** broken and shattered is the hammer of 375
50:23 **H** desolate is Babylon among the nations! 375
50:28 declaring in Zion **h** the LORD our God NIH
51:41 **"H** Sheshach will be captured, 375
La 1: 1 **H** deserted lies the city, 377
1: 1 **H** like a widow is she, NIH
1:20 "See, O LORD, **h** distressed I am! 3954
2: 1 **H** the Lord has covered the Daughter 377
4: 1 **H** the gold has lost its luster, 377
4: 2 **H** the precious sons of Zion, 377
Eze 6: 9 **h** I have been grieved 889
14:21 **H much worse** will it be when I send 677+3954
15: 2 **h** is the wood of a vine better than that of 4537
15: 5 **h much less** can it be made 677+3954
16:30 **" 'H** weak-willed you are, 4537
22: 6 " 'See **h** each of the princes NIH
26:17 **" 'H** you are destroyed, O city of renown, 375
33:10 **H** then can we live?" ' 375
35:15 **that is h** I will treat you. 4027
44:23 **show them h to distinguish** 3359
Da 4: 3 **H** great are his signs, 10341+10408
4: 3 **h** mighty his wonders! 10341+10408
8:13 **"H long** will it take *for* the vision to 5503+6330
10:17 **H** can I, your servant, talk with you, 2120
12: 6 **"H long** will it be 5503+6330
Hos 4:16 **H** then can the LORD pasture them NIH
8: 5 **H long** will they be incapable of purity? 5503
11: 8 **"H** can I give you up, Ephraim? 375
11: 8 **H** can I hand you over, Israel? NIH
11: 8 **H** can I treat you like Admah? 375
11: 8 **H** can I make you like Zeboiim? NIH
Joel 1:18 **H** the cattle moan! 4537
Am 3:10 *"They do* not **know h** to do right," 3359
5:12 For I know **h** many are your offenses and NIH
5:12 how many are your offenses and **h** NIH
7: 2 **H** can Jacob survive? 4769
Am 7: 5 **H** can Jacob survive? 4769
Ob 1: 6 But **h** Esau will be ransacked, 375
Jnh 1: 6 **"H** can you sleep? 4537
3:10 and **h** they turned from their evil ways, 3954
Mic 6: 3 **H** have I burdened you? 4537
Hab 1: 2 **H long,** O LORD, must I call for help, 625+2025+6330
2: 6 **H long** must this go on?' 5503+6330
Hag 2: 3 **H** does it look to you now? 4537
2:15 consider **h** things were before one stone NIH
Zec 1:12 **h long** will you withhold mercy 5503+6330
2: 2 to find out **h** wide and how long it is." 3869+4537
2: 2 to find out how wide and **h** long it is." 3869+4537
7:14 This is **h** they made the pleasant land NIH
9:17 **H** attractive and beautiful they will be! 4537
Mal 1: 2 "But you ask, **'H** have you loved us?' 928+4537
1: 6 **'H** have we shown contempt 928+4537
1: 7 "But you ask, **'H** have we defiled you?' 928+4537
2:17 **"H** have we wearied him?" 928+4537
3: 7 "But you ask, **'H** are we to return?' 928+4537
3: 8 "But you ask, **'H** do we rob you?' 928+4537
Mt 1:18 **This is h** the birth of Jesus Christ came *4048*
5:13 **h** can it be made salty again? *1877+5515*
6: 9 **"This,** then, **is h** you should pray: *4048*
6:23 **h great** is that darkness! *4531*
6:28 See **h** the lilies of the field grow. *4802*
6:30 If **that is h** God clothes the grass of *4048*
7: 4 **H can** you say to your brother, *4802*
7:11 know **h** to give good gifts to your children, *NIG*
7:11 **h much** more will your Father *4531*
9:14 **"H is it that** we and the Pharisees fast, *1328+5515*
9:15 **"H** can the guests of the bridegroom mourn *3590*
10:19 not worry about what to say or **h** to say it. *4802*
10:25 **h much** more the members of his household! *4531*
12:12 **H much more** valuable is a man than a sheep! *4531*
12:14 But the Pharisees went out and plotted **h** *3968*
12:26 **H** then can his kingdom stand? *4802*
12:29 **h** can anyone enter a strong man's house *4802*
12:34 **h** can you who are evil say anything good? *4802*
12:45 **That is h** it will be with this wicked *4048*
13:49 **This is h** it will be at the end of the age. *4048*
15:34 **"H many** loaves do you have?" *4531*
16: 3 *You* **know h** to interpret the appearance of *1182*
16: 9 and **h many** basketfuls you gathered? *4531*
16:10 and **h many** basketfuls you gathered? *4531*
16:11 **H** is it you don't understand that I was *4802*
17:17 **"h long** shall I stay with you? *2401+4536*
17:17 **H long** shall I put up with you? *2401+4536*
18:21 **h many times** shall I forgive my brother *4529*
18:35 **"This is h** my heavenly Father will treat each of you unless you forgive *4048*
21:20 **"H** did the fig tree wither so quickly?" *4802*
22:12 **'h** did you get in here *4802*
22:43 He said to them, **"H is it** then that David, *4802*
22:45 **h can** he be his son?" *4802*
23:33 **H** will you escape being condemned to hell? *4802*
23:37 **h often** I have longed to gather your children together, *4529*
24:19 **H dreadful** it will be in those days *4026*
24:39 **That is h** it will be at the coming of the Son *4048*
26:54 But **h** then would the Scriptures be fulfilled *4802*
27:65 make the tomb as secure as you know **h."** *NIG*
Mk 2:18 **"H is it that** John's disciples and *1328+5515*
2:19 **"H** can the guests of the bridegroom fast *3590*
3: 6 with the Herodians **h** they might kill Jesus. *3968*
3:23 **"H** can Satan drive out Satan? *4802*
4:13 **H** then will you understand any parable? *4802*
4:27 though he does not know **h.** *NIG*
5:19 and tell them **h much** the Lord has done *4012*
5:19 and **h** he has had mercy on you." *NIG*
5:20 in the Decapolis **h much** Jesus had done *4012*
6:38 **"H many** loaves do you have?" *4531*
8: 5 **"H many** loaves do you have?" *4531*
8:19 for the five thousand, **h many** basketfuls *4531*
8:20 for the four thousand, **h many** basketfuls *4531*
9:19 Jesus replied, **"h** long shall I stay with you? *2401*
9:19 **H** long shall I put up with you? *2401*
9:21 **"H** long has he been like this?" *4531*
9:50 **h** can you make it salty again? *1877+5515*
10:23 **"H** hard it is for the rich to enter *4802*
10:24 **h** hard it is to enter the kingdom of God! *4802*
12:26 **h** God said to him, *4802*
12:35 **"H is it** that the teachers of the law say that *4802*
12:37 **H** then **can** he be his son?" *4470*
13:17 **H dreadful** it will be in those days *4026*
15: 4 See **h many** *things* they are accusing you of. *4531*
15:39 heard his cry and saw **h** he died, he said, *4048*
Lk 1:18 **"H** can I be sure of this? *2848+5515*
1:34 **"H** will this be," Mary asked the angel, *4802*
6:23 **that is h** their fathers treated the prophets. *899+2848+3836*
6:26 for **that is h** their fathers treated *899+2848+3836*
6:42 **H** can you say to your brother, 'Brother, *4802*
8:18 Therefore consider carefully **h** you listen. *4802*
8:36 Those who had seen it told the people **h** *4802*
8:39 and tell **h much** God has done for you." *4012*
8:39 over town **h much** Jesus had done for him. *4012*
8:47 she told why she had touched him and **h** *6055*
9:41 **"h** long shall I stay with you and put up *2401*
10:26 **"H** do you read it?" *4802*
11:13 know **h** to give good gifts to your children, *NIG*
11:13 **h much** more will your Father in heaven give the Holy Spirit *4531*
11:18 **h** can his kingdom stand? *4802*
12:11 about **h** you will defend yourselves *4802*
Lk 12:21 **"This is h** it will be with anyone who stores *4048*
12:24 **h much** more valuable you are than birds! *4531*
12:27 "Consider **h** the lilies grow. *4802*
12:28 If **that is h** God clothes the grass of *4048*
12:28 **h much** more will he clothe you, *4531*
12:49 and **h** I wish it were already kindled! *NIG*
12:50 and **h** distressed I am until it is completed! *4802*
12:56 You know **h** to interpret the appearance of *NIG*
12:56 **H is it** that you don't know how *4802*
12:56 don't know **h** *to* **interpret** this present time? *1507*
13:34 **h often** I have longed to gather your children together, *4529*
14: 7 When he noticed **h** the guests picked *4802*
14:34 **h** can it be made salty again? *1877+5515*
15:17 **H many** of my father's hired men have food *4531*
16: 5 **'H much** do you owe my master?' *4531*
16: 7 'And **h much** do you owe?' *4531*
18:24 **"H** hard it is for the rich to enter *4802*
20:41 **"H is it** that they say the Christ is the Son *4802*
20:44 **H** then can he be his son?" *4802*
21: 5 of his disciples were remarking about **h** *4022*
21:14 up your mind not to worry beforehand **h** *NIG*
21:23 **H dreadful** it will be in those days *4026*
22: 4 the temple guard and discussed with them **h** *4802*
23:55 and saw the tomb and **h** his body was laid *6055*
24: 6 Remember **h** he told you, *6055*
24:25 He said to them, **"H foolish you are,** *485+6043*
24:25 and **h slow** of heart to believe all that *1096*
24:35 and **h** Jesus was recognized by them *6055*
Jn 1:48 **"H** do you know me?" *4470*
2:16 **H dare you** turn my Father's house into *3590*
3: 4 **"H** can a man be born when he is old?" *4802*
3: 9 **"H** can this be?" Nicodemus asked. *4802*
3:12 **h** then will you believe if I speak *4802*
4: 9 **H** can you ask me for a drink?" *4802*
5:44 **H** can you believe if you accept praise *4802*
5:47 **h** are you going to believe what I say?" *4802*
6: 9 but **h far will they go** among so *1639+4047+5515*
6:42 **H can** he now say, *4802*
6:52 **"H** can this man give us his flesh to eat?" *4802*
7:15 **"H** did this man get such learning *4802*
7:41 **"H** can the Christ come from Galilee? *1142+3590*
8:33 **H** can you say that we shall be set free?" *4802*
9:10 **"H** then were your eyes opened?" *4802*
9:15 also asked him **h** he had received his sight. *4802*
9:16 **"H** can a sinner do such miraculous signs?" *4802*
9:19 **H is it** that now he can see?" *4802*
9:21 But **h** he can see now, *4802*
9:26 **H** did he open your eyes?" *4802*
9:34 **h** dare you lecture us!" *NIG*
10:24 **"H long** will you keep us in suspense? *2401+4536*
11:31 noticed **h** quickly she got up and went out, *4022*
11:36 Then the Jews said, "See **h** he loved him!" *4802*
12:19 Look **h** the whole world has gone *NIG*
12:34 so **h** can you say, *4802*
12:49 to say and **h** to say it. *5515*
14: 5 so **h** can we know the way?" *4802*
14: 9 **H** can you say, 'Show us the Father'? *4802*
Ac 2: 8 Then **h is it** that each of us hears them *4802*
3:18 But **this is h** God fulfilled what he had *4048*
4: 9 cripple and are asked **h** he was healed, *1877+5515*
4:21 They could not decide **h** to punish them, *4802*
5: 3 **h is it that** Satan has so filled your heart that you have lied to the Holy Spirit *1328+5515*
5: 9 **"H** could you agree to test the Spirit of the Lord? *4022+5515*
8:31 **"H** can I," he said, *4802*
9:16 I will show him **h much** he must suffer *4012*
9:27 He told them **h** Saul on his journey had seen *4802*
9:27 and **h** in Damascus he had preached *4802*
10:34 "I now realize **h true** it is that God does *237+2093*
10:38 **h** God anointed Jesus of Nazareth with *6055*
10:38 and **h** he went around doing good *NIG*
11:13 He told us **h** he had seen an angel appear *4802*
12:17 for them to be quiet and described **h** *4802*
14:27 through them and **h** he had opened the door *4022*
15: 3 *they* **told h** the Gentiles had been coverted. *1687*
15:14 to us **h** God at first showed his concern *2777*
15:36 of the Lord and see **h** they are doing." *4802*
19:26 and hear **h** this fellow Paul has convinced *4022*
20:18 "You know **h** I lived the whole time I was *4802*
21:20 **h many** thousands of Jews have believed, *4531*
25:20 I was at a loss **h** to investigate such matters; *NIG*
Ro 1: 9 is my witness **h** constantly I remember you *6055*
3: 6 **h** could God judge the world? *4802*
5: 9 **h much** more shall we be saved *4498*
5:10 **h much** more, having been reconciled, *4498*
5:15 **h much** more did God's grace and the gift *4498*
5:17 **h much** more will those who receive God's abundant provision *4498*
6: 2 **h** can we live in it any longer? *4802*
8:32 **h** will he not also, along with him, *4802*
9: 9 For this was **h** the promise was stated: *NIG*
10:14 **H,** then, can they call on the one they have *4802*
10:14 And **h** can they believe in the one *4802*
10:14 And **h** can they hear without someone *4802*
10:15 And **h** can they preach unless they are sent? *4802*
10:15 **"H** beautiful are the feet *6055*
11: 2 **h** he appealed to God against Israel: *6055*
11:12 **h much** greater riches will their fullness bring! *4531*
11:24 **h much** more readily will these, *4531*
11:33 **H** unsearchable his judgments, *6055*
13:14 not think about **h** to gratify the desires of *NIG*
1Co 3:10 But each one should be careful **h** he builds. *4802*
4: 8 **H I wish that** you really had become kings *4054*
4:19 not only **h** these arrogant people are talking, *NIG*

1Co 6: 3 **H much more** the things of this life! *3615*
7:16 **H** do you know, wife, *5515*
7:16 Or, **h** do you know, husband, *5515*
7:32 **h** he can please the Lord. *4802*
7:33 **h** he can please his wife— *4802*
7:34 **h** she can please her husband. *4802*
14: 7 **h** will anyone know what tune *4802*
14: 9 **h** will anyone know what you are saying? *4802*
14:16 **h** can one who finds himself *4802*
15:12 **h can** some of you say *4802*
15:35 someone may ask, **"H** are the dead raised? *4802*
15:36 **H** foolish! What you sow does *NIG*
2Co 1:20 no matter **h many** promises God has made, *4012*
3: 9 **h** much more glorious is the ministry *NIG*
3:11 **h** much **greater** is the glory of *3437*
7:12 **h** devoted to us you are. *NIG*
7:13 delighted to see **h** happy Titus was, *NIG*
12:13 **H** were you inferior to the other churches, *5515*
Gal 1:13 **h** intensely I persecuted the church of God *4022*
2:14 **H is it,** then, that you force Gentiles *4802*
4: 9 **h is it** that you are turning back *4802*
4:20 **h** I wish I could be with you now *NIG*
Eph 3:18 to grasp **h** wide and long and high *5515*
5:15 Be very careful, then, **h** you live— *4802*
6:21 know **h** I am and what I am doing. *2848+3836*
6:22 that you may know **h** we are, *3836+4309*
Php 1: 8 God can testify **h** I long for all of you with *6055*
2:23 to send him as soon as I see **h** things go *NIG*
4: 1 **that is h** you should stand firm in the Lord, *4048*
Col 2: 1 to know **h much** I am struggling for you *2462*
2: 5 in spirit and delight to see **h** orderly you are *NIG*
2: 5 how orderly you are and **h** firm your faith *NIG*
4: 6 that you may know **h** to answer everyone. *4802*
1Th 1: 5 You know **h** we lived among you *3888*
1: 9 They tell **h** you turned to God from idols *4802*
2:10 You are witnesses, and so is God, of **h** holy, *6055*
3: 9 **H** can we thank God enough for you *5515*
4: 1 we instructed you **h** to live in order *4802*
2Th 3: 7 For you yourselves know **h** you ought *4802*
3:17 **This is h** I write. *4048*
1Ti 3: 5 not know **h** to manage his own family, *NIG*
3: 5 **h** can he take care of God's church?) *4802*
3:15 you will know **h** people ought to conduct *4802*
2Ti 1:18 in **h many** *ways* he helped me in Ephesus. *4012*
3:15 and **h** from infancy you have known *4022*
Heb 2: 3 **h** shall we escape if we ignore such *4802*
7: 4 Just think **h great** he was: *4383*
9:14 **H much** more, then, will the blood of Christ *4531*
10:24 let us consider **h** we may spur one another *NIG*
10:29 **H much** more severely do you think *4531*
12: 9 **H** much more should we submit to *NIG*
12:25 **h** much less will we, if we turn away *NIG*
Jas 5: 7 **See h** the farmer waits for the land *2627*
5: 7 to yield its valuable crop and **h** patient he is *NIG*
1Pe 2:20 But **h is it** to your credit if you receive *4481*
2Pe 2: 9 then the Lord knows **h** to rescue godly men *NIG*
1Jn 2: 5 **This is h** we know we are in him: *1877+4047*
2:18 **This is h** we know it is the last hour. *3854*
3: 1 **H great** is the love the Father has lavished *4534*
3:10 **This is h** we know who the children *1877+4047*
3:16 **This is h** we know what love is: *1877+4047*
3:17 **h can** the love of God be in him? *4802*
3:19 This then is **h** we know that we belong to *1877*
3:19 **h** we set our hearts at rest in his presence *NIG*
3:24 And this is **h** we know that he lives in us: *1877*
4: 2 **This is h** you can recognize the Spirit *1877+4047*
4: 6 **This is h** we recognize the Spirit of truth and the spirit of falsehood. *1666+4047*
4: 9 **This is h** God showed his love among us: *1877+4047*
5: 2 **This is h** we know that we love the children of God: *1877+4047*
3Jn 1: 3 and **h** you continue to walk in the truth. *NIG*
Rev 6:10 called out in a loud voice, **"H long,** *2401+4536*
11: 5 **This is h** anyone who wants to harm *4048*

HOWBEIT (KJV) See ALTHOUGH, BUT, HOWEVER, NEVERTHELESS, THOUGH, YET

HOWEVER (145) [HOW]

Ge 15:10 the birds, **h,** he did not cut in half. 2256
15:15 **h,** will go to your fathers in peace and 2256
30:37 **h,** took fresh-cut branches from poplar, 2256
31: 7 **H,** God has not allowed him to harm me. 2256
33:17 Jacob, **h,** went to Succoth, 2256
40:23 The chief cupbearer, **h,** did not remember 2256
47:13 There was no food, **h,** in the whole region 2256
47:22 **H,** he did not buy the land of the priests, 8370
Ex 1:17 **h,** feared God and did not do what the king 2256
9:32 The wheat and spelt, **h,** were not destroyed, 2256
16:20 **H,** some of them paid no attention to Moses; 2256
21:13 **H,** if he does not do it intentionally, 2256
21:19 **h,** he must pay the injured man for the loss 8370
21:29 **h,** the bull has had the habit of goring and 2256
21:30 **H,** if payment is demanded of him, NIH
21:36 **H,** if it was known that the bull had NIH
32:34 **H,** when the time comes for me to punish, 2256
Lev 5:11 " 'If, **h,** he cannot afford two doves 2256
7:16 " 'If, **h,** his offering is the result of a vow 2256
11:21 **h,** some winged creatures that walk 421
11:36 A spring, **h,** or a cistern 421
13:28 **h,** the spot is unchanged and has not spread 2256
13:37 If, **h,** in his judgment it is unchanged 2256
14:21 "If, **h,** he is poor and cannot afford these, 2256
Lev 19:21 **h,** must bring a ram to the entrance to 2256
22:13 No unauthorized person, **h,** 2256
22:23 **h,** present as a freewill offering an ox or 2256
25:26 If, **h,** a man has no one to redeem it for him 2256
27:20 If, **h,** he does not redeem the field, 2256
27:26 **h,** may dedicate the firstborn of an animal, 421
Nu 1:47 The families of the tribe of Levi, **h,** 2256
1:53 The Levites, **h,** are to set up their tents 2256
2:33 The Levites, **h,** were not counted along with 2256
3: 4 and Abihu, **h,** fell dead before the LORD 2256
5:28 If, **h,** the woman has not defiled herself 2256
11:26 **H,** two men, whose names were Eldad 2256
21:24 **h,** put him to the sword and took 2256
26:11 The line of Korah, **h,** did not die out. 2256
30:15 If, **h,** he nullifies them some time 2256
Dt 3:19 **H,** your wives, your children 8370
14: 7 **H,** of those that chew the cud or that have 421
15: 4 **H,** there should be no poor among you, 700+3954
20:16 **H,** in the cities of the nations 8370
20:20 **H,** you may cut down trees 8370
22:20 If, **h,** the charge is true and no proof of 2256
23: 5 **H,** the LORD your God would not listen 2256
25: 7 **H,** if a man does not want 2256
28:15 **H,** if you do not obey the LORD your God 2256
Jos 9: 3 **H,** when the people of Gibeon 2256
14: 8 I, **h,** followed the LORD my God wholeheartedly. 2256
17:13 **H,** when the Israelites grew stronger, 2256
18: 7 **h,** do not get a portion among you, 3954
Jdg 1:21 **h,** failed to dislodge the Jebusites, 2256
4:17 Sisera, **h,** fled on foot to the tent of Jael, 2256
9:51 Inside the city, **h,** was a strong tower, 2256
11:20 **h,** did not trust Israel to pass 2256
11:28 The king of Ammon, **h,** 2256
1Sa 2:25 **h,** did not listen to their father's rebuke, 2256
21: 4 **h,** there is some consecrated bread here 561+3954
26:19 If, **h,** men have done it, 2256
30:22 **H,** each man may take his wife and 561+3954
2Sa 2:10 The house of Judah, **h,** followed David. 421
3:16 Her husband, **h,** went with her, 2256
24: 4 **h,** overruled Joab and 2256
1Ki 3: 2 **h,** were still sacrificing at the high places, 8370
7: 1 It took Solomon thirteen years, **h,** 2256
11: 1 Solomon, **h,** loved many foreign women 2256
11:37 **H,** as for you, I will take you, 2256
12:18 **h,** managed to get into his chariot 2256
15:23 In his old age, **h,** his feet became diseased. 8370
22:43 The high places, **h,** were not removed, 421
2Ki 8:21 his army, **h,** fled back home. 2256
10:29 **H,** he did not turn away from the sins 8370
12: 3 The high places, **h,** were not removed; 8370
14: 4 The high places, **h,** were not removed; 8370
14:11 Amaziah, **h,** would not listen, 2256
15: 4 The high places, **h,** were not removed; 8370
15:35 The high places, **h,** were not removed; 8370
17:40 They would not listen, **h,** 2256
25:25 In the seventh month, **h,** 2256
1Ch 21: 4 The king's word, **h,** overruled Joab; 2256
2Ch 10:18 **h,** managed to get into his chariot 2256
12: 8 They will, **h,** become subject to him, 3954
19: 3 There is, **h,** some good in you, 66
20:33 The high places, **h,** were not removed, 421
25:20 Amaziah, **h,** would not listen, 2256
27: 2 people, **h,** continued their corrupt practices. 2256
29:34 priests, **h,** were too few to skin all 8370
33:17 **h,** continued to sacrifice at the high places, 66
35:22 Josiah, **h,** would not turn away from him, 2256
Ezr 5:13 **"H,** in the first year of Cyrus king 10124
Ne 13: 2 **h,** turned the curse into a blessing.) 2256
Est 9:18 The Jews in Susa, **h,** had assembled 2256
Job 13: 4 You, **h,** smear me with lies; 219+2256
27:14 **H** many his children, their fate is the sword; 561
Ps 58: 5 **h** skillful the enchanter may be. NIH
Pr 6:35 he will refuse the bribe, **h** great it is. 3954
Ecc 11: 8 **H** many years a man may live, 561+3954
Jer 16:14 **"H,** the days are coming," 4027+4200
26:15 Be assured, **h,** that if you put me to death, 421
26:22 **h,** sent Elnathan son of Acbor to Egypt, 2256
27: 8 " ' "If, **h,** any nation or kingdom will 2256
29:29 Zephaniah the priest, **h,** read the letter 2256
34:14 **h,** did not listen to me or pay attention 2256
37: 3 **h,** sent Jehucal son of Shelemiah with 2256
40: 5 **H,** before Jeremiah turned to go, 2256
42:13 **"H,** if you say, 'We will not stay 2256
46:26 **H,** Egypt will be inhabited as in times past," 2256
Eze 16:53 " **'H,** I will restore the fortunes of Sodom 2256
44:25 **h,** if the dead person was his father 3954
46:17 **h,** he makes a gift from his inheritance 2256
Da 2:10 No king, **h** great and mighty, NIH
11:20 In a few years, **h,** he will be destroyed, NIH
Mt 25: 4 **h,** took oil in jars along with their lamps. *1254*
Lk 10:20 **H,** do not rejoice that the spirits submit *4440*
18: 8 **H,** when the Son of Man comes, *4440*
19:15 "He was made king, **h,** and returned home. *NIG*
24:12 Peter, **h,** got up and ran to the tomb. *1254*
Jn 7:10 **H,** after his brothers had left for the Feast, *1254*
15:22 Now, **h,** they have no excuse for their sin. *1254*
Ac 2:13 Some, **h,** made fun of them and said, *1254*
6: 9 **h,** from members of the Synagogue of *1254*
7:48 **"H,** the Most High does not live *247*
8:40 **h,** appeared at Azotus and traveled about, *1254*
11:20 **h,** men from Cyprus and Cyrene, *1254*
20:24 **H,** I consider my life worth nothing to me, *247*
24:14 **H,** I admit that I worship the God *1254*
25:11 If, **h,** I am guilty of anything *3525+4036*
Ro 4: 5 **H,** to the man who does not work *1254*
8: 9 **h,** are controlled not by the sinful nature but *1254*
Ro 15:25 Now, **h,** I am on my way to Jerusalem in *1254*
1Co 2: 6 **h,** speak a message of wisdom among *1254*
2: 9 **H,** as it is written: *247*
8: 9 **h,** that the exercise of your freedom does *1254*
11:11 **h,** woman is not independent of man, *4440*
14:22 prophecy, **h,** is for believers, *1254*
2Co 10:13 We, **h,** will not boast beyond proper limits, *1254*
Gal 3:20 **h,** does not represent just one party; *1254*
Eph 4:20 **h,** did not come to know Christ that way. *1254*
5:33 **H,** each one of you also must love his wife *4440*
Col 2:17 the reality, **h,** is found in Christ. *1254*
2Ti 3:10 You, **h,** know all about my teaching, *1254*
Heb 7: 6 **h,** did not trace his descent from Levi, *1254*
12:11 **h,** it produces a harvest of righteousness *1254*
1Pe 4:16 **H,** if you suffer as a Christian, *1254*

HOWL (4) [HOWLING]

Ps 59:15 for food and **h** if not satisfied. 4296
Isa 13:22 Hyenas *will* **h** in her strongholds, 6702
14:31 Wail, O gate! **H,** O city! 2410
Mic 1: 8 *I will* **h** like a jackal and moan like 5027+6913

HOWLING (1) [HOWL]

Dt 32:10 in a barren and **h** waste. 3537

HOWSOEVER (KJV) See COME WHAT MAY

HUBBAH (1)

1Ch 7:34 Ahi, Rohgah, **H** and Aram. 2465

HUBS (1)

1Ki 7:33 rims, spokes and **h** were all of cast metal. 3141

HUDDLED (1)

Job 30: 7 among the bushes and **h** in the undergrowth. 6202

HUG (1)

Job 24: 8 They are drenched by mountain rains and **h** 2485

HUGE (12)

Ge 41:49 Joseph stored up **h** quantities of grain, 4394
Jos 11: 4 a **h** army, as numerous as the sand on 8041
2Sa 21:20 a **h** man with six fingers on each hand 4500
23:21 And he struck down a **h** Egyptian. 5260
1Ch 20: 6 a **h** man with six fingers on each hand 4500
2Ch 16:14 and they made a **h** fire in his honor. 1524+4200+4394+6330
Ecc 9:14 surrounded it and built **h** siegeworks 1524
Da 2:35 that struck the statue became a **h** mountain 10647
11:13 with a **h** army fully equipped. 1524
Mt 12:40 and three nights in the belly *of* a **h fish,** *3063*
Rev 8: 8 and something like a **h** mountain, all ablaze, *3489*
16:21 From the sky **h** hailstones of about *3489*

HUKKOK (1)

Jos 19:34 through Aznoth Tabor and came out at **H.** 2982

HUKOK (1)

1Ch 6:75 **H** and Rehob, together 2577

HUL (2)

Ge 10:23 Uz, **H,** Gether and Meshech. 2566
1Ch 1:17 Uz, **H,** Gether and Meshech. 2566

HULDAH (2)

2Ki 22:14 to speak to the prophetess **H,** 2701
2Ch 34:22 with him went to speak to the prophetess **H,** 2701

HUMAN (50) [HUMANITY]

Lev 5: 3 " 'Or if he touches **h** uncleanness— 132
7:21 whether **h** uncleanness or an unclean animal 132
24:17 " 'If anyone takes the life of a **h being,** 132
Nu 19:16 or anyone who touches a **h** bone or a grave, 132
19:18 a **h** bone or a grave NIH
1Ki 13: 2 and **h** bones will be burned on you.' " 132
2Ki 23:14 and covered the sites with **h** bones. 132
23:20 on the altars and burned **h** bones on them. 132
Job 34:20 the mighty are removed without **h** hand. NIH
Ps 73: 5 they are not plagued by **h** ills. 132
Isa 37:19 fashioned by **h** hands. 132
52:14 his form marred beyond **h** likeness— 132+1201
Eze 4:12 using **h** excrement for fuel." 132
4:15 over cow manure instead of **h** excrement." 132
39:15 the land and one of them sees a **h** bone, 132
Da 2:34 a rock was cut out, but not by **h** hands. NIH
2:45 but not by **h** hands— NIH
5: 5 a **h** hand appeared and wrote on the plaster 10050
8:25 he will be destroyed, but not by **h** power. NIH
Hos 11: 4 I led them with cords of **h** kindness, 132
13: 2 "They offer **h** sacrifice and kiss 132
Jn 1:13 nor of **h** decision or a husband's will, *4922*
5:34 Not that I accept **h** testimony; *476*
8:15 You judge by **h standards;** *3836+4922*
Ac 5:38 For if their purpose or activity is of **h** origin, *476*
14:11 "The gods have come down to us *in* **h** form!" *476*
14:15 We too are only men, **h like** you. *3926*
17:25 And he is not served by **h** hands, *474*

Ro 1: 3 to his **h nature** was a descendant of David, *4922*
2: 9 distress for every **h being** who does evil: *476*
3: 5 (I am using a **h** argument.) *476+2848*
6:19 **I put this in h terms** because *474+3306*
9: 5 from them is traced the **h ancestry** of Christ *4922*
1Co 1:17 not with words of **h** wisdom, *NIG*
1:26 Not many of you were wise by **h** standards; *4922*
2:13 not in words taught us *by* **h** wisdom but *474*
4: 3 if I am judged by you or by any **h** court; *474*
9: 8 **from** a **h point of view?** *476+2848*
15:32 in Ephesus for merely **h reasons,** *476*
2Co 3: 3 of stone but on tablets **of h** hearts. *4921*
5: 1 house in heaven, **not built by h hands.** *942*
Gal 3: 3 to attain your goal *by* **h effort?** *4922*
3:15 a **h** covenant that has been duly established, *476*
Php 2: 7 being made in **h** likeness. *476*
Col 2: 8 on **h** tradition and the basic principles *476*
2:22 because they are based on **h** commands *476*
Heb 12: 9 we have all had **h** fathers who disciplined us *4922*
1Pe 4: 2 the rest of his earthly life *for* evil **h** desires, *476*
2Pe 2:18 to the lustful desires *of* **sinful h nature,** *4922*
Rev 9: 7 and their faces resembled **h** faces. *476*

HUMANITY (1) [HUMAN]

Heb 2:14 he too shared in their **h** so that *NIG*

HUMBLE (40) [HUMBLED, HUMBLES, HUMBLY, HUMILIATE, HUMILIATED, HUMILIATION, HUMILITY]

Ex 10: 3 'How long will you refuse to **h yourself** 6700
Nu 12: 3 (Now Moses was a very **h** man, 6705
12: 3 more **h** than anyone else on the face of NIH
Dt 8: 2 to **h** you and to test you in order 6700
8:16 to **h** and to test you so that in 6700
2Sa 22:28 You save the **h**, but your eyes are on 6639+6714
1Ki 11:39 *I will* **h** David's descendants because 6700
2Ch 7:14 *will* **h themselves** and pray 4044
33:23 *he did* not **h himself** before the LORD; 4044
36:12 of the LORD his God and *did* not **h himself** 4044
Ezr 8:21 that we *might* **h ourselves** before our God 6700
Job 8: 7 Your beginnings will seem **h,** 5203
40:12 look at every proud man and **h** him, 4044
Ps 18:27 You save the **h** but bring low 6639+6714
25: 9 He guides the **h** in what is right 6705
147: 6 The LORD sustains the **h** but casts the 6705
149: 4 he crowns the **h** with salvation. 6705
Pr 3:34 but gives grace to the **h.** 6705
6: 3 Go and **h yourself;** 8346
Isa 13:11 to the arrogance of the haughty and *will* **h** 9164
23: 9 and to **h** all who are renowned on the earth. 7837
29:19 Once more the **h** will rejoice in the LORD; 6705
58: 5 only a day for a man *to* **h** himself? 6700
66: 2 *he who* is **h** and contrite in spirit, 6714
Da 4:37 those who walk in pride he is able to **h.** 10737
5:19 and those he wanted to **h,** he humbled. NIH
10:12 to gain understanding and to **h yourself** 6700
Zep 2: 3 Seek the LORD, all you **h** *of* the land, 6705
3:12 But I will leave within you the meek and **h,** 1924
Mt 11:29 for I am gentle and **h** in heart, *5424*
Lk 1:48 for he has been mindful of the **h state** *5428*
1:52 from their thrones but has lifted up the **h.** *5424*
2Co 12:21 that when I come again my God *will* **h** me *5427*
Eph 4: 2 Be completely **h** and gentle; *5425*
Jas 1: 9 The brother **in h circumstances** ought *5424*
4: 6 the proud but gives grace *to* the **h.**" *5424*
4:10 **H** *yourselves* before the Lord, *5427*
1Pe 3: 8 love as brothers, be compassionate and **h.** *5426*
5: 5 the proud but gives grace *to* the **h.**" *5424*
5: 6 **H** *yourselves,* therefore, under God's *5427*

HUMBLED (34) [HUMBLE]

Lev 26:41 then when their uncircumcised hearts **are h** 4044
Dt 8: 3 *He* **h** you, causing you to hunger and 6700
1Ki 21:29 "Have you noticed how Ahab *has* **h himself** 4044
21:29 Because *he has* **h himself,** 4044
2Ki 22:19 and *you* **h yourself** before the LORD 4044
2Ch 12: 6 leaders of Israel and the king **h themselves** 4044
12: 7 the LORD saw that *they* **h themselves,** 4044
12: 7 "Since *they have* **h themselves,** 4044
12:12 Because Rehoboam **h himself,** 4044
28:19 The LORD *had* **h** Judah because 4044
30:11 Manasseh and Zebulun **h themselves** 4044
33:12 of the LORD his God and **h himself** greatly 4044
33:19 and idols before he **h himself—** 4044
34:27 and *you* **h yourself** before God 4044
34:27 and because *you* **h yourself** before me 4044
Ps 35:13 on sackcloth and **h** myself with fasting. 6700
44: 9 But now you have rejected and **h** us; 4007
68:30 **H,** may it bring bars of silver. 8346
107:39 and *they were* **h** by oppression, 8820
Isa 2: 9 man will be brought low and mankind **h—** 9164
2:11 The eyes of the arrogant man *will be* **h** and 9164
2:12 for all that is exalted (and *they will be* **h**), 9164
2:17 be brought low and the pride of men **h;** 9164
5:15 So man will be brought low and mankind **h,** 9164
5:15 the eyes of the arrogant **h.** 9164
9: 1 past *he* **h** the land of Zebulun and the land 7837
58: 3 Why *have we* **h** ourselves, 6700
Jer 44:10 To this day *they have* not **h themselves** 1917
Da 5:19 and those he wanted to humble, *he* **h.** 10737
5:22 O Belshazzar, *have* not **h** yourself, 10737
Mt 23:12 For whoever exalts himself *will be* **h,** *5427*
Lk 14:11 For everyone who exalts himself *will be* **h,** *5427*
18:14 For everyone who exalts himself *will be* **h,** *5427*

Php 2: 8 *he* **h** himself and became obedient *5427*

HUMBLES (6) [HUMBLE]

1Sa 2: 7 *he* **h** and he exalts. 9164
Isa 26: 5 *He* **h** those who dwell on high, 8820
Mt 18: 4 whoever **h** himself like this child is *5427*
23:12 and whoever **h** himself will be exalted. *5427*
Lk 14:11 and he who **h** himself will be exalted." *5427*
18:14 and he who **h** himself will be exalted." *5427*

HUMBLY (4) [HUMBLE]

2Sa 16: 4 "*I* **h bow,**" Ziba said. 2556
Isa 38:15 *I will* **walk h** all my years because 1844
Mic 6: 8 to love mercy and to walk **h** with your God. 7570
Jas 1:21 and **h** accept the word planted in you, *1877+4559*

HUMILIATE (2) [HUMBLE]

Pr 25: 7 than for him *to* **h** you before a nobleman. 9164
1Co 11:22 of God and **h** those who have nothing? *2875*

HUMILIATED (10) [HUMBLE]

2Sa 6:22 and I will be **h** in my own eyes. 9166
10: 5 for they were greatly **h.** 4007
19: 5 "Today *you have* **h** all your men, 1017
1Ch 19: 5 for they were greatly **h.** 4007
Isa 54: 4 Do not fear disgrace; *you will* not *be* **h.** 2917
Jer 15: 9 she will be disgraced and **h.** 2917
31:19 I was ashamed and **h** because I bore 4007
Mal 2: 9 "So I have caused you to be despised and **h** 9166
Lk 13:17 When he said this, all his opponents *were* **h,** *2875*
14: 9 Then, **h,** you will have to take *158+3552*

HUMILIATION (4) [HUMBLE]

Ezr 9: 7 and **h** at the hand of foreign kings, 1425+7156
Job 19: 5 above me and use my **h** against me, 3075
Eze 16:63 because of your **h,** 4009
Ac 8:33 In his **h** he was deprived of justice. *5428*

HUMILITY (14) [HUMBLE]

Ps 45: 4 in behalf of truth, **h** and righteousness; 6708
Pr 11: 2 but with **h** comes wisdom. 7560
15:33 and **h** comes before honor. 6708
18:12 but **h** comes before honor. 6708
22: 4 **H** and the fear of the LORD bring wealth 6708
Zep 2: 3 Seek righteousness, seek **h;** 6708
Ac 20:19 the Lord with **great h** and with tears, *4246+5425*
Php 2: 3 *in* **h** consider others better than yourselves. *5425*
Col 2:18 not let anyone who delights in false **h** and *5425*
2:23 their false **h** and their harsh treatment of *5425*
3:12 kindness, **h,** gentleness and patience. *5425*
Tit 3: 2 and to show **true h** toward all men. *4559*
Jas 3:13 by deeds done in the **h** that comes *4559*
1Pe 5: 5 with **h** toward one another, *5425*

HUMPS (1)

Isa 30: 6 their treasures on the **h** *of* camels, 1832

HUMTAH (1)

Jos 15:54 **H,** Kiriath Arba (that is, Hebron) and Zior— 2794

HUNCHBACKED (1)

Lev 21:20 or who is **h** or dwarfed, 1492

HUNDRED (291) [HUNDREDFOLD, HUNDREDS, HUNDREDTH, 100]

Ge 6: 3 his days will be a **h** and twenty years." 4395
7: 6 Noah was six **h** years old when 4395
7:24 flooded the earth for a **h** and fifty days. 4395
8: 3 of the **h** and fifty days the water had gone 4395
8:13 first month of Noah's six **h** and first year, 4395
15:13 be enslaved and mistreated four **h** years. 4395
17:17 "Will a son be born to a man a **h** years old? 4395
21: 5 a **h** years old when his son Isaac was born 4395
23: 1 to be a **h** and twenty-seven years old. 4395
23:15 the land is worth four **h** shekels of silver, 4395
23:16 four **h** shekels of silver, 4395
25: 7 Abraham lived a **h** and seventy-five years. 4395
25:17 Ishmael lived a **h** and thirty-seven years. 4395
32: 6 and four **h** men are with him." 4395
32:14 *two* **h** female goats and twenty male goats, 4395
32:14 *two* **h** ewes and twenty rams, 4395
33: 1 coming with his four **h** men; 4395
33:19 For a **h** pieces of silver, 4395
35:28 Isaac lived a **h** and eighty years. 4395
45:22 but to Benjamin he gave three **h** shekels 4395
47: 9 years of my pilgrimage are a **h** and thirty. 4395
47:28 years of his life were a **h** and forty-seven. 4395
50:22 He lived a **h** and ten years 4395
50:26 So Joseph died at the age of a **h** and ten. 4395
Ex 12:37 There were about six **h** thousand men 4395
14: 7 He took six **h** *of* the best chariots, 4395
27: 9 be a **h** cubits long and is to have curtains 4395
27:11 The north side shall also be a **h** cubits long 4395
27:18 be a **h** cubits long and fifty cubits wide, 4395
38: 9 The south side was a **h** cubits long 4395
38:11 also a **h** cubits long and had twenty posts 4395
Lev 26: 8 Five of you will chase a **h,** 4395
26: 8 and a **h** of you will chase ten thousand, 4395
Nu 7:13 silver plate weighing a **h** and thirty shekels, 4395
7:19 silver plate weighing a **h** and thirty shekels, 4395
7:25 silver plate weighing a **h** and thirty shekels, 4395
7:31 silver plate weighing a **h** and thirty shekels, 4395
7:37 silver plate weighing a **h** and thirty shekels, 4395
7:43 silver plate weighing a **h** and thirty shekels, 4395
7:49 silver plate weighing a **h** and thirty shekels, 4395
7:55 silver plate weighing a **h** and thirty shekels, 4395
7:61 silver plate weighing a **h** and thirty shekels, 4395
7:67 silver plate weighing a **h** and thirty shekels, 4395
7:73 silver plate weighing a **h** and thirty shekels, 4395
7:79 silver plate weighing a **h** and thirty shekels, 4395
7:85 Each silver plate weighed a **h** and thirty 4395
7:85 dishes weighed two thousand four **h** shekels 4395
7:86 gold dishes weighed a **h** and twenty shekels. 4395
11:21 "Here I am among six **h** thousand men 4395
31:28 for the LORD one out of every five **h,** 4395
33:39 a **h** and twenty-three years old when he died 4395
35: 4 the Levites will extend out **fifteen h feet** 547+564
Dt 22:19 They shall fine him a **h** shekels of silver 4395
31: 2 "I am now a **h** and twenty years old 4395
34: 7 a **h** and twenty years old when he died, 4395
Jos 7:21 *two* **h** shekels of silver and a wedge 4395
24:29 died at the age of a **h** and ten. 4395
24:32 a **h** pieces of silver from the sons of Hamor, 4395
Jdg 2: 8 died at the age of a **h** and ten. 4395
3:31 who struck down six **h** Philistines with 4395
4: 3 Because he had nine **h** iron chariots 4395
4:13 gathered together his nine **h** iron chariots 4395
7: 6 Three **h** men lapped with their hands 4395
7: 7 the three **h** men that lapped I will save you 4395
7: 8 to their tents but kept the three **h,** 4395
7:16 the three **h** men into three companies, 4395
7:19 and the **h** men with him reached the edge of 4395
7:22 When the three **h** trumpets sounded, 4395
8: 4 Gideon and his three **h** men, 4395
8:10 a **h** and twenty thousand swordsmen had 4395
8:26 to **seventeen h** shekels, 547+2256+4395+8679
11:26 For three **h** years Israel occupied Heshbon, 4395
15: 4 and caught three **h** foxes and tied them tail 4395
16: 5 will give you **eleven h** shekels 547+2256+4395
17: 2 "The **eleven h** shekels of silver 547+2256+4395
17: 3 the **eleven h** shekels of silver 547+2256+4395
17: 4 and she took *two* **h** shekels of silver 4395
18:11 six **h** men from the clan of the Danites, 4395
18:16 The six **h** Danites, armed for battle, 4395
18:17 the six **h** armed men stood at the entrance to 4395
20: 2 four **h** thousand soldiers armed with swords. 4395
20:10 We'll take ten men out of every **h** from all 4395
20:10 and a **h** from a thousand, 4395
20:15 to seven **h** chosen men from those living 4395
20:16 seven **h** chosen men who were left-handed, 4395
20:17 mustered four **h** thousand swordsmen, 4395
20:47 But six **h** men turned and fled into 4395
21:12 in Jabesh Gilead four **h** young women who
had never slept with a man, 4395
1Sa 11: 8 men of Israel numbered three **h** thousand 4395
13:15 They numbered about six **h.** 4395
14: 2 With him were about six **h** men, 4395
15: 4 *two* **h** thousand foot soldiers 4395
17: 7 and its iron point weighed six **h** shekels. 4395
18:25 for the bride than a **h** Philistine foreskins, 4395
18:27 and killed *two* **h** Philistines. 4395
22: 2 About four **h** men were with him. 4395
23:13 David and his men, about six **h** in number, 4395
25:13 About four **h** men went up with David, 4395
25:13 while *two* **h** stayed with the supplies. 4395
25:18 She took *two* **h** loaves of bread, 4395
25:18 a **h** cakes of raisins and two hundred cakes 4395
25:18 a hundred cakes of raisins and *two* **h** cakes 4395
27: 2 the six **h** men with him left and went over 4395
30: 9 David and the six **h** men with him came to 4395
30:10 for *two* **h** men were too exhausted to cross 4395
30:10 and four **h** men continued the pursuit. 4395
30:17 except four **h** young men who rode off 4395
30:21 the *two* **h** men who had been too exhausted 4395
2Sa 2:31 But David's men had killed three **h** 4395
3:14 for the price of a **h** Philistine foreskins." 4395
8: 4 but a **h** of the chariot horses. 4395
10:18 and David killed seven **h** of their charioteers 4395
14:26 and its weight was *two* **h** shekels by 4395
15:11 *Two* **h** men from Jerusalem 4395
15:18 the six **h** Gittites who had accompanied him 4395
16: 1 and loaded with *two* **h** loaves of bread, 4395
16: 1 a **h** cakes of raisins, 4395
16: 1 a **h** cakes of figs and a skin of wine. 4395
21:16 bronze spearhead weighed three **h** shekels 4395
23: 8 he raised his spear against eight **h** men, 4395
23:18 He raised his spear against three **h** men, 4395
24: 3 the troops a **h** times over, 4395
24: 9 In Israel there were eight **h** thousand
able-bodied men who could handle 4395
24: 9 and in Judah five **h** thousand. 4395
1Ki 4:23 twenty of pasture-fed cattle and a **h** sheep 4395
5:16 as **thirty-three h** foremen who supervised
547+2256+4395+8993+8993
6: 1 In the four **h** and eightieth year after 4395
7: 2 of the Forest of Lebanon a **h** cubits long, 4395
7:20 the *two* **h** pomegranates in rows all around. 4395
7:42 the four **h** pomegranates for the two sets 4395
8:63 a **h** and twenty thousand sheep and goats. 4395
10:16 King Solomon made *two* **h** large shields 4395
10:16 six **h** bekas of gold went into each shield. 4395
10:17 He also made three **h** small shields 4395
10:26 he had **fourteen h** chariots 547+752+2256+4395
10:29 from Egypt for six **h** shekels of silver, 4395
10:29 and a horse for a **h** and fifty. 4395
11: 3 He had seven **h** wives of royal birth 4395
11: 3 of royal birth and three **h** concubines, 4395

1Ki 12:21 a **h** and eighty thousand fighting men— 4395
18: 4 a **h** prophets and hidden them in two caves, 4395
18:13 a **h** of the LORD's prophets in two caves, 4395
18:19 the four **h** and fifty prophets of Baal and 4395
18:19 of Baal and the four **h** prophets of Asherah, 4395
18:22 but Baal has four **h** and fifty prophets. 4395
20:29 a **h** thousand casualties on the Aramean 4395
22: 6 about four **h** men— 4395
2Ki 3: 4 with a **h** thousand lambs and with the wool 4395
3: 4 and with the wool of a **h** thousand rams. 4395
3:26 with him seven **h** swordsmen to break 4395
4:43 "How can I set this before a **h** men?" 4395
11: 4 for the commanders of **units of a h,** 4395
11: 9 The commanders of **units of a h** did just 4395
11:15 the commanders of **units of a h,** who were 4395
14:13 a section **about six h feet** long. 564+752+4395
18:14 from Hezekiah king of Judah three **h** talents 4395
19:35 of the LORD went out and put to death a **h** 4395
23:33 of a **h** talents of silver and a talent of gold. 4395
1Ch 4:42 And five **h** of these Simeonites, 4395
5:21 *two* **h** fifty thousand sheep 4395
5:21 also took *one* **h** thousand people captive, 4395
11:11 he raised his spear against three **h** men, 4395
11:20 He raised his spear against three **h** men, 4395
12:14 the least was a match for a **h,** 4395
18: 4 but a **h** of the chariot horses. 4395
21: 3 the LORD multiply his troops a **h** times over. 4395
21: 5 In all Israel there were one million *one* **h**
thousand men who could handle a sword, 4395
21: 5 including four **h** and seventy thousand 4395
21:25 So David paid Araunah six **h** shekels 4395
22:14 of the LORD a **h** thousand talents of gold, 4395
26:30 **seventeen h** able men— 547+2256+4395+8679
26:32 Jeriah had **twenty-seven h** relatives,
547+2256+4395+8679
29: 7 of bronze and a **h** thousand talents of iron. 4395
2Ch 1:14 he had **fourteen h** chariots 547+752+2256+4395
1:17 from Egypt for six **h** shekels of silver, 4395
1:17 and a horse for a **h** and fifty. 4395
2: 2 and **thirty-six h** as 547+2256+4395+8993+9252
3: 8 the inside with six **h** talents of fine gold. 4395
3:16 a **h** pomegranates and attached them to 4395
4: 8 He also made a **h** gold sprinkling bowls. 4395
4:13 the four **h** pomegranates for the two sets 4395
7: 5 of cattle and a **h** and twenty thousand sheep 4395
8:10 *two* **h** and fifty officials supervising 4395
8:18 and brought back four **h** and fifty talents 4395
9:15 King Solomon made *two* **h** large shields 4395
9:15 six **h** bekas of hammered gold went 4395
9:16 He also made three **h** small shields 4395
9:16 with three **h** bekas of gold in each shield. 4395
11: 1 a **h** and eighty thousand fighting men— 4395
12: 3 With **twelve h** chariots 547+2256+4395
13: 3 of four **h** thousand able fighting men, 4395
13: 3 with eight **h** thousand able troops. 4395
13:17 so that there were five **h** thousand casualties 4395
14: 8 Asa had an army of three **h** thousand men 4395
14: 8 *two* **h** and eighty thousand from Benjamin, 4395
14: 9 with a vast army and three **h** chariots, 4395
15:11 to the LORD seven **h** head of cattle 4395
17:11 seven thousand seven **h** rams 4395
17:11 and seven thousand seven **h** goats. 4395
18: 5 brought together the prophets—four **h** men 4395
23: 1 with the commanders of **units of a h:** 4395
23: 9 the commanders of **units of a h** the spears 4395
23:14 the commanders of **units of a h,** who were 4395
24:15 and he died at the age of a **h** and thirty. 4395
25: 5 that there were three **h** thousand men ready 4395
25: 6 a **h** thousand fighting men from Israel for 4395
25: 6 from Israel for a **h** talents of silver. 4395
25: 9 "But what about the **h** talents I paid 4395
25:23 a section **about six h feet** long. 564+752+4395
27: 5 the Ammonites paid him a **h** talents 4395
28: 6 a **h** and twenty thousand soldiers in Judah— 4395
28: 8 from their kinsmen *two* **h** thousand wives, 4395
29:32 a **h** rams and two hundred male lambs— 4395
29:32 a hundred rams and *two* **h** male lambs— 4395
29:33 to six **h** bulls and three thousand sheep 4395
35: 8 the priests **twenty-six h** Passover offerings
547+2256+4395+9252
35: 8 and three **h** cattle. 4395
35: 9 and five **h** head of cattle for the Levites. 4395
36: 3 and imposed on Judah a levy of a **h** talents 4395
Ezr 6:17 of this house of God they offered a **h** bulls, 10395
6:17 *two* **h** rams, four hundred male lambs and, 10395
6:17 two hundred rams, four **h** male lambs and, 10395
7:22 up to a **h** talents of silver, 10395
7:22 a **h** cors of wheat, a hundred baths of wine, 10395
7:22 a hundred cors of wheat, a **h** baths of wine, 10395
7:22 a **h** baths of olive oil, and salt without limit. 10395
Ne 3: 1 building as far as the Tower of the **H,** 4396
3:13 also repaired **five h yards** of the wall 547+564
5:17 a **h** and fifty Jews and officials ate 4395
12:39 of Hananel and the Tower of the **H,** 4396
Est 9: 6 the Jews killed and destroyed five **h** men. 4395
9:12 and destroyed five **h** men and the ten sons 4395
9:15 and they put to death in Susa three **h** men, 4395
Job 1: 3 five **h** yoke of oxen 4395
1: 3 of oxen and five **h** donkeys, 4395
42:16 After this, Job lived a **h** and forty years; 4395
Pr 17:10 of discernment more than a **h** lashes a fool. 4395
Ecc 6: 3 a **h** children and live many years; 4395
8:12 Although a wicked man commits a **h** crimes 4395
SS 8:12 and *two* **h** are for those who tend its fruit. 4395
Isa 37:36 of the LORD went out and put to death a **h** 4395
65:20 dies at a **h** will be thought a mere youth; 4395
65:20 to reach a **h** will be considered accursed. 4395
Jer 52:23 above the surrounding network was a **h.** 4395
Eze 40:19 it was a **h** cubits on the east side as well as 4395
40:23 it was a **h** cubits. 4395
40:27 it was a **h** cubits. 4395
40:47 a **h** cubits long and a hundred cubits wide. 4395
40:47 a hundred cubits long and a **h** cubits wide. 4395
41:13 it was a **h** cubits long, 4395
41:13 with its walls were also a **h** cubits long. 4395
41:14 was a **h** cubits. 4395
41:15 it was a **h** cubits. 4395
42: 2 a **h** cubits long and fifty cubits wide. 4395
42: 4 and a **h** cubits long. 4395
42: 8 the sanctuary was a **h** cubits long. 4395
42:16 it was five **h** cubits. 4395
42:17 it was five **h** cubits by the measuring rod. 4395
42:18 it was five **h** cubits by the measuring rod. 4395
42:19 it was five **h** cubits by the measuring rod. 4395
42:20 five **h** cubits long 4395
42:20 and five **h** cubits wide, 4395
45:15 to be taken from every flock of *two* **h** from 4395
Am 5: 3 for Israel will have only a **h** left; 4395
5: 3 a **h** strong will have only ten left." 4395
Jnh 4:11 **h and twenty thousand** people who cannot
tell their right hand from 6926+8052+9109
Mt 13: 8 a **h,** sixty or thirty *times* what was sown. *1669*
13:23 He produces a crop, yielding a **h,** *1669*
18:12 If a man owns a **h** sheep, *1669*
18:28 fellow servants who owed him a **h** denarii. *1669*
19:29 for my sake will receive a **h** times as much *1671*
Mk 4: 8 multiplying thirty, sixty, or even a **h** *times."* *1669*
4:20 sixty or even a **h** *times* what was sown." *1669*
10:30 will fail to receive a **h times** as much *1671*
Lk 7:41 One owed him **five h** denarii, *4296*
8: 8 a **h times** more than was sown." *1671*
15: 4 of you has a **h** sheep and loses one of them. *1669*
16: 6 " **'Eight h gallons** of olive oil,' *1004+1669*
16: 6 sit down quickly, and make it **four h.'** *4299*
16: 7 'Take your bill and make it **eight h.'** *3837*
Jn 21: 8 not far from shore, about a **h yards.** *1357+4388*
Ac 1:15 (a group numbering about a **h** and twenty) *1669*
5:36 and about **four h** men rallied to him. *5484*
7: 6 be enslaved and mistreated **four h** years. *5484*
23:23 "Get ready a detachment of **two h** soldiers, *1357*
23:23 seventy horsemen and **two h** spearmen to go *1357*
27:28 **a h and twenty feet deep.** *1633+3976*
Ro 4:19 since he was about a **h years old—** *1670*
1Co 15: 6 *to* more than **five h** of the brothers at *4296*
Rev 9:16 mounted troops was **two h million.** *1490+3689*
16:21 of about a **h pounds** each fell upon men. *5418*

HUNDREDFOLD (1) [HUNDRED]

Ge 26:12 land and the same year reaped a **h,** 4395+9134

HUNDREDS (21) [HUNDRED]

Ex 18:21 appoint them as officials over thousands, **h,** 4395
18:25 officials over thousands, **h,** fifties and tens. 4395
Nu 31:14 of thousands and commanders of **h—** 4395
31:48 of thousands and commanders of **h—** 4395
31:52 of **h** that Moses and Eleazar presented as 4395
31:54 of **h** and brought it into the Tent of Meeting 4395
Dt 1:15 as commanders of thousands, of **h,** 4395
1Sa 22: 7 of thousands and commanders of **h?** 4395
29: 2 with their **units of h** and thousands, 4395
2Sa 18: 1 of thousands and commanders of **h.** 4395
18: 4 while all the men marched out in **units of h** 4395
2Ki 11:19 He took with him the commanders of **h,** 4395
1Ch 13: 1 of thousands and commanders of **h,** 4395
26:26 of thousands and commanders of **h,** 4395
27: 1 of thousands and commanders of **h,** 4395
28: 1 of thousands and commanders of **h,** 4395
29: 6 of thousands and commanders of **h,** 4395
2Ch 1: 2 and commanders of **h,** to the judges and 4395
23:20 He took with him the commanders of **h,** 4395
25: 5 of thousands and commanders of **h** 4395
Mk 6:40 So they sat down in groups of **h** and fifties. *1669*

HUNDREDTH (2) [HUNDRED]

Ge 7:11 In the six **h** year of Noah's life, 4395
Ne 5:11 the **h** *part of* the money, grain, 4395

HUNG (16) [HANG]

Ex 40:21 the tabernacle and **h** the shielding curtain 8492
Dt 21:22 to death and his body *is* **h** on a tree, 9434
21:23 *who* is **h** on a tree is under God's curse. 9434
Jos 8:29 *He* **h** the king of Ai on a tree 9434
10:26 the kings and **h** them on five trees, 9434
2Sa 4:12 and **h** the bodies by the pool in Hebron. 9434
21:12 where the Philistines *had* **h** them 9428
1Ch 10:10 and **h up** his head *in* the temple of Dagon. 9546
Ps 137: 2 There on the poplars *we* **h** our harps, 9434
La 5:12 Princes *have* **been h up** by their hands; 9434
Eze 27:10 *They* **h** their shields and helmets 9434
27:11 *They* **h** their shields around your walls; 9434
Mt 18: 6 be better for him to *have* a large millstone **h** *3203*
Lk 19:48 because all the people **h on** his words. *1717*
23:39 of the criminals who **h** there hurled insults *3203*
Gal 3:13 "Cursed is everyone who *is* **h** on a tree." *3203*

HUNGER (22) [HUNGRY]

Dt 8: 3 **causing** you to **h** and then feeding you 8279
28:48 therefore in **h** and thirst, 8280
1Sa 2: 5 but those who were hungry **h** no more. NIH
2Ch 32:11 to let you die of **h** and thirst. 8280
Ne 9:15 In their **h** you gave them bread from heaven 8280
Job 30: 3 Haggard from want and **h,** 4103
38:39 for the lioness and satisfy the **h** *of* the lions 2652
Ps 17:14 *You* **still** *the* **h** *of* those you cherish; 1061+4848
Pr 6:30 to satisfy his **h** when he is starving. 5883
16:26 his **h** drives him on. 7023
Isa 5:13 of rank will die of **h** and their masses will 8280
29: 8 but he awakens, and his **h** remains; 5883+8199
49:10 *They will* neither **h** nor thirst, 8279
La 2:19 who faint from **h** at the head of every street. 8280
4: 9 **racked with h,** they waste away for lack 1991
5:10 Our skin is hot as an oven, feverish from **h.** 8280
Eze 7:19 not satisfy their **h** or fill their stomachs 5883
Mt 5: 6 Blessed are those who **h** and thirst *4277*
Lk 6:21 Blessed are you who **h** now, *4277*
2Co 6: 5 in hard work, sleepless nights and **h;** *3763*
11:27 I have known **h** and thirst *3350*
Rev 7:16 Never again *will they* **h;** *4277*

HUNGRY (52) [HUNGER]

1Sa 2: 5 but *those who were* **h** hunger no more. 8281
2Sa 17:29 "The people have become **h** and tired 8281
Job 5: 5 The **h** consume his harvest, 8281
18:12 Calamity is **h** *for* him; 8281
22: 7 and you withheld food from the **h,** 8281
24:10 they carry the sheaves, but still go **h.** 8281
Ps 17:12 They are like a lion **h** for prey, 4083
34:10 The lions may grow weak and **h,** 8279
50:12 If *I were* **h** I would not tell you, 8279
107: 5 *They* were **h** and thirsty, 8281
107: 9 and fills the **h** with good things. 5883+8281
107:36 there he brought the **h** to live, 8281
146: 7 of the oppressed and gives food to the **h.** 8281
Pr 10: 3 The LORD *does* not **let** the righteous **go h** 8279
13:25 but the stomach of the wicked **goes h.** 2893
19:15 and the shiftless man **goes h.** 8279
25:21 If your enemy is **h,** give him food to eat; 8281
27: 7 but to the **h** even what is bitter tastes sweet. 8281
Isa 8:21 Distressed and **h,** they will roam through 8281
9:20 they will devour, but *still be* **h;** 8279
29: 8 as when a **h** *man* dreams that he is eating, 8281
32: 6 the **h** he leaves empty and from 5883+8281
44:12 *He gets* **h** and loses his strength; 8279
58: 7 to share your food with the **h** and to provide 8281
58:10 the **h** and satisfy the needs of the oppressed, 8281
65:13 "My servants will eat, but you *will go* **h;** 8279
Jer 42:14 not see war or hear the trumpet or *be* **h** 8279
Eze 18: 7 to the **h** and provides clothing for the naked. 8281
18:16 to the **h** and provides clothing for the naked. 8281
Mt 4: 2 and forty nights, *he was* **h.** *4277*
12: 1 His disciples *were* **h** and began *4277*
12: 3 when *he* and his companions *were* **h?** *4277*
15:32 I do not want to send them away **h,** *3765*
21:18 on his way back to the city, *he was* **h.** *4277*
25:35 *I was* **h** and you gave me something to eat, *4277*
25:37 'Lord, when did we see you **h** and feed you, *4277*
25:42 *I was* **h** and you gave me nothing to eat, *4277*
25:44 when did we see you **h** or thirsty or *4277*
Mk 2:25 and his companions *were* **h** and in need? *4277*
8: 3 If I send them home **h,** *3765*
11:12 as they were leaving Bethany, Jesus *was* **h.** *4277*
Lk 1:53 He has filled the **h** with good things *4277*
4: 2 and at the end of them *he was* **h.** *4277*
6: 3 when he and his companions *were* **h?** *4277*
6:25 who are well fed now, for *you will* **go h.** *4277*
Jn 6:35 He who comes to me *will* never **go h,** *4277*
Ac 10:10 He became **h** and wanted something to eat, *4698*
Ro 12:20 "If your enemy *is* **h,** feed him; *4277*
1Co 4:11 To this very hour *we* **go h** and thirsty, *4277*
11:21 One *remains* **h,** another gets drunk. *4277*
11:34 If anyone *is* **h,** he should eat at home, *4277*
Php 4:12 whether well fed or **h,** *4277*

HUNT (7) [HUNTED, HUNTER, HUNTERS, HUNTING, HUNTS]

Ge 27: 3 to the open country *to* **h** some wild game 7421
27: 5 for the open country to **h** game 7421
31:36 that *you* **h** me **down?** 1944
Job 38:39 *"Do you* **h** the prey for the lioness and 7421
Ps 140:11 *may* disaster **h down** men of violence.
4200+4511+7421
Jer 16:16 and *they will* **h** them **down** 7421
Am 9: 3 there *I will* **h** them **down** and seize them. 2924

HUNTED (3) [HUNT]

Ge 27:33 then, that **h** game and brought it to me? 7421
Isa 13:14 Like a **h** gazelle, 5615
La 3:52 without cause **h** me like a bird. 7421+7421

HUNTER (4) [HUNT]

Ge 10: 9 He was a mighty **h** before the LORD; 7473
10: 9 Nimrod, a mighty **h** before the LORD." 7473
25:27 and Esau became a skillful **h,** 408+7473
Pr 6: 5 like a gazelle from the hand of the **h,** NIH

HUNTERS (1) [HUNT]

Jer 16:16 After that I will send for many **h,** 7475

HUNTING (2) [HUNT]

Ge 27:30 his brother Esau came in from **h.** 7473
1Sa 24:11 but you *are* **h** me **down** to take my life. 7399

HUNTS (4) [HUNT]
Lev 17:13 among you who **h** any animal or bird 7421
1Sa 26:20 as *one* **h** a partridge in the mountains." 8103
Ps 10: 2 In his arrogance the wicked man **h down** 1944
Mic 7: 2 each **h** his brother with a net. 7421

HUPHAM (1) [HUPHAMITE]
Nu 26:39 through **H,** the Huphamite clan. 2573

HUPHAMITE (1) [HUPHAM]
Nu 26:39 through Hupham, the **H** clan. 2574

HUPHAMITES (KJV) See HUPHAM

HUPPAH (1)
1Ch 24:13 the thirteenth to **H,** 2904

HUPPIM (1)
Ge 46:21 Naaman, Ehi, Rosh, Muppim, **H** and Ard. 2907

HUPPITES (2)
1Ch 7:12 The Shuppites and **H** were the descendants 2907
7:15 a wife from among the **H** and Shuppites. 2907

HUR (15) [BEN-HUR]
Ex 17:10 Aaron and **H** went to the top of the hill. 2581
17:12 Aaron and **H** held his hands up— 2581
24:14 Aaron and **H** are with you, 2581
31: 2 the son of **H,** of the tribe of Judah, 2581
35:30 the son of **H,** of the tribe of Judah, 2581
38:22 (Bezalel son of Uri, the son of **H,** 2581
Nu 31: 8 Zur, **H** and Reba—the five kings of Midian. 2581
Jos 13:21 Evi, Rekem, Zur, **H** and Reba— 2581
1Ch 2:19 Caleb married Ephrath, who bore him **H.** 2581
2:20 **H** was the father of Uri, 2581
2:50 The sons of **H** the firstborn of Ephrathah: 2581
4: 1 Perez, Hezron, Carmi, **H** and Shobal. 2581
4: 4 These were the descendants of **H,** 2581
2Ch 1: 5 of **H,** had made was in Gibeon in front of 2581
Ne 3: 9 Rephaiah son of **H,** 2581

HURAI (1)
1Ch 11:32 **H** from the ravines of Gaash, 2584

HURAM (6)
1Ki 7:13 King Solomon sent to Tyre and brought **H,** 2671
7:14 **H** was highly skilled and experienced NIH
7:40 So **H** finished all the work he had 2671
7:45 that **H** made for King Solomon for 2671
1Ch 8: 5 Gera, Shephuphan and **H.** 2586
2Ch 4:11 So **H** finished the work he had undertaken 2586

HURAM-ABI (2)
2Ch 2:13 "I am sending you **H,** a man of great skill, 2587
4:16 the objects that **H** made for King Solomon 2587

HURI (1)
1Ch 5:14 These were the sons of Abihail son of **H,** 2585

HURL (8) [HURLED, HURLS]
1Sa 25:29 the lives of your enemies *he will* **h away** as 7843
2Ch 26:15 to shoot arrows and **h** large stones. NIH
Ps 22: 7 *they* **h insults,** shaking their heads: 928+7080+8557
Isa 22:17 take firm hold of you and **h** you **away,** 3214+3232
Jer 10:18 "At this time I *will* **h out** those who live 7843
22:26 *I will* **h** you and the mother who gave 3214
Eze 32: 4 and **h** you on the open field. 3214
Mic 7:19 and **h** all our iniquities into the depths of 8959

HURLED (23) [HURL]
Ex 15: 1 The horse and its rider *he has* **h** into the sea. 8227
15: 4 Pharaoh's chariots and his army *he has* **h** 3721
15:21 horse and its rider *he has* **h** into the sea." 8227
Jos 10:11 **h** large hailstones **down** 8959
1Sa 18:11 and he **h** it, saying to himself, 3214
20:33 But Saul **h** his spear at him to kill him. 3214
25:14 but *he* **h insults** at them. 6512
Ne 9:11 but *you* **h** their pursuers into the depths, 8959
Ps 79:12 the reproach *they have* **h** *at* you, 3070
Jer 22:28 Why *will* he and his children **be h out,** 3214
La 2: 1 *He has* **h down** the splendor of Israel 8959
Jnh 2: 3 *You* **h** me into the deep, 8959
Mt 27:39 Those who passed by **h insults at** him, *1059*
Mk 15:29 Those who passed by **h insults at** him, *1059*
Lk 23:39 the criminals who hung there **h insults at** *1059*
Jn 9:28 Then *they* **h insults at** him and said, *3366*
1Pe 2:23 *When they* **h** *their* **insults at** him, *3366*
Rev 8: 5 and **h** it on the earth; *965*
8: 7 and *it was* **h** down upon the earth. *965*
12: 9 The great dragon *was* **h down—** *965*
12: 9 *He was* **h** to the earth, and his angels *965*
12:10 *has been* **h down.** *965*
12:13 When the dragon saw that *he had been* **h** to *965*

HURLS (2) [HURL]
Job 27:22 *It* **h** *itself* against him without mercy 8959
Ps 147:17 *He* **h down** his hail like pebbles. 8959

HURRICANE (1)
Ac 27:14 Before very long, a wind **of h force,** *5607*

HURRIED (25) [HURRY]
Ge 18: 2 *he* **h** from the entrance of his tent 8132
18: 6 So Abraham **h** into the tent to Sarah. 4554
18: 7 *who* **h** to prepare it. 4554
24:17 The servant **h** to meet her and said, 8132
24:29 and he **h** out to the man at the spring. 8132
29:13 his sister's son, *he* **h** to meet him. 8132
43:15 *They* **h** down to Egypt 7756
43:30 Joseph **h** *out* and looked for a place 4554
Ex 9:20 of the LORD **h to bring** their slaves 5674
Jos 4:10 The people **h** over, 4554
8:14 he and all the men of the city **h** out early in 4554
Jdg 13:10 The woman **h** to tell her husband, 4554
1Sa 4:14 The man **h** over to Eli, 4554
2Sa 4: 4 but as she **h** to leave, 2905
19:16 **h** down with the men of Judah 4554
2Ki 5:21 So Gehazi **h** after Naaman. 8103
9:13 *They* **h** and took their cloaks 4554
2Ch 26:20 so *they* **h** him out. 987
Est 6:14 and **h** Haman away to 987
Job 31: 5 in falsehood or my foot *has* **h** after deceit— 2590
Da 6:19 the king got up and **h** to the lions' den. 10097
Mt 28: 8 So the women **h away from** the tomb, *599+5444*
Mk 6:25 the girl **h** in to the king with the request: *1656+3552+5082*
Lk 1:39 Mary got ready and **h** to a town *3552+4513+5082*
2:16 *they* **h off** and found Mary and Joseph, *2262+5067*

HURRIEDLY (1) [HURRY]
Jdg 9:54 **H** he called to his armor-bearer, 4559

HURRIES (1) [HURRY]
Ecc 1: 5 and **h back** to where it rises. 8634

HURRY (15) [HURRIED, HURRIES, HURRIEDLY, HURRYING]
Ge 19:14 He said, **"H** and get out of this place, 7756
19:15 the angels urged Lot, saying, **"H!** 7756
45: 9 Now **h** back to my father and say to him, 4554
Ex 12:33 the people to **h** and leave the country. 4554
Nu 16:46 **h** to the assembly to make atonement 2143+4559
1Sa 9:12 "He's ahead of you. **H** now; 4554
17:17 for your brothers and **h** to their camp. 8132
20: 6 'David earnestly asked my permission to **h** 8132
20:38 Then he shouted, **"H!** 4559
2Ch 35:21 God has told me to **h;** 987
Ps 55: 8 *I would* **h** *to* my place of shelter, 2590
Ecc 8: 3 not *be* **in a h** to leave the king's presence. 987
SS 1: 4 Take me away with you—*let us* **h!** 8132
Isa 5:19 *"Let* God **h,** let him hasten his work 4554
Ac 20:16 for *he was* **in a h** to reach Jerusalem, *5067*

HURRYING (1) [HURRY]
1Sa 23:26 **h** to get away from Saul. 2905

HURT (9) [HURTS]
Ps 69:26 and talk about the pain of *those* you **h.** 2728
Pr 23:35 you will say, "but *I'm* not **h!** 2703
Ecc 8: 9 a man lords it over others to his own **h.** 8273
Da 6:22 *They have* not **h** me, 10243
Mk 16:18 *it will* not **h** them at all; *1055*
Jn 21:17 Peter *was* **h** because Jesus asked him *3382*
Ac 7:26 why *do you* want to **h** each other?' *92*
2Co 7: 8 I see that my letter **h** you, *3382*
Rev 2:11 He who overcomes *will* not *be* **h** at all by *92*

HURTLING (1)
Eze 13:11 and I will send hailstones **h down,** 5877

HURTS (2) [HURT]
Ps 15: 4 who keeps his oath even when *it* **h,** 8317
Pr 26:28 A lying tongue hates *those* it **h,** 1916

HUSBAND (116) [HUSBAND'S, HUSBANDS]
Ge 3: 6 She also gave some to her **h,** 408
3:16 Your desire will be for your **h,** 408
16: 3 and gave her to her **h** to be his wife. 408
29:32 Surely my **h** will love me now." 408
29:34 at last my **h** will become attached to me, 408
30:15 that you took away my **h?** 408
30:18 for giving my maidservant to my **h."** 408
30:20 This time my **h** will treat me with honor, 408
Ex 21:22 be fined whatever the woman's **h** demands 1251
Lev 21: 3 on him since she has no **h—** 408
Nu 5:13 from her **h** and her impurity is undetected 408
5:14 and if feelings of jealousy come over **her h** 2257S
5:19 while married to your **h,** 408
5:20 to your **h** and you have defiled yourself 408
5:20 by sleeping with a man other than your **h"** 408
5:27 to her **h,** then when she is made to drink 408
5:29 and defiles herself while married to her **h,** 408
5:31 The **h** will be innocent of any wrongdoing, 408
30: 7 her **h** hears about it but says nothing to her, 408
30: 8 if her **h** forbids her when he hears about it, 408
30:10 with her **h** makes a vow or obligates herself 408
30:11 and her **h** hears about it but says nothing 408
Nu 30:12 But if her **h** nullifies them when he hears 408
30:12 Her **h** has nullified them, 408
30:13 Her **h** may confirm or nullify any vow 408
30:14 But if her **h** says nothing to her about it 408
Dt 21:13 and *be* her **h** and she shall be your wife. 1249
24: 3 and her second **h** dislikes her and writes her 408
24: 4 then her first **h,** who divorced her, 1251
25:11 of one of them comes to rescue her **h** 408
28:56 the **h** she loves and her own son or daughter 408
Jdg 13: 6 the woman went to her **h** and told him, 408
13: 9 but her **h** Manoah was not with her. 408
13:10 The woman hurried to tell her **h,** 408
14:15 "Coax your **h** into explaining the riddle 408
19: 3 her **h** went to her to persuade her to return. 408
20: 4 the Levite, the **h** *of* the murdered woman, 408
Ru 1: 3 Now Elimelech, Naomi's **h,** died, 408
1: 5 without her two sons and her **h.** 408
1: 9 in the home of another **h."** 408
1:12 I am too old to have another **h.** 408
1:12 even if I had a **h** tonight and then gave birth 408
2:11 since the death of your **h—** 408
1Sa 1: 8 Elkanah her **h** would say to her, "Hannah, 408
1:22 She said to her **h,** "After the boy is weaned, 408
1:23 Elkanah her **h** told her. 408
2:19 to him when she went up with her **h** to offer 408
4:19 that her father-in-law and her **h** were dead, 408
4:21 the deaths of her father-in-law and her **h.** 408
25: 3 but her **h,** a Calebite, was surly and mean 408
25:19 But she did not tell her **h** Nabal. 408
2Sa 3:15 from her **h** Paltiel son of Laish. 408
3:16 Her **h,** however, went with her, 408
11:26 Uriah's wife heard that her **h** was dead, 408
14: 5 "I am indeed a widow; my **h** is dead. 408
14: 7 leaving my **h** neither name nor descendant 408
2Ki 4: 1 "Your servant my **h** is dead, 408
4: 9 She said to her **h,** 408
4:14 "Well, she has no son and her **h** is old." 408
4:22 She called her **h** and said, 408
4:26 Is your **h** all right? 408
Pr 7:19 My **h** is not at home; 408
31:11 Her **h** has full confidence in her 1251
31:23 Her **h** is respected at the city gate, 1251
31:28 her **h** also, and he praises her: 1251
Isa 54: 1 desolate woman than of *her who* **has a h,"** 1249
54: 5 For your Maker *is* your **h—** 1249
Jer 3:14 declares the LORD, "for I *am* your **h.** 1249
3:20 But like a woman unfaithful to her **h,** 8276
6:11 both **h** and wife will be caught in it, 408
31:32 though I *was a* **h** to them," 1249
Eze 16:32 You prefer strangers to your own **h!** 408
16:45 who despised her **h** and her children; 408
Hos 2: 2 for she is not my wife, and I am not her **h.** 408
2: 7 'I will go back to my **h** as at first, 408
2:16 "you will call me 'my **h';** 408
Joel 1: 8 in sackcloth grieving for the **h** *of* her youth. 1251
Mt 1:16 the **h** of Mary, of whom was born Jesus, *467*
1:19 Because Joseph her **h** was a righteous man *467*
19:10 "If this is the situation between a **h** *476*
Mk 10:12 she divorces her **h** and marries another man, *467*
Lk 2:36 with *her* **h** seven years after her marriage, *467*
Jn 4:16 "Go, call your **h** and come back." *467*
4:17 "I have no **h,"** she replied. *467*
4:17 "You are right when you say you have no **h.** *467*
4:18 and the man you now have is not your **h.** *467*
Ac 5: 9 the men who buried your **h** are at the door, *467*
5:10 carried her out and buried her beside her **h.** *467*
Ro 7: 2 a married woman is bound *to* her **h** as long *467*
7: 2 but if her **h** dies, she is released from the *467*
7: 3 if she marries another man while her **h** is still alive, *467*
7: 3 But if her **h** dies, she is released from that *467*
1Co 7: 2 and each woman her own **h.** *467*
7: 3 **h** should fulfill his marital duty to his wife, *467*
7: 3 and likewise the wife *to* her **h.** *467*
7: 4 not belong to her alone but also to her **h.** *467*
7:10 A wife must not separate from her **h.** *467*
7:11 or else be reconciled *to* her **h.** *467*
7:11 And a **h** must not divorce his wife. *467*
7:13 a **h** who is not a believer and he is willing *467*
7:14 For the unbelieving **h** has been sanctified *467*
7:14 sanctified through her believing **h.** *467*
7:16 wife, whether you will save your **h?** *467*
7:16 Or, how do you know, **h,** *467*
7:34 how she can please her **h.** *467*
7:39 woman is bound to her **h** as long as he lives. *467*
7:39 But if her **h** dies, she is free to marry *467*
2Co 11: 2 I promised you *to* one **h,** to Christ, *467*
Gal 4:27 desolate woman than of her who has a **h."** *467*
Eph 5:23 For the **h** is the head of the wife as Christ is *467*
5:33 and the wife must respect her **h.** *467*
1Ti 3: 2 overseer must be above reproach, the **h** of but one wife, temperate, *467*
3:12 A deacon must be the **h** of but one wife *467*
5: 9 has been **faithful to her h,** *467+1222+1651*
Tit 1: 6 An elder must be blameless, the **h** of but one wife, *467*
Rev 21: 2 as a bride beautifully dressed *for* her **h.** *467*

HUSBAND'S (7) [HUSBAND]
Dt 25: 5 Her **h brother** shall take her and marry her 3303
25: 7 "My **h brother** refuses to carry 3303
Ru 2: 1 Now Naomi had a relative on her **h** side, 408
Pr 6:34 for jealousy arouses a **h** fury, 1505
12: 4 A wife of noble character is her **h** crown, 1251
Jn 1:13 nor of human decision or a **h** will, *467*
1Co 7: 4 the **h** body does not belong to him alone but *467*

HUSBANDMAN (KJV) See FARMER, GARDENER, MAN OF THE SOIL

HUSBANDS (20) [HUSBAND]
Lev 21: 7 by prostitution or divorced from their **h,** 408
Ru 1:11 who could become your **h?** 408
Est 1:17 and so they will despise their **h** and say, 1251
1:20 all the women will respect their **h,** 1251
Jer 44:19 not our **h** know that we were making cakes 408
Eze 16:45 who despised their **h** and their children. 408
Am 4: 1 and crush the needy and say to your **h,** 123
Jn 4:18 The fact is, you have had five **h,** *467*
1Co 14:35 they should ask their own **h** at home; *467*
Eph 5:22 Wives, submit *to* your **h** as to the Lord. *467*
5:24 so also wives should submit *to* their **h** *467*
5:25 **H,** love your wives, just as Christ loved *467*
5:28 **h** ought to love their wives *467*
Col 3:18 Wives, submit *to* your **h,** *467*
3:19 **H,** love your wives and do not be harsh *467*
Tit 2: 4 the younger women to **love their h** *5791*
2: 5 to be kind, and to be subject *to* their **h,** *467*
1Pe 3: 1 in the same way be submissive *to* your **h** so *467*
3: 5 They were submissive *to* their own **h,** *467*
3: 7 **H,** in the same way be considerate *467*

HUSH (1) [HUSHED]
Am 6:10 and he says, "No," then he will say, **"H!** 2187

HUSHAH (1)
1Ch 4: 4 and Ezer the father of **H.** 2592

HUSHAI (12)
2Sa 15:32 **H** the Arkite was there to meet him, 2593
15:37 So David's friend **H** arrived at Jerusalem 2593
16:16 Then **H** the Arkite, David's friend, 2593
16:17 Absalom asked **H,** "Is this the love you 2593
16:18 **H** said to Absalom, "No, 2593
17: 5 Absalom said, "Summon also **H** the Arkite, 2593
17: 6 When **H** came to him, Absalom said, 2593
17: 7 **H** replied to Absalom, "The advice 2593
17:14 "The advice of **H** the Arkite is better than 2593
17:15 **H** told Zadok and Abiathar, the priests, 2593
1Ki 4:16 Baana son of **H**—in Asher and in Aloth; 2593
1Ch 27:33 **H** the Arkite was the king's friend. 2593

HUSHAM (4)
Ge 36:34 **H** from the land of the Temanites 2595
36:35 When **H** died, Hadad son of Bedad, 2595
1Ch 1:45 **H** from the land of the Temanites 2595
1:46 When **H** died, Hadad son of Bedad, 2595

HUSHATHITE (5)
2Sa 21:18 At that time Sibbecai the **H** killed Saph, 3144
23:27 Abiezer from Anathoth, Mebunnai the **H,** 3144
1Ch 11:29 Sibbecai the **H,** Ilai the Ahohite, 3144
20: 4 At that time Sibbecai the **H** killed Sippai, 3144
27:11 for the eighth month, was Sibbecai the **H,** 3144

HUSHED (4) [HUSH]
Job 4:16 and I heard a **h** voice: 1960
29:10 the voices of the nobles *were* **h,** 7461
37:17 when the land **lies h** under the south wind, 9200
Ps 107:29 the waves of the sea *were* **h.** 3120

HUSHIM (3)
Ge 46:23 The son of Dan: **H.** 3123
1Ch 8: 8 in Moab after he had divorced his wives **H** 2594
8:11 By **H** he had Abitub and Elpaal. 2594

HUSHITES (1)
1Ch 7:12 and the **H** the descendants of Aher. 3131

HUSK (KJV) See GRAIN, SKIN

HUT (3)
Job 27:18 like a **h** made by a watchman. 6109
Isa 1: 8 like a **h** in a field of melons, 4870
24:20 it sways like a **h** in the wind; 4870

HUZ (KJV) See UZ

HUZOTH See KIRIATH HUZOTH

HUZZAB (KJV) See DECREED

HYENAS (3)
Isa 13:22 **H** will howl in her strongholds, 363
34:14 Desert creatures will meet with **h,** 363
Jer 50:39 "So desert creatures and **h** will live there, 363

HYMENAEUS (2)
1Ti 1:20 Among them are **H** and Alexander, *5628*
2Ti 2:17 Among them are **H** and Philetus, *5628*

HYMN (4) [HYMNS]
Ps 40: 3 in my mouth, a **h of praise** to our God. 9335
Mt 26:30 *When they had* **sung a h,** they went out *5630*
Mk 14:26 *When they had* **sung a h,** they went out *5630*
1Co 14:26 When you come together, everyone has a **h,** *6011*

HYMNS (4) [HYMN]
Ac 16:25 Silas *were* praying and **singing h** to God, *5630*
Ro 15: 9 *I will* **sing h** to your name." *6010*
Eph 5:19 psalms, **h** and spiritual songs. *5631*
Col 3:16 psalms, **h** and spiritual songs with gratitude *5631*

HYPOCRISY (6) [HYPOCRITE, HYPOCRITES, HYPOCRITICAL]
Mt 23:28 the inside you are full *of* **h** and wickedness. *5694*
Mk 12:15 But Jesus knew their **h.** *5694*
Lk 12: 1 the yeast of the Pharisees, which is **h.** *5694*
Gal 2:13 The other Jews **joined** him **in** his **h,** *5347*
2:13 *by* their **h** even Barnabas was led astray. *5694*
1Pe 2: 1 **h,** envy, and slander of every kind. *5694*

HYPOCRITE (2) [HYPOCRISY]
Mt 7: 5 *You* **h,** first take the plank out of your own *5695*
Lk 6:42 *You* **h,** first take the plank out of your eye, *5695*

HYPOCRITES (16) [HYPOCRISY]
Ps 26: 4 nor do I consort with **h;** 6623
Mt 6: 2 as the **h** do in the synagogues and on *5695*
6: 5 "And when you pray, do not be like the **h,** *5695*
6:16 do not look somber as the **h** do, *5695*
15: 7 *You* **h!** Isaiah was right when he prophesied *5695*
22:18 Jesus, knowing their evil intent, said, *"You* **h,** why are you trying to trap me? *5695*
23:13 teachers of the law and Pharisees, *you* **h!** *5695*
23:15 teachers of the law and Pharisees, *you* **h!** *5695*
23:23 teachers of the law and Pharisees, *you* **h!** *5695*
23:25 teachers of the law and Pharisees, *you* **h!** *5695*
23:27 teachers of the law and Pharisees, *you* **h!** *5695*
23:29 teachers of the law and Pharisees, *you* **h!** *5695*
24:51 to pieces and assign him a place with the **h,** *5695*
Mk 7: 6 when he prophesied about you **h;** *5695*
Lk 12:56 **H!** You know how to interpret *5695*
13:15 The Lord answered him, *"You* **h!** *5695*

HYPOCRITICAL (1) [HYPOCRISY]
1Ti 4: 2 Such teachings come through **h** liars, *5694*

HYSSOP (12)
Ex 12:22 Take a bunch of **h,** dip it in the blood 257
Lev 14: 4 and **h** be brought for the one to be cleansed. 257
14: 6 the scarlet yarn and the **h,** 257
14:49 scarlet yarn and **h.** 257
14:51 Then he is to take the cedar wood, the **h,** 257
14:52 the cedar wood, the **h** and the scarlet yarn. 257
Nu 19: 6 **h** and scarlet wool and throw them onto 257
19:18 to take *some* **h,** dip it in the water 257
1Ki 4:33 the cedar of Lebanon to the **h** that grows out 257
Ps 51: 7 Cleanse me with **h,** and I will be clean; 257
Jn 19:29 put the sponge *on* a stalk of the **h plant,** *5727*
Heb 9:19 scarlet wool and **branches of h,** *5727*

I

I (8747) [I'LL, I'M, I'VE, ME, MINE, MYSELF] See Index of Articles Etc.

I AM (61 of 1036) See Index of Articles Etc. for Exhaustive Listings of I and AM (See Introduction, pages x-xi)
Ge 15: 1 "Do not be afraid, Abram. **I am** your shield, your very great reward." 644
17: 1 "**I am** God Almighty; walk before me and be blameless. 638
Ex 3:14 God said to Moses, "**I AM WHO I AM.** 2118
3:14 God said to Moses, "I AM WHO I AM. 2118
3:14 This is what you are to say to the Israelites: '**I AM** has sent me to you.' " 2118
Ps 46:10 "Be still, and know that **I am** God; 644
Isa 41:10 So do not fear, for **I am** with you; 638
41:10 do not be dismayed, for **I am** your God. 638
43: 3 For **I am** the LORD, your God, the Holy One of Israel, your Savior; 638
43:11 **I, even I, am** the LORD, and apart from me there is no savior. 644+644
43:15 **I am** the LORD, your Holy One, Israel's Creator, your King." 638
44: 6 **I am** the first and I am the last; apart from me there is no God. 638
44: 6 I am the first and **I am** the last; apart from me there is no God. 638
48:12 **I am** the first and I am the last. 638
Isa 48:12 I am the first and **I am** the last. 638
Jer 3:14 "Return, faithless people," declares the LORD, "for **I am** your husband. 644
32:27 "**I am** the LORD, the God of all mankind. Is anything too hard for me? 638
Mt 16:15 he asked. "Who do you say **I am**?" *1609+1639*
28:20 And surely **I am** with you always, to the very end of the age." *1609+1639*
Mk 8:29 he asked. "Who do you say **I am**?" *1609+1639*
14:62 "**I am,**" said Jesus. "And you will see the Son of Man sitting at the right hand *1609+1639*
Jn 6:35 Jesus declared, "**I am** the bread of life. *1609+1639*
6:41 because he said, "**I am** the bread that came down from heaven." *1609+1639*
6:48 **I am** the bread of life. *1609+1639*
6:51 **I am** the living bread that came down from heaven. *1609+1639*
8:12 "**I am** the light of the world. *1609+1639*
8:24 if you do not believe that **I am** [the one I claim to be], you will indeed die in your sins." *1609+1639*
8:28 said, "When you have lifted up the Son of Man, then you will know that **I am** *1609+1639*
8:58 "before Abraham was born, **I am**!" *1609+1639*
9: 5 **I am** the light of the world." *1639*
10: 7 **I am** the gate for the sheep. *1609+1639*
10: 9 **I am** the gate; whoever enters through me will be saved. *1609+1639*
10:11 "**I am** the good shepherd. *1609+1639*
10:14 "**I am** the good shepherd; *1609+1639*
10:36 Why then do you accuse me of blasphemy because I said, '**I am** God's Son'? *1639*
11:25 Jesus said to her, "**I am** the resurrection and the life. *1609+1639*
13:19 so that when it does happen you will believe that **I am** He. *1609+1639*
14: 6 Jesus answered, "**I am** the way and the truth and the life. *1609+1639*
14:10 Don't you believe that **I am** in the Father, and that the Father is in me? *1609*
14:11 Believe me when I say that **I am** in the Father and the Father is in me; *1609*
14:20 On that day you will realize that **I am** in my Father, *1609*
14:20 and you are in me, and **I am** in you. *1609*
15: 1 "**I am** the true vine, and my Father is the gardener. *1609+1639*
15: 5 "**I am** the vine; you are the branches. *1609+1639*
18: 5 "Jesus of Nazareth," they replied. "**I am** he," Jesus said. *1609+1639*
18: 6 When Jesus said, "**I am** he," they drew back and fell to the ground. *1609+1639*
18: 8 "I told you that **I am** he," Jesus *1609+1639*
Ac 9: 5 "**I am** Jesus, whom you are persecuting," he replied. *1609+1639*
18:10 For **I am** with you, and no one is going to attack and harm you, *1609+1639*
22: 8 " '**I am** Jesus of Nazareth, whom you are persecuting,' he replied. *1609+1639*
26:15 " '**I am** Jesus, whom you are persecuting,' the Lord replied. *1609+1639*
Rev 1: 8 "**I am** the Alpha and the Omega," says the Lord God, "who is, and who was, and who is to come, the Almighty." *1609+1639*
1:17 "Do not be afraid. **I am** the First and the Last. *1609+1639*
1:18 I am the Living One; I was dead, and behold **I am** alive for ever and ever! *1639*
3:11 *I am* **coming** soon. *AIT*
21: 6 **I am** the Alpha and the Omega, the Beginning and the End. *1609+1639*
22: 7 "Behold, *I am* **coming** soon! *AIT*
22:12 "Behold, *I am* **coming** soon! *AIT*
22:13 **I am** the Alpha and the Omega, the First and the Last, the Beginning and the End. *1609*
22:16 **I am** the Root and the Offspring of David, and the bright Morning Star." *1609+1639*
22:20 He who testifies to these things says, "Yes, *I am* **coming** soon." Amen. Come, Lord Jesus. *AIT*

I'LL (38) [I, WILL] See Index of Articles Etc.

I'M (24) [BE, I] See Index of Articles Etc.

I'VE (9) [HAVE, I]
Ge 30:26 You know how much work **I** done 3276
31: 6 You know that *I* **worked for** your father AIT
Ru 2:11 "**I** been told all about what you have done 3276
1Ki 22:34 *I* **been wounded."** AIT
2Ch 18:33 *I* **been wounded."** AIT
Job 19: 7 "Though I cry, '**I** been wronged!' NIH
Pr 30:20 '*I* **done** nothing wrong.' AIT
Lk 13: 7 'For three years now *I been* **coming** *AIT*
15:29 All these years *I been* **slaving** for you *AIT*

IBEX (1)
Dt 14: 5 the **i,** the antelope and the mountain sheep. 1913

IBHAR (3)
2Sa 5:15 **I,** Elishua, Nepheg, Japhia, 3295
1Ch 3: 6 There were also **I,** Elishua, Eliphelet, 3295
14: 5 **I,** Elishua, Elpelet, 3295

IBLEAM (3)
Jos 17:11 I and the people of Dor, Endor, 3300
Jdg 1:27 of Beth Shan or Taanach or Dor or I 3300
2Ki 9:27 in his chariot on the way up to Gur near I, 3300

IBNEIAH (1)
1Ch 9: 8 I son of Jeroham; 3307

IBNIJAH (1)
1Ch 9: 8 the son of Reuel, the son of I. 3308

IBRI (1)
1Ch 24:27 Beno, Shoham, Zaccur and I. 6304

IBSAM (1)
1Ch 7: 2 Rephaiah, Jeriel, Jahmai, I and Samuel— 3311

IBZAN (3)
Jdg 12: 8 After him, I of Bethlehem led Israel. 83
12: 9 I led Israel seven years. NIH
12:10 Then I died, and was buried in Bethlehem. 83

ICE (4) [ICY]
Job 6:16 when darkened by thawing i and swollen 7943
37:10 The breath of God produces i, 7943
38:29 From whose womb comes the i? 7943
Eze 1:22 sparkling like i, and awesome. 7943

ICHABOD (1) [ICHABOD'S]
1Sa 4:21 She named the boy I, saying, 376

ICHABOD'S (1) [ICHABOD]
1Sa 14: 3 a son of I brother Ahitub son of Phinehas, 376

ICONIUM (6)
Ac 13:51 in protest against them and went to I. *2658*
14: 1 At I Paul and Barnabas went as usual into *2658*
14:19 Then some Jews came from Antioch and I *2658*
14:21 they returned to Lystra, I and Antioch, *2658*
16: 2 The brothers at Lystra and I spoke well *2658*
2Ti 3:11 I and Lystra, the persecutions I endured. *2658*

ICY (1) [ICE]
Ps 147:17 Who can withstand his i **blast?** 7938

IDALAH (1)
Jos 19:15 Nahalal, Shimron, I and Bethlehem. 3339

IDBASH (1)
1Ch 4: 3 Jezreel, Ishma and I. 3340

IDDO (13) [IDDO'S]
1Ki 4:14 Ahinadab son of I—in Mahanaim; 6333
1Ch 6:21 I his son, Zerah his son 6341
27:21 I son of Zechariah; 3346
2Ch 9:29 the Shilonite and in the visions of I the seer 3587
12:15 of Shemaiah the prophet and of I the seer 6341
13:22 in the annotations of the prophet I. 6341
Ezr 5: 1 Zechariah the prophet, a descendant of I, 10529
6:14 Zechariah, a descendant of I. 10529
8:17 and I sent them to I, 120
8:17 to say to I and his kinsmen, 120
Ne 12: 4 I, Ginnethon, Abijah, 6342
Zec 1: 1 Zechariah son of Berekiah, the son of I: 6341
1: 7 Zechariah son of Berekiah, the son of I. 6342

IDDO'S (1) [IDDO]
Ne 12:16 of I, Zechariah; of Ginnethon's, 6342

IDEA (8) [IDEAS]
Nu 16:28 and that it was not my **i:** 4213+4946
Dt 1:23 The i seemed good to me; 1821
Est 3: 6 he **scorned the i** of killing only Mordecai. 928+1022+6524
Jn 5:13 man who was healed *had* no i who it was, *3857*
8:14 But you *have* no i where I come from or *3857*
18:34 "Is that your own i," Jesus asked, *NIG*
Ac 12: 9 but *he* **had** no i that what the angel was *3857*
2Pe 2:13 *Their* i of pleasure *is* to carouse *2451*

IDEAS (3) [IDEA]
Ac 17:20 You are bringing some **strange** *i* *AIT*
17:21 about and listening to the latest **i.)** *5516*^{S}
1Ti 6:20 from godless chatter and the **opposing i** *509*

IDENTICAL (2)
1Ki 6:25 the two cherubim were **i** in size and shape. 285
7:37 in the same molds and were **i** in size 285

IDLE (11) [IDLENESS, IDLERS]
Dt 32:47 They are not just i words for you— 8199
Job 11: 3 Will your **i talk** reduce men to silence? 966
Ecc 10:18 if his hands are i, the house leaks. 9170
11: 6 at evening **let** not your hands **be i,** 5663
Isa 58:13 as you please or speaking i words, NIH
Col 2:18 unspiritual mind puffs up *with* **i notions.** *1632*
1Th 5:14 warn those who are i, encourage the timid, *864*
2Th 3: 6 to keep away from every brother who is i *865*
3: 7 *We were* not i when we were with you, *863*
3:11 We hear that some among you *are* i. *865+4344*
1Ti 5:13 they get into the habit of being i and going *734*

IDLENESS (1) [IDLE]
Pr 31:27 and does not eat the bread of i. 6791

IDLERS (1) [IDLE]
1Ti 5:13 And not only do they become i, *734*

IDOL (39) [CALF-IDOL, CALF-IDOLS, IDOL'S, IDOLATER, IDOLATERS, IDOLATRIES, IDOLATROUS, IDOLATRY, IDOLS]
Ex 20: 4 "You shall not make for yourself an i in 7181
32: 4 and made it into an **i cast** in the shape of 5011
32: 8 and have made themselves an **i cast** in 5011
Dt 4:16 and make for yourselves an i, 7181
4:23 do not make for yourselves an i *in* the form 7181
4:25 and make any kind of i, 7181
5: 8 for yourself an i in the form *of* anything 7181
9:12 and have made a **cast i** for themselves." 5011
9:16 you had made for yourselves an **i cast** in 5011
27:15 the man who carves an image or casts an **i**— 5011
Jdg 17: 3 to make a carved image and a **cast i.** 5011
17: 4 who made them into the image and the **i.** 5011
18:14 a carved image and a **cast i?** 5011
18:17 the other household gods and the **cast i** 5011
18:18 the other household gods and the **cast i,** 5011
1Sa 19:13 Michal took an i and laid it on the bed, 9572
19:16 the men entered, there was the i in the bed, 9572
Ps 24: 4 up his soul to an i or swear by what is false. 8736
106:19 a calf and worshiped an **i cast from metal.** 5011
Isa 40:19 As for an i, a craftsman casts it, 7181
40:20 a skilled craftsman to set up an i that will 7181
41: 7 He nails down **the i** so it will not topple. 2084^S
44:10 Who shapes a god and casts an **i,** 7181
44:12 he shapes an i with hammers, 2084^S
44:15 he makes an i and bows down to it. 7181
44:17 From the rest he makes a god, his **i;** 7181
66: 3 like one who worships an **i.** 224
Eze 8: 3 where the i that provokes to jealousy stood. 6166
8: 5 the gate of the altar I saw this i *of* jealousy. 6166
8:12 each at the shrine of his own **i?** 5381
Hos 3: 4 without ephod or **i.** 9572
4:12 They consult a **wooden i** and are answered 6770
9:10 to that **shameful i** and became as vile as 1425
Hab 2:18 "Of what value is an **i,** 7181
Ac 7:41 the time they made an i in the form of *NIG*
1Co 8: 4 that an i is nothing at all in the world and *1631*
8: 7 of it as having been sacrificed to an **i,** *NIG*
10:19 that a **sacrifice offered to an i** is anything, *1628*
10:19 or that an i is anything? *1631*

IDOL'S (1) [IDOL]
1Co 8:10 eating in an **i temple,** *1627*

IDOLATER (2) [IDOL]
1Co 5:11 immoral or greedy, an i or a slanderer, *1629*
Eph 5: 5 or greedy person—such a man is an **i**— *1629*

IDOLATERS (5) [IDOL]
1Co 5:10 or the greedy and swindlers, or **i.** *1629*
6: 9 the sexually immoral nor i nor adulterers *1629*
10: 7 Do not be **i,** as some of them were; *1629*
Rev 21: 8 practice magic arts, the i and all liars— *1629*
22:15 the i and everyone who loves and *1629*

IDOLATRIES (1) [IDOL]
Jer 14:14 **i** and the delusions of their own minds. 496

IDOLATROUS (3) [IDOL]
Jer 3:23 Surely the **[i]** commotion on the hills NIH
Hos 10: 5 and so will its **i priests,** 4024
Zep 1: 4 the names of the pagan and the **i priests**— 3913

IDOLATRY (8) [IDOL]
1Sa 15:23 and arrogance like the evil of **i.** 9572
2Ki 9:22 "as long as all the i and witchcraft 2393
Eze 14: 4 in keeping with his great **i.** 1658
23:49 and bear the consequences of your sins of **i.** 1658
1Co 10:14 Therefore, my dear friends, flee from **i.** *1630*
Gal 5:20 **i** and witchcraft; hatred, *1630*
Col 3: 5 lust, evil desires and greed, which is **i.** *1630*
1Pe 4: 3 orgies, carousing and detestable **i.** *1630*

IDOLS (173) [IDOL]
Ex 34:17 "Do not make **cast i.** 466
Lev 17: 7 offer any of their sacrifices to the **goat i** 8539
19: 4 not turn to i or make gods of cast metal 496
26: 1 " 'Do not make i or set up an image or 496
26:30 on the lifeless forms of your **i,** 1658
Nu 33:52 carved images and their cast **i,** 7512
Dt 7: 5 down their Asherah poles and burn their i 7178
12: 3 the i *of* their gods and wipe out their names 7178
29:17 among them their detestable images and i 1658
32:16 and angered him with their **detestable i.** 9359
32:21 and angered me with their **worthless i.** 2039
Jdg 3:19 At the **i** near Gilgal he himself turned back 7178
3:26 He passed by the **i** and escaped to Seirah. 7178
17: 5 and *some* **i** and installed one of his sons 9572
18:30 the Danites set up for themselves the **i,** 7181
18:31 to use the **i** Micah had made, 7181
1Sa 12:21 Do not turn away after **useless i.** 9332
31: 9 to proclaim the news in the temple of their **i** 6773
2Sa 5:21 The Philistines abandoned their **i** there, 6773
1Ki 14: 9 other gods, **i made of metal;** 5011
15:12 and got rid of all the **i** his fathers had made. 1658
16:13 to anger by their **worthless i.** 2039
16:26 to anger by their **worthless i.** 2039
21:26 in the vilest manner by going after **i,** 1658
2Ki 11:18 and **i** to pieces and killed Mattan the priest 7512
17:12 They worshiped **i,** though 1658
17:15 They followed **worthless i** 2039
17:16 and made for themselves two **i cast** in 5011
17:41 they were serving their **i.** 7178
21:11 and has led Judah into sin with his **i.** 1658
21:21 the **i** his father had worshiped, 1658
22:17 **i** their hands have **made,** 5126
23:24 the **i** and all the other detestable things seen 1658
1Ch 10: 9 the news among their **i** and their people. 6773
16:26 For all the gods of the nations are **i,** 496
2Ch 11:15 and for the **goat** and calf **i** he had made. 8539
15: 8 the **detestable i** from the whole land 9199
23:17 the altars and **i** and killed Mattan the priest 7512
24:18 and worshiped Asherah poles and **i.** 6773
28: 2 also made **cast i** for worshiping the Baals. 5011
33:19 and **i** before he humbled himself— 7178
33:22 to all the **i** Manasseh had made. 7178
34: 3 Asherah poles, **carved i** and cast images. 7178
34: 4 the **i** and the images. 7178
34: 7 and the Asherah poles and crushed the **i** 7178
34:33 Josiah removed all the **detestable i** 9359
Ps 31: 6 I hate those who cling to **worthless i;** 2039+8736
78:58 they aroused his jealousy with their **i.** 7178
96: 5 For all the gods of the nations are **i,** 496
97: 7 those who boast in **i**— 496
106:36 They worshiped their **i,** 6773
106:38 whom they sacrificed to the **i** *of* Canaan, 6773
115: 4 But their **i** are silver and gold, 6773
135:15 The **i** *of* the nations are silver and gold, 6773
Isa 2: 8 Their land is full of **i;** 496
2:18 and the **i** will totally disappear. 496
2:20 and bats their **i** *of* silver and idols of gold, 496
2:20 and bats their idols of silver and **i** *of* gold, 496
10:10 As my hand seized the kingdoms of the **i,** 496
10:11 as I dealt with Samaria and her **i?'** " 496
19: 1 The **i** *of* Egypt tremble before him, 496
19: 3 they will consult the **i** and the spirits of 496
30:22 Then you will defile your **i** overlaid 7178
31: 7 in that day every one of you will reject the **i** 496
41:22 "Bring in **[your i]** to tell us what is going NIH
42: 8 to another or my praise to **i.** 7178
42:17 But those who trust in **i,** 7181
44: 9 All who make **i** are nothing, 7181
45:16 All the makers of **i** will be put to shame 7497
45:20 Ignorant are those who carry about **i** 7181
46: 1 their **i** are borne by beasts of burden. 6773
48: 5 so that you could not say, 'My **i** did them; 6777
48:14 Which of **[the i]** has foretold these things? 2157^S
57: 6 **[The i]** among the smooth stones of NIH
57:13 let your collection **[of i]** save you! NIH
Jer 2: 5 They followed **worthless i** 2039
2: 8 following **worthless i.** 3603+4202
2:11 But my people have exchanged their Glory for **worthless i.** 3603+4202
4: 1 "If you put your **detestable i** out 9199
7:30 They have set up their **detestable i** in 9199
8:19 with their **worthless** foreign **i?"** 2039
10: 5 **their i** cannot speak; 2156^S
10: 8 they are taught by **worthless** wooden **i.** 2039
10:14 every goldsmith is shamed by his **i.** 7181
14:22 of the **worthless i** *of* the nations bring rain? 2039
16:18 with their **detestable i."** 9359
16:19 **worthless i** that did them no good. 2039
18:15 they burn incense to **worthless i,** 8736
32:34 They set up their **abominable i** in the house 9199
50: 2 be put to shame and her **i** filled with terror.' 1658
50:38 For it is a land of **i,** 7178
50:38 **i** that will go mad with terror. NIH
51:17 every goldsmith is shamed by his **i.** 7181
51:47 when I will punish the **i** *of* Babylon; 7178
51:52 "when I will punish her **i,** 7178
Eze 5: 9 Because of all your **detestable i,** 9359
6: 4 I will slay your people in front of your **i.** 1658
6: 5 of the Israelites in front of their **i,** 1658
6: 6 your **i** smashed and ruined, 1658
6: 9 which have lusted after their **i.** 1658
6:13 when their people lie slain among their **i** 1658
6:13 fragrant incense to all their **i.** 1658
7:20 to make their detestable **i** and vile images. 7512
8:10 and detestable animals and all the **i** *of* 1658
11:18 remove all its vile images and **detestable i.** 9359
11:21 to their vile images and **detestable i,** 9359
14: 3 these men have set up **i** in their hearts 1658
14: 4 When any Israelite sets up **i** in his heart 1658
14: 5 who have all deserted me for their **i.'** 1658
14: 6 Turn from your **i** and renounce all your 1658
14: 7 from me and sets up **i** in his heart and puts 1658
16:17 and you made for yourself male **i** 7512
16:20 to me and sacrificed them as food to **the i.** 2157^S
16:21 and sacrificed them to **the i.** 2157^S
16:36 and because of all your detestable **i,** 1658

Eze 18: 6 at the mountain shrines or look to the i *of* 1658
18:12 He looks to the i. 1658
18:15 at the mountain shrines or look to the i *of* 1658
20: 7 not defile yourselves with the i *of* Egypt. 1658
20: 8 nor did they forsake the i *of* Egypt. 1658
20:16 For their hearts were devoted to their i. 1658
20:18 or defile yourselves with their i. 1658
20:24 and their eyes [lusted] after their fathers' i. 1658
20:31 to defile yourselves with all your i 1658
20:39 Go and serve your i, every one of you! 1658
20:39 with your gifts and i. 1658
21:21 he will consult his i, 9572
22: 3 and defiles herself by making i, 1658
22: 4 by the i you have made. 1658
23: 7 with all the i *of* everyone she lusted after. 1658
23:30 the nations and defiled yourself with their i. 1658
23:37 They committed adultery with their i; 1658
23:39 to their i, they entered my sanctuary 1658
30:13 " 'I will destroy the i and put an end to 1658
33:25 with the blood still in it and look to your i 1658
36:18 and because they had defiled it with their i. 1658
36:25 and from all your i. 1658
37:23 with their i and vile images or with any 1658
43: 7 by their prostitution and the **lifeless i** 7007
43: 9 and the **lifeless i** *of* their kings, 7007
44:10 after their i must bear the consequences 1658
44:12 the presence of their i and made the house 1658
Hos 4:17 Ephraim is joined to i; leave him alone! 6773
5:11 trampled in judgment, intent on pursuing i. 7417
8: 4 With their silver and gold they make i 6773
10: 6 Israel will be ashamed of its **wooden i**. 6785
13: 2 they make i for themselves 5011
14: 8 what more have I to do with i? 6773
Am 5:26 the pedestal of your i, 7512
Jnh 2: 8 to worthless i forfeit the grace that could 8736
Mic 1: 7 All her i will be broken to pieces; 7178
Na 1:14 I will destroy the carved images and **cast i** 5011
Hab 2:18 he makes i that cannot speak. 496
Zec 10: 2 The i speak deceit, diviners see visions 9572
13: 2 I will banish the names of the i from 6773
Ac 7:43 the i you made to worship. *5596*
15:20 to abstain from food polluted *by* i, *1631*
15:29 to abstain from **food sacrificed to i**, *1628*
17:16 to see that the city was **full of i**. *2977*
21:25 from **food sacrificed to i**, *1628*
Ro 2:22 You who abhor i, do you rob temples? *1631*
1Co 8: 1 Now about **food sacrificed to i**: *1628*
8: 4 So then, about eating food **sacrificed to i**: *1628*
8: 7 to i that when they eat such food they think *1631*
8:10 to eat what *has been* **sacrificed to i**? *1628*
12: 2 and led astray to mute i. *1631*
2Co 6:16 between the temple of God and i? *1631*
1Th 1: 9 They tell how you turned to God from i *1631*
1Jn 5:21 Dear children, keep yourselves from i. *1631*
Rev 2:14 to sin by eating **food sacrificed to i** and *1628*
2:20 and the eating of **food sacrificed to i**. *1628*
9:20 and i of gold, silver, bronze, *1631*
9:20 i that cannot see or hear or walk. *NIG*

IDUMEA (1)

Mk 3: 8 from Judea, Jerusalem, I, and the regions *2628*

IEZER (1) [IEZERITE]

Nu 26:30 through I, the Iezerite clan; 404

IEZERITE (1) [IEZER]

Nu 26:30 through Iezer, the I clan; 405

IF (1784)

Ge 4: 7 I you do what is right, 561
4: 7 But i you do not do what is right, 561
4:15 i anyone kills Cain, he will suffer vengeance NIH
4:24 I Cain is avenged seven times, 3954
8: 8 a dove to see i the water had receded from 2022
11: 6 "I as one people speaking 2176
13: 9 I you go to the left, I'll go to the right; 561
13: 9 i you go to the right, I'll go to the left." 561
13:16 so that i anyone could count the dust, 561
15: 5 **i indeed** you can count them." 561
17:18 "**I only** Ishmael might live under your 4273
18: 3 He said, "I I have found favor in your eyes, 561
18:21 and see i what they have done is as bad as 2022
18:21 I not, I will know." 561
18:24 **What i** there are fifty righteous people in 218
18:26 "I I find fifty righteous people in the city 561
18:28 **what i** the number of 218
18:28 "I I find forty-five there," he said, 561
18:29 "**What i** only forty can be found there?" 218
18:30 **What i** only thirty can be found there?" 218
18:30 "I will not do it i I find thirty there." 561
18:31 **what i** only twenty can be found there?" 218
18:32 **What i** only ten can be found there?" 218
20: 7 But i you do not return her, 561
23: 8 "I you are willing to let me bury my dead, 561
23:13 "Listen to me, i you will. 561
24: 5 "**What i** the woman is unwilling 218
24: 8 I the woman is unwilling to come back 561
24:39 '**What i** the woman will not come back 218
24:41 be released from my oath even i they refuse 561
24:42 God of my master Abraham, i you will, 561
24:43 i a maiden comes out to draw water NIH
24:44 and i she says to me, NIH
24:49 Now i you will show kindness 561
24:49 and i not, tell me, so I may know 561
Ge 27:12 **What i** my father touches me? 218
27:46 I Jacob takes a wife from among 561
28:20 "I God will be with me and will watch 561
30:27 "I I have found favor in your eyes, 561
30:31 "**But i** you will do this one thing for me, 561
30:42 but i the animals were weak, 928
31: 8 I he said, 'The speckled ones will 561+3907
31: 8 and i he said, 'The streaked ones will 561+3907
31:32 But i you find anyone who has your gods, NIH
31:32 and i so, take it." NIH
31:42 I the God of my father, the God of
Abraham and the Fear of Isaac, had **not** 4295
31:50 I you mistreat my daughters or 561
31:50 If you mistreat my daughters or i 561
32: 8 "I Esau comes and attacks one group, 561
33:10 "I I have found favor in your eyes, 561
33:13 I they are driven hard just one day, 2256
34:17 But i you will not agree to be circumcised, 561
34:30 and *i they* **join forces** against me AIT
37:14 "Go and see i all is well with your brothers NIH
37:26 "What will we gain i we kill our brother 3954
38:25 *"See i you* **recognize** whose seal and cord AIT
42:16 be tested to see i you are telling the truth. 2022
42:16 I you are not, 561
42:19 I you are honest men, 561
42:37 to death i I do not bring him back to you. 561
42:38 I harm comes to him on 2256
43: 4 I you will send our brother along with us, 561
43: 5 But i you will not send him, 561
43: 9 I I do not bring him back to you 561
43:10 As it is, i we had **not** delayed, 3954+4295
43:11 "I it must be, then do this: 561
43:14 i I am bereaved, I am bereaved." 889+3869
44: 9 I any of your servants is found to have it, NIH
44:22 i he leaves him, his father will die.' 2256
44:26 **Only i** our youngest brother is 561
44:29 I you take this one from me too 2256
44:30 i the boy is not with us when I go back 2256
44:30 to your servant my father and i my father, NIH
44:32 I said, 'I I do not bring him back to you, 561
44:34 How can I go back to my father i the boy is 2256
47: 6 And i you know of any among them 561
47:29 "I I have found favor in your eyes, 561
50: 4 "I I have found favor in your eyes, 561
50:15 "**What i** Joseph holds a grudge against us 4273
Ex 1:10 i war breaks out, will join our enemies, 3954
1:16 i it is a boy, kill him; 561
1:16 but i it is a girl, let her live." 561
4: 1 "**What i** they do not believe me or listen 2176
4: 8 "I they do not believe you or pay attention 561
4: 9 But i they do not believe these two signs 561
4:16 and it will be **as i** he were your mouth and 4200
4:16 be as if he were your mouth and **as i** 4200
4:18 to my own people in Egypt to see i any 2022
6:12 "I the Israelites will not listen to me, 2176
8: 2 I you refuse to let them go, 561
8:21 I you do not let my people go, 561+3954
8:26 And i we offer sacrifices that are detestable 2176
9: 2 I you refuse to let them go and continue 561+3954
10: 4 I you refuse to let them go, 561+3954
10:10 i I let you go, along with your women 889+3869
12: 4 I any household is too small for a whole 561
12:10 i some is left till morning, you must burn it. 2256
13:13 but i you do not redeem it, break its neck. 561
13:17 For God said, "I they face war, 928
15:26 "I you listen carefully to the voice of 561
15:26 i you pay attention to his commands 2256
16: 3 "**I only** we had died by the LORD's hand 4769+5989
18:23 I you do this and God so commands, 561
19: 5 Now i you obey me fully 561
20:25 I you make an altar of stones for me, 561
20:25 for you will defile it i you use a tool on it. NIH
21: 2 "I you buy a Hebrew servant, 3954
21: 3 I he comes alone, he is to go free alone; 561
21: 3 **but i** he has a wife when he comes, 561
21: 4 I his master gives him a wife 561
21: 5 "But i the servant declares, 561
21: 7 "I a man sells his daughter as a servant, 3954
21: 8 I she does not please 561
21: 9 I he selects her for his son, 561
21:10 I he marries another woman, 561
21:11 I he does not provide her with these three 561
21:13 However, i he does not do it intentionally, NIH
21:14 But i a man schemes and kills another 3954
21:18 "I men quarrel and one hits the other with 3954
21:19 not be held responsible i the other gets up 561
21:20 "I a man beats his male or female slave 3954
21:21 but he is not to be punished i the slave gets 561
21:22 "I men who are fighting hit a pregnant 3954
21:23 But i there is serious injury, 561
21:26 "I a man hits a manservant or maidservant 3954
21:27 And i he knocks out the tooth of 561
21:28 "I a bull gores a man or a woman to death, 3954
21:29 I, however, the bull has had the habit 561
21:30 However, i payment is demanded of him, 561
21:31 This law also applies i the bull gores a son 196
21:32 I the bull gores a male or female slave, 561
21:33 "I a man uncovers a pit or digs one 3954
21:35 "I a man's bull injures the bull of another 3954
21:36 i it was known that the bull had the habit 196
22: 1 "I a man steals an ox or a sheep 3954
22: 2 "I a thief is caught breaking in and is struck 561
22: 3 **but i** it happens after sunrise, 561
22: 3 **but i** he has nothing, 561
22: 4 "I the stolen animal is found alive 561
22: 5 "I a man grazes his livestock in a field 3954
Ex 22: 6 "I a fire breaks out and spreads 3954
22: 7 "I a man gives his neighbor silver or goods 3954
22: 7 i he is caught, must pay back double. 561
22: 8 **But i** the thief is not found, 561
22:10 "I a man gives a donkey, an ox, 3954
22:12 i the animal was stolen from the neighbor, 561
22:13 I it was torn to pieces by a wild animal, 561
22:14 "I a man borrows an animal 3954
22:15 **But i** the owner is with the animal, 561
22:15 I the animal was hired, 561
22:16 "I a man seduces a virgin who is not 3954
22:17 I her father absolutely refuses to give her 561
22:23 I you do and they cry out to me, 561
22:25 "I you lend money to one of my people 561
22:26 I you take your neighbor's cloak as 561
23: 4 "I you come across your enemy's ox 3954
23: 5 I you see the donkey of someone 3954
23:22 I you listen carefully to what he says 561+3954
29:34 And i any of the meat of the ordination ram 561
32:32 but i not, then blot me out of the book 561
33: 5 *I I were to* **go** with you even for a moment AIT
33:13 I you are pleased with me, 561
33:15 "I your Presence does not go with us, 561
34: 9 i I have found favor in your eyes," he said, 561
34:20 but i you do not redeem it, break its neck. 561
40:37 but i the cloud did not lift, they did 561
Lev 1: 3 " 'I the offering is a burnt offering from 561
1:10 " 'I the offering is a burnt offering from 561
1:14 " 'I the offering to the LORD is 561
2: 4 " 'I you bring a grain offering baked in 3954
2: 5 I your grain offering is prepared on 561
2: 7 I your grain offering is cooked in a pan, 561
2:14 " 'I you bring a grain offering of firstfruits 561
3: 1 " 'I someone's offering is a fellowship 561
3: 6 " 'I he offers an animal from the flock as 561
3: 7 I he offers a lamb, 561
3:12 " 'I his offering is a goat, 561
4: 3 " 'I the anointed priest sins, 561
4:13 " 'I the whole Israelite community sins
unintentionally 561
4:27 " 'I a member of the community sins
unintentionally 561
4:32 " 'I he brings a lamb as his sin offering, 561
5: 1 " 'I a person sins because he does 3954
5: 2 " 'Or i a person touches anything
ceremonially unclean— 889
5: 3 " 'Or i he touches human uncleanness— 3954
5: 4 " 'Or i a person thoughtlessly takes an oath 3954
5: 7 " 'I he cannot afford a lamb, 561
5:11 " 'I, however, he cannot afford two doves 561
5:17 "I a person sins and does what is forbidden 561
6: 2 "I anyone sins and is unfaithful to 3954
6: 2 or i he cheats him, NIH
6: 3 or i he finds lost property and lies about it, NIH
6: 3 or i he swears falsely, NIH
6: 3 or i he commits any such sin NIH
6:27 and i any of the blood is spattered on 889
6:28 but i it is cooked in a bronze pot, 561
7:12 " 'I he offers it as an expression 561
7:16 " 'I, however, his offering is the result of 561
7:18 I any meat of the fellowship offering 561
7:20 But I anyone who is unclean eats any meat NIH
7:21 I anyone touches something unclean— 3954
7:27 I anyone eats blood, NIH
10:19 i I had eaten the sin offering today?" 2256
11:33 I one of them falls into a clay pot, 2256
11:37 I a carcass falls on any seeds that are to 3954
11:38 But i water has been put on the seed and 3954
11:39 " 'I an animal that you are allowed 3954
12: 5 I she gives birth to a daughter, 561
12: 8 I she cannot afford a lamb, 561
13: 3 and i the hair in the sore has turned white NIH
13: 4 I the spot on his skin is white but does 561
13: 5 and i he sees that the sore is unchanged 2180
13: 6 and i the sore has faded and has not spread 2180
13: 7 But i the rash does spread in his skin 561
13: 8 and i the rash has spread in the skin, 2180
13:10 and i there is a white swelling in the skin 2180
13:10 the skin that has turned the hair white and i NIH
13:12 "I the disease breaks out all over his skin 561
13:13 i the disease has covered his whole body, 2180
13:17 and i the sores have turned white, 2180
13:20 and i it appears to be more than skin deep 2180
13:21 But i, when the priest examines it, 561
13:22 I it is spreading in the skin, 561
13:23 i the spot is unchanged and has not spread, 561
13:25 and i the hair in it has turned white, 2180
13:26 But i the priest examines it 561
13:26 the spot and i it is not more than skin deep NIH
13:27 and i it is spreading in the skin, 561
13:28 I, however, the spot is unchanged and has 561
13:29 "I a man or woman has a sore on the head 3954
13:30 and i it appears to be more than skin deep 2180
13:31 But i, when the priest examines this kind NIH
13:32 and i the itch has not spread 2180
13:34 and i it has not spread in the skin 2180
13:35 But i the itch does spread in the skin 561
13:36 and i the itch has spread in the skin, 2180
13:37 I, however, in his judgment it is unchanged 561
13:39 and i the spots are dull white, 2180
13:41 I he has lost his hair from the front 561
13:42 But i he has a reddish-white sore 3954
13:43 and i the swollen sore on his head 2180
13:47 "I any clothing is contaminated 3954
13:49 and i the contamination in the clothing, NIH
13:51 and i the mildew has spread in the clothing, 3954
13:53 "But i, when the priest examines it, 561

Lev 13:55 and **i** the mildew has not changed 2180
13:56 **I**, when the priest examines it, 561
13:57 But **i** it reappears in the clothing, 561
14: 3 **I** the person has been healed 2180
14:21 "**I**, however, he is poor 561
14:37 and **i** it has greenish or reddish depressions 2180
14:39 **I** the mildew has spread on the walls, 2180
14:43 "**I** the mildew reappears in the house after 561
14:44 **i** the mildew has spread in the house, 2180
14:48 "But **i** the priest comes to examine it and 561
15: 8 " '**I** the man with the discharge spits 3954
15:24 " '**I** a man lies with her 561
17:16 But **i** he does not wash his clothes 561
18:28 And **i** you defile the land, 928
19: 7 **I** any of it is eaten on the third day, 561
19:20 " '**I** a man sleeps with a woman who is 3954
20: 4 **I** the people of the community close their 561
20: 9 " '**I** anyone curses his father or mother, 3954
20:10 " '**I** a man commits adultery 2256
20:11 " '**I** a man sleeps with his father's wife, 2256
20:12 " '**I** a man sleeps with his daughter-in-law, 2256
20:13 " '**I** a man lies with a man as one lies with 2256
20:14 " '**I** a man marries both a woman 2256
20:15 " '**I** a man has sexual relations with 2256
20:16 " '**I** a woman approaches an animal 2256
20:17 " '**I** a man marries his sister, 2256
20:18 " '**I** a man lies with a woman 2256
20:20 " '**I** a man sleeps with his aunt, 2256
20:21 " '**I** a man marries his brother's wife, 2256
21: 9 " '**I** a priest's daughter defiles herself 3954
22: 3 'For the generations to come, **i** any 889
22: 4 " '**I** a descendant of Aaron has NIH
22: 4 be unclean **i** he touches something defiled NIH
22: 5 or **i** he touches any crawling thing NIH
22:11 But **i** a priest buys a slave with money, 3954
22:11 or **i** a slave is born in his household, NIH
22:12 **I** a priest's daughter marries anyone other than a priest, 3954
22:13 But **i** a priest's daughter becomes a widow 3954
22:14 " '**I** anyone eats a sacred offering 3954
22:18 '**I** any of you—either a Israelite or an alien 889
24:15 '**I** anyone curses his God, 3954
24:17 " '**I** anyone takes the life of a human being, 3954
24:19 **I** anyone injures his neighbor, 3954
25:14 " '**I** you sell land to one of your countrymen 3954
25:20 "What will we eat in the seventh year **i** 2176
25:25 " '**I** one of your countrymen becomes poor 3954
25:26 **I**, however, a man has no one to redeem it 3954
25:28 But **i** he does not acquire the means 561
25:29 " '**I** a man sells a house in a walled city, 3954
25:30 **I** it is not redeemed before a full year 561
25:35 " '**I** one of your countrymen becomes poor 3954
25:39 " '**I** one of your countrymen becomes poor 3954
25:47 " '**I** an alien or a temporary resident 3954
25:49 Or **i** he prospers, he may redeem himself. NIH
25:51 **I** many years remain, 561
25:52 **I** only a few years remain until the Year 561
25:54 **i** he is not redeemed in any of these ways, 561
26: 3 " '**I** you follow my decrees and are careful 561
26:14 " 'But **i** you will not listen to me 561
26:15 and **i** you reject my decrees 561
26:18 " '**I** after all this you will not listen to me, 561
26:21 " '**I** you remain hostile toward me 561
26:23 " '**I** in spite of these things you do 561
26:27 " '**I** in spite of this you still do not listen 561
26:40 " 'But **i** they will confess their sins and NIH
27: 2 '**I** anyone makes a special vow 3954
27: 4 and **i** it is a female, 561
27: 5 **I** it is a person between the ages of five 561
27: 6 **I** it is a person between one month 561
27: 7 **I** it is a person sixty years old or more, 561
27: 8 **I** anyone making the vow is too poor to pay 561
27: 9 " '**I** what he vowed is an animal 561
27:10 **i** he should substitute one animal 561
27:11 **I** what he vowed is 561
27:13 **I** the owner wishes to redeem the animal, 561
27:14 " '**I** a man dedicates his house 3954
27:15 **I** the man who dedicates his house redeems 561
27:16 " '**I** a man dedicates to the LORD part 561
27:17 **I** he dedicates his field during the Year 561
27:18 But **i** he dedicates his field after the Jubilee, 561
27:19 **I** the man who dedicates the field wishes 561
27:20 **I**, however, he does not redeem the field, 561
27:20 or **i** he has sold it to someone else, 561
27:22 " '**I** a man dedicates to the LORD 561
27:27 **I** it is one of the unclean animals, 561
27:27 **I** he does not redeem it, 561
27:31 **I** a man redeems any of his tithe, 561
27:33 **I** he does make a substitution, 561
Nu 5: 8 But **i** that person has no close relative 561
5:12 '**I** a man's wife goes astray 3954
5:14 and **i** feelings of jealousy come NIH
5:14 or **i** he is jealous and suspects her even NIH
5:19 "**I** no other man has slept with you 561
5:20 But **i** you have gone astray while married 3954
5:27 **I** she has defiled herself 561
5:28 **I**, however, the woman has 561
6: 2 '**I** a man or woman wants to make 3954
6: 7 **Even i** his own father or mother or brother 928
6: 9 " '**I** someone dies suddenly in his presence, 3954
9:13 But **i** a man who is ceremonially clean and NIH
10: 4 **I** only one is sounded, the leaders— 561
10:32 **I** you come with us, 3954
11: 4 "**I only** we had meat to eat! 4769
11:15 **I** this is how you are going to treat me, 561
11:15 **i** I have found favor in your eyes— 561
11:18 "**I only** we had meat to eat! 4769
Nu 11:22 Would they have enough **i** flocks 2022
11:22 Would they have enough **i** all the fish in 561
12:14 "**I** her father had spit in her face, 2256
14: 2 "**I only** we had died in Egypt! 4273
14: 8 **I** the LORD is pleased with us, 561
14:15 **I** you put these people to death all 2256
15:22 " 'Now **i** you unintentionally fail 3954
15:24 and **i** this is done unintentionally without 561
15:27 **i** just one person sins unintentionally, 561
16:29 **I** these men die a natural death 561
16:30 But **i** the LORD brings about something 561
19:12 But **i** he does not purify himself on 561
19:20 But **i** a person who is unclean does 2256
20: 3 "**I only** we had died 4273
20:18 **i** you try, we will march out and attack you 7153
20:19 "We will go along the main road, and **i** we 561
21: 2 "**I** you will deliver these people 561
22:18 "**Even i** Balak gave me his palace filled 561
22:29 **I** I had a sword in my hand, 4273
22:33 **I** she had **not** turned away, 218
22:34 Now **i** you are displeased, I will go back." 561
24:13 '**Even i** Balak gave me his palace filled 561
27: 8 '**I** a man dies and leaves no son, 3954
27: 9 **I** he has no daughter, 561
27:10 **I** he has no brothers, 561
27:11 **I** his father had no brothers, 561
30: 5 But **i** her father forbids her when he hears 561
30: 6 "**I** she marries after she makes a vow or 561
30: 8 But **i** her husband forbids her 561
30:10 "**I** a woman living with her husband makes 561
30:12 But **i** her husband nullifies them 561
30:14 But **i** her husband says nothing to her 561
30:15 **I**, however, he nullifies them some time 561
32: 5 **I** we have found favor in your eyes," 561
32:15 **I** you turn away from following him, 3954
32:20 Moses said to them, "**I** you will do this— 561
32:20 **i** you will arm yourselves before 561
32:21 and **i** all of you will go armed over NIH
32:23 "But **i** you fail to do this, 561
32:29 "**I** the Gadites and Reubenites, 561
32:30 **i** they do not cross over with you armed, 561
33:55 " 'But **i** you do not drive out the inhabitants 561
35:16 " '**I** a man strikes someone with 561
35:17 Or **i** anyone has a stone in his hand 561
35:18 Or **i** anyone has a wooden object NIH
35:20 **I** anyone with malice aforethought shoves 561
35:21 or **i** in hostility he hits him with his fist so NIH
35:22 " 'But **i** without hostility 561
35:26 " 'But **i** the accused ever goes outside 561
Dt 4:25 **i** you **then** become corrupt 2256
4:29 But **i** from there you seek the LORD NIH
4:29 you will find him **i** you look for him 3954
4:42 a person could flee **i** he had unintentionally NIH
5:24 a man can live even **i** God speaks with him. NIH
5:25 and we will die **i** we hear the voice of 561
6:25 And **i** we are careful to obey all this law 3954
7:12 **I** you pay attention to these laws 6813
8:19 **I** you ever forget the LORD your God 561
11:13 So **i** you faithfully obey 561
11:22 **I** you carefully observe all these commands 561
11:27 the blessing **i** you obey the commands of 889
11:28 the curse **i** you disobey the commands of 561
12:15 **as i** it were gazelle or deer, 3869
12:21 **I** the place where the LORD your God 3954
13: 1 **I** a prophet, or one who foretells 3954
13: 2 and **i** the sign or wonder NIH
13: 6 **I** your very own brother, 3954
13:12 **I** you hear it said about one of the towns 3954
13:14 And **i** it is true and it has been proved 2180
14:24 But **i** that place is too distant 3954
15: 5 **i** only you fully obey the LORD your God 561
15: 7 **I** there is a poor man among your brothers 3954
15:12 **I** a fellow Hebrew, a man or a woman, 3954
15:16 But **i** your servant says to you, 3954
15:21 **I** an animal has a defect, is lame or blind, 3954
15:22 **as i** it were gazelle or deer. 3869
17: 2 **I** a man or woman living among you in one 3954
17: 4 **I** it is true and it has been proved 2180
17: 8 **I** cases come before your courts 3954
18: 6 **I** a Levite moves from one of your towns 3954
18:19 **I** anyone does not listen to my words that 889
18:22 **I** what a prophet proclaims in the name of 2256
19: 6 overtake him **i** the distance is too great, 3954
19: 8 **I** the LORD your God enlarges your territory, 561
19:11 But **i** a man hates his neighbor and lies 3954
19:16 **I** a malicious witness takes the stand 3954
19:18 and **i** the witness proves to be a liar, 2180
20:11 **I** they accept and open their gates, 561
20:12 **I** they refuse to make peace 561
21: 1 **I** a man is found slain, 3954
21:11 **i** you notice among the captives 2256
21:14 **I** you are not pleased with her, 561
21:15 **I** a man has two wives, 3954
21:18 **I** a man has a stubborn and rebellious son 3954
21:22 **I** a man guilty of a capital offense is put 3954
22: 1 **I** you see your brother's ox NIH
22: 2 **I** the brother does not live near you or 561
22: 2 near you or **i** you do not know who he is, NIH
22: 3 the same **i** you find your brother's donkey NIH
22: 4 **I** you see your brother's donkey NIH
22: 6 **I** you come across a bird's nest beside 3954
22: 8 of bloodshed on your house **i** someone falls 3954
22: 9 **i** you do, not only the crops you plant but 7153
22:13 **I** a man takes a wife and, after lying with 3954
22:20 **I**, however, the charge is true and no proof 561
22:22 **I** a man is found sleeping with another 3954
22:23 **I** a man happens to meet in a town 3954
Dt 22:25 But **i** out in the country a man happens 561
22:28 **I** a man happens to meet a virgin who is 3954
23:10 **I** one of your men is unclean because of 3954
23:15 **I** a slave has taken refuge with you, 889
23:21 **I** you make a vow to the LORD your God, 3954
23:22 But **i** you refrain from making a vow, 3954
23:24 **I** you enter your neighbor's vineyard, 3954
23:25 **I** you enter your neighbor's grainfield, 3954
24: 1 **I** a man marries a woman who becomes 3954
24: 2 **i** after she leaves his house she becomes the wife of another NIH
24: 3 sends her from his house, or **i** he dies, 3954
24: 5 **I** a man has recently married, 3954
24: 7 **I** a man is caught kidnapping one 3954
24:12 **I** the man is poor, 561
25: 2 **I** the guilty man deserves to be beaten, 561
25: 3 **I** he is flogged more than that, 7153
25: 5 **I** brothers are living together and one 3954
25: 7 **i** a man does not want to marry his brother's 561
25: 8 **I** he persists in saying, 2256
25:11 **I** two men are fighting and the wife of one 3954
28: 1 **I** you fully obey the LORD your God 561
28: 2 upon you and accompany you **i** you obey 3954
28: 9 **i** you keep the commands of 3954
28:13 **I** you pay attention to the commands of 3954
28:15 **i** you do not obey the LORD your God 561
28:58 **I** you do not carefully follow all the words 561
28:67 "**I only** it were evening!" 4769+5989
28:67 "**I only** it were morning!"— 4769+5989
30: 4 **Even i** you have been banished to 561
30:10 **i** you obey the LORD your God 3954
30:17 But **i** your heart turns away and you are 561
30:17 and **i** you are drawn away to bow down NIH
31:27 **I** you have been rebellious against 2176
32:29 **I only** they were wise and would understand 4273
Jos 2:14 "**I** you don't tell what we are doing, 561
2:19 **I** anyone goes outside your house into 889
2:19 be on our head **i** a hand is laid on him. 561
2:20 But **i** you tell what we are doing, 561
7: 7 **I only** we had been content to stay on 4273
17:15 "**I** you are so numerous," Joshua answered, 561
17:15 "and **i** the hill country of Ephraim is too 3954
20: 5 **I** the avenger of blood pursues him, 3954
22:18 " '**I** you rebel against the LORD today, 2256
22:19 **I** the land you possess is defiled, 561
22:22 **I** this has been in rebellion or disobedience 561
22:23 **I** we have built our own altar to turn away 561
22:28 "And we said, '**I** they ever say this to us, 3954
23:12 "But **i** you turn away and ally yourselves 561
23:12 among you and **i** you intermarry with them NIH
23:16 **I** you violate the covenant of the LORD 928
24:15 But **i** serving the LORD seems undesirable 561
24:20 **I** you forsake the LORD and serve foreign 3954
24:27 against you **i** you are untrue to your God." 7153
Jdg 4: 8 Barak said to her, "**I** you go with me, 561
4: 8 but **i** you don't go with me, I won't go." 561
4:20 "**I** someone comes by and asks you, 561
6:13 Gideon replied, "**i** the LORD is with us, 2256
6:17 "**I** now I have found favor in your eyes, 561
6:31 **I** Baal really is a god, 561
6:36 "**I** you will save Israel by my hand 561
6:37 **I** there is dew only on the fleece and all 561
7: 4 **I** I say, 'This one shall go with you,' 889
7: 4 but **i** I say, 'This one shall not go with you,' 889
7:10 **I** you are afraid to attack, 561
8:19 LORD lives, **i** you had spared their lives, 4273
9:15 '**I** you really want to anoint me king 561
9:15 but **i** not, then let fire come out of 561
9:16 "Now **i** you have acted honorably and 561
9:16 and **i** you have been fair to Jerub-Baal 561
9:16 **i** you have treated him as he deserves— 561
9:19 **i** then you have acted honorably and 561
9:20 But **i** you have not, let fire come out 561
9:29 **I only** this people were under my 4769+5989
11:30 "**I** you give the Ammonites into my hands, 561
12: 5 "Are you an Ephraimite?" **I** he replied, 2256
12: 6 **I** he said, "Sibboleth," 2256
13:16 But **i** you prepare a burnt offering, 561
13:23 "**I** the LORD had meant to kill us, 4273
14:12 "**I** you can give me the answer within 561
14:13 **I** you can't tell me the answer, 561
14:18 "**I** you had **not** plowed with my heifer, 4295
16: 5 *"See i you can* **lure** him into showing AIT
16: 7 "**I** anyone ties me with seven fresh thongs 561
16:11 "**I** anyone ties me securely with new ropes 561
16:12 But he snapped the ropes off his arms **as i** 3869
16:13 "**I** you weave the seven braids of my head 561
16:17 **I** my head were shaved, 561
Ru 1:12 **Even i** I thought there was still hope 3954
1:12 even **i** I had a husband tonight and NIH
1:17 **i anything but** death separates you 3954
2:15 "**Even i** she gathers among the sheaves, 1685
3:13 and in the morning **i** he wants to redeem, 561
3:13 But **i** he is not willing, 561
4: 4 **I** you will redeem it, do so. 561
4: 4 But **i** you will not, tell me, so I will know. 561
1Sa 1:11 **i** you will only look upon your servant's 561
2:16 **I** the man said to him, 2256
2:16 **i** you don't, I'll take it by force." 561
2:25 **I** a man sins against another man, 561
2:25 but **i** a man sins against the LORD, 561
3: 9 "Go and lie down, and **i** he calls you, say, 561
3:17 **i** you hide from me anything he told you." 561
6: 3 "**I** you return the ark of the god of Israel, 561
6: 9 **I** it goes up to its own territory, 561
6: 9 But **i** it does not, then we will know that 561
7: 3 "**I** you are returning to the LORD 561

1Sa 9: 7 Saul said to his servant, "I we go, 2180
9: 9 i a man went to inquire of God, 928
9:20 i not to you and all your father's family?" 2022
11: 3 i no one comes to rescue us, 561
12: 3 I I have done any of these, NIH
12:14 I you fear the LORD and serve 561
12:14 and i both you and the king who reigns NIH
12:15 But i you do not obey the LORD, 561
12:15 and i you rebel against his commands, NIH
12:25 Yet i you persist in doing evil, 561
13:13 not kept the command the LORD your God gave you; i you had, 3954
14: 9 I they say to us, 'Wait there 561
14:10 But i they say, 'Come up to us,' 561
14:30 How much better it would have been i 4273
14:39 even i it lies with my son Jonathan, 561
14:44 be it ever so severely, i you do not die, 3954
17: 9 I he is able to fight and kill me, 561
17: 9 but i I overcome him and kill him, 561
19:11 "I you don't run for your life tonight, 561
20: 6 I your father misses me at all, tell him, 561
20: 7 I he says, 'Very well,' 561
20: 7 But i he loses his temper, 561
20: 8 I I am guilty, then kill me yourself! 561
20: 9 "I I had the least inkling 561+3954
20:10 "Who will tell me i your father answers 196+4537
20:12 I he is favorably disposed toward you, 2180
20:13 But i my father is inclined to harm you, 3954
20:13 i I do not let you know 2256
20:21 I I say to him, 'Look, 561
20:22 But i I say to the boy, 'Look, 561
20:29 I I have found favor in your eyes, 561
21: 9 I you want it, take it; 561
23: 3 i we go to Keilah against the Philistine 3954
23:23 Then I will go with you; i he is in the area, 561
25:22 i by morning I leave alive one male 561
25:34 i you had not come quickly to meet 3954+4295
26:19 I the LORD has incited you against me, 561
26:19 I, however, men have done it, 561
27: 5 "I I have found favor in your eyes, 561
2Sa 2:27 i you had not spoken, 3954+4295
3: 9 i I do not do for David what 3954
3:35 i I taste bread or anything else 561+3954
4: 6 of the house as i to get some wheat, NIH
7:19 And as i this were not enough in your sight, NIH
10:11 "I the Arameans are too strong for me, 561
10:11 but i the Ammonites are too strong for you, 561
11:21 I he asks you this, then say to him, 'Also, NIH
12: 8 And i all this had been too little, 561
13:26 Then Absalom said, "I not, 2256
14:10 "I anyone says anything to you, NIH
14:32 be better for me i I were still there!" ' NIH
14:32 and i I am guilty of anything, 561
15: 4 "I only I were appointed judge in 4769
15: 8 'I the LORD takes me back to Jerusalem, 561
15:25 I I find favor in the LORD's eyes, 561
15:26 But i he says, 'I am not pleased with you,' 561
15:33 David said to him, "I you go with me, 561
15:34 i you return to the city and say to Absalom, 561
16:10 I he is cursing because the LORD said 3954
17: 6 I not, give us your opinion." 561
17: 9 I he should attack your troops first, 3869
17:13 I he withdraws into a city, 561
18: 3 i we are forced to flee, 561+3954
18: 3 Even i half of us die, they won't care; 561
18:12 But the man replied, "Even i 4273
18:13 And i I had put my life in jeopardy— 196
18:25 The king said, "I he is alone, 561
18:33 I only I had died instead of you— 4769+5989
19: 6 be pleased i Absalom were alive today 4273
19: 7 by the LORD that i you don't go out, 3954
19:13 i from now on you are not the commander 561
1Ki 1:52 "I he shows himself to be a worthy man, 561
1:52 but i evil is found in him, he will die." 561
2: 4 'I your descendants watch how they live, 561
2: 4 how they live, and i they walk faithfully NIH
2: 5 shedding their blood in peacetime *as i* AIT
2:23 be it ever so severely, i Adonijah does not 3954
3:14 And i you walk in my ways 561
6:12 i you follow my decrees, 561
8:25 i only your sons are careful in all they do 561
8:47 and i they have a change of heart in NIH
8:48 and i they turn back to you NIH
9: 4 i you walk before me in integrity of heart 561
9: 6 "But i you or your sons turn away from me 561
11:38 I you do whatever I command you 561
12: 7 "I today you will be a servant 561
12:27 I these people go up to offer sacrifices at 561
13: 8 "Even i you were to give me half 561
18:12 I I go and tell Ahab 2256
18:21 I the LORD is God, follow him; 561
18:21 but i Baal is God, follow him." 561
19: 2 i by this time tomorrow I do not make your 3954
20:10 i enough dust remains in Samaria 561
20:18 He said, "I they have come out for peace, 561
20:18 i they have come out for war, 561
20:23 But i we fight them on the plains, 219
20:39 I he is missing, it will be your life 561
21: 2 or, i you prefer, I will pay you 561
21: 6 or i you prefer, I will give you another 561
22:28 Micaiah declared, "I you ever return safely, 561
2Ki 1: 2 to see i I will recover from this injury." 561
1:10 "I I am a man of God, 561
1:12 "I I am a man of God," Elijah replied, 561
2:10 "yet i you see me when I am taken 561
3:14 i I did not have respect for the 3954+4295
4:29 I you meet anyone, do not greet him, 3954
2Ki 4:29 do not greet him, and i anyone greets you, 3954
5: 3 "I only my master would see 332
5:13 i the prophet had told you to do some 2022
5:17 "I you will not," said Naaman, 2256
6:27 "I the LORD does not help you, NIH
6:31 i the head of Elisha son of Shaphat remains 561
7: 2 *i* the LORD *should* open the floodgates AIT
7: 4 I we say, 'We'll go into the city'— 561
7: 4 And i we stay here, we will die. 561
7: 4 I they spare us, we live; 561
7: 4 i they kill us, then we die." 561
7: 9 I we wait until daylight, 2256
7:19 *i* the LORD *should* open the floodgates AIT
9:15 Jehu said, "I this is the way you feel, 561
10: 4 "I two kings could not resist him, 2180
10: 6 "I you are on my side and will obey me, 561
10:15 "I so," said Jehu, "give me your hand." 2256
10:24 "I one of you lets any of the men NIH
18:21 a man's hand and wounds him i he leans 889
18:22 And i you say to me, 3954
18:23 i you can put riders on them! 561
21: 8 i only they will be careful 561
1Ch 12:17 "I you have come to me in peace, 561
12:17 But i you have come to betray me 561
12:19 "It will cost us our heads *i he* deserts AIT
13: 2 "I it seems good to you and if it is the will 561
13: 2 "If it seems good to you and i it is the will NIH
17:17 And as i this were not enough in your sight, NIH
19:12 "I the Arameans are too strong for me, 561
19:12 but i the Ammonites are too strong for you, 561
22:13 Then you will have success i you are careful 561
28: 7 I will establish his kingdom forever i he is 561
28: 9 I you seek him, he will be found by you; 561
28: 9 but i you forsake him, 561
2Ch 6:16 i only your sons are careful in all they do 561
6:37 and i they have a change of heart in NIH
6:38 and i they turn back to you NIH
7:14 i my people, who are called by my name, 2256
7:17 i you walk before me 561
7:19 "But i you turn away and forsake 561
10: 7 "I you will be kind to these people 561
15: 2 I you seek him, he will be found by you, 561
15: 2 but i you forsake him, he will forsake you. 561
18:27 Micaiah declared, "I you ever return safely, 561
20: 9 'I calamity comes upon us, 561
25: 8 i you go and fight courageously in battle, 561
30: 9 I you return to the LORD, 3954
30: 9 not turn his face from you i you return 561
30:19 even i he is not clean according to the rules 2256
33: 8 i only they will be careful to do 561
Ezr 4:13 the king should know that i this city is built 10213
4:16 We inform the king that i this city is built 10213
5:17 Now i it pleases the king, 10213
5:17 in the royal archives of Babylon to see i 10213
6:11 I decree that i anyone changes this edict, 10168
Ne 1: 8 saying, 'I you are unfaithful, NIH
1: 9 i you return to me and obey my commands, NIH
1: 9 then even i your exiled people are at 561
2: 5 "I it pleases the king and 561
2: 5 the king and i your servant has found favor 561
2: 7 I also said to him, "I it pleases the king, 561
4: 3 i even a fox climbed up on it, 561
9:29 by which a man will live i he obeys them. 2256
13:21 I you do this again, 561
Est 1:19 "Therefore, i it pleases the king, 561
3: 9 I it pleases the king, 561
4:14 For i you remain silent at this time, 561
4:16 And i I perish, I perish." 889+3869
5: 4 "I it pleases the king," replied Esther, 561
5: 8 I the king regards me with favor and 561
5: 8 and i it pleases the king to grant 561
7: 3 "I I have found favor with you, O king, 561
7: 3 O king, and i it pleases your majesty, 561
7: 4 I we had merely been sold as male 467
8: 5 "I it pleases the king," she said, 561
8: 5 "and i he regards me with favor 561
8: 5 and i he is pleased with me, NIH
9:13 "I it pleases the king," Esther answered, 561
Job 4: 2 "I someone ventures a word with you, 2022
4:18 I God places no trust in his servants, 2176
4:18 i he charges his angels with error, NIH
5: 1 "Call i you will, 5528
5: 8 "But i it were I, I would appeal to God; 219
6: 2 "I only my anguish could be weighed 4273
7:20 I I have sinned, what have I done to you, NIH
8: 5 But i you will look to God and plead with 561
8: 6 i you are pure and upright, 561
9:12 I he snatches away, who can stop him? 2176
9:16 Even i I summoned him and he responded, 561
9:19 I it is a matter of strength, he is mighty! 561
9:19 And i it is a matter of justice, 561
9:20 Even i I were innocent, 561
9:20 i I were blameless, NIH
9:24 I it is not he, then who is it? 561
9:27 I I say, 'I will forget my complaint, 561
9:30 Even i I washed myself with soap 561
9:33 I only there were someone to arbitrate 4273
10:14 I I sinned, you would be watching me 561
10:15 I I am guilty—woe to me! 561
10:15 Even i I am innocent, I cannot lift my head, 2256
10:16 I I hold my head high, 2256
10:19 I only I had never come into being, 889+3869
11:10 "I he comes along and confines you 561
11:13 "Yet i you devote your heart to him 561
11:14 i you put away the sin that is in your hand 561
12:15 I he holds back the waters, there is drought; 2176
12:15 i he lets them loose, 2256
Job 13: 5 I only you would be altogether silent! 4769+5989
13: 9 Would it turn out well i he examined you? 3954
13:10 rebuke you i you secretly showed partiality. 561
13:19 I so, I will be silent and die. 3954+6964
14: 7 I it is cut down, it will sprout again, 561
14:13 I only you would hide me in the grave 4769+5989
14:13 I only you would set me a time and NIH
14:14 I a man dies, will he live again? 561
14:21 I his sons are honored, he does not know it; NIH
14:21 i they are brought low, he does not see it. 2256
15:15 I God places no trust in his holy ones, 2176
15:15 i even the heavens are not pure in his eyes, NIH
16: 4 i you were in my place; 4273
16: 6 "Yet i I speak, my pain is not relieved; 561
16: 6 and i I refrain, it does not go away. NIH
17: 5 I a man denounces his friends for reward, NIH
17:13 I the only home I hope for is the grave, 561
17:13 i I spread out my bed in darkness, NIH
17:14 i I say to corruption, NIH
19: 4 I it is true that I have gone astray, 677
19: 5 I indeed you would exalt yourselves 561
19:28 "I you say, 'How we will hound him, 3954
22: 3 What pleasure would it give the Almighty i 3954
22: 3 What would he gain i your ways were 3954
22:23 I you return to the Almighty, 561
22:23 I you remove wickedness far NIH
23: 3 I only I knew where to find him; 4769+5989
23: 3 i only I could go to his dwelling! NIH
23: 8 "But i I go to the east, he is not there; 2176
23: 8 i I go to the west, I do not find him. 2256
24:25 "I this is not so, 561
25: 5 I even the moon is not bright and 2176
30: 5 shouted at as i they were thieves. 3869
31: 5 "I I have walked in falsehood 561
31: 7 i my steps have turned from the path, 561
31: 7 i my heart has been led by my eyes, 2256
31: 7 or i my hands have been defiled, NIH
31: 9 "I my heart has been enticed by a woman, 561
31: 9 or i I have lurked at my neighbor's door, NIH
31:13 "I I have denied justice to my menservants 561
31:16 "I I have denied the desires of the poor 561
31:17 i I have kept my bread to myself, 2256
31:19 i I have seen anyone perishing for lack 561
31:21 i I have raised my hand against 561
31:24 "I I have put my trust in gold or said 561
31:25 i I have rejoiced over my great wealth, 561
31:26 i I have regarded the sun in its radiance or 561
31:29 "I I have rejoiced at my enemy's misfortune 561
31:31 i the men of my household have never said, 561
31:33 i I have concealed my sin as men do, 561
31:38 "i my land cries out against me 561
31:39 i I have devoured its yield without payment 561
32:22 for i I were skilled in flattery, 4202
33: 5 Answer me then, i you can; 561
33:23 "Yet i there is an angel on his side as 561
33:32 I you have anything to say, answer me; 561
33:33 But i not, then listen to me; 561
34:14 I it were his intention 561
34:16 "I you have understanding, hear this; 561
34:29 i he remains silent, who can condemn him? NIH
34:29 I he hides his face, who can see him? 2256
34:32 I I have done wrong, 561
35: 6 I you sin, how does that affect him? 561
35: 6 I your sins are many, 2256
35: 7 I you are righteous, 561
36: 8 But i men are bound in chains, 561
36:11 I they obey and serve him, 561
36:12 But i they do not listen, 561
38: 4 Tell me, i you understand. 561
38:18 Tell me, i you know all this. 561
39:16 as i they were not hers; 4200
41: 8 I you lay a hand on him, NIH
Ps 7: 3 i I have done this and there is guilt 561
7: 4 i I have done evil to him who is at peace 561
7:12 I he does not relent, 561
14: 2 to see i there are any who understand, 2022
28: 1 For i you remain silent, 7153
37:23 I the LORD delights in a man's way, 2256
44:20 I we had forgotten the name of our God 561
50:12 I I were hungry I would not tell you, 561
53: 2 to see i there are any who understand, 2022
55:12 I an enemy were insulting me, 4273
55:12 i a foe were raising himself against me, 4273
59:15 and howl i not satisfied. 561
62: 9 i weighed on a balance, they are nothing; NIH
66:18 I I had cherished sin in my heart, 561
73:15 I I had said, "I will speak thus," 561
81: 8 i you would but listen to me, O Israel! 561
81:13 "I my people would but listen to me, 4273
81:13 i Israel would follow my ways, NIH
89:30 "I his sons forsake my law and do 561
89:31 i they violate my decrees and fail 561
90:10 or eighty, i we have the strength; 561
91: 9 I you make the Most High your dwelling— 3954
95: 7 Today, i you hear his voice, 561
119:92 I your law had not been my delight, 4295
124: 1 I the LORD had not been on our side— 4295
124: 2 i the LORD had not been on our side 4295
130: 3 I you, O LORD, kept a record of sins, 561
132:12 i your sons keep my covenant and 561
133: 3 It is as i the dew of Hermon were falling 3869
137: 5 I I forget you, O Jerusalem, 561
137: 6 of my mouth i I do not remember you, 561
137: 6 of my mouth if I do not remember you, i 561
139: 8 I I go up to the heavens, you are there; 561
139: 8 i I make my bed in the depths, 2256
139: 9 I I rise on the wings of the dawn, NIH

Ps 139: 9 i I settle on the far side of the sea, NIH
139:11 I I say, "Surely the darkness will hide me 2256
139:19 I only you would slay the wicked, O God! 561
139:24 See i there is any offensive way in me, 561
Pr 1:10 My son, i sinners entice you, 561
1:11 I they say, "Come along with us; 561
1:23 I you had responded to my rebuke, NIH
2: 1 i you accept my words and store 561
2: 3 and i you call out for insight and cry aloud 561
2: 4 and i you look for it as for silver and search 561
6: 1 i you have put up security 561
6: 1 i you have struck hands in pledge NIH
6: 2 i you have been trapped by what you said, NIH
6:30 a thief i he steals to satisfy his hunger 3954
6:31 Yet i he is caught, he must pay sevenfold, NIH
9:12 I you are wise, your wisdom will reward 561
9:12 i you are a mocker, you alone will suffer." 2256
11:31 I the righteous receive their due on earth, 2176
17:13 I a man pays back evil for good, NIH
17:28 a fool is thought wise i he keeps silent, NIH
17:28 and discerning i he holds his tongue. NIH
19:19 i you rescue him, 561+3954
20:16 hold it in pledge i he does it for 2256
20:18 i you wage war, obtain guidance. 2256
20:20 I a man curses his father or mother, NIH
21:13 I a man shuts his ears to the cry of NIH
22:27 i you lack the means to pay, 561
23: 2 to your throat i you are given to gluttony. 561
23:13 i you punish him with the rod, 3954
23:15 My son, i your heart is wise, 561
24:10 I you falter in times of trouble, NIH
24:12 I you say, "But we knew nothing 3954
24:14 i you find it, there is a future hope for you, 561
25: 8 the end i your neighbor puts you to shame? 928
25: 9 I you argue your case with a neighbor, NIH
25:16 I you find honey, eat just enough— NIH
25:21 I your enemy is hungry, 561
25:21 i he is thirsty, give him water to drink. 561
26:27 I a man digs a pit, he will fall into it; NIH
26:27 i a man rolls a stone, NIH
27:13 hold it in pledge i he does it for 2256
27:14 I a man loudly blesses his neighbor early in NIH
28: 9 I anyone turns a deaf ear to the law, NIH
29: 9 I a wise man goes to court with a fool, NIH
29:12 I a ruler listens to lies, NIH
29:14 I a king judges the poor with fairness, NIH
29:21 I a man pampers his servant from youth, NIH
30: 4 Tell me i you know! 3954
30:32 "I you have played the fool 561
30:32 or i you have planned evil, 561
Ecc 3:21 Who knows i the spirit of man rises upward NIH
3:21 and i the spirit of the animal goes down NIH
4:10 I one falls down, 561+3954
4:11 Also, i two lie down together, 561
5: 8 I you see the poor oppressed in a district, 561
6: 3 i he cannot enjoy his prosperity and does 2256
6: 6 even i he lives a thousand years twice over 467
8:17 Even i a wise man claims he knows, 561
10: 4 I a ruler's anger rises against you, 561
10:10 I the ax is dull and its edge unsharpened, 561
10:11 I a snake bites before it is charmed, 561
10:18 I a man is lazy, the rafters sag; 928
10:18 i his hands are idle, the house leaks. 928
11: 3 I clouds are full of water, 561
SS 1: 8 I you do not know, 561
5: 8 i you find my lover, what will you tell him? 561
6:11 to see i the vines had budded or 2022
7:12 Let us go early to the vineyards to see i 561
7:12 i their blossoms have opened, NIH
7:12 and i the pomegranates are in bloom— NIH
8: 1 I only you were to me like a brother, 4769+5989
8: 1 Then, i I found you outside, NIH
8: 7 I one were to give all the wealth 561
8: 9 I she is a wall, we will build towers 561
8: 9 I she is a door, we will enclose her 561
Isa 1:15 i you offer many prayers, I will not listen. 3954
1:19 I you are willing and obedient, 561
1:20 but i you resist and rebel, 561
5:30 And i one looks at the land, NIH
7: 9 I you do not stand firm in your faith, 561
8:20 I they do not speak according to this word, 561
10:15 As i a rod were to wield him who lifts it up, 3869
21:12 I you would ask, then ask; 561
27: 4 I only there were briers 4769+5989
29:11 And i you give the scroll NIH
29:12 Or i you give the scroll NIH
29:16 as i the potter were thought to be like 561
33:12 The peoples will be burned *as i to* lime; AIT
36: 6 a man's hand and wounds him i he leans 889
36: 7 And i you say to me, 3954
36: 8 i you can put riders on them! 561
41:25 He treads on rulers as *i* they were mortar, AIT
41:25 as *i* he were a potter treading the clay. AIT
48:18 I only you had paid attention 4273
54: 6 The LORD will call you back as i 3869
54:15 I anyone does attack you, 2176
58: 2 to know my ways, as i they were a nation 3869
58: 9 "I you do away with the yoke 561
58:10 and i you spend yourselves in behalf of NIH
58:13 "I you keep your feet from breaking 561
58:13 i you call the Sabbath a delight and NIH
58:13 i you honor it by not going your own way NIH
59:10 At midday we stumble as i it were twilight; 3869
Jer 2:10 see i there has ever been anything like this: 2176
2:28 Let them come i they can save you 561
3: 1 "I a man divorces his wife 2176
4: 1 "I you will return, O Israel, return to me," 561

Jer 4: 1 "I you put your detestable idols out 561
4: 2 and i in a truthful, just and righteous way NIH
5: 1 I you can find but one person who deals 561
7: 5 I you really change your ways 561+3954
7: 6 i you do not oppress the alien, NIH
7: 6 and i you do not follow other gods NIH
12: 5 "I you have raced with men on foot 3954
12: 5 I you stumble in safe country, 2256
12:16 And i they learn well the ways 561
12:17 But i any nation does not listen, 561
13:12 And i they say to you, NIH
13:17 But i you do not listen, 561
13:22 And i you ask yourself, 3954
14:18 I I go into the country, 561
14:18 i I go into the city, 561
15: 1 "Even i Moses and Samuel were to stand 561
15: 2 And i they ask you, 'Where shall we go?' 3954
15:19 "I you repent, I will restore you 561
15:19 i you utter worthy, not worthless, words, 561
17:24 But i you are careful to obey me, 561
17:27 But i you do not obey me to keep 561
18: 7 I at any time I announce that a nation NIH
18: 8 i that nation I warned repents of its evil, NIH
18: 9 And i at another time I announce that NIH
18:10 and i it does evil in my sight and does NIH
20: 9 But i I say, "I will not mention him NIH
22: 4 For i you are careful to carry out 561
22: 5 But i you do not obey these commands, 561
22:24 I live," declares the LORD, "even i you, 561
22:30 "Record this man as i childless, NIH
23:22 But i they had stood in my council, 561
23:34 I a prophet or a priest or anyone else claims NIH
25:28 But i they refuse to take the cup 3954
26: 4 I you do not listen to me 561
26: 5 and i you do not listen to the words NIH
26:15 however, that i you put me to death, 561
27: 8 " ' "I, however, any nation or kingdom NIH
27:11 But i any nation will bow its neck under NIH
27:18 I they are prophets and have the word of 561
28: 9 as one truly sent by the LORD only i 928
29: 7 because i it prospers, you too will prosper." 928
31:36 "Only i these decrees vanish 561
31:37 "Only i the heavens above can 561
32: 5 I you fight against the Babylonians, 3954
33:20 'I you can break my covenant with the day 561
33:25 'I I have not established my covenant 561
37:10 Even i you were to defeat 561
38:15 "I I give you an answer, 3954
38:15 Even i I did give you counsel, 3954
38:17 'I you surrender to the officers of the king 561
38:18 But i you will not surrender to the officers 561
38:21 But i you refuse to surrender, 561
38:25 I the officials hear that I talked with you, 3954
40: 4 Come with me to Babylon, i you like, 561
40: 4 but i you do not want to, then don't come. 561
42: 5 be a true and faithful witness against us i 561
42:10 'I you stay in this land, I will build you up 561
42:13 i you say, 'We will not stay in this land,' 561
42:14 and i you say, 'No we will go NIH
42:15 'I you are determined to go to Egypt 561
49: 9 I grape pickers came to you, 561
49: 9 I thieves came during the night, 561
49:12 "I those who do not deserve to drink 2180
51:53 Even i Babylon reaches the sky 3954
La 3:37 Who can speak and have it happen i NIH
Eze 1:27 like glowing metal, as i full of fire, 3869
3: 6 Surely i I had sent you to them, 561
3:19 But i you do warn the wicked man 3954
3:21 But i you do warn the righteous man not 3954
14: 9 i the prophet is enticed to utter a prophecy, 3954
14:13 i a country sins against me 3954
14:14 even i these three men—Noah, Daniel and 2256
14:15 "Or i I send wild beasts through 4273
14:16 even i these three men were in it, NIH
14:17 "Or i I bring a sword against that country NIH
14:18 even i these three men were in it, 2256
14:19 "Or i I send a plague into that land NIH
14:20 even i Noah, Daniel and Job were in it, 2256
15: 5 I it was not useful for anything 2180
17:10 Even i it is transplanted, will it thrive? 2180
18:21 "But i a wicked man turns away from all 3954
18:24 "But i a righteous man turns 928
18:26 I a righteous man turns 928
18:27 But i a wicked man turns away from 928
21:13 And what i the scepter [of Judah], 561
33: 4 then i anyone hears the trumpet but does NIH
33: 5 I he had taken warning, 2256
33: 6 But i the watchman sees the sword coming 3954
33: 9 But i you do warn the wicked man to turn 3954
33:12 The righteous man, i he sins, 928+3427
33:13 I I tell the righteous man that he will 928
33:14 And i I say to the wicked man, 928
33:15 i he gives back what he took in pledge for NIH
33:18 I a righteous man turns 928
33:19 And i a wicked man turns away 928
39:18 the princes of the earth as i they were rams NIH
43:11 and i they are ashamed 561
44:25 i the dead person was his father or mother, NIH
46:16 I the prince makes a gift 3954
46:17 I, however, he makes a gift 3954
Da 2: 5 I you do not tell me what my dream was 10213
2: 6 But i you tell me the dream and explain it, 10213
2: 9 I you do not tell me the dream, 10213
3:15 i you are ready to fall down and worship 10213
3:15 But i you do not worship it, 10213
3:17 I we are thrown into the blazing furnace, 10213
3:18 But even i he does not, 10213

Da 4:19 i only the dream applied to your enemies NIH
5:16 I you can read this writing 10213
Hos 9: 6 Even i they escape from destruction, 3954
9:12 Even i they rear children, 561
9:16 Even i they bear children, 3954
10: 3 i we had a king, what could he do for us?" NIH
11: 7 Even *i they* call to the Most High, AIT
Joel 3: 4 I you are paying me back, 561
Am 2: 1 Because he burned, as i to lime, NIH
6: 9 I ten men are left in one house, 561
6:10 And i a relative who is to burn NIH
Ob 1: 5 "I thieves came to you, 561
1: 5 i robbers in the night— 561
1: 5 I grape pickers came to you, 561
1:16 and drink and be as i they had never been. 3869
Mic 2:11 I a liar and deceiver comes and says, 4273
3: 5 i one feeds them, they proclaim 'peace'; NIH
3: 5 i he does not, they prepare to wage war 2256
Hab 1: 5 not believe, even i you were told. 3954
Hag 2:12 I a person carries consecrated meat in 2176
2:13 "I a person defiled by contact with 561
Zec 3: 7 'I you will walk in my ways 561
6:15 This will happen i you diligently obey 561
11:12 I told them, "I you think it best, 561
11:12 but i not, keep it." 561
13: 3 And i anyone still prophesies, 3954
13: 6 I someone asks him, 2256
14:17 I any of the peoples of the earth do not go 889
14:18 I the Egyptian people do not go up 561
Mal 1: 6 I I am a father, where is the honor due me? 561
1: 6 I I am a master, where is the respect due 561
2: 2 I you do not listen, 561
2: 2 and i you do not set your heart 561
3:10 "and see i I will not throw open the 561
Mt 4: 3 "I you are the Son of God, *1623*
4: 6 "I you are the Son of God," he said, *1623*
4: 9 "i you will bow down and worship me." *1569*
5:13 But i the salt loses its saltiness, *1569*
5:23 i you are offering your gift at the altar *1569*
5:29 I your right eye causes you to sin, *1623*
5:30 And i your right hand causes you to sin, *1623*
5:39 I someone strikes you on the right cheek, *247*
5:40 And i someone wants to sue you *NIG*
5:41 I someone forces you to go one mile, *2779*
5:46 I you love those who love you, *1569*
5:47 And i you greet only your brothers, *1569*
6: 1 I you do, you will have no reward *1623*
6:14 For i you forgive men when they sin *1569*
6:15 But i you do not forgive men their sins, *1569*
6:22 I your eyes are good, your whole body *1569*
6:23 But i your eyes are bad, your whole body *1569*
6:23 I then the light within you is darkness, *1623*
6:30 I that is how God clothes the grass of *1623*
7: 6 I you do, they may trample them *3607*
7: 9 "Which of you, i his son asks for bread, *1569*
7:10 i he asks for a fish, will give him a snake? *2779*
7:11 I you, then, though you are evil, *1623*
8: 2 i you are willing, you can make me clean." *1569*
8:31 "I you drive us out, *1623*
9:17 I they do, the skins will burst, *1623*
9:21 "I I only touch his cloak, I will be healed." *1569*
10:13 I the home is deserving, let your peace *1569*
10:13 i it is not, let your peace return to you. *1569*
10:14 I anyone will not welcome you or listen *323*
10:25 I the head of the house has been called *1623*
10:42 And i anyone gives even a cup of cold water *323*
11: 8 I not, what did you go out to see? *247*
11:14 And i you are willing to accept it, *1623*
11:21 I the miracles that were performed *1623*
11:23 I the miracles that were performed *1623*
12: 7 I you had known what these words mean, *1623*
12:11 "I any of you has a sheep and it falls into *1569*
12:26 I Satan drives out Satan, *1623*
12:27 And i I drive out demons by Beelzebub, *1623*
12:28 i I drive out demons by the Spirit of God, *1623*
14:28 "Lord, i it's you," Peter replied, *1623*
15: 5 But you say that i a man says to his father *323*
15:14 I a blind man leads a blind man, *1569*
16:24 "I anyone would come after me, *1623*
16:26 What good will it be for a man i he gains *1569*
17: 4 I you wish, I will put up three shelters— *1623*
17:20 i you have faith as small as a mustard seed, *1569*
18: 6 But i anyone causes one of these little ones *323*
18: 8 I your hand or your foot causes you to sin, *1623*
18: 9 And i your eye causes you to sin, *1623*
18:12 I a man owns a hundred sheep, *1569*
18:13 And i he finds it, I tell you the truth, *1569*
18:15 "I your brother sins against you, *1569*
18:15 I he listens to you, you have won your *1569*
18:16 But i he will not listen, take one or two *1569*
18:17 I he refuses to listen to them, tell it to *1569*
18:17 i he refuses to listen even to the church, *1569*
18:19 I tell you that i two of you on earth agree *1569*
19:10 "I this is the situation between a husband *1623*
19:17 I you want to enter life, obey *1623*
19:21 Jesus answered, "I you want to be perfect, *1623*
21: 3 I anyone says anything to you, *1569*
21:21 i you have faith and do not doubt, *1569*
21:22 I you believe, you will receive whatever *323*
21:24 I you answer me, I will tell you *1569*
21:25 "I we say, 'From heaven,' he will ask, *1569*
21:26 But i we say, 'From men'— *1569*
22:24 that i a man dies without having children, *1569*
22:45 I then David calls him 'Lord,' *1623*
23:16 You say, 'I anyone swears by the temple, *323*
23:16 i anyone swears by the gold of the temple, *323*
23:18 'I anyone swears by the altar, *323*

Mt 23:18 but **i** anyone swears by the gift on it, 323
23:30 'I we had lived in the days 1623
24:22 **I** those days had not been cut short, 1623
24:23 At that time **i** anyone says to you, 'Look, 1569
24:24 **i** that were possible. 1623
24:26 "So **i** anyone tells you, 'There he is, 1569
24:43 **I** the owner of the house had known 1623
26:15 to give me **i** I hand him over to you?" 2779
26:24 be better for him **i** he had not been born." 1623
26:33 "Even **i** all fall away on account of you, 1623
26:35 "Even **i** I have to die with you, 1569
26:39 "My Father, **i** it is possible, 1623
26:42 **i** it is not possible for this cup to 1623
26:63 Tell us **i** you are the Christ, 1623
27:40 **i** you are the Son of God!" 1623
27:43 Let God rescue him now **i** he wants him, 1623
27:49 Let's see **i** Elijah comes to save him." 1623
28:14 **I** this report gets to the governor, 1569
Mk 1:40 "**I** you are willing, you can make me clean." 1569
2:21 **I he does,** the new piece will pull away
from the old, 1254+1623+3590
2:22 **I he does,** the wine will burst the skins,
1254+1623+3590
3:2 to see **i** he would heal him on the Sabbath. 1623
3:24 **I** a kingdom is divided against itself, 1569
3:25 **I** a house is divided against itself, 1569
3:26 **i** Satan opposes himself and is divided, 1623
4:23 **I** anyone has ears to hear, let him hear." 1623
4:38 "Teacher, don't you care **i** we drown?" 4022
5:28 "**I** I just touch his clothes, I will be healed." 1569
6:11 And **i any** place will not welcome you 323+4005
7:11 But you say that **i** a man says to his father 1569
8:3 **I** I send them home hungry, 1569
8:34 "**I** anyone would come after me, 1623
8:38 **I** anyone is ashamed of me and my words 1569
9:22 But **i** you can do anything, 1623
9:23 "'**I** you can'?" 1623
9:35 "**I** anyone wants to be first, he must be 1623
9:42 And **i** anyone causes one of these little ones 323
9:43 **I** your hand causes you to sin, cut it off. 1569
9:45 And **i** your foot causes you to sin, cut it off. 1569
9:47 **i** your eye causes you to sin, pluck it out. 1569
9:50 "Salt is good, but **i** it loses its saltiness, 1569
10:12 And **i** she divorces her husband 1569
11:3 **I** anyone asks you, 'Why are you doing this 1569
11:13 he went to find out **i** it had any fruit. 1623
11:23 **i** anyone says to this mountain, 'Go, 323
11:25 **i** you hold anything against anyone, 1623
11:31 "**I** we say, 'From heaven,' he will ask, 1569
11:32 But **i** we say, 'From men'...." NIG
12:19 for us that **i** a man's brother dies and leaves 1569
13:20 **I** the Lord had not cut short those days, 1623
13:21 At that time **i** anyone says to you, 'Look, 1569
13:22 deceive the elect—**i** that were possible. 1623
13:36 **I** he comes suddenly, 3590
14:21 be better for him **i** he had not been born." 1623
14:29 Peter declared, "Even **i** all fall away, 1623
14:31 "Even **i** I have to die with you, 1569
14:35 to the ground and prayed that **i** possible 1623
15:36 Let's see **i** Elijah comes to take him down," 1623
15:44 he asked him **i** Jesus had already died. 1623
Lk 3:15 and were all wondering in their hearts **i** 3607
4:3 "**I** you are the Son of God, 1623
4:7 So **i** you worship me, it will all be yours." 1569
4:9 "**I** you are the Son of God," he said, 1623
5:12 **i** you are willing, you can make me clean." 1569
5:36 **I** he does, he will have torn 1623
5:37 **I** he does, the new wine will burst 1623
6:7 to see **i** he would heal on the Sabbath. 1623
6:29 *I* someone **strikes** you on one cheek, AIT
6:29 *I* someone **takes** your cloak, AIT
6:30 and *i* anyone **takes** what belongs to you, AIT
6:32 "**I** you love those who love you, 1623
6:33 And **i** you do good to those who are good 1569
6:34 And **i** you lend to those from whom you 1569
7:25 **I not,** what did you go out to see? 247
7:39 "**I** this man were a prophet, 1623
9:5 **I** people do not welcome you, 323
9:23 "**I** anyone would come after me, 1623
9:26 **I** anyone is ashamed of me and my words, 323
10:6 **I** a man of peace is there, 1569
10:6 **i** not, it will return to you. 1623
10:13 For **i** the miracles that were performed 1623
11:11 *i* your son **asks for** a fish, AIT
11:12 Or *i he* **asks for** an egg, AIT
11:13 **I** you then, though you are evil, 1623
11:18 **I** Satan is divided against himself, 1623
11:19 Now **i** I drive out demons by Beelzebub, 1623
11:20 **i** I drive out demons by the finger of God, 1623
11:36 **i** your whole body is full of light, 1623
12:28 **I** that is how God clothes the grass of 1623
12:38 even **i** he comes in the second or third 1569
12:39 **I** the owner of the house had known 1623
13:9 **I** it bears fruit next year, fine! 1569
13:9 **I** not, then cut it down.'" 1623
14:5 "**I** one of you has a son or an ox that falls NIG
14:9 **I so,** the host who invited both 2779
14:12 **i you do,** they may invite you back and 3607
14:26 "**I** anyone comes to me and does 1623
14:28 the cost **to see i** he has enough money 1623
14:29 **For i** he lays the foundation and 2671+3607
14:32 **I** he is not able, 1623
14:34 "Salt is good, but **i** it loses its saltiness, 1569
16:11 So **i** you have not been trustworthy 1623
16:12 And **i** you have not been trustworthy 1623
16:30 'but **i** someone from the dead goes to them, 1569
16:31 '**I** they do not listen to Moses and 1623

Lk 16:31 be convinced even **i** someone rises from 1569
17:3 "**I** your brother sins, rebuke him, 1569
17:3 rebuke him, and **i** he repents, forgive him. 1569
17:4 **I** he sins against you seven times in a day, 1569
17:6 "**I** you have faith as small as 1623
19:8 **i** I have cheated anybody out of anything, 1623
19:31 **I** anyone asks you, 'Why are you untying 1569
19:40 "I tell you," he replied, "**i** they keep quiet, 1569
19:42 "**I** you, even you, had only known 1623
20:5 "**I** we say, 'From heaven,' he will ask, 1569
20:6 But **i** we say, 'From men,' 1569
20:28 for us that **i** a man's brother dies and leaves 1569
22:36 "But now *i you* **have** a purse, take it, AIT
22:36 and *i you* don't **have** a sword, AIT
22:42 **i** you are willing, take this cup from me; 1623
22:67 "**I** you are the Christ," they said, "tell us." 1623
22:67 Jesus answered, "**I** I tell you, 1569
22:68 and **i** I asked you, you would not answer. 1569
23:6 Pilate asked **i** the man was a Galilean. 1623
23:31 For **i** men do these things when 1623
23:35 let him save himself **i** he is the Christ 1623
23:37 "**I** you are the king of the Jews, 1623
24:28 Jesus **acted as i** he were going farther. 4701
Jn 1:25 "Why then do you baptize **i** you are not 1623
3:2 the miraculous signs you are doing **i** 1569
3:12 how then will you believe **i** I speak 1569
4:10 "**I** you knew the gift of God and who it is 1623
5:31 "**I** I testify about myself, 1569
5:43 but **i** someone else comes in his own name, 1569
5:44 How can you believe *i you* **accept** praise AIT
5:46 **I** you believed Moses, you would believe
me, 1623
6:51 **I** anyone eats of this bread, 1569
6:62 What **i** you see the Son of Man ascend to 1569
7:17 **I** anyone chooses to do God's will, 1569
7:23 Now **i** a child can be circumcised on 1569
7:37 "**I** anyone is thirsty, let him come to me 1569
8:7 "**I** any one of you is without sin, NIG
8:14 "Even **i** I testify on my own behalf, 1569
8:16 But **i** I do judge, my decisions are right, 1569
8:19 "**I** you knew me, you would know my 1623
8:24 **i** you do not believe that I am 1569
8:31 Jesus said, "**I** you hold to my teaching, 1569
8:36 So **i** the Son sets you free, you will be free 1569
8:39 "**I** you were Abraham's children," 1623
8:42 "**I** God were your Father, you would love 1623
8:46 **I** I am telling the truth, 1623
8:51 **i** anyone keeps my word, 1569
8:52 yet you say that **i** anyone keeps your word, 1569
8:54 Jesus replied, "**I** I glorify myself, 1569
8:55 **I** I said I did not, I would be a liar like you, 1569
9:33 **I** this man were not from God, 1623
9:41 Jesus said, "**I** you were blind, 1623
10:24 **I** you are the Christ, tell us plainly." 1623
10:35 **I** he called them 'gods,' 1623
10:38 But **i** I do it, even though you do not 1623
11:12 His disciples replied, "Lord, **i** he sleeps, 1623
11:21 Martha said to Jesus, "**i** you had been here, 1623
11:32 "Lord, **i** you had been here, 1623
11:40 "Did I not tell you that **i** you believed, 1569
11:48 **I** we let him go on like this, 1569
11:57 that **i** anyone found out where Jesus was, 1569
12:24 But **i** it dies, it produces many seeds. 1569
13:17 you will be blessed **i** you do them. 1569
13:32 **I** God is glorified in him, 1623
13:35 **i** you love one another." 1569
14:2 **i** it were not so, I would have told you. 1623
14:3 And **i** I go and prepare a place for you, 1569
14:7 **I** you really knew me, 1623
14:15 "**I** you love me, you will obey what I 1569
14:23 Jesus replied, "**I** anyone loves me, 1569
14:28 **I** you loved me, you would be glad 1623
15:5 *I* a man **remains** in me and I in him, AIT
15:6 **I** anyone does not remain in me, 1569
15:7 **I** you remain in me and my words remain 1569
15:10 **I** you obey my commands, 1569
15:14 You are my friends **i** you do what I
command. 1569
15:18 "**I** the world hates you, 1623
15:19 **I** you belonged to the world, 1623
15:20 **I** they persecuted me, 1623
15:20 **I** they obeyed my teaching, 1623
15:22 **I** I had not come and spoken to them, 1623
15:24 **I** I had not done among them what 1623
16:7 but **i** I go, I will send him to you. 1569
18:8 "**I** you are looking for me, 1623
18:14 that it would be good *i* one man **died** for AIT
18:23 "**I** I said something wrong," Jesus replied, 1623
18:23 **i** I spoke the truth, why did you strike me?" 1623
18:30 "**I** he were not a criminal," they replied, 1623
18:36 **I** it were, my servants would fight 1623
19:11 "You would have no power over me **i** 1623
19:12 "**I** you let this man go, 1569
20:15 she said, "Sir, **i** you have carried him away, 1623
20:23 **I** you forgive anyone his sins, 323
20:23 **i** you do not forgive them, 323
21:22 "**I** I want him to remain alive until I return, 1569
21:23 "**I** I want him to remain alive until I return, 1569
21:25 **I** every one of them were written down, 1569
Ac 3:12 you stare at us **as i** by our own power 6055
4:9 **I** we are being called to account today for 1623
5:38 For **i** their purpose or activity is 1569
5:39 But **i** it is from God, you will not be able 1623
9:2 so that **i** he found any there who belonged 1569
10:18 asking **i** Simon who was known 1623
11:17 So **i** God gave them the same gift 1623
13:15 **i** you have a message of encouragement for 1623

Ac 13:41 even **i** someone told you.'" 1569
16:15 "**I** you consider me a believer in the Lord," 1623
17:11 to see **i** what Paul said was true. 1623
17:25 *as i he* **needed** anything, AIT
18:14 "**I** you Jews were making a complaint 1623
18:21 "I will come back *i it is* God's **will."** AIT
19:38 **I,** then, Demetrius and his fellow 1623
19:39 **I** there is anything further you want 1623
20:16 **i** possible, by the day of Pentecost. 1623
20:24 **i only** I may finish the race and complete 6055
23:9 "**What i** a spirit or an angel has spoken 1623
24:19 to be here before you and bring charges **i** 1623
25:5 **i** he has done anything wrong." 1623
25:11 **I,** however, I am guilty 1623
25:11 But **i** the charges brought against me 1623
25:20 so I asked **i** he would be willing to go 1623
26:5 can testify, **i** they are willing, 1569
26:32 "This man could have been set free **i** he had 1623
27:39 to run the ship aground **i** they could. 1623
Ro 2:17 Now you, **i** you call yourself a Jew; 1623
2:17 **i** you rely on the law and brag NIG
2:18 **i** you know his will and approve NIG
2:19 **i** you are convinced that you are a guide for NIG
2:25 Circumcision has value **i** you observe 1569
2:25 but **i** you break the law, 1569
2:26 **I** those who are not circumcised keep 1569
2:28 not a Jew **i** he is only one outwardly, NIG
2:29 No, a man is a Jew **i** he is one inwardly; NIG
3:3 What **i** some did not have faith? 1623
3:5 But **i** our unrighteousness brings out God's
righteousness more clearly, 1623
3:6 **I that were so,** how could God judge 2075
3:7 Someone might argue, "**I** my falsehood 1623
4:2 **I,** in fact, Abraham was justified by works, 1623
4:14 For **i** those who live by law are heirs, 1623
5:10 For **i,** when we were God's enemies, 1623
5:15 For **i** the many died by the trespass of 1623
5:17 For **i,** by the trespass of the one man, 1623
6:5 **I** we have been united with him like this 1623
6:8 Now **i** we died with Christ, 1623
7:2 but **i** her husband dies, 1569
7:3 **i** she marries another man 1569
7:3 But **i** her husband dies, 1569
7:7 not have known what coveting really was **i** 1623
7:16 And **i** I do what I do not want to do, 1623
7:20 Now **i** I do what I do not want to do, 1623
8:9 **i** the Spirit of God lives in you. 1642
8:9 **i** anyone does not have the Spirit of Christ, 1623
8:10 But **i** Christ is in you, 1623
8:11 And **i** the Spirit of him who raised Jesus 1623
8:13 **i** you live according to the sinful nature, 1623
8:13 but **i** by the Spirit you put to death 1623
8:17 Now **i** we are children, then we are heirs— 1623
8:17 and co-heirs with Christ, **i indeed** we share 1642
8:25 But **i** we hope for what we do not yet have, 1623
8:31 **I** God is for us, who can be against us? 1623
9:22 What **i** God, choosing to show his wrath 1623
9:23 What **i** he did this to make the riches NIG
9:32 Because they pursued it not by faith but **as i** 6055
10:9 That **i** you confess with your mouth, 1569
11:6 **i** by grace, then it is no longer by works; 1623
11:6 **i it were,** grace would no longer be grace. 2075
11:12 But **i** their transgression means riches for 1623
11:15 For **i** their rejection is the reconciliation of 1623
11:16 **I** the part of the dough offered 1623
11:16 **i** the root is holy, so are the branches. 1623
11:17 **I** some of the branches have been broken off 1623
11:18 **I** you do, consider this: 1623
11:21 **i** God did not spare the natural branches, 1623
11:23 And **i** they do not persist in unbelief, 1569
11:24 **i** you were cut out of an olive tree 1623
12:6 **I** a man's gift is prophesying, 1664
12:7 **I** it is serving, let him serve; 1664
12:7 **i** it is teaching, let him teach; 1664
12:8 **i** it is encouraging, let him encourage; 1664
12:8 **i** it is contributing to the needs of others, NIG
12:8 **i** it is leadership, let him govern diligently; NIG
12:8 **i** it is showing mercy, let him do it NIG
12:18 **I** it is possible, as far as it depends on you, 1623
12:20 "**I** your enemy is hungry, feed him; 1569
12:20 **i** he is thirsty, give him something to drink. 1569
13:4 But **i** you do wrong, be afraid, 1569
13:7 **I** you owe taxes, pay taxes; NIG
13:7 **i** revenue, then revenue; NIG
13:7 **i** respect, then respect; if honor, then honor. NIG
13:7 if respect, then respect; **i** honor, then honor. NIG
14:8 **I** we live, we live to the Lord; 1569
14:8 and **i** we die, we die to the Lord. 1569
14:14 But **i** anyone regards something as unclean, 1623
14:15 **I** your brother is distressed because 1623
14:23 the man who has doubts is condemned **i** 1569
15:15 **as i** to remind you of them again, 6055
15:27 For **i** the Gentiles have shared in 1623
1Co 1:16 I don't remember **i** I baptized anyone else.) 1623
2:8 for **i** they had, they would not have crucified 1623
3:12 **I** any man builds on this foundation 1623
3:14 **I** what he has built survives, 1623
3:15 **I** it is burned up, he will suffer loss; 1623
3:17 **I** anyone destroys God's temple, 1623
3:18 **I** any one of you thinks he is wise by 1623
4:3 I care very little **i** I am judged by you or 2671
4:7 And **i** you did receive it, 1623
4:18 **as i** I were not coming to you. 6055
4:19 come to you very soon, **i** the Lord is willing, 1569
5:3 **just as i** I were present. 4048
6:1 *I* any of you **has** a dispute with another, AIT
6:2 And **i** you are to judge the world, 1623

1Co 6: 4 **i** you have disputes about such matters, *1569*
7: 9 But **i** they cannot control themselves, *1623*
7: 11 But **i** she does, she must remain unmarried *1569*
7: 12 **I** any brother has a wife who is not *1623*
7: 13 And **i** a woman has a husband who is not *1623*
7: 15 But **i** the unbeliever leaves, let him do so. *1623*
7: 21 **i** you can gain your freedom, do so. *1623*
7: 28 But **i** you do marry, you have not sinned; *1569*
7: 28 and **i** a virgin marries, she has not sinned. *1569*
7: 29 on those who have wives should live **as i** *6055*
7: 30 those who mourn, **as i** they did not; *6055*
7: 30 those who are happy, **as i** they were not; *6055*
7: 30 **as i** it were not theirs to keep; *6055*
7: 31 **as i** not engrossed in them. *6055*
7: 36 **I** anyone thinks he is acting improperly *1623*
7: 36 and **i** she is getting along in years *1569*
7: 39 But **i** her husband dies, she is free to marry *1569*
7: 40 she is happier **i** she stays as she is— *1569*
8: 5 For even **i** there are so-called gods, *1642*
8: 8 we are no worse **i** we do not eat, *1569*
8: 8 and no better **i** we do. *1569*
8: 10 For **i** anyone with a weak conscience *1569*
8: 13 **i** what I eat causes my brother to fall *1569*
9: 11 **I** we have sown spiritual seed among you, *1623*
9: 11 is it too much **i** we reap a material harvest *1623*
9: 12 **I** others have this right of support *1623*
9: 16 Woe to me **i** I do not preach the gospel! *1569*
9: 17 **I** I preach voluntarily, I have a reward; *1623*
9: 17 **i** not voluntarily, I am simply discharging *1623*
10: 12 So, *i you* **think** you are standing firm, *AIT*
10: 27 **I** some unbeliever invites you to a meal *1623*
10: 28 But **i** anyone says to you, *1569*
10: 30 **I** I take part in the meal with thankfulness, *1623*
11: 6 **I** a woman does not cover her head, *1623*
11: 6 and **i** it is a disgrace for a woman *1623*
11: 14 the very nature of things teach you that **i** *1569*
11: 15 but that **i** a woman has long hair, *1569*
11: 16 **I** anyone wants to be contentious *1623*
11: 31 But **i** we judged ourselves, *1623*
11: 34 **I** anyone is hungry, he should eat at home, *1623*
12: 15 **I** the foot should say, *1569*
12: 16 And **i** the ear should say, *1569*
12: 17 **I** the whole body were an eye, *1623*
12: 17 **I** the whole body were an ear, *1623*
12: 19 **I** they were all one part, *1623*
12: 26 **I** one part suffers, every part suffers with it; *1664*
12: 26 **i** one part is honored, *1664*
13: 1 **I** I speak in the tongues of men and *1569*
13: 2 **I** I have the gift of prophecy *1569*
13: 2 **i** I have a faith that can move mountains, *1569*
13: 3 **I** I give all I possess to the poor *1569*
14: 6 **i** I come to you and speak in tongues, *1569*
14: 8 **i** the trumpet does not sound a clear call, *1569*
14: 11 **I** then I do not grasp the meaning *1569*
14: 14 For **i** I pray in a tongue, my spirit prays, *1569*
14: 16 **I** you are praising God with your spirit, *1569*
14: 23 So **i** the whole church comes together *1569*
14: 24 But **i** an unbeliever or someone who does *1569*
14: 27 **I** anyone speaks in a tongue, two— *1664*
14: 28 **I** there is no interpreter, *1569*
14: 30 And **i** a revelation comes to someone *1569*
14: 35 **I** they want to inquire about something, *1623*
14: 37 **I** anybody thinks he is a prophet *1623*
14: 38 **I** he ignores this, he himself will be *1623*
15: 2 **i** you hold firmly to the word I preached *1623*
15: 12 But **i** it is preached that Christ *1623*
15: 13 **I** there is no resurrection of the dead, *1623*
15: 14 And **i** Christ has not been raised, *1623*
15: 15 not raise him **i in fact** the dead are *726+1642*
15: 16 For **i** the dead are not raised, *1623*
15: 17 And **i** Christ has not been raised, *1623*
15: 19 **I** only for this life we have hope in Christ, *1623*
15: 29 **Now i** there is no resurrection, *2075*
15: 29 **I** the dead are not raised at all, *1623*
15: 32 **I** I fought wild beasts in Ephesus *1623*
15: 32 **I** the dead are not raised, *1623*
15: 44 **I** there is a natural body, *1623*
16: 4 **I** it seems advisable for me to go also, *1569*
16: 7 I hope to spend some time with you, **i** *1569*
16: 10 **I** Timothy comes, see to it that *1569*
16: 22 **I** anyone does not love the Lord— *1623*
2Co 1: 6 **I** we are distressed, it is for your comfort *1664*
1: 6 **i** we are comforted, it is for your comfort, *1664*
2: 2 For **i** I grieve you, who is left to make me *1623*
2: 5 **I** anyone has caused grief, *1623*
2: 9 to **see i** you would stand the test and *1182*
2: 10 **I** you forgive anyone, I also forgive him. *1254*
2: 10 **i** there was anything to forgive— *1623*
3: 7 Now **i** the ministry that brought death, *1623*
3: 9 **I** the ministry that condemns men is glorious, *1623*
3: 11 **i** what was fading away came with glory, *1623*
4: 3 And even **i** our gospel is veiled, *1623*
5: 1 Now we know that **i** the earthly tent we live *1569*
5: 13 **I** we are out of our mind, it is for the sake of *1664*
5: 13 **i** we are in our right mind, it is for you. *1664*
5: 17 **i** anyone is in Christ, he is a new creation; *1623*
7: 8 Even **i** I caused you sorrow by my letter, *1623*
8: 12 For **i** the willingness is there, *1623*
9: 4 For **i** any Macedonians come with me *1569*
10: 7 **I** anyone is confident that he belongs *1623*
10: 8 For even **i** I boast somewhat freely about *1569*
10: 14 as would be the case **i** we had not come *NIG*
11: 4 For **i** someone comes to you and preaches *1623*
11: 4 or **i** you receive a different spirit from *NIG*
11: 15 **i** his servants masquerade as servants *1623*
11: 16 But **i** you do, then receive me just as *1623*
2Co 11: 30 **I** I must boast, I will boast of *1623*
12: 6 **Even i** I should choose to boast, *1569*
12: 15 **I** I love you more, will you love me less? *1623*
Gal 1: 8 But even **i** we or an angel *1569*
1: 9 **I** anybody is preaching to you *1623*
1: 10 **I** I were still trying to please men, *1623*
2: 17 **"I,** while we seek to be justified in Christ, *1623*
2: 18 **I** I rebuild what I destroyed, *1623*
2: 21 for **i** righteousness could be gained through *1623*
3: 4 **i** it really was for nothing? *1623*
3: 18 For **i** the inheritance depends on the law, *1623*
3: 21 For **i** a law had been given that could *1623*
3: 29 **I** you belong to Christ, *1623*
4: 14 you welcomed me **as i** I were an angel *6055*
4: 14 **as i** I were Christ Jesus himself. *6055*
4: 15 I can testify that, **i** you could have done so, *1623*
5: 2 that **i** you let yourselves be circumcised, *1569*
5: 11 **i** I am still preaching circumcision, *1623*
5: 15 **I** you keep on biting and devouring each *1623*
5: 18 But **i** you are led by the Spirit, *1623*
6: 1 Brothers, **i** someone is caught in a sin, *1569*
6: 3 **I** anyone thinks he is something *1623*
6: 9 a harvest *i we do* not **give up.** *AIT*
Eph 6: 7 **as i** you were serving the Lord, not men, *6055*
Php 1: 22 **I** I am to go on living in the body, *1623*
2: 1 **I** you have any encouragement *1623*
2: 1 **i** any comfort from his love, *1623*
2: 1 **i** any fellowship with the Spirit, *1623*
2: 1 **i** any tenderness and compassion, *1623*
2: 17 But even **i** I am being poured out like *1623*
3: 4 **I** anyone else thinks he has reasons *1623*
3: 15 And **i** on some point you think differently, *1623*
4: 8 **i** anything is excellent or praiseworthy— *1623*
Col 1: 23 **i** you continue in your faith, *1623*
4: 10 **i** he comes to you, welcome him.) *1569*
2Th 3: 10 **"I** a man will not work, he shall not eat." *1623*
3: 14 **I** anyone does not obey our instruction *1623*
1Ti 1: 8 that the law is good **i** one uses it properly. *1569*
2: 15 **i** they continue in faith, love and holiness *1569*
3: 1 **I** anyone sets his heart on being an overseer *1623*
3: 5 (**I** anyone does not know how to manage *1623*
3: 10 and then *i there* **is** nothing against them, *AIT*
3: 15 **i** I am delayed, you will know how *1569*
4: 4 nothing is to be rejected *i it* **is received** *AIT*
4: 6 *I you* **point** these things **out** *AIT*
4: 16 Persevere in them, because *i you* **do,** *AIT*
5: 1 but exhort him **as i** he were your father. *6055*
5: 4 **i** a widow has children or grandchildren, *1623*
5: 8 **I** anyone does not provide for his relatives, *1623*
5: 16 **I** any woman who is a believer has widows *1623*
6: 3 **I** anyone teaches false doctrines and does *1623*
6: 8 But *i we* **have** food and clothing, *AIT*
2Ti 2: 5 Similarly, **i** anyone competes as an athlete, *1569*
2: 11 **I** we died with him, we will also live with *1623*
2: 12 **i** we endure, we will also reign *1623*
2: 12 **I** we disown him, he will also disown us; *1623*
2: 13 **i** we are faithless, he will remain faithful, *1623*
2: 21 **I** a man cleanses himself from the latter, *1569*
Phm 1: 17 So **i** you consider me a partner, *1623*
1: 18 **I** he has done you any wrong *1623*
Heb 2: 2 For **i** the message spoken *1623*
2: 3 how shall we escape *i we* **ignore** such *AIT*
3: 6 **i** we hold on to our courage and the hope *1570*
3: 7 "Today, **i** you hear his voice, *1569*
3: 14 to share in Christ **i** we hold firmly till *1570*
3: 15 "Today, **i** you hear his voice, *1569*
3: 18 that they would never enter his rest **i** not *1623*
4: 7 "Today, **i** you hear his voice, *1569*
4: 8 For **i** Joshua had given them rest, *1623*
6: 6 *i they* **fall away,** to be brought back *AIT*
7: 11 **I** perfection could have been attained *1623*
7: 15 And what we have said is even more clear **i** *1623*
8: 4 **I** he were on earth, he would not be a priest, *1623*
8: 7 For **i** there had been nothing wrong with *1623*
10: 2 **I** it **could,** would they not have stopped *2075*
10: 26 *I* we deliberately *keep on* **sinning** *AIT*
10: 38 And **i** he shrinks back, I will not be pleased *1569*
11: 15 **I** they had been thinking of the *1623+3525*
12: 8 **I** you are not disciplined *1623*
12: 20 **"I** even an animal touches the mountain, *1569*
12: 25 **I** they did not escape when they refused *1623*
12: 25 *i* we **turn away from** him who warns us *AIT*
13: 3 Remember those in prison **as i** *6055*
13: 3 and those who are mistreated **as i** *6055*
13: 23 **I** he arrives soon, *1569*
Jas 1: 5 **I** any of you lacks wisdom, he should ask *1623*
1: 26 **I** anyone considers himself religious and *1623*
2: 3 *I you* **show special attention to** the man *AIT*
2: 8 **I** you really keep the royal law found *1623*
2: 9 But **i** you show favoritism, you sin *1623*
2: 11 **I** you do not commit adultery *1623*
2: 14 **i** a man claims to have faith but has no *1569*
2: 16 *I* one of you **says** to him, "Go, *AIT*
2: 17 **i** it is not accompanied by action, is dead. *1569*
3: 2 **I** anyone is never at fault in what he says, *1623*
3: 14 But **i** you harbor bitter envy *1623*
4: 15 you ought to say, **"I** it is the Lord's will, *1569*
5: 15 **I** he has sinned, he will be forgiven. *1569*
5: 19 **i** one of you should wander from the truth *1569*
1Pe 2: 19 For it is commendable **i** a man bears up *1623*
2: 20 But how is it to your credit **i** you receive *1623*
2: 20 But **i** you suffer for doing good *1623*
3: 1 **i** any of them do not believe the word, *1623*
3: 6 *i you* **do what is right** and do not give way *AIT*
3: 13 Who is going to harm you **i** you are eager *1569*
3: 14 even **i** you should suffer for what is right, *1623*
3: 17 It is better, **i** it is God's will, *1623*
1Pe 4: 11 **I** anyone speaks, he should do it *1623*
4: 11 **I** anyone serves, he should do it with *1623*
4: 14 **I** you are insulted because of the name *1623*
4: 15 **I** you suffer, it should not be as a murderer *1142*
4: 16 However, **i** you suffer as a Christian, *1623*
4: 17 and **i** it begins with us, *1623*
4: 18 **"I** it is hard for the righteous to be saved, *1623*
2Pe 1: 8 For *i you* **possess** these qualities *AIT*
1: 9 *i* anyone *does* not **have** them, *AIT*
1: 10 For *i you* **do** these things, *AIT*
2: 4 For **i** God did not spare angels *1623*
2: 5 **i** he did not spare the ancient world *NIG*
2: 6 **i** he condemned the cities of Sodom *NIG*
2: 7 and **i** he rescued Lot, *NIG*
2: 9 **i** this is so, then the Lord knows how *NIG*
2: 20 **I** they have escaped the corruption of *1623*
1Jn 1: 6 **I** we claim to have fellowship with him *1569*
1: 7 But **i** we walk in the light, as he is in *1569*
1: 8 **I** we claim to be without sin, we deceive *1569*
1: 9 **I** we confess our sins, he is faithful and just *1569*
1: 10 **I** we claim we have not sinned, *1569*
2: 1 But **i** anybody does sin, we have one who *1569*
2: 3 come to know him **i** we obey his commands. *1569*
2: 5 But **i** anyone obeys his word, *323*
2: 15 **I** anyone loves the world, *1569*
2: 19 For **i** they had belonged to us, *1623*
2: 24 **I** it does, you also will remain in the Son *1569*
2: 29 **I** you know that he is righteous, *1569*
3: 13 my brothers, **i** the world hates you. *1623*
3: 17 **I** anyone has material possessions *323*
3: 21 **i** our hearts do not condemn us, *1569*
4: 12 but **i** we love one another, *1569*
4: 15 **I** anyone acknowledges that Jesus is *1569*
4: 20 **I** anyone says, "I love God," *1569*
5: 14 that **i** we ask anything according to his will, *1569*
5: 15 And **i** we know that he hears us— *1569*
5: 16 **I** anyone sees his brother commit a sin *1569*
2Jn 1: 10 **I** anyone comes to you and does not bring *1623*
3Jn 1: 10 So **i** I come, I will call attention to what *1569*
Rev 2: 5 **I** you do not repent, I will come to you *1623*
3: 3 But **i** you do not wake up, I will come like *1569*
3: 20 **I** anyone hears my voice and opens *1569*
5: 6 a Lamb, looking **as i** it had been slain, *6055*
11: 5 **I** anyone tries to harm them, *1623*
13: 10 **I** anyone is to go into captivity, *1623*
13: 10 **I** anyone is to be killed with the sword, *1623*
13: 18 *I* anyone **has** insight, let him calculate *AIT*
14: 9 **"I** anyone worships the beast and his image *1623*
20: 15 **I** anyone's name was not found written in *1623*
22: 18 **I** anyone adds anything to them, *1569*
22: 19 And **i** anyone takes words away *1569*

IGAL (3)

Nu 13: 7 from the tribe of Issachar, **I** son of Joseph; 3319
2Sa 23: 36 **I** son of Nathan from Zobah, 3319
1Ch 3: 22 Hattush, **I,** Bariah, Neariah and Shaphat— 3319

IGDALIAH (1)

Jer 35: 4 the sons of Hanan son of **I** the man of God. 3323

IGEAL (KJV) See IGAL

IGNOBLE (1)

2Ti 2: 20 for noble purposes and some for **i.** *871*

IGNOMINY (KJV) See SHAME

IGNORANCE (7) [IGNORE]

Eze 45: 20 who sins unintentionally or through **i;** 7344
Ac 3: 17 "Now, brothers, I know that you acted in **i,** *53*
17: 30 In the past God overlooked such **i,** *53*
Eph 4: 18 of the **i** that is in them due to the hardening *53*
1Ti 1: 13 I was shown mercy because I acted in **i** *51*
Heb 9: 7 **sins** the people had **committed in i.** *52*
1Pe 1: 14 when you lived in **i.** *53*

IGNORANT (12) [IGNORE]

Ps 73: 22 I was senseless and **i;** 3359+4202
Pr 30: 2 "*I am the* most **i** of men; 1280
Isa 44: 9 *they are* **i,** to their own shame. 1153+3359
45: 20 **I** *are* those who carry about idols of wood, 3359+4202
Ro 11: 25 I do not want you *to be* **i** of this mystery, *51*
1Co 10: 1 For I do not want you *to be* **i** of the fact, *51*
12: 1 brothers, I do not want you *to be* **i.** *51*
15: 34 for there are some who **are i** of God— *57+2400*
1Th 4: 13 *to be* **i** about those who fall asleep, *51*
Heb 5: 2 *with* those who *are* **i** and are going astray, *51*
1Pe 2: 15 by doing good you should silence the **i** talk *57*
2Pe 3: 16 which **i** and unstable people distort, *276*

IGNORE (10) [IGNORANCE, IGNORANT, IGNORED, IGNORES, IGNORING]

Dt 22: 1 *do* not **i** it but be sure to take it back to him. 6623
22: 3 or anything he loses. *Do* not **i** it. 6623
22: 4 or his ox fallen on the road, *do* not **i** it. 6623
Ps 9: 12 *he does* not **i** the cry of the afflicted. 8894
55: 1 O God, *do* not **i** my plea; 6623
74: 23 *Do* not **i** the clamor of your adversaries, 8894
119: 139 for my enemies **i** your words. 8894
Pr 8: 33 to my instruction and be wise; *do* not **i** it. 7277

Hos 4: 6 I also *will* **i** your children. 8894
Heb 2: 3 how shall we escape *if we* **i** such a great salvation? *288*

IGNORED (5) [IGNORE]
Ex 9:21 But those who **i** the word of 4202+4213+8492
Pr 1:25 since *you* **i** all my advice and would 7277
2:17 who has left the partner of her youth and **i** 8894
Hos 4: 6 because *you have* **i** the law of your God, 8894
1Co 14:38 If he ignores this, *he* himself *will be* **i.** *51*

IGNORES (4) [IGNORE]
Pr 10:17 but *whoever* **i** correction leads others astray. 6440
13:18 *He who* **i** discipline comes to poverty 7277
15:32 *He who* **i** discipline despises himself, 7277
1Co 14:38 If he **i** this, he himself will be ignored. *51*

IGNORING (1) [IGNORE]
Mk 5:36 **I** what they said, Jesus told the synagogue *4159*

IIM (1)
Jos 15:29 Baalah, **I,** Ezem, 6517

IJE-ABARIM (KJV) See IYE ABARIM

IJON (3)
1Ki 15:20 He conquered **I,** Dan, Abel Beth Maacah 6510
2Ki 15:29 of Assyria came and took **I,** 6510
2Ch 16: 4 They conquered **I,** Dan, 6510

IKKESH (3)
2Sa 23:26 Helez the Paltite, Ira son of **I** from Tekoa, 6837
1Ch 11:28 Ira son of **I** from Tekoa, 6837
27: 9 was Ira the son of **I** the Tekoite. 6837

ILAI (1)
1Ch 11:29 Sibbecai the Hushathite, **I** the Ahohite, 6519

ILL (24) [ILLNESS, ILLNESSES, ILLS]
Ge 48: 1 "Your father *is* **i.**" 2703
Dt 15: 9 *do* not **show i will** toward your needy brother 6524+8317
1Sa 19:14 Michal said, "He *is* **i.**" 2703
30:13 when *I became* **i** three days ago. 2703
2Sa 12:15 and *he became* **i.** 653
13: 5 "Go to bed and **pretend to be i,**" 2703
13: 6 So Amnon lay down and **pretended to be i.** 2703
1Ki 14: 1 that time Abijah son of Jeroboam *became* **i,** 2703
14: 5 to ask you about her son, for he *is* **i,** 2703
17:17 the woman who owned the house *became* **i.** 2703
2Ki 8: 7 and Ben-Hadad king of Aram *was* **i.** 2703
20: 1 In those days Hezekiah *became* **i** and was at 2703
2Ch 21:15 be very **i** with a lingering disease of 2716
32:24 In those days Hezekiah *became* **i** and was at 2703
Ne 2: 2 so sad when you *are* not **i?** 2703
Job 6: 7 I refuse to touch it; such food makes me **i.** 1867
Ps 35:13 Yet when they *were* **i,** 2703
Isa 33:24 No one living in Zion will say, *"I am* **i";** 2703
38: 1 In those days Hezekiah *became* **i** and was at 2703
Da 8:27 was exhausted and **lay i** for several days. 2703
Mt 4:24 all who **were i** with various diseases, *2400+2809*
Ac 28: 5 into the fire and suffered no **i effects.** *2805*
Php 2:26 because you heard *he was* **i.** *820*
2:27 Indeed *he was* **i,** and almost died. *820*

ILL-GOTTEN (5) [GET]
Pr 1:19 is the end of all *who* **go after i gain;** 1298+1299
10: 2 **I** treasures are of no value, 8400
28:16 he who hates **i gain** will enjoy a long life. 1299
Mic 4:13 You will devote their **i gains** to the LORD, 1299
6:10 your **i** treasures and the short ephah, 8400

ILL-TEMPERED (1) [TEMPER]
Pr 21:19 a desert than with a quarrelsome and **i** wife. 4088

ILL-TREAT, ILL-TREATED, ILL-TREATING (Anglicized) See MISTREAT, MISTREATED, MISTREATING

ILLEGAL (1) [LEGAL]
Ex 22: 9 In all cases of **i possession** of an ox, 7322

ILLEGITIMATE (3)
Hos 5: 7 they give birth to **i** children. 2424
Jn 8:41 "We *are* not **i children,"** *1164+1666+4518*
Heb 12: 8 then you are **i children** and not true sons. *3785*

ILLICIT (1)
Eze 16:33 to you from everywhere for your **i favors.** 9373

ILLNESS (11) [ILL]
2Sa 13: 2 Amnon became frustrated to the point of **i** 2703
2Ki 8: 8 ask him, 'Will I recover from this **i?'** " 2716
8: 9 'Will I recover from this **i?'** " 2716
13:14 Now Elisha was suffering from the **i** 2716
20:12 because he had heard of Hezekiah's **i.** 2703
2Ch 16:12 even in his **i** he did not seek help from 2716
Ps 41: 3 and restore him from his bed of **i.** 2716
Isa 38: 9 of Hezekiah king of Judah after his **i** 2703
39: 1 because he had heard of *his* **i** and recovery. 2703
Gal 4:13 an **i** that I first preached the gospel to you. *819+3836+4922*
4:14 Even though my **i** was a trial to you, *NIG*

ILLNESSES (3) [ILL]
Dt 28:59 and severe and lingering **i.** 2716
Ac 19:12 and their **i** were cured and *3798*
1Ti 5:23 of your stomach and your frequent **i.** *819*

ILLS (1) [ILL]
Ps 73: 5 they are not plagued by human **i.** NIH

ILLUMINATED (1)
Rev 18: 1 and the earth *was* **i** by his splendor. *5894*

ILLUSIONS (1)
Isa 30:10 Tell us pleasant things, prophesy **i.** 4562

ILLUSTRATION (1)
Heb 9: 9 This is an **i** for the present time, *4130*

ILLYRICUM (1)
Ro 15:19 So from Jerusalem all the way around to **I,** *2665*

IMAGE (47) [IMAGES]
Ge 1:26 Then God said, "Let us make man in our **i,** 7512
1:27 So God created man in his own **i,** 7512
1:27 in the **i** *of* God he created him; 7512
5: 3 in his own **i;** and he named him Seth. 7512
9: 6 for in the **i** *of* God has God made man. 7512
Lev 26: 1 up an **i** or a sacred stone for yourselves, 7181
Dt 4:16 an idol, an **i** *of* any shape, 9454
27:15 "Cursed is the man who carves an **i** or casts 7181
Jdg 17: 3 the LORD for my son to make a **carved i** 7181
17: 4 who made them into the **i** and the idol. 7181
18:14 a **carved i** and a cast idol? 7181
18:17 the land went inside and took the **carved i,** 7181
18:18 into Micah's house and took the **carved i,** 7181
18:20 the other household gods and the **carved i** 7181
2Ch 33: 7 He took the carved **i** he had made and put it 6166
33:15 of the foreign gods and removed the **i** from 6166
Ne 9:18 when they cast for themselves an **i** of a calf 5011
Ps 106:20 They exchanged their Glory for an **i** *of* 9322
Isa 40:18 What **i** will you compare him to? 1952
48: 5 my wooden **i** and metal god ordained 7181
Jer 44:19 that we were making cakes **like** her **i** 6771
Da 3: 1 King Nebuchadnezzar made an **i** of gold, 10614
3: 2 to the dedication of the **i** he had set up. 10614
3: 3 the **i** that King Nebuchadnezzar had set up, 10614
3: 5 you must fall down and worship the **i** 10614
3: 7 down and worshiped the **i** *of* gold 10614
3:10 of music must fall down and worship the **i** 10614
3:12 nor worship the **i** *of* gold you have set up." 10614
3:14 or worship the **i** *of* gold I have set up? 10614
3:15 to fall down and worship the **i** I made, 10614
3:18 or worship the **i** *of* gold you have set up." 10614
Hab 2:18 Or an **i** that teaches lies? 5011
Ac 17:29 an **i** made by man's design and skill. *5916*
19:35 and of her **i, which fell from heaven?** *1479*
1Co 11: 7 since he is the **i** and glory of God; *1635*
2Co 4: 4 who is the **i** of God. *1635*
Col 1:15 He is the **i** of the invisible God, *1635*
3:10 in knowledge in the **i** of its Creator. *1635*
Rev 13:14 He ordered them to set up an **i** in honor of *1635*
13:15 He was given power to give breath *to* the **i** *1635*
13:15 and cause all who refused to worship the **i** *1635*
14: 9 the beast and his **i** and receives his mark on *1635*
14:11 for those who worship the beast and his **i,** *1635*
15: 2 and his **i** and over the number of his name *1635*
16: 2 the mark of the beast and worshiped his **i.** *1635*
19:20 the mark of the beast and worshiped his **i.** *1635*
20: 4 They had not worshiped the beast or his **i** *1635*

IMAGES (35) [IMAGE]
Nu 33:52 Destroy all their **carved i** 5381
Dt 7:25 **i** *of* their gods you are to burn in the fire. 7178
29:17 among them their **detestable i** and idols 9199
2Ch 34: 3 Asherah poles, carved idols and **cast i.** 5011
34: 4 Asherah poles, the idols and the **i.** 5011
Ps 97: 7 All who worship **i** are put to shame, 7181
Isa 10:10 kingdoms whose **i** excelled those 7178
10:11 not deal with Jerusalem and her **i** as I dealt 6773
21: 9 All the **i** *of* its gods lie shattered on 7178
30:22 with silver and your **i** covered with gold; 5011
41:29 their **i** are but wind and confusion. 5822
42:17 But those who trust in idols, who say to **i,** 5011
46: 1 **i that are carried about** are burdensome, 5953
Jer 8:19 they provoked me to anger with their **i,** 7178
10:14 His **i** are a fraud; 5822
16:18 with the lifeless forms of their **vile i** 9199
50: 2 Her **i** will be put to shame 6773
51:17 His **i** are a fraud; 5822
Eze 5:11 with all your **vile i** and detestable practices, 9199
7:20 to make their detestable idols and **vile i.** 9199
11:18 to it and remove all its **vile i** 9199
11:21 to their **vile i** and detestable idols, 9199
20: 7 get rid of the **vile i** you have set your eyes 9199
20: 8 of the **vile i** they had set their eyes on, 9199
Eze 20:30 and lust after their **vile i?** 9199
30:13 and put an end to the **i** in Memphis. 496
37:23 and **vile i** or with any of their offenses, 9199
Da 4: 5 the **i** and visions that passed 10217
11: 8 their **metal i** and their valuable articles 5816
Hos 11: 2 to the Baals and they burned incense to **i.** 7178
13: 2 from their silver, cleverly fashioned **i,** 6773
Mic 1: 7 I will destroy all her **i.** 6773
5:13 I will destroy your **carved i** 7178
Na 1:14 I will destroy the **carved i** and cast idols 7181
Ro 1:23 the glory of the immortal God for **i** made *1635*

IMAGINATION (2) [IMAGINE]
Eze 13: 2 to those who prophesy out of their own **i:** 4213
13:17 who prophesy out of their own **i.** 4213

IMAGINATIONS (2) [IMAGINE]
Isa 65: 2 pursuing their own **i—** 4742
66:18 "And I, because of their actions and their **i,** 4742

IMAGINE (4) [IMAGINATION, IMAGINATIONS]
Ps 41: 7 *they* **i** the worst for me, saying, 3108
Pr 18:11 they **i** it an unscalable wall. 928+5381
23:33 and your mind **i** confusing things. 1819
Eph 3:20 or **i,** according to his power that is at work *3783*

IMITATE (6) [IMITATED, IMITATORS]
Dt 18: 9 to **i** the detestable ways of the nations 3869+6913
Eze 23:48 may take warning and not **i** you. 3869+6913
1Co 4:16 Therefore I urge you to **i** me. *1181+3629*
Heb 6:12 but to **i** those who through faith *3629*
13: 7 of their way of life and **i** their faith. *3628*
3Jn 1:11 *do* not **i** what is evil but what is good. *3628*

IMITATED (1) [IMITATE]
2Ki 17:15 They **i** the nations around them although 339

IMITATORS (3) [IMITATE]
Eph 5: 1 Be **i** of God, therefore, *3629*
1Th 1: 6 You became **i** of us and of the Lord; *3629*
2:14 became **i** of God's churches in Judea, *3629*

IMLAH (4)
1Ki 22: 8 He is Micaiah son of **I."** 3551
22: 9 "Bring Micaiah son of **I** at once." 3551
2Ch 18: 7 He is Micaiah son of **I."** 3550
18: 8 "Bring Micaiah son of **I** at once," 3550

IMMANUEL (3)
Isa 7:14 give birth to a son, and will call him **I.** 6672
8: 8 the breadth of your land, O **I!"** 6672
Mt 1:23 **I"**—which means, "God with us." *1842*

IMMEASURABLY (1) [MEASURE]
Eph 3:20 to do **i** more than all we ask or imagine, *5655*

IMMEDIATE (1) [IMMEDIATELY]
1Ti 5: 8 and especially for his **i family,** *3858*

IMMEDIATELY (55) [IMMEDIATE]
1Sa 28:20 **I** Saul fell full length on the ground, 4554
2Sa 15:14 *We must* leave **i,** or he will move quickly 4554
17:16 Now send a message **i** and tell David, 4559
Ezr 4:23 they went **i** to the Jews in Jerusalem 10089+10096
Ne 5:11 Give back to them **i** their fields, 2021+3427+3869
Est 2: 9 **I** *he* provided her with her beauty treatments 987
Da 3: 6 and worship will **i** be thrown into a blazing furnace. 10002+10734
3:15 you will be thrown **i** into a blazing furnace. 10191+10734
4:33 **I** what had been said about 10002+10734
Mt 4:22 and **i** they left the boat and their father *2311*
8: 3 **I** he was cured of his leprosy. *2311*
14:22 **I** Jesus made the disciples get into the boat *2311*
14:27 But Jesus **i** said to them: "Take courage! *2317*
14:31 **I** Jesus reached out his hand *2311*
20:34 **I** they received their sight *2311*
21:19 **I** the tree withered. *4202*
24:29 **"I** after the distress of those days *2311*
26:74 **I** a rooster crowed. *2311*
27:48 **I** one of them ran and got a sponge. *2311*
Mk 1:42 **I** the leprosy left him and he was cured. *2317*
2: 8 **I** Jesus knew in his spirit that this was what *2317*
5:29 **I** her bleeding stopped and she felt *2317*
5:42 **I** the girl stood up and walked *2317*
6:27 So he **i** sent an executioner with orders *2317*
6:45 **I** Jesus made his disciples get into the boat *2317*
6:50 **I** he spoke to them and said, *2317*
9:20 it **i** threw the boy into a convulsion. *2317*
9:24 **I** the boy's father exclaimed, "I do believe; *2317*
10:52 **I** he received his sight and followed Jesus *2317*
14:72 **I** the rooster crowed the second time. *2317*
Lk 1:64 **I** his mouth was opened *4202*
5:13 And **i** the leprosy left him. *2311*
5:25 **I** he stood up in front of them, *4202*
8:44 and **i** her bleeding stopped. *4202*
12:36 when he comes and knocks they can **i** open *2311*
12:54 **i** you say, 'It's going to rain,' and it does. *2311*

Lk 13:13 and i she straightened up and praised God. 4202
14:5 will you not i pull him out?" 2311
18:43 I he received his sight and followed Jesus, 4202
19:5 "Zacchaeus, come down i. 5067
20:19 for a way to arrest him i, 899+1877+3836+6052
Jn 6:21 and i the boat reached the shore 2311
Ac 9:18 I, something like scales fell from Saul's 2311
9:34 I Aeneas got up. 2311
10:16 and i the sheet was taken back to heaven. 2317
10:33 So I sent for you i, 1994
12:23 I, because Herod did not give praise 4202
13:11 I mist and darkness came over him, 4202
16:33 then i he and all his family were baptized. 4202
17:14 The brothers i sent Paul to the coast, 2311
21:30 and i the gates were shut. 2311
22:18 'Leave Jerusalem i, because they will 1877+5443
22:29 about to question him withdrew i. 2311
Gal 1:17 but I went i into Arabia and later returned NIG
Jas 1:24 goes away and i forgets what he looks like. 2311

IMMENSE (1)

Eze 1:4 an i cloud with flashing lightning 1524

IMMER (10)

1Ch 9:12 the son of Meshillemith, the son of I. 612
24:14 the fifteenth to Bilgah, the sixteenth to I, 612
Ezr 2:37 of I 1,052 612
2:59 Tel Harsha, Kerub, Addon and I, 613
10:20 From the descendants of I: 612
Ne 3:29 of I made repairs opposite his house. 612
7:40 of I 1,052 612
7:61 Tel Harsha, Kerub, Addon and I, 613
11:13 the son of Meshillemoth, the son of I, 612
Jer 20:1 When the priest Pashhur son of I, 612

IMMORAL (10) [IMMORALITY]

Pr 6:24 keeping you from the i woman, 8273
1Co 5:9 not to associate with **sexually** i *people*— 4521
5:10 the people of this world who are i, 4521
5:11 a brother but is **sexually** i or greedy, 4521
6:9 the **sexually** i nor idolaters nor adulterers 4521
Eph 5:5 No i, impure or greedy person— 4521
Heb 12:16 See that no one *is* **sexually** i, 4521
13:4 the adulterer and all the **sexually** i. 4521
Rev 21:8 the vile, the murderers, the **sexually** i, 4521
22:15 the **sexually** i, the murderers, 4521

IMMORALITY (23) [IMMORAL]

Nu 25:1 the men began to **indulge in sexual** i 2388
Jer 3:9 Because Israel's i mattered so little to her, 2394
Mt 15:19 adultery, **sexual** i, theft, false testimony, 4518
Mk 7:21 come evil thoughts, **sexual** i, theft, 4518
Ac 15:20 from food polluted by idols, from **sexual** i, 4518
15:29 of strangled animals and *from* **sexual** i. 4518
21:25 of strangled animals and from **sexual** i." 4518
Ro 13:13 not *in* **sexual** i and debauchery, 3130
1Co 5:1 It is actually reported that there is **sexual** i 4518
6:13 The body is not *meant for* **sexual** i, 4518
6:18 Flee from **sexual** i. 4518
7:2 But since there is so much i, 4518
10:8 *We should* not **commit sexual** i, 4519
Gal 5:19 **sexual** i, impurity and debauchery; 4518
Eph 5:3 not be even a hint of **sexual** i, 4518
Col 3:5 **sexual** i, impurity, lust, 4518
1Th 4:3 that you should avoid **sexual** i; 4518
Jude 1:4 the grace of our God into a **license for** i 816
1:7 **gave** themselves **up to sexual** i 1745
Rev 2:14 to idols and by **committing sexual** i. 4519
2:20 into **sexual** i and the eating 4519
2:21 I have given her time to repent of her i, 4518
9:21 their **sexual** i or their thefts. 4518

IMMORTAL (3) [IMMORTALITY]

Ro 1:23 exchanged the glory *of* the i God for images 915
1Ti 1:17 Now to the King eternal, i, invisible, 915
6:16 who alone is i and who lives 114

IMMORTALITY (5) [IMMORTAL]

Pr 12:28 along that path is i. 440+4638
Ro 2:7 honor and i, he will give eternal life. 914
1Co 15:53 and the mortal with i. 114
15:54 and the mortal with i, 114
2Ti 1:10 and has brought life and i to light through 914

IMMOVABLE (2)

Job 41:23 they are firm and i. 1153+4572
Zec 12:3 I will make Jerusalem an i rock for all 5098

IMMUTABILITY, IMMUTABLE (KJV) See UNCHANGEABLE

IMNA (1)

1Ch 7:35 Zophah, I, Shelesh and Amal. 3557

IMNAH (4) [IMNITE]

Ge 46:17 I, Ishvah, Ishvi and Beriah. 3555
Nu 26:44 through I, the Imnite clan; 3555
1Ch 7:30 sons of Asher: I, Ishvah, Ishvi and Beriah. 3555
2Ch 31:14 Kore son of I the Levite, 3555

IMNITE (1) [IMNAH]

Nu 26:44 through Imnah, the I clan; 3555

IMPALED (1)

Ezr 6:11 and he is to be lifted up and i on it. 10411

IMPART (2) [IMPARTED, IMPARTS]

Ro 1:11 so that *I may* i to you some spiritual gift 3556
Gal 3:21 if a law had been given that could i **life,** 2443

IMPARTED (1) [IMPART]

Ecc 12:9 but also *he* i knowledge to the people. 4340

IMPARTIAL (1) [IMPARTIALLY]

Jas 3:17 full of mercy and good fruit, i and sincere. 88

IMPARTIALLY (2) [IMPARTIAL]

1Ch 24:5 divided them i by drawing lots, 465+465+6640
1Pe 1:17 on a Father who judges each man's work i, 719

IMPARTS (1) [IMPART]

Pr 29:15 The rod of correction i wisdom, 5989

IMPATIENT (3)

Nu 21:4 But the people *grew* i on the way; 5883+7918
Job 4:2 ventures a word with you, *will you be* i? 4206
21:4 Why *should* I not *be* i? 7918

IMPEDIMENT (KJV) See HARDLY TALK

IMPENITENT (KJV) See UNREPENTANT

IMPERFECT (1)

1Co 13:10 perfection comes, the i disappears. 1666+3538

IMPERIAL (13) [EMPIRE]

2Ki 25:8 Nebuzaradan commander of the i **guard,** 3184
25:10 under the commander of the i **guard,** 3184
25:15 The commander of the i **guard** took away 3184
Jer 39:9 of the i **guard** carried into exile to Babylon 3184
39:11 commander of the i **guard:** 3184
40:1 of the i **guard** had released him at Ramah. 3184
41:10 of the i **guard** had appointed Gedaliah son 3184
43:6 of the i **guard** had left with Gedaliah son 3184
52:12 Nebuzaradan commander of the i **guard,** 3184
52:14 under the commander of the i **guard** broke 3184
52:19 The commander of the i **guard** took away 3184
52:30 the commander of the i **guard.** 3184
Ac 27:1 who belonged to the I Regiment. 4935

IMPERISHABLE (6)

1Co 15:42 that is sown is perishable, it is raised i; 914+1877
15:50 nor does the perishable inherit the i. 914
15:52 the dead will be raised i, 915
15:53 the perishable must clothe itself with the i, 914
15:54 with the i, and the mortal with immortality, 914
1Pe 1:23 not of perishable seed, but *of* i, 915

IMPETUOUS (2)

Job 6:3 no wonder my words *have been* i. 4362
Hab 1:6 that ruthless and i people, 4554

IMPLACABLE (KJV) See RUTHLESS

IMPLANTED (1) [PLANT]

Ps 94:9 Does he *who* i the ear not hear? 5749

IMPLEAD (KJV) See PRESS CHARGES

IMPLORE (2)

Mal 1:9 "Now i God to be gracious to us. 2704+7156
2Co 5:20 *We* i you on Christ's behalf: 1289

IMPORTANCE (1) [IMPORTANT]

1Co 15:3 I passed on to you **as of first** i: 1877+4755

IMPORTANT (19) [IMPORTANCE]

Jos 10:2 because Gibeon was an i city, 1524
1Ki 3:4 for that was the **most** i high place, 1524
2Ki 25:9 Every i building he burned down. 1524
Jer 52:13 Every i building he burned down. 1524
Jnh 3:3 Now Nineveh was a very i city— 1524
Mt 6:25 Is not life **more** *i than* food, AIT
6:25 and the body more i than clothes? NIG
23:6 and the **most** i **seats** in the synagogues; 4751
23:23 But you have neglected the *more* i **matters** 987
Mk 12:28 which is the **most** i?" 4755
12:29 "The **most** i *one*," answered Jesus, "is this: 4755
12:33 is **more** i **than** all burnt offerings 4358
12:39 and have the **most** i **seats** in the synagogues 4751
Lk 11:43 because you love the **most** i **seats** in 4751
14:9 you will have to take the **least** i place. 2274
20:46 and have the **most** i **seats** in the synagogues 4751
Ac 8:27 an i **official** in charge of all the treasury 1541

Gal 2:6 As for those who seemed to be i— 5516
Php 1:18 The i **thing** is that in every way, 4440

IMPORTED (7)

1Ki 10:12 So much almugwood *has* never *been* i 995
10:28 Solomon's horses were i from Egypt and 4604
10:29 *They* i a chariot from Egypt 2256+3655+6590
2Ch 1:16 Solomon's horses were i from Egypt and 4604
1:17 *They* i a chariot from Egypt 2256+3655+6590
9:28 Solomon's horses *were* i from Egypt and 3655
Isa 17:10 the finest plants and plant i vines, 2424

IMPORTUNITY (KJV) See BOLDNESS

IMPOSE (2) [IMPOSED, IMPOSING, SELF-IMPOSED]

Ezr 7:24 that you have no authority to i taxes, 10667
Rev 2:24 not i any other burden on you): 965

IMPOSED (5) [IMPOSE]

2Ki 23:33 and *he* i on Judah a levy of a hundred talents 5989
2Ch 24:6 in from Judah and Jerusalem the **tax** *i* AIT
36:3 i *on* Judah **a levy** of a hundred talents 6740
Est 10:1 King Xerxes i tribute throughout 8492
Jer 19:9 during the stress of the siege i on them *by* 7439

IMPOSING (4) [IMPOSE]

Jos 22:10 and the half-tribe of Manasseh built an i altar 1524+4200+5260
1Ki 9:8 And though this temple is now i, 6609
2Ch 7:21 And though this temple is now *so* i, 6609
Da 7:20 the horn that looked more i than the others 10647

IMPOSSIBLE (13)

Ge 11:6 then nothing they plan to do *will be* i 1307
Jdg 6:5 **It was** i to count the men and their camels; 401
2Sa 13:2 it seemed i *for* him to do anything to her. 7098
Mt 17:20 Nothing *will be* i for you." 104
19:26 "With man this is i, but with God all things 105
Mk 10:27 "With man this is i, but not with God; 105
Lk 1:37 For nothing *is* i with God." 104
18:27 "What *is* i with men is possible with God." 105
Ac 2:24 i for death to keep its hold on him. 1543+4024
Heb 6:4 *It is* i for those who have once been enlightened, 105
6:18 by two unchangeable things in which it is i 105
10:4 because it is i for the blood of bulls 105
11:6 And without faith *it is* i to please God, 105

IMPOSTORS (2)

2Co 6:8 genuine, yet regarded as i; 4418
2Ti 3:13 while evil men and i will go from bad 1200

IMPOTENT (KJV) See CRIPPLE, CRIPPLED, DISABLED, INVALID

IMPOVERISHED (1) [POOR]

Jdg 6:6 Midian so i the Israelites that they cried out 1937

IMPRESS (1) [IMPRESSED, IMPRESSES, IMPRESSION, IMPRESSIVE]

Dt 6:7 I them on your children. 9112

IMPRESSED (1) [IMPRESS]

Ecc 9:13 of wisdom that greatly i me: 448

IMPRESSES (1) [IMPRESS]

Pr 17:10 A rebuke i a man of discernment more than 5737

IMPRESSION (1) [IMPRESS]

Gal 6:12 *to* **make a good** i outwardly are trying 2349

IMPRESSIVE (1) [IMPRESS]

1Sa 9:2 an i young man without equal among 3202

IMPRISON (1) [PRISON]

Ac 22:19 to another *to* i and beat those who believe 5872

IMPRISONED (4) [PRISON]

Ge 41:10 and *he* i me and the chief baker 928+5464+5989
1Sa 23:7 for David *has* i **himself** by entering a town 6037
Jer 32:3 Zedekiah king of Judah *had* i him there, 3973
37:15 and had him beaten and i 657+1074+2021+5989

IMPRISONMENT (3) [PRISON]

Ezr 7:26 banishment, confiscation of property, or i. 10054
Ac 23:29 against him that deserved death or i. 1301
26:31 not doing anything that deserves death or i." 1301

IMPRISONMENTS (1) [PRISON]

2Co 6:5 in beatings, i and riots; 5871

IMPRISONS (1) [PRISON]

Job 12:14 the man *he* i cannot be released. 6037

IMPROPER (1) [IMPROPERLY]
Eph 5: 3 because these are **i** for God's holy people. *NIG*

IMPROPERLY (1) [IMPROPER]
1Co 7:36 If anyone thinks *he is* **acting i** toward *858*

IMPROVISE (1)
Am 6: 5 like David and **i** on musical instruments. 3108

IMPUDENT (KJV) See BRAZEN, OBSTINATE, HARDENED

IMPURE (16) [IMPURITIES, IMPURITY]
Lev 7:18 for it is **i**; the person who eats any of it 7002
19: 7 it is **i** and will not be accepted. 7002
Nu 5:14 and he suspects his wife and she *is* **i**— 3237
5:14 and suspects her even though she *is* not **i**— 3237
5:19 not gone astray and become **i** while married 3240
Dt 23: 9 keep away from everything **i**. 8273
Job 14: 4 Who can bring what is pure from the **i**? 3238
Ac 10:14 "I have never eaten anything **i** or unclean." *3123*
10:15 *"Do* not **call** anything **i** that God has made *3123*
10:28 that I should not call any man **i** or unclean. *3123*
11: 8 Nothing **i** or unclean has ever entered my *3123*
11: 9 *'Do* not **call** anything **i** that God has made *3123*
Eph 5: 5 No immoral, **i** or greedy person— *176*
1Th 2: 3 not spring from error or **i** motives, *174*
4: 7 For God did not call us **to be i**, *174+2093*
Rev 21:27 Nothing **i** will ever enter it, *3123*

IMPURITIES (3) [IMPURE]
Isa 1:25 and remove all your **i**. 975
Eze 24:11 and its copper glows so its **i** may be melted 3240
36:25 from all your **i** and from all your idols. 3240

IMPURITY (16) [IMPURE]
Lev 15:19 **i of** her **monthly period** 5614
20:21 marries his brother's wife, it is an **act of i**; 5614
Nu 5:13 from her husband and *her* **i** is undetected 3237
5:28 not defiled herself and is **free from i**, 3196
Ezr 9:11 with their **i** from one end to the other. 3240
Eze 24:13 " 'Now your **i** is lewdness. 3240
24:13 but you would not be cleansed from your **i**, 3240
Zec 13: 1 to cleanse them from sin and **i**. 5614
13: 2 both the prophets and the spirit of **i** from 3240
Ro 1:24 of their hearts to **sexual i** for the degrading *174*
6:19 the parts of your body in slavery *to* **i** and *174*
2Co 12:21 and have not repented of the **i**, *174*
Gal 5:19 sexual immorality, **i** and debauchery; *174*
Eph 4:19 so as to indulge in every kind *of* **i**, *174*
5: 3 or of any kind of **i**, or of greed, *174*
Col 3: 5 sexual immorality, **i**, lust, *174*

IMPUTE, IMPUTED, IMPUTETH, IMPUTING (KJV) See ACCUSE, COUNT, COUNTING, CREDIT, CREDITED, CREDITS, HOLD GUILTY, TAKEN INTO ACCOUNT

IMRAH (1)
1Ch 7:36 Suah, Harnepher, Shual, Beri, **I**, 3559

IMRI (2)
1Ch 9: 4 the son of Omri, the son of **I**, 617
Ne 3: 2 and Zaccur son of **I** built next to them. 617

IN (11277) [INASMUCH, INMOST, INNER, INNERMOST, INSIDE, WITHIN] See Index of Articles Etc.

INASMUCH (1) [IN]
Ro 11:13 **I as** I am the apostle to the Gentiles, *2093+3525+4012+4036*

INCAPABLE (1)
Hos 8: 5 How long *will they be* **i** *of* purity? 3523+4202

INCENSE (150) [FRANKINCENSE, INCENSED]
Ex 25: 6 for the anointing oil and for the fragrant **i**; 7792
30: 1 an altar of acacia wood for burning **i**. 7792
30: 7 "Aaron must burn fragrant **i** on 7792
30: 8 He must burn **i** again when he lights 5626[S]
30: 8 so **i** will burn regularly before the LORD 7792
30: 9 Do not offer on this altar any other **i** 7792
30:27 and its accessories, the altar of **i**, 7792
30:35 and make a fragrant blend of **i**, 7792
30:37 Do not make any **i** with this formula 7792
31: 8 and all its accessories, the altar of **i**, 7792
31:11 and the anointing oil and fragrant **i** for 7792
35: 8 for the anointing oil and for the fragrant **i**; 7792
35:15 the altar of **i** with its poles, the anointing oil 7792
35:15 the anointing oil and the fragrant **i**; 7792
35:28 for the anointing oil and for the fragrant **i**. 7792
37:25 made the altar of **i** out of acacia wood. 7792
Ex 37:29 fragrant **i**—the work of a perfumer. 7792
39:38 the anointing oil, the fragrant **i**, 7792
40: 5 Place the gold altar of **i** in front of the ark 7792
40:27 and burned fragrant **i** on it, 7792
Lev 2: 1 He is to pour oil on it, put **i** on it 4247
2: 2 together with all the **i**, 4247
2:15 Put oil and **i** on it; it is a grain offering. 4247
2:16 together with all the **i**, 4247
4: 7 on the horns of the altar of fragrant **i** that is 7792
5:11 He must not put oil or **i** on it, 4247
6:15 together with all the **i** on the grain offering, 4247
10: 1 put fire in them and added **i**; 7792
16:12 of finely ground fragrant **i** and take them 7792
16:13 to put the **i** on the fire before the LORD, 7792
16:13 of the **i** will conceal the atonement cover 7792
24: 7 Along each row put *some* pure **i** as 4247
26:30 cut down your **i altars** 2802
Nu 4:16 the fragrant **i**, the regular grain offering and 7792
5:15 He must not pour oil on it or put **i** on it, 4247
7:14 gold dish weighing ten shekels, filled with **i**; 7792
7:20 gold dish weighing ten shekels, filled with **i**; 7792
7:26 gold dish weighing ten shekels, filled with **i**; 7792
7:32 gold dish weighing ten shekels, filled with **i**; 7792
7:38 gold dish weighing ten shekels, filled with **i**; 7792
7:44 gold dish weighing ten shekels, filled with **i**; 7792
7:50 gold dish weighing ten shekels, filled with **i**; 7792
7:56 gold dish weighing ten shekels, filled with **i**; 7792
7:62 gold dish weighing ten shekels, filled with **i**; 7792
7:68 gold dish weighing ten shekels, filled with **i**; 7792
7:74 gold dish weighing ten shekels, filled with **i**; 7792
7:80 gold dish weighing ten shekels, filled with **i**; 7792
7:86 with **i** weighed ten shekels each, 7792
16: 7 and tomorrow put fire and **i** in them before 7792
16:17 Each man is to take his censer and put **i** 7792
16:18 put fire and **i** in it, 7792
16:35 the 250 men who were offering the **i**. 7792
16:40 of Aaron should come to burn **i** before 7792
16:46 "Take your censer and put **i** in it, 7792
16:47 the **i** and made atonement for them. 7792
Dt 33:10 He offers **i** before you 7777
1Sa 2:28 to go up to my altar, to burn **i**, 7792
1Ki 3: 3 that he offered sacrifices and **burned i** on 7787
9:25 **burning i** before the LORD along 7787
11: 8 *who* **burned i** and offered sacrifices 7787
22:43 to offer sacrifices and **burn i** there. 7787
2Ki 12: 3 to offer sacrifices and **burn i** there. 7787
14: 4 to offer sacrifices and **burn i** there. 7787
15: 4 to offer sacrifices and **burn i** there. 7787
15:35 to offer sacrifices and **burn i** there. 7787
16: 4 He offered sacrifices and **burned i** at 7787
17:11 At every high place *they* **burned i**, 7787
18: 4 that time the Israelites had been **burning i** 7787
22:17 **burned i** to other gods and provoked me 7787
23: 5 *to* **burn i** on the high places of the towns 7787
23: 5 those *who* **burned i** to Baal, 7787
23: 8 where the priests *had* **burned i**. 7787
1Ch 6:49 of **i** in connection with all that was done in 7792
9:29 and the oil, **i** and spices. 4247
28:18 of the refined gold for the altar of **i**. 7792
2Ch 2: 4 to dedicate it to him for burning fragrant **i** 7792
13:11 and fragrant **i** to the LORD. 7792
14: 5 the high places and **i altars** in every town 2802
26:16 the LORD to **burn i** on the altar of incense. 7787
26:16 to burn incense on the altar of **i**. 7792
26:18 Uzziah, to **burn i** to the LORD. 7787
26:18 who have been consecrated to **burn i**. 7787
26:19 a censer in his hand *ready* to **burn i**, 7787
26:19 before the **i** altar in the LORD's temple, 7792
28: 4 He offered sacrifices and **burned i** at 7787
29: 7 not burn **i** or present any burnt offerings at 7792
29:11 to minister before him and *to* **burn i**." 7787
30:14 in Jerusalem and cleared away the **i altars** 5232
34: 4 he cut to pieces the **i altars** that were 2802
34: 7 to powder and cut to pieces all the **i altars** 2802
34:25 **burned i** to other gods and provoked me 7787
Ne 13: 5 to store the grain offerings and **i** 4247
13: 9 with the grain offerings and the **i**. 4247
Ps 141: 2 May my prayer be set before you like **i**; 7792
Pr 27: 9 Perfume and **i** bring joy to the heart, 7792
SS 3: 6 with myrrh and **i** made from all the spices 4247
4: 6 the mountain of myrrh and to the hill of **i**. 4247
4:14 with every kind of **i** tree, 4247
Isa 1:13 Your **i** is detestable to me. 7792
17: 8 and the **i altars** their fingers have made. 2802
27: 9 no Asherah poles or **i altars** will 2802
43:23 nor wearied you with demands for **i**. 4247
60: 6 bearing gold and **i** and proclaiming 4247
65: 3 offering sacrifices in gardens and **burning i** 7787
66: 3 and whoever burns memorial **i**, 4247
Jer 1:16 *in* **burning i** to other gods and 7787
6:20 about **i** from Sheba or sweet calamus from 4247
7: 9 adultery and perjury, **burn i** to Baal 7787
11:12 to the gods to whom they **burn i**, 7787
11:13 up to **burn i** to that shameful god Baal are 7787
11:17 and provoked me to anger by **burning i** 7787
17:26 **i** and thank offerings to the house of 4247
18:15 *they* **burn i** to worthless idols, 7787
19:13 the houses where *they* **burned i** on the roofs 7787
32:29 to anger by **burning i** on the roofs to Baal 7787
41: 5 and **i** with them to the house of the LORD. 4247
44: 3 by **burning i** and by worshiping other gods 7787
44: 5 from their wickedness or stop **burning i** 7787
44: 8 **burning i** to other gods in Egypt, 7787
44:15 that their wives *were* **burning i** 7787
44:17 We *will* **burn i** to the Queen of Heaven 7787
44:18 since we stopped **burning i** to the Queen 7787
44:19 When we **burned i** to the Queen of Heaven 7787
Jer 44:21 and think about the **i** burned in the towns 7789
44:23 Because *you have* **burned i** and have sinned 7787
44:25 to **burn i** and pour out drink offerings to 7787
48:35 on the high places and **burn i** to their gods," 7787
Eze 6: 4 be demolished and your **i altars** will 2802
6: 6 your **i altars** broken down, 2802
6:13 places where they offered **fragrant i** 5767+8194
8:11 and a fragrant cloud of **i** was rising. 7792
16:18 and you offered my oil and **i** before them. 7792
16:19 you offered as **fragrant i** before them. 5767+8194
20:28 presented their **fragrant i** 5767+8194
20:41 as **fragrant i** when I bring you out 5767+8194
23:41 before it on which you had placed the **i** 7792
Da 2:46 that an offering and **i** be presented to him. 10478
Hos 2:13 I will punish her for the days *she* **burned i** to the Baals; 7787
11: 2 to the Baals and *they* **burned i** to images. 7787
Hab 1:16 to his net and **burns i** to his dragnet, 7787
Mal 1:11 In every place **i** and pure offerings will 5231
Mt 2:11 with gifts of gold and of **i** and of myrrh. *3337*
Lk 1: 9 into the temple of the Lord and **burn i**. *2594*
1:10 when the time *for* the **burning of i** came, *2592*
1:11 standing at the right side of the altar *of* **i**. *2592*
Heb 9: 4 which had the golden **altar of i** and *2593*
Rev 5: 8 *of* **i**, which are the prayers of the saints. *2592*
8: 3 He was given much **i** to offer, *2592*
8: 4 smoke *of* the **i**, together with the prayers *2592*
18:13 of **i**, myrrh and frankincense, *2592*

INCENSED (1) [INCENSE]
Ne 4: 1 he became angry and *was* greatly **i**. 4087

INCHES (1)
Ge 6:16 a roof for it and finish the ark to within **18 i** 564

INCIDENT (1)
1Ki 21: 1 Some time later there was an **i** involving NIH

INCITED (6) [INCITING]
1Sa 22: 8 that my son *has* **i** my servant to lie in wait 7756
26:19 If the LORD *has* **i** you against me, 6077
2Sa 24: 1 and *he* **i** David against them, saying, 6077
1Ch 21: 1 against Israel and **i** David to take a census 6077
Job 2: 3 though *you* **i** me against him to ruin him 6077
Ac 13:50 But the Jews **i** the God-fearing women *4241*

INCITING (2) [INCITED]
Jer 43: 3 son of Neriah *is* **i** you against us to hand us 6077
Lk 23:14 **who** *was* **i** the people **to rebellion.** *695*

INCLINATION (2) [INCLINATIONS, INCLINED, INCLINES]
Ge 6: 5 and that every **i** *of* the thoughts 3671
8:21 every **i** *of* his heart is evil from childhood. 3671

INCLINATIONS (1) [INCLINATION]
Jer 7:24 instead, they followed the stubborn **i** 4600

INCLINED (3) [INCLINATION]
Dt 5:29 that their hearts *would be* **i** to fear me 2118+2296
Jdg 9: 3 they *were* **i** to follow Abimelech, 4213+5742
1Sa 20:13 But if my father *is* **i** to harm you, 3512

INCLINES (1) [INCLINATION]
Ecc 10: 2 The heart of the wise **i** to the right, 4200

INCLOSE (KJV) See ENCLOSE

INCLUDE (18) [INCLUDED, INCLUDES, INCLUDING]
Nu 1:49 **i** them **in the census** 906+5951+8031
28:22 **I** one male goat as a sin offering 2256
28:30 **I** one male goat to make atonement for you. NIH
29: 5 **I** one male goat as a sin offering 2256
29:11 **I** one male goat as a sin offering, NIH
29:16 **I** one male goat as a sin offering, 2256
29:19 **I** one male goat as a sin offering, 2256
29:22 **I** one male goat as a sin offering, 2256
29:25 **I** one male goat as a sin offering, 2256
29:28 **I** one male goat as a sin offering, 2256
29:31 **I** one male goat as a sin offering, 2256
29:34 **I** one male goat as a sin offering, 2256
29:38 **I** one male goat as a sin offering, 2256
34: 3 " 'Your southern side *will* **i** some of 2118
Jos 17: 7 The boundary ran southward from there to **i** 448
1Ch 21: 6 not **i** Levi and Benjamin in the numbering, 928+9348
Eze 16:29 to **i** Babylonia, a land of merchants, but 448
1Co 15:27 it is clear that this does **not i** God himself, *1760*

INCLUDED (18) [INCLUDE]
Dt 4:49 **and i** all the Arabah east of the Jordan, 2256
Jos 12: 2 This **i** half of Gilead. 2256
13: 9 **and i** the whole plateau of Medeba as far 2256
13:11 It **also i** Gilead, the territory of the people 2256
16: 9 It **also i** all the towns and their villages NIH
19: 2 It **i**: Beersheba (or Sheba), Moladah, 2118
19:15 **I** were Kattath, Nahalal, Shimron, 2256
19:18 Their territory **i**: Jezreel, 2118

Jos 19:25 Their territory i: Helkath, 2118
19:41 The territory of their inheritance i: 2118
2Sa 23:19 even though *he was* not i among them. 995
23:23 but *he was* not i among the Three. 995
1Ch 7:28 Their lands and settlements i Bethel NIH
11:21 even though *he was* not i among them. 995
11:25 but *he was* not i among the Three. 995
2Ch 31:18 They i all the little ones, the wives, NIH
Job 3: 6 *may it* not **be** i among the days of the year 2526
Eph 1:13 also were i in Christ when you heard *NIG*

INCLUDES (1) [INCLUDE]

2Th 1:10 all those who have believed. This i you, *NIG*

INCLUDING (66) [INCLUDE]

Ge 17:12 i those born in your household or bought NIH
17:27 i those born in his household or bought NIH
19:25 i all those living in the cities— 2256
Ex 10: 5 i every tree that is growing in your fields. 2256
27:19 i all the tent pegs for it and those for 2256
34:19 i all the firstborn males of your livestock, 2256
Lev 1: 8 i the head **and** the fat, 2256
1:12 i the head and the fat, 2256
9:13 i the head, and he burned them on the altar. 2256
Nu 3:39 i every male a month old or more, NIH
4:14 i the firepans, meat forks, NIH
4:16 i its holy furnishings and articles." 928
21:25 and occupied them, i Heshbon 928
31:11 i the people and animals, 928
Dt 3:12 i half the hill country of Gilead, 2256
Jos 8:35 i the women and children, 2256
10: 7 i all the best fighting men. 2256
10:40 i the hill country, the Negev, 2256
12: 1 i all the eastern side of the Arabah: 2256
13:17 i Dibon, Bamoth Baal, Beth Baal Meon, NIH
13:30 from Mahanaim and i all of Bashan, NIH
24: 2 i Terah the father of Abraham and Nahor, NIH
24:18 i the Amorites, who lived in the land. 2256
Jdg 20:48 the towns to the sword, i the animals 6330
21:10 i the women and children. 2256
1Sa 30:18 i his two wives. 2256
1Ki 4:31 i Ethan the Ezrahite— 4946
10:15 **not** i the revenues from merchants and traders 963+4200+4946
14:26 i all the gold shields Solomon had made. 2256
22:39 other events of Ahab's reign, i all he did, 2256
2Ki 8: 6 i all the income from her land from 2256
13:12 i his war against Amaziah king of Judah, 889
14:15 i his war against Amaziah king of Judah, 2256
14:28 i how he recovered for Israel both 2256
15:29 i all the land of Naphtali, NIH
21:17 and all he did, i the sin he committed, 2256
24: 4 i the shedding of innocent blood. 1685+2256
1Ch 12:27 i Jehoiada, leader of the family of Aaron, 2256
21: 5 i four hundred and seventy thousand in 2256
2Ch 8:15 i that of the treasuries. 2256
9:14 **not** i the revenues brought in by merchants 963+4200+4946
12: 9 i the gold shields Solomon had made. 2256
27: 7 i all his wars and the other things he did, 2256
30:25 i the aliens who had come from Israel 2256
33:18 i his prayer to his God and the words 2256
Ezr 7: 7 Some of the Israelites, i priests, Levites, 2256
7:13 i priests and Levites, 10221
9: 1 i the priests and the Levites, 2256
Ne 1: 6 i myself and my father's house, 2256
10:39 The people of Israel, i the Levites, 2256
Est 4: 7 i the exact amount of money Haman had 2256
Ecc 12:14 deed into judgment, i every hidden thing, 6584
Jer 10:16 for he is the Maker of all things, i Israel, 2256
13:13 i the kings who sit on David's throne, 2256
42: 1 i Johanan son of Kareah and Jezaniah son 2256
44:24 the people, i the women, "Hear the word of 2256
51:19 i the tribe of his inheritance— 2256
Eze 10:12 Their entire bodies, i their backs, 2256
41:14 i the front of the temple, 2256
41:15 i its galleries on each side; 2256
41:16 and i the threshold was covered with wood. NIH
Mt 8:33 i what had happened to *2779*
Lk 23:27 i women who mourned and wailed for him. *2779*
23:49 i the women who had followed him *2779*
Ro 16: 2 a great help to many people, i me. *2779*
2Ti 1:15 i Phygelus and Hermogenes. *1639+4005*

INCOME (6)

2Ki 8: 6 the i *from* her land from the day she left 9311
Pr 10:16 i *of* the wicked brings them punishment. 9311
15: 6 but the i *of* the wicked brings them trouble. 9311
Ecc 5:10 whoever loves wealth is never satisfied with his **i.** 9311
Ac 19:25 "Men, you know we receive a **good i** *2345*
1Co 16: 2 **in keeping with** *his* **i,** *1569+2338+4005+5516*

INCOMPARABLE (1) [INCOMPARABLY]

Eph 2: 7 the coming ages he might show the i riches *5650*

INCOMPARABLY (1) [INCOMPARABLE]

Eph 1:19 and his i great power for us who believe. *5650*

INCOMPREHENSIBLE (1)

Isa 33:19 with their strange, i tongue. 401+1069

INCONTINENCY (KJV) See LACK OF SELF-CONTROL

INCORRUPTIBLE, INCORRUPTION (KJV) See IMPERISHABLE, LAST FOREVER, NEVER PERISH

INCREASE (54) [EVER-INCREASING, INCREASED, INCREASES, INCREASING]

Ge 1:22 and i **in number** and fill the water in 8049
1:22 and *let* the birds i on the earth." 8049
1:28 "Be fruitful and i **in number;** 8049
3:16 *"I will* **greatly** i your pains in childbearing; 8049+8049
6: 1 men began to i **in number** on the earth 8045
8:17 on the earth and be fruitful and i **in number** 8049
9: 1 "Be fruitful and i **in number** and fill 8049
9: 7 As for you, be fruitful and i **in number;** 8049
9: 7 multiply on the earth and i upon it." 8049
16:10 *"I will* **so** i your descendants that they 8049+8049
17: 2 and you and *will* greatly i your **numbers."** 8049
17:20 and *will* greatly i his **numbers.** 8049
24:60 *may* you i to thousands upon thousands; 2118
26:24 and *will* i **the number** *of* your descendants 8049
28: 3 and make you fruitful and i your **numbers** 8049
35:11 be fruitful and i **in number.** 8049
48: 4 and *will* i your **numbers.** 8049
48:16 and *may they* i greatly upon the earth." 1835
Lev 25:16 the years are many, *you are to* i the price, 8049
26: 9 and make you fruitful and i your **numbers,** 8049
Dt 1:11 i you a thousand times and bless you 3578+6584
6: 3 and that *you may* i greatly in a land flowing 8049
7:13 and bless you and i your **numbers.** 8049
8: 1 and i and may enter and possess the land 8049
8:13 and gold i and all you have is multiplied, 8049
13:17 on you, and i your **numbers,** 8049
28:63 to make you prosper and i **in number,** 8049
30:16 then you will live and **i,** 8049
Job 10:17 against me and i your anger toward me; 8049
Ps 16: 4 of those *will* i who run after other gods. 8049
61: 6 **I** the days of the king's life, 3578
62:10 though your riches **i,** do not set your heart 5649
71:21 *You will* i my honor and comfort me 8049
73:12 always carefree, *they* i in wealth. 8436
115:14 *May* the LORD **make** you **i,** 3578
144:13 Our sheep *will* **i by thousands,** 545
Pr 22:16 He who oppresses the poor to i his wealth 8049
Ecc 5: 9 The i *from* the land is taken by all; 3862
5:11 As goods **i,** so do those who consume them. 8049
Isa 9: 7 Of the i *of* his government and peace 5269
Jer 23: 3 where they will be fruitful and i **in number.** 8049
29: 6 **I in number** there; do not decrease. 8049
Eze 36:11 *I will* i **the number** *of* men and animals 8049
36:30 *I will* i the fruit of the trees and the crops 8049
37:26 I will establish them and i their **numbers,** 8049
Da 12: 4 and there *to* i knowledge." 8049
Hos 4:10 they will engage in prostitution but not **i,** 7287
Mt 24:12 Because of the i of wickedness, *4437*
Lk 17: 5 The apostles said to the Lord, **"I** our faith!" *4707*
Ac 12:24 word of God *continued to* i and spread. *889*
Ro 5:20 law was added so that the trespass *might* **i.** *4429*
6: 1 go on sinning so that grace *may* **i?** *4429*
2Co 9:10 for food will also supply and i your store *4437*
1Th 3:12 *May* the Lord **make** your love i and *4429*

INCREASED (32) [INCREASE]

Ge 7:17 and *as* the waters i they lifted the ark high 8049
7:18 The waters rose and i greatly on the earth, 8049
30:30 little you had before I came *has* i greatly, 7287
47:27 and were fruitful and i greatly **in number.** 8049
Ex 1:20 the midwives and the people i and became 8049
23:30 until *you have* **i** *enough* to take possession 7238
Lev 19:25 In this way your harvest *will be* **i.** 3578
Dt 1:10 The LORD your God *has* i your **numbers** so 8049
Jdg 1:35 when the power of the house of Joseph **i,** 3877
1Sa 14:19 tumult in the Philistine camp **i more and more.** 2143+2143+2256+8041
1Ch 4:38 Their families i greatly, 7287
5: 9 because their livestock *had* i in Gilead. 8049
2Ch 33:23 Amon i his guilt. 8049
Ps 25:19 See how my enemies *have* i and 8045
39: 2 even saying anything good, my anguish **i.** 6579
107:38 and *their* **numbers** greatly **i,** 8049
107:41 and i their families like flocks. 8492
Ecc 1:16 I have grown and i in wisdom more than 3578
Isa 9: 3 have enlarged the nation and i their joy; 1540
57: 9 with olive oil and i your perfumes. 8049
Jer 3:16 *your* **numbers** *have* **i greatly** 2256+7238+8049
Eze 16:29 Then *you* i your promiscuity 8049
28: 5 in trading *you have* i your wealth, 8049
31: 5 its boughs i and its branches grew long, 8049
Hos 4: 7 The more the priests **i,** 8045
10: 1 As his fruit **i,** he built more altars; 8044
Na 3:16 *You have* i **the number** *of* your merchants 8049
Lk 11:29 *As* the crowds **i,** Jesus said, *2044*
Ac 6: 7 of disciples in Jerusalem i rapidly, *4437*
7:17 of our people in Egypt **greatly i.** *889+2779+4437*
Ro 5:20 But where sin **i,** grace increased all the *4429*
5:20 where sin increased, grace **i all the more,** *5668*

INCREASES (5) [INCREASE]

Ps 49:16 when the splendor of his house **i;** 8049
Pr 24: 5 and a man of knowledge i strength; 599
28: 8 *He who* i his wealth by exorbitant interest 8049
Isa 40:29 to the weary and i the power of the weak. 8049
Ro 3: 7 and so i his glory, why am I still condemned *NIG*

INCREASING (7) [INCREASE]

2Sa 15:12 and Absalom's following kept on **i.** 8041
Job 21: 7 growing old and i *in* power? 1504
Eze 16:25 offering your body *with* i promiscuity 8049
16:26 to anger with your i promiscuity. 8049
Ac 6: 1 *when* the number of disciples *was* **i,** *4437*
2Th 1: 3 of you has for each other *is* **i.** *4429*
2Pe 1: 8 if you possess these qualities in i measure, *4429*

INCREDIBLE (1)

Ac 26: 8 Why should any of you consider it i *603*

INCUR (1) [INCURS]

Ex 28:43 so that *they will* not i guilt and die. 5951

INCURABLE (7)

2Ch 21:18 with an i disease of the bowels. 401+5340
Job 34: 6 his arrow inflicts an i **wound.'** 631
Isa 17:11 as nothing in the day of disease and i pain. 631
Jer 10:19 My wound *is* **i!** 2703
15:18 and my wound grievous and **i?** 4412+8324
30:12 " 'Your wound is **i,** 631
Mic 1: 9 For her wound is **i;** it has come to Judah. 631

INCURS (2) [INCUR]

Pr 9: 7 whoever rebukes a wicked man i abuse. NIH
14:35 but a shameful servant i his wrath. 2118

INDECENT (3)

Dt 23:14 that he will not see among you anything i 6872
24: 1 because he finds something i about her, 6872
Ro 1:27 Men committed i **acts** with other men, *859*

INDECISIVE (1)

2Ch 13: 7 and i and not strong enough to resist 4222+8205

INDEED (64)

Ge 15: 5 **if** i you can count them." 561
27:33 **and** i he will be blessed!" 1685
Ex 3: 7 *"I have* i **seen** the misery of my people 8011+8011
Nu 22: 3 **I,** Moab was filled with dread because of 2256
Dt 9:13 and they are a stiff-necked people **i!** 2180
18: 1 i the whole tribe of Levi— NIH
Jdg 5:29 The wisest of her ladies answer her; **i,** 677
1Sa 21: 5 **"I** women have been kept from us, 561+3954
2Sa 3:36 **i,** everything the king did pleased them. 3869
14: 5 She said, "I am i a widow; 66
1Ki 8:13 *I have* i **built** a magnificent temple 1215+1215
10: 7 **I,** not even half was told me; 2180
2Ki 14:10 *You have* i **defeated** Edom and 5782+5782
1Ch 16:19 When they were but few in number, few **i,** 3869
2Ch 9: 6 **I,** not even half the greatness 2180
12:12 **I,** there was some good in Judah. 1685+2256
13: 8 You are i a vast army and have with you 2256
20: 4 **i,** they came from every town in Judah 1685
26:20 **I,** he himself was eager to leave, 1685+2256
Job 9: 2 **"I,** I know that this is true. 597
13:16 **I,** this will turn out for my deliverance, 1685
19: 5 If i you would exalt yourselves above me 597
35:13 **I,** God does not listen to their empty plea; 421
Ps 58: 1 Do you rulers i speak justly? 598
85:12 The LORD will i give what is good, 1685
87: 5 **I,** of Zion it will be said, 2256
89:18 **I,** our shield belongs to the LORD, 3954
105:12 When they were but few in number, few **i,** NIH
121: 4 **i,** he who watches over Israel 2180
Jer 2:20 **I,** on every high hill and 3954
14:13 **I,** I will give you lasting peace 3954
14:20 we have i sinned against you. 3954
20: 9 I am weary of holding it in; **i,** I cannot. 2256
23:32 **I,** I am against those 2180
25:29 and *will* you **i go unpunished?** 5927+5927
32:30 **i,** the people of Israel have done nothing 3954
42:17 **I,** all who are determined to go to Egypt 2256
La 3: 3 **i,** he has turned his hand against me again 421
Eze 33:32 **I,** to them you are nothing more than one who sings love songs with a 2180
Hab 2: 5 **i,** wine betrays him; 677+2256+3954
Mt 20:23 "You will i drink from my cup, *3525*
Lk 12: 7 **I,** the very hairs of your head *247+2779*
13:30 **I** there are those who are last who will *2627+2779*
18:25 **I,** it is easier for a camel to go through *1142*
Jn 4:14 **I,** the water I give him will become in him *247*
8:24 you will i die in your sins." *NIG*
8:36 if the Son sets you free, you will be free **i.** *3953*
Ac 3:24 **"I,** all the prophets from Samuel on, *1254+2779*
4:27 **I** Herod and Pontius Pilate met together *1142*
7:34 *I have* i **seen** the oppression of my people *3972+3972*
Ro 2:14 **(I,** when Gentiles, who do not have the law *1142*
7: 7 **I** I would not have known what sin was *247*
8:17 with Christ, **if** i we share in his sufferings *1642*
15:27 **and** i they owe it to them. *2779*
1Co 3: 2 **I,** you are still not ready. *247*
4: 3 **i,** I do not even judge myself. *247*
8: 5 or on earth (**as** i there are many "gods" *6061*
14: 2 **I,** no one understands him; *1142*

1Co 15:20 But Christ has **i** been raised from the dead, *3815*
2Co 1: 9 **I**, in our hearts we felt the sentence *247*
Php 2:27 **I** he was ill, and almost died. *1142*
4:10 **I**, you have been concerned, *2779*
Col 2:23 Such regulations **i** have an appearance *3525*
1Th 2:20 **I**, you are our glory and joy. *1142*

INDEPENDENT (2)
1Co 11:11 however, woman is not **i of** man, *6006*
11:11 nor is man **i** of woman. *NIG*

INDESCRIBABLE (1)
2Co 9:15 Thanks be to God for his **i** gift! *442*

INDESTRUCTIBLE (1)
Heb 7:16 but on the basis of the power *of* an **i** life. *186*

INDIA (2)
Est 1: 1 over 127 provinces stretching from **I** 2064
8: 9 of the 127 provinces stretching from **I** 2064

INDICATE (3) [INDICATED, INDICATING]
1Sa 16: 3 You are to anoint for me the one *I* **i**." 606
Jn 21:19 Jesus said this *to* **i** the kind of death *4955*
Heb 12:27 The words "once more" **i** the removing *1317*

INDICATED (2) [INDICATE]
Nu 1:18 The people **i** *their* **ancestry** by their clans 3528
2Ki 6:10 So the king of Israel checked on the place **i** 606

INDICATING (2) [INDICATE]
Jn 18:32 that the words Jesus had spoken **i** the kind *4955*
Heb 9: 9 **i that** the gifts and sacrifices being *2848+4005*

INDICTMENT (1)
Job 31:35 let my accuser put his **i** in writing. 6219

INDIGNANT (6) [INDIGNANTLY, INDIGNATION]
Mt 20:24 *they were* **i** with the two brothers. *24*
21:15 to the Son of David," *they were* **i**. *24*
26: 8 When the disciples saw this, *they were* **i**. *24*
Mk 10:14 When Jesus saw this, *he was* **I**. *24*
10:41 they became **i** with James and John. *24*
Lk 13:14 **I** because Jesus had healed on the Sabbath, *24*

INDIGNANTLY (1) [INDIGNANT]
Mk 14: 4 Some of those present were **saying i** *24*

INDIGNATION (6) [INDIGNANT]
Ps 78:49 his wrath, **i** and hostility— 2405
90: 7 by your anger and terrified by your **i**. 2779
119:53 **I** grips me because of the wicked, 2363
Jer 15:17 on me and you had filled me with **i**. 2405
Na 1: 6 Who can withstand his **i**? 2405
2Co 7:11 what eagerness to clear yourselves, what **i**, *25*

INDISPENSABLE (1)
1Co 12:22 of the body that seem to be weaker are **i**, *338*

INDIVIDUALLY (1)
1Ch 23:24 under their names and counted **i**, 1653+4200

INDOORS (2)
Mt 9:28 When he had gone **i**, *1650+3836+3864*
Mk 9:28 After Jesus had gone **i**, *1650+3875*

INDULGE (7) [INDULGED, INDULGENCE, INDULGING, SELF-INDULGENCE]
Ex 32: 6 to eat and drink and got up to **i in revelry**. 7464
Nu 25: 1 the men began to **i in sexual immorality** 2388
Lk 7:25 those who wear expensive clothes and **i** *5639*
1Co 10: 7 and got up *to* **i in pagan revelry**." *4089*
Gal 5:13 not use your freedom to **i** the sinful nature; *929*
Eph 4:19 over to sensuality so as to **i** in every kind *2238*
2Ti 2:16 because *those who* **i** in it will become more *4621*

INDULGED (1) [INDULGE]
2Co 12:21 and debauchery in which *they have* **i**. *4556*

INDULGENCE (1) [INDULGE]
Col 2:23 they lack any value in restraining sensual **i**. *4447*

INDULGING (1) [INDULGE]
1Ti 3: 8 sincere, not **i** in much wine, *4668*

INEFFECTIVE (1)
2Pe 1: 8 they will keep you from being **i** *734*

INEXCUSABLE (KJV) See NO EXCUSE

INEXPERIENCED (2)
1Ch 22: 5 "My son Solomon is young and **i**, 8205
29: 1 one whom God has chosen, is young and **i**. 8205

INEXPRESSIBLE (2)
2Co 12: 4 He heard **i** *things*, things that man is not *777*
1Pe 1: 8 you believe in him and are filled with an **i** *443*

INFALLIBLE (KJV) See CONVINCING

INFAMOUS (1) [INFAMY]
Eze 22: 5 O **i** city, full of turmoil. 2021+3238+9005

INFAMY (1) [INFAMOUS]
Isa 44:11 they will be brought down to terror and **i**. 1017

INFANCY (1) [INFANT]
2Ti 3:15 from **i** you have known the holy Scriptures, *1100*

INFANT (7) [INFANCY, INFANT'S, INFANTS]
Nu 11:12 as a nurse carries an **i**, 3437
12:12 not let her be like a **stillborn i** coming 4637
Job 3:16 like an **i** who never saw the light of day? 6407
24: 9 the **i** *of* the poor is seized for a debt. 6403
Isa 11: 8 The **i** will play near the hole of the cobra, 3437
65:20 be in it an **i** who lives but a few days, or 6403
Heb 5:13 Anyone who lives on milk, being still an **i**, *3758*

INFANT'S (1) [INFANT]
La 4: 4 the **i** tongue sticks to the roof of its mouth; 3437

INFANTS (15) [INFANT]
Dt 32:25 **i** and gray-haired men. 3437
1Sa 15: 3 children and **i**, cattle and sheep, 3437
22:19 with its men and women, its children and **i**, 3437
Ps 8: 2 of children and **i** you have ordained praise 3437
137: 9 he who seizes your **i** and dashes them 6408
Isa 13:16 Their **i** will be dashed to pieces 6407
13:18 they will have no mercy on **i** 1061+7262
Jer 44: 7 the men and women, the children and **i**, 3437
La 2:11 children and **i** faint in the streets of the city. 3437
Na 3:10 Her **i** were dashed to pieces at the head 6408
Mt 21:16 and **i** you have ordained praise'?" *2558*
Ro 2:20 a teacher *of* **i**, because you have in the law *3758*
1Co 3: 1 but as worldly—mere **i** in Christ. *3758*
14:20 In regard to evil *be* **i**, *3757*
Eph 4:14 Then we will no longer be **i**, *3758*

INFECTED (4) [INFECTION]
Lev 13: 4 the priest is to put the **i person** in isolation 5596
13:12 the skin of the **i person** from head to foot, 5596
13:17 shall pronounce the **i person** clean; 5596
13:31 is to put the **i person** in isolation 5596+5999

INFECTION (1) [INFECTED, INFECTIOUS]
Lev 13:46 As long as he has the **i** he remains unclean. 5596

INFECTIOUS (21) [INFECTION]
Lev 13: 2 that may become an **i** skin disease, 5596
13: 3 it is an **i** skin disease. 5596
13: 8 it is an **i disease**. 7669
13: 9 "When anyone has an **i** skin disease, 5596
13:15 raw flesh is unclean; he has an **i disease**. 7669
13:20 an **i** skin disease that has broken out where 5596
13:22 priest shall pronounce him unclean; it is **i**. 5596
13:25 an **i disease** that has broken out in the burn. 7669
13:25 it is an **i** skin disease. 5596
13:27 it is an **i** skin disease. 5596
13:30 it is an itch, an **i disease** *of* the head or chin. 7669
13:42 it is an **i disease** breaking out on his head 7669
13:43 like an **i** skin **disease**, 7669
13:45 The person with such an **i** disease must wear 5596
14: 3 of his **i** skin disease, 5596
14: 7 of the **i disease** and pronounce him clean. 7669
14:32 an **i** skin disease and who cannot afford 5596
14:54 the regulations for any **i** skin disease, 5596
14:57 **i skin diseases and mildew.** 7669
22: 4 a descendant of Aaron **has an i skin disease** 7665
Nu 5: 2 anyone who **has an i skin disease** 7665

INFERIOR (6)
Job 12: 3 I *am* not **i** to you. 5877
13: 2 I *am* not **i** to you. 5877
Da 2:39 another kingdom will rise, **i** to yours. 10075
2Co 11: 5 But I do not think *I am* in the least **i to** *5728*
12:11 not in the least **i** to the "super-apostles," *5728*
12:13 How were *you* **i** to the other churches, *2273*

INFIDEL (KJV) See UNBELIEVER

INFILTRATED (1)
Gal 2: 4 some false brothers *had* **i** *our* **ranks** *4207+4209*

INFINITE (KJV) See BOUNDLESS, ENDLESS, NO LIMIT

INFIRMITIES (2) [INFIRMITY]
Isa 53: 4 he took up our **i** and carried our sorrows, 2716
Mt 8:17 "He took up our **i** and carried our diseases." *819*

INFIRMITY (1) [INFIRMITIES]
Lk 13:12 "Woman, you are set free *from* your **i**." *819*

INFLAMED (3) [INFLAMMATION]
Isa 5:11 up late at night *till* they *are* **i** *with* wine. 1944
Hos 7: 5 the princes *become* **i** *with* wine, 2703+2779
Ro 1:27 and *were* **i** with lust for one another. *1706*

INFLAMMATION (1) [INFLAMED]
Dt 28:22 with fever and **i**, with scorching heat 1945

INFLICT (22) [INFLICTED, INFLICTS]
Dt 7:15 not **i** on you the horrible diseases you knew 8492
7:15 but *he will* **i** them on all who hate you. 5989
28:53 of the suffering that your enemy *will* **i** 7439
28:55 because of the suffering your enemy *will* **i** 7439
28:57 the distress that your enemy *will* **i** on you 7439
Jdg 20:31 to **i** casualties on the Israelites as before, so 5782
20:39 The Benjamites had begun to **i** casualties 5782
Ps 149: 7 to **i** vengeance on the nations 6913
Jer 18: 8 and not **i** on it the disaster I had planned. 6913
36: 3 about every disaster I plan to **i** on them, 6913
Eze 5: 8 and *I will* **i** punishment on you in 6913
5:10 *I will* **I** punishment on you 6913
5:15 when I **i** punishment on you in anger and 6913
11: 9 over to foreigners and **i** punishment on you. 6913
16:41 down your houses and **i** punishment on you 6913
25:11 and *I will* **i** punishment on Moab. 6913
28:22 when I **i** punishment on her 6913
28:26 they will live in safety when I **i** punishment 6913
30:14 to Zoan and **i** punishment on Thebes. 6913
30:19 So *I will* **i** punishment on Egypt, 6913
39:21 the nations will see the punishment *I* **i** and 6913
Rev 9:19 having heads with which *they* **i injury.** *92*

INFLICTED (16) [INFLICT]
Ge 12:17 the LORD **i** serious diseases *on* Pharaoh 5595
1Sa 14:47 *he* **i punishment** on them. 8399
23: 5 He **i** heavy losses on the Philistines 5782
2Sa 7:14 the rod of men, with **floggings** *i by* men. AIT
1Ki 20:21 the horses and chariots and **i** heavy losses 5782
20:29 **i** a hundred thousand **casualties** 5782
2Ki 8:29 the wounds the Arameans *had* **i** *on* him 5782
9:15 the wounds the Arameans *had* **i** *on* him 5782
2Ch 13:17 Abijah and his men **i** heavy losses on them, 5782
22: 6 the wounds *they had* **i** *on* him at Ramoth 5782
28: 5 *who* **i** heavy casualties on him, 5782
Isa 30:26 of his people and heals the wounds he **i** 4804
Jer 42:10 for I am grieved over the disaster *I have* **i** 6913
La 1:12 Is any suffering like my suffering that **was i** 6618
Eze 23:10 and punishment *was* **i** on her. 6913
2Co 2: 6 The punishment **i** on him by *NIG*

INFLICTS (2) [INFLICT]
Job 34: 6 his arrow **i** an incurable wound.' NIH
Zec 14:18 the plague *he* **i** on the nations that do not go 5597

INFLUENCE (1) [INFLUENCED, INFLUENTIAL]
Job 31:21 knowing that I had **i** in court, 6476

INFLUENCED (1) [INFLUENCE]
1Co 12: 2 somehow or other *you were* **i** and led astray *72*

INFLUENTIAL (1) [INFLUENCE]
1Co 1:26 not many were **i**; *1543*

INFORM (8) [INFORMATION, INFORMED]
Ex 18:16 and I decide between the parties and **i** them 3359
1Sa 27:11 for he thought, *"They* might **i** on us and say, 5583
2Sa 15:28 until word comes from you to **i** me." 5583
17:17 A servant girl was to go and **i** them, 5583
17:21 of the well and went *to* **i** King David. 5583
Ezr 4:14 we are sending this message *to* **i** the king, 10313
4:16 We **i** the king that if this city is built 10313
Job 12: 8 or *let* the fish of the sea **i** you. 6218

INFORMATION (4) [INFORM]
1Sa 23:23 and come back to me with **definite i.** 3922
Ezr 5:10 down the names of their leaders *for* your **i**. 10313
Ac 23:15 of wanting more accurate **i** about his case. *1336*
23:20 on the pretext of wanting more accurate **i** *4785*

INFORMED (6) [INFORM]
2Ki 22:10 Then Shaphan the secretary **i** the king, 5583
2Ch 34:18 Then Shaphan the secretary **i** the king, 5583
Da 1: 4 **well i**, quick to understand, 1981+3359
Ac 21:21 *They have been* **i** that you teach all *2994*
23:30 *When* I *was* **i** of a plot to be carried out *3606*
1Co 1:11 some from Chloe's household *have* **i** me *1317*

INGATHERING (2) [GATHER]
Ex 23:16 "Celebrate the Feast of **I** at the end of the year, 658
34:22 and the Feast of **I** at the turn of the year. 658

INHABIT (2) [HABITAT, INHABITANT, INHABITANTS, INHABITED]

Job 15:28 *he will* **i** ruined towns and houses 8905
Ac 17:26 that *they should* **i** the whole earth; 2997

INHABITANT (3) [INHABIT]

Isa 6:11 "Until the cities lie ruined and without **i**, 3782
Jer 4: 7 Your towns will lie in ruins without **i**. 3782
46:19 be laid waste and lie in ruins without **i**. 3782

INHABITANTS (41) [INHABIT]

Lev 18:25 and the land vomited out its **i**. 3782
25:10 throughout the land to all its **i**. 3782
Nu 14:14 And they will tell the **i** *of* this land about it. 3782
32:17 for protection from the **i** *of* the land. 3782
33:52 drive out all the **i** *of* the land before you. 3782
33:55 if you do not drive out the **i** *of* the land, 3782
Jos 9:24 the whole land and to wipe out all its **i** from 3782
13: 6 "As for all the **i** *of* the mountain regions 3782
Jdg 1:32 of Asher lived among the Canaanite **i** *of* 3782
1:33 among the Canaanite **i** *of* the land, 3782
1Ki 9:16 He killed its Canaanite **i** and then gave it 3782
2Ki 16: 9 He deported **its i** to Kir and put Rezin 2023S
1Ch 8:13 in Aijalon and who drove out the **i** *of* Gath. 3782
10:11 the **i** of Jabesh Gilead heard of everything NIH
22:18 he has handed the **i** *of* the land over to me, 3782
2Ch 15: 5 the **i** *of* the lands were in great turmoil. 3782
20: 7 the **i** *of* this land before your people Israel 3782
34: 9 the people of Judah and Benjamin and the **i** 3782
Isa 9: 9 Ephraim and the **i** *of* Samaria— 3782
24: 1 he will ruin its face and scatter its **i**— 3782
24: 6 Therefore earth's **i** are burned up, 3782
51: 6 like a garment and its **i** die like flies. 3782
Jer 25: 9 against this land and its **i** and against all 3782
44:22 of cursing and a desolate waste without **i**, 3782
48:18 O **i** *of* the Daughter of Dibon, 3782
49: 3 Cry out, O **i** *of* Rabbah! 1426
51:35 be upon Babylon," say the **i** *of* Zion. 3782
Mic 7:13 earth will become desolate because of its **i**, 3782
Zec 8:20 and the **i** *of* many cities will yet come, 3782
8:21 the **i** *of* one city will go to another and say, 3782
12: 7 of Jerusalem's **i** may not be greater than 3782
12:10 the house of David and the **i** *of* Jerusalem 3782
13: 1 the house of David and the **i** *of* Jerusalem, 3782
Rev 6:10 the **i** of the earth and avenge our blood?" 2997
8:13 Woe *to* the **i** of the earth, 2997
11:10 The **i** of the earth will gloat over them 2997
13: 8 All **i** of the earth will worship the beast— 2997
13:12 the earth and its **i** worship the first beast, 2997
13:14 he deceived the **i** of the earth. 2997
17: 2 and the **i of** the earth were intoxicated with 2997
17: 8 The **i** of the earth whose names have 2997

INHABITED (16) [INHABIT]

Isa 13:20 *be* **i** or lived in through all generations; 3782
44:26 who says of Jerusalem, *'It shall* **be i**,' 3782
45:18 but formed it to *be* **i**— 3782
Jer 17:25 and this city *will be* **i** forever. 3782
22: 6 like a desert, like towns not **i**. 3782
33:10 **i** *by* neither men nor animals, 3782
46:26 however, Egypt *will be* **i** as in times past," 8905
50:13 not *be* **i** but will be completely desolate. 3782
50:39 *It will* never again *be* **i** or lived in 3782
Eze 12:20 The **i** towns will be laid waste and 3782
26:19 like cities no longer **i**, 3782
35: 9 your towns *will* not *be* **i**. 3782
36:10 The towns *will* **be i** and the ruins rebuilt. 3782
36:35 *are now* fortified and **i**." 3782
Joel 3:20 Judah *will be* **i** forever and Jerusalem 3782
Zec 14:11 It *will be* **i**; never again will it be destroyed. 3782

INHERIT (45) [CO-HEIRS, HEIR, HEIRS, HERITAGE, INHERITANCE, INHERITANCES, INHERITED, INHERITS]

Ge 15: 2 the **one who will i** my estate is Eliezer 1201+5479
48: 6 the **territory** they **i** they will be reckoned 5709
Nu 14:24 and his descendants *will* **i** it. 3769
32:32 but the property we **i** will be on this side of 5709
Dt 1:38 because he *will* **lead** Israel **to i** it. 5706
3:28 across and *will* **cause** them **to i** the land 5706
33:23 *he will* **i** southward to the lake." 3769
Jos 1: 6 *you will* **lead** these people **to i** 5706
1Sa 2: 8 he seats them with princes and **has** them **i** 5706
2Ki 2: 9 *Let* me **i** a double portion of your spirit, 448+2118
1Ch 16:18 of Canaan as the portion you will **i**." 5709
Job 13:26 and **make** me **i** the sins of my youth. 3769
Ps 25:13 and his descendants *will* **i** the land. 3769
37: 9 but those who hope in the LORD *will* **i** 3769
37:11 But the meek *will* **i** the land 3769
37:22 those the LORD blesses *will* **i** the land, 3769
37:29 the righteous *will* **i** the land and dwell 3769
37:34 He will exalt you to **i** the land; 3769
69:36 the children of his servants *will* **i** it, 5706
105:11 of Canaan as the portion you *will* **i**." 5709
Pr 3:35 The wise **i** honor, 5706
11:29 trouble on his family *will* **i** only wind, 5706
14:18 The simple **i** folly, 5706
Isa 14:21 not to rise *to* **i** the land and cover the earth 3769
57:13 the man who makes me his refuge *will* **i** 5706
61: 7 and so *they will* **i** a double portion 3769
65: 9 my chosen people *will* **i** them, 3769
Zep 2: 9 survivors of my nation *will* **i** their **land.**" 5706
Zec 2:12 The LORD *will* **i** Judah as his portion in 5706
Mt 5: 5 for they *will* **i** the earth. 3099
19:29 as much and *will* **i** eternal life. 3099
Mk 10:17 he asked, "what must I do to **i** eternal life?" 3099
Lk 10:25 "what must I do *to* **i** eternal life?" 3099
18:18 what must I do *to* **i** eternal life?" 3099
1Co 6: 9 the wicked *will* not **i** the kingdom of God? 3099
6:10 nor swindlers *will* **i** the kingdom of God. 3099
15:50 that flesh and blood cannot **i** the kingdom 3099
15:50 nor *does* the perishable **i** the imperishable. 3099
Gal 5:21 like this *will* not **i** the kingdom of God. 3099
Heb 1:14 to serve those who will **i** salvation? 3099
6:12 and patience **i** what has been promised. 3099
12:17 when he wanted *to* **i** this blessing, 3099
Jas 2: 5 of the world to be rich in faith and to **i** 3101
1Pe 3: 9 to this you were called so that *you may* **i** 3099
Rev 21: 7 He who overcomes *will* **i** all this, 3099

INHERITANCE (238) [INHERIT]

Ge 21:10 slave woman's son *will* never **share in the i** 3769
31:14 "Do we still have any share in the **i** 5709
Ex 15:17 and plant them on the mountain of your **i**— 5709
32:13 and *it will be their* **i** forever.' " 5706
34: 9 and **take** us **as** *your* **i**." 5706
Lev 20:24 I will give it to you as an **i**, 3769
Nu 16:14 or given us an **i** *of* fields and vineyards. 5709
18:20 *"You will* **have** no **i** in their land, 5706
18:20 I am your share and your **i** among 5709
18:21 the Levites all the tithes in Israel as their **i** 5709
18:23 *They will* **receive** no **i** among 5706+5709
18:24 as their **i** the tithes that the Israelites present 5709
18:24 *'They will* **have** no **i** among 5706+5709
18:26 the Israelites the tithe I give you as your **i**, 5709
26:53 as an **i** based on the number of names. 5709
26:54 To a larger group give a larger **i**, 5709
26:54 to receive its **i** according to the number 5709
26:56 Each **i** is to be distributed by lot among 5709
26:62 because they received no **i** among them. 5709
27: 7 as an **i** among their father's relatives 5709
27: 7 and turn their father's **i** over to them. 5709
27: 8 turn his **i** over to his daughter. 5709
27: 9 give his **i** to his brothers. 5709
27:10 give his **i** to his father's brothers. 5709
27:11 give his **i** to the nearest relative in his clan, 5709
32:18 until every Israelite has received his **i**. 5709
32:19 *We will* not **receive** *any* **i** with them on 5706
32:19 because our **i** has come to us on 5709
33:54 To a larger group give a larger **i**, 5709
34: 2 to you as an **i** will have these boundaries: 5709
34:13 **"Assign** this land by lot **as an i**. 5706
34:14 of Manasseh have received their **i**. 5709
34:15 two and a half tribes have received their **i** 5709
34:17 **assign** the land for you **as an i**: 5706
34:29 the LORD commanded to **assign** *the* **i** *to* 5706
35: 2 in from the **i** the Israelites will possess. 5709
35: 8 in proportion to the **i** *of* each tribe: 5709
36: 2 to give the land as an **i** to the Israelites 5709
36: 2 to give the **i** *of* our brother Zelophehad 5709
36: 3 then their **i** will be taken 5709
36: 3 be taken from our ancestral **i** and added to 5709
36: 3 of the **i** allotted *to* us will be taken away. 5709
36: 4 their **i** will be added to that of the tribe 5709
36: 4 from the tribal **i** *of* our forefathers." 5709
36: 7 No **i** in Israel is to pass from tribe to tribe, 5709
36: 8 so that every Israelite will possess the **i** 5709
36: 9 No **i** may pass from tribe to tribe, 5709
36:12 and their **i** remained in their father's clan 5709
Dt 4:20 to be the people of his **i**, as you now are. 5709
4:21 and enter the good land the LORD your God is giving you as your **i**. 5709
4:38 into their land to give it to you for your **i**, 5709
9:26 your own **i** that you redeemed 5709
9:29 your **i** that you brought out 5709
10: 9 That is why the Levites have no share or **i** 5709
10: 9 the LORD is their **i**, 5709
12: 9 not yet reached the resting place and the **i** 5709
12:10 the LORD your God *is* **giving** you **as an i**, 5706
12:12 who have no allotment or **i** *of* their own. 5709
14:27 they have no allotment or **i** of their own. 5709
14:29 that the Levites (who have no allotment or **i** 5709
15: 4 your God is giving you to possess as your **i**, 5709
18: 1 are to have no allotment or **i** with Israel. 5709
18: 1 for that is their **i**. 5709
18: 2 They shall have no **i** among their brothers; 5709
18: 2 the LORD is their **i**, as he promised them. 5709
19: 3 the LORD your God *is* **giving** you **as an i**, 5706
19:10 as your **i**, and so that you will not be guilty 5709
19:14 by your predecessors in the **i** you receive in 5709
20:16 the LORD your God is giving you as an **i**, 5709
21:23 the LORD your God is giving you as an **i**. 5709
24: 4 the LORD your God is giving you as an **i**. 5709
25:19 the land he is giving you to possess as an **i**, 5709
26: 1 the LORD your God is giving you as an **i** 5709
29: 8 We took their land and gave it as an **i** to 5709
31: 7 **divide** it *among* them **as** their **i**. 5706
32: 8 the Most High **gave** the nations their **i**, 5706
32: 9 Jacob his allotted **i**. 5709
Jos 11:23 and he gave it as an **i** to Israel according 5709
12: 7 toward Seir (their lands Joshua gave as an **i** 3772
13: 6 to allocate this land to Israel for an **i**, 5709
13: 7 and divide it as an **i** among the nine tribes 5709
13: 8 the **i** that Moses had given them east of 5709
13:14 But to the tribe of Levi he gave no **i**, 5709
13:14 are their **i**, as he promised them. 5709
13:23 These towns and their villages were the **i** 5709
13:28 and their villages were the **i** *of* the Gadites, 5709
13:32 This is *the* **i** Moses *had* **given** when he was 5706
13:33 to the tribe of Levi, Moses had given no **i**; 5709
13:33 the LORD, the God of Israel, is their **i**, 5709
14: 1 the areas the Israelites **received as an i** in 5706
14: 3 the two-and-a-half tribes their **i** east of 5709
14: 3 not granted the Levites an **i** among the rest, 5709
14: 9 be your **i** and that of your children forever, 5709
14:13 and gave him Hebron as his **i**. 5709
15:20 This is the **i** *of* the tribe of Judah, 5709
16: 4 the descendants of Joseph, **received** *their* **i**. 5706
16: 5 of their **i** went from Ataroth Addar in 5709
16: 8 the **i** *of* the tribe of the Ephraimites, 5709
16: 9 for the Ephraimites within the **i** *of* 5709
17: 4 to give us an **i** among our brothers." 5709
17: 4 an **i** along with the brothers of their father, 5709
17: 6 of Manasseh received an **i** among the sons. 5709
17:14 and one portion for an **i**? 5709
18: 2 not yet received their **i**. 5709
18: 4 according to the **i** *of* each. 5709
18: 7 the priestly service of the LORD is their **i**. 5709
18: 7 of Manasseh have already received their **i** 5709
18:20 the **i** of the clans of Benjamin on all sides. 5709
18:28 This was the **i** *of* Benjamin for its clans. 5709
19: 1 Their **i** lay within the territory of Judah. 5709
19: 8 the **i** *of* the tribe of the Simeonites, 5709
19: 9 The **i** *of* the Simeonites was taken from 5709
19: 9 So the Simeonites **received** *their* **i** within 5706
19:10 The boundary of their **i** went as far 5709
19:16 These towns and their villages were the **i** 5709
19:23 These towns and their villages were the **i** 5709
19:31 These towns and their villages were the **i** 5709
19:39 These towns and their villages were the **i** 5709
19:41 The territory of their **i** included: 5709
19:48 These towns and their villages were the **i** 5709
19:49 the Israelites gave Joshua son of Nun an **i** 5709
21: 3 and pasturelands out of their own **i**: 5709
23: 4 Remember how I have allotted as an **i** 5709
24:28 each to his own **i**. 5709
24:30 And they buried him in the land of his **i**, 5709
24:32 This became the **i** of Joseph's descendants. 5709
Jdg 2: 6 each to his own **i**. 5709
2: 9 And they buried him in the land of his **i**, 5709
11: 2 not *going to* **get** *any* **i** in our family," 5706
18: 1 because they had not yet come into an **i** 5709
20: 6 to each region of Israel's **i**, 5709
21:23 to their **i** and rebuilt the towns and settled 5709
21:24 each to his own **i**. 5709
1Sa 10: 1 not the LORD anointed you leader over his **i**? 5709
26:19 from my share in the LORD's **i** 5709
2Sa 14:16 and my son from the **i** God gave us.' 5709
20:19 to swallow up the LORD's **i**?" 5709
21: 3 so that you will bless the LORD's **i**?" 5709
1Ki 8:36 on the land you gave your people for an **i**. 5709
8:51 for they are your people and your **i**, 5709
8:53 the nations of the world to be your own **i**, 5709
21: 3 that I should give you the **i** *of* my fathers." 5709
21: 4 "I will not give you the **i** *of* my fathers." 5709
2Ki 21:14 the remnant of my **i** and hand them over 5709
1Ch 28: 8 and **pass** *it* **on as an i** to your descendants 5706
2Ch 6:27 on the land you gave your people for an **i**. 5709
20:11 the possession *you* **gave** us **as an i**. 3769
Ezr 9:12 **leave** it to your children **as an** everlasting **i**.' 3769
Job 42:15 and their father granted them an **i** along 5709
Ps 2: 8 and I will make the nations your **i**, 5709
16: 6 surely I have a delightful **i**. 5709
28: 9 Save your people and bless your **i**; 5709
33:12 the people he chose for his **i**. 5709
37:18 and their **i** will endure forever. 5709
47: 4 He chose our **i** for us, the pride of Jacob, 5709
68: 9 you refreshed your weary **i**. 5709
74: 2 the tribe of your **i**, whom you redeemed— 5709
78:55 and allotted their lands to them as an **i**; 5709
78:62 he was very angry with his **i**. 5709
78:71 of his people Jacob, of Israel his **i**. 5709
79: 1 O God, the nations have invaded your **i**; 5709
82: 8 for all the nations *are* your **i**. 5706
94: 5 they oppress your **i**. 5709
94:14 he will never forsake his **i**. 5709
106: 5 in the joy of your nation and join your **i** 5709
106:40 with his people and abhorred his **i**. 5709
135:12 and he gave their land as an **i**, 5709
135:12 an **i** to his people Israel. 5709
136:21 and gave their land as an **i**, 5709
136:22 an **i** to his servant Israel; 5709
Pr 13:22 A good man **leaves an i** 5706
17: 2 and will share the **i** as one of the brothers. 5709
20:21 An **i** quickly gained at the beginning will 5709
28:10 but the blameless *will* **receive** a good **i**. 5706
Ecc 7:11 Wisdom, like an **i**, is a good thing 5709
Isa 19:25 Assyria my handiwork, and Israel my **i**." 5709
47: 6 with my people and desecrated my **i**; 5709
58:14 the heights of the land and to feast on the **i** 5709
61: 7 of disgrace they will rejoice in their **i**; 2750
63:17 the tribes that are your **i**. 5709
Jer 2: 7 and made my **i** detestable. 5709
3:18 **gave** your forefathers *as an* **i**. 5706
3:19 the most beautiful **i** *of* any nation.' 5709
10:16 including Israel, the tribe of his **i**— 5709
12: 7 "I will forsake my house, abandon my **i**; 5709
12: 8 My **i** has become to me like a lion in 5709
12: 9 not my **i** become to me like a speckled bird 5709
12:14 the **i** I gave my people Israel, 5709
12:15 to his own **i** and his own country. 5709
16:18 of their vile images and have filled my **i** 5709
17: 4 the **i** I gave you. 5709
50:11 you who pillage my **i**, 5709
51:19 including the tribe of his **i**— 5709

La 5: 2 Our i has been turned over to aliens, 5709
Eze 35:15 Because you rejoiced when the i *of* 5709
36:12 and you will be their i; 5709
44:28 " 'I am to be the only i the priests have. 5709
45: 1 " 'When you allot the land as an i, 5709
46:16 If the prince makes a gift from his i to one 5709
46:16 it is to be their property by i. 5709
46:17 a gift from his i to one of his servants, 5709
46:17 His i belongs to his sons only; it is theirs. 5709
46:18 The prince must not take any of the i *of* 5709
46:18 **give** his sons their i out of his own 5706
47:13 **divide** the land **for an** i among the twelve 5706
47:14 this land will become your i. 5709
47:22 You are to allot it as an i for yourselves and 5709
47:22 with you they are to be allotted an i among 5709
47:23 there you are to give him his i," 5709
48:29 the land you are to allot as an i to the tribes 5709
Da 12:13 to receive your **allotted** i." 1598
Joel 2:17 Do not make your i an object of scorn, 5709
3: 2 against them concerning my i, 5709
Ob 1:17 and the house of Jacob will possess its i. 4625
Mic 2: 2 a man of his home, a fellowman of his i. 5709
7:14 the flock of your i, which lives by itself 5709
7:18 the transgression of the remnant of his i? 5709
Zec 8:12 **give** all these things **as an** i 5706
Mal 1: 3 and left his i to the desert jackals." 5709
Mt 21:38 Come, let's kill him and take his i.' *3100*
25:34 **take** *your* i, the kingdom prepared for you *3099*
Mk 12: 7 Come, let's kill him, and the i will be ours.' *3100*
Lk 12:13 tell my brother to divide the i with me." *3100*
20:14 'Let's kill him, and the i will be ours.' *3100*
Ac 7: 5 He gave him no i here, *3100*
13:19 **gave** their land **to** his people **as** their i. *2883*
20:32 which can build you up and give you an i *3100*
Gal 3:18 For if the i depends on the law, *3100*
4:30 slave woman's son *will* never **share in the** i *3099*
Eph 1:14 who is a deposit guaranteeing our i until *3100*
1:18 the riches *of* his glorious i in the saints, *3100*
5: 5 has any i in the kingdom of Christ and *3100*
Col 1:12 who has qualified you to share *in* the i of *3102*
3:24 that you will receive an i from the Lord as *3100*
Heb 9:15 may receive the promised eternal i— *3100*
11: 8 to a place he would later receive as his i, *3100*
12:16 sold his **i rights as the oldest son.** *4757*
1Pe 1: 4 an i that can never perish, spoil or fade— *3100*

INHERITANCES (2) [INHERIT]

Jos 14: 2 Their i were assigned by lot to 5709
Isa 49: 8 the land and to reassign its desolate i, 5709

INHERITED (4) [INHERIT]

Lev 25:46 as i property and can make them slaves 3769
Nu 36: 7 the tribal **land** i *from* his forefathers. 5709
Pr 19:14 Houses and wealth are i *from* parents, 5709
Heb 1: 4 to the angels as the name *he has* i is superior *3099*

INHERITS (3) [INHERIT]

Nu 26:55 What each group i will be according to 5706
36: 8 Every daughter *who* i land in any 3769
36: 9 every Israelite tribe is to keep the **land** it i." 5709

INIQUITIES (11) [INIQUITY]

Ps 78:38 he forgave their i and did not destroy them. 6411
90: 8 You have set our i before you, 6411
103:10 or repay us according to our i. 6411
107:17 and suffered affliction because of their i. 6411
Isa 53: 5 he was crushed for our i; 6411
53:11 and he will bear their i. 6411
59: 2 your i have separated you from your God; 6411
59:12 and we acknowledge our i: 6411
La 4:13 because of the sins of her prophets and the i 6411
Da 9:16 the i *of* our fathers have made Jerusalem 6411
Mic 7:19 and hurl all our i into the depths of the sea. 2633

INIQUITY (14) [INIQUITIES]

Ps 25:11 O LORD, forgive my i, though it is great. 6411
32: 5 to you and did not cover up my i. 6411
38:18 I confess my i; I am troubled by my sin. 6411
51: 2 Wash away all my i and cleanse me 6411
51: 9 from my sins and blot out all my i. 6411
73: 7 From their callous hearts comes i; 6411
85: 2 You forgave the i *of* your people 6411
89:32 their i with flogging; 6411
109:14 the i *of* his fathers be remembered before 6411
Isa 53: 6 the LORD has laid on him the i *of* us all. 6411
61: 8 I hate robbery and i. 6406
Hos 12: 8 not find in me any i or sin." 6411
Mic 2: 1 Woe to those who plan i, 224
Zec 5: 6 the i *of* the people throughout the land." 6411

INITIATIVE (1)

2Co 8:17 with much enthusiasm and **on** *his* **own** i. *882*

INJURE (1) [INJURED, INJURES, INJURING, INJURY]

Zec 12: 3 who try to move it *will* **i themselves.** 8581+8581

INJURED (16) [INJURE]

Ex 21:19 he must pay **the i man** for the loss 2257[S]
22:10 and it dies or **is** i or is taken away 8689
22:14 from his neighbor and *it* **is** i or dies while 8689
Lev 22:22 the blind, the i or the maimed, 8653
24:20 As *he has* i the other, so he is to be injured. 4583+5989
24:20 he has injured the other, so he *is to* **be** i. 5989
2Ki 1: 2 in Samaria and i *himself.* 2703
Ecc 10: 9 Whoever quarries stones *may* **be** i by them; 6772
Isa 1: 5 Your whole head is i, 2716
28:13 **be** i and snared and captured. 8689
Eze 34: 4 or healed the sick or bound up the i. 8689
34:16 I will bind up the i and strengthen 8689
Hos 6: 1 *he has* i us but he will bind up our wounds. 5782
Zec 11:16 or heal the i, or feed the healthy, 8689
Mal 1:13 "When you bring i, crippled or diseased 1608
2Co 7:12 the one who did the wrong or of the i party, *92*

INJURES (3) [INJURE]

Ex 21:35 "If a man's bull i the bull of another 5597
Lev 24:19 If anyone i his neighbor, 4583+5989
Job 5:18 *he* i, but his hands also heal. 4730

INJURING (2) [INJURE]

Ge 4:23 for wounding me, a young man for i me. 2467
Lk 4:35 before them all and came out without i him. *1055*

INJURY (7) [INJURE]

Ex 21:22 but there is no **serious** i, 656
21:23 But if there is **serious** i, 656
2Ki 1: 2 to see if I will recover from this i." 2716
Jer 10:19 Woe to me because of my i! 8691
30:12 your i beyond healing. 4804
Na 3:19 your i is fatal. 4804
Rev 9:19 having heads with which *they* **inflict** i. *92*

INJUSTICE (10)

2Ch 19: 7 for with the LORD our God there is no i 6406
Job 5:16 the poor have hope, and i shuts its mouth. 6637
Ps 58: 2 No, in your heart you devise i, 6406
64: 6 They plot i and say, 6406
Pr 13:23 but i sweeps it away. 4202+5477
16: 8 righteousness than much gain with i. 4202+5477
Isa 58: 6 to loose the chains of i and untie the cords 8400
Jer 22:13 his upper rooms by i, 4202+5477
Eze 9: 9 of bloodshed and the city is full of i. 4754
Hab 1: 3 Why do you make me look at i? 224

INK (4)

Jer 36:18 and I wrote them in i on the scroll." 1902
2Co 3: 3 *with* i but with the Spirit of the living God, *3506*
2Jn 1:12 but I do not want to use paper and i. *3506*
3Jn 1:13 but I do not want to do so with pen and i. *3506*

INKHORN (KJV) See WRITING KIT

INKLING (1)

1Sa 20: 9 "If *I* **had the least** i that my father 3359+3359

INLAID (6)

1Ki 10:18 the king made a great **throne** *i with* ivory AIT
22:39 the palace he built and i with ivory, NIH
2Ch 9:17 the king made a great **throne** *i with* ivory AIT
SS 3:10 its interior lovingly i by the daughters 8362
Eze 27: 6 the coasts of Cyprus they made your deck, i NIH
Am 6: 4 You lie on **beds** *i with* ivory and lounge AIT

INMOST (10) [IN, MOST]

Ps 51: 6 you teach me wisdom in the i **place.** 6258
103: 1 all my i **being,** praise his holy name. 7931
139:13 For you created my i **being;** 4000
Pr 18: 8 they go down to a man's i **parts.** 1061+2540
20:27 it searches out his i **being.** 1061+2540
20:30 and beatings purge the i **being.** 1061+2540
23:16 my i **being** will rejoice 4000
26:22 they go down to a man's i **parts.** 1061+2540
Isa 16:11 my i **being** for Kir Hareseth. 7931
Lk 1:51 are proud in their i thoughts. *2840*

INN (2) [INNKEEPER]

Lk 2: 7 there was no room for them in the i. *2906*
10:34 took him to an i and took care of him. *4106*

INNER (84) [IN]

Ge 30:37 the bark and exposing the white i wood of 6584
Ex 12: 9 head, legs and i **parts.** 7931
29:13 Then take all the fat around the i **parts,** 7931
29:17 the ram into pieces and wash the i **parts** 7931
29:22 the fat tail, the fat around the i **parts,** 7931
Lev 1: 9 to wash the i **parts** and the legs with water, 7931
1:13 to wash the i **parts** and the legs with water, 7931
3: 3 that covers the i **parts** or is connected 7931
3: 9 that covers the i **parts** or is connected 7931
3:14 that covers the i **parts** or is connected 7931
4: 8 that covers the i **parts** or is connected 7931
4:11 the i **parts** and offal— 7931
7: 3 and the fat that covers the i **parts,** 7931
8:16 also took all the fat around the i **parts,** 7931
8:21 He washed the i **parts** and the legs 7931
8:25 the fat tail, all the fat around the i **parts,** 7931
9:14 the i **parts** and the legs and burned them 7931
Dt 18: 3 the shoulder, the jowls and the i **parts.** 7687
Jdg 3:24 "He must be relieving himself in the i **room** 2540
2Sa 4: 6 They went into the i **part** *of* the house as if 9348
18:24 between the i **and outer** gates, 9109[S]
1Ki 6: 5 and i **sanctuary** he built a structure around 1808
6:16 to form within the temple an i **sanctuary,** 1808
6:19 the i **sanctuary** within the temple to set 1808
6:20 The i **sanctuary** was twenty cubits long, 1808
6:21 across the front of the i **sanctuary,** 1808
6:22 the altar that belonged to the i **sanctuary.** 1808
6:23 the i **sanctuary** he made a pair of cherubim 1808
6:29 in both the i and outer rooms, 4200+7156
6:30 the i and outer rooms of the temple 4200+7163
6:31 of the i **sanctuary** he made doors 1808
6:36 the i courtyard of three courses 7164
7: 9 and trimmed with a saw on their i and outer 1074
7:12 the i courtyard of the temple of the LORD 7164
7:49 in front of the i **sanctuary);** 1808
8: 6 in the i **sanctuary** *of* the temple, 1808
8: 8 the Holy Place in front of the i **sanctuary,** 1808
20:30 to the city and hid in an i **room.** 928+2540+2540
22:25 you go to hide in an i **room."** 928+2540+2540
2Ki 9: 2 and take him into an i **room.** 928+2540+2540
10:25 the bodies out and then entered the i **shrine** 6551
1Ch 28:11 its i rooms and the place of atonement. 7164
2Ch 4:20 in front of the i **sanctuary** as prescribed; 1808
4:22 the i doors to the Most Holy Place and 7164
5: 7 in the i **sanctuary** *of* the temple, 1808
5: 9 be seen from in front of the i **sanctuary,** 1808
18:24 you go to hide in an i **room."** 928+2540+2540
Est 4:11 in the i court without being summoned 7164
5: 1 on her royal robes and stood in the i court 7164
Ps 51: 6 Surely you desire truth in the i **parts;** 3219
Eze 8: 3 the entrance to the north gate of the i court, 7164
8:16 into the i court of the house of the LORD, 7164
10: 3 and a cloud filled the i court. 7164
40:19 to the outside of the i court; 7164
40:23 a gate to the i court facing the north gate, 7164
40:27 The i court also had a gate facing south, 7164
40:28 into the i court through the south gate, 7164
40:30 the i court were twenty-five cubits wide NIH
40:32 Then he brought me to the i court on 7164
40:38 by the portico in each of the i gateways, NIH
40:44 Outside the i gate, within the inner court, 7164
40:44 Outside the inner gate, within the i court, 6584
41: 3 the i **sanctuary** and measured the jambs of 7163
41: 4 he measured the length of the i **sanctuary;** 2257[S]
41:15 the i **sanctuary** and the portico facing 7164
41:17 of the entrance to the i sanctuary and on 7164
41:17 around the i and outer **sanctuary** 7164
42: 3 in the section twenty cubits from the i court 7164
42: 4 an i passageway ten cubits wide and 7164
43: 5 up and brought me into the i court, 7164
44:17 " 'When they enter the gates of the i court, 7164
44:17 the gates of the i court or inside the temple. 7164
44:21 to drink wine when he enters the i court. 7164
44:27 into the i court of the sanctuary to minister 7164
45:19 the altar and on the gateposts of the i court. 7164
46: 1 of the i court facing east is to be shut on 7164
Mt 24:26 or, 'Here he is, in the i **rooms,'** *5421*
Lk 12: 3 in the ear in the i **rooms** will be proclaimed *5421*
Ac 16:24 in the i cell and fastened their feet in *2278*
Ro 7:22 For in my i being I delight in God's law; *2276*
Eph 3:16 through his Spirit in your i being, *2276*
Heb 6:19 It enters the i sanctuary behind the curtain, *2278*
9: 7 But only the high priest entered the i room, *1311*
1Pe 3: 4 Instead, it should be that of your i self, *3220*

INNERMOST (2) [IN, MOST]

1Ki 6:27 He placed the cherubim inside the i *room* of 7164
7:50 the gold sockets for the doors of the i room, 7164

INNKEEPER (1) [INN]

Lk 10:35 two silver coins and gave them *to* the i. *4107*

INNOCENCE (6) [INNOCENT]

Ge 44:16 How *can we* **prove** *our* i? 7405
1Ki 8:32 and so establish his i. 7407
2Ch 6:23 not guilty and so establish his i. 7407
Ps 26: 6 I wash my hands in i, 5931
73:13 in vain have I washed my hands in i. 5931
Isa 43:26 state the *case for* your i. 7405

INNOCENT (69) [INNOCENCE, INNOCENTLY]

Ge 20: 4 "Lord, will you destroy an i nation? 7404
Ex 23: 7 to do with a false charge and do not put an i 5929
Nu 5:31 The husband *will be* i of any wrongdoing, 5927
Dt 19:10 that i blood will not be shed in your land, 5929
19:13 from Israel the guilt of shedding i blood, 5929
21: 8 guilty of the blood of an i *man.*" 5929
21: 9 the guilt of shedding i blood, 5929
25: 1 acquitting the i and condemning the guilty. 7404
27:25 a bribe to kill an i person." 5929
Jdg 21:22 and *you are* i, since you did not give 870
1Sa 19: 5 then would you do wrong to an i **man** 1947+5929
2Sa 3:28 "I and my kingdom are forever i before 5929
4:11 when wicked men have killed an i man 7404
1Ki 2: 9 But now, *do* not **consider** him i. 5927
2:31 of the guilt of the i blood that Joab shed. 2855
8:32 Declare the i not guilty, 7404
2Ki 10: 9 before all the people and said, "You are i. 7404
21:16 so much i blood that he filled Jerusalem 5929
24: 4 including the shedding of i blood. 5929
24: 4 For he had filled Jerusalem with i blood, 5929
2Ch 6:23 Declare the i not guilty and 7404

Job 4: 7 Who, being **i**, has ever perished? 5929
9:15 Though *I were* **i**, I could not answer him; 7405
9:20 if *I were* **i**, my mouth would condemn me; 7405
9:23 he mocks the despair of the **i**. 5929
9:28 for I know *you will* not **hold** me **i**. 5927
10:15 Even if *I am* **i**, I cannot lift my head, 7405
17: 8 the **i** are aroused against the ungodly. 5929
22:19 the **i** mock them, saying, 5929
22:30 He will deliver even *one who* is not **i**, 5929
27:17 and the **i** will divide his silver. 5929
34: 5 "Job says, *'I am* **i**, but God denies me 7404
Ps 10: 8 from ambush he murders the **i**, 5929
15: 5 and does not accept a bribe against the **i**. 5929
19:13 will I be blameless, **i** of great transgression. 5927
64: 4 They shoot from ambush at the **i** *man;* 9447
94:21 the righteous and condemn the **i** to death. 5929
106:38 They shed **i** blood, the blood of their sons 5929
Pr 6:17 a lying tongue, hands that shed **i** blood, 5929
16: 2 All a man's ways seem **i** to him, 2341
17:15 Acquitting the guilty and condemning the **i** 7404
17:26 It is not good to punish an **i** *man,* 7404
18: 5 to the wicked or to deprive the **i** of justice. 7404
21: 8 but the conduct of the **i** is upright. 3838
24:24 to the guilty, "You are **i**"— 7404
Isa 5:23 but deny justice to the **i**. 7404
29:21 and with false testimony deprive the **i** 7404
59: 7 they are swift to shed **i** blood. 5929
Jer 2:34 the lifeblood of the **i** poor, 5929
2:35 *'I am* **i**; he is not angry with me.' 5927
7: 6 or the widow and do not shed **i** blood 5929
19: 4 with the blood of the **i**. 5929
22: 3 and do not shed **i** blood in this place. 5929
22:17 on shedding **i** blood and on oppression 5929
26:15 of **i** blood on yourselves and on this city 5929
Da 6:22 because I was found **i** in his sight. 10229
Joel 3:19 in whose land they shed **i** blood. 5929
Jnh 1:14 not hold us accountable for killing an **i** *man,* 5929
Mt 10:16 be as shrewd as snakes and as **i** as doves. *193*
12: 5 the temple desecrate the day and yet are **i**? *360*
12: 7 you would not have condemned the **i**. *360*
27: 4 he said, "for I have betrayed **i** blood." *127*
27:19 "Don't have anything to do *with* that **i** *man,* *1465*
27:24 "I am **i** of this man's blood," he said. *127*
Ac 20:26 to you today that I am **i** of the blood *2754*
Ro 16:19 about what is good, and **i** about what is evil. *193*
1Co 4: 4 but that *does* not **make** *me* **i**. *1467*
2Co 7:11 proved yourselves to be **i** in this matter. *54*
Jas 5: 6 You have condemned and murdered **i** *men,* *1465*

INNOCENTLY (1) [INNOCENT]
2Sa 15:11 invited as guests and went **quite i**, 4200+9448

INNUMERABLE (1)
2Ch 12: 3 and the **i** troops of Libyans, 401+5031

INORDINATE (KJV) See LUST

INQUIRE (37) [INQUIRED, INQUIRES, INQUIRING, INQUIRY]
Ge 25:22 So she went to **i** of the LORD. 2011
Dt 13:14 then *you must* **i**, probe and investigate it 2011
17: 9 **I** of them and they will give you 2011
Jos 9:14 but *did* not **i** of the LORD. 906+7023+8626
Jdg 18: 5 "Please **i** of God to learn whether 928+8626
1Sa 9: 9 if a man went to **i** of God, he would say, 2011
14:36 the priest said, *"Let us* **i** of God here." 448+7928
28: 7 so I may go and **i** of her." 928+2011
1Ki 22: 7 LORD here whom *we can* **i** of?" 907+2011+4946
22: 8 through whom we *can* **i** of the LORD, 2011
2Ki 3:11 that *we may* **i** of the LORD through him?" 2011
22:13 "Go and **i** of the LORD for me and for 2011
22:18 who sent you to **i** of the LORD, 2011
1Ch 10:14 and *did* not **i** of the LORD. 928+2011
13: 3 *we did* not **i** of it during the reign of Saul." 2011
15:13 *We did* not **i** of him *about* how to do it in 2011
21:30 David could not go before it to **i** of God, 2011
2Ch 18: 6 of the LORD here whom *we can* **i** of?" 2011
18: 7 through whom we *can* **i** of the LORD, 2011
20: 3 Jehoshaphat resolved to **i** of the LORD, 2011+4200
34:21 "Go and **i** of the LORD for me and for 2011
34:26 who sent you to **i** of the LORD, 928+2011
Ezr 7:14 to **i** about Judah and Jerusalem with regard 10118
Isa 8:19 *should* not a people **i** of their God? 448+2011
Jer 10:21 The shepherds are senseless and *do* not **i** of 2011
18:13 "**I** among the nations: 8626
21: 2 "**I** now of the LORD for us 2011
37: 7 who sent you to **i** of me, 'Pharaoh's army, 2011
Eze 14: 3 *Should I* **let** them **i** of *me* **at all**? 2011+2011+4200
14: 7 and then goes to a prophet to **i** of me, 928+2011
20: 1 some of the elders of Israel came to **i** of 2011
20: 3 Have you come to **i** of me? 2011
20: 3 as I live, *I will* not **let** you **i** of *me,* 2011
20:31 *Am* I *to* **let** you **i** of *me,* O house of Israel? 2011+4200
20:31 *I will* not **let** you **i** of *me.* 2011+4200
Zep 1: 6 and neither seek the LORD nor **i** of him. 2011
1Co 14:35 If they want *to* **i** about something, *3443*

INQUIRED (21) [INQUIRE]
Lev 10:16 When Moses **i** about the goat of 2011+2011
Jdg 13:17 Then Manoah **i** of the angel of the LORD, 448+606
20:18 Israelites went up to Bethel and **i** of 928+8626
20:23 and *they* **i** of the LORD. 928+8626
20:27 And the Israelites **i** of the LORD. 928+8626
1Sa 10:22 So *they* **i** further of the LORD, 928+8626
22:10 Ahimelech **i** of the LORD for him; 928+8626
22:15 the first time I **i** of God for him? 928+8626
23: 2 he **i** of the LORD, 928+8626
23: 4 Once again David **i** of the LORD, 928+8626
28: 6 He **i** of the LORD, 928+8626
30: 8 and David **i** of the LORD, 928+8626
2Sa 2: 1 David **i** of the LORD. 928+8626
5:19 so David **i** of the LORD, 928+8626
5:23 so David **i** of the LORD, 928+8626
1Ch 14:10 so David **i** of God: 928+8626
14:14 so David **i** of God again, 928+8626
2Ch 1: 5 Solomon and the assembly **i** of him there. 2011
Ps 77: 6 My heart mused and my spirit **i**: 2924
Mt 19:18 "Which ones?" the man **i**. *3306*
Jn 4:52 When *he* **i** as to the time when his son *4785*

INQUIRES (1) [INQUIRE]
2Sa 16:23 like that of one *who* **i** of God. 928+1821+8626

INQUIRING (4) [INQUIRE]
Ex 33: 7 Anyone **i** of the LORD would go to 1335
Nu 27:21 obtain decisions for him by **i** *of* the Urim 5477
Dt 12:30 not to be ensnared *by* **i** about their gods, 2011
1Sa 22:13 him bread and a sword and **i** of God 928+8626

INQUIRY (1) [INQUIRE]
Job 34:24 Without **i** he shatters the mighty and sets 2984

INQUISITION (KJV) See AVENGES, INVESTIGATION

INSANE (5)
1Sa 21:13 *he* **pretended to be i** in their presence; 3248+9101
21:14 "Look at the man! *He is* **i**! 8713
Ps 34: T **pretended to be i** before Abimelech, 3248+9101
Ac 26:24 "Your great learning is driving you **i**." *3444*
26:25 *"I am* not **i**, most excellent Festus," *3419*

INSATIABLE (1)
Eze 16:28 because you *were* **i**; 1194+8425

INSCRIBE (1) [INSCRIBED, INSCRIPTION]
Isa 30: 8 write it on a tablet for them, **i** it on a scroll, 2980

INSCRIBED (6) [INSCRIBE]
Ex 31:18 the tablets of stone **i** by the finger of God. 4180
32:15 They *were* **i** on both sides, front and back. 4180
Dt 9:10 The LORD gave me two stone tablets **i** by 4180
Job 19:24 that they were **i** with an iron tool on lead, NIH
Jer 17: 1 **i** with a flint point, 3086
Zec 14:20 be *i* **on** the bells of the horses, AIT

INSCRIPTION (9) [INSCRIBE]
Ex 39:30 like an **i** *on* a seal: 4844+7334
Da 5:24 Therefore he sent the hand that wrote the **i**. 10375
5:25 "This is the **i** that was written: 10375
Zec 3: 9 and I will engrave an **i** *on it,'* 7334
Mt 22:20 "Whose portrait is this? And whose **i**?" *2107*
Mk 12:16 "Whose portrait is this? And whose **i**?" *2107*
Lk 20:24 Whose portrait and **i** are on it?" *2107*
Ac 17:23 I even found an altar with **this i**: *2108+4005*
2Ti 2:19 sealed with this **i**: "The Lord knows who *NIG*

INSECTS (2)
Lev 11:20 " 'All flying **i** that walk on all fours are to 9238
Dt 14:19 All flying **i that swarm** are unclean to you; 9238

INSERT (1) [INSERTED]
Ex 25:14 **I** the poles into the rings on the sides of 995

INSERTED (6) [INSERT]
Ex 27: 7 *to* **be i** into the rings so they will be 995
37: 5 And *he* **i** the poles into the rings on 995
38: 7 *They* **i** the poles into the rings 995
40:18 **i** the crossbars and set up the posts. 5989
1Ki 6: 6 the temple so that nothing *would be* **i** into 296
Eze 41: 6 so that the supports were not **i into** the wall 928

INSIDE (80) [IN]
Ge 6:14 and coat it with pitch **i** and out. 1074+4946
9:21 he became drunk and lay uncovered **i** 928+9348
19:10 the men **i** reached out and pulled Lot back 448
31:34 the household gods and put them **i** 928
39:11 of the household servants was **i**. 928+1074+2021
44: 8 of Canaan the silver we found **i** the mouths 928
Ex 4: 6 LORD said, "Put your hand **i** your cloak." 928
9:20 their slaves and their livestock **i**. 448+1074+2021
12:46 "It must be eaten **i** one house; 928
25:11 Overlay it with pure gold, both **i** and 1074+4946
28:26 of the breastpiece on the **i** edge next to 1074+2025
37: 2 with pure gold, both **i** and out, 1074+4946
39:19 of the breastpiece on the **i** edge next to 1074+2025
Lev 14:41 the **i** walls of the house scraped and 1074+4946
Nu 18: 7 at the altar and **i** the curtain. 1074+4200+4946
Jos 7:21 are hidden in the ground **i** my tent, 928+9348
Jdg 7:16 the hands of all of them, with torches **i**. 928+9348
9:49 and set it on fire over the people **i**. NIH
9:51 **I** the city, however, was a strong tower, 928+9348
18:17 went **i** and took the carved image, 2025+9004[S]
1Sa 26: 5 Saul was lying **i** the camp, 928
26: 7 lying asleep **i** the camp with his spear stuck 928
2Sa 6:17 in its place **i** the tent that David had 928+9348
10:14 they fled before Abishai and **went i** the city. 995
1Ki 6:18 The **i** of the temple was cedar, 7163
6:20 He overlaid the **i** with pure gold, 4200+7156
6:21 Solomon covered the **i** *of* the temple 4946+7163
6:27 the cherubim **i** the innermost room of 928+9348
7:31 On the **i** of the stand there was an opening 1074
2Ki 4: 4 Then **go** *i* and shut the door behind you AIT
6:20 and there they were, **i** Samaria. 928+9348
1Ch 16: 1 set it **i** the tent that David had pitched 928+9348
19:15 before his brother Abishai and went **i** 2025
2Ch 3: 4 He overlaid the **i** with pure gold. 7163
3: 8 He overlaid the **i** with six hundred talents 2084[S]
Ne 4:22 and his helper stay **i** Jerusalem at night, 928+9348
6:10 **i** the temple, and let us close 448+9348
Job 30:27 The churning **i** me never stops; 5055
32:19 **i** I am like bottled-up wine, 1061
Ps 78:28 He made them come down **i** their camp, 928+7931
Jer 21: 4 And I will gather them **i** this city. 448+9348
49: 3 rush here and there **i** the walls, 928
La 1:20 **i**, there is only death. 928+1074+2021
Eze 3:24 "Go, shut yourself **i** your house. 928+9348
5: 2 a third of the hair with fire **i** the city. 928+9348
5:12 of the plague or perish by famine **i** you; 928+9348
7:15 **i** are plague and famine; 1074+4946
22:18 tin, iron and lead left **i** a furnace. 928+9348
22:20 in my anger and my wrath and put you **i** NIH
22:21 and you will be melted **i** her. 928+9348
22:22 so you will be melted **i** her, 928+9348
40:10 **I** the east gate were three alcoves NIH
40:14 of the projecting walls all around the **i** of NIH
40:16 The alcoves and the projecting walls **i** 4200+7163
40:19 the **i** *of* the lower gateway to the 4200+7156
42:15 he had finished measuring what was **i** 7164
43: 6 I heard someone speaking to me **from i** 4946
44: 3 the only one who may sit **i** the gateway 928
44:17 the gates of the inner court or **i** the temple. 2025
46:23 Around the **i** of each of the four courts was 928
Jnh 1:17 and Jonah was **i** the fish three days 928+5055
2: 1 From **i** the fish Jonah prayed to 5055
Mt 23:25 **i** they are full of greed and self-indulgence. *2277*
23:26 First clean the **i** of the cup and dish, *1955*
23:27 but **on the i** are full of dead men's bones *2277*
23:28 but **on the i** you are full of hypocrisy *2277*
Mk 7:23 All these evils come **from i** and make *2277*
Lk 11: 7 "Then the one **i** answers, 'Don't bother me. *2277*
11:39 but **i** you are full of greed and wickedness. *2277*
11:40 the one who made the outside make the **i** *2277*
11:41 But give what *is* **i** [the dish] to the poor, *1913*
17:31 on the roof of his house, with his goods **i**, *1877*
Jn 18:33 Pilate then **went** back **i** the palace, *1656*
19: 9 and *he* **went** back **i** the palace. *1656*
20: 8 who had reached the tomb first, also **went i**. *1656*
Ac 5:23 when we opened them, we found no one **i**." *2276*
10:27 Peter **went i** and found a large gathering *1656*
1Co 5:12 Are you not to judge those **i**? *2276*
Rev 5: 3 could open the scroll or even look **i** it. *NIG*
5: 4 worthy to open the scroll or look **i**. *NIG*

INSIGHT (16) [INSIGHTS]
1Ki 4:29 gave Solomon wisdom and very great **i**, 9312
1Ch 27:32 was a counselor, a man of **i** and a scribe. 1067
Job 26: 3 And what great **i** you have displayed! 9370
34:35 speaks without knowledge; his words lack **i**. 8505
Ps 119:99 *I* **have** more **i** than all my teachers, 8505
Pr 1: 2 for understanding words of **i**; 1069
2: 3 for **i** and cry aloud for understanding, 1069
5: 1 listen well to my **words of i**, 9312
21:30 There is no wisdom, no **i**, 9312
Da 5:11 to have **i** and intelligence and wisdom like 10467
5:14 of the gods is in you and that you have **i**, 10467
9:22 now come to **give** you **i** and understanding. 8505
Eph 3: 4 be able to understand my **i** into the mystery *5304*
Php 1: 9 and more in knowledge and depth of **i**, *151*
2Ti 2: 7 for the Lord will give you **i** into all this. *5304*
Rev 13:18 If anyone has **i**, let him calculate *3808*

INSIGHTS (1) [INSIGHT]
Job 15: 9 What **i** *do you* **have** that we do not have? 1067

INSIST (3) [INSISTED, INSISTING, INSISTENTLY]
2Sa 24:24 **i on paying you for** 928+4697+7864+7864
1Ch 21:24 "No, *I* **i on paying** the full price. 7864+7864
Eph 4:17 So I tell you this, and **i on** it in the Lord, *3458*

INSISTED (7) [INSIST]
Ge 19: 3 But *he* **i** so strongly that they did go 7210
33:11 And because Jacob **i**, Esau accepted it. 7210
1Ki 3:22 But the first one **i**, "No! 606
Mk 14:31 But Peter **i** emphatically, *3281*
Lk 23: 5 But they **i**, "He stirs up the people all *2196*
Jn 9: 9 But he himself **i**, "I am the man." *3306*
19: 7 The Jews **i**, "We have a law, *646*

INSISTENTLY (1) [INSIST]
Lk 23:23 with loud shouts they **i** demanded that he *2130*

INSISTING (1) [INSIST]

Ac 12:15 When she *kept* **i that** it was so, they said, *1462*

INSOLENCE (6) [INSOLENT]

2Ki 19:28 against me and your **i** has reached my ears, 8633
Isa 16: 6 her pride and her **i**— 6301
37:29 and because your **i** has reached my ears, 8633
Jer 48:30 I know her **i** but it is futile," 6301
Da 11:18 but a commander will put an end to his **i** 3075
11:18 to his insolence and will turn his **i** back 3075

INSOLENT (3) [INSOLENCE]

Nu 16: 1 On son of Peleth—*became* **i** 3689
Hos 7:16 by the sword because of their **i** words. 2405
Ro 1:30 God-haters, **i**, arrogant and boastful; *5616*

INSOMUCH (KJV) See AS A RESULT, BECAUSE, SO MUCH

INSPECT (2) [INSPECTED, INSPECTION]

Lev 14:36 the priest is to go in and **i** the house. 8011
14:39 the seventh day the priest shall return *to* **i** 8011

INSPECTED (1) [INSPECT]

Ex 39:43 Moses **i** the work and saw that they had 8011

INSPECTION (1) [INSPECT]

Ne 3:31 opposite the **I** Gate, and as far as the room 5152

INSPIRE (2) [INSPIRED, INSPIRES]

Jer 32:40 and *I will* **i** them to fear me, 928+4222+5989
49:16 The terror you **i** and the pride NIH

INSPIRED (2) [INSPIRE]

Hos 9: 7 the **i** man a maniac. 8120
1Th 1: 3 and your endurance *i by* **hope** *AIT*

INSPIRES (1) [INSPIRE]

Job 20: 3 and my understanding **i** me to reply. 8120

INSTALLED (5)

Jdg 17: 5 some idols and **i** one of his sons 906+3338+4848
17:12 Then Micah **i** the Levite, 906+3338+4848
1Ki 12:32 And at Bethel *he* also **i** priests at 6641
Ezr 6:18 And *they* **i** the priests in their divisions and 10624
Ps 2: 6 "I *have* **i** my King on Zion, my holy hill." 5820

INSTANCE (1)

Dt 19: 5 **For i**, a man may go into the forest 2256

INSTANT (9) [INSTANTLY]

Job 7:19 or let me alone even **for an i?** 1180+6330+8371
34:20 They die **in an i**, in the middle of the night; 8092
Pr 6:15 Therefore disaster will overtake him **in an i**; 7328
Isa 29: 5 like blown chaff. Suddenly, in an **i**, 7353
30:13 that collapses suddenly, in an **i**. 7353
Jer 4:20 **In an i** my tents are destroyed, 7328
49:19 I will chase Edom from its land *in an* **i**. 8088
50:44 I will chase Babylon from its land **in an i**. 8088
Lk 4: 5 showed him in an **i** all the kingdoms *5117+5989*

INSTANTLY (2) [INSTANT]

Lk 8:47 and how she had been **i** healed. *4202*
Ac 3: 7 **i** the man's feet and ankles became strong. *4202*

INSTEAD (102) [STEAD]

Ge 11: 3 They used brick **i of** stone, 4200
22:13 sacrificed it as a burnt offering **i of** his son. 9393
Ex 7:23 **I**, he turned and went into his palace, 2256
Lev 17: 4 **i of** bringing it to the entrance to the Tent 4202
Nu 1:50 **I**, appoint the Levites to be in charge of 2256
18:24 **I**, I give to the Levites as their inheritance 3954
Dt 12:18 **I**, you are to eat them in the presence of 561+3954
Jos 23:13 **I**, they will become snares and traps 2256
Jdg 15: 2 Take her **i**." 9393
2Sa 6:10 **I**, he took it aside to the house 2256
12: 4 **I**, he took the ewe lamb that belonged to 2256
14:14 But God does not take away life; **i**, 2256
18:33 If only I had died **i of** you— 9393
23:16 **i**, he poured it out before the LORD. 2256
1Ch 11:18 **i**, he poured it out before the LORD. 2256
13:13 **I**, he took it aside to the house 2256
2Ch 28:20 but he gave him trouble **i of** help. 4202
Ne 5:16 **I**, I devoted myself to the work 1685+2256
Est 2: 4 the girl who pleases the king be queen **i of** 9393
2:17 on her head and made her queen **i of** Vashti. 9393
3: 6 **I** Haman looked for a way to destroy all 2256
4: 4 She sent clothes for him to put on **i of** 6073
Job 3:24 For sighing comes to me **i of** food; 4200+7156
31:40 up **i of** wheat and weeds instead of barley." 9393
31:40 up instead of wheat and weeds **i of** barley." 9393
Pr 8:10 Choose my instruction **i of** silver, 440
11: 8 and it comes on the wicked **i**. 9393
Ecc 6: 2 and a stranger enjoys them **i**. 3954
Isa 3:24 **I of** fragrance there will be a stench; 9393
3:24 **i of** a sash, a rope; 9393
3:24 **i of** well-dressed hair, baldness; 9393
3:24 **i of** fine clothing, sackcloth; 9393
3:24 sackcloth; **i of** beauty, 9393
55:13 **I** *of* the thornbush will grow the pine tree, 9393
55:13 and **i of** briers the myrtle will grow. 9393
60:17 **I of** bronze I will bring you gold, 9393
60:17 **I of** wood I will bring you bronze, 9393
61: 3 to bestow on them a crown of beauty **i of** 9393
61: 3 the oil of gladness **i of** mourning, 9393
61: 3 a garment of praise **i of** a spirit of despair. 9393
61: 7 **I of** their shame my people will receive 9393
61: 7 and **i of** disgrace they will rejoice NIH
Jer 7:24 But they did not listen or pay attention; **i**, 2256
9:14 **I**, they have followed the stubbornness 2256
11: 8 But they did not listen or pay attention; **i**, 2256
14:12 **I**, I will destroy them with the sword, 3954
16:12 the stubbornness of his evil heart **i of** 1194+4200
30: 9 **I**, they will serve the LORD their God 2256
31:13 I will give them comfort and joy **i of** 4946
31:30 **I**, everyone will die for his own sin; 561+3954
36:26 **I**, the king commanded Jerahmeel, 2256
37:14 But Irijah would not listen to him; **i**, 2256
43: 5 **I**, Johanan son of Kareah and all 2256
Eze 4:15 over cow manure **i** *of* human excrement." 9393
36:34 be cultivated **i of** lying desolate in 889+9393
44: 8 **I of** carrying out your duty in regard 4202
Da 1:16 to drink and gave them vegetables **i**. NIH
5:23 **I**, you have set yourself up against the Lord 10221
11:38 **I of** them, he will honor a god 4030+6584
Jnh 1:13 **I**, the men did their best to row back 2256
Hab 2:16 You will be filled with shame **i of** glory. 4946
Mt 5:15 **I** they put it on its stand, *247*
18:30 **I**, he went off and had the man thrown *247*
20:26 **I**, whoever wants to become great *247*
25: 9 **I**, go to those who sell oil and buy some *3437*
27:24 but that **i** an uproar was starting, *3437*
Mk 1:45 **I** he went out and began to talk freely, *1254*
4:21 **I**, don't you put it on its stand? *NIG*
5:26 yet **i of** getting better she grew worse. *3437*
7: 5 according to the tradition of the elders **i of** *247*
10:43 **I**, whoever wants to become great *247*
15:11 the crowd to have Pilate release Barabbas **i**. *3437*
Lk 8:16 **I**, he puts it on a stand, *247*
11:11 will give him a snake **i?** *505*
11:33 **I** he puts it on its stand, *247*
22:26 **I**, the greatest among you should be like *247*
Jn 3:19 but men loved darkness **i of** light *2445+3437*
11:54 **I** he withdrew to a region near the desert, *247*
15:15 **I**, I have called you friends, *1254*
19:34 **I**, one of the soldiers pierced Jesus' side *247*
20:17 Go **i** to my brothers and tell them, *1254*
Ac 7:39 **I**, they rejected him and *247*
15:20 **I** we should write to them, *247*
25:19 **I**, they had some points of dispute with him *1254*
27:11 **i of** listening to what Paul said, *2445+3437*
Ro 14:13 **I**, make up your mind not to put any *247*
1Co 6: 1 the ungodly for judgment **i of** before *2779+4049*
6: 6 **But i**, one brother goes to law against *247*
6: 8 **I**, you yourselves cheat and do wrong, *247*
2Co 2: 7 Now **i**, you ought to forgive *1883+3437+3836*
Gal 4:14 **I**, you welcomed me as if I were an angel *247*
Eph 4:15 **I**, speaking the truth in love, *1254*
5:18 **I**, be filled with the Spirit. *247*
6: 4 Fathers, do not exasperate your children; **i**, *247*
1Ti 6: 2 **I**, they are to serve them even better, *247+3437*
2Ti 2:24 And the Lord's servant must not quarrel; **i**, *247*
4: 3 **I**, to suit their own desires, *247*
Heb 11:16 **I**, they were longing for a better country— *1254+3814*
Jas 4:15 **I**, you ought to say, "If it is the Lord's will, *505*
1Pe 2:23 **I**, he entrusted himself to him who judges *1254*
3: 4 **I**, it should be that of your inner self, *247*
2Jn 1:12 **I**, I hope to visit you and talk with you face *247*

INSTINCT (2) [INSTINCTS]

2Pe 2:12 They are like brute beasts, **creatures of i**, *5879*
Jude 1:10 and what things they do understand *by* **i**, *5880*

INSTINCTS (1) [INSTINCT]

Jude 1:19 **follow mere natural i** and do not have *6035*

INSTITUTED (5)

Nu 28: 6 the regular burnt offering **i** at Mount Sinai 6913
1Ki 12:32 He **i** a festival on the fifteenth day of 6913
12:33 So *he* **i** the festival for the Israelites 6913
Ro 13: 2 is rebelling against what God *has* **i**, *1411*
1Pe 2:13 for the Lord's sake to every authority **i** *NIG*

INSTRUCT (12) [INSTRUCTED, INSTRUCTING, INSTRUCTION, INSTRUCTIONS, INSTRUCTOR, INSTRUCTORS, INSTRUCTS]

Dt 24: 8 who are Levites, **i** you. 3723
Ne 9:20 You gave your good Spirit to **i** them. 8505
Job 8:10 *Will* they not **i** you and tell you? 3723
Ps 25:12 *He will* **i** him in the way chosen for him. 3723
32: 8 *I will* **i** you and teach you in 8505
105:22 to **i** his princes as he pleased 673
Pr 9: 9 **I** a wise man and he will be wiser still; 5989
Da 11:33 "Those who are wise *will* **i** many, 1067
Ro 15:14 and competent *to* **i** one another. *3805*
1Co 2:16 the mind of the Lord that he *may* **i** him?" *5204*
14:19 to **i** others than ten thousand words in *2994*
2Ti 2:25 Those who oppose him *he must* gently **i**, *4084*

INSTRUCTED (33) [INSTRUCT]

Ge 32: 4 *He* **i** them: "This is what you are to say 7422
32:17 *He* **i** the one in the lead: 7422
32:19 *He* also **i** the second, 7422
Ex 12:35 The Israelites did as Moses **i** and asked 1821
Nu 5: 4 They did just as the LORD *had* **i** Moses. 1819
27:23 as the LORD **i** through Moses. 1819
Jos 8:27 as the LORD *had* **i** Joshua. 7422
13: 6 Israel for an inheritance, as *I have* **i** you, 7422
18: 8 Joshua **i** them, "Go and make a survey of 7422
20: 2 as *I* **i** you through Moses, 1819
Jdg 21:20 So *they* **i** the Benjamites, saying, 7422
2Sa 11:19 *He* **i** the messenger: 7422
14:19 it was your servant Joab *who* **i** me to do this 7422
2Ki 12: 2 the years Jehoiada the priest **i** him. 3723
2Ch 26: 5 who **i** him in the fear of God. 1067
35: 3 He said to the Levites, who **i** all Israel 1067
Ne 8: 7 **i** the people in the Law while 1067
Est 1: 8 for the king **i** all the wine stewards 3569
4:10 Then she **i** him to say to Mordecai, 606
Job 4: 3 Think how *you have* **i** many, 3579
Pr 21:11 when a wise man *is* **i**, he gets knowledge. 8505
Isa 40:13 or **i** him as his counselor? 3359
50: 4 an **i** tongue, to know the word that sustains 4341
Jer 9:12 Who *has been* **i** *by* the LORD 1819+7023
Da 9:22 *He* **i** me and said to me, "Daniel, 1067
Mt 13:52 *who has been* **i** about the kingdom of heaven *3411*
17: 9 coming down the mountain, Jesus **i** them, *1948*
21: 6 and did as Jesus *had* **i** them. *5332*
28:15 the money and did as *they were* **i**. *1438*
Ac 18:25 He had been **i in** the way of the Lord, *2994*
Ro 2:18 of what is superior *because you are* **i** by *2994*
1Co 14:31 so that everyone *may be* **i** and encouraged. *3443*
1Th 4: 1 we **i** *you* how to live in order *4161*

INSTRUCTING (2) [INSTRUCT]

Ne 8: 9 and the Levites who *were* **i** the people said 1067
Mt 11: 1 Jesus had finished **i** his twelve disciples, *1411*

INSTRUCTION (33) [INSTRUCT]

Ex 24:12 and commands I have written for their **i**." 3723
Dt 33: 3 and from you receive **i**, 1830
Ne 1: 8 the **i** you gave your servant Moses, 1821
Job 22:22 Accept **i** from his mouth and lay 9368
Ps 50:17 You hate my **i** and cast my words 4592
Pr 1: 8 Listen, my son, to your father's **i** and do 4592
4: 1 Listen, my sons, to a father's **i**; 4592
4:13 Hold on to **i**, do not let it go; 4592
8:10 Choose my **i** instead of silver, 4592
8:33 Listen to my **i** and be wise; do not ignore it. 4592
13: 1 A wise son heeds his father's **i**, 4592
13:13 He who scorns **i** will pay for it, 1821
16:20 Whoever gives heed to **i** prospers, 1821
16:21 and pleasant words promote **i**. 4375
16:23 and his lips promote **i**. 4375
19:20 Listen to advice and accept **i**, 4592
19:27 Stop listening to **i**, my son, 4592
23:12 to **i** and your ears to words of knowledge. 4592
31:26 and faithful **i** is on her tongue. 9368
Isa 29:24 those who complain will accept **i**." *4375*
30: 9 to listen to the LORD's **i**. 9368
Mal 2: 6 True **i** was in his mouth 9368
2: 7 and from his mouth men should seek **i**— 9368
1Co 14: 6 or knowledge or prophecy or word of **i?** *1439*
14:26 everyone has a hymn, or a word of **i**, *1439*
Gal 6: 6 Anyone who **receives i in** the word *2994*
Eph 6: 4 instead, bring them up in the training and **i** *3804*
1Th 4: 8 he who rejects this **i** does not reject man *NIG*
2Th 3:14 If anyone does not obey our **i** in this letter, *3364*
1Ti 1:18 I give you this **i** in keeping with *4132*
6: 3 to the sound **i** of our Lord Jesus Christ and *3364*
2Ti 4: 2 with great patience and **careful i**. *1439*
Heb 6: 2 **i** about baptisms, the laying on of hands, *1439*

INSTRUCTIONS (31) [INSTRUCT]

Ge 44: 1 Now Joseph **gave** *these* **i** *to* the steward 7422
49:29 Then *he* **gave** them *these* **i**: 7422
49:33 Jacob had finished **giving i** *to* his sons, 7422
50:16 "Your father **left** *these* **i** before he died: 7422
Ex 12:24 "Obey these **i** as a lasting ordinance for you 1821
16: 4 and see whether they will follow my **i**. 9368
16:28 to keep my commands and my **i?** 9368
Jos 8:33 when he gave **i** to bless the people of Israel. NIH
Jdg 21:10 with **i** to go to Jabesh Gilead and put to 7422
1Sa 15:11 from me and has not carried out my **i**." 1821
15:13 I have carried out the LORD's **i**." 1821
15:24 the LORD's command and your **i**. 1821
21: 2 about your mission and your **i**.' 7422
1Ch 23:27 According to the last **i** *of* David, 1821
28:13 He gave him **i** for the divisions of NIH
Est 2:20 for she continued to follow Mordecai's **i** 4411
4:17 and carried out all of Esther's **i**. 7422
Pr 19:16 He who obeys **i** guards his life, 5184
Jer 32:13 "In their presence *I* **gave** Baruch *these* **i**: 7422
35:18 and have followed all his **i** 5184
Mt 10: 5 Jesus sent out *with* the following **i**: *4133*
Mk 6: 8 These *were his* **i**: "Take nothing for the *4133*
Ac 1: 2 *after* **giving i** through the Holy Spirit to *1948*
17:15 then left **with i** for Silas and Timothy *1953+3284*
19:33 and *some* of the crowd shouted **i to** him. *5204*
Col 4:10 (You have received **i** about him; *1953*
1Th 4: 2 For you know what **i** we gave you by *4132*
1Ti 3:14 I am writing you these **i** so that, *NIG*
5: 7 **Give** the people these **i**, *4133*

1Ti 5:21 to keep these i without partiality, NIG
Heb 11:22 from Egypt and gave i about his bones. 1948

INSTRUCTOR (2) [INSTRUCT]
Ro 2:20 an i of the foolish, a teacher of infants, 4083
Gal 6: 6 word must share all good things with his i. 2994

INSTRUCTORS (1) [INSTRUCT]
Pr 5:13 not obey my teachers or listen to my i. 4340

INSTRUCTS (3) [INSTRUCT]
Ps 16: 7 even at night my heart i me. 3579
25: 8 therefore he i sinners in his ways. 3723
Isa 28:26 His God i him and teaches him 3579

INSTRUMENT (3) [INSTRUMENTS]
Eze 33:32 with a beautiful voice and plays an i well, 5594
Ac 9:15 This man is my chosen i to carry my name 5007
2Ti 2:21 he will be an i for noble purposes, 5007

INSTRUMENTS (23) [INSTRUMENT]
1Ch 15:16 accompanied by musical i: 3998
16:42 the playing of the other i for sacred song. 3998
23: 5 with the musical i I have provided for 3998
2Ch 5:13 and other i, they raised their voices 3998+8877
7: 6 the Levites with the LORD's musical i, 3998
23:13 and singers with musical i were leading 3998
29:26 So the Levites stood ready with David's i, 3998
29:27 by trumpets and the i of David king 3998
30:21 accompanied by the LORD's i of praise. 3998
34:12 all who were skilled in playing musical i— 3998
Ne 12:36 with musical i [prescribed by] David 3998
Ps 4: T With stringed i. 5593
6: T With stringed i. 5593
54: T With stringed i. 5593
55: T With stringed i. 5593
61: T With stringed i. 5593
67: T With stringed i. 5593
76: T With stringed i. 5593
Isa 38:20 and we will sing with stringed i all the days 5593
Am 6: 5 like David and improvise on musical i. 3998
Hab 3:19 On my stringed i. 5593
Ro 6:13 parts of your body to sin, as i of wickedness, 3960
6:13 of your body to him as i of righteousness. 3960

INSULT (15) [INSULTED, INSULTING, INSULTS]
2Ki 19:16 to the words Sennacherib has sent to i 3070
Ps 69: 9 the insults of those who i you fall on me. 3070
Pr 9: 7 "Whoever corrects a mocker invites i; 7830
12:16 but a prudent man overlooks an i. 7830
Isa 37:17 to all the words Sennacherib has sent to i 3070
Jer 20: 8 the word of the LORD has brought me i 3075
Mt 5:11 "Blessed are you when people i you, 3943
Lk 6:22 and i you and reject your name as evil, 3943
11:45 when you say these things, you i us also." 5614
18:32 They will mock him, i him, spit on him, 5614
Ac 23: 4 "You dare to i God's high priest?" 3366
Ro 15: 3 "The insults of those who i you have fallen 3943
Heb 10:33 Sometimes you were publicly exposed to i 3944
1Pe 3: 9 Do not repay evil with evil or i with insult, 3367
3: 9 Do not repay evil with evil or insult with i, 3367

INSULTED (8) [INSULT]
2Ki 19:22 Who is it you have i and blasphemed? 3070
Isa 37:23 Who is it you have i and blasphemed? 3070
Jer 51:51 we have been i and shame covers our faces, 3075
Zep 2: 8 who i my people and made threats 3070
1Th 2: 2 We had previously suffered and been i 5614
Heb 10:29 and who has i the Spirit of grace? 1964
Jas 2: 6 But you have i the poor. 869
1Pe 4:14 If you are i because of the name of Christ, 3943

INSULTING (4) [INSULT]
2Ch 32:17 The king also wrote letters i the LORD, 3070
Ps 55:12 If an enemy were i me, I could endure it; 3070
Zep 2:10 for i and mocking the people of 3070
Lk 22:65 And they said many other i things to him. 1059

INSULTS (21) [INSULT]
1Sa 25:14 but he hurled i at them. 6512
2Ki 19:23 By your messengers you have heaped i on 3070
Ne 4: 4 Turn their i back on their own heads. 3075
4: 5 for they have thrown i in the face of 4087
Ps 22: 7 they hurl i, shaking their heads: 928+7080+8557
69: 9 the i of those who insult you fall on me. 3075
Pr 22:10 quarrels and i are ended. 7830
Isa 37:24 By your messengers you have heaped i on 3070
51: 7 of men or be terrified by their i. 1528
La 3:61 O LORD, you have heard their i, 3075
Eze 21:28 about the Ammonites and their i: 3075
Zep 2: 8 "I have heard the i of Moab and the taunts 3075
Mt 27:39 Those who passed by hurled i at him, 1059
27:44 with him also heaped i on him. 3943
Mk 15:29 Those who passed by hurled i at him, 1059
15:32 Those crucified with him also heaped i on 3943
Lk 23:39 of the criminals who hung there hurled i at 1059
Jn 9:28 Then they hurled i at him and said, 3366
Ro 15: 3 "The i of those who insult you have fallen 3944
2Co 12:10 I delight in weaknesses, in i, in hardships, 5615
1Pe 2:23 When they hurled their i at him, 3366

INSURRECTION (2) [INSURRECTIONISTS]
Lk 23:19 into prison for an i in the city, 5087
23:25 into prison for i and murder, 5087

INSURRECTIONISTS (1) [INSURRECTION]
Mk 15: 7 with the i who had committed murder in 5086

INTACT (2)
Pr 15:25 keeps the widow's boundaries i. 5893
Zec 12: 6 but Jerusalem will remain i in her place. 3782

INTEGRITY (22)
Dt 9: 5 not because of your righteousness or your i 3841+4222
1Ki 9: 4 before me in i of heart and uprightness, 9448
1Ch 29:17 you test the heart and are pleased with i. 4797
Ne 7: 2 because he was a man of i 622
Job 2: 3 And he still maintains his i, 9450
2: 9 "Are you still holding on to your i? 9450
6:29 reconsider, for my i is at stake. 7406
27: 5 till I die, I will not deny my i. 9450
Ps 7: 8 according to my i, O Most High. 9448
25:21 May i and uprightness protect me, 9448
41:12 In my i you uphold me and set me 9448
78:72 David shepherded them with i of heart; 9448
Pr 10: 9 The man of i walks securely, 9448
11: 3 The i of the upright guides them, 9450
13: 6 Righteousness guards the man of i, 2006+9448
17:26 or to flog officials for their i. 3841
29:10 Bloodthirsty men hate a man of i and seek 9447
Isa 45:23 in all i a word that will not be revoked: 7407
59: 4 no one pleads his case with i. 575
Mt 22:16 man of i and that you teach the way of God 239
Mk 12:14 "Teacher, we know you are a man of i. 239
Tit 2: 7 In your teaching show i, 917

INTELLIGENCE (5) [INTELLIGENT]
2Ch 2:12 endowed with i and discernment, 8507
Isa 29:14 the i of the intelligent will vanish." 1069
Da 5:11 to have insight and i and wisdom like that 10684
5:14 i and outstanding wisdom. 10684
1Co 1:19 the i of the intelligent I will frustrate." 5304

INTELLIGENT (4) [INTELLIGENCE]
1Sa 25: 3 She was an i and beautiful woman, 3202+8507
Isa 29:14 the intelligence of the i will vanish." 1067
Ac 13: 7 The proconsul, an i man, 5305
1Co 1:19 the intelligence of the i I will frustrate." 5305

INTELLIGIBLE (2)
1Co 14: 9 you speak i words with your tongue, 2358
14:19 in the church I would rather speak five i words 1609+3808+3836

INTEND (11) [INTENDED, INTENDING, INTENDS, INTENT, INTENTION, INTENTIONAL, INTENTIONALLY, INTENTLY]
Ge 37: 8 "Do you i to reign over us? 4887+4887
Nu 35:23 not his enemy and he did not i to harm him, 1335
1Sa 25:26 and all who i to harm my master be 1335
1Ki 5: 5 I i, therefore, to build a temple for the Name 606
2Ch 28:10 now you i to make the men and women 606
28:13 Do you i to add to our sin and guilt? 606
29:10 I i to make a covenant with the LORD, 4222+6640
Ps 62: 4 They fully i to topple him 3619
Jn 7:35 "Where does this man i to go 3516
14:22 why do you i to show yourself to us and 3516
Ac 5:35 of Israel, consider carefully what you i 3516

INTENDED (14) [INTEND]
Ge 50:20 You i to harm me, but God intended it for 3108
50:20 but God i it for good to accomplish what is 3108
Dt 19:19 then do to him as he i to do to his brother. 2372
1Sa 14: 4 of the pass that Jonathan i to cross to reach 1335
20:33 Then Jonathan knew that his father i 3983
2Ch 32: 2 that Sennacherib had come and that he i 7156
Jer 18:10 then I will reconsider the good I had i to do 606
Hos 2: 9 i to cover her nakedness. NIH
Jn 6:15 that they i to come and make him king 3516
12: 7 [It was i] that she should save this perfume 2671
Ac 12: 4 Herod i to bring him out for public trial 1089
20: 7 because he i to leave the next day, 3516
Ro 7:10 was i to bring life actually brought death. 1650
2Co 7: 9 For you became sorrowful as God i and 2848

INTENDING (2) [INTEND]
Jdg 20: 5 surrounded the house, i to kill me. 1948
Ac 12: 1 Herod arrested some who belonged to the church, i to persecute them. AIT

INTENDS (2) [INTEND]
Dt 28:57 For she i to eat them secretly during AIT
Isa 10: 7 But this is not what he i, 1948

INTENSE (3) [INTENSELY]
2Sa 13:15 Then Amnon hated her with i hatred. 1524+4394
1Th 2:17 out of our i longing we made every effort 4498
Rev 16: 9 the i heat and they cursed the name of God, 3489

INTENSELY (3) [INTENSE]
Gal 1:13 how i I persecuted the church of God 2848+5651
Jas 4: 5 the spirit he caused to live in us envies i? 2160
Rev 2:22 who commit adultery with her suffer i, 3489

INTENT (8) [INTEND]
Ex 32:12 with evil i that he brought them out, 8288
1Ch 29:17 given willingly and with honest i. 4222
Ps 139:20 They speak of you with evil i; 4659
Pr 7:10 dressed like a prostitute and with crafty i. 4213
21:27 much more so when brought with evil i! 2365
Hos 5:11 trampled in judgment, i on pursuing idols. 3283
Mt 22:18 But Jesus, knowing their evil i, said, NIG
Eph 3:10 His i was that now, through the church, 2671

INTENTION (2) [INTEND]
2Sa 13:32 This has been Absalom's expressed i ever 8461
Job 34:14 If it were his i and he withdrew his spirit 4213+8492

INTENTIONAL (1) [INTEND]
Nu 15:25 for it was not i and they have brought to 8705

INTENTIONALLY (2) [INTEND]
Ex 21:13 However, if he does not do it i, 7399
Nu 35:20 something at him i so that he dies 928+7402

INTENTLY (4) [INTEND]
Ac 1:10 They were looking i up into the sky 867
6:15 in the Sanhedrin looked i at Stephen, 867
Jas 1:25 the man who looks i into the perfect law 4160
1Pe 1:10 searched i and with the greatest care, 1699+2001+2779

INTERCEDE (5) [INTERCEDED, INTERCEDES, INTERCEDING, INTERCESSION, INTERCESSOR]
Ge 23: 8 then listen to me and i with Ephron son 7003
1Sa 2:25 sins against the LORD, who will i for him?" 7137
7: 5 at Mizpah and I will i with the LORD 7137
1Ki 13: 6 "I with the LORD your God and 906+2704+7156
Heb 7:25 because he always lives to i for them. 1961

INTERCEDED (1) [INTERCEDE]
1Ki 13: 6 the man of God i with the LORD, 906+2704+7156

INTERCEDES (2) [INTERCEDE]
Ro 8:26 but the Spirit himself i for us with groans 5659
8:27 the Spirit i for the saints in accordance 1961

INTERCEDING (1) [INTERCEDE]
Ro 8:34 the right hand of God and is also i for us. 1961

INTERCESSION (2) [INTERCEDE]
Isa 53:12 and made i for the transgressors. 7003
1Ti 2: 1 i and thanksgiving be made for everyone— 1950

INTERCESSOR (1) [INTERCEDE]
Job 16:20 My i is my friend as my eyes pour out tears 4885

INTEREST (16) [INTERESTS]
Ex 22:25 charge him no i. 5968
Lev 25:36 Do not take i of any kind from 2256+5968+9552
25:37 not lend him money at i or sell him food at 5968
Dt 23:19 Do not charge your brother i, 5967+5968
23:19 or food or anything else that may earn i. 5967
23:20 You may charge a foreigner i, 5967
Est 3: 8 it is not in the king's best i 8750
Pr 28: 8 his wealth by exorbitant i 2256+5968+9552
Eze 18: 8 not lend at usury or take excessive i. 9552
18:13 He lends at usury and takes excessive i. 9552
18:17 from sin and takes no usury or excessive i. 9552
22:12 and excessive i and make unjust gain 9552
Mt 25:27 I would have received it back with i. 5527
Lk 19:23 I could have collected it with i?' 5527
Php 2:20 who takes a genuine i in your welfare. 3534
1Ti 6: 4 an unhealthy i in controversies and quarrels 4309

INTERESTS (5) [INTEREST]
Ezr 4:22 to the detriment of the royal i? 10421
1Co 7:34 and his i are divided. An unmarried NIG
Php 2: 4 of you should look not only to your own i, 3836
2: 4 but also to the i of others. 3836
2:21 For everyone looks out for his own i, 3836

INTERFERE (1) [INTERFERED]
Ezr 6: 7 Do not i with the work on this temple 10697

INTERFERED (1) [INTERFERE]
1Ki 1: 6 (His father had never i with him by asking, 6772

INTERIOR (4)

1Ki 6:15 He lined its **i** walls with cedar 1074+2025+4946
6:22 So he overlaid the whole **i** with gold. 1074
SS 3:10 its **i** lovingly inlaid by the daughters 9348
Ac 19: 1 Paul took the road through the **i** and *541+3538*

INTERMARRY (5) [MARRY]

Ge 34: 9 **I** *with* us; give us your daughters 3161
Dt 7: 3 *Do* not **i** with them. 3161
Jos 23:12 if *you* **i** with them and associate with them, 3161
1Ki 11: 2 *"You must* not **i** with them, 995
Ezr 9:14 Shall we again break your commands and **i** 3161

INTERMEDDLE (KJV) See SHARE

INTERMITTENT (1)

Job 6:15 as undependable as **i streams,** 5707

INTERPRET (25) [INTERPRETATION, INTERPRETATIONS, INTERPRETED, INTERPRETER, INTERPRETERS, INTERPRETS]

Ge 40: 8 "but there is no *one to* **i** them." 7354
41: 8 but no *one could* **i** them for him. 7354
41:15 "I had a dream, and no *one can* **i** it. 7354
41:15 that when you hear a dream *you can* **i** it." 7354
Da 2: 4 the dream, and *we will* **i** it." 10252+10600
2: 5 not tell me what my dream was and **i** it, 10600
2: 6 So tell me the dream and **i** it for me." 10600
2: 7 the dream, and *we will* **i** it." 10252+10600
2: 9 I will know that *you can* **i** it *for* me. 10252+10600
2:16 that he *might* **i** the dream for him. 10252+10600
2:24 and *I will* **i** his dream for him." 10252+10600
2:26 in my dream and **i** it?" 10600
2:36 and now *we will* **i** it to the king. 10042+10600
4: 6 before me *to* **i** the dream for me. 10313+10600
4: 7 but *they could* not **i** it for me. 10313+10600
4: 9 Here is my dream; **i** it for me. 10042+10600
4:18 wise men in my kingdom can **i** it 10313+10600
5:12 and also the *ability to* **i** dreams, 10599
Mt 16: 3 You know how *to* **i** the appearance of *1359*
16: 3 but *you* cannot **i** the signs of the times. *NIG*
Lk 12:56 how *to* **i** the appearance of the earth and *1507*
12:56 you don't know **how** *to* **i** this present time? *1507*
1Co 12:30 Do all speak in tongues? Do all **i?** *1450*
14:13 that *he may* **i** what he says. *1450*
14:27 one at a time, and someone *must* **i.** *1450*

INTERPRETATION (11) [INTERPRET]

Ge 40:16 that Joseph *had* **given** *a* favorable **i,** he said 7354
40:22 **said** to them **in** *his* **i.** 7354
41:12 **giving** each man *the* **i** of his dream. 7354
Jdg 7:15 When Gideon heard the dream and its **i,** 8694
Da 2:30 O king, may know the **i** and 10600
2:45 The dream is true and the **i** is trustworthy." 10600
4:24 "This is the **i,** O king, 10600
7:16 and gave me the **i** *of* these things: 10600
1Co 12:10 and to still another the **i** of tongues. *2255*
14:26 a revelation, a tongue or an **i.** *2255*
2Pe 1:20 about by the prophet's own **i.** *2146*

INTERPRETATIONS (2) [INTERPRET]

Ge 40: 8 "Do not **i** belong to God? 7355
Da 5:16 able to **give i** and to solve difficult problems. 10599+10600

INTERPRETED (2) [INTERPRET]

Ge 41:12 and *he* **i** them for us, 7354
41:13 things turned out exactly as *he* **i** them to us: 7354

INTERPRETER (2) [INTERPRET]

Ge 42:23 since he was using an **i.** 4885
1Co 14:28 If there is no **i,** *1449*

INTERPRETERS (1) [INTERPRET]

Jer 27: 9 your diviners, your **i of dreams,** 2706

INTERPRETS (2) [INTERPRET]

Dt 18:10 **I omens,** engages in witchcraft, 5727
1Co 14: 5 unless *he* **i,** so that the church may *1450*

INTERRUPTED (1)

Ac 26:24 At this point Festus **i** Paul's defense. *NIG*

INTERSECTING (2)

Eze 1:16 appeared to be made like a wheel **i** 928+9348
10:10 each was like a wheel **i** a wheel. 928+9348

INTERVALS (1)

Eze 41:17 the walls **at regular i** all around the inner 4500

INTERVENE (1) [INTERVENED]

Isa 59:16 he was appalled that there was no *one to* **i;** 7003

INTERVENED (1) [INTERVENE]

Ps 106:30 But Phinehas stood up and **i,** 7136

INTERWOVEN (3) [WEAVE]

1Ki 7:17 A network of **i chains** festooned the 5126+9249
2Ch 3:16 He made **i** chains and put them 928+2021+8054
Ps 45:13 her gown is **i** *with* gold. 5401

INTESTINES (2)

2Sa 20:10 and his **i** spilled out on the ground. 5055
Ac 1:18 his body burst open and all his **i** spilled out. *5073*

INTIMATE (4)

1Ki 1: 4 **had** no **i relations with** her. 3359
Job 19:19 All my **i** friends detest me; 6051
29: 4 when God's **i friendship** blessed my house, 6051
Hos 3: 3 you must not be a prostitute or be **i with** 4200

INTIMIDATE (3)

Ne 6:13 to **i** *me* so that I would commit a sin 3707
6:14 the prophets who have been *trying to* **i** me. 3707
6:19 And Tobiah sent letters to **i** me. 3707

INTO (1286)

Ge 2: 7 and breathed **i** his nostrils the breath of life, 928
2:10 from there it was separated **i** four 4200
2:21 **caused** the man **to fall** *i* a deep sleep; AIT
6:19 to bring **i** the ark two of all living creatures, 448
7: 1 LORD then said to Noah, "Go **i** the ark, 448
9: 2 they are given **i** your hands. 928
10: 5 the maritime peoples spread out **i** their 928
12: 2 "I will make you **i** a great nation 4200
12:15 and she **was taken** *i* his palace. AIT
14:10 of the men fell **i** them and the rest fled to 2025
14:20 who delivered your enemies **i** your hand." 928
15:12 Abram **fell** *i* a deep sleep, AIT
17:20 and I will make him **i** a great nation. 4200
18: 6 So Abraham hurried **i** the tent to Sarah. 2025
19:10 and pulled Lot back **i** the house and shut 2025
20: 1 on from there **i** the region of the Negev 2025
21:13 the son of the maidservant **i** a nation also, 4200
21:18 for I will make him **i** a great nation." 4200
24:20 So she quickly emptied her jar **i** the trough, 448
24:67 Isaac brought her **i** the tent 2025
30:14 Reuben went out **i** the fields 928
31:33 So Laban went **i** Jacob's tent and 928
31:33 into Jacob's tent and **i** Leah's tent and into 928
31:33 into Jacob's tent and into Leah's tent and **i** 928
32: 7 the people who were with him **i** two groups 4200
37:20 and throw him **i** one of these cisterns 928
37:22 Throw him **i** this cistern here in the desert, 448
37:24 they took him and threw him **i** the cistern. 2025
39:11 One day he went **i** the house to attend 2025
40:10 and its clusters **ripened** *i* grapes. AIT
40:11 squeezed them **i** Pharaoh's cup and put 448
40:21 he once again put the cup **i** Pharaoh's hand, 6584
43:12 the silver that was put back **i** the mouths 928
43:18 that was put back **i** our sacks the first time. 928
43:24 The steward took the men **i** Joseph's house, 2025
43:26 the gifts they had brought **i** the house, 2025
43:30 He went **i** his private room and wept there. 2025
45: 4 the one you sold **i** Egypt! 2025
46: 3 for I will make you **i** a great nation there. 4200
49:33 he drew his feet up **i** the bed, 448
Ex 1:22 "Every boy that is born you must throw **i** 2025
3: 8 to bring them up out of that land **i** a good 448
3:17 up out of your misery in Egypt **i** the land of 448
3:18 Let us take a three-day journey **i** the desert 928
4: 4 the snake and *it* **turned** *back* **i** a staff 2118+4200
4: 6 So Moses put his hand **i** his cloak, 928
4: 7 "Now put it back **i** your cloak," he said. 448
4: 7 So Moses put his hand back **i** his cloak, 448
4:27 "Go **i** the desert to meet Moses." 2025
5: 3 Now let us take a three-day journey **i** 928
7:15 hand the staff that was changed **i** a snake. 4200
7:17 and it will be changed **i** blood. 4200
7:20 and all the water was changed **i** blood. 4200
7:23 Instead, he turned and went **i** his palace, 448
8: 3 up **i** your palace and your bedroom 928
8: 3 **i** the houses of your officials and 928
8: 3 and **i** your ovens and kneading troughs. 928
8:14 They *were* **piled** *i* heaps, AIT
8:21 on your people and **i** your houses. 928
8:24 of flies poured **i** Pharaoh's palace and into 2025
8:24 of flies poured into Pharaoh's palace and **i** NIH
8:27 We must take a three-day journey **i** 928
9: 8 a furnace and have Moses toss it **i** the air in 2025
9:10 Moses tossed it **i** the air, 2025
10: 4 I will bring locusts **i** your country 928
10:19 the locusts and carried them **i** the Red Sea. 2025
12: 4 having **taken i account** the number 928
12:11 **cloak tucked i** your **belt,** 2520+5516
12:22 dip it **i** the blood in the basin and put some 928
13: 5 When the LORD brings you **i** the land of 448
13:11 "After the LORD brings you **i** the land of 448
14:21 a strong east wind and turned it **i** dry land. 4200
14:23 and horsemen followed them **i** the sea. 448+9348
14:24 the Egyptian army and **threw** it **i confusion.** 2169
14:27 and the LORD swept them **i** the sea. 928+9348
14:28 of Pharaoh that had followed the Israelites **i** 928
15: 1 The horse and its rider he has hurled **i** 928
15: 4 and his army he has hurled **i** the sea. 928
15:19 chariots and horsemen went **i** the sea, 928
15:21 The horse and its rider he has hurled **i** 928
15:22 the Red Sea and they went **i** the Desert 448
15:25 He threw it **i** the water, 448
16: 3 but you have brought us out **i** this desert 448
Ex 18: 7 They greeted each other and then went **i** 2025
21:33 to cover it and an ox or a donkey falls **i** it, 2025
22: 6 a fire breaks out and **spreads** *i* thornbushes AIT
23:23 and bring you **i** the land of the Amorites, 448
23:27 **throw i confusion** every nation you encounter. 2169
25:14 Insert the poles **i** the rings on the sides of 928
26: 1 with cherubim **worked** *i* them *by* AIT
26: 9 five of the curtains together **i one set** 963+4200
26: 9 one set and the other six **i another set.** 963+4200
26:24 and fitted **i** a single ring; 448
26:31 with cherubim **worked** *i* it *by* AIT
27: 7 to be inserted **i** the rings so they will be 928
29:17 the ram **i** pieces and wash the inner parts 4200
30:25 **Make** these *i* a sacred anointing oil, AIT
32: 4 and **made** it *i* an idol cast in the shape of AIT
32:10 Then I will make you **i** a great nation." 4200
32:21 that *you* **led** them **i** such great sin?" 995
32:24 and I threw it **i** the fire, 928
33: 9 As Moses went **i** the tent, 2025
36: 8 with cherubim **worked** *i* them *by* AIT
36:16 of the curtains **i** one set and the other six 4200
36:16 the curtains into one set and the other six **i** 4200
36:29 the way to the top and fitted **i** a single ring; 448
36:35 with cherubim **worked** *i* it *by* AIT
37: 5 the poles **i** the rings on the sides of the ark 928
38: 7 the poles **i** the rings so they would be on 928
39: 3 and cut strands to be worked **i** the blue, 928+9348
40:21 Then he brought the ark **i** the tabernacle 448
Lev 1: 6 to skin the burnt offering and cut it **i** pieces. 4200
1:12 He is to cut it **i** pieces, 4200
4: 5 of the bull's blood and carry it **i** the Tent 448
4: 6 He is to dip his finger **i** the blood 928
4:16 to take some of the bull's blood **i** the Tent 448
4:17 He shall dip his finger **i** the blood 4946
6:30 any sin offering whose blood is brought **i** 448
8:20 the ram **i** pieces and burned the head, 4200
9: 9 and he dipped his finger **i** the blood 928
9:23 and Aaron then went **i** the Tent of Meeting. 448
10: 9 or other fermented drink whenever you go **i** 448
10:18 its blood was not taken **i** the Holy Place, 448+7163
11:33 If one of them falls **i** a clay pot, 448+9348
14: 6 **i** the blood of the bird that was killed over 928
14: 8 After this he may come **i** the camp, 448
14:16 dip his right forefinger **i** the oil in his palm, 4946
14:26 of the oil **i** the palm of his own left hand, 6584
14:40 and thrown **i** an unclean place outside 448
14:41 the material that is scraped off dumped **i** 448
14:46 "Anyone who goes **i** the house 448
14:51 dip them **i** the blood of the dead bird and 928
16: 2 not to come whenever he chooses **i** 448
16:10 by sending it **i** the desert as a scapegoat. 2025
16:21 He shall send the goat away **i** the desert in 2025
16:23 "Then Aaron is to go **i** the Tent of Meeting 448
16:26 afterward he may come **i** the camp. 448
16:27 whose blood was brought **i** 928
16:28 afterward he may come **i** the camp. 448
26:25 When you withdraw **i** your cities, 448
26:25 and you will be given **i** enemy hands. 928
26:31 *I will* **turn** your cities **i** ruins 5989
26:41 toward them so that I sent them **i** the land 928
Nu 4:19 and his sons *are to* **go i** the sanctuary 995
5:17 from the tabernacle floor **i** the water. 448
5:23 and then wash them off **i** the bitter water. 448
5:27 it will go **i** her and cause bitter suffering; 928
10: 9 When *you* **go i** battle in your own land 995
11: 8 They cooked it in a pot or **made** it *i* cakes. AIT
13:17 the Negev and on *i* the hill country. AIT
13:27 "We went **i** the land to which you sent us, 448
14: 8 he will lead us **i** that land, 448
14:12 but I will make you **i** a nation greater 4200
14:16 not able to bring these people **i** 448
14:24 I will bring him **i** the land he went to, 448
16:14 you haven't brought us **i** a land flowing 448
16:30 and they go down alive **i** the grave, 2025
16:33 They went down alive **i** the grave, 2025
16:38 **Hammer** the censers *i* sheets to overlay AIT
16:47 and ran **i** the midst of the assembly. 448
19: 7 He may then come **i** the camp, 448
19:17 from the burned purification offering **i** a jar 448
20: 4 the LORD's community **i** this desert, 448
20:12 you will not bring this community **i** 448
20:15 Our forefathers went down **i** Egypt, 2025
21: 2 "If you will deliver these people **i** 928
21:13 in the desert extending **i** Amorite territory. 4946
21:22 not turn aside **i** any field or vineyard, 928
21:23 and marched out **i** the desert against Israel. 2025
22:23 she turned off the road **i** a field. 928
25: 8 and followed the Israelite **i** the tent. 448
25: 8 the Israelite and **i** the woman's body. 448
31: 4 Send **i** battle a thousand men from each of 4200
31: 6 Moses sent them **i** battle, 4200
31:21 the soldiers who had gone **i** battle, "This is 4200
31:24 Then you may come **i** the camp." 448
31:54 and brought it **i** the Tent of Meeting as 448
32: 7 over **i** the land the LORD has given them? 448
32:32 **cross over** before the LORD *i* AIT
33: 8 and passed through the sea **i** the desert, 2025
33:51 'When you cross the Jordan **i** Canaan, 448
35:10 'When you cross the Jordan **i** Canaan, 2025
36: 3 added to that of the tribe *they* **marry i.** 2118+4200
36: 4 that of the tribe **i** which *they* **marry,** 2118+4200
Dt 1: 7 Break camp and **advance** *i* the hill country AIT
1:24 They left and went up **i** the hill country, 2025
1:27 to deliver us **i** the hands of the Amorites 928
1:41 thinking it easy to go up **i** the hill country. 2025
1:43 in your arrogance you marched up **i** the hill 2025

Dt 2:24 I have given i your hand Sihon 928
2:29 until we cross the Jordan i the land 448
2:30 in order to give him i your hands, 928
3: 3 also gave i our hands Og king of Bashan 928
4:19 *do* not **be enticed** *i* bowing down to them AIT
4:38 to **bring** you i their land to give it to you 995
4:42 He could flee i one of these cities 448
6:10 When the LORD your God brings you i 448
7: 1 When the LORD your God brings you i 448
7:23 **throwing** them i great **confusion** 2169+4539
7:24 He will give their kings i your hand, 928
7:26 not bring a detestable thing i your house 448
8: 7 For the LORD your God is bringing you i 448
9:14 And I will make you i a nation stronger 4200
9:21 as fine as dust and threw the dust i a stream 448
9:28 the LORD was not able to take them i 448
10:22 Your forefathers who went down i 2025
11:29 the LORD your God has brought you i 448
13:16 the town i the middle of the public square 448
15:17 and push it through his ear lobe i the door, 928
19: 3 Build roads to them and **divide** i **three** parts 8992
19: 5 a man may go i the forest with his neighbor 928
20: 2 When you are about to go i battle, 448
20: 3 "Hear, O Israel, today you are going i battle 4200
20:13 LORD your God delivers it i your hand, 928
21:10 and the LORD your God delivers them i 928
21:12 Bring her i your home 448+9348
23: 5 to Balaam but turned the curse i a blessing 4200
23:18 a female prostitute or of a male prostitute i NIH
24:10 not go i his house to get what he is offering 448
26: 5 a wandering Aramean, and he went down i 2025
27: 2 When you have crossed the Jordan i 448
28:24 **turn** the rain of your country i dust and 5989
28:41 because they will go i captivity. 928
29:12 You are standing here in order to enter i 928
29:28 from their land and thrust them i 448
30:12 "Who will ascend i heaven to get it 2025
31: 7 for you must go with this people i the land 448
31:20 When I have brought them i the land 448
31:21 even before I bring them i the land 448
31:23 the Israelites i the land I promised them 448
32:49 "Go up i the Abarim Range to Mount Nebo 448
34: 4 but you will not cross over i it." 2025
Jos 1: 2 to cross the Jordan River i the land I am 448
2:18 your brothers and all your family i your 2025
2:19 If anyone goes outside your house i the 2025
2:22 they went i the hills 2025
2:24 surely given the whole land i our hands; 928
3:11 the Lord of all the earth will go i the Jordan 928
4: 5 before the ark of the LORD your God i 448
6: 2 "See, I have delivered Jericho i your hands, 928
6:19 to the LORD and *must* **go** i his treasury." 995
6:22 "**Go** i the prostitute's house 995
6:24 **put** the silver and gold and the articles of bronze and iron *i* AIT
7: 7 across the Jordan to deliver us i the hands 928
8: 1 For I have delivered i your hands the king 928
8: 7 The LORD your God will give it i your hand. 928
8:13 That night Joshua went i the valley. 928+9348
8:18 for i your hand I will deliver the city." 928
10: 8 I have given them i your hand. 928
10:10 **threw** them i **confusion** before Israel. 2169
10:19 for the LORD your God has given them i 928
10:27 from the trees and threw them i the cave 448
10:30 that city and its king i Israel's hand. 928
11: 8 the LORD gave them i the hand of Israel. 928
16: 1 and went up from there through the desert i 928
17:15 go up i the forest and clear land 2025
18: 5 You are to divide the land i seven parts. 4200
18:12 and headed west i the hill country, 928
18:18 of Beth Arabah and on down i the Arabah. 2025
19:49 When they had finished dividing the land i 4200
20: 4 Then they are to admit him i their city 2025
24: 8 but I gave them i your hands. 928
24:11 but I gave them i your hands. 928
Jdg 1: 2 I have given the land i their hands." 928
1: 3 "Come up with us i the territory allotted 928
1: 3 We in turn will go with you i yours." 928
1: 4 and Perizzites i their hands and they struck 928
1:24 "Show us **how to get** i the city 4427
1:28 they pressed the Canaanites i forced labor 4200
1:34 not allowing them to come down i 4200
1:35 they too were pressed i forced labor. 4200
2: 1 of Egypt and led you i the land that I swore 448
2:23 not drive them out at once by giving them i 928
3: 8 against Israel so that he sold them i 928
3:10 of Aram i the hands of Othniel, 928
3:21 from his right thigh and plunged it i 928
3:28 your enemy, i your hands." 928
4: 2 the LORD sold them i the hands of Jabin, 928
4: 7 to the Kishon River and give him i 928
4:14 the LORD has given Sisera i your hands. 928
4:21 the peg through his temple i the ground, 928
5:15 rushing after him i the valley. 928
6: 1 for seven years he gave them i the hands of 928
6:13 the LORD has abandoned us and put us i 928
6:35 and also i Asher, Zebulun and Naphtali, 928
7: 2 for me to deliver Midian i their hands. 928
7: 7 and give the Midianites i your hands. 928
7: 9 because I am going to give it i your hands. 928
7:13 of barley bread came tumbling i 928
7:14 the Midianites and the whole camp i 928
7:15 The LORD has given the Midianite camp i 928
7:16 the three hundred men i three companies, NIH
8: 3 the Midianite leaders, i your hands. 928
8: 7 and Zalmunna i my hand, 928
8:27 Gideon made the gold i an ephod, 4200
Jdg 9:26 moved with his brothers i Shechem, 928
9:27 After *they had* **gone out** *i* the fields AIT
9:43 divided them i three companies and set 4200
9:46 the tower of Shechem went i the stronghold 448
10: 7 He sold them i the hands of the Philistines 928
11:21 gave Sihon and all his men i Israel's hands, 928
11:30 "If you give the Ammonites i my hands, 928
11:32 and the LORD gave them i his hands. 928
11:38 She and the girls went i the hills and wept 6584
13: 1 so the LORD delivered them i the hands 928
14:15 "**Coax** your husband *i* explaining AIT
15:18 Must I now die of thirst and fall i the hands 928
16: 5 *"See if you can* **lure** him *i* showing you AIT
16:13 the seven braids of my head i the fabric [on 6640
16:13 wove them i the fabric 6640
16:23 our enemy, i our hands." 928
16:24 "Our god has delivered our enemy i 928
17: 4 *who* **made** them *i* the image and the idol. AIT
18: 1 **come** i an inheritance among the tribes 928+5877
18:10 and a spacious land that God has put i 928
18:18 When these men **went** i Micah's house 995
19: 3 *She* **took** him i her father's house, 995
19:12 We won't go i an alien city, 448
19:15 no one took them i his home for the night. 2025
19:18 No one has taken me i his house. 2025
19:21 So he took him i his house 4200
19:29 i twelve parts and sent them into all 4200
19:29 and sent them i all the areas of Israel. 928
20: 6 **cut** her i **pieces** and sent one piece 5983
20:28 tomorrow I will give them i your hands." 928
20:37 in ambush made a sudden dash i Gibeah, 448
20:40 the smoke of the whole city going up i 2025
20:47 and fled i the desert to the rock of Rimmon, 2025
Ru 2: 7 *She* **went** i the field 995
3:15 **poured** i it six **measures** of barley 4499
4:11 the woman who is coming i your home 448
1Sa 2:14 He would plunge it i the pan or kettle 928
4: 5 of the LORD's covenant came i the camp, 448
4: 6 the ark of the LORD had come i the camp, 448
4: 7 "A god has come i the camp," they said. 448
4:19 *she* **went** i **labor** and gave birth, 4156
5: 2 Then they **carried** the ark *i* Dagon's temple AIT
5: 9 throwing it i a great panic. NIH
6:19 of them to death because they had looked i 928
7:10 **threw** them i *such* **a panic** 2169
9: 4 They went on i the district of Shaalim, 928
9:22 Then Samuel brought Saul and his servant i 2025
10: 6 you will be changed i a different person. 4200
11: 7 He took a pair of oxen, **cut** them i **pieces,** 5983
11:11 The next day Saul **separated** his men *i* AIT
11:11 the last watch of the night they broke i 928+9348
12: 9 so he sold them i the hand of Sisera, 928
12: 9 the commander of the army of Hazor, and i 928
14:10 the LORD has given them i our hands." 928
14:12 the LORD has given them i the hand 928
14:26 When they went i the woods, 448
14:27 the staff that was in his hand and dipped it i 928
14:37 Will you give them i Israel's hand?" 928
14:52 **took** him i his **service.** 665
17:47 and he will give all of you i our hands." 928
17:49 Reaching i his bag and taking out a stone, 448
17:49 The stone sank i his forehead, 928
19: 2 go i hiding and stay there. 928
19:10 as Saul drove the spear i the wall. 928
20: 8 for you have brought him i a covenant 928
20:11 Jonathan said, *"let's* **go out** *i* the field." AIT
21:15 Must this man come i my house?" 448
22: 5 Go i the land of Judah." 995
23: 4 for I am going to give the Philistines i 928
23:14 but God did not give David i his hands. 928
23:25 **went** *i* the Desert of Maon **in pursuit** AIT
24: 4 'I will give your enemy i your hands 928
24:10 how the LORD delivered you i my hands 928
24:18 the LORD delivered me i your hands, 928
25: 1 David moved down i the Desert of Maon. 448
25:20 As she came riding her donkey i 928
26: 6 "Who will go down i the camp with me 448
26: 8 "Today God has delivered your enemy i 928
26:10 or he will go i battle and perish. 928
26:12 the LORD *had* **put** them *i* a deep sleep. AIT
26:23 The LORD delivered you i my hands today, 928
29: 4 He must not go with us i battle, 928
29: 9 'He must not go up with us i battle.' 928
2Sa 2:16 and thrust his dagger i his opponent's side, 928
2:23 the butt of his spear i Asahel's stomach, 448
2:25 They formed themselves i a group 4200
3:13 *Do* not **come** i my **presence** 906+7156+8011
3:27 Joab took him aside i the gateway, 448+9348
4: 6 They went i the inner part of the house as if 6330
4: 7 *They had* **gone** i the house 995
12: 8 and your master's wives i your arms. 928
12:16 He fasted and **went** i his house and spent 995
12:20 *he* **went** i the house of the LORD 995
13:10 "**Bring** the food here i my bedroom 995
14: 6 *They* **got** i **a fight** *with* each other in 5897
14:19 and who put all these words i the mouth 928
15:25 "**Take** the ark of God **back** *i* the city. AIT
15:31 **turn** Ahithophel's counsel i **foolishness."** 6118
17:11 with you yourself leading them i battle. 928
17:13 If he withdraws i a city, 448
17:18 and *they* **climbed down** *i* it. AIT
18: 6 The army **marched** i the field to fight Israel, 3655
18:12 if a thousand shekels were weighed out i 6584
18:14 and plunged them i Absalom's heart 928
18:17 threw him i a big pit in the forest and piled 448
19: 2 that day *was* **turned** i mourning, 2118+4200
19: 3 The men **stole** i the city that day 995+1704+4200
2Sa 19: 5 Joab went i the house to the king and said, 448
20:10 and Joab plunged it i his belly, 448
20:12 **dragged** him from the road *i* AIT
22:20 He brought me out i a spacious place; 4200
22:29 **turns** my darkness i **light.** 5585
23:20 also went down i a pit on a snowy day 928+9348
24:14 Let us fall i the hands of the LORD, 928
24:14 but do not let me fall i the hands of men." 928
1Ki 1:28 So she came *i* the king's **presence** and stood AIT
6: 6 so that nothing would be inserted i 928
8: 1 King Solomon summoned i his **presence** 448
10:16 six hundred bekas of gold went i 6584
11:30 the new cloak he was wearing and **tore** it *i* AIT
12:18 to get i his chariot and escape to Jerusalem. 928
15:15 *He* **brought** i the temple of the LORD 995
16:18 he went i the citadel of the royal palace 448
16:21 people of Israel were split i two factions; 4200
17:23 and carried him down from the room i 2025
18:23 and *let them* **cut** it i **pieces** and put it on 5983
18:33 **cut** the bull i **pieces** 5983
18:46 **tucking** his **cloak** i *his* **belt,** 5516+9113
19: 4 while he himself went a day's journey i 928
19: 9 There he went i a cave and spent the night. 448
20: 2 He sent messengers i the city to Ahab king 2025
20:13 I will give it i your hand today, 928
20:28 I will deliver this vast army i your hands, 928
20:33 Ahab had him come up i his chariot. 6584
20:39 "Your servant went i the thick of the battle, 928
22: 6 "for the Lord will give it i the king's hand." 928
22:12 the LORD will give it i the king's hand." 928
22:15 the LORD will give it i the king's hand." 928
22:20 'Who *will* **entice** Ahab *i* attacking AIT
22:30 of Israel disguised himself and went i 928
2Ki 2:21 to the spring and threw the salt **i it,** 9004[S]
4: 4 Pour oil i all the jars, and as each is filled, 6584
4:29 "**Tuck** your **cloak** i your **belt,** 2520+5516
4:39 of them went out i the fields to gather herbs 448
4:39 he cut them up i the pot of stew, 448
4:41 He put it i the pot and said, 448
6: 5 the iron axhead fell i the water. 448
7: 4 If we say, *'We'll* **go** i the city'— 995
7:10 "We went i the Aramean camp and not 448
7:12 and then we will take them alive and get i 448
9: 1 "**Tuck** *your* **cloak** i your **belt,** 2520+5516
9: 2 from his companions and **take** him i 995
9: 6 Jehu got up and went i the house. 2025
9:16 he **got** i *his* **chariot** and rode to Jezreel, 8206
10:15 and Jehu helped him up i the chariot. 448
10:21 *They* **crowded** i the temple of Baal 995
10:23 of Recab **went** i the temple of Baal. 995
11:19 from the temple of the LORD and **went** i 995
12: 9 The priests who guarded the entrance put i 2025
12:10 counted the money that *had* **been brought** *i* AIT
12:10 the temple of the LORD and **put** it i **bags.** 7443
12:13 The money **brought** i the temple was 995
12:16 and sin offerings **was** not **brought** i 995
13:21 they threw the man's body i Elisha's tomb. 928
16: 6 then **moved** i Elath and have lived there 995
17:20 he afflicted them and gave them i the hands 928
17:23 **taken** from their homeland i **exile** 1655
18: 4 *He* **broke** i **pieces** the bronze snake 4198
18:30 be given i the hand of the king of Assyria.' 928
19: 1 and put on sackcloth and **went** i the temple 995
19:18 They have thrown their gods i the fire 928
19:25 **turned** fortified cities i piles of stone. 8615
20:20 and the tunnel by which he brought water i 2025
21:11 and *has* **led** Judah i **sin** with his idols. 2627
22: 4 that *has* **been brought** i the temple of 995
23:12 and threw the rubble i the Kidron Valley. 448
24:14 *He* **carried** i **exile** all Jerusalem: 1655+1655
25:11 the commander of the guard **carried** i **exile** 1655
25:21 So Judah **went** i **captivity,** 1655
1Ch 5: 6 king of Assyria **took** i **exile.** 1655
5:26 **took** the Reubenites, the Gadites and the half-tribe of Manasseh i **exile.** 1655
6:15 **sent** Judah and Jerusalem i **exile** 1655
11:22 also went down i a pit on a snowy day 928+9348
21:13 Let me fall i the hands of the LORD, 928
21:13 but do not let me fall i the hands of men." 928
21:27 and he put his sword back i its sheath. 448
22:19 and the sacred articles belonging to God i 4200
23: 6 David **divided** the Levites *i* groups AIT
24: 3 David **separated** them i **divisions** 2745
2Ch 3:14 with cherubim worked i it. 6584
9:15 six hundred bekas of hammered gold went i 6584
10:18 to get i his chariot and escape to Jerusalem. 928
13: 3 Abijah **went** i battle with a force 673
13:16 and God delivered them i their hands. 928
15:12 They entered i a covenant to seek 928
15:18 *He* **brought** i the temple of God the silver 995
16: 8 he delivered them i your hand. 928
18: 5 "for God will give it i the king's hand." 928
18:11 the LORD will give it i the king's hand." 928
18:14 "for they will be given i your hand." 928
18:19 **entice** Ahab king of Israel *i* attacking AIT
18:29 of Israel disguised himself and went i 928
22: 1 who came with the Arabs i the camp, 4200
23:20 *They* **went** i the palace through 995
24: 7 wicked woman Athaliah *had* **broken** i 7287
24:10 dropping them i the chest until it was full. 4200
24:18 the LORD delivered i their hands 928
28: 5 also given i the hands of the king of Israel, 928
28: 9 he gave them i your hand. 928
29:16 The priests went i the sanctuary of 4200+7163
30:14 and threw them i the Kidron Valley. 4200
32:21 And when *he* **went** i the temple of his god, 995
34: 9 money that *had* **been brought** i the temple 995

2Ch 34:11 kings of Judah *had* **allowed to fall i ruin.** 8845
34:14 the money that *had* **been taken i** the temple 995
36:20 *He* **carried i exile** to Babylon the remnant, 1655
Ezr 7:27 who has put it **i** the king's heart 928
8:33 and gold and the sacred articles **i** the hands 6584
Ne 6:11 like me go **i** the temple to save his life? 448
7:5 So my God put it **i** my heart to assemble 448
8:15 **"Go out** *i* the hill country AIT
9:11 but you hurled their pursuers **i** the depths, 928
9:11 like a stone **i** mighty waters. 928
9:23 and you brought them **i** the land 448
12:44 around the towns they were to bring **i** 928
13:1 or Moabite should ever be admitted **i** 928
13:2 however, turned the curse **i** a blessing.) 4200
13:9 and then *I* **put back** *i* them the equipment AIT
13:12 new wine and oil **i** the storerooms. 4200
13:15 And *they were* **bringing** all this **i** Jerusalem 995
13:26 even he *was* **led i sin** *by* foreign women. 2627
Est 2:3 to bring all these beautiful girls **i** the harem 448
2:6 *had* **been carried i exile** from Jerusalem 1655
2:9 and her maids **i** the best place in the harem. 4200
3:9 of silver **i** the royal treasury for 448
4:1 and went out **i** the city, 928+9348
4:7 of money Haman had promised to pay **i** 6584
4:8 urge her to go **i** the king's **presence** to beg 448
7:7 and went out **i** the palace garden. 448
8:1 And Mordecai came **i** the presence of 4200
9:22 the month when their sorrow was turned **i** 4200
9:22 and their mourning **i** a day of celebration. 4200
Job 6:18 they go up **i** the wasteland and perish. 928
9:24 a land falls **i** the hands of the wicked, 928
9:31 you would plunge me **i** a slime pit so that 928
10:19 If only *I had* never **come i being,** 2118+2118
12:22 of darkness and brings deep shadows **i** 4200
16:11 and thrown me **i** the clutches of the wicked. 6584
17:12 These men turn night **i** day; 4200
17:16 Will we descend together **i** the dust?" 6584
18:8 His feet thrust him **i** a net and he wanders 928
18:8 into a net and he wanders **i** its mesh. 6584
18:18 from light **i** darkness and is banished from 448
24:4 **force** all the poor of the land **i hiding.** 2461
24:16 In the dark, *men* **break i** houses, 3168
30:19 He throws me **i** the mud, 4200
39:21 and charges **i** the fray. 7925
Ps 4:2 O men, will you **turn** my glory **i** shame? 4200
5:7 by your great mercy, *will* **come i** your house; 995
7:15 and scoops it out falls **i** the pit he has made. 928
9:15 nations have fallen **i** the pit they have dug; 928
18:6 my cry came before him, **i** his ears. 928
18:19 He brought me out **i** a spacious place; 4200
18:28 my God **turns** my darkness **i light.** 5585
19:4 Their voice goes out **i** all the earth, 928
30:3 you spared me from **going down** *i* the pit. AIT
30:9 in my going down **i** the pit? 448
30:11 You turned my wailing **i** dancing; 4200
31:5 **I** your hands I commit my spirit; 928
33:7 He gathers the waters of the sea **i** jars; 3869
33:7 he puts the deep **i** storehouses. 928
35:8 may they fall **i** the pit, to their ruin. 928
46:2 and the mountains fall **i** the heart of the sea, 928
55:23 down the wicked **i** the pit of corruption; 4200
57:T When he had fled from Saul **i** the cave. 928
57:6 but they have fallen **i** it themselves. 928+9348
66:6 He turned the sea **i** dry land, 4200
66:11 You brought us **i** prison and laid burdens 928
68:17 Lord [has come] from Sinai **i** his sanctuary. 928
68:24 Your procession *has* **come i view,** O God, 8011
68:24 the procession of my God and King **i** 928
69:2 I have come **i** the deep waters; 928
73:24 and afterward *you will* **take** me *i* glory. AIT
78:61 He sent [the ark of] his might **i** captivity, 4200
78:61 his splendor **i** the hands of the enemy. 928
79:12 Pay back **i** the laps 448
96:8 bring an offering and come **i** his courts. 4200
98:4 **burst** *i* jubilant song with music; AIT
104:8 *they* **went down** *i* the valleys, AIT
104:10 He makes springs pour water **i** the ravines; 928
105:29 He turned their waters **i** blood, 4200
105:30 up **i** the bedrooms of their rulers. 928
105:32 *He* **turned** their rain **i** hail, 5989
107:33 He turned rivers **i** a desert, 4200
107:33 flowing springs **i** thirsty ground, 4200
107:34 and fruitful land **i** a salt waste, 4200
107:35 He turned the desert **i** pools of water and 4200
107:35 and the parched ground **i** flowing springs; 4200
109:18 it entered **i** his body like water, 928
109:18 like water, **i** his bones like oil. 928
114:8 who **turned** the rock **i** a pool, 2200
114:8 the hard rock **i** springs of water. 4200
135:9 He sent his signs and wonders **i** your midst, 928
136:15 swept Pharaoh and his army **i** the Red Sea; 928
140:10 may they be thrown **i** the fire, 928
140:10 **i** miry pits, never to rise. 928
141:10 Let the wicked fall **i** their own nets, 928
143:2 Do not bring your servant **i** judgment, 928
144:14 no **going i captivity,** 3448
Pr 1:16 for their feet rush **i** sin, 4200
3:32 but takes the upright **i** his confidence. 907
6:3 you have fallen **i** your neighbor's hands: 928
6:18 feet that are quick to rush **i** evil, 4200
6:27 Can a man scoop fire **i** his lap 928
7:22 like a deer stepping **i** a noose 448
7:23 like a bird darting **i** a snare, 448
7:25 not let your heart turn to her ways or stray **i** 928
8:3 beside the gates **leading i** the city, at 4200+7023
13:17 A wicked messenger falls **i** trouble, 928
16:33 The lot is cast **i** the lap, 928
Pr 17:20 he whose tongue is deceitful falls **i** trouble. 928
18:16 for the giver and ushers him **i** the presence 4200
22:14 under the LORD's wrath *will* **fall** *i* it. AIT
26:27 If a man digs a pit, he will fall **i** it; 928
28:10 along an evil path will fall **i** his own trap, 928
28:12 the wicked rise to power, men **go i hiding.** 2924
28:14 but he who hardens his heart falls **i** trouble. 928
28:28 wicked rise to power, people **go i hiding;** 6259
Ecc 1:7 All streams flow **i** the sea, 448
2:19 the work *i* **which** I have poured my effort AIT
3:21 and if the spirit of the animal goes down **i** 4200
5:6 Do not let your mouth **lead** you **i sin.** 2627
7:7 Extortion **turns** a wise man **i a fool,** 2147
10:8 Whoever digs a pit may fall **i** it; 928
12:14 For God will bring every deed **i** judgment, 928
SS 1:4 *Let* the king **bring** me **i** his chambers. 995
4:16 Let my lover come **i** his garden 4200
5:1 I have come **i** my garden, my sister, 4200
Isa 2:4 They will beat their swords **i** plowshares 4200
2:4 into plowshares and their spears **i** 4200
2:10 Go **i** the rocks, hide in the ground 928
3:14 The LORD enters **i** judgment against 928
5:13 Therefore my people *will* **go i exile** 1655
5:14 **i** it will descend their nobles and masses 928
8:8 and sweep on **i** Judah, 928
8:22 and *they will* **be thrust** *i* utter darkness. AIT
10:14 As one reaches **i** a nest, 3869
11:8 young child put his hand **i** the viper's nest. 6584
11:15 up **i** seven streams so that men can cross 4200
14:7 *they* **break** *i* singing. AIT
14:23 "I will turn her **i** a place for owls and 4200
14:23 "I will turn her into a place for owls and **i** NIH
19:8 all who cast hooks **i** the Nile; 928
19:14 The LORD has poured **i** them a spirit 928+7931
22:18 like a ball and throw you **i** a large country. 448
22:23 I will drive him like a peg **i** a firm place; 928
22:25 peg driven **i** the firm place will give way; 928
23:13 and turned it **i** a ruin. 4200
24:18 at the sound of terror will fall **i** a pit; 448
28:15 *"We have* **entered** *i* a covenant with death, AIT
29:17 will not Lebanon be turned **i** a fertile field 4200
34:9 Edom's streams will be turned **i** pitch, 4200
34:9 her dust **i** burning sulfur; 4200
35:2 *it will* **burst i bloom;** 7255+7255
36:15 be given **i** the hand of the king of Assyria.' 928
37:1 and put on sackcloth and **went i** the temple 995
37:19 They have thrown their gods **i** the fire 928
37:26 **turned** fortified cities **i** piles of stone. 8615
41:15 "See, I will make you **i** a threshing sledge, 4200
41:18 I will turn the desert **i** pools of water, 4200
41:18 and the parched ground **i** springs. 4200
42:9 before *they* **spring i being** I announce them 7541
42:15 I will turn rivers **i** islands and dry up 4200
42:16 I will turn the darkness **i** light before them 4200
44:23 **Burst** *i* song, *you* mountains, AIT
44:25 of the wise and **turns** it **i nonsense,** 6118
45:16 they will go off **i** disgrace together. 928
46:2 they themselves go off **i** captivity. 928
46:6 they hire a goldsmith *to* **make** it *i* a god, AIT
47:5 "Sit in silence, go **i** darkness, 928
47:6 I gave them **i** your hand, 928
49:2 he made me **i** a polished arrow 4200
49:11 I will turn all my mountains **i** roads, 4200
49:13 **burst** *i* song, O mountains! AIT
50:2 *I* **turn** rivers **i** a desert; 8492
51:23 I will put it **i** the hands of your tormentors, 928
52:9 **Burst** *i* songs of joy together, AIT
54:1 **burst** *i* song, shout for joy, AIT
54:16 the blacksmith *who* **fans** the coals *i* flame AIT
55:12 the mountains and hills *will* **burst** *i* song AIT
57:2 Those who walk uprightly **enter** *i* peace; AIT
57:8 *you* **climbed** *i* it and opened it wide; AIT
59:7 Their feet rush **i** sin; 4200
59:8 **turned** them *i* **crooked** AIT
65:6 I will pay it back **i** their laps— 6584
65:7 I will measure **i** their laps the full payment 448
66:2 and so they **came i being?"** 2118
66:7 "Before *she* **goes i labor,** she gives birth; 2655
66:17 and purify themselves to go **i** the gardens, 448
Jer 1:3 when the people of Jerusalem **went i exile.** 1655
2:7 I brought you **i** a fertile land to eat its fruit 448
2:21 then *did you* **turn** against me **i** a corrupt, 2200
4:29 Some go **i** the thickets; 928
8:6 like a horse charging **i** battle. 928
12:7 the one I love **i** the hands of her enemies. 928
12:10 they will turn my pleasant field **i** 4200
13:19 All Judah *will* **be carried i exile,** 1655
14:16 be thrown out **i** the streets of Jerusalem 928
14:18 If *I* **go i** the country, 3655
14:18 if *I* **go i** the city, 995
16:13 So I will throw you out of this land **i** 6584
18:4 so the potter **formed** it *i* another pot, AIT
20:6 in your house will go **i** exile to Babylon. 928
21:10 It will be given **i** the hands of the king 928
22:7 up your fine cedar beams and throw them **i** 6584
22:22 and your allies will go **i** exile. 928
22:26 and the mother who gave you birth **i** 6584
22:28 cast **i** a land they do not know? 6584
24:1 the artisans of Judah *were* **carried i exile** 1655
26:23 down with a sword and his body thrown **i** 448
27:20 **carried** Jehoiachin son of Jehoiakim king
of Judah **i exile** 1655
29:1 people Nebuchadnezzar *had* **carried i exile** 1655
29:2 the craftsmen and the artisans had gone **i** NIH
29:4 says to all those *I* **carried i exile** 1655
29:7 to which *I have* **carried** you **i exile.** 1655
29:14 from which *I* **carried** you **i exile."** 1655
Jer 29:16 your countrymen who did not go with you **i** 928
29:26 like a prophet **i** the stocks and neck-irons. 448
30:16 all your enemies will go **i** exile. 928
31:13 I will turn their mourning **i** gladness; 4200
32:18 the fathers' sins **i** the laps of their children 448
34:10 the officials and people who entered **i** 928
35:4 I brought them **i** the house of the LORD, NIH
35:4 **i** the room of the sons of Hanan son 448
36:23 with a scribe's knife and threw them **i** 448
37:15 which they had made **i** a prison. 4200
37:16 Jeremiah was put **i** a vaulted cell in 448
38:6 and put him **i** the cistern of Malkijah, 448
38:6 They lowered Jeremiah by ropes **i** 928
38:6 and Jeremiah sank down **i** the mud. 928
38:7 that they had put Jeremiah **i** the cistern. 448
38:9 They have thrown him **i** a cistern, 448
39:9 of the imperial guard **carried i exile** 1655
40:1 and Judah who *were* **being carried i exile** 1655
40:7 and who *had* not **been carried i exile** 1655
41:7 When they went **i** the city, 448+9348
41:7 and threw them **i** a cistern. 448+9348
42:16 the famine you dread *will* **follow** you *i* AIT
43:3 so they may kill us or **carry** us **i exile** 1655
48:7 and Chemosh will go **i** exile, 928
48:11 she has not gone **i** exile. 928
48:44 "Whoever flees from the terror will fall **i** 448
48:46 your sons are taken **i** exile 928
48:46 into exile and your daughters **i** captivity. 928
49:3 for Molech will go **i** exile, 928
51:34 *he has* **thrown** us **i confusion,** 2169
51:63 stone to it and throw it **i** the Euphrates. 448+9348
52:15 of the guard **carried i exile** some of 1655
52:27 So Judah **went i captivity,** 1655
52:28 the people Nebuchadnezzar **carried i exile:** 1655
52:30 745 Jews **taken i exile** *by* Nebuzaradan 1655
La 1:3 Judah *has* **gone i exile.** 1655
1:5 Her children *have* **gone** *i* exile, AIT
1:7 When her people fell **i** enemy hands, 928
1:13 sent it down **i** my bones. 928
1:14 "My sins *have* **been bound** *i* a yoke; AIT
1:18 My young men and maidens have gone **i** 928
2:9 Her gates have sunk **i** the ground; 928
Eze 2:2 the Spirit came **i** me and raised me 928
3:24 Spirit came **i** me and raised me to my feet. 928
5:4 throw them **i** the fire and burn them up. 448+9348
7:11 Violence has grown **i** a rod 4200
7:14 no one will go **i** battle, 4200
7:19 They will throw their silver **i** the streets, 928
7:19 for it has made them **stumble** *i* sin. AIT
7:20 Therefore I will turn these **I** 4200
8:8 "Son of man, now dig **i** the wall." 928
8:8 I dug **i** the wall and saw a doorway there. 928
8:16 He then brought me **i** the inner court of 448
10:7 He took up some of it and put it **i** the hands 448
12:4 go out like *those who* **go** *i* exile. AIT
12:11 They will go **i** exile as captives. 928
14:19 a plague **i** that land and pour out my wrath 448
15:5 be made **i** something useful when 4200
16:5 you were thrown out **i** the open field, 448
16:8 I gave you my solemn oath and entered **i** 928
19:9 With hooks they pulled him **i** a cage 928
20:6 that I would bring them out of Egypt **i** 448
20:10 of Egypt and brought them **i** the desert. 448
20:15 in the desert that I would not bring them **i** 448
20:28 When I brought them **i** the land I had sworn 448
20:35 I will bring you **i** the desert of the nations 448
20:37 I will bring you **i** the bond of the covenant. 928
20:42 when I bring you **i** the land of Israel, 448
21:22 **I** his right hand will come the lot 928
22:19 I will gather you **i** Jerusalem. 448+9348
22:20 lead and tin **i** a furnace to melt it with 448+9348
23:31 so I will put her cup **i** your hand. 928
24:3 put it on and pour water **i** it. 928
24:4 Put **i** it the pieces of meat, 448
25:3 the people of Judah when they went **i** exile, 928
25:5 I will turn Rabbah **i** a pasture for camels 4200
25:5 for camels and Ammon **i** a resting place 4200
26:12 timber and rubble **i** the sea. 928+9348
27:27 on board will sink **i** the heart of the sea on 928
30:17 the cities themselves will go **i** captivity. 928
30:18 and her villages will go **i** captivity. 928
30:25 when I put my sword **i** the hand of the king 928
33:31 but *they do* not **put** them **i practice.** 6913
33:32 but *do* not **put** them **i practice.** 6913
34:13 and I will bring them **i** their own land. 448
35:4 *I will* **turn** your towns **i** ruins 8492
36:24 from all the countries and bring you back **i** 448
37:9 O breath, and breathe **i** these slain, 928
37:17 Join them together **i** one stick so 4200
37:21 from all around and bring them back **i** 448
37:22 or be divided **i** two kingdoms. 4200
38:10 On that day thoughts will come **i** your mind 6584
39:23 that the people of Israel **went i exile** 1655
39:28 I **sent** them **i exile** among the nations, 1655
40:17 Then he brought me **i** the outer court. 448
40:20 **leading i** the outer court. 4200
40:28 Then he brought me **i** the inner court 448
41:3 Then he went **i** the inner sanctuary 4200
41:6 the supports were not **inserted i** the wall of 928
42:1 the man led me northward **i** the outer court 448
42:14 not to go **i** the outer court until they leave 448
43:5 the Spirit lifted me up and brought me **i** 448
44:7 in heart and flesh **i** my sanctuary, 928
44:12 **made** the house of Israel **fall** *i* AIT
44:19 When they go out **i** the outer court where 448
44:27 On the day he goes **i** the inner court of 448
46:20 to avoid bringing them **i** the outer court 448

Eze 47: 8 toward the eastern region and goes down **i** 6584
47: 8 When it empties **i** the Sea, 448
48:14 of the land and *must* not **pass i other hands,** 6296
Da 1: 2 Jehoiakim king of Judah **i** his hand, 928
2: 5 and interpret it, I *will have you* **cut i** 10522
2: 5 into pieces and your houses **turned i** piles 10682
3: 6 will immediately be thrown **i** a 10135+10378
3:11 and worship will be thrown **i** a 10135+10378
3:15 immediately **i** a blazing furnace. 10135+10378
3:17 If we are thrown **i** the blazing furnace, NIH
3:20 Meshach and Abednego and throw them **i** 10378
3:21 and thrown **i** the blazing furnace. 10135+10378
3:23 tied, fell **i** the blazing furnace. 10135+10378
3:24 we tied up and threw **i** the fire?" 10135+10378
3:29 Meshach and Abednego **be cut i** pieces 10522
3:29 their houses **be turned i** piles of rubble, 10702
4: 8 Daniel **came i** my presence and I told him 10549
5:10 came **i** the banquet hall. 10378
6: 7 O king, shall be thrown **i** the lions' den. 10378
6:12 O king, would be thrown **i** the lions' den?" 10378
6:16 and they brought Daniel and threw him **i** 10378
6:24 in and thrown **i** the lions' den, 10378
7:11 and its body destroyed and thrown **i** 10378
7:13 of Days and was led **i** his **presence.** 10621
10: 9 *I* **fell i a deep sleep,** 8101
Hos 2: 3 turn her **i** a parched land, 3869
2:14 I will lead her **i** the desert NIH
7: 1 They practice deceit, thieves **break i** houses, 995
9: 4 not **come i** the temple of the LORD. 995
9: 9 *They have* **sunk deep** *i* corruption, AIT
10: 5 **taken** from them **i exile.** 1655
Joel 2: 9 They climb **i** the houses; 928
2:20 pushing it **i** a parched and barren land, 448
2:20 its front columns going **i** the eastern sea 448
2:20 sea and those in the rear **i** the westsern sea. 448
3: 2 There *I will* **enter i judgment** 9149
3:10 Beat your plowshares **i** swords 4200
3:10 and your pruning hooks **i** spears. 4200
3:12 let them advance **i** the Valley 448
Am 1: 5 The people of Aram *will* **go i exile** 1655
1:15 Her king will go **i** exile, 928
3: 5 Does a bird fall **i** a trap on the ground 6584
5: 5 For Gilgal *will* **surely go i exile,** 1655+1655
5: 7 You who turn justice **i** bitterness 4200
5: 8 who turns blackness **i** dawn 4200
5: 8 and **darkens** day *i* night, who calls for AIT
5:27 Therefore *I will* **send** you **i exile** 1655
6: 7 be among the first to **go i exile;** 1655+1655
6:11 **smash** the great house *i* bits. AIT
6:11 into pieces and the small house **i** bits. NIH
6:12 But you have turned justice **i** poison and 4200
6:12 and the fruit of righteousness **i** bitterness— 4200
7:11 and Israel *will* **surely go i exile,** 1655+1655
7:17 Israel *will* **certainly go i exile,** 1655+1655
8:10 I will turn your religious feasts **i** mourning 4200
8:10 into mourning and all your singing **i** 4200
9: 4 Though they are driven **i** exile 928
Jnh 1: 5 the cargo **i** the sea to lighten the ship. 448
1: 5 lay down and **fell i a deep sleep.** 8101
1:12 "Pick me up and throw me **i** the sea," 448
2: 3 You hurled me **i** the deep, NIH
2: 3 **i** the very heart of the seas, 928
3: 4 On the first day, Jonah started **i** the city. 928
Mic 1: 6 I will pour her stones **i** the valley 4200
1:16 **go** from you **i exile.** 1655
4: 3 They will beat their swords **i** plowshares 4200
4: 3 into plowshares and their spears **i** 4200
5: 6 when he invades our land and marches **i** 928
7: 9 He will bring me out **i** the light; 4200
7:19 and hurl all our iniquities **i** the depths of 928
Na 1: 8 he will pursue his foes **i** darkness. NIH
3:10 Yet she was taken captive and went **i** exile. 928
3:11 *you will* **go** *i* hiding and seek refuge from AIT
3:12 the figs fall **i** the mouth of the eater. 6584
Hab 3:16 decay crept **i** my bones, 928
Hag 1: 8 **Go up** *i* the mountains and bring AIT
Zec 5: 8 and he pushed her back **i** the basket 448+9348
11:13 the thirty pieces of silver and **threw** them *i* AIT
13: 9 This third I will bring **i** the fire; 928
14: 2 Half of the city will go **i** exile, 928
Mal 1: 3 **turned** his mountains **i** a wasteland 8492
3:10 Bring the whole tithe **i** the storehouse, 448
Mt 3:10 be cut down and thrown **i** the fire. 1650
3:12 gathering his wheat **i** the barn and burning 1650
4: 1 Then Jesus was led by the Spirit **i** the desert 1650
4:18 They were casting a net **i** the lake, 1650
5:25 and you may be thrown **i** prison. 1650
5:29 for your whole body to be thrown **i** hell. 1650
5:30 for your whole body to go **i** hell. 1650
6: 6 But when you pray, **go i** your room, 1656
6:13 And **lead** us not **i** temptation, 1662
6:30 and tomorrow is thrown **i** the fire, 1650
7:19 down and thrown **i** the fire. 1650
7:24 of mine and **puts** them **i practice** is like 4472
7:26 and *does* not **put** them **i practice** is like 4472
8:12 **i** the darkness, where there will be weeping 1650
8:14 When Jesus came **i** Peter's house, 1650
8:23 Then he got **i** the boat 1650
8:31 send us **i** the herd of pigs." 1650
8:32 So they came out and went **i** the pigs, 1650
8:32 down the steep bank **i** the lake and died in 1650
8:33 went **i** the town and reported all this, 1650
9: 1 Jesus stepped **i** a boat, 1650
9:17 Neither do men pour new wine **i** old 1650
9:17 No, they pour new wine **i** new wineskins, 1650
9:38 to send out workers **i** his harvest field." 1650
11: 7 "What did you go out **i** the desert to see? 1650

Mt 12: 9 he went **i** their synagogue, 1650
12:11 "If any of you has a sheep and it falls **i** a pit 1650
13: 2 around him that he got **i** a boat and sat in it, 1650
13:30 the wheat and bring it **i** my barn.' " 1650
13:33 a woman took and mixed **i** a large amount 1650
13:36 he left the crowd and went **i** the house. 1650
13:42 They will throw them **i** the fiery furnace, 1650
13:47 down **i** the lake and caught all kinds of fish. 1650
13:50 and throw them **i** the fiery furnace, 1650
14:22 the disciples get **i** the boat and go on ahead 1650
14:32 And when they climbed **i** the boat, 1650
15:11 What **goes i** a man's mouth does not 1656
15:14 both will fall **i** a pit." 1650
15:17 the mouth goes **i** the stomach and then out 1650
15:39 *he* **got i** the boat and went to the vicinity 1832
17:15 He often falls **i** the fire or into the water. 1650
17:15 He often falls into the fire or **i** the water. 1650
17:22 of Man is going to be betrayed **i** the hands 1650
17:25 When Peter came **i** the house, 1650
18: 8 or two feet and be thrown **i** eternal fire. 1650
18: 9 to have two eyes and be thrown **i** the fire 1650
18:30 the man thrown **i** prison until he could pay 1650
19: 1 he left Galilee and went **i** the region 1650
20: 2 for the day and sent them **i** his vineyard. 1650
21:21 'Go, throw yourself **i** the sea,' 1650
22:10 So the servants went out **i** the streets 1650
22:13 and throw him outside, **i** the darkness, 1650
24:43 not have let his house *be* **broken i.** 1482
25:30 **i** the darkness, where there will be weeping 1650
25:41 **i** the eternal fire prepared for the devil 1650
26:18 "Go **i** the city to a certain man and tell him, 1650
26:23 "The one who has dipped his hand **i** 1877
26:32 I will go ahead of you **i** Galilee." 1650
26:41 so that *you will* not **fall i** temptation. 1656
26:45 and the Son of Man is betrayed **i** the hands 1650
27: 5 So Judas threw the money **i** the temple 1650
27: 6 against the law to put this **i** the treasury, 1650
27:27 Then the governor's soldiers took Jesus **i** 1650
27:53 and after Jesus' resurrection *they* **went i** 1656
28: 7 from the dead and is going ahead of you **i** 1650
28:11 of the guards went **i** the city and reported to 1650
Mk 1:12 At once the Spirit sent him out **i** the desert, 1650
1:14 Jesus went **i** Galilee, 1650
1:16 and his brother Andrew casting a net **i** 1877
1:21 Jesus **went i** the synagogue and began 1656
2:22 no one pours new wine **i** old wineskins. 1650
2:22 No, he pours new wine **i** new wineskins." 1650
3: 1 Another time *he* **went i** the synagogue, 1656
4: 1 around him was so large that he got **i** a boat 1650
4:22 to be brought out **i** the open. 1650
5:12 allow *us to* **go i** them." 1656
5:13 the evil spirits came out and **went i** the pigs. 1656
5:13 the steep bank **i** the lake and were drowned. 1650
5:18 As Jesus was getting **i** the boat, 1650
6:45 Immediately Jesus made his disciples get **i** 1650
6:51 Then he climbed **i** the boat with them, 1650
6:56 And wherever *he* **went—i** villages, 1660
7:15 a man can make him 'unclean' *by* **going i** 1660
7:19 For *it* doesn't **go i** his heart but 1660
7:19 For it doesn't go into his heart but **i** NIG
7:31 and **i** the region of the Decapolis. 324+3545
7:33 Jesus put his fingers **i** the man's ears. 1650
8:10 he got **i** the boat with his disciples and went 1650
8:13 got back **i** the boat and crossed to 1650
8:26 saying, "Don't **go i** the village." 1656
9:20 **threw** the boy **i a convulsion.** 5360
9:22 "It has often thrown him **i** fire or water 1650
9:31 of Man is going to be betrayed **i** the hands 1650
9:42 it would be better for him to be thrown **i** 1650
9:43 with two hands to go **i** hell, 1650
9:45 to have two feet and be thrown **i** hell. 1650
9:47 to have two eyes and be thrown **i** hell, 1650
10: 1 and went **i** the region of Judea and across 1650
11:23 'Go, throw yourself **i** the sea,' 1650
12:41 the crowd putting their money **i** 1650
12:43 this poor widow has put more **i** 1650
14:13 telling them, "Go **i** the city, 1650
14:16 went **i** the city and found things just 1650
14:20 "one who dips bread **i** the bowl with me. 1650
14:28 I will go ahead of you **i** Galilee." 1650
14:38 Watch and pray so that you will not fall **i** 1650
14:41 of Man is betrayed **i** the hands of sinners. 1650
14:54 **right i** the courtyard of the high 1650+2276+2401
14:68 he said, and went out **i** the entryway. 1650
15:16 The soldiers led Jesus away **i** the palace 2276
16: 7 'He is going ahead of you **i** Galilee. 1650
16:15 "Go **i** all the world and preach 1650
16:19 up **i** heaven and he sat at the right hand 1650
Lk 1: 9 to **go i** the temple of the Lord 1656
1:79 to guide our feet **i** the path of peace." 1650
2:15 the angels had left them and gone **i** heaven, 1650
2:27 he went **i** the temple courts. 1650
3: 3 He went **i** all the country around 1650
3: 9 be cut down and thrown **i** the fire." 1650
3:17 and to gather the wheat **i** his barn, 1650
4:16 on the Sabbath day *he* **went i** the synagogue 1656
5: 3 He got **i** one of the boats, 1650
5: 4 he said to Simon, "Put out **i** deep water, 1650
5:18 and tried *to* **take** him **i** the house to lay him 1662
5:19 through the tiles **i** the middle of the crowd, 1650
5:37 no one pours new wine **i** old wineskins. 1650
5:38 new wine must be poured **i** new wineskins. 1650
6: 6 On another Sabbath he **went i** 1656
6:38 will be poured **i** your lap. 1650
6:39 Will they not both fall **i** a pit? 1650
6:47 and **puts** them **i practice.** 4472
6:49 and *does* not **put** them **i practice** is like 4472

Lk 7:24 "What did you go out **i** the desert to see? 1650
7:44 *I* **came i** your house. 1656
8:17 not be known or brought out **i** the open. 1650
8:21 and **put** it **i practice."** 4472
8:22 So they got **i** a boat and set out. 1650
8:29 and had been driven by the demon **i** 1650
8:30 because many demons *had* **gone i** him. 1656
8:31 not to order them to go **i** the Abyss. 1650
8:32 The demons begged Jesus to let them **go i** 1656
8:33 *they* **went i** the pigs, 1656
8:33 the steep bank **i** the lake and was drowned. 1650
8:37 So he got **i** the boat and left. 1650
9:39 **throws** him **i convulsions** 5057
9:44 of Man is going to be betrayed **i** the hands 1650
9:52 *who* **went i** a Samaritan village 1656+4513
10: 2 to send out workers **i** his harvest field. 1650
10:10 go **i** its streets and say, 1650
10:30 **fell i the hands of** robbers. 4346
10:36 a neighbor to the man who fell **i** the hands 1650
11: 4 And **lead** us not **i** temptation.' " 1662
12: 5 has power to throw you **i** hell. 1650
12:28 and tomorrow is thrown **i** the fire, 1650
12:39 would not have let his house *be* **broken i.** 1482
12:58 and the officer throw you **i** prison. 1650
13:21 a woman took and mixed **i** a large amount 1650
14: 5 "If one of you has a son or an ox that falls **i** 1650
14:21 'Go out quickly **i** the streets and alleys of 1650
16: 4 people will welcome me **i** their houses.' 1650
16: 9 you will be welcomed **i** eternal dwellings. 1650
16:16 and everyone is forcing his way **i** it. 1650
17: 2 to be thrown **i** the sea with a millstone tied 1650
17:12 *As* he *was* **going i** a village, 1656
21: 1 Jesus saw the rich putting their gifts **i** 1650
22:40 that *you will* not **fall i** temptation." 1656
22:46 so that *you will* not **fall i** temptation." 1656
22:54 they led him away and **took** him **i** the house 1652
23:19 (Barabbas had been thrown **i** prison for 1877
23:25 He released the man who had been thrown **i** 1650
23:42 when you come **i** your kingdom." 1650
23:46 "Father, **i** your hands I commit my spirit." 1650
24: 7 be delivered **i** the hands of sinful men, 1650
24:51 he left them and was taken up **i** heaven. 1650
Jn 1: 9 that gives light to every man was coming **i** 1650
2: 9 the water *that had* **been turned i** wine. 1181
2:16 **turn** my Father's house **i** a market!" 4472
3: 4 **enter** a second time **i** his mother's womb 1656
3:13 No one has ever gone **i** heaven except 1650
3:17 For God did not send his Son **i** the world 1650
3:19 Light has come **i** the world, 1650
3:20 and will not come **i** the light for fear 4639
3:21 But whoever lives by the truth comes **i** 4639
3:22 Jesus and his disciples went out **i** 1650
4: 8 (His disciples had gone **i** the town 1650
4:46 where *he had* **turned** the water **i** wine. 4472
5: 7 "I have no one to help me **i** the pool when 1650
5:13 for Jesus had slipped away **i** the crowd NIG
6:14 "Surely this is the Prophet who is to come **i** 1650
6:17 where they got **i** a boat and set off across 1650
6:21 they were willing to take him **i** the boat, 1650
6:24 they got **i** the boats and went to Capernaum 1650
7:52 **Look i** it, and you will find that 2236
9:39 "For judgment I have come **i** this world, 1650
10:36 as his very own and sent **i** the world? 1650
11:27 who was to come **i** the world." 1650
12: 6 he used to help himself to what was put **i** it. NIG
12:46 I have come **i** the world as a light, 1650
13: 5 he poured water **i** a basin and began 1650
13:27 Satan **entered i** him. 1656
15: 6 thrown **i** the fire and burned. 1650
16:13 comes, he will guide you **i** all truth. 1877
16:21 of her joy that a child is born **i** the world. 1650
17:18 As you sent me **i** the world, 1650
17:18 I have sent them **i** the world. 1650
18: 1 and he and his disciples **went i** it. 1656
18:15 *he* **went with** Jesus **i** the high priests' 5291
18:37 and for this I came **i** the world, 1650
19:23 **dividing** them **i** four **shares,** 3538+4472
19:27 this disciple took her **i** his home. 1650
20: 6 arrived and **went i** the tomb. 1656
20:11 she bent over to look **i** the tomb 1650
20:25 and put my hand **i** his side, 1650
20:27 Reach out your hand and put it **i** my side. 1650
21: 3 So they went out and **got i** the boat, 1832
21: 7 (for he had taken it off) and jumped **i** 1650
Ac 1:10 They were looking intently up **i** the sky 1650
1:11 "why do you stand here looking **i** the sky? 1650
1:11 who has been taken from you **i** heaven, 1650
1:11 in the same way you have seen him go **i** 1650
3: 2 to beg from those **going i** the temple courts. 1660
3: 8 Then *he* **went** with them **i** the temple courts, 1656
5:15 the sick **i** the streets and laid them on beds 1650
7: 9 they sold him as a slave **i** Egypt. 1650
7:43 Therefore *I will* **send** you **i exile'** 3579
7:53 that was **put i effect** through angels 1408
8:16 they had simply been baptized **i** the name 1650
8:38 down **i** the water and Philip baptized him. 1650
9: 6 "Now get up and **go i** the city, 1656
9: 8 **led** him by the hand **i** Damascus. 1652
10:10 he **fell i a trance.** 1181+1749+2093
10:23 Then Peter invited the men **i** the house to NIG
11: 3 *"You* **went i** the house of uncircumcised 1656
11: 6 I looked **i** it and saw four-footed animals of 1650
14: 1 Paul and Barnabas **went** as usual **i** 1656
14:14 they tore their clothes and rushed out **i** 1650
14:20 *he* got up and **went** back **i** the city. 1656
14:24 they came **i** Pamphylia, 1650
15: 2 Paul and Barnabas **i** sharp dispute and NIG

Ac 16:19 and dragged them **i** the marketplace to face *1650*
16:20 **throwing** our city **i an uproar** *1752*
16:23 they were thrown **i** prison, *1650*
16:34 The jailer brought them **i** his house and set *1650*
16:37 and threw us **i** prison. *1650*
17: 2 Paul **went i** the synagogue, *1656*
17: 7 **welcomed** them **i** *his* **house.** *5685*
17: 8 the city officials *were* **thrown i turmoil.** *5429*
18:12 a united attack on Paul and brought him **i** *2093*
18:19 *He* himself **went i** the synagogue *1656*
19: 5 they were baptized **i** the name of *1650*
19:29 and rushed as one man **i** the theater. *1650*
19:31 a message begging him not to venture **i** *1650*
20: 9 who was sinking *i* a **deep sleep** *AIT*
20:18 the first day I came **i** the province of Asia. *1650*
21:28 *he has* **brought** Greeks **i** the temple area *1652*
21:29 Paul *had* **brought** him **i** the temple area. *1652*
21:34 he ordered that Paul be taken **i** the barracks. *1650*
21:37 As the soldiers were about to **take** Paul **i** *1652*
21:38 and led four thousand terrorists out **i** *1650*
22: 4 both men and women and throwing them **i** *1650*
22:10 the Lord said, 'and go **i** Damascus. *1650*
22:11 My companions led me by the hand **i** *1650*
22:17 I fell **i** a trance *1877*
22:23 and flinging dust **i** the air, *1650*
22:24 the commander ordered Paul *to be* **taken i** *1652*
23:10 by force and bring him **i** the barracks. *1650*
23:16 he **went i** the barracks and told Paul. *1656*
27:15 by the storm and could not **head i** the wind; *535*
27:30 the sailors let the lifeboat down **i** the sea, *1650*
27:38 the ship by throwing the grain **i** the sea. *1650*
28: 5 But Paul shook the snake off **i** the fire *1650*
Ro 5: 2 by faith **i** this grace in which we now stand. *1650*
5: 5 because God has poured out his love **i** *1877*
5:13 not **taken i account** when there is no law. *1824*
6: 3 that all of us who were baptized **i** Christ *1650*
6: 3 into Christ Jesus were baptized **i** his death? *1650*
6: 4 with him through baptism **i** death in order *1650*
8:21 to decay and brought **i** the glorious freedom *1650*
10: 6 'Who will ascend **i** heaven?' " *1650*
10: 7 "or 'Who will descend **i** the deep?' " *1650*
10:18 "Their voice has gone out **i** all the earth, *1650*
11:24 and contrary to nature were grafted **i** *1650*
11:24 *be* **grafted i** their own olive tree! *1596*
1Co 1: 9 who has called you **i** fellowship *1650*
1:13 Were you baptized **i** the name of Paul? *1650*
1:15 no one can say that you were baptized **i** my *1650*
8:13 **causes** my brother *to* **fall i sin,** *4997*
9:25 in the games **goes i** strict **training.** *1603*
10: 2 They were all baptized **i** Moses in the cloud *1650*
12:13 For we were all baptized by one Spirit **i** *1650*
14: 9 You will just be speaking **i** the air. *1650*
2Co 1: 5 as the sufferings of Christ flow over **i** *1650*
3:18 *are being* **transformed i** his likeness *3565*
7: 5 For when we came **i** Macedonia, *1650*
8:16 who put **i** the heart of Titus *1877*
11:29 Who *is* **led i sin,** and I do not inwardly *4997*
Gal 1: 7 **throwing** you **i confusion** *5429*
1:17 but I went immediately **i** Arabia *1650*
3:19 The law *was* **put i effect** through angels *1411*
3:27 for all of you who were baptized **i** *1650*
4: 6 God sent the Spirit of his Son **i** our hearts, *1650*
5:10 the one who *is* **throwing** you **i confusion** *5429*
Eph 1:10 to be **put i effect** when the times *3873*
3: 4 you will be able to understand my insight **i** *1877*
4:15 we will in all things grow up **i** him who is *1650*
Php 4: 9 **put** it **i practice.** *4556*
Col 1:13 the dominion of darkness and brought us **i** *1650*
2:18 **goes i great detail about** what he has seen *1836*
1Th 2:12 who calls you **i** his kingdom and glory. *1650*
2Th 3: 5 the Lord direct your hearts **i** God's love *1650*
1Ti 1: 3 As I urged you when I went **i** Macedonia, *1650*
1:15 Christ Jesus came **i** the world *1650*
3: 7 not fall **i** disgrace and into the devil's trap. *1650*
3: 7 not fall into disgrace and **i** the devil's trap. *NIG*
5: 4 **put** *their* **religion i practice by caring for** *2355*
5:13 **get i the habit of being** idle *3443*
6: 7 For *we* **brought** nothing **i** the world, *1662*
6: 9 to get rich fall **i** temptation and a trap and *1650*
6: 9 and **i** many foolish and harmful desires *NIG*
6: 9 and harmful desires that plunge men **i** ruin *1650*
2Ti 1: 6 *to* **fan i flame** the gift of God, *351*
2: 7 for the Lord will give you insight **i** all this. *1877*
3: 6 They are the kind who worm their way **i** *1650*
Heb 1: 6 God **brings** his firstborn **i** the world, *1650+1652*
9: 6 the priests **entered** regularly **i** the outer *1655*
9: 8 that the way **i** the Most Holy Place had not *NIG*
9:18 even the first covenant *was* not **put i effect** *1590*
10: 5 *when* Christ **came i** the world, he said: *1656*
10:31 It is a dreadful thing to fall **i** the hands of *1650*
13:11 the blood of animals **i** the Most Holy Place *1650*
Jas 1:25 But the man who looks intently **i** *1650*
2: 2 a man **comes i** your meeting wearing *1656*
2: 6 not the ones who are dragging you **i** court? *1650*
3: 3 When we put bits **i** the mouths of horses *1650*
1Pe 1: 3 he has given us new birth **i** a living hope *1650*
1: 4 and **i** an inheritance that can never perish, *1650*
1:12 Even angels long to look **i** these things. *1650*
2: 5 are being built **i** a spiritual house to be *NIG*
2: 9 of him who called you out of darkness **i** *1650*
3:22 who has gone **i** heaven and is *1650*
4: 4 with them **i** the same flood of dissipation, *1650*
2Pe 1:11 and you will receive a rich **welcome i** *1658*
2: 2 **bring** the way of truth **i disrepute.** *1059*
2: 4 **putting** them **i** gloomy dungeons to *4140*
1Jn 4: 1 many false prophets have gone out **i** *1650*
4: 9 and only Son **i** the world that we might live *1650*

2Jn 1: 7 have gone out **i** the world. *1650*
1:10 not take him **i** your house or welcome him. *1650*
Jude 1: 4 of our God **i** a license for immorality *1650*
1:11 for profit *i* Balaam's **error;** *AIT*
Rev 2:20 By her teaching she misleads my servants **i** *NIG*
5: 6 the seven spirits of God sent out **i** all *1650*
8: 8 all ablaze, was thrown **i** the sea. *1650*
8: 8 A third of the sea **turned i** blood, *1181*
9: 9 of many horses and chariots rushing **i** *1650*
11: 6 the waters **i** blood and to strike the earth *1650*
12: 6 The woman fled **i** the desert to *1650*
13:10 If anyone is to go **i** captivity, *1650*
13:10 **i** captivity he will go. *1650*
14:10 which has been poured full strength **i** *1877*
14:19 and threw them **i** the great winepress *1650*
16: 3 *it* **turned i** blood like that of a dead man, *1181*
16:10 and his kingdom *was* **plunged i** darkness. *1181*
16:17 The seventh angel poured out his bowl **i** *2093*
16:19 The great city split **i** three parts, *1650*
17: 3 the angel carried me away in the Spirit **i** *1650*
17:17 For God has put it **i** their hearts *1650*
18:21 the size of a large millstone and threw it **i** *1650*
19:20 of them were thrown alive **i** the fiery lake *1650*
20: 3 He threw him **i** the Abyss, *1650*
20:10 was thrown **i** the lake of burning sulfur, *1650*
20:14 and Hades were thrown **i** the lake of fire. *1650*
20:15 he was thrown **i** the lake of fire. *1650*
21:24 of the earth will bring their splendor **i** it. *1650*
21:26 and honor of the nations will be brought **i** *1650*
22:14 and *may* **go** through the gates **i** the city. *1656*

INTOXICATED (1)

Rev 17: 2 and the inhabitants of the earth *were* **i** with *3499*

INTREAT, INTREATED, INTREATIES, INTREATY (KJV) See ANSWER, ANSWERED, ASK, CURRY FAVOR, ENTREATY, EXHORT, INTERCEDE, INTERCEDED, PRAY, PRAYED, SEEK, URGE

INTRIGUE (3) [INTRIGUES]

Da 8:23 a stern-faced king, a master of **i**, will arise. 2648
11:21 and he will seize it through **i.** 2761
Hos 7: 6 they approach him with **i.** 744

INTRIGUES (2) [INTRIGUE]

Ps 5:10 Let their **i** be their downfall. 4600
31:20 of your presence you hide them from the **i** 8222

INTRODUCE (1) [INTRODUCED, INTRODUCTION]

2Pe 2: 1 They *will* **secretly i** destructive heresies, *4206*

INTRODUCED (4) [INTRODUCE]

2Ki 17: 8 as the practices that the kings of Israel *had* **i.** 6913
17:19 They followed the practices Israel *had* **i.** 6913
Gal 3:17 The law, **i** 430 years later, *1181*
Heb 7:19 and a better hope is **i,** *2081*

INTRODUCTION (1) [INTRODUCE]

1Co 16: 3 of **i** to the men you approve and send them *NIG*

INVADE (14) [INVADED, INVADER, INVADERS, INVADES, INVADING]

Dt 12:29 the nations you *are about to* **i** 995+2025+9004
1Sa 7:13 and *did* not **i** Israelite territory again. 928+995
2Ch 20:10 not allow Israel to **i** when they came 928+995
Isa 7: 6 *"Let us* **i** Judah; 928+6590
Eze 38: 8 In future years *you will* **i** a land 448+995
38:11 *"I will* **i** a land of unwalled villages; 6584+6590
Da 11: 9 the king of the North *will* **i** the realm 928+995
11:21 *He will* **i** the kingdom 995
11:24 *he will* **i** them 995
11:29 "At the appointed time *he will* **i** 928+995
11:40 *He will* **i** many countries and sweep 928+995
11:41 *He will* also **i** the Beautiful Land. 928+995
Joel 3:17 never again *will* foreigners **i** her. 928+6296
Na 1:15 No more *will* the wicked **i** you; 6296

INVADED (15) [INVADE]

Ex 10:14 they **i** all Egypt and settled down 6584+6590
Jdg 6: 3 other eastern peoples **i** the country. 6584+6590
6: 5 *they* **i** the land to ravage it. 928+995
2Ki 3:24 the Israelites **i** the land and slaughtered 928+995
15:19 Then Pul king of Assyria **i** the land, 995+6584
17: 5 The king of Assyria **i** the entire land, 928+6590
24: 1 Nebuchadnezzar king of Babylon **i** 6590
1Ch 4:42 sons of Ishi, **i** the hill country of Seir. 2143+4200
2Ch 21:17 **i** it and carried off all the goods found in 1324
24:23 *it* **i** Judah and Jerusalem and killed all 448+995
32: 1 of Assyria came and **i** Judah. 928+995
Ps 79: 1 O God, the nations *have* **i** your inheritance; 928+995
Jer 35:11 of Babylon **i** this land, 448+6590
48:15 Moab will be destroyed and her towns **i**; 6590
Joel 1: 6 A nation *has* **i** my land, 6584+6590

INVADER (2) [INVADE]

Isa 21: 1 *an i* **comes** from the desert, AIT
Da 11:16 The **i** will do as he pleases; 448+995

INVADERS (1) [INVADE]

Jer 18:22 when you suddenly bring **i** against them, 1522

INVADES (2) [INVADE]

Mic 5: 5 When the Assyrian **i** our land and 928+995
5: 6 from the Assyrian when *he* **i** our land 928+995

INVADING (2) [INVADE]

2Ch 20:22 and Mount Seir who *were* **i** Judah, 995+4200
Hab 3:16 of calamity to come on the nation **i** us. 1574

INVALID (2)

Jn 5: 5 One who was there had been an **i** *819*
5: 7 the **i** replied, "I have no one to help me into *820*

INVENT (1) [INVENTED]

Ro 1:30 they **i** ways of doing evil; *2388*

INVENTED (1) [INVENT]

2Pe 1:16 We did not follow **cleverly i** stories *5054*

INVENTORY (1)

Ezr 1: 9 This was the **i:** 5031

INVESTIGATE (6) [INVESTIGATED, INVESTIGATION]

Ex 9: 7 Pharaoh sent men to **i** and found that not NIH
Dt 13:14 probe and **i** it thoroughly. 8626
17: 4 then *you must* **i** it thoroughly. 2011
Ezr 10:16 of the tenth month they sat down to **i** 2011
Ecc 7:25 to **i** and to search out wisdom and 9365
Ac 25:20 I was at a loss how to **i** such matters; *2428*

INVESTIGATED (3) [INVESTIGATE]

Jdg 6:29 When *they* **carefully i,** 1335+2011+2256
Est 2:23 when the report **was i** and found to be true, 1335
Lk 1: 3 since *I* myself *have* carefully **i** everything *4158*

INVESTIGATION (2) [INVESTIGATE]

Dt 19:18 The judges *must* **make** *a* thorough **i,** 2011
Ac 25:26 as a result *of* this **i** I may have something *374*

INVISIBLE (5)

Ro 1:20 creation of the world God's **i** *qualities*— *548*
Col 1:15 He is the image *of* the **i** God, *548*
1:16 things in heaven and on earth, visible and **i,** *548*
1Ti 1:17 Now to the King eternal, immortal, **i,** *548*
Heb 11:27 because he saw him who *is* **i.** *548*

INVITATION (1) [INVITE]

2Sa 11:13 *At* David's **i,** he ate and drank with him, 7924

INVITE (15) [INVITATION, INVITED, INVITES, INVITING]

Ex 2:20 **I** him to have something to eat." 7924
34:15 and sacrifice to them, *they will* **i** you 7924
Jdg 14:15 *Did you* **i** us here to rob us?" 7924
1Sa 16: 3 **I** Jesse to the sacrifice, 7924
1Ki 1:10 not **i** Nathan the prophet or Benaiah or 7924
1:26 and your servant Solomon *he did* not **i.** 7924
Job 1: 4 and *they would* **i** their three sisters to eat 2256+7924+8938
Jer 35: 2 to the Recabite family and **i** them to come 1819
Zec 3:10 that day each of you *will* **i** his neighbor 7924
Mt 22: 9 and **i** to the banquet anyone you find.' *2813*
25:38 a stranger and **i** you **in,** *5251*
25:43 I was a stranger and *you did* not **i** me **in,** *5251*
Lk 14:12 *do* not **i** your friends, *5888*
14:12 they *may* **i** you **back** and so you will *511*
14:13 But when you give a banquet, **i** the poor, *2813*

INVITED (37) [INVITE]

Ge 31:54 in the hill country and **i** his relatives to 7924
Nu 25: 2 *who* **i** them to the sacrifices to their gods. 7924
1Sa 9:13 afterward, those *who are* **i** will eat. 7924
9:22 at the head of those *who* **were i**— 7924
9:24 from the time I said, *'I have* **i** guests.' " 7924
16: 5 and his sons and **i** them to the sacrifice. 7924
2Sa 13:23 he **i** all the king's sons to come there. 7924
15:11 *They had* **been i as guests** 7924
1Ki 1: 9 *He* **i** all his brothers, the king's sons, 7924
1:19 and sheep, and *has* **i** all the king's sons, 7924
1:19 but *he has* not **i** Solomon your servant. 7924
1:25 *He has* **i** all the king's sons, 7924
Est 5:12 "I'm the only person Queen Esther **i** 995
5:12 And she *has* **i** me along with 7924
Zep 1: 7 he has consecrated *those* he *has* **i.** 7924
Mt 22: 3 He sent his servants to those who *had been* **i** *2813*
22: 4 'Tell those who *have been* **i** *2813*
22: 8 but those I **i** did not deserve to come. *2813*
22:14 "For many are **i,** but few are chosen." *3105*
25:35 I was a stranger and *you* **i** me **in,** *5251*
Lk 7:36 of the Pharisees **i** Jesus to have dinner *2263*

Lk 7:39 When the Pharisee who *had* **i** him saw this, *2813*
11:37 a Pharisee **i** him to eat with him; *2263*
14: 8 distinguished than you may have been **i**. *2813*
14: 9 **host who i** both of you will come and say *2813*
14:10 But when *you are* **i**, take the lowest place, *2813*
14:16 a great banquet and **i** many guests. *2813*
14:17 to tell those who *had been* **i**, *2813*
14:24 not one of those men who *were* **i** will get *2813*
Jn 2: 2 and Jesus and his disciples *had* also *been* **i** *2813*
Ac 8:31 So *he* **i** Philip to come up and sit with him. *4151*
10:23 Then Peter **i** the men into the house to *1657*
13:42 the *people* **i** them to speak further *4151*
16:15 *she* **i** us to her home. *4151*
18:26 **i** him **to** *their* **home** *4689*
28:14 There we found some brothers who **i** *us* *4151*
Rev 19: 9 'Blessed are those who *are* **i** to *2813*

INVITES (6) [INVITE]
Pr 9: 7 "Whoever corrects a mocker **i** insult; 4374
10:14 but the mouth of a fool **i** ruin. 7940
17:19 he who builds a high gate **i** destruction. 1335
18: 6 and his mouth **i** a beating. 7924
Lk 14: 8 "When someone **i** you to a wedding feast, *2813*
1Co 10:27 If some unbeliever **i** you to a meal *2813*

INVITING (1) [INVITE]
2Ch 30: 1 **i** them to come to the temple of the LORD NIH

INVOKE (6) [INVOKED, INVOKES, INVOKING]
Ex 23:13 *Do* not **i** the names of other gods; 2349
Jos 23: 7 *do* not **i** the names of their gods or swear 2349
2Sa 14:11 "Then *let* the king **i** the LORD his God 2349
Isa 48: 1 in the name of the LORD and **i** the God 2349
Jer 44:26 Egypt *will* ever again **i** my name 928+7023+7924
Ac 19:13 *to* **i the name** of the Lord Jesus *3950+3951*

INVOKED (1) [INVOKE]
Hos 2:17 no longer *will* their names **be i**. 2349

INVOKES (2) [INVOKE]
Dt 29:19 *he* **i a blessing on himself** 1385
Isa 65:16 Whoever **i a blessing** in the land will do so 1385

INVOKING (1) [INVOKE]
Job 31:30 not allowed my mouth to sin by **i** a curse 8626

INVOLVE (1) [INVOLVED, INVOLVES, INVOLVING]
Jn 2: 4 "Dear woman, **why do** you **i** me?" *2779+5515*

INVOLVED (7) [INVOLVE]
Ex 24:14 and anyone **i in** a dispute can go to them." 1251
28:38 and he will bear the **guilt** *i in* AIT
Nu 15:26 because all the people were **i in** 928
Dt 19:17 the two men **i in** the dispute must stand in 4200
Ac 23:13 More than forty men were **i in** this plot. *4472*
24:18 nor was I **i** in any disturbance. *3552*
2Ti 2: 4 as a soldier *gets* **i in** civilian affairs— *1861*

INVOLVES (1) [INVOLVE]
Ac 18:15 since *it* **i** questions about words and names *1639*

INVOLVING (2) [INVOLVE]
2Sa 3: 8 of an **offense** *i* this woman! AIT
1Ki 21: 1 Some time later there was an incident **i** NIH

INWARD (2) [INWARDLY]
2Sa 5: 9 from the supporting terraces **i**. 1074+2025
Eze 40:16 the openings all around faced **i**. 7163

INWARDLY (5) [INWARD]
Mt 7:15 but **i** they are ferocious wolves. *2277*
Ro 2:29 a man is a Jew if he is one **i**; *1877+3220+3836*
8:23 groan **i** as we wait eagerly for our adoption
as sons, *1571+1877*
2Co 4:16 yet **i** we are being renewed day by day. *2276+3836*
11:29 Who is led into sin, and I do not **i burn?** *4792*

INWARDS (KJV) See INNER PARTS

IPHDEIAH (1)
1Ch 8:25 **I** and Penuel were the sons of Shashak. 3635

IPHTAH (1) [IPHTAH EL]
Jos 15:43 **I**, Ashnah, Nezib, 3652

IPHTAH EL (2) [IPHTAH]
Jos 19:14 and ended at the Valley of **I**. 3654
19:27 touched Zebulun and the Valley of **I**, 3654

IR (1)
1Ch 7:12 and Huppites were the descendants of **I**, 6553

IR NAHASH (1) [NAHASH]
1Ch 4:12 and Tehinnah the father of **I**. 6560

IR SHEMESH (1)
Jos 19:41 Zorah, Eshtaol, **I**, 6561

IRA (6)
2Sa 20:26 and **I** the Jairite was David's priest. 6562
23:26 **I** son of Ikkesh from Tekoa, 6562
23:38 **I** the Ithrite, Gareb the Ithrite 6562
1Ch 11:28 **I** son of Ikkesh from Tekoa, 6562
11:40 **I** the Ithrite, Gareb the Ithrite, 6562
27: 9 was **I** the son of Ikkesh the Tekoite. 6562

IRAD (2)
Ge 4:18 To Enoch was born **I**, 6563
4:18 and **I** was the father of Mehujael, 6563

IRAM (2)
Ge 36:43 and **I**. These were the chiefs of Edom, 6566
1Ch 1:54 and **I**. These were the chiefs of Edom. 6566

IRI (1)
1Ch 7: 7 Ezbon, Uzzi, Uzziel, Jerimoth and **I**, 6565

IRIJAH (2)
Jer 37:13 whose name was **I** son of Shelemiah, 3713
37:14 But **I** would not listen to him; 3713

IRON (95) [IRON-SMELTING, IRONS, NECK-IRONS]
Ge 4:22 of tools out of bronze and **i**. 1366
Lev 26:19 and make the sky above you like **i** and 1366
Nu 31:22 Gold, silver, bronze, **i**, tin, lead 1366
35:16 " 'If a man strikes someone with an **i** object 1366
Dt 3:11 of **i** and was more than thirteen feet long 1366
8: 9 the rocks are **i** and you can dig copper out 1366
27: 5 Do not use any **i tool** upon them. 1366
28:23 the ground beneath you **i**. 1366
28:48 He will put an **i** yoke on your neck 1366
33:25 bolts of your gates will be **i** and bronze, 1366
Jos 6:19 and **i** are sacred to the LORD and must go 1366
6:24 the articles of bronze and **i** into the treasury 1366
8:31 on which no **i tool** had been used. 1366
17:16 in the plain have **i** chariots, 1366
17:18 though the Canaanites have **i** chariots and 1366
19:38 **I**, Migdal El, Horem, Beth Anath 3712
22: 8 with silver, gold, bronze and **i**, 1366
Jdg 1:19 because they had **i** chariots. 1366
4: 3 Because he had nine hundred **i** chariots 1366
4:13 Sisera gathered together his nine hundred **i**
chariots 1366
1Sa 17: 7 and its **i** point weighed six hundred shekels. 1366
2Sa 12:31 with saws and with **i** picks and axes, 1366
23: 7 Whoever touches thorns uses a **tool of i** 1366
1Ki 6: 7 chisel or any other **i** tool was heard at 1366
22:11 of Kenaanah had made **i** horns 1366
2Ki 6: 5 the **i axhead** fell into the water. 1366
6: 6 and made the **i** float. 1366
1Ch 20: 3 with saws and with **i** picks and axes. 1366
22: 3 a large amount of **i** to make nails for 1366
22:14 of bronze and **i** too great to be weighed, 1366
22:16 bronze and **i**—craftsmen beyond number. 1366
29: 2 **i** for the iron and wood for the wood, 1366
29: 2 iron for the **i** and wood for the wood, 1366
29: 7 and a hundred thousand talents of **i**. 1366
2Ch 2: 7 bronze and **i**, and in purple, 1366
2:14 bronze and **i**, stone and wood, 1366
18:10 of Kenaanah had made **i** horns, 1366
24:12 and also workers in **i** and bronze to repair 1366
Job 19:24 they were inscribed with an **i** tool on lead, 1366
20:24 Though he flees from an **i** weapon, 1366
28: 2 **I** is taken from the earth, 1366
40:18 his limbs like rods of **i**. 1366
41:27 **I** he treats like straw and bronze 1366
Ps 2: 9 You will rule them with an **i** scepter; 1366
107:10 prisoners suffering in **i chains**, 1366
107:16 of bronze and cuts through bars of **i**. 1366
149: 8 their nobles with shackles of **i**, 1366
Pr 27:17 As **i** sharpens iron, so one man sharpens 1366
27:17 As iron sharpens **i**, so one man sharpens 1366
Isa 45: 2 of bronze and cut through bars of **i**. 1366
48: 4 the sinews of your neck were **i**, 1366
60:17 and silver in place of **i**. 1366
60:17 and **i** in place of stones. 1366
Jer 1:18 an **i** pillar and a bronze wall to stand 1366
6:28 They are bronze and **i**; 1366
15:12 "Can a man break **i**— 1366
15:12 **i** from the north—or bronze? 1366
17: 1 "Judah's sin is engraved with an **i** tool, 1366
28:13 but in its place you will get a yoke of **i**. 1366
28:14 an **i** yoke on the necks of all these nations 1366
Eze 4: 3 Then take an **i** pan, 1366
4: 3 as an **i** wall between you and the city 1366
22:18 tin, **i** and lead left inside a furnace. 1366
22:20 As men gather silver, copper, **i**, 1366
27:12 they exchanged silver, **i**, 1366
27:19 they exchanged wrought **i**, 1366
Da 2:33 its legs of **i**, its feet partly of iron 10591
2:33 its feet partly of **i** and partly of baked clay. 10591
2:34 on its feet of **i** and clay and smashed them. 10591
2:35 Then the **i**, the clay, the bronze, 10591
2:40 there will be a fourth kingdom, strong as **i** 10591
2:40 for **i** breaks and smashes everything— 10591
2:40 and as **i** breaks things to pieces, 10591
2:41 of baked clay and partly of **i**, so this will be 10591
2:41 it will have some of the strength of **i** in it, 10591
2:41 even as you saw **i** mixed with clay. 10591
2:42 As the toes were partly **i** and partly clay, 10591
2:43 as you saw the **i** mixed with baked clay, 10591
2:43 any more than **i** mixes with clay. 10591
2:45 a rock that broke the **i**, the bronze, the clay, 10591
4:15 bound with **i** and bronze, 10591
4:23 bound with **i** and bronze, 10591
5: 4 of bronze, **i**, wood and stone. 10591
5:23 of bronze, **i**, wood and stone. 10591
7: 7 It had large **i** teeth; 10591
7:19 with its **i** teeth and bronze claws— 10591
Am 1: 3 with sledges having **i** teeth, 1366
Mic 4:13 for I will give you horns of **i**; 1366
Ac 12:10 and came to the **i** gate leading to the city. *4969*
1Ti 4: 2 **seared as with a hot i**. *3013*
Rev 2:27 'He will rule them with an **i** scepter; *4969*
9: 9 They had breastplates like breastplates **of i**, *4969*
12: 5 the nations with an **i** scepter. *4969*
18:12 costly wood, bronze, **i** and marble; *4970*
19:15 "He will rule them with an **i** scepter." *4969*

IRON-SMELTING (3) [IRON]
Dt 4:20 and brought you out of the **i** furnace, 1366
1Ki 8:51 out of Egypt, out of that **i** furnace. 1366
Jer 11: 4 out of Egypt, out of the **i** furnace.' 1366

IRONS (2) [IRON]
Ps 105:18 his neck was put in **i**, 1366
Mk 5: 4 the chains apart and broke the **i on** his **feet.** *4267*

IRPEEL (1)
Jos 18:27 Rekem, **I**, Taralah, 3761

IRRELIGIOUS (1)
1Ti 1: 9 the ungodly and sinful, the unholy and **i**; *1013*

IRRESISTIBLE (1)
Da 11:10 on like an **i** flood and carry the battle as far 6296

IRREVERENT (1)
2Sa 6: 7 burned against Uzzah because of his **i act**; 8915

IRREVOCABLE (1)
Ro 11:29 for God's gifts and his call are **i**. *294*

IRRIGATED (1) [IRRIGATE]
Dt 11:10 and **i** it by foot as in a vegetable garden. 9197

IRRITATE (1)
1Sa 1: 6 rival kept provoking her in order to **i** her. 8307

IRU (1)
1Ch 4:15 The sons of Caleb son of Jephunneh: **I**, 6564

IS (7214) [BE] See Index of Articles Etc.

ISAAC (132) [ISAAC'S]
Ge 17:19 and you will call him **I**. 3663
17:21 But my covenant I will establish with **I**, 3663
21: 3 the name **I** to the son Sarah bore him. 3663
21: 4 When his son **I** was eight days old, 3663
21: 5 when his son **I** was born to him. 3663
21: 8 and on the day **I** was weaned Abraham held 3663
21:10 in the inheritance with my son **I**." 3663
21:12 through **I** that your offspring will 3663
22: 2 God said, "Take your son, your only son, **I**, 3663
22: 3 with him two of his servants and his son **I**. 3663
22: 6 and placed it on his son **I**, 3663
22: 7 **I** spoke up and said to his father Abraham, 3663
22: 7 "The fire and wood are here," **I** said, NIH
22: 9 He bound his son **I** and laid him on 3663
24: 4 and get a wife for my son **I**." 3663
24:14 the one you have chosen for your servant **I**. 3663
24:62 Now **I** had come from Beer Lahai Roi, 3663
24:64 Rebekah also looked up and saw **I**. 3663
24:66 Then the servant told **I** all he had done. 3663
24:67 **I** brought her into the tent 3663
24:67 **I** was comforted after his mother's death. 3663
25: 5 Abraham left everything he owned to **I**. 3663
25: 6 and sent them away from his son **I** to 3663
25: 9 His sons **I** and Ishmael buried him in 3663
25:11 God blessed his son **I**, 3663
25:19 This is the account of Abraham's son **I**. 3663
25:19 Abraham became the father of **I**, 3663
25:20 and **I** was forty years old 3663
25:21 **I** prayed to the LORD on behalf 3663
25:26 **I** was sixty years old 3663
25:28 **I**, who had a taste for wild game, 3663
26: 1 and **I** went to Abimelech king of 3663
26: 2 The LORD appeared to **I** and said, 2257[S]
26: 6 So **I** stayed in Gerar. 3663
26: 8 When **I** had been there a long time, 2257[S]
26: 8 and saw **I** caressing his wife Rebekah. 3663

Ge 26: 9 So Abimelech summoned I and said, 3663
26: 9 'She is my sister'?" I answered him, 3663
26:12 I planted crops in that land and 3663
26:16 Abimelech said to I, "Move away from us; 3663
26:17 So I moved away from there and encamped 3663
26:18 I reopened the wells that had been dug in 3663
26:25 I built an altar there and called on the name NIH
26:27 I asked them, "Why have you come to me, 3663
26:30 I then made a feast for them, NIH
26:31 Then I sent them on their way, 3663
26:35 a source of grief to I and Rebekah. 3663
27: 1 When I was old and his eyes were so weak 3663
27: 2 I said, "I am now an old man NIH
27: 5 Now Rebekah was listening as I spoke 3663
27:20 I asked his son, "How did you find it 3663
27:21 Then I said to Jacob, 3663
27:22 Jacob went close to his father I, 3663
27:26 Then his father I said to him, "Come here, 3663
27:27 When I caught the smell of his clothes, NIH
27:30 After I finished blessing him 3663
27:32 His father I asked him, "Who are you?" 3663
27:33 I trembled violently and said, "Who was it, 3663
27:37 I answered Esau, "I have made him lord 3663
27:39 His father I answered him, 3663
27:46 Then Rebekah said to I, 3663
28: 1 So I called for Jacob and blessed him 3663
28: 5 Then I sent Jacob on his way, 3663
28: 6 Now Esau learned that I had blessed Jacob 3663
28: 8 the Canaanite women were to his father I; 3663
28:13 of your father Abraham and the God of I. 3663
31:18 to go to his father I in the land of Canaan. 3663
31:42 the God of Abraham and the Fear of I, 3663
31:53 in the name of the Fear of his father I. 3663
32: 9 God of my father I, O LORD, 3663
35:12 to Abraham and I I also give to you, 3663
35:27 Jacob came home to his father I in Mamre, 3663
35:27 Hebron), where Abraham and I had stayed. 3663
35:28 I lived a hundred and eighty years. 3663
46: 1 to the God of his father I. 3663
48:15 before whom my fathers Abraham and I walked, 3663
48:16 the names of my fathers Abraham and I, 3663
49:31 there I and his wife Rebekah were buried, 3663
50:24 the land he promised on oath to Abraham, I 3663
Ex 2:24 with Abraham, with I and with Jacob. 3663
3: 6 the God of I and the God of Jacob." 3663
3:15 the God of I and the God of Jacob— 3663
3:16 the God of Abraham, I and Jacob— 3663
4: 5 the God of I and the God of Jacob— 3663
6: 3 to I and to Jacob as God Almighty, 3663
6: 8 give to Abraham, to I and to Jacob. 3663
32:13 I and Israel, to whom you swore 3663
33: 1 the land I promised on oath to Abraham, I 3663
Lev 26:42 and my covenant with I and my covenant 3663
Nu 32:11 the land I promised on oath to Abraham, I 3663
Dt 1: 8 to Abraham, I and Jacob— 3663
6:10 to Abraham, I and Jacob, to give you 3663
9: 5 to Abraham, I and Jacob. 3663
9:27 Remember your servants Abraham, I and 3663
29:13 Abraham, I and Jacob. 3663
30:20 Abraham, I and Jacob. 3663
34: 4 Abraham, I and Jacob when I said, 3663
Jos 24: 3 gave him many descendants. I gave him I, 3663
24: 4 and to I I gave Jacob and Esau. 3663
1Ki 18:36 "O LORD, God of Abraham, I and Israel, 3663
2Ki 13:23 of his covenant with Abraham, I and Jacob. 3663
1Ch 1:28 The sons of Abraham: I and Ishmael. 3663
1:34 Abraham was the father of I. 3663
1:34 The sons of I: Esau and Israel. 3663
16:16 the oath he swore to I. 3663
29:18 God of our fathers Abraham, I and Israel, 3663
2Ch 30: 6 the God of Abraham, I and Israel, 3663
Ps 105: 9 the oath he swore to I. 3773
Jer 33:26 to rule over the descendants of Abraham, I 3773
Am 7: 9 "The high places of I will be destroyed and 3663
7:16 and stop preaching against the house of I.' 3663
Mt 1: 2 Abraham was the father of I, *2693*
1: 2 I the father of Jacob, *2693*
8:11 I and Jacob in the kingdom of heaven. *2693*
22:32 the God *of* I, and the God of Jacob'? *2693*
Mk 12:26 'I am the God of Abraham, the God *of* I, *2693*
Lk 3:34 the son *of* I, the son of Abraham, *2693*
13:28 I and Jacob and all the prophets in *2693*
20:37 and the God *of* I, and the God of Jacob.' *2693*
Ac 3:13 The God of Abraham, I and Jacob, *2693*
7: 8 And Abraham became the father of I *2693*
7: 8 Later I became the father of Jacob, *2693*
7:32 the God *of* Abraham, I and Jacob.' *2693*
Ro 9: 7 "It is through I that your offspring will *2693*
9:10 and the same father, our father I. *2693*
Gal 4:28 Now you, brothers, like I, *2693*
Heb 11: 9 he lived in tents, as did I and Jacob, *2693*
11:17 offered I as a sacrifice. *2693*
11:18 "It is through I that your offspring will *2693*
11:19 he did receive I back from death. *899S*
11:20 By faith I blessed Jacob and Esau in regard *2693*
Jas 2:21 for what he did when he offered his son I *2693*

ISAAC'S (3) [ISAAC]

Ge 26:19 I servants dug in the valley and discovered 3663
26:20 of Gerar quarreled with I herdsmen 3663
26:32 That day I servants came and told him 3663

ISAIAH (53)

2Ki 19: 2 to the prophet I son of Amoz. 3833
19: 5 When King Hezekiah's officials came to I, 3833
19: 6 I said to them, "Tell your master, 3833
19:20 I son of Amoz sent a message to Hezekiah: 3833
20: 1 The prophet I son of Amoz went to him 3833
20: 4 Before I had left the middle court, 3833
20: 7 Then I said, "Prepare a poultice of figs." 3833
20: 8 Hezekiah had asked I, 3833
20: 9 I answered, "This is the LORD's sign 3833
20:11 Then the prophet I called upon the LORD, 3833
20:14 Then I the prophet went to King Hezekiah 3833
20:16 Then I said to Hezekiah, 3833
2Ch 26:22 are recorded by the prophet I son of Amoz. 3833
32:20 and the prophet I son of Amoz cried out 3833
32:32 of the prophet I son of Amoz in the book of 3833
Isa 1: 1 concerning Judah and Jerusalem that I son 3833
2: 1 This is what I son of Amoz saw 3833
7: 3 Then the LORD said to I, "Go out, 3833
7:13 I said, "Hear now, you house of David! NIH
13: 1 An oracle concerning Babylon that I son 3833
20: 2 at that time the LORD spoke through I son 3833
20: 3 "Just as my servant I has gone stripped 3833
37: 2 to the prophet I son of Amoz. 3833
37: 5 When King Hezekiah's officials came to I, 3833
37: 6 I said to them, "Tell your master, 3833
37:21 I son of Amoz sent a message to Hezekiah: 3833
38: 1 The prophet I son of Amoz went to him 3833
38: 4 Then the word of the LORD came to I: 3833
38:21 I had said, "Prepare a poultice of figs 3833
39: 3 Then I the prophet went to King Hezekiah 3833
39: 5 Then I said to Hezekiah, 3833
Mt 3: 3 spoken of through the prophet I: *2480*
4:14 what was said through the prophet I: *2480*
8:17 what was spoken through the prophet I: *2480*
12:17 what was spoken through the prophet I: *2480*
13:14 In them is fulfilled the prophecy *of* I: *2480*
15: 7 I was right when he prophesied about you: *2480*
Mk 1: 2 It is written in I the prophet: *2480*
7: 6 "I was right when he prophesied *2480*
Lk 3: 4 As is written in the book of the words *of* I *2480*
4:17 The scroll *of* the prophet I was handed *2480*
Jn 1:23 John replied in the words of I the prophet, *2480*
12:38 to fulfill the word *of* I the prophet: *2480*
12:39 because, as I says elsewhere: *2480*
12:41 I said this because he saw Jesus' glory *2480*
Ac 8:28 in his chariot reading the book of I *2480*
8:30 to the chariot and heard the man reading I *2480*
28:25 to your forefathers when he said through I *2480*
Ro 9:27 I cries out concerning Israel: *2480*
9:29 It is just as I said previously: *2480*
10:16 For I says, "Lord, who have believed our *2480*
10:20 And I boldly says, "I was found *2480*
15:12 I says, "The Root of Jesse will spring up, *2480*

ISCAH (1)

Ge 11:29 the father of both Milcah and I. 3576

ISCARIOT (11)

Mt 10: 4 Simon the Zealot and Judas I, *2697*
26:14 the one called Judas I— *2697*
Mk 3:19 and Judas I, who betrayed him. *2697*
14:10 Then Judas I, one of the Twelve, *2697*
Lk 6:16 and Judas I, who became a traitor. *2697*
22: 3 Then Satan entered Judas, called I, *2697*
Jn 6:71 (He meant Judas, the son of Simon I, who, *2697*
12: 4 But one of his disciples, Judas I, *2697*
13: 2 the devil had already prompted Judas I, *2697*
13:26 he gave it to Judas I, son of Simon. *2697*
14:22 Then Judas (not Judas I) said, "But, Lord, *2697*

ISH-BOSHETH (14) [ESH-BAAL]

2Sa 2: 8 had taken I son of Saul and brought him 410
2:10 I son of Saul was forty years old 410
2:12 together with the men of I son of Saul, 410
2:15 twelve men for Benjamin and I son of Saul, 410
3: 7 And I said to Abner, NIH
3: 8 because of what I said and he answered, 410
3:11 I did not dare to say another word NIH
3:14 David sent messengers to I son of Saul, 410
3:15 So I gave orders and had her taken away 410
4: 1 When I son of Saul heard NIH
4: 5 set out for the house of I, 410
4: 8 the head of I to David at Hebron and said 410
4: 8 "Here is the head of I son of Saul, 410
4:12 the head of I and buried it in Abner's tomb 410

ISHBAH (1)

1Ch 4:17 Shammai and I the father of Eshtemoa. 3786

ISHBAK (2)

Ge 25: 2 Jokshan, Medan, Midian, I and Shuah. 3791
1Ch 1:32 Jokshan, Medan, Midian, I and Shuah. 3791

ISHBI-BENOB (1)

2Sa 21:16 And I, one of the descendants of Rapha, 3787

ISHHOD (1)

1Ch 7:18 His sister Hammoleketh gave birth to I, 412

ISHI (4)

1Ch 2:31 I, who was the father of Sheshan. 3831
4:20 The descendants of I: 3831
4:42 Rephaiah and Uzziel, the sons of I, 3831
5:24 Epher, I, Eliel, Azriel, Jeremiah, 3831

ISHIAH (KJV) See ISSHIAH

ISHIJAH (1)

Ezr 10:31 From the descendants of Harim: Eliezer, I, 3807

ISHMA (1)

1Ch 4: 3 Jezreel, I and Idbash. 3816

ISHMAEL (47) [ISHMAELITE, ISHMAELITES]

Ge 16:11 You shall name him I, 3817
16:15 the name I to the son she had borne. 3817
16:16 when Hagar bore him I. 3817
17:18 "If only I might live under your blessing!" 3817
17:20 And as for I, I have heard you: 3817
17:23 On that very day Abraham took his son I 3817
17:25 and his son I was thirteen; 3817
17:26 and his son I were both circumcised on 3817
25: 9 His sons Isaac and I buried him in the cave 3817
25:12 This is the account of Abraham's son I, 3817
25:13 These are the names of the sons of I, 3817
25:13 Nebaioth the firstborn of I, Kedar, Adbeel, 3817
25:16 These were the sons of I, 3817
25:17 I lived a hundred and thirty-seven years. 3817
28: 9 so he went to I and married Mahalath, 3817
28: 9 the sister of Nebaioth and daughter of I son 3817
36: 3 also Basemath daughter of I and sister 3817
2Ki 25:23 I son of Nethaniah, Johanan son of Kareah, 3817
25:25 I son of Nethaniah, the son of Elishama, 3817
1Ch 1:28 The sons of Abraham: Isaac and I. 3817
1:29 Nebaioth the firstborn of I, Kedar, Adbeel, 3817
1:31 These were the sons of I. 3817
8:38 Azrikam, Bokeru, I, Sheariah, 3817
9:44 Azrikam, Bokeru, I, Sheariah, 3817
2Ch 19:11 and Zebadiah son of I, 3817
23: 1 I son of Jehohanan, Azariah son of Obed, 3817
Ezr 10:22 Elioenai, Maaseiah, I, Nethanel, 3817
Jer 40: 8 I son of Nethaniah, 3817
40:14 the Ammonites has sent I son of Nethaniah 3817
40:15 "Let me go and kill I son of Nethaniah, 3817
40:16 What you are saying about I is not true." 3817
41: 1 In the seventh month I son of Nethaniah, 3817
41: 2 I son of Nethaniah and 3817
41: 3 I also killed all the Jews who were 3817
41: 6 I son of Nethaniah went out from Mizpah 3817
41: 7 I son of Nethaniah and the men who were 3817
41: 8 But ten of them said to I, "Don't kill us! 3817
41: 9 I son of Nethaniah filled it with the dead. 3817
41:10 I made captives of all the rest of 3817
41:10 I son of Nethaniah took them captive 3817
41:11 with him heard about all the crimes I son 3817
41:12 and went to fight I son of Nethaniah. 3817
41:13 the people I had with him saw Johanan son 3817
41:14 All the people I had taken captive 3817
41:15 But I son of Nethaniah and eight 3817
41:16 from I son of Nethaniah 3817
41:18 They were afraid of them because I son 3817

ISHMAELITE (2) [ISHMAEL]

1Ch 2:17 whose father was Jether the I. 3818
27:30 Obil the I was in charge of the camels. 3818

ISHMAELITES (6) [ISHMAEL]

Ge 37:25 a caravan of I coming from Gilead. 3818
37:27 let's sell him to the I and not lay our hands 3818
37:28 for twenty shekels of silver to the I, 3818
39: 1 from the I who had taken him there. 3818
Jdg 8:24 the custom of the I to wear gold earrings.) 3818
Ps 83: 6 the tents of Edom and the I, 3818

ISHMAIAH (2)

1Ch 12: 4 and I the Gibeonite, a mighty man among 3819
27:19 I son of Obadiah; 3820

ISHMEELITE, ISHMEELITES (KJV) See ISHMAELITE, ISHMAELITES

ISHMERAI (1)

1Ch 8:18 I, Izliah and Jobab were the sons of Elpaal. 3821

ISHOD (KJV) See ISHHOD

ISHPAH (1)

1Ch 8:16 I and Joha were the sons of Beriah. 3834

ISHPAN (1)

1Ch 8:22 I, Eber, Eliel, 3836

ISHTOB (KJV) See MEN OF TOB

ISHUAH (KJV) See ISHVAH

ISHUAI (KJV) See ISHUI, ISHVI

ISHUI (KJV) See ISHVI

ISHVAH (2)

Ge 46:17 Imnah, I, Ishvi and Beriah. 3796
1Ch 7:30 sons of Asher: Imnah, I, Ishvi and Beriah. 3796

ISHVI (4) [ISHVITE]

Ge 46:17 Imnah, Ishvah, I and Beriah. 3798
Nu 26:44 through I, the Ishvite clan; 3798
1Sa 14:49 Saul's sons were Jonathan, I and 3798
1Ch 7:30 sons of Asher: Imnah, Ishvah, I and Beriah. 3798

ISHVITE (1) [ISHVI]

Nu 26:44 through Ishvi, the I clan; 3799

ISLAND (13) [ISLANDERS, ISLANDS]

Isa 23: 2 you people of the i and you merchants 362
23: 6 wail, you people of the i. 362
Ac 13: 6 the whole I until they came to Paphos. *3762*
27:14 swept down from the i. *899S*
27:16 to the lee of a small i called Cauda, *3761*
27:26 we must run aground on some i." *3762*
28: 1 we found out that the i was called Malta. *3762*
28: 7 the chief official *of* the i. *3762*
28: 9 of the sick on the i came and were cured. *3762*
28:11 to sea in a ship that had wintered in the i. *3762*
Rev 1: 9 was on the i of Patmos because of the word *3762*
6:14 and every mountain and i was removed *3762*
16:20 Every i fled away and the mountains could *3762*

ISLANDERS (2) [ISLAND]

Ac 28: 2 The i showed us unusual kindness. *975*
28: 4 the i saw the snake hanging from his hand, *975*

ISLANDS (15) [ISLAND]

Isa 11:11 from Hamath and from the i *of* the sea. 362
24:15 the God of Israel, in the i *of* the sea. 362
40:15 the i as though they were fine dust. 362
41: 1 "Be silent before me, you i! 362
41: 5 The i have seen it and fear; 362
42: 4 In his law the i will put their hope." 362
42:10 you i, and all who live in them. 362
42:12 the LORD and proclaim his praise in the i. 362
42:15 I will turn rivers into i and dry up the pools. 362
49: 1 Listen to me, you i; 362
51: 5 The i will look to me and wait in hope 362
59:18 he will repay the i their due. 362
60: 9 Surely the i look to me; 362
66:19 the distant i that have not heard of my fame 362
Eze 26:18 the i in the sea are terrified 362

ISMACHIAH (KJV) See ISMAKIAH

ISMAIAH (KJV) See ISHMAIAH

ISMAKIAH (1)

2Ch 31:13 Nahath, Asahel, Jerimoth, Jozabad, Eliel, I, 3577

ISN'T (32) [BE, NOT] See Index of Articles Etc.

ISOLATE (2) [ISOLATION]

Lev 13:50 The priest is to examine the mildew and i 6037
13:54 Then *he is to* i it for another seven days. 6037

ISOLATION (7) [ISOLATE]

Lev 13: 4 priest *is to* **put** the infected person **in i** 6037
13: 5 he *is to* **keep** him **in i** another seven days. 6037
13:11 *He is* not *to* **put** him **in i,** 6037
13:21 priest *is to* **put** him **in i** for seven days. 6037
13:26 priest *is to* **put** him **in i** for seven days. 6037
13:31 priest *is to* **put** the infected person **in i** 6037
13:33 *to* **keep** him **in i** another seven days. 6037

ISPAH (KJV) See ISHPAH

ISRAEL (1840) [ISRAEL'S, ISRAELITE, ISRAELITES, ISRAELITES']

Ge 32:28 "Your name will no longer be Jacob, but I, 3776
34: 7 in I by lying with Jacob's daughter— 3776
35:10 your name will be I." 3776
35:10 So he named him I. 3776
35:21 I moved on again and pitched his tent 3776
35:22 While I was living in that region, 3776
35:22 and I heard of it. 3776
37: 3 Now I loved Joseph more than any 3776
37:13 and I said to Joseph, 3776
43: 6 I asked, "Why did you bring this trouble 3776
43: 8 Then Judah said to I his father, 3776
43:11 Then their father I said to them, 3776
45:21 So the sons of I did this. 3776
45:28 And I said, "I'm convinced! 3776
Ge 46: 1 So I set out with all that was his, 3776
46: 2 God spoke to I in a vision at night and said, 3776
46: 8 These are the names of the sons of I (Jacob 3776
46:29 and went to Goshen to meet his father I. 3776
46:30 I said to Joseph, "Now I am ready to die, 3776
47:29 When the time drew near for I to die, 3776
47:31 and I worshiped as he leaned on the top 3776
48: 2 I rallied his strength and sat up on the bed. 3776
48: 8 When I saw the sons of Joseph, he asked, 3776
48: 9 Then I said, "Bring them to me NIH
48:11 I said to Joseph, "I never expected to see 3776
48:14 But I reached out his right hand and put it 3776
48:20 In your name will I pronounce this blessing: 3776
48:21 Then I said to Joseph, "I am about to die, 3776
49: 2 listen to your father I. 3776
49: 7 in Jacob and disperse them in I. 3776
49:16 for his people as one of the tribes of I. 3776
49:24 because of the Shepherd, the Rock of I, 3776
49:28 All these are the twelve tribes of I, 3776
50: 2 in his service to embalm his father I. 3776
50:25 And Joseph made the sons of I swear 3776
Ex 1: 1 of I who went to Egypt with Jacob, each 3776
3:16 assemble the elders of I and say to them, 3776
3:18 "The elders of I will listen to you. 3776
4:22 I is my firstborn son, 3776
5: 1 "This is what the LORD, the God of I, 3776
5: 2 that I should obey him and let I go? 3776
5: 2 the LORD and I will not let I go." 3776
6:14 the firstborn son of I were Hanoch 3776
9: 4 a distinction between the livestock of I and 3776
11: 7 a distinction between Egypt and I. 3776
12: 3 Tell the whole community of I that on 3776
12: 6 of the community of I must slaughter them 3776
12:15 through the seventh must be cut off from I. 3776
12:19 be cut off from the community of I, 3776
12:21 Then Moses summoned all the elders of I 3776
12:47 whole community of I must celebrate it. 3776
13:19 the sons of I swear an oath. 3776
14:20 coming between the armies of Egypt and I. 3776
14:30 the LORD saved I from the hands of 3776
14:30 and I saw the Egyptians lying dead on 3776
15:22 Then Moses led I from the Red Sea 3776
16:31 The people of I called the bread manna. 3776
17: 5 with you some of the elders of I and take 3776
17: 6 in the sight of the elders of I. 3776
18: 1 for Moses and for his people I, 3776
18: 1 the LORD had brought I out of Egypt. 3776
18: 9 the LORD had done for I in rescuing them 3776
18:11 to those who had treated I arrogantly." 2157S
18:12 of I to eat bread with Moses' father-in-law 3776
18:25 from all I and made them leaders of 3776
19: 2 and I camped there in the desert in front of 3776
19: 3 and what you are to tell the people of I: 3776
24: 1 and seventy of the elders of I. 3776
24: 4 the twelve tribes of I. 3776
24: 9 and the seventy elders of I went up 3776
24:10 and saw the God of I. 3776
28: 9 on them the names of the sons of I 3776
28:11 of the sons of I on the two stones the way 3776
28:12 as memorial stones for the sons of I. 3776
28:21 one for each of the names of the sons of I, 3776
28:29 the names of the sons of I over his heart on 3776
32: 4 Then they said, "These are your gods, O I, 3776
32: 8 O I, who brought you up out of Egypt.' 3776
32:13 Isaac and I, to whom you swore 3776
32:27 "This is what the LORD, the God of I, 3776
34:23 the Sovereign LORD, the God of I. 3776
34:27 a covenant with you and with I." 3776
39: 6 like a seal with the names of the sons of I. 3776
39: 7 as memorial stones for the sons of I, 3776
39:14 one for each of the names of the sons of I, 3776
40:38 of all the house of I during all their travels. 3776
Lev 9: 1 and his sons and the elders of I. 3776
10: 6 But your relatives, all the house of I, 3776
16:17 and the whole community of I. 3776
19: 2 to the entire assembly of I and say 1201+3776
20: 2 or any alien living in I who gives any 3776
22:18 either an Israelite or an alien living in I— 3776
Nu 1: 3 in I twenty years old or more who are able 3776
1:16 They were the heads of the clans of I. 3776
1:20 of Reuben the firstborn son of I: 3776
1:44 and Aaron and the twelve leaders of I, 3776
3:13 I set apart for myself every firstborn in I, 3776
3:45 the Levites in place of all the firstborn of I, 1201+3776
4:46 and the leaders of I counted all the Levites 3776
7: 2 Then the leaders of I, 3776
8:17 Every firstborn male in I, 1201+3776
8:18 in place of all the firstborn sons in I. 1201+3776
10: 4 the heads of the clans of I— 3776
10:29 the LORD has promised good things to I." 3776
10:36 O LORD, to the countless thousands of I." 3776
11:30 Then Moses and the elders of I returned to 3776
16: 9 for you that the God of I has separated you 3776
16:25 and the elders of I followed him. 3776
18:14 in I that is devoted to the LORD is yours. 3776
18:21 the tithes in I as their inheritance in return 3776
19:13 That person must be cut off from I. 3776
20:14 "This is what your brother I says: 3776
20:21 I turned away from them. 3776
20:29 of I mourned for him thirty days. 3776
21: 1 heard that I was coming along the road 3776
21: 2 Then I made this vow to the LORD: 3776
21:17 Then I sang this song: "Spring up, O well! 3776
21:21 I sent messengers to say to Sihon king of 3776
21:23 not let I pass through his territory. 3776
21:23 and marched out into the desert against I. 3776
Nu 21:23 When he reached Jahaz, he fought with I. 3776
21:24 I, however, put him to the sword and took 3776
21:25 I captured all the cities of the Amorites 3776
21:31 So I settled in the land of the Amorites. 3776
22: 2 of Zippor saw all that I had done to 3776
23: 7 for me; come, denounce I.' 3776
23:10 of Jacob or number the fourth part of I? 3776
23:21 no misery observed in I. 3776
23:23 no divination against I. 3776
23:23 It will now be said of Jacob and of I, 3776
24: 1 that it pleased the LORD to bless I, 3776
24: 2 and saw I encamped tribe by tribe, 3776
24: 5 O Jacob, your dwelling places, O I! 3776
24:17 a scepter will rise out of I. 3776
24:18 will be conquered, but I will grow strong. 3776
25: 1 While I was staying in Shittim, 3776
25: 3 So I joined in worshiping the Baal of Peor. 3776
25: 4 LORD's fierce anger may turn away from I." 3776
25: 6 Moses and the whole assembly of I 1201+3776
26: 2 to serve in the army of I." 3776
26: 5 the firstborn son of I, were: 3776
26:51 total number of the men of I was 601,730. 3776
30: 1 said to the heads of the tribes of I: 1201+3776
31: 4 from each of the tribes of I." 3776
31: 5 were supplied from the clans of I. 3776
32: 4 the LORD subdued before the people of I— 3776
32:13 against I and he made them wander in 3776
32:14 the LORD even more angry with I. 3776
32:22 to the LORD and to I. 3776
36: 7 No inheritance in I is to pass from 1201+3776
Dt 1: 1 These are the words Moses spoke to all I in 3776
1:38 because he will lead I to inherit it. 3776
2:12 as I did in the land the LORD gave them 3776
4: 1 now, O I, the decrees and laws I am about 3776
5: 1 Moses summoned all I and said: 3776
5: 1 Hear, O I, the decrees and laws I declare 3776
6: 3 Hear, O I, and be careful to obey so 3776
6: 4 Hear, O I: The LORD our God, the LORD is one. 3776
9: 1 Hear, O I. You are now about to cross 3776
10:12 O I, what does the LORD your God ask 3776
11: 6 the middle of all I and swallowed them up 3776
13:11 Then all I will hear and be afraid, 3776
17: 4 that this detestable thing has been done in I, 3776
17:12 You must purge the evil from I. 3776
17:20 a long time over his kingdom in I. 3776
18: 1 to have no allotment or inheritance with I. 3776
18: 6 from one of your towns anywhere in I 3776
19:13 You must purge from I the guilt 3776
20: 3 He shall say: "Hear, O I, 3776
21: 8 Accept this atonement for your people I, 3776
21:21 All I will hear of it and be afraid. 3776
22:21 in I by being promiscuous while still 3776
22:22 You must purge the evil from I. 3776
25: 6 that his name will not be blotted out from I. 3776
25: 7 to carry on his brother's name in I. 3776
25:10 That man's line shall be known in I as 3776
26:15 and bless your people I and 3776
27: 1 and the elders of I commanded the people: 3776
27: 9 said to all I, "Be silent, O Israel, and listen! 3776
27: 9 said to all Israel, "Be silent, O I, and listen! 3776
27:14 to all the people of I in a loud voice: 3776
29:10 and all the other men of I, 3776
29:21 from all the tribes of I for disaster, 3776
31: 1 and spoke these words to all I: 3776
31: 7 and said to him in the presence of all I, 3776
31: 9 and to all the elders of I. 3776
31:11 when all I comes to appear before 3776
31:30 in the hearing of the whole assembly of I: 3776
32: 8 according to the number of the sons of I. 3776
32:45 When Moses finished reciting all these words to all I, 3776
32:52 the land I am giving to the people of I." 3776
33: 5 along with the tribes of I. 3776
33:10 to Jacob and your law to I. 3776
33:21 and his judgments concerning I." 3776
33:28 So I will live in safety alone; 3776
33:29 Blessed are you, O I! 3776
34:10 no prophet has risen in I like Moses, 3776
34:12 that Moses did in the sight of all I. 3776
Jos 3: 7 to exalt you in the eyes of all I, 3776
3:12 choose twelve men from the tribes of I, 3776
3:17 while all I passed by until 3776
4: 7 be a memorial to the people of I forever." 3776
4:14 in the sight of all I; 3776
4:22 'I crossed the Jordan on dry ground.' 3776
6:18 of I liable to destruction and bring trouble 3776
6:23 in a place outside the camp of I. 3776
7: 1 So the LORD's anger burned against I. 1201+3776
7: 6 The elders of I did the same, 3776
7: 8 now that I has been routed by its enemies? 3776
7:11 I has sinned; they have violated my covenant, 3776
7:13 this is what the LORD, the God of I, says: 3776
7:13 That which is devoted is among you, O I. 3776
7:15 and has done a disgraceful thing in I!' " 3776
7:16 next morning Joshua had I come forward 3776
7:19 give glory to the LORD, the God of I, 3776
7:20 sinned against the LORD, the God of I. 3776
7:24 Then Joshua, together with all I, 3776
7:25 Then all I stoned him, 3776
8:10 the leaders of I marched before them to Ai. 3776
8:14 in the morning to meet I in battle at 3776
8:15 and all I let themselves be driven back 3776
8:17 in Ai or Bethel who did not go after I. 3776
8:17 the city open and went in pursuit of I. 3776
8:21 and all I saw that the ambush had taken 3776

Jos 8:22 I cut them down, NIH
8:24 When I had finished killing all the men 3776
8:27 But I did carry off for themselves 3776
8:30 an altar to the LORD, the God of I, 3776
8:33 All I, aliens and citizens alike, 3776
8:33 to bless the people of I. 3776
8:35 not read to the whole assembly of I, 3776
9: 2 to make war against Joshua and I. 3776
9: 6 at Gilgal and said to him and the men of I, 3776
9: 7 The men of I said to the Hivites, 3776
9:14 The men of I sampled their provisions NIH
9:18 an oath to them by the LORD, the God of I. 3776
9:19 our oath by the LORD, the God of I, 3776
10: 1 of peace with I and were living near them. 3776
10:10 threw into confusion before I, 3776
10:10 I pursued them along the road going up NIH
10:11 before I on the road down from Beth Horon 3776
10:12 the LORD gave the Amorites over to I, 1201+3776
10:12 to the LORD in the presence of I: 3776
10:14 Surely the LORD was fighting for I! 3776
10:15 Then Joshua returned with all I to the camp 3776
10:24 he summoned all the men of I and said to 3776
10:29 Then Joshua and all I with him moved on 3776
10:31 Then Joshua and all I with him moved on 3776
10:32 The LORD handed Lachish over to I, 3776
10:34 and all I with him moved on from Lachish 3776
10:36 Then Joshua and all I with him went up 3776
10:38 Then Joshua and all I with him turned 3776
10:40 just as the LORD, the God of I, 3776
10:42 because the LORD, the God of I, 3776
10:42 the God of Israel, fought for I, 3776
10:43 Then Joshua returned with all I to the camp 3776
11: 5 at the Waters of Merom, to fight against I. 3776
11: 6 I will hand all of them over to I, 3776
11: 8 the LORD gave them into the hand of I. 3776
11:13 Yet I did not burn any of the cities built 3776
11:16 and the mountains of I with their foothills, 3776
11:20 to wage war against I, 3776
11:21 and from all the hill country of I. 3776
11:23 to I according to their tribal divisions. 3776
12: 7 an inheritance to the tribes of I according 3776
13: 6 to allocate this land to I for an inheritance, 3776
13:14 the God of I, are their inheritance, 3776
13:33 the LORD, the God of I, 3776
14: 1 heads of the tribal clans of I allotted 1201+3776
14:10 while I moved about in the desert. 3776
14:14 the God of I, wholeheartedly. 3776
19:51 heads of the tribal clans of I assigned 1201+3776
21: 1 heads of the other tribal families of I 1201+3776
21:43 So the LORD gave I all the land he had 3776
21:45 good promises to the house of I failed; 3776
22:12 assembly of I gathered at Shiloh 1201+3776
22:14 one for each of the tribes of I, 3776
22:16 with the God of I like this? 3776
22:18 be angry with the whole community of I. 3776
22:20 upon the whole community of I? 3776
22:21 to the heads of the clans of I: 3776
22:22 And let I know! 3776
22:24 have to do with the LORD, the God of I? 3776
23: 1 and the LORD had given I rest 3776
23: 2 summoned all I—their elders, 3776
24: 1 Then Joshua assembled all the tribes of I 3776
24: 1 leaders, judges and officials of I, 3776
24: 2 "This is what the LORD, the God of I, 3776
24: 9 prepared to fight against I, 3776
24:23 hearts to the LORD, the God of I." 3776
24:31 I served the LORD throughout the lifetime 3776
24:31 the LORD had done for I. 3776
Jdg 1:28 When I became strong, 3776
2: 7 the great things the LORD had done for I. 3776
2:10 the LORD nor what he had done for I. 3776
2:14 against I the LORD handed them over 3776
2:15 Whenever I went out to fight, NIH
2:20 the LORD was very angry with I and said, 3776
2:22 to test I and see whether they will keep 3776
3: 8 The anger of the LORD burned against I 3776
3:12 gave Eglon king of Moab power over I. 3776
3:13 Eglon came and attacked I, 3776
3:30 That day Moab was made subject to I, 3776
3:31 He too saved I. 3776
4: 4 was leading I at that time. 3776
4: 6 the God of I, commands you: 3776
5: 2 "When the princes in I take the lead, when 3776
5: 3 to the LORD, the God of I. 3776
5: 5 before the LORD, the God of I. 3776
5: 7 Village life in I ceased, ceased until I, 3776
5: 7 Deborah, arose, arose a mother in I. 3776
5: 8 among forty thousand in I. 3776
5:11 the righteous acts of his warriors in I. 3776
6: 4 and did not spare a living thing for I, 3776
6: 8 "This is what the LORD, the God of I, 3776
6:14 "Go in the strength you have and save I out 3776
6:15 Gideon asked, "how can I save I? 3776
6:36 "If you will save I by my hand 3776
6:37 then I will know that you will save I 3776
7: 2 In order that I may not boast against me 3776
7:15 He returned to the camp of I and called out, 3776
8:27 All I prostituted themselves 3776
9:22 Abimelech had governed I three years, 3776
10: 1 the son of Dodo, rose to save I. 3776
10: 2 He led I twenty-three years; 3776
10: 3 who led I twenty-two years. 3776
10: 9 and I was in great distress. 3776
11: 4 when the Ammonites made war on I, 3776
11:13 "When I came up out of Egypt, 3776
11:15 I did not take the land of Moab or the land 3776
11:16 I went through the desert to the Red Sea 3776
Jdg 11:17 I sent messengers to the king of Edom, 3776
11:17 So I stayed at Kadesh. 3776
11:19 "Then I sent messengers to Sihon king of 3776
11:20 did not trust I to pass through his territory. 3776
11:20 and encamped at Jahaz and fought with I. 3776
11:21 "Then the LORD, the God of I, 3776
11:21 I took over all the land of the Amorites 3776
11:23 "Now since the LORD, the God of I, 3776
11:23 the Amorites out before his people I, 3776
11:25 Did he ever quarrel with I or fight 3776
11:26 three hundred years I occupied Heshbon, 3776
11:33 Thus I subdued Ammon. 1201+3776
11:40 that each year the young women of I go out 3776
12: 7 Jephthah led I six years. 3776
12: 8 After him, Ibzan of Bethlehem led I. 3776
12: 9 Ibzan led I seven years. 3776
12:11 Elon the Zebulunite led I ten years. 3776
12:13 Abdon son of Hillel, from Pirathon, led I. 3776
12:14 He led I eight years. 3776
13: 5 and he will begin the deliverance of I from 3776
14: 4 for at that time they were ruling over I.) 3776
15:20 Samson led I for twenty years in the days 3776
16:31 He had led I twenty years. 3776
17: 6 In those days I had no king; 3776
18: 1 In those days I had no king. 3776
18: 1 into an inheritance among the tribes of I. 3776
18:19 that you serve a tribe and clan in I 3776
18:29 who was born to I— 3776
19: 1 In those days I had no king. 3776
19:29 and sent them into all the areas of I. 3776
20: 2 of I took their places in the assembly of 3776
20: 6 and disgraceful act in I. 3776
20:10 of every hundred from all the tribes of I, 3776
20:10 for all this vileness done in I." 3776
20:11 So all the men of I got together and united 3776
20:12 The tribes of I sent men throughout 3776
20:13 to death and purge the evil from I." 3776
20:17 I, apart from Benjamin, mustered 408+3776
20:20 of I went out to fight the Benjamites 3776
20:22 of I encouraged one another and again took 3776
20:29 Then I set an ambush around Gibeah. 3776
20:33 All the men of I moved from their places 3776
20:35 The LORD defeated Benjamin before I, 3776
20:36 men of I had given way before Benjamin, 3776
20:38 of I had arranged with the ambush 3776
20:39 then the men of I would turn in the battle. 3776
20:39 to inflict casualties on the men of I 3776
20:41 Then the men of I turned on them, 3776
20:42 of I who came out of the towns cut them NIH
20:48 of I went back to Benjamin and put all 3776
21: 1 The men of I had taken an oath at Mizpah: 3776
21: 3 "O LORD, the God of I," they cried, 3776
21: 3 they cried, "why has this happened to I? 3776
21: 3 should one tribe be missing from I today?" 3776
21: 5 the tribes of I has failed to assemble before 3776
21: 6 "Today one tribe is cut off from I," 3776
21: 8 of the tribes of I failed to assemble before 3776
21:15 LORD had made a gap in the tribes of I. 3776
21:17 "so that a tribe of I will not be wiped out. 3776
21:25 In those days I had no king; 3776
Ru 2:12 rewarded by the LORD, the God of I, 3776
4: 7 (Now in earlier times in I, 3776
4: 7 the method of legalizing transactions in I.) 3776
4:11 who together built up the house of I. 3776
4:14 May he become famous throughout I! 3776
1Sa 1:17 of I grant you what you have asked 3776
2:22 to all I and how they slept with 3776
2:28 I chose your father out of all the tribes of I 3776
2:29 of every offering made by my people I?' 3776
2:30 "Therefore the LORD, the God of I, 3776
2:32 Although good will be done to I, 3776
3:11 to do something in I that will make the ears 3776
3:20 And all I from Dan to Beersheba 3776
4: 1 And Samuel's word came to all I. 3776
4: 1 Philistines deployed their forces to meet I, 3776
4: 2 I was defeated by the Philistines, 3776
4: 3 the elders of I asked, 3776
4: 5 all I raised such a great shout that 3776
4:10 I lost thirty thousand foot soldiers. 3776
4:17 "I fled before the Philistines, 3776
4:18 He had led I forty years. 3776
4:21 saying, "The glory has departed from I"— 3776
4:22 She said, "The glory has departed from I, 3776
5: 7 "The ark of the god of I must not stay here 3776
5: 8 with the ark of the god of I?" 3776
5: 8 the ark of the god of I moved to Gath." 3776
5: 8 So they moved the ark of the God of I. 3776
5:10 of I around to us to kill us and our people." 3776
5:11 "Send the ark of the god of I away; 3776
6: 3 "If you return the ark of the god of I, 3776
7: 2 and all the people of I mourned and sought 3776
7: 3 And Samuel said to the whole house of I, 3776
7: 5 "Assemble all I at Mizpah 3776
7: 6 Samuel was leader of I at Mizpah. 1201+3776
7: 7 Philistines heard that I had assembled 1201+3776
7:10 the Philistines drew near to engage I 3776
7:11 of I rushed out of Mizpah and pursued 3776
7:14 from I were restored to her, 3776
7:14 and I delivered the neighboring territory 3776
7:14 And there was peace between I and 3776
7:15 as judge over I all the days of his life. 3776
7:16 judging I in all those places. 3776
7:17 and there he also judged I. 3776
8: 1 he appointed his sons as judges for I. 3776
8: 4 of I gathered together and came to Samuel 3776
8:22 Then Samuel said to the men of I, 3776
9: 9 (Formerly in I, if a man went to inquire 3776
1Sa 9:16 Anoint him leader over my people I; 3776
9:20 And to whom is all the desire of I turned, 3776
9:21 from the smallest tribe of I, 3776
10:17 the people of I to the LORD at Mizpah NIH
10:18 "This is what the LORD, the God of I, 3776
10:18 'I brought I up out of Egypt, 3776
10:20 Samuel brought all the tribes of I near, 3776
11: 2 of you and so bring disgrace on all I." 3776
11: 3 so we can send messengers throughout I; 3776
11: 7 the pieces by messengers throughout I, 3776
11: 8 of I numbered three hundred thousand and 3776
11:13 for this day the LORD has rescued I." 3776
12: 1 Samuel said to all I, 3776
13: 1 and he reigned over I [forty-]two years. 3776
13: 2 Saul chose three thousand men from I; 3776
13: 4 So all I heard the news: 3776
13: 4 I has become a stench to the Philistines." 3776
13: 5 The Philistines assembled to fight I, 3776
13: 6 of I saw that their situation was critical and 3776
13:13 over I for all time. 3776
13:19 be found in the whole land of I, 3776
13:20 So all I went down to the Philistines 3776
14:12 into the hand of I." 3776
14:23 So the LORD rescued I that day, 3776
14:24 Now the men of I were in distress that day, 3776
14:39 surely as the LORD who rescues I lives, 3776
14:41 Saul prayed to the LORD, the God of I, 3776
14:45 about this great deliverance in I? 3776
14:47 After Saul had assumed rule over I, 3776
14:48 delivering I from the hands 3776
15: 1 to anoint you king over his people I; 3776
15: 2 to I when they waylaid them as they came 3776
15:17 not become the head of the tribes of I? 3776
15:17 The LORD anointed you king over I. 3776
15:26 the LORD has rejected you as king over I!" 3776
15:28 of I from you today and has given it to one 3776
15:29 He who is the Glory of I does not lie 3776
15:30 the elders of my people and before I; 3776
15:35 that he had made Saul king over I. 3776
16: 1 since I have rejected him as king over I? 3776
17: 8 Goliath stood and shouted to the ranks of I, 3776
17:10 "This day I defy the ranks of I! 3776
17:19 with Saul and all the men of I in the Valley 3776
17:21 I and the Philistines were drawing 3776
17:25 He comes out to defy I. 3776
17:25 exempt his father's family from taxes in I." 3776
17:26 and removes this disgrace from I? 3776
17:45 the LORD Almighty, the God of the armies of I, 3776
17:46 will know that there is a God in I. 3776
17:52 of I and Judah surged forward with a shout 3776
18: 6 from all the towns of I to meet King Saul 3776
18:16 But all I and Judah loved David, 3776
18:18 what is my family or my father's clan in I, 3776
19: 5 The LORD won a great victory for all I, 3776
20:12 "By the LORD, the God of I, 3776
23:10 David said, "O LORD, God of I, 3776
23:11 O LORD, God of I, tell your servant." 3776
23:17 You will be king over I, 3776
24: 2 from all I and set out to look for David 3776
24:14 "Against whom has the king of I come out? 3776
24:20 that the kingdom of I will be established 3776
25: 1 and all I assembled and mourned for him; 3776
25:30 and has appointed him leader over I, 3776
25:32 "Praise be to the LORD, the God of I, 3776
25:34 as surely as the LORD, the God of I, 3776
26: 2 with his three thousand chosen men of I, 3776
26:15 And who is like you in I? 3776
26:20 The king of I has come out to look for 3776
27: 1 up searching for me anywhere in I, 3776
28: 1 gathered their forces to fight against I. 3776
28: 3 and all I had mourned for him 3776
28:19 The LORD will hand over both I and you 3776
28:19 over the army of I to the Philistines." 3776
29: 1 and I camped by the spring in Jezreel. 3776
29: 3 who was an officer of Saul king of I? 3776
30:25 a statute and ordinance for I from that day 3776
31: 1 Now the Philistines fought against I; 3776
2Sa 1:12 the army of the LORD and the house of I, 3776
1:19 O I, lies slain on your heights. 3776
1:24 "O daughters of I, weep for Saul, 3776
2: 9 and also over Ephraim, Benjamin and all I. 3776
2:10 when he became king over I, 3776
2:17 and Abner and the men of I were defeated 3776
2:28 they no longer pursued I, 3776
3:10 of Saul and establish David's throne over I 3776
3:12 and I will help you bring all I over to you." 3776
3:17 Abner conferred with the elders of I 3776
3:18 'By my servant David I will rescue my people I 3776
3:19 to Hebron to tell David everything that I 3776
3:21 and assemble all I for my lord the king, 3776
3:37 So on that day all the people and all I knew 3776
3:38 and a great man has fallen in I this day? 3776
4: 1 he lost courage, and all I became alarmed. 3776
5: 1 All the tribes of I came to David at Hebron 3776
5: 2 you were the one who led I 3776
5: 2 'You will shepherd my people I, 3776
5: 3 of I had come to King David at Hebron, 3776
5: 3 and they anointed David king over I. 3776
5: 5 over all I and Judah thirty-three years. 3776
5:12 as king over I and had exalted his kingdom 3776
5:12 for the sake of his people I. 3776
5:17 that David had been anointed king over I, 3776
6: 1 brought together out of I chosen men, 3776
6: 5 and the whole house of I were celebrating 3776
6:15 and the entire house of I brought up the ark 3776

2Sa 6:20 king of I has distinguished himself today, 3776
6:21 ruler over the LORD's people I— 3776
7: 7 to shepherd my people I, 3776
7: 8 the flock to be ruler over my people I. 3776
7:10 a place for my people I and will plant them 3776
7:11 I appointed leaders over my people I. 3776
7:23 And who is like your people I— 3776
7:24 You have established your people I 3776
7:26 'The LORD Almighty is God over I!' 3776
7:27 "O LORD Almighty, God of I, 3776
8:15 David reigned over all I, 3776
10: 9 so he selected some of the best troops in I 3776
10:15 that they had been routed by I, 3776
10:17 David was told of this, he gathered all I, 3776
10:18 But they fled before I, 3776
10:19 that they had been defeated by I, 3776
11:11 ark and I and Judah are staying in tents, 3776
12: 7 This is what the LORD, the God of I, 3776
12: 7 'I anointed you king over I, 3776
12: 8 I gave you the house of I and Judah. 3776
12:12 in broad daylight before all I.' " 3776
13:12 Such a thing should not be done in I! 3776
13:13 be like one of the wicked fools in I. 3776
14:25 In all I there was not a man 3776
15: 2 Your servant is from one of the tribes of I. 3776
15: 6 and so he stole the hearts of the men of I. 3776
15:10 throughout the tribes of I to say, 3776
15:13 hearts of the men of I are with Absalom." 3776
16: 3 the house of I will give me back my grandfather's kingdom.' " 3776
16:15 and all the men of I came to Jerusalem, 3776
16:18 by these people, and by all the men of I— 3776
16:21 Then all I will hear 3776
16:22 in the sight of all I. 3776
17: 4 to Absalom and to all the elders of I. 3776
17:10 for all I knows that your father is a fighter 3776
17:11 Let all I, from Dan to Beersheba— 3776
17:13 then all I will bring ropes to that city, 3776
17:14 Absalom and all the men of I said, 3776
17:15 and the elders of I to do such and such, 3776
17:24 the Jordan with all the men of I. 3776
18: 6 The army marched into the field to fight I, 3776
18: 7 of I was defeated by David's men, and 3776
18:16 and the troops stopped pursuing I, 3776
19: 9 Throughout the tribes of I, 3776
19:11 throughout I has reached the king 3776
19:22 Should anyone be put to death in I today? 3776
19:22 not know that today I am king over I?" 3776
19:40 of Judah and half the troops of I had taken 3776
19:41 of I were coming to the king and saying 3776
19:42 the men of Judah answered the men of I, 3776
19:43 the men of I answered the men of Judah, 3776
19:43 even more harshly than the men of I. 3776
20: 1 Every man to his tent, O I!" 3776
20: 2 of I deserted David to follow Sheba son 3776
20:14 the tribes of I to Abel Beth Maacah and 3776
20:19 We are the peaceful and faithful in I. 3776
20:19 to destroy a city that is a mother in I. 3776
21: 2 the Gibeonites were not a part of I 1201+3776
21: 2 but Saul in his zeal for I and Judah 1201+3776
21: 4 nor do we have the right to put anyone in I 3776
21: 5 and have no place anywhere in I, 3776
21:15 a battle between the Philistines and I. 3776
21:17 that the lamp of I will not be extinguished." 3776
21:21 When he taunted I, 3776
23: 3 The God of I spoke, 3776
23: 3 the Rock of I said to me: 3776
23: 9 Then the men of I retreated, 3776
24: 1 the anger of the LORD burned against I, 3776
24: 1 "Go and take a census of I and Judah." 3776
24: 2 "Go throughout the tribes of I from Dan 3776
24: 4 of the king to enroll the fighting men of I. 3776
24: 9 In I there were eight hundred thousand able-bodied men who could handle 3776
24:15 on I from that morning until the end of 3776
24:25 and the plague on I was stopped. 3776
1Ki 1: 3 Then they searched throughout I for 3776
1:20 the eyes of all I are on you, 3776
1:30 the God of I: 3776
1:34 the prophet anoint him king over I. 3776
1:35 I have appointed him ruler over I 3776
1:48 'Praise be to the LORD, the God of I, 3776
2: 4 to have a man on the throne of I.' 3776
2:11 He had reigned forty years over I— 3776
2:15 All I looked to me as their king. 3776
3:28 all I heard the verdict the king had given, 3776
4: 1 So King Solomon ruled over all I. 3776
4: 7 over all I, who supplied provisions for 3776
4:20 and I were as numerous as the sand on 3776
4:25 During Solomon's lifetime Judah and I, 3776
5:13 Solomon conscripted laborers from all I— 3776
6: 1 the fourth year of Solomon's reign over I, 3776
6:13 and will not abandon my people I." 3776
8: 1 at Jerusalem the elders of I, 3776
8: 2 of I came together to King Solomon at 3776
8: 3 When all the elders of I had arrived, 3776
8: 5 the entire assembly of I that had gathered 3776
8:14 whole assembly of I was standing there, 3776
8:15 "Praise be to the LORD, the God of I, 3776
8:16 the day I brought my people I out of Egypt, 3776
8:16 of I to have a temple built for my Name to 3776
8:16 I have chosen David to rule my people I.' 3776
8:17 I swore to you by the LORD, the God of I. 3776
8:20 and now I sit on the throne of I, 3776
8:20 for the Name of the LORD, the God of I. 3776
8:22 in front of the whole assembly of I, 3776
8:23 "O LORD, God of I, 3776
1Ki 8:25 "Now LORD, God of I, 3776
8:25 a man to sit before me on the throne of I, 3776
8:26 And now, O God of I, 3776
8:30 and of your people I when they pray 3776
8:33 "When your people I have been defeated 3776
8:34 of your people I and bring them back to 3776
8:36 the sin of your servants, your people I. 3776
8:38 or plea is made by any of your people I— 3776
8:41 not belong to your people I but has come 3776
8:43 as do your own people I, 3776
8:52 and to the plea of your people I, 3776
8:55 the whole assembly of I in a loud voice, 3776
8:56 who has given rest to his people I just 3776
8:59 of his servant and the cause of his people I 3776
8:62 and all I with him offered sacrifices before 3776
8:65 and all I with him— 3776
8:66 for his servant David and his people I. 3776
9: 5 I will establish your royal throne over I forever, 3776
9: 5 to have a man on the throne of I.' 3776
9: 7 then I will cut off I from 3776
9: 7 I will then become a byword and an object 3776
10: 9 in you and placed you on the throne of I. 3776
10: 9 Because of the LORD's eternal love for I, 3776
11: 9 the LORD, the God of I, 3776
11:25 in Aram and was hostile toward I. 3776
11:31 for this is what the LORD, the God of I, 3776
11:32 of all the tribes of I, 3776
11:37 you will be king over I. 3776
11:38 as the one I built for David and will give I 3776
11:42 in Jerusalem over all I forty years. 3776
12: 3 the whole assembly of I went to Rehoboam 3776
12:16 When all I saw that the king refused 3776
12:16 To your tents, O I! 3776
12:18 but all I stoned him to death. 3776
12:19 So I has been in rebellion against the house 3776
12:20 the assembly and made him king over all I. 3776
12:21 the house of I and to regain the kingdom 3776
12:28 Here are your gods, O I, 3776
14: 7 what the LORD, the God of I, says: 3776
14: 7 and made you a leader over my people I. 3776
14:10 from Jeroboam every last male in I— 3776
14:13 All I will mourn for him and bury him. 3776
14:13 the God of I, has found anything good. 3776
14:14 for himself a king over I who will cut off 3776
14:15 And the LORD will strike I, 3776
14:15 He will uproot I from this good land 3776
14:16 And he will give I up because of 3776
14:16 and has caused I to commit." 3776
14:18 and all I mourned for him, 3776
14:19 in the book of the annals of the kings of I. 3776
14:21 the tribes of I in which to put his Name. 3776
15: 9 In the twentieth year of Jeroboam king of I, 3776
15:16 between Asa and Baasha king of I 3776
15:17 Baasha king of I went up against Judah 3776
15:19 with Baasha king of I so he will withdraw 3776
15:20 of his forces against the towns of I. 3776
15:25 Nadab son of Jeroboam became king of I 3776
15:25 and he reigned over I two years. 3776
15:26 which he had caused I to commit. 3776
15:27 while Nadab and all I were besieging it. 3776
15:30 and had caused I to commit, 3776
15:30 provoked the LORD, the God of I, to anger. 3776
15:31 in the book of the annals of the kings of I? 3776
15:32 between Asa and Baasha king of I 3776
15:33 Baasha son of Ahijah became king of all I 3776
15:34 which he had caused I to commit. 3776
16: 2 and made you leader of my people I, 3776
16: 2 of Jeroboam and caused my people I to sin 3776
16: 5 in the book of the annals of the kings of I? 3776
16: 8 Elah son of Baasha became king of I, 3776
16:13 and had caused I to commit, 3776
16:13 provoked the LORD, the God of I, to anger 3776
16:14 in the book of the annals of the kings of I? 3776
16:16 king over I that very day there in the camp. 3776
16:19 the sin he had committed and had caused I 3776
16:20 in the book of the annals of the kings of I? 3776
16:21 the people of I were split into two factions; 3776
16:23 Omri became king of I, 3776
16:26 which he had caused I to commit, 3776
16:26 provoked the LORD, the God of I, to anger 3776
16:27 in the book of the annals of the kings of I? 3776
16:29 Ahab son of Omri became king of I, 3776
16:29 in Samaria over I twenty-two years. 3776
16:33 provoke the LORD, the God of I, to anger 3776
16:33 to anger than did all the kings of I 3776
17: 1 "As the LORD, the God of I, lives, 3776
17:14 this is what the LORD, the God of I, says: 3776
18:17 "Is that you, you troubler of I?" 3776
18:18 "I have not made trouble for I," 3776
18:19 Now summon the people from all over I 3776
18:20 So Ahab sent word throughout all I 1201+3776
18:31 saying, "Your name shall be I." 3776
18:36 "O LORD, God of Abraham, Isaac and I, 3776
18:36 let it be known today that you are God in I 3776
19:16 anoint Jehu son of Nimshi king over I, 3776
19:18 Yet I reserve seven thousand in I— 3776
20: 2 into the city to Ahab king of I, 3776
20: 4 The king of I answered, "Just as you say, 3776
20: 7 The king of I summoned all the elders of 3776
20:11 The king of I answered, "Tell him: 3776
20:13 of I and announced, "This is what 3776
20:21 of I advanced and overpowered the horses 3776
20:22 the prophet came to the king of I and said, 3776
20:25 so we can fight I on the plains. 4392S
20:26 and went up to Aphek to fight against I. 3776
20:28 up and told the king of I, "This is what 3776
1Ki 20:31 the kings of the house of I are merciful. 3776
20:31 Let us go to the king of I with sackcloth 3776
20:32 they went to the king of I and said, 3776
20:40 "That is your sentence," the king of I said. 3776
20:41 of I recognized him as one of the prophets. 3776
20:43 the king of I went to his palace in Samaria. 3776
21: 7 "Is this how you act as king over I? 3776
21:18 "Go down to meet Ahab king of I, 3776
21:21 cut off from Ahab every last male in I— 3776
21:22 to anger and have caused I to sin.' 3776
21:26 the LORD drove out before I.) 1201+3776
22: 1 there was no war between Aram and I. 3776
22: 2 of Judah went down to see the king of I. 3776
22: 3 The king of I had said to his officials, 3776
22: 4 Jehoshaphat replied to the king of I, 3776
22: 5 But Jehoshaphat also said to the king of I, 3776
22: 6 king of I brought together the prophets— 3776
22: 8 The king of I answered Jehoshaphat, 3776
22: 9 So the king of I called one of his officials 3776
22:10 the king of I and Jehoshaphat king 3776
22:17 "I saw all I scattered on the hills like sheep 3776
22:18 The king of I said to Jehoshaphat, 3776
22:26 The king of I then ordered, 3776
22:29 of I and Jehoshaphat king of Judah went up 3776
22:30 The king of I said to Jehoshaphat, 3776
22:30 So the king of I disguised himself and went 3776
22:31 small or great, except the king of I." 3776
22:32 they thought, "Surely this is the king of I." 3776
22:33 not the king of I and stopped pursuing him. 3776
22:34 and hit the king of I between the sections 3776
22:39 in the book of the annals of the kings of I? 3776
22:41 in the fourth year of Ahab king of I. 3776
22:44 also at peace with the king of I. 3776
22:51 of Ahab became king of I in Samaria in 3776
22:51 and he reigned over I two years. 3776
22:52 Jeroboam son of Nebat, who caused I to sin. 3776
22:53 provoked the LORD, the God of I, to anger, 3776
2Ki 1: 1 Ahab's death, Moab rebelled against I. 3776
1: 3 'Is it because there is no God in I 3776
1: 6 Is it because there is no God in I 3776
1:16 Is it because there is no God in I for you 3776
1:18 in the book of the annals of the kings of I? 3776
2:12 The chariots and horsemen of I!" 3776
3: 1 Joram son of Ahab became king of I 3776
3: 3 which he had caused I to commit; 3776
3: 4 of I with a hundred thousand lambs and 3776
3: 5 of Moab rebelled against the king of I. 3776
3: 6 from Samaria and mobilized all I. 3776
3: 9 the king of I set out with the king of Judah 3776
3:10 exclaimed the king of I. 3776
3:11 An officer of the king of I answered, 3776
3:12 the king of I and Jehoshaphat and the king 3776
3:13 Elisha said to the king of I, 3776
3:13 "No," the king of I answered, 3776
3:24 when the Moabites came to the camp of I, 3776
3:27 The fury against I was great; 3776
5: 2 had taken captive a young girl from I, 824+3776
5: 4 told him what the girl from I had said. 824+3776
5: 5 "I will send a letter to the king of I." 3776
5: 6 The letter that he took to the king of I read: 3776
5: 7 As soon as the king of I read the letter, 3776
5: 8 that the king of I had torn his robes, 3776
5: 8 that there is a prophet in I." 3776
5:12 better than any of the waters of I? 3776
5:15 in all the world except in I. 3776
6: 8 Now the king of Aram was at war with I. 3776
6: 9 The man of God sent word to the king of I: 3776
6:10 the king of I checked on the place indicated 3776
6:11 of us is on the side of the king of I?" 3776
6:12 "but Elisha, the prophet who is in I, 3776
6:12 tells the king of I the very words you speak 3776
6:21 When the king of I saw them, 3776
6:26 the king of I was passing by on the wall, 3776
7: 6 the king of I has hired the Hittite 3776
8:16 of Joram son of Ahab king of I, 3776
8:18 He walked in the ways of the kings of I, 3776
8:25 of Joram son of Ahab king of I, 3776
8:26 a granddaughter of Omri king of I. 3776
9: 3 I anoint you king over I.' 3776
9: 6 "This is what the LORD, the God of I, 3776
9: 6 over the LORD's people I. 3776
9: 8 from Ahab every last male in I— 3776
9:12 I anoint you king over I.' " 3776
9:14 all I had been defending Ramoth Gilead 3776
9:21 of I and Ahaziah king of Judah rode out, 3776
10:21 Then he sent word throughout I, 3776
10:28 So Jehu destroyed Baal worship in I. 3776
10:29 which he had caused I to commit— 3776
10:30 on the throne of I to the fourth generation." 3776
10:31 the God of I, with all his heart. 3776
10:31 which he had caused I to commit. 3776
10:32 the LORD began to reduce the size of I. 3776
10:34 in the book of the annals of the kings of I? 3776
10:36 over I in Samaria was twenty-eight years. 3776
13: 1 Jehoahaz son of Jehu became king of I 3776
13: 2 which he had caused I to commit, 3776
13: 3 So the LORD's anger burned against I, 3776
13: 4 the king of Aram was oppressing I. 3776
13: 5 The LORD provided a deliverer for I, 3776
13: 6 which he had caused I to commit; 3776
13: 8 in the book of the annals of the kings of I? 3776
13:10 Jehoash son of Jehoahaz became king of I 3776
13:11 which he had caused I to commit; 3776
13:12 in the book of the annals of the kings of I? 3776
13:13 in Samaria with the kings of I. 3776
13:14 Jehoash king of I went down to see him 3776
13:14 "The chariots and horsemen of I!" 3776

2Ki 13:16 he said to the king of I. 3776
13:22 of Aram oppressed I throughout the reign 3776
14: 1 of Jehoash son of Jehoahaz king of I, 3776
14: 8 king of I, with the challenge: 3776
14: 9 of I replied to Amaziah king of Judah: 3776
14:11 so Jehoash king of I attacked. 3776
14:12 Judah was routed by I, 3776
14:13 Jehoash king of I captured Amaziah king 3776
14:15 in the book of the annals of the kings of I? 3776
14:16 in Samaria with the kings of I. 3776
14:17 of Jehoash son of Jehoahaz king of I. 3776
14:23 of Jehoash king of I became king 3776
14:24 which he had caused I to commit. 3776
14:25 the boundaries of I from Lebo Hamath to 3776
14:25 the word of the LORD, the God of I, 3776
14:26 in I, whether slave or free, was suffering; 3776
14:27 not said he would blot out the name of I 3776
14:28 how he recovered for I both Damascus 3776
14:28 in the book of the annals of the kings of I? 3776
14:29 rested with his fathers, the kings of I. 3776
15: 1 of Jeroboam king of I, 3776
15: 8 of Jeroboam became king of I in Samaria, 3776
15: 9 which he had caused I to commit. 3776
15:11 in the book of the annals of the kings of I. 3776
15:12 on the throne of I to the fourth generation." 3776
15:15 in the book of the annals of the kings of I. 3776
15:17 Menahem son of Gadi became king of I, 3776
15:18 which he had caused I to commit. 3776
15:20 Menahem exacted this money from I. 3776
15:21 in the book of the annals of the kings of I? 3776
15:23 of Menahem became king of I in Samaria, 3776
15:24 which he had caused I to commit. 3776
15:26 in the book of the annals of the kings of I. 3776
15:27 of Remaliah became king of I in Samaria, 3776
15:28 which he had caused I to commit. 3776
15:29 In the time of Pekah king of I, 3776
15:31 in the book of the annals of the kings of I? 3776
15:32 of Pekah son of Remaliah king of I, 3776
16: 3 He walked in the ways of the kings of I and 3776
16: 5 of I marched up to fight against Jerusalem 3776
16: 7 of the king of Aram and of the king of I, 3776
17: 1 Hoshea son of Elah became king of I 3776
17: 2 not like the kings of I who preceded him. 3776
17: 8 that the kings of I had introduced. 3776
17:13 The LORD warned I and Judah 3776
17:18 So the LORD was very angry with I 3776
17:19 the practices I had introduced. 3776
17:20 the LORD rejected all the people of I; 3776
17:21 he tore I away from the house of David, 3776
17:21 Jeroboam enticed I away from following 3776
17:23 of I were taken from their homeland 3776
17:34 descendants of Jacob, whom he named I. 3776
18: 1 of Hoshea son of Elah king of I, 3776
18: 5 Hezekiah trusted in the LORD, the God of I. 3776
18: 9 of Hoshea son of Elah king of I, 3776
18:10 the ninth year of Hoshea king of I. 3776
18:11 The king of Assyria deported I to Assyria 3776
19:15 "O LORD, God of I, 3776
19:20 "This is what the LORD, the God of I, 3776
19:22 Against the Holy One of I! 3776
21: 3 as Ahab king of I had done. 3776
21: 7 chosen out of all the tribes of I, 3776
21:12 the LORD, the God of I, says: 3776
22:15 "This is what the LORD, the God of I, 3776
22:18 'This is what the LORD, the God of I, 3776
23:13 the ones Solomon king of I had built 3776
23:15 who had caused I to sin— 3776
23:19 the high places that the kings of I had built 3776
23:22 Not since the days of the judges who led I, 3776
23:22 throughout the days of the kings of I and 3776
23:27 also from my presence as I removed I, 3776
24:13 that Solomon king of I had made for 3776
1Ch 1:34 The sons of Isaac: Esau and I. 3776
2: 1 These were the sons of I: 3776
2: 7 who brought trouble on I by violating 3776
4:10 Jabez cried out to the God of I, "Oh, 3776
5: 1 the firstborn of I (he was the firstborn, but 3776
5: 1 to the sons of Joseph son of I; 3776
5: 3 the sons of Reuben the firstborn of I: 3776
5:17 of Judah and Jeroboam king of I. 3776
5:26 the God of I stirred up the spirit of Pul king 3776
6:38 the son of Levi, the son of I; 3776
6:49 making atonement for I, 3776
7:29 The descendants of Joseph son of I lived 3776
9: 1 All I was listed in the genealogies recorded 3776
9: 1 in the book of the kings of I. 3776
10: 1 Now the Philistines fought against I; 3776
11: 1 All I came together to David at Hebron 3776
11: 2 you were the one who led I 3776
11: 2 'You will shepherd my people I, 3776
11: 3 of I had come to King David at Hebron, 3776
11: 3 and they anointed David king over I, 3776
11:10 they, together with all I, 3776
12:32 the times and knew what I should do— 3776
12:38 to make David king over all I. 3776
12:40 oil, cattle and sheep, for there was joy in I. 3776
13: 2 He then said to the whole assembly of I, 3776
13: 2 throughout the territories of I, 3776
14: 2 established him as king over I and 3776
14: 2 for the sake of his people I. 3776
14: 8 over all I, they went up in full force 3776
15: 3 David assembled all I in Jerusalem to bring 3776
15:12 up the ark of the LORD, the God of I, 3776
15:14 the ark of the LORD, the God of I. 3776
15:25 the elders of I and the commanders of units 3776
15:28 So all I brought up the ark of the covenant 3776
16: 4 and to praise the LORD, the God of I: 3776
1Ch 16:13 O descendants of I his servant, 3776
16:17 to I as an everlasting covenant: 3776
16:36 Praise be to the LORD, the God of I, 3776
16:40 law of the LORD, which he had given I. 3776
17: 5 in a house from the day I brought I up out 3776
17: 7 to be ruler over my people I. 3776
17: 9 a place for my people I and will plant them 3776
17:10 I appointed leaders over my people I. 3776
17:21 And who is like your people I— 3776
17:22 You made your people I your very own
forever, 3776
17:24 'The LORD Almighty, the God over I, 3776
18:14 David reigned over all I, 3776
19:10 so he selected some of the best troops in I 3776
19:16 that they had been routed by I, 3776
19:17 he gathered all I and crossed the Jordan; 3776
19:18 But they fled before I, 3776
19:19 that they had been defeated by I, 3776
20: 7 When he taunted I, 3776
21: 1 against I and incited David to take a census 3776
21: 1 and incited David to take a census of I. 3776
21: 3 Why should he bring guilt on I?" 3776
21: 4 and went throughout I and then came back 3776
21: 5 In all I there were one million one hundred
thousand men who could handle a sword, 3776
21: 7 evil in the sight of God, so he punished I. 3776
21:12 angel of the LORD ravaging every part of I. 3776
21:14 So the LORD sent a plague on I, 3776
21:14 and seventy thousand men of I fell dead. 3776
22: 1 and also the altar of burnt offering for I." 3776
22: 2 to assemble the aliens living in I, 824+3776
22: 6 a house for the LORD, the God of I. 3776
22: 9 and I will grant I peace and quiet 3776
22:10 the throne of his kingdom over I forever.' 3776
22:12 when he puts you in command over I, 3776
22:13 and laws that the LORD gave Moses for I. 3776
22:17 the leaders of I to help his son Solomon. 3776
23: 1 he made his son Solomon king over I. 3776
23: 2 also gathered together all the leaders of I, 3776
23:25 "Since the LORD, the God of I, 3776
24:19 the God of I, had commanded him. 3776
26:29 as officials and judges over I. 3776
26:30 in I west of the Jordan for all the work of 3776
27:16 The officers over the tribes of I: 3776
27:22 These were the officers over the tribes of I. 3776
27:23 to make I as numerous as the stars in 3776
27:24 on I on account of this numbering, 3776
28: 1 the officials of I to assemble at Jerusalem: 3776
28: 4 "Yet the LORD, the God of I, 3776
28: 4 to be king over I forever. 3776
28: 4 to make me king over all I. 3776
28: 5 of the kingdom of the LORD over I. 3776
28: 8 now I charge you in the sight of all I and of 3776
29: 6 the officers of the tribes of I, 3776
29:10 O LORD, God of our father I, 3776
29:18 God of our fathers Abraham, Isaac and I, 3776
29:21 and other sacrifices in abundance for all I. 3776
29:23 He prospered and all I obeyed him. 3776
29:25 in the sight of all I and bestowed 3776
29:25 as no king over I ever had before. 3776
29:26 David son of Jesse was king over all I. 3776
29:27 He ruled over I forty years— 3776
29:30 that surrounded him and I and 3776
2Ch 1: 2 Then Solomon spoke to all I— 3776
1: 2 to the judges and to all the leaders in I, 3776
1:13 And he reigned over I. 3776
2: 4 This is a lasting ordinance for I. 3776
2:12 "Praise be to the LORD, the God of I, 3776
2:17 a census of all the aliens who were in I, 824+3776
5: 2 to Jerusalem the elders of I, 3776
5: 3 of I came together to the king at the time of 3776
5: 4 When all the elders of I had arrived, 3776
5: 6 the entire assembly of I that had gathered 3776
6: 3 whole assembly of I was standing there, 3776
6: 4 "Praise be to the LORD, the God of I, 3776
6: 5 of I to have a temple built for my Name to 3776
6: 5 to be the leader over my people I. 3776
6: 6 I have chosen David to rule my people I.' 3776
6: 7 for the Name of the LORD, the God of I. 3776
6:10 and now I sit on the throne of I, 3776
6:10 for the Name of the LORD, the God of I. 3776
6:11 that he made with the people of I." 3776
6:12 in front of the whole assembly of I 3776
6:13 down before the whole assembly of I 3776
6:14 He said: "O LORD, God of I, 3776
6:16 "Now LORD, God of I, 3776
6:16 a man to sit before me on the throne of I, 3776
6:17 And now, O LORD, God of I, 3776
6:21 and of your people I when they pray 3776
6:24 "When your people I have been defeated 3776
6:25 of your people I and bring them back to 3776
6:27 the sin of your servants, your people I. 3776
6:29 or plea is made by any of your people I— 3776
6:32 not belong to your people I but has come 3776
6:33 as do your own people I, 3776
7: 8 and all I with him—a vast assembly 3776
7:10 and Solomon and for his people I. 3776
7:18 to have a man to rule over I.' 3776
7:20 then I will uproot I from my land, 4392S
8:11 not live in the palace of David king of I, 3776
9: 8 for I and his desire to uphold them forever, 3776
9:30 in Jerusalem over all I forty years. 3776
10: 3 and all I went to Rehoboam and said 3776
10:16 When all I saw that the king refused 3776
10:16 To your tents, O I! 3776
10:19 So I has been in rebellion against the house 3776
11: 1 against I and to regain the kingdom 3776
2Ch 11:13 from all their districts throughout I sided 3776
11:16 from every tribe of I who set their hearts 3776
11:16 seeking the LORD, the God of I, 3776
12: 1 he and all I with him abandoned the law of 3776
12: 6 of I and the king humbled themselves 3776
12:13 the tribes of I in which to put his Name. 3776
13: 4 and said, "Jeroboam and all I, listen to me! 3776
13: 5 know that the LORD, the God of I, 3776
13: 5 of I to David and his descendants forever 3776
13:12 Men of I, do not fight against the LORD, 3776
13:15 and all I before Abijah and Judah. 3776
13:18 of I were subdued on that occasion, 3776
15: 3 For a long time I was without the true God, 3776
15: 4 the LORD, the God of I, and sought him, 3776
15: 9 over to him from I when they saw that 3776
15:13 the God of I, were to be put to death, 3776
15:17 not remove the high places from I, 3776
16: 1 of Asa's reign Baasha king of I went up 3776
16: 3 with Baasha king of I so he will withdraw 3776
16: 4 of his forces against the towns of I. 3776
16:11 in the book of the kings of Judah and I. 3776
17: 1 as king and strengthened himself against I. 3776
17: 4 rather than the practices of I. 3776
18: 3 Ahab king of I asked Jehoshaphat king 3776
18: 4 But Jehoshaphat also said to the king of I, 3776
18: 5 king of I brought together the prophets— 3776
18: 7 The king of I answered Jehoshaphat, 3776
18: 8 So the king of I called one of his officials 3776
18: 9 the king of I and Jehoshaphat king 3776
18:16 "I saw all I scattered on the hills like sheep 3776
18:17 The king of I said to Jehoshaphat, 3776
18:19 of I into attacking Ramoth Gilead 3776
18:25 The king of I then ordered, 3776
18:28 of I and Jehoshaphat king of Judah went up 3776
18:29 The king of I said to Jehoshaphat, 3776
18:29 So the king of I disguised himself and went 3776
18:30 small or great, except the king of I." 3776
18:31 they thought, "This is the king of I." 3776
18:32 that he was not the king of I, 3776
18:33 and hit the king of I between the sections 3776
18:34 and the king of I propped himself up 3776
20: 7 before your people I and give it forever to 3776
20:10 whose territory you would not allow I 3776
20:19 the God of I, with very loud voice. 3776
20:29 LORD had fought against the enemies of I. 3776
20:34 in the book of the kings of I. 3776
20:35 an alliance with Ahaziah king of I, 3776
21: 2 of Jehoshaphat king of I. 3776
21: 4 along with some of the princes of I. 3776
21: 6 He walked in the ways of the kings of I, 3776
21:13 in the ways of the kings of I, 3776
22: 5 with Joram son of Ahab king of I to war 3776
24: 5 the money due annually from all I, 3776
24: 6 of the LORD and by the assembly of I for 3776
24: 9 the servant of God had required of I in 3776
24:16 because of the good he had done in I 3776
25: 6 a hundred thousand fighting men from I for 3776
25: 7 from I must not march with you, for 3776
25: 7 for the LORD is not with I— 3776
25:17 king of I: "Come, meet me face to face." 3776
25:18 of I replied to Amaziah king of Judah: 3776
25:21 So Jehoash king of I attacked. 3776
25:22 Judah was routed by I, 3776
25:23 Jehoash king of I captured Amaziah king 3776
25:25 of Jehoash son of Jehoahaz king of I. 3776
25:26 in the book of the kings of Judah and I? 3776
27: 7 are written in the book of the kings of I 3776
28: 2 He walked in the ways of the kings of I and 3776
28: 5 also given into the hands of the king of I, 3776
28:13 and his fierce anger rests on I." 3776
28:19 because of Ahaz king of I, 3776
28:23 and the downfall of all I. 3776
28:26 in the book of the kings of Judah and I. 3776
28:27 not placed in the tombs of the kings of I. 3776
29: 7 at the sanctuary to the God of I. 3776
29:10 covenant with the LORD, the God of I, 3776
29:24 the altar for a sin offering to atone for all I, 3776
29:24 and the sin offering for all I. 3776
29:27 and the instruments of David king of I. 3776
30: 1 Hezekiah sent word to all I and Judah and 3776
30: 1 Passover to the LORD, the God of I. 3776
30: 5 to send a proclamation throughout I, 3776
30: 5 Passover to the LORD, the God of I. 3776
30: 6 throughout I and Judah with letters from 3776
30: 6 "People of I, return to the LORD, 3776
30: 6 the God of Abraham, Isaac and I, 3776
30:25 and all who had assembled from I, 3776
30:25 the aliens who had come from I 824+3776
30:26 of David king of I there had been nothing 3776
31: 6 of I and Judah who lived in the towns 3776
31: 8 the LORD and blessed his people I. 3776
32:17 the God of I, and saying this against him: 3776
32:32 in the book of the kings of Judah and I. 3776
33: 7 of all the tribes of I, 3776
33:16 to serve the LORD, the God of I. 3776
33:18 the name of the LORD, the God of I, 3776
33:18 are written in the annals of the kings of I. 3776
34: 7 all the incense altars throughout I. 824+3776
34: 9 Ephraim and the entire remnant of I and 3776
34:21 the LORD for me and for the remnant in I 3776
34:23 "This is what the LORD, the God of I, 3776
34:26 'This is what the LORD, the God of I, 3776
34:33 and he had all who were present in I serve 3776
35: 3 the Levites, who instructed all I 3776
35: 3 that Solomon son of David king of I built. 3776
35: 3 the LORD your God and his people I. 3776
35: 4 to the directions written by David king of I 3776

2Ch 35:18 in I since the days of the prophet Samuel; 3776
35:18 of the kings of I had ever celebrated such 3776
35:18 and all Judah and I who were there with 3776
35:25 in I and are written in the Laments. 3776
35:27 are written in the book of the kings of I 3776
36: 8 are written in the book of the kings of I 3776
36:13 would not turn to the LORD, the God of I. 3776
Ezr 1: 3 the God of I, the God who is in Jerusalem. 3776
2: 2 The list of the men of the people of I: 3776
2:59 that their families were descended from I: 3776
3: 2 of the God of I to sacrifice burnt offerings 3776
3:10 as prescribed by David king of I. 3776
3:11 his love to I endures forever." 3776
4: 1 a temple for the LORD, the God of I, 3776
4: 3 of the heads of the families of I answered, 3776
4: 3 the LORD, the God of I, as King Cyrus, 3776
5: 1 and Jerusalem in the name of the God of I, 10335
5:11 one that a great king of I built and finished. 10335
6:14 according to the command of the God of I 10335
6:16 Then the people of I— 10335
6:17 as a sin offering for all I, 10335
6:17 one for each of the tribes of I. 10335
6:21 to seek the LORD, the God of I. 3776
6:22 the house of God, the God of I. 3776
7: 6 which the LORD, the God of I, had given. 3776
7:10 and to teaching its decrees and laws in I. 3776
7:11 and decrees of the LORD for I: 3776
7:15 advisers have freely given to the God of I, 10335
7:28 and gathered leading men from I to go up 3776
8:18 the son of I, and Sherebiah's sons 3776
8:25 and all I present there had donated for 3776
8:29 and the Levites and the family heads of I." 3776
8:35 offerings to the God of I: 3776
8:35 twelve bulls for all I, ninety-six rams, 3776
9: 1 "The people of I, including the priests 3776
9: 4 the God of I gathered around me because 3776
9:15 O LORD, God of I, you are righteous! 3776
10: 2 But in spite of this, there is still hope for I. 3776
10: 5 the leading priests and Levites and all I 3776
Ne 1: 6 for your servants, the people of I. 3776
7: 7 The list of the men of I: 3776+6639
7:61 that their families were descended from I: 3776
8: 1 which the LORD had commanded for I. 3776
10:33 for sin offerings to make atonement for I; 3776
10:39 The people of I, including the Levites, 3776
12:47 all I contributed the daily portions for 3776
13: 3 from I all who were of foreign descent. 3776
13:18 up more wrath against I by desecrating 3776
13:26 like these that Solomon king of I sinned? 3776
13:26 and God made him king over all I, 3776
Ps 14: 7 that salvation for I would come out 3776
14: 7 let Jacob rejoice and I be glad! 3776
22: 3 you are the praise of I. 3776
22:23 Revere him, all you descendants of I! 3776
25:22 Redeem I, O God, from all their troubles! 3776
41:13 Praise be to the LORD, the God of I, 3776
50: 7 O my people, and I will speak, O I, 3776
53: 6 salvation for I would come out of Zion! 3776
53: 6 let Jacob rejoice and I be glad! 3776
59: 5 O LORD God Almighty, the God of I, 3776
68: 8 the One of Sinai, before God, the God of I. 3776
68:26 praise the LORD in the assembly of I. 3776
68:34 whose majesty is over I, 3776
68:35 of I gives power and strength to his people. 3776
69: 6 be put to shame because of me, O God of I. 3776
71:22 O Holy One of I. 3776
72:18 Praise be to the LORD God, the God of I, 3776
73: 1 Surely God is good to I, 3776
76: 1 his name is great in I. 3776
78: 5 for Jacob and established the law in I, 3776
78:21 and his wrath rose against I, 3776
78:31 cutting down the young men of I. 3776
78:41 they vexed the Holy One of I. 3776
78:55 he settled the tribes of I in their homes. 3776
78:59 he rejected I completely. 3776
78:71 of I his inheritance. 3776
80: 1 Hear us, O Shepherd of I, 3776
81: 4 this is a decree for I, 3776
81: 8 if you would but listen to me, O I! 3776
81:11 I would not submit to me. 3776
81:13 if I would follow my ways, 3776
83: 4 the name of I be remembered no more." 3776
89:18 our king to the Holy One of I. 3776
98: 3 and his faithfulness to the house of I; 3776
99: 8 you were to I a forgiving God, 2157S
103: 7 his deeds to the people of I: 3776
105:10 to I as an everlasting covenant: 3776
105:23 Then I entered Egypt; 3776
105:37 He brought out I, 4392S
105:38 because dread of I had fallen on them. 4392S
106:48 Praise be to the LORD, the God of I, 3776
114: 1 When I came out of Egypt, 3776
114: 2 Judah became God's sanctuary, I his dominion. 3776
115: 9 O house of I, trust in the LORD— 3776
115:12 He will bless the house of I, 3776
118: 2 Let I say: "His love endures forever." 3776
121: 4 he who watches over I will neither slumber 3776
122: 4 according to the statute given to I. 3776
124: 1 on our side—let I say— 3776
125: 5 Peace be upon I. 3776
128: 6 Peace be upon I. 3776
129: 1 oppressed me from my youth—let I say— 3776
130: 7 O I, put your hope in the LORD, 3776
130: 8 He himself will redeem I 3776
131: 3 O I, put your hope in the LORD both now 3776
135: 4 I to be his treasured possession. 3776
Ps 135:12 an inheritance to his people I. 3776
135:19 O house of I, praise the LORD; 3776
136:11 and brought I out from 3776
136:14 and brought I through the midst of it, 3776
136:22 an inheritance to his servant I; 3776
147: 2 he gathers the exiles of I. 3776
147:19 his laws and decrees to I. 3776
148:14 of I, the people close to his heart. 1201+3776
149: 2 Let I rejoice in their Maker; 3776
Pr 1: 1 of Solomon son of David, king of I: 3776
Ecc 1:12 the Teacher, was king over I in Jerusalem. 3776
SS 3: 7 escorted by sixty warriors, the noblest of I, 3776
Isa 1: 3 but I does not know, 3776
1: 4 the Holy One of I and turned their backs 3776
1:24 the LORD Almighty, the Mighty One of I, 3776
4: 2 be the pride and glory of the survivors in I. 3776
5: 7 of the LORD Almighty is the house of I, 3776
5:19 let the plan of the Holy One of I come, 3776
5:24 and spurned the word of the Holy One of I. 3776
7: 1 of I marched up to fight against Jerusalem, 3776
8:14 but for both houses of I he will be a stone 3776
8:18 We are signs and symbols in I from 3776
9: 8 it will fall on I. 3776
9:12 have devoured I with open mouth. 3776
9:14 from I both head and tail, both palm branch 3776
10:17 The Light of I will become a fire, 3776
10:20 In that day the remnant of I, 3776
10:20 rely on the LORD, the Holy One of I. 3776
10:22 Though your people, O I, 3776
11:12 for the nations and gather the exiles of I; 3776
11:16 as there was for I when they came up 3776
12: 6 for great is the Holy One of I among you." 3776
14: 1 once again he will choose I 3776
14: 2 of I will possess the nations as menservants 3776
17: 6 declares the LORD, the God of I. 3776
17: 7 and turn their eyes to the Holy One of I. 3776
19:24 In that day I will be the third, 3776
19:25 and I my inheritance." 3776
21:10 the LORD Almighty, from the God of I. 3776
21:17 The LORD, the God of I, has spoken. 3776
24:15 exalt the name of the LORD, the God of I, 3776
27: 6 I will bud and blossom and fill all 3776
29:19 the needy will rejoice in the Holy One of I. 3776
29:23 and will stand in awe of the God of I. 3776
30:11 stop confronting us with the Holy One of I! 3776
30:12 this is what the Holy One of I says: 3776
30:15 the Holy One of I, says: 3776
30:29 mountain of the LORD, to the Rock of I. 3776
31: 1 but do not look to the Holy One of I, 3776
37:16 God of I, enthroned between the cherubim, 3776
37:21 "This is what the LORD, the God of I, 3776
37:23 Against the Holy One of I! 3776
40:27 O I, "My way is hidden from the LORD; 3776
41: 8 "But you, O I, my servant, Jacob, 3776
41:14 Do not be afraid, O worm Jacob, O little I, 3776
41:14 your Redeemer, the Holy One of I. 3776
41:16 the LORD and glory in the Holy One of I. 3776
41:17 I, the God of I, will not forsake them. 3776
41:20 that the Holy One of I has created it. 3776
42:24 and I to the plunderers? 3776
43: 1 O Jacob, he who formed you, O I: 3776
43: 3 your God, the Holy One of I, your Savior; 3776
43:14 your Redeemer, the Holy One of I: 3776
43:22 not wearied yourselves for me, O I. 3776
43:28 to destruction and I to scorn. 3776
44: 1 "But now listen, O Jacob, my servant, I, 3776
44: 5 'The LORD's,' and will take the name I. 3776
44:21 O Jacob, for you are my servant, O I. 3776
44:21 O I, I will not forget you. 3776
44:23 he displays his glory in I. 3776
45: 3 the God of I, who summons you by name. 3776
45: 4 sake of Jacob my servant, of I my chosen, 3776
45:11 the Holy One of I, and its Maker: 3776
45:15 O God and Savior of I. 3776
45:17 But I will be saved by the LORD with 3776
45:25 of I will be found righteous and will exult. 3776
46: 3 all you who remain of the house of I, 3776
46:13 my splendor to I. 3776
47: 4 is the Holy One of I. 3776
48: 1 by the name of I and come from the line 3776
48: 1 of the LORD and invoke the God of I— 3776
48: 2 of the holy city and rely on the God of I— 3776
48:12 "Listen to me, O Jacob, I, 3776
48:17 your Redeemer, the Holy One of I: 3776
49: 3 He said to me, "You are my servant, I, 3776
49: 5 and gather I to himself, for I am honored in 3776
49: 6 and bring back those of I I have kept. 3776
49: 7 the Redeemer and Holy One of I— 3776
49: 7 the Holy One of I, who has chosen you." 3776
52:12 the God of I will be your rear guard. 3776
54: 5 the Holy One of I is your Redeemer; 3776
55: 5 the LORD your God, the Holy One of I, 3776
56: 8 he who gathers the exiles of I: 3776
57:19 on the lips of the mourners in I. 2257S
60: 9 the LORD your God, the Holy One of I, 3776
60:14 Zion of the Holy One of I. 3776
63: 7 for the house of I, 3776
63:16 not know us or I acknowledge us; 3776
Jer 2: 3 I was holy to the LORD, 3776
2: 4 all you clans of the house of I. 3776
2:14 Is I a servant, a slave by birth? 3776
2:26 so the house of I is disgraced— 3776
2:31 a desert to I or a land of great darkness? 3776
3: 6 "Have you seen what faithless I has done? 3776
3: 8 I gave faithless I her certificate of divorce 3776
3:11 "Faithless I is more righteous than unfaithful Judah. 3776
Jer 3:12 " 'Return, faithless I,' declares the LORD, 3776
3:18 the house of Judah will join the house of I, 3776
3:20 O house of I," declares the LORD. 3776
3:21 weeping and pleading of the people of I, 3776
3:23 in the LORD our God is the salvation of I. 3776
4: 1 "If you will return, O I, return to me," 3776
5:11 The house of I and the house 3776
5:15 O house of I," declares the LORD, 3776
6: 9 the remnant of I as thoroughly as a vine; 3776
7: 3 the LORD Almighty, the God of I, says: 3776
7:12 because of the wickedness of my people I. 3776
7:21 the LORD Almighty, the God of I, says: 3776
9:15 the LORD Almighty, the God of I, says: 3776
9:26 even the whole house of I is uncircumcised 3776
10: 1 the LORD says to you, O house of I. 3776
10:16 including I, the tribe of his inheritance— 3776
11: 3 the LORD, the God of I, says: 3776
11:10 of I and the house of Judah have broken 3776
11:17 of I and the house of Judah have done evil 3776
12:14 the inheritance I gave my people I, 3776
13:11 of I and the whole house of Judah to me,' 3776
13:12 'This is what the LORD, the God of I, 3776
14: 8 O Hope of I, its Savior in times of distress, 3776
16: 9 the LORD Almighty, the God of I, says: 3776
17:13 O LORD, the hope of I, 3776
18: 6 "O house of I, can I not do with you as 3776
18: 6 so are you in my hand, O house of I. 3776
18:13 A most horrible thing has been done by Virgin I. 3776
19: 3 LORD Almighty, the God of I, says: Listen! 3776
19:15 LORD Almighty, the God of I, says: 'Listen! 3776
21: 4 the LORD the God of I, says: 3776
23: 2 the LORD the God of I, says to 3776
23: 6 be saved and I will live in safety. 3776
23: 8 who brought the descendants of I up 1074+3776
23:13 by Baal and led my people I astray. 3776
24: 5 the LORD, the God of I, says: 3776
25:15 This is what the LORD, the God of I, 3776
25:27 the LORD Almighty, the God of I, says: 3776
27: 4 the LORD Almighty, the God of I, says: 3776
27:21 the LORD Almighty, the God of I, says 3776
28: 2 the God of I, says: 3776
28:14 the LORD Almighty, the God of I, says: 3776
29: 4 the LORD Almighty, of I, says 3776
29: 8 the LORD Almighty, the God of I, says: 3776
29:21 God of I, says about Ahab son of Kolaiah 3776
29:23 For they have done outrageous things in I; 3776
29:25 the LORD Almighty, the God of I, says: 3776
30: 2 the LORD, the God of I, says: 3776
30: 3 'when I will bring my people I 3776
30: 4 the LORD spoke concerning I and Judah: 3776
30:10 do not be dismayed, O I,' 3776
31: 1 "I will be the God of all the clans of I, 3776
31: 2 I will come to give rest to I." 3776
31: 4 and you will be rebuilt, O Virgin I. 3776
31: 7 save your people, the remnant of I.' 3776
31:10 'He who scattered I will gather them 3776
31:21 Return, O Virgin I, return to your towns. 3776
31:23 the LORD Almighty, the God of I, says: 3776
31:27 the house of I and the house of Judah with 3776
31:31 the house of I and with the house of Judah. 3776
31:33 with the house of I after that time," 3776
31:36 "will the descendants of I ever cease to be 3776
31:37 of I because of all they have done," 3776
32:14 the LORD Almighty, the God of I, says: 3776
32:15 the LORD Almighty, the God of I, says: 3776
32:20 both in I and among all mankind, 3776
32:21 You brought your people I out of Egypt 3776
32:30 of I and Judah have done nothing but evil 3776
32:30 indeed, the people of I have done nothing 3776
32:32 of I and Judah have provoked me by all 3776
32:36 but this is what the LORD, the God of I, 3776
33: 4 For this is what the LORD, the God of I, 3776
33: 7 I will bring Judah and I back from captivity 3776
33:14 to the house of I and to the house of Judah. 3776
33:17 a man to sit on the throne of the house of I, 3776
34: 2 the LORD, the God of I, says: 3776
34:13 the LORD, the God of I, says: 3776
35:13 the LORD Almighty, the God of I, says: 3776
35:17 LORD Almighty, the God of I, says: 'Listen! 3776
35:18 the LORD Almighty, the God of I, says: 3776
35:19 the LORD Almighty, the God of I, says: 3776
36: 2 to you concerning I, Judah and all 3776
37: 7 the LORD, the God of I, says: 3776
38:17 the LORD Almighty, the God of I, says: 3776
39:16 the LORD Almighty, the God of I, says: 3776
41: 9 of his defense against Baasha king of I. 3776
42: 9 "This is what the LORD, the God of I, 3776
42:15 the LORD Almighty, the God of I, says: 3776
42:18 the LORD Almighty, the God of I, says: 3776
43:10 the LORD Almighty, the God of I, says: 3776
44: 2 the LORD Almighty, the God of I, says: 3776
44: 7 the LORD Almighty, the God of I, says: 3776
44:11 the LORD Almighty, the God of I, says: 3776
44:25 the LORD Almighty, the God of I, says: 3776
45: 2 the LORD, the God of I, says to you, Baruch: 3776
46:25 The LORD Almighty, the God of I, says: 3776
46:27 do not be dismayed, O I. 3776
48: 1 the LORD Almighty, the God of I, says: 3776
48:13 house of I was ashamed when they trusted 3776
48:27 Was not I the object of your ridicule? 3776
49: 1 "Has I no sons? 3776
49: 2 I will drive out those who drove her out," 3776
50: 4 "the people of I and the people 3776
50:17 "I is a scattered flock 3776
50:18 the LORD Almighty, the God of I, says: 3776
50:19 But I will bring I back to his own pasture 3776

Jer 50:29 the LORD, the Holy One of I. 3776
50:33 "The people of I are oppressed, 3776
51: 5 For I and Judah have not been forsaken 3776
51: 5 of guilt before the Holy One of I. 3776
51:33 the LORD Almighty, the God of I, says: 3776
La 2: 1 the splendor of I from heaven to earth; 3776
2: 3 fierce anger he has cut off every horn of I. 3776
2: 5 he has swallowed up I. 3776
Eze 3: 1 then go and speak to the house of I." 3776
3: 4 the house of I and speak my words to them. 3776
3: 5 but to the house of I— 3776
3: 7 the house of I is not willing to listen to you 3776
3: 7 whole house of I is hardened and obstinate. 3776
3:17 a watchman for the house of I; 3776
4: 3 This will be a sign to the house of I. 3776
4: 4 the sin of the house of I upon yourself. 3776
4: 5 the sin of the house of I. 3776
4:13 of I will eat defiled food among the nations 3776
5: 4 from there to the whole house of I. 3776
6: 2 set your face against the mountains of I; 3776
6: 3 'O mountains of I, 3776
6:11 and detestable practices of the house of I, 3776
7: 2 the Sovereign LORD says to the land of I: 3776
8: 4 before me was the glory of the God of I, 3776
8: 6 the house of I is doing here, 3776
8:10 and all the idols of the house of I. 3776
8:11 elders of the house of I, 3776
8:12 of the house of I are doing in the darkness, 3776
9: 3 of I went up from above the cherubim, 3776
9: 8 the entire remnant of I in this outpouring 3776
9: 9 of I and Judah is exceedingly great; 3776
10:19 the glory of the God of I was above them. 3776
10:20 the God of I by the Kebar River, 3776
11: 5 That is what you are saying, O house of I, 3776
11:10 on you at the borders of I. 3776
11:11 on you at the borders of I. 3776
11:13 the remnant of I?" 3776
11:15 and the whole house of I— 3776
11:17 the land of I again.' 3776
11:22 the glory of the God of I was above them. 3776
12: 6 I have made you a sign to the house of I." 3776
12: 9 did not that rebellious house of I ask you, 3776
12:10 and the whole house of I who are there.' 3776
12:19 in Jerusalem and in the land of I: 3776
12:22 proverb you have in the land of I: 3776
12:23 and they will no longer quote it in I.' 3776
12:24 among the people of I. 3776
12:27 the house of I is saying, 3776
13: 2 the prophets of I who are now prophesying. 3776
13: 4 O I, are like jackals among ruins. 3776
13: 5 of I so that it will stand firm in the battle on 3776
13: 9 or be listed in the records of the house of I, 3776
13: 9 nor will they enter the land of I. 3776
13:16 those prophets of I who prophesied 3776
14: 1 Some of the elders of I came to me and sat 3776
14: 5 to recapture the hearts of the people of I, 3776
14: 6 "Therefore say to the house of I, 3776
14: 7 or any alien living in I separates himself 3776
14: 9 and destroy him from among my people I. 3776
14:11 people of I will no longer stray from me, 3776
17: 2 set forth an allegory and tell the house of I 3776
17:23 On the mountain heights of I I will plant it; 3776
18: 2 by quoting this proverb about the land of I: 3776
18: 3 you will no longer quote this proverb in I. 3776
18: 6 or look to the idols of the house of I. 3776
18:15 or look to the idols of the house of I. 3776
18:25 Hear, O house of I: Is my way unjust? 3776
18:29 Yet the house of I says, 3776
18:29 Are my ways unjust, O house of I? 3776
18:30 "Therefore, O house of I, I will judge you, 3776
18:31 Why will you die, O house of I? 3776
19: 1 up a lament concerning the princes of I 3776
19: 9 on the mountains of I. 3776
20: 1 some of the elders of I came to inquire of 3776
20: 3 speak to the elders of I and say to them, 3776
20: 5 On the day I chose I, 3776
20:13 " 'Yet the people of I rebelled against me 3776
20:27 speak to the people of I and say to them, 3776
20:30 "Therefore say to the house of I: 3776
20:31 let you inquire of me, O house of I? 3776
20:38 yet they will not enter the land of I. 3776
20:39 " 'As for you, O house of I, 3776
20:40 my holy mountain, the high mountain of I, 3776
20:40 the entire house of I will serve me, 3776
20:42 when I bring you into the land of I, 3776
20:44 your corrupt practices, O house of I, 3776
21: 2 Prophesy against the land of I 3776
21:12 it is against all the princes of I. 3776
21:25 " 'O profane and wicked prince of I, 3776
22: 6 " 'See how each of the princes of I who are 3776
22:18 the house of I has become dross to me; 3776
24:21 Say to the house of I, 'This is what 3776
25: 3 over the land of I when it was laid waste 3776
25: 6 of your heart against the land of I, 3776
25:14 the hand of my people I, and they will deal 3776
27:17 " 'Judah and I traded with you; 824+3776
28:24 the people of I have malicious neighbors 3776
28:25 When I gather the people of I from 3776
29: 6 a staff of reed for the house of I. 3776
29:16 of confidence for the people of I but will be 3776
29:21 a horn grow for the house of I, 3776
33: 7 a watchman for the house of I; 3776
33:10 "Son of man, say to the house of I, 3776
33:11 Why will you die, O house of I?' 3776
33:20 Yet, O house of I, you say, 3776
33:24 in those ruins in the land of I are saying, 3776
33:28 the mountains of I will become desolate so 3776
Eze 34: 2 prophesy against the shepherds of I; 3776
34: 2 to the shepherds of I who only take care 3776
34:13 I will pasture them on the mountains of I, 3776
34:14 and the mountain heights of I will 3776
34:14 in a rich pasture on the mountains of I. 3776
34:30 am with them and that they, the house of I, 3776
35:12 against the mountains of I. 3776
35:15 of the house of I became desolate, 3776
36: 1 prophesy to the mountains of I and say, 3776
36: 1 'O mountains of I, hear the word of 3776
36: 4 O mountains of I, hear the word of 3776
36: 6 of I and say to the mountains and hills, to 3776
36: 8 " 'But you, O mountains of I, 3776
36: 8 and fruit for my people I, 3776
36:10 even the whole house of I. 3776
36:12 I will cause people, my people I, 3776
36:17 people of I were living in their own land, 3776
36:21 the house of I profaned among the nations 3776
36:22 "Therefore say to the house of I, 3776
36:22 It is not for your sake, O house of I, 3776
36:32 disgraced for your conduct, O house of I! 3776
36:37 to the plea of the house of I and do this 3776
37:11 these bones are the whole house of I. 3776
37:12 I will bring you back to the land of I. 3776
37:16 and all the house of I associated with him.' 3776
37:22 on the mountains of I. 3776
37:28 that I the LORD make I holy, 3776
38: 8 from many nations to the mountains of I, 3776
38:14 when my people I are living in safety, 3776
38:16 against my people I like a cloud that covers 3776
38:17 by my servants the prophets of I? 3776
38:18 When Gog attacks the land of I, 3776
38:19 be a great earthquake in the land of I. 3776
39: 2 and send you against the mountains of I. 3776
39: 4 On the mountains of I you will fall, 3776
39: 7 my holy name among my people I. 3776
39: 7 that I the LORD am the Holy One in I. 3776
39: 9 of I will go out and use the weapons 3776
39:11 that day I will give Gog a burial place in I, 3776
39:12 the house of I will be burying them in order 3776
39:17 the great sacrifice on the mountains of I. 3776
39:22 that day forward the house of I will know 3776
39:23 the people of I went into exile for their sin, 3776
39:25 have compassion on all the people of I, 3776
39:29 I will pour out my Spirit on the house of I, 3776
40: 2 of I and set me on a very high mountain, 3776
40: 4 Tell the house of I everything you see." 3776
43: 2 and I saw the glory of the God of I coming 3776
43: 7 of I will never again defile my holy name— 3776
43:10 describe the temple to the people of I, 3776
44: 2 the God of I, has entered through it. 3776
44: 6 Say to the rebellious house of I, 3776
44: 6 of your detestable practices, O house of I! 3776
44:10 when I went astray and who wandered 3776
44:12 of their idols and made the house of I fall 3776
44:28 You are to give them no possession in I; 3776
44:29 in I devoted to the LORD will belong 3776
45: 6 it will belong to the whole house of I. 3776
45: 8 This land will be his possession in I. 3776
45: 8 the house of I to possess the land according 3776
45: 9 You have gone far enough, O princes of I! 3776
45:15 from the well-watered pastures of I. 3776
45:16 for the use of the prince in I. 3776
45:17 at all the appointed feasts of the house of I. 3776
45:17 to make atonement for the house of I. 3776
47:13 an inheritance among the twelve tribes of I, 3776
47:18 between Gilead and the land of I, 3776
47:21 according to the tribes of I. 3776
47:22 an inheritance among the tribes of I. 3776
48:19 from all the tribes of I. 3776
48:29 to allot as an inheritance to the tribes of I, 3776
48:31 the city will be named after the tribes of I. 3776
Da 9: 7 of Judah and people of Jerusalem and all I, 3776
9:11 All I has transgressed your law 3776
9:20 of my people I and making my request to 3776
Hos 1: 1 of Jeroboam son of Jehoash king of I: 3776
1: 4 I will put an end to the kingdom of I. 1074+3776
1: 6 no longer show love to the house of I, 3776
1:11 and the people of I will be reunited, 3776
4:15 "Though you commit adultery, O I, 3776
5: 3 I is not hidden from me. 3776
5: 3 to prostitution; I is corrupt. 3776
5: 9 the tribes of I I proclaim what is certain. 3776
6:10 a horrible thing in the house of I. 3776
6:10 to prostitution and I is defiled. 3776
7: 1 whenever I would heal I, 3776
8: 2 I cries out to me, 'O our God, 3776
8: 3 But I has rejected what is good; 3776
8: 6 They are from I! 3776
8: 8 I is swallowed up; 3776
8:14 I has forgotten his Maker and built palaces; 3776
9: 1 Do not rejoice, O I; 3776
9: 7 Let I know this. Because your sins are so 3776
9:10 "When I found I, it was like finding grapes 3776
10: 1 I was a spreading vine; 3776
10: 6 I will be ashamed of its wooden idols. 3776
10: 8 it is the sin of I. 3776
10: 9 the days of Gibeah, you have sinned, O I, 3776
10:15 the king of I will be completely destroyed. 3776
11: 1 "When I was a child, I loved him, 3776
11: 2 But the more I called I, 2157S
11: 8 How can I hand you over, I? 3776
11:12 the house of I with deceit. 3776
12:12 I served to get a wife, 3776
12:13 The LORD used a prophet to bring I up 3776
13: 1 he was exalted in I. 3776
13: 9 "You are destroyed, O I, 3776
Hos 14: 1 Return, O I, to the LORD your God. 3776
14: 5 I will be like the dew to I; 3776
Joel 2:27 Then you will know that I am in I, 3776
3: 2 my people I, for they scattered my people 3776
3:16 a stronghold for the people of I. 3776
Am 1: 1 what he saw concerning I two years before 3776
1: 1 of Jehoash was king of I. 3776
2: 6 "For three sins of I, even for four, 3776
2:11 Is this not true, people of I?" 3776
3: 1 O people of I—against the whole family 3776
3:14 "On the day I punish I for her sins, 3776
4:12 "Therefore this is what I will do to you, I, 3776
4:12 prepare to meet your God, O I." 3776
5: 1 Hear this word, O house of I, 3776
5: 2 "Fallen is Virgin I, never to rise again, 3776
5: 3 a thousand strong for I will have only 1074+3776
5: 4 the LORD says to the house of I: 3776
5:25 O house of I? 3776
6: 1 to whom the people of I come! 3776
6:14 O house of I, 3776
7: 8 a plumb line among my people I; 3776
7: 9 be destroyed and the sanctuaries of I will 3776
7:10 a message to Jeroboam king of I: 3776
7:10 against you in the very heart of I. 1074+3776
7:11 and I will surely go into exile, 3776
7:15 'Go, prophesy to my people I.' 3776
7:16 You say, " 'Do not prophesy against I, 3776
7:17 And I will certainly go into exile, 3776
8: 2 "The time is ripe for my people I; 3776
9: 7 "Did I not bring I up from Egypt, 3776
9: 9 and I will shake the house of I among all 3776
9:14 I will bring back my exiled people I; 3776
9:15 I will plant I in their own land, 4392S
Mic 1: 5 because of the sins of the house of I. 3776
1:13 the transgressions of I were found in you. 3776
1:14 will prove deceptive to the kings of I. 3776
1:15 the glory of I will come to Adullam. 3776
2:12 surely bring together the remnant of I. 3776
3: 1 you rulers of the house of I. 3776
3: 8 to Jacob his transgression, to I his sin. 3776
3: 9 you rulers of the house of I, 3776
5: 2 for me one who will be ruler over I, 3776
5: 3 Therefore I will be abandoned until 4392S
6: 2 he is lodging a charge against I. 3776
Na 2: 2 the splendor of Jacob like the splendor of I, 3776
Zep 2: 9 the God of I, "surely Moab will become 3776
3:13 The remnant of I will do no wrong; 3776
3:14 shout aloud, O I! 3776
3:15 The LORD, the King of I, is with you; 3776
Zec 1:19 that scattered Judah, I and Jerusalem." 3776
8:13 O Judah and I, so will I save you, 1074+3776
9: 1 and all the tribes of I are on the LORD— 3776
11:14 the brotherhood between Judah and I. 3776
12: 1 the word of the LORD concerning I. 3776
Mal 1: 1 word of the LORD to I through Malachi. 3776
1: 5 even beyond the borders of I!' 3776
2:11 A detestable thing has been committed in I 3776
2:16 "I hate divorce," says the LORD God of I, 3776
4: 4 and laws I gave him at Horeb for all I. 3776
Mt 2: 6 be the shepherd of my people I.' " 2702
2:20 and his mother and go to the land *of* I, 2702
2:21 and his mother and went to the land *of* I. 2702
8:10 not found anyone in I with such great faith. 2702
9:33 "Nothing like this has ever been seen in I." 2702
10: 6 Go rather to the lost sheep *of* I. 2702+3875
10:23 not finish going through the cities *of* I 2702
15:24 I was sent only to the lost sheep *of* I. 2702+3875
15:31 And they praised the God *of* I. 2702
19:28 judging the twelve tribes *of* I. 2702
27: 9 price set on him by the people *of* I, 2702+5626
27:42 He's the King *of* I! 2702
Mk 12:29 'Hear, O I, the Lord our God, 2702
15:32 Let this Christ, this King *of* I, 2702
Lk 1:16 Many of the people *of* I will he bring back 2702
1:54 He has helped his servant I, 2702
1:68 "Praise be to the Lord, the God *of* I, 2702
1:80 in the desert until he appeared publicly to I. 2702
2:25 He was waiting for the consolation *of* I, 2702
2:32 the Gentiles and for glory to your people I." 2702
2:34 to cause the falling and rising of many in I, 2702
4:25 that there were many widows in I 2702
4:27 And there were many in I with leprosy in 2702
7: 9 I have not found such great faith even in I." 2702
22:30 judging the twelve tribes *of* I. 2702
24:21 the one who was going to redeem I. 2702
Jn 1:31 that he might be revealed *to* I." 2702
1:49 you are the King *of* I." 2702
12:13 "Blessed is the King *of* I!" 2702
Ac 1: 6 to restore the kingdom *to* I?" 2702
2:22 "Men of I, listen to this: 2703
2:36 "Therefore let all I be assured of this: 2702+3875
3:12 "Men of I, why does this surprise you? 2703
4:10 you and all the people *of* I: 2702
4:27 the Gentiles and the people of I in this city 2702
5:21 the full assembly of the elders *of* I— 2702+5626
5:31 and forgiveness of sins *to* I. 2702
5:35 Then he addressed them: "Men of I, 2703
7:42 in the desert, O house *of* I? 2702
9:15 and their kings and before the people *of* I. 2702
10:36 the message God sent to the people *of* I, 2702
13:16 "Men of I and you Gentiles who worship God, 2703
13:17 God of the people *of* I chose our fathers; 2702
13:23 God has brought *to* I the Savior Jesus, 2702
13:24 and baptism to all the people *of* I. 2702
21:28 "Men of I, help us! 2703
28:20 because of the hope *of* I that I am bound 2702

Ro 9: 4 the people of I. Theirs is the adoption as *2703*
9: 6 not all who are descended from I are Israel. *2702*
9: 6 not all who are descended from Israel are I. *2702*
9:27 Isaiah cries out concerning I: *2702*
9:31 but I, who pursued a law of righteousness *2702*
10:19 Again I ask: Did I not understand? *2702*
10:21 But concerning I he says, *2702*
11: 2 how he appealed to GOD against I: *2702*
11: 7 What I sought so earnestly it did not obtain, *2702*
11:11 come to the Gentiles to make I envious. *899*[S]
11:25 I has experienced a hardening in part until *2702*
11:26 And so all I will be saved, as it is written: *2702*
1Co 10:18 Consider the people of I: *2702*
Gal 6:16 even to the I of God. *2702*
Eph 2:12 *in* I and foreigners to the covenants of *2702*
3: 6 the Gentiles are heirs together with I, *NIG*
Php 3: 5 of the people *of* I, of the tribe of *2702*
Heb 8: 8 the house *of* I and with the house of Judah. *2702*
8:10 with the house *of* I after that time, *2702*
11:28 not touch the firstborn of I. *NIG*
Rev 7: 4 144,000 from all the tribes *of* I. *2702+5626*
21:12 the names of the twelve tribes *of* I. *2702+5626*

ISRAEL'S (44) [ISRAEL]

Ge 42: 5 So I sons were among those who went 3776
46: 5 and I sons took their father Jacob 3776
48:10 I eyes were failing because of old age, 3776
48:12 Then Joseph removed them from I knees 2257[S]
48:13 toward I left hand and Manasseh on his left 3776
48:13 on his left toward I right hand, 3776
Ex 14:19 who had been traveling in front of I army, 3776
18: 8 to Pharaoh and the Egyptians for I sake and 3776
Nu 1:45 able to serve in I army were counted 928+3776
11:16 of I elders who are known to you as leaders 3776
21: 3 The LORD listened to I plea and gave 3776
25: 5 So Moses said to I judges, 3776
Jos 10:30 also gave that city and its king into I hand. 3776
Jdg 3:10 so that he became I judge and went to war. 3776
5: 9 My heart is with I princes, 3776
10:16 And he could bear I misery no longer. 3776
11:21 gave Sihon and all his men into I hands, 3776
20: 6 to each region of I inheritance, 3776
20:34 Then ten thousand of I finest men made 3776
1Sa 6: 5 and pay honor to I god. 3776
7: 9 He cried out to the LORD on I behalf, 3776
14:37 Will you give them into I hand?" 3776
2Sa 20:23 Joab was over I entire army; 3776
23: 1 by the God of Jacob, I singer of songs: 3776
23:11 I troops fled from them. 2021[S]
1Ki 2: 5 to the two commanders of I armies, 3776
2:32 Abner son of Ner, commander of I army, 3776
11:25 Rezon was I adversary as long 3776+4200
2Ki 6:23 from Aram stopped raiding I territory. 3776
1Ch 17:24 the God over Israel, is I God!' 3776+4200
2Ch 13:17 casualties among I able men. 3776
Ezr 10:10 married foreign women, adding to I guilt. 3776
Isa 43:15 I am the LORD, your Holy One, I Creator, 3776
44: 6 I King and Redeemer, the LORD Almighty 3776
56:10 I watchmen are blind, 2257[S]
Jer 3: 9 I immorality mattered so little to her, 2023[S]
31: 9 because I am I father, 3776+4200
50:20 "search will be made for I guilt, 3776
51:49 "Babylon must fall because of I slain, 3776
Hos 1: 5 In that day I will break I bow in the Valley 3776
5: 5 I arrogance testifies against them; 3776
7:10 I arrogance testifies against him, 3776
Mic 5: 1 They will strike I ruler on the cheek with 3776
Jn 3:10 "You are I teacher," said Jesus, *2702*

ISRAELITE (96) [ISRAEL]

Ge 36:31 in Edom before any I king reigned: 1201+3776
Ex 5:14 The I foremen appointed 1201+3776
5:15 I foremen went and appealed to Pharaoh: 1201+3776
5:19 The I foremen realized they were in trouble 1201+3776
12:40 the I *people* lived in Egypt was 430 years. 1201+3776
16: 1 whole I community set out from Elim 1201+3776
16: 9 "Say to the entire I community, 1201+3776
16:10 to the whole I community, 1201+3776
17: 1 The whole I community set out from 1201+3776
24: 5 Then he sent young I men, 1201+3776
35: 1 Moses assembled the whole I community 1201+3776
35: 4 Moses said to the whole I community, 1201+3776
35:20 Then the whole I community withdrew 1201+3776
35:29 All the I men and women who were 1201+3776
Lev 4:13 the whole I community sins unintentionally 3776
16: 5 From the I community he is 1201+3776
17: 3 I who sacrifices an ox, 408+1074+3776+4946
17: 8 Any I or any alien living 408+1074+3776+4946
17:10 Any I or any alien living 408+1074+3776+4946
17:13 Any I or any alien living 408+1201+3776+4946
20: 2 Any I or any alien living 408+1201+3776+4946
22:18 an I or an alien living in 408+1074+3776+4946
24:10 Now the son of an I mother and 3778
24:10 the camp between him and an I. 408+2021+3778
24:11 son of the I woman blasphemed the Name 3778
Nu 1: 2 "Take a census of the whole I community 1201+3776
1:53 that wrath will not fall on the I community. 1201+3776
3:12 first male offspring of every I woman. 1201+3776
3:40 firstborn I males who are a month old 1201+3776
7:84 the I leaders for the dedication of the altar 3776
8: 9 and assemble the whole I community. 1201+3776
8:16 first male offspring from every I woman. 1201+3776
8:20 Aaron and the whole I community did 1201+3776
10:28 for the I divisions as they set out. 1201+3776
13:26 the whole I community at Kadesh in 1201+3776
14: 5 the whole I assembly gathered there. 1201+3776
14: 7 and said to the entire I assembly, 1201+3776
15:25 for the whole I community, 1201+3776
15:26 The whole I community and 1201+3776
15:29 he is a native-born I or an alien. 928+1201+3776
16: 2 With them were 250 I men, 1201+3776
16: 9 of the I community and brought you 3776
16:41 the whole I community grumbled 1201+3776
19: 9 the I community for use in the water 1201+3776
20: 1 the whole I community arrived at 1201+3776
20:22 The whole I community set out 1201+3776
25: 6 an I man brought to his family 1201+3776+4946
25: 8 and followed the I into the tent. 408+3776
25: 8 the I and into the woman's body. 408+3776
25:14 The name of the I who was killed with 408+3776
26: 2 "Take a census of the whole I community 1201+3776
27:20 the whole I community will obey him. 1201+3776
31:12 priest and the I assembly at their camp 1201+3776
32:18 until every I has received his inheritance. 1201+3776
32:28 and to the family heads of the I tribes. 1201+3776
36: 1 the heads of the I families. 1201+3776
36: 3 from other I tribes; 1201+3776
36: 7 for every I shall keep 1201+3776
36: 8 in any I tribe must marry someone 1201+3776
36: 8 every I will possess the inheritance 1201+3776
36: 9 for each I tribe is to keep 1201+3776
Dt 15: 2 the loan he has made to his fellow I. 8276
15: 2 not require payment from his fellow I 8276
17:15 one who is not a brother I. 3870[S]
22:19 this man has given an I virgin a bad name. 3776
23:17 No I man or woman is to become 3776+4946
23:20 but not a brother I, 278
24:14 whether he is a brother I or an alien living 278
Jos 11:22 No Anakites were left in I territory; 1201+3776
18: 2 but there were still seven I tribes who 1201+3776
22:11 Geliloth near the Jordan on the I side, 1201+3776
22:14 of a family division among the I clans. 3776
Jdg 7:14 sword of Gideon son of Joash, the I. 408+3776
11:39 From this comes the I custom 928+3776
20:33 and the I ambush charged out of its place 3776
1Sa 7:13 and did not invade I territory again. 3776
31: 7 the Jordan saw that the I army had fled and 3776
2Sa 1: 3 "I have escaped from the I camp." 3776
11: 1 with the king's men and the whole I army. 3776
17:25 an I who had married Abigail, 3778
1Ki 8: 1 tribes and the chiefs of the I families, 1201+3776
2Ki 13:25 and so he recovered the I towns. 3776
1Ch 1:43 before any I king reigned: 1201+3776+4200
16: 3 a cake of raisins to each I man and 408+3776
2Ch 5: 2 tribes and the chiefs of the I families, 1201+3776
19: 8 priests and heads of I families to administer 3776
23: 2 the heads of I families from all the towns. 3776
25: 9 for these I troops?" 3776
Ne 9: 2 of I descent had separated themselves 3776
Eze 14: 4 When any I sets up idols in his heart 408+1074+3776+4946
14: 7 When any I or any alien 408+1074+3776+4946
37:19 and of the I tribes associated with him, 3776
44:22 may marry only virgins of I descent 1074+3776
Ob 1:20 of I exiles who are in Canaan 1201+3776
Jn 1:47 he said of him, "Here is a true I, *2703*
Ro 11: 1 I am an I myself, a descendant of Abraham, *2703*

ISRAELITES (611) [ISRAEL]

Ge 32:32 the I do not eat the tendon attached to 1201+3776
47:27 I settled in Egypt in the region of Goshen. 3776
Ex 1: 7 I were fruitful and multiplied greatly 1201+3776
1: 9 I have become much too numerous for us. 1201+3776+6639
1:12 so the Egyptians came to dread the I 1201+3776
2:23 The I groaned in their slavery 1201+3776
2:25 So God looked on the I and was concerned about them. 1201+3776
3: 9 now the cry of the I has reached me, 1201+3776
3:10 Pharaoh to bring my people the I out 1201+3776
3:11 Pharaoh and bring the I out of Egypt? 1201+3776
3:13 Suppose I go to the I and say to them, 1201+3776
3:14 This is what you are to say to the I: 1201+3776
3:15 God also said to Moses, "Say to the I, 1201+3776
4:29 the elders of the I, 1201+3776
6: 5 I have heard the groaning of the I, 1201+3776
6: 6 "Therefore, say to the I: 1201+3776
6: 9 Moses reported this to the I, 1201+3776
6:11 to let the I go out of his country." 1201+3776
6:12 "If the I will not listen to me, 1201+3776
6:13 to Moses and Aaron about the I 1201+3776
6:13 he commanded them to bring the I out 1201+3776
6:26 the I out of Egypt by their divisions." 1201+3776
6:27 about bringing the I out of Egypt. 1201+3776
7: 2 to tell Pharaoh to let the I go out 1201+3776
7: 4 my people the I. 1201+3776
7: 5 against Egypt and bring the I out of it. 1201+3776
9: 4 no animal belonging to the I will die. 1201+3776
9: 6 not one animal belonging to the I died. 1201+3776
9: 7 even one of the animals of the I had died. 3776
9:26 Goshen, where the I were. 1201+3776
9:35 and he would not let the I go, 1201+3776
Ex 10:20 and he would not let the I go. 1201+3776
10:23 Yet all the I had light in the places 1201+3776
11: 7 the I not a dog will bark at any man 1201+3776
11:10 not let the I go out of his country. 1201+3776
12:27 the I in Egypt and spared our homes 1201+3776
12:28 The I did just what the LORD 1201+3776
12:31 Leave my people, you and the I! 1201+3776
12:35 The I did as Moses instructed and 1201+3776
12:37 The I journeyed from Rameses to 1201+3776
12:42 I are to keep vigil to honor the LORD 1201+3776
12:50 All the I did just what 1201+3776
12:51 very day the LORD brought the I out 1201+3776
13: 2 first offspring of every womb among the I belongs to me, 1201+3776
13:18 The I went up out of Egypt armed 1201+3776
14: 2 "Tell the I to turn back and encamp 1201+3776
14: 3 'The I are wandering around the land 1201+3776
14: 4 So the I did this. NIH
14: 5 the I go and have lost their services!" 3776
14: 8 so that he pursued the I, 1201+3776
14: 9 pursued the I and overtook them 2157[S]
14:10 Pharaoh approached, the I looked up, 1201+3776
14:15 Tell the I to move on. 1201+3776
14:16 the I can go through the sea on dry ground. 1201+3776
14:22 the I went through the sea on dry ground, 1201+3776
14:25 "Let's get away from the I! 3776
14:28 of Pharaoh that had followed the I into 2157[S]
14:29 the I went through the sea on dry ground, 1201+3776
14:31 And when the I saw the great power 3776
15: 1 Then Moses and the I sang this song to 1201+3776
15:19 the I walked through the sea on dry ground. 1201+3776
16: 3 The I said to them, 1201+3776
16: 6 So Moses and Aaron said to all the I, 1201+3776
16:12 "I have heard the grumbling of the I. 1201+3776
16:15 When the I saw it, they said to each 1201+3776
16:17 The I did as they were told; 1201+3776
16:35 The I ate manna forty years, 1201+3776
17: 7 and Meribah because the I quarreled 1201+3776
17: 8 The Amalekites came and attacked the I 3776
17:11 the I were winning, 3776
19: 1 the third month after the I left Egypt 1201+3776
19: 6 the words you are to speak to the I." 1201+3776
20:22 the LORD said to Moses, "Tell the I 1201+3776
24:11 against these leaders of the I; 1201+3776
24:17 the I the glory of the LORD looked like 1201+3776
25: 2 "Tell the I to bring me an offering. 1201+3776
25:22 give you all my commands for the I. 1201+3776
27:20 the I to bring you clear oil of pressed olives 1201+3776
27:21 the I for the generations to come. 1201+3776
28: 1 to you from among the I, 1201+3776
28:30 decisions for the I over his heart 1201+3776
28:38 in the sacred gifts the I consecrate, 1201+3776
29:28 the regular share from the I for Aaron 1201+3776
29:28 It is the contribution the I are to make 1201+3776
29:43 there also I will meet with the I, 1201+3776
29:45 I will dwell among the I and be their God. 1201+3776
30:12 take a census of the I to count them, 1201+3776
30:16 the atonement money from the I and 1201+3776
30:16 a memorial for the I before the LORD, 1201+3776
30:31 Say to the I, 1201+3776
31:13 "Say to the I, 1201+3776
31:16 The I are to observe the Sabbath, 1201+3776
31:17 a sign between me and the I forever, 1201+3776
32:20 on the water and made the I drink it. 1201+3776
33: 5 LORD had said to Moses, "Tell the I, 1201+3776
33: 6 So the I stripped off their ornaments 1201+3776
34:30 When Aaron and all the I saw Moses, 1201+3776
34:32 Afterward all the I came near him, 1201+3776
34:34 the I what he had been commanded, 1201+3776
35:30 Then Moses said to the I, "See, 1201+3776
36: 3 offerings the I had brought to 1201+3776
39:32 The I did everything just as 1201+3776
39:42 The I had done all the work just as 1201+3776
40:36 In all the travels of the I, 1201+3776
Lev 1: 2 "Speak to the I and say to them: 1201+3776
4: 2 "Say to the I: 1201+3776
7:23 "Say to the I: 1201+3776
7:29 "Say to the I: 1201+3776
7:34 From the fellowship offerings of the I 1201+3776
7:34 as their regular share from the I.' " 1201+3776
7:36 the I give this to them as their regular share 1201+3776
7:38 I to bring their offerings to the LORD, 1201+3776
9: 3 Then say to the I: 1201+3776
10:11 you must teach the I all the decrees 1201+3776
11: 2 "Say to the I: 1201+3776
12: 2 "Say to the I: 1201+3776
15: 2 "Speak to the I and say to them: 1201+3776
15:31 " 'You must keep the I separate 1201+3776
16:16 the uncleanness and rebellion of the I, 1201+3776
16:19 from the uncleanness of the I. 1201+3776
16:21 the wickedness and rebellion of the I 1201+3776
16:34 a year for all the sins of the I." 1201+3776
17: 2 to Aaron and his sons and to all the I 1201+3776
17: 5 This is so the I will bring to the LORD 1201+3776
17:12 Therefore I say to the I, 1201+3776
17:14 That is why I have said to the I, 1201+3776
18: 2 "Speak to the I and say to them: 1201+3776
20: 2 "Say to the I: 1201+3776
21:24 to Aaron and his sons and to all the I. 1201+3776
22: 2 sacred offerings the I consecrate to 1201+3776

Lev 22: 3 sacred offerings that the I consecrate 1201+3776
22:15 the sacred offerings the I present to 1201+3776
22:18 to Aaron and his sons and to all the I 1201+3776
22:32 I must be acknowledged as holy by the I. 1201+3776
23: 2 "Speak to the I and say to them: 1201+3776
23:10 "Speak to the I and say to them: 1201+3776
23:24 "Say to the I: 1201+3776
23:34 "Say to the I: 1201+3776
23:42 All native-born I are to live in booths 3776
23:43 that I had the I live in booths 1201+3776
23:44 the I the appointed feasts of the LORD. 1201+3776
24: 2 "Command the I to bring you clear oil of pressed olives 1201+3776
24: 8 after Sabbath, on behalf of the I, 1201+3776
24:10 went out among the I, 1201+3776
24:15 Say to the I: 1201+3776
24:23 Then Moses spoke to the I, 1201+3776
24:23 The I did as the LORD commanded 1201+3776
25: 2 "Speak to the I and say to them: 1201+3776
25:33 Levites are their property among the I. 1201+3776
25:42 Because the I are my servants, 2156S
25:46 not rule over your fellow I ruthlessly. 1201+3776
25:55 for the I belong to me as servants. 1201+3776
26:46 Sinai between himself and the I 1201+3776
27: 2 "Speak to the I and say to them: 1201+3776
27:34 on Mount Sinai for the I. 1201+3776
Nu 1: 1 of the second year after the I came out 4392S
1:45 All the I twenty years old 1201+3776
1:49 them in the census of the other I. 1201+3776
1:52 I are to set up their tents by divisions, 1201+3776
1:54 The I did all this just as 1201+3776
2: 2 "The I are to camp around the Tent 1201+3776
2:32 These are the I, 1201+3776
2:33 not counted along with the other I, 1201+3776
2:34 So the I did everything 1201+3776
3: 8 fulfilling the obligations of the I by 1201+3776
3: 9 are the I who are to be given wholly 1201+3776
3:12 "I have taken the Levites from among the I 1201+3776
3:38 of the sanctuary on behalf of the I. 1201+3776
3:41 in place of all the firstborn of the I, 1201+3776
3:41 the firstborn of the livestock of the I. 1201+3776
3:42 So Moses counted all the firstborn of the I, 1201+3776
3:46 273 firstborn I who exceed the number 1201+3776
3:48 the redemption of the additional I to Aaron 2157S
3:50 firstborn of the I he collected silver 1201+3776
5: 2 "Command the I to send away from 1201+3776
5: 4 The I did this; 1201+3776
5: 6 "Say to the I: 1201+3776
5: 9 All the sacred contributions the I bring 1201+3776
5:12 "Speak to the I and say to them: 1201+3776
6: 2 "Speak to the I and say to them: 1201+3776
6:23 'This is how you are to bless the I. 1201+3776
6:27 "So they will put my name on the I, 1201+3776
8: 6 the Levites from among the other I 1201+3776
8:10 the I are to lay their hands on them. 1201+3776
8:11 LORD as a wave offering from the I, 1201+3776
8:14 set the Levites apart from the other I, 1201+3776
8:16 are the I who are to be given wholly 1201+3776
8:19 Of all the I, 1201+3776
8:19 the I and to make atonement for them 1201+3776
8:19 so that no plague will strike the I 1201+3776
9: 2 "Have the I celebrate the Passover at 1201+3776
9: 4 told the I to celebrate the Passover, 1201+3776
9: 5 The I did everything just as 1201+3776
9: 7 the LORD's offering with the other I at 1201+3776
9:10 "Tell the I: 'When any of you 1201+3776
9:17 from above the Tent, the I set out; 1201+3776
9:17 the cloud settled, the I encamped. 1201+3776
9:18 At the LORD's command the I set out, 1201+3776
9:19 the I obeyed the LORD's order and did 1201+3776
9:22 the I would remain in camp and not 1201+3776
10:12 the I set out from the Desert of Sinai 1201+3776
11: 4 again the I started wailing and said, 1201+3776
13: 2 which I am giving to the I. 1201+3776
13: 3 All of them were leaders of the I. 1201+3776
13:24 cluster of grapes the I cut off there. 1201+3776
13:32 they spread among the I a bad report 1201+3776
14: 2 I grumbled against Moses and Aaron, 1201+3776
14:10 at the Tent of Meeting to all the I. 1201+3776
14:27 the complaints of these grumbling I. 1201+3776
14:39 When Moses reported this to all the I, 1201+3776
15: 2 "Speak to the I and say to them: 1201+3776
15:18 "Speak to the I and say to them: 1201+3776
15:32 While the I were in the desert, 1201+3776
15:38 "Speak to the I and say to them: 1201+3776
16:34 At their cries, all the I around them fled, 3776
16:38 Let them be a sign to the I." 1201+3776
16:40 to remind the I that no one except 1201+3776
17: 2 the I and get twelve staffs from them, 1201+3776
17: 5 grumbling against you by the I." 1201+3776
17: 6 So Moses spoke to the I, 1201+3776
17: 9 from the LORD's presence to all the I. 1201+3776
17:12 The I said to Moses, "We will die! 1201+3776
18: 5 that wrath will not fall on the I again. 1201+3776
18: 6 from among the I as a gift to you, 1201+3776
18: 8 all the holy offerings the I give me 1201+3776
18:11 gifts of all the wave offerings of the I. 1201+3776
18:19 the I present to the LORD I give to you 1201+3776
18:20 and your inheritance among the I. 1201+3776
18:22 the I must not go near the Tent of Meeting, 1201+3776
18:23 receive no inheritance among the I. 1201+3776
18:24 tithes that the I present as an offering 1201+3776
18:24 will have no inheritance among the I. 1201+3776
Nu 18:26 'When you receive from the I 1201+3776
18:28 all the tithes you receive from the I. 1201+3776
18:32 not defile the holy offerings of the I, 1201+3776
19: 2 Tell the I to bring you a red heifer 1201+3776
19:10 a lasting ordinance both for the I and 1201+3776
20:12 honor me as holy in the sight of the I, 1201+3776
20:13 the I quarreled with the LORD and 1201+3776
20:19 The I replied: "We will go along the 1201+3776
20:24 He will not enter the land I give the I, 1201+3776
21: 1 he attacked the I and captured some 3776
21: 6 they bit the people and many I died. 3776+4946
21:10 The I moved on and camped at Oboth 1201+3776
21:32 the I captured its surrounding settlements NIH
22: 1 the I traveled to the plains of Moab 1201+3776
22: 3 with dread because of the I. 1201+3776
25: 8 the plague against the I was stopped; 1201+3776
25:11 has turned my anger away from the I; 1201+3776
25:13 God and made atonement for the I." 1201+3776
26: 4 were the I who came out of Egypt: 1201+3776
26:62 not counted along with the other I 1201+3776
26:63 the I on the plains of Moab by the 1201+3776
26:64 when they counted the I in the Desert 1201+3776
26:65 For the LORD had told those I they would 2157S
27: 8 "Say to the I, 1201+3776
27:11 is to be a legal requirement for the I, 1201+3776
27:12 and see the land I have given the I. 1201+3776
27:21 entire community of the I will go out, 1201+3776
28: 2 "Give this command to the I and say 1201+3776
29:40 I all that the LORD commanded him. 1201+3776
31: 2 on the Midianites for the I. 1201+3776
31: 9 The I captured the Midianite women 1201+3776
31:16 were the means of turning the I away 1201+3776
31:42 The half belonging to the I, 1201+3776
31:54 of Meeting as a memorial for the I 1201+3776
32: 7 do you discourage the I from going 1201+3776
32: 9 they discouraged the I from entering 1201+3776
32:17 of the I until we have brought them 1201+3776
33: 1 journey of the I when they came out 1201+3776
33: 3 The I set out from Rameses on 1201+3776
33: 5 The I left Rameses and camped at 1201+3776
33:38 the fortieth year after the I came out 1201+3776
33:40 heard that the I were coming. 1201+3776
33:51 "Speak to the I and say to them: 1201+3776
34: 2 "Command the I and say to them: 1201+3776
34:13 Moses commanded the I: 1201+3776
34:29 the inheritance to the I in the land 1201+3776
35: 2 the I to give the Levites towns 1201+3776
35: 2 in from the inheritance the I will possess. 4392S
35: 8 the land the I possess are to be given 1201+3776
35:10 "Speak to the I and say to them: 1201+3776
35:15 be a place of refuge for I, 1201+3776
35:34 for I, the LORD, dwell among the I.'" 1201+3776
36: 2 give the land as an inheritance to the I 1201+3776
36: 4 the Year of Jubilee for the I comes, 1201+3776
36: 5 Moses gave this order to the I: 1201+3776
36:13 the LORD gave through Moses to the I 1201+3776
Dt 1: 3 Moses proclaimed to the I all that 1201+3776
1:16 between brother I or between one of them 278
3:18 cross over ahead of your brother I. 1201+3776
4:44 This is the law Moses set before the I. 1201+3776
4:46 and was defeated by Moses and the I 1201+3776
10: 6 (The I traveled from the wells of 1201+3776
24: 7 of his brother I and treats him as a slave 1201+3776+4946
29: 1 to make with the I in Moab, 1201+3776
29: 2 Moses summoned all the I and said 3776
31:19 this song and teach it to the I 1201+3776
31:22 that day and taught it to the I. 1201+3776
31:23 you will bring the I into the land I promised them on oath, 1201+3776
32:49 the I as their own possession. 1201+3776
32:51 the I at the waters of Meribah Kadesh 1201+3776
32:51 not uphold my holiness among the I. 1201+3776
33: 1 the man of God pronounced on the I 1201+3776
34: 8 The I grieved for Moses in the plains 1201+3776
34: 9 So the I listened to him and did what 1201+3776
Jos 1: 2 to give to them—to the I. 1201+3776
2: 2 Some of the I have come here tonight to spy out 1201+3776
3: 1 and all the I set out from Shittim and 1201+3776
3: 9 Joshua said to the I, 1201+3776
4: 4 men he had appointed from the I, 1201+3776
4: 5 to the number of the tribes of the I, 1201+3776
4: 8 So the I did as Joshua commanded 1201+3776
4: 8 of the I, as the LORD had told Joshua; 1201+3776
4:12 armed, in front of the I, 1201+3776
4:21 He said to the I, 1201+3776
5: 1 before the I until we had crossed 1201+3776
5: 1 the courage to face the I. 1201+3776
5: 2 and circumcise the I again." 1201+3776
5: 3 circumcised the I at Gibeath Haaraloth 1201+3776
5: 6 The I had moved about in 1201+3776
5:10 the I celebrated the Passover. 1201+3776
5:12 was no longer any manna for the I, 1201+3776
6: 1 shut up because of the I. 1201+3776
6:25 and she lives among the I to this day. 3776
7: 1 the I acted unfaithfully in regard to 1201+3776
7: 5 They chased the I from the city gate as far 4392S
7:12 I cannot stand against their enemies; 1201+3776
7:23 brought them to Joshua and all the I 1201+3776
8:20 for the I who had been fleeing toward 6639S
8:22 with I on both sides. 3776
8:24 all the I returned to Ai 3776
8:31 of the LORD had commanded the I. 1201+3776
8:32 There, in the presence of the I, 1201+3776
9:16 the I heard that they were neighbors, NIH
9:17 the I set out and on the third day came 1201+3776
Jos 9:18 But the I did not attack them, 1201+3776
9:26 So Joshua saved them from the I, 1201+3776
10: 4 made peace with Joshua and the I." 1201+3776
10:11 by the swords of the I. 1201+3776
10:20 the I destroyed them completely— 1201+3776
10:21 no one uttered a word against the I. 1201+3776
11:14 The I carried off for themselves all 1201+3776
11:19 city made a treaty of peace with the I, 1201+3776
12: 1 of the land whom the I had defeated 1201+3776
12: 6 and the I conquered them. 1201+3776
12: 7 land that Joshua and the I conquered 1201+3776
13: 6 will drive them out before the I. 1201+3776
13:13 the I did not drive out the people of Geshur 1201+3776
13:13 so they continue to live among the I 3776
13:22 the I had put to the sword Balaam son 1201+3776
14: 1 areas the I received as an inheritance 1201+3776
14: 5 So the I divided the land, 1201+3776
17:13 However, when the I grew stronger, 1201+3776
18: 1 the I gathered at Shiloh and set up the Tent of Meeting 1201+3776
18: 3 So Joshua said to the I: 1201+3776
18:10 I according to their tribal divisions. 1201+3776
19:49 the I gave Joshua son of Nun 1201+3776
20: 2 the I to designate the cities of refuge, 1201+3776
20: 9 Any of the I or any alien living 1201+3776
21: 3 the I gave the Levites the following 1201+3776
21: 8 I allotted to the Levites these towns 1201+3776
21:41 the territory held by the I were 1201+3776
22: 9 of Manasseh left the I at Shiloh 1201+3776
22:11 the I heard that they had built the altar 1201+3776
22:13 So the I sent Phinehas son of Eleazar, 1201+3776
22:30 the heads of the clans of the I— 3776
22:31 Now you have rescued the I from 1201+3776
22:32 in Gilead and reported to the I. 1201+3776
24:32 the I had brought up from Egypt, 1201+3776
Jdg 1: 1 the I asked the LORD, 1201+3776
2: 4 to all the I, 1201+3776
2: 6 After Joshua had dismissed the I, 1201+3776
2:11 the I did evil in the eyes of the LORD 1201+3776
3: 1 the LORD left to test all those I who had 3776
3: 2 to the descendants of the I who had 1201+3776
3: 4 to test the I to see whether they would obey 3776
3: 5 The I lived among the Canaanites, 1201+3776
3: 7 The I did evil in the eyes of the LORD; 1201+3776
3: 8 the I were subject for eight years. 1201+3776
3:12 the I did evil in the eyes of the LORD, 1201+3776
3:14 I were subject to Eglon king of Moab 1201+3776
3:15 Again the I cried out to the LORD, 1201+3776
3:15 The I sent him with tribute to Eglon 1201+3776
3:27 I went down with him from the hills, 1201+3776
4: 1 the I once again did evil in the eyes of 1201+3776
4: 3 and had cruelly oppressed the I 1201+3776
4: 5 and the I came to her 1201+3776
4:23 the Canaanite king, before the I. 1201+3776
4:24 And the hand of the I grew stronger 1201+3776
6: 1 the I did evil in the eyes of the LORD, 1201+3776
6: 2 the I prepared shelters for themselves 1201+3776
6: 3 Whenever the I planted their crops, 3776
6: 6 so impoverished the I that they cried out to 3776
6: 7 When the I cried to the LORD because 1201+3776
7: 8 the rest of the I to their tents but kept 408+3776
7:23 I from Naphtali, Asher 408+3776
8:22 The I said to Gideon, "Rule over us— 408+3776
8:28 Thus Midian was subdued before the I 1201+3776
8:33 the I again prostituted themselves to 1201+3776
9:55 the I saw that Abimelech was dead, 408+3776
10: 6 the I did evil in the eyes of the LORD. 1201+3776
10: 6 And because the I forsook the LORD NIH
10: 8 eighteen years they oppressed all the I 1201+3776
10:10 Then the I cried out to the LORD, 1201+3776
10:15 I said to the LORD, "We have sinned. 1201+3776
10:17 I assembled and camped at Mizpah. 1201+3776
11:27 the dispute this day between the I 1201+3776
13: 1 the I did evil in the eyes of the LORD, 1201+3776
19:12 whose people are not I. 1201+3776+4946
19:30 the day the I came up out of Egypt. 1201+3776
20: 1 Then all the I from Dan to Beersheba 1201+3776
20: 3 Benjamites heard that the I had gone 1201+3776
20: 3 Then the I said, 1201+3776
20: 7 you I, speak up and give your verdict. 1201+3776
20:13 not listen to their fellow I. 1201+3776
20:14 at Gibeah to fight against the I. 1201+3776
20:18 The I went up to Bethel and inquired 1201+3776
20:19 the I got up and pitched camp 1201+3776
20:21 and cut down twenty-two thousand I on 3776
20:23 I went up and wept before the LORD 1201+3776
20:24 I drew near to Benjamin the second 1201+3776
20:25 cut down another eighteen thousand I, 1201+3776
20:26 Then the I, all the people, 1201+3776
20:27 And the I inquired of the LORD. 1201+3776
20:31 the I as before, so that about thirty men fell 6639S
20:32 the I were saying, 1201+3776
20:35 on that day the I struck down 25,100 1201+3776
20:42 So they fled before the I in the direction 408+3776
20:45 the I cut down five thousand men along NIH
21: 5 Then the I asked, 1201+3776
21: 6 I grieved for their brothers, the Benjamites. 1201+3776
21:18 since we I have taken this oath: 1201+3776
21:24 the I left that place and went home 1201+3776
1Sa 2:14 This is how they treated all the I who came 3776
2:28 the offerings made with fire by the I. 1201+3776
4: 1 I went out to fight against the Philistines. 3776
4: 1 The I camped at Ebenezer, NIH
4:10 and the I were defeated and every man fled 3776
6: 6 did they not send the I out so they could go 4392S

1Sa 7: 4 the I put away their Baals and 1201+3776
7: 7 And when the I heard of it, 1201+3776
7:10 a panic that they were routed before the I. 3776
9: 2 without equal among the I— 1201+3776
11:15 and all the I held a great celebration. 408+3776
14:18 (At that time it was with the I.) 1201+3776
14:21 to the I who were with Saul and Jonathan. 3776
14:22 the I who had hidden in the hill country 408+3776
14:31 after the I had struck down the Philistines 6639[S]
14:40 Saul then said to all the I, 3776
15: 6 the I when they came up out of Egypt 1201+3776
17: 2 the I assembled and camped in the 408+3776
17: 3 occupied one hill and the I another, 3776
17:11 and all the I were dismayed and terrified. 3776
17:24 When the I saw the man, 408+3776
17:25 Now the I had been saying, 408+3776
17:53 the I returned from chasing the Philistines, 1201+3776
27:12 the I, that he will be my servant forever." 3776
28: 4 while Saul gathered all the I and set 3776
31: 1 the I fled before them, 408+3776
31: 7 the I along the valley and those across 408+3776
2Sa 6:19 to each person in the whole crowd of I, 3776
7: 6 from the day I brought the I up out 1201+3776
7: 7 Wherever I have moved with all the I, 1201+3776
10:19 with the I and became subject to them. 3776
15: 6 in this way toward all the I who came to 3776
17:26 The I and Absalom camped in the land 3776
18:17 Meanwhile, all the I fled to their homes. 3776
19: 8 Meanwhile, the I had fled to their homes. 3776
21: 2 the I had sworn to [spare] them, 1201+3776
1Ki 6: 1 after the I had come out of Egypt, 1201+3776
6:13 And I will live among the I and will 1201+3776
8: 9 covenant with the I after they came 1201+3776
8:63 king and all the I dedicated the temple 1201+3776
9:20 Jebusites (these peoples were not I), 1201+3776
9:21 whom the I could not exterminate— 1201+3776
9:22 not make slaves of any of the I; 1201+3776
11: 2 about which the LORD had told the I, 1201+3776
11:16 and all the I stayed there for six months, 3776
12: 1 all the I had gone there to make him king. 3776
12:16 So the I went home. 3776
12:17 the I who were living in the towns of Judah, 1201+3776
12:20 the I heard that Jeroboam had returned, 3776
12:24 up to fight against your brothers, the I. 1201+3776
12:33 So he instituted the festival for the I 1201+3776
14:24 the LORD had driven out before the I. 1201+3776
16:16 When the I in the camp heard 6639[S]
16:17 Then Omri and all the I with him withdrew 3776
19:10 The I have rejected your covenant, 1201+3776
19:14 The I have rejected your covenant, 1201+3776
20:15 Then he assembled the rest of the I, 1201+3776
20:20 the Arameans fled, with the I in pursuit. 3776
20:27 the I were also mustered and given 1201+3776
20:27 The I camped opposite them 1201+3776
20:29 The I inflicted a hundred thousand casualties on the Aramean foot soldiers 1201+3776
2Ki 3:24 the I rose up and fought them 3776
3:24 And the I invaded the land and slaughtered NIH
7:13 be like that of all the I left here— 3776
7:13 be like all these I who are doomed. 3776
8:12 the harm you will do to the I," 1201+3776
10:32 the I throughout their territory 3776
13: 5 So the I lived in their own homes 1201+3776
13:21 Once while *some* I were burying a man, 2156[S]
16: 3 the LORD had driven out before the I. 1201+3776
17: 6 and deported the I to Assyria. 3776
17: 7 took place because the I had sinned 1201+3776
17: 9 The I secretly did things against 1201+3776
17:22 I persisted in all the sins of Jeroboam 1201+3776
17:24 the towns of Samaria to replace the I. 1201+3776
17:35 the LORD made a covenant with **the I,** 4392[S]
18: 4 the I had been burning incense to it. 1201+3776
21: 2 the LORD had driven out before the I. 1201+3776
21: 8 not again make the feet of the I wander 3776
21: 9 the LORD had destroyed before the I. 1201+3776
1Ch 6:64 So the I gave the Levites these towns 1201+3776
6:70 of Manasseh the I gave Aner and Bileam, NIH
9: 2 in their own towns were *some* I, 3776
10: 1 the I fled before them, 408+3776
10: 7 When all the I in the valley saw that 408+3776
11: 4 and all the I marched to Jerusalem (that is, 3776
12:38 All the rest of the I were also of one mind 3776
13: 5 So David assembled all the I, 3776
13: 6 and all the I with him went to Baalah 3776
13: 8 the I were celebrating with all their might 3776
17: 6 Wherever I have moved with all the I, 3776
21: 2 and count the I from Beersheba to Dan. 3776
27: 1 This is the list of the I— 1201+3776
2Ch 5:10 covenant with the I after they came 1201+3776
7: 3 all the I saw the fire coming down 1201+3776
7: 6 and all the I were standing. 3776
8: 2 and settled I in them. 1201+3776
8: 7 and Jebusites (these peoples were not I), 3776
8: 8 whom the I had not destroyed— 1201+3776
8: 9 Solomon did not make slaves of the I 1201+3776
10: 1 all the I had gone there to make him king. 3776
10:16 So all the I went home. 3776
10:17 as for the I who were living in the towns of Judah, 1201+3776
10:18 but the I stoned him to death. 1201+3776
11: 3 of Solomon king of Judah and to all the I 3776
13:16 The I fled before Judah, 1201+3776
28: 3 the LORD had driven out before the I. 1201+3776
28: 8 The I took captive from their kinsmen 1201+3776
30:21 The I who were present 1201+3776
2Ch 31: 1 the I who were there went out to the towns 3776
31: 1 the I returned to their own towns and 1201+3776
31: 5 the I generously gave the firstfruits 1201+3776
33: 2 the LORD had driven out before the I. 1201+3776
33: 8 I will not again make the feet of the I leave 3776
33: 9 the LORD had destroyed before the I. 1201+3776
34:33 all the territory belonging to the I, 1201+3776
35:17 The I who were present celebrated 1201+3776
Ezr 2:70 and the rest of the I settled in their towns. 3776
3: 1 and the I had settled in their towns, 1201+3776
6:21 the I who had returned from the exile 1201+3776
7: 7 Some of the I, including priests, 1201+3776
7:13 that any of the I in my kingdom, 10335+10553
10: 1 a large crowd of I— 3776
10:25 And among the other I: 3776
Ne 1: 6 I confess the sins we I, 1201+3776
2:10 to promote the welfare of the I. 1201+3776
7:73 of the people and the rest of the I, 3776
7:73 and the I had settled in their towns, 1201+3776
8:14 the I were to live in booths during the 1201+3776
8:17 the I had not celebrated it like this. 1201+3776
9: 1 the I gathered together, 1201+3776
11: 3 who settled in Jerusalem (now *some* I, 3776
11:20 The rest of the I, 3776
13: 2 they had not met the I with food 1201+3776
Isa 17: 3 Aram will be like the glory of the I," 1201+3776
17: 9 which they left because of the I, 1201+3776
27:12 O I, will be gathered up one by one. 1201+3776
31: 6 so greatly revolted against, O I. 1201+3776
66:20 as the I bring their grain offerings, 1201+3776
Jer 16:14 who brought the I up out of Egypt,' 1201+3776
16:15 the I up out of the land of the north 1201+3776
23: 7 who brought the I up out of Egypt,' 1201+3776
Eze 2: 3 Son of man, I am sending you to the I, 1201+3776
6: 5 I will lay the dead bodies of the I in 1201+3776
20: 9 to **the I** by bringing them out of Egypt. 2157[S]
35: 5 delivered the I over to the sword 1201+3776
37:16 'Belonging to Judah and the I 1201+3776
37:21 I will take the I out of the nations 1201+3776
43: 7 where I will live among the I forever. 1201+3776
44: 9 the foreigners who live among the I. 1201+3776
44:15 when the I went astray from me, 1201+3776
47:22 to consider them as native-born I; 1201+3776
48:11 the Levites did when the I went astray. 1201+3776
Da 1: 3 some of the I from the royal family 1201+3776
Hos 1:10 the I will be like the sand on the seashore, 1201+3776
3: 1 Love her as the LORD loves the I, 1201+3776
3: 4 the I will live many days without king 1201+3776
3: 5 Afterward the I will return and seek 1201+3776
4: 1 Hear the word of the LORD, you I, 1201+3776
4:16 The I are stubborn, like a stubborn heifer. 3776
5: 1 Pay attention, you I! 1074+3776
5: 5 the I, even Ephraim, stumble in their sin; 3776
Am 3:12 so will the I be saved, 1201+3776
4: 5 boast about them, you I, 1201+3776
9: 7 you I the same to me as the Cushites? 1201+3776
Mic 5: 3 rest of his brothers return to join the I. 1201+3776
Ac 7:23 he decided to visit his fellow I. *2702+3836+5626*
7:26 Moses came upon **two I** who were fighting. *899[S]*
7:37 "This is that Moses who told the I, *2702+5626*
Ro 9:27 the number of the I be like the sand by the sea, *2702+5626*
10: 1 and prayer to God for **the I** is that they may *899[S]*
10:16 But not all the I accepted the good news. *NIG*
2Co 3: 7 the I could not look steadily at the face of Moses because of its glory, *2702+5626*
3:13 veil over his face to keep the I from *2702+5626*
11:22 Are they I? So am I. *2703*
Heb 11:22 about the exodus *of* the I from Egypt *2702+5626*
Rev 2:14 who taught Balak to entice the I *2702+5626*

ISRAELITES' (3) [ISRAEL]

Lev 10:14 share of the I' fellowship offerings. 1201+3776
Nu 31:30 From the I' half, select one out of 1201+3776
31:47 From the I' half, Moses selected one 1201+3776

ISSACHAR (43)

Ge 30:18 So she named him I. 3779
35:23 Simeon, Levi, Judah, I and Zebulun. 3779
46:13 The sons of I: 3779
49:14 "I is a rawboned donkey lying down 3779
Ex 1: 3 I, Zebulun and Benjamin; 3779
Nu 1: 8 from I, Nethanel son of Zuar; 3779
1:28 From the descendants of I: 3779
1:29 The number from the tribe of I was 54,400. 3779
2: 5 The tribe of I will camp next to them. 3779
2: 5 of the people of I is Nethanel son of Zuar. 3779
7:18 the leader of I, brought his offering. 3779
10:15 over the division of the tribe of I, 1201+3779
13: 7 from the tribe of I, Igal son of Joseph; 3779
26:23 The descendants of I by their clans were: 3779
26:25 These were the clans of I; 3779
34:26 the leader from the tribe of I; 1201+3779
Dt 27:12 Simeon, Levi, Judah, I, 3779
33:18 in your going out, and you, I, in your tents. 3779
Jos 17:10 and bordered Asher on the north and I on 3779
17:11 Within I and Asher, 3779
19:17 The fourth lot came out for I, clan by 1201+3779
19:23 the inheritance of the tribe of I, 1201+3779
21: 6 from the clans of the tribes of I, 3779
21:28 from the tribe of I, Kishion, Daberath, 3779
Jdg 5:15 The princes of I were with Deborah; 3779
5:15 yes, I was with Barak, 3779
10: 1 After the time of Abimelech a man of I, 3779
1Ki 4:17 Jehoshaphat son of Paruah—in I; 3779
15:27 of the house of I plotted against him, 3779
1Ch 2: 1 Reuben, Simeon, Levi, Judah, I, Zebulun, 3779
6:62 from the tribes of I, 3779
6:72 from the tribe of I they received Kedesh, 3779
7: 1 The sons of I: 3779
7: 5 to all the clans of I, 3779
12:32 men of I, who understood the times 3779
12:40 Also, their neighbors from as far away as I, 3779
26: 5 I the seventh and Peullethai the eighth. 3779
27:18 a brother of David; over I: 3779
2Ch 30:18 I and Zebulun had not purified themselves, 3779
Eze 48:25 "I will have one portion; 3779
48:26 it will border the territory of I from east 3779
48:33 the gate of I and the gate of Zebulun. 3779
Rev 7: 7 from the tribe *of* I 12,000, *2704*

ISSHIAH (6)

1Ch 7: 3 Michael, Obadiah, Joel and I. 3807
12: 6 I, Azarel, Joezer and Jashobeam 3808
23:20 Micah the first and I the second. 3807
24:21 for Rehabiah, from his sons: I was the first. 3807
24:25 I; from the sons of Isshiah: Zechariah. 3807
24:25 from the sons of I: Zechariah. 3807

ISSUE (10) [ISSUED, ISSUES, ISSUING]

Ex 22:11 the i between them will be settled by NIH
2Sa 14: 8 and I *will* **i an order** in your behalf." 7422
Ezr 4:21 Now i an order *to* these men to stop work, 10682
5:17 to see if King Cyrus *did* in fact i a decree 10682
Est 1:19 *let* him i a royal decree and let it 3655
Isa 10: 1 to *those who* i oppressive **decrees,** 4180+4180
Da 2:15 did the king i such a harsh decree?" 10427+10621
6: 7 that the king *should* i an edict and enforce 10624
6: 8 i the decree and put it in writing so 10624
6:26 "I i a decree that in every part 10682

ISSUED (19) [ISSUE]

1Ki 15:22 Then King Asa **i an order** *to* all Judah— 9048
2Ch 24: 9 A proclamation *was* then i in Judah 5989
Ezr 4:19 I i an order and a search was made, 10682
5:13 King Cyrus i a decree to rebuild this house 10682
6: 1 King Darius then i an order, 10682
6: 3 the king i a decree concerning the temple 10682
10: 7 then i throughout Judah and Jerusalem 6296
Est 3: 9 *let a* **decree be i** to destroy them, 4180
3:14 A copy of the text of the edict *was to* **be i** 5989
3:15 and the edict **was i** in the citadel of Susa. 5989
8:13 A copy of the text of the edict *was to* **be i** 5989
8:14 the edict **was** also **i** in the citadel of Susa. 5989
9:14 An edict **was i** in Susa, 5989
9:25 *he* **i** written **orders** that the evil scheme 606
Da 2:13 decree *was* i to put the wise men to death, 10485
3:10 You *have* i a decree, O king, 10682
4:24 and this is the decree the Most High *has* i 10413
Jnh 3: 7 Then *he* **i a proclamation** in Nineveh: 2410
Lk 2: 1 In those days Caesar Augustus i a decree *2002*

ISSUES (1) [ISSUE]

Da 6:15 or edict that the king i can be changed." 10624

ISSUING (1) [ISSUE]

Da 9:25 From the i *of* the decree to restore and 4604

ISUAH (KJV) See ISHUAH

ISUI (KJV) See ISHUI

IT (5147) [IT'S, ITS, ITSELF] See Index of Articles Etc.

IT'S (20) [BE, IT] See Index of Articles Etc.

ITALIAN (1) [ITALY]

Ac 10: 1 in what was known as the I Regiment. *2713*

ITALY (4) [ITALIAN]

Ac 18: 2 who had recently come from I *2712*
27: 1 that we would sail for I, *2712*
27: 6 an Alexandrian ship sailing for I and put us *2712*
Heb 13:24 Those from I send you their greetings. *2712*

ITCH (8) [ITCHING]

Lev 13:30 it is an i, an infectious disease 5999
13:32 and if the i has not spread 5999
13:34 the priest is to examine the i, 5999
13:35 But if the i does spread in the skin 5999
13:36 and if the i has spread in the skin, 5999
13:37 the i is healed. He is clean, 5999
14:54 for any infectious skin disease, for an i, 5999
Dt 28:27 festering sores and the i, 3063

ITCHING (1) [ITCH]

2Ti 4: 3 teachers to say what their i ears want to hear *3117*

ITHAI (2)

2Sa 23:29 I son of Ribai from Gibeah in Benjamin, 915
1Ch 11:31 I son of Ribai from Gibeah in Benjamin, 416

ITHAMAR (19) [ITHAMAR'S]
Ex 6:23 and Abihu, Eleazar and **I.** 418
28: 1 Eleazar and **I,** so they may serve me 418
38:21 by the Levites under the direction of **I** son 418
Lev 10: 6 to Aaron and his sons Eleazar and **I,** 418
10:12 Eleazar and **I,** "Take the grain offering left 418
10:16 he was angry with Eleazar and **I,** 418
Nu 3: 2 the firstborn and Abihu, Eleazar and **I.** 418
3: 4 and **I** served as priests during the lifetime 418
4:28 to be under the direction of **I** son of Aaron, 418
4:33 of Meeting under the direction of **I** son 418
7: 8 They were all under the direction of **I** son 418
26:60 of Nadab and Abihu, Eleazar and **I.** 418
1Ch 6: 3 Nadab, Abihu, Eleazar and **I.** 418
24: 1 of Aaron were Nadab, Abihu, Eleazar and **I.** 418
24: 2 so Eleazar and **I** served as the priests. 418
24: 3 and Ahimelech a descendant of **I,** 418
24: 5 the descendants of both Eleazar and **I.** 418
24: 6 from Eleazar and then one from **I.** 418
Ezr 8: 2 of the descendants of **I,** Daniel; 418

ITHAMAR'S (2) [ITHAMAR]
1Ch 24: 4 among Eleazar's descendants than among **I,** 418
24: 4 of families from **I** descendants. 418

ITHIEL (3)
Ne 11: 7 the son of Maaseiah, the son of **I,** 417
Pr 30: 1 This man declared to **I,** 417
30: 1 to **I** and to Ucal: 417

ITHLAH (1)
Jos 19:42 Shaalabbin, Aijalon, **I,** 3849

ITHMAH (1)
1Ch 11:46 and Joshaviah the sons of Elnaam, **I** 3850

ITHNAN (1)
Jos 15:23 Kedesh, Hazor, **I,** 3854

ITHRAN (3)
Ge 36:26 Hemdan, Eshban, **I** and Keran. 3864
1Ch 1:41 Hemdan, Eshban, **I** and Keran. 3864
7:37 Hod, Shamma, Shilshah, **I** and Beera. 3864

ITHREAM (2)
2Sa 3: 5 **I** the son of David's wife Eglah. 3865
1Ch 3: 3 and the sixth, **I,** by his wife Eglah. 3865

ITHRITE (4) [ITHRITES]
2Sa 23:38 Ira the **I,** Gareb the Ithrite 3863
23:38 Ira the Ithrite, Gareb the **I** 3863
1Ch 11:40 Ira the **I,** Gareb the Ithrite, 3863
11:40 Ira the Ithrite, Gareb the **I,** 3863

ITHRITES (1) [ITHRITE]
1Ch 2:53 the **I,** Puthites, Shumathites and Mishraites. 3863

ITS (1008) [IT] See Index of Articles Etc.

ITSELF (53) [IT, SELF] See Index of Articles Etc.

ITTAH-KAZIN (KJV) See ETH KAZIN

ITTAI (7)
2Sa 15:19 The king said to **I** the Gittite, 915
15:21 But **I** replied to the king, 915
15:22 David said to **I,** "Go ahead, march on." 915
15:22 So **I** the Gittite marched on 915
18: 2 and a third under **I** the Gittite. 915
18: 5 The king commanded Joab, Abishai and **I,** 915
18:12 and Abishai and **I,** 915

ITUREA (1)
Lk 3: 1 brother Philip tetrarch *of* **I** and Traconitis, *2714*

IVAH (KJV) See IVVAH

IVORY (13)
1Ki 10:18 the king made a great throne inlaid with **i** 9094
10:22 silver and **i,** and apes and baboons. 9105
22:39 the palace he built and inlaid with **i,** 9094
2Ch 9:17 the king made a great throne inlaid with **i** 9094
9:21 silver and **i,** and apes and baboons. 9105
Ps 45: 8 from palaces adorned with **i** the music of 9094
SS 5:14 like polished **i** decorated with sapphires. 9094
7: 4 Your neck is like an **i** tower. 9094
Eze 27: 6 Cyprus they made your deck, inlaid with **i.** 9094
27:15 they paid you with **i** tusks and ebony. 9094
Am 3:15 the houses adorned with **i** will be destroyed 9094
6: 4 You lie on beds inlaid with **i** and lounge 9094
Rev 18:12 and articles of every kind *made of* **i,** *1804*

IVVAH (3)
2Ki 18:34 are the gods of Sepharvaim, Hena and **I?** 6394
19:13 Sepharvaim, or of Hena or **I?"** 6394
Isa 37:13 Sepharvaim, or of Hena or **I?"** 6394

IYE ABARIM (2) [ABARIM]
Nu 21:11 from Oboth and camped in **I,** 6516
33:44 They left Oboth and camped at **I,** 6516

IYIM (1)
Nu 33:45 They left **I** and camped at Dibon Gad. 6517

IZEHAR (KJV) See IZHAR

IZEHARITES (KJV) See IZHARITES

IZHAR (9) [IZHARITES]
Ex 6:18 The sons of Kohath were Amram, **I,** 3659
6:21 The sons of **I** were Korah, 3659
Nu 3:19 Amram, **I,** Hebron and Uzziel. 3659
16: 1 Korah son of **I,** the son of Kohath, 3659
1Ch 6: 2 Amram, **I,** Hebron and Uzziel. 3659
6:18 Amram, **I,** Hebron and Uzziel. 3659
6:38 of **I,** the son of Kohath, the son of Levi, 3659
23:12 Amram, **I,** Hebron and Uzziel—four in all. 3659
23:18 The sons of **I:** Shelomith was the first. 3659

IZHARITES (4) [IZHAR]
Nu 3:27 **I,** Hebronites and Uzzielites; 3660
1Ch 24:22 From the **I:** Shelomoth; 3660
26:23 From the Amramites, the **I,** 3660
26:29 From the **I:** Kenaniah 3660

IZLIAH (1)
1Ch 8:18 **I** and Jobab were the sons of Elpaal. 3468

IZRAHIAH (2)
1Ch 7: 3 The son of Uzzi: **I.** 3474
7: 3 The sons of **I:** Michael, Obadiah, Joel 3474

IZRAHITE (1)
1Ch 27: 8 was the commander Shamhuth the **I.** 3473

IZRI (1)
1Ch 25:11 the fourth to **I,** his sons and relatives, 12 3673

IZZIAH (1)
Ezr 10:25 Ramiah, **I,** Malkijah, Mijamin, Eleazar, 3466

J

JAAKAN See BENE JAAKAN

JAAKANITES (1) [BENE JAAKAN]
Dt 10: 6 from the wells of the **J** to Moserah. 1201+3622

JAAKOBAH (1)
1Ch 4:36 **J,** Jeshohaiah, Asaiah, Adiel, Jesimiel, 3621

JAALA (2)
Ezr 2:56 **J,** Darkon, Giddel, 3608
Ne 7:58 **J,** Darkon, Giddel, 3606

JAALAM (KJV) See JALAM

JAAN See DAN JAAN

JAANAI (KJV) See JANAI

JAAR (1)
Ps 132: 6 we came upon it in the fields of **J:** 3625

JAARE-OREGIM (1)
2Sa 21:19 of **J** the Bethlehemite killed Goliath 3629

JAARESHIAH (1)
1Ch 8:27 **J,** Elijah and Zicri were the sons 3631

JAASAU (KJV) See JAASU

JAASIEL (2)
1Ch 11:47 Eliel, Obed and **J** the Mezobaite. 3634
27:21 **J** son of Abner; 3634

JAASU (1)
Ezr 10:37 Mattaniah, Mattenai and **J.** 3632

JAAZANIAH (5)
2Ki 25:23 **J** the son of the Maacathite, and their men. 3280
Jer 35: 3 So I went to get **J** son of Jeremiah, 3279
40: 8 and **J** the son of the Maacathite, 3471
Eze 8:11 and **J** son of Shaphan was standing 3280
11: 1 and I saw among them **J** son of Azzur 3279

JAAZER (KJV) See JAZER

JAAZIAH (2)
1Ch 24:26 The son of **J:** Beno. 3596
24:27 from **J:** Beno, Shoham, Zaccur and Ibri. 3596

JAAZIEL (1)
1Ch 15:18 Zechariah, **J,** Shemiramoth, Jehiel, Unni, 3595

JABAL (1)
Ge 4:20 Adah gave birth to **J;** 3299

JABBOK (7)
Ge 32:22 and crossed the ford of the **J.** 3309
Nu 21:24 over his land from the Arnon to the **J,** 3309
Dt 2:37 the **J** nor that around the towns in the hills. 3309
3:16 the border) and out to the **J** River, 3309
Jos 12: 2 the middle of the gorge—to the **J** River, 3309
Jdg 11:13 from the Arnon to the **J,** 3309
11:22 to the **J** and from the desert to the Jordan. 3309

JABESH (11) [JABESH GILEAD]
1Sa 11: 1 And all the men of **J** said to him, 3315
11: 3 The elders of **J** said to him, 3315
11: 5 to him what the men of **J** had said. 3315
11: 9 and reported this to the men of **J,** 3315
31:12 from the wall of Beth Shan and went to **J,** 3315
31:13 and buried them under a tamarisk tree at **J,** 3315
2Ki 15:10 of **J** conspired against Zechariah. 3314
15:13 of **J** became king in the thirty-ninth year 3314
15:14 He attacked Shallum son of **J** in Samaria, 3314
1Ch 10:12 and his sons and brought them to **J.** 3315
10:12 under the great tree in **J,** 3315

JABESH GILEAD (12) [GILEAD, JABESH]
Jdg 21: 8 from **J** had come to the camp for 3316
21: 9 of the people of **J** were there. 3316
21:10 with instructions to go to **J** and put 3316
21:12 in **J** four hundred young women who had never slept with a man, 3316
21:14 the women of **J** who had been spared. 3316
1Sa 11: 1 the Ammonite went up and besieged **J.** 3316
11: 9 "Say to the men of **J,** 3316
31:11 When the people of **J** heard of what 3316
2Sa 2: 4 the men of **J** who had buried Saul, 3316
2: 5 he sent messengers to the men of **J** 3316
21:12 from the citizens of **J.** 3316
1Ch 10:11 When all the inhabitants of **J** heard 3316

JABEZ (4)
1Ch 2:55 and the clans of scribes who lived at **J:** 3583
4: 9 **J** was more honorable than his brothers. 3584
4: 9 His mother had named him **J,** saying, 3584
4:10 **J** cried out to the God of Israel, "Oh, 3584

JABIN (6) [JABIN'S]
Jos 11: 1 When **J** king of Hazor heard of this, 3296
Jdg 4: 2 the LORD sold them into the hands of **J,** 3296
4:17 between **J** king of Hazor and the clan 3296
4:23 On that day God subdued **J,** 3296
4:24 and stronger against **J,** 3296
Ps 83: 9 you did to Sisera and **J** at the river Kishon, 3296

JABIN'S (1) [JABIN]
Jdg 4: 7 the commander of **J** army, 3296

JABNEEL (2)
Jos 15:11 along to Mount Baalah and reached **J.** 3305
19:33 and **J** to Lakkum and ending at the Jordan. 3305

JABNEH (1)
2Ch 26: 6 down the walls of Gath, **J** and Ashdod. 3306

JACAN (1)
1Ch 5:13 Michael, Meshullam, Sheba, Jorai, **J,** 3602

JACHIN, JACHINITES (KJV) See JAKIN, JAKINITE

JACINTH (3)
Ex 28:19 the third row a **j,** an agate and an amethyst; 4385
39:12 the third row a **j,** an agate and an amethyst; 4385
Rev 21:20 the eleventh **j,** and the twelfth amethyst. *5611*

JACKAL (2) [JACKALS]

Ne 2:13 through the Valley Gate toward the J Well 9490
Mic 1:8 I will howl like a j and moan like an owl. 9478

JACKALS (17) [JACKAL]

Job 30:29 I have become a brother of j, 9478
Ps 44:19 and made us a haunt for j and covered us 9478
63:10 over to the sword and become food for j. 8785
Isa 13:21 j will fill her houses; 280
13:22 j in her luxurious palaces. 9478
34:13 She will become a haunt for j, 9478
35:7 In the haunts where j once lay, 9478
43:20 wild animals honor me, the j and the owls, 9478
Jer 9:11 a haunt of j; 9478
10:22 a haunt of j. 9478
14:6 on the barren heights and pant like j; 9478
49:33 "Hazor will become a haunt of j, 9478
51:37 a haunt of j, an object of horror and scorn, 9478
La 4:3 j offer their breasts to nurse their young, 9478
5:18 with j prowling over it. 8785
Eze 13:4 O Israel, are like j among ruins. 8785
Mal 1:3 and left his inheritance to the desert j." 9478

JACOB (363) [JACOB'S]

Ge 25:26 so he was named J. 3620
25:27 while J was a quiet man, 3620
25:28 loved Esau, but Rebekah loved J. 3620
25:29 Once when J was cooking some stew, 3620
25:30 He said to J, "Quick, let me have some 3620
25:31 J replied, "First sell me your birthright." 3620
25:33 But J said, "Swear to me first." 3620
25:33 selling his birthright to J. 3620
25:34 Then J gave Esau some bread 3620
27:6 Rebekah said to her son J, 3620
27:11 J said to Rebekah his mother, 3620
27:15 and put them on her younger son J. 3620
27:17 to her son J the tasty food and 3620
27:19 J said to his father, "I am Esau 3620
27:21 Then Isaac said to J, "Come near so I can 3620
27:22 J went close to his father Isaac, 3620
27:22 "The voice is the voice of J, but the hands 3620
27:25 J brought it to him and he ate; NIH
27:30 J had scarcely left his father's presence, 3620
27:36 Esau said, "Isn't he rightly named J? 3620
27:41 Esau held a grudge against J because of 3620
27:41 then I will kill my brother J." 3620
27:42 she sent for her younger son J and said 3620
27:46 If J takes a wife from among the women 3620
28:1 So Isaac called for J and blessed him 3620
28:5 Then Isaac sent J on his way, 3620
28:5 who was the mother of J and Esau. 3620
28:6 Now Esau learned that Isaac had blessed J 3620
28:7 that J had obeyed his father and mother 3620
28:10 J left Beersheba and set out for Haran. 3620
28:16 When J awoke from his sleep, he thought, 3620
28:18 Early the next morning J took the stone 3620
28:20 Then J made a vow, saying, 3620
29:1 Then J continued on his journey and came 3620
29:4 J asked the shepherds, "My brothers, 3620
29:6 Then J asked them, "Is he well?" NIH
29:10 When J saw Rachel daughter of Laban, 3620
29:11 J kissed Rachel and began to weep aloud. 3620
29:13 As soon as Laban heard the news about J, 3620
29:13 and there J told him all these things. NIH
29:14 After J had stayed with him for NIH
29:18 J was in love with Rachel and said, 3620
29:20 So J served seven years to get Rachel, 3620
29:21 Then J said to Laban, "Give me my wife. 3620
29:23 his daughter Leah and gave her to J, 2257S
29:23 and J lay with her. NIH
29:25 So J said to Laban, "What is this you have NIH
29:28 And J did so. 3620
29:30 J lay with Rachel also, and he loved Rachel NIH
30:1 that she was not bearing J any children, 3620
30:1 So she said to J, "Give me children, 3620
30:2 J became angry with her and said, 3620
30:4 Bilhah as a wife. J slept with her, 3620
30:7 and bore J a second son. 3620
30:9 Zilpah and gave her to J as a wife. 3620
30:10 Leah's servant Zilpah bore J a son. 3620
30:12 Leah's servant Zilpah bore J a second son. 3620
30:16 J came in from the fields that evening, 3620
30:17 and she became pregnant and bore J 3620
30:19 Leah conceived again and bore J 3620
30:25 J said to Laban, "Send me on my way 3620
30:29 J said to him, "You know how I NIH
30:31 "Don't give me anything," J replied. 3620
30:36 between himself and J, 3620
30:36 while J continued to tend the rest 3620
30:37 J, however, took fresh-cut branches 3620
30:40 J set apart the young of the flock 3620
30:41 J would place the branches in the troughs 3620
30:42 to Laban and the strong ones to J. 3620
31:1 J heard that Laban's sons were saying, NIH
31:1 "J has taken everything our father owned 3620
31:2 And J noticed that Laban's attitude 3620
31:3 Then the LORD said to J, "Go back 3620
31:4 So J sent word to Rachel and Leah 3620
31:11 of God said to me in the dream, 'J.' 3620
31:17 J put his children and his wives on camels, 3620
31:20 J deceived Laban the Aramean by 3620
31:22 Laban was told that J had fled. 3620
31:23 he pursued J for seven days and caught up 2257S
31:24 "Be careful not to say anything to J, 3620
31:25 J had pitched his tent in the hill country 3620
Ge 31:26 Laban said to J, "What have you done? 3620
31:29 'Be careful not to say anything to J, 3620
31:31 J answered Laban, "I was afraid, 3620
31:32 Now J did not know that Rachel had stolen 3620
31:36 J was angry and took Laban to task. 3620
31:43 Laban answered J, "The women are my daughters, 3620
31:45 So J took a stone and set it up as a pillar. 3620
31:47 and J called it Galeed. 3620
31:51 Laban also said to J, "Here is this heap, 3620
31:53 So J took an oath in the name of the Fear 3620
32:1 J also went on his way, 3620
32:2 When J saw them, he said, 3620
32:3 J sent messengers ahead of him 3620
32:4 'Your servant J says, I have been staying 3620
32:6 When the messengers returned to J, 3620
32:7 J divided the people who were with him 3620
32:9 Then J prayed, "O God of my father 3620
32:18 'They belong to your servant J. 3620
32:20 'Your servant J is coming behind us.'" 3620
32:22 That night J got up and took his two wives NIH
32:24 So J was left alone, 3620
32:26 But J replied, "I will not let you go NIH
32:27 "J," he answered. 3620
32:28 man said, "Your name will no longer be J, 3620
32:29 J said, "Please tell me your name." 3620
32:30 So J called the place Peniel, saying, 3620
33:1 J looked up and there was Esau, 3620
33:4 But Esau ran to meet J and embraced him; 2257S
33:5 J answered, "They are the children NIH
33:10 "No, please!" said J. 3620
33:11 And because J insisted, Esau accepted it. NIH
33:13 But J said to him, "My lord knows NIH
33:15 "But why do that?" J asked. NIH
33:17 J, however, went to Succoth, 3620
33:18 After J came from Paddan Aram, 3620
34:1 Dinah, the daughter Leah had borne to J, 3620
34:3 His heart was drawn to Dinah daughter of J, 3620
34:5 When J heard that his daughter Dinah had been defiled, 3620
34:6 Hamor went out to talk with J. 3620
34:27 of J came upon the dead bodies and looted 3620
34:30 Then J said to Simeon and Levi, 3620
35:1 Then God said to J, "Go up to Bethel 3620
35:2 So J said to his household and 3620
35:4 So they gave J all the foreign gods 3620
35:4 J buried them under the oak at Shechem. 3620
35:6 J and all the people with him came to Luz 3620
35:9 After J returned from Paddan Aram, 3620
35:10 God said to him, "Your name is J, 3620
35:10 but you will no longer be called J; 3620
35:14 J set up a stone pillar at the place 3620
35:15 J called the place where God had talked 3620
35:20 Over her tomb J set up a pillar, 3620
35:22 J had twelve sons: 3620
35:23 Reuben the firstborn of J, Simeon, Levi, 3620
35:26 These were the sons of J, 3620
35:27 J came home to his father Isaac in Mamre, 3620
35:29 And his sons Esau and J buried him. 3620
36:6 to a land some distance from his brother J. 3620
37:1 J lived in the land where his father had 3620
37:2 This is the account of J. 3620
37:34 Then J tore his clothes, 3620
42:1 J learned that there was grain in Egypt, 3620
42:4 But J did not send Benjamin, 3620
42:29 to their father J in the land of Canaan, 3620
42:36 Their father J said to them, 3620
42:38 But J said, "My son will not go NIH
45:25 up out of Egypt and came to their father J 3620
45:26 J was stunned; he did not believe them. 2257S
45:27 the spirit of their father J revived. 3620
46:2 to Israel in a vision at night and said, "J! 3620
46:2 at night and said, "Jacob! J!" 3620
46:5 Then J left Beersheba, 3620
46:5 and Israel's sons took their father J 3620
46:6 and J and all his offspring went to Egypt. 3620
46:8 of Israel (J and his descendants) who went 3620
46:8 Reuben the firstborn of J. 3620
46:15 the sons Leah bore to J in Paddan Aram, 3620
46:18 to J by Zilpah, whom Laban had given 3620
46:22 the sons of Rachel who were born to J— 3620
46:25 These were the sons born to J by Bilhah, 3620
46:26 All those who went to Egypt with J— 3620
46:28 Now J sent Judah ahead of him to Joseph NIH
47:7 Then Joseph brought his father J in 3620
47:7 After J blessed Pharaoh, 3620
47:9 And J said to Pharaoh, 3620
47:10 Then J blessed Pharaoh and went out 3620
47:28 J lived in Egypt seventeen years, 3620
48:2 When J was told, "Your son Joseph has 3620
48:3 J said to Joseph, "God Almighty appeared 3620
49:1 Then J called for his sons and said: 3620
49:2 "Assemble and listen, sons of J; 3620
49:7 I will scatter them in J and disperse them 3620
49:24 of the hand of the Mighty One of J, 3620
49:33 When J had finished giving instructions 3620
50:24 on oath to Abraham, Isaac and J." 3620
Ex 1:1 of Israel who went to Egypt with J, each 3620
1:5 The descendants of J numbered seventy 3620
2:24 with Isaac and with J. 3620
3:6 the God of Isaac and the God of J." 3620
3:15 the God of Isaac and the God of J— 3620
3:16 the God of Abraham, Isaac and J— 3620
4:5 the God of Isaac and the God of J— 3620
6:3 to Isaac and to J as God Almighty, 3620
6:8 give to Abraham, to Isaac and to J. 3620
19:3 to say to the house of J and what you are 3620
Ex 33:1 Isaac and J, saying, 'I will give it 3620
Lev 26:42 I will remember my covenant with J 3620
Nu 23:7 'Come,' he said, 'curse J for me; 3620
23:10 of J or number the fourth part of Israel? 3620
23:21 "No misfortune is seen in J, 3620
23:23 There is no sorcery against J, 3620
23:23 It will now be said of J and of Israel, 3620
24:5 O J, your dwelling places, O Israel! 3620
24:17 A star will come out of J; 3620
24:19 of J and destroy the survivors of the city." 3620
32:11 on oath to Abraham, Isaac and J— 3620
Dt 1:8 to Abraham, Isaac and J— 3620
6:10 to Abraham, Isaac and J, to give you— 3620
9:5 to Abraham, Isaac and J. 3620
9:27 Remember your servants Abraham, Isaac and J. 3620
29:13 Abraham, Isaac and J. 3620
30:20 Abraham, Isaac and J. 3620
32:9 J his allotted inheritance. 3620
33:4 the possession of the assembly of J. 3620
33:10 He teaches your precepts to J and your law 3620
34:4 Abraham, Isaac and J when I said, 3620
Jos 24:4 and to Isaac I gave J and Esau. 3620
24:4 but J and his sons went down to Egypt. 3620
24:32 that J bought for a hundred pieces of silver 3620
1Sa 12:8 "After J entered Egypt, 3620
2Sa 23:1 the man anointed by the God of J, 3620
1Ki 18:31 for each of the tribes descended from J, 3620
2Ki 13:23 with Abraham, Isaac and J. 3620
17:34 that the LORD gave the descendants of J, 3620
1Ch 16:13 O sons of J, his chosen ones. 3620
16:17 He confirmed it to J as a decree, 3620
Ps 14:7 let J rejoice and Israel be glad! 3620
20:1 may the name of the God of J protect you. 3620
22:23 All you descendants of J, honor him! 3620
24:6 who seek your face, O God of J. 3620
44:4 who decrees victories for J. 3620
46:7 the God of J is our fortress. 3620
46:11 the God of J is our fortress. 3620
47:4 the pride of J, whom he loved. 3620
53:6 let J rejoice and Israel be glad! 3620
59:13 the ends of the earth that God rules over J. 3620
75:9 I will sing praise to the God of J. 3620
76:6 At your rebuke, O God of J, 3620
77:15 the descendants of J and Joseph. 3620
78:5 He decreed statutes for J and established 3620
78:21 his fire broke out against J, 3620
78:71 to be the shepherd of his people J, 3620
79:7 for they have devoured J 3620
81:1 shout aloud to the God of J! 3620
81:4 an ordinance of the God of J. 3620
84:8 listen to me, O God of J. 3620
85:1 you restored the fortunes of J. 3620
87:2 of Zion more than all the dwellings of J. 3620
94:7 the God of J pays no heed." 3620
99:4 in J you have done what is just and right. 3620
105:6 O sons of J, his chosen ones. 3620
105:10 He confirmed it to J as a decree, 3620
105:23 J lived as an alien in the land of Ham. 3620
114:1 of J from a people of foreign tongue, 3620
114:7 at the presence of the God of J, 3620
132:2 and made a vow to the Mighty One of J: 3620
132:5 a dwelling for the Mighty One of J." 3620
135:4 the LORD has chosen J to be his own, 3620
146:5 Blessed is he whose help is the God of J, 3620
147:19 He has revealed his word to J, 3620
Isa 2:3 to the house of the God of J. 3620
2:5 Come, O house of J, let us walk in the 3620
2:6 abandoned your people, the house of J. 3620
8:17 who is hiding his face from the house of J. 3620
9:8 The Lord has sent a message against J; 3620
10:20 the survivors of the house of J, 3620
10:21 of J will return to the Mighty God. 3620
14:1 The LORD will have compassion on J; 3620
14:1 and unite with the house of J. 3620
17:4 "In that day the glory of J will fade; 3620
27:6 In days to come J will take root, 3620
29:22 says to the house of J: 3620
29:22 "No longer will J be ashamed; 3620
29:23 the holiness of the Holy One of J, 3620
40:27 Why do you say, O J, and complain, 3620
41:8 "But you, O Israel, my servant, J, 3620
41:14 Do not be afraid, O worm J, O little Israel, 3620
42:24 Who handed J over to become loot, 3620
43:1 he who created you, O J, 3620
43:22 "Yet you have not called upon me, O J, 3620
43:28 and I will consign J to destruction 3620
44:1 "But now listen, O J, my servant, Israel, 3620
44:2 Do not be afraid, O J, my servant, 3620
44:5 another will call himself by the name of J; 3620
44:21 "Remember these things, O J, 3620
44:23 for the LORD has redeemed J, 3620
45:4 For the sake of J my servant, 3620
46:3 "Listen to me, O house of J, 3620
48:1 "Listen to this, O house of J, 3620
48:12 "Listen to me, O J, Israel, 3620
48:20 "The LORD has redeemed his servant J." 3620
49:5 the womb to be his servant to bring J back 3620
49:6 to be my servant to restore the tribes of J 3620
49:26 your Redeemer, the Mighty One of J." 3620
58:1 and to the house of J their sins. 3620
58:14 to feast on the inheritance of your father J." 3620
59:20 to those in J who repent of their sins," 3620
60:16 your Redeemer, the Mighty One of J. 3620
65:9 I will bring forth descendants from J, 3620
Jer 2:4 Hear the word of the LORD, O house of J, 3620
5:20 to the house of J and proclaim it in Judah: 3620

Jer 10:16 He who is the Portion of **J** is not like these, 3620
10:25 For they have devoured **J;** 3620
30: 7 It will be a time of trouble for **J,** 3620
30:10 " 'So do not fear, O **J** my servant; 3620
30:10 **J** will again have peace and security, 3620
31: 7 "Sing with joy for **J;** 3620
31:11 For the LORD will ransom **J** 3620
33:26 the descendants of **J** and David my servant 3620
33:26 the descendants of Abraham, Isaac and **J.** 3620
46:27 "Do not fear, O **J** my servant; 3620
46:27 **J** will again have peace and security, 3620
46:28 Do not fear, O **J** my servant, 3620
51:19 He who is the Portion of **J** is not like these, 3620
La 1:17 for **J** that his neighbors become his foes; 3620
2: 2 up all the dwellings of **J;** 3620
2: 3 He has burned in **J** like a flaming fire 3620
Eze 20: 5 the house of **J** and revealed myself to them 3620
28:25 which I gave to my servant **J.** 3620
37:25 in the land I gave to my servant **J,** 3620
39:25 I will now bring **J** back from captivity 3620
Hos 10:11 and **J** must break up the ground. 3620
12: 2 he will punish **J** according to his ways 3620
12:12 **J** fled to the country of Aram; 3620
Am 3:13 and testify against the house of **J,"** 3620
6: 8 the pride of **J** and detest his fortresses; 3620
7: 2 How can **J** survive? 3620
7: 5 How can **J** survive? 3620
8: 7 The LORD has sworn by the Pride of **J:** 3620
9: 8 I will not totally destroy the house of **J,"** 3620
Ob 1:10 of the violence against your brother **J,** 3620
1:17 the house of **J** will possess its inheritance. 3620
1:18 The house of **J** will be a fire and the house 3620
Mic 2: 7 Should it be said, O house of **J:** 3620
2:12 "I will surely gather all of you, O **J;** 3620
3: 1 Then I said, "Listen, you leaders of **J,** 3620
3: 8 to declare to **J** his transgression, 3620
3: 9 Hear this, you leaders of the house of **J,** 3620
4: 2 to the house of the God of **J.** 3620
5: 7 of **J** will be in the midst of many peoples 3620
5: 8 The remnant of **J** will be among 3620
7:20 You will be true to **J,** 3620
Na 2: 2 The LORD will restore the splendor of **J** 3620
Mal 1: 2 "Yet I have loved **J,** 3620
2:12 the LORD cut him off from the tents of **J—** 3620
3: 6 So you, O descendants of **J,** 3620
Mt 1: 2 Isaac the father of **J,** *2609*
1: 2 **J** the father of Judah and his brothers, *2609*
1:15 Matthan the father of **J,** *2609*
1:16 and **J** the father of Joseph, *2609*
8:11 Isaac and **J** in the kingdom of heaven. *2609*
22:32 the God of Isaac, and the God *of* **J'?** *2609*
Mk 12:26 the God of Isaac, and the God *of* **J'?** *2609*
Lk 1:33 he will reign over the house *of* **J** forever; *2609*
3:34 the son *of* **J,** the son of Isaac, *2609*
13:28 and **J** and all the prophets in the kingdom *2609*
20:37 and the God of Isaac, and the God *of* **J.'** *2609*
Jn 4: 5 of ground **J** had given to his son Joseph. *2609*
4:12 Are you greater than our father **J,** *2609*
Ac 3:13 The God of Abraham, Isaac and **J,** *2609*
7: 8 Later Isaac became the father of **J,** *2609*
7: 8 and **J** became the father of the twelve *2609*
7:12 When **J** heard that there was grain *2609*
7:14 for his father **J** and his whole family, *2609*
7:15 Then **J** went down to Egypt, *2609*
7:32 the God *of* Abraham, Isaac and **J.'** *2609*
7:46 a dwelling place for the God *of* **J.** *2609*
Ro 9:13 **"J I loved, but Esau I hated."** *2609*
11:26 he will turn godlessness away from **J.** *2609*
Heb 11: 9 he lived in tents, as did Isaac and **J,** *2609*
11:20 By faith Isaac blessed **J** and Esau in regard *2609*
11:21 By faith **J,** when he was dying, *2609*

JACOB'S (21) [JACOB]

Ge 31:33 into **J** tent and into Leah's tent and into 3620
32:21 So **J** gifts went on ahead of him, 2021[S]
32:25 of **J** hip so that his hip was wrenched 3620
32:32 because the socket of **J** hip was touched 3620
34: 7 Now **J** sons had come in from the fields 3620
34: 7 in Israel by lying with **J** daughter— 3620
34:13 **J** sons replied deceitfully as they spoke 3620
34:19 because he was delighted with **J** daughter. 3620
34:25 two of **J** sons, Simeon and Levi, 3620
46:19 The sons of **J** wife Rachel: 3620
46:27 the members of **J** family, 3620
50:12 So **J** sons did as he had commanded them: 2257[S]
Dt 33:28 **J** spring is secure in a land of grain 3620
Isa 27: 9 By this, then, will **J** guilt be atoned for, 3620
41:21 "Set forth your arguments," says **J** King. 3620
45:19 I have not said to **J** descendants, 3620
Jer 30:18 " 'I will restore the fortunes of **J** tents 3620
Mic 1: 5 All this is because of **J** transgression, 3620
1: 5 What is **J** transgression? 3620
Mal 1: 2 "Was not Esau **J** brother?" 3620+4200
Jn 4: 6 **J** well was there, and Jesus, *2609*

JADA (2)

1Ch 2:28 The sons of Onam: Shammai and **J.** 3360
2:32 The sons of **J,** Shammai's brother: 3360

JADAH (2)

1Ch 9:42 Ahaz was the father of **J,** 3586
9:42 **J** was the father of Alemeth, 3586

JADAU (KJV) See JADDAI

JADDAI (1)

Ezr 10:43 Jeiel, Mattithiah, Zabad, Zebina, **J,** 3350

JADDUA (3)

Ne 10:21 Meshezabel, Zadok, **J,** 3348
12:11 and Jonathan the father of **J.** 3348
12:22 Joiada, Johanan and **J,** 3348

JADON (1)

Ne 3: 7 Melatiah of Gibeon and **J** of Meronoth— 3347

JAEL (6)

Jdg 4:17 however, fled on foot to the tent of **J,** 3605
4:18 **J** went out to meet Sisera and said to him, 3605
4:21 But **J,** Heber's wife, picked up a tent peg 3605
4:22 and **J** went out to meet him. 3605
5: 6 in the days of **J,** the roads were abandoned; 3605
5:24 "Most blessed of women be **J,** 3605

JAGGED (1)

Job 41:30 His undersides are **j** potsherds, 2529

JAGUR (1)

Jos 15:21 of Edom were: Kabzeel, Eder, **J,** 3327

JAH (KJV) See †LORD

JAHATH (7)

1Ch 4: 2 Reaiah son of Shobal was the father of **J,** 3511
4: 2 and **J** the father of Ahumai and Lahad. 3511
6:43 of **J,** the son of Gershon, the son of Levi; 3511
23:10 sons of Shimei: **J,** Ziza, Jeush and Beriah. 3511
23:11 **J** was the first and Ziza the second, 3511
24:22 from the sons of Shelomoth: **J.** 3511
2Ch 34:12 to direct them were **J** and Obadiah, 3511

JAHAZ (7)

Nu 21:23 When he reached **J,** he fought with Israel. 3403
Dt 2:32 to meet us in battle at **J,** 3403
Jos 13:18 **J,** Kedemoth, Mephaath, 3403
21:36 from the tribe of Reuben, Bezer, **J,** 3403
Jdg 11:20 and encamped at **J** and fought with Israel. 3403
Isa 15: 4 their voices are heard all the way to **J.** 3403
Jer 48:34 from Heshbon to Elealeh and **J,** 3403

JAHAZA, JAHAZAH (KJV) See JAHAZ

JAHAZIAH (KJV) See JAHZEIAH

JAHAZIEL (6)

1Ch 12: 4 Jeremiah, **J,** Johanan, 3487
16: 6 and Benaiah and **J** the priests were to blow 3487
23:19 **J** the third and Jekameam the fourth. 3487
24:23 **J** the third and Jekameam the fourth. 3487
2Ch 20:14 the LORD came upon **J** son of Zechariah, 3487
Ezr 8: 5 of **J,** and with him 300 men; 3487

JAHDAI (1)

1Ch 2:47 The sons of **J:** 3367

JAHDIEL (1)

1Ch 5:24 Eliel, Azriel, Jeremiah, Hodaviah and **J.** 3484

JAHDO (1)

1Ch 5:14 the son of Jeshishai, the son of **J,** 3482

JAHLEEL (2) [JAHLEELITE]

Ge 46:14 The sons of Zebulun: Sered, Elon and **J.** 3499
Nu 26:26 through **J,** the Jahleelite clan. 3499

JAHLEELITE (1) [JAHLEEL]

Nu 26:26 through Jahleel, the **J** clan. 3500

JAHMAI (1)

1Ch 7: 2 Uzzi, Rephaiah, Jeriel, **J,** 3503

JAHZAH (2)

1Ch 6:78 Jericho they received Bezer in the desert, **J,** 3404
Jer 48:21 to Holon, **J** and Mephaath, 3404

JAHZEEL (1) [JAHZEELITE]

Nu 26:48 through **J,** the Jahzeelite clan; 3505

JAHZEELITE (1) [JAHZEEL]

Nu 26:48 through Jahzeel, the **J** clan; 3506

JAHZEIAH (1)

Ezr 10:15 Only Jonathan son of Asahel and **J** son 3488

JAHZERAH (1)

1Ch 9:12 and Maasai son of Adiel, the son of **J,** 3492

JAHZIEL (2)

Ge 46:24 **J,** Guni, Jezer and Shillem. 3505
1Ch 7:13 **J,** Guni, Jezer and Shillem— 3507

JAIL (7) [JAILER, JAILERS]

Ac 4: 3 they put them in **j** until the next day. *5499*
5:18 the apostles and put them in the public **j.** *5499*
5:19 the doors *of* the **j** and brought them out. *5871*
5:21 and sent to the **j** for the apostles. *1303*
5:22 But on arriving at the **j,** *5871*
5:23 "We found the **j** securely locked, with *1303*
5:25 The men you put in **j** are standing in *5871*

JAILER (7) [JAIL]

Ac 16:23 **j** was commanded to guard them carefully. *1302*
16:27 The **j** woke up, and when he saw the *1302*
16:29 The **j** called for lights, *NIG*
16:33 the **j** took them and washed their wounds; *NIG*
16:34 The **j** brought them into his house and set *NIG*
16:35 the magistrates sent their officers to the **j** *NIG*
16:36 The **j** told Paul, "The magistrates have *1302*

JAILERS (1) [JAIL]

Mt 18:34 turned him over *to* the **j to be tortured,** *991*

JAIR (9) [JAIRITE, HAVVOTH JAIR]

Nu 32:41 **J,** a descendant of Manasseh, 3281
Dt 3:14 **J,** a descendant of Manasseh, 3281
Jos 13:30 all the settlements of **J** in Bashan, 3281
Jdg 10: 3 He was followed by **J** of Gilead, 3281
10: 5 When **J** died, he was buried in Kamon. 3281
1Ki 4:13 in Ramoth Gilead (the settlements of **J** son 3281
1Ch 2:22 Segub was the father of **J,** 3281
20: 5 Elhanan son of **J** killed Lahmi the brother 3600
Est 2: 5 named Mordecai son of **J,** 3281

JAIRITE (1) [JAIR]

2Sa 20:26 and Ira the **J** was David's priest. 3285

JAIRUS (6)

Mk 5:22 one of the synagogue rulers, named **J,** *2608*
5:35 some men came from the house of **J,** *NIG*
Lk 8:41 a man named **J,** a ruler of the synagogue, *2608*
8:49 someone came from the house of **J,** *NIG*
8:50 Hearing this, Jesus said *to* **J,** *899[S]*
8:51 When he arrived at the house of **J,** *NIG*

JAKAN (KJV) See AKAN

JAKEH (1)

Pr 30: 1 The sayings of Agur son of **J—** 3681

JAKIM (2)

1Ch 8:19 **J,** Zicri, Zabdi, 3691
24:12 the eleventh to Eliashib, the twelfth to **J,** 3691

JAKIN (8) [JAKINITE]

Ge 46:10 Jemuel, Jamin, Ohad, **J,** 3520
Ex 6:15 of Simeon were Jemuel, Jamin, Ohad, **J,** 3520
Nu 26:12 through **J,** the Jakinite clan; 3520
1Ki 7:21 to the south he named **J** and the one to 3521
1Ch 9:10 Of the priests: Jedaiah; Jehoiarib; **J;** 3520
24:17 the twenty-first to **J,** 3520
2Ch 3:17 to the south he named **J** and the one to 3521
Ne 11:10 the son of Joiarib; **J;** 3520

JAKINITE (1) [JAKIN]

Nu 26:12 through Jakin, the **J** clan; 3522

JALAM (4)

Ge 36: 5 and Oholibamah bore Jeush, **J** and Korah. 3609
36:14 Jeush, **J** and Korah. 3609
36:18 Chiefs Jeush, **J** and Korah. 3609
1Ch 1:35 Eliphaz, Reuel, Jeush, **J** and Korah. 3609

JALON (1)

1Ch 4:17 Jether, Mered, Epher and **J.** 3534

JAMBRES (1)

2Ti 3: 8 Just as Jannes and **J** opposed Moses, *2612*

JAMBS (12)

1Ki 6:31 of olive wood with five-sided **j.** 382+4647
6:33 In the same way he made four-sided **j** 4647
Eze 40: 9 and its **j** were two cubits thick. 382
40:24 He measured its **j** and its portico, 382
40:31 palm trees decorated its **j,** 382
40:34 palm trees decorated the **j** on either side, 382
40:37 palm trees decorated the **j** on either side, 382
40:48 of the temple and measured the **j** *of* 382
40:49 and there were pillars on each side of the **j.** 382
41: 1 to the outer sanctuary and measured the **j;** 382
41: 1 width of the **j** was six cubits on each side. NIH
41: 3 into the inner sanctuary and measured the **j** 382

JAMES (42)
Mt 4:21 J son of Zebedee and his brother John. 2610
10: 2 J son of Zebedee, and his brother John; 2610
10: 3 J son of Alphaeus, and Thaddaeus; 2610
13:55 and aren't his brothers J, Joseph, 2610
17: 1 J and John the brother of James, 2610
17: 1 James and John the brother of J, 899S
27:56 Mary the mother of J and Joses, 2610
Mk 1:19 he saw J son of Zebedee 2610
1:29 they went with J and John to the home 2610
3:17 J son of Zebedee and his brother John 2610
3:18 Thomas, J son of Alphaeus, Thaddaeus, 2610
5:37 J and John the brother of James. 2610
5:37 James and John the brother of J. 2610
6: 3 Isn't this Mary's son and the brother of J, 2610
9: 2 J and John with him and led them up 2610
10:35 Then J and John, the sons of Zebedee, 2610
10:41 they became indignant with J and John. 2610
13: 3 J, John and Andrew asked him privately, 2610
14:33 He took Peter, J and John along with him, 2610
15:40 the mother of J the younger and of Joses, 2610
16: 1 Mary Magdalene, Mary the mother of J, 2610
Lk 5:10 and so were J and John, 2610
6:14 his brother Andrew, J, John, Philip, 2610
6:15 Thomas, J son of Alphaeus, 2610
6:16 Judas son of J, and Judas Iscariot, 2610
8:51 in with him except Peter, John and J, and 2610
9:28 John and J with him and went up onto 2610
9:54 When the disciples J and John saw this, 2610
24:10 Joanna, Mary the mother of J, 2610
Ac 1:13 present were Peter, John, J and Andrew; 2610
1:13 J son of Alphaeus and Simon the Zealot, 2610
1:13 and Judas son of J. 2610
12: 2 He had J, the brother of John, 2610
12:17 "Tell J and the brothers about this," 2610
15:13 When they finished, J spoke up: 2610
21:18 and the rest of us went to see J, 2610
1Co 15: 7 Then he appeared to J, then to all the 2610
Gal 1:19 only J, the Lord's brother. 2610
2: 9 J, Peter and John, those reputed to 2610
2:12 Before certain men came from J, 2610
Jas 1: 1 J, a servant of God and of the Lord Jesus 2610
Jude 1: 1 servant of Jesus Christ and a brother of J, 2610

JAMIN (6) [JAMINITE]
Ge 46:10 The sons of Simeon: Jemuel, J, Ohad, 3546
Ex 6:15 The sons of Simeon were Jemuel, J, Ohad, 3546
Nu 26:12 through J, the Jaminite clan; 3546
1Ch 2:27 Maaz, J and Eker. 3546
4:24 Nemuel, J, Jarib, Zerah and Shaul; 3546
Ne 8: 7 The Levites—Jeshua, Bani, Sherebiah, J, 3546

JAMINITE (1) [JAMIN]
Nu 26:12 through Jamin, the J clan; 3547

JAMLECH (1)
1Ch 4:34 Meshobab, J, Joshah son of Amaziah, 3552

JANAI (1)
1Ch 5:12 Shapham the second, then J and Shaphat, 3614

JANGLING (KJV) See TALK

JANIM (1)
Jos 15:53 J, Beth Tappuah, Aphekah, 3565

JANNAI (1)
Lk 3:24 the son of J, the son of Joseph, 2613

JANNES (1)
2Ti 3: 8 Just as J and Jambres opposed Moses, 2614

JANOAH (3)
Jos 16: 6 passing by it to J on the east. 3562
16: 7 Then it went down from J to Ataroth 3562
2Ki 15:29 Abel Beth Maacah, J, Kedesh and Hazor. 3562

JANUM (KJV) See JANIM

JAPHETH (12)
Ge 5:32 he became the father of Shem, Ham and J. 3651
6:10 Noah had three sons: Shem, Ham and J. 3651
7:13 and J, together with his wife and the wives 3651
9:18 of the ark were Shem, Ham and J. 3651
9:23 But Shem and J took a garment and laid it 3651
9:27 May God extend the territory of J; 3651
9:27 may J live in the tents of Shem, NIH
10: 1 This is the account of Shem, Ham and J, 3651
10: 2 The sons of J: Gomer, Magog, Madai, 3651
10:21 whose older brother was J; 3651
1Ch 1: 4 The sons of Noah: Shem, Ham and J. 3651
1: 5 The sons of J: Gomer, Magog, Madai, 3651

JAPHIA (5)
Jos 10: 3 J king of Lachish and Debir king of Eglon. 3644
19:12 and went on to Daberath and up to J. 3643
2Sa 5:15 Ibhar, Elishua, Nepheg, J, 3644
1Ch 3: 7 Nogah, Nepheg, J, 3644
14: 6 Nogah, Nepheg, J, 3644

JAPHLET (2) [JAPHLET'S, JAPHLETITES]
1Ch 7:32 Heber was the father of J, 3646
7:33 The sons of J: 3646

JAPHLET'S (1) [JAPHLET]
1Ch 7:33 These were J sons. 3646

JAPHLETITES (1) [JAPHLET]
Jos 16: 3 to the territory of the J as far as the region 3647

JAPHO (KJV) See JOPPA

JAR (37) [JARS]
Ge 24:14 'Please let down your j that I may have 3902
24:15 Rebekah came out with her j 3902
24:16 filled her j and came up again. 3902
24:17 "Please give me a little water from your j." 3902
24:18 the j to her hands and gave him a drink. 3902
24:20 she quickly emptied her j into the trough, 3902
24:43 a little water from your j," 3902
24:45 with her j on her shoulder. 3902
24:46 "She quickly lowered her j 3902
Ex 16:33 "Take a j and put an omer of manna in it. 7573
Nu 5:17 in a clay j and put some dust from 3998
19:17 into a j and pour fresh water over them. 3998
1Ki 14: 3 some cakes and a j of honey, 1318
17:10 a little water in a j so I may have a drink?" 3998
17:12 only a handful of flour in a j and a little oil 3902
17:14 'The j of flour will not be used up and 3902
17:16 the j of flour was not used up and the jug 3902
19: 6 bread baked over hot coals, and a j of water. 7608
2Ki 4: 6 But he replied, "There is not a j left." 3998
Jer 19: 1 "Go and buy a clay j from a potter. 1318
19:10 "Then break the j while those who go 1318
19:11 as this potter's j is smashed and cannot 3998
32:14 and put them in a clay j so they will last 3998
48:11 not poured from one j to another— 3998
48:38 for I have broken Moab like a j 3998
51:34 he has made us an empty j. 3998
Eze 4: 9 in a storage j and use them to make bread 3998
Mt 26: 7 an alabaster j of very expensive perfume, 223
Mk 14: 3 an alabaster j of very expensive perfume, 223
14: 3 the j and poured the perfume on his head. 223
14:13 a man carrying a j of water will meet you. 3040
Lk 7:37 she brought an alabaster j of perfume, 223
8:16 a lamp and hides it in a j or puts it under 5007
22:10 a man carrying a j of water will meet you. 3040
Jn 4:28 Then, leaving her water j, 5620
19:29 A j of wine vinegar was there, 5007
Heb 9: 4 This ark contained the gold j of manna, 5085

JAREB (KJV) See GREAT

JARED (7)
Ge 5:15 he became the father of J. 3719
5:16 And after he became the father of J, 3719
5:18 When J had lived 162 years, 3719
5:19 J lived 800 years and had other sons 3719
5:20 Altogether, J lived 962 years, 3719
1Ch 1: 2 Kenan, Mahalalel, J, 3719
Lk 3:37 the son of J, the son of Mahalalel, 2616

JARESIAH (KJV) See JAARESHIAH

JARHA (2)
1Ch 2:34 He had an Egyptian servant named J. 3739
2:35 in marriage to his servant J, 3739

JARIB (3)
1Ch 4:24 Nemuel, Jamin, J, Zerah and Shaul; 3743
Ezr 8:16 Shemaiah, Elnathan, J, Elnathan, Nathan, 3743
10:18 Maaseiah, Eliezer, J and Gedaliah. 3743

JARKON See ME JARKON

JARMUTH (7)
Jos 10: 3 Piram king of J, 3754
10: 5 the kings of Jerusalem, Hebron, J, 3754
10:23 the kings of Jerusalem, Hebron, J, 3754
12:11 the king of J one the king of Lachish one 3754
15:35 J, Adullam, Socoh, Azekah, 3754
21:29 J and En Gannim, together 3754
Ne 11:29 in En Rimmon, in Zorah, in J, 3754

JAROAH (1)
1Ch 5:14 the son of J, the son of Gilead, 3726

JARS (23) [JAR]
Ex 7:19 even in the wooden buckets and stone j." AIT
Nu 4: 7 and the j for drink offerings; 7987
4: 9 and all its j for the oil used to supply it. 3998
Jdg 7:16 and empty j in the hands of all of them, 3902
7:19 They blew their trumpets and broke the j 3902
7:20 the trumpets and smashed the j. 3902
Ru 2: 9 from the water j the men have filled." 3998
1Ki 18:33 "Fill four large j with water and pour it 3902
2Ki 4: 3 and ask all your neighbors for empty j. 3998
4: 4 Pour oil into all the j, and as each is filled, 3998
2Ki 4: 5 the j to her and she kept pouring. NIH
4: 6 When all the j were full, 3998
Job 38:37 Who can tip over the water j of the heavens 5574
Ps 33: 7 He gathers the waters of the sea into j; 5532
Isa 22:24 from the bowls to all the j. 5574
Jer 14: 3 They return with their j unfilled; 3998
40:10 and put them in your storage j, 3998
48:12 "when I will send men who pour from j, NIH
48:12 they will empty her j and smash her jugs. 3998
Mt 25: 4 took oil in j along with their lamps. 31
Jn 2: 6 Nearby stood six stone water j, 5620
2: 7 "Fill the j with water"; 5620
2Co 4: 7 But we have this treasure in j of clay 5007

JASHAR (2)
Jos 10:13 as it is written in the Book of J. 3839
2Sa 1:18 of the bow (it is written in the Book of J): 3839

JASHEN (1)
2Sa 23:32 the sons of J, 3826

JASHER (KJV) See JASHAR

JASHOBEAM (3)
1Ch 11:11 J, a Hacmonite, was chief of the officers; 3790
12: 6 Azarel, Joezer and J the Korahites; 3790
27: 2 for the first month, was J son of Zabdiel. 3790

JASHUB (4) [JASHUBITE]
Ge 46:13 Tola, Puah, J and Shimron. 3793
Nu 26:24 through J, the Jashubite clan; 3793
1Ch 7: 1 Tola, Puah, J and Shimron—four in all. 3793
Ezr 10:29 Meshullam, Malluch, Adaiah, J, 3793

JASHUBI LEHEM (1)
1Ch 4:22 who ruled in Moab and J. 3788

JASHUBITE (1) [JASHUB]
Nu 26:24 through Jashub, the J clan; 3795

JASIEL (KJV) See JAASIEL

JASON (4) [JASON'S]
Ac 17: 6 they dragged J and some other brothers 2619
17: 7 and J has welcomed them into his house. 2619
17: 9 Then they made J and the others post bond 2619
Ro 16:21 as do Lucius, J and Sosipater, 2619

JASON'S (1) [JASON]
Ac 17: 5 They rushed to J house in search of Paul 2619

JASPER (8)
Ex 28:20 an onyx and a j. 3835
39:13 an onyx and a j. 3835
Job 28:18 Coral and j are not worthy of mention; 1486
Eze 28:13 topaz and emerald, chrysolite, onyx and j, 3835
Rev 4: 3 the appearance of j and carnelian. 2618
21:11 like a j, clear as crystal. 2618+3345
21:18 The wall was made of j, 2618
21:19 The first foundation was j, 2618

JATHNIEL (1)
1Ch 26: 2 Zebadiah the third, J the fourth, 3853

JATTIR (4)
Jos 15:48 In the hill country: Shamir, J, Socoh, 3848
21:14 J, Eshtemoa, 3848
1Sa 30:27 Ramoth Negev and J; 3848
1Ch 6:57 and Libnah, J, Eshtemoa, 3848

JAVAN (4)
Ge 10: 2 Gomer, Magog, Madai, J, Tubal, 3430
10: 4 The sons of J: Elishah, Tarshish, 3430
1Ch 1: 5 Gomer, Magog, Madai, J, Tubal, 3430
1: 7 The sons of J: Elishah, Tarshish, 3430

JAVELIN (7) [JAVELINS]
Jos 8:18 toward Ai the j that is in your hand, 3959
8:18 So Joshua held out his j toward Ai. 3959
8:26 not draw back the hand that held out his j 3959
1Sa 17: 6 and a bronze j was slung on his back. 3959
17:45 against me with sword and spear and j, 3959
Job 41:26 nor does the spear or the dart or the j. 9233
Ps 35: 3 and j against those who pursue me. 6038

JAVELINS (1) [JAVELIN]
2Sa 18:14 So he took three j in his hand 8657

JAW (2) [JAWBONE, JAWS]
Job 41: 2 a cord through his nose or pierce his j with 4305
Ps 3: 7 Strike all my enemies on the j; 4305

JAWBONE (4) [JAW]
Jdg 15:15 Finding a fresh j of a donkey, 4305
15:16 a donkey's j I have made donkeys of them. 4305
15:16 With a donkey's j I have killed 4305

Jdg 15:17 he threw away the j; 4305

JAWS (5) [JAW]

Job 36:16 "He is wooing you from the j *of* distress to 7023
Pr 30:14 and whose j are set with knives to devour 5506
Isa 30:28 he places in the j *of* the peoples a bit 4305
Eze 29: 4 But I will put hooks in your j and make 4305
38: 4 put hooks in your j and bring you out 4305

JAZER (13)

Nu 21:32 After Moses had sent spies to J, 3597
32: 1 that the lands of J and Gilead were suitable 3597
32: 3 J, Nimrah, Heshbon, Elealeh, Sebam, 3597
32:35 Atroth Shophan, J, Jogbehah, 3597
Jos 13:25 The territory of J, all the towns of Gilead 3597
21:39 and J, together with their pasturelands— 3597
2Sa 24: 5 and then went through Gad and on to J. 3597
1Ch 6:81 Heshbon and J, together 3597
26:31 the Hebronites were found at J *in* Gilead. 3597
Isa 16: 8 which once reached J and spread toward 3597
16: 9 So I weep, as J weeps, 3597
Jer 48:32 I weep for you, as J weeps, 3597
48:32 they reached as far as the sea of J. 3597

JAZIZ (1)

1Ch 27:31 J the Hagrite was in charge of the flocks. 3467

JEALOUS (28) [JEALOUSY]

Ge 30: 1 she *became* j of her sister. 7861
37:11 His brothers *were* j of him, 7861
Ex 20: 5 for I, the LORD your God, am a j God, 7862
34:14 whose name is J, is a jealous God. 7862
34:14 whose name is Jealous, is a j God. 7862
Nu 5:14 or if he *is* j and suspects her even though she is not impure— 6296+6584+7863+8120
11:29 But Moses replied, *"Are* you j for my sake? 7861
Dt 4:24 your God is a consuming fire, a j God. 7862
5: 9 for I, the LORD your God, am a j God, 7862
6:15 is a j God and his anger will burn 7862
32:16 *They* **made** him j with their foreign gods 7861
32:21 They **made** me j by what is no god 7861
Jos 24:19 He is a holy God; he is a j God. 7868
1Sa 18: 9 Saul **kept a** j **eye on** David. 6523
1Ki 14:22 *they* **stirred up** his j **anger** more than 7861
Isa 11:13 Ephraim *will* not *be* j *of* Judah, 7861
Eze 16:38 of my wrath and j **anger.** 7863
16:42 and my j **anger** will turn away from you; 7863
23:25 I will direct my j **anger** against you, 7863
36: 6 in my j wrath because you have suffered 7863
Joel 2:18 Then the LORD *will be* j for his land 7861
Na 1: 2 The LORD is a j and avenging God; 7868
Zep 3: 8 be consumed by the fire of my j **anger.** 7863
Zec 1:14 *'I am* very j for Jerusalem and Zion, 7861+7863
8: 2 *"I am* very j for Zion; 7861+7863
Ac 7: 9 *"Because* the patriarchs *were* j **of** Joseph, *2420*
17: 5 But the Jews *were* j; *2420*
2Co 11: 2 *I am* j for you with a godly jealousy. *2420*

JEALOUSY (26) [JEALOUS]

Nu 5:14 and if feelings of j come over her husband 7863
5:15 because it is a grain offering for j, 7863
5:18 the grain offering for j, 7863
5:25 from her hands the grain offering for j, 7863
5:29 is the law of j when a woman goes astray 7863
5:30 or when feelings of j come over a man 7863
Ps 78:58 *they* **aroused** his j with their idols. 7861
79: 5 How long will your j burn like fire? 7863
Pr 6:34 for j arouses a husband's fury, 7863
27: 4 but who can stand before j? 7863
Ecc 9: 6 and their j have long since vanished; 7863
SS 8: 6 its j unyielding as the grave. 7863
Isa 11:13 Ephraim's j will vanish, 7863
Eze 8: 3 where the idol that **provokes to** j stood. 7861
8: 5 of the gate of the altar I saw this idol of j. 7863
35:11 the anger and j you showed in your hatred 7863
Zep 1:18 of his j the whole world will be consumed, 7863
Zec 8: 2 *I am* burning with j for her." 7861
Ac 5:17 of the Sadducees, were filled *with* j. *2419*
13:45 they were filled *with* j and talked abusively *2419*
Ro 13:13 not in dissension and j. *2419*
1Co 3: 3 since there is j and quarreling among you, *2419*
10:22 *Are we trying to* **arouse** the Lord's j? *4143*
2Co 11: 2 I am jealous for you *with* a godly j. *2419*
12:20 I fear that there may be quarreling, j, *2419*
Gal 5:20 hatred, discord, j, fits of rage, *2419*

JEARIM (1) [KESALON, KIRIATH JEARIM]

Jos 15:10 ran along the northern slope of Mount J 3630

JEATHERAI (1)

1Ch 6:21 Iddo his son, Zerah his son and J his son. 3290

JEBERECHIAH (KJV) See JEBEREKIAH

JEBEREKIAH (1)

Isa 8: 2 in Uriah the priest and Zechariah son of J 3310

JEBUS (3) [JEBUSITE, JEBUSITES, JERUSALEM]

Jdg 19:10 and went toward J (that is, Jerusalem), 3293
19:11 near J and the day was almost gone, 3293
1Ch 11: 4 to Jerusalem (that is, J). 3293

JEBUSI (KJV) See JEBUSITES

JEBUSITE (9) [JEBUS]

Jos 15: 8 the southern slope of the J city (that is, 3294
18:16 along the southern slope of the J *city* and 3294
18:28 Haeleph, the J *city* (that is, Jerusalem), 3294
2Sa 24:16 at the threshing floor of Araunah the J. 3294
24:18 on the threshing floor of Araunah the J." 3294
1Ch 21:15 at the threshing floor of Araunah the J. 3294
21:18 on the threshing floor of Araunah the J. 3294
21:28 on the threshing floor of Araunah the J, 3294
2Ch 3: 1 on the threshing floor of Araunah the J, 3294

JEBUSITES (33) [JEBUS]

Ge 10:16 J, Amorites, Girgashites, 3294
15:21 Amorites, Canaanites, Girgashites and J." 3294
Ex 3: 8 Amorites, Perizzites, Hivites and J. 3294
3:17 Amorites, Perizzites, Hivites and J— 3294
13: 5 Hittites, Amorites, Hivites and J— 3294
23:23 Hivites and J, and I will wipe them out. 3294
33: 2 Hittites, Perizzites, Hivites and J. 3294
34:11 Hittites, Perizzites, Hivites and J. 3294
Nu 13:29 J and Amorites live in the hill country; 3294
Dt 7: 1 Canaanites, Perizzites, Hivites and J, 3294
20:17 Canaanites, Perizzites, Hivites and J— 3294
Jos 3:10 Perizzites, Girgashites, Amorites and J. 3294
9: 1 Canaanites, Perizzites, Hivites and J)— 3294
11: 3 Perizzites and J in the hill country; 3294
12: 8 Canaanites, Perizzites, Hivites and J): 3294
15:63 Judah could not dislodge the J, 3294
15:63 to this day the J live there with the people 3294
24:11 Hittites, Girgashites, Hivites and J, 3294
Jdg 1:21 however, failed to dislodge the J, 3294
1:21 the J live there with the Benjamites. 3294
3: 5 Amorites, Perizzites, Hivites and J. 3294
19:11 at this city of the J and spend the night." 3294
2Sa 5: 6 to Jerusalem to attack the J, 3294
5: 6 The J said to David, NIH
5: 8 "Anyone who conquers the J will have 3294
1Ki 9:20 and J (these peoples were not Israelites), 3294
1Ch 1:14 J, Amorites, Girgashites, 3294
11: 4 The J who lived there 3294
11: 6 the J will become commander-in-chief." 3294
2Ch 8: 7 and J (these peoples were not Israelites), 3294
Ezr 9: 1 Perizzites, J, Ammonites, Moabites, 3294
Ne 9: 8 Amorites, Perizzites, J and Girgashites. 3294
Zec 9: 7 and Ekron will be like the J. 3294

JECAMIAH (KJV) See JEKAMIAH

JECHOLIAH (KJV) See JECOLIAH

JECHONIAS (KJV) See JECONIAH

JECOLIAH (2)

2Ki 15: 2 His mother's name was J; 3525
2Ch 26: 3 His mother's name was J; 3524

JECONIAH (2)

Mt 1:11 the father of J and his brothers at the time *2651*
1:12 J was the father of Shealtiel, *2651*

JEDAIAH (11) [JEDAIAH'S]

1Ch 4:37 the son of J, the son of Shimri, 3355
9:10 Of the priests: J; Jehoiarib; Jakin; 3361
24: 7 the second to J, 3361
Ezr 2:36 the descendants of J (through the family 3361
Ne 3:10 Adjoining this, J son of Harumaph 3355
7:39 the descendants of J (through the family 3361
11:10 From the priests: J; the son of Joiarib; 3361
12: 6 Shemaiah, Joiarib, J, 3361
12: 7 Amok, Hilkiah and J. 3361
Zec 6:10 from the exiles Heldai, Tobijah and J, 3361
6:14 J and Hen son of Zephaniah as a memorial 3361

JEDAIAH'S (2) [JEDAIAH]

Ne 12:19 of Joiarib's, Mattenai; of J, Uzzi; 3361
12:21 of Hilkiah's, Hashabiah; of J, Nethanel. 3361

JEDIAEL (6)

1Ch 7: 6 Bela, Beker and J. 3356
7:10 The son of J: Bilhan. 3356
7:11 All these sons of J were heads of families. 3356
11:45 J son of Shimri, 3356
12:20 Adnah, Jozabad, J, Michael, Jozabad, 3356
26: 2 Zechariah the firstborn, J the second, 3356

JEDIDAH (1)

2Ki 22: 1 His mother's name was J daughter of 3352

JEDIDIAH (1)

2Sa 12:25 through Nathan the prophet to name him J. 3354

JEDUTHUN (16)

1Ch 9:16 the son of Galal, the son of J; 3349
16:38 Obed-Edom son of J, and also Hosah, 3357
16:41 With them were Heman and J and the rest 3349
16:42 and J were responsible for the sounding of 3349
16:42 The sons of J were stationed at the gate. 3349
25: 1 and J for the ministry of prophesying, 3349
25: 3 As for J, from his sons: 3349
25: 3 under the supervision of their father J, 3349
25: 6 J and Heman were under the supervision 3349
2Ch 5:12 Heman, J and their sons and relatives— 3349
29:14 from the descendants of J, 3349
35:15 Asaph, Heman and J the king's seer. 3349
Ne 11:17 the son of Galal, the son of J. 3349
Ps 39: T For the director of music. For J. 3349
62: T For the director of music. For J. 3349
77: T For the director of music. For J. 3349

JEER (1) [JEERED, JEERS]

Job 16:10 Men open their mouths to j at me; NIH

JEERED (1) [JEER]

2Ki 2:23 some youths came out of the town and j 7840

JEERS (1) [JEER]

Heb 11:36 Some faced j and flogging, *1849*

JEEZER (KJV) See IEZER

JEEZERITES (KJV) See IEZERITE

JEGAR SAHADUTHA (1)

Ge 31:47 Laban called it J, and Jacob called it Galeed 3337

JEHALLELEL (2)

1Ch 4:16 The sons of J: 3401
2Ch 29:12 Kish son of Abdi and Azariah son of J; 3401

JEHATH (1)

1Ch 6:20 Libni his son, J his son, Zimmah his son, 3511

JEHDEIAH (2)

1Ch 24:20 from the sons of Shubael: J. 3485
27:30 J the Meronothite was in charge of 3485

JEHEZKEL (1)

1Ch 24:16 the twentieth to J, 3489

JEHIAH (1)

1Ch 15:24 and J were also to be doorkeepers for 3496

JEHIEL (14)

1Ch 15:18 Zechariah, Jaaziel, Shemiramoth, J, Unni, 3493
15:20 Aziel, Shemiramoth, J, Unni, Eliab, 3493
16: 5 then Jeiel, Shemiramoth, J, Mattithiah, 3493
23: 8 J the first, Zetham and Joel—three in all. 3493
27:32 J son of Hacmoni took care of 3493
29: 8 in the custody of J the Gershonite. 3493
2Ch 21: 2 the sons of Jehoshaphat, were Azariah, J, 3493
29:14 the descendants of Heman, J and Shimei; 3493
31:13 J, Azaziah, Nahath, Asahel, Jerimoth, 3493
35: 8 Hilkiah, Zechariah and J, 3493
Ezr 8: 9 Obadiah son of J, and with him 218 men; 3493
10: 2 Then Shecaniah son of J, 3493
10:21 Maaseiah, Elijah, Shemaiah, J and Uzziah. 3493
10:26 Mattaniah, Zechariah, J, Abdi, 3493

JEHIELI (2)

1Ch 26:21 to Ladan the Gershonite, were J, 3494
26:22 the sons of J, 3494

JEHIZKIAH (1)

2Ch 28:12 of Meshillemoth, J son of Shallum, 3491

JEHOADDAH (2)

1Ch 8:36 Ahaz was the father of J, 3389
8:36 J was the father of Alemeth, 3389

JEHOADDIN (2)

2Ki 14: 2 His mother's name was J; 3390
2Ch 25: 1 His mother's name was J; 3391

JEHOAHAZ (22)

2Ki 10:35 And J his son succeeded him as king. 3370
13: 1 J son of Jehu became king of Israel 3370
13: 4 Then J sought the LORD's favor, 3370
13: 7 of the army of J except fifty horsemen, 3370
13: 8 As for the other events of the reign of J, 3370
13: 9 J rested with his fathers and was buried 3370
13:10 Jehoash son of J became king of Israel 3370
13:22 throughout the reign of J. 3370
13:25 of J recaptured from Ben-Hadad son 3370
13:25 in battle from his father J. 3370
14: 1 In the second year of Jehoash son of J king 3407
14: 8 to Jehoash son of J, the son of Jehu, king 3370
14:17 after the death of Jehoash son of J king 3370
23:30 the people of the land took J son of Josiah 3370
23:31 J was twenty-three years old 3370

2Ki 23:34 But he took **J** and carried him off to Egypt. 3370
2Ch 25:17 he sent this challenge to Jehoash son of **J**, 3370
25:25 after the death of Jehoash son of **J** king 3370
36: 1 the people of the land took **J** son of Josiah 3370
36: 2 **J** was twenty-three years old 3407
36: 4 made Eliakim, a brother of **J**, king over 2257^S
36: 4 But Neco took Eliakim's brother **J** 3407

JEHOASH (28) [JOASH]

2Ki 13: 9 And **J** his son succeeded him as king. 3409
13:10 **J** son of Jehoahaz became king of Israel 3371
13:12 As for the other events of the reign of **J**, 3409
13:13 **J** rested with his fathers, 3409
13:13 **J** was buried in Samaria with the kings 3409
13:14 **J** king of Israel went down to see him 3409
13:25 Then **J** son of Jehoahaz recaptured 3371
13:25 Three times **J** defeated him, 3409
14: 1 the second year of **J** son of Jehoahaz king 3409
14: 8 to **J** son of Jehoahaz, the son of Jehu, king 3371
14: 9 But **J** king of Israel replied 3371
14:11 so **J** king of Israel attacked. 3371
14:13 **J** king of Israel captured Amaziah king 3371
14:13 Then **J** went to Jerusalem and broke down NIH
14:15 As for the other events of the reign of **J**, 3371
14:16 **J** rested with his fathers and was buried 3371
14:17 after the death of **J** son of Jehoahaz king 3371
14:23 of **J** king of Israel became king in Samaria, 3409
14:27 by the hand of Jeroboam son of **J**. 3409
2Ch 25:17 he sent this challenge to **J** son of Jehoahaz, 3409
25:18 But **J** king of Israel replied 3409
25:20 that he might hand them over to [**J**], NIH
25:21 So **J** king of Israel attacked. 3409
25:23 **J** king of Israel captured Amaziah king 3409
25:23 Then **J** brought him to Jerusalem NIH
25:25 after the death of **J** son of Jehoahaz king 3409
Hos 1: 1 during the reign of Jeroboam son of **J** king 3409
Am 1: 1 and Jeroboam son of **J** was king of Israel. 3409

JEHOHANAN (9)

1Ch 26: 3 **J** the sixth and Eliehoenai the seventh. 3380
2Ch 17:15 next, **J** the commander, with 280,000; 3380
23: 1 Azariah son of Jeroham, Ishmael son of **J**, 3380
28:12 Azariah son of **J**, Berekiah son 3380
Ezr 10: 6 and went to the room of **J** son of Eliashib. 3380
10:28 **J**, Hananiah, Zabbai and Athlai. 3380
Ne 6:18 and his son **J** had married the daughter 3380
12:13 of Ezra's, Meshullam; of Amariah's, **J**; 3380
12:42 Eleazar, Uzzi, **J**, Malkijah, Elam and Ezer. 3380

JEHOIACHIN (26) [JEHOIACHIN'S]

2Ki 24: 6 And **J** his son succeeded him as king. 3382
24: 8 **J** was eighteen years old when he became 3382
24:12 **J** king of Judah, his mother, his attendants, 3382
24:12 he took **J** prisoner. 2257^S
24:15 Nebuchadnezzar took **J** captive 3382
25:27 of the exile of **J** king of Judah, 3382
25:27 he released **J** from prison 3382
25:29 So **J** put aside his prison clothes and for NIH
25:30 the king gave **J** a regular allowance as long 2257^S
1Ch 3:16 **J** his son, and Zedekiah. 3526
3:17 The descendants of **J** the captive: 3526
2Ch 36: 8 And **J** his son succeeded him as king. 3382
36: 9 **J** was eighteen years old whe he became 3382
Est 2: 6 among those taken captive with **J** king 3526
Jer 22:24 **J** son of Jehoiakim king of Judah, 4037
22:28 Is this man **J** a despised, broken pot, 4037
24: 1 After **J** son of Jehoiakim king of Judah 3527
27:20 when he carried **J** son of Jehoiakim king 3526
28: 4 I will also bring back to this place **J** son 3526
29: 2 after King **J** and the queen mother, 3526
37: 1 he reigned in place of **J** son of Jehoiakim. 4037
52:31 of the exile of **J** king of Judah, 3382
52:31 he released **J** king of Judah and freed him 3382
52:33 So **J** put aside his prison clothes and for NIH
52:34 Day by day the king of Babylon gave **J** 2257^S
Eze 1: 2 it was the fifth year of the exile of King **J**— 3422

JEHOIACHIN'S (2) [JEHOIACHIN]

2Ki 24:17 He made Mattaniah, **J** uncle, 2257^S
2Ch 36:10 and he made **J** uncle, Zedekiah, 2257^S

JEHOIADA (53)

2Sa 8:18 Benaiah son of **J** was over the Kerethites 3381
20:23 Benaiah son of **J** was over the Kerethites 3381
23:20 of **J** was a valiant fighter from Kabzeel, 3381
23:22 the exploits of Benaiah son of **J**; 3381
1Ki 1: 8 But Zadok the priest, Benaiah son of **J**, 3381
1:26 and Benaiah son of **J**, 3381
1:32 Nathan the prophet and Benaiah son of **J**." 3381
1:36 Benaiah son of **J** answered the king, 3381
1:38 Nathan the prophet, Benaiah son of **J**, 3381
1:44 Nathan the prophet, Benaiah son of **J**, 3381
2:25 to Benaiah son of **J**, 3381
2:29 Then Solomon ordered Benaiah son of **J**, 3381
2:34 So Benaiah son of **J** went up and struck 3381
2:35 of **J** over the army in Joab's position 3381
2:46 king gave the order to Benaiah son of **J**, 3381
4: 4 Benaiah son of **J**— 3381
2Ki 11: 4 In the seventh year **J** sent for 3381
11: 9 a hundred did just as **J** the priest ordered. 3381
11: 9 and came to **J** the priest. 3381
11:12 **J** brought out the king's son and put NIH
11:15 **J** the priest ordered the commanders 3381
11:17 **J** then made a covenant between 3381
11:18 Then **J** the priest posted guards at NIH
12: 2 in the eyes of the LORD all the years **J** 3381
12: 7 Therefore King Joash summoned **J** 3381
12: 9 **J** the priest took a chest and bored a hole 3381
1Ch 11:22 of **J** was a valiant fighter from Kabzeel, 3381
11:24 the exploits of Benaiah son of **J**; 3381
12:27 including **J**, leader of the family of Aaron, 3381
18:17 Benaiah son of **J** was over the Kerethites 3381
27: 5 was Benaiah son of **J** the priest. 3381
27:34 by **J** son of Benaiah and by Abiathar. 3381
2Ch 22:11 of King Jehoram and wife of the priest **J**, 3381
23: 1 In the seventh year **J** showed his strength. 3381
23: 3 **J** said to them, "The king's son shall reign, NIH
23: 8 of Judah did just as **J** the priest ordered. 3381
23: 8 for **J** the priest had not released any of 3381
23:11 **J** and his sons brought out the king's son 3381
23:14 **J** the priest sent out the commanders 3381
23:16 **J** then made a covenant that he and 3381
23:18 Then **J** placed the oversight of the temple 3381
24: 2 in the eyes of the LORD all the years of **J** 3381
24: 3 **J** chose two wives for him, 3381
24: 6 the king summoned **J** the chief priest 3381
24:12 and **J** gave it to the men who carried out 3381
24:14 and **J**, and with it were made articles for 3381
24:14 As long as **J** lived, burnt offerings were 3381
24:15 Now **J** was old and full of years, 3381
24:17 After the death of **J**, the officials of Judah 3381
24:20 of God came upon Zechariah son of **J** 3381
24:22 Joash did not remember the kindness
Zechariah's father **J** had shown him 3381
24:25 against him for murdering the son of **J** 3381
Jer 29:26 in place of **J** to be in charge of the house 3381

JEHOIAKIM (34) [ELIAKIM, JEHOIAKIM'S]

2Ki 23:34 and changed Eliakim's name to **J**. 3383
23:35 **J** paid Pharaoh Neco the silver 3383
23:36 **J** was twenty-five years old 3383
24: 1 and **J** became his vassal for three years. 3383
24: 6 **J** rested with his fathers. 3383
24:19 just as **J** had done. 3383
1Ch 3:15 Johanan the firstborn, **J** the second son, 3383
3:16 The successors of **J**: 3383
2Ch 36: 4 and changed Eliakim's name to **J**. 3383
36: 5 **J** was twenty-five years old 3383
Jer 1: 3 the reign of **J** son of Josiah king of Judah, 3383
22:18 the LORD says about **J** son of Josiah king 3383
22:24 Jehoiachin son of **J** king of Judah, 3383
24: 1 After Jehoiachin son of **J** king of Judah 3383
25: 1 in the fourth year of **J** son of Josiah king 3383
26: 1 the reign of **J** son of Josiah king of Judah, 3383
26:21 When King **J** and all his officers 3383
26:22 King **J**, however, sent Elnathan son 3383
26:23 of Egypt and took him to King **J**, 3383
27:20 when he carried Jehoiachin son of **J** king 3383
28: 4 of **J** king of Judah and all the other exiles 3383
35: 1 from the LORD during the reign of **J** son 3383
36: 1 In the fourth year of **J** son of Josiah king 3383
36: 9 the ninth month of the fifth year of **J** son 3383
36:28 which **J** king of Judah burned up. 3383
36:29 Also tell **J** king of Judah, 3383
36:30 this is what the LORD says about **J** king 3383
36:32 that **J** king of Judah had burned in the fire. 3383
37: 1 he reigned in place of Jehoiachin son of **J**. 3383
45: 1 in the fourth year of **J** son of Josiah king 3383
46: 2 in the fourth year of **J** son of Josiah king 3383
52: 2 just as **J** had done. 3383
Da 1: 1 In the third year of the reign of **J** king 3383
1: 2 And the Lord delivered **J** king of Judah 3383

JEHOIAKIM'S (3) [JEHOIAKIM]

2Ki 24: 1 During **J** reign, Nebuchadnezzar king 2257^S
24: 5 As for the other events of **J** reign, 3383
2Ch 36: 8 The other events of **J** reign, 3383

JEHOIARIB (2)

1Ch 9:10 Of the priests: Jedaiah; **J**; Jakin; 3384
24: 7 The first lot fell to **J**, 3384

JEHONADAB (3)

2Ki 10:15 he left there, he came upon **J** son of Recab, 3386
10:15 "I am," **J** answered. 3386
10:23 and **J** son of Recab went into the temple 3386

JEHONATHAN (2)

2Ch 17: 8 **J**, Adonijah, Tobijah and Tob-Adonijah— 3387
Ne 12:18 of Bilgah's, Shammua; of Shemaiah's, **J**; 3387

JEHORAM (29) [JEHORAM'S, JORAM]

1Ki 22:50 And **J** his son succeeded him. 3393
2Ki 1:17 of **J** son of Jehoshaphat king of Judah. 3393
8:16 **J** son of Jehoshaphat began his reign 3393
8:20 In the time of **J**, Edom rebelled 2257^S
8:21 So **J** went to Zair with all his chariots. 3456
8:24 **J** rested with his fathers and was buried 3456
8:25 Ahaziah son of **J** king of Judah began 3393
8:29 Then Ahaziah son of **J** king of Judah went 3393
11: 2 daughter of King **J** and sister of Ahaziah, 3456
12:18 Jehoshaphat, **J** and Ahaziah, 3393
1Ch 3:11 **J** his son, Ahaziah his son, Joash his son, 3456
2Ch 17: 8 and the priests Elishama and **J**. 3393
21: 1 And **J** his son succeeded him as king. 3393
21: 3 to **J** because he was his firstborn son. 3393
21: 4 When **J** established himself firmly 3393
21: 5 **J** was thirty-two years old 3393
21: 8 In the time of **J**, Edom rebelled 2257^S
21: 9 So **J** went there with his officers 3393
21:10 because **J** had forsaken the LORD, NIH
21:12 **J** received a letter from Elijah the prophet, 2257^S
21:16 against **J** the hostility of the Philistines and 3393
21:18 the LORD afflicted **J** with an incurable 2257^S
21:20 **J** was thirty-two years old NIH
22: 1 So Ahaziah son of **J** king of Judah began 3393
22: 6 Then Ahaziah son of **J** king of Judah went 3393
22:11 But Jehosheba, the daughter of King **J**, NIH
22:11 of King **J** and wife of the priest Jehoiada, 3393
Mt 1: 8 Jehoshaphat the father of **J**, *2732*
1: 8 **J** the father of Uzziah, *2732*

JEHORAM'S (3) [JEHORAM]

2Ki 8:23 As for the other events of **J** reign, 3456
2Ch 21: 2 **J** brothers, the sons of Jehoshaphat, 2257^S
22: 1 **J** youngest son, king in his place, 2257^S

JEHOSHAPHAT (85) [JEHOSHAPHAT'S]

2Sa 8:16 **J** son of Ahilud was recorder; 3398
20:24 **J** son of Ahilud was recorder; 3398
1Ki 4: 3 **J** son of Ahilud—recorder; 3398
4:17 **J** son of Paruah—in Issachar; 3398
15:24 And **J** his son succeeded him as king. 3398
22: 2 But in the third year **J** king of Judah went 3398
22: 4 So he asked **J**, 3398
22: 4 **J** replied to the king of Israel, 3398
22: 5 But **J** also said to the king of Israel, 3398
22: 7 But **J** asked, "Is there not a prophet of 3398
22: 8 The king of Israel answered **J**, 3398
22: 8 "The king should not say that," **J** replied. 3398
22:10 of Israel and **J** king of Judah were sitting 3398
22:18 The king of Israel said to **J**, 3398
22:29 the king of Israel and **J** king of Judah went 3398
22:30 The king of Israel said to **J**, 3398
22:32 When the chariot commanders saw **J**, 3398
22:32 but when **J** cried out, 3398
22:41 **J** son of Asa became king of Judah in 3398
22:42 **J** was thirty-five years old 3398
22:44 **J** was also at peace with the king of Israel. 3398
22:48 Now **J** built a fleet of trading ships to go 3398
22:49 that time Ahaziah son of Ahab said to **J**, 3398
22:49 with your men," but **J** refused. 3398
22:50 Then **J** rested with his fathers 3398
22:51 in the seventeenth year of **J** king of Judah, 3398
2Ki 1:17 the second year of Jehoram son of **J** king 3398
3: 1 in Samaria in the eighteenth year of **J** king 3398
3: 7 also sent this message to **J** king of Judah: 3398
3:11 **J** asked, "Is there no prophet of the LORD 3398
3:12 **J** said, "The word of the LORD is 3398
3:12 of Israel and **J** and the king of Edom went 3398
3:14 not have respect for the presence of **J** king 3398
8:16 when **J** was king of Judah, 3398
8:16 Jehoram son of **J** began his reign as king 3398
9: 2 you get there, look for Jehu son of **J**, 3398
9:14 So Jehu son of **J**, the son of Nimshi, 3398
12:18 **J**, Jehoram and Ahaziah, 3398
1Ch 3:10 Abijah his son, Asa his son, **J** his son, 3398
18:15 **J** son of Ahilud was recorder; 3398
2Ch 17: 1 **J** his son succeeded him as king 3398
17: 3 with **J** because in his early years he walked 3398
17: 5 and all Judah brought gifts to **J**, 3398
17:10 so that they did not make war with **J**. 3398
17:11 Some Philistines brought **J** gifts and silver 3398
17:12 **J** became more and more powerful; 3398
18: 1 Now **J** had great wealth and honor, 3398
18: 3 Ahab king of Israel asked **J** king of Judah, 3398
18: 3 **J** replied, "I am as you are, NIH
18: 4 But **J** also said to the king of Israel, 3398
18: 6 **J** asked, "Is there not a prophet of the LORD 3398
18: 7 The king of Israel answered **J**, 3398
18: 7 "The king should not say that," **J** replied. 3398
18: 9 of Israel and **J** king of Judah were sitting 3398
18:17 The king of Israel said to **J**, 3398
18:28 the king of Israel and **J** king of Judah went 3398
18:29 The king of Israel said to **J**, 3398
18:31 When the chariot commanders saw **J**, 3398
18:31 they turned to attack him, but **J** cried out, 3398
19: 1 When **J** king of Judah returned safely 3398
19: 4 **J** lived in Jerusalem, 3398
19: 8 **J** appointed some of the Levites, 3398
20: 1 of the Meunites came to make war on **J**. 3398
20: 2 Some men came and told **J**, 3398
20: 3 **J** resolved to inquire of the LORD, 3398
20: 5 Then **J** stood up in the assembly of Judah 3398
20:15 "Listen, King **J** and all who live in Judah 3398
20:18 **J** bowed with his face to the ground, 3398
20:20 As they set out, **J** stood and said, 3398
20:21 **J** appointed men to sing to the LORD and NIH
20:25 So **J** and his men went 3398
20:27 Then, led by **J**, all the men of Judah 3398
20:30 And the kingdom of **J** was at peace, 3398
20:31 So **J** reigned over Judah. 3398
20:35 **J** king of Judah made an alliance 3398
20:37 of Mareshah prophesied against **J**, 3398
21: 1 Then **J** rested with his fathers 3398
21: 2 Jehoram's brothers, the sons of **J**, 3398
21: 2 All these were sons of **J** king of Israel. 3398
21:12 in the ways of your father **J** or of Asa king 3398
22: 9 for they said, "He was a son of **J**, 3398
Joel 3: 2 and bring them down to the Valley of **J**. 3399
3:12 let them advance into the Valley of **J**, 3399
Mt 1: 8 Asa the father of **J**, *2734*

Mt 1: 8 J the father of Jehoram, *2734*

JEHOSHAPHAT'S (2) [JEHOSHAPHAT]
1Ki 22:45 As for the other events of J reign, 3398
2Ch 20:34 The other events of J reign, 3398

JEHOSHEBA (3)
2Ki 11: 2 But J, the daughter of King Jehoram 3394
2Ch 22:11 But J, the daughter of King Jehoram, 3395
22:11 Because J, the daughter of King Jehoram 3395

JEHOSHUA, JEHOSHUAH (KJV) See JOSHUA

JEHOVAH (KJV) See †LORD

JEHOVAH-JIREH (KJV) See †LORD WILL PROVIDE

JEHOVAH-NISSI (KJV) See †LORD IS MY BANNER

JEHOVAH-SHALOM (KJV) See †LORD IS PEACE

JEHOZABAD (4)
2Ki 12:21 of Shimeath and J son of Shomer. 3379
1Ch 26: 4 Shemaiah the firstborn, J the second, 3379
2Ch 17:18 J, with 180,000 men armed for battle. 3379
24:26 and J, son of Shimrith a Moabite woman. 3379

JEHOZADAK (8)
1Ch 6:14 and Seraiah the father of J. 3392
6:15 J was deported when the LORD sent Judah 3392
Hag 1: 1 governor of Judah, and to Joshua son of J, 3392
1:12 Joshua son of J, the high priest, 3392
1:14 and the spirit of Joshua son of J, 3392
2: 2 governor of Judah, to Joshua son of J, 3392
2: 4 'Be strong, O Joshua son of J, 3392
Zec 6:11 Joshua son of J. 3392

JEHU (74) [JEHU'S]
1Ki 16: 1 word of the LORD came to J son of Hanani 3369
16: 7 the prophet J son of Hanani to Baasha 3369
16:12 against Baasha through the prophet J— 3369
19:16 anoint J son of Nimshi king over Israel, 3369
19:17 J will put to death any who escape 3369
19:17 to death any who escape the sword of J. 3369
2Ki 9: 2 look for J son of Jehoshaphat, 3369
9: 5 "For which of us?" asked J. 3369
9: 6 J got up and went into the house. NIH
9:11 When J went out to his fellow officers, 3369
9:11 and the sort of things he says," J replied. NIH
9:12 J said, "Here is what he told me: NIH
9:13 the trumpet and shouted, "J is king!" 3369
9:14 So J son of Jehoshaphat, 3369
9:15 J said, "If this is the way you feel, 3369
9:18 The horseman rode off to meet J and said, 2257S
9:18 do you have to do with peace?" J replied. 3369
9:19 J replied, "What do you have to do 3369
9:20 The driving is like that of J son 3369
9:21 each in his own chariot, to meet J. 3369
9:22 When Joram saw J he asked, 3369
9:22 "Have you come in peace, J?" 3369
9:22 "How can there be peace," J replied, NIH
9:24 Then J drew his bow and shot Joram 3369
9:25 J said to Bidkar, his chariot officer, NIH
9:27 J chased him, shouting, "Kill him too!" 3369
9:30 Then J went to Jezreel. 3369
9:31 As J entered the gate, she asked, 3369
9:33 "Throw her down!" J said. NIH
9:34 J went in and ate and drank. NIH
9:36 They went back and told J, who said, 2257S
10: 1 J wrote letters and sent them to Samaria: 3369
10: 5 and the guardians sent this message to J: 3369
10: 6 Then J wrote them a second letter, saying, NIH
10: 7 in baskets and sent them to J in Jezreel. 2257S
10: 8 When the messenger arrived, he told J, 2257S
10: 8 Then J ordered, "Put them in two piles at NIH
10: 9 The next morning J went out. NIH
10:11 So J killed everyone in Jezreel who 3369
10:12 J then set out and went toward Samaria. NIH
10:15 J greeted him and said, NIH
10:15 "If so," said J, "give me your hand." NIH
10:15 and J helped him up into the chariot. NIH
10:16 J said, "Come with me and see my zeal for NIH
10:17 When J came to Samaria, NIH
10:18 Then J brought all the people together 3369
10:18 J will serve him much. 3369
10:19 But J was acting deceptively in order 3369
10:20 J said, "Call an assembly in honor 3369
10:22 And J said to the keeper of the wardrobe, NIH
10:23 Then J and Jehonadab son of Recab went 3369
10:23 J said to the ministers of Baal, NIH
10:24 Now J had posted eighty men outside 3369
10:25 As soon as J had finished making 3369
10:28 So J destroyed Baal worship in Israel. 3369
10:30 The LORD said to J, 3369
10:31 Yet J was not careful to keep the law of 3369
2Ki 10:35 J rested with his fathers and was buried 3369
10:36 The time that J reigned over Israel 3369
12: 1 In the seventh year of J, 3369
13: 1 Jehoahaz son of J became king of Israel 3369
14: 8 the son of J, king of Israel, 3369
15:12 of the LORD spoken to J was fulfilled: 3369
1Ch 2:38 Obed the father of J, 3369
2:38 J the father of Azariah, 3369
4:35 J son of Joshibiah, the son of Seraiah, 3369
12: 3 Beracah, J the Anathothite, 3369
2Ch 19: 2 J the seer, the son of Hanani, went out 3369
20:34 are written in the annals of J son 3369
22: 7 he went out with Joram to meet J son 3369
22: 8 While J was executing judgment on 3369
22: 9 He was brought to J and put to death. 3369
25:17 the son of J, king of Israel: 3369
Hos 1: 4 the house of J for the massacre at Jezreel, 3369

JEHU'S (3) [JEHU]
2Ki 9: 6 Then the prophet poured the oil on J head 2257S
9:17 in Jezreel saw J troops approaching, 3369
10:34 As for the other events of J reign, 3369

JEHUBBAH (KJV) See HUBBAH

JEHUCAL (2)
Jer 37: 3 sent J son of Shelemiah with the priest 3385
38: 1 J son of Shelemiah, and Pashhur son of 3426

JEHUD (1)
Jos 19:45 J, Bene Berak, Gath Rimmon, 3372

JEHUDI (4)
Jer 36:14 all the officials sent J son of Nethaniah, 3375
36:21 The king sent J to get the scroll, 3375
36:21 and J brought it from the room 3375
36:23 Whenever J had read three or four columns 3375

JEHUDIJAH (KJV) See JUDEAN

JEHUSH (KJV) See JEUSH

JEIEL (13)
1Ch 5: 7 J the chief, Zechariah, 3599
8:29 J the father of Gibeon lived in Gibeon. 3599
9:35 J the father of Gibeon lived in Gibeon. 3599
11:44 and J the sons of Hotham the Aroerite, 3599
15:18 Eliphelehu, Mikneiah, Obed-Edom and J, 3599
15:21 J and Azaziah were to play the harps, 3599
16: 5 Zechariah second, then J, Shemiramoth, 3599
16: 5 Eliab, Benaiah, Obed-Edom and J. 3599
2Ch 20:14 the son of J, the son of Mattaniah, 3599
26:11 by J the secretary and Maaseiah the officer 3599
29:13 of Elizaphan, Shimri and J; 3599
35: 9 J and Jozabad, the leaders of the Levites, 3599
Ezr 10:43 J, Mattithiah, Zabad, Zebina, Jaddai, 3599

JEKABZEEL (1)
Ne 11:25 in J and its villages, 3677

JEKAMEAM (2)
1Ch 23:19 Jahaziel the third and J the fourth. 3694
24:23 Jahaziel the third and J the fourth. 3694

JEKAMIAH (3)
1Ch 2:41 Shallum the father of J, 3693
2:41 and J the father of Elishama. 3693
3:18 Shenazzar, J, Hoshama and Nedabiah. 3693

JEKUTHIEL (1)
1Ch 4:18 and J the father of Zanoah.) 3688

JEMIMAH (1)
Job 42:14 The first daughter he named J, 3544

JEMUEL (2)
Ge 46:10 The sons of Simeon: J, Jamin, Ohad, 3543
Ex 6:15 The sons of Simeon were J, Jamin, Ohad, 3543

JEOPARDED (KJV) See RISKED

JEOPARDY (2)
2Sa 18:13 And if *I had* **put** my life **in** j— 6913+9214
Job 13:14 Why *do I* **put** myself **in** j and take my life 928+1414+5951+9094

JEPHTHAE (KJV) See JEPHTHAH

JEPHTHAH (23) [JEPHTHAH'S]
Jdg 11: 1 J the Gileadite was a mighty warrior. 3653
11: 2 they drove J away. 3653
11: 3 So J fled from his brothers and settled in 3653
11: 5 the elders of Gilead went to get J from 3653
11: 7 J said to them, "Didn't you hate me 3653
11: 9 J answered, "Suppose you take me back 3653
11:11 So J went with the elders of Gilead, 3653
Jdg 11:12 Then J sent messengers to the Ammonite 3653
11:14 J sent back messengers to the Ammonite 3653
11:15 "This is what J says: 3653
11:28 to the message J sent him. 3653
11:29 the Spirit of the LORD came upon J. 3653
11:30 And J made a vow to the LORD: 3653
11:32 Then J went over to fight the Ammonites, 3653
11:34 When J returned to his home in Mizpah, 3653
11:40 to commemorate the daughter of J 3653
12: 1 crossed over to Zaphon and said to J, 3653
12: 2 J answered, "I and my people were 3653
12: 4 J then called together the men of Gilead 3653
12: 7 J led Israel six years. 3653
12: 7 Then J the Gileadite died, 3653
1Sa 12:11 Barak, J and Samuel, 3653
Heb 11:32 J, David, Samuel and the prophets, *2650*

JEPHTHAH'S (1) [JEPHTHAH]
Jdg 11:13 of the Ammonites answered J messengers, 3653

JEPHUNNEH (16)
Nu 13: 6 from the tribe of Judah, Caleb son of J; 3648
14: 6 Joshua son of Nun and Caleb son of J, 3648
14:30 except Caleb son of J and Joshua son 3648
14:38 of Nun and Caleb son of J survived. 3648
26:65 of them was left except Caleb son of J 3648
32:12 of J the Kenizzite and Joshua son of Nun, 3648
34:19 Caleb son of J, from the tribe of Judah; 3648
Dt 1:36 except Caleb son of J. 3648
Jos 14: 6 Caleb son of J the Kenizzite said to him, 3648
14:13 Then Joshua blessed Caleb son of J 3648
14:14 to Caleb son of J the Kenizzite ever since, 3648
15:13 Joshua gave to Caleb son of J a portion 3648
21:12 the city they had given to Caleb son of J 3648
1Ch 4:15 The sons of Caleb son of J: 3648
6:56 the city were given to Caleb son of J. 3648
7:38 The sons of Jether: J, Pispah and Ara. 3648

JERAH (2)
Ge 10:26 Sheleph, Hazarmaveth, J, 3733
1Ch 1:20 Sheleph, Hazarmaveth, J, 3733

JERAHMEEL (9) [JERAHMEELITES]
1Sa 27:10 "Against the Negev of J" or 3738
1Ch 2: 9 The sons born to Hezron were: J, 3737
2:25 The sons of J the firstborn of Hezron: 3737
2:26 J had another wife, 3737
2:27 The sons of Ram the firstborn of J: 3737
2:33 These were the descendants of J. 3737
2:42 The sons of Caleb the brother of J: 3737
24:29 From Kish: the son of Kish: J. 3737
Jer 36:26 Instead, the king commanded J, 3737

JERAHMEELITES (1) [JERAHMEEL]
1Sa 30:29 in the towns of the J and the Kenites; 3738

JERED (1)
1Ch 4:18 (His Judean wife gave birth to J the father 3719

JEREMAI (1)
Ezr 10:33 Mattenai, Mattattah, Zabad, Eliphelet, J, 3757

JEREMIAH (145) [JEREMIAH'S]
2Ki 23:31 mother's name was Hamutal daughter of J; 3759
24:18 mother's name was Hamutal daughter of J; 3759
1Ch 5:24 Epher, Ishi, Eliel, Azriel, J, 3758
12: 4 J, Jahaziel, Johanan, Jozabad 3758
12:10 Mishmannah the fourth, J the fifth, 3758
12:13 J the tenth and Macbannai the eleventh. 3759
2Ch 35:25 J composed laments for Josiah, 3759
36:12 not humble himself before J the prophet, 3759
36:21 of the word of the LORD spoken by J. 3759
36:22 the word of the LORD spoken by J, 3759
Ezr 1: 1 the word of the LORD spoken by J, 3758
Ne 10: 2 Seraiah, Azariah, J, 3758
12: 1 with Jeshua: Seraiah, J, 3758
12:34 Judah, Benjamin, Shemaiah, J, 3758
Jer 1: 1 The words of J son of Hilkiah, 3759
1:11 "What do you see, J?" 3759
7: 1 the word that came to J from the LORD: 3759
11: 1 the word that came to J from the LORD: 3759
14: 1 of the LORD to J concerning the drought: 3759
18: 1 the word that came to J from the LORD: 3759
18:18 "Come, let's make plans against J; 3759
19:14 J then returned from Topheth, 3759
20: 1 heard J prophesying these things, 3759
20: 2 he had J the prophet beaten and put in 3759
20: 3 J said to him, "The LORD's name for you 3759
21: 1 The word came to J from the LORD 3759
21: 3 But J answered them, "Tell Zedekiah, 3759
24: 3 LORD asked me, "What do you see, J?" 3759
25: 1 to J concerning all the people of Judah in 3759
25: 2 So J the prophet said to all the people 3759
25:13 and prophesied by J against all the nations. 3759
26: 7 the people heard J speak these words in 3759
26: 8 But as soon as J finished telling all 3759
26: 9 the people crowded around J in the house 3759
26:12 J said to all the officials and all the people: 3759
26:20 against this city and this land as J did. 3759
26:24 Ahikam son of Shaphan supported J, 3759
27: 1 this word came to J from the LORD: 3758
28: 5 Then the prophet J replied to 3758

Jer 28:10 the neck of the prophet J and broke it, 3758
28:11 At this, the prophet J went on his way. 3758
28:12 the yoke off the neck of the prophet J, 3758
28:12 the word of the LORD came to J: 3758
28:15 the prophet J said to Hananiah the prophet, 3758
29: 1 the text of the letter that the prophet J sent 3758
29:27 So why have you not reprimanded J 3759
29:29 however, read the letter to J the prophet. 3759
29:30 Then the word of the LORD came to J: 3759
30: 1 the word that came to J from the LORD: 3759
32: 1 the word that came to J from the LORD 3759
32: 2 and J the prophet was confined in 3759
32: 6 J said, "The word of the LORD came 3759
32:26 Then the word of the LORD came to J: 3759
33: 1 While J was still confined in the courtyard 3759
33:19 The word of the LORD came to J: 3759
33:23 The word of the LORD came to J: 3759
34: 1 this word came to J from the LORD: 3759
34: 6 Then J the prophet told all this 3759
34: 8 The word came to J from the LORD 3759
34:12 Then the word of the LORD came to J: 3759
35: 1 the word that came to J from the LORD 3759
35: 3 So I went to get Jaazaniah son of J, 3759
35:12 the word of the LORD came to J, saying: 3759
35:18 Then J said to the family of the Recabites, 3759
36: 1 this word came to J from the LORD: 3759
36: 4 So J called Baruch son of Neriah, 3759
36: 4 and while J dictated all the words 3759
36: 5 Then J told Baruch, "I am restricted; 3759
36: 8 Baruch son of Neriah did everything J 3759
36:10 the LORD's temple the words of J from 3759
36:17 Did J dictate it?" 2257S
36:19 the officials said to Baruch, "You and J, 3759
36:26 of Abdeel to arrest Baruch the scribe and J 3759
36:27 the word of the LORD came to J: 3759
36:32 So J took another scroll and gave it to 3759
36:32 and as J dictated, Baruch wrote on it 3759
37: 2 the LORD had spoken through J 3759
37: 3 the priest Zephaniah son of Maaseiah to J 3759
37: 4 Now J was free to come and go among 3759
37: 6 word of the LORD came to J the prophet: 3759
37:12 J started to leave the city to go to 3759
37:14 "That's not true!" J said. 3759
37:14 instead, he arrested J and brought him to 3759
37:15 with J and had him beaten and imprisoned 3759
37:16 J was put into a vaulted cell in a dungeon, 3759
37:17 J replied, "you will be handed over to 3759
37:18 Then J said to King Zedekiah, 3759
37:21 King Zedekiah then gave orders for J to 3759
37:21 J remained in the courtyard of the guard. 3759
38: 1 of Malkijah heard what J was telling all 3759
38: 6 So they took J and put him into the cistern 3759
38: 6 They lowered J by ropes into the cistern; 3759
38: 6 only mud, and J sank down into the mud. 3759
38: 7 heard that they had put J into the cistern. 3759
38: 9 in all they have done to J the prophet. 3759
38:10 and lift J the prophet out of the cistern 3759
38:11 and let them down with ropes to J in 3759
38:12 Ebed-Melech the Cushite said to J, 3759
38:12 to pad the ropes." J did so, 3759
38:13 J remained in the courtyard of the guard. 3759
38:14 Then King Zedekiah sent for J the prophet 3759
38:14 the king said to J. "Do not hide anything 3759
38:15 J said to Zedekiah, "If I give you an answer 3759
38:16 Zedekiah swore this oath secretly to J: 3759
38:17 Then J said to Zedekiah, "This is what 3759
38:19 King Zedekiah said to J, 3759
38:20 "They will not hand you over," J replied. 3759
38:24 Then Zedekiah said to J, 3759
38:27 All the officials did come to J 3759
38:28 And J remained in the courtyard of 3759
39:11 of Babylon had given these orders about J 3759
39:14 sent and had J taken out of the courtyard 3759
39:15 While J had been confined in 3759
40: 1 The word came to J from the LORD 3759
40: 1 He had found J bound in chains among all 2257S
40: 2 the commander of the guard found J, 3759
40: 5 However, before J turned to go, 5647S
40: 6 So J went to Gedaliah son of Ahikam 3759
42: 2 J the prophet and said to him, 3759
42: 4 "I have heard you," replied J the prophet. 3759
42: 5 Then they said to J, 3759
42: 7 the word of the LORD came to J. 3759
43: 1 When J finished telling the people all 3759
43: 2 and all the arrogant men said to J, 3759
43: 6 J the prophet and Baruch son of Neriah. 3759
43: 8 the word of the LORD came to J: 3759
44: 1 This word came to J concerning all 3759
44:15 in Lower and Upper Egypt, said to J, 3759
44:20 Then J said to all the people, 3759
44:24 Then J said to all the people, 3759
45: 1 This is what J the prophet told Baruch son 3759
45: 1 on a scroll the words J was then dictating: 3759
46: 1 of the LORD that came to J the prophet 3759
46:13 This is the message the LORD spoke to J 3759
47: 1 to J the prophet concerning the Philistines 3759
49:34 to J the prophet concerning Elam, early in 3759
50: 1 through J the prophet concerning Babylon 3759
51:59 This is the message J gave to the staff 3759
51:60 J had written on a scroll about all the disasters that would come upon Babylon 3759
51:64 The words of J end here. 3759
52: 1 mother's name was Hamutal daughter of J; 3759
Da 9: 2 of the LORD given to J the prophet, 3758
Mt 2:17 through the prophet J was fulfilled: *2635*
16:14 and still others, J or one of the prophets." *2635*
27: 9 by J the prophet was fulfilled: *2635*

JEREMIAH'S (2) [JEREMIAH]

Ne 12:12 Meraiah; of J, Hananiah; 3758
Jer 36:27 that Baruch had written at J dictation, 3759

JEREMIAS, JEREMY (KJV) See JEREMIAH

JEREMOTH (5)

1Ch 7: 8 Zemirah, Joash, Eliezer, Elioenai, Omri, J, 3756
8:14 Ahio, Shashak, J, 3756
Ezr 10:26 Zechariah, Jehiel, Abdi, J and Elijah. 3756
10:27 Elioenai, Eliashib, Mattaniah, J, 3756
10:29 Malluch, Adaiah, Jashub, Sheal and J. 3756

JERIAH (4)

1Ch 23:19 J the first, Amariah the second, 3746
24:23 J the first, Amariah the second, 3746
26:31 J was their chief according to 3745
26:32 J had twenty-seven hundred relatives, 2257S

JERIBAI (1)

1Ch 11:46 J and Joshaviah the sons of Elnaam, 3744

JERICHO (62)

Nu 22: 1 along the Jordan across from J. 3735
26: 3 plains of Moab by the Jordan across from J, 3735
26:63 plains of Moab by the Jordan across from J. 3735
31:12 by the Jordan across from J. 3735
33:48 plains of Moab by the Jordan across from J. 3735
33:50 the Jordan across from J the LORD said 3735
34:15 on the east side of the Jordan of J, 3735
35: 1 plains of Moab by the Jordan across from J, 3735
36:13 plains of Moab by the Jordan across from J. 3735
Dt 32:49 across from J, and view Canaan, 3735
34: 1 to the top of Pisgah, across from J. 3735
34: 3 and the whole region from the Valley of J, 3735
Jos 2: 1 look over the land," he said, "especially J." 3735
2: 2 The king of J was told, "Look! 3735
2: 3 the king of J sent this message to Rahab: 3735
3:16 So the people crossed over opposite J. 3735
4:13 over before the LORD to the plains of J 3735
4:19 at Gilgal on the eastern border of J. 3735
5:10 while camped at Gilgal on the plains of J, 3735
5:13 Now when Joshua was near J, 3735
6: 1 Now J was tightly shut up because of 3735
6: 2 "See, I have delivered J into your hands, 3735
6:25 the men Joshua had sent as spies to J— 3735
6:26 who undertakes to rebuild this city, J: 3735
7: 2 Now Joshua sent men from J to Ai, 3735
8: 2 and its king as you did to J and its king, 3735
9: 3 what Joshua had done to J and Ai, 3735
10: 1 to Ai and its king as he had done to J 3735
10:28 as he had done to the king of J. 3735
10:30 to its king as he had done to the king of J. 3735
12: 9 of J one the king of Ai (near Bethel) one 3735
13:32 of Moab across the Jordan east of J. 3735
16: 1 for Joseph began at the Jordan of J, 3735
16: 1 east of the waters of J, 3735
16: 7 touched J and came out at the Jordan. 3735
18:12 of J and headed west into the hill country, 3735
18:21 J, Beth Hoglah, Emek Keziz, 3735
20: 8 of the Jordan of J they designated Bezer in 3735
24:11 you crossed the Jordan and came to J. 3735
24:11 The citizens of J fought against you, 3735
2Sa 10: 5 "Stay at J till your beards have grown, 3735
1Ki 16:34 In Ahab's time, Hiel of Bethel rebuilt J. 3735
2Ki 2: 4 the LORD has sent me to J." 3735
2: 4 So they went to J. 3735
2: 5 The company of the prophets at J went up 3735
2:15 The company of the prophets from J, 3735
2:18 who was staying in J, he said to them, 3735
25: 5 and overtook him in the plains of J. 3735
1Ch 6:78 the Jordan east of J they received Bezer in 3735
19: 5 "Stay at J till your beards have grown, 3735
2Ch 28:15 to their fellow countrymen at J, 3735
Ezr 2:34 of J 345 3735
Ne 3: 2 The men of J built the adjoining section, 3735
7:36 of J 345 3735
Jer 39: 5 and overtook Zedekiah in the plains of J. 3735
52: 8 and overtook him in the plains of J. 3735
Mt 20:29 As Jesus and his disciples were leaving J, *2637*
Mk 10:46 Then they came to J. *2637*
Lk 10:30 man was going down from Jerusalem to J, *2637*
18:35 As Jesus approached J, *2637*
19: 1 Jesus entered J and was passing through. *2637*
Heb 11:30 By faith the walls *of* J fell, *2637*

JERIEL (1)

1Ch 7: 2 The sons of Tola: Uzzi, Rephaiah, J, 3741

JERIJAH (KJV) See JERIAH

JERIMOTH (9)

1Ch 7: 7 Ezbon, Uzzi, Uzziel, J and Iri, 3748
12: 5 J, Bealiah, Shemariah and Shephatiah 3748
23:23 The sons of Mushi: Mahli, Eder and J— 3756
24:30 And the sons of Mushi: Mahli, Eder and J. 3748
25: 4 Mattaniah, Uzziel, Shubael and J; 3748
25:22 the fifteenth to J, his sons and relatives, 12 3756
27:19 J son of Azriel; 3748
2Ch 11:18 who was the daughter of David's son J 3748
31:13 Jehiel, Azaziah, Nahath, Asahel, J, 3748

JERIOTH (1)

1Ch 2:18 by his wife Azubah (and by J). 3750

JEROBOAM (95) [JEROBOAM'S]

1Ki 11:26 J son of Nebat rebelled against the king. 3716
11:28 Now J was a man of standing, 3716
11:29 that time J was going out of Jerusalem, 3716
11:31 Then he said to J, "Take ten pieces 3716
11:40 Solomon tried to kill J, but Jeroboam fled 3716
11:40 but J fled to Egypt, to Shishak the king, 3716
12: 2 When J son of Nebat heard this 3716
12: 3 So they sent for J, 3716
12:12 Three days later J and all the people 3716
12:15 the word the LORD had spoken to J son 3716
12:20 the Israelites heard that J had returned, 3716
12:25 Then J fortified Shechem in the hill 3716
12:26 J thought to himself, 3716
12:31 J built shrines on high places NIH
13: 1 as J was standing by the altar to make 3716
13: 4 When King J heard what the man 3716
13:33 after this, J did not change his evil ways, 3716
13:34 This was the sin of the house of J that led 3716
14: 1 At that time Abijah son of J became ill, 3716
14: 2 and J said to his wife, "Go, disguise 3716
14: 2 you won't be recognized as the wife of J. 3716
14: 6 he said, "Come in, wife of J. 3716
14: 7 Go, tell J that this is what the LORD, 3716
14:10 to bring disaster on the house of J. 3716
14:10 I will cut off from J every last male 3716
14:10 up the house of J as one burns dung, 3716
14:11 Dogs will eat those belonging to J who die 3716
14:13 He is the only one belonging to J who will 3716
14:13 the only one in the house of J in whom 3716
14:14 who will cut off the family of J. 3716
14:16 up because of the sins J has committed 3716
14:30 warfare between Rehoboam and J. 3716
15: 1 In the eighteenth year of the reign of J son 3716
15: 6 There was war between Rehoboam and J 3716
15: 7 There was war between Abijah and J. 3716
15: 9 In the twentieth year of J king of Israel, 3716
15:25 Nadab son of J became king of Israel in 3716
15:29 He did not leave J anyone that breathed, 3716
15:30 because of the sins J had committed 3716
15:34 walking in the ways of J and in his sin, 3716
16: 2 of J and caused my people Israel to sin and 3716
16: 3 like that of J son of Nebat. 3716
16: 7 and becoming like the house of J— 3716
16:19 the LORD and walking in the ways of J 3716
16:26 the ways of J son of Nebat and in his sin, 3716
16:31 to commit the sins of J son of Nebat, 3716
21:22 of J son of Nebat and that of Baasha son 3716
22:52 and mother and in the ways of J son 3716
2Ki 3: 3 he clung to the sins of J son of Nebat, 3716
9: 9 the house of Ahab like the house of J son 3716
10:29 he did not turn away from the sins of J son 3716
10:31 He did not turn away from the sins of J, 3716
13: 2 the LORD by following the sins of J son 3716
13: 6 the house of J, which he had caused Israel 3716
13:11 not turn away from any of the sins of J son 3716
13:13 and J succeeded him on the throne. 3716
14:16 And J his son succeeded him as king. 3716
14:23 J son of Jehoash king of Israel 3716
14:24 not turn away from any of the sins of J son 3716
14:27 he saved them by the hand of J son 3716
14:29 J rested with his fathers, 3716
15: 1 the twenty-seventh year of J king of Israel, 3716
15: 8 Zechariah son of J became king of Israel 3716
15: 9 not turn away from the sins of J son 3716
15:18 not turn away from the sins of J son 3716
15:24 not turn away from the sins of J son 3716
15:28 not turn away from the sins of J son 3716
17:21 they made J son of Nebat their king. 3716
17:21 J enticed Israel away from following 3716
17:22 The Israelites persisted in all the sins of J 3716
23:15 the high place made by J son of Nebat, 3716
1Ch 5:17 of Jotham king of Judah and J king 3716
2Ch 9:29 the seer concerning J son of Nebat? 3716
10: 2 When J son of Nebat heard this (he was 3716
10: 3 So they sent for J, 3716
10:12 Three days later J and all Israel went to 3716
10:15 the word the LORD had spoken to J son 3716
11: 4 and turned back from marching against J. 3716
11:14 because J and his sons had rejected them 3716
12:15 warfare between Rehoboam and J. 3716
13: 1 In the eighteenth year of the reign of J, 3716
13: 2 There was war between Abijah and J. 3716
13: 3 and J drew up a battle line against him 3716
13: 4 and said, "J and all Israel, listen to me! 3716
13: 6 Yet J son of Nebat, an official of Solomon 3716
13: 8 with you the golden calves that J made to 3716
13:13 Now J had sent troops around to the rear, 3716
13:15 God routed J and all Israel before Abijah 3716
13:19 Abijah pursued J and took from him 3716
13:20 J did not regain power during the time 3716
Hos 1: 1 during the reign of J son of Jehoash king 3716
Am 1: 1 when Uzziah was king of Judah and J son 3716
7: 9 against the house of J." 3716
7:10 of Bethel sent a message to J king 3716
7:11 " 'J will die by the sword, 3716

JEROBOAM'S (6) [JEROBOAM]

1Ki 14: 4 So J wife did what he said and went 3716
14: 5 "J wife is coming to ask you 3716

1Ki 14:17 J wife got up and left and went to Tirzah. 3716
14:19 The other events of J reign, 3716
15:29 he killed J whole family. 3716
2Ki 14:28 As for the other events of J reign, 3716

JEROHAM (10)

1Sa 1: 1 whose name was Elkanah son of J, 3736
1Ch 6:27 J his son, Elkanah his son 3736
6:34 the son of J, the son of Eliel, 3736
8:27 Elijah and Zicri were the sons of J. 3736
9: 8 Ibneiah son of J; 3736
9:12 Adaiah son of J, the son of Pashhur, 3736
12: 7 and Zebadiah the sons of J from Gedor. 3736
27:22 Azarel son of J. 3736
2Ch 23: 1 Azariah son of J, 3736
Ne 11:12 Adaiah son of J, the son of Pelaliah, 3736

JERUB-BAAL (11) [GIDEON, JERUB-BAAL'S, JERUB-BESHETH]

Jdg 6:32 So that day they called Gideon "J," saying, 3715
7: 1 Early in the morning, J (that is, Gideon) 3715
8:29 J son of Joash went back home to live. 3715
8:35 to show kindness to the family of J 3715
9: 1 of J went to his mother's brothers 3715
9: 5 murdered his seventy brothers, the sons of J 3715
9: 5 But Jotham, the youngest son of J, 3715
9:16 if you have been fair to J and his family, 3715
9:19 toward J and his family today, 3715
9:57 The curse of Jotham son of J came 3715
1Sa 12:11 Then the LORD sent J, Barak, 3715

JERUB-BAAL'S (3) [JERUB-BAAL]

Jdg 9: 2 to have all seventy of J sons rule over you, 3715
9:24 that the crime against J seventy sons, 3715
9:28 Isn't he J son, and isn't Zebul his deputy? 3715

JERUB-BESHETH (1) [JERUB-BAAL]

2Sa 11:21 Who killed Abimelech son of J? 3717

JERUEL (1)

2Ch 20:16 at the end of the gorge in the Desert of J. 3725

JERUSALEM (804) [JEBUS, JERUSALEM'S]

Jos 10: 1 king of J heard that Joshua had taken Ai 3731
10: 3 king of J appealed to Hoham king of Hebron, 3731
10: 5 the kings of J, Hebron, Jarmuth, 3731
10:23 the kings of J, Hebron, Jarmuth, 3731
12:10 the king of J one the king of Hebron one 3731
15: 8 of the Jebusite city (that is, J). 3731
15:63 who were living in J; 3731
18:28 Haeleph, the Jebusite city (that is, J), 3731
Jdg 1: 7 They brought him to J, and he died there. 3731
1: 8 men of Judah attacked J also and took it. 3731
1:21 who were living in J; 3731
19:10 (that is, J), with his two saddled donkeys 3731
1Sa 17:54 the Philistine's head and brought it to J, 3731
2Sa 5: 5 and in J he reigned over all Israel 3731
5: 6 The king and his men marched to J 3731
5:13 David took more concubines and wives in J, 3731
8: 7 of Hadadezer and brought them to J. 3731
9:13 And Mephibosheth lived in J, 3731
10:14 the Ammonites and came to J. 3731
11: 1 But David remained in J. 3731
11:12 Uriah remained in J that day and the next. 3731
12:31 David and his entire army returned to J. 3731
14:23 to Geshur and brought Absalom back to J. 3731
14:28 in J without seeing the king's face. 3731
15: 8 'If the LORD takes me back to J, 3731
15:11 from J had accompanied Absalom. 3731
15:14 to all his officials who were with him in J, 3731
15:29 and Abiathar took the ark of God back to J 3731
15:37 at J as Absalom was entering the city. 3731
16: 3 Ziba said to him, "He is staying in J, 3731
16:15 and all the men of Israel came to J, 3731
17:20 so they returned to J. 3731
19:19 on the day my lord the king left J. 3731
19:25 When he came from J to meet the king, 3731
19:33 over with me and stay with me in J, 3731
19:34 that I should go up to J with the king? 3731
20: 2 the way from the Jordan to J. 3731
20: 3 When David returned to his palace in J, 3731
20: 7 from J to pursue Sheba son of Bicri. 3731
20:22 And Joab went back to the king in J. 3731
24: 8 they came back to J at the end 3731
24:16 angel stretched out his hand to destroy J, 3731
1Ki 2:11 in Hebron and thirty-three in J. 3731
2:36 "Build yourself a house in J and live there, 3731
2:38 And Shimei stayed in J for a long time. 3731
2:41 that Shimei had gone from J to Gath 3731
3: 1 temple of the LORD, and the wall around J. 3731
3:15 He returned to J, 3731
8: 1 into his presence at J the elders of Israel, 3731
9:15 the supporting terraces, the wall of J, 3731
9:19 whatever he desired to build in J, 3731
10: 2 Arriving at J with a very great caravan— 3731
10:26 in the chariot cities and also with him in J. 3731
10:27 The king made silver as common in J 3731
11: 7 hill east of J, Solomon built a high place 3731
11:13 of David my servant and for the sake of J, 3731
11:29 that time Jeroboam was going out of J, 3731
11:32 sake of my servant David and the city of J, 3731
11:36 may always have a lamp before me in J, 3731
11:42 in J over all Israel forty years. 3731
12:18 to get into his chariot and escape to J. 3731
12:21 When Rehoboam arrived in J, 3731
12:27 at the temple of the LORD in J, 3731
12:28 "It is too much for you to go up to J. 3731
14:21 and he reigned seventeen years in J, 3731
14:25 Shishak king of Egypt attacked J. 3731
15: 2 and he reigned in J three years. 3731
15: 4 in J by raising up a son to succeed him and 3731
15: 4 to succeed him and by making J strong. 3731
15:10 and he reigned in J forty-one years. 3731
22:42 and he reigned in J twenty-five years. 3731
2Ki 8:17 and he reigned in J eight years. 3731
8:26 and he reigned in J one year. 3731
9:28 His servants took him by chariot to J 3731
12: 1 and he reigned in J forty years. 3731
12:17 Then he turned to attack J. 3731
12:18 who then withdrew from J. 3731
14: 2 and he reigned in J twenty-nine years. 3731
14: 2 Jehoaddin; she was from J. 3731
14:13 to J and broke down the wall of Jerusalem 3731
14:13 to Jerusalem and broke down the wall of J 3731
14:19 They conspired against him in J, 3731
14:20 and was buried in J with his fathers, 3731
15: 2 and he reigned in J fifty-two years. 3731
15: 2 Jecoliah; she was from J. 3731
15:33 and he reigned in J sixteen years. 3731
16: 2 and he reigned in J sixteen years. 3731
16: 5 up to fight against J and besieged Ahaz, 3731
18: 2 and he reigned in J twenty-nine years. 3731
18:17 from Lachish to King Hezekiah at J. 3731
18:17 up to J and stopped at the aqueduct of 3731
18:22 saying to Judah and J, 3731
18:22 "You must worship before this altar in J"? 3731
18:35 can the LORD deliver J from my hand?" 3731
19:10 when he says, 'J will not be handed over 3731
19:21 Daughter of J tosses her head as you flee. 3731
19:31 For out of J will come a remnant, 3731
21: 1 and he reigned in J fifty-five years. 3731
21: 4 "In J I will put my Name." 3731
21: 7 "In this temple and in J, 3731
21:12 to bring such disaster on J and Judah that 3731
21:13 over J the measuring line used 3731
21:13 I will wipe out J as one wipes a dish, 3731
21:16 so much innocent blood that he filled J 3731
21:19 and he reigned in J two years. 3731
22: 1 and he reigned in J thirty-one years. 3731
22:14 She lived in J, in the Second District. 3731
23: 1 the elders of Judah and J. 3731
23: 2 of J, the priests and the prophets— 3731
23: 4 He burned them outside J in the fields of 3731
23: 5 the towns of Judah and on those around J— 3731
23: 6 the LORD to the Kidron Valley outside J 3731
23: 9 not serve at the altar of the LORD in J, 3731
23:13 that were east of J on the south of the Hill 3731
23:20 Then he went back to J. 3731
23:23 Passover was celebrated to the LORD in J. 3731
23:24 detestable things seen in Judah and J. 3731
23:27 and I will reject J, the city I chose, 3731
23:30 to J and buried him in his own tomb. 3731
23:31 and he reigned in J three months. 3731
23:33 of Hamath so that he might not reign in J, 3731
23:36 and he reigned in J eleven years. 3731
24: 4 For he had filled J with innocent blood, 3731
24: 8 and he reigned in J three months. 3731
24: 8 daughter of Elnathan; she was from J. 3731
24:10 of Babylon advanced on J and laid siege 3731
24:14 He carried into exile all J: 3731
24:15 from J to Babylon the king's mother, 3731
24:18 and he reigned in J eleven years. 3731
24:20 that all this happened to J and Judah, 3731
25: 1 against J with his whole army. 3731
25: 8 of the king of Babylon, came to J. 3731
25: 9 the royal palace and all the houses of J. 3731
25:10 broke down the walls around J. 3731
1Ch 3: 4 David reigned in J thirty-three years, 3731
6:10 in the temple Solomon built in J), 3731
6:15 the LORD sent Judah and J into exile by 3731
6:32 the temple of the LORD in J. 3731
8:28 and they lived in J. 3731
8:32 They too lived near their relatives in J. 3731
9: 3 and Manasseh who lived in J were: 3731
9:34 and they lived in J. 3731
9:38 They too lived near their relatives in J. 3731
11: 4 all the Israelites marched to J (that is, Jebus) 3731
14: 3 In J David took more wives and became 3731
15: 3 David assembled all Israel in J to bring up 3731
18: 7 of Hadadezer and brought them to J. 3731
19:15 So Joab went back to J. 3731
20: 1 but David remained in J. 3731
20: 3 David and his entire army returned to J. 3731
21: 4 throughout Israel and then came back to J. 3731
21:15 And God sent an angel to destroy J. 3731
21:16 in his hand extended over J. 3731
23:25 and has come to dwell in J forever, 3731
28: 1 the officials of Israel to assemble at J: 3731
29:27 seven in Hebron and thirty-three in J. 3731
2Ch 1: 4 because he had pitched a tent for it in J. 3731
1:13 to J from the high place at Gibeon, 3731
1:14 in the chariot cities and also with him in J. 3731
1:15 and gold as common in J as stones, 3731
2: 7 in Judah and J with my skilled craftsmen, 3731
2:16 You can then take them up to J." 3731
3: 1 to build the temple of the LORD in J 3731
5: 2 Then Solomon summoned to J the elders 3731
6: 6 I have chosen J for my Name to be there, 3731
8: 6 whatever he desired to build in J, 3731
9: 1 to J to test him with hard questions. 3731
9:25 in the chariot cities and also with him in J. 3731
9:27 The king made silver as common in J 3731
9:30 in J over all Israel forty years. 3731
10:18 to get into his chariot and escape to J. 3731
11: 1 When Rehoboam arrived in J, 3731
11: 5 Rehoboam lived in J and built up towns 3731
11:14 to Judah and J because Jeroboam 3731
11:16 followed the Levites to J to offer sacrifices 3731
12: 2 Shishak king of Egypt attacked J in 3731
12: 4 of Judah and came as far as J. 3731
12: 5 of Judah who had assembled in J for fear 3731
12: 7 not be poured out on J through Shishak. 3731
12: 9 When Shishak king of Egypt attacked J, 3731
12:13 in J and continued as king. 3731
12:13 and he reigned seventeen years in J, 3731
13: 2 and he reigned in J three years. 3731
14:15 Then they returned to J. 3731
15:10 at J in the third month of the fifteenth year 3731
17:13 also kept experienced fighting men in J. 3731
19: 1 of Judah returned safely to his palace in J, 3731
19: 4 Jehoshaphat lived in J, 3731
19: 8 In J also, Jehoshaphat appointed some of 3731
19: 8 And they lived in J. 3731
20: 5 of Judah and J at the temple of the LORD 3731
20:15 and all who live in Judah and J! 3731
20:17 the LORD will give you, O Judah and J. 3731
20:18 and all the people of Judah and J fell down 3731
20:20 "Listen to me, Judah and people of J! 3731
20:27 the men of Judah and J returned joyfully 3731
20:27 and Jerusalem returned joyfully to J, 3731
20:28 They entered J and went to the temple of 3731
20:31 and he reigned in J twenty-five years. 3731
21: 5 and he reigned in J eight years. 3731
21:11 of Judah and had caused the people of J 3731
21:13 and you have led Judah and the people of J 3731
21:20 and he reigned in J eight years. 3731
22: 1 The people of J made Ahaziah, 3731
22: 2 and he reigned in J one year. 3731
23: 2 When they came to J, 3731
24: 1 and he reigned in J forty years. 3731
24: 6 the Levites to bring in from Judah and J 3731
24: 9 and J that they should bring to the LORD 3731
24:18 God's anger came upon Judah and J. 3731
24:23 it invaded Judah and J and killed all 3731
25: 1 and he reigned in J twenty-nine years. 3731
25: 1 Jehoaddin; she was from J. 3731
25:23 to J and broke down the wall of Jerusalem 3731
25:23 to Jerusalem and broke down the wall of J 3731
25:27 they conspired against him in J and he fled 3731
26: 3 and he reigned in J fifty-two years 3731
26: 3 Jecoliah; she was from J. 3731
26: 9 Uzziah built towers in J at the Corner Gate, 3731
26:15 In J he made machines designed 3731
27: 1 and he reigned in J sixteen years. 3731
27: 8 and he reigned in J sixteen years. 3731
28: 1 and he reigned in J sixteen years. 3731
28:10 and women of Judah and J your slaves. 3731
28:24 and set up altars at every street corner in J. 3731
28:27 and was buried in the city of J, 3731
29: 1 and he reigned in J twenty-nine years. 3731
29: 8 of the LORD has fallen on Judah and J; 3731
30: 1 the LORD in J and celebrate the Passover 3731
30: 2 in J decided to celebrate the Passover in 3731
30: 3 and the people had not assembled in J. 3731
30: 5 to come to J and celebrate the Passover to 3731
30:11 humbled themselves and went to J. 3731
30:13 of people assembled in J to celebrate 3731
30:14 in J and cleared away the incense altars 3731
30:21 in J celebrated the Feast 3731
30:26 There was great joy in J, 3731
30:26 there had been nothing like this in J. 3731
31: 4 He ordered the people living in J to give 3731
32: 2 and that he intended to make war on J, 3731
32: 9 he sent his officers to J with this message 3731
32:10 that you remain in J under siege? 3731
32:12 saying to Judah and J, 3731
32:18 in Hebrew to the people of J who were on 3731
32:19 They spoke about the God of J as they did 3731
32:22 of J from the hand of Sennacherib king 3731
32:23 to J for the LORD and valuable gifts 3731
32:25 on him and on Judah and J. 3731
32:26 as did the people of J; 3731
32:33 the people of J honored him when he died. 3731
33: 1 and he reigned in J fifty-five years. 3731
33: 4 "My Name will remain in J forever." 3731
33: 7 "In this temple and in J, 3731
33: 9 and the people of J astray, 3731
33:13 so he brought him back to J and 3731
33:15 on the temple hill and in J; 3731
33:21 and he reigned in J two years. 3731
34: 1 and he reigned in J thirty-one years. 3731
34: 3 to purge Judah and J of high places, 3731
34: 5 and so he purged Judah and J. 3731
34: 7 Then he went back to J. 3731
34: 9 and Benjamin and the inhabitants of J. 3731
34:22 She lived in J, in the Second District. 3731
34:29 the elders of Judah and J. 3731
34:30 of J, the priests and the Levites— 3731
34:32 in J and Benjamin pledge themselves to it; 3731
34:32 the people of J did this in accordance with 3731
35: 1 the Passover to the LORD in J, 3731
35:18 who were there with the people of J. 3731
35:24 and brought him to J, where he died. 3731
35:24 and all Judah and J mourned for him. 3731

2Ch 36: 1 of Josiah and made him king in J in place 3731
36: 2 and he reigned in J three months. 3731
36: 3 of Egypt dethroned him in J and imposed 3731
36: 4 king over Judah and J and changed 3731
36: 5 and he reigned in J eleven years. 3731
36: 9 he reigned in J three months and ten days. 3731
36:10 Zedekiah, king over Judah and J. 3731
36:11 and he reigned in J eleven years. 3731
36:14 which he had consecrated in J. 3731
36:19 and broke down the wall of J; 3731
36:23 to build a temple for him at J in Judah. 3731
Ezr 1: 2 to build a temple for him at J in Judah. 3731
1: 3 with him, and let him go up to J in Judah 3731
1: 3 the God of Israel, the God who is in J. 3731
1: 4 for the temple of God in J.' " 3731
1: 5 up and build the house of the LORD in J. 3731
1: 7 from J and had placed in the temple 3731
1:11 the exiles came up from Babylon to J. 3731
2: 1 to Babylon (they returned to J and Judah, 3731
2:68 at the house of the LORD in J, 3731
3: 1 the people assembled as one man in J. 3731
3: 8 after their arrival at the house of God in J, 3731
3: 8 from the captivity to J) began the work, 3731
4: 6 against the people of Judah and J. 3731
4: 8 a letter against J to Artaxerxes the king 10332
4:12 to J and are rebuilding that rebellious 10332
4:20 J has had powerful kings ruling over 10332
4:23 the Jews in J and compelled them by force 10332
4:24 the work on the house of God in J came to 10332
5: 1 to the Jews in Judah and J in the name of 10332
5: 2 to work to rebuild the house of God in J. 10332
5:14 in J and brought to the temple in Babylon. 10332
5:15 and go and deposit them in the temple in J. 10332
5:16 the foundations of the house of God in J. 10332
5:17 a decree to rebuild this house of God in J. 10332
6: 3 concerning the temple of God in J: 10332
6: 5 the temple in J and brought to Babylon, 10332
6: 5 to their places in the temple in J; 10332
6: 9 as requested by the priests in J— 10332
6:12 or to destroy this temple in J. 10332
6:18 in their groups for the service of God at J, 10332
7: 7 also came up to J in the seventh year 3731
7: 8 in J in the fifth month of the seventh year 3731
7: 9 in J on the first day of the fifth month, 3731
7:13 who wish to go to J with you, may go. 10332
7:14 to inquire about Judah and J with regard to 10332
7:15 whose dwelling is in J, 10332
7:16 for the temple of their God in J. 10332
7:17 on the altar of the temple of your God in J. 10332
7:19 to the God of J all the articles entrusted 10332
7:27 to the house of the LORD in J in this way 3731
8:29 the LORD in J before the leading priests 3731
8:30 to be taken to the house of our God in J. 3731
8:31 from the Ahava Canal to go to J. 3731
8:32 So we arrived in J, where we rested 3731
9: 9 a wall of protection in Judah and J. 3731
10: 7 then issued throughout Judah and J for all 3731
10: 7 for all the exiles to assemble in J. 3731
10: 9 of Judah and Benjamin had gathered in J. 3731
Ne 1: 2 that survived the exile, and also about J. 3731
1: 3 The wall of J is broken down, 3731
2:11 I went to J, and after staying there three 3731
2:12 God had put in my heart to do for J. 3731
2:13 examining the walls of J, which had been 3731
2:17 J lies in ruins, and its gates have been 3731
2:17 Come, let us rebuild the wall of J, 3731
2:20 in J or any claim or historic right to it." 3731
3: 8 They restored J as far as the Broad Wall. 3731
3: 9 ruler of a half-district of J, 3731
3:12 ruler of a half-district of J, 3731
4: 8 against J and stir up trouble against it. 3731
4:22 and his helper stay inside J at night, 3731
6: 7 to make this proclamation about you in J: 3731
7: 2 I put in charge of J my brother Hanani, 3731
7: 3 "The gates of J are not to be opened until 3731
7: 3 Also appoint residents of J as guards, 3731
7: 6 (they returned to J and Judah, 3731
8:15 throughout their towns and in J: 3731
11: 1 Now the leaders of the people settled in J, 3731
11: 1 to bring one out of every ten to live in J, 3731
11: 2 the men who volunteered to live in J. 3731
11: 3 the provincial leaders who settled in J 3731
11: 4 from both Judah and Benjamin lived in J): 3731
11: 6 who lived in J totaled 468 able men. 3731
11:22 of the Levites in J was Uzzi son of Bani, 3731
12:27 At the dedication of the wall of J, 3731
12:27 and were brought to J to celebrate joyfully 3731
12:28 from the region around J— 3731
12:29 built villages for themselves around J. 3731
12:43 of rejoicing in J could be heard far away. 3731
13: 6 while all this was going on, I was not in J, 3731
13: 7 and came back to J. 3731
13:15 And they were bringing all this into J on 3731
13:16 from Tyre who lived in J were bringing 2023S
13:16 in J on the Sabbath to the people of Judah. 3731
13:19 on the gates of J before the Sabbath, 3731
13:20 all kinds of goods spent the night outside J. 3731
Est 2: 6 into exile from J by Nebuchadnezzar king 3731
Ps 51:18 build up the walls of J. 3731
68:29 at J kings will bring you gifts. 3731
79: 1 they have reduced J to rubble. 3731
79: 3 poured out blood like water all around J, 3731
102:21 be declared in Zion and his praise in J 3731
116:19 in your midst, O J. 3731
122: 2 Our feet are standing in your gates, O J. 3731
122: 3 J is built like a city that is closely 3731
122: 6 Pray for the peace of J: "May those who 3731
Ps 125: 2 As the mountains surround J, 3731
128: 5 may you see the prosperity of J, 3731
135:21 to him who dwells in J. 3731
137: 5 If I forget you, O J, 3731
137: 6 if I do not consider J my highest joy. 3731
137: 7 what the Edomites did on the day J fell. 3731
147: 2 The LORD builds up J; 3731
147:12 Extol the LORD, O J; 3731
Ecc 1: 1 the Teacher, son of David, king in J: 3731
1:12 I, the Teacher, was king over Israel in J. 3731
1:16 anyone who has ruled over J before me; 3731
2: 7 and flocks than anyone in J before me. 3731
2: 9 I became greater by far than anyone in J 3731
SS 1: 5 Dark am I, yet lovely, O daughters of J, 3731
2: 7 Daughters of J, I charge you by the gazelles 3731
3: 5 Daughters of J, I charge you by the gazelles 3731
3:10 by the daughters of J. 3731
5: 8 O daughters of J, I charge you— 3731
5:16 this my friend, O daughters of J. 3731
6: 4 my darling, as Tirzah, lovely as J, 3731
8: 4 Daughters of J, I charge you: 3731
Isa 1: 1 and J that Isaiah son of Amoz saw during 3731
2: 1 of Amoz saw concerning Judah and J: 3731
2: 3 the word of the LORD from J. 3731
3: 1 from J and Judah both supply and support: 3731
3: 8 J staggers, Judah is falling; 3731
4: 3 who remain in J, will be called holy, 3731
4: 3 all who are recorded among the living in J. 3731
4: 4 from J by a spirit of judgment and a spirit 3731
5: 3 "Now you dwellers in J and men of Judah, 3731
7: 1 of Israel marched up to fight against J, 3731
8:14 people of J he will be a trap and a snare. 3731
10:10 excelled those of J and Samaria— 3731
10:11 not deal with J and her images as I dealt 3731
10:12 against Mount Zion and J, 3731
10:32 the Daughter of Zion, at the hill of J. 3731
22:10 the buildings in J and tore down houses 3731
22:21 He will be a father to those who live in J 3731
24:23 on Mount Zion and in J, 3731
27:13 the LORD on the holy mountain in J. 3731
28:14 you scoffers who rule this people in J. 3731
30:19 O people of Zion, who live in J, 3731
31: 5 the LORD Almighty will shield J; 3731
31: 9 whose furnace is in J. 3731
33:20 your eyes will see J, a peaceful abode, 3731
36: 2 from Lachish to King Hezekiah at J. 3731
36: 7 saying to Judah and J, 3731
36:20 can the LORD deliver J from my hand?" 3731
37:10 when he says, 'J will not be handed over 3731
37:22 Daughter of J tosses her head as you flee. 3731
37:32 For out of J will come a remnant, 3731
40: 2 Speak tenderly to J, and proclaim to her 3731
40: 9 You who bring good tidings to J, 3731
41:27 I gave to J a messenger of good tidings. 3731
44:26 who says of J, 'It shall be inhabited,' 3731
44:28 he will say of J, "Let it be rebuilt," 3731
51:17 O J, you who have drunk from the hand of 3731
52: 1 Put on your garments of splendor, O J, 3731
52: 2 rise up, sit enthroned, O J. 3731
52: 9 into songs of joy together, you ruins of J, 3731
52: 9 comforted his people, he has redeemed J. 3731
62: 6 O J; they will never be silent day or night. 3731
62: 7 and give him no rest till he establishes J 3731
64:10 even Zion is a desert, J a desolation. 3731
65:18 for I will create J to be a delight 3731
65:19 over J and take delight in my people; 3731
66:10 "Rejoice with J and be glad for her, 3731
66:13 and you will be comforted over J." 3731
66:20 to my holy mountain in J as an offering to 3731
Jer 1: 3 when the people of J went into exile. 3731
1:15 in the entrance of the gates of J; 3731
2: 2 "Go and proclaim in the hearing of J: 3731
3:17 they will call J The Throne of the LORD, 3731
3:17 and all nations will gather in J to honor 3731
4: 3 to the men of Judah and to J: 3731
4: 4 you men of Judah and people of J, 3731
4: 5 "Announce in Judah and proclaim in J 3731
4:10 and J by saying, 'You will have peace,' 3731
4:11 At that time this people and J will be told, 3731
4:14 O J, wash the evil from your heart and 3731
4:16 "Tell this to the nations, proclaim it to J: 3731
5: 1 "Go up and down the streets of J, 3731
6: 1 Flee from J! Sound the trumpet 3731
6: 6 the trees and build siege ramps against J. 3731
6: 8 O J, or I will turn away from you 3731
7:17 the towns of Judah and in the streets of J? 3731
7:34 in the towns of Judah and the streets of J, 3731
8: 1 of J will be removed from their graves. 3731
8: 5 Why does J always turn away? 3731
9:11 "I will make J a heap of ruins, 3731
11: 2 of Judah and to those who live in J. 3731
11: 6 the towns of Judah and in the streets of J: 3731
11: 9 of Judah and those who live in J. 3731
11:12 and the people of J will go and cry out to 3731
11:13 as many as the streets of J.' 3731
13: 9 the pride of Judah and the great pride of J. 3731
13:13 the prophets and all those living in J. 3731
13:27 Woe to you, O J! 3731
14: 2 and a cry goes up from J. 3731
14:16 be thrown out into the streets of J because 3731
15: 4 son of Hezekiah king of Judah did in J. 3731
15: 5 "Who will have pity on you, O J? 3731
17:19 stand also at all the other gates of J. 3731
17:20 living in J who come through these gates. 3731
17:21 or bring it through the gates of J. 3731
17:25 by the men of Judah and those living in J, 3731
17:26 towns of Judah and the villages around J, 3731
Jer 17:27 through the gates of J on the Sabbath day, 3731
17:27 of J that will consume her fortresses.' " 3731
18:11 the people of Judah and those living in J, 3731
19: 3 O kings of Judah and people of J. 3731
19: 7 the plans of Judah and J. 3731
19:13 in J and those of the kings of Judah will 3731
21:13 I am against you, [J,] NIH
22:19 and thrown outside the gates of J." 3731
23:14 of J I have seen something horrible: 3731
23:14 the people of J are like Gomorrah." 2023S
23:15 the prophets of J ungodliness has spread 3731
24: 1 of Judah were carried into exile from J 3731
24: 8 his officials and the survivors from J, 3731
25: 2 of Judah and to all those living in J: 3731
25:18 J and the towns of Judah, its kings 3731
26:18 J will become a heap of rubble, 3731
27: 3 through the envoys who have come to J 3731
27:18 the palace of the king of Judah and in J not 3731
27:20 of Judah into exile from J to Babylon, 3731
27:20 along with all the nobles of Judah and J— 3731
27:21 in the palace of the king of Judah and in J: 3731
29: 1 that the prophet Jeremiah sent from J to 3731
29: 1 into exile from J to Babylon. 3731
29: 2 and the leaders of Judah and J, 3731
29: 2 the artisans had gone into exile from J.) 3731
29: 4 says to all those I carried into exile from J 3731
29:20 sent them away from J to Babylon. 3731
29:25 in your own name to all the people in J, 3731
32: 2 the king of Babylon was then besieging J, 3731
32:32 the men of Judah and the people of J. 3731
32:44 in the villages around J, 3731
33:10 in the towns of Judah and the streets of J 3731
33:13 in the villages around J and in the towns 3731
33:16 be saved and J will live in safety. 3731
34: 1 the empire he ruled were fighting against J 3731
34: 6 to Zedekiah king of Judah, in J, 3731
34: 7 the king of Babylon was fighting against J 3731
34: 8 in J to proclaim freedom for the slaves. 3731
34:19 The leaders of Judah and J, 3731
35:11 we must go to J to escape the Babylonian 3731
35:11 So we have remained in J." 3731
35:13 the men of Judah and the people of J, 3731
35:17 in J every disaster I pronounced 3731
36: 9 the people in J and those who had come 3731
36:31 I will bring on them and those living in J 3731
37: 5 Babylonians who were besieging J heard 3731
37: 5 they withdrew from J. 3731
37:11 from J because of Pharaoh's army, 3731
38:28 of the guard until the day J was captured. 3731
38:28 This is how J was taken: 3731
39: 1 against J with his whole army 3731
39: 8 the people and broke down the walls of J. 3731
40: 1 from J and Judah who were being carried 3731
42:18 on those who lived in J, 3731
44: 2 the great disaster I brought on J and on all 3731
44: 6 the towns of Judah and the streets of J 3731
44: 9 in the land of Judah and the streets of J? 3731
44:13 famine and plague, as I punished J. 3731
44:17 the towns of Judah and in the streets of J. 3731
44:21 in the towns of Judah and the streets of J 3731
51:35 on those who live in Babylonia," says J. 3731
51:50 in a distant land, and think on J." 3731
52: 1 and he reigned in J eleven years. 3731
52: 3 that all this happened to J and Judah, 3731
52: 4 against J with his whole army. 3731
52:12 the king of Babylon, came to J. 3731
52:13 the royal palace and all the houses of J. 3731
52:14 broke down all the walls around J. 3731
52:29 832 people from J; 3731
La 1: 7 J remembers all the treasures that were hers 3731
1: 8 J has sinned greatly and so has become 3731
1:17 J has become an unclean thing 3731
2:10 of J have bowed their heads to the ground. 3731
2:13 what can I compare you, O Daughter of J? 3731
2:15 and shake their heads at the Daughter of J: 3731
4:12 and foes could enter the gates of J. 3731
Eze 4: 1 put it in front of you and draw the city of J 3731
4: 7 the siege of J and with bared arm prophesy 3731
4:16 I will cut off the supply of food in J. 3731
5: 5 This is J, which I have set in the center of 3731
5: 8 I myself am against you, J, NIH
8: 3 and in visions of God he took me to J, 3731
9: 4 throughout the city of J and put a mark on 3731
9: 8 in this outpouring of your wrath on J?" 3731
11:15 of J have said, 'They are far away from 3731
12:10 This oracle concerns the prince in J and 3731
12:19 about those living in J and in the land 3731
13:16 to J and saw visions of peace for her 3731
14:21 against J my four dreadful judgments— 3731
14:22 the disaster I have brought upon J— 3731
15: 6 so will I treat the people living in J. 3731
16: 2 confront J with her detestable practices 3731
16: 3 the Sovereign LORD says to J: 3731
17:12 'The king of Babylon went to J 3731
21: 2 against J and preach against the sanctuary. 3731
21:20 and another against Judah and fortified J. 3731
21:22 Into his right hand will come the lot for J, 3731
22:19 I will gather you into J. 3731
23: 4 Oholah is Samaria, and Oholibah is J. 3731
24: 2 has laid siege to J this very day. 3731
26: 2 because Tyre has said of J, 'Aha! 3731
33:21 a man who had escaped from J came to me 3731
36:38 as numerous as the flocks for offerings at J 3731
Da 1: 1 king of Babylon came to J and besieged it. 3731
5: 2 had taken from the temple in J, 10332
5: 3 taken from the temple of God in J, 10332
6:10 where the windows opened toward J. 10332

Da 9: 2 desolation of J would last seventy years. 3731
9: 7 of Judah and people of J and all Israel, 3731
9:12 like what has been done to J. 3731
9:16 and your wrath from J, 3731
9:16 the iniquities of our fathers have made J 3731
9:25 of the decree to restore and rebuild J until 3731
Joel 2:32 Zion and in J there will be deliverance, 3731
3: 1 when I restore the fortunes of Judah and J, 3731
3: 6 the people of Judah and J to the Greeks, 3731
3:16 from Zion and thunder from J; 3731
3:17 J will be holy; never again will foreigners 3731
3:20 Judah will be inhabited forever and J 3731
Am 1: 2 from Zion and thunders from J; 3731
2: 5 that will consume the fortresses of J." 3731
Ob 1:11 entered his gates and cast lots for J, 3731
1:20 from J who are in Sepharad will possess 3731
Mic 1: 1 concerning Samaria and J. 3731
1: 5 What is Judah's high place? Is it not J? 3731
1: 9 the very gate of my people, even to J itself. 3731
1:12 come from the LORD, even to the gate of J. 3731
3:10 and J with wickedness. 3731
3:12 J will become a heap of rubble, 3731
4: 2 the word of the LORD from J. 3731
4: 8 kingship will come to the Daughter of J." 3731
Zep 1: 4 against Judah and against all who live in J. 3731
1:12 At that time I will search J with lamps 3731
3:14 rejoice with all your heart, O Daughter of J! 3731
3:16 On that day they will say to J, 3731
Zec 1:12 how long will you withhold mercy from J 3731
1:14 'I am very jealous for J and Zion, 3731
1:16 'I will return to J with mercy, 3731
1:16 measuring line will be stretched out over J,' 3731
1:17 LORD will again comfort Zion and choose J. 3731
1:19 the horns that scattered Judah, Israel and J." 3731
2: 2 He answered me, "To measure J, 3731
2: 4 "Run, tell that young man, 'J will be a city 3731
2:12 in the holy land and will again choose J. 3731
3: 2 The LORD, who has chosen J, 3731
7: 7 when J and its surrounding towns were 3731
8: 3 "I will return to Zion and dwell in J. 3731
8: 3 Then J will be called the City of Truth, 3731
8: 4 of ripe old age will sit in the streets of J, 3731
8: 8 I will bring them back to live in J; 3731
8:15 to do good again to J and Judah. 3731
8:22 to J to seek the LORD Almighty and 3731
9: 9 Shout, Daughter of J! 3731
9:10 from Ephraim and the war-horses from J, 3731
12: 2 "I am going to make J a cup that sends all 3731
12: 2 Judah will be besieged as well as J. 3731
12: 3 I will make J an immovable rock for all 3731
12: 5 'The people of J are strong, 3731
12: 6 but J will remain intact in her place. 3731
12: 8 the LORD will shield those who live in J, 3731
12: 9 to destroy all the nations that attack J. 3731
12:10 the house of David and the inhabitants of J 3731
12:11 On that day the weeping in J will be great, 3731
13: 1 of David and the inhabitants of J, 3731
14: 2 I will gather all the nations to J to fight 3731
14: 4 of J, and the Mount of Olives will be split 3731
14: 8 that day living water will flow out from J, 3731
14:10 south of J, will become like the Arabah. 3731
14:10 J will be raised up and remain in its place, NIH
14:11 J will be secure. 3731
14:12 the nations that fought against J: 3731
14:14 Judah too will fight at J. 3731
14:16 the nations that have attacked J will go 3731
14:17 the peoples of the earth do not go up to J 3731
14:21 Every pot in J and Judah will be holy to 3731
Mal 2:11 has been committed in Israel and in J: 3731
3: 4 and J will be acceptable to the LORD, 3731
Mt 2: 1 Magi from the east came to J 2647
2: 3 he was disturbed, and all J with him. 2647
3: 5 from J and all Judea and the whole region 2647
4:25 from Galilee, the Decapolis, J, Judea and 2647
5:35 or by J, for it is the city of the Great King. 2647
15: 1 teachers of the law came to Jesus from J 2647
16:21 to J and suffer many things at the hands of 2647
20:17 Now as Jesus was going up to J, 2647
20:18 "We are going up to J, 2647
21: 1 As they approached J and came 2647
21:10 When Jesus entered J, 2647
23:37 "*O* J, Jerusalem, you who kill the prophets 2647
23:37 J, you who kill the prophets and stone those 2647
Mk 1: 5 and all the people of J went out to him. 2643
3: 8 many people came to him from Judea, J, 2647
3:22 teachers of the law who came down from J 2647
7: 1 teachers of the law who had come from J 2647
10:32 They were on their way up to J, 2647
10:33 "We are going up to J," he said, 2647
11: 1 As they approached J and came 2647
11:11 Jesus entered J and went to the temple. 2647
11:15 On reaching J, Jesus entered 2647
11:27 They arrived again in J, 2647
15:41 had come up with him to J were also there. 2647
Lk 2:22 and Mary took him to J to present him to 2647
2:25 Now there was a man in J called Simeon, 2647
2:38 looking forward to the redemption *of* J. 2647
2:41 Every year his parents went to J for 2647
2:43 the boy Jesus stayed behind in J, 2647
2:45 they went back to J to look for him. 2647
4: 9 to J and had him stand on the highest point 2647
5:17 of Galilee and from Judea and J, 2647
6:17 of people from all over Judea, from J, and 2647
9:31 about to bring to fulfillment at J. 2647
9:51 Jesus resolutely set out for J. 2647
9:53 because he was heading for J. 2647
10:30 "A man was going down from J to Jericho, 2647
Lk 13: 4 more guilty than all the others living in J? 2647
13:22 teaching as he made his way to J. 2647
13:33 for surely no prophet can die outside J! 2647
13:34 "*O* J, Jerusalem, you who kill the prophets 2647
13:34 J, you who kill the prophets and stone those 2647
17:11 Now on his way to J, 2647
18:31 "We are going up to J, 2647
19:11 near J and the people thought that 2647
19:28 he went on ahead, going up to J. 2647
19:41 As he approached J and saw the city, NIG
21:20 "When you see J being surrounded 2647
21:24 J will be trampled on by the Gentiles until 2647
23: 7 who was also in J at that time. 2647
23:28 "Daughters *of* J, do not weep for me; 2647
24:13 Emmaus, about seven miles from J. 2647
24:18 Are you only a visitor to J and do not know 2647
24:33 They got up and returned at once to J. 2647
24:47 in his name to all nations, beginning at J. 2647
24:52 Then they worshiped him and returned to J 2647
Jn 1:19 when the Jews of J sent priests and Levites 2647
2:13 Jesus went up to J. 2647
2:23 while he was in J at the Passover Feast, 2647
4:20 the place where we must worship is in J." 2647
4:21 neither on this mountain nor in J. 2647
4:45 that he had done in J at the Passover Feast, 2647
5: 1 Jesus went up to J for a feast of the Jews. 2647
5: 2 there is in J near the Sheep Gate a pool, 2647
7:25 that point some of the people of J began 2643
10:22 Then came the Feast of Dedication at J. 2647
11:18 Bethany was less than two miles from J, 2647
11:55 to J for their ceremonial cleansing before 2647
12:12 that Jesus was on his way to J. 2647
Ac 1: 4 "Do not leave J, but wait for the gift 2647
1: 8 and you will be my witnesses in J, 2647
1:12 Then they returned to J from the hill called 2647
1:19 Everyone in J heard about this, 2647
2: 5 in J God-fearing Jews from every nation 2647
2:14 "Fellow Jews and all of you who live in J, 2647
4: 5 elders and teachers of the law met in J. 2647
4:16 *in* J knows they have done an outstanding 2647
5:16 also from the towns around J, 2647
5:28 "Yet you have filled J with your teaching 2647
6: 7 number of disciples in J increased rapidly, 2647
8: 1 broke out against the church at J, 2647
8:14 in J heard that Samaria had accepted 2647
8:25 Peter and John returned to J, 2647
8:26 that goes down from J to Gaza." 2647
8:27 This man had gone to J to worship, 2647
9: 2 he might take them as prisoners to J. 2647
9:13 the harm he has done to your saints in J. 2647
9:21 in J among those who call on this name? 2647
9:26 When he came to J, he tried to join 2647
9:28 with them and moved about freely in J, 2647
10:39 in the country of the Jews and in J. 2647
11: 2 So when Peter went up to J, 2647
11:22 of this reached the ears of the church at J, 2647
11:27 prophets came down from J to Antioch. 2647
12:25 they returned from J, taking with them John 2647
13:13 where John left them to return to J. 2647
13:27 The people of J and their rulers did 2647
13:31 traveled with him from Galilee to J. 2647
15: 2 to go up to J to see the apostles and elders 2647
15: 4 When they came to J, they were welcomed 2647
16: 4 the apostles and elders in J for the people 2647
19:21 Paul decided to go to J, 2647
20:16 for he was in a hurry to reach J, 2647
20:22 compelled by the Spirit, I am going to J, 2647
21: 4 Spirit they urged Paul not to go on to J. 2647
21:11 Jews of J will bind the owner of this belt 2647
21:12 pleaded with Paul not to go up to J. 2647
21:13 to die in J for the name of the Lord Jesus." 2647
21:15 After this, we got ready and went up to J. 2647
21:17 When we arrived at J, the brothers 2647
21:31 that the whole city of J was in an uproar. 2647
22: 5 to bring these people as prisoners to J to 2647
22:17 "When I returned to J and was praying at 2647
22:18 'Leave J immediately, because they will not 2647
23:11 As you have testified about me in J, 2647
24:11 I went up to J to worship. 2647
24:17 to J to bring my people gifts for the poor NIG
25: 1 Festus went up from Caesarea to J, 2647
25: 3 to have Paul transferred to J, 2647
25: 7 had come down from J stood around him, 2647
25: 9 up to J and stand trial before me there 2647
25:15 When I went to J, the chief priests and 2647
25:20 so I asked if he would be willing to go to J 2647
25:24 about him in J and here in Caesarea, 2647
26: 4 in my own country, and also in J. 2647
26:10 And that is just what I did in J. 2647
26:20 then to those *in* J and in all Judea, 2647
28:17 I was arrested in J and handed over to 2647
Ro 15:19 So from J all the way around to Illyricum, 2647
15:25 I am on my way to J in the service of 2647
15:26 for the poor among the saints in J. 2647
15:31 and that my service in J may be acceptable 2647
1Co 16: 3 and send them with your gift to J. 2647
Gal 1:17 up to J to see those who were apostles 2647
1:18 I went up to J to get acquainted with Peter 2647
2: 1 Fourteen years later I went up again to J, 2647
4:25 and corresponds *to* the present city of J, 2647
4:26 But the J that is above is free, 2647
Heb 12:22 to Mount Zion, to the heavenly J, 2647
Rev 3:12 the new J, which is coming down out of heaven from my God; 2647
21: 2 I saw the Holy City, the new J, 2647
21:10 the Holy City, J, coming down out of heaven from God. 2647

JERUSALEM'S (3) [JERUSALEM]

Ne 4: 7 that the repairs to J walls had gone ahead 3731
Isa 62: 1 for J sake I will not remain quiet, 3731
Zec 12: 7 of J inhabitants may not be greater than 3731

JERUSHA (2)

2Ki 15:33 His mother's name was J daughter 3729
2Ch 27: 1 His mother's name was J daughter 3730

JESAIAH (KJV) See JESHAIAH

JESARELAH (1)

1Ch 25:14 the seventh to J, his sons and relatives, 12 3777

JESHAIAH (7)

1Ch 3:21 Pelatiah and J, and the sons of Rephaiah, 3832
25: 3 Gedaliah, Zeri, J, Shimei, 3833
25:15 the eighth to J, his sons and relatives, 12 3833
26:25 Rehabiah his son, J his son, Joram his son, 3833
Ezr 8: 7 J son of Athaliah, and with him 70 men; 3832
8:19 with J from the descendants of Merari, 3832
Ne 11: 7 the son of Ithiel, the son of J, 3832

JESHANAH (3)

2Ch 13:19 and took from him the towns of Bethel, J 3827
Ne 3: 6 The J Gate was repaired by Joiada son 3827
12:39 the J Gate, the Fish Gate, 3827

JESHARELAH (KJV) See JESARELAH

JESHEBEAB (1)

1Ch 24:13 the fourteenth to J, 3784

JESHER (1)

1Ch 2:18 J, Shobab and Ardon. 3840

JESHIMON (4)

1Sa 23:19 on the hill of Hakilah, south of J? 3810
23:24 in the Arabah south of J. 3810
26: 1 on the hill of Hakilah, which faces J?" 3810
26: 3 the road on the hill of Hakilah facing J, 3810

JESHIMOTH See BETH JESHIMOTH

JESHISHAI (1)

1Ch 5:14 the son of Michael, the son of J, 3814

JESHOHAIAH (1)

1Ch 4:36 Jaakobah, J, Asaiah, Adiel, Jesimiel, 3797

JESHUA (29)

1Ch 24:11 the ninth to J, the tenth to Shecaniah, 3800
2Ch 31:15 Eden, Miniamin, J, Shemaiah, 3800
Ezr 2: 2 J, Nehemiah, Seraiah, Reelaiah, Mordecai, 3800
2: 6 of Pahath-Moab (through the line of J 3800
2:36 of Jedaiah (through the family of J) 973 3800
2:40 the descendants of J and Kadmiel (through 3800
3: 2 Then J son of Jozadak 3800
3: 8 J son of Jozadak and the rest 3800
3: 9 J and his sons and brothers and Kadmiel 3800
4: 3 J and the rest of the heads of the families 3800
5: 2 and J son of Jozadak set to work to rebuild 10336
8:33 and so were the Levites Jozabad son of J 3800
10:18 From the descendants of J son of Jozadak, 3800
Ne 3:19 Next to him, Ezer son of J, 3800
7: 7 J, Nehemiah, Azariah, Raamiah, 3800
7:11 of Pahath-Moab (through the line of J 3800
7:39 of Jedaiah (through the family of J) 973 3800
7:43 of J (through Kadmiel through the line 3800
8: 7 The Levites—J, Bani, Sherebiah, Jamin, 3800
9: 4 J, Bani, Kadmiel, Shebaniah, Bunni, 3800
9: 5 J, Kadmiel, Bani, Hashabneiah, Sherebiah, 3800
10: 9 The Levites: J son of Azaniah, 3800
11:26 in J, in Moladah, in Beth Pelet, 3801
12: 1 of Shealtiel and with J: 3800
12: 7 and their associates in the days of J. 3800
12: 8 The Levites were J, Binnui, Kadmiel, 3800
12:10 J was the father of Joiakim, 3800
12:24 J son of Kadmiel, and their associates, 3800
12:26 in the days of Joiakim son of J, 3800

JESHURUN (4)

Dt 32:15 J grew fat and kicked; 3843
33: 5 He was king over J when the leaders of 3843
33:26 "There is no one like the God of J, 3843
Isa 44: 2 Do not be afraid, O Jacob, my servant, J, 3843

JESIAH (KJV) See ISSHIAH

JESIMIEL (1)

1Ch 4:36 Jaakobah, Jeshohaiah, Asaiah, Adiel, J, 3774

JESSE (42) [JESSE'S]

Ru 4:17 He was the father of J, the father of David. 3805
4:22 Obed the father of J, 3805
4:22 and J the father of David. 3805

1Sa 16: 1 I am sending you to J of Bethlehem. 3805
16: 3 Invite J to the sacrifice, 3805
16: 5 Then he consecrated J and his sons 3805
16: 8 Then J called Abinadab and had him pass 3805
16: 9 J then had Shammah pass by, 3805
16:10 J had seven of his sons pass before Samuel, 3805
16:11 So he asked J, "Are these all the sons you 3805
16:11 "There is still the youngest," J answered, NIH
16:18 of J of Bethlehem who knows how to play 3805
16:19 Then Saul sent messengers to J and said, 3805
16:20 So J took a donkey loaded with bread, 3805
16:22 Then Saul sent word to J, saying, 3805
17:12 the son of an Ephrathite named J, 3805
17:12 J had eight sons, and in Saul's time 2257S
17:17 Now J said to his son David, 3805
17:20 loaded up and set out, as J had directed. 3805
17:58 the son of your servant J of Bethlehem." 3805
20:27 "Why hasn't the son of J come to 3805
20:30 sided with the son of J to your own shame 3805
20:31 As long as the son of J lives on this earth, 3805
22: 7 Will the son of J give all of you fields and 3805
22: 8 a covenant with the son of J. 3805
22: 9 "I saw the son of J come to Ahimelech son 3805
22:13 conspired against me, you and the son of J, 3805
25:10 Who is this son of J? 3805
2Sa 23: 1 "The oracle of David son of J, 3805
1Ch 2:12 of Obed and Obed the father of J. 3805
2:13 J was the father of Eliab his firstborn; 414
10:14 the kingdom over to David son of J. 3805
12:18 We are with you, O son of J! 3805
29:26 David son of J was king over all Israel. 3805
Ps 72:20 the prayers of David son of J. 3805
Isa 11: 1 A shoot will come up from the stump of J; 3805
11:10 the Root of J will stand as a banner for the peoples; 3805
Mt 1: 5 Obed the father of J, 2649
1: 6 and J the father of King David. 2649
Lk 3:32 the son of J, the son of Obed, 2649
Ac 13:22 'I have found David son of J a man 2649
Ro 15:12 Isaiah says, "The Root of J will spring up, 2649

JESSE'S (5) [JESSE]

1Sa 17:13 J three oldest sons had followed Saul to 3805
2Sa 20: 1 have no share in David, no part in J son! 3805
1Ki 12:16 do we have in David, what part in J son? 3805
2Ch 10:16 do we have in David, what part in J son? 3805
11:18 the daughter of J son Eliab. 3805

JESTING (KJV) See COARSE JOKING

JESUI, JESUITES (KJV) See ISHVI, ISHVITE

JESURUN (KJV) See JESHURUN

JESUS (1241) [JESUS']

Mt 1: 1 A record of the genealogy of J Christ 2652
1:16 of whom was born J, who is called Christ. 2652
1:18 how the birth of J Christ came about: 2652
1:21 and you are to give him the name J, 2652
1:25 And he gave him the name J. 2652
2: 1 After J was born in Bethlehem in Judea, 2652
3:13 Then J came from Galilee to the Jordan to 2652
3:15 J replied, "Let it be so now; 2652
3:16 As soon as J was baptized, 2652
4: 1 Then J was led by the Spirit into the desert 2652
4: 4 J answered, "It is written: 1254+3836S
4: 7 J answered him, "It is also written: 2652
4:10 J said to him, "Away from me, Satan! 2652
4:12 When J heard that John had been put NIG
4:17 From that time on J began to preach, 2652
4:18 As J was walking beside the Sea NIG
4:19 "Come, follow me," J said, NIG
4:21 preparing their nets. J called them, NIG
4:23 J went throughout Galilee, NIG
7:28 When J had finished saying these things, 2652
8: 3 J reached out his hand and touched NIG
8: 4 Then J said to him, "See that you don't tell 2652
8: 5 When J had entered Capernaum, 899S
8: 7 J said to him, "I will go and heal him." NIG
8:10 When J heard this, he was astonished 2652
8:13 Then J said to the centurion, "Go! 2652
8:14 When J came into Peter's house, 2652
8:18 When J saw the crowd around him, 2652
8:20 J replied, "Foxes have holes and birds of 2652
8:22 But J told him, "Follow me, 2652
8:24 But J was sleeping. 899S
8:31 The demons begged J, 899S
8:34 Then the whole town went out to meet J. 2652
9: 1 J stepped into a boat, crossed over 2652
9: 2 When J saw their faith, he said 2652
9: 4 Knowing their thoughts, J said, 2652
9: 9 As J went on from there, 2652
9:10 While J was having dinner 2652
9:12 On hearing this, J said, 3836S
9:15 J answered, "How can the guests of 2652
9:19 J got up and went with him, 2652
9:22 J turned and saw her. 2652
9:23 When J entered the ruler's house and saw 2652
9:27 As J went on from there, 2652
9:30 J warned them sternly, "See that no one 2652
9:32 and could not talk was brought to J. 899S
9:35 J went through all the towns and villages, 2652
Mt 10: 5 These twelve J sent out with the following 2652
11: 1 After J had finished instructing his twelve disciples, 2652
11: 4 J replied, "Go back and report 2652
11: 7 J began to speak to the crowd about John: 2652
11:20 Then J began to denounce the cities 2652
11:25 At that time J said, "I praise you, Father, 2652
12: 1 that time J went through the grainfields on 2652
12:10 Looking for a reason to accuse J, 899S
12:14 and plotted how they might kill J. 899S
12:15 Aware of this, J withdrew from that place. 2652
12:22 J healed him, so that he could both talk and NIG
12:25 J knew their thoughts and said to them, NIG
12:46 While J was still talking to the crowd, 899S
13: 1 That same day J went out of the house 2652
13:24 J told them another parable: NIG
13:34 J spoke all these things to the crowd 2652
13:51 "Have you understood all these things?" J asked. 2652
13:53 When J had finished these parables, 2652
13:57 But J said to them, "Only in his hometown 2652
14: 1 Herod the tetrarch heard the reports about J, 2652
14:12 Then they went and told J. 2652
14:13 When J heard what had happened, 2652
14:14 When J landed and saw a large crowd, NIG
14:16 J replied, "They do not need to go away. 2652
14:22 Immediately J made the disciples get into NIG
14:25 the fourth watch of the night J went out NIG
14:27 But J immediately said to them: 2652
14:29 walked on the water and came toward J. 2652
14:31 Immediately J reached out his hand 2652
14:35 when the men of that place recognized J, 899S
15: 1 of the law came to J from Jerusalem 2652
15: 3 J replied, "And why do you break 1254+3836S
15:10 J called the crowd to him and said, NIG
15:16 "Are you still so dull?" J asked them. 1254+3836S
15:21 J withdrew to the region of Tyre 2652
15:23 J did not answer a word. 1254+3836S
15:28 J answered, "Woman, you have great faith! 2652
15:29 J left there and went along the Sea 2652
15:32 J called his disciples to him and said, 2652
15:34 "How many loaves do you have?" J asked. 2652
15:39 After J had sent the crowd away, NIG
16: 1 and Sadducees came to J and tested him NIG
16: 4 J then left them and went away. NIG
16: 6 "Be careful," J said to them. 2652
16: 8 Aware of their discussion, J asked, 2652
16:13 When J came to the region of Caesarea 2652
16:17 J replied, "Blessed are you, 2652
16:21 J began to explain to his disciples that 2652
16:23 J turned and said to Peter, "Get behind me, Satan! 1254+3836S
16:24 Then J said to his disciples, 2652
17: 1 After six days J took with him Peter, 2652
17: 3 Moses and Elijah, talking with J. 899S
17: 4 Peter said to J, "Lord, it is good for us 2652
17: 7 But J came and touched them. 2652
17: 8 they saw no one except J. 2652
17: 9 down the mountain, J instructed them, 2652
17:11 J replied, "To be sure, Elijah comes 1254+3836S
17:14 a man approached J and knelt before him. 899S
17:17 J replied, "how long shall I stay with you? 2652
17:18 J rebuked the demon, and it came out 2652
17:19 disciples came to J in private and asked, 2652
17:24 After J and his disciples arrived 899S
17:25 J was the first to speak. 2652
17:26 "Then the sons are exempt," J said to him. 2652
18: 1 At that time the disciples came to J 2652
18:21 Then Peter came to J and asked, "Lord, 899S
18:22 J answered, "I tell you, not seven times, 2652
19: 1 When J had finished saying these things, 2652
19: 8 J replied, "Moses permitted you NIG
19:11 J replied, "Not everyone can accept this word, 1254+3836S
19:13 to J for him to place his hands on them 899S
19:14 J said, "Let the little children come to me, 2652
19:16 Now a man came up to J and asked, 899S
19:17 about what is good?" J replied. 1254+3836S
19:18 J replied, " 'Do not murder, 2652
19:21 J answered, "If you want to be perfect, go, 2652
19:23 Then J said to his disciples, 2652
19:26 J looked at them and said, 2652
19:28 J said to them, "I tell you the truth, 2652
20:17 Now as J was going up to Jerusalem, 2652
20:20 of Zebedee's sons came to J with her sons 899S
20:22 what you are asking," J said to them. 2652
20:23 J said to them, "You will indeed drink NIG
20:25 J called them together and said, 2652
20:29 As J and his disciples were leaving Jericho, 899S
20:30 and when they heard that J was going by, 2652
20:32 J stopped and called them. 2652
20:34 J had compassion on them 2652
21: 1 J sent two disciples, 2652
21: 6 went and did as J had instructed them. 2652
21: 7 their cloaks on them, and J sat on them. NIG
21:10 When J entered Jerusalem, 899S
21:11 The crowds answered, "This is J, 2652
21:12 J entered the temple area and drove out 2652
21:16 "Yes," replied J, "have you never read, 2652
21:21 J replied, "I tell you the truth, 2652
21:23 J entered the temple courts, and, 899S
21:24 J replied, "I will also ask you one question. 2652
21:27 So they answered J, "We don't know." 2652
21:31 J said to them, "I tell you the truth, 2652
21:42 J said to them, "Have you never read in 2652
22: 1 J spoke to them again in parables, saying: 2652
22:18 But J, knowing their evil intent, said, 2652
Mt 22:29 J replied, "You are in error because you do 2652
22:34 Hearing that J had silenced the Sadducees, NIG
22:37 J replied: " 'Love the Lord your God with all your heart 1254+3836S
22:41 Pharisees were gathered together, J asked 2652
23: 1 J said to the crowds and to his disciples: 2652
24: 1 J left the temple and was walking away 2652
24: 3 As J was sitting on the Mount of Olives, 899S
24: 4 J answered: "Watch out that no one 2652
26: 1 When J had finished saying all these things, 2652
26: 4 to arrest J in some sly way and kill him. 2652
26: 6 While J was in Bethany in the home of 2652
26:10 Aware of this, J said to them, 2652
26:17 the disciples came to J and asked, 2652
26:19 So the disciples did as J had directed them 2652
26:20 J was reclining at the table with NIG
26:23 J replied, "The one who has dipped his hand into the bowl with me 1254+3836S
26:25 J answered, "Yes, it is you." NIG
26:26 While they were eating, J took bread, 2652
26:31 Then J told them, "This very night you will 2652
26:34 "I tell you the truth," J answered, 2652
26:36 Then J went with his disciples to a place 2652
26:49 Going at once to J, Judas said, "Greetings, 2652
26:50 J replied, "Friend, do what you came for." 2652
26:50 seized J and arrested him. 2652
26:52 sword back in its place," J said to him, 2652
26:55 At that time J said to the crowd, 2652
26:57 Those who had arrested J took him 2652
26:59 against J so that they could put him 2652
26:62 the high priest stood up and said to J, 899S
26:63 But J remained silent. 2652
26:64 "Yes, it is as you say," J replied. 2652
26:69 "You also were with J of Galilee," 2652
26:71 "This fellow was with J of Nazareth." 2652
26:75 Peter remembered the word J had spoken: 2652
27: 1 of the people came to the decision to put J 2652
27: 3 saw that J was condemned, NIG
27:11 Meanwhile J stood before the governor, 2652
27:11 "Yes, it is as you say," J replied. 2652
27:14 But J made no reply, NIG
27:17 Barabbas, or J who is called Christ?" 2652
27:18 of envy that they had handed J over 899S
27:20 for Barabbas and to have J executed. 2652
27:22 then, with J who is called Christ?" 2652
27:26 But he had J flogged, 2652
27:27 Then the governor's soldiers took J into 2652
27:34 There they offered J wine to drink, 899S
27:37 THIS IS J, THE KING OF THE JEWS. 2652
27:46 the ninth hour J cried out in a loud voice, 2652
27:48 and offered it to J to drink. 899S
27:50 when J had cried out again in a loud voice, 2652
27:54 with him who were guarding J saw 2652
27:55 They had followed J from Galilee to care 2652
27:57 who had himself become a disciple of J. 2652
28: 5 for I know that you are looking for J, 2652
28: 9 Suddenly J met them. 2652
28:10 Then J said to them, "Do not be afraid. 2652
28:16 the mountain where J had told them to go. 2652
28:18 Then J came to them and said, 2652
Mk 1: 1 beginning of the gospel about J Christ, 2652
1: 9 that time J came from Nazareth in Galilee 2652
1:10 As J was coming up out of the water, NIG
1:14 J went into Galilee, proclaiming the good 2652
1:16 As J walked beside the Sea of Galilee, NIG
1:17 "Come, follow me," J said, 2652
1:21 J went into the synagogue and began NIG
1:24 "What do you want with us, J of Nazareth? 2652
1:25 said J sternly. "Come out of him!" 2652
1:30 and they told J about her. 899S
1:32 after sunset the people brought to J all 899S
1:34 J healed many who had various diseases. NIG
1:35 while it was still dark, J got up, NIG
1:38 J replied, "Let us go somewhere else— NIG
1:41 J reached out his hand and touched NIG
1:43 J sent him away at once with a strong NIG
1:45 J could no longer enter a town openly 899S
2: 1 when J again entered Capernaum, NIG
2: 4 Since they could not get him to J because 899S
2: 4 they made an opening in the roof above J NIG
2: 5 When J saw their faith, he said 2652
2: 8 Immediately J knew in his spirit 2652
2:13 Once again J went out beside the lake. NIG
2:14 "Follow me," J told him, NIG
2:15 While J was having dinner 899S
2:17 On hearing this, J said to them, 2652
2:18 Some people came and asked J, 899S
2:19 J answered, "How can the guests of 2652
2:23 One Sabbath J was going through 899S
3: 2 looking for a reason to accuse J, 899S
3: 3 J said to the man with the shriveled hand, NIG
3: 4 Then J asked them, "Which is lawful on NIG
3: 6 with the Herodians how they might kill J. 899S
3: 7 J withdrew with his disciples to the lake, 2652
3:13 J went up on a mountainside and called NIG
3:20 Then J entered a house, NIG
3:23 So J called them and spoke to them NIG
4: 1 Again J began to teach by the lake. NIG
4: 9 Then J said, "He who has ears to hear, NIG
4:13 Then J said to them, "Don't you understand NIG
4:33 With many similar parables J spoke NIG
4:38 J was in the stern, sleeping on a cushion. 899S
5: 2 When J got out of the boat, 899S
5: 6 When he saw J from a distance, 2652
5: 7 "What do you want with me, J, 2652
5: 8 For J had said to him, "Come out of him, NIG
5: 9 Then J asked him, "What is your name?" NIG

Mk 5:10 And he begged J again and again not 899S
5:12 The demons begged J, "Send us among 899S
5:15 When they came to J, they saw the man 2652
5:17 Then the people began to plead with J 899S
5:18 As J was getting into the boat, 899S
5:19 J did not let him, but said, NIG
5:20 in the Decapolis how much J had done 2652
5:21 When J had again crossed over by boat to 2652
5:22 Seeing J, he fell at his feet 899S
5:24 So J went with him. NIG
5:27 When she heard about J, she came up 2652
5:30 At once J realized that power had gone out 2652
5:32 But J kept looking around to see who NIG
5:35 While J was still speaking, 899S
5:36 J told the synagogue ruler, 2652
5:38 J saw a commotion, with people crying NIG
6:1 J left there and went to his hometown, NIG
6:4 J said to them, "Only in his hometown, 2652
6:6 Then J went around teaching from village NIG
6:30 The apostles gathered around J 2652
6:34 When J landed and saw a large crowd, NIG
6:39 Then J directed them to have all NIG
6:45 Immediately J made his disciples get into NIG
6:54 of the boat, people recognized J. 899S
7:1 from Jerusalem gathered around J and 899S
7:5 Pharisees and teachers of the law asked J, 899S
7:14 Again J called the crowd to him and said, NIG
7:19 (In saying this, J declared all foods "clean.") NIG
7:24 J left that place and went to the vicinity NIG
7:26 She begged J to drive the demon out 899S
7:31 Then J left the vicinity of Tyre and went NIG
7:33 J put his fingers into the man's ears. NIG
7:36 J commanded them not to tell anyone. NIG
8:1 J called his disciples to him and said, NIG
8:5 "How many loaves do you have?" J asked. NIG
8:11 Pharisees came and began to question J. 899S
8:15 "Be careful," J warned them. NIG
8:17 Aware of their discussion, J asked them: 2652
8:22 a blind man and begged J to touch him. 899S
8:23 J asked, "Do you see anything?" NIG
8:25 Once more J put his hands on the man's eyes NIG
8:26 J sent him home, saying, NIG
8:27 J and his disciples went on to the villages 2652
8:30 J warned them not to tell anyone NIG
8:33 when J turned and looked at his disciples, 3836S
9:2 After six days J took Peter, 2652
9:4 Elijah and Moses, who were talking with J. 2652
9:5 Peter said *to* J, "Rabbi, it is good for us 2652
9:8 no longer saw anyone with them except J. 2652
9:9 J gave them orders not to tell anyone NIG
9:12 J replied, "To be sure, Elijah does 1254+3836S
9:15 As soon as all the people saw J, 899S
9:19 "O unbelieving generation," J replied 1254+3836S
9:20 When the spirit saw J, it immediately 899S
9:21 J asked the boy's father, NIG
9:23 " 'If you can'?" said J. 2652
9:25 When J saw that a crowd was running to 2652
9:27 But J took him by the hand and lifted him 2652
9:28 After J had gone indoors, 899S
9:30 J did not want anyone to know NIG
9:35 Sitting down, J called the Twelve and said, NIG
9:39 "Do not stop him," J said. 2652
10:1 J then left that place and went into NIG
10:5 that Moses wrote you this law," J replied. 2652
10:10 the disciples asked J about this. 899S
10:13 People were bringing little children *to* J 899S
10:14 When J saw this, he was indignant. 2652
10:17 As J started on his way, 899S
10:18 "Why do you call me good?" J answered. 2652
10:21 J looked at him and loved him. 2652
10:23 J looked around and said to his disciples, 2652
10:24 But J said again, "Children, how hard it is 2652
10:27 J looked at them and said, "With man this is 2652
10:29 "I tell you the truth," J replied, 2652
10:32 to Jerusalem, with J leading the way, 2652
10:38 don't know what you are asking," J said. 2652
10:39 J said to them, "You will drink the cup 2652
10:42 J called them together and said, 2652
10:46 As J and his disciples, 899S
10:47 When he heard that it was J of Nazareth, 2652
10:47 "J, Son of David, have mercy on me!" 2652
10:49 J stopped and said, "Call him." 2652
10:50 he jumped to his feet and came to J. 2652
10:51 do want me to do for you?" J asked him. 2652
10:52 "Go," said J, "your faith has healed you." 2652
10:52 and followed J along the road. 899S
11:1 J sent two of his disciples, NIG
11:6 They answered as J had told them to, 2652
11:7 the colt to J and threw their cloaks over it, 2652
11:11 J entered Jerusalem and went to NIG
11:12 they were leaving Bethany, J was hungry. NIG
11:15 J entered the temple area and began NIG
11:21 Peter remembered and said *to* J, "Rabbi, 899S
11:22 "Have faith in God," J answered. 2652
11:27 while J was walking in the temple courts, 899S
11:29 J replied, "I will ask you one question. 2652
11:33 So they answered J, "We don't know." 2652
11:33 J said, "Neither will I tell you 2652
12:13 of the Pharisees and Herodians to J 899S
12:15 But J knew their hypocrisy. 3836S
12:17 Then J said to them, "Give to Caesar 2652
12:24 J replied, "Are you not in error 2652
12:28 that J had given them a good answer, NIG
12:29 "The most important one," answered J, 2652
12:34 When J saw that he had answered wisely, 2652
12:35 While J was teaching in the temple courts, 2652
12:38 As he taught, J said, "Watch out for NIG

Mk 12:41 J sat down opposite the place where NIG
12:43 Calling his disciples to him, J said, NIG
13:2 you see all these great buildings?" replied J. 2652
13:3 As J was sitting on the Mount 899S
13:5 J said to them: "Watch out that no one 2652
14:1 for some sly way to arrest J and kill him. 899S
14:6 "Leave her alone," said J. 2652
14:10 to the chief priests to betray J to them. 899S
14:16 and found things just as J had told them. NIG
14:17 J arrived with the Twelve. NIG
14:22 While they were eating, J took bread, 2652
14:27 "You will all fall away," J told them, 2652
14:30 "I tell you the truth," J answered, "today— 2652
14:32 and J said to his disciples, NIG
14:45 Going at once *to* J, Judas said, "Rabbi!" 899S
14:46 The men seized J and arrested him. 899S
14:48 "Am I leading a rebellion," said J, 2652
14:51 but a linen garment, was following J. 899S
14:53 They took J to the high priest, 2652
14:55 against J so that they could put him 2652
14:60 up before them and asked J, 2652
14:61 But J remained silent and gave no answer. 3836S
14:62 "I am," said J. 2652
14:67 "You also were with that Nazarene, J," 2652
14:72 the word J had spoken to him: 2652
15:1 They bound J, led him away 2652
15:2 "Yes, it is as you say," J replied. 1254+3836S
15:5 But J still made no reply, 2652
15:10 the chief priests had handed J over to him. 899S
15:15 He had J flogged, and handed him over 2652
15:16 The soldiers led J away into the palace 899S
15:22 brought J to the place called Golgotha 899S
15:34 the ninth hour J cried out in a loud voice, 2652
15:36 and offered it *to* J to drink. 899S
15:37 With a loud cry, J breathed his last. 2652
15:39 centurion, who stood there in front of J, 899S
15:44 he asked him if J had already died. NIG
16:6 "You are looking for J the Nazarene, 2652
16:9 When J rose early on the first day of NIG
16:11 that J was alive and that she had seen him, NIG
16:12 Afterward J appeared in a different form NIG
16:14 Later J appeared to the Eleven NIG
16:19 After the Lord J had spoken to them, 2652
Lk 1:31 and you are to give him the name J. 2652
2:21 he was named J, the name the angel had 2652
2:27 the child J to do for him what the custom 2652
2:43 the boy J stayed behind in Jerusalem, 2652
2:52 And J grew in wisdom and stature, 2652
3:21 J was baptized too. 2652
3:23 Now J himself was about thirty years old 2652
4:1 J, full of the Holy Spirit, returned from 2652
4:4 J answered, "It is written: 2652
4:8 J answered, "It is written: 2652
4:12 J answered, "It says: 2652
4:14 J returned to Galilee in the power of 2652
4:23 J said to them, "Surely you will quote NIG
4:34 What do you want with us, J of Nazareth? 2652
4:35 J said sternly, "Come out of him!" 2652
4:38 J left the synagogue and went to the home NIG
4:38 and they asked J to help her. 899S
4:40 to J all who had various kinds of sickness, 899S
4:42 At daybreak J went out to a solitary place. NIG
5:1 One day as J was standing by the Lake 899S
5:10 Then J said to Simon, "Don't be afraid; 2652
5:12 While J was in one of the towns, 899S
5:12 When he saw J, he fell with his face to 2652
5:13 J reached out his hand and touched NIG
5:14 Then J ordered him, "Don't tell anyone, 899S
5:16 But J often withdrew to lonely places 899S
5:18 into the house to lay him before J. 899S
5:19 middle of the crowd, right in front of J. 2652
5:20 When J saw their faith, he said, "Friend, NIG
5:22 J knew what they were thinking 2652
5:27 J went out and saw a tax collector by NIG
5:27 "Follow me," J said to him, NIG
5:29 Then Levi held a great banquet *for* J 899S
5:31 J answered them, "It is not the healthy 2652
5:34 J answered, "Can you make the guests of 2652
6:1 One Sabbath J was going through 899S
6:3 J answered them, "Have you never read 2652
6:5 Then J said to them, "The Son of Man is NIG
6:7 looking for a reason to accuse J, 899S
6:8 But J knew what they were thinking 899S
6:9 Then J said to them, "I ask you, 2652
6:11 with one another what they might *do to* J. 2652
6:12 of those days J went out to a mountainside 899S
7:1 When J had finished saying all this in 899S
7:3 of J and sent some elders of the Jews 2652
7:4 When they came to J, they pleaded 2652
7:6 So J went with them. 2652
7:9 When J heard this, he was amazed at him, 2652
7:11 J went to a town called Nain, NIG
7:15 and J gave him back to his mother. NIG
7:17 about J spread throughout Judea and 899S
7:20 When the men came to J, they said, 899S
7:21 very time J cured many who had diseases, NIG
7:24 J began to speak to the crowd about John: NIG
7:36 of the Pharisees invited J to have dinner 899S
7:37 that J was eating at the Pharisee's house, NIG
7:40 J answered him, "Simon, I have something 2652
7:43 "You have judged correctly," J said. 1254+3836S
7:48 J said to her, "Your sins are forgiven." NIG
7:50 J said to the woman, "Your faith has saved NIG
8:1 J traveled about from one town and village 899S
8:4 and people were coming to J from town 899S
8:22 One day J said to his disciples, NIG
8:27 When J stepped ashore, he was met by NIG

Lk 8:28 When he saw J, he cried out and fell at 2652
8:28 "What do you want with me, J, 2652
8:29 For J had commanded the evil spirit NIG
8:30 J asked him, "What is your name?" 2652
8:32 The demons begged J to let them go 899S
8:35 When they came to J, they found the man 2652
8:37 of the Gerasenes asked J to leave them, 899S
8:38 but J sent him away, saying, NIG
8:39 over town how much J had done for him. 2652
8:40 Now when J returned, a crowd welcomed 2652
8:42 As J was on his way, 899S
8:45 "Who touched me?" J asked. 2652
8:46 But J said, "Someone touched me; 2652
8:49 While J was still speaking, 899S
8:50 Hearing this, J said to Jairus, 2652
8:52 "Stop wailing," J said. 1254+3836S
8:55 J told them to give her something to eat. NIG
9:1 When J had called the Twelve together, NIG
9:10 they reported *to* J what they had done. 899S
9:18 Once when J was praying in private 899S
9:21 J strictly warned them not to tell this 1254+3836S
9:28 About eight days after J said this, NIG
9:31 in glorious splendor, talking with J. 899S
9:33 As the men were leaving J, 2652
9:36 they found that J was alone. 2652
9:41 J replied, "how long shall I stay with you 2652
9:42 But J rebuked the evil spirit, healed the boy 2652
9:43 was marveling at all that J did, NIG
9:47 J, knowing their thoughts, 2652
9:50 "Do not stop him," J said, 2652
9:51 J resolutely set out for Jerusalem. 899S
9:55 But J turned and rebuked them, NIG
9:58 J replied, "Foxes have holes and birds of 2652
9:60 J said to him, "Let the dead bury their own NIG
9:62 J replied, "No one who puts his hand to 2652
10:21 J, full of joy through the Holy Spirit NIG
10:25 an expert in the law stood up to test J. 899S
10:28 "You have answered correctly," J replied. NIG
10:29 so he asked J, "And who is my neighbor?" 2652
10:30 In reply J said: "A man was going down 2652
10:37 J told him, "Go and do likewise." 2652
10:38 As **J and his disciples** were on their way, 899S
11:1 One day J was praying in a certain place. 899S
11:14 J was driving out a demon that was mute. NIG
11:17 J knew their thoughts and said to them: 899S
11:27 As J was saying these things, 899S
11:29 As the crowds increased, J said, NIG
11:37 When J had finished speaking, NIG
11:38 that J did not first wash before the meal, NIG
11:46 J replied, "And you experts in the law 1254+3836S
11:53 When J left there, the Pharisees and the 899S
12:1 J began to speak first to his disciples, NIG
12:14 J replied, "Man, who appointed me 1254+3836S
12:22 Then J said to his disciples: NIG
13:1 some present at that time who told J about 899S
13:2 J answered, "Do you think that these NIG
13:10 On a Sabbath J was teaching in one of NIG
13:12 When J saw her, he called her forward 2652
13:14 because J had healed on the Sabbath, 2652
13:18 Then J asked, "What is the kingdom NIG
13:22 J went through the towns and villages, NIG
13:31 At that time some Pharisees came to J NIG
14:1 when J went to eat in the house of 899S
14:3 J asked the Pharisees and experts in 2652
14:12 Then J said to his host, "When you give a NIG
14:15 he said *to* J, "Blessed is the man who will 899S
14:16 J replied: "A certain man was preparing a great banquet 1254+3836S
14:25 Large crowds were traveling with J, 899S
15:3 Then J told them this parable: NIG
15:11 J continued: "There was a man who had two sons. NIG
16:1 J told his disciples: "There was a rich man NIG
16:14 heard all this and were sneering at J. 899S
17:1 J said to his disciples: NIG
17:11 J traveled along the border 899S
17:13 "J, Master, have pity on us!" 2652
17:17 J asked, "Were not all ten cleansed? 2652
17:20 J replied, "The kingdom of God does NIG
18:1 Then J told his disciples a parable NIG
18:9 J told this parable: NIG
18:15 People were also bringing babies *to* J 899S
18:16 But J called the children to him and said, 2652
18:19 "Why do you call me good?" J answered. 2652
18:22 When J heard this, he said to him, 2652
18:24 J looked at him and said, "How hard it is 2652
18:27 J replied, "What is impossible 1254+3836S
18:29 "I tell you the truth," J said to them, 1254+3836S
18:31 J took the Twelve aside and told them, NIG
18:35 As J approached Jericho, 899S
18:37 "J of Nazareth is passing by." 2652
18:38 He called out, "J, Son of David, 2652
18:40 J stopped and ordered the man to 2652
18:40 When he came near, J asked him, NIG
18:42 J said to him, "Receive your sight; 2652
18:43 he received his sight and followed J, 899S
19:1 J entered Jericho and was passing through. NIG
19:3 He wanted to see who J was, 2652
19:4 since J was coming that way. NIG
19:5 When J reached the spot, 2652
19:9 J said to him, "Today salvation has come 2652
19:28 After J had said this, he went on ahead, NIG
19:35 They brought it to J, 2652
19:35 threw their cloaks on the colt and put J 2652
19:39 of the Pharisees in the crowd said to J, 899S
20:8 J said, "Neither will I tell you 2652
20:17 J looked directly at them and asked, 1254+3836S

Lk	20:20	to catch **J** in something he said so	899S
	20:27	came to **J** with a question.	899S
	20:34	**J** replied, "The people of this age marry	2652
	20:41	Then **J** said to them, "How is it that they say	NIG
	20:45	**J** said to his disciples,	NIG
	21: 1	**J** saw the rich putting their gifts into	NIG
	21: 5	with gifts dedicated to God. But **J** said,	NIG
	21:37	Each day **J** was teaching at the temple,	NIG
	22: 2	looking for some way to get rid of **J**,	899S
	22: 4	with them how he might betray **J**.	899S
	22: 6	for an opportunity to hand **J** over to them	899S
	22: 8	**J** sent Peter and John, saying,	NIG
	22:13	and found things just as **J** had told them.	NIG
	22:14	**J** and his apostles reclined at the table.	899S
	22:25	**J** said to them, "The kings of	1254+3836S
	22:34	**J** answered, "I tell you, Peter,	1254+3836S
	22:35	Then **J** asked them, "When I sent you	NIG
	22:39	**J** went out as usual to the Mount of Olives,	NIG
	22:47	He approached **J** to kiss him,	2652
	22:48	but **J** asked him, "Judas, are you betraying	2652
	22:51	But **J** answered, "No more of this!"	2652
	22:52	Then **J** said to the chief priests,	2652
	22:63	The men who were guarding **J** began mocking and beating him.	899S
	22:66	met together, and **J** was led before them.	899S
	22:67	**J** answered, "If I tell you,	NIG
	23: 3	So Pilate asked **J**, "Are you the king of	899S
	23: 3	"Yes, it is as you say," **J** replied.	1254+3836S
	23: 7	that **J** was under Herod's jurisdiction,	NIG
	23: 8	When Herod saw **J**, he was greatly pleased,	2652
	23: 9	but **J** gave him no answer.	899S
	23:20	Wanting to release **J**, Pilate appealed to	2652
	23:25	and surrendered **J** to their will.	2652
	23:26	on him and made him carry it behind **J**.	2652
	23:28	**J** turned and said to them, "Daughters of	2652
	23:34	**J** said, "Father, forgive them,	2652
	23:42	"**J**, remember me when you come	2652
	23:43	**J** answered him, "I tell you the truth,	NIG
	23:46	**J** called out with a loud voice, "Father,	2652
	23:55	with **J** from Galilee followed Joseph	NIG
	24: 3	they did not find the body *of* the Lord **J**.	2652
	24:15	**J** himself came up and walked along	2652
	24:19	"About **J** of Nazareth," they replied.	2652
	24:28	**J** acted as if he were going farther.	899S
	24:35	and how **J** was recognized by them	NIG
	24:36	**J** himself stood among them and said	899S
Jn	1:17	grace and truth came through **J** Christ.	2652
	1:29	The next day John saw **J** coming toward	2652
	1:36	When he saw **J** passing by, he said, "Look,	2652
	1:37	When the two disciples heard him say this, they followed **J**.	2652
	1:38	**J** saw them following and asked,	2652
	1:40	what John had said and who had followed **J**.	899S
	1:42	And he brought him to **J**.	2652
	1:42	**J** looked at him and said, "You are Simon	2652
	1:43	next day **J** decided to leave for Galilee.	NIG
	1:45	**J** of Nazareth, the son of Joseph."	2652
	1:47	When **J** saw Nathanael approaching,	2652
	1:48	**J** answered, "I saw you while you were	2652
	1:50	**J** said, "You believe because I told you	2652
	2: 2	**J** and his disciples had also been invited	2652
	2: 4	why do you involve me?" **J** replied.	2652
	2: 7	**J** said to the servants, "Fill the jars with	2652
	2:11	**J** performed at Cana in Galilee.	2652
	2:13	**J** went up to Jerusalem.	2652
	2:19	**J** answered them, "Destroy this temple,	2652
	2:22	and the words that **J** had spoken.	2652
	2:24	**J** would not entrust himself to them,	899+2652
	3: 2	He came to **J** at night and said, "Rabbi,	899S
	3: 3	In reply **J** declared, "I tell you the truth,	2652
	3: 5	**J** answered, "I tell you the truth,	2652
	3:10	"You are Israel's teacher," said **J**,	2652
	3:22	**J** and his disciples went out into the Judean	2652
	4: 1	The Pharisees heard that **J** was gaining	2652
	4: 2	although in fact it was not **J** who baptized,	2652
	4: 6	Jacob's well was there, and **J**,	2652
	4: 7	**J** said to her, "Will you give me a drink?"	2652
	4:10	**J** answered her, "If you knew the gift	2652
	4:13	**J** answered, "Everyone who drinks this water will be thirsty again,	2652
	4:17	**J** said to her, "You are right when you say	2652
	4:21	**J** declared, "Believe me, woman,	2652
	4:26	**J** declared, "I who speak to you am he."	2652
	4:34	said **J**, "is to do the will of him who sent me	2652
	4:44	(Now **J** himself had pointed out that	2652
	4:47	that **J** had arrived in Galilee from Judea,	2652
	4:48	**J** told him, "you will never believe."	2652
	4:50	**J** replied, "You may go.	2652
	4:50	The man took **J** at his word and departed.	2652
	4:53	the exact time at which **J** had said to him,	2652
	4:54	that **J** performed, having come from Judea	2652
	5: 1	**J** went up to Jerusalem for a feast of	2652
	5: 6	When **J** saw him lying there and learned	2652
	5: 8	Then **J** said to him, "Get up!	2652
	5:13	for **J** had slipped away into the crowd	2652
	5:14	Later **J** found him at the temple and said	2652
	5:15	that it was **J** who had made him well.	2652
	5:16	**J** was doing these things on the Sabbath,	2652
	5:17	**J** said to them, "My Father is always at work	2652
	5:19	**J** gave them this answer:	2652
	6: 1	**J** crossed to the far shore of the Sea	2652
	6: 3	Then **J** went up on a mountainside and sat	2652
	6: 5	When **J** looked up and saw a great crowd	2652
	6:10	**J** said, "Have the people sit down."	2652
	6:11	**J** then took the loaves, gave thanks,	2652
	6:14	people saw the miraculous sign that **J** did,	NIG
	6:15	**J**, knowing that they intended to come	2652
Jn	6:17	and **J** had not yet joined them.	2652
	6:19	they saw **J** approaching the boat,	2652
	6:22	that **J** had not entered it with his disciples,	2652
	6:24	that neither **J** nor his disciples were there,	2652
	6:24	and went to Capernaum in search of **J**.	2652
	6:26	**J** answered, "I tell you the truth,	2652
	6:29	**J** answered, "The work of God is this:	2652
	6:32	**J** said to them, "I tell you the truth,	2652
	6:35	Then **J** declared, "I am the bread of life.	2652
	6:42	They said, "Is this not **J**, the son of Joseph,	2652
	6:43	among yourselves," **J** answered.	2652
	6:53	**J** said to them, "I tell you the truth,	2652
	6:61	**J** said to them, "Does this offend you?	2652
	6:64	For **J** had known from the beginning	2652
	6:67	to leave too, do you?" **J** asked the Twelve.	2652
	6:70	Then **J** replied, "Have I not chosen you,	2652
	7: 1	After this, **J** went around in Galilee,	2652
	7: 6	Therefore **J** told them, "The right time	2652
	7:14	until halfway through the Feast did **J** go up	2652
	7:16	**J** answered, "My teaching is not my own.	2652
	7:21	**J** said to them, "I did one miracle,	2652
	7:28	Then **J**, still teaching in the temple courts,	2652
	7:33	**J** said, "I am with you for only a short time,	2652
	7:37	**J** stood and said in a loud voice,	2652
	7:39	since **J** had not yet been glorified.	2652
	7:43	the people were divided because of **J**.	899S
	7:50	to **J** earlier and who was one	899S
	8: 1	But **J** went to the Mount of Olives.	2652
	8: 4	said *to* **J**, "Teacher, this woman was caught	899S
	8: 6	But **J** bent down and started to write on	2652
	8: 9	the older ones first, until only **J** was left,	NIG
	8:10	**J** straightened up and asked her, "Woman,	2652
	8:11	neither do I condemn you," **J** declared.	2652
	8:12	When **J** spoke again to the people, he said,	2652
	8:14	**J** answered, "Even if I testify	2652
	8:19	not know me or my Father," **J** replied.	2652
	8:21	Once more **J** said to them, "I am going	NIG
	8:25	"Just what I have been claiming all along," **J** replied.	2652
	8:28	So **J** said, "When you have lifted up	2652
	8:31	To the Jews who had believed him, **J** said,	2652
	8:34	**J** replied, "I tell you the truth,	2652
	8:39	"If you were Abraham's children," said **J**,	2652
	8:42	**J** said to them, "If God were your Father,	2652
	8:49	"I am not possessed by a demon," said **J**,	2652
	8:54	**J** replied, "If I glorify myself,	2652
	8:58	"I tell you the truth," **J** answered,	2652
	8:59	but **J** hid himself, slipping away from	2652
	9: 3	said **J**, "but this happened so that the work	2652
	9:11	"The man they call **J** made some mud	2652
	9:14	on which **J** had made the mud and opened	2652
	9:22	that anyone who acknowledged that **J** was	899S
	9:35	**J** heard that they had thrown him out,	2652
	9:37	**J** said, "You have now seen him;	2652
	9:39	**J** said, "For judgment I have come	2652
	9:41	**J** said, "If you were blind,	2652
	10: 6	**J** used this figure of speech,	2652
	10: 7	Therefore **J** said again,	2652
	10:23	and **J** was in the temple area walking	2652
	10:25	**J** answered, "I did tell you,	2652
	10:32	but **J** said to them, "I have shown you many	2652
	10:34	**J** answered them, "Is it not written	2652
	10:40	Then **J** went back across the Jordan to	NIG
	10:42	And in that place many believed in **J**.	899S
	11: 3	So the sisters sent word to **J**, "Lord,	899S
	11: 4	When he heard this, **J** said,	2652
	11: 5	**J** loved Martha and her sister and Lazarus.	2652
	11: 9	**J** answered, "Are there not twelve hours	2652
	11:13	**J** had been speaking of his death,	2652
	11:17	**J** found that Lazarus had already been in	2652
	11:20	When Martha heard that **J** was coming,	2652
	11:21	"Lord," Martha said to **J**,	2652
	11:23	**J** said to her, "Your brother will rise again."	2652
	11:25	**J** said to her, "I am the resurrection and	2652
	11:30	Now **J** had not yet entered the village,	2652
	11:32	When Mary reached the place where **J** was	2652
	11:33	When **J** saw her weeping,	2652
	11:35	**J** wept.	2652
	11:38	**J**, once more deeply moved, came to	2652
	11:40	Then **J** said, "Did I not tell you that	2652
	11:41	Then **J** looked up and said, "Father,	2652
	11:43	**J** called in a loud voice, "Lazarus, come out!"	NIG
	11:44	**J** said to them, "Take off the grave clothes	2652
	11:45	to visit Mary, and had seen what **J** did,	NIG
	11:46	and told them what **J** had done.	2652
	11:51	that year he prophesied that **J** would die	2652
	11:54	Therefore **J** no longer moved about publicly	2652
	11:56	They kept looking for **J**,	2652
	11:57	that if anyone found out where **J** was,	NIG
	12: 1	**J** arrived at Bethany, where Lazarus lived,	2652
	12: 1	whom **J** had raised from the dead.	2652
	12: 7	"Leave her alone," **J** replied.	2652
	12: 9	of Jews found out that **J** was there	NIG
	12:11	over to **J** and putting their faith in him.	2652
	12:12	for the Feast heard that **J** was on his way	2652
	12:14	**J** found a young donkey and sat upon it,	2652
	12:16	Only after **J** was glorified did they realize	2652
	12:21	"Sir," they said, "we would like to see **J**."	2652
	12:22	Andrew and Philip in turn told **J**.	2652
	12:23	**J** replied, "The hour has come for the Son	2652
	12:30	**J** said, "This voice was for your benefit,	2652
	12:35	Then **J** told them, "You are going to have	2652
	12:36	**J** left and hid himself from them.	2652
	12:37	after **J** had done all these miraculous signs	899S
	12:44	Then **J** cried out, "When a man believes	2652
	13: 1	**J** knew that the time had come for him	2652
Jn	13: 2	Judas Iscariot, son of Simon, to betray **J**.	899S
	13: 3	**J** knew that the Father had put all things	NIG
	13: 7	**J** replied, "You do not realize now what	2652
	13: 8	**J** answered, "Unless I wash you,	2652
	13:10	**J** answered, "A person who has had	2652
	13:21	**J** was troubled in spirit and testified,	2652
	13:23	One of them, the disciple whom **J** loved,	2652
	13:25	Leaning back against **J**, he asked him,	2652
	13:26	**J** answered, "It is the one to whom I will	2652
	13:27	you are about to do, do quickly," **J** told him,	2652
	13:28	at the meal understood why **J** said this	NIG
	13:29	some thought **J** was telling him	2652
	13:31	When he was gone, **J** said,	2652
	13:36	**J** replied, "Where I am going,	2652
	13:38	Then **J** answered, "Will you really lay	2652
	14: 6	**J** answered, "I am the way and the truth	2652
	14: 9	**J** answered: "Don't you know me,	2652
	14:23	**J** replied, "If anyone loves me,	2652
	16:19	**J** saw that they wanted to ask him	2652
	16:31	"You believe at last!" **J** answered.	2652
	17: 1	After **J** said this, he looked toward heaven	2652
	17: 3	and **J** Christ, whom you have sent.	2652
	18: 1	**J** left with his disciples and crossed	2652
	18: 2	**J** had often met there with his disciples.	2652
	18: 4	**J**, knowing all that was going to happen	2652
	18: 5	"**J** of Nazareth," they replied.	2652
	18: 5	"I am he," **J** said.	NIG
	18: 6	When **J** said, "I am he,"	NIG
	18: 7	And they said, "**J** of Nazareth."	2652
	18: 8	"I told you that I am he," **J** answered.	2652
	18:11	**J** commanded Peter, "Put your sword away!	2652
	18:12	and the Jewish officials arrested **J**.	2652
	18:15	and another disciple were following **J**.	2652
	18:15	with **J** into the high priest's courtyard,	2652
	18:19	the high priest questioned **J**	2652
	18:20	have spoken openly to the world," **J** replied.	2652
	18:22	When **J** said this, one of the officials	899S
	18:23	"If I said something wrong," **J** replied,	2652
	18:28	the Jews led **J** from Caiaphas to the palace	2652
	18:32	the words **J** had spoken indicating the kind	2652
	18:33	summoned **J** and asked him,	2652
	18:34	"Is that your own idea," **J** asked,	2652
	18:36	**J** said, "My kingdom is not of this world.	2652
	18:37	**J** answered, "You are right in saying I am	2652
	19: 1	Then Pilate took **J** and had him flogged.	2652
	19: 5	When **J** came out wearing the crown	2652
	19: 9	he asked **J**, but Jesus gave him no answer.	2652
	19: 9	he asked Jesus, but **J** gave him no answer.	2652
	19:11	**J** answered, "You would have no power	2652
	19:12	From then on, Pilate tried to set **J** free,	899S
	19:13	he brought **J** out and sat down on	2652
	19:16	So the soldiers took charge of **J**.	2652
	19:18	one on each side and **J** in the middle.	2652
	19:19	**J** OF NAZARETH, THE KING OF THE JEWS.	2652
	19:20	the place where **J** was crucified was near	2652
	19:23	When the soldiers crucified **J**,	2652
	19:25	Near the cross *of* **J** stood his mother,	2652
	19:26	When **J** saw his mother there,	2652
	19:28	**J** said, "I am thirsty."	2652
	19:30	When he had received the drink, **J** said,	2652
	19:32	man who had been crucified with **J**,	899S
	19:33	to **J** and found that he was already dead,	2652
	19:38	asked Pilate for the body *of* **J**.	2652
	19:38	Now Joseph was a disciple *of* **J**,	2652
	19:39	the man who earlier had visited **J** at night.	899S
	19:41	At the place where **J** was crucified,	NIG
	19:42	the tomb was nearby, they laid **J** there.	2652
	20: 2	other disciple, the one **J** loved, and said,	2652
	20: 9	not understand from Scripture that **J** had	899S
	20:14	turned around and saw **J** standing there,	2652
	20:14	but she did not realize that it was **J**.	2652
	20:16	**J** said to her, "Mary."	2652
	20:17	**J** said, "Do not hold on to me,	2652
	20:19	**J** came and stood among them and said,	2652
	20:21	Again **J** said, "Peace be with you!	2652
	20:24	was not with the disciples when **J** came.	2652
	20:26	**J** came and stood among them and said,	2652
	20:29	**J** told him, "Because you have seen me,	2652
	20:30	**J** did many other miraculous signs in	2652
	20:31	that you may believe that **J** is the Christ,	2652
	21: 1	Afterward **J** appeared again	2652
	21: 4	Early in the morning, **J** stood on the shore,	2652
	21: 4	the disciples did not realize that it was **J**.	2652
	21: 7	the disciple whom **J** loved said to Peter,	2652
	21:10	**J** said to them, "Bring some of the fish	2652
	21:12	**J** said to them, "Come and have breakfast."	2652
	21:13	**J** came, took the bread and gave it to them,	2652
	21:14	the third time **J** appeared to his disciples	2652
	21:15	**J** said to Simon Peter, "Simon son of John,	2652
	21:15	**J** said, "Feed my lambs."	NIG
	21:16	Again **J** said, "Simon son of John,	NIG
	21:16	**J** said, "Take care of my sheep."	NIG
	21:17	Peter was hurt because **J** asked him	NIG
	21:17	**J** said, "Feed my sheep.	2652
	21:19	**J** said this to indicate the kind of death	NIG
	21:20	disciple whom **J** loved was following them.	2652
	21:20	the one who had leaned back against **J** at	899S
	21:22	**J** answered, "If I want him to remain alive	2652
	21:23	But **J** did not say that he would not die;	2652
	21:25	**J** did many other things as well.	2652
Ac	1: 1	about all that **J** began to do and to teach	2652
	1:11	This same **J**, who has been taken from you	2652
	1:14	the women and Mary the mother *of* **J**,	2652
	1:16	as guide for those who arrested **J**—	2652
	1:21	the whole time the Lord **J** went in and out	2652
	1:22	to the time when **J** was taken up from us.	NIG
	2:22	**J** of Nazareth was a man accredited	2652

Ac 2:32 God has raised this **J** to life, 2652
2:36 God has made this **J**, whom you crucified, 2652
2:38 in the name *of* **J** Christ for the forgiveness 2652
3: 6 In the name *of* **J** Christ of Nazareth, 2652
3:13 has glorified his servant **J**. 2652
3:16 By faith in the name *of* **J**, 899S
3:20 who has been appointed for you—even **J**. 2652
4: 2 and proclaiming in **J** the resurrection of 2652
4:10 It is by the name *of* **J** Christ of Nazareth, 2652
4:13 that these men had been with **J**. 2652
4:18 to speak or teach at all in the name *of* **J**. 2652
4:27 to conspire against your holy servant **J**, 2652
4:30 through the name *of* your holy servant **J**." 2652
4:33 to testify to the resurrection *of* the Lord **J**, 2652
5:30 of our fathers raised **J** from the dead— 2652
5:40 not to speak in the name *of* **J**, 2652
5:42 and proclaiming the good news that **J** is 2652
6:14 For we have heard him say that this **J** 2652
7:55 and **J** standing at the right hand of God. 2652
7:59 "Lord **J**, receive my spirit." 2652
8:12 of God and the name *of* **J** Christ, 2652
8:16 baptized into the name *of* the Lord **J**. 2652
8:35 and told him the good news about **J**. 2652
9: 5 "I am **J**, whom you are persecuting," 2652
9:17 **J**, who appeared to you on the road 2652
9:20 in the synagogues that **J** is the Son of God. 2652
9:22 in Damascus by proving that **J** is 4047S
9:27 preached fearlessly in the name *of* **J**. 2652
9:34 Peter said to him, "**J** Christ heals you. 2652
10:36 the good news of peace through **J** Christ, 2652
10:38 how God anointed **J** of Nazareth with 2652
10:48 be baptized in the name *of* **J** Christ. 2652
11:17 who believed in the Lord **J** Christ, 2652
11:20 the good news about the Lord **J**. 2652
13:23 God has brought to Israel the Savior **J**, 2652
13:24 Before the coming *of* **J**, 899S
13:27 and their rulers did not recognize **J**, 4047S
13:33 their children, by raising up **J**. 2652
13:38 to know that through **J** the forgiveness 4047S
15:11 the grace *of* our Lord **J** that we are saved, 2652
15:26 for the name *of* our Lord **J** Christ. 2652
16: 7 the Spirit *of* **J** would not allow them to. 2652
16:18 "In the name *of* **J** Christ I command you 2652
16:31 They replied, "Believe in the Lord **J**, 2652
17: 3 "This **J** I am proclaiming to you is 2652
17: 7 that there is another king, one called **J**." 2652
17:18 *about* **J** and the resurrection. 2652
18: 5 testifying to the Jews that **J** was the Christ. 2652
18:25 and taught about **J** accurately, 2652
18:28 from the Scriptures that **J** was the Christ. 2652
19: 4 in the one coming after him, that is, in **J**." 2652
19: 5 baptized into the name *of* the Lord **J**. 2652
19:13 to invoke the name *of* the Lord **J** 2652
19:13 They would say, "In the name *of* **J**, 2652
19:15 "**J** I know, and I know about Paul, 2652
19:17 name *of* the Lord **J** was held in high honor. 2652
20:21 in repentance and have faith in our Lord **J**. 2652
20:24 the task the Lord **J** has given me— 2652
20:35 the words the Lord **J** himself said: 2652
21:13 in Jerusalem for the name *of* the Lord **J**." 2652
22: 8 'I am **J** of Nazareth, whom you are persecuting,' 2652
24:24 to him as he spoke about faith in Christ **J**. 2652
25:19 about a dead man named **J** who Paul claimed was alive. 2652
26: 9 that was possible to oppose the name *of* **J** 2652
26:15 " 'I am **J**, whom you are persecuting,' 2652
28:23 of God and tried to convince them about **J** 2652
28:31 of God and taught about the Lord **J** Christ. 2652
Ro 1: 1 Paul, a servant *of* Christ **J**, 2652
1: 4 from the dead: **J** Christ our Lord. 2652
1: 6 called to *belong to* **J** Christ. 2652
1: 7 and from the Lord **J** Christ. 2652
1: 8 I thank my God through **J** Christ for all 2652
2:16 when God will judge men's secrets through **J** Christ, 2652
3:22 from God comes through faith *in* **J** Christ 2652
3:24 the redemption that came by Christ **J**. 2652
3:26 one who justifies those who have faith *in* **J**. 2652
4:24 in him who raised **J** our Lord from 2652
5: 1 with God through our Lord **J** Christ, 2652
5:11 in God through our Lord **J** Christ, 2652
5:15 **J** Christ, overflow to the many! 2652
5:17 in life through the one man, **J** Christ. 2652
5:21 through **J** Christ our Lord. 2652
6: 3 into Christ **J** were baptized into his death? 2652
6:11 to sin but alive to God in Christ **J**. 2652
6:23 of God is eternal life in Christ **J** our Lord. 2652
7:25 through **J** Christ our Lord! 2652
8: 1 for those who are in Christ **J**, 2652
8: 2 through Christ **J** the law of the Spirit 2652
8:11 of him who raised **J** from the dead is living 2652
8:34 Christ **J**, who died—more than that, 2652
8:39 love of God that is in Christ **J** our Lord. 2652
10: 9 with your mouth, "**J** is Lord," and believe 2652
13:14 clothe yourselves with the Lord **J** Christ, 2652
14:14 As one who is in the Lord **J**, 2652
15: 5 among yourselves as you follow Christ **J**, 2652
15: 6 the God and Father *of* our Lord **J** Christ. 2652
15:16 to be a minister *of* Christ **J** to the Gentiles 2652
15:17 I glory in Christ **J** in my service to God. 2652
15:30 by our Lord **J** Christ and by the love of 2652
16: 3 my fellow workers in Christ **J**. 2652
16:20 The grace *of* our Lord **J** be with you. 2652
16:25 and the proclamation *of* **J** Christ, 2652
16:27 be glory forever through **J** Christ! 2652
1Co 1: 1 an apostle *of* Christ **J** by the will of God, 2652
1: 2 to those sanctified in Christ **J** and called to 2652
1: 2 on the name *of* our Lord **J** Christ— 2652
1: 3 God our Father and the Lord **J** Christ. 2652
1: 4 because of his grace given you in Christ **J**. 2652
1: 7 as you eagerly wait for our Lord **J** Christ 2652
1: 8 on the day *of* our Lord **J** Christ. 2652
1: 9 with his Son **J** Christ our Lord, 2652
1:10 brothers, in the name *of* our Lord **J** Christ, 2652
1:30 that you are in Christ **J**, who has become 2652
2: 2 while I was with you except **J** Christ 2652
3:11 one already laid, which is **J** Christ. 2652
4:15 in Christ **J** I became your father through 2652
4:17 of my way of life in Christ **J**, 2652
5: 4 the name *of* our Lord **J** and I am with you 2652
5: 4 and the power *of* our Lord **J** is present, 2652
6:11 in the name *of* the Lord **J** Christ and by 2652
8: 6 and there is but one Lord, **J** Christ, 2652
9: 1 Have I not seen **J** our Lord? 2652
11:23 The Lord **J**, on the night he was betrayed, 2652
12: 3 "**J** be cursed," and no one can say, 2652
12: 3 "**J** is Lord," except by the Holy Spirit. 2652
15:31 as I glory over you in Christ **J** our Lord. 2652
15:57 the victory through our Lord **J** Christ. 2652
16:23 The grace *of* the Lord **J** be with you. 2652
16:24 My love to all of you in Christ **J**. Amen. 2652
2Co 1: 1 an apostle *of* Christ **J** by the will of God, 2652
1: 2 God our Father and the Lord **J** Christ. 2652
1: 3 the God and Father *of* our Lord **J** Christ, 2652
1:14 of you in the day of the Lord **J**. 2652
1:19 For the Son of God, **J** Christ, 2652
4: 5 not preach ourselves, but **J** Christ as Lord, 2652
4:10 carry around in our body the death *of* **J**, 2652
4:10 life *of* **J** may also be revealed in our body. 2652
4:14 the Lord **J** from the dead will also raise us 2652
4:14 from the dead will also raise us with **J** 2652
8: 9 you know the grace *of* our Lord **J** Christ, 2652
11: 4 a **J** other than the Jesus we preached, 2652
11: 4 a Jesus other than **the J** we preached, 4005S
11:31 The God and Father *of* the Lord **J**, 2652
13: 5 Do you not realize that Christ **J** is in you— 2652
13:14 May the grace *of* the Lord **J** Christ, 2652
Gal 1: 1 but by **J** Christ and God the Father, 2652
1: 3 God our Father and the Lord **J** Christ, 2652
1:12 I received it by revelation *from* **J** Christ. 2652
2: 4 to spy on the freedom we have in Christ **J** 2652
2:16 observing the law, but by faith *in* **J** Christ. 2652
2:16 have put our faith in Christ **J** that we may 2652
3: 1 Before your very eyes **J** Christ was clearly portrayed as crucified. 2652
3:14 might come to the Gentiles through Christ **J** 2652
3:22 being given through faith *in* **J** Christ, 2652
3:26 all sons of God through faith in Christ **J**, 2652
3:28 for you are all one in Christ **J**. 2652
4:14 angel of God, as if I were Christ **J** himself. 2652
5: 6 For in Christ **J** neither circumcision 2652
5:24 *to* Christ **J** have crucified the sinful nature 2652
6:14 in the cross *of* our Lord **J** Christ, 2652
6:17 for I bear on my body the marks *of* **J**. 2652
6:18 *of* our Lord **J** Christ be with your spirit, 2652
Eph 1: 1 an apostle *of* Christ **J** by the will of God, 2652
1: 1 the faithful in Christ **J**: 2652
1: 2 God our Father and the Lord **J** Christ. 2652
1: 3 the God and Father *of* our Lord **J** Christ, 2652
1: 5 as his sons through **J** Christ, in accordance 2652
1:15 since I heard about your faith in the Lord **J** 2652
1:17 that the God *of* our Lord **J** Christ, 2652
2: 6 in the heavenly realms in Christ **J**, 2652
2: 7 expressed in his kindness to us in Christ **J**. 2652
2:10 created in Christ **J** to do good works, 2652
2:13 in Christ **J** you who once were far away have been brought near 2652
2:20 Christ **J** himself as the chief cornerstone. 2652
3: 1 *of* Christ **J** for the sake of you Gentiles— 2652
3: 6 sharers together in the promise in Christ **J**. 2652
3:11 accomplished in Christ **J** our Lord. 2652
3:21 and in Christ **J** throughout all generations, 2652
4:21 in accordance with the truth that is in **J**. 2652
5:20 in the name *of* our Lord **J** Christ. 2652
6:23 from God the Father and the Lord **J** Christ. 2652
6:24 Grace to all who love our Lord **J** Christ 2652
Php 1: 1 Paul and Timothy, servants *of* Christ **J**, 2652
1: 1 To all the saints in Christ **J** at Philippi, 2652
1: 2 God our Father and the Lord **J** Christ. 2652
1: 6 on to completion until the day *of* Christ **J**. 2652
1: 8 of you with the affection *of* Christ **J**. 2652
1:11 righteousness that comes through **J** Christ— 2652
1:19 the help given by the Spirit *of* **J** Christ, 2652
1:26 in Christ **J** will overflow on account of me. 2652
2: 5 be the same as that of Christ **J**: 2652
2:10 at the name *of* **J** every knee should bow, 2652
2:11 every tongue confess that **J** Christ is Lord, 2652
2:19 in the Lord **J** to send Timothy to you soon, 2652
2:21 his own interests, not those *of* **J** Christ. 2652
3: 3 glory in Christ **J**, and put no confidence 2652
3: 8 of knowing Christ **J** my Lord, 2652
3:12 of that for which Christ **J** took hold of me. 2652
3:14 the prize for which God has called me heavenward in Christ **J**. 2652
3:20 a Savior from there, the Lord **J** Christ, 2652
4: 7 your hearts and your minds in Christ **J**. 2652
4:19 according to his glorious riches in Christ **J**. 2652
4:21 Greet all the saints in Christ **J**. 2652
4:23 The grace *of* the Lord **J** Christ be with your spirit. 2652
Col 1: 1 an apostle *of* Christ **J** by the will of God, 2652
1: 3 God, the Father *of* our Lord **J** Christ, 2652
1: 4 we have heard of your faith in Christ **J** 2652
Col 2: 6 then, just as you received Christ **J** as Lord, 2652
3:17 do it all in the name *of* the Lord **J**, 2652
4:11 **J**, who is called Justus, also sends 2652
4:12 one of you and a servant *of* Christ **J**, 2652
1Th 1: 1 in God the Father and the Lord **J** Christ: 2652
1: 3 inspired by hope *in* our Lord **J** Christ. 2652
1:10 **J**, who rescues us from the coming wrath. 2652
2:14 churches in Judea, which are in Christ **J**: 2652
2:15 who killed the Lord **J** and the prophets and 2652
2:19 presence *of* our Lord **J** when he comes? 2652
3:11 and Father himself and our Lord **J** clear 2652
3:13 God and Father when our Lord **J** comes 2652
4: 1 and urge you in the Lord **J** to do this more 2652
4: 2 by the authority of the Lord **J**. 2652
4:14 We believe that **J** died and rose again and 2652
4:14 with **J** those who have fallen asleep 899S
5: 9 salvation through our Lord **J** Christ. 2652
5:18 for this is God's will for you in Christ **J**. 2652
5:23 at the coming *of* our Lord **J** Christ. 2652
5:28 grace *of* our Lord **J** Christ be with you. 2652
2Th 1: 1 in God our Father and the Lord **J** Christ: 2652
1: 2 from God the Father and the Lord **J** Christ. 2652
1: 7 when the Lord **J** is revealed from heaven 2652
1: 8 and do not obey the gospel *of* our Lord **J**. 2652
1:12 the name *of* our Lord **J** may be glorified 2652
1:12 the grace of our God and the Lord **J** Christ. 2652
2: 1 the coming *of* our Lord **J** Christ 2652
2: 8 the Lord **J** will overthrow with the breath 2652
2:14 in the glory *of* our Lord **J** Christ. 2652
2:16 May our Lord **J** Christ himself 2652
3: 6 In the name *of* the Lord **J** Christ, 2652
3:12 the Lord **J** Christ to settle down and earn 2652
3:18 grace *of* our Lord **J** Christ be with you all. 2652
1Ti 1: 1 an apostle *of* Christ **J** by the command 2652
1: 1 God our Savior and of Christ **J** our hope, 2652
1: 2 God the Father and Christ **J** our Lord. 2652
1:12 I thank Christ **J** our Lord, 2652
1:14 with the faith and love that are in Christ **J**. 2652
1:15 Christ **J** came into the world to save 2652
1:16 Christ **J** might display his unlimited patience as an example 2652
2: 5 between God and men, the man Christ **J**, 2652
3:13 assurance in their faith in Christ **J**. 2652
4: 6 you will be a good minister *of* Christ **J**, 2652
5:21 of God and Christ **J** and the elect angels, 2652
6: 3 the sound instruction *of* our Lord **J** Christ 2652
6:13 and *of* Christ **J**, who while testifying 2652
6:14 until the appearing *of* our Lord **J** Christ, 2652
2Ti 1: 1 an apostle *of* Christ **J** by the will of God, 2652
1: 1 to the promise of life that is in Christ **J**, 2652
1: 2 God the Father and Christ **J** our Lord. 2652
1: 9 This grace was given us in Christ **J** before 2652
1:10 the appearing *of* our Savior, Christ **J**, 2652
1:13 with faith and love in Christ **J**. 2652
2: 1 be strong in the grace that is in Christ **J**. 2652
2: 3 with us like a good soldier *of* Christ **J**. 2652
2: 8 Remember **J** Christ, raised from the dead, 2652
2:10 the salvation that is in Christ **J**, 2652
3:12 a godly life in Christ **J** will be persecuted, 2652
3:15 for salvation through faith in Christ **J**. 2652
4: 1 In the presence of God and *of* Christ **J**, 2652
Tit 1: 1 a servant of God and an apostle *of* **J** Christ 2652
1: 4 God the Father and Christ **J** our Savior. 2652
2:13 *of* our great God and Savior, **J** Christ, 2652
3: 6 generously through **J** Christ our Savior, 2652
Phm 1: 1 Paul, a prisoner *of* Christ **J**, 2652
1: 3 God our Father and the Lord **J** Christ. 2652
1: 5 I hear about your faith in the Lord **J** 2652
1: 9 and now also a prisoner *of* Christ **J**— 2652
1:23 Epaphras, my fellow prisoner in Christ **J**, 2652
1:25 The grace *of* the Lord **J** Christ be with your spirit. 2652
Heb 2: 9 But we see **J**, who was made a little lower 2652
2:11 So **J** is not ashamed to call them brothers. *NIG*
3: 1 fix your thoughts on **J**, the apostle and 2652
3: 3 **J** has been found worthy of greater honor 4047S
4:14 through the heavens, **J** the Son of God, 2652
6:20 where **J**, who went before us, has entered 2652
7:22 **J** has become the guarantee of a better covenant. 2652
7:24 but because **J** lives forever, 899S
8: 6 the ministry **J** has received is as superior *NIG*
10:10 the sacrifice of the body *of* **J** Christ once 2652
10:19 the Most Holy Place by the blood *of* **J**, 2652
12: 2 Let us fix our eyes on **J**, the author 2652
12:24 *to* **J** the mediator of a new covenant, 2652
13: 8 **J** Christ is the same yesterday and today 2652
13:12 And so **J** also suffered outside the city gate 2652
13:15 Through **J**, therefore, let us continually 899S
13:20 brought back from the dead our Lord **J**, 2652
13:21 to him, through **J** Christ, to whom be glory 2652
Jas 1: 1 a servant of God and *of* the Lord **J** Christ, 2652
2: 1 as believers *in* our glorious Lord **J** Christ, 2652
1Pe 1: 1 Peter, an apostle *of* **J** Christ, 2652
1: 2 for obedience *to* **J** Christ and sprinkling 2652
1: 3 the God and Father *of* our Lord **J** Christ! 2652
1: 3 the resurrection *of* **J** Christ from the dead, 2652
1: 7 glory and honor when **J** Christ is revealed. 2652
1:13 to be given you when **J** Christ is revealed. 2652
2: 5 acceptable to God through **J** Christ. 2652
3:21 saves you by the resurrection *of* **J** Christ, 2652
4:11 God be praised through **J** Christ. 2652
2Pe 1: 1 Peter, a servant and apostle *of* **J** Christ, 2652
1: 1 and Savior **J** Christ have received a faith 2652
1: 2 the knowledge of God and *of* **J** our Lord. 2652
1: 8 in your knowledge *of* our Lord **J** Christ. 2652
1:11 of our Lord and Savior **J** Christ. 2652

2Pe 1:14 as our Lord J Christ has made clear to me. 2652
1:16 and coming *of* our Lord J Christ, 2652
2:20 by knowing our Lord and Savior J Christ 2652
3:18 *of* our Lord and Savior J Christ. 2652
1Jn 1:3 with the Father and with his Son, J Christ. 2652
1:7 and the blood *of* J, his Son, 2652
2:1 J Christ, the Righteous One. 2652
2:6 to live in him must walk as J did. 1697S
2:22 the man who denies that J is the Christ. 2652
3:16 **J Christ** laid down his life for us. 1697S
3:23 to believe in the name of his Son, J Christ, 2652
4:2 that acknowledges that J Christ has come 2652
4:3 not acknowledge J is not from God. 2652
4:15 If anyone acknowledges that J is the Son 2652
5:1 that J is the Christ is born of God, 2652
5:5 Only he who believes that J is the Son 2652
5:6 who came by water and blood—J Christ. 2652
5:20 even in his Son J Christ. 2652
2Jn 1:3 from God the Father and from J Christ, 2652
1:7 not acknowledge J Christ as coming in 2652
Jude 1:1 servant *of* J Christ and a brother of James, 2652
1:1 by God the Father and kept *by* J Christ: 2652
1:4 and deny J Christ our only Sovereign 2652
1:17 the apostles *of* our Lord J Christ foretold. 2652
1:21 for the mercy *of* our Lord J Christ 2652
1:25 through J Christ our Lord, before all ages, 2652
Rev 1:1 The revelation *of* J Christ, 2652
1:2 word of God and the testimony *of* J Christ. 2652
1:5 J Christ, who is the faithful witness 2652
1:9 and patient endurance that are ours in J, 2652
1:9 of the word of God and the testimony *of* J. 2652
12:17 and hold to the testimony *of* J. 2652
14:12 and remain faithful *to* J. 2652
17:6 of those who bore testimony *to* J. 2652
19:10 who hold to the testimony *of* J. 2652
19:10 testimony *of* J is the spirit of prophecy." 2652
20:4 of their testimony *for* J and because of 2652
22:16 J, have sent my angel to give you this 2652
22:20 Come, Lord J. 2652
22:21 grace *of* the Lord J be with God's people. 2652

JESUS' (33) [JESUS]

Mt 21:45 and the Pharisees heard J' parables, 899S
26:51 of J' companions reached for his sword, 2652
27:53 and after J' resurrection they went into 899S
27:58 Going to Pilate, he asked for J' body, 2652
Mk 3:31 Then J' mother and brothers arrived. 899S
6:14 for J' name had become well known. 899S
14:12 J' disciples asked him, 899S
15:43 to Pilate and asked for J' body. 2652
16:1 so that they might go to anoint **J' body.** 899S
Lk 5:8 he fell at J' knees and said, 2652
7:29 when they heard J' words, NIG
8:19 J' mother and brothers came to see him, 899S
8:35 at J' feet, dressed and in his right mind; 2652
8:41 came and fell at J' feet, 2652
17:16 at J' feet and thanked him— 899S
22:49 **J' followers** saw what was going 1254+3836S
23:52 Going to Pilate, he asked for J' body. 2652
Jn 2:1 J' mother was there, 2652
2:3 J' mother said to him, "They have no more 2652
7:3 J' brothers said to him, "You ought to 899S
12:2 Here a dinner was given *in* J' *honor*. 899S
12:3 on J' feet and wiped his feet with her hair. 2652
12:41 Isaiah said this because he saw J' glory 899S
16:29 Then J' disciples said, "Now you are 899S
19:29 hyssop plant, and lifted it *to* J' lips. 3836S
19:34 of the soldiers pierced J' side with a spear, 899S
19:40 Taking J' body, the two of them wrapped 2652
20:7 burial cloth that had been around J' head. 899S
20:12 seated where J' body had been, 2652
Ac 3:16 It is J' name and the faith that comes 899S
2Co 4:5 and ourselves as your servants for J' sake. 2652
4:11 being given over to death for J' sake, 2652
Heb 5:7 During the days *of* J' life on earth, 899S

JETHER (10)

Jdg 8:20 Turning to J, his oldest son, he said, 3858
8:20 But J did not draw his sword, 2021+5853S
2Sa 17:25 Amasa was the son of a man named J, 3859
1Ki 2:5 Abner son of Ner and Amasa son of J. 3858
2:32 and Amasa son of J, 3858
1Ch 2:17 whose father was J the Ishmaelite. 3858
2:32 Shammai's brother: J and Jonathan. 3858
2:32 J died without children. 3858
4:17 J, Mered, Epher and Jalon. 3858
7:38 The sons of J: Jephunneh, Pispah and Ara. 3858

JETHETH (2)

Ge 36:40 and regions: Timna, Alvah, J, 3867
1Ch 1:51 of Edom were: Timna, Alvah, J, 3867

JETHLAH (KJV) See ITHLAH

JETHRO (11)

Ex 3:1 tending the flock of J his father-in-law, 3861
4:18 to J his father-in-law and said to him, 3858
4:18 J said, "Go, and I wish you well." 3861
18:1 Now J, the priest of Midian 3861
18:2 his father-in-law J received her 3861
18:5 J, Moses' father-in-law, together with 3861
18:6 J had sent word to him, "I, your NIH
18:6 "I, your father-in-law J, am coming 3861
18:9 J was delighted to hear about all the good 3861
Ex 18:12 Then J, Moses' father-in-law, brought a 3861
18:27 and J returned to his own country. 2257S

JETUR (3)

Ge 25:15 Hadad, Tema, J, Naphish and Kedemah. 3515
1Ch 1:31 J, Naphish and Kedemah. 3515
5:19 They waged war against the Hagrites, J, 3515

JEUEL (2)

1Ch 9:6 Of the Zerahites: J. 3590
Ezr 8:13 J and Shemaiah, and with them 60 men; 3590

JEUSH (9)

Ge 36:5 and Oholibamah bore J, 3593
36:14 she bore to Esau: J, Jalam and 3593
36:18 Chiefs J, Jalam and Korah. 3593
1Ch 1:35 Eliphaz, Reuel, J, Jalam and Korah. 3593
7:10 The sons of Bilhan: J, Benjamin, Ehud, 3593
8:39 J the second son and Eliphelet the third. 3593
23:10 sons of Shimei: Jahath, Ziza, J and Beriah. 3593
23:11 but J and Beriah did not have many sons; 3593
2Ch 11:19 J, Shemariah and Zaham. 3593

JEUZ (1)

1Ch 8:10 J, Sakia and Mirmah. 3591

JEW (32) [JEWESS, JEWISH, JEWS, JEWS', JUDAISM]

Est 2:5 Now there was in the citadel of Susa a J of 3374
3:4 for he had told them he was a J. 3374
5:13 that J Mordecai sitting at the king's gate." 3374
6:10 as you have suggested for Mordecai the J, 3374
8:7 to Queen Esther and to Mordecai the J, 3374
9:29 along with Mordecai the J, 3374
9:31 the J and Queen Esther had decreed 3374
10:3 the J was second in rank to King Xerxes, 3374
Jer 34:9 no one was to hold a fellow J in bondage. 3374
Zec 8:23 and nations will take firm hold of one J by 3374
Jn 3:25 of John's disciples and a certain J over 2681
4:9 "You are a J and I am a Samaritan woman. 2681
18:35 "Am I a J?" Pilate replied. 2681
Ac 10:28 a J to associate with a Gentile or visit 467+2681
18:2 There he met a J named Aquila, 2681
18:24 Meanwhile a J named Apollos, 2681
19:34 But when they realized he was a J, 2681
21:39 Paul answered, "I am a J, from Tarsus 476+2681
22:3 "I am a J, born in Tarsus of Cilicia, 467+2681
Ro 1:16 first *for* the J, then for the Gentile. 2681
2:9 first for the J, then for the Gentile; 2681
2:10 first for the J, then for the Gentile. 2681
2:17 Now you, if you call yourself a J; 2681
2:28 not a J if he is only one outwardly, 2681
2:29 No, a man is a J if he is one inwardly; 2681
3:1 advantage, then, is there *in* being a J, 2681
10:12 For there is no difference between J 2681
1Co 9:20 To the Jews I became like a J, 2681
Gal 2:14 "You are a J, yet you live like a Gentile 2681
2:14 yet you live like a Gentile and not **like a J.** 2680
3:28 There is neither J nor Greek, 2681
Col 3:11 Here there is no Greek or J, 2681

JEWEL (4) [JEWELRY, JEWELS]

Pr 20:15 but lips that speak knowledge are a rare j. 3998
SS 4:9 with one j of your necklace. 6736
Isa 13:19 Babylon, the j *of* kingdoms, 7382
Rev 21:11 brilliance was like that of a very precious j, 3345

JEWELRY (13) [JEWEL]

Ge 24:53 the servant brought out gold and silver j 3998
Ex 32:24 So I told them, 'Whoever has any gold j, NIH
35:22 came and brought gold j *of* all kinds: 3998
Jer 2:32 Does a maiden forget her j, 6344
Eze 7:20 They were proud of their **beautiful** j 6344+7382
16:11 I adorned you with j: 6344
16:17 You also took the fine j I gave you, 3998
16:17 the j made of my gold and silver, NIH
16:39 and take your fine j and leave you naked 3998
23:26 of your clothes and take your fine j. 3998
23:40 painted your eyes and **put on** *your* j. 6335+6344
Hos 2:13 she decked herself with rings and j, 2719
1Pe 3:3 as braided hair and the wearing *of* **gold** j 5992

JEWELS (9) [JEWEL]

Job 28:17 nor can it be had for j *of* gold. 3998
SS 1:10 your neck with **strings of** j. 3016
5:12 washed in milk, **mounted like** j 3782+4859+6584
7:1 Your graceful legs are like j, 2717
Isa 54:12 your gates of **sparkling** j, 74+734
61:10 and as a bride adorns herself with her j. 3998
Jer 4:30 Why dress yourself in scarlet and put on j 6344
Eze 16:7 and became the **most beautiful of** j. 6344+6344
Zec 9:16 They will sparkle in his land like j *in* 74

JEWESS (2) [JEW]

Ac 16:1 whose mother was a J and a believer, 2681
24:24 his wife Drusilla, who was a J. 2681

JEWISH (27) [JEW]

Ezr 6:7 and the J elders rebuild this house of God 10316
Ne 1:2 and I questioned them about the J remnant 3374
Ne 5:1 a great outcry against their J brothers. 3374
5:8 bought back our J brothers who were sold 3374
Est 6:13 is of J origin, you cannot stand 3374
Jn 2:13 it was almost time for the J Passover, 2681
3:1 a member of the J ruling council. 2681
6:4 The J Passover Feast was near. 2681
7:2 when the J Feast of Tabernacles was near, 2681
11:51 that Jesus would die for the J nation, NIG
11:55 it was almost time for the J Passover, 2681
18:12 and the J officials arrested Jesus. 2681
19:40 in accordance with J burial customs. 2681
19:42 Because it was the J day of Preparation 2681
Ac 10:22 who is respected by all the J people. 2681
12:11 the J people were anticipating." 2681
13:5 the word of God in the J synagogues. 2681
13:6 they met a J sorcerer named Bar-Jesus, 2681
14:1 went as usual into the J synagogue. 2681
17:1 where there was a J synagogue. 2681
17:10 they went to the J synagogue. 2681
19:14 Seven sons of Sceva, a J chief priest, 2681
25:2 the chief priests and J leaders appeared 2681
25:24 whole **J community** has petitioned me 2681+4436
26:3 with all the J customs and controversies. 2681
Gal 2:14 force Gentiles *to* **follow J customs?** 2678
Tit 1:14 and will pay no attention *to* J myths or to 2679

JEWRY (KJV) See JUDAH, JUDEA

JEWS (243) [JEW]

Ezr 4:12 The king should know that the J who came 10316
4:23 to the J in Jerusalem and compelled them 10316
5:1 prophesied to the J in Judah and Jerusalem 10316
5:5 over the elders of the J, 10316
6:7 Let the governor of the J and 10316
6:8 for these elders of the J in the construction 10316
6:14 the J continued to build and prosper under 10316
7:18 You and your **brother** J may 10017
Ne 2:16 to the J or the priests or nobles or officials 3374
4:1 He ridiculed the J, 3374
4:2 he said, "What are those feeble J doing? 3374
4:12 Then the J who lived near them came 3374
5:17 and fifty J and officials ate at my table, 3374
6:6 that you and the J are plotting to revolt, 3374
Est 3:6 to destroy all Mordecai's people, the J, 3374
3:10 the Agagite, the enemy of the J. 3374
3:13 kill and annihilate all the J— 3374
4:3 there was great mourning among the J, 3374
4:7 for the destruction of the J. 3374
4:13 you alone of all the J will escape. 3374
4:14 relief and deliverance for the J will arise 3374
4:16 gather together all the J who are in Susa, 3374
8:1 Haman, the enemy of the J. 3374
8:3 which he had devised against the J. 3374
8:5 to destroy the J in all the king's provinces. 3374
8:7 "Because Haman attacked the J, 3374
8:8 the J as seems best to you, and seal it with 3374
8:9 to the J, and to the satraps, governors 3374
8:9 to the J in their own script and language. 3374
8:11 The king's edict granted the J in every city 3374
8:12 for the J to do this in all the provinces NIH
8:13 so that the J would be ready on that day 3374
8:16 the J it was a time of happiness and joy, 3374
8:17 there was joy and gladness among the J, 3374
8:17 of other nationalities **became** J because fear 3366
8:17 because fear of the J had seized them. 3374
9:1 On this day the enemies of the J had hoped 3374
9:1 now the tables were turned and the J got 3374
9:2 The J assembled in their cities in all 3374
9:3 and the king's administrators helped the J, 3374
9:5 The J struck down all their enemies with 3374
9:6 J killed and destroyed five hundred men. 3374
9:10 son of Hammedatha, the enemy of the J. 3374
9:12 "The J have killed and destroyed 3374
9:13 "give the J in Susa permission to carry out 3374
9:15 The J in Susa came together on the 3374
9:16 of the J who were in the king's provinces 3374
9:18 The J in Susa, however, had assembled 3374
9:19 That is why rural J— 3374
9:20 and he sent letters to all the J throughout 3374
9:22 when the J got relief from their enemies, 3374
9:23 So the J agreed to continue the celebration 3374
9:24 the Agagite, the enemy of all the J, 3374
9:24 against the J to destroy them and had cast 3374
9:25 the J should come back onto his own head, 3374
9:27 the J took it upon themselves to establish 3374
9:28 never cease to be celebrated by the J, 3374
9:30 the J in the 127 provinces of the kingdom 3374
10:3 preeminent among the J, and held in high 3374
10:3 in high esteem by his many **fellow** J, 278
10:3 and spoke up for the welfare of all the J. 2446S
Jer 32:12 the J sitting in the courtyard of the guard. 3374
38:19 "I am afraid of the J who have gone over 3374
40:11 When all the J in Moab, Ammon, 3374
40:15 the J who are gathered around you to 3373
41:3 the J who were with Gedaliah at Mizpah, 3374
43:9 "While the J are watching, 3374
44:1 to Jeremiah concerning all the J living 3374
44:26 all J living in Egypt: 3373
44:27 the J in Egypt will perish by sword 3373
52:28 in the seventh year, 3,023 J; 3374
52:30 745 J taken into exile by Nebuzaradan 3374
Da 3:8 came forward and denounced the J. 10316
3:12 But there are some J whom you have set 10316
Mt 2:2 the one who has been born king *of* the J? 2681
27:11 "Are you the king *of* the J?" 2681

Mt 27:29 "Hail, king *of* the **J**!" *2681*
27:37 THIS IS JESUS, THE KING OF THE **J**. *2681*
28:15 among the **J** to this very day. *2681*
Mk 7: 3 (The Pharisees and all the **J** do not eat *2681*
15: 2 "Are you the king *of* the **J**?" *2681*
15: 9 to release to you the king *of* the **J**?" *2681*
15:12 with the one you call the king *of* the **J**?" *2681*
15:18 "Hail, king *of* the **J**!" *2681*
15:26 THE KING OF THE **J**. *2681*
Lk 7: 3 and sent some elders *of* the **J** to him, *2681*
23: 3 "Are you the king *of* the **J**?" *2681*
23:37 "If you are the king *of* the **J**, *2681*
23:38 THIS IS THE KING OF THE **J**. *2681*
Jn 1:19 Now this was John's testimony when the **J** *2681*
2: 6 kind used by the **J** for ceremonial washing, *2681*
2:18 Then the **J** demanded of him, *2681*
2:20 The **J** replied, "It has taken forty-six years *2681*
4: 9 (For **J** do not associate with Samaritans.) *2681*
4:20 but you **J** claim that the place where we *NIG*
4:22 for salvation is from the **J**. *2681*
5: 1 went up to Jerusalem for a feast *of* the **J**. *2681*
5:10 the **J** said to the man who had been healed, *2681*
5:15 The man went away and told the **J** *2681*
5:16 things on the Sabbath, the **J** persecuted him. *2681*
5:18 For this reason the **J** tried all the harder *2681*
6:41 At this the **J** began to grumble about him *2681*
6:52 Then the **J** began to argue sharply *2681*
7: 1 the **J** there were waiting to take his life. *2681*
7:11 the **J** were watching for him and asking, *2681*
7:13 anything publicly about him for fear *of* the **J** *2681*
7:15 The **J** were amazed and asked, *2681*
7:35 The **J** said to one another, *2681*
8:22 This made the **J** ask, "Will he kill himself? *2681*
8:31 To the **J** who had believed him, Jesus said, *2681*
8:48 The **J** answered him, "Aren't we right *2681*
8:52 At this the **J** exclaimed, "Now we know *2681*
8:57 the **J** said to him, "and you have seen *2681*
9:18 The **J** still did not believe *2681*
9:22 because they were afraid of the **J**, *2681*
9:22 for already the **J** had decided that *2681*
10:19 At these words the **J** were again divided. *2681*
10:24 The **J** gathered around him, saying, *2681*
10:31 Again the **J** picked up stones to stone him, *2681*
10:33 replied the **J**, "but for blasphemy, *2681*
11: 8 "a short while ago the **J** tried to stone you, *2681*
11:19 and many **J** had come to Martha and Mary *2681*
11:31 **J** who had been with Mary in the house, *2681*
11:33 and the **J** who had come along with her *2681*
11:36 Then the **J** said, "See how he loved him!" *2681*
11:45 many of the **J** who had come to visit Mary, *2681*
11:54 moved about publicly among the **J**. *2681*
12: 9 Meanwhile a large crowd of **J** found out *2681*
12:11 of him many of the **J** were going over *2681*
13:33 and just as I told the **J**, so I tell you now: *2681*
18:14 the **J** that it would be good if one man died *2681*
18:20 where all the **J** come together. *2681*
18:28 the **J** led Jesus from Caiaphas to the palace *NIG*
18:28 to avoid ceremonial uncleanness **the J** did *899S*
18:31 to execute anyone," the **J** objected. *2681*
18:33 "Are you the king *of* the **J**?" *2681*
18:36 to prevent my arrest *by* the **J**. *2681*
18:38 With this he went out again to the **J** *2681*
18:39 to release 'the king *of* the **J**'?" *2681*
19: 3 saying, "Hail, king *of* the **J**!" *2681*
19: 4 Pilate came out and said *to* **the J**, *899S*
19: 7 The **J** insisted, "We have a law, *2681*
19:12 to set Jesus free, but the **J** kept shouting, *2681*
19:14 "Here is your king," Pilate said *to* the **J**. *2681*
19:19 JESUS OF NAZARETH, THE KING OF THE **J**. *2681*
19:20 Many *of* the **J** read this sign, *2681*
19:21 The chief priests *of* the **J** protested *2681*
19:21 "Do not write 'The King *of* the **J**,' *2681*
19:21 that this man claimed to be king *of* the **J**." *2681*
19:31 Because the **J** did not want the bodies left *2681*
19:38 but secretly because he feared the **J**. *2681*
20:19 with the doors locked for fear *of* the **J**, *2681*
Ac 2: 5 in Jerusalem God-fearing **J** from every *2681*
2:11 (both **J** and converts to Judaism); *2681*
2:14 "Fellow **J** and all of you who live *467+2681*
6: 1 the **Grecian J** among them complained *1821*
6: 1 against the **Hebraic J** because their widows *1578*
6: 9 **J** of Cyrene and Alexandria as well as *NIG*
9:22 and more powerful and baffled the **J** living *2681*
9:23 the **J** conspired to kill him, *2681*
9:29 He talked and debated with the **Grecian J**, *1821*
10:39 in the country *of* the **J** and in Jerusalem. *2681*
11:19 telling the message only *to* **J**. *2681*
12: 3 When he saw that this pleased the **J**, *2681*
13:43 many *of* the **J** and devout converts *2681*
13:45 When the **J** saw the crowds, *2681*
13:50 But the **J** incited the God-fearing women *2681*
14: 1 a great number *of* **J** and Gentiles believed. *2681*
14: 2 But the **J** who refused to believe stirred up *2681*
14: 4 were divided; some sided with the **J**, *2681*
14: 5 a plot afoot *among* the Gentiles and **J**, *2681*
14:19 Then some **J** came from Antioch *2681*
16: 3 because of the **J** who lived in that area, *2681*
16:20 "These men are **J**, and are throwing our city *2681*
17: 4 of **the J** were persuaded and joined Paul *899S*
17: 5 But the **J** were jealous; *2681*
17:12 Many of **the J** believed, *899S*
17:13 When the **J** in Thessalonica learned *2681*
17:17 *with* the **J** and the God-fearing Greeks, *2681*
18: 2 because Claudius had ordered all the **J** *2681*
18: 4 trying to persuade **J** and Greeks. *2681*
18: 5 testifying *to* the **J** that Jesus was the Christ. *2681*
18: 6 **the J** opposed Paul and became abusive, *899S*
Ac 18:12 the **J** made a united attack on Paul *2681*
18:14 Gallio said to the **J**, "If you Jews were *2681*
18:14 "If you **J** were making a complaint *2681*
18:19 the synagogue and reasoned *with* the **J**. *2681*
18:28 For he vigorously refuted the **J** *2681*
19:10 the **J** and Greeks who lived in the province *2681*
19:13 Some **J** who went around driving out *2681*
19:17 *to* the **J** and Greeks living in Ephesus, *2681*
19:33 The **J** pushed Alexander to the front, *2681*
20: 3 Because the **J** made a plot against him just *2681*
20:19 severly tested by the plots *of* the **J**. *2681*
20:21 *to* both **J** and Greeks that they must turn *2681*
21:11 'In this way the **J** of Jerusalem will bind *2681*
21:20 how many thousands of **J** have believed, *2681*
21:21 that you teach all the **J** who live among *2681*
21:27 some **J** from the province of Asia saw Paul *2681*
22:12 highly respected by all the **J** living there. *2681*
22:30 by the **J**, he released him and ordered *2681*
23:12 The next morning the **J** formed *2681*
23:20 "The **J** have agreed to ask you *2681*
23:27 by the **J** and they were about to kill him, *2681*
24: 5 up riots *among* the **J** all over the world. *2681*
24: 9 The **J** joined in the accusation, *2681*
24:19 But there are some **J** from the province *2681*
24:27 Felix wanted to grant a favor *to* the **J**, *2681*
25: 7 the **J** who had come down from Jerusalem *2681*
25: 8 the law *of* the **J** or against the temple or *2681*
25: 9 Festus, wishing to do the **J** a favor, *2681*
25:10 I have not done any wrong to the **J**, *2681*
25:11 against me by these **J** are not true, *NIG*
25:15 *of* the **J** brought charges against him *2681*
26: 2 against all the accusations of the **J**, *2681*
26: 4 "The **J** all know the way I have lived ever *2681*
26: 7 of this hope that the **J** are accusing me. *2681*
26:21 the **J** seized me in the temple courts *2681*
28:17 he called together the leaders *of* the **J**. *2681*
28:19 But when the **J** objected, *2681*
Ro 3: 9 the charge that **J** and Gentiles alike are all *2681*
3:29 Is God the God *of* **J** only? *2681*
9:24 only from the **J** but also from the Gentiles? *2681*
15: 8 a servant *of* the **J** on behalf of God's truth, *4364*
15:27 they owe it to the **J** to share with them *NIG*
1Co 1:22 **J** demand miraculous signs *2681*
1:23 a stumbling block *to* **J** and foolishness *2681*
1:24 God has called, both **J** and Greeks, *2681*
9:20 *To* the **J** I became like a Jew, *2681*
9:20 I became like a Jew, to win the **J**. *2681*
10:32 whether **J**, Greeks or the church of God— *2681*
12:13 whether **J** or Greeks, slave or free— *2681*
2Co 11:24 from the **J** the forty lashes minus one. *2681*
Gal 1:14 advancing in Judaism beyond many **J** of my own age *1169+1609+1877+3836*
2: 7 just as Peter had been *to* the **J**. *4364*
2: 8 of Peter as an apostle *to* the **J**, *4364*
2: 9 should go to the Gentiles, and they *to* the **J**. *4364*
2:13 The other **J** joined him in his hypocrisy, *2681*
2:15 "We who are **J** by birth and not *2681*
Col 4:11 the only **J** among my fellow workers *1666+4364*
1Th 2:14 things those churches suffered from the **J**, *2681*
Rev 2: 9 of those who say they are **J** and are not, *2681*
3: 9 who claim to be **J** though they are not, *2681*

JEWS' (1) [JEW]

Ro 15:27 have shared in the **J'** spiritual blessings, *899S*

JEZANIAH (1)

Jer 42: 1 including Johanan son of Kareah and **J** son 3470

JEZEBEL (19) [JEZEBEL'S]

1Ki 16:31 also married **J** daughter of Ethbaal king of 374
18: 4 **J** was killing off the LORD's prophets, 374
18:13 what I did while **J** was killing the prophets 374
19: 1 Ahab told **J** everything Elijah had done 374
19: 2 So **J** sent a messenger to Elijah to say, 374
21: 5 His wife **J** came in and asked him, 374
21: 7 **J** his wife said, "Is this how you act as king 374
21:11 as **J** directed in the letters she had written 374
21:14 Then they sent word to **J**: 374
21:15 as **J** heard that Naboth had been stoned 374
21:23 "And also concerning **J** the LORD says: 374
21:23 'Dogs will devour **J** by the wall 374
21:25 urged on by **J** his wife. 374
2Ki 9: 7 of all the LORD's servants shed by **J**. 374
9:10 As for **J**, dogs will devour her on the plot 374
9:22 and witchcraft of your mother **J** abound?" 374
9:30 When **J** heard about it, she painted her eyes 374
9:37 that no one will be able to say, 'This is **J**.' " 374
Rev 2:20 You tolerate that woman **J**, *2630*

JEZEBEL'S (3) [JEZEBEL]

1Ki 18:19 prophets of Asherah, who eat at **J** table." 374
2Ki 9:36 at Jezreel dogs will devour **J** flesh. 374
9:37 **J** body will be like refuse on the ground in 374

JEZER (3) [JEZERITE]

Ge 46:24 Jahziel, Guni, **J** and Shillem. 3672
Nu 26:49 through **J**, the Jezerite clan; 3672
1Ch 7:13 Jahziel, Guni, **J** and Shillem— 3672

JEZERITE (1) [JEZER]

Nu 26:49 through Jezer, the **J** clan; 3673

JEZIAH (KJV) See IZZIAH

JEZIEL (1)

1Ch 12: 3 **J** and Pelet the sons of Azmaveth; 3465

JEZLIAH (KJV) See IZLIAH

JEZOAR (KJV) See ZOHAR

JEZRAHIAH (1)

Ne 12:42 The choirs sang under the direction of **J**. 3474

JEZREEL (41) [JEZREELITE]

Jos 15:56 **J**, Jokdeam, Zanoah, 3476
17:16 and those in the Valley of **J**." 3476
19:18 Their territory included: **J**, Kesulloth, 3476
Jdg 6:33 the Jordan and camped in the Valley of **J**. 3476
1Sa 25:43 David had also married Ahinoam of **J**, 3476
27: 3 Ahinoam **of J** and Abigail of Carmel, 3477
29: 1 and Israel camped by the spring in **J**. 3476
29:11 and the Philistines went up to **J**. 3476
30: 5 Ahinoam **of J** and Abigail, 3477
2Sa 2: 2 Ahinoam **of J** and Abigail, 3477
2: 9 Ashuri and **J**, and also over Ephraim, 3476
3: 2 the son of Ahinoam **of J**; 3477
4: 4 about Saul and Jonathan came from **J**. 3476
1Ki 4:12 of Beth Shan next to Zarethan below **J**, 3476
18:45 heavy rain came on and Ahab rode off to **J**. 3476
18:46 he ran ahead of Ahab all the way to **J**. 3476
21: 1 The vineyard was in **J**, close to the palace 3476
21:23 'Dogs will devour Jezebel by the wall of **J**.' 3476
2Ki 8:29 so King Joram returned to **J** to recover 3476
8:29 of Judah went down to **J** to see Joram son 3476
9:10 on the plot of ground at **J**, 3476
9:15 but King Joram had returned to **J** 3476
9:15 of the city to go and tell the news in **J**." 3476
9:16 Then he got into his chariot and rode to **J**, 3476
9:17 in **J** saw Jehu's troops approaching, 3476
9:30 Then Jehu went to **J**. 3476
9:36 at **J** dogs will devour Jezebel's flesh. 3476
9:37 like refuse on the ground in the plot at **J**, 3476
10: 1 to the officials of **J**, to the elders 3476
10: 6 of your master's sons and come to me in **J** 3476
10: 7 in baskets and sent them to Jehu in **J**. 3476
10:11 So Jehu killed everyone in **J** who remained 3476
1Ch 3: 1 Amnon the son of Ahinoam **of J**; 3477
4: 3 These were the sons of Etam: **J**, 3475
2Ch 22: 6 so he returned to **J** to recover from 3476
22: 6 of Judah went down to **J** to see Joram son 3476
Hos 1: 4 the LORD said to Hosea, "Call him **J**, 3475
1: 4 the house of Jehu for the massacre at **J**, 3476
1: 5 break Israel's bow in the Valley of **J**." 3476
1:11 for great will be the day of **J**. 3476
2:22 and they will respond to **J**. 3476

JEZREELITE (7) [JEZREEL]

1Ki 21: 1 a vineyard belonging to Naboth the **J**. 3477
21: 4 and angry because Naboth the **J** had said, 3477
21: 6 "Because I said to Naboth the **J**, 3477
21: 7 I'll get you the vineyard of Naboth the **J**." 3477
21:15 of Naboth the **J** that he refused to sell you. 3477
2Ki 9:21 that had belonged to Naboth the **J**. 3477
9:25 on the field that belonged to Naboth the **J**. 3477

JEZREELITESS (KJV) See JEZREELITE

JIBSAM (KJV) See IBSAM

JIDLAPH (1)

Ge 22:22 Kesed, Hazo, Pildash, **J** and Bethuel." 3358

JIMNA, JIMNAH (KJV) See IMNAH

JIMNITES (KJV) See IMNITE

JINGLING (1)

Isa 3:16 with **ornaments j** on their ankles. 6576

JIPHTAH (KJV) See IPHTAH

JIPHTHAH-EL (KJV) See IPHTAH EL

JOAB (141) [JOAB'S, ATROTH BETH JOAB]

2Sa 2:13 **J** son of Zeruiah and David's men went out 3405
2:14 Then Abner said to **J**, "Let's have some of 3405
2:14 "All right, let them do it," **J** said. 3405
2:18 **J**, Abishai and Asahel. 3405
2:22 How could I look your brother **J** in 3405
2:24 But **J** and Abishai pursued Abner, 3405
2:26 Abner called out to **J**, "Must the sword 3405
2:27 **J** answered, "As surely as God lives, 3405
2:28 So **J** blew the trumpet, 3405
2:30 Then **J** returned from pursuing Abner 3405
2:32 Then **J** and his men marched all night 3405
3:22 Just then David's men and **J** returned from 3405
3:23 **J** and all the soldiers with him arrived, 3405
3:24 So **J** went to the king and said, 3405

2Sa 3:26 J then left David and sent messengers 3405
3:27 J took him aside into the gateway, 3405
3:27 J stabbed him in the stomach, and he died. NIH
3:29 May his blood fall upon the head of J and 3405
3:30 (J and his brother Abishai murdered Abner 3405
3:31 Then David said to J and all the people 3405
8:16 J son of Zeruiah was over the army; 3405
10: 7 David sent J out with the entire army 3405
10: 9 J saw that there were battle lines in front 3405
10:11 J said, "If the Arameans are too strong NIH
10:13 Then J and the troops with him advanced 3405
10:14 So J returned from fighting 3405
11: 1 David sent J out with the king's men and 3405
11: 6 So David sent this word to J: 3405
11: 6 And J sent him to David. 3405
11: 7 David asked him how J was, 3405
11:11 and my master J and my lord's men 3405
11:14 In the morning David wrote a letter to J 3405
11:16 So while J had the city under siege, 3405
11:17 of the city came out and fought against J, 3405
11:18 J sent David a full account of the battle. 3405
11:22 he told David everything J had sent him 3405
11:25 David told the messenger, "Say this to J: 3405
11:25 Say this to encourage J." 2084[S]
12:26 Meanwhile J fought against Rabbah of 3405
12:27 J then sent messengers to David, saying, 3405
14: 1 J son of Zeruiah knew that 3405
14: 2 So J sent someone to Tekoa and had 3405
14: 3 And J put the words in her mouth. 3405
14:19 "Isn't the hand of J with you in all this?" 3405
14:19 it was your servant J who instructed me 3405
14:20 Your servant J did this to change 3405
14:21 The king said to J, "Very well, I will do it. 3405
14:22 J fell with his face to the ground 3405
14:22 J said, "Today your servant knows 3405
14:23 Then J went to Geshur 3405
14:29 for J in order to send him to the king, 3405
14:29 but J refused to come to him. NIH
14:31 Then J did go to Absalom's house 3405
14:32 Absalom said to J, "Look, 3405
14:33 So J went to the king and told him this. 3405
17:25 over the army in place of J. 3405
17:25 and sister of Zeruiah the mother of J. 3405
18: 2 a third under the command of J, 3405
18: 5 The king commanded J, Abishai and Ittai, 3405
18:10 When one of the men saw this, he told J, 3405
18:11 J said to the man who had told him this, 3405
18:14 J said, "I'm not going to wait like this 3405
18:16 Then J sounded the trumpet, 3405
18:16 stopped pursuing Israel, for J halted them. 3405
18:20 to take the news today," J told him. 3405
18:21 Then J said to a Cushite, "Go, 3405
18:21 The Cushite bowed down before J 3405
18:22 Ahimaaz son of Zadok again said to J, 3405
18:22 But J replied, "My son, why do you want 3405
18:23 So J said, "Run!" NIH
18:29 "I saw great confusion just as J was about 3405
19: 1 J was told, "The king is weeping 3405
19: 5 J went into the house to the king and said, 3405
19:13 the commander of my army in place of J.'" 3405
20: 8 J was wearing his military tunic, 3405
20: 9 J said to Amasa, "How are you, 3405
20: 9 Then J took Amasa by the beard 3405
20:10 and J plunged it into his belly, NIH
20:10 Amasa died. Then J and his brother 3405
20:11 "Whoever favors J, and whoever is 3405
20:11 whoever is for David, let him follow J!" 3405
20:13 on with J to pursue Sheba son of Bicri. 3405
20:15 the troops with J came and besieged Sheba 3405
20:16 Tell J to come here so I can speak to him." 3405
20:17 and she asked, "Are you J?" 3405
20:20 J replied, "Far be it from me to swallow 3405
20:21 The woman said to J, "His head will be 3405
20:22 head of Sheba son of Bicri and threw it to J. 3405
20:22 And J went back to the king in Jerusalem. 3405
20:23 J was over Israel's entire army; 3405
23:18 of J son of Zeruiah was chief of the Three. 3405
23:24 Asahel the brother of J, 3405
23:37 the armor-bearer of J son of Zeruiah, 3405
24: 2 to J and the army commanders with him, 3405
24: 3 But J replied to the king, 3405
24: 4 overruled J and the army commanders; 3405
24: 9 J reported the number of the fighting men 3405
1Ki 1: 7 Adonijah conferred with J son of Zeruiah 3405
1:19 Abiathar the priest and J the commander 3405
1:41 the sound of the trumpet, J asked, "What's 3405
2: 5 "Now you yourself know what J son 3405
2:22 and for Abiathar the priest and J son 3405
2:28 When the news reached J, 3405
2:29 King Solomon was told that J had fled to 3405
2:30 the tent of the LORD and said to J, 2257[S]
2:30 "This is how J answered me." 3405
2:31 the guilt of the innocent blood that J shed. 3405
2:33 the head of J and his descendants forever. 3405
2:34 of Jehoiada went up and struck down J 2257[S]
11:15 J the commander of the army, 3405
11:16 J and all the Israelites stayed there 3405
11:21 and that J the commander of the army was 3405
1Ch 2:16 Zeruiah's three sons were Abishai, J and Asahel. 3405
4:14 Seraiah was the father of J, 3405
11: 6 J son of Zeruiah went up first, 3405
11: 8 while J restored the rest of the city. 3405
11:20 the brother of J was chief of the Three. 3405
11:26 Asahel the brother of J, 3405
11:39 the armor-bearer of J son of Zeruiah, 3405
18:15 J son of Zeruiah was over the army; 3405
19: 8 David sent J out with the entire army 3405
19:10 J saw that there were battle lines in front 3405
19:12 J said, "If the Arameans are too strong NIH
19:14 Then J and the troops with him advanced 3405
19:15 So J went back to Jerusalem. 3405
20: 1 J led out the armed forces. 3405
20: 1 J attacked Rabbah and left it in ruins. 3405
21: 2 So David said to J and the commanders of 3405
21: 3 But J replied, "May the LORD multiply his 3405
21: 4 The king's word, however, overruled J; 3405
21: 4 so J left and went throughout Israel and 3405
21: 5 J reported the number of the fighting men 3405
21: 6 But J did not include Levi and Benjamin 3405
26:28 Abner son of Ner and J son of Zeruiah, 3405
27: 7 was Asahel the brother of J; 3405
27:24 J son of Zeruiah began to count the men 3405
27:34 J was the commander of the royal army. 3405
Ezr 2: 6 (through the line of Jeshua and J) 2,812 3405
8: 9 of the descendants of J, Obadiah son 3405
Ne 7:11 (through the line of Jeshua and J) 2,818 3405
Ps 60: T and when J returned and struck 3405

JOAB'S (9) [JOAB]

1Sa 26: 6 of Zeruiah, J brother, "Who will go down 3405
2Sa 3:29 May J house never be without someone 3405
14:30 "Look, J field is next to mine, 3405
18: 2 under J brother Abishai son of Zeruiah, 3405
18:15 of J armor-bearers surrounded Absalom, 3405
20: 7 So J men and the Kerethites and Pelethites 3405
20:10 on his guard against the dagger in J hand, 3405
20:11 of J men stood beside Amasa and said, 3405
1Ki 2:35 of Jehoiada over the army in J position 2257[S]

JOAH (11)

2Ki 18:18 and J son of Asaph the recorder went out 3406
18:26 Shebna and J said to the field commander, 3406
18:37 Shebna the secretary and J son of Asaph 3406
1Ch 6:21 J his son, Iddo his son, Zerah his son 3406
26: 4 Jehozabad the second, J the third, 3406
2Ch 29:12 J son of Zimmah and Eden son of Joah; 3406
29:12 Joah son of Zimmah and Eden son of J; 3406
34: 8 with J son of Joahaz, the recorder, 3406
Isa 36: 3 and J son of Asaph the recorder went out 3406
36:11 Shebna and J said to the field commander, 3406
36:22 and J son of Asaph the recorder went 3406

JOAHAZ (1)

2Ch 34: 8 with Joah son of J, the recorder, 3407

JOANAN (1)

Lk 3:27 the son *of* J, *2720*

JOANNA (2)

Lk 8: 3 J the wife of Cuza, the manager *2721*
24:10 It was Mary Magdalene, J, *2721*

JOASH (42) [JEHOASH]

Jdg 6:11 under the oak in Ophrah that belonged to J 3409
6:29 they were told, "Gideon son of J did it." 3409
6:30 The men of the town demanded of J, 3409
6:31 J replied to the hostile crowd around him, 3409
7:14 the sword of Gideon son of J, 3409
8:13 of J then returned from the battle by 3409
8:29 Jerub-Baal son of J went back home 3409
8:32 of J died at a good old age and was buried 3409
8:32 of his father J in Ophrah of the Abiezrites. 3409
1Ki 22:26 the ruler of the city and to J the king's son 3409
2Ki 11: 2 took J son of Ahaziah and stole him away 3409
11:21 J was seven years old when he began 3371
12: 1 In the seventh year of Jehu, J became king, 3371
12: 2 J did what was right in the eyes of the LORD 3371
12: 4 J said to the priests, "Collect all the money 3371
12: 6 of King J the priests still had not repaired 3371
12: 7 Therefore King J summoned Jehoiada 3371
12:18 But J king of Judah took all 3371
12:19 As for the other events of the reign of J, 3409
12:20 of J son of Ahaziah king of Judah, 3409
13:10 the thirty-seventh year of J king of Judah, 3409
14: 1 Amaziah son of J king of Judah began 3409
14: 3 the example of his father J. 3409
14:13 the son of J, the son of Ahaziah, 3371
14:17 of J king of Judah lived for fifteen years 3409
14:23 the fifteenth year of Amaziah son of J king 3409
1Ch 3:11 Ahaziah his son, J his son, 3409
4:22 the men of Cozeba, and J and Saraph, 3409
7: 8 The sons of Beker: Zemirah, J, Eliezer, 3447
12: 3 and J the sons of Shemaah the Gibeathite; 3409
27:28 J was in charge of the supplies of olive oil. 3447
2Ch 18:25 the ruler of the city and to J the king's son, 3409
22:11 took J son of Ahaziah and stole him away 3409
24: 1 J was seven years old 3409
24: 2 J did what was right in the eyes of the LORD 3409
24: 4 Some time later J decided to restore 3409
24:22 King J did not remember 3409
24:23 the army of Aram marched against J; 2257[S]
24:24 judgment was executed on J. 3409
24:25 they left J severely wounded. 2257[S]
25:23 the son of J, the son of Ahaziah, 3409
25:25 of J king of Judah lived for fifteen years 3409

JOATHAM (KJV) See JOTHAM

JOB (55) [JOB'S]

2Ch 34:13 and supervised all the workers from j 6275
34:13 the workers from job to j. 6275
Job 1: 1 a man whose name was J. 373
1: 5 J would send and have them purified. 373
1: 8 "Have you considered my servant J? 373
1: 9 "Does J fear God for nothing?" 373
1:14 a messenger came to J and said, 373
1:20 J got up and tore his robe 373
1:22 J did not sin by charging God 373
2: 3 "Have you considered my servant J? 373
2: 7 the presence of the LORD and afflicted J 373
2: 8 Then J took a piece of broken pottery 2257[S]
2:10 In all this, J did not sin in what he said. 373
3: 1 J opened his mouth and cursed the day 373
6: 1 Then J replied: 373
9: 1 Then J replied: 373
12: 1 Then J replied: 373
16: 1 Then J replied: 373
19: 1 Then J replied: 373
21: 1 Then J replied: 373
23: 1 Then J replied: 373
26: 1 Then J replied: 373
27: 1 And J continued his discourse: 373
29: 1 J continued his discourse: 373
31:40 The words of J are ended. 373
32: 1 So these three men stopped answering J, 373
32: 2 became very angry with J 373
32: 3 because they had found no way to refute J, 373
32: 4 to J because they were older than he. 373
32:12 But not one of you has proved J wrong; 373
32:14 J has not marshaled his words against me, NIH
33: 1 "But now, J, listen to my words; 373
33:31 "Pay attention, J, and listen to me; 373
34: 5 "J says, 'I am innocent, 373
34: 7 What man is like J, 373
34:35 'J speaks without knowledge; 373
34:36 that J might be tested to the utmost 373
35:16 So J opens his mouth with empty talk; 373
37:14 J; stop and consider God's wonders. 373
38: 1 the LORD answered J out of the storm. 373
40: 1 The LORD said to J: 373
40: 3 Then J answered the LORD: 373
40: 6 the LORD spoke to J out of the storm: 373
42: 1 Then J replied to the LORD: 373
42: 7 the LORD had said these things to J, 373
42: 7 of me what is right, as my servant J has. 373
42: 8 and seven rams and go to my servant J 373
42: 8 My servant J will pray for you, 373
42: 8 of me what is right, as my servant J has." 373
42:10 After J had prayed for his friends, 373
42:16 J lived a hundred and forty years; 373
Eze 14:14 Noah, Daniel and J— 373
14:20 even if Noah, Daniel and J were in it, 373
Lk 16: 3 My master is taking away my j. *3873*
16: 4 when I lose my j here, *3873*

JOB'S (8) [JOB]

Job 1: 5 This was J regular custom. 373
1:13 when J sons and daughters were feasting 2257[S]
2:11 When J three friends, Eliphaz the 373
31:31 'Who has not had his fill of J meat?'— 2257[S]
42: 9 and the LORD accepted J prayer. 373
42:12 the latter part of J life more than the first. 373
42:15 as beautiful as J daughters, 373
Jas 5:11 of J perseverance and have seen what *2724*

JOBAB (9)

Ge 10:29 Ophir, Havilah and J. 3411
36:33 J son of Zerah from Bozrah succeeded him 3412
36:34 When J died, Husham from the land of 3412
Jos 11: 1 he sent word to J king of Madon, 3412
1Ch 1:23 Ophir, Havilah and J. 3411
1:44 J son of Zerah from Bozrah succeeded him 3412
1:45 When J died, Husham from the land of 3412
8: 9 By his wife Hodesh he had J, Zibia, 3412
8:18 Izliah and J were the sons of Elpaal. 3412

JOCHEBED (2)

Ex 6:20 Amram married his father's sister J, 3425
Nu 26:59 the name of Amram's wife was J, 3425

JODA (1)

Lk 3:26 the son of Josech, the son *of* J, *2726*

JOED (1)

Ne 11: 7 Sallu son of Meshullam, the son of J, 3444

JOEL (21)

1Sa 8: 2 The name of his firstborn was J and 3408
1Ch 4:35 J, Jehu son of Joshibiah, the son 3408
5: 4 The descendants of J: 3408
5: 8 the son of Shema, the son of J. 3408
5:12 J was the chief, 3408
6:28 J the firstborn and Abijah the second son. 3408
6:33 Heman, the musician, the son of J, 3408
6:36 the son of J, the son of Azariah, 3408
7: 3 Michael, Obadiah, J and Isshiah. 3408
11:38 J the brother of Nathan, 3408
15: 7 J the leader and 130 relatives; 3408
15:11 and Uriel, Asaiah, J, Shemaiah, 3408
15:17 So the Levites appointed Heman son of J; 3408

1Ch 23: 8 Jehiel the first, Zetham and J—three in all. 3408
26:22 Zetham and his brother **J.** 3408
27:20 **J** son of Pedaiah; 3408
2Ch 29:12 Mahath son of Amasai and J son 3408
Ezr 10:43 Zabad, Zebina, Jaddai, J and Benaiah. 3408
Ne 11: 9 **J** son of Zicri was their chief officer, 3408
Joel 1: 1 The word of the LORD that came to J son 3408
Ac 2:16 this is what was spoken by the prophet **J:** *2727*

JOELAH (1)

1Ch 12: 7 and J and Zebadiah the sons of Jeroham 3443

JOEZER (1)

1Ch 12: 6 Azarel, J and Jashobeam the Korahites; 3445

JOGBEHAH (2)

Nu 32:35 Atroth Shophan, Jazer, **J,** 3322
Jdg 8:11 and J and fell upon the unsuspecting army. 3322

JOGLI (1)

Nu 34:22 Bukki son of **J,** the leader from the tribe 3332

JOHA (2)

1Ch 8:16 Ishpah and J were the sons of Beriah. 3418
11:45 his brother J the Tizite, 3418

JOHANAN (24)

2Ki 25:23 Ishmael son of Nethaniah, J son 3419
1Ch 3:15 **J** the firstborn, Jehoiakim the second son, 3419
3:24 Hodaviah, Eliashib, Pelaiah, Akkub, **J,** 3419
6: 9 Azariah the father of **J,** 3419
6:10 **J** the father of Azariah (it was he who 3419
12: 4 Jeremiah, Jahaziel, **J,** 3419
12:12 **J** the eighth, Elzabad the ninth, 3419
Ezr 8:12 **J** son of Hakkatan, and with him 110 men; 3419
Ne 12:22 the days of Eliashib, Joiada, J and Jaddua, 3419
12:23 the time of J son of Eliashib were recorded 3419
Jer 40: 8 **J** and Jonathan the sons of Kareah, 3419
40:13 **J** son of Kareah and all the army officers 3419
40:15 Then J son of Kareah said privately 3419
40:16 But Gedaliah son of Ahikam said to J son 3419
41:11 When J son of Kareah and all 3419
41:13 the people Ishmael had with him saw J son 3419
41:14 at Mizpah turned and went over to J son 3419
41:15 of his men escaped from J and fled to 3419
41:16 Then J son of Kareah and all the army 3419
42: 1 including J son of Kareah 3419
42: 8 So he called together J son of Kareah 3419
43: 2 of Hoshaiah and J son of Kareah and all 3419
43: 4 So J son of Kareah and all the army 3419
43: 5 **J** son of Kareah and all the army officers 3419

JOHN (138) [JOHN'S]

Mt 3: 1 In those days J the Baptist came, *2722*
3:13 to the Jordan to be baptized by **J.** *2722*
3:14 But J tried to deter him, saying, *2722*
3:15 Then J consented. *NIG*
4:12 When Jesus heard that J had been put *2722*
4:21 James son of Zebedee and his brother **J.** *2722*
10: 2 James son of Zebedee, and his brother **J;** *2722*
11: 2 **J** heard in prison what Christ was doing, *2722*
11: 4 "Go back and report *to* J what you hear *2722*
11: 7 Jesus began to speak to the crowd about **J:** *2722*
11:11 not risen anyone greater than J the Baptist; *2722*
11:12 From the days *of* J the Baptist until now, *2722*
11:13 and the Law prophesied until **J.** *2722*
11:18 For J came neither eating nor drinking, *2722*
14: 2 "This is J the Baptist; *2722*
14: 3 Now Herod had arrested J and bound him *2722*
14: 4 for J had been saying to him: *2722*
14: 5 Herod wanted to kill **J,** *899S*
14: 8 "Give me here on a platter the head *of* J *2722*
14:10 and had J beheaded in the prison. *2722*
16:14 They replied, "Some say J the Baptist; *2722*
17: 1 James and J the brother of James, *2722*
17:13 that he was talking to them about **J** *2722*
21:26 for they all hold that J was a prophet." *2722*
21:32 For J came to you to show you the way *2722*
Mk 1: 4 And so J came, baptizing in the desert *2722*
1: 6 **J** wore clothing made of camel's hair, *2722*
1: 9 and was baptized by J in the Jordan. *2722*
1:14 After J was put in prison, *2722*
1:19 of Zebedee and his brother J in a boat, *2722*
1:29 and J to the home of Simon and Andrew. *2722*
3:17 James son of Zebedee and his brother **J** *2722*
5:37 James and J the brother of James. *2722*
6:14 "**J** the Baptist has been raised from *2722*
6:16 But when Herod heard this, he said, "**J,** *2722*
6:17 had give orders to have J arrested, *2722*
6:18 For J had been saying to Herod, *2722*
6:19 a grudge against J and wanted to kill him. *899S*
6:20 because Herod feared J and protected him, *2722*
6:20 When Herod heard **J,** he was greatly *899S*
6:24 "The head *of* J the Baptist," she answered. *2722*
6:25 the head *of* J the Baptist on a platter." *2722*
6:27 The man went, beheaded J in the prison, *899S*
8:28 They replied, "Some say J the Baptist; *2722*
9: 2 James and J with him and led them up *2722*
9:38 said **J,** "we saw a man driving out demons *2722*
10:35 Then James and **J,** the sons of Zebedee, *2722*
10:41 they became indignant with James and **J.** *2722*
11:32 everyone held that J really was a prophet.) *2722*
Mk 13: 3 James, J and Andrew asked him privately, *2722*
14:33 James and J along with him, *2722*
Lk 1:13 and you are to give him the name **J.** *2722*
1:60 He is to be called **J.**" *2722*
1:63 "His name is **J.**" *2722*
3: 2 word of God came to J son of Zechariah in *2722*
3: 7 **J** said to the crowds coming out to *NIG*
3:11 **J** answered, "The man with two tunics *NIG*
3:15 if J might possibly be the Christ. *2722*
3:16 **J** answered them all, "I baptize you with *2722*
3:18 And with many other words J exhorted *NIG*
3:19 when J rebuked Herod the tetrarch because *899S*
3:20 He locked J up in prison. *2722*
5:10 and so were James and **J,** *2722*
6:14 his brother Andrew, James, **J,** Philip, *2722*
7:20 "**J** the Baptist sent us to you to ask, *2722*
7:22 *to* J what you have seen and heard: *2722*
7:24 Jesus began to speak to the crowd about **J:** *2722*
7:28 of women there is no one greater than **J;** *2722*
7:29 because they had been baptized by **J.** *2722*
7:30 because they had not been baptized by **J.**) *899S*
7:33 For J the Baptist came neither eating bread *2722*
8:51 in with him except Peter, J and James, and *2722*
9: 7 that J had been raised from the dead, *2722*
9: 9 But Herod said, "I beheaded **J.** *2722*
9:19 They replied, "Some say J the Baptist; *2722*
9:28 **J** and James with him and went up onto *2722*
9:49 said **J,** "we saw a man driving out demons *2722*
9:54 When the disciples James and J saw this, *2722*
11: 1 just as J taught his disciples." *2722*
16:16 and the Prophets were proclaimed until **J.** *2722*
20: 6 they are persuaded that J was a prophet." *2722*
22: 8 Jesus sent Peter and **J,** saying, *2722*
Jn 1: 6 who was sent from God; his name was **J.** *2722*
1:15 **J** testifies concerning him. *2722*
1:23 **J** replied in the words of Isaiah *NIG*
1:26 "I baptize with water," J replied, *2722*
1:28 side of the Jordan, where J was baptizing. *2722*
1:29 The next day J saw Jesus coming *NIG*
1:32 Then J gave this testimony: *2722*
1:35 The next day J was there again with two *2722*
1:40 of the two who heard what J had said *2722*
1:42 "You are Simon son *of* **J.** *2722*
3:23 **J** also was baptizing at Aenon near Salim, *2722*
3:24 (This was before J was put in prison.) *2722*
3:26 They came to J and said to him, "Rabbi, *2722*
3:27 To this J replied, "A man can receive only *2722*
4: 1 and baptizing more disciples than **J,** *2722*
5:33 "You have sent to J and he has testified to *2722*
5:35 **J** was a lamp that burned and gave light, *1697S*
5:36 "I have testimony weightier than that *of* **J.** *2722*
10:40 to the place where J had been baptizing in *2722*
10:41 "Though J never performed *2722*
10:41 all that J said about this man was true." *2722*
21:15 "Simon *son of* **J,** do you truly love me *2722*
21:16 Again Jesus said, "Simon *son of* **J,** *2722*
21:17 "Simon *son of* **J,** do you love me?" *2722*
Ac 1: 5 For J baptized with water, *2722*
1:13 Those present were Peter, **J,** *2722*
3: 1 One day Peter and J were going up to *2722*
3: 3 When he saw Peter and J about to enter, *2722*
3: 4 Peter looked straight at him, as did **J.** *2722*
3:11 While the beggar held on to Peter and **J,** *2722*
4: 1 to **Peter and J** while they were speaking to *899S*
4: 3 They seized **Peter and J,** *899S*
4: 6 and so were Caiaphas, **J,** Alexander and *2722*
4: 7 They had **Peter and J** brought before them *899S*
4:13 When they saw the courage of Peter and J *2722*
4:19 But Peter and J replied, "Judge for *2722*
4:23 Peter and J went back to their own people *NIG*
8:14 they sent Peter and J to them. *2722*
8:17 Peter and J placed their hands on them, *NIG*
8:25 **Peter and J** returned to Jerusalem, *3525+3836S*
10:37 after the baptism that J preached— *2722*
11:16 'J baptized with water, *2722*
12: 2 He had James, the brother *of* **J,** *2722*
12:12 to the house of Mary the mother *of* **J,** *2722*
12:25 taking with them **J,** also called Mark *2722*
13: 5 **J** was with them as their helper. *2722*
13:13 where J left them to return to Jerusalem. *2722*
13:24 **J** preached repentance and baptism to all *2722*
13:25 As J was completing his work, he said: *2722*
15:37 Barnabas wanted to take **J,** *2722*
18:25 though he knew only the baptism *of* **J.** *2722*
Gal 2: 9 Peter and **J,** those reputed to be pillars, *2722*
Rev 1: 1 by sending his angel to his servant **J,** *2722*
1: 4 **J,** To the seven churches in the province *2722*
1: 9 **J,** your brother and companion in *2722*
22: 8 **J,** am the one who heard and saw *2722*

JOHN'S (19) [JOHN]

Mt 3: 4 **J** clothes were made of camel's hair, *899+2722*
9:14 Then J disciples came and asked him, *2722*
11: 7 As **J disciples** were leaving, *4047S*
14:12 **J** disciples came and took his body *899S*
21:25 **J** baptism—where did it come from? *2722*
Mk 2:18 **J** disciples and the Pharisees were fasting. *2722*
2:18 "How is it that J disciples and the disciples *2722*
6:27 an executioner with orders to bring J head. *899S*
6:29 **J** disciples came and took his body *899S*
11:30 **J** baptism—was it from heaven, *2722*
Lk 5:33 "**J** disciples often fast and pray, *2722*
7:18 **J** disciples told him about all these things. *2722*
7:24 After J messengers left, *2722*
20: 4 **J** baptism—was it from heaven, *2722*
Jn 1:19 Now this was J testimony when the Jews *2722*
Jn 3:25 of J disciples and a certain Jew over *2722*
Ac 1:22 beginning from J baptism to the time *2722*
19: 3 "**J** baptism," they replied. *2722*
19: 4 "**J** baptism was a baptism of repentance. *2722*

JOIADA (5)

Ne 3: 6 The Jeshanah Gate was repaired by J son 3421
12:10 Eliashib the father of **J,** 3421
12:11 **J** the father of Jonathan, 3421
12:22 **J,** Johanan and Jaddua, 3421
13:28 One of the sons of J son of Eliashib 3421

JOIAKIM (4)

Ne 12:10 Jeshua was the father of **J,** 3423
12:10 **J** the father of Eliashib, 3423
12:12 In the days of **J,** these were the heads of 3423
12:26 They served in the days of J son of Jeshua, 3423

JOIARIB (4) [JOIARIB'S]

Ezr 8:16 who were leaders, and J and Elnathan, 3424
Ne 11: 5 the son of **J,** the son of Zechariah, 3424
11:10 From the priests: Jedaiah; the son of **J;** 3424
12: 6 Shemaiah, **J,** Jedaiah, 3424

JOIARIB'S (1) [JOIARIB]

Ne 12:19 of **J,** Mattenai; of Jedaiah's, Uzzi; 3424

JOIN (42) [ADJOINING, JOINED, JOINING, JOINS, JUNCTION, REJOINED]

Ge 34:30 *if they* **j forces** against me and attack me, 665
49: 6 *let* me not **j** their assembly, 3479
Ex 1:10 if war breaks out, *will* **j** our enemies, 3578
26: 3 **J** five of the curtains together, 2489
26: 9 **J** five of the curtains **together** 2489
Nu 18: 2 from your ancestral tribe *to* **j** you 4277
18: 4 *to* **j** you and be responsible for the care of 4277
34: 5 **j** the Wadi of Egypt and end at the Sea. 2025
Jdg 3:13 the Ammonites and Amalekites *to* **j** him, 665
21:21 When the girls of Shiloh come out to **j** in 2565
1Sa 13: 4 people were summoned to **j** Saul at Gilgal. 339
22:20 escaped and fled to **j** David. 339
2Sa 13:24 the king and his officials please **j** me?" 2143+6640
1Ki 1: 8 David's special guard did not **j** Adonijah. 6640
1Ch 13: 2 towns and pasturelands, *to* **come and j** us. 7695
2Ch 18: 3 we will **j** you in the war." 6640
Ne 4:20 the sound of the trumpet, **j** us there. 7695
10:29 *these* now **j** their brothers the nobles, 2616+6584
Est 9:27 and all who **j** them should 4277
Job 37:18 can you **j** him in spreading out the skies, 6640
Ps 49:19 *he will* **j** the generation of his fathers, 995+6330
50:18 When you see a thief, *you* **j** with him; 8354
106: 5 and **j** your inheritance in giving praise. 6640
118:27 **j in** the festal procession up to the horns of 673
Pr 23:20 *Do* not **j** those who drink too much wine 928+2118
24:21 my son, and *do* not **j** with the rebellious, 6843
Ecc 9: 3 and afterward they **j** the dead. 448
Isa 5: 8 to you who add house to house and **j** field 7928
14: 1 Aliens *will* **j** them and unite with 4277
14:20 *you will* not **j** them in burial, 3479
Jer 3:18 In those days the house of Judah *will* **j** 2143+6584
Eze 37:17 **J** them together into one stick so 7928
37:19 and **j** it to Judah's stick, 5989
Da 11:34 and many who are not sincere *will* **j** them. 4277
Mic 5: 3 of his brothers return to **j** the Israelites. NIH
Ac 5:13 No one else dared **j** them, *3140*
9:26 he tried *to* **j** the disciples, *3140*
17:15 Timothy to **j** him as soon as possible. *2262+4639*
21:24 **j in** their purification rites *5250*
Ro 15:30 **j** me **in** my **struggle** by praying to God *5253*
Php 3:17 **J with others** in **following** my **example,** *1181+5213*
2Ti 1: 8 **j** with me **in suffering** for the gospel, *5155*

JOINED (34) [JOIN]

Ge 14: 3 All these latter kings **j forces** in the Valley 2489
Ex 36:10 *They* **j** five of the curtains together and did 2489
36:16 *They* **j** five of the curtains into one set and 2489
Nu 25: 3 So Israel **j in worshiping** the Baal of Peor. 7537
25: 5 *of* your men who *have* **j in worshiping** 7537
Jos 10: 5 Jarmuth, Lachish and Eglon—**j forces.** 665
10: 6 the hill country *have* **j forces** against us." 7695
11: 5 All these kings **j forces** 3585
15: 4 along to Azmon and **j** the Wadi of Egypt, 3655
Jdg 6:33 and other eastern peoples **j forces** 665+3481
1Sa 10:10 and he **j in** their prophesying. 928+9348
14:22 they **j** the battle in hot pursuit. 1815
28:23 his men **j** the woman in urging him, 1685+2256
1Ki 20:29 and on the seventh day the battle *was* **j.** 7928
2Ch 5:13 The trumpeters and singers **j** in unison, 2118
Ezr 3: 9 **j together** in supervising those 285+3869+6641
Job 41:17 *They* **are j fast** to one another; 1815
41:23 The folds of his flesh *are* **tightly j;** 1815
Ps 48: 4 When the kings **j forces,** 3585
83: 8 Even Assyria *has* **j** them to lend strength to 4277
Hos 4:17 Ephraim *is* **j to** idols; leave him alone! 2489
Zec 2:11 "Many nations *will* **be j** with the LORD 4277
Mt 19: 6 Therefore what God *has* **j together,** *5183*
Mk 10: 9 Therefore what God *has* **j together,** *5183*
Jn 6:17 and Jesus *had* not yet **j** them. *2262+4639*
Ac 1:14 **j** together **constantly** in prayer, along with *4674*
12:20 now **j together** and sought an audience *3924*
16:22 The crowd **j in the attack** against Paul *5308*
17: 4 of the Jews were persuaded and **j** Paul *4677*

Ac 20: 6 five days later j the others at Troas, 2262+4639
24: 9 The Jews j **in the accusation,** 5298
Gal 2:13 j him **in his hypocrisy,** 5347
Eph 2:21 the whole building is j **together** and rises 5274
4:16 the whole body, j and held together 5274

JOINING (1) [JOIN]
Eze 31:17 j those killed by the sword. 448

JOINS (2) [JOIN]
Hos 7: 5 and he j hands with the mockers. 5432
1Co 16:16 as these and *to* everyone who j **in the work,** 5300

JOINT (2) [JOINTED, JOINTS]
Job 31:22 let it be broken off at the j. 7866
Ps 22:14 and all my bones *are* **out of** j. 7233

JOINTED (1) [JOINT]
Lev 11:21 that have j legs for hopping on the ground. 4200+4946+5087+8079

JOINTS (1) [JOINT]
Heb 4:12 to dividing soul and spirit, j and marrow; 765

JOISTS (1)
2Ch 34:11 for j and beams for the buildings that 4677

JOKDEAM (1)
Jos 15:56 Jezreel, J, Zanoah, 3680

JOKIM (1)
1Ch 4:22 J, the men of Cozeba, and Joash 3451

JOKING (3)
Ge 19:14 But his sons-in-law thought he was j. 7464
Pr 26:19 "I *was* only j!" 8471
Eph 5: 4 foolish talk or **coarse** j, 2365

JOKMEAM (2)
1Ki 4:12 to Abel Meholah across to J; 3695
1Ch 6:68 J, Beth Horon, 3695

JOKNEAM (4)
Jos 12:22 the king of J in Carmel one 3696
19:11 and extended to the ravine near J. 3696
21:34 from the tribe of Zebulun, J, Kartah, 3696
1Ch 6:77 From the tribe of Zebulun they received J, 3696

JOKSHAN (4)
Ge 25: 2 She bore him Zimran, J, Medan, Midian, 3705
25: 3 J was the father of Sheba and Dedan; 3705
1Ch 1:32 Zimran, J, Medan, Midian, 3705
1:32 The sons of J: Sheba and Dedan. 3705

JOKTAN (6)
Ge 10:25 his brother was named J. 3690
10:26 J was the father of Almodad, Sheleph, 3690
10:29 All these were sons of J. 3690
1Ch 1:19 his brother was named J. 3690
1:20 J was the father of Almodad, Sheleph, 3690
1:23 All these were sons of J. 3690

JOKTHEEL (2)
Jos 15:38 Dilean, Mizpah, J, 3706
2Ki 14: 7 calling it J, the name it has to this day. 3706

JOLTING (1)
Na 3: 2 galloping horses and j chariots! 8376

JONA (KJV) See JOHN

JONADAB (12)
2Sa 13: 3 Now Amnon had a friend named J son 3432
13: 3 J was a very shrewd man. 3432
13: 5 "Go to bed and pretend to be ill," J said. 3386
13:32 But J son of Shimeah, David's brother, 3432
13:35 J said to the king, "See, 3432
Jer 35: 6 because our forefather J son 3432
35: 8 We have obeyed everything our forefather J son of Recab commanded 3386
35:10 fully obeyed everything our forefather J 3432
35:14 'J son of Recab ordered his sons not to drink wine 3386
35:16 of J son of Recab have carried out 3386
35:18 obeyed the command of your forefather J 3386
35:19 'J son of Recab will never fail to have 3432

JONAH (28) [JONAH'S]
2Ki 14:25 through his servant J son of Amittai, 3434
Jnh 1: 1 of the LORD came to J son of Amittai: 3434
1: 3 But J ran away from the LORD 3434
1: 5 But J had gone below deck, 3434
1: 7 They cast lots and the lot fell on J. 3434
1:15 they took J and threw him overboard, 3434
1:17 LORD provided a great fish to swallow J, 3434
1:17 and J was inside the fish three days 3434
Jnh 2: 1 From inside the fish J prayed to the LORD 3434
2:10 and it vomited J onto dry land. 3434
3: 1 Then the word of the LORD came to J 3434
3: 3 J obeyed the word of the LORD and went 3434
3: 4 On the first day, J started into the city. 3434
4: 1 But J was greatly displeased 3434
4: 5 J went out and sat down at a place east of 3434
4: 6 and made it grow up over J to give shade 3434
4: 6 and J was very happy about the vine. 3434
4: 9 But God said to J, 3434
Mt 12:39 the sign *of* the prophet J. 2731
12:40 For as J was three days and three nights in 2731
12:41 for they repented at the preaching *of* J, 2731
12:41 and now one greater than J is here. 2731
16: 4 none will be given it except the sign *of* J." 2731
16:17 "Blessed are you, Simon **son of** J, 980
Lk 11:29 none will be given it except the sign *of* J. 2731
11:30 For as J was a sign to the Ninevites, 2731
11:32 for they repented at the preaching *of* J, 2731
11:32 and now one greater than J is here. 2731

JONAH'S (1) [JONAH]
Jnh 4: 8 sun blazed on J head so that he grew faint. 3434

JONAM (1)
Lk 3:30 the son *of* J, the son of Eliakim, 2729

JONAN (KJV) See JONAM

JONAS (KJV) See JONAH

JONATHAN (112) [JONATHAN'S]
Jdg 18:30 and J son of Gershom, the son of Moses, 3387
1Sa 13: 2 of Bethel, and a thousand were with J 3440
13: 3 J attacked the Philistine outpost at Geba, 3440
13:16 Saul and his son J and the men 3440
13:22 the battle not a soldier with Saul and J had 3440
13:22 only Saul and his son J had them. 3440
14: 1 One day J son of Saul said to 3440
14: 3 No one was aware that J had left. 3440
14: 4 of the pass that J intended to cross to reach 3440
14: 6 J said to his young armor-bearer, "Come, 3387
14: 8 J said, "Come, then; 3387
14:12 The men of the outpost shouted to J 3440
14:12 So J said to his armor-bearer, 3440
14:13 J climbed up, using his hands and feet, 3440
14:13 The Philistines fell before J, 3440
14:14 In that first attack J and his armor-bearer 3440
14:17 it was J and his armor-bearer who were 3440
14:21 to the Israelites who were with Saul and J. 3440
14:27 But J had not heard that his father 3440
14:29 J said, "My father has made trouble for 3440
14:39 even if it lies with my son J, he must die." 3440
14:40 I and J my son will stand over here." 3440
14:41 And J and Saul were taken by lot, 3440
14:42 "Cast the lot between me and J my son." 3440
14:42 And J was taken. 3440
14:43 Then Saul said to J, "Tell me what you 3440
14:43 So J told him, "I merely tasted a little 3440
14:44 be it ever so severely, if you do not die, J." 3440
14:45 But the men said to Saul, "Should J die— 3440
14:45 So the men rescued J, 3440
14:49 Saul's sons were J, Ishvi and Malki-Shua. 3440
18: 1 J became one in spirit with David, 3387
18: 3 And J made a covenant with David 3387
18: 4 J took off the robe he was wearing 3387
19: 1 Saul told his son J and all the attendants 3440
19: 1 But J was very fond of David 3387
19: 4 J spoke well of David to Saul his father 3387
19: 6 Saul listened to J and took this oath: 3387
19: 7 So J called David and told him 3387
20: 1 from Naioth at Ramah and went to J 3387
20: 2 "Never!" J replied. "You are not going to NIH
20: 3 'J must not know this or he will 3387
20: 4 J said to David, "Whatever you want me 3387
20: 9 "Never!" J said. "If I had the least inkling 3387
20:11 J said, "let's go out into the field." 3387
20:12 Then J said to David: 3387
20:16 So J made a covenant with the house 3387
20:17 And J had David reaffirm his oath out 3387
20:18 Then J said to David: 3387
20:25 opposite J, and Abner sat next to Saul, 3387
20:27 Then Saul said to his son J, 3387
20:28 J answered, "David earnestly asked me 3387
20:30 Saul's anger flared up at J and he said 3387
20:32 What has he done?" J asked his father. 3387
20:33 Then J knew that his father intended 3387
20:34 J got up from the table in fierce anger; 3387
20:35 In the morning J went out to the field 3387
20:37 J called out after him, 3387
20:39 only J and David knew.) 3387
20:40 J gave his weapons to the boy and said, 3387
20:41 and bowed down before J three times, NIH
20:42 J said to David, "Go in peace, 3387
20:42 David left, and J went back to the town. 3387
23:16 And Saul's son J went to David at Horesh 3387
23:18 Then J went home, 3387
31: 2 and they killed his sons J, Abinadab and 3387
2Sa 1: 4 And Saul and his son J are dead." 3387
1: 5 that Saul and his son J are dead?" 3387
1:12 till evening for Saul and his son J, 3387
1:17 concerning Saul and his son J, 3387
1:22 the bow of J did not turn back, 3387
1:23 "Saul and J—in life they were loved 3387
2Sa 1:25 J lies slain on your heights. 3387
1:26 I grieve for you, J my brother; 3387
4: 4 (J son of Saul had a son who was lame in 3387
4: 4 when the news about Saul and J came 3387
9: 3 "There is still a son of J; 3387
9: 6 When Mephibosheth son of J, 3387
9: 7 for the sake of your father J. 3387
15:27 with your son Ahimaaz and J son 3387
15:36 Ahimaaz son of Zadok and J son 3387
17:17 J and Ahimaaz were staying at En Rogel. 3387
17:20 they asked, "Where are Ahimaaz and J?" 3387
21: 7 The king spared Mephibosheth son of J, 3387
21: 7 the LORD between David and J son 3387
21:12 and took the bones of Saul and his son J 3387
21:13 the bones of Saul and his son J from there, 3387
21:14 the bones of Saul and his son J in the tomb 3387
21:21 When he taunted Israel, J son of Shimeah, 3387
23:32 the Shaalbonite, the sons of Jashen, J 3387
1Ki 1:42 J son of Abiathar the priest arrived. 3440
1:43 "Not at all!" J answered. 3440
1Ch 2:32 Shammai's brother: Jether and J. 3440
2:33 The sons of J: Peleth and Zaza. 3440
8:33 and Saul the father of J, Malki-Shua, 3387
8:34 The son of J: Merib-Baal, 3387
9:39 and Saul the father of J, Malki-Shua, 3387
9:40 The son of J: Merib-Baal, 3387
10: 2 and they killed his sons J, Abinadab 3440
11:34 J son of Shagee the Hararite, 3440
20: 7 When he taunted Israel, J son of Shimea, 3387
27:25 J son of Uzziah was in charge of 3387
27:32 J, David's uncle, was a counselor, 3387
Ezr 8: 6 Ebed son of J, and with him 50 men; 3440
10:15 Only J son of Asahel and Jahzeiah son 3440
Ne 12:11 Joiada the father of J, 3440
12:11 and J the father of Jaddua. 3440
12:14 of Malluch's, J; of Shecaniah's, Joseph; 3440
12:35 and also Zechariah son of J, 3440
Jer 37:15 and imprisoned in the house of J 3387
37:20 Do not send me back to the house of J 3387
40: 8 Johanan and J the sons of Kareah, 3440

JONATHAN'S (3) [JONATHAN]
1Sa 20:37 to the place where J arrow had fallen, 3387
2Sa 9: 1 to whom I can show kindness for J sake?" 3387
Jer 38:26 to send me back to J house to die there.' " 3387

JOPPA (14)
Jos 19:46 with the area facing J. 3639
2Ch 2:16 will float them in rafts by sea down to J. 3639
Ezr 3: 7 bring cedar logs by sea from Lebanon to J, 3639
Jnh 1: 3 He went down to J, where he found a ship 3639
Ac 9:36 In J there was a disciple named Tabitha 2673
9:38 Lydda was near J; 2673
9:42 This became known all over J, 2673
9:43 Peter stayed in J for some time with 2673
10: 5 Now send men to J to bring back 2673
10: 8 that had happened and sent them to J. 2673
10:23 some of the brothers from J went along. 2673
10:32 Send to J for Simon who is called Peter. 2673
11: 5 "I was in the city *of* J praying, 2673
11:13 'Send to J for Simon who is called Peter. 2673

JORAH (1)
Ezr 2:18 of J 112 3454

JORAI (1)
1Ch 5:13 Michael, Meshullam, Sheba, J, Jacan, 3455

JORAM (28) [JEHORAM]
2Sa 8:10 he sent his son J to King David 3456
8:10 J brought with him articles of silver NIH
2Ki 1:17 J succeeded him as king in the second year 3393
3: 1 J son of Ahab became king of Israel 3393
3: 6 at that time King J set out from Samaria 3393
8:16 In the fifth year of J son of Ahab king 3456
8:25 In the twelfth year of J son of Ahab king 3456
8:28 Ahaziah went with J son of Ahab to war 3456
8:28 The Arameans wounded J; 3456
8:29 so King J returned to Jezreel to recover 3456
8:29 of Judah went down to Jezreel to see J son 3456
9:14 the son of Nimshi, conspired against J. 3456
9:14 against Joram. (Now J and all Israel 3456
9:15 but King J had returned to Jezreel 3393
9:16 because J was resting there 3456
9:17 "Get a horseman," J ordered. 3393
9:21 "Hitch up my chariot," J ordered. 3393
9:21 J king of Israel and Ahaziah king 3393
9:22 When J saw Jehu he asked, 3393
9:23 J turned about and fled, 3393
9:24 Then Jehu drew his bow and shot J 3393
9:29 (In the eleventh year of J son of Ahab, 3456
1Ch 26:25 Jeshaiah his son, J his son, 3456
2Ch 22: 5 with J son of Ahab king of Israel to war 3393
22: 5 The Arameans wounded J; 3456
22: 6 of Judah went down to Jezreel to see J son 3393
22: 7 Through Ahaziah's visit to J, 3456
22: 7 he went out with J to meet Jehu son 3393

JORDAN (193) [JORDAN'S]
Ge 13:10 the whole plain of the J was well watered, 3720
13:11 the whole plain of the J and set out toward 3720
32:10 I had only my staff when I crossed this J, 3720
50:10 the J, they lamented loudly and bitterly; 3720

Ge 50:11 near the J is called Abel Mizraim. 3720
Nu 13:29 near the sea and along the J." 3720
22:1 the plains of Moab and camped along the J 3720
26:3 So on the plains of Moab by the J *across* 3720
26:63 of Moab by the J *across from* Jericho. 3720
31:12 by the J *across from* Jericho. 3720
32:5 Do not make us cross the J." 3720
32:19 with them on the other side of the J, 3720
32:19 to us on the east side of the J." 3720
32:21 and if all of you will go armed over the J 3720
32:29 over the J with you before the LORD, 3720
32:32 be on this side of the J." 3720
33:48 and camped on the plains of Moab by the J 3720
33:49 the J from Beth Jeshimoth to Abel Shittim. 3720
33:50 the J *across from* Jericho the LORD said 3720
33:51 'When you cross the J into Canaan, 3720
34:12 down along the J and end at the Salt Sea. 3720
34:15 on the east side of the J *of* Jericho, 3720
35:1 On the plains of Moab by the J *across* 3720
35:10 'When you cross the J into Canaan, 3720
35:14 Give three on this side of the J and three 3720
36:13 of Moab by the J *across from* Jericho. 3720
Dt 1:1 to all Israel in the desert east of the J— 3720
1:5 East of the J in the territory of Moab, 3720
2:29 until we cross the J into the land 3720
3:8 of the Amorites the territory east of the J, 3720
3:17 Its western border was the J in the Arabah, 3720
3:20 land that the LORD your God is giving them, across the J. 3720
3:25 over and see the good land beyond the J— 3720
3:27 since you are not going to cross this J. 3720
4:14 you are crossing the J to possess. 2025+9004S
4:21 not cross the J and enter the good land 3720
4:22 I will not cross the J; 3720
4:26 from the land that you are crossing the J 3720
4:41 Moses set aside three cities east of the J, 3720
4:46 in the valley near Beth Peor east of the J, 3720
4:47 the two Amorite kings east of the J. 3720
4:49 and included all the Arabah east of the J, 3720
6:1 you are crossing the J to possess, 2025+9004S
9:1 You are now about to cross the J to go in 3720
11:8 the land that you are crossing the J 2025+9004S
11:11 But the land you are crossing the J 2025+9004S
11:30 these mountains are across the J, 3720
11:31 to cross the J to enter and take possession 3720
12:10 But you will cross the J and settle in 3720
27:2 When you have crossed the J into the land 3720
27:4 And when you have crossed the J, 3720
27:12 When you have crossed the J, 3720
30:18 in the land you are crossing the J to enter 3720
31:2 'You shall not cross the J.' 3720
31:13 the land you are crossing the J to possess." 3720
32:47 the land you are crossing the J to possess." 3720
Jos 1:2 the J River into the land I am about to give 3720
1:11 from now you will cross the J here to go in 3720
1:14 the land that Moses gave you east of the J, 3720
1:15 the LORD gave you east of the J toward 3720
2:7 on the road that leads to the fords of the J, 3720
2:10 of the Amorites east of the J, 3720
3:1 from Shittim and went to the J, 3720
3:11 the Lord of all the earth will go into the J 3720
3:13 set foot in the J, its waters flowing 3720
3:14 the people broke camp to cross the J, 3720
3:15 the J is at flood stage all during harvest. 3720
3:15 the ark reached the J and their feet touched 3720
3:17 on dry ground in the middle of the J, 3720
4:1 finished crossing the J, the LORD said 3720
4:3 of the J from right where the priests stood 3720
4:5 into the middle of the J. 3720
4:7 the flow of the J was cut off before the ark 3720
4:7 When it crossed the J, the waters 3720
4:7 the waters of the J were cut off. 3720
4:8 the J, according to the number of the tribes 3720
4:9 in the middle of the J at the spot where 3720
4:10 in the middle of the J until everything 3720
4:16 of the Testimony to come up out of the J." 3720
4:17 "Come up out of the J." 3720
4:18 the waters of the J returned to their place 3720
4:19 the people went up from the J and camped 3720
4:20 twelve stones they had taken out of the J. 3720
4:22 'Israel crossed the J on dry ground.' 3720
4:23 For the LORD your God dried up the J 3720
4:23 the J just what he had done to the Red Sea NIH
5:1 of the J and all the Canaanite kings along 3720
5:1 how the LORD had dried up the J before 3720
7:7 across the J to deliver us into the hands of 3720
7:7 to stay on the other side of the J! 3720
9:1 when all the kings west of the J heard 3720
9:10 the two kings of the Amorites east of the J 3720
12:1 over east of the J, from the Arnon Gorge 3720
12:7 on the west side of the J, from Baal Gad in 3720
13:8 that Moses had given them east of the J, 3720
13:23 of the Reubenites was the bank of the J. 3720
13:27 of Heshbon (the east side of the J, 3720
13:32 in the plains of Moab across the J east 3720
14:3 of the J but had not granted the Levites 3720
15:5 the Salt Sea as far as the mouth of the J. 3720
15:5 the bay of the sea at the mouth of the J, 3720
16:1 The allotment for Joseph began at the J 3720
16:7 touched Jericho and came out at the J. 3720
17:5 and Bashan east of the J, 3720
18:7 on the east side of the J. 3720
18:12 the J, passed the northern slope of Jericho 3720
18:19 at the mouth of the J in the south. 3720
18:20 The J formed the boundary on the eastern 3720
19:22 and ended at the J. 3720
19:33 to Lakkum and ending at the J. 3720
Jos 19:34 Asher on the west and the J on the east. 3720
20:8 of the J *of* Jericho they designated Bezer 3720
22:4 on the other side of the J. 3720
22:7 the west side of the J with their brothers.) 3720
22:10 When they came to Geliloth near the J in 3720
22:10 an imposing altar there by the J. 3720
22:11 the border of Canaan at Geliloth near the J 3720
22:25 the J a boundary between us and you— 3720
23:4 the J and the Great Sea in the west. 3720
24:8 of the Amorites who lived east of the J. 3720
24:11 you crossed the J and came to Jericho. 3720
Jdg 3:28 taking possession of the fords of the J 3720
5:17 Gilead stayed beyond the J. 3720
6:33 the J and camped in the Valley of Jezreel. NIH
7:24 the Midianites and seize the waters of the J 3720
7:24 the waters of the J as far as Beth Barah. 3720
7:25 to Gideon, who was by the J. 3720
8:4 came to the J and crossed it. 3720
10:8 the Israelites on the east side of the J 3720
10:9 The Ammonites also crossed the J to fight 3720
11:13 all the way to the J. 3720
11:22 to the Jabbok and from the desert to the J. 3720
12:5 the fords of the J leading to Ephraim, 3720
12:6 and killed him at the fords of the J. 3720
1Sa 13:7 even crossed the J to the land of Gad 3720
31:7 along the valley and those across the J saw 3720
2Sa 2:29 They crossed the J, continued through 3720
10:17 crossed the J and went to Helam. 3720
17:22 with him set out and crossed the J. 3720
17:22 no one was left who had not crossed the J. 3720
17:24 and Absalom crossed the J with all 3720
19:15 the king returned and went as far as the J. 3720
19:15 the king and bring him across the J. 3720
19:17 They rushed to the J, where the king was. 3720
19:18 When Shimei son of Gera crossed the J, 3720
19:31 from Rogelim to cross the J with the king 3720
19:36 the J with the king for a short distance, 3720
19:39 So all the people crossed the J, 3720
19:41 and his household across the J, 3720
20:2 by their king all the way from the J 3720
24:5 After crossing the J, they camped 3720
1Ki 2:8 When he came down to meet me at the J, 3720
7:46 of the J between Succoth and Zarethan. 3720
17:3 in the Kerith Ravine, east of the J. 3720
17:5 east of the J, and stayed there. 3720
2Ki 2:6 the LORD has sent me to the J." 3720
2:7 and Elisha had stopped at the J. 3720
2:13 and stood on the bank of the J. 3720
5:10 "Go, wash yourself seven times in the J, 3720
5:14 and dipped himself in the J seven times, 3720
6:2 Let us go to the J, where each of us can get 3720
6:4 to the J and began to cut down trees. 3720
7:15 They followed them as far as the J, 3720
10:33 the J in all the land of Gilead (the region 3720
1Ch 6:78 the J east of Jericho they received Bezer in 3720
12:15 It was they who crossed the J in 3720
12:37 from east of the J, men of Reuben, Gad 3720
19:17 he gathered all Israel and crossed the J; 3720
26:30 of the J for all the work of the LORD and 3720
2Ch 4:17 of the J between Succoth and Zarethan. 3720
Job 40:23 the J should surge against his mouth. 3720
Ps 42:6 the land of the J, the heights of Hermon— 3720
114:3 The sea looked and fled, the J turned back; 3720
114:5 Why was it, O sea, that you fled, O J, 3720
Isa 9:1 by the way of the sea, along the J— 3720
Jer 12:5 in the thickets by the J? 3720
Eze 47:18 along the J between Gilead and the land 3720
Zec 11:3 the lush thicket of the J is ruined! 3720
Mt 3:5 and the whole region *of* the J. *2674*
3:6 they were baptized by him in the J River. *2674*
3:13 Then Jesus came from Galilee to the J to *2674*
4:15 along the J, Galilee of the Gentiles— *2674*
4:25 and the region across the J followed him. *2674*
19:1 of Judea to the other side *of* the J. *2674*
Mk 1:5 they were baptized by him in the J River. *2674*
1:9 and was baptized by John in the J. *2674*
3:8 the regions across the J and around Tyre *2674*
10:1 into the region of Judea and across the J. *2674*
Lk 3:3 He went into all the country around the J, *2674*
4:1 from the J and was led by the Spirit in *2674*
Jn 1:28 at Bethany on the other side *of* the J, *2674*
3:26 with you on the other side *of* the J— *2674*
10:40 Then Jesus went back across the J to *2674*

JORDAN'S (3) [JORDAN]

Jos 3:8 'When you reach the edge of the J waters, 3720
Jer 49:19 "Like a lion coming up from J thickets to 3720
50:44 Like a lion coming up from J thickets to 3720

JORIM (1)

Lk 3:29 the son *of* J, the son of Matthat, *2733*

JORKEAM (1)

1Ch 2:44 and Raham the father of J. 3767

JORKOAM (KJV) See JORKEAM

JOSABAD (KJV) See JOZABAD

JOSAPHAT (KJV) See JEHOSHAPHAT

JOSE (KJV) See JOSHUA

JOSECH (1)

Lk 3:26 the son of Semein, the son *of* J, *2738*

JOSEDECH (KJV) See JEHOZADAK

JOSEPH (237) [JOSEPH'S]

Ge 30:24 She named him J, and said, 3441
30:25 After Rachel gave birth to J, 3441
33:2 and Rachel and J in the rear. 3441
33:7 Last of all came J and Rachel, 3441
35:24 The sons of Rachel: J and Benjamin. 3441
37:2 J, a young man of seventeen, 3441
37:3 Now Israel loved J more than any 3441
37:5 J had a dream, and when he told it to 3441
37:13 and Israel said to J, "As you know, 3441
37:14 When J arrived at Shechem, NIH
37:17 So J went after his brothers 3441
37:23 So when J came to his brothers, 3441
37:28 his brothers pulled J up out of the cistern 3441
37:29 to the cistern and saw that J was not there, 3441
37:33 J has surely been torn to pieces." 3441
37:36 the Midianites sold J in Egypt to Potiphar, 2257S
39:1 Now J had been taken down to Egypt. 3441
39:2 The LORD was with J and he prospered, 3441
39:4 J found favor in his eyes 3441
39:5 of the Egyptian because of J. 3441
39:6 with J in charge, he did not concern himself 2257S
39:6 Now J was well-built and handsome, 3441
39:7 a while his master's wife took notice of J 3441
39:10 And though she spoke to J day after day, 3441
39:20 But while J was there in the prison, NIH
39:22 the warden put J in charge of all those held 3441
39:23 because the LORD was with J 2257S
40:3 in the same prison where J was confined. 3441
40:4 of the guard assigned them to J, 3441
40:6 When J came to them the next morning, 3441
40:8 Then J said to them, 3441
40:9 So the chief cupbearer told J his dream. 3441
40:12 "This is what it means," J said to him. 3441
40:16 When the chief baker saw that J had given NIH
40:16 he said to J, "I too had a dream: 3441
40:18 "This is what it means," J said. 3441
40:22 as J had said to them in his interpretation. 3441
40:23 did not remember J; he forgot him. 3441
41:14 So Pharaoh sent for J, 3441
41:15 Pharaoh said to J, "I had a dream, 3441
41:16 "I cannot do it," J replied to Pharaoh, 3441
41:17 Then Pharaoh said to J, "In my dream 3441
41:25 Then J said to Pharaoh, "The dreams of 3441
41:39 Then Pharaoh said to J, "Since God has 3441
41:41 So Pharaoh said to J, "I hereby put you 3441
41:44 Then Pharaoh said to J, "I am Pharaoh, 3441
41:45 Pharaoh gave J the name Zaphenath-Paneah 3441
41:45 And J went throughout the land of Egypt. 3441
41:46 J was thirty years old when he entered 3441
41:46 And J went out from Pharaoh's presence 3441
41:48 J collected all the food produced NIH
41:49 J stored up huge quantities of grain, 3441
41:50 to J by Asenath daughter of Potiphera, 3441
41:51 J named his firstborn Manasseh and said, 3441
41:54 years of famine began, just as J had said. 3441
41:55 "Go to J and do what he tells you." 3441
41:56 J opened the storehouses and sold grain to 3441
41:57 to Egypt to buy grain from J, 3441
42:6 Now J was the governor of the land, 3441
42:7 As soon as J saw his brothers, 3441
42:8 Although J recognized his brothers, 3441
42:14 J said to them, "It is just as I told you: 3441
42:18 On the third day, J said to them, 3441
42:23 not realize that J could understand them, 3441
42:25 J gave orders to fill their bags with grain, 3441
42:36 J is no more and Simeon is no more, 3441
43:15 to Egypt and presented themselves to J. 3441
43:16 When J saw Benjamin with them, 3441
43:17 The man did as J told him and took 3441
43:26 When J came home, 3441
43:30 J hurried out and looked for a place 3441
44:1 Now J gave these instructions to NIH
44:2 And he did as J said. 3441
44:4 from the city when J said to his steward, 3441
44:14 J was still in the house when Judah 3441
44:15 J said to them, "What is this you have done? 3441
44:17 But J said, "Far be it from me to do such NIH
45:1 Then J could no longer control himself 3441
45:1 with J when he made himself known 3441
45:3 J said to his brothers, "I am Joseph! 3441
45:3 Joseph said to his brothers, "I am J! 3441
45:4 J said to his brothers, "Come close to me." 3441
45:4 he said, "I am your brother J, 3441
45:9 'This is what your son J says: 3441
45:17 Pharaoh said to J, "Tell your brothers, 3441
45:21 J gave them carts, as Pharaoh had 3441
45:26 They told him, "J is still alive! 3441
45:27 when they told him everything J had said 3441
45:27 the carts J had sent to carry him back, 3441
45:28 My son J is still alive. 3441
46:19 of Jacob's wife Rachel: J and Benjamin. 3441
46:20 to J by Asenath daughter of Potiphera, 3441
46:27 With the two sons who had been born to J 3441
46:28 Now Jacob sent Judah ahead of him to J 3441
46:29 J had his chariot made ready and went 3441
46:29 As soon as J appeared before him, NIH
46:30 Israel said to J, "Now I am ready to die, 3441
46:31 Then J said to his brothers and 3441
47:1 J went and told Pharaoh, 3441

Ge 47: 5 Pharaoh said to J, "Your father and 3441
47: 7 Then J brought his father Jacob in 3441
47:11 So J settled his father and his brothers 3441
47:12 J also provided his father and his brothers 3441
47:14 J collected all the money that was to 3441
47:15 all Egypt came to J and said, 3441
47:16 "Then bring your livestock," said J. 3441
47:17 So they brought their livestock to J, 3441
47:20 J bought all the land in Egypt for Pharaoh. 3441
47:21 and J reduced the people to servitude, NIH
47:23 J said to the people, "Now that I have 3441
47:26 So J established it as a law 3441
47:29 he called for his son J and said to him, 3441
47:31 Then J swore to him, and Israel NIH
48: 1 Some time later J was told, 3441
48: 2 "Your son J has come to you," 3441
48: 3 Jacob said to J, "God Almighty appeared 3441
48: 8 When Israel saw the sons of J, he asked, 3441
48: 9 J said to his father. 3441
48:10 So J brought his sons close to him, NIH
48:11 Israel said to J, "I never expected to see 3441
48:12 Then J removed them from Israel's knees 3441
48:13 And J took both of them, 3441
48:15 Then he blessed J and said, 3441
48:17 J saw his father placing his right hand 3441
48:18 J said to him, "No, my father, 3441
48:21 Then Israel said to J, "I am about to die, 3441
49:22 "J is a fruitful vine, a fruitful vine near a 3441
49:26 Let all these rest on the head of J, 3441
50: 1 J threw himself upon his father and wept 3441
50: 2 Then J directed the physicians 3441
50: 4 J said to Pharaoh's court, 3441
50: 7 So J went up to bury his father. 3441
50:10 and there J observed a seven-day period NIH
50:14 burying his father, J returned to Egypt, 3441
50:15 "What if J holds a grudge against us 3441
50:16 So they sent word to J, saying, 3441
50:17 'This is what you are to say to J: 3441
50:17 When their message came to him, J wept. 3441
50:19 But J said to them, "Don't be afraid. 3441
50:22 J stayed in Egypt, along with all 3441
50:24 J said to his brothers, "I am about to die. 3441
50:25 And J made the sons of Israel swear 3441
50:26 So J died at the age of a hundred and ten. 3441
Ex 1: 5 J was already in Egypt. 3441
1: 6 Now J and all his brothers and all 3441
1: 8 a new king, who did not know about J, 3441
13:19 of J with him because Joseph had made 3441
13:19 of Joseph with him because J had made NIH
Nu 1:10 from the sons of J: 3441
1:32 From the sons of J: 3441
13: 7 from the tribe of Issachar, Igal son of J; 3441
13:11 from the tribe of Manasseh (a tribe of J), 3441
26:28 of J by their clans through Manasseh 3441
26:37 the descendants of J by their clans. 3441
27: 1 to the clans of Manasseh son of J. 3441
32:33 and the half-tribe of Manasseh son of J 3441
34:23 from the tribe of Manasseh son of J; 3441
34:24 leader from the tribe of Ephraim son of J; NIH
36: 1 from the clans of the descendants of J, 3441
36: 5 of the descendants of J is saying is right. 3441
36:12 of the descendants of Manasseh son of J, 3441
Dt 27:12 Levi, Judah, Issachar, J and Benjamin. 3441
33:13 About J he said: "May the LORD bless 3441
33:16 Let all these rest on the head of J, 3441
Jos 14: 4 for the sons of J had become two tribes— 3441
16: 1 allotment for J began at the Jordan 1201+3441
16: 4 the descendants of J, 3441
17: 2 of Manasseh son of J by their clans. 3441
17:14 The people of J said to Joshua, 3441
17:16 The people of J replied, 3441
17:17 But Joshua said to the house of J— 3441
18: 5 the south and the house of J in its territory 3441
18:11 between the tribes of Judah and J: 1201+3441
Jdg 1:22 Now the house of J attacked Bethel, 3441
1:35 the power of the house of J increased, 3441
2Sa 19:20 as the first of the whole house of J to come 3441
1Ki 11:28 of the whole labor force of the house of J. 3441
1Ch 2: 2 J, Benjamin, Naphtali, Gad and Asher. 3441
5: 1 as firstborn were given to the sons of J son 3441
5: 2 the rights of the firstborn belonged to J)— 3441
7:29 The descendants of J son of Israel lived 3441
25: 2 Zaccur, J, Nethaniah and Asarelah. 3441
25: 9 fell to J, his sons and relatives, 3441
Ezr 10:42 Shallum, Amariah and J. 3441
Ne 12:14 of Malluch's, Jonathan; of Shecaniah's, J; 3441
Ps 77:15 the descendants of Jacob and J. 3441
78:67 Then he rejected the tents of J, 3441
80: 1 you who lead J like a flock; 3441
81: 5 for J when he went out against Egypt, 3388
105:17 sent a man before them—J, sold as a slave. 3441
Eze 37:16 to J and all the house of Israel associated 3441
37:19 I am going to take the stick of J— 3441
47:13 with two portions for J. 3441
48:32 the gate of J, the gate of Benjamin, 3441
Am 5: 6 or he will sweep through the house of J 3441
5:15 have mercy on the remnant of J. 3441
6: 6 but you do not grieve over the ruin of J. 3441
Ob 1:18 of Jacob will be a fire and the house of J 3441
Zec 10: 6 of Judah and save the house of J. 3441
Mt 1:16 and Jacob the father of J, *2737*
1:18 Mary was pledged to be married *to* J, *2737*
1:19 Because J her husband was a righteous man *2737*
1:20 "J son of David, do not be afraid to take *2737*
1:24 When J woke up, he did what the angel *2737*
2:13 angel of the Lord appeared *to* J in a dream. *2737*
2:19 angel of the Lord appeared in a dream *to* J *2737*
Mt 13:55 and aren't his brothers James, J, *2737*
27:57 a rich man from Arimathea, named J, *2737*
27:59 J took the body, wrapped it in a clean linen *2737*
Mk 6: 3 and the brother *of* James, J, Judas *2736*
15:43 J of Arimathea, a prominent member of *2737*
15:45 he gave the body *to* J. *2737*
15:46 So J bought some linen cloth, *NIG*
Lk 1:27 pledged to be married to a man named J, *2737*
2: 4 So J also went up from the town *2737*
2:16 So they hurried off and found Mary and J, *2737*
2:22 J and Mary took him to Jerusalem *NIG*
2:39 When J and Mary had done everything *NIG*
3:23 He was the son, so it was thought, *of* J, *2737*
3:24 the son of Jannai, the son *of* J, *2737*
3:30 the son *of* J, the son of Jonam, *2737*
23:50 Now there was a man named J, *2737*
23:55 from Galilee followed J and saw the tomb *899*[S]
Jn 1:45 Jesus of Nazareth, the son *of* J." *2737*
4: 5 of ground Jacob had given to his son J. *2737*
6:42 They said, "Is this not Jesus, the son *of* J, *2737*
19:38 J of Arimathea asked Pilate for the body *2737*
19:38 Now J was a disciple of Jesus, *NIG*
Ac 1:23 J called Barsabbas (also known as Justus) *2737*
4:36 J, a Levite from Cyprus, *2737*
7: 9 "Because the patriarchs were jealous of J, *2737*
7:10 He gave J wisdom and enabled him *899*[S]
7:13 J told his brothers who he was, *2737*
7:14 J sent for his father Jacob *2737*
7:18 another king, who knew nothing about J, *2737*
Heb 11:22 By faith J, when his end was near, *2737*
Rev 7: 8 from the tribe *of* J 12,000, *2737*

JOSEPH'S (24) [JOSEPH]

Ge 37:31 Then they got J robe, 3441
39: 6 So he left in J care everything he had; 3441
39:20 J master took him and put him in prison, 3441
39:23 to anything under J care, 2257[S]
41:42 from his finger and put it on J finger. 3441
42: 3 of J brothers went down to buy grain 3441
42: 4 Jacob did not send Benjamin, J brother, 3441
42: 6 So when J brothers arrived, 3441
43:17 and took the men to J house. 3441
43:19 So they went up to J steward and spoke 3441
43:24 The steward took the men into J house, 3441
43:25 They prepared their gifts for J arrival 3441
43:34 portions were served to them from J table, 2257[S]
45:16 that J brothers had come, 3441
46: 4 And J own hand will close your eyes." 3441
50: 8 besides all the members of J household 3441
50:15 J brothers saw that their father was dead, 3441
50:23 were placed at birth on J knees. 3441
Jos 17: 1 for the tribe of Manasseh as J firstborn, 3441
24:32 And J bones, which the Israelites had brought up from Egypt, 3441
24:32 the inheritance of J descendants. 3441
Lk 4:22 "Isn't this J son?" *2737*
Ac 7:13 and Pharaoh learned about J family. *2737*
Heb 11:21 blessed each *of* J sons, *2737*

JOSES (3)

Mt 27:56 Mary the mother *of* James and J, *2736*
Mk 15:40 the mother of James the younger and *of* J, *2736*
15:47 the mother *of* J saw where he was laid. *2736*

JOSHAH (1)

1Ch 4:34 Meshobab, Jamlech, J son of Amaziah, 3459

JOSHAPHAT (2)

1Ch 11:43 Hanan son of Maacah, J the Mithnite, 3461
15:24 Shebaniah, J, Nethanel, Amasai, 3461

JOSHAVIAH (1)

1Ch 11:46 Jeribai and J the sons of Elnaam, 3460

JOSHBEKASHAH (2)

1Ch 25: 4 J, Mallothi, Hothir and Mahazioth. 3792
25:24 the seventeenth to J, 3792

JOSHEB-BASSHEBETH (1)

2Sa 23: 8 J, a Tahkemonite, was chief of the Three; 3783

JOSHIBIAH (1)

1Ch 4:35 Jehu son of J, the son of Seraiah, 3458

JOSHUA (218) [HOSHEA]

Ex 17: 9 Moses said to J, "Choose some of our men 3397
17:10 So J fought the Amalekites 3397
17:13 So J overcame the Amalekite army with 3397
17:14 and make sure that J hears it, 3397
24:13 Then Moses set out with J his aide, 3397
32:17 J heard the noise of the people shouting, 3397
33:11 but his young aide J son of Nun did 3397
Nu 11:28 J son of Nun, who had been Moses' aide 3397
13:16 Moses gave Hoshea son of Nun the name J. 3397
14: 6 J son of Nun and Caleb son of Jephunneh, 3397
14:30 except Caleb son of Jephunneh and J son 3397
14:38 only J son of Nun and Caleb son 3397
26:65 of Jephunneh and J son of Nun. 3397
27:18 "Take J son of Nun, a man in whom 3397
27:22 He took J and had him stand 3397
32:12 of Jephunneh the Kenizzite and J son 3397
Nu 32:28 to Eleazar the priest and J son of Nun and 3397
34:17 Eleazar the priest and J son of Nun. 3397
Dt 1:38 your assistant, J son of Nun, will enter it. 3397
3:21 At that time I commanded J: 3397
3:28 But commission J, and encourage 3397
31: 3 J also will cross over ahead of you, 3397
31: 7 Then Moses summoned J and said to him 3397
31:14 Call J and present yourselves at the Tent 3397
31:14 and J came and presented themselves at 3397
31:23 The LORD gave this command to J son 3397
32:44 with J son of Nun and spoke all the words 2107
34: 9 Now J son of Nun was filled with 3397
Jos 1: 1 the LORD said to J son of Nun, 3397
1:10 So J ordered the officers of the people: 3397
1:12 and the half-tribe of Manasseh, J said, 3397
1:16 Then they answered J, 3397
2: 1 Then J son of Nun secretly sent two spies 3397
2:23 forded the river and came to J son of Nun 3397
2:24 to J, "The LORD has surely given 3397
3: 1 the morning J and all the Israelites set out 3397
3: 5 J told the people, "Consecrate yourselves, 3397
3: 6 J said to the priests, "Take up the ark 3397
3: 7 And the LORD said to J, "Today I will begin 3397
3: 9 J said to the Israelites, "Come here and 3397
4: 1 crossing the Jordan, the LORD said to J, 3397
4: 4 So J called together the twelve men 3397
4: 8 the Israelites did as J commanded them. 3397
4: 8 as the LORD had told J; 3397
4: 9 J set up the twelve stones that had been in 3397
4:10 the LORD had commanded J was done 3397
4:10 just as Moses had directed J. 3397
4:14 That day the LORD exalted J in the sight 3397
4:15 Then the LORD said to J, 3397
4:17 So J commanded the priests, 3397
4:20 And J set up at Gilgal the twelve stones 3397
5: 2 At that time the LORD said to J, 3397
5: 3 So J made flint knives and circumcised 3397
5: 7 and these were the ones J circumcised. 3397
5: 9 Then the LORD said to J, 3397
5:13 Now when J was near Jericho, 3397
5:13 J went up to him and asked, 3397
5:14 J fell facedown to the ground in reverence, 3397
5:15 And J did so. 3397
6: 2 Then the LORD said to J, "See, 3397
6: 6 So J son of Nun called the priests and said 3397
6: 8 When J had spoken to the people, 3397
6:10 But J had commanded the people, 3397
6:12 J got up early the next morning and 3397
6:16 J commanded the people, "Shout! 3397
6:22 J said to the two men who had spied out 3397
6:25 But J spared Rahab the prostitute, 3397
6:25 the men J had sent as spies to Jericho— 3397
6:26 that time J pronounced this solemn oath: 3397
6:27 So the LORD was with J, 3397
7: 2 Now J sent men from Jericho to Ai, 3397
7: 3 When they returned to J, they said, 3397
7: 6 Then J tore his clothes and fell facedown 3397
7: 7 And J said, "Ah, Sovereign LORD, 3397
7:10 The LORD said to J, "Stand up! 3397
7:16 next morning J had Israel come forward 3397
7:18 J had his family come forward man NIH
7:19 Then J said to Achan, "My son, 3397
7:22 So J sent messengers, 3397
7:23 brought them to J and all the Israelites 3397
7:24 Then J, together with all Israel, 3397
7:25 J said, "Why have you brought this trouble 3397
8: 1 the LORD said to J, "Do not be afraid; 3397
8: 3 So J and the whole army moved out 3397
8: 9 Then J sent them off, 3397
8: 9 but J spent that night with the people. 3397
8:10 the next morning J mustered his men, 3397
8:12 J had taken about five thousand men NIH
8:13 That night J went into the valley. 3397
8:15 J and all Israel let themselves 3397
8:16 and they pursued J and were lured away 3397
8:18 Then the LORD said to J, 3397
8:18 So J held out his javelin toward Ai. 3397
8:21 For when J and all Israel saw that 3397
8:23 the king of Ai alive and brought him to J. 3397
8:26 For J did not draw back the hand 3397
8:27 as the LORD had instructed J. 3397
8:28 So J burned Ai and made it a permanent 3397
8:29 J ordered them to take his body from 3397
8:30 Then J built on Mount Ebal an altar to 3397
8:32 J copied on stones the law of Moses, NIH
8:34 J read all the words of the law— NIH
8:35 that J did not read to the whole assembly 3397
9: 2 they came together to make war against J 3397
9: 3 of Gibeon heard what J had done 3397
9: 6 Then they went to J in the camp at Gilgal 3397
9: 8 "We are your servants," they said to J. 3397
9: 8 But J asked, "Who are you and 3397
9:15 Then J made a treaty of peace with them 3397
9:22 Then J summoned the Gibeonites and said, 3397
9:24 They answered J, "Your servants were 3397
9:26 So J saved them from the Israelites, NIH
10: 1 that J had taken Ai and totally destroyed it, 3397
10: 4 "because it has made peace with J and 3397
10: 6 then sent word to J in the camp at Gilgal: 3397
10: 7 So J marched up from Gilgal 3397
10: 8 The LORD said to J, 3397
10: 9 J took them by surprise. 3397
10:12 J said to the LORD in the presence 3397
10:15 Then J returned with all Israel to the camp 3397
10:17 When J was told that the five kings 3397
10:20 So J and the Israelites destroyed them completely— 3397

Jos 10:21 The whole army then returned safely to J 3397
10:22 J said, "Open the mouth of the cave 3397
10:24 When they had brought these kings to J, 3397
10:25 J said to them, "Do not be afraid; 3397
10:26 Then J struck and killed the kings 3397
10:27 At sunset J gave the order 3397
10:28 That day J took Makkedah. 3397
10:29 Then J and all Israel with him moved on 3397
10:30 and everyone in it J put to the sword. NIH
10:31 Then J and all Israel with him moved on 3397
10:32 and J took it on the second day. NIH
10:33 but J defeated him and his army— 3397
10:34 Then J and all Israel with him moved on 3397
10:36 Then J and all Israel with him went up 3397
10:38 Then J and all Israel with him turned 3397
10:40 So J subdued the whole region, 3397
10:41 J subdued them from Kadesh Barnea 3397
10:42 All these kings and their lands J conquered 3397
10:43 Then J returned with all Israel to the camp 3397
11: 6 The LORD said to J, "Do not be afraid 3397
11: 7 So J and his whole army came 3397
11: 9 J did to them as the LORD had directed: 3397
11:10 that time J turned back and captured Hazor 3397
11:12 J took all these royal cities and their kings 3397
11:13 except Hazor, which J burned. 3397
11:15 so Moses commanded J, and Joshua did it; 3397
11:15 so Moses commanded Joshua, and J did it; 3397
11:16 So J took this entire land: 3397
11:18 J waged war against all these kings for 3397
11:21 At that time J went and destroyed 3397
11:21 J totally destroyed them and their towns. 3397
11:23 So J took the entire land, 3397
12: 7 the land that J and the Israelites conquered 3397
12: 7 which rises toward Seir (their lands J gave 3397
13: 1 J was old and well advanced in years, 3397
14: 1 J son of Nun and the heads of 3397
14: 6 the men of Judah approached J at Gilgal, 3397
14:13 Then J blessed Caleb son of Jephunneh 3397
15:13 J gave to Caleb son of Jephunneh 3397
17: 4 J son of Nun, and the leaders and said, 3397
17: 4 So J gave them an inheritance along with NIH
17:14 The people of Joseph said to J, 3397
17:15 "If you are so numerous," J answered, 3397
17:17 But J said to the house of Joseph— 3397
18: 3 So J said to the Israelites: 3397
18: 8 the land, J instructed them, "Go and make 3397
18: 9 and returned to J in the camp at Shiloh. 3397
18:10 J then cast lots for them in Shiloh in 3397
19:49 the Israelites gave J son of Nun 3397
19:51 J son of Nun and the heads of 3397
20: 1 Then the LORD said to J: 3397
21: 1 Eliezer the priest, J son of Nun, 3397
22: 1 Then J summoned the Reubenites, 3397
22: 6 Then J blessed them and sent them away, 3397
22: 7 to the other half of the tribe J gave land on 3397
22: 7 When J sent them home, he blessed them, 3397
23: 1 J, by then old and well advanced in years, 3397
24: 1 Then J assembled all the tribes of Israel 3397
24: 2 J said to all the people, "This is what 3397
24:19 J said to the people, "You are not able to 3397
24:21 But the people said to J, "No! 3397
24:22 Then J said, "You are witnesses 3397
24:23 said J, "throw away the foreign gods NIH
24:24 And the people said to J, 3397
24:25 that day J made a covenant for the people, 3397
24:26 And J recorded these things in the Book of 3397
24:28 Then J sent the people away, 3397
24:29 After these things, J son of Nun, 3397
24:31 Israel served the LORD throughout the lifetime of J 3397
Jdg 1: 1 After the death of J, the Israelites asked 3397
2: 6 After J had dismissed the Israelites, 3397
2: 7 The people served the LORD throughout the lifetime of J 3397
2: 8 J son of Nun, the servant of the LORD, 3397
2:21 before them any of the nations J left 3397
2:23 at once by giving them into the hands of J. 3397
1Sa 6:14 to the field of J of Beth Shemesh, 3397
6:18 is a witness to this day in the field of J 3397
1Ki 16:34 the word of the LORD spoken by J son 3397
2Ki 23: 8 at the entrance to the Gate of J, 3397
1Ch 7:27 Nun his son and J his son. 3397
Ne 8:17 the days of J son of Nun until that day, 3800
Hag 1: 1 and to J son of Jehozadak, the high priest: 3397
1:12 J son of Jehozadak, the high priest, 3397
1:14 and the spirit of J son of Jehozadak, 3397
2: 2 governor of Judah, to J son of Jehozadak, 3397
2: 4 'Be strong, O J son of Jehozadak, 3397
Zec 3: 1 Then he showed me J the high priest 3397
3: 3 Now J was dressed in filthy clothes 3397
3: 4 Then he said to J, "See, I have taken 2257^S
3: 6 of the LORD gave this charge to J: 3397
3: 8 O high priest J and your associates seated 3397
3: 9 See, the stone I have set in front of J! 3397
6:11 J son of Jehozadak. 3397
Lk 3:29 the son *of* J, the son of Eliezer, *2652*
Ac 7:45 our fathers under J brought it with them *2652*
Heb 4: 8 For if J had given them rest, *2652*

JOSIAH (56) [JOSIAH'S]

1Ki 13: 2 'A son named J will be born to the house 3288
2Ki 21:24 and they made J his son king in his place. 3288
21:26 And J his son succeeded him as king. 3288
22: 1 J was eight years old when he became king 3288
22: 3 King J sent the secretary, 3288
23: 8 J brought all the priests from the towns NIH
23:11 J then burned the chariots dedicated to NIH
23:14 J smashed the sacred stones and cut down NIH
23:16 Then J looked around, and when he saw 3288
23:19 J removed and defiled all the shrines at 3288
23:20 J slaughtered all the priests NIH
23:23 But in the eighteenth year of King J, 3288
23:24 J got rid of the mediums and spiritists, 3288
23:25 Neither before nor after J was there a king 2257^S
23:29 While J was king, Pharaoh Neco of Egypt 2257^S
23:29 King J marched out to meet him in battle, 3288
23:30 of J and anointed him and made him king 3288
23:34 Pharaoh Neco made Eliakim son of J king 3288
23:34 of Josiah king in place of his father J 3288
1Ch 3:14 Amon his son, J his son. 3288
3:15 The sons of J: Johanan the firstborn, 3288
2Ch 33:25 and they made J his son king in his place. 3288
34: 1 J was eight years old when he became king 3288
34:33 J removed all the detestable idols from all 3288
35: 1 J celebrated the Passover to the LORD 3288
35: 7 J provided for all the lay people 3288
35:16 as King J had ordered. 3288
35:18 celebrated such a Passover as did J, 3288
35:20 all this, when J had set the temple in order, 3288
35:20 and J marched out to meet him in battle. 3288
35:22 J, however, would not turn away 3288
35:23 Archers shot King J, and he told his officers 3288
35:25 Jeremiah composed laments for J, 3288
35:25 and women singers commemorate J in 3288
36: 1 of J and made him king in Jerusalem 3288
Jer 1: 2 the reign of J son of Amon king of Judah, 3288
1: 3 of Jehoiakim son of J king of Judah, 3288
1: 3 of Zedekiah son of J king of Judah, 3288
3: 6 During the reign of King J, 3288
22:11 the LORD says about Shallum son of J, 3288
22:18 about Jehoiakim son of J king of Judah: 3288
25: 1 the fourth year of Jehoiakim son of J king 3288
25: 3 the thirteenth year of J son of Amon king 3288
26: 1 of J king of Judah, this word came from 3288
27: 1 in the reign of Zedekiah son of J king 3288
35: 1 of Jehoiakim son of J king of Judah: 3288
36: 1 the fourth year of Jehoiakim son of J king 3288
36: 2 to you in the reign of J till now. 3288
36: 9 of the fifth year of Jehoiakim son of J king 3288
37: 1 Zedekiah son of J was made king of Judah 3288
45: 1 the fourth year of Jehoiakim son of J king 3288
46: 2 the fourth year of Jehoiakim son of J king 3288
Zep 1: 1 the reign of J son of Amon king of Judah: 3288
Zec 6:10 Go the same day to the house of J son 3287
Mt 1:10 Amon the father of J, *2739*
1:11 and J the father of Jeconiah *2739*

JOSIAH'S (5) [JOSIAH]

2Ki 23:28 As for the other events of J reign, 3288
23:30 J servants brought his body in a chariot 2257^S
2Ch 34: 8 In the eighteenth year of J reign, 2257^S
35:19 in the eighteenth year of J reign. 3288
35:26 The other events of J reign and his acts 3288

JOSIAS (KJV) See JOSIAH

JOSIBIAH (KJV) See JOSHIBIAH

JOSIPHIAH (1)

Ezr 8:10 of J, and with him 160 men; 3442

JOSTLE (1) [JOSTLED]

Joel 2: 8 *They do* not j each other; 1895

JOSTLED (1) [JOSTLE]

Ge 25:22 The babies j **each other** within her, 8368

JOT (KJV) See SMALLEST LETTER

JOTBAH (1)

2Ki 21:19 daughter of Haruz; she was from J. 3513

JOTBATH (KJV) See JOTBATHAH

JOTBATHAH (3)

Nu 33:33 They left Hor Haggidgad and camped at J. 3514
33:34 They left J and camped at Abronah. 3514
Dt 10: 7 to Gudgodah and on to J, 3514

JOTHAM (27) [JOTHAM'S]

Jdg 9: 5 But J, the youngest son of Jerub-Baal, 3462
9: 7 When J was told about this, 3462
9:21 Then J fled, escaping to Beer, 3462
9:57 The curse of J son of Jerub-Baal came 3462
2Ki 15: 5 J the king's son had charge of the palace 3462
15: 7 And J his son succeeded him as king. 3462
15:30 in the twentieth year of J son of Uzziah. 3462
15:32 J son of Uzziah king of Judah began 3462
15:35 J rebuilt the Upper Gate of the temple of 2085^S
15:38 J rested with his fathers and was buried 3462
16: 1 Ahaz son of J king of Judah began 3462
1Ch 2:47 The sons of Jahdai: Regem, J, Geshan, 3462
3:12 Azariah his son, J his son, 3462
5:17 of J king of Judah and Jeroboam king 3462
2Ch 26:21 J his son had charge of the palace 3462
26:23 And J his son succeeded him as king. 3462
27: 1 J was twenty-five years old 3462
27: 3 J rebuilt the Upper Gate of the temple of 2085^S
27: 5 J made war on the king of the Ammonites 2085^S
27: 6 J grew powerful because he walked 3462
27: 9 J rested with his fathers and was buried in 3462
Isa 1: 1 J, Ahaz and Hezekiah, kings of Judah. 3462
7: 1 When Ahaz son of J, the son of Uzziah, 3462
Hos 1: 1 J, Ahaz and Hezekiah, kings of Judah, 3462
Mic 1: 1 of J, Ahaz and Hezekiah, kings of Judah— 3462
Mt 1: 9 Uzziah the father of J, *2718*
1: 9 J the father of Ahaz, *2718*

JOTHAM'S (2) [JOTHAM]

2Ki 15:36 As for the other events of J reign, 3462
2Ch 27: 7 The other events in J reign, 3462

JOURNEY (56) [JOURNEYED, JOURNEYS]

Ge 24:21 or not the LORD had made his j successful. 2006
24:27 the LORD has led me on the j to 2006
24:40 with you and make your j a success, 2006
24:42 to the j on which I have come. 2006
24:56 the LORD has granted success to my j. 2006
28:20 on this j I am taking and will give me food 2006
29: 1 Then Jacob **continued on** his j and 5951+8079
30:36 Then he put a three-day j between himself 2006
42:25 and to give them provisions for their j. 2006
42:38 harm comes to him on the j you are taking, 2006
45:21 he also gave them provisions for their j. 2006
45:23 and bread and other provisions for his j. 2006
Ex 3:18 Let us take a three-day j into the desert 2006
5: 3 Now let us take a three-day j into 2006
8:27 We must take a three-day j into the desert 2006
Nu 9:10 because of a dead body or are away on a j, 2006
9:13 not on a j fails to celebrate the Passover, 2006
33: 1 Here are the **stages in** the j *of* the Israelites 5023
33: 2 Moses recorded the stages in their j. 5023
33: 2 This is their j by stages: 5023
Dt 1:33 who went ahead of you on your j, 2006
2: 7 over your j *through* this vast desert. 2143
25:18 they met you on your j 2006
28:68 on a j I said you should never make again. 2006
Jos 5: 5 the desert during the j from Egypt had not. 2006
9:11 'Take provisions for your j; 2006
9:13 worn out by the very long j." 2006
24:17 on our entire j and among all the nations 2006
Jdg 18: 5 to learn whether our j will be successful." 2006
18: 6 Your j has the LORD's approval." 2006
1Ki 13:26 who had brought him back from his j 2006
19: 4 he himself went a day's j into the desert. 2006
19: 7 for the j is too much for you." 2006
Ezr 7: 9 He had begun his j from Babylon on 5092
8:21 before our God and ask him for a safe j 2006
Ne 2: 6 asked me, "How long will your j take, 4511
Job 16:22 a few years will pass before I go on the j 784
Pr 7:19 he has gone on a long j. 2006
Isa 35: 8 The unclean *will* not j *on* it; 6296
Am 5: 5 do not go to Gilgal, *do* not j *to* Beersheba. 6296
Mic 6: 5 Remember [your j] from Shittim to Gilgal, NIH
Mt 10:10 the j, or extra tunic, or sandals or a staff; *3847*
21:33 to some farmers and **went away on a** j. *623*
25:14 "Again, it will be like a man **going on a** j, *623*
25:15 Then *he* **went on** *his* j. *623*
Mk 6: 8 "Take nothing for the j except a staff— *3847*
12: 1 to some farmers and **went away on a** j. *623*
Lk 9: 3 He told them: "Take nothing for the j— *3847*
11: 6 a friend of mine **on a** j has come to me, *3847*
Jn 4: 6 and Jesus, tired as he was from the j, *3845*
Ac 9: 3 As he neared Damascus **on his** j, *1877+4513*
9:27 He told them how Saul on his j had seen *3847*
10: 9 the following day *as* they *were* **on their** j *3844*
16: 3 Paul wanted to take him along on the j, *NIG*
Ro 15:24 *to have* you **assist** me **on** my j there, *4636*
1Co 16: 6 so that you can **help** me **on** my j, *4636*

JOURNEYED (3) [JOURNEY]

Ex 12:37 The Israelites j from Rameses to Succoth. 5825
1Sa 31:12 all their valiant men j through the night 2143
Job 38:16 *"Have you* j to the springs of the sea 995

JOURNEYS (1) [JOURNEY]

Ac 26:12 "On **one of these** j I was going to Damascus *4005*^S

JOWLS (1)

Dt 18: 3 the shoulder, the j and the inner parts. 4305

JOY (218) [ENJOY, ENJOYED, ENJOYING, ENJOYMENT, ENJOYS, JOYFUL, JOYOUS, JOYFULLY, OVERJOYED, REJOICE, REJOICED, REJOICES, REJOICING]

Ge 31:27 so I could send you away with j 8525
Lev 9:24 *they* **shouted for** j and fell facedown. 8264
Dt 16:15 and your j will be complete. 8524
Jdg 9:19 *may* Abimelech *be your* j, 8523
1Ch 12:40 cattle and sheep, for there was j in Israel. 8525
16:27 strength and j in his dwelling place. 2530
16:33 *they will* **sing for** j before the LORD, 8264
29:17 And now I have seen with j 8525
29:22 with great j in the presence of the LORD 8525
2Ch 30:26 There was great j in Jerusalem, 8525
Ezr 3:12 while many others shouted for j. 8525

Ezr 3:13 the sound of the shouts of j from the sound 8525
6:16 the dedication of the house of God with j. 10250
6:22 with j the Feast of Unleavened Bread, 8525
6:22 because the LORD *had* filled them with j 8523
Ne 8:10 for the j *of* the LORD is your strength." 2530
8:12 of food and to celebrate with great j, 8525
8:17 And their j was very great. 8525
12:43 because God *had* given them great j. 8523+8525
Est 8:16 the Jews it was a time of happiness and j, 8525
8:17 there was j and gladness among the Jews, 8525
9:17 and made it a day of feasting and j. 8525
9:18 and made it a day of feasting and j. 8525
9:19 of the month of Adar as a day of j 8525
9:22 when their sorrow was turned into j 8525
9:22 of feasting and j and giving presents 8525
Job 3:7 may no shout of j be heard in it. 8265
6:10 *my* j in unrelenting pain— 6134
8:21 and your lips with shouts of j. 9558
9:25 they fly away without a glimpse of j. 3208
10:20 from me so *I can* have a moment's j 1158
20:5 the j *of* the godless lasts but a moment. 8525
33:26 he sees God's face and shouts for j; 9558
38:7 and all the angels shouted for j? 8131
Ps 4:7 You have filled my heart with greater j 8525
5:11 *let them* ever sing for j. 8264
16:11 you will fill me with j in your presence, 8525
19:8 giving j *to* the heart. 8523
20:5 *We will* shout for j when you are victorious 8264
21:1 How great *is his* j in the victories you give! 1635
21:6 made him glad with the j of his presence. 8525
27:6 I will sacrifice with shouts of j; 9558
28:7 My heart leaps for j 6600
30:11 and clothed me with j, 8525
33:3 play skillfully, and shout for j. 9558
35:27 in my vindication shout for j and gladness; 8264
42:4 with shouts of j and thanksgiving 7754+8262
43:4 to God, my j and my delight. 8525
45:7 by anointing you with the oil of j. 8607
45:15 They are led in with j and gladness; 8525
47:1 shout to God with cries of j. 8262
47:5 God has ascended amid shouts of j, 9558
48:2 the j *of* the whole earth. 5375
51:8 Let me hear j and gladness; 8607
51:12 Restore to me the j *of* your salvation 8607
65:8 *you* call forth songs of j. 8264
65:13 *they* shout for j and sing. 8131
66:1 Shout with j to God, all the earth! 8131
67:4 May the nations be glad and sing for j, 8264
71:23 My lips *will* shout for j 8264
81:1 Sing for j to God our strength; 8264
86:4 Bring j *to* your servant, for to you, 8523
89:12 Tabor and Hermon sing for j at your name. 8264
90:14 *we may* sing for j and be glad all our days. 8264
92:4 *I* sing for j at the works of your hands. 8264
94:19 your consolation brought j *to* my soul. 9130
95:1 Come, *let us* sing for j to the LORD; 8264
96:12 all the trees of the forest *will* sing for j; 8264
97:11 the righteous and j on the upright in heart. 8525
98:4 Shout for j to the LORD, all the earth, 8131
98:6 shout for j before the LORD, the King. 8131
98:8 *let* the mountains sing together for j; 8264
100:1 Shout for j to the LORD, all the earth. 8131
105:43 his chosen ones with shouts of j; 8262
106:5 that I *may* share in the j *of* your nation 8523+8525
107:22 and tell of his works with songs of j. 8262
118:15 Shouts of j and victory resound in the tents 8262
119:111 they are the j *of* my heart. 8607
126:2 our tongues with songs of j. 8262
126:3 and we are filled with j. 8524
126:5 in tears will reap with songs of j. 8262
126:6 will return with songs of j, 8262
132:9 *may* your saints sing for j." 8264
132:16 and her saints *will* ever sing for j. 8264+8264
137:3 our tormentors demanded songs of j; 8525
137:6 I do not consider Jerusalem my highest j. 8525
149:5 in this honor and sing for j on their beds. 8264
Pr 10:1 A wise son brings j *to* his father, 8523
10:28 The prospect of the righteous is j, 8525
11:10 the wicked perish, there are shouts of j. 8262
12:20 but j for those who promote peace. 8525
14:10 and no one else can share its j. 8525
14:13 and j may end in grief. 8525
15:20 A wise son brings j *to* his father, 8523
15:23 A man finds j in giving an apt reply— 8525
15:30 A cheerful look brings j *to* the heart, 8523
17:21 *there is* no j *for* the father of a fool. 8523
21:15 it brings j to the righteous but terror 8525
23:24 father of a righteous man *has* great j; 1635+1635
27:9 Perfume and incense bring j *to* the heart, 8523
27:11 Be wise, my son, and bring j *to* my heart; 8523
29:3 A man who loves wisdom brings j 8523
Ecc 8:15 Then j will accompany him in his work all 2085[S]
11:9 and *let* your heart give you j in the days 3512
Isa 9:3 the nation and increased their j; 8525
12:3 With j you will draw water from the wells 8607
12:6 Shout aloud and sing for j, people of Zion, 8264
16:9 The shouts of j over your ripened fruit and 2116
16:10 J and gladness are taken away from 8525
22:13 But see, there is j and revelry, 8607
24:11 all j turns to gloom, 8525
24:14 They raise their voices, *they* shout for j; 8264
26:19 wake up and shout for j. 8264
35:2 it will rejoice greatly and shout for j. 8264
35:6 and the mute tongue shout for j. 8264
35:10 everlasting j will crown their heads. 8525
35:10 Gladness and j will overtake them, 8525
42:11 *Let* the people of Sela sing for j; 8264
Isa 44:23 Sing for j, O heavens, 8264
48:20 with shouts of j and proclaim it. 7754+8262
49:13 Shout for j, O heavens; 8264
51:3 J and gladness will be found in her, 8607
51:11 everlasting j will crown their heads. 8525
51:11 Gladness and j will overtake them, 8525
52:8 together *they* shout for j. 8264
52:9 Burst into songs of j together, 8264
54:1 burst into song, shout for j, 7412
55:12 You will go out in j and be led forth 8525
56:7 and give them j in my house of prayer. 8523
58:14 then *you will* find *your* j in the LORD, 6695
60:5 your heart will throb and swell with j; 8143
60:15 the everlasting pride and the j 5375
61:7 and everlasting j will be theirs. 8525
65:14 My servants will sing out of the j 3206
65:18 to be a delight and its people a j. 5375
66:5 that we may see your j!' 8525
Jer 7:34 bring an end to the sounds of j and gladness 8607
15:16 they were my j and my heart's delight, 8607
16:9 bring an end to the sounds of j and gladness 8607
25:10 from them the sounds of j and gladness, 8607
31:7 "Sing with j for Jacob; 8525
31:12 and shout for j on the heights of Zion; 8264
31:13 I will give them comfort and j instead 8523
33:9 Then this city will bring me renown, j, 8607
33:11 the sounds of j and gladness, the voices 8607
48:33 J and gladness are gone from the orchards 8525
48:33 no one treads them with shouts of j. 2116
48:33 there are shouts, they are not shouts of j. 2116
51:48 in them *will* shout for j over Babylon, 8264
La 2:15 the j of the whole earth?" 5375
5:15 J is gone from our hearts; 5375
Eze 7:7 there is panic, not j, *upon* the mountains. 2059
24:25 their j and glory, the delight of their eyes, 5375
Joel 1:12 Surely the j of mankind is withered away. 8607
1:16 j and gladness from the house of our God? 8525
Mt 13:20 the word and at once receives it with j. *5915*
13:44 and then in his j went and sold all he had *5915*
28:8 afraid yet filled with j, *3489+5915*
Mk 4:16 hear the word and at once receive it with j. *5915*
Lk 1:14 He will be a j and delight to you, *5915*
1:44 the baby in my womb leaped for j. *21*
1:58 and *they* shared her j. *5176*
2:10 I bring you good news of great j that will *5915*
6:23 "Rejoice in that day and leap for j, *5015*
8:13 the ones who receive the word with j *5915*
10:17 The seventy-two returned with j and said, *5915*
10:21 full of j through the Holy Spirit, said, *22*
24:41 not believe it because of j and amazement, *5915*
24:52 and returned to Jerusalem with great j. *5915*
Jn 3:29 and *is* full of j when he hears *5897+5915*
3:29 That j is mine, and it is now complete. *5915*
15:11 I have told you this so that my j may be *5915*
15:11 be in you and that your j may be complete. *5915*
16:20 but your grief will turn to j. *5915*
16:21 of her j that a child is born into the world. *5915*
16:22 and no one will take away your j. *5915*
16:24 and your j will be complete. *5915*
17:13 the full measure of my j within them. *5915*
Ac 2:28 you will fill me *with* j in your presence.' *2372*
8:8 So there was great j in that city. *5915*
13:52 the disciples were filled *with* j and with *5915*
14:17 fills your hearts with j." *2372*
16:34 *he was* filled with j because he had come *22*
Ro 14:17 peace and j in the Holy Spirit, *5915*
15:13 *with* all j and peace as you trust in him, *5915*
15:32 with j and together with you be refreshed. *5915*
16:19 so *I am* full of j over you; *5897*
2Co 1:24 but we work with you *for* your j, *5915*
2:3 that you would all share my j. *5915*
7:4 in all our troubles my j knows no bounds. *5915*
7:7 so that my j *was* greater than ever. *5897*
8:2 of the most severe trial, their overflowing j *5915*
Gal 4:15 What has happened to all your j? *3422*
5:22 But the fruit of the Spirit is love, j, peace, *5915*
Php 1:4 I always pray with j *5915*
1:25 of you for your progress and j in the faith, *5915*
1:26 through my being with you again your j *3017*
2:2 make my j complete by being like-minded, *5915*
2:29 Welcome him in the Lord with great j, *5915*
4:1 my j and crown, *5915*
1Th 1:6 with the j given by the Holy Spirit. *5915*
2:19 For what is our hope, our j, *5915*
2:20 Indeed, you are our glory and j. *5915*
3:9 j *we* have in the presence of our God *5897+5915*
2Ti 1:4 so that I may be filled *with* j. *5915*
Phm 1:7 Your love has given me great j *5915*
Heb 1:9 by anointing you with the oil *of* j." *21*
12:2 for the j set before him endured the cross, *5915*
13:17 Obey them so that their work will be a j, *5915*
Jas 1:2 Consider it pure j, my brothers, *5915*
4:9 to mourning and your j to gloom. *5915*
1Pe 1:8 filled with an inexpressible and glorious j, *22+5915*
1Jn 1:4 We write this to make our j complete. *5915*
2Jn 1:4 *It has given me* great j to find some *5897*
1:12 so that our j may be complete. *5915*
3Jn 1:3 *It gave me* great j to have some brothers *5897*
1:4 I have no greater j than to hear *5915*
Jude 1:24 without fault and with great j— *21*

JOYFUL (16) [JOY]

Dt 16:14 *Be* j at your Feast— 8523
1Sa 18:6 with j songs and with tambourines 8525
1Ki 8:66 j and glad in heart for all the good things 8524
1Ch 15:16 as singers to sing j songs, accompanied 8525
2Ch 7:10 j and glad in heart for the good things 8524
Ps 68:3 may they be happy and j. 8525
100:2 come before him with j songs. 8265
Ecc 9:7 and drink your wine with a j heart, 3202
Isa 24:8 the j harp is silent. 5375
Jer 31:4 and go out to dance with the j. 8471
Hab 3:18 *I will be* j in God my Savior. 1635
Zec 8:19 seventh and tenth months will become j 8607
10:7 Their children will see it and *be* j; 8523
Ro 12:12 Be j in hope, patient in affliction, *5897*
1Th 5:16 *Be* j always; *5897*
Heb 12:22 upon thousands of angels *in* j assembly, *4108*

JOYFULLY (11) [JOY]

Dt 28:47 you did not serve the LORD your God j 928+8525
2Ch 20:27 men of Judah and Jerusalem returned j 928+8525
30:23 so for another seven days they celebrated j. 8525
Ne 12:27 to Jerusalem to celebrate j the dedication 8525
Job 39:13 "The wings of the ostrich flap j, 6632
Ps 33:1 Sing j to the LORD, *you* righteous; 8264
145:7 and j sing *of* your righteousness. 8264
Lk 15:5 he j puts it on his shoulders *5897*
19:37 the whole crowd of disciples began j *5897*
Col 1:11 great endurance and patience, and j *3552+5915*
Heb 10:34 j accepted the confiscation of your *3552+5915*

JOYOUS (1) [JOY]

Est 8:15 And the city of Susa held a j celebration. 8523

JOZABAD (11)

2Ki 12:21 The officials who murdered him were J son 3416
1Ch 12:4 Jahaziel, Johanan, J the Gederathite, 3416
12:20 Adnah, J, Jediael, Michael, Jozabad, 3416
12:20 Adnah, Jozabad, Jediael, Michael, J, 3416
2Ch 31:13 Azaziah, Nahath, Asahel, Jerimoth, J, 3416
35:9 his brothers, and Hashabiah, Jeiel and J, 3416
Ezr 8:33 and so were the Levites J son of Jeshua 3416
10:22 Ishmael, Nethanel, J and Elasah. 3416
10:23 J, Shimei, Kelaiah (that is, Kelita), 3416
Ne 8:7 Kelita, Azariah, J, Hanan and Pelaiah— 3416
11:16 Shabbethai and J, two of the heads of 3416

JOZACHAR (KJV) See JEHOZABAD

JOZADAK (5)

Ezr 3:2 Then Jeshua son of J and his fellow priests 3449
3:8 of J and the rest of their brothers 3449
5:2 and Jeshua son of J set to work to rebuild 10318
10:18 From the descendants of Jeshua son of J, 3449
Ne 12:26 Joiakim son of Jeshua, the son of J, 3449

JUBAL (1)

Ge 4:21 His brother's name was J; 3415

JUBILANT (5)

1Ch 16:32 *let* the fields *be* j, 6636
Ps 94:3 how long *will* the wicked *be* j? 6600
96:12 *let* the fields *be* j, 6600
98:4 all the earth, burst into j song with music; 8264
Hos 9:1 *do* not *be* j like the other nations. 1637

JUBILEE (21)

Lev 25:10 It shall be a j for you; 3413
25:11 The fiftieth year shall be a j for you; 3413
25:12 For it is a j and is to be holy for you; 3413
25:13 " 'In this Year of J everyone is to return 3413
25:15 of the number of years since the J. 3413
25:28 of the buyer until the Year of J. 3413
25:28 It will be returned in the J, 3413
25:30 It is not to be returned in the J. 3413
25:31 and they are to be returned in the J. 3413
25:33 and is to be returned in the J, 3413
25:40 he is to work for you until the Year of J. 3413
25:50 up to the Year of J. 3413
25:52 a few years remain until the Year of J, 3413
25:54 to be released in the Year of J, 3413
27:17 he dedicates his field during the Year of J, 3413
27:18 But if he dedicates his field after the J, 3413
27:18 that remain until the next Year of J, 3413
27:21 When the field is released in the J, 3413
27:23 determine its value up to the Year of J, 3413
27:24 In the Year of J the field will revert to 3413
Nu 36:4 the Year of J for the Israelites comes, 3413

JUDAH (828) [JUDAH'S, JUDEA, JUDEAN]

Ge 29:35 So she named him J. 3373
35:23 Simeon, Levi, J, Issachar and Zebulun. 3373
37:26 J said to his brothers, "What will we gain 3373
38:1 J left his brothers and went down to stay 3373
38:2 There J met the daughter of a Canaanite 3373
38:6 J got a wife for Er, his firstborn, 3373
38:8 Then J said to Onan, 3373
38:11 J then said to his daughter-in-law Tamar, 3373
38:12 When J had recovered from his grief, 3373
38:15 When J saw her, he thought she was a 3373
38:20 Meanwhile J sent the young goat 3373
38:22 So he went back to J and said, 3373
38:23 Then J said, "Let her keep what she has, 3373
38:24 About three months later J was told, 3373
38:24 J said, "Bring her out and have her burned 3373

Ge	38:26	J recognized them and said,	3373
	43: 3	But J said to him, "The man warned us	3373
	43: 8	Then J said to Israel his father,	3373
	44:14	the house when J and his brothers came in,	3373
	44:16	"What can we say to my lord?" J replied.	3373
	44:18	Then J went up to him and said:	3373
	46:12	The sons of J: Er, Onan, Shelah,	3373
	46:28	Now Jacob sent J ahead of him to Joseph	3373
	49: 8	"J, your brothers will praise you;	3373
	49: 9	You are a lion's cub, O J;	3373
	49:10	The scepter will not depart from J,	3373
Ex	1: 2	Reuben, Simeon, Levi and J;	3373
	31: 2	the son of Hur, of the tribe of J,	3373
	35:30	the son of Hur, of the tribe of J,	3373
	38:22	the son of Hur, of the tribe of J,	3373
Nu	1: 7	from J, Nahshon son of Amminadab;	3373
	1:26	From the descendants of J:	3373
	1:27	number from the tribe of J was 74,600.	3373
	2: 3	of J are to encamp under their standard.	3373
	2: 3	of J is Nahshon son of Amminadab.	3373
	2: 9	All the men assigned to the camp of J,	3373
	7:12	of Amminadab of the tribe of J.	3373
	10:14	divisions of the camp of J went first,	1201+3373
	13: 6	the tribe of J, Caleb son of Jephunneh;	3373
	26:19	Er and Onan were sons of J,	3373
	26:20	The descendants of J by their clans were:	3373
	26:22	These were the clans of J;	3373
	34:19	from the tribe of J;	3373
Dt	27:12	Simeon, Levi, J, Issachar,	3373
	33: 7	And this he said about J:	3373
	33: 7	"Hear, O LORD, the cry of J;	3373
	34: 2	all the land of J as far as the western sea,	3373
Jos	7: 1	of the tribe of J, took some of them.	3373
	7:16	came forward by tribes, and J was taken.	3373
	7:17	The clans of J came forward,	3373
	7:18	the son of Zerah, of the tribe of J,	3373
	11:21	from all the hill country of J,	3373
	14: 6	the men of J approached Joshua at Gilgal,	3373
	15: 1	The allotment for the tribe of J,	1201+3373
	15:12	the boundaries around the people of J	3373
	15:13	Caleb son of Jephunneh a portion in J	1201+3373
	15:20	the inheritance of the tribe of J,	1201+3373
	15:21	southernmost towns of the tribe of J	1201+3373
	15:63	J could not dislodge the Jebusites,	1201+3373
	15:63	with the people of J.	3373
	18: 5	J is to remain in its territory on the south	3373
	18:11	between the tribes of J and Joseph:	3373
	18:14	Kiriath Jearim), a town of the people of J.	3373
	19: 1	within the territory of J.	1201+3373
	19: 9	from the share of J,	1201+3373
	19: 9	within the territory of J.	4392S
	20: 7	Hebron) in the hill country of J.	3373
	21: 4	from the tribes of J,	3373
	21: 9	tribes of J and Simeon they allotted	1201+3373
	21:11	in the hill country of J.	3373
Jdg	1: 2	The LORD answered, "J is to go;	3373
	1: 3	of J said to the Simeonites their brothers,	3373
	1: 4	When J attacked, the LORD gave	3373
	1: 8	of J attacked Jerusalem also and took it.	3373
	1: 9	the men of J went down to fight against	3373
	1:16	with the men of J to live among the people	3373
	1:16	to live among the people of the Desert of J	3373
	1:17	Then the men of J went with	3373
	1:18	The men of J also took Gaza,	3373
	1:19	The LORD was with the men of J.	3373
	10: 9	the Jordan to fight against J, Benjamin and	3373
	15: 9	The Philistines went up and camped in J,	3373
	15:10	The men of J asked,	3373
	15:11	from J went down to the cave in the rock	3373
	17: 7	A young Levite from Bethlehem in J,	3373
	17: 7	who had been living within the clan of J,	3373
	17: 9	"I'm a Levite from Bethlehem in J,"	3373
	18:12	up camp near Kiriath Jearim in J.	3373
	19: 1	a concubine from Bethlehem in J.	3373
	19: 2	to her father's house in Bethlehem, J.	3373
	19:18	"We are on our way from Bethlehem in J	3373
	19:18	to Bethlehem in J and now I am going to	3373
	20:18	The LORD replied, "J shall go first."	3373
Ru	1: 1	and a man from Bethlehem in J,	3373
	1: 2	They were Ephrathites from Bethlehem, J.	3373
	1: 7	that would take them back to the land of J.	3373
	4:12	Perez, whom Tamar bore to J."	3373
1Sa	11: 8	and the men of J thirty thousand.	3373
	15: 4	and ten thousand men from J.	3373
	17: 1	for war and assembled at Socoh in J.	3373
	17:12	who was from Bethlehem in J.	3373
	17:52	of Israel and J surged forward with a shout	3373
	18:16	But all Israel and J loved David,	3373
	22: 5	Go into the land of J."	3373
	23: 3	"Here in J we are afraid.	3373
	23:23	down among all the clans of J."	3373
	27: 6	belonged to the kings of J ever since.	3373
	27:10	David would say, "Against the Negev of J"	3373
	30:14	the territory belonging to J and the Negev	3373
	30:16	from the land of the Philistines and from J.	3373
	30:26	of the plunder to the elders of J,	3373
2Sa	1:18	that the men of J be taught this lament of	3373
	2: 1	"Shall I go up to one of the towns of J?"	3373
	2: 4	Then the men of J came to Hebron	3373
	2: 4	anointed David king over the house of J.	3373
	2: 7	and the house of J has anointed me king	3373
	2:10	The house of J, however, followed David.	3373
	2:11	of J was seven years and six months.	3373
	3:10	over Israel and J from Dan to Beersheba."	3373
	5: 5	In Hebron he reigned over J seven years	3373
	5: 5	over all Israel and J thirty-three years.	3373
	6: 2	of J to bring up from there the ark of God,	3373
2Sa	11:11	ark and Israel and J are staying in tents,	3373
	12: 8	I gave you the house of Israel and J.	3373
	19:11	"Ask the elders of J,	3373
	19:14	the men of J as though they were one man.	3373
	19:15	of J had come to Gilgal to go out and meet	3373
	19:16	with the men of J to meet King David.	3373
	19:40	of J and half the troops of Israel had taken	3373
	19:41	"Why did our brothers, the men of J,	3373
	19:42	the men of J answered the men of Israel,	3373
	19:43	the men of Israel answered the men of J,	3373
	19:43	of J responded even more harshly than	3373
	20: 2	of J stayed by their king all the way from	3373
	20: 4	"Summon the men of J to come to me	3373
	20: 5	But when Amasa went to summon J,	3373
	21: 2	in his zeal for Israel and J had tried	3373
	24: 1	"Go and take a census of Israel and J."	3373
	24: 7	on to Beersheba in the Negev of J.	3373
	24: 9	and in J five hundred thousand.	3373
1Ki	1: 9	all the men of J who were royal officials,	3373
	1:35	appointed him ruler over Israel and J."	3373
	4:20	of J and Israel were as numerous as	3373
	4:25	During Solomon's lifetime J and Israel,	3373
	12:17	living in the towns of J,	3373
	12:20	of J remained loyal to the house of David.	3373
	12:21	he mustered the whole house of J and	3373
	12:23	to Rehoboam son of Solomon king of J,	3373
	12:23	to the whole house of J and Benjamin,	3373
	12:27	Rehoboam king of J.	3373
	12:32	like the festival held in J,	3373
	13: 1	of the LORD a man of God came from J	3373
	13:12	the man of God from J had taken.	3373
	13:14	the man of God who came from J?"	3373
	13:21	to the man of God who had come from J,	3373
	14:21	Rehoboam son of Solomon was king in J.	3373
	14:22	J did evil in the eyes of the LORD.	3373
	14:29	the book of the annals of the kings of J?	3373
	15: 1	Abijah became king of J,	3373
	15: 7	the book of the annals of the kings of J?	3373
	15: 9	Asa became king of J,	3373
	15:17	Baasha king of Israel went up against J	3373
	15:17	or entering the territory of Asa king of J.	3373
	15:22	Then King Asa issued an order to all J—	3373
	15:23	the book of the annals of the kings of J?	3373
	15:25	in the second year of Asa king of J,	3373
	15:28	in the third year of Asa king of J and	3373
	15:33	In the third year of Asa king of J,	3373
	16: 8	In the twenty-sixth year of Asa king of J,	3373
	16:10	the twenty-seventh year of Asa king of J.	3373
	16:15	the twenty-seventh year of Asa king of J,	3373
	16:23	In the thirty-first year of Asa king of J,	3373
	16:29	In the thirty-eighth year of Asa king of J,	3373
	19: 3	When he came to Beersheba in J,	3373
	22: 2	the third year Jehoshaphat king of J went	3373
	22:10	and Jehoshaphat king of J were sitting	3373
	22:29	of Israel and Jehoshaphat king of J went	3373
	22:41	of Asa became king of J in the fourth year	3373
	22:45	the book of the annals of the kings of J?	3373
	22:51	year of Jehoshaphat king of J,	3373
2Ki	1:17	of Jehoram son of Jehoshaphat king of J.	3373
	3: 1	year of Jehoshaphat king of J,	3373
	3: 7	to Jehoshaphat king of J:	3373
	3: 9	the king of Israel set out with the king of J	3373
	3:14	for the presence of Jehoshaphat king of J,	3373
	8:16	when Jehoshaphat was king of J,	3373
	8:16	of Jehoshaphat began his reign as king of J.	3373
	8:19	the LORD was not willing to destroy J.	3373
	8:20	against J and set up its own king.	3373
	8:22	in rebellion against J.	3373
	8:23	the book of the annals of the kings of J?	3373
	8:25	Ahaziah son of Jehoram king of J began	3373
	8:29	of J went down to Jezreel to see Joram son	3373
	9:16	and Ahaziah king of J had gone down	3373
	9:21	of Israel and Ahaziah king of J rode out,	3373
	9:27	Ahaziah king of J saw what had happened,	3373
	9:29	Ahaziah had become king of J.)	3373
	10:13	he met some relatives of Ahaziah king of J	3373
	12:18	of J took all the sacred objects dedicated	3373
	12:18	Jehoram and Ahaziah, the kings of J—	3373
	12:19	the book of the annals of the kings of J?	3373
	13: 1	of Joash son of Ahaziah king of J,	3373
	13:10	the thirty-seventh year of Joash king of J,	3373
	13:12	against Amaziah king of J,	3373
	14: 1	Amaziah son of Joash king of J began	3373
	14: 9	of Israel replied to Amaziah king of J:	3373
	14:10	your own downfall and that of J also?"	3373
	14:11	and Amaziah king of J faced each other	3373
	14:11	at Beth Shemesh in J.	3373
	14:12	J was routed by Israel,	3373
	14:13	of Israel captured Amaziah king of J,	3373
	14:15	against Amaziah king of J,	3373
	14:17	of J lived for fifteen years after the death	3373
	14:18	the book of the annals of the kings of J?	3373
	14:21	Then all the people of J took Azariah,	3373
	14:22	to J after Amaziah rested with his fathers.	3373
	14:23	of Amaziah son of Joash king of J,	3373
	15: 1	Azariah son of Amaziah king of J began	3373
	15: 6	the book of the annals of the kings of J?	3373
	15: 8	the thirty-eighth year of Azariah king of J,	3373
	15:13	the thirty-ninth year of Uzziah king of J,	3373
	15:17	the thirty-ninth year of Azariah king of J,	3373
	15:23	In the fiftieth year of Azariah king of J,	3373
	15:27	the fifty-second year of Azariah king of J,	3373
	15:32	Jotham son of Uzziah king of J began	3373
	15:36	the book of the annals of the kings of J?	3373
	15:37	and Pekah son of Remaliah against J.)	3373
	16: 1	Ahaz son of Jotham king of J began	3373
	16: 6	for Aram by driving out the **men of J**.	3374
2Ki	16:19	the book of the annals of the kings of J?	3373
	17: 1	In the twelfth year of Ahaz king of J,	3373
	17:13	and J through all his prophets and seers:	3373
	17:18	Only the tribe of J was left,	3373
	17:19	and even J did not keep the commands of	3373
	18: 1	Hezekiah son of Ahaz king of J began	3373
	18: 5	like him among all the kings of J,	3373
	18:13	the fortified cities of J and captured them.	3373
	18:14	So Hezekiah king of J sent this message to	3373
	18:14	of J three hundred talents of silver	3373
	18:16	Hezekiah king of J stripped off the gold	3373
	18:22	saying to J and Jerusalem,	3373
	19:10	"Say to Hezekiah king of J:	3373
	19:30	of the house of J will take root below	3373
	20:20	the book of the annals of the kings of J?	3373
	21:11	of J has committed these detestable sins.	3373
	21:11	and has led J into sin with his idols.	3373
	21:12	and J that the ears of everyone who hears	3373
	21:16	the sin that he had caused J to commit,	3373
	21:17	the book of the annals of the kings of J?	3373
	21:25	the book of the annals of the kings of J?	3373
	22:13	for all J about what is written in this book	3373
	22:16	in the book the king of J has read.	3373
	22:18	Tell the king of J, who sent you to inquire	3373
	23: 1	the king called together all the elders of J	3373
	23: 2	the LORD with the men of J, the people	3373
	23: 5	of J to burn incense on the high places of	3373
	23: 5	on the high places of the towns of J and	3373
	23: 8	of J and desecrated the high places,	3373
	23:11	the horses that the kings of J had dedicated	3373
	23:12	the kings of J had erected on the roof near	3373
	23:17	of God who came from J and pronounced	3373
	23:22	of the kings of Israel and the kings of J,	3373
	23:24	all the other detestable things seen in J	824+3373
	23:26	which burned against J because of all	3373
	23:27	"I will remove J also from my presence	3373
	23:28	the book of the annals of the kings of J?	3373
	23:33	J a levy of a hundred talents of silver	824+2021S
	24: 2	He sent them to destroy J,	3373
	24: 3	to J according to the LORD's command,	3373
	24: 5	the book of the annals of the kings of J?	3373
	24:12	Jehoiachin king of J, his mother,	3373
	24:20	that all this happened to Jerusalem and J,	3373
	25:21	So J went into captivity,	3373
	25:22	over the people he had left behind in J.	824+3373
	25:25	and also the **men of J** and	3374
	25:27	of the exile of Jehoiachin king of J,	3373
1Ch	2: 1	Reuben, Simeon, Levi, J, Issachar,	3373
	2: 3	The sons of J: Er, Onan and Shelah.	3373
	2: 4	J had five sons in all.	3373
	2:10	the leader of the people of J.	3373
	4: 1	The descendants of J: Perez, Hezron,	3373
	4:21	The sons of Shelah son of J:	3373
	4:27	as numerous as the people of J.	3373
	4:41	in the days of Hezekiah king of J.	3373
	5: 2	though J was the strongest of his brothers	3373
	5:17	of Jotham king of J and Jeroboam king	3373
	6:15	the LORD sent J and Jerusalem into exile	3373
	6:55	in J with its surrounding pasturelands.	824+3373
	6:65	From the tribes of J,	1201+3373
	9: 1	The people of J were taken captive	3373
	9: 3	Those from J, from Benjamin,	1201+3373
	9: 4	a descendant of Perez son of J.	3373
	9: 6	The **people from** J numbered 690.	278+2157
	12:16	and some men from J also came to David	3373
	12:24	men of J, carrying shield and spear—	3373
	13: 6	of J (Kiriath Jearim) to bring up from there	3373
	21: 5	and seventy thousand in J.	3373
	27:18	over J: Elihu, a brother of David;	3373
	28: 4	He chose J as leader,	3373
	28: 4	from the house of J he chose my family,	3373
2Ch	2: 7	to work in J and Jerusalem	3373
	9:11	like them had ever been seen in J.)	824+3373
	10:17	living in the towns of J,	3373
	11: 1	the house of J and Benjamin—	3373
	11: 3	to Rehoboam son of Solomon king of J	3373
	11: 3	and to all the Israelites in J and Benjamin,	3373
	11: 5	and built up towns for defense in J:	3373
	11:10	These were fortified cities in J	3373
	11:12	So J and Benjamin were his.	3373
	11:14	to J and Jerusalem because Jeroboam	3373
	11:17	They strengthened the kingdom of J	3373
	11:23	throughout the districts of J and Benjamin,	3373
	12: 4	the fortified cities of J and came as far	3373
	12: 5	and to the leaders of J who had assembled	3373
	12:12	Indeed, there was some good in J.	3373
	13: 1	Abijah became king of J,	3373
	13:13	in front of J the ambush was behind them.	3373
	13:14	J turned and saw that they were	3373
	13:15	and the men of J raised the battle cry.	3373
	13:15	and all Israel before Abijah and J.	3373
	13:16	The Israelites fled before J,	3373
	13:18	of J were victorious because they relied on	3373
	14: 4	He commanded J to seek the LORD,	3373
	14: 5	and incense altars in every town in J,	3373
	14: 6	He built up the fortified cities of J,	3373
	14: 7	"Let us build up these towns," he said to J,	3373
	14: 8	of three hundred thousand men from J,	3373
	14:12	down the Cushites before Asa and J.	3373
	14:13	of J carried off a large amount of plunder.	NIH
	15: 2	"Listen to me, Asa and all J and Benjamin.	3373
	15: 8	from the whole land of J and Benjamin	3373
	15: 9	Then he assembled all J and Benjamin and	3373
	15:15	All J rejoiced about the oath	3373
	16: 1	up against J and fortified Ramah	3373
	16: 1	or entering the territory of Asa king of J.	3373
	16: 6	Then King Asa brought all the men of J,	3373

2Ch 16: 7 the seer came to Asa king of J and said 3373
16:11 are written in the book of the kings of J 3373
17: 2 the fortified cities of J and put garrisons 3373
17: 2 and put garrisons in J and in the towns 824+3373
17: 5 and all J brought gifts to Jehoshaphat, 3373
17: 6 and the Asherah poles from J. 3373
17: 7 and Micaiah to teach in the towns of J. 3373
17: 9 They taught throughout J, 3373
17: 9 to all the towns of J and taught the people. 3373
17:10 the kingdoms of the lands surrounding J, 3373
17:12 he built forts and store cities in J 3373
17:13 and had large supplies in the towns of J. 3373
17:14 From J, commanders of units of 1,000: 3373
17:19 in the fortified cities throughout J. 3373
18: 3 of Israel asked Jehoshaphat king of J, 3373
18: 9 and Jehoshaphat king of J were sitting 3373
18:28 of Israel and Jehoshaphat king of J went 3373
19: 1 of J returned safely to his palace 3373
19: 5 in each of the fortified cities of J. 3373
19:11 the leader of the tribe of J, 3373
20: 3 and he proclaimed a fast for all J. 3373
20: 4 The people of J came together to seek help 3373
20: 4 indeed, they came from every town in J 3373
20: 5 up in the assembly of J and Jerusalem at 3373
20:13 All the men of J, with their wives and 3373
20:15 King Jehoshaphat and all who live in J 3373
20:17 the LORD will give you, O J 3373
20:18 and all the people of J and Jerusalem fell 3373
20:20 "Listen to me, J and people of Jerusalem! 3373
20:22 and Mount Seir who were invading J, 3373
20:24 When the men of J came to the place 3373
20:27 of J and Jerusalem returned joyfully 3373
20:31 So Jehoshaphat reigned over J. 3373
20:31 when he became king of J, NIH
20:35 of J made an alliance with Ahaziah king 3373
21: 3 as well as fortified cities in J, 3373
21: 8 Edom rebelled against J and set up its own 3373
21:10 Edom has been in rebellion against J. 3373
21:11 on the hills of J and had caused the people 3373
21:11 and had led J astray. 3373
21:12 Jehoshaphat or of Asa king of J. 3373
21:13 and you have led J and the people 3373
21:17 They attacked J, invaded it 3373
22: 1 of Jehoram king of J began to reign. 3373
22: 6 of J went down to Jezreel to see Joram son 3373
22: 8 of J and the sons of Ahaziah's relatives, 3373
22:10 the whole royal family of the house of J. 3373
23: 2 throughout J and gathered the Levites and 3373
23: 8 of J did just as Jehoiada the priest ordered. 3373
24: 5 of J and collect the money due annually 3373
24: 6 in from J and Jerusalem the tax imposed 3373
24: 9 in J and Jerusalem that they should bring 3373
24:17 the officials of J came and paid homage to 3373
24:18 God's anger came upon J and Jerusalem. 3373
24:23 it invaded J and Jerusalem and killed all 3373
24:24 Because J had forsaken the LORD, NIH
25: 5 the people of J together and assigned them 3373
25: 5 and commanders of hundreds for all J 3373
25:10 They were furious with J and left for home 3373
25:12 of J also captured ten thousand men alive, 3373
25:17 Amaziah king of J consulted his advisers, 3373
25:18 of Israel replied to Amaziah king of J: 3373
25:19 your own downfall and that of J also?" 3373
25:21 and Amaziah king of J faced each other 3373
25:21 at Beth Shemesh in J. 3373
25:22 J was routed by Israel, 3373
25:23 of Israel captured Amaziah king of J, 3373
25:25 of J lived for fifteen years after the death 3373
25:26 not written in the book of the kings of J 3373
25:28 with his fathers in the City of J. 3373
26: 1 Then all the people of J took Uzziah, 3373
26: 2 to J after Amaziah rested with his fathers. 3373
27: 7 in the book of the kings of Israel and J. 3373
28: 6 and twenty thousand soldiers in J— 3373
28: 6 because J had forsaken the LORD, 4392[S]
28: 9 the God of your fathers, was angry with J, 3373
28:10 to make the men and women of J 1201+3373
28:17 and attacked J and carried away prisoners, 3373
28:18 in the foothills and in the Negev of J. 3373
28:19 The LORD had humbled J because 3373
28:19 for he had promoted wickedness in J 3373
28:25 in J he built high places to burn sacrifices 3373
28:26 are written in the book of the kings of J 3373
29: 8 the LORD has fallen on J and Jerusalem; 3373
29:21 for the sanctuary and for J. 3373
30: 1 Hezekiah sent word to all Israel and J and 3373
30: 6 throughout Israel and J with letters from 3373
30:12 in J the hand of God was on the people 3373
30:24 of J provided a thousand bulls 3373
30:25 The entire assembly of J rejoiced, 3373
30:25 from Israel and those who lived in J. 3373
31: 1 went out to the towns of J, 3373
31: 1 the high places and the altars throughout J 3373
31: 6 and J who lived in the towns of Judah 3373
31: 6 and Judah who lived in the towns of J 3373
31:20 This is what Hezekiah did throughout J, 3373
32: 1 of Assyria came and invaded J. 3373
32: 8 from what Hezekiah the king of J said. 3373
32: 9 with this message for Hezekiah king of J 3373
32: 9 and for all the people of J who were there: 3373
32:12 saying to J and Jerusalem, 3373
32:23 and valuable gifts for Hezekiah king of J. 3373
32:25 the LORD's wrath was on him and on J 3373
32:32 in the book of the kings of J and Israel. 3373
32:33 All J and the people of Jerusalem 3373
33: 9 But Manasseh led J and the people 3373
33:14 in all the fortified cities in J. 3373
2Ch 33:16 and told J to serve the LORD, 3373
34: 3 to purge J and Jerusalem of high places, 3373
34: 5 and so he purged J and Jerusalem. 3373
34: 9 from all the people of J and Benjamin and 3373
34:11 the kings of J had allowed to fall into ruin. 3373
34:21 for me and for the remnant in Israel and J 3373
34:24 in the presence of the king of J. 3373
34:26 Tell the king of J, who sent you to inquire 3373
34:29 the king called together all the elders of J 3373
34:30 the LORD with the men of J, the people 3373
35:18 and all J and Israel who were there with 3373
35:21 between you and me, O king of J? 3373
35:24 and all J and Jerusalem mourned for him. 3373
35:27 in the book of the kings of Israel and J. 3373
36: 3 J a levy of a hundred talents of silver 824+2021[S]
36: 4 king over J and Jerusalem 3373
36: 8 in the book of the kings of Israel and J. 3373
36:10 Zedekiah, king over J and Jerusalem. 3373
36:23 to build a temple for him at Jerusalem in J. 3373
Ezr 1: 2 to build a temple for him at Jerusalem in J. 3373
1: 3 up to Jerusalem in J and build the temple 3373
1: 5 Then the family heads of J and Benjamin, 3373
1: 8 to Sheshbazzar the prince of J. 3373
2: 1 they returned to Jerusalem and J, 3373
4: 1 the enemies of J and Benjamin heard that 3373
4: 4 the people of J and make them afraid to go 3373
4: 6 against the people of J and Jerusalem. 3373
5: 1 the Jews in J and Jerusalem in the name of 10315
5: 8 that we went to the district of J, 10315
7:14 and his seven advisers to inquire about J 10315
9: 9 a wall of protection in J and Jerusalem. 3373
10: 7 then issued throughout J and Jerusalem 3373
10: 9 the men of J and Benjamin had gathered 3373
10:23 Kelita), Pethahiah, J and Eliezer. 3373
Ne 1: 2 came from J with some other men, 3373
2: 5 to the city in J where my fathers are buried 3373
2: 7 provide me safe-conduct until I arrive in J? 3373
4:10 Meanwhile, the people in J said, 3373
4:16 behind all the people of J 3373
5:14 to be their governor in the land of J, 3373
6: 7 'There is a king in J!' 3373
6:17 of J were sending many letters to Tobiah, 3373
6:18 For many in J were under oath to him, 3373
7: 6 they returned to Jerusalem and J, 3373
11: 3 lived in the towns of J, 3373
11: 4 both J and Benjamin lived in Jerusalem): 3373
11: 4 From the descendants of J: 3373
11: 9 and J son of Hassenuah was over 3373
11:20 were in all the towns of J, 3373
11:24 one of the descendants of Zerah son of J, 3373
11:25 of the people of J lived in Kiriath Arba 3373
11:36 of the divisions of the Levites of J settled 3373
12: 8 Sherebiah, J, and also Mattaniah, who, 3373
12:31 the leaders of J go up on top of the wall. 3373
12:32 and half the leaders of J followed them, 3373
12:34 J, Benjamin, Shemaiah, Jeremiah, 3373
12:36 Gilalai, Maai, Nethanel, J and Hanani— 3373
12:44 for J was pleased with 3373
13:12 All J brought the tithes of grain, 3373
13:15 in J treading winepresses on the Sabbath 3373
13:16 on the Sabbath to the people of J. 3373
13:17 I rebuked the nobles of J and said to them, 3373
13:23 I saw **men of J** who had married women 3374
13:24 how to speak the **language of J**. 3376
Est 2: 6 taken captive with Jehoiachin king of J. 3373
Ps 48:11 of J are glad because of your judgments. 3373
60: 7 Ephraim is my helmet, J my scepter. 3373
63: T When he was in the Desert of J. 3373
69:35 and rebuild the cities of J. 3373
76: 1 In J God is known; 3373
78:68 but he chose the tribe of J, 3373
97: 8 and rejoices and the villages of J are glad 3373
108: 8 Ephraim is my helmet, J my scepter. 3373
114: 2 J became God's sanctuary, 3373
Pr 25: 1 copied by the men of Hezekiah king of J: 3373
Isa 1: 1 concerning J and Jerusalem that Isaiah son 3373
1: 1 Jotham, Ahaz and Hezekiah, kings of J. 3373
2: 1 of Amoz saw concerning J and Jerusalem: 3373
3: 1 to take from Jerusalem and J both supply 3373
3: 8 Jerusalem staggers, J is falling; 3373
5: 3 in Jerusalem and men of J, 3373
5: 7 the men of J are the garden of his delight. 3373
7: 1 the son of Uzziah, was king of J, 3373
7: 6 "Let us invade J; 3373
7:17 since Ephraim broke away from J— 3373
8: 8 and sweep on into J, 3373
9:21 together they will turn against J. 3373
11:12 he will assemble the scattered people of J 3373
11:13 Ephraim will not be jealous of J, 3373
11:13 nor J hostile toward Ephraim. 3373
19:17 land of J will bring terror to the Egyptians; 3373
19:17 to whom J is mentioned will be terrified, 2023[S]
22: 8 the defenses of J are stripped away. 3373
22:21 in Jerusalem and to the house of J. 3373
26: 1 be sung in the land of J: 3373
36: 1 the fortified cities of J and captured them. 3373
36: 7 saying to J and Jerusalem, 3373
37:10 "Say to Hezekiah king of J: 3373
37:31 of the house of J will take root below 3373
38: 9 of Hezekiah king of J after his illness 3373
40: 9 say to the towns of J, "Here is your God!" 3373
44:26 'It shall be inhabited,' of the towns of J, 3373
48: 1 from the line of J, you who take oaths in 3373
65: 9 J those who will possess my mountains; 3373
Jer 1: 2 the reign of Josiah son of Amon king of J, 3373
1: 3 of Jehoiakim son of Josiah king of J, 3373
1: 3 of Zedekiah son of Josiah king of J, 3373
Jer 1:15 and against all the towns of J. 3373
1:18 against the kings of J, its officials, 3373
2:28 as many gods as you have towns, O J. 3373
3: 7 and her unfaithful sister J saw it. 3373
3: 8 that her unfaithful sister J had no fear; 3373
3:10 her unfaithful sister J did not return to me 3373
3:11 "Faithless Israel is more righteous than unfaithful J. 3373
3:18 the house of J will join the house of Israel, 3373
4: 3 the LORD says to the men of J and 3373
4: 4 you men of J and people of Jerusalem, 3373
4: 5 "Announce in J and proclaim in Jerusalem 3373
4:16 raising a war cry against the cities of J. 3373
5:11 the house of J have been utterly unfaithful 3373
5:20 to the house of Jacob and proclaim it in J: 3373
7: 2 the LORD, all you people of J who come 3373
7:17 of J and in the streets of Jerusalem? 3373
7:30 " 'The people of J have done evil 3373
7:34 the towns of J and the streets of Jerusalem, 3373
8: 1 the bones of the kings and officials of J, 3373
9:11 the towns of J so no one can live there." 3373
9:26 J, Edom, Ammon, Moab and all who live 3373
10:22 It will make the towns of J desolate, 3373
11: 2 of J and to those who live in Jerusalem. 3373
11: 6 "Proclaim all these words in the towns of J 3373
11: 9 among the people of J and those who live 3373
11:10 of Israel and the house of J have broken 3373
11:12 of J and the people of Jerusalem will go 3373
11:13 as many gods as you have towns, O J; 3373
11:17 of Israel and the house of J have done evil 3373
12:14 and I will uproot the house of J from 3373
13: 9 the same way I will ruin the pride of J and 3373
13:11 of Israel and the whole house of J to me,' 3373
13:19 All J will be carried into exile, 3373
14: 2 "J mourns, her cities languish; 3373
14:19 Have you rejected J completely? 3373
15: 4 of Hezekiah king of J did in Jerusalem. 3373
17:19 through which the kings of J go in and out; 3373
17:20 O kings of J and all people of Judah 3373
17:20 and all people of J and everyone living 3373
17:25 the men of J and those living in Jerusalem, 3373
17:26 People will come from the towns of J and 3373
18:11 "Now therefore say to the people of J 3373
19: 3 O kings of J and people of Jerusalem. 3373
19: 4 nor the kings of J ever knew, 3373
19: 7 " 'In this place I will ruin the plans of J 3373
19:13 and those of the kings of J will be defiled 3373
20: 4 I will hand all J over to the king 3373
20: 5 and all the treasures of the kings of J. 3373
21: 7 I will hand over Zedekiah king of J, 3373
21:11 "Moreover, say to the royal house of J, 3373
22: 1 "Go down to the palace of the king of J 3373
22: 2 of J, you who sit on David's throne— 3373
22: 6 about the palace of the king of J: 3373
22:11 as king of J but has gone from this place: 3373
22:18 about Jehoiakim son of Josiah king of J: 3373
22:24 Jehoiachin son of Jehoiakim king of J, 3373
22:30 the throne of David or rule anymore in J." 3373
23: 6 In his days J will be saved 3373
24: 1 of Jehoiakim king of J and the officials, 3373
24: 1 and the artisans of J were carried into exile 3373
24: 5 I regard as good the exiles from J, 3373
24: 8 'so will I deal with Zedekiah king of J, 3373
25: 1 to Jeremiah concerning all the people of J 3373
25: 1 of Jehoiakim son of Josiah king of J, 3373
25: 2 to all the people of J and to all those living 3373
25: 3 of Amon king of J until this very day— 3373
25:18 and the towns of J, its kings and officials, 3373
26: 1 of Josiah king of J, this word came from 3373
26: 2 of the towns of J who come to worship in 3373
26:10 the officials of J heard about these things, 3373
26:18 in the days of Hezekiah king of J. 3373
26:18 He told all the people of J, 3373
26:19 "Did Hezekiah king of J or anyone else 3373
26:19 or anyone else in J put him to death? 3373
27: 1 of J, this word came to Jeremiah from 3373
27: 3 to Jerusalem to Zedekiah king of J. 3373
27:12 the same message to Zedekiah king of J. 3373
27:18 the king of J and in Jerusalem not be taken 3373
27:20 of J into exile from Jerusalem to Babylon, 3373
27:20 with all the nobles of J and Jerusalem— 3373
27:21 and in the palace of the king of J and 3373
28: 1 early in the reign of Zedekiah king of J, 3373
28: 4 of Jehoiakim king of J and all 3373
28: 4 and all the other exiles from J who went 3373
29: 2 the court officials and the leaders of J 3373
29: 3 of J sent to King Nebuchadnezzar 3373
29:22 all the exiles from J who are in Babylon 3373
30: 3 and J back from captivity and restore them 3373
30: 4 the LORD spoke concerning Israel and J: 3373
31:23 from captivity, the people in the land of J 3373
31:24 People will live together in J 3373
31:27 the house of Israel and the house of J with 3373
31:31 the house of Israel and with the house of J. 3373
32: 1 in the tenth year of Zedekiah king of J, 3373
32: 2 of the guard in the royal palace of J. 3373
32: 3 king of J had imprisoned him there, 3373
32: 4 Zedekiah king of J will not escape out of 3373
32:30 of Israel and J have done nothing but evil 3373
32:32 of Israel and J have provoked me by all 3373
32:32 the men of J and the people of Jerusalem. 3373
32:35 a detestable thing and so make J sin. 3373
32:44 of J and in the towns of the hill country, 3373
33: 4 the royal palaces of J that have been torn 3373
33: 7 I will bring J and Israel back 3373
33:10 the towns of J and the streets of Jerusalem 3373
33:13 around Jerusalem and in the towns of J, 3373

Jer 33:14 to the house of Israel and to the house of J. 3373
33:16 In those days J will be saved 3373
34: 2 Go to Zedekiah king of J and tell him, 3373
34: 4 O Zedekiah king of J, 3373
34: 6 told all this to Zedekiah king of J, 3373
34: 7 against Jerusalem and the other cities of J 3373
34: 7 the only fortified cities left in J. 3373
34:19 The leaders of J and Jerusalem, 3373
34:21 "I will hand Zedekiah king of J 3373
34:22 the towns of J so no one can live there." 3373
35: 1 of Jehoiakim son of Josiah king of J: 3373
35:13 the men of J and the people of Jerusalem, 3373
35:17 to bring on J and on everyone living 3373
36: 1 of J, this word came to Jeremiah from 3373
36: 2 J and all the other nations from 3373
36: 3 of J hear about every disaster I plan 3373
36: 6 Read them to all the people of J who come 3373
36: 9 of Jehoiakim son of Josiah king of J, 3373
36: 9 who had come from the towns of J. 3373
36:28 which Jehoiakim king of J burned up. 3373
36:29 Also tell Jehoiakim king of J, 3373
36:30 about Jehoiakim king of J: 3373
36:31 the people of J every disaster I pronounced 3373
36:32 scroll that Jehoiakim king of J had burned 3373
37: 1 Zedekiah son of Josiah was made king of J 824+3373
37: 7 Tell the king of J, who sent you to inquire 3373
38:22 of J will be brought out to the officials of 3373
39: 1 In the ninth year of Zedekiah king of J, 3373
39: 4 of J and all the soldiers saw them, 3373
39: 6 and also killed all the nobles of J. 3373
39:10 the guard left behind in the land of J some 3373
40: 1 and J who were being carried into exile 3373
40: 5 has appointed over the towns of J, 3373
40:11 the king of Babylon had left a remnant in J 3373
40:12 they all came back to the land of J, 3373
40:15 to be scattered and the remnant of J 3373
42:15 O remnant of J. 3373
42:19 "O remnant of J, the LORD has told you, 3373
43: 4 to stay in the land of J. 3373
43: 5 of J who had come back to live in the land 3373
43: 5 to live in the land of J from all the nations 3373
44: 2 on Jerusalem and on all the towns of J. 3373
44: 6 the towns of J and the streets of Jerusalem 3373
44: 7 by cutting off from J the men and women, 3373
44: 9 of J and the wickedness committed by you 3373
44: 9 by you and your wives in the land of J and 3373
44:11 on you and to destroy all J. 3373
44:12 of J who were determined to go to Egypt 3373
44:14 of the remnant of J who have gone to live 3373
44:14 of J, to which they long to return and live; 3373
44:17 and our officials did in the towns of J and 3373
44:21 the towns of J and the streets of Jerusalem 3373
44:24 all you people of J in Egypt. 3373
44:26 'that no one from J living anywhere 3373
44:28 and return to the land of J from Egypt will 3373
44:28 the whole remnant of J who came to live 3373
44:30 just as I handed Zedekiah king of J over 3373
45: 1 of J, after Baruch had written on a scroll 3373
46: 2 of Jehoiakim son of Josiah king of J: 3373
49:34 early in the reign of Zedekiah king of J: 3373
50: 4 the people of J together will go in tears 3373
50:20 and for the sins of J, 3373
50:33 and the people of J as well. 3373
51: 5 and J have not been forsaken by their God, 3373
51:59 with Zedekiah king of J in the fourth year 3373
52: 3 that all this happened to Jerusalem and J, 3373
52:10 he also killed all the officials of J. 3373
52:27 So J went into captivity, 3373
52:31 of the exile of Jehoiachin king of J, 3373
52:31 of J and freed him from prison on 3373
La 1: 3 J has gone into exile. 3373
1:15 has trampled the Virgin Daughter of J. 3373
2: 2 down the strongholds of the Daughter of J. 3373
2: 5 and lamentation for the Daughter of J. 3373
5:11 and virgins in the towns of J. 3373
Eze 4: 6 and bear the sin of the house of J. 3373
8: 1 and the elders of J were sitting before me, 3373
8:17 Is it a trivial matter for the house of J to do 3373
9: 9 of Israel and J is exceedingly great; 3373
21:10 in the scepter of my son [J]? NIH
21:13 And what if the scepter [of J], NIH
21:20 of the Ammonites and another against J 3373
25: 3 the people of J when they went into exile, 3373
25: 8 of J has become like all the other nations," 3373
25:12 on the house of J and became very guilty 3373
25:15 with ancient hostility sought to destroy J, NIH
27:17 " 'J and Israel traded with you; 3373
37:16 to J and the Israelites associated 3373
48: 7 "J will have one portion; 3373
48: 8 the territory of J from east to west will be 3373
48:22 the prince will lie between the border of J 3373
48:31 the gate of J and the gate of Levi. 3373
Da 1: 1 of the reign of Jehoiakim king of J, 3373
1: 2 the Lord delivered Jehoiakim king of J 3373
1: 6 Among these were some from J: 3373
2:25 among the exiles from J who can tell 10315
5:13 the king brought from J? 10315
6:13 "Daniel, who is one of the exiles from J, 10315
9: 7 of J and people of Jerusalem and all Israel, 3373
Hos 1: 1 Jotham, Ahaz and Hezekiah, kings of J, 3373
1: 7 Yet I will show love to the house of J; 3373
1:11 people of J and the people of Israel will 3373
4:15 O Israel, let not J become guilty. 3373
5: 5 J also stumbles with them. 3373
5:12 like rot to the people of J. 3373
5:13 Ephraim saw his sickness, and J his sores, 3373

Hos 5:14 like a great lion to J. 1074+3373
6: 4 "What can I do with you, J? 3373
6:11 "Also for you, J, a harvest is appointed. 3373
8:14 J has fortified many towns. 3373
10:11 I will drive Ephraim, J must plow, 3373
11:12 And J is unruly against God, 3373
12: 2 a charge to bring against J; 3373
Joel 3: 1 I restore the fortunes of J and Jerusalem, 3373
3: 6 You sold the people of J and Jerusalem to 3373
3: 8 and daughters to the people of J, 3373
3:18 all the ravines of J will run with water. 3373
3:19 of violence done to the people of J, 3373
3:20 J will be inhabited forever and Jerusalem 3373
Am 1: 1 the earthquake, when Uzziah was king of J 3373
2: 4 "For three sins of J, even for four, 3373
2: 5 I will send fire upon J that will consume 3373
7:12 Go back to the land of J. 3373
Ob 1:12 nor rejoice over the people of J in the day 3373
Mic 1: 1 Ahaz and Hezekiah, kings of J— 3373
1: 9 her wound is incurable; it has come to J. 3373
5: 2 you are small among the clans of J, 3373
Na 1:12 Although I have afflicted you, [O J,] NIH
1:15 Celebrate your festivals, O J, 3373
Zep 1: 1 the reign of Josiah son of Amon king of J: 3373
1: 4 "I will stretch out my hand against J and 3373
2: 7 to the remnant of the house of J; 3373
Hag 1: 1 of J, and to Joshua son of Jehozadak, 3373
1:14 governor of J, and the spirit of Joshua son 3373
2: 2 governor of J, to Joshua son of Jehozadak, 3373
2:21 of J that I will shake the heavens and 3373
Zec 1:12 from Jerusalem and from the towns of J, 3373
1:19 "These are the horns that scattered J, 3373
1:21 "These are the horns that scattered J so 3373
1:21 against the land of J to scatter its people." 3373
2:12 The LORD will inherit J as his portion in 3373
8:13 O J and Israel, so will I save you, 1074+3373
8:15 to do good again to Jerusalem and J. 1074+3373
8:19 and happy festivals for J. 1074+3373
9: 7 to our God and become leaders in J, 3373
9:13 I will bend J as I bend my bow and fill it 3373
10: 3 for his flock, the house of J, 3373
10: 4 From J will come the cornerstone, 5647[S]
10: 6 "I will strengthen the house of J and save 3373
11:14 the brotherhood between J and Israel. 3373
12: 2 J will be besieged as well as Jerusalem. 3373
12: 4 a watchful eye over the house of J, 3373
12: 5 the leaders of J will say in their hearts, 3373
12: 6 "On that day I will make the leaders of J 3373
12: 7 will save the dwellings of J first, 3373
12: 7 not be greater than that of J. 3373
14: 5 in the days of Uzziah king of J. 3373
14:14 J too will fight at Jerusalem. 3373
14:21 Every pot in Jerusalem and J will be holy 3373
Mal 2:11 J has broken faith. 3373
2:11 J has desecrated the sanctuary 3373
3: 4 and the offerings of J and Jerusalem will 3373
Mt 1: 2 Jacob the father of J and his brothers, 2683
1: 3 J the father of Perez and Zerah, 2683
2: 6 Bethlehem, in the land of J, 2683
2: 6 by no means least among the rulers of J; 2683
Lk 3:30 the son of J, the son of Joseph, 2683
3:33 the son of Perez, the son of J, 2683
Heb 7:14 it is clear that our Lord descended from J, 2683
8: 8 of Israel and with the house of J. 2683
Rev 5: 5 See, the Lion of the tribe of J, 2683
7: 5 From the tribe of J 12,000 were sealed, 2683

JUDAH'S (13) [JUDAH]

Ge 38: 7 But Er, J firstborn, was wicked in 3373
38:12 After a long time J wife, 3373
Jos 19: 9 J portion was more than they needed. 1201+3373
2Sa 3: 8 "Am I a dog's head—on J side? 3373
1Ki 2:32 Amasa son of Jether, commander of J army 3373
1Ch 2: 3 Er, J firstborn, was wicked in 3373
2: 4 Tamar, J daughter-in-law, 2257[S]
Ps 68:27 there the great throng of J princes, 3373
Isa 11:13 and J enemies will be cut off; 3373
Jer 17: 1 "J sin is engraved with an iron tool, 3373
Eze 37:19 and join it to J stick, making them a single 3373
Hos 5:10 J leaders are like those who move 3373
Mic 1: 5 What is J high place? Is it not Jerusalem? 3373

JUDAISM (5) [JEW]

Ac 2:11 (both Jews and converts to J); 4670
6: 5 Nicolas from Antioch, a convert to J. 4670
13:43 and devout converts to J followed Paul 4670
Gal 1:13 heard of my previous way of life in J, 2682
1:14 I was advancing in J beyond many Jews 2682

JUDAS (41)

Mt 10: 4 Simon the Zealot and J Iscariot, 2683
13:55 Joseph, Simon and J? 2683
26:14 the one called J Iscariot— 2683
26:16 From then on J watched for an opportunity NIG
26:25 Then J, the one who would betray him, 2683
26:47 While he was still speaking, J, 2683
26:49 Going at once to Jesus, J said, "Greetings, NIG
27: 3 When J, who had betrayed him, 2683
27: 5 J threw the money into the temple and left. NIG
Mk 3:19 and J Iscariot, who betrayed him. 2683
6: 3 Joseph, J and Simon? 2683
14:10 Then J Iscariot, one of the Twelve, 2683
14:43 Just as he was speaking, J, 2683
14:45 Going at once to Jesus, J said, "Rabbi!" NIG
Lk 6:16 J son of James, and Judas Iscariot, 2683

Lk 6:16 and J Iscariot, who became a traitor. 2683
22: 3 Then Satan entered J, called Iscariot, 2683
22: 4 And J went to the chief priests and NIG
22:47 and the man who was called J, 2683
22:48 but Jesus asked him, "J, are you betraying 2683
Jn 6:71 (He meant J, the son of Simon Iscariot, 2683
12: 4 But one of his disciples, J Iscariot, 2683
13: 2 the devil had already prompted J Iscariot, 2683
13:26 he gave it to J Iscariot, son of Simon. 2683
13:27 As soon as J took the bread, NIG
13:29 Since J had charge of the money, 2683
13:30 As soon as J had taken the bread, 1697[S]
14:22 Then J (not Judas Iscariot) said, "But, 2683
14:22 Then Judas (not J Iscariot) said, "But, NIG
18: 2 Now J, who betrayed him, knew the place, 2683
18: 3 So J came to the grove, 2683
18: 5 (And J the traitor was standing there 2683
Ac 1:13 and J son of James. 2683
1:16 through the mouth of David concerning J, 2683
1:18 J bought a field; 4047[S]
1:25 which J left to go where he belongs." 2683
5:37 J the Galilean appeared in the days of 2683
9:11 of J on Straight Street and ask for a man 2683
15:22 They chose J (called Barsabbas) and Silas, 2683
15:27 Therefore we are sending J and Silas 2683
15:32 J and Silas, who themselves were prophets, 2683

JUDE (1)

Jude 1: 1 J, a servant of Jesus Christ and a brother 2683

JUDEA (44) [JUDAH]

Mt 2: 1 After Jesus was born in Bethlehem in J, 2677
2: 5 "In Bethlehem in J," they replied, 2677
2:22 that Archelaus was reigning in J in place 2677
3: 1 preaching in the Desert of J 2677
3: 5 to him from Jerusalem and all J and 2677
4:25 J and the region across the Jordan 2677
19: 1 into the region of J to the other side of 2677
24:16 then let those who are in J flee to 2677
Mk 3: 8 many people came to him from J, 2677
10: 1 into the region of J and across the Jordan. 2677
13:14 then let those who are in J flee to 2677
Lk 1: 5 of J there was a priest named Zechariah, 2677
1:39 to a town in the hill country of J, 2683
1:65 the hill country of J people were talking 2677
2: 4 from the town of Nazareth in Galilee to J, 2677
3: 1 when Pontius Pilate was governor of J, 2677
4:44 on preaching in the synagogues of J. 2677
5:17 from every village of Galilee and from J 2677
6:17 a great number of people from all over J, 2677
7:17 This news about Jesus spread throughout J 2677
21:21 Then let those who are in J flee to 2677
23: 5 up the people all over J by his teaching. 2677
Jn 4: 3 he left J and went back once more 2677
4:47 that Jesus had arrived in Galilee from J, 2677
4:54 having come from J to Galilee. 2677
7: 1 purposely staying away from J because 2677
7: 3 "You ought to leave here and go to J, 2677
11: 7 "Let us go back to J." 2677
Ac 1: 8 and in all J and Samaria, 2677
2: 9 J and Cappadocia, Pontus and Asia, 2677
8: 1 the apostles were scattered throughout J 2677
9:31 Then the church throughout J, 2677
10:37 throughout J, beginning in Galilee after 2677
11: 1 and the brothers throughout J heard that 2677
11:29 to provide help for the brothers living in J. 2677
12:19 Then Herod went from J to Caesarea 2677
15: 1 down from J to Antioch and were teaching 2677
21:10 prophet named Agabus came down from J. 2677
26:20 then to those in Jerusalem and in all J, 2677
28:21 "We have not received any letters from J 2677
Ro 15:31 in J and that my service in Jerusalem may 2677
2Co 1:16 then to have you send me on my way to J. 2677
Gal 1:22 to the churches of J that are in Christ. 2677
1Th 2:14 became imitators of God's churches in J, 2677

JUDEAN (6) [JUDAH]

1Ch 4:18 (His J wife gave birth to Jered the father 3374
2Ch 25:13 in the war raided J towns from Samaria 3373
27: 4 He built towns in the J hills and forts 3373
Mk 1: 5 The whole J countryside and all the people 2677
Lk 23:51 He came from the J town of Arimathea 2681
Jn 3:22 went out into the J countryside, 2681

JUDGE (153) [JUDGE'S, JUDGED, JUDGES, JUDGING, JUDGMENT, JUDGMENTS]

Ge 16: 5 May the LORD j between you and me." 9149
18:25 Will not the J of all the earth do right?" 9149
19: 9 and now he wants to play the j! 9149+9149
31:37 and let them j between the two of us. 3519
31:53 the God of their father, j between us." 9149
Ex 2:14 "Who made you ruler and j over us? 9149
5:21 the LORD look upon you and j you! 9149
18:13 to serve as j for the people, 9149
18:14 Why do you alone sit as j, 3782
Lev 19:15 but j your neighbor fairly. 9149
27:12 who will j its quality as good or bad. 6885
27:14 the priest will j its quality as good 6885
Nu 35:24 the assembly must j between him and 9149
Dt 1:16 between your brothers and j fairly, 9149
16:18 and they shall j the people fairly. 5477+9149
17: 8 that are too difficult for you to j— 5477

Dt 17: 9 and to the j who is in office 9149
17:12 The man who shows contempt for the j or 9149
25: 2 the j shall make him lie down 9149
32:36 The LORD will j his people 1906
Jdg 2:18 the LORD raised up a j for them, he was 9149
2:18 with the j and saved them out of the hands 9149
2:18 of their enemies as long as the j lived; 9149
2:19 But when the j died, 9149
3:10 that he became Israel's j and went to war. 9149
11:27 Let the LORD, the J, decide the dispute 9149
1Sa 2:10 the LORD will j the ends of the earth. 1906
3:13 that I would j his family forever because of 9149
7:15 Samuel continued as j over Israel all 9149
24:12 May the LORD j between you and me. 9149
24:15 May the LORD be our j and decide 1908
2Sa 15: 4 "If only I were appointed j in the land! 9149
1Ki 7: 7 the Hall of Justice, where he was to j, 9149
8:32 J between your servants, 9149
1Ch 12:17 the God of our fathers see it and j you." 3519
16:33 for he comes to j the earth. 9149
2Ch 6:23 J between your servants, 9149
19: 7 J carefully, for with the LORD our God
there is no injustice 6913S
20:12 O our God, will you not j them? 9149
Job 9:15 I could only plead with my J for mercy. 9149
22:13 Does he j through such darkness? 9149
23: 7 I would be delivered forever from my j. 9149
Ps 7: 8 let the LORD j the peoples. 1906
7: 8 J me, O LORD, according 9149
7:11 God is a righteous j, 9149
9: 8 He will j the world in righteousness; 9149
50: 4 and the earth, that he may j his people: 1906
50: 6 for God himself is j. 9149
51: 4 when you speak and justified when you j. 9149
58: 1 Do you j uprightly among men? 9149
72: 2 He will j your people in righteousness, 1906
75: 2 it is I who j uprightly. 9149
76: 9 when you, O God, rose up to j, 5477
82: 8 Rise up, O God, j the earth, 9149
94: 2 Rise up, O J of the earth; 9149
96:10 he will j the peoples with equity. 1906
96:13 for he comes, he comes to j the earth. 9149
96:13 He will j the world in righteousness and 9149
98: 9 for he comes to j the earth. 9149
98: 9 He will j the world in righteousness and 9149
110: 6 He will j the nations, 1906
Pr 20: 8 When a king sits on his throne to j, 1907
31: 9 Speak up and j fairly; 9149
Isa 2: 4 He will j between the nations 9149
3: 2 the j and prophet, the soothsayer and elder, 9149
3:13 he rises to j the people. 1906
5: 3 j between me and my vineyard. 9149
11: 3 not j by what he sees with his eyes, 9149
11: 4 but with righteousness he will j the needy, 9149
33:22 For the LORD is our j, 9149
Jer 11:20 you who j righteously and test the heart 9149
Eze 7: 3 I will j you according to your conduct 9149
7: 8 I will j you according to your conduct 9149
7:27 and by their own standards I will j them. 9149
18:30 O house of Israel, I will j you, 9149
20: 4 "Will you j them? Will you judge them, 9149
20: 4 Will you j them, son of man? 9149
20:36 so I will j you, declares the Sovereign 9149
21:30 in the land of your ancestry, I will j you. 9149
22: 2 will you j her? Will you judge this city 9149
22: 2 Will you j this city of bloodshed? 9149
23:36 will you j Oholah and Oholibah? 9149
33:20 But I will j each of you according 9149
34:17 I will j between one sheep and another, 9149
34:20 See, I myself will j between the fat sheep 9149
34:22 I will j between one sheep and another. 9149
35:11 known among them when I j you. 9149
Joel 3:12 of Jehoshaphat, for there I will sit to j all 9149
Mic 3:11 Her leaders j for a bribe, 9149
4: 3 He will j between many peoples 9149
7: 3 ruler demands gifts, the j accepts bribes, 9149
Mt 5:25 or he may hand you over to the j, 3216
5:25 and the j may hand you over to the officer, 3216
7: 1 "Do not j, or you too will be judged. 3212
7: 2 For in the same way you j others, 3212
Lk 6:37 "Do not j, and you will not be judged. 3212
12:14 who appointed me a j or an arbiter 3216
12:57 "Why don't you j for yourselves 3212
12:58 or he may drag you off to the j, 3216
12:58 and the j turn you over to the officer, 3216
18: 2 a j who neither feared God nor cared 3216
18: 6 "Listen to what the unjust j says. 3216
19:22 'I will j you by your own words, 3212
Jn 5:27 And he has given him authority to j 3213+4472
5:30 I j only as I hear, and my judgment is just, 3212
8:15 You j by human standards; 3212
8:16 But if I do j, my decisions are right, 3212
8:50 there is one who seeks it, and he is the j. 3212
12:47 but does not keep them, I do not j him. 3212
12:47 I did not come to j the world, but to save it. 3212
12:48 There is a j for the one who rejects me and
does not accept my words; 2400+3212+3836
18:31 "Take him yourselves and j him 3212
Ac 4:19 "J for yourselves whether it is right 3212
7:27 'Who made you ruler and j over us? 1471
7:35 'Who made you ruler and j?' 1471
10:42 that he is the one whom God appointed as j 3216
17:31 a day when he will j the world with justice 3212
18:15 I will not be a j of such things." 3216
23: 3 You sit there to j me according to the law, 3212
24:10 of years you have been a j over this nation; 3216
Ro 2: 1 for at whatever point you j the other, 3212
Ro 2:16 on the day when God will j men's secrets 3212
3: 4 when you speak and prevail when you j." 3212
3: 6 how could God j the world? 3212
14: 4 Who are you to j someone else's servant? 3212
14:10 You, then, why do you j your brother? 3212
1Co 4: 3 indeed, I do not even j myself. 373
4: 5 j nothing before the appointed time; 3212
5:12 of mine to j those outside the church? 3212
5:12 Are you not to j those inside? 3212
5:13 God will j those outside. 3212
6: 2 not know that the saints will j the world? 3212
6: 2 And if you are to j the world, 3212
6: 2 are you not competent to j trivial cases? 3215
6: 3 Do you not know that we will j angels? 3212
6: 5 among you wise enough to j a dispute 1359
10:15 j for yourselves what I say. 3212
11:13 J for yourselves: Is it proper 3212
Gal 2: 6 not j by external appearance— 476+3284+4725
Col 2:16 not let anyone j you by what you eat 3212
2Ti 4: 1 who will j the living and the dead, 3212
4: 8 which the Lord, the righteous J, 3216
Heb 10:30 and again, "The Lord will j his people." 3212
12:23 You have come to God, the j of all men, 3216
13: 4 for God will j the adulterer and all 3212
Jas 4:11 When you j the law, you are not keeping it, 3212
4:12 There is only one Lawgiver and J, 3216
4:12 But you—who are you to j your neighbor? 3212
5: 9 The J is standing at the door! 3216
1Pe 4: 5 to give account to him who is ready to j 3212
Jude 1:15 to j everyone, and to convict all 3213+4472
Rev 6:10 until you j the inhabitants of the earth 3212+4024
20: 4 those who had been given authority to j. 3210

JUDGE'S (2) [JUDGE]

Mt 27:19 While Pilate was sitting on the j seat, 1037
Jn 19:13 sat down on the j seat at a place known as 1037

JUDGED (25) [JUDGE]

1Sa 7:17 and there he also j Israel. 9149
Job 31:11 would have been shameful, a sin to be j. 7132
31:28 then these also would be sins to be j, 7132
Ps 9:19 let the nations be j in your presence. 9149
Eze 20:36 As I j your fathers in the desert of the land 9149
24:14 You will be j according to your conduct 9149
36:19 I j them according to their conduct 9149
Mt 7: 1 "Do not judge, or you too will be j. 3212
7: 2 same way you judge others, you will be j, 3212
Lk 6:37 "Do not judge, and you will not be j. 3212
7:43 "You have j correctly," Jesus said. 3212
Ro 2:12 who sin under the law will be j by the law. 3212
1Co 4: 3 if I am j by you or by any human court; 373
10:29 For why should my freedom be j 3212
11:31 But if we j ourselves, we would not come 1359
11:32 When we are j by the Lord, 3212
14:24 that he is a sinner and will be j by all, 373
Jas 2:12 as those who are going to be j by the law 3212
3: 1 we who teach will be j more strictly. 3210+3284
5: 9 brothers, or you will be j. 3212
1Pe 4: 6 so that they might be j according to men 3212
Rev 16: 5 the Holy One, because you have so j; 3212
18:20 God has j her for the way she treated you.' 3212
20:12 The dead were j according to what 3212
20:13 and each person was j according to what 3212

JUDGES (53) [JUDGE]

Ex 18:22 Have them serve as j for the people 9149
18:26 They served as j for the people at all times. 9149
21: 6 then his master must take him before the j. 466
22: 8 of the house must appear before the j 466
22: 9 parties are to bring their cases before the j. 466
22: 9 the j declare guilty must pay back double 466
Nu 25: 5 So Moses said to Israel's j, 9149
Dt 1:16 And I charged your j at that time: 9149
16:18 Appoint j and officials for each 9149
19:17 and the j who are in office 9149
19:18 The j must make a thorough investigation, 9149
21: 2 and j shall go out and measure the distance 9149
25: 1 to take it to court and the j will decide 9149
Jos 8:33 with their elders, officials and j, 9149
23: 2 their elders, leaders, j and officials— 9149
24: 1 leaders, j and officials of Israel, 9149
Jdg 2:16 Then the LORD raised up j, 9149
2:17 to their j but prostituted themselves 9149
Ru 1: 1 In the days when the j ruled, 9149
1Sa 8: 1 he appointed his sons as j for Israel. 9149
2Ki 23:22 Not since the days of the j who led Israel, 9149
1Ch 23: 4 and six thousand are to be officials and j. 9149
26:29 as officials and j over Israel. 9149
2Ch 1: 2 to the j and to all the leaders in Israel, 9149
19: 5 He appointed j in the land, 9149
Ezr 4: 9 j and officials over the men from Tripolis, 10171
7:25 and j to administer justice to all the people 10171
10:14 along with the elders and j of each town, 9149
Job 9:24 he blindfolds its j. 9149
12:17 and makes fools of j. 9149
21:22 since he j even the highest? 9149
Ps 58:11 surely there is a God who j the earth." 9149
75: 7 But it is God who j: 9149
Pr 29:14 If a king j the poor with fairness, 9149
Isa 1:26 I will restore your j as in days of old, 9149
Eze 18: 8 and j fairly between man and man. 5477+6913
44:24 the priests are to serve as j and decide it 9149
Da 3: 2 prefects, governors, advisers, treasurers, j, 10188
3: 3 prefects, governors, advisers, treasurers, j, 10188
Mt 12:27 So then, they will be your j. 3216
Lk 11:19 So then, they will be your j. 3216
Jn 5:22 Moreover, the Father j no one, 3212
Ac 13:20 God gave them j until the time of Samuel 3216
1Co 4: 4 It is the Lord who j me. 373
6: 4 appoint as j even men of little account in 2767
Heb 4:12 it j the thoughts and attitudes of the heart. 3217
Jas 2: 4 and become j with evil thoughts? 3216
4:11 against his brother or j him speaks against 3212
4:11 against the law and j it. 3212
1Pe 1:17 Father who j each man's work impartially, 3212
2:23 he entrusted himself to him who j justly. 3212
Rev 18: 8 for mighty is the Lord God who j her. 3212
19:11 With justice he j and makes war. 3212

JUDGING (10) [JUDGE]

Dt 1:17 Do not show partiality in j; 5477
1Sa 7:16 j Israel in all those places. 9149
2Ch 19: 6 you are not j for man but for the LORD, 9149
Ps 9: 4 you have sat on your throne, j righteously. 9149
Pr 24:23 To show partiality in j is not good: 5477
Isa 16: 5 in j seeks justice and speeds the cause 9149
Mt 19:28 j the twelve tribes of Israel. 3212
Lk 22:30 j the twelve tribes of Israel. 3212
Jn 7:24 Stop j by mere appearances, 3212
Rev 11:18 The time has come for j the dead, 3212

JUDGMENT (132) [JUDGE]

Ex 6: 6 outstretched arm and with mighty acts of j. 9150
7: 4 with mighty acts of j I will bring out my
divisions, 9150
12:12 and I will bring j on all the gods of Egypt. 9150
Lev 13:37 If, however, in his j it is unchanged 6524
Nu 33: 4 for the LORD had brought j on their gods. 9150
Dt 1:17 for j belongs to God. 5477
32:41 and my hand grasps it in j, 5477
1Sa 25:33 May you be blessed for your good j and 3248
2Ch 20: 9 whether the sword of j, 9144
22: 8 While Jehu was executing j on the house 9149
24:24 j was executed on Joash. 9150
Job 14: 3 Will you bring him before you for j? 5477
19:29 and then you will know that there is j." 8723
24: 1 the Almighty not set times for j? NIH
34:23 that they should come before him for j. 5477
36:17 you are laden with the j due the wicked; 1907
36:17 j and justice have taken hold of you. 1907
Ps 1: 5 the wicked will not stand in the j, 5477
9: 7 he has established his throne for j. 5477
76: 8 From heaven you pronounced j, 1907
82: 1 he gives j among the "gods": 9149
94:15 J will again be founded on righteousness, 5477
119:66 Teach me knowledge and good j, 3248
122: 5 There the thrones for j stand, 5477
143: 2 Do not bring your servant into j, 5477
Pr 3:21 My son, preserve sound j and discernment, 9370
6:32 But a man who commits adultery lacks j; 4213
7: 7 a youth who lacked j. 4213
8:14 Counsel and sound j are mine; 9370
9: 4 she says to those who lack j. 4213
9:16 she says to those who lack j. 4213
10:13 a rod is for the back of him who lacks j. 4213
10:21 but fools die for lack of j. 4213
11:12 A man who lacks j derides his neighbor, 4213
12:11 but he who chases fantasies lacks j. 4213
15:21 Folly delights a man who lacks j, 4213
17:18 A man lacking in j strikes hands in pledge 4213
18: 1 he defies all sound j. 9370
24:30 past the vineyard of the man who lacks j; 4213
28:16 A tyrannical ruler lacks j, 9312
Ecc 3:16 In the place of j—wickedness was there 5477
3:17 "God will bring to j both the righteous 9149
11: 9 for all these things God will bring you to j. 5477
12:14 For God will bring every deed into j, 5477
Isa 3:14 The LORD enters into j against the elders 5477
4: 4 from Jerusalem by a spirit of j and a spirit 5477
28: 6 be a spirit of justice to him who sits in j, 5477
34: 5 see, it descends in j on Edom, 5477
41: 1 let us meet together at the place of j. 5477
53: 8 By oppression and j he was taken away. 5477
66:16 with his sword the LORD will execute j 9149
Jer 2:35 But I will pass j on you because you say, 9149
10:15 when their j comes, they will perish. 7213
25:31 he will bring j on all mankind and put 9149
48:21 J has come to the plateau— 5477
48:47 Here ends the j on Moab. 5477
51: 9 for her j reaches to the skies, 5477
51:18 when their j comes, they will perish. 7213
Eze 11:10 and I will execute j on you at the borders 9149
11:11 I will execute j on you at the borders 9149
17:20 I will bring him to Babylon and execute j 9149
20:35 face to face, I will execute j upon you. 9149
38:22 I will execute j upon him with plague 9149
Da 7:22 of Days came and pronounced j in favor of 10170
Hos 5: 1 This j is against you: 5477
5:11 Ephraim is oppressed, trampled in j, 5477
Joel 3: 2 There I will enter into j against them 9149
Am 7: 4 The Sovereign LORD was calling for j 8189
Hab 1:12 you have appointed them to execute j; 5477
Zec 8:16 render true and sound j 5477+9149
Mal 3: 5 "So I will come near to you for j. 5477
Mt 5:21 anyone who murders will be subject to j.' 3213
5:22 with his brother will be subject to j. 3213
10:15 and Gomorrah on the day of j than for 3213
11:22 for Tyre and Sidon on the day of j than 3213
11:24 for Sodom on the day of j than for you." 3213
12:36 to give account on the day of j 3213

Mt 12:41 the j with this generation and condemn it; 3213
12:42 the j with this generation and condemn it; 3213
Lk 10:14 for Tyre and Sidon at the j than for you. 3213
11:31 of the South will rise at the j with the men 3213
11:32 the j with this generation and condemn it; 3213
Jn 5:22 but has entrusted all j to the Son, 3213
5:30 I judge only as I hear, and my j is just, 3213
7:24 and make a right j." 3212+3213
8:15 by human standards; I pass j on no one. 3212
8:26 "I have much to say in j of you. 3212
9:39 "For j I have come into this world, 3210
12:31 Now is the time for j on this world; 3213
16:8 in regard to sin and righteousness and j: 3213
16:11 and in regard to j, because the prince of this 3213
Ac 15:19 "*It is* my j, therefore, that we should 3212
24:25 self-control and the j to come, 3210
Ro 2:1 you who pass j on someone else, 3212
2:1 because you who pass j do the same things. 3212
2:2 Now we know that God's j against those 3210
2:3 pass j on them and yet do the same things, 3212
2:3 do you think you will escape God's j? 3210
2:5 when his righteous j will be revealed. 1464
5:16 The j followed one sin and brought 3210
12:3 but rather think of yourself with sober j, 5404
13:2 and those who do so will bring j 3210
14:1 without passing j on disputable matters. 1360
14:10 For we will all stand before God's j seat. 1037
14:13 *let us* stop passing j on one another. 3212
1Co 2:15 he himself *is* not subject to any man's j: 373
5:3 And *I have* already passed j on 3212
6:1 take it before the ungodly *for* j 3212
7:25 from the Lord, but I give a j as one who by 1191
7:40 In my j, she is happier if she stays 1191
9:3 This is my defense *to* those who sit in j on 373
11:29 of the Lord eats and drinks j on himself. 3210
11:31 *we* would not come under j. 3212
11:34 you meet together it may not result in j. 3210
2Co 5:10 For we must all appear before the j seat 1037
2Th 1:5 All this is evidence that God's j is right, 3213
1Ti 3:6 and fall under the same j as the devil. 3210
5:12 Thus they bring j on themselves, 3210
5:24 reaching the place of j ahead of them; 3213
Heb 6:2 the resurrection of the dead, and eternal j. 3210
9:27 to die once, and after that to face j, 3213
10:27 a fearful expectation *of* j and of raging fire 3213
Jas 2:13 because j without mercy will be shown 3213
2:13 Mercy triumphs over j! 3213
4:11 you are not keeping it, but sitting in j on it. 3216
1Pe 4:17 For it is time for j to begin with the family 3210
2Pe 2:4 into gloomy dungeons to be held for j; 3213
2:9 to hold the unrighteous for the day *of* j, 3213
3:7 being kept for the day *of* j and destruction 3213
1Jn 4:17 have confidence on the day *of* j, 3213
Jude 1:6 bound with everlasting chains for j on 3213
Rev 14:7 because the hour *of* his j has come. 3213

JUDGMENTS (18) [JUDGE]

Dt 33:21 and his j concerning Israel." 5477
1Ch 16:12 his miracles, and the j he pronounced, 5477
16:14 his j are in all the earth. 5477
Ps 48:11 villages of Judah are glad because of your j. 5477
97:8 villages of Judah are glad because of your j, 5477
105:5 his miracles, and the j he pronounced, 5477
105:7 his j are in all the earth. 5477
Isa 26:9 When your j come upon the earth, 5477
Jer 1:16 I will pronounce my j on my people 5477
4:12 Now I pronounce my j against them." 5477
Eze 14:21 against Jerusalem my four dreadful j— 9150
Da 9:11 "Therefore the curses and sworn j written 8652
Hos 6:5 my j flashed like lightning upon you. 5477
Ro 11:33 How unsearchable his j, 3210
1Co 2:15 The spiritual man makes j about all things, 373
Rev 16:5 "You are just in these j, NIG
16:7 true and just are your j." 3213
19:2 for true and just are his j. 3213

JUDITH (1)

Ge 26:34 he married J daughter of Beeri the Hittite, 3377

JUG (6) [JUGS]

1Sa 26:11 the spear and water j that are near his head, 7608
26:12 the spear and water j near Saul's head, 7608
26:16 Where are the king's spear and water j 7608
1Ki 17:12 of flour in a jar and a little oil in a j. 7608
17:14 be used up and the j *of* oil will not run dry 7608
17:16 the jar of flour was not used up and the j 7608

JUGS (1) [JUG]

Jer 48:12 they will empty her jars and smash her j. 5574

JUICE (3)

Nu 6:3 not drink grape j or eat grapes or raisins. 5489
18:27 the threshing floor or j from the winepress. 4852
Isa 65:8 when j is still found in a cluster of grapes 9408

JULIA (1)

Ro 16:15 Greet Philologus, J, Nereus and his sister, 2684

JULIUS (2)

Ac 27:1 over *to* a centurion named J, 2685
27:3 The next day we landed at Sidon; and J, 2685

JUMP (1) [JUMPED, JUMPING]

Ac 27:43 to j overboard first and get to land. 681

JUMPED (5) [JUMP]

Mk 10:50 he j to his feet and came to Jesus. 403
Jn 21:7 and j into the water. 965+1571
Ac 3:8 He j to his feet and began to walk. 1982
14:10 At that, the *man* j up and began to walk. 256
19:16 Then the man who had the evil spirit j on 2383

JUMPING (1) [JUMP]

Ac 3:8 walking and j, and praising God. 256

JUNCTION (1) [JOIN]

Eze 21:21 at the j *of* the two roads, to seek an omen: 8031

JUNIAS (1)

Ro 16:7 Greet Andronicus and J, 2687

JUPITER (KJV) See ZEUS

JURISDICTION (1)

Lk 23:7 that Jesus was under Herod's j, 2026

JUSHAB-HESED (1)

1Ch 3:20 Ohel, Berekiah, Hasadiah and J. 3457

JUST (393) [JUSTICE, JUSTIFICATION, JUSTIFIED, JUSTIFIES, JUSTIFY, JUSTIFYING, JUSTLY]

Ge 6:22 Noah did everything j as God had 3869
9:3 J as I gave you the green plants, 3869
18:19 of the LORD by doing what is right and j, 5477
18:32 but let me speak j once more. 421
26:29 j as we did not molest you 889+3869
27:9 j the way he likes it. 889+3869
27:13 J do what I say; go and get them for me." 421
27:14 j the way his father liked it. 889+3869
27:33 I ate it j before you came 928+3270
29:15 "J because you are a relative of mine, 3954
33:13 If they are driven hard j one day, NIH
33:15 "*J let me* find favor in the eyes AIT
38:11 "He may die too, j like his brothers." 3869
40:13 j as you used to do 3869
40:22 j as Joseph had said to them 889+3869
41:21 they looked j as ugly as before. 889+3869
41:28 "It is j as I said to Pharaoh: 889
41:54 j as Joseph had said. 889+3869
42:1 *j keep* looking at each other?" AIT
42:14 Joseph said to them, "It is j as I told you: 889
46:34 j as our fathers did.' 1685
47:3 "j as our fathers were." 1685
48:5 j as Reuben and Simeon are mine. 3869
Ex 5:13 j as when you had straw." 889+3869
7:6 Moses and Aaron did j as 889+3869+4027
7:10 Aaron went to Pharaoh and did j as the LORD commanded. 889+3869+4027
7:13 j as the LORD had said. 889+3869
7:20 Moses and Aaron did j as 889+3869+4027
7:22 j as the LORD had said. 889+3869
8:15 j as the LORD had said. 889+3869
8:19 j as the LORD had said. 889+3869
9:12 j as the LORD had said to Moses. 889+3869
9:35 j as the LORD had said through Moses. 889+3869
10:8 "But j who will be going?" 2256+4769+4769
10:29 "J as you say," Moses replied, 4027
12:28 The Israelites did j what 889+3869+4027
12:50 All the Israelites did j what 889+3869+4027
27:8 be made j as you were shown on 889+3869+4027
28:27 to the seam j above the waistband of 4946+5087
31:11 them j as I commanded you." 889+3869+3972
36:1 j as the LORD has commanded." 889+3972+4200
39:20 to the seam j above the waistband of 4946+5087
39:32 The Israelites did everything j as 889+3869+4027
39:42 The Israelites had done all the work j as the LORD had commanded 889+3869+4027
39:43 saw that they had done it j as 889+3869+4027
40:15 Anoint them j as you anointed their father, 889+3869
40:16 Moses did everything j as 889+3869+4027
Lev 4:10 j as the fat is removed from 889+3869
4:20 this bull j as he did with the bull 889+3869+4027
4:31 j as the fat is removed from the 889+3869
4:35 j as the fat is removed from the lamb of 889+3869
12:2 j as she is unclean during her monthly 3869
15:25 j as in the days of her period. 3869
Nu 1:54 The Israelites did all this j as 889+3869+4027
5:4 They did j as the LORD had 889+3869+4027
8:3 j as the LORD commanded Moses. 889+3869
8:20 the Levites j as the LORD 889+3869+3972+4027
8:22 They did with the Levites j as 889+3869+4027
9:5 The Israelites did everything j as 889+3869+4027
11:19 You will not eat it for j one day, NIH
14:17 j as you have declared: 889+3869
14:19 j as you have pardoned them from 889+3869
15:27 " 'But if j one person sins unintentionally, NIH
17:11 Moses did j as the LORD 889+3869+4027
18:18 j as the breast of the wave offering and 3869
20:9 j as he commanded him. 889+3869
22:38 "But can I say j anything? NIH
32:27 j as our lord says." 889+3869
Dt 2:12 j as Israel did in the land 889+3869
6:3 j as the LORD, the God of your fathers, 889+3869
27:3 j as the LORD, the God of your fathers, 889+3869
28:63 J as it pleased the LORD 889+3869
30:9 j as he delighted in your fathers, 889+3869
32:4 and all his ways are j. 5477
32:4 upright and j is he. 3838
32:47 They are not j idle words for you— 3954
32:50 j as your brother Aaron died on Mount Hor 889+3869
Jos 1:17 J as we fully obeyed Moses, 3869
4:10 j as Moses had directed Joshua. 889+3869+3972
4:14 j as they had revered Moses. 889+3869
4:23 to the Jordan j what he had done to 889+3869
8:34 j as it is written in the Book of the Law. 3869
10:32 j as he had done to Libnah. 889+3869+3972
10:35 j as they had done to Lachish. 889+3869+3972
10:37 J as at Eglon, they totally 889+3869+3972
10:40 j as the LORD, the God of Israel, 889+3869
11:23 j as the LORD had directed 889+3869+3972
14:5 j as the LORD had commanded 889+3869+4027
14:10 "Now then, j as the LORD promised, 889+3869
14:11 I'm j as vigorous to go out to battle now 3869
14:12 I will drive them out j as he said." 889+3869
21:44 j as he had sworn to their forefathers. 889+3869+3972
23:10 fights for you, j as he promised. 889+3869
23:15 But j as every good promise of 889+3869
Jdg 2:15 j as he had sworn to them. 889+3869
6:39 Let me make j one more request. 421
7:13 Gideon arrived j as a man was telling 2180
7:19 j after they had changed the guard. 421
8:7 Then Gideon replied, "J for that, 4027+4200
9:2 sons rule over you, or j one man?' NIH
9:35 the entrance to the city gate j as Abimelech 2256
11:36 Do to me j as you promised, 889+3869
16:28 O God, please strengthen me j once more, 421
18:19 priest rather than j one man's household?" NIH
Ru 2:4 J then Boaz arrived from Bethlehem 2180+2256
1Sa 4:16 "I *have j* come from the battle line; AIT
9:12 he has j come to our town today, 3954
11:5 J then Saul was returning from the fields, 2180
13:10 J as he finished making the offering, 3869
24:18 You have j now told me of 2021+3427
25:21 David *had j* said, "It's been useless— AIT
25:25 is j like his name—his name is Fool, 3869+4027
2Sa 3:22 J then David's men and Joab returned 2180+2256
8:15 doing what was j and right for all 5477
10:2 j as his father showed kindness to me." 889+3869
11:10 "Haven't you *j* come from a distance? AIT
13:35 has happened j as your servant said." 3869+4027
16:19 J as I served your father, 889+3869
18:10 "I j saw Absalom hanging in an oak tree." 2180
18:29 "I saw great confusion j as Joab was about NIH
19:5 your men, who have j saved your life 2021+3427
21:9 j as the barley harvest was beginning. 928
1Ki 5:12 j as he had promised him. 889+3869
8:20 j as the LORD promised, 889+3869
8:53 j as you declared through your 889+3869
8:56 rest to his people Israel j as 889+3869+3972
20:4 The king of Israel answered, "J as you say, 3869
22:53 to anger, j as his father had done. 889+3869+3972
2Ki 4:3 Don't ask for j a few. 5070
4:17 j as Elisha had told her, 889
5:22 company of the prophets have j come 2296+6964
7:10 and the tents left j as they were." 889+3869
7:17 j as the man of God had foretold when 889+3869
8:5 J as Gehazi was telling the king 2256
11:9 of a hundred did j as Jehoiada 889+3869+3972
15:3 j as his father Amaziah had done. 889+3869+3972
15:34 j as his father Uzziah had done. 889+3869+3972
16:16 did j as King Ahaz had ordered. 889+3869+3972
18:3 j as his father David had done. 889+3869+3972
23:19 J as he had done at Bethel, 3869+3972
23:32 j as his fathers had done. 889+3869+3972
23:37 j as his fathers had done. 889+3869+3972
24:9 j as his father had done. 889+3869+3972
24:19 j as Jehoiakim had done. 889+3869+3972
1Ch 9:19 for guarding the thresholds of the Tent j as 2256
18:14 doing *what* was j and right for all 5477
24:31 j as their brothers the descendants 4200+6645
26:12 j as their relatives had. 4200+6645
2Ch 6:10 j as the LORD promised, 889+3869
12:6 "The LORD is j." 7404
21:13 j as the house of Ahab did. 3869
23:8 men of Judah did j as Jehoiada 889+3869+3972
26:4 j as his father Amaziah had done. 889+3869+3972
27:2 j as his father Uzziah had done, 889+3869+3972
29:2 j as his father David had done. 889+3869+3972
32:17 "J as the gods of the peoples of the other 3869
Ne 6:8 you are j making it up out of your head." 3954
9:13 and laws that are j and right, 3838
9:33 all that has happened to us, you have been j; 7404
Est 2:20 nationality j as Mordecai had told her 889+3869
6:4 Now Haman *had j* entered the outer court AIT
6:10 and do j as you have suggested 889+3869+4027
7:8 J as the king returned from 2256
Job 33:6 I am j like you before God; 3869+7023
34:17 Will you condemn the j and mighty One? 7404
35:2 "Do you think this is j? 5477
Ps 35:25 "Aha, j what we wanted!" 5883
37:28 the j and will not forsake his faithful ones. 5477
37:30 and his tongue speaks *what* is j. 5477
90:4 like a day that *has j* gone by, AIT
99:4 in Jacob you have done *what* is j and right. 5477
111:7 The works of his hands are faithful and j; 5477

Ps 119:121 I have done what is righteous and j; 5477
Pr 1: 3 doing what is right and j and fair; 5477
2: 8 the course of the j and protects the way 5477
2: 9 what is right and j and fair— 5477
8: 8 All the words of my mouth are j; 7406
8:15 and rulers make laws that are j; 7406
12: 5 The plans of the righteous are j, 5477
21: 3 what is right and j is more acceptable to 5477
25:16 If you find honey, eat j enough— 1896
Ecc 2:13 j as light is better than darkness. 3869
12:10 Teacher searched to find j the right words, 2914
SS 4: 2 Your teeth are like a flock of sheep j shorn, 7892
Isa 20: 3 "J as my servant Isaiah has gone stripped and barefoot 889+3869
28: 9 to those j taken from the breast? AIT
32: 7 even when the plea of the needy is j. 5477
52:14 J as there were many who were appalled at him— 889+3869
58: 2 for j decisions and seem eager for God 7406
Jer 3: 4 Have you not j called to me: 4946+6964
4: 2 j and righteous way you swear, 5477
7:15 j as I did all your brothers, 889+3869
7:22 I did not j give them commands AIT
19:11 will smash this nation and this city j as 889+3869
22: 3 Do what is j and right. 5477
22:15 He did what was right and j, 7407
23: 5 and do what is j and right in the land. 5477
23:27 j as their fathers forgot my name 889+3869
31:28 J as I watched over them to uproot 889+3869
32: 8 "Then, j as the LORD had said, 3869
33:15 he will do what is j and right in the land. 5477
40: 3 he has done j as he said he would. 889+3869
44:17 will pour out drink offerings to her j as 889+3869
44:30 j as I handed Zedekiah king of Judah 889+3869
51:49 j as the slain in all the earth have fallen 1685
52: 2 j as Jehoiakim had done. 889+3869+3972
Eze 18: 5 a righteous man who does what is j 5477
18:19 Since the son has done what is j and right 5477
18:21 and keeps all my decrees and does what is j 5477
18:25 you say, 'The way of the Lord is not j.' 9419
18:27 and does what is j and right, 5477
18:29 'The way of the Lord is not j,' 9419
20:49 'Isn't he j telling parables?' " AIT
23:18 j as I had turned away from her sister. 889+3869
24:24 you will do j as he has done. 889+3869+3972
33:14 from his sin and does what is j and right— 5477
33:16 He has done what is j and right; 5477
33:17 'The way of the Lord is not j.' 9419
33:17 But it is their way that is not j. 9419
33:19 from his wickedness and does what is j 5477
33:20 you say, 'The way of the Lord is not j.' 9419
40:23 j as there was on the east. 2256
45: 9 and oppression and do what is j and right. 5477
Da 2: 9 there is j one penalty for you. NIH
2:41 J as you saw that the feet and toes were 10168
2:43 And j as you saw the iron mixed 10168
4:37 and all his ways are j. 10170
6:10 j as he had done before. 10168+10353+10619
9:13 J as it is written in the Law of Moses, 889+3869
Am 5:14 j as you say he is. 889+3869+4027
7: 1 and j as the second crop was coming up. 928
Ob 1:16 J as you drank on my holy hill, 889+3869
Mic 2:11 he would be j the prophet for this people! NIH
Zec 1: 6 j as he determined to do.' " 889+3869
7: 6 were you not j feasting for yourselves? AIT
8:14 "J as I had determined to bring disaster 889+3869
Mal 3:17 j as in compassion a man spares his 889+3869
Mt 8: 8 But j say the word, and my servant will be 3667
8:13 It will be done j as you believed it would." 6055
9:18 "My daughter has j died. 785
9:20 J then a woman who had been subject 2627+2779
12:13 j as sound as the other. 6055
14:36 to let the sick j touch the edge of his cloak, 3668
17: 3 J then there appeared before them Moses 2627
18:15 j between the two of you. 3668
18:33 on your fellow servant j as I had on you?' 6055
20:28 j as the Son of Man did not come to 6061
26:24 Son of Man will go j as it is written about 2777
28: 6 He is not here; he has risen, j as he said. 2777
Mk 1:23 J then a man in their synagogue 2317
4:36 they took him along, j as he was, 6055
5:28 If I j touch his clothes, I will be healed 1569+2779
5:36 "Don't be afraid; j believe." 3668
9:13 j as it is written about him." 2777
11: 2 and j as you enter it, you will find 2317
13:11 J say whatever is given you at the time, 247
14:16 and found things j as Jesus had told them. 2777
14:21 Son of Man will go j as it is written about 2777
14:43 J as he was speaking, Judas, 2285+2317
16: 2 j after sunrise, they were on their way to the tomb. 422+2463+3836
16: 7 There you will see him, j as he told you.' " 2777
Lk 1: 2 j as they were handed down to us 2777
2:20 which were j as they had been told. NIG
6:36 Be merciful, j as your Father is merciful. 2777
8:50 j believe, and she will be healed." 3668
11: 1 j as John taught his disciples." 2777
14:18 The first said, 'I have j bought a field, NIG
14:19 'I have j bought five yoke of oxen, NIG
14:20 "Still another said, 'I j got married, NIG
17:26 "J as it was in the days of Noah, 2777
17:30 "It will be j like this on the day the Son of Man is revealed. 899+2848+3836
19:32 and found it j as he had told them. 2777
22:13 and found things j as Jesus had told them. 2777
22:29 j as my Father conferred one on me, 2777
22:60 J as he was speaking, the rooster crowed. 4202
Lk 24:24 and found it j as the women had said, 2777+4048
Jn 3:14 J as Moses lifted up the snake in 2777
4:18 What you have j said is quite true." NIG
4:27 J then his disciples returned 2093+4047
4:42 "We no longer believe j because NIG
5:21 For j as the Father raises the dead 6061
5:23 that all may honor the Son j as they honor 2777
5:30 and my judgment is j, 1465
6:57 J as the living Father sent me and I live 2777
8:25 "J what I have been claiming all along," NIG
8:28 but speak j what the Father has taught me. 2777
10:15 j as the Father knows me and I know 2777
12:35 "You are going to have the light j a little NIG
12:50 whatever I say is j what the Father told me 2777
13: 1 It was j before the Passover Feast. NIG
13: 9 "not j my feet but my hands and my head 3667
13:33 and j as I told the Jews, so I tell you now: 2777
14:10 The words I say to you are not j my own. NIG
15:10 j as I have obeyed my Father's commands 2777
17:21 Father, j as you are in me and I am in you. 2777
21:10 some of the fish you have j caught." 3814
Ac 7:51 You are j like your fathers: 6055
10:47 They have received the Holy Spirit j 6055
14:13 whose temple was j outside the city, 4574
15: 8 the Holy Spirit to them, j as he did to us. 2777
15:11 we are saved, j as they are." 2848+4005+5573
18:14 J as Paul was about to speak, 1254
20: 3 a plot against him j as he was about to sail NIG
22: 3 of our fathers and was j as zealous for God NIG
26:10 And that is j what I did in Jerusalem. NIG
27:25 happen j as he told me. 2848+4005+4048+5573
27:33 J before dawn Paul urged them all 948+4005
Ro 1:13 j as I have had among the other Gentiles. 2777
1:17 j as it is written: "The righteous will live by 2777
3:26 so as to be j and the one who justifies 1465
4:18 j as it had been said to him, 2848
5: 6 at j the right time, when we were 2789+2848
5:12 j as sin entered the world through one man, 6061
5:18 j as the result of one trespass was 6055
5:19 For j as through the disobedience of the one 6061
5:21 j as sin reigned in death, 6061
6: 4 j as Christ was raised from the dead 6061
6:19 J as you used to offer the parts of your body 6061
9:13 J as it is written: "Jacob I loved, 2777
9:29 j as Isaiah said previously: "Unless 2777
11:30 J as you who were at one time disobedient 6061
12: 4 J as each of us has one body 2749
15: 7 then, j as Christ accepted you, 2777
1Co 5: 3 j as if I were present. 4048
9:18 then is my reward? J this: that in preaching NIG
11: 2 j as I passed them on to you. 2777
11: 5 it is j as though her head were shaved. 899+1651+2779+3836
12:11 j as he determines. 2777
12:18 j as he wanted them to be. 2777
14: 9 You will j be speaking into the air. NIG
15:31 I mean that, brothers—j as surely 3755
15:37 but j a seed, perhaps of wheat or NIG
15:49 And j as we have borne the likeness of 2777
16:10 carrying on the work of the Lord, j as I am. 6055
2Co 1: 5 For j as the sufferings of Christ flow over 2777
1: 7 because we know that j as you share 6055
1:14 of us j as we will boast of you in the day of 2749
7:14 j as everything we said to you was true, 6055
8: 7 But j as you excel in everything— 6061
10: 7 that we belong to Christ j as much as he. 2777
11: 3 But I am afraid that j as Eve was deceived 6055
11:16 then receive me j as you would a fool, 6055
Gal 2: 7 j as Peter had been to the Jews. 2777
3: 2 like to learn j one thing from you: 3668+4047
3:15 J as no one can set aside or add to 3940
3:20 however, does not represent j one party; NIG
4:18 so always and not j when I am with you. 3667
Eph 4: 4 j as you were called to one hope 2777
4:32 j as in Christ God forgave you. 2777
5: 2 j as Christ loved us and gave himself up 2777
5:25 j as Christ loved the church 2777
5:29 j as Christ does the church— 2777+2779
6: 5 j as you would obey Christ. 6055
Col 1: 6 j as it has been doing among you since 2777
2: 6 j as you received Christ Jesus as Lord, 6055
1Th 3: 6 But Timothy has j now come to us 785
3: 6 j as we also long to see you. 2749
3:12 j as ours does for you. 2749
4:11 to work with your hands, j as we told you, 2777
5:11 j as in fact you are doing. 2777
2Th 1: 6 God is j: He will pay back trouble to those 1465
3: 1 j as it was with you. 2777
2Ti 3: 8 J as Jannes and Jambres opposed Moses, 4005+5573
Heb 2: 2 disobedience received its j punishment, 1899
3: 2 j as Moses was faithful in all God's house. 6055
3: 3 j as the builder of a house has 2848+4012
3:15 As has j been said: "Today, if 1877+3306+3836
4: 2 preached to us, j as they did; 2749
4: 3 j as God has said, "So I declared on oath 2777
4:10 from his own work, j as God did from his. 6061
4:15 j as we are—yet was without sin. 2848
5: 4 he must be called by God, j as Aaron was. 2778
7: 4 J think how great he was: 1254
9:27 J as man is destined to die once, 2848+4012
10:37 For in j a very little while, NIG
Jas 2:10 at j one point is guilty of breaking all of it. NIG
5:17 Elijah was a man j like us. 3926
1Pe 1:15 But j as he who called you is holy, 2848
2Pe 2: 1 j as there will be false teachers among you. 6055
2:18 they entice people who are j escaping 3903
2Pe 3:15 j as our dear brother Paul also wrote you 2777
1Jn 1: 9 and j and will forgive us our sins 1465
2:27 j as it has taught you, remain in him. 2777
3: 3 purifies himself, j as he is pure. 2777
3: 7 right is righteous, j as he is righteous. 2777
2Jn 1: 4 j as the Father commanded us. 2777
Rev 2:27 j as I have received authority from my Father. 6055
3:21 j as I overcame and sat down with my Father on his throne. 6055
10: 7 j as he announced to his servants 6055
15: 3 J and true are your ways, King of the ages. 1465
16: 5 "You are j in these judgments, 1465
16: 7 true and j are your judgments." 1465
19: 2 for true and j are his judgments. 1465

JUSTICE (134) [JUST]

Ge 49:16 "Dan will provide j for his people as one 1906
Ex 23: 2 do not pervert j by siding with the crowd, NIH
23: 6 "Do not deny j to your poor people 5477
Lev 19:15 " 'Do not pervert j; 5477
Dt 16:19 Do not pervert j or show partiality. 5477
16:20 Follow j and justice alone, 7406
16:20 Follow justice and j alone, 7406
24:17 not deprive the alien or the fatherless of j, 5477
27:19 "Cursed is the man who withholds j from 5477
1Sa 8: 3 and accepted bribes and perverted j. 5477
2Sa 15: 4 see that he gets j." 7405
15: 6 to the king asking for j, 5477
1Ki 3:11 but for discernment in administering j, 5477
3:28 he had wisdom from God to administer j. 5477
7: 7 He built the throne hall, the Hall of J, 5477
10: 9 to maintain j and righteousness." 5477
2Ch 9: 8 to maintain j and righteousness." 5477
Ezr 7:25 and judges to administer j to all the people 10169
Est 1:13 to consult experts in matters of law and j, 1907
Job 8: 3 Does God pervert j? 5477
9:19 And if it is a matter of j, 5477
19: 7 though I call for help, there is no j. 5477
27: 2 who has denied me j, the Almighty, 5477
29:14 j was my robe and my turban. 5477
31:13 "If I have denied j to my menservants 5477
34: 5 'I am innocent, but God denies me j. 5477
34:12 that the Almighty would pervert j. 5477
34:17 Can he who hates j govern? 5477
36: 3 I will ascribe j to my Maker. 7406
36:17 judgment and j have taken hold of you. 5477
37:23 in his j and great righteousness, 5477
40: 8 "Would you discredit my j? 5477
Ps 7: 6 Awake, my God; decree j. 5477
9: 8 he will govern the peoples with j. 4797
9:16 The LORD is known by his j; 5477
11: 7 For the LORD is righteous, he loves j; 7407
33: 5 The LORD loves righteousness and j; 5477
36: 6 your j like the great deep. 5477
37: 6 the j of your cause like the noonday sun. 5477
45: 6 of j will be the scepter of your kingdom. 4793
72: 1 Endow the king with your j, O God, 5477
72: 2 your afflicted ones with j. 5477
89:14 and j are the foundation of your throne; 5477
97: 2 righteousness and j are the foundation 5477
99: 4 The King is mighty, he loves j— 5477
101: 1 I will sing of your love and j; 5477
103: 6 The LORD works righteousness and j 5477
106: 3 Blessed are they who maintain j, 5477
112: 5 who conducts his affairs with j. 5477
140:12 that the LORD secures j for the poor 1907
Pr 8:20 along the paths of j, 5477
16:10 and his mouth should not betray j. 5477
17:23 a bribe in secret to pervert the course of j. 5477
18: 5 the wicked or to deprive the innocent of j. 5477
19:28 A corrupt witness mocks at j, 5477
21:15 When j is done, it brings joy to the 5477
28: 5 Evil men do not understand j, 5477
29: 4 By j a king gives a country stability, 5477
29: 7 The righteous care about j for the poor, 1907
29:26 but it is from the LORD that man gets j. 5477
Ecc 3:16 wickedness was there, in the place of j— 7406
5: 8 and j and rights denied, 5477
Isa 1:17 Seek j, encourage the oppressed. 5477
1:21 She once was full of j; 5477
1:27 Zion will be redeemed with j, 5477
5: 7 And he looked for j, but saw bloodshed; 5477
5:16 LORD Almighty will be exalted by his j, 5477
5:23 but deny j to the innocent. 7407
9: 7 with j and righteousness from that time on 5477
10: 2 the poor of their rights and withhold j from 5477
11: 4 with j he will give decisions for the poor of 4793
16: 5 in judging seeks j and speeds the cause 5477
28: 6 be a spirit of j to him who sits in judgment, 5477
28:17 I will make j the measuring line 5477
29:21 false testimony deprive the innocent of j. NIH
30:18 For the LORD is a God of j. 5477
32: 1 in righteousness and rulers will rule with j. 5477
32:16 J will dwell in the desert 5477
33: 5 he will fill Zion with j and righteousness. 5477
42: 1 on him and he will bring j to the nations. 5477
42: 3 In faithfulness he will bring forth j; 5477
42: 4 or be discouraged till he establishes j 5477
51: 4 my j will become a light to the nations. 5477
51: 5 and my arm will bring j to the nations. 9149
56: 1 "Maintain j and do what is right, 5477
59: 4 No one calls for j; 7406
59: 8 there is no j in their paths. 5477
59: 9 So j is far from us, 5477
59:11 We look for j, but find none; 5477

Isa 59:14 So j is driven back, 5477
59:15 and was displeased that there was no j. 5477
61: 8 "For I, the LORD, love j; 5477
Jer 9:24 j and righteousness on earth, 5477
10:24 Correct me, LORD, but only with j— 5477
12: 1 Yet I would speak with you about your j: 5477
21:12 " 'Administer j every morning; 5477
30:11 I will discipline you but only with j; 5477
46:28 I will discipline you but only with j; 5477
La 3:36 to deprive a man of j— 8190
Eze 22:29 and mistreat the alien, denying them j. 5477
34:16 I will shepherd the flock with j. 5477
Hos 2:19 I will betroth you in righteousness and j, 5477
12: 6 maintain love and j, 5477
Am 2: 7 of the ground and deny j to the oppressed. 2006
5: 7 You who turn j into bitterness 5477
5:12 deprive the poor of j in the courts. 5742
5:15 maintain j in the courts. 5477
5:24 But let j roll on like a river, 5477
6:12 But you have turned j into poison and 5477
Mic 3: 1 Should you not know j, 5477
3: 8 and with j and might, 5477
3: 9 who despise j and distort all that is right; 5477
Hab 1: 4 and j never prevails. 5477
1: 4 so that j is perverted. 5477
Zep 3: 5 Morning by morning he dispenses his j, 5477
Zec 7: 9 "This is what the LORD Almighty says: 'Administer true j; 5477
Mal 2:17 or "Where is the God of j?" 5477
3: 5 and deprive aliens of j, 5742
Mt 12:18 and he will proclaim j to the nations. 3213
12:20 till he leads j to victory. 3213
23:23 j, mercy and faithfulness. 3213
Lk 11:42 but you neglect j and the love of God. 3213
18: 3 'Grant me j against my adversary.' 1688
18: 5 I will see that she gets j, 1688
18: 7 not God bring about j for his chosen ones, 1689
18: 8 I tell you, he will see that they get j, 1689
Ac 8:33 In his humiliation he was deprived of j. 3213
17:31 a day when he will judge the world with j 1466
28: 4 J has not allowed him to live." 1472
Ro 3:25 He did this to demonstrate his j, 1466
3:26 to demonstrate his j at the present time, 1466
2Co 7:11 readiness to see j done. 1689
Heb 11:33 through faith conquered kingdoms, administered j, 1466
Rev 19:11 With j he judges and makes war. 1466

JUSTIFICATION (4) [JUST]

Eze 16:52 you have furnished some j for your sisters. 7136
Ro 4:25 for our sins and was raised to life for our j. 1470
5:16 but the gift followed many trespasses and brought j. 1468
5:18 the result of one act of righteousness was j 1470

JUSTIFIED (22) [JUST]

Ps 51: 4 when you speak and j when you judge. 2342
Lk 18:14 went home j before God. 1467
Ac 13:39 Through him everyone who believes is j 1467
13:39 from everything you could not be j from 1467
Ro 3:24 and are j freely by his grace through 1467
3:28 a man is j by faith apart from observing 1467
4: 2 If, in fact, Abraham was j by works, 1467
5: 1 since we have been j through faith, 1467
5: 9 Since we have now been j by his blood, 1467
8:30 those he called, he also j; 1467
8:30 those he j, he also glorified. 1467
10:10 your heart that you believe and are j, 1466+1650
1Co 6:11 you were j in the name of the Lord Jesus 1467
Gal 2:16 that a man is not j by observing the law, 1467
2:16 be j by faith in Christ and not by observing 1467
2:16 by observing the law no one will be j. 1467
2:17 "If, while we seek to be j in Christ, 1467
3:11 Clearly no one is j before God by the law, 1467
3:24 to lead us to Christ that we might be j 1467
5: 4 trying to be j by law have been alienated 1467
Tit 3: 7 having been j by his grace, 1467
Jas 2:24 You see that a person is j by what he does 1467

JUSTIFIES (3) [JUST]

Ro 3:26 the one who j those who have faith in Jesus. 1467
4: 5 not work but trusts God who j the wicked, 1467
8:33 It is God who j. 1467

JUSTIFY (7) [JUST]

Est 7: 4 no such distress would j disturbing 8750
Job 40: 8 Would you condemn me to j yourself? 7405
Isa 53:11 by his knowledge my righteous servant will j many, 7405
Lk 10:29 But he wanted to j himself, 1467
16:15 "You are the ones who j yourselves in 1467
Ro 3:30 who will j the circumcised by faith and 1467
Gal 3: 8 The Scripture foresaw that God would j 1467

JUSTIFYING (1) [JUST]

Job 32: 2 angry with Job for j himself rather than God 7405

JUSTLE (KJV) See RUSHING

JUSTLY (6) [JUST]

Ps 58: 1 Do you rulers indeed speak j? 7406
67: 4 the peoples j and guide the nations of 4793
Jer 7: 5 and deal with each other j, 5477
Mic 6: 8 To act j and to love mercy and 5477
Lk 23:41 We are punished j, 1469
1Pe 2:23 he entrusted himself to him who judges j. 1469

JUSTUS (3) [BARSABBAS, JESUS, TITIUS]

Ac 1:23 Joseph called Barsabbas (also known as J) 2688
18: 7 to the house of Titius J, 2688
Col 4:11 Jesus, who is called J, 2688

JUTTAH (3)

Jos 15:55 Maon, Carmel, Ziph, J, 3420
21:16 J and Beth Shemesh, together 3420
1Ch 6:59 J and Beth Shemesh, 3420

K

KABZEEL (3)

Jos 15:21 toward the boundary of Edom were: K, 7696
2Sa 23:20 of Jehoiada was a valiant fighter from K, 7696
1Ch 11:22 of Jehoiada was a valiant fighter from K, 7696

KADESH (14) [EN MISHPAT, KADESH BARNEA, MERIBAH KADESH]

Ge 14: 7 went to En Mishpat (that is, K), 7729
16:14 it is still there, between K and Bered. 7729
20: 1 the Negev and lived between K and Shur. 7729
Nu 13:26 and the whole Israelite community at K in 7729
20: 1 and they stayed at K. 7729
20:14 Moses sent messengers from K to the king 7729
20:16 "Now we are here at K, 7729
20:22 from K and came to Mount Hor. 7729
33:36 They left Ezion Geber and camped at K, 7729
33:37 They left K and camped at Mount Hor, 7729
Dt 1:46 And so you stayed in K many days— 7729
Jdg 11:16 the desert to the Red Sea and on to K. 7729
11:17 So Israel stayed at K. 7729
Ps 29: 8 the LORD shakes the Desert of K. 7729

KADESH BARNEA (10) [KADESH]

Nu 32: 8 when I sent them from K to look 7732
34: 4 on to Zin and go south of K. 7732
Dt 1: 2 to K by the Mount Seir road.) 7732
1:19 and so we reached K. 7732
2:14 from the time we left K until we crossed 7732
9:23 the LORD sent you out from K, 7732
Jos 10:41 Joshua subdued them from K 7732
14: 6 said to Moses the man of God at K about 7732
14: 7 the servant of the LORD sent me from K 7732
15: 3 and went over to the south of K. 7732

KADMIEL (8)

Ezr 2:40 the descendants of Jeshua and K (through 7718
3: 9 Jeshua and his sons and brothers and K 7718
Ne 7:43 of Jeshua (through K through the line 7718
9: 4 Jeshua, Bani, K, Shebaniah, Bunni, 7718
9: 5 Jeshua, K, Bani, Hashabneiah, Sherebiah, 7718
10: 9 Binnui of the sons of Henadad, K, 7718
12: 8 The Levites were Jeshua, Binnui, K, 7718
12:24 Jeshua son of K, and their associates, 7718

KADMONITES (1)

Ge 15:19 the land of the Kenites, Kenizzites, K, 7720

KAIN (1)

Jos 15:57 K, Gibeah and Timnah— 7805

KALLAI (1)

Ne 12:20 of Sallu's, K; of Amok's, Eber; 7834

KAMAI See LEB KAMAI

KAMON (1)

Jdg 10: 5 When Jair died, he was buried in K. 7852

KANAH (3)

Jos 16: 8 the border went west to the K Ravine 7867
17: 9 boundary continued south to the K Ravine. 7867
19:28 It went to Abdon, Rehob, Hammon and K, 7867

KAREAH (14)

2Ki 25:23 of Nethaniah, Johanan son of K, 7945
Jer 40: 8 Johanan and Jonathan the sons of K, 7945
40:13 son of K and all the army officers still in 7945
40:15 of K said privately to Gedaliah in Mizpah, 7945
40:16 of Ahikam said to Johanan son of K, 7945
41:11 son of K and all the army officers who were 7945
41:13 son of K and the army officers who were 7945
41:14 and went over to Johanan son of K. 7945
41:16 son of K and all the army officers who were 7945
42: 1 son of K and Jezaniah son of Hoshaiah, 7945
42: 8 son of K and all the army officers who were 7945
43: 2 of Hoshaiah and Johanan son of K and all 7945
43: 4 son of K and all the army officers and all 7945
43: 5 of K and all the army officers led away all 7945

KARKA (1)

Jos 15: 3 up to Addar and curved around to K. 7978

KARKOR (1)

Jdg 8:10 Now Zebah and Zalmunna were in K with 7980

KARNAIM (1)

Am 6:13 "Did we not take K by our own strength?" 7969

KARTAH (2)

Jos 21:34 from the tribe of Zebulun, Jokneam, K, 7985
1Ch 6:77 K, Rimmono and Tabor, 7985

KARTAN (1)

Jos 21:32 and K, together with their pasturelands— 7986

KATTATH (1)

Jos 19:15 Included were K, Nahalal, Shimron, 7793

KATYDID (1)

Lev 11:22 Of these you may eat any kind of locust, k, 6155

KAZIN See ETH KAZIN

KEBAR (8)

Eze 1: 1 I was among the exiles by the K River, 3894
1: 3 the K River in the land of the Babylonians. 3894
3:15 at Tel Abib near the K River. 3894
3:23 like the glory I had seen by the K River, 3894
10:15 I had seen by the K River. 3894
10:20 the God of Israel by the K River, 3894
10:22 as those I had seen by the K River. 3894
43: 3 like the visions I had seen by the K River, 3894

KEDAR (11) [KEDAR'S]

Ge 25:13 Nebaioth the firstborn of Ishmael, K, 7723
1Ch 1:29 Nebaioth the firstborn of Ishmael, K, 7723
Ps 120: 5 that I live among the tents of K! 7723
SS 1: 5 dark like the tents of K, 7723
Isa 21:16 all the pomp of K will come to an end. 7723
21:17 the warriors of K, will be few." 1201+7723
42:11 let the settlements where K lives rejoice. 7723
Jer 2:10 send to K and observe closely; 7723
49:28 Concerning K and the kingdoms of Hazor, 7723
49:28 attack K and destroy the people of the East. 7723
Eze 27:21 the princes of K were your customers; 7723

KEDAR'S (1) [KEDAR]

Isa 60: 7 All K flocks will be gathered to you, 7723

KEDEMAH (2)

Ge 25:15 Hadad, Tema, Jetur, Naphish and K. 7715
1Ch 1:31 and K. These were the sons of Ishmael. 7715

KEDEMOTH (4)

Dt 2:26 From the desert of K I sent messengers 7717
Jos 13:18 Jahaz, K, Mephaath, 7717
21:37 K and Mephaath, together 7717
1Ch 6:79 K and Mephaath, together 7717

KEDESH (11)

Jos 12:22 the king of K one 7730
15:23 K, Hazor, Ithnan, 7730
19:37 K, Edrei, En Hazor, 7730
20: 7 So they set apart K in Galilee in 7730
21:32 K in Galilee (a city of refuge 7730
Jdg 4: 6 She sent for Barak son of Abinoam from K 7730
4: 9 So Deborah went with Barak to K, 7730
4:11 by the great tree in Zaanannim near K. 7730
2Ki 15:29 Abel Beth Maacah, Janoah, K and Hazor. 7730
1Ch 6:72 from the tribe of Issachar they received K, 7730
6:76 from the tribe of Naphtali they received K 7730

KEDORLAOMER (5)

Ge 14: 1 K king of Elam and Tidal king of Goiim 3906
14: 4 twelve years they had been subject to K, 3906
14: 5 K and the kings allied with him went out 3906
14: 9 against K king of Elam, Tidal king 3906
14:17 After Abram returned from defeating K and 3906

KEEN (1)

Da 5:12 k mind and knowledge and understanding, 10339

KEEP (325) [KEEPER, KEEPERS, KEEPING, KEEPS, KEPT, SAFEKEEPING]

Ge 6:19 to k them alive with you. 2649
7: 3 to k their various kinds alive 2649
14:21 the people and k the goods for yourself." 4374
17: 9 "As for you, you must k my covenant, 9068

Ge 17:10 the covenant *you are to* **k:** 9068
18:19 and his household after him *to* **k** the way of 9068
31:49 the LORD **k watch** between you and me 7595
32:16 and **k** some space between the herds." 8492
33: 9 **K** what you have for yourself." 2118
38: 9 the ground to **k from** producing offspring 1194
38:23 Then Judah said, *"Let her* **k** what she has, 4374
42: 1 "Why *do you k* **looking at each other?"** AIT
47:24 other four-fifths you *may* **k** as seed for 2118+4200
Ex 5: 9 so that *they k* **working** and pay no attention AIT
5:17 That is why you *k* **saying,** AIT
12:42 on this night all the Israelites are to **k** vigil 4200
13:10 *You must* **k** this ordinance at the appointed 9068
15:26 to his commands and **k** all his decrees, 9068
16:19 "No one *is to* **k** any of it until morning." 3855
16:23 Save whatever is left and **k** it until morning. 5466
16:28 to **k** my commands and my instructions? 9068
16:32 of manna and **k** it for the generations 5466
19: 5 if you obey me fully and **k** my covenant, 9068
20: 6 and **k** my commandments. 9068
20:20 will be with you to **k** you **from** sinning." 1194
21:36 yet the owner *did* not **k** it **penned up,** 9068
27:21 *to* **k** the lamps burning before the LORD 6885
Lev 7: 8 a burnt offering for anyone *may* **k** its hide 2118
13: 5 *to* **k** him **in isolation** another seven days. 6037
13:33 *to* **k** him **in isolation** another seven days. 6037
15:31 **k** the Israelites **separate** from things that 5692
18: 5 **K** my decrees and laws, 9068
18:26 But you *must* **k** my decrees and my laws. 9068
18:30 **K** my requirements and do not follow any 9068
19:19 " '**K** my decrees. 9068
19:37 " '**K** all my decrees and all my laws 9068
20: 8 **K** my decrees and follow them. 9068
20:22 " '**K** all my decrees and laws 9068
22: 9 " 'The priests *are to* **k** my requirements so 9068
22:31 "**K** my commands and follow them. 9068
26: 9 and *I will* **k** my covenant with you. 7756
Nu 6:24 " ' "The LORD bless you and **k** you; 9068
11:13 *They k* **wailing** to me, AIT
15:22 " 'Now if you unintentionally fail *to* **k** any 6913
22:16 not *let anything* **k** *you* from coming to me, 4979
36: 7 for every Israelite *shall* **k** the tribal land 1815
36: 9 for each Israelite tribe *is to* **k** the land 1815
Dt 4: 2 but **k** the commands of the LORD 9068
4:40 **K** his decrees and commands, 9068
5:10 and **k** my commandments. 9068
5:29 to fear me and **k** all my commands always, 9068
6:17 **Be sure to k** the commands of 9068+9068
7: 9 of those who love him and **k** his commands. 9068
7:12 the LORD your God *will* **k** his covenant 9068
7:15 LORD *will* **k** you **free** from every disease. 6073
8: 2 whether or not *you would* **k** his commands. 9068
11: 1 and **k** his requirements, 9068
13: 4 **K** his commands and obey him; 9068
22: 2 with you and **k** it until he comes looking 2118
23: 9 **k** away from everything impure. 9068
26:17 that you *will* **k** his decrees, 9068
26:18 and that you *are to* **k** all his commands. 9068
27: 1 "**K** all these commands 9068
28: 9 if *you* **k** the commands of the LORD 9068
28:41 and daughters but you *will* not **k** them, 2118+4200
30:10 the LORD your God and **k** his commands 9068
30:16 to walk in his ways, and to **k** his commands, 9068
Jos 3: 4 But **k** a distance of about a thousand yards 2118
6:18 But **k away** from the devoted things, 9068
7:11 which I commanded them to **k.** NIH
22: 5 But be very careful to **k** the commandment 6913
Jdg 2:22 to test Israel and see whether they *will* **k** 9068
6:11 in a winepress to **k** it from the Midianites. 5674
1Sa 1:14 "How long *will you* **k on getting drunk?** 8910
2: 3 *"Do* not **k** talking so proudly 8049
6: 9 but *k* **watching** it. AIT
2Sa 7:25 **k** forever the promise you have made 7756
13:13 not **k** me from being married to you." 4979
14:18 *"Do* not **k** from me the answer 3948
1Ki 1: 1 not *k* **warm** even when they put covers AIT
1: 2 so that our lord the king *may k* **warm."** AIT
2: 3 and **k** his decrees and commands, 9068
2: 4 that the LORD *may* **k** his promise to me: 7756
2:43 then *did you* not **k** your oath to the LORD 9068
6:12 and **k** all my commands and obey them, 9068
8:23 you *who* **k** your covenant of love 9068
8:25 **k** for your servant David my father 9068
8:58 in all his ways and to **k** the commands, 9068
11:10 Solomon *did* not **k** the LORD's command. 9068
15: 5 *had* not **failed to k** any of the LORD's 4946+6073
18: 5 **k** the horses and mules **alive** 2649
2Ki 10:31 Yet Jehu was not careful to **k** the law of 928+2143
17:19 and even Judah *did* not **k** the commands of 9068
17:37 You must always be careful to **k** the decrees 6913
21: 8 and will **k** the whole Law NIH
23: 3 to follow the LORD and **k** his commands, 9068
1Ch 4:10 and **k** me from harm so that I will be free 6913
10:13 *he did* not **k** the word of the LORD and 9068
22:12 so that you *may* **k** the law of the LORD 9068
29:18 **k** this desire in the hearts 9068
29:18 and **k** their hearts **loyal** to you. 3922
29:19 wholehearted devotion to **k** your commands 9068
2Ch 2:18 foremen over them to **k** the people **working** 6268
6:14 you *who* **k** your covenant of love 9068
6:16 **k** for your servant David my father 9068
23: 4 on the Sabbath are to **k watch** *at* the doors, 8788
34:31 to follow the LORD and **k** his commands, 9068
Ne 5:13 *who does* not **k** this promise. 7756
13:22 **k** the Sabbath day **holy.** 7727
Est 3:11 "**K** the money," the king said to Haman, 5989
Job 4: 2 But who can **k** from speaking? 6806

Job 7:11 "Therefore I *will* not **k silent;** 3104+7023
13:13 "*K* **silent** and let me speak; AIT
13:27 *you* **k close watch on** all my paths 9068
14:16 but not **k track of** my sin. 9068
16: 3 What ails you that *you k on* **arguing?** AIT
22:15 *Will you* **k** *to* the old path 9068
30:10 They detest me and **k** *their* **distance;** 8178
33:17 to turn man from wrongdoing and **k** him 4059
34:30 to **k** a godless man from ruling, NIH
36: 6 *He does* not **k** the wicked **alive** but gives 2649
41: 3 *Will he* **k** begging you for mercy? 8049
Ps 12: 7 you *will* **k** us **safe** and protect us 9068
16: 1 **K** me **safe,** O God, for in you I take refuge. 9068
17: 8 **K** me as the apple of your eye; 9068
18:28 You, O LORD, **k** my lamp **burning;** 239
19:13 **K** your servant also from willful sins; 3104
22:29 *those who* cannot **k** themselves **alive.** 2649
25:10 and faithful for *those who* **k** the demands 5915
27: 5 of trouble *he will* **k** me **safe** in his dwelling; 7621
31:20 in your dwelling *you* **k** them **safe** 7621
33:19 from death and **k** them **alive** in famine. 2649
34:13 **k** your tongue from evil and your lips 5915
37:34 Wait for the LORD and **k** his way. 9068
39: 1 "I will watch my ways and **k** my tongue NIH
78: 7 but *would* **k** his commands. 5915
78:10 *they did* not **k** God's covenant and refused 9068
78:56 *they did* not **k** his statutes. 9068
83: 1 O God, do not **k** silent; NIH
89:31 and fail *to* **k** my commands, 9068
103:18 with *those who* **k** his covenant 9068
105:45 that *they might* **k** his precepts 9068
106:23 in the breach before him to **k** his wrath 8740
119: 2 Blessed are *they who* **k** his statutes 5915
119: 9 How *can* a young man **k** his way **pure?** 2342
119:22 for *I* **k** your statutes. 5915
119:29 **K** me from deceitful ways; 6073
119:33 then *I will* **k** them to the end. 5915
119:34 and *I will* **k** your law and obey it 5915
119:55 O LORD, and *I will* **k** your law. 9068
119:69 I **k** your precepts with all my heart. 5915
119:115 that *I may* **k** the commands of my God! 5915
119:146 save me and *I will* **k** your statutes. 9068
121: 7 The LORD *will* **k** you from all harm— 9068
132:12 if your sons **k** my covenant and 9068
140: 4 **K** me, O LORD, from the hands of 9068
141: 3 **k** watch over the door of my lips. NIH
141: 9 **K** me from the snares they have laid for me, 9068
Pr 2:20 the ways of good men and **k** *to* the paths of 9068
3: 1 but **k** my commands *in* your heart, 5915
3:26 be your confidence and *will* **k** your foot 9068
4: 4 **k** my commands and you will live. 9068
4:21 **k** them within your heart; 9068
4:24 **k** corrupt talk **far** from your lips. 8178
4:27 **k** your foot from evil. 6073
5: 8 **K** *to* a path **far** from her, 8178
6:20 **k** your father's commands and do not 5915
7: 1 **k** my words and store up my commands 9068
7: 2 **K** my commands and you will live; 9068
7: 5 they *will* **k** you from the adulteress, 9068
8:32 blessed are *those who* **k** my ways. 9068
15:24 for the wise to **k** him from going down to 6073
20:28 Love and faithfulness **k** a king **safe;** 5915
22: 3 but the simple *k* **going** and suffer for it. AIT
22:12 of the LORD **k watch over** knowledge, 5915
22:18 when *you* **k** them in your heart and have all 9068
23:19 **k** your heart on the **right** 886
23:26 give me your heart and *let* your eyes **k** to 5915
27:12 but the simple *k* **going** and suffer for it. AIT
28: 4 but *those who* **k** the law resist them. 9068
30: 8 **K** falsehood and lies **far** from me; 8178
Ecc 3: 6 a time to **k** and a time to throw away, 9068
4:11 if two lie down together, they will *k* **warm.** AIT
4:11 But how *can* one *k* **warm** alone? AIT
12:13 Fear God and **k** his commandments, 9068
Isa 7: 4 'Be careful, *k* **calm** and don't be afraid. AIT
7:21 a man *will* **k alive** a young cow 2649
19:21 to the LORD and **k** them. 8966
26: 3 *You will* **k** *in* perfect peace him whose mind 5915
28:24 *Does he* **k on breaking up** and harrowing AIT
29:23 *they will* **k** my name **holy;** 7727
42: 6 *I will* **k** you and will make you to be 5915
47:12 "**K on,** then, with your magic spells and 6641
49: 8 *I will* **k** you and will make you to be 5915
56: 4 "To the eunuchs who **k** my Sabbaths, 9068
56: 6 all *who* **k** the Sabbath without desecrating it 9068
58:13 "If *you* **k** your feet from breaking 8740
62: 1 For Zion's sake *I will* not *k* **silent,** AIT
64:12 *Will you k* **silent** and punish us AIT
65: 5 say, '**K away;** don't come near 448+3870+7928
65: 6 *I will* not *k* **silent** but will pay back AIT
Jer 4:19 *I* cannot *k* **silent.** AIT
11: 8 to follow but that *they did* not **k.'** " 6913
13:14 or mercy or compassion to **k** me **from** 4946
14:13 the prophets *k* **telling** them, AIT
15: 6 *"You* **k on** backsliding. 2143
16:11 They forsook me and *did* not **k** my law. 9068
17:15 They *k* **saying** to me, AIT
17:18 but *k* me from **shame;** AIT
17:18 let them be terrified, but *k* me from **terror.** AIT
17:22 **k** the Sabbath day **holy,** 7727
17:24 **k** the Sabbath day **holy** 7727
17:27 **k** the Sabbath day **holy** 7727
23:17 *They* **k saying** to those who despise me, 606+606
23:37 This is what *you k* **saying** to a prophet: AIT
42: 4 the LORD says and *will* **k** nothing **back** 4979
44:25 **K** your vows! 7756+7756
50: 2 **k** nothing **back,** but say, 3948

La 1:11 for food to **k themselves alive.** 5883+8740
1:19 food *to* **k themselves alive** 906+4392+5883+8740
Eze 11:20 and be careful *to* **k** my laws. 6913
18:19 and has been careful *to* **k** all my decrees, 6913
20: 9 I did what would **k** it **from** being profaned 1194
20:14 I did what would **k** it **from** being profaned 1194
20:18 the statutes of your fathers or **k** their laws 9068
20:19 and be careful *to* **k** my laws. 6913
20:20 **K** my Sabbaths **holy,** 7727
20:21 they were not careful to **k** my laws— 6913
20:22 of my name I did what would **k** it **from** 1194
24:17 *K* your turban **fastened** AIT
24:23 You will **k** your turbans on your heads NIH
36:27 and be careful *to* **k** my laws. 6913
37:24 and be careful *to* **k** my decrees. 6913
44:20 **k** *the* **hair** of their heads **trimmed.** 4080+4080
44:24 *They are to* **k** my laws and my decrees 9068
44:24 and *they are to* **k** my Sabbaths **holy.** 7727
46:17 the servant *may* **k** it until the year 2118+4200
Da 5:17 "You *may* **k** your gifts for yourself 10201
Hab 1:17 Is he to **k on** emptying his net, 9458
Zec 3: 7 in my ways and **k** my requirements, 9068
11:12 give me my pay; but if not, **k** it." 2532
12: 4 *"I will* **k** a **watchful** eye over the house 7219
Mt 5:33 but **k** the oaths you have made to the Lord.' *625*
6: 7 *do* not *k on* **babbling** like pagans, *AIT*
10:10 for the worker is worth his **k.** *5575*
24:42 "Therefore **k watch,** because you do *1213*
25:13 "Therefore **k watch,** because you do *1213*
26:38 Stay here and **k watch** with me." *1213*
26:40 "Could you men not **k watch** with me *1213*
28:14 we will satisfy him and **k** you out *4472*
Mk 3: 9 **to k** the people **from** crowding him. *2671+3590*
7:24 yet he could not **k** his presence **secret.** *3291*
13:34 and tells the one at the door to **k watch.** *1213*
13:35 "Therefore **k watch** because you do *1213*
14:34 "Stay here and **k watch."** *1213*
14:37 Could you not **k watch** for one hour? *1213*
Lk 4:42 *they tried* to **k** him from leaving them. *2988*
12:35 *k* your lamps **burning,** *AIT*
13:33 I must **k going** today and tomorrow and *AIT*
17:33 Whoever tries *to* **k** his life will lose it, *4347*
18: 7 *k* **putting** them **off?** *AIT*
19:40 "I tell you," he replied, "if they *k* **quiet,** *AIT*
Jn 4:15 and have to *k* **coming** here to draw water." *AIT*
8:55 but I do know him and **k** his word. *5498*
9:16 for *he does* not **k** the Sabbath." *5498*
10:24 "How long *will you* **k** us **in suspense?** *149+3836+6034*
12:25 in this world *will* **k** it for eternal life. *5875*
12:47 hears my words but *does* not **k** them, *5875*
15:18 **k in mind** that it hated me first. *1182*
18:18 around a fire they had made *to* **k warm.** *2548*
Ac 2:24 for death *to k* its **hold on** him. *AIT*
10:47 "Can anyone **k** these people **from** *3266*
18: 9 *k on* **speaking,** do not be silent. *AIT*
20:28 **K watch over** yourselves and all the flock *4668*
24:16 So I strive always *to* **k** my conscience clear *2400*
24:23 the centurion *to* **k** Paul **under guard** but *5498*
27:22 But now I urge you *to* **k up** your **courage,** *2313*
27:25 So **k up** *your* **courage,** men, *2313*
Ro 2:26 not circumcised **k** the law's requirements, *5875*
7:19 this *I k on* **doing.** *AIT*
12:11 *k* your spiritual **fervor,** *AIT*
14:22 about these things **k** between yourself *2400*
16:17 *K* **away** from them. *AIT*
1Co 1: 8 He *will* **k** you **strong** to the end, *1011*
5: 8 Therefore *let us* **k the Festival,** *2037*
7:30 as if *it were* not **theirs to k;** *2988*
10: 6 to **k** us from setting our hearts on evil things *1639*
14:28 the speaker *should k* **quiet** in the church *AIT*
2Co 3:13 **to k** the Israelites **from** *3590+3836+4639*
11:12 And *I will k on* **doing** what I am doing *AIT*
12: 7 To **k** me **from** becoming conceited because *3590*
Gal 5:15 If *you k on* **biting** and **devouring** *AIT*
5:25 *let us* **k in step** with the Spirit. *5123*
Eph 1:17 I **k** asking that the God of our Lord Jesus *NIG*
4: 3 *to* **k** the unity of the Spirit through the bond *5498*
6:18 and always **k on** praying for all the saints. *4675*
1Th 2:16 to **k** us **from** speaking to the Gentiles so *3266*
2Th 3: 6 *to* **k away** from every brother who is idle *5097*
1Ti 3: 9 They must **k hold of** the deep truths of *2400*
5:21 to **k** these instructions without partiality, *5875*
5:22 **K** yourself pure. *5498*
6:14 *to* **k** this command without spot or blame *5498*
2Ti 1:13 **k** as the pattern of sound teaching, *2400*
2:14 *K* **reminding** them **of** these things. *AIT*
4: 5 But you, **k** your **head** in all situations, *3768*
Phm 1:13 I would have liked *to* **k** him with me so *2988*
Heb 9:20 which God *has* **commanded** you **to k."** *1948*
10:26 *If* we deliberately *k on* **sinning** *AIT*
13: 1 **K on** loving each other as brothers. *3531*
13: 5 **K** your lives free from the love of money *NIG*
13:17 They **k watch** over you *70*
Jas 1:26 not **k a tight rein on** his tongue, *5902*
1:27 and *to* **k** oneself from being polluted by *5498*
2: 8 If *you* really **k** the royal law found *5464*
2:16 *k* **warm** and **well fed,"** *AIT*
3: 2 **k** his whole body **in check.** *5902*
1Pe 3:10 and see good days *must* **k** his tongue *4264*
2Pe 1: 8 *they will* **k** you from being ineffective *2770*
1Jn 5:21 Dear children, **k** yourselves from idols. *5875*
Jude 1: 6 And the angels who *did* not **k** their positions *5498*
1:21 **K** yourselves in God's love as you wait for *5498*
1:24 To him who is able *to* **k** you **from** falling *5875*
Rev 3:10 I will also **k** you from the hour of trial *5498*
20: 3 to **k** him **from** deceiving the nations *3590*

Rev 22: 9 and *of* all who **k** the words of this book. *5498*

KEEPER (8) [KEEP]

Ge 4: 9 "Am I my brother's **k**?" 9068
1Sa 17:22 David left his things with the **k** *of* supplies, 9068
2Ki 10:22 Jehu said to the **k** *of* the wardrobe, 889+6584S
22:14 the son of Harhas, **k** *of* the wardrobe. 9068
2Ch 31:14 the Levite, **k of the East Gate,** 8788
34:22 the son of Hasrah, **k** *of* the wardrobe. 9068
Ne 2: 8 Asaph, **k** *of* the king's forest, 9068
Jn 12: 6 as **k of the money bag,** he used to *1186+2400*

KEEPERS (1) [KEEP]

Ecc 12: 3 when the **k** *of* the house tremble, and 9068

KEEPING (39) [KEEP]

Ge 41:49 it was so much that he stopped **k records** 6218
Ex 20: 8 "Remember the Sabbath day by **k** it **holy.** 7727
Dt 5:12 "Observe the Sabbath day by **k** it **holy,** 7727
6: 2 as long as you live by **k** all his decrees 9068
7: 9 the faithful God, **k** his covenant of love to 9068
13:18 **k** all his commands that I am giving you 9068
Jdg 8: 4 exhausted yet *k up the* **pursuit,** AIT
1Sa 6:12 **k** on the road and lowing **all the way;** 2143+2143
17:34 "Your servant has been **k** his father's sheep. 8286
25:33 and for **k** me from bloodshed this day and 3973
1Ki 11:38 in my eyes by **k** my statutes and commands, 9068
17:16 **in k with** the word of the LORD spoken 3869
2Ki 7: 9 of good news and we *are* **k it to ourselves.** 3120
2Ch 8:14 **In k with** the ordinance of his father David, 3869
Est 1: 7 **in k with** the king's liberality. 3869
Ps 19:11 in **k** them there is great reward. 9068
119:112 My heart is set on **k** your decrees to 6913
Pr 6:24 **k** you from the immoral woman, 9068
15: 3 **k watch** *on* the wicked and the good. 7595
Isa 65: 4 and spend their nights **k secret vigil;** 5915
Eze 14: 4 LORD will answer him myself **in k with** 928
17:14 surviving only by **k** his treaty. 9068
22:26 they shut their eyes to the **k** of my Sabbaths, NIH
Da 9:16 O Lord, **in k with** all your righteous acts, 3869
Zec 9: 8 for now I *am* **k watch.** 928+6524+8011
Mt 3: 8 Produce fruit **in k with** repentance. *545*
Lk 2: 8 **k watch** over their flocks at night. *5871+5875*
2:24 to offer a sacrifice **in k with** what is said *2848*
3: 8 Produce fruit **in k with** repentance. *545*
20:20 **K a close watch** on him, they sent spies, *4190*
Ac 14:18 *they* had difficulty **k** the crowd from *2924*
1Co 7:19 **K** God's commands is what counts. *5499*
16: 2 **in k with** *his* **income,** *1569+2338+4005+5516*
2Co 8: 5 and then to us **in k with** God's will. *1328*
1Ti 1:18 I give you this instruction **in k with** *2848*
Jas 4:11 When you judge the law, you are not **k** it, *4475*
1Pe 3:16 **k** a clear conscience, *2400*
2Pe 3: 9 The Lord is not slow in **k** his promise, *NIG*
3:13 But **in k with** his promise we are looking *2848*

KEEPS (44) [KEEP]

Jdg 5:29 indeed, she **k saying** to herself, 609+8740
1Sa 17:25 "Do you see how this man *k* **coming out?** AIT
Ne 1: 5 and awesome God, *who* **k** his covenant 9068
9:32 *who* **k** his covenant of love, 9068
Job 20:13 though he cannot bear to let it go and **k** it 4979
24:15 and *he* **k** his face concealed. 8492
33:11 *he* **k close watch** *on* all my paths.' 9068
34: 8 *He* **k company** with evildoers; 782+2495+4200
Ps 15: 4 *who* **k** his oath even when it hurts, 4202+4614
Pr 11:13 but a trustworthy man **k** a secret. 4059
12:23 prudent man **k** his knowledge *to himself,* 4059
15:21 a man of understanding **k** a **straight** course. 3837
15:25 **k** the widow's boundaries **intact.** 5893
17:24 A discerning man **k** wisdom in view, NIH
17:28 Even a fool is thought wise if *he* **k silent,** 3087
18:18 **k** strong opponents **apart.** 7233
21:23 and his tongue **k** himself from calamity. 9068
28: 7 *He who* **k** the law is a discerning son, 5915
29:11 but a wise man **k** himself under control. 8656
29:18 but blessed is he *who* **k** the law. 9068
Ecc 5:20 God **k** him **occupied** with gladness of heart. 6701
Isa 26: 2 nation may enter, the nation *that* **k** faith. 9068
33:15 and **k** his hand from accepting bribes, 5850
56: 2 *who* **k** the Sabbath without desecrating it, 9068
56: 2 and **k** his hand from doing any evil." 9068
65: 5 a fire *that k* **burning** all day. AIT
Jer 23:35 of *you k on* **saying** to his friend or relative: AIT
48:10 on *him who* **k** his sword from bloodshed! 4979
Eze 18: 9 my decrees and faithfully **k** my laws. 9068
18:17 *He* **k** my laws and follows my decrees. 6913
18:21 and **k** all my decrees and does what is just 9068
Da 9: 4 and awesome God, *who* **k** his covenant 9068
Am 5:13 the prudent man **k quiet** in such times, 1957
Mt 15:23 for *she k* **crying out** after us." *AIT*
Lk 18: 5 yet because this widow *k* **bothering** me, *AIT*
Jn 7:19 Yet not one of you **k** the law. *4472*
8:51 I tell you the truth, if anyone **k** my word, *5498*
8:52 yet you say that if anyone **k** your word, *5498*
1Co 13: 5 *it k* **no record of** wrongs. *AIT*
Jas 2:10 For whoever **k** the whole law and *5498*
1Jn 3: 6 No one who lives in him *k on* **sinning.** *AIT*
5:18 the one who was born of God **k** him **safe,** *5498*
Rev 16:15 and **k** his clothes with him, *5498*
22: 7 Blessed is he who **k** the words of *5498*

KEHELATHAH (2)

Nu 33:22 They left Rissah and camped at **K.** 7739
33:23 They left **K** and camped at Mount Shepher. 7739

KEILAH (18)

Jos 15:44 **K,** Aczib and Mareshah— 7881
1Sa 23: 1 the Philistines are fighting against **K** 7881
23: 2 "Go, attack the Philistines and save **K.**" 7881
23: 3 if we go to **K** against the Philistine forces!" 7881
23: 4 "Go down to **K,** for I am going to give 7881
23: 5 So David and his men went to **K,** 7881
23: 5 the Philistines and saved the people of **K.** 7881
23: 6 with him when he fled to David at **K.**) 7881
23: 7 Saul was told that David had gone to **K,** 7881
23: 8 down to **K** to besiege David and his men. 7881
23:10 that Saul plans to come to **K** and destroy 7881
23:11 Will the citizens of **K** surrender me to him? 7881
23:12 the citizens of **K** surrender me and my men 7881
23:13 left **K** and kept moving from place to place. 7881
23:13 that David had escaped from **K,** 7881
1Ch 4:19 the father of **K** the Garmite, 7881
Ne 3:17 Hashabiah, ruler of half the district of **K,** 7881
3:18 ruler of the other half-district of **K.** 7881

KELAIAH (1) [KELITA]

Ezr 10:23 Jozabad, Shimei, **K** (that is, Kelita), 7835

KELAL (1)

Ezr 10:30 Adna, **K,** Benaiah, Maaseiah, Mattaniah, 4006

KELITA (3) [KELAIAH]

Ezr 10:23 Jozabad, Shimei, Kelaiah (that is, **K**), 7836
Ne 8: 7 Shabbethai, Hodiah, Maaseiah, **K,** Azariah, 7836
10:10 Shebaniah, Hodiah, **K,** Pelaiah, Hanan, 7836

KELUB (2)

1Ch 4:11 **K,** Shuhah's brother, was the father 3991
27:26 Ezri son of **K** was in charge of 3991

KELUHI (1)

Ezr 10:35 Benaiah, Bedeiah, **K,** 3988

KEMUEL (3)

Ge 22:21 Buz his brother, **K** (the father of Aram), 7851
Nu 34:24 **K** son of Shiphtan, the leader from the tribe 7851
1Ch 27:17 Hashabiah son of **K;** 7851

KENAANAH (5)

1Ki 22:11 of **K** had made iron horns and he declared, 4049
22:24 of **K** went up and slapped Micaiah in 4049
1Ch 7:10 Jeush, Benjamin, Ehud, **K,** Zethan, 4049
2Ch 18:10 Zedekiah son of **K** had made iron horns, 4049
18:23 of **K** went up and slapped Micaiah in 4049

KENAN (7)

Ge 5: 9 he became the father of **K.** 7809
5:10 And after he became the father of **K,** 7809
5:12 When **K** had lived 70 years, 7809
5:13 **K** lived 840 years and had other sons 7809
5:14 Altogether, **K** lived 910 years, 7809
1Ch 1: 2 **K,** Mahalalel, Jared, 7809
Lk 3:37 the son of Mahalalel, the son *of* **K,** *2783*

KENANI (1)

Ne 9: 4 Shebaniah, Bunni, Sherebiah, Bani and **K**— 4039

KENANIAH (3)

1Ch 15:22 **K** the head Levite was in charge of 4041
15:27 and as were the singers, and **K,** 4040
26:29 **K** and his sons were assigned duties away 4041

KENATH (2)

Nu 32:42 And Nobah captured **K** 7875
1Ch 2:23 as **K** with its surrounding settlements— 7875

KENAZ (11)

Ge 36:11 Teman, Omar, Zepho, Gatam and **K.** 7869
36:15 Chiefs Teman, Omar, Zepho, **K,** 7869
36:42 **K,** Teman, Mibzar, 7869
Jos 15:17 Othniel son of **K,** Caleb's brother, took it; 7869
Jdg 1:13 Othniel son of **K,** Caleb's younger brother, 7869
3: 9 Othniel son of **K,** Caleb's younger brother, 7869
3:11 until Othniel son of **K** died. 7869
1Ch 1:36 Teman, Omar, Zepho, Gatam and **K;** 7869
1:53 **K,** Teman, Mibzar, 7869
4:13 The sons of **K:** Othniel and Seraiah. 7869
4:15 The son of Elah: **K.** 7869

KENEZITE (KJV) See KENIZZITE

KENITE (5) [KENITES]

Jdg 1:16 the **K,** went up from the City of Palms with 7808
4:11 Heber the **K** had left the other Kenites, 7808
4:17 the wife of Heber the **K,** 7808
4:17 of Hazor and the clan of Heber the **K.** 7808
5:24 the wife of Heber the **K,** 7808

KENITES (9) [KENITE]

Ge 15:19 the land of the **K,** Kenizzites, Kadmonites, 7808
Nu 24:21 Then he saw the **K** and uttered his oracle: 7808
24:22 yet you **K** will be destroyed 7804
Jdg 4:11 Now Heber the Kenite had left the other **K,** 7804
1Sa 15: 6 Then he said to the **K,** "Go away, 7808
15: 6 So the **K** moved away from the Amalekites. 7808
27:10 or "Against the Negev of the **K.**" 7808
30:29 the towns of the Jerahmeelites and the **K;** 7808
1Ch 2:55 These are the **K** who came from Hammath, 7808

KENIZZITE (3) [KENIZZITES]

Nu 32:12 of Jephunneh the **K** and Joshua son of Nun, 7870
Jos 14: 6 Caleb son of Jephunneh the **K** said to him, 7870
14:14 to Caleb son of Jephunneh the **K** ever since, 7870

KENIZZITES (1) [KENIZZITE]

Ge 15:19 the land of the Kenites, **K,** Kadmonites, 7870

KEPHAR AMMONI (1)

Jos 18:24 **K,** Ophni and Geba— 4112

KEPHIRAH (4)

Jos 9:17 Gibeon, **K,** Beeroth and Kiriath Jearim. 4098
18:26 Mizpah, **K,** Mozah, 4098
Ezr 2:25 of Kiriath Jearim, **K** and Beeroth 743 4098
Ne 7:29 of Kiriath Jearim, **K** and Beeroth 743 4098

KEPT (178) [KEEP]

Ge 4: 2 Abel **k** flocks, and Cain worked the soil. 8286
6:20 the ground will come to you to *be* **k alive.** 2649
7:17 For forty days the flood *k* **coming** on AIT
8: 7 and *it k* **flying** back and forth until AIT
16: 2 "The LORD *has* **k** me from having children. 6806
19: 9 *They* **k bringing pressure** on Lot 4394+7210
20: 6 so I *have* **k** you from sinning against me. 3104
26: 5 and **k** my requirements, 9068
30: 2 who *has* **k** you from having children?" 4979
34: 5 he **k quiet** *about* it until they came home. 3087
37:11 his father **k** the matter **in mind.** 9068
39:16 *She* **k** his cloak beside **her** 5663
41:35 *to be* **k** in the cities *for* food. 9068
42:16 the rest of you *will* **be k in prison,** 673
Ex 5:13 The slave drivers *k* **pressing** them, saying, AIT
12:42 Because the LORD **k** vigil that night 4200
16:20 *they* **k** part of it until morning, 3855
16:33 Then place it before the LORD to be **k** for 5466
16:34 in front of the Testimony, that it might be **k.** 5466
21:29 *has* not **k** it **penned up** and it kills a man 9068
23:18 of my festival offerings *must* not *be* **k** 4328
27:20 so that the lamps may be **k** burning. 9458
Lev 6: 9 and the fire *must* **be k burning** on the altar. 3678
6:12 The fire on the altar *must* **be k burning;** 3678
6:13 The fire *must* **be k burning** on the altar 3678
24: 2 the lamps *may be* **k burning** continually. 6590
Nu 9: 7 *should we* **be k from** presenting 1194+1757+4200
15:34 and *they* **k** him in custody, 5663
17:10 to be **k** as a sign to the rebellious. 5466
18: 9 of the most holy offerings that is **k from** 4946
19: 9 *They shall be* **k** by the Israelite community 2118
24:11 the LORD *has* **k** you from being rewarded 4979
Dt 6:24 we might always prosper and *be* **k alive,** 2649
7: 8 and **k** the oath he swore to your forefathers 9068
32:34 "*Have* I not **k this in reserve** and sealed it 4022
33:21 the leader's portion **was k** for him. 6211
Jos 6:13 while the trumpets **k** sounding. 2143
9:21 **promise** to them *was k.* AIT
14:10 *he has* **k** me **alive** for forty-five years since 2649
Jdg 7: 8 the rest of the Israelites to their tents but **k** 2616
20:45 *They k* **pressing** after the Benjamites as far AIT
1Sa 1: 6 her rival **k provoking** her 1685+4087+4088
1:12 As *she* **k on** praying to the LORD, 8049
9:24 "Here is what *has* **been k** for you. 8636
10:27 But Saul **k** silent. 2118
13:13 "*You have* not **k** the command 9068
13:14 *you have* not **k** the LORD's command." 9068
17:41 **k coming** closer to David. 2143+2143
18: 2 that day Saul **k** David with him and did 4374
18: 9 Saul **k** a **jealous eye on** David. 6523
21: 4 the men *have* **k themselves** from women." 9068
21: 5 "Indeed women *have* **been k** from us, 6806
23:13 *k* **moving from place to place.** AIT
25:26 "Now since the LORD *has* **k** you, 4979
25:34 lives, who *has* **k** me from harming you, 4979
25:39 *He has* **k** his servant from doing wrong 3104
2Sa 15:12 and Absalom's following **k on** increasing. 2143
18: 9 while the mule he was riding **k on going.** 6296
18:13 you *would have* **k** *your* **distance** *from* me." 3656+4946+5584
20: 3 They were **k in confinement** till the day 7674
22:22 For *I have* **k** the ways of the LORD; 9068
22:24 before him and *have* **k myself** from sin. 9068
1Ki 5:10 In this way Hiram *k* Solomon **supplied** AIT
8:20 "The LORD *has* **k** the promise he made: 7756
8:24 *You have* **k** your promise 9068
10:26 and twelve thousand horses, which *he* **k** in 5663
11:11 not **k** my covenant and my decrees, 9068
11:33 nor **k** my statutes and laws as David, NIH
13:21 of the LORD and *have* not **k** the command 9068
14: 8 who **k** my commands and followed me 9068
2Ki 4: 5 the jars to her and she *k* **pouring.** AIT
13: 3 for a long time *he* **k** them under the power 5989
18: 6 *he* **k** the commands the LORD had given 9068
25: 2 The city *was* **k** under siege until 995
1Ch 4:33 And *they* **k a genealogical record.** 3509
2Ch 1:14 and twelve thousand horses, which *he* **k** in 5663

2Ch 6:10 "The LORD *has* **k** the promise he made. 7756
6:15 You *have* **k** your promise 9068
9:25 which *he* **k** in the chariot cities and also 5663
17:13 He also **k** experienced fighting men NIH
34:21 because our fathers *have* not **k** the word of 9068
Ezr 9:1 *have* not **k themselves separate** from 976
Ne 5:8 *They k* **quiet,** because they could not find AIT
6:17 and replies from Tobiah *k* **coming** to them. AIT
6:19 *they* **k** reporting to me his good deeds and 2118
9:8 *You have* **k** your promise 7756
10:39 where the articles for the sanctuary are **k** NIH
11:19 who **k watch** at the gates—172 men. 9068
Est 2:20 Esther *had* **k secret** her family background and nationality 401+5583
7:4 *I would have k* **quiet,** because no such AIT
Job 21:32 and **watch** *is* **k** over his tomb. 9193
23:11 *I have* **k** *to* his way without turning aside. 9068
31:17 if *I have* **k** my bread to myself, 430
31:34 that *I k* **silent** and would not go outside AIT
Ps 17:4 *I have* **k** *myself from* the ways of the violent. 9068
18:21 For *I have* **k** the ways of the LORD; 9068
18:23 before him and *have* **k myself** from sin. 9068
32:3 When *I k* **silent,** my bones wasted away AIT
50:21 These thing you have done and *I k* **silent;** AIT
66:9 he has preserved our lives and **k** our feet 5989
73:13 Surely in vain *have I* **k** my heart **pure;** 2342
77:4 **k** my eyes **from closing;** 296+9073
78:32 In spite of all this, they **k on** sinning; 6388
99:7 *they* **k** his statutes and the decrees 9068
119:101 *I have* **k** my feet from every evil path so 3973
130:3 If *you,* O LORD, **k a record** *of* sins, 9068
Pr 20:9 Who can say, *"I have* **k** my heart **pure;** 2342
28:18 He whose walk is blameless *is* **k safe,** 3828
28:26 but he who walks in wisdom **is k safe.** 4880
29:25 but whoever trusts in the LORD **is k safe.** 8435
Isa 38:17 **In** *your* **love** you **k** me from the pit 3137
42:14 "For a long time *I have k* **silent,** AIT
49:6 and bring back *those of* Israel I *have* **k.** 5915
57:17 yet *he* **k on** in his willful ways. 2143+8743
Jer 5:25 Your wrongdoings *have* **k** these **away;** 5742
35:14 to drink wine and this command *has* **been k.** 7756
52:5 The city *was* **k** under siege until 995
Eze 5:7 not followed my decrees or **k** my laws. 6913
11:12 not followed my decrees or **k** my laws 6913
Da 7:11 *I* **k** looking until the beast was slain 10201
7:28 but *I* **k** the matter to myself." 10476
9:10 not obeyed the LORD our God or **k** 928+2143
Hos 13:12 his sins *are* **k on record.** 7621
Am 2:4 of the LORD and *have* not **k** his decrees, 9068
Mal 3:7 from my decrees and *have* not **k** them. 9068
Mt 19:20 "All these *I have* **k,"** the young man said. *5875*
24:43 thief was coming, *he* would *have* **k watch** *1213*
27:36 sitting down, *they* **k watch over** him there. *5498*
Mk 5:32 But Jesus *k* **looking around** *AIT*
7:36 the more they *k* **talking about** it. *AIT*
9:10 *They* **k** the matter to themselves, *3195*
9:34 But *they k* **quiet** because on the way *AIT*
10:20 "all these *I have* **k** since I was a boy." *5875*
Lk 1:22 for he *k* **making signs** to them *AIT*
4:44 And *he* **k on** preaching in the synagogues *1639*
8:29 and foot and **k under guard,** *5875*
9:36 The disciples **k this to themselves,** *4967*
13:16 whom Satan *has k* **bound** *AIT*
18:3 a widow in that town *who k* **coming** to him *AIT*
18:21 "All these *I have* **k** since I was a boy," *5875*
19:20 *I* **have k** it laid away in a piece of cloth. *2400*
23:21 But they *k* **shouting,** "Crucify him! *AIT*
24:16 but they *were* **k from** recognizing him. *3195*
Jn 8:7 When *they* **k on** questioning him, *2152*
11:37 *have* **k** this man from dying?" *4472*
11:56 *They* **k looking for** Jesus, *AIT*
16:18 *They* **k asking,** "What does he mean by *AIT*
17:12 and **k** them **safe** by that name you gave me. *5875*
19:12 but the Jews *k* **shouting,** *AIT*
Ac 5:2 *he* **k back** part of the money for himself, *3802*
5:3 and *have* **k** *for yourself* some of the money *3802*
9:24 Day and night *they* **k close watch on** *4190*
12:5 So Peter *was* **k** in prison, *5498*
12:15 When she *k* **insisting that** it was so, *AIT*
12:16 But Peter **k on** knocking, *2152*
16:6 **k** by the Holy Spirit **from** preaching *3266*
16:18 *She* **k** this **up** for many days. *4472*
20:7 **k on** talking until midnight. *4189*
21:36 The crowd that followed *k* **shouting,** *AIT*
23:35 he ordered that Paul *be* **k under guard** *5875*
27:43 and **k** them **from** carrying out their plan. *3266*
2Co 11:9 *I have* **k** myself from being a burden to you *5498*
Gal 5:7 and **k** you **from** obeying the truth? *3590*
Eph 3:9 which for ages past *was k* **hidden** in God, *AIT*
Col 1:26 the mystery that *has been* **k hidden for** ages *648*
1Th 3:4 *we k* **telling** you that we would *AIT*
5:23 soul and body *be* **k** blameless at the coming *5498*
2Ti 4:7 I have finished the race, *I have* **k** the faith. *5498*
Heb 11:28 By faith *he* **k** the Passover and *4472*
13:4 and the marriage bed **k** pure, *NIG*
1Pe 1:4 **k** in heaven for you, *5498*
2Pe 3:7 *being* **k** for the day of judgment *5498*
Jude 1:1 by God the Father and **k** by Jesus Christ: *5498*
1:6 these *he has* **k** in darkness, *5498*
Rev 3:8 yet *you have* **k** my word and have *5498*
3:10 Since *you have* **k** my command *5498*
9:15 And the four angels who *had been* **k ready** *2286*
14:4 for they **k** themselves pure. *NIG*

KERAMIM See ABEL KERAMIM

KERAN (2)
Ge 36:26 Hemdan, Eshban, Ithran and **K.** 4154
1Ch 1:41 Hemdan, Eshban, Ithran and **K.** 4154

KERCHIEFS (KJV) See VEILS

KEREN-HAPPUCH (1)
Job 42:14 the second Keziah and the third **K.** 7968

KERETHITE (1) [KERETHITES]
Zep 2:5 to you who live by the sea, O **K** people; 4165

KERETHITES (10) [KERETHITE]
1Sa 30:14 the **K** and the territory belonging to Judah 4165
2Sa 8:18 of Jehoiada was over the **K** and Pelethites; 4165
15:18 along with all the **K** and Pelethites; 4165
20:7 So Joab's men and the **K** and Pelethites 4165
20:23 of Jehoiada was over the **K** and Pelethites; 4165
1Ki 1:38 the **K** and the Pelethites went down 4165
1:44 the **K** and the Pelethites, 4165
1Ch 18:17 of Jehoiada was over the **K** and Pelethites; 4165
Eze 25:16 the **K** and destroy those remaining along 4165
Zep 2:6 The land by the sea, where the **K** dwell, 4165

KERIOTH (3)
Jer 48:24 to **K** and Bozrah—to all the towns of Moab 7954
48:41 **K** will be captured and the strongholds 7954
Am 2:2 that will consume the fortresses of **K.** 7954

KERIOTH HEZRON (1) [HAZOR, HEZRON]
Jos 15:25 Hazor Hadattah, **K** (that is, Hazor), 7955

KERITH (2)
1Ki 17:3 turn eastward and hide in the **K** Ravine, 4134
17:5 He went to the **K** Ravine, 4134

KERNEL (2) [KERNELS]
Mk 4:28 then the head, then the full **k** in the head. *4992*
Jn 12:24 a **k** of wheat falls to the ground and dies, *3133*

KERNELS (3) [KERNEL]
Dt 23:25 you may pick **k** with your hands, 4884
32:14 with choice rams of Bashan and the finest **k** 4000
Lk 6:1 rub them in their hands and eat the **k.** *NIG*

KEROS (2)
Ezr 2:44 **K,** Siaha, Padon, 7820
Ne 7:47 **K,** Sia, Padon, 7820

KERUB (2)
Ezr 2:59 Tel Harsha, **K,** Addon and Immer, 4132
Ne 7:61 Tel Harsha, **K,** Addon and Immer, 4132

KESALON (1) [JEARIM]
Jos 15:10 of Mount Jearim (that is, **K**), continued 4076

KESED (1)
Ge 22:22 **K,** Hazo, Pildash, Jidlaph and Bethuel." 4168

KESIL (1)
Jos 15:30 Eltolad, **K,** Hormah, 4069

KESULLOTH (1)
Jos 19:18 Their territory included: Jezreel, **K,** 4063

KETTLE (1) [KETTLES]
1Sa 2:14 He would plunge it into the pan or **k** 1857

KETTLES (1) [KETTLE]
Mk 7:4 as the washing of cups, pitchers and **k.)** *5908*

KETURAH (4)
Ge 25:1 took another wife, whose name was **K.** 7778
25:4 All these were descendants of **K.** 7778
1Ch 1:32 The sons born to **K,** Abraham's concubine: 7778
1:33 All these were descendants of **K.** 7778

KEY (8) [KEYS]
Jdg 3:25 they took a **k** and unlocked them. 5158
1Ch 9:27 of the **k for opening** it each morning. 5158
Isa 22:22 on his shoulder the **k** *to* the house of David; 5158
33:6 fear of the LORD is **the k** to this treasure. 2085S
Lk 11:52 you have taken away the **k** to knowledge. *3090*
Rev 3:7 who holds the **k** of David. *3090*
9:1 The star was given the **k** to the shaft of *3090*
20:1 the **k** to the Abyss and holding in his hand *3090*

KEYS (2) [KEY]
Mt 16:19 I will give you the **k** of the kingdom *3090*
Rev 1:18 And I hold the **k** of death and Hades. *3090*

KEZIAH (1)
Job 42:14 the second **K** and the third Keren-Happuch. 7905

KEZIB (1)
Ge 38:5 It was at **K** that she gave birth to him. 3945

KEZIZ See EMEK KEZIZ

KIBROTH HATTAAVAH (5)
Nu 11:34 Therefore the place was named **K,** 7701
11:35 From **K** the people traveled to Hazeroth 7701
33:16 left the Desert of Sinai and camped at **K.** 7701
33:17 They left **K** and camped at Hazeroth. 7701
Dt 9:22 LORD angry at Taberah, at Massah and at **K.** 7701

KIBZAIM (1)
Jos 21:22 **K** and Beth Horon, together 7698

KICK (1) [KICKED, KICKING]
Ac 26:14 It is hard for you *to* **k** against the goads.' *3280*

KICKED (1) [KICK]
Dt 32:15 Jeshurun grew fat and **k;** 1246

KICKING (2) [KICK]
Eze 16:6 " 'Then I passed by and saw you **k about** 1008
16:22 **k about** in your blood. 1008

KIDNAPPER (1) [KIDNAPPING, KIDNAPS]
Dt 24:7 as a slave or sells him, the **k** must die. 1705

KIDNAPPING (1) [KIDNAPPER]
Dt 24:7 If a man is caught **k** one of his brother 1704+5883

KIDNAPS (1) [KIDNAPPER]
Ex 21:16 *"Anyone who* **k** another and either sells him 1704

KIDNEYS (18)
Ex 29:13 and both **k** with the fat on them, 4000
29:22 both **k** with the fat on them, 4000
Lev 3:4 both **k** with the fat on them near the loins, 4000
3:4 which he will remove with the **k.** 4000
3:10 both **k** with the fat on them near the loins, 4000
3:10 which he will remove with the **k.** 4000
3:15 both **k** with the fat on them near the loins, 4000
3:15 which he will remove with the **k.** 4000
4:9 both **k** with the fat on them near the loins, 4000
4:9 which he will remove with the **k—** 4000
7:4 both **k** with the fat on them near the loins, 4000
7:4 which is to be removed with the **k.** 4000
8:16 and both **k** and their fat, 4000
8:25 both **k** and their fat and the right thigh. 4000
9:10 the **k** and the covering of the liver from 4000
9:19 the **k** and the covering of the liver— 4000
Job 16:13 he pierces my **k** and spills my gall on 4000
Isa 34:6 fat from the **k** *of* rams. 4000

KIDON (1)
1Ch 13:9 they came to the threshing floor of **K,** 3961

KIDRON (11)
2Sa 15:23 The king also crossed the **K** Valley, 7724
1Ki 2:37 The day you leave and cross the **K** Valley, 7724
15:13 down and burned it in the **K** Valley. 7724
2Ki 23:4 the **K** Valley and took the ashes to Bethel. 7724
23:6 to the **K** Valley outside Jerusalem 7724
23:12 and threw the rubble into the **K** Valley. 7724
2Ch 15:16 broke it up and burned it in the **K** Valley. 7724
29:16 and carried it out to the **K** Valley. 7724
30:14 and threw them into the **K** Valley. 7724
Jer 31:40 the **K** Valley on the east as far as the corner 7724
Jn 18:1 with his disciples and crossed the **K** Valley. *3022*

KILEAB (1)
2Sa 3:3 **K** the son of Abigail the widow of Nabal 3976

KILION (3)
Ru 1:2 names of his two sons were Mahlon and **K.** 4002
1:5 both Mahlon and **K** also died, 4002
4:9 the property of Elimelech, **K** and Mahlon. 4002

KILL (186) [KILLED, KILLING, KILLS]
Ge 4:14 and whoever finds me *will* **k** me." 2222
4:15 so that no one who found him *would* **k** him. 5782
12:12 Then *they will* **k** me but will let you live. 2222
18:25 to **k** the righteous with the wicked, 4637
20:11 and *they will* **k** me because of my wife.' 2222
26:7 of this place might **k** me on account 2222
27:41 then *I will* **k** my brother Jacob." 2222
37:18 they plotted to **k** him. 4637
37:20 *let's* **k** him and throw him into one 2222
37:26 if *we* **k** our brother and cover up his blood? 2222
Ex 1:16 if it is a boy, **k** him; but if it is a girl, 4637
2:15 Pharaoh heard of this, he tried to **k** Moses, 2222
4:19 all the men who **wanted to k** you are dead." 906+1335+5883

Ex 4:23 so I *will* **k** your firstborn son.' " 2222
4:24 and was about to **k** him. 4637
5:21 and have put a sword in their hand to **k** us." 2222
22:24 and *I will* **k** you with the sword; 2222
32:12 to **k** them in the mountains and 2222
Lev 14:50 *He shall* **k** one of the birds over fresh water 8821
20:15 and *you must* **k** the animal. 2222
20:16 **k** both the woman and the animal. 2222
Nu 16:13 a land flowing with milk and honey to **k** us 4637
22:29 *I would* **k** you right now." 2222
25:4 **k** them **and expose** them in broad daylight 3697
25:17 the Midianites as enemies and **k** them, 5782
31:17 Now **k** all the boys. 2222
31:17 And **k** every woman who has slept with 2222
35:17 anyone has a stone in his hand that *could* **k,** 4637
35:18 a wooden object in his hand that *could* **k,** 4637
35:23 drops a stone on him that *could* **k** him, 4637
35:27 the avenger of blood *may* **k** the accused 8357
Dt 19:5 and hit his neighbor and **k** him. 4637
19:6 and **k** him even though he is not deserving
of death, 5782+5883
27:25 "Cursed is the man who accepts a bribe to
k an innocent person." 5782+5883
Jos 9:26 and *they did* not **k** them. 2222
Jdg 8:18 "What kind of men *did you* **k** at Tabor?" 2222
8:19 *I would* not **k** you." 2222
8:20 his oldest son, he said, **"K** them!" 2222
9:54 "Draw your sword and **k** me, 4637
13:23 "If the LORD had meant to **k** us, 4637
15:12 to me that *you* won't **k** me yourselves." 7003
15:13 *We will* not **k** you." 4637+4637
16:2 saying, "At dawn *we'll* **k** him." 2222
20:5 surrounded the house, intending to **k** me. 2222
21:11 **"K** every male and every woman who is not 3049
1Sa 5:10 ark of the god of Israel around to us to **k** us 4637
5:11 or *it will* **k** us and our people." 4637
16:2 Saul will hear about it and **k** me." 2222
17:9 If he is able to fight and **k** me, 5782
17:9 but if I overcome him and **k** him, 5782
19:1 and all the attendants to **k** David. 4637
19:2 Saul is looking for a chance to **k** you. 4637
19:11 to David's house to watch it and to **k** him in 4637
19:15 up to me in his bed so that I *may* **k** him." 4637
19:17 Why *should I* **k** you?' " 4637
20:8 If I am guilty, then **k** me yourself! 4637
20:33 But Saul hurled his spear at him to **k** him. 5782
20:33 that his father intended to **k** David. 4637
22:17 "Turn and **k** the priests of the LORD, 4637
24:10 Some urged me to **k** you, but I spared you; 2222
24:11 the corner of your robe but *did* not **k** you. 2222
24:18 but *you did* not **k** me. 2222
30:15 to me before God that *you will* not **k** me 4637
2Sa 1:9 he said to me, 'Stand over me and **k** me! 4637
13:28 'Strike Amnon down,' then **k** him. 4637
21:16 said he *would* **k** David. 5782
1Ki 3:26 Don't **k** him!" 4637+4637
3:27 *Do* not **k** him; she is his mother." 4637+4637
11:40 Solomon tried to **k** Jeroboam, 4637
12:27 *They will* **k** me and return to King 2222
17:18 to remind me of my sin and **k** my son?" 4637
18:5 not *have to* **k** any of our animals." 4162
18:12 and doesn't find you, *he will* **k** me. 2222
18:14 *He will* **k** me!" 2222
19:10 and now they are trying to **k** me too." 4374+5883
19:14 and now they are trying to **k** me too." 4374+5883
20:36 as soon as you leave me a lion *will* **k** you." 5782
2Ki 5:7 *Can I* **k** and bring back to life? 4637
6:21 he asked Elisha, *"Shall I* **k** them, 5782
6:21 *Shall I* **k** them?" 5782
6:22 *"Do* not **k** them," he answered. 5782
6:22 *"Would* you **k** men you have captured 5782
7:4 if *they* **k** us, then we die." 4637
8:12 **k** their young men with the sword, 2222
9:27 Jehu chased him, shouting, **"K** him too!" 5782
10:25 "Go in and **k** them; let no one escape." 5782
2Ch 22:11 from Athaliah so *she could* not **k** him. 4637
30:17 the Levites had to **k** the Passover lambs 8824
Ne 4:11 be right there among them and *will* **k** them 2222
6:10 because men are coming to **k** you— 2222
6:10 by night they are coming to **k** you." 2222
Est 3:13 destroy, **k** and annihilate all the Jews— 2222
8:11 to destroy, **k** and annihilate any armed force 2222
Job 20:16 the fangs of an adder *will* **k** him. 2222
Ps 59:T to watch David's house in order to **k** him. 4637
59:11 But *do* not **k** them, O Lord our shield, 2222
71:10 *those who* **wait to k** me conspire together.
5883+9068
Pr 1:32 waywardness of the simple *will* **k** them, 2222
29:10 a man of integrity and seek to **k** the upright. 5883
Ecc 3:3 a time to **k** and a time to heal, 2222
Jer 15:3 "the sword to **k** and the dogs to drag away 2222
18:23 O LORD, all their plots to **k** me. 4638
20:17 For *he did* not **k** me in the womb, 4637
38:15 *will you* not **k** me? 4637+4637
38:16 *I will* neither **k** you nor hand you over 4637
38:25 do not hide it from us or *we will* **k** you,' 4637
40:15 "Let me go and **k** Ishmael son of Nethaniah, 5782
41:8 ten of them said to Ishmael, "Don't **k** us! 4637
41:8 So he let them alone and *did* not **k** them 4637
43:3 so they *may* **k** us or carry us into exile 4637
50:21 Pursue, **k** and completely destroy them," 2991
50:27 **K** all her young bulls; 2991
Eze 9:5 "Follow him through the city and **k,** 5782
14:13 upon it and **k** its men and their animals, 4162
14:17 and *I* **k** its men and their animals, 4162
14:21 to **k** its men and their animals! 4162
22:27 and **k** people to make unjust gain. 6
Eze 23:47 *they will* **k** their sons and daughters 2222
25:13 and **k** its men and their animals. 4162
26:11 *he will* **k** your people with the sword, 2222
28:9 in the presence of *those who* **k** you? 2222
29:8 a sword against you and **k** your men 4162
Am 2:3 I will destroy her ruler and **k** all her officials 2222
9:1 those who are left *I will* **k** with the sword. 2222
Na 2:12 filling his lairs with the **k** and his dens with 3272
Mt 2:13 to search for the child *to* **k** him." *660+3836*
2:16 and he gave orders *to* **k** all the boys *359*
10:28 Do not be afraid of those who **k** the body *650*
10:28 of those who kill the body but cannot **k** *650*
12:14 and plotted how *they might* **k** Jesus. *660*
14:5 Herod wanted *to* **k** John, *650*
17:23 *They will* **k** him, and on the third day *650*
21:38 *let's* **k** him and take his inheritance.' *650*
23:34 Some of them *you will* **k** and crucify; *650*
23:37 you who **k** the prophets and stone those sent *650*
26:4 to arrest Jesus in some sly way and **k** him. *650*
Mk 3:4 to save life or *to* **k?"** *650*
3:6 with the Herodians how *they might* **k** Jesus. *660*
6:19 a grudge against John and wanted *to* **k** him. *650*
9:22 thrown him into fire or water to **k** him. *660*
9:31 *They will* **k** him, and after three days *650*
10:34 spit on him, flog him and **k** him. *650*
11:18 and began looking for a way *to* **k** him, *660*
12:7 *let's* **k** him, and the inheritance will *650*
12:9 He will come and **k** those tenants and give *660*
14:1 for some sly way to arrest Jesus and **k** him. *650*
Lk 11:49 some of whom *they will* **k** and others *650*
12:4 be afraid of those who **k** the body and after *650*
13:31 Herod wants *to* **k** you." *650*
13:34 you who **k** the prophets and stone those sent *650*
15:23 Bring the fattened calf and **k** it. *2604*
15:30 *you* **k** the fattened calf for him!' *2604*
18:32 insult him, spit on him, flog him and **k** him. *650*
19:27 bring them here and **k** them in front *2956*
19:47 among the people were trying *to* **k** him. *660*
20:14 *'Let's* **k** him, and the inheritance will *650*
20:16 He will come and **k** those tenants and give *660*
Jn 5:18 the Jews tried all the harder *to* **k** him; *650*
7:19 Why are you trying *to* **k** me?" *650*
7:20 "Who is trying *to* **k** you?" *650*
7:25 "Isn't this the man they are trying *to* **k?** *650*
8:22 This made the Jews ask, *"Will he* **k** himself? *650*
8:37 Yet you are ready *to* **k** me, *650*
8:40 As it is, you are determined *to* **k** me, *650*
10:10 thief comes only to steal and **k** and destroy; *2604*
12:10 So the chief priests made plans to **k** Lazarus *650*
Ac 7:28 Do you want *to* **k** me as you killed *359*
9:23 the Jews conspired *to* **k** him, *359*
9:24 on the city gates in order to **k** him. *359*
9:29 but they tried *to* **k** him. *359*
10:13 "Get up, Peter. **K** and eat." *2604*
11:7 'Get up, Peter. **K** and eat.' *2604*
16:27 about *to* **k** himself because he thought *359*
21:31 While they were trying *to* **k** him, *650*
23:15 We are ready *to* **k** him before he gets here." *359*
23:27 by the Jews and they were about to **k** him, *359*
25:3 an ambush *to* **k** him along the way. *359*
26:21 in the temple courts and tried *to* **k** me. *1429*
27:42 to **k** the prisoners to prevent any of them *650*
Ro 11:3 and *they are* **trying to k** me"? *2426+3836+6034*
1Ti 1:9 *for those who* **k their fathers** or mothers, *4260*
Jas 4:2 *You* **k** and covet, *5839*
Rev 6:8 over a fourth of the earth *to* **k** by sword, *650*
9:5 They were not given power to **k** them, *650*
9:15 and month and year were released to **k** *650*
11:7 and overpower and **k** them. *650*

KILLED (211) [KILL]

Ge 4:8 Cain attacked his brother Abel and **k** him. 2222
4:23 *I have* **k** a man for wounding me, 2222
4:25 child in place of Abel, since Cain **k** him." 2222
49:6 for *they have* **k** men in their anger 2222
Ex 2:12 *he* **k** the Egyptian and hid him in the sand. 5782
2:14 Are you thinking of killing me as *you* **k** 2222
13:15 the LORD **k** every firstborn in Egypt, 2222
Lev 14:5 that one of the birds *be* **k** over fresh water in 8821
14:6 of the bird that **was k** over the fresh water. 8821
Nu 16:41 "You *have* **k** the LORD's people," 4637
19:16 open who touches someone *who* has been **k** 2728
19:18 or a grave or someone who has been **k** 2728
22:33 *I would* certainly *have* **k** you by now, 2222
25:14 The name of the Israelite who *was* **k** with 5782
25:18 the *woman who* **was k** when the plague 5782
31:7 LORD commanded Moses, and **k** every man. 2222
31:8 also **k** Balaam son of Beor with the sword. 2222
31:19 "All of you *who have* **k** anyone 2222
31:19 touched anyone who was **k** must stay
outside 2728
35:6 a *person who has* **k** someone may flee. 8357
35:11 *person who has* **k** someone accidentally
may flee. 5782+8357
35:15 anyone *who has* **k** another accidentally can
flee there. 5782
Dt 4:42 to which *anyone* who *had* **k a person** could
flee 8357
4:42 if he had unintentionally **k** his neighbor 8357
21:1 and it is not known who **k** him, 5782
Jos 7:5 who **k** about thirty-six of them. 5782
8:24 Israelites returned to Ai and **k** those who
were in it. 2995+4200+5782+7023
10:11 the hailstones than *were* **k** by the swords 2222
10:26 and **k** the kings and hung them on five trees, 4637
20:5 because *he* **k** his neighbor unintentionally 5782
Jos 20:9 *who* **k** someone accidentally could flee 5782
20:9 and not *be* **k** by the avenger of blood prior 4637
Jdg 7:25 *They* **k** Oreb at the rock of Oreb, 2222
8:17 also pulled down the tower of Peniel and **k** 2222
8:21 So Gideon stepped forward and **k** them, 2222
9:45 until he had captured it and **k** its people. 2222
9:54 so that they can't say, 'A woman **k** him.' " 2222
12:6 they seized him and **k** him at the fords of 8821
12:6 Forty-two thousand Ephraimites *were* **k** at 5877
15:16 With a donkey's jawbone *I have* **k** 5782
16:30 Thus *he* **k** many more when he died than 4637
1Sa 4:2 *who* **k** about four thousand of them on 5782
14:13 and his armor-bearer followed and **k** 4637
14:14 and his armor-bearer **k** some twenty men in 5782
17:35 I seized it by its hair, struck it and **k** it. 4637
17:36 Your servant *has* **k** both the lion and 5782
17:50 down the Philistine and **k** him. 4637
17:51 *he* **k** him, he cut off his head with the sword 4637
18:6 after David *had* **k** the Philistine, 5782
18:27 and **k** two hundred Philistines. 5782
19:5 He took his life in his hands when *he* **k** 5782
19:11 tomorrow you'll **be k."** 4637
20:14 so that *I may* not *be* **k,** 4637
21:9 whom *you* **k** in the Valley of Elah, 5782
22:18 That day *he* **k** eighty-five men who wore 4637
22:21 He told David that Saul *had* **k** the priests of 2222
30:2 *They* **k** none of them, 4637
31:2 and they **k** his sons Jonathan, 5782
2Sa 1:10 "So I stood over him and **k** him, 4637
1:16 'I **k** the LORD's anointed.' " 4637
2:31 But David's men *had* **k** three hundred 4637+5782
3:30 because *he had* **k** their brother Asahel in 4637
4:7 After they stabbed and **k** him, 4637
4:11 when wicked men *have* **k** an innocent man 2222
4:12 gave an order to his men, and *they* **k** them. 2222
10:18 and David **k** seven hundred of their 2222
11:21 Who **k** Abimelech son of Jerub-Besheth? 5782
12:9 *You* **k** him with the sword of the 2222
13:32 "My lord should not think that *they* **k** all 4637
14:6 One struck the other and **k** him. 4637
14:7 for the life of his brother whom *he* **k;** 2222
18:15 Absalom, struck him and **k** him. 4637
21:6 to us *to be* **k and exposed** before the LORD 3697
21:9 *who* **k and exposed** them on a hill before 3697
21:13 *who had* **been k and exposed** were gathered 3697
21:17 he struck the Philistine down and **k** him. 4637
21:18 that time Sibbecai the Hushathite **k** Saph. 5782
21:19 of Jaare-Oregim the Bethlehemite **k** Goliath 5782
21:21 David's brother, **k** him. 5782
23:8 whom he **k** in one encounter. 2728
23:18 against three hundred men, whom he **k,** 2728
23:20 down into a pit on a snowy day and **k** a lion. 5782
23:21 from the Egyptian's hand and **k** him 2222
1Ki 2:5 *He* **k** them, shedding their blood 2222
2:32 and **k** them with the sword. 2222
2:34 up and struck down Joab and **k** him, 4637
2:46 and struck Shimei down and **k** him. 4637
9:16 *He* **k** its Canaanite inhabitants and 2222
13:24 a lion met him on the road and **k** him, 4637
13:26 which has mauled him and **k** him, 4637
15:28 Baasha **k** Nadab in the third year 4637
15:29 *he* **k** Jeroboam's whole family. 5782
16:10 down and **k** him in the twenty-seventh year 4637
16:11 *he* **k off** Baasha's whole family. 5782
19:1 *he had* **k** all the prophets with the sword. 2222
20:36 a lion found him and **k** him. 5782
2Ki 10:9 against my master and **k** him, 2222
10:9 but who **k** all these? 5782
10:11 So Jehu **k** everyone in Jezreel who remained 5782
10:17 *he* **k** all who were left there of Ahab's 5782
11:2 so *he* **was** not **k.** 4637
11:18 and **k** Mattan the priest of Baal 2222
14:19 after him to Lachish and **k** him there. 4637
15:25 So Pekah **k** Pekahiah and succeeded him 4637
17:25 among them and *they* **k** some of the people. 2222
21:24 the people of the land **k** all who had plotted 5782
23:29 but Neco faced him and **k** him at Megiddo. 4637
25:7 *They* **k** the sons of Zedekiah 8821
1Ch 4:43 *They* **k** the remaining Amalekites who had 5782
7:21 and Elead *were* **k** *by* the native-born men 2222
10:2 and they **k** his sons Jonathan, 5782
11:11 whom he **k** in one encounter. 2728
11:20 *whom* he **k,** and so he became as famous as 2728
11:22 down into a pit on a snowy day and **k** a lion. 5782
11:23 from the Egyptian's hand and **k** him 2222
19:18 and David **k** seven thousand 2222
19:18 *He* also **k** Shophach the commander 4637
20:4 that time Sibbecai the Hushathite **k** Sippai, 5782
20:5 Elhanan son of Jair **k** Lahmi the brother 5782
20:7 David's brother, **k** him. 5782
2Ch 22:1 *had* **k** all the older sons. 2222
22:8 been attending Ahaziah, and *he* **k** them. 2222
23:17 the altars and idols and **k** Mattan the priest 2222
24:22 but **k** his son, who said as he lay dying, 2222
24:23 it invaded Judah and Jerusalem and **k** all 8845
24:25 and *they* **k** him in his bed. 2222
25:11 where *he* **k** ten thousand men of Seir. 5782
25:13 *They* **k** three thousand people 5782
25:27 after him to Lachish and **k** him there. 4637
28:6 In one day Pekah son of Remaliah **k** 2222
28:7 **k** Maaseiah the king's son, 2222
33:25 the people of the land **k** all who had plotted 5782
36:17 *who* **k** their young men with the sword in 2222
Ne 9:26 *They* **k** your prophets, 2222
Est 9:6 the Jews **k** and destroyed five hundred men. 2222
9:7 *They* also **k** Parshandatha, Dalphon, 2222
9:12 "The Jews *have* **k** and destroyed 2222

Est 9:16 They **k** seventy-five thousand of them 2222
Ps 135:10 down many nations and **k** mighty kings— 2222
136:18 **k** mighty kings—His love endures forever. 2222
Isa 14:20 destroyed your land and **k** your people. 2222
22: 2 Your slain were not **k** *by* the sword, 2728
27: 7 *Has she* **been k** as those were killed who 2222
27: 7 killed as those were **k** who killed her? 2223
27: 7 killed as *those* were killed *who* **k** her? 2222
Jer 39: 6 of Zedekiah before his eyes and also **k** all 8821
41: 3 also **k** all the Jews who were with Gedaliah 5782
41: 9 of the men *he had* **k** along with Gedaliah 5782
41:18 Nethaniah *had* **k** Gedaliah son of Ahikam, 5782
52:10 *he* also **k** all the officials of Judah. 8821
La 2:20 and prophet **be k** in the sanctuary of 2222
4: 9 *Those* **k** *by* the sword are better off than 2728
Eze 11: 6 You have **k** many *people* in this city 2728
13:19 you *have* **k** those who should not have died 4637
23:10 took away her sons and daughters and **k** her 2222
31:17 joining *those* **k** *by* the sword. 2728
31:18 with *those* **k** *by* the sword. 2728
32:20 They will fall among *those* **k** *by* the sword. 2728
32:21 with *those* **k** *by* the sword.' 2728
32:25 are uncircumcised, **k** *by* the sword. 2728
32:26 are uncircumcised, **k** *by* the sword 2726
32:28 with *those* **k** *by* the sword. 2728
32:29 they are laid with *those* **k** *by* the sword. 2728
32:30 They lie uncircumcised with *those* **k** *by* 2728
32:31 for all his hordes *that* were **k** by the sword, 2728
32:32 with *those* **k** *by* the sword, 2728
35: 8 *those* **k** *by* the sword will fall on your hills 2728
Da 3:22 flames of the fire **k** the soldiers who took 10625
Hos 6: 5 *I* **k** you with the words of my mouth; 2222
Am 4:10 *I* **k** your young men with the sword, 2222
Na 2:12 The lion **k** enough for his cubs 3271
Mt 16:21 and that he must *be* **k** and on the third day *650*
21:35 they beat one, **k** another, and stoned a third. *650*
21:39 of the vineyard and **k** him. *650*
22: 6 mistreated them and **k** them. *650*
Mk 8:31 *he* must *be* **k** and after three days rise again. *650*
12: 5 He sent still another, and that one *they* **k.** *650*
12: 5 some of them they beat, others *they* **k.** *650*
12: 8 So *they* took him and **k** him, *650*
Lk 9:22 *be* **k** and on the third day be raised to life." *650*
11:47 and it was your forefathers who **k** them. *650*
11:48 they **k** the prophets, *650*
11:51 who *was* **k** between the altar and *660*
15:27 'and your father *has* **k** the fattened calf *2604*
20:15 of the vineyard and **k** him. *650*
Ac 3:13 You handed him over to be **k**, *NIG*
3:15 *You* **k** the author of life, but God raised him *650*
5:30 whom you *had* **k** by hanging him on a tree. *1429*
5:36 He *was* **k**, all his followers were dispersed, *359*
5:37 He too *was* **k**, and all his followers were *660*
7:28 as *you* **k** the Egyptian yesterday?' *359*
7:52 even **k** those who predicted the coming of *650*
10:39 *They* **k** him by hanging him on a tree, *359*
23:12 not to eat or drink until *they had* **k** Paul. *650*
23:14 not to eat anything until we *have* **k** Paul. *650*
23:21 not to eat or drink until *they have* **k** him. *359*
Ro 11: 3 *they have* **k** your prophets and torn down *650*
1Co 10: 9 some of them did—and *were* **k** by snakes. *660*
10:10 and *were* **k** by the destroying angel. *660*
2Co 6: 9 beaten, and yet not **k;** *2506*
1Th 2:15 who **k** the Lord Jesus and the prophets and *650*
Heb 11:31 *was* not **k with** those who were disobedient. *5272*
Rev 6:11 to be **k** as they had been was completed. *650*
9:18 third of mankind *was* **k** by the three plagues *650*
9:20 not **k** by these plagues still did not repent of *650*
11:13 Seven thousand people *were* **k** in *650*
13:10 If anyone *is to be* **k** with the sword, *650*
13:10 with the sword he *will be* **k.** *650*
13:15 refused to worship the image *to be* **k.** *650*
18:24 and *of* all who *have been* **k** on the earth." *5377*
19:21 *were* **k** with the sword that came out of *650*

KILLING (21) [KILL]

Ge 27:42 with the thought of **k** you. 2222
34:25 the unsuspecting city, **k** every male. 2222
Ex 2:14 Are you thinking of **k** me as you killed 2222
32:27 each **k** his brother and friend 2222
Jos 8:24 When Israel had finished **k** all the men 2222
1Sa 17:57 as David returned from **k** the Philistine, 5782
19: 5 to an innocent man like David by **k** him 4637
1Ki 18: 4 Jezebel *was* **k off** the LORD's prophets, 4162
18:13 what I did while Jezebel *was* **k** the prophets 2222
2Ki 17:26 lions among them, which *are* **k** them **off,** 4637
Est 3: 6 the idea of **k** only Mordecai. 928+3338+8938
9: 5 with the sword, **k** and destroying them, 2223
Isa 22:13 slaughtering of cattle and **k** *of* sheep, 8821
Jer 41: 2 **k** the one whom the king of Babylon 4637
Eze 9: 7 So they went out and *began* **k** throughout 5782
9: 8 While they *were* **k** and I was left alone, 5782
14:19 **k** its men and their animals, 4162
Jnh 1:14 Do not hold us accountable for **k** an 1947
Lk 12: 5 Fear him who, after the **k** of the body, *650*
Ac 7:24 to his defense and avenged him *by* **k** *4250*
22:20 the clothes *of* those who *were* **k** him.' *359*

KILLS (21) [KILL]

Ge 4:15 if anyone **k** Cain, he will suffer vengeance 2222
Ex 21:12 "Anyone who strikes a man and **k** him shall 4637
21:14 and **k** another man deliberately, 2222
21:29 but has not kept it penned up and *it* **k** 4637
Lev 24:21 *Whoever* **k** an animal must make restitution, 5782
24:21 but *whoever* **k** a man must be put to death. 5782
Nu 35:30 " 'Anyone *who* **k** a person is to be put 5782
Dt 19: 3 so that anyone *who* **k a man** may flee there. 8357
19: 4 the rule concerning the *man who* **k another** 8357
19: 4 *one* who **k** his neighbor unintentionally, 8357
19:11 assaults and **k** him, 2256+4637+5782+5883
27:24 the man *who* **k** his neighbor secretly." 5782
Jos 20: 3 so that anyone *who* **k** a person accidentally 5782
1Sa 17:25 great wealth to the man who **k** him. 5782
17:26 be done for the man who **k** this Philistine 5782
17:27 be done for the man who **k** him." 5782
Job 5: 2 Resentment **k** a fool, 2222
24:14 murderer rises up and **k** the poor and needy; 7779
Isa 66: 3 like *one who* **k** a man, and whoever offers 5782
Jn 16: 2 anyone who **k** you will think he is offering *650*
2Co 3: 6 for the letter **k**, but the Spirit gives life. *650*

KILMAD (1)

Eze 27:23 Asshur and **K** traded with you. 4008

KIMHAM (3) [GERUTH KIMHAM]

2Sa 19:37 But here is your servant **K.** 4016
19:38 The king said, "**K** shall cross over with me, 4016
19:40 **K** crossed with him. 4016

KIN (1) [KINSMAN, KINSMEN]

Ru 3:12 Although it is true that I *am* **near of k,** 1457

KINAH (1)

Jos 15:22 **K,** Dimonah, Adadah, 7807

KIND (112) [KINDEST, KINDHEARTED, KINDLY, KINDNESS, KINDNESSES, KINDS]

Ge 1:21 and every winged bird according to its **k.** 4786
1:24 and wild animals, each according to its **k."** 4786
6:20 Two of every **k** *of* bird, 4786
6:20 of every **k** *of* animal and of every kind 4786
6:20 and of every **k** *of* creature that moves along 4786
6:21 to take **every** *k of* food that is to be eaten AIT
7: 2 with you seven of **every** *k of* clean animal, AIT
7: 2 and two of every **k** of unclean animal, NIH
7: 3 and also seven of every **k** of bird, NIH
7:14 every wild animal according to its **k,** 4786
7:14 the ground according to its **k** and every bird 4786
7:14 to its kind and every bird according to its **k,** 4786
8:17 Bring out **every** *k of* living creature that is AIT
8:19 came out of the ark, **one k after another.** 2157+4200+5476
9:15 and you and all living creatures of every **k.** 1414
9:16 and all living creatures of every **k** on 1414
27: 4 the **k** *of* tasty food I like and bring it 889+3869
37: 4 and could not speak a **k** word to him. 8934
Ex 1:20 So God *was* **k** to the midwives and 3512
Lev 7:14 He is to bring one of **each** *k* as an offering, AIT
11:14 the red kite, any **k** *of* black kite, 4786
11:15 any **k** *of* raven, 4786
11:16 the screech owl, the gull, any **k** *of* hawk, 4786
11:19 any **k** *of* heron, the hoopoe and the bat. 4786
11:22 Of these you may eat any **k** *of* locust, 4786
11:29 the weasel, the rat, any **k** *of* great lizard, 4786
13:31 if, when the priest examines **this k of sore,** 2021+5596+5999
19:23 " 'When you enter the land and plant **any** *k* AIT
25:36 Do not take **interest of any k** 2256+5968+9552
Nu 5: 2 or a discharge *of* **any** *k*, AIT
13:19 **What** *k of* land do they live in? AIT
13:19 **What** *k of* towns do they live in? AIT
28: 8 along with the **same** *k of* grain offering AIT
Dt 4:15 *of* **any** *k* the day the LORD spoke to you AIT
4:25 if you then become corrupt and make any **k** 9454
14:13 the red kite, the black kite, any **k** *of* falcon, 4786
14:14 any **k** *of* raven, 4786
14:15 the screech owl, the gull, any **k** *of* hawk, 4786
14:18 any **k** *of* heron, the hoopoe and the bat. 4786
24:10 you make a loan of **any k** to your neighbor, 4399
28:61 The LORD will also bring on you **every** *k* AIT
Jdg 6:26 a **proper k** of altar to the LORD your God 5120
8:18 "What **k** of men did you kill at Tabor?" NIH
2Sa 13:18 for **this was the k** *of* garment 4027
1Ki 9:13 "What **k** of towns are these you have given NIH
2Ki 1: 7 "What **k** *of* man was it who came 5477
1Ch 22:15 as well as men skilled in **every** *k of* work AIT
2Ch 10: 7 be **k** to these people and please them 3202
15: 6 troubling them with **every** *k of* distress. AIT
Job 6:28 "But now **be so k as** to look at me. 3283
Ps 144:13 Our barns will be filled with **every k** of provision. 448+2385+2385+4946
Pr 11:17 A **k** man benefits himself, 2876
12:25 but a **k** word cheers him up. 3202
14:21 but blessed is he *who is* **k** *to* the needy. 2858
14:31 but *whoever is* **k** *to* the needy honors God. 2858
19:17 *He who is* **k** *to* the poor lends to the LORD, 2858
23: 7 the **k** *of* man who is always thinking about 4017
28: 8 *who will be* **k** *to* the poor. 2858
SS 4:14 with **every** *k of* incense tree, AIT
Isa 44:11 He and his **k** will be put to shame; 2492
58: 5 Is this the **k** of fast I have chosen, 3869
58: 6 "Is not this the **k** of fasting I have chosen: NIH
Jer 8: 9 **what k** *of* wisdom do they have? 4537
Eze 17:23 Birds *of* **every** *k* will nest in it; AIT
39:17 to every **k** *of* bird and all the wild animals: 4053S
39:20 mighty men and soldiers of **every** *k*,' AIT
Da 1: 4 showing aptitude for **every** *k of* learning, AIT
Da 4:27 and your wickedness by *being* **k** *to* 10274
Zep 2:14 will lie down there, creatures of every **k.** 1580
Zec 1:13 the LORD spoke **k** and comforting words 3202
Mt 8:27 **"What k of** *man* is this? *4534*
Mk 9:29 "This **k** can come out only by prayer." *1169*
Lk 1:29 and wondered **what k of** greeting this might *4534*
6:35 he is **k** to the ungrateful and wicked. *5982*
7:39 and **what k of** woman she is— *4534*
16: 8 with their own **k** than are the people of *1155*
Jn 2: 6 **k** used by the Jews for ceremonial washing, *NIG*
4:23 for **they are the k** of worshipers *5525*
12:33 to show the **k of** death he was going to die. *4481*
16:25 will no longer use **this k of** language *1877+4231S*
18:32 the **k** of death he was going to die would *4481*
21:19 Jesus said this to indicate the **k of** death *4481*
Ac 7:49 **What k of** house will you build for me? *4481*
20:35 that **by this k** of hard work we must help *4048*
24: 4 that you be **k** enough to hear us briefly. *2116*
Ro 1:29 They have become filled *with* **every** *k* *AIT*
7: 8 produced in me **every** *k* of covetous desire. *AIT*
1Co 5: 1 and **of a k** that does not occur even *5525*
13: 4 Love is patient, love *is* **k.** *5980*
15:35 *With* **what k of** body will they come?" *4481*
15:38 *to* **each** *k* of seed he gives its own body. *AIT*
15:39 Men have one **k** of flesh, *NIG*
15:40 of the heavenly bodies is one **k,** *NIG*
15:41 The sun has one **k** of splendor, *NIG*
Gal 5: 8 That **k** of persuasion does not come from *NIG*
Eph 4:19 to sensuality so as to indulge in **every** *k* *AIT*
4:32 Be **k** and compassionate to one another, *5982*
5: 3 or of **any** *k* of impurity, or of greed, *AIT*
1Th 1: 9 for they themselves report **what k of** *3961*
5:15 to be **k** to each other and to everyone else. *19*
5:22 Avoid every **k** of evil. *1626*
2Ti 2:24 instead, he must be **k** to everyone, *2473*
3: 6 **They are the k** who worm their way *1666+4047*
Tit 2: 5 to be **k,** and to be subject to their husbands, *19*
Jas 1:18 be **a k** of firstfruits of all he created. *5516*
1Pe 2: 1 hypocrisy, envy, and slander of **every** *k*. *AIT*
4:15 not be as a murderer or thief or any other **k** *NIG*
5: 9 the world are undergoing the **same** *k* *AIT*
2Pe 3:11 **what k of** *people* ought you to be? *4534*
Rev 11: 6 to strike the earth with **every** *k* of plague *AIT*
18:12 and articles of every **k** made of ivory, *5007*
21:19 the city walls were decorated *with* **every** *k* *AIT*

KINDEST (1) [KIND]

Pr 12:10 but the **k acts** *of* the wicked are cruel. 8171

KINDHEARTED (1) [KIND, HEART]

Pr 11:16 A **k** woman gains respect, 2834

KINDLE (5) [KINDLED, KINDLES, KINDLING]

Jer 15:14 for my anger *will* **k** a fire that will burn 7706
17:27 then *I will* **k** an unquenchable fire in 3675
21:14 *I will* **k** a fire in your forests 3675
50:32 *I will* **k** a fire in her towns 3675
Eze 24:10 So heap on the wood and **k** the fire. 1944

KINDLED (7) [KINDLE]

Dt 32:22 For a fire *has been* **k** by my wrath, 7706
Isa 10:16 a fire *will be* **k** like a blazing flame. 3678
Jer 17: 4 for *you have* **k** my anger, 836+7706
La 4:11 *He* **k** a fire in Zion 3675
Eze 20:48 that I the LORD *have* **k** it; 1277
Lk 12:49 and how I wish *it were* already **k!** *409*
22:55 But *when they had* **k** a fire in the middle of *4312*

KINDLES (1) [KINDLE]

Isa 44:15 *he* **k a fire** and bakes bread. 5956

KINDLING (1) [KINDLE]

Pr 26:21 so is a quarrelsome man for **k** strife. 3081

KINDLY (6) [KIND]

Ge 50:21 And he reassured them and spoke **k** to them. 4213
Jos 2:14 we will treat you **k** and faithfully when 2876
Ru 2:13 *have* **spoken k** *to* your servant 1819+4213+6584
2Ki 25:28 He spoke **k** to him and gave him a seat 3208
Jer 52:32 He spoke **k** to him and gave him a seat 3208
1Co 4:13 when we are slandered, *we* **answer k.** *4151*

KINDNESS (64) [KIND]

Ge 19:19 and you have shown great **k** to me 2876
21:23 an alien the same **k** I have shown to you." 2876
24:12 and show **k** to my master Abraham. 2876
24:14 By this I will know that you have shown **k** 2876
24:27 not abandoned his **k** and faithfulness 2876
24:49 Now if you will show **k** and faithfulness 2876
32:10 I am unworthy of all the **k** 2876
39:21 he showed him **k** and granted him favor in 2876
40:14 remember me and show me **k;** 2876
47:29 that you will show me **k** and faithfulness. 2876
Jos 2:12 to me by the LORD that you will show **k** 2876
2:12 because I have shown **k** to you. 2876
Jdg 8:35 They also failed to show **k** to the family 2876
21:22 **'Do** us **a k** by helping them, 2858
Ru 1: 8 May the LORD show **k** to you, 2876
2:20 not stopped showing his **k** to the living and 2876
3:10 "This **k** is greater than that which you 2876

1Sa 15: 6 for you showed **k** to all the Israelites 2876
20: 8 As for you, show **k** to your servant, 2876
20:14 But show me **unfailing k** *like that of* 2876
20:15 not ever cut off your **k** from my family— 2876
2Sa 2: 5 "The LORD bless you for showing this **k** 2876
2: 6 May the LORD now show you **k** 2876
9: 1 to whom I can show **k** for Jonathan's sake?" 2876
9: 3 of Saul to whom I can show God's **k?"** 2876
9: 7 "for I will surely show you **k** for the sake 2876
10: 2 "I will show **k** to Hanun son of Nahash, 2876
10: 2 just as his father showed **k** to me." 2876
15:20 May **k** and faithfulness be with you." 2876
22:51 he shows **unfailing k** to his anointed, 2876
1Ki 2: 7 "But show **k** to the sons of Barzillai 2876
3: 6 "You have shown great **k** to your servant, 2876
3: 6 You have continued this great **k** to him 2876
1Ch 19: 2 "I will show **k** to Hanun son of Nahash, 2876
19: 2 because his father showed **k** to me." 2876
2Ch 1: 8 "You have shown great **k** 2876
24:22 **k** Zechariah's father Jehoiada had shown 2876
32:25 and he did not respond to the **k** *shown* him; 1691
Ezr 9: 9 He has shown us **k** in the sight of the kings 2876
Job 10:12 You gave me life and showed me **k,** 2876
24:21 and *to* the widow **show** no **k.** 3512
Ps 18:50 he shows **unfailing k** to his anointed, 2876
109:12 May no one extend **k** to him or take pity 2876
109:16 For he never thought of doing a **k,** 2876
141: 5 Let a righteous man strike me—it is a **k;** 2876
Isa 54: 8 with everlasting **k** I will have compassion 2876
Jer 9:24 that I am the LORD, who exercises **k,** 2876
Hos 11: 4 I led them with cords of human **k,** NIH
Ac 4: 9 an **act of k shown to** a cripple *2307*
14:17 *He has* **shown k** by giving you rain *14*
27: 3 and Julius, **in k** to Paul, *5793+5968*
28: 2 The islanders showed us unusual **k.** *5792*
Ro 2: 4 for the riches *of* his **k,** *5983*
2: 4 that God's **k** leads you toward repentance? *5982*
11:22 Consider therefore the **k** and sternness *5983*
11:22 sternness to those who fell, but **k** to you, *5983*
11:22 provided that you continue in his **k.** *5983*
2Co 6: 6 understanding, patience and **k;** *5983*
Gal 5:22 peace, patience, **k,** goodness, faithfulness, *5983*
Eph 2: 7 expressed in his **k** to us in Christ Jesus. *5983*
Col 3:12 clothe yourselves with compassion, **k,** *5983*
Tit 3: 4 the **k** and love of God our Savior appeared, *5983*
2Pe 1: 7 and to godliness, **brotherly k;** *5789*
1: 7 and to **brotherly k,** love. *5789*

KINDNESSES (3) [KIND]

Ps 106: 7 they did not remember your many **k,** 2876
Isa 63: 7 I will tell of the **k** *of* the LORD, 2876
63: 7 according to his compassion and many **k.** 2876

KINDRED, KINDREDS (KJV) See BLOOD RELATIVES, CLAN, FAMILY, KINSMAN, KINSMEN, NATIVE, PEOPLE, RELATIVES, TRIBE

KINDS (77) [KIND]

Ge 1:11 according to their **various k."** 4786
1:12 according to their **k** and trees bearing fruit 4786
1:12 with seed in it according to their **k.** 4786
1:21 according to their **k,** 4786
1:24 according to their **k:** 4786
1:25 the wild animals according to their **k,** 4786
1:25 the livestock according to their **k,** 4786
1:25 along the ground according to their **k.** 4786
2: 9 And the LORD God made **all** *k* AIT
4:22 who forged **all** *k of* tools out of bronze AIT
7: 3 to keep their **various k** alive throughout 2446
7:14 all livestock according to their **k,** 4786
24:10 taking with him **all** *k of* good things AIT
40:17 top basket were **all k** *of* baked goods 3972+4946
Ex 1:14 and mortar and with **all** *k of* work in AIT
31: 3 and knowledge in **all** *k of* crafts— AIT
31: 5 and to engage in **all** *k of* craftsmanship. AIT
35:22 came and brought gold jewelry of **all** *k:* AIT
35:31 and knowledge in **all** *k of* crafts— AIT
35:33 to engage in all **k** *of* artistic craftsmanship. 4856
35:35 He has filled them with skill to do **all** *k* AIT
Lev 19:19 " 'Do not mate **different k** *of* animals. 3977
19:19 not plant your field with **two k** *of* seed. 3977
19:19 " 'Do not wear clothing woven of **two k** 3977
Dt 6:11 with **all** *k of* good things you did AIT
12:31 they do **all** *k of* detestable things AIT
22: 9 Do not plant **two k** of seed in your vineyard; 3977
1Sa 4: 8 the Egyptians with **all** *k of* plagues in AIT
1Ki 7:14 in **all** *k of* bronze work. AIT
1Ch 18:10 Hadoram brought **all** *k of* articles AIT
28:14 be used in **various k of service,** 2256+6275+6275
28:14 be used in **various k of service:** 2256+6275+6275
29: 2 and **all** *k of* fine stone and marble— AIT
2Ch 2:14 He is experienced in **all** *k of* engraving AIT
32:27 spices, shields and all **k** *of* valuables. 3998
32:28 made stalls for various **k of cattle,** 989+989+2256
Ne 5:18 an abundant supply of wine of **all** *k.* AIT
9:25 houses filled with **all** *k of* good things, AIT
13:15 grapes, figs and **all** *other k* of loads. AIT
13:16 in fish and **all** *k of* merchandise AIT
13:20 and sellers of **all** *k of* goods spent AIT
Ecc 2: 5 and parks and planted **all** *k of* fruit trees AIT
Jer 15: 3 "I will send four **k** of destroyers 5476
Eze 8:10 and I saw portrayed all over the walls all **k** 9322
27:22 of **all** *k of* spices and precious stones, AIT
Eze 39: 4 as food to all **k** *of* carrion birds and to 4053[S]
47:10 The fish will be of many **k—** 4786
47:12 of **all** *k* will grow on both banks of AIT
Da 1:17 and understanding of **all** *k of* literature AIT
1:17 understand visions and dreams of **all** *k.* AIT
3: 5 zither, lyre, harp, pipes and all **k** *of* music, 10235
3: 7 flute, zither, lyre, harp and all **k** *of* music, 10235
3:10 pipes and all **k** *of* music must fall down 10235
3:15 zither, lyre, harp, pipes and all **k** *of* music, 10235
Mt 5:11 and falsely say **all** *k* of evil against you *AIT*
13:47 down into the lake and caught all **k** of fish. *1169*
Lk 4:40 to Jesus all who had **various k** of sickness, *4476*
11:42 rue and **all** other *k* of garden herbs, *AIT*
12:15 Be on your guard against **all** *k* of greed; *AIT*
Ac 10:12 It contained **all** *k* of four-footed animals, *AIT*
13:10 full *of* **all** *k of* deceit and trickery. *AIT*
1Co 12: 4 There are **different** *k* of gifts, *AIT*
12: 5 There are **different** *k* of service, *AIT*
12: 6 There are **different** *k* of working, *AIT*
12:10 to another speaking in different **k** *1169*
12:28 those speaking in different **k** of tongues. *1169*
Eph 6:18 in the Spirit on all occasions with **all** *k* *AIT*
2Th 2: 9 the work of Satan displayed in **all** *k* *AIT*
1Ti 5:10 in trouble and devoting herself *to* **all** *k* *AIT*
6:10 love of money is a root *of* **all** *k* of evil. *AIT*
2Ti 3: 6 and are swayed *by* **all k of** evil desires, *4476*
3:11 **what k of** *things* happened to me *3888*
Tit 3: 3 *by* **all k of** passions and pleasures. *4476*
Heb 13: 9 Do not be carried away *by* **all k of** *4476*
Jas 1: 2 whenever you face trials of **many k,** *4476*
3: 7 All **k** of animals, birds, *5882*
1Pe 1: 6 to suffer grief in **all k of** trials. *4476*

KINE (KJV) See COW, COWS

KING (2314) [KING'S, KINGDOM, KINGDOMS, KINGS, KINGS', KINGSHIP]

Ge 14: 1 At this time Amraphel **k** *of* Shinar, 4889
14: 1 Arioch **k** *of* Ellasar, 4889
14: 1 Kedorlaomer **k** *of* Elam and Tidal king 4889
14: 1 Kedorlaomer king of Elam and Tidal **k** 4889
14: 2 went to war against Bera **k** *of* Sodom, 4889
14: 2 Birsha **k** *of* Gomorrah, 4889
14: 2 Shinab **k** *of* Admah, 4889
14: 2 Shemeber **k** *of* Zeboiim, 4889
14: 2 and the **k** *of* Bela (that is, Zoar). 4889
14: 8 Then the **k** *of* Sodom, 4889
14: 8 the king of Sodom, the **k** *of* Gomorrah, 4889
14: 8 the king of Gomorrah, the **k** *of* Admah, 4889
14: 8 the **k** *of* Zeboiim and the king of Bela 4889
14: 8 the king of Zeboiim and the **k** *of* Bela 4889
14: 9 against Kedorlaomer **k** *of* Elam, Tidal king 4889
14: 9 Tidal **k** *of* Goiim, Amraphel king of Shinar 4889
14: 9 Amraphel **k** *of* Shinar and Arioch king 4889
14: 9 Amraphel king of Shinar and Arioch **k** 4889
14:17 the **k** *of* Sodom came out to meet him in 4889
14:18 Then Melchizedek **k** *of* Salem 4889
14:21 The **k** *of* Sodom said to Abram, 4889
14:22 But Abram said to the **k** *of* Sodom, 4889
20: 2 Then Abimelech **k** *of* Gerar sent for Sarah 4889
26: 1 to Abimelech **k** *of* the Philistines in Gerar. 4889
26: 8 Abimelech **k** *of* the Philistines looked down 4889
36:31 in Edom before any Israelite **k** reigned: 4889
36:32 Bela son of Beor *became* **k** of Edom. 4887
36:33 of Zerah from Bozrah succeeded him *as* **k.** 4887
36:34 of the Temanites succeeded him *as* **k.** 4887
36:35 succeeded him *as* **k.** 4887
36:36 Samlah from Masrekah succeeded him *as* **k.** 4887
36:37 on the river succeeded him *as* **k.** 4887
36:38 son of Acbor succeeded him *as* **k.** 4887
36:39 Hadad succeeded him *as* **k.** 4887
40: 1 and the baker of the **k** *of* Egypt offended 4889
40: 1 offended their master, the **k** *of* Egypt. 4889
40: 5 cupbearer and the baker of the **k** *of* Egypt, 4889
41:46 when he entered the service of Pharaoh **k** 4889
49:20 he will provide delicacies fit for a **k.** 4889
Ex 1: 8 Then a new **k,** who did not know about 4889
1:15 **k** *of* Egypt said to the Hebrew midwives, 4889
1:17 not do what the **k** *of* Egypt had told them 4889
1:18 the **k** *of* Egypt summoned the midwives 4889
2:23 that long period, the **k** *of* Egypt died. 4889
3:18 Then you and the elders are to go to the **k** 4889
3:19 the **k** *of* Egypt will not let you go unless 4889
5: 4 But the **k** *of* Egypt said, "Moses and Aaron, 4889
6:11 "Go, tell Pharaoh **k** *of* Egypt to let 4889
6:13 about the Israelites and Pharaoh **k** *of* Egypt, 4889
6:27 They were the ones who spoke to Pharaoh **k** 4889
6:29 Pharaoh **k** *of* Egypt everything I tell you." 4889
14: 5 When the **k** *of* Egypt was told that 4889
14: 8 hardened the heart of Pharaoh **k** *of* Egypt, 4889
Nu 20:14 from Kadesh to the **k** *of* Edom, saying: 4889
21: 1 When the Canaanite **k** *of* Arad, 4889
21:21 Israel sent messengers to say to Sihon **k** *of* 4889
21:26 the city of Sihon **k** *of* the Amorites, 4889
21:26 against the former **k** *of* Moab and had taken 4889
21:29 and his daughters as captives to Sihon **k** *of* 4889
21:33 and Og **k** *of* Bashan and his whole army 4889
21:34 Do to him what you did to Sihon **k** *of* 4889
22: 4 who was **k** of Moab at that time, 4889
22:10 "Balak son of Zippor, **k** *of* Moab, 4889
23: 7 the **k** *of* Moab from the eastern mountains. 4889
23:21 the shout of the **K** is among them. 4889
24: 7 "Their **k** will be greater than Agag; 4889
32:33 the kingdom of Sihon **k** *of* the Amorites 4889
32:33 of the Amorites and the kingdom of Og **k** 4889
Nu 33:40 The Canaanite **k** *of* Arad, 4889
Dt 1: 4 This was after he had defeated Sihon **k** *of* 4889
1: 4 and at Edrei had defeated Og **k** *of* Bashan, 4889
2:24 **k** *of* Heshbon, and his country. 4889
2:26 of Kedemoth I sent messengers to Sihon **k** 4889
2:30 But Sihon **k** *of* Heshbon refused 4889
3: 1 and Og **k** *of* Bashan and his whole army 4889
3: 2 Do to him what you did to Sihon **k** *of* 4889
3: 3 also gave into our hands Og **k** *of* Bashan 4889
3: 6 as we had done with Sihon **k** *of* Heshbon, 4889
3:11 (Only Og **k** *of* Bashan was left of 4889
4:46 in the land of Sihon **k** *of* the Amorites, 4889
4:47 of his land and the land of Og **k** *of* Bashan, 4889
7: 8 from the power of Pharaoh **k** *of* Egypt. 4889
11: 3 both to Pharaoh **k** *of* Egypt and 4889
17:14 a **k** over us like all the nations around us," 4889
17:15 the **k** the LORD your God chooses. 4889
17:16 The **k,** moreover, must not acquire great NIH
28:36 the **k** you set over you to a nation unknown 4889
29: 7 Sihon **k** *of* Heshbon and Og king of 4889
29: 7 of Heshbon and Og **k** *of* Bashan came out 4889
33: 5 He was **k** over Jeshurun when the leaders of 4889
Jos 2: 2 The **k** *of* Jericho was told, "Look! 4889
2: 3 the **k** *of* Jericho sent this message to Rahab: 4889
6: 2 along with its **k** and its fighting men. 4889
8: 1 For I have delivered into your hands the **k** 4889
8: 2 and its **k** as you did to Jericho and its king, 4889
8: 2 and its king as you did to Jericho and its **k,** 4889
8:14 When the **k** *of* Ai saw this, 4889
8:23 the **k** *of* Ai alive and brought him 4889
8:29 the **k** *of* Ai on a tree and left him there 4889
9:10 Sihon **k** *of* Heshbon, 4889
9:10 and Og **k** *of* Bashan, 4889
10: 1 Now Adoni-Zedek **k** *of* Jerusalem heard 4889
10: 1 to Ai and its **k** as he had done to Jericho 4889
10: 1 as he had done to Jericho and its **k,** 4889
10: 3 So Adoni-Zedek **k** *of* Jerusalem appealed 4889
10: 3 Jerusalem appealed to Hoham **k** of Hebron, 4889
10: 3 Piram **k** *of* Jarmuth, 4889
10: 3 Japhia **k** *of* Lachish and Debir king of 4889
10: 3 king of Lachish and Debir **k** *of* Eglon. 4889
10:28 He put the city and its **k** to the sword 4889
10:28 to the **k** *of* Makkedah as he had done to 4889
10:28 of Makkedah as he had done to the **k** *of* 4889
10:30 The LORD also gave that city and its **k** 4889
10:30 And he did to its **k** as he had done to 4889
10:30 as he had done to the **k** *of* Jericho. 4889
10:33 Horam **k** *of* Gezer had come up 4889
10:37 to the sword, together with its **k,** 4889
10:39 They took the city, its **k** and its villages, 4889
10:39 They did to Debir and its **k** as they had done 4889
10:39 as they had done to Libnah and its **k** and 4889
11: 1 When Jabin **k** *of* Hazor heard of this, 4889
11: 1 he sent word to Jobab **k** *of* Madon, 4889
11:10 and captured Hazor and put its **k** to 4889
12: 2 Sihon **k** *of* the Amorites, 4889
12: 4 And the territory of Og **k** *of* Bashan, 4889
12: 5 and half of Gilead to the border of Sihon **k** 4889
12: 9 the **k** *of* Jericho one the king of Ai 4889
12: 9 of Jericho one the **k** *of* Ai (near Bethel) one 4889
12:10 **k** *of* Jerusalem one the king of Hebron one 4889
12:10 king of Jerusalem one the **k** *of* Hebron one 4889
12:11 **k** *of* Jarmuth one the king of Lachish one 4889
12:11 king of Jarmuth one the **k** *of* Lachish one 4889
12:12 the **k** *of* Eglon one the king of Gezer one 4889
12:12 the king of Eglon one the **k** *of* Gezer one 4889
12:13 the **k** *of* Debir one the king of Geder one 4889
12:13 the king of Debir one the **k** *of* Geder one 4889
12:14 the **k** *of* Hormah one the king of Arad one 4889
12:14 the king of Hormah one the **k** *of* Arad one 4889
12:15 **k** *of* Libnah one the king of Adullam one 4889
12:15 king of Libnah one the **k** *of* Adullam one 4889
12:16 **k** *of* Makkedah one the king of Bethel one 4889
12:16 king of Makkedah one the **k** *of* Bethel one 4889
12:17 **k** *of* Tappuah one the king of Hepher one 4889
12:17 king of Tappuah one the **k** *of* Hepher one 4889
12:18 **k** *of* Aphek one the king of Lasharon one 4889
12:18 king of Aphek one the **k** *of* Lasharon one 4889
12:19 the **k** *of* Madon one the king of Hazor one 4889
12:19 the king of Madon one the **k** *of* Hazor one 4889
12:20 the **k** *of* Shimron Meron one the king 4889
12:20 the king of Shimron Meron one the **k** 4889
12:21 **k** *of* Taanach one the king of Megiddo one 4889
12:21 king of Taanach one the **k** *of* Megiddo one 4889
12:22 the **k** *of* Kedesh one the king of Jokneam 4889
12:22 the king of Kedesh one the **k** *of* Jokneam 4889
12:23 the **k** *of* Dor (in Naphoth Dor) one the king 4889
12:23 the king of Dor (in Naphoth Dor) one the **k** 4889
12:24 the **k** *of* Tirzah one thirty-one kings in all. 4889
13:10 all the towns of Sihon **k** *of* the Amorites, 4889
13:21 the entire realm of Sihon **k** *of* the Amorites, 4889
13:27 the rest of the realm of Sihon **k** *of* Heshbon 4889
13:30 the entire realm of Og **k** *of* Bashan— 4889
24: 9 When Balak son of Zippor, the **k** *of* Moab, 4889
Jdg 3: 8 into the hands of Cushan-Rishathaim **k** 4889
3:10 The LORD gave Cushan-Rishathaim **k** 4889
3:12 the LORD gave Eglon **k** *of* Moab power 4889
3:14 to Eglon **k** *of* Moab for eighteen years. 4889
3:15 with tribute to Eglon **k** *of* Moab. 4889
3:17 He presented the tribute to Eglon **k** 4889
3:19 "I have a secret message for you, O **k."** 4889
3:19 The **k** said, "Quiet!" NIH
3:20 As the **k** rose from his seat, NIH
4: 2 a **k** *of* Canaan, who reigned in Hazor. 4889
4:17 between Jabin **k** *of* Hazor and the clan 4889
4:23 the Canaanite **k,** before the Israelites. 4889
4:24 the Canaanite **k,** until they destroyed him. 4889

Jdg 9: 6 in Shechem to crown Abimelech **k.** 4889
9: 8 One day the trees went out to anoint a **k** 4889
9: 8 They said to the olive tree, *'Be* our **k.'** 4887
9: 10 'Come and *be* our **k.'** 4887
9: 12 trees said to the vine, 'Come and *be* our **k.'** 4887
9: 14 'Come and *be* our **k.'** 4887
9: 15 'If you really want to anoint me **k** over you, 4889
9: 16 in good faith when *you* **made** Abimelech **k,** 4887
9: 18 **made** Abimelech, the son of his slave girl, **k** 4887
11: 12 to the Ammonite **k** with the question: 4889
11: 13 **k** *of* the Ammonites answered Jephthah's 4889
11: 14 messengers to the Ammonite **k,** 4889
11: 17 Israel sent messengers to the **k** *of* Edom, 4889
11: 17 but the **k** *of* Edom would not listen. 4889
11: 17 They sent also to the **k** *of* Moab, 4889
11: 19 "Then Israel sent messengers to Sihon **k** *of* 4889
11: 25 of Zippor, **k** *of* Moab? 4889
11: 28 The **k** *of* Ammon, however, 4889
17: 6 In those days Israel had no **k;** 4889
18: 1 In those days Israel had no **k.** 4889
19: 1 In those days Israel had no **k.** 4889
21: 25 In those days Israel had no **k;** 4889
1Sa 2: 10 to his **k** and exalt the horn of his anointed." 4889
8: 5 now appoint a **k** to lead us, 4889
8: 6 when they said, "Give us a **k** to lead us," 4889
8: 7 but they have rejected me as their **k.** 4887
8: 9 the **k** who will reign over them will do." 4889
8: 10 to the people who were asking him for a **k.** 4889
8: 11 the **k** who will reign over you will do: 4889
8: 18 for relief from the **k** you have chosen, 4889
8: 19 "We want a **k** over us. 4889
8: 20 with a **k** to lead us and to go out before us 4889
8: 22 "Listen to them and **give** them a **k."** 4887+4889
10: 19 And you have said, 'No, set a **k** over us.' 4889
10: 24 Then the people shouted, "Long live the **k!"** 4889
11: 15 and **confirmed** Saul **as k** in the presence of 4887
12: 1 to me and *have* **set** a **k** over you. 4887+4889
12: 2 Now you have a **k** as your leader. 4889
12: 9 into the hands of the Philistines and the **k** 4889
12: 12 "But when you saw that Nahash **k** *of* 4889
12: 12 'No, we want a **k** to rule over us'— 4889
12: 12 though the LORD your God was your **k.** 4889
12: 13 Now here is the **k** you have chosen, 4889
12: 13 see, the LORD has set a **k** over you. 4889
12: 14 and the **k** who reigns over you follow 4889
12: 17 of the LORD when you asked for a **k."** 4889
12: 19 the evil of asking for a **k."** 4889
12: 25 both you and your **k** will be swept away." 4889
13: 1 when he *became* **k,** and he reigned over 4887
15: 1 the one the LORD sent to anoint you **k** 4889
15: 8 He took Agag **k** *of* the Amalekites alive, 4889
15: 11 I am grieved that *I have* **made** Saul **k,** 4887+4889
15: 17 The LORD anointed you **k** over Israel. 4889
15: 20 and brought back Agag their **k.** 4889
15: 23 he has rejected you as **k."** 4889
15: 26 LORD has rejected you as **k** over Israel!" 4889
15: 32 "Bring me Agag **k** *of* the Amalekites." 4889
15: 35 that *he had* **made** Saul **k** over Israel. 4887
16: 1 since I have rejected him as **k** over Israel? 4887
16: 1 I have chosen one of his sons to be **k."** 4889
17: 25 The **k** will give great wealth to the man 4889
17: 55 Abner replied, "As surely as you live, O **k,** 4889
17: 56 The **k** said, "Find out whose son this young man is." 4889
18: 6 from all the towns of Israel to meet **K** Saul 4889
18: 22 'Look, the **k** is pleased with you, 4889
18: 25 'The **k** wants no other price for 4889
18: 27 and presented the full number to the **k** so 4889
19: 4 not the **k** do wrong to his servant David; 4889
20: 5 and I am supposed to dine with the **k;** 4889
20: 24 the **k** sat down to eat. 4889
21: 2 "The **k** charged me with a certain matter 4889
21: 10 from Saul and went to Achish **k** *of* Gath. 4889
21: 11 "Isn't this David, the **k** *of* the land? 4889
21: 12 was very much afraid of Achish **k** *of* Gath. 4889
22: 3 to Mizpah in Moab and said to the **k** 4889
22: 4 So he left them with the **k** *of* Moab, 4889
22: 11 the **k** sent for the priest Ahimelech son 4889
22: 11 and they all came to the **k.** 4889
22: 14 Ahimelech answered the **k,** 4889
22: 15 Let not the **k** accuse your servant or any 4889
22: 16 But the **k** said, "You will surely die, 4889
22: 17 Then the **k** ordered the guards at his side: 4889
22: 18 The **k** then ordered Doeg, 4889
23: 17 You *will be* **k** over Israel, 4887
23: 20 O **k,** come down whenever it pleases you 4889
23: 20 for handing him over to the **k."** 4889
24: 8 "My lord the **k!"** 4889
24: 14 "Against whom has the **k** *of* Israel 4889
24: 20 I know that *you will* **surely be k** and 4887+4887
25: 36 the house holding a banquet like that of a **k.** 4889
26: 14 "Who are you who calls to the **k?"** 4889
26: 15 Why didn't you guard your lord the **k?** 4889
26: 15 Someone came to destroy your lord the **k.** 4889
26: 17 David replied, "Yes it is, my lord the **k."** 4889
26: 19 the **k** listen to his servant's words. 4889
26: 20 The **k** *of* Israel has come out to look for 4889
27: 2 and went over to Achish son of Maoch **k** 4889
28: 13 The **k** said to her, "Don't be afraid. 4889
29: 3 who was an officer of Saul **k** *of* Israel? 4889
29: 8 against the enemies of my lord the **k?"** 4889
2Sa 2: 4 to Hebron and there they anointed David **k** 4889
2: 7 and the house of Judah has anointed me **k** 4889
2: 9 *He* **made** him **k** over Gilead, 4887
2: 10 when he *became* **k** over Israel, 4887
2: 11 The length of time David was **k** in Hebron 4889
3: 3 of Maacah daughter of Talmai **k** *of* Geshur; 4889
2Sa 3: 17 have wanted to make David your **k.** 4889
3: 21 and assemble all Israel for my lord the **k,** 4889
3: 23 to the **k** and that the king had sent him away 4889
3: 23 to the king and that the **k** had sent him away NIH
3: 24 So Joab went to the **k** and said, 4889
3: 31 **K** David himself walked behind the bier. 4889
3: 32 and the **k** wept aloud at Abner's tomb. 4889
3: 33 The **k** sang this lament for Abner: 4889
3: 36 indeed, everything the **k** did pleased them. 4889
3: 37 and all Israel knew that the **k** had no part in 4889
3: 38 Then the **k** said to his men, 4889
3: 39 And today, though I am the anointed **k,** 4889
4: 8 to David at Hebron and said to the **k,** 4889
4: 8 the LORD has avenged my lord the **k** 4889
5: 2 In the past, while Saul was **k** over us, 4889
5: 3 of Israel had come to **K** David at Hebron, 4889
5: 3 the **k** made a compact with them at Hebron 4889
5: 3 and they anointed David **k** over Israel. 4889
5: 4 thirty years old when he *became* **k,** 4887
5: 6 The **k** and his men marched to Jerusalem 4889
5: 11 Hiram **k** *of* Tyre sent messengers to David, 4889
5: 12 that the LORD had established him as **k** 4889
5: 17 that David had been anointed **k** over Israel, 4889
6: 12 Now **K** David was told, 4889
6: 16 when she saw **K** David leaping and dancing 4889
6: 20 **k** *of* Israel has distinguished himself today, 4889
7: 1 After the **k** was settled in his palace and 4889
7: 3 Nathan replied to the **k,** 4889
7: 18 **K** David went in and sat before the LORD, 4889
8: 3 of Rehob, **k** *of* Zobah, when he went 4889
8: 5 of Damascus came to help Hadadezer **k** 4889
8: 8 **K** David took a great quantity of bronze. 4889
8: 9 When Tou **k** *of* Hamath heard 4889
8: 10 he sent his son Joram to **K** David 4889
8: 11 **K** David dedicated these articles to 4889
8: 12 from Hadadezer son of Rehob, **k** *of* Zobah. 4889
9: 2 and the **k** said to him, "Are you Ziba?" 4889
9: 3 The **k** asked, "Is there no one still left of 4889
9: 3 Ziba answered the **k,** "There is still a son 4889
9: 4 "Where is he?" the **k** asked. 4889
9: 5 **K** David had him brought from Lo Debar, 4889
9: 9 Then the **k** summoned Ziba, Saul's servant, 4889
9: 11 Then Ziba said to the **k,** 4889
9: 11 the **k** commands his servant to do." 4889
10: 1 the **k** *of* the Ammonites died, 4889
10: 1 and his son Hanun succeeded him *as* **k.** 4887
10: 5 The **k** said, "Stay at Jericho 4889
10: 6 as the **k** *of* Maacah with a thousand men, 4889
11: 8 and a gift from the **k** was sent after him. 4889
11: 19 the **k** this account of the battle, 4889
12: 7 'I anointed you **k** over Israel, 4889
12: 30 He took the crown from the head of their **k** 4889
13: 6 When the **k** came to see him, 4889
13: 13 Please speak to the **k;** 4889
13: 18 the virgin daughters of the **k** wore. 4889
13: 21 **K** David heard all this, he was furious. 4889
13: 24 Absalom went to the **k** and said, 4889
13: 24 Will the **k** and his officials please join me?" 4889
13: 25 "No, my son," the **k** replied. 4889
13: 26 The **k** asked him, "Why should he go 4889
13: 31 The **k** stood up, tore his clothes and lay 4889
13: 33 My lord the **k** should not be concerned 4889
13: 34 The watchman went and told the **k,** 4889
13: 35 Jonadab said to the **k,** "See, 4889
13: 36 wailing loudly. The **k,** too, and all 4889
13: 37 Talmai son of Ammihud, the **k** *of* Geshur. 4889
13: 37 **K** David mourned for his son every day. NIH
13: 39 the spirit of the **k** longed to go to Absalom, 4889
14: 3 go to the **k** and speak these words to him." 4889
14: 4 the woman from Tekoa went to the **k,** 4889
14: 4 and she said, "Help me, O **k!"** 4889
14: 5 The **k** asked her, "What is troubling you?" 4889
14: 8 The **k** said to the woman, "Go home, 4889
14: 9 "My lord the **k,** let the blame rest on me 4889
14: 9 let the **k** and his throne be without guilt." 4889
14: 10 The **k** replied, "If anyone says anything 4889
14: 11 the **k** invoke the LORD his God to prevent 4889
14: 12 speak a word to my lord the **k."** 4889
14: 13 When the **k** says this, 4889
14: 13 **k** has not brought back his banished son? 4889
14: 15 to say this to my lord the **k** because 4889
14: 15 'I will speak to the **k;** 4889
14: 16 the **k** will agree to deliver his servant from 4889
14: 17 the word of my lord the **k** bring me rest, 4889
14: 17 for my lord the **k** is like an angel of God 4889
14: 18 Then the **k** said to the woman, 4889
14: 18 "Let my lord the **k** speak," the woman said. 4889
14: 19 The **k** asked, "Isn't the hand of Joab 4889
14: 19 "As surely as you live, my lord the **k,** 4889
14: 19 to the left from anything my lord the **k** says. 4889
14: 21 The **k** said to Joab, "Very well, I will do it. 4889
14: 22 to pay him honor, and he blessed the **k.** 4889
14: 22 favor in your eyes, my lord the **k,** 4889
14: 22 the **k** has granted his servant's request." 4889
14: 24 the **k** said, "He must go to his own house; 4889
14: 24 and did not see the face of the **k.** 4889
14: 29 for Joab in order to send him to the **k,** 4889
14: 32 'Come here so I can send you to the **k** 4889
14: 33 So Joab went to the **k** and told him this. 4889
14: 33 Then the **k** summoned Absalom, 4889
14: 33 with his face to the ground before the **k.** 4889
14: 33 And the **k** kissed Absalom. 4889
15: 2 with a complaint to be placed before the **k** 4889
15: 3 but there is no representative of the **k** 4889
15: 6 the Israelites who came to the **k** asking 4889
15: 7 Absalom said to the **k,** 4889
15: 9 The **k** said to him, "Go in peace." 4889
2Sa 15: 10 then say, 'Absalom *is* **k** in Hebron.'" 4887
15: 15 to do whatever our lord the **k** chooses." 4889
15: 16 The **k** set out, with his entire household 4889
15: 17 So the **k** set out, with all the people 4889
15: 18 from Gath marched before the **k.** 4889
15: 19 The **k** said to Ittai the Gittite, 4889
15: 19 Go back and stay with **K** Absalom. 4889
15: 21 But Ittai replied to the **k,** 4889
15: 21 and as my lord the **k** lives, 4889
15: 21 wherever my lord the **k** may be, 4889
15: 23 The **k** also crossed the Kidron Valley, 4889
15: 25 Then the **k** said to Zadok, 4889
15: 27 The **k** also said to Zadok the priest, 4889
15: 34 'I will be your servant, O **k;** 4889
16: 2 The **k** asked Ziba, 4889
16: 3 The **k** then asked, 4889
16: 4 Then the **k** said to Ziba, 4889
16: 4 find favor in your eyes, my lord the **k."** 4889
16: 5 As **K** David approached Bahurim, 4889
16: 9 Then Abishai son of Zeruiah said to the **k,** 4889
16: 9 "Why should this dead dog curse my lord the **k?** 4889
16: 10 But the **k** said, 4889
16: 14 The **k** and all the people with him arrived 4889
16: 16 "Long live the **k!** 4889
16: 16 Long live the **k!"** 4889
17: 2 I would strike down only the **k** 4889
17: 16 over without fail, or the **k** and all the people 4889
17: 17 and they were to go and tell **K** David, 4889
17: 21 of the well and went to inform **K** David. 4889
18: 2 The **k** told the troops, 4889
18: 4 **k** answered, "I will do whatever seems best 4889
18: 4 So the **k** stood beside the gate while all 4889
18: 5 The **k** commanded Joab, Abishai and Ittai, 4889
18: 5 And all the troops heard the **k** giving orders 4889
18: 12 the **k** commanded you and Abishai and Ittai, 4889
18: 13 and nothing is hidden from the **k—** 4889
18: 19 "Let me run and take the news to the **k** that 4889
18: 21 "Go, tell the **k** what you have seen." 4889
18: 25 The watchman called out to the **k** 4889
18: 25 The **k** said, "If he is alone, 4889
18: 26 The **k** said, "He must be bringing good 4889
18: 27 "He's a good man," the **k** said. 4889
18: 28 Ahimaaz called out to the **k,** "All is well!" 4889
18: 28 He bowed down before the **k** with his face 4889
18: 28 lifted their hands against my lord the **k."** 4889
18: 29 The **k** asked, "Is the young man Absalom safe?" 4889
18: 30 The **k** said, "Stand aside and wait here." 4889
18: 31 "My lord the **k,** hear the good news! 4889
18: 32 The **k** asked the Cushite, 4889
18: 32 the **k** and all who rise up to harm you be 4889
18: 33 The **k** was shaken. 4889
19: 1 "The **k** is weeping and mourning 4889
19: 2 "The **k** is grieving for his son." 4889
19: 4 The **k** covered his face and cried aloud, 4889
19: 5 Joab went into the house to the **k** and said, 4889
19: 8 **k** got up and took his seat in the gateway. 4889
19: 8 "The **k** is sitting in the gateway," 4889
19: 9 "The **k** delivered us from the hand 4889
19: 10 about bringing the **k** back?" 4889
19: 11 **K** David sent this message to Zadok 4889
19: 11 be the last to bring the **k** back to his palace, 4889
19: 11 throughout Israel has reached the **k** 4889
19: 12 be the last to bring back the **k?'** 4889
19: 14 They sent word to the **k,** "Return, 4889
19: 15 the **k** returned and went as far as the Jordan. 4889
19: 15 to go out and meet the **k** and bring him 4889
19: 16 with the men of Judah to meet **K** David. 4889
19: 17 They rushed to the Jordan, where the **k** was. 4889
19: 18 he fell prostrate before the **k** 4889
19: 19 on the day my lord the **k** left Jerusalem. 4889
19: 19 May the **k** put it out of his mind. 4889
19: 20 to come down and meet my lord the **k."** 4889
19: 22 not know that today I am **k** over Israel?" 4889
19: 23 So the **k** said to Shimei, "You shall not die." 4889
19: 23 And the **k** promised him on oath. 4889
19: 24 also went down to meet the **k.** 4889
19: 24 or washed his clothes from the day the **k** left 4889
19: 25 from Jerusalem to meet the **k,** 4889
19: 25 the **k** asked him, "Why didn't you go with 4889
19: 26 He said, "My lord the **k,** 4889
19: 26 ride on it, so I can go with the **k.'** 4889
19: 27 slandered your servant to my lord the **k.** 4889
19: 27 My lord the **k** is like an angel of God; 4889
19: 28 but death from my lord the **k,** 4889
19: 28 to make any more appeals to the **k?"** 4889
19: 29 The **k** said to him, "Why say more? 4889
19: 30 Mephibosheth said to the **k,** 4889
19: 30 that my lord the **k** has arrived home safely." 4889
19: 31 from Rogelim to cross the Jordan with the **k** 4889
19: 32 He had provided for the **k** during his stay 4889
19: 33 The **k** said to Barzillai, 4889
19: 34 But Barzillai answered the **k,** 4889
19: 34 I should go up to Jerusalem with the **k?** 4889
19: 35 be an added burden to my lord the **k?** 4889
19: 36 the Jordan with the **k** for a short distance, 4889
19: 36 why should the **k** reward me in this way? 4889
19: 37 Let him cross over with my lord the **k.** 4889
19: 38 The **k** said, "Kimham shall cross over 4889
19: 39 and then the **k** crossed over. 4889
19: 39 The **k** kissed Barzillai and gave him 4889
19: 40 When the **k** crossed over to Gilgal, 4889
19: 40 the troops of Israel had taken the **k** over. 4889
19: 41 of Israel were coming to the **k** and saying 4889
19: 41 the **k** away and bring him and his household 4889
19: 42 "We did this because the **k** is closely related 4889

2Sa 19:43 "We have ten shares in the **k**; 4889
19:43 the first to speak of bringing back our **k**?" 4889
20: 2 of Judah stayed by their **k** all the way from 4889
20: 4 Then the **k** said to Amasa, 4889
20: 5 he took longer than the time the **k** had set NIH
20:21 has lifted up his hand against the **k**, 4889
20:22 And Joab went back to the **k** in Jerusalem. 4889
21: 2 The **k** summoned the Gibeonites and spoke 4889
21: 5 They answered the **k**, 4889
21: 6 So the **k** said, "I will give them to you." 4889
21: 7 The **k** spared Mephibosheth son 4889
21: 8 But the **k** took Armoni and Mephibosheth, 4889
21:14 and did everything the **k** commanded. 4889
22:51 He gives his **k** great victories; 4889
24: 2 So the **k** said to Joab and 4889
24: 3 But Joab replied to the **k**, 4889
24: 3 and may the eyes of my lord the **k** see it. 4889
24: 3 But why does my lord the **k** want to do such 4889
24: 4 of the **k** to enroll the fighting men of Israel. 4889
24: 9 the number of the fighting men to the **k**: 4889
24:20 the **k** and his men coming toward him, 4889
24:20 and bowed down before the **k** with his face 4889
24:21 "Why has my lord the **k** come 4889
24:22 the **k** take whatever pleases him 4889
24:23 O **k**, Araunah gives all this to the king." 4889
24:23 O king, Araunah gives all this to the **k**." 4889
24:24 But the **k** replied to Araunah, "No, 4889
1Ki 1: 1 When **K** David was old and well advanced 4889
1: 2 a young virgin to attend the **k** and take care 4889
1: 2 so that our lord the **k** may keep warm." 4889
1: 3 a Shunammite, and brought her to the **k**. 4889
1: 4 she took care of the **k** and waited on him, 4889
1: 4 but the **k** had no intimate relations with her. 4889
1: 5 put himself forward and said, "I *will be* **k**." 4887
1:11 Adonijah, the son of Haggith, *has become* **k** 4887
1:13 Go in to **K** David and say to him, 4889
1:13 the **k**, did you not swear to me your servant: 4889
1:13 "Surely Solomon your son *shall be* **k** 4887
1:13 Why then *has* Adonijah *become* **k**?' 4887
1:14 While you are still there talking to the **k**, 4889
1:15 So Bathsheba went to see the aged **k** 4889
1:16 and knelt before the **k**. 4889
1:16 "What is it your want?" the **k** asked. 4889
1:17 'Solomon your son *shall be* **k** after me, 4887
1:18 But now Adonijah *has become* **k**, and you, 4887
1:18 my lord the **k**, do not know about it. 4889
1:20 My lord the **k**, the eyes of all Israel are on 4889
1:20 on the throne of my lord the **k** after him. 4889
1:21 as soon as my lord the **k** is laid to rest 4889
1:22 While she was still speaking with the **k**, 4889
1:23 And they told the **k**, 4889
1:23 before the **k** and bowed with his face to 4889
1:24 Nathan said, "Have you, my lord the **k**, 4889
1:24 declared that Adonijah *shall be* **k** after you, 4887
1:25 'Long live **K** Adonijah!' 4889
1:27 Is this something my lord the **k** has done 4889
1:27 on the throne of my lord the **k** after him?" 4889
1:28 Then **K** David said, "Call in Bathsheba." 4889
1:29 The **k** then took an oath: 4889
1:30 Solomon your son *shall be* **k** after me, 4887
1:31 kneeling before the **k**, said, 4889
1:31 said, "May my lord **K** David live forever!" 4889
1:32 **K** David said, "Call in Zadok the priest, 4889
1:32 When they came before the **k**, 4889
1:34 and Nathan the prophet anoint him **k** 4889
1:34 'Long live **K** Solomon!' 4889
1:36 Benaiah son of Jehoiada answered the **k**, 4889
1:36 May the LORD, the God of my lord the **k**, 4889
1:37 As the LORD was with my lord the **k**, 4889
1:37 the throne of my lord **K** David!" 4889
1:38 down and put Solomon on **K** David's mule 4889
1:39 "Long live **K** Solomon!" 4889
1:43 "Our lord **K** David has made Solomon king. 4889
1:43 Our lord King David *has* **made** Solomon **k**. 4887
1:44 The **k** has sent with him Zadok the priest, 4889
1:45 and Nathan the prophet have anointed him **k** 4889
1:47 to congratulate our lord **K** David, 4889
1:47 And the **k** bowed in worship on his bed 4889
1:51 of **K** Solomon and is clinging to the horns 4889
1:51 'Let **K** Solomon swear to me today 4889
1:53 Then **K** Solomon sent men, 4889
1:53 and bowed down to **K** Solomon, 4889
2:15 All Israel looked to me as their **k**. 4887
2:17 So he continued, "Please ask **K** Solomon— 4889
2:18 "I will speak to the **k** for you." 4889
2:19 to **K** Solomon to speak to him for Adonijah, 4889
2:19 the **k** stood up to meet her, 4889
2:20 The **k** replied, "Make it, my mother; 4889
2:22 **K** Solomon answered his mother, 4889
2:23 Then **K** Solomon swore by the LORD: 4889
2:25 So **K** Solomon gave orders to Benaiah son 4889
2:26 To Abiathar the priest the **k** said, 4889
2:29 **K** Solomon was told that Joab had fled to 4889
2:30 "The **k** says, 'Come out!' " 4889
2:30 Benaiah reported to the **k**, 4889
2:31 the **k** commanded Benaiah, "Do as he says. 4889
2:35 The **k** put Benaiah son of Jehoiada over 4889
2:36 Then the **k** sent for Shimei and said to him, 4889
2:38 Shimei answered the **k**, 4889
2:38 as my lord the **k** has said." 4889
2:39 **k** *of* Gath, and Shimei was told, 4889
2:42 the **k** summoned Shimei and said to him, 4889
2:44 The **k** also said to Shimei, 4889
2:45 But **K** Solomon will be blessed, 4889
2:46 **k** gave the order to Benaiah son of Jehoiada, 4889
3: 1 Solomon made an alliance with Pharaoh **k** 4889
3: 4 The **k** went to Gibeon to offer sacrifices, 4889
1Ki 3: 7 you *have* **made** your servant **k** in place 4887
3:16 Now two prostitutes came to the **k** 4889
3:22 And so they argued before the **k**. 4889
3:23 The **k** said, "This one says, 4889
3:24 Then the **k** said, "Bring me a sword." 4889
3:24 So they brought a sword for the **k**. 4889
3:26 for her son and said to the **k**, 4889
3:27 Then the **k** gave his ruling: 4889
3:28 all Israel heard the verdict the **k** had given, 4889
3:28 they held the **k** in awe, 4889
4: 1 So **K** Solomon ruled over all Israel. 4889
4: 5 a priest and personal adviser to the **k**; 4889
4: 7 who supplied provisions for the **k** and 4889
4:19 (the country of Sihon **k** *of* the Amorites and 4889
4:19 of the Amorites and the country of Og **k** 4889
4:27 for **K** Solomon and all who came to 4889
5: 1 When Hiram **k** *of* Tyre heard 4889
5: 1 that Solomon had been anointed **k** 4889
5:13 **K** Solomon conscripted laborers 4889
6: 2 The temple that **K** Solomon built for 4889
7:13 **K** Solomon sent to Tyre and brought Huram 4889
7:14 to **K** Solomon and did all the work assigned 4889
7:40 for **K** Solomon in the temple of the LORD: 4889
7:45 that Huram made for **K** Solomon for 4889
7:46 The **k** had them cast in clay molds in 4889
7:51 When all the work **K** Solomon had done for 4889
8: 1 Then **K** Solomon summoned into his 4889
8: 2 to **K** Solomon at the time of the festival in 4889
8: 5 and **K** Solomon and the entire assembly 4889
8:14 the **k** turned around and blessed them. 4889
8:62 Then the **k** and all Israel 4889
8:63 So the **k** and all the Israelites dedicated 4889
8:64 the **k** consecrated the middle part of 4889
8:66 They blessed the **k** and then went home, 4889
9:11 **K** Solomon gave twenty towns in Galilee 4889
9:11 in Galilee to Hiram **k** *of* Tyre, 4889
9:14 Hiram had sent to the **k** 120 talents of gold. 4889
9:15 of the forced labor **K** Solomon conscripted 4889
9:16 (Pharaoh **k** *of* Egypt had attacked 4889
9:26 **K** Solomon also built ships at Ezion Geber, 4889
9:28 which they delivered to **K** Solomon. 4889
10: 3 nothing was too hard for the **k** to explain 4889
10: 6 She said to the **k**, "The report I heard 4889
10: 9 eternal love for Israel, he has made you **k**, 4889
10:10 And she gave the **k** 120 talents of gold, 4889
10:10 the queen of Sheba gave to **K** Solomon. 4889
10:12 The **k** used the almugwood 4889
10:13 **K** Solomon gave the queen of Sheba 4889
10:16 **K** Solomon made two hundred large shields 4889
10:17 The **k** put them in the Palace of the Forest 4889
10:18 the **k** made a great throne inlaid with ivory 4889
10:21 All **K** Solomon's goblets were gold, 4889
10:22 The **k** had a fleet of trading ships at sea 4889
10:23 **K** Solomon was greater in riches 4889
10:27 The **k** made silver as common in Jerusalem 4889
11: 1 **K** Solomon, however, loved many foreign
women besides Pharaoh's daughter— 4889
11:18 they went to Egypt, to Pharaoh **k** *of* Egypt, 4889
11:23 Hadadezer **k** *of* Zobah. 4889
11:26 Jeroboam son of Nebat rebelled against
the **k**. 4889
11:27 of how he rebelled against the **k**: 4889
11:37 you will be **k** over Israel. 4889
11:40 to Shishak the **k**, and stayed there 4889
11:43 And Rehoboam his son succeeded him *as* **k**. 4887
12: 1 the Israelites had gone there to **make** him **k**. 4887
12: 2 where he had fled from **K** Solomon), 4889
12: 6 Then **K** Rehoboam consulted 4889
12:12 as the **k** had said, 4889
12:13 The **k** answered the people harshly. 4889
12:15 So the **k** did not listen to the people, 4889
12:16 When all Israel saw that the **k** refused 4889
12:16 they answered the **k**: 4889
12:18 **K** Rehoboam sent out Adoniram, 4889
12:18 **K** Rehoboam, however, managed to get 4889
12:20 assembly and **made** him **k** over all Israel. 4887
12:23 to Rehoboam son of Solomon **k** *of* Judah, 4889
12:27 Rehoboam **k** *of* Judah. 4889
12:27 and return to **K** Rehoboam." 4889
12:28 the **k** made two golden calves. 4889
13: 4 When **K** Jeroboam heard what the man 4889
13: 6 Then the **k** said to the man of God, 4889
13: 7 The **k** said to the man of God, 4889
13: 8 But the man of God answered the **k**, 4889
13:11 told their father what he had said to the **k**. 4889
14: 2 the one who told me I would be **k** 4889
14:14 for himself a **k** over Israel who will cut off 4889
14:20 And Nadab his son succeeded him *as* **k**. 4887
14:21 Rehoboam son of Solomon *was* **k** in Judah. 4887
14:21 forty-one years old when he *became* **k**, 4887
14:25 In the fifth year of **K** Rehoboam, 4889
14:25 Shishak **k** *of* Egypt attacked Jerusalem. 4889
14:27 So **K** Rehoboam made bronze shields 4889
14:28 the **k** went to the LORD's temple, 4889
14:31 And Abijah his son succeeded him *as* **k**. 4887
15: 1 Abijah *became* **k** of Judah, 4887
15: 8 And Asa his son succeeded him *as* **k**. 4887
15: 9 the twentieth year of Jeroboam **k** *of* Israel, 4889
15: 9 Asa *became* **k** *of* Judah, 4887+4889
15:16 There was war between Asa and Baasha **k** 4889
15:17 Baasha **k** *of* Israel went up against Judah 4889
15:17 or entering the territory of Asa **k** *of* Judah. 4889
15:18 the son of Hezion, the **k** *of* Aram, 4889
15:19 with Baasha **k** *of* Israel so he will withdraw 4889
15:20 Ben-Hadad agreed with **K** Asa and sent 4889
15:22 Then **K** Asa issued an order to all Judah— 4889
15:22 With them **K** Asa built up Geba 4889
1Ki 15:24 Jehoshaphat his son succeeded him *as* **k**. 4887
15:25 Nadab son of Jeroboam *became* **k** of Israel 4887
15:25 in the second year of Asa **k** *of* Judah, 4889
15:28 of Asa **k** *of* Judah and succeeded him 4889
15:28 of Judah and succeeded him *as* **k**. 4887
15:32 There was war between Asa and Baasha **k** 4889
15:33 In the third year of Asa **k** *of* Judah, 4889
15:33 Baasha son of Ahijah *became* **k** of all Israel 4887
16: 6 And Elah his son succeeded him *as* **k**. 4887
16: 8 In the twenty-sixth year of Asa **k** *of* Judah, 4889
16: 8 Elah son of Baasha *became* **k** of Israel, 4887
16:10 the twenty-seventh year of Asa **k** *of* Judah. 4889
16:10 Then *he* succeeded him *as* **k**. 4887
16:15 the twenty-seventh year of Asa **k** *of* Judah, 4889
16:16 that Zimri had plotted against the **k** 4889
16:16 **proclaimed** Omri, the commander of the
army, **k** over Israel 4887
16:21 half supported Tibni son of Ginath for **k**, 4887
16:22 So Tibni died and Omri *became* **k**. 4887
16:23 In the thirty-first year of Asa **k** *of* Judah, 4889
16:23 Omri *became* **k** of Israel, 4887
16:28 And Ahab his son succeeded him *as* **k**. 4887
16:29 In the thirty-eighth year of Asa **k** *of* Judah, 4889
16:29 Ahab son of Omri *became* **k** of Israel, 4887
16:31 also married Jezebel daughter of Ethbaal **k** 4889
19:15 you get there, anoint Hazael **k** over Aram. 4889
19:16 anoint Jehu son of Nimshi **k** over Israel, 4889
20: 1 Now Ben-Hadad **k** *of* Aram 4889
20: 2 He sent messengers into the city to Ahab **k** 4889
20: 4 The **k** *of* Israel answered, "Just as you say, 4889
20: 4 "Just as you say, my lord the **k**. 4889
20: 7 The **k** *of* Israel summoned all the elders of 4889
20: 9 "Tell my lord the **k**, 4889
20:11 The **k** *of* Israel answered, "Tell him: 4889
20:13 Meanwhile a prophet came to Ahab **k** 4889
20:20 But Ben-Hadad **k** *of* Aram escaped 4889
20:21 The **k** *of* Israel advanced and overpowered 4889
20:22 the prophet came to the **k** *of* Israel and said, 4889
20:22 the **k** *of* Aram will attack you again." 4889
20:23 the officials of the **k** *of* Aram advised him, 4889
20:28 up and told the **k** *of* Israel, "This is what 4889
20:31 Let us go to the **k** *of* Israel with sackcloth 4889
20:32 they went to the **k** *of* Israel and said, 4889
20:32 The **k** answered, "Is he still alive? NIH
20:33 "Go and get him," the **k** said. NIH
20:38 and stood by the road waiting for the **k**. 4889
20:39 As the **k** passed by, 4889
20:40 "That is your sentence," the **k** *of* Israel said. 4889
20:41 and the **k** *of* Israel recognized him as one of 4889
20:42 He said to **the k**, 2257
20:43 **k** *of* Israel went to his palace in Samaria. 4889
21: 1 close to the palace of Ahab **k** *of* Samaria. 4889
21: 7 "Is this how you act as **k** over Israel? 4867
21:10 that he has cursed both God and the **k**. 4889
21:13 "Naboth has cursed both God and the **k**." 4889
21:18 "Go down to meet Ahab **k** *of* Israel, 4889
22: 2 the third year Jehoshaphat **k** *of* Judah went 4889
22: 2 of Judah went down to see the **k** *of* Israel. 4889
22: 3 The **k** *of* Israel had said to his officials, 4889
22: 3 to retake it from the **k** *of* Aram?" 4889
22: 4 Jehoshaphat replied to the **k** *of* Israel, 4889
22: 5 But Jehoshaphat also said to the **k** *of* Israel, 4889
22: 6 **k** *of* Israel brought together the prophets— 4889
22: 8 The **k** *of* Israel answered Jehoshaphat, 4889
22: 8 "The **k** should not say that," 4889
22: 9 So the **k** *of* Israel called one of his officials 4889
22:10 the **k** *of* Israel and Jehoshaphat king 4889
22:10 and Jehoshaphat **k** *of* Judah were sitting 4889
22:13 prophets are predicting success for the **k**. 4889
22:15 When he arrived, the **k** asked him, 4889
22:16 The **k** said to him, 4889
22:18 The **k** *of* Israel said to Jehoshaphat, 4889
22:26 The **k** *of* Israel then ordered, 4889
22:27 'This is what the **k** says: 4889
22:29 So the **k** *of* Israel and Jehoshaphat king 4889
22:29 of Israel and Jehoshaphat **k** *of* Judah went 4889
22:30 The **k** *of* Israel said to Jehoshaphat, 4889
22:30 the **k** *of* Israel disguised himself and went 4889
22:31 Now the **k** *of* Aram had ordered his 4889
22:31 small or great, except the **k** *of* Israel." 4889
22:32 "Surely this is the **k** *of* Israel." 4889
22:33 the **k** *of* Israel and stopped pursuing him. 4889
22:34 and hit the **k** *of* Israel between the sections 4889
22:34 The **k** told his chariot driver, NIH
22:35 the **k** was propped up in his chariot facing 4889
22:37 So the **k** died and was brought to Samaria, 4889
22:40 And Ahaziah his son succeeded him *as* **k**. 4887
22:41 of Asa *became* **k** of Judah in the fourth year 4887
22:41 in the fourth year of Ahab **k** *of* Israel. 4889
22:42 thirty-five years old when he *became* **k**, 4887
22:44 Jehoshaphat was also at peace with the **k** 4889
22:47 There was then no **k** in Edom; 4889
22:51 of Ahab *became* **k** of Israel in Samaria in 4887
22:51 in the seventeenth year of Jehoshaphat **k** 4889
2Ki 1: 3 "Go up and meet the messengers of the **k** 4889
1: 5 When the messengers returned to **the k**, 2257S
1: 6 to the **k** who sent you and tell him, 4889
1: 7 The **k** asked them, "What kind of man NIH
1: 8 The **k** said, "That was Elijah the Tishbite." NIH
1: 9 "Man of God, the **k** says, 'Come down!' " 4889
1:11 At this the **k** sent to Elijah another captain NIH
1:11 "Man of God, this is what the **k** says, 4889
1:13 the **k** sent a third captain with his fifty men. NIH
1:15 up and went down with him to the **k**. 4889
1:16 He told **the k**, "This is what 2257S
1:17 *as* **k** in the second year of Jehoram son 4887
1:17 of Jehoram son of Jehoshaphat **k** *of* Judah. 4889

2Ki 3: 1 of Ahab *became* **k** of Israel in Samaria in 4887
3: 1 in the eighteenth year of Jehoshaphat **k** 4889
3: 4 Now Mesha **k** *of* Moab raised sheep, 4889
3: 4 and he had to supply the **k** *of* Israel with 4889
3: 5 the **k** *of* Moab rebelled against the king 4889
3: 5 of Moab rebelled against the **k** *of* Israel. 4889
3: 6 at that time **K** Joram set out from Samaria 4889
3: 7 He also sent this message to Jehoshaphat **k** 4889
3: 7 "The **k** *of* Moab has rebelled against me. 4889
3: 9 So the **k** *of* Israel set out with the king 4889
3: 9 with the **k** *of* Judah and the king of Edom. 4889
3: 9 with the king of Judah and the **k** *of* Edom. 4889
3:10 exclaimed the **k** *of* Israel. 4889
3:11 An officer of the **k** *of* Israel answered, 4889
3:12 the **k** *of* Israel and Jehoshaphat and the king 4889
3:12 the king of Israel and Jehoshaphat and the **k** 4889
3:13 Elisha said to the **k** *of* Israel, 4889
3:13 "No," the **k** *of* Israel answered, 4889
3:14 for the presence of Jehoshaphat **k** *of* Judah, 4889
3:26 the **k** *of* Moab saw that the battle had gone 4889
3:26 to break through to the **k** *of* Edom, 4889
3:27 who *was to* succeed him *as* **k,** 4887
4:13 on your behalf to the **k** or the commander of 4889
5: 1 of the army of the **k** *of* Aram. 4889
5: 5 "By all means, go," the **k** *of* Aram replied. 4889
5: 5 "I will send a letter to the **k** *of* Israel." 4889
5: 6 that he took to the **k** *of* Israel read: 4889
5: 7 As soon as the **k** *of* Israel read the letter, 4889
5: 8 that the **k** *of* Israel had torn his robes, 4889
6: 8 Now the **k** *of* Aram was at war with Israel. 4889
6: 9 of God sent word to the **k** *of* Israel: 4889
6:10 So the **k** *of* Israel checked on 4889
6:10 Time and again Elisha warned **the k,** 2257[S]
6:11 This enraged the **k** *of* Aram. 4889
6:11 of us is on the side of the **k** *of* Israel?" 4889
6:12 "None of us, my lord the **k,"** 4889
6:12 the **k** *of* Israel the very words you speak 4889
6:13 "Go, find out where he is," the **k** ordered, NIH
6:21 When the **k** *of* Israel saw them, 4889
6:24 Some time later, Ben-Hadad **k** 4889
6:26 the **k** *of* Israel was passing by on the wall, 4889
6:26 "Help me, my lord the **k!"** 4889
6:27 The **k** replied, "If the LORD does NIH
6:30 When the **k** heard the woman's words, 4889
6:32 **The k** sent a messenger ahead, 2257[S]
6:33 **k]** said, "This disaster is from the LORD. NIH
7: 2 the **k** was leaning said to the man of God, 4889
7: 6 the **k** *of* Israel has hired the Hittite 4889
7:12 The **k** got up in the night and said 4889
7:14 the **k** sent them after the Aramean army. 4889
7:15 messengers returned and reported to the **k.** 4889
7:17 Now the **k** had put the officer 4889
7:17 of God had foretold when the **k** came down 4889
7:18 as the man of God had said to the **k:** 4889
8: 3 the land of the Philistines and went to the **k** 4889
8: 4 The **k** was talking to Gehazi, 4889
8: 5 the **k** how Elisha had restored the dead 4889
8: 5 to life came to beg the **k** for her house 4889
8: 5 "This is the woman, my lord the **k,** 4889
8: 6 The **k** asked the woman about it, 4889
8: 7 and Ben-Hadad **k** *of* Aram was ill. 4889
8: 7 When **the k** was told, 2257[S]
8: 9 "Your son Ben-Hadad **k** *of* Aram 4889
8:13 that you will become **k** of Aram," 4889
8:15 Then Hazael succeeded him *as* **k.** 4887
8:16 In the fifth year of Joram son of Ahab **k** 4889
8:16 when Jehoshaphat was **k** *of* Judah, 4889
8:16 of Jehoshaphat began his reign as **k** 4889
8:17 thirty-two years old when he *became* **k,** 4887
8:20 and **set up** its own **k.** 4887+4889
8:24 And Ahaziah his son succeeded him *as* **k.** 4887
8:25 In the twelfth year of Joram son of Ahab **k** 4889
8:25 Ahaziah son of Jehoram **k** *of* Judah began 4889
8:26 twenty-two years old when he *became* **k,** 4887
8:26 a granddaughter of Omri **k** *of* Israel. 4889
8:28 of Ahab to war against Hazael **k** *of* Aram 4889
8:29 so **K** Joram returned to Jezreel to recover 4889
8:29 at Ramoth in his battle with Hazael **k** 4889
8:29 of Jehoram **k** *of* Judah went down 4889
9: 3 I anoint you **k** over Israel.' 4889
9: 6 'I anoint you **k** over of the LORD's people 4889
9:12 I anoint you **k** over Israel.' " 4889
9:13 the trumpet and shouted, "Jehu *is* **k!"** 4887
9:14 against Hazael **k** *of* Aram, 4889
9:15 but **K** Joram had returned to Jezreel 4889
9:15 in the battle with Hazael **k** *of* Aram.) 4889
9:16 and Ahaziah **k** *of* Judah had gone down 4889
9:18 "This is what the **k** says: 4889
9:19 So the **k** sent out a second horseman. NIH
9:19 "This is what the **k** says: 4889
9:21 Joram **k** *of* Israel and Ahaziah king 4889
9:21 of Israel and Ahaziah **k** *of* Judah rode out, 4889
9:27 When Ahaziah **k** *of* Judah 4889
9:29 Ahaziah *had become* **k** of Judah.) 4887
10: 5 *We will* not **appoint** anyone **as k;** 4887
10:13 he met some relatives of Ahaziah **k** 4889
10:13 down to greet the families of the **k** and of 4889
10:35 And Jehoahaz his son succeeded him *as* **k.** 4887
11: 2 the daughter of **K** Jehoram and sister 4889
11: 7 to guard the temple for the **k.** 4889
11: 8 Station yourselves around the **k,** 4889
11: 8 Stay close to the **k** wherever he goes." 4889
11:10 that had belonged to **K** David and that were 4889
11:11 stationed themselves around the **k—** 4889
11:12 of the covenant and **proclaimed** him **k.** 4887
11:12 "Long live the **k!"** 4889
11:14 She looked and there was the **k,** 4889

2Ki 11:14 and the trumpeters were beside the **k,** 4889
11:17 between the LORD and the **k** and people 4889
11:17 He also made a covenant between the **k** and 4889
11:19 and together they brought the **k** down from 4889
11:19 **k** then took his place on the royal throne, NIH
12: 1 In the seventh year of Jehu, Joash *became* **k,** 4887
12: 6 of **K** Joash the priests still had not repaired 4889
12: 7 Therefore **K** Joash summoned Jehoiada 4889
12:17 About this time Hazael **k** *of* Aram went up 4889
12:18 But Joash **k** *of* Judah took all 4889
12:18 and he sent them to Hazael **k** *of* Aram, 4889
12:21 And Amaziah his son succeeded him *as* **k.** 4887
13: 1 of Joash son of Ahaziah **k** *of* Judah, 4889
13: 1 Jehoahaz son of Jehu *became* **k** of Israel 4887
13: 3 under the power of Hazael **k** *of* Aram 4889
13: 4 the **k** *of* Aram was oppressing Israel. 4889
13: 7 for the **k** *of* Aram had destroyed the rest 4889
13: 9 And Jehoash his son succeeded him *as* **k.** 4887
13:10 the thirty-seventh year of Joash **k** *of* Judah, 4889
13:10 Jehoash son of Jehoahaz *became* **k** of Israel 4887
13:12 including his war against Amaziah **k** 4889
13:14 Jehoash **k** *of* Israel went down to see him 4889
13:16 he said to the **k** *of* Israel. 4889
13:18 "Take the arrows," and the **k** took them. 4889
13:22 Hazael **k** *of* Aram oppressed Israel 4889
13:24 Hazael **k** *of* Aram died, 4889
13:24 and Ben-Hadad his son succeeded him *as* **k.** 4887
14: 1 of Jehoash son of Jehoahaz **k** *of* Israel, 4889
14: 1 Amaziah son of Joash **k** *of* Judah began 4889
14: 2 twenty-five years old when he *became* **k,** 4887
14: 5 he executed the officials who had murdered
his father the **k.** 4889
14: 8 **k** *of* Israel, with the challenge: 4889
14: 9 But Jehoash **k** *of* Israel replied 4889
14: 9 of Israel replied to Amaziah **k** *of* Judah: 4889
14:11 so Jehoash **k** *of* Israel attacked. 4889
14:11 and Amaziah **k** *of* Judah faced each other 4889
14:13 Jehoash **k** *of* Israel captured Amaziah king 4889
14:13 Jehoash king of Israel captured Amaziah **k** 4889
14:15 including his war against Amaziah **k** 4889
14:16 And Jeroboam his son succeeded him *as* **k.** 4887
14:17 of Joash **k** *of* Judah lived for fifteen years 4889
14:17 after the death of Jehoash son of Jehoahaz **k** 4889
14:21 and **made him k** in place of his father 4887
14:23 the fifteenth year of Amaziah son of Joash **k** 4889
14:23 of Jehoash **k** *of* Israel became king 4889
14:23 of Jehoash king of Israel *became* **k** 4887
14:29 And Zechariah his son succeeded him *as* **k.** 4887
15: 1 In the twenty-seventh year of Jeroboam **k** 4889
15: 1 Azariah son of Amaziah **k** *of* Judah began 4889
15: 2 was sixteen years old when he *became* **k,** 4887
15: 5 The LORD afflicted the **k** with leprosy 4889
15: 7 And Jotham his son succeeded him *as* **k.** 4887
15: 8 the thirty-eighth year of Azariah **k** *of* Judah, 4889
15: 8 of Jeroboam *became* **k** of Israel in Samaria, 4887
15:10 assassinated him and succeeded him *as* **k.** 4887
15:10 of Jabesh *became* **k** in the thirty-ninth year 4887
15:13 the thirty-ninth year of Uzziah **k** *of* Judah, 4889
15:14 assassinated him and succeeded him *as* **k.** 4887
15:17 the thirty-ninth year of Azariah **k** *of* Judah, 4889
15:17 Menahem son of Gadi *became* **k** of Israel, 4887
15:19 Then Pul **k** *of* Assyria invaded the land, 4889
15:20 of silver to be given to the **k** *of* Assyria. 4889
15:20 So the **k** *of* Assyria withdrew and stayed in 4889
15:22 And Pekahiah his son succeeded him *as* **k.** 4887
15:23 In the fiftieth year of Azariah **k** *of* Judah, 4889
15:23 of Menahem *became* **k** of Israel in Samaria, 4887
15:25 killed Pekahiah and succeeded him *as* **k.** 4887
15:27 the fifty-second year of Azariah **k** *of* Judah, 4889
15:27 of Remaliah *became* **k** of Israel in Samaria, 4887
15:29 In the time of Pekah **k** *of* Israel, 4889
15:29 Tiglath-Pileser **k** *of* Assyria came 4889
15:30 *as* **k** in the twentieth year of Jotham son 4887
15:32 the second year of Pekah son of Remaliah **k** 4889
15:32 Jotham son of Uzziah **k** *of* Judah began 4889
15:33 twenty-five years old when he *became* **k,** 4887
15:37 the LORD began to send Rezin **k** *of* Aram 4889
15:38 And Ahaz his son succeeded him *as* **k.** 4887
16: 1 Ahaz son of Jotham **k** *of* Judah began 4889
16: 2 twenty years old when he *became* **k,** 4887
16: 5 Then Rezin **k** *of* Aram and Pekah son 4889
16: 5 of Remaliah **k** *of* Israel marched up to fight 4889
16: 6 Rezin **k** *of* Aram recovered Elath for Aram 4889
16: 7 to say to Tiglath-Pileser **k** *of* Assyria, 4889
16: 7 of the **k** *of* Aram and of the king of Israel, 4889
16: 7 of the hand of the king of Aram and of the **k** 4889
16: 8 the royal palace and sent it as a gift to the **k** 4889
16: 9 The **k** *of* Assyria complied by attacking 4889
16:10 Then **K** Ahaz went to Damascus 4889
16:10 to Damascus to meet Tiglath-Pileser **k** 4889
16:11 with all the plans that **K** Ahaz had sent 4889
16:11 and finished it before **K** Ahaz returned. 4889
16:12 the **k** came back from Damascus and saw 4889
16:15 **K** Ahaz then gave these orders to Uriah 4889
16:16 the priest did just as **K** Ahaz had ordered. 4889
16:17 **K** Ahaz took away the side panels 4889
16:18 in deference to the **k** *of* Assyria. 4889
16:20 And Hezekiah his son succeeded him *as* **k.** 4887
17: 1 In the twelfth year of Ahaz **k** *of* Judah, 4889
17: 1 Hoshea son of Elah *became* **k** of Israel 4887
17: 3 Shalmaneser **k** *of* Assyria came up 4889
17: 4 But the **k** *of* Assyria discovered 4889
17: 4 for he had sent envoys to So **k** *of* Egypt, 4889
17: 4 and he no longer paid tribute to the **k** 4889
17: 5 The **k** *of* Assyria invaded the entire land, 4889
17: 6 the **k** *of* Assyria captured Samaria 4889
17: 7 of Egypt from under the power of Pharaoh **k** 4889

2Ki 17:21 **made** Jeroboam son of Nebat *their* **k.** 4887
17:24 The **k** *of* Assyria brought people 4889
17:26 It was reported to the **k** *of* Assyria: 4889
17:27 Then the **k** *of* Assyria gave this order: 4889
18: 1 In the third year of Hoshea son of Elah **k** 4889
18: 1 Hezekiah son of Ahaz **k** *of* Judah began 4889
18: 2 twenty-five years old when he *became* **k,** 4887
18: 7 He rebelled against the **k** *of* Assyria and did 4889
18: 9 In **K** Hezekiah's fourth year, 4889
18: 9 the seventh year of Hoshea son of Elah **k** 4889
18: 9 Shalmaneser **k** *of* Assyria marched 4889
18:10 which was the ninth year of Hoshea **k** 4889
18:11 The **k** *of* Assyria deported Israel to Assyria 4889
18:13 the fourteenth year of **K** Hezekiah's reign, 4889
18:13 Sennacherib **k** *of* Assyria attacked all 4889
18:14 So Hezekiah **k** *of* Judah sent this message 4889
18:14 of Judah sent this message to the **k** 4889
18:14 The **k** *of* Assyria exacted from Hezekiah 4889
18:14 exacted from Hezekiah **k** *of* Judah 4889
18:16 At this time Hezekiah **k** *of* Judah 4889
18:16 and gave it to the **k** *of* Assyria. 4889
18:17 **k** *of* Assyria sent his supreme commander, 4889
18:17 from Lachish to **K** Hezekiah at Jerusalem. 4889
18:18 They called for the **k;** 4889
18:19 " 'This is what the great **k,** 4889
18:19 the **k** *of* Assyria, says: 4889
18:21 Such is Pharaoh **k** *of* Egypt 4889
18:23 bargain with my master, the **k** *of* Assyria: 4889
18:28 "Hear the word of the great **k,** 4889
18:28 the word of the great king, the **k** *of* Assyria! 4889
18:29 This is what the **k** says: 4889
18:30 be given into the hand of the **k** *of* Assyria.' 4889
18:31 This is what the **k** *of* Assyria says: 4889
18:33 from the hand of the **k** *of* Assyria? 4889
18:36 because the **k** had commanded, 4889
19: 1 When **K** Hezekiah heard this, 4889
19: 4 whom his master, the **k** *of* Assyria, 4889
19: 5 **K** Hezekiah's officials came to Isaiah, 4889
19: 6 of the **k** *of* Assyria have blasphemed me. 4889
19: 8 When the field commander heard that the **k** 4889
19: 8 and found the **k** fighting against Libnah. NIH
19: 9 Tirhakah, the Cushite **k** [of Egypt], 4889
19:10 "Say to Hezekiah **k** *of* Judah: 4889
19:10 'Jerusalem will not be handed over to the **k** 4889
19:13 Where is the **k** *of* Hamath, 4889
19:13 is the king of Hamath, the **k** *of* Arpad, 4889
19:13 the **k** of the city of Sepharvaim, 4889
19:20 concerning Sennacherib **k** *of* Assyria. 4889
19:32 the LORD says concerning the **k** 4889
19:36 So Sennacherib **k** *of* Assyria broke camp 4889
19:37 Esarhaddon his son succeeded him *as* **k.** 4887
20: 6 and this city from the hand of the **k** 4889
20:12 Merodach-Baladan son of Baladan **k** *of* 4889
20:14 the prophet went to **K** Hezekiah and asked, 4889
20:18 in the palace of the **k** *of* Babylon." 4889
20:21 And Manasseh his son succeeded him *as* **k.** 4887
21: 1 twelve years old when he *became* **k,** 4887
21: 3 as Ahab **k** *of* Israel had done. 4889
21:11 "Manasseh **k** *of* Judah has committed 4889
21:18 And Amon his son succeeded him *as* **k.** 4887
21:19 twenty-two years old when he *became* **k,** 4887
21:23 and assassinated the **k** in his palace. 4889
21:24 killed all who had plotted against **K** Amon, 4889
21:24 **made** Josiah his son **k** in his place. 4887
21:26 And Josiah his son succeeded him *as* **k.** 4887
22: 1 eight years old when he *became* **k,** 4887
22: 3 **K** Josiah sent the secretary, 4889
22: 9 Then Shaphan the secretary went to the **k** 4889
22:10 Then Shaphan the secretary informed the **k,** 4889
22:10 from it in the presence of the **k.** 4889
22:11 **k** heard the words of the Book of the Law, 4889
22:16 to everything written in the book the **k** 4889
22:18 Tell the **k** *of* Judah, 4889
22:20 So they took her answer back to the **k.** 4889
23: 1 the **k** called together all the elders of Judah 4889
23: 3 The **k** stood by the pillar and renewed 4889
23: 4 The **k** ordered Hilkiah the high priest, 4889
23:13 The **k** also desecrated the high places 4889
23:13 the ones Solomon **k** *of* Israel had built 4889
23:17 The **k** asked, "What is that tombstone NIH
23:21 The **k** gave this order to all the people: 4889
23:23 But in the eighteenth year of **K** Josiah, 4889
23:25 Neither before nor after Josiah was there a **k** 4889
23:29 While Josiah was **k,** Pharaoh Neco NIH
23:29 Pharaoh Neco **k** *of* Egypt went up to 4889
23:29 up to the Euphrates River to help the **k** 4889
23:29 **K** Josiah marched out to meet him in battle, 4889
23:30 of Josiah and anointed him and **made** him **k** 4887
23:31 twenty-three years when he *became* **k,** 4887
23:34 **made** Eliakim son of Josiah **k** in place of 4887
23:36 twenty-five years old when he *became* **k,** 4887
24: 1 Nebuchadnezzar **k** *of* Babylon invaded 4889
24: 6 And Jehoiachin his son succeeded him *as* **k.** 4887
24: 7 The **k** *of* Egypt did not march out 4889
24: 7 the **k** *of* Babylon had taken all his territory, 4889
24: 8 eighteen years old when he *became* **k,** 4887
24:10 of Nebuchadnezzar **k** *of* Babylon advanced 4889
24:12 Jehoiachin **k** *of* Judah, his mother, 4889
24:12 In the eighth year of the reign of the **k** 4889
24:13 that Solomon **k** *of* Israel had made for 4889
24:16 The **k** *of* Babylon also deported to Babylon 4889
24:17 **made** Mattaniah, Jehoiachin's uncle, **k** 4887
24:18 twenty-one years old when he *became* **k,** 4887
24:20 Zedekiah rebelled against the **k** *of* Babylon. 4889
25: 1 Nebuchadnezzar **k** *of* Babylon marched 4889
25: 2 until the eleventh year of **K** Zedekiah. 4889
25: 5 but the Babylonian army pursued the **k** 4889

2Ki 25: 6 He was taken to the **k** *of* Babylon at Riblah, 4889
25: 8 in the nineteenth year of Nebuchadnezzar **k** 4889
25: 8 an official of the **k** *of* Babylon, 4889
25:11 and those who had gone over to the **k** 4889
25:20 and brought them to the **k** *of* Babylon 4889
25:21 the **k** had them executed. 4889
25:22 Nebuchadnezzar **k** *of* Babylon 4889
25:23 the **k** *of* Babylon had appointed Gedaliah 4889
25:24 "Settle down in the land and serve the **k** 4889
25:27 of the exile of Jehoiachin **k** *of* Judah, 4889
25:27 in the year Evil-Merodach *became* **k** 4887
25:30 the **k** gave Jehoiachin a regular allowance 4889
1Ch 1:43 in Edom before any Israelite **k** reigned: 4889
1:44 of Zerah from Bozrah succeeded him *as* **k**. 4887
1:45 of the Temanites succeeded him *as* **k**. 4887
1:46 succeeded him *as* **k**. 4887
1:47 Samlah from Masrekah succeeded him *as* **k**. 4887
1:48 on the river succeeded him *as* **k**. 4887
1:49 son of Acbor succeeded him *as* **k**. 4887
1:50 Hadad succeeded him *as* **k**. 4887
3: 2 of Maacah daughter of Talmai **k** *of* Geshur; 4889
4:23 they stayed there and worked for the **k**. 4889
4:41 in the days of Hezekiah **k** *of* Judah. 4889
5: 6 whom Tiglath-Pileser **k** *of* Assyria took 4889
5:17 of Jotham **k** *of* Judah and Jeroboam king 4889
5:17 of Jotham king of Judah and Jeroboam **k** 4889
5:26 stirred up the spirit of Pul **k** *of* Assyria 4889
5:26 Tiglath-Pileser **k** *of* Assyria), 4889
11: 2 In the past, even while Saul was **k**, 4889
11: 3 of Israel had come to **K** David at Hebron, 4889
11: 3 and they anointed David **k** over Israel, 4889
12:31 by name to come and **make** David **k—** 4887
12:38 Hebron fully determined to **make** David **k** 4887
12:38 also of one mind to **make** David **k**. 4887
14: 1 Hiram **k** *of* Tyre sent messengers to David, 4889
14: 2 that the LORD had established him as **k** 4889
14: 8 that David had been anointed **k** 4889
15:29 she saw **K** David dancing and celebrating, 4889
17:16 **K** David went in and sat before the LORD, 4889
18: 3 David fought Hadadezer **k** *of* Zobah, 4889
18: 5 of Damascus came to help Hadadezer **k** 4889
18: 9 When Tou **k** *of* Hamath heard 4889
18: 9 the entire army of Hadadezer **k** *of* Zobah, 4889
18:10 he sent his son Hadoram to **K** David 4889
18:11 **K** David dedicated these articles to 4889
19: 1 Nahash **k** *of* the Ammonites died, 4889
19: 1 and his son succeeded him *as* **k**. 4887
19: 5 The **k** said, "Stay at Jericho 4889
19: 7 as well as the **k** *of* Maacah with his troops, 4889
20: 2 the crown from the head of their **k—** 4889
21: 3 My lord the **k**, are they not all my lord's 4889
21:23 Let my lord the **k** do whatever pleases him. 4889
21:24 But **K** David replied to Araunah, "No, 4889
23: 1 *he* **made** his son Solomon **k** over 4887
24: 6 in the presence of the **k** and of the officials: 4889
24:31 in the presence of **K** David and of Zadok, 4889
25: 6 under the supervision of the **k**. 4889
26:26 for the things dedicated by **K** David, 4889
26:32 and **K** David put them in charge of 4889
26:32 to God and for the affairs of the **k**. 4889
27: 1 and their officers, who served the **k** in all 4889
27:24 in the book of the annals of **K** David. 4889
27:31 in charge of **K** David's property. 4889
28: 1 of the divisions in the service of the **k**, 4889
28: 1 and livestock belonging to the **k** 4889
28: 2 **K** David rose to his feet and said: 4889
28: 4 chose me from my whole family to be **k** 4889
28: 4 to **make** me **k** over all Israel. 4887
29: 1 Then **K** David said to the whole assembly: 4889
29: 9 David the **k** also rejoiced greatly. 4889
29:20 before the LORD and the **k**. 4889
29:22 **acknowledged** Solomon son of David **as k** 4887
29:23 on the throne of the LORD as **k** in place 4889
29:24 as well as all of **K** David's sons, 4889
29:24 pledged their submission to **K** Solomon. 4889
29:25 as no **k** over Israel ever had before. 4889
29:26 David son of Jesse *was* **k** over all Israel. 4887
29:28 His son Solomon succeeded him *as* **k**. 4887
29:29 As for the events of **K** David's reign, 4889
2Ch 1: 8 to David my father and *have* **made** me **k** 4887
1: 9 for you *have* **made** me **k** over 4887
1:11 over whom *I have* **made** you **k**, 4887
1:12 such as no **k** who was before you ever had 4889
1:15 The **k** made silver and gold as common 4889
2: 3 Solomon sent this message to Hiram **k** 4889
2:11 Hiram **k** *of* Tyre replied by letter 4889
2:11 he has made you their **k**." 4889
2:12 He has given **K** David a wise son, 4889
4:11 the work he had undertaken for **K** Solomon 4889
4:16 that Huram-Abi made for **K** Solomon for 4889
4:17 The **k** had them cast in clay molds in 4889
5: 3 of Israel came together to the **k** at the time 4889
5: 6 and **K** Solomon and the entire assembly 4889
6: 3 the **k** turned around and blessed them. 4889
7: 4 the **k** and all the people offered sacrifices 4889
7: 5 And **K** Solomon offered a sacrifice 4889
7: 5 So the **k** and all the people dedicated 4889
7: 6 which **K** David had made for praising 4889
8:10 also **K** Solomon's chief officials— 4889
8:11 not live in the palace of David **k** *of* Israel, 4889
8:18 which they delivered to **K** Solomon. 4889
9: 5 She said to the **k**, "The report I heard 4889
9: 8 and placed you on his throne as **k** to rule for 4889
9: 8 he has made you **k** over them, 4889
9: 9 Then she gave the **k** 120 talents of gold, 4889
9: 9 the queen of Sheba gave to **K** Solomon. 4889
9:11 The **k** used the algumwood to make steps 4889
2Ch 9:12 **K** Solomon gave the queen of Sheba 4889
9:15 **K** Solomon made two hundred large shields 4889
9:16 The **k** put them in the Palace of the Forest 4889
9:17 the **k** made a great throne inlaid with ivory 4889
9:20 All **K** Solomon's goblets were gold, 4889
9:21 The **k** had a fleet of trading ships manned 4889
9:22 **K** Solomon was greater in riches 4889
9:27 The **k** made silver as common in Jerusalem 4889
9:31 And Rehoboam his son succeeded him *as* **k**. 4887
10: 1 the Israelites had gone there to **make** him **k**. 4887
10: 2 where he had fled from **K** Solomon), 4889
10: 6 Then **K** Rehoboam consulted the elders 4889
10:12 as the **k** had said, 4889
10:13 The **k** answered them harshly. 4889
10:15 So the **k** did not listen to the people, 4889
10:16 When all Israel saw that the **k** refused 4889
10:16 they answered the **k**: 4889
10:18 **K** Rehoboam sent out Adoniram, 4889
10:18 **K** Rehoboam, however, managed to get 4889
11: 3 to Rehoboam son of Solomon **k** *of* Judah 4889
11:22 in order to **make** him **k**. 4887
12: 1 Rehoboam's **position as k** was established 4895
12: 2 Shishak **k** *of* Egypt attacked Jerusalem in 4889
12: 2 in the fifth year of **K** Rehoboam. 4889
12: 6 and the **k** humbled themselves and said, 4889
12: 9 Shishak **k** *of* Egypt attacked Jerusalem, 4889
12:10 So **K** Rehoboam made bronze shields 4889
12:11 the **k** went to the LORD's temple, 4889
12:13 **K** Rehoboam established himself firmly 4889
12:13 in Jerusalem and *continued as* **k**. 4887
12:13 forty-one years old when he *became* **k**, 4887
12:16 And Abijah his son succeeded him *as* **k**. 4887
13: 1 Abijah *became* **k** of Judah, 4887
14: 1 Asa his son succeeded him *as* **k**, 4887
15:16 **K** Asa also deposed his grandmother
Maacah from her position 4889
16: 1 the thirty-sixth year of Asa's reign Baasha **k** 4889
16: 1 or entering the territory of Asa **k** *of* Judah. 4889
16: 2 and sent it to Ben-Hadad **k** *of* Aram, 4889
16: 3 with Baasha **k** *of* Israel so he will withdraw 4889
16: 4 Ben-Hadad agreed with **K** Asa and sent 4889
16: 6 Then **K** Asa brought all the men of Judah, 4889
16: 7 At that time Hanani the seer came to Asa **k** 4889
16: 7 "Because you relied on the **k** *of* Aram and 4889
16: 7 the **k** *of* Aram has escaped from your hand. 4889
17: 1 Jehoshaphat his son succeeded him *as* **k** 4887
17:19 These were the men who served the **k**, 4889
18: 3 Ahab **k** *of* Israel asked Jehoshaphat king 4889
18: 3 Ahab king of Israel asked Jehoshaphat **k** 4889
18: 4 But Jehoshaphat also said to the **k** *of* Israel, 4889
18: 5 **k** *of* Israel brought together the prophets— 4889
18: 7 The **k** *of* Israel answered Jehoshaphat, 4889
18: 7 "The **k** should not say that," 4889
18: 8 So the **k** *of* Israel called one of his officials 4889
18: 9 the **k** *of* Israel and Jehoshaphat king 4889
18: 9 and Jehoshaphat **k** *of* Judah were sitting 4889
18:12 prophets are predicting success for the **k**. 4889
18:14 When he arrived, the **k** asked him, 4889
18:15 The **k** said to him, "How many times 4889
18:17 The **k** *of* Israel said to Jehoshaphat, 4889
18:19 'Who will entice Ahab **k** *of* Israel 4889
18:25 The **k** *of* Israel then ordered, 4889
18:26 'This is what the **k** says: 4889
18:28 So the **k** *of* Israel and Jehoshaphat king 4889
18:28 of Israel and Jehoshaphat **k** *of* Judah went 4889
18:29 The **k** *of* Israel said to Jehoshaphat, 4889
18:29 the **k** *of* Israel disguised himself and went 4889
18:30 Now the **k** *of* Aram had ordered 4889
18:30 small or great, except the **k** *of* Israel." 4889
18:31 they thought, "This is the **k** *of* Israel." 4889
18:32 that he was not the **k** *of* Israel, 4889
18:33 and hit the **k** *of* Israel between the sections 4889
18:33 The **k** told the chariot driver, NIH
18:34 and the **k** *of* Israel propped himself up 4889
19: 1 When Jehoshaphat **k** *of* Judah 4889
19: 2 went out to meet him and said to the **k**, 4889
19:11 be over you in any matter concerning the **k**, 4889
20:15 **K** Jehoshaphat and all who live in Judah 4889
20:31 when he *became* **k** *of* Judah, 4887
20:35 Jehoshaphat **k** *of* Judah made an alliance 4889
20:35 of Judah made an alliance with Ahaziah **k** 4889
21: 1 And Jehoram his son succeeded him *as* **k**. 4887
21: 2 All these were sons of Jehoshaphat **k** 4889
21: 5 thirty-two years old when he *became* **k**, 4887
21: 8 and **set up** its own **k**. 4887+4889
21:12 of your father Jehoshaphat or of Asa **k** 4889
21:20 when he *became* **k**, 4887
22: 1 **made** Ahaziah, Jehoram's youngest son, **k** 4887
22: 1 of Jehoram **k** *of* Judah began to reign. 4889
22: 2 thirty-two years old when he *became* **k**, 4887
22: 5 with Joram son of Ahab **k** *of* Israel to war 4889
22: 5 of Israel to war against Hazael **k** *of* Aram 4889
22: 6 at Ramoth in his battle with Hazael **k** 4889
22: 6 of Jehoram **k** *of* Judah went down 4889
22:11 But Jehosheba, the daughter of **K** Jehoram, 4889
22:11 the daughter of **K** Jehoram and wife of 4889
23: 3 a covenant with the **k** at the temple of God. 4889
23: 7 to station themselves around the **k**, 4889
23: 7 Stay close to the **k** wherever he goes." 4889
23: 9 that had belonged to **K** David and that were 4889
23:10 with his weapon in his hand, around the **k—** 4889
23:11 of the covenant and **proclaimed** him **k**. 4887
23:11 "Long live the **k!"** 4889
23:12 of the people running and cheering the **k**, 4889
23:13 She looked, and there was the **k**, 4889
23:13 and the trumpeters were beside the **k**, 4889
23:16 that he and the people and the **k** would be 4889
2Ch 23:20 the **k** down from the temple of the LORD. 4889
23:20 through the Upper Gate and seated the **k** on 4889
24: 1 seven years old when he *became* **k**, 4887
24: 6 the **k** summoned Jehoiada the chief priest 4889
24:12 The **k** and Jehoiada gave it to 4889
24:14 the rest of the money to the **k** and Jehoiada, 4889
24:17 of Judah came and paid homage to the **k**, 4889
24:21 by order of the **k** they stoned him to death 4889
24:22 **K** Joash did not remember the kindness 4889
24:23 the plunder to their **k** *in* Damascus. 4889
24:27 And Amaziah his son succeeded him *as* **k**. 4887
25: 1 twenty-five years old *when he became* **k**, 4887
25: 3 he executed the officials who had murdered
his father the **k**. 4889
25: 7 a man of God came to him and said, "O **k**, 4889
25:16 the **k** said to him, NIH
25:16 appointed you an adviser to the **k**? 4889
25:17 Amaziah **k** *of* Judah consulted his advisers, 4889
25:17 **k** *of* Israel: "Come, meet me face to face." 4889
25:18 But Jehoash **k** *of* Israel replied 4889
25:18 of Israel replied to Amaziah **k** *of* Judah: 4889
25:21 So Jehoash **k** *of* Israel attacked. 4889
25:21 and Amaziah **k** *of* Judah faced each other 4889
25:23 Jehoash **k** *of* Israel captured Amaziah king 4889
25:23 Jehoash king of Israel captured Amaziah **k** 4889
25:25 of Joash **k** *of* Judah lived for fifteen years 4889
25:25 after the death of Jehoash son of Jehoahaz **k** 4889
26: 1 **made** him **k** in place of his father Amaziah. 4887
26: 3 sixteen years old when he *became* **k**, 4887
26:13 to support the **k** against his enemies. 4889
26:21 **K** Uzziah had leprosy until the day he died. 4889
26:23 And Jotham his son succeeded him *as* **k**. 4887
27: 1 twenty-five years old when he *became* **k**, 4887
27: 5 Jotham made war on the **k** *of* 4889
27: 8 twenty-five years old when he *became* **k**, 4887
27: 9 And Ahaz his son succeeded him *as* **k**. 4887
28: 1 twenty years old when he *became* **k**, 4887
28: 5 over to the **k** *of* Aram. 4889
28: 5 also given into the hands of the **k** *of* Israel, 4889
28: 7 and Elkanah, second to the **k**. 4889
28:16 that time **K** Ahaz sent to the king of Assyria 4889
28:16 At that time King Ahaz sent to the **k** 4889
28:19 because of Ahaz **k** *of* Israel, 4889
28:20 Tiglath-Pileser **k** *of* Assyria came to him, 4889
28:21 and presented them to the **k** *of* Assyria, 4889
28:22 In his time of trouble **K** Ahaz became 4889
28:27 And Hezekiah his son succeeded him *as* **k**. 4887
29: 1 twenty-five years old *when he became* **k**, 4887
29:15 as the **k** had ordered, 4889
29:18 they went in to **K** Hezekiah and reported: 4889
29:19 that **K** Ahaz removed in his unfaithfulness 4889
29:19 in his unfaithfulness while he was **k**. 4895
29:20 the next morning **K** Hezekiah gathered 4889
29:21 The **k** commanded the priests, NIH
29:23 the sin offering were brought before the **k** 4889
29:24 because the **k** had ordered the burnt offering 4889
29:27 by trumpets and the instruments of David **k** 4889
29:29 the **k** and everyone present with him knelt 4889
29:30 **K** Hezekiah and his officials ordered 4889
30: 2 The **k** and his officials and 4889
30: 4 The plan seemed right both to the **k** and to 4889
30: 6 the **k** and from his officials, which read: 4889
30:12 the **k** and his officials had ordered, 4889
30:24 Hezekiah **k** *of* Judah provided 4889
30:26 of David **k** *of* Israel there had been nothing 4889
31: 3 The **k** contributed from his own possessions 4889
31:13 by appointment of **K** Hezekiah and Azariah 4889
32: 1 Sennacherib **k** *of* Assyria came 4889
32: 7 or discouraged because of the **k** *of* Assyria 4889
32: 8 from what Hezekiah the **k** *of* Judah said. 4889
32: 9 when Sennacherib **k** *of* Assyria 4889
32: 9 with this message for Hezekiah **k** *of* Judah 4889
32:10 "This is what Sennacherib **k** 4889
32:11 from the hand of the **k** *of* Assyria,' 4889
32:17 **k** also wrote letters insulting the LORD, NIH
32:20 **K** Hezekiah and the prophet Isaiah son 4889
32:21 and officers in the camp of the Assyrian **k**. 4889
32:22 from the hand of Sennacherib **k** *of* Assyria 4889
32:23 and valuable gifts for Hezekiah **k** *of* Judah. 4889
32:33 And Manasseh his son succeeded him *as* **k**. 4887
33: 1 twelve years old when he *became* **k**, 4887
33:11 against them the army commanders of the **k** 4889
33:20 And Amon his son succeeded him *as* **k**. 4887
33:21 twenty-two years old when he *became* **k**, 4887
33:25 killed all who had plotted against **K** Amon, 4889
33:25 **made** Josiah his son **k** 4887
34: 1 eight years old when he *became* **k**, 4887
34:16 the book to the **k** and reported to him: 4889
34:18 Then Shaphan the secretary informed the **k**, 4889
34:18 from it in the presence of the **k**. 4889
34:19 When the **k** heard the words of the Law, 4889
34:22 the **k** had sent with him went to speak to 4889
34:24 that has been read in the presence of the **k** 4889
34:26 Tell the **k** *of* Judah, 4889
34:28 So they took her answer back to the **k**. 4889
34:29 the **k** called together all the elders of Judah 4889
34:31 The **k** stood by his pillar and renewed 4889
35: 3 that Solomon son of David **k** *of* Israel built. 4889
35: 4 the directions written by David **k** *of* Israel 4889
35:10 in their divisions as the **k** had ordered. 4889
35:16 as **K** Josiah had ordered. 4889
35:20 Neco **k** *of* Egypt went up to fight 4889
35:21 O **k** *of* Judah? It is not you I am attacking 4889
35:23 Archers shot **K** Josiah, 4889
36: 1 of Josiah and **made** him **k** in Jerusalem 4887
36: 2 twenty-three years old when he *became* **k**, 4887
36: 3 The **k** *of* Egypt dethroned him in Jerusalem 4889

2Ch 36: 4 The **k** *of* Egypt made Eliakim, 4889
36: 4 **made** Eliakim, a brother of Jehoahaz, **k** 4887
36: 5 twenty-five years old when he *became* **k**, 4887
36: 6 Nebuchadnezzar **k** *of* Babylon attacked him 4889
36: 8 And Jehoiachin his son succeeded him *as* **k**. 4887
36: 9 eighteen years old when he *became* **k**, 4887
36:10 **K** Nebuchadnezzar sent for him 4889
36:10 **made** Jehoiachin's uncle, Zedekiah, **k** 4887
36:11 twenty-one years old when he *became* **k**, 4887
36:13 also rebelled against **K** Nebuchadnezzar, 4889
36:17 up against them the **k** *of* the Babylonians, 4889
36:18 and the treasures of the **k** and his officials. 4889
36:22 In the first year of Cyrus **k** *of* Persia, 4889
36:22 the LORD moved the heart of Cyrus **k** 4889
36:23 "This is what Cyrus **k** *of* Persia says: 4889
Ezr 1: 1 In the first year of Cyrus **k** *of* Persia, 4889
1: 1 the LORD moved the heart of Cyrus **k** 4889
1: 2 "This is what Cyrus **k** *of* Persia says: 4889
1: 7 **K** Cyrus brought out the articles belonging 4889
1: 8 Cyrus **k** *of* Persia had them brought 4889
2: 1 Nebuchadnezzar **k** *of* Babylon had taken 4889
3: 7 as authorized by Cyrus **k** *of* Persia. 4889
3:10 as prescribed by David **k** *of* Israel. 4889
4: 2 since the time of Esarhaddon **k** *of* Assyria, 4889
4: 3 as **K** Cyrus, the king of Persia, 4889
4: 3 the **k** *of* Persia, commanded us." 4889
4: 5 during the entire reign of Cyrus **k** *of* Persia 4889
4: 5 and down to the reign of Darius **k** *of* Persia. 4889
4: 7 And in the days of Artaxerxes **k** *of* Persia, 4889
4: 8 against Jerusalem to Artaxerxes the **k** 10421
4:11 To **K** Artaxerxes, From your servants, 10421
4:12 The **k** should know that the Jews who came 10421
4:13 the **k** should know that if this city is built 10421
4:14 not proper for us to see the **k** dishonored, 10421
4:14 sending this message to inform the **k**, 10421
4:16 We inform the **k** that if this city is built 10421
4:17 The **k** sent this reply: 10421
4:23 of the letter of **K** Artaxerxes was read 10421
4:24 the second year of the reign of Darius **k** 10421
5: 6 sent to **K** Darius. 10421
5: 7 To **K** Darius: Cordial greetings. 10421
5: 8 The **k** should know that we went to 10421
5:11 that a great **k** of Israel built and finished. 10421
5:12 **k** *of* Babylon, who destroyed this temple 10421
5:13 in the first year of Cyrus **k** of Babylon, 10421
5:13 **K** Cyrus issued a decree 10421
5:14 "Then **K** Cyrus gave them to 10421
5:17 Now if it pleases the **k**, 10421
5:17 to see if **K** Cyrus did in fact issue a decree 10421
5:17 let the **k** send us his decision in this matter. 10421
6: 1 **K** Darius then issued an order, 10421
6: 3 In the first year of **K** Cyrus, the king issued 10421
6: 3 the **k** issued a decree concerning the temple 10421
6:10 for the well-being of the **k** and his sons. 10421
6:12 overthrow any **k** or people who lifts a hand 10421
6:13 because of the decree **K** Darius had sent, 10421
6:15 in the sixth year of the reign of **K** Darius. 10421
6:22 by changing the attitude of the **k** *of* Assyria, 4889
7: 1 during the reign of Artaxerxes **k** *of* Persia, 4889
7: 6 The **k** had granted him everything he asked, 4889
7: 7 in the seventh year of **K** Artaxerxes. 4889
7: 8 the fifth month of the seventh year of the **k**. 4889
7:11 of the letter **K** Artaxerxes had given to Ezra 4889
7:12 **k** *of* kings, To Ezra the priest, 10421
7:14 You are sent by the **k** and his seven advisers 10421
7:15 that the **k** and his advisers have freely given 10421
7:21 **K** Artaxerxes, order all the treasurers 10421
7:23 against the realm of the **k** and of his sons? 10421
7:26 of the **k** must surely be punished by death, 10421
7:28 to me before the **k** and his advisers and all 4889
8: 1 during the reign of **K** Artaxerxes: 4889
8:22 I was ashamed to ask the **k** for soldiers 4889
8:22 because we had told the **k**, 4889
8:25 of silver and gold and the articles that the **k**, 4889
Ne 1:11 I was cupbearer to the **k**. 4889
2: 1 in the twentieth year of **K** Artaxerxes, 4889
2: 1 I took the wine and gave it to the **k**. 4889
2: 2 so the **k** asked me, "Why does your face 4889
2: 3 but I said to the **k**, "May the king live 4889
2: 3 "May the **k** live forever! 4889
2: 4 The **k** said to me, "What is it you want?" 4889
2: 5 and I answered the **k**, 4889
2: 5 the **k** and if your servant has found favor 4889
2: 6 Then the **k**, with the queen sitting 4889
2: 6 It pleased the **k** to send me; so I set a time. 4889
2: 7 I also said to him, "If it pleases the **k**, 4889
2: 8 the **k** granted my requests. 4889
2: 9 The **k** had also sent army officers 4889
2:18 of my God upon me and what the **k** had said 4889
2:19 "Are you rebelling against the **k?**" 4889
5:14 from the twentieth year of **K** Artaxerxes, 4889
6: 6 reports that you are about to become their **k** 4889
6: 7 'There is a **k** in Judah!' 4889
6: 7 Now this report will get back to the **k**; 4889
7: 6 of the exiles whom Nebuchadnezzar **k** 4889
9:22 over the country of Sihon **k** *of* Heshbon and 4889
9:22 of Heshbon and the country of Og **k** 4889
13: 6 for in the thirty-second year of Artaxerxes **k** 4889
13: 6 of Babylon I had returned to the **k**. 4889
13:26 like these that Solomon **k** *of* Israel sinned? 4889
13:26 the many nations there was no **k** like him. 4889
13:26 and God made him **k** over all Israel, 4889
Est 1: 2 At that time **K** Xerxes reigned 4889
1: 5 the **k** gave a banquet, lasting seven days, 4889
1: 8 for the **k** instructed all the wine stewards 4889
1: 9 the women in the royal palace of **K** Xerxes. 4889
1:10 **K** Xerxes was in high spirits from wine, 4889
Est 1:12 **k** became furious and burned with anger. 4889
1:13 for the **k** to consult experts in matters of law 4889
1:14 and were closest to **the k**— 2257S
1:14 and Media who had special access to the **k** 4889
1:15 not obeyed the command of **K** Xerxes that 4889
1:16 in the presence of the **k** and the nobles, 4889
1:16 against the **k** but also against all the nobles 4889
1:16 of all the provinces of **K** Xerxes. 4889
1:17 '**K** Xerxes commanded Queen Vashti to 4889
1:19 "Therefore, if it pleases the **k**, 4889
1:19 to enter the presence of **K** Xerxes. 4889
1:19 Also let the **k** give her royal position 4889
1:21 The **k** and his nobles were pleased 4889
1:21 so the **k** did as Memucan proposed. 4889
2: 1 when the anger of **K** Xerxes had subsided, 4889
2: 2 for beautiful young virgins for the **k**. 4889
2: 3 Let the **k** appoint commissioners 4889
2: 4 the girl who pleases the **k** be queen instead 4889
2: 4 This advice appealed to the **k**, 4889
2: 6 from Jerusalem by Nebuchadnezzar **k** 4889
2: 6 with Jehoiachin **k** *of* Judah. 4889
2:12 a girl's turn came to go in to **K** Xerxes, 4889
2:13 And this is how she would go to the **k**: 4889
2:14 not return to the **k** unless he was pleased 4889
2:15 of his uncle Abihail) to go to the **k**, 4889
2:16 to **K** Xerxes in the royal residence in 4889
2:17 Now the **k** was attracted to Esther more than 4889
2:18 And the **k** gave a great banquet, 4889
2:21 and conspired to assassinate **K** Xerxes. 4889
2:22 who in turn reported it to the **k**, 4889
2:23 of the annals in the presence of the **k**. 4889
3: 1 **K** Xerxes honored Haman son 4889
3: 2 the **k** had commanded this concerning him. 4889
3: 7 In the twelfth year of **K** Xerxes, 4889
3: 8 Then Haman said to **K** Xerxes, 4889
3: 9 If it pleases the **k**, 4889
3:10 So the **k** took his signet ring from his finger 4889
3:11 "Keep the money," the **k** said to Haman, 4889
3:12 in the name of **K** Xerxes himself and sealed 4889
3:15 The **k** and Haman sat down to drink, 4889
4: 3 to which the edict and order of the **k** came, 4889
4:11 or woman who approaches the **k** in 4889
4:11 **the k** has but one law: 2257S
4:11 to this is for the **k** to extend the gold scepter 4889
4:11 since I was called to go to the **k**." 4889
4:16 When this is done, I will go to the **k**, 4889
5: 1 The **k** was sitting on his royal throne in 4889
5: 3 the **k** asked, "What is it, Queen Esther? 4889
5: 4 "If it pleases the **k**," replied Esther, 4889
5: 4 "let the **k**, together with Haman, 4889
5: 5 "Bring Haman at once," the **k** said, 4889
5: 5 So the **k** and Haman went to 4889
5: 6 the **k** again asked Esther, 4889
5: 8 the **k** regards me with favor and if it pleases 4889
5: 8 and if it pleases the **k** to grant my petition 4889
5: 8 let the **k** and Haman come tomorrow to 4889
5:11 and all the ways the **k** had honored him and 4889
5:12 to accompany the **k** to the banquet she gave. 4889
5:12 along with the **k** tomorrow. 4889
5:14 and ask the **k** in the morning 4889
5:14 go with the **k** to the dinner and be happy." 4889
6: 1 That night the **k** could not sleep; 4889
6: 2 who had conspired to assassinate **K** Xerxes. 4889
6: 3 Mordecai received for this?" the **k** asked. 4889
6: 4 The **k** said, "Who is in the court?" 4889
6: 4 to speak to the **k** about hanging Mordecai 4889
6: 5 "Bring him in," the **k** ordered. 4889
6: 6 When Haman entered, the **k** asked him, 4889
6: 6 for the man the **k** delights to honor?" 4889
6: 6 that the **k** would rather honor than me?" 4889
6: 7 So he answered the **k**, 4889
6: 7 "For the man the **k** delights to honor, 4889
6: 8 have them bring a royal robe the **k** has worn 4889
6: 8 and a horse the **k** has ridden, 4889
6: 9 Let them robe the man the **k** delights 4889
6: 9 for the man the **k** delights to honor!' " 4889
6:10 "Go at once," the **k** commanded Haman. 4889
6:11 for the man the **k** delights to honor!" 4889
7: 1 So the **k** and Haman went to dine 4889
7: 2 the **k** again asked, "Queen Esther, 4889
7: 3 "If I have found favor with you, O **k**, 4889
7: 4 because no such distress would justify
disturbing the **k**." 4889
7: 5 **K** Xerxes asked Queen Esther, "Who is he? 4889
7: 6 Haman was terrified before the **k** and queen. 4889
7: 7 The **k** got up in a rage, 4889
7: 7 that the **k** had already decided his fate, 4889
7: 8 as the **k** returned from the palace garden to 4889
7: 8 The **k** exclaimed, "Will he even molest 4889
7: 9 one of the eunuchs attending the **k**, said, 4889
7: 9 who spoke up to help the **k**." 4889
7: 9 The **k** said, "Hang him on it!" 4889
8: 1 That same day **K** Xerxes gave Queen Esther 4889
8: 1 into the presence of the **k**, 4889
8: 2 The **k** took off his signet ring, 4889
8: 3 Esther again pleaded with the **k**, 4889
8: 4 the **k** extended the gold scepter to Esther 4889
8: 5 "If it pleases the **k**," she said, 4889
8: 7 **K** Xerxes replied to Queen Esther and 4889
8:10 Mordecai wrote in the name of **K** Xerxes, 4889
8:10 rode fast horses especially bred **for the k**. 350
8:12 of **K** Xerxes was the thirteenth day of 4889
8:17 wherever the edict of the **k** went, 4889
9: 1 the edict commanded by the **k** was to 4889
9: 2 in all the provinces of **K** Xerxes 4889
9:11 of Susa was reported to the **k** that same day. 4889
9:12 The **k** said to Queen Esther, 4889
Est 9:13 "If it pleases the **k**," Esther answered, 4889
9:14 So the **k** commanded that this be done. 4889
9:20 throughout the provinces of **K** Xerxes, 4889
10: 1 **K** Xerxes imposed tribute throughout 4889
10: 2 of Mordecai to which the **k** had raised him, 4889
10: 3 the Jew was second in rank to **K** Xerxes, 4889
Job 15:24 like a **k** poised to attack, 4889
18:14 and marched off to the **k** *of* terrors. 4889
29:25 I dwelt as a **k** among his troops; 4889
41:34 he is **k** over all that are proud." 4889
Ps 2: 6 "I have installed my **K** on Zion, 4889
5: 2 my **K** and my God, for to you I pray. 4889
10:16 The LORD is **K** for ever and ever; 4889
18:50 He gives his **k** great victories; 4889
20: 9 O LORD, save the **k**! 4889
21: 1 O LORD, the **k** rejoices in your strength. 4889
21: 7 For the **k** trusts in the LORD; 4889
24: 7 that the **K** *of* glory may come in. 4889
24: 8 Who is this **K** *of* glory? 4889
24: 9 that the **K** *of* glory may come in. 4889
24:10 Who is he, this **K** *of* glory? 4889
24:10 LORD Almighty—he is the **K** *of* glory. 4889
29:10 the LORD is enthroned as **K** forever. 4889
33:16 No **k** is saved by the size of his army; 4889
44: 4 You are my **K** and my God, 4889
45: 1 as I recite my verses for the **k**; 4889
45:11 The **k** is enthralled by your beauty; 4889
45:14 In embroidered garments she is led to the **k**; 4889
45:15 they enter the palace of the **k**. 4889
47: 2 the great **K** over all the earth! 4889
47: 6 sing praises to our **K**, sing praises. 4889
47: 7 For God is the **K** *of* all the earth; 4889
48: 2 the city of the Great **K**. 4889
63:11 But the **k** will rejoice in God; 4889
68:24 the procession of my God and **K** into 4889
72: 1 Endow the **k** with your justice, O God, 4889
74:12 But you, O God, are my **k** from of old; 4889
84: 3 O LORD Almighty, my **K** and my God. 4889
89:18 our **k** to the Holy One of Israel. 4889
95: 3 the great **K** above all gods. 4889
98: 6 shout for joy before the LORD, the **K**. 4889
99: 4 The **K** is mighty, he loves justice— 4889
105:20 The **k** sent and released him, 4889
135:11 Sihon **k** *of* the Amorites, Og king 4889
135:11 Og **k** *of* Bashan and all the kings 4889
136:19 Sihon **k** *of* the Amorites 4889
136:20 Og **k** *of* Bashan— 4889
145: 1 I will exalt you, my God the **K**; 4889
149: 2 let the people of Zion be glad in their **K**. 4889
Pr 1: 1 The proverbs of Solomon son of David, **k** 4889
14:35 A **k** delights in a wise servant, 4889
16:10 The lips of a **k** speak as an oracle, 4889
20: 8 When a **k** sits on his throne to judge, 4889
20:26 A wise **k** winnows out the wicked; 4889
20:28 Love and faithfulness keep a **k** safe; 4889
22:11 will have the **k** for his friend. 4889
24:21 Fear the LORD and the **k**, my son, 4889
25: 1 copied by the men of Hezekiah **k** *of* Judah: 4889
29: 4 By justice a **k** gives a country stability, 4889
29:14 If a **k** judges the poor with fairness, 4889
30:22 a servant *who becomes* **k**, 4887
30:27 locusts have no **k**, yet they advance together 4889
30:31 and a **k** with his army around him. 4889
31: 1 The sayings of **K** Lemuel— 4889
Ecc 1: 1 son of David, **k** in Jerusalem: 4889
1:12 the Teacher, was **k** over Israel in Jerusalem. 4889
4:13 an old but foolish **k** who no longer knows 4889
5: 9 the **k** himself profits from the fields. 4889
9:14 And a powerful **k** came against it, 4889
10:16 O land whose **k** was a servant 4889
10:17 O land whose **k** is of noble birth 4889
10:20 Do not revile the **k** even in your thoughts, 4889
SS 1: 4 Let the **k** bring me into his chambers. 4889
1:12 While the **k** was at his table, 4889
3: 9 **K** Solomon made for himself the carriage; 4889
3:11 and look at **K** Solomon wearing the crown, 4889
7: 5 the **k** is held captive by its tresses. 4889
Isa 6: 1 In the year that **K** Uzziah died, 4889
6: 5 and my eyes have seen the **K**, 4889
7: 1 the son of Uzziah, was **k** *of* Judah, 4889
7: 1 **K** Rezin *of* Aram and Pekah son 4889
7: 1 of Remaliah **k** *of* Israel marched up to fight 4889
7: 6 and **make** the son of Tabeel **k** 4887+4889
7:17 he will bring the **k** *of* Assyria." 4889
7:20 the **k** *of* Assyria— 4889
8: 4 of Samaria will be carried off by the **k** 4889
8: 7 the **k** *of* Assyria with all his pomp. 4889
8:21 will curse their **k** and their God. 4889
10:12 the **k** *of* Assyria for the willful pride 4889
14: 4 you will take up this taunt against the **k** 4889
14:28 This oracle came in the year **K** Ahaz died: 4889
19: 4 and a fierce **k** will rule over them," 4889
20: 1 sent by Sargon **k** *of* Assyria, 4889
20: 4 so the **k** *of* Assyria will lead away stripped 4889
20: 6 and deliverance from the **k** *of* Assyria! 4889
30:33 it has been made ready for the **k**. 4889
32: 1 a **k** will reign in righteousness 4889
33:17 Your eyes will see the **k** in his beauty 4889
33:22 the LORD is our **k**; it is he who will save us. 4889
36: 1 the fourteenth year of **K** Hezekiah's reign, 4889
36: 1 Sennacherib **k** *of* Assyria attacked all 4889
36: 2 the **k** *of* Assyria sent his field commander 4889
36: 2 from Lachish to **K** Hezekiah at Jerusalem. 4889
36: 4 "Tell Hezekiah, " 'This is what the great **k**, 4889
36: 4 the **k** *of* Assyria, says: 4889
36: 6 Such is Pharaoh **k** *of* Egypt 4889
36: 8 bargain with my master, the **k** *of* Assyria: 4889

Isa 36:13 "Hear the words of the great **k**, 4889
36:13 the great king, the **k** *of* Assyria! 4889
36:14 This is what the **k** says: 4889
36:15 be given into the hand of the **k** *of* Assyria.' 4889
36:16 This is what the **k** *of* Assyria says: 4889
36:18 from the hand of the **k** *of* Assyria? 4889
36:21 because the **k** had commanded, 4889
37: 1 When **K** Hezekiah heard this, 4889
37: 4 whom his master, the **k** *of* Assyria, 4889
37: 5 **K** Hezekiah's officials came to Isaiah, 4889
37: 6 of the **k** *of* Assyria have blasphemed me. 4889
37: 8 When the field commander heard that the **k** 4889
37: 8 and found the **k** fighting against Libnah. NIH
37: 9 Tirhakah, the Cushite **k** [of Egypt], 4889
37:10 "Say to Hezekiah **k** *of* Judah: 4889
37:10 'Jerusalem will not be handed over to the **k** 4889
37:13 Where is the **k** *of* Hamath, 4889
37:13 is the king of Hamath, the **k** *of* Arpad, 4889
37:13 the **k** of the city of Sepharvaim, 4889
37:21 to me concerning Sennacherib **k** *of* Assyria, 4889
37:33 the LORD says concerning the **k** 4889
37:37 So Sennacherib **k** *of* Assyria broke camp 4889
37:38 Esarhaddon his son succeeded him *as* **k.** 4887
38: 6 and this city from the hand of the **k** 4889
38: 9 of Hezekiah **k** *of* Judah after his illness 4889
39: 1 Merodach-Baladan son of Baladan **k** 4889
39: 3 the prophet went to **K** Hezekiah and asked, 4889
39: 7 in the palace of the **k** *of* Babylon." 4889
41:21 "Set forth your arguments," says Jacob's **K.** 4889
43:15 your Holy One, Israel's Creator, your **K."** 4889
44: 6 Israel's **K** and Redeemer, 4889
Jer 1: 2 the reign of Josiah son of Amon **k** *of* Judah, 4889
1: 3 of Jehoiakim son of Josiah **k** *of* Judah, 4889
1: 3 of Zedekiah son of Josiah **k** *of* Judah, 4889
3: 6 During the reign of **K** Josiah, 4889
4: 9 "the **k** and the officials will lose heart, 4889
8:19 Is her **K** no longer there?" 4889
10: 7 O **K** *of* the nations? 4889
10:10 he is the living God, the eternal **K.** 4889
13:18 Say to the **k** and to the queen mother, 4889
15: 4 of Hezekiah **k** *of* Judah did in Jerusalem. 4889
20: 4 I will hand all Judah over to the **k** 4889
21: 1 when **K** Zedekiah sent to him Pashhur son 4889
21: 2 for us because Nebuchadnezzar **k** 4889
21: 4 which you are using to fight the **k** 4889
21: 7 I will hand over Zedekiah **k** *of* Judah, 4889
21: 7 to Nebuchadnezzar **k** *of* Babylon and 4889
21:10 be given into the hands of the **k** *of* Babylon, 4889
22: 1 "Go down to the palace of the **k** *of* Judah 4889
22: 2 O **k** *of* Judah, you who sit 4889
22: 6 the LORD says about the palace of the **k** 4889
22:10 not weep for the dead [**k**] or mourn his loss; NIH
22:11 *as* **k** *of* Judah but has gone from this place: 4887
22:15 "*Does it make you a* **k** to have more 4887
22:18 about Jehoiakim son of Josiah **k** *of* Judah: 4889
22:24 Jehoiachin son of Jehoiakim **k** *of* Judah, 4889
22:25 to Nebuchadnezzar **k** *of* Babylon and to 4889
23: 5 a **K** who will reign wisely 4889
24: 1 of Jehoiakim **k** *of* Judah and the officials, 4889
24: 1 by Nebuchadnezzar **k** *of* Babylon, 4889
24: 8 'so will I deal with Zedekiah **k** *of* Judah, 4889
25: 1 the fourth year of Jehoiakim son of Josiah **k** 4889
25: 1 the first year of Nebuchadnezzar **k** 4889
25: 3 the thirteenth year of Josiah son of Amon **k** 4889
25: 9 the north and my servant Nebuchadnezzar **k** 4889
25:11 and these nations will serve the **k** 4889
25:12 the **k** *of* Babylon and his nation, 4889
25:19 Pharaoh **k** *of* Egypt, 4889
25:26 the **k** *of* Sheshach will drink it too. 4889
26: 1 of Josiah **k** *of* Judah, this word came from 4889
26:18 in the days of Hezekiah **k** *of* Judah. 4889
26:19 "Did Hezekiah **k** *of* Judah or anyone else 4889
26:21 When **K** Jehoiakim and all his officers 4889
26:21 the **k** sought to put him to death. 4889
26:22 **K** Jehoiakim, however, sent Elnathan 4889
26:23 of Egypt and took him to **K** Jehoiakim, 4889
27: 1 in the reign of Zedekiah son of Josiah **k** 4889
27: 3 to Jerusalem to Zedekiah **k** *of* Judah. 4889
27: 6 over to my servant Nebuchadnezzar **k** 4889
27: 8 not serve Nebuchadnezzar **k** *of* Babylon 4889
27: 9 'You will not serve the **k** *of* Babylon.' 4889
27:11 the yoke of the **k** *of* Babylon and serve him, 4889
27:12 the same message to Zedekiah **k** *of* Judah. 4889
27:12 "Bow your neck under the yoke of the **k** 4889
27:13 that will not serve the **k** *of* Babylon? 4889
27:14 'You will not serve the **k** *of* Babylon,' 4889
27:17 Serve the **k** *of* Babylon, and you will live. 4889
27:18 of the LORD and in the palace of the **k** 4889
27:20 which Nebuchadnezzar **k** *of* Babylon did 4889
27:20 of Jehoiakim **k** *of* Judah into exile 4889
27:21 of the LORD and in the palace of the **k** 4889
28: 1 early in the reign of Zedekiah **k** *of* Judah, 4889
28: 2 'I will break the yoke of the **k** *of* Babylon. 4889
28: 3 the LORD's house that Nebuchadnezzar **k** 4889
28: 4 to this place Jehoiachin son of Jehoiakim **k** 4889
28: 4 I will break the yoke of the **k** *of* Babylon.' " 4889
28:11 of Nebuchadnezzar **k** *of* Babylon off 4889
28:14 to make them serve Nebuchadnezzar **k** 4889
29: 2 after **K** Jehoiachin and the queen mother, 4889
29: 3 whom Zedekiah **k** *of* Judah sent 4889
29: 3 of Judah sent to **K** Nebuchadnezzar 4889
29:16 the **k** who sits on David's throne and all 4889
29:21 "I will hand them over to Nebuchadnezzar **k** 4889
29:22 whom the **k** *of* Babylon burned in the fire.' 4889
30: 9 the LORD their God and David their **k,** 4889
32: 1 the LORD in the tenth year of Zedekiah **k** 4889
32: 2 The army of the **k** *of* Babylon was 4889
Jer 32: 3 Now Zedekiah **k** *of* Judah 4889
32: 3 to hand this city over to the **k** *of* Babylon, 4889
32: 4 Zedekiah **k** *of* Judah will not escape out of 4889
32: 4 but will certainly be handed over to the **k** 4889
32:28 the Babylonians and to Nebuchadnezzar **k** 4889
32:36 and plague it will be handed over to the **k** 4889
34: 1 While Nebuchadnezzar **k** *of* Babylon 4889
34: 2 Go to Zedekiah **k** *of* Judah and tell him, 4889
34: 2 to hand this city over to the **k** *of* Babylon, 4889
34: 3 the **k** *of* Babylon with your own eyes, 4889
34: 4 O Zedekiah **k** *of* Judah. 4889
34: 6 the prophet told all this to Zedekiah **k** 4889
34: 7 the army of the **k** *of* Babylon was fighting 4889
34: 8 the LORD after **K** Zedekiah had made 4889
34:21 "I will hand Zedekiah **k** *of* Judah 4889
34:21 to the army of the **k** *of* Babylon, 4889
35: 1 of Jehoiakim son of Josiah **k** *of* Judah: 4889
35:11 But when Nebuchadnezzar **k** 4889
36: 1 the fourth year of Jehoiakim son of Josiah **k** 4889
36: 9 the fifth year of Jehoiakim son of Josiah **k** 4889
36:16 "We must report all these words to the **k."** 4889
36:20 they went to the **k** in the courtyard 4889
36:21 The **k** sent Jehudi to get the scroll, 4889
36:21 the secretary and read it to the **k** and all 4889
36:22 It was the ninth month and the **k** was sitting 4889
36:23 the **k** cut them off with a scribe's knife NIH
36:24 The **k** and all his attendants who heard all these words showed no fear, 4889
36:25 Delaiah and Gemariah urged the **k** not 4889
36:26 Instead, the **k** commanded Jerahmeel, 4889
36:26 Jerahmeel, a son of the **k,** 4889
36:27 the **k** burned the scroll containing the words 4889
36:28 which Jehoiakim **k** *of* Judah burned up. 4889
36:29 Also tell Jehoiakim **k** *of* Judah, 4889
36:29 that the **k** *of* Babylon would certainly come 4889
36:30 the LORD says about Jehoiakim **k** 4889
36:32 that Jehoiakim **k** *of* Judah had burned in 4889
37: 1 Zedekiah son of Josiah *was* **made k** of Judah 4887
37: 1 of Judah by Nebuchadnezzar **k** *of* Babylon; 4889
37: 3 **K** Zedekiah, however, sent Jehucal son 4889
37: 7 Tell the **k** *of* Judah, 4889
37:17 Then **K** Zedekiah sent for him 4889
37:17 be handed over to the **k** *of* Babylon." 4889
37:18 Then Jeremiah said to **K** Zedekiah, 4889
37:19 'The **k** *of* Babylon will not attack you 4889
37:20 But now, my lord the **k,** please listen. 4889
37:21 **K** Zedekiah then gave orders for Jeremiah 4889
38: 3 over to the army of the **k** *of* Babylon, 4889
38: 4 Then the officials said to the **k,** 4889
38: 5 **K** Zedekiah answered, 4889
38: 5 "The **k** can do nothing to oppose you." 4889
38: 7 the **k** was sitting in the Benjamin Gate, 4889
38: 9 "My lord the **k,** these men have acted 4889
38:10 **k** commanded Ebed-Melech the Cushite, 4889
38:14 Then **K** Zedekiah sent for Jeremiah 4889
38:14 the **k** said to Jeremiah. 4889
38:16 But **K** Zedekiah swore this oath secretly 4889
38:17 of the **k** *of* Babylon, your life will be spared 4889
38:18 the **k** *of* Babylon, this city will be handed 4889
38:19 **K** Zedekiah said to Jeremiah, 4889
38:22 All the women left in the palace of the **k** 4889
38:22 be brought out to the officials of the **k** 4889
38:23 but will be captured by the **k** *of* Babylon; 4889
38:25 'Tell us what you said to the **k** and what 4889
38:25 to the king and what the **k** said to you; 4889
38:26 with the **k** not to send me back 4889
38:27 the **k** had ordered him to say. 4889
38:27 had heard his conversation with the **k.** NIH
39: 1 In the ninth year of Zedekiah **k** *of* Judah, 4889
39: 1 Nebuchadnezzar **k** *of* Babylon marched 4889
39: 3 of the **k** *of* Babylon came and took seats in 4889
39: 3 the other officials of the **k** *of* Babylon. 4889
39: 4 When Zedekiah **k** *of* Judah and all 4889
39: 5 to Nebuchadnezzar **k** *of* Babylon at Riblah 4889
39: 6 at Riblah the **k** *of* Babylon slaughtered 4889
39:11 Now Nebuchadnezzar **k** *of* Babylon 4889
39:13 the other officers of the **k** *of* Babylon 4889
40: 5 whom the **k** *of* Babylon has appointed over 4889
40: 7 in the open country heard that the **k** 4889
40: 9 "Settle down in the land and serve the **k** 4889
40:11 and all the other countries heard that the **k** 4889
40:14 "Don't you know that Baalis **k** *of* 4889
41: 2 the **k** *of* Babylon had appointed as governor 4889
41: 9 with Gedaliah was the one **K** Asa had made 4889
41: 9 of his defense against Baasha **k** *of* Israel. 4889
41:18 the **k** *of* Babylon had appointed as governor 4889
42:11 Do not be afraid of the **k** *of* Babylon, 4889
43:10 for my servant Nebuchadnezzar **k** 4889
44:30 to hand Pharaoh Hophra **k** *of* Egypt over 4889
44:30 just as I handed Zedekiah **k** *of* Judah over 4889
44:30 over to Nebuchadnezzar **k** *of* Babylon, 4889
45: 1 the fourth year of Jehoiakim son of Josiah **k** 4889
46: 2 the army of Pharaoh Neco **k** *of* Egypt, 4889
46: 2 the Euphrates River by Nebuchadnezzar **k** 4889
46: 2 the fourth year of Jehoiakim son of Josiah **k** 4889
46:13 about the coming of Nebuchadnezzar **k** 4889
46:17 'Pharaoh **k** *of* Egypt is only a loud noise; 4889
46:18 "As surely as I live," declares the **K,** 4889
46:26 to Nebuchadnezzar **k** *of* Babylon 4889
48:15 down in the slaughter," declares the **K,** 4889
49:28 which Nebuchadnezzar **k** *of* Babylon 4889
49:30 "Nebuchadnezzar **k** *of* Babylon has plotted 4889
49:34 early in the reign of Zedekiah **k** *of* Judah: 4889
49:38 in Elam and destroy her **k** and officials," 4889
50:17 first to devour him was the **k** *of* Assyria; 4889
50:17 to crush his bones was Nebuchadnezzar **k** 4889
Jer 50:18 "I will punish the **k** *of* Babylon and his land 4889
50:18 and his land as I punished the **k** *of* Assyria. 4889
50:43 **k** *of* Babylon has heard reports about them, 4889
51:31 to announce to the **k** *of* Babylon 4889
51:34 "Nebuchadnezzar **k** *of* Babylon 4889
51:57 and not awake," declares the **K,** 4889
51:59 with Zedekiah **k** *of* Judah in the fourth year 4889
52: 1 twenty-one years old when he *became* **k,** 4887
52: 3 Zedekiah rebelled against the **k** *of* Babylon. 4889
52: 4 Nebuchadnezzar **k** *of* Babylon marched 4889
52: 5 until the eleventh year of **K** Zedekiah. 4889
52: 8 the Babylonian army pursued **K** Zedekiah 4889
52: 9 He was taken to the **k** *of* Babylon at Riblah 4889
52:10 at Riblah the **k** *of* Babylon slaughtered 4889
52:12 in the nineteenth year of Nebuchadnezzar **k** 4889
52:12 who served the **k** *of* Babylon, 4889
52:15 and those who had gone over to the **k** 4889
52:20 which **K** Solomon had made for the temple 4889
52:26 and brought them to the **k** *of* Babylon 4889
52:27 the **k** had them executed. 4889
52:31 of the exile of Jehoiachin **k** *of* Judah, 4889
52:31 in the year Evil-Merodach **became k** 4895
52:31 he released Jehoiachin **k** *of* Judah 4889
52:34 by day the **k** *of* Babylon gave Jehoiachin 4889
La 2: 6 in his fierce anger he has spurned both **k** 4889
2: 9 Her **k** and her princes are exiled among 4889
Eze 1: 2 the fifth year of the exile of **K** Jehoiachin— 4889
7:27 The **k** will mourn, the prince will be 4889
17:12 'The **k** *of* Babylon went to Jerusalem 4889
17:12 and carried off her **k** and her nobles, 4889
17:15 But the **k** rebelled against him NIH
17:16 the land of the **k** who put him on the throne, 4889
19: 9 and brought him to the **k** *of* Babylon. 4889
21:19 for the sword of the **k** *of* Babylon to take, 4889
21:21 For the **k** *of* Babylon will stop at the fork in 4889
24: 2 because the **k** *of* Babylon has laid siege 4889
26: 7 against Tyre Nebuchadnezzar **k** *of* Babylon, 4889
26: 7 **k** *of* kings, with horses and chariots, 4889
28:12 a lament concerning the **k** *of* Tyre and say 4889
29: 2 against Pharaoh **k** *of* Egypt and prophesy 4889
29: 3 " 'I am against you, Pharaoh **k** *of* Egypt, 4889
29:18 Nebuchadnezzar **k** *of* Babylon 4889
29:19 to give Egypt to Nebuchadnezzar **k** 4889
30:10 the hand of Nebuchadnezzar **k** *of* Babylon. 4889
30:21 I have broken the arm of Pharaoh **k** 4889
30:22 I am against Pharaoh **k** *of* Egypt. 4889
30:24 of the **k** *of* Babylon and put my sword 4889
30:25 I will strengthen the arms of the **k** 4889
30:25 when I put my sword into the hand of the **k** 4889
31: 2 to Pharaoh **k** *of* Egypt and to his hordes: 4889
32: 2 up a lament concerning Pharaoh **k** *of* Egypt 4889
32:11 " 'The sword of the **k** *of* Babylon will come 4889
37:22 There will be one **k** over all of them 4889
37:24 " 'My servant David will be **k** over them, 4889
Da 1: 1 In the third year of the reign of Jehoiakim **k** 4889
1: 1 Nebuchadnezzar **k** *of* Babylon came 4889
1: 2 the Lord delivered Jehoiakim **k** *of* Judah 4889
1: 3 Then the **k** ordered Ashpenaz, 4889
1: 5 The **k** assigned them a daily amount of food 4889
1:10 "I am afraid of my lord the **k,** 4889
1:10 The **k** would then have my head because 4889
1:18 of the time set by the **k** to bring them in, 4889
1:19 The **k** talked with them, 4889
1:20 about which the **k** questioned them, 4889
1:21 until the first year of **K** Cyrus. 4889
2: 2 So the **k** summoned the magicians, 4889
2: 2 When they came in and stood before the **k,** 4889
2: 4 the astrologers answered the **k** in Aramaic, 4889
2: 4 the king in Aramaic, "O **k,** 10421
2: 5 The **k** replied to the astrologers, 10421
2: 7 "Let the **k** tell his servants the dream, 10421
2: 8 Then the **k** answered, "I am certain 10421
2:10 The astrologers answered the **k,** 10421
2:10 a man on earth who can do what the **k** asks! 10421
2:10 No **k,** however great and mighty, 10421
2:11 What the **k** asks is too difficult. 10421
2:11 No one can reveal it to the **k** except 10421
2:12 the **k** so angry and furious that he ordered 10421
2:15 "Why did the **k** issue such a harsh decree?" 10421
2:16 Daniel went in to the **k** and asked for time, 10421
2:23 to us the dream of the **k."** 10421
2:24 the **k** had appointed to execute the wise men 10421
2:24 Take me to the **k,** 10421
2:25 Arioch took Daniel to the **k** at once 10421
2:25 the **k** what his dream means." 10421
2:26 **k** asked Daniel (also called Belteshazzar), 10421
2:27 to the **k** the mystery he has asked about, 10421
2:28 **K** Nebuchadnezzar what will happen 10421
2:29 O **k,** your mind turned to things to come, 10421
2:30 but so that you, O **k,** may know 10421
2:31 O **k,** and there before you stood 10421
2:36 and now we will interpret it to the **k.** 10421
2:37 You, O **k,** are the king of kings. 10421
2:37 You, O king, are the **k** *of* kings. 10421
2:45 the **k** what will take place in the future. 10421
2:46 Then **K** Nebuchadnezzar fell prostrate 10421
2:47 The **k** said to Daniel, 10421
2:48 Then the **k** placed Daniel in a high position 10421
2:49 the **k** appointed Shadrach, Meshach 10421
3: 1 **K** Nebuchadnezzar made an image of gold, 10421
3: 3 the image that **K** Nebuchadnezzar had set 10421
3: 5 of gold that **K** Nebuchadnezzar has set up. 10421
3: 7 of gold that **K** Nebuchadnezzar had set up. 10421
3: 9 They said to **K** Nebuchadnezzar, "O king, 10421
3: 9 They said to King Nebuchadnezzar, "O **k,** 10421
3:10 You have issued a decree, O **k,** 10421
3:12 who pay no attention to you, O **k.** 10421

Da 3:13 So these men were brought before the **k**, 10421
3:16 Meshach and Abednego replied to the **k**, 10421
3:17 and he will rescue us from your hand, O **k**. 10421
3:18 if he does not, we want you to know, O **k**, 10421
3:24 Then **K** Nebuchadnezzar leaped to his feet 10421
3:24 They replied, "Certainly, O **k**." 10421
3:30 Then the **k** promoted Shadrach, 10421
4: 1 **K** Nebuchadnezzar, To the peoples, 10421
4:18 **K** Nebuchadnezzar, had. 10421
4:19 So the **k** said, "Belteshazzar, 10421
4:22 O **k**, are that tree! 10421
4:23 "You, O **k**, saw a messenger, a holy one, 10421
4:24 "This is the interpretation, O **k**, 10421
4:24 against my lord the **k**: 10421
4:27 O **k**, be pleased to accept my advice: 10421
4:28 All this happened to **K** Nebuchadnezzar. 10421
4:29 as the **k** was walking on the roof of NIH
4:31 for you, **K** Nebuchadnezzar: 10421
4:37 and exalt and glorify the **K** *of* heaven, 10421
5: 1 **K** Belshazzar gave a great banquet for 10421
5: 2 so that the **k** and his nobles, 10421
5: 3 and the **k** and his nobles, 10421
5: 5 The **k** watched the hand as it wrote. 10421
5: 7 The **k** called out for the enchanters, 10421
5: 8 the writing or tell the **k** what it meant. 10421
5: 9 So **K** Belshazzar became even more 10421
5:10 hearing the voices of the **k** and his nobles, 10421
5:10 "O **k**, live forever!" 10421
5:11 **K** Nebuchadnezzar your father— 10421
5:11 your father the **k**, I say— 10421
5:12 whom the **k** called Belteshazzar, 10421
5:13 So Daniel was brought before the **k**, 10421
5:13 and the **k** said to him, "Are you Daniel, 10421
5:13 one of the exiles my father the **k** brought 10421
5:17 Then Daniel answered the **k**, 10421
5:17 for the **k** and tell him what it means. 10421
5:18 "O **k**, the Most High God gave your father Nebuchadnezzar sovereignty 10421
5:19 Those the **k** wanted to put to death, NIH
5:30 **k** *of* the Babylonians, was slain, 10421
6: 2 to them so that the **k** might not suffer loss. 10421
6: 3 that the **k** planned to set him over 10421
6: 6 and the satraps went as a group to the **k** 10421
6: 6 "O **K** Darius, live forever! 10421
6: 7 that the **k** should issue an edict and enforce 10421
6: 7 O **k**, shall be thrown into the lions' den. 10421
6: 8 O **k**, issue the decree and put it in writing so 10421
6: 9 So **K** Darius put the decree in writing. 10421
6:12 So they went to the **k** and spoke to him 10421
6:12 O **k**, would be thrown into the lions' den?" 10421
6:12 The **k** answered, "The decree stands— 10421
6:13 Then they said to the **k**, "Daniel, 10421
6:13 O **k**, or to the decree you put in writing. 10421
6:14 When the **k** heard this, 10421
6:15 the men went as a group to the **k** and said 10421
6:15 O **k**, that according to the law of the Medes 10421
6:15 or edict that the **k** issues can be changed." 10421
6:16 So the **k** gave the order, 10421
6:16 The **k** said to Daniel, "May your God, 10421
6:17 and the **k** sealed it with his own signet ring 10421
6:18 Then the **k** returned to his palace and spent 10421
6:19 the **k** got up and hurried to the lions' den. 10421
6:21 Daniel answered, "O **k**, live forever! 10421
6:22 Nor have I ever done any wrong before you, O **k**." 10421
6:23 The **k** was overjoyed and gave orders 10421
6:25 Then **K** Darius wrote to all the peoples, 10421
7: 1 In the first year of Belshazzar **k** *of* Babylon, 10421
7:24 After them another **k** will arise, NIH
8: 1 In the third year of **K** Belshazzar's reign, I, 4889
8:21 The shaggy goat is the **k** *of* Greece, 4889
8:21 large horn between his eyes is the first **k**. 4889
8:23 a stern-faced **k**, a master of intrigue, 4889
10: 1 In the third year of Cyrus **k** *of* Persia, 4889
10:13 I was detained there with the **k** *of* Persia. 4889
11: 3 Then a mighty **k** will appear, 4889
11: 5 "The **k** *of* the South will become strong, 4889
11: 6 of the **k** *of* the South will go to the king of 4889
11: 6 of the king of the South will go to the **k** *of* 4889
11: 7 of the **k** *of* the North and enter his fortress; 4889
11: 8 For some years he will leave the **k** *of* 4889
11: 9 the **k** of the North will invade the realm of NIH
11: 9 the North will invade the realm of the **k** *of* 4889
11:11 "Then the **k** *of* the South will march out in 4889
11:11 a rage and fight against the **k** *of* the North, 4889
11:12 **the k of the South** will be filled with pride 2257S
11:13 **k** *of* the North will muster another army, 4889
11:14 "In those times many will rise against the **k** 4889
11:15 the **k** *of* the North will come and build 4889
11:17 alliance with **the k of the South.** 2257S
11:25 up his strength and courage against the **k** *of* 4889
11:25 The **k** *of* the South will wage war with 4889
11:28 The **k** of the North will return NIH
11:36 "The **k** will do as he pleases. 4889
11:40 the **k** *of* the South will engage him in battle, 4889
11:40 and the **k** *of* the North will storm out 4889
Hos 1: 1 of Jeroboam son of Jehoash **k** *of* Israel: 4889
3: 4 the Israelites will live many days without **k** 4889
3: 5 the LORD their God and David their **k**. 4889
5:13 and sent to the great **k** for help. 4889
7: 3 "They delight the **k** with their wickedness, 4889
7: 5 of our **k** the princes become inflamed 4889
8:10 under the oppression of the mighty **k**. 4889
10: 3 "We have no **k** because we did not revere 4889
10: 3 if we had a **k**, what could he do for us?" 4889
10: 6 to Assyria as tribute for the great **k**. 4889
10: 7 Samaria and its **k** will float away like a twig 4889
Hos 10:15 **k** *of* Israel will be completely destroyed. 4889
13:10 Where is your **k**, that he may save you? 4889
13:10 'Give me a **k** and princes'? 4889
13:11 So in my anger I gave you a **k**, 4889
Am 1: 1 before the earthquake, when Uzziah was **k** 4889
1: 1 and Jeroboam son of Jehoash was **k** 4889
1: 5 I will destroy the **k** *who is* in the Valley 3782
1: 8 the **k** of Ashdod and the one who holds 3782
1:15 Her **k** will go into exile, 4889
2: 1 as if to lime, the bones of Edom's **k**, 4889
5:26 You have lifted up the shrine of your **k**, 4889
7:10 of Bethel sent a message to Jeroboam **k** 4889
Jnh 3: 6 When the news reached the **k** *of* Nineveh, 4889
3: 7 "By the decree of the **k** and his nobles: 4889
Mic 2:13 Their **k** will pass through before them, 4889
4: 9 Why do you cry aloud—have you no **k**? 4889
6: 5 remember what Balak **k** *of* Moab counseled 4889
Na 3:18 O **k** *of* Assyria, your shepherds slumber; 4889
Zep 1: 1 the reign of Josiah son of Amon **k** *of* Judah: 4889
3:15 The LORD, the **K** *of* Israel, is with you; 4889
Hag 1: 1 In the second year of **K** Darius, 4889
1:15 in the second year of **K** Darius. 4889
Zec 7: 1 In the fourth year of **K** Darius, 4889
9: 5 Gaza will lose her **k** and Ashkelon will 4889
9: 9 See, your **k** comes to you, 4889
11: 6 over to his neighbor and his **k**. 4889
14: 5 from the earthquake in the days of Uzziah **k** 4889
14: 9 The LORD will be **k** over the whole earth. 4889
14:16 up year after year to worship the **K**, 4889
14:17 not go up to Jerusalem to worship the **K**, 4889
Mal 1:14 For I am a great **k**," 4889
Mt 1: 6 and Jesse the father of **K** David. *995*
2: 1 during the time *of* **K** Herod, *995*
2: 2 is the one who has been born **k** of the Jews? *995*
2: 3 When **K** Herod heard this he was disturbed, *995*
2: 9 After they had heard the **k**, *995*
5:35 for it is the city *of* the Great **K**. *995*
14: 9 The **k** was distressed, *995*
18:23 like a **k** who wanted to settle accounts *476+995*
21: 5 'See, your **k** comes to you, *995*
22: 2 like a **k** who prepared a wedding banquet *476+995*
22: 7 The **k** was enraged. *995*
22:11 "But when the **k** came in to see the guests, *995*
22:13 "Then the **k** told the attendants, *995*
25:34 "Then the **K** will say to those on his right, *995*
25:40 "The **K** will reply, 'I tell you the truth, *995*
27:11 "Are you the **k** of the Jews?" *995*
27:29 "Hail, **k** of the Jews!" *995*
27:37 THIS IS JESUS, THE **K** OF THE JEWS. *995*
27:42 He's the **K** of Israel! *995*
Mk 6:14 **K** Herod heard about this, *995*
6:22 The **k** said to the girl, *995*
6:25 the girl hurried in to the **k** with the request: *995*
6:26 The **k** was greatly distressed, *995*
15: 2 "Are you the **k** of the Jews?" *995*
15: 9 "Do you want me to release to you the **k** of *995*
15:12 with the one you call the **k** of the Jews?" *995*
15:18 "Hail, **k** of the Jews!" *995*
15:26 THE **K** OF THE JEWS. *995*
15:32 Let this Christ, this **K** of Israel, *995*
Lk 1: 5 In the time of Herod **k** of Judea there was *995*
14:31 "Or suppose a **k** is about to go to war *995*
14:31 about to go to war *against* another **k**. *995*
19:12 to have himself appointed **k** and then *993*
19:14 'We don't want this man *to be* our **k**.' *996*
19:15 "He *was* **made k**, however, *993+3284+3836*
19:27 of mine who did not want me *to be* **k** *996*
19:38 "Blessed is the **k** who comes in the name of *995*
23: 2 to Caesar and claims to be Christ, a **k**." *995*
23: 3 "Are you the **k** of the Jews?" *995*
23:37 "If you are the **k** of the Jews, *995*
23:38 THIS IS THE **K** OF THE JEWS. *995*
Jn 1:49 you are the **K** of Israel." *995*
6:15 that they intended to come and make him **k** *995*
12:13 "Blessed is the **K** of Israel!" *995*
12:15 see, your **k** is coming, *995*
18:33 "Are you the **k** of the Jews?" *995*
18:37 "You are a **k**, then!" *995*
18:37 "You are right in saying I am a **k**. *995*
18:39 Do you want me to release 'the **k** of *995*
19: 3 saying, "Hail, **k** of the Jews!" *995*
19:12 to be a **k** opposes Caesar." *995*
19:14 "Here is your **k**," Pilate said to the Jews. *995*
19:15 "Shall I crucify your **k**?" *995*
19:15 "We have no **k** but Caesar," *995*
19:19 JESUS OF NAZARETH, THE **K** OF THE JEWS. *995*
19:21 "Do not write 'The **K** of the Jews,' *995*
19:21 that this man claimed to be **k** of the Jews." *995*
Ac 7:10 to gain the goodwill of Pharaoh **k** of Egypt; *995*
7:18 Then another **k**, who knew nothing about *995*
12: 1 that **K** Herod arrested some who belonged *995*
12:20 a trusted personal servant *of* the **k**, *995*
13:21 Then the people asked for a **k**, *995*
13:22 he made David their **k**. *995*
17: 7 saying that there is another **k**, *995*
25:13 A few days later **K** Agrippa *995*
25:14 Festus discussed Paul's case *with* the **k**. *995*
25:24 Festus said: "**K** Agrippa, *995*
25:26 and especially before you, **K** Agrippa, *995*
26: 2 "**K** Agrippa, I consider myself fortunate *995*
26: 7 *O* **k**, it is because of this hope that *995*
26:13 About noon, *O* **k**, as I was on the road, *995*
26:19 "So then, **K** Agrippa, I was not disobedient *995*
26:26 The **k** is familiar with these things, *995*
26:27 **K** Agrippa, do you believe the prophets? *995*
26:30 The **k** rose, and with him the governor *995*
2Co 11:32 the governor *under* **K** Aretas had the city of *995*
1Ti 1:17 Now *to* the **K** eternal, immortal, invisible, *995*
6:15 the **K** of kings and Lord of lords, *995*
Heb 7: 1 This Melchizedek was **k** of Salem and priest *995*
7: 2 First, his name means "**k** of righteousness"; *995*
7: 2 "**k** of Salem" means "king of peace." *995*
7: 2 "king of Salem" means "**k** of peace." *995*
1Pe 2:13 whether *to* the **k**, as the supreme authority, *995*
2:17 fear God, honor the **k**. *995*
Rev 9:11 as **k** over them the angel of the Abyss, *995*
15: 3 Just and true are your ways, **K** of the ages. *995*
17:11 and now is not, is an eighth **k**. *NIG*
17:14 because he is Lord of lords and **K** *995*
19:16 **K** OF KINGS AND LORD OF LORDS. *995*

KING'S (197) [KING]

Ge 14:17 the Valley of Shaveh (that is, the **K** Valley). 4889
39:20 where the **k** prisoners were confined. 4889
Nu 20:17 the **k** highway and not turn to the right or to 4889
21:22 along the **k** highway until we have passed 4889
Jdg 3:21 and plunged it into **the k** belly. 2257
1Sa 18:18 I should become the **k** son-in-law?" 4200+4889
18:23 matter to become the **k** son-in-law? 928+4889
18:26 pleased to become the **k** son-in-law. 928+4889
18:27 that he might become the **k** son-in-law. 928+4889
20:29 That is why he has not come to the **k** table." 4889
21: 8 because the **k** business was urgent." 4889
22:14 the **k** son-in-law, captain of your bodyguard 4889
22:17 But the **k** officials were not willing to raise 4889
26:16 Where are the **k** spear and water jug 4889
26:22 "Here is the **k** spear," David answered. 4889
2Sa 9:11 at David's table like one of the **k** sons. 4889
9:13 because he always ate at the **k** table, 4889
11: 1 **the k** men and the whole Israelite army. 2257S
11:20 the **k** anger may flare up, 4889
11:24 and some of the **k** men died. 4889
13: 4 He asked Amnon, "Why do you, the **k** son, 4889
13:23 he invited all the **k** sons to come there. 4889
13:27 with him Amnon and the rest of the **k** sons. 4889
13:29 Then all the **k** sons got up, 4889
13:30 "Absalom has struck down all the **k** sons; 4889
13:33 about the report that all the **k** sons are dead. 4889
13:35 "See, the **k** sons are here; 4889
13:36 As he finished speaking, the **k** sons came in, 4889
14: 1 of Zeruiah knew that the **k** heart longed 4889
14:28 in Jerusalem without seeing the **k** face. 4889
14:32 Now then, I want to see the **k** face, 4889
15:15 The **k** officials answered him, 4889
15:35 Tell them anything you hear in the **k** palace. 4889
16: 2 donkeys are for the **k** household to ride on, 4889
16: 6 He pelted David and all the **k** officials 4889
18:12 I would not lift my hand against the **k** son. 4889
18:18 in the **K** Valley as a monument to himself, 4889
18:20 because the **k** son is dead." 4889
18:29 as Joab was about to send the **k** servant 4889
19:18 at the ford to take the **k** household over and 4889
19:42 Have we eaten any of the **k** provisions? 4889
24: 4 The **k** word, however, overruled Joab and 4889
1Ki 1: 9 He invited all his brothers, the **k** sons, 4889
1:19 and sheep, and has invited all the **k** sons, 4889
1:25 He has invited all the **k** sons, 4889
1:28 So she came into the **k** presence and stood 4889
1:44 and they have put him on the **k** mule, 4889
2:19 He had a throne brought for the **k** mother, 4889
4:27 and all who came to the **k** table. 4889
5:17 At the **k** command they removed from 4889
13: 6 and the **k** hand was restored and became 4889
22: 6 "for the Lord will give it into the **k** hand." 4889
22:12 the LORD will give it into the **k** hand." 4889
22:15 the LORD will give it into the **k** hand." 4889
22:26 the ruler of the city and to Joash the **k** son 4889
2Ki 8:15 in water and spread it over **the k** face, 2257S
9:34 "and bury her, for she was a **k** daughter." 4889
11: 4 Then he showed them the **k** son. 4889
11:12 Jehoiada brought out the **k** son and put 4889
13:16 Elisha put his hands on the **k** hands. 4889
15: 5 Jotham the **k** son had charge of the palace 4889
16:15 the **k** burnt offering and his grain offering, 4889
22:12 the secretary and Asaiah the **k** attendant: 4889
24:15 from Jerusalem to Babylon the **k** mother, 4889
25: 4 between the two walls near the **k** garden, 4889
25:29 of his life ate regularly at **the k** table. 2257S
1Ch 9:18 being stationed at the **K** Gate on the east, 4889
18:17 sons were chief officials at the **k** side. 4889
21: 4 The **k** word, however, overruled Joab; 4889
21: 6 the **k** command was repulsive to him. 4889
25: 2 who prophesied under the **k** supervision. 4889
25: 5 All these were sons of Heman the **k** seer. 4889
26:30 of the LORD and for the **k** service. 4889
27:32 of Hacmoni took care of the **k** sons. 4889
27:33 Ahithophel was the **k** counselor. 4200+4889
27:33 Hushai the Arkite was the **k** friend. 4889
29: 6 in charge of the **k** work gave willingly. 4889
2Ch 8:15 They did not deviate from the **k** commands 4889
18: 5 "for God will give it into the **k** hand." 4889
18:11 the LORD will give it into the **k** hand." 4889
18:25 the ruler of the city and to Joash the **k** son, 4889
21:17 the goods found in the **k** palace, 4889
23: 3 "The **k** son shall reign, 4889
23:11 Jehoiada and his sons brought out the **k** son 4889
24: 8 At the **k** command, 4889
24:11 the **k** officials and they saw that there was 4889
28: 7 killed Maaseiah the **k** son, 4889
29:25 and Gad the **k** seer and Nathan the prophet; 4889
30: 6 At the **k** command, couriers went 4889
34:20 the secretary and Asaiah the **k** attendant: 4889
35: 7 all from the **k** *own* possessions. 4889

2Ch 35:15 Asaph, Heman and Jeduthun the **k** seer. 4889
Ezr 7:27 into the **k** heart to bring honor to the house 4889
7:28 and all the **k** powerful officials. 4889
8:36 the **k** orders to the royal satraps and to 4889
Ne 2: 8 Asaph, keeper of the **k** forest, 4200+4889
2: 9 and gave them the **k** letters. 4889
2:14 the **K** Pool, but there was not enough room 4889
3:15 Pool of Siloam, by the **K** Garden, 4889
5: 4 to pay the **k** tax on our fields and vineyards. 4889
11:23 The singers were under the **k** orders, 4889
11:24 was the **k** agent in all affairs relating to 4889
Est 1: 5 in the enclosed garden of the **k** palace, 4889
1: 7 in keeping with the **k** liberality. 4889
1: 8 By the **k** command each guest was allowed NIH
1:12 the attendants delivered the **k** command, 4889
1:18 to all the **k** nobles in the same way. 4889
1:20 Then when the **k** edict is proclaimed 4889
2: 2 Then the **k** personal attendants proposed, 4889
2: 3 **k** eunuch, who is in charge of the women; 4889
2: 8 the **k** order and edict had been proclaimed, 4889
2: 8 also was taken to the **k** palace and entrusted 4889
2: 9 the **k** palace and moved her and her maids 4889
2:13 with her from the harem to the **k** palace. 4889
2:14 the **k** eunuch who was in charge of 4889
2:15 **k** eunuch who was in charge of the harem, 4889
2:19 Mordecai was sitting at the **k** gate. 4889
2:21 the time Mordecai was sitting at the **k** gate, 4889
2:21 of the **k** officers who guarded the doorway, 4889
3: 2 the royal officials at the **k** gate knelt down 4889
3: 3 royal officials at the **k** gate asked Mordecai, 4889
3: 3 "Why do you disobey the **k** command?" 4889
3: 8 and who do not obey the **k** laws; 4889
3: 8 not in the **k** best interest to tolerate them. 4889
3:12 Haman's orders to the **k** satraps, 4889
3:13 the **k** provinces with the order to destroy, 4889
3:15 Spurred on by the **k** command, 4889
4: 2 But he went only as far as the **k** gate, 4889
4: 5 one of the **k** eunuchs assigned to attend her, 4889
4: 6 of the city in front of the **k** gate. 4889
4: 8 to urge her to go into the **k** presence to beg 4889
4:11 "All the **k** officials and the people of 4889
4:13 because you are in the **k** house you alone 4889
5: 1 in front of the **k** hall. 4889
5: 8 Then I will answer the **k** question." 4889
5: 9 the **k** gate and observed that he neither rose 4889
5:13 that Jew Mordecai sitting at the **k** gate." 4889
6: 2 of the **k** officers who guarded the doorway, 4889
6: 9 to one of the **k** most noble princes. 4889
6:10 Mordecai the Jew, who sits at the **k** gate. 4889
6:12 Afterward Mordecai returned to the **k** gate. 4889
6:14 the **k** eunuchs arrived and 4889
7: 8 As soon as the word left the **k** mouth, 4889
7:10 Then the **k** fury subsided. 4889
8: 5 to destroy the Jews in all the **k** provinces. 4889
8: 8 Now write another decree in the **k** name 4889
8: 8 and seal it with the **k** signet ring— 4889
8: 8 in the **k** name and sealed with his ring can 4889
8:10 sealed the dispatches with the **k** signet ring, 4889
8:11 The **k** edict granted the Jews in every city 4889
8:14 raced out, spurred on by the **k** command. 4889
8:15 the **k** presence wearing royal garments 4889
9: 3 the **k** administrators helped the Jews, 4200+4889
9:12 in the rest of the **k** provinces? 4889
9:16 of the Jews who were in the **k** provinces 4889
9:25 But when the plot came to the **k** attention, 4889
Ps 45: 5 the hearts of the **k** enemies; 4889
61: 6 Increase the days of the **k** life, 4889
Pr 14:28 A large population is a **k** glory, 4889
16:14 A **k** wrath is a messenger of death, 4889
16:15 When a **k** face brightens, it means life; 4889
19:12 A **k** rage is like the roar of a lion, 4889
20: 2 A **k** wrath is like the roar of a lion; 4889
21: 1 The **k** heart is in the hand of the LORD; 4889
25: 5 remove the wicked from the **k** presence, 4889
25: 6 Do not exalt yourself in the **k** presence, 4889
Ecc 2:12 What more can the **k** successor do than what has already been done? 4889
4:15 sun followed the youth, **the k** successor. 2257[S]
8: 2 Obey the **k** command, I say, 4889
8: 3 not be in a hurry to leave **the k** presence. 2257[S]
8: 4 Since a **k** word is supreme, 4889
Isa 23:15 seventy years, the span of a **k** life. 4889
Jer 38: 6 the **k** son, which was in the courtyard of 4889
39: 4 the city at night by way of the **k** garden, 4889
41: 1 and had been one of the **k** officers, 4889
41:10 the **k** daughters along with all 4889
43: 6 and the **k** daughters whom Nebuzaradan 4889
52: 7 between the two walls near the **k** garden, 4889
52:33 of his life ate regularly at **the k** table. 2257[S]
Da 1: 4 and qualified to serve in the **k** palace. 4889
1: 5 of food and wine from the **k** table. 4889
1: 5 after that they were to enter the **k** service. 4889
1:19 so they entered the **k** service. 4889
2:14 Arioch, the commander of the **k** guard, 10421
2:15 He asked the **k** officer, 10421
3:22 The **k** command was so urgent and 10421
3:28 and defied the **k** command and were willing 10421
5: 8 Then all the **k** wise men came in, 10421
6:24 At the **k** command, the men who had 10421
8:27 I got up and went about the **k** business. 4889
11:26 Those who eat from **the k** provisions will 2257[S]
Am 7: 1 after the **k** *share* had been harvested and 4889
7:13 because this is the **k** sanctuary and 4889
Zep 1: 8 the princes and the **k** sons and all those clad 4889
Ac 12:20 because they depended on the **k** country *997*
Heb 11:23 and they were not afraid of the **k** edict. *995*
11:27 not fearing the **k** anger; *995*

KINGDOM (302) [KING]

Ge 10:10 The first centers of his **k** were Babylon, 4930
20: 9 upon me and my **k?** 4930
Ex 19: 6 be for me a **k** *of* priests and a holy nation.' 4930
Nu 24: 7 their **k** will be exalted. 4895
32:33 the **k** *of* Sihon king of the Amorites and 4930
32:33 of Sihon king of the Amorites and the **k** 4930
Dt 3: 4 whole region of Argob, Og's **k** in Bashan. 4930
3:10 towns of Og's **k** in Bashan. 4930
3:13 all of Bashan, the **k** *of* Og, 4930
17:18 When he takes the throne of his **k,** 4930
17:20 a long time over his **k** in Israel. 4930
Jos 13:12 the whole **k** *of* Og in Bashan, 4931
1Sa 13:13 he would have established your **k** 4930
13:14 But now your **k** will not endure; 4930
15:28 "The LORD has torn the **k** *of* Israel 4931
18: 8 What more can he get but the **k?"** 4867
20:31 neither you nor your **k** will be established. 4895
24:20 surely be king and that the **k** *of* Israel will 4930
28:17 the **k** out of your hands and given it to one 4930
2Sa 3:10 and transfer the **k** from the house of Saul 4930
3:28 "I and my **k** are forever innocent before 4930
5:12 as king over Israel and had exalted his **k** for 4930
7:12 and I will establish his **k.** 4930
7:13 I will establish the throne of his **k** forever. 4930
7:16 Your house and your **k** will endure forever 4930
8: 6 He put garrisons in the **Aramean k** 806
16: 3 Israel will give me back my grandfather's **k.** 4931
16: 8 The LORD has handed the **k** over 4867
1Ki 2:15 "As you know," he said, "the **k** was mine. 4867
2:15 and the **k** has gone to my brother; 4867
2:22 You might as well request the **k** for him— 4867
2:46 The **k** was now firmly established 4930
10:20 like it had ever been made for any other **k.** 4930
11:11 the **k** away from you and give it to one 4930
11:13 Yet I will not tear the whole **k** from him, 4930
11:31 to tear the **k** out of Solomon's hand 4930
11:34 " 'But I will not take the whole **k** out 4930
11:35 I will take the **k** from his son's hands 4867
12:21 and to regain the **k** for Rehoboam son 4867
12:26 "The **k** will now likely revert to the house 4930
14: 8 I tore the **k** away from the house of David 4930
18:10 or **k** where my master has not sent someone 4930
18:10 a nation or **k** claimed you were not there, 4930
2Ki 14: 5 After the **k** was firmly in his grasp, 4930
15:19 and strengthen his own hold on the **k.** 4930
20:13 or in all his **k** that Hezekiah did 4939
1Ch 10:14 and turned the **k** over to David son of Jesse. 4867
12:23 at Hebron to turn Saul's **k** over to him, as 4895
14: 2 and that his **k** had been highly exalted for 4895
16:20 nation to nation, from one **k** to another. 4930
17:11 and I will establish his **k.** 4895
17:14 over my house and my **k** forever; 4895
18: 6 He put garrisons in the **Aramean k** 806
22:10 the throne of his **k** over Israel forever.' 4895
28: 5 to sit on the throne of the **k** *of* the LORD 4895
28: 7 I will establish his **k** forever 4867
29:11 Yours, O LORD, is the **k;** 4867
2Ch 1: 1 over his **k,** for the LORD his God was 4895
9:19 like it had ever been made for any other **k.** 4930
11: 1 and to regain the **k** for Rehoboam. 4930
11:17 They strengthened the **k** *of* Judah 4895
13: 8 now you plan to resist the **k** *of* the LORD, 4930
14: 5 and the **k** was at peace under him. 4930
17: 5 The LORD established the **k** 4930
20:30 And the **k** *of* Jehoshaphat was at peace, 4895
21: 3 but he had given the **k** to Jehoram 4930
21: 4 Jehoram established himself firmly over his father's **k,** 4930
22: 9 of Ahaziah powerful enough to retain the **k.** 4930
25: 3 After the **k** was firmly in his control, 4930
29:21 as a sin offering for the **k,** 4930
32:15 for no god of any nation or **k** has been able 4930
33:13 to Jerusalem and to his **k.** 4895
36:20 and his sons until the **k** *of* Persia came 4895
Ezr 7:13 I decree that any of the Israelites in my **k,** 10424
Ne 9:35 Even while they were in their **k,** 4895
Est 1: 4 the vast wealth of his **k** and the splendor 4895
1:14 to the king and were highest in the **k.** 4895
1:22 He sent dispatches to all parts of the **k,** 4889
3: 6 throughout the whole **k** *of* Xerxes. 4895
3: 8 of your **k** whose customs are different 4895
5: 3 Even up to half the **k,** it will be given you." 4895
5: 6 Even up to half the **k,** it will be granted." 4895
7: 2 Even up to half the **k,** it will be granted." 4895
9:30 to all the Jews in the 127 provinces of the **k** 4895
Ps 45: 6 of justice will be the scepter of your **k.** 4895
103:19 and his **k** rules over all. 4895
105:13 from *one* **k** to another. 4930
145:11 the glory of your **k** and speak of your might, 4895
145:12 and the glorious splendor of your **k.** 4895
145:13 Your **k** is an everlasting kingdom, 4895
145:13 Your kingdom is an everlasting **k,** 4895
Ecc 4:14 born in poverty within his **k.** 4895
Isa 9: 7 on David's throne and over his **k,** 4930
19: 2 city against city, **k** against kingdom. 4930
19: 2 city against city, kingdom against **k.** 4930
34:12 have nothing there to be called a **k,** 4867
39: 2 or in all his **k** that Hezekiah did 4939
60:12 or **k** that will not serve you will perish; 4930
Jer 18: 7 at any time I announce that a nation or **k** is 4930
18: 9 a nation or **k** is to be built up and planted, 4930
27: 8 or **k** will not serve Nebuchadnezzar king 4930
La 2: 2 He has brought her **k** and its princes down 4930
Eze 17:14 so that the **k** would be brought low, 4930
29:14 There they will be a lowly **k.** 4930
Da 1:20 and enchanters in his whole **k.** 4895
2:39 "After you, another **k** will rise, 10424
2:39 Next, a third **k,** one of bronze, 10424
2:40 Finally, there will be a fourth **k,** 10424
2:41 so this will be a divided **k;** 10424
2:42 **k** will be partly strong and partly brittle. 10424
2:44 of heaven will set up a **k** that will never 10424
4: 3 His **k** is an eternal kingdom; 10424
4: 3 His kingdom is an eternal **k;** 10424
4:18 of the wise men in my **k** can interpret it 10424
4:26 the tree with its roots means that your **k** 10424
4:34 **k** endures from generation to generation. 10424
4:36 to me for the glory of my **k.** 10424
5: 7 be made the third highest ruler in the **k."** 10424
5:11 your **k** who has the spirit of the holy gods 10424
5:16 be made the third highest ruler in the **k."** 10424
5:28 Your **k** is divided and given to the Medes 10424
5:29 the third highest ruler in the **k.** 10424
5:31 and Darius the Mede took over the **k,** 10424
6: 1 to rule throughout the **k,** 10424
6: 3 to set him over the whole **k.** 10424
6:26 that in every part of my **k** people must fear 10424
6:26 his **k** will not be destroyed, 10424
7:14 his **k** is one that will never be destroyed. 10424
7:18 of the Most High will receive the **k** 10424
7:22 the time came when they possessed the **k.** 10424
7:23 a fourth **k** that will appear on earth. 10424
7:24 The ten horns are ten kings who will come from this **k.** 10424
7:27 His **k** will be an everlasting kingdom, 10424
7:27 His kingdom will be an everlasting **k,** 10424
9: 1 who was made ruler over the Babylonian **k** 4895
10:13 the Persian **k** resisted me twenty-one days. 4895
11: 2 up everyone against the **k** *of* Greece. 4895
11: 5 and will rule his own **k** with great power. 4939
11:17 with the might of his entire **k** and will make 4895
11:17 in marriage in order to overthrow **the k,** 2023[S]
11:21 the **k** when its people feel secure, 4895
Hos 1: 4 and I will put an end to the **k** *of* Israel. 4931
Am 7:13 and the temple of the **k."** 4930
9: 8 of the Sovereign LORD are on the sinful **k.** 4930
Ob 1:21 And the **k** will be the LORD's. 4867
Mt 3: 2 "Repent, for the **k** of heaven is near." *993*
4:17 "Repent, for the **k** of heaven is near." *993*
4:23 preaching the good news *of* the **k,** *993*
5: 3 for theirs is the **k** of heaven. *993*
5:10 for theirs is the **k** of heaven. *993*
5:19 to do the same will be called least in the **k** *993*
5:19 be called great in the **k** of heaven. *993*
5:20 you will certainly not enter the **k** of heaven. *993*
6:10 your **k** come, your will be done on earth *993*
6:33 But seek first his **k** and his righteousness, *993*
7:21 'Lord, Lord,' will enter the **k** of heaven, *993*
8:11 Isaac and Jacob in the **k** of heaven. *993*
8:12 the subjects *of* the **k** will be thrown outside, *993*
9:35 *of* the **k** and healing every disease *993*
10: 7 'The **k** of heaven is near.' *993*
11:11 in the **k** of heaven is greater than he. *993*
11:12 **k** of heaven has been forcefully advancing, *993*
12:25 "Every **k** divided against itself will *993*
12:26 How then can his **k** stand? *993*
12:28 then the **k** of God has come upon you. *993*
13:11 *of* the **k** of heaven has been given to you, *993*
13:19 *about* the **k** and does not understand it, *993*
13:24 "The **k** of heaven is like a man who *993*
13:31 "The **k** of heaven is like a mustard seed, *993*
13:33 "The **k** of heaven is like yeast that *993*
13:38 the good seed stands for the sons *of* the **k.** *993*
13:41 and they will weed out of his **k** everything *993*
13:43 the righteous will shine like the sun in the **k** *993*
13:44 **k** of heaven is like treasure hidden in a field. *993*
13:45 the **k** of heaven is like a merchant looking *993*
13:47 the **k** of heaven is like a net that was let *993*
13:52 *about* the **k** of heaven is like the owner of *993*
16:19 I will give you the keys *of* the **k** of heaven; *993*
16:28 the Son of Man coming in his **k."** *993*
18: 1 "Who is the greatest in the **k** of heaven?" *993*
18: 3 you will never enter the **k** of heaven. *993*
18: 4 like this child is the greatest in the **k** *993*
18:23 the **k** of heaven is like a king who wanted *993*
19:12 because of the **k** of heaven. *993*
19:14 the **k** of heaven belongs to such as these." *993*
19:23 for a rich man to enter the **k** of heaven. *993*
19:24 of a needle than for a rich man to enter the **k** *993*
20: 1 "For the **k** of heaven is like a landowner *993*
20:21 and the other at your left in your **k."** *993*
21:31 and the prostitutes are entering the **k** of God *993*
21:43 "Therefore I tell you that the **k** of God will *993*
22: 2 "The **k** of heaven is like a king who *993*
23:13 You shut the **k** of heaven in men's faces. *993*
24: 7 and **k** against kingdom. *993*
24: 7 and kingdom against **k.** *993*
24:14 the **k** will be preached in the whole world as *993*
25: 1 "At that time the **k** of heaven will be *993*
25:34 the **k** prepared for you since the creation of *993*
26:29 with you in my Father's **k."** *993*
Mk 1:15 "The **k** of God is near. *993*
3:24 If a **k** is divided against itself, *993*
3:24 against itself, that **k** cannot stand. *993*
4:11 "The secret *of* the **k** of God has been given *993*
4:26 "This is what the **k** of God is like. *993*
4:30 "What shall we say the **k** of God is like, *993*
6:23 I will give you, up to half my **k."** *993*
9: 1 not taste death before they see the **k** *993*
9:47 It is better for you to enter the **k** of God *993*
10:14 for the **k** of God belongs to such as these. *993*
10:15 anyone who will not receive the **k** of God *993*

Mk 10:23 hard it is for the rich to enter the **k** of God!" *993*
10:24 how hard it is to enter the **k** of God! *993*
10:25 of a needle than for a rich man to enter the **k** *993*
11:10 the coming **k** of our father David!" *993*
12:34 "You are not far from the **k** of God." *993*
13: 8 and **k** against kingdom. *993*
13: 8 and kingdom against **k.** *993*
14:25 until that day when I drink it anew in the **k** *993*
15:43 who was himself waiting for the **k** of God, *993*
Lk 1:33 his **k** will never end." *993*
4:43 of the **k** of God to the other towns also, *993*
6:20 for yours is the **k** of God. *993*
7:28 in the **k** of God is greater than he." *993*
8: 1 proclaiming the good news of the **k** of God. *993*
8:10 *of* the **k** of God has been given to you, but *993*
9: 2 and he sent them out to preach the **k** of God *993*
9:11 and spoke to them about the **k** of God, *993*
9:27 not taste death before they see the **k** *993*
9:60 but you go and proclaim the **k** of God." *993*
9:62 and looks back is fit for service *in* the **k** *993*
10: 9 'The **k** of God is near you.' *993*
10:11 Yet be sure of this: The **k** of God is near.' *993*
11: 2 hallowed be your name, your **k** come. *993*
11:17 "Any **k** divided against itself will be ruined, *993*
11:18 how can his **k** stand? *993*
11:20 then the **k** of God has come to you. *993*
12:31 But seek his **k,** and these things will be *993*
12:32 pleased to give you the **k.** *993*
13:18 Jesus asked, "What is the **k** of God like? *993*
13:20 "What shall I compare the **k** of God to? *993*
13:28 Isaac and Jacob and all the prophets in the **k** *993*
13:29 at the feast in the **k** of God. *993*
14:15 the man who will eat at the feast in the **k** *993*
16:16 of the **k** of God is being preached, *993*
17:20 when the **k** of God would come, *993*
17:20 "The **k** of God does not come *993*
17:21 because the **k** of God is within you." *993*
18:16 for the **k** of God belongs to such as these. *993*
18:17 anyone who will not receive the **k** of God *993*
18:24 hard it is for the rich to enter the **k** of God! *993*
18:25 of a needle than for a rich man to enter the **k** *993*
18:29 or parents or children for the sake *of* the **k** *993*
19:11 the **k** of God was going to appear at once. *993*
21:10 and **k** against kingdom. *993*
21:10 and kingdom against **k.** *993*
21:31 you know that the **k** of God is near. *993*
22:16 until it finds fulfillment in the **k** of God." *993*
22:18 of the vine until the **k** of God comes." *993*
22:29 And I confer on you a **k,** *993*
22:30 at my table in my **k** and sit on thrones, *993*
23:42 remember me when you come into your **k."** *993*
23:51 of Arimathea and he was waiting for the **k** *993*
Jn 3: 3 the **k** of God unless he is born again." *993*
3: 5 the **k** of God unless he is born of water and *993*
18:36 Jesus said, "My **k** is not of this world. *993*
18:36 But now my **k** is from another place." *993*
Ac 1: 3 a period of forty days and spoke about the **k** *993*
1: 6 at this time going to restore the **k** to Israel?" *993*
8:12 the good news of the **k** of God and the name *993*
14:22 through many hardships to enter the **k** *993*
19: 8 arguing persuasively about the **k** of God. *993*
20:25 the **k** will ever see me again. *993*
28:23 and declared to them the **k** of God and tried *993*
28:31 without hindrance he preached the **k** of God *993*
Ro 14:17 For the **k** of God is not a matter of eating *993*
1Co 4:20 For the **k** of God is not a matter of talk but *993*
6: 9 the wicked will not inherit the **k** of God? *993*
6:10 nor swindlers will inherit the **k** of God. *993*
15:24 when he hands over the **k** to God the Father *993*
15:50 flesh and blood cannot inherit the **k** of God, *993*
Gal 5:21 like this will not inherit the **k** of God. *993*
Eph 2: 2 of this world and of the ruler *of* the **k** of *2026*
5: 5 has any inheritance in the **k** of Christ and *993*
Col 1:12 the inheritance of the saints in the **k** of light. *NIG*
1:13 of darkness and brought us into the **k** of *993*
4:11 among my fellow workers for the **k** of God, *993*
1Th 2:12 who calls you into his **k** and glory. *993*
2Th 1: 5 a result you will be counted worthy *of* the **k** *993*
2Ti 4: 1 and in view of his appearing and his **k,** *993*
4:18 and will bring me safely to his heavenly **k.** *993*
Heb 1: 8 righteousness will be the scepter *of* your **k.** *993*
12:28 we are receiving a **k** that cannot be shaken, *993*
Jas 2: 5 the **k** he promised those who love him? *993*
2Pe 1:11 a rich welcome into the eternal **k** *993*
Rev 1: 6 and has made us to be a **k** and priests *993*
1: 9 in the suffering and **k** and patient endurance *993*
5:10 You have made them to be a **k** and priests *993*
11:15 "The **k** of the world has become *993*
11:15 the world has become the **k** of our Lord and *NIG*
12:10 the salvation and the power and the **k** *993*
16:10 and his **k** was plunged into darkness. *993*
17:12 ten kings who have not yet received a **k,** *993*

KINGDOMS (61) [KING]

Dt 3:21 to all the **k** over there where you are going. 4930
28:25 a thing of horror to all the **k** *on* earth. 4930
Jos 11:10 (Hazor had been the head of all these **k.**) 4930
1Sa 10:18 of Egypt and all the **k** that oppressed you.' 4930
1Ki 4:21 over all the **k** from the River to the land of 4930
4:24 For he ruled over all the **k** west of the River, 4889
2Ki 19:15 you alone are God over all the **k** *of* 4930
19:19 that all **k** *on* earth may know that you alone, 4930
1Ch 29:30 and Israel and the **k** *of* all the other lands. 4930
2Ch 17:10 on all the **k** *of* the lands surrounding Judah, 4930
20: 6 You rule over all the **k** *of* the nations. 4930
20:29 of God came upon all the **k** *of* the countries 4930
36:23 the **k** *of* the earth and he has appointed me 4930
Ezr 1: 2 the **k** *of* the earth and he has appointed me 4930
Ne 9:22 "You gave them **k** and nations, 4930
Ps 46: 6 Nations are in uproar, **k** fall; 4930
68:32 Sing to God, O **k** *of* the earth, 4930
79: 6 on the **k** that do not call on your name; 4930
102:22 and the **k** assemble to worship the LORD. 4930
Isa 10:10 As my hand seized the **k** *of* the idols, 4930
10:10 **k** whose images excelled those of Jerusalem NIH
13: 4 Listen, an uproar among the **k,** 4930
13:19 Babylon, the jewel of **k,** 4930
14:16 the earth and made **k** tremble, 4930
23:11 over the sea and made its **k** tremble. 4930
23:17 and will ply her trade with all the **k** on 4930
37:16 you alone are God over all the **k** *of* 4930
37:20 that all **k** *on* earth may know that you alone, 4930
47: 5 no more will you be called queen of **k.** 4930
Jer 1:10 over nations and **k** to uproot and tear down, 4930
1:15 the peoples of the northern **k,"** 4930
10: 7 of the nations and in all their **k,** 4895
15: 4 I will make them abhorrent to all the **k** *of* 4930
24: 9 and an offense to all the **k** *of* the earth, 4930
25:26 all the **k** on the face of the earth. 4930
28: 8 against many countries and great **k.** 4930
29:18 and will make them abhorrent to all the **k** *of* 4930
33:24 the two **k** he chose'? 5476
34: 1 and all his army and all the **k** and peoples in 4930
34:17 I will make you abhorrent to all the **k** *of* 4930
49:28 Concerning Kedar and the **k** *of* Hazor, 4930
51:20 with you I destroy **k,** 4930
51:27 summon against her these **k:** 4930
Eze 29:15 of **k** and will never again exalt itself above 4930
37:22 be two nations or be divided into two **k.** 4930
Da 2:44 It will crush all those **k** and bring them to 10424
4:17 that the Most High is sovereign over the **k** 10424
4:25 that the Most High is sovereign over the **k** 10424
4:32 that the Most High is sovereign over the **k** 10424
5:21 the Most High God is sovereign over the **k** 10424
7:17 'The four great beasts are four **k** 10421
7:23 the other **k** and will devour the whole earth, 10424
7:27 of the **k** under the whole heaven will 10424
8:22 the one that was broken off represent four **k** 4895
Am 6: 2 Are they better off than your two **k?** 4930
Na 3: 5 and the **k** your shame. 4930
Zep 3: 8 the **k** and to pour out my wrath on them— 4930
Hag 2:22 and shatter the power of the foreign **k.** 4930
Mt 4: 8 and showed him all the **k** of the world *993*
Lk 4: 5 and showed him in an instant all the **k** of *993*
Heb 11:33 who through faith conquered **k,** *993*

KINGS (324) [KING]

Ge 14: 3 All these latter **k** joined forces in the Valley NIH
14: 5 the **k** allied with him went out and defeated 4889
14: 9 four **k** against five. 4889
14:10 when the **k** *of* Sodom and Gomorrah fled, 4889
14:11 The four **k** seized all the goods of Sodom NIH
14:17 and the **k** allied with him, 4889
17: 6 and **k** will come from you. 4889
17:16 **k** *of* peoples will come from her." 4889
35:11 and **k** will come from your body. 4889
36:31 These were the **k** who reigned in Edom 4889
Nu 31: 8 the five **k** *of* Midian. 4889
Dt 3: 8 So at that time we took from these two **k** *of* 4889
3:21 LORD your God has done to these two **k.** 4889
4:47 the two Amorite **k** east of the Jordan. 4889
7:24 He will give their **k** into your hand, 4889
31: 4 Sihon and Og, the **k** *of* the Amorites, 4889
Jos 2:10 the two **k** *of* the Amorites east of 4889
5: 1 when all the Amorite **k** west of the Jordan 4889
5: 1 of the Jordan and all the Canaanite **k** along 4889
9: 1 when all the **k** west of the Jordan heard 4889
9: 1 of the Great Sea as far as Lebanon (the **k** of NIH
9:10 that he did to the two **k** *of* the Amorites east 4889
10: 5 Then the five **k** *of* the Amorites— 4889
10: 5 the **k** *of* Jerusalem, Hebron, Jarmuth, 4889
10: 6 because all the Amorite **k** *from* 4889
10:16 the five **k** had fled and hidden in the cave 4889
10:17 the five **k** had been found hiding in the cave 4889
10:22 the cave and bring those five **k** out to me." 4889
10:23 So they brought the five **k** out of the cave— 4889
10:23 the **k** *of* Jerusalem, Hebron, Jarmuth, 4889
10:24 When they had brought these **k** to Joshua, 4889
10:24 and put your feet on the necks of these **k."** 4889
10:26 killed **the k** and hung them on five trees, 4392S
10:40 together with all their **k.** 4889
10:42 All these **k** and their lands Joshua conquered in one campaign, 4889
11: 1 to the **k** *of* Shimron and Acshaph, 4889
11: 2 the northern **k** who were in the mountains, 4889
11: 5 All these **k** joined forces 4889
11:12 Joshua took all these royal cities and their **k** 4889
11:17 He captured all their **k** and struck them 4889
11:18 Joshua waged war against all these **k** for 4889
12: 1 These are the **k** *of* the land whom 4889
12: 7 These are the **k** *of* the land that Joshua and 4889
12:24 the king of Tirzah one thirty-one **k** in all. 4889
24:12 also the two Amorite **k.** 4889
Jdg 1: 7 "Seventy **k** with their thumbs 4889
5: 3 "Hear this, you **k!** 4889
5:19 "**K** came, they fought; 4889
5:19 the **k** *of* Canaan fought at Taanach by 4889
8: 5 and Zalmunna, the **k** *of* Midian." 4889
8:12 Zebah and Zalmunna, the two **k** *of* Midian, 4889
8:26 by the **k** *of* Midian or the chains that were 4889
1Sa 14:47 Edom, the **k** *of* Zobah, and the Philistines. 4889
27: 6 belonged to the **k** *of* Judah ever since. 4889
2Sa 10:19 the **k** who were vassals of Hadadezer saw 4889
11: 1 at the time when **k** go off to war, 4889
1Ki 3:13 in your lifetime you will have no equal among **k.** 4889
4:34 sent by all the **k** *of* the world, 4889
10:15 the Arabian **k** and the governors of the land. 4889
10:23 in riches and wisdom than all the other **k** *of* 4889
10:29 the **k** *of* the Hittites and of the Arameans. 4889
14:19 are written in the book of the annals of the **k** 4889
14:29 in the book of the annals of the **k** *of* Judah? 4889
15: 7 in the book of the annals of the **k** *of* Judah? 4889
15:23 in the book of the annals of the **k** *of* Judah? 4889
15:31 in the book of the annals of the **k** *of* Israel? 4889
16: 5 in the book of the annals of the **k** *of* Israel? 4889
16:14 in the book of the annals of the **k** *of* Israel? 4889
16:20 in the book of the annals of the **k** *of* Israel? 4889
16:27 in the book of the annals of the **k** *of* Israel? 4889
16:33 to anger than did all the **k** *of* Israel 4889
20: 1 by thirty-two **k** with their horses 4889
20:12 and the **k** were drinking in their tents, 4889
20:16 while Ben-Hadad and the 32 **k** allied 4889
20:24 Remove all the **k** from their commands 4889
20:31 the **k** *of* the house of Israel are merciful. 4889
22:39 in the book of the annals of the **k** *of* Israel? 4889
22:45 in the book of the annals of the **k** *of* Judah? 4889
2Ki 1:18 in the book of the annals of the **k** *of* Israel? 4889
3:10 the LORD called us three **k** together only 4889
3:13 the LORD who called us three **k** together 4889
3:21 the Moabites had heard that the **k** had come 4889
3:23 "Those **k** must have fought 4889
7: 6 the Hittite and Egyptian **k** to attack us!" 4889
8:18 He walked in the ways of the **k** *of* Israel, 4889
8:23 in the book of the annals of the **k** *of* Judah? 4889
10: 4 "If two **k** could not resist him, 4889
10:34 in the book of the annals of the **k** *of* Israel? 4889
12:18 Jehoram and Ahaziah, the **k** *of* Judah— 4889
12:19 in the book of the annals of the **k** *of* Judah? 4889
13: 8 in the book of the annals of the **k** *of* Israel? 4889
13:12 in the book of the annals of the **k** *of* Israel? 4889
13:13 Jehoash was buried in Samaria with the **k** 4889
14:15 in the book of the annals of the **k** *of* Israel? 4889
14:16 and was buried in Samaria with the **k** 4889
14:18 in the book of the annals of the **k** *of* Judah? 4889
14:28 in the book of the annals of the **k** *of* Israel? 4889
14:29 rested with his fathers, the **k** *of* Israel. 4889
15: 6 in the book of the annals of the **k** *of* Judah? 4889
15:11 in the book of the annals of the **k** *of* Israel. 4889
15:15 are written in the book of the annals of the **k** 4889
15:21 in the book of the annals of the **k** *of* Israel? 4889
15:26 are written in the book of the annals of the **k** 4889
15:31 in the book of the annals of the **k** *of* Israel? 4889
15:36 in the book of the annals of the **k** *of* Judah? 4889
16: 3 the **k** *of* Israel and even sacrificed his son in 4889
16:19 in the book of the annals of the **k** *of* Judah? 4889
17: 2 not like the **k** *of* Israel who preceded him. 4889
17: 8 that the **k** *of* Israel had introduced. 4889
18: 5 There was no one like him among all the **k** 4889
19:11 Surely you have heard what the **k** 4889
19:17 the Assyrian **k** have laid waste these nations 4889
20:20 in the book of the annals of the **k** *of* Judah? 4889
21:17 in the book of the annals of the **k** *of* Judah? 4889
21:25 in the book of the annals of the **k** *of* Judah? 4889
23: 5 with the pagan priests appointed by the **k** 4889
23:11 that the **k** *of* Judah had dedicated to the sun. 4889
23:12 the **k** *of* Judah had erected on the roof near 4889
23:19 the high places that the **k** *of* Israel had built 4889
23:22 throughout the days of the **k** *of* Israel and 4889
23:22 of the kings of Israel and the **k** *of* Judah, 4889
23:28 in the book of the annals of the **k** *of* Judah? 4889
24: 5 in the book of the annals of the **k** *of* Judah? 4889
25:28 the other **k** who were with him in Babylon. 4889
1Ch 1:43 These were the **k** who reigned in Edom 4889
9: 1 in the book of the **k** *of* Israel. 4889
16:21 for their sake he rebuked **k:** 4889
19: 9 the **k** who had come were by themselves in 4889
20: 1 at the time when **k** go off to war, 4889
2Ch 1:17 the **k** *of* the Hittites and of the Arameans. 4889
9:14 Also all the **k** *of* Arabia and the governors 4889
9:22 in riches and wisdom than all the other **k** *of* 4889
9:23 All the **k** *of* the earth sought audience 4889
9:26 over all the **k** from the River to the land of 4889
12: 8 between serving me and serving the **k** 4930
16:11 are written in the book of the **k** of Judah 4889
20:34 which are recorded in the book of the **k** 4889
21: 6 He walked in the ways of the **k** *of* Israel, 4889
21:13 But you have walked in the ways of the **k** 4889
21:20 but not in the tombs of the **k.** 4889
24:16 He was buried with the **k** in the City 4889
24:25 but not in the tombs of the **k.** 4889
24:27 in the annotations on the book of the **k.** 4889
25:26 not written in the book of the **k** *of* Judah 4889
26:23 in a field for burial that belonged to the **k,** 4889
27: 7 are written in the book of the **k** *of* Israel 4889
28: 2 of the **k** *of* Israel and also made cast idols 4889
28:23 gods of the **k** *of* Aram have helped them, 4889
28:26 are written in the book of the **k** *of* Judah 4889
28:27 but he was not placed in the tombs of the **k** 4889
30: 6 who have escaped from the hand of the **k** 4889
32: 4 the **k** *of* Assyria come and find plenty 4889
32:32 in the book of the **k** *of* Judah and Israel. 4889
33:18 are written in the annals of the **k** *of* Israel. 4889
34:11 the **k** *of* Judah had allowed to fall into ruin. 4889
35:18 of the **k** *of* Israel had ever celebrated such 4889
35:27 are written in the book of the **k** *of* Israel 4889
36: 8 are written in the book of the **k** *of* Israel 4889
Ezr 4:15 troublesome to **k** and provinces, 10421
4:19 against **k** and has been a place of rebellion 10421

Ezr 4:20 Jerusalem has had powerful **k** ruling over 10421
6:14 Darius and Artaxerxes, **k** *of* Persia. 10421
7:12 king of **k,** To Ezra the priest, 10421
9: 7 we and our **k** and our priests 4889
9: 7 and humiliation at the hand of foreign **k,** 4889
9: 9 in the sight of the **k** *of* Persia: 4889
Ne 9:24 to them, along with their **k** and the peoples 4889
9:32 upon our **k** and leaders, 4889
9:32 and all your people, from the days of the **k** 4889
9:34 Our **k,** our leaders, our priests 4889
9:37 to the **k** you have placed over us. 4889
Est 10: 2 of the annals of the **k** *of* Media and Persia? 4889
Job 3:14 with **k** and counselors of the earth, 4889
12:18 the shackles put on by **k** and ties a loincloth 4889
34:18 Is he not the One who says to **k,** 4889
36: 7 with **k** and exalts them forever. 4889
Ps 2: 2 The **k** *of* the earth take their stand and 4889
2:10 Therefore, you **k,** be wise; 4889
45: 9 of **k** are among your honored women; 4889
47: 9 for the **k** *of* the earth belong to God; 4482
48: 4 When the **k** joined forces, 4889
68:12 "**K** and armies flee in haste; 4889
68:14 the Almighty scattered the **k** in the land, 4889
68:29 at Jerusalem **k** will bring you gifts. 4889
72:10 The **k** *of* Tarshish and of distant shores 4889
72:10 **k** *of* Sheba and Seba will present him gifts. 4889
72:11 All **k** will bow down to him 4889
76:12 he is feared by the **k** *of* the earth. 4889
89:27 the most exalted of the **k** *of* the earth. 4889
102:15 all the **k** *of* the earth will revere your glory. 4889
105:14 for their sake he rebuked **k:** 4889
110: 5 he will crush **k** on the day of his wrath. 4889
119:46 of your statutes before **k** and will not be put 4889
135:10 down many nations and killed mighty **k**— 4889
135:11 of Bashan and all the **k** *of* Canaan— 4930
136:17 who struck down great **k,** 4889
136:18 killed mighty **k**—His love endures forever. 4889
138: 4 May all the **k** *of* the earth praise you, 4889
144:10 to the One who gives victory to **k,** 4889
148:11 **k** *of* the earth and all nations, 4889
149: 8 to bind their **k** with fetters, 4889
Pr 8:15 By me **k** reign and rulers make laws 4889
16:12 **K** detest wrongdoing, for a throne is 4889
16:13 **K** take pleasure in honest lips; 4889
22:29 He will serve before **k;** 4889
25: 2 to search out a matter is the glory of **k.** 4889
25: 3 so the hearts of **k** are unsearchable. 4889
31: 3 your vigor on those who ruin **k.** 4889
31: 4 "It is not for **k,** O Lemuel— 4889
31: 4 not for **k** to drink wine, 4889
Ecc 2: 8 and the treasure of **k** and provinces. 4889
Isa 1: 1 Jotham, Ahaz and Hezekiah, **k** *of* Judah. 4889
7:16 of the two **k** you dread will be laid waste. 4889
10: 8 'Are not my commanders all **k?**' he says. 4889
10:13 like a mighty one I subdued their **k.** 3782
14: 9 all *those who* were **k** *over* the nations. 4889
14:18 All the **k** *of* the nations lie in state, 4889
19:11 a disciple of the ancient **k**"? 4889
24:21 the powers in the heavens above and the **k** 4889
37:11 Surely you have heard what the **k** 4889
37:18 Assyrian **k** have laid waste all these peoples 4889
41: 2 He hands nations over to him and subdues **k** 4889
45: 1 to subdue nations before him and to strip **k** 4889
49: 7 "**K** will see you and rise up, 4889
49:23 **K** will be your foster fathers, 4889
52:15 and **k** will shut their mouths because of him. 4889
60: 3 and **k** to the brightness of your dawn. 4889
60:10 and their **k** will serve you. 4889
60:11 their **k** led in triumphal procession. 4889
62: 2 and all **k** your glory; 4889
Jer 1:15 "Their **k** will come and set up their thrones 408[S]
1:18 against the **k** *of* Judah, its officials, 4889
2:26 they, their **k** and their officials, 4889
8: 1 the bones of the **k** and officials of Judah, 4889
13:13 including the **k** who sit on David's throne, 4889
17:19 through which the **k** *of* Judah go in and out; 4889
17:20 O **k** *of* Judah and all people of Judah 4889
17:25 then **k** who sit on David's throne will come 4889
19: 3 O **k** *of* Judah and people of Jerusalem. 4889
19: 4 that neither they nor their fathers nor the **k** 4889
19:13 The houses in Jerusalem and those of the **k** 4889
20: 5 all its valuables and all the treasures of the **k** 4889
22: 4 then **k** who sit on David's throne will come 4889
25:14 be enslaved by many nations and great **k;** 4889
25:18 its **k** and officials, to make them a ruin and 4889
25:20 the foreign people there; all the **k** *of* Uz; 4889
25:20 the **k** *of* the Philistines (those of Ashkelon, 4889
25:22 all the **k** *of* Tyre and Sidon; 4889
25:22 the **k** *of* the coastlands across the sea; 4889
25:24 all the **k** *of* Arabia and all the kings of 4889
25:24 and all the **k** *of* the foreign people who live 4889
25:25 all the **k** *of* Zimri, Elam and Media; 4889
25:26 and all the **k** *of* the north, near and far, one 4889
27: 3 Then send word to the **k** *of* Edom, Moab, 4889
27: 7 and great **k** will subjugate him. 4889
32:32 they, their **k** and officials, 4889
34: 5 the former **k** who preceded you, 4889
44: 9 by your fathers and by the **k** and queens 4889
44:17 and our fathers, our **k** and our officials did 4889
44:21 your **k** and your officials and the people of 4889
46:25 on Egypt and her gods and her **k,** 4889
50:41 a great nation and many **k** are being stirred 4889
51:11 LORD has stirred up the **k** *of* the Medes, 4889
51:28 the **k** *of* the Medes, their governors 4889
52:32 the other **k** who were with him in Babylon. 4889
La 4:12 The **k** *of* the earth did not believe, 4889
Eze 26: 7 king of **k,** with horses and chariots, 4889
Eze 27:33 and your wares you enriched the **k** *of* 4889
27:35 their **k** shudder with horror 4889
28:17 I made a spectacle of you before **k.** 4889
32:10 and their **k** will shudder with horror because 4889
32:29 "Edom is there, her **k** and all her princes; 4889
43: 7 neither they nor their **k**— 4889
43: 7 and the lifeless idols of their **k** 4889
43: 9 and the lifeless idols of their **k,** 4889
Da 2:21 he sets up **k** and deposes them. 10421
2:37 You, O king, are the king of **k.** 10421
2:44 "In the time of those **k,** 10421
2:47 the Lord of **k** and a revealer of mysteries, 10421
7:24 The ten horns are ten **k** who will come 10421
7:24 he will subdue three **k.** 10421
8:20 that you saw represents the **k** *of* Media 4889
9: 6 who spoke in your name to our **k,** 4889
9: 8 O LORD, we and our **k,** 4889
11: 2 Three more **k** will appear in Persia, 4889
11:27 The two **k,** with their hearts bent on evil, 4889
Hos 1: 1 Jotham, Ahaz and Hezekiah, **k** *of* Judah, 4889
7: 7 All their **k** fall, 4889
8: 4 They **set up k** without my consent; 4887
Mic 1: 1 Ahaz and Hezekiah, **k** *of* Judah— 4889
1:14 of Aczib will prove deceptive to the **k** 4889
Hab 1:10 They deride **k** and scoff at rulers. 4889
Mt 10:18 before governors and **k** as witnesses to them *995*
17:25 the **k** of the earth collect duty and taxes— *995*
Mk 13: 9 of me you will stand before governors and **k** *995*
Lk 10:24 and **k** wanted to see what you see but did *995*
21:12 you will be brought before **k** and governors, *995*
22:25 "The **k** of the Gentiles lord it over them; *995*
Ac 4:26 The **k** of the earth take their stand and *995*
9:15 and their **k** and before the people of Israel. *995*
1Co 4: 8 *You have become* **k**—and that without us! *996*
4: 8 How I wish that *you* really *had become* **k** so *996*
4: 8 so that we *might be* **k with** you! *5203*
1Ti 2: 2 for **k** and all those in authority, *995*
6:15 the King *of* **k** and Lord of lords, *996*
Heb 7: 1 from the defeat *of* the **k** and blessed him, *995*
Rev 1: 5 and the ruler *of* the **k** of the earth. *995*
6:15 Then the **k** of the earth, the princes, *995*
10:11 nations, languages and **k.**" *995*
16:12 to prepare the way *for* the **k** from the East. *995*
16:14 and they go out to the **k** of the whole world, *995*
16:16 Then they gathered **the k** together to *899[S]*
17: 2 the **k** of the earth committed adultery and *995*
17:10 They are also seven **k.** *995*
17:12 "The ten horns you saw are ten **k** who have *995*
17:12 for one hour will receive authority as **k** *995*
17:14 because he is Lord of lords and King *of* **k**— *995*
17:18 the great city that rules over the **k** of *995*
18: 3 The **k** of the earth committed adultery *995*
18: 9 the **k** of the earth who committed adultery *995*
19:16 KING OF K AND LORD OF LORDS. *995*
19:18 so that you may eat the flesh *of* **k,** *995*
19:19 Then I saw the beast and the **k** of the earth *995*
21:24 the **k** of the earth will bring their splendor *995*

KINGS' (2) [KING]

Pr 30:28 yet it is found in **k'** palaces. 4889
Mt 11: 8 who wear fine clothes are in **k'** palaces. *995*

KINGSHIP (7) [KING]

1Sa 10:16 not tell his uncle what Samuel had said about the **k.** 4867
10:25 to the people the regulations of the **k.** 4867
11:14 let us go to Gilgal and there reaffirm the **k.**" 4867
1Ch 11:10 gave his **k** strong support to extend it over 4895
2Ch 13: 5 has given the **k** of Israel to David 4930
Ecc 4:14 youth may have come from prison to the **k,** 4887
Mic 4: 8 **k** will come to the Daughter of Jerusalem." 4930

KINNERETH (7)

Nu 34:11 along the slopes east of the Sea of **K.** 4055
Dt 3:17 from **K** to the Sea of the Arabah 4055
Jos 11: 2 in the Arabah south of **K,** 4054
12: 3 of **K** to the Sea of the Arabah (the Salt Sea), 4054
13:27 the territory up to the end of the Sea of **K).** 4055
19:35 Zer, Hammath, Rakkath, **K,** 4055
1Ki 15:20 Abel Beth Maacah and all **K** in addition 4054

KINSMAN (2) [KIN]

Ru 3: 2 you have been, a **k** *of* ours? 4531
Pr 7: 4 and call understanding your **k;** 4530

KINSMAN-REDEEMER (7) [REDEEM]

Ru 3: 9 since you *are a* **k.**" 1457
3:12 there is a **k** nearer than I. 1457
4: 1 When the **k** he had mentioned came along, 1457
4: 3 Then he said to the **k,** "Naomi, 1457
4: 6 At this, the **k** said, "Then I cannot redeem 1457
4: 8 So the **k** said to Boaz, "Buy it yourself." 1457
4:14 who this day has not left you without a **k.** 1457

KINSMAN-REDEEMERS (1) [REDEEM]

Ru 2:20 our close relative; he is one of our **k.**" 1457

KINSMEN (6) [KIN]

1Ch 12: 2 they were **k** *of* Saul from the tribe 278
12:29 men of Benjamin, Saul's **k**— 278
2Ch 28: 8 from their **k** two hundred thousand wives, 278
29:34 so their **k** the Levites helped them until 278
Ezr 8:17 I told them what to say to Iddo and his **k,** 278
Job 19:14 My **k** have gone away; 7940

KIOS (1)

Ac 20:15 from there and arrived off **K.** *5944*

KIR (5) [KIR HARESETH]

2Ki 16: 9 He deported its inhabitants to **K** 7817
Isa 15: 1 **K** *in* Moab is ruined, destroyed in a night! 7816
22: 6 **K** uncovers the shield. 7817
Am 1: 5 people of Aram will go into exile to **K,**" 7817
9: 7 from Caphtor and the Arameans from **K?** 7817

KIR HARESETH (5) [KIR]

2Ki 3:25 Only **K** was left with its stones 7819
Isa 16: 7 and grieve for the men of **K.** 7819
16:11 my inmost being for **K.** 7818
Jer 48:31 I moan for the men of **K.** 7818
48:36 like a flute for the men of **K.** 7818

KIR-HARASETH, KIR-HARESH, KIR-HERES (KJV) See KIR HARESETH

KIRIATH (1)

Jos 18:28 (that is, Jerusalem), Gibeah and **K**— 7956

KIRIATH ARBA (9) [ARBA, HEBRON]

Ge 23: 2 She died at **K** (that is, Hebron) 7957
35:27 near **K** (that is, Hebron), 7959
Jos 14:15 (Hebron used to be called **K** after Arba, 7957
15:13 **K,** that is, Hebron. 7957
15:54 **K** (that is, Hebron) and Zior— 7957
20: 7 and **K** (that is, Hebron) 7957
21:11 They gave them **K** (that is, Hebron) 7957
Jdg 1:10 in Hebron (formerly called **K**) 7957
Ne 11:25 in **K** and its surrounding settlements, 7959

KIRIATH BAAL (2) [BAAL, KIRIATH JEARIM]

Jos 15:60 **K** (that is, Kiriath Jearim) 7958
18:14 the western side and came out at **K** 7958

KIRIATH HUZOTH (1) [HUZOTH]

Nu 22:39 Balaam went with Balak to **K.** 7960

KIRIATH JEARIM (19) [BAALAH, JEARIM, KIRIATH BAAL]

Jos 9:17 Gibeon, Kephirah, Beeroth and **K.** 7961
15: 9 down toward Baalah (that is, **K**). 7961
15:60 (that is, **K**) and Rabbah— 7961
18:14 (that is, **K**), a town of the people of Judah. 7961
18:15 at the outskirts of **K** on the west, 7961
Jdg 18:12 up camp near **K** in Judah. 7961
18:12 of **K** is called Mahaneh Dan 7961
1Sa 6:21 messengers to the people of **K,** 7961
7: 1 So the men of **K** came and took up 7961
7: 2 that the ark remained at **K,** 7961
1Ch 2:50 Shobal the father of **K,** 7961
2:52 of Shobal the father of **K** were: 7961
2:53 and the clans of **K:** 7961
13: 5 to bring the ark of God from **K.** 7961
13: 6 Baalah of Judah (**K**) to bring up from there 7961
2Ch 1: 4 from **K** to the place he had prepared 7961
Ezr 2:25 of **K,** Kephirah and Beeroth 743 7961
Ne 7:29 of **K,** Kephirah and Beeroth 743 7961
Jer 26:20 from **K** was another man who prophesied 7961

KIRIATH SANNAH (1) [DEBIR, SANNAH]

Jos 15:49 Dannah, **K** (that is, Debir), 7962

KIRIATH SEPHER (4) [SEPHER]

Jos 15:15 living in Debir (formerly called **K**). 7963
15:16 the man who attacks and captures **K.**" 7963
Jdg 1:11 living in Debir (formerly called **K**). 7963
1:12 the man who attacks and captures **K.**" 7963

KIRIATHAIM (6) [SHAVEH KIRIATHAIM]

Nu 32:37 Reubenites rebuilt Heshbon, Elealeh and **K,** 7964
Jos 13:19 **K,** Sibmah, Zereth Shahar on the hill in 7964
1Ch 6:76 in Galilee, Hammon and **K,** together 7964
Jer 48: 1 **K** will be disgraced and captured; 7964
48:23 to **K,** Beth Gamul and Beth Meon, 7964
Eze 25: 9 Beth Jeshimoth, Baal Meon and **K**— 7964

KIRIOTH (KJV) See KERIOTH

KIRJATH (KJV) See KIRIATH

KIRJATH-ARBA (KJV) See KIRIATH ARBA

KIRJATH-ARIM (KJV) See KIRIATH ARIM

KIRJATH-BAAL (KJV) See KIRIATH BAAL

KIRJATH-HUZOTH (KJV) See KIRIATH HUZOTH

KIRJATH-JEARIM (KJV) See KIRIATH JEARIM

KIRJATH-SANNAH (KJV) See KIRIATH SANNAH

KIRJATH-SEPHER (KJV) See KIRIATH SEPHER

KIRJATHAIM (KJV) See KIRIATHAIM

KISH (22)

1Sa 9: 1 whose name was **K** son of Abiel, 7821
9: 3 to Saul's father **K** were lost, 7821
9: 3 and **K** said to his son Saul, 7821
10:11 that has happened to the son of **K?** 7821
10:21 Finally Saul son of **K** was chosen. 7821
14:51 Saul's father **K** and Abner's father Ner 7821
2Sa 21:14 in the tomb of Saul's father **K,** 7821
1Ch 8:30 followed by Zur, **K,** Baal, Ner, Nadab, 7821
8:33 Ner was the father of **K,** 7821
8:33 **K** the father of Saul, 7821
9:36 followed by Zur, **K,** Baal, Ner, Nadab, 7821
9:39 Ner was the father of **K,** 7821
9:39 **K** the father of Saul, 7821
12: 1 the presence of Saul son of **K** (they were 7821
23:21 The sons of Mahli: Eleazar and **K.** 7821
23:22 Their cousins, the sons of **K,** married them. 7821
24:29 From **K:** the son of Kish: Jerahmeel. 7821
24:29 From Kish: the son of **K:** Jerahmeel. 7821
26:28 by Samuel the seer and by Saul son of **K,** 7821
2Ch 29:12 from the Merarites, **K** son of Abdi 7821
Est 2: 5 the son of Shimei, the son of **K,** 7821
Ac 13:21 and he gave them Saul son *of* **K,** *3078*

KISHI (1)

1Ch 6:44 Ethan son of **K,** the son of Abdi, 7823

KISHION (2)

Jos 19:20 Rabbith, **K,** Ebez, 8002
21:28 from the tribe of Issachar, **K,** Daberath, 8002

KISHON (6)

Jdg 4: 7 and his troops to the **K** River and give him 7822
4:13 from Harosheth Haggoyim to the **K** River. 7822
5:21 The river **K** swept them away, 7822
5:21 the age-old river, the river **K.** 7822
1Ki 18:40 down to the **K** Valley and slaughtered there. 7822
Ps 83: 9 you did to Sisera and Jabin at the river **K,** 7822

KISLEV (2)

Ne 1: 1 In the month of **K** in the twentieth year, 4075
Zec 7: 1 the ninth month, the month of **K.** 4075

KISLON (1)

Nu 34:21 of **K,** from the tribe of Benjamin; 4077

KISLOTH TABOR (1) [TABOR]

Jos 19:12 of **K** and went on to Daberath and up 4079

KISON (KJV) See KISHON

KISS (22) [KISSED, KISSES, KISSING]

Ge 27:26 "Come here, my son, and **k** me." 5975
31:28 **k** my grandchildren and my daughters **good-by.** 5975
2Sa 15: 5 take hold of him and **k** him. 5975
20: 9 by the beard with his right hand to **k** him. 5975
1Ki 19:20 **k** my father and mother **good-by,"** 5975
Job 31:27 **offered** them **a k of homage,** 4200+5975+7023
Ps 2:12 **K** the Son, lest he be angry and you 5975
85:10 righteousness and peace **k** *each other.* 5975
Pr 24:26 An honest answer *is* like a **k** *on* the lips. 5975
SS 1: 2 *Let him* **k** me with the kisses 5975
8: 1 if I found you outside, *I would* **k** you, 5975
Hos 13: 2 offer human sacrifice and **k** the calf-idols." 5975
Mt 26:48 "The one *I* **k** is the man; arrest him." *5797*
Mk 14:44 "The one *I* **k** is the man; arrest him and *5797*
Lk 7:45 You did not give me a **k,** but this woman, *5799*
22:47 He approached Jesus *to* **k** him, *5797*
22:48 the Son of Man *with* a **k?"** *5799*
Ro 16:16 Greet one another with a holy **k.** *5799*
1Co 16:20 Greet one another with a holy **k.** *5799*
2Co 13:12 Greet one another with a holy **k.** *5799*
1Th 5:26 Greet all the brothers with a holy **k.** *5799*
1Pe 5:14 Greet one another with a **k** of love. *5799*

KISSED (23) [KISS]

Ge 27:27 So he went to him and **k** him. 5975
29:11 Jacob **k** Rachel and began to weep aloud. 5975
29:13 and **k** him and brought him to his home, 5975
31:55 the next morning Laban **k** his grandchildren 5975
33: 4 around his neck and **k** him. 5975
45:15 *he* **k** all his brothers and wept over them. 5975
48:10 and his father **k** them and embraced them. 5975
50: 1 and wept over him and **k** him. 5975
Ex 4:27 at the mountain of God and **k** him. 5975
18: 7 and bowed down and **k** him. 5975
Ru 1: 9 Then *she* **k** them and they wept aloud 5975
1:14 **k** her mother-in-law **good-by,** 5975
1Sa 10: 1 and poured it on Saul's head and **k** him, 5975
20:41 Then *they* **k** each other and wept together— 5975
2Sa 14:33 And the king **k** Absalom. 5975
19:39 The king **k** Barzillai and gave him his 5975
1Ki 19:18 and all whose mouths *have* not **k** him." 5975
Pr 7:13 and **k** him and with a brazen face she said: 5975
Mt 26:49 Judas said, "Greetings, Rabbi!" and **k** him. *2968*
Mk 14:45 Judas said, "Rabbi!" and **k** him. *2968*
Lk 7:38 **k** them and poured perfume on them. *2968*
15:20 threw his arms around him and **k** him. *2968*
Ac 20:37 as they embraced him and **k** him. *2968*

KISSES (2) [KISS]

Pr 27: 6 but an enemy multiplies **k.** 5965
SS 1: 2 Let him kiss me with the **k** *of* his mouth— 5965

KISSING (1) [KISS]

Lk 7:45 has not stopped **k** my feet. *2968*

KIT (3)

Eze 9: 2 a man clothed in linen who had a writing **k** 7879
9: 3 in linen who had the writing **k** at his side 7879
9:11 the **writing k** at his side brought back word, 7879

KITCHENS (1)

Eze 46:24 the **k** where those who minister 1074+1418

KITE (4)

Lev 11:14 the **red k,** any kind of black kite, 1798
11:14 the red kite, any kind of **black k,** 370
Dt 14:13 the **red k,** the black kite, any kind of falcon, 8012
14:13 the **black k,** any kind of falcon, 370

KITLISH (1)

Jos 15:40 Cabbon, Lahmas, **K,** 4186

KITRON (1)

Jdg 1:30 the Canaanites living in **K** or Nahalol, 7790

KITTIM (4)

Ge 10: 4 Elishah, Tarshish, the **K** and the Rodanim. 4183
Nu 24:24 Ships will come from the shores of **K;** 4183
1Ch 1: 7 Elishah, Tarshish, the **K** and the Rodanim. 4183
Jer 2:10 Cross over to the coasts of **K** and look, 4183

KNEAD (2) [KNEADED, KNEADING, WELL-KNEADED]

Ge 18: 6 of fine flour and **k** it and bake some bread." 4297
Jer 7:18 and the women **k** the dough and make cakes 4297

KNEADED (2) [KNEAD]

1Sa 28:24 **k** it and baked bread without yeast. 4297
2Sa 13: 8 She took some dough, **k** it, 4297

KNEADING (5) [KNEAD]

Ex 8: 3 and into your ovens and **k troughs.** 5400
12:34 on their shoulders in **k troughs** wrapped 5400
Dt 28: 5 Your basket and your **k trough** will 5400
28:17 Your basket and your **k trough** will 5400
Hos 7: 4 not stir from the **k** *of* the dough till it rises. 4297

KNEE (6) [KNEE-DEEP, KNEES]

Isa 45:23 Before me every **k** will bow; 1386
Eze 7:17 and every **k** will become as weak as water. 1386
21: 7 and every **k** become as weak as water.' 1386
Ro 11: 4 not bowed the **k** to Baal." *1205*
14:11 says the Lord, 'every **k** will bow before me; *1205*
Php 2:10 at the name of Jesus every **k** should bow, *1205*

KNEE-DEEP (1) [KNEE]

Eze 47: 4 and led me through water that was **k.** 1386

KNEEL (7) [KNEELING, KNELT]

Ge 24:11 *He* **had** the camels **k down** 1384
Jdg 7: 5 a dog from those who **k** down to drink." 1386
Est 3: 2 But Mordecai *would* not **k down** 4156
3: 5 that Mordecai *would* not **k down** 4156
Ps 22:29 down to the dust *will* **k** before him— 4156
95: 6 *let us* **k** before the LORD our Maker; 1384
Eph 3:14 this reason *I* **k** before the Father, *1205+2828+3836*

KNEELING (3) [KNEEL]

1Ki 1:31 and, **k** before the king, said, 2556
8:54 where *he had been* **k** 1386+4156+6584
Mt 20:20 and, **k down,** asked a favor of him. *4686*

KNEES (28) [KNEE]

Ge 48:12 Then Joseph removed them from Israel's **k** 1386
50:23 were placed at birth on Joseph's **k.** 1386
Dt 28:35 The LORD will afflict your **k** and legs 1386
Jdg 7: 6 All the rest got down on their **k** to drink. 1386
1Ki 18:42 the ground and put his face between his **k.** 1386
19:18 all whose **k** have not bowed down to Baal 1386
2Ki 1:13 This third captain went up and fell on his **k** 1386
Ezr 9: 5 and fell on my **k** with my hands spread out 1386
Job 3:12 Why were there **k** to receive me and breasts 1386
4: 4 you have strengthened faltering **k.** 1386
Ps 20: 8 They *are* **brought to** *their* **k** and fall, 4156
109:24 My **k** give way from fasting; 1386
Isa 35: 3 steady the **k** that give way; 1386
66:12 be carried on her arm and dandled on her **k.** 1386
Da 5: 6 so frightened that his **k** knocked together 10072
6:10 Three times a day he got down on his **k** 10123
10:10 and set me trembling on my hands and **k.** 1386
Na 2:10 Hearts melt, **k** give way, bodies tremble, 1386
Mt 18:26 "The servant fell **on** *his* **k before** him. *4686*
18:29 "His fellow servant fell to his **k** *NIG*
Mk 1:40 to him and begged him **on** his **k,** *1206*
5: 6 he ran and **fell on** his **k in front of** *4686*
10:17 ran up to him and **fell on** his **k before** *1206*
15:19 Falling on their **k,** they paid homage to him. *1205*
Lk 5: 8 he fell at Jesus' **k** and said, *1205*
Ac 7:60 Then he fell on his **k** and cried out, "Lord, *1205*
9:40 then he got down *on* his **k** and prayed. *1205*
Heb 12:12 strengthen your feeble arms and weak **k.** *1205*

KNELT (13) [KNEEL]

1Ki 1:16 Bathsheba bowed low and **k** before 2556
2Ch 6:13 and then **k down** before the whole assembly 1384+1386+6584
7: 3 *they* **k** on the pavement with their faces to 4156
29:29 and everyone present with him **k down** 4156
Est 3: 2 the royal officials at the king's gate **k down** 4156
Mt 8: 2 A man with leprosy came and **k before** him *4686*
9:18 a ruler came and **k before** him and said, *4686*
15:25 The woman came and **k before** him. *4686*
17:14 a man approached Jesus and **k before** him. *1206*
27:29 They put a staff in his right hand and **k** *1206*
Lk 22:41 beyond them, **k down** and prayed, *1205+5502*
Ac 20:36 he **k down** with all of them and prayed. *1205+3836+5502*
21: 5 there on the beach *we* **k** to pray. *1205+3836+5502*

KNEW (83) [KNOW]

Ge 8:11 Then Noah **k** that the water had receded 3359
16: 4 When *she* **k** she was pregnant, 8011
38: 9 Onan **k** that the offspring would not be his; 3359
Dt 7:15 the horrible diseases *you* **k** in Egypt, 3359
34:10 whom the LORD **k** face to face, 3359
Jdg 2:10 who **k** neither the LORD 3359
1Sa 3:13 because of the sin *he* **k about;** 3359
20:33 Then Jonathan **k** that his father intended 3359
20:39 (The boy **k** nothing *of* all this; 3359
20:39 only Jonathan and David **k.)** 3359
22:17 *They* **k** he was fleeing, 3359
22:22 *I* **k** he would be sure to tell Saul. 3359
26:12 No one saw or **k about** it, 3359
28:14 Then Saul **k** it was Samuel, 3359
2Sa 1:10 and killed him, because *I* **k** that 3359
3:37 So on that day all the people and all Israel **k** 3359
5:12 And David **k** that the LORD had established 3359
11:16 where *he* **k** the strongest defenders were. 3359
14: 1 of Zeruiah **k** that the king's heart longed 3359
17:19 No *one* **k** anything **about** it. 3359
1Ki 9:27 sailors *who* **k** the sea— 3359
2Ki 4:39 though no *one* **k** what they were. 3359
1Ch 12:32 the times and **k** what Israel should do— 3359
14: 2 And David **k** that the LORD had established 3359
2Ch 8:18 men *who* **k** the sea. 3359
33:13 Then Manasseh **k** that the LORD is God. 3359
Ne 9:10 for *you* **k** how arrogantly the Egyptians 3359
Job 23: 3 If only *I* **k** where to find him; 3359
Ps 31: 7 for you saw my affliction and **k** the anguish 3359
Pr 24:12 If you say, "But *we* **k** nothing **about** this," 3359
Ecc 6: 5 Though it never saw the sun or **k** anything, 3359
Isa 48: 4 For I **k** how stubborn you were; 3359
48: 7 So you cannot say, 'Yes, *I* **k** *of* them.' 3359
Jer 1: 5 "Before I formed you in the womb *I* **k** you, 3359
11:18 the LORD revealed their plot to me, *I* **k** it, 3359
19: 4 nor the kings of Judah *ever* **k,** 3359
32: 8 "*I* **k** that this was the word of the LORD; 3359
41: 4 before anyone **k about** it, 3359
44: 3 nor you nor your fathers *ever* **k.** 3359
44:15 Then all the men who **k** that their wives 3359
50:24 and you were caught before you **k** it; 3359
Eze 28:19 the nations *who* **k** you are appalled at you; 3359
Da 5:22 though *you* **k** all this. 10313
Jnh 1:10 (They **k** he was running away from 3359
4: 2 *I* **k** that you are a gracious and compassionate God, 3359
Zec 11:11 of the flock who were watching me **k** it was 3359
Mt 7:23 '*I* never **k** you. Away from me, *1182*
12:25 Jesus **k** their thoughts and said to them, *3857*
21:45 *they* **k** he was talking about them. *1182*
24:39 and *they* **k** nothing **about** what would *1182*
25:24 he said, '*I* **k** that you are a hard man, *1182*
25:26 So *you* **k** that I harvest where I have *3857*
27:18 For *he* **k** it was out of envy *3857*
Mk 1:34 because *they* **k who he was.** *3857*
2: 8 Immediately Jesus **k** in his spirit *2105*
12:12 to arrest him because *they* **k** he had spoken *1182*
12:15 But Jesus **k** their hypocrisy. *3857*
Lk 4:41 because *they* **k** he was the Christ. *3857*
5:22 Jesus **k** what they were thinking and asked, *2105*

Lk 6: 8 But Jesus **k** what they were thinking *3857*
11:17 Jesus **k** their thoughts and said to them: *3857*
19:22 *You* **k**, did you, that I am a hard man, *3857*
20:19 because *they* **k** he had spoken this parable *1182*
23:49 But all those who **k** him, *1196*
Jn 2: 9 the servants who had drawn the water **k.** *3857*
2:24 not entrust himself to them, for he **k** all men *1182*
2:25 for he **k** what was in a man. *1182*
4:10 "If *you* **k** the gift of God and who it is *3857*
8:19 "If *you* **k** me, you would know my Father *3857*
11:42 I **k** that you always hear me, *3857*
13: 1 Jesus **k** that the time had come for him *3857*
13: 3 Jesus **k** that the Father had put all things *3857*
13:11 For *he* **k** who was going to betray him, *3857*
14: 7 If *you* really **k** me, you would know my *1182*
17: 8 *They* **k** with certainty that I came from you, *1182*
18: 2 Now Judas, who betrayed him, **k** the place, *3857*
21:12 *They* **k** it was the Lord. *3857*
Ac 2:30 a prophet and **k** that God had promised him *3857*
7:18 another king, who **k** nothing **about** Joseph, *3857*
16: 3 for *they* all **k** that his father was a Greek. *3857*
18:25 *though he* **k** only the baptism of John. *2179*
Ro 1:21 For *although they* **k** God, *1182*
Heb 10:34 *because you* **k** that you yourselves had *1182*

KNIFE (6) [KNIVES]

Ge 22: 6 and he himself carried the fire and the **k.** 4408
22:10 Then he reached out his hand and took the **k** 4408
Ex 4:25 But Zipporah took a **flint k,** 7644
Jdg 19:29 he took a **k** and cut up his concubine, 4408
Pr 23: 2 and put a **k** to your throat if you are given 8501
Jer 36:23 a scribe's **k** and threw them into the firepot, 9509

KNIT (2) [CLOSE-KNIT, KNITTED]

Job 10:11 and **k** me **together** with bones and sinews? 6115
Ps 139:13 *you* **k** me **together** in my mother's womb. 6115

KNITTED (9) [KNIT]

Lev 13:48 or **k material** of linen or wool, any leather 6849
13:49 or leather, or woven or **k material,** 6849
13:51 or the woven or **k material,** or the leather, 6849
13:52 the woven or **k material** of wool or linen, 6849
13:53 or the woven or **k material,** 6849
13:56 or the leather, or the woven or **k material.** 6849
13:57 or in the woven or **k material,** 6849
13:58 The clothing, or the woven or **k material,** 6849
13:59 woven or **k material,** or any leather article, 6849

KNIVES (4) [KNIFE]

Jos 5: 2 "Make flint **k** and circumcise 2995
5: 3 So Joshua made flint **k** and circumcised 2995
Pr 30:14 with **k** to devour the poor from the earth, 4408
Isa 18: 5 he will cut off the shoots with **pruning k,** 4661

KNOCK (3) [KNOCKED, KNOCKING, KNOCKS]

Mt 7: 7 **k** and the door will be opened to you. *3218*
Lk 11: 9 **k** and the door will be opened to you. *3218*
Rev 3:20 Here I am! I stand at the door and **k.** *3218*

KNOCKED (3) [KNOCK]

Da 5: 6 so frightened that his knees **k** together 10491
8: 7 the goat **k** him to the ground and trampled 8959
Ac 12:13 Peter **k at** the outer entrance, *3218*

KNOCKING (3) [KNOCK]

SS 5: 2 My lover *is* **k**: "Open to me, 1985
Lk 13:25 *you will* stand outside **k** and pleading, *3218*
Ac 12:16 But Peter kept on **k,** and when they opened *3218*

KNOCKS (4) [KNOCK]

Ex 21:27 And if *he* **k out** the tooth of a manservant 5877
Mt 7: 8 and *to* him who **k,** the door will be opened. *3218*
Lk 11:10 and *to* him who **k,** the door will be opened. *3218*
12:36 and **k** they can immediately open the door *3218*

KNOP, KNOPS (KJV) See BUD, BUDS

KNOTTED (1) [KNOT]

Eze 27:24 with cords twisted and **tightly k.** 775

KNOW (852) [FOREKNEW, FOREKNOWLEDGE, KNEW, KNOWING, KNOWLEDGE, KNOWN, KNOWS, WELL-KNOWN]

Ge 4: 9 *"I* don't **k,"** he replied. 3359
12:11 *"I* **k** what a beautiful woman you are. 3359
15: 8 how *can I* **k** that I will gain possession 3359
15:13 **"K for certain** that your descendants 3359+3359
18:21 If not, *I will* **k."** 3359
20: 6 I **k** you did this with a clear conscience, 3359
21:26 *"I* don't **k** who has done this. 3359
22:12 Now *I* **k** that you fear God, 3359
24:14 By this *I will* **k** that you have shown 3359
24:49 *k* which way *to* **turn."** AIT
27: 2 an old man and don't **k** the day of my death. 3359
27:21 to **k** whether you really are my son Esau NIH
29: 5 He said to them, *"Do you* **k** Laban, 3359
Ge 29: 5 "Yes, *we* **k** him," they answered. 3359
30:26 You **k** how much work I've done for you." 3359
30:29 "You **k** how I have worked for you and 3359
31: 6 You **k** that I've worked for your father 3359
31:32 Now Jacob *did* not **k** that Rachel had stolen 3359
37:13 **"As you k,** your brothers are grazing 2022+4202
42:33 how *I will* **k** whether you are honest men: 3359
42:34 to me so *I will* **k** that you are not spies 3359
43: 7 *How were we to* **k** he would say, 3359+3359
43:22 *We* don't **k** who put our silver in our sacks." 3359
44:15 Don't *you* **k** that a man like me can find 3359
44:27 'You **k** that my wife bore me two sons. 3359
47: 6 And if *you* **k** *of* any among them 3359
48:19 But his father refused and said, *"I* **k,** 3359
48:19 "I know, my son, *I* **k.** 3359
Ex 1: 8 a new king, who *did* not **k about** Joseph, 3359
3:19 But I **k** that the king of Egypt will 3359
4:14 *I* **k** he can speak well. 3359
5: 2 *I do* not **k** the LORD and I will 3359
6: 7 *you will* **k** that I am the LORD your God, 3359
7: 5 the Egyptians *will* **k** that I am the LORD 3359
7:17 By this *you will* **k** that I am the LORD: 3359
8:10 so that *you may* **k** there is no one like 3359
8:22 so that *you will* **k** that I, the LORD, 3359
9:14 so *you may* **k** that there is no one like me 3359
9:29 so *you may* **k** that the earth is the LORD's. 3359
9:30 But *I* **k** that you and your officials still do 3359
10: 2 and that *you may* **k** that I am the LORD." 3359
10:26 not **k** what we are to use to worship 3359
11: 7 Then *you will* **k** that the LORD makes 3359
14: 4 Egyptians *will* **k** that I am the LORD." 3359
14:18 The Egyptians *will* **k** that I am the LORD 3359
16: 6 "In the evening *you will* **k** that it was 3359
16: 8 "You will **k** that it was the LORD NIH
16:12 Then *you will* **k** that I am the LORD your 3359
16:15 For *they did* not **k** what it was. 3359
18:11 Now *I* **k** that the LORD is greater than all 3359
23: 9 *you* yourselves **k** how it feels to be aliens, 3359
29:46 *They will* **k** that I am the LORD their God, 3359
31:13 so *you may* **k** that I am the LORD, 3359
32: 1 *we* don't **k** what has happened to him." 3359
32:22 "You **k** how prone these people are to evil. 3359
32:23 *we* don't **k** what has happened to him.' 3359
33:12 not **let** me **k** whom you will send with me. 3359
33:12 *'I* **k** you by name and you have found favor 3359
33:13 so *I may* **k** you and continue to find favor 3359
33:16 How *will anyone* **k** that you are pleased 3359
33:17 because I am pleased with you and *I* **k** you 3359
36: 1 ability to **k how** to carry out all the work 3359
Lev 5:17 even though *he does* not **k** it, 3359
23:43 so your descendants *will* **k** that I had 3359
Nu 10:31 *You* **k** where we should camp in the desert, 3359
14:34 suffer for your sins and **k what it is like** 3359
16:28 "This is how *you will* **k** that 3359
16:30 then *you will* **k** that these men 3359
20:14 You **k about** all the hardships 3359
22: 6 For *I* **k** that those you bless are blessed, 3359
Dt 1:39 your children who *do* not yet **k** good 3359
3:19 *(I* **k** you have much livestock) may stay 3359
4:35 so that *you might* **k** that the LORD is God; 3359
7: 9 **K** therefore that the LORD your God is God; 3359
8: 2 and to test you in order to **k** what was 3359
8: 5 **K** then in your heart that as 3359
9: 2 You **k about** them and have heard it said: 3359
11:30 **As you k,** these mountains are across 2022+4202
18:21 "How *can we* **k** when a message has 3359
20:20 that *you* **k** are not fruit trees and use them 3359
22: 2 near you or if *you do* not **k** who he is, 3359
28:33 that *you do* not **k** will eat what your land 3359
29: 6 I did this so that *you might* **k** that I am 3359
29:16 *You* yourselves **k** how we lived in Egypt 3359
29:26 gods *they did* not **k,** gods he had not given 3359
31:13 Their children, who *do* not **k** this law, 3359
31:21 *I* **k** what they are disposed to do, 3359
31:27 I **k** how rebellious and stiff-necked you are. 3359
31:29 For *I* **k** that after my death you are sure 3359
Jos 2: 4 but *I did* not **k** where they had come from. 3359
2: 5 *I* don't **k** which way they went. 3359
2: 9 *"I* **k** that the LORD has given this land 3359
3: 4 Then *you will* **k** which way to go, 3359
3: 7 so *they may* **k** that I am with you as I was 3359
3:10 how *you will* **k** that the living God is 3359
4:24 that all the peoples of the earth *might* **k** that 3359
8:14 not **k** that an ambush had been set 3359
14: 6 "You **k** what the LORD said to Moses 3359
22:22 And *let* Israel **k!** 3359
22:31 "Today *we* **k** that the LORD is with us, 3359
23:14 *You* **k** with all your heart and soul that 3359
Jdg 6:37 then *I will* **k** that you will save Israel 3359
14: 4 (His parents *did* not **k** that this was from 3359
16:20 he *did* not **k** that the LORD had left him. 3359
17:13 *I* **k** that the LORD will be good to me, 3359
18:14 *"Do you* **k** that one of these houses has 3359
18:14 Now *you* **k** what to do." 3359
Ru 2:11 to live with a people *you did* not **k** before. 3359
3: 3 but don't **let** him **k** *you* are there 3359
3:11 All my fellow townsmen **k** that you are 3359
4: 4 But if you will not, tell me, so *I will* **k.** 3359
1Sa 3: 7 Now Samuel *did* not yet **k** the LORD: 3359
6: 3 and you *will* **k** why his hand has 3359
6: 9 then *we will* **k** that it was not his hand 3359
8: 9 and **let** them **k** what the king who will reign 5583
17:28 I **k** how conceited you are and 3359
17:46 the whole world *will* **k** that there is a God 3359
17:47 All those gathered here *will* **k** that it is not 3359
17:55 "As surely as you live, O king, *I* don't **k."** 3359
20: 3 'Jonathan *must* not **k** this or he will 3359
1Sa 20:12 I not send you word and **let** you **k?** 265+906+1655
20:13 not **let** you **k** and send you away 265+906+1655
20:30 Don't *I* **k** that you have sided with the son 3359
21: 2 *to* **k** anything **about** your mission 3359
24:20 *I* **k** that you will surely be king and that 3359
28: 9 "Surely you **k** what Saul has done. 3359
29: 9 *"I* **k** that you have been as pleasing 3359
2Sa 1: 5 "How *do you* **k** that Saul 3359
3:25 *You* **k** Abner son of Ner; 3359
3:26 But David *did* not **k** it. 3359
7:20 you **k** your servant, O Sovereign LORD. 3359
11:20 Didn't *you* **k** they would shoot arrows from 3359
15:20 when I **do not k where I am going?** 889+2143+2143+6584
17: 8 You **k** your father and his men; 3359
18:29 your servant, but *I* don't **k** what it was." 3359
19:20 For I your servant **k** that I have sinned, 3359
19:22 not **k** that today I am king over Israel?" 3359
22:44 People *I did* not **k** are subject to me, 3359
24: 2 so that *I may* **k** how many there are." 3359
1Ki 1:18 my lord the king, *do* not **k about** it. 3359
1:27 **letting** his servants **k** who should sit on 3359
2: 5 "Now *you* yourself **k** what Joab son 3359
2: 9 *you will* **k** what to do to him. 3359
2:15 *"As* you **k,"** he said, "the kingdom was 3359
2:44 "You **k** in your heart all the wrong you did 3359
3: 7 But I am only a little child and *do* not **k how** 3359
5: 3 "You **k** that because of the wars waged 3359
5: 6 You **k** that we have no one so skilled 3359
8:39 since *you* **k** his heart (for you alone know 3359
8:39 since you know his heart (for you alone **k** 3359
8:43 of the earth *may* **k** your name and fear you, 3359
8:43 as do your own people Israel, and *may* **k** 3359
8:60 so that all the peoples of the earth *may* **k**
that the LORD is God 3359
17:24 "Now *I* **k** that you are a man of God and 3359
18:12 *I* don't **k** where the Spirit of 3359
18:37 answer me, so these people *will* **k** that you, 3359
20:13 then *you will* **k** that I am the LORD.' " 3359
20:28 and *you will* **k** that I am the LORD.' " 3359
22: 3 "Don't *you* **k** that Ramoth Gilead belongs 3359
2Ki 2: 3 *"Do you* **k** that the LORD is going 3359
2: 3 "Yes, I **k,"** Elisha replied, 3359
2: 5 *"Do you* **k** that the LORD is going 3359
2: 5 "Yes, I **k,"** he replied, 3359
4: 1 and you **k** that he revered the LORD. 3359
4: 9 to her husband, *"I* **k** that this man 3359
5: 8 to me and *he will* **k** that there is a prophet 3359
5:15 "Now *I* **k** that there is no God in all 3359
7:12 *They* **k** we are starving; 3359
8:12 "Because *I* **k** the harm you will do to 3359
9:11 "You **k** the man and the sort of things he 3359
10:10 **K** then, that not a word the LORD has 3359
17:26 not **k** what the god of that country requires. 3359
17:26 the people *do* not **k** what he requires." 3359
19:19 all kingdoms on earth *may* **k** that you alone, 3359
19:27 " 'But *I* **k** where you stay and 3359
1Ch 17:18 For you **k** your servant, 3359
21: 2 to me so that *I may* **k** how many there are." 3359
29:17 *I* **k,** my God, that you test the heart 3359
2Ch 2: 8 for **I k** that your men are skilled 3359
6:30 since *you* **k** his heart (for you alone know 3359
6:30 since you know his heart (for you alone **k** 3359
6:33 of the earth *may* **k** your name and fear you, 3359
6:33 as do your own people Israel, and *may* **k** 3359
13: 5 Don't you **k** that the LORD, 3359
20:12 We *do* not **k** what to do, 3359
25:16 *I* **k** that God has determined to destroy you, 3359
32:13 not **k** what I and my fathers have done to all 3359
32:31 God left him to test him and to **k** everything 3359
Ezr 4:12 The king *should* **k** that the Jews who came 10313
4:13 the king *should* **k** that if this city is built 10313
5: 8 The king *should* **k** that we went to 10313
7:24 also *to* **k** that you have no authority 10313
7:25 all *who* **k** the laws of your God. 10313
7:25 you are to teach any who *do* not **k** them. 10313
Ne 2:16 not **k** where I had gone or what I was doing, 3359
4:11 "Before *they* **k** it or see us, 3359
13:24 not **k how** to speak the language of Judah. 5795
Est 4:11 and the people of the royal provinces **k** that 3359
Job 5:24 *You will* **k** that your tent is secure; 3359
5:25 *You will* **k** that your children will be many, 3359
7:10 his place *will* **k** him no more. 5795
8: 9 we were born only yesterday and **k** nothing, 3359
9: 2 *I* **k** that this is true. 3359
9:28 for *I* **k** you will not hold me innocent. 3359
10: 7 though you **k** that I am not guilty and 1981
10:13 and *I* **k** that this was in your mind: 3359
11: 6 for true wisdom has two sides. **K** this: 3359
11: 8 depths of the grave—what *can you* **k?** 3359
12: 3 Who does not **k** all these things? 907
12: 9 Which of all these *does* not **k** that the hand 3359
13: 2 What you **k,** I also know; 1981
13: 2 What you know, I also **k;** 3359
13:18 *I* **k** I will be vindicated. 3359
14:21 If his sons are honored, *he does* not **k** it; 3359
15: 9 What *do you* **k** that we do not know? 3359
15: 9 What do you know that we *do* not **k?** 3359
19: 6 then **k** that God has wronged me 3359
19:25 I **k** that my Redeemer lives, 3359
19:29 then *you will* **k** that there is judgment." 3359
20: 4 "Surely *you* **k** how it has been from of old, 3359
21:14 We have no desire to **k** your ways. 1981
21:19 so that *he will* **k** it! 3359
21:27 *"I* **k** full well what you are thinking, 3359
22:13 Yet you say, 'What *does* God **k?** 3359
24: 1 Why must *those who* **k** him look in vain 3359

Job 24:13 *who do* not **k** its ways or stay in its paths. 5795
30:23 *I* **k** you will bring me down to death, 3359
31: 6 and *he will* **k** that I am blameless— 3359
32: 6 not daring to tell you **what I k.** 1976
32:10 I too will tell you **what I k.** 1976
32:17 I too will tell **what I k.** 1976
33: 3 my lips sincerely speak **what I k.** 1981
34:33 so tell me what *you* **k.** 3359
37: 7 that all men he has made *may* **k** his work, 3359
37:15 *Do you* **k** how God controls the clouds 3359
37:16 *Do you* **k** how the clouds hang poised, 3359
38: 5 marked off its dimensions? Surely *you* **k!** 3359
38:18 Tell me, if *you* **k** all this. 3359
38:20 *Do you* **k** the paths to their dwellings? 1067
38:21 Surely *you* **k,** for you were already born! 3359
38:33 *Do you* **k** the laws of the heavens? 3359
39: 1 *"Do you* **k** when the mountain goats 3359
39: 2 *Do you* **k** the time they give birth? 3359
42: 2 *"I* **k** that you can do all things; 3359
42: 3 things too wonderful for me *to* **k.** 3359
Ps 4: 3 **K** that the LORD has set apart the godly 3359
9:10 *Those who* **k** your name will trust in you, 3359
9:20 *let* the nations **k** they are but men. 3359
18:43 people *I did* not **k** are subject to me. 3359
20: 6 *I* **k** that the LORD saves his anointed; 3359
35:11 on things *I* **k** nothing **about.** 3359
36:10 Continue your love to *those who* **k** you, 3359
39: 4 *let me* **k** how fleeting is my life. 3359
40: 9 I do not seal my lips, *as* you **k,** O LORD. 3359
41:11 *I* **k** that you are pleased with me, 3359
46:10 "Be still, and **k** that I am God; 3359
50:11 *I* **k** every bird in the mountains, 3359
51: 3 For I **k** my transgressions, 3359
56: 9 By this *I will* **k** that God is for me. 3359
69: 5 You **k** my folly, O God; 3359
69:19 You **k** how I am scorned, 3359
71:15 though *I* **k** not its measure. 3359
73: 7 the evil conceits of their minds **k no limits.** 6296
73:11 They say, "How *can* God **k?** 3359
78: 6 so the next generation *would* **k** them, 3359
82: 5 *"They* **k** nothing, they understand nothing. 3359
83:18 *Let them* **k** that you, 3359
92: 6 The senseless man *does* not **k,** 3359
100: 3 **K** that the LORD is God. 3359
109:27 *Let them* **k** that it is your hand, that you, 3359
119:75 *I* **k,** O LORD, that your laws are righteous, 3359
135: 5 I **k** that the LORD is great, 3359
139: 1 you have searched me and *you* **k** me. 3359
139: 2 You **k** when I sit and when I rise; 3359
139: 4 on my tongue *you* **k** it completely, 3359
139:14 your works are wonderful, I **k** that full well. 3359
139:23 Search me, O God, and **k** my heart; 3359
139:23 test me and **k** my anxious thoughts. 3359
140:12 *I* **k** that the LORD secures justice for 3359
142: 3 it is you *who* **k** my way. 3359
145:12 that all men *may* **k** *of* your mighty acts and 3359
147:20 *they do* not **k** his laws. 3359
Pr 4:19 *they do* not **k** what makes them stumble. 3359
9:18 But little *do they* **k** that the dead are there, 3359
10:32 The lips of the righteous **k** what is fitting, 3359
24:12 *Does* not he who guards your life **k** it? 3359
24:14 **K** also that wisdom is sweet to your soul; 3359
27: 1 *you do* not **k** what a day may bring forth. 3359
27:23 **Be sure** *you* **k** the condition of your flocks, 3359+3359
30: 4 the name of his son? Tell me if *you* **k!** 3359
Ecc 3:12 *I* **k** that there is nothing better for men than 3359
3:14 *I* **k** that everything God does will endure forever; 3359
5: 1 who *do* not **k** that they do wrong. 3359
7:22 for *you* **k** in your heart that many times 3359
8: 5 and the wise heart *will* **k** the proper time 3359
8:12 I **k** that it will go better with God-fearing 3359
8:16 When I applied my mind to **k** wisdom and 3359
9: 5 For the living **k** that they will die, 3359
9: 5 but the dead **k** nothing; 3359
10:15 *he does* not **k** the way to town. 3359
11: 2 for *you do* not **k** what disaster may come 3359
11: 5 As you *do* not **k** the path of the wind, 3359
11: 6 for you *do* not **k** which will succeed, 3359
11: 9 and whatever your eyes see, but **k** that 3359
SS 1: 8 If *you do* not **k,** most beautiful of women, 3359
Isa 1: 3 but Israel *does* not **k,** 3359
5:19 so *we may* **k** it." 3359
9: 9 All the people *will* **k** it— 3359
29:12 will answer, *"I* don't **k how to read."** 3359+6219
29:15 "Who sees us? Who *will* **k?"** 3359
32: 4 of the rash *will* **k** and understand, 3359
37:20 all kingdoms on earth *may* **k** that you alone, 3359
37:28 "But *I* **k** where you stay and 3359
40:21 *Do you* not **k?** Have you not heard? 3359
40:28 *Do you* not **k?** Have you not heard? 3359
41:20 so that people may see and **k,** 3359
41:22 and **k** their final outcome. 3359
41:23 so *we may* **k** that you are gods. 3359
41:26 so *we could* **k,** or beforehand, 3359
43:10 so that *you may* **k** and believe me 3359
44: 8 No, there is no other Rock; *I* **k** not one." 3359
44:18 *They* **k** nothing, they understand nothing; 3359
45: 3 so that *you may* **k** that I am the LORD, 3359
45: 6 *men may* **k** there is none besides me. 3359
47:11 and *you will* not **k how** to conjure it away. 3359
48: 8 Well *do I* **k** how treacherous you are; 3359
49:23 Then *you will* **k** that I am the LORD; 3359
49:26 Then all mankind *will* **k** that I, the LORD, 3359
50: 4 to **k** the word that sustains the weary. 3359
50: 7 and *I* **k** I will not be put to shame. 3359

Isa 51: 7 "Hear me, *you who* **k** what is right, 3359
52: 6 Therefore my people *will* **k** my name; 3359
52: 6 therefore in that day they will **k** NIH
55: 5 Surely you will summon nations *you* **k** not, 3359
55: 5 nations *that do* not **k** you will hasten to you, 3359
58: 2 they seem eager to **k** my ways, 1981
59: 8 The way of peace *they do* not **k;** 3359
59: 8 no one who walks in them *will* **k** peace. 3359
60:16 Then *you will* **k** that I, the LORD, 3359
63:16 not **k** us or Israel acknowledge us; 3359
Jer 1: 6 *"I do* not **k how** to speak; I am only a child. 3359
2: 8 Those who deal with the law *did* not **k** me; 3359
4:22 "My people are fools; *they do* not **k** me. 3359
4:22 *they* **k** not **how** to do good." 3359
5: 4 for *they do* not **k** the way of the LORD, 3359
5: 5 surely they **k** the way of the LORD, 3359
5:15 a people whose language *you do* not **k,** 3359
6:15 *they do* not even **k how** to blush. 3359
8: 7 But my people *do* not **k** the requirements of 3359
8:12 *they do* not even **k how** to blush. 3359
10:23 *I* **k,** O LORD, that a man's life is 3359
12: 3 Yet you **k** me, O LORD; 3359
13:12 'Don't *we* **k** that every wineskin 3359+3359
14:18 and priest have gone to a land *they* **k** not.' " 3359
15:14 to your enemies in a land *you do* not **k,** 3359
16:21 Then *they will* **k** that my name is the LORD 3359
17: 4 to your enemies in a land *you do* not **k,** 3359
17:16 you **k** I have not desired the day of despair. 3359
18:23 you **k,** O LORD, all their plots to kill me. 3359
22:16 Is that not what it means to **k** me?" 1981
22:28 cast into a land *they do* not **k?** 3359
24: 7 I will give them a heart to **k** me, 3359
29:11 For I **k** the plans I have for you," 3359
29:23 I **k** it and am a witness to it," 3359
31:34 saying, '**K** the LORD,' 3359
31:34 because they *will* all **k** me, 3359
33: 3 and unsearchable things *you do* not **k.'** 3359
36:19 Don't *let* anyone **k** where you are." 3359
38:24 not *let* anyone **k** about this conversation, 3359
40:14 "Don't *you* **k** that Baalis king of 3359+3359
40:15 and no one *will* **k** it. 3359
44:19 did not our husbands **k** that we were NIH
44:28 in Egypt *will* **k** whose word will stand— 3359
44:29 'so that *you will* **k** that my threats of harm 3359
48:17 all who live around her, all *who* **k** her fame; 3359
48:30 I **k** her insolence but it is futile," 3359
Eze 2: 5 *they will* **k** that a prophet has been 3359
5:13 *they will* **k** that I the LORD have spoken 3359
6: 7 and *you will* **k** that I am the LORD. 3359
6:10 And *they will* **k** that I am the LORD; 3359
6:13 And *they will* **k** that I am the LORD, 3359
6:14 Then *they will* **k** that I am the LORD.' " 3359
7: 4 Then *you will* **k** that I am the LORD. 3359
7: 9 Then *you will* **k** that it is I 3359
7:27 Then *they will* **k** that I am the LORD." 3359
11: 5 but I **k** what is going through your mind. 3359
11:10 Then *you will* **k** that I am the LORD. 3359
11:12 And *you will* **k** that I am the LORD, 3359
12:15 *"They will* **k** that I am the LORD, 3359
12:16 Then *they will* **k** that I am the LORD." 3359
12:20 Then *you will* **k** that I am the LORD.' " 3359
13: 9 *you will* **k** that I am the Sovereign LORD 3359
13:14 and *you will* **k** that I am the LORD. 3359
13:21 Then *you will* **k** that I am the LORD. 3359
13:23 then *you will* **k** that I am the LORD.' " 3359
14: 8 Then *you will* **k** that I am the LORD. 3359
14:23 for *you will* **k** that I have done nothing 3359
15: 7 *you will* **k** that I am the LORD. 3359
16:62 and *you will* **k** that I am the LORD. 3359
17:12 *'Do you* not **k** what these things mean?' 3359
17:21 *you will* **k** that I the LORD have spoken. 3359
17:24 of the field *will* **k** that I the LORD bring 3359
20:12 so they *would* **k** that I the LORD made them 3359
20:20 Then *you will* **k** that I am the LORD. 3359
20:26 so *they would* **k** that I am the LORD.' 3359
20:38 Then *you will* **k** that I am the LORD. 3359
20:42 Then *you will* **k** that I am the LORD, 3359
20:44 *You will* **k** that I am the LORD, 3359
21: 5 Then all people *will* **k** that I the LORD have 3359
22:16 *you will* **k** that I am the LORD.' " 3359
22:22 and *you will* **k** that I the LORD have poured 3359
23:49 *you will* **k** that I am the Sovereign LORD. 3359
24:24 *you will* **k** that I am the Sovereign LORD. 3359
24:27 and *they will* **k** that I am the LORD." 3359
25: 5 Then *you will* **k** that I am the LORD. 3359
25: 7 and *you will* **k** that I am the LORD.' " 3359
25:11 Then *they will* **k** that I am the LORD.' " 3359
25:14 *they will* **k** my vengeance, 3359
25:17 Then *they will* **k** that I am the LORD, 3359
26: 6 Then *they will* **k** that I am the LORD. 3359
28:22 *They will* **k** that I am the LORD, 3359
28:23 Then *they will* **k** that I am the LORD. 3359
28:24 *they will* **k** that I am the Sovereign LORD. 3359
28:26 *they will* **k** that I am the LORD their God. 3359
29: 6 Then all who live in Egypt *will* **k** that I am 3359
29: 9 Then *they will* **k** that I am the LORD. 3359
29:16 *they will* **k** that I am the Sovereign LORD. 3359
29:21 Then *they will* **k** that I am the LORD." 3359
30: 8 Then *they will* **k** that I am the LORD, 3359
30:19 and *they will* **k** that I am the LORD.' " 3359
30:25 Then *they will* **k** that I am the LORD, 3359
30:26 Then *they will* **k** that I am the LORD." 3359
32:15 then *they will* **k** that I am the LORD.' 3359
33:29 Then *they will* **k** that I am the LORD, 3359
33:33 then *they will* **k** that a prophet has been 3359
34:27 *They will* **k** that I am the LORD, 3359
34:30 *they will* **k** that I, the LORD their God, 3359

Eze 35: 4 Then *you will* **k** that I am the LORD. 3359
35: 9 Then *you will* **k** that I am the LORD. 3359
35:12 Then *you will* **k** that I the LORD have heard 3359
35:15 Then *they will* **k** that I am the LORD.' " 3359
36:11 Then *you will* **k** that I am the LORD. 3359
36:23 the nations *will* **k** that I am the LORD, 3359
36:32 *to* **k** that I am not doing this for your sake, 3359
36:36 the nations around you that remain *will* **k** 3359
36:38 Then *they will* **k** that I am the LORD." 3359
37: 3 I said, "O Sovereign LORD, you alone **k."** 3359
37: 6 Then *you will* **k** that I am the LORD.' " 3359
37:13 my people, *will* **k** that I am the LORD, 3359
37:14 *you will* **k** that I the LORD have spoken, 3359
37:28 the nations *will* **k** that I the LORD made 3359
38:16 so that the nations *may* **k** me 3359
38:23 Then *they will* **k** that I am the LORD.' 3359
39: 6 and *they will* **k** that I am the LORD. 3359
39: 7 and the nations *will* **k** that I the LORD am 3359
39:22 that day forward the house of Israel *will* **k** 3359
39:23 And the nations *will* **k** that the people 3359
39:28 *they will* **k** that I am the LORD their God, 3359
Da 2: 3 and I want to **k what it means."** 3359
2: 9 *I will* **k** that you can interpret it for me." 10313
2:30 *may* **k** the interpretation and that you 10313
3:18 But even if he does not, we *want* you *to* **k,** 10313
4: 9 I **k** that the spirit of the holy gods is in you, 10313
4:17 so that the living *may* **k** that the Most High 10313
7:19 to **k the true meaning** of the fourth beast, 10326
7:20 to **k** about the ten horns on its head and NIH
9:25 "**K** and understand this: From the issuing 3359
10:20 said, *"Do you* **k** why I have come to you? 3359
11:32 but people *who* **k** their God will firmly resist him. 3359
Hos 5: 3 I **k all about** Ephraim; Israel is not hidden 3359
9: 7 *Let* Israel **k** this. Because your sins are so 3359
Joel 2:27 Then *you will* **k** that I am in Israel, 3359
3:17 "Then *you will* **k** that I, the LORD your God, 3359
Am 3:10 *"They do* not **k how** to do right," 3359
5:12 For *I* **k** how many are your offenses and 3359
Jnh 1:12 I **k** that it is my fault that this great storm 3359
Mic 3: 1 *Should* you not **k** justice, 3359
4:12 they *do* not **k** the thoughts of the LORD; 3359
6: 5 that *you may* **k** the righteous acts of 3359
Zep 3: 5 yet the unrighteous **k** no shame. 3359
Zec 2: 9 Then *you will* **k** that the LORD Almighty 3359
2:11 I will live among you and *you will* **k** that 3359
4: 5 *"Do you* not **k** what these are?" 3359
4: 9 Then *you will* **k** that the LORD Almighty 3359
4:13 He replied, *"Do you* not **k** what these are?" 3359
6:15 and *you will* **k** that the LORD Almighty 3359
Mal 2: 4 And *you will* **k** that I have sent you this 3359
Mt 6: 3 not *let* your left hand **k** what your right hand is doing, *1182*
7:11 **k** how to give good gifts to your children, *3857*
9: 6 But so that *you may* **k** that the Son of Man *3857*
15:12 *"Do you* **k** that the Pharisees were offended *3857*
16: 3 *You* **k how** to interpret the appearance of *1182*
20:22 *"You* don't **k** what you are asking," *3857*
20:25 *"You* **k** that the rulers of the Gentiles lord it *3857*
21:27 So they answered Jesus, *"We* don't **k."** *3857*
22:16 *"we* **k** you are a man of integrity and *3857*
22:29 not **k** the Scriptures or the power of God. *3857*
24:32 *you* **k** that summer is near. *1182*
24:33 you see all these things, you **k** that it is near, *1182*
24:42 not **k** on what day your Lord will come. *3857*
25:12 'I tell you the truth, *I* don't **k** you.' *3857*
25:13 because *you do* not **k** the day or the hour. *3857*
26: 2 *you* **k,** the Passover is two days away— *3857*
26:70 *"I* don't **k** what you're talking about," *3857*
26:72 *"I* don't **k** the man!" *3857*
26:74 *"I* don't **k** the man!" *3857*
27:65 make the tomb as secure as *you* **k** how." *3857*
28: 5 for *I* **k** that you are looking for Jesus, *3857*
Mk 1:24 *I* **k** who you are—the Holy One of God!" *3857*
2:10 But that *you may* **k** that the Son of Man *3857*
4:27 though he *does* not **k** how. *3857*
5:43 not to let anyone **k about** this, *1182*
7:24 a house and did not want anyone *to* **k** it; *1182*
9: 6 (*He did* not **k** what to say, *3857*
9:30 not want anyone *to* **k** where they were, *1182*
10:19 *You* **k** the commandments: *3857*
10:38 *"You* don't **k** what you are asking," *3857*
10:42 *"You* **k** that those who are regarded as rulers *3857*
11:33 So they answered Jesus, *"We* don't **k."** *3857*
12:14 "Teacher, *we* **k** you are a man of integrity. *3857*
12:24 in error because *you do* not **k** the Scriptures *3857*
13:28 *you* **k** that summer is near. *1182*
13:29 *you* **k** that it is near, right at the door. *1182*
13:33 *You do* not **k** when that time will come. *3857*
13:35 because *you do* not **k** when the owner of *3857*
14:40 *They did* not **k** what to say to him. *3857*
14:68 *"I* don't **k** or understand what you're talking *3857*
14:71 *"I* don't **k** this man you're talking about." *3857*
Lk 1: 4 so that *you may* **k** the certainty of the things *2105*
2:49 "Didn't *you* **k** I had to be in my Father's *3857*
4:34 *I* **k** who you are—the Holy One of God!" *3857*
5:24 But that *you may* **k** that the Son of Man *3857*
7:39 *he* would **k** who is touching him *1182*
8:46 I **k that** power has gone out from me." *1182*
9:33 (*He did* not **k** what he was saying.) *3857*
11:13 **k** how to give good gifts to your children, *3857*
12:48 But the one who *does* not **k** *1182*
12:56 *You* **k** how to interpret the appearance of *3857*
12:56 How is it that *you* don't **k** how *3857*
13:25 *'I* don't **k** you or where you come from.' *3857*
13:27 *'I* don't **k** you or where you come from. *3857*
16: 4 *I* **k** what I'll do so that, when I lose my job *1182*

Lk 18:20 *You* **k** the commandments: *3857*
18:34 *they did* not **k** what he was talking about. *1182*
20: 7 *"We* don't **k** where it was from." *3857*
20:21 *we* **k** that you speak and teach what is right, *3857*
21:20 *you will* **k** that its desolation is near. *1182*
21:30 for yourselves and **k** that summer is near. *1182*
21:31 *you* **k** that the kingdom of God is near. *1182*
22:34 you will deny three times that *you* **k** me." *3857*
22:57 "Woman, *I* don't **k** him," he said. *3857*
22:60 *I* don't **k** what you're talking about!" *3857*
23:34 for *they do* not **k** what they are doing." *3857*
24:18 visitor to Jerusalem and *do* not **k** the things *1182*
Jn 1:26 "but among you stands one you *do* not **k.** *3857*
1:31 I myself *did* not **k** him, *3857*
1:48 "How *do you* **k** me?" *1182*
3: 2 *we* **k** you are a teacher who has come *3857*
3:11 I tell you the truth, we speak of what *we* **k,** *3857*
4:22 You Samaritans worship what *you do* not **k;** *3857*
4:22 we worship what *we do* **k,** *3857*
4:25 The woman said, *"I* **k** that the Messiah" *3857*
4:32 to eat that you **k** nothing about." *3857*
4:42 and *we* **k** that this man really is the Savior *3857*
5:32 *I* **k** that his testimony about me is valid. *3857*
5:42 but *I* **k** you. I know that you do not have *1182*
5:42 I **k** that you do not have the love of God *NIG*
6:42 whose father and mother we **k?** *3857*
6:69 We believe and **k** that you are the Holy One *1182*
7:27 But *we* **k** where this man is from; *3857*
7:27 no one *will* **k** where he is from." *1182*
7:28 *you* **k** me, and you know where I am from. *3857*
7:28 you know me, and *you* **k** where I am from. *3857*
7:28 You *do* not **k** him, *3857*
7:29 but I **k** him because I am from him *3857*
8:14 for *I* **k** where I came from and *3857*
8:19 *"You do* not **k** me or my Father," *3857*
8:19 *you* would **k** my Father also." *3857*
8:28 then *you will* **k** that I am [the one I claim *1182*
8:32 Then *you will* **k** the truth, *1182*
8:37 *I* **k** you are Abraham's descendants. *3857*
8:52 "Now *we* **k** that you are demon-possessed! *1182*
8:55 Though *you do* not **k** him, I know him. *1182*
8:55 Though you do not know him, I **k** him. *3857*
8:55 but *I do* **k** him and keep his word. *3857*
9:12 *"I* don't **k,"** he said. *3857*
9:20 *"We* **k** he is our son," the parents answered, *3857*
9:20 "and we **k** he was born blind. *NIG*
9:21 or who opened his eyes, we don't **k.** *3857*
9:24 "We **k** this man is a sinner." *3857*
9:25 "Whether he is a sinner or not, *I* don't **k.** *3857*
9:25 One thing *I do* **k.** I was blind but now I see! *3857*
9:29 We **k** that God spoke to Moses, *3857*
9:29 we don't even **k** where he comes from." *3857*
9:30 You don't **k** where he comes from, *3857*
9:31 *We* **k** that God does not listen to sinners. *3857*
10: 4 because *they* **k** his voice. *3857*
10:14 *I* **k** my sheep and my sheep know me— *1182*
10:14 I know my sheep and my sheep **k** me— *1182*
10:15 as the Father knows me and I **k** the Father— *1182*
10:27 I **k** them, and they follow me. *1182*
10:38 that *you may* **k** and understand that *1182*
11:22 But *I* **k** that even now God will give you *3857*
11:24 *"I* **k** he will rise again in the resurrection at *3857*
11:49 spoke up, "You **k** nothing at all! *3857*
12:35 The man who walks in the dark *does* not **k** *3857*
12:50 *I* **k** that his command leads to eternal life. *3857*
13:17 Now that *you* **k** these things, *3857*
13:18 I **k** those I have chosen. *3857*
13:22 at a loss to **k** which of them he meant. *NIG*
13:35 By this all men *will* **k** that you are my disciples, if you love one another." *1182*
14: 4 *You* **k** the way to the place *3857*
14: 5 "Lord, *we* don't **k** where you are going, *3857*
14: 5 so how can *we* **k** the way?" *3857*
14: 7 *you would* **k** my Father as well. *1182*
14: 7 *you do* **k** him and have seen him." *1182*
14: 9 Jesus answered: "Don't *you* **k** me, Philip, *1182*
14:17 But you **k** him, for he lives with you *1182*
15:15 a servant *does* not **k** his master's business. *3857*
15:21 for *they do* not **k** the One who sent me. *3857*
16:30 Now we can see that *you* **k** all things and *3857*
17: 3 Now this is eternal life: that *they may* **k** you, *1182*
17: 7 Now *they* **k** that everything you have given me comes from you. *1182*
17:23 to let the world **k** that you sent me *1182*
17:25 though the world *does* not **k** you, *1182*
17:25 not know you, I **k** you, and they know *1182*
17:25 and they **k** that you have sent me. *1182*
18:21 Surely they **k** what I said." *3857*
19: 4 to let *you* **k** that I find no basis for a charge *1182*
20: 2 and *we* don't **k** where they have put him!" *3857*
20:13 "and *I* don't **k** where they have put him." *3857*
21:15 Lord," he said, "you **k** that I love you." *3857*
21:16 "Yes, Lord, you **k** that I love you." *3857*
21:17 He said, "Lord, you **k** all things; *3857*
21:17 you **k** that I love you." *1182*
21:24 *We* **k** that his testimony is true. *3857*
Ac 1: 7 *to* **k** the times or dates the Father has set *1182*
1:24 they prayed, "Lord, you **k** everyone's **heart.** *2841*
2:22 through him, as *you* yourselves **k.** *3857*
3:16 man whom you see and **k** was made strong. *3857*
3:17 brothers, *I* **k** that you acted in ignorance, *3857*
4:10 **k** *this*, you and all the people of Israel: *1196+1639*
7:40 *we* don't **k** what has happened to him!' *3857*
10:36 You **k** the message God sent to the people *NIG*
10:37 You **k** what has happened throughout Judea, *3857*
12:11 "Now *I* **k** without a doubt that *3857*
13:38 to **k** that through Jesus the forgiveness *1196*
15: 7 you **k** that some time ago God made *2179*
17:19 "May we **k** what this new teaching is *1182*
17:20 and we want *to* **k** what they mean." *1182*
19:15 "Jesus *I* **k,** and I know about Paul, *1182*
19:15 and *I* **k about** Paul, but who are you?" *2179*
19:25 "Men, *you* **k** we receive a good income *2179*
19:32 not even **k** why they were there. *3857*
19:35 of Ephesus, doesn't all the world **k that** *1182*
20:18 "You **k** how I lived the whole time I was *2179*
20:20 You **k** that I have not hesitated *NIG*
20:23 I only **k** that in every city the Holy Spirit *NIG*
20:25 "Now I **k** that none of you *3857*
20:29 I **k** that after I leave, savage wolves will *3857*
20:34 *You* yourselves **k** that these hands *1182*
21:24 Then everybody *will* **k** there is no truth *1182*
22:14 of our fathers has chosen you *to* **k** his will *1182*
22:19 'these men **k** that I went from one *2179*
23:28 I wanted *to* **k** why they were accusing him, *2105*
24:10 *"I* **k that** for a number of years *2179*
25:10 as *you* yourself **k** very well. *2105*
26: 4 "The Jews all **k** the way I have lived ever *3857*
26:27 do you believe the prophets? *I* **k** you do." *3857*
28:22 **k** that people everywhere are talking *1196+1639*
28:28 *to* **k** that God's salvation has been sent *1196+1639*
Ro 1:32 *Although* they **k** God's righteous decree *2105*
2: 2 Now *we* **k** that God's judgment against *3857*
2:18 if *you* **k** his will and approve of what *1182*
3:17 and the way of peace *they do* not **k."** *1182*
3:19 Now *we* **k** that whatever the law says, *3857*
5: 3 *we* **k** that suffering produces perseverance; *3857*
6: 3 Or **don't** *you* **k** that all of us who *51*
6: 6 For *we* **k** that our old self was crucified *1182*
6: 9 *For we* **k** that since Christ was raised from *3857*
6:16 Don't *you* **k** that when you offer yourselves *3857*
7: 1 *Do you* **not k,** brothers— *51*
7: 1 for I am speaking *to men who* **k** the law— *1182*
7:14 *We* **k** that the law is spiritual; *3857*
7:18 *I* **k** that nothing good lives in me, that is, *3857*
8:22 *We* **k** that the whole creation has been groaning as in the pains of childbirth *3857*
8:26 *We do* not **k** what we ought to pray for, *3857*
8:28 And *we* **k** that in all things God works for *3857*
10: 3 *Since they did* **not k** the righteousness *51*
11: 2 Don't *you* **k** what the Scripture says in *3857*
15:29 *I* **k** that when I come to you, *3857*
1Co 1:21 the world through its wisdom *did* not **k** him, *1182*
2: 2 For I resolved *to* **k** nothing while I was *3857*
3:16 Don't *you* **k** that you yourselves are God's temple *3857*
5: 6 Don't *you* **k** that a little yeast works *3857*
6: 2 not **k** that the saints will judge the world? *3857*
6: 3 *Do you* not **k** that we will judge angels? *3857*
6: 9 not **k** that the wicked will not inherit *3857*
6:15 *Do you* not **k** that your bodies are members *3857*
6:16 *Do you* not **k** that he who unites himself *3857*
6:19 *Do you* not **k** that your body is a temple of *3857*
7:16 How *do you* **k,** wife, whether you will save *3857*
7:16 Or, how *do you* **k,** husband, whether you *3857*
8: 1 *We* **k** that we all possess knowledge. *3857*
8: 2 not yet **k** as he ought to know. *1182*
8: 2 not yet know as he ought *to* **k.** *1182*
8: 4 *We* **k** that an idol is nothing at all in *3857*
9:13 Don't *you* **k** that those who work in *3857*
9:24 not **k** that in a race all the runners run, *3857*
12: 2 *You* **k** that when you were pagans, *3857*
13: 9 For *we* **k** in part and we prophesy in part, *1182*
13:12 Now *I* **k** in part; than I shall know fully *1182*
13:12 then *I shall* **k fully,** even as I am fully *2105*
14: 7 *will* anyone **k** what tune is being played *1182*
14: 9 how *will* anyone **k** what you are saying? *1182*
14:16 since *he does* not **k** what you are saying? *3857*
15:58 *because you* **k** that your labor in *3857*
16:15 *You* **k** that the household of Stephanas were *3857*
2Co 1: 7 *we* **k** that just as you share in our sufferings, *3857*
2: 4 not to grieve you but to let *you* **k** the depth *1182*
4:14 *because we* **k** that the one who raised *3857*
5: 1 Now *we* **k** that if the earthly tent we live *3857*
5: 6 Therefore *we* are always confident and **k** *3857*
5:11 then, *we* **k** what it is to fear the Lord, *3857*
8: 1 *to* **k about** the grace that God has given *1192*
8: 9 *you* **k** the grace of our Lord Jesus Christ, *1182*
9: 2 For *I* **k** your eagerness to help, *3857*
12: 2 *I* **k** a man in Christ who *3857*
12: 2 in the body or out of the body *I do* not **k—** *3857*
12: 3 And *I* **k** that this man— *3857*
12: 3 from the body *I do* not **k,** but God knows— *3857*
Gal 1:11 *I want* you *to* **k,** brothers, that the gospel *1192*
2:16 **k** that a man is not justified by observing *3857*
4: 8 Formerly, *when you did* not **k** God, *3857*
4: 9 But now *that you* **k** God— *1182*
4:13 As *you* **k,** it was because of an illness *3857*
Eph 1:17 so that you may **k** him **better.** *2106*
1:18 be enlightened in order that you *may* **k** *3857*
3:19 *to* **k** this love that surpasses knowledge— *1182*
4:20 however, *did* not *come to* **k** Christ that way. *3443*
6: 8 *because* you **k** that the Lord will reward *3857*
6: 9 *since you* **k** that he who is both their Master *3857*
6:21 also *may* **k** how I am and what I am doing. *3857*
6:22 that *you may* **k** how we are, *1182*
Php 1:12 Now I want you *to* **k,** brothers, *1182*
1:19 for *I* **k** that through your prayers and *3857*
1:22 Yet what shall I choose? *I do* not **k!** *1192*
1:25 Convinced of this, *I* **k** that I will remain, *3857*
1:27 I will **k** that you stand firm in one spirit, *NIG*
2:22 But *you* **k** that Timothy has proved himself, *1182*
3:10 I *want to* **k** Christ and the power *1182*
4:12 *I* **k** what it is to be in need, *3857*
Php 4:12 and *I* **k** what it is to have plenty. *3857*
4:15 Moreover, as you Philippians **k,** *3857*
Col 2: 1 *to* **k** how much I am struggling for you and *3857*
2: 2 in order that they may **k** the mystery *2106*
3:24 *since you* **k** that you will receive *3857*
4: 1 *because you* **k** that you also have a Master *3857*
4: 6 *so that* you *may* **k** how to answer everyone. *3857*
4: 8 that *you may* **k** about our circumstances and *1182*
1Th 1: 4 *For we* **k,** brothers loved by God, *3857*
1: 5 *You* **k** how we lived among you *3857*
2: 1 You **k,** brothers, that our visit to you was *3857*
2: 2 and been insulted in Philippi, as *you* **k,** but *3857*
2: 5 *You* **k** we never used flattery, *3857*
2:11 For *you* **k** that we dealt with each of you as *3857*
3: 3 You **k** quite well that we were destined *3857*
3: 4 And it turned out that way, as *you* well **k.** *3857*
4: 2 For *you* **k** what instructions we gave you by *3857*
4: 5 who *do* not **k** God; *3857*
5: 2 for you **k** very well that the day of the Lord *3857*
2Th 1: 8 He will punish those who *do* not **k** God *3857*
2: 6 And now *you* **k** what is holding him back, *3857*
3: 7 For *you* yourselves **k** how you ought *3857*
1Ti 1: 7 but *they do* not **k** what they are talking *3783*
1: 8 *We* **k** that the law is good if one uses *3857*
1: 9 also **k** that law is made not for the righteous *3857*
3: 5 not **k** how to manage his own family, *3857*
3:15 *you will* **k** how people ought to conduct *3857*
4: 3 *by* those who believe and who **k** the truth. *2105*
2Ti 1:12 because *I* **k** whom I have believed, *3857*
1:15 *You* **k** that everyone in the province *3857*
1:18 You **k** very well in how many ways *1182*
2:23 *because you* **k** they produce quarrels. *3857*
3:10 You, however, **k all about** my teaching, *4158*
3:14 *you* **k** those from whom you learned it, *3857*
Tit 1:16 They claim *to* **k** God, but by their actions *3857*
Heb 8:11 or a man his brother, saying, **'K** the Lord,' *1182*
8:11 because *they will* all **k** me, from the least *3857*
10:30 *we* **k** him who said, "It is mine to avenge; *3857*
11: 8 *though he did* not **k** where he was going. *2179*
12:17 as *you* **k,** when he wanted to inherit *3857*
13:23 I *want you to* **k** that our brother Timothy *1182*
Jas 1: 3 *because you* **k** that the testing of your faith *1182*
3: 1 *because you* **k** that we who teach will *3857*
4: 4 don't *you* **k** that friendship with the world *3857*
4:14 not even **k** what will happen tomorrow. *2179*
5:11 **As** *you* **k,** we consider blessed those who have persevered. *2627*
1Pe 1:18 *For you* **k** that it was not with perishable *3857*
5: 9 *because you* **k** that your brothers *3857*
2Pe 1:12 even though *you* **k** them *3857*
1:14 *because I* **k** that I will soon put it aside, *3857*
3:17 dear friends, *since* you **already k** this, *4589*
1Jn 2: 3 *We* **k** that we have come to know him *1182*
2: 3 We know that *we have come to* **k** him *1182*
2: 4 The man who says, *"I* **k** him," *1182*
2: 5 This is how *we* **k** we are in him: *1182*
2:11 *he does* not **k** where he is going, *3857*
2:18 This is how *we* **k** it is the last hour. *1182*
2:20 and all of *you* **k** the truth. *3857*
2:21 I do not write to you because *you do* not **k** *3857*
2:21 but because *you do* **k** it and *3857*
2:29 If *you* **k** that he is righteous, *3857*
2:29 If you know that he is righteous, *you* **k** *1182*
3: 1 The reason the world *does* not **k** us is *1182*
3: 1 not know us is that *it did* not **k** him. *1182*
3: 2 But *we* **k** that when he appears, *3857*
3: 5 But *you* **k** that he appeared so *3857*
3:10 how we **k** who the children of God are *1639+5745*
3:14 We **k** that we have passed from death *3857*
3:15 and *you* **k** that no murderer has eternal life *3857*
3:16 This is how *we* **k** what love is: *1182*
3:19 then is how *we* **k** that we belong to the truth, *1182*
3:24 And this is how *we* **k** that he lives in us: *1182*
3:24 We **k** it by the Spirit he gave us. *NIG*
4: 8 Whoever does not love *does* not **k** God, *1182*
4:13 *We* **k** that we live in him and he in us, *1182*
4:16 so we **k** and rely on the love God has for us. *1182*
5: 2 how *we* **k** that we love the children of God: *1182*
5:13 so that *you may* **k** that you have eternal life. *3857*
5:15 And if *we* **k** that he hears us— *3857*
5:15 *we* **k** that we have what we asked of him. *3857*
5:18 *We* **k** that anyone born of God does not *3857*
5:19 *We* **k** that we are children of God, *3857*
5:20 *We* **k** also that the Son of God has come *3857*
5:20 so that *we may* **k** him who is true. *1182*
2Jn 1: 1 not I only, but also all who **k** the truth— *1182*
3Jn 1:12 and *you* **k** that our testimony is true. *3857*
Jude 1: 5 **Though** you already **k** all this, *3857*
Rev 2: 2 *I* **k** your deeds, your hard work and *3857*
2: 2 I **k** that you cannot tolerate wicked men, *NIG*
2: 9 *I* **k** your afflictions and your poverty— *3857*
2: 9 *I* **k** the slander of those who say they are *NIG*
2:13 *I* **k** where you live—where Satan has his *3857*
2:19 *I* **k** your deeds, your love and faith, *3857*
2:23 Then all the churches *will* **k** that I am he *1182*
3: 1 *I* **k** your deeds; you have a reputation *3857*
3: 3 not **k** at what time I will come to you. *1182*
3: 8 *I* **k** your deeds. See, I have placed before *3857*
3: 8 I **k** that you have little strength, *NIG*
3:15 *I* **k** your deeds, that you are neither cold *3857*
7:14 I answered, "Sir, you **k."** *3857*

KNOWING (28) [KNOW]

Ge 3: 5 and you will be like God, **k** good and evil." 3359
3:22 has become like one of us, **k** good and evil. 3359
2Sa 15:11 **k** nothing **about** the matter. 3359

1Ki 1:11 without our lord David's k it? 3359
Job 9: 5 He moves mountains without *their* k it 3359
31:21 k that I had influence in court, 8011
Ps 39: 6 he heaps up wealth, not k who will get it. 3359
Pr 7:23 little k it will cost him his life. 3359
Ecc 6: 8 poor man gain *by* k how to conduct himself 3359
Mt 9: 4 K their thoughts, Jesus said, *3857*
22:18 But Jesus, k their evil intent, said, *1182*
Mk 5:33 the woman, k what had happened to her, *3857*
6:20 k him to be a righteous and holy man. *3857*
15:10 k it was out of envy that the chief priests *1182*
Lk 8:53 They laughed at him, k that she was dead. *3857*
9:47 Jesus, k their thoughts, *3857*
11:44 which men walk over without k it." *3857*
Jn 6:15 k that they intended to come *1182*
18: 4 Jesus, k all that was going to happen to him, *3857*
19:28 Later, k that all was now completed, *3857*
Ac 5: 7 not k what had happened. *3857*
20:22 not k what will happen to me there. *3857*
23: 6 k that some of them were Sadducees and *1182*
Php 1:16 k that I am put here for the defense of *3857*
3: 8 *of* k Christ Jesus my Lord, *1194*
Phm 1:21 k that you will do even more than I ask. *3857*
Heb 13: 2 people have entertained angels **without** k it. *3291*
2Pe 2:20 the corruption of the world by k our Lord *2106*

KNOWLEDGE (132) [KNOW]

Ge 2: 9 the tree of life and the tree of the k *of* good 1981
2:17 but you must not eat from the tree of the k 1981
Ex 31: 3 ability and k in all kinds of crafts— 1981
35:31 ability and k in all kinds of crafts— 1981
Nu 24:16 *who* **has** k *from* the Most High, 1981+3359
1Ki 2:32 because without the k of my father David 3359
2Ch 1:10 Give me wisdom and k, 4529
1:11 but for wisdom and k to govern my people 4529
1:12 therefore wisdom and k will be given you. 4529
Job 21:22 "Can anyone teach k to God, 1981
34:35 'Job speaks without k; 1981
35:16 without k he multiplies words." 1981
36: 3 I get my k from afar; 1976
36: 4 one perfect in k is with you. 1978
36:12 by the sword and die without k. 1981
37:16 those wonders of him who is perfect in k? 1976
38: 2 darkens my counsel with words without k? 1981
42: 3 that obscures my counsel without k?' 1981
Ps 19: 2 night after night they display k. 1981
73:11 Does the Most High have k?" 1978
94:10 Does he who teaches man lack k? 1981
119:66 Teach me k and good judgment, 1981
139: 6 *Such* k is too wonderful for me, 1981
Pr 1: 4 k and discretion to the young— 1981
1: 7 fear of the LORD is the beginning of k, 1981
1:22 in mockery and fools hate k? 1981
1:29 Since they hated k and did not choose 1981
2: 5 fear of the LORD and find the k *of* God. 1981
2: 6 from his mouth come k and understanding. 1981
2:10 and k will be pleasant to your soul. 1981
3:20 by his k the deeps were divided, 1981
5: 2 and your lips may preserve k. 1981
8: 9 they are faultless to those who have k. 1981
8:10 k rather than choice gold, 1981
8:12 I possess k and discretion. 1981
9:10 and k *of* the Holy One is understanding. 1981
9:13 she is undisciplined and without k. 3359
10:14 Wise men store up k, 1981
11: 9 but through k the righteous escape. 1981
12: 1 Whoever loves discipline loves k, 1981
12:23 A prudent man keeps his k to himself, 1981
13:16 Every prudent man acts out of k, 1981
14: 6 but k comes easily to the discerning. 1981
14: 7 for you will not find k on his lips. 1981
14:18 but the prudent are crowned with k. 1981
15: 2 The tongue of the wise commends k, 1981
15: 7 The lips of the wise spread k; 1981
15:14 The discerning heart seeks k, 1981
17:27 A **man of** k uses words with restraint, 1981+3359
18:15 The heart of the discerning acquires k; 1981
19: 2 It is not good to have zeal without k, 1981
19:25 rebuke a discerning man, and he will gain k. 1981
19:27 and you will stray from the words of k. 1981
20:15 but lips that speak k are a rare jewel. 1981
21:11 when a wise man is instructed, he gets k. 1981
22:12 The eyes of the LORD keep watch over k, 1981
22:20 sayings of counsel and k, 1981
23:12 to instruction and your ears to words of k. 1981
24: 4 through k its rooms are filled with rare 1981
24: 5 and a man of k increases strength; 1981
28: 2 of understanding and k maintains order. 3359
30: 3 nor **have** *I* k *of* the Holy One. 1981+3359
Ecc 1:16 I have experienced much of wisdom and k." 1981
1:18 the more k, the more grief. 1981
2:21 For a man may do his work with wisdom, k 1981
2:26 God gives wisdom, k and happiness, 1981
7:12 but the advantage of k is this: 1981
9:10 there is neither working nor planning nor k 1981
12: 9 but also he imparted k *to* the people. 1981
Isa 11: 2 Spirit of k and of the fear of the LORD— 1981
11: 9 the earth will be full of the k *of* the LORD 1978
33: 6 a rich store of salvation and wisdom and k; 1981
40:14 that taught him k or showed him the path 1981
44:19 no one has the k or understanding to say, 1981
47:10 and k mislead you when you say 1981
53:11 by his k my righteous servant will justify many, 1981
56:10 Israel's watchmen are blind, they all lack k; 3359
Jer 3:15 with k and understanding. 1978
10:14 Everyone is senseless and without k; 1981
51:17 "Every man is senseless and without k; 1981
Da 1:17 To these four young men God gave k 4529
2:21 He gives wisdom to the wise and k to 10430
5:12 a keen mind and k and understanding, 10430
12: 4 Many will go here and there to increase k." 1981
Hos 4: 6 my people are destroyed from lack of k. 1981
4: 6 "Because you have rejected k, 1981
Hab 2:14 For the earth will be filled with the k *of* 3359
Mal 2: 7 "For the lips of a priest ought to preserve k, 1981
Mt 13:11 "The k of the secrets of the kingdom *1182*
Lk 1:77 to give his people the k of salvation through *1194*
8:10 "The k of the secrets of the kingdom *1182*
11:52 because you have taken away the key *to* k. *1194*
Ac 5: 2 *With* his wife's **full** k he kept back part *5323*
18:24 with a thorough k of the Scriptures. *NIG*
Ro 1:28 not think it worthwhile to retain the k of *2106*
2:20 in the law the embodiment *of* k and truth— *1194*
10: 2 but their zeal is not based on k. *2106*
11:33 the depth of the riches of the wisdom and k *1194*
15:14 *in* k and competent to instruct one another. *1194*
1Co 1: 5 in all your speaking and in all your k— *1194*
8: 1 We know that we all possess k. *1194*
8: 1 K puffs up, but love builds up. *1194*
8:10 weak conscience sees you who have this k eating in an idol's temple, *1194*
8:11 is destroyed by your k. *1194*
12: 8 to another the message *of* k by means of *1194*
13: 2 and can fathom all mysteries and all k, *1194*
13: 8 where there is k, it will pass away. *1194*
14: 6 or k or prophecy or word of instruction? *1194*
2Co 2:14 the fragrance *of* the k of him. *1194*
4: 6 in our hearts to give us the light *of* the k of *1194*
8: 7 in faith, in speech, *in* k, *1194*
10: 5 that sets itself up against the k of God, *1194*
11: 6 not be a trained speaker, but I do have k. *1194*
Eph 3:19 and to know this love that surpasses k— *1194*
4:13 the k of the Son of God and become mature, *2106*
Php 1: 9 and more in k and depth of insight, *2106*
Col 1: 9 and asking God to fill you with the k *2106*
1:10 growing *in* the k of God, *2106*
2: 3 the treasures *of* wisdom and k. *1194*
3:10 which is being renewed in k in the image *2106*
1Ti 2: 4 to be saved and to come to a k of the truth. *2106*
6:20 *of* what is falsely called k, *1194*
2Ti 2:25 repentance leading to a k of the truth, *2106*
Tit 1: 1 the k of the truth that leads to godliness— *2106*
1: 2 and k resting on the hope of eternal life, *NIG*
Heb 10:26 on sinning after we have received the k of *2106*
2Pe 1: 2 be yours in abundance through the k of God *2106*
1: 3 for life and godliness through our k *2106*
1: 5 and to goodness, k; *1194*
1: 6 and to k, self-control; *1194*
1: 8 in your k of our Lord Jesus Christ. *2106*
3:18 and k of our Lord and Savior Jesus Christ. *1194*

KNOWN (147) [KNOW]

Ge 41:39 "Since God *has* **made** all this k *to* you, 3359
45: 1 when he **made himself** k to his brothers. 3359
Ex 2:14 "What I did *must have* **become** k." 3359
6: 3 the LORD *I did* not **make myself** k to them. 3359
21:36 if *it* **was** k that the bull had the habit 3359
Nu 11:16 of Israel's elders who *are* k *to you* 3359
Dt 3:13 of Argob in Bashan *used to* **be** k **as** a land 7924
8: 3 which neither *you* nor your fathers *had* k, 3359
8:16 something your fathers *had* never k, 3359
9:24 against the LORD ever since I *have* k you. 3359
11:28 other gods, which *you have* not k. 3359
13: 2 not k) "and let us worship them," 3359
13: 6 that neither you nor your fathers *have* k, 3359
13:13 worship other gods" (gods *you have* not k), 3359
21: 1 and *it* **is** not k who killed him, 3359
25:10 man's line *shall* **be** k in Israel **as** 7924+9005
28:64 which neither you nor your fathers *have* k. 3359
32:17 gods *they had* not k, 3359
Ru 3:14 "Don't *let it* **be** k that a woman came to 3359
1Sa 10:11 When all *those who had* formerly k him saw him prophesying 3359
18:23 I'm only a poor man and **little** k." 7829
18:30 and his name *became* **well** k. 3700+4394
2Sa 7:21 have done this great thing and **made** it k 3359
1Ki 18:36 *let it* **be** k today that you are God in Israel 3359
1Ch 16: 8 **make** k among the nations what he has done. 3359
17:19 and **made** k all these great promises. 3359
Ne 8:12 the words that *had been* **made** k to them. 3359
9:14 *You* **made** k to them your holy Sabbath 3359
Est 1:17 the queen's conduct *will* **become** k to all 3655
2: 7 This girl, who was also k as Esther, NIH
3:14 **made** k to the people of every nationality 1655
8:13 **made** k to the people of every nationality 1655
Job 36:33 even the cattle make k its approach. NIH
42:11 and everyone *who had* k him before came 3359
Ps 9:16 The LORD **is** k *by* his justice; 3359
16:11 *You have* **made** k *to* me the path of life; 3359
25:14 he **makes** his covenant k *to* them. 3359
37:18 days of the blameless *are* k *to* the LORD, 3359
59:13 *be* k to the ends of the earth that God rules 3359
67: 2 that your ways *may be* k on earth, 3359
76: 1 In Judah God **is** k; 3359
78: 3 what we have heard and k, 3359
79:10 **make** k among the nations that you avenge 3359
88:12 **Are** your wonders k in the place 3359
89: 1 **make** your faithfulness k 3359
95:10 and they *have* not k my ways." 3359
98: 2 The LORD *has* **made** his salvation k 3359
Ps 103: 7 *He* **made** k his ways to Moses, 3359
105: 1 **make** k among the nations what he has done. 3359
106: 8 **make** his mighty power k. 3359
119:168 for all my ways are k to you. 5584
Pr 1:23 to you and **made** my thoughts k *to* you. 3359
14:33 even among fools *she* **lets** *herself* **be** k. 3359
20:11 Even a child **is** k by his actions, 5795
24: 8 He who plots evil *will be* k **as** a schemer. 7924
Ecc 6:10 and what man is *has* **been** k; 3359
Isa 12: 4 **make** k among the nations what he has done, 3359
12: 5 *let* this **be** k to all the world. 3359
19:12 Let them show you and **make** k what 3359
19:21 So the LORD *will* **make himself** k to 3359
42:16 the blind by ways *they have* not k, 3359
46:10 I **make** k the end from the beginning, 5583
48: 3 and *I* **made** them k; 9048
61: 9 Their descendants *will* **be** k among 3359
64: 2 down to **make** your name k to your enemies 3359
66:14 the LORD *will* **be made** k *to* his servants, 3359
Jer 7: 9 and follow other gods *you have* not k, 3359
9:16 that neither they nor their fathers *have* k, 3359
16:13 a land neither you nor your fathers *have* k, 3359
Eze 20:11 I gave them my decrees and **made** k 3359
32: 9 among lands *you have* not k. 3359
35:11 and *I will* **make myself** k among them 3359
38:23 and *I will* **make myself** k in the sight 3359
39: 7 " *'I will* **make** k my holy name 3359
43:11 **make** k *to* them the design of the temple— 3359
Da 2:23 *you have* **made** k *to* me what we asked 10313
2:23 of you, *you have* **made** k *to* us the dream of 10313
Hab 3: 2 in our time **make** them k; 3359
Zec 14: 7 a day k to the LORD. 3359
Mt 10:26 or hidden that *will* not *be* **made** k. *1182*
12: 7 If *you had* k what these words mean, *1182*
24:43 If the owner of the house *had* k at what time *3857*
26: 6 in the home of a man k as Simon the Leper, *NIG*
Mk 6:14 for Jesus' name had become **well** k. *5745*
14: 3 reclining at the table in the home of a man k *NIG*
Lk 8:17 and nothing concealed that *will* not *be* k *1182*
12: 2 or hidden that *will* not *be* **made** k. *1182*
12:39 If the owner of the house *had* k at what hour *3857*
19:42 and said, "If *you*, even you, *had* only k *1182*
Jn 1:18 who is at the Father's side, *has* **made** him k. *2007*
1:33 I *would* not *have* k him, *3857*
6:64 For Jesus *had* k from the beginning which *3857*
15:15 I learned from my Father *I have* **made** k *1192*
16: 3 because *they have* not k the Father or me. *1182*
16:14 taking from what is mine and **making** it k *334*
16:15 from what is mine and **make** it k to you. *334*
17:26 *I have* **made** you k to them, *1192*
17:26 and *will continue to* **make** you k in order *1192*
18:15 this disciple was k to the high priest, *1196*
18:16 who *was* k to the high priest, came back, *1196*
19:13 at a place k **as** the Stone Pavement (which *3306*
Ac 1:23 Joseph called Barsabbas (also k **as** Justus) *2813*
2:28 *You have* **made** k to me the paths of life; *1192*
6: 3 among you *who are* k to be full of the Spirit *3455*
8:10 the divine power k **as** the Great Power." *2813*
9:42 This became k all over Joppa, *1196*
10: 1 in what **was** k **as** the Italian Regiment. *2813*
10:18 asking if Simon who *was* k **as** Peter *2126*
15:18 *that have been* k for ages. *1196*
19:17 When this became k to the Jews *1196*
26: 5 *They have* k me for a long time *4589*
Ro 1:19 what may be k about God is plain to them, *1196*
3:21 apart from law, *has been* **made** k, *5746*
7: 7 not *have* k what sin was except through *1182*
7: 7 not *have* k what coveting really was if *3857*
9:22 to show his wrath and **make** his power k, *1192*
9:23 **make** the riches of his glory k *1192*
11:34 "Who *has* k the mind of the Lord? *1182*
15:20 to preach the gospel where Christ *was* not k, *3951*
16:26 and **made** k through the prophetic writings *1192*
1Co 2:16 "For who *has* k the mind of the Lord *1182*
8: 3 But the man who loves God *is* k by God. *1182*
13:12 I shall know fully, even as *I am* **fully** k. *2105*
2Co 3: 2 on our hearts, k and read by everybody. *1182*
6: 9 k, yet regarded as unknown; *2105*
11:27 I have k hunger and thirst *NIG*
Gal 4: 9 or rather *are* k by God— *1182*
Eph 1: 9 And he *made* k to us the mystery of his will *1192*
3: 3 the mystery *made* k to me by revelation, *1192*
3: 5 not **made** k to men in other generations *1192*
3:10 *be made* k to the rulers and authorities in *1192*
6:19 so that I will fearlessly **make** k the mystery *1192*
Col 1:27 To them God has chosen to **make** k among *1192*
1Th 1: 8 your faith in God *has become* k everywhere. *2002*
1Ti 5:10 and *is* **well** k for her good deeds, *3455*
2Ti 3:15 and how from infancy *you have* k *3857*
Heb 3:10 and they *have* not k my ways.' *1182*
11:24 *to be* k **as** the son of Pharaoh's daughter. *3306*
2Pe 2:21 not *to have* k the way of righteousness, *2105*
2:21 than *to have* k it and then to turn their backs *2105*
1Jn 2:13 *you have* k him who is from the beginning. *1182*
2:13 because *you have* k the Father. *1182*
2:14 *you have* k him who is from the beginning. *1182*
3: 2 what we will be *has* not yet *been* **made** k. *5746*
3: 6 to sin has either seen him or k him. *1182*
Rev 1: 1 *He* **made** it k by sending his angel *4955*
2:17 k only to him who receives it. *3857*

KNOWS (91) [KNOW]

Ge 3: 5 "For God k that when you eat 3359
16: 5 and now that *she* k she is pregnant, 8011

Ge 33:13 "My lord **k** that the children are tender and 3359
Dt 34: 6 but to this day no one **k** where his grave is. 3359
Jos 22:22 The Mighty One, God, the LORD! He **k**! 3359
1Sa 2: 3 for the LORD is a God who **k**, 1978
16:18 of Bethlehem *who* **k how** to play the harp. 3359
20: 3 "Your father **k very well** 3359+3359
22:15 for your servant **k** nothing at all 3359
23:17 Even my father Saul **k** this." 3359
25:11 give it to men coming from who **k** where?" 3359
2Sa 12:22 I thought, 'Who **k**? 3359
14:20 he **k** everything that happens in the land." 3359
14:22 "Today your servant **k** that he has found 3359
17:10 for all Israel **k** that your father is a fighter 3359
Est 4:14 And who **k** but that you have come 3359
Job 15:23 *he* **k** the day of darkness is at hand. 3359
18:21 such is the place of *one who* **k** not God." 3359
23:10 But *he* **k** the way that I take; 3359
28: 7 No bird of prey **k** that hidden path, 3359
28:23 the way to it and he alone **k** where it dwells, 3359
Ps 37:13 for *he* **k** their day is coming. 8011
44:21 since he **k** the secrets of the heart? 3359
74: 9 and none of us **k** how long this will be. 3359
90:11 Who **k** the power of your anger? 3359
94:11 The LORD **k** the thoughts of man; 3359
94:11 he **k** that they are futile. NIH
103:14 for he **k how** we are formed, 3359
104:19 and the sun **k** when to go down. 3359
138: 6 but the proud *he* **k** from afar. 3359
Pr 5: 6 her paths are crooked, but *she* **k** it not. 3359
14:10 Each heart **k** its own bitterness, 3359
24:22 and who **k** what calamities they can bring? 3359
Ecc 2:19 And who **k** whether he will be a wise man 3359
3:21 Who **k** if the spirit of man rises upward and 3359
4:13 old but foolish king who no longer **k how** 3359
6:12 For who **k** what is good for a man in life, 3359
8: 1 Who **k** the explanation of things? 3359
8: 7 Since no man **k** the future, 3359
8:17 Even if a wise man claims he **k**, 3359
9: 1 no man **k** whether love or hate awaits him. 3359
9:12 no man **k** when his hour will come: 3359
10:14 No one **k** what is coming— 3359
Isa 1: 3 The ox **k** his master, 3359
7:15 when he **k** *enough* to reject the wrong and 3359
7:16 before the boy **k** *enough* to reject the wrong 3359
8: 4 Before the boy **k how** to say 'My father' 3359
29:16 the pot say of the potter, *"He* **k** nothing"? 1067
Jer 8: 7 the stork in the sky **k** her appointed seasons, 3359
9:24 that he understands and **k** me, 3359
Da 2:22 *he* **k** what lies in darkness, 10313
Joel 2:14 Who **k**? He may turn and have pity 3359
Jnh 3: 9 Who **k**? God may yet relent 3359
Na 3:17 and no *one* **k** where. 3359
Mt 6: 8 for your Father **k** what you need *3857*
6:32 your heavenly Father **k** that you need them. *3857*
9:30 "See that no one **k about** this." *1182*
11:27 No one **k** the Son except the Father, *2105*
11:27 and no one **k** the Father except the Son *2105*
24:36 "No one **k** about that day or hour, *3857*
Mk 13:32 "No one **k** about that day or hour, *3857*
Lk 10:22 No one **k** who the Son is except the Father, *1182*
10:22 and no one **k** who the Father is except *NIG*
12:30 and your Father **k** that you need them. *3857*
12:47 "That servant who **k** his master's will *1182*
16:15 but God **k** your hearts. *1182*
Jn 7:49 But this mob that **k** nothing of the law— *1182*
10:15 as the Father **k** me and I know the Father— *1182*
14:17 because it neither sees him nor **k** him. *1182*
19:35 He **k** that he tells the truth, *3857*
Ac 4:16 living in Jerusalem **k** they have done *5745*
15: 8 God, who **k the heart,** *2841*
Ro 8:27 And he who searches our hearts **k** the mind *3857*
1Co 2:11 among men **k** the **thoughts** of a man except *3857*
2:11 In the same way no one **k** the **thoughts** *1182*
3:20 "The Lord **k** that the thoughts of *1182*
8: 2 The man who thinks *he* **k** something does *1182*
8: 7 But not everyone **k** this. *1194*
2Co 7: 4 in all our troubles my joy **k no bounds.** *5668*
11:11 Because I do not love you? God **k** I do! *3857*
11:31 **k** that I am not lying. *3857*
12: 2 of the body I do not know—God **k.** *3857*
12: 3 from the body I do not know, but God **k**— *3857*
2Ti 2:19 "The Lord **k** those who are his," and, *1182*
Jas 4:17 **who k** the good he ought to do *3857*
2Pe 2: 9 then the Lord **k** how to rescue godly men *3857*
1Jn 3:20 and *he* **k** everything. *1182*
4: 6 and whoever **k** God listens to us; *1182*
4: 7 who loves has been born of God and **k** God. *1182*
Rev 12:12 *because he* **k** that his time is short." *3857*
19:12 He has a name written on him that no one **k** *3857*

KOA (1)

Eze 23:23 the men of Pekod and Shoa and **K,** 7760

KOHATH (19) [KOHATH'S, KOHATHITE, KOHATHITES]

Ge 46:11 The sons of Levi: Gershon, **K** and Merari. 7740
Ex 6:16 Gershon, **K** and Merari. 7740
6:18 The sons of **K** were Amram, Izhar, 7740
6:18 **K** lived 133 years. 7740
Nu 3:17 Gershon, **K** and Merari. 7740
3:27 To **K** belonged the clans of the Amramites, 7740
16: 1 Korah son of Izhar, the son of **K,** 7740
26:57 through **K,** the Kohathite clan; 7740
26:58 (**K** was the forefather of Amram; 7740
1Ch 6: 1 The sons of Levi: Gershon, **K** and Merari. 7740
6: 2 The sons of **K:** Amram, Izhar, Hebron 7740
6:16 The sons of Levi: Gershon, **K** and Merari. 7740
6:18 The sons of **K:** Amram, Izhar, Hebron 7740
6:22 The descendants of **K:** 7740
6:38 the son of **K,** the son of Levi, 7740
15: 5 From the descendants of **K,** Uriel the leader 7740
23: 6 Gershon, **K** and Merari. 7740
23:12 The sons of **K:** Amram, Izhar, Hebron 7740
2Ch 34:12 and Meshullam, descended from **K.** 7741

KOHATH'S (2) [KOHATH]

Jos 21: 5 of **K** descendants were allotted ten towns 7740
1Ch 6:61 of **K** descendants were allotted ten towns 7740

KOHATHITE (16) [KOHATH]

Nu 3:19 The **K** clans: Amram, Izhar, 1201+7740
3:27 these were the **K** clans. 7741
3:29 **K** clans were to camp on the south 1201+7740
3:30 of the **K** clans was Elizaphan son of Uzziel. 7741
4: 2 **K** branch of the Levites by their clans 1201+7740
4:18 that the **K** tribal clans are not cut off from 7741
4:37 of all those in the **K** clans who served in 7741
26:57 through Kohath, the **K** clan; 7741
Jos 21:10 from the **K** clans of the Levites, because 7741
21:20 The rest of the **K** clans of 1201+7740
21:26 to the rest of the **K** clans. 1201+7740
1Ch 6:54 from the **K** clan, because the first lot was 7741
6:60 which were distributed among **the K** clans, 2157[S]
6:66 Some of the **K** clans were given 1201+7740
6:70 to the rest of the **K** clans. 1201+7740
9:32 of their **K** brothers were in charge 1201+7741

KOHATHITES (12) [KOHATH]

Nu 3:28 The **K** were responsible for the care of NIH
4: 4 work of the **K** in the Tent of Meeting: 1201+7740
4:15 the **K** are to come to do the carrying. 1201+7740
4:15 The **K** are to carry those things 1201+7740
4:20 **K** must not go in to look at the holy things, NIH
4:34 counted the **K** by their clans 1201+7741
7: 9 But Moses did not give any to the **K,** 1201+7740
10:21 the **K** set out, carrying the holy things. 7741
Jos 21: 4 The first lot came out for the **K,** 7741
1Ch 6:33 with their sons: From the **K:** 7741
2Ch 20:19 **K** and Korahites stood up and praised 1201+7741
29:12 these Levites set to work: from the **K,** 1201+7741

KOLAIAH (2)

Ne 11: 7 the son of **K,** the son of Maaseiah, 7755
Jer 29:21 says about Ahab son of **K** and Zedekiah son 7755

KORAH (35) [KORAH'S, KORAHITE, KORAHITES]

Ge 36: 5 and Oholibamah bore Jeush, Jalam and **K.** 7946
36:14 Jeush, Jalam and **K.** 7946
36:16 **K,** Gatam and Amalek. 7946
36:18 Chiefs Jeush, Jalam and **K.** 7946
Ex 6:21 The sons of Izhar were **K,** 7946
6:24 The sons of **K** were Assir, 7946
Nu 16: 1 **K** son of Izhar, the son of Kohath, 7946
16: 5 Then he said to **K** and all his followers: 7946
16: 6 **K,** and all your followers are to do this: 7946
16: 8 Moses also said to **K,** "Now listen, 7946
16:16 to **K,** "You and all your followers are 7946
16:19 When **K** had gathered all his followers 7946
16:24 'Move away from the tents of **K,** 7946
16:27 So they moved away from the tents of **K,** 7946
16:40 he would become like **K** and his followers. 7946
16:49 to those who had died because of **K.** 7946
26:10 and swallowed them along with **K,** 7946
26:11 The line of **K,** however, did not die out. 7946
1Ch 1:35 Eliphaz, Reuel, Jeush, Jalam and **K.** 7946
2:43 **K,** Tappuah, Rekem and Shema. 7946
6:22 Amminadab his son, **K** his son, 7946
6:37 the son of Ebiasaph, the son of **K,** 7946
9:19 the son of Ebiasaph, the son of **K,** 7946
26:19 the gatekeepers who were descendants of **K** 7948
Ps 42: T A maskil of the Sons of **K.** 7946
44: T Of the Sons of **K.** 7946
45: T Of the Sons of **K.** 7946
46: T Of the Sons of **K.** 7946
47: T Of the Sons of **K.** 7946
48: T A song. A psalm of the Sons of **K.** 7946
49: T Of the Sons of **K.** 7946
84: T Of the Sons of **K.** 7946
85: T Of the Sons of **K.** 7946
87: T Of the Sons of **K.** A psalm. A song. 7946
88: T A psalm of the Sons of **K.** 7946

KORAH'S (4) [KORAH]

Nu 16:32 all **K** men and all their possessions. 4200+7946
26: 9 and Aaron and were among **K** followers 7946
27: 3 He was not among **K** followers, 7946
Jude 1:11 they have been destroyed in **K** rebellion. *3169*

KORAHITE (3) [KORAH]

Ex 6:24 These were the **K** clans. 7948
Nu 26:58 the Mushite clan, the **K** clan. 7948
1Ch 9:31 the firstborn son of Shallum the **K,** 7948

KORAHITES (4) [KORAH]

1Ch 9:19 from his family (the **K**) were responsible 7948
12: 6 Azarel, Joezer and Jashobeam the **K;** 7948
26: 1 of the gatekeepers: From the **K:** 7948
2Ch 20:19 Kohathites and **K** stood up and praised 1201+7948

KORATHITES, KORHITES (KJV) See KORAHITE, KORAHITES

KORAZIN (2)

Mt 11:21 "Woe to you, **K!** *5960*
Lk 10:13 "Woe to you, **K!** *5960*

KORE (3)

1Ch 9:19 Shallum son of **K,** the son of Ebiasaph, 7927
26: 1 Meshelemiah son of **K,** 7927
2Ch 31:14 **K** son of Imnah the Levite, 7927

KOUM (1)

Mk 5:41 by the hand and said to her, "Talitha **k!**" *3182*

KOZ (1)

1Ch 4: 8 and **K,** who was the father of Anub 7766

KUE (4)

1Ki 10:28 from Egypt and from **K**— 7750
10:28 royal merchants purchased them from **K.** 7750
2Ch 1:16 from Egypt and from **K**— 7745
1:16 royal merchants purchased them from **K.** 7745

KUSHAIAH (1)

1Ch 15:17 the Merarites, Ethan son of **K;** 7773

L

LAADAH (1)

1Ch 4:21 **L** the father of Mareshah and the clans of 4355

LAADAN (KJV) See LADAN

LABAN (49) [LABAN'S]

Ge 24:29 Now Rebekah had a brother named **L,** 4238
24:33 "Then tell us," [**L**] said. NIH
24:50 **L** and Bethuel answered, 4238
25:20 from Paddan Aram and sister of **L** 4238
27:43 Flee at once to my brother **L** in Haran. 4238
28: 2 from among the daughters of **L,** 4238
28: 5 to **L** son of Bethuel the Aramean, 4238
29: 5 He said to them, "Do you know **L,** 4238
29:10 When Jacob saw Rachel daughter of **L,** 4238
29:13 As soon as **L** heard the news about Jacob, 4238
29:14 Then **L** said to him, "You are my own flesh 4238
29:15 **L** said to him, "Just because you are a 4238
29:16 Now **L** had two daughters; 4238
29:19 **L** said, "It's better that I give her 4238
29:21 Then Jacob said to **L,** "Give me my wife. 4238
29:22 So **L** brought together all the people of 4238
29:24 And **L** gave his servant girl Zilpah 4238
29:25 So Jacob said to **L,** "What is this you have 4238
29:26 **L** replied, "It is not our custom here 4238
29:28 and then **L** gave him his daughter Rachel NIH
29:29 **L** gave his servant girl Bilhah 4238
29:30 And he worked for **L** another seven years. 2257[S]
30:25 Jacob said to **L,** "Send me on my way 4238
30:27 But **L** said to him, "If I have found favor 4238
30:34 said **L.** "Let it be as you have said." 4238
30:40 dark-colored animals that belonged to **L.** 4238
30:42 So the weak animals went to **L** and 4238
31:12 for I have seen all that **L** has been doing 4238
31:19 When **L** had gone to shear his sheep, 4238
31:20 Jacob deceived **L** the Aramean by 4238
31:22 On the third day **L** was told 4238
31:24 to **L** the Aramean in a dream at night 4238
31:25 of Gilead when **L** overtook him, 4238
31:25 and **L** and his relatives camped there too. 4238
31:26 **L** said to Jacob, "What have you done? 4238
31:31 Jacob answered **L,** "I was afraid, 4238
31:33 So **L** went into Jacob's tent and 4238
31:34 **L** searched through everything in the tent 4238
31:36 Jacob was angry and took **L** to task. 4238
31:36 he asked **L.** "What sin have I committed 4238
31:43 **L** answered Jacob, "The women are my daughters, 4238
31:47 **L** called it Jegar Sahadutha, 4238
31:48 **L** said, "This heap is a witness 4238
31:51 **L** also said to Jacob, "Here is this heap, 4238
31:55 next morning **L** kissed his grandchildren 4238
32: 4 with **L** and have remained there till now. 4238
46:18 whom **L** had given to his daughter Leah— 4238
46:25 whom **L** had given to his daughter Rachel 4238
Dt 1: 1 between Paran and Tophel, **L,** 4239

LABAN'S (5) [LABAN]

Ge 29:10 his mother's brother, and L sheep, 4238
30:36 to tend the rest of L flocks. 4238
30:40 and did not put them with L animals. 4238
31: 1 Jacob heard that L sons were saying, 4238
31: 2 And Jacob noticed that L attitude 4238

LABOR (93) [LABORED, LABORER, LABORER'S, LABORERS, LABORING, LABORS]

Ge 5:29 the l and painful toil of our hands caused 5126
49:15 to the burden and submit to **forced l.** 4989
Ex 1:11 over them to oppress them with **forced l,** 6026
1:14 They made their lives bitter with hard l 6275
1:14 in all their hard l the Egyptians used them 6275
2:11 and watched them at their **hard l.** 6026
5: 4 the people away from their l? 5126
20: 9 Six days *you shall* l and do all your work, 6268
34:21 "Six days *you shall* l, but on the seventh 6268
Dt 5:13 Six days *you shall* l and do all your work, 6268
20:11 the people in it shall be subject to **forced l** 4989
26: 6 made us suffer, putting us to hard l. 6275
28:33 and l produce, and you will have nothing 3330
Jos 16:10 but are required to do **forced l.** 4989
17:13 they subjected the Canaanites to **forced l** 4989
Jdg 1:28 they pressed the Canaanites into **forced l** 4989
1:30 but they did subject them to **forced l.** 4989
1:35 they too were pressed into **forced l.** 4989
1Sa 4:19 *she* **went into** l and gave birth, 4156
4:19 but was overcome by her **l pains.** 7496
2Sa 12:31 **consigning** them **to** l with saws and with 8492
20:24 Adoniram was in charge of **forced l;** 4989
1Ki 4: 6 son of Abda—in charge of **forced l.** 4989
5:14 Adoniram was in charge of the **forced l.** 4989
9:15 of the **forced** l King Solomon conscripted 4989
9:21 Solomon conscripted for his slave **l force,** 4989
11:28 the whole **l** *force of* the house of Joseph. 6023
12: 4 the harsh l and the heavy yoke he put 6275
12:18 who was in charge of **forced l,** 4989
1Ch 20: 3 **consigning** them **to** l with saws and with 8492
2Ch 8: 8 Solomon conscripted for his **slave l force,** 4989
10: 4 the harsh l and the heavy yoke he put 6275
10:18 who was in charge of **forced l,** 4989
Job 24: 5 the poor go about their l of foraging food; 7189
37: 7 he stops every man from his l. 3338
39: 3 their **l pains** are ended. 2477
39:16 she cares not that her l was in vain, 3330
Ps 48: 6 pain like that of a *woman* **in l.** 3528
104:23 to his l until evening. 6275
107:12 So he subjected them to **bitter l;** 6662
109:11 may strangers plunder the **fruits of** his l. 3330
127: 1 its builders l in vain. 6661
128: 2 You will eat the **fruit of** your l; 3330+4090
Pr 12:24 but laziness ends in **slave l.** 4989
Ecc 1: 3 from all his l at which he toils under 6662
2:10 and this was the reward for all my l. 6662
2:20 to despair over all my toilsome l under 6661
4: 4 that all l and all achievement spring 6662
5:15 from his l that he can carry in his hand. 6662
5:18 to find satisfaction in his toilsome l under 6661
8:16 to know wisdom and to observe man's l 6721
9: 9 and in your toilsome l under the sun. 6662
SS 8: 5 there *she who was* **in** l gave you birth. 2473
Isa 13: 8 they will writhe like a *woman* **in l.** 3528
21: 3 pangs seize me, like those of a *woman* **in l;** 3528
23: 4 *"I have* neither *been* **in** l nor given birth; 2655
31: 8 their young men will be put to **forced l.** 4989
54: 1 shout for joy, you *who were* never **in l;** 2655
55: 2 and your l on what does not satisfy? 3330
66: 7 "Before *she* **goes into l,** she gives birth; 2655
66: 8 no sooner *is* Zion **in l** than she gives birth 2655
Jer 3:24 **fruits of** our fathers' **l**—their flocks and 3330
4:31 I hear a cry as of a *woman* **in l,** 2655
6:24 pain like that of a *woman* **in l.** 3528
13:21 like that of a woman **in l?** 4256
22:13 not paying them for their l. 7189
22:23 pain like that of a *woman* **in l!** 3528
30: 6 on his stomach like a *woman* **in l,** 3528
31: 8 expectant mothers and *women* **in l;** 3528
48:41 be like the heart of a woman **in l.** 7674
49:22 be like the heart of a woman **in l.** 7674
49:24 pain like that of a *woman* **in l.** 3528
50:43 pain like that of a *woman* **in l.** 3528
51:58 the nations' l is only fuel for the flames." 3615
La 1: 3 After affliction and harsh **l,** 6275
Mic 4: 9 pain seizes you like that of a *woman* **in l?** 3528
4:10 O Daughter of Zion, like a *woman* **in l,** 3528
5: 3 the time when *she who is* **in** l gives birth 3528
Hab 2:13 that the people's l is only fuel for the fire, 3333
Hag 1:11 and on the **l** *of* your hands." 3330
Mt 6:28 *They do* not l or spin. *3159*
Lk 12:27 *They do* not l or spin. *3159*
Jn 4:38 you have reaped the benefits of their **l."** *3160*
1Co 3: 8 be rewarded according to his own **l.** *3160*
15:58 that your l in the Lord is not in vain. *3160*
Gal 4:27 you who **have** no **l pains;** *6048*
Php 1:22 this will mean fruitful l for me. *2240*
2:16 on the day of Christ that I did not run or l *3159*
Col 1:29 To this end *I* **l,** struggling with all his energy *3159*
1Th 1: 3 your l prompted by love, *3160*
5: 3 as **l pains** on a pregnant woman, *6047*
1Ti 4:10 (and for this *we* l and strive), *3159*
Rev 14:13 says the Spirit, "they will rest from their l, *3160*

LABORED (4) [LABOR]

Isa 47:12 which *you have* l at since childhood. 3333
47:15 these *you have* l *with* and trafficked with 3333
49: 4 But I said, *"I have* l to no purpose; 3333
2Co 11:27 I have l and toiled and have often gone *3160*

LABORER (1) [LABOR]

Ecc 5:12 The sleep of a l is sweet, 6268

LABORER'S (1) [LABOR]

Pr 16:26 The l appetite works for him; 6664

LABORERS (5) [LABOR]

Jdg 1:33 and Beth Anath became **forced** l for them. 4989
1Ki 5:13 King Solomon conscripted l from all Israel 4989
2Ch 34:13 of the l and supervised all the workers 6025
Ne 4:10 "The strength of the l is giving out, 6025
Mal 3: 5 against those who defraud l 8502

LABORING (1) [LABOR]

2Th 3: 8 l and toiling so that we would not be *3160*

LABORS (2) [LABOR]

Ecc 2:22 and anxious striving with which he l 6665
1Co 16:16 who joins in the work, and l at it. *3159*

LACE (KJV) See CORD

LACHISH (24)

Jos 10: 3 Japhia king of L and Debir king of Eglon. 4337
10: 5 Jarmuth, L and Eglon—joined forces. 4337
10:23 Hebron, Jarmuth, L and Eglon. 4337
10:31 with him moved on from Libnah to L; 4337
10:32 The LORD handed L over to Israel, 4337
10:33 up to help L, but Joshua defeated him 4337
10:34 and all Israel with him moved on from L 4337
10:35 just as they had done to L. 4337
12:11 the king of Jarmuth one the king of L one 4337
15:39 L, Bozkath, Eglon, 4337
2Ki 14:19 against him in Jerusalem and he fled to L, 4337
14:19 after him to L and killed him there. 4337
18:14 to the king of Assyria at L: 4337
18:17 from L to King Hezekiah at Jerusalem. 4337
19: 8 that the king of Assyria had left L, 4337
2Ch 11: 9 Adoraim, L, Azekah, 4337
25:27 against him in Jerusalem and he fled to L, 4337
25:27 after him to L and killed him there. 4337
32: 9 and all his forces were laying siege to L, 4337
Ne 11:30 in L and its fields, 4337
Isa 36: 2 from L to King Hezekiah at Jerusalem. 4337
37: 8 that the king of Assyria had left L, 4337
Jer 34: 7 that were still holding out—L and Azekah. 4337
Mic 1:13 You who live in L, harness the team to 4337

LACK (40) [LACKED, LACKING, LACKS]

Dt 8: 9 not be scarce and *you will* l nothing; 2893
Job 4:11 The lion perishes for l *of* prey, 1172
24: 8 by mountain rains and hug the rocks for l 1172
31:19 if I have seen anyone perishing for l *of* 1172
34:35 his words l insight.' 928+4202
38:41 to God and wander about for l *of* food? 1172
Ps 34: 9 for those who fear him l nothing. 4728
34:10 who fear the LORD l no good thing. 2893
94:10 Does he who teaches man l knowledge? NIH
Pr 5:23 He will die for l *of* discipline, 401
9: 4 she says to those who l judgment. 2894
9:16 she says to those *who* l judgment. 2894
10:21 but fools die for l *of* judgment. 2894
11:14 For l *of* guidance a nation falls, 401
15:22 Plans fail for l *of* counsel, 401
22:27 if you l the means to pay, 401+4200
28:27 He who gives to the poor will l nothing, 4728
Isa 5:13 into exile for l *of* understanding; 1172
34:16 not one *will* l her mate. 7212
50: 2 Do I l the strength to rescue you? 401+928
50: 2 their fish rot for l *of* water and die 401
51:14 nor *will they* l bread. 2893
56:10 they all l knowledge; 4202
56:11 They are shepherds who l understanding; 4202
Jer 14: 6 their eyesight fails for l *of* pasture." 401
La 4: 9 with hunger, they waste away **for l of** 4946
Hos 4: 6 people are destroyed from l *of* knowledge. 1172
Am 4: 6 in every city and l *of* bread in every town, 2896
Zec 10: 2 like sheep oppressed for l *of* a shepherd. 401
Mt 13:58 because of their **l of faith.** *602*
19:20 "What *do I* still **l?"** *5728*
Mk 6: 6 And he was amazed at their **l of faith.** *602*
10:21 "One thing you **l,"** he said. *5728*
16:14 he rebuked them for their **l of faith** *602*
Lk 18:22 he said to him, "You still l one thing. *3309*
22:35 bag or sandals, *did you* l anything?" *5728*
Ro 3: 3 their **l of faith** nullify God's faithfulness? *602*
1Co 1: 7 not l any spiritual gift as you eagerly wait *5728*
7: 5 because of your **l of self-control.** *202*
Col 2:23 but they l any value in restraining sensual *4024*

LACKED (6) [LACK]

Dt 2: 7 and *you have* not l anything. 2893
Jdg 18: 7 their land l nothing, they were prosperous. 4007
1Ki 11:22 "What *have* you l here that you want 2894
Ne 9:21 *they* l nothing, their clothes did not wear out 2893
Pr 7: 7 a youth who l judgment. 2894
1Co 12:24 *to* the parts *that* l it, *5728*

LACKING (10) [LACK]

1Ki 4:27 **saw to it that** nothing **was l.** 6372
Job 24: 7 L clothes, they spend the night naked; 1172+4946
24:10 L clothes, they go about naked; 1172
Pr 17:18 A man l *in* judgment strikes hands in pledge 2894
Ecc 1:15 *what* is l cannot be counted. 2898
Ro 12:11 Never be l in zeal, *3891*
1Co 16:17 they have supplied what was l from you. *5729*
Col 1:24 fill up in my flesh **what is** still l in regard *5729*
1Th 3:10 and supply what *is* l in your faith. *5729*
Jas 1: 4 be mature and complete, not l anything. *3309*

LACKS (16) [LACK]

Jdg 18:10 a land that l nothing whatever." 4728
2Sa 3:29 or who falls by the sword or who l food." 2894
Pr 6:32 a man who commits adultery l judgment; 2894
10:13 rod is for the back of him who l judgment. 2894
11:12 man who l judgment derides his neighbor, 2894
12:11 but he who chases fantasies l judgment. 2894
15:21 Folly delights a *man who* l judgment, 2894
24:30 the vineyard of the man who l judgment; 2894
25:28 broken down is a man who l self-control. 401
28:16 A tyrannical ruler l judgment, 2894
31:11 in her and l nothing of value. 2893
Ecc 6: 2 so that he l nothing his heart desires, 2894
10: 3 the fool l sense and shows everyone 2893
SS 7: 2 *that* never l blended wine. 2893
Eze 34: 8 because my flock l a shepherd and 401
Jas 1: 5 If any of you l wisdom, *3309*

LAD (KJV) See BOY, SERVANT, YOUNG MAN

LADAN (7)

1Ch 7:26 L his son, Ammihud his son, 4356
23: 7 to the Gershonites: L and Shimei. 4356
23: 8 The sons of L: 4356
23: 9 These were the heads of the families of L. 4356
26:21 The descendants of L, 4356
26:21 who were Gershonites through L 4356
26:21 of families belonging to L the Gershonite, 4356

LADE, LADED, LADING (KJV) See LAID, LOAD

LADEN (3) [LOAD]

Job 36:16 to the comfort of your table **l with** 4848
36:17 But now *you are* **l with** the judgment due 4848
Ps 105:37 He brought out Israel, **l with** silver and gold, 928

LADIES (1) [LADY]

Jdg 5:29 The wisest of her l answer her; 8576

LADY (2) [LADIES]

2Jn 1: 1 elder, *To* the chosen l and her children, *3257*
1: 5 And now, **dear l,** I am not writing you *3257*

LAEL (1)

Nu 3:24 of the Gershonites was Eliasaph son of L. 4210

LAGGING (1)

Dt 25:18 and cut off all who *were* l behind; 3129

LAHAD (1)

1Ch 4: 2 and Jahath the father of Ahumai and L. 4262

LAHAI-ROI (KJV) See BEER LAHAI ROI

LAHMAS (1)

Jos 15:40 Cabbon, L, Kitlish, 4314

LAHMI (1)

1Ch 20: 5 Elhanan son of Jair killed L the brother 4313

LAID (147) [LAY]

Ge 9:23 a garment and l it across their shoulders; 8492
22: 9 He bound his son Isaac and l him on 8492
Ex 19:13 not a hand *is to be* l on him. 5595
22: 8 to determine whether *he has* l his hands on 8938
Lev 8:14 and his sons l their hands on its head. 6164
8:18 and his sons l their hands on its head. 6164
8:22 and his sons l their hands on its head. 6164
9:20 these *they* l on the breasts, 8492
26:33 Your land will be **l waste,** 9039
Nu 27:23 Then *he* l his hands on him 6164
Dt 24: 5 not be sent to war or *have* any other duty l 6296
34: 9 of wisdom because Moses *had* l his hands 6164
Jos 2: 6 the stalks of flax she *had* **l out** on the roof.) 6885
2:19 his blood will be on our head if a hand is l NIH
Jdg 2:20 that *I* **l down** *for* their forefathers and has 7422
16:24 the *one who* **l waste** our land 2990
Ru 4:16 l him in her lap and cared for him. 8883
1Sa 19:13 Michal took an idol and l it on the bed, 8492
2Sa 22:16 and the foundations of the earth **l bare** at 1655

1Ki 1:21 as soon as my lord the king *is* **l to rest** 8886
6:37 **The foundation** of the temple of the LORD **was l** 3569
7:10 **The foundations were l** with large stones 3569
12:11 My father **l** on you a heavy yoke; 6673
13:29 **l** it on the donkey, 5663
13:30 Then *he* **l** the body in his own tomb, 5663
16:17 from Gibbethon and **l siege** to Tirzah. 7443
16:34 *He* **l** its **foundations** at the cost of his 3569
17:19 and **l** him on his bed. 8899
18:33 the bull into pieces and **l** it on the wood. 8492
2Ki 4:21 and **l** him on the bed of the man of God, 8886
4:31 on ahead and **l** the staff on the boy's face, 8492
6:24 and marched up and **l siege** to Samaria. 7443
17:5 marched against Samaria and **l siege** to it 7443
18:9 against Samaria and **l siege** to it. 7443
19:17 Assyrian kings *have* **l waste** these nations 2990
22:19 they would become accursed and **l waste,** 9014
24:10 Jerusalem and **l siege** *to it,* 928+995+2021+5189
1Ch 6:32 according to the **regulations** *l down* AIT
20:1 *He* **l waste** the land of the Ammonites 8845
2Ch 3:3 **The foundation** Solomon **l** for building 3569
8:16 **foundation** *of* the temple of the LORD was **l** 4586
10:11 My father **l** on you a heavy yoke; 6673
16:14 *They* **l** him on a bier covered with spices 8886
29:23 and *they* **l** their hands on them. 6164
32:1 *He* **l siege to** the fortified cities, 2837+6584
Ezr 3:6 **the foundation** of the LORD's temple *had* not *yet* **been l.** 3569
3:10 When the builders **l the foundation** *of* 3569
3:11 **the foundation** *of* the house of the LORD **was l.** 3569
3:12 **the foundation** *of* this temple *being* **l,** 3569
5:16 and **l** the foundations of the house of God 10314
6:3 and *let* its foundations **be l.** 10502
Ne 3:3 They **l** its **beams** and put its doors and bolts 7936
3:6 They **l** its **beams** and put its doors and bolts 7936
Job 14:10 But man dies and *is* **l low;** 2764
16:18 may my cry never be **l** to rest! NIH
38:4 **l the** earth's **foundation?** 3569
38:6 or who **l** its cornerstone— 3721
Ps 18:15 and the foundations of the earth **l bare** 1655
66:11 You brought us into prison and **l** burdens 8492
102:25 In the beginning *you* **l the foundations** *of* 3569
119:4 You *have* **l down** precepts that are to 7422
119:25 *I am* **l low** in the dust; 1815
119:138 statutes *you have* **l down** are righteous; 7422
139:5 *you have* **l** your hand upon me. 8883
141:9 Keep me from the snares *they have* **l** 3704
Pr 3:19 **l the** earth's **foundations,** 3569
Ecc 1:13 What a heavy burden God *has* **l** on men! 5989
3:10 I have seen the burden God *has* **l** on men 5989
Isa 1:7 **l waste** as when overthrown by strangers. 9039
6:13 it will again be **l waste.** 1278
7:16 the two kings you dread *will* **be l waste.** 6440
14:8 "Now that *you have been* **l low,** 8886
14:12 *you who once* **l low** the nations! 2765
24:3 The earth *will* **be completely l waste** 1327+1327
28:1 the pride of *those* **l low** *by* wine! 2150
37:18 Assyrian kings *have* **l waste** all these peoples 2990
44:28 *"Let its* **foundations be l."** ' 3569
47:6 on the aged *you* **l** a very **heavy** yoke. 3877
48:13 My own hand **l the foundations** *of* 3569
49:17 *those who* **l** you **waste** depart from you. 2238+2256+2990
49:19 and made desolate and your land **l** waste, NIH
51:13 and **l the foundations** *of* the earth, 3569
51:16 *who* **l the foundations** *of* the earth, 3569
53:6 LORD *has* **l** on him the iniquity of us all. 7003
Jer 2:15 *They have* **l** waste his land; 8883
9:12 Why has the land been ruined and **l waste** 5898
12:11 the whole land *will* **be l waste** 9037
18:16 Their land *will be* **l** waste, 8492
25:37 The peaceful meadows *will* **be l waste** 1959
39:1 with his whole army and **l siege** to it. 7443
46:15 Why *will* your warriors **be l low?** 6085
46:19 for Memphis will be **l waste** and lie 9014
48:9 salt on Moab, for *she will be* **l waste;** 5898+5898
La 1:10 The enemy **l** hands on all her treasures; 7298
2:6 *He has* **l waste** his dwelling like a garden; 2803
3:28 for the LORD *has* **l** it on him. 5747
Eze 6:6 *be* **l waste** and the high places demolished, 2990
6:6 so that your altars *will be* **l waste** 2990
12:20 The inhabited towns *will be* **l waste** and 2990
13:14 so that its foundation *will* **be l bare.** 1655
21:29 *be* **l** on the necks of the wicked who are to 5989
24:2 because the king of Babylon *has* **l siege** 6164
25:3 over the land of Israel when *it* **was l waste** 9037
32:19 down and **be l** among the uncircumcised.' 8886
32:25 *they* **are l** among the slain. 5989
32:29 *they are* **l** with those killed by the sword. 5989
32:32 Pharaoh and all his hordes *will* **be l** 8886
35:12 *"They have been* **l waste** 9037
36:35 "This land that **was l waste** has become 9037
Hos 5:9 be **l waste** on the day of reckoning. 9014
Joel 1:7 *It has* **l** waste my vines 8492
Mic 5:1 for a siege *is* **l** against us. 8492
Na 2:2 though destroyers *have* **l** them **waste** 1327
Hag 2:15 how things were before one stone *was* **l** 8492
2:18 **the foundation** of the LORD's temple **was l.** 3569
Zec 4:9 of Zerubbabel *have* **l the foundation** 3569
8:9 when **the foundation was l** *for* the house 3569
Mt 15:30 and **l** them at his feet; and he healed them. *4849*
22:15 the Pharisees went out and **l plans** *3284+5206*
Mk 6:29 and took his body and **l** it in a tomb. *5502*
15:47 the mother of Joses saw where *he was* **l.** *5502*
16:6 See the place where *they* **l** him. *5502*
Lk 6:48 who dug down deep and **l** the foundation *5502*
12:19 "You have plenty of good things **l up** *3023*
16:20 At his gate *was* **l** a beggar named Lazarus, *965*
19:20 I have kept it **l away** in a piece of cloth. *641*
23:53 one in which no one had yet been **l.** *3023*
23:55 and saw the tomb and how his body *was* **l** *5502*
Jn 7:30 but no one **l** a hand **on** him, *2095*
7:44 but no one **l** a hand **on** him. *2095*
11:34 "Where *have you* **l** him?" *5502*
11:38 a cave with a stone **l across** the entrance. *2130*
19:41 in which no one had ever been **l.** *5502*
19:42 the tomb was nearby, *they* **l** Jesus there. *5502*
Ac 5:15 the sick into the streets and **l** them on beds *5502*
6:6 who prayed and **l** their hands **on** them. *2202*
7:58 the witnesses **l** their clothes at the feet of *700*
13:29 down from the tree and **l** him in a tomb. *5502*
1Co 3:10 *I* **l** a foundation as an expert builder, *5502*
3:11 foundation other than the one *already* **l,** *3023*
14:25 and the secrets of his heart will be **l bare.** *5745*
1Ti 4:14 when the body of elders **l** their hands **on** *2120*
Heb 1:10 you **l the foundations of** the earth, *2530*
4:13 and **l bare** before the eyes of him *5548*
2Pe 3:10 earth and everything in it *will be* **l bare.** *2351*
1Jn 3:16 Jesus Christ **l down** his life for us. *5502*
Rev 21:16 The city *was* **l out** like a square, *3023*

LAIN (2) [LAY]

Ge 24:16 no man *had ever* **l with** her. 3359
1Sa 26:5 the commander of the army, *had* **l down.** 8886

LAIR (3) [LAIRS]

Jer 4:7 A lion has come out of his **l;** 6020
25:38 Like a lion he will leave his **l,** 6108
Zep 2:15 a **l** for wild beasts! 5271

LAIRS (1) [LAIR]

Na 2:12 filling his **l** with the kill and his dens with 2986

LAISH (6) [DAN]

Jdg 18:7 So the five men left and came to **L,** 4332
18:14 the land of **L** said to their brothers, 4332
18:27 and his priest, and went on to **L,** 4332
18:29 though the city used to be called **L.** 4332
1Sa 25:44 to Paltiel son of **L,** who was from Gallim. 4331
2Sa 3:15 from her husband Paltiel son of **L.** 4331

LAISHAH (1)

Isa 10:30 Listen, O **L!** 4333

LAKE (39)

Dt 33:23 he will inherit southward to the **l.**" 3542
Mt 4:13 which was **by the l** in the area of Zebulun *4144*
4:18 They were casting a net into the **l,** *2498*
8:18 to cross to the other side of the **l.** *NIG*
8:24 a furious storm came up on the **l,** *2498*
8:32 down the steep bank into the **l** and died in *2498*
13:1 of the house and sat by the **l.** *2498*
13:47 into the **l** and caught all kinds of fish. *2498*
14:25 Jesus went out to them, walking on the **l.** *2498*
14:26 the disciples saw him walking on the **l,** *2498*
16:5 When they went across the **l,** *NIG*
17:27 go to the **l** and throw out your line. *2498*
Mk 1:16 Andrew casting a net into the **l,** *2498*
2:13 Once again Jesus went out beside the **l.** *2498*
3:7 Jesus withdrew with his disciples to the **l,** *2498*
4:1 Again Jesus began to teach by the **l.** *2498*
4:1 into a boat and sat in it out *on* the **l,** *2498*
5:1 across the **l** to the region of the Gerasenes. *2498*
5:13 rushed down the steep bank into the **l** *2498*
5:21 over by boat to the other side of the **l,** *NIG*
5:21 around him while he was by the **l.** *2498*
6:47 the boat was in the middle *of* the **l,** *2498*
6:48 he went out to them, walking on the **l.** *2498*
6:49 but when they saw him walking on the **l,** *2498*
Lk 5:1 One day as Jesus was standing by the **L** *3349*
8:22 "Let's go over to the other side of the **l.**" *3349*
8:23 A squall came down on the **l,** *3349*
8:26 which is across the **l** from Galilee. *NIG*
8:33 the steep bank into the **l** and was drowned. *3349*
Jn 6:16 his disciples went down to the **l,** *2498*
6:17 and set off across the **l** for Capernaum. *2498*
6:22 on the opposite shore *of* the **l** realized *2498*
6:25 on the other side *of* the **l,** *2498*
Rev 19:20 of them were thrown alive into the fiery **l** *3349*
20:10 was thrown into the **l** of burning sulfur, *3349*
20:14 and Hades were thrown into the **l** of fire. *3349*
20:14 The **l** of fire is the second death. *3349*
20:15 he was thrown into the **l** of fire. *3349*
21:8 be in the fiery **l** of burning sulfur. *3349*

LAKKUM (1)

Jos 19:33 and Jabneel to **L** and ending at the Jordan. 4373

LAMA (2)

Mt 27:46 "Eloi, Eloi, **l** sabachthani?"— *3316*
Mk 15:34 "Eloi, Eloi, **l** sabachthani?"— *3316*

LAMB (103) [LAMB'S, LAMBS]

Ge 22:7 "but where is the **l** for the burnt offering?" 8445
22:8 "God himself will provide the **l** for 8445
30:32 every dark-colored **l** and 928+2021+4166+8445
30:33 or any **l** that is not dark-colored, 4166
Ex 12:3 of this month each man is to take a **l** 8445
12:4 any household is too small for a *whole* **l,** 8445
12:4 the amount of **l** needed in accordance 8445
12:21 and slaughter the **Passover l.** 7175
13:13 Redeem with a **l** every firstborn donkey, 8445
29:40 With the first **l** offer a tenth of an ephah 3897
29:41 Sacrifice the other **l** at twilight with 3897
34:20 Redeem the firstborn donkey with a **l,** 8445
Lev 3:7 If he offers a **l,** he is to present it 4166
4:32 " 'If he brings a **l** as his sin offering, 3897
4:35 just as the fat is removed from the **l** *of* 4166
5:6 he must bring to the LORD a female **l** 4167
5:7 " 'If he cannot afford a **l,** he is to bring 8445
9:3 a calf and a **l**—both a year old and without 3897
12:6 to the Tent of Meeting a year-old **l** for 3897
12:8 If she cannot afford a **l,** she is to bring 8445
14:10 and one **ewe l** a year old, 3898
14:13 to slaughter the **l** in the holy place where 3897
14:21 he must take one **male l** as a guilt offering 3897
14:24 to take the **l** *for* the guilt offering, 3897
14:25 the **l** *for* the guilt offering and take some 3897
17:3 a **l** or a goat in the camp or outside of it 4166
22:27 "When a calf, a **l** or a goat is born, 4166
23:12 to the LORD a **l** a year old without defect, 3897
Nu 6:12 a year-old **male l** as a guilt offering. 3897
6:14 a year-old **male l** without defect for 3897
6:14 for a burnt offering, a year-old **ewe l** 3898
7:15 one ram and one **male l** a year old, 3897
7:21 one ram and one **male l** a year old, 3897
7:27 one ram and one **male l** a year old, 3897
7:33 one ram and one **male l** a year old, 3897
7:39 one ram and one **male l** a year old, 3897
7:45 one ram and one **male l** a year old, 3897
7:51 one ram and one **male l** a year old, 3897
7:57 one ram and one **male l** a year old, 3897
7:63 one ram and one **male l** a year old, 3897
7:69 one ram and one **male l** a year old, 3897
7:75 one ram and one **male l** a year old, 3897
7:81 one ram and one **male l** a year old, 3897
9:11 They are to eat **the l,** 2084S
15:5 With each **l** for the burnt offering or 3897
15:11 Each bull or ram, each **l** or young goat, 928+2021+3897+8445
28:4 Prepare one **l** in the morning and the other 3897
28:7 of a hin of fermented drink with each **l.** 3897
28:8 Prepare the second **l** at twilight, 3897
28:13 and with each **l,** a grain offering of a tenth 3897
28:14 and with each **l,** a quarter of a hin. 3897
1Sa 7:9 a suckling **l** and offered it up as 3231
2Sa 12:3 poor man had nothing except one little **ewe l** he had bought. 3898
12:4 the **ewe l** *that belonged to* the poor man 3898
12:6 He must pay for that **l** four times over, 3898
2Ch 30:15 the **Passover l** on the fourteenth day of 7175
35:1 and the **Passover l** was slaughtered on 7175
Ezr 6:20 The Levites slaughtered the **Passover l** 7175
Isa 11:6 The wolf will live with the **l,** 3897
53:7 he was led like a **l** to the slaughter, 8445
65:25 The wolf and the **l** will feed together, 3231
66:3 and whoever offers a **l,** 8445
Jer 11:19 like a gentle **l** led to the slaughter; 3897
Eze 46:13 to provide a year-old **l** without defect for 3897
46:15 So the **l** and the grain offering and 3897
Mk 14:12 to sacrifice the **Passover l,** *4247*
Lk 22:7 the **Passover l** had to be sacrificed. *4247*
Jn 1:29 "Look, the **L** of God, who takes away the sin *303*
1:36 he said, "Look, the **L** of God!" *303*
Ac 8:32 and as a **l** before the shearer is silent, *303*
1Co 5:7 For Christ, our **Passover l,** *4247*
1Pe 1:19 a **l** without blemish or defect. *303*
Rev 5:6 I saw a **L,** looking as if it had been slain, *768*
5:8 twenty-four elders fell down before the **L.** *768*
5:12 "Worthy is the **L,** who was slain, *768*
5:13 and *to* the **L** be praise and honor and glory *768*
6:1 as the **L** opened the first of the seven seals. *768*
6:3 When the **L** opened the second seal, *NIG*
6:5 When the **L** opened the third seal, *NIG*
6:7 When the **L** opened the fourth seal, *NIG*
6:16 on the throne and from the wrath *of* the **L!** *768*
7:9 before the throne and in front of the **L.** *768*
7:10 who sits on the throne, and *to* the **L.**" *768*
7:14 made them white in the blood *of* the **L.** *768*
7:17 For the **L** at the center of the throne will *768*
12:11 They overcame him by the blood *of* the **L** *768*
13:8 *to* the **L** that was slain from the creation of *768*
13:11 He had two horns like a **l,** *768*
14:1 I looked, and there before me was the **L,** *768*
14:4 They follow the **L** wherever he goes. *768*
14:4 and offered as firstfruits *to* God and the **L.** *768*
14:10 of the holy angels and *of* the **L.** *768*
15:3 the servant of God and the song *of* the **L:** *768*
17:14 They will make war against the **L,** *768*
17:14 but the **L** will overcome them *768*
19:7 For the wedding *of* the **L** has come, *768*
19:9 to the wedding supper *of* the **L!**" *768*
21:9 show you the bride, the wife *of* the **L.**" *768*
21:14 the names of the twelve apostles *of* the **L.** *768*
21:22 Lord God Almighty and the **L** are its temple. *768*
21:23 of God gives it light, and the **L** is its lamp. *768*
22:1 from the throne of God and *of* the **L** *768*
22:3 The throne of God and *of* the **L** will be in *768*

LAMB'S (1) [LAMB]

Rev 21:27 names are written in the **L** book of life. *768*

LAMBS (92) [LAMB]

Ge 21:28 Abraham set apart seven **ewe l** *from* 3898
21:29 of these seven **ewe l** you have set apart 3898
21:30 "Accept these seven **l** from my hand as 3898
30:35 on them) and all the dark-colored **l,** 4166
Ex 12: 7 of the houses where they eat **the l.** 2257[S]
29:38 regularly each day: two **l** a year old. 3897
Lev 14:10 the eighth day he must bring two **male l** 3897
14:12 the **male l** and offer it as a guilt offering, 3897
23:18 Present with this bread seven **male l,** 3897
23:19 for a sin offering and two **l,** 3897
23:20 to wave the two **l** before the LORD as 3897
Nu 7:17 five male goats and five **male l** a year old, 3897
7:23 five male goats and five **male l** a year old, 3897
7:29 five male goats and five **male l** a year old, 3897
7:35 five male goats and five **male l** a year old, 3897
7:41 five male goats and five **male l** a year old, 3897
7:47 five male goats and five **male l** a year old, 3897
7:53 five male goats and five **male l** a year old, 3897
7:59 five male goats and five **male l** a year old, 3897
7:65 five male goats and five **male l** a year old, 3897
7:71 five male goats and five **male l** a year old, 3897
7:77 five male goats and five **male l** a year old, 3897
7:83 five male goats and five **male l** a year old, 3897
7:87 twelve rams and twelve **male l** a year old, 3897
7:88 sixty male goats and sixty **male l** 3897
28: 3 two **l** a year old without defect, 3897
28: 9 make an offering of two **l** a year old 3897
28:11 one ram and seven **male l** a year old, 3897
28:19 one ram and seven **male l** a year old, 3897
28:21 and with each of the seven **l,** one-tenth. 3897
28:27 one ram and seven **male l** a year old as 3897
28:29 and with each of the seven **l,** one-tenth. 3897
29: 2 one ram and seven **male l** a year old, 3897
29: 4 and with each of the seven **l,** one-tenth. 3897
29: 8 one ram and seven **male l** a year old, 3897
29:10 and with each of the seven **l,** one-tenth. 3897
29:13 two rams and fourteen **male l** a year old, 3897
29:15 and with each of the fourteen **l,** one-tenth. 3897
29:17 two rams and fourteen **male l** a year old, 3897
29:18 With the bulls, rams and **l,** 3897
29:20 two rams and fourteen **male l** a year old, 3897
29:21 With the bulls, rams and **l,** 3897
29:23 two rams and fourteen **male l** a year old, 3897
29:24 With the bulls, rams and **l,** 3897
29:26 two rams and fourteen **male l** a year old, 3897
29:27 With the bulls, rams and **l,** 3897
29:29 two rams and fourteen **male l** a year old, 3897
29:30 With the bulls, rams and **l,** 3897
29:32 two rams and fourteen **male l** a year old, 3897
29:33 With the bulls, rams and **l,** 3897
29:36 one ram and seven **male l** a year old, 3897
29:37 With the bull, the ram and the **l,** 3897
Dt 7:13 of your herds and the **l** *of* your flocks in 6957
28: 4 of your herds and the **l** *of* your flocks. 6957
28:18 of your herds and the **l** *of* your flocks. 6957
28:51 or **l** *of* your flocks until you are ruined. 6957
32:14 and flock and with fattened **l** and goats, 4119
1Sa 15: 9 the fat calves and **l**— 4119
2Ki 3: 4 a hundred thousand **l** and with the wool of 4119
1Ch 29:21 a thousand rams and a thousand **male l,** 3897
2Ch 29:21 seven **male l** and seven male goats as 3897
29:22 the **l** and sprinkled their blood on the altar. 3897
29:32 a hundred rams and two hundred **male l**— 3897
30:17 the **Passover l** for all those who were 7175
30:17 not consecrate [their **l**] to the LORD. NIH
35: 6 Slaughter the **Passover l,** 7175
35: 6 consecrate yourselves and prepare [the **l**] NIH
35:11 The **Passover l** were slaughtered, 7175
Ezr 6: 9 **male l** for burnt offerings to the God 10043
6:17 four hundred **male l** and, 10043
7:17 to buy bulls, rams and **male l,** 10043
8:35 seventy-seven **male l** and, 3897
Ps 114: 4 skipped like rams, the hills like **l.** 1201+7366
114: 6 skipped like rams, you hills, like **l?** 1201+7366
Pr 27:26 the **l** will provide you with clothing, 3897
Isa 1:11 in the blood of bulls and **l** and goats. 3897
5:17 **l** will feed among the ruins of the rich. 1531
16: 1 Send **l** as tribute to the ruler of the land, 4119
34: 6 the blood of **l** and goats, 4119
40:11 the **l** in his arms and carries them close 3231
Jer 51:40 "I will bring them down like **l** to 4119
Eze 27:21 they did business with you in **l,** 4119
39:18 if they were rams and **l,** goats and bulls— 4119
46: 4 on the Sabbath day is to be six **male l** and 3897
46: 5 with the **l** is to be as much as he pleases, 3897
46: 6 six **l** and a ram, all without defect. 3897
46: 7 with the **l** as much as he wants to give, 3897
46:11 and with the **l** as much as one pleases, 3897
Hos 4:16 then can the LORD pasture them like **l** in 3897
Am 6: 4 You dine on **choice l** and fattened calves. 4119+4946+7366
Lk 10: 3 I am sending you out like **l** among wolves. *748*
Jn 21:15 Jesus said, "Feed my **l.**" *768*

LAME (26)

Lev 21:18 no man who is blind or **l,** 7177
Dt 15:21 If an animal has a defect, is **l** or blind, 7177
2Sa 4: 4 (Jonathan son of Saul had a son who was **l** 5783
5: 6 the blind and the **l** can ward you off." 7177
5: 8 to use the water shaft to reach those '**l** 7177
5: 8 'blind and **l**' will not enter the palace." 7177
19:26 since I your servant am **l,** I said, 7177
Job 29:15 I was eyes to the blind and feet to the **l.** 7177
Pr 25:19 Like a bad tooth or a **l** foot is reliance on 5048
Pr 26: 7 Like a **l** *man's* legs that hang limp is 7177
Isa 33:23 and even the **l** will carry off plunder. 7177
35: 6 Then will the **l** leap like a deer, 7177
Jer 31: 8 Among them will be the blind and the **l,** 7177
Mic 4: 6 declares the LORD, "I will gather the **l;** 7519
4: 7 I will make the **l** a remnant, 7519
Zep 3:19 I will rescue the **l** and gather those 7519
Mt 11: 5 The blind receive sight, the **l** walk, *6000*
15:30 Great crowds came to him, bringing the **l,** *6000*
15:31 the **l** walking and the blind seeing. *6000*
21:14 and the **l** came to him at the temple, *6000*
Lk 7:22 The blind receive sight, the **l** walk, *6000*
14:13 invite the poor, the crippled, the **l,** *6000*
14:21 the crippled, the blind and the **l.**' *6000*
Jn 5: 3 the blind, the **l,** the paralyzed. *6000*
Ac 14: 8 crippled in his feet, who was **l** from birth *6000*
Heb 12:13 so that the **l** may not be disabled, *6000*

LAMECH (12)

Ge 4:18 and Methushael was the father of **L.** 4347
4:19 **L** married two women, 4347
4:23 **L** said to his wives, "Adah and Zillah, 4347
4:23 wives of **L,** hear my words. 4347
4:24 then **L** seventy-seven times." 4347
5:25 he became the father of **L.** 4347
5:26 And after he became the father of **L,** 4347
5:28 When **L** had lived 182 years, he had a son. 4347
5:30 **L** lived 595 years and had other sons 4347
5:31 Altogether, **L** lived 777 years, 4347
1Ch 1: 3 Enoch, Methuselah, **L,** Noah. 4347
Lk 3:36 the son of Noah, the son *of* **L,** *3285*

LAMENT (29) [LAMENTATION, LAMENTED, LAMENTS]

2Sa 1:17 David **took up** this **l** concerning Saul 7801+7806
1:18 the men of Judah be taught this **l** of the bow NIH
3:33 The king **sang** *this* **l** for Abner: 7801
Ps 56: 8 Record my **l;** list my tears on your 5654
102: T When he is faint and pours out his **l** before 8490
Isa 3:26 The gates of Zion *will* **l** and mourn; 627
15: 5 to Horonaim *they* **l** their destruction. 2411+6424
16: 7 **L** and grieve for the men of Kir Hareseth. 2047
19: 8 The fishermen will groan and **l,** 61
29: 2 she will mourn and **l,** 640
Jer 4: 8 So put on sackcloth, **l** and wail, 6199
7:29 take up a **l** on the barren heights, 7806
9:10 and wail for the mountains and take up a **l** 7806
9:20 teach one another a **l.** 7806
34: 5 they will make a fire in your honor and **l,** 6199
La 2: 8 **made** ramparts and walls **l;** 61
Eze 2:10 On both sides of it were written words of **l** 7806
9: 4 on the foreheads of those who grieve and **l** 650
19: 1 up a **l** concerning the princes of Israel 7806
19:14 This is a **l** and is to be used as a lament." 7806
19:14 This is a lament and is to be used as a **l.**" 7806
24:16 Yet *do* not **l** or weep or shed any tears. 6199
26:17 Then they will take up a **l** concerning you 7806
27: 2 "Son of man, take up a **l** concerning Tyre. 7806
27:32 *they will* **take up a l** concerning you: 7801
28:12 up a **l** concerning the king of Tyre and say 7806
32: 2 up a **l** concerning Pharaoh king of Egypt 7806
32:16 "This is the **l** they will chant for her. 7806
Am 5: 1 this **l** I take up concerning you: 7806

LAMENTATION (3) [LAMENT]

Est 9:31 in regard to their times of fasting and **l.** 2411
Isa 15: 8 their **l** as far as Beer Elim. 3538
La 2: 5 He has multiplied mourning and **l** for 640

LAMENTATIONS (KJV) See LAMENTS

LAMENTED (1) [LAMENT]

Ge 50:10 the Jordan, *they* **l** loudly and bitterly; 5027+6199

LAMENTS (6) [LAMENT]

2Ch 35:25 Jeremiah **composed l** for Josiah, 7801
35:25 women singers commemorate Josiah in the **l** 7806
35:25 in Israel and are written in the **L.** 7806
Isa 16:11 My heart **l** for Moab like a harp, 2159
Jer 48:36 "So my heart **l** for Moab like a flute; 2159
48:36 it **l** like a flute for the men of Kir Hareseth. 2159

LAMP (35) [LAMPS, LAMPSTAND, LAMPSTANDS]

1Sa 3: 3 The **l** *of* God had not yet gone out, 5944
2Sa 21:17 the **l** *of* Israel will not be extinguished." 5944
22:29 You are my **l,** O LORD; 5944
1Ki 11:36 a **l** before me in Jerusalem, 5775
15: 4 a **l** in Jerusalem by raising up a son 5775
2Ki 4:10 a chair and a **l** for him. 4963
8:19 He had promised to maintain a **l** for David 5775
2Ch 21: 7 He had promised to maintain a **l** for him 5775
Job 18: 5 "The **l** *of* the wicked is snuffed out; 240
18: 6 the **l** beside him goes out. 5944
21:17 the **l** *of* the wicked snuffed out? 5944
29: 3 when his **l** shone upon my head and 5944
Ps 18:28 You, O LORD, keep my **l** burning; 5944
119:105 Your word is a **l** to my feet and a light 5944
132:17 a horn grow for David and set up a **l** 5944
Pr 6:23 For these commands are a **l,** 5944
13: 9 but the **l** *of* the wicked is snuffed out. 5944
20:20 his **l** will be snuffed out in pitch darkness. 5944
Pr 20:27 The **l** *of* the LORD searches the spirit of 5944
21: 4 the **l** *of* the wicked, are sin! 5775
24:20 the **l** *of* the wicked will be snuffed out. 5944
31:18 and her **l** does not go out at night. 5944
Jer 25:10 sound of millstones and the light of the **l.** 5944
Mt 5:15 Neither do people light a **l** and put it under *3394*
6:22 "The eye is the **l** of the body. *3394*
Mk 4:21 "Do you bring in a **l** to put it under a bowl *3394*
Lk 8:16 a **l** and hides it in a jar or puts it under *3394*
11:33 "No one lights a **l** and puts it in a place *3394*
11:34 Your eye is the **l** of your body. *3394*
11:36 as when the light of a **l** shines on you." *3394*
15: 8 Does she not light a **l,** *3394*
Jn 5:35 John was a **l** that burned and gave light, *3394*
Rev 18:23 *of* a **l** will never shine in you again. *3394*
21:23 God gives it light, and the Lamb is its **l.** *3394*
22: 5 not need the light *of* a **l** or the light of *3394*

LAMPS (33) [LAMP]

Ex 25:37 "Then make its seven **l** and set them up 5944
27:20 the light so that the **l** may be kept burning. 5944
27:21 to keep **the l** burning before the LORD 2257[S]
30: 7 when he tends the **l.** 5944
30: 8 when he lights the **l** at twilight 5944
35:14 **l** and oil for the light; 5944
37:23 They made its seven **l,** 5944
39:37 *of* **l** and all its accessories, and the oil for 5944
40: 4 bring in the lampstand and set up its **l.** 5944
40:25 and set up the **l** before the LORD, 5944
Lev 24: 2 that the **l** may be kept burning continually. 5944
24: 3 Aaron is to tend **the l** before the LORD 2257[S]
24: 4 The **l** on the pure gold lampstand before 5944
Nu 4: 9 together with its **l,** 5944
8: 2 'When you set up the seven **l,** 5944
8: 3 he set up the **l** so that they faced forward 5944
1Ki 7:49 the gold floral work and **l** and tongs; 5944
1Ch 28:15 for the gold lampstands and their **l,** with 5944
28:15 the weight for each lampstand and its **l;** 5944
28:15 for each silver lampstand and its **l,** 5944
2Ch 4:20 of pure gold with their **l,** to burn in front 5944
4:21 and **l** and tongs (they were solid gold); 5944
13:11 the ceremonially clean table and light the **l** 5944
29: 7 the doors of the portico and put out the **l.** 5944
Zep 1:12 At that time I will search Jerusalem with **l** 5944
Mt 25: 1 be like ten virgins who took their **l** *3286*
25: 3 The foolish ones took their **l** but did *3286*
25: 4 took oil in jars along with their **l.** *3286*
25: 7 the virgins woke up and trimmed their **l.** *3286*
25: 8 some of your oil; our **l** are going out.' *3286*
Lk 12:35 for service and keep your **l** burning, *3394*
Ac 20: 8 There were many **l** in the upstairs room *3286*
Rev 4: 5 Before the throne, seven **l** were blazing. *3286*

LAMPSTAND (37) [LAMP]

Ex 25:31 "Make a **l** of pure gold and hammer it out, 4963
25:32 to extend from the sides of the **l**— 4963
25:33 for all six branches extending from the **l.** 4963
25:34 on the **l** there are to be four cups shaped 4963
25:35 the **l,** a second bud under the second pair, 4963
25:36 be of one piece with **the l,** 5626[S]
25:39 A talent of pure gold is to be used for the **l** NIH
26:35 and put the **l** opposite it on the south side. 4963
30:27 the **l** and its accessories, 4963
31: 8 the pure gold **l** and all its accessories, 4963
35:14 the **l** that is *for* light with its accessories, 4963
37:17 the **l** of pure gold and hammered it out, 4963
37:18 from the sides of the **l**— 4963
37:19 for all six branches extending from the **l.** 4963
37:20 And on the **l** were four cups shaped 4963
37:21 of branches extending from **the l,** 5626[S]
37:22 of one piece with **the l,** 5626[S]
37:24 They made **the l** and all its accessories 2023[S]
39:37 the pure gold **l** with its row of lamps 4963
40: 4 Then bring in the **l** and set up its lamps. 4963
40:24 the **l** in the Tent of Meeting opposite 4963
Lev 24: 4 on the pure gold **l** before the LORD must 4963
Nu 3:31 the table, the **l,** the altars, 4963
4: 9 to take a blue cloth and cover the **l** that is 4963
8: 2 they are to light the area in front of the **l.**' " 4963
8: 3 so that they faced forward on the **l,** 4963
8: 4 This is how the **l** was made: 4963
8: 4 The **l** was made exactly like the pattern 4963
1Ch 28:15 with the weight for **each l** and 2256+4963+4963
28:15 for **each** silver **l** and its lamps, 4963+4963
28:15 according to the use of **each l;** 2256+4963+4963
2Ch 13:11 the lamps on the gold **l** every evening. 4963
Da 5: 5 near the **l** in the royal palace. 10456
Zec 4: 2 "I see a solid gold **l** with a bowl at the top 4963
4:11 on the right and the left of the **l?**" 4963
Heb 9: 2 In its first room were the **l,** *3393*
Rev 2: 5 to you and remove your **l** from its place. *3393*

LAMPSTANDS (11) [LAMP]

1Ki 7:49 the **l** of pure gold (five on the right 4963
1Ch 28:15 weight of gold for the gold **l** and their lamps, 4963
2Ch 4: 7 He made ten gold **l** according to 4963
4:20 the **l** of pure gold with their lamps, to burn 4963
Jer 52:19 censers, sprinkling bowls, pots, **l,** 4963
Rev 1:12 And when I turned I saw seven golden **l,** *3393*
1:13 and among the **l** was someone "like a son of man," *3393*
1:20 and of the seven golden **l** is this: *3393*
1:20 and the seven **l** are the seven churches. *3393*
2: 1 and walks among the seven golden **l:** *3393*
11: 4 the two olive trees and the two **l** that stand *3393*

LANCE (2)

Job 39:23 along with the flashing spear and **l.** 3959
41:29 he laughs at the rattling of the **l.** 3959

LANCETS (KJV) See SPEARS

LAND (1462) [BORDERLAND, GRASSLANDS, LAND'S, LANDED, LANDOWNER, LANDS, MAINLAND, SHORELANDS, WASTELAND, WASTELANDS]

Ge 1:10 God called the dry ground "**l,**" 824
1:11 God said, "Let the **l** produce vegetation: 824
1:11 and trees on the **l** that bear fruit with seed 824
1:12 The **l** produced vegetation: 824
1:24 the **l** produce living creatures according 824
2:11 it winds through the entire **l** of Havilah, 824
2:12 (The gold of that **l** is good; 824
2:13 it winds through the entire **l** *of* Cush. 824
4:14 Today you are driving me from the **l,** 141
4:16 the LORD's presence and lived in the **l** 824
7:22 Everything on **dry l** that had the breath 3000
10:11 From that **l** he went to Assyria, 824
11:28 in the **l** *of* his birth. 824
12:1 and go to the **l** I will show you. 824
12:5 and they set out for the **l** *of* Canaan, 824
12:6 Abram traveled through the **l** as far as 824
12:6 At that time the Canaanites were in the **l.** 824
12:7 "To your offspring I will give this **l.**" 824
12:10 Now there was a famine in the **l,** 824
13:6 But the **l** could not support them 824
13:7 and Perizzites were also living in the **l** at 824
13:9 Is not the whole **l** before you? 824
13:10 like the **l** *of* Egypt, toward Zoar. 824
13:12 Abram lived in the **l** *of* Canaan, 824
13:15 All the **l** that you see I will give to you 824
13:17 through the length and breadth of the **l,** 824
15:7 to give you this **l** to take possession of it." 824
15:18 "To your descendants I give this **l,** 824
15:19 the **l** of the Kenites, NIH
17:8 The whole **l** *of* Canaan, 824
19:23 the sun had risen over the **l.** 824
19:25 and also the vegetation in the **l.** 141
19:28 toward all the **l** *of* the plain, 824
19:28 and he saw dense smoke rising from the **l,** 824
20:15 And Abimelech said, "My **l** is before you; 824
21:32 his forces returned to the **l** *of* the Philistines. 824
21:34 in the **l** *of* the Philistines for a long time. 824
23:2 Hebron) in the **l** *of* Canaan, 824
23:7 down before the people of the **l,** 824
23:12 down before the people of the **l** 824
23:15 **l** is worth four hundred shekels of silver, 824
23:19 near Mamre (which is at Hebron) in the **l** 824
24:5 to come back with me to this **l?** 824
24:7 of my father's household and my native **l** 824
24:7 'To your offspring I will give this **l**'— 824
24:37 Canaanites, in whose **l** I live, 824
25:6 from his son Isaac to the **l** *of* the east. 824
26:1 Now there was a famine in the **l**— 824
26:2 live in the **l** where I tell you to live. 824
26:3 Stay in this **l** for a while, 824
26:12 in that **l** and the same year reaped 824
26:22 and we will flourish in the **l.**" 824
27:46 a wife from among the women of this **l,** 824
28:4 so that you may take possession of the **l** 824
28:4 **the l** God gave to Abraham." 889^{S}
28:13 I will give you and your descendants the **l** 824
28:15 and I will bring you back to this **l.** 141
29:1 and came to the **l** *of* the eastern peoples. 824
31:3 the **l** *of* your fathers and to your relatives, 824
31:13 Now leave this **l** at once and go back 824
31:13 at once and go back to your native **l.**' " 824
31:18 to his father Isaac in the **l** *of* Canaan. 824
32:3 of him to his brother Esau in the **l** *of* Seir, 824
34:1 went out to visit the women of the **l.** 824
34:10 settle among us; the **l** is open to you. 824
34:21 "Let them live in our **l** and trade in it; 824
34:21 the **l** has plenty of room for them. 824
34:30 the people living in this **l.** 824
35:6 Bethel) in the **l** *of* Canaan. 824
35:12 The **l** I gave to Abraham and Isaac I 824
35:12 and I will give this **l** to your descendants 824
36:6 a **l** some distance from his brother Jacob. 824
36:7 the **l** *where* they were staying could 824
36:30 in the **l** *of* Seir. 824
36:34 the **l** *of* the Temanites succeeded him 824
36:43 to their settlements in the **l** they occupied. 824
37:1 in the **l** *where* his father had stayed, 824
37:1 his father had stayed, the **l** *of* Canaan. 824
40:15 For I was forcibly carried off from the **l** 824
41:19 such ugly cows in all the **l** *of* Egypt. 824
41:29 coming throughout the **l** *of* Egypt, 824
41:30 and the famine will ravage the **l.** 824
41:31 in the **l** will not be remembered, 824
41:33 and put him in charge of the **l** *of* Egypt. 824
41:34 the **l** to take a fifth of the harvest of Egypt 824
41:41 "I hereby put you in charge of the whole **l** 824
41:43 Thus he put him in charge of the whole **l** 824
41:45 Joseph went throughout the **l** *of* Egypt. 824
41:47 of abundance the **l** produced plentifully. 824
41:52 because God has made me fruitful in the **l** 824
41:54 in the whole **l** *of* Egypt there was food. 824
42:5 the famine was in the **l** *of* Canaan also. 824
Ge 42:6 Now Joseph was the governor of the **l,** 824
42:7 "From the **l** *of* Canaan," they replied, 824
42:9 to see where our **l** is unprotected." 824
42:12 to see where our **l** is unprotected." 824
42:13 who lives in the **l** *of* Canaan. 824
42:29 to their father Jacob in the **l** *of* Canaan, 824
42:30 the **l** spoke harshly to us and treated us as 824
42:30 as though we were spying on the **l.** 824
42:33 the man who is lord over the **l** said to us, 824
42:34 and you can trade in the **l.**' " 824
43:1 Now the famine was still severe in the **l.** 824
43:11 of the **l** in your bags and take them down 824
44:8 the **l** *of* Canaan the silver we found inside 824
45:6 now there has been famine in the **l,** 824
45:17 Load your animals and return to the **l** 824
45:18 I will give you the best of the **l** *of* Egypt 824
45:18 and you can enjoy the fat of the **l.**' 824
45:25 to their father Jacob in the **l** *of* Canaan. 824
46:12 and Onan had died in the **l** *of* Canaan). 824
46:31 who were living in the **l** *of* Canaan, 824
47:1 the **l** *of* Canaan and are now in Goshen." 824
47:6 and the **l** *of* Egypt is before you; 824
47:6 and your brothers in the best part of the **l.** 824
47:11 in the best part of the **l,** 824
47:18 for our lord except our bodies and our **l.** 141
47:19 we and our **l** as well? 141
47:19 Buy us and our **l** in exchange for food, 141
47:19 with our **l** will be in bondage to Pharaoh. 141
47:19 and that the **l** may not become desolate." 141
47:20 So Joseph bought all the **l** *in* Egypt 141
47:20 The **l** became Pharaoh's, 824
47:22 he did not buy the **l** *of* the priests, 141
47:22 That is why they did not sell their **l.** 141
47:23 that I have bought you and your **l** today 141
47:26 as a law concerning **l** *in* Egypt— 141
47:26 It was only the **l** *of* the priests that did 141
48:3 to me at Luz in the **l** *of* Canaan, 824
48:4 I will give this **l** as an everlasting possession 824
48:7 in the **l** *of* Canaan while we were still on 824
48:21 and take you back to the **l** *of* your fathers. 824
48:22 the **ridge of l** I took from the Amorites 8900
49:15 and how pleasant is his **l,** 824
50:5 in the tomb I dug for myself in the **l** 824
50:13 to the **l** *of* Canaan and buried him in 824
50:24 to your aid and take you up out of this **l** to 824
50:24 to the **l** he promised on oath to Abraham, 824
Ex 1:7 so that the **l** was filled with them. 824
2:22 "I have become an alien in a foreign **l.**" 824
3:8 to bring them up out of that **l** into a good 824
3:8 into a good and spacious **l,** a land flowing 824
3:8 a **l** flowing with milk and honey— 824
3:17 up out of your misery in Egypt into the **l** 824
3:17 a **l** flowing with milk and honey.' 824
5:5 the people of the **l** are now numerous, 824
6:4 with them to give them the **l** *of* Canaan, 824
6:8 to the **l** I swore with uplifted hand to give 824
8:5 make frogs come up on the **l** *of* Egypt.' " 824
8:6 and the frogs came up and covered the **l.** 824
8:7 they also made frogs come up on the **l** 824
8:14 and the **l** reeked of them. 824
8:16 and throughout the **l** *of* Egypt 824
8:17 throughout the **l** *of* Egypt became gnats. 824
8:22 that day I will deal differently with the **l** 824
8:22 know that I, the LORD, am in this **l.** 824
8:24 and throughout Egypt the **l** was ruined by 824
8:25 "Go, sacrifice to your God here in the **l.**" 824
9:5 the LORD will do this in the **l.**" 824
9:9 It will become fine dust over the whole **l** 824
9:9 on men and animals throughout the **l.**" 824
9:23 the LORD rained hail on the **l** *of* Egypt; 824
9:24 in all the **l** *of* Egypt since it had become 824
9:26 The only place it did not hail was the **l** 824
9:33 the rain no longer poured down on the **l.** 824
10:6 the day they settled in this **l** till now.' " 141
10:12 over the **l** and devour everything growing 824
10:13 an east wind blow across the **l** all that day 824
10:15 on tree or plant in all the **l** *of* Egypt. 824
12:23 the LORD goes through the **l** to strike NIH
12:25 the **l** that the LORD will give you 824
12:48 he may take part like one born in the **l.** 824
13:3 out of Egypt, out of the **l** *of* slavery, 1074
13:5 When the LORD brings you into the **l** *of* 824
13:5 **the l** he swore to your forefathers 889^{S}
13:5 a **l** flowing with milk and honey— 824
13:11 the **l** *of* the Canaanites and gives it to you, 824
13:14 out of Egypt, out of the **l** *of* slavery. 1074
14:3 'The Israelites are wandering around the **l** 824
14:21 a strong east wind and turned it into **dry l.** 3000
16:35 until they came to a **l** that was settled; 824
18:3 "I have become an alien in a foreign **l**"; 824
20:2 out of Egypt, out of the **l** *of* slavery. 1074
20:12 the **l** the LORD your God is giving you. 141
23:11 the seventh year let **the l** lie unplowed 5626^{S}
23:23 and bring you into the **l** of the Amorites, NIH
23:26 none will miscarry or be barren in your **l.** 824
23:29 because the **l** would become desolate and 824
23:30 to take possession of the **l.** 824
23:31 over to you the people who live in the **l** 824
23:33 Do not let them live in your **l,** 824
32:13 I will give your descendants all this **l** I promised them, 824
33:1 to the **l** I promised on oath to Abraham, 824
33:3 up to the **l** flowing with milk and honey. 824
34:12 a treaty with those who live in the **l** 824
34:15 a treaty with those who live in the **l;** 824
34:24 and no one will covet your **l** when you go 824
Lev 11:2 'Of all the animals that live on **l,** 824
Lev 14:34 "When you enter the **l** *of* Canaan, 824
14:34 a spreading mildew in a house in that **l,** 824
18:3 and you must not do as they do in the **l** 824
18:25 Even the **l** was defiled; 824
18:25 and the **l** vomited out its inhabitants. 824
18:27 the people who lived in the **l** before you, 824
18:27 and the **l** became defiled. 824
18:28 And if you defile the **l,** 824
19:9 " 'When you reap the harvest of your **l,** 824
19:23 the **l** and plant any kind of fruit tree, 824
19:29 the **l** will turn to prostitution and be filled 824
19:33 " 'When an alien lives with you in your **l,** 824
20:22 the **l** where I am bringing you to live may 824
20:24 I said to you, "You will possess their **l;** 141
20:24 a **l** flowing with milk and honey." 824
22:24 You must not do this in your own **l,** 824
23:10 'When you enter the **l** I am going 824
23:22 " 'When you reap the harvest of your **l,** 824
23:39 after you have gathered the crops of the **l,** 824
25:2 you enter the **l** I am going to give you, 824
25:2 the **l** itself must observe a sabbath to 824
25:4 the seventh year the **l** is to have a sabbath 824
25:5 The **l** is to have a year of rest. 824
25:6 the **l** yields during the sabbath year will 824
25:7 and the wild animals in your **l.** 824
25:7 Whatever **the l** produces may be eaten. 2023^{S}
25:9 the trumpet throughout your **l.** 824
25:10 throughout the **l** to all its inhabitants. 824
25:14 If *you* **sell l** to one of your countrymen 4835+4928
25:18 and you will live safely in the **l.** 824
25:19 Then the **l** will yield its fruit, 824
25:21 that the **l** will yield enough for three years. NIH
25:23 " 'The **l** must not be sold permanently, 824
25:23 the **l** is mine and you are but aliens 824
25:24 for the redemption of the **l.** 824
25:38 of Egypt to give you the **l** *of* Canaan and 824
26:1 not place a carved stone in your **l** to bow 824
26:5 and live in safety in your **l.** 824
26:6 " 'I will grant peace in the **l,** 824
26:6 I will remove savage beasts from the **l,** 824
26:20 nor will the trees of the **l** yield their fruit. 824
26:32 I will lay waste the **l,** 824
26:33 Your **l** will be laid waste, 824
26:34 Then the **l** will enjoy its sabbath years all 824
26:34 then the **l** will rest and enjoy its sabbaths. 824
26:35 the **l** will have the rest it did not have NIH
26:38 the **l** *of* your enemies will devour you. 824
26:41 toward them so that I sent them into the **l** 824
26:42 and I will remember the **l.** 824
26:43 For the **l** will be deserted by them 824
26:44 when they are in the **l** *of* their enemies, 824
27:16 of his **family l,** its value is to be set 299+8441
27:22 which is not part of his **family l,** 299+8441
27:24 the one whose **l** it was 299+824
27:28 whether man or animal or **family l**— 299+8441
27:30 " 'A tithe of everything from the **l,** 824
Nu 10:9 When you go into battle in your own **l** 824
10:30 to my own **l** and my own people." 824
11:12 to the **l** you promised on oath 141
13:2 "Send some men to explore the **l** 824
13:16 of the men Moses sent to explore the **l.** 824
13:18 See what the **l** is like and whether 824
13:19 What kind of **l** do they live in? 824
13:20 to bring back some of the fruit of the **l.**" 824
13:21 and explored the **l** from the Desert of Zin 824
13:25 they returned from exploring the **l.** 824
13:26 and showed them the fruit of the **l.** 824
13:27 "We went into the **l** to which you sent us, 824
13:30 up and take possession of **the l,** 2023^{S}
13:32 a bad report about the **l** they had explored. 824
13:32 **l** we explored devours those living in it. 824
14:3 to this **l** only to let us fall by the sword? 824
14:6 among those who had explored the **l,** 824
14:7 "The **l** we passed through and explored 824
14:8 he will lead us into that **l,** 824
14:8 a **l** flowing with milk and honey, 824
14:9 do not be afraid of the people of the **l,** 824
14:14 And they will tell the inhabitants of this **l** 824
14:16 into the **l** he promised them on oath; 824
14:23 of them will ever see the **l** I promised 824
14:24 I will bring him into the **l** he went to, 824
14:30 Not one of you will enter the **l** I swore 824
14:31 in to enjoy the **l** you have rejected. 824
14:34 of the forty days you explored the **l**— 824
14:36 the men Moses had sent to explore the **l,** 824
14:37 about the **l** were struck down and died of 824
14:38 Of the men who went to explore the **l,** 824
15:2 you enter the **l** I am giving you as a home 824
15:18 you enter the **l** to which I am taking you 824
15:19 and you eat the food of the **l,** 824
16:13 up out of a **l** flowing with milk and honey 824
16:14 you haven't brought us into a **l** flowing 824
18:20 "You will have no inheritance in their **l,** 824
20:12 this community into the **l** I give them." 824
20:24 He will not enter the **l** I give the Israelites, 824
21:24 over his **l** from the Arnon to the Jabbok, 824
21:26 of Moab and had taken from him all his **l** 824
21:31 So Israel settled in the **l** *of* the Amorites. 824
21:34 with his whole army and his **l.** 824
21:35 And they took possession of his **l.** 824
22:5 near the River, in his native **l.** 824
22:5 cover the face of the **l** and have settled next 824
22:11 come out of Egypt covers the face of the **l.** 824
26:53 "The **l** is to be allotted to them as 824
26:55 Be sure that the **l** is distributed by lot. 824
27:12 and see the **l** I have given the Israelites. 824
32:4 the **l** the LORD subdued before the people 824

Nu 32: 5 "let this l be given to your servants 824
32: 7 the Israelites from going over into the l 824
32: 8 from Kadesh Barnea to look over the l. 824
32: 9 to the Valley of Eshcol and viewed the l, 824
32: 9 the l the LORD had given them. 824
32:11 of Egypt will see the l I promised on oath 141
32:17 protection from the inhabitants of the l. 824
32:22 when the l is subdued before the LORD, 824
32:22 And this l will be your possession before 824
32:29 then when the l is subdued before you, 824
32:29 the l *of* Gilead as their possession. 824
32:33 the whole l with its cities and the territory 824
33:52 drive out all the inhabitants of the l 824
33:53 Take possession of the l and settle in it, 824
33:53 for I have given you the l to possess. 824
33:54 Distribute the l by lot, 824
33:55 not drive out the inhabitants of the l, 824
33:55 They will give you trouble in the l 824
34: 2 'When you enter Canaan, the l that will 824
34:12 " 'This will be your l, 824
34:13 "Assign this l by lot as an inheritance. 824
34:17 the men who are to assign the l for you as 824
34:18 from each tribe to help assign the l. 824
34:29 the inheritance to the Israelites in the l 824
35: 8 The towns you give the Levites from the l NIH
35:32 and live on his own l before the death of 824
35:33 " 'Do not pollute the l where you are. 824
35:33 Bloodshed pollutes the l, 824
35:33 and atonement cannot be made for the l 824
35:34 the l where you live and where I dwell, 824
36: 2 the l as an inheritance to the Israelites 824
36: 7 the tribal **l inherited** *from* his forefathers. 5709
36: 8 Every daughter who inherits l in any 5709
36: 9 tribe is to keep the **l it inherits."** 5709
Dt 1: 7 to the l *of* the Canaanites and to Lebanon, 824
1: 8 See, I have given you this l. 824
1: 8 the l that the LORD swore he would give 824
1:21 the LORD your God has given you the l. 824
1:22 the l for us and bring back a report about 824
1:25 with them some of the fruit of the l, 824
1:25 "It is a good l that the LORD our God 824
1:35 the good l I swore to give your forefathers. 824
1:36 and his descendants the l he set his feet 824
1:39 they will enter **the l.** 2025+9004[S]
2: 5 for I will not give you any of their l, 824
2: 9 for I will not give you any part of their l. 824
2:12 in the l the LORD gave them 824
2:19 of any l *belonging to* the Ammonites. 824
2:20 too was considered a l *of* the Rephaites, 824
2:29 the l the LORD our God is giving us." 824
2:31 Now begin to conquer and possess his l." 824
2:37 you did not encroach on any of the l *of* 824
2:37 the l along the course of the Jabbok nor NIH
3: 2 over to you with his whole army and his l. 824
3:12 Of the l that we took over at that time, 824
3:13 in Bashan used to be known as a l *of* 824
3:18 "The LORD your God has given you this l 824
3:20 and they too have taken over the l that 824
3:25 Let me go over and see the good l beyond 824
3:27 Look at the l with your own eyes, NIH
3:28 across and will cause them to inherit the l 824
4: 1 and may go in and take possession of the l 824
4: 5 in the l you are entering to take possession 824
4:10 to revere me as long as they live in the l 141
4:14 in the l that you are crossing the Jordan 824
4:21 not cross the Jordan and enter the good l 824
4:22 I will die in this l; I will not cross the Jordan 824
4:22 over and take possession of that good l. 824
4:25 and grandchildren and have lived in the l 824
4:26 from the l that you are crossing the Jordan 824
4:38 to bring you into their l to give it to you 824
4:40 in the l the LORD your God gives you 141
4:46 in the l *of* Sihon king of the Amorites, 824
4:47 of his l and the land of Og king of Bashan, 824
4:47 They took possession of his land and the l 824
4:48 This l extended from Aroer on the rim of NIH
5: 6 out of Egypt, out of the l *of* slavery. 1074
5:16 the l the LORD your God is giving you. 141
5:21 on your neighbor's house or l, 8441
5:31 in the l I am giving them to possess." 824
5:33 and prosper and prolong your days in the l 824
6: 1 in the l that you are crossing the Jordan 824
6: 3 in a l flowing with milk and honey, 824
6:10 into the l he swore to your fathers, 824
6:10 a l with large, flourishing cities NIH
6:12 out of Egypt, out of the l *of* slavery. 1074
6:15 he will destroy you from the face of the l. 141
6:18 over the good l that the LORD promised 824
6:23 and give us the l that he promised on oath 824
7: 1 into the l you are entering to possess 824
7: 8 and redeemed you from the l *of* slavery, 1074
7:13 the crops of your l—your grain, new wine 141
7:13 in the l that he swore to your forefathers 141
8: 1 the l that the LORD promised on oath 824
8: 7 into a good l—a land with streams 824
8: 7 a l *with* streams and pools of water, 824
8: 8 a l *with* wheat and barley, vines 824
8: 9 a l where bread will not be scarce 824
8: 9 a l where the rocks are iron 824
8:10 your God for the good l he has given you. 824
8:14 out of Egypt, out of the l *of* slavery. 1074
8:15 that thirsty and waterless l, NIH
9: 4 of this l because of my righteousness." 824
9: 5 in to take possession of their l; 824
9: 6 LORD your God is giving you this good l 824
9:23 take possession of the l I have given you." 824
9:28 into the l he had promised them, 824
Dt 10: 7 a l *with* streams of water. 824
10:11 so that they may enter and possess the l 824
11: 8 in and take over the l that you are crossing 824
11: 9 and so that you may live long in the l that 141
11: 9 a l flowing with milk and honey. 824
11:10 The l you are entering to take over is not 824
11:10 to take over is not like the l *of* Egypt, 824
11:11 But the l you are crossing the Jordan 824
11:11 to take possession of is a l *of* mountains 824
11:12 It is a l the LORD your God cares for; 824
11:14 I will send rain on your l in its season, 824
11:17 from the good l the LORD is giving you. 824
11:21 of your children may be many in the l that 141
11:25 the terror and fear of you on the whole l, 824
11:29 into the l you are entering to possess, 824
11:31 the l the LORD your God is giving you. 824
12: 1 to follow in the l that the LORD, the God 824
12: 1 as long as you live in the l. 141
12:10 the l the LORD your God is giving you 824
12:19 the Levites as long as you live in your l. 141
12:29 driven them out and settled in their l, 824
13: 5 and redeemed you from the l *of* slavery; 1074
13: 7 from one end of the l to the other), 824
13:10 out of Egypt, out of the l *of* slavery. 1074
15: 4 the l the LORD your God is giving you 824
15: 7 in any of the towns of the l that 824
15:11 There will always be poor people in the l. 824
15:11 and toward the poor and needy in your l. 824
16: 4 be found in your possession in all your l 1473
16:20 the l the LORD your God is giving you. 824
17:14 the l the LORD your God is giving you 824
18: 9 the l the LORD your God is giving you, 824
19: 1 the nations whose l he is giving you, 824
19: 2 the l the LORD your God is giving you 824
19: 3 the l the LORD your God is giving you 824
19: 8 gives you the whole l he promised them, 824
19:10 innocent blood will not be shed in your l, 824
19:14 the l the LORD your God is giving you 824
21: 1 the l the LORD your God is giving you 141
21:23 the l the LORD your God is giving you 141
23:20 to in the l you are entering to possess. 824
24: 4 the l the LORD your God is giving you 824
25:15 the l the LORD your God is giving you. 141
25:19 in the l he is giving you to possess as 824
26: 1 the l the LORD your God is giving you 824
26: 2 the l the LORD your God is giving you 824
26: 3 the l the LORD swore to our forefathers 824
26: 9 and gave us this l, a land flowing 824
26: 9 a l flowing with milk and honey; 824
26:15 the l you have given us as you promised 141
26:15 a l flowing with milk and honey." 824
27: 2 the l the LORD your God is giving you, 824
27: 3 when you have crossed over to enter the l 824
27: 3 a l flowing with milk and honey, 824
28: 4 and the crops of your l and the young 141
28: 8 bless you in the l he is giving you. 824
28:11 in the l he swore to your forefathers 141
28:12 to send rain on your l in season and 824
28:18 will be cursed, and the crops of your l, 141
28:21 from the l you are entering to possess. 141
28:33 that you do not know will eat what your l 141
28:42 over all your trees and the crops of your l. 141
28:51 the crops of your l until you are destroyed. 141
28:52 to all the cities throughout your l until 824
28:52 the l the LORD your God is giving you. 824
28:63 be uprooted from the l you are entering 141
29: 2 to all his officials and to all his l. 824
29: 8 We took their l and gave it as 824
29:19 This will bring disaster on the **watered l** 8116
29:22 the calamities that have fallen on the l and 824
29:23 The whole l will be a burning waste 824
29:24 "Why has the LORD done this to this l? 824
29:27 the LORD's anger burned against this l, 824
29:28 the LORD uprooted them from their l 141
29:28 and thrust them into another l, 824
30: 4 to the **most distant l** *under* the heavens, 7895
30: 5 He will bring you to the l that belonged 824
30: 9 of your livestock and the crops of your l. 141
30:16 in the l you are entering to possess. 824
30:18 the l you are crossing the Jordan to enter 141
30:20 in the l he swore to give to your fathers, 141
31: 3 and you will take possession of their l. NIH
31: 4 whom he destroyed along with their l. 824
31: 7 for you must go with this people into the l 824
31:13 as you live in the l you are crossing 141
31:16 the foreign gods of the l they are entering. 824
31:20 into the l flowing with milk and honey, 141
31:20 **the l** I promised on oath 889[S]
31:21 into the l I promised them on oath." 824
31:23 the Israelites into the l I promised them 824
32:10 In a desert l he found him, 824
32:13 He made him ride on the heights of the l 824
32:43 and make atonement for his l and people. 141
32:47 in the l you are crossing the Jordan 141
32:49 the l I am giving the Israelites 824
32:52 you will see the l only from a distance; 824
32:52 the l I am giving to the people of Israel." 824
33:13 "May the LORD bless his l with 824
33:21 He chose the best l for himself; NIH
33:28 Jacob's spring is secure in a l *of* grain 824
34: 1 There the LORD showed him the whole l— 824
34: 2 all the l *of* Judah as far as the western sea, 824
34: 4 the l I promised on oath to Abraham, 824
34:11 and to all his officials and to his whole l. 824
Jos 1: 2 to cross the Jordan River into the l I am 824
1: 6 to inherit the l I swore to their forefathers 824
1:11 the l the LORD your God is giving you 824
Jos 1:13 and has granted you this l.' 824
1:14 and your livestock may stay in the l 824
1:15 taken possession of the l that the LORD 824
1:15 you may go back and occupy your own l, 824
2: 1 "Go, look over the l," he said, 824
2: 2 tonight to spy out the l." 824
2: 3 they have come to spy out the whole l." 824
2: 9 "I know that the LORD has given this l 824
2:14 when the LORD gives us the l." 824
2:18 when we enter the l, 824
2:24 "The LORD has surely given the whole l 824
5: 6 to them that they would not see the l 824
5: 6 a l flowing with milk and honey. 824
5:11 they ate some of the produce of the l: 824
5:12 the day after they ate this food from the l; 824
6:22 to the two men who had spied out the l, 824
6:27 and his fame spread throughout the l. 824
8: 1 his people, his city and his l. 824
9:24 his servant Moses to give you the whole l 824
11:16 So Joshua took this entire l: 824
11:23 So Joshua took the entire l, 824
11:23 Then the l had rest from war. 824
12: 1 of the l whom the Israelites had defeated 824
12: 6 the LORD gave **their l** to the Reubenites, 2023[S]
12: 7 These are the kings of the l that Joshua 824
13: 1 and there are still very large **areas of l** to 824
13: 2 "This is the l that remains: 824
13: 4 all the l *of* the Canaanites, 824
13: 6 Be sure to allocate **this l** to Israel for 2023[S]
13:12 and taken over their l. NIH
14: 1 as an inheritance in the l *of* Canaan, 824
14: 4 The Levites received no share of the l 824
14: 5 So the Israelites divided the l, 824
14: 7 from Kadesh Barnea to explore the l. 824
14: 9 So on that day Moses swore to me, 'The l 824
14:15 Then the l had rest from war. 824
15:19 Since you have given me l *in* the Negev, 824
17: 5 of ten **tracts of l** besides Gilead 824
17: 6 The l *of* Gilead belonged to the rest of 824
17: 8 (Manasseh had the l *of* Tappuah, 824
17:10 On the south the l belonged to Ephraim, NIH
17:15 the forest and **clear l** for yourselves there 1345
17:15 and clear land for yourselves there in the l 824
18: 3 to take possession of the l that the LORD 824
18: 4 a survey of the l and to write a description 824
18: 5 You are to divide **the l** into seven parts. 2023[S]
18: 6 descriptions of the seven parts of the l, 824
18: 8 on their way to map out the l, 824
18: 8 "Go and make a survey of the l and write 824
18: 9 So the men left and went through the l. 824
18:10 and there he distributed the l to the Israelites 824
19:49 When they had finished dividing the l 824
19:51 And so they finished dividing the l. 824
21:43 the l he had sworn to give their forefathers, 824
22: 4 return to your homes in the l that Moses 299+824
22: 7 half-tribe of Manasseh Moses had given l NIH
22: 7 the other half of the tribe Joshua gave l on NIH
22: 9 Canaan to return to Gilead, their own l, 299+824
22:10 near the Jordan in the l *of* Canaan, 824
22:13 the priest, to the l *of* Gilead— 824
22:19 If the l you possess is defiled, 824
22:19 come over to the LORD's l, 299+824
22:19 and share the l with us. NIH
23: 4 as an inheritance for your tribes all the l of NIH
23: 5 and you will take possession of their l, 824
23:13 until you perish from this good l, 141
23:15 from this good l he has given you. 141
23:16 from the good l he has given you." 824
24: 3 from the **l beyond** the River and led him 6298
24: 8 to the l *of* the Amorites who lived east of 824
24: 8 and you took possession of their l. 824
24:13 So I gave you a l on which you did 824
24:15 the Amorites, in whose l you are living. 824
24:17 out of Egypt, from that l *of* slavery, 1074
24:18 including the Amorites, who lived in the l. 824
24:30 they buried him in the l *of* his inheritance, 1473
24:32 were buried at Shechem in the tract of l 8441
Jdg 1: 2 I have given the l into their hands." 824
1:15 Since you have given me l in the Negev, 824
1:26 He then went to the l *of* the Hittites, 824
1:27 Canaanites were determined to live in that l. 824
1:32 among the Canaanite inhabitants of the l. 824
1:33 among the Canaanite inhabitants of the l, 824
2: 1 and led you into the l that I swore to give 824
2: 2 a covenant with the people of this l, 824
2: 6 they went to take possession of the l, 824
2: 9 they buried him in the l *of* his inheritance, 1473
3:11 So the l had peace for forty years, 824
3:30 and the l had peace for eighty years. 824
5: 4 when you marched from the l *of* Edom, 8441
5:31 Then the l had peace forty years. 824
6: 4 on the l and ruined the crops all the way 824
6: 5 they invaded the l to ravage it. 824
6: 8 out of Egypt, out of the l *of* slavery. 1074
6: 9 from before you and gave you their l. 824
6:10 the Amorites, in whose l you live.' 824
8:28 the l enjoyed peace forty years. 824
9:37 down from the center of the l, 824
10: 8 the l *of* the Amorites. 824
11: 3 from his brothers and settled in the l 824
11: 5 went to get Jephthah from the l *of* Tob. 824
11:13 they took away my l from the Arnon to 824
11:15 not take the l *of* Moab or the land of 824
11:15 the land of Moab or the l *of* the Ammonites. 824
11:21 over all the l *of* the Amorites who lived in 824
12:12 and was buried in Aijalon in the l 824
16:24 the one who laid waste our l 824

Jdg 18: 2 and Eshtaol to spy out the l and explore it. 824
18: 2 They told them, "Go, explore the l." 824
18: 7 And since their l lacked nothing, 824
18: 9 We have seen that the l is very good. 824
18:10 an unsuspecting people and a spacious l 824
18:10 a l that lacks nothing whatever." 5226
18:14 Then the five men who had spied out the l 824
18:17 who had spied out the l went inside and 824
18:30 until the time of the captivity of the l. 824
20: 1 from the l of Gilead came out as one man 824
21:21 from the girls of Shiloh and go to the l 824
Ru 1: 1 there was a famine in the l, 824
1: 7 that would take them back to the l 824
4: 3 is selling the piece of l that belonged 8441
4: 5 "On the day you buy the l from Naomi 8441
1Sa 6: 5 from you and your gods and your l. 824
9:16 a man from the l of Benjamin. 824
13: 3 the trumpet blown throughout the l 824
13: 7 even crossed the Jordan to the l of Gad 824
13:19 be found in the whole l of Israel, 824
14:46 and they withdrew to their own l. 5226
21:11 "Isn't this David, the king of the l? 824
22: 5 Go into the l of Judah." 824
23:27 The Philistines are raiding the l." 824
27: 1 to escape to the l of the Philistines. 824
27: 8 in the l extending to Shur and Egypt.) 824
28: 3 the mediums and spiritists from the l. 824
28: 9 the mediums and spiritists from the l. 824
29:11 up early in the morning to go back to the l 824
30:16 of plunder they had taken from the l of 824
31: 9 and they sent messengers throughout the l 824
2Sa 3:12 to say to David, "Whose l is it? 824
9: 7 I will restore to you all the l that belonged 8441
9:10 and your servants are to farm the l for him 141
10: 2 When David's men came to the l of 824
14:20 he knows everything that happens in the l." 824
15: 4 "If only I were appointed judge in the l! 824
17:26 and Absalom camped in the l of Gilead. 824
21:14 God answered prayer in behalf of the l. 824
24: 8 After they had gone through the entire l, 824
24:13 upon you three years of famine in your l? 824
24:13 Or three days of plague in your l? 824
24:25 the LORD answered prayer in behalf of the l, 824
1Ki 2:34 he was buried on his own l in the desert. 1074
4:10 and all the l of Hepher were his); 824
4:21 from the River to the l of the Philistines, 824
8:34 and bring them back to the l you gave 141
8:36 on the l you gave your people for 824
8:37 "When famine or plague comes to the l, 824
8:40 in the l you gave our fathers. 141
8:41 from a distant l because of your name— 824
8:46 who takes them captive to his own l, 824
8:47 and if they have a change of heart in the l 824
8:47 and repent and plead with you in the l 824
8:48 to you with all their heart and soul in the l 824
8:48 toward the l you gave their fathers, toward 824
9: 7 from the l I have given them 141
9: 8 the LORD done such a thing to this l and 824
9:13 And he called them the l of Cabul, 824
9:18 and Tadmor in the desert, within his l, 824
9:21 their descendants remaining in the l, 824
10:15 and the governors of the l. 824
11:18 a house and l and provided him with food. 824
14:15 He will uproot Israel from this good l 141
14:24 even male shrine prostitutes in the l; 824
15:12 the male shrine prostitutes from the l 824
17: 7 up because there had been no rain in the l. 824
17:14 the day the LORD gives rain on the l.' " 141
18: 1 and I will send rain on the l." 141
18: 5 through the l to all the springs and valleys. 824
18: 6 So they divided the l they were to cover, 824
20: 7 of Israel summoned all the elders of the l 824
22:36 everyone to his l!" 824
22:46 He rid the l of the rest of the male shrine 824
2Ki 2:19 water is bad and the l is unproductive." 824
2:21 or make the l unproductive.' " NIH
3:20 And the l was filled with water. 824
3:24 the Israelites invaded the l and slaughtered 2023S
3:27 they withdrew and returned to their own l. 824
8: 1 the LORD has decreed a famine in the l 824
8: 2 in the l of the Philistines seven years. 824
8: 3 the seven years she came back from the l 824
8: 3 to the king to beg for her house and l. 8441
8: 5 to beg the king for her house and l. 8441
8: 6 including all the income from her l from 8441
10:33 in all the l of Gilead (the region of Gad, 824
11: 3 for six years while Athaliah ruled the l. 824
11:14 the l were rejoicing and blowing trumpets. 824
11:18 All the people of the l went to the temple 824
11:19 the guards and all the people of the l, 824
11:20 and all the people of the l rejoiced. 824
15: 5 and governed the people of the l. 824
15:19 Then Pul king of Assyria invaded the l, 824
15:20 and stayed in the l no longer. 824
15:29 including all the l of Naphtali, 824
16:15 burnt offering of all the people of the l, 824
17: 5 The king of Assyria invaded the entire l, 824
17:27 the people what the god of the l requires." 824
18:32 and take you to a l like your own, 824
18:32 a l of grain and new wine, 824
18:32 a l of bread and vineyards, 824
18:32 a l of olive trees and honey. 824
18:33 the god of any nation ever delivered his l 824
18:35 has been able to save his l from me? 824
19:37 and they escaped to the l of Ararat. 824
20:14 "From a distant l," Hezekiah replied. 824
21: 8 from the l I gave their forefathers, 141

2Ki 21:24 of the l killed all who had plotted 824
23:30 And the people of the l took Jehoahaz son 824
23:33 the l of Hamath so that he might not reign 824
23:35 the l and exacted the silver and gold from 824
23:35 of the l according to their assessments. 824
24: 1 king of Babylon invaded the l, NIH
24:14 Only the poorest people of the l were left. 824
24:15 his officials and the leading men of the l. 824
25:12 behind some of the poorest people of the l 824
25:19 the l and sixty of his men who were found 824
25:21 There at Riblah, in the l of Hamath, 824
25:21 Judah went into captivity, away from her l. 141
25:24 "Settle down in the l and serve the king 824
1Ch 1:45 the l of the Temanites succeeded him 824
4:40 and the l was spacious, peaceful and quiet. 824
5: 9 the east they occupied the l up to the edge NIH
5:22 And they occupied the l until the exile. 9393S
5:23 in the l from Bashan to Baal Hermon, 824
5:25 to the gods of the peoples of the l, 824
10: 9 and sent messengers throughout the l of 824
11:10 to extend it over the whole l, as 3776S
14:17 David's fame spread throughout every l, 824
16:18 "To you I will give the l of Canaan as 824
19: 2 to Hanun in the l of the Ammonites 824
20: 1 He laid waste the l of the Ammonites 824
21:12 days of plague in the l, with the angel of 824
22:18 For he has handed the inhabitants of the l 824
22:18 and the l is subject to the LORD and 824
27:26 of the field workers who farmed the l. 141
28: 8 that you may possess this good l 824
2Ch 6:25 to the l you gave to them and their fathers. 141
6:27 on the l you gave your people for 824
6:28 "When famine or plague comes to the l, 824
6:31 in the l you gave our fathers. 141
6:32 a distant l because of your great name 824
6:36 who takes them captive to a l far away 824
6:37 and if they have a change of heart in the l 824
6:37 and repent and plead with you in the l 824
6:38 to you with all their heart and soul in the l 824
6:38 toward the l you gave their fathers, toward 824
7:13 the l or send a plague among my people, 824
7:14 forgive their sin and will heal their l. 824
7:20 then I will uproot Israel from my l, 141
7:21 the LORD done such a thing to this l and 824
8: 8 their descendants remaining in the l, 824
9:14 the l brought gold and silver to Solomon. 824
9:26 from the River to the l of the Philistines, 824
14: 6 since the l was at peace. 824
14: 7 The l is still ours, because we have sought 824
15: 8 from the whole l of Judah and Benjamin 824
19: 3 for you have rid the l of the Asherah poles 824
19: 5 He appointed judges in the l, 824
20: 7 not drive out the inhabitants of this l 824
22:12 for six years while Athaliah ruled the l. 824
23:13 the l were rejoicing and blowing trumpets, 824
23:20 of the l and brought the king down from 824
23:21 and all the people of the l rejoiced. 824
26:21 and governed the people of the l. 824
30: 9 and will come back to this l, 824
32: 4 and the stream that flowed through the l. 824
32:13 of those nations ever able to deliver their l 824
32:21 So he withdrew to his own l in disgrace. 824
32:31 miraculous sign that had occurred in the l, 824
33: 8 of the Israelites leave the l I assigned 141
33:25 people of the l killed all who had plotted 824
34: 8 to purify the l and the temple, 824
36: 1 And the people of the l took Jehoahaz son 824
36:21 The l enjoyed its sabbath rests; 824
Ezr 9:11 'The l you are entering to possess is 824
9:11 to possess is a l polluted by the corruption 824
9:12 be strong and eat the good things of the l 824
Ne 4: 4 over as plunder in a l of captivity. 824
5:14 to be their governor in the l of Judah, 824
5:16 we did not acquire any l. 8441
9: 8 to his descendants the l of the Canaanites, 824
9:10 and all the people of his l, 824
9:15 of the l you had sworn with uplifted hand 824
9:23 the l that you told their fathers to enter 824
9:24 in and took possession of the l. 824
9:24 the Canaanites, who lived in the l; 824
9:24 with their kings and the peoples of the l, 824
9:25 They captured fortified cities and fertile l; 141
9:35 the spacious and fertile l you gave them, 824
9:36 slaves in the l you gave our forefathers 824
10:31 the l and will cancel all debts. NIH
Job 1: 1 In the l of Uz there lived a man 824
1:10 and herds are spread throughout the l. 824
9:24 a l falls into the hands of the wicked, 824
10:21 to the l of gloom and deep shadow, 824
10:22 to the l of deepest night, 824
12:15 if he lets them loose, they devastate the l. 824
15:19 the l was given when no alien passed 824
15:29 nor will his possessions spread over the l. 824
18:17 he has no name in the l. 2575
22: 8 owning l—an honored man, living on it. 824
24: 4 and force all the poor of the l into hiding. 824
24:18 their portion of the l is cursed, 824
28:13 it cannot be found in the l of the living. 824
30: 3 the parched l in desolate wastelands 7480
30: 8 they were driven out of the l. 824
31:38 "if my l cries out against me 141
37:17 the l lies hushed under the south wind, 824
38:26 to water a l where no man lives, 824
42:15 the l were there found women as beautiful 824
Ps 10:16 the nations will perish from his l. 824
16: 3 As for the saints who are in the l, 824
25:13 and his descendants will inherit the l. 824

Ps 27:13 goodness of the LORD in the l of the living. 824
35:20 against those who live quietly in the l. 824
37: 3 dwell in the l and enjoy safe pasture. 824
37: 9 who hope in the LORD will inherit the l. 824
37:11 But the meek will inherit the l 824
37:22 those the LORD blesses will inherit the l, 824
37:27 then you will dwell in the l forever. NIH
37:29 the righteous will inherit the l and dwell 824
37:34 He will exalt you to inherit the l; 824
41: 2 in the l and not surrender him to the desire 824
42: 6 therefore I will remember you from the l 824
44: 3 not by their sword that they won the l, 824
45:16 you will make them princes throughout the l. 824
52: 5 will uproot you from the l of the living. 824
60: 2 You have shaken the l and torn it open; 824
63: 1 a dry and weary l where there is no water. 824
65: 9 You care for the l and water it; 824
66: 6 He turned the sea into dry l, 3317
67: 6 Then the l will yield its harvest, and God, 824
68: 6 but the rebellious live in a sun-scorched l. 7461
68:14 the Almighty scattered the kings in the l, 2023S
72:16 Let grain abound throughout the l; 824
74: 8 where God was worshiped in the l. 824
74:20 of violence fill the dark places of the l. 824
76: 8 and the l feared and was quiet— 824
76: 9 to save all the afflicted of the l. 824
78:12 the sight of their fathers in the l of Egypt, 824
78:54 to the border of his holy l, NIH
80: 9 and it took root and filled the l. 824
85: 1 You showed favor to your l, O LORD; 824
85: 9 that his glory may dwell in our l. 824
85:12 and our l will yield its harvest. 824
88:12 your righteous deeds in the l of oblivion? 824
95: 5 and his hands formed the dry l. 3318
101: 6 My eyes will be on the faithful in the l, 824
101: 8 to silence all the wicked in the l; 824
105:11 "To you I will give the l of Canaan as 824
105:16 on the l and destroyed all their supplies 824
105:23 Jacob lived as an alien in the l of Ham. 824
105:27 his wonders in the l of Ham. 824
105:28 He sent darkness and made the l dark— NIH
105:30 Their l teemed with frogs, 824
105:32 with lightning throughout their l; 824
105:35 they ate up every green thing in their l, 824
105:36 he struck down all the firstborn in their l, 824
106:22 in the l of Ham and awesome deeds by 824
106:24 Then they despised the pleasant l; 824
106:38 and the l was desecrated by their blood. 824
107:34 and fruitful l into a salt waste, 824
112: 2 His children will be mighty in the l; 824
116: 9 that I may walk before the LORD in the l 824
125: 3 over the l allotted to the righteous, AIT
135:12 and he gave their l as an inheritance, 824
136:21 and gave their l as an inheritance, 824
137: 4 of the LORD while in a foreign l? 141
140:11 Let slanderers not be established in the l; 824
142: 5 my portion in the l of the living." 824
143: 6 my soul thirsts for you like a parched l. 824
Pr 2:21 For the upright will live in the l, 824
2:22 but the wicked will be cut off from the l, 824
10:30 but the wicked will not remain in the l. 824
12:11 He who works his l will have abundant food, 141
25:25 is good news from a distant l. 824
28:19 He who works his l will have abundant food, 141
30:16 l, which is never satisfied with water, 824
31:23 he takes his seat among the elders of the l. 824
Ecc 5: 9 The increase from the l is taken by all; 824
10:16 Woe to you, O l whose king was a servant 824
10:17 Blessed are you, O l whose king is of noble birth 824
11: 2 not know what disaster may come upon the l. 824
SS 2:12 the cooing of doves is heard in our l. 824
Isa 1:19 you will eat the best from the l; 824
2: 7 Their l is full of silver and gold; 824
2: 7 Their l is full of horses; 824
2: 8 Their l is full of idols; they bow down to 824
4: 2 of the l will be the pride and glory of 824
5: 8 and you live alone in the l. 824
5:30 And if one looks at the l, 824
6:12 and the l is utterly forsaken. 824
6:13 And though a tenth remains in the l, 2023S
6:13 so the holy seed will be the stump in the l." 2023S
7:16 the l of the two kings you dread will 141
7:18 and for bees from the l of Assyria. 824
7:22 All who remain in the l will eat curds 824
7:24 l will be covered with briers and thorns. 824
8: 8 cover the breadth of your l, O Immanuel!" 824
8:21 they will roam through the l; 2023S
9: 1 the l of Zebulun and the land of Naphtali, 824
9: 1 the land of Zebulun and the l of Naphtali, 824
9: 2 on those living in the l of the shadow 824
9:19 the l will be scorched and the people will 824
10:23 the destruction decreed upon the whole l. 824
13: 9 the l desolate and destroy the sinners 824
13:14 each will flee to his native l. 824
14: 1 and will settle them in their own l. 141
14: 2 and maidservants in the LORD's l. 141
14:20 for you have destroyed your l 824
14:21 the l and cover the earth with their cities. 824
14:25 I will crush the Assyrian in my l; 824
15: 9 and upon those who remain in the l. 141
16: 1 Send lambs as tribute to the ruler of the l, 824
16: 4 the aggressor will vanish from the l. 824
18: 1 to the l of whirring wings along the rivers 824
18: 2 whose l is divided by rivers. 824
18: 7 whose l is divided by rivers— 824
19:17 And the l of Judah will bring terror to 141

Isa	19:20	to the LORD Almighty in the l *of* Egypt.	824
	21: 1	comes from the desert, from a l *of* terror.	824
	23: 1	From the l *of* Cyprus word has come	824
	23:10	Till your l as along the Nile,	824
	23:13	Look at the l *of* the Babylonians,	824
	26: 1	In that day this song will be sung in the l	824
	26:10	in a l *of* uprightness they go on doing evil	824
	26:15	you have extended all the borders of the l.	824
	28:22	destruction decreed against the whole l.	824
	30: 6	Through a l *of* hardship and distress,	824
	30:23	the food that comes from the l will be rich	141
	32: 2	the shadow of a great rock in a thirsty l.	824
	32:13	for the l *of* my people, a land overgrown	141
	32:13	a l overgrown with thorns and briers—	NIH
	33: 9	The l mourns and wastes away,	824
	33:17	the king in his beauty and view a l	824
	34: 7	Their l will be drenched with blood,	824
	34: 9	her l will become blazing pitch!	824
	35: 1	The desert and the **parched** l will be glad;	7480
	36:10	have I come to attack and destroy this l	824
	36:17	and take you to a l like your own—	824
	36:17	a l *of* grain and new wine,	824
	36:17	a l *of* bread and vineyards.	824
	36:18	the god of any nation ever delivered his l	824
	36:20	has been able to save his l from me?	824
	37:38	and they escaped to the l *of* Ararat.	824
	38:11	the LORD, in the l *of* the living;	824
	39: 3	"From a distant l," Hezekiah replied.	824
	44: 3	For I will pour water on the thirsty l,	NIH
	45:19	from somewhere in a l *of* darkness;	824
	46:11	from a far-off l, a man to fulfill my purpose.	824
	49: 8	a covenant for the people, to restore the l	824
	49:19	and made desolate and your l laid waste,	824
	53: 8	he was cut off from the l *of* the living;	824
	57:13	the l and possess my holy mountain."	824
	58:11	satisfy your needs in a **sun-scorched** l	7463
	58:14	to ride on the heights of the l and to feast	824
	60: 6	Herds of camels will cover your l,	NIH
	60:18	No longer will violence be heard in your l,	824
	60:21	and they will possess the l forever.	824
	61: 7	inherit a double portion in their l,	824
	62: 4	call you Deserted, or name your l Desolate.	824
	62: 4	called Hephzibah, and your l Beulah;	824
	62: 4	and your l will be married.	824
	65:16	a blessing in the l will do so by the God	824
	65:16	he who takes an oath in the l will swear	824
Jer	1:14	be poured out on all who live in the l.	824
	1:18	a bronze wall to stand against the whole l—	824
	1:18	its priests and the people of the l.	824
	2: 2	through the desert, through a l not sown.	824
	2: 6	through a l *of* deserts and rifts,	824
	2: 6	a l *of* drought and darkness,	824
	2: 6	a l where no one travels and no one lives?'	824
	2: 7	I brought you into a fertile l to eat its fruit	824
	2: 7	But you came and defiled my l	824
	2:15	They have laid waste his l;	824
	2:31	a desert to Israel or a l *of* great darkness?	824
	3: 1	Would not the l be completely defiled?	824
	3: 2	You have defiled the l with your prostitution	824
	3: 9	she defiled the l and committed adultery	824
	3:16	numbers have increased greatly in the l,"	824
	3:18	they will come from a northern l to	824
	3:18	to the l I gave your forefathers as	824
	3:19	like sons and give you a desirable l,	824
	4: 5	'Sound the trumpet throughout the l!'	824
	4: 7	He has left his place to lay waste your l.	824
	4:16	besieging army is coming from a distant l,	824
	4:20	the whole l lies in ruins.	824
	4:26	I looked, and the **fruitful** l was a desert;	4149
	4:27	"The whole l will be ruined,	824
	5:19	and served foreign gods in your own l,	824
	5:19	so now you will serve foreigners in a l	824
	5:30	and shocking thing has happened in the l:	824
	6: 8	away from you and make your l desolate	824
	6:12	against those who live in the l,"	824
	6:20	or sweet calamus from a distant l?	824
	6:22	an army is coming from the l *of* the north;	824
	7: 7	in the l I gave your forefathers for ever	824
	7:34	for the l will become desolate.	824
	8:16	of their stallions the whole l trembles.	824
	8:16	to devour the l and everything in it,	824
	8:19	to the cry of my people from a l far away:	824
	9: 3	it is not by truth that they triumph in the l.	824
	9:12	Why has the l been ruined and laid waste	824
	9:19	We must leave our l because our houses	824
	10:17	Gather up your belongings to leave the l,	824
	10:18	I will hurl out those who live in this l;	824
	10:22	a great commotion from the l *of* the north!	824
	11: 5	a l flowing with milk and honey'—	824
	11: 5	the l you possess today."	NIH
	11:19	let us cut him off from the l *of* the living,	824
	12: 4	How long will the l lie parched and	824
	12:11	the whole l will be laid waste	824
	12:12	from one end of the l to the other;	824
	13:13	with drunkenness all who live in this l,	824
	14: 2	they wail for the l, and a cry goes up from	824
	14: 4	because there is no rain in the l;	824
	14: 8	why are you like a stranger in the l,	824
	14:15	'No sword or famine will touch this l.'	824
	14:18	and priest have gone to a l they know not.' "	824
	15: 7	a winnowing fork at the city gates of the l.	824
	15:10	a man with whom the whole l strives	824
	15:14	to your enemies in a l you do not know,	824
	16: 3	about the sons and daughters born in this l	5226
	16: 6	"Both high and low will die in this l.	824
	16:13	So I will throw you out of this l into	824
	16:13	into a l neither you nor your fathers have	824
Jer	16:15	who brought the Israelites up out of the l	824
	16:15	to the l I gave their forefathers.	141
	16:18	because they have defiled my l with	824
	17: 3	My mountain in the l and your wealth	8441
	17: 4	to your enemies in a l you do not know,	824
	17: 6	in a salt l where no one lives.	824
	18:16	Their l will be laid waste,	824
	22:10	nor see his native l again.	824
	22:12	he will not see this l again."	824
	22:27	to the l you long to return to."	824
	22:28	cast into a l they do not know?	824
	22:29	O l, land, land, hear the word of the LORD!	824
	22:29	l, land, hear the word of the LORD!	824
	22:29	land, l, hear the word of the LORD!	824
	23: 5	and do what is just and right in the l.	824
	23: 8	the descendants of Israel up out of the l *of*	824
	23: 8	Then they will live in their own l."	141
	23:10	The l is full of adulterers;	824
	23:10	because of the curse the l lies parched and	824
	23:15	ungodliness has spread throughout the l."	824
	24: 5	whom I sent away from this place to the l	824
	24: 6	and I will bring them back to this l.	824
	24: 8	whether they remain in this l or live	824
	24:10	until they are destroyed from the l I gave	141
	25: 5	and you can stay in the l the LORD gave	141
	25: 9	against this l and its inhabitants and	824
	25:12	the l *of* the Babylonians, for their guilt,"	824
	25:13	upon that l all the things I have spoken	824
	25:30	and roar mightily against his l.	5659
	25:38	and their l will become desolate because	824
	26:17	of the elders of the l stepped forward	824
	26:20	against this city and this l as Jeremiah did.	824
	27: 7	until the time for his l comes;	824
	27:11	that nation remain in its own l to till it and	141
	30: 3	to the l I gave their forefathers to possess,'	824
	30:10	your descendants from the l *of* their exile.	824
	31: 8	I will bring them from the l *of* the north	824
	31:16	"They will return from the l *of* the enemy.	824
	31:17	"Your children will return to their own l.	1473
	31:23	from captivity, the people in the l	824
	32:15	vineyards will again be bought in this l.'	824
	32:22	You gave them this l you had sworn	824
	32:22	a l flowing with milk and honey.	824
	32:41	and will assuredly plant them in this l	824
	32:43	Once more fields will be bought in this l	824
	33:11	the fortunes of the l as they were before,'	824
	33:15	he will do what is just and right in the l.	824
	34:13	out of Egypt, out of the l *of* slavery.	1074
	34:19	and all the people of the l	824
	35: 7	Then you will live a long time in the l	141
	35:11	king of Babylon invaded this l,	824
	35:15	Then you will live in the l I have given	141
	36:29	and destroy this l and cut off both men	824
	37: 2	nor the people of the l paid any attention	824
	37: 7	will go back to its own l, to Egypt.	824
	37:19	of Babylon will not attack you or this l'?	824
	39: 5	of Babylon at Riblah in the l *of* Hamath,	824
	39:10	in the l *of* Judah some of the poor people,	824
	40: 6	the people who were left behind in the l.	824
	40: 7	over the l and had put him in charge of	824
	40: 7	and children who were the poorest in the l	824
	40: 9	"Settle down in the l and serve the king	824
	40:12	they all came back to the l *of* Judah,	824
	41: 2	had appointed as governor over the l.	824
	41:18	had appointed as governor over the l.	824
	42:10	'If you stay in this l, I will build you up	824
	42:12	on you and restore you to your l.'	141
	42:13	if you say, 'We will not stay in this l,'	824
	43: 4	the LORD's command to stay in the l	824
	43: 5	in the l *of* Judah from all the nations	824
	44: 9	by you and your wives in the l *of* Judah	824
	44:14	or survive to return to the l *of* Judah,	824
	44:21	and the people of the l?	824
	44:22	your l became an object of cursing and	824
	44:28	the sword and return to the l *of* Judah	824
	45: 4	uproot what I have planted, throughout the l.	824
	46:10	will offer sacrifice in the l *of* the north by	824
	46:27	your descendants from the l *of* their exile.	824
	47: 2	They will overflow the l and everything	824
	47: 2	all who dwell in the l will wail	824
	49:19	I will chase Edom from **its** l in an instant.	2023^S
	50: 1	the prophet concerning Babylon and the l	824
	50: 3	and lay waste her l.	824
	50: 8	leave the l *of* the Babylonians,	824
	50: 9	an alliance of great nations from the l *of*	824
	50:12	a wilderness, a **dry** l, a desert.	7480
	50:16	let everyone flee to his own l.	824
	50:18	of Babylon and his l as I punished	824
	50:21	the l *of* Merathaim and those who live	824
	50:22	The noise of battle is in the l,	824
	50:25	to do in the l *of* the Babylonians.	824
	50:34	so that he may bring rest to their l,	824
	50:38	For it is a l *of* idols,	824
	50:44	I will chase Babylon from **its** l in	2023^S
	50:45	what he has purposed against the l *of*	824
	51: 2	to winnow her and to devastate her l;	824
	51: 5	though their l is full of guilt before	824
	51: 9	let us leave her and each go to his own l,	824
	51:27	"Lift up a banner in the l!	824
	51:29	The l trembles and writhes,	824
	51:29	to lay waste the l *of* Babylon so	824
	51:43	towns will be desolate, a dry and desert l,	824
	51:43	a l where no one lives,	NIH
	51:46	be afraid when rumors are heard in the l;	824
	51:46	the next, rumors of violence in the l and	824
	51:47	her whole l will be disgraced	824
	51:50	Remember the LORD in a **distant** *l*,	AIT
Jer	51:52	throughout her l the wounded will groan.	824
	51:54	the sound of great destruction from the l	824
	52: 9	of Babylon at Riblah in the l *of* Hamath,	824
	52:16	of the l to work the vineyards and fields.	824
	52:25	the l and sixty of his men who were found	824
	52:27	There at Riblah, in the l *of* Hamath,	824
	52:27	Judah went into captivity, away from her l.	141
La	3:34	To crush underfoot all prisoners in the l,	824
	4:21	you who live in the l *of* Uz.	824
Eze	1: 3	the Kebar River in the l *of* the Babylonians.	824
	6:14	and make the l a desolate waste from	824
	7: 2	the Sovereign LORD says to the l	141
	7: 2	upon the four corners of the l.	824
	7: 7	you who dwell in the l.	824
	7:13	not recover the l he has **sold** as long as	4928
	7:23	because the l is full of bloodshed and	824
	7:27	hands of the people of the l will tremble.	824
	8:12	the LORD has forsaken the l.' "	824
	8:17	Must they also fill the l with violence	824
	9: 9	the l is full of bloodshed and	824
	9: 9	'The LORD has forsaken the l;	824
	11:15	this l was given to us as our possession.'	824
	11:17	and I will give you back the l	141
	12: 6	so that you cannot see the l,	824
	12:12	so that he cannot see the l.	824
	12:13	the l *of* the Chaldeans,	824
	12:19	Say to the people of the l:	824
	12:19	in Jerusalem and in the l *of* Israel:	141
	12:19	for their l will be stripped of everything	824
	12:20	be laid waste and the l will be desolate.	824
	12:22	what is this proverb you have in the l	141
	13: 9	nor will they enter the l *of* Israel.	141
	14:16	but the l would be desolate.	824
	14:17	'Let the sword pass throughout the l,'	824
	14:19	a plague into that l and pour out my wrath	824
	15: 8	I will make the l desolate	824
	16: 3	and birth were in the l *of* the Canaanites;	824
	16:29	Babylonia, a l *of* merchants,	824
	17: 4	and carried it away to a l *of* merchants,	824
	17: 5	the seed of your l and put it in fertile soil.	824
	17:13	also carried away the leading men of the l,	824
	17:16	in the l *of* the king who put him on	5226
	18: 2	by quoting this proverb about the l	141
	19: 4	They led him with hooks to the l	824
	19: 7	The l and all who were in it were terrified	824
	19:13	in the desert, in a dry and thirsty l.	824
	20: 6	into a l I had searched out for them,	824
	20: 6	a l flowing with milk and honey,	NIH
	20:15	into the l I had given them—	824
	20:15	a l flowing with milk and honey,	NIH
	20:28	into the l I had sworn to give them	824
	20:36	in the desert of the l *of* Egypt,	824
	20:38	Although I will bring them out of the l	824
	20:38	yet they will not enter the l *of* Israel.	141
	20:40	there in the l the entire house of Israel will	824
	20:42	when I bring you into the l *of* Israel,	141
	20:42	the l I had sworn with uplifted hand	824
	21: 2	Prophesy against the l *of* Israel	141
	21:30	in the l *of* your ancestry, I will judge you.	824
	21:32	your blood will be shed in your l,	824
	22:24	say to **the** l, 'You are a land that has had	2023^S
	22:24	a l that has had no rain or showers in	824
	22:29	The people of the l practice extortion	824
	22:30	of the l so I would not have to destroy it,	824
	23: 3	In **that** l their breasts were fondled	9004^S
	23:48	"So I will put an end to lewdness in the l,	824
	25: 3	over the l *of* Israel when it was laid waste	141
	25: 6	the malice of your heart against the l	141
	25: 9	and Kiriathaim—the glory of that l.	824
	26:20	or take your place in the l *of* the living.	824
	28:25	Then they will live in their own l,	141
	29:10	the l *of* Egypt a ruin and a desolate waste	824
	29:12	I will make the l *of* Egypt desolate	824
	29:14	to Upper Egypt, the l *of* their ancestry.	824
	29:19	and plunder **the** l as pay for his army.	2023^S
	30: 5	the covenant l will fall by the sword along	824
	30:11	will be brought in to destroy the l.	824
	30:11	against Egypt and fill the l with the slain.	824
	30:12	up the streams of the Nile and sell the l	824
	30:12	of foreigners I will lay waste the l	824
	30:13	and I will spread fear throughout the l.	824
	31:12	lay broken in all the ravines of the l.	824
	32: 4	I will throw you on the l and hurl you on	824
	32: 6	the l with your flowing blood all the way	824
	32: 8	I will bring darkness over your l,	824
	32:15	and strip the l of everything in it,	824
	32:23	All who had spread terror in the l *of*	824
	32:24	All who had spread terror in the l *of*	824
	32:25	Because their terror had spread in the l *of*	824
	32:26	because they spread their terror in the l *of*	824
	32:27	of these warriors had stalked through the l	824
	32:32	Although I had him spread terror in the l	824
	33: 2	'When I bring the sword against a l,	824
	33: 2	a land, and the people of the l choose one	824
	33: 3	the sword coming against the l and blows	824
	33:24	in those ruins in the l *of* Israel are saying,	141
	33:24	yet he possessed the l.	824
	33:24	l has been given to us as our possession.'	824
	33:25	should you then possess the l?	824
	33:26	Should you then possess the l?'	824
	33:28	I will make the l a desolate waste,	824
	33:29	when I have made the l a desolate waste	824
	34:13	and I will bring them into their own l.	141
	34:13	and in all the settlements in the l.	824
	34:14	heights of Israel will be their **grazing** l.	5659
	34:14	they will lie down in good **grazing** l,	5659
	34:25	the l of wild beasts so that they may live	824

Eze 34:27 the people will be secure in their **l.** 141
34:29 **l** renowned **for** its **crops,** 4760
34:29 in the **l** or bear the scorn of the nations. 824
36: 5 hearts they made my **l** their own possession 824
36: 6 the **l** *of* Israel and say to the mountains 141
36:17 people of Israel were living in their own **l,** 141
36:18 because they had shed blood in the **l** and 824
36:20 and yet they had to leave his **l.'** 824
36:24 and bring you back into your own **l.** 141
36:28 in the **l** I gave your forefathers; 824
36:34 The desolate **l** will be cultivated instead 824
36:35 "This **l** that was laid waste has become 824
37:12 I will bring you back to the **l** *of* Israel. 141
37:14 and I will settle you in your own **l.** 141
37:21 and bring them back into their own **l.** 141
37:22 I will make them one nation in the **l,** 824
37:25 in the **l** I gave to my servant Jacob, 824
37:25 **the l** where your fathers lived. 2023[S]
38: 2 against Gog, of the **l** *of* Magog, 824
38: 8 In future years you will invade a **l** 824
38: 9 you will be like a cloud covering the **l.** 824
38:11 "I will invade a **l** *of* unwalled villages; 824
38:12 living at the center of the **l."** 824
38:16 like a cloud that covers the **l.** 824
38:16 O Gog, I will bring you against my **l,** 824
38:18 When Gog attacks the **l** *of* Israel, 141
38:19 be a great earthquake in the **l** *of* Israel. 141
39:12 be burying them in order to cleanse the **l.** 824
39:13 All the people of the **l** will bury them, 824
39:14 be regularly employed to cleanse **the l.** 2023[S]
39:14 Some will go throughout the **l** and, 824
39:15 the **l** and one of them sees a human bone, 824
39:16 And so they will cleanse the **l.'** 824
39:26 in their **l** with no one to make them afraid. 141
39:28 I will gather them to their own **l,** 141
40: 2 In visions of God he took me to the **l** 824
43: 2 and the **l** was radiant with his glory. 824
45: 1 " 'When you allot the **l** as an inheritance, 824
45: 1 to present to the LORD a portion of the **l** 824
45: 2 with 50 cubits around it for **open l.** 4494
45: 4 the sacred portion of the **l** for the priests, 824
45: 7 the **l** bordering each side of the area NIH
45: 8 This **l** will be his possession in Israel. 824
45: 8 to possess the **l** according to their tribes. 824
45:16 the **l** will participate in this special gift for 824
45:22 for himself and for all the people of the **l.** 824
46: 3 of the **l** are to worship in the presence of 824
46: 9 " 'When the people of the **l** come before 824
47:13 to divide the **l** for an inheritance among 824
47:14 this **l** will become your inheritance. 824
47:15 "This is to be the boundary of the **l:** 824
47:18 along the Jordan between Gilead and the **l** 824
47:21 to distribute this **l** among yourselves 824
48:12 to them from the sacred portion of the **l,** 824
48:14 This is the best of the **l** and must not pass 824
48:29 the **l** you are to allot as an inheritance to 824
Da 4:10 a tree in the middle of the **l.** 10075
6:25 of every language throughout the **l:** 10075
8: 9 and to the east and toward the Beautiful **L.** NIH
9: 6 and to all the people of the **l.** 824
11:16 in the Beautiful **L** and will have the power 824
11:39 over many people and will distribute the **l** 141
11:41 He will also invade the Beautiful **L.** 824
Hos 1: 2 the **l** is guilty of the vilest adultery 824
1:11 and will come up out of the **l,** 824
2: 3 turn her into a parched **l,** 824
2:18 sword and battle I will abolish from the **l,** 824
2:23 I will plant her for myself in the **l;** 824
4: 1 to bring against you who live in the **l:** 824
4: 1 no acknowledgment of God in the **l.** 824
4: 3 Because of this the **l** mourns, 824
7:16 For this they will be ridiculed in the **l** 824
9: 3 They will not remain in the LORD's **l;** 824
10: 1 as his **l** prospered, he adorned his sacred stones. 824
13: 5 in the desert, in the **l** *of* burning heat. 824
Joel 1: 2 listen, all who live in the **l.** 824
1: 6 A nation has invaded my **l,** 824
1:14 the **l** to the house of the LORD your God, 824
2: 1 Let all who live in the **l** tremble, 824
2: 3 Before them the **l** is like the garden 824
2:18 Then the LORD will be jealous for his **l** 824
2:20 pushing it into a parched and barren **l,** 824
2:21 Be not afraid, O **l;** be glad and rejoice. 141
3: 2 among the nations and divided up my **l.** 824
3:19 in whose **l** they shed innocent blood. 824
Am 2:10 to give you the **l** *of* the Amorites. 824
3:11 "An enemy will overrun the **l;** 824
5: 2 never to rise again, deserted in her own **l,** 141
5: 8 and pours them out over the face of the **l**— 824
6: 2 Is their **l** larger than yours? 1473
7: 2 When they had stripped the **l** clean, 824
7: 4 up the great deep and devoured the **l.** 2750
7:10 The **l** cannot bear all his words. 824
7:11 away from their **native l.'** " 141
7:12 Go back to the **l** *of* Judah. 824
7:17 Your **l** will be measured and divided up, 141
7:17 go into exile, away from their **native l.'** " 141
8: 4 and do away with the poor of the **l,** 824
8: 8 "Will not the **l** tremble for this, 824
8: 8 The whole **l** will rise like the Nile; 2023[S]
8:11 "when I will send a famine through the **l**— 824
9: 5 the whole **l** rises like the Nile, 2023[S]
9: 6 and pours them out over the face of the **l**— 824
9:15 I will plant Israel in their own **l,** 141
9:15 from the **l** I have given them," 141
Ob 1:19 from the foothills will possess the **l** of NIH
Ob 1:20 in Canaan will possess [the **l**] as far as NIH
Jnh 1: 9 who made the sea and the **l."** 3317
1:13 the men did their best to row back to **l.** 3317
2:10 and it vomited Jonah onto **dry l.** 3317
Mic 2: 5 the assembly of the LORD to divide the **l** 2475
5: 5 the Assyrian invades our **l** and marches 824
5: 6 They will rule the **l** *of* Assyria with 824
5: 6 the **l** *of* Nimrod with drawn sword. 824
5: 6 from the Assyrian when he invades our **l** 824
5:11 I will destroy the cities of your **l** and tear 824
6: 4 and redeemed you from the **l** *of* slavery. 1074
7: 2 The godly have been swept from the **l;** 824
Na 3:13 of your **l** are wide open to your enemies; 824
3:16 but like locusts they strip the **l** and NIH
Hab 3:13 the leader of the **l** *of* wickedness, 1074
Zep 2: 3 Seek the LORD, all you humble of the **l,** 824
2: 5 O Canaan, **l** *of* the Philistines. 824
2: 6 The **l** *by* the sea, where the Kerethites 2475
2: 8 and made threats against their **l.** 1473
2: 9 of my nation *will* **inherit** their **l."** 5706
2:11 when he destroys all the gods of the **l.** 824
2:11 every one in its own **l.** 5226
3:19 and honor in every **l** *where* they were put 824
Hag 2: 4 Be strong, all you people of the **l,'** 824
2: 6 and the earth, the sea and the **dry l.** 3000
Zec 1:21 up their horns against the **l** *of* Judah 824
2: 6 Flee from the **l** *of* the north," 824
2:12 inherit Judah as his portion in the holy **l** 141
3: 9 'and I will remove the sin of this **l** in 824
5: 3 that is going out over the whole **l;** 824
5: 6 the iniquity of the people throughout the **l."** 824
6: 8 given my Spirit rest in the **l** *of* the north." 824
7: 5 the people of the **l** and the priests, 824
7:14 The **l** was left so desolate behind them 824
7:14 how they made the pleasant **l** desolate.' " 824
9: 1 of the LORD is against the **l** *of* Hadrach 824
9:16 They will sparkle in his **l** like jewels in 141
11: 6 no longer have pity on the people of the **l,"** 824
11: 6 They will oppress the **l,** 824
11:16 a shepherd over the **l** who will not care for 824
12:12 The **l** will mourn, each clan by itself, 824
13: 2 the names of the idols from the **l,** 824
13: 2 and the spirit of impurity from the **l.** 824
13: 5 the **l** has been my livelihood since my youth. 141
13: 8 In the whole **l,"** declares the LORD, 824
14:10 The whole **l,** from Geba to Rimmon, 824
Mal 1: 4 They will be called the Wicked **L,** 1473
3:12 for yours will be a delightful **l,"** 824
4: 6 or else I will come and strike the **l** with 824
Mt 2: 6 Bethlehem, in the **l** of Judah, *1178*
2:20 and his mother and go to the **l** of Israel, *1178*
2:21 and his mother and went to the **l** of Israel. *1178*
4:15 "**L** of Zebulun and land of Naphtali, *1178*
4:15 of Zebulun and **l** of Naphtali, the way to *1178*
4:16 on those living in the **l** of the shadow *6001*
14:24 a considerable distance from **l,** *1178*
23:15 over **l** and sea to win a single convert, *3831*
27:45 the ninth hour darkness came over all the **l.** *1178*
Mk 6:47 and he was alone on **l.** *1178*
15:33 over the whole **l** until the ninth hour. *1178*
Lk 4:25 a severe famine throughout the **l.** *1178*
21:23 in the **l** and wrath against this people. *1178*
23:44 and darkness came over the whole **l** until *1178*
Ac 5: 3 of the money you received *for* the **l?** *6005*
5: 8 the price you and Ananias got for the **l?"** *6005*
7: 3 'and go to the **l** I will show you.' *1178*
7: 4 left the **l** of the Chaldeans and settled *1178*
7: 4 God sent him to this **l** where you are *1178*
7: 5 after him would possess **the l,** *899[S]*
7:45 with them when they took the **l** from *NIG*
7:45 It remained in the **l** until the time *NIG*
13:19 in Canaan and gave their **l** to his people *1178*
27:27 sailors sensed they were approaching **l.** *6001*
27:39 they did not recognize the **l,** *1178*
27:43 to jump overboard first and get to **l.** *1178*
27:44 In this way everyone reached **l** in safety. *1178*
Heb 6: 7 **L** that drinks in the rain often falling on it *1178*
6: 8 But **l** that produces thorns and thistles *NIG*
11: 9 home in the promised **l** like a stranger in *1178*
11:29 passed through the Red Sea as on dry **l;** *1178*
Jas 5: 7 for the **l** to yield its valuable crop and *1178*
5:17 not rain on the **l** for three and a half years. *1178*
Rev 7: 1 to prevent any wind from blowing on the **l** *1178*
7: 2 given power to harm the **l** and the sea: *1178*
7: 3 "Do not harm the **l** or the sea or the trees *1178*
10: 2 on the sea and his left foot on the **l,** *1178*
10: 5 the sea and on the **l** raised his right hand *1178*
10: 8 standing on the sea and on the **l."** *1178*
16: 2 and poured out his bowl on the **l,** *1178*

LAND'S (1) [LAND]

Nu 18:13 All the **l** firstfruits that they bring to 824+928

LANDMARK (KJV) See BOUNDARY STONE

LANDED (11) [LAND]

Mt 14:14 *When* Jesus **l** and saw a large crowd, *2002*
14:34 *they* **l** at Gennesaret. *1178+2093+2262+3836*
Mk 6:34 *When* Jesus **l** and saw a large crowd, *2002*
6:53 *they* **l** at Gennesaret and *1178+2093+2262+3836*
Jn 6:23 Then some boats from Tiberias **l** near *2262*
21: 9 When *they* **l,** they saw a *609+1178+1650+3836*
Ac 18:22 *When he* **l** at Caesarea, he went up *2982*
Ac 21: 3 *We* **l** at Tyre, where our ship was to unload *2982*
21: 7 We continued our voyage from Tyre and **l** *2918*
27: 3 The next day *we* **l** at Sidon; *2864*
27: 5 *we* **l** at Myra in Lycia. *2982*

LANDOWNER (3) [LAND]

Mt 20: 1 a **l** who went out early in the morning *476+3867*
20:11 they began to grumble against the **l.** *3867*
21:33 There was a **l** who planted a vineyard. *476+3867*

LANDS (50) [LAND]

Ge 26: 3 your descendants I will give all these **l** 824
26: 4 in the sky and will give them all these **l,** 824
41:54 There was famine in all the other **l,** 824
Lev 26:36 in the **l** *of* their enemies that the sound of 824
26:39 in the **l** *of* their enemies because 824
Nu 32: 1 the **l** *of* Jazer and Gilead were suitable 824
Dt 29:22 from distant **l** will see the calamities 824
Jos 10:42 and their **l** Joshua conquered 824
12: 7 toward Seir (**their l** Joshua gave as 2023[S]
12: 8 the **l** of the Hittites, Amorites, Canaanites, NIH
Jdg 11:18 skirted the **l** *of* Edom and Moab, 824
2Ki 19:17 have laid waste these nations and their **l.** 824
19:24 I have dug wells in **foreign** *l* and drunk AIT
1Ch 7:28 Their **l** and settlements included Bethel 299
29:30 and the kingdoms of all the other **l.** 824
2Ch 12: 8 and serving the kings of other **l."** 824
13: 9 of your own as the peoples of other **l** do? 824
15: 5 for all the inhabitants of the **l** were 824
17:10 the kingdoms of the **l** surrounding Judah, 824
26:10 in the hills and in the **fertile l,** 4149
31:19 on the farm **l** around their towns or 8441
32:13 to all the peoples of the other **l?** 824
32:17 the gods of the peoples of the other **l** did 824
Ps 49:11 though they had named **l** after themselves. 141
76:11 the **neighboring** *l* bring gifts to the One to AIT
78:55 and allotted their **l** to them as an inheritance 2475
105:44 he gave them the **l** *of* the nations, 824
106:27 and scatter them throughout the **l.** 824
107: 3 those he gathered from the **l,** 824
111: 6 giving them the **l** *of* other nations. 5709
Isa 8: 9 Listen, all you distant **l.** 824
13: 5 They come from faraway **l,** 824
14: 7 All the **l** are at rest and at peace; 824
23: 7 have taken her to settle in far-off **l?** NIH
37:18 have laid waste all these peoples and their **l.** 824
37:25 I have dug wells in foreign **l** and drunk NIH
Jer 12:14 from their **l** and I will uproot the house 141
27:10 to remove you far from your **l;** 141
32:37 I will surely gather them from all the **l** 824
46:16 to our own people and our native **l,** 824
Eze 6: 8 when you are scattered among the **l** 824
20: 6 the most beautiful of all **l.** 824
20:15 most beautiful of all **l**— 824
29:12 land of Egypt desolate among devastated **l,** 824
30: 7 " 'They will be desolate among desolate **l,** 824
32: 9 among **l** you have not known. 824
Hab 2: 8 you have destroyed **l** and cities 824
2:17 you have destroyed **l** and cities 824
Zec 10: 9 yet in **distant l** they will remember me. 5305
Ac 4:34 For from time to time those who owned **l** *6005*

LANES (1)

Lk 14:23 and **country l** and make them come in, *5850*

LANGUAGE (41) [LANGUAGES]

Ge 10: 5 within their nations, each with its own **l.)** 4383
11: 1 Now the whole world had one **l** and 8557
11: 6 the same **l** they have begun to do this, 8557
11: 7 down and confuse their **l** so they will 8557
11: 9 because there the LORD confused the **l** 8557
Dt 28:49 a nation whose **l** you will not understand, 4383
Ezr 4: 7 in Aramaic script and in the Aramaic **l.** 9553
Ne 13:24 of their children spoke the **l of Ashdod** or 848
13:24 Ashdod or the **l** *of* one of the other peoples 4383
13:24 not know how to speak the **l of Judah.** 3376
Est 1:22 and to each people in its own **l,** 4383
3:12 the **l** *of* each people all Haman's orders to 4383
8: 9 of each province and the **l** *of* each people 4383
8: 9 also to the Jews in their own script and **l.** 4383
Ps 19: 3 or **l** where their voice is not heard. 1821
81: 5 where we heard a **l** we did not understand. 8557
Isa 19:18 cities in Egypt will speak the **l** *of* Canaan 8557
Jer 5:15 a people whose **l** you do not know, 4383
Eze 3: 5 and difficult **l,** but to the house of Israel— 4383
3: 6 of obscure speech and difficult **l,** 4383
Da 1: 4 He was to teach them the **l** and literature 4383
3: 4 O peoples, nations and **men of every l:** 10392
3: 7 nations and **men of every l** fell down 10392
3:29 or **l** who say anything against the God 10392
4: 1 nations and **men of every l,** 10392
5:19 and nations and **men of every l** dreaded 10392
6:25 and **men of every l** throughout the land: 10392
7:14 nations and **men of every l** worshiped him. 10392
Jn 8:43 Why is my **l** not clear to you? *3282*
8:44 When he lies, he speaks **his native l,** *1666+2625+3836*
16:25 *I will* no longer **use** this kind of **l** *3281*
Ac 1:19 they called that field in their **l** Akeldama, *1365*
2: 6 each one heard them speaking *in* his own **l.** *1365*
2: 8 each of us hears them *in* his own native **l?** *1365*
14:11 they shouted *in* **the Lycaonian l,** *3378*
Col 3: 8 slander, and **filthy l** from your lips. *155*
Rev 5: 9 for God from every tribe and **l** and people *1185*

Rev 7: 9 from every nation, tribe, people and **l**, *1185*
11: 9 **l** and nation will gaze on their bodies *1185*
13: 7 over every tribe, people, **l** and nation. *1185*
14: 6 to every nation, tribe, **l** and people. *1185*

LANGUAGES (6) [LANGUAGE]
Ge 10:20 the sons of Ham by their clans and **l**, 4383
10:31 the sons of Shem by their clans and **l**, 4383
Zec 8:23 from all **l** and nations will take firm hold 4383
1Co 14:10 Undoubtedly there are all sorts *of* **l** in *5889*
Rev 10:11 nations, **l** and kings." *1185*
17:15 are peoples, multitudes, nations and **l**. *1185*

LANGUISH (2) [LANGUISHES]
Isa 24: 4 the exalted of the earth **l**. 581
Jer 14: 2 "Judah mourns, her cities **l**; 581

LANGUISHES (1) [LANGUISH]
Isa 24: 4 the world **l** and withers, 581

LANTERNS (1)
Jn 18: 3 They were carrying torches, **l** and weapons. *3286*

LAODICEA (6) [LAODICEANS]
Col 2: 1 for you and for those at **L**, *3293*
4:13 for you and for those at **L** and Hierapolis. *3293*
4:15 Give my greetings to the brothers at **L**, *3293*
4:16 and that you in turn read the letter from **L**. *3293*
Rev 1:11 Thyatira, Sardis, Philadelphia and **L**." *3293*
3:14 "To the angel of the church in **L** write: *3293*

LAODICEANS (1) [LAODICEA]
Col 4:16 *of* the **L** and that you in turn read the letter *3294*

LAPIDOTH (KJV) See LAPPIDOTH

LAP (8) [LAPPED, LAPS]
Jdg 7: 5 "Separate those who **l** the water 4379
16:19 Having put him to sleep on her **l**, 1386
Ru 4:16 laid him in her **l** and cared for him. 2668
2Ki 4:20 the boy sat on her **l** until noon, 1386
Pr 6:27 Can a man scoop fire into his **l** 2668
16:33 The lot is cast into the **l**, 2668
Ecc 7: 9 for anger resides in the **l** *of* fools. 2668
Lk 6:38 will be poured into your **l**. *3146*

LAPPED (2) [LAP]
Jdg 7: 6 Three hundred men **l** with their hands 4379
7: 7 men that **l** I will save you and give 4379

LAPPIDOTH (1)
Jdg 4: 4 Deborah, a prophetess, the wife of **L**, 4366

LAPS (4) [LAP]
Ps 79:12 into the **l** *of* our neighbors seven times 2668
Isa 65: 6 I will pay it back into their **l**— 2668
65: 7 I will measure into their **l** the full payment 2668
Jer 32:18 the fathers' sins into the **l** *of* their children 2668

LAPWING (KJV) See HOOPOE

LARGE (154) [ENLARGE, ENLARGED, ENLARGES, LARGER, LARGEST]
Ge 29: 2 stone over the mouth of the well was **l**. 1524
30:43 and came to own **l** flocks, 8041
50: 9 It was a very **l** company. 3878
Ex 12:38 as well as **l** droves of livestock, 3878+4394
Nu 13:28 and the cities are fortified and very **l**. 1524
20:20 against them with a **l** and powerful army. 3878
32: 1 who had very **l** herds and flocks, 8041
Dt 1:28 the cities are **l**, with walls up to the sky. 1524
6:10 a land with **l**, flourishing cities 1524
8:13 and when your herds and flocks **grow l** 8049
9: 1 with **l** cities that have walls up to the sky. 1524
17:17 **accumulate l amounts** of silver and 4394+8049
25:14 measures in your house—one **l**, one small. 1524
27: 2 set up some **l** stones and coat them 1524
Jos 7:26 Over Achan they heaped up a **l** pile 1524
8:29 And they raised a **l** pile of rocks over it, 1524
10:11 the LORD hurled **l** hailstones down 1524
10:18 "Roll **l** rocks up to the mouth of the cave, 1524
10:27 the mouth of the cave they placed **l** rocks, 1524
11: 4 and a **l** number of horses and chariots— 4394
13: 1 and there are still very **l** areas of land to 2221
14:12 and their cities were **l** and fortified, 1524
19:33 from Heleph and the **l tree** in Zaanannim, 471
22: 8 with **l** herds of livestock, with silver, 4394+8041
24:26 a **l** stone and set it up there under the oak 1524
1Sa 6:14 and there it stopped beside a **l** rock. 1524
6:15 and placed them on the **l** rock. 1524
6:18 The **l** rock, on which they set the ark of 1524
14:33 "Roll a **l** stone over here at once." 1524
2Sa 12: 2 The rich man had a very **l number** *of* sheep 2221
18: 9 under the thick branches of a **l** oak, 1524
18:17 pit in the forest and piled up a **l** heap 1524+4394
1Ki 4:13 in Bashan and its sixty **l** walled cities 1524
5:17 from the quarry **l** blocks of quality stone 1524
7:10 The foundations were laid with **l** stones 1524
1Ki 10: 2 **l** quantities of gold, and precious stones— 4394
10:10 **l** quantities of spices, and precious stones. 4394
10:16 King Solomon made two hundred **l shields** 7558
18:32 and he dug a trench around it **l enough** 3869
18:33 "Fill four **l jars** with water and pour it on 3902
2Ki 4:38 "Put on the **l** pot and cook some stew 1524
12:10 that there was a **l amount** *of* money in 8041
16:15 "On the **l** new altar, offer the morning burnt 1524
18:17 and his field commander with a **l** army, 3878
1Ch 22: 3 a **l amount** of iron to make nails for 4200+8044
22: 4 Tyrians had brought **l numbers** of 4200+8044
29: 2 all of these *in* **l quantities**. 4200+8044
2Ch 2: 9 temple I build must be **l** and magnificent. 1524
4: 9 and the **l** court and the doors for the court, 1524
9: 1 **l quantities** of gold, and precious 4200+8044
9: 9 **l** quantities of spices, and precious stones. 4394
9:15 King Solomon made two hundred **l shields** 7558
14: 8 equipped with **l shields** and with spears, 7558
14:13 carried off a **l amount** of plunder. 2221+4394
15: 9 for **l numbers** had come over to him 4200+8044
17:13 and had **l** supplies in the towns of Judah. 8041
23: 9 the **l** and small shields that had belonged 4482[S]
24:11 and they saw that there was a **l amount** 8041
26:15 to shoot arrows and hurl **l** stones. 1524
30: 5 not been celebrated **in l numbers** 4200+8044
30:13 A very **l** crowd of people assembled 8041
32: 4 A **l** force of men assembled, 8041
32: 5 He also made **l numbers** of weapons 4200+8044
36:18 from the temple of God, both **l** and small, 1524
Ezr 5: 8 are building it with **l stones** and 10006+10146
6: 4 with three courses of **l stones** and 10006+10146
10: 1 a **l** crowd of Israelites—men, women 4394+8041
Ne 5: 7 So I called together a **l** meeting to deal 1524
7: 4 Now the city was **l** and spacious, 1524
12:31 I also assigned two **l** choirs to give thanks. 1524
13: 5 with a **l** room formerly used to store 1524
Est 8:15 a **l** crown of gold and a purple robe 1524
Job 1: 3 and had a **l** number of servants. 4394
36:18 do not let a **l** bribe turn you aside. 8044
Ps 104:25 living things both **l** and small. 1524
Pr 14:28 A **l** population is a king's glory, 8044
Isa 8: 1 "Take a **l** scroll and write on it with 1524
22:18 a ball and throw you into a **l** country. 3338+8146
36: 2 a **l** army from Lachish to King Hezekiah 3878
Jer 22:14 So *he* **makes l** windows in it, 7973
43: 9 take some **l** stones with you 1524
44:15 women who were present—a **l** assembly— 1524
46: 3 both **l** and small, and march out for battle! 7558[S]
49:32 and their **l** herds will be booty. 2162
Eze 17:15 to Egypt to get horses and a **l** army. 8041
23:24 with **l** and small shields and with helmets. 7558[S]
23:32 drink your sister's cup, a cup **l** and deep; 8146
38: 4 and a great horde with **l** and small shields, 7558[S]
39: 9 burn them up—the small and **l** shields, 7558[S]
47: 9 There will be **l** numbers of fish, 4394
Da 2:31 and there before you stood a **l** statue— 10678
4:11 The tree **grew l** and strong 10648
4:20 The tree you saw, which **grew l** and strong, 10648
7: 7 It had **l** iron teeth; it crushed and 10647
8: 8 of his power his **l** horn was broken off, 1524
8:21 **l** horn between his eyes is the first king. 1524
11:11 who will raise a **l** army, 8041
11:25 "With a **l** army he will stir up his strength 1524
11:25 of the South will wage war with a **l** 1524
Joel 2: 2 the mountains a **l** and mighty army comes, 8041
Mt 4:25 **L** crowds from Galilee, the Decapolis, *4498*
8: 1 **l** crowds followed him. *4498*
8:30 from them a **l** herd of pigs was feeding. *4498*
13: 2 Such **l** crowds gathered around him *4498*
13:33 into a **l** amount of flour until it worked all *5552*
14:14 When Jesus landed and saw a **l** crowd, *4498*
18: 6 a **l millstone** hung around his neck *3685+3948*
19: 2 **L** crowds followed him, *4498*
20:29 a **l** crowd followed him. *4498*
21: 8 A *very* **l** crowd spread their cloaks on *4498*
26:47 a **l** crowd armed with swords and clubs, *4498*
28:12 they gave the soldiers a **l sum** of money, *2653*
Mk 2:13 A **l** crowd came to him, *NIG*
3: 7 and a **l** crowd from Galilee followed. *4498*
4: 1 around him was so **l** that he got into a boat *4498*
5:11 A **l** herd of pigs was feeding on *3489*
5:21 a **l** crowd gathered around him *4498*
5:24 A **l** crowd followed and pressed *4498*
6:34 When Jesus landed and saw a **l** crowd, *4498*
8: 1 During those days another **l** crowd gathered. *4498*
9:14 a **l** crowd around them and the teachers of *4498*
9:42 with a **l** millstone tied around his neck. *3948*
10:46 together with a **l** crowd, *2653*
12:37 The **l** crowd listened to him with delight. *4498*
12:41 Many rich people threw in **l** *amounts.* *4498*
14:15 He will show you a **l** upper room, *3489*
16: 4 they saw that the stone, which was very **l**, *3489*
Lk 5: 6 a **l** number of fish that their nets began *4498*
5:29 and a **l** crowd of tax collectors *4498*
6:17 A **l** crowd of his disciples was there and *4498*
7:11 and his disciples and a **l** crowd went along *4498*
7:12 a **l** crowd from the town was with her. *2653*
8: 4 While a **l** crowd was gathering *4498*
8:32 A **l** herd of pigs was feeding there on *2653*
9:37 a **l** crowd met him. *4498*
13:21 a **l amount of flour** until it *236+4929+5552*
14:25 **L** crowds were traveling with Jesus, *4498*
22:12 He will show you a **l** upper room, *3489*
23:27 A **l** number of people followed him, *4498*
Jn 12: 9 Meanwhile a **l** crowd of Jews found out *4498*
21: 6 the net in because of the **l number** of fish. *4436*
21:11 It was full of **l** fish, 153, *3489*
Ac 6: 7 and a **l** number of priests became obedient *4498*
10:11 and something like a **l** sheet being let *3489*
10:27 Peter went inside and found a **l** gathering *4498*
11: 5 like a **l** sheet being let down from heaven *3489*
14:21 that city and won **a l number** *of* disciples. *2653*
17: 4 a **l** number of God-fearing Greeks and not *4498*
19:26 led astray **l numbers of people** here *2653+4063*
Gal 6:11 See **what l** letters I use as I write to you *4383*
2Ti 2:20 In a **l** house there are articles not only *3489*
Jas 3: 4 Although they are **so l** and are driven *5496*
Rev 6: 4 To him was given a **l** sword. *3489*
18:21 the size of a **l** millstone and threw it into *3489*

LARGER (15) [LARGE]
Lev 25:51 he must pay for his redemption a **l share of** 4946
Nu 26:54 To a **l** *group* give a larger inheritance, 8041
26:54 To a larger group **give** a **l** inheritance, 8049
26:56 by lot among the **l** and smaller groups." 8041
33:54 To a **l** *group* give a larger inheritance, 8041
33:54 To a larger group **give a l** inheritance, 8049
Dt 7: 1 seven nations **l** and stronger than you— 8041
11:23 and you will dispossess nations **l** 1524
Jos 10: 2 it was **l** than Ai, and all its men 1524
1Ch 24: 4 A **l number** of leaders were found 8041
2Ch 24:24 into their hands a much **l** army. 4200+8044
Eze 43:14 up to the **l** ledge it is four cubits high and 1524
Da 11:13 will muster another army, **l** than the first; 8041
Am 6: 2 Is their land **l** than yours? 8041
Ac 28:23 and came in even **l** *numbers* to the place *4498*

LARGEST (2) [LARGE]
Mt 13:32 the **l** of garden plants and becomes a tree, *3505*
Mk 4:32 and becomes the **l** of all garden plants, *3505*

LASCIVIOUSNESS (KJV) See DEBAUCHERY, IMMORALITY, LEWDNESS, SENSUALITY

LASEA (1)
Ac 27: 8 called Fair Havens, near the town of **L**. *3297*

LASH (2) [LASHED, LASHES]
Job 5:21 be protected from the **l** *of* the tongue, 8765
Isa 10:26 The LORD Almighty *will* **l** them *with* 6424

LASHA (1)
Ge 10:19 Admah and Zeboiim, as far as **L**. 4388

LASHARON (1)
Jos 12:18 the king of Aphek one the king of **L** one 4389

LASHED (1) [LASH]
Isa 54:11 **l by storms** and not comforted, 6192

LASHES (4) [LASH]
Dt 25: 2 with the number of **l** his crime deserves, NIH
25: 3 *he must* not **give** him more than forty **l**. 5782
Pr 17:10 more than a hundred **l** a fool. 5782
2Co 11:24 from the Jews the forty **l** minus one. *NIG*

LAST (113) [LASTED, LASTING, LASTS, LATTER]
Ge 19:34 **"L night** I lay with my father. 621
25: 8 Then Abraham **breathed his l** and died at 1588
25:17 *He* **breathed his l** and died, 1588
29:34 **at l** my husband will become attached 2021+7193
31:29 **l night** the God of your father said to me, 621
31:42 and **l night** he rebuked you." 621
33: 7 **L of all** came Joseph and Rachel, 339
35:18 As she **breathed her l**— 3655+5883
35:29 Then he **breathed his l** and died 1588
49:33 **breathed** *his* **l** and was gathered 1588
Ex 14:24 During the **l watch of the night** 874+1332
Lev 8:33 for your ordination will **l** seven days. NIH
15:19 of her monthly period *will* **l** seven days, 2118
26:10 will still be eating **l year's harvest** 3823+3824
Nu 2:31 They will set out **l**, under their standards. 340
14:33 the **l** *of* your bodies lies in the desert. 9448
24:20 but he will come to ruin **at l**." 344
Dt 2:16 when the **l** *of* these fighting men among 9462
Jos 12: 4 one of the **l** *of* the Rephaites, 3856
13:12 and had survived as one of the **l** of the 3856
1Sa 11:11 during the **l watch of the night** 874+1332+2021
15:16 the LORD said to me **l night**." 2021+4326
2Sa 19:11 the **l** to bring the king back to his palace, 340
19:12 So why should you be the **l** to bring back 340
23: 1 These are the **l** words of David: 340
1Ki 14:10 I will cut off from Jeroboam **every l male** 928+7815+8874
21:21 cut off from Ahab **every l male** 928+7815+8874
2Ki 8: 1 in the land *that will* **l** seven years." 995
9: 8 I will cut off from Ahab **every l male** 928+7815+8874
1Ch 23:27 According to the **l** instructions of David, 340
Ezr 8:13 the **l** *ones,* whose names were Eliphelet, 340
Ne 8:18 Day after day, from the first day to the **l**, 340
Job 14:10 he **breathes his l** and is no more. 1588
Ps 45: 6 O God, will **l** for ever and ever; NIH
76: 5 men lie plundered, they sleep their **l** sleep; NIH

Ps 81:15 and their punishment *would* **l** forever. 2118
119:152 that you established them to **l** forever. NIH
Isa 2: 2 In the **l** days the mountain of the LORD's 344
41: 4 with the first of them and with the **l**— 340
44: 6 I am the first and I am the **l**; 340
48:12 I am the first and I am the **l**. 340
51: 6 But my salvation *will* **l** forever, 2118
51: 8 But my righteousness *will* **l** forever, 2118
Jer 15: 9 will grow faint and **breathe** her **l**. 5870+5883
32:14 and put them in a clay jar so *they will* **l** 6641
50:17 **l** to crush his bones was Nebuchadnezzar 340
Da 9: 2 of Jerusalem *would* **l** seventy years. 4848
11: 6 and *he* and his power *will* not **l**. 6641
Hos 3: 5 and to his blessings in the **l** days. 344
Am 1: 8 till the **l** *of* the Philistines is dead," 8642
4: 2 the **l** *of* you with fishhooks. 344
Mic 4: 1 In the **l** days the mountain of the LORD's 344
Mt 5:26 until you have paid the **l** penny. *2274*
19:30 But many who are first will be **l**, *2274*
19:30 and many who are **l** will be first. *2274*
20: 8 beginning with the **l** *ones* hired and going *2274*
20:12 'These men who were hired **l** worked only *2274*
20:14 to give the man who was hired **l** the same *2274*
20:16 **l** will be first, and the first will be last." *2274*
20:16 the last will be first, and the first will be **l**." *2274*
21:37 **L of all,** he sent his son to them. *5731*
27:64 This **l** deception will be worse than *2274*
Mk 4:17 they have no root, *they* **l** only a short time. *1639*
9:35 wants to be first, he must be the very **l**, *2274*
10:31 But many who are first will be **l**, *2274*
10:31 first will be last, and the **l** first." *2274*
12: 6 He sent him **l of all,** saying, *2274*
12:22 **L** of all, the woman died too. *2274*
15:37 With a loud cry, Jesus **breathed his l.** *1743*
Lk 12:59 until you have paid the **l** penny." *2274*
13:30 Indeed there are *those who are* **l** who will *2274*
13:30 and first who will be **l**." *2274*
23:46 When he had said this, *he* **breathed** *his* **l**. *1743*
Jn 6:39 but raise them up at the **l** day. *2274*
6:40 and I will raise him up at the **l** day." *2274*
6:44 and I will raise him up at the **l** day. *2274*
6:54 and I will raise him up *at* the **l** day. *2274*
7:37 On the **l** and greatest day of the Feast, *2274*
11:24 rise again in the resurrection at the **l** day." *2274*
12:48 will condemn him at the **l** day. *2274*
15:16 go and bear fruit—fruit that *will* **l**. *3531*
16:31 "You believe **at l!**" Jesus answered. *785*
Ac 2:17 " 'In the **l** days, God says, I will pour out *2274*
27:23 **L night** an angel of the God *3816+3836+4047*
27:33 "For the **l** fourteen days," he said, *1412*
Ro 1:10 that **now at l** by God's will the way *2453+4537*
1:17 is by **faith from first to l**, *1650+4411+4411*
1Co 9:25 They do it to get a crown that will **not l**; *5778*
9:25 we do it to get a crown that will **l forever.** *915*
15: 8 and **l** of all he appeared to me also, *2274*
15:26 The **l** enemy to be destroyed is death. *2274*
15:45 the **l** Adam, a life-giving spirit. *2274*
15:52 in the twinkling of an eye, at the **l** trumpet. *2274*
2Co 8:10 **L year** you were the first not only to give *4373*
9: 2 that since **l year** you in Achaia were ready *4373*
Php 4:10 **at l** you have renewed your concern *2453+4537*
1Th 2:16 of God has come upon them at **l**. *5465*
2Ti 3: 1 There will be terrible times in the **l** days. *2274*
Heb 1: 2 but in these **l** days he has spoken to us *2274*
1: 8 O God, will **l** for ever and ever, *NIG*
Jas 5: 3 You have hoarded wealth in the **l** days. *2274*
1Pe 1: 5 that is ready to be revealed in the **l** time. *2274*
1:20 but was revealed in these **l** times *2274*
2Pe 3: 3 that in the **l** days scoffers will come, *2274*
1Jn 2:18 Dear children, this is the **l** hour; *2274*
2:18 This is how we know it is the **l** hour. *2274*
Jude 1:18 "In the **l** times there will be scoffers *2274*
Rev 1:17 I am the First and the **L**. *2274*
2: 8 of him who is the First and the **L**, *2274*
15: 1 seven angels with the seven **l** plagues— *2274*
15: 1 **l**, because with them God's wrath is completed. *NIG*
21: 9 the seven bowls full of the seven **l** plagues *2274*
22:13 the First and the **L**, the Beginning and *2274*

LASTED (2) [LAST]

2Sa 3: 1 the house of Saul and the house of David **l** 2118
2Ki 6:25 the siege **l so long** that a donkey's head 6330

LASTING (35) [LAST]

Ex 12:14 to the LORD—a **l** ordinance. 6409
12:17 a **l** ordinance for the generations to come. 6409
12:24 these instructions as a **l** ordinance 6330+6409
27:21 be a **l** ordinance among the Israelites for 6409
28:43 "This is to be a **l** ordinance for Aaron 6409
29: 9 The priesthood is theirs by a **l** ordinance. 6409
30:21 This is to be a **l** ordinance for Aaron 6409
31:16 the generations to come as a **l** covenant. 6409
Lev 3:17 " 'This is a **l** ordinance for the generations 6409
10: 9 a **l** ordinance for the generations to come. 6409
16:29 "This is to be a **l** ordinance for you: 6409
16:31 must deny yourselves; it is a **l** ordinance. 6409
16:34 "This is to be a **l** ordinance for you: 6409
17: 7 This is to be a **l** ordinance for them and 6409
23:14 a **l** ordinance for the generations to come, 6409
23:21 a **l** ordinance for the generations to come, 6409
23:31 a **l** ordinance for the generations to come, 6409
23:41 a **l** ordinance for the generations to come; 6409
24: 3 a **l** ordinance for the generations to come. 6409
24: 8 on behalf of the Israelites, as a **l** covenant. 6409
Nu 10: 8 a **l** ordinance for you and the generations 6409
15:15 a **l** ordinance for the generations to come. 6409
18:23 a **l** ordinance for the generations to come. 6409
19:10 a **l** ordinance both for the Israelites and for 6409
19:21 This is a **l** ordinance for them. 6409
25:13 a covenant of a **l** priesthood, 6409
Dt 11: 4 how the LORD brought **l** ruin on them. 2021+2021+2296+3427+6330
1Sa 25:28 a **l** dynasty for my master, 586
2Ch 2: 4 This is a **l** ordinance for Israel. 4200+6409
Est 1: 5 the king gave a banquet, **l** seven days, NIH
Jer 14:13 I will give you **l** peace in this place.' " 622
18:16 will be laid waste, an object of **l** scorn; 6409
Eze 45:21 Passover, a **feast** *l* seven days, AIT
46:14 to the LORD is a **l** ordinance. 6409+9458
Heb 10:34 you yourselves had better and **l** possessions. *3531*

LASTS (7) [LAST]

Lev 23:34 Tabernacles begins, and it **l** for seven days. NIH
Job 20: 5 the joy of the godless **l** but a moment. 6330
Ps 30: 5 For his anger **l** only a moment, NIH
30: 5 but his favor **l** a lifetime; NIH
Pr 12:19 but a lying tongue **l** only a moment. 6330
Mt 13:21 since he has no root, *he* **l** only a short time. *1639*
2Co 3:11 much greater is the glory of that which **l**! *3531*

LATCH-OPENING (1)

SS 5: 4 My lover thrust his hand through the **l**; 2986

LATCHET (KJV) See THONGS

LATE (8) [LATELY, LATER, LATEST]

Ps 127: 2 In vain you rise early and stay up **l**, 336
Isa 5:11 *who* **stay up l** at night till they are inflamed 336
Mt 14:15 and it's already getting **l**. *6052*
Mk 6:35 By this time it was **l in the day,** *4498+6052*
6:35 they said, "and it's already **very l**. *4498+6052*
11:11 but since it was already **l**, *4070*
Lk 9:12 **L in the afternoon** the Twelve *806+2465+3111*
Rev 6:13 as **l** figs drop from a fig tree when shaken *3913*

LATELY (2) [LATE]

Isa 52: 4 **l**, Assyria has oppressed them. 700+928
Mic 2: 8 **L** my people have risen up like an enemy. 919

LATER (82) [LATE]

Ge 4: 2 **L** she gave birth to his brother Abel. 3578
10:18 **L** the Canaanite clans scattered 339
22: 1 **Some time l** God tested Abraham. 339+465+1821+2021+2021
22:20 **Some time l** Abraham was told, "Milcah is also a mother; 339+465+1821+2021+2021
30:21 **Some time l** she gave birth to a daughter 339
32:20 **l**, when I see him, perhaps he will 339+4027
34:25 Three days **l**, while all of them were still 928
38:24 About three months **l** Judah was told, 4946
40: 1 **Some time l**, the cupbearer and the baker of the king of Egypt 339+465+1821+2021+2021
48: 1 **Some time l** Joseph was told, "Your father is ill. 339+465+1821+2021+2021
Ex 9:32 were not destroyed, because they **ripen l**.) 689
Dt 4:30 then in **l** days you will return to 344
29:22 in **l** generations and foreigners who come 340
Jdg 11: 4 **Some time l**, when the Ammonites made war on Israel, 3427+4946
14: 8 **Some time l**, when he went back 3427+4946
15: 1 **L on**, at the time of wheat harvest, 3427+4946
16: 4 **Some time l**, he fell in love with a woman 339+4027
1Sa 25:38 About ten days **l**, the LORD struck Nabal NIH
2Sa 3:28 **L**, when David heard about this, 339+4027+4946
13:23 Two years **l**, when Absalom's sheepshearers were at Baal Hazor 4200
1Ki 2:39 But three years **l**, two of Shimei's 4946+7891
12:12 Three days **l** Jeroboam and all the people 928
17: 7 Some time **l** the brook dried up 4946+7891
17:17 **Some time l** the son of the woman 339+465+1821+2021+2021
21: 1 **Some time l** there was an incident involving a vineyard 339+465+1821+2021+2021
2Ki 6:24 **Some time l**, Ben-Hadad king 339+4027
1Ch 2:21 **L**, Hezron lay with the daughter of Makir 339
2Ch 10:12 Three days **l** Jeroboam and all the people 928
18: 2 **Some years l** he went down to visit Ahab in Samaria. 4200+7891+9102
20:35 **L**, Jehoshaphat king of Judah made 339+4027
24: 4 **Some time l** Joash decided to restore 339+4027
32: 9 **L**, when Sennacherib king of Assyria 339+2296
Ne 13: 6 Some time **l** I asked his permission 4200+7891
Est 2: 1 **L** when the anger of King Xerxes had subsided, 339+465+1821+2021+2021
Pr 3:28 not say to your neighbor, "Come back **l**; NIH
20:25 rashly and only **l** to consider his vows. 339
Ecc 4:16 But those *who* came **l** were not pleased 340
Jer 13: 6 Many days **l** the LORD said to me, 4946+7891
42: 7 Ten days **l** the word of the LORD came 4946+7891
46:26 **L**, however, Egypt will be inhabited as 339+4027
Eze 16: 8 " '**L** I passed by, and when I looked at you 2256
Da 4:29 Twelve months **l**, as the king was walking on the roof 10378+10636
8: 3 the other but grew up **l**. 340+928+2021
8:19 to tell you what will happen **l in the time** 344+928
Mt 21:29 but **l** he changed his mind and went. *5731*
25:11 "**L** the others also came. *5731*
Mk 2: 1 A few days **l**, when Jesus again entered *NIG*
10:34 Three days **l** he will rise." *3552*
12:13 **L** they sent some of the Pharisees *2779*
16:14 **L** Jesus appeared to the Eleven *5731*
Lk 22:58 A little **l** someone else saw him and said, *3552*
22:59 About an hour **l** another asserted, *1460*
Jn 5: 1 **Some time l**, Jesus went up to Jerusalem for a feast *3552+4047*
5:14 **L** Jesus found him at the temple and *3552+4047*
6:71 one of the Twelve, *was* **l** to betray him.) *3516*
7:39 whom those who believed in him were **l** *3516*
12: 4 Judas Iscariot, who *was* **l** to betray him, *3516*
13: 7 but **l** you will understand." *3552+4047*
13:36 but you will follow **l**." *5731*
19:28 **L**, knowing that all was now completed, *3552+4047*
19:38 **L**, Joseph of Arimathea asked Pilate *3552+4047*
20:26 **A week l** his disciples were in *2465+3552+3893*
Ac 5: 7 About three hours **l** his wife came in, *1404*
7: 8 **L** Isaac became the father of Jacob, *2779*
15:36 Some time **l** Paul said to Barnabas, *3552*
20: 6 and five days **l** joined the others at Troas, *948*
24: 1 Five days **l** the high priest Ananias went *3552*
24:24 Several days **l** Felix came with his wife *3552*
25:13 A few days **l** King Agrippa and Bernice *1335*
27:28 A short time **l** they took soundings again *NIG*
28:17 Three days **l** he called together the leaders *3552*
Gal 1:17 into Arabia and **l** returned to Damascus. *4099*
1:21 **L** I went to Syria and Cilicia. *2083*
2: 1 Fourteen years **l** I went up again *2083*
3:17 The law, introduced 430 years **l**, *3552*
1Ti 4: 1 that in **l** times some will abandon the faith *5731*
Heb 4: 7 **when** a long time **l** he spoke through David, *3552*
4: 8 not have spoken **l** about another day. *3552+4047*
11: 8 to go to a place *he would* **l** receive *3516*
12:11 **L on**, however, it produces a harvest *5731*
Jude 1: 5 but **l** destroyed those who did not believe. *1309*
Rev 1:19 what is now and what will take place **l**. *3552+4047*

LATEST (1) [LATE]

Ac 17:21 about and listening to the **l** ideas.) *2785*

LATIN (1)

Jn 19:20 and the sign was written in Aramaic, **L** *4872*

LATRINE (1)

2Ki 10:27 and people have used it for a **l** to this day. 4738

LATTER (7) [LAST]

Ge 14: 3 All these **l** kings joined forces in NIH
Job 42:12 The LORD blessed **l part of** Job's **life** 344
Da 8:23 "In the **l part** *of* their reign, 344
Mt 23:23 You should have practiced **the l**, *4047*[S]
Lk 11:42 You should have practiced the **l** *4047*[S]
Php 1:16 The **l** do so in love, knowing that I *3525*
2Ti 2:21 If a man cleanses himself from **the l**, *4047*[S]

LATTICE (4)

Jdg 5:28 behind the **l** she cried out, 876
2Ki 1: 2 Now Ahaziah had fallen through the **l** 8422
Pr 7: 6 of my house I looked out through the **l**. 876
SS 2: 9 peering through the **l**. 3048

LAUD (KJV) See SING PRAISES

LAUGH (13) [LAUGHED, LAUGHINGSTOCK, LAUGHS, LAUGHTER]

Ge 18:13 "Why *did* Sarah **l** and say, 7464
18:15 so she lied and said, *"I did* not **l**." 7464
18:15 But he said, "Yes, *you did* **l**." 7464
21: 6 and everyone who hears about this *will* **l** 7464
Job 5:22 *You will* **l** at destruction and famine, 8471
Ps 52: 6 *they will* **l** at him, saying, 8471
59: 8 But you, O LORD, **l** at them; 8471
Pr 1:26 I in turn *will* **l** at your disaster; 8471
31:25 *she can* **l** at the days to come. 8471
Ecc 3: 4 a time to weep and a time to **l**, 8471
Hab 1:10 They **l** at all fortified cities; 8471
Lk 6:21 are you who weep now, for *you will* **l**. *1151*
6:25 Woe to you who **l** now, *1151*

LAUGHED (6) [LAUGH]

Ge 17:17 *he* **l** and said to himself, "Will a son be 7464
18:12 So Sarah **l** to herself as she thought, 7464
La 1: 7 Her enemies looked at her and **l** 8471
Mt 9:24 But *they* **l** at him. *2860*
Mk 5:40 But *they* **l** at him. *2860*
Lk 8:53 *They* **l** at him, knowing that she was dead. *2860*

LAUGHINGSTOCK (6) [LAUGH]

Ge 38:23 or we will become a **l**. 997
Ex 32:25 and so become a **l** to their enemies. 9067
Job 12: 4 "I have become a **l** to my friends, 8468
12: 4 a mere **l**, though righteous and blameless! 8468
La 3:14 I became the **l** of all my people; 8468
Eze 22: 4 to the nations and a **l** to all the countries. 7842

LAUGHS (6) [LAUGH]

Job 39: 7 *He* **l** at the commotion in the town; 8471

Job 39:18 *she* l at horse and rider. 8471
39:22 *He* l at fear, afraid of nothing; 8471
41:29 *he* l at the rattling of the lance. 8471
Ps 2: 4 The One enthroned in heaven **l**; 8471
37:13 but the Lord l at the wicked, 8471

LAUGHTER (10) [LAUGH]

Ge 21: 6 Sarah said, "God has brought me **l**, 7465
Job 8:21 He will yet fill your mouth with **l** 8468
Ps 126: 2 Our mouths were filled with **l**, 8468
Pr 14:13 Even in **l** the heart may ache, 8468
Ecc 2: 2 "**L**," I said, "is foolish. 8468
7: 3 Sorrow is better than **l**, 8468
7: 6 so is the **l** *of* fools. 8468
10:19 A feast is made for **l**, 8468
Jer 51:39 so that *they* **shout with l**— 6600
Jas 4: 9 Change your **l** to mourning and your joy *1152*

LAUNCH (1)

Jdg 10:18 "Whoever *will* **l** the attack against 2725

LAUNDERER'S (1)

Mal 3: 2 he will be like a refiner's fire or a **l** soap. 3891

LAVER (KJV) See BASIN

LAVISHED (6)

Isa 43:24 or **l on** me the fat of your sacrifices. 8115
Eze 16:15 *You* **l** your favors on anyone who passed 9161
Da 2:48 in a high position and **l** many gifts on him. 10314
Hos 2: 8 *who* **l** on her the silver and gold— 8049
Eph 1: 8 that *he* **l** on us with all wisdom *4355*
1Jn 3: 1 How great is the love the Father *has* **l** *1443*

LAW (467) [LAW'S, LAWFUL, LAWGIVER, LAWS, LAWYER]

Ge 47:26 as a **l** concerning land in Egypt— 2976
Ex 12:49 The same **l** applies to the native-born and 9368
13: 9 and a reminder on your forehead that the **l** 9368
15:25 There the LORD made a decree and a **l** 5477
21:31 This **l** also applies if the bull gores a son 5477
24:12 with the **l** and commands I have written 9368
Lev 7: 7 " 'The same **l** applies to both 9368
24:22 You are to have the same **l** for the alien 5477
Nu 5:29 the **l** *of* jealousy when a woman goes astray 9368
5:30 the LORD and is to apply this entire **l** 9368
6:13 " 'Now this is the **l** *for* the Nazirite when 9368
6:21 " 'This is the **l** *of* the Nazirite 9368
6:21 according to the **l** *of* the Nazirite.' " 9368
15:29 One and the same **l** applies 9368
19: 2 of the **l** that the LORD has commanded: 9368
19:14 the **l** that applies when a person dies in 9368
31:21 of the **l** that the LORD gave Moses: 9368
Dt 1: 5 Moses began to expound this **l**, saying: 9368
4:44 the **l** Moses set before the Israelites. 9368
6:25 if we are careful to obey all this **l** before 5184
17:11 Act according to the **l** they teach you and 9368
17:18 for himself on a scroll a copy of this **l**, 9368
17:19 and follow carefully all the words of this **l** 9368
17:20 and turn from the **l** to the right or to 5184
27: 3 the words of this **l** when you have crossed 9368
27: 8 of this **l** on these stones you have set up." 9368
27:26 the words of this **l** by carrying them out." 9368
28:58 not carefully follow all the words of this **l**, 9368
28:61 not recorded in this Book of the **L**, 9368
29:21 the covenant written in this Book of the **L**. 9368
29:29 that we may follow all the words of this **l**. 9368
30:10 of the **L** and turn to the LORD your God 9368
31: 9 So Moses wrote down this **l** and gave it to 9368
31:11 you shall read this **l** before them 9368
31:12 follow carefully all the words of this **l**. 9368
31:13 Their children, who do not know this **l**, NIH
31:24 the words of this **l** from beginning to end, 9368
31:26 of the **L** and place it beside the ark of 9368
32:46 to obey carefully all the words of this **l**. 9368
33: 4 the **l** that Moses gave us, 9368
33:10 to Jacob and your **l** to Israel. 9368
Jos 1: 7 the **l** my servant Moses gave you; 9368
1: 8 Do not let this Book of the **L** depart 9368
8:31 to what is written in the Book of the **L** 9368
8:32 Joshua copied on stones the **l** *of* Moses, 9368
8:34 Joshua read all the words of the **l**— 9368
8:34 just as it is written in the Book of the **L**. 9368
22: 5 the commandment and the **l** that Moses 9368
23: 6 that is written in the Book of the **L** 9368
24:26 in the Book of the **L** *of* God. 9368
1Ki 2: 3 as written in the **L** *of* Moses, 9368
2Ki 10:31 Yet Jehu was not careful to keep the **l** *of* 9368
14: 6 with what is written in the Book of the **L** 9368
17:13 the entire **L** that I commanded your fathers 9368
21: 8 and will keep the whole **L** 9368
22: 8 of the **L** in the temple of the LORD." 9368
22:11 the words of the Book of the **L**, 9368
23:24 to fulfill the requirements of the **l** written 9368
23:25 in accordance with all the **L** *of* Moses. 9368
1Ch 16:40 with everything written in the **L** *of* 9368
22:12 the **l** *of* the LORD your God. 9368
2Ch 6:16 to walk before me according to my **l**, 9368
12: 1 and all Israel with him abandoned the **l** *of* 9368
15: 3 without a priest to teach and without the **l**. 9368
17: 9 taking with them the Book of the **L** *of* 9368
19: 8 the **l** *of* the LORD and to settle disputes. 5477
19:10 the **l**, commands, decrees or ordinances— 9368
2Ch 23:18 the LORD as written in the **L** *of* Moses, 9368
25: 4 with what is written in the **L**, in the Book 9368
30:16 as prescribed in the **L** *of* Moses the man 9368
31: 3 and appointed feasts as written in the **L** *of* 9368
31: 4 so they could devote themselves to the **L** 9368
31:21 of God's temple and in obedience to the **l** 9368
34:14 Hilkiah the priest found the Book of the **L** 9368
34:15 Book of the **L** in the temple of the LORD." 9368
34:19 When the king heard the words of the **L**, 9368
35:26 according to what is written in the **L** *of* 9368
Ezr 3: 2 in accordance with what is written in the **L** 9368
7: 6 a teacher well versed in the **L** *of* Moses, 9368
7:10 and observance of the **L** *of* the LORD, 9368
7:12 a teacher of the **L** of the God of heaven: 10186
7:14 and Jerusalem with regard to the **L** 10186
7:21 a teacher of the **L** of the God of heaven, 10186
7:26 Whoever does not obey the **l** of your God 10186
7:26 not obey the law of your God and the **l** of 10186
10: 3 Let it be done according to the **L**. 9368
Ne 8: 1 to bring out the Book of the **L** *of* Moses, 9368
8: 2 the priest brought the **L** before 9368
8: 3 listened attentively to the Book of the **L**. 9368
8: 7 the **L** while the people were standing there. 9368
8: 8 They read from the Book of the **L** *of* God, 9368
8: 9 as they listened to the words of the **L**. 9368
8:13 to give attention to the words of the **L**. 9368
8:14 They found written in the **L**, 9368
8:18 Ezra read from the Book of the **L** *of* God. 9368
9: 3 the Book of the **L** *of* the LORD their God 9368
9:26 they put your **l** behind their backs. 9368
9:29 "You warned them to return to your **l**, 9368
9:34 and our fathers did not follow your **l**; 9368
10:28 of the **L** *of* God, together with their wives 9368
10:29 and an oath to follow the **L** *of* God given 9368
10:34 as it is written in the **L**. 9368
10:36 "As it is also written in the **L**, 9368
12:44 by the **L** for the priests and the Levites, 9368
13: 3 When the people heard this **l**, 9368
Est 1:13 the king to consult experts in *matters of* **l** 2017
1:15 "According to **l**, what must be done 2017
3:14 as **l** in every province and made known to 2017
4:11 the king has but one **l**: 2017
4:16 even though it is against the **l**. 2017
8:13 as **l** in every province and made known to 2017
Ps 1: 2 But his delight is in the **l** *of* the LORD, 9368
1: 2 and on his **l** he meditates day and night. 9368
19: 7 The **l** *of* the LORD is perfect, 9368
37:31 The **l** *of* his God is in his heart; 9368
40: 8 your **l** is within my heart." 9368
78: 5 for Jacob and established the **l** in Israel, 9368
78:10 and refused to live by his **l**. 9368
89:30 "If his sons forsake my **l** and do 9368
94:12 the man you teach from your **l**; 9368
119: 1 according to the **l** *of* the LORD. 9368
119:18 that I may see wonderful things in your **l**. 9368
119:29 be gracious to me through your **l**. 9368
119:34 and I will keep your **l** and obey it 9368
119:44 I will always obey your **l**, 9368
119:51 but I do not turn from your **l**. 9368
119:53 who have forsaken your **l**. 9368
119:55 O LORD, and I will keep your **l**. 9368
119:61 I will not forget your **l**. 9368
119:70 but I delight in your **l**. 9368
119:72 The **l** *from* your mouth is more precious 9368
119:77 for your **l** is my delight. 9368
119:85 contrary to your **l**. 9368
119:92 If your **l** had not been my delight, 9368
119:97 Oh, how I love your **l**! 9368
119:109 I will not forget your **l**. 9368
119:113 but I love your **l**. 9368
119:126 O LORD; your **l** is being broken. 9368
119:136 for your **l** is not obeyed. 9368
119:142 and your **l** is true. 9368
119:150 but they are far from your **l**. 9368
119:153 for I have not forgotten your **l**. 9368
119:163 and abhor falsehood but I love your **l**. 9368
119:165 Great peace have they who love your **l**, 9368
119:174 O LORD, and your **l** is my delight. 9368
Pr 28: 4 Those who forsake the **l** praise the wicked, 9368
28: 4 but those who keep the **l** resist them. 9368
28: 7 He who keeps the **l** is a discerning son, 9368
28: 9 If anyone turns a deaf ear to the **l**, 9368
29:18 but blessed is he who keeps the **l**. 9368
31: 5 and forget what the **l** decrees, NIH
Isa 1:10 listen to the **l** *of* our God, 9368
2: 3 The **l** will go out from Zion, 9368
5:24 the **l** *of* the LORD Almighty and spurned 9368
8:16 Bind up the testimony and seal up the **l** 9368
8:20 To the **l** and to the testimony! 9368
42: 4 In his **l** the islands will put their hope." 9368
42:21 of his righteousness to make his **l** great 9368
42:24 they did not obey his **l**. 9368
51: 4 The **l** will go out from me; 9368
51: 7 you people who have my **l** in your hearts: 9368
Jer 2: 8 Those who deal with the **l** did not know me; 9368
6:19 to my words and have rejected my **l**. 9368
8: 8 for we have the **l** *of* the LORD," 9368
9:13 "It is because they have forsaken my **l**, 9368
9:13 they have not obeyed me or followed **my l**. 2023[S]
16:11 They forsook me and did not keep my **l**. 9368
18:18 the **teaching of** the **l** by the priest will not 9368
26: 4 you do not listen to me and follow my **l**, 9368
31:33 "I will put my **l** in their minds and write it 9368
32:23 they did not obey you or follow your **l**; 9368
44:10 nor have they followed my **l** and 9368
44:23 and have not obeyed him or followed his **l** 9368
La 2: 9 the **l** is no more, 9368
Eze 7:26 the **teaching of the l** by the priest will 9368
22:26 to my **l** and profane my holy things; 9368
43:12 "This is the **l** *of* the temple: 9368
43:12 Such is the **l** *of* the temple. 9368
Da 6: 5 unless it has something to do with the **l** 10186
6:15 the **l** of the Medes and Persians no decree 10186
9:11 All Israel has transgressed your **l** 9368
9:11 and sworn judgments written in the **L** 9368
9:13 Just as it is written in the **L** *of* Moses, 9368
Hos 4: 6 you have ignored the **l** *of* your God, 9368
8: 1 and rebelled against my **l**. 9368
8:12 I wrote for them the many things of my **l**, 9368
Am 2: 4 Because they have rejected the **l** *of* 9368
Mic 4: 2 The **l** will go out from Zion, 9368
Hab 1: 4 Therefore the **l** is paralyzed, 9368
1: 7 they are a **l** to themselves 5477
Zep 3: 4 the sanctuary and do violence to the **l**. 9368
Hag 2:11 'Ask the priests what the **l** says: 9368
Zec 7:12 as flint and would not listen to the **l** or to 9368
Mal 2: 9 shown partiality in **matters of the l**." 9368
4: 4 "Remember the **l** *of* my servant Moses, 9368
Mt 2: 4 chief priests and **teachers of the l**, *1208*
5:17 not think that I have come to abolish the **L** *3795*
5:18 will by any means disappear from the **L** *3795*
5:20 *of* the Pharisees and the **teachers of the l**, *1208*
7:12 for this sums up the **L** and the Prophets. *3795*
7:29 and not as their **teachers of the l**. *1208*
8:19 a **teacher of the l** came to him and said, *1208*
9: 3 *of* the **teachers of the l** said to themselves, *1208*
11:13 For all the Prophets and the **L** prophesied *3795*
12: 5 in the **L** that on the Sabbath the priests in *3795*
12:38 of the Pharisees and **teachers of the l** said *1208*
13:52 "Therefore every **teacher of the l** who has been instructed *1208*
15: 1 and **teachers of the l** came to Jesus *1208*
16:21 chief priests and **teachers of the l**, *1208*
17:10 "Why then do the **teachers of the l** say *1208*
20:18 the chief priests and the **teachers of the l**. *1208*
21:15 and the **teachers of the l** saw *1208*
22:35 One of them, an **expert in the l**, *3788*
22:36 the greatest commandment in the **L**?" *3795*
22:40 All the **L** and the Prophets hang *3795*
23: 2 "The **teachers of the l** and the Pharisees sit *1208*
23:13 **teachers of the l** and Pharisees, *1208*
23:15 **teachers of the l** and Pharisees, *1208*
23:23 **teachers of the l** and Pharisees, *1208*
23:23 the more important matters *of* the **l**— *3795*
23:25 **teachers of the l** and Pharisees, *1208*
23:27 **teachers of the l** and Pharisees, *1208*
23:29 **teachers of the l** and Pharisees, *1208*
26:57 where the **teachers of the l** and *1208*
27: 6 against **the l** to put this into the treasury, *2003*
27:41 the **teachers of the l** and *1208*
Mk 1:22 not as the **teachers of the l**. *1208*
2: 6 some **teachers of the l** were sitting there, *1208*
2:16 **teachers of the l** who were Pharisees saw him eating *1208*
3:22 And the **teachers of the l** who came down *1208*
7: 1 *of* the **teachers of the l** who had come *1208*
7: 5 and **teachers of the l** asked Jesus, *1208*
8:31 chief priests and **teachers of the l**, *1208*
9:11 "Why do the **teachers of the l** say *1208*
9:14 the **teachers of the l** arguing with them. *1208*
10: 5 that Moses wrote you this **l**," *1953*
10:33 *to* the chief priests and **teachers of the l**. *1208*
11:18 and the **teachers of the l** heard this *1208*
11:27 the **teachers of the l** and the elders came *1208*
12:28 One *of* the **teachers of the l** came *1208*
12:35 the **teachers of the l** say that the Christ is *1208*
12:38 "Watch out for the **teachers of the l**. *1208*
14: 1 and the **teachers of the l** were looking *1208*
14:43 the **teachers of the l**, and the elders. *1208*
14:53 elders and **teachers of the l** came together. *1208*
15: 1 the **teachers of the l** and the whole *1208*
15:31 and the **teachers of the l** mocked him *1208*
Lk 2:22 to the **L** of Moses had been completed, *3795*
2:23 (as it is written in the **L** of the Lord, *3795*
2:24 in keeping with what is said in the **L** of *3795*
2:27 for him what the custom *of* the **L** required, *3795*
2:39 everything required by the **L** of the Lord, *3795*
5:17 Pharisees and **teachers of the l**, *3791*
5:21 and the **teachers of the l** began thinking *1208*
5:30 and the **teachers of the l** who belonged *1208*
6: 7 and the **teachers of the l** were looking for *1208*
7:30 and **experts in the l** rejected God's purpose *3788*
9:22 chief priests and **teachers of the l**, *1208*
10:25 On one occasion an **expert in the l** stood *3788*
10:26 "What is written in the **L**?" *3795*
10:37 **The expert in the l** replied, *1254+3836*[S]
11:45 One *of* the **experts in the l** answered him, *3788*
11:46 Jesus replied, "And you **experts in the l**, *3788*
11:52 "Woe to you **experts in the l**, *3788*
11:53 and the **teachers of the l** began *1208*
14: 3 the Pharisees and **experts in the l**, *3788*
15: 2 and the **teachers of the l** muttered, *1208*
16:16 "The **L** and the Prophets were proclaimed *3795*
16:17 least stroke of a pen to drop out *of* the **L**. *3795*
19:47 the **teachers of the l** and the leaders among *1208*
20: 1 the chief priests and the **teachers of the l**, *1208*
20:19 The **teachers of the l** and the chief priests *1208*
20:39 Some *of* the **teachers of the l** responded, *1208*
20:46 "Beware of the **teachers of the l**. *1208*
22: 2 and the **teachers of the l** were looking *1208*
22:66 both the chief priests and **teachers of the l**, *1208*
23:10 the **teachers of the l** were standing there, *1208*
24:44 that is written about me in the **L** of Moses, *3795*
Jn 1:17 For the **l** was given through Moses; *3795*

Jn 1:45 the one Moses wrote about in the L, and 3795
5:10 the l forbids you to carry your mat." 2003+4024
7:19 Has not Moses given you the l? 3795
7:19 Yet not one of you keeps the l. 3795
7:23 the Sabbath so that the l of Moses may not 3795
7:49 But this mob that knows nothing of the l— 3795
7:51 "Does our l condemn anyone 3795
8:3 The teachers of the l and the Pharisees 1208
8:5 In the L Moses commanded us to stone such 3795
8:17 In your own L it is written that 3795
10:34 "Is it not written in your L, 3795
12:34 the L that the Christ will remain forever, 3795
15:25 this is to fulfill what is written in their L: 3795
18:31 and judge him by your own l." 3795
19:7 The Jews insisted, "We have a l, 3795
19:7 and according to that l he must die, 3795
Ac 4:5 and teachers of the l met in Jerusalem. 1208
5:34 Gamaliel, a teacher of the l, 3791
6:12 and the elders and the teachers of the l. 1208
6:13 against this holy place and against the l. 3795
7:53 you who have received the l that was put 3795
10:28 that it is against our l for a Jew 116
13:15 the reading *from* the L and the Prophets, 3795
13:39 not be justified from by the l of Moses. 3795
15:5 be circumcised and required to obey the l 3795
18:13 to worship God in ways contrary to the l." 3795
18:15 about words and names and your own l— 3795
21:20 and all of them are zealous *for* the l. 3795
21:24 are living in obedience to the l. 3795
21:28 against our people and our l and this place. 3795
22:3 the l of our fathers and was just as zealous 3795
22:12 He was a devout observer of the l 2848+3795
23:3 to judge me according to the l, 3795
23:3 yet you yourself violate the l 4174
23:9 teachers of the l who were Pharisees stood 1208
23:29 to do with questions *about* their l, 3795
24:14 that agrees with the L and that is written in 3795
25:8 "I have done nothing wrong against the l 3795
28:23 about Jesus from the L of Moses and from 3795
Ro 2:12 All who sin apart from the l will also perish 492
2:12 the law will also perish apart from the l, 492
2:12 and all who sin under the l will be judged 3795
2:12 under the law will be judged by the l. 3795
2:13 not those who hear the l who are righteous 3795
2:13 but it is those who obey the l who will 3795
2:14 when Gentiles, who do not have the l, 3795
2:14 do by nature things *required by* the l, 3795
2:14 they are a l for themselves, 3795
2:14 even though they do not have the l, 3795
2:15 that the requirements *of* the l are written 3795
2:17 on the l and brag about your relationship 3795
2:18 because you are instructed by the l; 3795
2:20 because you have in the l the embodiment 3795
2:23 You who brag about the l, 3795
2:23 do you dishonor God by breaking the l? 3795
2:25 has value if you observe the l, 3795
2:25 but if you break the l, you become as though 3795
2:27 yet obeys the l will condemn you who, 3795
3:19 Now we know that whatever the l says, 3795
3:19 it says *to* those who are under the l, 3795
3:20 in his sight by observing the l; 3795
3:20 through the l we become conscious of sin. 3795
3:21 a righteousness from God, apart from l, 3795
3:21 to which the L and the Prophets testify. 3795
3:27 On that of observing the l? NIG
3:28 by faith apart from observing the l. 3795
3:31 Do we, then, nullify the l by this faith? 3795
3:31 Rather, we uphold the l. 3795
4:13 It was not through l that Abraham and his 3795
4:14 For if those who live by l are heirs, 3795
4:15 because l brings wrath. 3795
4:15 there is no l there is no transgression. 3795
4:16 not only *to* those who are of the l but also 3795
5:13 for before the l was given, sin was in the 3795
5:13 not taken into account when there is no l. 3795
5:20 The l was added so that the trespass 3795
6:14 because you are not under l, but under grace 3795
6:15 Shall we sin because we are not under l 3795
7:1 for I am speaking to men who know the l— 3795
7:1 the l has authority over a man only as long 3795
7:2 *by* l a married woman is bound to her 3795
7:2 she is released from the l of marriage. 3795
7:3 she is released from that l and is not 3795
7:4 you also died *to* the l through the body 3795
7:5 the sinful passions aroused by the l were 3795
7:6 from the l so that we serve in the new way 3795
7:7 Is the l sin? Certainly not! 3795
7:7 I would not have known what sin was except through the l. 3795
7:7 if the l had not said, "Do not covet." 3795
7:8 For apart from l, sin is dead. 3795
7:9 Once I was alive apart from l; 3795
7:12 So then, the l is holy, and the commandment 3795
7:14 We know that the l is spiritual; 3795
7:16 I agree that the l is good. 3795
7:21 So I find this l at work: 3795
7:22 in my inner being I delight *in* God's l; 3795
7:23 but I see another l at work in the members 3795
7:23 against the l of my mind and making me 3795
7:23 the l of sin at work within my members. 3795
7:25 in my mind am a slave *to* God's l, 3795
7:25 in the sinful nature a slave *to* the l of sin. 3795
8:2 the l of the Spirit of life set me free from 3795
8:2 of the Spirit of life set me free from the l 3795
8:3 For what the l was powerless to do in 3795
8:4 the righteous requirements *of* the l might 3795
8:7 It does not submit *to* God's l, 3795
Ro 9:4 the covenants, the receiving of the l, 3792
9:31 who pursued a l of righteousness, 3795
10:4 *of* the l so that there may be righteousness 3795
10:5 the righteousness that is by the l: 3795
13:8 who loves his fellowman has fulfilled the l. 3795
13:10 Therefore love is the fulfillment *of* the l. 3795
1Co 6:6 one brother goes to l against another— 3212
9:8 Doesn't the L say the same thing? 3795
9:9 For it is written in the L of Moses: 3795
9:20 To those under the l I became like one 3795
9:20 under the l (though I myself am not under 3795
9:20 (though I myself am not under the l), 3795
9:20 so as to win those under the l. 3795
9:21 *To* those not having the l I became 491
9:21 the law I became like one not having the l 491
9:21 the law (though I am not free from God's l 491
9:21 from God's law but am under Christ's l), 1937
9:21 so as to win those not having the l. 491
14:21 In the L it is written: 3795
14:34 but must be in submission, as the L says. 3795
15:56 and the power of sin is the l. 3795
Gal 2:16 a man is not justified by observing the l, 3795
2:16 faith in Christ and not by observing the l, 3795
2:16 by observing the l no one will be justified. 3795
2:19 the l I died to the law so that I might live 3795
2:19 the law I died *to* the l so that I might live 3795
2:21 righteousness could be gained through the l, 3795
3:2 Did you receive the Spirit by observing the l 3795
3:5 among you because you observe the l, 3795
3:10 All who rely on observing the l are under 3795
3:10 everything written in the Book *of* the L." 3795
3:11 no one is justified before God by the l, 3795
3:12 The l is not based on faith; 3795
3:13 Christ redeemed us from the curse *of* the l 3795
3:17 The l, introduced 430 years later, 3795
3:18 For if the inheritance depends on the l, 3795
3:19 What, then, was the purpose of the l? 3795
3:19 The l was put into effect through angels NIG
3:21 the l, therefore, opposed to the promises 3795
3:21 a l had been given that could impart life, 3795
3:21 then righteousness would certainly have come by the l. 3795
3:23 we were held prisoners by the l, 3795
3:24 the l was put in charge to lead us to Christ 3795
3:25 under the supervision of the l. NIG
4:4 born of a woman, born under l, 3795
4:5 to redeem those under l, 3795
4:21 Tell me, you who want to be under the l, 3795
4:21 are you not aware of what the l says? 3795
5:3 that he is obligated to obey the whole l. 3795
5:4 to be justified by l have been alienated 3795
5:14 The entire l is summed up in a single 3795
5:18 led by the Spirit, you are not under l. 3795
5:23 Against such things there is no l. 3795
6:2 in this way you will fulfill the l of Christ. 3795
6:13 the l, yet they want you to be circumcised 3795
Eph 2:15 in his flesh the l with its commandments 3795
Php 3:5 in regard to the l, a Pharisee; 3795
3:9 from the l, but that which is through faith 3795
1Ti 1:7 They want to be teachers of the l, 3791
1:8 that the l is good if one uses it properly. 3795
1:9 that l is made not for the righteous but 3795
Tit 3:9 and arguments and quarrels about the l, 3788
Heb 7:5 Now the l requires the descendants 3795
7:11 (for on the basis of it the l was given to 3793
7:12 there must also be a change *of* the l. 3795
7:19 (for the l made nothing perfect), 3795
7:28 For the l appoints as high priests men who 3795
7:28 but the oath, which came after the l, 3795
8:4 the gifts prescribed by the l. 3795
9:19 commandment of the l to all the people, 3795
9:22 the l requires that nearly everything 3795
10:1 The l is only a shadow of the good things 3795
10:8 (although the l required them to be made). 3795
10:28 Anyone who rejected the l of Moses died 3795
Jas 1:25 into the perfect l that gives freedom, 3795
2:8 If you really keep the royal l found 3795
2:9 and are convicted by the l as lawbreakers. 3795
2:10 For whoever keeps the whole l and 3795
2:12 to be judged by the l that gives freedom, 3795
4:11 or judges him speaks against the l 3795
4:11 When you judge the l, you are not keeping it 3795
1Jn 3:4 Everyone who sins breaks the l; 490+4472

LAW'S (1) [LAW]

Ro 2:26 not circumcised keep the l requirements, 3795

LAWBREAKER (3) [BREAK]

Ro 2:27 written code and circumcision, are a l. 3795+4127
Gal 2:18 I prove that I am a l. 4127
Jas 2:11 you have become a l. 3795+4127

LAWBREAKERS (2) [BREAK]

1Ti 1:9 not for the righteous but *for* l and rebels, 491
Jas 2:9 you sin and are convicted by the law as l. 4127

LAWFUL (12) [LAW]

Mt 12:4 which was not l for them to do, 2003
12:10 *"Is it* l to heal on the Sabbath?" 2003
12:12 *it is* l to do good on the Sabbath." 2003
14:4 *"It is* not l for you to have her." 2003
19:3 *"Is it* l for a man to divorce his wife 2003
Mk 2:26 which *is* l only for priests to eat. 2003+4024
3:4 "Which *is* l on the Sabbath: 2003
Mk 6:18 not l for you to have your brother's wife." 2003
10:2 *"Is it* l for a man to divorce his wife?" 2003
Lk 6:4 he ate what *is* l only for priests to eat. 2003
6:9 "I ask you, which *is* l on the Sabbath: 2003
14:3 *"Is it* l to heal on the Sabbath or not?" 2003

LAWGIVER (2) [LAW]

Isa 33:22 LORD is our judge, the LORD *is* our l, 2980
Jas 4:12 There is only one L and Judge, 3794

LAWLESS (7) [LAWLESSNESS]

2Sa 3:33 "Should Abner have died as the l die? 5572
2Th 2:8 And then the l *one* will be revealed, 491
2:9 *of* the l one will be in accordance with 4005[S]
Heb 10:17 and l acts I will remember no more." 490
2Pe 2:7 distressed by the filthy lives *of* l *men* 118
2:8 in his righteous soul *by* the l deeds he saw 491
3:17 not be carried away by the error *of* l *men* 118

LAWLESSNESS (3) [LAWLESS]

2Th 2:3 and the man *of* l is revealed, 490
2:7 the secret power *of* l is already at work; 490
1Jn 3:4 who sins breaks the law; in fact, sin is l. 490

LAWS (113) [LAW]

Ge 26:5 my commands, my decrees and my l." 9368
Ex 18:16 and inform them of God's decrees and l." 9368
18:20 Teach them the decrees and l, 9368
21:1 the l you are to set before them: 5477
24:3 the people all the LORD's words and l, 5477
Lev 18:4 You must obey my l and be careful 5477
18:5 Keep my decrees and l, 5477
18:26 But you must keep my decrees and my l. 5477
19:37 " 'Keep all my decrees and all my l 5477
20:22 " 'Keep all my decrees and l 5477
25:18 and be careful to obey my l, 5477
26:15 if you reject my decrees and abhor my l 5477
26:43 for their sins because they rejected my l 5477
26:46 the l and the regulations that 5477
Nu 15:16 The same l and regulations will apply 9368
Dt 4:1 the decrees and l I am about to teach you. 5477
4:5 I have taught you decrees and l as 5477
4:8 as to have such righteous decrees and l 5477
4:8 and laws as this body of l I am setting 9368
4:14 to teach you the decrees and l you are 5477
4:45 decrees and l Moses gave them 5477
5:1 Hear, O Israel, the decrees and l I declare 5477
5:31 and l you are to teach them to follow in 5477
6:1 and l the LORD your God directed me 5477
6:20 of the stipulations, decrees and l 5477
7:11 decrees and l I give you today. 5477
7:12 to these l and are careful to follow them, 5477
8:11 his l and his decrees 5477
11:1 his l and his commands always. 5477
11:32 and l I am setting before you today. 5477
12:1 and l you must be careful to follow in 5477
19:9 you carefully follow all these l I command 5184
26:16 to follow these decrees and l; 5477
26:17 commands and l, and 5477
30:16 and to keep his commands, decrees and l; 5477
Jos 24:25 up for them decrees and l. 5477
2Sa 22:23 All his l are before me; 5477
1Ki 2:3 his l and requirements, 5477
9:4 and observe my decrees and l, 5477
11:33 nor kept my statutes and l as David, 5477
2Ki 17:34 the l and commands that the LORD gave 9368
17:37 the l and commands he wrote for you. 9368
1Ch 22:13 and l that the LORD gave Moses 5477
28:7 in carrying out my commands and l, 5477
2Ch 7:17 and observe my decrees and l, 5477
14:4 and to obey his l and commands. 9368
33:8 concerning all the l, decrees and 9368
Ezr 7:10 and to teaching its decrees and l in Israel. 5477
7:25 all who know the l *of* your God. 10186
Ne 1:7 and l you gave your servant Moses. 5477
9:13 You gave them regulations and l 9368
9:14 decrees and l through your servant Moses. 9368
Est 1:19 a royal decree and let it be written in the l 2017
3:8 and who do not obey the king's l; 2017
Job 38:33 Do you know the l *of* the heavens? 2978
Ps 10:5 he is haughty and your l are far from him; 5477
18:22 All his l are before me; 5477
50:16 "What right have you to recite my l 2976
105:45 keep his precepts and observe his l. 9368
119:7 as I learn your righteous l. 5477
119:13 With my lips I recount all the l *that come* 5477
119:20 with longing for your l at all times. 5477
119:30 I have set my heart on your l. 5477
119:39 for your l are good. 5477
119:43 for I have put my hope in your l. 5477
119:52 I remember your ancient l, O LORD, 5477
119:62 to give you thanks for your righteous l. 5477
119:75 O LORD, that your l are righteous, 5477
119:91 Your l endure to this day, 5477
119:102 I have not departed from your l, 5477
119:106 that I will follow your righteous l. 5477
119:108 and teach me your l. 5477
119:120 I stand in awe of your l. 5477
119:137 O LORD, and your l are right. 5477
119:149 O LORD, according to your l. 5477
119:156 preserve my life according to your l. 5477
119:160 all your righteous l are eternal. 5477
119:164 a day I praise you for your righteous l. 5477
119:175 and may your l sustain me. 5477

Ps 147:19 his **l** and decrees to Israel. 5477
147:20 they do not know his **l.** 5477
Pr 8:15 By me kings reign and rulers **make l** 2980
Isa 10: 1 Woe to those *who* **make** unjust **l,** 2976+2980
24: 5 they have disobeyed the **l,** 9368
26: 8 LORD, walking in the way of your **l,** 5477
Jer 33:25 and the **fixed l** *of* heaven and earth, 2978
Eze 5: 6 against my **l** and decrees more than 5477
5: 6 She has rejected my **l** and has 5477
5: 7 not followed my decrees or kept my **l.** 5477
11:12 not followed my decrees or kept my **l** 5477
11:20 and be careful to keep my **l.** 5477
18: 9 and faithfully keeps my **l.** 5477
18:17 He keeps my **l** and follows my decrees. 5477
20:11 and made known to them my **l,** 5477
20:13 not follow my decrees but rejected my **l**— 5477
20:16 because they rejected my **l** and did 5477
20:18 the statutes of your fathers or keep their **l** 5477
20:19 and be careful to keep my **l.** 5477
20:21 they were not careful to keep my **l**— 5477
20:24 because they had not obeyed my **l** 5477
20:25 not good and **l** they could not live by; 5477
36:27 and be careful to keep my **l.** 5477
37:24 They will follow my **l** and be careful 5477
43:11 and all its regulations and **l.** 9368
44:24 They are to keep my **l** and my decrees 9368
Da 6: 8 in accordance with the **l** *of* the Medes 10186
6:12 in accordance with the **l** *of* the Medes 10186
7:25 and try to change the set times and the **l.** 10186
9: 5 turned away from your commands and **l.** 5477
9:10 the **l** he gave us through his servants 9368
Mal 4: 4 and **l** I gave him at Horeb for all Israel. 5477
Heb 8:10 I will put my **l** in their minds *3795*
10:16 I will put my **l** in their hearts, *3795*

LAWSUIT (2) [LAWSUITS]

Ex 23: 2 When you give testimony in a **l,** 8190
23: 3 not show favoritism to a poor man in his **l.** 8190

LAWSUITS (4) [LAWSUIT]

Ex 23: 6 to your poor people in their **l.** 8190
Dt 17: 8 whether bloodshed, **l** or assaults 1907+1907+4200
Hos 10: 4 therefore **l** spring up like poisonous weeds 5477
1Co 6: 7 The very fact that you have **l** *3210*

LAWYER (2) [LAW]

Ac 24: 1 of the elders and a **l** named Tertullus, *4842*
Tit 3:13 Do everything you can to help Zenas the **l** *3788*

LAX (1)

Jer 48:10 "A curse on him who is **l** in doing 8244

LAY (168) [LAID, LAIN, LAYER, LAYING, LAYS]

Ge 4: 1 Adam **l with** his wife Eve, 3359
4:17 Cain **l with** his wife, 3359
4:25 Adam **l with** his wife again, 3359
9:21 he became drunk and *l* **uncovered** AIT
19:33 older daughter went in and **l with** him. 907+8886
19:33 He was not aware of it when she **l down** or 8886
19:34 "Last night *I* **l with** my father. 907+8886
19:35 younger daughter went and **l with** him. 6640+8886
19:35 of it when she **l down** or when she got up. 8886
22:12 *"Do* not **l** a hand on the boy," he said. 8938
28:11 under his head and **l down to sleep.** 8886
29:23 and Jacob **l with** her. 448+995
29:30 Jacob **l with** Rachel also, 448+995
37:22 but don't **l** a hand on him." 8938
37:27 to the Ishmaelites and not **l** our hands 2118
38: 2 He married her and **l with** her; 448+995
38: 9 so whenever *he* **l with** his brother's wife, 448+995
Ex 7: 4 Then *I will* **l** my hand on Egypt and 5989
22:11 not **l** hands on the other person's property. 8938
29:10 and Aaron and his sons *shall* **l** their hands 6164
29:15 and Aaron and his sons *shall* **l** their hands 6164
29:19 and Aaron and his sons *shall* **l** their hands 6164
Lev 1: 4 *He is to* **l** his hand on the head of 6164
3: 2 *to* **l** his hand on the head of his offering 6164
3: 8 *to* **l** his hand on the head of his offering 6164
3:13 *to* **l** his hand on its head and slaughter it 6164
4: 4 *to* **l** his hand on its head and slaughter it 6164
4:15 *to* **l** their hands on the bull's head before 6164
4:24 *He is to* **l** his hand on the goat's head 6164
4:29 *He is to* **l** his hand on the head of 6164
4:33 *to* **l** his hand on its head and slaughter it 6164
16:21 He *is to* **l** both hands on the head of 6164
24:14 *to* **l** their hands on his head, 6164
26:31 into ruins and **l waste** your sanctuaries, 9037
26:32 I *will* **l waste** the land, 9037
Nu 8:10 the Israelites *are to* **l** their hands on them. 6164
8:12 the Levites **l** their hands on the heads of 6164
22:27 *she* **l down** under Balaam, and he was 8069
27:18 and **l** your hand on him. 6164
Dt 9:25 *I* **l prostrate** before the LORD 5877
20:12 **l siege** to that city. 7443
20:19 When *you* **l siege** to a city for a long time, 7443
28:52 *They will* **l siege** to all the cities 7674
Jos 2: 8 Before the spies **l down** for the night, 8886
6:26 his firstborn son *will he* **l** its **foundations;** 3569
8: 9 of ambush and **l in wait** between Bethel 3782
18:11 Their allotted territory **l** between the tribes 3655
19: 1 Their inheritance **l** within the territory 2118
Jdg 4:21 to him while he **l fast asleep,** 8101
4:22 and there **l** Sisera with the tent peg 5877
5:27 At her feet he sank, he fell; there *he* **l.** 8886
7: 8 camp of Midian **l** below him in the valley. 2118
16: 2 So they surrounded the place and **l in wait** 741
16: 3 But Samson **l** there only until the middle 8886
19:26 at the door and **l** there until daylight. NIH
19:27 there **l** his concubine, fallen in the doorway NIH
Ru 3: 7 uncovered his feet and **l down.** 8886
3:14 So *she* **l** at his feet until morning, 8886
1Sa 1:19 Elkanah **l with** Hannah his wife, 3359
3: 5 So he went and **l down.** 8886
3: 9 So Samuel went and **l down** in his place. 8886
3:15 Samuel **l down** until morning and 8886
9:23 the one I told you *to* **l** aside." 8492
19:24 *He* **l** that way all that day and night. 5877
23:17 "My father Saul *will* not **l** a hand **on** you. 5162
26: 9 Who *can* **l** a hand on the LORD's anointed 8938
26:11 the LORD forbid that I *should* **l** a hand 8938
26:23 not **l** a hand on the LORD's anointed. 8938
2Sa 12:24 and he went to her and **l with** her. 6640+8886
13: 6 So Amnon **l down** and pretended to be ill. 8886
13:31 tore his clothes and **l down** on the ground; 8886
16:22 and he **l with** his father's concubines in 448+995
20:12 Amasa **l wallowing** in his blood in 1670
1Ki 3:19 woman's son died because *she* **l** on him. 8886
13:31 **l** my bones beside his bones. 5663
19: 5 *he* **l down** under the tree and fell asleep. 8886
19: 6 He ate and drank and then **l down** again. 8886
21: 4 *He* **l** on his bed sulking and refused to eat. 8886
21:27 *He* **l** in sackcloth and went around meekly. 8886
2Ki 4:11 he went up to his room and **l down** there. 8886
4:29 **L** my staff on the boy's face." 8492
4:34 he got on the bed and **l** upon the boy, 8886
1Ch 2:21 Hezron **l with** the daughter of Makir 448+995
7:23 Then *he* **l with** his wife again, 448+995
2Ch 24:22 killed his son, who said as he **l** dying, NIH
35: 5 your fellow countrymen, the **l people.** 1201+6639
35: 7 for all the **l people** who were there 1201+6639
Ne 13:21 do this again, *I will* **l** hands on you." 8938
Est 4: 3 Many **l** *in* sackcloth and ashes. 3667
9:10 *they did* not **l** their hands on the plunder. 8938
9:15 *they did* not **l** their hands on the plunder. 8938
9:16 but *did* not **l** their hands on the plunder. 8938
Job 1:12 but on the man himself *do* not **l** a finger." 8938
5: 8 *I would* **l** my cause before him. 8492
9:33 *to* **l** his hand upon us both, 8883
22:22 from his mouth and **l up** his words 8492
30:12 *they* **l snares** *for* my feet, 8938
41: 8 If *you* **l** a hand on him, you will remember 8492
Ps 5: 3 in the morning *I* **l** my requests before you 6885
21: 8 Your hand *will* **l hold** on all your enemies; 5162
22:15 *you* **l** me in the dust of death. 9189
73: 9 Their mouths **l claim** to heaven, 9286
Pr 3:18 *those who* **l hold** *of* her will be blessed. 9461
4: 4 **"L hold** *of* my words *with* all your heart; 9461
Ecc 10: 4 calmness *can* **l** great errors **to rest.** 5663
Isa 11:14 They *will* **l** hands *on* Edom and Moab, 5447
21: 2 Elam, attack! Media, **l siege!** 7443
24: 1 the LORD *is going to* **l waste** the earth 1327
25:12 your high fortified walls and **l** *them* **low;** 9164
28:16 "See, I **l** a stone in Zion, a tested stone, 3569
34:15 The owl will nest there and **l eggs,** 4880
35: 7 In the haunts **where** jackals once **l,** 8070
42:15 *I will* **l waste** the mountains and hills 2990
43:17 and *they* **l** there, never to rise again, 8886
44: 7 and **l out** before me what has happened 6885
52:10 The LORD *will* **l bare** his holy arm in 3106
64: 7 on your name or strives to **l hold** of you; 2616
Jer 2:20 and under every spreading tree you **l down** 7579
4: 7 He has left his place to **l** waste your land. 8492
4:26 all its towns **l in ruins** before the LORD, 5997
9:11 and *I will* **l** waste the towns of Judah 5989
15: 6 *I will* **l** hands on you and destroy you; 5742
17:11 a partridge that hatches eggs *it did* not **l** is 3528
34:22 And *I will* **l** waste the towns of Judah 5989
50: 3 and **l** waste her land. 8883
51:29 to **l** waste the land of Babylon so 8492
La 4:19 over the mountains and **l in wait** for us in 741
Eze 4: 2 Then **l** siege to it: 5989
6: 5 *I will* **l** the dead bodies of the Israelites 5989
16: 6 as you **l** there in your blood I said to you, NIH
19: 2 *She* **l down** among the young lions 8069
25:13 *I will* **l** it waste, 5989
26:16 from their thrones and **l aside** their robes 6073
30:12 by the hand of foreigners *I will* **l waste** 9037
30:14 *I will* **l waste** Upper Egypt, 9037
31:12 its branches *l* **broken** in all the ravines of AIT
39:21 the punishment I inflict and the hand *I* **l** 8492
Da 2:28 that passed through your mind as you **l** NIH
8:27 was exhausted and **l ill** for several days. 2703
Jnh 1: 5 where *he* **l down** and fell into a deep sleep. 8886
Mic 1: 6 into the valley and **l bare** her foundations. 1655
7:16 *They will* **l** their hands on their mouths 8492
Mt 8:20 Son of Man has no place to **l** his head." *3111*
11:12 and forceful men **l hold of** it. *773*
28: 6 Come and see the place where *he* **l.** *3023*
Mk 6: 5 except **l** his hands **on** a few sick people *2202*
Lk 5:18 into the house *to* **l** him before Jesus. *5502*
9:58 Son of Man has no place *to* **l** his head." *3111*
21:12 *they will* **l** hands **on** you *2095*
22:53 and *you did* not **l** a hand on me. *1753*
Jn 4:46 a certain royal official whose son **l sick** *820*
10:15 and *I* **l down** my life for the sheep. *5502*
10:17 Father loves me is that I **l down** my life— *5502*
10:18 but I **l** it **down** of my own accord. *5502*
10:18 I have authority *to* **l** it **down** and authority *5502*
11: 2 whose brother Lazarus now **l sick,** *820*
13:37 *I will* **l down** my life for you." *5502*
13:38 *"Will you* really **l down** your life for me? *5502*
15:13 that he **l down** his life for his friends. *5502*
Ac 8:19 everyone **on** whom *I* **l** my hands may receive the Holy Spirit." *2202*
Ro 9:33 "See, *I* **l** in Zion a stone that causes men *5502*
1Co 3:11 no one can **l** any foundation other than *5502*
7:17 **the rule** *I* **l down** in all the churches. *1411*
1Ti 6:19 In this way *they will* **l up treasure** *631*
1Pe 2: 6 "See, *I* **l** a stone in Zion, *5502*
1Jn 3:16 *to* **l down** our lives for our brothers. *5502*
Rev 4:10 *They* **l** their crowns before the throne *965*
10: 2 a little scroll, *which* **l open** in his hand. *487*

LAYER (2) [LAY]

Ex 16:13 the morning there was a **l** *of* dew around 8887
Lev 9:19 the fat tail, the **l of fat,** 4833

LAYING (8) [LAY]

2Ch 32: 9 and all his forces were **l** siege to Lachish, NIH
Job 34:30 from **l** snares for the people. NIH
Lk 4:40 and **l** his hands **on** each one, *2202*
Ac 8:18 the Spirit was given at the **l on** of the apostles' hands, *2120*
1Ti 5:22 *Do* not be hasty in the **l on of** hands, *2202*
2Ti 1: 6 in you through the **l on** of my hands. *2120*
Heb 6: 1 not **l** again the foundation of repentance *2850*
6: 2 about baptisms, the **l on** of hands, *2120*

LAYS (10) [LAY]

Job 27:17 what *he* **l up** the righteous will wear, 3922
28: 9 and **l bare** the roots of the mountains. 2200
30:24 "Surely no *one* **l** a hand on a broken man 8938
39:14 *She* **l** her eggs on the ground 6440
Ps 104: 3 and **l** *the* **beams** *of* his upper chambers 7936
Isa 26: 5 **l** the lofty city **low;** 9164
30:32 Every stroke the LORD **l** on them 5663
Zec 12: 1 *who* **l the foundation** *of* the earth, 3569
Lk 14:29 For if he **l** the foundation and is not able *5502*
Jn 10:11 The good shepherd **l down** his life for *5502*

LAZARUS (18)

Lk 16:20 At his gate was laid a beggar named **L,** *3276*
16:23 saw Abraham far away, with **L** by his side. *3276*
16:24 have pity on me and send **L** to dip the tip *3276*
16:25 while **L** received bad things, *3276*
16:27 father, send **L** to my father's house, *899S*
Jn 11: 1 Now a man named **L** was sick. *3276*
11: 2 This Mary, whose brother **L** now lay sick, *3276*
11: 5 Jesus loved Martha and her sister and **L.** *3276*
11: 6 Yet when he heard that **L** was sick, *NIG*
11:11 "Our friend **L** has fallen asleep; *3276*
11:14 So then he told them plainly, **"L** is dead, *3276*
11:17 Jesus found that **L** had already been in *899S*
11:43 Jesus called in a loud voice, **"L,** *3276*
12: 1 Jesus arrived at Bethany, where **L** lived, *3276*
12: 2 while **L** was among those reclining at *3276*
12: 9 not only because of him but also to see **L,** *3276*
12:10 chief priests made plans to kill **L** as well, *3276*
12:17 with him when he called **L** from the tomb *3276*

LAZINESS (2) [LAZY]

Pr 12:24 but **l** ends in slave labor. 8244
19:15 **L** brings on deep sleep, 6790

LAZY (10) [LAZINESS]

Ex 5: 8 don't reduce the quota. They *are* **l;** 8332
5:17 Pharaoh said, **"L,** that's what you are— 8332
5:17 that's what you are—**l!** 8332
Pr 10: 4 **L** hands make a man poor, 8244
12:27 The **l** *man* does not roast his game, 8244
26:15 *he is too* **l** to bring it back to his mouth. 4206
Ecc 10:18 If a man is **l,** the rafters sag; 6792
Mt 25:26 *'You* wicked, **l** servant! *3891*
Tit 1:12 always liars, evil brutes, **l** gluttons." *734*
Heb 6:12 We do not want you to become **l,** *3821*

LEAD (89) [LEADER, LEADER'S, LEADERS, LEADERS', LEADERSHIP, LEADING, LEADS, LED, RINGLEADER]

Ge 32:17 He instructed the **one in the l:** 8037
Ex 13:17 God *did* not **l** them *on* the road through 5697
15:10 They sank like **l** in the mighty waters. 6769
15:13 "In your unfailing love *you will* **l** 5697
32:34 **l** the people to the place I spoke of, 5697
33:12 **'L** these people,' but you have 6590
34:16 **l** your sons **to do the same.** 339+466+2177+2388S
Nu 14: 8 *he will* **l** us into that land, 995
21:15 the ravines that **l** to the site of Ar and lie 5742
27:17 *one* who *will* **l** them **out** and bring them 3655
31:22 Gold, silver, bronze, iron, tin, **l** 6769
Dt 1:38 because he *will* **l** Israel **to inherit** it. 5706
3:28 for he *will* **l** this people **across** 4200+6296+7156
10:11 "and **l** the people on their way, 2143+4200+7156
21: 4 and **l** her **down** to a valley that has 3718
31: 2 and I am no longer able to **l** you. 995+2256+3655
Jos 1: 6 because you *will* **l** these people **to inherit** 5706
Jdg 4: 6 of Naphtali and Zebulun and **l the way** 5432
5: 2 "When the princes in Israel **take the l,** 7276
7:17 **"Follow** my **l.** 4027+6913
1Sa 8: 5 now appoint a king to **l** us, 9149
8: 6 when they said, "Give us a king to **l** us," 9149

1Sa 8:20 with a king *to* l us and to go out before us 9149
30:15 "*Can you* l me **down** to this raiding party?" 3718
2Ki 4:24 and said to her servant, "**L on;** 2143+2256+5627
6:19 and *I will* l you to the man you are looking 2143
2Ch 1:10 wisdom and knowledge, that *I may* l this people, 995+2256+3655+4200+7156
8:14 and the Levites to l the praise and to assist 5466
Est 6:9 and l him on the horse through 8206
Job 19:24 they were inscribed with an iron tool on **l,** 6769
38:32 the constellations in their seasons or **l out** 5697
Ps 5:8 **L** me, O LORD, in your righteousness 5697
26:11 But I l a blameless **life;** 928+2143
27:11 l me in a straight path because 5697
31:3 for the sake of your name l and guide me. 5697
60:9 Who *will* l me to Edom? 5697
61:2 l me to the rock that is higher than I. 5697
80:1 you *who* l Joseph like a flock; 5627
101:2 I will be careful to l a blameless life— NIH
108:10 Who *will* l me to Edom? 5697
139:24 and l me in the way everlasting. 5697
143:10 *may* your good Spirit l me on level ground. 5697
Pr 4:11 of wisdom and l you along straight paths. 2005
5:5 her steps **l straight** *to* the grave. 9461
21:5 The plans of the diligent **l to** profit as 4200
Ecc 5:6 Do not let your mouth l you **into sin.** 2627
SS 8:2 *I would* l you and bring you my mother's 5627
Isa 3:12 O my people, your guides l you **astray;** 9494
11:6 and a little child *will* l them. 5627
20:4 the king of Assyria *will* **l away** stripped 5627
42:16 *I will* l the blind by ways they have 2143
43:8 **L out** those who have eyes but are blind, 3655
49:10 on them will guide them and l them 5633
60:9 in the l are the ships of Tarshish, 8037
Jer 3:15 *who will* l you *with* knowledge 8286
6:29 the l with fire, but the refining goes on 6769
23:32 "They tell them and l my people **astray** 9494
31:9 *I will* l them beside streams of water on 2143
31:32 by the hand to l them **out** of Egypt, 3655
50:8 and be like the goats that l the flock. 4200+7156
Eze 13:10 " 'Because *they* l my people **astray,** 3246
22:18 tin, iron and l left inside a furnace. 6769
22:20 l and tin into a furnace to melt it with 6769
27:12 iron, tin and l for your merchandise. 6769
Da 12:3 l many **to righteousness,** 7405
Hos 2:14 *I will* l her into the desert 2143
5:8 Raise the battle cry in Beth Aven; **l on,** 339+3870
Mic 3:5 for the prophets *who* l my people **astray,** 9494
6:4 I sent Moses to l you, 7156
Zec 5:7 Then the cover of l was raised, 6769
5:8 the basket and pushed the l cover down 6769
Mt 6:13 And l us not **into** temptation, *1662*
Mk 14:44 arrest him and l him **away** under guard." *552*
Lk 6:39 "Can a blind man l a blind man? *3842*
11:4 And l us not **into** temptation.' " *1662*
13:15 from the stall and l it **out** to give it water? *552*
Jn 21:18 and someone else will dress you and l you *5770*
Ac 13:11 **someone to l him by the hand.** *5933*
Gal 3:24 law *was* **put in charge** *to* l us to Christ *4080*
1Th 4:11 Make it your ambition *to* **l a quiet life,** *2483*
Heb 6:1 of repentance from acts that **l** to death, *NIG*
8:9 by the hand *to* l them **out** of Egypt, *1974*
9:14 cleanse our consciences from acts that l *NIG*
1Jn 2:26 who *are trying to* l you **astray.** *4414*
3:7 *do* not *let* anyone l you **astray.** *4414*
5:16 a sin that does not **l to** death, *4639*
5:16 I refer to those whose sin does not **l to** *4639*
5:17 and there is sin that does not **l to** death. *4639*
Rev 7:17 *he will* l them to springs of living water. *3842*

LEADER (79) [LEAD]

Lev 4:22 " 'When a l sins unintentionally 5954
Nu 2:3 The l of the people of Judah is Nahshon 5954
2:5 The l of the people of Issachar is Nethanel 5954
2:7 The l of the people of Zebulun is Eliab 5954
2:10 The l of the people of Reuben is Elizur 5954
2:12 The l of the people of Simeon is Shelumiel 5954
2:14 The l of the people of Gad is Eliasaph 5954
2:18 The l of the people of Ephraim is Elishama 5954
2:20 The l of the people of Manasseh is Gamaliel 5954
2:22 The l of the people of Benjamin is Abidan 5954
2:25 The l of the people of Dan is Ahiezer 5954
2:27 The l of the people of Asher is Pagiel 5954
2:29 The l of the people of Naphtali is Ahira 5954
3:24 The l *of* the families of the Gershonites 5954
3:30 The l *of* the families of the Kohathite 5954
3:32 The **chief** l *of* the Levites was Eleazar 5954+5954
3:35 The l *of* the families of the Merarite clans 5954
7:3 ox from each l and a cart from every two. 5954
7:11 "Each day one l is to bring his offering for 5954
7:18 the l *of* Issachar, brought his offering. 5954
7:24 the l of the people of Zebulun, 5954
7:30 the l of the people of Reuben, 5954
7:36 the l of the people of Simeon, 5954
7:42 the l of the people of Gad, 5954
7:48 the l of the people of Ephraim, 5954
7:54 the l of the people of Manasseh, 5954
7:60 the l of the people of Benjamin, 5954
7:66 the l of the people of Dan, 5954
7:72 the l of the people of Asher, 5954
7:78 the l of the people of Naphtali, 5954
14:4 "We should choose a l and go back 8031
17:2 from the l *of* each of their ancestral tribes. 5954
17:6 for the l of each of their ancestral tribes, 5954
25:14 the l of a Simeonite family. 5954
25:18 the daughter of a Midianite **l,** 5954
34:18 And appoint one l from each tribe 5954
34:22 the l from the tribe of Dan; 5954
34:23 the l from the tribe of Manasseh son 5954
34:24 l from the tribe of Ephraim son of Joseph; 5954
34:25 the l from the tribe of Zebulun; 5954
34:26 the l from the tribe of Issachar; 5954
34:27 the l from the tribe of Asher; 5954
34:28 the l from the tribe of Naphtali." 5954
1Sa 7:6 And Samuel *was* l *of* Israel at Mizpah. 9149
9:16 Anoint him l over my people Israel; 5592
10:1 "Has not the LORD anointed you l 5592
12:2 Now you have a king *as* your **l.** 2143+4200+7156
12:2 *have been* your l from my youth 2143+4200+7156
13:14 after his own heart and appointed him l 5592
19:20 with Samuel standing there *as* their **l,** 5893
22:2 gathered around him, and he became their **l.** 8569
25:30 concerning him and has appointed him l 5592
1Ki 11:24 around him and became the l *of* a band 8569
14:7 from among the people and made you a l 5592
16:2 and made you l of my people Israel, 5592
2Ki 20:5 Hezekiah, the l *of* my people, 5592
1Ch 2:10 Nahshon, the l *of* the people of Judah. 5954
5:6 Beerah was a l of the Reubenites. 5954
12:4 who was a l *of* the Thirty; 6584
12:27 l of the family of Aaron, with 3,700 men, 5592
15:5 Uriel the l and 120 relatives; 8569
15:6 Asaiah the l and 220 relatives; 8569
15:7 Joel the l and 130 relatives; 8569
15:8 Shemaiah the l and 200 relatives; 8569
15:9 Eliel the l and 80 relatives; 8569
15:10 Amminadab the l and 112 relatives. 8569
27:4 Mikloth was the l of his division. 5592
28:4 He chose Judah as **l,** 5592
2Ch 6:5 nor have I chosen anyone to be the l 5592
13:12 God is with us; he is our **l.** 8031
19:11 the l of the tribe of Judah, 5592
Ezr 8:17 Iddo, the l in Casiphia. 8031
Ne 9:17 in their rebellion appointed a l in order 8031
Isa 3:6 and say, "You have a cloak, you be our **l;** 7903
3:7 do not make me the l *of* the people." 7903
55:4 a l and commander of the peoples. 5592
Jer 30:21 Their l will be one of their own; 129
Hos 1:11 and they will appoint one l and will come 8031
Hab 3:13 the l of the land of wickedness, 8031

LEADER'S (1) [LEAD]

Dt 33:21 the l portion was kept for him. 2980

LEADERS (120) [LEAD]

Ex 15:15 l *of* Moab will be seized with trembling, 380
16:22 and the l *of* the community came 5954
18:25 from all Israel and made them l of 8031
24:11 not raise his hand against these l *of* 722
34:31 the l of the community came back to him, 5954
35:27 The l brought onyx stones and other gems 5954
Nu 1:16 the l *of* their ancestral tribes. 5954
1:44 by Moses and Aaron and the twelve l 5954
4:34 and the l *of* the community counted 5954
4:46 and the l *of* Israel counted all the Levites 5954
7:2 Then the l *of* Israel, the heads of families 5954
7:2 the heads of families who were the tribal l 5954
7:10 the l brought their offerings 5954
7:84 These were the offerings of the Israelite l 5954
10:4 If only one is sounded, the l— 5954
11:16 to you as l and officials among the people. 2418
13:2 From each ancestral tribe send one of its **l."** 5954
13:3 All of them were l *of* the Israelites. 408+8031
16:2 well-known community l who had been 5954
17:6 and their l gave him twelve staffs, 5954
25:4 "Take all the l *of* these people, 8031
27:2 the l and the whole assembly, and said, 5954
31:13 and all the l *of* the community went 5954
32:2 the priest and to the l *of* the community, 5954
36:1 came and spoke before Moses and the **l,** 5954
Dt 29:10 your l and chief men, your elders and 8031
32:42 the heads of the enemy **l."** 7278
33:5 He was king over Jeshurun when the l *of* 8031
Jos 8:10 the l *of* Israel marched before them to Ai. 2418
9:15 the l *of* the assembly ratified it by oath. 5954
9:18 because the l *of* the assembly had sworn 5954
9:18 The whole assembly grumbled against the **l,** 5954
9:19 but all the l answered, 5954
17:4 Joshua son of Nun, and the l and said, 5954
22:30 the priest and the l *of* the community— 5954
22:32 and the l returned to Canaan 5954
23:2 their elders, **l,** judges and officials— 8031
24:1 He summoned the elders, **l,** 8031
Jdg 7:25 They also captured two of the Midianite **l,** 8569
8:3 God gave Oreb and Zeeb, the Midianite **l,** 8569
10:18 The l *of* the people of Gilead said 8569
20:2 The l *of* all the people of the tribes 7157
1Sa 14:38 all you who are l *of* the army, 7157
2Sa 4:2 Now Saul's son had two men who were l 8569
7:11 since the time I appointed l 9149
1Ch 4:38 The men listed above by name were l 5954
7:40 brave warriors and outstanding **l.** 5954
12:18 So David received them and made them l 8031
12:20 l *of* units of a thousand in Manasseh. 8031
15:16 David told the l *of* the Levites 8569
17:6 to any of their l whom I commanded 9149
17:10 since the time I appointed l 9149
22:17 the l *of* Israel to help his son Solomon. 8569
23:2 also gathered together all the l *of* Israel, 8569
24:4 A larger number of l were found 8031
26:6 who were l in their father's family 4938
29:6 Then the l *of* families, the officers 8569
29:9 at the willing response of **their l,** 4392[S]
2Ch 1:2 to the judges and to all the l in Israel, 5954
12:5 and to the l *of* Judah who had assembled 8569
12:6 The l *of* Israel and the king humbled 8569
24:23 and Jerusalem and killed all the l *of* 8569
26:12 The total number of family l over 8031
28:12 Then some of the l *in* Ephraim— 8031
32:21 the fighting men and the l and officers in 5592
35:9 Jeiel and Jozabad, the l *of* the Levites, 8569
36:14 all the l *of* the priests and 8569
Ezr 5:10 the names of their l for your information. 10646
8:16 Zechariah and Meshullam, *who* were **l,** 8031
9:1 the l came to me and said, 8569
9:2 And the l and officials have led the way 8569
Ne 9:32 upon our kings and **l,** 8569
9:34 our **l,** our priests and our fathers did 8569
9:38 putting it in writing, and our **l,** 8569
10:14 The l *of* the people: 8031
11:1 the l *of* the people settled in Jerusalem, 8569
11:3 the provincial l who settled in Jerusalem 8031
12:7 the l *of* the priests and their associates in 8031
12:24 And the l *of* the Levites were Hashabiah, 8031
12:31 the l *of* Judah go up on top of the wall. 8569
12:32 and half the l *of* Judah followed them, 8569
Est 1:3 The **military** l *of* Persia and Media, 2657
Job 12:24 the l *of* the earth of their reason; 6639+8031
Isa 3:14 against the elders and l *of* his people: 8569
14:9 all *those who* were l *in* the world; 6966
19:13 the l *of* Memphis are deceived; 8569
22:3 All your l have fled together; 7903
Jer 2:8 the l rebelled against me. 8286
5:5 So I will go to the l and speak to them; 1524
25:34 roll in the dust, you l *of* the flock. 129
25:35 the l *of* the flock no place to escape. 129
25:36 the wailing of the l *of* the flock, 129
29:2 the court officials and the l *of* Judah 8569
34:19 The l *of* Judah and Jerusalem, 8569
Eze 11:1 l *of* the people. 8569
32:21 the grave the mighty l will say of Egypt 1475
Da 11:41 and the l *of* Ammon will be delivered 8040
Hos 5:10 Judah's l are like those who move boundary 8569
7:16 Their l will fall by the sword because 8569
9:15 all their l are rebellious. 8569
Mic 3:1 Then I said, "Listen, you l *of* Jacob, 8031
3:9 Hear this, you l *of* the house of Jacob, 8031
3:11 Her l judge for a bribe, 8031
5:5 even eight l *of* men. 5817
Zec 9:7 to our God and become l in Judah, 477
10:3 and I will punish the **l;** 6966
12:5 the l *of* Judah will say in their hearts, 477
12:6 the l *of* Judah like a firepot in a woodpile, 477
Lk 19:47 the teachers of the law and the l among *4755*
Jn 12:42 even among the l believed in him. *807*
Ac 3:17 you acted in ignorance, as did your **l.** *807*
14:5 together with their **l,** to mistreat them *807*
15:22 two men *who were* l among the brothers. *2451*
25:2 the chief priests and Jewish l appeared *4755*
25:5 of your l come with me and press charges *1543*
28:17 later he called together the l of *1639+4755*
Gal 2:2 *to* those who **seemed to be l,** *1506*
Heb 13:7 Remember your **l,** who spoke the word *2451*
13:17 Obey your l and submit to their authority. *2451*
13:24 Greet all your l and all God's people. *2451*

LEADERS' (1) [LEAD]

Jos 9:21 So the l' promise to them was kept. 5954

LEADERSHIP (4) [LEAD]

Nu 33:1 by divisions under the l *of* Moses 3338
Ps 109:8 may another take his **place of l.** 7213
Ac 1:20 and, " 'May another take his **place of l.'** *2175*
Ro 12:8 if it is l, let him govern diligently; *4613*

LEADING (38) [LEAD]

Dt 1:15 So I took the l *men of* your tribes, 8031
5:23 all the l **men** *of* your tribes 8031
Jdg 3:27 from the hills, with him l them. 4200+7156
4:4 *was* l Israel at that time. 9149
12:5 the fords of the Jordan **l to** Ephraim, 4200
20:31 the one **l to** Bethel and the other 6590
2Sa 10:16 of Hadadezer's army l them. 4200+7156
15:2 and stand by the side of the **road** *l to* the AIT
17:11 with you yourself l them into battle. 2143
2Ki 10:6 were with the l *men of* the city, 1524
19:2 Shebna the secretary and the l priests, 2418
24:15 his officials and the l **men** *of* the land. 380
1Ch 19:16 of Hadadezer's army l them. 4200+7156
2Ch 23:13 with musical instruments *were* l 3359
Ezr 7:28 and gathered l *men* from Israel to go up 8031
8:24 Then I set apart twelve of the l priests, 8569
8:29 before the l priests and the Levites and 8569
10:5 the l priests and Levites and all Israel 8569
Ps 42:4 l the procession to the house of God, 1844
68:27 the little tribe of Benjamin, l them, there 8097
Pr 7:27 **l down** to the chambers of death. 3718
8:3 beside the gates **l into** the city, at 4200+7023
Isa 37:2 and the l priests, all wearing sackcloth, 2418
Eze 17:13 He also carried away the l **men** *of* the land, 380
40:20 **l into** the outer court. 4200
Mt 26:55 Jesus said to the crowd, "Am I l **a rebellion,** *3334*
Mk 6:21 and military commanders and the l *men* *4755*
10:32 up to Jerusalem, with Jesus l the way, *4575*
14:48 "Am I l **a rebellion,"** said Jesus, *3334*
Lk 22:47 Judas, one of the Twelve, *was* l them. *4601*
22:52 "Am I l **a rebellion,** that you have come *3334*

Ac 12:10 and came to the iron gate l to the city. 5770
13:50 of high standing and the l men of the city. 4755
16:12 the l city of that district of Macedonia. 4755
25:23 the high ranking officers and the l men of 2029
Ro 6:19 in slavery to righteousness l to holiness. 1650
15:18 through me in l the Gentiles to obey God 1650
2Ti 2:25 God will grant them repentance l them to 1650

LEADS (40) [LEAD]

Dt 27:18 "Cursed is the man who l the blind astray 8706
Jos 2:7 in pursuit of the spies on the road that l to 6584
1Ch 11:6 "Whoever l the attack on 928+2021+8037
Job 12:17 He l counselors away stripped 2143
12:19 He l priests away stripped 2143
Ps 23:2 he l me beside quiet waters, 5633
37:8 do not fret—it l only to evil. 8317
68:6 he l forth the prisoners with singing; 3655
Pr 2:18 For her house l down to death 8755
10:17 whoever ignores correction l others astray. 9494
12:26 but the way of the wicked l them astray. 9494
14:12 but in the end it l to death. 2006
14:23 but mere talk l only to poverty. 4200
15:24 of life l upward for the wise to keep him NIH
16:25 but in the end it l to death. 2006
16:29 and l him down a path that is not good. 2143
19:23 The fear of the LORD l to life: 4200
20:7 The righteous man l a blameless life; 2143
21:5 to profit as surely as haste l to poverty. 4200
28:10 He who l the upright along 8706
Isa 30:28 of the peoples a bit that l them astray. 9494
40:11 he gently l those that have young. 5633
Hos 4:12 A spirit of prostitution l them astray; 9494
Mt 7:13 and broad is the road that l to destruction, 552
7:14 the gate and narrow the road that l to life, 552
12:20 till he l justice to victory. 1675
15:14 If a blind man l a blind man, 3842
Jn 10:3 by name and l them out. 1974
12:50 I know that his command l to eternal life. 1639
Ro 2:4 not realizing that God's kindness l you 72
6:16 which l to death, or to obedience, 1650
6:16 or to obedience, which l to righteousness? 1650
6:22 the benefit you reap l to holiness, 1650
14:19 therefore make every effort to do what l NIG
2Co 2:14 l us in triumphal procession 2581
7:10 Godly sorrow brings repentance that l to 1650
Eph 5:18 Do not get drunk on wine, which l to
debauchery. 1639
Tit 1:1 knowledge of the truth that l to godliness— 2848
1Jn 5:16 There is a sin that l to death. 4639
Rev 12:9 Satan, who l the whole world astray. 4414

LEAF (7) [LEAFY, LEAVES]

Ge 8:11 in its beak was a freshly plucked olive l! 6591
Lev 26:36 the sound of a windblown l will put them 6591
Job 13:25 Will you torment a windblown l? 6591
Ps 1:3 in season and whose l does not wither. 6591
Pr 11:28 but the righteous will thrive like a green l. 6591
Isa 64:6 we all shrivel up like a l, 6591
Mk 11:13 Seeing in the distance a fig tree in l, 2400+5877

LEAFY (4) [LEAF]

Lev 23:40 and palm fronds, l branches and poplars, 6290
Eze 6:13 every spreading tree and every l oak— 6290
17:6 produced branches and put out l boughs. 6997
20:28 and they saw any high hill or any l tree, 6290

LEAGUE (KJV) See TREATY

LEAH (29) [LEAH'S]

Ge 29:16 the name of the older was L, 4207
29:17 L had weak eyes, but Rachel was lovely 4207
29:23 he took his daughter L and gave her 4207
29:25 When morning came, there was L! 4207
29:28 He finished the week with L, 2296[S]
29:30 and he loved Rachel more than L. 4207
29:31 the LORD saw that L was not loved, 4207
29:32 L became pregnant and gave birth to a son. 4207
30:9 L saw that she had stopped having children, 4207
30:11 Then L said, "What good fortune!" 4207
30:13 Then L said, "How happy I am! 4207
30:14 which he brought to his mother L. 4207
30:14 Rachel said to L, "Please give me some of 4207
30:16 L went out to meet him. 4207
30:17 God listened to L, and she became pregnant 4207
30:18 Then L said, "God has rewarded me 4207
30:19 L conceived again and bore Jacob 4207
30:20 Then L said, "God has presented me with 4207
31:4 to Rachel and L to come out to the fields 4207
31:14 Then Rachel and L replied, 4207
33:1 so he divided the children among L, 4207
33:2 L and her children next, 4207
33:7 L and her children came and bowed down. 4207
34:1 Dinah, the daughter L had borne to Jacob, 4207
35:23 The sons of L: Reuben the firstborn 4207
46:15 the sons L bore to Jacob in Paddan Aram, 4207
46:18 whom Laban had given to his daughter L— 4207
49:31 and there I buried L. 4207
Ru 4:11 into your home like Rachel and L, 4207

LEAH'S (5) [LEAH]

Ge 30:10 L servant Zilpah bore Jacob a son. 4207
30:12 L servant Zilpah bore Jacob a second son. 4207
31:33 into Jacob's tent and into L tent and into 4207
31:33 After he came out of L tent, 4207
35:26 The sons of L maidservant Zilpah: 4207

LEAKS (1) [LEAK]

Ecc 10:18 if his hands are idle, the house l. 1940

LEAN (7) [LEANED, LEANING, LEANS]

Ge 41:19 scrawny and very ugly and l. 1414+8369
41:20 The l, ugly cows ate up the seven fat cows 8369
41:27 The seven l, ugly cows that came 8369
Jdg 16:26 so that I may l against them." 9128
Pr 3:5 in the LORD with all your heart and l not 9128
Eze 34:20 between the fat sheep and the l sheep. 8136
Mic 3:11 Yet they l upon the LORD and say, 9128

LEANED (5) [LEAN]

Ge 47:31 and Israel worshiped as he l on the top 2556
2Ki 7:17 the officer on whose arm he l in charge of 9128
Eze 29:7 when they l on you, you broke 9128
Jn 21:20 the one who had l back against Jesus at 404
Heb 11:21 worshiped as he l on the top of his staff. NIG

LEANFLESHED (KJV) See GAUNT, LEAN

LEANING (6) [LEAN]

2Sa 1:6 "and there was Saul, l on his spear, 9128
2Ki 5:18 of Rimmon to bow down and he is l 9128
7:2 the king was l said to the man of God, 9128
Ps 62:3 this l wall, this tottering fence? 5742
SS 8:5 Who is this coming up from the desert l 8345
Jn 13:25 L back against Jesus, he asked him, "Lord, 404

LEANNOTH (1)

Ps 88:T According to mahalath l. 4361

LEANS (4) [LEAN]

2Sa 3:29 or leprosy or who l on a crutch or who falls 2616
2Ki 18:21 a man's hand and wounds him if he l on it! 6164
Job 8:15 He l on his web, but it gives way; 9128
Isa 36:6 a man's hand and wounds him if he l on it! 6164

LEAP (6) [LEAPED, LEAPING, LEAPS]

Job 39:20 Do you make him l like a locust, 8321
Isa 13:21 and there the wild goats will l about. 8376
35:6 Then will the lame l like a deer, 1925
Joel 2:5 of chariots they l over the mountaintops, 8376
Mal 4:2 and l like calves released from the stall. 7055
Lk 6:23 "Rejoice in that day and l for joy, 5015

LEAPED (3) [LEAP]

Da 3:24 Then King Nebuchadnezzar l to his feet 10624
Lk 1:41 the baby l in her womb, 5015
1:44 the baby in my womb l for joy. 5015

LEAPING (2) [LEAP]

2Sa 6:16 when she saw King David l and dancing 7060
SS 2:8 Here he comes, l across the mountains, 1925

LEAPS (2) [LEAP]

Job 37:1 "At this my heart pounds and l 6001
Ps 28:7 My heart l for joy and I will give thanks 6600

LEARN (42) [LEARNED, LEARNING, LEARNS]

Ge 24:21 the man watched her closely to l whether 3359
Dt 4:10 so that they may l to revere me as long 4340
5:1 L them and be sure to follow them. 4340
14:23 so that you may l to revere the LORD your 4340
17:19 that he may l to revere the LORD his God 4340
18:9 do not l to imitate the detestable ways of 4340
31:12 and l to fear the LORD your God 4340
31:13 and l to fear the LORD your God as long 4340
Jdg 18:5 of God to l whether our journey will 3359
1Sa 22:3 with you until I l what God will do 3359
1Ki 1:20 to l from you who will sit on the throne 5583
2Ch 12:8 l the difference between serving me and 3359
Job 34:4 let us l together what is good. 3359
Ps 14:4 Will evildoers never l— 3359
53:4 Will the evildoers never l— 3359
119:7 an upright heart as I l your righteous laws. 4340
119:71 be afflicted so that I might l your decrees. 4340
119:73 give me understanding to l your commands. 4340
141:6 and the wicked will l that my words were 9048
Pr 19:25 and the simple will l prudence; 6891
22:25 or you may l his ways and get yourself 544
Isa 1:17 l to do right! Seek justice, encourage the 4340
26:9 the people of the world l righteousness. 4340
26:10 they do not l righteousness; 4340
Jer 2:33 the worst of women can l from your ways. 4340
10:2 not l the ways of the nations or be terrified 4340
12:16 if they l well the ways of my people 4340+4340
35:13 'Will you not l a lesson and obey my words 4374
Mt 9:13 But go and l what this means: 3443
11:29 Take my yoke upon you and l from me, 3443
24:32 "Now l this lesson from the fig tree: 3443
Mk 13:28 "Now l this lesson from the fig tree: 3443
Jn 14:31 but the world must l that I love the Father 1182
Ac 24:8 be able to l the truth about all these charges 2105
1Co 4:6 so that you may l from us the meaning of 3443
Gal 3:2 I would like to l just one thing from you: 3443
1Th 4:4 of you should l to control his own body in 3857
1Ti 2:11 A woman should l in quietness 3443
5:4 these should l first of all 3443
Tit 3:14 Our people must l to devote themselves 3443
Heb 5:11 to explain because you are slow to l. 198
Rev 14:3 No one could l the song except 3443

LEARNED (49) [LEARN]

Ge 28:6 Now Esau l that Isaac had blessed Jacob 8011
30:27 I have l by divination that the LORD has 5727
42:1 Jacob l that there was grain in Egypt, 8011
Lev 5:1 something he has seen or l about, he will 3359
Nu 20:29 whole community l that Aaron had died, 8011
1Sa 4:6 When they l that the ark of the LORD 3359
23:9 When David l that Saul was plotting 3359
23:15 he l that Saul had come out 8011
26:4 and l that Saul had definitely arrived. 3359
Ezr 7:11 a man l in matters concerning 6221
Ne 13:7 Here I l about the evil thing Eliashib 1067
13:10 I also l that the portions assigned to 3359
Est 3:6 having l who Mordecai's people were, 4200+5583
4:1 Mordecai l of all that had been done, 3359
Job 8:8 and find out what their fathers l, 2984
Ps 89:15 Blessed are those who have l 3359
119:152 Long ago I l from your statutes 3359
Pr 24:32 to what I observed and l a lesson 4374
30:3 I have not l wisdom, 4340
Ecc 1:17 I l that this, too, is a chasing after the wind. 3359
9:11 or wealth to the brilliant or favor to the l; 3359
Eze 19:3 He l to tear the prey and he devoured men. 4340
19:6 He l to tear the prey and he devoured men. 4340
Da 6:10 Now when Daniel l that the decree 10313
Mt 2:16 in accordance with the time he had l from 208
11:25 from the wise and l, 5305
Mk 15:45 When he l from the centurion that it was so, 1182
Lk 7:37 in that town l that Jesus was eating at 2105
9:11 the crowds l about it and followed him. 1182
10:21 hidden these things from the wise and l, 5305
23:7 When he l that Jesus was eating at 2105
Jn 4:3 When the Lord l of this, 1182
5:6 and l that he had been in this condition for 1182
15:15 for everything that I l from my Father 201
Ac 7:13 and Pharaoh l about Joseph's family. 1181+5745
9:24 but Saul l of their plan. 1182
9:30 When the brothers l of this, 2105
17:13 in Thessalonica l that Paul was preaching 1182
18:24 He was a l man, with a thorough knowledge 3360
23:27 for I had l that he is a Roman citizen. 3443
Ro 16:17 contrary to the teaching you have l. 3443
Php 4:9 Whatever you have l or received or heard 3443
4:11 for I have l to be content whatever 3443
4:12 I have l the secret of being content in any 3679
Col 1:7 You l it from Epaphras, 3443
2Ti 3:14 continue in what you have l 3443
3:14 you know those from whom you l it, 3443
Heb 5:8 he l obedience from what he suffered 3443
Rev 2:24 not l Satan's so-called deep secrets 1182

LEARNING (12) [LEARN]

Ezr 8:16 Joiarib and Elnathan, who were men of l, 1067
Job 34:2 listen to me, you men of l. 3359
Pr 1:5 the wise listen and add to their l, and let 4375
4:2 I give you sound l, 4375
9:9 a righteous man and he will add to his l. 4375
Isa 44:25 who overthrows the l of the wise 1981
Da 1:4 showing aptitude for every kind of l, 2683
1:17 of all kinds of literature and l. 2683
Jn 7:15 "How did this man get such l 1207+3857
Ac 23:34 L that he was from Cilicia, 4785
26:24 "Your great l is driving you insane." 1207
2Ti 3:7 always l but never able to acknowledge 3443

LEARNS (3) [LEARN]

Lev 5:3 when he l of it he will be guilty. 3359
5:4 of it, in any case when he l of it he will 3359
Jn 6:45 to the Father and l from him comes to me. 3443

LEASH (1)

Job 41:5 or put him on a l for your girls? 8003

LEASING (KJV) See FALSE GODS, LIES

LEAST (41) [LESS]

Jdg 6:15 and I am the l in my family." 7582
1Sa 9:21 and is not my clan the l of all the clans of 7582
20:9 "If I had the l inkling that 3359+3359
2Ki 18:24 How can you repulse one officer of the l 7783
23:2 all the people from the l to the greatest. 7785
25:26 all the people from the l to the greatest, 7785
1Ch 12:14 the l was a match for a hundred, 7783
2Ch 34:30 all the people from the l to the greatest. 7783
Est 1:5 all the people from the l to the greatest, 7783
1:20 from the l to the greatest." 7783
Job 14:7 "At l there is hope for a tree: 3954
35:15 not take the l notice of wickedness. 4394
Isa 36:9 then can you repulse one officer of the l 7783
60:22 The l of you will become a thousand, 7785
Jer 6:13 "From the l to the greatest, 7783
8:10 From the l to the greatest, 7785
23:32 not benefit these people in the l," 3603+3603
31:34 from the l of them to the greatest," 7783
42:1 from the l to the greatest approached 7785

Jer 42: 8 with him and all the people from the l to 7785
44:12 From the l to the greatest, 7785
50:12 She will be the l *of* the nations— 344
Jnh 3: 5 and all of them, from the greatest to the l, 7783
Mt 2: 6 by no means l among the rulers of Judah; *1788*
5:18 not the **l stroke of a pen,** *3037*
5:19 *of* the l of these commandments *1788*
5:19 the same will be called l in the kingdom *1788*
11:11 yet he who is l in the kingdom *3625*
25:40 for one *of* the l of these brothers of mine, *1788*
25:45 whatever you did not do for one *of* the l *1788*
Lk 7:28 yet the one who is l in the kingdom *3625*
9:48 For he who is l among you all— *3625*
14: 9 to take the **l important** place. *2274*
16:17 than for the **l stroke of a pen** *3037*
Jn 14:11 **or at l** believe on the evidence *1254+1623+3590*
Ac 5:15 so that at l Peter's shadow might fall *1569+2779*
1Co 15: 9 For I am the l of the apostles and do not *1788*
2Co 11: 5 **not** think I am **in the l** inferior to *3594*
12:11 for I am **not in the l** inferior to *4029*
Eph 3: 8 I am *less than* the l of all God's people, *1788*
Heb 8:11 from the l of them to the greatest. *3625*

LEATHER (17)

Lev 13:48 any l or anything made of leather— 6425
13:48 any leather or anything made of **l—** 6425
13:49 or l, or woven or knitted material, 6425
13:49 or any l article, is greenish or reddish, 6425
13:51 or the woven or knitted material, or the **l,** 6425
13:52 or any l article that has the contamination 6425
13:53 woven or knitted material, or the l article, 6425
13:56 or the **l,** or the woven or knitted material. 6425
13:57 or in the l article, it is spreading, 6425
13:58 or any l article that has been washed 6425
13:59 woven or knitted material, or any l article, 6425
15:17 or l that has semen on it must be washed 6425
Nu 31:20 as well as everything made of **l,** 6425
2Ki 1: 8 of hair and with a l belt around his waist." 6425
Eze 16:10 an embroidered dress and put l sandals 9391
Mt 3: 4 and he had a l belt around his waist. *1294*
Mk 1: 6 with a l belt around his waist, *1294*

LEATHERN (KJV) See LEATHER

LEAVE (207) [LEAVES, LEAVING]

Ge 2:24 a man *will* l his father and mother and 6440
12: 1 Abram, **"L** your country, your people 2143+4946
18:16 When the men got up to **l,** 4946+9004
28:15 *I will* not l you until I have done what 6440
31:13 Now l this land at once and go back 3655
33:15 *let me* l some of my men with you." 3657
42:15 *you will* not l this place unless 3655
42:33 **L** one of your brothers here with me, 5663
44:22 'The boy cannot l his father; 6440
45: 1 **"Have** everyone l my presence!" 3655
Ex 1:10 fight against us and l the country." 4946+6590
2:20 "Why *did you* l him? 6440
3:21 so that when *you* l you will 2143
8: 9 l *to you* **the honor** of setting the time 6995
8:11 The frogs *will* l you and your houses, 6073
8:29 Moses answered, "As soon as I l you, 3655
8:29 the flies *will* l Pharaoh and his officials 6073
10:23 or l his place for three days. 4946+7756
10:24 l your flocks and herds **behind."** 3657
11: 8 After that *I will* **l."** 3655
12:10 *Do* not l any of it till morning; 3855
12:31 **L** my people, you and the Israelites! 3655
12:33 the people to hurry and l the country. 8938
14:12 **L** us **alone;** let us serve the Egyptians 2532+4946
23: 5 do not l it there; be sure you help him 6440
23:11 and the wild animals may eat *what* they **l.** 3856
32:10 Now l me **alone** so that my anger 5663
33: 1 the LORD said to Moses, **"L** this place, 2143+4946
33:11 Joshua son of Nun *did* not l the tent. 4631
34: 7 not l **the guilty unpunished;** 5927+5927
Lev 2:13 *Do* not l the salt of the covenant 8697
7:15 *he must* l none of it till morning. 5663
8:33 not l the entrance to the Tent of Meeting 3655
10: 7 not l the entrance to the Tent of Meeting 3655
16:23 and *he is to* l them there. 5663
19:10 **L** them for the poor and the alien. 6440
21:12 nor l the sanctuary of his God 3655
22:30 l none of it till morning. 3855
23:22 **L** them for the poor and the alien. 6440
Nu 9:12 not l any of it till morning or break any 8636
10:31 But Moses said, "Please *do* not l us. 6440
11:20 saying, "Why *did we ever* l Egypt?" '" 3655
14:18 not l **the guilty unpunished;** 5927+5927
24:11 Now l **at once** and go home! 1368
32:15 he will again l all this people in the desert, 5663
Dt 15:16 *"I do* not *want to* l you," 3655
20:16 *do* not l **alive** anything that breathes. 2649
21:23 l his body on the tree **overnight.** 4328
24:19 **L** it for the alien, 2118
24:20 **L** what remains for the alien, 2118
24:21 **L** what remains for the alien, 2118
28:51 *They will* l you no grain, 8636
31: 6 *he will* never l you nor forsake you." 8332
31: 8 *he will* never l you nor forsake you. 8332
Jos 1: 5 *I will* never l you nor forsake you. 8332
Jdg 7: 3 may turn back and l Mount Gilead.' " 7629
16:17 head were shaved, my strength *would* l me, 6073
19: 5 up early and he prepared to **l,** but 2143
19: 9 got up to l, his father-in-law, 2143
Ru 1:16 "Don't urge me to l you or to turn back 6440
2:16 the bundles and l them for her to pick up, 6440
1Sa 10: 2 When you l me today, 2143+4946+6643
10: 9 As Saul turned to l Samuel, 2143+4946+6640
14:36 *let us* not l one of them **alive."** 8636
15: 6 l the Amalekites so that I do 3718+4946+9348
15:27 As Samuel turned to **l,** 2143
16:23 and the evil spirit *would* l him. 6073
17:28 And with whom *did you* l those few sheep 5759
25:22 if by morning *I* l **alive** one male 8636
27: 9 *he did* not l a man or woman **alive,** 2649
27:11 *He did* not l a man or woman **alive** 2649
29:10 and l in the morning as soon as it is light." 2143
2Sa 4: 4 but as she hurried to **l,** 5674
15:14 We must l immediately, 2143
16:11 this Benjamite! **L** him **alone;** 5663
1Ki 2:37 The day you l and cross the Kidron Valley 3655
2:42 'On the day you l to go anywhere else, 3655
8:57 *may he* never l us nor forsake us. 6440
15:29 not l Jeroboam anyone that breathed, 8636
17: 3 **"L** here, turn eastward and hide in 2143+4946
18:12 where the Spirit of the LORD may carry you
when I l you. 907+2143+4946
20:36 as you l me a lion will kill you." 907+2143+4946
2Ki 1: 4 *will* not l the bed you are lying on. 3718+4946
1: 6 *will* not l the bed you are lying on. 3718+4946
1:16 *will* never l the bed you are lying on. 3718+4946
2: 2 *I will* not l you." 6440
2: 4 *I will* not l you." 6440
2: 6 *I will* not l you." 6440
4:27 but the man of God said, **"L** her **alone!** 8332
4:30 *I will* not l you." 6440
23:18 **"L** it **alone,"** he said. 5663
2Ch 26:18 to burn incense. **L** the sanctuary, 3655
26:20 Indeed, he himself was eager to **l,** 3655
33: 8 **make** the feet of the Israelites l 6073
35:15 at each gate *did* not *need to* l their posts, 6073
Ezr 9:12 l it to your children **as an** everlasting
inheritance.' 3769
Ne 6: 3 the work stop while *I* l it and go down 8332
Job 21:14 Yet they say to God, **'L** us **alone!** 4946+6073
22:17 They said to God, **'L** us **alone!** 4946+6073
39: 4 *they* l and do not return. 3655
39:11 *Will you* l your heavy work to him? 6440
Ps 35:12 for good and l my soul forlorn. NIH
37:33 the LORD *will* not l them in their power 6440
49:10 and l their wealth to others. 6440
55:11 threats and lies never l its streets. 4631
119:121 *do* not l me to my oppressors. 5663
Pr 2:13 who l the straight paths to walk 6440
3: 3 *Let* love and faithfulness never l you; 6440
9: 6 **L** your simple ways and you will live; 6440
17:13 evil *will* never l his house. 4631
Ecc 2:18 because *I must* l them to the one who comes 5663
2:21 and then *he must* l all he owns to someone 5989
8: 3 Do not be in a hurry *to* l the king's presence.
2143+4946
10: 4 anger rises against you; *do* not l your post; 5663
Isa 6:13 and oak l stumps when they are cut down, 928
10: 3 Where *will you* l your riches? 6440
30:11 **L** this way, get off this path, 6073
48:20 **L** Babylon, flee from the Babylonians! 3655
52:12 *you will* not l in haste or go in flight; 3655
65:15 *You will* l your name to my chosen ones 5663
Jer 2:37 *You will* also l that place with your hands 3655
9: 2 so that *I might* l my people and go away 6440
9:19 *We must* l our land because our houses 6440
10:17 Gather up your belongings to l the land, 4946
25:38 Like a lion *he will* l his lair, 6440
37: 9 'The Babylonians *will* **surely** l us.'
2143+2143+4946+6584
37:12 Jeremiah *started to* l the city to go to 3655
44: 7 and so l yourselves without a remnant? 3855
49: 9 *would they* not l a few grapes? 8636
49:11 **L** your orphans; I will protect their lives. 6440
50: 8 l the land of the Babylonians, 3655
50:26 and l her no remnant. 2118
51: 9 *let us* l her and each go to his own land, 6440
51:50 l and do not linger! 2143
Eze 5:17 and *they will* l you **childless.** 8897
10:16 the wheels *did* not l their side. 4946+6015
12:12 on his shoulder at dusk and **l,** 3655
14:15 that country and *they* l it **childless** 8897
16:39 and l you naked and bare. 5663
23:29 *They will* l you naked and bare, 6440
29: 5 *I will* l you in the desert, 5759
36:20 and yet *they had to* l his land.' 3655
42:14 not to go into the outer court until *they* l 5663
44:19 in and *are to* l them in the sacred rooms, 5663
Da 4:23 and destroy it, but l the stump, 10697
4:26 The command to l the stump of the tree 10697
11: 8 l the king of the North **alone.** 4946+6641
Hos 4:17 Ephraim is joined to idols; l him **alone!** 5663
12:14 his Lord *will* l upon him the guilt 5759
Joel 2:14 He may turn and have pity and l behind 8636
2:16 *Let* the bridegroom l his room and 3655
Ob 1: 5 *would they* not l a few grapes? 8636
Mic 4:10 for now *you must* l the city to camp in 3655
Na 1: 3 not l **the guilty unpunished.** 5927+5927
2:13 *I will* l you **no** prey on the earth. 4162
Zep 3: 3 *who* l nothing for the morning. 1750
3:12 But *I will* l within you the meek 8636
Mt 5:24 l your gift there in front of the altar. *918*
8:34 they pleaded with him to l their region. *3553*
10:11 and stay at his house until *you* **l.** *2002*
10:14 shake the dust off your feet *when you* l *2002+2032*
15:14 **L** them; they are blind guides. *918*
18:12 *will he* not l the ninety-nine on the hills *918*
19: 5 'For this reason a man *will* l his father *2901*
27:49 The rest said, "Now l him **alone.** *918*
Mk 5:17 to plead with Jesus *to* l their region. *599*
6:10 stay there until *you* l that town. *2002*
6:11 shake the dust off your feet *when you* **l,** *1744*
10: 7 'For this reason a man *will* l his father *2901*
14: 6 **"L** her **alone,"** said Jesus. *918*
15:36 "Now l him **alone.** *918*
Lk 8:37 of the Gerasenes asked Jesus *to* l them, *599*
9: 4 stay there until you l that town. *2002*
9: 5 *when you* l their town, *2002*
13: 8 **'l** it **alone** for one more year, *918*
13:31 **"L** this place and go somewhere else. *2002*
15: 4 not l the ninety-nine in the open country *2901*
19:44 *They will* not l one stone on another, *918*
Jn 1:43 next day Jesus decided *to* l for Galilee. *2002*
6:67 "You do not want *to* l too, do you?" *5632*
7: 3 *"You ought to* l here and go to Judea, *3553*
8:11 "Go now and l **your life of sin."** *279+3600*
12: 7 **"L** her **alone,"** Jesus replied. *918*
13: 1 the time had come for *him to* l this world *3553*
14:18 *I will* not l you as orphans; *918*
14:27 Peace *I* l with you; my peace I give you. *918*
14:31 "Come now; *let us* **l.** *72+1949*
16:32 *You will* l me all alone. *918*
Ac 1: 4 *"Do* not l Jerusalem, *6004*
5:38 **L** these men **alone!** *923*
7: 3 **'L** your country and your people,' *2002*
16:10 we got ready at once *to* l for Macedonia, *2002*
16:36 Now *you can* **l.** *2002*
16:39 requesting them *to* l the city. *599*
18: 2 had ordered all the Jews *to* l Rome. *6004*
20: 7 because he intended to l the next day, *1996*
20:29 I know that after I **l,** savage wolves *922*
22:18 'L Jerusalem immediately, *2002*
24:25 "That's enough for now! *You may* **l.** *4513*
28:25 among themselves and *began to* l *668*
Ro 12:19 my friends, but l room for God's wrath, *1443*
1Co 5:10 that case you would have *to* l this world. *2002*
Eph 5:31 "For this reason a man *will* l his father *2901*
Heb 6: 1 Therefore let us l the elementary teachings *918*
13: 5 "Never *will I* l you; never will I forsake you. *479*
Rev 3:12 Never again *will he* l it. *2002+2032*
17:16 They will bring her to ruin and l her naked; *NIG*

LEAVED (KJV) See DOORS

LEAVEN (KJV) See YEAST

LEAVENED (1)

Am 4: 5 Burn l **bread** as a thank offering and brag 2809

LEAVES (36) [LEAF, LEAVE]

Ge 3: 7 so they sewed fig l together 6591
44:22 if *he* l him, his father will die.' 6440
Nu 27: 8 'If a man dies and l no son, 4200
Dt 24: 2 after *she* l his house she becomes the wife 3655
1Ki 6:34 each having two l that turned in sockets. 7521
Job 21:21 does he care about the family he l **behind** 339
41:32 Behind him *he* l a **glistening** wake; 239
Pr 13:22 A good man l **an inheritance** 5706
15:10 Stern discipline awaits *him who* l the path; 6440
28: 3 like a driving rain that l no crops. NIH
Isa 1:30 You will be like an oak with fading **l,** 6591
32: 6 the hungry he l **empty** and from 8197
33: 9 and Bashan and Carmel **drop** *their* **l.** 5850
34: 4 all the starry host will fall like withered l 6591
Jer 3: 1 "If a man divorces his wife and *she* l him
907+2143+4946
8:13 and their l will wither. 6591
17: 8 its l are always green. 6591
Eze 41:24 Each door had two **l—** 1946
41:24 two hinged l for each door. 1946
47:12 Their l will not wither, 6591
47:12 Their fruit will serve for food and their l 6591
Da 4:12 Its l were beautiful, its fruit abundant, 10564
4:14 strip off its l and scatter its fruit. 10564
4:21 with beautiful l and abundant fruit, 10564
Mt 21:19 up to it but found nothing on it except **l.** *5877*
24:32 as its twigs get tender and its l come out, *5877*
Mk 11:13 he found nothing but **l,** *5877*
12:19 that if a man's brother dies and l a wife *2901*
13:28 as its twigs get tender and its l come out, *5877*
13:34 *He* l his house and puts his servants *918*
Lk 9:39 *It* scarcely ever l him and is destroying him. *713*
20:28 if a man's brother dies and l a **wife** *1222+2400*
21:30 When *they* **sprout l,** you can see *4582*
1Co 7:15 But if the unbeliever **l,** let him do so. *6004*
2Co 7:10 that leads to salvation and l no regret, *NIG*
Rev 22: 2 And the l of the tree are for the healing of *5877*

LEAVING (44) [LEAVE]

Ge 45:24 and *as they were* l he said to them, 2143
Ex 13: 4 Today, in the month of Abib, you *are* **l.** 3655
13:20 After l Succoth they camped at Etham 4946+5825
Nu 21:35 l them no survivors. 8636
Dt 3: 3 We struck them down, l no survivors. 8636
Jos 5: 4 died in the desert on the way after l Egypt. 3655
8:22 l them neither survivors nor fugitives. 8636
2Sa 14: 7 l my husband neither name nor descendant 8492
15:24 all the people had finished l the city. 4946+6296
1Ki 15:17 from l or entering the territory of Asa king 3655
2Ki 10:11 and his priests, l him no survivor. 8636
2Ch 16: 1 from l or entering the territory of Asa king 3655

Ezr 9: 8 in l us a remnant and giving us a firm place 8636
9:14 l us no remnant or survivor? NIH
Job 22: 6 of their clothing, l them naked. NIH
41:30 l a trail in the mud like a threshing sledge. 8331
Isa 17: 6 l two or three olives on the topmost NIH
Eze 39:28 to their own land, not l any behind. 3855
Da 2:35 The wind swept them away without l 10708
Joel 1: 7 l their branches white. 4235
Zep 2:13 l Nineveh utterly desolate and dry as 8492
Mt 4:13 L Nazareth, he went and lived 2901
11: 7 As John's disciples were l, 4513
15:21 L that place, Jesus withdrew to the region 2002
20:29 As Jesus and his disciples were l Jericho, 1744
Mk 4:36 L the crowd behind, they took him along, 918
6:33 many who saw them l recognized them 5632
6:46 After l them, he went up on 698
10:46 were l the city, a blind man, 1744
11:12 The next day as they were l Bethany, 2002
12:20 and died without l any children. 918
12:21 but he also died, l no child. 2901
13: 1 As he was l the temple, 1744
14:52 he fled naked, l his garment behind. 2901
Lk 4:42 they tried to keep him from l them. 608+4513
9:33 As the men were l Jesus, Peter said to him, 1431
10:30 beat him and went away, l him half dead. 918
11:42 the latter without l the former undone. 4205
20:31 the seven died, l no children. 2901
Jn 4:28 Then, l her water jar, the woman went back 918
16:28 now I am l the world and going back to 918
Ac 13:42 and Barnabas were l the synagogue, 1996
21: 8 L the next day, we reached Caesarea 2002
1Pe 2:21 l you an example, that you should follow 5701

LEB KAMAI (1)

Jer 51: 1 and the people of L. 4214

LEBANA (1)

Ne 7:48 L, Hagaba, Shalmai, 4245

LEBANAH (1)

Ezr 2:45 L, Hagabah, Akkub, 4245

LEBANON (70)

Dt 1: 7 to the land of the Canaanites and to L, 4248
3:25 that fine hill country and L." 4248
11:24 extend from the desert to L, 4248
Jos 1: 4 the desert to L, and from the great river, 4248
9: 1 the entire coast of the Great Sea as far as L 4248
11:17 in the Valley of L below Mount Hermon. 4248
12: 7 in the Valley of L to Mount Halak, 4248
13: 5 and all L to the east, 4248
13: 6 of the mountain regions from L 4248
Jdg 3: 3 the L mountains from Mount Baal Hermon 4248
9:15 and consume the cedars of L!' 4248
1Ki 4:33 the cedar of L to the hyssop that grows out 4248
5: 6 give orders that cedars of L be cut for me. 4248
5: 9 My men will haul them down from L to 4248
5:14 to L in shifts of ten thousand a month, 4248
5:14 so that they spent one month in L 4248
7: 2 of the Forest of L a hundred cubits long, 4248
9:19 in Jerusalem, in L and throughout all 4248
10:17 in the Palace of the Forest of L. 4248
10:21 Palace of the Forest of L were pure gold. 4248
2Ki 14: 9 in L sent a message to a cedar in Lebanon, 4248
14: 9 in Lebanon sent a message to a cedar in L, 4248
14: 9 a wild beast in L came along and trampled 4248
19:23 the utmost heights of L. 4248
2Ch 2: 8 pine and algum logs from L, 4248
2:16 from L that you need and will float them 4248
8: 6 in Jerusalem, in L and throughout all 4248
9:16 in the Palace of the Forest of L. 4248
9:20 Palace of the Forest of L were pure gold. 4248
25:18 in L sent a message to a cedar in Lebanon, 4248
25:18 in Lebanon sent a message to a cedar in L, 4248
25:18 a wild beast in L came along and trampled 4248
Ezr 3: 7 by sea from L to Joppa, 4248
Ps 29: 5 in pieces the cedars of L. 4248
29: 6 He makes L skip like a calf, 4248
72:16 Let its fruit flourish like L; 4248
92:12 they will grow like a cedar of L; 4248
104:16 the cedars of L that he planted. 4248
SS 3: 9 he made it of wood from L. 4248
4: 8 Come with me from L, my bride, 4248
4: 8 my bride, come with me from L. 4248
4:11 of your garments is like that of L. 4248
4:15 of flowing water streaming down from L. 4248
5:15 His appearance is like L, 4248
7: 4 the tower of L looking toward Damascus. 4248
Isa 2:13 for all the cedars of L, 4248
10:34 L will fall before the Mighty One. 4248
14: 8 and the cedars of L exult over you and say, 4248
29:17 will not L be turned into a fertile field and 4248
33: 9 L is ashamed and withers; 4248
35: 2 The glory of L will be given to it, 4248
37:24 the utmost heights of L. 4248
40:16 L is not sufficient for altar fires, 4248
60:13 "The glory of L will come to you, the pine, 4248
Jer 18:14 of L ever vanish from its rocky slopes? 4248
22: 6 like the summit of L, 4248
22:20 "Go up to L and cry out, 4248
22:23 You who live in 'L,' 4248
Eze 17: 3 of varied colors came to L. 4248
27: 5 they took a cedar from L to make a mast 4248
31: 3 Consider Assyria, once a cedar in L, 4248
31:15 Because of it I clothed L with gloom, 4248
31:16 the choicest and best of L, 4248
Hos 14: 5 a cedar of L he will send down his roots; 4248
14: 6 his fragrance like a cedar of L. 4248
14: 7 and his fame will be like the wine from L. 4248
Na 1: 4 and the blossoms of L fade. 4248
Hab 2:17 to L will overwhelm you, 4248
Zec 10:10 I will bring them to Gilead and L, 4248
11: 1 Open your doors, O L, 4248

LEBAOTH (1) [BETH LEBAOTH]

Jos 15:32 L, Shilhim, Ain and Rimmon— 4219

LEBBAEUS (KJV) See THADDAEUS

LEBO HAMATH (12)

Nu 13:21 of Zin as far as Rehob, toward L. 4217
34: 8 and from Mount Hor to L. 4217
Jos 13: 5 from Baal Gad below Mount Hermon to L. 4217
Jdg 3: 3 from Mount Baal Hermon to L. 4217
1Ki 8:65 a vast assembly, people from L to 4217
2Ki 14:25 the boundaries of Israel from L to 4217
1Ch 13: 5 the Shihor River in Egypt to L, 4217
2Ch 7: 8 a vast assembly, people from L to 4217
Eze 47:15 the Hethlon road past L to Zedad, 4217
47:20 to a point opposite L. 4217
48: 1 the Hethlon road to L; 4217
Am 6:14 oppress you all the way from L to 4217

LEBONAH (1)

Jdg 21:19 and to the south of L." 4228

LECAH (1)

1Ch 4:21 Er the father of L, 4336

LECTURE (2)

Jn 9:34 how dare you l us!" 1438
Ac 19: 9 and had discussions daily in the l hall 5391

LED (153) [LEAD]

Ge 19:16 of his two daughters and l them safely out 3655
24:27 the LORD has l me on the journey to 5697
24:48 who had l me on the right road to get 5697
Ex 3: 1 and he l the flock to the far side of 5627
13:18 So God l the people around by 6015
15:22 Then Moses l Israel from the Red Sea 5825
19:17 Then Moses l the people out of the camp 3655
32:21 that you l them into such great sin?" 995
Dt 8: 2 the LORD your God l you all the way in 2143
8:15 He l you through the vast 2143
13:13 l the people of their town astray, 5615
17:17 or his heart will be l astray. 6073
29: 5 the forty years that I l you through 2143
32:12 The LORD alone l him; 5697
Jos 24: 3 from the land beyond the River and l him 2143
Jdg 2: 1 and l you into the land that I swore to give 995
3:28 of the fords of the Jordan that l to Moab, 4200
9:39 So Gaal l out the citizens of Shechem 3655+4200+7156
10: 2 He l Israel twenty-three years; 9149
10: 3 Jair of Gilead, who l Israel twenty-two years 9149
12: 7 Jephthah l Israel six years. 9149
12: 8 After him, Ibzan of Bethlehem l Israel. 9149
12: 9 Ibzan l Israel seven years. 9149
12:11 Elon the Zebulunite l Israel ten years. 9149
12:13 Abdon son of Hillel, from Pirathon, l Israel. 9149
12:14 He l Israel eight years. 9149
15:13 with two new ropes and l him up from 6590
15:20 Samson l Israel for twenty years in 9149
16:31 He had l Israel twenty years. 9149
1Sa 4:18 He had l Israel forty years. 9149
18:13 David l the troops in their campaigns. 995+2256+3655+4200+7156
18:16 because he l them in their campaigns. 995+2256+3655+4200+7156
30:16 He l David down, and there they were, 3718
2Sa 5: 2 l Israel on their military campaigns. 995+2256+3655
1Ki 6: 8 a stairway l up to the middle level and AIT
11: 3 and his wives l him astray. 4213+5742
13:34 of Jeroboam that l to its downfall and 3948
2Ki 6:19 And he l them to Samaria. 2143
15:15 and the conspiracy he l, 8003+8004
21: 9 Manasseh l them astray. 9494
21:11 and has l Judah into sin with his idols. 2627
23:22 since the days of the judges who l Israel, 9149
1Ch 4:42 l by Pelatiah, Neariah, 928+8031
11: 2 l Israel on their military campaigns. 995+2256+3655
20: 1 Joab l out the armed forces. 5627
2Ch 20:27 Then, l by Jehoshaphat, 928+8031
21:11 and had l Judah astray. 5615
21:13 l Judah and the people of Jerusalem to prostitute themselves, 2388
25:11 then marshaled his strength and l his army 5627
26:16 his pride l to his downfall. 6330
33: 9 l Judah and the people of Jerusalem astray, 9494
Ezr 9: 2 and officials have l the way 2118+3338+8037
Ne 9:12 By day you l them with a pillar of cloud, 5697
11:17 who l in thanksgiving and prayer; 3344+9378
12:36 Ezra the scribe l the procession. 4200+7156
13:26 even he was l into sin by foreign women. 2627
Est 6:11 l him on horseback through the city streets, 8206
Job 31: 7 if my heart has been l by my eyes, 339+2143
Ps 26: 1 O LORD, for I have l a blameless life; 928+2143
45:14 In embroidered garments she is l to 3297
45:15 They are l in with joy and gladness; 3297
68:18 l captives in your train; 8647
77:19 Your path l through the sea, NIH
77:20 You l your people like a flock by the hand 5697
78:13 He divided the sea and l them through; 6296
78:26 and l forth the south wind by his power. 5627
78:52 he l them like sheep through the desert. 5627
78:72 with skillful hands he l them. 5697
106: 9 he l them through the depths as through 2143
107: 7 He l them by a straight way to a city 2005
136:16 to him who l his people through the desert, 2143
Pr 5:23 l astray by his own great folly. 8706
7:21 With persuasive words she l him astray; 5742
20: 1 whoever is l astray by them is not wise. 8706
24:11 Rescue those being l away to death; 4374
Isa 9:16 and those who are guided are l astray. 1182
19:13 of her peoples have l Egypt astray. 9494
48:21 They did not thirst when he l them through 2143
53: 7 he was l like a lamb to the slaughter, 3297
55:12 You will go out in joy and be l forth 3297
60:11 l in triumphal procession. 5627
63:13 who l them through the depths? 2143
Jer 2: 6 who brought us up out of Egypt and l us 2143
2:17 the LORD your God when he l you in 2143
11:19 like a gentle lamb l to the slaughter; 3297
22:12 the place where they have l him captive; 1655
23:13 l my people Israel astray. 9494
29:31 and has l you to believe a lie, 1053
41:16 with him l away all the survivors 4374
43: 5 the army officers l away all the remnant 4374
43: 6 They also l away all the men, NIH
50: 6 their shepherds have l them astray 9494
Eze 19: 4 They l him with hooks to the land 995
20:10 Therefore I l them out of Egypt 3655
29:18 from the campaign he l against Tyre. 6268
37: 2 He l me back and forth among them, 6296
40:22 Seven steps l up to it, 6590
40:24 Then he l me to the south side and I saw 2143
40:26 Seven steps l up to it, 6590
40:31 and eight steps l up to it. 6590
40:34 and eight steps l up to it. 6590
40:37 and eight steps l up to it. 6590
42: 1 Then the man l me northward into 3655
42:15 he l me out by the east gate and measured 3655
46:21 and l me around to its four corners, 6296
47: 2 the north gate and l me around the outside 6015
47: 3 a thousand cubits and then l me 6296
47: 4 and l me through water that was knee-deep. 6296
47: 4 and l me through water that was up to 6296
47: 6 Then he l me back to the bank of the river. 2143
Da 7:13 Ancient of Days and was l into his presence 10638
Hos 11: 4 I l them with cords of human kindness, 5432
Am 2: 4 they have been l astray by false gods, 9494
2:10 and I l you forty years in the desert 2143
Mt 4: 1 Then Jesus was l by the Spirit into 343
17: 1 l them up a high mountain by themselves. 429
27: 2 l him away and handed him over to Pilate. 552
27:31 Then they l him away to crucify him. 552
Mk 8:23 by the hand and l him outside the village. 1766
9: 2 with him and l them up a high mountain, 429
15: 1 l him away and handed him over to Pilate. 708
15:16 The soldiers l Jesus away into the palace 552
15:20 Then they l him out to crucify him. 1974
Lk 4: 1 from the Jordan and was l by the Spirit in 72
4: 5 The devil l him up to a high place 343
4: 9 The devil l him to Jerusalem 72
18:39 Those who l the way rebuked him 4575
22:54 they l him away and took him into 72
22:66 met together, and Jesus was l before them. 552
23: 1 the whole assembly rose and l him off 72
23:26 As they l him away, they seized Simon from 552
23:32 were also l out with him to be executed. 72
24:50 When he had l them out to the vicinity 1974
Jn 18:28 Then the Jews l Jesus from Caiaphas to 72
Ac 5:37 and l a band of people in revolt. 923
7:36 He l them out of Egypt and did wonders 1974
7:40 As for this fellow Moses who l us out 1974
8:32 "He was l like a sheep to the slaughter, 72
9: 8 l him by the hand into 1652
13:17 with mighty power he l them out of 1974
19:26 and l astray large numbers of people here 3496
21:38 l four thousand terrorists out 1974
22:11 l me by the hand into Damascus. 5932
Ro 8:14 because those who are l by the Spirit 72
1Co 12: 2 or other you were influenced and l astray 552
2Co 7: 9 because your sorrow l you to repentance. 1650
11: 3 your minds may somehow be l astray 5780
11:29 Who is l into sin, and I do not inwardly 4997
Gal 2:13 even Barnabas was l astray. 5270
5:18 But if you are l by the Spirit, 72
Eph 4: 8 l captives in his train and gave gifts 168+169
Heb 3:16 Were they not all those Moses l out 2002
Rev 18:23 the nations were l astray. 4414

LEDGE (10) [LEDGES]

Ex 27: 5 the l of the altar so that it is halfway up 4136
38: 4 to be under its l, halfway up the altar. 4136
Eze 43:14 up to the lower l it is two cubits high and 6478
43:14 and from the smaller l up to the larger 6478
43:14 up to the larger l it is four cubits high and 6478
43:17 The upper l also is square, 6478
43:20 on the four corners of the upper l and all 6478

Eze 45:19 the four corners of the upper l of the altar 6478
46:23 of each of the four courts was a l **of stone,** 3215
46:23 for fire built all around under the l. 3227

LEDGES (2) [LEDGE]

1Ki 6: 6 He made **offset** l around the outside of 4492
Eze 41: 6 There were l all around the wall of 995

LEE (3)

Ac 27: 4 **passed to the l of** Cyprus *5709*
27: 7 **sailed to the l of** Crete, *5709*
27:16 **passed to the l of** a small island called *5720*

LEECH (1)

Pr 30:15 "The l has two daughters. 'Give!' 'Give!' 6598

LEEKS (1)

Nu 11: 5 also the cucumbers, melons, l, 2946

LEES (KJV) See AGED, DREGS

LEFT (556) [LEFT-HANDED, LEFTOVER]

Ge 7:23 Only Noah *was* l, and those with him 8636
12: 4 So Abram l, as the LORD had told him; 2143
13: 9 If you go to the l, I'll go to the right; 8520
13: 9 if you go to the right, *I'll* **go to the l."** 8521
18:33 *he* l, and Abraham returned home. 2143
19:30 Lot and his two daughters l Zoar and 4946+6590
24:10 of his master's camels and l, 2143
24:61 So the servant took Rebekah and l. 2143
25: 5 Abraham l everything he owned to Isaac. 5989
25:34 He ate and drank, and then got up and l. 2143
26:31 and *they* l him in peace. 2143
27: 5 When Esau l *for* the open country 2143
27:30 Jacob *had* scarcely l his father's 3655+3655
28:10 Jacob l Beersheba and set out for Haran. 3655
31:55 Then he l and returned home. 2143
32: 8 the group that *is* l may escape." 8636
32:24 So Jacob *was* l alone, 3855
34:26 from Shechem's house and l. 3655
38: 1 Judah l his brothers and went down 907+4946
38:19 After *she* l, she took off her veil and put 2143
39: 6 So *he* l in Joseph's care everything he had; 6440
39:12 But *he* l his cloak in her hand and ran out 6440
39:13 When she saw that *he had* l his cloak 6440
39:15 *he* l his cloak beside me and ran out of 6440
39:18 *he* l his cloak beside me and ran out of 6440
42:26 loaded their grain on their donkeys and l. 2143
42:38 and he *is* the only one l. 8636
44:20 he *is* the only one of his mother's sons l, 3855
46: 5 Then Jacob l Beersheba, 4946+7756
47:18 *there is* nothing l for our lord except 8636
48:13 toward Israel's l hand and Manasseh 8520
48:13 on his l toward Israel's right hand, 8520
48:14 he put his l hand on Manasseh's head, 8520
50: 8 and their flocks and herds *were* l 6440
50:16 "Your father l *these* **instructions** 7422
Ex 5:20 When they l Pharaoh, 3655
8:12 After Moses and Aaron l Pharaoh, 3655
8:30 Then Moses l Pharaoh and prayed to 3655
8:31 The flies l Pharaoh and his officials 6073
9:21 of the LORD l their slaves and livestock 6440
9:33 Moses l Pharaoh and went out of the city. 3655
10: 5 They will devour what **little** you have l 3856+7129+8636
10: 6 Then Moses turned and l Pharaoh. 3655
10:12 everything l *by* the hail." 8636
10:15 They devoured all that *was* l after 3855
10:18 then l Pharaoh and prayed to the LORD. 3655
10:19 Not a locust *was* l anywhere in Egypt. 8636
10:26 not a hoof *is to be* **l behind.** 8636
11: 8 Then Moses, hot with anger, l Pharaoh. 3655
12:10 some *is* l till morning, you must burn it. 3855
12:41 all the LORD's divisions l Egypt. 3655
13:22 nor the pillar of fire by night l **its place** 4631
14:22 of water on their right and on their l. 8520
14:29 of water on their right and on their l. 8520
16:23 Save whatever *is* l and keep it 6369
19: 1 after the Israelites l Egypt— 3655
26:12 that *is* **l over** is to hang down at the rear 6369
26:13 what *is* l will hang over the sides of 6369
29:34 the ordination ram or any bread *is* **l over** 3855
36: 4 the work on the sanctuary l their work 995+4946
Lev 6: 2 about something entrusted to him or l 9582
7:16 but anything **l over** may be eaten on 3855
7:17 the sacrifice **l over** till the third day must 3855
10:12 "Take the grain offering **l over** from 3855
14:15 pour it in the palm of his own l hand, 8522
14:26 of the oil into the palm of his own l hand, 8522
19: 6 anything **l over** until the third day must 3855
25:15 to you on the basis of the number of **years** *l* AIT
26:36 " 'As for those of you *who are* l, 8636
26:39 Those of you *who are* l will waste away in 8636
Nu 12: 9 LORD burned against them, and *he* l them. 2143
12:16 the people l Hazeroth and encamped 4946+5825
14:19 from the time they l Egypt until now." NIH
20:17 the right or to the l until we have passed 8520
22: 7 The elders of Moab and Midian l, 2143
22:26 either to the right or to the l. 8520
25: 7 saw this, *he* l the assembly, 4946+7756+9348
26:65 not one of them *was* l except Caleb son 3855
27: 3 he died for his own sin and l no sons. 2118+4200
33: 5 The Israelites l Rameses and camped 5825

Nu 33: 6 *They* l Succoth and camped at Etham, 5825
33: 7 *They* l Etham, turned back to Pi Hahiroth, 5825
33: 8 *They* l Pi Hahiroth and passed through 5825
33: 9 *They* l Marah and went to Elim, 5825
33:10 *They* l Elim and camped by the Red Sea. 5825
33:11 *They* l the Red Sea and camped in 5825
33:12 *They* l the Desert of Sin and camped 5825
33:13 *They* l Dophkah and camped at Alush. 5825
33:14 *They* l Alush and camped at Rephidim, 5825
33:15 *They* l Rephidim and camped in 5825
33:16 *They* l the Desert of Sinai and camped 5825
33:17 *They* l Kibroth Hattaavah and camped 5825
33:18 *They* l Hazeroth and camped at Rithmah. 5825
33:19 *They* l Rithmah and camped 5825
33:20 *They* l Rimmon Perez and camped 5825
33:21 *They* l Libnah and camped at Rissah. 5825
33:22 *They* l Rissah and camped at Kehelathah. 5825
33:23 *They* l Kehelathah and camped 5825
33:24 *They* l Mount Shepher and camped 5825
33:25 *They* l Haradah and camped at Makheloth. 5825
33:26 *They* l Makheloth and camped at Tahath. 5825
33:27 *They* l Tahath and camped at Terah. 5825
33:28 *They* l Terah and camped at Mithcah. 5825
33:29 *They* l Mithcah and camped 5825
33:30 *They* l Hashmonah and camped 5825
33:31 *They* l Moseroth and camped 5825
33:32 *They* l Bene Jaakan and camped 5825
33:33 *They* l Hor Haggidgad and camped 5825
33:34 *They* l Jotbathah and camped at Abronah. 5825
33:35 *They* l Abronah and camped 5825
33:36 *They* l Ezion Geber and camped 5825
33:37 *They* l Kadesh and camped at Mount Hor, 5825
33:41 *They* l Mount Hor and camped 5825
33:42 *They* l Zalmonah and camped at Punon. 5825
33:43 *They* l Punon and camped at Oboth. 5825
33:44 *They* l Oboth and camped at Iye Abarim, 5825
33:45 *They* l Iyim and camped at Dibon Gad. 5825
33:46 *They* l Dibon Gad and camped 5825
33:47 *They* l Almon Diblathaim and camped in 5825
33:48 *They* l the mountains of Abarim 5825
Dt 1:24 *They* l and went up into the hill country, 7155
2:14 from the time *we* l Kadesh Barnea 2143+4946
2:27 not turn aside to the right or to the l. 8520
2:34 *We* l no survivors. 8636
3:11 Og king of Bashan *was* l of the remnant 8636
5:32 do not turn aside to the right or to the l. 8520
9: 7 From the day *you* l Egypt 3655
16: 3 because *you* l Egypt in haste— 3655
17:11 to the right or to the l. 8520
17:20 from the law to the right or to the l. 8520
28:14 to the right or to the l, following other gods 8520
28:55 It will be all he has l because of 8636
28:62 as the stars in the sky *will be* l but few 8636
32:36 and no one is l, slave or free. NIH
Jos 1: 7 do not turn from it to the right or to the l, 8520
2: 5 to close the city gate, the men l. 3655
2:22 When *they* l, they went into the hills 2143
5: 6 of military age *when* they l Egypt had died, 3655
8:17 *They* l the city open and went in pursuit 6440
8:29 the king of Ai on a tree and l him there NIH
9:12 at home on the day we l to come to you. 3655
10:20 few *who* were l reached their fortified cities. 8572
10:26 and they were *l* **hanging** on the trees AIT
10:28 *He* l no survivors. 8636
10:30 *He* l no survivors there. 8636
10:33 until no survivors *were* l. 8636
10:37 *They* l no survivors. 8636
10:39 *They* l no survivors. 8636
10:40 *He* l no survivors. 8636
11: 8 until no survivors *were* l. 8636
11:15 *he* l nothing **undone** of all that 6073
11:22 No Anakites *were* l in Israelite territory; 3855
18: 9 So the men l and went through the land. 2143
19:27 passing Cabul on the l. 8520
22: 9 the half-tribe of Manasseh l the Israelites at Shiloh 907+2143+4946
23: 6 turning aside to the right or to the l. 8520
Jdg 2:21 before them any of the nations Joshua l 6440
3: 1 These are the nations the LORD l 5663
3: 4 *They were* l to test the Israelites 2118
3:19 And all his attendants l him. 3655
3:21 Ehud reached with his l hand, 8520
4:11 Heber the Kenite *had* l the other Kenites, 7233
4:16 not a man *was* l. 8636
5:13 **men who were** l came down to the nobles; 8586
7: 3 So twenty-two thousand men l, 8740
7:20 the torches in their l hands and holding 8520
8:10 all that *were* l of the armies of 3855
16:19 And his strength l him. 6073
16:20 he did not know that the LORD *had* l him. 6073
16:29 his right hand on the one and his l hand on 8520
17: 8 l that town in search of some other 2143+4946
18: 7 So the five men l and came to Laish, 2143
18:21 they turned away and l. 2143
19: 2 *She* l him and went back 907+2143+4946
19:10 the man l and went toward Jebus (that is, 2143
21: 7 can we provide wives for those who *are* l, 3855
21:16 for the *men who are* l? 3855
21:24 Israelites l that place and went home 2143+4946
Ru 1: 3 and she *was* l with her two sons. 8636
1: 5 and Naomi *was* l without her two sons 8636
1: 7 With her two daughters-in-law *she* l 3655
2:11 how *you* l your father and mother 6440
2:14 She ate all she wanted and **had some l over.** 3855
2:18 and gave her what *she* **had l over** 3855
4:14 not l you **without** a kinsman-redeemer. 8697
1Sa 2:36 Then everyone l in your family line 3855

1Sa 6:12 they did not turn to the right or to the l. 8520
11:11 so that no two of them *were* l together. 8636
13:15 Then Samuel l Gilgal and went up 4946+7756
14: 3 No one was aware that Jonathan *had* l. 2143
14:17 "Muster the forces and see who *has* l us." 2143+4946+6640
15:34 Then Samuel l for Ramah, 2143
17:20 Early in the morning David l the flock 5759
17:22 David l his things with the keeper 5759
18:12 the LORD was with David but *had* l Saul. 6073
19:22 *he* himself l for Ramah and went to 2143
20:42 Then David l, and Jonathan went back to 2143
22: 1 David l Gath and escaped to the cave 2143+4946
22: 4 So *he* l them with the king of Moab, 5663
22: 5 David l and went to the forest of Hereth. 2143
23:13 l Keilah and kept moving from place 3655
24: 7 And Saul l the cave and went his way. 4946+7756
25:34 belonging to Nabal *would have* **been l alive** 3855
26:12 near Saul's head, and *they* l. 2143
27: 2 the six hundred men with him l and went 7756
28:25 That same night they got up and l. 2143
29: 3 and from the day he l Saul until now, 5877
30: 4 until they had no strength l to weep. NIH
30:21 and who *were* **l behind** at the Besor Ravine. 8740
2Sa 2:12 l Mahanaim and went to Gibeon. 3655
2:19 to the right nor to the l as he pursued him. 8520
2:21 "Turn aside to the right or to the l; 8520
3:26 Joab then l David and sent messengers 3655
5:13 After he l Hebron, 995+4946
9: 1 "Is there anyone still l of the house 3855
9: 3 "Is there no one still l of the house of Saul NIH
11: 8 So Uriah l the palace, 3655
13: 9 So everyone l him. 3655
13:30 not one of them *is* l." 3855
14: 7 the only burning coal I *have* l, 8636
14:19 the right or **to the l** from anything my lord 8521
15:16 but he l ten concubines to take care of 6440
16: 6 special guard were on David's right and l. 8520
16:21 with your father's concubines whom *he* l 5663
17:12 nor any of his men *will* **be l alive.** 3855
17:18 of them l quickly and went to the house of 2143
17:22 no one *was* l who had not crossed 6372
18: 9 *He* **was l hanging** in midair, 5989
19: 7 not a man *will be* l with you by nightfall. 4328
19:19 on the day my lord the king l Jerusalem. 3655
19:24 the king l until the day he returned safely. 2143
20: 3 the ten concubines *he had* l to take care of 5663
24: 4 so they l the presence of the king to enroll 3655
1Ki 7:47 l all these things **unweighed,** 5663
7:49 on the l, in front of the inner sanctuary); 8520
9:20 All the people l from the Amorites, 3855
10:13 Then *she* l and returned with her retinue 7155
14:17 Then Jeroboam's wife got up and l 2143
15:18 then took all the silver and gold that *was* l 3855
18:22 the only one *of* the LORD's prophets l, 3855
19: 3 *he* l his servant there, 5663
19:10 *I am* the only one l, 3855
19:14 *I am* the only one l, 3855
19:20 Elisha then l his oxen and ran after Elijah. 6440
19:21 So Elisha l him and went back. 339+4946
20: 9 They l and took the answer back 2143
22:19 around him on his right and on his l. 8520
2Ki 2: 8 to the right and *to the* l, 2178[S]
2:14 it divided to the right and *to the* l, 2178[S]
3:25 Only Kir Hareseth *was* l with its stones 8636
4: 5 *She* l him and afterward shut the 907+2143+4946
4: 6 But he replied, "There is not a jar l." 6388
4: 7 You and your sons can live on what *is* l." 3855
4:43 'They will eat and **have** *some* **l over.'** " 3855
4:44 and they ate and **had** *some* **l over,** 3855
5: 5 So Naaman l, taking with him ten talents 2143
5:24 He sent the men away and *they* l. 2143
7: 7 They l the camp as it was and ran NIH
7:10 and the tents l just as they were." NIH
7:12 so *they have* l the camp to hide in 3655
7:13 of the horses that *are* l in the city. 8636
7:13 be like that of all the Israelites l here— 8636
8: 6 from the day *she* l the country until now." 6440
8:14 Hazael l Elisha and returned to 907+2143+4946
10:14 *He* l no **survivor.** 8636
10:15 After *he* l there, 2143+4946
10:17 he killed all who *were* l there of Ahab's 8636
13: 7 Nothing *had been* l *of* the army 8636
17:18 Only the tribe of Judah *was* l, 8636
19: 8 that the king of Assyria *had* l Lachish, 5825
20: 4 Before Isaiah *had* l the middle court, 3655
20:17 Nothing *will* **be l,** says the LORD. 3855
22: 2 not turning aside to the right or to the l. 8520
23: 8 which is on the l of the city gate. 8520
24:14 Only the poorest people of the land *were* l. 8636
25:12 But the commander **l behind** some of 8636
25:22 over the people *he had* **l behind** in Judah. 8636
1Ch 6:44 the Merarites, at his l hand: 8520
16:37 David l Asaph and his associates before 6440
16:38 He also l Obed-Edom NIH
16:39 David l Zadok the priest NIH
16:43 Then all the people l, 2143
20: 1 Joab attacked Rabbah and l it **in ruins.** 2238
21: 4 so Joab l and went throughout Israel and 3655
21:21 *he* l the threshing floor and bowed down 3655
2Ch 8: 7 All the people l from the Hittites, 3855
9:12 Then she l and returned with her retinue 2200
18:18 on his right and on his l. 8520
20:20 Early in the morning *they* l for the Desert 3655
21:17 Not a son *was* l to him except Ahaziah, 8636
24:25 *they* l Joash severely wounded. 6440
25:10 with Judah and l for home in a great rage. 8740

2Ch 30: 6 that he may return to you who are l, 8636
31:10 and this great amount is l over." 3855
32:31 God l him to test him and to know 6440
34: 2 not turning aside to the right or to the l. 8520
Ezr 4:16 you will be l with nothing 10029+10378
9:15 We are l this day as a remnant. 8636
Ne 6: 1 the wall and not a gap was l in it— 3855
8: 4 and on his l were Pedaiah, Mishael, 8520
Est 7: 7 l his wine and went out into the palace 4946
7: 8 As soon as the word l the king's mouth, 3655
8:15 Mordecai l the king's presence wearing royal garments of blue 3655
Job 20:19 the poor and l them destitute; 6440
20:21 Nothing is l for him to devour; 8586
20:26 and devour what is l in his tent. 8586
21:34 Nothing is l of your answers 8636
Ps 34: T who drove him away, and he l. 2143
69:20 and has l me helpless; AIT
74: 9 no prophets are l, 6388
105:38 Egypt was glad when they l, 3655
Pr 2:17 who has l the partner of her youth 6440
3:16 in her l hand are riches and honor. 8520
4:27 Do not swerve to the right or the l; 8520
29:15 a child l to himself disgraces his mother. 8938
Ecc 5:14 that when he has a son there is nothing l NIH
10: 2 but the heart of the fool to the l. 8520
SS 2: 6 His l arm is under my head, 8520
5: 6 I opened for my lover, but my lover had l; 2811
8: 3 His l arm is under my head 8520
Isa 1: 8 The Daughter of Zion is l like a shelter in 3855
1: 9 LORD Almighty had l us some survivors, 3855
4: 3 Those who are l in Zion, 8636
5: 8 to field till no space is l and you live alone NIH
5: 9 the fine mansions l without occupants. NIH
6:11 until the houses are l deserted and NIH
9:20 on the l they will eat, but not be satisfied. 8520
11:11 that is l of his people from Assyria, 8636
11:16 for the remnant of his people that is l 8636
15: 6 vegetation is gone and nothing green is l. 2118
17: 2 The cities of Aroer will be deserted and l 2118
17: 9 which they l because of the Israelites, 6440
18: 6 They will all be l to the mountain birds 6440
21:11 "Watchman, what is l of the night? 4946
21:11 Watchman, what is l of the night?" 4946
23: 1 For Tyre is destroyed and l without house NIH
24: 6 and very few are l. 8636
24:12 The city is l in ruins, 8636
24:13 gleanings are l after the grape harvest. NIH
27: 9 or incense altars will be l standing. AIT
30:17 till you are l like a flagstaff on 3855
30:21 Whether you turn to the right or to the l, 8521
37: 8 that the king of Assyria had l Lachish, 5825
39: 6 Nothing will be l, says the LORD. 3855
44:19 a detestable thing from what is l? 3856
49:21 I was l all alone, but these— 8636
54: 3 to the right and to the l; 8520
Jer 4: 7 He has l his place to lay waste your land. 3655
7:25 From the time your forefathers l Egypt 3655
10:20 no one is l now to pitch my tent or to set 6388
11:23 Not even a remnant will be l to them, 2118
25:20 Gaza, Ekron, and the people l at Ashdod); 8642
27:19 the other furnishings that are l in this city, 3855
27:21 about the things that are l in the house of 3855
29:32 He will have no one l among this people, 3782
34: 7 These were the only fortified cities l 8636
37:10 and only wounded men were l 8636
38: 4 He is discouraging the soldiers who are l 8636
38:22 All the women l in the palace of the king 8636
39: 4 they l the city at night by way of 3655
39:10 the commander of the guard l behind in 8636
40: 6 the people who were l behind in the land. 8636
40:11 that the king of Babylon had l a remnant 5989
41:10 along with all the others who were l there, 8636
42: 2 now only a few are l. 8636
43: 6 the imperial guard had l with Gedaliah son 5663
48:11 like wine l on its dregs, 9200
52: 7 They l the city at night through the gate 3655
52:16 But Nebuzaradan l behind the rest of 8636
La 3:11 from the path and mangled me and l me 8492
Eze 1:10 and on the l the face of an ox; 8520
4: 4 on your l side and put the sin of the house 8522
7:11 none of the people will be l, NIH
9: 8 and I was l alone, 8636
19:14 No strong branch is l on it fit for 2118
21:16 O sword, slash to the right, then to the l, 8521
22:18 tin, iron and lead l inside a furnace. NIH
23:25 of you who are l will fall by the sword. 344
23:25 of you who are l will be consumed by fire. 344
24:21 and daughters you l behind will fall by 6440
31:12 of foreign nations cut it down and l it. 5759
31:12 from under its shade and l it. 5759
33:27 those who are l in the ruins will fall by NIH
39: 3 I will strike your bow from your l hand 8520
47:11 they will be l for salt. 5989
Da 2:44 nor will it be l to another people. 10697
7: 7 and trampled underfoot whatever was l. 10692
7:19 and trampled underfoot whatever was l. 10692
10: 8 I was l alone, gazing at this great vision; 8636
10: 8 I had no strength l, 8636
12: 7 lifted his right hand and his l hand 8520
Joel 1: 4 What the locust swarm has l 3856
1: 4 what the great locusts have l 3856
1: 4 young locusts have l other locusts have 3856
Am 5: 3 will have only a hundred l; 8636
5: 3 a hundred strong will have only ten l." 8636
6: 9 If ten men are l in one house, 3855
9: 1 those who are l I will kill with the sword. 344
Jnh 4:11 from their l, and many cattle 8520
Hab 2: 8 the peoples who are l will plunder you. 3856
Zep 1:12 who are like wine l on its dregs, NIH
2: 4 Gaza will be abandoned and Ashkelon l NIH
2: 5 "I will destroy you, and none will be l." 3782
3: 6 I have l their streets deserted, 2990
3: 6 no one will be l—no one at all. 3782
Hag 2: 3 'Who of you is l who saw this house 8636
2:19 Is there yet any seed l in the barn? NIH
Zec 2: 3 Then the angel who was speaking to me l, 3655
4: 3 the right of the bowl and the other on its l." 8520
4:11 on the right and the l of the lampstand?" 8520
7:14 The land was l so desolate behind them 9037
9: 7 Those who are l will belong to our God 8636
11: 9 Let those who are l eat one another's flesh." 8636
12: 6 and l all the surrounding peoples, 8520
13: 8 yet one-third will be l in it. 3855
Mal 1: 3 and l his inheritance to the desert jackals." NIH
4: 1 "Not a root or a branch will be l to them. 6440
Mt 2:14 and his mother during the night and l 432
4:11 Then the devil l him, 918
4:20 At once they l their nets and followed him. 918
4:22 and immediately they l the boat 918
6: 3 do not let your l hand know what your right hand is doing, 754
8:15 He touched her hand and the fever l her, 918
12:44 it says, 'I will return to the house I l.' 2002
13:36 he l the crowd and went into the house. 918
14:20 of broken pieces that were l over. 4355
15:29 Jesus l there and went along the Sea 1696+3553
15:37 of broken pieces that were l over. 4355
16: 4 Jesus then l them and went away. 2901
19: 1 he l Galilee and went into the region 3558
19:27 "We have l everything to follow you! 918
19:29 And everyone who has l houses 918
20:21 and the other at your l in your kingdom." 2381
20:23 but to sit at my right or l is not for me 2381
21:17 And he l them and went out of the city 2901
22:22 So they l him and went away. 918
22:25 he l his wife to his brother. 918
23:38 Look, your house is l to you desolate. 918
24: 1 Jesus l the temple and was walking away 2002
24: 2 not one stone here will be l on another; 918
24:40 one will be taken and the other l. 918
24:41 one will be taken and the other l. 918
25:33 on his right and the goats on his l. 2381
25:41 "Then he will say to those on his l, 2381
26:44 So he l them and went away once more 918
27: 5 the money into the temple and l. 432
27:38 one on his right and one on his l. 2381
Mk 1:18 At once they l their nets and followed him. 918
1:20 and they l their father Zebedee in the boat 918
1:29 As soon as they l the synagogue, 2002
1:31 The fever l her and she began to wait 918
1:35 l the house and went off to a solitary place, 2002
1:42 the leprosy l him and he was cured. 599
2: 2 that there was no room l, NIG
6: 1 Jesus l there and went to his hometown, 2002
7:17 After he had l the crowd and entered 608
7:24 Jesus l that place and went to 1696
7:29 the demon has l your daughter." 2002
7:31 Then Jesus l the vicinity of Tyre and went 2002
8: 8 of broken pieces that were l over. 4354
8:13 Then he l them, got back into the boat 918
9:30 They l that place and passed through 2002
10: 1 then l that place and went into the region 482
10:28 "We have l everything to follow you!" 918
10:29 "no one who has l home or brothers 918
10:37 and the other at your l in your glory." 754
10:40 but to sit at my right or l is not for me 2381
12: 6 "He had one l to send, a son, 2285
12:12 so they l him and went away. 918
12:22 In fact, none of the seven l any children. 918
13: 2 "Not one stone here will be l on another; 918
14:16 The disciples l, went into the city 2002
15:27 one on his right and one on his l. 2381
Lk 1:38 Then the angel l her. 599
2:15 When the angels had l them and gone 599
2:37 She never l the temple 918
4:13 he l him until an opportune time. 923
4:38 Jesus l the synagogue and went to 482+608
4:39 rebuked the fever, and it l her. 918
5: 2 l there by the fishermen, 609
5:11 l everything and followed him. 918
5:13 And immediately the leprosy l him. 599
5:28 l everything and followed him. 2901
7:24 After John's messengers l, 599
8:37 So he got into the boat and l. 5715
9:17 of broken pieces that were l over. 4355
10:40 that my sister has l me to do the work 2901
11:14 When the demon l, the man who had been 2002
11:24 it says, 'I will return to the house I l.' 2002+3854
11:53 When Jesus l there, 2002
13:35 Look, your house is l to you desolate. 918
17:29 But the day Lot l Sodom, 2002
17:34 one will be taken and the other l. 918
17:35 one will be taken and the other l." 918
18:28 "We have l all we had to follow you!" 918
18:29 "no one who has l home or wife 918
21: 6 when not one stone will be l on another; 918
22:13 They l and found things just as Jesus had 599
23:33 one on his right, the other on his l. 754
24:51 he l them and was taken up into heaven. 1460
Jn 4: 3 he l Judea and went back once more 918
4:43 After the two days he l for Galilee. 1696+2002
4:52 "The fever l him yesterday at 918
6:12 "Gather the pieces that are l over. 4355
Jn 6:13 the pieces of the five barley loaves l over 4355
7:10 after his brothers had l for the Feast, 326
8: 9 the older ones first, until only Jesus was l, 2901
8:29 he has not l me alone, 918
12:36 Jesus l and hid himself from them. 599
18: 1 Jesus l with his disciples and crossed 2002
19:31 the Jews did not want the bodies l on 3531
Ac 1:25 which Judas l to go where he belongs." 4124
5:41 The apostles l the Sanhedrin, 4513
7: 4 "So he l the land of the Chaldeans 2002
12:10 suddenly the angel l him. 923
12:17 he said, and then he l for another place. 4513
13:13 where John l them to return to Jerusalem. 713
14:17 Yet he has not l himself without testimony: 918
14:20 The next day he and Barnabas l for Derbe. 2002
15:40 but Paul chose Silas and l, 2002
16:18 At that moment the spirit l her. 2002
16:40 and encouraged them. Then they l. 2002
17:15 then l with instructions for Silas and 1996
17:33 At that, Paul l the Council. 2002
18: 1 this, Paul l Athens and went to Corinth. 6004
18: 7 Then Paul l the synagogue 3553
18:18 he l the brothers and sailed for Syria, 698
18:19 where Paul l Priscilla and Aquila. 2901
18:21 But as he l, he promised, 698
19: 9 So Paul l them. 923
19:12 were cured and the evil spirits l them. 1744
20:11 After talking until daylight, he l. 2002
21: 5 we l and continued on our way. 2002
24:27 a favor to the Jews, he l Paul in prison. 2901
25:14 a man here whom Felix l as a prisoner. 2901
26:31 They l the room, and while talking 432
27:40 they l them in the sea and at the same time 1572
Ro 3:25 he had l the sins committed beforehand unpunished— 4217
9:29 the Lord Almighty had l us descendants, 1593
11: 3 I am the only one l, 5699
2Co 2: 2 who is l to make me glad but you NIG
6: 7 in the right hand and in the l; 754
1Th 3: 1 we thought it best to be l by ourselves 2901
4:15 who are l till the coming of the Lord, 4335
4:17 and are l will be caught up together 4335
1Ti 5: 5 in need and l all alone puts her hope 3670
2Ti 4:13 the cloak that I l with Carpus at Troas, 657
4:20 and I l Trophimus sick in Miletus. 657
Tit 1: 5 The reason I l you in Crete was 657
1: 5 might straighten out what was l unfinished 3309
Heb 2: 8 God l nothing that is not subject to him. 918
10:26 no sacrifice for sins is l, 657
11:15 of the country they had l, 1674
11:27 By faith he l Egypt, not fearing the king's 2901
2Pe 2:15 They have l the straight way 2901
Rev 10: 2 on the sea and his l foot on the land, 2381

LEFT-HANDED (3) [HAND]

Jdg 3:15 Ehud, a l man, the son of Gera 360+3338+3545
20:16 Among all these soldiers there were seven hundred chosen men who were l, 360+3338+3545
1Ch 12: 2 or to sling stones right-handed or l; 8521

LEFTOVER (1) [LEFT]

Ru 2: 2 and pick up the l grain behind anyone 8672

LEG (3) [LEGS]

1Sa 9:24 the l with what was on it and set it in front 8797
Eze 24: 4 the choice pieces—the l and the shoulder. 3751
Am 3:12 from the lion's mouth only two l bones or 4157

LEGAL (4) [ILLEGAL, LEGALISTIC, LEGALIZING]

Nu 27:11 to be a l requirement for the Israelites, 5477
35:29 " 'These are to be l requirements for you 5477
Ac 19:39 it must be settled in a l assembly. 1937
22:25 "Is it l for you to flog a Roman citizen 2003

LEGALISTIC (1) [LEGAL]

Php 3: 6 as for l righteousness, faultless. 1877+3795

LEGALIZING (1) [LEGAL]

Ru 4: 7 the method of l transactions in Israel.) 9496

LEGALLY MADE OVER (Anglicized) See DEEDED

LEGION (3) [LEGIONS]

Mk 5: 9 "My name is L," he replied, 3305
5:15 the l of demons, sitting there, dressed and 3305
Lk 8:30 "What is your name?" "L," he replied, 3305

LEGIONS (1) [LEGION]

Mt 26:53 at my disposal more than twelve l 3305

LEGS (28) [LEG]

Ex 12: 9 head, l and inner parts. 4157
25:26 where the four l are. 8079
29:17 and wash the inner parts and the l, 4157
37:13 where the four l were. 8079
Lev 1: 9 He is to wash the inner parts and the l 4157
1:13 He is to wash the inner parts and the l 4157
4:11 as well as the head and l, 4157

Lev 8:21 the l with water and burned the whole ram 4157
9:14 the inner parts and the l and burned them 4157
11:21 those that have jointed l for hopping on 4157
11:23 that have four l you are to detest. 8079
Dt 28:35 The LORD will afflict your knees and l 8797
1Sa 17:6 on his l he wore bronze greaves, 8079
Ps 147:10 nor his delight in the l *of* a man; 8797
Pr 26:7 a lame man's l that hang limp is a proverb 8797
SS 5:15 His l are pillars of marble set on bases 8797
7:1 Your graceful l are like jewels, 3751
Isa 7:20 to shave your head and the hair of your l, 8079
47:2 Lift up your skirts, bare your l, 8797
Eze 1:7 Their l were straight; 8079
Da 2:33 its l of iron, its feet partly of iron 10741
5:6 and his l gave way. 10284+10626
10:6 and l like the gleam of burnished bronze, 5274
Hab 3:16 into my bones, and my l trembled. 9393
Jn 19:31 they asked Pilate to have the l broken and *5003*
19:32 came and broke the l of the first man *5003*
19:33 they did not break his l. *5003*
Rev 10:1 and his l were like fiery pillars. *4546*

LEHABITES (2)

Ge 10:13 Anamites, L, Naphtuhites, 4260
1Ch 1:11 Anamites, L, Naphtuhites, 4260

LEHEM See JASHUBI LEHEM

LEHI (4) [RAMATH LEHI]

Jdg 15:9 spreading out near L. 4306
15:14 As he approached L, the Philistines 4306
15:19 God opened up the hollow place in L, 4306
15:19 and it is still there in L. 4306

LEISURE (KJV) See CHANCE

LEMUEL (2)

Pr 31:1 The sayings of King L— 4345
31:4 "It is not for kings, O L— 4345

LEND (14) [LENDER, LENDING, LENDS, LENT, MONEYLENDER]

Ex 22:25 "If *you* l money *to* one of my people 4278
Lev 25:37 *You must* not l him money at interest 5989
Dt 15:6 and you *will* l *to* many nations 6292
15:8 and **freely** l him whatever he needs. 6292+6292
28:12 *You will* l *to* many nations 4278
28:44 He *will* l *to* you, but you will not lend 4278
28:44 but you *will* not l *to* him. 4278
Ps 37:26 They are always generous and l **freely**; 4278
83:8 *to* l strength to the descendants of Lot. 2118
Eze 18:8 not l at usury or take excessive interest. 5989
Lk 6:34 if *you* l to those from whom you expect *1247*
6:34 Even 'sinners' l to 'sinners,' *1247*
6:35 and l to them without expecting *1247*
11:5 'Friend, l me three loaves of bread, *3079*

LENDER (2) [LEND]

Pr 22:7 and the borrower is servant to the l. 4278
Isa 24:2 for borrower as for l, 4278

LENDING (1) [LEND]

Ne 5:10 and my men *are* also l the people money 5957

LENDS (4) [LEND]

Ps 15:5 *who* l his money without usury and does 5989
112:5 to him who is generous and l **freely**, 4278
Pr 19:17 He who is kind to the poor l *to* the LORD, 4278
Eze 18:13 *He* l at usury and takes excessive interest. 5989

LENGTH (27) [LONG]

Ge 13:17 walk through the l and breadth of the land, 802
Ex 12:40 the **l of time** the Israelite people lived 4632
26:12 As for the additional l of the tent curtains, 6245
Lev 19:35 when measuring l, weight or 4500
1Sa 28:20 Immediately Saul fell full l on the ground, 7757
2Sa 2:11 The l *of* time David was king in Hebron 5031
8:2 and measured them off with a **l of cord.** 2475
8:2 and the third l was allowed to live. 2475
2Ch 3:8 its l corresponding to the width of 802
Ps 21:4 l *of* days, for ever and ever. 802
90:10 The **l of our days** is seventy years— 3427+9102
Pr 10:27 The fear of the LORD **adds** l *to* life, 3578
Eze 40:5 The l of the measuring rod in NIH
40:11 and its l was thirteen cubits. 802
40:20 the l and width of the gate facing north, 802
41:4 he measured the l *of* the inner sanctuary; 802
41:8 It was the l *of* the rod, six long cubits. 4850
41:12 and its l was ninety cubits. 802
41:15 the l *of* the building facing the courtyard 802
42:10 along the l *of* the wall of the outer court, 8145
42:11 they had the same l and width, 802
48:8 and its l from east to west will equal one 802
48:13 Its total l will be 25,000 802
48:18 the sacred portion and running the l of it, 802
48:21 the l *of* the tribal portions will belong 4200+6645
Ac 12:10 When they had walked *the l of* **one street,** *AIT*
Rev 21:16 and found it to be 12,000 stadia in l, and *NIG*

LENGTHEN (2) [LONG]

Ecc 8:13 and their days *will* not l like a shadow. 799
Isa 54:2 l your cords, strengthen your stakes. 799

LENGTHS (2) [LONG]

2Sa 8:2 Every two l of them were put to death, 2475
Eze 13:18 and make veils of various l for their heads 7757

LENGTHWISE (1) [LONG]

Eze 45:7 running l from the western to 802

LENGTHY (2) [LONG]

Mk 12:40 and for a show make l prayers. *3431*
Lk 20:47 and for a show make l prayers. *3431*

LENT (1) [LEND]

Jer 15:10 *I have* neither l nor borrowed, 5957

LENTIL (1) [LENTILS]

Ge 25:34 gave Esau some bread and some l stew. 6378

LENTILS (3) [LENTIL]

2Sa 17:28 flour and roasted grain, beans and l, 6378
23:11 at a place where there was a field full of l, 6378
Eze 4:9 "Take wheat and barley, beans and l, 6378

LEOPARD (6) [LEOPARDS]

Isa 11:6 the l will lie down with the goat, 5807
Jer 5:6 a l will lie in wait near their towns to tear 5807
13:23 or the l its spots? 5807
Da 7:6 one that looked like a l. 10480
Hos 13:7 like a l I will lurk by the path. 5807
Rev 13:2 The beast I saw resembled a l, *4203*

LEOPARDS (2) [LEOPARD]

SS 4:8 and the mountain haunts of the l. 5807
Hab 1:8 Their horses are swifter than l, 5807

LEPER (2) [LEPROSY]

Mt 26:6 the home of a man known as Simon the L, *3320*
Mk 14:3 the home of a man known as Simon the L, *3320*

LEPROSY (26) [LEPER, LEPROUS]

Nu 12:10 toward her and saw that *she* **had** l; 7665
2Sa 3:29 or l or who leans on a crutch or who falls 7665
2Ki 5:1 He was a valiant soldier, but *he* **had** l. 7665
5:3 He would cure him of his l." 7669
5:6 to you so that you may cure him of his l." 7669
5:7 to me to be cured of his l? 7669
5:11 over the spot and cure me of my l. 7665
5:27 Naaman's l will cling to you and 7669
7:3 *with* l at the entrance of the city gate. 7665
7:8 The *men who* **had** l reached the edge of 7665
15:5 The LORD afflicted the king with l until 7665
2Ch 26:19 l broke out on his forehead. 7669
26:20 they saw that he **had** l on his forehead, 7665
26:21 King Uzziah **had** l until the day he died. 7665
26:23 for people said, "He **had** l." 7665
Mt 8:2 A **man with** l came and knelt before him *3320*
8:3 Immediately he was cured of his l. *3319*
10:8 cleanse **those who have** l, drive out demons *3320*
11:5 the lame walk, *those* **who have** l are cured, *3320*
Mk 1:40 A **man with** l came to him and begged him *3320*
1:42 the l left him and he was cured. *3319*
Lk 4:27 And there were many in Israel **with** l in *3320*
5:12 along who was covered *with* l. *3319*
5:13 And immediately the l left him. *3319*
7:22 the lame walk, *those who* **have** l are cured, *3320*
17:12 ten men who **had** l met him. *3320*

LEPROUS (5) [LEPROSY]

Ex 4:6 and when he took it out, it *was* l, 7665
Nu 12:10 there stood Miriam—l, 7665
Dt 24:8 of l diseases be very careful to do exactly 7669
2Ki 5:27 from Elisha's presence and *he was* l, 7665
2Ch 26:21 He lived in a separate house—l, 7665

LESHEM (2) [DAN]

Jos 19:47 so they went up and attacked L, took it, 4386
19:47 They settled in L and named it Dan 4386

LESS (23) [LEAST, LESSER]

Ge 18:28 **number** of the righteous **is** five **l than** 2893
Ex 30:15 the poor *are* not *to* **give** l when you make 5070
Nu 11:32 **No** one gathered **l than** ten homers. 5070
1Ki 8:27 **How much** l this temple I have built! 677+3954
1Ch 27:23 of the men twenty years old or l, 4752
2Ch 6:18 **How much** l this temple I have built! 677+3954
32:15 **How much** l will your god deliver you 677+3954+4202
Ezr 9:13 you *have* **punished** us l than our sins have deserved 3104+4200+4752
Job 15:16 **how much** l man, who is vile and 677+3954
25:6 **how much** l man, who is but a maggot—677+3954
35:14 **How much** l, then, will he listen 677+3954
Ecc 6:11 more the words, the l the **meaning,** 2039+8049
Isa 40:17 by him as worthless and l **than** nothing. 4946
41:24 But you are l **than** nothing 4946
Eze 15:5 **how much** l can it be made into 677+3954
Jn 3:30 He must become greater; I must *become* l. *1783*
11:18 Bethany was l than two miles from Jerusalem *NIG*
1Co 12:23 parts that we think are l **honorable** we treat *872*
2Co 12:15 If I love you more, will you love me l? *2482*
Eph 3:8 I am *l than* the **least** of all God's people, *AIT*
Php 2:28 be glad and I may have l **anxiety.** *267*
1Ti 6:2 not *to* **show** l **respect** for them *2969*
Heb 12:25 how much l will we, if we turn away *3437*

LESSER (3) [LESS]

Ge 1:16 to govern the day and the l light to govern 7785
Isa 22:24 all its l vessels, from the bowls to all the 7783
Heb 7:7 And without doubt the l *person* is blessed *1781*

LESSON (6)

Jdg 8:16 **taught** the men of Succoth **a l** 3359
1Sa 14:12 "Come up to us and we'll teach you a l." 1821
Pr 24:32 to what I observed and learned a l 4592
Jer 35:13 people of Jerusalem, 'Will you not learn a l 4592
Mt 24:32 "Now learn this l from the fig tree: *4130*
Mk 13:28 "Now learn this l from the fig tree: *4130*

LEST (10)

Ex 20:26 l your nakedness be exposed on it.' 889+4202
Dt 32:27 l the adversary misunderstand and say, 7153
2Sa 1:20 l the daughters of the Philistines be glad, 7153
1:20 l the daughters of the uncircumcised rejoice. 7153
Ps 2:12 l he be angry and you be destroyed 7153
Pr 5:9 l you give your best strength to others 7153
5:10 l strangers feast on your wealth 7153
31:5 l they drink and forget what 7153
Jer 10:24 in your anger, l you reduce me to nothing. 7153
1Co 1:17 human wisdom, l the cross of Christ *2671+3590*

LET (1045) [LET'S, LETS, LETTING]

Ge 1:3 And God said, "*L there* **be** light," AIT
1:6 "*L there* **be** an expanse between the waters AIT
1:9 "*L* the water under the sky **be gathered** AIT
1:9 and *l* dry ground **appear.**" AIT
1:11 God said, "*L* the land **produce** vegetation: AIT
1:14 "*L there* **be** lights in the expanse of the sky AIT
1:14 and *l them* **serve** as signs to mark seasons AIT
1:15 and *l them* **be** lights in the expanse of AIT
1:20 "*L* the water **teem** *with* living creatures, AIT
1:20 and *l* birds **fly** above the earth across AIT
1:22 and *l* the birds **increase** on the earth." AIT
1:24 "*L* the land **produce** living creatures AIT
1:26 God said, "*L us* **make** man in our image, AIT
1:26 and *l them* **rule over** the fish of the sea and AIT
11:4 "Come, *l us* **build** ourselves a city, AIT
11:7 *l us* **go down** and confuse their language AIT
12:12 they will kill me but *will* l you **live.** 2649
14:24 *L* them **have** their share." AIT
18:4 *L* a little water **be brought,** AIT
18:5 *L me* **get** you something to eat, AIT
18:30 "May the Lord not be angry, but *l me* **speak.** AIT
18:32 but *l me* **speak** just once more. AIT
19:8 *L me* **bring** them **out** AIT
19:20 *L me* **flee** to it—it is very small, isn't it? AIT
20:6 That is why *I did* not l you touch her. 5989
23:8 "If you are willing to *l me* **bury** my dead, AIT
24:14 'Please l **down** your jar that I may have 5742
24:14 l her be the one you have chosen NIH
24:43 to her, "Please l me **drink** a little water 9197
24:44 l her be the one the LORD has chosen NIH
24:51 *l her* **become** the wife of your master's son, AIT
24:55 "*L* the girl **remain** with us ten days or so; AIT
25:30 "Quick, l me **have** some of that red stew! 4358
26:28 *L us* **make** a treaty with you AIT
27:13 "My son, l the curse fall on me. NIH
30:32 *L me* **go** through all your flocks today AIT
30:34 "**L it be** as you have said." 4273
31:28 even l me kiss my grandchildren 5759
31:37 and *l them* **judge** between the two of us. AIT
31:44 and *l it* **serve** as a witness between us." AIT
32:26 man said, "**L me go,** for it is daybreak." 8938
32:26 "*I will* not l you go unless you bless me." 8938
33:12 "*L us* **be on** *our* **way;** AIT
33:14 *l* my lord **go on** ahead of his servant, AIT
33:15 *l me* **leave** some of my men with you." AIT
33:15 "*Just l me* **find** favor in the eyes AIT
34:11 "*L me* **find** favor in your eyes, AIT
34:21 "*L them* **live** in our land and trade in it; AIT
34:23 *l us* **give** *our* **consent** to them, AIT
35:3 Then come, *l us* **go up** *to* Bethel, AIT
38:16 "Come now, *l me* **sleep with** you." AIT
38:23 Then Judah said, "*L her* **keep** what she has, AIT
41:33 "And now *l* Pharaoh **look for** a discerning AIT
41:34 *L* Pharaoh **appoint** commissioners over AIT
42:19 *l* one of your brothers **stay** here in prison, AIT
43:14 *l* your other brother and Benjamin **come back** with you. AIT
44:10 then," he said, "**l it be** as you say. 2085+4027
44:18 *l* your servant **speak** a word to my lord. AIT
44:33 please *l* your servant **remain** here AIT
44:33 and *l* the boy **return** with his brothers. AIT
44:34 *Do* not *l me* **see** the misery that would come AIT
47:4 *l* your servants **settle** in Goshen." AIT
47:6 *L them* **live** in Goshen. AIT
49:6 *L* me not **enter** their council, AIT
49:6 *l* me not **join** their assembly, AIT
49:26 *L all these* **rest** on the head of Joseph, AIT
50:5 Now *l me* **go up** and bury my father; AIT

Ex 1:16 but if it is a girl, *l her* **live."** AIT
1:17 *they* l the boys **live.** 2649
1:18 Why *have you* l the boys **live?"** 2649
1:22 But l every girl **live."** 2649
3:18 *L us* **take** a three-day journey into AIT
3:19 the king of Egypt *will* not l you go unless 5989
3:20 After that, *he will* l you **go.** 8938
4:18 *"L me* **go** back to my own people in Egypt AIT
4:21 so that *he will* not l the people **go.** 8938
4:23 **"L** my son **go,** so he may worship me." 8938
4:23 But you refused to l him **go;** 8938
4:26 So the LORD l him **alone.** 8332
5:1 **'L** my people **go,** 8938
5:2 that I should obey him and l Israel **go?** 8938
5:2 the LORD and *I will* not l Israel **go."** 8938
5:3 Now *l us* **take** a three-day journey into AIT
5:7 *l* them go and gather their own straw. AIT
5:8 *'L us* **go** and sacrifice to our God.' AIT
5:17 *'L us* **go** and sacrifice to the LORD.' AIT
6:1 of my mighty hand *he will* l them **go;** 8938
6:11 *to* l the Israelites **go** out of his country." 8938
7:2 to tell Pharaoh *to* l the Israelites **go** out 8938
7:14 he refuses to l the people **go.** 8938
7:16 **L** my people **go,** 8938
8:1 **L** my people **go,** 8938
8:2 If you refuse to l them **go,** 8938
8:8 and *I will* l your people **go** 8938
8:20 **L** my people **go,** 8938
8:21 If you *do* not l my people **go,** 8938
8:28 "I *will* l you **go** to offer sacrifices to 8938
8:32 and *would* not l the people **go.** 8938
9:1 **"L** my people **go,** 8938
9:2 If you refuse to l them **go** and continue 8938
9:7 and *he would* not l the people **go.** 8938
9:13 **L** my people **go,** 8938
9:17 and *will* not l them **go.** 8938
9:28 *I will* l you **go;** 8938
9:35 and *he would* not l the Israelites **go,** 8938
10:3 **L** my people **go,** 8938
10:4 If you refuse to l them **go,** 8938
10:7 **L** the people **go,** 8938
10:10 if *I* l you **go,** 8938
10:20 and *he would* not l the Israelites **go.** 8938
10:27 and he was not willing to l them **go.** 8938
11:1 After that, *he will* l you **go** from here, 8938
11:10 not l the Israelites **go** out of his country. 8938
13:15 Pharaoh stubbornly refused to l us **go,** 8938
13:17 When Pharaoh l the people **go,** 8938
14:5 *We have* l the Israelites **go** 8938
14:12 *l us* **serve** the Egyptians'? AIT
21:8 *he must* l her **be redeemed.** 7009
21:26 *he must* l the servant **go** free 8938
21:27 *he must* l the servant **go** free 8938
22:30 *L them* **stay** with their mothers AIT
23:11 *l* the land **lie unplowed** AIT
23:13 *do* not *l them* **be heard** on your lips. AIT
23:33 *Do* not *l them* **live** in your land, AIT
32:25 Aaron *had l* them **get out of control** AIT
33:12 not l me **know** whom you will send 3359
34:9 he said, "then *l* the Lord **go** with us. AIT
34:25 not *l* any of the sacrifice from the Passover Feast **remain** AIT
Lev 10:6 *"Do* not *l* your hair *become* **unkempt,** AIT
13:45 *l* his hair **be** unkempt, AIT
21:10 *l* his hair *become* **unkempt** AIT
Nu 6:5 *l* the hair of his head **grow long.** AIT
11:15 and *do* not *l me* **face** my own ruin." AIT
12:12 *Do* not *l her* **be** like a stillborn infant AIT
14:3 to this land only to *l us* **fall** by AIT
16:38 *L them* **be** a sign to the Israelites." AIT
20:17 Please *l us* **pass** through your country. AIT
20:21 *to* l them go through their territory, 5989
21:22 *"L us* **pass** through your country. AIT
21:23 not l Israel pass through his territory. 5989
21:27 "Come to Heshbon and *l it* **be rebuilt;** AIT
21:27 *l* Sihon's city **be restored.** AIT
22:13 LORD has refused to l me go with you." 5989
22:16 *Do* not *l anything* **keep** *you* from coming AIT
23:10 *L* me **die** the death of the righteous, AIT
23:27 "Come, *l me* **take** you to another place. AIT
23:27 *to l you* **curse** them for me from there." AIT
24:14 *l me* **warn** you of what this people will do AIT
32:5 *"l* this land **be given** AIT
Dt 1:22 *"L us* **send** men ahead to spy out the land AIT
2:27 *"L us* **pass** through your country. AIT
2:28 Only *l us* **pass through** on foot— AIT
2:30 of Heshbon refused *to* l us **pass** through. 6296
3:25 *L me* **go over** and see the good land beyond AIT
4:9 or *l them* **slip** from your heart as long AIT
9:14 **L** me **alone,** so that I may destroy them 8332
13:2 *"L us* **follow** other gods" (gods you have AIT
13:2 not known) "and *l us* **worship** them," AIT
13:6 *"L us* **go** and worship other gods" (gods AIT
13:13 astray, saying, *"L us* **go** and worship other AIT
15:12 the seventh year *you must* l him **go** free. 8938
16:4 *L* no yeast **be found** AIT
16:4 not *l* any of the meat you sacrifice on the evening of the first day **remain** AIT
17:14 *"L us* **set** a king over us like all the nations AIT
18:10 *L* no *one* **be found** among you who AIT
18:16 *"L us* not **hear** the voice of the LORD AIT
20:5 *L him* **go** home, or he may die in battle AIT
20:6 *L him* **go** home, or he may die in battle AIT
20:7 *L him* **go** home, or he may die in battle AIT
20:8 *L him* **go** home so that his brothers will not AIT
21:14 l her **go** wherever she wishes. 8938
22:7 **be sure to** l the mother **go,** 8938+8938
Dt 23:16 *L him* **live** among you wherever he likes AIT
24:11 *l* the man to whom you are making the loan **bring** the pledge **out** AIT
32:2 *L* my teaching **fall** like rain AIT
32:38 *L them* **rise up** to help you! AIT
32:38 *L them* **give** you **shelter!** AIT
33:6 *"L* Reuben **live** and not die, AIT
33:12 *"L* the beloved of the LORD **rest** AIT
33:16 *L all these* **rest** on the head of Joseph, AIT
33:24 *l him* **be** favored by his brothers, AIT
33:24 and *l him* **bathe** his feet in oil. AIT
34:4 *I have* l you **see** it with your eyes, 8011
Jos 1:8 *Do* not *l* this Book of the Law **depart** AIT
2:15 So *she* l them **down** by a rope through 3718
2:18 the window through which *you* l us **down,** 3718
2:21 **"L** it be as you say." NIH
8:15 **l themselves be driven back** before them, 5595
9:15 of peace with them to l them **live,** 2649
9:20 *We will* l them **live,** 2649
9:21 They continued, *"L them* **live,** AIT
9:21 but *l them* **be** woodcutters AIT
10:19 the rear and don't l them reach their cities, 5989
22:22 And *l* Israel **know!** AIT
22:26 *'L us* **get ready** and build an altar— AIT
Jdg 6:32 saying, *"L* Baal **contend** with him," AIT
6:39 *L me* **make** just one more **request.** AIT
7:7 *L* all the other men **go,** AIT
9:15 if not, then *l* fire **come out** of the thornbush AIT
9:20 *l* fire **come out** from Abimelech AIT
9:20 and *l* fire **come out** from you, AIT
10:14 *L* them **save** you when you are in trouble!" AIT
11:19 *'L us* **pass** through your country AIT
11:27 *L* the LORD, the Judge, **decide** *the* **dispute** AIT
11:38 And *he* l her **go** for two months. 8938
12:5 *"L me* **cross over,"** AIT
13:8 *l* the man of God you sent to us **come** AIT
14:12 *"L me* **tell** you a riddle," AIT
15:1 But her father *would* not l him go in. 5989
15:5 and l the foxes **loose** in the standing grain 8938
16:28 *l me with* one blow **get revenge** AIT
16:30 *"L* me **die** with the Philistines!" AIT
19:20 **"L** me supply whatever you need. NIH
19:25 and at dawn *they* l her **go.** 8938
Ru 2:2 *"L me* **go** *to* the fields and pick up AIT
2:7 'Please *l me* **glean** and gather among AIT
3:3 but don't l him **know** *you* are there 3359
3:13 to redeem, good; *l him* **redeem.** AIT
3:14 "Don't *l it* **be known** that a woman came to AIT
1Sa 2:3 or *l* your mouth **speak** such arrogance, AIT
2:16 *"L* the fat **be burned up** AIT
3:18 *l him* **do** what is good in his eyes." AIT
3:19 l none of his words **fall** to the ground. 5877
4:3 *L us* **bring** the ark of the LORD's AIT
5:11 *l* it **go back** to its own place, AIT
8:9 and l them **know** what the king 5583
9:9 he would say, "Come, *l us* **go** to the seer," AIT
9:19 and in the morning *I will* l you **go** 8938
11:14 *l us* **go** *to* Gilgal and there reaffirm AIT
13:3 *"L* the Hebrews **hear!"** AIT
14:8 over toward the men and l them **see** *us.* 1655
14:36 *"L us* **go down** after the Philistines by night AIT
14:36 *l us* not **leave** one of them **alive."** AIT
14:36 the priest said, *"L us* **inquire** *of* God here." AIT
14:38 *l us* **find out** what sin has been committed AIT
15:16 *"L me* **tell** you what the LORD said AIT
16:16 *L* our lord **command** his servants here AIT
17:10 Give me a man and *l us* **fight** each other." AIT
17:32 *"L* no one **lose** heart on account AIT
18:2 not l him return to his father's house. 5989
18:17 *L* the Philistines **do that!"** AIT
19:4 *"L* not the king **do wrong** AIT
19:12 Michal l David **down** through a window, 3718
19:17 "He said to me, **'L** me **get away.** 8938
20:5 but l me **go** and hide in the field until 8938
20:12 send you word and l you **know?** 265+906+1655
20:13 if *I do* not l you **know** and 265+906+1655
20:29 He said, **'L** me **go,** 8938
20:29 *l* me **get away** to see my brothers.' 4880
22:3 *l* my father and mother **come** AIT
22:15 *L* not the king **accuse** your servant AIT
24:19 his enemy, *does he* l him **get away** unharmed? 928+2006+8938
25:24 "My lord, l the blame be on me alone. NIH
25:24 Please *l* your servant **speak** to you; AIT
25:27 *l* this gift, which your servant has brought to my master, **be given** AIT
25:28 *L* no wrongdoing **be found** AIT
26:8 Now *l me* **pin** him to the ground AIT
26:19 *l* my lord the king **listen** AIT
26:20 not *l* my blood **fall** to the ground far AIT
26:22 *"L* one of your young men **come over** AIT
27:5 *l* a place *be* **assigned** AIT
28:22 and *l me* **give** you some food AIT
2Sa 2:14 **"All right,** *l them* **do it,"** AIT
3:21 *"L me* **go** at once and assemble all Israel AIT
3:24 Why *did you* l him **go?** 8938
10:12 and *l us* **fight bravely** for our people and AIT
11:25 'Don't *l* this **upset** you; AIT
12:22 be gracious to me and *l* the child **live.'** AIT
13:5 *L her* **prepare** the food in my sight AIT
13:26 *l* my brother Amnon **come** AIT
14:9 l the blame rest on me and NIH
14:9 l the king and his throne be without guilt." NIH
14:11 "Then *l* the king **invoke** AIT
14:12 *"L* your servant **speak** a word to my lord AIT
14:18 *"L* my lord the king **speak,"** AIT
14:32 *l him* **put** me **to death."** AIT
2Sa 15:7 *"L me* **go** to Hebron and fulfill a vow AIT
15:25 he will bring me back and l me **see** it 8011
15:26 *l him* **do** to me whatever seems good AIT
16:9 *L me* **go over** and cut off his head." AIT
16:11 Leave him alone; *l* him **curse,** AIT
17:11 *L* all Israel, from Dan to Beersheba—as numerous as the sand on the seashore—**be gathered** AIT
18:19 *"L me* **run** and take the news to the king AIT
18:22 please *l* me **run** behind the Cushite." AIT
19:30 *"L him* **take** everything, AIT
19:37 *L* your servant **return,** AIT
19:37 *L him* **cross over** with my lord the king. AIT
20:11 l him follow Joab!" NIH
21:6 *l* seven of his male descendants **be given** AIT
21:10 not l the birds of the air touch them 5989
24:14 *L us* **fall** into the hands of the LORD, AIT
24:14 *do* not *l me* **fall** into the hands of men." AIT
24:17 *L* your hand **fall** upon me AIT
24:22 *"L* my lord the king **take** AIT
1Ki 1:2 *"L us* **look for** a young virgin to attend AIT
1:12 *l me* **advise** you how you can save your own AIT
1:51 *'L* King Solomon **swear** to me AIT
2:6 l his gray head **go down** 3718
2:7 the sons of Barzillai of Gilead and *l them* **be** AIT
2:21 *"L* Abishag the Shunammite **be given in marriage** AIT
8:26 *l* your word that you promised your servant David my father **come true.** AIT
11:21 Then Hadad said to Pharaoh, **"L** me **go,** 8938
11:22 Hadad replied, "but **do** l me **go!"** 8938+8938
15:19 **"L** there be a treaty between me and you," NIH
17:21 *l* this boy's life **return** AIT
18:23 *L them* **choose** one for themselves, AIT
18:23 *l them* **cut it into pieces** AIT
18:36 *l it* **be known** today that you are God AIT
18:40 Don't l anyone **get away!"** 4880
19:20 *"L me* **kiss** my father and mother **good-by,"** AIT
20:31 *L us* **go** to the king of Israel AIT
20:32 'Please *l* me **live.'** " AIT
20:34 he made a treaty with him, and l him **go.** 8938
21:2 **"L** me **have** your vineyard to use for 5989
22:13 *L* your word **agree** with theirs, AIT
22:17 *L* each one **go** home in peace.' " AIT
22:49 *"L* my men **sail** with your men," AIT
2Ki 2:9 *L me* **inherit** a double portion of your spirit, AIT
2:16 *L them* **go** and look for your master. AIT
5:17 *l me,* your servant, **be given** as much AIT
6:2 *L us* **go** to the Jordan, AIT
6:2 *l us* **build** a place there for us to live." AIT
7:13 *l us* **send** them to find out what happened." AIT
9:15 don't *l* anyone **slip out** of the city to go AIT
10:25 *l* no one **escape."** AIT
12:5 *L* every priest **receive** the money AIT
12:5 *l it be used to* **repair** whatever damage AIT
18:29 *Do* not l Hezekiah **deceive** you. 5958
18:30 *Do* not l Hezekiah **persuade** you **to trust** 1053
19:10 *Do* not l the god you depend on **deceive** 5958
23:18 "Don't *l* anyone **disturb** his bones." AIT
1Ch 4:10 *L* your hand **be** with me, AIT
13:2 *l us* **send word** far and wide to the rest AIT
13:3 *L us* **bring** the ark of our God **back** AIT
16:10 *l* the hearts of those who seek the LORD **rejoice.** AIT
16:31 *L* the heavens **rejoice,** AIT
16:31 *l* the earth *be* **glad;** AIT
16:31 *l them* **say** among the nations, AIT
16:32 *L* the sea **resound,** and all that is in it; AIT
16:32 *l* the fields *be* **jubilant,** AIT
17:23 *l* the promise you have made concerning your servant and his house **be established** AIT
19:13 and *l us* **fight bravely** for our people and AIT
21:13 *L me* **fall** into the hands of the LORD, AIT
21:13 *do* not *l me* **fall** into the hands of men." AIT
21:17 *l* your hand **fall** upon me and my family, AIT
21:17 but do not l this plague remain on your people." NIH
21:22 *"L me* **have** the site of your threshing floor AIT
21:23 *L* my lord the king **do** whatever pleases AIT
2Ch 1:9 *l* your promise to my father David **be confirmed,** AIT
2:15 "Now *l* my lord **send** his servants the wheat AIT
6:17 *l* your word that you promised your servant David **come true.** AIT
14:7 *"L us* **build up** these towns," AIT
14:11 *do* not *l* man **prevail** against you." AIT
16:3 **"L** there be a treaty between me and you," NIH
18:12 *L* your word **agree** with theirs, AIT
18:16 *L* each one **go** home in peace.' " AIT
19:7 *l* the fear of the LORD **be** upon you. AIT
32:11 to l you die of hunger and thirst. 5989
32:15 Now *do* not *l* Hezekiah **deceive** you AIT
36:23 his God be with him, and *l him* **go up.'** " AIT
Ezr 1:3 may his God be with him, and *l him* **go up** AIT
4:2 *"L us* help you **build** AIT
4:22 Why *l* this threat **grow,** AIT
5:17 *l* **a search be made** in the royal archives AIT
5:17 Then *l* the king **send** us his decision AIT
6:3 *L* the temple **be rebuilt** AIT
6:3 *l* its foundations **be laid.** AIT
6:7 *L* the governor of the Jews and the Jewish elders **rebuild** AIT
6:12 *L it* **be carried out** with diligence. AIT
7:23 *l it* **be done** with diligence for the temple AIT
10:3 Now *l us* **make** a covenant before our God AIT
10:3 *L it* **be done** according to the Law. AIT
10:14 *L* our officials **act** for the whole assembly. AIT

Ezr 10:14 *l* everyone in our towns who has married a foreign woman **come** at a set time, AIT
Ne 1: 6 *l* your ear **be** attentive and your eyes open AIT
1:11 *l* your ear **be** attentive to the prayer AIT
2: 5 *l him* **send** me to the city in Judah AIT
2:17 Come, *l us* **rebuild** the wall of Jerusalem, AIT
2:18 They replied, "*L us* **start** rebuilding." AIT
5:10 *l* the exacting of usury **stop!** AIT
6: 2 *l us* **meet** together in one of the villages on AIT
6: 7 so come, *l us* **confer** together." AIT
6:10 He said, "*L us* **meet** in the house of God, AIT
6:10 and *l us* **close** the temple doors, AIT
9:32 *do* not *l* all this hardship *seem* **trifling** AIT
Est 1:19 *l* him **issue** a royal decree and let it AIT
1:19 and *l it* **be written** in the laws of Persia AIT
1:19 Also *l* the king **give** her royal position AIT
2: 2 "*L a* **search** *be* **made for** beautiful young AIT
2: 3 *L* the king **appoint** commissioners AIT
2: 3 **L** them be placed under the care of Hegai, NIH
2: 3 *l* beauty treatments *be* **given** AIT
2: 4 *l* the girl who pleases the king *be* **queen** AIT
3: 9 *l a* **decree be issued** to destroy them, AIT
5: 4 "*l* the king, together with Haman, **come** AIT
5: 8 *l* the king and Haman **come** AIT
6: 9 *l* the robe and horse *be* **entrusted** AIT
6: 9 *L them* **robe** the man the king delights AIT
8: 5 *l an* **order be written** overruling AIT
9:13 *l* Haman's ten sons *be* **hanged** AIT
Job 6: 9 *to* **l loose** his hand and cut me off! 6000
7:16 **L** me **alone;** my days have no meaning. 2532
7:19 or **l** me **alone** even for an instant? 8332
9:18 *He would* not **l** me regain my breath 5989
10:14 and *would* not **l** my offense **go unpunished.** 5927
12: 8 *l* the fish of the sea **inform** you. AIT
13:13 "Keep silent and *l me* **speak;** AIT
13:13 then *l* **come** to me what may. AIT
13:17 **l** your ears take in what I say. NIH
13:22 or *l me* **speak,** and you reply. AIT
14: 6 So look away from him and **l** him **alone,** 2532
15:17 *l me* **tell** you what I have seen, AIT
15:31 *L him* not **deceive himself** AIT
17: 4 therefore *you will* not **l** them **triumph.** 8123
20:13 *to l* it **go** and keeps it in his mouth, AIT
21: 2 *l* this **be** the consolation you give me. AIT
21:19 *L him* **repay** the man himself, AIT
21:20 *L* his own eyes **see** his destruction; AIT
21:20 *l him* **drink** of the wrath of the Almighty. AIT
24:23 *He may* **l** them rest in a feeling of security, 5989
27: 6 and never **l go** *of* it; 8332
31: 6 *l* God **weigh** me in honest scales AIT
31:16 *l* the eyes of the widow **grow weary,** AIT
31:22 then *l* my arm **fall** from the shoulder, AIT
31:22 *l* it **be broken off** at the joint. AIT
31:35 *l* the Almighty **answer** AIT
31:35 *l* my accuser **put** *his* indictment **in writing.** AIT
31:40 then *l* briers **come up** instead of wheat AIT
31:?? *l* God **refute** him, not man.' AIT
34: 4 *L us* **discern** for ourselves what is right; AIT
34: 4 *l* us **learn** together what is good. AIT
36:18 *l* a large bribe **turn** you **aside.** AIT
39: 5 "Who **l** the wild donkey **go** free? 8938
40: 2 *L him* who accuses God **answer** AIT
Ps 2: 3 "*L us* **break** their chains," they say, AIT
4: 6 **L** the light of your face **shine** 5951
5:10 *L* their intrigues *be their* **downfall.** AIT
5:11 *l* all who take refuge in you *be* **glad;** AIT
5:11 *l them* ever **sing for joy.** AIT
7: 5 then *l* my enemy **pursue** and overtake me; AIT
7: 5 *l him* **trample** my life to the ground AIT
7: 7 *L* the assembled peoples **gather around** AIT
7: 8 *l* the LORD **judge** the peoples. AIT
9:19 Arise, O LORD, *l* not man **triumph;** AIT
9:19 *l* the nations **be judged** AIT
9:20 *l* the nations **know** they are but men. AIT
14: 7 *l* Jacob **rejoice** and Israel be glad! AIT
16:10 nor *will you* **l** your Holy One see decay. 5989
22: 8 *l* the LORD **rescue** him. AIT
22: 8 *L him* **deliver** him, AIT
25: 2 *l me be* **put to shame,** AIT
25: 2 nor *l* my enemies **triumph** over me. AIT
25:20 *l me* not *be* **put to shame,** AIT
30: 1 and *did* not **l** my enemies **gloat** 8523
31: 1 *l me* never *be* **put to shame;** AIT
31:16 *L* your face **shine** on your servant; AIT
31:17 *L me* not *be* **put to shame,** AIT
31:17 *l* the wicked *be* **put to shame** AIT
31:18 *L* their lying lips **be silenced,** AIT
32: 6 *l* everyone who is godly **pray** AIT
33: 8 *L* all the earth **fear** the LORD; AIT
33: 8 *l* all the people of the world **revere** him. AIT
34: 2 *l* the afflicted **hear** and rejoice. AIT
34: 3 *l us* **exalt** his name together. AIT
35:19 *L* not *those* **gloat** over me AIT
35:19 *l* not those who hate me without reason **maliciously wink** AIT
35:24 *do* not *l them* **gloat** over me. AIT
35:25 *Do* not *l them* **think,** "Aha, AIT
37:33 in their power or **l** them **be condemned** 8399
38:16 "*Do* not *l them* **gloat** or exalt themselves AIT
39: 4 *l me* **know** how fleeting is my life. AIT
43: 3 and your truth, *l* them **guide** me; AIT
43: 3 *l them* **bring** me to your holy mountain, AIT
45: 4 *l* your right hand **display** awesome deeds. AIT
45: 5 **L** your sharp arrows pierce the hearts of NIH
45: 5 *l* the nations **fall** beneath your feet. AIT
51: 8 **L** me **hear** joy and gladness; 9048
51: 8 *l* the bones you have crushed **rejoice.** AIT
Ps 53: 6 *l* Jacob **rejoice** and Israel be glad! AIT
54: 5 *L* evil **recoil** on those who slander me; AIT
55:15 *L* death **take** my enemies **by surprise;** AIT
55:15 *l them* **go down** alive to the grave, AIT
55:22 *he will* never **l** the righteous fall. 5989
56: 7 On no account **l** them **escape;** 7117
57: 5 **l** your glory be over all the earth. NIH
57:11 **l** your glory be over all the earth. NIH
58: 7 *L them* **vanish** like water that flows away; AIT
58: 7 *l* their arrows **be blunted.** AIT
59:10 before me and *will* **l** me **gloat** 8011
59:12 *l them* **be caught** in their pride. AIT
64:10 *L* the righteous **rejoice** AIT
64:10 *l* all the upright in heart **praise** AIT
66: 6 *come, l us* **rejoice** in him. AIT
66: 7 *l* not the rebellious **rise up** AIT
66: 8 **l** the sound of his praise **be heard;** 9048
66:12 *You* **l** men **ride** over our heads; 8206
66:16 *l me* **tell** you what he has done for me. AIT
69:14 Rescue me from the mire, *do* not *l me* **sink;** AIT
69:15 *Do* not *l* the floodwaters **engulf** me AIT
69:24 *l* your fierce anger **overtake** them. AIT
69:25 *l there* **be** no one to dwell in their tents. AIT
69:27 *do* not *l them* **share** in your salvation. AIT
69:34 *L* heaven and earth **praise** him, AIT
70: 4 "*L* God *be* **exalted!"** AIT
71: 1 *l me* never *be* **put to shame.** AIT
72:16 *L* grain **abound** throughout the land; AIT
72:16 *L* its fruit **flourish** like Lebanon; AIT
72:16 *l it* **thrive** like the grass of the field. AIT
74:21 *l* the oppressed **retreat** in disgrace; AIT
76:11 *l* all the neighboring lands **bring** gifts AIT
78:26 *He* **l loose** the east wind from the heavens 5825
80:17 *L* your hand **rest** on the man at your right AIT
83: 4 they say, "*l us* **destroy** them as a nation, AIT
83:12 "*L us* **take possession** *of* the pasturelands AIT
83:18 *L them* **know** that you, AIT
85: 8 but *l them* not **return** to folly. AIT
95: 1 *l us* **sing for joy** AIT
95: 1 *l us* **shout aloud** to the Rock AIT
95: 2 *L us* **come** before him with thanksgiving AIT
95: 6 Come, *l us* **bow down** in worship, AIT
95: 6 *l us* **kneel** before the LORD our Maker; AIT
96:11 *L* the heavens **rejoice,** AIT
96:11 *l* the earth *be* **glad;** AIT
96:11 *l* the sea **resound,** and all that is in it, AIT
96:12 *l* the fields *be* **jubilant,** AIT
97: 1 *l* the earth *be* **glad;** AIT
97: 1 *l* the distant shores **rejoice.** AIT
97:10 *L those who* **love** the LORD hate evil, AIT
98: 7 *L* the sea **resound,** and everything in it, AIT
98: 8 *L* the rivers **clap** their hands, AIT
98: 8 *l* the mountains **sing** together **for joy;** AIT
98: 9 **l** them sing before the LORD, NIH
99: 1 *l* the nations **tremble;** AIT
99: 1 between the cherubim, *l* the earth **shake.** AIT
99: 3 *L them* **praise** your great and awesome name AIT
102: 1 *l* my cry for help **come** to you. AIT
102:18 *L* this **be written** for a future generation, AIT
105: 3 *l* the hearts of those who seek the LORD **rejoice.** AIT
106:48 *L* all the people **say,** AIT
107: 2 *L* the redeemed of the LORD **say** AIT
107: 8 *L them* **give thanks** to the LORD AIT
107:15 *L them* **give thanks** to the LORD AIT
107:21 *L them* **give thanks** to the LORD AIT
107:22 *L them* **sacrifice** thank offerings and tell AIT
107:31 *L them* **give thanks** to the LORD AIT
107:32 *L them* **exalt** him in the assembly of AIT
107:38 and *he did* not **l** their herds **diminish.** 5070
107:43 *l him* **heed** these things and consider AIT
108: 5 and **l** your glory be over all the earth. NIH
109: 6 *l* an accuser **stand** at his right hand. AIT
109: 7 When he is tried, *l him be* **found** guilty, AIT
109:27 *L them* **know** that it is your hand, that you, AIT
113: 2 *L* the name of the LORD **be** praised, AIT
118: 2 *L* Israel **say:** "His love endures forever." AIT
118: 3 *L* the house of Aaron **say:** AIT
118: 4 *L* those who fear the LORD **say:** AIT
118:24 *l us* **rejoice** and be glad in it. AIT
119:10 *do* not **l** me **stray** from your commands. 8706
119:27 **L** me **understand** the teaching 1067
119:31 *do* not **l** me **be put to shame.** 1017
119:77 *L* your compassion **come** to me AIT
119:116 *do* not **l** my hopes **be dashed.** 1017
119:122 *l* not the arrogant **oppress** AIT
119:133 **l** no sin **rule** over me. 8948
119:175 *L* me **live** that I may praise you, AIT
121: 3 *He will* not **l** your foot slip— 5989
122: 1 "*L us* **go** *to* the house of the LORD." AIT
124: 1 on our side—*l* Israel **say—** AIT
124: 6 who *has* not **l** us be torn by their teeth. 5989
129: 1 from my youth—*l* Israel **say—** AIT
130: 2 *L* your ears be attentive to my cry AIT
132: 7 "*L us* **go** to his dwelling place; AIT
132: 7 *l us* **worship** at his footstool— AIT
140: 8 *do* not **l** their plans **succeed,** 7049
140: 9 *L* the heads of those who surround me *be* **covered** with the trouble AIT
140:10 **L** burning coals **fall** upon them; 4572
140:11 *L* slanderers not **be established** in the land; AIT
141: 4 **L** not my heart **be drawn** to what is evil, 5742
141: 4 *l me* not **eat** of their delicacies. AIT
141: 5 *L* a righteous man **strike** me— AIT
141: 5 *l him* **rebuke** me—it is oil on my head. AIT
141:10 *L* the wicked **fall** into their own nets, AIT
143: 8 *L* the morning **bring** me **word** AIT
Ps 145:21 *L* every creature **praise** his holy name AIT
148: 5 *L them* **praise** the name of the LORD, AIT
148:13 *L them* **praise** the name of the LORD, AIT
149: 2 *L* Israel **rejoice** in their Maker; AIT
149: 2 *l* the people of Zion *be* **glad** AIT
149: 3 *L them* **praise** his name with dancing AIT
149: 5 *L* the saints **rejoice** in this honor and sing AIT
150: 6 *L* everything that has breath **praise** AIT
Pr 1: 5 *l* the wise **listen** and add to their learning, AIT
1: 5 and *l* the discerning **get** guidance— AIT
3: 3 *L* love and faithfulness never **leave** you; AIT
3:20 and the clouds **l drop** the dew. 8319
3:21 *do* not *l them* **out** of your sight; 4279
4:13 Hold on to instruction, *do* not **l** it **go;** 8332
4:21 *Do* not **l** *them* **out** of your sight, 4279
4:25 **L** your eyes **look** straight ahead, 5564
5:17 *L them* **be** yours alone, AIT
6:25 after her beauty or *l her* **captivate** you AIT
7:25 not *l* your heart **turn** to her ways or stray AIT
9: 4 "*L all* who are simple **come in** AIT
9:16 "*L all* who are simple **come in** AIT
10: 3 *does* not **l** the righteous **go hungry** 8279
23:17 *Do* not *l* your heart **envy** sinners, AIT
23:26 give me your heart and *l* your eyes **keep** AIT
24:17 *do* not *l* your heart **rejoice,** AIT
27: 2 *L* another **praise** you, and AIT
28:17 *l* no *one* **support** him. AIT
31: 7 *l them* **drink** and forget their poverty AIT
31:31 *l* her works **bring** her **praise** AIT
Ecc 5: 2 so *l* your words **be** few. AIT
5: 6 *Do* not **l** your mouth lead you into sin. 5989
7:18 It is good to grasp the one and not **l go** of the other. 906+3338+5663
11: 6 and at evening **l** not your hands **be idle,** 5663
11: 8 *l him* **enjoy** them all. AIT
11: 8 But *l him* **remember** the days of darkness, AIT
11: 9 *l* your heart **give** you **joy** AIT
SS 1: 2 *L him* **kiss** me with the kisses of his mouth AIT
1: 4 Take me away with you—*l us* **hurry!** AIT
1: 4 *L* the king **bring** me **into** his chambers. AIT
2:14 show me your face, **l** me **hear** your voice; 9048
3: 4 I held him and *would* not **l** him **go** 8332
4:16 *L* my lover **come** into his garden AIT
7:11 my lover, *l us* **go** *to* the countryside, AIT
7:11 *l us* **spend the night** in the villages. AIT
7:12 *L us* **go early** to the vineyards to see if AIT
8:11 *he* **l out** his vineyard to tenants. 5989
8:13 **l** me **hear** your voice! 9048
Isa 1:18 "Come now, *l us* **reason together,"** AIT
2: 3 *l us* **go up** to the mountain of the LORD, AIT
2: 5 *l us* **walk** in the light of the LORD. AIT
4: 1 only *l us* **be called** *by* your name. AIT
5:19 "*L* God **hurry,** let him hasten his work AIT
5:19 *l him* **hasten** his work so we may see it. AIT
5:19 *L it* **approach,** let the plan of AIT
5:19 *l* the plan of the Holy One of Israel **come,** AIT
7: 6 "*L us* **invade** Judah; AIT
7: 6 *l us* **tear it apart** and divide it AIT
12: 5 *l* this **be known** to all the world. AIT
14:17 and *would* not *l* his captives **go** home?" AIT
16: 4 *L* the Moabite fugitives **stay** with you; AIT
19:12 *L them* **show** you and make known what AIT
21: 7 *l him be* **alert,** fully alert." AIT
22: 4 *l me* **weep bitterly.** AIT
22:13 "*L* us **eat** and drink," you say, AIT
25: 9 *l us* **rejoice** and be glad in his salvation." AIT
26:11 *L them* **see** your zeal for your people and AIT
26:11 *l* the fire reserved for your enemies **consume** them. AIT
27: 5 Or else *l them* **come** *to* me for refuge; AIT
27: 5 *l them* **make** peace with me, yes, AIT
27: 5 yes, *l them* **make** peace with me." AIT
28:12 "This is the resting place, *l* the weary **rest";** AIT
29: 1 *l* your **cycle** of festivals **go on.** AIT
34: 1 *L* the earth **hear,** and all that is in it, AIT
36:14 *Do* not **l** Hezekiah **deceive** you. 5958
36:15 *Do* not **l** Hezekiah **persuade** you **to trust** 1053
36:18 not **l** Hezekiah **mislead** you when he says, 6077
37:10 *Do* not **l** the god you depend on **deceive** 5958
38:16 You restored me to health and **l** me **live.** 2649
41: 1 **L** the nations **renew** their strength! 2736
41: 1 *L them* **come forward** and speak; AIT
41: 1 *l us* **meet** together at the place AIT
42:11 *L* the desert and its towns **raise** AIT
42:11 *l* the settlements where Kedar lives **rejoice.** AIT
42:11 *L* the people of Sela **sing for joy;** AIT
42:11 *l them* **shout** from the mountaintops. AIT
42:12 *L them* **give** glory to the LORD AIT
43: 9 *L them* **bring** *in* their witnesses AIT
43:26 *l us* **argue** *the matter* together; AIT
44: 7 *L him* **proclaim** it. AIT
44: 7 *L him* **declare** and lay out AIT
44: 7 yes, *l him* **foretell** what will come. AIT
44:11 *L* them all **come together** AIT
44:14 *He* **l** it **grow** among the trees of the forest, 599
44:28 he will say of Jerusalem, "*L it* **be rebuilt,"** AIT
44:28 "*L its* **foundations be laid."'** AIT
45: 8 *l* the clouds **shower** it **down.** AIT
45: 8 *L* the earth **open wide,** AIT
45: 8 *l* salvation **spring up,** AIT
45: 8 *l* righteousness **grow** with it; AIT
45:21 *l them* **take counsel** together. AIT
47:13 *L* your astrologers **come forward,** AIT
47:13 *l them* **save** you from what is coming AIT
48:11 How *can* I *l* myself **be defamed?** AIT
50: 8 *L us* **face** each other! AIT
50: 8 *L him* **confront** me! AIT

Isa 50:10 L him who walks in the dark, who has no light, trust in the name AIT
55: 7 L the wicked forsake his way and AIT
55: 7 L him turn to the LORD, AIT
56: 3 L no foreigner who has bound himself to the LORD say, AIT
56: 3 l not any eunuch complain, AIT
56:12 "Come," each one cries, "l me get wine! AIT
56:12 L us drink our fill AIT
57:13 l your collection [of idols] save you! AIT
66: 5 'L the LORD be glorified, AIT
Jer 2:28 L them come if they can save you AIT
3:25 L us lie down in our shame, AIT
3:25 and l our disgrace cover us. AIT
4: 5 L us flee to the fortified cities!' AIT
5:13 l what they say be done AIT
5:24 'L us fear the LORD our God, AIT
6: 4 Arise, l us attack at noon! AIT
6: 5 l us attack at night AIT
6: 9 "L them glean the remnant of Israel as thoroughly as a vine; AIT
7: 3 and I will l you live in this place. 8905
7: 7 then I will l you live in this place, 8905
8:14 L us flee to the fortified cities AIT
9:18 L them come quickly and wail over us AIT
9:23 "L not the wise man boast AIT
9:24 but l him who boasts boast about this: AIT
11:19 saying, "L us destroy the tree and its fruit; AIT
11:19 l us cut him off from the land of the living, AIT
11:20 l me see your vengeance upon them, AIT
13: 1 but do not l it touch water." 928+995
14:17 "L my eyes overflow with tears AIT
15: 1 L them go! AIT
15:19 L this people turn to you, AIT
17:15 L it now be fulfilled!" AIT
17:18 L my persecutors be put to shame, AIT
17:18 l them be terrified, AIT
18:21 L their wives be made childless and widows; AIT
18:21 l their men be put to death, AIT
18:22 L a cry be heard from their houses AIT
18:23 L them be overthrown before you; AIT
20:12 l me see your vengeance upon them, AIT
22:20 l your voice be heard in Bashan, 5989
23:28 L the prophet who has a dream tell AIT
23:28 l the one who has my word speak AIT
27:11 I will l that nation remain in its own land 5663
27:18 l them plead with the LORD Almighty AIT
29: 8 Do not l the prophets and diviners among you deceive you. AIT
30:11 l you go entirely unpunished.' 5927+5927
31: 6 'Come, l us go up to Zion, AIT
32:37 to this place and l them live in safety. 3782
33: 6 and will l them enjoy abundant peace 1655
34:14 you must l him go free.' 8938
36:19 Don't l anyone know where you are." AIT
37:20 L me bring my petition before you: AIT
38:11 and l them down with ropes to Jeremiah in 8938
38:24 not l anyone know about this conversation, AIT
40: 5 and a present and l him go. 8938
40:15 "L me go and kill Ishmael son of Nethaniah, AIT
41: 8 So he l them alone and did not kill them 2532
45: 5 but wherever you go I will l you escape 5989
46:16 l us go back to our own people AIT
46:28 l you go entirely unpunished." 5927+5927
48: 2 l us put an end to that nation.' AIT
48:26 L Moab wallow in her vomit; AIT
48:26 l her be an object of ridicule. AIT
50:16 of the oppressor l everyone return AIT
50:16 l everyone flee to his own land. AIT
50:27 l them go down to the slaughter! AIT
50:29 Encamp all around her; l no one escape. 2118
50:33 refusing to l them go. 8938
51: 3 L not the archer string his bow, AIT
51: 3 nor l him put on his armor. AIT
51: 9 l us leave her and each go AIT
51:10 come, l us tell in Zion what AIT
La 1:22 "L all their wickedness come AIT
2:17 he has l the enemy gloat over you, 8523
2:18 l your tears flow like a river day 3718
3:28 L him sit alone in silence, AIT
3:29 L him bury his face in the dust— AIT
3:30 L him offer his cheek to the one AIT
3:30 and l him be filled with disgrace. AIT
3:40 L us examine our ways and test them, AIT
3:40 and l us return to the LORD. AIT
3:41 L us lift up our hearts and our hands AIT
Eze 3:27 Whoever will listen l him listen, AIT
3:27 and whoever will refuse l him refuse; AIT
4:15 "I will l you bake your bread 5989
7:12 L not the buyer rejoice AIT
14: 3 l them inquire of me at all? 2011+2011+4200
14:17 'L the sword pass throughout the land,' AIT
20: 3 as I live, I will not l you inquire of me, 2011
20:26 I l them become defiled through their gifts 3237
20:31 Am I to l you inquire of me, 2011+4200
20:31 I will not l you inquire of me. 2011+4200
21:14 L the sword strike twice, AIT
23:43 l them use her as a prostitute, AIT
24:10 l the bones be charred. AIT
32: 4 l all the birds of the air settle 8905
32:14 Then I will l her waters settle 9205
32:20 l her be dragged off AIT
39: 7 l my holy name be profaned, 2725
43: 9 Now l them put away AIT
43:10 L them consider the plan, AIT
44:20 or l their hair grow long, 8938
Da 2: 7 "L the king tell his servants the dream, AIT
Da 4:14 L the animals flee from under it and AIT
4:15 l the stump and its roots, bound with iron and bronze, remain AIT
4:15 "'L him be drenched with the dew AIT
4:15 and l him live with the animals among NIH
4:16 L his mind be changed AIT
4:16 and l him be given the mind of an animal, AIT
4:19 l the dream or its meaning alarm AIT
4:23 L him be drenched with the dew of heaven; AIT
4:23 l him live like the wild animals, NIH
Hos 2: 2 L her remove the adulterous look AIT
4: 4 l no man bring a charge, AIT
4: 4 l no man accuse another, AIT
4:15 l not Judah become guilty. AIT
6: 1 "Come, l us return to the LORD. AIT
6: 3 L us acknowledge the LORD; AIT
6: 3 l us press on to acknowledge him. AIT
9: 7 L Israel know this. AIT
Joel 1: 3 and l your children tell it to their children, NIH
2: 1 L all who live in the land tremble, AIT
2:16 L the bridegroom leave his room AIT
2:17 L the priests, who minister before the LORD, weep AIT
2:17 L them say, "Spare your people, O LORD. AIT
3: 9 L all the fighting men draw near AIT
3:10 L the weakling say, "I am strong!" AIT
3:12 "L the nations be roused; AIT
3:12 l them advance into the Valley AIT
Am 5:24 But l justice roll on like a river, AIT
Ob 1: 1 and l us go against her for battle"— AIT
Jnh 1: 7 l us cast lots to find out AIT
1:14 not l us die for taking this man's life. AIT
3: 7 l any man or beast, herd or flock, taste AIT
3: 7 do not l them eat or drink. AIT
3: 8 l man and beast be covered AIT
3: 8 L everyone call urgently on God. AIT
3: 8 L them give up their evil ways AIT
Mic 4: 2 l us go up to the mountain of the LORD, AIT
4:11 They say, "L her be defiled, AIT
4:11 l our eyes gloat over Zion!" AIT
6: 1 l the hills hear what you have to say. AIT
7:14 L them feed in Bashan and Gilead as AIT
Hab 2:20 l all the earth be silent AIT
Zep 3:16 do not l your hands hang limp. AIT
Zec 8: 9 l your hands be strong AIT
8:13 l your hands be strong." AIT
8:21 'L us go at once to entreat the LORD AIT
8:23 'L us go with you, AIT
11: 9 L the dying die, and the perishing perish. AIT
11: 9 L those who are left eat one another's AIT
Mt 3:15 Jesus replied, "L it be so now; 918
5:16 l your light shine before men, AIT
5:37 Simply l your 'Yes' be 'Yes,' AIT
5:40 l him have your cloak as well. 918
6: 3 do not l your left hand know what AIT
7: 4 'L me take the speck out of your eye,' 918
8:21 "Lord, first l me go and bury my father." 2205
8:22 and l the dead bury their own dead." 918
10:13 l your peace rest on it; AIT
10:13 if it is not, l your peace return to you. AIT
11:15 He who has ears, l him hear. AIT
13: 9 He who has ears, l him hear." AIT
13:30 L both grow together until the harvest. 918
13:43 He who has ears, l him hear. AIT
13:47 of heaven is like a net that was l down into 965
14:36 and begged him to l the sick just touch 2671
18:27 canceled the debt and l him go. 668
19: 6 God has joined together, l man not separate. AIT
19:14 "L the little children come to me, 918
23:13 will you l those enter who are trying to. 918
24:15 l the reader understand— AIT
24:16 l those who are in Judea flee AIT
24:17 L no one on the roof of his house go down AIT
24:18 L no one in the field go back AIT
24:43 not have l his house be broken into. 1572
26:46 Rise, l us go! Here comes my betrayer!" AIT
27:25 "L his blood be on us and NIG
27:42 L him come down now from the cross, AIT
27:43 L God rescue him now if he wants him, AIT
Mk 1:34 but he would not l the demons speak 918
1:38 Jesus replied, "L us go somewhere else— AIT
4: 9 "He who has ears to hear, l him hear." AIT
4:23 If anyone has ears to hear, l him hear." AIT
4:35 "L us go over to the other side." AIT
5:19 Jesus did not l him, but said, 918
5:37 not l anyone follow him except Peter, 918
5:43 not to l anyone know about this, 2671
6:56 They begged him to l them touch even 2671
7: 8 You have l go of the commands of God 918
7:12 then you no longer l him do anything 918
7:27 "First l the children eat all they want," 918
9: 5 L us put up three shelters— AIT
10: 9 God has joined together, l man not separate. AIT
10:14 "L the little children come to me, 918
10:37 "L one of us sit at your right and the other 1443
11: 6 and the people l them go. 918
12:15 "Bring me a denarius and l me look at it." 2671
13:14 l the reader understand— AIT
13:14 l those who are in Judea flee AIT
13:15 L no one on the roof of his house go down AIT
13:16 L no one in the field go back AIT
13:36 do not l him find you sleeping. NIG
14:42 Rise! L us go! Here comes my betrayer!" AIT
15:32 L this Christ, this King of Israel, come down AIT
Lk 5: 4 and l down the nets for a catch." 5899
5: 5 you say so, I will l down the nets." 5899
Lk 6:42 l me take the speck out of your eye,' 918
8: 8 "He who has ears to hear, l him hear." AIT
8:32 The demons begged Jesus to l them go 2205
8:51 not l anyone go in with him except Peter, 918
9:33 L us put up three shelters— AIT
9:59 "Lord, first l me go and bury my father." 2205
9:60 "L the dead bury their own dead, 918
9:61 but first l me go back and say good-by 2205
12:39 not have l his house be broken into. 918
14:35 "He who has ears to hear, l him hear." AIT
16:28 L him warn them, AIT
16:29 l them listen to them.' AIT
18:16 "L the little children come to me, 918
21:21 l those who are in Judea flee AIT
21:21 l those in the city get out, AIT
21:21 l those in the country not enter AIT
23:35 l him save himself if he is the Christ AIT
Jn 6:12 L nothing be wasted." 2671
7:37 l him come to me and drink. AIT
8: 7 l him be the first to throw AIT
11: 7 "L us go back to Judea." AIT
11:15 But l us go to him." AIT
11:16 "L us also go, that we may die with him." AIT
11:44 "Take off the grave clothes and l him go." 918
11:48 If we l him go on like this, 918
14: 1 not l your hearts be troubled. Trust in God; AIT
14:27 Do not l your hearts be troubled AIT
14:31 "Come now; l us leave. AIT
17:23 to complete unity to l the world know 2671
18: 8 then l these men go." 918
19: 4 to you to l you know that I find no basis 2671
19:12 "If you l this man go, 668
Ac 1:20 l there be no one to dwell in it,' and, AIT
2:14 l me explain this to you; AIT
2:27 nor will you l your Holy One see decay. 1443
2:36 l all Israel be assured AIT
3:13 though he had decided to l him go. AIT
4:21 After further threats they l them go. 668
5:38 L them go! 918
5:40 and l them go. 668
10:11 like a large sheet being l down to earth 2768
11: 5 a large sheet being l down from heaven 2768
13:35 not l your Holy One see decay.' 1443
14:16 he l all nations go their own way. 1572
15:36 "L us go back and visit AIT
16:37 L them come themselves and escort us out." AIT
17: 9 and the others post bond and l them go. AIT
19:30 but the disciples would not l him. 1572
21:39 Please l me speak to the people." 2205
23:32 The next day they l the cavalry go on 1572
25: 5 L some of your leaders come with me and press charges against the man AIT
27:17 l the ship be driven along. 5770
27:30 the sailors l the lifeboat down into the sea, 5899
27:32 that held the lifeboat and l it fall away. 1572
Ro 3: 4 L God be true, and every man a liar. AIT
3: 8 "L us do evil that good may result"? AIT
6:12 not l sin reign in your mortal body so AIT
12: 6 l him use it in proportion to his faith. NIG
12: 7 If it is serving, l him serve; NIG
12: 7 if it is teaching, l him teach; NIG
12: 8 if it is encouraging, l him encourage; NIG
12: 8 l him give generously; NIG
12: 8 if it is leadership, l him govern diligently; NIG
12: 8 l him do it cheerfully. NIG
13: 8 L no debt remain outstanding, AIT
13:12 l us put aside the deeds of darkness and AIT
13:13 L us behave decently, as in the daytime, AIT
14:13 l us stop passing judgment on AIT
14:19 L us therefore make every effort AIT
1Co 1:31 "L him who boasts boast AIT
5: 8 l us keep the Festival, AIT
7:15 But if the unbeliever leaves, l him do so. AIT
7:21 Don't l it trouble you— AIT
10:13 he will not l you be tempted 1572
14:37 l him acknowledge that what I am writing AIT
15:32 "L us eat and drink, AIT
15:58 L nothing move you. NIG
2Co 2: 4 to grieve you but to l you know the depth 2671
4: 6 who said, "L light shine out of darkness," AIT
7: 1 l us purify ourselves from everything AIT
10:17 But, "L him who boasts boast in the Lord." AIT
11:16 L no one take me for AIT
Gal 1: 8 l him be eternally condemned! AIT
1: 9 l him be eternally condemned! AIT
3:15 l me take an example AIT
5: 1 l yourselves be burdened AIT
5: 2 l yourselves be circumcised, AIT
5:25 l us keep in step AIT
5:26 L us not become conceited, AIT
6: 9 L us not become weary AIT
6:10 l us do good to all people, 2237
6:17 Finally, l no one cause me trouble, AIT
Eph 4:26 l the sun go down AIT
4:29 l any unwholesome talk come out AIT
5: 6 L no one deceive you with empty words, AIT
Php 3:16 Only l us live up NIG
4: 5 L your gentleness be evident AIT
Col 2:16 not l anyone judge you by what you eat AIT
2:18 l anyone who delights in false humility and the worship of angels disqualify you for the prize. AIT
3:15 L the peace of Christ rule in your hearts, AIT
3:16 L the word of Christ dwell in AIT
4: 6 L your conversation be always full NIG
1Th 5: 6 l us not be like others, who are asleep, AIT

1Th 5: 6 l us be alert and self-controlled. AIT
5: 8 l us be self-controlled, AIT
2Th 2: 3 Don't l anyone deceive you in any way, AIT
1Ti 3:10 l them serve as deacons. AIT
4:12 Don't l anyone look down on you AIT
5:16 not l the church be burdened with them, AIT
Tit 2:15 Do not l anyone despise you. AIT
Heb 1: 6 "L all God's angels worship AIT
4: 1 l us be careful that none of you be found AIT
4:11 L us, therefore, make every effort AIT
4:14 l us hold firmly to the faith we profess. AIT
4:16 L us then approach the throne of grace AIT
6: 1 l us leave the elementary teachings about Christ and go on AIT
10:22 l us draw near to God with a sincere heart AIT
10:23 L us hold unswervingly to the hope AIT
10:24 And l us consider how we may spur one AIT
10:25 L us not give up meeting together, AIT
10:25 but l us encourage one another— NIG
12: 1 l us throw off everything that hinders and AIT
12: 1 and l us run with perseverance AIT
12: 2 L us fix our eyes on Jesus AIT
12:28 l us be thankful, AIT
13:13 L us, then, go to him outside the camp, AIT
13:15 l us continually offer to God AIT
Jas 3:13 L him show it by his good life, AIT
5:12 L your "Yes" be yes, and your "No," no, 1639
5:13 L him sing songs of praise. AIT
1Jn 3: 7 do not l anyone lead you astray. AIT
3:18 l us not love with words or tongue but AIT
4: 7 Dear friends, l us love one another, AIT
Rev 2: 7 l him hear what the Spirit says to AIT
2:11 l him hear what the Spirit says to AIT
2:17 l him hear what the Spirit says to AIT
2:29 l him hear what the Spirit says to AIT
3: 6 l him hear what the Spirit says to AIT
3:13 l him hear what the Spirit says to AIT
3:22 l him hear what the Spirit says to AIT
13: 9 He who has an ear, l him hear. AIT
13:18 l him calculate the number of the beast, AIT
19: 7 L us rejoice and be glad and give AIT
22:11 L him who does wrong continue to do wrong; AIT
22:11 l him who is vile continue to be vile; AIT
22:11 l him who does right continue to do AIT
22:11 l him who is holy continue to be holy." AIT
22:17 l him who hears say, AIT
22:17 Whoever is thirsty, l him come; AIT
22:17 l him take the free gift of the water of life. AIT

LET (Anglicized) See also HAVE

LET'S (48) [LET, WE]

Ge 4: 8 "L go out to the field." AIT
11: 3 l make bricks and bake them thoroughly." AIT
13: 8 "L not have any quarreling between you AIT
13: 9 L part company. AIT
19:32 L get our father to drink wine AIT
19:34 L get him to drink wine AIT
24:57 "L call the girl and ask her about it." AIT
31:44 Come now, l make a covenant, you and I, AIT
37:17 "I heard them say, 'L go to Dothan.' " AIT
37:20 l kill him and throw him into one AIT
37:21 "L not take his life," he said. AIT
37:27 l sell him to the Ishmaelites and AIT
Ex 14:25 "L get away from the Israelites! AIT
Jdg 14:13 "L hear it." AIT
18: 9 They answered, "Come on, l attack them! AIT
19:11 l stop at this city of the Jebusites AIT
19:13 l try to reach Gibeah or Ramah and spend AIT
19:28 He said to her, "Get up; l go." AIT
20:32 "L retreat and draw them away from AIT
1Sa 9: 5 l go back, or my father will stop thinking AIT
9: 6 L go there now. AIT
9:10 "Come, l go." AIT
14: 1 l go over to the Philistine outpost on AIT
14: 6 l go over to the outpost AIT
20:11 Jonathan said, "l go out into the field." AIT
26:11 that are near his head, and l go." AIT
2Sa 2:14 "L have some of the young men get up AIT
2Ki 4:10 L make a small room on the roof and put AIT
7: 4 So l go over to the camp of the Arameans AIT
7: 9 L go at once and report this to AIT
Pr 1:11 l lie in wait for someone's blood, AIT
1:11 l waylay some harmless soul; AIT
1:12 l swallow them alive, like the grave, AIT
7:18 Come, l drink deep of love till morning; AIT
7:18 l enjoy ourselves with love! AIT
Jer 18:18 "Come, l make plans against Jeremiah; AIT
18:18 l attack him with our tongues AIT
20:10 L report him!" AIT
Mt 21:38 l kill him and take his inheritance.' AIT
27:49 L see if Elijah comes to save him." AIT
Mk 12: 7 l kill him, and the inheritance will AIT
15:36 L see if Elijah comes to take him down," AIT
Lk 2:15 "L go to Bethlehem and see this thing AIT
8:22 "L go over to the other side of the lake." AIT
15:23 L have a feast and celebrate. AIT
20:14 'L kill him, and the inheritance will AIT
Jn 19:24 "L not tear it," they said to one another. AIT
19:24 "L decide by lot who will get it." AIT

LETHEK (1)

Hos 3: 2 and about a homer and a l of barley. 4390

LETS (7) [LET]

Ex 21:13 but God l it happen, 628+3338+4200
22: 5 in a field or vineyard and l them stray 8938
2Ki 10:24 of you l any of the men I am placing NIH
Job 12:15 if he l them loose, they devastate the land. 8938
39:14 on the ground and l them warm in the sand, 2801
Pr 14:33 even among fools she l herself be known. 3359
Gal 5: 3 l himself be circumcised AIT

LETTER (49) [LETTERS]

2Sa 11:14 In the morning David wrote a l to Joab 6219
2Ki 5: 5 "I will send a l to the king of Israel." 6219
5: 6 The l that he took to the king 6219
5: 6 "With this l I am sending my servant Naaman 6219
5: 7 As soon as the king of Israel read the l, 6219
10: 2 "As soon as this l reaches you, 6219
10: 6 Then Jehu wrote them a second l, saying, 6219
10: 7 When the l arrived, 6219
19:14 the l from the messengers and read it. 6219
2Ch 2:11 of Tyre replied by l to Solomon: 4181
21:12 a l from Elijah the prophet, which said: 4844
Ezr 4: 7 of his associates wrote a l to Artaxerxes. NIH
4: 7 The l was written in Aramaic script and in 10496
4: 8 the secretary wrote a l against Jerusalem 10007
4:11 (This is a copy of the l they sent him.) 10007
4:18 The l you sent us has been read 10496
4:23 of the l of King Artaxerxes was read 10496
5: 6 This is a copy of the l that Tattenai, 10007
7:11 of the l King Artaxerxes had given to Ezra 10496
Ne 2: 8 And may I have a l to Asaph, 115
6: 5 and in his hand was an unsealed l 115
Est 9:26 Because of everything written in this l and 115
9:29 with full authority to confirm this second l 115
Isa 37:14 the l from the messengers and read it. 6219
Jer 29: 1 of the l that the prophet Jeremiah sent 6219
29: 3 the l to Elasah son of Shaphan and NIH
29:29 read the l to Jeremiah the prophet. 6219
Mt 5:18 not the smallest l, 2740
Ac 15:23 With them they sent the following l: 1211
15:30 the church together and delivered the l. 2186
23:25 He wrote a l as follows: 2186
23:33 the l to the governor and handed Paul over 2186
23:34 The governor read the l NIG
Ro 16:22 I, Tertius, who wrote down this l, 2186
1Co 5: 9 I have written you in my l not to associate 2186
2Co 3: 2 You yourselves are our l, 2186
3: 3 You show that you are a l from Christ, 2186
3: 6 not of the l but of the Spirit; 1207
3: 6 for the l kills, but the Spirit gives life. 1207
7: 8 Even if I caused you sorrow by my l, 2186
7: 8 I see that my l hurt you, 2186
Col 4:16 After this l has been read to you, 2186
4:16 that you in turn read the l from Laodicea. NIG
1Th 5:27 before the Lord to have this l read to all 2186
2Th 2: 2 or l supposed to have come from us, 2186
2:15 whether by word of mouth or by l. 2186
3:14 not obey our instruction in this l, 2186
Heb 13:22 for I have written you only a short l. NIG
2Pe 3: 1 this is now my second l to you. 2186

LETTERS (29) [LETTER]

1Ki 21: 8 So she wrote l in Ahab's name, 6219
21: 9 In those l she wrote: 6219
21:11 as Jezebel directed in the l she had written 6219
2Ki 10: 1 So Jehu wrote l and sent them to Samaria: 6219
20:12 of Babylon sent Hezekiah l and a gift, 6219
2Ch 30: 1 also wrote l to Ephraim and Manasseh, 115
30: 6 throughout Israel and Judah with l from 115
32:17 king also wrote l insulting the LORD, 6219
Ne 2: 7 may I have l to the governors 115
2: 9 and gave them the king's l. 115
6:17 of Judah were sending many l to Tobiah, 115
6:19 And Tobiah sent l to intimidate me. 115
Est 9:20 and he sent l to all the Jews throughout 6219
9:30 And Mordecai sent l to all the Jews in 6219
Isa 39: 1 of Babylon sent Hezekiah l and a gift, 6219
Jer 29:25 You sent l in your own name to all 6219
Ac 9: 2 and asked him for l to the synagogues 2186
22: 5 I even obtained l from them 2186
28:21 "We have not received any l from Judea 1207
1Co 16: 3 I will give l of introduction to 2186
2Co 3: 1 l of recommendation to you or from you? 2186
3: 7 which was engraved in l on stone, 1207
10: 9 to be trying to frighten you with my l. 2186
10:10 some say, "His l are weighty and forceful, 2186
10:11 in our l when we are absent, 2186
Gal 6:11 See what large l I use as I write to you 1207
2Th 3:17 the distinguishing mark in all my l. 2186
2Pe 3:16 He writes the same way in all his l, 2186
3:16 His l contain some things that are hard NIG

LETTING (4) [LET]

Ex 8:29 by not l the people go to offer sacrifices to 8938
1Sa 21:13 of the gate and l saliva run down his beard. 3718
1Ki 1:27 without l his servants know who should sit 3359
Isa 32:20 l your cattle and donkeys range free. 8079+8938

LETUSHITES (1)

Ge 25: 3 the L and the Leummites. 4322

LEUMMITES (1)

Ge 25: 3 the Letushites and the L. 4212

LEVEL (15) [LEVELED, LEVELS]

1Ki 6: 8 to the middle l and from there to the third. AIT
Ps 26:12 My feet stand on l ground; 4793
65:10 You drench its furrows and l its ridges; 5737
143:10 may your good Spirit lead me on l ground. 4793
Pr 4:26 Make l paths for your feet 7142
Isa 26: 7 The path of the righteous is l; 4797
40: 4 the rough ground shall become l, 4793
45: 2 before you and will l the mountains; 3837
Jer 31: 9 on a l path where they will not stumble, 3838
Eze 13:14 with whitewash and will l it to 5595
41: 6 one above another, thirty on each l. 7193
41: 7 temple were wider at each successive l. 2025+2025+4200+4200+5087+5087
Zec 4: 7 Zerubbabel you will become l ground. 4793
Lk 6:17 down with them and stood on a l place. 4268
Heb 12:13 "Make l paths for your feet," 3981

LEVELED (3) [LEVEL]

Isa 28:25 When he has l the surface, 8750
32:19 the forest and the city is l completely, 928+2021+9164+9168
Jer 51:58 "Babylon's thick wall will be l 6910+6910

LEVELS (3) [LEVEL]

Isa 26: 5 he l it to the ground and casts it down to 9164
Eze 41: 6 The side rooms were on three l, NIH
42: 3 gallery faced gallery at the three l. AIT

LEVI (59) [LEVI'S, LEVITE, LEVITES, LEVITICAL]

Ge 29:34 So he was named L. 4290
34:25 two of Jacob's sons, Simeon and L, 4290
34:30 Then Jacob said to Simeon and L, 4290
35:23 Reuben the firstborn of Jacob, Simeon, L, 4290
46:11 The sons of L: Gershon, Kohath and 4290
49: 5 "Simeon and L are brothers— 4290
Ex 1: 2 Reuben, Simeon, L and Judah; 4290
2: 1 of the house of L married a Levite woman, 4290
6:16 of the sons of L according to their records: 4290
6:16 L lived 137 years. 4290
6:19 the clans of L according to their records. 4290
Nu 1:47 The families of the tribe of L, however, 4291
1:49 the tribe of L or include them in the census 4290
3: 6 of L and present them to Aaron the priest 4290
3:17 These were the names of the sons of L: 4290
16: 1 the son of L, and certain Reubenites— 4290
17: 3 On the staff of L write Aaron's name, 4290
17: 8 which represented the house of L, 4290
26:59 Jochebed, a descendant of L, 4290
Dt 10: 8 the LORD set apart the tribe of L to carry 4290
18: 1 indeed the whole tribe of L— 4290
21: 5 The priests, the sons of L, 4290
27:12 Simeon, L, Judah, Issachar, 4290
31: 9 the priests, the sons of L, 4290
33: 8 About L he said: 4290
Jos 13:14 to the tribe of L he gave no inheritance, 4291
13:33 But to the tribe of L, 4291
1Ch 2: 1 Reuben, Simeon, L, Judah, Issachar, 4290
6: 1 sons of L: Gershon, Kohath and Merari. 4290
6:16 sons of L: Gershon, Kohath and Merari. 4290
6:38 the son of Kohath, the son of L, 4290
6:43 the son of Gershon, the son of L; 4290
6:47 the son of Merari, the son of L. 4290
12:26 men of L—4,600, 4291
21: 6 But Joab did not include L and Benjamin 4290
23: 6 into groups corresponding to the sons of L: 4290
23:14 as part of the tribe of L. 4290
23:24 the descendants of L by their families— 4290
24:20 As for the rest of the descendants of L: 4290
27:17 over L: Hashabiah son of Kemuel; 4290
Ezr 8:18 from the descendants of Mahli son of L, 4291
Ne 12:23 among the descendants of L up to the time 4290
Ps 135:20 O house of L, praise the LORD; 4290
Eze 48:31 the gate of Judah and the gate of L. 4290
Zec 12:13 the clan of the house of L and their wives, 4290
Mal 2: 4 that my covenant with L may continue," 4290
2: 8 you have violated the covenant with L," 4290
Mk 2:14 he saw L son of Alphaeus sitting at 3322
2:14 and L got up and followed him. NIG
Lk 3:24 the son of L, the son of Melki, 3322
3:29 the son of Matthat, the son of L, 3322
5:27 by the name of L sitting at his tax booth. 3322
5:28 and L got up, left everything and followed NIG
5:29 Then L held a great banquet for Jesus 3322
Heb 7: 5 of L who become priests to collect a tenth 3322
7: 6 however, did not trace his descent from L, 899S
7: 9 One might even say that L, 3322
7:10 L was still in the body of his ancestor. NIG
Rev 7: 7 from the tribe of L 12,000, 3322

LEVI'S (1) [LEVI]

Mk 2:15 While Jesus was having dinner at L house, 899S

LEVIATHAN (6)

Job 3: 8 those who are ready to rouse L. 4293
41: 1 "Can you pull in the l with a fishhook 4293
Ps 74:14 of L and gave him as food to the creatures 4293
104:26 There the ships go to and fro, and the l, 4293
Isa 27: 1 L the gliding serpent, 4293
27: 1 L the coiling serpent; 4293

LEVITE (30) [LEVI]

Ex 2: 1 of the house of Levi married a L woman, 4290
4:14 "What about your brother, Aaron the L? 4291
6:25 These were the heads of the L families, 4291
Nu 3:20 These were the L clans, 4291
26:58 These also were L clans: 4290
Dt 18: 6 If a L moves from one of your towns 4291
26:12 you shall give it to the L, the alien, 4291
26:13 and have given it to the L, 4291
Jos 21:27 The L clans of the Gershonites were given: 4291
Jdg 17: 7 A young L from Bethlehem in Judah, 4291
17: 9 "I'm a L from Bethlehem in Judah," 4291
17:11 So the L agreed to live with him, 4291
17:12 Then Micah installed the L, 4291
17:13 since this L has become my priest." 4291
18: 3 they recognized the voice of the young L; 4291
18:15 the house of the young L *at* Micah's place 4291
19: 1 Now a L who lived in a remote area in 4291
20: 4 So the L, the husband of the murdered 4291
1Ch 9:31 A L named Mattithiah, 4291
9:33 heads of L families, 4291
9:34 All these were heads of L families, 4291
15:22 the head L was in charge of the singing; 4291
24: 6 The scribe Shemaiah son of Nethanel, a L, 4291
2Ch 20:14 a L and descendant of Asaph, 4291
31:12 a L, was in charge of these things, 4291
31:14 Kore son of Imnah the L, 4291
Ezr 10:15 by Meshullam and Shabbethai the L, 4291
Ne 13:13 and a L named Pedaiah in charge of 4291
Lk 10:32 So too, a L, when he came to the place *3324*
Ac 4:36 Joseph, a L from Cyprus, *3324*

LEVITES (282) [LEVI]

Ex 32:26 And all the L rallied to him. 1201+4290
32:28 The L did as Moses commanded, 1201+4290
38:21 by the L under the direction of Ithamar son 4291
Lev 25:32 " 'The L always have the right 4291
25:33 So the property of the L is redeemable— 4291
25:33 in the towns of the L are their property 4291
Nu 1:50 the L to be in charge of the tabernacle of 4291
1:51 the L are to take it down, 4291
1:51 the L shall do it. 4291
1:53 The L, however, are to set up their tents 4291
1:53 The L are to be responsible for the care of 4291
2:17 of the L will set out in the middle of 4291
2:33 The L, however, were not counted along 4291
3: 9 Give the L to Aaron and his sons; 4291
3:12 the L from among the Israelites in place of 4291
3:12 The L are mine, 4291
3:15 "Count the L by their families and 1201+4290
3:32 The chief leader of the L was Eleazar son 4291
3:39 of L counted at the LORD's command 4291
3:41 the L for me in place of all the firstborn of 4291
3:41 and the livestock of the L in place of all 4291
3:45 the L in place of all the firstborn of Israel, 4291
3:45 of the L in place of their livestock. 4291
3:45 The L are to be mine. 4291
3:46 the number of the L, 4291
3:49 the number redeemed by the L. 4291
4: 2 of the Kohathite branch of the L 1201+4290
4:18 not cut off from the L. 4291
4:46 and the leaders of Israel counted all the L 4291
7: 5 to the L as each man's work requires." 4291
7: 6 the carts and oxen and gave them to the L. 4291
8: 6 the L from among the other Israelites 4291
8: 9 the L to the front of the Tent of Meeting 4291
8:10 You are to bring the L before the LORD, 4291
8:11 to present the L before the LORD as 4291
8:12 L lay their hands on the heads of the bulls, 4291
8:12 to make atonement for the L. 4291
8:13 the L stand in front of Aaron and his sons 4291
8:14 In this way you are to set the L apart from 4291
8:14 and the L will be mine. 4291
8:15 "After you have purified the L 4291
8:18 the L in place of all the firstborn sons 4291
8:19 the L as gifts to Aaron and his sons to do 4291
8:20 with the L just as the LORD commanded 4291
8:21 The L purified themselves 4291
8:22 the L came to do their work at the Tent 4291
8:22 They did with the L just as 4291
8:24 "This applies to the L: 4291
8:26 to assign the responsibilities of the L." 4291
16: 7 You L have gone too far!" 1201+4290
16: 8 said to Korah, "Now listen, you L! 1201+4290
16:10 has brought you and all your fellow L 1201+4290
18: 2 Bring your fellow L from your 4290+4751
18: 6 I myself have selected your fellow L from 4291
18:21 "I give to the L all the tithes in Israel 1201+4290
18:23 the L who are to do the work at the Tent 4291
18:24 to the L as their inheritance the tithes that 4291
18:26 "Speak to the L and say to them: 4291
18:30 "Say to the L: 'When you present 4291
26:57 the L who were counted by their clans: 4291
26:59 who was born to the L in Egypt. 4290
26:62 All the male L a month old NIH
31:30 Give them to the L, 4291
31:47 and gave them to the L, 4291
35: 2 the L towns to live in from the inheritance 4291
35: 4 the L will extend out fifteen hundred feet 4291
35: 6 of the towns you give the L will be cities 4291
35: 7 the L forty-eight towns, 4291
35: 8 The towns you give the L from the land 4291
Dt 10: 9 the L have no share or inheritance 4290
12:12 and the L from your towns, 4291
12:18 and the L from your towns— 4291
Dt 12:19 not to neglect the L as long as you live 4291
14:27 do not neglect the L living in your towns, 4291
14:29 so that the L (who have no allotment 4291
16:11 the L in your towns, and the aliens, 4291
16:14 and the L, the aliens, 4291
17: 9 Go to the priests, who are L, 4291
17:18 taken from that of the priests, who are L. 4291
18: 1 The priests, who are L— 4291
18: 7 like all his fellow L who serve there in 4291
24: 8 who are L, instruct you. 4291
26:11 And you and the L and the aliens 4291
27: 9 Then Moses and the priests, who are L, 4291
27:14 The L shall recite to all the people of Israel 4291
31:25 the L who carried the ark of the covenant 4291
Jos 3: 3 and the priests, who are L, carrying it, 4291
8:33 the priests, who were L. 4291
14: 3 but had not granted the L an inheritance 4291
14: 4 The L received no share of the land 4291
18: 7 The L, however, do not get a portion 4291
21: 1 of the L approached Eleazar the priest, 4291
21: 3 the L the following towns 4291
21: 4 The L who were descendants of Aaron 4291
21: 8 the Israelites allotted to the L these towns 4291
21:10 from the Kohathite clans of the L, 1201+4290
21:20 of the L were allotted towns from the tribe 4291
21:34 (the rest of the L) were given: 4291
21:40 were the rest of the L, were twelve. 4291+5476
21:41 The towns of the L in the territory held by 4291
1Sa 6:15 The L took down the ark of the LORD, 4291
2Sa 15:24 the L who were with him were carrying 4291
1Ki 8: 4 The priests and L carried them up, 4291
12:31 even though they were not L. 1201+4290
1Ch 6:19 of the L listed according to their fathers: 4291
6:48 Their fellow L were assigned to all 4291
6:64 the L these towns and their pasturelands. 4291
6:77 (the rest of the L) received the following: NIH
9: 2 priests, L and temple servants. 4291
9:14 Of the L: Shemaiah son of Hasshub, 4291
9:18 to the camp of the L. 1201+4290
9:26 four principal gatekeepers, who were L, 4291
13: 2 also to the priests and L who are with them 4291
15: 2 "No one but the L may carry the ark 4291
15: 4 the descendants of Aaron and the L: 4291
15:11 Shemaiah, Eliel and Amminadab the L. 4291
15:12 you and your **fellow** L are to consecrate 278
15:13 It was because you, the L, NIH
15:14 the priests and L consecrated themselves 4291
15:15 the L carried the ark of God with 1201+4291
15:16 of the L to appoint their brothers as singers 4291
15:17 So the L appointed Heman son of Joel; 4291
15:26 the L who were carrying the ark of 4291
15:27 were all the L who were carrying the ark, 4291
16: 4 He appointed some of the L to minister 4291
23: 2 as well as the priests and L. 4291
23: 3 The L thirty years old or more 4291
23: 6 David divided **the** L into groups 4392[S]
23:26 the L no longer need to carry 4291
23:27 the L were counted 1201+4290
23:28 of **the** L was to help Aaron's descendants 4392[S]
23:32 the L carried out their responsibilities for NIH
24: 6 of families of the priests and of the L— 4291
24:30 These were the L, 1201+4290
24:31 of families of the priests and of the L. 4291
26:17 There were six L a day on the east, 4291
26:20 Their fellow L were in charge of 4291
28:13 for the divisions of the priests and L, 4291
28:21 the priests and L are ready for all the work 4291
2Ch 5: 4 the L took up the ark, 4291
5: 5 The priests, who were L, carried them up; 4291
5:12 All the L who were musicians— 4291
7: 6 as did the L with the LORD's musical 4291
7: 6 Opposite **the** L, the priests blew their 4392[S]
8:14 and the L to lead the praise and to assist 4291
8:15 to the priests or to the L in any matter, 4291
11:13 The priests and L from all their districts 4291
11:14 The L even abandoned their pasturelands 4291
11:16 followed **the** L to Jerusalem 2157[S]
13: 9 the sons of Aaron, and the L, 4291
13:10 and the L assist them. 4291
17: 8 With them were certain L— 4291
19: 8 Jehoshaphat appointed some of the L, 4291
19:11 the L will serve as officials before you. 4291
20:19 Then some L from the Kohathites 4291
23: 2 throughout Judah and gathered the L and 4291
23: 4 of you priests and L who are going on duty 4291
23: 6 of the LORD except the priests and L 4291
23: 7 The L are to station themselves around 4291
23: 8 The L and all the men of Judah did just 4291
23:18 in the hands of the priests, who were L, 4291
24: 5 He called together the priests and L 4291
24: 5 But the L did not act at once. 4291
24: 6 the L to bring in from Judah and Jerusalem 4291
24:11 the L to the king's officials and they saw 4291
29: 4 He brought in the priests and the L, 4291
29: 5 "Listen to me, L! 4291
29:12 Then these L set to work: 4291
29:16 The L took it and carried it out to 4291
29:25 He stationed the L in the temple of 4291
29:26 L stood ready with David's instruments, 4291
29:30 the L to praise the LORD with the words 4291
29:34 so their kinsmen the L helped them until 4291
29:34 for the L had been more conscientious 4291
30:15 The priests and the L were ashamed 4291
30:16 the blood handed to them by the L. 4291
30:17 the L had to kill the Passover lambs 4291
30:21 while the L and priests sang to 4291
30:22 Hezekiah spoke encouragingly to all the L, 4291
2Ch 30:25 and L and all who had assembled 4291
30:27 The priests and the L stood to bless 4291
31: 2 Hezekiah assigned the priests and L 4291
31: 2 according to their duties as priests or L— 4291
31: 4 and L so they could devote themselves to 4291
31: 9 Hezekiah asked the priests and L about 4291
31:17 and likewise to the L twenty years old 4291
31:19 in the genealogies of the L. 4291
34: 9 which the L who were the doorkeepers 4291
34:12 L descended from Merari, 4291
34:12 descended from Kohath. The L— 4291
34:13 Some of the L were secretaries, 4291
34:30 the priests and the L— 4291
35: 3 He said to the L, who instructed all Israel 4291
35: 5 "Stand in the holy place with a group of L 4291
35: 8 to the people and the priests and L. 4291
35: 9 Jeiel and Jozabad, the leaders of the L, 4291
35: 9 and five hundred head of cattle for the L. 4291
35:10 in their places with the L in their divisions 4291
35:11 while the L skinned the animals. 4291
35:14 So the L made preparations for themselves 4291
35:15 their fellow L made the preparations 4291
35:18 as did Josiah, with the priests, the L 4291
Ezr 1: 5 and the priests and L— 4291
2:40 The L: the descendants of Jeshua 4291
2:70 The priests, the L, the singers, 4291
3: 8 and the L and all who had returned from 4291
3: 8 appointing L twenty years of age and older 4291
3: 9 and their sons and brothers—all L— 4291
3:10 the L (the sons of Asaph) with cymbals, 4291
3:12 the older priests and L and family heads, 4291
6:16 priests, the L and the rest of the exiles— 10387
6:18 the L in their groups for the service of God 10387
6:20 The priests and L had purified themselves 4291
6:20 The L slaughtered the Passover lamb NIH
7: 7 including priests, L, singers, 4291
7:13 including priests and L, 10387
7:24 tribute or duty on any of the priests, L, 10387
8:15 I found no L there. 1201+4291
8:20 the officials had established to assist the L. 4291
8:29 and the L and the family heads of Israel." 4291
8:30 Then the priests and L received the silver 4291
8:33 and so were the L Jozabad son of Jeshua 4291
9: 1 including the priests and the L, 4291
10: 5 the leading priests and L and all Israel 4291
10:23 Among the L: Jozabad, 4291
Ne 3:17 by the L under Rehum son of Bani. 4291
7: 1 and the singers and the L were appointed. 4291
7:43 The L: the descendants of Jeshua 4291
7:73 The priests, the L, the gatekeepers, 4291
8: 7 The L—Jeshua, Bani, Sherebiah, 4291
8: 9 the L who were instructing the people said 4291
8:11 The L calmed all the people, saying, 4291
8:13 along with the priests and the L, 4291
9: 4 Standing on the stairs were the L— 4291
9: 5 And the L—Jeshua, Kadmiel, 4291
9:38 in writing, and our leaders, our L 4291
10: 9 The L: Jeshua son of Azaniah, 4291
10:28 "The rest of the people—priests, L, 4291
10:34 "We—the priests, the L and the people— 4291
10:37 we will bring a tithe of our crops to the L, 4291
10:37 the L who collect the tithes in all the towns 4291
10:38 to accompany the L when they receive 4291
10:38 the L are to bring a tenth of the tithes up to 4291
10:39 The people of Israel, including the L, 1201+4291
11: 3 L, temple servants and descendants 4291
11:15 From the L: Shemaiah son of Hasshub, 4291
11:16 two of the heads of the L, 4291
11:18 The L in the holy city totaled 284. 4291
11:20 with the priests and L, 4291
11:22 the L in Jerusalem was Uzzi son of Bani, 4291
11:36 of the divisions of the L *of* Judah settled 4291
12: 1 These were the priests and L who returned 4291
12: 8 The L were Jeshua, Binnui, Kadmiel, 4291
12:22 The family heads of the L in the days 4291
12:24 And the leaders of the L were Hashabiah, 4291
12:27 the L were sought out from 4291
12:30 L had purified themselves ceremonially, 4291
12:44 by the Law for the priests and the L, 4291
12:44 with the ministering priests and L. 4291
12:47 also set aside the portion for the other L, 4291
12:47 and the L set aside the portion for 4291
13: 5 new wine and oil prescribed for the L, 4291
13:10 that the portions assigned to the L had 4291
13:10 and that all the L and singers responsible 4291
13:22 the L to purify themselves and go 4291
13:29 of the priesthood and of the L. 4291
13:30 the priests and the L of everything foreign, 4291
Isa 66:21 of them also to be priests and L," 4291
Jer 33:18 who are L, ever fail to have a man to stand 4291
33:21 with the L who are priests ministering 4291
33:22 the L who minister before me as countless 4291
Eze 40:46 the only L who may draw near to 1201+4290
43:19 who are L, of the family of Zadok, 4291
44:10 " 'The L who went far from me 4291
44:15 who are L and descendants of Zadok 4291
45: 5 cubits wide will belong to the L, 4291
48:11 the L did when the Israelites went astray. 4291
48:12 bordering the territory of the L. 4291
48:13 the L will have an allotment 25,000 4291
48:22 So the property of the L and the property 4291
Mal 3: 3 the L and refine them like gold and 1201+4290
Jn 1:19 the Jews of Jerusalem sent priests and L *3324*

LEVITICAL (3) [LEVI]

Lev 25:32 to redeem their houses in the L towns, 4291

1Ch 15:12 "You are the heads of the **L** families; 4291
Heb 7:11 through the **L** priesthood (for on the basis *3325*

LEVY (2)

2Ki 23:33 on Judah a **l** of a hundred talents of silver 6741
2Ch 36: 3 **imposed** *on* Judah a **l** of a hundred talents 6740

LEWD (4) [LEWDNESS]

Jdg 20: 6 **l** and disgraceful **act** in Israel. 2365
Eze 16:27 who were shocked by your **l** conduct. 2365
22: 9 the mountain shrines and commit **l acts.** 2365
23:44 so they slept with those **l** women, 2365

LEWDNESS (11) [LEWD]

Eze 16:43 Did you not add **l** to all your other 2365
16:58 bear the **consequences of** your **l** 2365
23:21 So you longed for the **l** *of* your youth, 2365
23:27 the **l** and prostitution you began in Egypt. 2365
23:29 Your **l** and promiscuity 2365
23:35 bear the **consequences of** your **l** 2365
23:48 "So I will put an end to **l** in the land, 2365
23:49 You will suffer the **penalty for** your **l** 2365
24:13 " 'Now your impurity is **l.** 2365
Hos 2:10 So now I will expose her **l** before the eyes 5578
Mk 7:22 **l,** envy, slander, arrogance and folly. *816*

LIABLE (2)

Jos 6:18 of Israel **l to** destruction and bring trouble 4200
7:12 and run because they have been made **l to** 4200

LIAR (14) [LIE]

Dt 19:18 and if the witness proves to be a **l,** 9214
Job 34: 6 Although I am right, *I am* **considered a l;** 3941
Pr 17: 4 a **l** pays attention to a malicious tongue. 9214
19:22 better to be poor than a **l.** 408+3942
30: 6 or he will rebuke you and **prove** *you* **a l.** 3941
Mic 2:11 If a **l** and deceiver comes and says, 3941+8120
Jn 8:44 for he is a **l** and the father of lies. *6026*
8:55 If I said I did not, I would be a **l** like you, *6026*
Ro 3: 4 Let God be true, and every man a **l.** *6026*
1Jn 1:10 make him out to be a **l** and his word *6026*
2: 4 but does not do what he commands is a **l,** *6026*
2:22 Who is the **l?** It is the man who denies *6026*
4:20 yet hates his brother, he is a **l.** *6026*
5:10 God has made him out to be a **l,** *6026*

LIARS (9) [LIE]

Ps 63:11 while the mouths of **l** will be silenced. 1819+9214
116:11 And in my dismay I said, "All men *are* **l.**" 3941
Isa 57: 4 the offspring of **l?** 9214
Mic 6:12 her people *are* **l** and their tongues 1819+9214
1Ti 1:10 *for* slave traders and **l** and perjurers— *6026*
4: 2 Such teachings come through hypocritical **l,** *6016*
Tit 1:12 "Cretans are always **l,** evil brutes, *6026*
Rev 3: 9 to be Jews though *they* are not, but *are* **l**— *6017*
21: 8 the idolaters and all **l**— *6014*

LIBATIONS (1)

Ps 16: 4 I will not pour out their **l** of blood or take 5821

LIBERAL (1) [LIBERALITY, LIBERALLY]

2Co 8:20 of the way we administer this **l** gift. *103*

LIBERALITY (2) [LIBERAL]

Est 1: 7 in keeping with the king's **l.** 3338
2:18 and distributed gifts with royal **l.** 3338

LIBERALLY (1) [LIBERAL]

Dt 15:14 **Supply** him **l** from your flock, 6735+6735

LIBERATED (1) [LIBERTY]

Ro 8:21 that the creation itself *will be* **l** *1802*

LIBERTINES (KJV) See FREEDMEN

LIBERTY (1) [LIBERATED]

Lev 25:10 Consecrate the fiftieth year and proclaim **l** 2002

LIBNAH (17) [LIBNITE, LIBNITES]

Nu 33:20 They left Rimmon Perez and camped at **L.** 4243
33:21 They left **L** and camped at Rissah. 4243
Jos 10:29 with him moved on from Makkedah to **L** 4243
10:31 and all Israel with him moved on from **L** 4243
10:32 just as he had done to **L.** 4243
10:39 to Debir and its king as they had done to **L** 4243
12:15 the king of **L** one the king of Adullam one 4243
15:42 **L,** Ether, Ashan, 4243
21:13 of refuge for one accused of murder), **L,** 4243
2Ki 8:22 **L** revolted at the same time. 4243
19: 8 and found the king fighting against **L.** 4243
23:31 daughter of Jeremiah; she was from **L.** 4243
24:18 daughter of Jeremiah; she was from **L.** 4243
1Ch 6:57 and **L,** Jattir, Eshtemoa, 4243
2Ch 21:10 **L** revolted at the same time, 4243
Isa 37: 8 and found the king fighting against **L.** 4243
Jer 52: 1 daughter of Jeremiah; she was from **L.** 4243

LIBNATH See SHIHOR LIBNATH

LIBNI (5)

Ex 6:17 by clans, were **L** and Shimei. 4249
Nu 3:18 of the Gershonite clans: **L** and Shimei. 4249
1Ch 6:17 of Gershon: **L** and Shimei. 4249
6:20 **L** his son, Jehath his son, Zimmah his son, 4249
6:29 Mahli, **L** his son, Shimei his son, 4249

LIBNITE (1) [LIBNAH]

Nu 26:58 These also were Levite clans: the **L** clan, 4250

LIBNITES (1) [LIBNAH]

Nu 3:21 To Gershon belonged the clans of the **L** 4250

LIBYA (3) [LIBYANS]

Eze 30: 5 **L** and the people of the covenant 4275
Na 3: 9 Put and **L** were among her allies. 4275
Ac 2:10 Egypt and the parts *of* **L** near Cyrene; *3340*

LIBYANS (4) [LIBYA]

2Ch 12: 3 and the innumerable troops of **L,** 4275
16: 8 and **L** a mighty army with great numbers 4275
Isa 66:19 to the **L** and Lydians (famous as archers), 4275
Da 11:43 with the **L** and Nubians in submission. 4275

LICE (KJV) See GNAT

LICENSE (1)

Jude 1: 4 grace of our God into a **l for immorality** *816*

LICK (6) [LICKED, LICKS]

Nu 22: 4 "This horde *is* going to **l up** everything 4308
1Ki 21:19 dogs *will* **l up** your blood— 4379
Ps 72: 9 before him and his enemies *will* **l** 4308
Isa 5:24 of fire **l up** straw and as dry grass sinks 430
49:23 *they will* **l** the dust at your feet. 4308
Mic 7:17 *They will* **l** dust like a snake, 4308

LICKED (4) [LICK]

1Ki 18:38 and also **l up** the water in the trench. 4308
21:19 the place where dogs **l up** Naboth's blood, 4379
22:38 and the dogs **l up** his blood, 4379
Lk 16:21 Even the dogs came and **l** his sores. *2143*

LICKS (1) [LICK]

Nu 22: 4 as an ox **l up** the grass of the field." 4308

LID (2)

Nu 19:15 without a **l** fastened on it will be unclean. 7544
2Ki 12: 9 a chest and bored a hole in its **l.** 1946

LIE (140) [LIAR, LIARS, LIED, LIES, LYING]

Ge 19:31 there is no man around here to **l with** us 995+6584
19:32 to drink wine and then **l with** him 6640+8886
19:34 and you go in and **l with** him 6640+8886
29:21 and *I want to* **l with** her." 448+995
38: 8 "**L with** your brother's wife 448+995
Ex 23:11 the seventh year *let* the land **l unplowed** 9023
Lev 18:22 " '*Do* not **l with** a man as one lies with a woman; 907+8886
19:11 " '*Do* not **l.** 3950
26: 6 and *you will* **l down** and no one will 8886
26:33 and your cities *will* **l** in ruins. 2118
Nu 21:15 the ravines that lead to the site of Ar and **l** 9128
23:19 God is not a man, that *he should* **l,** 3941
24: 9 Like a lion they crouch and **l down,** 8886
Dt 6: 7 when you **l down** and when you get up. 8886
11:19 when you **l down** and when you get up. 8886
25: 2 the judge *shall* **make** him **l down** 5877
33:13 and with the deep waters *that* **l** below; 8069
Jdg 9:32 and your men should come and **l in wait** 741
Ru 3: 4 Then go and uncover his feet and **l down.** 8886
3: 7 to **l down** at the far end of the grain pile. 8886
3:13 **L** here until morning." 8886
1Sa 3: 5 go back and **l down."** 8886
3: 6 go back and **l down."** 8886
3: 9 So Eli told Samuel, "Go and **l down,** 8886
15:29 He who is the Glory of Israel *does* not **l** 9213
22: 8 to **l in wait** for me, 741
2Sa 8: 2 *He* **made** them **l down** on the ground 8886
11:11 my house to eat and drink and **l with** 6640+8886
12:11 and *he will* **l with** your wives 6640+8886
16:21 Ahithophel answered, "**L with** 448+995
20: 3 but *did* not **l with** them. 448+995
23: 7 they are burned up where they **l."** 8699
1Ki 1: 2 *She can* **l** beside him so that our lord 8886
Job 6:28 *Would I* **l** to your face? 3941
7: 4 When *I* **l down** I think, 8886
7:21 For *I will* soon **l down** in the dust; 8886
11:19 *You will* **l down,** 8069
20:11 *will* **l** with him in the dust. 8886
21:26 Side by side *they* **l** in the dust, 8886
29:19 dew *will* **l all night** on my branches. 4328
38:40 when they crouch in their dens or **l** in wait 3782
Ps 3: 5 **I l down** and sleep; 8886
4: 8 *I will* **l down** and sleep in peace, 8886
23: 2 *He* **makes** me **l down** in green pastures, 8069
31:17 the wicked be put to shame and *l* **silent** in AIT
36:12 See how the evildoers **l fallen—** 5877
37:32 The wicked **l in wait** for the righteous, 7595
38: 9 All my longings **l** open before you, NIH
57: 4 *I* **l** among ravenous beasts— 8886
59: 3 See how *they* **l in wait** for me! 741
62: 9 the highborn are but a **l;** 3942
76: 5 Valiant men *l* **plundered,** AIT
76: 6 both horse and chariot **l still.** 8101
88: 5 like the slain *who* **l** *in* the grave, 8905
89:35 and *I will* not **l** to David— 3941
102: 7 *I* **l awake;** I have become like a 9193
104:22 they return and **l down** in their dens. 8069
Pr 1:11 *let's* **l in wait** for someone's blood, 741
1:18 These men **l in wait** for their own blood; 741
3:24 when *you* **l down,** you will not be afraid; 8886
3:24 *you* **l down,** your sleep will be sweet. 8886
6: 9 How long *will you* **l** there, 8886
12: 6 words of the wicked **l in wait** *for* blood, 741
15:11 Death and Destruction **l** open before NIH
22: 5 In the paths of the wicked **l** thorns NIH
24:15 *Do* not **l in wait** like an outlaw against 741
Ecc 4:11 two **l down** *together,* they will keep warm. 8886
11: 3 in the place where it falls, there *will it* **l.** 2093
Isa 6:11 the cities **l ruined** and without inhabitant, 8615
11: 6 the leopard *will* **l down** with the goat, 8069
11: 7 their young *will* **l down** together, 8069
13:21 But desert creatures *will* **l** there, 8069
14:18 the kings of the nations **l in state,** 928+3883+8886
14:30 and the needy *will* **l down** in safety. 8069
17: 2 *which will* **l down,** with no one to 8069
21: 9 All the images of its gods *l* **shattered** on AIT
27:10 there the calves graze, there *they* **l down;** 8069
28:15 for we have made a **l** our refuge 3942
28:17 hail will sweep away your refuge, the **l,** 3942
34:10 to generation *it will* **l desolate;** AIT
44:20 "Is not this thing in my right hand a **l?"** 9214
50:11 *You will* **l down** in torment. 8886
51:20 *they* **l** at the head of every street, 8886
56:10 *they* **l around** and dream, 8886
57: 2 they find rest as they **l in death.** 5435
Jer 3:25 *Let us* **l down** in our shame, 8886
4: 7 Your towns *will* **l in ruins** 5898
5: 6 a leopard *will* **l in wait** near their towns 9193
5:26 "Among my people are wicked men *who* **l in wait** 8800
9: 5 They have taught their tongues *to* **l;** 1819+9214
9:22 " 'The dead bodies of men *will* **l** 5877
12: 4 How long *will* the land *l* **parched** and AIT
23:14 They commit adultery and live a **l.** 9214
29:31 and has led you to believe a **l,** 9214
44: 2 Today they *l* **deserted** and in ruins AIT
46:19 and **l in ruins** without inhabitant. 5898
51:47 and her slain *will* all **l fallen** 5877
La 2:21 Young and old **l** *together* in the dust of 8886
4: 5 Those nurtured in purple now **l** on ash heaps 2485
Eze 4: 4 "Then **l** on your left side and put the sin of 8886
4: 4 for the number of days *you* **l** on your side. 8886
4: 6 you have finished this, **l down** again, 8886
4: 9 You are to eat it during the 390 days you **l** 8886
6:13 when their people **l** slain among 2118
13: 6 and their divinations a **l.** 3942
18: 6 not defile his neighbor's wife or **l with** 448+7928
29:12 and her cities *will* **l** desolate forty years 2118
30: 7 their cities *will* **l** among ruined cities. 2118
31:18 *you will* **l** among the uncircumcised, 8886
32:21 down and *they* **l** *with* the uncircumcised, 8886
32:27 *Do they* not **l** with the other uncircumcised 8886
32:28 and *will* **l** among the uncircumcised, 8886
32:29 They **l** with the uncircumcised, 8886
32:30 *They* **l** uncircumcised with those killed by 8886
34:14 There *they will* **l down** 8069
34:15 and **have them l down,** 8069
48:22 of the city *will* **l** in the center of the area 2118
48:22 The area belonging to the prince *will* **l** 2118
Da 11:27 at the same table and **l** *to each other,* 1819+3942
Hos 2:18 so that all *may* **l down** in safety. 8886
6: 9 As marauders **l in ambush** *for* a man, 2675
Am 2: 8 *They* **l down** beside every altar 5742
6: 4 *You* **l** on beds inlaid with ivory and lounge 8886
Mic 7: 2 All men **l** in wait to shed blood; 741
Na 3:18 your nobles **l down to rest.** 8905
Zep 2: 7 In the evening *they will* **l down** in 8069
2:14 Flocks and herds *will* **l down** there, 8069
3:13 They will eat and **l down** 8069
Zec 10: 2 diviners see visions that **l;** 9214
Jn 5: 3 of disabled people *used to* **l**— *2879*
Ro 1:25 They exchanged the truth of God for a **l,** *6022*
Gal 1:20 that what I am writing you *is* no **l.** *6017*
Col 3: 9 *Do* not **l** to each other, *6017*
2Th 2:11 so that they will believe the **l** *6022*
Tit 1: 2 which God, who *does* **not l,** *950*
Heb 6:18 in which it is impossible for God *to* **l,** *6017*
1Jn 1: 6 *we* **l** and do not live by the truth. *6017*
2:21 and because no **l** comes from the truth. *6022*
Rev 11: 8 Their bodies will **l** in the street of *NIG*
14: 5 No **l** was found in their mouths; *6022*

LIED (6) [LIE]

Ge 18:15 Sarah was afraid, so *she* **l** and said, 3950
Jos 7:11 they have stolen, *they have* **l,** 3950
Jdg 16:10 made a fool of me; *you* **l** to me. 1819+3942
Jer 5:12 *They have* **l** about the LORD; 3950
Ac 5: 3 heart *that* you *have* **l to** the Holy Spirit *6017*
5: 4 *You have* not **l** to men but to God." *6017*

LIEN (KJV) See SLEEP, SLEPT, RAVISHED

LIES (106) [LIE]

Ge 21:17 the boy crying as he **l** there. NIH
49: 9 Like a lion he crouches and **l down,** 8069
49:25 blessings of the deep *that* **l** below, 8069
Ex 5: 9 and pay no attention to **l.**" 1821+9214
Lev 6: 3 or if he finds lost property and **l** about it, 3950
15: 4 " 'Any bed the man with a discharge **l** 8886
15:18 When a man **l with** a woman and 907+8886
15:20 " 'Anything *she* **l** on during her period 8886
15:24 " 'If a man **l with** her and her 907+8886+8886
15:24 any bed *he* **l** on will be unclean. 8886
15:26 Any bed *she* **l** on while her discharge 8886
15:33 and for a man who **l with** a woman 6640+8886
18:22 not lie with a man as one **l with** a woman; 5435
20:13 'If a man **l with** a man as one lies with 907+8886
20:13 'If a man lies with a man as one **l with** 5435
20:18 'If a man **l with** a woman during her 907+8886
26:34 the time that *it* **l desolate** and you are in 9037
26:35 All the time *that it* **l desolate,** 9037
26:43 while *it* **l desolate** without them. 9037
Nu 14:33 until the last of your bodies **l** in the desert. NIH
Dt 19:11 if a man hates his neighbor and **l in wait** 741
Ru 3: 4 When he **l down,** note the place where 8886
1Sa 14:39 even if it **l** with my son Jonathan, 3780
22:13 against me and **l in wait** for me, 741
2Sa 1:19 O Israel, **l** slain on your heights. NIH
1:25 Jonathan **l** slain on your heights. NIH
Ne 2: 3 where my fathers are buried **l** in ruins, NIH
2:17 Jerusalem **l** in ruins, NIH
Job 13: 4 You, however, smear me with **l;** 9214
14:12 so man **l down** and does not rise; 8886
18:10 a trap **l** in his path. NIH
19:28 since the root of the trouble **l** in him,' 5162
20:26 total darkness **l in wait** for his treasures. 3243
26: 6 Destruction **l** uncovered. NIH
27:19 *He* **l down** wealthy, but will do so no more; 8886
37:17 the land **l hushed** under the south wind, 9200
40:21 Under the lotus plants *he* **l,** 8886
Ps 5: 6 You destroy those who tell **l;** 3942
10: 7 His mouth is full of curses and **l** 5327
10: 8 *He* **l** in wait near the villages; 3782
10: 9 *He* **l in wait** like a lion in cover; 741
10: 9 *he* **l in wait** to catch the helpless; 741
12: 2 Everyone **l** to his neighbor; 1819+8736
34:13 from evil and your lips from speaking **l.** 5327
41: 8 up from the place where *he* **l.**" 8886
55:11 threats and **l** never leave its streets. 5327
58: 3 the womb they are wayward and speak **l.** 3942
59:12 For the curses and **l** they utter, 3951
62: 4 they take delight in **l.** 3942
88: 7 Your wrath **l heavily** upon me; 6164
119:69 the arrogant have smeared me with **l,** 9214
144: 8 whose mouths are full of **l,** 8736
144:11 of foreigners whose mouths are full of **l,** 8736
Pr 6:19 a false witness who pours out **l** and 3942
12:17 but a false witness tells **l.** 5327
14: 5 but a false witness pours out **l.** 3942
19: 5 and he who pours out **l** will not go free. 3942
19: 9 and he who pours out **l** will perish. 3942
23:28 Like a bandit she **l in wait,** 741
29:12 If a ruler listens to **l,** 1821+9214
30: 8 Keep falsehood and **l** far from me; 1821+3942
Isa 9:15 the prophets who teach **l** are the tail. 9214
24:10 The ruined city *l* **desolate;** AIT
32: 7 to destroy the poor with **l,** 609+9214
59: 3 Your lips have spoken **l,** 9214
59: 4 on empty arguments and speak **l;** 8736
59:13 uttering **l** our hearts have conceived. 1821+9214
64:11 and all that we treasured **l** in ruins. 2118
Jer 4:20 the whole land **l in ruins.** 8720
5:31 The prophets prophesy **l,** 9214
9: 3 ready their tongue like a bow, to shoot **l;** 9214
14:14 prophets are prophesying **l** in my name. 9214
20: 6 to whom you have prophesied **l.**' " 9214
23:10 because of the curse the land *l* **parched** and AIT
23:25 the prophets say who prophesy **l** 9214
23:32 lead my people astray with their reckless **l,** 9214
27:10 They prophesy **l** to you 9214
27:14 for they are prophesying **l** to you. 9214
27:15 'They are prophesying **l** in my name. 9214
27:16 They are prophesying **l** to you. 9214
28:15 persuaded this nation to trust in **l.** 9214
29: 9 They are prophesying **l** to you 9214
29:21 who are prophesying **l** to you in my name: 9214
29:23 and in my name have spoken **l,** 9214
40: 4 Look, the whole country **l** before you; NIH
La 1: 1 deserted **l** the city, once so full of people! 3782
5:18 which **l desolate,** with jackals prowling 9037
Eze 13:19 By lying to my people, who listen to **l,** 3942
13:22 disheartened the righteous with your **l,** 9214
26: 2 now that *she* **l in ruins** I will prosper,' 2990
32:23 of the pit and her army **l** around her grave. 2118
47:16 and Sibraim (which **l** on the border NIH
Da 2:22 he knows what **l** in darkness, NIH
Hos 7: 3 the princes with their **l.** 3951
7:13 I long to redeem them but they speak **l** 3942
11:12 Ephraim has surrounded me with **l,** 3951
12: 1 the east wind all day and multiplies **l** 3942
Mic 7: 5 with *her who* **l** *in* your embrace be careful 8886
Na 3: 1 Woe to the city of blood, full of **l,** 3951
Hab 2:18 Or an image that teaches **l?** 9214
Zep 3:13 they will speak no **l,** 3942
Zec 13: 3 because you have told **l** in the LORD's name 9214
Mt 8: 6 "my servant **l** at home paralyzed and *965*
Jn 8:44 When *he* **l,** he speaks his native language, *3281+3836+6022*
8:44 for he is a liar and the father *of* **l.** *899S*
Rev 10: 8 "Go, take the scroll that *l* **open** in the hand *AIT*

LIEUTENANTS (KJV) See SATRAP

LIFE (589) [LIVE]

Ge 1:30 everything that has the breath of **l** in it— 2645
2: 7 into his nostrils the breath of **l,** 2644
2: 9 of **l** and the tree of the knowledge of good 2644
3:14 you will eat dust all the days of your **l.** 2644
3:17 you will eat of it all the days of your **l.** 2644
3:22 and take also from the tree of **l** and eat, 2644
3:24 and forth to guard the way to the tree of **l.** 2644
6:17 to destroy all **l** under the heavens, 1414
6:17 every creature that has the breath of **l** in it. 2644
7:11 In the six hundredth year of Noah's **l,** 2644
7:15 of all creatures that have the breath of **l** 2644
7:22 that had the breath of **l** in its nostrils died. 2644
9: 5 an accounting for the **l** of his fellow man. 5883
9:11 Never again will all **l** be cut off by 1414
9:15 the waters become a flood to destroy all **l.** 1414
9:17 between me and all **l** on the earth." 1414
12:13 be treated well for your sake and my **l** will 5883
19:19 great kindness to me in sparing my **l.** 5883
19:20 Then my **l** will be spared." 5883
26: 9 "Because I thought *I* might **lose** *my* **l** 4637
27:46 my **l will not be worth living.**" 2644+4200+4537
32:30 and yet my **l** was spared." 5883
37:21 "Let's not take his **l,**" he said. 5883
42:21 with us for his **l,** but we would not listen; 5883
43: 9 I will bear the blame before you all my **l.** 3427
44:30 whose **l** is closely bound up with 5883
44:30 closely bound up with the boy's **l,** 5883
44:32 blame before you, my father, all my **l!**' 3427
47:28 of his **l** were a hundred and forty-seven. 2644
48:15 God who has been my shepherd **all** my **l** 4946+6388
Ex 21: 6 Then he will be his servant **for l.** 4200+6409
21:23 you are to take **l** for life, 5883
21:23 you are to take life for **l,** 5883
21:30 he may redeem his **l** by paying whatever 5883
23:26 I will give you a full **l span.** 3427+5031
30:12 for his **l** at the time he is counted. 5883
Lev 17:11 For the **l** *of* a creature is in the blood, 5883
17:11 that makes atonement for one's **l.** 5883
17:14 the **l** *of* every creature is its blood. 5883
17:14 the **l** *of* every creature is its blood; 5883
19:16 *Do* not **do anything that endangers** your neighbor's **l.** 1947+6584+6641
24:17 If anyone **takes** the **l** *of* a human being 5782+5883
24:18 *Anyone who* **takes** the **l** of someone's 5782+5883
24:18 animal must make restitution—**l** for life. 5883
24:18 animal must make restitution—life for **l.** 5883
25:46 and can make them slaves for **l,** 6409
26:16 and drain away your **l.** 5883
Nu 35:31 " 'Do not accept a ransom for the **l** *of* 5883
Dt 4:42 into one of these cities and **save** *his* **l.** 2649
6: 2 and so that you *may* **enjoy long l.** 799+3427
12:23 because the blood is the **l,** 5883
12:23 and you must not eat the **l** with the meat. 5883
15:17 and he will become your servant **for l.** 6409
16: 3 the days of your **l** you may remember 2644
17:19 and he is to read it all the days of his . so 2644
19: 4 and flees there *to* **save** *his* **l**— 2649
19: 5 to one of these cities and **save** *his* **l.** 2649
19:21 **l** for life, eye for eye, tooth for tooth, 5883
19:21 life for **l,** eye for eye, tooth for tooth, 5883
22: 7 with you and you may have a long **l.** 3427
28:66 never sure of your **l.** 2644
30:15 I set before you today **l** and prosperity, 2644
30:19 that I have set before you **l** and death, 2644
30:19 Now choose **l,** so that you 2644
30:20 For the LORD is your **l,** 2644
32:39 I put to death and *I* **bring to l,** 2649
32:47 not just idle words for you—they are your **l.** 2644
Jos 1: 5 up against you all the days of your **l.** 2644
4:14 and they revered him all the days of his **l,** 2644
Jdg 5: 7 **Village l** in Israel ceased, 7251
9:17 risked his **l** to rescue you from the hand 5883
12: 3 I took my **l** in my hands and crossed over 5883
13:12 to be the rule for the boy's **l** and work?" NIH
Ru 1:20 the Almighty has made **my l** very bitter. 3276
4:15 He will renew your **l** and sustain you 5883
1Sa 1:11 to the LORD for all the days of his **l,** 2644
1:28 *For* his whole **l** he will be given 889+2118+3427
2:33 descendants will die **in the prime of l.** 408
7:15 as judge over Israel all the days of his **l.** 2644
19: 5 He took his **l** in his hands when he killed 5883
19:11 "If you don't run for your **l** tonight, 5883
20: 1 that he is trying to take my **l?**" 5883
22:23 who is seeking your **l** is seeking mine also. 5883
23:15 that Saul had come out to take his **l.** 5883
24:11 but you are hunting me down to take my **l.** 5883
25: 6 Say to him: **'Long l** to you! 2021+2644+4200
25:29 someone is pursuing you to take your **l,** 5883
25:29 the **l** *of* my master will be bound securely 5883
26:21 you considered my **l** precious today, 5883
26:24 As surely as I valued your **l** today, 5883
26:24 the LORD value my **l** and deliver me 5883
28: 2 make you my bodyguard **for l.**" 2021+3427+3972
28: 9 Why have you set a trap for my **l** to bring 5883
28:21 I took my **l** in my hands 5883
2Sa 1:23 in **l** they were loved and gracious, 2644
4: 8 your enemy, who tried to take your **l.** 5883
14: 7 so that we may put him to death for the **l** 5883
14:14 But God does not take away **l;** 5883
15:21 whether it means **l** or death, 2644
16:11 is trying to take my **l.** 5883
18:13 And if I had put my **l** in jeopardy— 5883
19: 5 who have just saved your **l** and the lives 5883
1Ki 1:12 how you can save your own **l** and the life 5883
1:12 how you can save your own life and the **l** 5883
2:23 if Adonijah does not pay with his **l** 5883
3:11 and not for long **l** or wealth for yourself, 3427
3:14 I will give you a long **l.**" 3427
4:21 and were Solomon's subjects all his **l.** 2644
4:33 He described **plant l,** 6770
11:34 I have made him ruler all the days of his **l** 2644
15: 5 LORD's commands all the days of his **l**— 2644
15:14 to the LORD all his **l.** 3427
17:21 let this boy's **l** return to him!" 5883
17:22 and the boy's **l** returned to him, 5883
19: 2 not make your **l** like that of one of them." 5883
19: 3 Elijah was afraid and ran for his **l.** 5883
19: 4 he said. "Take my **l;** 5883
20:31 Perhaps he will spare your **l.**" 5883
20:39 he is missing, it will be your **l** for his life, 5883
20:39 he is missing, it will be your life for his **l,** 5883
20:42 Therefore it is your **l** for his life, 5883
20:42 Therefore it is your life for his **l,** 5883
2Ki 1:13 "please have respect for my **l** and the lives 5883
1:14 But now have respect for my **l!**" 5883
4:17 Can I kill and **bring back to l?** 2649
8: 1 the woman whose son *he had* **restored to l,** 2649
8: 5 **restored** the dead **to l,** 2649
8: 5 the woman whose son Elisha *had* **brought back to l** came 2649
8: 5 this is her son whom Elisha **restored to l.**" 2649
10:24 it will be your **l** for his life." 5883
10:24 it will be your life for his **l.**" 5883
13:21 the man **came to l** and stood up 2649
18:32 **Choose l** and not death! 2649
20: 6 I will add fifteen years to your **l.** 3427
25:29 of his **l** ate regularly at the king's table. 2644
1Ch 29:28 having **enjoyed long l,** wealth and 3427+8428
2Ch 1:11 and since you have not asked for a long **l** 3427
15:17 committed [to the LORD] all his **l.** 3427
Ezr 9: 9 He has granted us **new l** to rebuild 4695
Ne 4: 2 **bring** the stones **back to l** 2649
6:11 like me go into the temple *to* **save** *his* **l?** 2649
9: 6 You **give l** *to* everything, 2649
Est 4:11 the gold scepter to him and **spare** *his* **l.** 2649
7: 3 grant me my **l**—this is my petition. 5883
7: 7 behind to beg Queen Esther for his **l.** 5883
Job 2: 4 "A man will give all he has for his own **l.** 5883
2: 6 but you must spare his **l.**" 5883
3:20 and **l** to the bitter of soul, 2644
3:23 Why is **l** given to a man whose way NIH
7: 7 O God, that my **l** is but a breath; 2644
7:16 I despise my **l;** I would not live forever. NIH
8:19 Surely its **l** withers away, 2006
9:21 I despise my own **l.** 2644
10: 1 "I loathe my very **l;** 2644
10:12 You gave me **l** and showed me kindness, 2644
11:17 **L** will be brighter than noonday, 2698
12:10 In his hand is the **l** *of* every creature and 5883
13:12 Does not long **l** bring understanding? 3427
13:14 in jeopardy and take my **l** in my hands? 5883
24:22 they have no assurance of **l.** 2644
27: 3 as long as I have **l** within me, 5972
27: 8 when God takes away his **l?** 5883
30:16 "And now my **l** ebbs away; 5883
31:30 to sin by invoking a curse against his **l**— 5883
33: 4 the breath of the Almighty **gives** me **l.** 2649
33:18 his **l** from perishing by the sword. 2652
33:22 and his **l** to the messengers of death. 2652
33:30 that the light of **l** may shine on him. 2644
41: 4 for you to take him as your slave **for l?** 6409
42:12 LORD blessed the **latter part of** Job's **l** 344
Ps 7: 5 let him trample my **l** to the ground 2644
16:11 have made known to me the path of **l;** 2644
17:14 of this world whose reward is in this **l.** 2645
21: 4 He asked you for **l,** 2644
22:20 Deliver my **l** from the sword, 5883
22:20 my **precious l** from the power of the dogs. 3495
23: 6 love will follow me all the days of my **l,** 2644
25:20 Guard my **l** and rescue me; 5883
26: 1 O LORD, for I *have* **led** a blameless **l;** 928+2143
26: 9 my **l** with bloodthirsty men, 2644
26:11 But I **lead** a blameless **l;** 928+2143
27: 1 The LORD is the stronghold of my **l**— 2644
27: 4 of the LORD all the days of my **l,** 2644
31:10 My **l** is consumed by anguish 2644
31:13 against me and plot to take my **l.** 5883
34:12 Whoever of you loves **l** and desires 2644
35: 4 May those who seek my **l** be disgraced 5883
35:17 Rescue my **l** from their ravages, 5883
35:17 my **precious l** from these lions. 3495
36: 9 For with you is the fountain of **l;** 2644
38:12 Those who seek my **l** set their traps, 5883
39: 4 let me know how fleeting is **my l.** 638
39: 5 Each man's **l** is but a breath. 5893
40:14 May all who seek to take my **l** be put 5883
41: 2 LORD will protect him and **preserve** his **l;** 2649
42: 8 a prayer to the God of my **l.** 2644
49: 7 the **l** of another or give to God a ransom NIH
49: 8 a **l** is costly, no payment is ever enough— 5883
49:15 But God will redeem my **l** from the grave; 5883
49:19 who will never see the light [of **l**]. NIH

Ps 54: 3 ruthless men seek my **l**— 5883
56: 6 they watch my steps, eager to take my **l.** 5883
56:13 I may walk before God in the light of **l.** 2644
61: 6 Increase the **days of** the king's **l,** 3427
63: 3 Because your love is better than **l,** 2644
63: 9 They who seek my **l** will be destroyed; 5883
64: 1 protect my **l** from the threat of the enemy. 2644
69:28 May they be blotted out of the book of **l** 2644
70: 2 May those who seek my **l** be put to shame 5883
71:20 *you will* **restore** my **l** again; 2649
74:19 over the **l** *of* your dove to wild beasts; 5883
86: 2 Guard my **l,** for I am devoted to you. 5883
86:14 a band of ruthless men seeks my **l**— 5883
88: 3 of trouble and my **l** draws near the grave. 2644
89:47 Remember how **fleeting** is my **l.** 2698
91:16 With long **l** will I satisfy him 3427
101: 2 I will be careful to lead a blameless **l**— 2006
102:23 the **course of** my **l** he broke my strength; 2006
103: 4 who redeems your **l** from the pit 2644
104:33 I will sing to the LORD all my **l;** 2644
109:31 to save his **l** from those who condemn him. 5883
119:25 **preserve** my **l** according to your word. 2649
119:37 **preserve** my **l** according to your word. 2649
119:40 **Preserve** my **l** in your righteousness. 2649
119:50 Your promise **preserves** my **l.** 2649
119:88 **Preserve** my **l** according to your love, 2649
119:93 for by them *you have* **preserved** my **l.** 2649
119:107 I have suffered much; **preserve** my **l,** 2649
119:109 I constantly take my **l** in my hands, 5883
119:149 **preserve** my **l,** O LORD, 2649
119:154 **preserve** my **l** according to your promise. 2649
119:156 **preserve** my **l** according to your laws. 2649
119:159 **preserve** my **l,** O LORD, 2649
121: 7 he will watch over your **l;** 5883
128: 5 from Zion all the days of your **l;** 2644
133: 3 For there the LORD bestows his blessing,
even **l** forevermore. 2644
138: 7 *you* **preserve** my **l;** 2649
142: 4 I have no refuge; no one cares for my **l.** 5883
143:11 O LORD, **preserve** my **l;** 2649
146: 2 I will praise the LORD all my **l;** 2644
Pr 1: 3 and **prudent** *l,* doing what is right and just AIT
2:19 to her return or attain the paths of **l.** 2644
3: 2 for they will prolong your **l** many years 2644
3:16 Long **l** is in her right hand; 3427
3:18 a tree of **l** to those who embrace her; 2644
3:22 they will be **l** for you, 2644
4:10 and the years of your **l** will be many. 2644
4:13 guard it well, for it is your **l.** 2644
4:22 for they are **l** to those who find them 2644
4:23 for it is the wellspring of **l.** 2644
5: 6 She gives no thought to the way of **l;** 2644
5:11 At the **end of** your **l** you will groan, 344
6:23 corrections of discipline are the way to **l,** 2644
6:26 and the adulteress preys upon your very **l.** 5883
7:23 little knowing it will cost him his **l.** 5883
8:35 For whoever finds me finds **l** 2644
9:11 and years will be added to your **l.** 2644
10:11 mouth of the righteous is a fountain of **l,** 2644
10:16 The wages of the righteous bring them **l,** 2644
10:17 who heeds discipline shows the way to **l,** 2644
10:27 The fear of the LORD adds length to **l,** 3427
11:19 The truly righteous man attains **l,** 2644
11:30 The fruit of the righteous is a tree of **l,** 2644
12:28 In the way of righteousness there is **l;** 2644
13: 3 He who guards his lips guards his **l,** 5883
13: 8 A man's riches may ransom his **l,** 5883
13:12 but a longing fulfilled is a tree of **l.** 2644
13:14 The teaching of the wise is a fountain of **l,** 2644
14:27 The fear of the LORD is a fountain of **l,** 2644
14:30 A heart at peace gives **l** *to* the body, 2644
15: 4 tongue that brings healing is a tree of **l,** 2644
15:24 of **l** leads upward for the wise to keep him 2644
16:15 When a king's face brightens, it means **l;** 2644
16:17 he who guards his way guards his **l.** 5883
16:22 a fountain of **l** to those who have it, 2644
16:31 it is attained by a righteous **l.** 2006
18:21 The tongue has the power of **l** and death, 2644
19: 3 A man's own folly ruins his **l,** 2006
19:16 He who obeys instructions guards his **l,** 5883
19:23 The fear of the LORD leads to **l:** 2644
20: 2 he who angers him forfeits his **l.** 5883
20: 7 The righteous man **leads a** blameless **l;** 2143
21:21 and love finds **l,** prosperity and honor. 2644
22: 4 the LORD bring wealth and honor and **l.** 2644
23:22 Listen to your father, who **gave** you **l,** 3528
24:12 Does not he who guards your **l** know it? 5883
28:16 he who hates ill-gotten gain *will* **enjoy a long l.** 799+3427
31:12 not harm, all the days of her **l.** 2644
Ecc 2:17 So I hated **l,** because the work that is done 2644
5:18 the few days of **l** God has given him— 2644
5:20 He seldom reflects on the days of his **l,** 2644
6:12 who knows what is good for a man in **l,** 2644
7:12 wisdom **preserves** *the* **l** *of* its possessor. 2649
7:15 In this meaningless **l** *of* mine I have seen 3427
8:15 So I commend the enjoyment of **l,** NIH
8:15 the days of the **l** God has given him under 2644
9: 9 Enjoy **l** with your wife, whom you love, 2644
9: 9 all the days of this meaningless **l** 2644
9: 9 in **l** and in your toilsome labor under 2644
10:19 and wine makes **l** merry, 2644
Isa 23:15 seventy years, the **span of** a king's **l.** 3427
38: 5 I will add fifteen years to your **l.** 3427
38:10 "In the prime of my **l** must I go through 3427
38:12 Like a weaver I have rolled up my **l,** 2644
38:16 and my spirit finds **l** in them too. 2644
Isa 42: 5 and **l** to those who walk on it: 8120
43: 4 and people in exchange for your **l.** 5883
53:10 the LORD makes his **l** a guilt offering, 5883
53:11 he will see the light [of **l**] and be satisfied; NIH
53:12 because he poured out his **l** unto death, 5883
Jer 4:30 Your lovers despise you; they seek your **l.** 5883
4:31 my **l** is given over to murderers." 5883
8: 3 of this evil nation will prefer death to **l,** 2644
10:23 O LORD, that a man's **l** is not his own; 2006
11:21 of Anathoth who are seeking your **l** 5883
17:11 When his **l** is half gone, 3427
20:13 the **l** *of* the needy from the hands of 5883
21: 8 See, I am setting before you the way of **l** 2644
21: 9 he will escape with his **l.** 5883
22:25 to those who want your **l,** those you fear— 5883
38: 2 He will escape with his **l;** he will live.' 5883
38:16 over to those who are seeking your **l.**' 5883
38:17 your **l** will be spared and this city will not 5883
38:20 and your **l** will be spared. 5883
39:18 by the sword but will escape with your **l,** 5883
40:14 of Nethaniah to take your **l?**" 5883
40:15 Why should he take your **l** and cause all 5883
44:30 over to his enemies who seek his **l,** 5883
44:30 the enemy who was seeking his **l.**' " 5883
45: 5 I will let you escape with your **l.**' " 5883
52:33 rest of his **l** ate regularly at the king's table. 2644
La 3:53 to end my **l** in a pit and threw stones 2644
3:58 you redeemed my **l.** 2644
4:20 The LORD's anointed, our very **l breath** 678+8120
Eze 3:18 from his evil ways in order to **save** his **l,** 2649
7:13 not one of them will preserve his **l.** 2652
18:27 he will save his **l.** 5883
32:10 of them will tremble every moment for his **l.** 5883
33: 4 and the sword comes and **takes** his **l,** 4374
33: 6 the sword comes and takes the **l** of one 5883
33:15 follows the decrees that give **l,** 2644
37: 5 and *you will* **come to l.** 2649
37: 6 and *you will* **come to l.** 2649
37:10 *they* **came to l** and stood up 2649
Da 5:23 the God who holds in his hand your **l** 10494
12: 2 will awake: some to everlasting **l,** 2644
Am 2:14 and the warrior will not save his **l.** 5883
2:15 and the horseman will not save his **l.** 5883
Jnh 1:14 not let us die for taking this man's **l.** 5883
2: 6 But you brought my **l** up from the pit, 2644
2: 7 "When my **l** was ebbing away, 5883
4: 3 Now, O LORD, take away my **l,** 5883
Hab 2:10 your own house and forfeiting your **l.** 5883
2:19 to him who says to wood, **'Come to l!'** 7810
Mal 2: 5 a covenant of **l** and peace, 2644
Mt 2:20 to take the child's **l** are dead." *6034*
6:25 I tell you, do not worry about your **l,** *6034*
6:25 Is not **l** more important than food, *6034*
6:27 by worrying can add a single hour to his **l?** *2461*
7:14 and narrow the road that leads to **l,** *2437*
10:39 Whoever finds his **l** will lose it, *6034*
10:39 and whoever loses his **l** for my sake *6034*
13:22 the worries *of* this **l** and the deceitfulness *172*
16:21 and on the third day *be* **raised to l.** *1586*
16:25 whoever wants to save his **l** will lose it, *6034*
16:25 but whoever loses his **l** for me will find it. *6034*
17:23 on the third day *he will be* **raised to l.**" *1586*
18: 8 for you to enter **l** maimed or crippled than *2437*
18: 9 for you to enter **l** with one eye than *2437*
19:16 good thing must I do to get eternal **l?**" *2437*
19:17 If you want to enter **l,** *2437*
19:29 as much and will inherit eternal **l.** *2437*
20:19 On the third day *he will be* **raised to l!**" *1586*
20:28 and to give his **l** as a ransom for many." *6034*
25:46 but the righteous to eternal **l.**" *2437*
27:52 holy people who had died *were* **raised to l.** *1586*
Mk 3: 4 to save **l** or to kill?" *6034*
4:19 but the worries *of* this **l,** *1050*
8:35 whoever wants to save his **l** will lose it, *6034*
8:35 but whoever loses his **l** for me and for *6034*
9:43 It is better for you to enter **l** maimed than *2437*
9:45 It is better for you to enter **l** crippled than *2437*
10:17 "what must I do to inherit eternal **l?**" *2437*
10:30 and in the age to come, eternal **l.** *2437*
10:45 and to give his **l** as a ransom for many." *6034*
Lk 6: 9 to save **l** or to destroy it?" *6034*
7:37 When a woman who had lived a **sinful l** *283*
9: 8 of long ago *had* **come back to l.** *482*
9:19 of long ago *has* **come back to l.**" *482*
9:22 and on the third day *be* **raised to l.**" *1586*
9:24 whoever wants to save his **l** will lose it, *6034*
9:24 but whoever loses his **l** for me will save it. *6034*
10:25 "what must I do to inherit eternal **l?**" *2437*
12:15 a man's **l** does not consist in the abundance *2437*
12:19 **Take l easy;** eat, drink and be merry." ' *399*
12:20 This very night your **l** will be demanded *6034*
12:22 do not worry about your **l,** *6034*
12:23 **L** is more than food, *6034*
12:25 by worrying can add a single hour to his **l?** *2461*
14:26 yes, even his own **l**— *6034*
17:33 Whoever tries to keep his **l** will lose it, *6034*
17:33 and whoever loses his **l** will preserve it. *NIG*
18:18 what must I do to inherit eternal **l?**" *2437*
18:30 in the age to come, eternal **l.**" *2437*
21:19 By standing firm you will gain **l.** *6034*
21:34 drunkenness and the anxieties *of* **l,** *1053*
Jn 1: 4 In him was **l,** and that life was the light *2437*
1: 4 and that **l** was the light of men. *2437*
3:15 who believes in him may have eternal **l.** *2437*
3:16 in him shall not perish but have eternal **l.** *2437*
3:36 Whoever believes in the Son has eternal **l,** *2437*
3:36 but whoever rejects the Son will not see **l,** *2437*
Jn 4:14 a spring of water welling up to eternal **l.**" *2437*
4:36 now he harvests the crop for eternal **l,** *2437*
5:21 the Father raises the dead and **gives** them **l,** *2443*
5:21 so the Son **gives l** to whom he is pleased *2443*
5:24 believes him who sent me has eternal **l** *2437*
5:24 he has crossed over from death to **l.** *2437*
5:26 For as the Father has **l** in himself, *2437*
5:26 so he has granted the Son to have **l** *2437*
5:39 that by them you possess eternal **l.** *2437*
5:40 yet you refuse to come to me to have **l.** *2437*
6:27 but for food that endures to eternal **l,** *2437*
6:33 from heaven and gives **l** to the world." *2437*
6:35 Then Jesus declared, "I am the bread *of* **l.** *2437*
6:40 and believes in him shall have eternal **l,** *2437*
6:47 he who believes has everlasting **l.** *2437*
6:48 I am the bread *of* **l.** *2437*
6:51 which I will give for the **l** of the world." *2437*
6:53 you have no **l** in you. *2437*
6:54 and drinks my blood has eternal **l,** *2437*
6:63 The Spirit **gives l;** *1639+2443*
6:63 to you are spirit and they are **l.** *2437*
6:68 You have the words *of* eternal **l.** *2437*
7: 1 the Jews there were waiting *to* **take** his **l.** *650*
8:11 "Go now and **leave your l of sin.**" *279+3600*
8:12 but will have the light *of* **l.**" *2437*
9: 3 of God might be displayed in his **l.** *NIG*
10:10 I have come that they may have **l,** *2437*
10:11 The good shepherd lays down his **l** for *6034*
10:15 and I lay down my **l** for the sheep. *6034*
10:17 my Father loves me is that I lay down my **l** *6034*
10:28 I give them eternal **l,** and they shall never *2437*
11:25 "I am the resurrection and the **l.** *2437*
11:53 from that day on they plotted to **take** *his* **l.** *650*
12:25 The man who loves his **l** will lose it, *6034*
12:25 while the man who hates his **l** *6034*
12:25 in this world will keep it for eternal **l.** *2437*
12:50 that his command leads to eternal **l.** *2437*
13:37 I will lay down my **l** for you." *6034*
13:38 "Will you really lay down your **l** for me? *6034*
14: 6 "I am the way and the truth and the **l.** *2437*
15:13 that he lay down his **l** for his friends. *6034*
17: 2 over all people that he might give eternal **l** *2437*
17: 3 this is eternal **l:** that they may know you, *2437*
20:31 by believing you may have **l** in his name. *2437*
Ac 2:28 made known to me the paths *of* **l;** *2437*
2:32 God has **raised** this Jesus **to l,** *482*
3:15 You killed the author *of* **l,** *2437*
5:20 the people the full message *of* this new **l.**" *2437*
8:33 For his **l** was taken from the earth." *2437*
11:18 granted even the Gentiles repentance unto **l.** *2437*
13:46 not consider yourselves worthy *of* eternal **l,** *2437*
13:48 appointed for eternal **l** believed. *2437*
17:25 because he himself gives all men **l** *2437*
20:24 I consider my **l** worth nothing to me, *6034*
26: 4 the beginning of my **l** in my own country, *NIG*
27:43 But the centurion wanted to spare Paul's **l** *NIG*
Ro 2: 7 he will give eternal **l.** *2437*
4:17 the God who **gives l** to the dead *2443*
4:25 and *was* **raised to l** for our justification. *1586*
5:10 shall we be saved through his **l!** *2437*
5:17 the gift of righteousness reign in **l** through *2437*
5:18 *that* **brings l** for all men. *2437*
5:21 through righteousness to bring eternal **l** *2437*
6: 4 we too may live a new **l.** *2437*
6:10 but **the l** he lives, he lives to God. *4005*[S]
6:13 **brought** from death **to l;** *2409*
6:22 and the result is eternal **l.** *2437*
6:23 the gift of God is eternal **l** in Christ Jesus *2437*
7: 9 sin **sprang to l** and I died. *348*
7:10 to bring **l** actually brought death. *2437*
8: 2 of the Spirit *of* **l** set me free from the law *2437*
8: 6 but the mind controlled by the Spirit is **l** *2437*
8:11 also **give l** to your mortal bodies *2443*
8:34 more than that, who *was* **raised to l**— *1586*
8:38 I am convinced that neither death nor **l,** *2437*
11:15 what will their acceptance be but **l** from *2437*
14: 9 and **returned to l** so that he might be *2409*
1Co 3:22 or the world or **l** or death or the present or *2437*
4:17 He will remind you of my **way of l** *3847*
6: 3 How much more the *things* **of this l!** *1053*
7:17 **retain the place in l** that the Lord assigned *4344*
7:28 who marry will face many troubles *in* this **l,** *4922*
15:19 If only for this **l** we have hope in Christ, *2437*
15:36 What you sow *does* not **come to l** *2443*
2Co 1: 8 so that we despaired even *of* **l.** *2409*
2:16 to the other, the fragrance of **l.** *2437*
3: 6 for the letter kills, but the Spirit **gives l.** *2443*
4:10 so that the **l** of Jesus may also be revealed *2437*
4:11 his **l** may be revealed in our mortal body. *2437*
4:12 but **l** is at work in you. *2437*
5: 4 what is mortal may be swallowed up by **l.** *2437*
Gal 1:13 of my previous **way of l** in Judaism, *419*
2:20 **The l l** live in the body, *4005*[S]
3:15 me take an example **from everyday l.** *476+2848*
3:21 a law had been given that could **impart l,** *2443*
6: 8 from the Spirit will reap eternal **l.** *2437*
Eph 4: 1 I urge you *to* **live a l** worthy of *4344*
4:18 and separated *from* the **l** of God because of *2437*
4:22 with regard to your former **way of l,** *419*
5: 2 and **live a l** of love, *4344*
6: 3 *you may* **enjoy long l** on the earth." *1639+3432*
Php 1:20 whether by **l** or by death. *2437*
2:16 as you hold out the word *of* **l**— *2437*
2:30 risking his **l** to make up for the help you *6034*
4: 3 whose names are in the book *of* **l.** *2437*
Col 1:10 *that* you *may* **live a l** worthy of the Lord *4344*
3: 3 your **l** is now hidden with Christ in God. *2437*

Col 3: 4 When Christ, who is your l, appears, 2437
3: 7 in the l you once lived. 4005S
1Th 4: 7 impure, but to live a holy l. 40
4:11 Make it your ambition to lead a quiet l, 2483
4:12 so that your daily l may win the respect 4344
1Ti 1:16 believe on him and receive eternal l. 2437
4: 8 holding promise for both the present l and 2437
4: 8 for both the present life and the l to come. NIG
4:12 in l, in love, in faith and in purity. 419
4:16 Watch your l and doctrine closely. 4932
6:12 of the eternal l to which you were called 2437
6:13 God, who gives l to everything, 2441
6:19 so that they may take hold of the l 2437
6:19 may take hold of the life that is truly l. NIG
2Ti 1: 1 to the promise of l that is in Christ Jesus, 2437
1: 9 who has saved us and called us to a holy l— 3104
1:10 who has destroyed death and has brought l 2437
3:10 know all about my teaching, my way of l, 73
3:12 everyone who wants to live a godly l 2357
Tit 1: 2 knowledge resting on the hope of eternal l, 2437
3: 7 heirs having the hope of eternal l. 2437
Heb 5: 7 During the days of Jesus' l on earth, 4922
7: 3 without beginning of days or end of l, 2437
7:16 of the power of an indestructible l. 2437
11: 5 By faith Enoch was taken from this l, NIG
11:35 received back their dead, raised to l again. 414
13: 7 of their way of l and imitate their faith. 419
Jas 1:12 the crown of l that God has promised 2437
1:20 about the righteous l that God desires. 1466
3: 6 sets the whole course of his l on fire, 1161
3:13 Let him show it by his good l, 419
4:14 What is your l? 2437
1Pe 1:18 the empty way of l handed down to you 419
3: 7 as heirs with you of the gracious gift of l, 2437
3:10 "Whoever would love l and see good days 2437
4: 2 he does not live the rest of his earthly l 5989
2Pe 1: 3 for l and godliness through our knowledge 2437
1Jn 1: 1 concerning the Word of l. 2437
1: 2 The l appeared; we have seen it 2437
1: 2 and we proclaim to you the eternal l, 2437
2:25 And this is what he promised us—even eternal l. 2437
3:14 that we have passed from death to l, 2437
3:15 that no murderer has eternal l in him. 2437
3:16 Jesus Christ laid down his l for us. 6034
5:11 God has given us eternal l, 2437
5:11 and this l is in his Son. 2437
5:12 He who has the Son has l; 2437
5:12 not have the Son of God does not have l. 2437
5:13 you may know that you have eternal l. 2437
5:16 he should pray and God will give him l. 2437
5:20 He is the true God and eternal l. 2437
Jude 1:21 to bring you to eternal l. 2437
Rev 2: 7 the right to eat from the tree of l, 2437
2: 8 who died and came to l again. 2409
2:10 and I will give you the crown of l. 2437
3: 5 never blot out his name from the book of l, 2437
11:11 after the three and a half days a breath of l 2437
13: 8 of l belonging to the Lamb that was slain 2437
17: 8 book of l from the creation of the world will 2437
20: 4 They came to l and reigned with Christ 2409
20: 5 (The rest of the dead did not come to l 2409
20:12 which is the book of l. 2437
20:15 not found written in the book of l, 2437
21: 6 from the spring of the water of l. 2437
21:27 names are written in the Lamb's book of l. 2437
22: 1 the river of the water of l, 2437
22: 2 of the river stood the tree of l, 2437
22:14 the tree of l and may go through the gates 2437
22:17 let him take the free gift of the water of l. 2437
22:19 from him his share in the tree of l and in 2437

LIFE'S (2) [LIVE]
Ps 39: 4 my l end and the number of my days; 3276
Lk 8:14 on their way they are choked by l worries, 1050

LIFE-GIVING (2) [GIVE]
Pr 15:31 to a l rebuke will be at home among 2644
1Co 15:45 the last Adam, a l spirit. 2443

LIFEBLOOD (3) [BLOOD]
Ge 9: 4 not eat meat that has its l still in it. 1947+5883
9: 5 I l will surely demand an accounting. 1947+5883
Jer 2:34 On your clothes men find the l of 1947+5883

LIFEBOAT (3) [BOAT]
Ac 27:16 we were hardly able to make the l secure. 5002
27:30 the sailors let the l down into the sea, 5002
27:32 So the soldiers cut the ropes that held the l 5002

LIFELESS (7) [LIVE]
Lev 26:30 and pile your dead bodies on the l forms 7007
Ps 106:28 and ate sacrifices offered to l gods; 4637
Jer 16:18 with the l forms of their vile images 5577
Eze 43: 7 by their prostitution and the l idols 7007
43: 9 from me their prostitution and the l idols 7007
Hab 2:19 Or to l stone, 'Wake up!' 1876
1Co 14: 7 in the case of l things that make sounds, 953

LIFETIME (17) [LIVE]
Nu 3: 4 and Ithamar served as priests during the l 7156
Jos 24:31 Israel served the LORD throughout the l 3427
Jdg 2: 7 the LORD throughout the l of Joshua 3427
Jdg 8:28 During Gideon's l, the land enjoyed peace 3427
1Sa 7:13 Throughout Samuel's l, the hand of the LORD was against 3427
2Sa 18:18 During his l Absalom had taken a pillar 2644
1Ki 3:13 that in your l you will have no equal 3427+3972
4:25 During Solomon's l Judah and Israel, 3427
11:12 I will not do it during your l. 3427
12: 6 had served his father Solomon during his l. 2645
15: 6 and Jeroboam throughout [Abijah's] l. 2644+3427
2Ki 20:19 not be peace and security in my l?" 3427
2Ch 10: 6 had served his father Solomon during his l. 2645
Ps 30: 5 but his favor lasts a l; 2644
Isa 39: 8 "There will be peace and security in my l." 3427
Jer 22:30 a man who will not prosper in his l, 3427
Lk 16:25 in your l you received your good things, 2437

LIFT (73) [LIFTED, LIFTING, LIFTS, UPLIFTED]
Ge 13:14 "L up your eyes from where you are 5951
21:18 L the boy up and take him by the hand, 5951
40:13 Within three days Pharaoh will l up 5951
40:19 Within three days Pharaoh will l off your head 5951
41:44 but without your word no one will l hand 8123
Ex 40:37 the cloud did not l, they did not set out— 6590
Dt 28:32 powerless to l a hand. NIH
32:40 I l my hand to heaven and declare: 5951
1Sa 6: 5 Perhaps he will l his hand from you 7837
24: 6 or l my hand against him; 8938
24:10 'I will not l my hand against my master, 8938
2Sa 1:14 "Why were you not afraid to l your hand 8938
18:12 not l my hand against the king's son. 8938
2Ki 6: 7 "L it out," he said. 8123
Ezr 9: 6 I am too ashamed and disgraced to l up 8123
Job 10:15 if I am innocent, I cannot l my head, 5951
11:15 then you will l up your face 5951
22:26 in the Almighty and will l up your face 5951
22:29 and you say, 'L them up!' 1575
Ps 3: 3 you bestow glory on me and l up 8123
9:13 Have mercy and l me up from the gates 8123
10:12 L up your hand, O God. 5951
20: 5 and will l up our banners in the name 1839
24: 4 who does not l up his soul to an idol 5951
24: 7 L up your heads, O you gates; 5951
24: 9 L up your heads, O you gates; 5951
24: 9 l them up, you ancient doors, 5951
25: 1 To you, O LORD, I l up my soul; 5951
28: 2 as I l up my hands toward your Most Holy 5951
63: 4 and in your name I will l up my hands. 5951
75: 4 'Do not l up your horns. 8123
75: 5 Do not l your horns against heaven; 8123
76: 5 not one of the warriors can l his hands. 5162
86: 4 for to you, O Lord, I l up my soul. 5951
91:12 they will l you up in their hands, 5951
110: 7 therefore he will l up his head. 8123
116:13 I will l up the cup of salvation and call 5951
119:48 I l up my hands to your commands, 5951
121: 1 I l up my eyes to the hills— 5951
123: 1 I l up my eyes to you, 5951
134: 2 L up your hands in the sanctuary 5951
142: 1 I l up my voice to the LORD for mercy. 2858
143: 8 for to you I l up my soul. 5951
Isa 10:24 who beat you with a rod and l up a club 5951
40: 9 l up your voice with a shout, lift it up, 8123
40: 9 lift up your voice with a shout, l it up, 8123
40:26 L your eyes and look to the heavens: 5951
46: 7 They l it to their shoulders and carry it; 5951
47: 2 L up your skirts, bare your legs, 3106
49:18 L up your eyes and look around; 5951
49:22 I will l up my banner to the peoples; 8123
51: 6 L up your eyes to the heavens, 5951
52: 8 Your watchmen l up their voices; 5951
60: 4 "L up your eyes and look about you: 5951
Jer 13:20 L up your eyes and see those who are 5951
38:10 and l Jeremiah the prophet out of the cistern 6590
50: 2 l up a banner and proclaim it; 5951
51:12 L up a banner against the walls 5951
51:27 "L up a banner in the land! 5951
La 2:19 L up your hands to him for the lives 5951
3:41 Let us l up our hearts and our hands 5951
Da 6:23 and gave orders to l Daniel out of 10513
Am 5: 2 with no one to l her up." 7756
Na 3: 5 "I will l your skirts over your face. 1655
Mt 4: 6 and they will l you up in their hands, 149
12:11 will you not take hold of it and l it out? 1586
23: 4 not willing to l a finger to move them. 1235
Lk 4:11 they will l you up in their hands, 149
11:46 and you yourselves will not l one finger 4718
21:28 stand up and l up your heads, 2048
1Ti 2: 8 I want men everywhere to l up holy hands 2048
Jas 4:10 and he will l you up. 5738
1Pe 5: 6 that he may l you up in due time. 5738

LIFTED (71) [LIFT]
Ge 7:17 as the waters increased they l the ark high 5951
40:20 He l up the heads of the chief cupbearer 5951
Ex 17:16 "For hands were l up to the throne of NIH
40:36 the cloud l from above the tabernacle, 6590
40:37 they did not set out—until the day it l. 6590
Lev 9:22 Then Aaron l his hands toward the people 5951
Nu 9:17 Whenever the cloud l from above 6590
9:21 and when it l in the morning, they set out. 6590
9:21 whenever the cloud l, they set out. 6590
9:22 but when it l, they would set out. 6590
10:11 the cloud l from above the tabernacle of 6590
Nu 12:10 When the cloud l from above the Tent, 6073
Jdg 9:48 which he l to his shoulders. 5951
16: 3 He l them to his shoulders 8492
1Sa 2: 1 in the LORD my horn is l high. 8123
6: 3 why his hand has not been l from you." 6073
2Sa 18:28 the men who l their hands against my lord 5951
20:21 has l up his hand against the king, 5951
1Ki 16: 2 "I l you up from the dust 8123
2Ki 4:20 the servant had l him up and carried him 5951
19:22 and l your eyes in pride? 5951
Ezr 6:11 and he is to be l up and impaled on it. 10238
Ne 8: 6 all the people l their hands and responded, 5089
Job 5:11 and those who mourn are l to safety. 8435
Ps 24: 7 be l up, you ancient doors, 5951
30: 1 l me out of the depths 1926
40: 2 He l me out of the slimy pit, 6590
41: 9 has l up his heel against me. 1540
75:10 the horns of the righteous will be l up. 8123
93: 3 The seas have l up, O LORD, 5951
93: 3 O LORD, the seas have l up their voice; 5951
93: 3 the seas have l up their pounding waves. 5951
107:25 and stirred up a tempest that l high 8123
107:41 But he l the needy out of their affliction 8435
112: 9 his horn will be l high in honor. 8123
118:16 The LORD's right hand is l high; 8123
Isa 10:27 their burden will be l from your shoulders, 6073
26:11 O LORD, your hand is l high, 8123
33:10 will I be exalted; now will I be l up. 5951
37:23 and l your eyes in pride? 5951
52:13 be raised and l up and highly exalted. 5951
63: 9 he l them up and carried them all the days 5747
Jer 38:13 with the ropes and l him out of the cistern. 6590
Eze 3:12 Then the Spirit l me up, 5951
3:14 Spirit then l me up and took me away, 5951
8: 3 The Spirit l me up between earth 5951
11: 1 Then the Spirit l me up and brought me to 5951
11:24 The Spirit l me up and brought me to 5951
43: 5 Then the Spirit l me up and brought me 5951
Da 6:23 And when Daniel was l from the den, 10513
7: 4 until its wings were torn off and it was l 10475
12: 7 l his right hand and his left hand 8123
Hos 11: 4 I l the yoke from their neck and bent 8123
Am 5:26 You have l up the shrine of your king, 5951
Mic 5: 9 be l up in triumph over your enemies, 8123
Hab 3:10 the deep roared and l its waves on high. 5951
Zec 1:21 of the nations who l up their horns against 5951
5: 9 and they l up the basket between heaven 5951
Mt 11:23 will you be l up to the skies? 5738
Mk 9:27 But Jesus took him by the hand and l him 1586
Lk 1:52 down rulers from their thrones but has l up 5738
10:15 will you be l up to the skies? 5738
24:50 he l up his hands and blessed them. 2048
Jn 3:14 Just as Moses l up the snake in the desert, 5738
3:14 so the Son of Man must be l up, 5738
8:28 "When you have l up the Son of Man, 5738
12:32 But I, when I am l up from the earth, 5738
12:34 'The Son of Man must be l up'? 5738
13:18 'He who shares my bread has l up his heel 2048
19:29 and l it to Jesus' lips. 4712
Ac 7:43 You have l up the shrine of Molech and 377

LIFTING (3) [LIFT]
Ps 141: 2 may the l up of my hands be like 5368
Eze 31:10 l its top above the thick foliage, 5989
31:14 l their tops above the thick foliage. 5989

LIFTS (8) [LIFT]
1Sa 2: 8 and l the needy from the ash heap; 8123
Ezr 6:12 overthrow any king or people who l 10714
Ps 46: 6 he l his voice, the earth melts. 5989
113: 7 and l the needy from the ash heap; 8123
145:14 and l up all who are bowed down. 2422
146: 8 the LORD l up those who are bowed down, 2422
Isa 5:26 He l up a banner for the distant nations, 5951
10:15 As if a rod were to wield him who l it up, 8123

LIGAMENT (1) [LIGAMENTS]
Eph 4:16 and held together by every supporting l, 913

LIGAMENTS (1) [LIGAMENT]
Col 2:19 and held together by its l and sinews, 913

LIGHT (232) [DAYLIGHT, ENLIGHTEN, ENLIGHTENED, LIGHTED, LIGHTEN, LIGHTENED, LIGHTER, LIGHTING, LIGHTLY, LIGHTS, LIT, SUNLIGHT, TWILIGHT]
Ge 1: 3 And God said, "Let there be l," 240
1: 3 "Let there be light," and there was l. 240
1: 4 God saw that the l was good, 240
1: 4 and he separated the l from the darkness. 240
1: 5 God called the l "day," 240
1:15 in the expanse of the sky to give l on 239
1:16 the greater l to govern the day and 4401
1:16 and the lesser l to govern the night. 4401
1:17 in the expanse of the sky to give l on 239
1:18 and to separate l from darkness. 240
Ex 10:23 Yet all the Israelites had l in the places 240
13:21 by night in a pillar of fire to give them l, 239
14:20 to the one side and l to the other side; 239
25: 6 olive oil for the l; 4401
25:37 on it so that they l the space in front of it. 239

Ex 27:20 of pressed olives for the **l** so that 4401
35:3 *Do* not **l** a fire in any of your dwellings on 1277
35:8 olive oil for the **l**; 4401
35:14 for **l** with its accessories, lamps and oil for 4401
35:14 accessories, lamps and oil for the **l**; 4401
35:28 also brought spices and olive oil for the **l** 4401
39:37 and the oil for the **l**; 4401
Lev 24:2 of pressed olives for the **l** so that 4401
Nu 4:9 and cover the lampstand that is for **l**, 4401
4:16 is to have charge of the oil for the **l**, 4401
8:2 *to* **l** the area in front of the lampstand.' " 239
Dt 25:13 weights in your bag—one heavy, one **l**. 7783
1Sa 29:10 leave in the morning as soon as *it is* **l**." 239
2Sa 22:29 **turns** my darkness **into l**. 5585
23:4 he is like the **l** *of* morning at sunrise on 240
1Ki 3:21 I looked at him closely in the **morning l**, 1332
18:25 but *do* not **l** the fire." 8492
2Ch 13:11 on the ceremonially clean table and **l** 1277
Ezr 9:8 and so our God **gives l** *to* our eyes and 239
Ne 4:21 **first l of dawn** till the stars came out. 6590+8840
9:12 by night with a pillar of fire to **give** them **l** 239
Job 3:4 may no **l** shine upon it. 5644
3:5 may blackness overwhelm its **l**. 3427
3:16 an infant who never saw the **l of day?** 240
3:20 "Why is **l** given to those in misery, 240
9:7 he seals off the **l** of the stars. NIH
10:22 where even the **l** is like darkness." 3649
12:22 and brings deep shadows into the **l**. 240
12:25 They grope in darkness with no **l**; 240
17:12 the face of darkness they say, '**L** is near.' 240
18:6 The **l** in his tent becomes dark; 240
18:18 from **l** into darkness and is banished from 240
22:28 and **l** will shine on your ways. 240
24:13 "There are those who rebel against the **l**, 240
24:16 they want nothing to do with the **l**. 240
25:3 Upon whom does his **l** not rise? 240
26:10 for a boundary between **l** and darkness. 240
28:11 of the rivers and brings hidden things to **l**. 240
29:3 and by his **l** I walked through darkness! 240
29:24 the **l** *of* my face was precious to them. 240
30:26 when I looked for **l**, then came darkness. 240
33:28 and I will live to enjoy the **l**.' 240
33:30 that the **l** *of* life may shine on him. 240
38:15 The wicked are denied their **l**, 240
38:19 "What is the way to the abode of **l**? 240
41:18 His snorting throws out flashes of **l**; 240
Ps 4:6 Let the **l** *of* your face shine upon us, 240
13:3 **Give l** *to* my eyes, 239
18:28 my God **turns** my darkness **into l**. 5585
19:8 **giving l** *to* the eyes. 239
27:1 The LORD is my **l** and my salvation— 240
36:9 in your **l** we see light. 240
36:9 in your light we see **l**. 240
38:10 even the **l** has gone from my eyes. 240
43:3 Send forth your **l** and your truth, 240
44:3 your arm, and the **l** *of* your face, 240
49:19 who will never see the **l** [of life] 240
56:13 I may walk before God in the **l** *of* life. 240
76:4 You *are* **resplendent with l**, 239
78:14 by day and with **l** *from* the fire all night. 240
89:15 who walk in the **l** *of* your presence, 240
90:8 our secret sins in the **l** *of* your presence. 4401
97:11 **L** is shed upon the righteous and joy on 240
104:2 He wraps himself in **l** as with a garment; 240
105:39 and a fire to **give l** at night. 239
112:4 Even in darkness **l** dawns for the upright, 240
118:27 and *he has* **made** *his* **l shine** upon us. 239
119:105 word is a lamp to my feet and a **l** for my path 240
119:130 The unfolding of your words **gives l**; 239
139:11 and the **l** become night around me," 240
139:12 for darkness is as **l** to you. 245
Pr 4:18 shining ever brighter till the full **l** of day. NIH
6:23 commands are a lamp, this teaching is a **l**, 240
13:9 The **l** *of* the righteous shines brightly, 240
Ecc 2:13 just as **l** is better than darkness. 240
11:7 **L** is sweet, and it pleases the eyes to see 240
12:2 before the sun and the **l** and the moon and 240
Isa 2:5 let us walk in the **l** *of* the LORD. 240
5:20 who put darkness for **l** and light 240
5:20 who put darkness for light and **l** 240
5:30 even the **l** will be darkened by the clouds. 240
8:20 they have no **l of dawn**. 8840
9:2 in darkness have seen a great **l**; 240
9:2 of the shadow of death a **l** has dawned. 240
10:17 The **L** *of* Israel will become a fire, 240
13:10 constellations will not show their **l**. 240
13:10 and the moon will not give its **l**. 240
30:26 like the **l** *of* seven full days, 240
42:6 a covenant for the people and a **l** *for* the Gentiles, 240
42:16 I will turn the darkness into **l** before them 240
45:7 I form the **l** and create darkness, 240
49:6 I will also make you a **l** *for* the Gentiles, 240
50:10 who walks in the dark, who has no **l**, 5586
50:11 all you *who* **l** fires and provide yourselves 7706
50:11 walk in the **l** *of* your fires and of 241
51:4 my justice will become a **l** *to* the nations. 240
53:11 he will see the **l** [of life] and be satisfied; NIH
57:6 **In the l of** these things, should I relent? 6584
58:8 Then your **l** will break forth like the dawn, 240
58:10 then your **l** will rise in the darkness, 240
59:9 We look for **l**, but all is darkness; 240
60:1 "Arise, shine, for your **l** has come, 240
60:3 Nations will come to your **l**, 240
60:19 The sun will no more be your **l** by day, 240
60:19 for the LORD will be your everlasting **l**, 240
60:20 the LORD will be your everlasting **l**, 240
Jer 4:23 and at the heavens, and their **l** was gone. 240
7:18 children gather wood, the fathers **l** the fire, 1277
13:16 You hope for **l**, but he will turn it to thick 240
25:10 sound of millstones and the **l** *of* the lamp. 240
La 3:2 in darkness rather than **l**; 240
Eze 1:4 and surrounded by **brilliant l**. 5586
1:27 and **brilliant l** surrounded him. 5586
32:7 and the moon *will* not **give** its **l**. 239+240
Da 2:22 and **l** dwells with him. 10466
6:19 At the **first l** of dawn, 10459
Am 5:18 That day will be darkness, not **l**. 240
5:20 the day of the LORD be darkness, not **l**— 240
Mic 2:1 At morning's **l** they carry it out 240
7:8 I sit in darkness, the LORD will be my **l**. 240
7:9 He will bring me out into the **l**; 240
Zec 14:6 On that day there will be no **l**, 240
14:7 When evening comes, there will be **l**. 240
Mal 1:10 *you would* not **l** useless **fires** *on* my altar! 239
Mt 4:16 in darkness have seen a great **l**; 5890
4:16 of the shadow of death a **l** has dawned." 5890
5:14 "You are the **l** of the world. 5890
5:15 Neither *do people* **l** a lamp and put it under 2794
5:15 and *it* **gives l** to everyone in the house. 3290
5:16 let your **l** shine before men, 5890
6:22 your whole body will be **full of l**. 5893
6:23 If then the **l** within you is darkness, 5890
11:30 For my yoke is easy and my burden is **l**." 1787
17:2 and his clothes became as white as the **l**. 5890
24:29 and the moon will not give its **l**; 5766
Mk 13:24 and the moon will not give its **l**; 5766
Lk 2:32 a **l** for revelation to the Gentiles and 5890
8:16 so that those who come in can see the **l**. 5890
11:33 so that those who come in may see the **l**. 5890
11:34 your whole body also is **full of l**. 5893
11:35 then, that the **l** within you is not darkness. 5890
11:36 if your whole body is **full of l**, 5893
11:36 as when the **l** of a lamp shines on you." 847
15:8 *Does she* not **l** a lamp, 721
16:8 than are the people *of* the **l**. 5890
Jn 1:4 and that life was the **l** of men. 5890
1:5 The **l** shines in the darkness, 5890
1:7 as a witness to testify concerning that **l**, 5890
1:8 He himself was not the **l**; 5890
1:8 he came only as a witness to the **l**. 5890
1:9 The true **l** that gives light 5890
1:9 that **gives l to** every man was coming into 5894
3:19 **L** has come into the world, 5890
3:19 but men loved darkness instead of **l** 5890
3:20 Everyone who does evil hates the **l**, 5890
3:20 into the **l** for fear that his deeds will 5890
3:21 by the truth comes into the **l**, 5890
5:35 John was a lamp that burned and **gave l**, 5743
5:35 and you chose for a time to enjoy his **l**. 5890
8:12 he said, "I am the **l** of the world. 5890
8:12 but will have the **l** of life." 5890
9:5 I am in the world, I am the **l** of the world." 5890
11:9 for he sees by this world's **l**. 5890
11:10 he stumbles, for he has no **l**." 5890
12:35 "You are going to have the **l** just a little 5890
12:35 Walk while you have the **l**, 5890
12:36 Put your trust in the **l** while you have it, 5890
12:36 so that you may become sons *of* **l**." 5890
12:46 I have come into the world as a **l**, 5890
Ac 9:3 a **l** from heaven flashed around him. 5890
12:7 of the Lord appeared and a **l** shone in 5890
13:11 for a time you will be unable to see the **l** NIG
13:47 " 'I have made you a **l** for the Gentiles, 5890
22:6 a bright **l** from heaven flashed around me. 5890
22:9 My companions saw the **l**, 5890
22:11 the brilliance *of* the **l** had blinded me. 5890
26:13 I saw a **l** from heaven, 5890
26:18 and turn them from darkness to **l**, 5890
26:23 would proclaim **l** to his own people and to 5890
Ro 2:19 a **l** for those who are in the dark, 5890
13:12 of darkness and put on the armor *of* **l**. 5890
1Co 3:13 because the Day *will* **bring** it **to l**. 1317
4:5 He *will* **bring to l** what is hidden 5894
2Co 4:4 so that they cannot see the **l** of the gospel 5895
4:6 who said, "Let **l** shine out of darkness," 5890
4:6 made his **l** shine in our hearts to give us NIG
4:6 the **l** of the knowledge of the glory of God 5895
4:17 For our **l** and momentary troubles are 1787
6:14 what fellowship can **l** have with darkness? 5890
11:14 Satan himself masquerades as an angel *of* **l**. 5890
Eph 5:8 but now you are **l** in the Lord. 5890
5:8 Live as children *of* **l** 5890
5:9 the fruit *of* the **l** consists in all goodness, 5890
5:13 everything exposed by the **l** becomes visible, 5890
5:14 for it is **l** that makes everything visible. 5890
Col 1:12 inheritance of the saints in the kingdom of **l**. 5890
1Th 5:5 You are all sons *of* the **l** and sons of the day. 5890
1Ti 6:16 and who lives in unapproachable **l**, 5890
2Ti 1:10 **brought** life and immortality **to l** 5894
Tit 1:3 **brought** his word **to l** through the preaching 5746
Heb 10:32 *after you had* **received** the **l**, 5894
12:5 *do* not **make l of** the Lord's discipline, 3902
1Pe 2:9 you out of darkness into his wonderful **l**. 5890
2Pe 1:19 as *to* a **l** shining in a dark place, 3394
1Jn 1:5 and declare to you: God is **l**; 5890
1:7 But if we walk in the **l**, as he is in the light, 5890
1:7 if we walk in the light, as he is in the **l**, 5890
2:8 and the true **l** is already shining. 5890
2:9 be in the **l** but hates his brother is still in 5890
2:10 Whoever loves his brother lives in the **l**, 5890
Rev 8:12 A third of the day *was* **without l**, 3590+5743
18:23 The **l** of a lamp will never shine 5890
21:23 for the glory of God **gives** it **l**, 5894
Rev 21:24 The nations will walk by its **l**, 5890
22:5 not need the **l** of a lamp or the light of 5890
22:5 the light of a lamp or the **l** of the sun, 5890
22:5 for the Lord God *will* **give** them **l**. 5894

LIGHTED (1) [LIGHT]

Lk 11:36 it will be completely **l**, 5893

LIGHTEN (5) [LIGHT]

1Ki 12:4 but now **l** the harsh labor and 7837
12:9 '**L** the yoke your father put on us'?" 7837
2Ch 10:4 but now **l** the harsh labor and 7837
10:9 '**L** the yoke your father put on us'?" 7837
Jnh 1:5 And they threw the cargo into the sea to **l** 7837

LIGHTENED (1) [LIGHT]

Ac 27:38 *they* **l** the ship by throwing the grain into 3185

LIGHTER (3) [LIGHT]

Ex 18:22 *That will* **make** your load **l**, 7837
1Ki 12:10 heavy yoke on us, but **make** our yoke **l**'— 7837
2Ch 10:10 heavy yoke on us, but **make** our yoke **l**'— 7837

LIGHTING (1) [LIGHT]

Mt 3:16 Spirit of God descending like a dove and **l** 2262

LIGHTLY (1) [LIGHT]

2Co 1:17 When I planned this, did I do it **l**? 1786

LIGHTNING (46)

Ex 9:23 and **l** flashed down to the ground. 836
9:24 hail fell and **l** flashed back and forth. 836
19:16 of the third day there was thunder and **l**, 1398
20:18 the thunder and **l** and heard the trumpet 4365
2Sa 22:13 of his presence bolts of **l** blazed forth. 836
22:15 **bolts of l** and routed them. 1398
Job 36:30 See how he scatters his **l** about him, 240
36:32 with **l** and commands it to strike its mark. 240
37:3 He unleashes his **l** beneath the whole heaven 240
37:11 he scatters his **l** through them. 240
37:15 the clouds and makes his **l** flash? 240
38:24 to the place where the **l** is dispersed, 240
38:35 Do you send the **l bolts** on their way? 1398
Ps 18:12 with hailstones and bolts of **l**. 836
18:14 great **bolts of l** and routed them. 1398
29:7 voice of the LORD strikes with flashes of **l**. 836
77:18 your **l** lit up the world; 1398
78:48 their livestock to **bolts of l**. 8404
97:4 His **l** lights up the world; 1398
105:32 with **l** throughout their land; 836+4259
135:7 he sends **l** with the rain and brings out 1398
144:6 **Send forth l** and scatter [the enemies]; 1397+1398
148:8 **l** and hail, snow and clouds, stormy winds 836
Jer 10:13 He sends **l** with the rain and brings out 1398
51:16 He sends **l** with the rain and brings out 1398
Eze 1:4 an immense cloud with flashing **l** 836
1:13 it was bright, and **l** flashed out of it. 1398
1:14 and forth like **flashes of l**. 1027
21:10 polished to **flash like l**! 1398
21:15 It is made to **flash like l**, 1398
21:28 polished to consume and to **flash like l**! 1398
Da 10:6 his face like **l**, his eyes like flaming torches, 1398
Hos 6:5 my judgments flashed like **l** upon you. 240
Na 2:4 they dart about like **l**. 1398
Hab 3:11 at the **l** *of* your flashing spear. 1398
Zec 9:14 his arrow will flash like **l**. 1398
Mt 24:27 For as **l** that comes from the east is visible 847
28:3 His appearance was like **l**, 847
Lk 9:29 as bright as a **flash of l**. 1993
10:18 "I saw Satan fall like **l** from heaven. 847
17:24 Son of Man in his day will be like the **l**, 847
24:4 in clothes **that gleamed like l** stood 848
Rev 4:5 From the throne came **flashes of l**, 847
8:5 **flashes of l** and an earthquake. 847
11:19 And there came **flashes of l**, rumblings, 847
16:18 Then there came **flashes of l**, rumblings, 847

LIGHTS (14) [LIGHT]

Ge 1:14 be **l** in the expanse of the sky to separate 4401
1:15 and let them be **l** in the expanse of the sky 4401
1:16 God made two great **l**— 4401
Ex 30:8 He must burn incense again when he **l** 6590
Ps 97:4 His lightning **l up** the world; 239
136:7 who made the great **l**— 240
Eze 32:8 the shining **l** in the heavens I will darken 4401
Zec 4:2 with a bowl at the top and seven **l** on it, 5944
4:2 with seven channels to the **l**. 5944
Lk 8:16 "No one **l** a lamp and hides it in a jar 721
11:33 "No one **l** a lamp and puts it in a place 721
17:24 and **l up** the sky from one end to the other. 3290
Ac 16:29 The jailer called for **l**, 5890
Jas 1:17 down from the Father *of* the heavenly **l**, 5890

LIGURE (KJV) See JACINTH

LIKE (1532) [ALIKE, LIKE-MINDED, LIKED, LIKELY, LIKEN, LIKENESS, LIKES, LIKEWISE]

Ge 3:5 and you will be **l** God, knowing good and 3869
3:22 "The man has now become **l** one of us, 3869

Ge 10: 9 that is why it is said, "L Nimrod, 3869
13:10 l the garden of the LORD, 3869
13:10 l the land of Egypt, toward Zoar. 3869
13:16 I will make your offspring l the dust of 3869
19: 8 you can do what you l with them. 928+3202+6524
19:28 l smoke from a furnace. 3869
20:15 live wherever you l." 928+3202+6524
25:25 and his whole body was l a hairy garment; 3869
27: 4 of tasty food *l* l and bring it to me to eat, 170
27:23 his hands were hairy l those of his brother 3869
27:27 of my son is l the smell of a field that 3869
27:46 from Hittite women l these, 3869
28:14 Your descendants will be l the dust of 3869
29:20 but they seemed l only a few days to him 3869
31:26 and you've carried off my daughters l 3869
31:41 It was *l* **this** for the twenty years I was AIT
32:12 and will make your descendants l the sand 3869
33:10 For to see your face is l seeing the face 3869
34:12 **Make** the price for the bride and the gift I
am to bring **as great as you l,** 4394+8049
34:15 that you become l us by circumcising all 4017
34:31 "Should he have treated our sister l 3869
38:11 "He may die too, **just** l his brothers." 3869
41:38 "Can we find anyone l this man, 3869
41:49 quantities of grain, l the sand of the sea; 3869
44: 7 from your servants to do anything l that! 3869
44:15 that a man l me can find things out 4017
48:20 'May God make you l Ephraim 3869
49: 9 L a lion he crouches and lies down, 3869
49: 9 l a lioness—who dares to rouse him? 3869
Ex 1:19 "Hebrew women are not l Egyptian 3869
4: 6 it was leprous, l snow. 3869
4: 7 it was restored, l the rest of his flesh. 3869
7: 1 "See, I have made you l God to Pharaoh, NIH
8:10 you may know there is no one l the LORD 3869
9:14 so you may know that there is no one l me 4017
12:48 then he may take part l one born in 3869
13: 9 This observance will be for you l a sign 4200
13:16 And it will be l a sign on your hand and 4200
15: 5 they sank to the depths l a stone. 4017
15: 7 it consumed them l stubble. 3869
15: 8 The surging waters stood firm l a wall; 4017
15:10 They sank l lead in the mighty waters. 3869
15:11 "Who among the gods is l you, 4017
15:11 Who is l you—majestic in holiness, 4017
16:14 thin flakes l frost on the ground appeared 3869
16:31 It was white l coriander seed and tasted 3869
16:31 and tasted l wafers made with honey. 3869
19:18 The smoke billowed up from it l smoke 3869
22:25 do not be l a moneylender; 3869
24:10 Under his feet was something l a pavement 3869
24:17 of the LORD looked l a consuming fire 3869
25: 9 all its furnishings **exactly l** 889+3869+3972+4027
25:33 cups **shaped l almond flowers** 5481
25:34 cups **shaped l almond flowers** 5481
26:24 both shall be **l that.** 4027
28: 8 skillfully woven waistband is to be l 3869+5126
28:14 and two braided chains of pure gold, l 5126
28:15 Make it l the ephod: 3869+5126
28:21 each **engraved** *l* a seal with the name AIT
28:22 braided chains of pure gold, l a rope. 5126
28:32 There shall be a woven edge l a collar 3869
30:33 Whoever makes perfume l it 4017
30:38 Whoever makes any l it 4017
34: 1 "Chisel out two stone tablets l 3869
34: 4 So Moses chiseled out two stone tablets l 3869
37:19 cups **shaped l almond flowers** 5481
37:20 cups **shaped l almond flowers** 5481
38:18 l the curtains of the courtyard, 4200+6645
39: 5 skillfully woven waistband was l it— 3869+5126
39: 6 and **engraved** them *l* a seal with the names AIT
39: 8 They made it l the ephod: 3869
39:14 each **engraved** *l* a seal with the name AIT
39:15 braided chains of pure gold, l a rope. 5126
39:23 with an opening in the center of the robe l 3869
39:30 l an inscription on a seal: NIH
Lev 6:17 L the sin offering and the guilt offering, 3869
13:43 his head or forehead is reddish-white l 3869+5260
14:13 L the sin offering, the guilt offering 3869
14:35 'I have seen something that looks l 3869
26:19 and make the sky above you l iron and 3869
26:19 like iron and the ground beneath you l 3869
27:21 l a field devoted to the LORD; 3869
Nu 8: 4 The lampstand was made **exactly l** 3869+4027
9:15 the cloud above the tabernacle looked l 3869
9:16 and at night it **looked** *l* fire. AIT
11: 7 The manna was l coriander seed 3869
11: 7 like coriander seed and looked l resin. 3869
11: 8 it tasted l something made with olive oil. 3869
12:10 there stood Miriam—leprous, l snow. 3869
12:12 not let her be l a stillborn infant coming 3869
13:18 See **what** the land is l and 4537
13:33 We seemed l grasshoppers 3869
14:34 **know what it is l** to have me against you.' 3359
16:40 or he would become l Korah 3869
23:10 and may my end be l theirs!" 4017
23:24 The people rise l a lioness; 3869
23:24 they rouse themselves l a lion that does 3869
24: 6 "L valleys they spread out, 3869
24: 6 l gardens beside a river, 3869
24: 6 l aloes planted by the LORD, 3869
24: 6 l cedars beside the waters. 3869
24: 9 L a lion they crouch and lie down, 3869
24: 9 l a lioness—who dares to rouse them? 3869
27:17 the LORD's people will not be l sheep 3869
32:16 *"We would l to* **build** pens here AIT
Dt 1:44 they chased you l a swarm of bees 889+3869

Dt 2:11 L the Anakites, they too were considered
Rephaites, 3869
4:16 whether **formed** *l* a man or a woman, AIT
4:17 or l any animal on earth or any bird NIH
4:18 or l any creature that moves along NIH
4:32 or has anything l it ever been heard of? 4017
4:34 l all the things the LORD your God did 3869
7:26 l it, will be set apart for destruction. 4017
8:20 L the nations the LORD destroyed 3869
9: 3 the one who goes across ahead of you l NIH
10: 1 "Chisel out two stone tablets l 3869
10: 3 and chiseled out two stone tablets l 3869
11:10 to take over is not l the land of Egypt, 3869
12:16 pour it out on the ground l water. 3869
12:20 *"I would* l some meat," 430
12:24 pour it out on the ground l water. 3869
14:26 Use the silver to buy whatever you l: 203
15:23 pour it out on the ground l water. 3869
17:14 a king over us l all the nations around us," 3869
18: 7 in the name of the LORD his God l 3869
18:15 up for you a prophet l me from 4017
18:18 I will raise up for them a prophet l you 4017
22:26 This case is l that of someone 889+3869+4027
28:29 At midday you will grope about l 889+3869
28:49 l an eagle swooping down, 889+3869
29:23 It will be l the destruction of Sodom 3869
32: 2 Let my teaching fall l rain 3869
32: 2 like rain and my words descend l dew, 3869
32: 2 l showers on new grass, 3869
32: 2 l abundant rain on tender plants. 3869
32:11 l an eagle that stirs up its nest and hovers 3869
32:31 For their rock is not l our Rock, 3869
33:17 In majesty he is l a firstborn bull; NIH
33:20 Gad lives there l a lion, 3869
33:26 "There is no one l the God of Jeshurun, 3869
33:29 Who is l you, a people saved by the LORD? 4017
34:10 no prophet has risen in Israel l Moses, 3869
Jos 7: 5 of the people melted and became l water. 4200
10: 2 l one of the royal cities; 3869
10:14 There has never been a day l it before or 3869
22:16 with the God of Israel l this? 889
Jdg 5:31 be l the sun when it rises in its strength." 3869
6: 5 up with their livestock and their tents l 3869
7: 5 the water with their tongues l a dog 889+3869
8: 1 "Why have you treated us l this? NIH
8:18 "Men l you," they answered, 4017
13: 6 He looked l an angel of God, 3869
13:15 *"We would l you to* **stay** until we prepare AIT
15: 7 "Since you've acted l this, 3869
15:14 on his arms became l charred flax, 889+3869
17:11 young man was to him l one of his sons. 3869
18: 7 l the Sidonians, unsuspecting and 3869+5477
Ru 4:11 into your home l Rachel and Leah, 3869
4:12 may your family be l that of Perez, 3869
1Sa 2: 2 "There is no one holy l the LORD; 3869
2: 2 there is no Rock l our God. 3869
4: 7 Nothing l this has happened before. 3869
8:20 Then we will be l all the other nations, 3869
10:24 There is no one l him among all 4017
15:23 For rebellion is l the sin of divination, NIH
15:23 and arrogance l the evil of idolatry. NIH
17: 7 His spear shaft was l a weaver's rod, 3869
17:36 this uncircumcised Philistine will be l one 3869
18:22 and his attendants all l you; 170
19: 5 to an innocent man l David by killing him NIH
19:17 "Why did you deceive me l **this** 3970
20:14 But show me **unfailing kindness** *l that of* AIT
21: 9 David said, "There is none l it; 4017
21:13 he was in their hands *he* **acted l a madman,** 2147
21:15 to bring this fellow here to carry on l this NIH
25:25 is **just** l his name—his name is Fool, 3869+4027
25:26 and all who intend to harm my master be l 3869
25:36 he was in the house holding a banquet l 3869
25:37 and his heart failed him and he became l 4200
26:15 And who is l you in Israel? 4017
26:21 Surely *I have* **acted l a fool** 6118
28:14 "What does he **look l?"** 9307
2Sa 7: 9 l the names of the greatest men of the earth. 3869
7:22 There is no one l you, and there is no God 4017
7:23 And who is l your people Israel— 3869
9: 8 that you should notice a dead dog l me?" 4017
9:11 at David's table l one of the king's sons. 3869
12: 3 It was l a daughter to him. 3869
13: 5 **'I would l** my sister Tamar to come 5528
13: 6 **"I would l** my sister Tamar to come 5528
13:13 You would be l one of the wicked fools 3869
14: 2 Act l a woman who has spent many days
grieving for 3869
14:13 "Why then have you devised a thing l this 3869
14:14 L water spilled on the ground, 3869
14:17 for my lord the king is l an angel of God 3869
14:20 My lord has wisdom l that of an angel 3869
16:23 the advice Ahithophel gave was l that 3869
17:10 whose heart is l the heart of a lion, 3869
18:14 "I'm not going to wait l **this** for you." 4027
18:27 to me that the first one runs l Ahimaaz son 3869
18:32 up to harm you be l that young man." 3869
19:27 My lord the king is l an angel of God; 3869
21:19 a spear with a shaft l a weaver's rod. 3869
22:34 He makes my feet l the feet of a deer; 3869
22:43 and trampled them l mud in the streets. 3869
23: 4 he is l the light of morning at sunrise on 3869
23: 4 l the brightness after rain that brings 4946
23: 6 evil men are all to be cast aside l thorns, 3869
1Ki 1:42 A worthy man l you must NIH
3:12 there will never have been anyone l you, 4017
7: 8 a palace l this hall for Pharaoh's daughter, 3869

1Ki 7:26 and its rim was l the rim of a cup, 3869+5126
7:26 l a lily blossom. NIH
7:33 wheels were made l chariot wheels; 3869+5126
8:23 of Israel, there is no God l you in heaven 4017
10:20 Nothing l it had ever been made 4027
12:32 l the festival held in Judah, 3869
14: 8 but you have not been l my servant David, 3869
14:15 it will be l a reed swaying in the water. 889+3869
16: 3 and I will make your house l that 3869
16: 7 and becoming l the house of Jeroboam— 3869
19: 2 not make your life l that of one of them." 3869
20:11 not boast l one who takes it off.' " 3869
20:25 also raise an army l the one you lost— 3869
20:27 The Israelites camped opposite them l 3869
21:22 I will make your house l that 3869
21:25 (There was never a man l Ahab, 3869
21:26 l the Amorites the LORD drove 889+3869+3972
22:17 on the hills l sheep without a shepherd, 3869
2Ki 3:22 the water looked red—l blood. 3869
5:14 and became clean l that of a young boy. 3869
7:13 be l that of all the Israelites left here— 3869
7:13 be l all these Israelites who are doomed. 3869
9: 9 I will make the house of Ahab l the house 3869
9: 9 of Jeroboam son of Nebat and l the house 3869
9:20 The driving is l that of Jehu son of Nimshi 3869
9:20 he drives l a madman." 928
9:37 be l refuse on the ground in the plot 3869
13: 7 the rest and made them l the dust 3869
17: 2 l the kings of Israel who preceded him. 3869
18: 5 There was no one l him among all 4017
18:27 who, l you, will have to eat their own filth 6640
18:32 until I come and take you to a land l 3869
19:26 They are l plants in the field, NIH
19:26 l tender green shoots, NIH
19:26 l grass sprouting on the roof, NIH
23:25 before nor after Josiah was there a king l 4017
1Ch 11:23 the Egyptian had a spear l a weaver's rod 3869
12:22 l the army of God. 3869
17: 8 Now I will make your name l the names 3869
17:20 "There is no one l you, O LORD, 4017
17:21 And who is l your people Israel— 3869
20: 5 a spear with a shaft l a weaver's rod. 3869
29:15 Our days on earth are l a shadow, 3869
2Ch 4: 5 and its rim was l the rim of a cup, 3869+5126
4: 5 l a lily blossom. NIH
6:14 of Israel, there is no God l you in heaven 4017
9:11 Nothing l them had ever been seen 3869
9:19 Nothing l it had ever been made 4027
14:11 there is no one l you to help the powerless 6640
18:16 on the hills l sheep without a shepherd, 3869
30: 7 Do not be l your fathers and brothers, 3869
30:26 of Israel there had been nothing l this 3869
32:15 and mislead you l this. 3869
35:18 The Passover had not been observed l this 4017
Ezr 4: 2 "Let us help you build because, l you, 3869
9: 1 l those of the Canaanites, Hittites, 4200
9:13 and have given us a remnant l this. 3869
Ne 5:15 of reverence for God I did not act **l that.** 4027
6: 8 l what you are saying is happening; 3869
6:11 But I said, "Should a man l me run away? 4017
6:11 Or should one l me go into the temple 4017
8:17 the Israelites had not celebrated it **l this.** 4027
9:11 l a stone into mighty waters. 4017
13:26 Was it not because of marriages l these NIH
13:26 the many nations there was no king l him. 4017
Job 1: 8 There is no one on earth l him; 4017
2: 3 There is no one on earth l him; 4017
2:10 "You are talking l a foolish woman. 3869
3:16 Or why was I not hidden in the ground l 3869
3:16 l an infant who never saw the light 3869
3:24 my groans pour out l water. 3869
5:25 your descendants l the grass of the earth. 3869
5:26 l sheaves gathered in season. 3869
7: 1 Are not his days l those of a hired man? 3869
7: 2 L a slave longing for the evening shadows, 3869
8:16 l a well-watered plant in the sunshine, NIH
9:26 They skim past l boats of papyrus, 6640
9:26 l eagles swooping down on their prey. 3869
9:32 not a man l me that I might answer him, 4017
10: 5 Are your days l those of a mortal 3869
10: 5 like those of a mortal or your years l those 3869
10: 9 Remember that you molded me l clay. 3869
10:10 not pour me out l milk and curdle me 3869
10:10 not pour me out like milk and curdle me l 3869
10:16 you stalk me l a lion 3869
10:22 where even the light is l darkness." 4017
11:17 and darkness will become l morning. 3869
12:25 he makes them stagger l drunkards. 3869
13:28 "So man wastes away l something rotten, 3869
13:28 l a garment eaten by moths. 3869
14: 2 up l a flower and withers away; 3869
14: 2 l a fleeting shadow, he does not endure. 3869
14: 6 till he has put in his time l a hired man. 3869
14: 9 of water it will bud and put forth shoots l 4017
15:16 who drinks up evil l water! 3869
15:24 l a king poised to attack, 3869
15:33 be l a vine stripped of its unripe grapes, 3869
15:33 l an olive tree shedding its blossoms. 3869
16: 2 "I have heard many things l these; 3869
16: 4 I also could speak l you, 3869
16:14 he rushes at me l a warrior. 3869
19:10 he uproots my hope l a tree. 3869
20: 7 l his own dung; 3869
20: 8 L a dream he flies away, 3869
20: 8 banished l a vision of the night. 3869
21:18 often are they l straw before the wind, 3869
21:18 l chaff swept away by a gale? 3869

Job 24: 5 L wild donkeys in the desert, NIH
24:14 in the night he steals forth l a thief. 3869
24:20 but are broken l a tree. 3869
24:24 they are brought low and gathered up l 3869
24:24 they are cut off l heads of grain. 3869
27: 7 "May my enemies be l the wicked, 3869
27: 7 my adversaries l the unjust! 3869
27:16 up silver l dust and clothes like piles 3869
27:16 up silver like dust and clothes l piles 3869
27:18 The house he builds is l a moth's cocoon, 3869
27:18 l a hut made by a watchman. 3869
27:20 Terrors overtake him l a flood; 3869
29:25 I was l one who comforts mourners. 889+3869
30:15 my safety vanishes l a cloud. 3869
30:18 In his great power [God] **becomes** l 2924
30:18 he binds me l the neck of my garment. 3869
31:36 I would put it on l a crown. NIH
31:37 l a prince I would approach him.)— 4017
32:19 inside I am l bottled-up wine, 3869
32:19 l new wineskins ready to burst. 3869
33: 6 I am **just** l you before God; 3869+7023
33:25 then his flesh is renewed l a child's; 4946
34: 7 What man is l Job, 3869
34: 7 who drinks scorn l water? 3869
34:36 the utmost for answering l a wicked man! 928
35: 4 "I *would l to* **reply** *to* you and AIT
35: 8 Your wickedness affects only a man l 4017
36:22 Who is a teacher l him? 4017
38: 3 Brace yourself l a man; 3869
38:14 The earth takes shape l clay under a seal; 3869
38:14 its features stand out l those of a garment. 4017
39:20 Do you make him leap l a locust, 3869
40: 7 "Brace yourself l a man; 3869
40: 9 Do you have an arm l God's, 3869
40: 9 and can your voice thunder l his? 4017
40:15 along with you and which feeds on grass l 3869
40:17 His tail sways l a cedar; 4017
40:18 his limbs l rods of iron. 3869
41: 5 a pet of him l a bird or put him on a leash 3869
41:18 his eyes are l the rays of dawn. 3869
41:27 Iron he treats l straw and bronze 4200
41:27 Iron he treats like straw and bronze l 4200
41:28 slingstones are l chaff to him. 4200
41:30 a trail in the mud l a threshing sledge. NIH
41:31 the depths churn l a boiling caldron 3869
41:31 like a boiling caldron and stirs up the sea l 3869
Ps 1: 3 He is l a tree planted by streams of water, 3869
1: 4 They are l chaff that the wind blows away. 3869
2: 9 you will dash them to pieces l pottery." 3869
7: 2 or they will tear me l a lion and rip me 3869
10: 9 He lies in wait l a lion in cover; 3869
11: 1 "Flee l a bird to your mountain. NIH
12: 6 l silver refined in a furnace of clay, NIH
17:12 They are l a lion hungry for prey, 1955
17:12 l a great lion crouching in cover. 3869
18:33 He makes my feet l the feet of a deer; 3869
18:42 I poured them out l mud in the streets. 3869
19: 5 which is l a bridegroom coming forth 3869
19: 5 l a champion rejoicing to run his course. 3869
21: 9 of your appearing you will make them l 3869
22:14 I am poured out l water, 3869
22:15 My strength is dried up l a potsherd, 3869
28: 1 *I will* **be** l those who have gone down to 5439
29: 6 He makes Lebanon skip l a calf, 4017
29: 6 Sirion l a young wild ox. 4017
31:12 I have become l broken pottery. 3869
32: 9 Do not be l the horse or the mule, 3869
35: 5 May they be l chaff before the wind, 3869
35:10 "Who is l you, O LORD? 4017
35:16 L the ungodly they maliciously mocked; 3869
36: 6 Your righteousness is l the mighty mountains, 3869
36: 6 your justice l the great deep. NIH
37: 2 for l the grass they will soon wither, 3869
37: 2 l green plants they will soon die away. 3869
37: 6 He will make your righteousness shine l 3869
37: 6 of your cause l the noonday sun. 3869
37:20 The LORD's enemies will be l the beauty of 3869
37:20 they will vanish—vanish l smoke. 928
37:35 and ruthless man flourishing l a green tree 3869
38: 4 My guilt has overwhelmed me l a burden 3869
38:13 I am l a deaf man, who cannot hear, 3869
38:13 l a mute, who cannot open his mouth; 3869
38:14 I have become l a man who does not hear, 3869
39:11 you consume their wealth l a moth— 3869
44:11 be devoured l sheep and have scattered us 3869
48: 2 L the utmost heights of Zaphon NIH
48: 6 pain l that of a woman in labor. 3869
48: 7 You destroyed them l ships of Tarshish NIH
48:10 L your name, O God, your praise reaches 3869
49:12 *he* **is** l the beasts that perish. 5439
49:14 L sheep they are destined for the grave, 3869
49:20 without understanding **is** l the beasts 5439
50:21 you thought I was altogether l you. 4017
52: 2 it is l a sharpened razor, 3869
52: 8 But I am l an olive tree flourishing in 3869
55:13 But it is you, a man l myself, 3869+6886
58: 4 Their venom is l the venom of a snake, 1952+3869
58: 4 l that of a cobra that has stopped its ears, 4017
58: 7 Let them vanish l water that flows away; 4017
58: 8 L a slug melting away as it moves along, 4017
58: 8 l a stillborn child, NIH
59: 6 snarling l dogs, and prowl about the city. 3869
59:14 snarling l dogs, and prowl about the city. 3869
64: 3 They sharpen their tongues l swords 3869
64: 3 and aim their words l deadly arrows. NIH
66:10 you refined us l silver. 3869

Ps 68:14 *it was l* **snow fallen** on Zalmon. AIT
71: 7 I have become l a portent to many, 3869
71:19 Who, O God, is l you? 4017
72: 6 He will be l rain falling on a mown field, 3869
72: 6 l showers watering the earth. 3869
72:16 Let its fruit flourish l Lebanon; 3869
72:16 let it thrive l the grass of the field. 3869
73:12 This is what the wicked are l— NIH
74: 5 They behaved l men wielding axes to cut 3869
77:20 You led your people l a flock by the hand 3869
78: 8 They would not be l their forefathers— 3869
78:13 he made the water stand firm l a wall. 4017
78:16 a rocky crag and made water flow down l 3869
78:27 He rained meat down on them l dust, 3869
78:27 flying birds l sand on the seashore. 3869
78:52 But he brought his people out l a flock; 3869
78:52 he led them l sheep through the desert. 3869
78:57 L their fathers they were disloyal 3869
78:69 He built his sanctuary l the heights, 4017
78:69 l the earth that he established forever. 3869
79: 3 They have poured out blood l water all 3869
79: 5 How long will your jealousy burn l fire? 4017
80: 1 you who lead Joseph l a flock; 3869
82: 7 But you will die l mere men; 3869
82: 7 you will fall l every other ruler." 3869
83:10 who perished at Endor and became l NIH
83:11 Make their nobles l Oreb and Zeeb, 3869
83:11 all their princes l Zebah and Zalmunna, 3869
83:13 Make them l tumbleweed, O my God, 3869
83:13 O my God, l chaff before the wind. 3869
86: 8 Among the gods there is none l you, 4017
88: 4 I am l a man without strength. 3869
88: 5 l the slain who lie in the grave, 4017
88:17 All day long they surround me l a flood; 3869
89: 6 *Who* **is** l the LORD among the heavenly 1948
89: 8 O LORD God Almighty, who is l you? 4017
89:10 You crushed Rahab l one of the slain; 3869
89:36 and his throne endure before me l the sun; 3869
89:37 it will be established forever l the moon, 3869
89:46 How long will your wrath burn l fire? 4017
90: 4 in your sight are l a day that has just gone 3869
90: 4 or l a watch in the night. NIH
90: 5 they are l the new grass of the morning— 3869
92: 7 that though the wicked spring up l grass 4017
92:10 You have exalted my horn l that of 3869
92:12 The righteous will flourish l a palm tree, 3869
92:12 they will grow l a cedar of Lebanon; 3869
97: 5 mountains melt l wax before the LORD, 3869
102: 3 For my days vanish l smoke; 928
102: 3 my bones burn l glowing embers. 3869
102: 4 My heart is blighted and withered l grass; 3869
102: 6 **I am** l a desert owl, 1948
102: 6 l an owl among the ruins. 3869
102: 7 I have become l a bird alone on a roof. 3869
102:11 My days are l the evening shadow; 3869
102:11 I wither away l grass. 3869
102:26 they will all wear out l a garment. 3869
102:26 L clothing you will change them 3869
103: 5 that your youth is renewed l the eagle's. 3869
103:15 As for man, his days are l grass, 3869
103:15 he flourishes l a flower of the field; 3869
104: 2 he stretches out the heavens l a tent 3869
105:41 l a river it flowed in the desert. NIH
107:27 They reeled and staggered l drunken men; 3869
107:41 and increased their families l flocks. 3869
109:18 it entered into his body l water, 3869
109:18 into his bones l oil. 3869
109:19 May it be l a cloak wrapped about him, 3869
109:19 l a belt tied forever around him. 4200
109:23 I fade away l an evening shadow; 3869
109:23 I am shaken off l a locust. 3869
113: 5 Who is l the LORD our God, 3869
114: 4 the mountains skipped l rams, 3869
114: 4 skipped like rams, the hills l lambs. 3869
114: 6 that you skipped l rams, you hills, 3869
114: 6 skipped like rams, you hills, l lambs? 3869
115: 8 Those who make them will be l them, 4017
118:12 They swarmed around me l bees, 3869
119:83 Though I am l a wineskin in the smoke, 3869
119:119 All the wicked of the earth you discard l NIH
119:162 I rejoice in your promise l one who finds 3869
119:176 I have strayed l a lost sheep. 3869
122: 3 Jerusalem is built l a city 3869
124: 7 We have escaped l a bird out of 3869
125: 1 Those who trust in the LORD are l 3869
126: 1 we were l men who dreamed. 3869
126: 4 O LORD, l streams in the Negev. 3869
127: 4 L arrows in the hands of a warrior 3869
128: 3 be l a fruitful vine within your house; 3869
128: 3 be l olive shoots around your table. 3869
129: 6 May they be l grass on the roof, 3869
131: 2 l a weaned child with its mother, 3869
131: 2 l a weaned child is my soul within me. 3869
133: 2 It is l precious oil poured on the head, 3869
135:18 Those who make them will be l them, 4017
139:12 the night will shine l the day, 3869
141: 2 May my prayer be set before you l NIH
141: 2 up of my hands be l the evening sacrifice. NIH
143: 3 he makes me dwell in darkness l 3869
143: 6 my soul thirsts for you l a parched land. 3869
143: 7 not hide your face from me or *I will* **be** l 5439
144: 4 Man *is* l a breath; 1948
144: 4 his days are l a fleeting shadow. 3869
144:12 Then our sons in their youth will be l 3869
144:12 and our daughters will be l pillars carved 3869
147:16 He spreads the snow l wool and scatters 3869
147:16 and scatters the frost l ashes. 3869

Ps 147:17 He hurls down his hail l pebbles. 3869
Pr 1:12 l the grave, and whole, 3869
1:12 l those who go down to the pit; 3869
1:27 when calamity overtakes you l a storm, 3869
1:27 disaster sweeps over you l a whirlwind, 3869
4:18 the righteous is l the first gleam of dawn, 3869
4:19 the way of the wicked is l deep darkness; 3869
6: 5 l a gazelle from the hand of the hunter, 3869
6: 5 l a bird from the snare of the fowler. 3869
6:11 and poverty will come on you l a bandit 3869
6:11 like a bandit and scarcity l an armed man. 3869
7:10 **dressed** *l* a prostitute and with crafty intent. AIT
7:22 All at once he followed her l an ox going 3869
7:22 l a deer stepping into a noose 3869
7:23 l a bird darting into a snare, 3869
11:22 L a gold ring in a pig's snout is NIH
11:28 but the righteous will thrive l a green leaf. 3869
12: 4 a disgraceful wife is l decay in his bones. 3869
12:18 Reckless words pierce l a sword, 3869
16:15 his favor is l a rain cloud in spring. 3869
16:27 and his speech is l a scorching fire. 3869
17:14 Starting a quarrel is l breaching a dam; NIH
18: 8 words of a gossip are l choice morsels; 3869
18:19 disputes are l the barred gates of a citadel. 3869
19:12 A king's rage is l the roar of a lion, 3869
19:12 but his favor is l dew on the grass. 3869
19:13 quarrelsome wife is l a constant dripping. NIH
20: 2 A king's wrath is l the roar of a lion; 3869
21: 1 he directs it l a watercourse wherever he NIH
23: 5 sprout wings and fly off to the sky l an eagle 3869
23:28 L a bandit she lies in wait, 3869
23:32 the end it bites l a snake and poisons like 3869
23:32 bites like a snake and poisons l a viper. 3869
23:34 be l one sleeping on the high seas, 3869
24:15 Do not lie in wait l an outlaw against NIH
24:26 An honest answer is l a kiss on the lips. NIH
24:34 and poverty will come on you l a bandit NIH
24:34 like a bandit and scarcity l an armed man. 3869
25:11 A word aptly spoken is l apples of gold NIH
25:12 L an earring of gold or an ornament NIH
25:13 L the coolness of snow at harvest time is 3869
25:14 L clouds and wind without rain is NIH
25:18 L a club or a sword or a sharp arrow is NIH
25:19 L a bad tooth or a lame foot is reliance on NIH
25:20 L one who takes away a garment on NIH
25:20 or l vinegar poured on soda, NIH
25:25 L cold water to a weary soul is good news NIH
25:26 L a muddied spring or a polluted well is NIH
25:28 L a city whose walls are broken down is NIH
26: 1 L snow in summer or rain in harvest, 3869
26: 2 L a fluttering sparrow or 3869
26: 4 or *you will* **be** l him yourself. 8750
26: 6 L cutting off one's feet NIH
26: 7 L a lame man's legs that hang limp is NIH
26: 8 L tying a stone in a sling is the giving 3869
26: 9 L a thornbush in a drunkard's hand is NIH
26:10 L an archer who wounds at random NIH
26:17 L one who seizes a dog by the ears is NIH
26:18 L a madman shooting firebrands 3869
26:22 words of a gossip are l choice morsels; 3869
26:23 L a coating of glaze over earthenware 3869
27: 8 L a bird that strays from its nest is 3869
27:15 A quarrelsome wife **is** l a constant dripping 8750
27:16 restraining her is l restraining the wind NIH
27:22 grinding him l grain with a pestle, 928+9348
28: 3 A ruler who oppresses the poor is l a NIH
28:15 L a roaring lion or a charging bear is NIH
31:14 She is l the merchant ships, 3869
Ecc 2:16 For the wise man, l the fool, will not be 6640
2:16 L the fool, the wise man too must die! 6640
3:18 they may see that they are l the animals. 4200
3:19 Man's fate is l that of the animals; NIH
6:12 and meaningless days he passes through l 3869
7: 6 L the crackling of thorns under the pot, 3869
7:11 Wisdom, l an inheritance, is a good thing 6640
8: 1 Who is l the wise man? 3869
8:13 their days will not lengthen l a shadow. 3869
10: 7 while princes go on foot l slaves. 3869
12:11 The words of the wise are l goads, 3869
12:11 their collected sayings l firmly embedded 3869
SS 1: 3 your name is l perfume poured out. NIH
1: 5 dark l the tents of Kedar, 3869
1: 5 l the tent curtains of Solomon. 3869
1: 7 Why should I be l a veiled woman beside 3869
2: 2 L a lily among thorns is my darling among 3869
2: 3 L an apple tree among the trees of 3869
2: 9 My lover **is** l a gazelle or a young stag. 1948
2:17 and **be** l a gazelle or like a young stag on 1948
2:17 and be like a gazelle or l a young stag on NIH
3: 6 up from the desert l a column of smoke, 3869
4: 1 Your hair is l a flock of goats descending 3869
4: 2 Your teeth are l a flock of sheep just shorn, 3869
4: 3 Your lips are l a scarlet ribbon; 3869
4: 3 Your temples behind your veil are l 3869
4: 4 Your neck is l the tower of David, 3869
4: 5 Your two breasts are l two fawns, 3869
4: 5 l twin fawns of a gazelle that browse NIH
4:11 The fragrance of your garments is l that 3869
5:12 His eyes are l doves by the water streams, 3869
5:12 in milk, **mounted l jewels.** 3782+4859+6584
5:13 His cheeks are l beds of spice 3869
5:13 His lips are l lilies dripping with myrrh. NIH
5:14 His body is l polished ivory decorated NIH
5:15 His appearance is l Lebanon, 3869
6: 5 Your hair is l a flock of goats descending 3869
6: 6 Your teeth are l a flock of sheep coming 3869
6: 7 Your temples behind your veil are l 3869

SS	6:10	Who is this that appears l the dawn,	4017
	7:1	Your graceful legs are l jewels,	4017
	7:3	Your breasts are l two fawns,	3869
	7:4	Your neck is l an ivory tower.	3869
	7:4	Your nose is l the tower of Lebanon	3869
	7:5	Your head crowns you l Mount Carmel.	3869
	7:5	Your hair is l royal tapestry;	3869
	7:7	Your stature **is** l that of the palm,	1948
	7:7	and your breasts l clusters of fruit.	NIH
	7:8	May your breasts be l the clusters of	3869
	7:8	the fragrance of your breath l apples,	3869
	7:9	and your mouth l the best wine.	3869
	8:1	If only you were to me l a brother,	3869
	8:6	Place me l a seal over your heart,	3869
	8:6	l a seal on your arm;	3869
	8:6	It burns l blazing fire, like a mighty flame.	NIH
	8:6	It burns like blazing fire, l a mighty flame.	NIH
	8:10	I am a wall, and my breasts are l towers.	3869
	8:10	in his eyes l one bringing contentment.	3869
	8:14	and **be** l a gazelle or like a young stag on	1948
	8:14	and be like a gazelle or l a young stag on	NIH
Isa	1:8	The Daughter of Zion is left l a shelter in	3869
	1:8	l a hut in a field of melons,	3869
	1:8	l a city under siege.	3869
	1:9	we would have become l Sodom,	3869
	1:9	*we would have* **been** l Gomorrah.	1948
	1:18	"Though your sins are l scarlet,	3869
	1:18	sins are like scarlet, they shall be l wool.	3869
	1:30	You will be l an oak with fading leaves,	3869
	1:30	l a garden without water.	3869
	2:6	they practice divination l the Philistines	3869
	3:9	they parade their sin l Sodom;	3869
	5:24	and their flowers blow away l dust;	3869
	5:25	the dead bodies are l refuse in the streets.	3869
	5:28	their horses' hoofs seem l flint,	3869
	5:28	their chariot wheels l a whirlwind.	3869
	5:29	Their roar is l that of the lion,	3869
	5:29	they roar l young lions;	3869
	5:30	that day they will roar over it l the roaring	3869
	9:18	Surely wickedness burns l a fire;	3869
	10:6	to trample them down l mud in the streets.	3869
	10:9	'Has not Calno **fared** l Carchemish?	3869
	10:9	Is not Hamath l Arpad,	3869
	10:9	and Samaria l Damascus?	3869
	10:13	l a mighty one I subdued their kings.	3869
	10:16	a fire will be kindled l a blazing flame.	3869
	10:22	O Israel, be l the sand by the sea,	3869
	11:7	and the lion will eat straw l the ox.	3869
	13:4	l *that of* a great multitude!	1952
	13:4	l nations massing together!	NIH
	13:6	it will come l destruction from	3869
	13:8	they will writhe l a woman in labor.	3869
	13:14	L a hunted gazelle,	3869
	13:14	l sheep without a shepherd,	3869
	13:19	will be overthrown by God l Sodom	3869
	14:10	*you have* **become** l us."	5439
	14:14	*I will* **make myself** l the Most High."	1948
	14:19	But you are cast out of your tomb l	3869
	14:19	L a corpse trampled underfoot,	3869
	16:2	L fluttering birds pushed from the nest,	3869
	16:3	Make your shadow l night—at high noon.	3869
	16:11	My heart laments for Moab l a harp,	3869
	17:3	the remnant of Aram will be l the glory of	3869
	17:9	will be l places abandoned to thickets	3869
	17:12	they rage l the raging sea!	3869
	17:12	they roar l the roaring of great waters!	3869
	17:13	peoples roar l the roar of surging waters,	3869
	17:13	driven before the wind l chaff on the hills,	3869
	17:13	l tumbleweed before a gale.	3869
	18:4	l shimmering heat in the sunshine,	3869
	18:4	l a cloud of dew in the heat of harvest."	3869
	19:16	In that day the Egyptians will be l women.	3869
	21:1	L whirlwinds sweeping through	3869
	21:3	l those of a woman in labor;	3869
	22:18	roll you up tightly l a ball and throw you	3869
	22:23	I will drive him l a peg into a firm place;	NIH
	24:20	The earth reels l a drunkard,	3869
	24:20	it sways l a hut in the wind;	3869
	24:22	be herded together l prisoners bound in	NIH
	25:4	of the ruthless is l a storm driving against	3869
	25:5	and l the heat of the desert.	3869
	26:19	Your dew is l the dew of the morning;	NIH
	27:9	When he makes all the altar stones to be l	3869
	27:10	forsaken l the desert;	3869
	28:2	L a hailstorm and a destructive wind,	3869
	28:2	l a driving rain and a flooding downpour,	3869
	28:4	will be l a fig ripe before harvest—	3869
	29:2	she will be to me l an altar hearth.	3869
	29:5	But your many enemies will become l	3869
	29:5	the ruthless hordes l blown chaff.	3869
	29:16	if the potter were thought to be l the clay!	3869
	29:17	a fertile field and the fertile field seem l	4200
	30:13	this sin will become for you l a high wall,	3869
	30:14	It will break in pieces l pottery,	3869
	30:17	till you are left l a flagstaff on	3869
	30:17	l a banner on a hill."	3869
	30:22	you will throw them away l a menstrual	4017
	30:26	The moon will shine l the sun,	3869
	30:26	l the light of seven full days,	3869
	30:28	His breath is l a rushing torrent,	3869
	30:33	l a stream of burning sulfur, sets it ablaze.	3869
	31:5	L birds hovering overhead,	3869
	32:2	Each man will be l a shelter from the wind	3869
	32:2	l streams of water in the desert and	3869
	32:15	and the fertile field seems l a forest.	4200
	33:4	l a swarm of locusts men pounce on it.	3869
	33:9	Sharon is l the Arabah,	3869
Isa	33:12	l cut thornbushes they will be set ablaze."	NIH
	33:21	be l a place of broad rivers and streams.	NIH
	34:4	and the sky rolled up l a scroll;	3869
	34:4	the starry host will fall l withered leaves	3869
	34:4	l shriveled figs from the fig tree.	3869
	35:1	and blossom. L the crocus,	3869
	35:6	Then will the lame leap l a deer,	3869
	36:12	who, l you, will have to eat their own filth	6640
	36:17	until I come and take you to a land l	3869
	37:27	They are l plants in the field,	NIH
	37:27	l tender green shoots,	NIH
	37:27	l grass sprouting on the roof,	NIH
	38:12	L a shepherd's tent my house has been	3869
	38:12	L a weaver I have rolled up my life,	3869
	38:13	but l a lion he broke all my bones;	3869
	38:14	I cried l a swift or thrush,	3869
	38:14	I moaned l a mourning dove.	3869
	40:6	"All men are l grass,	NIH
	40:6	all their glory is l the flowers of the field.	3869
	40:11	He tends his flock l a shepherd:	3869
	40:15	Surely the nations are l a drop in a bucket;	3869
	40:22	and its people are l grasshoppers.	3869
	40:22	He stretches out the heavens l a canopy,	3869
	40:22	and spreads them out l a tent to live in.	3869
	40:24	a whirlwind sweeps them away l chaff.	3869
	40:31	They will soar on wings l eagles;	3869
	42:13	LORD will march out l a mighty man,	3869
	42:13	l a warrior he will stir up his zeal;	3869
	42:14	But now, l a woman in childbirth,	3869
	42:19	and deaf l the messenger I send?	3869
	42:19	Who is blind l the one committed to me,	3869
	42:19	blind l the servant of the LORD?	3869
	43:17	extinguished, snuffed out l a wick:	3869
	44:4	They will spring up l grass in a meadow,	NIH
	44:4	l poplar trees by flowing streams.	3869
	44:7	Who then is l me?	4017
	44:22	I have swept away your offenses l a cloud,	3869
	44:22	your sins l the morning mist.	3869
	46:9	I am God, and there is none l me.	4017
	47:14	Surely they are l stubble;	3869
	48:18	your peace would have been l a river,	3869
	48:18	your righteousness l the waves of the sea.	3869
	48:19	Your descendants would have been l	3869
	48:19	your children l its numberless grains;	3869
	49:2	He made my mouth l a sharpened sword,	3869
	49:18	you will put them on, l a bride.	3869
	50:4	to listen l one being taught.	3869
	50:7	Therefore have I set my face l flint,	3869
	50:9	They will all wear out l a garment;	3869
	51:3	he will make her deserts l Eden,	3869
	51:3	her wastelands l the garden of the LORD.	3869
	51:6	the heavens will vanish l smoke,	3869
	51:6	like smoke, the earth will wear out l	3869
	51:6	a garment and its inhabitants die l flies.	4017
	51:8	For the moth will eat them up l a garment;	3869
	51:8	the worm will devour them l wool.	3869
	51:20	l antelope caught in a net.	3869
	51:23	And you made your back l the ground,	3869
	51:23	l a street to be walked over."	3869
	53:2	He grew up before him l a tender shoot,	3869
	53:2	and l a root out of dry ground.	3869
	53:3	L one from whom men hide their faces he was despised,	3869
	53:6	We all, l sheep, have gone astray,	3869
	53:7	he was led l a lamb to the slaughter,	3869
	54:9	"To me this is l the days of Noah,	3869
	56:12	And tomorrow will be l today,	3869
	57:20	But the wicked are l the tossing sea,	3869
	58:1	Raise your voice l a trumpet.	3869
	58:5	Is it only for bowing one's head l a reed	3869
	58:8	your light will break forth l the dawn,	3869
	58:10	and your night will become l the noonday.	3869
	58:11	You will be l a well-watered garden,	3869
	58:11	l a spring whose waters never fail.	3869
	59:10	L the blind we grope along the wall,	3869
	59:10	feeling our way l men without eyes.	3869
	59:10	among the strong, we are l the dead.	3869
	59:11	We all growl l bears;	3869
	59:11	we moan mournfully l doves.	3869
	59:19	For he will come l a pent-up flood that	3869
	60:8	"Who are these that fly along l clouds,	3869
	60:8	l doves to their nests?	3869
	61:10	as a bridegroom adorns his head *l a* **priest**,	AIT
	62:1	till her righteousness shines out l the dawn,	3869
	62:1	her salvation l a blazing torch.	3869
	63:2	l those *of* one treading the winepress?	3869
	63:13	L a horse in open country,	3869
	63:14	l cattle that go down to the plain,	3869
	64:6	of us have become l one who is unclean,	3869
	64:6	and all our righteous acts are l filthy rags;	3869
	64:6	we all shrivel up l a leaf,	3869
	64:6	and l the wind our sins sweep us away.	3869
	65:25	and the lion will eat straw l the ox,	3869
	66:3	sacrifices a bull is l one who kills a man,	NIH
	66:3	l one who breaks a dog's neck;	NIH
	66:3	whoever makes a grain offering is l	NIH
	66:3	l one who worships an idol.	NIH
	66:12	"I will extend peace to her l a river,	3869
	66:12	the wealth of nations l a flooding stream;	3869
	66:14	and you will flourish l grass;	3869
	66:15	and his chariots are l a whirlwind;	3869
Jer	2:10	see if there has ever been anything l this:	3869
	2:21	I had planted you l a choice vine of sound	NIH
	2:30	Your sword has devoured your prophets l	3869
	3:2	sat l a nomad in the desert.	3869
	3:19	" 'How gladly would I treat you l sons	928
	3:20	But l a woman unfaithful to her husband,	NIH
Jer	4:4	or my wrath will break out and burn l fire	3869
	4:13	He advances l the clouds,	3869
	4:13	his chariots come l a whirlwind,	3869
	4:17	They surround her l men guarding a field,	3869
	5:16	Their quivers are l an open grave;	3869
	5:26	in wait l men who snare birds and	3869
	5:26	and l those who set traps to catch men.	NIH
	5:27	L cages full of birds,	3869
	6:9	l one gathering grapes."	3869
	6:23	They sound l the roaring sea as they ride	3869
	6:23	they come l men in battle formation	3869
	6:24	pain l that of a woman in labor.	3869
	8:2	but will be l refuse lying on the ground.	4200
	8:6	pursues his own course l a horse charging	3869
	9:3	"They make ready their tongue l a bow,	NIH
	9:12	the land been ruined and laid waste l	3869
	9:22	" 'The dead bodies of men will lie l refuse	3869
	9:22	l cut grain behind the reaper,	3869
	10:5	L a scarecrow in a melon patch,	3869
	10:6	No one is l you, O LORD;	4017
	10:7	there is no one l you.	4017
	10:16	of Jacob is not l these, for he is the Maker	3869
	11:19	I had been l a gentle lamb led to	3869
	12:3	Drag them off l sheep to be butchered!	3869
	12:8	My inheritance has become to me l a lion	3869
	12:9	Has not my inheritance become to me l	NIH
	13:10	will be l this belt—completely useless!	3869
	13:21	Will not pain grip you l that of a woman	4017
	13:24	"I will scatter you l chaff driven by	3869
	14:6	on the barren heights and pant l jackals;	3869
	14:8	why are you l a stranger in the land,	3869
	14:8	l a traveler who stays only a night?	3869
	14:9	Why are you l a man taken by surprise,	3869
	14:9	l a warrior powerless to save?	3869
	15:18	Will you be to me l a deceptive brook,	4017
	15:18	l a spring that fails?	NIH
	16:4	but will be l refuse lying on the ground.	4200
	17:6	He will be l a bush in the wastelands;	3869
	17:8	He will be l a tree planted by the water	3869
	17:11	L a partridge that hatches eggs it did	NIH
	18:6	"L clay in the hand of the potter,	3869
	18:13	Who has ever heard anything l this?	3869
	18:17	L a wind from the east,	3869
	19:12	I will make this city l Topheth.	3869
	19:13	of the kings of Judah will be defiled l	3869
	20:9	his word is in my heart l a fire,	3869
	20:11	the LORD is with me l a mighty warrior;	3869
	20:16	be l the towns the LORD overthrew	3869
	21:12	or my wrath will break out and burn l fire	3869
	22:6	"Though you are l Gilead to me,	NIH
	22:6	l the summit of Lebanon,	NIH
	22:6	I will surely make you l a desert,	NIH
	22:6	like a desert, l towns not inhabited.	NIH
	22:23	pain l that of a woman in labor!	3869
	23:9	I am l a drunken man,	3869
	23:9	l a man overcome by wine,	3869
	23:14	They are all l Sodom to me;	3869
	23:14	the people of Jerusalem are l Gomorrah."	3869
	23:29	"Is not my word l fire,"	3869
	23:29	l a hammer that breaks a rock in pieces?	3869
	24:2	l those that ripen early;	3869
	24:5	'L these good figs,	3869
	24:8	" 'But l the poor figs,	3869
	25:30	He will shout l those who tread	3869
	25:33	but will be l refuse lying on the ground.	4200
	25:34	you will fall and be shattered l	3869
	25:38	L a lion he will leave his lair,	3869
	26:6	then I will make this house l Shiloh	3869
	26:9	be l Shiloh and this city will be desolate	3869
	26:18	" 'Zion will be plowed l a field,	NIH
	29:17	and I will make them l poor figs that are	3869
	29:22	'The LORD treat you l Zedekiah	3869
	29:26	you should put any madman *who* **acts l a prophet** into the stocks	5547
	30:6	hands on his stomach l a woman in labor,	3869
	30:7	None will be l it.	4017
	31:10	and will watch over his flock l	3869
	31:12	They will be l a well-watered garden,	3869
	31:18	'You disciplined me l an unruly calf,	3869
	31:32	It will not be l the covenant I made	3869
	34:18	*I will* **treat** *l* the calf they cut in two and	AIT
	40:4	with me to Babylon, if you l,	928+3202+6524
	44:19	that we were making cakes l her **image**	6771
	46:7	"Who is this that rises l the Nile,	3869
	46:7	l rivers of surging waters?	3869
	46:8	Egypt rises l the Nile,	3869
	46:8	l rivers of surging waters.	3869
	46:18	"one will come who is l Tabor among	3869
	46:18	l Carmel by the sea.	3869
	46:21	mercenaries in her ranks are l fattened	3869
	46:22	Egypt will hiss l a fleeing serpent as	3869
	46:22	l men who cut down trees.	3869
	48:6	become l a bush in the desert.	3869
	48:11	l wine left on its dregs,	NIH
	48:28	Be l a dove that makes its nest at the mouth	3869
	48:36	"So my heart laments for Moab l a flute;	3869
	48:36	it laments l a flute for the men of	3869
	48:38	for I have broken Moab l a jar	3869
	48:41	Moab's warriors will be l the heart of	3869
	49:19	"L a lion coming up from Jordan's thickets	3869
	49:19	Who is l me and who can challenge me?	4017
	49:22	of Edom's warriors will be l the heart of	3869
	49:23	troubled l the restless sea.	3869
	49:24	pain l that of a woman in labor.	3869
	50:8	and be l the goats that lead the flock.	3869
	50:9	be l skilled warriors who do	3869
	50:11	because you frolic l a heifer threshing grain	3869

Jer 50:11 like a heifer threshing grain and neigh l 3869
50:26 pile her up l heaps of grain. 4017
50:42 They sound l the roaring sea as they ride 3869
50:42 they come l men in battle formation 3869
50:43 pain l that of a woman in labor. 3869
50:44 L a lion coming up from Jordan's thickets 3869
50:44 Who is l me and who can challenge me? 4017
51:19 of Jacob is not l these, for he is the Maker 3869
51:27 send up horses l a swarm of locusts. 3869
51:30 they have become l women. 4200
51:33 of Babylon is l a threshing floor at the time 3869
51:34 L a serpent he has swallowed us 3869
51:38 Her people all roar l young lions, 3869
51:38 they growl l lion cubs. 3869
51:40 "I will bring them down l lambs to 3869
51:40 l rams and goats. 3869
51:55 [of enemies] will rage l great waters; 3869
La 1: 1 How l a widow is she, 3869
1: 6 Her princes are l deer that find no pasture; 3869
1:12 Is any suffering l my suffering 3869
1:21 so they may become l me. 4017
2: 3 He has burned in Jacob l a flaming fire 3869
2: 4 L an enemy he has strung his bow; 3869
2: 4 L a foe he has slain all who were pleasing 3869
2: 4 he has poured out his wrath l fire on 3869
2: 5 The Lord is l an enemy; 3869
2: 6 He has laid waste his dwelling l a garden; 3869
2:12 as they faint l wounded men in the streets 3869
2:18 let your tears flow l a river day and night; 3869
2:19 pour out your heart l water in the presence 3869
2:20 Whom have you ever treated **l this?** 3907
3: 6 He has made me dwell in darkness l 3869
3:10 L a bear lying in wait, like a lion in hiding, NIH
3:10 l a lion in hiding, NIH
3:52 without cause hunted me l a bird. 3869
4: 3 but my people have become heartless l 3869
4: 7 their appearance l sapphires. NIH
4:14 through the streets l men who are blind. NIH
5: 3 our mothers l widows. 3869
Eze 1: 4 of the fire looked l glowing metal, 3869
1: 5 and in the fire was *what* **looked l** 1952
1: 7 their feet were l those of a calf 3869
1: 7 and gleamed l burnished bronze. 3869+6524
1:10 Their faces **looked l** this: 1952
1:13 of the living creatures was l burning coals 1952
1:13 like burning coals of fire or l torches. 3869
1:14 The creatures sped back and forth l 3869
1:16 They sparkled l chrysolite, 3869
1:16 be made l a wheel intersecting a wheel. 889+3869
1:22 of the living creatures was *what* **looked l** 1952
1:22 sparkling l ice, and awesome. 3869
1:24 l the roar of rushing waters, 3869
1:24 l the voice of the Almighty, 3869
1:24 l the tumult of an army. NIH
1:26 over their heads was what looked l 1952
1:26 on the throne was a figure l that of a man. 3869
1:27 he his waist up he looked l glowing metal, 3869
1:27 and that from there down he looked l fire; 3869
1:28 L the appearance of a rainbow in 3869
2: 8 Do not rebel l that rebellious house; 3869
3: 9 I will make your forehead l the hardest 3869
3:23 l the glory I had seen by the Kebar River, 3869
7:16 moaning l doves of the valleys, 3869
8: 2 and I saw a figure l that of a man. 3869
8: 2 to be his waist down he was l fire, NIH
8: 3 He stretched out *what* **looked l** a hand 9322
10: 5 l the voice of God Almighty 3869
10: 8 be seen *what* **looked l** the hands of a man.) 9322
10: 9 the wheels sparkled l chrysolite. 3869
10:10 each was l a wheel intersecting a wheel. 889+3869
10:21 and under their wings was *what* **looked l** 1952
12: 4 go out l those who go into exile. 3869
13: 4 O Israel, are l jackals among ruins. 3869
13:20 with which you ensnare people l birds 4200
13:20 I will set free the people that you ensnare l 4200
16: 7 I made you grow l a plant of the field. 3869
16:30 **acting** *l* a brazen prostitute! AIT
16:44 **"L** mother, like daughter." 3869
16:44 "Like mother, l daughter." NIH
17: 5 He planted it l a willow by abundat water, NIH
19:10 'Your mother was l a vine in your vineyard 3869
20:32 " 'You say, "We want to be l the nations, 3869
20:32 l the peoples of the world, 3869
21:10 polished to **flash l lightning!** 1398
21:15 It is made to **flash l lightning,** 1398
21:23 It will seem l a false omen 3869
21:28 to consume and to **flash l lightning!** 1398
22:25 within her l a roaring lion tearing its prey; 3869
22:27 within her are l wolves tearing their prey; 3869
23:15 all of them looked l Babylonian chariot 1952
23:20 whose genitals were l those of donkeys NIH
23:20 of donkeys and whose emission was l that NIH
25: 8 Judah has become l all the other nations," 3869
26: 3 l the sea casting up its waves. 3869
26:19 l cities no longer inhabited, 3869
27:32 "Who was ever silenced l Tyre, 3869
30:24 before him l a mortally wounded man. NIH
32: 2 " *'You* **are l** a lion among the nations; 1948
32: 2 you are l a monster in the seas thrashing 3869
32:14 and make her streams flow l oil, 3869
36:17 Their conduct was l a woman's monthly 3869
36:35 waste has become l the garden of Eden; 3869
38: 9 advancing l a storm; 3869
38: 9 you will be l a cloud covering the land. 3869
38:16 against my people Israel l a cloud 3869
40: 2 that looked l a city. 3869
40: 3 and I saw a man whose appearance was l 3869
Eze 40:25 l the openings of the others. 3869
41:25 palm trees l those carved on the walls, 889+3869
42:11 These were l the rooms on the north; 3869+5260
43: 2 His voice was l the roar of rushing waters, 3869
43: 3 The vision I saw was l the vision I had seen 3869
43: 3 and l the visions I had seen by the Kebar 3869
47:10 l the fish of the Great Sea. 3869
Da 2:35 and became l chaff on a threshing floor in 10341
3:25 and the fourth looks l a son of the gods." 10179
4:23 let him live l the wild animals, 10554
4:25 you will eat grass l cattle and be drenched 10341
4:32 you will eat grass l cattle. 10341
4:33 from people and ate grass l cattle. 10341
4:33 of heaven until his hair grew l the feathers 10341
4:33 an eagle and his nails l the claws of a bird. 10341
5:11 and intelligence and wisdom l that of 10341
5:21 the wild donkeys and ate grass l cattle; 10341
7: 4 "The first was l a lion, 10341
7: 4 the ground so that it stood on two feet l 10341
7: 5 which **looked l** a bear. 10179
7: 6 one that looked l a leopard. 10341
7: 6 And on its back it had four wings l those NIH
7: 8 This horn had eyes l the eyes of a man 10341
7: 9 the hair of his head was white l wool. 10341
7:13 and there before me was one l a son 10341
8:15 before me stood one who looked l a man. 3869
9:12 whole heaven nothing has ever been done l 3869
9:26 The end will come l a flood: 928
10: 6 His body was l chrysolite, 3869
10: 6 his face l lightning, 3869+5260
10: 6 his eyes l flaming torches, 3869
10: 6 and legs l the gleam of burnished bronze, 3869
10: 6 and his voice l the sound of a multitude. 3869
10:16 one who looked l a man touched my lips, 3869
10:18 the one who looked l a man touched me 3869
11:10 which will sweep on l an irresistible flood NIH
11:40 and sweep through them l a flood. NIH
12: 3 who are wise will shine l the brightness 3869
12: 3 l the stars for ever and ever. 3869
Hos 1:10 "Yet the Israelites will be l the sand on 3869
2: 3 I will make her l a desert, 3869
4: 4 your people are l those who bring charges 3869
4: 9 And it will be: L people, like priests. 3869
4: 9 And it will be: Like people, l priests. 3869
4:16 l a stubborn heifer. 3869
4:16 then can the LORD pasture them l lambs 3869
5:10 Judah's leaders are l those who move 3869
5:10 I will pour out my wrath on them l a flood 3869
5:12 I am l a moth to Ephraim, 3869
5:12 l rot to the people of Judah. 3869
5:14 For I will be l a lion to Ephraim, 3869
5:14 l a great lion to Judah. 3869
6: 3 he will come to us l the winter rains, 3869
6: 3 l the spring rains that water the earth." 3869
6: 4 Your love is l the morning mist, 3869
6: 4 l the early dew that disappears. 3869
6: 5 my judgments flashed l lightning NIH
6: 7 L Adam, they have broken the covenant— 3869
7: 4 burning l an oven whose fire 4017
7: 6 Their hearts are l an oven; 3869
7: 6 in the morning it blazes l a flaming fire. 3869
7:11 "Ephraim is l a dove, 3869
7:12 I will pull them down l birds of the air. 3869
7:16 they are l a faulty bow. 3869
8: 8 among the nations l a worthless thing. 3869
8: 9 gone up to Assyria l a donkey wandering NIH
9: 1 do not be jubilant l the other nations. 3869
9: 4 Such sacrifices will be to them l the bread 3869
9:10 it was l finding grapes in the desert; 3869
9:10 when I saw your fathers, it was l seeing 3869
9:11 Ephraim's glory will fly away l a bird— 3869
9:13 I have seen Ephraim, l Tyre, 889+3869
10: 4 up l poisonous weeds in a plowed field. 3869
10: 7 and its king will float away l a twig on 3869
11: 8 How can I treat you l Admah? 3869
11: 8 How can I make you l Zeboiim? 3869
11:10 he will roar l a lion. 3869
11:11 They will come trembling l birds 3869
11:11 l doves from Assyria. 3869
12:11 Their altars will be l piles of stones on 3869
13: 3 Therefore they will be l the morning mist, 3869
13: 3 l the early dew that disappears, 3869
13: 3 l chaff swirling from a threshing floor, 3869
13: 3 l smoke escaping through a window. 3869
13: 7 So I will come upon them l a lion, 4017
13: 7 l a leopard I will lurk by the path. 3869
13: 8 L a bear robbed of her cubs, 3869
13: 8 L a lion I will devour them; 3869
14: 5 I will be l the dew to Israel; 3869
14: 5 he will blossom l a lily. 3869
14: 5 L a cedar of Lebanon he will send 3869
14: 6 His splendor will be l an olive tree, 3869
14: 6 his fragrance l a cedar of Lebanon. 3869
14: 7 He will flourish l the grain. NIH
14: 7 He will blossom l a vine, 3869
14: 7 his fame will be l the wine from Lebanon. 3869
14: 8 I am l a green pine tree; 3869
Joel 1: 2 Has anything l this ever happened NIH
1: 8 Mourn l a virgin in sackcloth grieving for 3869
1:15 come l destruction from the Almighty. 3869
2: 2 L dawn spreading across the mountains 3869
2: 3 Before them the land is l the garden 3869
2: 4 they gallop along l cavalry. 3869
2: 5 With a noise l that of chariots they leap 3869
2: 5 l a crackling fire consuming stubble, 3869
2: 5 l a mighty army drawn up for battle. 3869
2: 7 They charge l warriors; 3869
Joel 2: 7 they scale walls l soldiers. 3869
2: 9 l thieves they enter through the windows. 3869
Am 4:11 You were l a burning stick snatched from 3869
5: 6 through the house of Joseph l a fire; 3869
5:24 But let justice roll on l a river, 3869
5:24 righteousness l a never-failing stream! 3869
6: 5 You strum away on your harps l David 3869
8: 8 The whole land will rise l the Nile; 3869
8: 8 be stirred up and then sink l the river 3869
8:10 that time l mourning for an only son and 3869
8:10 an only son and the end of it l a bitter day. 3869
9: 5 the whole land rises l the Nile, 3869
9: 5 then sinks l the river of Egypt— 3869
Ob 1: 4 Though you soar l the eagle 3869
1:11 you were l one of them. 3869
Mic 1: 4 l wax before the fire, 3869
1: 4 l water rushing down a slope. 3869
1: 8 I will howl l a jackal and moan like 3869
1: 8 like a jackal and moan l an owl. 3869
2: 8 Lately my people have risen up l 4200
2: 8 l men returning from battle. NIH
2:12 I will bring them together l sheep in a pen, 3869
2:12 l a flock in its pasture; 3869
3: 3 who chop them up l meat for the pan, 889+3869
3: 3 l flesh for the pot?" 3869
3:12 Zion will be plowed l a field, NIH
4: 9 that pain seizes you l that of a woman 3869
4:10 O Daughter of Zion, l a woman in labor, 3869
4:12 he who gathers them l sheaves to 3869
5: 7 of many peoples l dew from the LORD, 3869
5: 7 l showers on the grass, 3869
5: 8 l a lion among the beasts of the forest, 3869
5: 8 l a young lion among flocks of sheep, 3869
7: 1 I am l one who gathers summer fruit at 3869
7: 4 The best of them is l a brier, 3869
7:10 even now she will be trampled underfoot l 3869
7:17 They will lick dust l a snake, 3869
7:17 l creatures that crawl on the ground. 3869
7:18 Who is a God l you, who pardons sin 4017
Na 1: 6 His wrath is poured out l fire; 3869
1:10 they will be consumed l dry stubble. 3869
2: 2 the splendor of Jacob l the splendor 3869
2: 4 They look l flaming torches; 3869
2: 4 they dart about l lightning. 3869
2: 7 Its slave girls moan l doves and beat 3869
2: 8 Nineveh is l a pool, 3869
3:12 All your fortresses are l fig trees NIH
3:15 and, l grasshoppers, consume you. 3869
3:15 Multiply l grasshoppers, 3869
3:15 like grasshoppers, multiply l locusts! 3869
3:16 but l locusts they strip the land and NIH
3:17 Your guards are l locusts, 3869
3:17 your officials l swarms of locusts 3869
Hab 1: 8 They fly l a vulture swooping to devour; 3869
1: 9 Their hordes advance l a desert wind NIH
1: 9 a desert wind and gather prisoners l sand. 3869
1:11 they sweep past l the wind and go on— NIH
1:14 You have made men l fish in the sea, 3869
1:14 l sea creatures that have no ruler. 3869
2: 5 Because he is as greedy as the grave and l 3869
3: 4 His splendor was l the sunrise; 3869
3:19 he makes my feet l the feet of a deer, 3869
Zep 1:12 who are l wine left on its dregs, NIH
1:17 the people and they will walk l blind men, 3869
1:17 be poured out l dust and their entrails 3869
1:17 and their entrails l filth. 3869
2: 2 and that day sweeps on l chaff, 3869
2: 9 "surely Moab will become l Sodom, 3869
2: 9 the Ammonites l Gomorrah— 3869
Hag 2: 3 Does it not seem to you l nothing? 3869
2:23 'and I will make you l my signet ring, 3869
Zec 1: 4 Do not be l your forefathers, 3869
5: 9 They had wings l those of a stork, 3869
9: 3 she has heaped up silver l dust, 3869
9: 3 and gold l the dirt of the streets. 3869
9: 7 and Ekron will be l the Jebusites. 3869
9:13 and make you l a warrior's sword. 3869
9:14 his arrow will flash l lightning. 3869
9:15 be full l a bowl used for sprinkling 3869
9:16 They will sparkle in his land l jewels in NIH
10: 2 the people wander l sheep oppressed 4017
10: 3 and make them l a proud horse in battle. 3869
10: 5 be l mighty men trampling 3869
10: 7 The Ephraimites will become l 3869
12: 6 that day I will make the leaders of Judah l 3869
12: 6 l a flaming torch among sheaves. 3869
12: 8 the feeblest among them will be l David, 3869
12: 8 and the house of David will be l God, 3869
12: 8 l the Angel of the LORD going 3869
12:11 l the weeping of Hadad Rimmon in 3869
13: 9 I will refine them l silver and test them 3869
13: 9 like silver and test them l gold. 3869
14:10 will become l the Arabah. 3869
14:20 be l the sacred bowls in front of the altar. 3869
Mal 3: 2 be l a refiner's fire or a launderer's soap. 3869
3: 3 the Levites and refine them l gold 3869
3:14 going about l mourners before the LORD NIH
4: 1 the day is coming; it will burn l a furnace. 3869
4: 2 and leap l calves released from the stall. 3869
Mt 3:16 the Spirit of God descending l a dove *6059*
6: 5 when you pray, do not be l the hypocrites, *6055*
6: 7 do not keep on babbling l pagans, *6061*
6: 8 *Do* not *be* l them, for your Father knows *3929*
6:29 his splendor was dressed l one of these. *6055*
7:24 puts them into practice *is* l a wise man who *3929*
7:26 does not put them into practice *is* l a foolish *3929*
9:33 "Nothing **l this** has ever been seen *4048*

Mt 9:36 l sheep without a shepherd. *6059*
10:16 I am sending you out l sheep *6055*
10:25 It is enough for the student to be l *6055*
10:25 and the servant l his master. *6055*
11:16 are l children sitting in the marketplaces *3927*
13:24 "The kingdom of heaven *is* l a man who *3929*
13:31 kingdom of heaven is l a mustard seed, *3927*
13:33 "The kingdom of heaven is l yeast that *3927*
13:43 Then the righteous will shine l the sun in *6055*
13:44 of heaven is l treasure hidden in a field. *3927*
13:45 of heaven is l a merchant looking *3927*
13:47 of heaven is l a net that was let down into *3927*
13:52 the kingdom of heaven is l the owner of *3927*
17: 2 His face shone l the sun, *6055*
18: 3 you change and become l little children, *6055*
18: 4 whoever humbles himself l this child is *6055*
18: 5 welcomes a little child l **this** in my name *5525*
18:23 kingdom of heaven *is* l a king who wanted *3929*
20: 1 kingdom of heaven is l a landowner who *3927*
22: 2 kingdom of heaven *is* l a king who prepared *3929*
22:30 they will be l the angels in heaven. *6055*
22:39 And the second is l it: *3927*
23:27 *You are* l whitewashed tombs, *4234*
25: 1 the kingdom of heaven *will be* l ten virgins *3929*
25:14 it will be l a man going on a journey, *6061*
28: 3 His appearance was l lightning, *6055*
28: 4 that they shook and became l dead men. *6055*
Mk 1:10 and the Spirit descending on him l a dove. *6055*
2: 7 "Why does this fellow talk l **that?** *4048*
2:12 "We have never seen anything l **this!"** *4048*
4:15 Some people are l seed along the path, *NIG*
4:16 Others, l seed sown on rocky places, *3931*
4:18 Still others, l seed sown among thorns, *NIG*
4:20 Others, l seed sown on good soil, *NIG*
4:26 "This is what the kingdom of God is l. *6055*
4:30 *shall we* **say** the kingdom of God **is** l, *3929*
4:31 It is l a mustard seed, *6055*
6:15 l one of the prophets of long ago." *6055*
6:34 they were l sheep without a shepherd. *6055*
7:13 And you do many things l that." *4235*
8:24 they look l trees walking around." *6055*
9:21 "How long has he been l this?" *6055*
9:26 The boy **looked so much** l a corpse *1181+6059*
10:15 of God l a little child will never enter it." *6055*
12:25 they will be l the angels in heaven. *6055*
12:38 *They* l to walk around in flowing robes *2527*
13:34 It's l a man going away: *6055*
Lk 1:62 to find out what *he* would l to name *2527*
2:48 "Son, why have you treated us l **this?** *4048*
3:22 descended on him in bodily form l a dove. *6055*
6:40 but everyone who is fully trained will be l *6055*
6:47 I will show you what he is l who comes *3927*
6:48 He is l a man building a house, *3927*
6:49 into practice is l a man who built a house *3927*
7:31 What are they l? *3927*
7:32 are l children sitting in the marketplace *3927*
10: 3 I am sending you out l lambs *6055*
10:18 "I saw Satan fall l lightning from heaven. *6055*
11:44 because you are l unmarked graves, *6055*
12:27 in all his splendor was dressed l one *6055*
12:36 l men waiting for their master to return *3927*
13:18 "What is the kingdom of God l? *3927*
13:19 It is l a mustard seed, *3927*
13:21 It is l yeast that a woman took and mixed *3927*
15:19 make me l one of your hired men.' *6055*
17:24 of Man in his day will be l the lightning, *6061*
17:30 "It will be **just** l **this** on the day the Son of Man is revealed. *899+2848+3836*
18:11 I thank you that I am not l other men— *6061*
18:11 or even l this tax collector. *6055*
18:17 of God l a little child will never enter it." *6055*
20:36 for they are l the **angels.** *2694*
20:46 They l to walk around in flowing robes *2527*
21:34 that day will close on you unexpectedly l *6055*
22:26 But you are not to be l **that.** *4048*
22:26 among you should be l the youngest, *6055*
22:26 the one who rules l the one who serves. *6055*
22:44 and his sweat was l drops of blood falling *6059*
24: 4 **that gleamed** l **lightning** stood beside them. *848*
24:11 their words seemed to them l nonsense. *6059*
Jn 1:44 Philip, l Andrew and Peter, was from *NIG*
8:55 If I said I did not, I would be a liar l you, *3927*
9: 9 Others said, "No, *he* only **looks** l him." *1639+3927*
11:48 If we let him go on l **this,** *4048*
12:21 "Sir," they said, *"we would* l to see Jesus." *2527*
15: 6 he is l a branch that is thrown away *6055*
Ac 2: 2 Suddenly a sound l the blowing of *6061*
3:22 raise up for you a prophet l me from *6055*
6:15 and they saw that his face was l the face *6059*
7:37 a prophet l me from your own people.' *6055*
7:51 You are **just** l your fathers: *6055*
8:32 "He was led l a sheep to the slaughter, *6055*
9:18 something l scales fell from Saul's eyes, *6055*
10:11 He saw heaven opened and something l *6055*
11: 5 I saw something l a large sheet being let *6055*
14:15 We too are only men, **human** l you. *3926*
17:29 not think that the divine being is l gold *3927*
22:24 the people were shouting at him l this. *4048*
25:22 *"I would* l to hear this man myself." *1089*
Ro 1:23 for images made to **look** l mortal man *3930*
5:15 But the gift is not l the trespass. *4048*
5:16 not l the result of the one man's sin: *6055*
6: 5 If we have been united with him l this *3930*
9:20 'Why did you make me l **this?"** ' *4048*
9:27 "Though the number of the Israelites be l *6055*
9:29 we would have become l Sodom, *6055*
9:29 *we* would *have been* l Gomorrah." *3929*
1Co 3: 3 Are you not acting l mere men? *2848*
4: 9 l men condemned to die in the arena. *6055*
7:32 *I would* l you to be free from concern. *2527*
9:20 To the Jews I became l a Jew, *6055*
9:20 To those under the law I became l one *6055*
9:21 the law I became l one not having the law *6055*
9:26 I do not run l a man running aimlessly; *6055*
9:26 I do not fight l a man beating the air. *6055*
13:11 When I was a child, I talked l a child, *6055*
13:11 I thought l a child, I reasoned like a child. *6055*
13:11 I thought like a child, I reasoned l a child. *6055*
14: 5 *I would* l every one of you to speak *2527*
14:20 Brothers, stop thinking *l* **children.** *AIT*
2Co 2:17 l men sent from God. *6055*
3: 1 Or do we need, l some people, *6055*
3:13 We are not l Moses, who would put a veil *2749*
11:23 (I am out of my mind to talk l this.) *NIG*
12: 5 I will boast about a **man** l **that,** *5525*
Gal 2:14 you live l **a Gentile** and not like a Jew. *1619*
2:14 yet you live like a Gentile and not l **a Jew.** *2680*
3: 2 *I would* l to learn just one thing *2527*
4:12 I plead with you, brothers, become l me, *6055*
4:12 become like me, for I became l you. *6055*
4:28 Now you, brothers, l Isaac, *2848*
5:21 drunkenness, orgies, and the l. *3927+4047*
5:21 that those who live l **this** will not inherit *5525*
Eph 1:19 That power is l the working *2848*
2: 3 L the rest, we were by nature objects *6055*
4:24 created to be l God in true righteousness *2848*
6: 6 but l slaves of Christ, *6055*
Php 2:15 in which you shine l stars in the universe *6055*
2:17 **poured out** l **a drink offering** *5064*
2:20 I have no one else l *him,* *2701*
2:29 and honor **men** l **him,** *5525*
3:10 **becoming** l him in his death, *5214*
3:21 so that they will be l his glorious body. *5215*
1Th 2: 7 l a mother caring for her little children *1569+6055*
4: 5 in passionate lust l the heathen, who do *2749*
4:13 or to grieve l the rest of men, *2777*
5: 2 that the day of the Lord will come l a thief *6055*
5: 4 that this day should surprise you l a thief. *6055*
5: 6 So then, let us not be l others, *6055*
2Ti 2: 3 Endure **hardship** with us l a good soldier *6055*
2: 9 to the point of being chained l a criminal. *6055*
2:17 Their teaching will spread l gangrene. *6055*
4: 6 **poured out** l **a drink offering,** *5064*
Heb 1:11 they will all wear out l a garment. *6055*
1:12 You will roll them up l a robe; *6059*
1:12 l a garment they will be changed. *6055*
2:17 *to be* **made** l his brothers in every way, *3929*
6: 9 Even though we speak l **this,** dear friends, *4048*
7: 3 l the Son of God he remains a priest forever. *926*
7:15 if another priest l Melchizedek appears, *3928*
8: 9 It will not be l the covenant I made *2848*
9: 6 When everything had been arranged l **this,** *4048*
11: 9 in the promised land l a stranger in *6055*
12:16 or is godless l Esau, *6055*
Jas 1: 6 he who doubts *is* l a wave of the sea, *2036*
1:10 because he will pass away l a wild flower. *6055*
1:17 who does not change l shifting shadows. *NIG*
1:23 the word but does not do what it says *is* l *2036*
1:24 and immediately forgets what *he* **looks** l. *1639*
5: 3 against you and eat your flesh l fire. *6055*
5:17 Elijah was a man **just** l us. *3926*
1Pe 1:24 For, "All men are l grass, *6055*
1:24 all their glory is l the flowers of the field; *6055*
2: 2 L newborn babies, crave pure spiritual milk, *6055*
2: 5 also, l living stones, are being built into *6055*
2:25 For you were l sheep going astray, *6055*
3: 6 l Sarah, who obeyed Abraham *6055*
5: 8 Your enemy the devil prowls around l *6055*
2Pe 2:12 They are l brute beasts, *6055*
2:12 and l beasts they too will perish. *NIG*
3: 8 With the Lord a day is l a thousand years, *6055*
3: 8 and a thousand years are l a day. *6055*
3:10 the day of the Lord will come l a thief. *6055*
1Jn 3: 2 when he appears, we shall be l him, *3927*
3:12 Do not be l Cain, who belonged to the evil *2777*
4:17 because in this world we are l him. *2777*
Jude 1:10 l unreasoning animals— *6055*
Rev 1:10 a loud voice l a trumpet, *6055*
1:13 lampstands was someone **"**l a son of man," *3927*
1:14 His head and hair were white l wool, *6055*
1:14 and his eyes were l blazing fire. *6055*
1:15 His feet were l bronze glowing in *3927*
1:15 his voice was l the sound of rushing waters. *6055*
1:16 His face was l the sun shining *6055*
2:18 Son of God, whose eyes are l blazing fire *6055*
2:18 and whose feet are l burnished bronze. *3927*
2:27 he will dash them to pieces l pottery'— *6055*
3: 3 you do not wake up, I will come l a thief, *6055*
3: 5 He who overcomes will, l them, *4048*
4: 1 speaking to me l a trumpet said, *6055*
4: 6 before the throne there was what **looked** l *6055*
4: 7 The first living creature was l a lion, *3927*
4: 7 the second was l an ox, *3927*
4: 7 the third had a face l a man, *6055*
4: 7 the fourth was l a flying eagle. *3927*
6: 1 four living creatures say in a voice l thunder *6055*
6: 6 Then I heard what sounded l a voice *6055*
6:12 The sun turned black l sackcloth made *6055*
6:14 The sky receded l a scroll, rolling up, *6055*
8: 8 and something l a huge mountain, *6055*
8:10 and a great star, blazing l a torch, *6055*
9: 2 smoke rose from it l the smoke from *6055*
9: 3 and were given power l **that of** scorpions *6055*
9: 5 And the agony they suffered was l **that of** *6055*
Rev 9: 7 The locusts **looked** l horses prepared *3927+3930*
9: 7 they wore something l crowns of gold, *3927*
9: 8 Their hair was l women's hair, *6055*
9: 8 and their teeth were l lions' teeth. *6055*
9: 9 They had breastplates l breastplates *6055*
9: 9 of their wings was l the thundering *6055*
9:10 They had tails and stings l scorpions, *3927*
9:17 and riders I saw in my vision looked l **this:** *4048*
9:19 for their tails were l snakes, *3927*
10: 1 his face was l the sun, *6055*
10: 1 and his legs were l fiery pillars. *6055*
10: 3 he gave a loud shout l the roar of a lion. *6061*
11: 1 a reed l a measuring rod and was told, *3927*
12:15 from his mouth the serpent spewed water l *6055*
13: 2 but had feet l those of a bear and a mouth *6055*
13: 2 like those of a bear and a mouth l that of *6055*
13: 4 "Who is l the beast? *3927*
13:11 He had two horns l a lamb, *3927*
13:11 but he spoke l a dragon. *6055*
14: 2 from heaven l the roar of rushing waters *6055*
14: 2 rushing waters and l a loud peal of thunder. *6055*
14: 2 The sound I heard was l that of harpists *6055*
14:14 on the cloud was one **"**l a son of man" *3927*
15: 2 And I saw what looked l a sea of glass *6055*
16: 3 it turned into blood l that of a dead man, *6055*
16:13 I saw three evil spirits that looked l frogs; *6055*
16:15 "Behold, I come l a thief! *6055*
16:18 No earthquake l *it* has ever occurred *3888*
18:18 'Was there ever a city l this great city?' *3927*
19: 1 After this I heard **what sounded** l the roar *6055*
19: 6 I heard what sounded l a great multitude, *6055*
19: 6 l the roar of rushing waters and *6055*
19: 6 rushing waters and l loud peals of thunder, *6055*
19:12 His eyes are l blazing fire, *6055*
20: 8 number they are l the sand on the seashore. *6055*
21:11 brilliance was l that of a very precious jewel *3927*
21:11 l a jasper, clear as crystal. *6055*
21:16 The city was laid out l a square, *NIG*
21:21 of pure gold, l transparent glass. *6055*

LIKE-MINDED (1) [LIKE, MIND]

Php 2: 2 then make my joy complete by **being** l, *899+3836+5858*

LIKED (5) [LIKE]

Ge 27:14 tasty food, just the way his father l it. 170
Jdg 14: 7 with the woman, and he l her. 928+3837+6524
1Sa 16:21 Saul l him very much, and David became 170
Mk 6:20 yet he l to listen to him. *2452*
Phm 1:13 I *would have* l to keep him with me so *1089*

LIKELY (1) [LIKE]

1Ki 12:26 "The kingdom *will* now *l* **revert** to AIT

LIKEN (3) [LIKE]

SS 1: 9 *I* l you, my darling, to a mare harnessed 1948
Isa 46: 5 To whom *will you* l me that we may 5439
La 2:13 To what *can I* l you, that I may comfort you, 8750

LIKENESS (14) [LIKE]

Ge 1:26 "Let us make man in our image, in our l, 1952
5: 1 he made him in the l *of* God. 1952
5: 3 he had a son in his own l, 1952
Ps 17:15 I will be satisfied with seeing your l. 9454
Isa 52:14 and his form marred beyond human l— NIH
Eze 1:28 appearance of the l *of* the glory of the LORD 1952
10: 1 and I saw the l *of* a throne of sapphire 1952
Ro 8: 3 in the l of sinful man to be a sin offering. *3930*
8:29 also predestined to be conformed *to* the l *1635*
1Co 15:49 as we have borne the l of the earthly man, *1635*
15:49 so shall we bear the l of the man *1635*
2Co 3:18 into his l with ever-increasing glory, *1635*
Php 2: 7 being made in human l. *3930*
Jas 3: 9 who have been made in God's l. *3932*

LIKES (2) [LIKE]

Ge 27: 9 food for your father, just the way *he* l it. 170
Dt 23:16 Let him live among you wherever he l and 928+2021+3202+4200

LIKEWISE (11) [LIKE]

Jdg 11:24 L, whatever the LORD our God has given us, 2256
2Ch 31:17 **and** l to the Levites twenty years old or 2256
Mt 7:17 L every good tree bears good fruit, *4048*
Lk 10:37 Jesus told him, "Go and do l." *3931*
17:31 L, no one in the field should go back *3931*
1Co 7: 3 and l the wife to her husband. *3931*
2Co 13: 4 L, we are weak in him, *1142+2779*
1Ti 3: 8 l, are to be men worthy of respect, *6058*
Tit 2: 3 L, teach the older women to be reverent in *6058*
Jas 3: 5 L the tongue is a small part of the *2779+4048*
Rev 2:15 L you also have those who hold to *4048*

LIKHI (1)

1Ch 7:19 Ahian, Shechem, L and Aniam. 4376

LILIES (13) [LILY]

1Ki 7:19 in the portico were in the shape of l, 8808
7:22 The capitals on top were in the shape of l. 8808
Ps 45: T To [the tune of] **"L."** 8808
69: T To [the tune of] **"L."** 8808

Ps 80: T To [the tune of] "The **L** *of* the Covenant." 8808
SS 2:16 he browses among the **l.** 8808
4: 5 of a gazelle that browse among the **l.** 8808
5:13 His lips are like **l** dripping with myrrh. 8808
6: 2 to browse in the gardens and to gather **l.** 8808
6: 3 he browses among the **l.** 8808
7: 2 a mound of wheat encircled by **l.** 8808
Mt 6:28 See how the **l** of the field grow. *3211*
Lk 12:27 "Consider how the **l** grow. *3211*

LILY (6) [LILIES]

1Ki 7:26 a cup, like a **l** blossom. 8808
2Ch 4: 5 a cup, like a **l** blossom. 8808
Ps 60: T To [the tune of] "The **L** *of* the Covenant." 8808
SS 2: 1 I am a rose of Sharon, a **l** *of* the valleys. 8808
2: 2 a **l** among thorns is my darling among 8808
Hos 14: 5 he will blossom like a **l.** 8808

LIMB (2) [LIMBS]

Jdg 19:29 **l** by limb, into twelve parts and sent them NIH
19:29 limb by **l,** into twelve parts and sent them 6795

LIMBER (1)

Ge 49:24 his strong arms *stayed* **l,** 7060

LIMBS (3) [LIMB]

Job 18:13 death's firstborn devours his **l.** 963
40:18 his **l** like rods of iron. 1752
41:12 "I will not fail to speak of his **l,** 963

LIME (2)

Isa 33:12 The peoples will be burned as if to **l;** 8487
Am 2: 1 Because he burned, as if to **l,** 8487

LIMIT (8) [LIMITS]

Ezr 7:22 olive oil, and salt without **l.** 10375
Job 15: 8 *Do you* **l** wisdom to yourself? 1757
Ps 119:96 To all perfection I see a **l;** 7891
147: 5 his understanding has no **l.** 5031
Isa 5:14 and opens its mouth without **l;** 2976
Jer 5:28 Their evil deeds **have no l;** 6296
Jn 3:34 for God gives the Spirit without **l.** *3586*
1Th 2:16 **heap up** their sins **to the l.** *405*

LIMITS (10) [LIMIT]

Ex 19:12 **Put l** *for* the people around the mountain 1487
19:23 **'Put l around** the mountain 1487
Nu 35:26 if the accused ever goes outside the **l** *of* 1473
Jos 17:18 Clear it, and its **farthest l** will be yours; 9362
Job 11: 7 Can you probe the **l** *of* the Almighty? 9417
14: 5 and have set **l** he cannot exceed. 2976
38:10 when I fixed **l** for it and set its doors 2976
Ps 73: 7 the evil conceits of their minds **know no l.** 6296
2Co 10:13 will not boast **beyond** proper **l,** *296+1650+3836*
10:15 we go **beyond** our **l** by boasting *296+1650+3836*

LIMP (9) [LIMPING]

Pr 26: 7 a lame man's legs *that* **hang l** is a proverb 1927
Isa 13: 7 Because of this, all hands *will* **go l,** 8332
Jer 6:24 and our hands **hang l.** 8332
47: 3 their hands will **hang l.** 8342
50:43 and his hands **hang l.** 8332
Eze 7:17 Every hand *will* **go l,** 8332
21: 7 and every hand **go l;** 8332
30:25 but the arms of Pharaoh *will* **fall l.** 5877
Zep 3:16 *do* not *let* your hands **hang l.** 8332

LIMPING (1) [LIMP]

Ge 32:31 and he *was* **l** because of his hip. 7519

LINE (55) [LINED, LINES]

Ge 5: 1 written **account of** Adam's **l.** 9352
19:32 with him and preserve our **family l** 2446
19:34 with him so we can preserve our **family l** 2446
Nu 26:11 The **l** *of* Korah, however, did not die out. 1201
34: 7 **run a l** from the Great Sea to Mount Hor 9292
34:10 **run a l** from Hazar Enan to Shepham, 204
Dt 25: 9 not build up his brother's **family l."** 1074
25:10 **That man's l** shall be known in Israel as 2257[S]
Ru 4: 4 and I am **next in l."** 339
4:18 This, then, is the **family l** *of* Perez: 9352
1Sa 2:31 not be an old man in your **family l** 1074
2:32 in your **family l** there will never be 1074
2:36 in your **family l** will come and bow down 1074
4:12 from the **battle l** and went to Shiloh, 5120
4:16 "I have just come from the **battle l;** 5120
17: 2 **drew up** their battle **l** to meet the Philistines 6885
17: 8 "Why do you come out and **l up** 6885
17:48 David ran quickly toward the **battle l** 5120
2Sa 11:15 "Put Uriah **in the front l** where 448+4578+7156
1Ki 7:15 and twelve cubits around, *by* **l.** 2562
7:23 a **l** of thirty cubits to measure around it. 7742
11:14 from the royal **l** of Edom. 2446
2Ki 21:13 the **measuring l** *used against* Samaria and 7742
21:13 and the **plumb l** *used against* the house 5487
2Ch 4: 2 a **l** of thirty cubits to measure around it. 7742
13: 3 Jeroboam **drew up** *a* battle **l** against him 6885
Ezr 2: 6 of Pahath-Moab (through the **l** *of* Jeshua 1201
2:40 of Jeshua and Kadmiel (through the **l** *of* 1201
Ne 7:11 of Pahath-Moab (through the **l** *of* Jeshua 1201
7:43 of Jeshua (through Kadmiel through the **l** 1201
Job 38: 5 Who stretched a **measuring l** across it? 7742
Ps 89: 4 'I will establish your **l** forever 2446
89:29 I will establish his **l** forever, 2446
89:36 that his **l** will continue forever 2446
Isa 28:17 I will make justice the **measuring l** 7742
28:17 and righteousness the **plumb l;** 5487
34:11 over Edom the **measuring l** *of* chaos and 7742
34:11 of chaos and the **plumb l** *of* desolation. 74
44:13 a **l** and makes an outline with a marker; 7742
48: 1 by the name of Israel and come from the **l** 5055
Jer 31:39 The measuring **l** will stretch from there 7742
33:15 a righteous Branch sprout from **David's l;** 1858
La 2: 8 He stretched out a **measuring l** and did 7742
Eze 47: 3 the man went eastward with a **measuring l** 7742
Da 11: 7 "One from her **family l** will arise 5916+9247
Joel 2: 7 They all march in **l,** 2006
Am 7: 7 with a **plumb l** in his hand. 643
7: 8 "A **plumb l,"** I replied. 643
7: 8 a **plumb l** among my people Israel; 643
Zec 1:16 And the **measuring l** will be stretched out 7742
2: 1 before me was a man with a measuring **l** 2475
4:10 the **plumb l** in the hand of Zerubbabel. 74+974
Mt 17:27 go to the lake and throw out your **l.** *45*
Lk 2: 4 he belonged to the house and **l** of David. *4255*
Gal 2:14 When I saw that *they were* not **acting in l** *3980*

LINEAGE (KJV) See LINE

LINED (1) [LINE]

1Ki 6:15 *He* **l** its interior walls with cedar boards, 1215

LINEN (105) [LINENS]

Ge 41:42 He dressed him in robes of **fine l** and put 9254
Ex 25: 4 purple and scarlet yarn and **fine l;** 9254
26: 1 with ten curtains of finely twisted **l** 9254
26:31 and scarlet yarn and finely twisted **l,** 9254
26:36 and scarlet yarn and finely twisted **l—** 9254
27: 9 and is to have curtains of finely twisted **l,** 9254
27:16 and scarlet yarn and finely twisted **l—** 9254
27:18 of finely twisted **l** five cubits high, 9254
28: 5 purple and scarlet yarn, and **fine l.** 9254
28: 6 and of finely twisted **l—** 9254
28: 8 and with finely twisted **l.** 9254
28:15 and of finely twisted **l.** 9254
28:39 of **fine l** and make the turban of fine linen. 9254
28:39 of fine linen and make the turban of **fine l.** 9254
28:42 "Make **l** undergarments as a covering for 965
35: 6 purple and scarlet yarn and **fine l;** 9254
35:23 purple or scarlet yarn or **fine l,** 9254
35:25 blue, purple or scarlet yarn or **fine l.** 9254
35:35 purple and scarlet yarn and **fine l,** 9254
36: 8 with ten curtains of finely twisted **l** 9254
36:35 and scarlet yarn and finely twisted **l,** 9254
36:37 and scarlet yarn and finely twisted **l—** 9254
38: 9 and had curtains of finely twisted **l,** 9254
38:16 the courtyard were of finely twisted **l.** 9254
38:18 and scarlet yarn and finely twisted **l—** 9254
38:23 purple and scarlet yarn and **fine l.)** 9254
39: 2 and of finely twisted **l.** 9254
39: 3 purple and scarlet yarn and **fine l—** 9254
39: 5 and with finely twisted **l,** 9254
39: 8 and of finely twisted **l.** 9254
39:24 and finely twisted **l** around the hem of NIH
39:27 they made tunics of **fine l—** 9254
39:28 and the turban of **fine l,** 9254
39:28 the **l** headbands and the undergarments 9254
39:28 and the undergarments of finely twisted **l.** 9254
39:29 The sash was of finely twisted **l** and blue, 9254
Lev 6:10 The priest shall then put on his **l** clothes, 965
6:10 with **l** undergarments next to his body, 965
13:47 any woolen or **l** clothing, 7324
13:48 of **l** or wool, any leather or anything made 7324
13:52 of wool or **l,** or any leather article that has 7324
13:59 by mildew in woolen or **l** clothing, 7324
16: 4 He is to put on the sacred **l** tunic, 965
16: 4 with **l** undergarments next to his body; 965
16: 4 he is to tie the **l** sash around him and put 965
16: 4 around him and put on the **l** turban. 965
16:23 the **l** garments he put on before he entered 965
16:32 He is to put on the sacred **l** garments 965
Dt 22:11 of wool and **l** woven together. 7324
Jdg 14:12 I will give you thirty **l garments** 6041
14:13 you must give me thirty **l garments** 6041
1Sa 2:18 a boy wearing a **l** ephod. 965
22:18 That day he killed eighty-five men who wore the **l** ephod. 965
2Sa 6:14 David, wearing a **l** ephod, danced before 965
1Ch 4:21 of Mareshah and the clans of the **l** workers 1009
15:27 David was clothed in a robe of **fine l,** 1009
15:27 David also wore a **l** ephod. 965
2Ch 2:14 and blue and crimson yarn and **fine l.** 1009
3:14 purple and crimson yarn and **fine l,** 1009
5:12 dressed in **fine l** and playing cymbals, 1009
Est 1: 6 **hangings of** white and blue **l,** 4158
1: 6 with cords of **white l** and purple material 1009
8:15 of gold and a purple robe of **fine l.** 1009
Pr 31:22 she is clothed in **fine l** and purple. 9254
31:24 She makes **l garments** and sells them, 6041
Isa 3:23 and the **l garments** and tiaras and shawls. 6041
19: 9 the weavers of **fine l** will lose hope. 2583
Jer 13: 1 a **l** belt and put it around your waist, 7324
Eze 9: 2 a man clothed in **l** who had a writing kit 965
9: 3 the man clothed in **l** who had the writing kit 965
9:11 Then the man in **l** with the writing kit 965
10: 2 The LORD said to the man clothed in **l,** 965
10: 6 the LORD commanded the man in **l,** 965
10: 7 and put it into the hands of the man in **l,** 965
16:10 I dressed you in **fine l** and covered you 9254
16:13 your clothes were of **fine l** 9254
27: 7 **Fine** embroidered **l** from Egypt 9254
27:16 purple fabric, embroidered work, **fine l,** 1009
40: 3 a **l** cord and a measuring rod in his hand. 7324
44:17 they are to wear **l** clothes; 7324
44:18 They are to wear **l** turbans on their heads 7324
44:18 and **l** undergarments around their waists. 7324
Da 10: 5 before me was a man dressed in **l,** 965
12: 6 One of them said to the man clothed in **l,** 965
12: 7 The man clothed in **l,** who was above 965
Hos 2: 5 my wool and my **l,** my oil and my drink.' 7324
2: 9 I will take back my wool and my **l,** 7324
Mt 27:59 wrapped it in a clean **l cloth,** *4984*
Mk 14:51 wearing nothing but a **l garment,** *4984*
15:46 So Joseph bought some **l cloth,** *4984*
15:46 took down the body, wrapped it in the **l,** *4984*
Lk 16:19 and **fine l** and lived in luxury every day. *1116*
23:53 *in* **l cloth** and placed it in a tomb cut in *4984*
24:12 he saw the **strips of l** lying by themselves, *3856*
Jn 11:44 and feet wrapped *with* **strips of l,** *3024*
19:40 with the spices, *in* **strips of l.** *3856*
20: 5 and looked in at the **strips of l** lying there *3856*
20: 6 He saw the **strips of l** lying there, *3856*
20: 7 folded up by itself, separate from the **l.** *3856*
Rev 15: 6 shining **l** and wore golden sashes *3351*
18:12 **fine l,** purple, silk and scarlet cloth; *1115*
18:16 Woe, O great city, dressed in **fine l,** *1115*
19: 8 **Fine l,** bright and clean, *1115*
19: 8 **(Fine l** stands for the righteous acts of the saints.) *1115*
19:14 on white horses and dressed in **fine l,** *1115*

LINENS (1) [LINEN]

Pr 7:16 I have covered my bed with colored **l** 355

LINES (13) [LINE]

Ge 10:32 according to their **l of descent,** 9352
14: 8 **drew up** their battle **l** in the Valley of 6885
1Sa 17:21 drawing up their **l** facing each other. 5120
17:22 to the **battle l** and greeted his brothers. 5120
17:23 from his **l** and shouted his usual defiance, 5120
2Sa 10: 9 Joab saw that there were **battle l** in front 4878
10:17 The Arameans **formed** *their* **battle l** 6885
23:16 mighty men broke through the Philistine **l,** 4722
1Ch 11:18 the Three broke through the Philistine **l,** 4722
19:10 Joab saw that there were **battle l** in front 4878
19:17 and **formed** *his* **battle l** opposite them. 6885
19:17 David **formed** *his* **l** to meet the Arameans 6885
Ps 16: 6 The **boundary l** have fallen for me 2475

LINGER (5) [LINGERING]

Jdg 5:17 And Dan, why *did he* **l** *by* the ships? 1591
Pr 23:30 Those *who* **l** over wine, 336
Jer 51:50 leave and *do* not **l!** 6641
Mic 5: 7 not wait for man or **l** for mankind. 3498
Hab 2: 3 Though *it* **l,** wait for it; 4538

LINGERING (2) [LINGER]

Dt 28:59 and severe and **l** illnesses. 586
2Ch 21:15 ill with a **l** disease of the bowels, 3427+3427+6584

LINTEL (KJV) See TOP

LINUS (1)

2Ti 4:21 Eubulus greets you, and so do Pudens, **L,** *3352*

LION (86) [LION'S, LIONESS, LIONESSES, LIONS, LIONS']

Ge 49: 9 Like a **l** he crouches and lies down, 793
Nu 23:24 they rouse themselves like a **l** that does 787
24: 9 Like a **l** they crouch and lie down, 787
Dt 33:20 Gad lives there like a **l,** 4233
Jdg 14: 5 a **young l** came roaring toward him. 787+4097
14: 6 that he tore **the l** apart with his bare hands 2084[S]
14:18 What is stronger than a **l?"** 787
1Sa 17:34 a **l** or a bear came and carried off a sheep 787
17:36 Your servant has killed both the **l** and 787
17:37 from the paw of the **l** and the paw of 787
2Sa 17:10 whose heart is like the heart of a **l,** 793
23:20 into a pit on a snowy day and killed a **l.** 787
1Ki 10:19 with a **l** standing beside each of them. 787
13:24 a **l** met him on the road and killed him, 793
13:24 with both the donkey and the **l** standing 793
13:25 with the **l** standing beside the body, 793
13:26 The LORD has given him over to the **l,** 793
13:28 the donkey and the **l** standing beside it. 793
13:28 The **l** had neither eaten the body 793
20:36 as soon as you leave me a **l** will kill you." 793
20:36 a **l** found him and killed him. 793
1Ch 11:22 into a pit on a snowy day and killed a **l.** 787
2Ch 9:18 with a **l** standing beside each of them. 787
Job 4:11 The **l** perishes for lack of prey, 4330
10:16 a **l** and again display your awesome power 8828
28: 8 and no **l** prowls there. 8828
Ps 7: 2 like a **l** and rip me to pieces with no one 793
10: 9 He lies in wait like a **l** in cover; 793
17:12 They are like a **l** hungry for prey, 793
17:12 like a **great l** crouching in cover. 4097

Ps 91:13 You will tread upon the l and the cobra; 8828
91:13 you will trample the **great l** and 4097
Pr 19:12 A king's rage is like the roar of a l, 4097
20: 2 A king's wrath is like the roar of a l; 4097
22:13 The sluggard says, "There is a l outside!" 787
26:13 sluggard says, "There is a l in the road, 8828
26:13 a **fierce l** roaming the streets!" 787
28: 1 but the righteous are as bold as a l. 4097
28:15 Like a roaring l or a charging bear is 787
30:30 a l, mighty among beasts, who retreats 4330
Ecc 9: 4 even a live dog is better off than a dead l! 793
Isa 5:29 Their roar is like that of the l, 4233
11: 6 and the l and the yearling together; 4097
11: 7 and the l will eat straw like the ox. 793
15: 9 a l upon the fugitives of Moab and 793
31: 4 a l growls, a great lion over his prey— 793
31: 4 a lion growls, a **great l** over his prey— 4097
35: 9 No l will be there, 793
38:13 but like a l he broke all my bones; 787
65:25 and the l will eat straw like the ox, 793
Jer 2:30 devoured your prophets like a ravening l. 793
4: 7 A l has come out of his lair; 793
5: 6 a l from the forest will attack them, 793
12: 8 My inheritance has become to me like a l 793
25:38 Like a l he will leave his lair, 4097
49:19 a l coming up from Jordan's thickets to 793
50:44 Like a l coming up from Jordan's thickets 793
51:38 they growl like l cubs. 787
La 3:10 like a l in hiding, 787
Eze 1:10 on the right side each had the face of a l, 793
10:14 the third the face of a l, 793
19: 3 and he became a **strong l.** 4097
19: 5 of her cubs and made him a **strong l.** 4097
19: 6 for he was now a **strong l.** 4097
22:25 within her like a roaring l tearing its prey; 787
32: 2 " 'You are like a l *among* the nations; 4097
41:19 and the face of a l toward the palm tree on 4097
Da 7: 4 "The first was like a l, 10069
Hos 5:14 For I will be like a l to Ephraim, 8828
5:14 like a **great l** to Judah. 4097
11:10 he will roar like a l. 793
13: 7 So I will come upon them like a l, 8828
13: 8 Like a l I will devour them; 4233
Joel 1: 6 it has the teeth of a l, 793
Am 3: 4 Does a l roar in the thicket 793
3: 8 The l has roared—who will not fear? 793
5:19 as though a man fled from a l only to meet 787
Mic 5: 8 like a l among the beasts of the forest, 793
5: 8 like a **young l** among flocks of sheep, 4097
Na 2:11 where the l and lioness went, 793
2:12 The l killed enough for his cubs 793
1Pe 5: 8 a roaring l looking for someone to devour. *3329*
Rev 4: 7 The first living creature was like a l, *3329*
5: 5 See, the L of the tribe of Judah, *3329*
10: 3 he gave a loud shout like the roar *of* a l. *3329*
13: 2 of a bear and a mouth like that *of* a l. *3329*

LION'S (6) [LION]

Ge 49: 9 You are a l cub, O Judah; 793
Dt 33:22 "Dan is a l cub, springing out of Bashan." 793
Jdg 14: 8 he turned aside to look at the l carcass. 793
14: 9 the honey from the l carcass. 793
Am 3:12 the l mouth only two leg bones or a piece 787
2Ti 4:17 And I was delivered from the l mouth. *3329*

LIONESS (8) [LION]

Ge 49: 9 like a l—who dares to rouse him? 4233
Nu 23:24 The people rise like a l; 4233
24: 9 like a l—who dares to rouse them? 4233
Job 4:11 and the cubs of the l are scattered. 4233
38:39 for the l and satisfy the hunger of the lions 4233
Eze 19: 2 a l was your mother among the lions! 4234
Joel 1: 6 it has the teeth of a lion, the fangs of a l. 4233
Na 2:11 where the lion and l went, and the cubs, 4233

LIONESSES (1) [LION]

Isa 30: 6 of hardship and distress, of lions and l, 4330

LIONLIKE (KJV) See BEST

LIONS (36) [LION]

2Sa 1:23 they were stronger than l. 787
1Ki 7:29 the uprights were l, bulls and cherubim— 787
7:29 and below the l and bulls were wreaths 787
7:36 l and palm trees on the surfaces of 787
10:20 Twelve l stood on the six steps, 787
2Ki 17:25 so he sent l among them 787
17:26 He has sent l among them, 787
1Ch 12: 8 Their faces were the faces of l, 793
2Ch 9:19 Twelve l stood on the six steps, 787
Job 4:10 The l may roar and growl, 793
4:10 yet the teeth of the **great l** are broken. 4097
38:39 the lioness and satisfy the hunger of the l 4097
Ps 22:13 Roaring l tearing their prey open their 793
22:21 Rescue me from the mouth of the l; 793
34:10 The l may grow weak and hungry, 4097
35:17 my precious life from these l. 4097
57: 4 I am in the midst of l; 4216
58: 6 tear out, O LORD, the fangs of the l! 4097
104:21 The l roar for their prey 4097
Isa 5:29 they roar like **young l;** 4097
30: 6 a land of hardship and distress, of l 4233
Jer 2:15 L have roared; they have growled at him. 4097
50:17 a scattered flock that l have chased away. 787
51:38 Her people all roar like **young l,** 4097
Eze 19: 2 a lioness was your mother among the l! 787
19: 2 among the **young l** and reared her cubs. 4097
19: 6 He prowled among the l, 787
Da 6:20 been able to rescue you from the l?" 10069
6:22 and he shut the mouths of the l. 10069
6:24 the l overpowered them and crushed all 10069
6:27 rescued Daniel from the power of the l. 10069
Na 2:13 and the sword will devour your **young l.** 4097
Zep 3: 3 Her officials are roaring l, 787
Zec 11: 3 Listen to the roar of the l; 4097
Heb 11:33 who shut the mouths *of* l, *3329*
Rev 9:17 of the horses resembled the heads *of* l, *3329*

LIONS' (8) [LION]

SS 4: 8 from the l' dens and the mountain haunts 787
Da 6: 7 O king, shall be thrown into the l' den. 10069
6:12 O king, would be thrown into the l' den?" 10069
6:16 and threw him into the l' den. 10069
6:19 the king got up and hurried to the l' den. 10069
6:24 brought in and thrown into the l' den, 10069
Na 2:11 Where now is the l' den, 787
Rev 9: 8 and their teeth were like l' teeth. *3329*

LIPS (125)

Ex 6:12 since I speak with faltering l?" 8557
6:30 "Since I speak with faltering l, 8557
13: 9 the law of the LORD is to be on your l. 7023
23:13 do not let them be heard on your l. 7023
Nu 30: 6 after she makes a vow or after her l utter 8557
30:12 or pledges that came from her l will stand. 8557
Dt 23:23 Whatever your l utter you must be sure 8557
1Sa 1:13 and her l were moving but her voice was 8557
Job 6:30 Is there any wickedness on my l? 4383
8:21 laughter and your l with shouts of joy. 8557
11: 5 that he would open his l against you 8557
12:20 He silences the l of trusted advisers 8557
13: 6 listen to the plea of my l. 8557
15: 6 your own l testify against you. 8557
16: 5 comfort from my l would bring you relief. 8557
23:12 not departed from the commands of his l; 8557
27: 4 my l will not speak wickedness, 8557
32:20 I must open my l and reply. 8557
33: 3 my l sincerely speak what I know. 8557
Ps 8: 2 From the l *of* children and infants 7023
12: 2 their flattering l speak with deception. 8557
12: 3 May the LORD cut off all flattering l 8557
12: 4 we own our l—who is our master?" 8557
16: 4 of blood or take up their names on my l. 8557
17: 1 it does not rise from deceitful l. 8557
17: 4 by the word of your l I have kept myself 8557
21: 2 and have not withheld the request of his l. 8557
31:18 Let their lying l be silenced, 8557
34: 1 his praise will always be on my l. 7023
34:13 from evil and your l from speaking lies. 8557
40: 9 I do not seal my l, as you know, 8557
45: 2 and your l have been anointed with grace, 8557
50:16 or take my covenant on your l? 7023
51:15 O Lord, open my l, 8557
59: 7 they spew out swords from their l, 8557
59:12 for the words of their l, 8557
63: 3 my l will glorify you. 8557
63: 5 with singing l my mouth will praise you. 8557
66:14 vows my l promised and my mouth spoke 8557
71:23 My l will shout for joy when I sing praise 8557
89:34 or alter what my l have uttered. 8557
106:33 and rash words came from Moses' l. 8557
119:13 With my l I recount all the laws that come 8557
119:171 May my l overflow with praise, 8557
120: 2 from lying l and from deceitful tongues. 8557
140: 3 the poison of vipers is on their l. 8557
140: 9 with the trouble their l have caused. 8557
141: 3 keep watch over the door of my l. 8557
Pr 4:24 keep corrupt talk far from your l. 8557
5: 2 and your l may preserve knowledge. 8557
5: 3 For the l *of* an adulteress drip honey, 8557
8: 6 I open my l to speak what is right. 8557
8: 7 for my l detest wickedness. 8557
10:13 Wisdom is found on the l *of* the discerning, 8557
10:18 He who conceals his hatred has lying l, 8557
10:21 The l *of* the righteous nourish many, 8557
10:32 l *of* the righteous know what is fitting, 8557
12:14 of his l a man is filled with good things as 7023
12:19 Truthful l endure forever, 8557
12:22 The LORD detests lying l, 8557
13: 2 the fruit of his l a man enjoys good things, 7023
13: 3 He who guards his l guards his life, 7023
14: 3 but the l *of* the wise protect them. 8557
14: 7 for you will not find knowledge on his l. 8557
15: 7 The l *of* the wise spread knowledge; 8557
16:10 The l *of* a king speak as an oracle, 8557
16:13 Kings take pleasure in honest l; 8557
16:23 and his l promote instruction. 8557
16:30 he who purses his l is bent on evil. 8557
17: 4 A wicked man listens to evil l; 8557
17: 7 Arrogant l are unsuited to a fool— 8557
17: 7 how much worse lying l to a ruler! 8557
18: 6 A fool's l bring him strife, 8557
18: 7 and his l are a snare to his soul. 8557
18:20 with the harvest from his l he is satisfied. 8557
19: 1 a fool whose l are perverse. 8557
20:15 l *that speak* knowledge are a rare jewel. 8557
22:18 and have all of them ready on your l. 8557
23:16 when your l speak what is right. 8557
24: 2 and their l talk about making trouble. 8557
Pr 24:26 An honest answer is like a kiss on the l. 8557
24:28 or use your l to deceive. 8557
26:23 earthenware are fervent l with an evil heart. 8557
26:24 malicious man disguises himself with his l, 8557
27: 2 someone else, and not your own l. 8557
Ecc 10:12 but a fool is consumed by his own l. 8557
SS 4: 3 Your l are like a scarlet ribbon; 8557
4:11 Your l drop sweetness as the honeycomb, 8557
5:13 His l are like lilies dripping with myrrh. 8557
7: 9 flowing gently over l and teeth. 8557
Isa 6: 5 For I am a man of unclean l, 8557
6: 5 and I live among a people of unclean l, 8557
6: 7 "See, this has touched your l; 8557
11: 4 the breath of his l he will slay the wicked. 8557
28:11 Very well then, with foreign l 8557
29:13 and honor me with their l, 8557
30:27 his l are full of wrath, 8557
57:19 creating praise on the l of the mourners 8557
59: 3 Your l have spoken lies, 8557
Jer 7:28 it has vanished from their l. 7023
12: 2 on their l but far from their hearts. 7023
17:16 What passes my l is open before you. 8557
Da 4:31 on his l when a voice came from heaven, 10588
10: 3 no meat or wine touched my l; 7023
10:16 one who looked like a man touched my l, 8557
Hos 2:17 the names of the Baals from her l; 7023
8: 1 "Put the trumpet to your l! 2674
14: 2 that we may offer the fruit of our l. 8557
Joel 1: 5 for it has been snatched from your l. 7023
Hab 3:16 my l quivered at the sound; 8557
Zep 3: 9 "Then will I purify the l *of* the peoples, 8557
Mal 2: 6 and nothing false was found on his l. 8557
2: 7 l *of* a priest ought to preserve knowledge, 8557
Mt 15: 8 " 'These people honor me *with* their l, *5927*
21:16 " 'From the l of children and infants *5125*
Mk 7: 6 " 'These people honor me *with* their l, *5927*
Lk 4:22 the gracious words that came from his l. *5125*
22:71 We have heard it from his own l." *5125*
Jn 19:29 and lifted it *to* Jesus' l. *5125*
Ac 15: 7 that the Gentiles might hear from my l *5125*
Ro 3:13 "The poison of vipers is on their l." *5927*
1Co 14:21 through the l of foreigners I will speak *5927*
Col 3: 8 slander, and filthy language from your l. *5125*
Heb 13:15 the fruit *of* l that confess his name. *5927*
1Pe 3:10 from evil and his l from deceitful speech. *5927*

LIQUID (2)

Ex 30:23 500 shekels of l myrrh, 2001
Lev 11:34 and any l that could be drunk 5482

LIQUOR (KJV) See BLENDED WINE, JUICE

LIST (10) [LISTED, LISTING]

Nu 3:40 or more and make a l *of* their names. 5031
Jos 17:11 (the third in the l is Naphoth). NIH
1Ch 11:11 this is the l *of* David's mighty men: 5031
25: 1 Here is the l *of* the men who performed this 5031
27: 1 This is the l *of* the Israelites— 5031
Ezr 2: 2 The l *of* the men of the people of Israel: 5031
Ne 7: 7 The l *of* the men of Israel: 5031
Ps 56: 8 l my tears on your scroll— 8492
1Ti 5: 9 No widow *may be* **put on the l** of widows unless *2899*
5:11 As for younger widows, *do* **not put** them **on such a l.** *4148*

LISTED (35) [LIST]

Ge 25:13 of Ishmael, *l* **in** the order of their birth: AIT
Nu 1:18 the men twenty years old or more were l 5031
1:20 to serve in the army were l by name, 5031
1:22 in the army were counted and l by name, 5031
1:24 to serve in the army were l by name, 5031
1:26 to serve in the army were l by name, 5031
1:28 to serve in the army were l by name, 5031
1:30 to serve in the army were l by name, 5031
1:32 to serve in the army were l by name, 5031
1:34 to serve in the army were l by name, 5031
1:36 to serve in the army were l by name, 5031
1:38 to serve in the army were l by name, 5031
1:40 to serve in the army were l by name, 5031
1:42 to serve in the army were l by name, 5031
3:43 l by name, was 22,273. 5031
11:26 They **were l** among the elders, 4180
26:54 according to the number of those l. 7212
1Ch 4:38 The men l above by name were leaders 995
4:41 The men whose names *were* l came in 4180
5: 1 *could* not **be l in the genealogical record** 3509
5: 7 l according to their genealogical records: 3509
6:19 of the Levites l according to their fathers: NIH
7: 2 the descendants of Tola l as fighting men 5031
7: 5 Issachar, as **l in** their **genealogy,** 3509
7: 7 **genealogical record l** 22,034 fighting men. 3509
7: 9 Their genealogical record l the heads 3509
7:40 as **l in** their **genealogy,** was 26,000. 3509
8:28 chiefs as l in their **genealogy,** 9352
9: 1 All Israel **was l in the genealogies** 3509
9: 9 as l in their **genealogy,** numbered 956. 9352
9:34 chiefs as l in their **genealogy,** 9352
2Ch 31:18 **l in** *these* **genealogical records.** 3509
Ps 69:28 of life and not **be l** with the righteous. 4180
Eze 13: 9 or **be l** in the records of the house of Israel, 4180
48: 1 "These are the tribes, l by name: NIH

LISTEN (352) [LISTENED, LISTENING, LISTENS]

Ge 4:10 “What have you done? **L**! 7754
4:23 “Adah and Zillah, **l** *to* me; 9048
21:12 **L** to whatever Sarah tells you, 9048
23: 6 “Sir, **l** *to* us. You are a mighty prince among 9048
23: 8 then **l** *to* me and intercede with Ephron 9048
23:11 he said. “**L** *to* me; 9048
23:13 “**L** *to* me, if you will. 9048
23:15 “**L** *to* me, my lord; 9048
27: 8 **l carefully** and do what I tell you: 928+7754+9048
37: 6 He said to them, “**L** *to* this dream I had: 9048
37: 9 “**L**,” he said, “I had another dream, 2180
42:21 but *we would* not **l**; 9048
42:22 But *you* wouldn't **l**! 9048
49: 2 “Assemble and **l**, sons of Jacob; 9048
49: 2 sons of Jacob; **l** to your father Israel. 9048
Ex 3:18 “The elders of Israel *will* **l** to you. 9048
4: 1 “What if they do not believe me or **l** to me 9048
4: 9 if they do not believe these two signs or **l** 9048
6: 9 but *they did* not **l** to him because 9048
6:12 “If the Israelites *will* not **l** to me, 9048
6:12 why *would* Pharaoh **l** *to* me, 9048
6:30 why *would* Pharaoh **l** to me?” 9048
7: 4 he *will* not **l** to you. 9048
7:13 heart became hard and *he would* not **l** to 9048
7:22 hard; *he would* not **l** to Moses and Aaron, 9048
8:15 he hardened his heart and *would* not **l** 9048
8:19 heart was hard and *he would* not **l**, 9048
9:12 and *he would* not **l** to Moses and Aaron, 9048
11: 9 “Pharaoh *will* refuse *to* **l** to you— 9048
15:26 “If *you* **l carefully** to the voice of 9048+9048
18:19 **L** now to me and I will give you some 9048
20:19 “Speak to us yourself and *we will* **l**. 9048
23:21 Pay attention to him and **l** to what he says. 9048
23:22 If *you* **l carefully** to what he says 9048+9048
Lev 26:14 “ ‘But if *you will* not **l** to me 9048
26:18 “ ‘If after all this *you will* not **l** to me, 9048
26:21 toward me and refuse to **l** to me, 9048
26:27 in spite of this *you still do* not **l** to me 9048
Nu 12: 6 “**L** *to* my words: 9048
16: 8 Moses also said to Korah, “Now **l**, 9048
20:10 of the rock and Moses said to them, “**L**, 9048
23:18 “Arise, Balak, and **l**; 9048
Dt 1:43 So I told you, but *you would* not **l**. 9048
3:26 with me and *would* not **l** to me. 9048
5:27 and **l** *to* all that the LORD our God says. 9048
5:27 *We will* **l** and obey.” 9048
13: 3 not **l** to the words of that prophet 9048
13: 8 do not yield to him or **l** to him. 9048
18:14 The nations you will dispossess **l** 9048
18:15 *You must* **l** to him. 9048
18:19 not **l** to my words that the prophet speaks 9048
21:18 not **l** to them when they discipline him, 9048
23: 5 not **l** to Balaam but turned the curse into 9048
27: 9 “Be silent, O Israel, and **l**! 9048
30:20 **l** to his voice, and hold fast to him. 9048
31:12 so *they can* **l** and learn to fear 9048
32: 1 **L**, O heavens, and I will speak; 263
Jos 3: 9 “Come here and **l** *to* the words of 9048
8: 4 with these orders: “**L carefully.** 8011
24:10 But I would not **l** to Balaam, 9048
Jdg 2:17 Yet *they would* not **l** to their judges 9048
5: 3 **L**, *you* rulers! 263
7:11 and **l** *to* what they are saying. 9048
9: 7 “**L** to me, citizens of Shechem, 9048
9: 7 so that God *may* **l** to you. 9048
11:17 but the king of Edom *would* not **l**. 9048
19:25 But the men would not **l** to him. 9048
20:13 But the Benjamites would not **l** 9048
Ru 2: 8 Boaz said to Ruth, “My daughter, **l** *to* me. 9048
1Sa 2:25 however, *did* not **l** to their father's rebuke, 9048
8: 7 “**L** to all that the people are saying to you; 9048
8: 9 Now **l** to them; but warn them solemnly 9048
8:19 But the people refused to **l** to Samuel. 9048
8:22 “**L** to them and give them a king.” 9048
15: 1 so **l** now to the message from the LORD 9048
22: 7 Saul said to them, “**L**, men of Benjamin! 9048
22:12 Saul said, “**L** now, son of Ahitub.” 9048
24: 9 “Why *do you* **l** when men say, 9048
26:19 the king **l** *to* his servant's words. 9048
28:22 Now please **l** to your servant 9048
30:24 Who *will* **l** to what you say? 9048
2Sa 12:18 we spoke to David but *he would* not **l** 9048
13:14 But he refused to **l** to her, 9048
13:16 But he refused to **l** to her. 9048
13:28 Absalom ordered his men, “**L**! 8011
20:16 a wise woman called from the city, “**L**! 9048
20:16 from the city, “Listen! **L**! 9048
20:17 “**L** *to* what your servant has to say.” 9048
1Ki 4:34 Men of all nations came to **l** 9048
8:52 and *may* you **l** to them whenever they cry 9048
12:15 So the king *did* not **l** to the people, 9048
12:16 *to* **l** to them, they answered the king: 9048
20: 8 “Don't **l** to him or agree to his demands.” 9048
2Ki 14:11 Amaziah, however, *would* not **l**, 9048
17:14 But *they would* not **l** and were 9048
17:40 They *would* not **l**, however, 9048
18:31 “*Do* not **l** to Hezekiah. 9048
18:32 “*Do* not **l** to Hezekiah, 9048
19: 7 **L**! I am going to put such a spirit in him 2180
19:16 **l** *to* the words Sennacherib has sent 9048
21: 9 But *the people did* not **l**. 9048
1Ch 28: 2 “**L** *to* me, my brothers and my people. 9048
2Ch 10:15 So the king *did* not **l** to the people, 9048
10:16 *to* **l** to them, they answered the king: 9048
2Ch 13: 4 “Jeroboam and all Israel, **l** *to* me! 9048
15: 2 to meet Asa and said to him, “**L** *to* me, 9048
20:15 “**L**, King Jehoshaphat and all who live 7992
20:20 “**L** *to* me, Judah and people of Jerusalem! 9048
24:19 *they would* not **l**. 263
25:20 Amaziah, however, *would* not **l**, 9048
28:11 Now **l** *to* me! 9048
29: 5 and said: “**L** *to* me, 9048
35:22 *He would* not **l** to what Neco had said 9048
Ne 9:17 They refused to **l** and failed to remember 9048
9:29 became stiff-necked and refused *to* **l**. 9048
Job 13: 6 **l** *to* the plea of my lips. 7992
13:17 **L carefully** *to* my words; 9048+9048
15: 8 *Do you* **l in** on God's council? 9048
15:17 “**L** to me and I will explain to you; 9048
21: 2 “**L carefully** *to* my words; 9048+9048
27: 9 *Does* God **l** *to* his cry when distress comes 9048
32:10 **L** to me; I too will tell you what I know. 9048
33: 1 “But now, Job, **l** *to* my words; 9048
33:31 “Pay attention, Job, and **l** to me; 9048
33:33 But if not, then **l** to me; 9048
34: 2 **l** to me, you men of learning. 263
34:10 “So **l** to me, you men of understanding. 9048
34:16 hear this; **l** to what I say. 263
35:13 God *does* not **l** *to* their empty plea; 9048
35:14 will he **l** when you say that you do NIH
36:10 *He* **makes** them **l** to correction 265+1655
36:12 But if *they do* not **l**, 9048
37: 2 **L**! Listen to the roar of his voice, 9048
37: 2 Listen! **L** to the roar of his voice, 9048
37:14 “**L** *to* this, Job; 263
42: 4 ‘**L** now, and I will speak; 9048
Ps 5: 2 **L** to my cry for help, 7992
10:17 and *you* **l** to their cry, 265+7992
17: 1 **l** *to* my cry. Give ear to my prayer— 7992
34:11 Come, my children, **l** to me; 9048
39:12 O LORD, **l** *to* my cry for help; 263
45:10 **L**, O daughter, consider and give ear: 9048
49: 1 Hear this, all you peoples; **l**, 263
54: 2 **l** to the words of my mouth. 263
55: 1 **L** *to* my prayer, O God, 263
61: 1 Hear my cry, O God; **l** *to* my prayer. 7992
66:16 Come and **l**, all *you* who fear God; 9048
78: 1 **l** to the words of my mouth. 265+5742
81: 8 if *you would but* **l** to me, O Israel! 9048
81:11 “But my people *would* not **l** to me; 9048
81:13 “If my people *would but* **l** to me, 9048
84: 8 **l** to me, O God of Jacob. 263
85: 8 *I will* **l** to what God 9048
86: 6 **l** to my cry for mercy. 7992
142: 6 **L** to my cry, for I am in desperate need; 7992
143: 1 hear my prayer, **l** to my cry for mercy; 263
Pr 1: 5 *let* the wise **l** and add to their learning, 9048
1: 8 **L**, my son, *to your* father's instruction 9048
4: 1 **L**, my sons, *to* a father's instruction; 9048
4:10 **L**, my son, accept what I say, 9048
4:20 **l closely** to my words. 265+5742
5: 1 **l well** to my words of insight, 265+5742
5: 7 Now then, my sons, **l** to me; 9048
5:13 I would not obey my teachers or **l** to my 265+5742
7:24 Now then, my sons, **l** to me; 9048
8: 6 **L**, for I have worthy things to say; 9048
8:32 “Now then, my sons, **l** to me; 9048
8:33 **L** *to* my instruction and be wise; 9048
13: 1 but a mocker *does* not **l** *to* rebuke. 9048
19:20 **L** *to* advice and accept instruction, 9048
22:17 Pay attention and **l** *to* the sayings of 9048
23:19 **L**, my son, and be wise, 9048
23:22 **L** to your father, who gave you life, 9048
Ecc 5: 1 near to **l** rather than to offer the sacrifice 9048
7: 5 a wise man's rebuke than *to* **l** *to* the song 9048
SS 2: 8 **L**! My lover! Look! Here he comes, 7754
5: 2 but my heart was awake. **L**! 7754
Isa 1: 2 **L**, O earth! 263
1:10 **l** *to* the law of our God, 263
1:15 if you offer many prayers, I *will* not **l**. 9048
8: 9 **L**, all *you* distant lands. 263
10:30 **L**, O Laishah! 7992
13: 4 **L**, a noise on the mountains, 7754
13: 4 **L**, an uproar among the kingdoms, 7754
28:12 but they would not **l**. 9048
28:23 **L** and hear my voice; 263
30: 9 *to* **l** *to* the LORD's instruction. 9048
32: 3 and the ears of those who hear *will* **l**. 7992
32: 9 rise up and **l** *to* me; 7754+9048
34: 1 Come near, you nations, and **l**; 7992
36:16 “*Do* not **l** to Hezekiah. 9048
37: 7 **L**! I am going to put such a spirit in him 2180
37:17 **l** *to* all the words Sennacherib has sent 9048
42:23 Which of you *will* **l** *to* this 263
44: 1 “But now **l**, O Jacob, my servant, Israel, 9048
46: 3 “**L** to me, O house of Jacob, 9048
46:12 **L** to me, *you* stubborn-hearted, 9048
47: 8 “Now then, **l**, *you* wanton creature, 9048
48: 1 “**L** *to* this, O house of Jacob, 9048
48:12 “**L** to me, O Jacob, Israel, 9048
48:14 “Come together, all of you, and **l**: 9048
48:16 “Come near me and **l** *to* this: 9048
49: 1 **L** to me, *you* islands; 9048
50: 4 wakens my ear to **l** like one being taught. 9048
51: 1 “**L** to me, you who pursue righteousness 9048
51: 4 “**L** to me, my people; 7992
52: 8 **L**! Your watchmen lift up their 7754
55: 2 **L**, listen to me, and eat what is good, 9048
55: 2 Listen, **l** to me, and eat what is good, 9048
65:12 I spoke but *you did* not **l**. 9048
Jer 6:10 *Who will* **l** *to* me? 9048
Jer 6:17 ‘**L** to the sound of the trumpet!’ 7992
6:17 But you said, ‘*We will* not **l**.’ 7992
7:13 but *you did* not **l**; 9048
7:16 for I *will* not **l** *to* you. 9048
7:24 But *they did* not **l** or pay attention; 9048
7:26 But *they did* not **l** to me or pay attention. 9048
7:27 *they will* not **l** to you; 9048
8:19 **L** *to* the cry of my people from 7754
10:22 **L**! The report is coming— 7754
11: 2 “**L** *to* the terms of this covenant 9048
11: 6 ‘**L** *to* the terms of this covenant 9048
11: 8 But *they did* not **l** or pay attention; 9048
11:10 who refused to **l** *to* my words. 9048
11:11 *I will* not **l** to them. 9048
11:14 because I *will* not **l** when they call to me 9048
12:17 But if any nation *does* not **l**, 9048
13:10 who refuse to **l** *to* my words, 9048
13:17 But if *you do* not **l**, 9048
14:12 they fast, I *will* not **l** to their cry; 9048
17:23 Yet *they did* not **l** or pay attention; 9048
17:23 and *would* not **l** or respond to discipline. 9048
18:19 **L** to me, O LORD; 7992
19: 3 the God of Israel, says: **L**! 2180
19:15 the God of Israel, says: ‘**L**! 2180
19:15 and *would* not **l** *to* my words.’ ” 9048
22:21 but you said, ‘*I will* not **l**!’ 9048
23:16 not **l** to what the prophets are prophesying 9048
25: 7 “But *you did* not **l** to me,” 9048
26: 3 Perhaps *they will* **l** and each will turn 9048
26: 4 If *you do* not **l** to me and follow my law, 9048
26: 5 if *you do* not **l** to the words of my servants 9048
27: 9 So *do* not **l** to your prophets, 9048
27:14 not **l** to the words of the prophets who say 9048
27:16 *Do* not **l** to the prophets who say, 9048
27:17 *Do* not **l** to them. 9048
28: 7 **l** *to* what I have to say in your hearing 9048
28:15 to Hananiah the prophet, “**L**, 9048
29: 8 *Do* not **l** to the dreams 9048
29:12 and *I will* **l** to you. 9048
32:33 they *would* not **l** or respond to discipline. 9048
34:14 *did* not **l** to me or pay attention to me. 9048
35:17 the God of Israel, says: ‘**L**! 2180
35:17 I spoke to them, but *they did* not **l**; 9048
36:25 *he would* not **l** to them. 9048
37:14 But Irijah *would* not **l** to him; 9048
37:20 But now, my lord the king, please **l**. 9048
38:15 *you would* not **l** to me.” 9048
44: 5 But *they did* not **l** or pay attention; 9048
44:16 not **l** to the message you have spoken 9048
48: 3 **L** *to* the cries from Horonaim, 7754
50:28 **L** *to* the fugitives and refugees 7754
La 1:18 **L**, all you peoples; 9048
Eze 2: 5 And whether they **l** or fail to listen— 9048
2: 5 And whether they listen or fail to **l**— NIH
2: 7 whether *they* **l** or fail to listen, 9048
2: 7 whether they listen or fail to **l**, NIH
2: 8 you, son of man, **l** *to* what I say to you. 9048
3: 7 But the house of Israel is not willing to **l** 9048
3: 7 to you because they are not willing to **l** 9048
3:10 **l carefully** and take to heart all 265+928+9048
3:11 whether *they* **l** or fail to listen.” 9048
3:11 whether they listen or fail to **l**.” NIH
3:27 Whoever *will* **l** let him listen, 9048
3:27 Whoever will listen *let him* **l**, 9048
8:18 *I will* not **l** to them.” 9048
13:19 By lying to my people, *who* **l** *to* lies, 9048
20: 8 against me and would not **l** to me; 9048
20:39 But afterward you *will* surely **l** to me 9048
33:31 and sit before you *to* **l** *to* your words, 9048
44: 5 **l closely** and give attention 265+928+9048
Da 9:19 O Lord, **l**! O Lord, forgive! 9048
Hos 5: 1 **L**, O royal house! 263
Joel 1: 2 **l**, all who live in the land. 263
Am 5:23 *I will* not **l** *to* the music of your harps. 9048
Mic 1: 2 Hear, O peoples, all of you, **l**, 7992
3: 1 Then I said, “**L**, you leaders of Jacob, 9048
6: 1 **L** *to* what the LORD says: 9048
6: 2 **l**, you everlasting foundations of the earth. NIH
6: 9 **L**! The LORD is calling to the NIH
Hab 1: 2 must I call for help, but *you do* not **l**? 9048
Zep 1:14 near and coming quickly, **L**! NIH
Zec 1: 4 But *they would* not **l** or pay attention 9048
3: 8 “ ‘**L**, O high priest Joshua 9048
7:12 as hard as flint and *would* not **l** *to* the law 9048
7:13 “ ‘When I called, *they did* not **l**; 9048
7:13 so when they called, *I would* not **l**,’ 9048
11: 3 **L** *to* the wail of the shepherds; 7754
11: 3 **L** *to* the roar of the lions; 7754
Mal 2: 2 If *you do* not **l**, and if you do not set your 9048
Mt 10:14 If anyone will not welcome you or **l** *to* your words, *201*
12:42 of the earth *to* **l** *to* Solomon's wisdom, *201*
13:18 “**L** then *to* what the parable of the sower *201*
15:10 to him and said, “**L** and understand. *201*
17: 5 with him I am well pleased. **L** *to* him!” *201*
18:16 But if *he will* not **l**, *201*
18:17 If *he* **refuses to l** *to* them, *4159*
18:17 and if *he* **refuses to l** even *to* the church, *4159*
21:33 “**L** *to* another parable: *201*
Mk 4: 3 “**L**! A farmer went out to sow his seed. *201*
6:11 if any place will not welcome you or **l** *to* *201*
6:20 yet *he* liked *to* **l** to him. *201*
7:14 “**L** *to* me, everyone, and understand this. *201*
9: 7 “This is my Son, whom I love. **L** *to* him!” *201*
15:35 they said, “**L**, he's calling Elijah.” *3972*
Lk 8:18 Therefore consider carefully how *you* **l**. *201*
9:35 whom I have chosen; **l** *to* him.” *201*

Lk 9:44 **“L carefully** *to* what I am about to tell you: 1650+3836+4044+5148+5148+5502
11:31 ends of the earth *to* **l** *to* Solomon's wisdom, *201*
16:29 Moses and the Prophets; *let them* **l** *to* them.' *201*
16:31 *they do* not **l** *to* Moses and the Prophets, *201*
18:6 **“L** *to* what the unjust judge says. *201*
Jn 9:27 told you already and *you did* not **l.** *201*
9:31 We know that God *does* not **l** *to* sinners. *201*
10:3 and the sheep **l** *to* his voice. *201*
10:8 but the sheep *did* not **l** *to* them. *201*
10:16 *They* too *will* **l** *to* my voice, *201*
10:20 Why **l** *to* him?" *201*
10:27 My sheep **l** *to* my voice; *201*
Ac 2:14 **l carefully** *to* what I say. *1969*
2:22 “Men of Israel, **l** *to* this: *201*
3:22 *you must* **l** *to* everything he tells you. *201*
3:23 not **l** *to* him will be completely cut off *201*
7:2 “Brothers and fathers, **l** *to* me! *201*
10:33 in the presence of God *to* **l** *to* everything *201*
13:16 and you Gentiles who worship God, **l** *201*
15:13 “Brothers, **l** *to* me. *201*
18:14 it would be reasonable for *me to* **l** *to* you. *462*
22:1 **l** now *to* my defense." *201*
26:3 Therefore, I beg *you to* **l** *to* me patiently. *201*
28:28 sent to the Gentiles, and they *will* **l!"** *201*
1Co 14:21 but even then *they will* not **l** *to* me," *1653*
15:51 **L,** I tell you a mystery: *2627*
2Co 13:11 Aim for perfection, **l to** my **appeal,** *4151*
Eph 4:29 that it may benefit those who **l.** *201*
2Ti 2:14 and only ruins those who **l.** *201*
Jas 1:19 Everyone should be quick to **l,** *201*
1:22 Do not merely **l** *to* the word, *212*
2:5 **L,** my dear brothers: Has not God chosen *201*
4:13 Now **l,** you who say, “Today or tomorrow *72*
5:1 Now **l,** you rich people, weep and wail *72*
1Jn 4:6 whoever is not from God *does* not **l** *to* us. *201*

LISTENED (52) [LISTEN]

Ge 3:17 “Because *you* **l** to your wife and ate from 9048
30:6 *he has* **l** to my plea and given me a son." 9048
30:17 God **l** to Leah, and she became pregnant 9048
30:22 he **l** to her and opened her womb. 9048
Ex 7:16 But until now *you have* not **l.** 9048
18:24 Moses **l** to his father-in-law 9048
Nu 21:3 The LORD **l** to Israel's plea and gave 9048
Dt 9:19 But again the LORD **l** to me. 9048
10:10 and the LORD **l** to me at this time also. 9048
34:9 So the Israelites **l** to him and did what 9048
Jos 10:14 a day when the LORD **l** to a man. 9048
Jdg 2:20 for their forefathers and *has* not **l** to me, 9048
6:10 But *you have* not **l** to me." 9048
1Sa 12:1 *“I have* **l** to everything you said to me 9048
19:6 Saul **l** to Jonathan and took this oath: 9048
28:23 in urging him, and *he* **l** to them. 9048
2Ki 13:4 and the LORD **l** to him, for he saw how 9048
18:12 *They* neither **l** to the commands nor 9048
2Ch 24:17 paid homage to the king, and he **l** to them. 9048
25:16 because you have done this and *have* not **l** 9048
33:13 by his entreaty and **l** *to* his plea; 9048
Ne 8:3 the people **l attentively to** the Book of 265+448
8:9 the people had been weeping as they **l** *to* 9048
Job 29:21 *“Men* **l** to me expectantly, 9048
32:11 *I* **l** to your reasoning; 263
Ps 22:24 not hidden his face from him but *has* **l** 9048
66:18 the Lord *would* not *have* **l;** 9048
66:19 but God *has* surely **l** and heard my voice 9048
Isa 66:4 no one answered, when I spoke, no *one* **l.** 9048
Jer 6:19 of their schemes, because *they have* not **l** 7992
8:6 *I have* **l** attentively, 9048
13:11 But *they have* not **l.'** 9048
23:18 Who *has* **l** and heard his word? 7992
25:3 but *you have* not **l.** 9048
25:4 *you have* not **l** or paid any attention. 9048
25:8 “Because *you have* not **l** *to* my words, 9048
26:5 and again (though *you have* not **l),** 9048
29:19 For *they have* not **l** to my words," 9048
29:19 And *you* exiles *have* not **l** either," 9048
35:15 But you have not paid attention or **l** to me. 9048
36:31 because *they have* not **l.' "** 9048
Eze 3:6 they *would have* **l** to you. 9048
9:5 As I **l,** he said to the others, 265+928
Da 9:6 not **l** to your servants the prophets, 9048
10:9 I heard him speaking, and as I **l** *to* him, 9048
Jnh 2:2 and *you* **l** to my cry. 9048
Mal 3:16 and the LORD **l** and heard. 7992
Mk 12:37 The large crowd **l** *to* him with delight. *201*
Ac 14:9 He **l** *to* Paul as he was speaking. *201*
15:12 as *they* **l** *to* Barnabas and Paul telling *201*
22:22 The crowd **l** *to* Paul until he said this. *201*
24:24 He sent for Paul and **l** *to* him as he spoke *201*

LISTENING (18) [LISTEN]

Ge 18:10 Sarah *was* **l** *at* the entrance to the tent, 9048
27:5 Now Rebekah *was* **l** as Isaac spoke 9048
1Sa 3:9 ‘Speak, LORD, for your servant *is* **l.'** " 9048
3:10 “Speak, for your servant *is* **l."** 9048
2Sa 20:17 “I'm **l,"** he said. 9048
Pr 18:13 He who answers before **l—** 9048
19:27 Stop **l** *to* instruction, my son, 9048
25:12 a wise man's rebuke to a **l** ear. 9048
Lk 2:46 **l** *to* them and asking them questions. *201*
5:1 the people crowding around him and **l** *to* *201*
10:39 at the Lord's feet **l** *to* what he said. *201*
19:11 *While* they *were* **l** *to* this, *201*
20:45 *While* all the people *were* **l,** *201*

Ac 16:14 of those **l** was a woman named Lydia, *201*
16:25 and the other prisoners *were* **l** *to* them. *2053*
17:21 but talking about and **l** *to* the latest ideas.) *201*
26:29 that not only you but all who *are* **l** *201*
27:11 centurion, instead of **l to** what Paul said, *4275*

LISTENS (17) [LISTEN]

Pr 1:33 but *whoever* **l** to me will live in safety and 9048
8:34 Blessed is the man *who* **l** to me, 9048
12:15 but a wise man **l** to advice. 9048
15:31 *He who* **l** *to* a life-giving rebuke will be 265+9048
17:4 A wicked man **l** to evil lips; 7992
21:28 and whoever **l** to him will be destroyed 9048
29:12 If a ruler **l** to lies, all his officials 7992
Mt 18:15 If *he* **l** *to* you, you have won your brother *201*
Lk 10:16 “He who **l** *to* you listens to me; *201*
10:16 “He who listens to you **l** *to* me; *201*
Jn 3:29 the bridegroom waits and **l** for him, *201*
6:45 Everyone who **l** *to* the Father and learns *201*
9:31 *He* **l** *to* the godly man who does his will. *201*
18:37 Everyone on the side of truth **l** *to* me." *201*
Jas 1:23 Anyone who **l** *to* the word but does *212+1639*
1Jn 4:5 and the world **l** *to* them. *201*
4:6 and whoever knows God **l** *to* us; *201*

LISTETH (KJV) See PLEASES, WANTS

LISTING (1) [LIST]

Nu 1:2 **l** every man by name, one by one. 5031

LIT (2) [LIGHT]

Jdg 15:5 **l** the torches and let the foxes loose in 836+1277
Ps 77:18 your lightning **l up** the world; 239

LITERATURE (2)

Da 1:4 He was to teach them the language and **l** 6219
1:17 and understanding of all kinds of **l** 6219

LITTERS (KJV) See WAGONS

LITTLE (171)

Ge 18:4 Let a **l** water be brought, 5071
24:17 “Please give me a **l** water from your jar." 5071
24:43 to her, “Please let me drink a **l** water 5071
30:30 The **l** you had before I came has increased 5071
43:2 “Go back and buy us a **l** more food." 5071
43:11 a **l** balm and a little honey, 5071
43:11 a little balm and a **l** honey, 5071
44:25 ‘Go back and buy a **l more** food.' 5071
48:7 a **l distance** from Ephrath. 824+3896
Ex 10:5 will devour what **l** you have **left** 3856+7129+8636
16:17 some gathered much, some **l.** 5070
16:18 he *who* **gathered l** did not have too little. 5070
16:18 he who gathered little *did* not **have too l.** 2893
23:30 **L** by little I will drive them out before you, 5071
23:30 Little *by* **l** I will drive them out before you, 5071
Lev 11:17 the **l owl,** the cormorant, the great owl, 3927
Nu 16:27 and **l ones** at the entrances to their tents. 3251
Dt 1:39 And the **l ones** that you said would 3251
7:22 drive out those nations before you, **l** *by* little 5071
7:22 drive out those nations before you, little by **l** 5071
14:16 the **l owl,** the great owl, the white owl, 3927
28:38 in the field but you will harvest **l,** 5071
Jdg 18:21 Putting their **l children,** their livestock 3251
1Sa 2:19 a **l** robe and took it to him when she went 7785
14:29 how my eyes brightened when I tasted a **l** 5071
14:43 “I merely tasted a **l** honey with the end 5071
18:23 I'm only a poor man and **l known."** 7829
2Sa 12:3 man had nothing except one **l** ewe lamb 7783
12:8 And if all this had been **too l,** 5071
1Ki 3:7 But I am only a **l** child and do not know 7785
10:21 silver was considered of **l value** 4202+4399
12:10 ‘My **l finger** is thicker than my father's waist. 7782
17:10 a **l** water in a jar so I may have a drink?" 5071
17:12 only a handful of flour in a jar and a **l** oil 5071
2Ki 4:2 she said, “except a **l** oil." 655[S]
8:12 dash their **l children** to the ground, 6407
10:18 “Ahab served Baal a **l;** 5071
2Ch 9:20 because silver was considered of **l value** 4399
10:10 ‘My **l finger** is thicker than my father's waist. 7782
20:13 with their wives and children and **l ones,** 3251
31:18 They included all the **l ones,** the wives, 3251
Ezr 9:8 to our eyes and a **l** relief in our bondage. 5071
Est 3:13 young and old, women and **l children—** 3251
Job 19:18 Even the **l boys** scorn me; 6396
21:11 their **l ones** dance about. 3529
24:24 *For a* **l while** they are exalted, 5071
36:2 with me a **l longer** and I will show you 10236
Ps 8:5 a **l** lower than the heavenly beings 5071
37:10 A **l while,** and the wicked will be no 5071+6388
37:16 Better the **l** that the righteous have than 5071
68:27 There is the **l** tribe of Benjamin, 7582
Pr 6:10 A **l** sleep, a little slumber, 5071
6:10 A little sleep, a **l** slumber, 5071
6:10 a **l** folding of the hands to rest— 5071
7:23 **l** knowing it will cost him his life. 4202
9:18 But **l** do they know that the dead are there, 4202
10:20 the heart of the wicked is **of l value.** 3869+5071
13:11 he who gathers money **l by little** makes it grow. 3338+6584

Pr 13:11 he who gathers money **little by l** makes it grow. 3338+6584
15:16 Better a **l** with the fear of the LORD than 5071
16:8 Better a **l** with righteousness than much 5071
23:8 You will vomit up the **l** you have eaten 7326
24:33 A **l** sleep, a little slumber, a little folding 5071
24:33 a **l** slumber, a little folding of the hands 5071
24:33 a **l** folding of the hands to rest— 5071
30:25 of **l** strength, yet they store up their food 4202
30:26 of **l** power, yet they make their home in 4202
Ecc 5:12 whether he eats **l** or much, 5071
10:1 so a **l** folly outweighs wisdom and honor. 5071
SS 2:15 the **l** foxes that ruin the vineyards, 7783
Isa 11:6 and a **l** child will lead them. 7785
26:20 a **l while** until his wrath has passed by. 5071+8092
28:10 a **l** here, a little there." 10236
28:10 a little here, a **l** there." 10236
28:13 a **l** here, a little there— 10236
28:13 a little here, a **l** there— 10236
32:10 **In l more than** a year you who feel 3427+6584
41:14 O **l** Israel, for I myself will help you," 5493
63:18 For a **l while** your people possessed 5203
Jer 3:9 Israel's immorality mattered so **l** to her, 7825
48:4 her **l** *ones* will cry out. 7582
Eze 11:16 the countries, yet *for* a **l while** I have been 5071
Da 7:8 there before me was another horn, a **l** *one,* 10236
11:34 When they fall, they will receive a **l** help, 5071
Hos 13:16 their **l ones** will be dashed to the ground, 6407
Hag 1:6 planted much, but have harvested **l.** 5071
1:9 but see, it turned out to be **l.** 5071
2:6 ‘In a **l while** I will once more shake 5071
Zec 1:15 I was **only a l** angry, 5071
13:7 and I will turn my hand against the **l ones.** 7592
Mt 6:30 *O you* **of l faith?** *3899*
8:26 He replied, *“You* **of l faith,** *3899*
10:42 *of* these **l** *ones* because he is my disciple, *3625*
11:25 and revealed them *to* **l children.** *3758*
14:31 *“You* **of l faith,"** he said, *3899*
16:8 Jesus asked, *“You* **of l** faith, *3899*
17:20 He replied, “Because you have so **l faith.** *3898*
18:2 a **l child** and had him stand among them. *4086*
18:3 you change and become like **l children,** *4086*
18:5 “And whoever welcomes a **l child** *4086*
18:6 of these **l** *ones* who believe in me to sin, *3625*
18:10 not look down on one *of* these **l** *ones.* *3625*
18:14 that any *of* these **l** *ones* should be lost. *3625*
19:13 Then **l children** were brought to Jesus *4086*
19:14 “Let the **l children** come to me, *4086*
26:39 Going a **l** farther, he fell with his face to *3625*
26:73 After a **l** *while,* those standing there *3625*
Mk 1:19 When he had gone a **l** farther, *3900*
5:23 “My **l daughter** is dying. *2589*
5:41 (which means, **“L girl,** I say to you, *3166*
7:25 a woman whose **l daughter** was possessed *2589*
9:36 a **l child** and had him stand among them. *4086*
9:37 welcomes one *of* these **l children** in my *4086*
9:42 *of* these **l** *ones* who believe in me to sin, *3625*
10:13 People were bringing **l children** to Jesus *4086*
10:14 “Let the **l children** come to me, *4086*
10:15 of God like a **l child** will never enter it." *4086*
14:35 Going a **l** farther, he fell to the ground *3625*
14:70 After a **l** *while,* those standing near said *3625*
Lk 5:3 and asked him to put out a **l** from shore. *3900*
7:47 he who has been forgiven **l** loves little." *3900*
7:47 he who has been forgiven little loves **l."** *3900*
9:47 a **l child** and had him stand beside him. *4086*
9:48 “Whoever welcomes this **l child** *4086*
10:21 and revealed them *to* **l children.** *3758*
12:26 Since you cannot do this **very l** *thing,* *1788*
12:28 *O you* **of l faith!** *3899*
12:32 “Do not be afraid, **l** flock, *3625*
16:10 with **very l** can also be trusted with much, *1788*
16:10 and whoever is dishonest with **very l** will *1788*
17:2 for him to cause one *of* these **l** *ones* *3625*
18:16 “Let the **l children** come to me, *4086*
18:17 of God like a **l child** will never enter it." *4086*
22:58 A **l** later someone else saw him and said, *1099*
Jn 12:35 “You are going to have the light just a **l** *3625*
13:33 I will be with you only a **l** longer. *3625*
16:16 *“In* **a l while** you will see me no more, *3625*
16:16 and then after **a l while** you will see me." *3625*
16:17 *‘In* **a l while** you will see me no more, *3625*
16:17 and then after **a l while** you will see me,' *3625*
16:18 “What does he mean by **‘a l while'?** *3625*
16:19 ‘In **a l while** you will see me no more, *3625*
16:19 and then after **a l while** you will see me'? *3625*
Ac 5:34 that the men be put outside **for a l while.** *1099*
19:22 while *he* **stayed** in the province of Asia **a l longer.** *2091+5989*
19:24 brought in no **l** business for the craftsmen. *3900*
1Co 4:3 **I care very l** if I am judged by *1639+1650+1788*
5:6 a **l** yeast works through the whole batch *3625*
6:4 appoint as judges even men of **l account** *2024*
2Co 7:8 but only for a **l while—** *6052*
8:15 he who gathered **l** did not have too little." *3900*
8:15 he who gathered little *did* not **have too l."** *1782*
11:1 I hope you will put up with a **l** of my *3625*
11:16 so that I may do a **l** boasting. *3625*
Gal 5:9 “A **l** yeast works through the whole batch *3625*
1Th 2:7 like a mother caring for her **l** children. *NIG*
1Ti 5:23 and use a **l** wine because of your stomach *3900*
Phm 1:15 separated from you **for a l while** was *4639+6052*
Heb 2:7 You made him a **l** lower than the angels; *1099*
2:9 who was made a **l** lower than the angels, *1099*
10:37 For in just a very **l** while, *3625*
12:10 Our fathers disciplined us for a **l while** *3900*
Jas 4:14 You are a mist that appears for a **l while** *3900*

1Pe 1: 6 a l while you may have had to suffer grief 3900
5:10 after you have suffered a l while, 3900
Rev 3: 8 I know that you have l strength, 3625
6:11 and they were told to wait a l longer, 3625
10: 2 He was holding a l scroll, 1044
10: 9 and asked him to give me the l scroll. 1044
10:10 I took the l scroll from the angel's hand 1044
17:10 he must remain *for* a l while. 3900

LIVE (650) [ALIVE, LIFE, LIFE'S, LIFELESS, LIFETIME, LIVED, LIVES, LIVING, OUTLIVED]

Ge 3:22 the tree of life and eat, and l forever." 2649
4:20 of *those who* l in tents and raise livestock. 3782
9:27 *may* Japheth l in the tents of Shem, 8905
12:10 went down to Egypt to l there for a while 1591
12:12 they will kill me but *will* let you l. 2649
13:18 So Abram moved his tents and went *to* l 3782
16:12 against him, and *he will* l in hostility 8905
17:18 only Ishmael *might* l under your blessing!" 2649
20: 7 and he will pray for you and *you will* l. 2649
20:15 l wherever you like." 3782
24:37 Canaanites, in whose land I l, 3782
26: 2 l in the land where I tell you to live. 8905
26: 2 live in the land where I tell you to l. NIH
27:40 *You will* l by the sword and you will serve 2649
28: 4 of the land where you now l as an alien, 4472
31:32 has your gods, *he shall* not l. 2649
34:10 L in it, trade in it, 3782
34:21 *"Let them* l in our land and trade in it; 3782
34:22 But the men will consent to l with us 3782
38:11 "L as a widow in your father's house 3782
38:11 So Tamar went *to* l in her father's house. 3782
42: 2 so that *we may* l and not die." 2649
42:18 "Do this and *you will* l, for I fear God: 2649
43: 8 so that we and you and our children *may* l 2649
45:10 *You shall* l in the region of Goshen and 3782
47: 4 "We have come to l here awhile, 1591
47: 6 *Let them* l in Goshen. 3782
47:19 Give us seed so that *we may* l and not die, 2649
49:13 "Zebulun *will* l by the seashore 8905
Ex 1:16 but if it is a girl, *let her* l." 2649
1:17 *they* let the boys l. 2649
1:18 Why *have you* let the boys l?" 2649
1:22 but let every girl l." 2649
2:15 from Pharaoh and went *to* l in Midian, 3782
8:22 the land of Goshen, where my people l; 6641
12:20 Wherever you l, you must eat unleavened 4632
18:20 and show them the way *to* l 2143
19:13 *he shall* not *be permitted to* l.' 2649
20:12 so that you *may* l long in the land 799+3427
21:35 to sell the l one and divide both the money 2645
22:18 *"Do* not allow a sorceress to l. 2649
23:31 I will hand over to you the *people who* l in 3782
23:33 *Do* not *let them* l in your land, 3782
33:20 for no one may see me and l." 2649
34:10 The people you l among will see NIH
34:12 not to make a treaty with *those who* l in 3782
34:15 not to make a treaty with *those who* l in 3782
Lev 3:17 the generations to come, wherever you l: 4632
7:26 And wherever you l, 4632
11: 2 'Of all the animals that l on land, NIH
13:46 *He must* l alone; 3782
13:46 he must l outside the camp. 4632
14: 4 the priest shall order that two l clean birds 2645
14: 6 He is then to take the l bird and dip it, 2645
14: 7 to release the l bird in the open fields. 2645
14:51 the hyssop, the scarlet yarn and the l bird, 2645
14:52 the fresh water, the l bird, the cedar wood, 2645
14:53 the l bird in the open fields outside 2645
16:20 he shall bring forward the l goat. 2645
16:21 to lay both hands on the head of the l goat 2645
18: 3 in Egypt, where *you used to* l, 3782
18: 5 the man who obeys them *will* l by them. 2649
20:22 the land where I am bringing you to l may 3782
20:23 *You must* not l according to the customs 2143
22:13 to l in her father's house as in her youth, NIH
23: 3 wherever you l, it is a Sabbath to 4632
23:14 the generations to come, wherever you l. 4632
23:17 From *wherever* you l, 4632
23:21 the generations to come, wherever you l. 4632
23:31 the generations to come, wherever you l. 4632
23:42 L in booths for seven days: 3782
23:42 All native-born Israelites *are to* l 3782
23:43 that *I* had the Israelites l in booths 3782
25: 6 and temporary resident who l among you, 1591
25:18 and *you will* l safely in the land. 3782
25:19 you will eat your fill and l there in safety. 3782
25:35 so *he can continue to* l among you. 2649
25:36 that your countryman *may continue to* l 2649
26: 5 the food you want and l in safety 3782
26:32 your enemies who l there will be appalled. 3782
Nu 4:19 So that *they may* l and not die 2649
13:18 the people who l there are strong or weak, 3782
13:19 What kind of land *do* they l in? 3782
13:19 What kind of towns *do* they l in? 3782
13:28 But the people who l there are powerful, 3782
13:29 The Amalekites l in the Negev; 3782
13:29 the Hittites, Jebusites and Amorites l in 3782
13:29 the Canaanites l near the sea and along 3782
14:21 Nevertheless, as surely as I l 2644
14:28 'As surely as I l, declares the LORD, 2644
21: 8 anyone who is bitten can look at it and l." 2649
23: 9 I see a people *who* l apart and do 8905
24:23 "Ah, who *can* l when God does this? 2649
Nu 31:15 *"Have you* allowed all the women to l?" 2649
32:17 and children *will* l in fortified cities, 3782
33:55 in the land where you *will* l. 3782
35: 2 to give the Levites towns to l in from 3782
35: 3 to l in and pasturelands for their cattle, 3782
35:29 the generations to come, wherever you l. 4632
35:32 and l on his own land before the death of 3782
35:34 the land where you l and where I dwell, 3782
Dt 2: 4 the descendants of Esau, who l in Seir. 3782
2: 8 the descendants of Esau, who l in Seir. 3782
2:10 (The Emites used to l there— 3782
2:12 Horites used to l in Seir, 3782
2:20 Rephaites, who used to l there; 3782
2:29 the descendants of Esau, who l in Seir, 3782
2:29 and the Moabites, who l in Ar, 3782
4: 1 Follow them so that *you may* l and may go 2649
4: 9 from your heart as long as you l. 2644
4:10 to revere me as long as they l in the land 2645
4:26 not l there long but will certainly 799+3427
4:40 after you and that *you may* l long in 799+3427
5:16 so that you *may* l long and 799+3427
5:24 Today we have seen that a man *can* l even 2649
5:33 so that *you may* l and prosper 2649
6: 2 as long as you l by keeping all his decrees 2644
8: 1 that *you may* l and increase and may enter 2649
8: 3 not l on bread alone but on every word 2649
11: 9 so that you *may* l long in the land that 799+3427
12: 1 as long as you l in the land. 2645
12:10 around you so that *you will* l in safety. 3782
12:19 as long as you l in your land. 3427+3972
13:12 the LORD your God is giving you to l in 3782
13:15 put to the sword all *who* l in that town. 3782
14:29 the fatherless and the widows who l NIH
16:14 and the widows who l in your towns. NIH
16:20 so that *you may* l and possess the land 2649
18: 1 *They shall* l on the offerings made to 430
22: 2 If the brother does not l near you or NIH
23: 6 as long as you l. 3427+3972+4200+6409
23:16 *Let him* l among you wherever he likes 3782
25:15 so that you *may* l long in the land 799+3427
28:30 but *you will* not l in it. 3782
28:66 You will l in constant suspense, 2644
30: 6 and with all your soul, and l. 2644
30:16 then *you will* l and increase, 2649
30:18 not l long in the land you are crossing 799+3427
30:19 so that you and your children *may* l 2649
31:13 the LORD your God as long as you l in 2645
32:40 As surely as I l forever, 2645
32:47 By them *you will* l long in the land 799+3427
33: 6 *"Let* Reuben l and not die, 2649
33:28 So Israel *will* l in safety alone; 8905
Jos 2: 9 so that all *who* l in this country are melting 3782
9: 7 "But perhaps you l near us. 3782
9:15 a treaty of peace with them to let them l, 2649
9:20 *We will* let them l, 2649
9:21 They continued, *"Let them* l, 2649
9:22 'We l a long way from you,' 3782
9:22 while actually you l near us? NIH
13:13 *to* l among the Israelites to this day. 3782
14: 4 of the land but only towns to l in, 3782
15:63 to this day the Jebusites l there with 3782
16:10 to this day the Canaanites l among 3782
17:12 for the Canaanites were determined to l in 3782
17:16 and all the Canaanites who l in the plain 3782
20: 4 into their city and give him a place *to* l 3782
21: 2 that you give us towns to l in, 3782
24:13 and *you* l in them and eat from vineyards 3782
Jdg 1:16 the men of Judah *to* l among the people 3782
1:21 the Jebusites l there with the Benjamites. 3782
1:27 for the Canaanites were determined to l in 3782
1:29 but the Canaanites *continued to* l there 3782
6:10 Amorites, in whose land you l.' 3782
8:29 of Joash went back home *to* l. 3782
11: 8 and you will be our head over all *who* l in 3782
17:10 "L with me and be my father and priest, 3782
17:11 So the Levite agreed to l with him, 3782
19:18 in the hill country of Ephraim where I l. NIH
Ru 1: 1 to l for a while in the country of Moab. 1591
2:11 and your homeland and came to l with NIH
1Sa 1:22 and *he will* l there always." 3782
1:26 "As surely as you l, my lord, 2644+5883
10:24 the people shouted, "Long l the king!" 2649
17:55 "As surely as you l, O king, 2644
20: 3 as surely as the LORD lives and as you l, 2644
20:14 like that of the LORD as long as I l, 2644
25:26 as surely as the LORD lives and as you l, 2644
25:28 be found in you as long as you l. 3427
27: 5 one of the country towns, that *I may* l there. 3782
27: 5 Why *should* your servant l in the royal city 3782
2Sa 8: 2 and the third length *was* allowed to l. 2649
11:11 As surely as you l, 2256+2644+2644+5883
12:22 be gracious to me and *let* the child l.' 2649
14:19 "As surely as you l, my lord the king, 2644+5883
16:16 "Long l the king! 2649
16:16 Long l the king!" 2649
19:34 "How many more years will I l, 2644
1Ki 1:25 'Long l King Adonijah!' 2649
1:31 said, *"May* my lord King David l forever!" 2649
1:34 'Long l King Solomon!' 2649
1:39 "Long l King Solomon!" 2649
2: 4 'If your descendants watch how they l, 2006
2:36 a house in Jerusalem and l there, 3782
3:17 this woman and I l in the same house. 3782
6:13 And *I will* l among the Israelites 8905
7: 8 And the palace in which *he was to* l, 3782
8:36 Teach them the right way *to* l, 2143
8:40 that they will fear you all the time they l 2645
1Ki 8:61 the LORD our God, to l by his decrees 2143
20:32 'Please *let* me l.' " 2649
2Ki 2: 2 surely as the LORD lives and as you l, 2644
2: 4 surely as the LORD lives and as you l, 2644
2: 6 surely as the LORD lives and as you l, 2644
4: 7 You and your sons *can* l on what is left." 2649
4:30 surely as the LORD lives and as you l, 2644
6: 2 and let us build a place there for us to l." 3782
7: 4 If they spare us, *we* l; 2649
10:19 to come *will* no *longer* l." 2649
11:12 "Long l the king!" 2649
17:27 from Samaria go back *to* l there and teach 3782
17:28 *to* l in Bethel and taught them how 3782
2Ch 2: 3 to build a palace to l in. 3782
6:27 Teach them the right way *to* l, 2143
6:31 and walk in your ways all the time they l 2645
8:11 not l in the palace of David king of Israel, 3782
19:10 from your fellow countrymen who l in 3782
20:15 "Listen, King Jehoshaphat and all *who* l in 3782
23:11 "Long l the king!" 2649
34:28 on this place and on *those who* l here.' " 3782
Ne 2: 3 *"May* the king l forever! 2649
8:14 the Israelites *were to* l in booths during 3782
9:29 by which a man *will* l if he obeys them. 2649
11: 1 bring one out of every ten to l in Jerusalem, 3782
11: 2 the men who volunteered to l in Jerusalem. 3782
Job 4:19 much more *those who* l in houses of clay, 8905
7:16 I despise my life; *I would* not l forever. 2649
14:14 If a man dies, *will he* l again? 2649
21: 7 Why *do* the wicked l on, 2649
26: 5 beneath the waters and *all that* l in them. 8905
27: 6 will not reproach me as long as I l. 3427+4946
30: 6 to l in the dry stream beds, 8905
33:28 and I will l to enjoy the light.' 2652
Ps 15: 1 Who *may* l on your holy hill? 8905
22:26 *may* your hearts l forever! 2649
24: 1 the world, and *all who* l in it; 3782
26: 8 I love the house where you l, O LORD, 5061
33:14 dwelling place he watches all *who* l on earth 3782
35:20 against *those who* l quietly *in* the land. 8091
49: 1 listen, all *who* l in this world, 3782
49: 9 *he should* l on forever and not see decay. 2649
55:23 not l out half their days. 2936
63: 4 I will praise you as long as I l, 2644
65: 4 and bring near *to* l in your courts! 8905
68: 6 but the rebellious l in a sun-scorched land. 8905
69:32 you who seek God, *may* your hearts l! 2649
72:15 Long *may he* l! 2649
78:10 God's covenant and refused to l by his law. 2143
89:48 What man *can* l and not see death, 2649
98: 7 the world, and *all who* l in it. 3782
102:28 of your servants *will* l in your presence; 3782
104:33 sing praise to my God as long as I l. 928+6388
107:36 there *he* brought the hungry to l, 3782
116: 2 I will call on him as long as I l. 3427
118:17 I will not die but l, 2649
119:17 Do good to your servant, and *I will* l; 2649
119:77 your compassion come to me that *I may* l, 2649
119:116 according to your promise and *I will* l; 2649
119:144 give me understanding that *I may* l. 2649
119:175 *Let* me l that I may praise you, 2649
120: 5 that *I* l among the tents of Kedar! 8905
128: 6 may you l to see your children's children. NIH
133: 1 *when* brothers l together in unity! 3782
140:13 and the upright *will* l before you. 3782
146: 2 sing praise to my God as long as I l. 928+6388
Pr 1:33 but whoever listens to me *will* l in safety 8905
2:21 For the upright *will* l in the land, 8905
4: 4 keep my commands and *you will* l. 2649
7: 2 Keep my commands and *you will* l; 2649
9: 6 Leave your simple ways and *you will* l; 2649
15:27 but he who hates bribes *will* l. 2649
16: 7 makes even his enemies l at peace with him 8966
19:10 It is not fitting for a fool to l in luxury— 9503
21: 9 Better to l on a corner of the roof than share 3782
21:19 Better *to* l in a desert than with a 3782
25:24 Better *to* l on a corner of the roof than share 3782
Ecc 3:12 to be happy and do good while they l. 2644
6: 3 a hundred children and l many years; 2649
9: 3 in their hearts while they l, 2644
9: 4 even a l dog is better off than a dead lion! 2645
11: 8 However many years a man *may* l, 2649
Isa 5: 8 to field till no space is left and *you* l alone 3782
6: 5 and I l among a people of unclean lips, 3782
6: 6 of the seraphs flew to me with a l coal 8365
10:24 "O my people *who* l in Zion, 3782
11: 6 The wolf *will* l with the lamb, 1591
18: 3 you *who* l *on* the earth, 8905
20: 6 the *people who* l *on* this coast will say, 3782
21:14 you *who* l in Tema, 3782
22:21 be a father to *those who* l in Jerusalem and 3782
23:18 Her profits will go to those *who* l before 3782
26:14 They are now dead, *they* l no more; 2649
26:19 your dead *will* l; their bodies will rise. 2649
30:19 O people of Zion, *who* l in Jerusalem, 3782
32:16 and righteousness l in the fertile field. 3782
32:18 My people *will* l in peaceful dwelling places 3782
38:16 Lord, by such things *men* l; 2649
38:16 You restored me to health and let me l. 2649
40:22 and spreads them out like a tent to l in. 3782
42:10 you islands, and *all who* l in them. 3782
49:18 As surely as I l," declares the LORD, 2644
49:20 give us more space *to* l in.' 3782
51:13 that *you* l in constant terror every day 7064
52: 4 my people went down to Egypt to l; 1591
55: 3 hear me, that your soul *may* l. 2649
57:15 *"I* l in a high and holy place, 8905

Isa	65: 9	and there *will* my servants **l.**	8905
	65:20	an old man who *does* not **l out** his years;	4848
	65:22	they build houses and others **l in** them,	3782
Jer	1:14	be poured out on all *who* **l in** the land.	3782
	6: 8	so no *one can* **l in** *it.*"	3782
	6:12	against *those who* **l in** the land,"	3782
	7: 3	and *I will* **let** you **l** in this place.	8905
	7: 7	then *I will* **let** you **l** in this place,	8905
	8:16	the city and *all who* **l** there."	3782
	9: 6	You **l** in the midst of deception;	3782
	9:11	the towns of Judah so no *one can* **l** there."	3782
	9:26	Moab and all who **l** in the desert	3782
	10:17	you *who* **l** under siege.	3782
	10:18	"At this time I will hurl out *those who* **l in**	3782
	11: 2	of Judah and to *those who* **l in** Jerusalem.	3782
	11: 9	of Judah and *those who* **l in** Jerusalem.	3782
	12: 1	Why *do* all the faithless **l at ease?**	8922
	12: 4	Because *those who* **l** in it are wicked,	3782
	13:13	with drunkenness all *who* **l in** this land,	3782
	19:12	to this place and to *those who* **l** here,	3782
	20: 6	and all *who* **l** in your house will go	3782
	21: 6	I will strike down *those who* **l in**	3782
	21: 9	Babylonians who are besieging you *will* **l;**	2649
	21:13	you *who* **l** *above* this valley *on*	3782
	22:23	You *who* **l** in 'Lebanon,'	3782
	22:24	**"As surely as I l,"** declares the LORD,	2644
	23: 6	be saved and Israel *will* **l** in safety.	8905
	23: 8	Then *they will* **l** in their own land."	3782
	23:14	They commit adultery and **l** a lie.	928+2143
	24: 8	whether they remain in this land or **l**	3782
	25:24	of the foreign people who **l** in the desert;	8905
	25:29	down a sword upon all *who* **l** *on* the earth,	3782
	25:30	shout against all *who* **l** *on* the earth.	3782
	26:15	and on this city and on *those who* **l in** it,	3782
	27:11	in its own land to till it and *to* **l** there,	3782
	27:12	serve him and his people, and *you will* **l.**	2649
	27:17	Serve the king of Babylon, and *you will* **l.**	2649
	31:24	*People will* **l** together in Judah	3782
	32:37	to this place and **let** them **l** in safety.	3782
	33:16	be saved and Jerusalem *will* **l** in safety.	8905
	34:22	the towns of Judah so no *one can* **l** there."	3782
	35: 7	but *must* always **l** in tents.	3782
	35: 7	Then *you will* **l** a long time in the land	2649
	35: 9	or built houses to **l in** or had vineyards,	3782
	35:15	Then *you will* **l** in the land I have given	3782
	38: 2	goes over to the Babylonians *will* **l.**	2649
	38: 2	He will escape with his life; *he will* **l.'**	2649
	38:17	you and your family *will* **l.**	2649
	40: 5	and **l** with him among the people,	3782
	40:10	and **l** in the towns you have taken over."	3782
	42:14	'No, we will go and **l in** Egypt,	3782
	43: 5	of Judah who had come back to **l** in	1591
	44: 8	where you have come to **l?**	1591
	44:13	I will punish those *who* **l** in Egypt with	3782
	44:14	the remnant of Judah who have gone to **l**	1591
	44:14	to which they long to return and **l;**	3782
	44:28	the whole remnant of Judah who came to **l**	1591
	46:18	**"As surely as I l,"** declares the King,	2644
	46:19	you *who* **l in** Egypt,	3782
	47: 2	the towns and *those who* **l** in them.	3782
	48: 9	with no *one to* **l** in them.	3782
	48:17	Mourn for her, all who **l** around her,	NIH
	48:19	*you who* **l in** Aroer.	3782
	48:28	you *who* **l in** Moab.	3782
	49: 1	Why *do* his people **l** in its towns?	3782
	49: 8	hide in deep caves, you *who* **l in** Dedan,	3782
	49:16	you *who* **l** in the clefts of the rocks,	8905
	49:18	says the LORD, "so no one *will* **l** there;	3782
	49:20	against *those who* **l in** Teman:	3782
	49:30	Stay in deep caves, you *who* **l in** Hazor,"	3782
	49:31	neither gates nor bars, its *people* **l** alone.	8905
	49:33	No one *will* **l** there; no man will dwell in it.	3782
	50: 3	No one *will* **l** in it; both men and animals	3782
	50:21	the land of Merathaim and *those who* **l in**	3782
	50:34	but unrest to *those who* **l in** Babylon.	3782
	50:35	"against *those who* **l in** Babylon and	3782
	50:39	and hyenas *will* **l** there,	3782
	50:40	"so no one *will* **l** there;	3782
	51:13	*You who* **l** by many waters and are rich	8905
	51:24	and all *who* **l** in Babylonia for all	3782
	51:29	of Babylon so that no *one will* **l** there.	3782
	51:35	"May our blood be on *those who* **l in**	3782
	51:62	that neither man nor animal *will* **l** in it;	3782
La	4:20	that under his shadow *we would* **l** among	2649
	4:21	you *who* **l** in the land of Uz.	3782
Eze	2: 6	around you and you **l** among scorpions.	3782
	3:21	*he will* **surely l** because he took warning,	2649+2649
	5:11	**as surely as I l,** declares the Sovereign	2644
	6: 6	Wherever you **l,** the towns will	4632
	6:14	to Diblah—wherever they **l.**	4632
	7:13	as long as both of them **l,**	928+2021+2644
	12:19	because of the violence of all who **l** there.	3782
	13:19	and have spared those who *should* not **l.**	2649
	14:16	**as surely as I l,** declares the Sovereign	2644
	14:18	**as surely as I l,** declares the Sovereign	2644
	14:20	**as surely as I l,** declares the Sovereign	2644
	16: 6	lay there in your blood I said to you, **"L!"**	2649
	16:48	**As surely as I l,** declares the Sovereign	2644
	17:16	" '**As surely as I l,** declares the Sovereign	2644
	17:19	the Sovereign LORD says: **As surely as I l,**	2644
	18: 3	"**As surely as I l,** declares the Sovereign	2644
	18: 9	That man is righteous; *he will* **surely l,**	2649+2649
	18:13	*Will such a man* **l?**	2649
	18:17	for his father's sin; *he will* **surely l.**	2649+2649
	18:19	keep all my decrees, *he will* **surely l.**	2649+2649
	18:21	*he will* **surely l;** he will not die.	2649+2649
Eze	18:22	the righteous things he has done, *he will* **l.**	2649
	18:23	when they turn from their ways and **l?**	2649
	18:24	the wicked man does, *will he* **l?**	2649
	18:28	*he will* **surely l;** he will not die.	2649+2649
	18:32	Repent and **l!**	2649
	20: 3	**As surely as I l,** I will not let you inquire	2644
	20:11	the man who obeys them *will* **l** by them.	2649
	20:13	man who obeys them *will* **l** by them—	2649
	20:21	although the man who obeys them *will* **l**	2649
	20:25	not good and laws *they could* not **l** by;	2649
	20:31	**As surely as I l,** declares the Sovereign	2644
	20:33	**As surely as I l,** declares the Sovereign	2644
	27:35	All *who* **l in** the coastlands are appalled	3782
	28:25	Then *they will* **l** in their own land,	3782
	28:26	*They will* **l** there in safety	3782
	28:26	*they will* **l** in safety	3782
	29: 6	Then all *who* **l in** Egypt will know	3782
	29:11	no *one will* **l** there for forty years.	3782
	32:15	when I strike down all *who* **l** there,	3782
	33:10	How then *can we* **l?"** '	2649
	33:11	'**As surely as I l,** declares the Sovereign	2644
	33:11	rather that they turn from their ways and **l.**	2649
	33:12	to **l** because of his former righteousness.'	2649
	33:13	the righteous man that *he will* **surely l,**	2649+2649
	33:15	and does no evil, *he will* **surely l;**	2649+2649
	33:16	what is just and right; *he will* **surely l.**	2649+2649
	33:19	just and right, *he will* **l** by doing so.	2649
	33:27	the Sovereign LORD says: **As surely as I l,**	2644
	34: 8	**As surely as I l,** declares the Sovereign	2644
	34:25	so that *they may* **l** in the desert and sleep in	3782
	34:28	*They will* **l** in safety,	3782
	35: 6	**as surely as I l,** declares the Sovereign	2644
	35:11	**as surely as I l,** declares the Sovereign	2644
	36:28	*You will* **l** in in the land I gave	3782
	37: 3	"Son of man, *can* these bones **l?"**	2649
	37: 9	into these slain, that *they may* **l.'** "	2649
	37:14	I will put my Spirit in you and *you will* **l,**	2649
	37:25	*They will* **l** in the land I gave	3782
	37:25	their children's children *will* **l** there forever,	3782
	38: 8	and now all of them **l** in safety.	3782
	39: 6	on *those who* **l** in safety **in** the coastlands,	3782
	39: 9	" 'Then *those who* **l in** the towns	3782
	43: 7	This is where *I will* **l** among	8905
	43: 9	and *I will* **l** among them forever.	8905
	44: 9	the foreigners who **l** among the Israelites.	NIH
	45: 5	as their possession for towns to **l in.**	3782
	47: 9	of living creatures *will* **l** wherever	2649
	47: 9	where the river flows everything *will* **l.**	2644
Da	2: 4	the king in Aramaic, "O king, **l** forever!	10262
	2:11	and they do not **l** among men."	10407
	2:38	Wherever *they* **l,** he has made you ruler	10163
	3: 9	King Nebuchadnezzar, "O king, **l** forever!	10262
	4: 1	who **l** in all the world:	10163
	4:15	and let him **l** with the animals among	10269
	4:23	let him **l** like the wild animals,	10269
	4:25	be driven away from people and will **l**	10403
	4:32	be driven away from people and will **l**	10403
	5:10	"O king, **l** forever!"	10262
	6: 6	"O King Darius, **l** forever!	10262
	6:21	Daniel answered, "O king, **l** forever!	10262
	7:12	but were allowed to **l** for a period of time.)	10073+10089+10261
Hos	3: 3	*"You are to* **l** with me many days;	3782
	3: 3	and I will **l** with you."	NIH
	3: 4	For the Israelites *will* **l** many days	3782
	4: 1	to bring against *you who* **l in** the land:	3782
	4: 3	and all *who* **l** in it waste away;	3782
	6: 2	that *we may* **l** in his presence.	2649
	10: 5	The **people who l in** Samaria fear for	8907
	12: 9	*I will* **make** you **l** in tents again,	3782
Joel	1: 2	listen, all *who* **l in** the land.	3782
	1:14	and all *who* **l in** the land to the house of	3782
	2: 1	Let all *who* **l in** the land tremble,	3782
Am	5: 4	"Seek me and **l;**	2649
	5: 6	Seek the LORD and **l,**	2649
	5:11	*you will* not **l** in them;	3782
	5:14	Seek good, not evil, that *you may* **l.**	2649
	8: 8	and all *who* **l** in it mourn?	3782
	9: 5	and all *who* **l** in it mourn—	3782
	9:14	they will rebuild the ruined cities and **l in**	3782
Ob	1: 3	you *who* **l** in the clefts of the rocks	8905
Jnh	4: 3	for it is better for me to die than to **l."**	2644
	4: 8	"It would be better for me to die than to **l."**	2644
Mic	1:11	*you who* **l in** Shaphir.	3782
	1:11	*Those who* **l in** Zaanan will not come out.	3782
	1:12	*Those who* **l in** Maroth writhe in pain,	3782
	1:13	*You who* **l in** Lachish,	3782
	1:15	a conqueror against you *who* **l in**	3782
	5: 4	And *they will* **l securely,**	3782
Na	1: 5	the world and all *who* **l** in it.	3782
Hab	2: 4	but the righteous *will* **l** by his faith—	2649
Zep	1: 4	against Judah and against all *who* **l in**	3782
	1:11	Wail, *you who* **l in** the market district;	3782
	1:13	They will build houses but not **l in** them;	3782
	1:18	a sudden end of all *who* **l in** the earth."	3782
	2: 5	Woe to *you who* **l** by the sea,	3782
	2: 9	**as surely as I l,"** declares the LORD	2644
Zec	1: 5	And the prophets, *do they* **l** forever?	2649
	2: 7	*you who* **l in** the Daughter of Babylon!"	3782
	2:10	I am coming, and *I will* **l** among you,"	8905
	2:11	*I will* **l** among you and you will know	8905
	8: 8	I will bring them back *to* **l** in Jerusalem;	8905
	12: 8	the LORD will shield *those who* **l in**	3782
Mt	4: 4	'Man *does* not **l** on bread alone,	*2409*
	9:18	put your hand on her, and *she will* **l."**	*2409*
	12:45	and they go in and **l** there.	*2997*
Mk	5:23	on her so that she will be healed and **l."**	*2409*
Mk	7: 5	"Why don't your disciples **l** according to	*4344*
	12:44	put in everything—all she had **to l on."**	*1050*
Lk	4: 4	'Man *does* not **l** on bread alone.' "	*2409*
	10:28	"Do this and *you will* **l."**	*2409*
	11:26	and *they* go in and **l** there.	*2997*
	21: 4	of her poverty put in all she had *to* **l on."**	*1050*
	21:35	For it will come upon all those who **l** on	*2764*
Jn	4:50	Your son *will* **l."**	*2409*
	4:53	"Your son *will* **l."**	*2409*
	5:25	Son of God and those who hear *will* **l.**	*2409*
	5:29	those who have done good will rise to **l,**	*2437*
	6:51	eats of this bread, *he will* **l** forever.	*2409*
	6:57	the living Father sent me and I **l** because	*2409*
	6:57	the one who feeds on me *will* **l** because	*2409*
	6:58	he who feeds on this bread *will* **l** forever."	*2409*
	7:35	**people l scattered among** the Greeks,	*1402+3836*
	11:25	He who believes in me *will* **l,**	*2409*
	14:19	Because I **l,** you also will live.	*2409*
	14:19	Because I live, you also *will* **l.**	*2409*
Ac	2:14	"Fellow Jews and all of you who **l in**	*2997*
	2:26	my body also *will* **l** in hope,	*2942*
	7:48	the Most High *does* not **l** in houses made	*2997*
	17:24	and *does* not **l** in temples built by hands.	*2997*
	17:26	and the exact places where they should **l.**	*3000*
	17:28	in him *we* **l** and move and have our being.'	*2409*
	21:21	that you teach all the Jews who **l** among	*NIG*
	21:21	to circumcise their children or **l** according	*4344*
	22:22	He's not fit *to* **l!"**	*2409*
	25:24	shouting that he ought not *to* **l** any longer.	*2409*
	28: 4	Justice has not allowed him *to* **l."**	*2409*
	28:16	Paul was allowed *to* **l** by himself,	*3531*
Ro	1:17	"The righteous *will* **l** by faith."	*2409*
	4:14	For if those who **l** by law are heirs,	*NIG*
	6: 2	how *can we* **l** in it any longer?	*2409*
	6: 4	we too *may* **l** a new life.	*4344*
	6: 8	we believe that *we will* also **l with** him.	*5182*
	8: 4	who *do* not **l** according to the sinful nature	*4344*
	8: 5	Those who **l** according to the sinful nature	*1639*
	8: 5	but those who **l** in accordance with	*NIG*
	8:12	not to the sinful nature, *to* **l** according to it.	*2409*
	8:13	For if *you* **l** according to the sinful nature,	*2409*
	8:13	the misdeeds of the body, *you will* **l,**	*2409*
	10: 5	"The man who does these things *will* **l**	*2409*
	12:16	**L in harmony** with one another.	*899+3836+5858*
	12:18	**l at peace** with everyone.	*1644*
	14: 8	If *we* **l,** we live to the Lord;	*2409*
	14: 8	If we live, *we* **l** to the Lord;	*2409*
	14: 8	So, whether *we* **l** or die,	*2409*
	14:11	" '**As surely as I l,**' says the Lord,	*1609+2409*
1Co	7:12	wife who is not a believer and she is willing *to* **l** with him, he must not divorce her.	*3861*
	7:13	husband who is not a believer and he is willing *to* **l** with her, she must not divorce	*3861*
	7:15	God has called us to **l** in peace.	*NIG*
	7:29	now on those who have wives *should* **l** as	*1639*
	7:35	but that you may **l** in a right way	*NIG*
	8: 6	and for whom we **l;**	*NIG*
	8: 6	and through whom we **l.**	*NIG*
2Co	5: 1	that if the earthly tent we **l in** is destroyed,	*3864*
	5: 7	*We* **l** by faith, not by sight.	*4344*
	5:15	that those who **l** should no longer live	*2409*
	5:15	that those who live *should* no longer **l**	*2409*
	6: 9	dying, and yet *we* **l on;**	*2409*
	6:16	*"I will* **l with** them and walk among them,	*1940*
	7: 3	a place in our hearts that we *would* **l**	*5182*
	10: 2	toward some people who think that we **l**	*4344*
	10: 3	For *though we* **l** in the world,	*4344*
	13: 4	yet by God's power *we will* **l** with him	*2409*
	13:11	be of one mind, **l in peace.**	*1644*
Gal	2:14	*you* **l** like a Gentile and not like a Jew.	*2409*
	2:19	the law I died to the law so that *I might* **l**	*2409*
	2:20	with Christ and I no longer **l,**	*2409*
	2:20	The life *I* **l** in the body,	*2409*
	2:20	*I* **l** by faith in the Son of God,	*2409*
	3:11	because, "The righteous *will* **l** by faith."	*2409*
	3:12	"The man who does these things *will* **l**	*2409*
	5:16	So I say, **l** by the Spirit,	*4344*
	5:21	that those who **l** like this will not inherit	*4556*
	5:25	Since *we* **l** by the Spirit,	*2409*
Eph	2: 2	in which *you* used to **l** when you followed	*4344*
	4: 1	I urge you *to* **l a life** worthy of	*4344*
	4:17	you *must* no longer **l** as the Gentiles do,	*4344*
	5: 2	and **l a life** of love,	*4344*
	5: 8	**L** as children of light	*4344*
	5:15	Be very careful, then, how *you* **l—**	*4344*
Php	1:21	For to me, *to* **l** is Christ and to die is gain.	*2409*
	3:16	Only let us **l up** to what we have already	*5123*
	3:17	and take note of those who **l** according to	*4344*
	3:18	many **l** as enemies of the cross of Christ.	*4344*
Col	1:10	*that* you *may* **l a life** worthy of the Lord	*4344*
	2: 6	Christ Jesus as Lord, *continue to* **l** in him,	*4344*
1Th	2:12	and urging you to **l lives** worthy of God,	*4344*
	3: 8	For now *we* really **l,** since you are standing	*2409*
	4: 1	we instructed you how *to* **l** in order	*4344*
	4: 7	but to **l** a holy life.	*NIG*
	5:10	*we may* **l** together with him.	*2409*
	5:13	**L in peace** with each other.	*1644*
2Th	3: 6	and *does* not **l** according to the teaching	*4344*
1Ti	2: 2	that *we may* **l** peaceful and quiet lives	*1341*
2Ti	2:11	If we died with him, *we will* also **l with** him;	*5182*
	3:12	everyone who wants *to* **l** a godly life	*2409*
Tit	2: 3	to be reverent in the **way** they **l,**	*2949*
	2:12	and *to* **l** self-controlled, upright and godly	*2409*
	3:14	and not **l** unproductive lives.	*1639*
Heb	10:38	But my righteous one *will* **l** by faith.	*2409*
	12: 9	to the Father of our spirits and **l!**	*2409*
	12:14	to **l** in peace with all men and to be holy;	*NIG*

Heb 13:18 and desire *to* l honorably in every way. *418*
Jas 4: 5 the spirit *he* caused to l in us envies *3001*
4:15 *we will* l and do this or that." *2409*
1Pe 1:17 l your lives as strangers here *418*
2:12 L such good lives among the pagans that, *2400*
2:16 L as free men, but do not use your *NIG*
2:16 l as servants of God. *NIG*
2:24 *we might* die to sins and l for righteousness; *2409*
3: 7 be considerate *as you* l **with** your wives, *5324*
3: 8 all of you, l **in harmony with** one another; *3939*
4: 2 *he does* not l the rest of his earthly life *1051*
4: 6 l according to God in regard to the spirit. *2409*
2Pe 1:13 to refresh your memory as long as *I* l in *1639*
2:18 from those who l in error. *418*
3:11 You ought to l holy and godly lives *419*
1Jn 1: 6 we lie and *do* not l **by** the truth. *4472*
2: 6 Whoever claims *to* l in him must walk *3531*
3:24 Those who obey his commands l in him, *3531*
4: 9 and only Son into the world that *we might* l *2409*
4:13 We know that *we* l in him and he in us, *3531*
Rev 2:13 I know where *you* l— *2997*
3:10 to test those who l on the earth. *2997*
11:10 these two prophets had tormented those who l on the earth. *2997*
13: 6 dwelling place and those who l in heaven. *5012*
14: 6 to proclaim to those who l on the earth— *2764*
21: 3 is with men, and *he will* l with them. *5012*

LIVED (247) [LIVE]

Ge 4:16 LORD's presence and l in the land of Nod, 3782
5: 3 When Adam *had* l 130 years, 2649
5: 4 Adam l 800 years and had other sons 2118+3427
5: 5 Altogether, Adam l 930 years, 2649
5: 6 When Seth *had* l 105 years, 2649
5: 7 Seth l 807 years and had other sons 2649
5: 8 Altogether, Seth l 912 years, 2118+3427
5: 9 When Enosh *had* l 90 years, 2649
5:10 Enosh l 815 years and had other sons 2649
5:11 Altogether, Enosh l 905 years, 2118+3427
5:12 When Kenan *had* l 70 years, 2649
5:13 Kenan l 840 years and had other sons 2649
5:14 Altogether, Kenan l 910 years, 2118+3427
5:15 When Mahalalel *had* l 65 years, 2649
5:16 Mahalalel l 830 years and had other sons 2649
5:17 Altogether, Mahalalel l 895 years, 2118+3427
5:18 When Jared *had* l 162 years, 2649
5:19 Jared l 800 years and had other sons 2649
5:20 Altogether, Jared l 962 years, 2118+3427
5:21 When Enoch *had* l 65 years, 2649
5:23 Altogether, Enoch l 365 years. 2118+3427
5:25 When Methuselah *had* l 187 years, 2649
5:26 Methuselah l 782 years and had other sons 2649
5:27 Altogether, Methuselah l 969 years, 2118+3427
5:28 Lamech *had* l 182 years, he had a son 2649
5:30 Lamech l 595 years and had other sons 2649
5:31 Altogether, Lamech l 777 years, 2118+3427
9:28 After the flood Noah l 350 years. 2649
9:29 Altogether, Noah l 950 years, 2118+3427
10:30 The **region where** they l stretched 4632
11:11 Shem l 500 years and had other sons 2649
11:12 When Arphaxad *had* l 35 years, 2649
11:13 Arphaxad l 403 years and had other sons 2649
11:14 When Shelah *had* l 30 years, 2649
11:15 Shelah l 403 years and had other sons 2649
11:16 When Eber *had* l 34 years, 2649
11:17 Eber l 430 years and had other sons 2649
11:18 When Peleg *had* l 30 years, 2649
11:19 Peleg l 209 years and had other sons 2649
11:20 When Reu *had* l 32 years, 2649
11:21 Reu l 207 years and had other sons 2649
11:22 When Serug *had* l 30 years, 2649
11:23 Serug l 200 years and had other sons 2649
11:24 When Nahor *had* l 29 years, 2649
11:25 Nahor l 119 years and had other sons 2649
11:26 After Terah *had* l 70 years, 2649
11:32 Terah l 205 years, and he died in 2118+3427
13:12 Abram l in the land of Canaan, 3782
13:12 while Lot l among the cities of the plain 3782
19:29 that overthrew the cities where Lot *had* l. 3782
19:30 He and his two daughters l in a cave. 3782
20: 1 Negev and l between Kadesh and Shur. 3782
21:20 *He* l in the desert and became an archer. 3782
23: 1 Sarah l to be a hundred and twenty-seven 2644
25: 7 Abraham l a hundred and seventy-five years 2649
25:11 who then l near Beer Lahai Roi. 3782
25:17 Ishmael l a hundred and thirty-seven 2644
25:18 l **in hostility toward** all their 5877+6584+7156
35:28 Isaac l a hundred and eighty years. 2118+3427
37: 1 Jacob l in the land where his father had 3782
38:21 He asked the **men** *who l* there, AIT
38:22 Besides, the **men** *who l* there said, AIT
39: 2 *he* l in the house of his Egyptian master. 2118
47:28 Jacob l in Egypt seventeen years, 2649
50:11 When the Canaanites *who* l there saw 3782
50:22 He l a hundred and ten years 2649
Ex 6: 4 land of Canaan, **where** they l as aliens. 4472
6:16 Levi l 137 years. 2644
6:18 Kohath l 133 years. 2644
6:20 Amram l 137 years. 2644
10:23 in the **places where** they l. 4632
12:40 the length of time the Israelite people l 3782
Lev 18:27 the people who l in the land before you, NIH
26:35 not have during the sabbaths you l in it. 3782
Nu 13:22 the descendants of Anak, l. NIH
14:45 the Amalekites and Canaanites who l in 3782
20:15 and *we* l there many years. 3782
21: 1 king of Arad, *who* l in the Negev, 3782
21: 9 and looked at the bronze snake, *he* l. 2649
33:40 who l in the Negev of Canaan, 3782
Dt 1:44 The Amorites who l in those hills 3782
2:22 descendants of Esau, who l in Seir, 3782
2:22 and *have* l in their place to this day. 3782
2:23 Avvites who l in villages as far as Gaza, 3782
4:25 l in the land **a long time—** 3823
4:33 speaking out of fire, as you have, and l? 2649
21:13 After *she has* l in your house 3782
23: 7 because *you* l as an alien in his country. 2118
26: 5 with a few people and l there and became 1591
29:16 You yourselves know how *we* l in Egypt 3782
Jos 2:15 house she l **in** was part of the city wall. 3782
8:26 until he had destroyed all *who* l in Ai. 3782
8:35 and the aliens who l among them. 2143
13:21 allied with Sihon—*who* l **in** that country. 3782
22:33 where the Reubenites and the Gadites l. 3782
24: 2 the father of Abraham and Nahor, l 3782
24: 7 Then *you* l in the desert for a long time. 3782
24: 8 of the Amorites who l east of the Jordan. 3782
24:18 including the Amorites, *who* l **in** the land. 3782
Jdg 1:32 and because of this the people of Asher l 3782
1:33 but the Naphtalites too l among 3782
2:18 of their enemies as long as the judge l; 3427
3: 5 The Israelites l among the Canaanites, 3782
4: 2 who l in Harosheth Haggoyim. 3782
8:31 His concubine, who l in Shechem, NIH
9:21 and *he* l there because he was afraid 3782
10: 1 He l in Shamir, in the hill country 3782
11:21 over all the land of the Amorites *who* l **in** 3782
16:30 when he died than while he l. 2644
17:12 the young man became his priest and l 2118
18: 7 they l a long way from the Sidonians NIH
18:22 the men who l near Micah 928+1074+2021
18:28 to rescue them because they l a long way NIH
19: 1 Now a Levite *who* l in a remote area in 1591
Ru 1: 2 And they went to Moab and l there. 2118
1: 4 After *they had* l there about ten years, 3782
2:23 And *she* l with her mother-in-law. 3782
1Sa 10:12 A man who l there answered, 4946
12:11 so that *you* l securely. 3782
23:29 And David went up from there and l in 3782
27: 7 David l in Philistine territory a year 3782
27: 8 (From ancient times these peoples *had* l **in** 3782
27:11 And such was his practice as long as *he* l 3782
2Sa 4: 3 of Beeroth fled to Gittaim and *have* l there 2118
5: 6 to attack the Jebusites, *who* l there. 3782
9:13 And Mephibosheth l in Jerusalem, 3782
13:20 And Tamar l in her brother Absalom's 3782
14:28 Absalom l two years in Jerusalem 3782
1Ki 4:25 from Dan to Beersheba, l in safety, 3782
11:20 Genubath l with Pharaoh's own children. 2118
11:25 adversary **as long as** Solomon l, 3427+3972
12:25 in the hill country of Ephraim and l there. 3782
13:25 in the city where the old prophet l. 3782
14: 9 You have done more evil than all who l 2118
17:22 the boy's life returned to him, and *he* l. 2649
21: 8 and nobles who l in Naboth's city 3782
21:11 and nobles who l in Naboth's city did 3782
2Ki 13: 5 So the Israelites l in their own homes 3782
14:17 of Judah l for fifteen years after the death 2649
15: 5 and *he* l in a separate house. 3782
16: 6 then moved into Elath and *have* l there 3782
17:24 They took over Samaria and l in its towns. 3782
17:25 When they first l there, 3782
22:14 She l in Jerusalem, in the Second District. 3782
25:30 a regular allowance as long as he l. 2644
1Ch 2:55 and the clans of scribes *who* l **at** Jabez: 3782
4:23 the potters *who* l **at** Netaim and Gederah; 3782
4:28 *They* l in Beersheba, Moladah, 3782
4:40 Some Hamites *had* l there formerly. 3782
4:43 and *they have* l there to this day. 3782
5:11 The Gadites l next to them in Bashan, 3782
5:16 The Gadites l in Gilead, 3782
7:29 The descendants of Joseph son of Israel l 3782
8:28 and they l in Jerusalem. 3782
8:29 Jeiel the father of Gibeon l in Gibeon. 3782
8:32 They too l near their relatives 3782
9: 3 and Manasseh *who* l in Jerusalem were: 3782
9:16 who l in the villages of the Netophathites. 3782
9:34 and they l in Jerusalem. 3782
9:35 Jeiel the father of Gibeon l in Gibeon. 3782
9:38 They too l near their relatives 3782
11: 4 The Jebusites *who* l there 3782
2Ch 11: 5 Rehoboam l in Jerusalem and built 3782
19: 4 Jehoshaphat l in Jerusalem, 3782
19: 8 And *they* l in Jerusalem. 3782
20: 8 *They have* l in it and have built in it 3782
21:16 the Philistines and of the Arabs who l near NIH
24:14 **As long as** Jehoiada l, 3427+3972
25:25 of Judah l for fifteen years after the death 2649
26: 7 the Philistines and against the Arabs who l 3782
26:21 *He* l **in** a separate house— 3782
30:25 from Israel and those *who* l in Judah. 3782
31: 6 and Judah who l in the towns of Judah 3782
31:19 who l on the farm lands NIH
34:22 She l in Jerusalem, in the Second District. 3782
34:33 **As long as** he l, they did not fail to 3427+3972
Ne 4:12 Then the Jews who l near them came 3782
8:17 from exile built booths and l in them. 3782
9:24 the Canaanites, *who* l **in** the land; 3782
11: 3 and descendants of Solomon's servants l 3782
11: 4 both Judah and Benjamin l in Jerusalem): 3782
11: 6 The descendants of Perez who l 3782
11:21 The temple servants l on the hill of Ophel, 3782
11:25 of the people of Judah l in Kiriath Arba 3782
11:31 the Benjamites from Geba l in Micmash, NIH
12:27 from **where** they l and were brought 5226
13:16 Men from Tyre *who* l in Jerusalem 3782
Job 1: 1 of Uz *there* l a man whose name was Job. 2118
18:19 no survivor where once he l. 4472
21:28 the tents where wicked men l?' 5438
38:21 You have l so many years! NIH
42:16 After this, Job l a hundred and forty years; 2649
Ps 49:18 while he l he counted himself blessed— 2644
105:23 Jacob l **as an alien** in the land of Ham. 1591
107:34 of the wickedness of *those who* l there. 3782
120: 6 Too long *have* I l among those who hate 8905
Ecc 4:15 I saw that all who l and walked under 2645
9:15 *there* l in that city a man poor but wise, 5162
Isa 13:20 She will never be inhabited or l **in** 8905
Jer 3: 1 But you *have l as a* **prostitute** AIT
35:10 *We have* l in tents and have fully obeyed 3782
42:18 poured out on *those who* l **in** Jerusalem, 3782
50:39 It will never again be inhabited or l **in** 8905
52:34 a regular allowance as long as he l, 2644
La 2:16 *we have* l to see it." 5162
Eze 3:15 I came to the exiles who l at Tel Abib near 3782
16:46 who l to the north of you 3782
16:46 and your younger sister, who l to 3782
20: 9 the eyes of the nations they l among and NIH
26:17 you put your terror on all *who* l there. 3782
31: 6 all the great nations l in its shade. 3782
31:17 Those *who* l in its shade, 3782
37:25 the land where your fathers l. 3782
39:26 when they l in safety in their land 3782
Da 4:12 and the birds of the air l in its branches; 10163
5:21 he l with the wild donkeys and ate grass 10403
Zep 2:15 This is the carefree city that l in safety. 3782
Mt 2:23 *he* went and l in a town called Nazareth. *2997*
4:13 *he* went and l in Capernaum, *2997*
23:30 'If *we had* l in the days of our forefathers, *1639*
Mk 5: 3 This man l in the tombs, *2400+2998+3836*
Lk 1:80 and *he* l in the desert until he appeared *1639*
2:36 *she had* l with her husband seven years *2409*
7:37 When a woman who *had* l a sinful life in *1639*
8:27 not worn clothes or l in a house, *3531*
8:27 but had l in the tombs. *NIG*
16:19 and fine linen and l in luxury every day. *2370*
Jn 7:42 the town where David l?" *1639*
12: 1 Jesus arrived at Bethany, where Lazarus l, *1639*
Ac 7: 2 before he l in Haran. *2997*
9:35 All those who l **in** Lydda and Sharon *2997*
16: 1 where a disciple named Timothy l, *1639+1695*
16: 3 because of the Jews who l in that area, *1639*
17:21 foreigners who l **there** spent their time *2111*
19:10 the Jews and Greeks who l **in** the province *2997*
20:18 "You know how *I* l the whole time I was *1181*
26: 4 "The Jews all know the **way** I have l ever *1052*
26: 5 *I* l as a Pharisee. *2409*
Eph 2: 3 All of us also l among them at one time, *418*
Col 3: 7 in these ways, in the life *you* once l. *2409*
1Th 1: 5 how *we* l among you for your sake. *1181*
2Ti 1: 5 which first l **in** your grandmother Lois and *1940*
Tit 3: 3 *We* l in malice and envy, *1341*
Heb 11: 9 *he* l in tents, as did Isaac and Jacob, *2997*
Jas 5: 5 l on earth **in luxury** and self-indulgence. *5587*
1Pe 1:14 to the evil desires you had when you l *NIG*
Rev 13:14 wounded by the sword and yet l. *2409*

LIVELIHOOD (2)

Dt 24: 6 that would be taking a man's l as security. 5883
Zec 13: 5 the land has been my l since my youth.' 7871

LIVELY (KJV) See LIVING, VIGOROUS

LIVER (14)

Ex 29:13 the covering of the l, 3879
29:22 the covering of the l, 3879
Lev 3: 4 and the covering of the l, 3879
3:10 and the covering of the l, 3879
3:15 and the covering of the l, 3879
4: 9 and the covering of the l, 3879
7: 4 and the covering of the l, 3879
8:16 the covering of the l, 3879
8:25 the covering of the l, 3879
9:10 the covering of the l from the sin offering, 3879
9:19 the kidneys and the covering of the l— 3879
Job 20:25 the gleaming point out of his l. 5355
Pr 7:23 till an arrow pierces his l, 3879
Eze 21:21 he will examine the l. 3879

LIVES (192) [LIVE]

Ge 9: 3 Everything that l and moves will be food 2645
19:17 one of them said, "Flee for your l! 5883
42:13 who l in the land of Canaan. NIH
42:15 **As surely** as Pharaoh l, 2644
42:16 **as surely** as Pharaoh l, 2644
45: 5 because it was to **save** l that God sent me 4695
45: 7 and to **save** your l by a great deliverance. 2649
47:25 *"You have* **saved** our l," they said. 2649
50:20 now being done, the saving of many l. 6639
Ex 1:14 They made their l bitter with hard labor 2644
30:15 offering to the LORD to atone for your l. 5883
30:16 making atonement for your l." 5883
Lev 19:33 " 'When an alien l with you in your land, 1591
Nu 16:38 the men who sinned at the cost of their l. 5883
Dt 22:19 not divorce her **as long as** he l. 3427+3972
22:29 never divorce her **as long as** he l. 3427+3972
28:43 The alien who l among you will rise NIH

Dt 33:20 Gad l there like a lion, 8905
Jos 2:13 that *you will* **spare** *the* l *of* my father 2649
2:14 "Our l for your lives!" 5883
2:14 "Our lives for your l!" NIH
6:25 and *she* l among the Israelites to this day. 3782
9:24 So we feared for our l because of you, 5883
Jdg 5:18 The people of Zebulun risked their very l; 5883
8:19 **As surely as** the LORD l, 2644
8:19 the LORD lives, if *you had* **spared** their l, 2649
18:25 and you and your family will lose your l." 5883
Ru 3:13 **as surely as** the LORD l 2644
1Sa 14:39 **As surely as** the LORD who rescues Israel l, 2644
14:45 **As surely as** the LORD l, 2644
19:6 "**As surely as** the LORD l, 2644
20:3 **as surely as** the LORD l 2644
20:21 **as surely as** the LORD l, 2644
20:31 As long as the son of Jesse l on this earth, 2644
25:26 **as surely as** the LORD l 2644
25:29 the l *of* your enemies he will hurl away as 5883
25:34 **as surely as** the LORD, the God of Israel, l, 2644
26:10 **As surely as** the LORD l," 2644
26:16 **As surely as** the LORD l, 2644
28:10 "**As surely as** the LORD l, 2644
29:6 "**As surely as** the LORD l, 2644
2Sa 2:27 "**As surely as** God l, 2644
4:9 "**As surely as** the LORD l, 2644
12:5 "**As surely as** the LORD l, 2644
14:11 "**As surely as** the LORD l," 2644
15:21 "**As surely as** the LORD l, 2644
15:21 **as** my lord the king l, 2644
18:8 the forest claimed more l that day than 6639
19:5 and the l *of* your sons and daughters and 5883
19:5 and the l *of* your wives and concubines. 5883
22:47 "The LORD l! Praise be to my Rock! 2644
23:17 of men who went at the risk of their l?" 5883
1Ki 1:29 "**As surely as** the LORD l, 2644
2:24 **as surely as** the LORD l— 2644
17:1 "**As** the LORD, the God of Israel, l, 2644
17:12 "**As surely as** the LORD your God l," 2644
18:10 **As surely as** the LORD your God l, 2644
18:15 "**As** the LORD Almighty l, 2644
22:14 "**As surely as** the LORD l, 2644
2Ki 1:13 "please have respect for my life and the l 5883
2:2 "**As surely as** the LORD l 2644
2:4 "**As surely as** the LORD l 2644
2:6 "**As surely as** the LORD l 2644
3:14 "**As surely as** the LORD Almighty l, 2644
4:30 "**As surely as** the LORD l 2644
5:16 "**As surely as** the LORD l, 2644
5:20 **As surely as** the LORD l, 2644
7:7 left the camp as it was and ran for their l. 5883
1Ch 11:19 these men who went at the risk of their l?" 5883
11:19 they risked their l to bring it back, 5883
2Ch 18:13 "**As surely as** the LORD l, 2644
Job 15:28 and houses where no *one* l, 3782
19:25 I know that my Redeemer l, 2645
27:2 "**As surely as** God l, who has denied me 2644
38:26 to water a land where no man l, NIH
Ps 18:46 The LORD l! Praise be to my Rock! 2644
37:32 seeking their very l; 4637
66:9 he has preserved our l and kept our feet 5883
74:19 the l *of* your afflicted people forever. 2652
97:10 for he guards the l *of* his faithful ones 5883
107:5 and their l ebbed away. 5883
Pr 1:19 it takes away the l *of* those who get it. 5883
3:29 your neighbor, who l trustfully near you. 3782
14:25 A truthful witness saves l, 5883
Ecc 2:3 during the few days of their l. 2644
6:3 yet no matter how long he l, 3427+9102
6:6 if *he* l a thousand years twice over but fails 2649
8:12 a hundred crimes and still l **a long time,** 799
Isa 38:20 of our l in the temple of the LORD. 2644
42:11 let the settlements where Kedar l rejoice. 3782
57:15 *he who* l forever, whose name is holy: 8905
65:20 be in it an infant who l but a few days, or NIH
Jer 2:6 where no one travels and no one l?' 3782
4:2 '**As surely as** the LORD l,' 2644
4:29 towns are deserted; no one l in them. 3782
5:2 '**As surely as** the LORD l,' 2644
12:16 '**As surely as** the LORD l'— 2644
16:14 '**As surely as** the LORD l, 2644
16:15 '**As surely as** the LORD l, 2644
17:6 in a salt land where no *one* l. 3782
19:7 at the hands of those who seek their l, 5883
19:9 on them by the enemies who seek their l.' 5883
21:7 and to their enemies who seek their l. 5883
23:7 '**As surely as** the LORD l, 2644
23:8 '**As surely as** the LORD l, 2644
34:20 over to their enemies who seek their l. 5883
34:21 over to their enemies who seek their l, 5883
38:16 "**As surely as** the LORD l, 2644
44:26 "**As surely as** the Sovereign LORD l." 2644
46:26 hand them over to those who seek their l, 5883
48:6 Run for your l; become like a bush in the 5883
49:11 I *will* **protect** their l. 2649
49:31 a nation at ease, *which* l in confidence," 3782
49:37 before those who seek their l; 5883
51:6 Run for your l! 5883
51:37 a place where no *one* l. 3782
51:43 a land where no one l, 3782
51:45 Run for your l! 5883
La 2:12 as their l ebb away in their mothers' arms. 5883
2:19 Lift up your hands to him for the l 5883
5:9 of our l because of the sword in the desert. 5883
Eze 13:18 the l of my people but preserve your own? 5883
13:22 from their evil ways and so **save** their l, 2649
17:17 siege works erected to destroy many l. 5883
Da 3:28 willing to give up their l rather than serve 10151
4:34 I honored and glorified *him who* l forever. 10261
12:7 I heard him swear by *him who* l forever, 2645
Hos 4:15 '**As surely as** the LORD l!' 2644
Am 8:14 '**As surely as** your god l, 2644
8:14 '**As surely as** the god of Beersheba l'— 2644
Mic 7:14 *which* l by itself **in** a forest, 8905
Hab 1:16 for by his net he l in luxury and enjoys 2750
Jn 3:21 But whoever l **by** the truth comes into *4472*
11:26 and whoever l and believes *2409*
14:17 for *he* l with you and will be in you. *3531*
Ac 10:32 Simon the tanner, who l by the sea.' *NIG*
15:26 men who have risked their l for the name *6034*
27:10 loss to ship and cargo, and to our own l also. *6034*
27:24 and God has graciously given you the l of *NIG*
Ro 6:10 but the life *he* l, he lives to God. *2409*
6:10 but the life he lives, *he* l to God. *2409*
7:1 over a man only as long as *he* l? *2409*
7:18 I know that nothing good l in me, that is, *3861*
8:9 if the Spirit of God l in you. *3861*
8:11 through his Spirit, who l **in** you. *1940*
14:7 For none of us l to himself alone and none *2409*
16:4 They **risked** their l for me. *5549+5719*
1Co 3:16 and that God's Spirit l in you? *3861*
7:39 bound to her husband as long as *he* l. *2409*
2Co 1:5 the sufferings of Christ flow over into our l, *NIG*
13:4 yet *he* l by God's power. *2409*
Gal 2:20 I no longer live, but Christ l in me. *2409*
Eph 2:22 a dwelling in which God l by his Spirit. *NIG*
Col 2:9 For in Christ all the fullness of the Deity l *2997*
1Th 2:8 not only the gospel of God but our l as *6034*
2:12 and urging you to **live** l worthy of God, *4344*
1Ti 2:2 and quiet l in all godliness and holiness. *1050*
5:6 But the widow who l **for pleasure** is dead *5059*
5:6 for pleasure is dead *even while she* l. *2409*
6:16 immortal and *who* l **in** unapproachable light *3861*
2Ti 1:5 I am persuaded, now l in you also. *NIG*
1:14 with the help *of* the Holy Spirit who l **in** us. *1940*
Tit 2:12 **upright** and **godly** *l* in this present age, *AIT*
3:14 and not live unproductive l. *NIG*
Heb 2:15 and free those who all their l were held *2409*
5:13 Anyone who l **on** milk, being still an infant, *3576*
7:24 but because Jesus l forever, *3531*
7:25 *because he* always l to intercede for them. *2409*
13:5 Keep your l free from the love of money *5573*
1Pe 1:17 live your l as strangers here *5989*
2:12 Live such good l among the pagans that *419+3836*
3:2 the purity and reverence of your l. *419*
2Pe 2:7 who was distressed by the filthy l *419*
3:11 You ought to live **holy** and **godly** *l* *AIT*
1Jn 1:10 a liar and his word has no place in our l. *NIG*
2:10 Whoever loves his brother l in the light, *3531*
2:14 and the word of God l in you, *3531*
2:17 man who does the will of God l forever. *3531*
3:6 No one who l in him keeps on sinning. *3531*
3:16 to lay down our l for our brothers. *6034*
3:24 And this is how we know that *he* l in us: *3531*
4:12 God l in us and his love is made complete *3531*
4:15 God l in him and he in God. *3531*
4:16 Whoever l in love lives in God, *3531*
4:16 Whoever lives in love l in God, *3531*
2Jn 1:2 which l in us and will be with us forever: *3531*
Rev 2:13 in your city—where Satan l. *2997*
4:9 on the throne and who l for ever and ever, *2409*
4:10 and worship him who l for ever and ever. *2409*
10:6 he swore by him who l for ever and ever, *2409*
12:11 not love their l so much as to shrink *6034*
15:7 who l for ever and ever. *2409*

LIVESTOCK (88)

Ge 1:24 l, creatures that move along the ground, 989
1:25 the l according to their kinds, 989
1:26 over the l, over all the earth, 989
2:20 So the man gave names to all the l, 989
3:14 above all the l and all the wild animals! 989
4:20 of those who live in tents and raise l. 5238
7:14 all l according to their kinds, 989
7:21 birds, l, wild animals, 989
8:1 and the l that were with him in the ark, 989
9:10 the birds, the l and all the wild animals, 989
13:2 Abram had become very wealthy in l and 5238
30:29 and how your l has fared under my care. 5238
31:9 So God has taken away your father's l 5238
31:18 and he drove all his l ahead of him, 5238
33:17 for himself and made shelters for his l. 5238
34:5 his sons were in the fields with his l; 5238
34:23 Won't their l, their property 5238
36:6 as well as his l and all his other animals 5238
36:7 not support them both because of their l. 5238
46:6 They also took with them their l and 5238
46:32 men are shepherds; *they* **tend** l, 408+2118+5238
46:34 'Your servants *have* **tended** l 408+2118+5238
47:6 put them in charge of my own l." 5238
47:16 "Then bring your l," said Joseph. 5238
47:16 sell you food in exchange for your l, 5238
47:17 So they brought their l to Joseph, 5238
47:17 with food in exchange for all their l. 5238
47:18 our money is gone and our l belongs 989+5238
Ex 9:3 a terrible plague on your l in the field— 5238
9:4 between the l *of* Israel and that of Egypt, 5238
9:6 All the l *of* the Egyptians died, 5238
9:19 to bring your l and everything you have in 5238
9:20 to bring their slaves and their l inside. 5238
9:21 left their slaves and l in the field. 5238
10:26 Our l too must go with us; 5238
12:29 and the firstborn of all the l as well. 989
Ex 12:38 as well as large **droves of l,** 5238
13:12 All the firstborn males of your l belong to 989
17:3 to make us and our children and l die 5238
22:5 a man grazes his l in a field or vineyard 1248
34:19 including all the firstborn males of your l, 5238
Lev 5:2 of unclean wild animals or of unclean l or 989
25:7 as well as for your l and the wild animals 989
Nu 3:41 and the l *of* the Levites in place of all 989
3:41 in place of all the firstborn of the l *of* 989
3:45 and the l *of* the Levites in place 989
3:45 of the Levites in place of their l. 989
20:4 that we and our l should die here? 1248
20:8 so they and their l can drink." 1248
20:11 and the community and their l drank. 1248
20:19 and if we or our l drink any of your water, 5238
32:1 of Jazer and Gilead were suitable for l. 5238
32:4 are suitable for l, and your servants have 5238
32:4 and your servants have l. 5238
32:16 like to build pens here for our l and cities 5238
35:3 flocks and all their *other* l. 2651
Dt 2:35 But the l and the plunder from the towns 989
3:7 But all the l and the plunder from their 989
3:19 your l (I know you have much livestock) 5238
3:19 (I know you have much l) may stay in 5238
7:14 nor any of your l without young. 989
13:15 both its people and its l. 989
20:14 the l and everything else in the city, 989
28:4 crops of your land and the young of your l 989
28:11 of your l and the crops of your ground— 989
28:51 They will devour the young of your l and 989
30:9 of your l and the crops of your land. 989
Jos 1:14 your children and your l may stay in 5238
8:2 that you may carry off their plunder and l 989
8:27 for themselves the l and plunder 989
11:14 for themselves all the plunder and l 989
21:2 with pasturelands for our l." 989
22:8 with large **herds of l,** with silver, gold, 5238
Jdg 6:5 up with their l and their tents like swarms 5238
18:21 their l and their possessions in front 5238
1Sa 23:5 the Philistines and carried off their l. 5238
30:20 his men drove them ahead of the other l, 5238
1Ch 5:9 because their l had increased in Gilead. 5238
5:21 They seized the l *of* the Hagrites— 5238
7:21 when they went down to seize their l. 5238
28:1 and l belonging to the king and his sons, 5238
2Ch 26:10 because he had much l in the foothills and 5238
Ezr 1:4 with silver and gold, with goods and l, 989
1:6 with goods and l, and with valuable gifts, 989
Ps 78:48 their l to bolts of lightning. 5238
Eze 38:12 from the nations, rich in l and goods, 5238
38:13 to take away l and goods and 5238
Zec 2:4 because of the great number of men and l 989

LIVING (323) [LIVE]

Ge 1:20 "Let the water teem with l creatures, 2645
1:21 and every l and moving thing with which 2645
1:24 the land produce l creatures according 2645
1:28 and over every l **creature** that moves on 2651
2:7 and the man became a l being. 2645
2:19 whatever the man called each l creature, 2645
3:20 she would become the mother of all the l. 2645
6:19 to bring into the ark two of all l creatures, 2644
7:4 the earth every l **creature** I have made." 3685
7:16 in were male and female of every l **thing,** 1414
7:21 Every l **thing** that moved on the earth 1414
7:23 Every l **thing** on the face of the earth 3685
8:17 Bring out every kind of l creature that is 2651
8:21 never again will I destroy all l **creatures,** 2645
9:10 with every l creature that was with you— 2651
9:10 every l **creature** *on* earth. 2651
9:12 and every l creature with you, a covenant 2651
9:15 and you and all l creatures of every kind. 2651
9:16 and all l creatures of every kind on 2651
13:7 The Canaanites and Perizzites *were* also l 3782
14:7 as well as the Amorites who *were* l 3782
14:12 since he *was* l in Sodom. 3782
14:13 Now Abram *was* l near the great trees 8905
16:3 Abram *had been* l in Canaan ten years, 3782
19:25 including all *those* l **in** the cities— 3782
21:21 While *he was* l in the Desert of Paran, 3782
21:23 the country where *you are* l **as an alien** 1591
24:3 the Canaanites, among whom I *am* l, 3782
24:62 for he *was* l in the Negev. 3782
25:6 But while he was still l, 2645
27:46 with l because of these Hittite women. 2644
27:46 **life will not be worth l."** 2644+4200+4537
34:30 and Perizzites, the *people* l **in** this land. 3782
35:22 While Israel *was* l in that region, 8905
36:20 *who were* l **in** the region: 3782
43:7 'Is your father still l?' 2645
43:27 Is he still l?" 2645
45:3 Is my father still l?" 2645
46:31 who were *l* in the land of Canaan, AIT
Ex 3:22 and *any woman* l *in* her house for articles 1591
12:48 "An alien l among you who wants 1591
12:49 to the native-born and to the alien l 1591
Lev 11:9 the creatures l in the water of the seas and NIH
11:10 or among all the other l creatures in 2651
11:12 Anything l in the water that does NIH
11:46 every l thing that moves in the water 2651
11:47 between l **creatures** that may be eaten 2651
16:29 whether native-born or an alien l 1591
17:8 or any alien l among them who offers 1591
17:10 " 'Any Israelite or any alien l 1591
17:12 nor may an alien l among you eat blood." 1591
17:13 " 'Any Israelite or any alien l 1591

Lev 18:18 with her while your wife is **l.** 2644
18:26 the aliens **l** among you must not do any 1591
19:34 The alien **l** with you must be treated 1591
20: 2 or any alien **l** in Israel who gives any 1591
22:18 either an Israelite or an alien **l** in Israel— NIH
25:45 also buy some of the temporary residents **l** 1591
25:47 and sells himself to the alien **l** among you 9369
Nu 9:14 " 'An alien **l** among you who wants 1591
13:32 land we explored devours *those* **l in** it. 3782
14:25 Since the Amalekites and Canaanites *are* **l** 3782
15:14 or anyone else **l** among you presents 1591
15:15 the same rules for you and for the alien **l** 1591
15:16 to you and to the alien **l** among you.' " 1591
15:26 the aliens **l** among them will be forgiven, 1591
16:48 He stood between the **l** and the dead, 2645
19:10 both for the Israelites and for the aliens **l** 1591
30: 3 "When a young woman still **l** NIH
30:10 a woman **l with** her husband makes a vow 1074
30:16 and his young daughter still **l** in his house. NIH
35:15 and any *other* **people l** among them, 9369
Dt 5:26 the voice of the **l** God speaking out of fire, 2645
11: 6 their tents and every **l thing** that belonged 3685
11:30 in the territory of those Canaanites **l** in 3782
11:31 you have taken it over and *are* **l** there, 3782
14: 9 Of all the creatures **l** in the water, NIH
14:21 You may give it to an alien **l** in any NIH
14:27 do not neglect the Levites **l** in your towns, NIH
16:11 the aliens, the fatherless and the widows **l** NIH
17: 2 If a man or woman **l** among you in one of NIH
18: 6 in Israel where he *is* **l,** 1591
24:14 a brother Israelite or an alien **l** in one NIH
25: 5 If brothers *are* **l** together and one 3782
29:11 and the aliens **l** in your camps NIH
31:12 and the aliens **l** in your towns— NIH
Jos 3:10 how you will know that the **l** God is 2645
6:21 with the sword every **l thing** in it— 889[S]
9:11 and all *those* **l in** our country said to us, 3782
9:16 that they were neighbors, **l** near them. 3782
10: 1 of peace with Israel and *were* **l** near them. 2118
11:19 Except for the Hivites **l in** Gibeon, 3782
15:15 against the *people* **l in** Debir 3782
15:63 *who were* **l in** Jerusalem; 3782
16:10 not dislodge the Canaanites **l** in Gezer; 3782
17: 7 to include the *people* **l at** En Tappuah. 3782
20: 9 Any of the Israelites or any alien **l** 1591
24:15 Amorites, in whose land you *are* **l.** 3782
Jdg 1: 9 down to fight against the Canaanites **l in** 3782
1:10 They advanced against the Canaanites **l** 3782
1:11 against the *people* **l in** Debir 3782
1:17 and attacked the Canaanites **l in** Zephath, 3782
1:21 the Jebusites, *who were* **l in** Jerusalem; 3782
1:29 the Canaanites **l** in Gezer, 3782
1:30 the Canaanites **l in** Kitron or Nahalol, 3782
1:31 Nor did Asher drive out *those* **l in** Acco 3782
1:33 Neither did Naphtali drive out *those* **l in** 3782
1:33 of the land, and *those* **l in** Beth Shemesh 3782
3: 3 the Hivites **l in** the Lebanon mountains 3782
6: 4 and did not spare a **l thing** for Israel, 4695
10:18 be the head of all *those* **l in** Gilead." 3782
17: 7 who *had been* **l** within the clan of Judah, 1591
18: 7 where they saw that the people *were* **l** 3782
19:16 who *was* **l** in Gibeah (the men of the place 1591
20:15 chosen men from *those* **l in** Gibeah. 3782
21:10 and put to the sword *those* **l** there, 3782
21:12 They found among the *people* **l in** 3782
Ru 1: 7 the place where *she had been* **l** and set out 2118
2:20 not stopped showing his kindness to the **l** 2645
4:17 *women* **l** there said, "Naomi has a son." 8907
1Sa 17:26 he should defy the armies of the **l** God?" 2645
17:36 he has defied the armies of the **l** God. 2645
25:29 be bound securely in the bundle of the **l** 2645
2Sa 7: 2 "Here I am, **l** in a palace of cedar, 3782
12:18 "While the child was still **l,** 2645
15: 8 While your servant *was* **l** at Geshur 3782
20: 3 in confinement till the day of their death, **l** 2654
1Ki 3:22 The **l** *one* is my son; 2645
3:22 The dead one is yours; the **l** *one* is mine." 2645
3:25 the **l** child in two and give half to one 2645
3:26 "Please, my lord, give her the **l** baby! 2645
3:27 "Give the **l** baby to the first woman. 2645
12:17 for the Israelites who *were* **l** in the towns 3782
13:11 *there was* a certain old prophet **l** in Bethel, 3782
2Ki 19: 4 has sent to ridicule the **l** God, 2645
19:16 Sennacherib has sent to insult the **l** God. 2645
1Ch 8: 6 who were heads of families of *those* **l in** 3782
8:13 who were heads of families of *those* **l in** 3782
12:15 and they put to flight **everyone** *l in* AIT
17: 1 "Here I am, **l** in a palace of cedar, 3782
22: 2 to assemble the aliens **l in** Israel, 928
2Ch 10:17 for the Israelites who *were* **l** in the towns 3782
31: 4 He ordered the people **l in** Jerusalem 3782
Ezr 1: 4 *now be* **l** are to provide him with silver 1591
4:17 the rest of their associates **l** in Samaria 10338
Ne 3:26 and the temple servants **l** on the hill 3782
3:30 made repairs opposite his **l quarters.** 5969
11:30 So *they were* **l** all the way from Beersheba 2837
Est 9:19 rural Jews—those **l** in villages— 3782
Job 22: 8 an honored man, **l** on it. 3782
28:13 it cannot be found in the land of the **l.** 2645
28:21 It is hidden from the eyes of every **l thing,** 2645
30:23 to the place appointed for all the **l.** 2645
Ps 27:13 of the LORD in the land of the **l.** 2645
42: 2 My soul thirsts for God, for the **l** God. 2645
52: 5 he will uproot you from the land of the **l.** 2645
65: 8 *Those* **l** far away fear your wonders; 3782
84: 2 and my flesh cry out for the **l** God. 2645
104:25 **l things** both large and small. 2651
Ps 116: 9 before the LORD in the land of the **l.** 2645
119: 9 *By* **l** according to your word. 9068
142: 5 my portion in the land of the **l.**" 2645
143: 2 for no one **l** is righteous before you. 2645
145:16 and satisfy the desires of every **l** *thing.* 2645
Ecc 4: 2 are happier than the **l,** who are still alive. 2645
7: 2 the **l** should take this to heart. 2645
7:15 a wicked man **l long** in his wickedness. 799
9: 4 Anyone who is among the **l** has hope— 2645
9: 5 For the **l** know that they will die, 2645
Isa 4: 3 all who are recorded among the **l** 2645
8:19 Why consult the dead on behalf of the **l?** 2645
9: 2 on *those* **l** in the land of the shadow 3782
33:24 No **one l** in Zion will say, "I am ill"; 8907
37: 4 has sent to ridicule the **l** God, 2645
37:17 Sennacherib has sent to insult the **l** God. 2645
38:11 the LORD, in the land of the **l;** 2645
38:19 The **l,** the living—they praise you, 2645
38:19 The living, the **l**—they praise you, 2645
53: 8 For he was cut off from the land of the **l;** 2645
Jer 2:13 forsaken me, the spring of **l** water, 2645
10:10 he is the **l** God, the eternal King. 2645
11:19 let us cut him off from the land of the **l,** 2645
13:13 the prophets and all *those* **l in** Jerusalem. 3782
17:13 forsaken the LORD, the spring of **l** water. 2645
17:20 and all people of Judah and everyone **l in** 3782
17:25 by the men of Judah and *those* **l in** 3782
18:11 and *those* **l in** Jerusalem, 'This is what 3782
23:36 and so you distort the words of the **l** God, 2645
25: 2 of Judah and to all *those* **l in** Jerusalem: 3782
35:17 to bring on Judah and on everyone **l in** 3782
36:31 and *those* **l in** Jerusalem and the people 3782
44: 1 to Jeremiah concerning all the Jews **l** 3782
44:15 the people **l** in Lower and Upper Egypt, 3782
44:26 all Jews **l** in Egypt: 3782
44:26 'that no one from Judah **l** anywhere NIH
La 3:39 Why should any **l** man complain 2645
Eze 1: 5 what looked like four **l creatures.** 2651
1:13 of the **l creatures** was like burning coals 2651
1:15 As I looked at the **l creatures,** 2651
1:19 When the **l creatures** moved, 2651
1:19 the **l creatures** rose from the ground, 2651
1:20 spirit of the **l creatures** was in the wheels. 2651
1:21 spirit of the **l creatures** was in the wheels. 2651
1:22 of the **l creatures** was what looked like 2651
3:13 the **l creatures** brushing against each other 2651
3:15 And there, where they *were* **l,** 3782
10:15 These were the **l creatures** I had seen by 2651
10:17 the spirit of the **l creatures** was in them. 2651
10:20 the **l creatures** I had seen beneath the God 2651
12: 2 you *are* **l** among a rebellious people. 3782
12:19 about *those* **l in** Jerusalem and in the land 3782
14: 7 or any alien **l** in Israel separates himself 1591
15: 6 so will I treat the *people* **l in** Jerusalem. 3782
18: 4 For every **l soul belongs** to me, 5883
20:38 of the land where they are **l,** 4472
26:20 or take your place in the land of the **l.** 2645
32:23 in the land of the **l** are slain, 2645
32:24 the land of the **l** went down uncircumcised 2645
32:25 their terror had spread in the land of the **l,** 2645
32:26 spread their terror in the land of the **l.** 2645
32:27 stalked through the land of the **l.** 2645
32:32 I had him spread terror in the land of the **l,** 2645
33:24 the *people* **l in** those ruins in the land 3782
36:17 people of Israel *were* **l** in their own land, 3782
38:11 of them **l** without walls and without gates 3782
38:12 **l** at the center of the land." 3782
38:14 when my people Israel *are* **l** in safety, 3782
47: 9 Swarms of **l** creatures will live wherever 2651
Da 2:30 I have greater wisdom than other **l** *men,* 10261
4:17 so that the **l** may know that the Most High 10261
6:20 servant of the **l** God, has your God, 10261
6:26 he is the **l** God and he endures forever; 10261
Hos 1:10 they will be called 'sons of the **l** God.' 2645
Hag 1: 4 "Is it a time for you yourselves to *be* **l** 3782
Zec 14: 8 On that day **l** water will flow out 2645
Mt 4:16 the people **l** in darkness have seen *2764*
4:16 *on* those **l** in the land of the shadow *2764*
16:16 the Son *of* the **l** God." *2409*
22:32 He is not the God of the dead but *of* the **l.**" *2409*
26:63 "I charge you under oath by the **l** God: *2409*
Mk 12:27 He is not the God of the dead, but *of* the **l.** *2409*
Lk 1:79 on those **l** in darkness and in the shadow *NIG*
2: 8 And there were shepherds **l out** in *64*
13: 4 the others **l in** Jerusalem? *2997*
15:13 and there squandered his wealth *in* wild **l.** *2409*
20:38 He is not the God of the dead, but *of* the **l,** *2409*
24: 5 "Why do you look for the **l** among *2409*
Jn 4:10 and he would have given you **l** water." *2409*
4:11 Where can you get this **l** water? *2409*
4:51 with the news that his boy *was* **l.** *2409*
6:51 I am the **l** bread that came down from
heaven. *2409*
6:57 the **l** Father sent me and I live because of *2409*
7:38 *of* **l** water will flow from within him." *2409*
14:10 Rather, it is the Father, **l** in me, *3531*
Ac 4:16 "Everybody **l** in Jerusalem knows they have
done an outstanding miracle, *2997*
7: 4 to this land where you *are* now **l.** *2997*
7:38 and he received **l** words to pass on to us. *2409*
9:22 and more powerful and baffled the Jews **l** *2997*
9:31 **l** in the fear of the Lord. *4513*
10:42 as judge *of* the **l** and the dead. *2409*
11:29 to provide help *for* the brothers **l** in Judea. *2997*
14:15 from these worthless things to the **l** God, *2409*
19:17 to the Jews and Greeks **l in** Ephesus, *2997*
21:24 *you* yourself *are* **l** in obedience to the law. *5123*
Ac 22:12 highly respected by all the Jews **l** there. *2997*
Ro 7:17 but it is sin **l** in me. *3861*
7:20 but it is sin **l** in me that does it. *3861*
8:11 who raised Jesus from the dead *is* **l** in you, *3861*
9:26 they will be called 'sons *of* the **l** God.' " *2409*
12: 1 to offer your bodies as **l** sacrifices, *2409*
14: 9 be the Lord *of* both the dead and the **l.** *2409*
1Co 9: 6 I and Barnabas who must **work for a l?** *2237*
9:14 *should* **receive** *their* **l** from the gospel. *2409*
15: 6 most of whom *are* still **l,** *3531*
15:45 "The first man Adam became a **l** being"; *2409*
2Co 3: 3 with ink but with the Spirit of the **l** God, *2409*
6:16 For we are the temple *of* the **l** God. *2409*
Php 1:22 If I am *to go on* **l** in the body, *2409*
4:12 whether **l in plenty** or in want. *4355*
1Th 1: 9 from idols to serve the **l** and true God, *2409*
4: 1 as in fact *you are* **l.** *4344*
1Ti 3:15 which is the church *of* the **l** God, *2409*
4:10 that we have put our hope in the **l** God, *2409*
2Ti 4: 1 who will judge the **l** and the dead, *2409*
Heb 3:12 that turns away from the **l** God. *2409*
4:12 For the word of God is **l** and active. *2409*
7: 8 by him who is declared to be **l.** *2409*
9:14 so that we may serve the **l** God! *2409*
9:17 while the one who made it *is* **l.** *2409*
10:20 by a new and **l** way opened for us through *2409*
10:31 to fall into the hands *of* the **l** God. *2409*
11:13 All these people were still **l** by faith *NIG*
12:22 heavenly Jerusalem, the city *of* the **l** God. *2409*
1Pe 1: 3 into a **l** hope through the resurrection *2409*
1:23 through the **l** and enduring word of God. *2409*
2: 4 As you come to him, the **l** Stone— *2409*
2: 5 also, like **l** stones, are being built into *2409*
4: 3 **l** in debauchery, lust, drunkenness, orgies, *4513*
4: 5 to him who is ready to judge the **l** and *2409*
2Pe 2: 8 **l among** them day after day, *1594*
Rev 1:18 I am the **L** *One;* I was dead, and behold *2409*
4: 6 around the throne, were four **l creatures,** *2442*
4: 7 The first **l creature** was like a lion, *2442*
4: 8 Each of the four **l creatures** had six wings *2442*
4: 9 Whenever the **l creatures** give glory, *2442*
5: 6 *by* the four **l creatures** and the elders. *2442*
5: 8 the four **l creatures** and the twenty-four *2442*
5:11 and the **l creatures** and the elders. *2442*
5:14 The four **l creatures** said, "Amen," *2442*
6: 1 of the four **l creatures** say in a voice *2442*
6: 3 I heard the second **l creature** say, *2442*
6: 5 I heard the third **l creature** say, "Come!" *2442*
6: 6 like a voice among the four **l creatures,** *2442*
6: 7 the voice *of* the fourth **l creature** say, *2442*
7: 2 having the seal *of* the **l** God. *2409*
7:11 around the elders and the four **l creatures.** *2442*
7:17 he will lead them to springs *of* **l** water. *2437*
8: 9 a third of the **l creatures** in the sea died,
2400+3836+6034
14: 3 before the four **l creatures** and the elders. *2442*
15: 7 Then one of the four **l creatures** gave to *2442*
16: 3 and every **l** thing in the sea died. *2437*
18:17 and all who **earn** *their* **l** from the sea, *2237*
19: 4 and the four **l creatures** fell down *2442*

LIZARD (4)

Lev 11:29 the weasel, the rat, any kind of **great l,** 7370
11:30 the **monitor l,** the wall lizard, 3947
11:30 the **wall l,** the skink and the chameleon. 4321
Pr 30:28 a **l** can be caught with the hand, 8532

LO DEBAR (4)

2Sa 9: 4 house of Makir son of Ammiel in **L."** 4274
9: 5 King David had him brought from **L,** 4274
17:27 and Makir son of Ammiel from **L,** 4203
Am 6:13 in the conquest of **L** and say, 4203

LO-AMMI (1)

Hos 1: 9 Then the LORD said, "Call him **L,** 4204

LO-RUHAMAH (2)

Hos 1: 6 the LORD said to Hosea, "Call her **L,** 4205
1: 8 After she had weaned **L,** 4205

LOAD (12) [CAMEL-LOADS, LADEN, LOADED, LOADING, LOADS, SPICE-LADEN]

Ge 45:17 **L** your animals and return to the land 3250
Ex 18:22 That will make your **l** lighter, 6584
23: 5 down under its **l,** do not leave it there; 5362
Ne 13:19 the gates so that no **l** could be brought in 5362
Job 35: 9 "Men cry out under a **l** *of* oppression; 8044
Isa 22:25 and the **l** hanging on it will be cut down." 5362
Jer 17:21 a **l** on the Sabbath day or bring it through 5362
17:22 a **l** out of your houses or do any work on 5362
17:24 and bring no **l** through the gates 5362
17:27 the Sabbath day holy by not carrying any **l** 5362
Lk 11:46 woe to you, because *you* **l** people **down** *5844*
Gal 6: 5 for each one should carry his own **l.** *5845*

LOADED (13) [LOAD]

Ge 37:25 Their camels *were* **l** *with* spices, 5951
42:26 *they* **l** their grain on their donkeys 5951
44:13 Then *they* all **l** their donkeys and returned 6673
45:23 ten donkeys **l** with the best things 5951
45:23 and ten female donkeys **l** *with* grain 5951

Jos 9: 4 as a delegation whose donkeys *were* **l** 4374
1Sa 16:20 So Jesse took a **donkey** *l with* bread, AIT
17:20 **l up** and set out, as Jesse had directed. 5951
25:18 and **l** them on donkeys. 8492
2Sa 16: 1 and **l with** two hundred loaves of bread, 6584
Isa 1: 4 Ah, sinful nation, a people **l** *with* guilt, 3878
Am 2:13 I will crush you as a cart crushes when **l** 4849
2Ti 3: 6 *who are* **l down** with sins and are swayed 5397

LOADING (1) [LOAD]
Ne 13:15 and bringing in grain and **l** it on donkeys, 6673

LOADS (5) [LOAD]
Ne 13:15 grapes, figs and all other kinds of **l.** 5362
Job 37:11 *He* **l** the clouds with moisture; 3267
Ps 144:14 our oxen *will* **draw heavy l.** 6022
La 5:13 boys stagger under **l of wood.** 6770
Mt 23: 4 They tie up heavy **l** and put them 5845

LOAF (9) [LOAVES]
Ex 29:23 which is before the LORD, take a **l,** 3971+4312
Lev 24: 5 using two-tenths of an ephah for each **l.** 2705
Jdg 7:13 "A **round l** *of* barley bread came tumbling 7501
2Sa 6:19 Then he gave a **l** *of* bread, 2705
1Ch 16: 3 Then he gave a **l** *of* bread, 3971
Pr 6:26 the prostitute reduces you to a **l** *of* bread, 3971
Mk 8:14 for one **l** they had with them in the boat. 788
1Co 10:17 Because there is one **l,** we, who are many, 788
10:17 for we all partake of the one **l.** 788

LOAN (6)
Dt 15: 2 *the* **l** *he has* **made** to his fellow Israelite. 5957
24:10 When *you* **make a l** of any kind to your neighbor, 5394+5957
24:11 to whom you *are* **making** *the* **l** bring 5957
Eze 18: 7 but returns what he took in pledge for a **l.** 2550
18:16 or **require a pledge for a l.** 2471+2478
33:15 gives back **what** he **took in pledge for a l,** 2478

LOATHE (5) [LOATHED, LOATHES, LOATHING, LOATHSOME]
Nu 11:20 comes out of your nostrils and you **l** it— 2426
Job 10: 1 "I **l** my very life; 7752
Eze 6: 9 *They will* **l** themselves for the evil 7752
20:43 and *you will* **l** yourselves for all the evil 7752
36:31 and *you will* **l** yourselves for your sins 7752

LOATHED (1) [LOATHE]
Ps 107:18 They **l** all food and drew near the gates 9493

LOATHES (2) [LOATHE]
Job 33:20 and his soul **l** the choicest meal. NIH
Pr 27: 7 He who is full **l** honey, 1008

LOATHING (1) [LOATHE]
Ps 119:158 I look on the faithless *with* **l,** 7752

LOATHSOME (5) [LOATHE]
Job 19:17 *I am* **l** to my own brothers. 2859
Ps 38: 5 and *are* **l** because of my sinful folly. 944
Isa 66:24 and they will be **l** to all mankind." 1994
Jer 6:15 Are they ashamed of their **l** conduct? 9359
8:12 Are they ashamed of their **l** conduct? 9359

LOAVES (32) [LOAF]
Lev 23:17 bring two **l** made of two-tenths of an ephah 4312
24: 5 and bake twelve **l of bread,** 2705
1Sa 10: 3 another three **l** *of* bread, 3971
10: 4 They will greet you and offer you two **l** NIH
17:17 and these ten **l of bread** for your brothers 4312
21: 3 Give me five **l of bread,** 4312
25:18 She took two hundred **l of bread,** 4312
2Sa 16: 1 and loaded with two hundred **l of bread,** 4312
1Ki 14: 3 Take ten **l of bread** with you, 4312
2Ki 4:42 of God twenty **l** of barley **bread** baked 4312
Mt 14:17 "We have here only five **l of bread** 788
14:19 the five **l** and the two fish and looking up 788
14:19 he gave thanks and broke the **l.** 788
15:34 "How many **l** do you have?" 788
15:36 Then he took the seven **l** and the fish, 788
16: 9 Don't you remember the five **l** for the five 788
16:10 Or the seven **l** for the four thousand, 788
Mk 6:38 "How many **l** do you have?" 788
6:41 the five **l** and the two fish and looking up 788
6:41 he gave thanks and broke the **l.** 788
6:52 for they had not understood about the **l;** 788
8: 5 "How many **l** do you have?" 788
8: 6 When he had taken the seven **l** and 788
8:19 I broke the five **l** for the five thousand, 788
8:20 I broke the seven **l** for the four thousand, NIG
Lk 9:13 "We have only five **l of bread** 788
9:16 the five **l** and the two fish and looking up 788
11: 5 'Friend, lend me three **l of bread,** 788
Jn 6: 9 "Here is a boy with five small barley **l** 788
6:11 Jesus then took the **l,** gave thanks, 788
6:13 with the pieces of the five barley **l** left 788
6:26 but because you ate the **l** and had your fill. 788

LOBE (6) [LOBES]
Lev 8:23 and put it on the **l** *of* Aaron's right ear, 9483
14:14 of the guilt offering and put it on the **l** *of* 9483
14:17 the oil remaining in his palm on the **l** *of* 9483
14:25 on the **l** *of* the right ear of the one to 9483
14:28 on the **l** *of* the right ear of the one to 9483
Dt 15:17 and push it through his **ear l** into the door, 265

LOBES (2) [LOBE]
Ex 29:20 take some of its blood and put it on the **l** 9483
Lev 8:24 of the blood on the **l** *of* their right ears, 9483

LOCAL (2)
Mt 10:17 they will hand you over to the **l councils** 5284
Mk 13: 9 You will be handed over to the **l** councils NIG

LOCATED (1) [LOCATIONS]
Dt 19: 2 three cities **centrally l in** the land 928+9348

LOCATIONS (1) [LOCATED]
1Ch 6:54 the **l** *of* their settlements allotted 3227

LOCK (1) [LOCKED]
SS 5: 5 on the handles of the **l.** 4980

LOCKED (11) [LOCK]
Jdg 3:23 of the upper room behind him and **l** them. 5835
3:24 and found the doors of the upper room **l.** 5835
9:51 *They* **l** themselves in and climbed up on 6037
SS 4:12 You are a garden **l up,** my sister, 5835
Lk 3:20 *He* **l** John up in prison. 2881
11: 7 The door *is* already **l,** 3091
Jn 20:19 with the doors **l** for fear of the Jews, 3091
20:26 *Though* the doors *were* **l,** Jesus came and 3091
Ac 5:23 "We found the jail securely **l,** with 3091
Gal 3:23 **l up** until faith should be revealed. 5168
Rev 20: 3 Abyss, and **l** and sealed it over him, 3091

LOCKS (KJV) See BOLTS, BRAIDS, HAIR, VEIL

LOCUST (9) [LOCUSTS]
Ex 10:19 Not a **l** was left anywhere in Egypt. 746
Lev 11:22 Of these you may eat any kind of **l,** 746
Job 39:20 Do you make him leap like a **l,** 746
Ps 78:46 their produce to the **l.** 746
109:23 I am shaken off like a **l.** 746
Joel 1: 4 What the **l swarm** has left 1612
2:25 the **great l** and the young locust, 746
2:25 the great locust and the **young l,** 3540
2:25 the other locusts and the **l swarm—** 1612

LOCUSTS (36) [LOCUST]
Ex 10: 4 I will bring **l** into your country tomorrow. 746
10:12 over Egypt so that **l** will swarm over 746
10:13 By morning the wind had brought the **l;** 746
10:14 before had there been such a plague of **l,** 746
10:19 the **l** and carried them into the Red Sea. 746
Dt 28:38 because **l** will devour it. 746
28:42 **Swarms of l** will take over all your trees 7526
Jdg 6: 5 and their tents like swarms of **l.** 746
7:12 had settled in the valley, thick as **l.** 746
1Ki 8:37 or blight or mildew, **l** or grasshoppers, 746
2Ch 6:28 or blight or mildew, **l** or grasshoppers, 746
7:13 or command **l** to devour the land or send 2506
Ps 105:34 He spoke, and the **l** came, 746
Pr 30:27 **l** have no king, yet they advance together 746
Isa 33: 4 O nations, is harvested as by **young l;** 2885
33: 4 like a swarm of **l** men pounce on it. 1466
Jer 46:23 They are more numerous than **l,** 746
51:14 fill you with men, as with a **swarm of l,** 3540
51:27 send up horses like a swarm of **l.** 3540
Joel 1: 4 swarm has left the **great l** have eaten; 746
1: 4 what the **great l** have left 746
1: 4 the **young l** have eaten; 3540
1: 4 **young l** have left other locusts have eaten. 3540
1: 4 young locusts have left other **l** have eaten. 2885
2:25 for the years the **l** have eaten— NIH
2:25 the other **l** and the locust swarm— 2885
Am 4: 9 **L** devoured your fig and olive trees, 1612
7: 1 He was preparing **swarms of l** after 1479
Na 3:15 like grasshoppers, multiply like **l!** 746
3:16 but like **l** they strip the land and 3540
3:17 Your guards are like **l,** 746
3:17 of **l** that settle in the walls on a cold day— 1479
Mt 3: 4 His food was **l** and wild honey. 210
Mk 1: 6 and he ate **l** and wild honey. 210
Rev 9: 3 out of the smoke **l** came down upon the earth 210
9: 7 The **l** looked like horses prepared for battle. 210

LOD (4)
1Ch 8:12 and **L** with its surrounding villages), 4254
Ezr 2:33 of **L,** Hadid and Ono 725 4254
Ne 7:37 of **L,** Hadid and Ono 721 4254
11:35 in **L** and Ono, 4254

LODGE (1) [LODGED, LODGING]
Ps 119:54 the theme of my song wherever **I l.** 1074+4472

LODGED (1) [LODGE]
Ezr 4: 6 *they* **l** an accusation against the people 4180

LODGING (6) [LODGE]
Ex 4:24 At a **l place** on the way, 4869
Ps 55:15 for evil finds **l** among them. 4472
Jer 9: 2 I had in the desert a **l place** *for* travelers, 4869
Mic 6: 2 *he is* **l a charge** against Israel. 3519
Lk 9:12 and countryside and find food and **l,** 2907
Jas 2:25 for what she did *when she* **gave l to** 5685

LOFT (KJV) See STORY, UPPER ROOM

LOFTINESS (1) [LOFTY]
Ps 48: 2 It is beautiful in its **l,** 5679

LOFTY (19) [LOFTINESS]
Job 22:12 And see how **l** *are* the highest stars! 8123
Ps 62: 4 to topple him from his **l place;** 8420
139: 6 too wonderful for me, too **l** for me to attain. 8435
Isa 2:12 a day in store for all the proud and **l,** 8123
2:13 tall and **l,** and all the oaks of Bashan, 5951
2:15 for every **l** tower and every fortified wall, 1469
10:33 The **l trees** will be felled, 7757+8123
26: 5 he lays the **l** city low; 8435
30:25 on every high mountain and every **l** hill. 5951
57: 7 made your bed on a high and **l** hill; 5951
57:15 For this is what the high and **l** One says— 5951
63:15 from heaven and see from your **l throne,** 2292
Jer 51:53 the sky and fortifies her **l** stronghold, 5294
Eze 16:24 and made a **l shrine** in every public square. 8229
16:25 of every street you built your **l shrines** 8229
16:31 of every street and made your **l shrines** 8229
16:39 and destroy your **l shrines.** 8229
17:22 and plant it on a high and **l** mountain. 9435
Am 9: 6 he who builds his **l palace** in the heavens 5092

LOG (5) [LOGS]
Lev 14:10 for a grain offering, and one **l** *of* oil. 4253
14:12 as a guilt offering, along with the **l** *of* oil; 4253
14:15 priest shall then take some of the **l** *of* oil, 4253
14:21 for a grain offering, a **l** *of* oil, 4253
14:24 guilt offering, together with the **l** *of* oil, 4253

LOGS (10) [LOG]
2Sa 5:11 along with cedar **l** and carpenters 6770
1Ki 5: 8 in providing the cedar and pine **l.** 6770
5:10 with all the cedar and pine **l** he wanted, 6770
1Ch 14: 1 messengers to David, along with cedar **l,** 6770
22: 4 He also provided more cedar **l** than could 6770
2Ch 2: 3 "Send me cedar **l** as you did NIH
2: 8 pine and algum **l** from Lebanon, 6770
2:16 and we will cut all the **l** from Lebanon 6770
Ezr 3: 7 so that they would bring cedar **l** by sea 6770
Ecc 10: 9 whoever splits **l** may be endangered 6770

LOINCLOTH (1)
Job 12:18 on by kings and ties a **l** around their waist. 258

LOINS (7)
Lev 3: 4 with the fat on them near the **l,** 4072
3:10 with the fat on them near the **l,** 4072
3:15 with the fat on them near the **l,** 4072
4: 9 on them near the **l,** and the covering of 4072
7: 4 with the fat on them near the **l,** 4072
Dt 33:11 the **l** *of* those who rise up against him; 5516
Job 40:16 What strength he has in his **l,** 5516

LOIS (1)
2Ti 1: 5 which first lived in your grandmother **L** 3396

LONELY (4) [ALONE]
Ps 25:16 for I am **l** and afflicted. 3495
68: 6 God sets the **l** in families, 3495
Mk 1:45 but stayed outside in **l** places. 2245
Lk 5:16 But Jesus often withdrew to **l places** 2245

LONG (434) [LENGTH, LENGTHEN, LENGTHS, LENGTHWISE, LENGTHY, LONGED, LONGER, LONGING, LONGINGS, LONGS]
Ge 6:15 The ark is to be 450 feet **l,** 802
8:22 **"As l as** the earth endures, 3972+6388
21:34 in the land of the Philistines for a **l** time. 8041
26: 8 When Isaac *had* **been** there *a* **l** time, 799
38:12 After a **l** time Judah's wife, 8049
46:29 around his father and wept *for a* **l time.** 6388
Ex 2:23 During that **l** period, the king of Egypt died. 8041
10: 3 **'How l** will you refuse to humble yourself before me? 5503+6330
10: 7 **"How l** will this man be a snare to us? 5503+6330
14:20 neither went near the other **all** night *l.* AIT
16:28 **"How l** will you refuse to keep 625+2025+6330
17:11 **As l as** Moses held up his hands, 889+3869
19:13 ram's horn **sounds a l blast** may they go 5432
20:12 so that you *may* **live l** in the land 799+3427
25:10 two and a half cubits **l,** 802
25:17 a half cubits **l** and a cubit and a half wide. 802

Ex 25:23 two cubits **l**, a cubit wide and a cubit and 802
26: 2 twenty-eight cubits **l** and four cubits wide. 802
26: 8 thirty cubits **l** and four cubits wide. 802
26:16 Each frame is to be ten cubits **l** and a cubit 802
27: 1 five cubits **l** and five cubits wide. 802
27: 9 The south side shall be a hundred cubits **l** 802
27:11 a hundred cubits **l** and is to have curtains, 802
27:14 Curtains fifteen cubits **l** are to be NIH
27:15 and curtains fifteen cubits **l** are to be on NIH
27:16 provide a curtain twenty cubits **l**, of blue, NIH
27:18 The courtyard shall be a hundred cubits **l** 802
28:16 a span **l** and a span wide— 802
30: 2 a cubit **l** and a cubit wide, 802
32: 1 that Moses *was so* **l** in coming down from 1018
36: 9 twenty-eight cubits **l** and four cubits wide. 802
36:15 thirty cubits **l** and four cubits wide. 802
36:21 Each frame was ten cubits **l** and a cubit 802
37: 1 two and a half cubits **l**, 802
37: 6 a half cubits **l** and a cubit and a half wide. 802
37:10 two cubits **l**, a cubit wide, 802
37:25 It was square, a cubit **l** and a cubit wide, 802
38: 1 five cubits **l** and five cubits wide. 802
38: 9 The south side was a hundred cubits **l** NIH
38:11 The north side was also a hundred cubits **l** NIH
38:14 Curtains fifteen cubits **l** were on one side NIH
38:15 and curtains fifteen cubits **l** were on NIH
38:18 It was twenty cubits **l** and, 802
39: 9 a span **l** and a span wide— 802
Lev 13:46 **As l as** he has the infection he remains 3427+3972
15:25 unclean **as l as** she has the discharge, 3427+3972
Nu 6: 4 **As l as** he is a Nazirite, 3427+3972
6: 5 *he must let* the hair of his head **grow l.** 1540
9:18 **As l as** the cloud stayed over 3427+3972
9:19 cloud remained over the tabernacle a **l** time, 8041
14:11 **"How l** will these people treat me with
contempt? 625+2025+6330
14:11 **How l** will they refuse to believe in me,
625+2025+6330
14:27 **"How l** will this wicked community
grumble against me? 5503+6330
36: 6 They may marry anyone they please **as l as** 421
Dt 1: 6 "You have stayed **l enough** 8041
2: 1 For a **l** time we made our way around 8041
2: 3 around this hill country **l enough;** 8041
3:11 of iron and was more than thirteen feet **l** 802
4: 9 or let them slip from your heart **as l as** 3427+3972
4:10 so that they may learn to revere me **as l as**
they live in the land 2021+3427+3972
4:25 and *have* **lived** in the land **a l time—** 3823
4:26 not **live** there **l** but will certainly 799+3427
4:32 the former days, **l** before your time, NIH
4:40 that *you may* **live l** in the land 799+3427
5:16 so that you *may* **live l** and 799+3427
6: 2 the LORD your God **as l as** you live 3427+3972
6: 2 and so that you *may* **enjoy l life.** 799+3427
11: 9 so that you *may* **live l** in the land that 799+3427
12: 1 **as l as** you live in the land. 2021+3427+3972
12:19 **as l as** you **live** in your land. 3427+3972
17:20 and his descendants *will* reign a **l** time 799
20:19 When you lay siege to a city for a **l** time, 8041
22: 7 with you and *you may* **have** *a* **l** life. 799
22:19 not divorce her **as l as he lives.** 3427+3972
22:29 never divorce her **as l as he lives.** 3427+3972
23: 6 with them **as l as** you **live.** 3427+3972+4200+6409
25:15 so that you *may* **live l** in the land 799+3427
30:18 not **live l** in the land you are crossing 799+3427
31:13 fear the LORD your God **as l as** you live in
the land 2021+3427+3972
32: 7 consider the **generations l past.**
1887+1887+2256+9102
32:47 By them *you will* **live l** in the land 799+3427
33:12 for he shields him all **day** *l*, AIT
Jos 6: 5 When you hear them **sound** a **l** blast on 5432
9:13 worn out by the very **l** journey." 8044
9:22 'We live a **l way** from you,' 4394+8158
11:18 against all these kings for a **l** time. 8041
18: 3 **"How l** will you wait before you 625+2025+6330
22: 3 For a **l** time now— 8041
23: 1 After a **l** time had passed and 8041
24: 2 **'L ago** your forefathers, 4946+6409
24: 7 Then you lived in the desert for a **l** time. 8041
Jdg 2:18 of their enemies **as l as** the judge lived; 3972
3:16 sword about a foot and a half **l**, 802
5:28 'Why *is* his chariot **so l** in coming? 1018
18: 7 they lived a **l way** from the Sidonians 8158
18:28 to rescue them because they lived a **l way** 8158
1Sa 1:14 **How l** will you keep on getting drunk? 5503+6330
7: 2 It was a **l** time, twenty years in all, 8049
10:24 the people shouted, **"L live** the king!" 2649
16: 1 **"How l** will you mourn for Saul, 5503+6330
20:14 like that of the LORD **as l as** I live, 561+6388
20:31 **As l as** the son of Jesse lives on this earth,
2021+3427+3972
22: 4 they stayed with him **as l as** David 3427+3972
25: 6 Say to him: **'L life** to you! 2021+2644+4200
25:28 Let no wrongdoing be found in you **as l as** 4946
27:11 And such was his practice **as l as** he lived
2021+3427+3972
2Sa 2:26 **How l** before you order your men 5503+6330
3: 1 and the house of David lasted a **l time.** 801
16:16 **"L live** the king! 2649
16:16 **L live** the king!" 2649
20:18 **"L ago** they used to say, 928+2021+8037
1Ki 1:25 **'L live** King Adonijah!' 2649
1:34 **'L live** King Solomon!' 2649
1:39 **"L live** King Solomon!" 2649
2:38 Shimei stayed in Jerusalem for a **l** time. 8041

1Ki 3:11 and not for **l** life or wealth for yourself, 8041
3:14 *I will* **give** you a **l** life." 799
6: 2 for the LORD was sixty cubits **l**, 802
6:17 in front of this room was forty cubits **l.** NIH
6:20 The inner sanctuary was twenty cubits **l**, 802
6:24 of the first cherub was five cubits **l**, and NIH
7: 2 the Forest of Lebanon a hundred cubits **l**, 802
7: 6 a colonnade fifty cubits **l** and thirty wide. 802
7:27 each was four cubits **l**, 802
8: 8 These poles *were so* **l** that their ends could 799
11:25 adversary **as l as** Solomon **lived,** 3427+3972
18: 1 After a **l** time, in the third year, 8041
18:21 **"How l** will you waver 5503+6330
22:35 **All day l** the battle raged,
928+2021+2021+2085+3427
2Ki 6:25 the siege **lasted so l** that 6330
9:22 **"as l as** all the idolatry and witchcraft 6330
11:12 **"L live** the king!" 2649
13: 3 for a **l** time he kept them under the power 3972
14:13 a section about six hundred feet **l.** NIH
19:25 **L ago** I ordained it. 4200+4946+8158
25:30 a regular allowance **as l as** he lived. 3427+3972
1Ch 29:28 **enjoyed l life,** wealth and honor. 3427+8428
2Ch 1:11 for a **l** life but for wisdom and knowledge 8041
3: 3 the temple of God was sixty cubits **l** 802
3: 4 the front of the temple was twenty cubits **l** 802
3: 8 twenty cubits **l** and twenty cubits wide. NIH
3:11 of the first cherub was five cubits **l** NIH
3:11 while its other wing, also five cubits **l**, NIH
3:12 of the second cherub was five cubits **l** NIH
3:12 and its other wing, also five cubits **l**, NIH
3:15 which [together] were thirty-five cubits **l**, 802
4: 1 He made a bronze altar twenty cubits **l**, 802
5: 9 These poles *were so* **l** that their ends, 799
6:13 a bronze platform, five cubits **l**, 802
15: 3 a **l** time Israel was without the true God, 8041
18:34 **All day l** the battle raged,
928+2021+2021+2085+3427
23:11 **"L live** the king!" 2649
24:14 **As l as** Jehoiada **lived,** burnt offerings 3427+3972
25:23 a section about six hundred feet **l.** NIH
26: 5 **As l as** he sought the LORD, God gave 928+3427
34:33 **As l as** he **lived,** they did not fail 3427+3972
Ezr 4:19 city has a **l history** of revolt 10317+10427+10550
Ne 2: 6 **"How l** will your journey take, 5503+6330
12:46 For **l ago,** in the days of David 4946+7710
Est 5:13 gives me no satisfaction **as l as** 928+3972+6961
Job 3:21 to those *who* **l for** death that does 2675
7: 4 I lie down I think, **'How l** *before* I get up?' 5503
8: 2 **"How l** will you say such things? 625+6330
12:12 Does not **l** life bring understanding? 802
12:19 and overthrows *men* **l established.** 419
14:15 *you will* **l for** the creature your hands have 4083
19: 2 **"How l** will you torment me and 625+2025+6330
27: 3 **as l as** I have life within me, 3972+6388
27: 6 will not reproach me **as l as I live.** 3427+4946
29: 2 **How I l for** the months gone by, 4769+5761+5989
36:20 *Do* not **l for** the night, 8634
Ps 4: 2 **How l,** O men, will you turn my glory 4537+6330
4: 2 How **l** will you love delusions NIH
6: 3 **How l,** O LORD, how long? 5503+6330
6: 3 How long, O LORD, how **l?** NIH
6: 6 **all** night *l* I flood my bed with weeping AIT
13: 1 **How l,** O LORD? 625+2025+6330
13: 1 **How l** will you hide your face from me?
625+2025+6330
13: 2 **How l** must I wrestle with my thoughts
625+2025+6330
13: 2 **How l** will my enemy triumph over me?
625+2025+6330
25: 5 and my hope is in you all **day** *l*. AIT
32: 3 through my groaning all **day** *l*. AIT
35:17 O Lord, **how l** will you look on? 3869+4537
35:28 and of your praises all **day** *l*. AIT
38: 6 all **day** *l* I go about mourning. AIT
38:12 all **day** *l* they plot deception. AIT
39: 1 I will put a muzzle on my mouth **as l as** 928+6388
42: 3 while men say to me all **day** *l*, AIT
42:10 saying to me all **day** *l*, AIT
44: 1 in their days, in days **l ago.** 7710
44: 8 In God we make our boast all **day** *l*, AIT
44:15 My disgrace is before me all **day** *l*, AIT
44:22 Yet for your sake we face death all **day** *l;* AIT
52: 1 Why do you boast all **day** *l*, AIT
56: 1 all **day** *l* they press their attack. AIT
56: 2 My slanderers pursue me all **day** *l;* AIT
56: 5 All **day** *l* they twist my words; AIT
61: 4 *I l to* **dwell** in your tent forever AIT
62: 3 **How l** will you assault a man? 625+2025+6330
63: 4 I will praise you **as l as** I live, 928
71: 8 declaring your splendor all **day** *l*. AIT
71:15 of your salvation all **day** *l*, AIT
71:24 of your righteous acts all **day** *l*, AIT
72: 5 He will endure **as l as** the sun, 6640
72: 5 as long as the sun, **as l as** the moon, 4200+7156
72:15 **L** *may he* **live!** 2649
72:15 for him and bless him all **day** *l*. AIT
72:17 may it continue **as l as** the sun. 4200+7156
73:14 All **day** *l* I have been plagued; AIT
74: 9 none of us knows **how l** this will be. 4537+6330
74:10 **How l** will the enemy mock you, O God?
5503+6330
74:22 remember how fools mock you all **day** *l*. AIT
77: 5 the former days, the years of **l ago;** 6409
77:11 I will remember your miracles of **l ago.** 7710
79: 5 **How l,** O LORD? 4537+6330
79: 5 How **l** will your jealousy burn like fire? NIH

Ps 80: 4 **how l** will your anger smolder against 5503+6330
82: 2 **"How l** will you defend the unjust 5503+6330
86: 3 O Lord, for I call to you all **day** *l*. AIT
88:17 All **day** *l* they surround me like a flood; AIT
89:16 They rejoice in your name all **day** *l;* AIT
89:29 **as l as** the heavens **endure.** 3427+3869
89:46 **How l,** O LORD? Will you hide yourself
forever? 4537+6330
89:46 How **l** will your wrath burn like fire? NIH
90:13 **How l** will it be? 5503+6330
91:16 With **l** life will I satisfy him 802
93: 2 Your throne was established **l ago;** 255+4946
94: 3 **How l** will the wicked, O LORD, 5503+6330
94: 3 **how l** will the wicked be jubilant? 5503+6330
102: 8 All **day** *l* my enemies taunt me; AIT
104:33 sing praise to my God **as l as I live.** 928+6388
116: 2 I will call on him **as l as** I live. 928
119:40 How *I* **l for** your precepts! 9289
119:84 **How l must** your servant **wait?** 3427+3869+4537
119:97 I meditate on it all **day** *l*. AIT
119:152 **L ago** I learned from your statutes 7710
119:174 *I* **l for** your salvation, O LORD, 9289
120: 6 **Too l** have I lived among those who hate 8041
129: 3 and **made** their furrows **l.** 799
143: 3 in darkness like those **l** dead. 6409
143: 5 I remember the days of **l ago;** 7710
146: 2 sing praise to my God **as l as I live.** 928+6388
Pr 1:22 **"How l** will you simple ones love your
simple ways? 5503+6330
1:22 How **l** will mockers delight in mockery NIH
3:16 **L** life is in her right hand; 802
6: 9 **How l** will you lie there, you sluggard? 5503+6330
7:19 he has gone on a **l** journey. 4946+8158
21:26 All **day** *l* he craves for more, AIT
28:16 he who hates ill-gotten gain *will* **enjoy a l
life.** 799+3427
Ecc 1:10 It was here already, **l ago;** 4200+6409
2:16 like the fool, will not be **l** remembered; 4200+6409
6: 3 yet no matter how **l** he lives, 8041
7:15 a wicked man **living l** in his wickedness. 799
8:12 a hundred crimes and still **lives a l time,** 799
9: 6 and their jealousy have **l since** vanished; 3893
SS 3: 1 **All night l** on my bed I looked 928+2021+4326
Isa 6:11 Then I said, **"For how l,** O Lord?" 5503+6330
22:11 for the One who planned it **l ago.** 4946+8158
25: 1 things planned **l ago.** 4946+8158
30:33 Topheth has **l** been prepared; 919+4946
33: 2 O LORD, be gracious to us; *we* **l for** you. 7747
37:26 **L ago** I ordained it. 4200+4946+8158
42:14 "For a **l time** I have kept silent, 6409
44: 8 not proclaim this and foretell it **l ago?** 255+4946
45:21 Who foretold this **l ago,** 4946+7710
46: 9 Remember the former things, those of **l ago;** 6409
48: 3 I foretold the former things **l ago,** 255+4946
48: 5 Therefore I told you these things **l ago;** 255+4946
48: 7 They are created now, and not **l ago;** 255+4946
52: 5 all **day** *l* my name is constantly blasphemed. AIT
57:11 because I have **l** been silent that you 4946+6409
61: 4 and restore the places **l** devastated; 8037
65: 2 All **day** *l* I have held out my hands to AIT
65:22 my chosen ones *will* **l enjoy** the works 1162
Jer 2:20 **"L ago** you broke off your yoke 4946+6409
4:14 **How l** will you harbor wicked thoughts?
5503+6330
4:21 **How l** must I see the battle standard 5503+6330
6: 4 and the shadows of evening **grow l.** 5742
12: 4 **How l** will the land lie parched and 5503+6330
13:27 **How l** will you be unclean?" 339+5503+6388
20: 7 I am ridiculed all **day** *l;* AIT
20: 8 brought me insult and reproach all **day** *l*. AIT
22:27 to the land you **l** to return to." 5883+5951
23:26 **How l** will this continue in the hearts 5503+6330
29:28 It will be a **l time.** 801
31:22 **How l** will you wander, 5503+6330
32:14 in a clay jar so they will last a **l** time. 8041
35: 7 Then you will live a **l** time in the land 8041
37:16 where he remained a **l** time. 8041
44:14 to which they **l** to return and live; 5883+5951
47: 5 **how l** will you cut yourselves? 5503+6330
47: 6 **'how l** till you rest? 625+2025+6330
52:34 a regular allowance **as l as** he lived, 3427+3972
La 1:13 He made me desolate, faint all the **day** *l*. AIT
2:17 which he decreed **l ago.** 3427+4946+7710
3: 3 against me again and again, all **day** *l*. AIT
3: 6 in darkness like those **l** dead. 6409
3:14 they mock me in song all **day** *l*. AIT
3:62 and mutter against me all **day** *l*. AIT
5:20 Why do you forsake us **so l?** 802+3427
Eze 7:13 not recover the land he has sold **as l as** 6388
17: 3 with powerful wings, **l** feathers 800
26:20 to the people of **l ago.** 6409
31: 5 and its branches *grew* **l**, 799
38: 8 which had **l** been desolate. 9458
40: 5 rod in the man's hand was six **l cubits,** 564
40: 7 The alcoves for the guards were one rod **l** 802
40:18 and was as wide as they were **l;** 802
40:21 It was fifty cubits **l** and twenty-five cubits 802
40:25 It was fifty cubits **l** and twenty-five cubits 802
40:29 It was fifty cubits **l** and twenty-five cubits 802
40:33 It was fifty cubits **l** and twenty-five cubits 802
40:36 It was fifty cubits **l** and twenty-five cubits 802
40:42 each a cubit and a half **l**, 802
40:43 each a handbreadth **l**, NIH
40:47 a square—a hundred cubits **l** and 802
41: 2 it was forty cubits **l** 802
41: 8 It was the length of the rod, six **l** cubits. 723
41:13 it was a hundred cubits **l**, 802

Eze 41:13 also a hundred cubits l. 802
42:2 a hundred cubits l and fifty cubits wide. 802
42:4 and a hundred cubits l. 2006
42:8 to the outer court was fifty cubits l, 802
42:8 the sanctuary was a hundred cubits l. NIH
42:20 five hundred cubits l 802
43:13 the measurements of the altar in l cubits, 564
43:16 twelve cubits l and twelve cubits wide. 802
43:17 fourteen cubits l and fourteen cubits wide, 802
44:20 or let their hair grow l, 7279
45:1 25,000 cubits l and 20,000 cubits wide; 802
45:3 25,000 cubits l and 10,000 cubits wide. 802
45:5 An area 25,000 cubits l and 10,000 802
45:6 25,000 cubits l, adjoining the sacred portion; 802
46:22 forty cubits l and thirty cubits wide; 802
48:9 25,000 cubits l and 10,000 cubits wide. 802
48:10 It will be 25,000 cubits l on the north side, NIH
48:10 25,000 cubits l on the south side. 802
48:13 25,000 cubits l and 10,000 cubits wide. 802
48:15 5,000 cubits wide and 25,000 cubits l, NIH
48:30 which is 4,500 cubits l, 4500
48:32 "On the east side, which is 4,500 cubits l, NIH
48:34 "On the west side, which is 4,500 cubits l, NIH
Da 8:3 and the horns were l. 1469
8:13 "How l will it take *for* the vision to 5503+6330
12:6 "How l will it be before these 5503+6330
Hos 7:13 I *l to* redeem them but they speak lies AIT
8:5 How l will they be incapable of purity? 5503
Am 5:18 to *you who* l for the day of the LORD! 203
5:18 Why *do* you l for the day of the LORD? 2296[S]
Mic 7:14 in Bashan and Gilead as in days l ago. 6409
7:20 on oath to our fathers in days l ago. 7710
Hab 1:2 How l, O LORD, must I call for help, 625+2025+6330
2:6 How l must this go on?' 5503+6330
Zec 1:12 how l will you withhold mercy 5503+6330
2:2 to find out how wide and how l it is." 802
5:2 thirty feet l and fifteen feet wide." 802
Mt 5:21 that it was said *to* the people l ago, 792
5:33 that it was said *to* the people l ago, 792
11:21 they would have repented l ago 4093
17:17 Jesus replied, "how l shall I stay with you? 2401+4536
17:17 How l shall I put up with you? 2401+4536
20:6 'Why have you been standing here all day *l* AIT
23:5 and the tassels on their garments l; 3486
24:48 'My master *is* staying away a l time,' 5988
25:5 The bridegroom *was* a l time in coming, 5988
25:19 "After a l time the master 4498
Mk 2:19 so l as they have him with them. 4012+5989
6:15 like one of the prophets of l ago." NIG
8:3 some of them have come a l distance." 3427
9:19 "how l shall I stay with you? 4536
9:19 How l shall I put up with you? 4536
9:21 "How l has he been like this?" 5989
Lk 1:21 and wondering why he stayed so l in 5988
1:70 through his holy prophets of l ago), 172
8:27 *For* a l time this man had not worn clothes 2653
9:8 of the prophets *of* l ago had come back 792
9:19 of the prophets *of* l ago has come back 792
9:41 "how l shall I stay with you and put up 4536
10:13 they would have repented l ago, 4093
12:45 'My master *is* taking a l time in coming,' 5988
13:16 Satan has kept bound for eighteen l years, NIG
14:32 the other is still a l way off and will ask 4522
15:13 "Not l after that, the younger son 2465+4498
15:20 "But while he was still a l way off, 3426
17:22 when *you will* l to see one of the days of 2121
20:9 and went away *for* a l time. 2653
23:8 a l time he had been wanting to see him. 2653
Jn 5:6 in this condition *for* a l time, 4498
9:4 As l as it is day, we must do the work of 2401
10:24 "How l will you keep us in suspense? 2401+4536
14:9 I have been among you such a l time? NIG
14:19 Before l, the world will not see me 2285+3625
Ac 1:16 the Holy Spirit spoke l ago through 4625
3:21 as he promised l ago through his holy 172+608
8:11 because he had amazed them *for* a l time 2653
14:28 And they stayed there a l time 3900+4024+5989
24:2 "We have enjoyed a l period of peace 4498
26:5 They have known me for a l time 540
26:29 Paul replied, "Short time or l— 3489
27:14 Before very l, a wind of 3552+4024+4498
27:21 the men had gone a l time without food, 4498
28:6 but after waiting a l time 2093+4498
Ro 1:11 *I* l to see you so that I may impart 2160
7:1 over a man only as l as he lives? 2093+4012+5989
7:2 bound to her husband *l as he is* alive, AIT
8:36 "For your sake we face death all day *l;* AIT
10:21 "All day l I have held out my hands to 3910
16:25 of the mystery hidden *for* l ages past, 5989
1Co 7:39 bound to her husband as l as 2093+4012+5989
11:14 of things teach you that if a man has l hair, 3150
11:15 but that if a woman has l hair, 3150
11:15 For l hair is given to her as a covering. 3151
2Co 5:6 *as l as we are* at home in the body AIT
Gal 4:1 that as l as the heir is a child, 2093+4012+5989
Eph 3:18 how wide and l and high and deep is 3601
6:3 and that *you may* enjoy l life on 1639+3432
Php 1:8 how *I* l for all of you with the affection 2160
4:1 my brothers, you whom I love and l for, 2162
1Th 3:6 and that *you* l to see us, just as we also 2160
3:6 just as we also l to see you. NIG
2Ti 1:4 Recalling your tears, *I* l to see you, 2160
Heb 3:13 as l as it is called Today, 948+4005
4:7 a l time later he spoke through David, 5537
9:8 as l as the first tabernacle was still 2285
1Pe 1:12 Even angels l to look into these things. 2121
3:20 who disobeyed l ago when God waited NIG
2Pe 1:13 refresh your memory as l as I live in 2093+4012
2:3 Their condemnation has l been hanging 1732
3:5 But they deliberately forget that l ago 1732
Jude 1:4 written about l ago have secretly slipped in 4093
Rev 6:10 called out in a loud voice, "How l, 2401+4536
9:6 *they will* l to die, but death will elude them. 2121
21:16 like a square, as l as it was wide. 3601
21:16 and as wide and high as it is l. 3601

LONG-SUFFERING (1) [SUFFER]

Jer 15:15 You are l—do not take me away; 678+800

LONG-WINDED (1) [WIND]

Job 16:3 Will your l speeches never end? 8120

LONGED (13) [LONG]

Ge 31:30 Now you have gone off because *you* l 4083+4083
2Sa 13:39 the spirit of the king l to go to Absalom, 3983
14:1 knew that the king's heart l for Absalom. 6584
23:15 David l for water and said, "Oh, 203
1Ch 11:17 David l for water and said, "Oh, 203
Isa 21:4 the twilight I l for has become a horror 3139
Eze 23:21 So *you* l for the lewdness of your youth, 7212
Mt 13:17 and righteous men l to see what you see 2121
23:37 how often *I have* l to gather your children 2527
Lk 13:34 how often *I have* l to gather your children 2527
15:16 *He* l to fill his stomach with the pods that 2121
2Ti 4:8 also *to* all who *have* l for his appearing. 26
Rev 18:14 'The fruit you l for is gone from you. 2123

LONGER (197) [LONG]

Ge 4:12 it will no l yield its crops for you. 3578
17:5 No l will you be called Abram; 6388
17:15 you are no *l* to call her Sarai; AIT
27:1 so weak *that* he could no *l* see, AIT
27:45 When your brother *is* no l angry with you 8740
32:28 man said, "Your name will no l be Jacob, 6388
35:10 but you will no l be called Jacob; 6388
45:1 Then Joseph could no *l* control himself AIT
49:4 you will no *l* excel, AIT
Ex 2:3 But when she could hide him no l, 6388
5:7 "*You are* no l to supply the people 3578
9:28 you don't have to stay any l." 3578
9:33 and the rain no *l* poured down on the land. AIT
26:13 The tent curtains will be a cubit l on 802
Lev 17:7 They must no l offer any of their sacrifices 6388
26:13 so that you would no *l* be slaves AIT
Nu 8:25 from their regular service and work no l. 6388
Dt 5:25 the voice of the LORD our God any l. 3578+6388
10:16 therefore, and do not be stiff-necked any l. 6388
31:2 and I am no l able to lead you. 6388
32:5 to their shame they are no *l* his children, AIT
Jos 5:1 and they no l had the courage to face 6388
5:12 there was no l any manna for the Israelites, 6388
23:13 the LORD your God *will* no l drive out these nations 3578
Jdg 2:14 whom they were no l able to resist. 6388
2:21 I *will* no l drive out before them any of 3578
10:6 forsook the LORD and no *l* served him, AIT
10:13 so *I will* no l save you. 3578
10:16 And he could bear Israel's misery no l. 7918
1Sa 1:18 and her face was no l downcast. 6388
27:4 *he* no l searched for him. 3578+6388
28:15 He no l answers me, 6388
2Sa 1:21 the shield of Saul—no l rubbed with oil. 1172
2:28 *they* no l pursued Israel, 6388
3:22 But Abner was no *l* with David in Hebron, AIT
7:10 a home of their own and no l be disturbed. 6388
20:5 *he* took l than the time the king had set 336
1Ki 21:15 He is no *l* alive, but dead." AIT
2Ki 6:33 Why should I wait for the LORD any l?" 6388
10:19 Anyone who fails to come *will* no *l* live." AIT
15:20 and stayed in the land no *l.* AIT
17:4 *he* no *l* paid tribute to the king of Assyria, AIT
1Ch 17:9 a home of their own and no l be disturbed. 6388
23:26 the Levites no *l need* to carry AIT
Ne 2:17 and we will no l be in disgrace." 6388
13:21 From that time on they no *l* came on AIT
Job 3:18 they no *l* hear the slave driver's shout. AIT
7:8 eye that now sees me will see me no *l;* AIT
11:9 Their measure is l than the earth 801
15:29 He will no *l* be rich and his wealth will AIT
24:20 evil men are no l remembered 6388
36:2 with me a little l and I will show you 10236
Ps 44:9 *you* no *l* go out with our armies. AIT
60:10 you who have rejected us and no *l* go out AIT
108:11 you who have rejected us and no *l* go out AIT
Ecc 4:13 an old but foolish king who no l knows 6388
9:16 and his words are no *l* heeded. AIT
12:5 along and desire no l *is* stirred. 7296
Isa 7:25 you will no *l* go there for fear of the briers AIT
10:20 *will* no l rely on him who struck them 3578+6388
17:1 "See, Damascus *will* no l be a city 4946+6073
23:10 for you no l have a harbor. 6388
24:9 No *l* do they drink wine with a song; AIT
26:21 she will conceal her slain no l. 6388
29:22 "No l will Jacob be ashamed; 6964
29:22 no l will their faces grow pale. 6964
32:3 of those who see *will* no *l be* closed, AIT
32:5 No l will the fool be called noble nor 6388
38:11 no l will I look on mankind, 6388
60:18 No l will violence be heard in your land, 6388
62:4 No l will they call you Deserted, 6388
62:12 the City No *L* Deserted. AIT
65:22 No *l* will they build houses and others live AIT
Jer 3:12 'I will frown on you no *l,* AIT
3:16 declares the LORD, "men will no l say, 6388
3:17 No l will they follow the stubbornness 6388
4:1 of my sight and no *l* go astray, AIT
7:32 when people will no l call it Topheth or 6388
8:19 Is her King no *l* there?" AIT
15:6 *I* can no l show compassion. 4206
16:14 "when men will no l say, 6388
19:6 people will no l call this place Topheth 6388
23:4 and they will no l be afraid or terrified, 6388
23:7 "when people will no l say, 6388
30:8 no l will foreigners enslave them. 6388
31:29 "In those days people will no l say, 6388
31:34 No l will a man teach his neighbor, 6388
33:20 and night no *l* come at their appointed time, AIT
33:21 can be broken and David will no *l* have AIT
33:24 and no l regard them as a nation. 6388
34:10 and female slaves and no l hold them 6388
38:9 when there is no l any bread in the city." 6388
44:22 LORD could no l endure your wicked actions 6388
49:7 "Is there no l wisdom in Teman? 6388
51:44 The nations will no l stream to him. 6388
La 2:9 and her prophets no *l* find visions from AIT
4:15 "They can stay here no l." 3578
4:16 *he* no l watches over them. 3578
Eze 12:23 and they will no l quote it in Israel.' 6388
12:28 None of my words will be delayed any l; 6388
13:21 and they will no l fall prey to your power. 6388
13:23 therefore you will no l see false visions 6388
14:11 people of Israel will no l stray from me, 6388
16:41 and you will no l pay your lovers. 6388
16:42 I will be calm and no l angry. 6388
18:3 you will no l quote this proverb in Israel. 6388
19:9 so his roar was heard no l on the mountains 6388
20:39 to me and no l profane my holy name 6388
24:27 speak with him and will no l be silent. 6388
26:19 like cities no *l* inhabited, AIT
28:24 " 'No l will the people of Israel have 6388
29:16 Egypt will no l be a source of confidence 6388
30:13 No l will there be a prince in Egypt, 6388
32:13 beside abundant waters no l to be stirred 6388
33:22 and I was no l silent. 6388
34:10 the shepherds can no l feed themselves. 6388
34:10 and it will no *l* be food for them. AIT
34:22 and they will no l be plundered. 6388
34:28 They will no l be plundered by 6388
34:29 and they will no l be victims of famine in 6388
36:14 therefore you will no l devour men 6388
36:15 No l will I make you hear the taunts of 6388
36:15 and no l will you suffer the scorn of 6388
36:30 that you will no l suffer disgrace among 6388
37:23 They will no l defile themselves 6388
39:7 I will no l let my holy name be profaned, 6388
39:29 I will no l hide my face from them, 6388
45:8 my princes will no l oppress my people 6388
Da 8:3 of the horns was l than the other but grew 1469
Hos 1:6 for I will no l show love to the house 3578+6388
2:16 you will no l call me 'my master.' 6388
2:17 no l will their names be invoked. 6388
9:15 I will no l love them; 3578
Joel 2:10 and the stars no l shine. 665+5586
3:15 and the stars no l shine. 665+5586
Am 7:8 I will spare them no l. 3578+6388
8:2 I will spare them no l. 3578+6388
Mic 2:3 You will no *l* walk proudly, AIT
5:12 and you will no l cast spells. NIH
5:13 you will no l bow down to the work 6388
Na 2:13 The voices of your messengers will no l 6388
Zec 11:6 For I will no l have pity on the people of 6388
14:21 on that day there will no l be a Canaanite 6388
Mal 2:13 and wail because he no l pays attention 6388
Mt 5:13 It is no l good for anything, 2285
19:6 So they are no l two, but one. 4033
Mk 1:45 Jesus could no l enter a town openly 3600
7:12 then you no l let him do anything 4033
9:8 they no l saw anyone with them 4033
10:8 So they are no l two, but one. 4033
Lk 15:19 I am no l worthy to be called your son; 4033
15:21 I am no l worthy to be called your son.' 4033
16:2 because you cannot be manager any l.' 2285
20:36 and they can no l die; 2285
Jn 4:42 "We no l believe just because of what you 4033
6:66 disciples turned back and no l followed him. 4033
11:54 Therefore Jesus no l moved about publicly 4033
12:35 to have the light just a little while l. 2285
13:33 I will be with you only a little l. 2285
14:30 I will not speak with you much l, 4033
15:15 I no l call you servants, 4033
16:10 where you can see me no l; 4033
16:23 In that day you will no l ask me anything. NIG
16:25 when I will no l use this kind of language 4033
17:11 I will remain in the world no l, 4033
Ac 4:17 we must warn these men to speak no l 3600
19:22 while *he* stayed in the province of Asia a little l. 2091+5989
25:24 shouting that he ought not to live any l. 3600
Ro 6:2 how can we live in it any l? 2285
6:6 that we should no l be slaves to sin— 3600
6:9 death no l has mastery over him. 4033
7:17 As it is, it is no l I myself who do it, 4033
7:20 is no l I who do it, but it is sin living in me 4033
11:6 And if by grace, then it is no l by works; 4033
11:6 if it were, grace would no l be grace. 4033
12:2 *Do* not conform *any l* to the pattern of AIT

Ro 14:15 you are **no l** acting in love. *4033*
2Co 5:15 that those who live should **no l** live for *3600*
5:16 regarded Christ in this way, we do so **no l.** *4033*
Gal 2:20 crucified with Christ and I **no l** live, *4033*
3:18 then it **no l** depends on a promise; *4033*
3:25 we are **no l** under the supervision of the law *4033*
4:7 So you are **no l** a slave, but a son; *4033*
Eph 2:19 you are **no l** foreigners and aliens, *4033*
4:14 Then we will **no l** be infants, *3600*
4:17 that you must **no l** live as the Gentiles do, *3600*
4:28 He who has been stealing must steal **no l,** *3600*
1Th 3:1 So when we could stand it **no l,** *3600*
3:5 For this reason, when I could stand it **no l,** *3600*
1Ti 1:3 not to teach false doctrines any **l** *NIG*
Phm 1:16 **no l** as a slave, but better than a slave, *4033*
Heb 8:11 **No l** will a man teach his neighbor, *3590+4024*
10:2 would no **l** have felt guilty for their sins. *2285*
10:18 there is **no l** any sacrifice for sin. *4033*
Rev 6:11 and they were told to wait a little **l,** *2285+5989*
21:1 and there was no **l** any sea. *2285*
22:3 No **l** will there be any curse. *2285*

LONGING (15) [LONG]

Dt 28:65 eyes **weary with l,** and a despairing heart. 4001
Job 7:2 Like a slave **l for** the evening shadows, 8634
Ps 119:20 My soul is consumed with **l** for your laws 9291
119:81 My soul **faints with l** for your salvation, 3983
119:131 **l for** your commands. 3277
Pr 13:12 but a **l** fulfilled is a tree of life. 9294
13:19 A **l** fulfilled is sweet to the soul, 9294
Eze 23:27 not **look** on these things **with l** 5951+6524
Lk 16:21 and **l** to eat what fell from the rich man's *2121*
Ro 15:23 I have been **l** for many years to see you, *2163*
2Co 5:2 **l** to be clothed with our heavenly dwelling, *2160*
7:7 He told us about your **l** for me, *2161*
7:11 what indignation, what alarm, what **l,** *2161*
1Th 2:17 out of our intense **l** we made every effort *2123*
Heb 11:16 Instead, *they were* **l for** a better country— *3977*

LONGINGS (2) [LONG]

Ps 38:9 All my **l** lie open before you, O Lord; 9294
112:10 the **l** *of* the wicked will come to nothing. 9294

LONGS (4) [LONG]

Ps 63:1 my body **l for** you, in a dry and weary land 4014
Isa 26:9 in the morning my spirit **l for** you. 8838
30:18 Yet the LORD **l** to be gracious to you; 2675
Php 2:26 For *he* **l for** all of you and is distressed *1639+2160*

LONGSUFFERING (KJV) See PATIENCE

LOOK (325) [FINE-LOOKING, LOOKED, LOOKING, LOOKOUT, LOOKOUTS, LOOKS]

Ge 4:5 and his offering *he did* not **l with favor.** 9120
13:14 from where you are and **l** north and south, 8011
15:5 **"L up** at the heavens and count the stars— 5564
19:8 **L,** I have two daughters who have never 2180
19:17 Don't **l** back, and don't stop anywhere in 5564
19:20 **L,** here is a town near enough to run to, 2180
25:32 **"L,** I am about to die," Esau said. 2180
27:6 **"L,** I overheard your father say 2180
29:7 **"L,"** he said, "the sun is still high; 2176
31:12 **'L** up and see that all the male goats 6524
39:14 **"L,"** she said to them, 8011
41:33 "And now *let* Pharaoh **l for** a discerning 8011
49:18 "*I* **l** for your deliverance, O LORD. 7747
Ex 1:9 **"L,"** he said to his people, 2180
3:4 the LORD saw that he had gone over to **l,** 8011
3:6 because he was afraid to **l** at God. 5564
5:5 Then Pharaoh said, **"L,** the people 2176
5:21 the LORD **l** upon you and judge you! 8011
Lev 13:36 priest *does* not *need to* **l** for yellow hair; 1329
26:9 " '*I will* **l** on you **with favor** 7155
Nu 4:20 But the Kohathites must not go in to **l** *at* 8011
15:39 You will have these tassels *to* **l** *at* and 8011
21:8 anyone who is bitten *can* **l** *at* it and live." 8011
32:8 from Kadesh Barnea to **l over** the land. 8011
Dt 3:27 Pisgah and **l** west and north and south 5951+6524
3:27 **L** at the land with your own eyes, 8011
4:19 when you **l** up to the sky and see the sun, 6524
4:29 if *you* **l for** him with all your heart and 2011
7:16 *Do* not **l** on them **with pity** 2571+6524
26:15 **L down** from heaven, 9207
Jos 2:1 "Go, **l over** the land," he said, 8011
2:2 The king of Jericho was told, **"L!** 2180
22:28 **L** *at* the replica of the LORD's altar, 8011
Jdg 6:37 **l,** I will place a wool fleece on 2180
9:36 Gaal saw them, he said to Zebul, **"L,** 2180
9:37 But Gaal spoke up again: **"L,** 2180
14:8 he turned aside to **l** *at* the lion's carcass. 8011
19:9 said, "Now **l,** it's almost evening. 2180
19:24 **L,** here is my virgin daughter, 2180
21:19 But **l,** there is the annual festival of 2180
Ru 1:15 **"L,"** said Naomi, "your sister-in-law is 2180
1Sa 1:11 "O LORD Almighty, *if you will* **only l** 8011+8011
9:3 the servants with you and go and **l for** 1335
9:6 But the servant replied, **"L,** 2180
9:8 **"L,"** he said, "I have a quarter of a shekel 2180
10:2 'The donkeys you set out to **l for** 1335
14:11 to the Philistine outpost. **"L!"** 2180
14:33 Then someone said to Saul, **"L,** 2180
16:7 LORD does not **l** at the things man looks at. NIH
1Sa 18:22 "Speak to David privately and say, **'L,** 2180
20:2 **L,** my father doesn't do anything, 2180
20:5 **"L,** tomorrow is the New Moon festival, 2180
20:21 If I say to him, **'L,** 2180
20:22 But if I say to the boy, **'L,** 2180
21:14 Achish said to his servants, **"L** *at* the man! 8011
23:1 When David was told, **"L,** 2180
24:2 to **l for** David and his men near the Crags 1335
24:11 **l** *at* this piece of your robe in my hand! 8011
26:16 **L around** you. 8011
26:20 The king of Israel has come out to **l for** 1335
28:14 "What does he **l like?"** 9307
28:21 **"L,** your maidservant has obeyed you. 2180
2Sa 2:22 **l** your brother Joab **in the face?"** 448+5951+7156
3:24 **L,** Abner came to you. 2180
13:4 **l** so haggard morning after morning? NIH
14:30 Then he said to his servants, **"L,** 8011
14:32 Absalom said to Joab, **"L,** 2180
15:3 Then Absalom would say to him, **"L,** 8011
18:26 and he called down to the gatekeeper, **"L,** 2180
1Ki 1:2 *"Let us* **l for** a young virgin to attend 1335
12:16 **L after** your own house, O David!" 8011
17:23 He gave him to his mother and said, **"L,** 8011
18:10 not sent someone to **l for** you. 1335
18:43 "Go and **l** toward the sea," 5564
20:31 His officials said to him, **"L,** 2180
22:13 to summon Micaiah said to him, **"L,** 2180
2Ki 2:16 **"L,"** they said, "we your servants have fifty 2180
2:16 Let them go and **l for** your master. 1335
2:19 The men of the city said to Elisha, **"L,** 2180
3:14 *I would* not **l** at you or even notice you. 5564
4:25 man of God said to his servant Gehazi, **"L!** 2180
6:1 the prophets said to Elisha, **"L,** the place 2180
6:32 **L,** when the messenger comes, 8011
7:2 **"L,** even if the LORD should open 2180
7:6 so that they said to one another, **"L,** 2180
7:19 **"L,** even if the LORD should open 2180
9:2 **l for** Jehu son of Jehoshaphat, 8011
10:23 **"L around** and see that no servants of 2924
18:21 **L** now, you are depending on Egypt, 2180
1Ch 16:11 **L to** the LORD and his strength; 2011
21:23 **L,** I will give the oxen for 8011
2Ch 10:16 **L after** your own house, O David!" 8011
18:12 to summon Micaiah said to him, **"L,** 2180
Ne 2:2 "Why does your face **l** *so* **sad** 8273
2:3 Why *should* my face not **l sad** when 8317
Est 1:11 for she was lovely to **l at.** 5260
Job 6:19 The caravans of Tema **l** for water, 5564
6:19 the traveling merchants of Sheba **l in hope.** 7747
6:28 "But now be so kind as *to* **l** at me. 7155
7:8 you will **l** for me, but I will be no more. 6524
7:19 *Will you* never **l** away from me, 9120
8:5 But if you *will* **l** to God and plead with 8838
11:18 *you will* **l about** you and take your rest 2916
14:6 So **l** away from him and let him alone, 9120
19:15 they **l** *upon* me as an alien. 928+6524
20:9 his place *will* **l** *on* him no more. 8800
21:5 **L** at me and be astonished; 7155
24:1 Why *must* those who know him **l** in vain 2600
30:20 I stand up, but *you merely* **l** at me. 1067
31:1 with my eyes not *to* **l lustfully** at a girl. 1067
35:5 **L up** *at* the heavens and see; 5564
37:21 Now no *one can* **l** *at* the sun, 8011
40:11 **l** *at* every proud man and bring him low, 8011
40:12 **l** *at* every proud man and humble him, 8011
40:15 **"L** *at* the behemoth, 2180
Ps 11:2 For **l,** the wicked bend their bows; 2180
13:3 **L** *on* me and answer, O LORD my God. 5564
25:18 **L** *upon* my affliction and my distress 8011
34:5 *Those who* **l** to him are radiant; 5564
35:17 O Lord, how long *will you* **l** *on?* 8011
37:10 *you* **l** for them, they will not be found. 1067
39:7 "But now, Lord, what *do I* **l for?** 7747
39:13 **L** away from me, 9120
40:4 *who does* not **l** to the proud, 7155
59:4 Arise to help me; **l** *on* my plight! 8011
80:14 **L down** from heaven and see! 5564
84:9 **L** *upon* our shield, O God; 8011
84:9 **l with favor** *on* your anointed one. 5564+7156
104:27 These all **l** to you to give them their food 8432
105:4 **L** *to* the LORD and his strength; 2011
112:8 in the end *he will* **l** in triumph on his foes. 8011
113:6 who stoops down to **l** on the heavens and 8011
118:7 I *will* **l** in triumph on my enemies. 8011
119:153 **L** *upon* my suffering and deliver me, 8011
119:158 *I* **l** *on* the faithless with loathing, 8011
123:2 of slaves **l** to the hand of their master, NIH
123:2 of a maid **l** to the hand of her mistress, NIH
123:2 so our eyes **l** to the LORD our God, NIH
142:4 **L** *to* my right and see; 5564
145:15 The eyes of all **l** to you, 8432
Pr 1:28 *they will* **l for** me but will not find me. 8838
2:4 and if *you* **l for** it as for silver and search 1335
4:25 **Let** your eyes **l** straight ahead, 5564
15:30 A cheerful **l** brings joy to the heart, 6524
Ecc 1:10 one can say, **"L!** This is something new"? 8011
1:16 I thought to myself, **"L,** I have grown and 2180
7:27 **"L,"** says the Teacher, 8011
SS 2:8 My lover! **L!** Here he comes, 2180
2:9 or a young stag. **L!** 2180
3:7 **L!** It is Solomon's carriage, 2180
3:11 and **l** at King Solomon wearing the crown, 8011
6:1 that *we may* **l for** him with you? 1335
6:11 I went down to the grove of nut trees to **l** 8011
Isa 3:9 The **l** *on* their faces testifies against them; 2129
8:22 Then *they will* **l** toward the earth 5564
10:12 of his heart and the haughty **l** *in* his eyes. 9514
Isa 13:8 *They will* **l aghast** at each other, 9449
13:18 nor *will* they **l with compassion** 2571+6524
17:7 In that day men *will* **l** to their Maker 9120
17:8 *They will* not **l** to the altars, 9120
18:4 and *will* **l on** from my dwelling place, 5564
21:9 **L,** here comes a man in a chariot with 2180
22:11 but *you did* not **l** to the One who made it, 5564
23:13 **L** *at* the land of the Babylonians, 2176
30:2 *who* **l for help** to Pharaoh's protection, 6395
31:1 but *do* not **l** to the Holy One of Israel, 9120
33:7 **L,** their brave men cry aloud in the streets; 2176
33:20 **L** *upon* Zion, the city of our festivals; 2600
34:16 **L** in the scroll of the LORD and read: 2011
36:6 **L** now, you are depending on Egypt, 2180
38:11 no longer *will I* **l** *on* mankind, 5564
40:26 Lift your eyes and **l** *to* the heavens: 8011
41:27 I was the first to tell Zion, **'L,** 2180
41:28 *I* **l** but there is no one— 8011
42:18 "Hear, you deaf; **l,** *you* blind, and see! 5564
48:6 **l** *at* them all. Will you not admit them? 2600
49:18 Lift up your eyes and **l** around; 8011
51:1 **L** to the rock from which you were cut and 5564
51:2 **l** to Abraham, your father, and 5564
51:3 and *will* **l with compassion** on all her ruins; 5714
51:5 The islands *will* **l** to me and wait in hope 7747
51:6 **l** at the earth beneath; 5564
59:9 *We* **l** for light, but all is darkness; 7747
59:11 *We* **l** for justice, but find none; 7747
60:4 "Lift up your eyes and **l** about you: 8011
60:5 Then *you will* **l** and be radiant, 8011
60:9 Surely the islands **l** to me; 7747
63:15 **L down** from heaven and see 5564
64:9 Oh, **l** *upon* us, we pray, 5564
66:24 "And they will go out and **l** upon 8011
Jer 2:10 Cross over to the coasts of Kittim and **l,** 8011
3:2 **"L** up to the barren heights and see. 6524
3:3 Yet you have the **brazen l** *of* a prostitute; 5195
4:13 **L!** He advances like the 2180
5:1 **l around** and consider, 8011
5:3 O LORD, do not your eyes **l** for truth? NIH
6:16 "Stand at the crossroads and **l;** 8011
6:22 This is what the LORD says: **"L,** 2180
7:8 But **l,** you are trusting in deceptive words 2180
18:11 'This is what the LORD says: **L!** 2180
25:32 This is what the LORD Almighty says: **"L!** 2180
39:12 "Take him and **l after** him; 6524+6584+8492
40:4 and I *will* **l after** you; 6524+6584+8492
40:4 **L,** the whole country lies before you; 8011
48:40 This is what the LORD says: **"L!** 2180
49:22 **L!** An eagle will soar and swoop down, 2180
50:41 **"L!** An army is coming from the north; 2180
La 1:9 **"L,** O LORD, *on* my affliction, 8011
1:11 **"L,** O LORD, and consider, 8011
1:12 **L around** and see. 5564
1:18 **l** *upon* my suffering. 8011
2:20 **"L,** O LORD, and consider: 8011
3:63 **L** *at* them! 5564
5:1 **l,** and see our disgrace. 5564
Eze 5:11 *I will* not **l** *on* you **with pity** 2571+6524
7:4 *I will* not **l** on you **with pity** 2571+6524
7:9 *I will* not **l** on you **with pity** 2571+6524
8:5 "Son of man, **l** toward the north." 5951+6524
8:17 **L** *at* them putting the branch to their nose! 2180
8:18 *I will* not **l** on them **with pity** 2571+6524
9:10 *I will* not **l** on them **with pity** 2571+6524
18:6 or **l** to the idols of the house of Israel. 5951+6524
18:15 or **l** to the idols of the house of Israel. 5951+6524
23:27 **l** on these things **with longing** 5951+6524
25:8 'Because Moab and Seir said, **"L,** 2180
33:25 the blood still in it and **l** to your idols 5951+6524
34:11 for my sheep and **l after** them. 1329
34:12 so *will I* **l after** my sheep. 1329
36:9 and *will* **l** on you **with favor;** 7155
40:4 **l** with your eyes and hear with your ears 8011
44:5 "Son of man, **l carefully,** 928+6524+8011
Da 2:13 *to* **l for** Daniel and his friends to put them 10114
3:25 He said, **"L!** I see four men walking around 10194
5:10 Don't be alarmed! Don't **l so pale!** 10228+10731
9:17 **l with favor** on your desolate sanctuary. 239+7156
Hos 2:2 the **adulterous l** from her face and 2393
2:7 *she will* **l for** them but not find them. 1335
Am 6:2 Go to Calneh and **l** *at* it; 8011
7:8 Then the Lord said, **"L,** I am setting 2180
Ob 1:12 *You should* not **l down on** your brother in 8011
1:13 nor **l down on** them in their calamity in 8011
Jnh 2:4 I will **l** again toward your holy temple.' 5564
Mic 1:3 **L!** The LORD is coming from his dwelling 2180
Na 1:15 **L,** there on the mountains, 2180
2:4 They **l** like flaming torches; 5260
3:13 **L** at your troops—they are all women! 2180
Hab 1:3 Why *do you* **make** me **l** *at* injustice? 8011
1:5 **"L** at the nations and watch— 8011
1:13 Your eyes are too pure *to* **l** *on* evil; 8011
2:1 *I will* **l** to see what he will say to me, 7595
Hag 2:3 How *does* it **l** to you now? 8011
Zec 5:5 **"L** up and see what this is 6524
6:8 Then he called to me, **"L,** those going 8011
12:10 *They will* **l** on me, the one they have pierced 5564
Mt 6:16 *do* not **l somber** as the hypocrites do, *1181+5034*
6:26 **L at** the birds of the air; *1838*
7:3 "Why *do you* **l** at the speck of sawdust *1063*
12:2 they said to him, **"L!** Your disciples are *2627*
18:10 not **l down on** one of these little ones. *2969*
18:12 and go *to* **l for** the one that wandered off? *2426*
23:27 which **l** beautiful on the outside but on the *5743*
23:38 **L,** your house is left to you desolate. *2627*
24:23 At that time if anyone says to you, **'L,** *2627*

Mt 25:43 and in prison and *you did* not **l after** me.' *2170*
26:45 **L,** the hour is near, the Son of Man *2627*
26:65 **L,** now you have heard the blasphemy. *3972*
28: 1 and the other Mary went *to* **l at** the tomb. *2555*
Mk 1:36 Simon and his companions *went to* **l for** *2870*
2:24 The Pharisees said to him, **"L,** *3972*
8:24 they **l** like trees walking around." *3972*
11:21 and said to Jesus, "Rabbi, **l!** *3972*
12:15 "Bring me a denarius and let *me* **l** at it." *3972*
13: 1 one of his disciples said to him, **"L,** *3972*
13:21 At that time if anyone says to you, **'L,** *3972*
13:21 or, **'L,** there he is!' *3972*
14:41 **L,** the Son of Man is betrayed into *2627*
Lk 2:45 they went back to Jerusalem *to* **l for** him. *349*
6:41 "Why *do you* **l at** the speck of sawdust *1063*
9:38 "Teacher, I beg you *to* **l at** my son, *2098*
10:35 **'L after** him,' he said, 'and when I return, *2150*
13: 6 and he went *to* **l for** fruit on it, *2426*
13: 7 now I've been coming *to* **l for** fruit *2426*
13:35 **L,** your house is left to you desolate. *2627*
15:29 But he answered his father, **'L!** *2627*
18:13 would not even **l up** to heaven, *2048+3836+4057*
19: 8 Zacchaeus stood up and said to the Lord, **"L** *2627*
21:29 **"L at** the fig tree and all the trees. *3972*
24: 5 "Why *do you* **l for** the living among *2426*
24:39 **L at** my hands and my feet. *3972*
Jn 1:29 **L,** the Lamb of God, who takes away the sin *3972*
1:36 he said, **"L,** the Lamb of God!" *3972*
4:35 open your eyes and **l at** the fields! *2517*
7:34 *You will* **l for** me, but you will not find me; *2426*
7:36 *'You will* **l for** me, but you will not find me, *2426*
7:52 **L into** it, and you will find that *2236*
8:21 and *you will* **l for** me, *2426*
12:19 **L** how the whole world has gone after him! *3972*
13:33 *You will* **l for** me, and just as I told the Jews, *2426*
19: 4 the Jews, **"L,** I am bringing him out to you *3972*
19:37 *"They will* **l** on the one they have pierced." *3972*
20:11 *she* **bent over** *to* **l** into the tomb *4160*
Ac 3: 4 Then Peter said, **"L** at us!" *1063*
5: 9 **L!** The feet of the men who buried your *2627*
5:25 Then someone came and said, **"L!** *2627*
7:31 As he went over *to* **l more closely,** *2917*
7:32 with fear and did not dare *to* **l.** *2917*
7:56 **"L,"** he said, "I see heaven open and *2627*
8:36 the eunuch said, **"L,** here is water. *2627*
11:25 Barnabas went to Tarsus *to* **l for** Saul, *349*
13:41 **" 'L,** you scoffers, wonder and perish, *3972*
Ro 1:23 for images made to **l like** mortal man *3930*
14: 3 not **l down on** him who does not, *2024*
14:10 Or why *do* you **l down on** your brother? *2024*
1Co 1:22 miraculous signs and Greeks **l for** wisdom, *2426*
7:27 Are you unmarried? *Do* not **l for** a wife. *2426*
2Co 3: 7 so that the Israelites could not **l steadily** *867*
Php 2: 4 Each of you *should* **l** not only **to** *5023*
1Ti 4:12 Don't *let* anyone **l down on you** *2969*
Jas 1:27 *to* **l after** orphans and widows *2170*
5: 4 **L!** The wages you failed to pay *2627*
1Pe 1:12 Even angels long *to* **l** into these things. *4160*
2Pe 3:12 *as you* **l forward to** the day of God *4659*
Rev 1: 7 **L,** he is coming with the clouds, *2627*
5: 3 could open the scroll or even **l** inside it. *1063*
5: 4 worthy *to* open the scroll or **l** inside. *1063*

LOOKED (208) [LOOK]

Ge 4: 4 The LORD **l with favor** on Abel 9120
13:10 Lot **l** up and saw that the whole plain of 6524
18: 2 Abraham **l** up and saw three men standing 6524
18:16 *they* **l down** toward Sodom, 9207
19:26 But Lot's wife **l** back, 5564
19:28 *He* **l down** toward Sodom and Gomorrah, 9207
22: 4 On the third day Abraham **l** up and saw 6524
22:13 Abraham **l** up and there in a thicket 6524
24:63 and *as* he **l** up, he saw camels approaching. 6524
24:64 Rebekah also **l** up and saw Isaac. 6524
26: 8 Abimelech king of the Philistines **l down** 9207
31:10 a dream in which I **l** up and saw that 6524
33: 1 Jacob **l** up and there was Esau, 6524
33: 5 Then Esau **l** up and saw the women 6524
37:25 they **l** up and saw a caravan 6524
41:21 they **l** just as ugly as before. 5260
43:29 **l about** and saw his brother Benjamin, 5951+6524
43:30 Joseph hurried out and **l for** a place 1335
43:33 **l** at each other **in astonishment.** 9449
Ex 2:25 God **l** *on* the Israelites and was concerned 8011
14:10 Pharaoh approached, the Israelites **l** up, 6524
14:24 the LORD **l down** from the pillar of fire 9207
16:10 *they* **l** toward the desert, 7155
24:17 To the Israelites the glory of the LORD **l** 5260
Nu 9:15 the cloud above the tabernacle **l** like fire. 5260
9:16 and at night it **l** *like* fire. 5260
11: 7 The manna was like coriander seed and **l** 6524
13:33 and *we* **l** the same *to* them." 928+2118+6524
17: 9 *They* **l** *at* them, and each man took his own 8011
21: 9 when anyone was bitten by a snake and **l** 5564
24: 2 When Balaam **l** out and saw Israel 6524
Dt 9:16 When *I* **l,** I saw that you had sinned 8011
Jos 5:13 he **l** up and saw a man standing in front 6524
8:20 The men of Ai **l** back and saw the smoke 8011
Jdg 13: 6 He **l** like an angel of God, very awesome. 5260
19:17 *he* **l** and saw the traveler in the city 5951+6524
1Sa 6:13 and when they **l** up and saw the ark, 6524
6:19 because *they had* **l** into the ark of the LORD. 8011
9:16 *I have* **l** *upon* my people, 8011
10:21 *they* **l for** him, he was not to be found. 1335
17:42 He **l** David **over** and saw that he was only 5564
24: 8 When Saul **l** behind him, David bowed 5564
2Sa 2:20 Abner **l** behind him and asked, 7155
13:34 Now the man standing watch **l** up 906+6524
18:24 As he **l** out, he saw a man running alone. 6524
24:20 When Araunah **l** and saw the king 9207
1Ki 2:15 All Israel **l** to me as their king. 7156+8492
3:21 *I* **l** at him **closely** in the morning light, 1067
18:43 And he went up and **l.** 5564
19: 6 *He* **l around,** and there by his head was 5564
2Ki 2:24 **l** *at* them and called down a curse 8011
3:22 the water **l** red—like blood. 8011
6:17 and *he* **l** and saw the hills full of horses 8011
6:20 the LORD opened their eyes and *they* **l,** 8011
6:30 As he went along the wall, the people **l,** 8011
9:30 arranged her hair and **l out** of a window. 9207
9:32 He **l** up at the window and called out, 7156
9:32 Two or three eunuchs **l down** at him. 9207
11:14 *She* **l** and there was the king, 8011
23:16 Then Josiah **l around,** 7155
1Ch 17:17 *You have* **l** *on* me as though I were 8011
21:16 David **l** up and saw the angel of 6524
21:21 and when Araunah **l** and saw him, 5564
2Ch 20:24 to the place that overlooks the desert and **l** 7155
23:13 *She* **l,** and there was the king, 8011
26:20 the chief priest and all the other priests **l** 7155
Ne 4:14 After *I* **l things over,** I stood up and said 8011
Est 3: 6 Instead Haman **l for** a way to destroy all 1335
Job 28:27 then *he* **l** *at* wisdom and appraised it; 8011
30:26 when *I* **l** for light, then came darkness. 3498
Ps 37:36 though *I* **l for** him, he could not be found. 1335
54: 7 and my eyes *have* **l** in triumph on my foes. 8011
69:20 *I* **l for** sympathy, but there was none, 7747
102:19 "The LORD **l down** from his sanctuary 9207
114: 3 The sea **l** and fled, the Jordan turned back; 8011
Pr 7: 6 the window of my house *I* **l out** through 9207
7:15 I **l for** you and have found you! 8838
Ecc 4: 1 Again I **l** and saw all the oppression NIH
SS 3: 1 on my bed *I* **l for** the one my heart loves; 1335
3: 1 *I* **l for** him but did not find him. 1335
3: 2 So *I* **l for** him but did not find him. 1335
5: 6 *I* **l for** him but did not find him. 1335
Isa 5: 2 Then *he* **l for** a crop of good grapes, 7747
5: 4 *When I* **l for** good grapes, 7747
5: 7 And *he* **l for** justice, but saw bloodshed; 7747
22: 8 And *you* **l** in that day to the weapons in 5564
38:14 My eyes grew weak as I **l** to the heavens. NIH
57: 8 and *you* **l** *on* their nakedness. 2600
59:15 The LORD **l** and was displeased 8011
63: 5 *I* **l,** but there was no one to help, 5564
Jer 4:23 *I* **l** *at* the earth, and it was formless and 8011
4:24 *I* **l** *at* the mountains, and they were quaking; 8011
4:25 *I* **l,** and there were no people; 8011
4:26 *I* **l,** and the fruitful land was a desert; 8011
31:26 At this I awoke and **l** *around.* 8011
36:16 *they* **l** at each other **in fear** 7064
La 1: 7 Her enemies **l** *at* her and laughed 8011
Eze 1: 4 *I* **l,** and I saw a windstorm coming out of 8011
1: 4 The center of the fire **l** like glowing metal, 6524
1: 5 and in the fire was *what* **l like** four living 1952
1:10 Their faces **l like** this: 1952
1:15 As *I* **l** *at* the living creatures, 8011
1:16 and all four **l** alike. 1952
1:22 of the living creatures was *what* **l like** 1952
1:26 over their heads was what **l** like a throne 5260
1:27 from what appeared to be his waist up he **l** 6524
1:27 and that from there down he **l** like fire; 5260
2: 9 *I* **l,** and I saw a hand stretched out to me. 8011
8: 2 *I* **l,** and I saw a figure like that of a man. 8011
8: 3 He stretched out *what* **l like** a hand 9322
8: 5 So I **l,** and in the entrance north of 5951+6524
8: 7 *I* **l,** and I saw a hole in the wall. 8011
8:10 So I went in and **l,** 8011
10: 1 *I* **l,** and I saw the likeness of a throne 8011
10: 8 of the cherubim could be seen *what* **l like** 9322
10: 9 *I* **l,** and I saw beside the cherubim 8011
10:10 their appearance, the four of them **l** alike; 1952
10:21 and under their wings was *what* **l like** 1952
16: 5 No one **l** on you **with pity** 2571+6524
16: 8 and when *I* **l** *at* you and saw 8011
20:17 Yet *I* **l** on them **with pity** 2571+6524
22:30 *"I* **l for** a man among them who would 1335
23:15 of them **l** like Babylonian chariot officers, 5260
34: 6 and no one searched or **l for** them. 1335
37: 8 *I* **l,** and tendons and flesh appeared 8011
40: 2 some buildings that **l** like a city. NIH
44: 4 *I* **l** and saw the glory of the LORD 8011
Da 1:15 the end of the ten days they **l** healthier 5260+8011
2:31 "You **l,** O king, and there before you 10255
4:10 I **l,** and there before me stood a tree in 10255
4:13 I **l,** and there before me was a messenger, 10255
7: 2 Daniel said: "In my vision at night *I* **l,** 10255
7: 5 second beast, which **l like** a bear. 10179
7: 6 I **l,** and there before me was another beast, 10255
7: 6 one that **l** like a leopard. NIH
7: 7 "After that, in my vision at night I **l,** 10255
7: 9 "As I **l,** "thrones were set in place, 10255
7:13 "In my vision at night I **l,** 10255
7:20 that **l** more imposing than the others and 10256
8: 3 I **l** up, and there before me was a ram 6524
8:15 before me stood one who **l** like a man. 5260
10: 5 I **l** up and there before me was 6524
10:16 one who **l** like a man touched my lips, 1952
10:18 the one who **l** like a man touched me 5260
12: 5 **l,** and there before me stood two others, 8011
Hab 3: 6 *he* **l,** and made the nations tremble. 8011
Zec 1:18 Then I **l** up—and there before me were 6524
2: 1 Then I **l** up—and there before me was 6524
5: 1 I **l** again—and there before me was 5951+6524
Zec 5: 9 Then I **l** up—and there before me were 6524
6: 1 I **l** up again—and there before me were 6524
Mt 17: 8 *When they* **l up,** they saw *2048+3836+4057*
19:26 Jesus **l** at them and said, *1838*
21:46 *They* **l for a way** to arrest him, *2426*
25:36 I was sick and *you* **l after** me, *2170*
Mk 3: 5 He **l around at** them in anger and, *4315*
3:34 Then he **l at** those seated in a circle *4315*
7:34 He **l up** to heaven and with a deep sigh *329*
8:24 He **l up** and said, "I see people; *329*
8:33 *when* Jesus turned and **l at** his disciples, *3972*
9: 8 Suddenly, *when they* **l around,** *4315*
9:26 The boy **l so much like** a corpse *1181+6059*
10:21 Jesus **l at** him and loved him. *1838*
10:23 Jesus **l around** and said to his disciples, *4315*
10:27 Jesus **l at** them and said, *1838*
11:11 *He* **l around at** everything, *4315*
12:12 Then *they* **l for a way** to arrest him *2426*
14:67 *she* **l closely** at him. *1838*
16: 4 But *when they* **l up,** they saw that the stone, *329*
Lk 6:10 He **l around at** them all, *4315*
16:23 he **l up** and saw Abraham far *2048+3836+4057*
18: 9 and **l down on** everybody else, *2024*
18:24 Jesus **l at** him and said, "How hard it is *3972*
19: 5 *he* **l up** and said to him, "Zacchaeus, *329*
20:17 Jesus **l directly at** them and asked, *1838*
20:19 of the law and the chief priests **l for a way** *2426*
21: 1 *As he* **l up,** Jesus saw the rich *329*
22:56 She **l closely** at him and said, *867*
22:61 The Lord turned and **l straight** at Peter. *1838*
Jn 1:42 Jesus **l at** him and said, "You are Simon *1838*
6: 5 *When* Jesus **l up** and saw *2048+3836+4057*
11:41 Then Jesus **l** up and said, "Father, *149+3836+4057*
17: 1 he **l** toward heaven and prayed: *2048+3836+4057*
20: 5 and **l** in **at** the strips of linen lying there *1063*
Ac 3: 4 Peter **l straight** at him, as did John. *867*
6:15 in the Sanhedrin **l intently** at Stephen, *867*
7:55 **l** up to heaven and saw the glory of God, *867*
11: 6 *I* **l** into it and saw four-footed animals *867+2917*
13: 9 **l straight** at Elymas and said, *867*
14: 9 Paul **l directly at** him, *867*
17:23 around and **l carefully** at your objects *355*
23: 1 Paul **l straight** at the Sanhedrin and said, *867*
1Jn 1: 1 which *we have* **l at** and our hands have *2517*
Rev 4: 1 After this *I* **l,** and there before me was a *3972*
4: 6 throne there was what **l like** a sea of glass, *6055*
5:11 *I* **l** and heard the voice of many angels, *3972*
6: 2 *I* **l,** and there before me was a white horse! *3972*
6: 5 *I* **l,** and there before me was a black horse! *3972*
6: 8 *I* **l,** and there before me was a pale horse! *3972*
7: 9 After this *I* **l** and there before me was *3972*
9: 7 The locusts **l like** horses prepared *3927+3930*
9:17 The horses and riders I saw in my vision **l** *NIG*
11:12 while their enemies **l on.** *2555*
14: 1 Then *I* **l,** and there before me was *3972*
14:14 *I* **l,** and there before me was *3972*
15: 2 And I saw what **l** like a sea of glass mixed *NIG*
15: 5 After this *I* **l** and in heaven the temple, *3972*
16:13 I saw three evil spirits that **l** like frogs; *NIG*

LOOKING (67) [LOOK]

Ge 37:15 "What *are you* **l for?"** 1335
37:16 He replied, "I'm **l for** my brothers. 1335
42: 1 "Why *do you just keep* **l at each other?"** 8011
Ex 22:10 or is taken away *while* no *one is* **l,** 8011
25:20 face each other, **l** toward the cover. 7156
37: 9 faced each other, **l** toward the cover. 7156
Dt 22: 2 with you and keep it until he **comes l for** it. 2011
Jdg 4:22 "I will show you the man you're **l for."** 1335
17: 9 he said, "and I'm **l for** a place to stay." 5162
1Sa 10:14 **"L for** the donkeys," he said. 1335
19: 2 "My father Saul *is* **l for a chance** 1335
1Ki 20: 7 "See how this man *is* **l for** trouble! 1335
2Ki 6:19 I will lead you to the man *you are* **l for."** 1335
Ps 69: 3 My eyes fail, **l** for my God. 3498
119:82 My eyes fail, **l** for your promise; NIH
119:123 My eyes fail, **l** for your salvation, NIH
119:123 **l** for your righteous promise. NIH
Ecc 12: 3 those **l** through the windows grow dim; 8011
SS 7: 4 the tower of Lebanon **l** toward Damascus. 7595
Isa 8:21 they will become enraged and, **l** upward, 7155
Jer 46: 5 They flee in haste without **l back,** 7155
La 4:17 our eyes failed, **l** in vain for help; NIH
Da 1:10 Why should he see you **l worse** than 2407
7:11 I kept **l** until the beast was slain 10255
Mt 12:10 **L** for a reason to accuse Jesus, *NIG*
13:45 kingdom of heaven is like a merchant **l for** *2426*
14:19 the five loaves and the two fish and **l up** *329*
26:59 and the whole Sanhedrin *were* **l for** *2426*
28: 5 for I know that you *are* **l for** Jesus, *2426*
Mk 1:37 "Everyone *is* **l for** you!" *2426*
3: 2 Some of them were **l** for a reason *NIG*
3:32 and brothers *are* outside **l for** you." *2426*
5:32 But Jesus *kept* **l around** *4315*
6:41 the five loaves and the two fish and **l up** *329*
11:18 the law heard this and *began* **l for** a way *2426*
14: 1 and the teachers of the law *were* **l for** *2426*
14:55 the whole Sanhedrin *were* **l for** evidence *2426*
16: 6 *"You are* **l for** Jesus the Nazarene, *2426*
Lk 2:38 the child *to* all who *were* **l forward to** *4657*
2:44 Then *they began* **l for** him *349*
4:42 The people *were* **l for** him and *2118*
6: 7 **were l for** a reason to accuse Jesus, *2351+2671*
6:20 **L** at his disciples, he said: *2048+3836+4057*
9:16 the five loaves and the two fish and **l up** *329*
17: 7 a servant plowing or **l after** the **sheep.** *4477*

Lk 22: 2 of the law *were* **l for** some way to get rid 2426
Jn 6:26 "I tell you the truth, *you are* **l for** me, 2426
11:56 *They kept* **l for** Jesus, 2426
18: 8 *you are* **l for** me, then let these men go." 2426
20:15 Who is it *you are* **l for?"** 2426
Ac 1:10 They were **l intently** up into the sky 867
1:11 "why do you stand here **l** into the sky? 1838
10:19 "Simon, three men *are* **l for** you. 2426
10:21 "I'm the one *you're* **l for.** 2426
2Co 10: 7 *You are* **l** only **on** the surface of things. 1063
Php 4:17 Not that *I am* **l for** a gift, 2118
4:17 but *I am* **l for** what may be credited 2118
1Th 2: 6 *We were* not **l for** praise from men, 2426
Heb 11:10 For *he was* **l forward to** the city 1683
11:14 that *they are* **l for** a country of their own. 2118
11:26 because *he was* **l ahead** to his reward. 611
13:14 but *we are* **l for** the city that is to come. 2118
Jas 1:24 *after* **l at** himself, goes away and 2917
1Pe 5: 8 like a roaring lion **l for** someone to devour. 2426
2Pe 3:13 with his promise *we are* **l forward to** 4659
3:14 *since* you *are* **l forward to** this, 4659
Rev 5: 6 I saw a Lamb, **l** as if it had been slain, NIG

LOOKINGGLASSES (KJV) See MIRROR

LOOKOUT (5) [LOOK]

2Ki 9:17 When the **l** standing on the tower 7595
9:18 The **l** reported, "The messenger has 7595
9:20 The **l** reported, "He has reached them, 7595
Isa 21: 6 post a **l** and have him report what he sees. 7595
21: 8 And the **l** shouted, "Day after day, 8011

LOOKOUTS (1) [LOOK]

1Sa 14:16 Saul's **l** at Gibeah in Benjamin saw 7595

LOOKS (33) [LOOK]

Lev 14:35 'I have seen something that **l** like mildew NIH
1Sa 16: 7 not look at the things man **l** *at.* 8011
16: 7 Man **l** at the outward appearance, 8011
16: 7 but the LORD **l** at the heart." 8011
Ezr 8:22 "The gracious hand of our God is on everyone *who* **l to** him, 1335
Job 8:17 and **l** *for* a place among the stones. 2600
41:34 *He* **l down on** all that are haughty; 8011
Ps 14: 2 The LORD **l down** from heaven on 9207
33:13 the LORD **l down** and sees all mankind; 5564
53: 2 God **l down** from heaven on the sons 9207
85:11 and righteousness **l down** from heaven. 9207
104:32 he *who* **l** at the earth, 5564
138: 6 LORD is on high, *he* **l** *upon* the lowly, 8011
Pr 20: 4 so at harvest time *he* **l** but finds nothing. 8626
25:23 so a sly tongue brings angry **l.** 7156
27:18 *he who* **l after** his master will be honored. 9068
Ecc 11: 4 *whoever* **l** at the clouds will not reap. 8011
Isa 5:30 And if *one* **l** at the land, 5564
40:20 *He* **l for** a skilled craftsman to set up 1335
La 3:50 the LORD **l down** from heaven and sees. 9207
Eze 18:12 He **l** to the idols. 5951+6524
34:12 As a shepherd **l after** his scattered flock 1333
Da 3:25 and the fourth **l** like a son of the gods." 10657
Mt 5:28 But I tell you that anyone who **l at** 1063
16: 4 A wicked and adulterous generation **l for** 2118
Lk 9:62 and **l** back is fit for service in the kingdom 1063
Jn 6:40 that everyone who **l** to the Son and believes 2555
9: 9 Others said, "No, *he* only **l like** him." 1639+3927
12:45 he **l at** me, he sees the one who sent me. 2555
Php 2:21 For everyone **l out for** his own interests, 2426
Jas 1:23 not do what it says is like a man *who* **l at** 2917
1:24 and immediately forgets what *he* **l like.** 1639
1:25 the man who **l intently** into the perfect law 4160

LOOM (3) [LOOMS]

Jdg 16:13 the fabric [on the **l**] and tighten it with NIH
16:14 and pulled up the pin and the **l,** 756
Isa 38:12 and he has cut me off from the **l;** 1929

LOOMS (1) [LOOM]

Jer 6: 1 For disaster **l** out of the north, 9207

LOOPS (11)

Ex 26: 4 Make **l** *of* blue material along the edge of 4339
26: 5 Make fifty **l** on one curtain and fifty loops 4339
26: 5 Make fifty loops on one curtain and fifty **l** 4339
26: 5 with the **l** opposite each other. 4339
26:10 Make fifty **l** along the edge of 4339
26:11 in the **l** to fasten the tent together as a unit. 4339
36:11 Then they made **l** *of* blue material along 4339
36:12 They also made fifty **l** on one curtain 4339
36:12 and fifty **l** on the end curtain of 4339
36:12 with the **l** opposite each other. 4339
36:17 Then they made fifty **l** along the edge of 4339

LOOSE (13) [LOOSED, LOOSEN, LOOSENED]

Jdg 15: 5 and **let** the foxes **l** in the standing grain 8938
16: 3 and **tore** them **l,** bar and all. 5825
Job 6: 9 *to* **let l** his hand and cut me off! 6000
12:15 if *he* **lets** them **l,** they devastate the land. 8938
38:31 *Can you* **l** the cords of Orion? 7337
Ps 78:26 *He* **let l** the east wind from the heavens 5825
Isa 7:25 **places where** cattle are **turned l** 5448
33:23 Your rigging **hangs l:** 5759
58: 6 *to* **l** the chains of injustice and untie 7337
Mt 16:19 whatever *you* **l** on earth will be loosed in heaven." 3395
18:18 whatever *you* **l** on earth will be loosed in heaven. 3395
Ac 16:26 and everybody's chains **came l.** 479
27:40 **Cutting l** the anchors, 4311

LOOSED (3) [LOOSE]

Mt 16:19 you loose on earth will be **l** in heaven." 3395
18:18 you loose on earth will be **l** in heaven. 3395
Lk 1:64 his mouth was opened and his tongue was **l,** NIG

LOOSEN (1) [LOOSE]

Nu 5:18 *he shall* **l** her hair and place in her hands 7277

LOOSENED (2) [LOOSE]

Isa 5:27 not a belt *is* **l** at the waist, 7337
Mk 7:35 his tongue *was* **l** and he began to speak 3395

LOOT (13) [LOOTED, LOOTER, LOOTING]

Isa 10: 6 to seize **l** and snatch plunder, 8965
17:14 This is the portion of *those who* **l** us, 9115
21: 2 The traitor betrays, the looter **takes l.** 8720
42:22 they have been made **l,** 5468
42:24 Who handed Jacob over to become **l,** 5468
Eze 7:21 over as plunder to foreigners and as **l** to 8965
26:12 and **l** your merchandise; 1024
29:19 *He will* **l** and plunder the land as pay 8964+8965
38:12 I will plunder and **l** and turn my hand 1020+1024
38:13 Have you gathered your hordes to **l,** 1020+1024
39:10 and **l** those who looted them, 1024
Da 11:24 **l** and wealth among his followers. 8965
Am 3:10 who hoard plunder and **l** in their fortresses. 8719

LOOTED (5) [LOOT]

Ge 34:27 of Jacob came upon the dead bodies and **l** 1024
2Ki 21:14 be **l** and plundered by all their foes, 1020
Isa 13:16 their houses *will* **be l** and their wives 9116
42:22 But this is a people plundered and **l,** 9115
Eze 39:10 and loot *those who* **l** them, 1024

LOOTER (1) [LOOT]

Isa 21: 2 The traitor betrays, the **l** takes loot. 8720

LOOTING (1) [LOOT]

1Sa 23: 1 and *are* **l** the threshing floors," 9115

LOP (1)

Isa 10:33 *will* **l off** the boughs with great power. 6188

*LORD (933) [*LORD'S, LORDED, LORDING, LORDS]

Ge 18: 3 "If I have found favor in your eyes, my **l,** 123
18:27 so bold as to speak to **the L,** 151
18:30 Then he said, "May **the L** not be angry, 151
18:31 so bold as to speak to **the L,** 151
18:32 Then he said, "May **the L** not be angry, 151
20: 4 **"L,** will you destroy an innocent nation? 151
23:11 "No, my **l,"** he said. 123
23:15 "Listen to me, my **l;** 123
24:18 "Drink, my **l,"** she said, 123
27:29 Be **l** over your brothers, 1484
27:37 "I have made him **l** over you 1484
31:35 "Don't be angry, my **l,** 123
32: 5 Now I am sending this message to my **l,** 123
32:18 They are a gift sent to my **l** Esau, 123
33: 8 "To find favor in your eyes, my **l,"** he said. 123
33:13 "My **l** knows that the children are tender 123
33:14 So let my **l** go on ahead of his servant, 123
33:14 until I come to my **l** in Seir." 123
33:15 "Just let me find favor in the eyes of my **l."** 123
42:10 "No, my **l,"** they answered. 123
42:30 "The man who is **l** *over* the land spoke 123
42:33 the man who is **l** *over* the land said to us, 123
44: 7 "Why does my **l** say such things? 123
44:16 "What can we say to my **l?"** 123
44:18 "Please, my **l,** let your servant speak 123
44:18 let your servant speak a word to my **l.** 123
44:19 My **l** asked his servants, 123
44:22 And we said to my **l,** 123
44:24 we told him what my **l** had said. 123
45: 8 **l** of his entire household and ruler 123
45: 9 God has made me **l** of all Egypt. 123
47:18 "We cannot hide from our **l** the fact that 123
47:18 left for our **l** except our bodies and our land. 123
47:25 "May we find favor in the eyes of our **l;** 123
Ex 4:10 Moses said to the LORD, "O **L,** 151
4:13 But Moses said, "O **L,** please send someone 151
5:22 "O **L,** why have you brought trouble 151
15:17 O **L,** your hands established. 151
32:22 "Do not be angry, my **l,"** Aaron answered. 123
34: 9 "O **L,** if I have found favor in your eyes," 151
34: 9 he said, "then let **the L** go with us. 151
Nu 11:28 spoke up and said, "Moses, my **l,** 123
12:11 and he said to Moses, "Please, my **l,** do 123
16:13 And now *you* also *want to* **l it** over us? 8606+8606
32:25 your servants will do as our **l** commands. 123
32:27 fight before the LORD, just as our **l** says." 123
36: 2 "When the LORD commanded my **l** 123
Dt 10:17 the LORD your God is God of gods and **L** *of* lords, 123
Jos 3:11 the ark of the covenant of the **L** *of* all 123
3:13 ark of the LORD—the **L** *of* all the earth— 123
5:14 "What message does my **L** have 123
7: 8 O **L,** what can I say, 151
Jdg 3:25 There they saw their **l** fallen to the floor, 123
4:18 "Come, my **l,** come right in. 123
6:15 **"But L,"** Gideon asked, 151
13: 8 "O **L,** I beg you, let the man of God 151
Ru 2:13 to find favor in your eyes, my **l,"** 123
1Sa 1:15 "Not so, my **l,"** Hannah replied, 123
1:26 "As surely as you live, my **l,** 123
16:16 Let our **l** command his servants here 123
22:12 "Yes, my **l,"** he answered. 123
24: 8 "My **l** the king!" 123
25:24 "My **l,** let the blame be on me alone. 123
25:25 May my **l** pay no attention to that wicked 123
26:15 Why didn't you guard your **l** the king? 123
26:15 Someone came to destroy your **l** the king. 123
26:17 David replied, "Yes it is, my **l** the king." 123
26:18 "Why is my **l** pursuing his servant? 123
26:19 Now let my **l** the king listen 123
29: 8 against the enemies of my **l** the king?" 123
2Sa 1:10 and have brought them here to my **l."** 123
3:21 and assemble all Israel for my **l** the king, 123
4: 8 This day the LORD has avenged my **l** 123
9:11 "Your servant will do whatever my **l** 123
10: 3 Ammonite nobles said to Hanun their **l,** 123
13:32 "My **l** should not think that they killed all 123
13:33 My **l** the king should not be concerned 123
14: 9 "My **l** the king, let the blame rest on me 123
14:12 "Let your servant speak a word to my **l** 123
14:15 "And now I have come to say this to my **l** 123
14:17 the word of my **l** the king bring me rest, 123
14:17 for my **l** the king is like an angel of God 123
14:18 "Let my **l** the king speak," 123
14:19 "As surely as you live, my **l** the king, 123
14:19 from anything my **l** the king says. 123
14:20 My **l** has wisdom like that of an angel 123
14:22 found favor in your eyes, my **l** the king, 123
15:15 to do whatever our **l** the king chooses." 123
15:21 and as my **l** the king lives, 123
15:21 wherever my **l** the king may be, 123
16: 4 find favor in your eyes, my **l** the king." 123
16: 9 "Why should this dead dog curse my **l** 123
18:28 against my **l** the king." 123
18:31 "My **l** the king, hear the good news! 123
18:32 of my **l** the king and all who rise up 123
19:19 "May my **l** not hold me guilty. 123
19:19 on the day my **l** the king left Jerusalem. 123
19:20 to come down and meet my **l** the king." 123
19:26 He said, "My **l** the king, 123
19:27 And he has slandered your servant to my **l** 123
19:27 My **l** the king is like an angel of God; 123
19:28 but death from my **l** the king, 123
19:30 now that my **l** the king has arrived home 123
19:35 be an added burden to my **l** the king? 123
19:37 Let him cross over with my **l** the king. 123
24: 3 and may the eyes of my **l** the king see it. 123
24: 3 But why does my **l** the king want 123
24:21 Why has my **l** the king come to his servant? 123
24:22 to David, "Let my **l** the king take whatever 123
1Ki 1: 2 so that our **l** the king may keep warm." 123
1:11 without our **l** David's knowing it? 123
1:13 'My **l** the king, did you not swear 123
1:17 She said to him, "My **l,** you yourself swore 123
1:18 my **l** the king, do not know about it. 123
1:20 My **l** the king, the eyes of all Israel are on 123
1:20 on the throne of my **l** the king after him. 123
1:21 as soon as my **l** the king is laid to rest 123
1:24 Nathan said, "Have you, my **l** the king, 123
1:27 Is this something my **l** the king has done 123
1:27 on the throne of my **l** the king after him?" 123
1:31 said, "May my **l** King David live forever!" 123
1:36 the God of my **l** the king, so declare it. 123
1:37 As the LORD was with my **l** the king, 123
1:37 the throne of my **l** King David!" 123
1:43 "Our **l** King David has made Solomon king. 123
1:47 to congratulate our **l** King David, 123
2:38 Your servant will do as my **l** the king 123
3:10 **The L** was pleased that Solomon had asked 151
3:17 One of them said, "My **l,** this woman and I 123
3:26 "Please, my **l,** give her the living baby! 123
12:27 to their **l,** Rehoboam king of Judah. 123
18: 7 and said, "Is it really you, my **l** Elijah?" 123
18:13 Haven't you heard, my **l,** 123
20: 4 "Just as you say, my **l** the king. 123
20: 9 "Tell my **l** the king, 123
22: 6 **the L** will give it into the king's hand." 151
2Ki 2:19 "Look, our **l,** this town is well situated, 123
4:16 "No, my **l,"** she objected. 123
4:28 "Did I ask you for a son, my **l?"** 123
6: 5 "Oh, my **l,"** he cried out, 123
6:12 "None of us, my **l** the king," 123
6:15 "Oh, my **l,** what shall we do?" 123
6:26 "Help me, my **l** the king!" 123
7: 6 for **the L** had caused the Arameans to hear 151
8: 5 "This is the woman, my **l** the king, 123
8:12 "Why is my **l** weeping?" 123
19:23 you have heaped insults on **the L.** 151
1Ch 21: 3 My **l** the king, are they not all my lord's 123
21: 3 Why does my **l** want to do this? 123
21:23 Let my **l** the king do whatever pleases him. 123
2Ch 2:14 and with those of my **l,** 123
2:15 "Now let my **l** send his servants the wheat 123
Ezr 10: 3 the counsel of my **l** and of those who fear 123

***LORD** distinguishes the words translated "Lord" and "lord" from the proper name of God, *Yahweh,* indicated in the NIV by "LORD" and indexed under the heading †**LORD**, pages 686-707.

Ne 1:11 O L, let your ear be attentive to the prayer 151
4:14 Remember the L, who is great 151
8:10 This day is sacred to our L. 151
10:29 and decrees of the LORD our L. 151
Job 28:28 And he said to man, 'The fear of the L— 151
Ps 2: 4 the L scoffs at them. 151
8: 1 our L, how majestic is your name in all 123
8: 9 our L, how majestic is your name in all 123
16: 2 I said to the LORD, "You are my L; 151
22:30 future generations will be told about the L. 151
30: 8 to the L I cried for mercy: 151
35:17 O L, how long will you look on? 151
35:22 Do not be far from me, O L. 151
35:23 Contend for me, my God and L. 151
37:13 but the L laughs at the wicked, 151
38: 9 All my longings lie open before you, O L; 151
38:15 you will answer, O L my God. 151
38:22 Come quickly to help me, O L my Savior. 151
39: 7 "But now, L, what do I look for? 151
40:17 may the L think of me. 151
44:23 Awake, O L! Why do you sleep? 151
45:11 honor him, for he is your l. 123
51:15 O L, open my lips, 151
54: 4 the L is the one who sustains me. 151
55: 9 Confuse the wicked, O L, 151
57: 9 I will praise you, O L, among the nations; 151
59:11 But do not kill them, O L our shield, 151
62:12 and that you, O L, are loving. 151
66:18 the L would not have listened; 151
68:11 The L announced the word, 151
68:17 the L [has come] from Sinai 151
68:19 Praise be to the L, to God our Savior, 151
68:22 The L says, "I will bring them 151
68:32 sing praise to the L, 151
69: 6 O L, the LORD Almighty; 151
73:20 O L, you will despise them as fantasies. 151
77: 2 When I was in distress, I sought the L; 151
77: 7 "Will the L reject forever? 151
78:65 Then the L awoke as from sleep, 151
79:12 the reproach they have hurled at you, O L. 151
86: 3 Have mercy on me, O L, 151
86: 4 Bring joy to your servant, for to you, O L, 151
86: 5 You are forgiving and good, O L, 151
86: 8 O L; no deeds can compare with yours. 151
86: 9 O L; they will bring glory to your name. 151
86:12 I will praise you, O L my God, 151
86:15 But you, O L, are a compassionate 151
89:49 O L, where is your former great love, 151
89:50 L, how your servant has been mocked, 151
90: 1 L, you have been our dwelling place 151
90:17 the favor of the L our God rest upon us; 151
97: 5 before the L *of* all the earth. 123
110: 1 The LORD says to my L: 123
110: 5 The L is at your right hand; 151
114: 7 Tremble, O earth, at the presence of the L, 123
130: 2 O L, hear my voice. 151
130: 3 you, O LORD, kept a record of sins, O L, 151
130: 6 for the L more than watchmen wait for 151
135: 5 that our L is greater than all gods. 151
136: 3 Give thanks to the L *of* lords: 151
147: 5 Great is our L and mighty in power; 151
Isa 1:24 Therefore the L, the LORD Almighty, 123
3: 1 See now, the L, the LORD Almighty, 123
3:15 declares the L, the LORD Almighty. 151
3:17 Therefore the L will bring sores on 151
3:18 day the L will snatch away their finery: 151
4: 4 The L will wash away the filth of 151
6: 1 I saw the L seated on a throne, 151
6: 8 Then I heard the voice of the L saying, 151
6:11 Then I said, "For how long, O L?" 151
7:14 Therefore the L himself will give you 151
7:20 that day the L will use a razor hired from 151
8: 7 therefore the L is about to bring 151
9: 8 The L has sent a message against Jacob; 151
9:17 Therefore the L will take no pleasure in 151
10:12 When the L has finished all his work 151
10:16 Therefore, the L, the LORD Almighty, 123
10:23 The L, the LORD Almighty, 151
10:24 Therefore, this is what the L, 151
10:33 See, the L, the LORD Almighty, 123
11:11 In that day the L will reach out his hand 151
19: 4 declares the L, the LORD Almighty. 123
21: 6 This is what the L says to me: 151
21: 8 the lookout shouted, "Day after day, my l, 123
21:16 This is what the L says to me: 151
22: 5 The L, the LORD Almighty, 151
22:12 The L, the LORD Almighty, 151
22:14 says the L, the LORD Almighty. 151
22:15 This is what the L, the LORD Almighty, 151
28: 2 the L has one who is powerful and strong. 151
28:22 the L, the LORD Almighty, 151
29:13 The L says: "These people come near to 151
30:20 Although the L gives you the bread 151
37:24 you have heaped insults on the L. 151
38:14 I am troubled; O L, come to my aid!" 151
38:16 L, by such things men live; 151
49:14 the L has forgotten me." 151
Jer 2:19 declares the L, the LORD Almighty. 151
37:20 But now, my l the king, please listen. 123
38: 9 "My l the king, these men have acted 123
46:10 But that day belongs to the L, 151
46:10 For the L, the LORD Almighty, 151
49: 5 declares the L, the LORD Almighty. 151
50:31 declares the L, the LORD Almighty, 151
La 1:14 and the L has sapped my strength. 151
1:15 "The L has rejected all the warriors 151
1:15 In his winepress the L has trampled 151
La 2: 1 How the L has covered the Daughter of Zion 151
2: 2 Without pity the L has swallowed up all 151
2: 5 The L is like an enemy; 151
2: 7 The L has rejected his altar 151
2:18 The hearts of the people cry out to the L. 151
2:19 like water in the presence of the L. 151
2:20 be killed in the sanctuary of the L? 151
3:31 For men are not cast off by the L forever. 151
3:36 would not the L see such things? 151
3:37 and have it happen if the L has 151
3:58 O L, you took up my case; 151
Eze 18:25 you say, 'The way of the L is not just.' 151
18:29 'The way of the L is not just.' 151
21: 9 prophesy and say, 'This is what the L says: 151
33:17 'The way of the L is not just.' 151
33:20 you say, 'The way of the L is not just.' 151
Da 1: 2 And the L delivered Jehoiakim king 151
1:10 "I am afraid of my l the king, 123
2:47 the L *of* kings and a revealer of mysteries, 10437
4:19 Belteshazzar answered, "My l, 10437
4:24 the Most High has issued against my l 10437
5:23 you have set yourself up against the L 10437
9: 3 So I turned to the L God and pleaded 151
9: 4 "O L, the great and awesome God, 151
9: 7 "L, you are righteous, 151
9: 9 The L our God is merciful and forgiving, 151
9:15 "Now, O L our God, who brought your 151
9:16 O L, in keeping with all your righteous 151
9:17 For your sake, O L, look with favor 151
9:19 O L, listen! 151
9:19 O L, forgive! 151
9:19 O L, hear and act! 151
10:16 my l, and I am helpless. 123
10:17 your servant, talk with you, my l? 123
10:19 my l, since you have given me strength." 123
12: 8 So I asked, "My l, what will the outcome 123
Hos 12:14 his L will leave upon him the guilt 151
Am 3:13 declares the L, the LORD God Almighty. 151
5:16 Therefore this is what the L, 151
7: 7 The L was standing by a wall 151
7: 8 Then the L said, "Look, I am setting 151
9: 1 I saw the L standing by the altar, 151
9: 5 The L, the LORD Almighty, 151
Mic 1: 2 the L from his holy temple. 151
4:13 their wealth to the L *of* all the earth. 123
Zec 1: 9 I asked, "What are these, my l?" 123
4: 4 "What are these, my l?" 123
4: 5 "No, my l," I replied. 123
4:13 "No, my l," I said. 123
4:14 the two who are anointed to serve the L 123
6: 4 "What are these, my l?" 123
6: 5 the presence of the L *of* the whole world. 123
9: 4 But the L will take away her possessions 151
Mal 1:14 sacrifices a blemished animal to the L. 151
3: 1 the L you are seeking will come 123
Mt 1:20 an angel of the L appeared to him in a dream *3261*
1:22 to fulfill what the L had said through *3261*
1:24 the angel *of* the L had commanded him *3261*
2:13 *of* the L appeared to Joseph in a dream. *3261*
2:15 And so was fulfilled what the L had said *3261*
2:19 an angel *of* the L appeared in a dream to Joseph *3261*
3: 3 'Prepare the way *for* the L, *3261*
4: 7 'Do not put the L your God to the test.' " *3261*
4:10 For it is written: 'Worship the L your God, *3261*
5:33 keep the oaths you have made *to* the L.' *3261*
7:21 "Not everyone who says to me, 'L, Lord,' *3261*
7:21 "Not everyone who says to me, 'Lord, L,' *3261*
7:22 Many will say to me on that day, 'L, Lord, *3261*
7:22 Many will say to me on that day, 'Lord, L, *3261*
8: 2 "L, if you are willing, you can make me *3261*
8: 6 "L," he said, "my servant lies at home *3261*
8: 8 The centurion replied, "L, I do not deserve *3261*
8:21 Another disciple said to him, "L, *3261*
8:25 and woke him, saying, "L, save us! *3261*
9:28 "Yes, L," they replied. *3261*
9:38 Ask the L of the harvest, therefore, *3261*
11:25 Father, L of heaven and earth, *3261*
12: 8 For the Son of Man is L of the Sabbath." *3261*
14:28 "L, if it's you," Peter replied, *3261*
14:30 beginning to sink, cried out, "L, save me!" *3261*
15:22 "L, Son of David, have mercy on me! *3261*
15:25 "L, help me!" she said. *3261*
15:27 L," she said, "but even the dogs eat *3261*
16:22 began to rebuke him. "Never, L!" *3261*
17: 4 Peter said to Jesus, "L, it is good for us *3261*
17:15 "L, have mercy on my son," he said. *3261*
18:21 Then Peter came to Jesus and asked, "L, *3261*
20:25 the rulers of the Gentiles l it over them, *2894*
20:30 "L, Son of David, have mercy on us!" *3261*
20:31 "L, Son of David, have mercy on us!" *3261*
20:33 "L," they answered, "we want our sight." *3261*
21: 3 tell him that the L needs them, *3261*
21: 9 he who comes in the name *of* the L!" *3261*
21:42 the L has done this, and it is marvelous *3261*
22:37 " 'Love the L your God with all your heart *3261*
22:43 speaking by the Spirit, calls him 'L'? *3261*
22:44 " 'The L said to my Lord: *3261*
22:44 " 'The Lord said *to* my L: *3261*
22:45 If then David calls him 'L,' *3261*
23:39 he who comes in the name *of* the L.' " *3261*
24:42 not know on what day your L will come. *3261*
25:37 "Then the righteous will answer him, 'L, *3261*
25:44 "They also will answer, 'L, *3261*
26:22 after the other, "Surely not I, L?" *3261*
27:10 potter's field, as the L commanded me." *3261*
28: 2 an angel *of* the L came down from heaven *3261*
Mk 1: 3 'Prepare the way *for* the L, *3261*
2:28 the Son of Man is L even of the Sabbath." *3261*
5:19 and tell them how much the L has done *3261*
7:28 L," she replied, "but even the dogs under *3261*
10:42 as rulers of the Gentiles l it over them, *2894*
11: 3 'The L needs it and will send it back here *3261*
11: 9 he who comes in the name *of* the L!" *3261*
12:11 the L has done this, and it is marvelous *3261*
12:29 'Hear, O Israel, the L our God, *3261*
12:29 O Israel, the Lord our God, the L is one. *3261*
12:30 Love the L your God with all your heart *3261*
12:36 " 'The L said to my Lord: *3261*
12:36 " 'The Lord said *to* my L: *3261*
12:37 David himself calls him 'L.' *3261*
13:20 If the L had not cut short those days, *3261*
16:19 After the L Jesus had spoken to them, *3261*
16:20 and the L worked with them *3261*
Lk 1: 9 into the temple *of* the L and burn incense. *3261*
1:11 Then an angel *of* the L appeared to him, *3261*
1:15 for he will be great in the sight of the L. *3261*
1:16 will he bring back to the L their God. *3261*
1:17 And he will go on before the L, *899S*
1:17 to make ready a people prepared *for* the L." *3261*
1:25 "The L has done this for me," she said. *3261*
1:28 The L is with you." *3261*
1:32 The L God will give him the throne *3261*
1:43 the mother *of* my L should come to me? *3261*
1:45 that what the L has said to her will *3261*
1:46 And Mary said: "My soul glorifies the L *3261*
1:58 that the L had shown her great mercy, *3261*
1:68 "Praise be to the L, the God of Israel *3261*
1:76 on before the L to prepare the way for him, *3261*
2: 9 An angel *of* the L appeared to them, *3261*
2: 9 and the glory *of* the L shone around them, *3261*
2:11 has been born to you; he is Christ the L. *3261*
2:15 which the L has told us about." *3261*
2:22 to Jerusalem to present him *to* the L *3261*
2:23 (as it is written in the Law *of* the L, *3261*
2:23 to be consecrated *to* the L"), *3261*
2:24 with what is said in the Law *of* the L: *3261*
2:29 "Sovereign L, as you have promised, you *1305*
2:39 required by the Law *of* the L, *3261*
3: 4 'Prepare the way for the L, *3261*
4: 8 Worship the L your God and serve him only *3261*
4:12 'Do not put the L your God to the test.' " *3261*
4:18 "The Spirit *of* the L is on me, *3261*
5: 8 "Go away from me, L; *3261*
5:12 "L, if you are willing, you can make me *3261*
5:17 the L was present for him to heal the sick. *3261*
6: 5 "The Son of Man is L of the Sabbath." *3261*
6:46 "Why do you call me, 'L, Lord,' *3261*
6:46 "Why do you call me, 'Lord, L,' *3261*
7: 6 "L, don't trouble yourself, *3261*
7:13 When the L saw her, his heart went out to *3261*
7:19 he sent them to the L to ask, *3261*
9:54 "L, do you want us to call fire down *3261*
9:59 But the man replied, "L, first let me go and *3261*
9:61 Still another said, "I will follow you, L; *3261*
10: 1 the L appointed seventy-two others *3261*
10: 2 Ask the L of the harvest, therefore, *3261*
10:17 and said, "L, even the demons submit *3261*
10:21 Father, L of heaven and earth, *3261*
10:27 " 'Love the L your God with all your heart *3261*
10:40 She came to him and asked, "L, *3261*
10:41 "Martha, Martha," the L answered, *3261*
11: 1 one of his disciples said to him, "L, *3261*
11:39 Then the L said to him, "Now then, *3261*
12:41 "L, are you telling this parable to us, *3261*
12:42 The L answered, "Who then is the faithful *3261*
13:15 The L answered him, "You hypocrites! *3261*
13:23 Someone asked him, "L, are only a few *3261*
13:35 he who comes in the name *of* the L.' " *3261*
17: 5 The apostles said *to* the L, "Increase our faith!" *3261*
17:37 "Where, L?" they asked. *3261*
18: 6 And the L said, "Listen to what *3261*
18:41 "L, I want to see," he replied. *3261*
19: 8 But Zacchaeus stood up and said to the L, *3261*
19: 8 up and said to the Lord, "Look, L! *3261*
19:31 tell him, 'The L needs it.' " *3261*
19:34 They replied, "The L needs it." *3261*
19:38 the king who comes in the name *of* the L!" *3261*
20:37 for he calls the L 'the God of Abraham, *3261*
20:42 " 'The L said to my Lord: *3261*
20:42 " 'The Lord said *to* my L: *3261*
20:44 David calls him 'L.' *3261*
22:25 "The kings of the Gentiles l it over them; *3259*
22:33 "L, I am ready to go with you to prison *3261*
22:38 The disciples said, "See, L, *3261*
22:49 "L, should we strike with our swords?" *3261*
22:61 The L turned and looked straight at Peter. *3261*
22:61 the word the L had spoken to him: *3261*
24: 3 they did not find the body *of* the L Jesus. *3261*
24:34 L has risen and has appeared to Simon." *3261*
Jn 1:23 'Make straight the way *for* the L.' " *3261*
4: 3 When the L learned of this, *3261*
6:23 the bread after the L had given thanks. *3261*
6:68 Simon Peter answered him, "L, *3261*
9:38 Then the man said, "L, I believe," *3261*
11: 2 on the L and wiped his feet with her hair. *3261*
11: 3 So the sisters sent word to Jesus, "L, *3261*
11:12 His disciples replied, "L, if he sleeps, *3261*
11:21 "L," Martha said to Jesus, *3261*
11:27 "Yes, L," she told him, *3261*
11:32 she fell at his feet and said, "L, *3261*
11:34 "Come and see, L," they replied. *3261*
11:39 "But, L," said Martha, *3261*

***LORD** distinguishes the words translated "Lord" and "lord" from the proper name of God, *Yahweh*, indicated in the NIV by "LORD" and indexed under the heading †**LORD**, pages 686-707.

Jn	12:13	he who comes in the name *of* the **L!"**	*3261*
	12:38	**"L,** who has believed our message and	*3261*
	12:38	has the arm *of* the **L** been revealed?"	*3261*
	13: 6	**"L,** are you going to wash my feet?"	*3261*
	13: 9	"Then, **L,"** Simon Peter replied,	*3261*
	13:13	"You call me 'Teacher' and **'L,'**	*3261*
	13:14	Now that I, your **L** and Teacher,	*3261*
	13:25	he asked him, **"L,** who is it?"	*3261*
	13:36	Simon Peter asked him, **"L,**	*3261*
	13:37	**"L,** why can't I follow you now?	*3261*
	14: 5	Thomas said to him, **"L,**	*3261*
	14: 8	**"L,** show us the Father and that will	*3261*
	14:22	Judas (not Judas Iscariot) said, "But, **L,**	*3261*
	20: 2	"They have taken the **L** out of the tomb,	*3261*
	20:13	"They have taken my **L** away," she said,	*3261*
	20:18	"I have seen the **L!"**	*3261*
	20:20	when they saw the **L.**	*3261*
	20:25	"We have seen the **L!"**	*3261*
	20:28	Thomas said to him, "My **L** and my God!"	*3261*
	21: 7	"It is the **L!"**	*3261*
	21: 7	"It is the **L,"**	*3261*
	21:12	They knew it was the **L.**	*3261*
	21:15	**L,"** he said, "you know that I love you."	*3261*
	21:16	He answered, "Yes, **L,**	*3261*
	21:17	He said, **"L,** you know all things;	*3261*
	21:20	**"L,** who is going to betray you?")	*3261*
	21:21	When Peter saw him, he asked, **"L,**	*3261*
Ac	1: 6	**"L,** are you at this time going to restore	*3261*
	1:21	the whole time the **L** Jesus went in and out	*3261*
	1:24	Then they prayed, **"L,** you know	*3261*
	2:20	of the great and glorious day *of* the **L.**	*3261*
	2:21	on the name *of* the **L** will be saved.'	*3261*
	2:25	" 'I saw the **L** always before me.	*3261*
	2:34	and yet he said, " 'The **L** said to my Lord:	*3261*
	2:34	and yet he said, " 'The Lord said *to* my **L:**	*3261*
	2:36	whom you crucified, both **L** and Christ."	*3261*
	2:39	for all whom the **L** our God will call."	*3261*
	2:47	And the **L** added to their number daily	*3261*
	3:19	times of refreshing may come from the **L,**	*3261*
	3:22	'The **L** your God will raise up for you	*3261*
	4:24	**"Sovereign L,"** they said, "you made the	*1305*
	4:26	the rulers gather together against the **L** and	*3261*
	4:29	Now, **L,** consider their threats	*3261*
	4:33	to testify to the resurrection *of* the **L** Jesus,	*3261*
	5: 9	to test the Spirit *of* the **L?**	*3261*
	5:14	*in* the **L** and were added to their number.	*3261*
	5:19	during the night an angel *of* the **L** opened	*3261*
	7:33	the **L** said to him, 'Take off your sandals;	*3261*
	7:49	house will you build for me? says the **L.**	*3261*
	7:59	**"L** Jesus, receive my spirit."	*3261*
	7:60	he fell on his knees and cried out, **"L,**	*3261*
	8:16	into the name *of* the **L** Jesus.	*3261*
	8:22	of this wickedness and pray *to* the **L.**	*3261*
	8:24	"Pray to the **L** for me so	*3261*
	8:25	and proclaimed the word *of* the **L,**	*3261*
	8:26	Now an angel *of* the **L** said to Philip,	*3261*
	8:39	Spirit *of* the **L** suddenly took Philip away,	*3261*
	9: 5	"Who are you, **L?"**	*3261*
	9:10	The **L** called to him in a vision,	*3261*
	9:10	"Yes, **L,"** he answered.	*3261*
	9:11	The **L** told him, "Go to the house of Judas	*3261*
	9:13	**"L,"** Ananias answered,	*3261*
	9:15	But the **L** said to Ananias, "Go!	*3261*
	9:17	he said, "Brother Saul, the **L—**	*3261*
	9:27	the **L** and that the Lord had spoken to him,	*3261*
	9:27	the Lord and that the **L** had spoken to him,	*NIG*
	9:28	speaking boldly in the name *of* the **L.**	*3261*
	9:31	living in the fear *of* the **L.**	*3261*
	9:35	and Sharon saw him and turned to the **L.**	*3261*
	9:42	and many people believed in the **L.**	*3261*
	10: 4	"What is it, **L?"** he asked.	*3261*
	10:14	"Surely not, **L!"** Peter replied.	*3261*
	10:33	to everything the **L** has commanded you	*3261*
	10:36	Jesus Christ, who is **L** of all.	*3261*
	11: 8	"I replied, 'Surely not, **L!**	*3261*
	11:16	Then I remembered what the **L** had said:	*3261*
	11:17	who believed in the **L** Jesus Christ,	*3261*
	11:20	the good news about the **L** Jesus.	*3261*
	11:21	of people believed and turned to the **L.**	*3261*
	11:23	remain true *to* the **L** with all their hearts.	*3261*
	11:24	of people were brought *to* the **L.**	*3261*
	12: 7	Suddenly an angel *of* the **L** appeared and	*3261*
	12:11	without a doubt that the **L** sent his angel	*3261*
	12:17	how the **L** had brought him out of prison.	*3261*
	12:23	an angel *of* the **L** struck him down,	*3261*
	13: 2	While they were worshiping the **L**	*3261*
	13:10	perverting the right ways *of* the **L?**	*3261*
	13:11	Now the hand *of* the **L** is against you.	*3261*
	13:12	at the teaching *about* the **L.**	*3261*
	13:44	to hear the word *of* the **L.**	*3261*
	13:47	For this is what the **L** has commanded us:	*3261*
	13:48	and honored the word *of* the **L;**	*3261*
	13:49	*of* the **L** spread through the whole region.	*3261*
	14: 3	speaking boldly for the **L,**	*3261*
	14:23	committed them *to* the **L,**	*3261*
	15:11	the grace *of* our **L** Jesus that we are saved,	*3261*
	15:17	that the remnant of men may seek the **L,**	*3261*
	15:17	Gentiles who bear my name, says the **L,**	*3261*
	15:26	for the name *of* our **L** Jesus Christ.	*3261*
	15:35	and preached the word *of* the **L.**	*3261*
	15:36	*of* the **L** and see how they are doing."	*3261*
	15:40	by the brothers to the grace *of* the **L.**	*3261*
	16:14	The **L** opened her heart to respond	*3261*
	16:15	"If you consider me a believer *in* the **L,"**	*3261*
	16:31	They replied, "Believe in the **L** Jesus,	*3261*
	16:32	Then they spoke the word *of* the **L** to him	*3261*
	17:24	the **L** of heaven and earth and does not live	*3261*
Ac	18: 8	his entire household believed *in* the **L;**	*3261*
	18: 9	One night the **L** spoke to Paul in a vision:	*3261*
	18:25	He had been instructed in the way *of* the **L,**	*3261*
	19: 5	baptized into the name *of* the **L** Jesus.	*3261*
	19:10	of Asia heard the word *of* the **L.**	*3261*
	19:13	to invoke the name *of* the **L** Jesus	*3261*
	19:17	name *of* the **L** Jesus was held in high honor.	*3261*
	19:20	*of* the **L** spread widely and grew in power.	*3261*
	20:19	the **L** with great humility and with tears,	*3261*
	20:21	and have faith in our **L** Jesus.	*3261*
	20:24	the task the **L** Jesus has given me—	*3261*
	20:35	the words the **L** Jesus himself said:	*3261*
	21:13	in Jerusalem for the name *of* the **L** Jesus."	*3261*
	22: 8	" 'Who are you, **L?'**	*3261*
	22:10	" 'What shall I do, **L?'**	*3261*
	22:10	" 'Get up,' the **L** said,	*3261*
	22:18	and saw **the L** speaking.	*899S*
	22:19	" **'L,'** I replied, 'these men know	*3261*
	22:21	"Then the **L** said to me, 'Go;	*NIG*
	23:11	The following night the **L** stood near Paul	*3261*
	26:15	"Then I asked, 'Who are you, **L?'**	*3261*
	26:15	whom you are persecuting,' the **L** replied.	*3261*
	28:31	and taught about the **L** Jesus Christ.	*3261*
Ro	1: 4	Jesus Christ our **L.**	*3261*
	1: 7	and from the **L** Jesus Christ.	*3261*
	4: 8	the man whose sin the **L** will never count	*3261*
	4:24	in him who raised Jesus our **L** from	*3261*
	5: 1	with God through our **L** Jesus Christ,	*3261*
	5:11	in God through our **L** Jesus Christ,	*3261*
	5:21	eternal life through Jesus Christ our **L.**	*3261*
	6:23	of God is eternal life in Christ Jesus our **L.**	*3261*
	7:25	through Jesus Christ our **L!**	*3261*
	8:39	love of God that is in Christ Jesus our **L.**	*3261*
	9:28	the **L** will carry out his sentence on earth	*3261*
	9:29	the **L** Almighty had left us descendants,	*3261*
	10: 9	with your mouth, "Jesus is **L,"** and believe	*3261*
	10:12	the same **L** is Lord of all	*3261*
	10:12	the same Lord is **L** of all	*NIG*
	10:13	calls on the name *of* the **L** will be saved."	*3261*
	10:16	**"L,** who has believed our message?"	*3261*
	11: 3	**"L,** they have killed your prophets	*3261*
	11:34	"Who has known the mind *of* the **L?**	*3261*
	12:11	but keep your spiritual fervor, serving the **L.**	*3261*
	12:19	I will repay," says the **L.**	*3261*
	13:14	clothe yourselves with the **L** Jesus Christ,	*3261*
	14: 4	for the **L** is able to make him stand.	*3261*
	14: 6	does so *to* the **L.**	*3261*
	14: 6	He who eats meat, eats *to* the **L,**	*3261*
	14: 6	does so *to* the **L** and gives thanks to God.	*3261*
	14: 8	If we live, we live *to* the **L;**	*3261*
	14: 8	and if we die, we die *to* the **L.**	*3261*
	14: 8	live or die, *we* **belong to** the **L.**	*1639+3261*
	14: 9	returned to life so that *he might be* the **L**	*3259*
	14:11	" 'As surely as I live,' says the **L,**	*3261*
	14:14	As one who is in the **L** Jesus,	*3261*
	15: 6	the God and Father *of* our **L** Jesus Christ.	*3261*
	15:11	And again, "Praise the **L,** all you Gentiles,	*3261*
	15:30	by our **L** Jesus Christ and by the love of	*3261*
	16: 2	in the **L** in a way worthy of the saints and	*3261*
	16: 8	Greet Ampliatus, whom I love in the **L.**	*3261*
	16:11	of Narcissus who are in the **L.**	*3261*
	16:12	those women who work hard in the **L.**	*3261*
	16:12	woman who has worked very hard in the **L.**	*3261*
	16:13	Greet Rufus, chosen in the **L,**	*3261*
	16:18	such people are not serving our **L** Christ,	*3261*
	16:20	The grace *of* our **L** Jesus be with you.	*3261*
	16:22	greet you in the **L.**	*3261*
1Co	1: 2	call on the name *of* our **L** Jesus Christ—	*3261*
	1: 2	their **L** and ours:	*NIG*
	1: 3	and the **L** Jesus Christ.	*3261*
	1: 7	as you eagerly wait for our **L** Jesus Christ	*3261*
	1: 8	on the day *of* our **L** Jesus Christ.	*3261*
	1: 9	with his Son Jesus Christ our **L,**	*3261*
	1:10	in the name *of* our **L** Jesus Christ,	*3261*
	1:31	"Let him who boasts boast in the **L."**	*3261*
	2: 8	they would not have crucified the **L**	*3261*
	2:16	"For who has known the mind *of* the **L**	*3261*
	3: 5	as the **L** has assigned to each his task.	*3261*
	3:20	"The **L** knows that the thoughts of the wise	*3261*
	4: 4	It is the **L** who judges me.	*3261*
	4: 5	wait till the **L** comes.	*3261*
	4:17	whom I love, who is faithful in the **L.**	*3261*
	4:19	come to you very soon, if the **L** is willing,	*3261*
	5: 4	the name *of* our **L** Jesus and I am with you	*3261*
	5: 4	and the power *of* our **L** Jesus is present,	*3261*
	5: 5	and his spirit saved on the day *of* the **L.**	*3261*
	6:11	in the name *of* the **L** Jesus Christ and by	*3261*
	6:13	but *for* the **L,** and the Lord for the body.	*3261*
	6:13	but for the Lord, and the **L** for the body.	*3261*
	6:14	By his power God raised the **L** from	*3261*
	6:17	*with* the **L** is one with him in spirit.	*3261*
	7:10	I give this command (not I, but the **L**):	*3261*
	7:12	To the rest I say this (I, not the **L**):	*3261*
	7:17	the place in life that the **L** assigned to him	*3261*
	7:22	a slave when he was called by the **L** is	*3261*
	7:25	I have no command *from* the **L,**	*3261*
	7:32	how he can please the **L.**	*3261*
	7:34	Her aim is to be devoted to the **L** in	*NIG*
	7:35	in undivided devotion *to* the **L.**	*3261*
	7:39	but he must belong to the **L.**	*3261*
	8: 6	and there is but one **L,** Jesus Christ,	*3261*
	9: 1	Have I not seen Jesus our **L?**	*3261*
	9: 1	not the result of my work in the **L?**	*3261*
	9: 2	you are the seal of my apostleship in the **L.**	*3261*
	9:14	the **L** has commanded that those who preach	*3261*
	10: 9	We should not test the **L,**	*3261*
	10:21	You cannot drink the cup *of* the **L** and	*3261*
1Co	11:11	the **L,** however, woman is not independent	*3261*
	11:23	from the **L** what I also passed on to you:	*3261*
	11:23	The **L** Jesus, on the night he was betrayed,	*3261*
	11:27	the **L** in an unworthy manner will be guilty	*3261*
	11:27	against the body and blood *of* the **L.**	*3261*
	11:29	without recognizing the body *of* the **L** eats	*3261*
	11:32	When we are judged by the **L,**	*3261*
	12: 3	"Jesus is **L,"** except by the Holy Spirit.	*3261*
	12: 5	different kinds of service, but the same **L.**	*3261*
	14:21	then they will not listen to me," says the **L.**	*3261*
	15:31	as I glory over you in Christ Jesus our **L.**	*3261*
	15:57	the victory through our **L** Jesus Christ.	*3261*
	15:58	give yourselves fully to the work *of* the **L,**	*3261*
	15:58	that your labor in the **L** is not in vain.	*3261*
	16: 7	spend some time with you, if the **L** permits.	*3261*
	16:10	for he is carrying on the work *of* the **L,**	*3261*
	16:19	and Priscilla greet you warmly in the **L,**	*3261*
	16:22	If anyone does not love the **L—**	*3261*
	16:22	**Come,** O **L!**	*3448*
	16:23	The grace *of* the **L** Jesus be with you.	*3261*
2Co	1: 2	and the **L** Jesus Christ.	*3261*
	1: 3	the God and Father *of* our **L** Jesus Christ,	*3261*
	1:14	of you in the day *of* the **L** Jesus.	*3261*
	1:24	Not that *we* **l it over** your faith,	*3259*
	2:12	of Christ and found that the **L** had opened	*3261*
	3:16	But whenever anyone turns to the **L,**	*3261*
	3:17	Now the **L** is the Spirit,	*3261*
	3:17	and where the Spirit *of* the **L** is,	*3261*
	3:18	which comes from the **L,** who is the Spirit.	*3261*
	4: 5	not preach ourselves, but Jesus Christ as **L,**	*3261*
	4:14	the **L** Jesus from the dead will also raise us	*3261*
	5: 6	in the body we are away from the **L.**	*3261*
	5: 8	from the body and at home with the **L.**	*3261*
	5:11	then, we know what it is to fear the **L,**	*3261*
	6:17	from them and be separate, says the **L.**	*3261*
	6:18	says the **L** Almighty."	*3261*
	8: 5	but they gave themselves first *to* the **L** and	*3261*
	8: 9	you know the grace *of* our **L** Jesus Christ,	*3261*
	8:19	the **L** himself and to show our eagerness	*3261*
	8:21	not only in the eyes *of* the **L** but also in	*3261*
	10: 8	about the authority the **L** gave us	*3261*
	10:17	But, "Let him who boasts boast in the **L."**	*3261*
	10:18	but the one whom the **L** commends.	*3261*
	11:17	not talking as the **L** would,	*3261*
	11:31	The God and Father *of* the **L** Jesus,	*3261*
	12: 1	on to visions and revelations *from* the **L.**	*3261*
	12: 8	with the **L** to take it away from me.	*3261*
	13:10	the **L** gave me for building you up,	*3261*
	13:14	May the grace *of* the **L** Jesus Christ,	*3261*
Gal	1: 3	and the **L** Jesus Christ,	*3261*
	5:10	in the **L** that you will take no other view.	*3261*
	6:14	in the cross *of* our **L** Jesus Christ,	*3261*
	6:18	*of* our **L** Jesus Christ be with your spirit,	*3261*
Eph	1: 2	and the **L** Jesus Christ.	*3261*
	1: 3	the God and Father *of* our **L** Jesus Christ,	*3261*
	1:15	the **L** Jesus and your love for all the saints,	*3261*
	1:17	that the God *of* our **L** Jesus Christ,	*3261*
	2:21	and rises to become a holy temple in the **L.**	*3261*
	3:11	he accomplished in Christ Jesus our **L.**	*3261*
	4: 1	As a prisoner for the **L,** then,	*3261*
	4: 5	one **L,** one faith, one baptism;	*3261*
	4:17	So I tell you this, and insist on it in the **L,**	*3261*
	5: 8	but now you are light in the **L.**	*3261*
	5:10	and find out what pleases the **L.**	*3261*
	5:19	and make music in your heart *to* the **L,**	*3261*
	5:20	in the name *of* our **L** Jesus Christ.	*3261*
	5:22	submit to your husbands as *to* the **L.**	*3261*
	6: 1	Children, obey your parents in the **L,**	*3261*
	6: 4	up in the training and instruction *of* the **L.**	*3261*
	6: 7	as if you were serving the **L,** not men,	*3261*
	6: 8	that the **L** will reward everyone for	*3261*
	6:10	in the **L** and in his mighty power.	*3261*
	6:21	and faithful servant in the **L,**	*3261*
	6:23	the Father and the **L** Jesus Christ.	*3261*
	6:24	Grace to all who love our **L** Jesus Christ	*3261*
Php	1: 2	and the **L** Jesus Christ.	*3261*
	1:14	the brothers in the **L** have been encouraged	*3261*
	2:11	every tongue confess that Jesus Christ is **L,**	*3261*
	2:19	the **L** Jesus to send Timothy to you soon,	*3261*
	2:24	in the **L** that I myself will come soon.	*3261*
	2:29	Welcome him in the **L** with great joy,	*3261*
	3: 1	Finally, my brothers, rejoice in the **L!**	*3261*
	3: 8	greatness of knowing Christ Jesus my **L,**	*3261*
	3:20	a Savior from there, the **L** Jesus Christ,	*3261*
	4: 1	that is how you should stand firm in the **L,**	*3261*
	4: 2	to agree with each other in the **L.**	*3261*
	4: 4	Rejoice in the **L** always.	*3261*
	4: 5	The **L** is near.	*3261*
	4:10	I rejoice greatly in the **L** that	*3261*
	4:23	*of* the **L** Jesus Christ be with your spirit.	*3261*
Col	1: 3	the Father *of* our **L** Jesus Christ,	*3261*
	1:10	*of* the **L** and may please him in every way:	*3261*
	2: 6	just as you received Christ Jesus as **L,**	*3261*
	3:13	Forgive as the **L** forgave you.	*3261*
	3:17	do it all in the name *of* the **L** Jesus,	*3261*
	3:18	as is fitting in the **L.**	*3261*
	3:20	for this pleases the **L.**	*3261*
	3:22	of heart and reverence for the **L.**	*3261*
	3:23	as working *for* the **L,** not for men,	*3261*
	3:24	an inheritance from the **L** as a reward.	*3261*
	3:24	It is the **L** Christ you are serving.	*3261*
	4: 7	and fellow servant in the **L.**	*3261*
	4:17	the work you have received in the **L."**	*3261*
1Th	1: 1	in God the Father and the **L** Jesus Christ:	*3261*
	1: 3	by hope *in* our **L** Jesus Christ.	*3261*
	1: 6	You became imitators of us and *of* the **L;**	*3261*
	2:15	who killed the **L** Jesus and the prophets	*3261*

***LORD** distinguishes the words translated "Lord" and "lord" from the proper name of God, *Yahweh*, indicated in the NIV by "LORD" and indexed under the heading **†LORD**, pages 686-707.

1Th 2:19 *of* our L Jesus when he comes? 3261
3: 8 since you are standing firm in the L. 3261
3:11 and Father himself and our L Jesus clear 3261
3:12 May the L make your love increase 3261
3:13 and Father when our L Jesus comes 3261
4: 1 and urge you in the L Jesus to do this more 3261
4: 2 by the authority of the L Jesus. 3261
4: 6 The L will punish men for all such sins, 3261
4:15 who are left till the coming *of* the L, 3261
4:16 L himself will come down from heaven, 3261
4:17 with them in the clouds to meet the L in 3261
4:17 And so we will be with the L forever. 3261
5: 2 *of* the L will come like a thief in the night. 3261
5: 9 through our L Jesus Christ. 3261
5:12 over you in the L and who admonish you. 3261
5:23 at the coming *of* our L Jesus Christ. 3261
5:27 before the L to have this letter read to all 3261
5:28 grace *of* our L Jesus Christ be with you. 3261
2Th 1: 1 in God our Father and the L Jesus Christ: 3261
1: 2 the Father and the L Jesus Christ. 3261
1: 7 when the L Jesus is revealed from heaven 3261
1: 8 and do not obey the gospel *of* our L Jesus. 3261
1: 9 the L and from the majesty of his power 3261
1:12 the name *of* our L Jesus may be glorified 3261
1:12 of our God and the L Jesus Christ. 3261
2: 1 the coming *of* our L Jesus Christ 3261
2: 2 that the day *of* the L has already come. 3261
2: 8 the L Jesus will overthrow with the breath 3261
2:13 brothers loved by the L, 3261
2:14 in the glory *of* our L Jesus Christ. 3261
2:16 May our L Jesus Christ himself 3261
3: 1 the L may spread rapidly and be honored, 3261
3: 3 But the L is faithful, 3261
3: 4 the L that you are doing and will continue 3261
3: 5 the L direct your hearts into God's love 3261
3: 6 In the name *of* the L Jesus Christ, 3261
3:12 the L Jesus Christ to settle down and earn 3261
3:16 the L of peace himself give you peace 3261
3:16 The L be with all of you. 3261
3:18 *of* our L Jesus Christ be with you all. 3261
1Ti 1: 2 the Father and Christ Jesus our L. 3261
1:12 I thank Christ Jesus our L, 3261
1:14 The grace *of* our L was poured out 3261
6: 3 the sound instruction *of* our L Jesus Christ 3261
6:14 until the appearing *of* our L Jesus Christ, 3261
6:15 the King of kings and L of lords, 3261
2Ti 1: 2 the Father and Christ Jesus our L. 3261
1: 8 do not be ashamed to testify *about* our L, 3261
1:16 May the L show mercy to the household 3261
1:18 the L grant that he will find mercy from 3261
1:18 that he will find mercy from the L on 3261
2: 7 for the L will give you insight into all this. 3261
2:19 "The L knows those who are his," and, 3261
2:19 the L must turn away from wickedness." 3261
2:22 along with those who call on the L out of 3261
3:11 Yet the L rescued me from all of them. 3261
4: 8 which the L, the righteous Judge, 3261
4:14 L will repay him for what he has done. 3261
4:17 L stood at my side and gave me strength, 3261
4:18 The L will rescue me from every evil attack 3261
4:22 The L be with your spirit. 3261
Phm 1: 3 and the L Jesus Christ. 3261
1: 5 the L Jesus and your love for all the saints. 3261
1:16 both as a man and as a brother in the L. 3261
1:20 some benefit from you in the L; 3261
1:25 *of* the L Jesus Christ be with your spirit. 3261
Heb 1:10 He also says, "In the beginning, *O* L, 3261
2: 3 which was first announced by the L, 3261
7:14 For it is clear that our L descended 3261
7:21 L has sworn and will not change his mind: 3261
8: 2 the true tabernacle set up by the L, 3261
8: 8 "The time is coming, declares the L, 3261
8: 9 turned away from them, declares the L. 3261
8:10 of Israel after that time, declares the L. 3261
8:11 saying, 'Know the L,' 3261
10:16 with them after that time, says the L. 3261
10:30 and again, "The L will judge his people." 3261
12: 6 because the L disciplines those he loves, 3261
12:14 without holiness no one will see the L. 3261
13: 6 "The L is my helper; I will not be afraid. 3261
13:20 brought back from the dead our L Jesus, 3261
Jas 1: 1 a servant of God and *of* the L Jesus Christ, 3261
1: 7 That man should not think he will receive
anything from the L; 3261
2: 1 as believers *in* our glorious L Jesus Christ, 3261
3: 9 the tongue we praise our L and Father, 3261
4:10 Humble yourselves before the L, 3261
5: 4 have reached the ears *of* the L Almighty. 3261
5:10 prophets who spoke in the name *of* the L. 3261
5:11 have seen what the L finally brought about. 3261
5:11 The L is full of compassion and mercy. 3261
5:14 anoint him with oil in the name *of* the L. 3261
5:15 the L will raise him up. 3261
1Pe 1: 3 the God and Father *of* our L Jesus Christ! 3261
1:25 but the word *of* the L stands forever." 3261
2: 3 that you have tasted that the L is good. 3261
3:12 For the eyes *of* the L are on the righteous 3261
3:12 *of* the L is against those who do evil." 3261
3:15 But in your hearts set apart Christ *as* L. 3261
2Pe 1: 2 the knowledge of God and *of* Jesus our L. 3261
1: 8 in your knowledge *of* our L Jesus Christ. 3261
1:11 into the eternal kingdom of our L 3261
1:14 our L Jesus Christ has made clear to me. 3261
1:16 power and coming *of* our L Jesus Christ, 3261
2: 1 denying the **sovereign** L who bought them 1305
2: 9 then the L knows how to rescue godly men 3261
2:11 against such beings in the presence *of* the L. 3261
2:20 by knowing our L and Savior Jesus Christ 3261
3: 2 *by* our L and Savior through your apostles. 3261
3: 8 With the L a day is like a thousand years, 3261
3: 9 The L is not slow in keeping his promise, 3261
3:10 But the day *of* the L will come like a thief. 3261
3:18 in the grace and knowledge *of* our L 3261
Jude 1: 4 deny Jesus Christ our only Sovereign and L. 3261
1: 5 the L delivered his people out of Egypt, 3261
1: 9 but said, "The L rebuke you!" 3261
1:14 "See, the L is coming with thousands 3261
1:17 the apostles *of* our L Jesus Christ foretold. 3261
1:21 for the mercy *of* our L Jesus Christ 3261
1:25 through Jesus Christ our L, 3261
Rev 1: 8 says the L God, "who is, and who was, 3261
4: 8 "Holy, holy, holy is the L God Almighty, 3261
4:11 "You are worthy, our L and God, 3261
6:10 "How long, **Sovereign** L, holy and true, 1305
11: 4 the two lampstands that stand before the L 3261
11: 8 where also their L was crucified. 3261
11:15 the kingdom *of* our L and of his Christ, 3261
11:17 "We give thanks to you, L God Almighty, 3261
14:13 Blessed are the dead who die in the L from 3261
15: 3 marvelous are your deeds, L God Almighty. 3261
15: 4 Who will not fear *you, O* L, 3261
16: 7 "Yes, L God Almighty, 3261
17:14 because he is L of lords and King 3261
18: 8 for mighty is the L God who judges her. 3261
19: 6 For our L God Almighty reigns. 3261
19:16 KING OF KINGS AND L OF LORDS. 3261
21:22 because the L God Almighty and 3261
22: 5 for *the* L God will give them light. 3261
22: 6 The L, the God of the spirits of 3261
22:20 Come, L Jesus. 3261
22:21 grace *of* the L Jesus be with God's people. 3261

*LORD'S (43) [*LORD]

Ge 44: 9 the rest of us will become my l slaves." 123+4200
44:16 We are now my l slaves— 123+4200
44:33 as my l slave in place of the boy, 123+4200
Nu 14:17 "Now may **the L** strength be displayed, 151
2Sa 11:11 and my l men are camped in the open fields. 123
1Ki 1:33 "Take your l servants with you 123
3:15 stood before the ark of **the L** covenant 151
1Ch 21: 3 are they not all my l subjects? 123+4200
Mal 1:12 you profane it by saying of **the L** table, 151
Lk 1: 6 observing all the L commandments 3261
1:38 "I am the L servant," Mary answered. 3261
1:66 For the L hand was with him. 3261
2:26 not die before he had seen the L Christ. 3261
4:19 to proclaim the year *of* the L favor." 3261
10:39 at the L feet listening to what he said. 3261
Ac 7:31 he heard the L voice: 3261
9: 1 murderous threats against the L disciples. 3261
11:21 The L hand was with them, 3261
21:14 "The L will be done." 3261
1Co 7:22 by the Lord is the L freedman; 3261
7:25 as one who by the L mercy is trustworthy. 3261
7:32 is concerned about the L affairs— 3261
7:34 or virgin is concerned about the L affairs: 3261
9: 5 as do the other apostles and the L brothers 3261
10:21 you cannot have a part in both the L table 3261
10:22 Are we trying to arouse the L jealousy? 3261
10:26 "The earth is the L, and everything in it." 3261
11:20 it is not the L Supper you eat, 3258
11:26 you proclaim the L death until he comes. 3261
14:37 what I am writing to you is the L command. 3261
2Co 3:18 with unveiled faces all reflect the L glory, 3261
Gal 1:19 only James, the L brother. 3261
Eph 5:17 but understand what the L will is. 3261
1Th 1: 8 The L message rang out from you not only 3261
4:15 According to the L own word, 3261
2Ti 2:24 And the L servant must not quarrel; 3261
Heb 12: 5 do not make light of the L discipline, 3261
Jas 4:15 you ought to say, "If it is the L will, 3261
5: 7 then, brothers, until the L coming. 3261
5: 8 because the L coming is near. 3261
1Pe 2:13 for the L sake to every authority instituted 3261
2Pe 3:15 that our L patience means salvation, 3261
Rev 1:10 On the L Day I was in the Spirit, 3258

†LORD (6551) [†LORD'S]

Ge 2: 4 When **the L** God made the earth and 3378
2: 5 for **the L** God had not sent rain on 3378
2: 7 **the L** God formed the man from the dust 3378
2: 8 Now **the L** God had planted a garden in 3378
2: 9 And **the L** God made all kinds 3378
2:15 **The L** God took the man and put him in 3378
2:16 And **the L** God commanded the man, 3378
2:18 **The L** God said, "It is not good for the man 3378
2:19 Now **the L** God had formed out of 3378
2:21 So **the L** God caused the man to fall into 3378
2:22 Then **the L** God made a woman from 3378
3: 1 of the wild animals **the L** God had made. 3378
3: 8 the sound of **the L** God as he was walking 3378
3: 8 and they hid from **the L** God among 3378
3: 9 But **the L** God called to the man, 3378
3:13 Then **the L** God said to the woman, 3378
3:14 So **the L** God said to the serpent, 3378
3:21 **The L** God made garments of skin 3378
3:22 And **the L** God said, "The man has now 3378
3:23 So **the L** God banished him from 3378
4: 1 the help of **the L** I have brought forth 3378
4: 3 of the soil as an offering to **the L**. 3378
4: 4 **The L** looked with favor on Abel 3378
4: 6 **the L** said to Cain, "Why are you angry? 3378
4: 9 Then **the L** said to Cain, "Where is 3378
4:10 The L said, "What have you done? NIH
4:13 Cain said to **the L**, "My punishment 3378
4:15 But **the L** said to him, "Not so; 3378
4:15 Then **the L** put a mark on Cain so 3378
4:26 to call on the name of **the L**. 3378
5:29 by the ground **the L** has cursed." 3378
6: 3 Then **the L** said, "My Spirit will not 3378
6: 5 **The L** saw how great man's wickedness 3378
6: 6 **The L** was grieved that he had made man 3378
6: 7 So **the L** said, "I will wipe mankind, 3378
6: 8 Noah found favor in the eyes of **the L**. 3378
7: 1 **The L** then said to Noah, "Go into the ark, 3378
7: 5 Noah did all that **the L** commanded him. 3378
7:16 Then **the L** shut him in. 3378
8:20 Then Noah built an altar to **the L** and, 3378
8:21 **The L** smelled the pleasing aroma 3378
9:26 He also said, "Blessed be **the L**, 3378
10: 9 He was a mighty hunter before **the L**; 3378
10: 9 a mighty hunter before **the L**." 3378
11: 5 But **the L** came down to see the city and 3378
11: 6 **The L** said, "If as one people speaking 3378
11: 8 So **the L** scattered them from there 3378
11: 9 because there **the L** confused the language 3378
11: 9 From there **the L** scattered them over 3378
12: 1 **The L** had said to Abram, "Leave your 3378
12: 4 So Abram left, as **the L** had told him; 3378
12: 7 **The L** appeared to Abram and said, 3378
12: 7 So he built an altar there to **the L**, 3378
12: 8 There he built an altar to **the L** and called 3378
12: 8 and called on the name of **the L**. 3378
12:17 But **the L** inflicted serious diseases 3378
13: 4 Abram called on the name of **the L**. 3378
13:10 like the garden of **the L**, 3378
13:10 (This was before **the L** destroyed Sodom 3378
13:13 and were sinning greatly against **the L**. 3378
13:14 **The L** said to Abram after Lot had parted 3378
13:18 where he built an altar to **the L**. 3378
14:22 "I have raised my hand to **the L**, 3378
15: 1 the word of **the L** came to Abram in 3378
15: 2 But Abram said, "O Sovereign **L**, 3378
15: 4 Then the word of **the L** came to him: 3378
15: 6 Abram believed **the L**, and he credited it 3378
15: 7 He also said to him, "I am **the L**, 3378
15: 8 But Abram said, "O Sovereign **L**, 3378
15: 9 So the L said to him, "Bring me a heifer, NIH
15:13 Then the L said to him, NIH
15:18 On that day **the L** made a covenant 3378
16: 2 "**The L** has kept me from having children. 3378
16: 5 May **the L** judge between you and me." 3378
16: 7 of **the L** found Hagar near a spring in 3378
16: 9 Then the angel of **the L** told her, 3378
16:11 The angel of **the L** also said to her: 3378
16:11 for **the L** has heard of your misery. 3378
16:13 She gave this name to **the L** who spoke 3378
17: 1 **the L** appeared to him and said, 3378
18: 1 **The L** appeared to Abraham near 3378
18:10 Then the L said, "I will surely return NIH
18:13 Then **the L** said to Abraham, 3378
18:14 Is anything too hard for **the L**? 3378
18:17 Then **the L** said, "Shall I hide from
Abraham what I am about to do? 3378
18:19 of **the L** by doing what is right and just, 3378
18:19 so that **the L** will bring about 3378
18:20 Then **the L** said, 3378
18:22 Abraham remained standing before **the L**. 3378
18:26 **The L** said, "If I find fifty righteous people 3378
18:33 When **the L** had finished speaking 3378
19:13 The outcry to **the L** against its people is 3378
19:14 **the L** is about to destroy the city!" 3378
19:16 for **the L** was merciful to them. 3378
19:24 Then **the L** rained down burning sulfur 3378
19:24 from **the L** out of the heavens. 3378
19:27 where he had stood before **the L**. 3378
20:18 for **the L** had closed up every womb 3378
21: 1 Now **the L** was gracious to Sarah 3378
21: 1 and **the L** did for Sarah what he had 3378
21:33 upon the name of **the L**, the Eternal God. 3378
22:11 But the angel of **the L** called out to him 3378
22:14 that place **The L** Will Provide. 3378
22:14 "On the mountain of **the L** it will 3378
22:15 of **the L** called to Abraham from heaven 3378
22:16 "I swear by myself, declares **the L**, 3378
24: 1 and **the L** had blessed him in every way. 3378
24: 3 I want you to swear by **the L**, 3378
24: 7 "**The L**, the God of heaven, 3378
24:12 Then he prayed, "O **L**, God of my master 3378
24:21 **the L** had made his journey successful. 3378
24:26 man bowed down and worshiped **the L**, 3378
24:27 "Praise be to **the L**, the God of my master 3378
24:27 **the L** has led me on the journey to 3378
24:31 "Come, you who are blessed by **the L**," 3378
24:35 **The L** has blessed my master abundantly, 3378
24:40 "He replied, '**The L**, before whom I 3378
24:42 I came to the spring today, I said, 'O **L**, 3378
24:44 let her be the one **the L** has chosen 3378
24:48 and I bowed down and worshiped **the L**. 3378
24:48 I praised **the L**, the God of my master 3378
24:50 "This is from **the L**; 3378
24:51 as **the L** has directed." 3378
24:52 down to the ground before **the L**. 3378
24:56 **the L** has granted success to my journey. 3378
25:21 Isaac prayed to **the L** on behalf 3378
25:21 **The L** answered his prayer, 3378
25:22 So she went to inquire of **the L**. 3378
25:23 **The L** said to her, "Two nations are in your 3378
26: 2 **The L** appeared to Isaac and said, 3378

***LORD'S** distinguishes the words translated "Lord's" and "lord's" from the proper name of God, *Yahweh's*, indicated in the NIV by "LORD's" and indexed under the heading **†LORD'S**, pp. 707-8.
†LORD distinguishes the proper name of God, *Yahweh*, indicated in the NIV by "LORD," from the words translated "Lord" and "lord," indexed under the heading ***LORD**, pages 683-86.

Ge 26:12 because **the L** blessed him. 3378
26:22 "Now **the L** has given us room 3378
26:24 That night **the L** appeared to him 3378
26:25 and called on the name of **the L.** 3378
26:28 "We saw clearly that **the L** was with you; 3378
26:29 And now you are blessed by **the L."** 3378
27: 7 in the presence of **the L** before I die.' 3378
27:20 **"The L** your God gave me success," 3378
27:27 the smell of a field that **the L** has blessed. 3378
28:13 There above it stood **the L,** and he said: 3378
28:13 "I am **the L,** the God of your father 3378
28:16 he thought, "Surely **the L** is in this place, 3378
28:21 then **the L** will be my God 3378
29:31 When **the L** saw that Leah was not loved, 3378
29:32 "It is because **the L** has seen my misery. 3378
29:33 "Because **the L** heard that I am not loved, 3378
29:35 "This time I will praise **the L."** 3378
30:24 "May **the L** add to me another son." 3378
30:27 by divination that **the L** has blessed me 3378
30:30 **the L** has blessed you wherever I have been. 3378
31: 3 Then **the L** said to Jacob, 3378
31:49 "May **the L** keep watch between you 3378
32: 9 God of my father Isaac, O **L,** 3378
38: 7 so **the L** put him to death. 3378
39: 2 **The L** was with Joseph and he prospered, 3378
39: 3 When his master saw that **the L** was with 3378
39: 3 with him and that **the L** gave him success 3378
39: 5 **the L** blessed the household of the Egyptian 3378
39: 5 of **the L** was on everything Potiphar had, 3378
39:21 **the L** was with him; 3378
39:23 because **the L** was with Joseph 3378
49:18 "I look for your deliverance, O **L.** 3378
Ex 3: 2 of **the L** appeared to him in flames of fire 3378
3: 4 **the L** saw that he had gone over to look, 3378
3: 7 **The L** said, "I have indeed seen 3378
3:15 **'The L,** the God of your fathers— 3378
3:16 **'The L,** the God of your fathers— 3378
3:18 **'The L,** the God of the Hebrews, 3378
3:18 to offer sacrifices to **the L** our God.' 3378
4: 1 **'The L** did not appear to you'?" 3378
4: 2 Then **the L** said to him, 3378
4: 3 The L said, "Throw it on the ground." NIH
4: 4 Then **the L** said to him, 3378
4: 5 said the L, "is so that they may believe NIH
4: 5 "is so that they may believe that **the L,** 3378
4: 6 Then **the L** said, "Put your hand inside 3378
4: 8 Then the L said, "If they do not believe NIH
4:10 Moses said to **the L,** "O Lord, 3378
4:11 **The L** said to him, "Who gave man his 3378
4:11 Is it not I, **the L?** 3378
4:19 Now **the L** had said to Moses in Midian, 3378
4:21 **The L** said to Moses, "When you return 3378
4:22 say to Pharaoh, 'This is what **the L** says: 3378
4:24 **the L** met [Moses] and was about 3378
4:26 So the L let him alone. NIH
4:27 **The L** said to Aaron, "Go into the desert 3378
4:28 Moses told Aaron everything **the L** had
sent him to say, 3378
4:30 Aaron told them everything **the L** had said 3378
4:31 that **the L** was concerned about them 3378
5: 1 "This is what **the L,** the God of Israel, 3378
5: 2 Pharaoh said, "Who is **the L,** 3378
5: 2 I do not know **the L** and I will not let 3378
5: 3 to offer sacrifices to **the L** our God, 3378
5:17 'Let us go and sacrifice to **the L.'** 3378
5:21 "May **the L** look upon you and judge 3378
5:22 Moses returned to **the L** and said, 3378
6: 1 Then **the L** said to Moses, 3378
6: 2 God also said to Moses, "I am **the L.** 3378
6: 3 but by my name **the L** I did not make 3378
6: 6 'I am **the L,** and I will bring you out 3378
6: 7 you will know that I am **the L** your God, 3378
6: 8 I am **the L.' "** 3378
6:10 Then **the L** said to Moses, 3378
6:12 But Moses said to **the L,** 3378
6:13 Now **the L** spoke to Moses and Aaron 3378
6:26 and Moses to whom **the L** said, 3378
6:28 when **the L** spoke to Moses in Egypt, 3378
6:29 "I am **the L.** Tell Pharaoh king of Egypt 3378
6:30 But Moses said to **the L,** 3378
7: 1 Then **the L** said to Moses, "See, 3378
7: 5 the Egyptians will know that I am **the L** 3378
7: 6 as **the L** commanded them. 3378
7: 8 **The L** said to Moses and Aaron, 3378
7:10 and did just as **the L** commanded. 3378
7:13 just as **the L** had said. 3378
7:14 Then **the L** said to Moses, 3378
7:16 Then say to him, **'The L,** 3378
7:17 This is what **the L** says: 3378
7:17 By this you will know that I am **the L:** 3378
7:19 **The L** said to Moses, "Tell Aaron, 3378
7:20 as **the L** had commanded. 3378
7:22 just as **the L** had said. 3378
7:25 Seven days passed after **the L** struck 3378
8: 1 Then **the L** said to Moses, 3378
8: 1 'This is what **the L** says: 3378
8: 5 Then **the L** said to Moses, "Tell Aaron, 3378
8: 8 to **the L** to take the frogs away from me 3378
8: 8 to offer sacrifices to **the L."** 3378
8:10 there is no one like **the L** our God. 3378
8:12 to **the L** about the frogs he had brought 3378
8:13 And **the L** did what Moses asked. 3378
8:15 just as **the L** had said. 3378
8:16 Then **the L** said to Moses, "Tell Aaron, 3378
8:19 just as **the L** had said. 3378
8:20 Then **the L** said to Moses, 3378
8:20 'This is what **the L** says: 3378
Ex 8:22 so that you will know that I, **the L,** 3378
8:24 And **the L** did this. 3378
8:26 The sacrifices we offer **the L** our God 3378
8:27 to offer sacrifices to **the L** our God, 3378
8:28 to offer sacrifices to **the L** your God in 3378
8:29 I will pray to **the L,** 3378
8:29 the people go to offer sacrifices to **the L."** 3378
8:30 Moses left Pharaoh and prayed to **the L,** 3378
8:31 and **the L** did what Moses asked: 3378
9: 1 Then **the L** said to Moses, 3378
9: 1 'This is what **the L,** the God of the Hebrews 3378
9: 3 hand of **the L** will bring a terrible plague 3378
9: 4 But **the L** will make a distinction between 3378
9: 5 **The L** set a time and said, 3378
9: 5 "Tomorrow **the L** will do this in 3378
9: 6 And the next day **the L** did it: 3378
9: 8 Then **the L** said to Moses and Aaron, 3378
9:12 But **the L** hardened Pharaoh's heart 3378
9:12 just as **the L** had said to Moses. 3378
9:13 Then **the L** said to Moses, 3378
9:13 'This is what **the L,** 3378
9:20 of **the L** hurried to bring their slaves 3378
9:21 of **the L** left their slaves and livestock in 3378
9:22 Then **the L** said to Moses, 3378
9:23 **the L** sent thunder and hail, 3378
9:23 So **the L** rained hail on the land of Egypt; 3378
9:27 **"The L** is in the right, 3378
9:28 Pray to **the L,** for we have had enough 3378
9:29 spread out my hands in prayer to **the L.** 3378
9:30 still do not fear **the L** God." 3378
9:33 He spread out his hands toward **the L;** 3378
9:35 just as **the L** had said through Moses. 3378
10: 1 Then **the L** said to Moses, 3378
10: 2 and that you may know that I am **the L."** 3378
10: 3 "This is what **the L,** 3378
10: 7 so that they may worship **the L** their God. 3378
10: 8 "Go, worship **the L** your God," he said. 3378
10: 9 to celebrate a festival to **the L."** 3378
10:10 Pharaoh said, **"The L** be with you— 3378
10:11 and worship **the L,** 3378
10:12 And **the L** said to Moses, 3378
10:13 and **the L** made an east wind blow across 3378
10:16 against **the L** your God and against you. 3378
10:17 and pray to **the L** your God 3378
10:18 then left Pharaoh and prayed to **the L.** 3378
10:19 And **the L** changed the wind to 3378
10:20 But **the L** hardened Pharaoh's heart, 3378
10:21 Then **the L** said to Moses, 3378
10:24 and said, "Go, worship **the L.** 3378
10:25 to present to **the L** our God. 3378
10:26 of them in worshiping **the L** our God, 3378
10:26 to use to worship **the L."** 3378
10:27 But **the L** hardened Pharaoh's heart, 3378
11: 1 Now **the L** had said to Moses, 3378
11: 3 (**The L** made the Egyptians favorably
disposed toward the people, 3378
11: 4 So Moses said, "This is what **the L** says: 3378
11: 7 Then you will know that **the L** makes 3378
11: 9 **The L** had said to Moses, 3378
11:10 but **the L** hardened Pharaoh's heart, 3378
12: 1 **The L** said to Moses and Aaron in Egypt, 3378
12:12 judgment on all the gods of Egypt. I am **the**
L. 3378
12:14 celebrate it as a festival to **the L—** 3378
12:23 When **the L** goes through the land 3378
12:25 that **the L** will give you as he promised, 3378
12:27 'It is the Passover sacrifice to **the L,** 3378
12:28 The Israelites did just what **the L**
commanded Moses 3378
12:29 At midnight **the L** struck down all 3378
12:31 Go, worship **the L** as you have requested. 3378
12:36 **The L** had made the Egyptians favorably
disposed toward the people, 3378
12:42 Because **the L** kept vigil that night 3378
12:42 to honor **the L** for the generations 3378
12:43 **The L** said to Moses and Aaron, 3378
12:50 Israelites did just what **the L** had
commanded Moses 3378
12:51 And on that very day **the L** brought 3378
13: 1 **The L** said to Moses, 3378
13: 3 because **the L** brought you out of it with 3378
13: 5 When **the L** brings you into the land of 3378
13: 6 the seventh day hold a festival to **the L.** 3378
13: 8 of what **the L** did for me when I came out 3378
13: 9 that the law of **the L** is to be on your lips. 3378
13: 9 For **the L** brought you out of Egypt 3378
13:11 "After **the L** brings you into the land of 3378
13:12 to give over to **the L** the first offspring 3378
13:12 of your livestock belong to **the L.** 3378
13:14 'With a mighty hand **the L** brought us out 3378
13:15 **the L** killed every firstborn in Egypt, 3378
13:15 to **the L** the first male offspring 3378
13:16 that **the L** brought us out of Egypt 3378
13:21 By day **the L** went ahead of them in 3378
14: 1 Then **the L** said to Moses, 3378
14: 4 the Egyptians will know that I am **the L."** 3378
14: 8 **The L** hardened the heart of Pharaoh king 3378
14:10 and cried out to **the L.** 3378
14:13 deliverance **the L** will bring you today. 3378
14:14 **The L** will fight for you; 3378
14:15 Then **the L** said to Moses, 3378
14:18 The Egyptians will know that I am **the L** 3378
14:21 and all that night **the L** drove the sea back 3378
14:24 the last watch of the night **the L** looked 3378
14:25 **The L** is fighting for them against Egypt." 3378
14:26 Then **the L** said to Moses, 3378
14:27 and **the L** swept them into the sea. 3378
Ex 14:30 That day **the L** saved Israel from 3378
14:31 the great power **the L** displayed against 3378
14:31 the people feared **the L** and put their trust 3378
15: 1 and the Israelites sang this song to **the L:** 3378
15: 1 "I will sing to **the L,** 3378
15: 2 **The L** is my strength and my song; 3363
15: 3 **The L** is a warrior; the LORD is his name. 3378
15: 3 LORD is a warrior; **the L** is his name. 3378
15: 6 "Your right hand, O **L,** was majestic 3378
15: 6 Your right hand, O **L,** shattered the enemy. 3378
15:11 "Who among the gods is like you, O **L?** 3378
15:16 until your people pass by, O **L,** 3378
15:17 O **L,** you made for your dwelling, 3378
15:18 **The L** will reign for ever and ever." 3378
15:19 **the L** brought the waters of the sea back 3378
15:21 "Sing to **the L,** for he is highly exalted. 3378
15:25 Then Moses cried out to **the L,** 3378
15:25 and **the L** showed him a piece of wood. 3378
15:25 the L made a decree and a law for them, NIH
15:26 of **the L** your God and do what is right 3378
15:26 for I am **the L,** who heals you." 3378
16: 4 Then **the L** said to Moses, 3378
16: 6 that it was **the L** who brought you out 3378
16: 7 you will see the glory of **the L,** 3378
16: 8 that it was **the L** when he gives you meat 3378
16: 8 grumbling against us, but against **the L."** 3378
16: 9 'Come before **the L,** 3378
16:10 the glory of **the L** appearing in the cloud. 3378
16:11 **The L** said to Moses, 3378
16:12 that I am **the L** your God.' " 3378
16:15 "It is the bread **the L** has given you to eat. 3378
16:16 This is what **the L** has commanded: 3378
16:23 "This is what **the L** commanded: 3378
16:23 a holy Sabbath to **the L.** 3378
16:25 "because today is a Sabbath to **the L.** 3378
16:28 Then **the L** said to Moses, 3378
16:29 Bear in mind that **the L** has given you 3378
16:32 "This is what **the L** has commanded: 3378
16:33 Then place it before **the L** to be kept for 3378
16:34 As **the L** commanded Moses, 3378
17: 1 from place to place as **the L** commanded. 3378
17: 2 Why do you put **the L** to the test?" 3378
17: 4 Then Moses cried out to **the L,** 3378
17: 5 **The L** answered Moses, 3378
17: 7 and because they tested **the L** saying, 3378
17: 7 "Is **the L** among us or not?" 3378
17:14 Then **the L** said to Moses, 3378
17:15 an altar and called it **The L** is my Banner. 3378
17:16 hands were lifted up to the throne of **the L.** 3363
17:16 **The L** will be at war against the Amalekites 3378
18: 1 **the L** had brought Israel out of Egypt. 3378
18: 8 about everything **the L** had done 3378
18: 8 the way and how **the L** had saved them. 3378
18: 9 the good things **the L** had done for Israel 3378
18:10 He said, "Praise be to **the L,** 3378
18:11 that **the L** is greater than all other gods, 3378
19: 3 and **the L** called to him from 3378
19: 7 the words **the L** had commanded him 3378
19: 8 "We will do everything **the L** has said." 3378
19: 8 Moses brought their answer back to **the L.** 3378
19: 9 **The L** said to Moses, 3378
19: 9 Then Moses told **the L** what the people 3378
19:10 And **the L** said to Moses, 3378
19:11 because on that day **the L** will come 3378
19:18 because **the L** descended on it in fire. 3378
19:20 **The L** descended to the top of Mount Sinai 3378
19:21 and **the L** said to him, 3378
19:21 not force their way through to see **the L** 3378
19:22 Even the priests, who approach **the L,** 3378
19:22 or **the L** will break out against them." 3378
19:23 Moses said to **the L,** 3378
19:24 **The L** replied, "Go down and bring Aaron 3378
19:24 through to come up to **the L,** 3378
20: 2 "I am **the L** your God, who brought you 3378
20: 5 for I, **the L** your God, am a jealous God, 3378
20: 7 not misuse the name of **the L** your God, 3378
20: 7 for **the L** will not hold anyone guiltless who 3378
20:10 a Sabbath to **the L** your God. 3378
20:11 in six days **the L** made the heavens and 3378
20:11 Therefore **the L** blessed the Sabbath day 3378
20:12 in the land **the L** your God is giving you. 3378
20:22 Then **the L** said to Moses, 3378
22:11 an oath before **the L** that the neighbor did 3378
22:20 to any god other than **the L** must 3378
23:17 to appear before the Sovereign **L.** 3378
23:19 to the house of **the L** your God. 3378
23:25 Worship **the L** your God, 3378
24: 1 he said to Moses, "Come up to **the L,** 3378
24: 2 but Moses alone is to approach **the L;** 3378
24: 3 "Everything **the L** has said we will do." 3378
24: 4 then wrote down everything **the L** had said. 3378
24: 5 as fellowship offerings to **the L.** 3378
24: 7 "We will do everything **the L** has said; 3378
24: 8 of the covenant that **the L** has made 3378
24:12 **The L** said to Moses, 3378
24:16 the glory of **the L** settled on Mount Sinai. 3378
24:16 on the seventh day the L called to Moses NIH
24:17 To the Israelites the glory of **the L** looked 3378
25: 1 **The L** said to Moses, 3378
27:21 before **the L** from evening till morning. 3378
28:12 as a memorial before **the L.** 3378
28:29 as a continuing memorial before **the L.** 3378
28:30 whenever he enters the presence of **the L.** 3378
28:30 the Israelites over his heart before **the L.** 3378
28:35 before **the L** and when he comes out, 3378
28:36 as on a seal: HOLY TO THE **L.** 3378
28:38 so that they will be acceptable to **the L.** 3378

†LORD distinguishes the proper name of God, *Yahweh*, indicated in the NIV by "LORD," from the words translated "Lord" and "lord," indexed under the heading ***LORD**, pages 683-86.

Ex 29:18 It is a burnt offering to **the L**, 3378
29:18 an offering made to **the L** by fire. 3378
29:23 which is before **the L**, take a loaf, 3378
29:24 and his sons and wave them before **the L** 3378
29:25 for a pleasing aroma to **the L**, 3378
29:25 an offering made to **the L** by fire. 3378
29:26 wave it before **the L** as a wave offering, 3378
29:28 to **the L** from their fellowship offerings. 3378
29:41 an offering made to **the L** by fire. 3378
29:42 to the Tent of Meeting before **the L**. 3378
29:46 They will know that I am **the L** their God, 3378
29:46 I am **the L** their God. 3378
30: 8 before **the L** for the generations to come. 3378
30:10 It is most holy to **the L**." 3378
30:11 Then **the L** said to Moses, 3378
30:12 each one must pay **the L** a ransom 3378
30:13 This half shekel is an offering to **the L**. 3378
30:14 are to give an offering to **the L**. 3378
30:15 when you make the offering to **the L** 3378
30:16 a memorial for the Israelites before **the L**, 3378
30:17 Then **the L** said to Moses, 3378
30:20 by presenting an offering made to **the L** 3378
30:22 Then **the L** said to Moses, 3378
30:34 Then **the L** said to Moses, 3378
30:37 consider it holy to **the L**. 3378
31: 1 Then **the L** said to Moses, 3378
31:12 Then **the L** said to Moses, 3378
31:13 so you may know that I am **the L**, 3378
31:15 a Sabbath of rest, holy to **the L**. 3378
31:17 in six days **the L** made the heavens and 3378
31:18 When **the L** finished speaking to Moses 2257[S]
32: 5 Tomorrow there will be a festival to **the L**. 3378
32: 7 Then **the L** said to Moses, "Go down, 3378
32: 9 **the L** said to Moses, 3378
32:11 Moses sought the favor of **the L** his God. 3378
32:11 favor of the LORD his God. "O **L**," 3378
32:14 Then **the L** relented and did not bring 3378
32:26 "Whoever is for **the L**, come to me." 3378
32:27 he said to them, "This is what **the L**, 3378
32:29 "You have been set apart to **the L** today, 3378
32:30 But now I will go up to **the L**; 3378
32:31 So Moses went back to **the L** and said, 3378
32:33 **The L** replied to Moses, 3378
32:35 And **the L** struck the people with a plague 3378
33: 1 Then **the L** said to Moses, 3378
33: 5 For **the L** had said to Moses, 3378
33: 7 Anyone inquiring of **the L** would go to 3378
33: 9 while **the L** spoke with Moses. NIH
33:11 **The L** would speak to Moses face to face, 3378
33:12 Moses said to **the L**, 3378
33:14 **The L** replied, "My Presence will go NIH
33:17 And **the L** said to Moses, 3378
33:19 And **the L** said, "I will cause all my NIH
33:19 and I will proclaim my name, **the L**, 3378
33:21 Then **the L** said, "There is a place near me 3378
34: 1 **The L** said to Moses, 3378
34: 4 as **the L** had commanded him; 3378
34: 5 Then **the L** came down in the cloud 3378
34: 5 with him and proclaimed his name, **the L**. 3378
34: 6 proclaiming, "**The L**, the LORD, 3378
34: 6 proclaiming, "The LORD, **the L**, 3378
34:10 Then **the L** said: "I am making a covenant NIH
34:10 the work that I, **the L**, will do for you. 3378
34:14 Do not worship any other god, for **the L**, 3378
34:23 to appear before the Sovereign **L**, 3378
34:24 to appear before **the L** your God. 3378
34:26 to the house of **the L** your God. 3378
34:27 Then **the L** said to Moses, 3378
34:28 Moses was there with **the L** forty days 3378
34:29 because he had spoken with **the L**. 2257[S]
34:32 the commands **the L** had given him 3378
34:35 until he went in to speak with **the L**. 2257[S]
35: 1 the things **the L** has commanded you 3378
35: 2 a Sabbath of rest to **the L**. 3378
35: 4 "This is what **the L** has commanded: 3378
35: 5 take an offering for **the L**. 3378
35: 5 to bring to **the L** an offering of gold, 3378
35:10 make everything **the L** has commanded: 3378
35:21 and brought an offering to **the L** for 3378
35:22 as a wave offering to **the L**. 3378
35:24 as an offering to **the L**, 3378
35:29 to **the L** freewill offerings for all the work 3378
35:29 for all the work **the L** 3378
35:30 **the L** has chosen Bezalel son of Uri, 3378
36: 1 to whom **the L** has given skill and ability 3378
36: 1 the work just as **the L** has commanded." 3378
36: 2 to whom **the L** had given ability 3378
36: 5 the work **the L** commanded to be done." 3378
38:22 made everything **the L** commanded Moses; 3378
39: 1 as **the L** commanded Moses. 3378
39: 5 as **the L** commanded Moses. 3378
39: 7 as **the L** commanded Moses. 3378
39:21 as **the L** commanded Moses. 3378
39:26 as **the L** commanded Moses. 3378
39:29 as **the L** commanded Moses. 3378
39:30 an inscription on a seal: HOLY TO THE **L**. 3378
39:31 as **the L** commanded Moses. 3378
39:32 as **the L** commanded Moses. 3378
39:42 as **the L** had commanded Moses. 3378
39:43 as **the L** had commanded. 3378
40: 1 Then **the L** said to Moses: 3378
40:16 as **the L** commanded him. 3378
40:19 as **the L** commanded him. 3378
40:21 as **the L** commanded him. 3378
40:23 and set out the bread on it before **the L**, 3378
40:23 as **the L** commanded him. 3378
40:25 and set up the lamps before **the L**, 3378

Ex 40:25 as **the L** commanded him. 3378
40:27 as **the L** commanded him. 3378
40:29 as **the L** commanded him. 3378
40:32 as **the L** commanded Moses. 3378
40:34 the glory of **the L** filled the tabernacle. 3378
40:35 the glory of **the L** filled the tabernacle. 3378
40:38 the cloud of **the L** was over the tabernacle 3378
Lev 1: 1 **The L** called to Moses and spoke to him 3378
1: 2 any of you brings an offering to **the L**, 3378
1: 3 so that it will be acceptable to **the L**. 3378
1: 5 to slaughter the young bull before **the L**, 3378
1: 9 an aroma pleasing to **the L**. 3378
1:11 at the north side of the altar before **the L**, 3378
1:13 an aroma pleasing to **the L**. 3378
1:14 the offering to **the L** is a burnt offering 3378
1:17 an aroma pleasing to **the L**. 3378
2: 1 a grain offering to **the L**, 3378
2: 2 an aroma pleasing to **the L**. 3378
2: 3 of the offerings made to **the L** by fire. 3378
2: 8 of these things to **the L**; 3378
2: 9 an aroma pleasing to **the L**. 3378
2:10 of the offerings made to **the L** by fire. 3378
2:11 to **the L** must be made without yeast, 3378
2:11 or honey in an offering made to **the L** 3378
2:12 to **the L** as an offering of the firstfruits, 3378
2:14 a grain offering of firstfruits to **the L**, 3378
2:16 as an offering made to **the L** by fire. 3378
3: 1 he is to present before **the L** an animal 3378
3: 3 to bring a sacrifice made to **the L** by fire: 3378
3: 5 an aroma pleasing to **the L**. 3378
3: 6 as a fellowship offering to **the L**, 3378
3: 7 he is to present it before **the L**. 3378
3: 9 to bring a sacrifice made to **the L** by fire: 3378
3:11 an offering made to **the L** by fire. 3378
3:12 he is to present it before **the L**. 3378
3:14 to make this offering to **the L** by fire: 3378
4: 1 **The L** said to Moses, 3378
4: 3 to **the L** a young bull without defect as 3378
4: 4 to the Tent of Meeting before **the L**. 3378
4: 4 on its head and slaughter it before **the L**. 3378
4: 6 of it seven times before **the L**, 3378
4: 7 of fragrant incense that is before **the L** in 3378
4:15 on the bull's head before **the L**, 3378
4:15 the bull shall be slaughtered before **the L**. 3378
4:17 and sprinkle it before **the L** seven times 3378
4:18 of the altar that is before **the L** in the Tent 3378
4:22 in any of the commands of **the L** his God, 3378
4:24 where the burnt offering is slaughtered
before **the L**. 3378
4:31 on the altar as an aroma pleasing to **the L**. 3378
4:35 of the offerings made to **the L** by fire. 3378
5: 6 he must bring to **the L** a female lamb 3378
5: 7 to **the L** as a penalty for his sin— 3378
5:12 of the offerings made to **the L** by fire. 3378
5:14 **The L** said to Moses: 3378
5:15 to **the L** as a penalty a ram from the flock, 3378
5:19 of wrongdoing against **the L**." 3378
6: 1 **The L** said to Moses: 3378
6: 2 "If anyone sins and is unfaithful to **the L** 3378
6: 6 that is, to **the L**, his guilt offering, 3378
6: 7 for him before **the L**, 3378
6: 8 **The L** said to Moses: 3378
6:14 Aaron's sons are to bring it before **the L**, 3378
6:15 on the altar as an aroma pleasing to **the L**. 3378
6:18 of the offerings made to **the L** by fire for 3378
6:19 **The L** also said to Moses, 3378
6:20 and his sons are to bring to **the L** on 3378
6:21 in pieces as an aroma pleasing to **the L**. 3378
6:24 **The L** said to Moses, 3378
6:25 be slaughtered before **the L** in the place 3378
7: 5 on the altar as an offering made to **the L** 3378
7:11 a person may present to **the L**: 3378
7:14 a contribution to **the L**; 3378
7:20 to **the L**, that person must be cut off 3378
7:21 to **the L**, that person must be cut off 3378
7:22 **The L** said to Moses, 3378
7:25 to **the L** must be cut off from his people. 3378
7:28 **The L** said to Moses, 3378
7:29 a fellowship offering to **the L** is 3378
7:29 to bring part of it as his sacrifice to **the L**. 3378
7:30 to bring the offering made to **the L** 3378
7:30 and wave the breast before **the L** as 3378
7:35 the portion of the offerings made to **the L** 3378
7:35 to serve **the L** as priests. 3378
7:36 **the L** commanded that the Israelites 3378
7:38 which **the L** gave Moses on Mount Sinai 3378
7:38 to bring their offerings to **the L**, 3378
8: 1 **The L** said to Moses, 3378
8: 4 Moses did as **the L** commanded him, 3378
8: 5 "This is what **the L** has commanded to 3378
8: 9 as **the L** commanded Moses. 3378
8:13 as **the L** commanded Moses. 3378
8:17 as **the L** commanded Moses. 3378
8:21 an offering made to **the L** by fire, 3378
8:21 as **the L** commanded Moses. 3378
8:26 which was before **the L**, 3378
8:27 and waved them before **the L** as 3378
8:28 an offering made to **the L** by fire. 3378
8:29 waved it before **the L** as a wave offering, 3378
8:29 as **the L** commanded Moses. 3378
8:34 by **the L** to make atonement for you. 3378
8:35 and do what **the L** requires, so you will 3378
8:36 his sons did everything **the L** commanded 3378
9: 2 and present them before **the L**. 3378
9: 4 to sacrifice before **the L**, 3378
9: 4 For today **the L** will appear to you.' " 3378
9: 5 near and stood before **the L**. 3378

Lev 9: 6 "This is what **the L** has commanded you 3378
9: 6 the glory of **the L** may appear to you." 3378
9: 7 as **the L** has commanded." 3378
9:10 as **the L** commanded Moses; 3378
9:21 and the right thigh before **the L** as 3378
9:23 glory of **the L** appeared to all the people. 3378
9:24 from the presence of **the L** and consumed 3378
10: 1 before **the L**, contrary to his command. 3378
10: 2 of **the L** and consumed them, 3378
10: 2 and they died before **the L**. 3378
10: 3 "This is what **the L** spoke of 3378
10: 6 or you will die and **the L** will be angry NIH
10: 6 may mourn for those **the L** has destroyed 3378
10: 8 Then **the L** said to Aaron, 3378
10:11 the decrees **the L** has given them 3378
10:12 from the offerings made to **the L** by fire 3378
10:13 of the offerings made to **the L** by fire; 3378
10:15 be waved before **the L** as a wave offering. 3378
10:15 as **the L** has commanded." 3378
10:17 atonement for them before **the L**. 3378
10:19 and their burnt offering before **the L**, 3378
10:19 Would **the L** have been pleased 3378
11: 1 **The L** said to Moses and Aaron, 3378
11:44 I am **the L** your God; 3378
11:45 I am **the L** who brought you up out 3378
12: 1 **The L** said to Moses, 3378
12: 7 before **the L** to make atonement for her, 3378
13: 1 **The L** said to Moses and Aaron, 3378
14: 1 **The L** said to Moses, 3378
14:11 be cleansed and his offerings before **the L** 3378
14:12 he shall wave them before **the L** as 3378
14:16 of it before **the L** seven times. 3378
14:18 make atonement for him before **the L**. 3378
14:23 to the Tent of Meeting, before **the L**. 3378
14:24 before **the L** as a wave offering. 3378
14:27 from his palm seven times before **the L**. 3378
14:29 to make atonement for him before **the L**. 3378
14:31 before **the L** on behalf of the one to 3378
14:33 **The L** said to Moses and Aaron, 3378
15: 1 **The L** said to Moses and Aaron, 3378
15:14 and come before **the L** to the entrance to 3378
15:15 before **the L** for the man because 3378
15:30 for her before **the L** for the uncleanness 3378
16: 1 **The L** spoke to Moses after the death of 3378
16: 1 when they approached **the L**. 3378
16: 2 **The L** said to Moses: 3378
16: 7 before **the L** at the entrance to the Tent 3378
16: 8 for **the L** and the other for the scapegoat. 3378
16: 9 to **the L** and sacrifice it for a sin offering. 3378
16:10 be presented alive before **the L** to be used 3378
16:12 the altar before **the L** and two handfuls 3378
16:13 the incense on the fire before **the L**, 3378
16:18 that is before **the L** and make atonement 3378
16:30 Then, before **the L**, you will be clean 3378
16:34 it was done, as **the L** commanded Moses. 3378
17: 1 **The L** said to Moses, 3378
17: 2 'This is what **the L** has commanded: 3378
17: 4 to **the L** in front of the tabernacle of 3378
17: 4 in front of the tabernacle of **the L**— 3378
17: 5 This is so the Israelites will bring to **the L** 3378
17: 5 bring them to the priest, that is, to **the L**, 3378
17: 6 against the altar of **the L** at the entrance 3378
17: 6 the fat as an aroma pleasing to **the L**. 3378
17: 9 the Tent of Meeting to sacrifice it to **the L** 3378
18: 1 **The L** said to Moses, 3378
18: 2 'I am **the L** your God. 3378
18: 4 I am **the L** your God. 3378
18: 5 follow my decrees. I am **the L**. 3378
18: 6 obeys them will live by them. I am **the L**. 3378
18:21 relative to have sexual relations. I am **the L**. 3378
18:30 I am **the L** your God.' " 3378
19: 1 **The L** said to Moses, 3378
19: 2 Be holy because I, **the L** your God, am holy 3378
19: 3 I am **the L** your God. 3378
19: 4 I am **the L** your God. 3378
19: 5 a fellowship offering to **the L**, 3378
19: 8 he has desecrated what is holy to **the L**; 3378
19:10 I am **the L** your God. 3378
19:12 profane the name of your God. I am **the L**. 3378
19:14 but fear your God. I am **the L**. 3378
19:16 endangers your neighbor's life. I am **the L**. 3378
19:18 love your neighbor as yourself. I am **the L**. 3378
19:21 Tent of Meeting for a guilt offering to **the L** 3378
19:22 before **the L** for the sin he has committed, 3378
19:24 an offering of praise to **the L**. 3378
19:25 I am **the L** your God. 3378
19:28 put tattoo marks on yourselves. I am **the L**. 3378
19:30 reverence for my sanctuary. I am **the L**. 3378
19:31 I am **the L** your God. 3378
19:32 revere your God. I am **the L**. 3378
19:34 I am **the L** your God. 3378
19:36 I am **the L** your God, who brought you out 3378
19:37 all my laws and follow them. I am **the L**.' " 3378
20: 1 **The L** said to Moses, 3378
20: 7 because I am **the L** your God. 3378
20: 8 I am **the L**, who makes you holy. 3378
20:24 I am **the L** your God, 3378
20:26 be holy to me because I, **the L**, am holy, 3378
21: 1 **The L** said to Moses, 3378
21: 6 the offerings made to **the L** by fire, 3378
21: 8 Consider them holy, because I **the L** am
holy— 3378
21:12 anointing oil of his God. I am **the L**. 3378
21:15 I am **the L**, who makes him holy.' " 3378
21:16 **The L** said to Moses, 3378
21:21 to present the offerings made to **the L** 3378
21:23 I am **the L**, who makes them holy.' " 3378

†LORD distinguishes the proper name of God, *Yahweh*, indicated in the NIV by "LORD," from the words translated "Lord" and "lord," indexed under the heading ***LORD**, pages 683-86.

Lev 22: 1 **The L** said to Moses, 3378
22: 2 not profane my holy name. I am **the L.** 3378
22: 3 that the Israelites consecrate to **the L,** 3378
22: 3 cut off from my presence. I am **the L.** 3378
22: 8 become unclean through it. I am **the L.** 3378
22: 9 I am **the L,** who makes them holy. 3378
22:15 the Israelites present to **the L** 3378
22:16 I am **the L,** who makes them holy.' " 3378
22:17 **The L** said to Moses, 3378
22:18 a gift for a burnt offering to **the L,** 3378
22:21 a fellowship offering to **the L** to fulfill 3378
22:22 Do not offer to **the L** the blind, 3378
22:22 on the altar as an offering made to **the L** 3378
22:24 You must not offer to **the L** 3378
22:26 **The L** said to Moses, 3378
22:27 as an offering made to **the L** by fire. 3378
22:29 a thank offering to **the L,** 3378
22:30 leave none of it till morning. I am **the L.** 3378
22:31 my commands and follow them. I am **the L.** 3378
22:32 I am **the L,** who makes you holy. 3378
22:33 to be your God. I am **the L."** 3378
23: 1 **The L** said to Moses, 3378
23: 2 the appointed feasts of **the L,** 3378
23: 3 it is a Sabbath to **the L.** 3378
23: 8 an offering made to **the L** by fire. 3378
23: 9 **The L** said to Moses, 3378
23:11 to wave the sheaf before **the L** so it will 3378
23:12 a burnt offering to **the L** a lamb a year old 3378
23:13 an offering made to **the L** by fire, 3378
23:16 present an offering of new grain to **the L.** 3378
23:17 as a wave offering of firstfruits to **the L.** 3378
23:18 They will be a burnt offering to **the L,** 3378
23:18 an aroma pleasing to **the L.** 3378
23:20 to wave the two lambs before **the L** as 3378
23:20 a sacred offering to **the L** for the priest. 3378
23:22 I am **the L** your God.' " 3378
23:23 **The L** said to Moses, 3378
23:25 but present an offering made to **the L** 3378
23:26 **The L** said to Moses, 3378
23:27 and present an offering made to **the L** 3378
23:28 for you before **the L** your God. 3378
23:33 **The L** said to Moses, 3378
23:36 an offering made to **the L** by fire, 3378
23:36 and present an offering made to **the L** 3378
23:37 for bringing offerings made to **the L** 3378
23:38 the freewill offerings you give to **the L.)** 3378
23:39 the festival to **the L** for seven days; 3378
23:40 before **the L** your God for seven days. 3378
23:41 Celebrate this as a festival to **the L** 3378
23:43 I am **the L** your God.' " 3378
23:44 the appointed feasts of **the L.** 3378
24: 1 **The L** said to Moses, 3378
24: 3 before **the L** from evening till morning, 3378
24: 4 before **the L** must be tended continually. 3378
24: 6 on the table of pure gold before **the L.** 3378
24: 7 to be an offering made to **the L** by fire. 3378
24: 8 to be set out before **the L** regularly, 3378
24: 9 of the offerings made to **the L** by fire." 3378
24:12 in custody until the will of **the L** should 3378
24:13 Then **the L** said to Moses: 3378
24:16 the name of **the L** must be put to death. 3378
24:22 I am **the L** your God.' " 3378
24:23 as **the L** commanded Moses. 3378
25: 1 **The L** said to Moses on Mount Sinai, 3378
25: 2 a sabbath to **the L.** 3378
25: 4 a sabbath to **the L.** 3378
25:17 but fear your God. I am **the L** your God. 3378
25:38 I am **the L** your God, who brought you out 3378
25:55 I am **the L** your God. 3378
26: 1 I am **the L** your God. 3378
26: 2 reverence for my sanctuary. I am **the L.** 3378
26:13 I am **the L** your God, who brought you out 3378
26:44 I am **the L** their God. 3378
26:45 to be their God. I am **the L.' "** 3378
26:46 and the regulations that **the L** established 3378
27: 1 **The L** said to Moses, 3378
27: 2 a special vow to dedicate persons to **the L** 3378
27: 9 that is acceptable as an offering to **the L,** 3378
27: 9 an animal given to **the L** becomes holy. 3378
27:11 not acceptable as an offering to **the L—** 3378
27:14 as something holy to **the L,** 3378
27:16 " 'If a man dedicates to **the L** part 3378
27:21 like a field devoted to **the L;** 3378
27:22 to **the L** a field he has bought, 3378
27:23 on that day as something holy to **the L.** 3378
27:26 the firstborn already belongs to **the L;** 3378
27:28 that a man owns and devotes to **the L—** 3378
27:28 so devoted is most holy to **the L.** 3378
27:30 or fruit from the trees, belongs to **the L;** 3378
27:30 it is holy to **the L.** 3378
27:32 will be holy to **the L.** 3378
27:34 the commands **the L** gave Moses 3378
Nu 1: 1 **The L** spoke to Moses in the Tent 3378
1:19 as **the L** commanded Moses. 3378
1:48 **The L** had said to Moses: 3378
1:54 as **the L** commanded Moses. 3378
2: 1 **The L** said to Moses and Aaron: 3378
2:33 as **the L** commanded Moses. 3378
2:34 Israelites did everything **the L** commanded Moses; 3378
3: 1 at the time **the L** talked with Moses 3378
3: 4 before **the L** when they made an offering 3378
3: 5 **The L** said to Moses, 3378
3:11 **The L** also said to Moses, 3378
3:13 They are to be mine. I am **the L."** 3378
3:14 **The L** said to Moses in the Desert 3378
3:16 he was commanded by the word of **the L.** 3378

Nu 3:40 **The L** said to Moses, 3378
3:41 of the livestock of the Israelites. I am **the L.** 3378
3:42 as **the L** commanded him. 3378
3:44 **The L** also said to Moses, 3378
3:45 The Levites are to be mine. I am **the L.** 3378
3:51 he was commanded by the word of **the L.** 3378
4: 1 **The L** said to Moses and Aaron: 3378
4:17 **The L** said to Moses and Aaron, 3378
4:21 **The L** said to Moses, 3378
4:49 as **the L** commanded Moses. 3378
5: 1 **The L** said to Moses, 3378
5: 4 as **the L** had instructed Moses. 3378
5: 5 **The L** said to Moses, 3378
5: 6 in any way and so is unfaithful to **the L,** 3378
5: 8 the restitution belongs to **the L** and must 3378
5:11 Then **the L** said to Moses, 3378
5:16 and have her stand before **the L.** 3378
5:18 the woman stand before **the L,** 3378
5:21 "may **the L** cause your people to curse 3378
5:25 before **the L** and bring it to the altar. 3378
5:30 to have her stand before **the L** and is 3378
6: 1 **The L** said to Moses, 3378
6: 2 a vow of separation to **the L** as a Nazirite, 3378
6: 5 of his separation to **the L** is over; 3378
6: 6 to **the L** he must not go near a dead body. 3378
6: 8 of his separation he is consecrated to **the L.** 3378
6:12 to **the L** for the period of his separation 3378
6:14 to present his offerings to **the L:** 3378
6:16 to present them before **the L** and make 3378
6:17 the ram as a fellowship offering to **the L,** 3378
6:20 before **the L** as a wave offering; 3378
6:21 Nazirite who vows his offering to **the L** 3378
6:22 **The L** said to Moses, 3378
6:24 " ' **"The L** bless you and keep you; 3378
6:25 **the L** make his face shine upon you and 3378
6:26 **the L** turn his face toward you 3378
7: 3 before **the L** six covered carts 3378
7: 4 **The L** said to Moses, 3378
7:11 For **the L** had said to Moses, 3378
7:89 the Tent of Meeting to speak with **the L,** 2257S
8: 1 **The L** said to Moses, 3378
8: 3 just as **the L** commanded Moses. 3378
8: 4 like the pattern **the L** had shown Moses. 3378
8: 5 **The L** said to Moses: 3378
8:10 You are to bring the Levites before **the L,** 3378
8:11 to present the Levites before **the L** as 3378
8:11 be ready to do the work of **the L.** 3378
8:12 to **the L** and the other for a burnt offering, 3378
8:13 as a wave offering to **the L.** 3378
8:20 as **the L** commanded Moses. 3378
8:21 before **the L** and made atonement 3378
8:22 as **the L** commanded Moses. 3378
8:23 **The L** said to Moses, 3378
9: 1 **The L** spoke to Moses in the Desert 3378
9: 5 as **the L** commanded Moses. 3378
9: 8 until I find out what **the L** commands 3378
9: 9 Then **the L** said to Moses, 3378
10: 1 **The L** said to Moses: 3378
10: 9 be remembered by **the L** your God 3378
10:10 I am **the L** your God." 3378
10:29 for the place about which **the L** said, 3378
10:29 for **the L** has promised good things 3378
10:32 whatever good things **the L** gives us." 3378
10:33 from the mountain of **the L** and traveled 3378
10:33 the covenant of **the L** went before them 3378
10:34 The cloud of **the L** was over them by day 3378
10:35 Moses said, "Rise up, **O L!** 3378
10:36 he said, "Return, **O L,** 3378
11: 1 complained about their hardships in the hearing of **the L,** 3378
11: 1 Then fire from **the L** burned among them 3378
11: 2 he prayed to **the L** and the fire died down. 3378
11: 3 fire from **the L** had burned among them. 3378
11:10 **The L** became exceedingly angry, 3378
11:11 He asked **the L,** 3378
11:16 **The L** said to Moses: 3378
11:18 **The L** heard you when you wailed, 3378
11:18 Now **the L** will give you meat, 3378
11:20 because you have rejected **the L,** 3378
11:23 **The L** answered Moses, 3378
11:24 and told the people what **the L** had said. 3378
11:25 Then **the L** came down in the cloud 3378
11:29 that **the L** would put his Spirit on them!" 3378
11:31 from **the L** and drove quail in from 3378
11:33 of **the L** burned against the people, 3378
12: 2 "Has **the L** spoken only through Moses?" 3378
12: 2 And **the L** heard this. 3378
12: 4 At once **the L** said to Moses, 3378
12: 5 **the L** came down in a pillar of cloud; 3378
12: 6 "When a prophet of **the L** is among you, 3378
12: 8 he sees the form of **the L.** 3378
12: 9 The anger of **the L** burned against them, 3378
12:13 So Moses cried out to **the L,** "O God, 3378
12:14 **The L** replied to Moses, 3378
13: 1 **The L** said to Moses, 3378
14: 3 Why is **the L** bringing us to this land only 3378
14: 8 If **the L** is pleased with us, 3378
14: 9 Only do not rebel against **the L.** 3378
14: 9 but **the L** is with us. 3378
14:10 of **the L** appeared at the Tent of Meeting 3378
14:11 **The L** said to Moses, 3378
14:13 Moses said to **the L,** 3378
14:14 They have already heard that you, **O L,** 3378
14:14 are with these people and that you, **O L,** 3378
14:16 **'The L** was not able to bring these people 3378
14:18 **'The L** is slow to anger, 3378
14:20 **The L** replied, "I have forgiven them, 3378

Nu 14:21 as the glory of **the L** fills the whole earth, 3378
14:26 **The L** said to Moses and Aaron: 3378
14:28 'As surely as I live, declares **the L,** 3378
14:35 I, **the L,** have spoken, 3378
14:37 down and died of a plague before **the L.** 3378
14:40 up to the place **the L** promised." 3378
14:42 because **the L** is not with you. 3378
14:43 you have turned away from **the L,** 3378
15: 1 **The L** said to Moses, 3378
15: 3 and you present to **the L** offerings made 3378
15: 3 as an aroma pleasing to **the L—** 3378
15: 4 to **the L** a grain offering of a tenth of 3378
15: 7 Offer it as an aroma pleasing to **the L.** 3378
15: 8 or a fellowship offering to **the L,** 3378
15:10 an aroma pleasing to **the L.** 3378
15:13 by fire as an aroma pleasing to **the L.** 3378
15:14 by fire as an aroma pleasing to **the L,** 3378
15:15 the alien shall be the same before **the L:** 3378
15:17 **The L** said to Moses, 3378
15:19 present a portion as an offering to **the L.** 3378
15:21 to give this offering to **the L** from the first 3378
15:22 of these commands **the L** gave Moses— 3378
15:23 the day **the L** gave them and continuing 3378
15:24 as an aroma pleasing to **the L,** 3378
15:25 to **the L** for their wrong an offering made 3378
15:28 to make atonement before **the L** for 3378
15:30 blasphemes **the L,** and that person must 3378
15:35 **the L** said to Moses, "The man must die. 3378
15:36 as **the L** commanded Moses. 3378
15:37 **The L** said to Moses, 3378
15:39 remember all the commands of **the L,** 3378
15:41 I am **the L** your God, 3378
15:41 I am **the L** your God.' " 3378
16: 3 and **the L** is with them. 3378
16: 5 the morning **the L** will show who belongs 3378
16: 7 and incense in them before **the L.** 3378
16: 7 The man **the L** chooses will be 3378
16:11 It is against **the L** that you 3378
16:15 and said to **the L,** 3378
16:16 to appear before **the L** tomorrow— 3378
16:17 and present it before **the L.** 3378
16:19 of **the L** appeared to the entire assembly. 3378
16:20 **The L** said to Moses and Aaron, 3378
16:23 Then **the L** said to Moses, 3378
16:28 how you will know that **the L** has sent me 3378
16:29 then **the L** has not sent me. 3378
16:30 **the L** brings about something totally new, 3378
16:30 these men have treated **the L** with contempt 3378
16:35 And fire came out from **the L** 3378
16:36 **The L** said to Moses, 3378
16:38 for they were presented before **the L** 3378
16:40 as **the L** directed him through Moses. 3378
16:40 to burn incense before **the L,** 3378
16:42 and the glory of **the L** appeared. 3378
16:44 and **the L** said to Moses, 3378
16:46 Wrath has come out from **the L;** 3378
17: 1 **The L** said to Moses, 3378
17: 7 before **the L** in the Tent of the Testimony. 3378
17:10 **The L** said to Moses, 3378
17:11 Moses did just as **the L** commanded him. 3378
17:13 near the tabernacle of **the L** will die. 3378
18: 1 **The L** said to Aaron, "You, your sons and 3378
18: 6 dedicated to **the L** to do the work at 3378
18: 8 Then **the L** said to Aaron, 3378
18:12 and grain they give **the L** as the firstfruits 3378
18:13 that they bring to **the L** will be yours. 3378
18:14 in Israel that is **devoted to** the **L** is yours. 3051
18:15 that is offered to **the L** is yours. 3378
18:17 an aroma pleasing to **the L.** 3378
18:19 to **the L** I give to you and your sons 3378
18:19 of salt before **the L** for both you 3378
18:20 **The L** said to Aaron, 3378
18:24 as an offering to **the L.** 3378
18:25 **The L** said to Moses, 3378
18:28 to **the L** from all the tithes you receive 3378
19: 1 **The L** said to Moses and Aaron: 3378
19: 2 of the law that **the L** has commanded: 3378
19:20 he has defiled the sanctuary of **the L.** 3378
20: 3 when our brothers fell dead before **the L!** 3378
20: 6 and the glory of **the L** appeared to them. 3378
20: 7 **The L** said to Moses, 3378
20:12 But **the L** said to Moses and Aaron, 3378
20:13 where the Israelites quarreled with **the L** 3378
20:16 but when we cried out to **the L,** 3378
20:23 **the L** said to Moses and Aaron, 3378
20:27 Moses did as **the L** commanded: 3378
21: 2 Then Israel made this vow to **the L:** 3378
21: 3 **The L** listened to Israel's plea and gave 3378
21: 6 **the L** sent venomous snakes among them; 3378
21: 7 "We sinned when we spoke against **the L** 3378
21: 7 Pray that **the L** will take the snakes away 3378
21: 8 **The L** said to Moses, 3378
21:14 the Book of the Wars of **the L** says: 3378
21:16 the well where **the L** said to Moses, 3378
21:34 **The L** said to Moses, 3378
22: 8 the answer **the L** gives me." 3378
22:13 **the L** has refused to let me go with you." 3378
22:18 beyond the command of **the L** my God. 3378
22:19 I will find out what else **the L** will tell me." 3378
22:22 of **the L** stood in the road to oppose him. 3378
22:23 the angel of **the L** standing in the road 3378
22:24 the angel of **the L** stood in a narrow path 3378
22:25 When the donkey saw the angel of **the L,** 3378
22:26 Then the angel of **the L** moved on ahead 3378
22:27 When the donkey saw the angel of **the L,** 3378
22:28 Then **the L** opened the donkey's mouth, 3378
22:31 Then **the L** opened Balaam's eyes, 3378

†LORD distinguishes the proper name of God, *Yahweh,* indicated in the NIV by "LORD," from the words translated "Lord" and "lord," indexed under the heading ***LORD**, pages 683-86.

Nu 22:31 and he saw the angel of **the L** standing in 3378
22:32 The angel of **the L** asked him, 3378
22:34 Balaam said to the angel of **the L,** 3378
22:35 The angel of **the L** said to Balaam, 3378
23: 3 Perhaps **the L** will come to meet with me. 3378
23: 5 **The L** put a message in Balaam's mouth 3378
23: 8 How can I denounce those whom **the L** has 3378
23:12 not speak what **the L** puts in my mouth?" 3378
23:16 **The L** met with Balaam and put 3378
23:17 Balak asked him, "What did **the L** say?" 3378
23:21 **The L** their God is with them; 3378
23:26 tell you I must do whatever **the L** says?" 3378
24: 1 when Balaam saw that it pleased **the L** 3378
24: 6 like aloes planted by **the L,** 3378
24:11 but **the L** has kept you 3378
24:13 to go beyond the command of **the L—** 3378
24:13 and I must say only what **the L** says'? 3378
25: 4 **The L** said to Moses, 3378
25: 4 in broad daylight before **the L,** 3378
25:10 **The L** said to Moses, 3378
25:16 **The L** said to Moses, 3378
26: 1 After the plague **the L** said to Moses 3378
26: 4 as **the L** commanded Moses." 3378
26: 9 when they rebelled against **the L.** 3378
26:52 **The L** said to Moses, 3378
26:61 when they made an offering before **the L** 3378
26:65 **the L** had told those Israelites they would 3378
27: 3 who banded together against **the L,** 3378
27: 5 So Moses brought their case before **the L** 3378
27: 6 and **the L** said to him, 3378
27:11 as **the L** commanded Moses.' " 3378
27:12 Then **the L** said to Moses, 3378
27:15 Moses said to **the L,** 3378
27:16 "May **the L,** the God of the spirits 3378
27:18 So **the L** said to Moses, 3378
27:21 by inquiring of the Urim before **the L.** 3378
27:22 Moses did as **the L** commanded him. 3378
27:23 as **the L** instructed through Moses. 3378
28: 1 **The L** said to Moses, 3378
28: 3 by fire that you are to present to **the L:** 3378
28: 6 an offering made to **the L** by fire. 3378
28: 7 Pour out the drink offering to **the L** at 3378
28: 8 an aroma pleasing to **the L.** 3378
28:11 present to **the L** a burnt offering 3378
28:13 an offering made to **the L** by fire. 3378
28:15 to be presented to **the L** as a sin offering. 3378
28:19 Present to **the L** an offering made by fire, 3378
28:24 as an aroma pleasing to **the L;** 3378
28:26 to **the L** an offering of new grain during 3378
28:27 a year old as an aroma pleasing to **the L.** 3378
29: 2 As an aroma pleasing to **the L,** 3378
29: 6 They are offerings made to **the L** 3378
29: 8 Present as an aroma pleasing to **the L** 3378
29:12 a festival to **the L** for seven days. 3378
29:13 by fire as an aroma pleasing to **the L,** 3378
29:36 by fire as an aroma pleasing to **the L,** 3378
29:39 for **the L** at your appointed feasts: 3378
29:40 that **the L** commanded him. 3378
30: 1 "This is what **the L** commands: 3378
30: 2 a man makes a vow to **the L** or takes 3378
30: 3 to **the L** or obligates herself by a pledge 3378
30: 5 **the L** will release her 3378
30: 8 and **the L** will release her. 3378
30:12 and **the L** will release her. 3378
30:16 the regulations **the L** gave Moses 3378
31: 1 **The L** said to Moses, 3378
31: 7 as **the L** commanded Moses, 3378
31:16 of turning the Israelites away from **the L** 3378
31:21 of the law that **the L** gave Moses: 3378
31:25 **The L** said to Moses, 3378
31:28 for **the L** one out of every five hundred, 3378
31:31 as **the L** commanded Moses. 3378
31:37 of which the tribute for **the L** was 675; 3378
31:38 of which the tribute for **the L** was 72; 3378
31:39 of which the tribute for **the L** was 61; 3378
31:40 of which the tribute for **the L** was 32. 3378
31:41 as **the L** commanded Moses. 3378
31:47 as **the L** commanded him, 3378
31:50 an offering to **the L** the gold articles each 3378
31:50 for ourselves before **the L."** 3378
31:52 as a gift to **the L** weighed 16,750 3378
31:54 a memorial for the Israelites before **the L.** 3378
32: 4 the land **the L** subdued before the people 3378
32: 7 over into the land **the L** has given them? 3378
32: 9 the land **the L** had given them. 3378
32:12 for they followed **the L** wholeheartedly.' 3378
32:14 and making **the L** even more angry 3378
32:20 if you will arm yourselves before **the L** 3378
32:21 over the Jordan before **the L** 3378
32:22 when the land is subdued before **the L,** 3378
32:22 be free from your obligation to **the L** and 3378
32:22 be your possession before **the L.** 3378
32:23 you will be sinning against **the L;** 3378
32:27 will cross over to fight before **the L,** 3378
32:29 over the Jordan with you before **the L,** 3378
32:31 "Your servants will do what **the L** has said. 3378
32:32 over before **the L** into Canaan armed, 3378
33: 4 whom **the L** had struck down 3378
33: 4 for **the L** had brought judgment 3378
33:50 the Jordan across from Jericho **the L** said 3378
34: 1 **The L** said to Moses, 3378
34:13 **The L** has ordered that it be given to 3378
34:16 **The L** said to Moses, 3378
34:29 These are the men **the L** commanded 3378
35: 1 **the L** said to Moses, 3378
35: 9 Then **the L** said to Moses: 3378
35:34 for I, **the L,** dwell among the Israelites.' " 3378

Nu 36: 2 "When **the L** commanded my lord to give 3378
36: 6 This is what **the L** commands 3378
36:10 as **the L** commanded Moses. 3378
36:13 the commands and regulations **the L** gave 3378
Dt 1: 3 that **the L** had commanded him 3378
1: 6 **The L** our God said to us at Horeb, 3378
1: 8 the land that **the L** swore he would give 3378
1:10 **The L** your God has increased your numbers 3378
1:11 May **the L,** the God of your fathers, 3378
1:19 Then, as **the L** our God commanded us, 3378
1:20 which **the L** our God is giving us. 3378
1:21 **the L** your God has given you the land. 3378
1:21 Go up and take possession of it as **the L,** 3378
1:25 that **the L** our God is giving us." 3378
1:26 against the command of **the L** your God. 3378
1:27 and said, **"The L** hates us; 3378
1:30 **The L** your God, who is going before you, 3378
1:31 how **the L** your God carried you, 3378
1:32 you did not trust in **the L** your God, 3378
1:34 When **the L** heard what you said, 3378
1:36 because he followed **the L** wholeheartedly." 3378
1:37 of you **the L** became angry with me also 3378
1:41 "We have sinned against **the L.** 3378
1:41 as **the L** our God commanded us." 3378
1:42 But **the L** said to me, "Tell them, 3378
1:45 You came back and wept before **the L,** 3378
2: 1 as **the L** had directed me. 3378
2: 2 Then **the L** said to me, 3378
2: 7 **The L** your God has blessed you in all 3378
2: 7 These forty years **the L** your God has been 3378
2: 9 Then **the L** said to me, 3378
2:12 as Israel did in the land **the L** gave them 3378
2:13 And the L said, "Now get up and cross NIH
2:14 as **the L** had sworn to them. 3378
2:17 **the L** said to me, 3378
2:21 **The L** destroyed them from before 3378
2:22 **The L** had done the same for NIH
2:29 into the land **the L** our God is giving us." 3378
2:30 For **the L** your God had made his spirit stubborn 3378
2:31 **The L** said to me, "See, I have begun 3378
2:33 **the L** our God delivered him over to us 3378
2:36 **The L** our God gave us all of them. 3378
2:37 with the command of **the L** our God, 3378
3: 2 **The L** said to me, "Do not be afraid of him, 3378
3: 3 So **the L** our God also gave 3378
3:18 **"The L** your God has given you this land 3378
3:20 until **the L** gives rest to your brothers 3378
3:20 that **the L** your God is giving them, 3378
3:21 that **the L** your God has done 3378
3:21 **The L** will do the same to all 3378
3:22 **the L** your God himself will fight 3378
3:23 At that time I pleaded with **the L:** 3378
3:24 "O Sovereign **L,** you have begun to show 3378
3:26 because of you **the L** was angry with me 3378
3:26 "That is enough," **the L** said. 3378
4: 1 take possession of the land that **the L,** 3378
4: 2 of **the L** your God that I give you. 3378
4: 3 with your own eyes what **the L** did 3378
4: 3 **The L** your God destroyed from 3378
4: 4 to **the L** your God are still alive today. 3378
4: 5 as **the L** my God commanded me, 3378
4: 7 near them the way **the L** our God is 3378
4:10 the day you stood before **the L** your God 3378
4:12 Then **the L** spoke to you out of the fire. 3378
4:14 And **the L** directed me at that time 3378
4:15 the day **the L** spoke to you at Horeb out 3378
4:19 worshiping things **the L** your God has 3378
4:20 **the L** took you and brought you out of 3378
4:21 **The L** was angry with me because of you, 3378
4:21 good land **the L** your God is giving you 3378
4:23 of **the L** your God that he made with you; 3378
4:23 of anything **the L** your God has forbidden. 3378
4:24 For **the L** your God is a consuming fire, 3378
4:25 doing evil in the eyes of **the L** your God 3378
4:27 **The L** will scatter you among the peoples, 3378
4:27 the nations to which **the L** will drive you. 3378
4:29 if from there you seek **the L** your God, 3378
4:30 to **the L** your God and obey him. 3378
4:31 For **the L** your God is a merciful God; 3378
4:34 the things **the L** your God did for you 3378
4:35 so that you might know that **the L** is God; 3378
4:39 that **the L** is God in heaven above and on 3378
4:40 in the land **the L** your God gives you 3378
5: 2 **The L** our God made a covenant with us 3378
5: 3 that **the L** made this covenant, 3378
5: 4 **The L** spoke to you face to face out of 3378
5: 5 between **the L** and you to declare to you 3378
5: 5 to declare to you the word of **the L,** 3378
5: 6 "I am **the L** your God, 3378
5: 9 for I, **the L** your God, am a jealous God, 3378
5:11 not misuse the name of **the L** your God, 3378
5:11 for **the L** will not hold anyone guiltless who 3378
5:12 as **the L** your God has commanded you. 3378
5:14 a Sabbath to **the L** your God. 3378
5:15 and that **the L** your God brought you out 3378
5:15 Therefore **the L** your God has commanded 3378
5:16 as **the L** your God has commanded you, 3378
5:16 in the land **the L** your God is giving you. 3378
5:22 the commandments **the L** proclaimed in 3378
5:24 **"The L** our God has shown us his glory 3378
5:25 the voice of **the L** our God any longer. 3378
5:27 and listen to all that **the L** our God says. 3378
5:27 tell us whatever **the L** our God tells you. 3378
5:28 **The L** heard you when you spoke to me 3378
5:28 when you spoke to me and **the L** said 3378

Dt 5:32 careful to do what **the L** your God has commanded you; 3378
5:33 that **the L** your God has commanded you, 3378
6: 1 and laws **the L** your God directed me 3378
6: 2 after them may fear **the L** your God 3378
6: 3 just as **the L,** the God of your fathers, 3378
6: 4 **The L** our God, the LORD is one. 3378
6: 4 The LORD our God, **the L** is one. 3378
6: 5 Love **the L** your God with all your heart 3378
6:10 When **the L** your God brings you into 3378
6:12 be careful that you do not forget **the L,** 3378
6:13 Fear **the L** your God, 3378
6:15 for **the L** your God, who is among you, 3378
6:16 Do not test **the L** your God as you did 3378
6:17 to keep the commands of **the L** your God 3378
6:18 the good land that **the L** promised on oath 3378
6:19 your enemies before you, as **the L** said. 3378
6:20 laws **the L** our God has commanded you?" 3378
6:21 but **the L** brought us out of Egypt with 3378
6:22 Before our eyes **the L** sent miraculous signs 3378
6:24 **The L** commanded us to obey all 3378
6:24 and to fear **the L** our God, 3378
6:25 to obey all this law before **the L** our God, 3378
7: 1 When **the L** your God brings you into 3378
7: 2 when **the L** your God has delivered them 3378
7: 6 you are a people holy to **the L** your God. 3378
7: 6 **The L** your God has chosen you out of all 3378
7: 7 **The L** did not set his affection on you 3378
7: 8 But it was because **the L** loved you 3378
7: 9 therefore that **the L** your God is God; 3378
7:12 **the L** your God will keep his covenant 3378
7:15 **The L** will keep you free from every disease. 3378
7:16 the peoples **the L** your God gives over 3378
7:18 remember well what **the L** your God did 3378
7:19 which **the L** your God brought you out. 3378
7:19 **The L** your God will do the same to all 3378
7:20 **the L** your God will send the hornet 3378
7:21 for **the L** your God, who is among you, 3378
7:22 **The L** your God will drive out those nations 3378
7:23 But **the L** your God will deliver them 3378
7:25 for it is detestable to **the L** your God. 3378
8: 1 and possess the land that **the L** promised 3378
8: 2 how **the L** your God led you all the way 3378
8: 3 that comes from the mouth of **the L.** 3378
8: 5 so **the L** your God disciplines you. 3378
8: 6 the commands of **the L** your God, 3378
8: 7 For **the L** your God is bringing you into 3378
8:10 praise **the L** your God for 3378
8:11 that you do not forget **the L** your God, 3378
8:14 and you will forget **the L** your God, 3378
8:18 But remember **the L** your God, 3378
8:19 If you ever forget **the L** your God 3378
8:20 the nations **the L** destroyed before you, 3378
8:20 for not obeying **the L** your God. 3378
9: 3 that **the L** your God is the one who goes 3378
9: 3 as **the L** has promised you. 3378
9: 4 After **the L** your God *has* driven them out 3378
9: 4 **"The L** has brought me here 3378
9: 4 that **the L** is going to drive them out 3378
9: 5 **the L** your God will drive them out 3378
9: 6 **the L** your God is giving you this good land 3378
9: 7 how you provoked **the L** your God 3378
9: 7 you have been rebellious against **the L.** 3378
9: 9 that **the L** had made with you, I stayed on 3378
9:10 **The L** gave me two stone tablets inscribed 3378
9:10 the commandments **the L** proclaimed 3378
9:11 **the L** gave me the two stone tablets, 3378
9:12 Then **the L** told me, "Go down from here 3378
9:13 And **the L** said to me, "I have seen this 3378
9:16 sinned against **the L** your God; 3378
9:16 the way that **the L** had commanded you. 3378
9:18 before **the L** for forty days 3378
9:19 I feared the anger and wrath of **the L,** 3378
9:19 But again **the L** listened to me. 3378
9:20 And **the L** was angry enough with Aaron 3378
9:22 You also made **the L** angry at Taberah, 3378
9:23 **the L** sent you out from Kadesh Barnea, 3378
9:23 against the command of **the L** your God. 3378
9:24 rebellious against **the L** ever since 3378
9:25 before **the L** those forty days 3378
9:25 **the L** had said he would destroy you. 3378
9:26 I prayed to **the L** and said, 3378
9:26 the LORD and said, "O Sovereign **L,** do 3378
9:28 'Because **the L** was not able to take them 3378
10: 1 At that time **the L** said to me, 3378
10: 4 **The L** wrote on these tablets 3378
10: 4 And **the L** gave them to me. 3378
10: 5 as **the L** commanded me, 3378
10: 8 that time **the L** set apart the tribe of Levi 3378
10: 8 to carry the ark of the covenant of **the L,** 3378
10: 8 to stand before **the L** to minister and 3378
10: 9 **the L** is their inheritance, 3378
10: 9 as **the L** your God told them.) 3378
10:10 and **the L** listened to me at this time also. 3378
10:11 "Go," **the L** said to me, 3378
10:12 what does **the L** your God ask of you but 3378
10:12 of you but to fear **the L** your God, 3378
10:12 to serve **the L** your God 3378
10:14 To **the L** your God belong the heavens, 3378
10:15 Yet **the L** set his affection on your 3378
10:17 For **the L** your God is God of gods 3378
10:20 Fear **the L** your God and serve him. 3378
10:22 and now **the L** your God has made you 3378
11: 1 Love **the L** your God and keep his 3378
11: 2 the discipline of **the L** your God: 3378
11: 4 how **the L** brought lasting ruin on them. 3378

†LORD distinguishes the proper name of God, *Yahweh*, indicated in the NIV by "LORD," from the words translated "Lord" and "lord," indexed under the heading ***LORD**, pages 683-86.

Dt 11: 7 saw all these great things **the L** has done. 3378
11: 9 that **the L** swore to your forefathers 3378
11:12 It is a land **the L** your God cares for; 3378
11:12 of **the L** your God are continually on it 3378
11:13 to love **the L** your God and to serve him 3378
11:17 from the good land **the L** is giving you. 3378
11:21 that **the L** swore to give your forefathers, 3378
11:22 to love **the L** your God, to walk in all his 3378
11:23 then **the L** will drive out all these nations 3378
11:25 **The L** your God, as he promised you, 3378
11:27 the commands of **the L** your God 3378
11:28 of **the L** your God and turn from the way 3378
11:29 When **the L** your God has brought you 3378
11:31 of the land **the L** your God is giving you. 3378
12: 1 be careful to follow in the land that **the L,** 3378
12: 4 not worship **the L** your God in their way. 3378
12: 5 the place **the L** your God will choose 3378
12: 7 There, in the presence of **the L** your God, 3378
12: 7 because **the L** your God has blessed you. 3378
12: 9 inheritance **the L** your God is giving you. 3378
12:10 the land **the L** your God is giving you as 3378
12:11 the place **the L** your God will choose as 3378
12:11 and all the choice possessions you have vowed to **the L.** 3378
12:12 And there rejoice before **the L** your God, 3378
12:14 at the place **the L** will choose in one 3378
12:15 to the blessing **the L** your God gives you. 3378
12:18 in the presence of **the L** your God at 3378
12:18 at the place **the L** your God will choose— 3378
12:18 to rejoice before **the L** your God 3378
12:20 **the L** your God has enlarged your territory 3378
12:21 the place where **the L** your God chooses 3378
12:21 the herds and flocks **the L** has given you, 3378
12:25 doing what is right in the eyes of **the L.** 3378
12:26 and go to the place **the L** will choose. 3378
12:27 on the altar of **the L** your God, 3378
12:27 beside the altar of **the L** your God, 3378
12:28 and right in the eyes of **the L** your God. 3378
12:29 **The L** your God will cut off before you 3378
12:31 not worship **the L** your God in their way, 3378
12:31 of detestable things **the L** hates. 3378
13: 3 **The L** your God is testing you 3378
13: 4 It is **the L** your God you must follow, 3378
13: 5 rebellion against **the L** your God, 3378
13: 5 the way **the L** your God commanded you 3378
13:10 to turn you away from **the L** your God, 3378
13:12 of the towns **the L** your God is giving you 3378
13:16 a whole burnt offering to **the L** your God. 3378
13:17 that **the L** will turn from his fierce anger; 3378
13:18 because you obey **the L** your God, 3378
14: 1 You are the children of **the L** your God. 3378
14: 2 you are a people holy to **the L** your God. 3378
14: 2 **the L** has chosen you to be his treasured 3378
14:21 you are a people holy to **the L** your God. 3378
14:23 in the presence of **the L** your God at 3378
14:23 to revere **the L** your God always. 3378
14:24 you have been blessed by **the L** your God 3378
14:24 the place where **the L** will choose 3378
14:25 to the place **the L** your God will choose. 3378
14:26 in the presence of **the L** your God 3378
14:29 and so that **the L** your God may bless you 3378
15: 4 in the land **the L** your God is giving you 3378
15: 5 if only you fully obey **the L** your God 3378
15: 6 For **the L** your God will bless you 3378
15: 7 that **the L** your God is giving you, 3378
15: 9 He may then appeal to **the L** against you, 3378
15:10 of this **the L** your God will bless you 3378
15:14 as **the L** your God has blessed you. 3378
15:15 and **the L** your God redeemed you. 3378
15:18 And **the L** your God will bless you 3378
15:19 for **the L** your God every firstborn male 3378
15:20 in the presence of **the L** your God at 3378
15:21 not sacrifice it to **the L** your God. 3378
16: 1 the Passover of **the L** your God, 3378
16: 2 the Passover to **the L** your God an animal 3378
16: 2 the place **the L** will choose as a dwelling 3378
16: 5 in any town **the L** your God gives you 3378
16: 7 at the place **the L** your God will choose. 3378
16: 8 to **the L** your God and do no work. 3378
16:10 Feast of Weeks to **the L** your God by giving 3378
16:10 blessings **the L** your God has given you. 3378
16:11 And rejoice before **the L** your God at 3378
16:15 the Feast to **the L** your God at the place 3378
16:15 at the place **the L** will choose. 3378
16:15 For **the L** your God will bless you 3378
16:16 before **the L** your God at 3378
16:16 before **the L** empty-handed: 3378
16:17 the way **the L** your God has blessed you. 3378
16:18 in every town **the L** your God is giving you, 3378
16:20 the land **the L** your God is giving you. 3378
16:21 the altar you build to **the L** your God, 3378
16:22 for these **the L** your God hates. 3378
17: 1 Do not sacrifice to **the L** your God an ox 3378
17: 2 towns **the L** gives you is found doing evil 3378
17: 2 in the eyes of **the L** your God in violation 3378
17: 8 to the place **the L** your God will choose. 3378
17:10 at the place **the L** will choose. 3378
17:12 to **the L** your God must be put to death. 3378
17:14 the land **the L** your God is giving you 3378
17:15 the king **the L** your God chooses. 3378
17:16 for **the L** has told you, 3378
17:19 that he may learn to revere **the L** his God 3378
18: 1 on the offerings made to **the L** by fire, 3378
18: 2 **the L** is their inheritance, 3378
18: 5 for **the L** your God has chosen them 3378
18: 6 to the place **the L** will choose, 3378
18: 7 in the name of **the L** his God 3378

Dt 18: 7 serve there in the presence of **the L.** 3378
18: 9 the land **the L** your God is giving you, 3378
18:12 who does these things is detestable to **the L,** 3378
18:12 of these detestable practices **the L** your God will drive out those nations 3378
18:13 be blameless before **the L** your God. 3378
18:14 **the L** your God has not permitted you 3378
18:15 **The L** your God will raise up for you 3378
18:16 of **the L** your God at Horeb on the day of 3378
18:16 not hear the voice of **the L** our God 3378
18:17 **The L** said to me: "What they say is good. 3378
18:21 not been spoken by **the L?"** 3378
18:22 of **the L** does not take place or come true, 3378
18:22 that is a message **the L** has not spoken. 3378
19: 1 When **the L** your God has destroyed 3378
19: 2 in the land **the L** your God is giving you 3378
19: 3 the land **the L** your God is giving you as 3378
19: 8 If **the L** your God enlarges your territory, 3378
19: 9 to love **the L** your God and to walk always 3378
19:10 which **the L** your God is giving you 3378
19:14 in the land **the L** your God is giving you 3378
19:17 in the presence of **the L** before the priests 3378
20: 1 because **the L** your God, 3378
20: 4 For **the L** your God is the one who goes 3378
20:13 **the L** your God delivers it into your hand, 3378
20:14 the plunder **the L** your God gives you 3378
20:16 the nations **the L** your God is giving you 3378
20:17 as **the L** your God has commanded you. 3378
20:18 and you will sin against **the L** your God. 3378
21: 1 in the land **the L** your God is giving you 3378
21: 5 for **the L** your God has chosen them 3378
21: 5 of **the L** and to decide all cases of dispute 3378
21: 8 whom you have redeemed, **O L,** 3378
21: 9 done what is right in the eyes of **the L.** 3378
21:10 and **the L** your God delivers them 3378
21:23 the land **the L** your God is giving you as 3378
22: 5 **the L** your God detests anyone who does this. 3378
23: 1 the assembly of **the L.** 3378
23: 2 the assembly of **the L,** 3378
23: 3 the assembly of **the L,** 3378
23: 5 **the L** your God would not listen 3378
23: 5 because **the L** your God loves you. 3378
23: 8 to them may enter the assembly of **the L.** 3378
23:14 For **the L** your God moves about 3378
23:18 of **the L** your God to pay any vow, 3378
23:18 **the L** your God detests them both. 3378
23:20 so that **the L** your God may bless you 3378
23:21 If you make a vow to **the L** your God, 3378
23:21 **the L** your God will certainly demand it 3378
23:23 to **the L** your God with your own mouth. 3378
24: 4 be detestable in the eyes of **the L.** 3378
24: 4 the land **the L** your God is giving you as 3378
24: 9 Remember what **the L** your God did 3378
24:13 in the sight of **the L** your God. 3378
24:15 Otherwise he may cry to **the L** 3378
24:18 and **the L** your God redeemed you 3378
24:19 that **the L** your God may bless you in all 3378
25:15 in the land **the L** your God is giving you. 3378
25:16 **the L** your God detests anyone who does these things. 3378
25:19 When **the L** your God gives you rest 3378
26: 1 the land **the L** your God is giving you as 3378
26: 2 of the land **the L** your God is giving you 3378
26: 2 the place **the L** your God will choose as 3378
26: 3 to **the L** your God that I have come to 3378
26: 3 to the land **the L** swore to our forefathers 3378
26: 4 in front of the altar of **the L** your God. 3378
26: 5 you shall declare before **the L** your God: 3378
26: 7 Then we cried out to **the L,** 3378
26: 7 and **the L** heard our voice 3378
26: 8 So **the L** brought us out of Egypt with 3378
26:10 **O L,** have given me." 3378
26:10 Place the basket before **the L** your God 3378
26:11 the good things **the L** your God has given 3378
26:13 Then say to **the L** your God: 3378
26:14 I have obeyed **the L** my God; 3378
26:16 **The L** your God commands you this day 3378
26:17 that **the L** is your God and 3378
26:18 And **the L** has declared this day 3378
26:19 be a people holy to **the L** your God, 3378
27: 2 the land **the L** your God is giving you, 3378
27: 3 the land **the L** your God is giving you, 3378
27: 3 just as **the L,** the God of your fathers, 3378
27: 5 Build there an altar to **the L** your God, 3378
27: 6 of **the L** your God with fieldstones 3378
27: 6 on it to **the L** your God. 3378
27: 7 in the presence of **the L** your God. 3378
27: 9 the people of **the L** your God. 3378
27:10 Obey **the L** your God and follow his 3378
27:15 a thing detestable to **the L,** 3378
28: 1 If you fully obey **the L** your God 3378
28: 1 **the L** your God will set you high 3378
28: 2 if you obey **the L** your God: 3378
28: 7 **The L** will grant that the enemies who 3378
28: 8 **The L** will send a blessing on your barns 3378
28: 8 **The L** your God will bless you in 3378
28: 9 **The L** will establish you as his holy people 3378
28: 9 of **the L** your God and walk in his ways. 3378
28:10 that you are called by the name of **the L,** 3378
28:11 **The L** will grant you abundant prosperity— 3378
28:12 **The L** will open the heavens, 3378
28:13 **The L** will make you the head, 3378
28:13 of **the L** your God that I give you this day 3378
28:15 if you do not obey **the L** your God and do 3378
28:20 **The L** will send on you curses, 3378
28:21 **The L** will plague you with diseases 3378

Dt 28:22 **The L** will strike you with wasting disease, 3378
28:24 **The L** will turn the rain of your country 3378
28:25 **The L** will cause you to be defeated 3378
28:27 **The L** will afflict you with the boils 3378
28:28 **The L** will afflict you with madness, 3378
28:35 **The L** will afflict your knees and legs 3378
28:36 **The L** will drive you and the king you set 3378
28:37 the nations where **the L** will drive you. 3378
28:45 because you did not obey **the L** your God 3378
28:47 not serve **the L** your God joyfully 3378
28:48 you will serve the enemies **the L** sends 3378
28:49 **The L** will bring a nation against you 3378
28:52 the land **the L** your God is giving you. 3378
28:53 daughters **the L** your God has given you. 3378
28:58 and awesome name—**the L** your God— 3378
28:59 **the L** will send fearful plagues on you 3378
28:61 **The L** will also bring on you every kind 3378
28:62 because you did not obey **the L** your God. 3378
28:63 as it pleased **the L** to make you prosper 3378
28:64 **the L** will scatter you among all nations, 3378
28:65 There **the L** will give you 3378
28:68 **The L** will send you back in ships 3378
29: 1 of the covenant **the L** commanded Moses 3378
29: 2 Your eyes have seen all that **the L** did 3378
29: 4 But to this day **the L** has not given you 3378
29: 6 that I am **the L** your God. 3378
29:10 in the presence of **the L** your God— 3378
29:12 into a covenant with **the L** your God, 3378
29:12 a covenant **the L** is making 3378
29:15 in the presence of **the L** our God but also 3378
29:18 from **the L** our God to go and worship 3378
29:20 **The L** will never be willing 3378
29:20 and **the L** will blot out his name from 3378
29:21 **The L** will single him out from all 3378
29:22 with which **the L** has afflicted it. 3378
29:23 which **the L** overthrew in fierce anger. 3378
29:24 "Why has **the L** done this to this land? 3378
29:25 the covenant of **the L,** the God of their 3378
29:28 and in great wrath **the L** uprooted them 3378
29:29 secret things belong to **the L** our God, 3378
30: 1 wherever **the L** your God disperses you 3378
30: 2 return to **the L** your God and obey him 3378
30: 3 **the L** your God will restore your fortunes 3378
30: 4 from there **the L** your God will gather you 3378
30: 6 **The L** your God will circumcise your hearts 3378
30: 7 **The L** your God will put all these curses 3378
30: 8 You will again obey **the L** 3378
30: 9 **the L** your God will make you most prosperous 3378
30: 9 **The L** will again delight in you 3378
30:10 if you obey **the L** your God 3378
30:10 to **the L** your God with all your heart and 3378
30:16 to love **the L** your God, to walk 3378
30:16 and **the L** your God will bless you in 3378
30:20 and that you may love **the L** your God, 3378
30:20 For **the L** is your life, 3378
31: 2 **The L** has said to me, 3378
31: 3 **The L** your God himself will cross over 3378
31: 3 cross over ahead of you, as **the L** said. 3378
31: 4 And **the L** will do to them what he did 3378
31: 5 **The L** will deliver them to you, 3378
31: 6 for **the L** your God goes with you; 3378
31: 7 that **the L** swore to their forefathers 3378
31: 8 **The L** himself goes before you and will 3378
31: 9 the ark of the covenant of **the L,** 3378
31:11 to appear before **the L** your God at 3378
31:12 and learn to fear **the L** your God 3378
31:13 to fear **the L** your God as long as you live 3378
31:14 **The L** said to Moses, 3378
31:15 Then **the L** appeared at the Tent in 3378
31:16 And **the L** said to Moses: 3378
31:23 The L gave this command to Joshua son NIH
31:25 the ark of the covenant of **the L:** 3378
31:26 of the covenant of **the L** your God. 3378
31:27 If you have been rebellious against **the L** 3378
31:29 in the sight of **the L** and provoke him 3378
32: 3 I will proclaim the name of **the L.** 3378
32: 6 Is this the way you repay **the L,** 3378
32:12 **The L** alone led him; 3378
32:19 **The L** saw this and rejected them 3378
32:27 **the L** has not done all this.' " 3378
32:30 unless **the L** had given them up? 3378
32:36 **The L** will judge his people 3378
32:48 On that same day **the L** told Moses, 3378
33: 2 **"The L** came from Sinai and dawned 3378
33: 7 "Hear, **O L,** the cry of Judah; 3378
33:11 Bless all his skills, **O L,** 3378
33:12 the beloved of **the L** rest secure in him, 3378
33:12 the L loves rests between his shoulders." NIH
33:13 "May **the L** bless his land with 3378
33:23 of **the L** and is full of his blessing; 3378
33:29 a people saved by **the L?** 3378
34: 1 There **the L** showed him the whole land— 3378
34: 4 Then **the L** said to him, 3378
34: 5 Moses the servant of **the L** died there in Moab, 3378
34: 5 as **the L** had said. 3378
34: 9 did what **the L** had commanded Moses. 3378
34:10 whom **the L** knew face to face, 3378
34:11 and wonders **the L** sent him to do 3378
Jos 1: 1 the death of Moses the servant of **the L,** 3378
1: 1 **the L** said to Joshua son of Nun, 3378
1: 9 be discouraged, for **the L** your God will 3378
1:11 of the land **the L** your God is giving you 3378
1:13 that Moses the servant of **the L** gave you: 3378
1:13 **'The L** your God is giving you rest 3378
1:15 until **the L** gives them rest, 3378

†LORD distinguishes the proper name of God, *Yahweh*, indicated in the NIV by "LORD," from the words translated "Lord" and "lord," indexed under the heading ***LORD**, pages 683-86.

Jos 1:15 that **the L** your God is giving them. 3378
1:15 the servant of **the L** gave you east of 3378
1:17 Only may **the L** your God be with you 3378
2: 9 that **the L** has given this land to you and 3378
2:10 We have heard how **the L** dried up 3378
2:11 for **the L** your God is God in heaven 3378
2:12 by **the L** that you will show kindness 3378
2:14 and faithfully when **the L** gives us 3378
2:24 **"The L** has surely given the whole land 3378
3: 3 of the covenant of **the L** your God, 3378
3: 5 tomorrow **the L** will do amazing things 3378
3: 7 And **the L** said to Joshua, 3378
3: 9 and listen to the words of **the L** your God. 3378
3:13 as the priests who carry the ark of **the L**— 3378
3:17 of **the L** stood firm on dry ground in 3378
4: 1 **the L** said to Joshua, 3378
4: 5 the ark of **the L** your God into the middle 3378
4: 7 before the ark of the covenant of **the L.** 3378
4: 8 as **the L** had told Joshua; 3378
4:10 until everything **the L** had commanded Joshua was done 3378
4:11 the ark of **the L** and the priests came to 3378
4:13 over before **the L** to the plains of Jericho 3378
4:14 That day **the L** exalted Joshua in the sight 3378
4:15 Then **the L** said to Joshua, 3378
4:18 the ark of the covenant of **the L.** 3378
4:23 For **the L** your God dried up the Jordan 3378
4:23 **The L** your God did to the Jordan 3378
4:24 that the hand of **the L** is powerful and so 3378
4:24 you might always fear **the L** your God." 3378
5: 1 along the coast heard how **the L** had dried 3378
5: 2 At that time **the L** said to Joshua, 3378
5: 6 since they had not obeyed **the L.** 3378
5: 6 For **the L** had sworn to them 3378
5: 9 Then **the L** said to Joshua, 3378
5:14 as commander of the army of **the L** I have 3378
6: 2 Then **the L** said to Joshua, "See, 3378
6: 6 "Take up the ark of the covenant of **the L** 3378
6: 7 ahead of the ark of **the L."** 3378
6: 8 before **the L** went forward, 3378
6:11 So he had the ark of **the L** carried around 3378
6:12 and the priests took up the ark of **the L.** 3378
6:13 before the ark of **the L** and blowing 3378
6:13 the rear guard followed the ark of **the L,** 3378
6:16 For **the L** has given you the city! 3378
6:17 that is in it are to be devoted to **the L.** 3378
6:19 and iron are sacred to **the L** and must go 3378
6:21 the city to **the L** and destroyed with NIH
6:26 before **the L** is the man who undertakes 3378
6:27 So **the L** was with Joshua, 3378
7: 6 to the ground before the ark of **the L,** 3378
7: 7 And Joshua said, "Ah, Sovereign **L,** 3378
7:10 **The L** said to Joshua, "Stand up! 3378
7:13 this is what **the L,** the God of Israel, says: 3378
7:14 that **the L** takes shall come forward clan 3378
7:14 **the L** takes shall come forward family 3378
7:14 that **the L** takes shall come forward man 3378
7:15 of **the L** and has done a disgraceful thing 3378
7:19 give glory to **the L,** the God of Israel, 3378
7:20 I have sinned against **the L,** 3378
7:23 and spread them out before **the L.** 3378
7:25 **The L** will bring trouble on you today." 3378
7:26 Then **the L** turned from his fierce anger. 3378
8: 1 **the L** said to Joshua, "Do not be afraid; 3378
8: 7 **The L** your God will give it 3378
8: 8 Do what **the L** has commanded. 3378
8:18 Then **the L** said to Joshua, 3378
8:27 as **the L** had instructed Joshua. 3378
8:30 on Mount Ebal an altar to **the L,** 3378
8:31 of **the L** had commanded the Israelites. 3378
8:31 On it they offered to **the L** burnt offerings 3378
8:33 of **the L,** facing those who carried it— 3378
8:33 of **the L** had formerly commanded 3378
9: 9 because of the fame of **the L** your God. 3378
9:14 but did not inquire of **the L.** 3378
9:18 had sworn an oath to them by **the L,** 3378
9:19 "We have given them our oath by **the L,** 3378
9:24 **the L** your God had commanded his servant Moses 3378
9:27 the community and for the altar of **the L** 3378
9:27 at the place **the L** would choose. NIH
10: 8 **The L** said to Joshua, 3378
10:10 **The L** threw them into confusion 3378
10:11 **the L** hurled large hailstones down 3378
10:12 On the day **the L** gave the Amorites over 3378
10:12 Joshua said to **the L** in the presence 3378
10:14 a day when **the L** listened to a man. 3378
10:14 Surely **the L** was fighting for Israel! 3378
10:19 for **the L** your God has given them 3378
10:25 This is what **the L** will do to all 3378
10:30 **The L** also gave that city and its king 3378
10:32 **The L** handed Lachish over to Israel, 3378
10:40 just as **the L,** the God of Israel, 3378
10:42 because **the L,** the God of Israel, 3378
11: 6 **The L** said to Joshua, 3378
11: 8 **the L** gave them into the hand of Israel. 3378
11: 9 Joshua did to them as **the L** had directed: 3378
11:12 the servant of **the L** had commanded. 3378
11:15 As **the L** commanded his servant Moses, 3378
11:15 of all that **the L** commanded Moses. 3378
11:20 was **the L** *himself* who hardened their hearts 3378
11:20 as **the L** had commanded Moses. 3378
11:23 just as **the L** had directed Moses, 3378
12: 6 Moses, the servant of **the L,** 3378
12: 6 of **the L** gave their land to the Reubenites, 3378
13: 1 **the L** said to him, "You are very old, 3378
13: 8 as he, the servant of **the L,** had assigned 3378

Jos 13:14 since the offerings made by fire to **the L,** 3378
13:33 **the L,** the God of Israel, 3378
14: 2 as **the L** had commanded through Moses. 3378
14: 5 just as **the L** had commanded Moses. 3378
14: 6 "You know what **the L** said to Moses 3378
14: 7 when Moses the servant of **the L** sent me 3378
14: 8 followed **the L** my God wholeheartedly. 3378
14: 9 you have followed **the L** my God wholeheartedly.' 3378
14:10 "Now then, just as **the L** promised, 3378
14:12 that **the L** promised me that day. 3378
14:12 but, **the L** helping me, 3378
14:14 because he followed **the L,** 3378
17: 4 **"The L** commanded Moses to give us 3378
17:14 and **the L** has blessed us abundantly." 3378
18: 3 to take possession of the land that **the L,** 3378
18: 6 for you in the presence of **the L** our God. 3378
18: 7 of **the L** is their inheritance. 3378
18: 7 the servant of **the L** gave it to them." 3378
18: 8 at Shiloh in the presence of **the L."** 3378
18:10 in Shiloh in the presence of **the L,** 3378
19:50 as **the L** had commanded. 3378
19:51 by lot at Shiloh in the presence of **the L** at 3378
20: 1 Then **the L** said to Joshua: 3378
21: 2 **"The L** commanded through Moses 3378
21: 3 So, as **the L** had commanded, 3378
21: 8 as **the L** had commanded through Moses. 3378
21:43 So **the L** gave Israel all the land 3378
21:44 **The L** gave them rest on every side, 3378
21:44 **the L** handed all their enemies over 3378
22: 2 the servant of **the L** commanded, 3378
22: 3 the mission **the L** your God gave you. 3378
22: 4 **the L** your God has given your brothers rest 3378
22: 4 that Moses the servant of **the L** gave you 3378
22: 5 that Moses the servant of **the L** gave you: 3378
22: 5 to love **the L** your God, to walk in all his 3378
22: 9 in accordance with the command of **the L** 3378
22:16 "The whole assembly of **the L** says: 3378
22:16 from **the L** and build yourselves an altar 3378
22:17 a plague fell on the community of **the L!** 3378
22:18 are you now turning away from **the L?** 3378
22:18 " 'If you rebel against **the L** today, 3378
22:19 against **the L** or against us by building 3378
22:19 other than the altar of **the L** our God. 3378
22:22 "The Mighty One, God, **the L!** 3378
22:22 The Mighty One, God, **the L!** 3378
22:22 in rebellion or disobedience to **the L,** 3378
22:23 from **the L** and to offer burnt offerings 3378
22:23 may **the L** himself call us to account. 3378
22:24 'What do you have to do with **the L,** 3378
22:25 **The L** has made the Jordan a boundary 3378
22:25 You have no share in **the L.'** 3378
22:25 to stop fearing **the L.** 3378
22:27 that we will worship **the L** 3378
22:27 'You have no share in **the L.'** 3378
22:29 "Far be it from us to rebel against **the L** 3378
22:29 the altar of **the L** our God that stands 3378
22:31 "Today we know that **the L** is with us, 3378
22:31 not acted unfaithfully toward **the L** 3378
22:34 A Witness Between Us that **the L** is God. 3378
23: 1 and **the L** had given Israel rest 3378
23: 3 You yourselves have seen everything **the L** your God has done 3378
23: 3 it was **the L** your God who fought 3378
23: 5 **The L** your God himself will drive them out 3378
23: 5 as **the L** your God promised you. 3378
23: 8 you are to hold fast to **the L** your God, 3378
23: 9 **"The L** has driven out before you great 3378
23:10 because **the L** your God fights for you, 3378
23:11 be very careful to love **the L** your God. 3378
23:13 **the L** your God will no longer drive out these nations 3378
23:13 which **the L** your God has given you. 3378
23:14 not one of all the good promises **the L** your God gave you has failed. 3378
23:15 of **the L** your God has come true, 3378
23:15 so **the L** will bring on you all 3378
23:16 the covenant of **the L** your God, 3378
24: 2 "This is what **the L,** the God of Israel, 3378
24: 7 But they cried to **the L** for help, 3378
24:14 "Now fear **the L** and serve him 3378
24:14 and serve **the L.** 3378
24:15 if serving **the L** seems undesirable to you, 3378
24:15 me and my household, we will serve **the L."** 3378
24:16 to forsake **the L** to serve other gods! 3378
24:17 was **the L** our God himself who brought us 3378
24:18 **the L** drove out before us all the nations, 3378
24:18 We too will serve **the L,** 3378
24:19 "You are not able to serve **the L.** 3378
24:20 you forsake **the L** and serve foreign gods, 3378
24:21 We will serve **the L."** 3378
24:22 that you have chosen to serve **the L."** 3378
24:23 and yield your hearts to **the L,** 3378
24:24 "We will serve **the L** our God 3378
24:26 the oak near the holy place of **the L.** 3378
24:27 It has heard all the words **the L** has said 3378
24:29 Joshua son of Nun, the servant of **the L,** 3378
24:31 Israel served **the L** throughout 3378
24:31 had experienced everything **the L** had done 3378
Jdg 1: 1 the Israelites asked **the L,** 3378
1: 2 **The L** answered, "Judah is to go; 3378
1: 4 **the L** gave the Canaanites and Perizzites 3378
1:19 **The L** was with the men of Judah. 3378
1:22 and **the L** was with them. 3378
2: 1 The angel of **the L** went up from Gilgal 3378
2: 4 of **the L** had spoken these things to all 3378
2: 5 There they offered sacrifices to **the L.** 3378

Jdg 2: 7 The people served **the L** throughout 3378
2: 7 the great things **the L** had done for Israel. 3378
2: 8 Joshua son of Nun, the servant of **the L,** 3378
2:10 who knew neither **the L** nor what he had 3378
2:11 in the eyes of **the L** and served the Baals. 3378
2:12 They forsook **the L,** the God of their fathers 3378
2:12 They provoked **the L** to anger 3378
2:14 against Israel **the L** handed them over 3378
2:15 of **the L** was against them to defeat them, 3378
2:16 Then **the L** raised up judges, 3378
2:18 Whenever **the L** raised up a judge 3378
2:18 for **the L** had compassion on them 3378
2:20 **the L** was very angry with Israel and said, 3378
2:22 the way of **the L** and walk in it 3378
2:23 **The L** had allowed those nations 3378
3: 1 These are the nations **the L** left 3378
3: 7 Israelites did evil in the eyes of **the L;** 3378
3: 7 they forgot **the L** their God and served 3378
3: 8 The anger of **the L** burned against Israel 3378
3: 9 But when they cried out to **the L,** 3378
3:10 The Spirit of **the L** came upon him, 3378
3:10 **The L** gave Cushan-Rishathaim king 3378
3:12 the Israelites did evil in the eyes of **the L,** 3378
3:12 they did this evil **the L** gave Eglon king 3378
3:15 Again the Israelites cried out to **the L,** 3378
3:28 "for **the L** has given Moab, your enemy, 3378
4: 1 again did evil in the eyes of **the L.** 3378
4: 2 **the L** sold them into the hands of Jabin, 3378
4: 3 they cried to **the L** for help. 3378
4: 6 **"The L,** the God of Israel, 3378
4: 9 **the L** will hand Sisera over to a woman." 3378
4:14 This is the day **the L** has given Sisera 3378
4:14 Has not **the L** gone ahead of you?" 3378
4:15 **the L** routed Sisera and all his chariots 3378
5: 2 when the people willingly offer themselves—praise **the L!** 3378
5: 3 I will sing to **the L,** I will sing; 3378
5: 3 I will make music to **the L,** 3378
5: 4 "O **L,** when you went out from Seir, 3378
5: 5 The mountains quaked before **the L,** 3378
5: 5 before **the L,** the God of Israel. 3378
5: 9 Praise **the L!** 3378
5:11 They recite the righteous acts of **the L,** 3378
5:11 "Then the people of **the L** went down to 3378
5:13 of **the L** came to me with the mighty. 3378
5:23 'Curse Meroz,' said the angel of **the L.** 3378
5:23 because they did not come to help **the L,** 3378
5:23 to help **the L** against the mighty.' 3378
5:31 "So may all your enemies perish, O **L!** 3378
6: 1 the Israelites did evil in the eyes of **the L,** 3378
6: 6 the Israelites that they cried out to **the L** 3378
6: 7 When the Israelites cried to **the L** because 3378
6: 8 "This is what **the L,** the God of Israel, 3378
6:10 I said to you, 'I am **the L** your God; 3378
6:11 of **the L** came and sat down under the oak 3378
6:12 the angel of **the L** appeared to Gideon, 3378
6:12 **"The L** is with you, mighty warrior." 3378
6:13 Gideon replied, "if **the L** is with us, 3378
6:13 'Did not **the L** bring us up out of Egypt?' 3378
6:13 now **the L** has abandoned us and put us 3378
6:14 **The L** turned to him and said, 3378
6:16 **The L** answered, "I will be with you, 3378
6:18 **the L** said, "I will wait until you return." NIH
6:21 the angel of **the L** touched the meat and 3378
6:21 And the angel of **the L** disappeared. 3378
6:22 that it was the angel of **the L,** 3378
6:22 he exclaimed, "Ah, Sovereign **L!** 3378
6:22 I have seen the angel of **the L** face 3378
6:23 But **the L** said to him, "Peace! 3378
6:24 So Gideon built an altar to **the L** there 3378
6:24 and called it **The L** is Peace. 3378
6:25 That same night **the L** said to him, 3378
6:26 a proper kind of altar to **the L** your God 3378
6:27 of his servants and did as **the L** told him. 3378
6:34 the Spirit of **the L** came upon Gideon, 3378
7: 2 **The L** said to Gideon, "You have too many 3378
7: 4 But **the L** said to Gideon, "There are still 3378
7: 5 There **the L** told him, "Separate those who 3378
7: 7 **The L** said to Gideon, 3378
7: 9 During that night **the L** said to Gideon, 3378
7:15 **The L** has given the Midianite camp 3378
7:18 'For **the L** and for Gideon.' " 3378
7:20 "A sword for **the L** and for Gideon!" 3378
7:22 **the L** caused the men throughout 3378
8: 7 when **the L** has given Zebah 3378
8:19 As surely as **the L** lives, 3378
8:23 **The L** will rule over you." 3378
8:34 and did not remember **the L** their God, 3378
10: 6 the Israelites did evil in the eyes of **the L.** 3378
10: 6 And because the Israelites forsook **the L** 3378
10:10 Then the Israelites cried out to **the L,** 3378
10:11 **The L** replied, "When the Egyptians, 3378
10:15 Israelites said to **the L,** "We have sinned. 3378
10:16 among them and served **the L.** 3378
11: 9 the Ammonites and **the L** gives them 3378
11:10 **"The L** is our witness; 3378
11:11 before **the L** in Mizpah. 3378
11:21 "Then **the L,** the God of Israel, 3378
11:23 "Now since **the L,** the God of Israel, 3378
11:24 whatever **the L** our God has given us, 3378
11:27 Let **the L,** the Judge, decide the dispute 3378
11:29 the Spirit of **the L** came upon Jephthah. 3378
11:30 And Jephthah made a vow to **the L:** 3378
11:32 and **the L** gave them into his hands. 3378
11:35 because I have made a vow to **the L** 3378
11:36 "you have given your word to **the L.** 3378
11:36 now that **the L** has avenged you 3378

†**LORD** distinguishes the proper name of God, *Yahweh*, indicated in the NIV by "LORD," from the words translated "Lord" and "lord," indexed under the heading ***LORD**, pages 683-86.

Jdg 12: 3 and **the L** gave me the victory over them. 3378
13: 1 the Israelites did evil in the eyes of **the L,** 3378
13: 1 so **the L** delivered them into the hands of 3378
13: 3 The angel of **the L** appeared to her 3378
13: 8 Then Manoah prayed to **the L:** 3378
13:13 The angel of **the L** answered, 3378
13:15 Manoah said to the angel of **the L,** 3378
13:16 The angel of **the L** replied, 3378
13:16 a burnt offering, offer it to **the L."** 3378
13:16 not realize that it was the angel of **the L.)** 3378
13:17 Manoah inquired of the angel of **the L,** 3378
13:19 and sacrificed it on a rock to **the L.** 3378
13:19 And the L did an amazing thing NIH
13:20 the angel of **the L** ascended in the flame. 3378
13:21 of **the L** did not show himself again 3378
13:21 that it was the angel of **the L.** 3378
13:23 "If **the L** had meant to kill us, 3378
13:24 He grew and **the L** blessed him, 3378
13:25 and the Spirit of **the L** began to stir him 3378
14: 4 from **the L,** who was seeking an occasion 3378
14: 6 Spirit of **the L** came upon him in power 3378
14:19 Spirit of **the L** came upon him in power. 3378
15:14 The Spirit of **the L** came upon him 3378
15:18 he was very thirsty, he cried out to **the L,** 3378
16:20 he did not know that **the L** had left him. 3378
16:28 Then Samson prayed to **the L,** 3378
16:28 "O Sovereign **L,** remember me. 3378
17: 2 Then his mother said, **"The L** bless you, 3378
17: 3 "I solemnly consecrate my silver to **the L** 3378
17:13 I know that **the L** will be good to me, 3378
19:18 and now I am going to the house of **the L.** 3378
20: 1 as one man and assembled before **the L** 3378
20:18 **The L** replied, "Judah shall go first." 3378
20:23 up and wept before **the L** until evening, 3378
20:23 and they inquired of **the L.** 3378
20:23 **The L** answered, "Go up against them." 3378
20:26 and there they sat weeping before **the L.** 3378
20:26 and fellowship offerings to **the L.** 3378
20:27 And the Israelites inquired of **the L.** 3378
20:28 **The L** responded, "Go, 3378
20:35 **The L** defeated Benjamin before Israel, 3378
21: 3 "O **L,** the God of Israel," they cried, 3378
21: 5 failed to assemble before **the L?"** 3378
21: 5 before **the L** at Mizpah should certainly 3378
21: 7 since we have taken an oath by **the L** not 3378
21: 8 of Israel failed to assemble before **the L** 3378
21:15 because **the L** had made a gap in 3378
21:19 the annual festival of **the L** in Shiloh, 3378
Ru 1: 6 in Moab that **the L** had come to the aid 3378
1: 8 May **the L** show kindness to you, 3378
1: 9 May **the L** grant that each of you will find 3378
1:17 May **the L** deal with me, 3378
1:21 but **the L** has brought me back empty. 3378
1:21 **The L** has afflicted me; the Almighty 3378
2: 4 **"The L** be with you!" 3378
2: 4 **"The L** bless you!" 3378
2:12 May **the L** repay you for what you have 3378
2:12 May you be richly rewarded by **the L,** 3378
2:20 **"The L** bless him!" 3378
3:10 **"The L** bless you, my daughter," 3378
3:13 as surely as **the L** lives I will do it. 3378
4:11 May **the L** make the woman who 3378
4:12 Through the offspring **the L** gives you 3378
4:13 and **the L** enabled her to conceive, 3378
4:14 "Praise be to **the L,** 3378
1Sa 1: 3 and sacrifice to **the L** Almighty at Shiloh, 3378
1: 3 the two sons of Eli, were priests of **the L.** 3378
1: 5 and **the L** had closed her womb. 3378
1: 6 And because **the L** had closed her womb, 3378
1: 7 Hannah went up to the house of **the L,** 3378
1:10 and prayed to **the L.** 3378
1:11 she made a vow, saying, "O **L** Almighty, 3378
1:11 then I will give him to **the L** for all 3378
1:12 As she kept on praying to **the L,** 3378
1:15 I was pouring out my soul to **the L.** 3378
1:19 before **the L** and then went back 3378
1:19 and **the L** remembered her. 3378
1:20 saying, "Because I asked **the L** for him." 3378
1:21 to offer the annual sacrifice to **the L** and 3378
1:22 and present him before **the L,** 3378
1:23 only may **the L** make good his word." 3378
1:24 and brought him to the house of **the L** 3378
1:26 beside you praying to **the L.** 3378
1:27 and **the L** has granted me what I asked 3378
1:28 So now I give him to **the L.** 3378
1:28 be given over to **the L."** 3378
1:28 And he worshiped **the L** there. 3378
2: 1 "My heart rejoices in **the L;** 3378
2: 1 in **the L** my horn is lifted high. 3378
2: 2 "There is no one holy like **the L;** 3378
2: 3 for **the L** is a God who knows, 3378
2: 6 **"The L** brings death and makes alive; 3378
2: 7 **The L** sends poverty and wealth; 3378
2:10 those who oppose **the L** will be shattered. 3378
2:10 **the L** will judge the ends of the earth. 3378
2:11 the boy ministered before **the L** under Eli 3378
2:12 they had no regard for **the L.** 3378
2:18 But Samuel was ministering before **the L—** 3378
2:20 "May **the L** give you children 3378
2:20 the one she prayed for and gave to **the L."** 3378
2:21 And **the L** was gracious to Hannah; 3378
2:21 Samuel grew up in the presence of **the L.** 3378
2:25 but if a man sins against **the L,** 3378
2:26 to grow in stature and in favor with **the L** 3378
2:27 "This is what **the L** says: 3378
2:30 "Therefore **the L,** the God of Israel, 3378
2:30 now **the L** declares: 'Far be it from me! 3378
1Sa 3: 1 The boy Samuel ministered before **the L** 3378
3: 1 In those days the word of **the L** was rare; 3378
3: 3 down in the temple of **the L,** 3378
3: 4 Then **the L** called Samuel. 3378
3: 6 Again **the L** called, "Samuel!" 3378
3: 7 Now Samuel did not yet know **the L:** 3378
3: 7 of **the L** had not yet been revealed to him. 3378
3: 8 **The L** called Samuel a third time, 3378
3: 8 Then Eli realized that **the L** was calling 3378
3: 9 and if he calls you, say, 'Speak, **L,** 3378
3:10 **The L** came and stood there, 3378
3:11 And **the L** said to Samuel: 3378
3:15 the doors of the house of **the L.** 3378
3:18 Then Eli said, "He is **the L;** 3378
3:19 **The L** was with Samuel as he grew up, 3378
3:20 Samuel was attested as a prophet of **the L.** 3378
3:21 **The L** continued to appear at Shiloh, 3378
4: 3 "Why did **the L** bring defeat 3378
4: 4 of the covenant of **the L** Almighty, 3378
4: 6 the ark of **the L** had come into the camp, 3378
5: 3 on the ground before the ark of **the L!** 3378
5: 4 on the ground before the ark of **the L!** 3378
6: 1 When the ark of **the L** had been 3378
6: 2 "What shall we do with the ark of **the L?** 3378
6: 8 the ark of **the L** and put it on the cart, 3378
6: 9 then **the L** has brought this great disaster 2085[S]
6:11 They placed the ark of **the L** on the cart 3378
6:14 the cows as a burnt offering to **the L.** 3378
6:15 The Levites took down the ark of **the L,** 3378
6:15 and made sacrifices to **the L.** 3378
6:17 as a guilt offering to **the L—** 3378
6:18 on which they set the ark of **the L,** 3378
6:19 into the ark of **the L.** 3378
6:19 of the heavy blow **the L** had dealt them, 3378
6:20 "Who can stand in the presence of **the L,** 3378
6:21 Philistines have returned the ark of **the L.** 3378
7: 1 and took up the ark of **the L.** 3378
7: 1 to guard the ark of **the L.** 3378
7: 2 of Israel mourned and sought after **the L.** 3378
7: 3 "If you are returning to **the L** 3378
7: 3 and commit yourselves to **the L** 3378
7: 4 and served **the L** only. 3378
7: 5 at Mizpah and I will intercede with **the L** 3378
7: 6 and poured it out before **the L.** 3378
7: 6 "We have sinned against **the L."** 3378
7: 8 "Do not stop crying out to **the L** our God 3378
7: 9 up as a whole burnt offering to **the L.** 3378
7: 9 He cried out to **the L** on Israel's behalf, 3378
7: 9 and **the L** answered him. 3378
7:10 But that day **the L** thundered 3378
7:12 saying, "Thus far has **the L** helped us." 3378
7:13 hand of **the L** was against the Philistines. 3378
7:17 And he built an altar there to **the L.** 3378
8: 6 so he prayed to **the L.** 3378
8: 7 And **the L** told him: "Listen to all that 3378
8:10 Samuel told all the words of **the L** to 3378
8:18 and **the L** will not answer you in 3378
8:21 he repeated it before **the L.** 3378
8:22 **The L** answered, "Listen to them 3378
9:15 **the L** had revealed this to Samuel: 3378
9:17 **the L** said to him, "This is the man 3378
10: 1 "Has not **the L** anointed you leader 3378
10: 6 The Spirit of **the L** will come upon you 3378
10:17 the people of Israel to **the L** at Mizpah 3378
10:18 "This is what **the L,** the God of Israel, 3378
10:19 So now present yourselves before **the L** 3378
10:22 So they inquired further of **the L,** 3378
10:22 And **the L** said, "Yes, 3378
10:24 "Do you see the man **the L** has chosen? 3378
10:25 on a scroll and deposited it before **the L.** 3378
11: 7 the terror of **the L** fell on the people, 3378
11:13 for this day **the L** has rescued Israel." 3378
11:15 as king in the presence of **the L.** 3378
11:15 before **the L,** and Saul and all 3378
12: 3 in the presence of **the L** and his anointed. 3378
12: 5 **"The L** is witness against you, 3378
12: 6 "It is **the L** who appointed Moses 3378
12: 7 with evidence before **the L** as to all 3378
12: 7 the righteous acts performed by **the L** 3378
12: 8 they cried to **the L** for help, 3378
12: 8 and **the L** sent Moses and Aaron, 3378
12: 9 "But they forgot **the L** their God; 3378
12:10 They cried out to **the L** and said, 3378
12:10 we have forsaken **the L** and served 3378
12:11 Then **the L** sent Jerub-Baal, Barak, 3378
12:12 though **the L** your God was your king. 3378
12:13 see, **the L** has set a king over you. 3378
12:14 If you fear **the L** and serve and obey him 3378
12:14 over you follow **the L** your God— 3378
12:15 But if you do not obey **the L,** 3378
12:16 stand still and see this great thing **the L** is 3378
12:17 I will call upon **the L** to send thunder 3378
12:17 an evil thing you did in the eyes of **the L** 3378
12:18 Then Samuel called upon **the L,** 3378
12:18 that same day **the L** sent thunder and rain. 3378
12:18 So all the people stood in awe of **the L** 3378
12:19 "Pray to **the L** your God for your servants 3378
12:20 yet do not turn away from **the L,** 3378
12:20 but serve **the L** with all your heart. 3378
12:22 For the sake of his great name **the L** will 3378
12:22 **the L** was pleased to make you his own. 3378
12:23 that I should sin against **the L** by failing 3378
12:24 to fear **the L** and serve him faithfully 3378
13:13 the command **the L** your God gave you; 3378
13:14 **the L** has sought out a man 3378
14: 6 Perhaps **the L** will act in our behalf. 3378
14: 6 Nothing can hinder **the L** from saving, 3378
1Sa 14:10 that **the L** has given them into our hands." 3378
14:12 **the L** has given them into the hand 3378
14:23 So **the L** rescued Israel that day, 3378
14:33 the men are sinning against **the L** 3378
14:34 Do not sin against **the L** by eating meat 3378
14:35 Then Saul built an altar to **the L;** 3378
14:39 surely as **the L** who rescues Israel lives, 3378
14:41 Then Saul prayed to **the L,** 3378
14:45 As surely as **the L** lives, 3378
15: 1 the one **the L** sent to anoint you king 3378
15: 1 so listen now to the message from **the L.** 3378
15: 2 This is what **the L** Almighty says: 3378
15:10 Then the word of **the L** came to Samuel: 3378
15:11 and he cried out to **the L** all that night. 3378
15:13 Saul said, **"The L** bless you! 3378
15:15 and cattle to sacrifice to **the L** your God, 3378
15:16 "Let me tell you what **the L** said 3378
15:17 **The L** anointed you king over Israel. 3378
15:19 Why did you not obey **the L?** 3378
15:19 and do evil in the eyes of **the L?"** 3378
15:20 "But I did obey **the L,"** Saul said. 3378
15:20 "I went on the mission **the L** assigned me. 3378
15:21 to sacrifice them to **the L** your God 3378
15:22 "Does **the L** delight in burnt offerings 3378
15:22 as in obeying the voice of **the L?** 3378
15:23 you have rejected the word of **the L,** 3378
15:25 so that I may worship **the L."** 3378
15:26 You have rejected the word of **the L,** 3378
15:26 and **the L** has rejected you as king 3378
15:28 **"The L** has torn the kingdom of Israel 3378
15:30 so that I may worship **the L** your God." 3378
15:31 and Saul worshiped **the L.** 3378
15:33 put Agag to death before **the L** at Gilgal. 3378
15:35 **the L** was grieved that he had made Saul 3378
16: 1 **The L** said to Samuel, 3378
16: 2 **The L** said, "Take a heifer with you 3378
16: 2 'I have come to sacrifice to **the L.'** 3378
16: 4 Samuel did what **the L** said. 3378
16: 5 I have come to sacrifice to **the L.** 3378
16: 6 "Surely the LORD's anointed stands here
before **the L."** 3378
16: 7 But **the L** said to Samuel, 3378
16: 7 The L does not look at the things man looks NIH
16: 7 but **the L** looks at the heart." 3378
16: 8 **"The L** has not chosen this one either." 3378
16: 9 "Nor has **the L** chosen this one." 3378
16:10 **"The L** has not chosen these." 3378
16:12 Then **the L** said, "Rise and anoint him; 3378
16:13 from that day on the Spirit of **the L** came 3378
16:14 Spirit of **the L** had departed from Saul, 3378
16:14 an evil spirit from **the L** tormented him. 3378
16:18 And **the L** is with him." 3378
17:37 **The L** who delivered me from the paw of 3378
17:37 "Go, and **the L** be with you." 3378
17:45 in the name of **the L** Almighty, 3378
17:46 This day **the L** will hand you over to me, 3378
17:47 not by sword or spear that **the L** saves; 3378
18:12 **the L** was with David but had left Saul. 3378
18:14 because **the L** was with him. 3378
18:17 and fight the battles of **the L."** 3378
18:28 When Saul realized that **the L** was 3378
19: 5 **The L** won a great victory for all Israel, 3378
19: 6 "As surely as **the L** lives, 3378
19: 9 an evil spirit from **the L** came upon Saul 3378
20: 3 as surely as **the L** lives and as you live, 3378
20: 8 into a covenant with you before **the L.** 3378
20:12 Then Jonathan said to David: *"By* **the L,** 3378
20:13 may **the L** deal with me, 3378
20:13 May **the L** be with you as he has been 3378
20:14 like that of **the L** as long as I live, 3378
20:15 not even when **the L** has cut off every one 3378
20:16 May **the L** call David's enemies to account. 3378
20:21 as surely as **the L** lives, you are safe; 3378
20:22 because **the L** has sent you away. 3378
20:23 remember, **the L** is witness between you 3378
20:42 with each other in the name of **the L,** 3378
20:42 **'The L** is witness between you and me, 3378
21: 6 before **the L** and replaced by hot bread on 3378
21: 7 detained before **the L;** 3378
22:10 Ahimelech inquired of **the L** for him; 3378
22:17 "Turn and kill the priests of **the L,** 3378
22:17 a hand to strike the priests of **the L.** 3378
22:21 that Saul had killed the priests of **the L.** 3378
23: 2 he inquired of **the L,** saying, 3378
23: 2 **The L** answered him, "Go, 3378
23: 4 Once again David inquired of **the L,** 3378
23: 4 and **the L** answered him, 3378
23:10 David said, "O **L,** God of Israel, 3378
23:11 O **L,** God of Israel, tell your servant." 3378
23:11 And **the L** said, "He will." 3378
23:12 And **the L** said, "They will." 3378
23:18 of them made a covenant before **the L.** 3378
23:21 **"The L** bless you for your concern for me. 3378
24: 4 the day **the L** spoke of when he said 3378
24: 6 **"The L** forbid that I should do such 3378
24: 6 for he is the anointed of **the L."** 3378
24:10 how **the L** delivered you into my hands in 3378
24:12 May **the L** judge between you and me. 3378
24:12 And may **the L** avenge the wrongs you 3378
24:15 May **the L** be our judge and decide 3378
24:18 **the L** delivered me into your hands, 3378
24:19 May **the L** reward you well for the way 3378
24:21 Now swear to me by **the L** that you will 3378
25:26 "Now since **the L** has kept you, 3378
25:26 as surely as **the L** lives and as you live, 3378
25:28 **the L** will certainly make a lasting dynasty 3378
25:29 bundle of the living by **the L** your God. 3378

†**LORD** distinguishes the proper name of God, *Yahweh*, indicated in the NIV by "LORD," from the words translated "Lord" and "lord," indexed under the heading *LORD, pages 683-86.

1Sa 25:30 When **the L** has done for my master 3378
25:31 **the L** has brought my master success, 3378
25:32 "Praise be to **the L,** the God of Israel, 3378
25:34 Otherwise, as surely as **the L,** 3378
25:38 **the L** struck Nabal and he died. 3378
25:39 he said, "Praise be to **the L,** 3378
26:10 As surely as **the L** lives," he said, 3378
26:10 he said, **"the L** himself will strike him; 3378
26:11 But **the L** forbid that I should lay a hand 3378
26:12 **the L** had put them into a deep sleep. 3378
26:16 As surely as **the L** lives, 3378
26:19 If **the L** has incited you against me, 3378
26:19 may they be cursed before **the L!** 3378
26:20 the ground far from the presence of **the L.** 3378
26:23 **The L** rewards every man for his 3378
26:23 **The L** delivered you into my hands today, 3378
26:24 so may **the L** value my life 3378
28: 6 He inquired of **the L,** 3378
28: 6 but **the L** did not answer him by dreams 3378
28:10 Saul swore to her by **the L,** 3378
28:10 "As surely as **the L** lives, 3378
28:16 now that **the L** has turned away from you 3378
28:17 **The L** has done what he predicted 3378
28:17 **The L** has torn the kingdom out 3378
28:18 Because you did not obey **the L** 3378
28:18 **the L** has done this to you today. 3378
28:19 **The L** will hand over both Israel and you 3378
28:19 **The L** will also hand over the army 3378
29: 6 "As surely as **the L** lives, 3378
30: 6 David found strength in **the L** his God. 3378
30: 8 and David inquired of **the L,** 3378
30:23 not do that with what **the L** has given us. 3378
2Sa 1:12 the army of **the L** and the house of Israel, 3378
2: 1 David inquired of **the L.** 3378
2: 1 **The L** said, "Go up." 3378
2: 1 "To Hebron," the L answered. NIH
2: 5 **"The L** bless you for showing this kindness 3378
2: 6 May **the L** now show you kindness 3378
3: 9 for David what **the L** promised him 3378
3:18 For **the L** promised David, 3378
3:28 before **the L** concerning the blood 3378
3:39 May **the L** repay the evildoer according 3378
4: 8 This day **the L** has avenged my lord 3378
4: 9 "As surely as **the L** lives, 3378
5: 2 And **the L** said to you, 3378
5: 3 with them at Hebron before **the L,** 3378
5:10 **the L** God Almighty was with him. 3378
5:12 that **the L** had established him as king 3378
5:19 so David inquired of **the L,** 3378
5:19 **The L** answered him, "Go, 3378
5:20 **the L** has broken out against my enemies 3378
5:23 so David inquired of **the L,** 3378
5:24 because that will mean **the L** has gone out 3378
5:25 So David did as **the L** commanded him, 3378
6: 2 the name of **the L** Almighty, 3378
6: 5 with all their might before **the L,** 3378
6: 9 David was afraid of **the L** that day 3378
6: 9 can the ark of **the L** ever come to me?" 3378
6:10 the ark of **the L** to be with him in the City 3378
6:11 The ark of **the L** remained in the house 3378
6:11 and **the L** blessed him 3378
6:12 **"The L** has blessed the household 3378
6:13 those who were carrying the ark of **the L** 3378
6:14 danced before **the L** with all his might, 3378
6:15 the ark of **the L** with shouts and the sound 3378
6:16 As the ark of **the L** was entering the City 3378
6:16 and dancing before **the L,** 3378
6:17 They brought the ark of **the L** and set it 3378
6:17 and fellowship offerings before **the L.** 3378
6:18 the people in the name of **the L** Almighty. 3378
6:21 "It was before **the L,** 3378
6:21 I will celebrate before **the L.** 3378
7: 1 in his palace and **the L** had given him rest 3378
7: 3 go ahead and do it, for **the L** is with you." 3378
7: 4 the word of **the L** came to Nathan, 3378
7: 5 'This is what **the L** says: 3378
7: 8 'This is what **the L** Almighty says: 3378
7:11 " **'The L** declares to you that 3378
7:11 that **the L** himself will establish a house 3378
7:18 King David went in and sat before **the L,** 3378
7:18 "Who am I, O Sovereign **L,** 3378
7:19 not enough in your sight, O Sovereign **L,** 3378
7:19 of dealing with man, O Sovereign **L?** 3378
7:20 you know your servant, O Sovereign **L.** 3378
7:22 "How great you are, O Sovereign **L!** 3378
7:24 and you, O **L,** have become their God. 3378
7:25 "And now, **L** God, keep forever 3378
7:26 **'The L** Almighty is God over Israel!' 3378
7:27 "O **L** Almighty, God of Israel, 3378
7:28 O Sovereign **L,** you are God! 3378
7:29 for you, O Sovereign **L,** have spoken, 3378
8: 6 **The L** gave David victory wherever he went 3378
8:11 to **the L,** as he had done with the silver 3378
8:14 **The L** gave David victory wherever he went 3378
10:12 **The L** will do what is good in his sight." 3378
11:27 thing David had done displeased **the L.** 3378
12: 1 **The L** sent Nathan to David. 3378
12: 5 "As surely as **the L** lives, 3378
12: 7 This is what **the L,** the God of Israel, 3378
12: 9 of **the L** by doing what is evil in his eyes? 3378
12:11 "This is what **the L** says: 3378
12:13 "I have sinned against **the L."** 3378
12:13 **"The L** has taken away your sin. 3378
12:14 the enemies of **the L** show utter contempt, 3378
12:15 **the L** struck the child that Uriah's wife 3378
12:20 into the house of **the L** and worshiped. 3378
12:22 **The L** may be gracious to me and let 3378
2Sa 12:24 named him Solomon. **The L** loved him; 3378
12:25 and because **the L** loved him, 3378
14:11 the king invoke **the L** his God to prevent 3378
14:11 "As surely as **the L** lives," he said, 3378
14:17 May **the L** your God be with you.' " 3378
15: 7 and fulfill a vow I made to **the L.** 3378
15: 8 'If **the L** takes me back to Jerusalem, 3378
15: 8 I will worship **the L** in Hebron.' " 3378
15:21 "As surely as **the L** lives, 3378
15:31 So David prayed, "O **L,** 3378
16: 8 **The L** has repaid you for all 3378
16: 8 **The L** has handed the kingdom over 3378
16:10 If he is cursing because **the L** said to him, 3378
16:11 let him curse, for **the L** has told him to. 3378
16:12 It may be that **the L** will see my distress 3378
16:18 the one chosen by **the L,** by these people, 3378
17:14 For **the L** had determined to frustrate 3378
18:19 to the king that **the L** has delivered him 3378
18:28 "Praise be to **the L** your God! 3378
18:31 **The L** has delivered you today 3378
19: 7 I swear by **the L** that if you don't go out, 3378
21: 1 so David sought the face of **the L.** 3378
21: 1 **The L** said, "It is on account of Saul 3378
21: 6 to be killed and exposed before **the L** 3378
21: 7 of the oath before **the L** between David 3378
21: 9 and exposed them on a hill before **the L.** 3378
22: 1 to **the L** the words of this song when 3378
22: 1 when **the L** delivered him from the hand 3378
22: 2 He said: **"The L** is my rock, 3378
22: 4 I call to **the L,** who is worthy of praise, 3378
22: 7 In my distress I called to **the L;** 3378
22:14 **The L** thundered from heaven; 3378
22:16 the earth laid bare at the rebuke of **the L,** 3378
22:19 but **the L** was my support. 3378
22:21 **"The L** has dealt with me according 3378
22:22 For I have kept the ways of **the L;** 3378
22:25 **The L** has rewarded me according 3378
22:29 You are my lamp, O **L;** 3378
22:29 **the L** turns my darkness into light. 3378
22:31 the word of **the L** is flawless. 3378
22:32 For who is God besides **the L?** 3378
22:42 to **the L,** but he did not answer. 3378
22:47 **"The L** lives! Praise be to my Rock! 3378
22:50 Therefore I will praise you, O **L,** 3378
23: 2 "The Spirit of **the L** spoke through me; 3378
23:10 **The L** brought about a great victory 3378
23:12 and **the L** brought about a great victory. 3378
23:16 instead, he poured it out before **the L.** 3378
23:17 "Far be it from me, O **L,** to do this!" 3378
24: 1 the anger of **the L** burned against Israel, 3378
24: 3 "May **the L** your God multiply the troops 3378
24:10 and he said to **the L,** 3378
24:10 Now, O **L,** I beg you, 3378
24:11 of **the L** had come to Gad the prophet, 3378
24:12 'This is what **the L** says: 3378
24:14 Let us fall into the hands of **the L,** 3378
24:15 So **the L** sent a plague on Israel from 3378
24:16 **the L** was grieved because of the calamity 3378
24:16 of **the L** was then at the threshing floor 3378
24:17 said to **the L,** "I am the one who has sinned 3378
24:18 to **the L** on the threshing floor of Araunah 3378
24:19 as **the L** had commanded through Gad. 3378
24:21 "so I can build an altar to **the L,** 3378
24:23 "May **the L** your God accept you." 3378
24:24 to **the L** my God burnt offerings 3378
24:25 David built an altar to **the L** there 3378
24:25 Then **the L** answered prayer in behalf of 3378
1Ki 1:17 to me your servant by **the L** your God: 3378
1:29 "As surely as **the L** lives, 3378
1:30 to you by **the L,** the God of Israel: 3378
1:36 May **the L,** the God of my lord the king, 3378
1:37 As **the L** was with my lord the king, 3378
1:48 'Praise be to **the L,** the God of Israel, 3378
2: 3 observe what **the L** your God requires: 3378
2: 4 that **the L** may keep his promise to me: 3378
2: 8 I swore to him by **the L:** 3378
2:15 for it has come to him from **the L.** 3378
2:23 Then King Solomon swore by **the L:** 3378
2:24 And now, as surely as **the L** lives— 3378
2:26 the ark of the Sovereign **L** 3378
2:27 from the priesthood of **the L,** 3378
2:27 the word **the L** had spoken at Shiloh 3378
2:28 he fled to the tent of **the L** and took hold 3378
2:29 the tent of **the L** and was beside the altar. 3378
2:30 So Benaiah entered the tent of **the L** 3378
2:32 **The L** will repay him for the blood 3378
2:42 "Did I not make you swear by **the L** 3378
2:43 then did you not keep your oath to **the L** 3378
2:44 Now **the L** will repay you for your 3378
2:45 will remain secure before **the L** forever." 3378
3: 1 and the temple of **the L,** 3378
3: 2 not yet been built for the Name of **the L.** 3378
3: 3 Solomon showed his love for **the L** 3378
3: 5 At Gibeon **the L** appeared to Solomon 3378
3: 7 "Now, O **L** my God, 3378
5: 3 a temple for the Name of **the L** his God 3378
5: 3 until **the L** put his enemies under his feet. 3378
5: 4 But now **the L** my God has given me rest 3378
5: 5 a temple for the Name of **the L** my God, 3378
5: 5 as **the L** told my father David, 3378
5: 7 "Praise be to **the L** today, 3378
5:12 **The L** gave Solomon wisdom, 3378
6: 1 he began to build the temple of **the L.** 3378
6: 2 for **the L** was sixty cubits long, 3378
6:11 The word of **the L** came to Solomon: 3378
6:19 the ark of the covenant of **the L** there. 3378
6:37 temple of **the L** was laid in the fourth year, 3378
1Ki 7:12 the inner courtyard of the temple of **the L** 3378
7:40 for King Solomon in the temple of **the L:** 3378
7:45 temple of **the L** were of burnished bronze. 3378
7:51 for the temple of **the L** was finished, 3378
8: 4 and they brought up the ark of **the L** and 3378
8: 9 where **the L** made a covenant with 3378
8:10 the cloud filled the temple of **the L.** 3378
8:11 for the glory of **the L** filled his temple. 3378
8:12 **"The L** has said that he would dwell in 3378
8:15 "Praise be to **the L,** the God of Israel, 3378
8:17 to build a temple for the Name of **the L,** 3378
8:18 But **the L** said to my father David, 3378
8:20 **"The L** has kept the promise he made: 3378
8:20 just as **the L** promised, 3378
8:20 the temple for the Name of **the L,** 3378
8:21 of **the L** that he made with our fathers 3378
8:22 of **the L** in front of the whole assembly 3378
8:23 "O **L,** God of Israel, 3378
8:25 "Now **L,** God of Israel, 3378
8:28 O **L** my God. 3378
8:44 to **the L** toward the city you have chosen 3378
8:53 O Sovereign **L,** brought our fathers out 3378
8:54 and supplications to **the L,** 3378
8:54 he rose from before the altar of **the L,** 3378
8:56 "Praise be to **the L,** 3378
8:57 May **the L** our God be with us as he was 3378
8:59 which I have prayed before **the L,** 3378
8:59 be near to **the L** our God day and night, 3378
8:60 the earth may know that **the L** is God and 3378
8:61 be fully committed to **the L** our God, 3378
8:62 with him offered sacrifices before **the L.** 3378
8:63 of fellowship offerings to **the L:** 3378
8:63 Israelites dedicated the temple of **the L.** 3378
8:64 in front of the temple of **the L,** 3378
8:64 before **the L** was too small to hold 3378
8:65 They celebrated it before **the L** our God 3378
8:66 for all the good things **the L** had done 3378
9: 1 the temple of **the L** and the royal palace, 3378
9: 2 **the L** appeared to him a second time, 3378
9: 3 **The L** said to him: 3378
9: 8 'Why has **the L** done such a thing 3378
9: 9 they have forsaken **the L** their God, 3378
9: 9 that is why **the L** brought all this disaster 3378
9:10 of **the L** and the royal palace— 3378
9:25 on the altar he had built for **the L,** 3378
9:25 burning incense before **the L** along 3378
10: 1 and his relation to the name of **the L,** 3378
10: 5 offerings he made at the temple of **the L,** 3378
10: 9 Praise be to **the L** your God, 3378
10:12 to make supports for the temple of **the L** 3378
11: 2 about which **the L** had told the Israelites, 3378
11: 4 not fully devoted to **the L** his God, 3378
11: 6 So Solomon did evil in the eyes of **the L;** 3378
11: 6 he did not follow **the L** completely, 3378
11: 9 **The L** became angry with Solomon 3378
11: 9 from **the L,** the God of Israel, 3378
11:11 So **the L** said to Solomon, 3378
11:14 Then **the L** raised up against Solomon 3378
11:31 for this is what **the L,** the God of Israel, 3378
12:15 for this turn of events was from **the L,** 3378
12:15 to fulfill the word **the L** had spoken 3378
12:24 'This is what **the L** says: 3378
12:24 the word of **the L** and went home again, 3378
12:24 as **the L** had ordered. 3378
12:27 to offer sacrifices at the temple of **the L** 3378
13: 1 By the word of **the L** a man of God came 3378
13: 2 against the altar by the word of **the L:** 3378
13: 2 This is what **the L** says: 3378
13: 3 "This is the sign **the L** has declared: 3378
13: 5 by the man of God by the word of **the L.** 3378
13: 6 "Intercede with **the L** your God and pray 3378
13: 6 So the man of God interceded with **the L,** 3378
13: 9 I was commanded by the word of **the L:** 3378
13:17 I have been told by the word of **the L:** 3378
13:18 an angel said to me by the word of **the L:** 3378
13:20 the word of **the L** came to the old prophet 3378
13:21 "This is what **the L** says: 3378
13:21 of **the L** and have not kept the command 3378
13:21 the command **the L** your God gave you. 3378
13:26 of God who defied the word of **the L.** 3378
13:26 **The L** has given him over to the lion, 3378
13:26 as the word of **the L** had warned him." 3378
13:32 of **the L** against the altar in Bethel and 3378
14: 5 But **the L** had told Ahijah, 3378
14: 7 Go, tell Jeroboam that this is what **the L,** 3378
14:11 **The L** has spoken!' 3378
14:13 in the house of Jeroboam in whom **the L,** 3378
14:14 **"The L** will raise up for himself a king 3378
14:15 And **the L** will strike Israel, 3378
14:15 because they provoked **the L** to anger 3378
14:18 as **the L** had said through his servant 3378
14:21 the city **the L** had chosen out of all 3378
14:22 Judah did evil in the eyes of **the L.** 3378
14:24 of the nations **the L** had driven out before 3378
14:26 of the temple of **the L** and the treasures of 3378
15: 3 not fully devoted to **the L** his God, 3378
15: 4 for David's sake **the L** his God gave him 3378
15: 5 of **the L** and had not failed to keep any of 3378
15:11 did what was right in the eyes of **the L,** 3378
15:14 fully committed to **the L** all his life. 3378
15:15 the temple of **the L** the silver and gold 3378
15:26 He did evil in the eyes of **the L,** 3378
15:29 of **the L** given through his servant Ahijah 3378
15:30 and because he provoked **the L,** 3378
15:34 He did evil in the eyes of **the L,** 3378
16: 1 Then the word of **the L** came to Jehu son 3378
16: 7 the word of **the L** came through 3378

†**LORD** distinguishes the proper name of God, *Yahweh,* indicated in the NIV by "LORD," from the words translated "Lord" and "lord," indexed under the heading ***LORD**, pages 683-86.

1Ki 16: 7 the eyes of **the L,** provoking him to anger 3378
16:12 the word of **the L** spoken against Baasha 3378
16:13 so that they provoked **the L,** 3378
16:19 the eyes of **the L** and walking in the ways 3378
16:25 of **the L** and sinned more than all those 3378
16:26 so that they provoked **the L,** 3378
16:30 of **the L** than any of those before him. 3378
16:33 and did more to provoke **the L,** 3378
16:34 the word of **the L** spoken by Joshua son 3378
17: 1 "As **the L,** the God of Israel, lives, 3378
17: 2 Then the word of **the L** came to Elijah: 3378
17: 5 So he did what **the L** had told him. 3378
17: 8 Then the word of **the L** came to him: 3378
17:12 "As surely as **the L** your God lives," 3378
17:14 this is what **the L,** the God of Israel, says: 3378
17:14 not run dry until the day **the L** gives rain 3378
17:16 in keeping with the word of **the L** spoken 3378
17:20 Then he cried out to **the L,** 3378
17:20 "O **L** my God, you have brought tragedy 3378
17:21 on the boy three times and cried to **the L,** 3378
17:21 "O **L** my God, let this boy's life return 3378
17:22 **The L** heard Elijah's cry, 3378
17:24 that the word of **the L** from your mouth is 3378
18: 1 the word of **the L** came to Elijah: 3378
18: 3 (Obadiah was a devout believer in **the L.** 3378
18:10 As surely as **the L** your God lives, 3378
18:12 of **the L** may carry you when I leave you. 3378
18:12 Yet I your servant have worshiped **the L** 3378
18:13 Jezebel was killing the prophets of **the L?** 3378
18:15 Elijah said, "As **the L** Almighty lives, 3378
18:21 If **the L** is God, follow him; 3378
18:24 and I will call on the name of **the L.** 3378
18:30 and he repaired the altar of **the L,** 3378
18:31 to whom the word of **the L** had come, 3378
18:32 an altar in the name of **the L,** 3378
18:36 "O **L,** God of Abraham, Isaac and Israel, 3378
18:37 Answer me, O **L,** answer me, 3378
18:37 so these people will know that you, O **L,** 3378
18:38 Then the fire of **the L** fell and burned up 3378
18:39 they fell prostrate and cried, "**The L—** 3378
18:39 **The L—**he is God!" 3378
18:46 The power of **the L** came upon Elijah 3378
19: 4 "I have had enough, **L,**" he said. 3378
19: 7 The angel of **the L** came back a second time 3378
19: 9 And the word of **the L** came to him: 3378
19:10 for **the L** God Almighty. 3378
19:11 The **L** said, "Go out and stand on NIH
19:11 on the mountain in the presence of **the L,** 3378
19:11 for **the L** is about to pass by." 3378
19:11 and shattered the rocks before **the L,** 3378
19:11 but **the L** was not in the wind. 3378
19:11 but **the L** was not in the earthquake. 3378
19:12 but **the L** was not in the fire. 3378
19:14 very zealous for **the L** God Almighty. 3378
19:15 **The L** said to him, 3378
20:13 "This is what **the L** says: 3378
20:13 and then you will know that I am **the L.'** " 3378
20:14 "This is what **the L** says: 3378
20:28 "This is what **the L** says: 3378
20:28 'Because the Arameans think **the L** is 3378
20:28 and you will know that I am **the L.'** " 3378
20:35 By the word of **the L** one of the sons of 3378
20:36 "Because you have not obeyed **the L,** 3378
20:42 "This is what **the L** says: 3378
21: 3 "**The L** forbid that I should give you 3378
21:17 word of **the L** came to Elijah the Tishbite: 3378
21:19 Say to him, 'This is what **the L** says: 3378
21:19 Then say to him, 'This is what **the L** says: 3378
21:20 to do evil in the eyes of **the L.** 3378
21:23 "And also concerning Jezebel **the L** says: 3378
21:25 to do evil in the eyes of **the L,** 3378
21:26 like the Amorites **the L** drove out 3378
21:28 word of **the L** came to Elijah the Tishbite: 3378
22: 5 "First seek the counsel of **the L.**" 3378
22: 7 of **the L** here whom we can inquire of?" 3378
22: 8 through whom we can inquire of **the L,** 3378
22:11 "This is what **the L** says: 3378
22:12 **the L** will give it into the king's hand." 3378
22:14 Micaiah said, "As surely as **the L** lives, 3378
22:14 I can tell him only what **the L** tells me." 3378
22:15 "for **the L** will give it into the king's hand. 3378
22:16 but the truth in the name of **the L?"** 3378
22:17 and **the L** said, 3378
22:19 "Therefore hear the word of **the L:** 3378
22:19 I saw **the L** sitting on his throne with all 3378
22:20 And **the L** said, 'These people have no 3378
22:21 stood before **the L** and said, 3378
22:22 " 'By what means?' **the L** asked. 3378
22:22 succeed in enticing him,' said the **L.** NIH
22:23 "So now **the L** has put a lying spirit in 3378
22:23 **The L** has decreed disaster for you." 3378
22:24 "Which way did the spirit from **the L** go 3378
22:28 **the L** has not spoken through me." 3378
22:38 as the word of **the L** had declared. 3378
22:43 he did what was right in the eyes of **the L.** 3378
22:52 He did evil in the eyes of **the L,** 3378
22:53 and worshiped Baal and provoked **the L,** 3378
2Ki 1: 3 angel of **the L** said to Elijah the Tishbite, 3378
1: 4 Therefore this is what **the L** says: 3378
1: 6 "This is what **the L** says: 3378
1:15 The angel of **the L** said to Elijah, 3378
1:16 "This is what **the L** says: 3378
1:17 the word of **the L** that Elijah had spoken. 3378
2: 1 When **the L** was about to take Elijah up 3378
2: 2 **the L** has sent me to Bethel." 3378
2: 2 "As surely as **the L** lives and as you live, 3378
2: 3 that **the L** is going to take your master 3378
2Ki 2: 4 **the L** has sent me to Jericho." 3378
2: 4 "As surely as **the L** lives and as you live, 3378
2: 5 that **the L** is going to take your master 3378
2: 6 **the L** has sent me to the Jordan." 3378
2: 6 "As surely as **the L** lives and as you live, 3378
2:14 "Where now is **the L,** the God of Elijah?" 3378
2:16 the Spirit of **the L** has picked him up and 3378
2:21 saying, "This is what **the L** says: 3378
2:24 a curse on them in the name of **the L.** 3378
3: 2 He did evil in the eyes of **the L,** 3378
3:10 "Has **the L** called us three kings together 3378
3:11 "Is there no prophet of **the L** here, 3378
3:11 we may inquire of **the L** through him?" 3378
3:12 "The word of **the L** is with him." 3378
3:13 "because it was **the L** who called us three kings together 3378
3:14 "As surely as **the L** Almighty lives, 3378
3:15 the hand of **the L** came upon Elisha 3378
3:16 "This is what **the L** says: 3378
3:17 For this is what **the L** says: 3378
3:18 This is an easy thing in the eyes of **the L;** 3378
4: 1 and you know that he revered **the L.** 3378
4:27 but **the L** has hidden it from me and has 3378
4:30 "As surely as **the L** lives and as you live, 3378
4:33 on the two of them and prayed to **the L.** 3378
4:43 For this is what **the L** says: 3378
4:44 according to the word of **the L.** 3378
5: 1 through him **the L** had given victory 3378
5:11 and call on the name of **the L** his God, 3378
5:16 "As surely as **the L** lives, whom I serve, 3378
5:17 and sacrifices to any other god but **the L.** 3378
5:18 But may **the L** forgive your servant 3378
5:18 may **the L** forgive your servant for this." 3378
5:20 As surely as **the L** lives, 3378
6:17 And Elisha prayed, "O **L,** open his eyes 3378
6:17 Then **the L** opened the servant's eyes, 3378
6:18 Elisha prayed to **the L,** 3378
6:20 the city, Elisha said, "**L,** open the eyes 3378
6:20 **the L** opened their eyes and they looked, 3378
6:27 "If **the L** does not help you, 3378
6:33 said, "This disaster is from **the L.** 3378
6:33 Why should I wait for **the L** any longer?" 3378
7: 1 Elisha said, "Hear the word of **the L.** 3378
7: 1 This is what **the L** says: 3378
7: 2 even if **the L** should open the floodgates 3378
7:16 as **the L** had said. 3378
7:19 even if **the L** should open the floodgates 3378
8: 1 because **the L** has decreed a famine in 3378
8: 8 Consult **the L** through him; 3378
8:10 but **the L** has revealed to me that he will 3378
8:13 "**The L** has shown me that you will become 3378
8:18 He did evil in the eyes of **the L.** 3378
8:19 **the L** was not willing to destroy Judah. 3378
8:27 of Ahab and did evil in the eyes of **the L,** 3378
9: 3 'This is what **the L** says: 3378
9: 6 "This is what **the L,** the God of Israel, 3378
9:12 'This is what **the L** says: 3378
9:25 when **the L** made this prophecy 3378
9:26 and the blood of his sons, declares **the L,** 3378
9:26 on this plot of ground, declares **the L.'** 3378
9:26 in accordance with the word of **the L.**" 3378
9:36 "This is the word of **the L** that he spoke 3378
10:10 that not a word **the L** has spoken against 3378
10:10 **The L** has done what he promised 3378
10:16 with me and see my zeal for **the L.**" 3378
10:17 according to the word of **the L** spoken 3378
10:23 and see that no servants of **the L** are here 3378
10:30 **The L** said to Jehu, "Because you have 3378
10:31 not careful to keep the law of **the L,** 3378
10:32 In those days **the L** began to reduce 3378
11: 3 with his nurse at the temple of **the L** 3378
11: 4 to him at the temple of **the L.** 3378
11: 4 under oath at the temple of **the L.** 3378
11:10 and that were in the temple of **the L.** 3378
11:13 to the people at the temple of **the L.** 3378
11:15 not be put to death in the temple of **the L.**" 3378
11:17 then made a covenant between **the L** and 3378
11:18 posted guards at the temple of **the L.** 3378
11:19 down from the temple of **the L** and went 3378
12: 2 in the eyes of **the L** all the years Jehoiada 3378
12: 4 as sacred offerings to the temple of **the L—** 3378
12: 9 as one enters the temple of **the L.** 3378
12: 9 that was brought to the temple of **the L.** 3378
12:10 the temple of **the L** and put it into bags. 3378
12:11 worked on the temple of **the L—** 3378
12:12 for the repair of the temple of **the L,** 3378
12:13 of gold or silver for the temple of **the L;** 3378
12:16 not brought into the temple of **the L;** 3378
12:18 the treasuries of the temple of **the L** and 3378
13: 2 in the eyes of **the L** by following the sins 3378
13: 4 and **the L** listened to him, 3378
13: 5 **The L** provided a deliverer for Israel, 3378
13:11 in the eyes of **the L** and did not turn away 3378
13:23 But **the L** was gracious to them 3378
14: 3 He did what was right in the eyes of **the L,** 3378
14: 6 of Moses where **the L** commanded: 3378
14:14 the temple of **the L** and in the treasuries 3378
14:24 in the eyes of **the L** and did not turn away 3378
14:25 in accordance with the word of **the L,** 3378
14:26 **The L** had seen how bitterly everyone 3378
14:27 since **the L** had not said he would blot out 3378
15: 3 He did what was right in the eyes of **the L,** 3378
15: 5 **The L** afflicted the king with leprosy until 3378
15: 9 He did evil in the eyes of **the L,** 3378
15:12 of **the L** spoken to Jehu was fulfilled: 3378
15:18 He did evil in the eyes of **the L.** 3378
15:24 Pekahiah did evil in the eyes of **the L.** 3378
2Ki 15:28 He did evil in the eyes of **the L.** 3378
15:34 He did what was right in the eyes of **the L,** 3378
15:35 the Upper Gate of the temple of **the L.** 3378
15:37 (In those days **the L** began 3378
16: 2 what was right in the eyes of **the L** his God. 3378
16: 3 of the nations **the L** had driven out before 3378
16: 8 and gold found in the temple of **the L** and 3378
16:14 before **the L** he brought from the front of 3378
16:14 the new altar and the temple of **the L—** 3378
16:18 royal entryway outside the temple of **the L,** 3378
17: 2 He did evil in the eyes of **the L,** 3378
17: 7 sinned against **the L** their God, 3378
17: 8 of the nations **the L** had driven out 3378
17: 9 against **the L** their God that were 3378
17:11 as the nations whom **the L** had driven out 3378
17:11 that provoked **the L** to anger. 3378
17:12 though **the L** had said, 3378
17:13 **The L** warned Israel and Judah 3378
17:14 who did not trust in **the L** their God. 3378
17:15 although **the L** had ordered them, 3378
17:15 the things the **L** had forbidden them NIH
17:16 the commands of **the L** their God 3378
17:17 to do evil in the eyes of **the L,** 3378
17:18 So **the L** was very angry with Israel 3378
17:19 the commands of **the L** their God. 3378
17:20 **the L** rejected all the people of Israel; 3378
17:21 from following **the L** and caused them 3378
17:23 until **the L** removed them from his presence 3378
17:25 they did not worship **the L;** 3378
17:28 and taught them how to worship **the L.** 3378
17:32 They worshiped **the L,** 3378
17:33 They worshiped **the L,** 3378
17:34 They neither worship **the L** nor adhere to 3378
17:34 that **the L** gave the descendants of Jacob, 3378
17:35 **the L** made a covenant with the Israelites, 3378
17:36 But **the L,** who brought you up out 3378
17:39 Rather, worship **the L** your God; 3378
17:41 these people were worshiping **the L,** 3378
18: 3 He did what was right in the eyes of **the L,** 3378
18: 5 Hezekiah trusted in **the L,** 3378
18: 6 to **the L** and did not cease to follow him; 3378
18: 6 the commands **the L** had given Moses. 3378
18: 7 And **the L** was with him; 3378
18:12 not obeyed **the L** their God, 3378
18:12 the servant of **the L** commanded. 3378
18:15 that was found in the temple of **the L** and 3378
18:16 and doorposts of the temple of **the L,** 3378
18:22 "We are depending on **the L** our God"— 3378
18:25 without word from **the L?** 3378
18:25 **The L** himself told me to march 3378
18:30 in **the L** when he says, 'The LORD will 3378
18:30 '**The L** will surely deliver us; 3378
18:32 '**The L** will deliver us.' 3378
18:35 How then can **the L** deliver Jerusalem 3378
19: 1 and went into the temple of **the L.** 3378
19: 4 be that **the L** your God will hear all 3378
19: 4 for the words **the L** your God has heard. 3378
19: 6 'This is what **the L** says: 3378
19:14 up to the temple of **the L** and spread it out 3378
19:14 and spread it out before **the L.** 3378
19:15 And Hezekiah prayed to **the L:** 3378
19:15 "O **L,** God of Israel, enthroned 3378
19:16 Give ear, O **L,** and hear; 3378
19:16 open your eyes, O **L,** and see; 3378
19:17 "It is true, O **L,** that the Assyrian kings 3378
19:19 Now, O **L** our God, deliver us 3378
19:19 on earth may know that you alone, O **L,** 3378
19:20 "This is what **the L,** the God of Israel, 3378
19:21 This is the word that **the L** has spoken 3378
19:31 of **the L** Almighty will accomplish this. 3378
19:32 "Therefore this is what **the L** says 3378
19:33 he will not enter this city, declares **the L.** 3378
19:35 That night the angel of **the L** went out 3378
20: 1 "This is what **the L** says: 3378
20: 2 to the wall and prayed to **the L,** 3378
20: 3 O **L,** how I have walked before you 3378
20: 4 the word of **the L** came to him: 3378
20: 5 'This is what **the L** says: 3378
20: 5 you will go up to the temple of **the L.** 3378
20: 8 the sign that **the L** will heal me and 3378
20: 8 that I will go up to the temple of **the L** on 3378
20: 9 that **the L** will do what he has promised: 3378
20:11 the prophet Isaiah called upon **the L,** 3378
20:11 and the **L** made the shadow go back NIH
20:16 "Hear the word of **the L:** 3378
20:17 Nothing will be left, says **the L.** 3378
20:19 of **the L** you have spoken is good," 3378
21: 2 He did evil in the eyes of **the L,** 3378
21: 2 of the nations **the L** had driven out before 3378
21: 4 He built altars in the temple of **the L,** 3378
21: 4 of which **the L** had said, 3378
21: 5 In both courts of the temple of **the L,** 3378
21: 6 He did much evil in the eyes of **the L,** 3378
21: 7 of which **the L** had said to David and 3378
21: 9 the nations **the L** had destroyed before 3378
21:10 **The L** said through his servants 3378
21:12 Therefore this is what **the L,** 3378
21:16 so that they did evil in the eyes of **the L.** 3378
21:20 He did evil in the eyes of **the L,** 3378
21:22 He forsook **the L,** the God of his fathers, 3378
21:22 and did not walk in the way of **the L.** 3378
22: 2 He did what was right in the eyes of **the L** 3378
22: 3 to the temple of **the L.** 3378
22: 4 brought into the temple of **the L,** 3378
22: 5 workers who repair the temple of **the L—** 3378
22: 8 of the Law in the temple of **the L.**" 3378
22: 9 the money that was in the temple of **the L** 3378

†LORD distinguishes the proper name of God, *Yahweh*, indicated in the NIV by "LORD," from the words translated "Lord" and "lord," indexed under the heading ***LORD**, pages 683-86.

2Ki 22:13	"Go and inquire of the L for me and for	3378
22:15	She said to them, "This is what the L,	3378
22:16	'This is what the L says:	3378
22:18	who sent you to inquire of the L,	3378
22:18	'This is what the L, the God of Israel,	3378
22:19	and you humbled yourself before the L	3378
22:19	I have heard you, declares the L.	3378
23: 2	He went up to the temple of the L with	3378
23: 2	found in the temple of the L.	3378
23: 3	the covenant in the presence of the L—	3378
23: 3	to follow the L and keep his commands,	3378
23: 4	the temple of the L all the articles made	3378
23: 6	the Asherah pole from the temple of the L	3378
23: 7	of the L and where women did weaving	3378
23: 9	at the altar of the L in Jerusalem,	3378
23:11	from the entrance to the temple of the L	3378
23:12	in the two courts of the temple of the L.	3378
23:16	the word of the L proclaimed by the man	3378
23:19	of Samaria that had provoked the L	NIH
23:21	the Passover to the L your God,	3378
23:23	this Passover was celebrated to the L	3378
23:24	had discovered in the temple of the L.	3378
23:25	like him who turned to the L as he did—	3378
23:26	the L did not turn away from the heat	3378
23:27	So the L said, "I will remove Judah also	3378
23:32	He did evil in the eyes of the L,	3378
23:37	And he did evil in the eyes of the L,	3378
24: 2	The L sent Babylonian, Aramean,	3378
24: 2	of the L proclaimed by his servants	3378
24: 4	and the L was not willing to forgive.	3378
24: 9	He did evil in the eyes of the L,	3378
24:13	As the L had declared,	3378
24:13	the treasures from the temple of the L and	3378
24:13	for the temple of the L.	3378
24:19	He did evil in the eyes of the L,	3378
25: 9	He set fire to the temple of the L,	3378
25:13	at the temple of the L and they carried	3378
25:16	for the temple of the L,	3378
1Ch 2: 3	so the L put him to death.	NIH
6:15	when the L sent Judah and Jerusalem	3378
6:31	of the L after the ark came to rest there.	3378
6:32	until Solomon built the temple of the L	3378
9:19	the entrance to the dwelling of the L.	3378
9:20	and the L was with him.	3378
9:23	the gates of the house of the L—	3378
10:13	because he was unfaithful to the L;	3378
10:13	of the L and even consulted a medium	3378
10:14	and did not inquire of the L.	3378
10:14	So the L put him to death and turned	NIH
11: 2	And the L your God said to you,	3378
11: 3	with them at Hebron before the L,	3378
11: 3	as the L had promised through Samuel.	3378
11: 9	because the L Almighty was with him.	3378
11:10	as the L had promised—	3378
11:14	and the L brought about a great victory.	3378
11:18	instead, he poured it out before the L.	3378
12:23	as the L had said:	3378
13: 2	and if it is the will of the L our God,	3378
13: 6	of God the L, who is enthroned between	3378
13:14	and the L blessed his household	3378
14: 2	that the L had established him as king	3378
14:10	The L answered him, "Go,	3378
14:17	and the L made all the nations fear him.	3378
15: 2	because the L chose them to carry the ark	3378
15: 2	to carry the ark of the L and to minister	3378
15: 3	in Jerusalem to bring up the ark of the L	3378
15:12	and bring up the ark of the L,	3378
15:13	the first time that the L our God broke out	3378
15:14	in order to bring up the ark of the L,	3378
15:15	in accordance with the word of the L.	3378
15:25	up the ark of the covenant of the L from	3378
15:26	the ark of the covenant of the L,	3378
15:28	of the covenant of the L with shouts,	3378
15:29	of the L was entering the City of David,	3378
16: 2	the people in the name of the L.	3378
16: 4	of the L, to make petition, to give thanks,	3378
16: 4	and to praise the L, the God of Israel:	3378
16: 7	of thanks to the L:	3378
16: 8	Give thanks to the L, call on his name;	3378
16:10	of those who seek the L rejoice.	3378
16:11	Look to the L and his strength;	3378
16:14	He is the L our God;	3378
16:23	Sing to the L, all the earth;	3378
16:25	great is the L and most worthy of praise;	3378
16:26	but the L made the heavens.	3378
16:28	Ascribe to the L, O families of nations,	3378
16:28	ascribe to the L glory and strength,	3378
16:29	ascribe to the L the glory due his name.	3378
16:29	worship the L in the splendor	3378
16:31	among the nations, "The L reigns!"	3378
16:33	they will sing for joy before the L,	3378
16:34	Give thanks to the L, for he is good;	3378
16:36	Praise be to the L, the God of Israel,	3378
16:36	and "Praise the L."	3378
16:37	before the ark of the covenant of the L	3378
16:39	the tabernacle of the L at the high place	3378
16:40	to present burnt offerings to the L on	3378
16:40	everything written in the Law of the L,	3378
16:41	by name to give thanks to the L,	3378
17: 1	of the covenant of the L is under a tent."	3378
17: 4	'This is what the L says:	3378
17: 7	'This is what the L Almighty says:	3378
17:10	" 'I declare to you that the L will build	3378
17:16	King David went in and sat before the L,	3378
17:16	"Who am I, O L God,	3378
17:17	the most exalted of men, O L God.	3378
17:19	O L. For the sake of your servant	3378
1Ch 17:20	"There is no one like you, O L,	3378
17:22	and you, O L, have become their God.	3378
17:23	now, L, let the promise you have made	3378
17:24	Then men will say, 'The L Almighty,	3378
17:26	O L, you are God!	3378
17:27	for you, O L, have blessed it,	3378
18: 6	The L gave David victory everywhere he went.	3378
18:11	David dedicated these articles to the L,	3378
18:13	The L gave David victory everywhere he went.	3378
19:13	The L will do what is good in his sight."	3378
21: 3	"May the L multiply his troops	3378
21: 9	The L said to Gad, David's seer,	3378
21:10	'This is what the L says:	3378
21:11	"This is what the L says:	3378
21:12	or three days of the sword of the L—	3378
21:12	of the L ravaging every part of Israel.'	3378
21:13	Let me fall into the hands of the L,	3378
21:14	So the L sent a plague on Israel,	3378
21:15	the L saw it and was grieved because of	3378
21:15	The angel of the L was then standing at	3378
21:16	up and saw the angel of the L standing	3378
21:17	O L my God, let your hand fall upon me	3378
21:18	of the L ordered Gad to tell David to go	3378
21:18	to the L on the threshing floor of Araunah	3378
21:19	that Gad had spoken in the name of the L.	3378
21:22	so I can build an altar to the L,	3378
21:24	I will not take for the L what is yours,	3378
21:26	David built an altar to the L there	3378
21:26	He called on the L,	3378
21:26	and the L answered him with fire	NIH
21:27	Then the L spoke to the angel,	3378
21:28	that the L had answered him on	3378
21:29	The tabernacle of the L,	3378
21:30	of the sword of the angel of the L.	3378
22: 1	"The house of the L God is to be here,	3378
22: 5	for the L should be of great magnificence	3378
22: 6	to build a house for the L,	3378
22: 7	a house for the Name of the L my God.	3378
22: 8	But this word of the L came to me:	3378
22:11	"Now, my son, the L be with you,	3378
22:11	and build the house of the L your God,	3378
22:12	May the L give you discretion	3378
22:12	the law of the L your God.	3378
22:13	and laws that the L gave Moses for Israel.	3378
22:14	temple of the L a hundred thousand talents	3378
22:16	begin the work, and the L be with you."	3378
22:18	"Is not the L your God with you?	3378
22:18	land is subject to the L and to his people.	3378
22:19	and soul to seeking the L your God.	3378
22:19	to build the sanctuary of the L God,	3378
22:19	of the L and the sacred articles belonging	3378
22:19	that will be built for the Name of the L."	3378
23: 4	the temple of the L and six thousand are	3378
23: 5	and four thousand are to praise the L with	3378
23:13	to offer sacrifices before the L,	3378
23:24	who served in the temple of the L.	3378
23:25	For David had said, "Since the L,	3378
23:28	in the service of the temple of the L:	3378
23:30	to thank and praise the L.	3378
23:31	to the L on Sabbaths and	3378
23:31	They were to serve before the L regularly	3378
23:32	for the service of the temple of the L.	3378
24:19	when they entered the temple of the L,	3378
24:19	as the L, the God of Israel,	3378
25: 3	the harp in thanking and praising the L.	3378
25: 6	for the music of the temple of the L,	3378
25: 7	and skilled in music for the L—	3378
26:12	for ministering in the temple of the L,	3378
26:22	of the treasuries of the temple of the L.	3378
26:27	for the repair of the temple of the L.	3378
26:30	of the Jordan for all the work of the L and	3378
27:23	because the L had promised	3378
28: 2	for the ark of the covenant of the L,	3378
28: 4	"Yet the L, the God of Israel,	3378
28: 5	and the L has given me many—	3378
28: 5	on the throne of the kingdom of the L	3378
28: 8	of all Israel and of the assembly of the L,	3378
28: 8	the commands of the L your God,	3378
28: 9	for the L searches every heart	3378
28:10	for the L has chosen you to build	3378
28:12	the courts of the temple of the L and all	3378
28:13	of serving in the temple of the L,	3378
28:18	the ark of the covenant of the L.	3378
28:19	"I have in writing from the hand of the L	3378
28:20	for the L God, my God, is with you.	3378
28:20	of the temple of the L is finished.	3378
29: 1	not for man but for the L God.	3378
29: 5	to consecrate himself today to the L?"	3378
29: 8	to the treasury of the temple of the L in	3378
29: 9	given freely and wholeheartedly to the L.	3378
29:10	David praised the L in the presence of	3378
29:10	saying, "Praise be to you, O L,	3378
29:11	O L, is the greatness and the power and	3378
29:11	Yours, O L, is the kingdom;	3378
29:16	O L our God, as for all this abundance	3378
29:18	O L, God of our fathers Abraham,	3378
29:20	"Praise the L your God."	3378
29:20	So they all praised the L,	3378
29:20	and fell prostrate before the L and	3378
29:21	to the L and presented burnt offerings	3378
29:22	with great joy in the presence of the L	3378
29:22	anointing him before the L to be ruler	3378
29:23	So Solomon sat on the throne of the L	3378
29:25	The L highly exalted Solomon in the sight	3378
2Ch 1: 1	for the L his God was with him	3378
2Ch 1: 5	in front of the tabernacle of the L;	3378
1: 6	the bronze altar before the L in the Tent	3378
1: 9	Now, L God, let your promise	3378
2: 1	for the Name of the L and a royal palace	3378
2: 4	of the L my God and to dedicate it to him	3378
2: 4	at the appointed feasts of the L our God.	3378
2:11	"Because the L loves his people,	3378
2:12	And Hiram added: "Praise be to the L,	3378
2:12	who will build a temple for the L and	3378
3: 1	to build the temple of the L in Jerusalem	3378
3: 1	the L had appeared to his father David.	NIH
4:16	temple of the L were of polished bronze.	3378
5: 1	for the temple of the L was finished,	3378
5:10	where the L made a covenant with	3378
5:13	to give praise and thanks to the L.	3378
5:13	they raised their voices in praise to the L	3378
5:13	temple of the L was filled with a cloud,	3378
5:14	glory of the L filled the temple of God.	3378
6: 1	"The L has said that he would dwell in	3378
6: 4	"Praise be to the L, the God of Israel,	3378
6: 7	to build a temple for the Name of the L,	3378
6: 8	But the L said to my father David,	3378
6:10	"The L has kept the promise he made.	3378
6:10	just as the L promised,	3378
6:10	the temple for the Name of the L,	3378
6:11	the covenant of the L that he made with	3378
6:12	of the L in front of the whole assembly	3378
6:14	He said: "O L, God of Israel,	3378
6:16	"Now L, God of Israel,	3378
6:17	And now, O L, God of Israel,	3378
6:19	his plea for mercy, O L my God.	3378
6:41	"Now arise, O L God,	3378
6:41	May your priests, O L God,	3378
6:42	O L God, do not reject your anointed one.	3378
7: 1	and the glory of the L filled the temple.	3378
7: 2	the temple of the L because the glory of	3378
7: 2	because the glory of the L filled it.	3378
7: 3	and the glory of the L above the temple,	3378
7: 3	they worshiped and gave thanks to the L,	3378
7: 4	the people offered sacrifices before the L.	3378
7: 6	for praising the L and which were used	3378
7: 7	in front of the temple of the L,	3378
7:10	the good things the L had done for David	3378
7:11	the temple of the L and the royal palace,	3378
7:11	the temple of the L and in his own palace,	3378
7:12	the L appeared to him at night and said:	3378
7:21	'Why has the L done such a thing	3378
7:22	'Because they have forsaken the L,	3378
8: 1	the temple of the L and his own palace,	3378
8:11	the ark of the L has entered are holy."	3378
8:12	the altar of the L that he had built in front	3378
8:12	Solomon sacrificed burnt offerings to the L,	3378
8:16	temple of the L was laid until its completion.	3378
8:16	So the temple of the L was finished.	3378
9: 4	offerings he made at the temple of the L,	3378
9: 8	Praise be to the L your God,	3378
9: 8	as king to rule for the L your God.	3378
9:11	to make steps for the temple of the L and	3378
10:15	to fulfill the word the L had spoken	3378
11: 2	But this word of the L came to Shemaiah	3378
11: 4	'This is what the L says:	3378
11: 4	of the L and turned back from marching	3378
11:14	rejected them as priests of the L.	3378
11:16	set their hearts on seeking the L,	3378
11:16	to Jerusalem to offer sacrifices to the L,	3378
12: 1	with him abandoned the law of the L.	3378
12: 2	Because they had been unfaithful to the L,	3378
12: 5	"This is what the L says,	3378
12: 6	"The L is just."	3378
12: 7	When the L saw that they humbled	3378
12: 7	this word of the L came to Shemaiah:	3378
12: 9	of the temple of the L and the treasures of	3378
12:13	the city the L had chosen out of all	3378
12:14	not set his heart on seeking the L.	3378
13: 5	Don't you know that the L,	3378
13: 8	you plan to resist the kingdom of the L,	3378
13: 9	you drive out the priests of the L,	3378
13:10	"As for us, the L is our God,	3378
13:10	The priests who serve the L are sons	3378
13:11	and fragrant incense to the L.	3378
13:11	the requirements of the L our God.	3378
13:12	Men of Israel, do not fight against the L,	3378
13:14	Then they cried out to the L.	3378
13:18	because they relied on the L,	3378
13:20	And the L struck him down and he died.	3378
14: 2	and right in the eyes of the L his God.	3378
14: 4	He commanded Judah to seek the L,	3378
14: 6	for the L gave him rest.	3378
14: 7	because we have sought the L our God;	3378
14:11	Asa called to the L his God and said,	3378
14:11	and said, "L, there is no one like you	3378
14:11	Help us, O L our God,	3378
14:11	O L, you are our God;	3378
14:12	The L struck down the Cushites	3378
14:13	they were crushed before the L	3378
14:14	the terror of the L had fallen upon them.	3378
15: 2	The L is with you when you are with him.	3378
15: 4	But in their distress they turned to the L,	3378
15: 8	of the L that was in front of the portico of	3378
15: 9	when they saw that the L his God was	3378
15:11	to the L seven hundred head of cattle	3378
15:12	into a covenant to seek the L,	3378
15:13	All who would not seek the L,	3378
15:14	an oath to the L with loud acclamation,	3378
15:15	So the L gave them rest on every side.	3378
15:17	fully committed [to the L] all his life.	NIH

†LORD distinguishes the proper name of God, *Yahweh*, indicated in the NIV by "LORD," from the words translated "Lord" and "lord," indexed under the heading *LORD, pages 683-86.

2Ch 16: 7 of Aram and not on **the L** your God, 3378
16: 8 Yet when you relied on **the L,** 3378
16: 9 For the eyes of **the L** range throughout 3378
16:12 not seek help from **the L,** 3378
17: 3 **The L** was with Jehoshaphat because 3378
17: 5 **The L** established the kingdom 3378
17: 6 devoted to the ways of **the L;** 3378
17: 9 with them the Book of the Law of **the L;** 3378
17:10 The fear of **the L** fell on all the kingdoms 3378
17:16 volunteered himself for the service of **the L,** 3378
18: 4 "First seek the counsel of **the L."** 3378
18: 6 of **the L** here whom we can inquire of?" 3378
18: 7 through whom we can inquire of **the L,** 3378
18:10 and he declared, "This is what **the L** says: 3378
18:11 **the L** will give it into the king's hand." 3378
18:13 Micaiah said, "As surely as **the L** lives, 3378
18:15 but the truth in the name of **the L?"** 3378
18:16 and **the L** said, 'These people have no 3378
18:18 "Therefore hear the word of **the L:** 3378
18:18 I saw **the L** sitting on his throne with all 3378
18:19 And **the L** said, 'Who will entice Ahab 3378
18:20 stood before **the L** and said, 3378
18:20 " 'By what means?' **the L** asked. 3378
18:21 succeed in enticing him,' said **the L.** NIH
18:22 "So now **the L** has put a lying spirit in 3378
18:22 **The L** has decreed disaster for you." 3378
18:23 "Which way did the spirit from **the L** go 3378
18:27 **the L** has not spoken through me." 3378
18:31 and **the L** helped him. 3378
19: 2 and love those who hate **the L?** 3378
19: 2 the wrath of **the L** is upon you. 3378
19: 4 and turned them back to **the L,** 3378
19: 6 you are not judging for man but for **the L,** 3378
19: 7 Now let the fear of **the L** be upon you. 3378
19: 7 with **the L** our God there is no injustice 3378
19: 8 the law of **the L** and to settle disputes. 3378
19: 9 and wholeheartedly in the fear of **the L.** 3378
19:10 to warn them not to sin against **the L;** 3378
19:11 over you in any matter concerning **the L,** 3378
19:11 may **the L** be with those who do well." 3378
20: 3 Jehoshaphat resolved to inquire of **the L,** 3378
20: 4 to seek help from **the L;** 3378
20: 5 of **the L** in the front of the new courtyard 3378
20: 6 "O **L,** God of our fathers, 3378
20:13 stood there before **the L.** 3378
20:14 of **the L** came upon Jahaziel son 3378
20:15 This is what **the L** says to you: 3378
20:17 the deliverance **the L** will give you, 3378
20:17 and **the L** will be with you.' " 3378
20:18 down in worship before **the L.** 3378
20:19 and Korahites stood up and praised **the L,** 3378
20:20 Have faith in **the L** your God and you will 3378
20:21 to sing to **the L** and to praise him for 3378
20:21 "Give thanks to **the L,** 3378
20:22 **the L** set ambushes against the men 3378
20:26 where they praised **the L.** 3378
20:27 for **the L** had given them cause to rejoice 3378
20:28 the temple of **the L** with harps and lutes 3378
20:29 how **the L** had fought against the enemies 3378
20:32 he did what was right in the eyes of **the L.** 3378
20:37 **the L** will destroy what you have made." 3378
21: 6 He did evil in the eyes of **the L.** 3378
21: 7 the covenant **the L** had made with David, 3378
21: 7 **the L** was not willing to destroy NIH
21:10 because Jehoram had forsaken **the L,** 3378
21:12 "This is what **the L,** the God of your father 3378
21:14 now **the L** is about to strike your people, 3378
21:16 **The L** aroused against Jehoram 3378
21:18 **the L** afflicted Jehoram with 3378
22: 4 He did evil in the eyes of **the L,** 3378
22: 7 whom **the L** had anointed to destroy 3378
22: 9 who sought **the L** with all his heart." 3378
23: 3 as **the L** promised concerning 3378
23: 5 in the courtyards of the temple of **the L.** 3378
23: 6 of **the L** except the priests and Levites 3378
23: 6 to guard what **the L** has assigned to them. 3378
23:12 she went to them at the temple of **the L.** 3378
23:14 to death at the temple of **the L."** 3378
23:18 the oversight of the temple of **the L** in 3378
23:18 of **the L** as written in the Law of Moses, 3378
23:20 the king down from the temple of **the L.** 3378
24: 2 the eyes of **the L** all the years of Jehoiada 3378
24: 4 to restore the temple of **the L.** 3378
24: 6 of **the L** and by the assembly of Israel for 3378
24: 8 at the gate of the temple of **the L.** 3378
24: 9 to **the L** the tax that Moses the servant 3378
24:12 the work required for the temple of **the L.** 3378
24:14 presented continually in the temple of **the L** 3378
24:18 They abandoned the temple of **the L,** 3378
24:19 Although **the L** sent prophets to the people 3378
24:20 Because you have forsaken **the L,** 3378
24:22 "May **the L** see this and call you 3378
24:24 **the L** delivered into their hands 3378
24:24 Because Judah had forsaken **the L,** 3378
25: 2 He did what was right in the eyes of **the L,** 3378
25: 4 where **the L** commanded: 3378
25: 7 for **the L** is not with Israel— 3378
25: 9 **"The L** can give you much more than that." 3378
25:15 of **the L** burned against Amaziah, 3378
25:27 turned away from following **the L,** 3378
26: 4 He did what was right in the eyes of **the L,** 3378
26: 5 As long as he sought **the L,** 3378
26:16 He was unfaithful to **the L** his God, 3378
26:16 the temple of **the L** to burn incense on 3378
26:17 priests of **the L** followed him in. 3378
26:18 Uzziah, to burn incense to **the L.** 3378
26:18 you will not be honored by **the L** God." 3378

2Ch 26:20 because **the L** had afflicted him. 3378
26:21 and excluded from the temple of **the L.** 3378
27: 2 He did what was right in the eyes of **the L,** 3378
27: 2 not enter the temple of **the L.** 3378
27: 3 the Upper Gate of the temple of **the L** 3378
27: 6 walked steadfastly before **the L** his God. 3378
28: 1 do what was right in the eyes of **the L.** 3378
28: 3 of the nations **the L** had driven out before 3378
28: 5 Therefore **the L** his God handed him over 3378
28: 6 because Judah had forsaken **the L,** 3378
28: 9 a prophet of **the L** named Oded was there, 3378
28: 9 He said to them, "Because **the L,** 3378
28:10 of sins against **the L** your God? 3378
28:13 "or we will be guilty before **the L.** 3378
28:19 **The L** had humbled Judah because 3378
28:19 and had been most unfaithful to **the L.** 3378
28:21 of the things from the temple of **the L** and 3378
28:22 even more unfaithful to **the L.** 3378
28:25 to other gods and provoked **the L,** 3378
29: 2 He did what was right in the eyes of **the L,** 3378
29: 3 of the temple of **the L** and repaired them. 3378
29: 5 now and consecrate the temple of **the L,** 3378
29: 6 they did evil in the eyes of **the L** our God 3378
29: 8 the anger of **the L** has fallen on Judah 3378
29:10 I intend to make a covenant with **the L,** 3378
29:11 for **the L** has chosen you to stand 3378
29:15 in to purify the temple of **the L,** 3378
29:15 following the word of **the L.** 3378
29:16 into the sanctuary of **the L** to purify it. 3378
29:16 that they found in the temple of **the L.** 3378
29:17 the portico of **the L.** 3378
29:17 the temple of **the L** itself, 3378
29:18 the entire temple of **the L,** 3378
29:20 and went up to the temple of **the L.** 3378
29:21 to offer these on the altar of **the L.** 3378
29:25 of **the L** with cymbals, harps and lyres in 3378
29:25 by **the L** through his prophets. 3378
29:27 singing to **the L** began also, 3378
29:30 the Levites to praise **the L** with the words 3378
29:31 now dedicated yourselves to **the L.** 3378
29:31 to the temple of **the L."** 3378
29:32 all of them for burnt offerings to **the L.** 3378
29:35 of the temple of **the L** was reestablished. 3378
30: 1 of **the L** in Jerusalem and celebrate 3378
30: 1 and celebrate the Passover to **the L,** 3378
30: 5 and celebrate the Passover to **the L,** 3378
30: 6 "People of Israel, return to **the L,** 3378
30: 7 who were unfaithful to **the L,** 3378
30: 8 as your fathers were; submit to **the L.** 3378
30: 8 Serve **the L** your God, 3378
30: 9 If you return to **the L,** 3378
30: 9 for **the L** your God is gracious and 3378
30:12 following the word of **the L.** 3378
30:15 burnt offerings to the temple of **the L.** 3378
30:17 not consecrate [their lambs] to **the L.** 3378
30:18 saying, "May **the L,** who is good, 3378
30:19 **the L,** the God of his fathers— 3378
30:20 And **the L** heard Hezekiah and healed 3378
30:21 and priests sang to **the L** every day, 3378
30:22 understanding of the service of **the L.** 3378
30:22 and praised **the L,** 3378
31: 3 as written in the Law of **the L.** 3378
31: 4 devote themselves to the Law of **the L.** 3378
31: 6 dedicated to **the L** their God, 3378
31: 8 they praised **the L** 3378
31:10 contributions to the temple of **the L,** 3378
31:10 because **the L** has blessed his people, 3378
31:11 storerooms in the temple of **the L,** 3378
31:14 the contributions made to **the L** and also 3378
31:16 all who would enter the temple of **the L** 3378
31:20 and faithful before **the L** his God. 3378
32: 8 with us is **the L** our God to help us and 3378
32:11 **'The L** our God will save us from 3378
32:16 spoke further against **the L** God and 3378
32:17 king also wrote letters insulting **the L,** 3378
32:21 And **the L** sent an angel, 3378
32:22 So **the L** saved Hezekiah and the people 3378
32:23 to Jerusalem for **the L** and valuable gifts 3378
32:24 He prayed to **the L,** 3378
33: 2 He did evil in the eyes of **the L,** 3378
33: 2 of the nations **the L** had driven out before 3378
33: 4 He built altars in the temple of **the L,** 3378
33: 4 of which **the L** had said, 3378
33: 5 In both courts of the temple of **the L,** 3378
33: 6 He did much evil in the eyes of **the L,** 3378
33: 9 the nations **the L** had destroyed before 3378
33:10 **The L** spoke to Manasseh and his people, 3378
33:11 So **the L** brought against them 3378
33:12 the favor of **the L** his God 3378
33:13 **the L** was moved by his entreaty NIH
33:13 Then Manasseh knew that **the L** is God. 3378
33:15 from the temple of **the L,** as well as all 3378
33:16 Then he restored the altar of **the L** 3378
33:16 and told Judah to serve **the L,** 3378
33:17 but only to **the L** their God. 3378
33:18 to him in the name of **the L,** 3378
33:22 He did evil in the eyes of **the L,** 3378
33:23 he did not humble himself before **the L;** 3378
34: 2 He did what was right in the eyes of **the L** 3378
34: 8 to repair the temple of **the L** his God. 3378
34:14 taken into the temple of **the L,** 3378
34:14 found the Book of the Law of **the L** 3378
34:15 the Book of the Law in the temple of **the L.** 3378
34:17 the money that was in the temple of **the L** 3378
34:21 "Go and inquire of **the L** for me and for 3378
34:21 our fathers have not kept the word of **the L;** 3378
34:23 She said to them, "This is what **the L,** 3378

2Ch 34:24 'This is what **the L** says: 3378
34:26 who sent you to inquire of **the L,** 3378
34:26 'This is what **the L,** the God of Israel, 3378
34:27 I have heard you, declares **the L.** 3378
34:30 He went up to the temple of **the L** with 3378
34:30 in the temple of **the L.** 3378
34:31 the covenant in the presence of **the L—** 3378
34:31 to follow **the L** and keep his commands, 3378
34:33 in Israel serve **the L** their God. 3378
34:33 they did not fail to follow **the L,** 3378
35: 1 Josiah celebrated the Passover to **the L** 3378
35: 3 and who had been consecrated to **the L:** 3378
35: 3 Now serve **the L** your God 3378
35: 6 doing what **the L** commanded 3378
35:12 of the people to offer to **the L,** 3378
35:16 the entire service of **the L** was carried out 3378
35:16 of burnt offerings on the altar of **the L,** 3378
35:26 to what is written in the Law of **the L—** 3378
36: 5 He did evil in the eyes of **the L** his God. 3378
36: 7 of **the L** and put them in his temple there. 3378
36: 9 He did evil in the eyes of **the L.** 3378
36:10 articles of value from the temple of **the L,** 3378
36:12 He did evil in the eyes of **the L** his God 3378
36:12 who spoke the word of **the L.** 3378
36:13 and would not turn to **the L,** 3378
36:14 and defiling the temple of **the L,** 3378
36:15 **The L,** the God of their fathers, 3378
36:16 of **the L** was aroused against his people 3378
36:21 in fulfillment of the word of **the L** spoken 3378
36:22 the word of **the L** spoken by Jeremiah, 3378
36:22 **the L** moved the heart of Cyrus king 3378
36:23 **" 'The L,** the God of heaven, 3378
36:23 may **the L** his God be with him, 3378
Ezr 1: 1 the word of **the L** spoken by Jeremiah, 3378
1: 1 **the L** moved the heart of Cyrus king 3378
1: 2 **" 'The L,** the God of heaven, 3378
1: 3 in Judah and build the temple of **the L,** 3378
1: 5 and build the house of **the L** in Jerusalem. 3378
1: 7 articles belonging to the temple of **the L,** 3378
2:68 When they arrived at the house of **the L** 3378
3: 3 sacrificed burnt offerings on it to **the L,** 3378
3: 5 the appointed sacred feasts of **the L,** 3378
3: 5 as freewill offerings to **the L.** 3378
3: 6 to offer burnt offerings to **the L,** 3378
3: 8 the building of the house of **the L.** 3378
3:10 the foundation of the temple of **the L,** 3378
3:10 took their places to praise **the L,** 3378
3:11 and thanksgiving they sang to **the L:** 3378
3:11 a great shout of praise to **the L,** 3378
3:11 foundation of the house of **the L** was laid. 3378
4: 1 a temple for **the L,** the God of Israel, 3378
4: 3 We alone will build it for **the L,** 3378
6:21 in order to seek **the L,** the God of Israel. 3378
6:22 because **the L** had filled them with joy 3378
7: 6 which **the L,** the God of Israel, had given. 3378
7: 6 for the hand of **the L** his God was on him. 3378
7:10 and observance of the Law of **the L,** 3378
7:11 the commands and decrees of **the L** 3378
7:27 Praise be to **the L,** the God of our fathers, 3378
7:27 to bring honor to the house of **the L** 3378
7:28 the hand of **the L** my God was on me, 3378
8:28 as these articles are consecrated to **the L.** 3378
8:28 and gold are a freewill offering to **the L,** 3378
8:29 of the house of **the L** in Jerusalem before 3378
8:35 All this was a burnt offering to **the L.** 3378
9: 5 my hands spread out to **the L** my God 3378
9: 8 **the L** our God has been gracious 3378
9:15 O **L,** God of Israel, you are righteous! 3378
10:11 Now make confession to **the L,** 3378
Ne 1: 5 Then I said: "O **L,** God of heaven, 3378
5:13 "Amen," and praised **the L.** 3378
8: 1 which **the L** had commanded for Israel. 3378
8: 6 Ezra praised **the L,** the great God; 3378
8: 6 and worshiped **the L** with their faces to 3378
8: 9 "This day is sacred to **the L** your God. 3378
8:10 for the joy of **the L** is your strength." 3378
8:14 which **the L** had commanded 3378
9: 3 the Law of **the L** their God for a quarter 3378
9: 3 and in worshiping **the L** their God. 3378
9: 4 with loud voices to **the L** their God. 3378
9: 5 "Stand up and praise **the L** your God, 3378
9: 6 You alone are **the L.** 3378
9: 7 "You are **the L** God, 3378
10:29 and decrees of **the L** our Lord. 3378
10:34 to burn on the altar of **the L** our God, 3378
10:35 the house of **the L** each year the firstfruits 3378
Job 1: 6 came to present themselves before **the L,** 3378
1: 7 **The L** said to Satan, "Where have you 3378
1: 7 Satan answered **the L,** "From roaming 3378
1: 8 **the L** said to Satan, "Have you considered 3378
1:12 **The L** said to Satan, "Very well, then, 3378
1:12 from the presence of **the L.** 3378
1:21 **The L** gave and the LORD has taken away; 3378
1:21 and **the L** has taken away; 3378
1:21 may the name of **the L** be praised." 3378
2: 1 came to present themselves before **the L,** 3378
2: 2 And **the L** said to Satan, "Where have you 3378
2: 2 Satan answered **the L,** "From roaming 3378
2: 3 **the L** said to Satan, "Have you considered 3378
2: 6 **The L** said to Satan, "Very well, then, 3378
2: 7 the presence of **the L** and afflicted Job 3378
12: 9 that the hand of **the L** has done this? 3378
38: 1 **the L** answered Job out of the storm. 3378
40: 1 **The L** said to Job: 3378
40: 3 Then Job answered **the L:** 3378
40: 6 Then **the L** spoke to Job out of the storm: 3378
42: 1 Then Job replied to **the L:** 3378

†**LORD** distinguishes the proper name of God, *Yahweh*, indicated in the NIV by "LORD," from the words translated "Lord" and "lord," indexed under the heading ***LORD**, pages 683-86.

Job 42: 7 After **the L** had said these things to Job, 3378
42: 9 the Naamathite did what **the L** told them; 3378
42: 9 and **the L** accepted Job's prayer. 3378
42:10 **the L** made him prosperous again 3378
42:11 the trouble **the L** had brought upon him, 3378
42:12 **The L** blessed the latter part of Job's life 3378
Ps 1: 2 But his delight is in the law of **the L**, 3378
1: 6 For **the L** watches over the way of 3378
2: 2 the rulers gather together against **the L** 3378
2: 7 I will proclaim the decree of **the L**: 3378
2:11 Serve **the L** with fear and rejoice 3378
3: 1 **O L**, how many are my foes! 3378
3: 3 But you are a shield around me, **O L**; 3378
3: 4 To **the L** I cry aloud, 3378
3: 5 I wake again, because **the L** sustains me. 3378
3: 7 Arise, **O L**! Deliver me, O my God! 3378
3: 8 From **the L** comes deliverance. 3378
4: 3 Know that **the L** has set apart the godly 3378
4: 3 **the L** will hear when I call to him. 3378
4: 5 Offer right sacrifices and trust in **the L**. 3378
4: 6 the light of your face shine upon us, **O L**. 3378
4: 8 **O L**, make me dwell in safety. 3378
5: 1 Give ear to my words, **O L**, 3378
5: 3 In the morning, **O L**, you hear my voice; 3378
5: 6 and deceitful men **the L** abhors. 3378
5: 8 **O L**, in your righteousness because 3378
5:12 For surely, **O L**, you bless the righteous; 3378
6: 1 **O L**, do not rebuke me in your anger 3378
6: 2 Be merciful to me, **L**, for I am faint; 3378
6: 2 **O L**, heal me, for my bones are in agony. 3378
6: 3 How long, **O L**, how long? 3378
6: 4 Turn, **O L**, and deliver me; 3378
6: 8 for **the L** has heard my weeping. 3378
6: 9 **The L** has heard my cry for mercy; 3378
6: 9 **the L** accepts my prayer. 3378
7: T which he sang to **the L** concerning Cush, 3378
7: 1 **O L** my God, I take refuge in you; 3378
7: 3 **O L** my God, if I have done this 3378
7: 6 Arise, **O L**, in your anger; 3378
7: 8 let **the L** judge the peoples. 3378
7: 8 **O L**, according to my righteousness, 3378
7:17 to **the L** because of his righteousness 3378
7:17 to the name of **the L** Most High. 3378
8: 1 **O L**, our Lord, how majestic is your name 3378
8: 9 **O L**, our Lord, how majestic is your name 3378
9: 1 I will praise you, **O L**, with all my heart; 3378
9: 7 **The L** reigns forever; 3378
9: 9 **The L** is a refuge for the oppressed, 3378
9:10 for you, **L**, have never forsaken those who seek you. 3378
9:11 Sing praises to **the L**, enthroned in Zion; 3378
9:13 **O L**, see how my enemies persecute me! 3378
9:16 **The L** is known by his justice; 3378
9:19 Arise, **O L**, let not man triumph; 3378
9:20 Strike them with terror, **O L**; 3378
10: 1 **O L**, do you stand far off? 3378
10: 3 he blesses the greedy and reviles **the L**. 3378
10:12 **L**! Lift up your hand, 3378
10:16 **The L** is King for ever and ever; 3378
10:17 You hear, **O L**, the desire of the afflicted; 3378
11: 1 In **the L** I take refuge. 3378
11: 4 **The L** is in his holy temple; 3378
11: 4 **the L** is on his heavenly throne. 3378
11: 5 **The L** examines the righteous, 3378
11: 7 For **the L** is righteous, he loves justice; 3378
12: 1 Help, **L**, for the godly are no more; 3378
12: 3 May **the L** cut off all flattering lips 3378
12: 5 I will now arise," says **the L**. 3378
12: 6 And the words of **the L** are flawless, 3378
12: 7 **O L**, you will keep us safe and protect us 3378
13: 1 How long, **O L**? 3378
13: 3 Look on me and answer, **O L** my God. 3378
13: 6 I will sing to **the L**, 3378
14: 2 **The L** looks down from heaven on 3378
14: 4 and who do not call on **the L**? 3378
14: 6 but **the L** is their refuge. 3378
14: 7 **the L** restores the fortunes of his people, 3378
15: 1 **L**, who may dwell in your sanctuary? 3378
15: 4 but honors those who fear **the L**, 3378
16: 2 I said to **the L**, "You are my Lord; 3378
16: 5 **L**, you have assigned me my portion 3378
16: 7 I will praise **the L**, who counsels me; 3378
16: 8 I have set **the L** always before me. 3378
17: 1 Hear, **O L**, my righteous plea; 3378
17:13 Rise up, **O L**, confront them, 3378
17:14 **O L**, by your hand save me 3378
18: T Of David the servant of **the L**. 3378
18: T He sang to **the L** the words of this song 3378
18: T when **the L** delivered him from the hand 3378
18: 1 I love you, **O L**, my strength. 3378
18: 2 **The L** is my rock, 3378
18: 3 I call to **the L**, who is worthy of praise, 3378
18: 6 In my distress I called to **the L**; 3378
18:13 **The L** thundered from heaven; 3378
18:15 at your rebuke, **O L**, at the blast of breath 3378
18:18 but **the L** was my support. 3378
18:20 **The L** has dealt with me according 3378
18:21 For I have kept the ways of **the L**; 3378
18:24 **The L** has rewarded me according 3378
18:28 You, **O L**, keep my lamp burning; 3378
18:30 the word of **the L** is flawless. 3378
18:31 For who is God besides **the L**? 3378
18:41 to **the L**, but he did not answer. 3378
18:46 **The L** lives! Praise be to my Rock! 3378
18:49 **O L**; I will sing praises to your name. 3378
19: 7 law of **the L** is perfect, reviving the soul. 3378
19: 7 The statutes of **the L** are trustworthy, 3378
Ps 19: 8 The precepts of **the L** are right, 3378
19: 8 The commands of **the L** are radiant, 3378
19: 9 fear of **the L** is pure, enduring forever. 3378
19: 9 of **the L** are sure and altogether righteous. 3378
19:14 **O L**, my Rock and my Redeemer. 3378
20: 1 May **the L** answer you when you are 3378
20: 5 May **the L** grant all your requests. 3378
20: 6 I know that **the L** saves his anointed; 3378
20: 7 we trust in the name of **the L** our God. 3378
20: 9 **O L**, save the king! 3378
21: 1 **O L**, the king rejoices in your strength. 3378
21: 7 For the king trusts in **the L**; 3378
21: 9 In his wrath **the L** will swallow them up, 3378
21:13 Be exalted, **O L**, in your strength; 3378
22: 8 "He trusts in **the L**; 3378
22: 8 let **the L** rescue him. NIH
22:19 But you, **O L**, be not far off; 3378
22:23 You who fear **the L**, praise him! 3378
22:26 they who seek **the L** will praise him— 3378
22:27 and turn to **the L**, 3378
22:28 to **the L** and he rules over the nations. 3378
23: 1 **The L** is my shepherd, I shall not be in want 3378
23: 6 I will dwell in the house of **the L** forever. 3378
24: 3 Who may ascend the hill of **the L**? 3378
24: 5 He will receive blessing from **the L** 3378
24: 8 **The L** strong and mighty, 3378
24: 8 **the L** mighty in battle. 3378
24:10 of glory? **The L** Almighty— 3378
25: 1 To you, **O L**, I lift up my soul; 3378
25: 4 Show me your ways, **O L**, 3378
25: 6 **O L**, your great mercy and love, 3378
25: 7 for you are good, **O L**. 3378
25: 8 Good and upright is **the L**; 3378
25:10 the ways of **the L** are loving and faithful 3378
25:11 For the sake of your name, **O L**, 3378
25:12 Who, then, is the man that fears **the L**? 3378
25:14 **The L** confides in those who fear him; 3378
25:15 My eyes are ever on **the L**, 3378
26: 1 **O L**, for I have led a blameless life; 3378
26: 1 I have trusted in **the L** without wavering. 3378
26: 2 Test me, **O L**, and try me, 3378
26: 6 and go about your altar, **O L**, 3378
26: 8 I love the house where you live, **O L**, 3378
26:12 in the great assembly I will praise **the L**. 3378
27: 1 **The L** is my light and my salvation— 3378
27: 1 **The L** is the stronghold of my life— 3378
27: 4 One thing I ask of **the L**, 3378
27: 4 the house of **the L** all the days of my life, 3378
27: 4 upon the beauty of **the L** and to seek him 3378
27: 6 I will sing and make music to **the L**. 3378
27: 7 Hear my voice when I call, **O L**; 3378
27: 8 Your face, **L**, I will seek. 3378
27:10 **the L** will receive me. 3378
27:11 Teach me your way, **O L**; 3378
27:13 the goodness of **the L** in the land of 3378
27:14 Wait for **the L**; be strong and take heart 3378
27:14 and take heart and wait for **the L**. 3378
28: 1 To you I call, **O L** my Rock; 3378
28: 5 of **the L** and what his hands have done, 3378
28: 6 Praise be to **the L**, 3378
28: 7 **The L** is my strength and my shield; 3378
28: 8 **The L** is the strength of his people, 3378
29: 1 Ascribe to **the L**, O mighty ones, 3378
29: 1 ascribe to **the L** glory and strength. 3378
29: 2 Ascribe to **the L** the glory due his name; 3378
29: 2 worship **the L** in the splendor 3378
29: 3 The voice of **the L** is over the waters; 3378
29: 3 **the L** thunders over the mighty waters. 3378
29: 4 The voice of **the L** is powerful; 3378
29: 4 the voice of **the L** is majestic. 3378
29: 5 The voice of **the L** breaks the cedars; 3378
29: 5 **the L** breaks in pieces the cedars 3378
29: 7 of **the L** strikes with flashes of lightning. 3378
29: 8 The voice of **the L** shakes the desert; 3378
29: 8 **the L** shakes the Desert of Kadesh. 3378
29: 9 The voice of **the L** twists the oaks 3378
29:10 **The L** sits enthroned over the flood; 3378
29:10 **the L** is enthroned as King forever. 3378
29:11 **The L** gives strength to his people; 3378
29:11 **the L** blesses his people with peace. 3378
30: 1 I will exalt you, **O L**, 3378
30: 2 **O L** my God, I called to you for help 3378
30: 3 **O L**, you brought me up from the grave; 3378
30: 4 Sing to **the L**, you saints of his; 3378
30: 7 **O L**, when you favored me, 3378
30: 8 To you, **O L**, I called; 3378
30:10 Hear, **O L**, and be merciful to me; 3378
30:10 **O L**, be my help." 3378
30:12 **O L** my God, I will give you thanks forever. 3378
31: 1 In you, **O L**, I have taken refuge; 3378
31: 5 redeem me, **O L**, the God of truth. 3378
31: 6 I trust in **the L**. 3378
31: 9 Be merciful to me, **O L**, 3378
31:14 But I trust in you, **O L**; 3378
31:17 Let me not be put to shame, **O L**, 3378
31:21 Praise be to **the L**, 3378
31:23 Love **the L**, all his saints! 3378
31:23 **The L** preserves the faithful, 3378
31:24 all you who hope in **the L**. 3378
32: 2 Blessed is the man whose sin **the L** does 3378
32: 5 "I will confess my transgressions to **the L**" 3378
32:11 Rejoice in **the L** and be glad, 3378
33: 1 Sing joyfully to **the L**, you righteous; 3378
33: 2 Praise **the L** with the harp; 3378
33: 4 For the word of **the L** is right and true; 3378
33: 5 **The L** loves righteousness and justice; 3378
33: 6 the word of **the L** were the heavens made, 3378
Ps 33: 8 Let all the earth fear **the L**; 3378
33:10 **The L** foils the plans of the nations; 3378
33:11 But the plans of **the L** stand firm forever, 3378
33:12 Blessed is the nation whose God is **the L**, 3378
33:13 From heaven **the L** looks down 3378
33:18 eyes of **the L** are on those who fear him, 3378
33:20 We wait in hope for **the L**; 3378
33:22 **O L**, even as we put our hope in you. 3378
34: 1 I will extol **the L** at all times; 3378
34: 2 My soul will boast in **the L**; 3378
34: 3 Glorify **the L** with me; 3378
34: 4 I sought **the L**, and he answered me; 3378
34: 6 and **the L** heard him; 3378
34: 7 The angel of **the L** encamps 3378
34: 8 Taste and see that **the L** is good; 3378
34: 9 Fear **the L**, you his saints, 3378
34:10 those who seek **the L** lack no good thing. 3378
34:11 I will teach you the fear of **the L**. 3378
34:15 The eyes of **the L** are on the righteous 3378
34:16 face of **the L** is against those who do evil, 3378
34:17 righteous cry out, and **the L** hears them; 3378
34:18 **The L** is close to the brokenhearted 3378
34:19 but **the L** delivers him from them all; 3378
34:22 **The L** redeems his servants; 3378
35: 1 **O L**, with those who contend with me; 3378
35: 5 the angel of **the L** driving them away; 3378
35: 6 with the angel of **the L** pursuing them. 3378
35: 9 in **the L** and delight in his salvation. 3378
35:10 "Who is like you, **O L**? 3378
35:22 **O L**, you have seen this; be not silent. 3378
35:24 Vindicate me in your righteousness, **O L** 3378
35:27 may they always say, "**The L** be exalted, 3378
36: T Of David the servant of **the L**. 3378
36: 5 Your love, **O L**, reaches to the heavens, 3378
36: 6 **O L**, you preserve both man and beast. 3378
37: 3 Trust in **the L** and do good; 3378
37: 4 in **the L** and he will give you the desires 3378
37: 5 Commit your way to **the L**; 3378
37: 7 before **the L** and wait patiently for him; 3378
37: 9 but those who hope in **the L** will inherit 3378
37:17 but **the L** upholds the righteous. 3378
37:18 days of the blameless are known to **the L**, 3378
37:22 those **the L** blesses will inherit the land, 2257[S]
37:23 If **the L** delights in a man's way, 3378
37:24 for **the L** upholds him with his hand. 3378
37:28 For **the L** loves the just and will 3378
37:33 but **the L** will not leave them 3378
37:34 Wait for **the L** and keep his way. 3378
37:39 of the righteous comes from **the L**; 3378
37:40 **The L** helps them and delivers them; 3378
38: 1 **O L**, do not rebuke me in your anger 3378
38:15 I wait for you, **O L**; 3378
38:21 **O L**, do not forsake me; 3378
39: 4 **O L**, my life's end and the number 3378
39:12 **O L**, listen to my cry for help; 3378
40: 1 I waited patiently for **the L**; 3378
40: 3 and fear and put their trust in **the L**. 3378
40: 4 the man who makes **the L** his trust, 3378
40: 5 Many, **O L** my God, are the wonders 3378
40: 9 I do not seal my lips, as you know, **O L**. 3378
40:11 not withhold your mercy from me, **O L**; 3378
40:13 Be pleased, **O L**, to save me; 3378
40:13 **O L**, come quickly to help me. 3378
40:16 "**The L** be exalted!" 3378
41: 1 **the L** delivers him in times of trouble. 3378
41: 2 **The L** will protect him and preserve his life; 3378
41: 3 **The L** will sustain him on his sickbed 3378
41: 4 I said, "**O L**, have mercy on me; 3378
41:10 But you, **O L**, have mercy on me; 3378
41:13 Praise be to **the L**, the God of Israel, 3378
42: 8 By day **the L** directs his love, 3378
46: 7 **The L** Almighty is with us; 3378
46: 8 Come and see the works of **the L**, 3378
46:11 **The L** Almighty is with us; 3378
47: 2 How awesome is **the L** Most High, 3378
47: 5 **the L** amid the sounding of trumpets. 3378
48: 1 Great is **the L**, and most worthy of praise, 3378
48: 8 of **the L** Almighty, in the city of our God: 3378
50: 1 The Mighty One, God, **the L**, 3378
54: 6 I will praise your name, **O L**, 3378
55:16 But I call to God, and **the L** saves me. 3378
55:22 on **the L** and he will sustain you; 3378
56:10 In God, whose word I praise, in **the L**, 3378
58: 6 tear out, **O L**, the fangs of the lions! 3378
59: 3 for no offense or sin of mine, **O L**. 3378
59: 5 **O L** God Almighty, the God of Israel, 3378
59: 8 But you, **O L**, laugh at them; 3378
64:10 Let the righteous rejoice in **the L** 3378
68: 4 his name is **the L**—and rejoice before him. 3363
68:16 where **the L** *himself* will dwell forever? 3378
68:18 that you, **O L** God, might dwell there. 3363
68:20 from **the** Sovereign **L** comes escape 3378
68:26 praise **the L** in the assembly of Israel. 3378
69: 6 O Lord, **the L** Almighty; 3378
69:13 But I pray to you, **O L**, 3378
69:16 **O L**, out of the goodness of your love; 3378
69:31 This will please **the L** more than an ox, 3378
69:33 **The L** hears the needy and does 3378
70: 1 **O L**, come quickly to help me. 3378
70: 5 **O L**, do not delay. 3378
71: 1 In you, **O L**, I have taken refuge; 3378
71: 5 you have been my hope, **O** Sovereign **L**, 3378
71:16 proclaim your mighty acts, **O** Sovereign **L**; 3378
72:18 Praise be to **the L** God, the God of Israel, 3378
73:28 I have made **the** Sovereign **L** my refuge; 3378
74:18 how the enemy has mocked you, **O L**, 3378
75: 8 In the hand of **the L** is a cup full 3378

†LORD distinguishes the proper name of God, *Yahweh*, indicated in the NIV by "LORD," from the words translated "Lord" and "lord," indexed under the heading ***LORD**, pages 683-86.

Ps 76:11 Make vows to **the L** your God and fulfill them; 3378
77:11 I will remember the deeds of **the L;** 3363
78: 4 the praiseworthy deeds of **the L,** 3378
78:21 When **the L** heard them, 3378
79: 5 How long, **O L?** 3378
80: 4 **O L** God Almighty, 3378
80:19 Restore us, **O L** God Almighty; 3378
81:10 I am **the L** your God, 3378
81:15 Those who hate **the L** would cringe 3378
83:16 so that men will seek your name, **O L.** 3378
83:18 whose name is **the L—** 3378
84: 1 How lovely is your dwelling place, **O L** Almighty! 3378
84: 2 even faints, for the courts of **the L;** 3378
84: 3 a place near your altar, **O L** Almighty, 3378
84: 8 Hear my prayer, **O L** God Almighty; 3378
84:11 For **the L** God is a sun and shield; 3378
84:11 **the L** bestows favor and honor; 3378
84:12 **O L** Almighty, blessed is the man who trusts in you. 3378
85: 1 You showed favor to your land, **O L;** 3378
85: 7 Show us your unfailing love, **O L,** 3378
85: 8 I will listen to what God **the L** will say; 3378
85:12 **The L** will indeed give what is good, 3378
86: 1 Hear, **O L,** and answer me, 3378
86: 6 Hear my prayer, **O L;** 3378
86:11 Teach me your way, **O L,** 3378
86:17 **O L,** have helped me and comforted me. 3378
87: 2 **the L** loves the gates of Zion more than 3378
87: 6 **The L** will write in the register of the 3378
88: 1 **O L,** the God who saves me, 3378
88: 9 I call to you, **O L,** every day; 3378
88:13 But I cry to you for help, **O L;** 3378
88:14 **O L,** do you reject me and hide your face 3378
89: 5 **O L,** your faithfulness too, 3378
89: 6 the skies above can compare with **the L?** 3378
89: 6 Who is like **the L** among the heavenly beings? 3378
89: 8 **O L** God Almighty, who is like you? 3378
89: 8 You are mighty, **O L,** 3363
89:15 in the light of your presence, **O L.** 3378
89:18 Indeed, our shield belongs to **the L,** 3378
89:46 How long, **O L?** Will you hide yourself forever? 3378
89:51 which your enemies have mocked, **O L,** 3378
89:52 Praise be to **the L** forever! 3378
90:13 Relent, **O L!** How long will it be? 3378
91: 2 I will say of **the L,** 3378
91: 9 even **the L,** who is my refuge— 3378
91:14 "Because he loves me," says the L, NIH
92: 1 It is good to praise **the L** and make music 3378
92: 4 you make me glad by your deeds, **O L;** 3378
92: 5 How great are your works, **O L,** 3378
92: 8 But you, **O L,** are exalted forever. 3378
92: 9 For surely your enemies, **O L,** 3378
92:13 planted in the house of **the L,** 3378
92:15 "**The L** is upright; he is my Rock, 3378
93: 1 **The L** reigns, he is robed in majesty; 3378
93: 1 **the L** is robed in majesty and is armed 3378
93: 3 The seas have lifted up, **O L,** 3378
93: 4 **the L** on high is mighty. 3378
93: 5 holiness adorns your house for endless days, **O L.** 3378
94: 1 **O L,** the God who avenges, 3378
94: 3 How long will the wicked, **O L,** 3378
94: 5 They crush your people, **O L;** 3378
94: 7 They say, "**The L** does not see; 3363
94:11 **The L** knows the thoughts of man; 3378
94:12 Blessed is the man you discipline, **O L,** 3363
94:14 For **the L** will not reject his people; 3378
94:17 Unless **the L** had given me help, 3378
94:18 your love, **O L,** supported me. 3378
94:22 But **the L** has become my fortress, 3378
94:23 **the L** our God will destroy them. 3378
95: 1 Come, let us sing for joy to **the L;** 3378
95: 3 For **the L** is the great God, 3378
95: 6 let us kneel before **the L** our Maker; 3378
96: 1 Sing to **the L** a new song; 3378
96: 1 sing to **the L,** all the earth. 3378
96: 2 Sing to **the L,** praise his name; 3378
96: 4 great is **the L** and most worthy of praise; 3378
96: 5 but **the L** made the heavens. 3378
96: 7 Ascribe to **the L,** O families of nations, 3378
96: 7 ascribe to **the L** glory and strength. 3378
96: 8 Ascribe to **the L** the glory due his name; 3378
96: 9 Worship **the L** in the splendor 3378
96:10 Say among the nations, "**The L** reigns." 3378
96:13 they will sing before **the L,** 3378
97: 1 **The L** reigns, let the earth be glad; 3378
97: 5 mountains melt like wax before **the L,** 3378
97: 8 because of your judgments, **O L.** 3378
97: 9 **O L,** are the Most High over all the earth; 3378
97:10 Let those who love **the L** hate evil, 3378
97:12 Rejoice in **the L,** you who are righteous, 3378
98: 1 Sing to **the L** a new song, 3378
98: 2 **The L** has made his salvation known 3378
98: 4 Shout for joy to **the L,** all the earth, 3378
98: 5 make music to **the L** with the harp, 3378
98: 6 shout for joy before **the L,** the King. 3378
98: 9 let them sing before **the L,** 3378
99: 1 **The L** reigns, let the nations tremble; 3378
99: 2 Great is **the L** in Zion; 3378
99: 5 Exalt **the L** our God and worship 3378
99: 6 on **the L** and he answered them. 3378
99: 8 **O L** our God, you answered them; 3378
99: 9 Exalt **the L** our God and worship 3378

Ps 99: 9 for **the L** our God is holy. 3378
100: 1 Shout for joy to **the L,** all the earth. 3378
100: 2 Worship **the L** with gladness; 3378
100: 3 Know that **the L** is God. 3378
100: 5 For **the L** is good and his love endures 3378
101: 1 to you, **O L,** I will sing praise. 3378
101: 8 from the city of **the L.** 3378
102: T and pours out his lament before **the L.** 3378
102: 1 Hear my prayer, **O L;** 3378
102:12 But you, **O L,** sit enthroned forever; 3378
102:15 The nations will fear the name of **the L,** 3378
102:16 For **the L** will rebuild Zion and appear 3378
102:18 a people not yet created may praise **the L:** 3363
102:19 "**The L** looked down from his sanctuary 3378
102:21 So the name of **the L** will be declared 3378
102:22 the kingdoms assemble to worship **the L.** 3378
103: 1 Praise **the L,** O my soul; 3378
103: 2 Praise **the L,** O my soul, 3378
103: 6 **The L** works righteousness and justice 3378
103: 8 **The L** is compassionate and gracious, 3378
103:13 so **the L** has compassion on those who fear him; 3378
103:19 **The L** has established his throne 3378
103:20 Praise **the L,** you his angels, 3378
103:21 Praise **the L,** all his heavenly hosts, 3378
103:22 Praise **the L,** all his works everywhere 3378
103:22 Praise **the L,** O my soul. 3378
104: 1 Praise **the L,** O my soul. 3378
104: 1 **O L** my God, you are very great; 3378
104:16 The trees of **the L** are well watered, 3378
104:24 How many are your works, **O L!** 3378
104:31 May the glory of **the L** endure forever; 3378
104:31 may **the L** rejoice in his works— 3378
104:33 I will sing to **the L** all my life; 3378
104:34 as I rejoice in **the L.** 3378
104:35 Praise **the L,** O my soul. 3378
104:35 O my soul. Praise **the L.** 3363
105: 1 Give thanks to **the L,** call on his name; 3378
105: 3 of those who seek **the L** rejoice. 3378
105: 4 Look to **the L** and his strength; 3378
105: 7 He is **the L** our God; 3378
105:19 till the word of **the L** proved him true. 3378
105:24 **The L** made his people very fruitful; NIH
105:45 Praise **the L.** 3363
106: 1 Praise **the L.** Give thanks to the LORD, 3363
106: 1 Give thanks to **the L,** for he is good; 3378
106: 2 of **the L** or fully declare his praise? 3378
106: 4 Remember me, **O L,** 3378
106:16 who was consecrated to **the L.** 3378
106:25 in their tents and did not obey **the L.** 3378
106:29 **the L** to anger by their wicked deeds, NIH
106:32 By the waters of Meribah they angered **the L** NIH
106:34 as **the L** had commanded them, 3378
106:40 Therefore **the L** was angry 3378
106:47 Save us, **O L** our God, 3378
106:48 Praise be to **the L,** the God of Israel, 3378
106:48 Praise **the L.** 3363
107: 1 Give thanks to **the L,** for he is good; 3378
107: 2 Let the redeemed of **the L** say this— 3378
107: 6 they cried out to **the L** in their trouble, 3378
107: 8 Let them give thanks to **the L** 3378
107:13 Then they cried to **the L** in their trouble, 3378
107:15 Let them give thanks to **the L** 3378
107:19 Then they cried to **the L** in their trouble, 3378
107:21 Let them give thanks to **the L** 3378
107:24 They saw the works of **the L,** 3378
107:28 they cried out to **the L** in their trouble, 3378
107:31 Let them give thanks to **the L** 3378
107:43 and consider the great love of **the L.** 3378
108: 3 I will praise you, **O L,** 3378
109:14 be remembered before **the L;** 3378
109:15 before **the L,** that he may cut off 3378
109:21 But you, O Sovereign **L,** 3378
109:26 Help me, **O L** my God; 3378
109:27 that you, **O L,** have done it. 3378
109:30 With my mouth I will greatly extol **the L;** 3378
110: 1 **The L** says to my Lord: 3378
110: 2 **The L** will extend your mighty scepter 3378
110: 4 **The L** has sworn and will 3378
111: 1 Praise **the L.** 3363
111: 1 I will extol **the L** with all my heart in 3378
111: 2 Great are the works of **the L;** 3378
111: 4 **the L** is gracious and compassionate. 3378
111:10 fear of **the L** is the beginning of wisdom; 3378
112: 1 Praise **the L.** 3363
112: 1 Blessed is the man who fears **the L,** 3378
112: 7 his heart is steadfast, trusting in **the L.** 3378
113: 1 Praise **the L.** 3363
113: 1 Praise, O servants of **the L,** 3378
113: 1 praise the name of **the L.** 3378
113: 2 Let the name of **the L** be praised, 3378
113: 3 the name of **the L** is to be praised. 3378
113: 4 **The L** is exalted over all the nations, 3378
113: 5 Who is like **the L** our God, 3378
113: 9 Praise **the L.** 3363
115: 1 Not to us, **O L,** 3378
115: 9 O house of Israel, trust in **the L—** 3378
115:10 O house of Aaron, trust in **the L—** 3378
115:11 You who fear him, trust in **the L—** 3378
115:12 **The L** remembers us and will bless us: 3378
115:13 he will bless those who fear **the L—** 3378
115:14 May **the L** make you increase, 3378
115:15 May you be blessed by **the L,** 3378
115:16 The highest heavens belong to **the L,** 3378
115:17 It is not the dead who praise **the L,** 3363
115:18 it is we who extol **the L,** 3363
115:18 Praise **the L.** 3363

Ps 116: 1 I love **the L,** for he heard my voice; 3378
116: 4 Then I called on the name of **the L:** 3378
116: 4 "**O L,** save me!" 3378
116: 5 **The L** is gracious and righteous; 3378
116: 6 **The L** protects the simplehearted; 3378
116: 7 for **the L** has been good to you. 3378
116: 8 **O L,** have delivered my soul from death, NIH
116: 9 that I may walk before **the L** in the land 3378
116:12 How can I repay **the L** 3378
116:13 and call on the name of **the L.** 3378
116:14 to **the L** in the presence of all his people. 3378
116:15 Precious in the sight of **the L** is the death 3378
116:16 **O L,** truly I am your servant; 3378
116:17 to you and call on the name of **the L.** 3378
116:18 to **the L** in the presence of all his people, 3378
116:19 in the courts of the house of **the L—** 3378
116:19 Praise **the L.** 3363
117: 1 Praise **the L,** all you nations; 3378
117: 2 the faithfulness of **the L** endures forever. 3378
117: 2 Praise **the L.** 3363
118: 1 Give thanks to **the L,** for he is good; 3378
118: 4 Let those who fear **the L** say: 3378
118: 5 In my anguish I cried to **the L,** 3363
118: 6 **The L** is with me; I will not be afraid. 3378
118: 7 **The L** is with me; he is my helper. 3378
118: 8 It is better to take refuge in **the L** than 3378
118: 9 It is better to take refuge in **the L** than 3378
118:10 but in the name of **the L** I cut them off. 3378
118:11 but in the name of **the L** I cut them off. 3378
118:12 in the name of **the L** I cut them off. 3378
118:13 but **the L** helped me. 3378
118:14 **The L** is my strength and my song; 3363
118:17 and will proclaim what **the L** has done. 3363
118:18 **The L** has chastened me severely, 3363
118:19 I will enter and give thanks to **the L.** 3363
118:20 This is the gate of **the L** through which 3378
118:23 **the L** has done this, 3378
118:24 This is the day **the L** has made; 3378
118:25 **O L,** save us; 3378
118:25 **O L,** grant us success. 3378
118:26 in the name of **the L.** 3378
118:26 From the house of **the L** we bless you. 3378
118:27 **The L** is God, he has made his light shine 3378
118:29 Give thanks to **the L,** for he is good; 3378
119: 1 who walk according to the law of **the L.** 3378
119:12 Praise be to you, **O L;** 3378
119:31 I hold fast to your statutes, **O L;** 3378
119:33 Teach me, **O L,** to follow your decrees; 3378
119:41 May your unfailing love come to me, **O L,** 3378
119:52 I remember your ancient laws, **O L,** 3378
119:55 In the night I remember your name, **O L,** 3378
119:57 You are my portion, **O L;** 3378
119:64 The earth is filled with your love, **O L;** 3378
119:65 according to your word, **O L.** 3378
119:75 **O L,** that your laws are righteous, 3378
119:89 Your word, **O L,** is eternal; 3378
119:107 preserve my life, **O L,** 3378
119:108 **O L,** the willing praise of my mouth, 3378
119:126 It is time for you to act, **O L;** 3378
119:137 Righteous are you, **O L,** 3378
119:145 I call with all my heart; answer me, **O L,** 3378
119:149 preserve my life, **O L,** 3378
119:151 Yet you are near, **O L,** 3378
119:156 Your compassion is great, **O L;** 3378
119:159 preserve my life, **O L,** 3378
119:166 I wait for your salvation, **O L,** 3378
119:169 May my cry come before you, **O L;** 3378
119:174 I long for your salvation, **O L,** 3378
120: 1 I call on **the L** in my distress, 3378
120: 2 **O L,** from lying lips and 3378
121: 2 My help comes from **the L,** 3378
121: 5 **The L** watches over you— 3378
121: 5 **the L** is your shade at your right hand; 3378
121: 7 **The L** will keep you from all harm— 3378
121: 8 **the L** will watch over your coming 3378
122: 1 "Let us go to the house of **the L.**" 3378
122: 4 where the tribes go up, the tribes of **the L,** 3363
122: 4 to praise the name of **the L** according to 3378
122: 9 the sake of the house of **the L** our God, 3378
123: 2 so our eyes look to **the L** our God, 3378
123: 3 Have mercy on us, **O L,** 3378
124: 1 If **the L** had not been on our side— 3378
124: 2 if **the L** had not been on our side 3378
124: 6 Praise be to **the L,** 3378
124: 8 Our help is in the name of **the L,** 3378
125: 1 who trust in **the L** are like Mount Zion, 3378
125: 2 so **the L** surrounds his people both now 3378
125: 4 Do good, **O L,** to those who are good, 3378
125: 5 to crooked ways **the L** will banish with 3378
126: 1 **the L** brought back the captives to Zion, 3378
126: 2 "**The L** has done great things for them." 3378
126: 3 **The L** has done great things for us, 3378
126: 4 Restore our fortunes, **O L,** 3378
127: 1 Unless **the L** builds the house, 3378
127: 1 Unless **the L** watches over the city, 3378
127: 3 Sons are a heritage from **the L,** 3378
128: 1 Blessed are all who fear **the L,** 3378
128: 4 Thus is the man blessed who fears **the L.** 3378
128: 5 May **the L** bless you from Zion all 3378
129: 4 But **the L** is righteous; 3378
129: 8 "The blessing of **the L** be upon you; 3378
129: 8 we bless you in the name of **the L.**" 3378
130: 1 Out of the depths I cry to you, **O L;** 3378
130: 3 If you, **O L,** kept a record of sins, 3363
130: 5 I wait for **the L,** my soul waits, 3378
130: 7 O Israel, put your hope in **the L,** 3378
130: 7 for with **the L** is unfailing love and 3378

†**LORD** distinguishes the proper name of God, *Yahweh*, indicated in the NIV by "LORD," from the words translated "Lord" and "lord," indexed under the heading ***LORD**, pages 683-86.

Ps 131: 1 My heart is not proud, O **L**, 3378
131: 3 O Israel, put your hope in **the L** 3378
132: 1 O **L**, remember David and all 3378
132: 2 He swore an oath to **the L** and made 3378
132: 5 till I find a place for **the L**, 3378
132: 8 O **L**, and come to your resting place, 3378
132:11 **The L** swore an oath to David, 3378
132:13 For **the L** has chosen Zion, 3378
133: 3 For there **the L** bestows his blessing, 3378
134: 1 Praise **the L**, all you servants of 3378
134: 1 all you servants of **the L** who minister 3378
134: 1 by night in the house of **the L**. 3378
134: 2 in the sanctuary and praise **the L**. 3378
134: 3 May **the L**, the Maker of heaven 3378
135: 1 Praise **the L**. 3363
135: 1 Praise the name of **the L**; 3378
135: 1 praise him, you servants of **the L**, 3378
135: 2 you who minister in the house of **the L**, 3378
135: 3 Praise **the L**, for the LORD is good; 3363
135: 3 Praise the LORD, for **the L** is good; 3378
135: 4 For **the L** has chosen Jacob to be his own, 3363
135: 5 I know that **the L** is great, 3378
135: 6 **The L** does whatever pleases him, 3378
135:13 Your name, O **L**, endures forever, 3378
135:13 endures forever, your renown, O **L**, 3378
135:14 For **the L** will vindicate his people 3378
135:19 O house of Israel, praise **the L**; 3378
135:19 O house of Aaron, praise **the L**; 3378
135:20 O house of Levi, praise **the L**; 3378
135:20 you who fear him, praise **the L**. 3378
135:21 Praise be to **the L** from Zion, 3378
135:21 Praise **the L**. 3363
136: 1 Give thanks to **the L**, for he is good. 3378
137: 4 How can we sing the songs of **the L** while 3378
137: 7 O **L**, what the Edomites did on 3378
138: 1 I will praise you, O **L**, with all my heart; NIH
138: 4 the earth praise you, O **L**, when they hear 3378
138: 5 May they sing of the ways of **the L**, 3378
138: 5 for the glory of **the L** is great. 3378
138: 6 Though **the L** is on high, 3378
138: 8 **The L** will fulfill [his purpose] for me; 3378
138: 8 your love, O **L**, endures forever— 3378
139: 1 O **L**, you have searched me 3378
139: 4 on my tongue you know it completely, O **L**. 3378
139:21 Do I not hate those who hate you, O **L**, 3378
140: 1 Rescue me, O **L**, from evil men; 3378
140: 4 O **L**, from the hands of the wicked; 3378
140: 6 O **L**, I say to you, 3378
140: 6 Hear, O **L**, my cry for mercy. 3378
140: 7 O Sovereign **L**, my strong deliverer, 3378
140: 8 not grant the wicked their desires, O **L**; 3378
140:12 that **the L** secures justice for the poor 3378
141: 1 O **L**, I call to you; come quickly to me. 3378
141: 3 Set a guard over my mouth, O **L**; 3378
141: 8 my eyes are fixed on you, O Sovereign **L**; 3378
142: 1 I cry aloud to **the L**; 3378
142: 1 I lift up my voice to **the L** for mercy. 3378
142: 5 I cry to you, O **L**; 3378
143: 1 O **L**, hear my prayer, 3378
143: 7 Answer me quickly, O **L**; my spirit fails. 3378
143: 9 Rescue me from my enemies, O **L**, 3378
143:11 your name's sake, O **L**, preserve my life; 3378
144: 1 Praise be to **the L** my Rock, 3378
144: 3 O **L**, what is man that you care for him, 3378
144: 5 Part your heavens, O **L**, and come down; 3378
144:15 the people whose God is **the L**. 3378
145: 3 Great is **the L** and most worthy of praise; 3378
145: 8 **The L** is gracious and compassionate, 3378
145: 9 **The L** is good to all; 3378
145:10 All you have made will praise you, O **L**; 3378
145:13 **The L** is faithful to all his promises 3378
145:14 **The L** upholds all those who fall and lifts 3378
145:17 **The L** is righteous in all his ways 3378
145:18 **The L** is near to all who call on him, 3378
145:20 **The L** watches over all who love him, 3378
145:21 My mouth will speak in praise of **the L**. 3378
146: 1 Praise **the L**. 3363
146: 1 Praise **the L**, O my soul. 3378
146: 2 I will praise **the L** all my life; 3378
146: 5 whose hope is in **the L** his God, 3378
146: 6 **the L**, who remains faithful forever. NIH
146: 7 **The L** sets prisoners free, 3378
146: 8 **the L** gives sight to the blind, 3378
146: 8 **the L** lifts up those who are bowed down, 3378
146: 8 **the L** loves the righteous. 3378
146: 9 **The L** watches over the alien and sustains 3378
146:10 **The L** reigns forever, your God, O Zion, 3378
146:10 Praise **the L**. 3363
147: 1 Praise **the L**. 3363
147: 2 **The L** builds up Jerusalem; 3378
147: 6 **The L** sustains the humble but casts 3378
147: 7 Sing to **the L** with thanksgiving; 3378
147:11 **the L** delights in those who fear him, 3378
147:12 Extol **the L**, O Jerusalem; 3378
147:20 Praise **the L**. 3363
148: 1 Praise **the L**. 3363
148: 1 Praise **the L** from the heavens, 3378
148: 5 Let them praise the name of **the L**, 3378
148: 7 Praise **the L** from the earth, 3378
148:13 Let them praise the name of **the L**, 3378
148:14 Praise **the L**. 3363
149: 1 Praise **the L**. 3363
149: 1 Sing to **the L** a new song, 3378
149: 4 For **the L** takes delight in his people; 3378
149: 9 Praise **the L**. 3363
150: 1 Praise **the L**. 3363
150: 6 Let everything that has breath praise **the L**. 3363
Ps 150: 6 Praise **the L**. 3363
Pr 1: 7 fear of **the L** is the beginning of knowledge, 3378
1:29 and did not choose to fear **the L**, 3378
2: 5 then you will understand the fear of **the L** 3378
2: 6 For **the L** gives wisdom, 3378
3: 5 Trust in **the L** with all your heart and lean 3378
3: 7 fear **the L** and shun evil. 3378
3: 9 Honor **the L** with your wealth, 3378
3:12 because **the L** disciplines those he loves, 3378
3:19 By wisdom **the L** laid the earth's
foundations, 3378
3:26 for **the L** will be your confidence 3378
3:32 for **the L** detests a perverse man but takes 3378
5:21 a man's ways are in full view of **the L**, 3378
6:16 There are six things **the L** hates, 3378
8:13 To fear **the L** is to hate evil; 3378
8:22 "**The L** brought me forth as the first 3378
8:35 and receives favor from **the L**. 3378
9:10 fear of **the L** is the beginning of wisdom, 3378
10: 3 **The L** does not let the righteous go hungry 3378
10:22 The blessing of **the L** brings wealth, 3378
10:27 The fear of **the L** adds length to life, 3378
10:29 way of **the L** is a refuge for the righteous, 3378
11: 1 **The L** abhors dishonest scales, 3378
11:20 **The L** detests men of perverse heart 3378
12: 2 A good man obtains favor from **the L**, 3378
12: 2 but **the L** condemns a crafty man. NIH
12:22 **The L** detests lying lips, 3378
14: 2 He whose walk is upright fears **the L**, 3378
14:16 A wise man fears **the L** and shuns evil, NIH
14:26 He who fears **the L** has a secure fortress, 3378
14:27 The fear of **the L** is a fountain of life, 3378
15: 3 The eyes of **the L** are everywhere, 3378
15: 8 **The L** detests the sacrifice of the wicked, 3378
15: 9 **The L** detests the way of the wicked 3378
15:11 and Destruction lie open before **the L**— 3378
15:16 Better a little with the fear of **the L** than 3378
15:25 **The L** tears down the proud man's house 3378
15:26 **The L** detests the thoughts of the wicked, 3378
15:29 **The L** is far from the wicked but he hears 3378
15:33 The fear of **the L** teaches a man wisdom, 3378
16: 1 from **the L** comes the reply of the tongue. 3378
16: 2 but motives are weighed by **the L**. 3378
16: 3 Commit to **the L** whatever you do, 3378
16: 4 **The L** works out everything for his own
ends— 3378
16: 5 **The L** detests all the proud of heart. 3378
16: 6 the fear of **the L** a man avoids evil. 3378
16: 7 a man's ways are pleasing to **the L**, 3378
16: 9 but **the L** determines his steps. 3378
16:11 and balances are from **the L**; 3378
16:20 and blessed is he who trusts in **the L**. 3378
16:33 but its every decision is from **the L**. 3378
17: 3 but **the L** tests the heart. 3378
17:15 **the L** detests them both. 3378
18:10 The name of **the L** is a strong tower; 3378
18:22 and receives favor from **the L**. 3378
19: 3 yet his heart rages against **the L**. 3378
19:14 but a prudent wife is from **the L**. 3378
19:17 He who is kind to the poor lends to **the L**, 3378
19:23 The fear of **the L** leads to life: 3378
20:10 **the L** detests them both. 3378
20:12 **the L** has made them both. 3378
20:22 Wait for **the L**, and he will deliver you. 3378
20:23 **The L** detests differing weights, 3378
20:24 A man's steps are directed by **the L**. 3378
20:27 The lamp of **the L** searches the spirit of 3378
21: 1 The king's heart is in the hand of **the L**; 3378
21: 2 but **the L** weighs the heart. 3378
21: 3 to **the L** than sacrifice. 3378
21:30 no plan that can succeed against **the L**. 3378
21:31 but victory rests with **the L**. 3378
22: 2 **The L** is the Maker of them all. 3378
22: 4 of **the L** bring wealth and honor and life. 3378
22:12 of **the L** keep watch over knowledge, 3378
22:19 So that your trust may be in **the L**, 3378
22:23 for **the L** will take up their case 3378
23:17 always be zealous for the fear of **the L**. 3378
24:18 or **the L** will see and disapprove 3378
24:21 Fear **the L** and the king, my son, 3378
25:22 and **the L** will reward you. 3378
28: 5 those who seek **the L** understand it fully. 3378
28:14 the man who always fears **the L**, NIH
28:25 but he who trusts in **the L** will prosper. 3378
29:13 **The L** gives sight to the eyes of both. 3378
29:25 but whoever trusts in **the L** is kept safe. 3378
29:26 but it is from **the L** that man gets justice. 3378
30: 7 "Two things I ask of you, O **L**; NIH
30: 9 and say, 'Who is **the L**?' 3378
31:30 a woman who fears **the L** is to be praised. 3378
Isa 1: 2 For **the L** has spoken: 3378
1: 4 They have forsaken **the L**; 3378
1: 9 **the L** Almighty had left us some survivors, 3378
1:10 Hear the word of **the L**, 3378
1:11 what are they to me?" says **the L**. 3378
1:18 let us reason together," says **the L**. 3378
1:20 For the mouth of **the L** has spoken. 3378
1:24 Therefore the Lord, **the L** Almighty, 3378
1:28 and those who forsake **the L** will perish. 3378
2: 3 let us go up to the mountain of **the L**, 3378
2: 3 the word of **the L** from Jerusalem. 3378
2: 5 let us walk in the light of **the L**. 3378
2:10 of **the L** and the splendor of his majesty! 3378
2:11 **the L** alone will be exalted in that day. 3378
2:12 **The L** Almighty has a day in store for all 3378
2:17 **the L** alone will be exalted in that day, 3378
2:19 to holes in the ground from dread of **the L** 3378
Isa 2:21 of **the L** and the splendor of his majesty, 3378
3: 1 See now, the Lord, **the L** Almighty, 3378
3: 8 their words and deeds are against **the L**, 3378
3:13 **The L** takes his place in court; 3378
3:14 **The L** enters into judgment against 3378
3:15 declares the Lord, **the L** Almighty. 3378
3:16 **The L** says, "The women of Zion 3378
3:17 **the L** will make their scalps bald." 3378
4: 2 of **the L** will be beautiful and glorious, 3378
4: 5 Then **the L** will create over all of Mount 3378
5: 7 of **the L** Almighty is the house of Israel, 3378
5: 9 **The L** Almighty has declared 3378
5:12 for the deeds of **the L**, 3378
5:16 But **the L** Almighty will be exalted 3378
5:24 of **the L** Almighty and spurned the word 3378
6: 3 "Holy, holy, holy is **the L** Almighty; 3378
6: 5 the King, **the L** Almighty." 3378
6:12 until **the L** has sent everyone far away 3378
7: 3 Then **the L** said to Isaiah, "Go out, 3378
7: 7 Yet this is what the Sovereign **L** says: 3378
7:10 Again **the L** spoke to Ahaz, 3378
7:11 "Ask **the L** your God for a sign, 3378
7:12 I will not put **the L** to the test." 3378
7:17 **The L** will bring on you and 3378
7:18 that day **the L** will whistle for flies from 3378
8: 1 **The L** said to me, 3378
8: 3 And **the L** said to me, 3378
8: 5 **The L** spoke to me again: 3378
8:11 **The L** spoke to me with his strong hand 3378
8:13 **The L** Almighty is the one you are 3378
8:17 I will wait for **the L**, 3378
8:18 and the children **the L** has given me. 3378
8:18 in Israel from **the L** Almighty, 3378
9: 7 of **the L** Almighty will accomplish this. 3378
9:11 But **the L** has strengthened Rezin's foes 3378
9:13 nor have they sought **the L** Almighty. 3378
9:14 So **the L** will cut off from Israel 3378
9:19 the wrath of **the L** Almighty the land will 3378
10:16 Therefore, the Lord, **the L** Almighty, 3378
10:20 down but will truly rely on **the L**, 3378
10:23 The Lord, **the L** Almighty, 3378
10:24 this is what the Lord, **the L** Almighty, 3378
10:26 **The L** Almighty will lash them with 3378
10:33 See, the Lord, **the L** Almighty, 3378
11: 2 The Spirit of **the L** will rest on him— 3378
11: 2 of knowledge and of the fear of **the L**— 3378
11: 3 and he will delight in the fear of **the L**. 3378
11: 9 of **the L** as the waters cover the sea. 3378
11:15 **The L** will dry up the gulf of the Egyptian 3378
12: 1 "I will praise you, O **L**. 3378
12: 2 **The L**, the LORD, is my strength 3363
12: 2 **the L**, is my strength and my song; 3378
12: 4 "Give thanks to **the L**, call on his name; 3378
12: 5 to **the L**, for he has done glorious things; 3378
13: 4 **The L** Almighty is mustering an army 3378
13: 5 **the L** and the weapons of his wrath— 3378
13: 6 Wail, for the day of **the L** is near; 3378
13: 9 See, the day of **the L** is coming— 3378
13:13 at the wrath of **the L** Almighty, 3378
14: 1 **The L** will have compassion on Jacob; 3378
14: 3 On the day **the L** gives you relief 3378
14: 5 **The L** has broken the rod of the wicked, 3378
14:22 declares **the L** Almighty. 3378
14:22 and descendants," declares **the L**. 3378
14:23 declares **the L** Almighty. 3378
14:24 **The L** Almighty has sworn, "Surely, 3378
14:27 For **the L** Almighty has purposed, 3378
14:32 "**The L** has established Zion, 3378
16:13 This is the word **the L** has already spoken 3378
16:14 But now **the L** says: 3378
17: 3 declares **the L** Almighty. 3378
17: 6 declares **the L**, the God of Israel. 3378
18: 4 This is what **the L** says to me: 3378
18: 7 to **the L** Almighty from a people tall 3378
18: 7 the place of the Name of **the L** Almighty. 3378
19: 1 **the L** rides on a swift cloud and is coming 3378
19: 4 declares the Lord, **the L** Almighty. 3378
19:12 make known what **the L** Almighty has
planned 3378
19:14 **The L** has poured into them a spirit 3378
19:16 that **the L** Almighty raises against them. 3378
19:17 of what **the L** Almighty is planning 3378
19:18 and swear allegiance to **the L** Almighty. 3378
19:19 be an altar to **the L** in the heart of Egypt, 3378
19:19 and a monument to **the L** at its border. 3378
19:20 and witness to **the L** Almighty in the land 3378
19:20 to **the L** because of their oppressors, 3378
19:21 So **the L** will make himself known to 3378
19:21 in that day they will acknowledge **the L**. 3378
19:21 they will make vows to **the L** 3378
19:22 **The L** will strike Egypt with a plague; 3378
19:22 They will turn to **the L**, 3378
19:25 **The L** Almighty will bless them, saying, 3378
20: 2 that time **the L** spoke through Isaiah son 3378
20: 3 Then **the L** said, 3378
21:10 from **the L** Almighty, 3378
21:17 **The L**, the God of Israel, has spoken. 3378
22: 5 The Lord, **the L** Almighty, 3378
22:12 The Lord, **the L** Almighty, 3378
22:14 **The L** Almighty has revealed this 3378
22:14 says the Lord, **the L** Almighty. 3378
22:15 This is what the Lord, **the L** Almighty, 3378
22:17 **the L** is about to take firm hold of you 3378
22:25 "In that day," declares **the L** Almighty, 3378
22:25 **The L** has spoken. 3378
23: 9 **The L** Almighty planned it, 3378
23:11 **The L** has stretched out his hand over 3378

†LORD distinguishes the proper name of God, *Yahweh*, indicated in the NIV by "LORD," from the words translated "Lord" and "lord," indexed under the heading ***LORD**, pages 683-86.

Isa 23:17	**the L** will deal with Tyre.	3378
23:18	her earnings will be set apart for **the L;**	3378
23:18	to those who live before **the L,**	3378
24: 1	**the L** is going to lay waste the earth	3378
24: 3	**The L** has spoken this word.	3378
24:15	Therefore in the east give glory to **the L;**	3378
24:15	exalt the name of **the L,**	3378
24:21	In that day **the L** will punish the powers	3378
24:23	for **the L** Almighty will reign	3378
25: 1	O **L,** you are my God;	3378
25: 6	On this mountain **the L** Almighty will prepare a feast	3378
25: 8	**The** Sovereign **L** will wipe away the tears	3378
25: 8	**The L** has spoken.	3378
25: 9	This is **the L,** we trusted in him;	3378
25:10	of **the L** will rest on this mountain;	3378
26: 4	Trust in **the L** forever, for the LORD,	3378
26: 4	Trust in the LORD forever, for **the L,**	3363
26: 4	**the L,** is the Rock eternal.	3378
26: 8	Yes, **L,** walking in the way of your laws,	3378
26:10	and regard not the majesty of **the L.**	3378
26:11	O **L,** your hand is lifted high,	3378
26:12	**L,** you establish peace for us;	3378
26:13	O **L,** our God, other lords besides you have ruled over us,	3378
26:15	You have enlarged the nation, O **L;**	3378
26:16	**L,** they came to you in their distress;	3378
26:17	so were we in your presence, O **L.**	3378
26:21	**the L** is coming out of his dwelling	3378
27: 1	**the L** will punish with his sword,	3378
27: 3	I, **the L,** watch over it;	3378
27: 7	Has [the L] struck her as he struck	NIH
27:12	In that day **the L** will thresh from	3378
27:13	in Egypt will come and worship **the L** on	3378
28: 5	In that day **the L** Almighty will be	3378
28:13	the word of **the L** to them will become:	3378
28:14	Therefore hear the word of **the L,**	3378
28:16	So this is what the Sovereign **L** says:	3378
28:21	**The L** will rise up as he did	3378
28:22	the Lord, **the L** Almighty,	3378
28:29	All this also comes from **the L** Almighty,	3378
29: 6	**the L** Almighty will come with thunder	3378
29:10	**The L** has brought over you a deep sleep:	3378
29:15	to hide their plans from **the L,**	3378
29:19	the humble will rejoice in **the L;**	3378
29:22	Therefore this is what **the L,**	3378
30: 1	to the obstinate children," declares **the L,**	3378
30:15	This is what the Sovereign **L,**	3378
30:18	Yet **the L** longs to be gracious to you;	3378
30:18	For **the L** is a God of justice.	3378
30:26	when **the L** binds up the bruises	3378
30:27	See, the Name of **the L** comes from afar,	3378
30:29	up with flutes to the mountain of **the L,**	3378
30:30	**The L** will cause men to hear his	3378
30:31	The voice of **the L** will shatter Assyria;	3378
30:32	Every stroke **the L** lays on them	3378
30:33	the breath of **the L,** like a stream of burning	3378
31: 1	or seek help from **the L.**	3378
31: 3	When **the L** stretches out his hand,	3378
31: 4	This is what **the L** says to me:	3378
31: 4	so **the L** Almighty will come down	3378
31: 5	**the L** Almighty will shield Jerusalem;	3378
31: 9	declares **the L,** whose fire is in Zion,	3378
32: 6	and spreads error concerning **the L;**	3378
33: 2	O **L,** be gracious to us; we long for you.	3378
33: 5	**The L** is exalted, for he dwells on high;	3378
33: 6	fear of **the L** is the key to this treasure.	3378
33:10	"Now will I arise," says **the L.**	3378
33:21	There **the L** will be our Mighty One.	3378
33:22	For **the L** is our judge,	3378
33:22	**the L** is our lawgiver,	3378
33:22	**the L** is our king;	3378
34: 2	**The L** is angry with all nations;	3378
34: 6	The sword of **the L** is bathed in blood,	3378
34: 6	For **the L** has a sacrifice in Bozrah and	3378
34: 8	For **the L** has a day of vengeance,	3378
34:16	Look in the scroll of **the L** and read:	3378
35: 2	they will see the glory of **the L,**	3378
35:10	and the ransomed of **the L** will return.	3378
36: 7	"We are depending on **the L** our God"—	3378
36:10	and destroy this land without **the L?**	3378
36:10	**The L** himself told me to march	3378
36:15	in **the L** when he says, 'The LORD will	3378
36:15	**'The L** will surely deliver us;	3378
36:18	**'The L** will deliver us.'	3378
36:20	How then can **the L** deliver Jerusalem	3378
37: 1	and went into the temple of **the L.**	3378
37: 4	that **the L** your God will hear the words	3378
37: 4	for the words **the L** your God has heard.	3378
37: 6	'This is what **the L** says:	3378
37:14	up to the temple of **the L** and spread it out	3378
37:14	and spread it out before **the L.**	3378
37:15	And Hezekiah prayed to **the L:**	3378
37:16	"O **L** Almighty, God of Israel, enthroned	3378
37:17	Give ear, O **L,** and hear;	3378
37:17	open your eyes, O **L,** and see;	3378
37:18	"It is true, O **L,** that the Assyrian kings	3378
37:20	Now, O **L** our God, deliver us	3378
37:20	on earth may know that you alone, O **L,**	3378
37:21	"This is what **the L,** the God of Israel,	3378
37:22	the word **the L** has spoken against him:	3378
37:32	zeal of **the L** Almighty will accomplish this.	3378
37:33	"Therefore this is what **the L** says	3378
37:34	he will not enter this city," declares **the L.**	3378
37:36	Then the angel of **the L** went out and put	3378
38: 1	"This is what **the L** says:	3378
38: 2	to the wall and prayed to **the L,**	3378
Isa 38: 3	"Remember, O **L,** how I have walked	3378
38: 4	Then the word of **the L** came to Isaiah:	3378
38: 5	'This is what **the L,**	3378
38: 7	that **the L** will do what he has promised:	3378
38:11	I said, "I will not again see **the L,**	3363
38:11	"I will not again see the LORD, **the L,**	3363
38:20	**The L** will save me,	3378
38:20	of our lives in the temple of **the L.**	3378
38:22	that I will go up to the temple of **the L?"**	3378
39: 5	"Hear the word of **the L** Almighty:	3378
39: 6	Nothing will be left, says **the L.**	3378
39: 8	of **the L** you have spoken is good,"	3378
40: 3	"In the desert prepare the way for **the L;**	3378
40: 5	And the glory of **the L** will be revealed,	3378
40: 5	For the mouth of **the L** has spoken."	3378
40: 7	the breath of **the L** blows on them.	3378
40:10	See, **the** Sovereign **L** comes with power,	3378
40:13	Who has understood the mind of **the L,**	3378
40:14	the L consult to enlighten him,	NIH
40:27	O Israel, "My way is hidden from **the L;**	3378
40:28	**The L** is the everlasting God,	3378
40:31	in **the L** will renew their strength.	3378
41: 4	from the beginning? I, **the L—**	3378
41:13	For I am **the L,** your God,	3378
41:14	declares **the L,** your Redeemer,	3378
41:16	But you will rejoice in **the L** and glory in	3378
41:17	But I **the L** will answer them;	3378
41:20	that the hand of **the L** has done this,	3378
41:21	"Present your case," says **the L.**	3378
42: 5	This is what God **the L** says—	3378
42: 6	**the L,** have called you in righteousness;	3378
42: 8	"I am **the L;** that is my name!	3378
42:10	Sing to **the L** a new song,	3378
42:12	to **the L** and proclaim his praise in	3378
42:13	**The L** will march out like a mighty man,	3378
42:19	blind like the servant of **the L?**	3378
42:21	It pleased **the L** for the sake	3378
42:24	Was it not **the L,**	3378
43: 1	But now, this is what **the L** says—	3378
43: 3	For I am **the L,** your God,	3378
43:10	"You are my witnesses," declares **the L,**	3378
43:11	I, even I, am **the L,**	3378
43:12	You are my witnesses," declares **the L,**	3378
43:14	This is what **the L** says—	3378
43:15	I am **the L,** your Holy One,	3378
43:16	This is what **the L** says—	3378
44: 2	This is what **the L** says—	3378
44: 5	One will say, 'I belong to **the L';**	3378
44: 6	"This is what **the L** says—	3378
44: 6	and Redeemer, **the L** Almighty:	3378
44:23	O heavens, for **the L** has done this;	3378
44:23	for **the L** has redeemed Jacob,	3378
44:24	"This is what **the L** says—	3378
44:24	I am **the L,** who has made all things,	3378
45: 1	"This is what **the L** says to his anointed,	3378
45: 3	so that you may know that I am **the L,**	3378
45: 5	I am **the L,** and there is no other;	3378
45: 6	I am **the L,** and there is no other.	3378
45: 7	I, **the L,** do all these things.	3378
45: 8	I, **the L,** have created it.	3378
45:11	"This is what **the L** says—	3378
45:13	says **the L** Almighty."	3378
45:14	This is what **the L** says:	3378
45:17	by **the L** with an everlasting salvation;	3378
45:18	For this is what **the L** says—	3378
45:18	"I am **the L,** and there is no other.	3378
45:19	I, **the L,** speak the truth;	3378
45:21	Was it not I, **the L?**	3378
45:24	'In **the L** alone are righteousness	3378
45:25	in **the L** all the descendants of Israel will	3378
47: 4	**the L** Almighty is his name—	3378
48: 1	in the name of **the L** and invoke the God	3378
48: 2	**the L** Almighty is his name:	3378
48:16	And now the Sovereign **L** has sent me,	3378
48:17	This is what **the L** says—	3378
48:17	"I am **the L** your God,	3378
48:20	**"The L** has redeemed his servant Jacob."	3378
48:22	"There is no peace," says **the L,** "for the wicked."	3378
49: 1	Before I was born **the L** called me;	3378
49: 5	And now **the L** says—	3378
49: 5	for I am honored in the eyes of **the L**	3378
49: 7	This is what **the L** says—	3378
49: 7	because of **the L,** who is faithful,	3378
49: 8	This is what **the L** says:	3378
49:13	For **the L** comforts his people	3378
49:14	But Zion said, **"The L** has forsaken me,	3378
49:18	As surely as I live," declares **the L,**	3378
49:22	This is what **the** Sovereign **L** says:	3378
49:23	Then you will know that I am **the L;**	3378
49:25	But this is what **the L** says:	3378
49:26	Then all mankind will know that I, **the L,**	3378
50: 1	This is what **the L** says:	3378
50: 4	**The** Sovereign **L** has given me	3378
50: 5	**The** Sovereign **L** has opened my ears,	3378
50: 7	Because **the** Sovereign **L** helps me,	3378
50: 9	It is **the** Sovereign **L** who helps me.	3378
50:10	Who among you fears **the L** and obeys	3378
50:10	in the name of **the L** and rely on his God.	3378
51: 1	and who seek **the L:**	3378
51: 3	**The L** will surely comfort Zion	3378
51: 3	her wastelands like the garden of **the L.**	3378
51: 9	O arm of **the L;**	3378
51:11	The ransomed of **the L** will return.	3378
51:13	that you forget **the L** your Maker,	3378
51:15	For I am **the L** your God,	3378
51:15	**the L** Almighty is his name.	3378
Isa 51:17	the hand of **the L** the cup of his wrath,	3378
51:20	with the wrath of **the L** and the rebuke	3378
51:22	This is what your Sovereign **L** says,	3378
52: 3	For this is what **the L** says:	3378
52: 4	For this is what **the** Sovereign **L** says:	3378
52: 5	what do I have here?" declares **the L.**	3378
52: 5	and those who rule them mock," declares **the L.**	3378
52: 8	When **the L** returns to Zion,	3378
52: 9	for **the L** has comforted his people,	3378
52:10	**The L** will lay bare his holy arm in	3378
52:11	you who carry the vessels of **the L.**	3378
52:12	for **the L** will go before you,	3378
53: 1	the arm of **the L** been revealed?	3378
53: 6	and **the L** has laid on him the iniquity	3378
53:10	the L makes his life a guilt offering,	NIH
53:10	the will of **the L** will prosper in his hand.	3378
54: 1	of her who has a husband," says **the L.**	3378
54: 5	**the L** Almighty is his name—	3378
54: 6	**The L** will call you back as if you were	3378
54: 8	says **the L** your Redeemer.	3378
54:10	says **the L,** who has compassion on you.	3378
54:13	All your sons will be taught by **the L,**	3378
54:17	the heritage of the servants of **the L,**	3378
54:17	vindication from me," declares **the L.**	3378
55: 5	because of **the L** your God,	3378
55: 6	Seek **the L** while he may be found;	3378
55: 7	Let him turn to **the L,**	3378
55: 8	neither are your ways my ways," declares **the L.**	3378
56: 1	This is what **the L** says:	3378
56: 3	who has bound himself to **the L** say,	3378
56: 3	**"The L** will surely exclude me	3378
56: 4	For this is what **the L** says:	3378
56: 6	to **the L** to serve him, to love the name of	3378
56: 6	to love the name of **the L,**	3378
56: 8	**The** Sovereign **L** declares—	3378
57:19	peace, to those far and near," says **the L.**	3378
58: 5	a day acceptable to **the L?**	3378
58: 8	the glory of **the L** will be your rear guard.	3378
58: 9	Then you will call, and **the L** will answer;	3378
58:11	**The L** will guide you always;	3378
58:14	then you will find your joy in **the L,**	3378
58:14	The mouth of **the L** has spoken.	3378
59: 1	the arm of **the L** is not too short to save,	3378
59:13	rebellion and treachery against **the L,**	3378
59:15	**The L** looked and was displeased	3378
59:19	men will fear the name of **the L,**	3378
59:19	that the breath of **the L** drives along.	3378
59:20	who repent of their sins," declares **the L.**	3378
59:21	my covenant with them," says **the L.**	3378
59:21	this time on and forever," says **the L.**	3378
60: 1	and the glory of **the L** rises upon you.	3378
60: 2	but **the L** rises upon you	3378
60: 6	and proclaiming the praise of **the L.**	3378
60: 9	to the honor of **the L** your God,	3378
60:14	and will call you the City of **the L,**	3378
60:16	Then you will know that I, **the L,**	3378
60:19	for **the L** will be your everlasting light,	3378
60:20	**the L** will be your everlasting light,	3378
60:22	I am **the L;**	3378
61: 1	The Spirit of **the** Sovereign **L** is on me,	3378
61: 1	because **the L** has anointed me	3378
61: 3	of **the L** for the display of his splendor.	3378
61: 6	And you will be called priests of **the L,**	3378
61: 8	"For I, **the L,** love justice;	3378
61: 9	that they are a people **the L** has blessed."	3378
61:10	I delight greatly in **the L;**	3378
61:11	so **the** Sovereign **L** will make righteousness	3378
62: 2	that the mouth of **the L** will bestow.	3378
62: 4	for **the L** will take delight in you,	3378
62: 6	You who call on **the L,**	3378
62: 8	**The L** has sworn by his right hand and	3378
62: 9	will eat it and praise **the L,**	3378
62:11	**The L** has made proclamation to the ends	3378
62:12	the Redeemed of **the L;**	3378
63: 7	I will tell of the kindnesses of **the L,**	3378
63: 7	according to all **the L** has done for us—	3378
63:14	by the Spirit of **the L.**	3378
63:16	you, O **L,** are our Father,	3378
63:17	O **L,** do you make us wander	3378
64: 8	Yet, O **L,** you are our Father.	3378
64: 9	Do not be angry beyond measure, O **L;**	3378
64:12	After all this, O **L,**	3378
65: 7	and the sins of your fathers," says **the L.**	3378
65: 8	This is what **the L** says:	3378
65:11	"But as for you who forsake **the L**	3378
65:13	Therefore this is what the Sovereign **L** says:	3378
65:15	**the** Sovereign **L** will put you to death,	3378
65:23	they will be a people blessed by **the L,**	3378
65:25	on all my holy mountain," says **the L.**	3378
66: 1	This is what **the L** says:	3378
66: 2	so they came into being?" declares **the L.**	3378
66: 5	Hear the word of **the L,**	3378
66: 5	have said, 'Let **the L** be glorified,	3378
66: 6	**the L** repaying his enemies all they deserve.	3378
66: 9	and not give delivery?" says **the L.**	3378
66:12	For this is what **the L** says:	3378
66:14	the hand of **the L** will be made known	3378
66:15	See, **the L** is coming with fire,	3378
66:16	with his sword **the L** will execute judgment	3378
66:16	and many will be those slain by **the L.**	3378
66:17	meet their end together," declares **the L.**	3378
66:20	in Jerusalem as an offering to **the L—**	3378
66:20	and on mules and camels," says **the L.**	3378
66:20	of **the L** in ceremonially clean vessels.	3378
66:21	to be priests and Levites," says **the L.**	3378

†LORD distinguishes the proper name of God, *Yahweh,* indicated in the NIV by "LORD," from the words translated "Lord" and "lord," indexed under the heading ***LORD**, pages 683-86.

Isa 66:22 declares **the L**, "so will your name 3378
66:23 and bow down before me," says **the L.** 3378
Jer 1: 2 The word of **the L** came to him in 3378
1: 4 The word of **the L** came to me, saying, 3378
1: 6 "Ah, Sovereign **L,"** I said, 3378
1: 7 But **the L** said to me, "Do not say, 3378
1: 8 and will rescue you," declares **the L.** 3378
1: 9 Then **the L** reached out his hand 3378
1:11 The word of **the L** came to me: 3378
1:12 **The L** said to me, 3378
1:13 The word of **the L** came to me again: 3378
1:14 **The L** said to me, 3378
1:15 the northern kingdoms," declares **the L.** 3378
1:19 and will rescue you," declares **the L.** 3378
2: 1 The word of **the L** came to me: 3378
2: 3 Israel was holy to **the L,** 3378
2: 3 disaster overtook them,' " declares **the L.** 3378
2: 4 Hear the word of **the L,** 3378
2: 5 This is what **the L** says: 3378
2: 6 They did not ask, 'Where is **the L,** 3378
2: 8 priests did not ask, 'Where is **the L?'** 3378
2: 9 against you again," declares **the L.** 3378
2:12 with great horror," declares **the L.** 3378
2:17 by forsaking **the L** your God 3378
2:19 for you when you forsake **the L** your God 3378
2:19 declares the Lord, **the L** Almighty. 3378
2:22 declares the Sovereign **L.** 3378
2:29 against me," declares **the L.** 3378
2:31 consider the word of **the L:** 3378
2:37 for **the L** has rejected those you trust; 3378
3: 1 you now return to me?" declares **the L.** 3378
3: 6 **the L** said to me, 3378
3:10 but only in pretense," declares **the L.** 3378
3:11 **The L** said to me, 3378
3:12 " 'Return, faithless Israel,' declares **the L,** 3378
3:12 for I am merciful,' declares **the L,** 3378
3:13 against **the L** your God, 3378
3:13 not obeyed me,' " declares **the L.** 3378
3:14 "Return, faithless people," declares **the L,** 3378
3:16 declares **the L,** "men will no longer say, 3378
3:16 'The ark of the covenant of **the L.'** 3378
3:17 will call Jerusalem The Throne of **the L,** 3378
3:17 in Jerusalem to honor the name of **the L.** 3378
3:20 O house of Israel," declares **the L.** 3378
3:21 and have forgotten **the L** their God. 3378
3:22 for you are **the L** our God. 3378
3:23 in **the L** our God is the salvation of Israel. 3378
3:25 We have sinned against **the L** our God, 3378
3:25 not obeyed **the L** our God." 3378
4: 1 O Israel, return to me," declares **the L.** 3378
4: 2 'As surely as **the L** lives,' 3378
4: 3 This is what **the L** says to the men 3378
4: 4 Circumcise yourselves to **the L,** 3378
4: 8 of **the L** has not turned away from us. 3378
4: 9 "In that day," declares **the L,** 3378
4:10 Then I said, "Ah, Sovereign **L,** 3378
4:17 against me,' " declares **the L.** 3378
4:26 all its towns lay in ruins before **the L,** 3378
4:27 This is what **the L** says: 3378
5: 2 'As surely as **the L** lives,' 3378
5: 3 **O L,** do not your eyes look for truth? 3378
5: 4 for they do not know the way of **the L,** 3378
5: 5 surely they know the way of **the L,** 3378
5: 9 punish them for this?" declares **the L.** 3378
5:10 for these people do not belong to **the L.** 3378
5:11 to me," declares **the L.** 3378
5:12 They have lied about **the L;** 3378
5:14 this is what **the L** God Almighty says: 3378
5:15 O house of Israel," declares **the L,** 3378
5:18 "Yet even in those days," declares **the L,** 3378
5:19 'Why has **the L** our God done all this 3378
5:22 Should you not fear me?" declares **the L.** 3378
5:24 'Let us fear **the L** our God, 3378
5:29 punish them for this?" declares **the L.** 3378
6: 6 This is what **the L** Almighty says: 3378
6: 9 This is what **the L** Almighty says: 3378
6:10 The word of **the L** is offensive to them; 3378
6:11 But I am full of the wrath of **the L,** 3378
6:12 who live in the land," declares **the L.** 3378
6:15 down when I punish them," says **the L.** 3378
6:16 This is what **the L** says: 3378
6:21 Therefore this is what **the L** says: 3378
6:22 This is what **the L** says: 3378
6:30 because **the L** has rejected them." 3378
7: 1 that came to Jeremiah from **the L:** 3378
7: 2 " 'Hear the word of **the L,** 3378
7: 2 through these gates to worship **the L.** 3378
7: 3 This is what **the L** Almighty, 3378
7: 4 "This is the temple of **the L,** 3378
7: 4 the temple of **the L,** 3378
7: 4 the temple of **the L!"** 3378
7:11 I have been watching! declares **the L.** 3378
7:13 declares **the L,** I spoke to you again 3378
7:19 the one they are provoking? declares **the L.** 3378
7:20 Therefore this is what the Sovereign **L** says: 3378
7:21 " 'This is what **the L** Almighty, 3378
7:28 not obeyed **the L** its God or responded 3378
7:29 the barren heights, for **the L** has rejected 3378
7:30 in my eyes, declares **the L.** 3378
7:32 the days are coming, declares **the L,** 3378
8: 1 " 'At that time, declares **the L,** 3378
8: 3 declares **the L** Almighty.' 3378
8: 4 "Say to them, 'This is what **the L** says: 3378
8: 7 not know the requirements of **the L.** 3378
8: 8 for we have the law of **the L,"** 3378
8: 9 they have rejected the word of **the L,** 3378
8:12 down when they are punished, says **the L.** 3378
Jer 8:13 " 'I will take away their harvest, declares **the L.** 3378
8:14 For **the L** our God has doomed us 3378
8:17 and they will bite you," declares **the L.** 3378
8:19 "Is **the L** not in Zion? 3378
9: 3 not acknowledge me," declares **the L.** 3378
9: 6 to acknowledge me," declares **the L.** 3378
9: 7 Therefore this is what **the L** Almighty says: 3378
9: 9 punish them for this?" declares **the L.** 3378
9:12 Who has been instructed by **the L** 3378
9:13 **The L** said, "It is because 3378
9:15 Therefore, this is what **the L** Almighty, 3378
9:17 This is what **the L** Almighty says: 3378
9:20 Now, O women, hear the word of **the L;** 3378
9:22 Say, "This is what **the L** declares: 3378
9:23 This is what **the L** says: 3378
9:24 that I am **the L,** who exercises kindness, 3378
9:24 for in these I delight," declares **the L.** 3378
9:25 "The days are coming," declares **the L,** 3378
10: 1 Hear what **the L** says to you, 3378
10: 2 This is what **the L** says: 3378
10: 6 No one is like you, **O L;** 3378
10:10 But **the L** is the true God; 3378
10:16 **the L** Almighty is his name. 3378
10:18 For this is what **the L** says: 3378
10:21 and do not inquire of **the L;** 3378
10:23 **O L,** that a man's life is not his own; 3378
10:24 Correct me, **L,** but only with justice— 3378
11: 1 that came to Jeremiah from **the L:** 3378
11: 3 Tell them that this is what **the L,** 3378
11: 5 I answered, "Amen, **L."** 3378
11: 6 **The L** said to me, 3378
11: 9 Then **the L** said to me, 3378
11:11 Therefore this is what **the L** says: 3378
11:16 **The L** called you a thriving olive tree 3378
11:17 **The L** Almighty, who planted you, 3378
11:18 Because **the L** revealed their plot to me, 3378
11:20 **O L** Almighty, you who judge righteously 3378
11:21 "Therefore this is what **the L** says about 3378
11:21 of **the L** or you will die by our hands'— 3378
11:22 therefore this is what **the L** Almighty says: 3378
12: 1 You are always righteous, **O L,** 3378
12: 3 Yet you know me, **O L;** 3378
12:12 sword of **the L** will devour from one end of 3378
12:14 This is what **the L** says: 3378
12:16 saying, 'As surely as **the L** lives'— 3378
12:17 and destroy it," declares **the L.** 3378
13: 1 This is what **the L** said to me: 3378
13: 2 So I bought a belt, as **the L** directed, 3378
13: 3 word of **the L** came to me a second time: 3378
13: 5 as **the L** told me. 3378
13: 6 Many days later **the L** said to me, 3378
13: 8 Then the word of **the L** came to me: 3378
13: 9 "This is what **the L** says: 3378
13:11 declares **the L,** 'to be my people for my 3378
13:12 'This is what **the L,** the God of Israel, 3378
13:13 then tell them, 'This is what **the L** says: 3378
13:14 fathers and sons alike, declares **the L.** 3378
13:15 do not be arrogant, for **the L** has spoken. 3378
13:16 to **the L** your God before he brings 3378
13:21 What will you say when [the L] sets NIH
13:25 I have decreed for you," declares **the L,** 3378
14: 1 the word of **the L** to Jeremiah concerning 3378
14: 7 Although our sins testify against us, **O L,** 3378
14: 9 You are among us, **O L,** 3378
14:10 This is what **the L** says about this people: 3378
14:10 So **the L** does not accept them; 3378
14:11 Then **the L** said to me, 3378
14:13 But I said, "Ah, Sovereign **L,** 3378
14:14 Then **the L** said to me, 3378
14:15 this is what **the L** says about 3378
14:20 **O L,** we acknowledge our wickedness 3378
14:22 No, it is you, **O L** our God. 3378
15: 1 Then **the L** said to me: 3378
15: 2 tell them, 'This is what **the L** says: 3378
15: 3 against them," declares **the L,** "the sword 3378
15: 6 You have rejected me," declares **the L.** 3378
15: 9 before their enemies," declares **the L.** 3378
15:11 **The L** said, "Surely I will deliver you for 3378
15:15 You understand, **O L;** 3378
15:16 for I bear your name, **O L** God Almighty. 3378
15:19 Therefore this is what **the L** says: 3378
15:20 to rescue and save you," declares **the L.** 3378
16: 1 Then the word of **the L** came to me: 3378
16: 3 For this is what **the L** says about the sons 3378
16: 5 For this is what **the L** says: 3378
16: 5 from this people," declares **the L.** 3378
16: 9 For this is what **the L** Almighty, 3378
16:10 'Why has **the L** decreed such 3378
16:10 against **the L** our God?' 3378
16:11 declares **the L,** 'and followed other gods 3378
16:14 the days are coming," declares **the L,** 3378
16:14 'As surely as **the L** lives, 3378
16:15 'As surely as **the L** lives, 3378
16:16 declares **the L,** "and they will catch them. 3378
16:19 **O L,** my strength and my fortress, 3378
16:21 that my name is **the L.** 3378
17: 5 This is what **the L** says: 3378
17: 5 and whose heart turns away from **the L.** 3378
17: 7 blessed is the man who trusts in **the L,** 3378
17:10 "I **the L** search the heart and examine 3378
17:13 **O L,** the hope of Israel, 3378
17:13 because they have forsaken **the L,** 3378
17:14 Heal me, **O L,** and I will be healed; 3378
17:15 "Where is the word of **the L?** 3378
17:19 This is what **the L** said to me: 3378
17:20 Say to them, 'Hear the word of **the L,** 3378
Jer 17:21 This is what **the L** says: 3378
17:24 declares **the L,** and bring no load through 3378
17:26 and thank offerings to the house of **the L.** 3378
18: 1 that came to Jeremiah from **the L:** 3378
18: 5 Then the word of **the L** came to me: 3378
18: 6 as this potter does?" declares **the L.** 3378
18:11 'This is what **the L** says: Look! 3378
18:13 Therefore this is what **the L** says: 3378
18:19 Listen to me, **O L;** 3378
18:23 you know, **O L,** all their plots to kill me. 3378
19: 1 This is what **the L** says: 3378
19: 3 'Hear the word of **the L,** 3378
19: 3 This is what **the L** Almighty, 3378
19: 6 the days are coming, declares **the L,** 3378
19:11 'This is what **the L** Almighty says: 3378
19:12 to those who live here, declares **the L.** 3378
19:14 where **the L** had sent him to prophesy, 3378
19:15 "This is what **the L** Almighty, the God 3378
20: 1 the chief officer in the temple of **the L,** 3378
20: 4 For this is what **the L** says: 3378
20: 7 **O L,** you deceived me, 3378
20: 8 the word of **the L** has brought me insult 3378
20:11 **the L** is with me like a mighty warrior; 3378
20:12 **O L** Almighty, you who examine 3378
20:13 Sing to **the L!** 3378
20:13 Give praise to **the L!** 3378
20:16 the towns **the L** overthrew without pity. 3378
21: 1 The word came to Jeremiah from **the L** 3378
21: 2 "Inquire now of **the L** for us 3378
21: 2 Perhaps **the L** will perform wonders 3378
21: 4 'This is what **the L,** the God 3378
21: 7 After that, declares **the L,** 3378
21: 8 tell the people, 'This is what **the L** says: 3378
21:10 and not good, declares **the L.** 3378
21:11 'Hear the word of **the L;** 3378
21:12 this is what **the L** says: 3378
21:13 on the rocky plateau, declares **the L**— 3378
21:14 as your deeds deserve, declares **the L.** 3378
22: 1 This is what **the L** says: 3378
22: 2 of **the L,** O king of Judah, you who sit 3378
22: 3 This is what **the L** says: 3378
22: 5 not obey these commands, declares **the L,** 3378
22: 6 For this is what **the L** says about 3378
22: 8 'Why has **the L** done such a thing 3378
22: 9 of **the L** their God and have worshiped 3378
22:11 For this is what **the L** says 3378
22:16 what it means to know me?" declares **the L.** 3378
22:18 Therefore this is what **the L** says 3378
22:24 "As surely as I live," declares **the L,** 3378
22:29 land, land, hear the word of **the L!** 3378
22:30 This is what **the L** says: 3378
23: 1 the sheep of my pasture!" declares **the L.** 3378
23: 2 Therefore this is what **the L,** 3378
23: 2 the evil you have done," declares **the L.** 3378
23: 4 nor will any be missing," declares **the L.** 3378
23: 5 "The days are coming," declares **the L,** 3378
23: 6 **The L** Our Righteousness. 3378
23: 7 the days are coming," declares **the L,** 3378
23: 7 'As surely as **the L** lives, 3378
23: 8 'As surely as **the L** lives, 3378
23: 9 because of **the L** and his holy words. 3378
23:11 in my temple I find their wickedness," declares **the L.** 3378
23:12 the year they are punished," declares **the L.** 3378
23:15 this is what **the L** Almighty says 3378
23:16 This is what **the L** Almighty says: 3378
23:16 not from the mouth of **the L.** 3378
23:17 **'The L** says: You will have peace.' 3378
23:18 of them has stood in the council of **the L** 3378
23:19 the storm of **the L** will burst out in wrath, 3378
23:20 The anger of **the L** will not turn back 3378
23:23 declares **the L,** "and not a God far away? 3378
23:24 I fill heaven and earth?" declares **the L.** 3378
23:24 I fill heaven and earth?" declares **the L.** 3378
23:28 straw to do with grain?" declares **the L.** 3378
23:29 "Is not my word like fire," declares **the L,** 3378
23:30 "Therefore," declares **the L,** 3378
23:31 Yes," declares **the L,** 3378
23:31 and yet declare, 'The L declares.' NIH
23:32 against those who prophesy false dreams," declares **the L.** 3378
23:32 in the least," declares **the L.** 3378
23:33 ask you, 'What is the oracle of **the L?'** 3378
23:33 I will forsake you, declares **the L.'** 3378
23:34 'This is the oracle of **the L,'** 3378
23:35 or 'What has **the L** spoken?' 3378
23:36 not mention 'the oracle of **the L'** again, 3378
23:36 **the L** Almighty, our God. 3378
23:37 or 'What has **the L** spoken?' 3378
23:38 'This is the oracle of **the L,'** 3378
23:38 this is what **the L** says: 3378
23:38 'This is the oracle of **the L,'** 3378
23:38 'This is the oracle of **the L.'** 3378
24: 1 **the L** showed me two baskets 3378
24: 1 in front of the temple of **the L.** 3378
24: 3 Then **the L** asked me, "What do you see, 3378
24: 4 Then the word of **the L** came to me: 3378
24: 5 "This is what **the L,** the God 3378
24: 7 a heart to know me, that I am **the L.** 3378
24: 8 so bad they cannot be eaten,' says **the L,** 3378
25: 3 the word of **the L** has come to me 3378
25: 4 And though **the L** has sent all his servants 3378
25: 5 and you can stay in the land **the L** gave 3378
25: 7 you did not listen to me," declares **the L,** 3378
25: 8 Therefore **the L** Almighty says this: 3378
25: 9 declares **the L,** "and I will bring them 3378
25:12 for their guilt," declares **the L,** 3378

†LORD distinguishes the proper name of God, *Yahweh*, indicated in the NIV by "LORD," from the words translated "Lord" and "lord," indexed under the heading ***LORD**, pages 683-86.

Jer 25:15 This is what **the L,** the God of Israel, 3378
25:27 tell them, 'This is what **the L** Almighty, 3378
25:28 'This is what **the L** Almighty says: 3378
25:29 who live on earth, declares **the L** Almighty. 3378
25:30 " '**The L** will roar from on high; 3378
25:31 for **the L** will bring charges against 3378
25:31 to the sword,' " declares **the L.** 3378
25:32 This is what **the L** Almighty says: "Look! 3378
25:33 At that time those slain by **the L** will 3378
25:36 for **the L** is destroying their pasture. 3378
25:37 because of the fierce anger of **the L.** 3378
26: 1 this word came from **the L:** 3378
26: 2 "This is what **the L** says: 3378
26: 2 to worship in the house of **the L,** 3378
26: 4 Say to them, 'This is what **the L** says: 3378
26: 7 these words in the house of **the L.** 3378
26: 8 everything **the L** had commanded him 3378
26: 9 around Jeremiah in the house of **the L.** 3378
26:10 to the house of **the L** and took their places 3378
26:12 "**The L** sent me to prophesy 3378
26:13 and obey **the L** your God. 3378
26:13 Then **the L** will relent and not bring 3378
26:15 for in truth **the L** has sent me to you 3378
26:16 to us in the name of **the L** our God." 3378
26:18 'This is what **the L** Almighty says: 3378
26:19 Did not Hezekiah fear **the L** 3378
26:19 And did not **the L** relent, 3378
26:20 prophesied in the name of **the L;** 3378
27: 1 this word came to Jeremiah from **the L:** 3378
27: 2 This is what **the L** said to me: 3378
27: 4 'This is what **the L** Almighty, 3378
27: 8 famine and plague, declares **the L,** 3378
27:11 till it and to live there, declares **the L.**" ' " 3378
27:13 with which **the L** has threatened any nation 3378
27:15 'I have not sent them,' declares **the L.** 3378
27:16 "This is what **the L** says: 3378
27:18 and have the word of **the L,** 3378
27:18 let them plead with **the L** Almighty that 3378
27:18 in the house of **the L** and in the palace of 3378
27:19 For this is what **the L** Almighty says 3378
27:21 this is what **the L** Almighty, 3378
27:21 in the house of **the L** and in the palace of 3378
27:22 the day I come for them,' declares **the L.** 3378
28: 1 in the house of **the L** in the presence of 3378
28: 2 "This is what **the L** Almighty, the God 3378
28: 4 declares **the L,** 'for I will break the yoke 3378
28: 5 in the house of **the L.** 3378
28: 6 May **the L** do so! 3378
28: 6 May **the L** fulfill the words 3378
28: 9 as one truly sent by **the L** only 3378
28:11 "This is what **the L** says: 3378
28:12 the word of **the L** came to Jeremiah: 3378
28:13 'This is what **the L** says: 3378
28:14 This is what **the L** Almighty, 3378
28:15 **The L** has not sent you, 3378
28:16 Therefore, this is what **the L** says: 3378
28:16 have preached rebellion against **the L.**' " 3378
29: 4 This is what **the L** Almighty, the God 3378
29: 7 Pray to **the L** for it, because if it prospers, 3378
29: 8 Yes, this is what **the L** Almighty, 3378
29: 9 I have not sent them," declares **the L.** 3378
29:10 This is what **the L** says: 3378
29:11 declares **the L,** "plans to prosper you and 3378
29:14 I will be found by you," declares **the L,** 3378
29:14 declares **the L,** "and will bring you back 3378
29:15 "**The L** has raised up prophets for us 3378
29:16 but this is what **the L** says about 3378
29:17 this is what **the L** Almighty says: 3378
29:19 not listened to my words," declares **the L,** 3378
29:19 not listened either," declares **the L.** 3378
29:20 Therefore, hear the word of **the L,** 3378
29:21 This is what **the L** Almighty, 3378
29:22 '**The L** treat you like Zedekiah and Ahab, 3378
29:23 and am a witness to it," declares **the L.** 3378
29:25 "This is what **the L** Almighty, the God 3378
29:26 '**The L** has appointed you priest in place 3378
29:26 to be in charge of the house of **the L;** 3378
29:30 Then the word of **the L** came to Jeremiah: 3378
29:31 'This is what **the L** says about Shemaiah 3378
29:32 this is what **the L** says: 3378
29:32 for my people, declares **the L,** 3378
30: 1 that came to Jeremiah from **the L:** 3378
30: 2 "This is what **the L,** the God 3378
30: 3 The days are coming,' declares **the L,** 3378
30: 3 to possess,' says **the L.**" 3378
30: 4 the words **the L** spoke concerning Israel 3378
30: 5 "This is what **the L** says: 3378
30: 8 " 'In that day,' declares **the L** Almighty, 3378
30: 9 they will serve **the L** their God 3378
30:10 O Israel,' declares **the L.** 3378
30:11 and will save you,' declares **the L.** 3378
30:12 "This is what **the L** says: 3378
30:17 and heal your wounds,' declares **the L,** 3378
30:18 "This is what **the L** says: 3378
30:21 to be close to me?" declares **the L.** 3378
30:23 the storm of **the L** will burst out in wrath, 3378
30:24 The fierce anger of **the L** will 3378
31: 1 "At that time," declares **the L,** 3378
31: 2 This is what **the L** says: 3378
31: 3 **The L** appeared to us in the past, saying: 3378
31: 6 let us go up to Zion, to **the L** our God.' " 3378
31: 7 This is what **the L** says: 3378
31: 7 Make your praises heard, and say, 'O **L,** 3378
31:10 "Hear the word of **the L,** O nations; 3378
31:11 For **the L** will ransom Jacob 3378
31:12 they will rejoice in the bounty of **the L—** 3378
31:14 be filled with my bounty," declares **the L.** 3378

Jer 31:15 This is what **the L** says: 3378
31:16 This is what **the L** says: 3378
31:16 work will be rewarded," declares **the L.** 3378
31:17 for your future," declares **the L.** 3378
31:18 because you are **the L** my God. 3378
31:20 great compassion for him," declares **the L.** 3378
31:22 **The L** will create a new thing on earth— 3378
31:23 This is what **the L** Almighty, 3378
31:23 '**The L** bless you, O righteous dwelling, 3378
31:27 "The days are coming," declares **the L,** 3378
31:28 to build and to plant," declares **the L.** 3378
31:31 "The time is coming," declares **the L,** 3378
31:32 a husband to them," declares **the L.** 3378
31:33 of Israel after that time," declares **the L.** 3378
31:34 saying, 'Know **the L,**' 3378
31:34 of them to the greatest," declares **the L.** 3378
31:35 This is what **the L** says, 3378
31:35 **the L** Almighty is his name: 3378
31:36 from my sight," declares **the L,** "will 3378
31:37 This is what **the L** says: 3378
31:37 of all they have done," declares **the L.** 3378
31:38 "The days are coming," declares **the L,** 3378
31:40 will be holy to **the L.** 3378
32: 1 to Jeremiah from **the L** in the tenth year 3378
32: 3 You say, 'This is what **the L** says: 3378
32: 5 until I deal with him, declares **the L.** 3378
32: 6 "The word of **the L** came to me: 3378
32: 8 "Then, just as **the L** had said, 3378
32: 8 "I knew that this was the word of **the L;** 3378
32:14 'This is what **the L** Almighty, the God 3378
32:15 For this is what **the L** Almighty, 3378
32:16 I prayed to **the L:** 3378
32:17 Sovereign **L,** you have made the heavens 3378
32:18 whose name is **the L** Almighty, 3378
32:25 you, O Sovereign **L,** say to me, 3378
32:26 Then the word of **the L** came to Jeremiah: 3378
32:27 "I am **the L,** the God of all mankind. 3378
32:28 Therefore, this is what **the L** says: 3378
32:30 what their hands have made, declares **the L.** 3378
32:36 but this is what **the L,** the God of Israel, 3378
32:42 "This is what **the L** says: 3378
32:44 because I will restore their fortunes,
declares **the L.**" 3378
33: 1 word of **the L** came to him a second time: 3378
33: 2 "This is what **the L** says, he who made 3378
33: 2 **the L** who formed it and established it— 3378
33: 2 **the L** is his name: 3378
33: 4 For this is what **the L,** the God of Israel, 3378
33:10 "This is what **the L** says: 3378
33:11 the house of **the L,** saying, "Give thanks 3378
33:11 saying, "Give thanks to **the L** Almighty, 3378
33:11 for **the L** is good; 3378
33:11 the land as they were before,' says **the L.** 3378
33:12 "This is what **the L** Almighty says: 3378
33:13 of the one who counts them,' says **the L.** 3378
33:14 " 'The days are coming,' declares **the L,** 3378
33:16 **The L** Our Righteousness.' 3378
33:17 For this is what **the L** says: 3378
33:19 The word of **the L** came to Jeremiah: 3378
33:20 "This is what **the L** says: 3378
33:23 The word of **the L** came to Jeremiah: 3378
33:24 '**The L** has rejected the two kingdoms 3378
33:25 This is what **the L** says: 3378
34: 1 this word came to Jeremiah from **the L:** 3378
34: 2 "This is what **the L,** the God 3378
34: 2 'This is what **the L** says: 3378
34: 4 " 'Yet hear the promise of **the L,** 3378
34: 4 This is what **the L** says concerning you: 3378
34: 5 I myself make this promise, declares **the L.** 3378
34: 8 from **the L** after King Zedekiah had made 3378
34:12 Then the word of **the L** came to Jeremiah: 3378
34:13 "This is what **the L,** the God 3378
34:17 "Therefore, this is what **the L** says: 3378
34:17 'freedom' for you, declares **the L—** 3378
34:22 declares **the L,** and I will bring them back 3378
35: 1 that came to Jeremiah from **the L** during 3378
35: 2 of the house of **the L** and give them wine 3378
35: 4 I brought them into the house of **the L,** 3378
35:12 word of **the L** came to Jeremiah, saying: 3378
35:13 "This is what **the L** Almighty, the God 3378
35:13 and obey my words?' declares **the L.** 3378
35:17 this is what **the L** God Almighty, 3378
35:18 "This is what **the L** Almighty, 3378
35:19 Therefore, this is what **the L** Almighty, 3378
36: 1 this word came to Jeremiah from **the L:** 3378
36: 4 the words **the L** had spoken to him, 3378
36: 6 So you go to the house of **the L** on a day 3378
36: 6 of **the L** that you wrote as I dictated. 3378
36: 7 before **the L,** and each will turn 3378
36: 7 against this people by **the L** are great." 3378
36: 8 the words of **the L** from the scroll. 3378
36: 9 of fasting before **the L** was proclaimed 3378
36:11 the words of **the L** from the scroll, 3378
36:26 But **the L** had hidden them. 3378
36:27 the word of **the L** came to Jeremiah: 3378
36:29 'This is what **the L** says: 3378
36:30 this is what **the L** says 3378
37: 2 to the words **the L** had spoken 3378
37: 3 "Please pray to **the L** our God for us." 3378
37: 6 Then the word of **the L** came to Jeremiah 3378
37: 7 "This is what **the L,** the God 3378
37: 9 "This is what **the L** says: 3378
37:17 "Is there any word from **the L?**" 3378
38: 2 "This is what **the L** says: 3378
38: 3 And this is what **the L** says: 3378
38:14 the third entrance to the temple of **the L.** 3378
38:16 "As surely as **the L** lives, 3378

Jer 38:17 "This is what **the L** God Almighty, 3378
38:20 "Obey **the L** by doing what I tell you. 3378
38:21 this is what **the L** has revealed to me: 3378
39:15 the word of **the L** came to him: 3378
39:16 'This is what **the L** Almighty, 3378
39:17 on that day, declares **the L;** 3378
39:18 because you trust in me, declares **the L.**' " 3378
40: 1 The word came to Jeremiah from **the L** 3378
40: 2 "**The L** your God decreed this disaster 3378
40: 3 And now **the L** has brought it about; 3378
40: 3 because you people sinned against **the L** 3378
41: 5 with them to the house of **the L.** 3378
42: 2 to **the L** your God for this entire remnant. 3378
42: 3 Pray that **the L** your God will tell us 3378
42: 4 to **the L** your God as you have requested; 3378
42: 4 I will tell you everything **the L** says 3378
42: 5 "May **the L** be a true and faithful witness 3378
42: 5 with everything **the L** your God sends you 3378
42: 6 we will obey **the L** our God, 3378
42: 6 for we will obey **the L** our God." 3378
42: 7 Ten days later the word of **the L** came 3378
42: 9 He said to them, "This is what **the L,** 3378
42:11 Do not be afraid of him, declares **the L,** 3378
42:13 and so disobey **the L** your God, 3378
42:15 then hear the word of **the L,** 3378
42:15 This is what **the L** Almighty, the God of 3378
42:18 This is what **the L** Almighty, the God of 3378
42:19 "O remnant of Judah, **the L** has told you, 3378
42:20 when you sent me to **the L** your God 3378
42:20 'Pray to **the L** our God for us; 3378
42:21 not obeyed **the L** your God 3378
43: 1 the words of **the L** their God— 3378
43: 1 everything **the L** had sent him 3378
43: 2 **The L** our God has not sent you to say, 3378
43: 7 in disobedience to **the L** and went as far 3378
43: 8 In Tahpanhes the word of **the L** came 3378
43:10 'This is what **the L** Almighty, the God of 3378
44: 2 "This is what **the L** Almighty, the God of 3378
44: 7 "Now this is what **the L** God Almighty, 3378
44:11 "Therefore, this is what **the L** Almighty, 3378
44:16 spoken to us in the name of **the L!** 3378
44:21 "Did not **the L** remember and think about 3378
44:22 **the L** could no longer endure your wicked
actions 3378
44:23 and have sinned against **the L** and have 3378
44:24 "Hear the word of **the L,** 3378
44:25 This is what **the L** Almighty, the God of 3378
44:26 But hear the word of **the L,** 3378
44:26 'I swear by my great name,' says **the L,** 3378
44:26 "As surely as **the** Sovereign **L** lives." 3378
44:29 declares **the L,** 'so that you will know 3378
44:30 This is what **the L** says: 3378
45: 2 "This is what **the L,** the God 3378
45: 3 **The L** has added sorrow to my pain; 3378
45: 4 [The L said,] "Say this to him: NIH
45: 4 'This is what **the L** says: 3378
45: 5 on all people, declares **the L,** 3378
46: 1 the word of **the L** that came to Jeremiah 3378
46: 5 on every side," declares **the L.** 3378
46:10 to the Lord, **the L** Almighty— 3378
46:10 For the Lord, **the L** Almighty, 3378
46:13 the message **the L** spoke to Jeremiah 3378
46:15 for **the L** will push them down. 3378
46:18 whose name is **the L** Almighty, 3378
46:23 declares **the L,** "dense though it be. 3378
46:25 **The L** Almighty, the God of Israel, says: 3378
46:26 as in times past," declares **the L.** 3378
46:28 for I am with you," declares **the L.** 3378
47: 1 the word of **the L** that came to Jeremiah 3378
47: 2 This is what **the L** says: 3378
47: 4 **The L** is about to destroy the Philistines, 3378
47: 6 " 'Ah, sword of **the L,**' 3378
47: 7 can it rest when **the L** has commanded it, 3378
48: 1 This is what **the L** Almighty, 3378
48: 8 because **the L** has spoken. 3378
48:12 But days are coming," declares **the L,** 3378
48:15 whose name is **the L** Almighty. 3378
48:25 her arm is broken," declares **the L.** 3378
48:26 for she has defied **the L.** 3378
48:30 but it is futile," declares **the L,** 3378
48:35 to their gods," declares **the L.** 3378
48:38 a jar that no one wants," declares **the L.** 3378
48:40 This is what **the L** says: "Look! 3378
48:42 as a nation because she defied **the L.** 3378
48:43 O people of Moab," declares **the L.** 3378
48:44 of her punishment," declares **the L.** 3378
48:47 of Moab in days to come," declares **the L.** 3378
49: 1 This is what **the L** says: 3378
49: 2 But the days are coming," declares **the L,** 3378
49: 2 Then Israel will drive out those who drove
her out," says **the L.** 3378
49: 5 declares the Lord, **the L** Almighty. 3378
49: 6 of the Ammonites," declares **the L.** 3378
49: 7 This is what **the L** Almighty says: 3378
49:12 This is what **the L** says: 3378
49:13 I swear by myself," declares **the L,** 3378
49:14 I have heard a message from **the L:** 3378
49:16 I will bring you down," declares **the L.** 3378
49:18 says **the L,** "so no one will live there; 3378
49:20 hear what **the L** has planned 3378
49:26 silenced in that day," declares **the L**
Almighty. 3378
49:28 This is what **the L** says: 3378
49:30 you who live in Hazor," declares **the L.** 3378
49:31 declares **the L,** "a nation that has neither 3378
49:32 on them from every side," declares **the L.** 3378
49:34 the word of **the L** that came to Jeremiah 3378

†LORD distinguishes the proper name of God, *Yahweh*, indicated in the NIV by "LORD," from the words translated "Lord" and "lord," indexed under the heading ***LORD**, pages 683-86.

Jer 49:35 This is what the L Almighty says: 3378
49:37 even my fierce anger," declares the L. 3378
49:38 her king and officials," declares the L. 3378
49:39 of Elam in days to come," declares the L. 3378
50: 1 the word the L spoke through Jeremiah 3378
50: 4 at that time," declares the L, 3378
50: 4 in tears to seek the L their God. 3378
50: 5 to the L in an everlasting covenant 3378
50: 7 for they sinned against the L, 3378
50: 7 the L, the hope of their fathers.' 3378
50:10 all who plunder her will have their fill," declares the L. 3378
50:14 for she has sinned against the L. 3378
50:15 Since this is the vengeance of the L, 3378
50:18 Therefore this is what the L Almighty, 3378
50:20 at that time," declares the L, 3378
50:21 completely destroy them," declares the L. 3378
50:24 and captured because you opposed the L. 3378
50:25 The L has opened his arsenal 3378
50:25 for the Sovereign L Almighty has work 3378
50:28 how the L our God has taken vengeance, 3378
50:29 For she has defied the L, 3378
50:30 be silenced in that day," declares the L. 3378
50:31 the L Almighty, "for your day has come, 3378
50:33 This is what the L Almighty says: 3378
50:34 the L Almighty is his name. 3378
50:35 against the Babylonians!" declares the L— 3378
50:40 declares the L, "so no one will live there; 3378
50:45 hear what the L has planned 3378
51: 1 This is what the L says: 3378
51: 5 the L Almighty, though their land is full 3378
51:10 " 'The L has vindicated us; 3378
51:10 in Zion what the L our God has done.' 3378
51:11 The L has stirred up the kings of 3378
51:11 The L will take vengeance, 3378
51:12 The L will carry out his purpose, 3378
51:14 The L Almighty has sworn by himself: 3378
51:19 the L Almighty is his name. 3378
51:24 in Zion," declares the L. 3378
51:25 the whole earth," declares the L. 3378
51:26 be desolate forever," declares the L. 3378
51:33 This is what the L Almighty, 3378
51:36 Therefore, this is what the L says: 3378
51:39 and not awake," declares the L. 3378
51:45 Run from the fierce anger of the L. 3378
51:48 out of the north destroyers will attack her," declares the L. 3378
51:50 Remember the L in a distant land, 3378
51:52 "But days are coming," declares the L, 3378
51:53 send destroyers against her," declares the L. 3378
51:55 The L will destroy Babylon; 3378
51:56 For the L is a God of retribution; 3378
51:57 whose name is the L Almighty. 3378
51:58 This is what the L Almighty says: 3378
51:62 Then say, 'O L, you have said you will destroy this place, 3378
52: 2 He did evil in the eyes of the L, 3378
52:13 He set fire to the temple of the L, 3378
52:17 at the temple of the L and they carried all 3378
52:20 for the temple of the L, 3378
La 1: 5 The L has brought her grief because 3378
1: 9 "Look, O L, on my affliction, 3378
1:11 "Look, O L, and consider, 3378
1:12 that the L brought on me in the day 3378
1:17 The L has decreed for Jacob 3378
1:18 "The L is righteous, 3378
1:20 "See, O L, how distressed I am! 3378
2: 6 The L has made Zion forget her appointed feasts 3378
2: 7 raised a shout in the house of the L 3378
2: 8 The L determined to tear down the wall 3378
2: 9 prophets no longer find visions from the L. 3378
2:17 The L has done what he planned; 3378
2:20 "Look, O L, and consider: 3378
3:18 and all that I had hoped from the L." 3378
3:24 I say to myself, "The L is my portion; 3378
3:25 The L is good to those whose hope is 3378
3:26 to wait quietly for the salvation of the L. 3378
3:28 for the L has laid it on him. NIH
3:40 and let us return to the L. 3378
3:50 until the L looks down from heaven 3378
3:55 I called on your name, O L, 3378
3:59 You have seen, O L, 3378
3:61 O L, you have heard their insults, 3378
3:64 Pay them back what they deserve, O L, 3378
3:66 from under the heavens of the L. 3378
4:11 The L has given full vent to his wrath; 3378
4:16 The L himself has scattered them; 3378+7156
5: 1 O L, what has happened to us; 3378
5:19 You, O L, reign forever; 3378
5:21 Restore us to yourself, O L, 3378
Eze 1: 3 word of the L came to Ezekiel the priest, 3378
1: 3 There the hand of the L was upon him. 3378
1:28 of the likeness of the glory of the L. 3378
2: 4 'This is what the Sovereign L says.' 3378
3:11 'This is what the Sovereign L says,' 3378
3:12 May the glory of the L be praised 3378
3:14 with the strong hand of the L upon me. 3378
3:16 of seven days the word of the L came 3378
3:22 The hand of the L was upon me there, 3378
3:23 the glory of the L was standing there, 3378
3:27 'This is what the Sovereign L says.' 3378
4:13 The L said, "In this way the people 3378
4:14 Then I said, "Not so, Sovereign L! 3378
5: 5 "This is what the Sovereign L says: 3378
5: 7 Therefore this is what the Sovereign L says: 3378
5: 8 Therefore this is what the Sovereign L says: 3378

Eze 5:11 declares the Sovereign L, 3378
5:13 they will know that I the L have spoken 3378
5:15 I the L have spoken. 3378
5:17 I the L have spoken." 3378
6: 1 The word of the L came to me: 3378
6: 3 hear the word of the Sovereign L. 3378
6: 3 This is what the Sovereign L says to 3378
6: 7 and you will know that I am the L. 3378
6:10 And they will know that I am the L; 3378
6:11 " 'This is what the Sovereign L says: 3378
6:13 And they will know that I am the L, 3378
6:14 Then they will know that I am the L.' " 3378
7: 1 The word of the L came to me: 3378
7: 2 this is what the Sovereign L says to 3378
7: 4 Then you will know that I am the L. 3378
7: 5 "This is what the Sovereign L says: 3378
7: 9 that it is I the L who strikes the blow. 3378
7:27 Then they will know that I am the L." 3378
8: 1 of the Sovereign L came upon me there. 3378
8:12 They say, 'The L does not see us; 3378
8:12 the L has forsaken the land.' " 3378
8:14 to the north gate of the house of the L, 3378
8:16 into the inner court of the house of the L, 3378
8:16 the temple of the L and their faces toward 3378
9: 3 Then the L called to the man clothed NIH
9: 8 crying out, "Ah, Sovereign L! 3378
9: 9 They say, 'The L has forsaken the land; 3378
9: 9 the L does not see.' 3378
10: 2 The L said to the man clothed in linen, NIH
10: 4 Then the glory of the L rose from above 3378
10: 4 of the radiance of the glory of the L. 3378
10: 6 When the L commanded the man 2257S
10:18 of the L departed from over the threshold 3378
11: 1 of the house of the L that faces east. 3378
11: 2 The L said to me, "Son of man, NIH
11: 5 Then the Spirit of the L came upon me, 3378
11: 5 "This is what the L says: 3378
11: 7 Therefore this is what the Sovereign L says: 3378
11: 8 declares the Sovereign L. 3378
11:10 Then you will know that I am the L. 3378
11:12 And you will know that I am the L, 3378
11:13 in a loud voice, "Ah, Sovereign L! 3378
11:14 The word of the L came to me: 3378
11:15 'They are far away from the L; 3378
11:16 'This is what the Sovereign L says: 3378
11:17 'This is what the Sovereign L says: 3378
11:21 declares the Sovereign L." 3378
11:23 The glory of the L went up from within 3378
11:25 exiles everything the L had shown me. 3378
12: 1 The word of the L came to me: 3378
12: 8 In the morning the word of the L came 3378
12:10 'This is what the Sovereign L says: 3378
12:15 "They will know that I am the L, 3378
12:16 Then they will know that I am the L." 3378
12:17 The word of the L came to me: 3378
12:19 'This is what the Sovereign L says 3378
12:20 Then you will know that I am the L.' " 3378
12:21 The word of the L came to me: 3378
12:23 'This is what the Sovereign L says: 3378
12:25 But I the L will speak what I will, 3378
12:25 declares the Sovereign L.' " 3378
12:26 The word of the L came to me: 3378
12:28 'This is what the Sovereign L says: 3378
12:28 declares the Sovereign L.' " 3378
13: 1 The word of the L came to me: 3378
13: 2 'Hear the word of the L! 3378
13: 3 This is what the Sovereign L says: 3378
13: 5 in the battle on the day of the L. 3378
13: 6 They say, "The L declares," 3378
13: 6 when the L has not sent them; 3378
13: 7 when you say, "The L declares," 3378
13: 8 Therefore this is what the Sovereign L says: 3378
13: 8 declares the Sovereign L. 3378
13: 9 you will know that I am the Sovereign L. 3378
13:13 Therefore this is what the Sovereign L says: 3378
13:14 and you will know that I am the L. 3378
13:16 declares the Sovereign L." ' 3378
13:18 'This is what the Sovereign L says: 3378
13:20 Therefore this is what the Sovereign L says: 3378
13:21 Then you will know that I am the L. 3378
13:23 And then you will know that I am the L.' " 3378
14: 2 Then the word of the L came to me: 3378
14: 4 'This is what the Sovereign L says: 3378
14: 4 I the L will answer him myself in keeping 3378
14: 6 'This is what the Sovereign L says: 3378
14: 7 I the L will answer him myself. 3378
14: 8 Then you will know that I am the L. 3378
14: 9 I the L have enticed that prophet, 3378
14:11 declares the Sovereign L.' " 3378
14:12 The word of the L came to me: 3378
14:14 declares the Sovereign L. 3378
14:16 declares the Sovereign L, 3378
14:18 declares the Sovereign L, 3378
14:20 declares the Sovereign L, even if Noah, 3378
14:21 "For this is what the Sovereign L says: 3378
14:23 declares the Sovereign L." 3378
15: 1 The word of the L came to me: 3378
15: 6 Therefore this is what the Sovereign L says: 3378
15: 7 you will know that I am the L. 3378
15: 8 declares the Sovereign L." 3378
16: 1 The word of the L came to me: 3378
16: 3 'This is what the Sovereign L says 3378
16: 8 declares the Sovereign L, 3378
16:14 declares the Sovereign L. 3378
16:19 declares the Sovereign L. 3378
16:23 Woe to you, declares the Sovereign L. 3378
16:30 declares the Sovereign L, 3378

Eze 16:35 you prostitute, hear the word of the L! 3378
16:36 This is what the Sovereign L says: 3378
16:43 declares the Sovereign L. 3378
16:48 surely as I live, declares the Sovereign L, 3378
16:58 your detestable practices, declares the L. 3378
16:59 " 'This is what the Sovereign L says: 3378
16:62 and you will know that I am the L. 3378
16:63 declares the Sovereign L.' " 3378
17: 1 The word of the L came to me: 3378
17: 3 'This is what the Sovereign L says: 3378
17: 9 'This is what the Sovereign L says: 3378
17:11 Then the word of the L came to me: 3378
17:16 surely as I live, declares the Sovereign L, 3378
17:19 Therefore this is what the Sovereign L says: 3378
17:21 you will know that I the L have spoken. 3378
17:22 " 'This is what the Sovereign L says: 3378
17:24 of the field will know that I the L bring 3378
17:24 " 'I the L have spoken, and I will do it.' " 3378
18: 1 The word of the L came to me: 3378
18: 3 surely as I live, declares the Sovereign L, 3378
18: 9 declares the Sovereign L. 3378
18:23 declares the Sovereign L. 3378
18:30 declares the Sovereign L. 3378
18:32 declares the Sovereign L. 3378
20: 1 of Israel came to inquire of the L, 3378
20: 2 Then the word of the L came to me: 3378
20: 3 'This is what the Sovereign L says: 3378
20: 3 declares the Sovereign L.' 3378
20: 5 'This is what the Sovereign L says: 3378
20: 5 "I am the L your God." 3378
20: 7 I am the L your God." 3378
20:12 that I the L made them holy. 3378
20:19 I am the L your God; 3378
20:20 that I am the L your God." 3378
20:26 so they would know that I am the L.' 3378
20:27 'This is what the Sovereign L says: 3378
20:30 'This is what the Sovereign L says: 3378
20:31 surely as I live, declares the Sovereign L, 3378
20:33 surely as I live, declares the Sovereign L, 3378
20:36 declares the Sovereign L. 3378
20:38 Then you will know that I am the L. 3378
20:39 this is what the Sovereign L says: 3378
20:40 declares the Sovereign L, 3378
20:42 Then you will know that I am the L, 3378
20:44 You will know that I am the L, 3378
20:44 declares the Sovereign L.' " 3378
20:45 The word of the L came to me: 3378
20:47 'Hear the word of the L. 3378
20:47 This is what the Sovereign L says: 3378
20:48 that I the L have kindled it; 3378
20:49 Then I said, "Ah, Sovereign L! 3378
21: 1 The word of the L came to me: 3378
21: 3 'This is what the L says: 3378
21: 5 that I the L have drawn my sword 3378
21: 7 declares the Sovereign L." 3378
21: 8 The word of the L came to me: 3378
21:13 declares the Sovereign L.' 3378
21:17 I the L have spoken." 3378
21:18 The word of the L came to me: 3378
21:24 Therefore this is what the Sovereign L says: 3378
21:26 this is what the Sovereign L says: 3378
21:28 'This is what the Sovereign L says about 3378
21:32 for I the L have spoken.' " 3378
22: 1 The word of the L came to me: 3378
22: 3 'This is what the Sovereign L says: 3378
22:12 declares the Sovereign L. 3378
22:14 I the L have spoken, and I will do it. 3378
22:16 you will know that I am the L.' " 3378
22:17 Then the word of the L came to me: 3378
22:19 Therefore this is what the Sovereign L says: 3378
22:22 that I the L have poured out my wrath 3378
22:23 Again the word of the L came to me: 3378
22:28 'This is what the Sovereign L says'— 3378
22:28 when the L has not spoken. 3378
22:31 declares the Sovereign L." 3378
23: 1 The word of the L came to me: 3378
23:22 this is what the Sovereign L says: 3378
23:28 "For this is what the Sovereign L says: 3378
23:32 "This is what the Sovereign L says: 3378
23:34 I have spoken, declares the Sovereign L. 3378
23:35 Therefore this is what the Sovereign L says: 3378
23:36 The L said to me: 3378
23:46 "This is what the Sovereign L says: 3378
23:49 you will know that I am the Sovereign L." 3378
24: 1 the word of the L came to me: 3378
24: 3 'This is what the Sovereign L says: 3378
24: 6 " 'For this is what the Sovereign L says: 3378
24: 9 Therefore this is what the Sovereign L says: 3378
24:14 " 'I the L have spoken. 3378
24:14 declares the Sovereign L.' " 3378
24:15 The word of the L came to me: 3378
24:20 "The word of the L came to me: 3378
24:21 'This is what the Sovereign L says: 3378
24:24 that I am the Sovereign L.' 3378
24:27 and they will know that I am the L." 3378
25: 1 The word of the L came to me: 3378
25: 3 'Hear the word of the Sovereign L. 3378
25: 3 This is what the Sovereign L says: 3378
25: 5 Then you will know that I am the L. 3378
25: 6 For this is what the Sovereign L says: 3378
25: 7 and you will know that I am the L.' " 3378
25: 8 "This is what the Sovereign L says: 3378
25:11 Then they will know that I am the L.' " 3378
25:12 "This is what the Sovereign L says: 3378
25:13 therefore this is what the Sovereign L says: 3378
25:14 declares the Sovereign L.' " 3378
25:15 "This is what the Sovereign L says: 3378

†LORD distinguishes the proper name of God, *Yahweh*, indicated in the NIV by "LORD," from the words translated "Lord" and "lord," indexed under the heading *LORD, pages 683-86.

Eze 25:16 therefore this is what **the Sovereign L** says: 3378
25:17 Then they will know that I am **the L,** 3378
26: 1 the word of **the L** came to me: 3378
26: 3 therefore this is what **the Sovereign L** says: 3378
26: 5 declares **the Sovereign L.** 3378
26: 6 Then they will know that I am **the L.** 3378
26: 7 "For this is what **the Sovereign L** says: 3378
26:14 for I **the L** have spoken, 3378
26:14 declares **the Sovereign L.** 3378
26:15 "This is what **the Sovereign L** says 3378
26:19 "This is what **the Sovereign L** says: 3378
26:21 declares **the Sovereign L."** 3378
27: 1 The word of **the L** came to me: 3378
27: 3 'This is what **the Sovereign L** says: 3378
28: 1 The word of **the L** came to me: 3378
28: 2 'This is what **the Sovereign L** says: 3378
28: 6 Therefore this is what **the Sovereign L** says: 3378
28:10 declares **the Sovereign L.'** " 3378
28:11 The word of **the L** came to me: 3378
28:12 'This is what **the Sovereign L** says: 3378
28:20 The word of **the L** came to me: 3378
28:22 'This is what **the Sovereign L** says: 3378
28:22 They will know that I am **the L,** 3378
28:23 Then they will know that I am **the L.** 3378
28:24 they will know that I am the Sovereign **L.** 3378
28:25 " 'This is what **the Sovereign L** says: 3378
28:26 they will know that I am **the L** their God.' " 3378
29: 1 the word of **the L** came to me: 3378
29: 3 'This is what **the Sovereign L** says: 3378
29: 6 in Egypt will know that I am **the L.** 3378
29: 8 Therefore this is what **the Sovereign L** says: 3378
29: 9 Then they will know that I am **the L.** 3378
29:13 " 'Yet this is what **the Sovereign L** says: 3378
29:16 that I am **the Sovereign L.'** " 3378
29:17 the word of **the L** came to me: 3378
29:19 Therefore this is what **the Sovereign L** says: 3378
29:20 declares **the Sovereign L.** 3378
29:21 Then they will know that I am **the L."** 3378
30: 1 The word of **the L** came to me: 3378
30: 2 'This is what **the Sovereign L** says: 3378
30: 3 the day is near, the day of **the L** is near— 3378
30: 6 " 'This is what **the L** says: 3378
30: 6 declares **the Sovereign L.** 3378
30: 8 Then they will know that I am **the L,** 3378
30:10 " 'This is what **the Sovereign L** says: 3378
30:12 I **the L** have spoken. 3378
30:13 " 'This is what **the Sovereign L** says: 3378
30:19 and they will know that I am **the L.'** " 3378
30:20 the word of **the L** came to me: 3378
30:22 Therefore this is what **the Sovereign L** says: 3378
30:25 Then they will know that I am **the L,** 3378
30:26 Then they will know that I am **the L."** 3378
31: 1 the word of **the L** came to me: 3378
31:10 Therefore this is what **the Sovereign L** says: 3378
31:15 " 'This is what **the Sovereign L** says: 3378
31:18 declares **the Sovereign L.'** " 3378
32: 1 the word of **the L** came to me: 3378
32: 3 " 'This is what **the Sovereign L** says: 3378
32: 8 declares **the Sovereign L.** 3378
32:11 " 'For this is what **the Sovereign L** says: 3378
32:14 declares **the Sovereign L.** 3378
32:15 then they will know that I am **the L.'** 3378
32:16 declares **the Sovereign L."** 3378
32:17 the word of **the L** came to me: 3378
32:31 declares **the Sovereign L.** 3378
32:32 declares **the Sovereign L."** 3378
33: 1 The word of **the L** came to me: 3378
33:11 declares **the Sovereign L,** 3378
33:22 the hand of **the L** was upon me, 3378
33:23 Then the word of **the L** came to me: 3378
33:25 'This is what **the Sovereign L** says: 3378
33:27 'This is what **the Sovereign L** says: 3378
33:29 Then they will know that I am **the L,** 3378
33:30 the message that has come from **the L.'** 3378
34: 1 The word of **the L** came to me: 3378
34: 2 'This is what **the Sovereign L** says: 3378
34: 7 you shepherds, hear the word of **the L:** 3378
34: 8 declares **the Sovereign L,** 3378
34: 9 O shepherds, hear the word of **the L:** 3378
34:10 This is what **the Sovereign L** says: 3378
34:11 " 'For this is what **the Sovereign L** says: 3378
34:15 declares **the Sovereign L.** 3378
34:17 this is what **the Sovereign L** says: 3378
34:20 Therefore this is what **the Sovereign L** says 3378
34:24 I **the L** will be their God, 3378
34:24 I **the L** have spoken. 3378
34:27 They will know that I am **the L,** 3378
34:30 they will know that I, **the L** their God, 3378
34:30 are my people, declares **the Sovereign L.** 3378
34:31 declares **the Sovereign L.'** " 3378
35: 1 The word of **the L** came to me: 3378
35: 3 'This is what **the Sovereign L** says: 3378
35: 4 Then you will know that I am **the L.** 3378
35: 6 declares **the Sovereign L,** 3378
35: 9 Then you will know that I am **the L.** 3378
35:10 even though I **the L** was there, 3378
35:11 declares **the Sovereign L,** 3378
35:12 that I **the L** have heard all 3378
35:14 This is what **the Sovereign L** says: 3378
35:15 Then they will know that I am **the L.'** " 3378
36: 1 hear the word of **the L.** 3378
36: 2 This is what **the Sovereign L** says: 3378
36: 3 'This is what **the Sovereign L** says: 3378
36: 4 hear the word of **the Sovereign L:** 3378
36: 4 This is what **the Sovereign L** says to 3378
36: 5 this is what **the Sovereign L** says: 3378
36: 6 'This is what **the Sovereign L** says: 3378

Eze 36: 7 Therefore this is what **the Sovereign L** says: 3378
36:11 Then you will know that I am **the L.** 3378
36:13 " 'This is what **the Sovereign L** says: 3378
36:14 declares **the Sovereign L.** 3378
36:15 declares **the Sovereign L.'** " 3378
36:16 Again the word of **the L** came to me: 3378
36:22 'This is what **the Sovereign L** says: 3378
36:23 the nations will know that I am **the L,** 3378
36:23 declares **the Sovereign L,** 3378
36:32 declares **the Sovereign L.** 3378
36:33 " 'This is what **the Sovereign L** says: 3378
36:36 I **the L** have rebuilt what was destroyed 3378
36:36 I **the L** have spoken, and I will do it.' 3378
36:37 "This is what **the Sovereign L** says: 3378
36:38 Then they will know that I am **the L."** 3378
37: 1 The hand of **the L** was upon me, 3378
37: 1 of **the L** and set me in the middle of 3378
37: 3 I said, "O **Sovereign L,** you alone know." 3378
37: 4 'Dry bones, hear the word of **the L!** 3378
37: 5 This is what **the Sovereign L** says 3378
37: 6 Then you will know that I am **the L.'** " 3378
37: 9 'This is what **the Sovereign L** says: 3378
37:12 'This is what **the Sovereign L** says: 3378
37:13 my people, will know that I am **the L,** 3378
37:14 you will know that I **the L** have spoken, 3378
37:14 and I have done it, declares **the L.'** " 3378
37:15 The word of **the L** came to me: 3378
37:19 'This is what **the Sovereign L** says: 3378
37:21 'This is what **the Sovereign L** says: 3378
37:28 that I **the L** make Israel holy, 3378
38: 1 The word of **the L** came to me: 3378
38: 3 'This is what **the Sovereign L** says: 3378
38:10 " 'This is what **the Sovereign L** says: 3378
38:14 'This is what **the Sovereign L** says: 3378
38:17 " 'This is what **the Sovereign L** says: 3378
38:18 declares **the Sovereign L.** 3378
38:21 declares **the Sovereign L.** 3378
38:23 Then they will know that I am **the L.'** 3378
39: 1 'This is what **the Sovereign L** says: 3378
39: 5 declares **the Sovereign L.** 3378
39: 6 and they will know that I am **the L.** 3378
39: 7 and the nations will know that I **the L** am 3378
39: 8 declares **the Sovereign L.** 3378
39:10 declares **the Sovereign L.** 3378
39:13 declares **the Sovereign L.** 3378
39:17 this is what **the Sovereign L** says: 3378
39:20 declares **the Sovereign L.** 3378
39:22 that I am **the L** their God. 3378
39:25 Therefore this is what **the Sovereign L** says: 3378
39:28 they will know that I am **the L** their God, 3378
39:29 declares **the Sovereign L."** 3378
40: 1 on that very day the hand of **the L** was 3378
40:46 near to **the L** to minister before him." 3378
41:22 "This is the table that is before **the L."** 3378
42:13 the priests who approach **the L** will eat 3378
43: 4 The glory of **the L** entered the temple 3378
43: 5 and the glory of **the L** filled the temple. 3378
43:18 this is what **the Sovereign L** says: 3378
43:19 declares **the Sovereign L.** 3378
43:24 You are to offer them before **the L,** 3378
43:24 as a burnt offering to **the L.** 3378
43:27 declares **the Sovereign L."** 3378
44: 2 **The L** said to me, 3378
44: 2 It is to remain shut because **the L,** 3378
44: 3 to eat in the presence of **the L.** 3378
44: 4 I looked and saw the glory of **the L** filling 3378
44: 4 of the LORD filling the temple of **the L,** 3378
44: 5 **The L** said to me, "Son of man, 3378
44: 5 regulations regarding the temple of **the L.** 3378
44: 6 'This is what **the Sovereign L** says: 3378
44: 9 This is what **the Sovereign L** says: 3378
44:12 declares **the Sovereign L.** 3378
44:15 declares **the Sovereign L.** 3378
44:27 declares **the Sovereign L.** 3378
44:29 in Israel devoted to **the L** will belong NIH
45: 1 to present to **the L** a portion of the land as 3378
45: 4 near to minister before **the L.** 3378
45: 9 " 'This is what **the Sovereign L** says: 3378
45: 9 declares **the Sovereign L.** 3378
45:15 declares **the Sovereign L.** 3378
45:18 " 'This is what **the Sovereign L** says: 3378
45:23 as a burnt offering to **the L,** 3378
46: 1 " 'This is what **the Sovereign L** says: 3378
46: 3 in the presence of **the L** at the entrance to 3378
46: 4 to **the L** on the Sabbath day is to 3378
46: 9 the people of the land come before **the L** 3378
46:12 a freewill offering to **the L—** 3378
46:13 for a burnt offering to **the L;** 3378
46:14 of this grain offering to **the L** is 3378
46:16 " 'This is what **the Sovereign L** says: 3378
47:13 This is what **the Sovereign L** says: 3378
47:23 declares **the Sovereign L.** 3378
48: 9 to offer to **the L** will be 25,000 3378
48:10 of it will be the sanctuary of **the L.** 3378
48:14 because it is holy to **the L.** 3378
48:29 declares **the Sovereign L.** 3378
48:35 THE L IS THERE." 3378
Da 9: 2 word of **the L** given to Jeremiah the prophet 3378
9: 4 I prayed to **the L** my God and confessed: 3378
9: 8 O **L,** we and our kings, 3378
9:10 we have not obeyed **the L** our God 3378
9:13 of **the L** our God by turning from our sins 3378
9:14 **The L** did not hesitate to bring 3378
9:14 for **the L** our God is righteous 3378
9:20 and making my request to **the L** my God 3378
Hos 1: 1 The word of **the L** that came to Hosea son 3378
1: 2 **the L** began to speak through Hosea, 3378

Hos 1: 2 **the L** said to him, "Go, take to yourself 3378
1: 2 adultery in departing from **the L."** 3378
1: 4 Then **the L** said to Hosea, 3378
1: 6 Then **the L** said to Hosea, NIH
1: 7 but by **the L** their God." 3378
1: 9 Then the L said, "Call him Lo-Ammi, NIH
2:13 but me she forgot," declares **the L.** 3378
2:16 "In that day," declares **the L,** 3378
2:20 and you will acknowledge **the L.** 3378
2:21 that day I will respond," declares **the L—** 3378
3: 1 **The L** said to me, "Go, show your love 3378
3: 1 Love her as **the L** loves the Israelites, 3378
3: 5 and seek **the L** their God 3378
3: 5 They will come trembling to **the L** and 3378
4: 1 Hear the word of **the L,** you Israelites, 3378
4: 1 because **the L** has a charge to bring 3378
4:10 because they have deserted **the L** 3378
4:15 'As surely as **the L** lives!' 3378
4:16 then can **the L** pasture them like lambs in 3378
5: 4 they do not acknowledge **the L.** 3378
5: 6 with their flocks and herds to seek **the L,** 3378
5: 7 They are unfaithful to **the L;** 3378
6: 1 "Come, let us return to **the L.** 3378
6: 3 Let us acknowledge **the L;** 3378
7:10 not return to **the L** his God or search 3378
8: 1 An eagle is over the house of **the L** 3378
8:13 but **the L** is not pleased with them. 3378
9: 4 not pour out wine offerings to **the L,** 3378
9: 4 it will not come into the temple of **the L.** 3378
9: 5 on the festival days of **the L?** 3378
9:14 Give them, O **L**—what will you give them? 3378
10: 2 **The L** will demolish their altars 2085[S]
10: 3 because we did not revere **the L.** 3378
10:12 for it is time to seek **the L,** 3378
11:10 They will follow **the L;** 3378
11:11 settle them in their homes," declares **the L.** 3378
12: 2 **The L** has a charge to bring 3378
12: 5 **the L** God Almighty, 3378
12: 5 **the L** is his name of renown! 3378
12: 9 "I am **the L** your God, 3378
12:13 **The L** used a prophet to bring Israel up 3378
13: 4 "But I am **the L** your God, 3378
13:15 An east wind from **the L** will come, 3378
14: 1 Return, O Israel, to **the L** your God. 3378
14: 2 Take words with you and return to **the L.** 3378
14: 9 The ways of **the L** are right; 3378
Joel 1: 1 The word of **the L** that came to Joel son of 3378
1: 9 from the house of **the L.** 3378
1: 9 those who minister before **the L.** 3378
1:14 the land to the house of **the L** your God, 3378
1:14 and cry out to **the L.** 3378
1:15 For the day of **the L** is near; 3378
1:19 To you, O **L,** I call, 3378
2: 1 for the day of **the L** is coming. 3378
2:11 **The L** thunders at the head of his army; 3378
2:11 The day of **the L** is great; it is dreadful. 3378
2:12 "Even now," declares **the L,** 3378
2:13 Return to **the L** your God, 3378
2:14 and drink offerings for **the L** your God. 3378
2:17 who minister before **the L,** 3378
2:17 Let them say, "Spare your people, O **L.** 3378
2:18 Then **the L** will be jealous for his land 3378
2:19 **The L** will reply to them: 3378
2:21 Surely **the L** has done great things. 3378
2:23 rejoice in **the L** your God, 3378
2:26 the name of **the L** your God, 3378
2:27 that I am **the L** your God, 3378
2:31 of the great and dreadful day of **the L.** 3378
2:32 on the name of **the L** will be saved; 3378
2:32 as **the L** has said, 3378
2:32 among the survivors whom **the L** calls. 3378
3: 8 **The L** has spoken. 3378
3:11 Bring down your warriors, O **L!** 3378
3:14 of **the L** is near in the valley of decision. 3378
3:16 **The L** will roar from Zion and thunder 3378
3:16 But **the L** will be a refuge for his people, 3378
3:17 you will know that I, **the L** your God, 3378
3:21 **The L** dwells in Zion! 3378
Am 1: 2 **"The L** roars from Zion and thunders 3378
1: 3 This is what **the L** says: 3378
1: 5 into exile to Kir," says **the L.** 3378
1: 6 This is what **the L** says: 3378
1: 8 says **the Sovereign L.** 3378
1: 9 This is what **the L** says: 3378
1:11 This is what **the L** says: 3378
1:13 This is what **the L** says: 3378
1:15 he and his officials together," says **the L.** 3378
2: 1 This is what **the L** says: 3378
2: 3 her officials with him," says **the L.** 3378
2: 4 This is what **the L** says: 3378
2: 4 of **the L** and have not kept his decrees, 3378
2: 6 This is what **the L** says: 3378
2:11 not true, people of Israel?" declares **the L.** 3378
2:16 on that day," declares **the L.** 3378
3: 1 Hear this word **the L** has spoken 3378
3: 6 has not **the L** caused it? 3378
3: 7 Surely **the Sovereign L** does nothing 3378
3: 8 **The Sovereign L** has spoken— 3378
3:10 declares **the L,** "who hoard plunder 3378
3:11 Therefore this is what **the Sovereign L** says: 3378
3:12 This is what **the L** says: 3378
3:13 declares the Lord, **the L** God Almighty. 3378
3:15 will be demolished," declares **the L** 3378
4: 2 **The Sovereign L** has sworn by his holiness 3378
4: 3 cast out toward Harmon," declares **the L.** 3378
4: 5 declares **the Sovereign L.** 3378
4: 6 not returned to me," declares **the L.** 3378

†LORD distinguishes the proper name of God, *Yahweh*, indicated in the NIV by "LORD," from the words translated "Lord" and "lord," indexed under the heading ***LORD**, pages 683-86.

Am	4: 8	not returned to me," declares **the L.**	3378
	4: 9	not returned to me," declares **the L.**	3378
	4:10	not returned to me," declares **the L.**	3378
	4:11	not returned to me," declares **the L.**	3378
	4:13	**the L** God Almighty is his name.	3378
	5: 3	This is what **the** Sovereign **L** says:	3378
	5: 4	This is what **the L** says to the house	3378
	5: 6	Seek **the L** and live,	3378
	5: 8	**the L** is his name—	3378
	5:14	**the L** God Almighty will be with you,	3378
	5:15	Perhaps **the L** God Almighty will have mercy	3378
	5:16	**the L** God Almighty, says:	3378
	5:17	pass through your midst," says **the L.**	3378
	5:18	to you who long for the day of **the L!**	3378
	5:18	Why do you long for the day of **the L?**	3378
	5:20	Will not the day of **the L** be darkness,	3378
	5:27	into exile beyond Damascus," says **the L,**	3378
	6: 8	**The** Sovereign **L** has sworn by himself—	3378
	6: 8	**the L** God Almighty declares:	3378
	6:10	We must not mention the name of **the L."**	3378
	6:11	For **the L** has given the command,	3378
	6:14	For **the L** God Almighty declares,	3378
	7: 1	This is what **the** Sovereign **L** showed me:	3378
	7: 2	I cried out, "Sovereign **L,** forgive!	3378
	7: 3	So **the L** relented.	3378
	7: 3	"This will not happen," **the L** said.	3378
	7: 4	This is what **the** Sovereign **L** showed me:	3378
	7: 4	**The** Sovereign **L** was calling	3378
	7: 5	Then I cried out, "Sovereign **L,** I beg you,	3378
	7: 6	So **the L** relented.	3378
	7: 6	**the** Sovereign **L** said.	3378
	7: 8	And **the L** asked me, "What do you see,	3378
	7:15	But **the L** took me from tending the flock	3378
	7:16	Now then, hear the word of **the L.**	3378
	7:17	"Therefore this is what **the L** says:	3378
	8: 1	This is what **the** Sovereign **L** showed me:	3378
	8: 2	Then **the L** said to me,	3378
	8: 3	"In that day," declares **the** Sovereign **L,**	3378
	8: 7	**The L** has sworn by the Pride of Jacob:	3378
	8: 9	"In that day," declares **the** Sovereign **L,**	3378
	8:11	declares **the** Sovereign **L,**	3378
	8:11	a famine of hearing the words of **the L.**	3378
	8:12	searching for the word of **the L,**	3378
	9: 5	The Lord, **the L** Almighty,	3378
	9: 6	**the L** is his name.	3378
	9: 7	to me as the Cushites?" declares **the L.**	3378
	9: 8	"Surely the eyes of **the** Sovereign **L** are	3378
	9: 8	the house of Jacob," declares **the L.**	3378
	9:12	declares **the L,** who will do these things.	3378
	9:13	"The days are coming," declares **the L,**	3378
	9:15	says **the L** your God.	3378
Ob	1: 1	This is what **the** Sovereign **L** says	3378
	1: 1	We have heard a message from **the L:**	3378
	1: 4	I will bring you down," declares **the L.**	3378
	1: 8	"In that day," declares **the L,**	3378
	1:15	"The day of **the L** is near for all nations.	3378
	1:18	**The L** has spoken.	3378
Jnh	1: 1	word of **the L** came to Jonah son of Amittai	3378
	1: 3	from **the L** and headed for Tarshish.	3378
	1: 3	and sailed for Tarshish to flee from **the L.**	3378
	1: 4	Then **the L** sent a great wind on the sea,	3378
	1: 9	"I am a Hebrew and I worship **the L,**	3378
	1:10	knew he was running away from **the L,**	3378
	1:14	Then they cried to **the L,** "O LORD,	3378
	1:14	Then they cried to the LORD, "O **L,**	3378
	1:14	for you, O **L,** have done as you pleased."	3378
	1:16	At this the men greatly feared **the L,**	3378
	1:16	and they offered a sacrifice to **the L**	3378
	1:17	But **the L** provided a great fish	3378
	2: 1	From inside the fish Jonah prayed to **the L**	3378
	2: 2	He said: "In my distress I called to **the L,**	3378
	2: 6	my life up from the pit, O **L** my God.	3378
	2: 7	**L,** and my prayer rose to you,	3378
	2: 9	Salvation comes from **the L."**	3378
	2:10	And **the L** commanded the fish,	3378
	3: 1	Then the word of **the L** came to Jonah	3378
	3: 3	Jonah obeyed the word of **the L** and went	3378
	4: 2	He prayed to **the L,** "O LORD,	3378
	4: 2	He prayed to the LORD, "O **L,**	3378
	4: 3	Now, O **L,** take away my life,	3378
	4: 4	But **the L** replied,	3378
	4: 6	Then **the L** God provided a vine	3378
	4:10	But **the L** said, "You have been concerned	3378
Mic	1: 1	The word of **the L** that came to Micah of	3378
	1: 2	**the** Sovereign **L** may witness against you,	3378
	1: 3	**The L** is coming from his dwelling place;	3378
	1:12	because disaster has come from **the L,**	3378
	2: 3	Therefore, **the L** says:	3378
	2: 5	the assembly of **the L** to divide the land	3378
	2: 7	"Is the Spirit of **the L** angry?	3378
	2:13	**the L** at their head."	3378
	3: 4	Then they will cry out to **the L,**	3378
	3: 5	This is what **the L** says:	3378
	3: 8	with the Spirit of **the L,**	3378
	3:11	Yet they lean upon **the L** and say,	3378
	3:11	"Is not **the L** among us?	3378
	4: 2	let us go up to the mountain of **the L,**	3378
	4: 2	the word of **the L** from Jerusalem.	3378
	4: 4	for **the L** Almighty has spoken.	3378
	4: 5	in the name of **the L** our God for ever	3378
	4: 6	"In that day," declares **the L,**	3378
	4: 7	**The L** will rule over them in Mount Zion	3378
	4:10	There **the L** will redeem you out of	3378
	4:12	they do not know the thoughts of **the L;**	3378
	4:13	to **the L,** their wealth to the Lord of all	3378
	5: 4	shepherd his flock in the strength of **the L,**	3378
Mic	5: 4	the majesty of the name of **the L** his God.	3378
	5: 7	of many peoples like dew from **the L,**	3378
	5:10	"In that day," declares **the L,**	3378
	6: 1	Listen to what **the L** says:	3378
	6: 2	For **the L** has a case against his people;	3378
	6: 5	the righteous acts of **the L."**	3378
	6: 6	With what shall I come before **the L**	3378
	6: 7	Will **the L** be pleased with thousands	3378
	6: 8	And what does **the L** require of you?	3378
	6: 9	**The L** is calling to the city—	3378
	7: 7	But as for me, I watch in hope for **the L,**	3378
	7: 8	I sit in darkness, **the L** will be my light.	3378
	7:10	"Where is **the L** your God?"	3378
	7:17	in fear to **the L** our God and will be afraid	3378
Na	1: 2	**The L** is a jealous and avenging God;	3378
	1: 2	**the L** takes vengeance and is filled	3378
	1: 2	**The L** takes vengeance on his foes	3378
	1: 3	**The L** is slow to anger and great	3378
	1: 3	**the L** will not leave the guilty unpunished.	3378
	1: 7	**The L** is good, a refuge in times of trouble.	3378
	1: 9	against **the L** he will bring to an end;	3378
	1:11	against **the L** and counsels wickedness.	3378
	1:12	This is what **the L** says:	3378
	1:14	**The L** has given a command	3378
	2: 2	**The L** will restore the splendor of Jacob	3378
	2:13	declares **the L** Almighty.	3378
	3: 5	declares **the L** Almighty.	3378
Hab	1: 2	How long, O **L,** must I call for help,	3378
	1:12	O **L,** are you not from everlasting?	3378
	1:12	O **L,** you have appointed them	3378
	2: 2	Then **the L** replied:	3378
	2:13	Has not **the L** Almighty determined that	3378
	2:14	with the knowledge of the glory of **the L,**	3378
	2:20	But **the L** is in his holy temple;	3378
	3: 2	**L,** I have heard of your fame;	3378
	3: 2	I stand in awe of your deeds, O **L.**	3378
	3: 8	Were you angry with the rivers, O **L?**	3378
	3:18	yet I will rejoice in **the L,**	3378
	3:19	**The** Sovereign **L** is my strength;	3378
Zep	1: 1	The word of **the L** that came to Zephaniah	3378
	1: 2	the face of the earth," declares **the L.**	3378
	1: 3	the face of the earth," declares **the L.**	3378
	1: 5	those who bow down and swear by **the L**	3378
	1: 6	those who turn back from following **the L**	3378
	1: 6	and neither seek **the L** nor inquire of him.	3378
	1: 7	Be silent before **the** Sovereign **L,**	3378
	1: 7	for the day of **the L** is near.	3378
	1: 7	**The L** has prepared a sacrifice;	3378
	1:10	"On that day," declares **the L,**	3378
	1:12	who think, '**The L** will do nothing,	3378
	1:14	"The great day of **the L** is near—	3378
	1:14	The cry on the day of **the L** will be bitter,	3378
	1:17	because they have sinned against **the L.**	3378
	2: 2	the fierce anger of **the L** comes upon you,	3378
	2: 3	Seek **the L,** all you humble of the land,	3378
	2: 5	the word of **the L** is against you,	3378
	2: 7	**The L** their God will care for them;	3378
	2: 9	declares **the L** Almighty,	3378
	2:10	the people of **the L** Almighty.	3378
	2:11	**The L** will be awesome to them	3378
	3: 2	She does not trust in **the L,**	3378
	3: 5	**The L** within her is righteous;	3378
	3: 8	Therefore wait for me," declares **the L,**	3378
	3: 9	call on the name of **the L** and serve him	3378
	3:12	who trust in the name of **the L.**	3378
	3:15	**The L** has taken away your punishment,	3378
	3:15	**The L,** the King of Israel, is with you;	3378
	3:17	**The L** your God is with you,	3378
	3:20	before your very eyes," says **the L.**	3378
Hag	1: 1	the word of **the L** came through the prophet Haggai to Zerubbabel	3378
	1: 2	This is what **the L** Almighty says:	3378
	1: 3	Then the word of **the L** came through	3378
	1: 5	Now this is what **the L** Almighty says:	3378
	1: 7	This is what **the L** Almighty says:	3378
	1: 8	in it and be honored," says **the L.**	3378
	1: 9	declares **the L** Almighty.	3378
	1:12	of **the L** their God and the message of	3378
	1:12	because **the L** their God had sent him.	3378
	1:12	And the people feared **the L.**	3378
	1:13	gave this message of **the L** to the people:	3378
	1:13	"I am with you," declares **the L.**	3378
	1:14	So **the L** stirred up the spirit of Zerubbabel	3378
	1:14	to work on the house of **the L** Almighty,	3378
	2: 1	the word of **the L** came through the prophet	3378
	2: 4	be strong, O Zerubbabel,' declares **the L.**	3378
	2: 4	declares **the L,** 'and work.	3378
	2: 4	I am with you,' declares **the L** Almighty.	3378
	2: 6	"This is what **the L** Almighty says:	3378
	2: 7	says **the L** Almighty.	3378
	2: 8	declares **the L** Almighty.	3378
	2: 9	says **the L** Almighty.	3378
	2: 9	declares **the L** Almighty."	3378
	2:10	word of **the L** came to the prophet Haggai:	3378
	2:11	"This is what **the L** Almighty says:	3378
	2:14	in my sight,' declares **the L.**	3378
	2:17	not turn to me,' declares **the L.**	3378
	2:20	The word of **the L** came to Haggai a second time	3378
	2:23	" 'On that day,' declares **the L** Almighty,	3378
	2:23	declares **the L,** 'and I will make you	3378
	2:23	declares **the L** Almighty."	3378
Zec	1: 1	the word of **the L** came to the prophet Zechariah	3378
	1: 2	"**The L** was very angry	3378
	1: 3	This is what **the L** Almighty says:	3378
	1: 3	'Return to me,' declares **the L** Almighty,	3378
Zec	1: 3	says **the L** Almighty.	3378
	1: 4	This is what **the L** Almighty says:	3378
	1: 4	or pay attention to me, declares **the L.**	3378
	1: 6	'**The L** Almighty has done to us what	3378
	1: 7	the word of **the L** came to the prophet Zechariah	3378
	1:10	the ones **the L** has sent to go throughout	3378
	1:11	And they reported to the angel of **the L,**	3378
	1:12	Then the angel of **the L** said,	3378
	1:12	angel of the LORD said, "**L** Almighty,	3378
	1:13	So **the L** spoke kind and comforting words	3378
	1:14	This is what **the L** Almighty says:	3378
	1:16	"Therefore, this is what **the L** says:	3378
	1:16	declares **the L** Almighty.	3378
	1:17	This is what **the L** Almighty says:	3378
	1:17	and **the L** will again comfort Zion	3378
	1:20	Then **the L** showed me four craftsmen.	3378
	2: 5	a wall of fire around it,' declares **the L,**	3378
	2: 6	declares **the L,** "for I have scattered you	3378
	2: 6	the four winds of heaven," declares **the L.**	3378
	2: 8	For this is what **the L** Almighty says:	3378
	2: 9	that **the L** Almighty has sent me.	3378
	2:10	among you," declares **the L.**	3378
	2:11	"Many nations will be joined with **the L**	3378
	2:11	that **the L** Almighty has sent me to you.	3378
	2:12	**The L** will inherit Judah as his portion in	3378
	2:13	Be still before **the L,** all mankind,	3378
	3: 1	before the angel of **the L,**	3378
	3: 2	**The L** said to Satan, "The LORD rebuke you	3378
	3: 2	"**The L** rebuke you, Satan!	3378
	3: 2	**The L,** who has chosen Jerusalem,	3378
	3: 5	while the angel of **the L** stood by.	3378
	3: 6	of **the L** gave this charge to Joshua:	3378
	3: 7	"This is what **the L** Almighty says:	3378
	3: 9	says **the L** Almighty,	3378
	3:10	declares **the L** Almighty."	3378
	4: 6	"This is the word of **the L** to Zerubbabel:	3378
	4: 6	but by my Spirit,' says **the L** Almighty.	3378
	4: 8	Then the word of **the L** came to me:	3378
	4: 9	that **the L** Almighty has sent me to you.	3378
	4:10	"(These seven are the eyes of **the L,**	3378
	5: 4	**The L** Almighty declares,	3378
	6: 9	The word of **the L** came to me:	3378
	6:12	Tell him this is what **the L** Almighty says:	3378
	6:12	and build the temple of **the L.**	3378
	6:13	he who will build the temple of **the L,**	3378
	6:14	as a memorial in the temple of **the L.**	3378
	6:15	and help to build the temple of **the L,**	3378
	6:15	that **the L** Almighty has sent me to you.	3378
	6:15	if you diligently obey **the L** your God."	3378
	7: 1	the word of **the L** came to Zechariah on	3378
	7: 2	together with their men, to entreat **the L**	3378
	7: 3	the priests of the house of **the L** Almighty	3378
	7: 4	the word of **the L** Almighty came to me:	3378
	7: 7	Are these not the words **the L** proclaimed	3378
	7: 8	word of **the L** came again to Zechariah:	3378
	7: 9	"This is what **the L** Almighty says:	3378
	7:12	to the words that **the L** Almighty had sent	3378
	7:12	So **the L** Almighty was very angry.	3378
	7:13	I would not listen,' says **the L** Almighty.	3378
	8: 1	the word of **the L** Almighty came to me.	3378
	8: 2	This is what **the L** Almighty says:	3378
	8: 3	This is what **the L** says:	3378
	8: 3	mountain of **the L** Almighty will be called	3378
	8: 4	This is what **the L** Almighty says:	3378
	8: 6	This is what **the L** Almighty says:	3378
	8: 6	declares **the L** Almighty.	3378
	8: 7	This is what **the L** Almighty says:	3378
	8: 9	This is what **the L** Almighty says:	3378
	8: 9	for the house of **the L** Almighty,	3378
	8:11	declares **the L** Almighty.	3378
	8:14	This is what **the L** Almighty says:	3378
	8:14	says **the L** Almighty,	3378
	8:17	I hate all this," declares **the L.**	3378
	8:18	the word of **the L** Almighty came to me.	3378
	8:19	This is what **the L** Almighty says:	3378
	8:20	This is what **the L** Almighty says:	3378
	8:21	'Let us go at once to entreat **the L**	3378
	8:21	the LORD and seek **the L** Almighty.	3378
	8:22	to Jerusalem to seek **the L** Almighty and	3378
	8:23	This is what **the L** Almighty says:	3378
	9: 1	The word of **the L** is against	3378
	9: 1	and all the tribes of Israel are on **the L—**	3378
	9:14	Then **the L** will appear over them;	3378
	9:14	**The** Sovereign **L** will sound the trumpet;	3378
	9:15	and **the L** Almighty will shield them.	3378
	9:16	**The L** their God will save them on	3378
	10: 1	Ask **the L** for rain in the springtime;	3378
	10: 1	it is **the L** who makes the storm clouds.	3378
	10: 3	for **the L** Almighty will care for his flock,	3378
	10: 5	Because **the L** is with them,	3378
	10: 6	for I am **the L** their God	3378
	10: 7	their hearts will rejoice in **the L.**	3378
	10:12	in **the L** and in his name they will walk,"	3378
	10:12	in his name they will walk," declares **the L.**	3378
	11: 4	This is what **the L** my God says:	3378
	11: 5	Those who sell them say, 'Praise **the L,**	3378
	11: 6	on the people of the land," declares **the L.**	3378
	11:11	knew it was the word of **the L.**	3378
	11:13	And **the L** said to me,	3378
	11:13	and threw them into the house of **the L** to	3378
	11:15	Then **the L** said to me,	3378
	12: 1	the word of **the L** concerning Israel.	3378
	12: 1	**The L,** who stretches out the heavens,	3378
	12: 4	its rider with madness," declares **the L.**	3378
	12: 5	because **the L** Almighty is their God.'	3378
	12: 7	"**The L** will save the dwellings	3378

†**LORD** distinguishes the proper name of God, *Yahweh*, indicated in the NIV by "LORD," from the words translated "Lord" and "lord," indexed under the heading ***LORD**, pages 683-86.

Zec 12: 8 that day **the L** will shield those who live 3378
12: 8 the Angel of **the L** going before them. 3378
13: 2 declares **the L** Almighty. 3378
13: 7 declares **the L** Almighty. 3378
13: 8 In the whole land," declares **the L,** 3378
13: 9 and they will say, '**The L** is our God.' " 3378
14: 1 A day of **the L** is coming 3378
14: 3 Then **the L** will go out and fight 3378
14: 5 Then **the L** my God will come, 3378
14: 7 a day known to **the L.** 3378
14: 9 **The L** will be king over the whole earth. 3378
14: 9 On that day there will be one **L,** 3378
14:12 the plague with which **the L** will strike all 3378
14:13 On that day men will be stricken by **the L** 3378
14:16 to worship the King, **the L** Almighty, and 3378
14:17 **the L** Almighty, they will have no rain. 3378
14:18 **The L** will bring on them 3378
14:20 HOLY TO THE **L** will be inscribed on 3378
14:21 and Judah will be holy to **the L** Almighty, 3378
14:21 in the house of **the L** Almighty. 3378
Mal 1: 1 word of **the L** to Israel through Malachi. 3378
1: 2 "I have loved you," says **the L.** 3378
1: 2 **the L** says. "Yet I have loved Jacob, 3378
1: 4 But this is what **the L** Almighty says: 3378
1: 4 a people always under the wrath of **the L.** 3378
1: 5 'Great is **the L**—even beyond the borders 3378
1: 6 the respect due me?" says **the L** Almighty. 3378
1: 8 he accept you?" says **the L** Almighty. 3378
1: 9 he accept you?"—says **the L** Almighty. 3378
1:10 not pleased with you," says **the L** Almighty, 3378
1:11 my name will be great among the nations," says **the L** Almighty. 3378
1:13 you sniff at it contemptuously, says **the L** Almighty. 3378
1:13 accept them from your hands?" says **the L.** 3378
1:14 I am a great king," says **the L** Almighty, 3378
2: 2 to honor my name," says **the L** Almighty, 3378
2: 4 covenant with Levi may continue," says **the L** Almighty. 3378
2: 7 he is the messenger of **the L** Almighty. 3378
2: 8 covenant with Levi," says **the L** Almighty. 3378
2:11 the sanctuary **the L** loves, 3378
2:12 may **the L** cut him off from the tents 3378
2:12 he brings offerings to **the L** Almighty. 3378
2:14 It is because **the L** is acting as the witness 3378
2:15 Has not [the L] made them one? NIH
2:16 "I hate divorce," says **the L** God of Israel, 3378
2:16 as with his garment," says **the L** Almighty. 3378
2:17 You have wearied **the L** with your words. 3378
2:17 who do evil are good in the eyes of **the L,** 3378
3: 1 will come," says **the L** Almighty. 3378
3: 3 **the L** will have men who will bring offerings in righteousness, 3378
3: 4 will be acceptable to **the L,** 3378
3: 5 but do not fear me," says **the L** Almighty. 3378
3: 6 "I **the L** do not change. 3378
3: 7 I will return to you," says **the L** Almighty. 3378
3:10 Test me in this," says **the L** Almighty, 3378
3:11 not cast their fruit," says **the L** Almighty. 3378
3:12 a delightful land," says **the L** Almighty. 3378
3:13 harsh things against me," says **the L.** 3378
3:14 like mourners before **the L** Almighty? 3378
3:16 Then those who feared **the L** talked 3378
3:16 and **the L** listened and heard. 3378
3:16 concerning those who feared **the L** 3378
3:17 "They will be mine," says **the L** Almighty, 3378
4: 1 set them on fire," says **the L** Almighty. 3378
4: 3 I do these things," says **the L** Almighty. 3378
4: 5 and dreadful day of **the L** comes. 3378

†LORD'S (278) [†LORD]

Ge 4:16 from **the L** presence and lived in the land 3378
38: 7 Judah's firstborn, was wicked in **the L** sight 3378
38:10 What he did was wicked in **the L** sight; 3378
Ex 4:14 Then **the L** anger burned against Moses 3378
9:29 you may know that the earth is **the L.** 3378+4200
12:11 Eat it in haste; it is **the L** Passover. 3378+4200
12:41 all **the L** divisions left Egypt. 3378
12:48 to celebrate **the L** Passover must 3378+4200
16: 3 only we had died by **the L** hand in Egypt! 3378
24: 3 the people all **the L** words and laws, 3378
29:11 in **the L** presence at the entrance to 3378
34:34 But whenever he entered **the L** presence 3378
Lev 3:16 All the fat is **the L.** 3378+4200
4: 2 forbidden in any of **the L** commands— 3378
4:13 forbidden in any of **the L** commands, 3378
4:27 forbidden in any of **the L** commands, 3378
5:15 in regard to any of **the L** holy things, 3378
5:17 forbidden in any of **the L** commands, 3378
6:22 It is **the L** regular share and is to 3378+4200
10: 7 because **the L** anointing oil is on you." 3378
23: 4 " 'These are **the L** appointed feasts, 3378
23: 5 **The L** Passover begins at twilight on 3378+4200
23: 6 **the L** Feast of Unleavened Bread 3378+4200
23:34 **the L** Feast of Tabernacles begins, 3378+4200
23:37 (" 'These are **the L** appointed feasts, 3378
23:38 in addition to those for **the L** Sabbaths 3378
27:26 whether an ox or a sheep, it is **the L.** 3378+4200
Nu 3:39 at **the L** command by Moses and Aaron 3378
4:37 to **the L** command through Moses. 3378
4:41 according to **the L** command. 3378
4:45 to **the L** command through Moses. 3378
4:49 At **the L** command through Moses, 3378
9: 7 be kept from presenting **the L** offering 3378
9:10 may still celebrate **the L** Passover. 3378+4200
9:13 because he did not present **the L** offering 3378
Nu 9:14 to celebrate **the L** Passover must do so 3378+4200
9:18 At **the L** command the Israelites set out, 3378
9:19 the Israelites obeyed **the L** order and did 3378
9:20 at **the L** command they would encamp, 3378
9:23 At **the L** command they encamped, 3378
9:23 and at **the L** command they set out. 3378
9:23 They obeyed **the L** order, 3378
10:13 at **the L** command through Moses. 3378
11:23 "Is **the L** arm too short? 3378
11:29 I wish that all **the L** people were prophets 3378
13: 3 at **the L** command Moses sent them out 3378
14:41 "Why are you disobeying **the L** command? 3378
14:44 nor the ark of **the L** covenant moved from 3378
15:23 of **the L** commands to you through him, 3378
15:31 Because he has despised **the L** word 3378
16: 3 you set yourselves above **the L** assembly?" 3378
16: 9 the work at **the L** tabernacle and to stand 3378
16:41 "You have killed **the L** people," 3378
17: 9 from **the L** presence to all the Israelites. 3378
18:26 a tenth of that tithe as **the L** offering. 3378
18:28 From these tithes you must give **the L** portion to Aaron 3378
18:29 as **the L** portion the best and holiest part 3378
19:13 to purify himself defiles **the L** tabernacle. 3378
20: 4 Why did you bring **the L** community 3378
20: 9 Moses took the staff from **the L** presence, 3378
25: 3 And **the L** anger burned against them. 3378
25: 4 so that **the L** fierce anger may turn away 3378
27:17 so **the L** people will not be like sheep 3378
28:16 of the first month **the L** Passover is to 3378+4200
31: 3 to carry out **the L** vengeance on them. 3378
31:16 so that a plague struck **the L** people. 3378
31:29 to Eleazar the priest as **the L** part. 3378
31:30 for the care of **the L** tabernacle." 3378
31:41 to Eleazar the priest as **the L** part, 3378
31:47 for the care of **the L** tabernacle. 3378
32:10 **The L** anger was aroused that day 3378
32:13 **The L** anger burned against Israel 3378
33: 2 At **the L** command Moses recorded 3378
33:38 At **the L** command Aaron the priest went 3378
36: 5 at **the L** command Moses gave this order 3378
Dt 1:43 You rebelled against **the L** command and 3378
2:15 **The L** hand was against them 3378
6:18 Do what is right and good in **the L** sight, 3378
7: 4 and **the L** anger will burn against you 3378
9: 8 At Horeb you aroused **the L** wrath so 3378
9:18 doing what was evil in **the L** sight and 3378
10:13 to observe **the L** commands and decrees 3378
11:17 Then **the L** anger will burn against you, 3378
15: 2 because **the L** time for canceling debts 3378+4200
18: 5 and minister in **the L** name always. 3378
29:27 **the L** anger burned against this land, 3378
32: 9 For **the L** portion is his people, 3378
33:21 he carried out **the L** righteous will, 3378
Jos 5:15 The commander of **the L** army replied, 3378
6: 8 the ark of **the L** covenant followed them. 3378
6:24 and iron into the treasury of **the L** house. 3378
7: 1 So **the L** anger burned against Israel. 3378
15:13 with **the L** command to him, Joshua gave 3378
17: 4 according to **the L** command. 3378
21:45 of all **the L** good promises to the house 3378
22:19 come over to **the L** land, 3378
22:19 where **the L** tabernacle stands, 3378
22:28 Look at the replica of **the L** altar, 3378
22:31 the Israelites from **the L** hand." 3378
23:16 **the L** anger will burn against you, 3378
Jdg 2:17 the way of obedience to **the L** commands. 3378
3: 4 to see whether they would obey **the L** commands, 3378
11:31 from the Ammonites will be **the L,** 3378+4200
18: 6 Your journey has **the L** approval." 3378
Ru 1:13 **the L** hand has gone out against me!" 3378
1Sa 1: 9 a chair by the doorpost of **the L** temple. 3378
2: 8 the foundations of the earth are **the L;** 3378+4200
2:17 was very great in **the L** sight, 3378
2:17 for they were treating **the L** offering 3378
2:24 that I hear spreading among **the L** people. 3378
2:25 for it was **the L** will to put them to death. 3378
4: 3 the ark of **the L** covenant from Shiloh, 3378
4: 5 of **the L** covenant came into the camp, 3378
5: 6 **The L** hand was heavy upon the people 3378
5: 9 **the L** hand was against that city, 3378
13:12 and I have not sought **the L** favor.' 3378
13:14 you have not kept **the L** command." 3378
14: 3 the son of Eli, **the L** priest in Shiloh. 3378
15:13 I have carried out **the L** instructions." 3378
15:24 I violated **the L** command 3378
16: 6 "Surely **the L** anointed stands here before 2257[S]
17:47 for the battle is **the L,** 3378+4200
24: 6 **the L** anointed, or lift my hand against him; 3378
24:10 because he is **the L** anointed.' 3378
25:28 because he fights **the L** battles. 3378
26: 9 Who can lay a hand on **the L** anointed 3378
26:11 that I should lay a hand on **the L** anointed. 3378
26:16 not guard your master, **the L** anointed. 3378
26:19 from my share in **the L** inheritance 3378
26:23 I would not lay a hand on **the L** anointed. 3378
30:26 from the plunder of **the L** enemies." 3378
2Sa 1:14 to destroy **the L** anointed?" 3378
1:16 'I killed **the L** anointed.' " 3378
6: 7 **The L** anger burned against Uzzah 3378
6: 8 because **the L** wrath had broken out 3378
6:21 over **the L** people Israel— 3378
15:25 If I find favor in **the L** eyes, 3378
19:21 He cursed **the L** anointed." 3378
20:19 to swallow up **the L** inheritance?" 3378
21: 3 so that you will bless **the L** inheritance?" 3378
2Sa 21: 6 of Saul—**the L** chosen one." 3378
1Ki 2:33 there be **the L** peace forever." 3378+4946+6640
7:48 the furnishings that were in **the L** temple: 3378
7:51 in the treasuries of **the L** temple. 3378
8: 1 up the ark of **the L** covenant from Zion, 3378
8: 6 the ark of **the L** covenant to its place in 3378
9:15 to build **the L** temple, 3378
10: 9 Because of **the L** eternal love for Israel, 3378
11:10 Solomon did not keep **the L** command. 3378
14:28 Whenever the king went to **the L** temple, 3378
15: 5 **the L** commands all the days of his life— NIH
15:18 of **the L** temple and of his own palace. 3378
18: 4 Jezebel was killing off **the L** prophets, 3378
18:13 a hundred of **the L** prophets in two caves, 3378
18:18 You have abandoned **the L** commands 3378
18:22 "I am the only one of **the L** prophets left, 3378+4200
2Ki 9: 6 'I anoint you king over **the L** people Israel. 3378
9: 7 and the blood of all **the L** servants shed 3378
11:17 that they would be **the L** people. 3378+4200
13: 3 So **the L** anger burned against Israel, 3378
13: 4 Then Jehoahaz sought **the L** favor, 3378
13:17 "**The L** arrow of victory, 3378+4200
20: 9 "This is **the L** sign to you that 907+3378+4946
22:13 Great is **the L** anger that burns against us 3378
24: 3 to Judah according to **the L** command, 3378
24:20 of **the L** anger that all this happened 3378
1Ch 2: 3 Judah's firstborn, was wicked in **the L** sight 3378
13:10 **The L** anger burned against Uzzah, 3378
13:11 because **the L** wrath had broken out 3378
2Ch 1: 3 which Moses **the L** servant had made in 3378
5: 2 up the ark of **the L** covenant from Zion, 3378
5: 7 the ark of **the L** covenant to its place in 3378
7: 6 with **the L** musical instruments, 3378
12:11 Whenever the king went to **the L** temple, 3378
12:12 **the L** anger turned from him, 3378
15: 8 in front of the portico of **the L** temple. 3378
16: 2 of **the L** temple and of his own palace 3378
23:16 and the king would be **the L** people. 3378+4200
23:19 of **the L** temple so that no one who was 3378
24:12 and carpenters to restore **the L** temple, 3378
24:14 made articles for **the L** temple: 3378
24:20 'Why do you disobey **the L** commands? 3378
24:21 to death in the courtyard of **the L** temple. 3378
26:19 before the incense altar in **the L** temple, 3378
28:11 for **the L** fierce anger rests on you." 3378
28:24 the doors of **the L** temple and set up altars 3378
29: 6 from **the L** dwelling place 3378
29:16 of **the L** temple everything unclean 3378
29:19 They are now in front of **the L** altar." 3378
30:21 accompanied by **the L** instruments 3378+4200
31: 2 at the gates of **the L** dwelling. 3378
32:25 therefore **the L** wrath was on him and NIH
32:26 therefore **the L** wrath did not come 3378
34:10 to supervise the work on **the L** temple. 3378
34:21 Great is **the L** anger that is poured out 3378
35: 2 in the service of **the L** temple. 3378
36:18 and the treasures of **the L** temple and 3378
Ezr 3: 6 the foundation of **the L** temple had not 3378
Ps 24: 1 The earth is **the L,** and everything in it 3378+4200
32:10 but **the L** unfailing love surrounds 3378
37:20 **The L** enemies will be like the beauty of 3378
89: 1 I will sing of **the L** great love forever; 3378
103:17 **the L** love is with those who fear him, 3378
109:20 **the L** payment to my accusers, 907+3378+4946
118:15 "**The L** right hand has done mighty things! 3378
118:16 **The L** right hand is lifted high; 3378
118:16 **the L** right hand has done mighty things!" 3378
Pr 3:11 do not despise **the L** discipline and do 3378
3:33 **The L** curse is on the house of the wicked, 3378
19:21 but it is **the L** purpose that prevails. 3378
22:14 he who is under **the L** wrath will fall into it. 3378
Isa 2: 2 the mountain of **the L** temple will be established 3378
5:25 Therefore **the L** anger burns 3378
14: 2 and maidservants in **the L** land. 3378
24:14 from the west they acclaim **the L** majesty. 3378
30: 9 to listen to **the L** instruction. 3378
38: 7 " 'This is **the L** sign to you that 907+3378+4946
40: 2 from **the L** hand double for all her sins. 3378
44: 5 '**The L,**' and will take the name Israel. 3378+4200
48:14 **The L** chosen ally will carry out his purpose 3378
49: 4 Yet what is due me is in **the L** hand, 3378
53:10 Yet it was **the L** will to crush him 3378
55:13 This will be for **the L** renown, 3378+4200
58:13 a delight and **the L** holy day honorable, 3378
61: 2 to proclaim the year of **the L** favor 3378+4200
62: 3 be a crown of splendor in **the L** hand, 3378
Jer 7: 2 "Stand at the gate of **the L** house 3378
12:13 because of **the L** fierce anger." 3378
13:17 because **the L** flock will be taken captive. 3378
19:14 in the court of **the L** temple and said to all 3378
20: 2 of Benjamin at **the L** temple. 3378
20: 3 "**The L** name for you is not Pashhur, 3378
23:35 'What is **the L** answer?' 3378
23:37 'What is **the L** answer to you?' 3378
25:17 from **the L** hand and made all the nations 3378
25:38 and because of **the L** fierce anger. 2257[S]
26: 2 of **the L** house and speak to all the people 3378
26: 9 Why do you prophesy in **the L** name 3378
26:10 of the New Gate of **the L** house. 3378
27:16 from **the L** house will be brought back 3378
28: 3 to this place all the articles of **the L** house 3378
28: 6 by bringing the articles of **the L** house 3378
36: 5 I cannot go to **the L** temple. 3378
36: 8 at **the L** temple he read the words of 3378
36:10 at **the L** temple the words of Jeremiah 3378

†LORD distinguishes the proper name of God, *Yahweh*, indicated in the NIV by "LORD," from the words translated "Lord" and "lord," indexed under the heading ***LORD**, pages 683-86.
†LORD'S distinguishes the proper name of God, *Yahweh's*, indicated in the NIV by "LORD's" from the words translated "Lord's" and "lord's," indexed under the heading ***LORD'S**, page 686.

Jer 43: 4 the people disobeyed **the L** command 3378
48:10 on him who is lax in doing **the L** work! 3378
50:13 of **the L** anger she will not be inhabited 3378
51: 6 It is time for **the L** vengeance; 3378+4200
51: 7 Babylon was a gold cup in **the L** hand; 3378
51:29 **the L** purposes against Babylon stand— 3378
51:51 the holy places of **the L** house." 3378
52: 3 because of **the L** anger that all this happened to Jerusalem 3378
La 2:22 In the day of **the L** anger no one escaped 3378
3:22 of **the L** great love we are not consumed, 3378
4:20 **The L** anointed, our very life breath, 3378
Eze 7:19 to save them in the day of **the L** wrath. 3378
10:19 to the east gate of **the L** house, 3378
36:20 'These are **the L** people, 3378
Hos 9: 3 They will not remain in **the L** land; 3378
Joel 3:18 of **the L** house and will water the valley 3378
Ob 1:21 And the kingdom will be **the L.** 3378+4200
Mic 4: 1 the mountain of **the L** temple will be established 3378
6: 2 Hear, O mountains, **the L** accusation; 3378
7: 9 I will bear **the L** wrath, 3378
Hab 2:16 The cup from **the L** right hand is coming 3378
Zep 1: 8 On the day of **the L** sacrifice I will punish 3378
1:18 to save them on the day of **the L** wrath. 3378
2: 2 the day of **the L** wrath comes upon you. 3378
2: 3 be sheltered on the day of **the L** anger. 3378
Hag 1: 2 yet come for **the L** house to be built.'" 3378
1:13 Then Haggai, **the L** messenger, 3378
2:15 stone was laid on another in **the L** temple. 3378
2:18 the foundation of **the L** temple was laid. 3378
Zec 13: 3 you have told lies in **the L** name.' 3378
14:20 cooking pots in **the L** house will be like 3378
Mal 1: 7 saying that **the L** table is contemptible. 3378
2:13 You flood **the L** altar with tears. 3378

LORDED (1) [*LORD]

Ne 5:15 Their assistants also **l it over** the people. 8948

LORDING (1) [*LORD]

1Pe 5: 3 not **l it over** those entrusted to you, *2894*

LORDS (10) [*LORD]

Ge 19: 2 "My **l,**" he said, "please turn aside 123
19:18 But Lot said to them, "No, my **l,** please! 123
Dt 10:17 your God is God of gods and Lord of **l,** 123
Ps 136: 3 Give thanks to the Lord of **l:** 123
Ecc 8: 9 a man **l it over** others to his own hurt. 8948
Isa 26:13 other **l** besides you have ruled over us, 123
1Co 8: 5 (as indeed there are many "gods" and many "**l**"), *3261*
1Ti 6:15 the King of kings and Lord *of* **l,** *3259*
Rev 17:14 because he is Lord *of* **l** and King of kings— *3261*
19:16 KING OF KINGS AND LORD OF **L.** *3261*

LORDSHIP (KJV) See LORD OVER

LOSE (36) [LOSES, LOSS, LOSSES, LOST]

Ge 26: 9 "Because I thought *I* might **l** *my* **life** 4637
27:45 Why *should I* **l** both of you in one day?" 8897
Dt 1:28 Our brothers *have* **made** us **l** heart. 5022
Jdg 18:25 *you* and your family *will* **l** your lives." 665
1Sa 17:32 *"Let* no one **l** heart on account 5877
2Sa 22:46 They all **l heart;** they come trembling 5570
Ps 18:45 They all **l heart;** they come trembling 5570
Pr 25:10 and *you will* never **l** your bad reputation. 8740
Isa 7: 4 *Do* not **l** heart because of these two 8216
19: 3 The Egyptians *will* **l heart,** 928+1327+7931+8120
19: 9 the weavers of fine linen will **l** hope. NIH
Jer 4: 9 "the king and the officials *will* **l** heart, 6
17: 4 Through your own fault *you will* **l** 9023
51:46 *Do* not **l** heart or be afraid 8216
Da 11:30 and *he will* **l heart.** 3874
Zec 9: 5 Gaza *will* **l** her king and Ashkelon will 6
Mt 5:29 better for you to **l** one part of your body than *660*
5:30 better for you to **l** one part of your body than *660*
10:39 Whoever finds his life **l** it, *660*
10:42 *he will* certainly not **l** his reward." *660*
16:25 whoever wants to save his life *will* **l** it, *660*
Mk 8:35 whoever wants to save his life *will* **l** it, *660*
9:41 to Christ *will* certainly not **l** his reward. *660*
Lk 9:24 whoever wants to save his life *will* **l** it, *660*
9:25 and yet **l** or forfeit his very self? *660*
16: 4 when *I* **l** my job here, *1666+3496*
17:33 Whoever tries to keep his life *will* **l** it, *660*
Jn 6:39 *I shall* **l** none of all that he has given me, *660*
12:25 The man who loves his life *will* **l** it, *660*
Ac 19:27 our trade *will* **l** its **good name,** *591+1650+2262*
27:34 of you *will* **l** a single hair from his head." *660*
2Co 4: 1 *we do* not **l heart.** *1591*
4:16 Therefore *we do* not **l heart.** *1591*
Heb 12: 3 that you will not grow weary and **l** heart. *1725*
12: 5 and *do* not **l heart** when he rebukes you, *1725*
2Jn 1: 8 that *you do* not **l** what you have worked *660*

LOSES (13) [LOSE]

Dt 22: 3 or his cloak or anything he **l.** 6+8
1Sa 20: 7 But if *he* **l** his **temper,** 3013+3013
Isa 44:12 He gets hungry and **l** his strength; 401
Mt 5:13 But if the salt **l its saltiness,** *3701*
10:39 whoever **l** his life for my sake will find it. *660*
16:25 but whoever **l** his life for me will find it. *660*
Mk 8:35 but whoever **l** his life for me and for *660*
9:50 "Salt is good, but if it **l** its saltiness, *1181*
Lk 9:24 but whoever **l** his life for me will save it. *660*
14:34 "Salt is good, but if *it* **l** its saltiness, *3701*
15: 4 of you has a hundred sheep and **l** one *660*
15: 8 a woman has ten silver coins and **l** one. *660*
17:33 and whoever **l** his life will preserve it. *660*

LOSS (18) [LOSE]

Ge 31:39 **I bore the l** myself. 2627
Ex 21:19 the injured man for the **l** of his **time** 8700
21:34 the owner of the pit *must* **pay for the l;** 8966
22:15 the money paid for the hire covers the **l.** NIH
Isa 47: 8 be a widow or suffer the **l of children.'** 8890
47: 9 **l of children** and widowhood. 8890
Jer 22:10 for the dead [king] or **mourn** his **l;** 5653
Da 6: 2 to them so that the king *might* not **suffer l.** 10472
Jn 11:19 to comfort them in the **l** of their brother. *NIG*
13:22 **at a l** to know which of them he meant. *679*
Ac 25:20 I *was* **at a l** how to investigate such matters *679*
27:10 and bring great **l** to ship and cargo, *2422*
27:21 have spared yourselves this damage and **l.** *2422*
Ro 11:12 and their **l** means riches for the Gentiles, *2488*
1Co 3:15 If it is burned up, *he will* **suffer l;** *2423*
Php 3: 7 to my profit I now consider **l** for the sake *2422*
3: 8 a **l** compared to the surpassing greatness *2422*
Heb 6: 6 because to their **l** they are crucifying *NIG*

LOSSES (4) [LOSE]

1Sa 4:17 and the army has suffered heavy **l.** 4487
23: 5 He inflicted heavy **l** on the Philistines 4804
1Ki 20:21 and inflicted heavy **l** on the Arameans. 4804
2Ch 13:17 and his men inflicted heavy **l** on them, 4804

LOST (45) [LOSE]

Ge 34:19 **l** no **time** in doing what they said, 336
Ex 14: 5 the Israelites go and have **l** their services!" 4946
22: 9 or any other **l** *property* 8
Lev 6: 3 or if he finds **l property** and lies about it, 8
6: 4 or the **l property** he found, 8
13:40 When a man *has* **l** his **hair** and is bald, 5307+8031
13:41 If *he has* **l** his **hair** from the front 5307+8031
Nu 11: 6 But now we *have* **l** our appetite; 3313
17:12 *We are* **l,** we are all lost! 6
17:12 We are lost, we *are* all **l!** 6
1Sa 4:10 Israel **l** thirty thousand foot soldiers. 4946+5877
9: 3 belonging to Saul's father Kish *were* **l,** 6
9:20 As for the donkeys you **l** three days ago, 6
25:18 Abigail **l no time.** 4554
2Sa 4: 1 had died in Hebron, he **l courage,** 3338+8332
1Ki 20:25 raise an army like the one you **l** 907+4946+5877
Ne 6:16 **l** their **self-confidence,** 928+4394+5877+6524
Ps 73: 2 I *had* nearly **l** my foothold. 9161
119:176 I have strayed like a **l** sheep. 6
Ecc 5:14 or wealth **l** through some misfortune, 6
Jer 18:18 of the law by the priest *will* not *be* **l,** 6
50: 6 "My people have been **l** sheep; 6
La 4: 1 How the gold *has* **l** *its* **luster,** 6670
Eze 7:26 of the law by the priest *will be* **l,** 6
34: 4 the strays or searched for the **l.** 6
34:16 I will search for the **l** and bring back 6
Zec 11:16 over the land who will not care for the **l,** 3948
Mt 10: 6 Go rather to the **l** sheep of Israel. *660*
15:24 "I was sent only to the **l** sheep of Israel." *660*
18:14 that any of these little ones *should be* **l.** *660*
Lk 15: 4 the open country and go after the **l** sheep *660*
15: 6 I have found my **l** sheep.' *660*
15: 9 I have found my **l** coin.' *660*
15:24 he was **l** and is found.' *660*
15:32 he was **l** and is found.'" *660*
19:10 to seek and to save what *was* **l."** *660*
Jn 17:12 None *has been* **l** except the one doomed *660*
18: 9 *"I have* not **l** one of those you gave me." *660*
Ac 27: 9 Much time *had been* **l,** *1335*
27:22 because not one of you will be **l;** *613*
1Co 15:18 also who have fallen asleep in Christ *are* **l.** *660*
Eph 4:19 *Having* **l all sensitivity,** they have given *556*
Php 3: 8 for whose sake *I have* **l** all things. *2423*
Col 2:19 He has **l connection with** the Head, *3195+4024*
Rev 12: 8 and they **l** their place in heaven. *NIG*

LOT (87) [LOT'S, LOTS, PUR]

Ge 11:27 And Haran became the father of **L.** 4288
11:31 his grandson **L** son of Haran, 4288
12: 4 and **L** went with him. 4288
12: 5 He took his wife Sarai, his nephew **L,** 4288
13: 1 and **L** went with him. 4288
13: 5 Now **L,** who was moving about 4288
13: 7 Abram's herdsmen and the herdsmen of **L.** 4288
13: 8 So Abram said to **L,** 4288
13:10 **L** looked up and saw that the whole plain 4288
13:11 So **L** chose for himself the whole plain of 4288
13:12 while **L** lived among the cities of the plain 4288
13:14 to Abram after **L** had parted from him, 4288
14:12 They also carried off Abram's nephew **L** 4288
14:16 the goods and brought back his relative **L** 4288
19: 1 **L** was sitting in the gateway of the city. 4288
19: 5 They called to **L,** "Where are the men 4288
19: 6 **L** went outside to meet them and shut 4288
19: 9 on **L** and moved forward to break down 4288
19:10 and pulled **L** back into the house and shut 4288
19:12 The two men said to **L,** 4288
19:14 **L** went out and spoke to his sons-in-law, 4288
19:15 the angels urged **L,** saying, "Hurry! 4288
19:18 But **L** said to them, "No, my lords, please! 4288
Ge 19:23 By the time **L** reached Zoar, 4288
19:29 and he brought **L** out of the catastrophe 4288
19:29 the cities where **L** had lived. 4288
19:30 **L** and his two daughters left Zoar 4288
Lev 16: 8 one **l** for the LORD and the other for 1598
16: 9 Aaron shall bring the goat whose **l** falls to 1598
16:10 the goat chosen by **l** as the scapegoat shall 1598
Nu 26:55 Be sure that the land is distributed by **l.** 1598
26:56 Each inheritance is to be distributed by **l** 1598
33:54 Distribute the land by **l,** 1598
33:54 Whatever falls to them by **l** will be theirs. 1598
34:13 "Assign this land by **l** as an inheritance. 1598
36: 2 as an inheritance to the Israelites by **l,** 1598
Dt 2: 9 I have given Ar to the descendants of **L** as 4288
2:19 as a possession to the descendants of **L."** 4288
Jos 14: 2 Their inheritances were assigned by **l** to 1598
18:11 The **l** came up *for* the tribe of Benjamin, 1598
19: 1 second **l** came out for the tribe of Simeon, 1598
19:10 The third **l** came up for Zebulun, 1598
19:17 The fourth **l** came out for Issachar, 1598
19:24 The fifth **l** came out for the tribe of Asher, 1598
19:32 The sixth **l** came out for Naphtali, 1598
19:40 seventh **l** came out for the tribe of Dan, 1598
19:51 of the tribal clans of Israel assigned by **l** 1598
21: 4 The first **l** came out for the Kohathites, 1598
21:10 because the first **l** fell to them): 1598
Jdg 20: 9 We'll go up against it as the **l** directs. 1598
1Sa 14:41 And Jonathan and Saul were taken by **l,** NIH
14:42 the **l** between me and Jonathan my son." NIH
1Ch 6:54 because the first **l** was for them): 1598
24: 7 The first **l** fell to Jehoiarib, 1598
25: 9 The first **l,** which was for Asaph, 1598
26:14 The **l** for the East Gate fell to Shelemiah. 1598
26:14 and the **l** for the North Gate fell to him. 1598
26:15 **l** for the South Gate fell to Obed-Edom, NIH
26:15 the **l** for the storehouse fell to his sons. NIH
Est 3: 7 they cast the pur (that is, the **l**) 1598
3: 7 And the **l** fell on the twelfth month, NIH
9:24 cast the pur (that is, the **l**) for their ruin 1598
Job 31: 2 For what is man's **l** *from* God above, 2750
Ps 11: 6 a scorching wind will be their **l.** 3926+4987
16: 5 you have made my **l** secure. 1598
50:18 you throw in your **l** with adulterers. 2750
83: 8 to lend strength to the descendants of **L.** 4288
Pr 1:14 throw in your **l** with us, and we will share 1598
6:33 Blows and disgrace *are his* **l,** 5162
16:33 The **l** is cast into the lap, but its every 1598
18:18 Casting the **l** settles disputes 1598
Ecc 3:22 because that is his **l.** 2750
5:18 life God has given him—for this is his **l.** 2750
5:19 to accept his **l** and be happy in his work— 2750
9: 9 For this is your **l** in life and 2750
Isa 17:14 the **l** of those who plunder us. 1598
57: 6 are your portion; they, they are your **l.** 1598
Jer 13:25 This is your **l,** the portion I have decreed 1598
Eze 21:22 Into his right hand will come the **l** 7877
Jnh 1: 7 They cast lots and the **l** fell on Jonah. 1598
Mic 2: 5 of the LORD to divide the land by **l.** 1598
Lk 1: 9 *he was* **chosen by l,** according to *3275*
17:28 "It was the same in the days *of* **L.** *3397*
17:29 But the day **L** left Sodom, *3397*
Jn 19:24 *"Let's* **decide by l** who will get it." *3275*
Ac 1:26 they cast lots, and the **l** fell to Matthias; *3102*
2Pe 2: 7 and if he rescued **L,** a righteous man, *3397*

LOT'S (3) [LOT]

Ge 19:26 But **L** wife looked back, 2257[S]
19:36 So both of **L** daughters became pregnant 4288
Lk 17:32 Remember **L** wife! *3397*

LOTAN (5) [LOTAN'S]

Ge 36:20 **L,** Shobal, Zibeon, Anah, 4289
36:22 The sons of **L:** Hori and Homam. 4289
36:29 These were the Horite chiefs: **L,** Shobal, 4289
1Ch 1:38 The sons of Seir: **L,** Shobal, Zibeon, 4289
1:39 The sons of **L:** Hori and Homam. 4289

LOTAN'S (2) [LOTAN]

Ge 36:22 Timna was **L** sister. 4289
1Ch 1:39 Timna was **L** sister. 4289

LOTHE (KJV) See LOATHE, NOT ABLE

LOTIONS (4)

2Sa 12:20 **put on l** and changed his clothes, 6057
14: 2 and don't use any **cosmetic l.** 9043
Da 10: 3 and *I* **used** no **l at all** 6057+6057
Am 6: 6 by the bowlful and use the finest **l,** 9043

LOTS (26) [LOT]

Lev 16: 8 He is to cast **l** for the two goats— 1598
Jos 18: 6 and I will cast **l** for you in the presence of 1598
18: 8 and I will cast **l** for you here at Shiloh in 1598
18:10 Joshua then cast **l** for them in Shiloh in 1598
1Ch 24: 5 by **drawing l,** for there were officials of 1598
24:31 They also cast **l,** just as their brothers 1598
25: 8 cast **l** for their duties. 1598
26:13 **L** were cast for each gate, 1598
26:14 Then **l** were cast for his son Zechariah, 1598
26:16 The **l** for the West Gate and NIH
Ne 10:34 have cast **l** to determine when each 1598
11: 1 of the people cast **l** to bring one out 1598
Job 6:27 You would even cast **l** for the fatherless NIH

†**LORD'S** distinguishes the proper name of God, *Yahweh's*, indicated in the NIV by "LORD's," from the words translated "Lord's" and "lord's," indexed under the heading ***LORD'S**, page 686.

Ps 22:18 among them and cast l for my clothing. 1598
Eze 21:21 *He will* cast l with arrows, 7837
24: 6 Empty it piece by piece without casting l 1598
Joel 3: 3 They cast l for my people and traded boys 1598
Ob 1:11 and foreigners entered his gates and cast l 1598
Jnh 1: 7 let us cast l to find out who is responsible 1598
1: 7 They cast l and the lot fell on Jonah. 1598
Na 3:10 L were cast for her nobles, 1598
Mt 27:35 they divided up his clothes by casting l. *3102*
Mk 15:24 they cast l to see what each would get. *3102*
Lk 23:34 they divided up his clothes by casting l. *3102*
Jn 19:24 among them and cast l for my clothing." *3102*
Ac 1:26 they cast l, and the lot fell to Matthias; *3102*

LOTUS (1) [LOTUSES]

Job 40:21 Under the **l plants** he lies, 7365

LOTUSES (1) [LOTUS]

Job 40:22 The l conceal him in their shadow; 7365

LOUD (61) [ALOUD, LOUDER, LOUDLY]

Ge 27:34 burst out with a l and bitter cry 1524+4394+6330
Ex 11: 6 be l wailing throughout Egypt— 1524
12:30 and there was l wailing in Egypt, 1524
19:16 and a very l trumpet blast. 2617
Dt 5:22 a l voice to your whole assembly there on 1524
27:14 to all the people of Israel in a l voice: 8123
Jos 6: 5 have all the people give a l shout; 1524
6:20 when the people gave a l shout, 1524
1Sa 7:10 the LORD thundered with l thunder 1524
1Ki 8:55 the whole assembly of Israel in a l voice, 1524
2Ch 15:14 an oath to the LORD with l acclamation, 1524
20:19 the God of Israel, with very l voice. 1524
Ezr 10:12 whole assembly responded with a l voice: 1524
Ne 9: 4 with l voices to the LORD their God. 1524
Ps 102: 5 Because of my l groaning I am reduced 7754
Pr 7:11 (She *is* l and defiant, 2159
9:13 The woman Folly *is* l; 2159
Jer 12: 6 they have raised a l cry against you. 4849
46:17 'Pharaoh king of Egypt is only a **l noise;** 8623
Eze 3:12 I heard behind me a l rumbling sound— 1524
3:13 a l rumbling sound. 1524
9: 1 Then I heard him call out in a l voice, 1524
11:13 I fell facedown and cried out in a l voice, 1524
Da 4:14 He called in a l *voice:* 10264
Zep 1:10 and a l crash from the hills. 1524
Mt 24:31 with a l trumpet call, *3489*
27:46 the ninth hour Jesus cried out *in* a l voice, *3489*
27:50 Jesus had cried out again *in* a l voice, *3489*
Mk 15:34 the ninth hour Jesus cried out *in* a l voice, *3489*
15:37 With a l cry, Jesus breathed his last. *3489*
Lk 1:42 *In* a l voice she exclaimed: *3489*
17:13 and **called out in a l voice,** *149+5889*
17:15 came back, praising God in a l voice. *3489*
19:37 to praise God *in* l voices for all *3489*
23:23 *with* l shouts they insistently demanded *3489*
23:46 Jesus called out *with* a l voice, "Father, *3489*
Jn 7:37 Jesus stood and said in **a l voice,** *3189*
11:43 Jesus called *in* a l voice, "Lazarus, *3489*
1Th 4:16 down from heaven, with a **l command,** *3026*
Heb 5: 7 and petitions with l cries and tears to *2708*
Rev 1:10 I heard behind me a l voice like a trumpet, *3489*
5: 2 a mighty angel proclaiming in a l voice, *3489*
5:12 *In* a l voice they sang: *3489*
6:10 They called out *in* a l voice, "How long, *3489*
7: 2 He called out *in* a l voice to the four angels *3489*
7:10 And they cried out *in* a l voice: *3489*
8:13 in midair call out in a l voice: *3489*
10: 3 he gave a l shout like the roar of a lion. *3489*
11:12 a l voice from heaven saying to them, *3489*
11:15 and there were l voices in heaven, *3489*
12:10 Then I heard a l voice in heaven say: *3489*
14: 2 the roar of rushing waters and like a l peal *3489*
14: 7 He said in a l voice, *3489*
14: 9 and said in a l voice: *3489*
14:15 in a l voice to him who was sitting on *3489*
14:18 came from the altar and called *in* a l voice *3489*
16: 1 a l voice from the temple saying to *3489*
16:17 the temple came a l voice from the throne, *3489*
19: 6 the roar of rushing waters and like l peals *2708*
19:17 a l voice to all the birds flying in midair, *3489*
21: 3 I heard a l voice from the throne saying, *3489*

LOUDER (7) [LOUD]

Ex 19:19 the sound of the trumpet **grew l and louder.** 2143+2256+2618+4394
19:19 the sound of the trumpet **grew louder and l.** 2143+2256+2618+4394
1Ki 18:27 Elijah began to taunt them. "Shout **l!**" 1524
18:28 So they shouted l and slashed themselves 1524
Mt 20:31 but they shouted **all the l,** "Lord, *3505*
27:23 But they shouted **all the l,** "Crucify him!" *4360*
Mk 15:14 But they shouted **all the l,** "Crucify him!" *4360*

LOUDLY (7) [LOUD]

Ge 45: 2 he **wept so l** that the Egyptians heard him, 906+928+1140+5989+7754
50:10 they lamented l and bitterly; 1524
2Sa 13:36 the king's sons came in, wailing l. 5951+7754
Est 4: 1 wailing l and bitterly. 1524
Pr 27:14 If a man l blesses his neighbor early in the morning, 928+1524+7754
Da 3: 4 Then the herald l proclaimed, 10089+10264
Mk 5:38 with people crying and wailing l. *4498*

LOUNGE (1) [LOUNGING]

Am 6: 4 You lie on beds inlaid with ivory and l 6242

LOUNGING (2) [LOUNGE]

Isa 47: 8 l in your security and saying to yourself, 3782
Am 6: 7 your feasting and l will end. 6242

LOVE (551) [BELOVED, LOVED, LOVELY, LOVER, LOVER'S, LOVERS, LOVES, LOVING, LOVING-KINDNESS, LOVINGLY]

Ge 20:13 'This is how you can show your l to me: 2876
22: 2 your only son, Isaac, whom *you* l, 170
29:18 Jacob *was* **in l with** Rachel and said, 170
29:20 a few days to him because of his l *for* her. 173
29:32 Surely my husband *will* l me now." 170
Ex 15:13 "In your **unfailing** l you will lead 2876
20: 6 but showing l to a thousand [generations] 2876
20: 6 a thousand [generations] of *those who* l me 170
21: 5 '*I* l my master and my wife and children 170
34: 6 abounding in l and faithfulness, 2876
34: 7 maintaining l to thousands, 2876
Lev 19:18 but l your neighbor as yourself. 170
19:34 L him as yourself, 170
Nu 14:18 in l and forgiving sin and rebellion. 2876
14:19 In accordance with your great l, 2876
Dt 5:10 but showing l to a thousand [generations] 2876
5:10 *those who* l me and keep my commandments 170
6: 5 L the LORD your God with all your heart 170
7: 9 the faithful God, keeping his covenant of l 2876
7: 9 a thousand generations of *those who* l him 170
7:12 will keep his covenant of l with you, 2876
7:13 *He will* l you and bless you 170
10:12 to walk in all his ways, to l him, 170
10:19 And *you are to* l those who are aliens, 170
11: 1 L the LORD your God and keep his 170
11:13 to l the LORD your God and to serve 170
11:22 to l the LORD your God, to walk in all his 170
13: 3 to find out whether you l him with all 170
13: 6 or your son or daughter, or the wife you l, 2668
19: 9 to l the LORD your God and to walk 170
21:15 the son of the wife *he does* **not l,** 8535
21:16 the son of the wife *he does* **not l.** 8533
30: 6 that you *may* l him with all your heart and 170
30:16 to l the LORD your God, to walk in his ways 170
30:20 and that you *may* l the LORD your God, 170
33: 3 Surely it is you *who* l the people; 2462
Jos 22: 5 to l the LORD your God, 170
23:11 be very careful to l the LORD your God. 170
Jdg 5:31 But *may they who* l you be like the sun 170
14:16 *You* don't really l me. 170
16: 4 *he* **fell in l with** a woman in the Valley 170
16:15 '*I* l you,' when you won't confide in me? 170
1Sa 18:20 Now Saul's daughter Michal *was* **in l with** 170
20:17 David reaffirm his oath out of l *for* him, 170
2Sa 1:26 Your l for me was wonderful, 173
7:15 my l will never be taken away from him, 2876
13: 1 Amnon son of David **fell in l with** Tamar, 170
13: 4 Amnon said to him, "I'm **in l with** Tamar, 170
16:17 "Is this the l you show your friend? 2876
19: 6 You l those who hate you 170
19: 6 and hate *those who* l you. 170
1Ki 3: 3 Solomon **showed** *his* l *for* the LORD 170
8:23 you who keep your covenant of l 2876
10: 9 of the LORD's eternal l *for* Israel, 173
11: 2 Solomon held fast to them in l. 173
1Ch 16:34 his l endures forever. 2876
16:41 "for his l endures forever." 2876
17:13 I will never take my l away from him, 2876
2Ch 5:13 his l endures forever." 2876
6:14 you who keep your covenant of l 2876
6:42 Remember the **great l** *promised* 2876
7: 3 his l endures forever." 2876
7: 6 saying, "His l endures forever." 2876
9: 8 the l *of* your God *for* Israel and his desire 170
19: 2 and l those who hate the LORD? 170
20:21 for his l endures forever." 2876
Ezr 3:11 his l to Israel endures forever." 2876
Ne 1: 5 his covenant of l with those who love him 2876
1: 5 his covenant of love with *those who* l him 170
9:17 slow to anger and abounding in l. 2876
9:32 who keeps his covenant of l, 2876
13:22 to me according to your great l. 2876
Job 15:34 the tents of **those who l bribes.** 8816
19:19 those *I* l have turned against me. 170
37:13 or to water his earth and show his l. 2876
Ps 4: 2 How long *will you* l delusions 170
5:11 *those who* l your name may rejoice in you. 170
6: 4 save me because of your **unfailing l.** 2876
11: 5 and *those who* l violence his soul hates. 170
13: 5 But I trust in your **unfailing l;** 2876
17: 7 Show the wonder of your **great l,** 2876
18: 1 *I* l you, O LORD, my strength. 8163
21: 7 through the **unfailing l** *of* the Most High 2876
23: 6 Surely goodness and l will follow me all 2876
25: 6 O LORD, your great mercy and l, 2876
25: 7 according to your l remember me, 2876
26: 3 for your l is ever before me, 2876
26: 8 *I* l the house where you live, O LORD, 170
31: 7 I will be glad and rejoice in your l, 2876
31:16 save me in your **unfailing l.** 2876
31:21 for he showed his wonderful l to me 2876
31:23 L the LORD, all his saints! 170
32:10 but the LORD's **unfailing l** surrounds 2876
33: 5 the earth is full of his **unfailing l.** 2876
Ps 33:18 those who hope in his **unfailing l,** 2876
33:22 May your **unfailing l** rest upon us, 2876
36: 5 Your l, O LORD, reaches to the heavens, 2876
36: 7 How priceless is your **unfailing l!** 2876
36:10 Continue your l to those who know you, 2876
40:10 not conceal your l and your truth from 2876
40:11 your l and your truth always protect 2876
40:16 may *those who* l your salvation always say, 170
42: 8 By day the LORD directs his l, 2876
44:26 redeem us because of your **unfailing l.** 2876
45: 7 *You* l righteousness and hate wickedness; 170
48: 9 O God, we meditate on your **unfailing l.** 2876
51: 1 O God, according to your **unfailing l;** 2876
52: 3 *You* l evil rather than good, 170
52: 4 *You* l every harmful word, 170
52: 8 in God's **unfailing l** for ever and ever. 2876
57: 3 God sends his l and his faithfulness. 2876
57:10 great is your l, reaching to the heavens; 2876
59:16 in the morning I will sing of your l; 2876
60: 5 that *those* you l may be delivered. 3351
61: 7 appoint your l and faithfulness 2876
63: 3 Because your l is better than life, 2876
66:20 not rejected my prayer or withheld his l 2876
69:13 in your great l, O God, 2876
69:16 O LORD, out of the goodness of your l; 2876
69:36 and *those who* l his name will dwell there. 170
70: 4 may *those who* l your salvation always say, 170
77: 8 Has his **unfailing** l vanished forever? 2876
85: 7 Show us your **unfailing l,** O LORD, 2876
85:10 L and faithfulness meet together; 2876
86: 5 abounding in l to all who call to you. 2876
86:13 For great is your l toward me; 2876
86:15 abounding in l and faithfulness. 2876
88:11 Is your l declared in the grave, 2876
89: 1 of the LORD's **great l** forever; 2876
89: 2 that your l stands firm forever, 2876
89:14 l and faithfulness go before you. 2876
89:24 My faithful l will be with him, 2876
89:28 I will maintain my l to him forever, 2876
89:33 but I will not take my l from him, 2876
89:49 where is your former **great l,** 2876
90:14 in the morning with your **unfailing l,** 2876
92: 2 to proclaim your l in the morning 2876
94:18 I said, "My foot is slipping," your l, 2876
97:10 *Let those who* l the LORD hate evil, 170
98: 3 He has remembered his l 2876
100: 5 LORD is good and his l endures forever; 2876
101: 1 I will sing of your l and justice; 2876
103: 4 and crowns you with l and compassion, 2876
103: 8 slow to anger, abounding in l. 2876
103:11 so great is his l for those who fear him; 2876
103:17 the LORD's l is with those who fear him; 2876
106: 1 for he is good; his l endures forever. 2876
106:45 and out of his great l he relented. 2876
107: 1 for he is good; his l endures forever. 2876
107: 8 give thanks to the LORD for his **unfailing l** 2876
107:15 give thanks to the LORD for his **unfailing l** 2876
107:21 give thanks to the LORD for his **unfailing l** 2876
107:31 give thanks to the LORD for his **unfailing l** 2876
107:43 and consider the **great l** *of* the LORD. 2876
108: 4 great is your l, higher than the heavens; 2876
108: 6 that *those* you l may be delivered. 3351
109:21 out of the goodness of your l, deliver me. 2876
109:26 save me in accordance with your l. 2876
115: 1 because of your l and faithfulness. 2876
116: 1 *I* l the LORD, for he heard my voice; 170
117: 2 For great is his l toward us, 2876
118: 1 for he is good; his l endures forever. 2876
118: 2 Let Israel say: "His l endures forever." 2876
118: 3 "His l endures forever." 2876
118: 4 "His l endures forever." 2876
118:29 for he is good; his l endures forever. 2876
119:41 May your **unfailing** l come to me, 2876
119:47 delight in your commands because *I* l them. 170
119:48 my hands to your commands, which *I* l, 170
119:64 The earth is filled with your l, O LORD; 2876
119:76 May your **unfailing l** be my comfort, 2876
119:88 Preserve my life according to your l, 2876
119:97 Oh, how *I* l your law! 170
119:113 but *I* l your law. 170
119:119 therefore *I* l your statutes. 170
119:124 Deal with your servant according to your l 2876
119:127 Because *I* l your commands more than gold, 170
119:132 you always do to *those who* l your name. 170
119:149 Hear my voice in accordance with your l; 2876
119:159 See how *I* l your precepts; 170
119:159 O LORD, according to your l. 2876
119:163 and abhor falsehood but *I* l your law. 170
119:165 Great peace have *they who* l your law, 170
119:167 I obey your statutes, for *I* l them greatly. 170
122: 6 "May *those who* l you be secure. 170
130: 7 for with the LORD is **unfailing l** and 2876
136: 1 His l endures forever. 2876
136: 2 His l endures forever. 2876
136: 3 His l endures forever. 2876
136: 4 His l endures forever. 2876
136: 5 His l endures forever. 2876
136: 6 His l endures forever. 2876
136: 7 His l endures forever. 2876
136: 8 His l endures forever. 2876
136: 9 His l endures forever. 2876
136:10 His l endures forever. 2876
136:11 His l endures forever. 2876
136:12 His l endures forever. 2876
136:13 His l endures forever. 2876
136:14 His l endures forever. 2876
136:15 His l endures forever. 2876

Ps 136:16 His l endures forever. 2876
136:17 His l endures forever. 2876
136:18 His l endures forever. 2876
136:19 His l endures forever. 2876
136:20 His l endures forever. 2876
136:21 His l endures forever. 2876
136:22 His l endures forever. 2876
136:23 His l endures forever. 2876
136:24 His l endures forever. 2876
136:25 His l endures forever. 2876
136:26 His l endures forever. 2876
138: 2 and will praise your name for your l 2876
138: 8 your l, O LORD, endures forever— 2876
143: 8 bring me word of your **unfailing l**, 2876
143:12 In your **unfailing l**, silence my enemies; 2876
145: 8 slow to anger and rich in l. 2876
145:20 The LORD watches over all *who* l him, 170
147:11 who put their hope in his **unfailing l**. 2876
Pr 1:22 "How long *will you* simple ones l your simple ways? 170
3: 3 Let l and faithfulness never leave you; 2876
4: 6 l her, and she will watch over you. 170
5:19 may you ever be captivated by her l. 173
7:18 Come, let's drink deep of l till morning; 1856
7:18 let's enjoy ourselves with l! 171
8:17 I l those who love me, 170
8:17 I love *those who* l me, 170
8:21 bestowing wealth on *those who* l me 170
8:36 all who hate me l death." 170
9: 8 rebuke a wise man and *he will* l you. 170
10:12 but l covers over all wrongs. 173
14:22 But those who plan what is good find l 2876
15:17 a meal of vegetables where there is l than 173
16: 6 Through l and faithfulness sin is atoned for; 2876
17: 9 He who covers over an offense promotes l, 173
18:21 and *those who* l it will eat its fruit. 170
19:22 What a man desires is **unfailing l**; 2876
20: 6 Many a man claims to have **unfailing l**, 2876
20:13 *Do* not l sleep or you will grow poor; 170
20:28 L and faithfulness keep a king safe; 2876
20:28 through l his throne is made secure. 2876
21:21 who pursues righteousness and l finds life, 2876
27: 5 Better is open rebuke than hidden l. 173
Ecc 3: 8 a time to l and a time to hate, 170
9: 1 but no man knows whether l or hate awaits 173
9: 6 Their l, their hate and their jealousy 173
9: 9 Enjoy life with your wife, whom *you* l, 170
SS 1: 2 for your l is more delightful than wine. 1856
1: 3 No wonder the maidens l you! 170
1: 4 we will praise your l more than wine. 1856
1: 7 Tell me, you whom I l, 170
2: 4 and his banner over me is l. 173
2: 5 for I am faint with l. 173
2: 7 not arouse or awaken l until it so desires. 173
3: 5 not arouse or awaken l until it so desires. 173
4:10 delightful is your l, my sister, my bride! 1856
4:10 much more pleasing is your l than wine, 1856
5: 8 Tell him I am faint with l. 173
7: 6 beautiful you are and how pleasing, O l, 173
7:12 there I will give you my l. 1856
8: 4 not arouse or awaken l until it so desires. 173
8: 6 for l is as strong as death, 173
8: 7 Many waters cannot quench l; 173
8: 7 to give all the wealth of his house for l, 173
Isa 1:23 they all l bribes and chase after gifts. 170
5: 1 for the *one* I l a song about his vineyard: 3351
16: 5 In l a throne will be established; 2876
38:17 **In** *your* l you **kept** me from the pit 3137
43: 4 honored in my sight, and because I l you, 170
54:10 yet my **unfailing** l for you will not 2876
55: 3 my faithful l *promised to* David. 2876
56: 6 to l the name of the LORD, 170
56:10 they lie around and dream, *they* l to sleep. 170
57: 8 a pact with those whose beds *you* l, 170
61: 8 "For I, the LORD, l justice; 170
63: 9 In his l and mercy he redeemed them; 173
66:10 be glad for her, all you *who* l her; 170
Jer 2:25 *I* l foreign gods, and I must go after them.' 170
2:33 How skilled you are at pursuing l! 173
5:31 and my people l it this way. 170
12: 7 the *one* I l into the hands of her enemies. 3342
14:10 *"They* greatly l to wander; 170
16: 5 my l and my pity from this people," 2876
31: 3 "I have loved you with an everlasting l; 173
32:18 You show l to thousands but bring 2876
33:11 the LORD is good; his l endures forever." 2876
La 3:22 Because of the LORD's **great** l we are 2876
3:32 so great is his **unfailing l**. 2876
Eze 16: 8 and saw that you were old enough for l, 1856
23:17 Babylonians came to her, to the bed of l, 1856
33:32 are nothing more than one who sings l songs 6312
Da 9: 4 who keeps his covenant of l with all who 2876
9: 4 his covenant of love with *all who* l him 170
Hos 1: 6 for *I will* no longer **show** l *to* the house 8163
1: 7 Yet *I will* **show** l *to* the house of Judah; 8163
2: 4 *I will* not **show** *my* l *to* her children, 8163
2:19 and justice, in l and compassion. 2876
2:23 *I will* **show** *my* l to the one I called 8163
3: 1 "Go, **show** *your* l *to* your wife again, 170
3: 1 L her as the LORD loves the Israelites, NIH
3: 1 though they turn to other gods and l 170
4: 1 "There is no faithfulness, no l, 2876
4:18 their rulers dearly l shameful ways. 170
6: 4 Your l is like the morning mist, 2876
9: 1 *you* l the wages of a prostitute 170
9:15 *I will* no longer l them; 170
10:12 reap the fruit of **unfailing l**, 2876

Hos 11: 4 with cords of human kindness, with ties of l; 173
12: 6 maintain l and justice, and wait for 2876
14: 4 heal their waywardness and l them freely, 170
Joel 2:13 slow to anger and abounding in l, 2876
Am 4: 5 for this is what *you* l to do," 170
5:15 l good; maintain justice in the courts. 170
Jnh 4: 2 slow to anger and abounding in l, 2876
Mic 3: 2 you who hate good and l evil; 170
6: 8 and *to* l mercy and to walk humbly 170
Zep 3:17 he will quiet you with his l, 173
Zec 8:17 and *do* not l to swear falsely. 170
8:19 Therefore l truth and peace." 170
Mt 3:17 Son, whom I l; with him I am well pleased." *28*
5:43 'L your neighbor and hate your enemy.' *26*
5:44 L your enemies and pray for those who *26*
5:46 If *you* l those who love you, *26*
5:46 If you love those who l you, *26*
6: 5 for *they* l to pray standing in the *5797*
6:24 Either he will hate the one and l the other, *26*
12:18 the one I l, in whom I delight; *28*
17: 5 whom I l; with him I am well pleased. *28*
19:19 and 'l your neighbor as yourself.' " *26*
22:37 " 'L the Lord your God with all your heart *26*
22:39 'L your neighbor as yourself.' *26*
23: 6 *they* l the place of honor at banquets and *5797*
23: 7 they l to be greeted in the marketplaces *NIG*
24:12 the l of most will grow cold, *27*
Mk 1:11 "You are my Son, whom I l; *28*
9: 7 "This is my Son, whom I l. *28*
12:30 L the Lord your God with all your heart *26*
12:31 'L your neighbor as yourself.' *26*
12:33 *To* l him with all your heart, *26*
12:33 and *to* l your neighbor as yourself.' *26*
Lk 3:22 "You are my Son, whom I l; *28*
6:27 L your enemies, do good to those who hate *26*
6:32 "If *you* l those who love you, *26*
6:32 "If you love those who l you, *26*
6:32 Even 'sinners' l those who love them. *26*
6:32 Even 'sinners' love those who l them. *26*
6:35 But l your enemies, do good to them, *26*
7:42 Now which of them *will* l him more?" *26*
10:27 " 'L the Lord your God with all your heart *26*
10:27 and, 'L your neighbor as yourself.' " *NIG*
11:42 but you neglect justice and the l of God. *27*
11:43 because *you* l the most important seats in *26*
16:13 Either he will hate the one and l the other, *26*
20:13 I will send my son, whom I l; *28*
20:46 like to walk around in flowing robes and l *5797*
Jn 5:42 I know that you do not have the l of God *27*
8:42 "If God were your Father, *you* would l me, *26*
11: 3 "Lord, the one *you* l is sick." *5797*
13: 1 **showed** them the full extent of *his* l. *26*
13:34 new command I give you: L one another. *26*
13:34 As I have loved you, so you *must* l one another. *26*
13:35 my disciples, if *you* l one another." *27+2400*
14:15 "If *you* l me, you will obey what I command. *26*
14:21 I too *will* l him and show myself to him." *26*
14:23 My Father *will* l him, and we will come *26*
14:24 *does* not l me will not obey my teaching. *26*
14:31 the world must learn that *I* l the Father *26*
15: 9 Now remain in my l. *27*
15:10 If you obey my commands, you will remain in my l, *27*
15:10 my Father's commands and remain in his l. *27*
15:12 L each other as I have loved you. *26*
15:13 Greater l has no one than this, *27*
15:17 This is my command: L each other. *26*
15:19 it would l you as its own. *5797*
17:26 in order that the l *you have* for me may be *26+27*
21:15 *do you* **truly** l me more than these?" *26*
21:15 Lord," he said, "you know that *I* l you." *5797*
21:16 "Simon son of John, *do you* **truly** l me?" *26*
21:16 "Yes, Lord, you know that *I* l you." *5797*
21:17 "Simon son of John, *do you* l me?" *5797*
21:17 asked him the third time, *"Do you* l me?" *5797*
21:17 you know all things; you know that *I* l you." *5797*
Ro 5: 5 because God has poured out his l *27*
5: 8 God demonstrates his own l for us in this: *27*
8:28 for the good *of* those who l him, *26*
8:35 Who shall separate us from the l of Christ? *27*
8:39 be able to separate us from the l of God *27*
12: 9 L must be sincere. *27*
12:10 Be devoted to one another *in* **brotherly l**. *5789*
13: 8 the continuing debt *to* l one another, *26*
13: 9 "L your neighbor as yourself." *26*
13:10 L does no harm to its neighbor. *27*
13:10 Therefore l is the fulfillment of the law. *27*
14:15 you are no longer acting in l. *27*
15:30 Lord Jesus Christ and by the l of the Spirit, *27*
16: 8 Greet Ampliatus, whom I l in the Lord. *28*
1Co 2: 9 God has prepared *for* those who l him"— *26*
4:17 Timothy, my son whom *I* l, *28*
4:21 or in l and with a gentle spirit? *27*
8: 1 Knowledge puffs up, but l builds up. *27*
13: 1 but have not l, I am only a resounding gong *27*
13: 2 but have not l, I am nothing. *27*
13: 3 but have not l, I gain nothing. *27*
13: 4 L is patient, love is kind. *27*
13: 4 Love is patient, l is kind. *27*
13: 6 L does not delight in evil but rejoices with *NIG*
13: 8 L never fails. *27*
13:13 now these three remain: faith, hope and l. *27*
13:13 But the greatest of these is l. *27*
14: 1 Follow the way of l and *27*
16:14 Do everything in l. *27*
16:22 If anyone *does* not l the Lord— *5797*

1Co 16:24 My l to all of you in Christ Jesus. Amen. *27*
2Co 2: 4 to let you know the depth of my l for you. *27*
2: 8 therefore, to reaffirm your l for him. *27*
5:14 For Christ's l compels us, *27*
6: 6 in the Holy Spirit and in sincere l; *27*
8: 7 in complete earnestness and in your l *27*
8: 8 but I want to test the sincerity *of* your l *27*
8:24 *of* your l and the reason for our pride *27*
11:11 Because *I do* not l you? *26*
12:15 If *I* l you more, will you love me less? *26*
12:15 If I love you more, *will* you l *me* less? *26*
13:11 the God *of* l and peace will be with you. *27*
13:14 and the l of God, and the fellowship of *27*
Gal 5: 6 counts is faith expressing itself through l. *27*
5:13 rather, serve one another in l. *27*
5:14 "L your neighbor as yourself." *26*
5:22 But the fruit of the Spirit is l, joy, peace, *27*
Eph 1: 4 holy and blameless in his sight. In l *27*
1:15 the Lord Jesus and your l for all the saints, *27*
2: 4 But because of his great l for us, God, *26+27*
3:17 being rooted and established in l, *27*
3:18 and high and deep is the l of Christ, *27*
3:19 to know this l that surpasses knowledge— *NIG*
4: 2 be patient, bearing with one another in l. *27*
4:15 Instead, speaking the truth in l, *27*
4:16 grows and builds itself up in l, *27*
5: 2 and live a life of l, just as Christ loved us *27*
5:25 Husbands, l your wives, just as Christ loved *26*
5:28 *to* l their wives as their own bodies. *26*
5:33 also *must* l his wife as he loves himself, *26*
6:23 and l with faith from God the Father and *27*
6:24 Grace to all who l our Lord Jesus Christ *26*
6:24 Lord Jesus Christ with an undying l. *NIG*
Php 1: 9 that your l may abound more and more *27*
1:16 The latter do so in l, *27*
2: 1 if any comfort *from* his l, *27*
2: 2 by being like-minded, having the same l, *27*
4: 1 my brothers, you whom I l and long for, *28*
Col 1: 4 and of the l you have for all the saints— *27*
1: 5 the faith and l that spring from the hope *NIG*
1: 8 who also told us of your l in the Spirit. *27*
2: 2 be encouraged in heart and united in l, *27*
3:14 And over all these virtues put on l, *27*
3:19 Husbands, l your wives and do not be harsh *26*
1Th 1: 3 your labor *prompted by* l, *27*
3: 6 good news about your faith and l. *27*
3:12 May the Lord make your l increase *27*
4: 9 about **brotherly** l we do not need to write *5789*
4: 9 have been taught by God to l each other. *26*
4:10 *you* do l all the brothers *899S*
5: 8 putting on faith and l as a breastplate, *27*
5:13 Hold them in the highest regard in l *27*
2Th 1: 3 and the l every one of you has for each *27*
2:10 because they refused to l the truth and so *27*
3: 5 the Lord direct your hearts into God's l *27*
1Ti 1: 5 The goal of this command is l, *27*
1:14 the faith and l that are in Christ Jesus. *27*
2:15 l and holiness with propriety. *27*
4:12 in life, in l, in faith and in purity. *27*
6:10 the **l of money** is a root of all kinds of evil. *5794*
6:11 faith, l, endurance and gentleness. *27*
2Ti 1: 7 a spirit of power, *of* l and of self-discipline. *27*
1:13 with faith and l in Christ Jesus. *27*
2:22 and pursue righteousness, faith, l and peace, *27*
3: 3 **without l**, unforgiving, slanderous, *845*
3:10 my purpose, faith, patience, l, endurance, *27*
Tit 2: 2 and sound in faith, *in* l and in endurance. *27*
2: 4 the younger women to **l their husbands** *5791*
3: 4 and l of God our Savior appeared, *5792*
3:15 Greet those who l us in the faith. *5797*
Phm 1: 5 the Lord Jesus and your l for all the saints. *27*
1: 7 Your l has given me great joy *27*
1: 9 yet I appeal to you on the basis of l. *27*
Heb 6:10 and the l you have shown him *27*
10:24 how we may spur one another on toward l *27*
13: 5 Keep your lives **free from the l of money** *921*
Jas 1:12 that God has promised *to* those who l him. *26*
2: 5 kingdom he promised those who l him? *26*
2: 8 "L your neighbor as yourself," *26*
1Pe 1: 8 Though you have not seen him, *you* l him; *26*
1:22 that you have sincere **l for your brothers,** *5789*
1:22 l one another deeply, from the heart. *26*
2:17 L the brotherhood of believers, fear God, *26*
3: 8 be sympathetic, **l as brothers,** *5790*
3:10 "Whoever would l life and see good days *26*
4: 8 Above all, l each other deeply, *27+2400*
4: 8 because l covers over a multitude of sins. *27*
5:14 Greet one another with a kiss *of* l. *27*
2Pe 1: 7 and to brotherly kindness, l. *27*
1:17 whom I l; with him I am well pleased." *28*
1Jn 2: 5 God's l is truly made complete in him. *27*
2:15 *Do* not l the world or anything in the world. *26*
2:15 the l of the Father is not in him. *27*
3: 1 How great is the l the Father has lavished *27*
3:10 nor is anyone who *does* not l his brother. *26*
3:11 *We should* l one another. *26*
3:14 because *we* l our brothers. *26*
3:14 Anyone *who does* not l remains in death. *26*
3:16 This is how we know what l is: *27*
3:17 how can the l of God be in him? *27*
3:18 *let us* not l with words or tongue but *26*
3:23 and to l one another as he commanded us. *26*
4: 7 Dear friends, *let us* l one another, *26*
4: 7 for l comes from God. *27*
4: 8 Whoever *does* not l does not know God, *26*
4: 8 because God is l. *27*
4: 9 This is how God showed his l among us: *27*

1Jn 4:10 This is l: not that we loved God, but that *27*
4:11 we also ought *to* l one another, *26*
4:12 but if *we* l one another, *26*
4:12 God lives in us and his l is made complete *27*
4:16 we know and rely on the l God has for us. *27*
4:16 God is l. *27*
4:16 Whoever lives in l lives in God, *27*
4:17 In this way, l is made complete among us *27*
4:18 There is no fear in l. *27*
4:18 But perfect l drives out fear, *27*
4:18 The one who fears is not made perfect in l. *27*
4:19 We l because he first loved us. *26*
4:20 If anyone says, *"I* l God," *26*
4:20 For anyone who *does* not l his brother, *26*
4:20 cannot l God, whom he has not seen. *26*
4:21 Whoever loves God must also l his brother. *26*
5:2 how we know that *we* l the children *26*
5:3 This is l for God: to obey his commands. *27*
2Jn 1:1 whom I l in the truth— *26*
1:3 will be with us in truth and l. *27*
1:5 I ask that *we* l one another. *26*
1:6 And this is l: *27*
1:6 his command is that you walk in l. *899S*
3Jn 1:1 and her children, whom I l in the truth. *26*
1:6 They have told the church about your l. *27*
Jude 1:2 peace and l be yours in abundance. *27*
1:12 These men are blemishes at your l **feasts,** *27*
1:21 Keep yourselves in God's l as you wait *27*
Rev 2:4 You have forsaken your first l. *27*
2:19 I know your deeds, your l and faith, *27*
3:19 Those whom I l I rebuke and discipline. *5797*
12:11 not l their lives so much as to shrink *26*

LOVED (94) [LOVE]

Ge 24:67 So she became his wife, and *he* l her; 170
25:28 who had a taste for wild game, l Esau, 170
25:28 loved Esau, but Rebekah l Jacob. 170
29:30 and *he* l Rachel more than Leah. 170
29:31 the LORD saw that Leah *was* **not l,** 8533
29:33 the LORD heard that I **am not l,** 8533
34:3 and *he* l the girl and spoke tenderly to her. 170
37:3 Now Israel l Joseph more than any 170
37:4 that their father l him more than any 170
Dt 4:37 Because *he* l your forefathers 170
7:8 But it was because the LORD l you 170
10:15 on your forefathers and l them, 170
1Sa 1:5 a double portion because *he* l her, 170
18:1 and he l him as himself. 170
18:3 with David because he l him as himself. 170
18:16 But all Israel and Judah l David, 170
18:28 and that his daughter Michal l David, 170
20:17 because *he* l him as he loved himself. 170
20:17 because he loved him as he l himself. 173
2Sa 1:23 in life they **were** l and gracious, 170
12:24 named him Solomon. The LORD l him; 170
12:25 and because the LORD l him, NIH
13:15 In fact, he hated her more than *he had* l her. 170
1Ki 11:1 Solomon l many foreign women besides
Pharaoh's daughter— 170
2Ch 11:21 Rehoboam l Maacah daughter 170
26:10 for *he* l the soil. 170
Ne 13:26 *He* **was** l by his God, 170
Ps 44:3 and the light of your face, for *you* l them. 8354
47:4 the pride of Jacob, whom *he* l. 170
78:68 Mount Zion, which *he* l. 170
88:18 and l *ones* from me; 170
109:17 *He* l to pronounce a curse— 170
Isa 5:1 My l **one** had a vineyard on 3351
Jer 2:2 how as a bride you l me and followed me 173
8:2 which *they have* l and served 170
31:3 *"I have* l you *with* an everlasting love; 170
Eze 16:37 those *you* l as well as those you hated. 170
Hos 2:1 and of your sisters, 'My l *one.'* 8163
2:23 to the one I called 'Not my l *one.'* 8163
3:1 *she is* l *by* another and is an adulteress. 170
9:10 and became as vile as the **thing** they l. 171
11:1 "When Israel was a child, *I* l him, 170
Mal 1:2 *"I have* l you," says the LORD. 170
1:2 "But you ask, 'How *have you* l us?' 170
1:2 "Yet *I have* l Jacob, 170
Mk 10:21 Jesus looked at him and l him. *26*
12:6 He had one left to send, a son, whom he l. *28*
Lk 7:47 sins have been forgiven—for *she* l much. *26*
16:14 The Pharisees, *who* l **money,** *5639+5795*
Jn 3:16 "For God so l the world that he gave his
one and only Son, *26*
3:19 but men l darkness instead of light *26*
11:5 Jesus l Martha and her sister and Lazarus. *26*
11:36 Then the Jews said, "See how *he* l him!" *5797*
12:43 for *they* l praise from men more than *26*
13:1 *Having* l his own who were in the world, *26*
13:23 One of them, the disciple whom Jesus l, *26*
13:34 As *I have* l you, so you must love *26*
14:21 He who loves me *will be* l by my Father, *26*
14:28 If *you* l me, you would be glad that I am *26*
15:9 the Father *has* l me, so have I loved you. *26*
15:9 the Father has loved me, so *have* I l you. *26*
15:12 Love each other as *I have* l you. *26*
16:27 because you *have* l me and have believed *5797*
17:23 that you sent me and *have* l them even *26*
17:23 even as *you have* l me. *26*
17:24 because *you* l me before the creation of *26*
19:26 the disciple whom *he* l standing nearby, *26*
20:2 other disciple, the one Jesus l, and said, *5797*
21:7 the disciple whom Jesus l said to Peter, *26*
21:20 disciple whom Jesus l was following them. *26*
Ro 1:7 in Rome who are l by God and called to *28*
8:37 more than conquerors through him who l us. *26*
9:13 "Jacob *I* l, but Esau I hated." *26*
9:25 and I will call her 'my l *one'* who is *26*
9:25 who is not my l *one,"* *26*
11:28 they are l on account of the patriarchs, *28*
Gal 2:20 who l me and gave himself for me. *26*
Eph 5:1 Be imitators of God, therefore, as **dearly l**
children *28*
5:2 as Christ l us and gave himself up for us *26*
5:25 as Christ l the church and gave himself up *26*
Col 3:12 God's chosen people, holy and dearly l, *26*
1Th 1:4 For we know, brothers l by God, *26*
2:8 *We* l you so much that we were delighted *3916*
2Th 2:13 thank God for you, brothers l by the Lord, *26*
2:16 God our Father, who l us and *26*
2Ti 4:10 for Demas, *because he* l this world, *26*
Heb 1:9 *You have* l righteousness and hated *26*
2Pe 2:15 who l the wages of wickedness. *26*
1Jn 4:10 This is love: not that we l God, *26*
4:10 not that we loved God, but that he l us *26*
4:11 Dear friends, since God so l us, *26*
4:19 We love because he first l us. *26*
Jude 1:1 *who are* l by God the Father and kept *26*
Rev 3:9 and acknowledge that I *have* l you. *26*

LOVELY (11) [LOVE]

Ge 29:17 but Rachel was l *in* form, and beautiful. 3637
Est 1:11 for she was l to look at. 3202
2:7 Esther was l *in* form and features, 3637
Ps 84:1 How l is your dwelling place, 3351
SS 1:5 Dark am I, yet l, 5534
2:14 for your voice is sweet, and your face is l. 5534
4:3 your mouth is l. 5534
5:16 he is altogether l. 4718
6:4 my darling, as Tirzah, l as Jerusalem, 5534
Am 8:13 "the l young women and strong young men 3637
Php 4:8 whatever is l, whatever is admirable— *4713*

LOVER (29) [LOVE]

SS 1:13 My l is to me a sachet of myrrh resting 1856
1:14 My l is to me a cluster of henna blossoms 1856
1:16 How handsome you are, my l! 1856
2:3 is my l among the young men. 1856
2:8 My l! Look! Here he comes, 1856
2:9 My l is like a gazelle or a young stag. 1856
2:10 My l spoke and said to me, "Arise, 1856
2:16 My l is mine and I am his; 1856
2:17 the shadows flee, turn, my l, and be like 1856
4:16 Let my l come into his garden 1856
5:2 My l is knocking: 1856
5:4 My l thrust his hand through 1856
5:5 I arose to open for my l, 1856
5:6 I opened for my l, but my lover had left; 1856
5:6 I opened for my lover, but my l had left; 1856
5:8 if you find my l, what will you tell him? 1856
5:10 My l is radiant and ruddy, 1856
5:16 This is my l, this my friend, 1856
6:1 Where has your l gone, 1856
6:1 Which way did your l turn, 1856
6:2 My l has gone down to his garden, 1856
6:3 I am my lover's and my l is mine; 1856
7:9 May the wine go straight to my l, 1856
7:10 I belong to my l, and his desire is for me. 1856
7:11 Come, my l, let us go to the countryside, 1856
7:13 that I have stored up for you, my l. 1856
8:5 up from the desert leaning on her l? 1856
8:14 Come away, my l, and be like a gazelle 1856
1Ti 3:3 not quarrelsome, **not a l of money.** *921*

LOVER'S (1) [LOVE]

SS 6:3 I am my l and my lover is mine; 1856+4200

LOVERS (25) [LOVE]

SS 5:1 drink your fill, O l. 1856
Jer 3:1 as a prostitute with many **l—** 8276
3:2 By the roadside you sat waiting for l, 2157S
4:30 Your l despise you; they seek your life. 6311
La 1:2 Among all her l there is none to comfort her. 170
Eze 16:33 but you give gifts to all your l, 170
16:36 in your promiscuity with your l, 170
16:37 therefore I am going to gather all your l, 170
16:39 Then I will hand you over to **your l,** 4392S
16:41 and you will no longer pay your l. NIH
23:5 and she lusted after her l, the Assyrians— 170
23:9 "Therefore I handed her over to her l, 170
23:20 There she lusted after her l, 7108
23:22 I will stir up your l against you, 170
Hos 2:5 She said, 'I will go after my l, 170
2:7 after her l but not catch them; 170
2:10 before the eyes of her l; 170
2:12 which she said were her pay from her l; 170
2:13 and went after her l, but me she forgot," 170
8:9 Ephraim has sold herself to l. 172
2Ti 3:2 People will be **l of themselves,** *5796*
3:2 **l of money,** boastful, proud, abusive, *5795*
3:3 self-control, brutal, **not l of the good,** *920*
3:4 **l of pleasure** rather than lovers of God— *5798*
3:4 lovers of pleasure rather than **l of God—** *5806*

LOVES (76) [LOVE]

Ge 44:20 and his father l him.' 170
Dt 10:18 the fatherless and the widow, and l the alien, 170
15:16 because *he* l you and your family 170
21:15 and he l one but not the other, 170
21:16 of the firstborn to the son of the wife *he* l 170
23:5 because the LORD your God l you. 170
28:54 or the wife he l or his surviving children, 2668
28:56 the husband she l and her own son 2668
33:12 the LORD l rests between his shoulders." NIH
Ru 4:15 daughter-in-law, who l you and who is better 170
2Ch 2:11 "Because the LORD l his people, 170
Ps 11:7 For the LORD is righteous, *he* l justice; 170
33:5 The LORD l righteousness and justice; 170
34:12 Whoever of you l life and desires 2913
37:28 For the LORD l the just and will 170
87:2 the LORD l the gates of Zion more than 170
91:14 "Because *he* l me," says the LORD, 3137
99:4 The King is mighty, *he* l justice— 170
119:140 and your servant l them. 170
127:2 for he grants sleep to *those* he l. 3351
146:8 the LORD l the righteous. 170
Pr 3:12 because the LORD disciplines those *he* l, 170
12:1 *Whoever* l discipline loves knowledge, 170
12:1 Whoever loves discipline l knowledge, 170
13:24 *he who* l him is careful to discipline him. 170
15:9 but *he* l those who pursue righteousness. 170
17:17 A friend l at all times, 170
17:19 *He who* l a quarrel loves sin; 170
17:19 He who loves a quarrel l sin; 170
19:8 He who gets wisdom l his own soul; 170
21:17 He *who* l pleasure will become poor; 170
21:17 *whoever* l wine and oil will never be rich. 170
22:11 *He who* l a pure heart 170
29:3 man *who* l wisdom brings joy to his father, 170
Ecc 5:10 *Whoever* l money never has money enough; 170
5:10 whoever l wealth is never satisfied 170
SS 3:1 I looked for the one my heart l; 170
3:2 I will search for the one my heart l. 170
3:3 "Have you seen the one my heart l?" 170
3:4 when I found the one my heart l. 170
Hos 3:1 Love her as the LORD l the Israelites, 170
10:11 Ephraim is a trained heifer *that* l to thresh; 170
12:7 uses dishonest scales; *he* l to defraud. 170
Mal 2:11 has desecrated the sanctuary the LORD l, 170
Mt 10:37 "Anyone who l his father or mother more *5797*
10:37 anyone who l his son or daughter more *5797*
Lk 7:5 because *he* l our nation and has built our *26*
7:47 he who has been forgiven little l little." *26*
Jn 3:35 The Father l the Son and has placed *26*
5:20 For the Father l the Son and shows him all *5797*
10:17 The reason my Father l me is that I lay *26*
12:25 The man who l his life will lose it, *5797*
14:21 he is the one who l me. *26*
14:21 He who l me will be loved by my Father, *26*
14:23 Jesus replied, "If anyone l me, *26*
16:27 the Father himself l you *5797*
Ro 13:8 for he who l his fellowman has fulfilled *26*
1Co 8:3 But the man who l God is known by God. *26*
2Co 9:7 for God l a cheerful giver. *26*
Eph 1:6 he has freely given us in the One *he* l. *26*
5:28 He who l his wife loves himself. *26*
5:28 He who loves his wife l himself. *26*
5:33 also must love his wife as *he* l himself, *NIG*
Col 1:13 into the kingdom of the Son he l, *27*
Tit 1:8 be hospitable, **one who l what is good,** *5787*
Heb 12:6 because the Lord disciplines those *he* l, *26*
1Jn 2:10 Whoever l his brother lives in the light, *26*
2:15 If anyone l the world, the love of the Father *26*
4:7 Everyone who l has been born of God *26*
4:21 Whoever l God must also love his brother. *26*
5:1 and everyone who l the father loves his *26*
5:1 who loves the father l his child as well. *26*
3Jn 1:9 but Diotrephes, who **l to be first,** *5812*
Rev 1:5 *To* him who l us and has freed us *26*
20:9 the camp of God's people, the city he l. *26*
22:15 and everyone *who* l and practices falsehood. *5797*

LOVING (10) [LOVE]

Ps 25:10 the ways of the LORD are l and faithful 2876
59:10 my l God. God will go before me 2876
59:17 you, O God, are my fortress, my l God. 2876
62:12 and that you, O Lord, are l. 2876
144:2 He is my l God and my fortress, 2876
145:13 and l toward all he has made. 2883
145:17 and l toward all he has made. 2883
Pr 5:19 A l doe, a graceful deer— 172
Heb 13:1 Keep on **l each other as brothers.** *5789*
1Jn 5:2 by l God and carrying out his commands. *26*

LOVING-KINDNESS (1) [LOVE]

Jer 31:3 I have drawn you with l. 2876

LOVINGKINDNESS (KJV) See LOVE, UNFAILING LOVE

LOVINGLY (1) [LOVE]

SS 3:10 its interior l inlaid by the daughters 173

LOW (45) [BELOW, LOWBORN, LOWER, LOWERED, LOWEST, LOWLIEST, LOWLY]

Ge 18:2 to meet them and **bowed** l to the ground. 2556
43:28 And *they* **bowed** l to pay him honor. 7702
Nu 22:31 So *he* **bowed** l and fell facedown. 7702
2Sa 22:28 on the haughty *to* **bring** them l. 9164
1Ki 1:16 Bathsheba **bowed** l and knelt before 7702
1:31 Then Bathsheba **bowed** l with her face to 7702

1Ch 29:20 *they* **bowed l** and fell prostrate before 7702
Job 14:10 But man dies and *is* **laid l;** 2764
14:21 if *they are* **brought l,** he does not see it. 7592
22:29 When *men are* **brought l** and you say, 9164
24:24 *they* **are brought l** and gathered up 4812
40:11 look at every proud man and **bring** him **l,** 9164
Ps 18:27 but **bring l** those whose eyes are haughty. 9164
36: 7 Both high and **l among men** find refuge in the shadow of your wings. 132+1201
38: 6 I am bowed down and **brought** very **l;** 8820
49: 2 both **l** and high, rich and poor alike: 132+1201
119:25 I *am* **laid l** in the dust; 1815
136:23 in our **l estate** His love endures forever. 9165
Pr 29:23 A man's pride **brings** him **l,** 9164
Ecc 10: 6 while the rich occupy the **l** *ones.* 9165
Isa 2: 9 So man *will* **be brought l** 8820
2:11 and the pride of men **brought l;** 8820
2:17 The arrogance of man *will* **be brought l** 8820
5:15 So man *will* **be brought l** 8820
10:33 the tall ones *will be* **brought l.** 9164
14: 8 "Now that *you have been* **laid l,** 8886
14:12 *you who once* **laid l** the nations! 2765
23: 9 to **bring l** the pride of all glory and 2725
25:12 your high fortified walls and **lay** *them* **l;** 9164
26: 5 *he* **lays** the lofty city **l;** 9164
28: 1 the pride of *those* **laid l** *by* wine! 2150
29: 4 **Brought l,** you will speak from the ground; 9164
40: 4 every mountain and hill *made* **l;** 9164
46: 1 Bel bows down, Nebo **stoops l;** 7970
Jer 16: 6 "Both high and **l** will die in this land. 7783
46:15 Why *will* your warriors **be laid l?** 6085
Eze 17: 6 and became a **l,** spreading vine. 7757+9166
17:14 so that the kingdom would be *brought* **l,** 9166
17:24 the tall tree and make the **l** tree grow tall. 9166
21:26 and the exalted *will be* **brought l.** 9164
Da 8:11 the place of his sanctuary **was brought l.** 8959
Lk 3: 5 every mountain and hill **made l.** *5427*
Ac 8:10 both high and **l,** gave him their attention *3625*
Ro 12:16 to associate *with people* **of l position.** *5424*
Jas 1:10 rich should take pride in his **l position,** *5428*

LOWBORN (1) [BEAR, LOW]

Ps 62: 9 **L men** are but a breath, 132+1201

LOWER (30) [LOW]

Ge 6:16 the ark and make **l,** middle and upper decks 9397
Lev 13:45 cover the **l part of** his **face** 8559
Dt 28:43 but you will sink **l** and lower. 4752
28:43 but you will sink lower and **l.** 4752
Jos 15:19 So Caleb gave her the upper and **l** springs. 9397
16: 3 as far as the region of **L** Beth Horon and 9396
18:13 on the hill south of **L** Beth Horon. 9396
Jdg 1:15 Caleb gave her the upper and **l** springs. 9397
1Ki 9:17 He built up **L** Beth Horon, 9396
1Ch 7:24 who built **L** and Upper Beth Horon as well 9396
2Ch 8: 5 and **L** Beth Horon as fortified cities, 9396
Job 41:24 hard as rock, hard as a **l** millstone. 9397
Ps 8: 5 **made** him a little **l** than the heavenly beings 2893
Isa 11:11 from **L Egypt,** from Upper Egypt, 5213
22: 9 you stored up water in the **L** Pool. 9396
Jer 44: 1 all the Jews living in **L Egypt—** 824+5213
44:15 people living in **L** and Upper **Egypt,** 824+5213
Eze 24:17 do not cover the **l part of** your **face** 8559
24:22 You will not cover the **l part of** your **face** 8559
40:18 this was the **l** pavement. 9396
40:19 the inside of the **l** gateway to the outside 9396
42: 5 from the rooms on the **l** and middle floors 9396
42: 6 in floor space than those *on* the **l** 9396
42: 9 The **l** rooms had an entrance on 4946+9393
43:14 up to the **l** ledge it is two cubits high and 9396
Ac 27:30 to **l** some anchors from the bow. *1753*
2Co 11: 7 for *me* to **l** myself in order to elevate you *5427*
Eph 4: 9 that he also descended to the **l,** *3005*
Heb 2: 7 *You* **made** him a little **l** than the angels; *1783*
2: 9 who *was* **made** a little **l** than the angels, *1783*

LOWERED (12) [LOW]

Ge 24:18 and quickly **l** the jar to her hands 3718
24:46 *"She* quickly **l** her jar from her shoulder 3718
44:11 of them quickly **l** his sack to the ground 3718
Ex 17:11 but whenever *he* **l** his hands, 5663
Jer 38: 6 *They* **l** Jeremiah by ropes into the cistern; 8938
Eze 1:24 When they stood still, *they* **l** their wings. 8332
1:25 as they stood with **l** wings. 8332
Mk 2: 4 **l** the mat the paralyzed man was lying on. *5899*
Lk 5:19 and **l** him on his mat through the tiles into *2768*
Ac 9:25 **l** him in a basket through an opening *2768+5899*
27:17 they **l** the sea anchor and let the ship *5899*
2Co 11:33 But *I was* **l** in a basket from a window in *5899*

LOWEST (7) [LOW]

Ge 9:25 **l of slaves** will he be to his brothers." 6269+6269
1Ki 6: 6 The **l** floor was five cubits wide, 9396
6: 8 to the **l** floor was on the south side of 9396
Ne 4:13 the people behind the **l** points of the wall 9397
Ps 88: 6 You have put me in the **l** pit, 9397
Eze 41: 7 from the **l** *floor* to the top floor through 9396
Lk 14:10 But when you are invited, take the **l** place, *2274*

LOWING (3)

1Sa 6:12 keeping on the road and **l** all the way; 1716
15:14 What is this **l** *of* cattle that I hear?" 7754
Jer 9:10 and the **l** *of* cattle is not heard. 7754

LOWLIEST (2) [LOW]

Eze 29:15 It will be the **l** of kingdoms 9166
Da 4:17 and sets over them the **l** *of* men.' 10738

LOWLY (11) [LOW]

Job 5:11 The **l** he sets on high, 9166
Ps 119:141 Though I am **l** and despised, 7582
138: 6 LORD is on high, he looks upon the **l,** 9166
Pr 16:19 Better to be **l** *in* spirit and among 9166
29:23 but a *man of* **l** spirit gains honor. 9166
Isa 57:15 with him who is contrite and **l** *in* spirit, 9166
57:15 the **l** and to revive the heart of the contrite. 9166
Eze 21:26 The **l** will be exalted and the exalted will 9166
29:14 There they will be a **l** kingdom. 9166
1Co 1:28 He chose the **l** *things* of this world and *38*
Php 3:21 will transform our **l** bodies so *5428*

LOWRING (KJV) See OVERCAST

LOYAL (8) [LOYALTY]

1Sa 22:14 "Who of all your servants *is* as **l** as David, 586
2Sa 3: 8 This very day I am **l** to the house 2876
1Ki 12:20 the tribe of Judah remained **l to** the house 339
1Ch 12:29 *had remained* **l** *to* Saul's house 5466+9068
29:18 and **keep** their hearts **l** to you. 3922
Ps 78: 8 whose hearts *were* not **l** to God, 3922
78:37 their hearts *were* not **l** to him, 3922
Php 4: 3 Yes, and I ask you, **l** yokefellow, *1188*

LOYALTY (1) [LOYAL]

1Ch 12:33 to help David with **undivided l—**50,000; 2256+4202+4213+4213

LUBIM, LUBIMS (KJV) See LIBYA, LIBYANS

LUCAS (KJV) See LUKE

LUCIFER (KJV) See MORNING STAR

LUCIUS (2)

Ac 13: 1 Simeon called Niger, **L** of Cyrene, *3372*
Ro 16:21 as do **L,** Jason and Sosipater, my relatives. *3372*

LUCRE (KJV) See DISHONEST GAIN, MONEY

LUD (2) [LUDITES]

Ge 10:22 Elam, Asshur, Arphaxad, **L** and Aram. 4276
1Ch 1:17 Elam, Asshur, Arphaxad, **L** and Aram. 4276

LUDITES (2) [LUD]

Ge 10:13 Mizraim was the father of the **L,** 4276
1Ch 1:11 Mizraim was the father of the **L,** 4276

LUHITH (2)

Isa 15: 5 They go up the way to **L,** 4284
Jer 48: 5 They go up the way to **L,** 4284

LUKE (3)

Col 4:14 Our dear friend **L,** the doctor, *3371*
2Ti 4:11 Only **L** is with me. *3371*
Phm 1:24 so do Mark, Aristarchus, Demas and **L,** *3371*

LUKEWARM (1) [WARM]

Rev 3:16 So, because you are **l—** *5950*

LUMBER (1)

2Ch 2: 9 to provide me with plenty of **l,** 6770

LUMP (1)

Ro 9:21 of the same **l of clay** some pottery *5878*

LUNATICK (KJV) See HAVING SEIZURES

LUNCHEON (1)

Lk 14:12 "When you give a **l** or dinner, *756*

LURE (2) [LURED]

Jdg 4: 7 *I will* **l** Sisera, the commander of Jabin's 5432
16: 5 *"See if you can* **l** him *into* showing you 7331

LURED (2) [LURE]

Jos 8: 6 until *we have* **l** them **away** from the city, 5998
8:16 and they pursued Joshua and **were l away** 5998

LURK (2) [LURKED, LURKS]

Ps 56: 6 They conspire, they **l,** 7621
Hos 13: 7 like a leopard *I will* **l** by the path. 8800

LURKED (1) [LURK]

Job 31: 9 or if *I have* **l** at my neighbor's door, 741

LURKS (1) [LURK]

Pr 7:12 now in the squares, at every corner *she* **l.**) 741

LUSH (2)

Am 5:11 though you have planted **l** vineyards, 2774
Zec 11: 3 the **l thicket** *of* the Jordan is ruined! 1454

LUST (13) [LUSTED, LUSTFUL, LUSTFULLY, LUSTS, LUSTY]

Pr 6:25 *Do* not **l** in your heart **after** her beauty 2773
Isa 57: 5 You **burn with l** among the oaks and 2801
Eze 20:30 the way your fathers did and **l after** 339+2388
23: 8 and poured out their **l** upon her. 9373
23:11 yet *in* her **l** and prostitution she was more 6312
23:17 and in their **l** they defiled her. 9373
Na 3: 4 all because of the **wanton l** *of* a harlot, 2393
Ro 1:27 and were inflamed with **l** for one another. *3979*
Eph 4:19 with a continual **l** for more. *4432*
Col 3: 5 sexual immorality, impurity, **l,** *4079*
1Th 4: 5 in passionate **l** like the heathen, who do *4079*
1Pe 4: 3 living in debauchery, **l,** drunkenness, *2123*
1Jn 2:16 of sinful man, the **l** of his eyes and *2123*

LUSTED (9) [LUST]

Eze 6: 9 which *have* **l** after their idols. 2388
20:24 and their eyes [**l**] after their fathers' idols. NIH
23: 5 *she* **l after** her lovers, the Assyrians— 6311+6584
23: 7 with all the idols of everyone *she* **l after.** 6311
23: 9 the Assyrians, for whom *she* **l.** 6311
23:12 *She* too **l after** the Assyrians— 448+6311
23:16 *she* **l after** them and sent messengers 6311+6584
23:20 There *she* **l after** her lovers, 6311+6584
23:30 because you **l after** the nations 339+2388

LUSTER (1)

La 4: 1 How the gold *has* **lost** *its* **l,** 6670

LUSTFUL (3) [LUST]

Jer 13:27 your adulteries and **l neighings,** 5177
Eze 16:26 with the Egyptians, your **l** neighbors, 1414+1541
2Pe 2:18 to the **l desires** of sinful human nature, *816+2123*

LUSTFULLY (2) [LUST]

Job 31: 1 a covenant with my eyes not *to* **look l** at 1067
Mt 5:28 who looks at a woman **l** has already committed adultery *2121+3836+4639*

LUSTS (2) [LUST]

Nu 15:39 after the **l** of your own hearts and eyes. NIH
Ro 1:26 of this, God gave them over to shameful **l.** *4079*

LUSTY (1) [LUST]

Jer 5: 8 They are well-fed, **l** stallions, 3469

LUTES (2) [LUTE]

1Sa 18: 6 and with tambourines and **l.** 8956
2Ch 20:28 the LORD with harps and **l** and trumpets. 4036

LUXURIES (1) [LUXURY]

Rev 18: 3 the earth grew rich from her excessive **l.**" *5140*

LUXURIOUS (1) [LUXURY]

Isa 13:22 jackals in her **l** palaces. 6696

LUXURY (7) [LUXURIES, LUXURIOUS]

Pr 19:10 It is not fitting for a fool to **live in l—** 9503
Hab 1:16 for by his net he lives in **l** and enjoys 9045
Lk 7:25 and indulge *in* **l** are in palaces. *5588*
16:19 and fine linen and lived **in l** every day. *3289*
Jas 5: 5 *You have* **lived** on earth **in l** *5587*
Rev 18: 7 as the glory and **l** she gave herself. *5139*
18: 9 with her and **shared** her **l** see the smoke *5139*

LUZ (7) [BETHEL]

Ge 28:19 though the city used to be called **L.** 4281
35: 6 the people with him came to **L** (that is, 4281
48: 3 "God Almighty appeared to me at **L** in 4281
Jos 16: 2 It went on from Bethel (that is, **L**), 4281
18:13 to the south slope of **L** (that is, 4281
Jdg 1:23 to spy out Bethel (formerly called **L**), 4281
1:26 where he built a city and called it **L,** 4281

LYCAONIAN (2)

Ac 14: 6 and fled to the **L** cities of Lystra and Derbe *3377*
14:11 they shouted *in* **the L language,** *3378*

LYCIA (1)

Ac 27: 5 we landed at Myra *in* **L.** *3379*

LYDDA (4)

Ac 9:32 he went to visit the saints in **L.** *3375*
9:35 in **L** and Sharon saw him and turned to *3375*
9:38 **L** was near Joppa; *3375*
9:38 the disciples heard that Peter was in **L,** *899*S

LYDIA (4) [LYDIA'S, LYDIANS]
Jer 46: 9 men of L who draw the bow. 4276
Eze 27:10 L and Put served as soldiers in your army. 4276
30: 5 Cush and Put, L and all Arabia, 4276
Ac 16:14 of those listening was a woman named L, 3376

LYDIA'S (1) [LYDIA]
Ac 16:40 they went to L house, 3376

LYDIANS (1) [LYDIA]
Isa 66:19 to the Libyans and L (famous as archers), 4276

LYING (82) [LIE]
Ge 28:13 the land on which you are l. 8886
29: 2 with three flocks of sheep l near it because 8069
34: 7 in Israel by l with Jacob's daughter— 907+8886
49:14 "Issachar is a rawboned donkey l down 8069
Ex 14:30 and Israel saw the Egyptians l dead on AIT
Dt 21: 1 If a man is found slain, l in a field 5877
22:13 If a man takes a wife and, after l with her, 448+995
Jos 17: 9 There were towns belonging to Ephraim l NIH
Jdg 16:13 making a fool of me and l to me. 1819+3942
Ru 3: 4 note the place where he is l. 8886
3: 8 and he turned and discovered a woman l 8886
1Sa 3: 2 was l down in his usual place. 8886
3: 3 and Samuel was l down in the temple of 8886
5: 4 and were l on the threshold; 448
26: 5 Saul was l inside the camp, 8886
26: 7 l asleep inside the camp 8886
26: 7 Abner and the soldiers were l around him. 8886
2Sa 4: 7 while he was l on the bed in his bedroom. 8886
12:16 into his house and spent the nights l on 8886
13: 8 her brother Amnon, who was l down. 8886
1Ki 13:18 (But he was l to him.) 3950
22:22 a l spirit in the mouths of all his prophets,' 9214
22:23 the LORD has put a l spirit in the mouths 9214
2Ki 1: 4 'You will not leave the bed you are l on. 6590
1: 6 not leave the bed you are l on. 6590
1:16 you will never leave the bed you are l on. 6590
4:32 there was the boy l dead on his couch. 8886
2Ch 18:21 a l spirit in the mouths of all his prophets,' 9214
18:22 the LORD has put a l spirit in the mouths 9214
20:24 they saw only dead bodies l on the ground; 5877
Job 3:13 For now I would be l down in peace; 8886
3:14 places now l in ruins, 2999
Ps 31:18 Let their l lips be silenced, 9214
78:36 l to him with their tongues; 3941
109: 2 they have spoken against me with l tongues. 9214
120: 2 from l lips and from deceitful tongues. 9214
139: 3 You discern my going out and my l down; 8061
Pr 6:17 haughty eyes, a l tongue, hands 9214
10:18 He who conceals his hatred has l lips, 9214
12:19 but a l tongue lasts only a moment. 9214
12:22 The LORD detests l lips, 9214
17: 7 how much worse l lips to a ruler! 9214
21: 6 A fortune made by a l tongue is a fleeting vapor 9214
23:34 l on top of the rigging. 8886
26:28 A l tongue hates those it hurts, 9214
Isa 58: 5 for bowing one's head like a reed and for l 3667
Jer 8: 2 but will be like refuse l on the ground. 6584+7156
8: 8 when actually the l pen of the scribes 9214
16: 4 but will be like refuse l on the ground. 2118
23:26 in the hearts of these l prophets, 9214
25:33 but will be like refuse l on the ground. 6584+7156
43: 2 said to Jeremiah, "You are l! 1819+9214
La 3:10 Like a bear l in wait, like a lion in hiding, 741
Eze 13: 7 and uttered l divinations when you say, 3942
13: 8 Because of your false words and l visions, 3942
13: 9 see false visions and utter l divinations. 3942
13:19 By l to my people, who listen to lies, 3941
21:29 concerning you and l divinations 3942
22:28 by false visions and l divinations. 3942
29: 3 you great monster l among your streams. 8069
36:34 instead of l desolate in the sight of all who 2118
36:35 the cities that were l in ruins, NIH
Da 2:29 "As you were l there, 10542
4: 5 As I was l in my bed, 10542
4:10 These are the visions I saw while l in 10542
4:13 "In the visions I saw while l in my bed, 10542
7: 1 through his mind as he was l on his bed. 10542
Hos 4: 2 There is only cursing, l and murder, 3950
Mt 8:14 he saw Peter's mother-in-law l in bed with 965
9: 2 brought to him a paralytic, l on a mat. 965
Mk 2: 4 the mat the paralyzed man was l on. 2879
7:30 She went home and found her child l on 965
Lk 2:12 a baby wrapped in cloths and l in 3023
2:16 and the baby, who was l in the manger. 3023
5:25 took what he had been l on 2879
24:12 he saw the strips of linen l by themselves, NIG
Jn 5: 6 When Jesus saw him l there and learned 2879
20: 5 the strips of linen l there but did not go in. 3023
20: 6 He saw the strips of linen l there, 3023
Ro 9: 1 I speak the truth in Christ—I am not l, 6017
2Co 11:31 knows that I am not l. 6017
1Ti 2: 7 I am telling the truth, I am not l— 6017

LYRE (12) [LYRES]
Ps 33: 2 make music to him on the ten-stringed l. 5575
57: 8 Awake, harp and l! 5575
71:22 I will sing praise to you with the l, 4036
81: 2 play the melodious harp and l. 5575
92: 3 to the music of the ten-stringed l and 5575
Ps 108: 2 Awake, harp and l! 5575
144: 9 on the ten-stringed l I will make music 5575
150: 3 praise him with the harp and l, 5575
Da 3: 5 l, harp, pipes and all kinds of music, 10676
3: 7 zither, l, harp and all kinds of music, 10676
3:10 of the horn, flute, zither, l, harp, pipes 10676
3:15 l, harp, pipes and all kinds of music, 10676

LYRES (15) [LYRE]
1Sa 10: 5 down from the high place with l, 5575
2Sa 6: 5 with songs and with harps, l, tambourines, 5575
1Ki 10:12 and to make harps and l for the musicians. 5575
1Ch 13: 8 with songs and with harps, l, tambourines, 5575
15:16 l, harps and cymbals. 5575
15:20 and Benaiah were to play the l according 5575
15:28 and the playing of l and harps. 5575
16: 5 They were to play the l and harps, 5575
25: 1 accompanied by harps, l and cymbals. 5575
25: 6 with cymbals, l and harps, 5575
2Ch 5:12 and playing cymbals, harps and l. 5575
9:11 and to make harps and l for the musicians. 5575
29:25 and l in the way prescribed by David 5575
Ne 12:27 with the music of cymbals, harps and l. 5575
Isa 5:12 They have harps and l at their banquets, 5575

LYSANIAS (1)
Lk 3: 1 and L tetrarch of Abilene— 3384

LYSIAS (2)
Ac 23:26 Claudius L, To His Excellency, 3385
24:22 "When L the commander comes," he said, 3385

LYSTRA (6)
Ac 14: 6 the Lycaonian cities of L and Derbe and to 3388
14: 8 In L there sat a man crippled in his feet, 3388
14:21 Then they returned to L, 3388
16: 1 He came to Derbe and then to L, 3388
16: 2 The brothers at L and Iconium spoke well 3388
2Ti 3:11 Iconium and L, the persecutions I endured. 3388

M

MAACAH (25) [ABEL BETH MAACAH, ARAM MAACAH, MAACATHITE, MAACATHITES]
Ge 22:24 Tebah, Gaham, Tahash and M. 5082
Jos 12: 5 the border of the people of Geshur and M, 5084
13:11 the territory of the people of Geshur and M, 5084
13:13 not drive out the people of Geshur and M, 5084
2Sa 3: 3 the third, Absalom the son of M daughter 5082
10: 6 well as the king of M with a thousand men, 5081
10: 8 and Rehob and the men of Tob and M were 5081
1Ki 2:39 ran off to Achish son of M, king of Gath, 5082
15: 2 His mother's name was M daughter 5082
15:10 His grandmother's name was M daughter 5082
15:13 He even deposed his grandmother M 5082
1Ch 2:48 Caleb's concubine M was the mother 5082
3: 2 of M daughter of Talmai king of Geshur; 5082
7:15 His sister's name was M. 5082
7:16 Makir's wife M gave birth to a son 5082
8:29 His wife's name was M, 5082
9:35 His wife's name was M, 5082
11:43 Hanan son of M, Joshaphat the Mithnite, 5082
19: 7 as well as the king of M with his troops, 5081
27:16 Shephatiah son of M; 5082
2Ch 11:20 Then he married M daughter of Absalom, 5082
11:21 Rehoboam loved M daughter 5082
11:22 Rehoboam appointed Abijah son of M to be 5082
13: 2 His mother's name was M, 5082
15:16 King Asa also deposed his grandmother M 5082

MAACATHITE (4) [MAACAH]
2Sa 23:34 Eliphelet son of Ahasbai the M, 1201+5084
2Ki 25:23 Jaazaniah the son of the M, and their men. 5084
1Ch 4:19 the Garmite, and Eshtemoa the M. 5084
Jer 40: 8 and Jaazaniah the son of the M, 5084

MAACATHITES (1) [MAACAH]
Dt 3:14 as the border of the Geshurites and the M; 5084

MAACHAH (KJV) See MAACAH

MAACHATHI, MAACHATHITE, MAACHATHITES (KJV) See MAACATHITE, MAACATHITES

MAADAI (1)
Ezr 10:34 From the descendants of Bani: M, Amram, 5049

MAAI (1)
Ne 12:36 Shemaiah, Azarel, Milalai, Gilalai, M, 5076

MAALEH-ACRABBIM (KJV) See SCORPION PASS

MAARATH (1)
Jos 15:59 M, Beth Anoth and Eltekon— 5125

MAASAI (1)
1Ch 9:12 and M son of Adiel, the son of Jahzerah, 5127

MAASEIAH (23)
1Ch 15:18 Jehiel, Unni, Eliab, Benaiah, M, Mattithiah, 5129
15:20 M and Benaiah were to play the lyres 5129
2Ch 23: 1 Azariah son of Obed, M son of Adaiah, 5129
26:11 as mustered by Jeiel the secretary and M 5129
28: 7 killed M the king's son, 5129
34: 8 he sent Shaphan son of Azaliah and M 5129
Ezr 10:18 M, Eliezer, Jarib and Gedaliah. 5128
10:21 M, Elijah, Shemaiah, Jehiel and Uzziah. 5128
10:22 Elioenai, M, Ishmael, Nethanel, 5128
10:30 Adna, Kelal, Benaiah, M, Mattaniah, 5128
Ne 3:23 and next to them, Azariah son of M, 5128
8: 4 Shema, Anaiah, Uriah, Hilkiah and M; 5128
8: 7 Shabbethai, Hodiah, M, Kelita, Azariah, 5128
10:25 Rehum, Hashabnah, M, 5128
11: 5 and M son of Baruch, 5128
11: 7 the son of Kolaiah, the son of M, 5128
12:41 Eliakim, M, Miniamin, Micaiah, Elioenai, 5128
12:42 also M, Shemaiah, Eleazar, 5128
Jer 21: 1 and the priest Zephaniah son of M. 5128
29:21 of M, who are prophesying lies to you 5128
29:25 to Zephaniah son of M the priest, 5128
35: 4 which was over that of M son of Shallum 5129
37: 3 the priest Zephaniah son of M to Jeremiah 5128

MAASIAI (KJV) See MAASAI

MAATH (1)
Lk 3:26 the son of M, the son of Mattathias, 3399

MAAZ (1)
1Ch 2:27 Ram the firstborn of Jerahmeel: M, Jamin 5106

MAAZIAH (2)
1Ch 24:18 to Delaiah and the twenty-fourth to M. 5069
Ne 10: 8 M, Bilgai and Shemaiah. 5068

MACBANNAI (1)
1Ch 12:13 Jeremiah the tenth and M the eleventh. 4801

MACBENAH (1)
1Ch 2:49 and to Sheva the father of M and Gibea. 4800

MACEDONIA (23) [MACEDONIAN, MACEDONIANS]
Ac 16: 9 of a man of M standing and begging him, 3424
16: 9 "Come over to M and help us." 3423
16:10 we got ready at once to leave for M, 3423
16:12 and the leading city of that district of M. 3423
18: 5 When Silas and Timothy came from M, 3423
19:21 passing through M and Achaia. 3423
19:22 Timothy and Erastus, to M, 3423
19:29 Paul's traveling companions from M, 3424
20: 1 said good-by and set out for M. 3423
20: 3 he decided to go back through M. 3423
Ro 15:26 For M and Achaia were pleased to make 3423
1Co 16: 5 After I go through M, I will come to you— 3423
16: 5 for I will be going through M. 3423
2Co 1:16 I planned to visit you on my way to M and 3423
1:16 and to come back to you from M, 3423
2:13 I said good-by to them and went on to M. 3423
7: 5 For when we came into M, 3423
11: 9 from M supplied what I needed. 3423
Php 4:15 when I set out from M, 3423
1Th 1: 7 to all the believers in M and Achaia. 3423
1: 8 from you not only in M and Achaia— 3423
4:10 you do love all the brothers throughout M. 3423
1Ti 1: 3 As I urged you when I went into M, 3423

MACEDONIAN (2) [MACEDONIA]
Ac 27: 2 Aristarchus, a M from Thessalonica, 3424
2Co 8: 1 that God has given the M churches. 3423

MACEDONIANS (2) [MACEDONIA]
2Co 9: 2 and I have been boasting about it to the M, 3424
9: 4 For if any M come with me 3424

MACHBANAI (KJV) See MACBANNAI

MACHBENAH (KJV) See MACBENAH

MACHI (KJV) See MAKI

MACHINES (1)

2Ch 26:15 In Jerusalem he made **m** designed by 3115

MACHIR, MACHIRITES (KJV) See MAKIR, MAKIRITE

MACHNADEBAI (KJV) See MACNADEBAI

MACHPELAH (6)

Ge 23: 9 so he will sell me the cave of **M,** 4834
23:17 So Ephron's field in **M** near Mamre— 4834
23:19 field of **M** near Mamre (which is at Hebron) 4834
25: 9 and Ishmael buried him in the cave of **M** 4834
49:30 the cave in the field of **M,** 4834
50:13 in the cave in the field of **M,** 4834

MACNADEBAI (1)

Ezr 10:40 **M,** Shashai, Sharai, 4827

MAD (5) [MADDENING, MADMAN, MADMEN, MADNESS]

Dt 28:34 The sights you see will **drive** you **m.** 8713
Jer 25:16 and **go m** because of the sword I will send 2147
50:38 idols *that will* go **m** with terror. 2147
51: 7 therefore they *have now* **gone m.** 2147
Jn 10:20 "He is demon-possessed and **raving m.** *3419*

MADAI (2)

Ge 10: 2 The sons of Japheth: Gomer, Magog, **M,** 4512
1Ch 1: 5 The sons of Japheth: Gomer, Magog, **M,** 4512

MADDENING (2) [MAD]

Rev 14: 8 which made all the nations drink the **m** wine *2596*
18: 3 For all the nations have drunk the **m** wine *2596*

MADE (1111) [MAKE]

Ge 1: 7 So God **m** the expanse and separated 6913
1:16 God **m** two great lights— 6913
1:16 He also **m** the stars. NIH
1:25 God **m** the wild animals according 6913
1:31 God saw all that *he had* **m,** 6913
2: 3 God blessed the seventh day and **m** it **holy,** 7727
2: 4 When the LORD God **m** the earth and 6913
2: 9 the LORD God **m** all kinds of trees **grow** 7541
2:22 the LORD God **m** a woman *from* the rib 1215
3: 1 of the wild animals the LORD God *had* **m.** 6913
3: 7 and **m** coverings for themselves. 6913
3:21 The LORD God **m** garments of skin 6913
5: 1 *he* **m** him in the likeness of God. 6913
6: 6 The LORD was grieved that *he had* **m** man 6913
6: 7 for I am grieved that *I have* **m** them." 6913
7: 4 of the earth every living creature *I have* **m."** 6913
8: 6 the window *he had* **m** in the ark 6913
9: 6 for in the image of God *has* God **m** man. 6913
14:23 'I **m** Abram **rich.'** 6947
15:18 the LORD **m** a covenant with Abram 4162
17: 5 for *I have* **m** you a father of many nations. 5989
21:27 and the two men **m** a treaty. 4162
21:32 After the treaty *had been* **m** at Beersheba, 4162
24:10 for Aram Naharaim and **m** *his* **way** to 2143
24:21 the LORD *had* **m** his journey **successful.** 7503
24:37 my master **m** me **swear an oath,** 8678
26:30 Isaac then **m** a feast for them, 6913
27:17 the tasty food and the bread *she had* **m.** 6913
27:37 "*I have* **m** him lord over you 8492
27:37 and *have* **m** all his relatives his servants, 5989
28:20 Then Jacob **m a vow,** saying, 5623+5624
30:37 *m* white stripes on them *by* **peeling** AIT
30:40 but **m** the rest **face** the streaked 5989+7156
30:40 Thus *he* **m** separate flocks for himself 8883
31:13 a pillar and where *you* **m a vow** to me. 5623+5624
33:17 for himself and **m** shelters for his livestock. 6913
37: 3 and *he* **m** a richly ornamented robe for him. 6913
39:22 and he was *m* **responsible** *for* all AIT
41:39 "Since God *has* **m** all this **known** *to* you, 3359
41:51 God *has* **m** me **forget** all my trouble 5960
41:52 because God *has* **m** me **fruitful** in the land 7238
45: 1 when he **m himself known** to his brothers. 3359
45: 8 *He* **m** me father to Pharaoh, 8492
45: 9 God *has* **m** me lord of all Egypt. 8492
46:29 Joseph *had* his chariot **m ready** and went 673
50: 5 'My father **m** me **swear an oath** 8678
50: 6 as *he* **m** you **swear** *to do*." 8678
50:25 Joseph **m** the sons of Israel **swear an oath** 8678
Ex 1:14 *They* **m** their lives **bitter** with hard labor 5352
2:14 "Who **m** you ruler and judge over us? 8492
5:21 *You have* **m** us a **stench** to Pharaoh 944+8194
7: 1 "See, *I have* **m** you like God to Pharaoh, 5989
8: 7 also **m** frogs **come up** on the land of Egypt. 6590
10:13 the LORD **m** an east wind **blow** 5627
11: 3 (The LORD **m** the Egyptians favorably disposed toward the people, 5989
12: 8 and **bread m without yeast.** 5174
12:15 to eat **bread m without yeast.** 5174
12:18 **bread m without yeast,** 5174
12:20 Eat nothing **m with yeast.** 4721
12:36 The LORD *had* **m** the Egyptians favorably disposed toward the people, 5989
13: 6 For seven days eat **bread m without yeast** 5174
13:19 **m** the sons of Israel **swear an oath.** 8678+8678
Ex 14: 6 So *he* **had** his chariot **m ready** 673
14:25 **m** the wheels of their chariots **come off** 6073
15:17 place, O LORD, *you* **m** for your dwelling, 7188
15:25 the LORD **m** a decree and a law for them, 8492
16:31 and tasted like wafers **m with** honey. 928
18:25 from all Israel and **m** them leaders of 5989
20:11 in six days the LORD **m** the heavens and 6913
20:11 the Sabbath day and **m** it **holy.** 7727
23:15 eat **bread m without yeast,** 5174
24: 8 the LORD *has* **m** with you in accordance 4162
24:10 like a pavement **m** *of* sapphire, 5126
27: 8 *It is to be* **m** just as you were shown on 6913
28: 8 of one piece with the ephod and **m** 2118
29:18 an **offering m** to the LORD **by fire.** 852
29:23 the basket of **bread m without yeast,** 5174
29:23 and a **cake** *m with* oil, and a wafer. AIT
29:25 an **offering m** to the LORD **by fire.** 852
29:33 by which **atonement was m** 4105
29:41 an **offering m** to the LORD **by fire.** 852
29:42 to be **m** regularly at the entrance to the Tent NIH
30:10 This annual **atonement** *must be* **m** with 4105
30:20 an **offering m** to the LORD **by fire,** 852
31:17 in six days the LORD **m** the heavens and 6913
32: 4 and **m** it *into* an idol cast in the shape of 6913
32: 8 and *have* **m** themselves an idol cast in 6913
32:20 the calf *they had* **m** and burned it in the fire; 6913
32:20 on the water and **m** the Israelites **drink** it. 9197
32:31 *They have* **m** themselves gods of gold. 6913
32:35 of what they did with the calf Aaron *had* **m.** 6913
34:18 eat **bread m without yeast,** 5174
34:27 in accordance with these words *I have* **m** 4162
36: 8 All the skilled men among the workmen **m** 6913
36:11 Then *they* **m** loops of blue material along 6913
36:12 *They* also **m** fifty loops on one curtain 6913
36:13 Then *they* **m** fifty gold clasps and used them 6913
36:14 *They* **m** curtains of goat hair for the tent 6913
36:17 Then *they* **m** fifty loops along the edge of 6913
36:18 *They* **m** fifty bronze clasps to fasten 6913
36:19 Then *they* **m** for the tent a covering 6913
36:20 *They* **m** upright frames of acacia wood for 6913
36:22 *They* **m** all the frames of the tabernacle 6913
36:23 *They* **m** twenty frames for the south side of 6913
36:24 and **m** forty silver bases to go under them— 6913
36:25 *they* **m** twenty frames 6913
36:27 *They* **m** six frames for the far end, that is, 6913
36:28 and two frames *were* **m** for the corners of 6913
36:29 both *were* **m** alike. 6913
36:31 *They* also **m** crossbars of acacia wood: 6913
36:33 *They* **m** the center crossbar so 6913
36:34 and **m** gold rings to hold the crossbars. 6913
36:35 *They* **m** the curtain *of* blue, 6913
36:36 *They* **m** four posts of acacia wood for it 6913
36:36 They **m** gold hooks for them NIH
36:37 For the entrance to the tent *they* **m** a curtain 6913
36:38 and they **m** five posts with hooks for them. NIH
36:38 with gold and **m** their five bases of bronze. NIH
37: 1 Bezalel **m** the ark *of* acacia wood— 6913
37: 2 and **m** a gold molding around it. 6913
37: 4 Then *he* **m** poles of acacia wood 6913
37: 6 *He* **m** the atonement cover *of* pure gold— 6913
37: 7 Then *he* **m** two cherubim *out* 6913
37: 8 He **m** one cherub on one end and NIH
37: 8 at the two ends *he* **m** them of one piece with 6913
37:10 *They* **m** the table *of* acacia wood— 6913
37:11 Then they overlaid it with pure gold and **m** 6913
37:12 also **m** around it a rim a handbreadth wide 6913
37:15 The poles for carrying the table *were* **m** 6913
37:16 And *they* **m** *from* pure gold the articles for 6913
37:17 *They* **m** the lampstand *of* pure gold 6913
37:23 *They* **m** its seven lamps, 6913
37:24 *They* **m** the lampstand and all its accessories 6913
37:25 *They* **m** the altar of incense *out* 6913
37:26 and **m** a gold molding around it. 6913
37:27 *They* **m** two gold rings below the molding— 6913
37:28 *They* **m** the poles of acacia wood 6913
37:29 also **m** the sacred anointing oil and the pure, 6913
38: 2 *They* **m** a horn at each of the four corners, 6913
38: 3 *They* **m** all its utensils of bronze— 6913
38: 4 *They* **m** a grating for the altar, 6913
38: 6 *They* **m** the poles *of* acacia wood 6913
38: 7 *They* **m** it hollow, out of boards. 6913
38: 8 *They* **m** the bronze basin 6913
38: 9 Next *they* **m** the courtyard. 6913
38:22 of Hur, of the tribe of Judah, **m** everything 6913
39: 1 and scarlet yarn *they* **m** woven garments 6913
39: 1 *They* also **m** sacred garments for Aaron, 6913
39: 2 *They* **m** the ephod *of* gold, and of blue, 6913
39: 4 *They* **m** shoulder pieces for the ephod, 6913
39: 5 of one piece with the ephod and **m** NIH
39: 8 They **m** it like the ephod: 5126
39:15 For the breastpiece *they* **m** braided chains 6913
39:16 *They* **m** two gold filigree settings 6913
39:19 *They* **m** two gold rings and attached them to 6913
39:20 Then *they* **m** two more gold rings 6913
39:22 *They* **m** the robe of the ephod entirely 6913
39:24 *They* **m** pomegranates of blue, 6913
39:25 And *they* **m** bells of pure gold 6913
39:27 *they* **m** tunics of fine linen— 6913
39:30 *They* **m** the plate, the sacred diadem, 6913
Lev 1: 9 It is a burnt offering, an **offering m by fire,** 852
1:13 It is a burnt offering, an **offering m by fire,** 852
1:17 It is a burnt offering, an **offering m by fire,** 852
2: 2 on the altar, an **offering m by fire,** 852
2: 3 of the **offerings m** *to* the LORD **by fire.** 852
2: 4 **cakes** *m* without yeast and mixed with oil, AIT
2: 4 **wafers** *m* without yeast and spread with oil. AIT
2: 5 it is to be **m** of fine flour mixed with oil, NIH
Lev 2: 7 *it is to* **be m** *of* fine flour and oil. 6913
2: 8 Bring the grain offering **m** of these things to 6913
2: 9 on the altar as an **offering m by fire,** 852
2:10 **offerings m** *to* the LORD **by fire.** 852
2:11 to the LORD *must* **be m** without yeast, 6913
2:11 **offering m** to the LORD **by fire.** 852
2:16 **offering m** to the LORD **by fire.** 852
3: 3 **sacrifice m** to the LORD **by fire:** 852
3: 5 as an **offering m by fire,** 852
3: 9 **sacrifice m** to the LORD **by fire:** 852
3:11 **offering m** to the LORD **by fire.** 852
3:16 an **offering m by fire,** a pleasing aroma. 852
4:23 he **is m aware** *of* the sin he committed, 3359
4:28 he **is m aware** *of* the sin he committed, 3359
4:35 **offerings m** *to* the LORD **by fire.** 852
5:12 **offerings m** *to* the LORD **by fire.** 852
6: 7 of these things he did that **m** him guilty." 928
6:17 **offerings m** *to* me **by fire.** 852
6:18 **offerings m** *to* the LORD **by fire** 852
7: 5 **offering m** to the LORD **by fire.** 852
7:12 to offer cakes of **bread m without yeast** 5174
7:12 wafers **m without yeast** and spread with oil, 5174
7:13 with cakes of bread **m with yeast.** 2809
7:25 from which an offering by fire *may be* **m** to 7928
7:30 **offering m** *to* the LORD **by fire;** 852
7:35 **offerings m** *to* the LORD **by fire** 852
8: 2 the basket of **bread m without yeast,** 5174
8:21 **offering m** to the LORD **by fire,** 852
8:26 the basket of **bread m without yeast,** 5174
8:26 he took a cake of bread, and one **m** with oil, NIH
8:28 **offering m** to the LORD **by fire.** 852
10:12 **offerings m** *to* the LORD **by fire** 852
10:13 **offerings m** *to* the LORD **by fire;** 852
10:15 the fat portions of the **offerings m by fire,** 852
11:32 will be unclean, whether it is **m of** wood, 4946
11:43 by means of them or **be m unclean** 3237
13:48 any leather or anything **m** *of* leather— 4856
15:32 for *anyone m* **unclean** by an emission AIT
16:17 *having* **m atonement** for himself, 4105
16:30 on this day **atonement** *will be* **m** for you, 4105
16:34 **Atonement** *is to be* **m** once a year 4105
21: 6 **offerings m** *to* the LORD **by fire,** 852
21:21 **offerings m** *to* the LORD **by fire.** 852
22:22 **offering m** to the LORD **by fire.** 852
22:27 **offering m** to the LORD **by fire.** 852+7933
23: 6 you must eat **bread m without yeast.** 5174
23: 8 **offering m** to the LORD **by fire.** 852
23:13 **offering m** to the LORD **by fire,** 852
23:17 bring two loaves **m** *of* two-tenths of 2118
23:18 an **offering m by fire,** 852
23:25 **offering m** to the LORD **by fire.' "** 852
23:27 **offering m** to the LORD **by fire.** 852
23:28 when **atonement** *is* **m** for you before 4105
23:36 **offerings m** to the LORD **by fire,** 852
23:36 **offering m** to the LORD **by fire.** 852
23:37 **offerings m** to the LORD **by fire—** 852
24: 7 **offering m** to the LORD **by fire.** 852
24: 9 **offerings m** *to* the LORD **by fire."** 852
24:12 of the LORD *should be* **m clear** to them. 7300
26:41 which **m** me hostile toward them so NIH
Nu 3: 4 before the LORD when they **m an offering** 7928
5: 8 to whom **restitution** *can be* **m** *for* 8740
5: 8 the ram with which **atonement** *is* **m** 4105+4113
5:27 then when she *is* **m to drink** the water 9197
6: 3 and must not drink **vinegar** *m from* wine or AIT
6:15 and a basket of **bread m without yeast—** 5174
6:15 **cakes** *m of* fine flour mixed with oil, AIT
6:19 both **m without yeast.** 5174
6:21 He must fulfill the **vow** *he has* **m,** 5623+5624
7: 2 of those who were counted, **m offerings.** 7928
8: 4 This is how the lampstand was **m:** 5126
8: 4 It was **m** of hammered gold— NIH
8: 4 The lampstand *was* **m** exactly like 6913
8:21 and **m atonement** for them to purify them. 4105
11: 8 They cooked it in a pot or **m** it *into* cakes. 6913
11: 8 it tasted like **something m** *with* olive oil. 4382
14:36 **m** the whole community **grumble** against 4296
15: 3 to the LORD **offerings m by fire,** from 852
15:10 It will be an **offering m by fire,** 852
15:13 an **offering m by fire** as an aroma pleasing 852
15:14 an **offering m by fire** as an aroma pleasing 852
15:25 for their wrong an offering **m by fire** and 852
15:28 and when **atonement** *has been* **m** for him, 4105
16:47 the incense and **m atonement** for them. 4105
18:17 and burn their fat as an **offering m by fire,** 852
21: 2 Then Israel **m** *this* **vow** to the LORD: 5623+5624
21: 9 So Moses **m** a bronze snake and put it up on 6913
22:29 "*You have* **m a fool** of me! 6618
25:13 the honor of his God and **m atonement** for 4105
26:61 when they **m an offering** before the LORD 7928
28: 2 the food for my offerings **m by fire,** 852
28: 3 'This is the **offering m by fire** that you are 852
28: 6 **offering m** to the LORD **by fire.** 852
28: 8 This is an **offering m by fire,** 852
28:13 **offering m** to the LORD **by fire.** 852
28:14 to be **m** at each new moon during the year. NIH
28:17 for seven days eat **bread m without yeast.** 5174
28:19 to the LORD an **offering m by fire,** 852
28:24 for the **offering m by fire** every day 852
29: 6 **offerings m** to the LORD **by fire—** 852
29:13 an **offering m by fire** as an aroma pleasing 852
29:36 an **offering m by fire** as an aroma pleasing 852
31:20 as well as everything **m** *of* leather, 5126
32:13 against Israel and *he* **m** them **wander** in 5675
35:33 **atonement** cannot be **m** for the land 4105
Dt 1:28 Our brothers *have* **m** us **lose** heart. 5022
2: 1 For a long time *we* **m** *our* **way around** 6015

Dt 2: 3 "You *have* **m** *your* **way around** 6015
2:30 LORD your God *had* **m** his spirit **stubborn** 7996
3:11 His **bed** was *m of* iron AIT
4:23 of the LORD your God that *he* **m** with you; 4162
4:36 From heaven *he* **m** you **hear** his voice 9048
5: 2 The LORD our God **m** a covenant with us 4162
5: 3 that the LORD **m** this covenant, 4162
9: 9 the covenant that the LORD *had* **m** with you, 4162
9:12 from what I commanded them and *have* **m** 6913
9:16 *you had* **m** for yourselves an idol cast in 6913
9:21 the calf *you had* **m**, and burned it in the fire. 6913
9:22 *You* also **m** the LORD **angry** at Taberah, 2118+7911
10: 3 So *I* **m** the ark *out of* acacia wood 6913
10: 5 and put the tablets in the ark *I had* **m**, 6913
10:22 and now the LORD your God *has* **m** you 8492
15: 2 *the* **loan** *he has* **m** to his fellow Israelite. 5957
16: 3 Do not eat it with **bread m with yeast,** 2809
18: 1 **offerings m** *to* the LORD **by fire,** 852
23:23 because *you* **m** *your* **vow** freely to 5623
26: 6 Egyptians mistreated us and **m** us **suffer,** 6700
26:19 the nations *he has* **m** and that you will be 6913
29: 1 the covenant *he had* **m** with them at Horeb. 4162
29:25 the covenant *he* **m** with them 4162
31:16 and break the covenant *I* **m** with them. 4162
31:29 to anger by **what** your hands have **m."** 5126
32: 6 your Creator, who **m** you and formed you? 6913
32:13 *He* **m** him **ride** on the heights of the land 8206
32:15 He abandoned the God *who* **m** him 6913
32:16 *They* **m** him **jealous** with their foreign gods 7861
32:21 They **m** me **jealous** by what is no god 7861
Jos 2:17 "This oath *you* **m** us **swear** will not 8678
2:20 be released from the oath *you* **m** us **swear."** 8678
5: 3 So Joshua **m** flint knives and circumcised 6913
7:12 and run because *they have been* **m** liable 2118
8:28 and **m** it a permanent heap of ruins, 8492
9:15 Then Joshua **m** a treaty of peace with them 4162
9:16 after *they* **m** the treaty with the Gibeonites, 4162
9:27 That day he **m** the Gibeonites woodcutters 5989
10: 1 Gibeon *had* **m a treaty of peace** with Israel 8966
10: 4 "because *it has* **m peace** with Joshua and 8966
11: 5 and **m camp** together at the Waters 2837
11:19 **m a treaty of peace** with the Israelites, 8966
13:14 since the **offerings m by fire** *to* the LORD, 852
14: 8 **m** the hearts of the people **melt with fear.** 4998
22:25 The LORD *has* **m** the Jordan a boundary 5989
24:25 that day Joshua **m** a covenant for the people, 4162
Jdg 3:16 Now Ehud *had* **m** a double-edged sword 6913
3:30 That day Moab *was* **m subject to** Israel, 3338+4044+9393
6:19 an ephah of flour he **m** bread without yeast. NIH
8: 8 to Peniel and **m** *the* same **request** of them, 1819
8:27 Gideon **m** the gold into an ephod, 6913
9:16 in good faith when *you* **m** Abimelech **king,** 4887
9:18 **m** Abimelech, the son of his slave girl, **king** 4887
9:57 **m** the men of Shechem **pay for** 928+8031+8740
11: 4 when the Ammonites **m war** on Israel, 4309
11:11 and the people **m** him head and commander 8492
11:30 And Jephthah **m a vow** to the LORD: 5623+5624
11:35 *have* **m** me **miserable** and wretched, 4156+4156
11:35 because I *have* **m a vow** to the LORD 7023+7198
14:10 And Samson **m** a feast there, 6913
15:16 a donkey's jawbone I have **m** donkeys NIH
16: 2 *They* **m no move** during the night, saying, 3087
16:10 "*You have* **m a fool of** me; you lied to me. 9438
16:15 This is the third time *you have* **m a fool of** 9438
17: 4 *who* **m** them *into* the image and the idol. 6913
17: 5 and *he* **m** an ephod and some idols 6913
18:24 He replied, "You took the gods *I* **m,** 6913
18:27 Then they took what Micah *had* **m,** 6913
18:31 to use the idols Micah *had* **m,** 6913
20:34 of Israel's finest men **m** a frontal **attack** 995
20:37 in ambush **m** a sudden **dash** into Gibeah, 7320
21:15 LORD *had* **m** a gap in the tribes of Israel. 6913
Ru 1:20 the Almighty *has* **m** my life very **bitter.** 5352
1Sa 1:11 And *she* **m a vow,** saying, 5623+5624
2:19 Each year his mother **m** him a little robe 6913
2:28 the **offerings m with fire** *by* the Israelites. 852
2:29 of every **offering** *m* by my people Israel?' AIT
3:13 **m** themselves **contemptible,** 7837
6:15 and **m sacrifices** to the LORD. 2284+2285
14:29 "My father *has* **m trouble** *for* the country. 6579
15:11 "I am grieved that *I have* **m** Saul **king,** 4887+4889
15:33 "As your sword *has* **m** women **childless,** 8897
15:35 that *he had* **m** Saul **king** over Israel. 4887
18: 3 And Jonathan **m** a covenant with David 4162
19:10 That night David **m good** *his* **escape.** 2256+4880+5674
19:18 When David had fled and **m** *his* **escape,** 4880
20: 6 because an annual sacrifice is being **m** there NIH
20:16 So Jonathan **m a covenant** with the house 4162
23:18 of them **m** a covenant before the LORD. 4162
26: 3 Saul **m** *his* **camp** beside the road on the hill 2837
30:25 David **m** this a statute and ordinance 8492
2Sa 2: 9 *He* **m** him **king** over Gilead, 4887
5: 3 the king **m** a compact with them at Hebron 4162
7:21 and **m** it **known** *to* your servant. 3359
7:25 keep forever the promise *you have* **m** 1819
8: 2 *He* **m** them **lie down** on the ground 8886
10:19 *they* **m peace** with the Israelites 8966
11:13 and David **m** him **drunk.** 8910
12:14 *you have* **m** the enemies of the LORD **show utter contempt,** 5540+5540
12:31 and *he* **m** them **work** at brickmaking. 6296
13: 8 **m** *the* **bread** in his sight and baked it. 4221
14:15 because the people *have* **m** me **afraid.** 3707
15: 7 go to Hebron and fulfill a **vow** *I* **m** 5623+5624
2Sa 15: 8 *I* **m** *this* **vow:** 5623+5624
16:21 that *you have* **m yourself a stench** 944
19: 6 *You have* **m** *it* **clear** today that 5583
22:12 *He* **m** darkness his canopy around him— 8883
22:40 *you* **m** my adversaries **bow** at my feet. 4156
22:41 *You* **m** my enemies **turn** their backs 5989
23: 5 not **m** with me an everlasting covenant, 8492
1Ki 1:43 "Our lord King David *has* **m** Solomon **king.** 4887
3: 1 Solomon **m an alliance** with Pharaoh 3161
3: 7 you *have* **m** your servant **king** in place 4887
5:12 and the two of them **m** a treaty. 4162
6: 4 *He* **m** narrow clerestory windows in 6913
6: 6 *He* **m** offset ledges around the outside of 5989
6:23 the inner sanctuary *he* **m** a pair of cherubim 6913
6:31 of the inner sanctuary *he* **m** doors 6913
6:33 In the same way *he* **m** four-sided jambs 6913
6:34 He also **m** two pine doors, NIH
7: 6 *He* **m** a colonnade fifty cubits long 6913
7: 8 Solomon also **m** a palace like this hall 6913
7: 9 were **m** of blocks of high-grade stone cut NIH
7:16 also **m** two capitals of cast bronze to set on 6913
7:18 *He* **m** pomegranates in two rows 6913
7:23 *He* **m** the Sea of cast metal, circular 6913
7:27 *He* also **m** ten movable stands of bronze; 6913
7:28 This is **how** the stands were **m:** 5126
7:33 The wheels were **m** like chariot wheels; 5126
7:37 This is the way *he* **m** the ten stands. 6913
7:38 *He* then **m** ten bronze basins, 6913
7:40 He also **m** the basins and shovels 6913
7:45 that Huram **m** for King Solomon for 6913
7:48 also **m** all the furnishings that were in 6913
8: 9 where the LORD **m a covenant** with 4162
8:20 "The LORD has kept the promise *he* **m:** 1819
8:21 of the LORD that *he* **m** with our fathers 4162
8:25 *the* **promises** *you* **m** to him when you said, 1819
8:38 or plea *is* **m** by any of your people Israel— 2118
9: 3 the prayer and plea *you have* **m** before me; 2858[S]
10: 5 and the burnt offerings *he* **m** at the temple 6590
10: 9 *he has* **m** you king, to maintain justice 8492
10:16 King Solomon **m** two hundred large shields 6913
10:17 He also **m** three hundred small shields NIH
10:18 the king **m** a great throne inlaid with ivory 6913
10:20 Nothing like it *had ever* **been m** 6913
10:21 Nothing was **m** of silver, NIH
10:27 The king **m** silver as common in Jerusalem 5989
11:34 *I have* **m** him ruler all the days of his life 8883
12:14 "My father **m** your yoke **heavy;** 3877
12:20 assembly and **m** him **king** over all Israel. 4887
12:28 the king **m** two golden calves. 6913
12:32 sacrificing to the calves *he had* **m.** 6913
12:32 priests at the high places *he had* **m.** 6913
14: 7 from among the people and **m** you a leader 5989
14: 9 *You have* **m** for yourself other gods, 6913
14: 9 other gods, **idols m of metal;** 5011
14:26 the gold shields Solomon *had* **m.** 6913
14:27 So King Rehoboam **m** bronze shields 6913
15:12 and got rid of all the idols his fathers *had* **m.** 6913
15:13 *she had* **m** a repulsive Asherah pole. 6913
16: 2 and **m** you leader of my people Israel, 5989
16:33 Ahab also **m** an Asherah pole and did more 6913
18:10 *he* **m** them **swear** they could not find you. 8678
18:18 "*I have* not **m trouble** *for* Israel," 6579
18:26 they danced around the altar *they had* **m.** 6913
20:34 So *he* **m** a treaty with him, and let him go. 4162
22:11 of Kenaanah *had* **m** iron horns 6913
2Ki 3: 2 of Baal that his father *had* **m.** 6913
6: 6 and **m** the iron **float.** 7429
9:25 the LORD **m** this prophecy about him: 5951
11: 4 *He* **m** a covenant with them and put them 4162
11:13 the **noise** *m by* the guards and the people, AIT
11:17 then **m** a covenant between the LORD and 4162
11:17 He also **m** a covenant between the king and NIH
13: 7 of Aram had destroyed the rest and **m** them 8492
14:21 and **m** him **king** in place of his father 4887
17:15 the covenant *he had* **m** with their fathers 4162
17:16 and **m** for themselves two idols cast in 6913
17:21 **m** Jeroboam son of Nebat *their* **king.** 4887
17:29 each national group **m** its own gods in 6913
17:29 in the shrines the people of Samaria *had* **m** 6913
17:30 The men from Babylon **m** Succoth Benoth, 6913
17:30 the men from Cuthah **m** Nergal, 6913
17:30 and the men from Hamath **m** Ashima; 6913
17:31 the Avvites **m** Nibhaz and Tartak, 6913
17:35 the LORD **m** a covenant with the Israelites, 4162
17:38 not forget the covenant *I have* **m** with you, 4162
18: 4 into pieces the bronze snake Moses *had* **m,** 6913
19:15 You *have* **m** heaven and earth. 6913
20:11 the LORD **m** the shadow **go back** 8740
20:20 all his achievements and how *he* **m** the pool 6913
21: 3 he also erected altars to Baal and **m** 6913
21: 7 the carved Asherah pole *he had* **m** and put it 6913
21:24 **m** Josiah his son **king** in his place. 4887
22:17 **idols** their hands have **m,** 5126
23: 4 the articles **m** for Baal and Asherah and all 6913
23:15 the high place **m** *by* Jeroboam son of Nebat, 6913
23:30 of Josiah and anointed him and **m** him **king** 4887
23:34 **m** Eliakim son of Josiah **king** 4887
24:13 of Israel *had* **m** for the temple of the LORD. 6913
24:17 **m** Mattaniah, Jehoiachin's uncle, **king** 4887
25:15 all that were **m** of pure gold or silver. NIH
25:16 which Solomon *had* **m** for the temple of 6913
1Ch 11: 3 *he* **m** a compact with them at Hebron before 4162
12:18 So David received them and **m** them leaders 5989
14:17 and the LORD **m** all the nations fear him. 5989
16:16 the covenant *he* **m** with Abraham, 4162
16:26 but the LORD **m** the heavens. 6913
17:19 and **m known** all these great promises. 3359
1Ch 17:22 *You* **m** your people Israel your very own forever, 5989
17:23 let the promise *you have* **m** concerning 1819
19:19 *they* **m peace** with David 8966
21:29 which Moses *had* **m** in the desert, 6913
22: 5 So David **m** extensive **preparations** 3922
23: 1 **m** his son Solomon **king** over Israel. 4887
26:31 of David's reign *a* **search was m** in 2011
28: 2 and *I* **m plans** to build it. 3922
29:21 The next day *they* **m sacrifices** to 2284+2285
2Ch 1: 1 and **m** him exceedingly **great.** 1540
1: 3 which Moses the LORD's servant *had* **m** in 6913
1: 5 *had* **m** was in Gibeon in front of 6913
1: 8 to David my father and *have* **m** me **king** 4887
1: 9 for you *have* **m** me **king** over a people 4887
1:11 over whom *I have* **m** you **king,** 4887
1:15 The king **m** silver and gold as common 5989
2:11 *he has* **m** you their king." 5989
2:12 the God of Israel, who **m** heaven and earth! 6913
3:10 In the Most Holy Place *he* **m** a pair of 6913
3:14 *He* **m** the curtain of blue, 6913
3:15 In the front of the temple *he* **m** two pillars, 6913
3:16 *He* **m** interwoven chains and put them 6913
3:16 *He* also **m** a hundred pomegranates 6913
4: 1 *He* **m** a bronze altar twenty cubits long, 6913
4: 2 *He* **m** the Sea of cast metal, circular in 6913
4: 6 *He* then **m** ten basins for washing 6913
4: 7 *He* **m** ten gold lampstands according to 6913
4: 8 *He* **m** ten tables and placed them in 6913
4: 8 *He* also **m** a hundred gold sprinkling bowls. 6913
4: 9 *He* **m** the courtyard of the priests, 6913
4:11 He also **m** the pots and shovels 6913
4:16 that Huram-Abi **m** for King Solomon for 6913
4:18 All these things that Solomon **m** amounted 6913
4:19 also **m** all the furnishings that were 6913
5:10 where the LORD **m a covenant** with 4162
6:10 "The LORD has kept the promise *he* **m.** 1819
6:11 the covenant of the LORD that *he* **m** with 4162
6:13 Now he *had* **m** a bronze platform, 6913
6:16 *the* **promises** *you* **m** to him when you said, 1819
6:29 or plea *is* **m** by any of your people Israel— 2118
7: 6 which King David *had* **m** for praising 6913
7: 7 the bronze altar he *had* **m** could not hold 6913
9: 4 and the burnt offerings *he* **m** at the temple 6590
9: 8 *he has* **m** you king over them, 5989
9:15 King Solomon **m** two hundred large shields 6913
9:16 He also **m** three hundred small shields NIH
9:17 the king **m** a great throne inlaid with ivory 6913
9:19 Nothing like it *had ever* **been m** 6913
9:20 Nothing was **m** of silver, NIH
9:27 The king **m** silver as common in Jerusalem 5989
10:14 "My father **m** your yoke **heavy;** 3877
11:12 and **m** them **very strong.** 2616
11:15 and for the goat and calf idols *he had* **m,** 6913
12: 9 including the gold shields Solomon *had* **m.** 6913
12:10 So King Rehoboam **m** bronze shields 6913
13: 8 with you the golden calves that Jeroboam **m** 6913
15:16 *she had* **m** a repulsive Asherah pole. 6913
16:14 and *they* **m** a huge fire in his honor. 8596
18:10 Zedekiah son of Kenaanah *had* **m** iron horns 6913
20:35 of Judah **m an alliance** with Ahaziah king 2489
20:37 you *have* **m an alliance** with Ahaziah, 2489
20:37 the LORD will destroy **what** you have **m."** 5126
21: 7 the covenant the LORD *had* **m** with David, 4162
21:19 His people **m** no fire in his honor, 6913
22: 1 **m** Ahaziah, Jehoram's youngest son, **king** 4887
23: 1 *He* **m** a covenant *with* the commanders 928+4374
23: 3 the whole assembly **m** a covenant with 4162
23:16 then **m** a covenant that he and the people 4162
23:18 *to* whom David *had* **m assignments** in 2745
24: 8 a chest *was* **m** and placed outside, 6913
24:14 and *with* it *were* **m** articles for 6913
26: 1 **m** him **king** in place of his father Amaziah. 4887
26:15 In Jerusalem *he* **m** machines designed 6913
27: 5 Jotham **m war** on the king of the Ammonites 4309
28: 2 also **m** cast idols for worshiping the Baals. 6913
29: 8 *he has* **m** them an object of dread and horror 5989
30: 7 so that *he* **m** them an object of horror, 5989
31:14 the **contributions** *m to* the LORD and also AIT
32: 5 *He* also **m** large numbers of weapons 6913
32:27 and *he* **m** treasuries for his silver and gold 6913
32:28 He also **m** buildings to store the harvest NIH
32:28 and he **m** stalls for various kinds of cattle, NIH
33: 3 to the Baals and **m** Asherah poles. 6913
33: 7 He took the carved image *he had* **m** and put 6913
33:14 *he* also **m** it much **higher.** 1467
33:22 to all the idols Manasseh *had* **m.** 6913
33:25 **m** Josiah his son **king** in his place. 4887
34:25 to anger by all **that** their hands have **m,** 5126
35:14 *they* **m preparations** for themselves and for 3922
35:14 the Levites **m preparations** for themselves 3922
35:15 their fellow Levites **m** *the* **preparations** 3922
36: 1 of Josiah and **m** him **king** in Jerusalem 4887
36: 4 **m** Eliakim, a brother of Jehoahaz, **king** 4887
36:10 **m** Jehoiachin's uncle, Zedekiah, **king** 4887
36:13 **m** him **take an oath** in God's name. 8678
Ezr 3:13 because the people **m** so much **noise.** 8131+9558
4:15 **a search** *may be* **m** in the royal archives 10118
4:19 I issued an order and **a search** *was* **m,** 10118
5:17 *let* **a search be m** in the royal archives 10118
6:11 for this crime his house *is to* **be m** a pile 10522
Ne 3: 4 the son of Meshezabel, **m repairs,** 2616
3: 4 to him Zadok son of Baana also **m repairs.** 2616
3: 7 **repairs** *were* **m** *by* men from Gibeon 2616
3: 8 perfume-makers, **m repairs** next to that. 2616
3:10 of Harumaph **m repairs** opposite his house, 2616
3:10 of Hashabneiah **m repairs** next to him. 2616

Ne 3:16 **m repairs** up to a point opposite the tombs 2616
3:17 *the* **repairs** *were* **m** *by* the Levites 2616
3:18 *the* **repairs** *were* **m** *by* their countrymen 2616
3:22 **repairs** next to him *were* **m** 2616
3:23 Benjamin and Hasshub **m repairs** in front 2616
3:23 **m repairs** beside his house. 2616
3:26 of Ophel **m** repairs up to a point opposite NIH
3:28 the Horse Gate, the priests **m repairs,** 2616
3:29 of Immer **m repairs** opposite his house. 2616
3:29 the guard at the East Gate, **m repairs.** 2616
3:30 **m repairs** opposite his living quarters. 2616
3:31 **m repairs** as far as the house of 2616
3:32 the goldsmiths and merchants **m repairs.** 2616
5:12 **m** the nobles and officials **take an oath** 8678
8:2 which was **m up of** men and women 4946
8:12 the words that *had been* **m known** to them. 3359
9:6 You **m** the heavens, 6913
9:8 and you **m** a covenant with him to give 4162
9:10 *You* **m** a name for yourself, 6913
9:14 *You* **m known** to them your holy Sabbath 3359
9:23 **m** their sons as **numerous** 8049
13:13 the storerooms and **m** Hanan son of Zaccur, NIH
13:13 They were **m** responsible for distributing NIH
13:25 **m** them **take an oath** 8678
13:26 and God **m** him king over all Israel, 5989
13:31 I also **m** provision for contributions of wood NIH
Est 2:2 *a* **search** *be* **m** *for* beautiful young virgins 1335
2:17 on her head and **m** her **queen** instead 4887
3:14 and **m known** to the people of every 1655
7:9 He *had* it **m** for Mordecai, 6913
8:13 and **m known** to the people of every 1655
9:17 on the fourteenth they rested and **m** it a day 6913
9:18 on the fifteenth they rested and **m** it a day 6913
Job 4:14 and **m** all my bones **shake.** 7064
7:20 Why *have you* **m** me your target? 8492
10:8 "Your hands shaped me and **m** me. 6913
14:15 the **creature** your hands have **m.** 5126
16:12 *He has* **m** me his target; 7756
17:6 "God *has* **m** me a byword *to* everyone, 3657
23:16 God *has* **m** my heart **faint;** 8216
27:2 *who has* **m** me **taste bitterness** of soul, 5352
27:18 like a hut **m** *by* a watchman. 6913
28:26 when he **m** a decree for the rain and a path 6913
29:13 *I* **m** the widow's heart **sing.** 8264
31:1 "*I* **m** a covenant with my eyes not 4162
31:15 not *he who* **m** me in the womb make them? 6913
33:4 The Spirit of God *has* **m** me; 6913
37:7 that all men he has **m** may know his work, 5126
38:9 when I **m** the clouds its garment 8492
40:15 which *I* **m** along with you and which feeds 6913
42:10 the LORD **m** him **prosperous again** 8654+8740
Ps 7:15 and scoops it out falls into the pit *he has* **m.** 7188
8:5 *You* **m** him a little **lower** than the heavenly beings 2893
8:6 *You* **m** him **ruler** over the works 5440
16:5 you *have* **m** my lot **secure.** 9461
16:11 *You have* **m known** *to* me the path of life; 3359
18:11 *He* **m** darkness his covering, 8883
18:39 *you* **m** my adversaries **bow** at my feet. 4156
18:40 *You* **m** my enemies **turn** their backs 5989
18:43 *you have* **m** me the head of nations; 8492
21:6 and **m** him **glad** with the joy 2525
22:9 you **m** me **trust** in you even 1053
30:7 *you* **m** my mountain **stand** firm; 6641
33:6 the word of the LORD **were** the heavens **m,** 6913
39:5 *You have* **m** my days a mere handbreadth; 5989
44:2 **m** our fathers **flourish.** 8938
44:10 *You* **m** us **retreat** before the enemy, 294+8740
44:13 *You have* **m** us a reproach to our neighbors, 8492
44:14 *You have* **m** us a byword among the nations; 8492
44:19 and **m** us a haunt for jackals and covered us 928
50:5 *who* **m** a covenant with me by sacrifice." 4162
71:20 Though *you have* **m** me **see** troubles, 8011
73:28 *I have* **m** the Sovereign LORD my refuge; 8883
74:17 you **m** both summer and winter. 3670
78:13 **m** the water **stand firm** 5893
78:16 of a rocky crag and **m** water **flow down** 3718
78:28 *He* **m** them **come down** inside their camp, 5877
80:5 *you have* **m** them **drink** tears by the bowlful 9197
80:6 *You have* **m** us a source of contention 8492
86:9 All the nations *you have* **m** will come 6913
88:8 and *have* **m** me repulsive to them. 8883
89:3 "*I have* **m** a covenant with my chosen one, 4162
89:42 **m** all his enemies **rejoice.** 8523
95:5 The sea is his, for he **m** it, 6913
96:5 but the LORD **m** the heavens. 6913
98:2 The LORD *has* **m** his salvation **known** 3359
100:3 It is *he who* **m** us, and we are his; 6913
103:7 *He* **m known** his ways to Moses, 3359
104:24 In wisdom *you* **m** them all; 6913
105:9 the covenant *he* **m** with Abraham, 4162
105:21 *He* **m** him master of his household, 8492
105:24 **m** his people very **fruitful;** 7238
105:24 *he* **m** them too **numerous** for their foes, 6793
105:28 He sent darkness and **m** the land **dark—** 3124
106:19 At Horeb *they* **m** a calf and worshiped 6913
107:40 **m** them **wander** in a trackless waste. 9494
115:4 **m** *by* the hands of men. 5126
118:24 This is the day the LORD *has* **m;** 6913
118:27 and *he has* **m** *his* **light shine** upon us. 239
119:73 Your hands **m** me and formed me; 6913
129:3 and **m** their furrows **long.** 799
132:2 and **m** a vow to the Mighty One of Jacob: 5623
135:15 **m** *by* the hands of men. 5126
136:5 *who* by his understanding **m** the heavens, 6913
136:7 *who* **m** the great lights— 6913
138:3 *you* **m** me **bold** and stouthearted. 8104
Ps 139:14 *I* **am** fearfully and **wonderfully m;** 7098
139:15 from you when *I* **was m** in the secret place. 6913
145:9 he has compassion on all he has **m.** 5126
145:10 All you have **m** will praise you, O LORD; 5126
145:13 and loving toward all he has **m.** 5126
145:17 and loving toward all he has **m.** 5126
Pr 1:23 to you and **m** my thoughts **known** *to* you. 3359
2:17 the **covenant** she **m** *before* God. AIT
8:26 before *he* **m** the earth or its fields or any of 6913
20:12 the LORD *has* **m** them both. 6913
20:28 through love his throne *is* **m secure.** 6184
21:6 A fortune **m** by a lying tongue is 7189
21:31 The horse **is m ready** for the day of battle, 3922
Ecc 2:5 *I* **m** gardens and parks and planted all kinds 6913
2:6 *I* **m** reservoirs to water groves 6913
3:11 *He has* **m** everything beautiful in its time. 6913
7:13 Who can straighten what *he has* **m crooked?** 6430
7:14 God *has* **m** the one as well as the other. 6913
7:29 God **m** mankind upright, 6913
10:19 A feast *is* **m** for laughter, 6913
SS 1:6 and **m** me take care of the vineyards; 8492
3:3 *as* they **m** *their* **rounds** in the city. 6015
3:6 perfumed with myrrh and incense **m from** 4946
3:9 King Solomon **m** for himself the carriage; 6913
3:9 he **m** it of wood from Lebanon. NIH
3:10 Its posts he **m** *of* silver, its base of gold. 6913
5:7 *as* they **m** *their* **rounds** in the city. 6015
Isa 2:8 to what their fingers *have* **m.** 6913
2:20 which *they* **m** to worship. 6913
14:16 the earth and **m** kingdoms **tremble,** 8321
14:17 *the man who* **m** the world a desert, 8492
17:8 and the incense altars their fingers *have* **m.** 6913
22:11 but you did not look to the *One who* **m** it, 6913
23:11 **m** its kingdoms **tremble.** 8074
23:13 The Assyrians *have* **m** it **a place** 3569
25:2 *You have* **m** the city a heap of rubble, 8492
28:15 with the grave *we have* **m** an agreement. 6913
28:15 for *we have* **m** a lie our refuge 8492
29:13 of me **is m** *up only of* rules taught by men. AIT
30:33 it *has* **been m ready** for the king. 3922
30:33 Its fire pit *has been* **m deep** and wide, 6676
31:7 of silver and gold your sinful hands *have* **m.** 6913
37:16 You *have* **m** heaven and earth. 6913
38:12 day and night *you* **m an end** *of* me. 8966
38:13 day and night *you* **m an end** *of* me. 8966
40:4 every mountain and hill *m* **low;** AIT
42:22 they have been **m** loot, with no one to say, NIH
43:7 whom I formed and **m."** 6913
43:16 *he who* **m** a way through the sea, 5989
44:2 *he who* **m** you, who formed you in the womb, 6913
44:14 or planted a pine, and the rain **m** it **grow.** 1540
44:21 *I have* **m** you, you are my servant; 3670
44:24 I am the LORD, *who has* **m** all things, 6913
45:12 It is I *who* **m** the earth and created mankind 6913
45:18 he who fashioned and **m** the earth, 6913
46:4 I *have* **m** you and I will carry you; 6913
48:3 and *I* **m** them **known;** 9048
48:21 *he* **m** water **flow** for them from the rock; 5688
49:1 from my birth *he has* **m mention of** 2349
49:2 *He* **m** my mouth like a sharpened sword, 8492
49:2 *he* **m** me into a polished arrow 8492
49:19 "Though you were ruined and **m desolate** 9037
51:2 and I blessed him and **m** him **many.** 8049
51:10 who **m** a road in the depths of the sea so that 8492
51:21 **m drunk,** but not with wine. 8912
51:22 of your hand the cup that **m** you **stagger;** 9570
51:23 And *you* **m** your back like the ground, 8492
53:12 and **m intercession** for the transgressors. 7003
55:4 See, *I have* **m** him a witness to the peoples, 5989
57:7 *You have* **m** your bed on a high 8492
57:8 *you* **m a pact** with those whose beds you 4162
62:11 The LORD *has* **m proclamation** to the ends 9048
63:6 in my wrath *I* **m** them **drunk** 8910
64:7 and **m** us **waste away** because of our sins. 4570
66:2 *Has* not my hand **m** all these things, 6913
66:14 the hand of the LORD *will* **be m known** 3359
Jer 1:16 worshiping **what** their hands have **m.** 5126
1:18 Today I *have* **m** you a fortified city, 5989
2:7 and **m** my inheritance detestable. 8492
2:28 then are the gods *you* **m** for yourselves? 6913
3:16 nor *will* another *one* **be m.** 6913
5:3 *They* **m** their faces **harder** than stone 2616
5:22 *I* **m** the sand a boundary for the sea, 8492
6:27 "*I have* **m** you a tester of metals 5989
7:12 where *I* first **m a dwelling** *for* my Name, 8905
10:9 **What** the craftsman and goldsmith have **m** 5126
10:9 all **m** *by* skilled workers. 5126
10:12 But God **m** the earth by his power; 6913
11:10 the covenant *I* **m** with their forefathers. 4162
12:11 It *will be* **m** a wasteland, 8492
15:17 never **m merry** with them; 6600
18:15 *which* **m** them **stumble** in their ways and in 4173
18:15 They *m* them **walk** *in* bypaths and on roads AIT
18:21 *Let* their wives **be** *m* childless and widows; AIT
19:4 **m** this a place of **foreign** 5796
20:15 *who* **m** him **very glad,** saying, 8523+8523
25:6 to anger with **what** your hands have **m.** 5126
25:7 provoked me with **what** your hands have **m,** 5126
25:17 **m** all the nations to whom he sent me **drink** 9197
27:5 and outstretched arm I **m** the earth 6913
31:32 like the covenant *I* **m** with their forefathers 4162
32:17 you *have* **m** the heavens and the earth 6913
32:30 provoke me with **what** their hands have **m,** 5126
33:2 *he who* **m** the earth, 6913
33:14 the gracious promise *I* **m** to the house 1819
Jer 34:5 As people **m** a funeral fire in honor NIH
34:8 after King Zedekiah *had* **m** a covenant 4162
34:13 I **m** a covenant with your forefathers 4162
34:15 even **m** a covenant before me in the house 4162
34:18 the terms of the covenant *they* **m** before me, 4162
37:1 Zedekiah son of Josiah *was* **m king** of Judah 4887
37:15 which *they had* **m** into a prison. 6913
41:9 with Gedaliah was the one King Asa *had* **m** 6913
41:10 Ishmael **m captives of** all the rest of 8647
42:20 that *you* **m a fatal mistake** 928+5883+9494
44:6 and the streets of Jerusalem and **m** them NIH
44:8 to anger with **what** your hands have **m,** 5126
44:25 'We will certainly carry out the **vows** *we* **m** 5623+5624
49:37 the sword until I *have* **m an end** *of* them. 3983
50:20 **"search** *will* **be m for** Israel's guilt, 1335
51:7 **m** the whole earth **drunk.** 8910
51:15 "*He* **m** the earth by his power; 6913
51:34 *he has* **m** us an empty jar. 3657
52:19 all that were **m** of pure gold or silver. NIH
52:20 which King Solomon *had* **m** for the temple 6913
La 1:13 *He* **m** me desolate, faint all the day long. 5989
2:6 LORD *has* **m** Zion **forget** her appointed feasts 8894
2:8 **m** ramparts and walls **lament;** 61
3:2 He has driven me away and **m** me **walk** 2143
3:4 **m** my skin and my flesh **grow old** 1162
3:6 *He has* **m** me **dwell** in darkness 3782
3:9 *he has* **m** my paths **crooked.** 6390
3:12 He drew his bow and **m** me the target 5893
3:45 *You have* **m** us scum and refuse among 8492
Eze 1:16 to be **m** like a wheel intersecting a wheel. 5126
3:17 *I have* **m** you a watchman for the house 5989
6:6 and **what** you have **m** wiped out. 5126
7:19 for *it has* **m** them stumble into sin. 2118
12:6 *I have* **m** you a sign to the house of Israel." 5989
15:5 how much less *can it* **be m** 6913
16:7 *I* **m** you grow like a plant of the field. 5989
16:14 splendor I had given you **m** your beauty perfect, NIH
16:17 the jewelry **m of** my gold and silver, 4946
16:17 and *you* **m** for yourself male idols 6913
16:24 and **m** a lofty shrine in every public square. 6913
16:31 of every street and **m** your lofty shrines 6913
16:51 **m** your sisters **seem righteous** 7405
16:52 **m** your sisters **appear righteous.** 7405
16:60 Yet I will remember the covenant I **m** NIH
17:13 a member of the royal family and **m** a treaty 4162
19:5 she took another of her cubs and **m** him 8492
19:12 The east wind **m** *it* **shrivel,** 3312
20:11 I gave them my decrees and **m known** 3359
20:12 that I the LORD **m** them **holy.** 7727
20:28 **m** offerings that provoked me to anger, 5989
21:11 **m ready** for the hand of the slayer. 5989
21:15 *It* **is m** to flash like lightning, 6913
22:4 by the idols *you have* **m.** 6913
22:13 at the unjust gain *you have* **m** and at 6913
27:5 *They* **m** all your timbers *of* pine trees 1215
27:6 *Of* oaks from Bashan *they* **m** your oars; 6913
27:6 the coasts of Cyprus *they* **m** your deck, 6913
28:13 Your settings and mountings were **m** NIH
28:17 *I* **m** a spectacle of you before kings. 5989
28:18 So *I* **m** a fire **come out** from you, 3655
29:3 I **m** it *for* myself." 6913
29:9 "The Nile is mine; I **m** it," 6913
29:18 and every shoulder **m raw.** 5307
31:4 deep springs **m** it **grow tall;** 8123
31:9 *I* **m** it beautiful with abundant branches, 6913
31:16 *I* **m** the nations **tremble** at the sound 8321
32:25 A bed *is* **m** for her among the slain, 5989
33:7 *I have* **m** you a watchman for the house 5989
33:29 when I *have* **m** the land a desolate waste 5989
36:5 *they* **m** my land their own possession 5989
44:12 **m** the house of Israel **fall** 2118+4200+4842
45:21 during which you shall eat **bread m without yeast.** 5174
Da 2:12 **This m** the king so angry 10180+10353+10619
2:23 *you have* **m known** *to* me what we asked 10313
2:23 *you have* **m known** *to* us the dream 10313
2:32 The head of the statue was **m** of pure gold, NIH
2:38 *he has* **m** you **ruler** over them all. 10715
2:48 *He* **m** him **ruler** over the entire province 10715
3:1 King Nebuchadnezzar **m** an image of gold, 10522
3:15 to fall down and worship the image *I* **m,** 10522
4:5 I had a dream *that* **m** me **afraid.** 10167
5:7 *m* the third highest **ruler** AIT
5:16 *m* the third highest **ruler** AIT
6:2 The satraps were **m** accountable to them so 10314
6:14 to rescue Daniel and **m every effort** 10700
9:1 who **was m ruler** over 4887
9:15 and *who* **m** for yourself a name that endures 6913
9:16 of our fathers have **m** Jerusalem 928
11:35 and **m spotless** until the time of the end, 4235
12:10 **m spotless** and refined, 4235
Hos 8:6 a craftsman *has* **m** it; it is not God. 6913
14:3 **what** our own hands have **m,** 5126
Am 2:12 "But *you* **m** the Nazirites **drink** wine 9197
5:8 (*he who* **m** the Pleiades and Orion, 6913
5:26 which *you* **m** for yourselves. 6913
Jnh 1:9 who **m** the sea and the land." 6913
1:16 a sacrifice to the LORD and **m vows** 5623+5624
4:5 There *he* **m** himself a shelter, 6913
4:6 and **m** it **grow up** over Jonah to give shade 6590
Na 2:3 on the day *they are* **m ready;** 3922
Hab 1:14 *You have* **m** men like fish in the sea, 6913
3:6 he looked, and **m** the nations **tremble.** 6001

Zep 2: 8 who insulted my people and m threats 1540
Zec 7:12 They m their hearts as hard as flint 8492
7:14 how they m the pleasant land desolate.' " 8492
11:10 the covenant I had m with all the nations. 4162
Mal 2:15 Has not [the LORD] m them one? 6913
Mt 3: 4 John's clothes were m of camel's hair, 2400
5:13 how can it be m salty again? 245
5:33 but keep the oaths you have m to the Lord.' NIG
10:26 or hidden that will not be m known. 1182
14:22 Immediately Jesus m the disciples get into 337
15:31 the mute speaking, the crippled m well, 5618
19: 4 at the beginning the Creator 'm them male 4472
19:12 others were m that way by men; 2335S+2336
20:12 'and you have m them equal 4472
27:14 But Jesus m no reply, 646
27:64 the tomb to be m secure until the third day. 856
27:66 and m the tomb secure by putting a seal on 856
Mk 1: 6 John wore clothing m of camel's hair, AIT
2: 4 they m an opening in the roof above Jesus 689
2:27 "The Sabbath was m for man, 1181
6:45 Immediately Jesus m his disciples get into 337
10: 6 of creation God 'm them male and female.' 4472
11:17 But you have m it 'a den of robbers.' " 4472
14: 3 very expensive perfume, m of pure nard. AIT
14:58 build another, not m by man.' " 942
15: 5 But Jesus still m no reply, 646
Lk 1:62 Then they m signs to his father, 1935
3: 5 every mountain and hill m low. 5427
10:40 preparations that had to be m. 1355
11:40 Did not the one who m the outside make the 4472
12: 2 or hidden that will not be m known. 1182
13:22 teaching as he m his way to Jerusalem. 4472
14:34 how can it be m salty again? 789
17:19 your faith has m you well." 5392
19:15 "He was m king, however, 993+3284+3836
19:46 but you have m it 'a den of robbers.' " 4472
23:26 and put the cross on him and m him carry it NIG
Jn 1: 3 Through him all things were m; 1181
1: 3 without him nothing was m that has been 1181
1: 3 nothing was made that has been m. 1181
1:10 and though the world was m through him, 1181
1:14 The Word became flesh and m his dwelling 5012
1:18 at the Father's side, has m him known. 2007
2:15 So he m a whip out of cords, 4472
4:30 They came out of the town and m their way 2262
5:11 "The man who m me well said to me, 4472
5:15 that it was Jesus who had m him well. 4472
8: 3 They m her stand before the group 2705
8:22 This m the Jews ask, "Will he kill himself? 4036
9: 6 m some mud with the saliva, 4472
9:11 "The man they call Jesus m some mud 4472
9:14 Now the day on which Jesus had m the mud 4472
12:10 So the chief priests m plans to kill Lazarus 1086
15:15 from my Father I have m known to you. 1192
17:26 I have m you known to them, 1192
18:18 and officials stood around a fire they had m 4472
Ac 2:13 Some, however, m fun of them and said, 1430
2:28 You have m known to me the paths of life; 1192
2:36 God has m this Jesus, whom you crucified, 4472
3:12 or godliness we had m this man walk? 4472
3:16 and know was m strong. AIT
3:25 prophets and of the covenant God m 1347+1416
4:24 "you m the heaven and the earth and 4472
5: 4 What m you think of doing such a thing? 1877+2840+3836+5502
5:27 they m them appear before the Sanhedrin to AIT
7:10 so he m him ruler over Egypt 2770
7:27 'Who m you ruler and judge over us? 2770
7:35 'Who m you ruler and judge?' 2770
7:41 m an idol in the form of a calf. 3674
7:41 in honor of what their hands had m. 2240
7:43 the idols you m to worship. 4472
7:44 It had been m as God directed Moses, 4472
7:48 the Most High does not live in houses m by men. 5935
7:50 Has not my hand m all these things?' 4472
9:39 that Dorcas had m while she was still 4472
10:15 call anything impure that God has m clean. 2751
10:26 But Peter m him get up. 1586
11: 9 call anything impure that God has m clean.' 2751
12:19 Herod had a thorough search m for him 2118
13:17 he m the people prosper during their stay 5738
13:22 After removing Saul, he m David their king. 1586
13:47 " 'I have m you a light for the Gentiles, 5502
14:15 who m heaven and earth and sea 4472
15: 3 This news m all the brothers very glad. 4472
15: 7 that some time ago God m a choice 1721
15: 9 He m no distinction between us and them, 1359
17: 9 Then they m Jason and the others post bond 3284
17:24 "The God who m the world and everything 4472
17:26 From one man he m every nation of men, 4472
17:29 an image m by man's design and skill. AIT
18:12 the Jews m a united attack on Paul 2987
19:24 who m silver shrines of Artemis, 4472
20: 3 Because the Jews m a plot against him just 1181
20:13 He had m this arrangement 1411
20:28 the Holy Spirit has m you overseers. 5502
21:23 There are four men with us who have m 2400
21:26 offering would be m for each of them. 4712+4714
25: 8 Then Paul m his defense: 664
25:21 When Paul m his appeal to be held over for 2126
25:25 but because he m his appeal to 2126
27: 7 We m slow headway for many days 1095
27:40 the foresail to the wind and m for the beach. 2988
28:25 after Paul had m this final statement: 3306+4839
Ro 1:19 because God has m it plain to them. 5746
1:20 being understood from what has been m, 4473

Ro 1:23 the glory of the immortal God for images m NIG
3: 9 We have already m the charge that Jews 4577
3:21 apart from law, has been m known, 5746
4:17 "I have m you a father of many nations." 5502
5:19 of the one man the many were m sinners, 2770
5:19 the one man the many will be m righteous. 2770
15: 8 to confirm the promises m to the patriarchs AIT
15:28 and have m sure that they have received 5381
16:26 m known through the prophetic writings 1192
1Co 1:20 Has not God m foolish the wisdom of 3701
3: 6 Apollos watered it, but God m it grow. 889
4: 9 We have been m a spectacle to the whole 1181
7:37 and who has m up his mind not to marry 3212
12:12 though it is m up of many parts; 2400
12:14 Now the body is not m up of one part but NIG
15:22 so in Christ all will be m alive. 2443
15:28 be m subject to him who put everything AIT
16: 2 I come no collections will have to be m. 1181
2Co 1:20 no matter how many promises God has m, NIG
2: 1 So I m up my mind that I would 3212
3: 6 He has m us competent as ministers of 2655
3:14 But their minds were m dull, 4800
4: 6 m his light shine in our hearts to give us 3290
5: 5 Now it is God who has m us 2981
5:21 God m him who had no sin to be sin for us, 4472
7: 9 not because you were m sorry, 3382
8: 6 since he had earlier m a beginning, 4599
9:11 You will be m rich in every way so 4457
11: 6 We have m this perfectly clear to you 5746
12: 9 for my power is m perfect in weakness." 5464
12:11 I have m a fool of myself, 1181
Gal 1:11 something that man m up. 476+2848
4: 7 you are a son, God has m you also an heir. NIG
Eph 1: 9 And he m known to us the mystery AIT
2: 5 m us alive with Christ even 5188
2:14 who has m the two one and has destroyed 4472
3: 3 the mystery m known to me by revelation, AIT
3: 5 not m known to men in other generations 1192
3:10 be m known to the rulers and authorities in AIT
4:23 to be m new in the attitude of your minds; 391
Php 2: 7 but m himself nothing, taking the very 3033
2: 7 being m in human likeness. 1181
3:12 or have already been m perfect, 5457
Col 2:13 God m you alive with Christ. 5188
2:15 he m a public spectacle of them, 1258
1Th 2:17 of our intense longing we m every effort 5079
1Ti 1: 9 that law is m not for the righteous but 3023
1:18 with the prophecies once m about you, 4575
2: 1 and thanksgiving be m for everyone— 4472
6:12 m your good confession 3933+3934
6:13 m the good confession, 3934
2Ti 2:21 an instrument for noble purposes, m holy, 39
Heb 1: 2 and through whom he m the universe. 4472
2: 7 You m him a little lower than the angels; 1783
2: 9 who was m a little lower than the angels, 1783
2:11 and those who are m holy are of 39
2:17 to be m like his brothers in every way, 3929
5: 9 and, once m perfect, he became the source 5457
6:13 When God m his promise to Abraham, 2040
7:19 (for the law m nothing perfect), 5457
7:28 who has been m perfect forever. 5457
8: 9 like the covenant I m with their forefathers 4472
8:13 By calling this covenant "new," m the first one obsolete; 4096
9:16 to prove the death of the one who m it, 1416
9:17 while the one who m it is living. 1416
10: 8 (although the law required them to be m). 4712S
10:10 we have been m holy through the sacrifice of the body of Jesus Christ 39+1639
10:13 for his enemies to be m his footstool, 5502
10:14 by one sacrifice he has m perfect forever those who are being made holy. 5457
10:14 by one sacrifice he has made perfect forever those who are being m holy. 39
11: 3 so that what is seen was not m out NIG
11: 9 By faith he m his home in the promised land 4228
11:11 he considered him faithful who had m the promise. 2040
11:40 with us would they be m perfect. 5457
12:23 to the spirits of righteous men m perfect, 5457
Jas 2:22 his faith was m complete by what he did. 5457
3: 9 who have been m in God's likeness. 1181
1Pe 2:23 when he suffered, he m no threats. 580
3:18 in the body but m alive by the Spirit, 2443
2Pe 1:14 as our Lord Jesus Christ has m clear to me. 1317
1:19 the word of the prophets m more certain, NIG
2: 3 with stories they have m up. 4422
2: 6 and m them an example of what is going 5502
1Jn 2: 5 God's love is truly m complete in him. 5457
3: 2 what we will be has not yet been m known. 5746
4:12 God lives in us and his love is m complete 5457
4:17 love is m complete among us so 5457
4:18 The one who fears is not m perfect in love. 5457
5:10 God has m him out to be a liar, 4472
Rev 1: 1 He m it known by sending his angel 4955
1: 6 and has m us to be a kingdom and priests 4472
5:10 You have m them to be a kingdom 4472
6:12 like sackcloth m of goat hair, 5570
7:14 and m them white in the blood of the Lamb. 3326
13:12 and m the earth and its inhabitants worship 4472
14: 7 Worship him who m the heavens, the earth, 4472
14: 8 m all the nations drink the maddening wine 4540
18:12 and articles of every kind m of ivory, AIT
19: 7 and his bride has m herself ready. 2286
21:18 The wall was m of jasper, NIG
21:21 each gate m of a single pearl. 1639

MADE (Anglicized) See also HAD

MADIAN (KJV) See MIDIAN

MADMAN (5) [MAD]

1Sa 21:13 he was in their hands he acted like a m, 2147
2Ki 9:11 Why did this m come to you?" 8713
9:20 he drives like a m." 8714
Pr 26:18 a m shooting firebrands or deadly arrows 4263
Jer 29:26 you should put any m who acts like 408+8713

MADMANNAH (2)

Jos 15:31 Ziklag, M, Sansannah, 4526
1Ch 2:49 of M and to Sheva the father of Macbenah 4525

MADMEN (2) [MAD]

1Sa 21:15 short of m that you have to bring this fellow 8713
Jer 48: 2 You too, O M, will be silenced; 4522

MADMENAH (1)

Isa 10:31 M is in flight; the people of Gebim take 4524

MADNESS (8) [MAD]

Dt 28:28 The LORD will afflict you with m, 8714
Ecc 1:17 and also of m and folly, 2099
2:12 and also m and folly. 2099
7:25 the stupidity of wickedness and the m 2099
9: 3 are full of evil and there is m in their hearts 2099
10:13 at the end they are wicked m— 2100
Zec 12: 4 with panic and its rider with m," 8714
2Pe 2:16 and restrained the prophet's m. 4197

MADON (2)

Jos 11: 1 he sent word to Jobab king of M, 4507
12:19 the king of M one the king of Hazor one 4507

MAGADAN (1)

Mt 15:39 into the boat and went to the vicinity of M. 3400

MAGBISH (1)

Ezr 2:30 of M 156 4455

MAGDALA (KJV) See MAGADAN

MAGDALENE (12)

Mt 27:56 Among them were Mary M, 3402
27:61 Mary M and the other Mary were sitting there opposite the tomb. 3402
28: 1 Mary M and the other Mary went to look at 3402
Mk 15:40 Among them were Mary M, 3402
15:47 Mary M and Mary the mother of Joses saw 3402
16: 1 When the Sabbath was over, Mary M, 3402
16: 9 he appeared first to Mary M, 3402
Lk 8: 2 (called M) from whom seven demons had come out; 3402
24:10 It was Mary M, Joanna, 3402
Jn 19:25 Mary the wife of Clopas, and Mary M. 3402
20: 1 Mary M went to the tomb and saw that 3402
20:18 Mary M went to the disciples with 3402

MAGDIEL (2)

Ge 36:43 M and Iram. These were the chiefs of Edom 4462
1Ch 1:54 M and Iram. These were the chiefs of Edom 4462

MAGGOT (1) [MAGGOTS]

Job 25: 6 how much less man, who is but a m— 8231

MAGGOTS (3) [MAGGOT]

Ex 16:20 but it was full of m and began to smell. 9357
16:24 and it did not stink or get m in it. 8231
Isa 14:11 m are spread out beneath you 8231

MAGI (4)

Mt 2: 1 M from the east came to Jerusalem 3407
2: 7 the M secretly and found out from them 3407
2:16 that he had been outwitted by the M, 3407
2:16 with the time he had learned from the M. 3407

MAGIC (8) [MAGICIAN, MAGICIANS]

Isa 47:12 with your m spells and 2490
Eze 13:18 Woe to the women who sew m charms 4086
13:20 I am against your m charms 4086
Ac 8:11 for a long time with his m. 3404
Rev 9:21 their m arts, their sexual immorality 5760
18:23 By your m spell all the nations were led 5758
21: 8 those who practice m arts, the idolaters 5761
22:15 the dogs, those who practice m arts, 5761

MAGICIAN (2) [MAGIC]

Da 2:10 a thing of any m or enchanter or astrologer. 10282
2:27 m or diviner can explain to the king 10282

MAGICIANS (13) [MAGIC]

Ge 41: 8 he sent for all the m and wise men of Egypt. 3033
41:24 I told this to the m, 3033

Ex 7:11 and the Egyptian m also did the same things 3033
7:22 But the Egyptian m did the same things 3033
8: 7 m did the same things by their secret arts; 3033
8:18 m tried to produce gnats by their secret arts, 3033
8:19 The m said to Pharaoh, 3033
9:11 The m could not stand before Moses 3033
Da 1:20 the m and enchanters in his whole kingdom. 3033
2: 2 So the king summoned the m, enchanters, 3033
4: 7 When the m, enchanters, 10282
4: 9 I said, "Belteshazzar, chief of the m, 10282
5:11 appointed him chief of the m, enchanters, 10282

MAGISTRATE (1) [MAGISTRATES]
Lk 12:58 with your adversary to the m, *807*

MAGISTRATES (8) [MAGISTRATE]
Ezr 7:25 appoint m and judges to administer justice 10735
Da 3: 2 m and all the other provincial officials 10767
3: 3 treasurers, judges, m and all 10767
Ac 16:20 They brought them before the m and said, *5130*
16:22 m ordered them to be stripped and beaten. *5130*
16:35 the m sent their officers to the jailer with *5130*
16:36 "The m have ordered that you and Silas *5130*
16:38 The officers reported this *to* the m, *5130*

MAGNIFICENCE (1) [MAGNIFY]
1Ch 22: 5 for the LORD should be of great m 2025+5087

MAGNIFICENT (5) [MAGNIFY]
1Ki 8:13 I have indeed built a m temple for you, 2292
2Ch 2: 9 the temple I build *must be* large and m. 7098
6: 2 I have built a m temple for you, 2292
Isa 28:29 wonderful in counsel and m *in* wisdom. 1540
Mk 13: 1 What m buildings!" *4534*

MAGNIFY (1) [MAGNIFICENCE, MAGNIFICENT]
Da 11:36 and m himself above every god 1540

MAGOG (5)
Ge 10: 2 The sons of Japheth: Gomer, M, Madai, 4470
1Ch 1: 5 The sons of Japheth: Gomer, M, Madai, 4470
Eze 38: 2 set your face against Gog, of the land of M, 4470
39: 6 I will send fire on M and on those who live 4470
Rev 20: 8 Gog and M—to gather them for battle. *3408*

MAGOR-MISSABIB (1)
Jer 20: 3 LORD's name for you is not Pashhur, but M. 4474

MAGPIASH (1)
Ne 10:20 M, Meshullam, Hezir, 4488

MAHALAH (KJV) See MAHLAH

MAHALALEL (8)
Ge 5:12 he became the father of M. 4546
5:13 And after he became the father of M, 4546
5:15 When M had lived 65 years, 4546
5:16 M lived 830 years and had other sons 4546
5:17 Altogether, M lived 895 years, 4546
1Ch 1: 2 Kenan, M, Jared, 4546
Ne 11: 4 the son of M, a descendant of Perez; 4546
Lk 3:37 the son *of* M, the son of Kenan, *3435*

MAHALATH (4)
Ge 28: 9 so he went to Ishmael and married M, 4715
2Ch 11:18 Rehoboam married M, 4715
Ps 53: T According to m. 4714
88: T According to m leannoth. 4714

MAHALI (KJV) See MAHLI

MAHANAIM (14)
Ge 32: 2 So he named that place M. 4724
Jos 13:26 and from M to the territory of Debir; 4724
13:30 from M and including all of Bashan, 4724
21:38 of refuge for one accused of murder), M, 4724
2Sa 2: 8 of Saul and brought him over to M. 4724
2:12 left M and went to Gibeon. 4724
2:29 through the whole Bithron and came to M. 4724
17:24 David went to M, 4724
17:27 When David came to M, 4724
19:32 for the king during his stay in M, 4724
1Ki 2: 8 on me the day I went to M. 4724
4:14 Ahinadab son of Iddo—in M; 4724
1Ch 6:80 of Gad they received Ramoth in Gilead, M, 4724
SS 6:13 on the Shulammite as on the dance of M? 4724

MAHANEH DAN (2) [DAN]
Jdg 13:25 the Spirit of the LORD to stir him while he was in M, 4723
18:12 place west of Kiriath Jearim is called M 4723

MAHARAI (3)
2Sa 23:28 Zalmon the Ahohite, M the Netophathite, 4560
1Ch 11:30 M the Netophathite, Heled son of Baanah 4560
27:13 was M the Netophathite, a Zerahite. 4560

MAHATH (3)
1Ch 6:35 the son of Elkanah, the son of M, 4744
2Ch 29:12 M son of Amasai and Joel son of Azariah; 4744
31:13 M and Benaiah were supervisors 4744

MAHAVITE (1)
1Ch 11:46 Eliel the M, Jeribai and Joshaviah the sons 4687

MAHAZIOTH (2)
1Ch 25: 4 Joshbekashah, Mallothi, Hothir and M. 4692
25:30 the twenty-third to M, 4692

MAHER-SHALAL-HASH-BAZ (2)
Isa 8: 1 write on it with an ordinary pen: M. 4561
8: 3 And the LORD said to me, "Name him M. 4561

MAHLAH (5) [MAHLITE, MAHLITES]
Nu 26:33 whose names were M, Noah, Hoglah, 4702
27: 1 The names of the daughters were M, Noah, 4702
36:11 M, Tirzah, Hoglah, Milcah and Noah— 4702
Jos 17: 3 whose names were M, Noah, Hoglah, 4702
1Ch 7:18 to Ishhod, Abiezer and M. 4702

MAHLI (12)
Ex 6:19 The sons of Merari were M and Mushi. 4706
Nu 3:20 The Merarite clans: M and Mushi. 4706
1Ch 6:19 The sons of Merari: M and Mushi. 4706
6:29 M, Libni his son, Shimei his son, 4706
6:47 the son of M, the son of Mushi, 4706
23:21 The sons of Merari: M and Mushi. 4706
23:21 The sons of M: Eleazar and Kish. 4706
23:23 M, Eder and Jerimoth—three in all. 4706
24:26 The sons of Merari: M and Mushi. 4706
24:28 From M: Eleazar, who had no sons. 4706
24:30 the sons of Mushi: M, Eder and Jerimoth. 4706
Ezr 8:18 from the descendants of M son of Levi, 4706

MAHLITE (1) [MAHLAH]
Nu 26:58 Libnite clan, the Hebronite clan, the M clan, 4707

MAHLITES (1) [MAHLAH]
Nu 3:33 To Merari belonged the clans of the M and 4707

MAHLON (3) [MAHLON'S]
Ru 1: 2 names of his two sons were M and Kilion. 4705
1: 5 both M and Kilion also died, 4705
4: 9 the property of Elimelech, Kilion and M. 4705

MAHLON'S (1) [MAHLON]
Ru 4:10 Ruth the Moabitess, M widow, as my wife, 4705

MAHOL (1)
1Ki 4:31 Calcol and Darda, the sons of M. 4689

MAHSEIAH (2)
Jer 32:12 Baruch son of Neriah, the son of M, 4729
51:59 Seraiah son of Neriah, the son of M, 4729

MAID (2) [MAIDEN, MAIDENS, MAIDS]
Ps 123: 2 eyes of a m look to the hand of her mistress, 9148
Isa 24: 2 for mistress as for m, for seller as for buyer, 9148

MAIDEN (5) [MAID]
Ge 24:43 if a m comes out to draw water and I say 6625
Pr 30:19 and the way of a man with a m. 6625
Isa 62: 5 As a young man marries a m, 1435
Jer 2:32 Does a m forget her jewelry, 1435
51:22 with you I shatter young man and m, 1435

MAIDENS (11) [MAID]
Ps 68:25 with them are the m playing tambourines. 6625
78:63 and their m had no wedding songs; 1435
148:12 young men and m, old men and children. 1435
SS 1: 3 No wonder the m love you! 6625
2: 2 among thorns is my darling among the m. 1426
6: 9 The m saw her and called her blessed; 1426
Jer 31:13 Then m will dance and be glad, 1435
La 1: 4 her m grieve, and she is in bitter anguish. 1435
1:18 My young men and m have gone into exile. 1435
2:21 my young men and m have fallen by 1435
Eze 9: 6 Slaughter old men, young men and m, 1435

MAIDS (7) [MAID]
Ge 24:61 Then Rebekah and her m got ready 5855
1Sa 25:42 attended by her five m, 5855
Est 2: 9 He assigned to her seven m selected from 5855
2: 9 and moved her and her m into the best place 5855
4: 4 When Esther's m and eunuchs came 5855
4:16 I and my m will fast as you do. 5855
Pr 9: 3 She has sent out her m, 5855

MAIDSERVANT (28) [SERVANT]
Ge 16: 1 But she had an Egyptian m named Hagar; 9148
16: 2 Go, sleep with my m; 9148
16: 3 Sarai his wife took her Egyptian m Hagar 9148
21:12 be so distressed about the boy and your m. 563
21:13 I will make the son of the m into a nation 563
25:12 whom Sarah's m, Hagar the Egyptian, 9148
29:24 to his daughter as her m. 9148
29:29 to his daughter Rachel as her m. 9148
30: 3 Then she said, "Here is Bilhah, my m. 563
30: 9 she took her m Zilpah and gave her to Jacob 9148
30:18 "God has rewarded me for giving my m 9148
35:25 The sons of Rachel's m Bilhah: 9148
35:26 The sons of Leah's m Zilpah: 9148
Ex 20:10 nor your manservant or m, 563
20:17 or his manservant or m, his ox or donkey, 563
21:26 "If a man hits a manservant or m in the eye 563
21:27 the tooth of a manservant or m, 563
Lev 25: 6 for yourself, your manservant and m, 563
Dt 5:14 nor your manservant or m, nor your ox, 563
5:14 so that your manservant and m may rest, 563
5:21 his manservant or m, his ox or donkey, 563
15:17 Do the same for your m. 563
Jdg 19:19 me, your m, and the young man with us. 563
1Sa 25:41 "Here is your m, ready to serve you 563
28:21 she said, "Look, your m has obeyed you. 9148
Ps 86:16 to your servant and save the son of your m. 563
116:16 I am your servant, the son of your m; 563
Pr 30:23 and a m who displaces her mistress. 9148

MAIDSERVANTS (21) [SERVANT]
Ge 12:16 menservants and m, and camels. 9148
24:35 silver and gold, menservants and m, 9148
30:43 and m and menservants, 9148
31:33 and into the tent of the two m, 563
32: 5 sheep and goats, menservants and m. 9148
32:22 his two m and his eleven sons and crossed 9148
33: 1 Rachel and the two m. 9148
33: 2 He put the m and their children in front, 9148
33: 6 Then the m and their children approached 9148
Dt 12:12 your menservants and m, 563
12:18 your menservants and m, 563
16:11 your menservants and m, 563
16:14 your menservants and m, and the Levites, 563
1Sa 8:16 Your menservants and m and the best 9148
2Ki 5:26 flocks, herds, or menservants and m? 9148
Ezr 2:65 besides their 7,337 menservants and m; 563
Ne 7:67 besides their 7,337 menservants and m; 563
Job 19:15 My guests and my m count me a stranger; 563
31:13 to my menservants and m when they had 563
Isa 14: 2 as menservants and m in the LORD's land. 9148
Lk 12:45 the menservants and m and to eat and drink *4087*

MAIL (KJV) See SCALE ARMOR

MAIM See ABEL MAIM, MISREPHOTH MAIM

MAIMED (3)
Lev 22:22 the injured or the m, 3024
Mt 18: 8 for you to enter life m or crippled than *3245*
Mk 9:43 for you to enter life m than with two hands *3245*

MAIN (11)
Nu 20:19 "We will go along the m road, 5019
Dt 2:27 We will stay on the m road; 2006+2006
1Ki 6: 3 The portico at the front of the m hall *of* 2121
6: 5 of the m hall and inner sanctuary he built 2121
6:17 The m hall in front 2121
6:33 for the entrance to the m hall. 2121
7:50 for the doors of the m hall of the temple. 2121
2Ch 3: 5 the m hall with pine and covered it 1524
3:13 facing the m hall. 1074
4:22 and the doors of the m hall. 2121
Eze 19:14 its m branches and consumed its fruit. 964+4751

MAINLAND (2) [LAND]
Eze 26: 6 on the m will be ravaged by the sword. 8441
26: 8 He will ravage your settlements on the m 8441

MAINSAIL (KJV) See FORESAIL

MAINSTAY (1)
Jer 49:35 the bow of Elam, the m *of* their might. 8040

MAINTAIN (16) [MAINTAINED, MAINTAINING, MAINTAINS]
Ru 4: 5 in order to m the name of the dead 7756
4:10 to m the name of the dead with his property, 7756
1Ki 10: 9 to m justice and righteousness." 6913
2Ki 8:19 He had promised to m a lamp for David 5989
2Ch 9: 8 to m justice and righteousness." 6913
21: 7 He had promised to m a lamp for him 5989
Job 27: 6 *I will* m my righteousness 2616
Ps 82: 3 m *the* rights *of* the poor and oppressed. 7405
89:28 *I will* m my love to him forever, 9068
106: 3 Blessed are *they who* m justice, 9068
Pr 5: 2 that you *may* m discretion 9068
Isa 56: 1 "M justice and do what is right, 9068
Da 11:20 a tax collector to m the royal splendor. NIH
Hos 12: 6 m love and justice, 9068
Am 5:15 Hate evil, love good; m justice in the courts. 3657
Ro 3:28 For *we* m that a man is justified *3357*

MAINTAINED (1) [MAINTAIN]
Rev 6: 9 of God and the testimony *they had* m. *2400*

MAINTAINING (1) [MAINTAIN]
Ex 34: 7 m love to thousands, and forgiving 5915

MAINTAINS (3) [MAINTAIN]
Job 2: 3 And he still m his integrity, 2616
Pr 28: 2 of understanding and knowledge m order. 799
Na 1: 2 and m his wrath against his enemies. 5757

MAJESTIC (14) [MAJESTY]
Ex 15: 6 Your right hand, O LORD, was m in power. 158
15:11 Who is like you—m in holiness, 158
Job 37: 4 he thunders with his m voice. 1454
Ps 8: 1 how m is your name in all the earth! 129
8: 9 how m is your name in all the earth! 129
29: 4 the voice of the LORD is m. 2077
68:15 The mountains of Bashan are m mountains; 466
76: 4 more m than mountains rich with game. 129
111: 3 Glorious and m are his deeds, 2077
SS 6: 4 m as troops with banners. 398
6:10 m as the stars in procession? 398
Isa 30:30 LORD will cause men to hear his m voice 2086
Eze 31: 7 It was m in beauty, 3636
2Pe 1:17 the voice came to him from the M Glory, 3485

MAJESTY (39) [MAJESTIC]
Ex 15: 7 In the greatness of your m you threw 1454
Dt 5:24 and his m, and we have heard his voice 1542
11: 2 his m, his mighty hand, 1542
33:17 In m he is like a firstborn bull; 2077
33:26 to help you and on the clouds in his m. 1452
1Ch 16:27 Splendor and m are before him; 2077
29:11 and the power and the glory and the m and 5905
Est 1: 4 and the splendor and glory of his m. 1525
7: 3 and if it pleases your m, grant me my life— 4889
Job 37:22 God comes in awesome m. 2086
40:10 and clothe yourself in honor and m. 2077
Ps 21: 5 you have bestowed on him splendor and m. 2077
45: 3 clothe yourself with splendor and m. 2077
45: 4 In your m ride forth victoriously in behalf 2077
68:34 whose m is over Israel, 1452
93: 1 The LORD reigns, he is robed in m; 1455
93: 1 the LORD is robed in m and is armed NIH
96: 6 Splendor and m are before him; 2077
104: 1 you are clothed with splendor and m. 2077
110: 3 Arrayed in holy m, 2077
145: 5 of the glorious splendor of your m, 2086
Isa 2:10 of the LORD and the splendor of his m! 1454
2:19 of the LORD and the splendor of his m, 1454
2:21 of the LORD and the splendor of his m, 1454
24:14 from the west they acclaim the LORD's m. 1454
26:10 on doing evil and regard not the m of 1455
53: 2 He had no beauty or m to attract us to him, 2077
Eze 31: 2 " 'Who can be compared with you in m? 1542
31:18 be compared with you in splendor and m? 1542
Da 4:30 and for the glory of my m?" 10199
Mic 5: 4 the m of the name of the LORD his God. 1454
Zec 6:13 with m and will sit and rule on his throne. 2086
Ac 19:27 will be robbed of her divine m." 3484
25:26 I have nothing definite to write to His M 3261
2Th 1: 9 of the Lord and from the m of his power 1518
Heb 1: 3 down at the right hand of the M in heaven. 3488
8: 1 at the right hand of the throne of the M 3488
2Pe 1:16 but we were eyewitnesses of his m. 3484
Jude 1:25 m, power and authority, 3488

MAJOR (1) [MAJORITY]
2Ki 3:19 every fortified city and every m town. 4435

MAJORITY (2) [MAJOR]
Ac 27:12 the m decided that we should sail on, 4498
2Co 2: 6 on him by the m is sufficient for him. 4498

MAKAZ (1)
1Ki 4: 9 in M, Shaalbim, Beth Shemesh 5242

MAKE (857) [MADE, MAKER, MAKERS, MAKES, MAKING, MAN-MADE]
Ge 1:26 God said, "Let us m man in our image, 6913
2:18 I will m a helper suitable for him." 6913
6:14 So m yourself an ark of cypress wood; 6913
6:14 m rooms in it and coat it with pitch inside 6913
6:16 M a roof for it and finish the ark to 6913
6:16 a door in the side of the ark and m lower, 6913
11: 3 let's m bricks and bake them 4236+4246
11: 4 that we may m a name for ourselves and not 6913
12: 2 "I will m you into a great nation 6913
12: 2 I will m your name great, 1540
13:16 I will m your offspring like the dust of 8492
17: 6 I will m you very fruitful; 7238
17: 6 I will m nations of you, 5989
17:20 I will m him fruitful 7238
17:20 and I will m him into a great nation. 5989
21:13 I will m the son of the maidservant into 8492
21:18 for I will m him into a great nation." 8492
22:17 m your descendants as numerous as 8049+8049
24: 6 "M sure that you do not take my son back 9068
24:40 m your journey a success, 7503
26: 4 m your descendants as numerous 8049
26:28 Let us m a treaty with you 4162
28: 3 God Almighty bless you and m you fruitful 7238
31:44 Come now, let's m a covenant, you and I, 4162
32: 9 and I will m you prosper,' 3512
32:12 'I will surely m you prosper 3512+3512
32:12 and will m your descendants like the sand 8492
34:12 M the price for the bride and the gift I am to bring as great as you like, 4394+8049
39:14 to us to m sport of us! 7464
39:17 to me to m sport of me. 7464
41:43 and men shouted before him, "M way!" 91
46: 3 for I will m you into a great nation there. 8492
48: 4 'I am going to m you fruitful 7238
48: 4 I will m you a community of peoples, 5989
48:20 'May God m you like Ephraim 8492
Ex 3:21 "And I will m the Egyptians favorably 5989
5: 8 to m the same number of bricks as before; 6913
5: 9 M the work harder for the men so AIT
5:16 yet we are told, 'M bricks!' 6913
6: 3 the LORD I did not m myself known 3359
8: 5 and m frogs come up on the land of Egypt.' 6590
8:23 I will m a distinction between my people 8492
9: 4 the LORD will m a distinction between 7111
10:28 M sure you do not appear before me again! 9068
17: 3 m us and our children and livestock die 4637
17:14 m sure that Joshua hears 265+928+8492
18:22 That will m your load lighter, 7837
20: 4 "You shall not m for yourself an idol in 6913
20:23 Do not m any gods to be alongside me; 6913
20:23 not m for yourselves gods of silver or gods 6913
20:24 " 'M an altar of earth for me and sacrifice 6913
20:25 If you m an altar of stones for me, 6913
22: 3 must certainly m restitution, 8966+8966
22: 5 he must m restitution from the best 8966
22: 6 one who started the fire must m restitution. 8966+8966
22:12 he must m restitution to the owner. 8966
22:14 he must m restitution. 8966+8966
23:27 m all your enemies turn their backs 448+5989
23:32 Do not m a covenant with them or 4162
25: 8 "Then have them m a sanctuary for me, 6913
25: 9 M this tabernacle and all its furnishings 6913
25:10 "Have them m a chest of acacia wood— 6913
25:11 and m a gold molding around it. 6913
25:13 Then m poles of acacia wood 6913
25:17 "M an atonement cover of pure gold— 6913
25:18 And m two cherubim out of hammered 6913
25:19 M one cherub on one end and 6913
25:19 m the cherubim of one piece with the cover, 6913
25:23 "M a table of acacia wood— 6913
25:24 with pure gold and m a gold molding 6913
25:25 Also m around it a rim a handbreadth wide 6913
25:26 M four gold rings for the table 6913
25:28 M the poles of acacia wood, 6913
25:29 And m its plates and dishes of pure gold, 6913
25:31 "M a lampstand of pure gold 6913
25:37 "Then m its seven lamps and set them up 6913
25:40 See that you m them according to 6913
26: 1 "M the tabernacle with ten curtains 6913
26: 4 M loops of blue material along the edge of 6913
26: 5 M fifty loops on one curtain and fifty loops 6913
26: 6 Then m fifty gold clasps and use them 6913
26: 7 "M curtains of goat hair for the tent over 6913
26:10 M fifty loops along the edge of 6913
26:11 Then m fifty bronze clasps and put them in 6913
26:14 M for the tent a covering 6913
26:15 "M upright frames of acacia wood for 6913
26:17 M all the frames of the tabernacle 6913
26:18 M twenty frames for the south side of 6913
26:19 and m forty silver bases to go under them— 6913
26:20 of the tabernacle, m twenty frames NIH
26:22 M six frames for the far end, that is, 6913
26:23 m two frames for the corners at the far end. 6913
26:26 "Also m crossbars of acacia wood: 6913
26:29 and m gold rings to hold the crossbars. 6913
26:31 "M a curtain of blue, 6913
26:36 the entrance to the tent m a curtain of blue, 6913
26:37 M gold hooks for this curtain and five posts 6913
27: 2 M a horn at each of the four corners, 6913
27: 3 M all its utensils of bronze— 6913
27: 4 M a grating for it, a bronze network, 6913
27: 4 and m a bronze ring at each of 6913
27: 6 M poles of acacia wood for the altar 6913
27: 8 M the altar hollow, out of boards. 6913
27: 9 "M a courtyard for the tabernacle. 6913
28: 2 M sacred garments for your brother Aaron, 6913
28: 3 in such matters that they are to m garments 6913
28: 4 These are the garments they are to m: 6913
28: 4 They are to m these sacred garments 6913
28: 6 "M the ephod of gold, and of blue, 6913
28:13 M gold filigree settings 6913
28:15 M it like the ephod: 6913
28:22 "For the breastpiece m braided chains 6913
28:23 M two gold rings for it and fasten them 6913
28:26 M two gold rings and attach them to 6913
28:27 M two more gold rings and attach them to 6913
28:31 "M the robe of the ephod entirely 6913
28:33 M pomegranates of blue, 6913
28:36 "M a plate of pure gold and engrave on it as 6913
28:39 of fine linen and m the turban of fine linen. 6913
28:40 M tunics, sashes and headbands 6913
28:42 "M linen undergarments as a covering for 6913
29: 2 m bread, and cakes mixed with oil, 6913
29:28 It is the contribution the Israelites are to m 2118
29:36 as a sin offering to m atonement. NIH
29:37 For seven days m atonement for the altar 4105
30: 1 "M an altar of acacia wood 6913
30: 3 and m a gold molding around it. 6913
30: 4 M two gold rings for the altar below 6913
30: 5 M the poles of acacia wood 6913
Ex 30:10 Once a year Aaron shall m atonement 4105
30:15 not to give less when you m the offering to 5989
30:18 "M a bronze basin, 6913
30:25 M these into a sacred anointing oil, 6913
30:32 and do not m any oil with the same formula. 6913
30:35 and m a fragrant blend of incense, 6913
30:37 Do not m any incense with this formula 6913
31: 4 to m artistic designs for work in gold, 3108
31: 6 to m everything I have commanded you: 6913
31:11 to m them just as I commanded you." 6913
32: 1 "Come, m us gods who will go before us. 6913
32:10 Then I will m you into a great nation." 6913
32:13 m your descendants as numerous 8049
32:23 'M us gods who will go before us. 6913
32:30 perhaps I can m atonement for your sin." 4105
34:12 not to m a treaty with those who live in 4162
34:15 not to m a treaty with those who live in 4162
34:17 "Do not m cast idols. 6913
35:10 among you are to come and m everything 6913
35:32 to m artistic designs for work in gold, 3108
36: 6 "No man or woman is to m anything else 6913
38:28 used the 1,775 shekels to m the hooks 6913
38:28 and to m their bands. 3138
38:30 They used it to m the bases for the entrance 6913
Lev 1: 4 be accepted on his behalf to m atonement 4105
3:14 to m this offering to the LORD by fire: 7928
4:20 In this way the priest will m atonement for 4105
4:26 In this way the priest will m atonement for 4105
4:31 In this way the priest will m atonement for 4105
4:35 In this way the priest will m atonement for 4105
5: 3 anything that would m him unclean— AIT
5: 6 and the priest shall m atonement for him 4105
5:10 in the prescribed way and m atonement 4105
5:13 the priest will m atonement for him for any 4105
5:16 He must m restitution for what 8966
5:16 who will m atonement for him with 4105
5:18 In this way the priest will m atonement 4105
6: 5 He must m restitution in full, 8966
6: 7 the priest will m atonement for him before 4105
6:30 into the Tent of Meeting to m atonement in 4105
8:15 So he consecrated it to m atonement for it. 4105
8:34 by the LORD to m atonement for you. 6913
9: 7 and your burnt offering and m atonement 4105
9: 7 for the people and m atonement for them, 4105
11:24 m yourselves unclean by these: 3237
11:43 Do not m yourselves unclean by 3237
11:44 Do not m yourselves unclean by 3237
12: 7 before the LORD to m atonement for her, 4105
12: 8 In this way the priest will m atonement 4105
14:18 be cleansed and m atonement for him 4105
14:19 and m atonement for the one to be cleansed 4105
14:20 and m atonement for him, 4105
14:21 guilt offering to be waved to m atonement 4105
14:29 to m atonement for him before the LORD. 4105
14:31 In this way the priest will m atonement 4105
14:53 In this way he will m atonement for 4105
15: 3 it will m him unclean. NIH
15:15 In this way he will m atonement before 4105
15:30 In this way he will m atonement for her 4105
15:31 things that m them unclean, 3240
16: 6 for his own sin offering to m atonement 4105
16:11 for his own sin offering to m atonement 4105
16:16 In this way he will m atonement for 4105
16:17 the time Aaron goes in to m atonement 4105
16:18 that is before the LORD and m atonement 4105
16:24 to m atonement for himself and for 4105
16:27 the Most Holy Place to m atonement, must 4105
16:32 as high priest is to m atonement. 4105
16:33 and m atonement for the Most Holy Place, 4105
17:11 to m atonement for yourselves on the altar; 4105
19: 4 not turn to idols or m gods of cast metal 6913
19:22 the priest is to m atonement for him before 4105
20:25 therefore m a distinction between clean 976
21: 1 m himself ceremonially unclean 3237
21: 3 for her he may m himself unclean. 3237
21: 4 not m himself unclean for people related 3237
21: 8 I who m you holy. 7727
21:11 He must not m himself unclean, 3237
22:14 he must m restitution to the priest for 5989
24:18 of someone's animal must m restitution— 8966
24:21 an animal must m restitution, 8966
25:39 do not m him work as a slave. 6268
25:46 and can m them slaves for life, 6268
26: 1 " 'Do not m idols or set up an image or 6913
26: 6 down and no one will m you afraid. 3006
26: 9 on you with favor and m you fruitful 7238
26:10 to move it out to m room for the new. 4946+7156
26:19 down your stubborn pride and m the sky 5989
26:22 m you so few in number 5070
26:36 I will m their hearts so fearful in the lands 995
27:33 from the bad or m any substitution. 4614
27:33 If he does m a substitution, 4614+4614
Nu 3:40 or more and m a list of their names. 5951
5: 7 He must m full restitution 928+8031+8740
6: 2 or woman wants to m a special vow, 5623+7098
6: 7 m himself ceremonially unclean 3237
6:11 as a burnt offering to m atonement for him 4105
6:16 before the LORD and m the sin offering 6913
6:25 the LORD m his face shine upon you and 239
8: 6 m them ceremonially clean. 3197
8:12 to m atonement for the Levites. 4105
8:19 the Israelites and to m atonement for them 4105
10: 2 "M two trumpets of hammered silver, 6913
14:12 but I will m you into a nation greater 6913
14:30 with uplifted hand to m your home, 8905
15:25 The priest is to m atonement for 4105
15:28 to m atonement before the LORD for 4105

Nu 15:38 to come *you are to* **m** tassels on the corners 6913
16:46 and hurry to the assembly *to* **m atonement** 4105
21: 8 "**M** a snake and put it up on a pole; 6913
22:28 *to* **m** *you* **beat** me these three times?" AIT
28: 9 **m** an offering of two lambs a year old NIH
28:22 as a sin offering to **m atonement** for you. 4105
28:30 Include one male goat to **m atonement** 4105
29: 5 as a sin offering to **m atonement** for you. 4105
31:50 to **m atonement** for ourselves before 4105
32: 5 *Do* not **m** us **cross** the Jordan." 6296
Dt 4:16 not become corrupt and **m** for yourselves 6913
4:23 *do* not **m** for yourselves an idol in the form 6913
4:25 then become corrupt and **m** any kind of idol, 6913
5: 8 "*You shall* not **m** for yourself an idol in 6913
7: 2 **M** no treaty with them, 4162
9:14 And *I will* **m** you into a nation stronger 6913
10: 1 Also **m** a wooden chest. 6913
17:16 or **m** the people **return** to Egypt to get 8740
19:18 **m** *a* thorough **investigation,** 2011
20:10 **m** its people **an offer** of peace. 7924
20:12 *to* **m peace** and they engage you in battle, 8966
22: 8 **m** a parapet around your roof so 6913
22:12 **M** tassels on the four corners of 6913
23:21 If *you* **m a vow** to the LORD your God, 5623+5624
24:10 When *you* **m a loan** of any kind 5394+5957
25: 2 the judge *shall* **m** him **lie down** 5877
28:13 The LORD *will* **m** you the head, 5989
28:63 the LORD to **m** you **prosper** and increase 3512
28:68 I said you *should* never **m again.** 3578+6388
29: 1 the LORD commanded Moses to **m** with 4162
29:18 **M** sure there is no man or woman, NIH
29:18 **m** sure there is no root among you NIH
30: 5 *He will* **m** you **more prosperous** 3512
30: 9 LORD your God *will m* you **most** prosperous AIT
30: 9 delight in you and **m** you prosperous, NIH
32:21 I *will* **m** them **envious** by those who are not 7861
32:21 *I will* **m** them **angry** by a nation 4087
32:25 the sword *will* **m** them **childless;** 8897
32:42 *I will* **m** my arrows **drunk** with blood, 8910
32:43 and **m atonement** *for* his land and people. 4105
Jos 5: 2 "**M** flint knives and circumcise 6913
6:18 Otherwise *you will* **m** the camp 8492
9: 2 they came together to **m war** against Joshua 4309
9: 6 **m** a treaty with us." 4162
9: 7 How then *can we* **m** a treaty with you?" 4162
9:11 **m** a treaty with us."' 4162
18: 4 *to* **m a survey of** the land and to write 928+2143
18: 8 "Go and **m a survey of** the land and 928+2143
24:20 and bring disaster on you and **m an end** 3983
Jdg 2: 2 and you *shall* not **m** a covenant with 4162
5: 3 *I will* **m music** to the LORD, 2376
6:39 **m** just one more **request.** 1819
6:39 This time **m** the fleece dry and 2118
17: 3 the LORD for my son to **m** a carved image 6913
Ru 4:11 the LORD **m** the woman who is coming 5989
1Sa 1:23 only *may* the LORD **m good** his word." 7756
3:11 that *will* **m** the ears of everyone who hears
of it **tingle.** AIT
6: 5 **M** models of the tumors and of the rats 6913
8:11 will take your sons and **m** them **serve** 4200+8492
8:12 to **m** weapons of war and equipment 6913
11: 1 "**M** a treaty with us, 4162
11: 2 "*I will* **m a treaty** with you only on 4162
12: 3 a bribe *to* **m** *me* **shut** my eyes? 6623
12: 3 *I will* **m** it **right."** 8740
12:22 the LORD was pleased to **m** you his own. 6913
13:19 "Otherwise the Hebrews *will* **m** swords 6913
15:18 **m war** on them until you have wiped them 4309
20:26 to David to **m** him ceremonially unclean— NIH
22: 7 *Will he* **m** all of you commanders 8492
23:22 Go and **m** further **preparation.** 3922
25:28 for the LORD *will* **certainly m** 6913+6913
28: 2 *I will* **m** you my bodyguard for life." 8492
2Sa 3:12 **M** an agreement with me, 4162
3:13 "I *will* **m** an agreement with you. 4162
3:17 "For some time *you have* **wanted to m**
David your king. 1335+4200
3:21 so that *they may* **m** a compact with you, 4162
7: 9 Now *I will* **m** your name great, 6913
7:23 and to **m** a name for himself, 8492
13: 6 **m** some **special bread** in my sight, 4221+4223
15:20 today *shall I* **m** you **wander about** with us, 5675
19:28 to **m** any more **appeals** to the king?" 2410
21: 3 How *shall I* **m amends** so 4105
22:36 you stoop down *to* **m** me **great.** 8049
1Ki 1:37 **m** his throne *even* **greater** 1540
1:47 **m** Solomon's name more **famous** 3512
2:16 Now *I* **have** one **request to m** 8626+8629
2:16 "*You may* **m** it," she said. 1819
2:20 "*I* **have** one small **request to m** 8626+8629
2:20 The king replied, "**M** it, my mother; 8626[S]
2:42 "*Did I* not **m** you **swear** by the LORD 8678
9:22 But Solomon did not **m** slaves of any of 5989
10:12 **used** the algumwood **to m** supports 6913
10:12 and to **m** harps and lyres for the musicians. NIH
12: 1 the Israelites had gone there to **m** him **king.** 4887
12:10 but **m** our yoke **lighter'**— 7837
12:11 I *will* **m** it **even heavier.** 3578
12:14 I *will* **m** it **even heavier.** 3578
12:21 to **m war** against the house of Israel and 4309
12:33 and went up to the altar to **m offerings.** 7787
13: 1 by the altar to **m** *an* **offering.** 7787
13: 2 the high places who now **m offerings** here, 7787
16: 3 and *I will* **m** your house like that 5989
17:12 a few sticks to take home and **m** a meal 6913
17:13 But first **m** a small cake of bread for me 6913
17:13 then **m** something for yourself and your son. 6913
1Ki 19: 2 *I do* not **m** your life like that of one of 8492
21:22 *I will* **m** your house like that 5989
22:16 "How many times *must* I **m** you **swear** 8678
2Ki 2:21 or **m** the land **unproductive.'"** 8897
3:16 **M** this valley full of ditches. 6913
4:10 *Let's* **m** a small room on the roof and put 6913
5:17 your servant *will* never again **m** burnt
offerings and sacrifices 6913
9: 9 *I will* **m** the house of Ahab like the house 5989
9:26 and *I will* surely **m** you **pay** *for* it 8966
10:24 in to **m** sacrifices and burnt offerings. 6913
18:23 " 'Come now, **m a bargain** with my master, 6842
18:31 **M** peace with me and come out to me. 6913
19:28 and *I will* **m** you **return** by 8740
21: 8 **m** the feet of the Israelites **wander** 5653
1Ch 12:31 by name to come and **m** David **king—** 4887
12:38 to Hebron fully determined to **m** David **king** 4887
12:38 also of one mind to **m** David **king.** 4887
16: 4 to **m petition,** to give thanks, 2349
16: 8 **m known** among the nations what he has
done. 3359
17: 8 Now *I will* **m** your name like the names of 6913
17:21 and to **m** a name for yourself, 8492
18: 8 which Solomon used to **m** the bronze Sea, 6913
22: 3 to **m** nails for the doors of the gateways and NIH
22: 5 Therefore *I will* **m preparations** for it." 3922
27:23 to **m** Israel as **numerous** as the stars in 8049
28: 4 to **m** me **king** over all Israel. 4887
2Ch 7:20 *I will* **m** it a byword and an object 5989
8: 9 not **m** slaves of the Israelites for his work; 5989
9:11 **used** the algumwood **to m** 6913
9:11 and to **m** harps and lyres for the musicians. NIH
10: 1 the Israelites had gone there to **m** him **king.** 4887
10:10 but **m** our yoke **lighter'**— 7837
10:11 I *will* **m** it **even heavier.** 3578
10:14 I *will* **m** it **even heavier.** 3578
11: 1 to **m war** against Israel and to regain 4309
11:22 in order to **m** him **king.** 4887
13: 9 and **m** priests of your own as the peoples 6913
17:10 that *they did* not **m war** with Jehoshaphat. 4309
18:15 "How many times *must* I **m** you **swear** 8678
20: 1 with some of the Meunites came to **m** war NIH
28:10 **m** the **men** and women of Judah and
Jerusalem your **slaves.** 3899+6269
29:10 I intend to **m** a covenant with the LORD, 4162
32: 2 and that he intended to *m* **war** on Jerusalem, AIT
32:18 to terrify them and **m** them **afraid** in order 987
33: 8 **m** the feet of the Israelites **leave** 6073
36:22 of Cyrus king of Persia *to* **m** a proclamation 6296
Ezr 1: 1 of Cyrus king of Persia *to* **m** a proclamation 6296
4: 4 the people of Judah and **m** them **afraid** 987
10: 3 Now *let us* **m** a covenant before our God 4162
10:11 Now **m** confession to the LORD, 5989
Ne 2: 8 to **m beams** *for* the gates of the citadel by 7936
6: 7 to **m** *this* **proclamation** about you 7924
8:15 palms and shade trees, to **m** booths"— 6913
10:33 for sin offerings to **m atonement** for Israel; 4105
Job 7:17 "What is man that *you* **m** *so* **much of** him, 1540
11:19 with no *one to* **m** you **afraid,** 3006
13:26 and **m** me **inherit** the sins of my youth. 3769
16: 4 *I could* **m fine speeches** against you
928+2488+4863
20:10 His children *must* **m amends** *to* the poor; 8355
20:15 **m** his stomach **vomit** them **up.** 3769
21:12 *they* **m merry** to the sound of the flute. 8523
24:17 *they* **m friends with** the terrors of darkness. 5795
31:15 not he who made me in the womb **m** them? 6913
36:33 even the cattle **m** known its approach. NIH
38:27 a desolate wasteland and **m** it **sprout** 7541
39:20 *Do you* **m** him **leap** like a locust, 8321
41: 4 *Will he* **m** an agreement with you for you 4162
41: 5 *Can you* **m a pet** of him like a bird 8471
41:28 Arrows *do* not **m** him **flee;** 1368
Ps 2: 8 and *I will* **m** the nations your inheritance, 5989
4: 8 O LORD, **m** me **dwell** in safety. 3782
5: 8 **m straight** your way before me. 3837
7: 5 to the ground and **m** me **sleep** in the dust. 8905
7: 9 **m** the righteous **secure.** 3922
18:35 you stoop down *to* **m** me **great.** 8049
20: 4 **m** all your plans **succeed.** 4848
21: 9 of your appearing *you will* **m** them like 8883
21:12 for *you will* **m** them **turn** their backs 8883
27: 6 I will sing and **m music** to the LORD. 2376
33: 2 **m music** to him on the ten-stringed lyre. 2376
37: 6 **m** your righteousness **shine** like the dawn, 3655
39: 8 *do* not **m** me the scorn of fools. 8492
44: 8 In God *we* **m** *our* **boast** all day long, 2146
45:16 *you will* **m** them princes throughout 8883
46: 4 There is a river whose streams **m glad** 8523
51:18 In your good pleasure **m** Zion **prosper;** 3512
52: 7 the man *who did* not **m** God his stronghold 8492
57: 7 I will sing and **m music.** 2376
59:11 In your might **m** them **wander about,** 5675
66: 2 **m** his praise glorious! 8492
67: 1 and bless us and **m** his face **shine** upon us, 239
69:11 people **m sport of** *me.* 2118+4200+5442
76:11 **M** vows to the LORD your God 5623
79:10 **m known** among the nations that you
avenge 3359
80: 3 **m** your face **shine** upon us, 239
80: 7 **m** your face **shine** upon us, 239
80:19 **m** your face **shine** upon us, 239
83:11 **M** their nobles like Oreb and Zeeb, 8883
83:13 **M** them like tumbleweed, O my God, 8883
84: 6 *they* **m** it a place of springs; 8883
87: 7 As *they* **m music** they will sing, 2727
89: 1 *I will* **m** your faithfulness **known** 3359
Ps 89: 4 and **m** your throne **firm** 1215
90:15 **M** us **glad** for as many days 8523
91: 9 If you **m** the Most High your dwelling— 8492
92: 1 It is good to praise the LORD and **m music** 2376
92: 4 *you* **m** me **glad** by your deeds, O LORD; 8523
98: 5 **m music** to the LORD with the harp, 2376
104:15 oil to **m** his face **shine,** 7413
104:17 There the birds **m** *their* **nests;** 7873
105: 1 **m known** among the nations what he has
done. 3359
106: 8 **m** his mighty power **known.** 3359
106:26 that he *would* **m** them **fall** in the desert, 5877
106:27 **m** their descendants **fall** 5877
108: 1 I will sing and **m music** *with* all my soul. 2376
110: 1 at my right hand until *I* **m** your enemies 8883
115: 8 *Those who* **m** them will be like them, 6913
115:14 *May* the LORD **m** you **increase,** 3578
119:98 Your commands **m** me **wiser** than my
enemies, 2681
119:135 **M** your face **shine** upon your servant 239
119:165 and nothing can **m** them **stumble.** 4842
132:17 "Here *I will* **m** a horn **grow** for David 7541
135:18 *Those who* **m** them will be like them, 6913
139: 8 if *I* **m** *my* **bed** *in* the depths, you are there. 3667
140: 3 **m** their tongues as **sharp** as a serpent's; 9111
144: 9 the ten-stringed lyre *I will* **m music** to you, 2376
147: 7 **m music** to our God on the harp. 2376
149: 3 and **m music** to him with tambourine 2376
Pr 3: 6 and he *will* **m** your paths **straight.** 3837
4:16 of slumber till *they* **m** someone **fall.** 4173
4:26 **M level** paths for your feet 7142
8:15 By me kings reign and rulers **m laws** 2980
10: 4 Lazy hands **m** a man poor, 6913
11:14 but many advisers **m** victory sure. NIH
20:18 **M** plans by seeking advice; 3922
22:24 *Do* not **m friends** with a hot-tempered man, 8287
30:26 yet *they* **m** their home in the crags; 8492
Ecc 5: 4 When *you* **m a vow** to God, 5623+5624
5: 5 It is better not to vow than *to* **m a vow** and 5623
SS 1:11 *We will* **m** you earrings of gold, 6913
Isa 1:16 wash and **m yourselves clean.** 2342
3: 4 *I will* **m** boys their officials; 5989
3: 7 *do* not **m** me the leader of the people." 8492
3:17 the LORD *will* **m** their scalps **bald."** 6867
5: 6 *I will* **m** it a wasteland, 8883
6:10 **M** the heart of this people **calloused;** 9042
6:10 **m** their ears **dull** and close their eyes. 3877
7: 6 **m** the son of Tabeel **king** over it." 4887+4889
10: 1 Woe to those *who* **m** unjust **laws,** 2976+2980
12: 4 **m known** among the nations what he has
done, 3359
13: 9 to **m** the land desolate and destroy 8492
13:12 *I will* **m** man **scarcer** than pure gold, 3700
13:13 Therefore *I will* **m** the heavens **tremble;** 8074
14: 2 *They will* **m captives** of their captors 8647
14:14 *I will* **m myself like** the Most High." 1948
16: 3 **M** your shadow like night—at high noon. 8883
17: 2 with no *one to* **m** them **afraid.** 3006
17:11 *you* **m** them **grow,** 8451
19:12 Let them show you and **m known** what 3359
19:14 *they* **m** Egypt **stagger** in all that she does, 9494
19:21 So the LORD *will* **m himself known** to 3359
19:21 *they will* **m** vows to the LORD 5623+5624
26: 7 **m** the way of the righteous **smooth.** 7142
27: 5 *let them* **m** peace with me, yes, 6913
27: 5 yes, *let them* **m** peace with me." 6913
27:11 and women come and **m fires** *with* them. 239
28:17 *I will* **m** justice the measuring line 8492
28:28 Grain must be ground to **m** bread; NIH
29:16 "*He did* not **m** me"? 6913
29:21 **m** a man **out to be guilty,** 2627
30:30 and *will* **m** them **see** his arm coming down 8011
36: 8 " 'Come now, **m a bargain** with my master, 6842
36:16 **M** peace with me and come out to me. 6913
37:29 *I will* **m** you **return** by the way you came. 8740
38: 8 **m** the shadow cast by the sun **go** 8740
40: 3 **m straight** in the wilderness a highway 3837
41:15 "See, *I will* **m** you into a threshing sledge, 8492
41:18 *I will* **m** rivers **flow** on barren heights, 7337
42: 6 I will keep you and *will* **m** you to be 5989
42:16 before them and **m** the rough places smooth. NIH
42:21 of his righteousness *to* **m** *his* law **great** 1540
44: 9 All who **m** idols are nothing, 3670
44:19 *Shall I* **m** a detestable thing 6913
45:13 **m** all his ways **straight.** 3837
46: 6 they hire a goldsmith *to* **m** it *into* a god, 6913
46:10 **I m known** the end from the beginning, 5583
47:13 those stargazers *who* **m predictions** month 3359
49: 6 *I will* also **m** you a light for the Gentiles, 5989
49: 8 I will keep you and *will* **m** you to be 5989
49:26 *I will* **m** your oppressors **eat** their own flesh; 430
50: 3 and **m** sackcloth its covering." 8492
51: 3 *he will* **m** her deserts like Eden, 8492
54:12 *I will* **m** your battlements *of* rubies, 8492
55: 3 *I will* **m** an everlasting covenant with you, 4162
59: 6 cannot cover themselves with **what** they **m.** 5126
60:15 *I will* **m** you the everlasting pride and 8492
60:17 *I will* **m** peace your governor 8492
61: 8 and **m** an everlasting covenant with them. 4162
61:11 **m** righteousness and praise **spring up** 7541
63:14 This is how you guided your people to **m** 6913
63:17 *do you* **m** us **wander** from your ways 9494
64: 2 to **m** your name **known** to your enemies 3359
66:22 and the new earth that I **m** will endure 6913
Jer 5:14 I *will* **m** my words in your mouth a fire 5989
6: 8 and **m** your land desolate so no one can live 8492
7:18 the women knead the dough and **m** cakes 6913

Jer 9: 3 **m ready** their tongue like a bow, **to shoot** 2005
9:11 *"I will* **m** Jerusalem a heap of ruins, 5989
9:15 *I will* **m** this people **eat** bitter **food** 430
10:11 who *did* not **m** the heavens and the earth, 10522
10:22 *It will* **m** the towns of Judah desolate, 8492
15: 4 *I will* **m** them abhorrent to all 5989
15: 8 *m* their widows more **numerous** AIT
15:11 **m** your enemies **plead** 7003
15:20 *I will* **m** you a wall to this people, 5989
16:20 *Do* men **m** their own gods? 6913
18:18 Come, *let's* **m plans** against Jeremiah; 3108+4742
19: 3 that *will* **m** the ears of everyone who hears of it **tingle.** 7509
19: 7 *I will* **m** them **fall** by the sword 5877
19: 8 *I will* devastate this city and **m** it an object 8492
19: 9 *I will* **m** them **eat** the flesh of their sons 430
19:12 I *will* **m** this city like Topheth. 5989
20: 4 'I *will* **m** you a terror to yourself and 5989
22: 6 *I will* surely **m** you like a desert, 8883
22:15 *"Does it* **m** *you a* **king** to have more AIT
23:15 *"I will* **m** them **eat** bitter **food** 430
23:27 dreams they tell one another *will* **m** my people **forget** my name, 8894
24: 9 *I will* **m** them abhorrent and an offense 5989
25: 9 I will completely destroy them and **m** them 8492
25:12 "and *will* **m** it desolate forever. 8492
25:15 **m** all the nations to whom I send you **drink** 9197
25:18 to **m** them a ruin and an object of horror 5989
26: 6 then *I will* **m** this house like Shiloh 5989
27: 2 **"M** a yoke out of straps and crossbars 6913
27: 6 *I will* **m** even the wild animals subject 5989
28:14 to *m* them **serve** Nebuchadnezzar king AIT
29:17 and *I will* **m** them like poor figs that are 5989
29:18 and plague and *will* **m** them abhorrent 5989
30:10 and no *one will* **m** him **afraid.** 3006
30:16 all *who* **m spoil** *of* you I will despoil. 1024
31: 7 **M** your praises **heard,** and say, 'O LORD, 9048
31:31 "when *I will* **m** a new covenant with 4162
31:33 the covenant *I will* **m** with the house 4162
32:35 a detestable thing and so **m** Judah **sin.** 2627
32:40 *I will* **m** an everlasting covenant 4162
33:15 *I will* **m** a righteous Branch **sprout** 7541
33:22 **m** the descendants of David my servant and the Levites who minister before me as **countless** as 889+4202+6218+8049
34: 5 so *they will* **m a fire** in your honor 8596
34: 5 *I* myself **m** *this* **promise,** 1819+1821
34:17 *I will* **m** you abhorrent to all the kingdoms 5989
44: 8 and **m** yourselves an object of cursing 2118
46:27 and no *one will* **m** him **afraid.** 3006
48:26 **"M** her **drunk,** for she has defied 8910
48:35 to *those who* **m offerings** *on* the high places 6590
49:15 "Now *I will* **m** you small among 5989
51:25 and **m** you a burned out mountain. 5989
51:36 I will dry up her sea and **m** her springs **dry.** 3312
51:39 a feast for them and **m** them **drunk,** so 8910
51:44 and **m** him **spew out** what he has swallowed. 3655+4946+7023
51:57 **m** her officials and wise men **drunk,** 8910
Eze 3: 8 But *I will* **m** you as unyielding 5989
3: 9 *I will* **m** your forehead like the hardest stone 5989
3:26 *I will* **m** your tongue **stick** to the roof 1815
4: 9 in a storage jar and **use** them **to m** bread 6913
5:14 *"I will* **m** you a ruin and a reproach among 5989
6:14 and **m** the land a desolate waste from 5989
7:20 *to* **m** their detestable idols and vile images. 6913
13:18 and **m** veils of various lengths 6913
14: 8 against that man and **m** him an example and 8492
15: 3 from it to **m** anything useful? 6913
15: 3 *Do they* **m** pegs from it to hang things on? 4374
15: 8 *I will* **m** the land desolate 5989
16: 4 with water to **m** you **clean,** 5470
16:16 of your garments *to* **m** gaudy high places, 6913
16:63 when I **m atonement** for you 4105
17:24 and **m** the low tree **grow tall.** 1467
17:24 and **m** the dry tree **flourish.** 7255
21:19 **M** a signpost where the road branches off to 1345
21:27 *I will* **m** it a ruin! 8492
22: 4 Therefore *I will* **m** you an object of scorn 5989
22:12 and excessive interest and **m unjust gain** 1298
22:25 and precious things and **m many** widows 8049
22:27 and kill people to **m unjust gain.** 1298+1299
26: 4 I will scrape away her rubble and **m** her 5989
26:14 *I will* **m** you a bare rock, 5989
26:19 When I **m** you a desolate city, 5989
26:20 *I will* **m** you **dwell** in the earth below, 3782
27: 5 they took a cedar from Lebanon to **m** a mast 6913
28:23 upon her and **m** blood flow in her streets. NIH
29: 4 **m** the fish of your streams **stick** 1815
29:10 and *I will* **m** the land of Egypt a ruin and 5989
29:12 *I will* **m** the land of Egypt desolate 5989
29:15 *I will* **m** it *so* **weak** 5070
29:21 "On that day *I will* **m** a horn **grow** for 7541
30:22 and **m** the sword **fall** from his hand. 5877
32:14 and **m** her streams **flow** like oil, 2143
32:15 When I **m** Egypt desolate and strip the land 5989
33: 2 of their men and **m** him their watchman, 5989
33:28 *I will* **m** the land a desolate waste, 5989
34:25 " *'I will* **m** a covenant of peace with them 4162
34:28 and no *one will* **m** them **afraid.** 3006
35: 3 against you and **m** you a desolate waste. 5989
35: 7 *I will* **m** Mount Seir a desolate waste 5989
35: 9 *I will* **m** you desolate forever; 5989
35:11 and *I will* **m myself known** among them 3359
35:14 *I will* **m** you desolate. 6913
36:11 and *will* **m** you **prosper** more than before. 3201
36:14 **m** your nation **childless,** 8897
Eze 36:15 No longer *will I* **m** you **hear** the taunts of 9048
36:29 I will call for the grain and **m** it **plentiful** 8049
36:37 *I will* **m** their people as **numerous** as 8049
37: 5 I *will* **m** breath **enter** you, 928+995
37: 6 and **m** flesh **come** upon you and cover you 6590
37:22 *I will* **m** them one nation in the land, 6913
37:26 *I will* **m** a covenant of peace with them; 4162
37:28 that I the LORD **m** Israel **holy,** 7727
38:23 and *I will* **m myself known** in the sight 3359
39: 3 your left hand and **m** your arrows **drop** 5877
39: 7 " *'I will* **m known** my holy name 3359
39:26 in their land with no *one to* **m** them **afraid.** 3006
43:11 **m known** *to* them the design of the temple 3359
43:20 so purify the altar and **m atonement** *for* it. 4105
43:26 For seven days *they are to* **m atonement** *for* 4105
45:15 fellowship offerings to **m atonement** for 4105
45:17 fellowship offerings to **m atonement** for 4105
45:20 so *you are to* **m atonement** *for* the temple. 4105
45:25 *to* **m** the same **provision** *for* sin offerings, 6913
Da 9:18 We *do* not **m** requests of you 5877
11: 6 to the king of the North to **m** an alliance, 6913
11:17 the might of his entire kingdom and *will* **m** 6913
11:39 *He will* **m** them **rulers** over many people 5440
Hos 2: 3 and **m** her as **bare** as on 3657
2: 3 *I will* **m** her like a desert, 8492
2:12 *I will* **m** them a thicket, 8492
2:15 will **m** the Valley of Achor a door of hope. NIH
2:18 that day *I will* **m** a covenant for them with 4162
8: 4 With their silver and gold *they* **m** idols 6913
10: 4 *They* **m many promises,** take false 1819+1821
10: 4 take false oaths and **m** agreements; 4162
11: 8 How *can I* **m** you like Zeboiim? 8492
12: 9 *I will* **m** you **live** in tents again, 3782
13: 2 *they* **m** idols for themselves 6913
Joel 2:17 not **m** your inheritance an object of scorn, 5989
2:19 never again *will I* **m** you an object 5989
Am 8: 9 *"I will* **m** the sun **go down** 995
8:10 **m** all of you **wear** sackcloth 5516+6584+6590
8:10 *I will* **m** that time like mourning for 8492
9:14 *they will* **m** gardens and eat their fruit. 6913
Ob 1: 2 *I will* **m** you small among the nations; 5989
1: 3 the clefts of the rocks and **m** your home on NIH
1: 4 the eagle and **m** your nest among the stars, 8492
Jnh 1:11 *m* the sea **calm down** for us?" AIT
2: 9 What I have vowed *I will* **m good.** 8966
4:10 though you did not tend it or **m** it **grow.** 1540
Mic 1: 6 *I will* **m** Samaria a heap of rubble, 8492
1:16 **m** yourselves as **bald** as the vulture, 7947+8143
4: 4 and no *one will* **m** them **afraid,** 3006
4: 7 *I will* **m** the lame a remnant, 8492
Na 1: 8 but with an overwhelming flood *he will* **m** 6913
3: 6 I will treat you with contempt and **m** you 8492
Hab 1: 3 Why *do you* **m** me **look** *at* injustice? 8011
2: 2 "Write down the revelation and **m** it **plain** 930
2: 7 Will they not wake up and **m** you **tremble?** 2316
3: 2 in our time **m** them **known;** 3359
Zep 1:18 for *he will* **m** a sudden end *of* all who live 6913
3:13 down and no *one will* **m** them **afraid."** 3006
Hag 2:23 'and *I will* **m** you like my signet ring, 8492
Zec 6:11 Take the silver and gold and **m** a crown, 6913
9:13 Greece, and **m** you like a warrior's sword. 8492
9:17 Grain *will* **m** the young men **thrive,** 5649
10: 3 and **m** them like a proud horse in battle. 8492
12: 2 *to* **m** Jerusalem a cup that sends all 8492
12: 3 *I will* **m** Jerusalem an immovable rock 8492
12: 6 "On that day *I will* **m** the leaders of Judah 8492
Mal 3:17 when I **m up** my treasured possession. 6913
Mt 2: 8 "Go and **m** a careful **search** for the child. *2004*
3: 3 **m** straight paths for him.' " *4472*
4:19 "and *I will* **m** you fishers of men." *4472*
5:36 you cannot **m** even one hair white or black. *4472*
8: 2 if you are willing, you can **m** me **clean."** *2751*
12:33 **"M** a tree good and its fruit will be good, *4472*
12:33 or **m** a tree bad and its fruit will be bad, *4472*
15:11 What goes into a man's mouth *does* not **m** him **'unclean,'** *3124*
15:18 and these **m** a man **'unclean.'** *3124*
15:20 These are what **m** a man **'unclean'**; *3124*
15:20 unwashed hands *does* not **m** him **'unclean.'** *3124*
23: 5 **m** their phylacteries **wide** *4425*
23:15 *you* **m** him twice as much a son of hell *4472*
26:17 "Where do you want *us to* **m preparations** *2286*
27:65 **m** the tomb as **secure** as you know how." *856*
28:19 Therefore go and **m disciples** of all nations, *3411*
Mk 1: 3 **m** straight paths for him.' " *4472*
1:17 "and *I will* **m** you fishers of men." *4472*
1:40 "If you are willing, you can **m** me **clean."** *2751*
7:15 a man can **m** him **'unclean'** by going *3124*
7:18 from the outside can **m** him **'unclean'?** *3124*
7:23 from inside and **m** a man **'unclean.' "** *3124*
9:50 how *can you* **m** it **salty** again? *789*
12:40 and for a show **m** lengthy **prayers.** *4667*
14:12 to go and **m preparations** for you to eat *2286*
14:15 **M preparations** for us there." *2286*
Lk 1:17 *to* **m ready** a people prepared for the Lord." *2286*
3: 4 **m** straight paths for him. *4472*
5:12 if you are willing, you can **m** me **clean."** *2751*
5:34 "Can you **m** the guests of the bridegroom *4472*
11:40 *Did* not the one who made the outside **m** the *4472*
13:24 **"M every effort** to enter through *76*
14:18 "But they all alike began *to* **m excuses.** *4148*
14:23 and country lanes and **m** them come in, *337*
15:19 **m** me like one of your hired men.' *4472*
16: 6 sit down quickly, and **m it** four hundred.' *1211*
16: 7 'Take your bill and **m it** eight hundred.' *1211*
20:43 until *I* **m** your enemies a footstool *5502*
20:47 and for a show **m** lengthy **prayers.** *4667*
Lk 21:14 But **m up** your **mind** not to worry beforehand *1877+2840+3836+5502*
22: 8 "Go and **m preparations** for us to eat *2286*
22:12 **M preparations** there." *2286*
Jn 1:23 **'M straight** the way for the Lord.' " *2316*
5:44 **m** no **effort to obtain** praise that comes *2426*
6:15 that they intended to come and **m** him king *4472*
7:24 and **m** a right **judgment."** *3212+3213*
11:52 bring them together and **m** them **one.** *1650+1651*
14:23 and we will come to him and **m** our home *4472*
16:15 from what is mine and **m it known** to you. *334*
17:26 and *will continue to* **m** you **known** *1192*
Ac 2:35 until *I* **m** your enemies a footstool *5502*
5:28 and are determined *to* **m** us **guilty of** *2042+2093*
7:40 **'M** us gods who will go before us. *4472*
15:19 that *we should* not **m it difficult for** *4214*
19:33 *in order to* **m a defense** before the people. *664+2527*
24:10 so *I* gladly **m** my **defense.** *664*
26: 2 as *I* **m** *my* **defense** against all the accusations *664*
27:16 we were hardly able *to* **m** the lifeboat secure *1181*
Ro 1:11 to you some spiritual gift to **m** you **strong** *5114*
9:20 'Why *did you* **m** me like this?' " *4472*
9:21 Does not the potter have the right *to* **m** out *4472*
9:22 to show his wrath and **m** his power **known,** *1192*
9:23 **m** the riches of his glory **known** *1192*
10:19 "I *will* **m** you **envious** by those who are not *4143*
10:19 *I will* **m** you **angry** by a nation *4239*
11:11 to the Gentiles to **m** Israel **envious.** *4143*
11:13 *I* **m much of** my ministry *1519*
14: 4 for the Lord is able *to* **m** him **stand.** *2705*
14:13 **m up** *your* **mind** not to put any stumbling *3212*
14:19 therefore **m every effort** to do what leads *1503*
15:26 *to* **m** a contribution for the poor among *4472*
1Co 4: 4 but that *does* not **m** *me* **innocent.** *1467*
9:18 so not **m use of** my rights in preaching it. *2974*
9:19 *I* **m** myself **a slave** to everyone, *1530*
9:27 I beat my body and **m** it my **slave** so that *1524*
14: 7 in the case of lifeless things *that* **m** sounds, *1443*
16: 7 to see you now and **m** only a passing visit; *NIG*
2Co 1:17 Or *do I* **m** *my* **plans** in a worldly manner so *1086*
2: 1 **m** another painful **visit** *2262*
2: 2 who is left to **m** me **glad** *2370*
2: 3 by those who ought *to* **m** me **rejoice.** *5897*
5: 9 So *we* **m it** *our* **goal** to please him, *5818*
7: 2 **M room for** us in your hearts. *6003*
9: 8 God is able *to* **m** all grace **abound** to you, *4355*
10: 5 to **m** it obedient to Christ. *NIG*
Gal 2: 4 in Christ Jesus and to **m** us **slaves.** *2871*
6:12 *to* **m a good impression** outwardly *2349*
Eph 3: 9 *to* **m plain** to everyone the administration *5894*
4: 3 **M every effort** to keep the unity of *5079*
5:19 Sing and **m music** in your heart to the Lord. *6010*
5:26 to **m** her **holy,** cleansing her by the washing *39*
6:19 so that I will fearlessly **m known** the *1192*
Php 2: 2 **m** my joy **complete** by being like-minded, *4444*
2:30 to **m up for** the help you could not give me. *405*
3:15 that too God *will* **m clear** to you. *636*
Col 1:27 To them God has chosen *to* **m known** *1192*
4: 5 toward outsiders; **m the most** of every **opportunity.** *1973+2789+3836*
1Th 2: 3 the appeal we **m** does not spring from error *NIG*
3:12 the Lord **m** your love **increase** and overflow *4429*
4:11 **M** it *your* **ambition** to lead a quiet life, *5818*
5:15 **M sure that** nobody pays back wrong *3972*
2Th 3: 9 but in order to **m** ourselves a model for you *1443*
2Ti 3:15 which are able *to* **m** you **wise** for salvation *5054*
Tit 2:10 *they will* **m** the teaching about God our Savior **attractive.** *3175*
Heb 1:13 at my right hand until *I* **m** your enemies *5502*
2:10 **m** the author of their salvation **perfect** *5457*
2:17 and that *he might* **m atonement for** the sins *2661*
4:11 therefore, **m every effort** to enter that rest, *5079*
6:11 in order to **m** your hope sure. *NIG*
6:17 **m** the unchanging nature of his purpose very **clear** *2109*
8: 5 "See to it that *you* **m** everything according *4472*
8: 8 the Lord, when *I will* **m** a new covenant *5334*
8:10 the **covenant** *I will* **m** with the house *1347+1416*
10: 1 **m perfect** those who draw near to worship. *5457*
10:16 the **covenant** *I will* **m** with them *1347+1416*
12: 5 *do* not **m light of** the Lord's discipline, *3902*
12:13 **"M** level paths for your feet," *4472*
12:14 **M every effort** to live in peace *1503*
13:12 the city gate to **m** the people **holy** *39*
Jas 3: 3 the mouths of horses to **m** them **obey** us, *4275*
4:13 carry on business and **m money."** *3045*
5:15 **m** the sick person **well;** *5392*
1Pe 3: 5 **m** themselves **beautiful.** *3175*
5:10 *will* himself restore you and **m** you **strong,** *5114*
2Pe 1: 5 **m** every effort to add to your faith *4210*
1:10 be all the more eager *to* **m** your calling *4472*
1:15 And *I will* **m every effort** to see that *5079*
3:14 **m every effort** to be found spotless, *5079*
1Jn 1: 4 We write this to **m** our joy **complete.** *1639+4444*
1:10 *we* **m** him **out to be** a liar and *4472*
2:10 there is nothing in him to **m** him stumble. *NIG*
Rev 2:22 and I will **m** those who commit adultery *NIG*
3: 9 *I will* **m** those who are of the synagogue *1443*
3: 9 *I will* **m** them come and fall down *4472*
3:12 Him who overcomes *I will* **m** a pillar in *4472*
6: 4 the earth and to **m** men slay each other. *NIG*
12:17 at the woman and went off *to* **m** war against *4472*
13: 4 Who can **m war** against him?" *4482*
13: 7 He was given power *to* **m** war against *4472*
17:14 They *will* **m war** against the Lamb, *4482*
19:19 and their armies gathered together *to* **m** war *4472*

MAKE (Anglicized) See also HAVE

MAKER (26) [MAKE]

Job 4:17 Can a man be more pure than his **M?** 6913
9: 9 *He is* the **M** *of* the Bear and Orion, 6913
32:22 my **M** would soon take me away. 6913
35:10 But no one says, 'Where is God my **M,** 6913
36: 3 I will ascribe justice to my **M.** 7188
40:19 yet his **M** can approach him with his sword. 6913
Ps 95: 6 let us kneel before the LORD our **M;** 6913
115:15 the LORD, the **M** *of* heaven and earth. 6913
121: 2 the LORD, the **M** *of* heaven and earth. 6913
124: 8 the LORD, the **M** *of* heaven and earth. 6913
134: 3 the LORD, the **M** *of* heaven and earth, 6913
146: 6 the **M** *of* heaven and earth, the sea, 6913
149: 2 Let Israel rejoice in their **M;** 6913
Pr 14:31 the poor shows contempt for their **M,** 6913
17: 5 the poor shows contempt for their **M;** 6913
22: 2 The LORD *is* the **M** *of* them all. 6913
Ecc 11: 5 the work of God, the **M** *of* all things. 6913
Isa 17: 7 In that day men will look to their **M** 6913
27:11 so their **M** has no compassion on them, 6913
45: 9 "Woe to him who quarrels with his **M,** 3670
45:11 the Holy One of Israel, and its **M:** 3670
51:13 that you forget the LORD your **M,** 6913
54: 5 For your **M** is your husband— 6913
Jer 10:16 for he *is* the **M** *of* all things, 3670
51:19 for he *is* the **M** *of* all things, 3670
Hos 8:14 Israel has forgotten his **M** and built palaces; 6913

MAKERS (1) [MAKE]

Isa 45:16 All the **m** *of* idols will be put to shame 3093

MAKES (118) [MAKE]

Ex 4:11 Who **m** him deaf or mute? 8492
4:11 Who gives him sight or **m** him blind? NIH
11: 7 the LORD **m a distinction** between Egypt 7111
30:33 Whoever **m perfume** like it 8379
30:38 Whoever **m** any like it 6913
31:13 I am the LORD, *who* **m** you **holy.** 7727
Lev 7: 7 They belong to the priest who **m atonement** 4105
17:11 the blood *that* **m atonement** for one's life. 4105
20: 8 I am the LORD, *who* **m** you **holy.** 7727
21:15 I am the LORD, *who* **m** him **holy.'** 7727
21:23 I am the LORD, *who* **m** them **holy.'** 7727
22: 5 that *m* him **unclean,** AIT
22: 5 or any person who *m* him **unclean,** AIT
22: 9 I am the LORD, *who* **m** them **holy.** 7727
22:16 I am the LORD, *who* **m** them **holy.'** 7727
22:32 I am the LORD, *who* **m** you **holy** 7727
27: 2 'If anyone **m a special vow** 5624+7098
Nu 30: 2 a man **m a vow** to the LORD or takes 5623+5624
30: 3 father's house **m a vow** to the LORD 5623+5624
30: 6 after she **m** a vow or after her lips utter NIH
30:10 a woman living with her husband **m a vow** 5623
30:13 or nullify any vow she **m** NIH
1Sa 2: 6 "The LORD brings death and **m alive;** 2649
22: 8 when my son **m a covenant** with the son 4162
2Sa 22:33 with strength and **m** my way perfect. 5989
22:34 *He* **m** my feet like the feet of a deer; 8751
Job 6: 7 I refuse to touch it; such food **m** me ill. NIH
9: 6 from its place and **m** its pillars **tremble.** 7145
12:17 and **m fools of** judges. 2147
12:23 *He* **m** nations **great,** and destroys them; 8434
12:25 *he* **m** them **stagger** like drunkards. 9494
35:11 and **m** us **wiser** than the birds of the air?' 2681
36:10 *He* **m** them **listen** to correction 265+1655
37:15 and **m** his lightning **flash?** 3649
41:31 *He* **m** the depths **churn** like a boiling caldron 8409
Ps 7:13 *he* **m ready** his flaming arrows. 7188
18:32 with strength and **m** my way perfect. 5989
18:33 *He* **m** my feet like the feet of a deer; 8751
19: 6 of the heavens and **m** its circuit to the other; NIH
23: 2 *He* **m** me **lie down** in green pastures, 8069
25:14 he **m** his covenant **known** *to* them. 3359
29: 6 *He* **m** Lebanon **skip** like a calf, 8376
37:23 he **m** his steps **firm;** 3922
40: 4 the man who **m** the LORD his trust, 8492
45: 8 the music of the strings **m** you **glad.** 8523
46: 9 *He* **m** wars **cease** to the ends of the earth; 8697
48: 8 God **m** her **secure** forever. 3922
60: 3 you have given us wine *that* **m** us **stagger.** 9570
104: 3 He **m** the clouds his chariot and rides on 8492
104: 4 *He* **m** winds his messengers, 6913
104:10 He **m** springs **pour** water into the ravines; 8938
104:14 *He* **m** grass **grow** for the cattle, 7541
135: 7 *He* **m** clouds **rise** from the ends of the earth; 6590
143: 3 *he* **m** me **dwell** in darkness 3782
147: 8 the earth with rain and **m** grass **grow** *on* 7541
Pr 1:21 in the gateways of the city *she* **m** her **speech:** 606+609
4:19 they do not know what *m them* **stumble.** AIT
11: 5 of the blameless **m** *a* **straight** way for them, 3837
13:11 by little **m** it **grow.** 8049
13:12 Hope deferred **m** the heart **sick,** 2703
15:13 A happy heart **m** the face **cheerful,** 3512
16: 7 **m** even his enemies **live at peace** 8966
31:22 *She* **m** coverings for her bed; 6913
31:24 *She* **m** linen garments and sells them, 6913
Ecc 7:19 Wisdom **m** one wise man more **powerful** 6451
10:19 and wine **m** life **merry,** 8523
Isa 8:14 to stumble and a rock that **m** them **fall.** 4842
14: 9 *it* **m** them **rise** from their thrones— 7756
Isa 21: 4 My heart falters, fear **m** me **tremble;** 1286
26: 1 God **m** salvation its walls and ramparts. 8883
27: 9 When he **m** all the altar stones to be 8492
32: 7 he **m up** evil schemes to destroy the poor 3619
32: 8 But the noble man **m** noble **plans,** 3619
44:13 a line and **m an outline** with a marker; 9306
44:15 *he* **m** an idol and bows down to it. 6913
44:17 *From* the rest *he* **m** a god, his idol; 6913
44:25 the signs of false prophets and **m fools of** 2147
51:17 to its dregs the goblet that **m** men **stagger.** 9570
53:10 the LORD **m** his life a guilt offering, 8492
57:13 the *man who* **m** me *his* **refuge** will inherit 2879
61:11 the soil **m** the sprout **come up** 3655
62: 7 till he establishes Jerusalem and **m** her 8492
66: 3 *whoever* **m** a grain **offering** is 6590
Jer 10:13 *he* **m** clouds **rise** from the ends of the earth. 6590
22:14 So *he* **m large** windows in it, 7973
48:28 Be like a dove *that* **m** *its* **nest** at the mouth 7873
51:16 *he* **m** clouds **rise** from the ends of the earth. 6590
Eze 44:18 not wear anything that **m** them perspire. 928
46:16 If the prince **m** a gift *from* his inheritance 5989
46:17 *he* **m** a gift from his inheritance to one 5989
47: 9 flows there and **m** the salt water **fresh;** 8324
Hos 12: 1 *He* **m** a treaty with Assyria 4162
Na 1: 4 **m** all the rivers **run dry.** 2990
Hab 2: 6 up stolen goods and **m** himself **wealthy** 3877
2:18 For *he who* **m** it trusts in his own creation; 3670
2:18 *he* **m** idols that cannot speak. 6913
3:19 *he* **m** my feet like the feet of a deer, 8492
Zec 10: 1 it is the LORD *who* **m** the storm clouds. 6913
Mt 15:11 that is **what m** him **'unclean.'"** *3124*
23:17 gold, or the temple that **m** the gold **sacred?** *39*
23:19 the gift, or the altar that **m** the gift **sacred?** *39*
Mk 7:15 comes out of a man that **m** him **'unclean.'"** *3124*
7:20 out of a man is what **m** him **'unclean.'** *3124*
7:37 even **m** the deaf hear and the mute speak." *4472*
Jn 16:30 **This m** us believe that you came from God." *1877+4047*
Ro 8:15 a spirit that **m** you **a slave** again to fear, *1525*
9:33 to stumble and a rock *that* **m** them **fall,** *4998*
1Co 2:15 The spiritual man **m judgments about** *373*
3: 7 but only God, who **m** things **grow.** *889*
4: 7 For who **m** you **different** from anyone else? *1359*
2Co 1:21 **m** both us and you **stand firm** *1011*
Gal 2: 6 whatever they were **m** no **difference** to me; *1422*
Eph 5:14 for it is light that **m** everything **visible.** *5746*
Heb 1: 7 "He **m** his angels winds, *4472*
2:11 Both the one who **m** men **holy** *39*
Jas 3: 5 but *it* **m** great **boasts.** *902*
1Pe 2: 8 to stumble and a rock *that* **m** them **fall."** *4998*
Rev 19:11 With justice *he* judges and **m war.** *4482*

MAKHELOTH (2)

Nu 33:25 They left Haradah and camped at **M.** 5221
33:26 They left **M** and camped at Tahath. 5221

MAKI (1)

Nu 13:15 from the tribe of Gad, Geuel son of **M.** 4809

MAKING (70) [MAKE]

Ge 9:12 of the covenant I *am* **m** between me and you 5989
34:30 on me by **m** me **a stench** to the Canaanites 944
Ex 5: 7 the people with straw for **m bricks;** 4236+4246
28:15 "Fashion a breastpiece for **m decisions**— 5477
28:30 the **means of m decisions** *for* the Israelites 5477
29:36 Purify the altar by **m atonement** for it, 4105
30:16 **m atonement** for your lives." 4105
34:10 LORD said: "*I am* **m** a covenant with you. 4162
Lev 10:17 of the community by **m atonement** for them 4105
16:10 be used for **m atonement** by sending it into 4105
16:20 When Aaron has finished **m atonement** *for* 4105
17: 5 the LORD the sacrifices they *are now* **m** in 2284
19:29 by **m** her **a prostitute,** 2388
27: 8 If anyone **m** the vow is too poor to pay NIH
27: 8 to what the *man the* **m** *the* **vow** can afford. 5623
Nu 25:12 Therefore tell him I *am* **m** my covenant 5989
32:14 **m** the LORD even **more** angry with Israel. 3578
Dt 23:22 But if you refrain from **m a vow,** 5623
24:11 the man to whom you *are* **m** *the* **loan** bring 5957
29:12 the LORD *is* **m** with you this day 4162
29:14 I *am* **m** this covenant, with its oath, 4162
Jdg 16:13 *you have been* **m a fool of** me and lying 9438
1Sa 13:10 Just as he finished **m** the offering, 6590
21:13 madman, **m marks** on the doors of the gate 9344
1Ki 8:33 and **m supplication** to you in this temple, 2858
14:15 the LORD to anger by **m** Asherah poles. 6913
15: 4 to succeed him and by **m** Jerusalem **strong.** 6641
2Ki 10:25 as Jehu had finished **m** the burnt offering, 6913
12:13 **was not spent for m** silver basins, 4946+6913
1Ch 6:49 **m atonement** for Israel, 4105
2Ch 2: 4 and for **m** burnt offerings every morning NIH
6:24 praying and **m supplication** before you 2858
Ezr 5: 8 on with diligence and *is* **m rapid progress** 10613
Ne 6: 8 you *are* just **m it up** out of your head." 968
8: 8 **m** it **clear** and giving the meaning so that 7300
9:38 we *are* **m** a binding agreement, 4162
Ps 19: 7 trustworthy, **m wise** the simple. 2681
Pr 8:21 and **m** their treasures **full.** 4848
14: 9 Fools mock at **m amends for sin,** 871
16:11 all the weights in the bag are of his **m.** 5126
24: 2 and their lips talk about **m trouble.** 6662
Ecc 12:12 Of **m** many books there is no end, 6913
Isa 10: 2 **m** widows their prey and robbing 2118
43:19 *I am* **m** a way in the desert and streams in 8492
45: 9 'What *are you* **m?'** 6913
Isa 55:10 without watering the earth and **m** it **bud** 3528
Jer 22:13 **m** his countrymen **work** for nothing, 6268
44:19 that *we were* **m** cakes like her image 6913
Eze 22: 3 in her midst and defiles herself by **m** idols, 6913
37:19 **m** them a single stick of wood, 6913
Da 9:20 and **m** my request to the LORD my God 5877
Jnh 1: 8 who is responsible for **m** all this trouble NIH
Mt 9:16 from the garment, **m** the tear worse. *1181*
13:22 of wealth choke it, **m** it unfruitful. *1181*
21:13 but you *are* **m** it a 'den of robbers.'" *4472*
Mk 2:21 pull away from the old, **m** the tear worse. *1181*
4:19 in and choke the word, **m** it unfruitful. *1181*
Lk 1:22 for he *kept* **m signs** to them *1377+1639*
Jn 5:18 **m** himself equal with God. *4472*
16:14 taking from what is mine and **m** it **known** *334*
Ac 16:19 that their hope *of* **m money** was gone, *2238*
18:14 "If you Jews *were* **m a complaint about** *1639*S
24:13 **charges** *they are* now **m against** *2989*
Ro 7:23 of my mind and **m** me **a prisoner** of the law *170*
2Co 5:20 though God *were* **m** *his* **appeal** through us. *4151*
6:10 poor, yet **m** many **rich;** *4457*
Eph 2:15 one new man out of the two, thus **m** peace, *4472*
5:16 **m the most of** every opportunity, *1973*
Col 1:20 *by* **m peace** through his blood, *1647*
Rev 21: 5 "*I am* **m** everything new!" *4472*

MAKIR (21) [MAKIR'S, MAKIRITE, MAKIRITES]

Ge 50:23 of **M** son of Manasseh were placed at birth 4810
Nu 26:29 through **M,** the Makirite clan (Makir was 4810
26:29 Makirite clan (**M** was the father of Gilead); 4810
27: 1 the son of **M,** the son of Manasseh, 4810
32:39 of **M** son of Manasseh went to Gilead, 4810
36: 1 of the clan of Gilead son of **M,** 4810
Dt 3:15 And I gave Gilead to **M.** 4810
Jos 13:31 the descendants of **M** son of Manasseh— 4810
13:31 for half of the sons of **M,** clan by clan. 4810
17: 1 that is, for **M,** Manasseh's firstborn. 4810
17: 1 **M** was the ancestor of the Gileadites, NIH
17: 3 the son of **M,** the son of Manasseh, 4810
Jdg 5:14 From **M** captains came down, 4810
2Sa 9: 4 "He is at the house of **M** son of Ammiel 4810
9: 5 from the house of **M** son of Ammiel. 4810
17:27 and **M** son of Ammiel from Lo Debar, 4810
1Ch 2:21 Hezron lay with the daughter of **M** 4810
2:23 All these were descendants of **M** the father 4810
7:14 She gave birth to **M** the father of Gilead. 4810
7:15 **M** took a wife from among the Huppites 4810
7:17 These were the sons of Gilead son of **M,** 4810

MAKIR'S (1) [MAKIR]

1Ch 7:16 **M** wife Maacah gave birth to a son 4810

MAKIRITE (1) [MAKIR]

Nu 26:29 **M** clan (Makir was the father of Gilead); 4811

MAKIRITES (2) [MAKIR]

Nu 32:40 So Moses gave Gilead to the **M,** 4810
Jos 17: 1 because **the M** were great soldiers. 2085S

MAKKEDAH (9)

Jos 10:10 down all the way to Azekah and **M.** 5218
10:16 and hidden in the cave at **M.** 5218
10:17 had been found hiding in the cave at **M,** 5218
10:21 to Joshua in the camp at **M,** 5218
10:28 That day Joshua took **M.** 5218
10:28 And he did to the king of **M** as he had done 5218
10:29 and all Israel with him moved on from **M** 5218
12:16 the king of **M** one the king of Bethel one 5218
15:41 Beth Dagon, Naamah and **M**— 5218

MAKTESH (KJV) See MARKET DISTRICT

MALACHI (1)

Mal 1: 1 word of the LORD to Israel through **M.** 4858

MALCAM (1)

1Ch 8: 9 he had Jobab, Zibia, Mesha, **M,** 4903

MALCHI-SHUA (KJV) See MALKI-SHUA

MALCHIAH (KJV) See MALKIJAH

MALCHIEL, MALCHIELITES (KJV) See MALKIEL, MALKIELITE

MALCHIJAH (KJV) See MALKIJAH

MALCHIRAM (KJV) See MALKIRAM

MALCHUS (1)

Jn 18:10 (The servant's name was **M.**) *3438*

MALE (184) [MALES]

Ge 1:27 **m** and female he created them. 2351
5: 2 He created them **m** and female 2351
6:19 **m** and female, to keep them alive with you. 2351

Ge 7: 2 a **m** and its mate, 408
7: 2 a **m** and its mate, 408
7: 3 and also seven of every kind of bird, **m** 2351
7: 9 **m** and female, came to Noah and entered 2351
7:16 were **m** and female of every living thing, 2351
12:16 **m** and female **donkeys,** 2789
17:10 Every **m** among you shall be circumcised. 2351
17:12 For the generations to come every **m** 2351
17:14 Any uncircumcised **m,** 2351
17:23 every **m** in his household, 2351
17:27 And every **m** *in* Abraham's household, 408
20:14 and **m** and female **slaves** and gave them 6269
30:35 That same day he removed all the **m goats** 9411
31:10 up and saw that the **m goats** mating with 6966
31:12 up and see that all the **m goats** mating with 6966
32:14 female goats and twenty **m goats,** 9411
32:15 twenty female donkeys and ten **m donkeys.** 6555
34:24 and every **m** in the city was circumcised. 2351
34:25 the unsuspecting city, killing every **m.** 2351
Ex 12:48 No **uncircumcised** *m* may eat of it. AIT
13: 2 "Consecrate to me every **firstborn** *m.* AIT
13:15 the first **m** offspring of every womb 2351
21:20 "If a man beats his **m** or female **slave** with 6269
21:32 If the bull gores a **m** or female **slave,** 6269
Lev 1: 3 he is to offer a **m** without defect. 2351
1:10 he is to offer a **m** without defect. 2351
3: 1 whether **m** or female, 2351
3: 6 he is to offer a **m** or female without defect. 2351
4:23 as his offering a **m** goat without defect. 2351
6:18 Any **m** descendant of Aaron may eat it. 2351
6:29 Any **m** in a priest's family may eat it; 2351
7: 6 Any **m** in a priest's family may eat it, 2351
9: 3 'Take a **m goat** for a sin offering, 6436+8538
14:10 the eighth day he must bring two **m lambs** 3897
14:12 the **m lambs** and offer it as a guilt offering, 3897
14:21 he must take one **m lamb** as a guilt offering 3897
16: 5 to take two **m goats** for a sin offering 6436+8538
22:19 you must present a **m** without defect from 2351
23:18 Present with this bread seven **m lambs,** 3897
23:19 sacrifice one **m goat** for a sin offering 6436+8538
25:44 " 'Your **m** and female **slaves** are to come 6269
27: 3 of a **m** between the ages of twenty and sixty 2351
27: 5 set the value of a **m** at twenty shekels and of 2351
27: 6 the value of a **m** at five shekels of silver and 2351
27: 7 set the value of a **m** at fifteen shekels and of 2351
Nu 3:12 in place of the **first m offspring** 1147+7081+8167
3:15 Count every **m** a month old or more." 2351
3:39 including every **m** a month old or more, 2351
5: 3 Send away **m** and female alike; 2351
6:12 a year-old **m lamb** as a guilt offering. 3897
6:14 a year-old **m lamb** without defect for 3897
7:15 one ram and one **m lamb** a year old, 3897
7:16 one **m goat** for a sin offering; 6436+8538
7:17 five **m goats** and five male lambs 6966
7:17 five male goats and five **m lambs** 3897
7:21 one ram and one **m lamb** a year old, 3897
7:22 one **m goat** for a sin offering; 6436+8538
7:23 five **m goats** and five male lambs 6966
7:23 five male goats and five **m lambs** 3897
7:27 one ram and one **m lamb** a year old, 3897
7:28 one **m goat** for a sin offering; 6436+8538
7:29 five **m goats** and five male lambs 6966
7:29 five male goats and five **m lambs** 3897
7:33 one ram and one **m lamb** a year old, 3897
7:34 one **m goat** for a sin offering; 6436+8538
7:35 five **m goats** and five male lambs 6966
7:35 five male goats and five **m lambs** 3897
7:39 one ram and one **m lamb** a year old, 3897
7:40 one **m goat** for a sin offering; 6436+8538
7:41 five **m goats** and five male lambs 6966
7:41 five male goats and five **m lambs** 3897
7:45 one ram and one **m lamb** a year old, 3897
7:46 one **m goat** for a sin offering; 6436+8538
7:47 five **m goats** and five male lambs 6966
7:47 five male goats and five **m lambs** 3897
7:51 one ram and one **m lamb** a year old, 3897
7:52 one **m goat** for a sin offering; 6436+8538
7:53 five **m goats** and five male lambs 6966
7:53 five male goats and five **m lambs** 3897
7:57 one ram and one **m lamb** a year old, 3897
7:58 one **m goat** for a sin offering; 6436+8538
7:59 five **m goats** and five male lambs 6966
7:59 five male goats and five **m lambs** 3897
7:63 one ram and one **m lamb** a year old, 3897
7:64 one **m goat** for a sin offering; 6436+8538
7:65 five **m goats** and five male lambs 6966
7:65 five male goats and five **m lambs** 3897
7:69 one ram and one **m lamb** a year old, 3897
7:70 one **m goat** for a sin offering; 6436+8538
7:71 five **m goats** and five male lambs 6966
7:71 five male goats and five **m lambs** 3897
7:75 one ram and one **m lamb** a year old, 3897
7:76 one **m goat** for a sin offering; 6436+8538
7:77 five **m goats** and five male lambs 6966
7:77 five male goats and five **m lambs** 3897
7:81 one ram and one **m lamb** a year old, 3897
7:82 one **m goat** for a sin offering; 6436+8538
7:83 five **m goats** and five male lambs 6966
7:83 five male goats and five **m lambs** 3897
7:87 twelve rams and twelve **m lambs** a year old, 3897
7:87 Twelve **m goats** were used for 6436+8538
7:88 sixty **m goats** and sixty male lambs 6966
7:88 sixty male goats and sixty **m lambs** 3897
8:16 the **first m offspring** from every Israelite 1147
8:17 Every **firstborn m** in Israel, 1147
15:24 and a **m goat** for a sin offering. 6436+8538
18:10 something most place; every **m** shall eat it. 2351
Nu 18:15 and every **firstborn m** *of* unclean animals. 1147
26:62 All the **m** Levites a month old 2351
28:11 one ram and seven **m lambs** a year old, 3897
28:15 one **m goat** is to be presented to 6436+8538
28:19 one ram and seven **m lambs** a year old, 3897
28:22 Include one **m goat** as a sin offering 8538
28:27 one ram and seven **m lambs** a year old as 3897
28:30 Include one **m goat** to make atonement 6436+8538
29: 2 one ram and seven **m lambs** a year old, 3897
29: 5 Include one **m goat** as a sin offering 6436+8538
29: 8 one ram and seven **m lambs** a year old, 3897
29:11 Include one **m goat** as a sin offering, 6436+8538
29:13 two rams and fourteen **m lambs** a year old, 3897
29:16 Include one **m goat** as a sin offering, 6436+8538
29:17 two rams and fourteen **m lambs** a year old, 3897
29:19 Include one **m goat** as a sin offering, 6436+8538
29:20 two rams and fourteen **m lambs** a year old, 3897
29:22 Include one **m goat** as a sin offering, 8538
29:23 two rams and fourteen **m lambs** a year old, 3897
29:25 Include one **m goat** as a sin offering, 6436+8538
29:26 two rams and fourteen **m lambs** a year old, 3897
29:28 Include one **m goat** as a sin offering, 8538
29:29 two rams and fourteen **m lambs** a year old, 3897
29:31 Include one **m goat** as a sin offering, 8538
29:32 two rams and fourteen **m lambs** a year old, 3897
29:34 Include one **m goat** as a sin offering, 8538
29:36 one ram and seven **m lambs** a year old, 3897
29:38 Include one **m goat** as a sin offering, 8538
Dt 15:19 for the LORD your God every firstborn **m** 2351
23:18 a female prostitute or of a **m prostitute** into 3978
28:68 to your enemies as **m** and female **slaves,** 6269
Jos 17: 2 the other **m** descendants of Manasseh son 2351
Jdg 21:11 "Kill every **m** and every woman who is not 2351
1Sa 25:22 if by morning I leave alive *one* **m** 928+7815+8874
25:34 not *one* **m** belonging to Nabal 928+7815+8874
2Sa 21: 6 let seven of his **m** descendants be given 408
1Ki 14:10 I will cut off from Jeroboam **every last m** 928+7815+8874
14:24 There were even *m* **shrine prostitutes** in AIT
15:12 He expelled the *m* **shrine prostitutes** from AIT
16:11 He did not spare a *single* **m,** 928+7815+8874
21:21 cut off from Ahab **every last m** 928+7815+8874
22:46 *m* **shrine prostitutes** who remained there AIT
2Ki 9: 8 I will cut off from Ahab **every last m** 928+7815+8874
23: 7 the quarters of the *m* **shrine prostitutes,** AIT
1Ch 29:21 a thousand rams and a thousand **m lambs,** 3897
2Ch 29:21 seven **m lambs** and seven male goats as 3897
29:21 seven male lambs and seven **m goats** 6436+7618
29:32 a hundred rams and two hundred **m lambs** 3897
31:19 to distribute portions to every **m** among 2351
Ezr 6: 9 **m lambs** for burnt offerings to the God 10043
6:17 four hundred **m lambs** and, 10043
6:17 for all Israel, twelve **m goats,** 10535+10615
7:17 rams and **m lambs,** 10043
8:35 seventy-seven **m lambs** and, 3897
8:35 as a sin offering, twelve **m goats.** 7618
Est 7: 4 as **m** and female **slaves,** 6269
Job 36:14 among *m* **prostitutes of the shrines.** AIT
Ecc 2: 7 I bought **m** and female **slaves** 6269
Jer 34: 9 to free his Hebrew **slaves,** both **m** 6269
34:10 they would free their **m** and female **slaves** 6269
34:16 the **m** and female **slaves** you had set free 6269
Eze 16:17 and you made for yourself **m** idols 2351
43:22 a **m goat** without defect for a sin offering, 6436+8538
43:25 to provide a **m goat** daily for a sin offering; 8538
45:23 and a **m goat** for a sin offering. 6436+8538
46: 4 on the Sabbath day is to be six **m lambs** and 3897
Mal 1:14 an acceptable **m** in his flock and vows 2351
Mt 19: 4 the Creator 'made them **m** and female,' *781*
Mk 10: 6 of creation God 'made them **m** and female.' *781*
Lk 2:23 "Every firstborn **m** is to be consecrated to *781*
1Co 6: 9 nor adulterers nor **m prostitutes** *3434*
Gal 3:28 slave nor free, **m** nor female, *781*
Rev 12: 5 She gave birth to a son, a **m** child, *781*
12:13 woman who had given birth to the **m** child. *781*

MALEFACTOR, MALEFACTORS (KJV)
See CRIMINAL, CRIMINALS

MALELEEL (KJV) See MAHALALEL

MALES (13) [MALE]

Ge 34:15 like us by circumcising all your **m.** 2351
34:22 on the condition that our **m** be circumcised, 2351
Ex 12: 5 The animals you choose must be year-old **m** 2351
12:48 the LORD's Passover must have all the **m** 2351
13:12 All the firstborn **m** of your livestock belong 2351
34:19 the firstborn **m** of your livestock, 2350
Nu 3:22 The number of all the **m** a month old 2351
3:28 of all the **m** a month old or more was 8,600. 2351
3:34 The number of all the **m** a month old 2351
3:40 "Count all the firstborn Israelite **m** who are 2351
3:43 The total number of firstborn **m** a month old 2351
2Ch 31:16 they distributed to the **m** three years old 2351
Jer 2:24 Any *m that* **pursue** her need AIT

MALICE (21) [MALICIOUS, MALICIOUSLY]

Nu 35:20 with **m aforethought** shoves another 8534
Dt 4:42 without **m aforethought.** 4946+8533+8997+9453
19: 4 without **m aforethought.** 4946+8533+8997+9453
19: 6 without **m aforethought.** 4946+8533+8997+9453
Jos 20: 5 without **m aforethought.** 4946+8533+8997+9453
Job 6:30 Can my mouth not discern **m?** 2095
Ps 28: 3 with their neighbors but harbor **m** 8288
41: 5 My enemies say of me *in* **m,** 8273
55:10 **m** and abuse are within it. 224
73: 8 They scoff, and speak with **m;** 8273
Pr 26:26 His **m** may be concealed by deception, 8534
Eze 25: 6 with all the **m** of your heart against the land 8624
25:15 and took revenge with **m** in their hearts, 8624
36: 5 against all Edom, for with glee and with **m** 8624
Mk 7:22 **m,** deceit, lewdness, envy, slander, *4504*
Ro 1:29 murder, strife, deceit and **m.** *2799*
1Co 5: 8 the yeast *of* **m** and wickedness, *2798*
Eph 4:31 along with every form of **m.** *2798*
Col 3: 8 anger, rage, **m,** slander, *2798*
Tit 3: 3 We lived in **m** and envy, *2798*
1Pe 2: 1 rid yourselves of all **m** and all deceit, *2798*

MALICIOUS (9) [MALICE]

Ex 23: 1 help a wicked man by being a **m** witness. 2805
Dt 19:16 a **m** witness takes the stand to accuse a man 2805
Pr 17: 4 a liar pays attention to a **m** tongue. 2095
26:24 A **m** *man* disguises himself with his lips, 8533
Isa 58: 9 with the pointing finger and **m** talk, 224
Eze 28:24 people of Israel have **m** neighbors who are painful briers 8764
36: 3 **object of** people's **m talk** 4383+6584+6590+8557
1Ti 3:11 not **m talkers** but temperate *1333*
6: 4 that result in envy, strife, **m talk,** *1060*

MALICIOUSLY (5) [MALICE]

Ps 35:16 Like the ungodly *they* **m mocked;** 4352+4352
35:19 without reason **m wink** the eye. 7975
Pr 10:10 *He who* **winks m** causes grief, 6524+7975
1Pe 3:16 so that those who **speak m against** *2092*
3Jn 1:10 gossiping **m** about us. *3364+4505*

MALIGN (2) [MALIGNED]

Ps 12: 5 from *those who* **m** them." 7032
Tit 2: 5 so that no one *will* **m** the word of God. *1059*

MALIGNED (2) [MALIGN]

Eze 28:26 on all their neighbors who **m** them. 8764
Ac 19: 9 they refused to believe and publicly **m** *2800*

MALIGNITY (KJV) See MALICE

MALKI-SHUA (5)

1Sa 14:49 Saul's sons were Jonathan, Ishvi and **M.** 4902
31: 2 killed his sons Jonathan, Abinadab and **M,** 4902
1Ch 8:33 and Saul the father of Jonathan, **M,** 4902
9:39 and Saul the father of Jonathan, **M,** 4902
10: 2 killed his sons Jonathan, Abinadab and **M.** 4902

MALKIEL (3) [MALKIELITE]

Ge 46:17 The sons of Beriah: Heber and **M.** 4896
Nu 26:45 through **M,** the Malkielite clan. 4896
1Ch 7:31 The sons of Beriah: Heber and **M,** 4896

MALKIELITE (1) [MALKIEL]

Nu 26:45 through Malkiel, the **M** clan. 4897

MALKIJAH (16)

1Ch 6:40 the son of Baaseiah, the son of **M,** 4898
9:12 the son of Pashhur, the son of **M;** 4898
24: 9 the fifth to **M,** the sixth to Mijamin, 4898
Ezr 10:25 Ramiah, Izziah, **M,** Mijamin, Eleazar, 4898
10:25 Mijamin, Eleazar, **M** and Benaiah. 4898
10:31 Eliezer, Ishijah, **M,** Shemaiah, Shimeon, 4898
Ne 3:11 **M** son of Harim and Hasshub son 4898
3:14 The Dung Gate was repaired by **M** son 4898
3:31 Next to him, **M,** one of the goldsmiths, 4898
8: 4 and on his left were Pedaiah, Mishael, **M,** 4898
10: 3 Pashhur, Amariah, **M,** 4898
11:12 the son of Pashhur, the son of **M,** 4898
12:42 Shemaiah, Eleazar, Uzzi, Jehohanan, **M,** 4898
Jer 21: 1 of **M** and the priest Zephaniah son 4898
38: 1 of **M** heard what Jeremiah was telling all 4898
38: 6 and put him into the cistern of **M,** 4899

MALKIRAM (1)

1Ch 3:18 **M,** Pedaiah, Shenazzar, 4901

MALLOTHI (2)

1Ch 25: 4 Joshbekashah, **M,** Hothir and Mahazioth. 4871
25:26 the nineteenth to **M,** 4871

MALLOWS (KJV) See SALT HERB

MALLUCH (6) [MALLUCH'S]

1Ch 6:44 the son of Abdi, the son of **M,** 4866
Ezr 10:29 Meshullam, **M,** Adaiah, Jashub, 4866
10:32 Benjamin, **M** and Shemariah. 4866
Ne 10: 4 Hattush, Shebaniah, **M,** 4866
10:27 **M,** Harim and Baanah. 4866
12: 2 Amariah, **M,** Hattush, 4866

MALLUCH'S (1) [MALLUCH]

Ne 12:14 of **M,** Jonathan; of Shecaniah's, Joseph; 4868

MALTA (1)

Ac 28: 1 we found out that the island was called M. 3514

MAMMON (KJV) See MONEY, WEALTH

MAMRE (10)

Ge 13:18 to live near the great trees of M at Hebron, 4934
14:13 near the great trees of M the Amorite, 4935
14:24 to Aner, Eshcol and M. 4935
18: 1 the great trees of M while he was sitting at 4934
23:17 So Ephron's field in Machpelah near M— 4934
23:19 in the field of Machpelah near M 4934
25: 9 in the cave of Machpelah near M, 4934
35:27 Jacob came home to his father Isaac in M, 4934
49:30 the field of Machpelah, near M in Canaan, 4934
50:13 the cave in the field of Machpelah, near M, 4934

MAN (2079) [COUNTRYMAN, COUNTRYMEN, FELLOWMAN, HORSEMAN, HORSEMEN, MAN'S, MAN-MADE, MANHOOD, MANKIND, MANNED, MEN, MEN'S, SPOKESMAN, SPOKESMEN, WOODSMAN, WOODSMEN, WORKMAN, WORKMAN'S, WORKMEN]

Ge 1:26 God said, "Let us make m in our image, 132
1:27 So God created m in his own image, 132
2: 5 on the earth and there was no m to work 132
2: 7 the LORD God formed the m from the dust 132
2: 7 and the m became a living being. 132
2: 8 and there he put the m he had formed. 132
2:15 The LORD God took the m and put him in 132
2:16 And the LORD God commanded the m, 132
2:18 "It is not good for the m to be alone. 132
2:19 to the m to see what he would name them; 132
2:19 whatever the m called each living creature, 132
2:20 So the m gave names to all the livestock, 132
2:21 So the LORD God caused the m to fall into 132
2:22 from the rib he had taken out of the m, 132
2:22 and he brought her to the m. 132
2:23 The m said, "This is now bone of my bones 132
2:23 for she was taken out of m." 408
2:24 a m will leave his father and mother and 408
2:25 The m and his wife were both naked, 132
3: 8 Then the m and his wife heard the sound of 132
3: 9 But the LORD God called to the m, 132
3:12 The m said, "The woman you put here 132
3:22 "The m has now become like one of us, 132
3:24 After he drove the m out, 132
4: 1 of the LORD I have brought forth a m." 408
4:23 I have killed a m for wounding me, 408
4:23 a young m for injuring me. 3529
5: 1 When God created m, he made him in 132
5: 2 they were created, he called them "m." 132
6: 3 "My Spirit will not contend with m forever, 132
6: 6 that he had made m on the earth, 132
6: 9 Noah was a righteous m, 408
8:21 will I curse the ground because of m, 132
9: 5 And from each m, too, 132
9: 5 an accounting for the life of his *fellow* m. 132
9: 6 "Whoever sheds the blood of m, 132
9: 6 by m shall his blood be shed; 132
9: 6 for in the image of God has God made m. 132
9:20 Noah, a m *of* the soil, 408
15: 4 "This *m* will not be your heir, AIT
16:12 He will be a wild donkey of a m; 132
17:17 *m* a hundred years old? AIT
19: 8 I have two daughters who have never slept with a m. 408
19:31 and there is no m around here to lie with us, 408
24:16 no m had ever lain with her. 408
24:21 the m watched her closely to learn whether 408
24:22 the m took out a gold nose ring weighing 408
24:26 m bowed down and worshiped the LORD, 408
24:29 and he hurried out to the m at the spring. 408
24:30 and had heard Rebekah tell what the m said 408
24:30 the m and found him standing by the camels 408
24:32 So the m went to the house, 408
24:58 "Will you go with this m?" 408
24:61 and went back with the m. 408
24:65 that m in the field coming to meet us?" 408
25: 8 an old *m* and full of years; AIT
25:27 a m *of* the open country, 408
25:27 while Jacob was a quiet m, 408
26:11 "Anyone who molests this m 408
26:13 The m became rich, 408
27: 2 "*I am* now *an* old *m* and don't know the day AIT
27:11 "But my brother Esau is a hairy m, 408
27:11 and I'm a m with smooth skin. 408
29:19 that I give her to you than to some other m. 408
30:43 the m grew exceedingly prosperous 408
32:24 and a m wrestled with him till daybreak. 408
32:25 the m saw that he could not overpower him, NIH
32:25 as he wrestled with the m. 2257S
32:26 the m said, "Let me go, for it is daybreak." NIH
32:27 The m asked him, "What is your name?" NIH
32:28 the m said, "Your name will no longer be NIH
34:14 we can't give our sister to a m who is 408
34:19 The young m, who was the most honored 5853
37: 2 Joseph, a young m of seventeen, 5853
37:15 a m found him wandering around in 408
37:17 they moved on from here," the m answered. 408

Ge 38: 1 to stay with a m of Adullam named Hirah. 408
38: 2 the daughter of a Canaanite m named Shua. 408
38:25 "I am pregnant by the m who owns these," 408
41:12 giving *each* m the interpretation 408
41:13 and the other m was hanged." 2257S
41:33 for a discerning and wise m and put him 408
41:38 "Can we find anyone like this m, 408
42:11 We are all the sons of one m. 408
42:13 twelve brothers, the sons of one m, 408
42:30 "The m who is lord over 408
42:33 the m who is lord over the land said to us, 408
43: 3 "The m warned us solemnly, 408
43: 5 because the m said to us, 408
43: 6 by telling the m you had another brother?" 408
43: 7 "The m questioned us closely 408
43:11 in your bags and take them down to the m 408
43:13 Take your brother also and go back to the m 408
43:14 the m so that he will let your other brother 408
43:17 The m did as Joseph told him and took 408
44:15 that a m like me can find things out 408
44:17 Only the m who was found to have 408
Ex 2: 1 Now a m of the house of Levi married 408
2:14 *The m* said, "Who made you ruler and judge AIT
2:21 Moses agreed to stay with the m, 408
4:11 "Who gave m his mouth? 132
9:19 the hail will fall on every m and animal 132
10: 7 "How long will this *m* be a snare to us? AIT
11: 7 the Israelites not a dog will bark at any m 408
12: 3 that on the tenth day of this month *each* m 408
13: 2 belongs to me, whether m or animal." 132
13:15 firstborn in Egypt, both m and animal. 132
19:13 Whether m or animal, 408
21: 4 and only the m shall go free. 2085S
21: 7 "If a m sells his daughter as a servant, 408
21:12 "Anyone who strikes a m and kills him shall 408
21:14 But if a m schemes and kills another man 408
21:14 and kills another *m* deliberately, AIT
21:19 however, he must pay the injured m for 2257S
21:20 "If a m beats his male or female slave with 408
21:26 "If a m hits a manservant or maidservant in 408
21:28 "If a bull gores a m or a woman to death, 408
21:29 but has not kept it penned up and it kills a m 408
21:33 "If a m uncovers a pit or digs one and fails 408
22: 1 a m steals an ox or a sheep and slaughters it 408
22: 5 "If a m grazes his livestock in a field 408
22: 7 "If a m gives his neighbor silver or goods 408
22:10 "If a m gives a donkey, an ox, 408
22:14 a m borrows an animal from his neighbor 408
22:16 "If a m seduces a virgin who is not pledged 408
23: 1 a wicked *m* by being a malicious witness. AIT
23: 3 and do not show favoritism to a poor *m* AIT
25: 2 from each m whose heart prompts him 408
32:27 'Each *m* strap a sword to his side. AIT
33:11 as a m speaks with his friend. 408
36: 6 "No m or woman is to make anything else 408
Lev 13: 6 The m must wash his clothes, NIH
13:29 "If a m or woman has a sore on the head or 408
13:38 a m or woman has white spots on the skin, 408
13:40 "When a m has lost his hair and is bald, 408
13:44 the m is diseased and is unclean. 408
15: 2 'When any m has a bodily discharge, 408+408
15: 4 " 'Any bed the *m with a* discharge lies AIT
15: 6 on anything that the *m with a* discharge sat AIT
15: 7 touches the *m who has a* discharge AIT
15: 8 " 'If the *m with the* discharge spits AIT
15: 9 'Everything the m sits on when riding will 2307S
15:11 " 'Anyone the *m with a* discharge touches AIT
15:12 " 'A clay pot that the m touches mus: 2307S
15:13 'When a m is cleansed from his discharge, 2307S
15:15 before the LORD for the m because 2257S
15:16 " 'When a m has an emission of semen, 408
15:18 When a m lies with a woman and there is 408
15:24 " 'If a m lies with her 408
15:32 the regulations for a *m with a* discharge, AIT
15:33 for a m or a woman with a discharge, 2351
15:33 and for a m who lies with 408
16:21 into the desert in the care of a m appointed 408
16:22 and the m shall release it in the desert. NIH
16:26 "The *m who* releases the goat as AIT
16:28 *m who* burns them must wash his clothes AIT
17: 4 that m shall be considered guilty 408
17: 9 that m must be cut off from his people. 408
18: 5 for the m who obeys them will live by them. 132
18:22 not lie with a m as one lies with a woman; 2351
19:13 the wages of a hired m overnight. 8502
19:20 " 'If a m sleeps with a woman who is 408
19:20 a slave girl promised to another m 408
19:21 The m, however, must bring a ram to 2257S
20: 3 against that m and I will cut him off 408
20: 4 that m gives one of his children to Molech 408
20: 5 that m and his family and will cut off 408
20:10 " 'If a m commits adultery 408
20:11 " 'If a m sleeps with his father's wife, 408
20:11 Both the m and the woman must be 2157S
20:12 " 'If a m sleeps with his daughter-in-law, 408
20:13 m lies with a man as one lies with a woman, 408
20:13 man lies with a m as one lies with a woman, 2351
20:14 a m marries both a woman and her mother, 408
20:15 a m has sexual relations with an animal, 408
20:17 " 'If a m marries his sister, 408
20:18 " 'If a m lies with a woman 408
20:20 " 'If a m sleeps with his aunt, 408
20:21 " 'If a m marries his brother's wife, 408
20:27 " 'A m or woman who is a medium 408
21:18 No m who has any defect may come near: 408
21:18 no m who is blind or lame, 408
21:19 no m with a crippled foot or hand, 408

Lev 24:21 but whoever kills a m must be put to death. 132
25:26 a m has no one to redeem it for him 408
25:27 the balance to the m to whom he sold it; 408
25:29 " 'If a m sells a house in a walled city, 408
25:50 the rate paid to a hired m for that number 8502
25:53 to be treated as a m hired *from* year to year; 8502
27: 8 to what the *m* making *the* vow can afford. AIT
27:14 a m dedicates his house as something holy 408
27:15 If the *m who* dedicates his house redeems it, AIT
27:16 " 'If a m dedicates to the LORD part 408
27:19 If the *m who* dedicates the field wishes AIT
27:22 " 'If a *m* dedicates to the LORD AIT
27:23 and the m must pay its value on that day NIH
27:28 " 'But nothing that a m owns and devotes to 408
27:28 whether m or animal or family land— 132
27:31 If a m redeems any of his tithe, 408
Nu 1: 2 listing every m by name, one by one. 2351
1: 4 One m from each tribe, 408
1:52 *each* m in his own camp 408
2: 2 *each* m under his standard with the banners 408
3:13 whether m or animal. 132
4:19 the sanctuary and assign to each m his work 408
4:32 Assign to each m the specific things he 928+9005
5: 6 a m or woman wrongs another in any way 408
5:13 by sleeping with another m, 408
5:19 "If no other m has slept with you 408
5:20 with a m other than your husband"— 408
5:30 or when feelings of jealousy come over a m 408
6: 2 a m or woman wants to make a special vow, 408
8:17 whether m or animal, is mine. 132
9:13 if a m who is ceremonially clean and not on 408
9:13 That m will bear the consequences 408
11:27 A young m ran and told Moses, 5853
12: 3 (Now Moses was a very humble m, 408
15:32 a m was found gathering wood on 408
15:35 the LORD said to Moses, "The m must die. 408
16: 5 The m he chooses he will cause to come 2257S
16: 7 The m the LORD chooses will be 408
16:17 *Each* m is to take his censer and put incense 408
16:18 So *each* m took his censer, 408
16:22 the entire assembly when only one m sins?" 408
17: 2 Write the name of *each* m on his staff. 408
17: 5 to the m I choose will sprout, 408
17: 9 and *each* m took his own staff. 408
18:15 both m and animal, 132
19: 8 The *m who* burns it must AIT
19: 9 "A m who is clean shall gather up the ashes 408
19:10 The *m who* gathers up the ashes of AIT
19:18 Then a m who is ceremonially clean is 408
19:19 The *m* who is clean is to sprinkle AIT
19:21 "The *m who* sprinkles the water AIT
23:19 God is not a m, that he should lie, 408
23:19 that he should lie, nor a son of m, 132
25: 6 Then an Israelite m brought to his family 408
27: 8 'If a m dies and leaves no son, 408
27:16 appoint a m over this community 408
27:18 a m in whom is the spirit, 408
30: 2 a m makes a vow to the LORD or takes 408
30:16 concerning relationships between a m 408
31: 7 and killed every m. 2351
31:17 kill every woman who has slept with a m, 2351
31:18 every girl who has never slept with a m. 2351
31:35 women who had never slept with a m. 5883
32:27 your servants, every *m* armed *for* battle, AIT
32:29 every *m* armed for battle, AIT
35:16 If *a m* strikes someone with an iron object AIT
Dt 1:17 Do not be afraid of any m, 408
1:23 one m from each tribe. 408
1:35 "Not a m of this evil generation shall see 408
4:16 whether formed like a m or a woman, 2351
4:32 from the day God created m on the earth; 132
5:24 Today we have seen that a m can live even 132
5:26 For what mortal m has ever heard 1414
8: 3 that m does not live on bread alone but 132
8: 5 in your heart that as a m disciplines his son, 408
11:25 No m will be able to stand against you. 408
15: 7 If there is a poor *m* among your brothers AIT
15:12 If a fellow Hebrew, a *m* or a woman, AIT
16:16 No m should appear before NIH
17: 2 If a m or woman living among you in one of 408
17: 5 take the m or woman who has done this 408
17: 6 or three witnesses a m shall be put to death, 4637S
17:12 The m who shows contempt for the judge or 408
19: 3 that anyone *who* kills a m may flee there. 8357
19: 4 the rule concerning the *m who* kills another AIT
19: 5 a m may go into the forest with his neighbor 889S
19: 5 That m may flee to one of these cities 2085S
19:11 if a m hates his neighbor and lies in wait 408
19:15 to convict a m accused of any crime 408
19:16 the stand to accuse a m of a crime, 408
20: 8 "Is any m afraid or fainthearted? 408+2021+4769
21: 1 If a *m* is found slain, AIT
21: 8 of the blood of an innocent *m*." AIT
21:15 If a m has two wives, 408
21:18 If a m has a stubborn and rebellious son 408
21:22 If a m guilty of a capital offense is put 408
22: 5 nor a m wear women's clothing, 1505
22:13 If a m takes a wife and, after lying with her, 408
22:16 "I gave my daughter in marriage to this m, 408
22:18 the elders shall take the m and punish him. 408
22:19 because this m has given an Israelite virgin NIH
22:22 If a m is found sleeping with another man's 408
22:22 both the m who slept with her and 408
22:23 If a m happens to meet in a town 408
22:24 and did not scream for help, and the m 408
22:25 if out in the country a m happens to meet 408
22:25 only the m who has done this shall die. 408

Dt 22:27 for the **m** found the girl out in the country, NIH
22:28 If a **m** happens to meet a virgin who is 408
22:30 A **m** is not to marry his father's wife; 408
23:17 No Israelite **m** or woman is to become 1201
24: 1 If a **m** marries a woman who becomes 408
24: 2 the wife of another **m,** 408
24: 5 If a **m** has recently married, 408
24: 7 If a **m** is caught kidnapping one 408
24:11 and let the **m** to whom you are making 408
24:12 If the **m** is poor, 408
24:14 not take advantage of a **hired** *m* who is poor AIT
25: 2 If the **guilty** *m* deserves to be beaten, AIT
25: 7 **m** does not want to marry his brother's wife, 408
25: 9 "This is what is done to the **m** who will 408
27:15 "Cursed is the **m** who carves an image 408
27:16 "Cursed is the **m** who dishonors his father NIH
27:17 "Cursed is **m** who moves his neighbor's boundary stone." NIH
27:18 "Cursed is the **m** who leads the blind astray NIH
27:19 "Cursed is the **m** who withholds justice from the alien, NIH
27:20 "Cursed is the **m** who sleeps with his father's wife, NIH
27:21 "Cursed is the **m** who has sexual relations NIH
27:22 "Cursed is the **m** who sleeps with his sister, NIH
27:23 "Cursed is the **m** who sleeps with his mother-in-law." NIH
27:24 "Cursed is the **m** who kills his neighbor secretly." NIH
27:25 "Cursed is the **m** who accepts a bribe to kill NIH
27:26 "Cursed is the **m** who does not uphold NIH
28:29 about like a **blind** *m* in the dark. AIT
28:54 Even the most gentle and sensitive **m** 408
29:18 Make sure there is no **m** or woman, 408
29:20 his wrath and zeal will burn against that **m.** 408
32:30 How could **one** *m* chase a thousand, AIT
33: 1 the **m** *of* God pronounced on the Israelites 408
33: 8 and Urim belong to the **m** you favored. 408
Jos 5:13 he looked up and saw a **m** standing in front 408
6: 5 the people will go up, every **m** straight in." 408
6:20 so every **m** charged straight in, 6639
6:26 before the LORD is the **m** who undertakes 408
7:14 that the LORD takes shall come forward **m** NIH
7:14 LORD takes shall come forward man by **m.** 1505
7:18 Joshua had his family come forward **m** NIH
7:18 by **m,** and Achan son of Carmi, the son 1505
8:17 Not a **m** remained in Ai or Bethel who did 408
10:14 a day when the LORD listened to a **m.** 408
10:20 completely—**almost to a m**— 4392+6330+9462
14: 6 the **m** *of* God at Kadesh Barnea about you 408
14:15 the greatest **m** among the Anakites.) 132
15:16 Acsah in marriage to **the m** who attacks 2257[S]
Jdg 1:12 Acsah in marriage to **the m** who attacks 2257[S]
1:24 a **m** coming out of the city and they said 408
1:25 but spared the **m** and his whole family. 408
3:15 Ehud, a left-handed **m,** the son of Gera 408
3:17 Eglon king of Moab, who was a very fat **m.** 408
3:29 not a **m** escaped. 408
4:16 not a **m** was left. 285[S]
4:22 "I will show you the **m** you're looking for." 408
5:30 a girl or two for each **m,** 1505
7:13 Gideon arrived just as a **m** was telling 408
7:21 *each* **m** held his position around the camp, 408
8:14 a young **m** of Succoth and questioned him, 408
8:14 the young **m** wrote down for him the names NIH
8:21 'As is the **m,** so is his strength.' " 408
8:25 *each* **m** threw a ring from his plunder onto 408
9: 2 sons rule over you, or just one **m?'** 408
10: 1 the time of Abimelech a **m** *of* Issachar, 408
13: 2 A certain **m** of Zorah, named Manoah, 408
13: 6 "A **m** *of* God came to me. 408
13: 8 let the **m** *of* God you sent to us come again 408
13:10 The **m** who appeared to me the other day!" 408
13:11 When he came to the **m,** he said, 408
16: 7 I'll become as weak as any other **m."** 132
16:11 I'll become as weak as any other **m."** 132
16:13 I'll become as weak as any other **m."** 132
16:17 I would become as weak as any other **m."** 132
16:19 a **m** to shave off the seven braids of his hair, 408
17: 1 a **m** named Micah from the hill country 408
17: 5 Now this **m** Micah had a shrine, 408
17:11 **young m** was to him like one of his sons. 5853
17:12 the **young m** became his priest and lived 5853
19: 7 And when the **m** got up to go, 408
19: 9 Then when the **m,** with his concubine 408
19:10 the **m** left and went toward Jebus (that is, 408
19:16 That evening an old **m** from the hill country 408
19:17 the old **m** asked, "Where are you going? 408
19:19 your maidservant, and the **young m** with us. 5853
19:20 welcome at my house," the old **m** said. 408
19:22 they shouted to the old **m** who owned 408
19:22 "Bring out the **m** who came to your house 408
19:23 Since this **m** is my guest, 408
19:24 But to this **m,** don't do such a disgraceful 408
19:25 So the **m** took his concubine 408
19:28 the **m** put her on his donkey and set out 408
20: 1 of Gilead came out as one **m** and assembled 408
20: 8 All the people rose as one **m,** saying, 408
20:11 of Israel got together and united as one **m** 408
21:12 with a **m,** and they took them to the camp 408
21:23 each **m** caught one and carried her off to 4392[S]
Ru 1: 1 and a **m** from Bethlehem in Judah, 408
2: 1 a **m** *of* standing, whose name was Boaz. 408
2:19 Blessed be the *m who* **took notice** *of* you!" AIT
2:19 of the **m** I worked with today is Boaz," 408
2:20 She added, "That **m** is our close relative; 408
3: 8 of the night something startled the **m,** 408
Ru 3:18 For the **m** will not rest until the matter 408
1Sa 1: 1 There was a certain **m** from Ramathaim, 408
1: 3 after year this **m** went up from his town 408
1:21 the **m** Elkanah went up with all his family 408
2:15 and say to the **m** who was sacrificing, "Give 408
2:16 If the **m** said to him, 408
2:25 If a **m** sins against another man, 408
2:25 If a man sins against another **m,** 408
2:25 but if a **m** sins against the LORD, 408
2:27 a **m** *of* God came to Eli and said to him, 408
2:31 not be an **old** *m* in your family line AIT
2:32 there will never be an **old** *m.* AIT
4:10 and *every* **m** fled to his tent. 408
4:13 When the **m** entered the town 408
4:14 The **m** hurried over to Eli, 408
4:17 *m who* **brought the news** AIT
4:18 for he was an old **m** and heavy. 408
9: 1 There was a Benjamite, a **m** *of* standing, 1475
9: 2 an impressive **young m** without equal 1033
9: 6 "Look, in this town there is a **m** *of* God; 408
9: 7 "If we go, what can we give the **m?** 408
9: 7 We have no gift to take to the **m** *of* God. 408
9: 8 I will give it to the **m** *of* God so 408
9: 9 if a **m** went to inquire of God, he would say, 408
9:10 So they set out for the town where the **m** 408
9:16 a **m** from the land of Benjamin. 408
9:17 "This is the **m** I spoke to you about; 408
10:12 A **m** who lived there answered, 408
10:22 "Has the **m** come here yet?" 408
10:24 "Do you see **the m** the LORD has chosen? 889[S]
11: 7 and they turned out as one **m.** 408
13:14 the LORD has sought out a **m** 408
14: 1 to the **young m** bearing his armor, 5853
14:24 "Cursed be any **m** who eats food 408
14:28 'Cursed be any **m** who eats food today!' 408
14:52 whenever Saul saw a mighty or brave **m,** 408
15:29 for he is not a **m,** that he should change his mind. 132
16: 7 LORD does not look at the things **m** looks at. 132
16: 7 **M** looks at the outward appearance, 132
16:18 He is a **brave m** and a warrior. 1475+2657
16:18 He speaks well and is a fine-looking **m.** 408
17: 8 Choose a **m** and have him come down 408
17:10 Give me a **m** and let us fight each other." 408
17:24 When the Israelites saw the **m,** 408
17:25 "Do you see how this **m** keeps coming out? 408
17:25 give great wealth to the **m** who kills him. 408
17:26 be done for the **m** who kills this Philistine 408
17:27 be done for the **m** who kills him." 408
17:33 he has been a fighting **m** from his youth." 408
17:55 "Abner, whose son is that **young m?"** 5853
17:56 "Find out whose son this **young m** is." 6624
17:58 "Whose son are you, **young m?"** 5853
18:23 I'm only a poor **m** and little known." 408
19: 5 would you do wrong to an **innocent m** 1947+5929
21:14 Achish said to his servants, "Look at the **m!** 408
21:15 Must **this** *m* come into my house?" AIT
22:23 *the m* who *is* **seeking** your life is seeking mine also. AIT
24:19 When a **m** finds his enemy, 408
25: 2 A certain **m** in Maon, 408
25:17 He is such a wicked **m** that no one can talk 1201
25:25 to that wicked **m** Nabal. 408
26:15 David said, "You're a **m,** aren't you? 408
26:23 The LORD rewards every **m** 408
27: 3 *Each* **m** had his family with him, 408
27: 9 he did not leave a **m** or woman alive, 408
27:11 not leave a **m** or woman alive to be brought 408
28:14 "An old **m** wearing a robe is coming up," 408
29: 4 "Send the **m** back, 408
30:22 *each* **m** may take his wife and children 408
30:24 of the *m who* **stayed** with the supplies AIT
2Sa 1: 2 the third day a **m** arrived from Saul's camp, 408
1: 5 to the **young m** who brought him the report, 5853
1: 6 the **young m** said, "and there was Saul, 5853
1:13 David said to the **young m** who brought 5853
2:16 Then *each* **m** grabbed his opponent by 408
2:23 And **every** *m* stopped when he came to AIT
3:38 and a **great** *m* has fallen in Israel this day? AIT
4:10 when a *m* **told** me, 'Saul is dead,' AIT
4:11 an innocent **m** in his own house and 408
7:19 Is this your usual way of dealing with **m,** 132
11: 3 *The m* **said,** "Isn't this Bathsheba, AIT
12: 2 The **rich** *m* had a very large number AIT
12: 3 **poor** *m* had nothing except one little ewe AIT
12: 4 "Now a traveler came to the rich **m,** 408
12: 4 but the rich **m** refrained from taking one NIH
12: 4 that belonged to the poor **m** and prepared it 408
12: 5 with anger against the **m** and said to Nathan, 408
12: 5 the **m** who did this deserves to die! 408
12: 7 Then Nathan said to David, "You are the **m!** 408
13: 3 Jonadab was a very shrewd **m.** 408
13:34 Now the **m** standing watch looked up 5853
14:16 the hand of the **m** who is trying to cut off 408
14:21 Go, bring back the **young m** Absalom." 5853
14:25 In all Israel there was not a **m** so highly 408
16: 5 a **m** from the same clan 408
16: 7 get out, you **m** *of* blood, you scoundrel! 408
16: 8 You have come to ruin because you are a **m** 408
17: 3 the **m** you seek will mean the return of all; 408
17:18 But a **young m** saw them and told Absalom. 5853
17:18 and went to the house of a **m** in Bahurim. 408
17:25 Amasa was the son of a **m** named Jether, 408
18: 5 with the **young m** Absalom for my sake." 5853
18:11 Joab said to the **m** who had told him this, 408
18:12 But the **m** replied, 408
18:12 Protect the **young m** Absalom for my sake. 5853
2Sa 18:24 As he looked out, he saw a **m** running alone. 408
18:25 And the **m** came closer and closer. NIH
18:26 Then the watchman saw another **m** running, 408
18:26 "Look, another **m** running alone!" 408
18:27 "He's a good **m,"** the king said. 408
18:29 "Is the **young m** Absalom safe?" 5853
18:32 "Is the **young m** Absalom safe?" 5853
18:32 up to harm you be like that **young m."** 5853
19: 7 not a **m** will be left with you by nightfall. 408
19:14 of Judah as though they were one **m.** 408
19:32 Now Barzillai *was* a very **old** *m,* AIT
19:32 for he was a very wealthy **m.** 408
20: 1 *Every* **m** to his tent, O Israel!" 408
20:12 and the **m** saw that all the troops came to 408
20:21 A **m** named Sheba son of Bicri, 408
20:21 Hand over this one **m,** 2257[S]
21: 5 "As for the **m** who destroyed us and plotted 408
21:20 a huge **m** with six fingers on each hand 408
23: 1 of Jesse, the oracle of the **m** exalted by 1505
23: 1 the **m** anointed by the God of Jacob, NIH
1Ki 1:42 A worthy **m** like you must 408
1:52 "If he shows himself to be a worthy **m,** 1201
2: 2 "So be strong, show yourself a **m,** 408
2: 4 you will never fail to have a **m** on the throne 408
2: 9 You are a **m** *of* wisdom; 408
4:25 *each* **m** under his own vine and fig tree. 408
4:31 He was wiser than any other **m,** 132
7:14 a **m** of Tyre and a craftsman in bronze. 408
8:25 a **m** to sit before me on the throne of Israel, 408
8:31 a **m** wrongs his neighbor and is required 408
8:39 deal with each **m** according to all he does, 408
9: 5 'You shall never fail to have a **m** on 408
11:28 Now Jeroboam was a **m** *of* standing, 408
11:28 how well the **young m** did his work, 5853
12:22 of God came to Shemaiah the **m** *of* God: 408
13: 1 of the LORD a **m** *of* God came from Judah 408
13: 3 That same day the **m** of God gave a sign: NIH
13: 4 When King Jeroboam heard what the **m** 408
13: 4 stretched out toward **the m** shriveled up, 2257[S]
13: 5 according to the sign given by the **m** *of* God 408
13: 6 Then the king said to the **m** *of* God, 408
13: 6 the **m** *of* God interceded with the LORD, 408
13: 7 The king said to the **m** *of* God, 408
13: 8 But the **m** *of* God answered the king, 408
13:11 whose sons came and told him all that the **m** 408
13:12 And his sons showed him which road the **m** 408
13:14 and rode after the **m** *of* God. 408
13:14 the **m** *of* God who came from Judah?" 408
13:16 The **m** of God said, "I cannot turn back NIH
13:19 So the **m** of God returned with him and ate NIH
13:21 He cried out to the **m** *of* God who had come 408
13:23 When the **m** of God had finished eating NIH
13:26 "It is the **m** *of* God who defied the word of 408
13:29 So the prophet picked up the body of the **m** 408
13:31 in the grave where the **m** *of* God is buried; 408
16: 9 **the m** in charge of the palace at Tirzah. 889[S]
17:18 "What do you have against me, **m** *of* God? 408
17:24 a **m** *of* God and that the word of the LORD 408
20: 7 "See how **this** *m* is looking for trouble! AIT
20:28 The **m** *of* God came up and told the king 408
20:35 but the **m** refused. 408
20:36 And after the **m** went away, NIH
20:37 The prophet found another **m** and said, 408
20:37 So the **m** struck him and wounded him. 408
20:39 with a captive and said, 'Guard this **m.** 408
20:40 and there, **the m** disappeared." 2085[S]
20:42 a **m** I had determined should die. 408
21:19 not murdered a **m** and seized his property?' NIH
21:25 (There was never a **m** like Ahab, NIH
22: 8 "There is still one **m** through whom we can 408
22:13 "Look, as one **m** the other prophets are 7023
22:36 *"Every* **m** to his town; everyone to his land! 408
2Ki 1: 6 "A **m** came to meet us," they replied. 408
1: 7 of **m** was it who came to meet you 408
1: 8 "He was a **m** with a garment of hair and 408
1: 9 **"M** *of* God, the king says, 'Come down!' " 408
1:10 "If I am a **m** *of* God, 408
1:11 The captain said to him, **"M** *of* God, 408
1:12 "If I am a **m** *of* God," Elijah replied, 408
1:13 **"M** *of* God," he begged, 408
3:21 so **every** *m,* young and old, AIT
3:25 and *each* **m** threw a stone 408
4: 1 The wife of a **m** from the company of NIH
4: 7 She went and told the **m** *of* God, 408
4: 9 that **this m** who often comes our way is 2085[S]
4: 9 a holy **m** *of* God. 408
4:16 "Don't mislead your servant, O **m** *of* God!" 408
4:21 up and laid him on the bed of the **m** *of* God, 408
4:22 to the **m** *of* God quickly and return." 408
4:25 So she set out and came to the **m** *of* God 408
4:25 the **m** *of* God said to his servant Gehazi, 408
4:27 she reached the **m** *of* God at the mountain, 408
4:27 but the **m** *of* God said, "Leave her alone! 408
4:40 "O **m** *of* God, there is death in the pot!" 408
4:42 A **m** came from Baal Shalishah, 408
4:42 bringing the **m** *of* God twenty loaves 408
5: 1 He was a great **m** in the sight of his master 408
5: 8 When Elisha the **m** *of* God heard that 408
5: 8 Have the **m** come to me and he will know NIH
5:14 as the **m** *of* God had told him, 408
5:15 and all his attendants went back to the **m** 408
5:20 the servant of Elisha the **m** *of* God, 408
5:26 not my spirit with you when the **m** got down 408
6: 6 The **m** *of* God asked, "Where did it fall?" 408
6: 7 the **m** reached out his hand and took it. NIH
6: 9 The **m** *of* God sent word to the king 408
6:10 on the place indicated by the **m** *of* God. 408

2Ki 6:15 of the **m** *of* God got up and went out early 408
6:19 to the **m** you are looking for." 408
7: 2 the king was leaning said to the **m** *of* God, 408
7: 5 not a **m** was there, 408
7:10 the Aramean camp and not a **m** was there— 408
7:17 just as the **m** *of* God had foretold when 408
7:18 It happened as the **m** *of* God had said to 408
7:19 The officer had said to the **m** *of* God, 408
7:19 The **m** of God had replied, NIH
8: 2 The woman proceeded to do as the **m** 408
8: 4 the servant of the **m** *of* God, and had said, 408
8: 7 "The **m** *of* God has come all the way 408
8: 8 "Take a gift with you and go to meet the **m** 408
8:11 Then the **m** *of* God began to weep. 408
9: 1 The prophet Elisha summoned a **m** from 285[S]
9: 4 So the **young m,** the prophet, 5853
9:11 the **m** and the sort of things he says," 408
11: 8 *each* **m** with his weapon in his hand. 408
13:19 The **m** *of* God was angry with him and said, 408
13:21 a **m,** suddenly they saw a band of raiders; 408
13:21 the **m** came to life and stood up on his feet. 408
14:12 and *every* **m** fled to his home. 408
15:20 Every wealthy **m** had to contribute 1475
22:15 Tell the **m** who sent you to me, 408
23:16 by the **m** *of* God who foretold these things. 408
23:17 of the **m** *of* God who came from Judah 408
1Ch 12: 4 a **mighty m** among the Thirty, 1475
16: 3 of raisins to each Israelite **m** and woman. 408
16:21 He allowed no **m** to oppress them; 408
20: 6 a huge **m** with six fingers on each hand 408
22: 9 a son who will be a **m** *of* peace and rest, 408
23:14 the **m** *of* God were counted as part of 408
27: 6 This was the Benaiah who was a **mighty m** 1475
27:32 a **m** *of* insight and a scribe. 408
28:21 and every **willing** *m* skilled AIT
29: 1 because this palatial structure is not for **m** 132
2Ch 2: 7 a **m** skilled to work in gold and silver, 408
2:13 Huram-Abi, a **m** *of* great skill, 408
6:16 a **m** to sit before me on the throne of Israel, 408
6:22 a **m** wrongs his neighbor and is required 408
6:30 deal with each **m** according to all he does, 408
7:18 'You shall never fail to have a **m** to rule 408
8:14 because this was what David the **m** 408
11: 2 of the LORD came to Shemaiah the **m** 408
14:11 do not let **m** prevail against you." 632
15:13 whether small or great, **m** or woman. 408
18: 7 "There is still one **m** through whom we can 408
18:12 "Look, as one **m** the other prophets are 7023
19: 6 because you are not judging for **m** but for 132
23: 7 *each* **m** with his weapons in his hand. 408
25: 7 But a **m** *of* God came to him and said, 408
25: 9 Amaziah asked the **m** *of* God, 408
25: 9 The **m** *of* God replied, 408
25:22 and *every* **m** fled to his home. 408
30:16 as prescribed in the Law of Moses the **m** 408
34:23 Tell the **m** who sent you to me, 408
36:17 spared neither **young m** nor young woman, 1033
36:17 **old** *m* or aged. AIT
Ezr 2:61 Hakkoz and Barzillai (a **m** who had married NIH
3: 1 the people assembled as one **m** 408
3: 2 in the Law of Moses the **m** *of* God. 408
5:14 to a **m** named Sheshbazzar, 10192[S]
7:11 a **m learned** *in* matters concerning 6221
8:18 they brought us Sherebiah, a capable **m,** 408
Ne 1:11 in the presence of this **m."** 408
4:18 *m who* **sounded** the trumpet stayed with me. AIT
4:22 "Have *every* **m** and his helper stay 408
5:13 and possessions every **m** who does 408
5:13 *a m* **be** shaken out and emptied!" AIT
6:11 But I said, "Should a **m** like me run away? 408
7: 2 because he was a **m** *of* integrity 408
7:63 Hakkoz and Barzillai (a **m** who had married NIH
8: 1 the people assembled as one **m** in the square 408
9:29 by which a **m** will live if he obeys them. 132
12:24 as prescribed by David the **m** *of* God. 408
12:36 David the **m** *of* God. 408
Est 1: 8 to serve *each* **m** what he wished. 408+408+2256
1:22 in each people's tongue that every **m** should 408
4:11 of the royal provinces know that for any **m** 408
6: 6 for the **m** the king delights to honor?" 408
6: 7 "For the **m** the king delights to honor, 408
6: 9 Let them robe the **m** the king delights 408
6: 9 for the **m** the king delights to honor!'" 408
6:11 for the **m** the king delights to honor!" 408
7: 5 Where is **the m** who has dared to do such 2085[S]
Job 1: 1 of Uz there lived a **m** whose name was Job. 408
1: 1 This **m** was blameless and upright; 408
1: 3 He was the greatest **m** among all the people 408
1: 8 a **m** who fears God and shuns evil." 408
1:12 but on **the m himself** do not lay a finger." 2257[S]
2: 3 a **m** who fears God and shuns evil. 408
2: 4 "A **m** will give all he has for his own life. 408
3:23 to a **m** whose way is hidden, 1505
4:17 Can a **m** be more pure than his Maker? 1505
5: 7 Yet **m** is born to trouble as surely 132
5:17 "Blessed is the **m** whom God corrects; 632
6:14 "A **despairing m** should have the devotion 4988
6:26 treat the words of a **despairing** *m* as wind? AIT
7: 1 "Does not **m** have hard service on earth? 632
7: 1 Are not his days like those of a **hired m?** 8502
7: 2 or a **hired m** waiting eagerly for his wages, 8502
7:17 "What is **m** that you make so much of him, 632
8:20 "Surely God does not reject a **blameless** *m* AIT
9:32 not a **m** like me that I might answer him, 408
10: 5 of a mortal or your years like those of a **m,** 1505
11:12 a witless **m** can no more become wise than 408
11:12 a wild donkey's colt can be born a **m.** 132
Job 12:14 the **m** he imprisons cannot be released. 408
13:16 no **godless** *m* would dare come before him! AIT
13:28 "So **m** wastes away like something rotten, 2085[S]
14: 1 "**M** born of woman is of few days and full 132
14: 6 till he has put in his time like a **hired m.** 8502
14:10 But **m** dies and is laid low; 1505
14:12 so **m** lies down and does not rise; 408
14:14 If a **m** dies, will he live again? 1505
15: 2 Would a **wise** *m* answer with empty notions AIT
15: 7 "Are you the first **m** ever born? 132
15:14 "What is **m,** that he could be pure, 632
15:16 how much less **m,** who is vile and corrupt, 408
15:20 All his days the **wicked** *m* suffers torment, AIT
16:21 of a **m** he pleads with God as a man pleads 1505
16:21 with God as a **m** pleads for his friend. 132+1201
17: 5 If *a m* **denounces** his friends for reward, AIT
17: 6 a **m** in whose face people spit. NIH
17:10 I will not find a **wise** *m* among you. AIT
18:21 Surely such is the dwelling of an **evil m;** 6405
20: 4 ever since **m** was placed on the earth, 132
21: 4 "Is my complaint directed to **m?** 132
21:19 Let him repay **the m himself,** 2257[S]
21:23 *One* **m** dies in full vigor, 2296[S]
21:25 *Another* **m** dies in bitterness of soul, 2296[S]
21:30 **evil** *m* is spared from the day of calamity, AIT
22: 2 "Can a **m** be of benefit to God? 1505
22: 2 Can even a **wise** *m* benefit him? AIT
22: 8 you were a powerful **m,** owning land— 408
22: 8 an **honored** *m,* living on it. AIT
23: 7 There an **upright** *m* could present his case AIT
25: 4 How then can a **m** be righteous before God? 632
25: 6 how much less **m,** who is but a maggot— 632
25: 6 a son of **m,** who is only a worm!" 132
27:13 a **ruthless** *m* receives from the Almighty: AIT
28: 3 *M* **puts** an end to the darkness; AIT
28: 4 in places forgotten by the foot of **m;** NIH
28:13 **M** does not comprehend its worth; 632
28:28 And he said to **m,** 'The fear of the Lord— 132
29:13 The *m who was* **dying** blessed me; AIT
30:24 no one lays a hand on a **broken m** when 6505
31:19 or a **needy** *m* without a garment, AIT
32: 8 But it is the spirit in a **m,** 632
32:13 let God refute him, not **m.'** 408
32:21 nor will I flatter *any* **m;** 132
33:12 for God is greater than **m.** 632
33:14 though *m may* not **perceive** it. AIT
33:17 to turn **m** from wrongdoing and keep him 132
33:19 Or a **m** may be chastened on a bed of pain NIH
33:23 to tell a **m** what is right for him, 132
33:29 "God does all these things to a **m—** 1505
34: 7 What **m** is like Job, 1505
34: 9 a **m** nothing when he tries to please God.' 1505
34:11 He repays a **m** for what he has done; 132
34:15 and **m** would return to the dust. 132
34:29 Yet he is over **m** and nation alike, 132
34:30 to keep a godless **m** from ruling, 132
34:31 "Suppose *a m* **says** to God, AIT
34:36 the utmost for answering like a wicked **m!** 408
35: 8 Your wickedness affects only a **m** 408
37: 7 he stops every **m** from his labor. 132
37:20 Would any **m** ask to be swallowed up? 408
38: 3 Brace yourself like a **m;** 1505
38:26 to water a land where no **m** lives, 408
40: 7 "Brace yourself like a **m;** 1505
40:11 look at every **proud** *m* and bring him low, AIT
40:12 look at every **proud** *m* and humble him, AIT
Ps 1: 1 Blessed is the **m** who does not walk in 408
8: 4 what is **m** that you are mindful of him, 632
8: 4 the son of **m** that you care for him? 132
9:19 Arise, O LORD, let not **m** triumph; 632
10: 2 In his arrogance the **wicked** *m* hunts down AIT
10:13 Why does the **wicked** *m* revile God? AIT
10:15 Break the arm of the wicked and **evil** *m;* AIT
10:18 in order that **m,** who is of the earth, 632
15: 4 a **vile** *m* but honors those who fear AIT
22: 6 But I am a worm and not a **m,** 408
25:12 Who, then, is the **m** that fears the LORD? 408
32: 2 Blessed is the **m** whose sin the LORD does 132
32:10 love surrounds the *m who* **trusts** in him. AIT
34: 6 This **poor** *m* called, and the LORD heard AIT
34: 8 blessed is the **m** who takes refuge in him. 1505
34:19 A **righteous** *m* may have many troubles, AIT
36: 6 O LORD, you preserve both **m** and beast. 132
37:30 mouth of the **righteous** *m* utters wisdom, AIT
37:35 and **ruthless** *m* flourishing like a green tree AIT
37:37 there is a future for the **m** *of* peace. 408
38:13 I am like a **deaf** *m,* who cannot hear, AIT
38:14 I have become like a **m** who does not hear, 408
39: 6 **M** is a mere phantom as he goes to and fro: 408
39:11 each **m** is but a breath. 132
40: 4 the **m** who makes the LORD his trust, 1505
49: 7 No **m** can redeem the life of another or give 408
49:12 But **m,** despite his riches, does not endure; 132
49:16 Do not be overawed when a **m** grows rich, 408
49:20 A **m** who has riches without understanding 132
52: 1 Why do you boast of evil, you **mighty m?** 1475
52: 7 the **m** who did not make God his stronghold 1505
55:13 But it is you, a **m** like myself, 632
56: 4 What can **mortal m** do to me? 1414
56:11 What can **m** do to me? 132
60:11 for the help of **m** is worthless. 132
62: 3 How long will you assault a **m?** 408
64: 4 from ambush at the **innocent** *m;* AIT
64: 6 Surely the mind and heart of **m** are cunning. 408
73: 5 from the burdens common to **m;** 632
75: 6 or the west or from the desert can exalt a **m.** NIH
78:65 as a **m** wakes from the stupor of wine. 1475
Ps 80:17 your hand rest on the **m** *at* your right hand, 408
80:17 the son of **m** you have raised up for yourself. 132
84:12 blessed is the **m** who trusts in you. 132
88: 4 I am like a **m** without strength. 1505
89:19 I have exalted a **young m** from among 1033
89:22 no wicked **m** will oppress him. 1201
89:48 What **m** can live and not see death, 1505
90: T A prayer of Moses the **m** *of* God. 408
92: 6 The senseless **m** does not know, 408
94:10 Does he who teaches **m** lack knowledge? 132
94:11 The LORD knows the thoughts of **m;** 132
94:12 Blessed is the **m** you discipline, O LORD, 1505
94:12 O LORD, **the m** you teach from your law; 5647[S]
102: T A prayer of an **afflicted** *m.* AIT
103:15 As for **m,** his days are like grass, 632
104:14 and plants for **m** to cultivate— 132
104:15 wine that gladdens the heart of **m,** 632
104:23 Then **m** goes out to his work, 132
105:17 and he sent a **m** before them— 408
108:12 for the help of **m** is worthless. 132
109: 4 but I am a **m** of prayer. NIH
109: 6 Appoint an **evil** *m* to oppose him; AIT
112: 1 Blessed is the **m** who fears the LORD, 408
112: 4 and compassionate and **righteous** *m.* AIT
112: 6 a **righteous** *m* will be remembered forever. AIT
112:10 The **wicked** *m* will see and be vexed, AIT
115:16 but the earth he has given to **m.** 132+1201
118: 6 What can **m** do to me? 132
118: 8 in the LORD than to trust in **m.** 132
119: 9 How can a **young m** keep his way pure? 5853
120: 7 I am a **m** of peace; NIH
127: 5 Blessed is the **m** whose quiver is full 1505
128: 4 the **m** blessed who fears the LORD. 1505
141: 5 Let a **righteous** *m* strike me— AIT
144: 3 O LORD, what is **m** that you care for him, 132
144: 3 the son of **m** that you think of him? 632
144: 4 **M** is like a breath; 132
147:10 nor his delight in the legs of a **m;** 408
Pr 3: 4 and a good name in the sight of God and **m.** 132
3:13 Blessed is the **m** who finds wisdom, 132
3:13 the **m** who gains understanding, 132
3:30 Do not accuse a **m** for no reason— 132
3:31 Do not envy a violent **m** or choose any 408
3:32 the LORD detests a **perverse** *m* but takes AIT
5:22 The evil deeds of a **wicked** *m* ensnare him; AIT
6:11 like a bandit and scarcity like an armed **m.** 408
6:19 *a m who* **stirs up** dissension among brothers. AIT
6:27 Can a **m** scoop fire into his lap 408
6:28 *Can* a **m** walk on hot coals 408
6:32 *m who* **commits adultery** lacks judgment; AIT
8:34 Blessed is the **m** who listens to me, 132
9: 7 whoever rebukes a **wicked** *m* incurs abuse. AIT
9: 8 rebuke a **wise** *m* and he will love you. AIT
9: 9 Instruct a **wise** *m* and he will be wiser still; AIT
9: 9 teach a **righteous** *m* and he will add AIT
10: 4 Lazy hands make *a m* **poor,** AIT
10: 9 The **m** of integrity walks securely, 2143[S]
10:23 a **m** *of* understanding delights in wisdom. 408
11: 7 When a wicked **m** dies, his hope perishes; 132
11: 8 The **righteous** *m* is rescued from trouble, AIT
11:12 **m** who lacks judgment derides his neighbor, NIH
11:12 but a **m** *of* understanding holds his tongue. 408
11:13 but a **trustworthy** *m* keeps a secret. AIT
11:17 A kind **m** benefits himself, 408
11:17 but a **cruel** *m* brings trouble on himself. AIT
11:18 The **wicked** *m* earns deceptive wages, AIT
11:19 The truly **righteous** *m* attains life, AIT
11:24 *One m* **gives freely,** yet gains even more; AIT
11:25 A generous **m** will prosper; 5883
11:26 People curse the *m who* **hoards** grain, AIT
12: 2 A **good** *m* obtains favor from the LORD, AIT
12: 2 but the LORD condemns a crafty **m.** 408
12: 3 A **m** cannot be established through wickedness, 132
12: 8 A **m** is praised according to his wisdom, 408
12:10 A **righteous** *m* cares for the needs AIT
12:13 An **evil** *m* is trapped by his sinful talk, AIT
12:13 but a **righteous** *m* escapes trouble. AIT
12:14 of his lips a **m** is filled with good things as 408
12:15 but a **wise** *m* listens to advice. AIT
12:16 but a **prudent** *m* overlooks an insult. AIT
12:23 prudent **m** keeps his knowledge to himself, 132
12:25 An anxious heart weighs a **m** down, 408
12:26 A **righteous** *m* is cautious in friendship, AIT
12:27 The **lazy** *m* does not roast his game, AIT
12:27 but the diligent **m** prizes his possessions. 132
13: 2 the fruit of his lips a **m** enjoys good things, 408
13: 6 Righteousness guards the **m of integrity,** 2006+9448
13: 7 *m* **pretends to be rich,** yet has nothing; AIT
13: 8 but a **poor** *m* hears no threat. AIT
13:14 turning a **m** from the snares of death. NIH
13:16 Every **prudent** *m* acts out of knowledge, AIT
13:22 A **good** *m* leaves an inheritance for his AIT
14: 7 Stay away from a foolish **m,** 408
14:12 There is a way that seems right to a **m,** 408
14:14 and the good **m** rewarded for his. 408
14:15 A **simple** *m* believes anything, AIT
14:15 but a **prudent** *m* gives thought to his steps. AIT
14:16 A **wise** *m* fears the LORD and shuns evil, AIT
14:17 A **quick-tempered** *m* does foolish things, AIT
14:17 and a crafty **m** is hated. 408
14:27 turning a **m** from the snares of death. NIH
14:29 A **patient** *m* has great understanding, AIT
14:29 but a **quick-tempered** *m* displays folly. AIT
15:18 A hot-tempered **m** stirs up dissension, 408
15:18 but a **patient** *m* calms a quarrel. AIT

Pr 15:20 but a foolish **m** despises his mother. 132
15:21 Folly delights a *m who* **lacks** judgment, AIT
15:21 **m** *of* understanding keeps a straight course. 408
15:23 A **m** finds joy in giving an apt reply— 408
15:27 A **greedy** *m* brings trouble to his family, AIT
15:33 The fear of the LORD teaches a **m** wisdom, NIH
16: 1 To **m** belong the plans of the heart, 132
16: 6 through the fear of the LORD *a m* **avoids** evil. AIT
16: 9 In his heart a **m** plans his course, 132
16:13 they value a *m who* **speaks** the truth. AIT
16:14 but a wise **m** will appease it. 408
16:25 There is a way that seems right to a **m,** 408
16:28 A perverse **m** stirs up dissension, 408
16:29 A violent **m** entices his neighbor 408
16:32 Better a **patient** *m* than a warrior, AIT
16:32 a *m who* **controls** his temper than AIT
17: 4 A **wicked** *m* listens to evil lips; AIT
17:10 A rebuke impresses a *m of* **discernment** AIT
17:11 An **evil** *m* is bent only on rebellion; AIT
17:13 If a *m* **pays back** evil for good, AIT
17:18 A **m** lacking in judgment strikes hands 132
17:20 A *m of* **perverse** heart does not prosper; AIT
17:23 A **wicked** *m* accepts a bribe in secret AIT
17:24 A **discerning** *m* keeps wisdom in view, AIT
17:26 It is not good to punish an **innocent** *m,* AIT
17:27 A **m of knowledge** uses words with restraint, 1981+3359
17:27 and a **m** *of* understanding is even-tempered. 408
18: 1 An **unfriendly** *m* pursues selfish ends, AIT
18:23 A **poor** *m* pleads for mercy, AIT
18:23 but a **rich** *m* answers harshly. AIT
18:24 **m** *of* many companions may come to ruin, 408
19: 1 a **poor** *m* whose walk is blameless than AIT
19: 6 the friend of a **m** *who gives* gifts. 408
19: 7 A **poor** *m* is shunned by all his relatives— AIT
19:15 and the shiftless **m** goes hungry. 5883
19:19 A **hot-tempered** *m* must pay the penalty; AIT
19:22 What a **m** desires is unfailing love; 132
19:25 rebuke a **discerning** *m,* AIT
20: 5 but a **m** *of* understanding draws them out. 408
20: 6 Many a **m** claims to have unfailing love, 132
20: 6 but a faithful **m** who can find? 408
20: 7 The **righteous** *m* leads a blameless life; AIT
20:17 Food gained by fraud tastes sweet to a **m,** 408
20:19 *m who* **talks too much.** AIT
20:20 If a *m* **curses** his father or mother, AIT
20:25 a trap for a **m** to dedicate something rashly 132
20:27 lamp of the LORD searches the spirit of a **m;** 132
21:10 The wicked **m** craves evil; 5883
21:11 when a **wise** *m* is instructed, AIT
21:13 If a *m* **shuts** his ears to the cry of the poor, AIT
21:16 A **m** who strays from the path 132
21:20 but a foolish **m** devours all he has. 132
21:22 A **wise** *m* attacks the city of the mighty AIT
21:24 The proud and **arrogant** *m*— AIT
21:29 A wicked **m** puts up a bold front, 408
21:29 but an **upright** *m* gives thought to his ways. AIT
22: 3 A **prudent** *m* sees danger and takes refuge, AIT
22: 9 **generous m** will himself be blessed, 3202+6524
22:24 not make friends with a hot-tempered **m,** 1251
22:26 *m who* **strikes** hands **in pledge** AIT
22:29 Do you see a **m** skilled in his work? 408
23: 6 Do not eat the food of a **stingy m,** 6524+8273
23: 7 *m who is always* **thinking** about the cost. AIT
23:24 The father of a **righteous** *m* has great joy; AIT
24: 5 A wise **m** has great power, 1505
24: 5 and a **m** *of* knowledge increases strength; 408
24:16 for though a **righteous** *m* falls seven times, AIT
24:20 for the **evil** *m* has no future hope, AIT
24:29 I'll pay that **m** back for what he did." 408
24:30 the vineyard of the **m** *who* lacks judgment; 132
24:34 like a bandit and scarcity like an armed **m.** 408
25:14 a **m** who boasts of gifts he does not give. 408
25:18 the **m** who gives false testimony 408
25:26 a **righteous** *m* who gives way to the wicked. AIT
25:28 down is a **m** who lacks self-control. 408
26:12 Do you see a **m** wise in his own eyes? 408
26:19 is a **m** who deceives his neighbor and says, 408
26:21 so is a quarrelsome **m** for kindling strife. 408
26:24 **malicious** *m* disguises himself with his lips, AIT
26:27 If a *m* **digs** a pit, he will fall into it; AIT
26:27 if a *m* **rolls** a stone, it will roll back on him. AIT
27: 8 that strays from its nest is a **m** who strays 408
27:14 If a *m* loudly **blesses** his neighbor early in AIT
27:17 sharpens iron, so *one* **m** sharpens another. 408
27:19 so a man's heart **reflects the m.** 132+2021+4200
27:20 and neither are the eyes of **m.** 132
27:21 but **m** is tested by the praise he receives. 408
28: 1 The **wicked** *m* flees though no one pursues, AIT
28: 2 but a **m** of understanding and knowledge 132
28: 6 a **poor** *m* whose walk is blameless than AIT
28: 6 a **rich** *m* whose ways are perverse. AIT
28:11 A rich **m** may be wise in his own eyes, 408
28:11 but a **poor** *m* who has discernment sees AIT
28:14 the **m** who always fears the LORD, 132
28:15 or a charging bear is a **wicked** *m* ruling over AIT
28:17 A **m** tormented by the guilt of murder will 132
28:20 A faithful **m** will be richly blessed, 408
28:21 yet a **m** will do wrong for a piece of bread. 1505
28:22 A stingy **m** is eager to get rich 408
28:23 He who rebukes a **m** will in the end gain 132
28:25 A **greedy m** stirs up dissension, 5883+8146
29: 1 A **m** who remains stiff-necked after many 408
29: 3 A **m** who loves wisdom brings joy 408
29: 6 An evil **m** is snared by his own sin, 408
29: 9 If a wise **m** goes to court with a fool, 408
29:10 Bloodthirsty men hate a *m of* **integrity** AIT

Pr 29:11 but a **wise** *m* keeps himself under control. AIT
29:13 The **poor** *m* and the oppressor have this AIT
29:20 Do you see a **m** who speaks in haste? 408
29:21 If a *m* **pampers** his servant from youth, AIT
29:22 An angry **m** stirs up dissension, 408
29:23 but a *m of* **lowly** spirit gains honor. AIT
29:25 Fear of **m** will prove to be a snare, 132
29:26 but it is from the LORD that **m** gets justice. 408
30: 1 This **m** declared to Ithiel, 1505
30:19 and the way of a **m** with a maiden. 1505
Ecc 1: 3 What does **m** gain from all his labor 132
2: 8 the delights of the heart of **m.** 132+1201
2:14 The **wise** *m* has eyes in his head, AIT
2:16 For the **wise** *m,* like the fool, AIT
2:16 Like the fool, the **wise** *m* too must die! AIT
2:19 who knows whether he will be a **wise** *m* AIT
2:21 For a **m** may do his work with wisdom, 132
2:22 a **m** get for all the toil and anxious striving 132
2:24 A **m** can do nothing better than to eat 132
2:26 To the **m** who pleases him, 132
3:19 **m** has no advantage over the animal. 132
3:21 knows if the spirit of **m** rises upward 132+1201
3:22 that there is nothing better for a **m** than 132
4: 8 There was a **m** all alone; 285S
4:10 But pity the **m** who falls and has no one 285S
5:12 abundance of a **rich** *m* permits him no sleep. AIT
5:15 Naked a *m* **comes** from his mother's womb, AIT
5:16 This too is a grievous evil: As a *m* **comes,** AIT
5:18 a **m** to eat and drink, and to find satisfaction NIH
5:19 God gives any **m** wealth and possessions, 132
6: 2 God gives a **m** wealth, 408
6: 3 A **m** may have a hundred children 408
6: 5 it has more rest than does **that** *m*— AIT
6: 8 What advantage has a **wise** *m* over a fool? AIT
6: 8 What does a **poor** *m* gain by knowing how AIT
6:10 and what **m** is has been known; 132
6:10 no **m** can contend with one who is stronger NIH
6:12 For who knows what is good for a **m** in life, 132
7: 2 for death is the destiny of every **m;** 132
7: 7 Extortion turns a **wise** *m* into a fool, AIT
7:14 a **m** cannot discover anything 132
7:15 a **righteous** *m* perishing in his righteousness, AIT
7:15 a **wicked** *m* living long in his wickedness. AIT
7:18 The *m who* **fears** God will avoid all AIT
7:19 Wisdom makes one **wise** *m* more powerful than ten rulers AIT
7:20 There is not a righteous **m** 132
7:26 The *m who* **pleases** God will escape her, AIT
7:28 I found one [upright] **m** among a thousand, 132
8: 1 Who is like the **wise** *m?* AIT
8: 7 Since no **m** knows the future, 5647S
8: 8 No **m** has power over the wind to contain it; 132
8: 9 a **m** lords it over others to his own hurt. 132
8:12 a **wicked** *m* commits a hundred crimes AIT
8:15 a **m** under the sun than to eat and drink and 132
8:17 **m** cannot discover its meaning. 132
8:17 Even if a **wise** *m* claims he knows, AIT
9: 1 but no **m** knows whether love or hate awaits 132
9: 2 As it is with the **good** *m,* so with the sinner; AIT
9:12 no **m** knows when his hour will come: 132
9:15 there lived in that city a **m** poor but wise, 408
9:15 But nobody remembered that poor **m.** 408
10:18 If a **m** is lazy, the rafters sag; NIH
11: 8 However many years a **m** may live, 132
11: 9 Be happy, **young m,** while you are young, 1033
12: 5 Then **m** goes to his eternal home 132
12:13 for this is the whole [duty] of **m.** 132
Isa 1:31 The **mighty** *m* will become tinder AIT
2: 9 So **m** will be brought low 132
2:11 The eyes of the arrogant **m** will be humbled 132
2:17 The arrogance of **m** will be brought low and 132
2:22 Stop trusting in **m,** 132
3: 3 the captain of fifty and **m of rank,** 5951+7156
3: 5 **m** against man, neighbor against neighbor. 408
3: 5 man against **m,** neighbor against neighbor. 408
3: 6 A **m** will seize one of his brothers 408
4: 1 seven women will take hold of one **m** 408
5:15 So **m** will be brought low 132
6: 5 For I am a **m** *of* unclean lips, 408
7:21 a **m** will keep alive a young cow 408
10:18 as when a **sick** *m* wastes away. AIT
13:12 I will make **m** scarcer than pure gold, 632
14:16 "Is this the **m** who shook the earth 408
14:17 *the m who* **made** the world a desert, AIT
16: 5 in faithfulness *a m will* **sit** on it— AIT
17: 5 *a m* **gleans** heads of grain in the Valley AIT
21: 9 here comes a **m** in a chariot *with* a team 408
22:17 O you **mighty m.** 1505
29: 8 when a **hungry** *m* dreams that he is eating, AIT
29: 8 when a **thirsty** *m* dreams that he is drinking, AIT
29:21 those who with a word make a **m** out to 132
31: 8 by a sword that is not *of* **m;** 408
32: 2 *Each* **m** will be like a shelter from the wind 408
32: 8 But the **noble** *m* makes noble plans, AIT
33:16 *the m who will* **dwell** on the heights, AIT
40:20 *A m* **too poor** *to* present such AIT
42:13 The LORD will march out like a **mighty m,** 1475
44:13 He shapes it in the form of **m,** 408
44:13 of **m** in all his glory, 132
46:11 a **m** *to fulfill* my purpose. 408
52:14 disfigured beyond that of *any* **m** and 408
53: 3 a **m** *of* sorrows, and familiar with suffering. 408
55: 7 and the evil **m** his thoughts. 408
56: 2 Blessed is the **m** who does this, 632
56: 2 the **m** who holds it fast, 132+1201
57:13 *m who* **makes** me *his* **refuge** AIT
57:16 spirit of **m** would grow faint before me— NIH

Isa 57:16 the breath of **m** that I have created. NIH
58: 5 only a day for a **m** to humble himself? 132
62: 5 As a **young m** marries a maiden, 1033
65:20 an **old** *m* who does not live out his years; AIT
66: 3 like one who kills a **m,** and whoever offers 408
Jer 3: 1 "If a **m** divorces his wife and she leaves him 408
3: 1 and she leaves him and marries another **m,** 408
7:20 be poured out on this place, on **m** and beast, 132
8: 4 When *a m* **turns away,** does he not return? AIT
9:12 What **m** is wise enough to understand this? 408
9:23 "Let not the **wise** *m* boast of his wisdom or AIT
9:23 or the **strong m** boast of his strength or 1475
9:23 of his strength or the **rich** *m* boast AIT
10:23 it is not for **m** to direct his steps. 408
11: 3 'Cursed is the **m** who does not obey 408
14: 9 Why are you like a **m** taken by surprise, 408
15:10 a **m** with whom the whole land strives 408
15:12 "*Can a m* **break** iron— AIT
17: 5 "Cursed is the one who trusts in **m,** 132
17: 7 blessed is the **m** who trusts in the LORD, 1505
17:10 to reward a **m** according to his conduct, 408
17:11 the *m who* **gains** riches by unjust means. AIT
20:15 be the **m** who brought my father the news, 408
20:16 May that **m** be like the towns 408
22: 7 *each* **m** with his weapons, 408
22:28 Is this **m** Jehoiachin a despised, broken pot, 408
22:30 "Record this **m** as if childless, 408
22:30 a **m** who will not prosper in his lifetime, 1505
23: 9 I am like a drunken **m,** 408
23: 9 like a **m** overcome by wine, 1505
23:34 I will punish that **m** and his household. 408
26:11 "This **m** should be sentenced to death 408
26:16 "This **m** should not be sentenced to death! 408
26:20 another **m** who prophesied in the name 408
30: 6 Ask and see: Can a **m** bear children? 2351
30: 6 Then why do I see every **strong m** 1505
31:22 a woman will surround a **m."** 1505
31:34 No longer will a **m** teach his neighbor, 408
31:34 or a **m** his brother, saying, 'Know the LORD,' 408
33:17 to have a **m** to sit on the throne of the house 408
33:18 to have a **m** to stand before me continually 408
35: 4 of the sons of Hanan son of Igdaliah the **m** 408
35:19 son of Recab will never fail to have a **m** 408
38: 4 "This **m** should be put to death. 408
38: 4 This **m** is not seeking the good 408
48:19 the *m* **fleeing** and the woman escaping, AIT
49:18 no **m** will dwell in it. 132+1201
49:33 no **m** will dwell in it." 132+1201
50:40 no **m** will dwell in it. 132+1201
51:17 "Every **m** is senseless and without 132
51:22 with you I shatter **m** and woman, 408
51:22 with you I shatter **old** *m* and youth, AIT
51:22 with you I shatter **young m** and maiden, 1033
51:43 through which no **m** travels, 132+1201
51:62 so that neither **m** nor animal will live in it; 132
La 3: 1 the **m** who has seen affliction by the rod 1505
3:27 for a **m** to bear the yoke while he is young. 1505
3:35 to deny a **m** his rights before the Most High, 1505
3:36 to deprive a **m** of justice— 132
3:39 Why should any living **m** complain 132
Eze 1: 5 In appearance their form was that of a **m,** 132
1: 8 they had the hands of a **m.** 132
1:10 Each of the four had the face of a **m,** 132
1:26 on the throne was a figure like that of a **m.** 132
2: 1 He said to me, "Son of **m,** 132
2: 3 He said: "Son of **m,** 132
2: 6 And you, son of **m,** 132
2: 8 you, son of **m,** listen to what I say to you. 132
3: 1 And he said to me, "Son of **m,** 132
3: 3 Then he said to me, "Son of **m,** 132
3: 4 He then said to me: "Son of **m,** 132
3:10 And he said to me, "Son of **m,** 132
3:17 "Son of **m,** I have made you a watchman for 132
3:18 When I say to a **wicked** *m,* AIT
3:18 that **wicked** *m* will die for his sin, AIT
3:19 But if you do warn the **wicked** *m* and AIT
3:20 a **righteous** *m* turns from his righteousness AIT
3:21 if you do warn the **righteous** *m* not to sin AIT
3:25 And you, son of **m,** they will tie with ropes; 132
4: 1 "Now, son of **m,** take a clay tablet, 132
4:16 He then said to me: "Son of **m,** 132
5: 1 son of **m,** take a sharp sword and use it as 132
6: 2 "Son of **m,** set your face against the 132
7: 2 "Son of **m,** this is what 132
8: 2 I looked, and I saw a figure like that of a **m.** 408
8: 5 Then he said to me, "Son of **m,** 132
8: 6 And he said to me, "Son of **m,** 132
8: 8 He said to me, "Son of **m,** 132
8:12 He said to me, "Son of **m,** 132
8:15 He said to me, "Do you see this, son of **m?** 132
8:17 "Have you seen this, son of **m?** 132
9: 2 a **m** clothed in linen who had a writing kit 408
9: 3 Then the LORD called to the **m** clothed 408
9:11 Then the **m** in linen with the writing kit 408
10: 2 The LORD said to the **m** clothed in linen, 408
10: 3 of the temple when the **m** went in, 408
10: 6 the LORD commanded the **m** in linen, 408
10: 6 the **m** went in and stood beside a wheel. NIH
10: 7 and put it into the hands of the **m** in linen, NIH
10: 8 be seen what looked like the hands of a **m.)** 132
10:14 the second the face of a **m,** 132
10:21 like the hands of a **m.** 132
11: 2 The LORD said to me, "Son of **m,** 132
11: 4 prophesy, son of **m."** 132
11:15 "Son of **m,** your brothers— 132
12: 2 "Son of **m,** you are living among 132
12: 3 "Therefore, son of **m,** pack your belongings 132

Eze 12: 9 “Son of **m,** did not that rebellious house 132
12:18 “Son of **m,** tremble as you eat your food, 132
12:22 “Son of **m,** what is this proverb you have in 132
12:27 “Son of **m,** the house of Israel is saying, 132
13: 2 “Son of **m,** prophesy against the prophets 132
13:17 son of **m,** set your face against the daughters 132
14: 3 “Son of **m,** these men have set up idols 132
14: 8 against that **m** and make him an example 408
14:13 “Son of **m,** if a country sins against me 132
15: 2 of **m,** how is the wood of a vine better than 132
16: 2 “Son of **m,** confront Jerusalem 132
17: 2 “Son of **m,** set forth an allegory and tell 132
18: 5 a righteous **m** who does what is just 408
18: 8 and judges fairly between **m** and man. 408
18: 8 and judges fairly between man and **m.** 408
18: 9 **That** *m* is righteous; AIT
18:13 *Will such a m* **live?** AIT
18:20 of the **righteous** *m* will be credited to him, AIT
18:21 “But if a **wicked** *m* turns away from all AIT
18:24 if a **righteous** *m* turns from his righteousness AIT
18:24 the **wicked** *m* does, AIT
18:26 If a **righteous** *m* turns from his righteousness AIT
18:27 But if a **wicked** *m* turns away from AIT
20: 3 of **m,** speak to the elders of Israel and say 132
20: 4 Will you judge them, son of **m?** 132
20:11 for the **m** who obeys them will live by them. 132
20:13 the **m** who obeys them will live by them— 132
20:21 the **m** who obeys them will live by them— 132
20:27 of **m,** speak to the people of Israel and say 132
20:46 “Son of **m,** set your face toward the south; 132
21: 2 “Son of **m,** set your face against Jerusalem 132
21: 6 “Therefore groan, son of **m!** 132
21: 9 “Son of **m,** prophesy and say, ‘This is what 132
21:12 Cry out and wail, son of **m,** 132
21:14 “So then, son of **m,** 132
21:19 “Son of **m,** mark out two roads for the sword 132
21:28 “And you, son of **m,** prophesy and say, 132
22: 2 “Son of **m,** will you judge her? 132
22:11 In you *one* **m** commits a detestable offense 408
22:18 “Son of **m,** the house of Israel has become 132
22:24 “Son of **m,** say to the land, ‘You are a land 132
22:30 for a **m** among them who would build up 408
23: 2 “Son of **m,** there were two women, daughters 132
23:36 The LORD said to me: “Son of **m,** 132
24: 2 “Son of **m,** record this date, this very date, 132
24:16 “Son of **m,** with one blow I am about 132
24:25 “And you, son of **m,** 132
25: 2 of **m,** set your face against the Ammonites 132
26: 2 “Son of **m,** because Tyre has said 132
27: 2 “Son of **m,** take up a lament 132
28: 2 “Son of **m,** say to the ruler of Tyre, ‘This 132
28: 2 But you are a **m** and not a god, 132
28: 9 You will be but a **m,** not a god, 132
28:12 “Son of **m,** take up a lament concerning 132
28:21 “Son of **m,** set your face against Sidon; 132
29: 2 “Son of **m,** set your face against Pharaoh 132
29:11 No foot of **m** or animal will pass through it; 132
29:18 “Son of **m,** Nebuchadnezzar king 132
30: 2 “Son of **m,** prophesy and say: 132
30:21 “Son of **m,** I have broken the arm 132
30:24 like a **mortally wounded m.** 2728
31: 2 “Son of **m,** say to Pharaoh king of Egypt 132
32: 2 “Son of **m,** take up a lament 132
32:13 to be stirred by the foot of **m** or muddied by 132
32:18 “Son of **m,** wail for the hordes of Egypt 132
33: 2 “Son of **m,** speak to your countrymen 132
33: 6 **that m** will be taken away because 2085[S]
33: 7 “Son of **m,** I have made you a watchman for 132
33: 8 When I say to the wicked, ‘O **wicked** *m,* AIT
33: 8 that **wicked** *m* will die for his sin, AIT
33: 9 But if you do warn the **wicked** *m* to turn AIT
33:10 “Son of **m,** say to the house of Israel, 132
33:12 son of **m,** say to your countrymen, 132
33:12 ‘The righteousness of the **righteous** *m* will AIT
33:12 of the **wicked** *m* will not cause him to fall AIT
33:12 The **righteous** *m,* if he sins, AIT
33:13 I tell the **righteous** *m* that he will surely live AIT
33:14 And if I say to the **wicked** *m,* AIT
33:18 If a **righteous** *m* turns from his righteousness AIT
33:19 a **wicked** *m* turns away from his wickedness AIT
33:21 a **m** who *had* **escaped** from Jerusalem came 7127
33:22 Now the evening before the **m** arrived, 7127[S]
33:22 and he opened my mouth before the **m** came NIH
33:24 “Son of **m,** the people living in those ruins 132
33:24 ‘Abraham was only **one** *m,* AIT
33:30 “As for you, son of **m,** 132
34: 2 “Son of **m,** prophesy against the shepherds 132
35: 2 of **m,** set your face against Mount Seir; 132
36: 1 of **m,** prophesy to the mountains of Israel 132
36:17 “Son of **m,** when the people of Israel were 132
37: 3 He asked me, “Son of **m,** 132
37: 9 prophesy, son of **m,** and say to it, 132
37:11 Then he said to me: “Son of **m,** 132
37:16 “Son of **m,** take a stick of wood and write 132
38: 2 “Son of **m,** set your face against Gog, 132
38:14 son of **m,** prophesy and say to Gog: 132
39: 1 “Son of **m,** prophesy against Gog and say: 132
39:17 “Son of **m,** this is what 132
40: 3 a **m** whose appearance was like bronze; 408
40: 4 The **m** said to me, “Son of man, 408
40: 4 The man said to me, “Son of **m,** 132
41: 1 the **m** brought me to the outer sanctuary NIH
41:19 of a **m** toward the palm tree on one side and 132
41:22 The **m** said to me, NIH
42: 1 the **m** led me northward into the outer court NIH
43: 1 the **m** brought me to the gate facing east, NIH
43: 6 While the **m** was standing beside me, 408
Eze 43: 7 He said: “Son of **m,** this is the place 132
43:10 of **m,** describe the temple to the people 132
43:18 Then he said to me, “Son of **m,** 132
44: 1 the **m** brought me back to the outer gate of NIH
44: 4 the **m** brought me by way of the north gate NIH
44: 5 The LORD said to me, “Son of **m,** 132
46:19 the **m** brought me through the entrance at NIH
47: 1 The **m** brought me back to the entrance of NIH
47: 3 the **m** went eastward with a measuring line 408
47: 6 He asked me, “Son of **m,** do you see this?” 132
Da 2:10 “There is not a **m** on earth who can do what 10050
2:25 “I have found a **m** among the exiles 10131
2:27 Daniel replied, “No **wise** *m,* enchanter, AIT
4:16 that of a **m** and let him be given the mind of 10050
5:11 a **m** in your kingdom who has the spirit of 10131
5:12 This **m** Daniel, whom the king called
Belteshazzar, NIH
6: 5 for charges against **this** *m* Daniel AIT
6: 7 to any god or **m** during the next thirty days, 10050
6:12 to any god or **m** except to you, 10050
7: 4 so that it stood on two feet like a **m,** 10050
7: 4 and the heart of a **m** was given to it. 10050
7: 8 This horn had eyes like the eyes of a **m** 10050
7:13 before me was one like a son of **m,** 10050
8:15 before me stood one who looked like a **m.** 1505
8:16 tell **this** *m* the meaning of the vision.” AIT
8:17 “Son of **m,**” he said to me, 132
9:21 the **m** I had seen in the earlier vision, 408
10: 5 up and there before me was a **m** dressed 408
10:16 who looked like a **m** touched my lips, 132+1201
10:18 like a **m** touched me and gave me strength. 132
10:19 “Do not be afraid, O **m** highly esteemed,” 408
12: 6 One of them said to the **m** clothed in linen, 408
12: 7 The **m** clothed in linen, 408
Hos 3: 3 be a prostitute or be intimate with any **m,** 408
4: 4 “But let no **m** bring a charge, 408
4: 4 let no **m** accuse another, 408
6: 9 As marauders lie in ambush for a **m,** 408
9: 7 the inspired **m** a maniac. 408
11: 9 For I am God, and not **m**— 408
12: 3 as a **m** he struggled with God. 226
Am 4:13 and reveals his thoughts to **m,** 132
5:13 the **prudent** *m* keeps quiet in such times, AIT
5:19 as though a **m** fled from a lion only to meet 408
Jnh 1:14 for killing an **innocent** *m.* AIT
3: 7 Do not let any **m** or beast, herd or flock, 132
3: 8 let **m** and beast be covered with sackcloth. 132
Mic 2: 2 They defraud a **m** of his home, 1505
4: 4 *Every* **m** will sit under his own vine and 408
5: 7 not wait for **m** or linger for mankind. 408
6: 8 He has showed you, O **m,** what is good. 132
6:11 Shall I acquit a **m** with dishonest scales, NIH
7: 2 not one upright **m** remains. 132
Hab 2:18 since a **m** has carved it? 3670
Zep 1: 3 when I cut off **m** from the face of the earth,” 132
Zec 1: 8 there before me was a **m** riding a red horse! 408
1:10 Then the **m** standing among the myrtle 408
2: 1 before me was a **m** with a measuring line 408
2: 4 “Run, tell that **young m,** 5853
3: 2 Is not **this** *m* a burning stick snatched from AIT
4: 1 as a **m** is wakened from his sleep. 408
6:12 ‘Here is the **m** whose name is the Branch, 408
8:10 Before that time there were no wages for **m** 132
8:10 I had turned every **m** against his neighbor. 132
12: 1 and who forms the spirit of **m** within him, 132
13: 7 against the **m** who is close to me!” 1505
14:13 *Each* **m** will seize the hand of another, 408
Mal 2:12 As for the **m** who does this, 408
3: 8 “Will a **m** rob God? 132
3:17 a **m** spares his son who serves him. 408
Mt 1:19 **righteous** *m* and did not want to expose her *AIT*
4: 4 ‘**M** does not live on bread alone, *476*
7:24 a wise **m** who built his house on the rock. *467*
7:26 a foolish **m** who built his house on sand. *467*
8: 2 A **m with leprosy** came and knelt *3320*
8: 3 his hand and touched **the m.** *899[S]*
8: 9 For I myself am a **m** under authority, *476*
8:20 the Son *of* **M** has no place to lay his head.” *476*
8:27 **“What kind of** *m* is this? *AIT*
9: 6 that the Son *of* **M** has authority on earth *476*
9: 7 And the **m** got up and went home. *NIG*
9: 9 he saw a **m** named Matthew sitting at *476*
9:32 a **m** who was demon-possessed and could *476*
9:33 **the m who had been mute** spoke. *3273*
10:23 cities of Israel before the Son *of* **M** comes. *476*
10:35 to turn “ ‘a **m** against his father, a daughter *476*
10:41 and anyone who receives a **righteous** *m* *AIT*
10:41 because he is a **righteous** *m* will receive *AIT*
11: 6 the **m** who does not fall away on account *1569*
11: 8 A **m** dressed in fine clothes? *476*
11:19 The Son *of* **M** came eating and drinking, *476*
12: 8 For the Son *of* **M** is Lord of the Sabbath.” *476*
12:10 and a **m** with a shriveled hand was there. *476*
12:12 How much more valuable is a **m** than *476*
12:13 he said *to* the **m,** “Stretch out your hand.” *476*
12:22 a **demon-possessed** *m* who was blind and *AIT*
12:29 unless he first ties up the **strong** *m?* *AIT*
12:32 against the Son *of* **M** will be forgiven, *476*
12:35 The good **m** brings good things out of *476*
12:35 and the evil **m** brings evil things out of *476*
12:40 Son *of* **M** will be three days and three nights *476*
12:43 “When an evil spirit comes out of a **m,** *476*
12:45 the final condition *of* that **m** is worse than *476*
13:20 on rocky places is **the** *m* **who** hears the word *AIT*
13:22 that fell among the thorns is the *m who* hears *AIT*
13:23 on good soil is **the** *m* **who** hears the word *AIT*
13:24 of heaven is like a **m** who sowed good seed *476*
Mt 13:31 which a **m** took and planted in his field. *476*
13:37 the good seed is the Son *of* **M.** *476*
13:41 The Son *of* **M** will send out his angels, *476*
13:44 When a **m** found it, he hid it again, *476*
13:54 “Where did **this** *m* get this wisdom *AIT*
13:56 Where then did **this** *m* get all these things?” *AIT*
15: 5 But you say that if a **m** says to his father *4005[S]*
15:14 If a **blind** *m* leads a blind man, *AIT*
15:14 If a blind man leads a **blind** *m,* *AIT*
15:18 and these make a **m** ‘unclean.’ *476*
15:20 These are what make a **m** ‘unclean’; *476*
16:13 “Who do people say the Son *of* **M** is?” *476*
16:17 was not revealed to you by **m,** *135+2779+4922*
16:26 What good will it be for a **m** if he gains *476*
16:26 what can a **m** give in exchange for his soul? *476*
16:27 the Son *of* **M** is going to come in his
Father's glory *476*
16:28 the Son *of* **M** coming in his kingdom.” *476*
17: 9 until the Son *of* **M** has been raised from *476*
17:12 In the same way the Son *of* **M** is going *476*
17:14 a **m** approached Jesus and knelt before him. *476*
17:22 “The Son *of* **M** is going to be betrayed into *476*
18: 7 but woe *to* the **m** through whom they come! *476*
18:12 If a **m** owns a hundred sheep, *476*
18:24 a **m** who owed him ten thousand talents *1651*
18:30 he went off and had **the m** thrown *899[S]*
19: 3 “Is it lawful *for* a **m** to divorce his wife *476*
19: 5 ‘For this reason a **m** will leave his father *476*
19: 6 God has joined together, let a **m** not separate. *476*
19: 7 “did Moses command that a **m** give his wife *NIG*
19:16 Now a **m** came up to Jesus and asked, *1651*
19:18 “Which ones?” the **m** inquired. *NIG*
19:20 “All these I have kept,” the **young m** said. *3734*
19:22 When the **young m** heard this, *3734*
19:23 for a **rich** *m* to enter the kingdom of heaven. *AIT*
19:24 for a **rich** *m* to enter the kingdom of God.” *AIT*
19:26 “With **m** this is impossible, *476*
19:28 the Son *of* **M** sits on his glorious throne, *476*
20:14 to give **the** *m* **who** was hired last the same *AIT*
20:18 the Son *of* **M** will be betrayed to the *476*
20:28 as the Son *of* **M** did not come to be served, *476*
21:28 There was a **m** who had two sons. *476*
22:11 he noticed a **m** there who was *476*
22:12 **The m** was speechless. *1254+3836[S]*
22:16 a *m of* **integrity** and that you teach the way *AIT*
22:24 that if a **m** dies without having children, *AIT*
24:27 so will be the coming of the Son *of* **M.** *476*
24:30 the sign of the Son *of* **M** will appear in *476*
24:30 They will see the Son *of* **M** coming on *476*
24:37 so it will be at the coming of the Son *of* **M.** *476*
24:39 be at the coming of the Son *of* **M.** *476*
24:44 because the Son *of* **M** will come at an hour *476*
25:14 it will be like a **m** going on a journey, *476*
25:16 **The** *m* **who** had received the five talents *AIT*
25:18 But **the** *m* **who** had received the one talent *AIT*
25:20 **The** *m* **who** had received the five talents *AIT*
25:22 **“The m** with the two talents also came. *3836*
25:24 **the** *m* **who** had received the one talent *AIT*
25:24 he said, ‘I knew that you are a hard **m,** *476*
25:31 “When the Son *of* **M** comes in his glory, *476*
26: 2 the Son *of* **M** will be handed over to be
crucified.” *476*
26: 6 the home of a **m** known as Simon the Leper, *NIG*
26:18 into the city to a **certain** *m* and tell him, *AIT*
26:24 Son *of* **M** will go just as it is written about *476*
26:24 woe *to* that **m** who betrays the Son of Man! *476*
26:24 woe to that man who betrays the Son *of* **M!** *476*
26:45 and the Son *of* **M** is betrayed into the hands *476*
26:48 “The one I kiss is **the m;** arrest him.” *899[S]*
26:64 the future you will see the Son *of* **M** sitting *476*
26:72 “I don't know the **m!”** *476*
26:74 “I don't know the **m!”** *476*
27:19 to do *with* that **innocent** *m,* *AIT*
27:32 they met a **m** from Cyrene, named Simon, *476*
27:57 there came a rich **m** from Arimathea, *476*
Mk 1:23 a **m** in their synagogue who was possessed *476*
1:26 The evil spirit shook **the m** violently *899[S]*
1:40 A **m with leprosy** came to him *3320*
1:41 his hand and touched **the m.** *NIG*
2: 4 the mat the **paralyzed** *m* was lying on. *AIT*
2:10 that the Son *of* **M** has authority on earth *476*
2:27 “The Sabbath was made for **m,** *476*
2:27 not **m** for the Sabbath. *476*
2:28 the Son *of* **M** is Lord even of the Sabbath.” *476*
3: 1 and a **m** with a shriveled hand was there. *476*
3: 3 Jesus said *to* the **m** with the shriveled hand, *476*
3: 5 said *to* the **m,** “Stretch out your hand.” *476*
3:27 unless he first ties up the **strong** *m.* *AIT*
4:26 A **m** scatters seed on the ground. *476*
5: 2 a **m** with an evil spirit came from the tombs *476*
5: 3 **This** *m* lived in the tombs, *AIT*
5: 8 Jesus had said to him, “Come out of this **m,** *476*
5:15 they saw **the** *m* **who** had been possessed by *AIT*
5:16 happened *to* the **demon-possessed** *m*— *AIT*
5:18 the *m* **who** had been demon-possessed *AIT*
5:20 So the *m* **went away** and began to tell in *AIT*
6: 2 “Where did **this** *m* get these things?” *AIT*
6:16 he said, “John, **the** *m* I beheaded, *AIT*
6:20 knowing him to be a righteous and holy **m.** *467*
6:27 The **m** went, beheaded John in the prison, *NIG*
7:11 But you say that if a **m** says to his father *476*
7:15 Nothing outside a **m** can make him ‘unclean’ *476*
7:15 comes out of a **m** that makes him ‘unclean.’ *476*
7:18 “Don't you see that nothing that enters a **m** *476*
7:20 out of a **m** is what makes him ‘unclean.’ *476*
7:23 from inside and make a **m** ‘unclean.’ ” *476*
7:32 a *m* who was **deaf** and could hardly talk, *AIT*

Mk 7:32 they begged him to place his hand on the m. NIG
8:22 a blind m and begged Jesus to touch him. AIT
8:23 He took the blind m by the hand AIT
8:31 that the Son of M must suffer many things 476
8:36 for a m to gain the whole world, 476
8:37 what can a m give in exchange for his soul? 476
8:38 the Son of M will be ashamed of him 476
9: 9 until the Son of M had risen from the dead. 476
9:12 Son of M must suffer much and be rejected? 476
9:17 A m in the crowd answered, "Teacher, 1651
9:31 "The Son of M is going to be betrayed into 476
9:38 "we saw a m driving out demons AIT
10: 2 "Is it lawful for a m to divorce his wife?" 467
10: 4 "Moses permitted a m to write a certificate NIG
10: 7 'For this reason a m will leave his father 476
10: 9 God has joined together, let m not separate. 476
10:12 and marries another m, AIT
10:17 a m ran up to him and fell on his knees 1651
10:25 for a rich m to enter the kingdom of God." AIT
10:27 "With m this is impossible, 476
10:33 the Son of M will be betrayed to the chief 476
10:45 the Son of M did not come to be served, 476
10:46 were leaving the city, a blind m, AIT
10:49 So they called to the blind m, "Cheer up! AIT
10:51 The blind m said, "Rabbi, I want to see." AIT
12: 1 "A m planted a vineyard. 476
12: 4 they struck this m on the head AIT
12:14 we know you are a m of integrity. AIT
12:19 the m must marry the widow 81
12:32 "Well said, teacher," the m replied. NIG
13:26 Son of M coming in clouds with great power 476
13:34 It's like a m going away: 476
14: 3 the home of a m known as Simon the Leper, NIG
14:13 a m carrying a jar of water will meet you. 476
14:21 Son of M will go just as it is written about 476
14:21 woe to that m who betrays the Son of Man! 476
14:21 woe to that man who betrays the Son of M! 476
14:41 the Son of M is betrayed into the hands of sinners. 476
14:44 "The one I kiss is the m; 899S
14:51 A young m, wearing nothing but 3734
14:58 will build another, not made by m.' " 942
14:62 "And you will see the Son of M sitting at 476
14:71 "I don't know this m you're talking about." 476
15: 7 A m called Barabbas was in prison with AIT
15:21 A certain m from Cyrene, Simon, AIT
15:36 One m ran, filled a sponge AIT
15:39 "Surely this m was the Son of God!" 476
16: 5 a young m dressed in a white robe sitting on 3734
Lk 1:18 I am an old m and my wife is well along 4566
1:27 to be married to a m named Joseph, 467
2:25 there was a m in Jerusalem called Simeon, 476
3:11 "The m with two tunics should share AIT
4: 4 'M does not live on bread alone.' " 476
4:33 the synagogue there was a m possessed by 476
4:35 Then the demon threw the m down 899S
5: 8 I am a sinful m!" 467
5:12 a m came along who was covered 467
5:13 his hand and touched the m. 899S
5:24 that the Son of M has authority on earth 476
5:24 He said to the paralyzed m, "I tell you, AIT
6: 5 "The Son of M is Lord of the Sabbath." 476
6: 6 m was there whose right hand was shriveled. 476
6: 8 and said to the m with the shriveled hand, 467
6:10 and then said to the m, 899S
6:22 your name as evil, because of the Son of M. 476
6:39 "Can a blind m lead a blind man? AIT
6:39 "Can a blind man lead a blind m? AIT
6:45 The good m brings good things out of 476
6:45 and the evil m brings evil things out of AIT
6:48 He is like a m building a house, 476
6:49 into practice is like a m who built a house 476
7: 4 "This m deserves to have you do this, AIT
7: 8 For I myself am a m under authority, 476
7:14 He said, "Young m, I say to you, get up!" 3734
7:15 The dead m sat up and began to talk, AIT
7:23 the m who does not fall away on account AIT
7:25 A m dressed in fine clothes? 476
7:34 The Son of M came eating and drinking, 476
7:39 he said to himself, "If this m were a prophet, AIT
8:27 he was met by a demon-possessed m from 467
8:27 For a long time this m had not worn clothes NIG
8:29 the evil spirit to come out of the m. 476
8:33 When the demons came out of the m, 476
8:35 the m from whom the demons had gone out, 476
8:36 how the demon-possessed m had been cured. AIT
8:38 The m from whom the demons had gone out 467
8:39 So the m went away and told all over town NIG
8:41 Then a m named Jairus, 467
9:22 "The Son of M must suffer many things 476
9:25 for a m to gain the whole world, 476
9:26 the Son of M will be ashamed of him 476
9:38 A m in the crowd called out, "Teacher, 467
9:44 The Son of M is going to be betrayed into 476
9:49 "we saw a m driving out demons AIT
9:57 a m said to him, "I will follow you AIT
9:58 the Son of M has no place to lay his head." 476
9:59 He said to another m, "Follow me." AIT
9:59 But the m replied, "Lord, 3836S
10: 6 If a m of peace is there, 5626
10:30 "A m was going down from Jerusalem 476
10:31 and when he saw the m, 899S
10:33 as he traveled, came where the m was; 899S
10:34 Then he put the m on his own donkey, 899S
10:36 to the m who fell into the hands of robbers? AIT
11:14 the m who had been mute spoke, 3273
11:21 "When a strong m, fully armed, AIT
Lk 11:22 the m trusted and divides up the spoils. AIT
11:24 "When an evil spirit comes out of a m, 476
11:26 the final condition of that m is worse than 476
11:30 will the Son of M be to this generation. 476
12: 8 the Son of M will also acknowledge him 476
12:10 against the Son of M will be forgiven, 476
12:14 "M, who appointed me a judge or an arbiter 476
12:16 "The ground of a certain rich m produced 476
12:40 because the Son of M will come at an hour 476
13: 6 "A m had a fig tree, planted in his vineyard, AIT
13: 7 to the m who took care of the vineyard, AIT
13: 8 the m replied, 'leave it alone 1254+3836S
13:19 which a m took and planted in his garden. 476
14: 2 There in front of him was a m suffering 476
14: 4 So taking hold of the m, NIG
14: 9 'Give this m your seat.' AIT
14:15 "Blessed is the m who will eat at the feast in AIT
14:16 "A certain m was preparing a great banquet 476
15: 2 "This m welcomes sinners and eats AIT
15:11 "There was a m who had two sons. 476
16: 1 a rich m whose manager was accused 476
16:18 and the m who marries a divorced woman AIT
16:19 "There was a rich m who was dressed 476
16:22 The rich m also died and was buried. AIT
17:22 to see one of the days of the Son of M, 476
17:24 Son of M in his day will be like the lightning, 476
17:26 also will it be in the days of the Son of M. 476
17:30 on the day the Son of M is revealed. 476
18: 8 However, when the Son of M comes, 476
18:14 "I tell you that this m, rather than the other, AIT
18:23 because he was a m of great wealth. AIT
18:25 for a rich m to enter the kingdom of God." AIT
18:31 by the prophets about the Son of M will 476
18:35 a blind m was sitting by the roadside AIT
18:40 and ordered the m to be brought to him. 899S
19: 2 A m was there by the name of Zacchaeus; 467
19: 3 but being a short m he could not, AIT
19: 9 because this m, too, is a son of Abraham. AIT
19:10 For the Son of M came to seek and 476
19:12 "A m of noble birth went to 476
19:14 'We don't want this m to be our king.' AIT
19:21 because you are a hard m. 476
19:22 You knew, did you, that I am a hard m, 476
20: 9 "A m planted a vineyard, 476
20:28 the m must marry the widow 81
21:27 the Son of M coming in a cloud with power 476
21:36 be able to stand before the Son of M." 476
22:10 a m carrying a jar of water will meet you. 476
22:22 of M will go as it has been decreed, 476
22:22 but woe to that m who betrays him." 476
22:47 and the m who was called Judas, AIT
22:48 are you betraying the Son of M with a kiss? 476
22:56 "This m was with him." AIT
22:58 "M, I am not!" Peter replied. 476
22:60 M, I don't know what you're talking about! 476
22:69 Son of M will be seated at the right hand of 476
23: 2 "We have found this m subverting our nation. AIT
23: 4 "I find no basis for a charge against this m." 476
23: 6 Pilate asked if the m was a Galilean. 476
23:14 "You brought me this m as one who 476
23:18 "Away with this m! AIT
23:22 What crime has this m committed? AIT
23:25 He released the m who had been thrown AIT
23:41 But this m has done nothing wrong." AIT
23:47 "Surely this was a righteous m." 476
23:50 Now there was a m named Joseph, 467
23:50 a good and upright m, 467
24: 7 Son of M must be delivered into the hands 476
Jn 1: 6 There came a m who was sent from God; 476
1: 9 that gives light to every m was coming into 476
1:30 'A m who comes after me has surpassed me 467
1:33 'The m on whom you see the Spirit come AIT
1:51 and descending on the Son of M." 476
2:25 He did not need man's testimony about m, 476
2:25 for he knew what was in a m. 476
3: 1 a m of the Pharisees named Nicodemus, 476
3: 4 "How can a m be born when he is old?" 476
3:13 who came from heaven—the Son of M. 476
3:14 so the Son of M must be lifted up, 476
3:26 that m who was with you on the other side NIG
3:27 "A m can receive only what is given him 476
3:33 The m who has accepted it has certified AIT
4:18 the m you now have is not your husband. 4005S
4:29 see a m who told me everything I ever did. 476
4:42 this m really is the Savior of the world." AIT
4:47 When this m heard that Jesus had arrived AIT
4:50 The m took Jesus at his word and departed. 476
5: 9 At once the m was cured; 476
5:10 the Jews said to the m who had been healed, AIT
5:11 "The m who made me well said to me, AIT
5:13 The m who was healed had no idea who it was, AIT
5:15 The m went away and told the Jews 476
5:27 authority to judge because he is the Son of M 476
6:27 which the Son of M will give you. 476
6:50 which a m may eat and not die. AIT
6:52 "How can this m give us his flesh to eat?" AIT
6:53 unless you eat the flesh of the Son of M 476
6:62 What if you see the Son of M ascend to 476
7:11 "Where is that m?" AIT
7:12 Some said, "He is a good m." AIT
7:15 "How did this m get such learning AIT
7:18 of the one who sent him is a m of truth; AIT
7:23 for healing the whole m on the Sabbath? 476
7:25 "Isn't this the m they are trying to kill? 4005S
7:27 But we know where this m is from; AIT
Jn 7:31 he do more miraculous signs than this m?" AIT
7:35 "Where does this m intend to go AIT
7:40 "Surely this m is the Prophet." AIT
7:46 "No one ever spoke the way this m does," 476
8:28 "When you have lifted up the Son of M, 476
8:40 a m who has told you the truth that I heard 476
9: 1 he saw a m blind from birth. 476
9: 2 "Rabbi, who sinned, this m or his parents, AIT
9: 3 "Neither this m nor his parents sinned," AIT
9: 7 m went and washed, and came home seeing. NIG
9: 8 "Isn't this the same m who used to sit AIT
9: 9 But he himself insisted, "I am the m." NIG
9:11 "The m they call Jesus made some mud 476
9:12 "Where is this m?" AIT
9:13 to the Pharisees the m who had been blind. 899S
9:15 put mud on my eyes," the m replied, 1254+3836S
9:16 "This m is not from God, 476
9:17 Finally they turned again to the blind m, AIT
9:17 The m replied, "He is a prophet." 1254+3836S
9:24 the m who had been blind. 476
9:24 "We know this m is a sinner." 476
9:30 The m answered, "Now that is remarkable! 476
9:31 to the godly m who does his will. 2538
9:32 of opening the eyes of a m born blind. AIT
9:33 If this m were not from God, AIT
9:35 he said, "Do you believe in the Son of M?" 476
9:36 "Who is he, sir?" the m asked. 1697S
9:38 Then the m said, "Lord, I believe," 3836S
10: 1 the m who does not enter the sheep pen by AIT
10: 2 The m who enters by the gate is the shepherd AIT
10:13 The m runs away because he is a hired hand NIG
10:21 m possessed by a demon. AIT
10:33 "but for blasphemy, because you, a mere m, 476
10:41 all that John said about this m was true." AIT
11: 1 Now a m named Lazarus was sick. AIT
11: 9 A m who walks by day will not stumble, AIT
11:37 the eyes of the blind m have kept this man AIT
11:37 the eyes of the blind man have kept this m AIT
11:39 Lord," said Martha, the sister of the dead m, AIT
11:44 The dead m came out, AIT
11:47 Here is this m performing many miraculous signs. 476
11:50 for you that one m die for the people than 476
12:23 "The hour has come for the Son of M to 476
12:25 The m who loves his life will lose it, AIT
12:25 while the m who hates his life AIT
12:34 'The Son of M must be lifted up'? 476
12:34 Who is this 'Son of M'?" 476
12:35 The m who walks in the dark does not know AIT
12:44 Jesus cried out, "When a m believes in me, AIT
13:31 the Son of M glorified and God is glorified 476
15: 5 If a m remains in me and I in him, 3836S
18:14 the Jews that it would be good if one m died 476
18:26 of the m whose ear Peter had cut off, 4005
18:29 "What charges are you bringing against this m?" 476
19: 5 Pilate said to them, "Here is the m!" 476
19:12 "If you let this m go, you are no friend of AIT
19:21 that this m claimed to be king of the Jews." AIT
19:32 of the first m who had been crucified AIT
19:35 The m who saw it has given testimony, AIT
19:39 the m who earlier had visited Jesus at night. AIT
Ac 2:22 a m accredited by God to you by miracles, 467
2:23 This m was handed over to you AIT
3: 2 a m crippled from birth was being carried to 467
3: 5 So the m gave them his attention, 3836S
3:10 they recognized him as the same m who AIT
3:12 or godliness we had made this m walk? 899S
3:16 this m whom you see and know was made AIT
4:10 that this m stands before you healed. AIT
4:14 the m who had been healed standing there 476
4:22 For the m who was miraculously healed was 476
5: 1 Now a m named Ananias, 467
6: 5 a m full of faith and of the Holy Spirit; 467
6: 8 Stephen, a m full of God's grace and power, NIG
7:27 "But the m who was mistreating AIT
7:56 and the Son of M standing at the right hand 476
7:58 at the feet of a young m named Saul. 3733
8: 9 a m named Simon had practiced sorcery in 467
8:10 "This m is the divine power known as AIT
8:27 This m had gone to Jerusalem to worship, 4005S
8:30 the chariot and heard the m reading Isaiah 899S
9:11 and ask for a m from Tarsus named Saul, 5432
9:12 a m named Ananias come and place his 467
9:13 about this m and all the harm he has done 467
9:15 This m is my chosen instrument AIT
9:21 "Isn't he the m who raised havoc AIT
9:33 There he found a m named Aeneas, 476
10: 1 a m named Cornelius, 467
10: 5 back a m named Simon who is called Peter. AIT
10:22 He is a righteous and God-fearing m, 467
10:26 he said, "I am only a m myself." 476
10:28 that I should not call any m impure 476
10:30 a m in shining clothes stood before me 467
11:24 He was a good m, 467
12:22 "This is the voice of a god, not of a m." 476
13: 7 The proconsul, an intelligent m, 467
13:22 'I have found David son of Jesse a m 467
14: 8 In Lystra there sat a m crippled in his feet, 467
14:10 m jumped up and began to walk. AIT
16: 9 During the night Paul had a vision of a m 467
17:26 From one m he made every nation of men, AIT
17:31 with justice by the m he has appointed. 467
18:13 "This m," they charged, "is persuading AIT
18:24 He was a learned m, with a thorough 467
19:16 Then the m who had the evil spirit jumped 476
19:29 and rushed as one m into the theater. 3924

Ac 20: 9 a window was a young m named Eutychus, 3733
20:10 on the young m and put his arms 899S
20:12 The people took the young m home alive 4090
21:16 He was a m from Cyprus and one of AIT
21:28 the m who teaches all men everywhere 476
22:12 "A m named Ananias came to see me. 467
22:26 "This m is a Roman citizen." 476
23: 9 "We find nothing wrong with this m," 476
23:17 "Take this young m to the commander; 3733
23:18 for me and asked me to bring this young m 3734
23:19 The commander took the young m by 899S
23:22 The commander dismissed the young m 3734
23:27 This m was seized by the Jews 467
23:30 of a plot to be carried out against the m, 467
24: 5 "We have found this m to be 467
24:16 conscience clear before God and m. 476
25: 5 and press charges against the m there, 899S
25:14 a m here whom Felix left as a prisoner. 467
25:16 over any m before he has faced his accusers 476
25:17 the court the next day and ordered the m to 467
25:19 about a dead m named Jesus who Paul claimed was alive. AIT
25:22 "I would like to hear this m myself." 476
25:24 with us, you see this m! AIT
26:31 "This m is not doing anything that deserves 476
26:32 "This m could have been set free if he had 476
28: 4 "This m must be a murderer; 476
Ro 1:23 to look like mortal m and birds and animals 476
2: 3 So when you, a mere m, 476
2:28 A m is not a Jew if he is only one outwardly AIT
2:29 No, a m is a Jew if he is one inwardly; 3836S
3: 4 Let God be true, and every m a liar. 476
3:28 For we maintain that a m is justified 476
4: 4 Now when a m works, 3836S
4: 5 to the m who does not work AIT
4: 6 when he speaks of the blessedness of the m 476
4: 8 the m whose sin the Lord will never count 467
5: 7 rarely will anyone die for a righteous m, AIT
5: 7 good m someone might possibly dare to die. AIT
5:12 just as sin entered the world through one m, 476
5:15 the many died by the trespass of the one m, AIT
5:15 that came by the grace of the one m, 476
5:17 For if, by the trespass of the one m, AIT
5:17 death reigned through that one m, AIT
5:17 reign in life through the one m, AIT
5:19 of the one m the many were made sinners, 476
5:19 the one m the many will be made righteous. AIT
7: 1 the law has authority over a m only as long 476
7: 3 if she marries another m while her husband 467
7: 3 even though she marries another m. 467
7:24 What a wretched m I am! 476
8: 3 the likeness of sinful m to be a sin offering. 4922
8: 3 And so he condemned sin in sinful m, 4922
8: 6 The mind of sinful m is death, 4922
9:20 But who are you, O m, to talk back to God? 476
10: 5 "The m who does these things will live 476
14: 2 but another m, whose faith is weak, 3836S
14: 3 The m who eats everything must not look AIT
14: 3 and the m who does not eat everything must AIT
14: 3 not condemn the m who does, AIT
14: 5 One m considers one day more sacred than another; AIT
14: 5 another m considers every day alike. 1254+4005
14:20 but it is wrong for a m to eat anything 476
14:22 Blessed is the m who does not condemn AIT
14:23 But the m who has doubts is condemned AIT
1Co 1:20 Where is the wise m? AIT
2:11 the thoughts of a m except the man's spirit 476
2:14 The m without the Spirit does not accept 476
2:15 The spiritual m makes judgments NIG
3: 8 The m who plants and the man who waters AIT
3: 8 and the m who waters have one purpose, AIT
3:12 If any m builds on this foundation AIT
4: 6 not take pride in one m over against another. AIT
5: 1 A m has his father's wife. AIT
5: 2 out of your fellowship the m who did this? AIT
5: 5 hand this m over to Satan, AIT
5:11 With such a m do not even eat. 5525
5:13 "Expel the wicked m from among you." AIT
6:18 other sins a m commits are outside his body, 476
7: 1 It is good for a m not to marry. 476
7: 2 each m should have his own wife, AIT
7: 7 But each m has his own gift from God; AIT
7:15 A believing m or woman is not bound 81
7:18 Was a m already circumcised when he was AIT
7:18 Was a m uncircumcised when he was called? AIT
7:22 similarly, he who was a free m AIT
7:24 Brothers, each m, as responsible to God, AIT
7:32 An unmarried m is concerned about AIT
7:33 a married m is concerned about the affairs AIT
7:37 But the m who has settled the matter AIT
7:37 this m also does the right thing. AIT
8: 2 The m who thinks he knows something does AIT
8: 3 But the m who loves God is known by God. AIT
9:19 I am free and belong to no m, 1666+1801+4246
9:26 I do not run like a m running aimlessly; NIG
9:26 I do not fight like a m beating the air. NIG
10:13 No temptation has seized you except what is common to m. 474
10:28 both for the sake of the m who told you 1697S
11: 3 to realize that the head of every m is Christ, 467
11: 3 and the head of the woman is m, 467
11: 4 Every m who prays or prophesies 467
11: 7 A m ought not to cover his head, 467
11: 7 but the woman is the glory of m. 467
11: 8 For m did not come from woman, 467
11: 8 from woman, but woman from m; 467
1Co 11: 9 neither was m created for woman, 467
11: 9 for woman, but woman for m. 467
11:11 however, woman is not independent of m, 467
11:11 nor is m independent of woman. 467
11:12 For as woman came from m, 467
11:12 so also m is born of woman. 467
11:14 of things teach you that if a m has long hair, 467
11:28 A m ought to examine himself 476
13:11 When I became a m, 467
14:17 but the other m is not edified. AIT
15:21 For since death came through a m, 476
15:21 of the dead comes also through a m. 476
15:45 "The first m Adam became a living being"; 476
15:47 The first m was of the dust of the earth, 476
15:47 the second m from heaven. 476
15:48 As was the earthly m, AIT
15:48 and as is the m from heaven, AIT
15:49 the likeness of the earthly m, AIT
15:49 the likeness of the m from heaven. AIT
2Co 9: 7 Each m should give what he has decided AIT
12: 2 I know a m in Christ who fourteen years ago 476
12: 3 And I know that this m— 476
12: 4 things that m is not permitted to tell. 476
12: 5 I will boast about a m like that, 5525
Gal 1: 1 sent not from men nor by m, 476
1:11 something that m made up. 476+2848
1:12 I did not receive it from any m, 476
1:16 I did not consult any m, 135+2779+4922
1:23 "The m who formerly persecuted us is AIT
2:16 a m is not justified by observing the law, 476
3: 9 along with Abraham, the m of faith. AIT
3:12 "The m who does these things will live AIT
5: 3 Again I declare to every m who lets himself 476
6: 7 A m reaps what he sows. 476
Eph 2:15 to create in himself one new m out of 476
5: 5 such a m is an idolater— 4005
5:31 "For this reason a m will leave his father 476
Php 1:27 contending as one m for the faith of 6034
2: 8 And being found in appearance as a m, 476
1Th 4: 8 does not reject m but God, 476
2Th 2: 3 and the m of lawlessness is revealed, 476
2: 3 the m doomed to destruction. 5626
3:10 "If a m will not work, he shall not eat." AIT
1Ti 1:13 and a persecutor and a violent m, 5616
2: 5 between God and men, the m Christ Jesus, 476
2:12 to teach or to have authority over a m; 467
5: 1 Do not rebuke an older m harshly, 4565
6:11 But you, m of God, flee from all this, 476
2Ti 2:21 If a m cleanses himself from the latter, AIT
3:17 the m of God may be thoroughly equipped 476
Tit 1: 6 a m whose children believe and are not open AIT
3:11 be sure that such a m is warped and sinful; 5525
Phm 1: 9 an old m and now also a prisoner 4566
1:16 as a m and as a brother in the Lord. 1877+4922
Heb 2: 6 "What is m that you are mindful of him, 476
2: 6 the son of m that you care for him? 476
7: 6 This m, however, did not trace his descent 3836S
8: 2 tabernacle set up by the Lord, not by m. 476
8:11 No longer will a m teach his neighbor, 1667S
8:11 a m his brother, saying, 'Know the Lord,' 1667S
9:27 Just as m is destined to die once, 476
10:29 do you think a m deserves to be punished AIT
11: 4 commended as a righteous m, AIT
11:12 And so from this one m, AIT
13: 6 What can m do to me?" 476
Jas 1: 7 That m should not think he will receive 476
1: 8 he is a double-minded m, 467
1:11 the rich m will fade away even AIT
1:12 Blessed is the m who perseveres under trial, 467
1:23 like a m who looks at his face in a mirror 467
1:25 But the m who looks intently into AIT
2: 2 a m comes into your meeting wearing 467
2: 2 a poor m in shabby clothes also comes in. AIT
2: 3 to the m wearing fine clothes and say, AIT
2: 3 but say to the poor m, "You stand there" AIT
2:14 a m claims to have faith but has no deeds? AIT
2:20 You foolish m, do you want evidence 476
3: 2 he is a perfect m, able to keep his whole 467
3: 7 and have been tamed by m, 474
3: 8 but no m can tame the tongue. 476
5:16 of a righteous m is powerful and effective. AIT
5:17 Elijah was a m just like us. 476
1Pe 2:19 For it is commendable if a m bears up under the pain of unjust suffering AIT
2Pe 1:21 For prophecy never had its origin in the will of m, 476
2: 7 a righteous m, who was distressed by AIT
2: 8 that righteous m, living among them day AIT
2:19 for a m is a slave to whatever has mastered AIT
1Jn 2: 4 The m who says, "I know him," AIT
2:16 the cravings of sinful m, 4922
2:17 the m who does the will of God lives forever. AIT
2:22 It is the m who denies that Jesus is the Christ. AIT
2:22 Such a m is the antichrist— AIT
Rev 1:13 was someone "like a son of m," dressed in 476
4: 7 the third had a face like a m, 476
6:15 and every free m hid in caves and among AIT
9: 5 the sting of a scorpion when it strikes a m. 476
14:14 one "like a son of m" with a crown of gold 476
16: 3 it turned into blood like that of a dead m, AIT
16:18 like it has ever occurred since m has been 476

MAN'S (140) [MAN]

Ge 2:21 he took one of the m ribs and closed up 2257S
Ge 6: 5 The LORD saw how great m wickedness 132
20: 7 Now return the m wife, for he is a prophet, 408
42:25 to put each m silver back in his sack, 2157S
42:35 in each m sack was his pouch of silver! 2257S
44: 1 put each m silver in the mouth of his sack. 408
44:26 the m face unless our youngest brother is 408
Ex 21:35 "If a m bull injures the bull of another 408
22: 5 and they graze in another m field, AIT
22: 8 on the other m property. AIT
Lev 4:26 priest will make atonement for the m sin, 2257S
20:10 commits adultery with another m wife— 408
Nu 5:10 Each m sacred gifts are his own, 408
5:12 m wife goes astray and is unfaithful to him 408
7: 5 to the Levites as each m work requires." 408
Dt 22:22 man is found sleeping with another m wife, 1251
22:24 because he violated another m wife. 8276
24: 6 would be taking a m livelihood as security. NIH
25:10 That m line shall be known in Israel as 2257S
Jdg 18:19 as priest rather than just one m household?" 408
Ru 1: 2 The m name was Elimelech, 408
4: 5 you acquire the dead m widow, AIT
2Sa 10: 4 shaved off half of each m beard, 4392S
1Ki 18:44 "A cloud as small as a m hand is rising from 408
2Ki 13:21 they threw the m body into Elisha's tomb. 408
18:21 a m hand and wounds him if he leans on it! 408
Job 14: 5 M days are determined; 2257S
14:19 so you destroy m hope. 632
21:19 up a m punishment for his sons.' 2257S
21:28 You say, 'Where now is the great m house, 5618
28: 9 M hand assaults the flinty rock 2257S
31: 2 For what is m lot from God above, NIH
31:10 then may my wife grind another m grain, AIT
33:13 to him that he answers none of m words? 2257S
Ps 37:23 If the LORD delights in a m way, 1505
39: 5 Each m life is but a breath. 132
66: 5 how awesome his works in m behalf! 132+1201
Pr 4:22 and health to a m whole body. 2257S
5:10 and your toil enrich another m house. 5799
5:20 the bosom of another m wife? AIT
5:21 a m ways are in full view of the LORD, 408
6:29 So is he who sleeps with another m wife; 8276
13: 8 A m riches may ransom his life, 408
13:23 A poor m field may produce abundant food, AIT
15:25 The LORD tears down the proud m house AIT
16: 2 All a m ways seem innocent to him, 408
16: 7 When a m ways are pleasing to the LORD, 408
16:23 A wise m heart guides his mouth, AIT
18: 4 The words of a m mouth are deep waters, 408
18: 8 they go down to a m inmost parts. NIH
18:12 Before his downfall a m heart is proud, 408
18:14 A m spirit sustains him in sickness, 408
18:20 the fruit of his mouth a m stomach is filled; 408
19: 3 A m own folly ruins his life, 132
19: 4 but a poor m friend deserts him. AIT
19:11 A m wisdom gives him patience; 132
19:21 Many are the plans in a m heart, 408
20: 3 It is to a m honor to avoid strife, 408
20: 5 The purposes of a m heart are deep waters, 408
20:24 A m steps are directed by the LORD. 1505
21: 2 All a m ways seem right to him, 408
24:15 like an outlaw against a righteous m house, AIT
25: 9 do not betray another m confidence, AIT
25:12 an ornament of fine gold is a wise m rebuke AIT
26: 7 a lame m legs that hang limp is a proverb in AIT
26:22 they go down to a m inmost parts. NIH
27:19 so a m heart reflects the man. 132
29:23 A m pride brings him low, 132
30: 2 I do not have a m understanding. 132
Ecc 3:19 M fate is like that of the animals; 132+1201
4: 4 and all achievement spring from m envy 408
6: 7 All m efforts are for his mouth, 132
7: 5 a wise m rebuke than to listen to the song AIT
8: 1 a m face and changes its hard appearance. 132
8: 6 a m misery weighs heavily upon him. 132
8:16 to know wisdom and to observe m labor 2021S
9:16 But the poor m wisdom is despised, AIT
10:12 Words from a wise m mouth are gracious, AIT
Isa 13: 7 every m heart will melt. 632
36: 6 a m hand and wounds him if he leans on it! 408
44:15 It is m fuel for burning; 132+4200
Jer 5: 8 each neighing for another m wife. AIT
10:23 O LORD, that a m life is not his own; 132+4200
13:11 For as a belt is bound around a m waist, 408
23:36 every m own word becomes his oracle 408
Eze 38:21 Every m sword will be against his brother. 408
40: 5 rod in the m hand was six long cubits, 408
Da 8:16 And I heard a m voice from the Ulai calling, 132
Jnh 1:14 not let us die for taking this m life. 408
Mic 7: 6 a m enemies are the members 408
Hab 2: 8 For you have shed m blood; 132
2:17 For you have shed m blood; 132
Mal 2:16 a m covering himself with violence as well AIT
Mt 10:36 a m enemies will be the members 476
10:41 will receive a righteous m reward. AIT
12:29 how can anyone enter a strong m house AIT
15:11 a m mouth does not make him 'unclean,' 476
27:24 "I am innocent of this m blood," he said. AIT
Mk 3:27 no one can enter a strong m house AIT
6:37 take eight months of a m wages! 1324+1357
7:33 Jesus put his fingers into the m ears. 899S
7:33 Then he spit and touched the m tongue. 899S
7:35 At this, the m ears were opened, 899S
8:23 on the m eyes and put his hands on him, 899S
8:25 Jesus put his hands on the m eyes. 899S
10:22 At this the m face fell. 1254+3836S
12:19 "Moses wrote for us that if a m brother dies AIT
Lk 11: 8 yet because of the m boldness he will get up 899S

Lk 12:15 **a m** life does not consist in the abundance *899[S]*
16:21 to eat what fell from the **rich** *m* table. *AIT*
20:28 "Moses wrote for us that if **a** *m* brother dies *AIT*
22:51 And he touched the **m** ear and healed him. *NIG*
Jn 2:25 He did not need **m** testimony about man, *5516[S]*
9: 6 and put it on **the m** eyes. *899[S]*
9:14 and opened **the m** eyes was a Sabbath. *899[S]*
9:18 until they sent for **the m** parents. *899[S]*
Ac 3: 7 and instantly **the m** feet and ankles became *899[S]*
5:28 to make us guilty of this **m** blood." *476*
11:12 and we entered the **m** house. *467*
13:23 "From **this** *m* descendants God has brought *AIT*
17:29 an image *made by* **m** design and skill. *476*
Ro 2:29 **Such a m** praise is not from men, *4005[S]*
5:16 the gift of God is not like the result of the **one** *m* sin: *AIT*
9:16 therefore, depend on **m** desire or effort, *3836[S]*
12: 6 If a **m** gift is prophesying, *NIG*
14: 2 **One** *m* faith allows him to eat everything, *AIT*
1Co 1:25 foolishness of God is wiser than **m** wisdom, *476*
1:25 weakness of God is stronger than **m** strength. *476*
2:11 the thoughts of a man except the **m** spirit *476*
2:15 **not** subject to **any** *m* judgment: *AIT*
3:13 the fire will test the quality *of* **each** *m* work. *AIT*
10:29 the **other** *m* conscience, I mean, not yours. *AIT*
2Co 4: 2 to every **m** conscience in the sight of God. *476*
10:16 work already done in **another** *m* territory. *AIT*
Jas 1:20 for **m** anger does not bring about *467*
1Pe 1:17 Father who judges **each** *m* work impartially, *AIT*
2Pe 2:16 who spoke with a **m** voice and restrained *476*
1Jn 5: 9 We accept **m** testimony, but God's *476*
Rev 13:18 for it is **m** number. His number is 666. *476*
21:17 144 cubits thick, by **m** measurement, *476*

MAN-MADE (5) [MAN, MAKE]
Dt 4:28 There you will worship **m** gods of wood 132+3338+5126
Mk 14:58 'I will destroy this **m** temple and *5935*
Ac 19:26 He says that **m** gods are no gods at all. *1181+1328+5931*
Heb 9:11 and more perfect tabernacle that is not **m**, *5935*
9:24 not enter a **m** sanctuary that was only a copy *5935*

MANAEN (1)
Ac 13: 1 **M** (who had been brought up with Herod *3441*

MANAGE (5) [MANAGED, MANAGEMENT, MANAGER]
Jer 12: 5 how *will you* **m** in the thickets by 6913
1Ti 3: 4 **m** his own family well **and see that** *4613*
3: 5 not know how *to* **m** his own family, *4613*
3:12 of but one wife and *must* **m** his children *4613*
5:14 to have children, *to* **m** *their* **homes** and *3866*

MANAGED (2) [MANAGE]
1Ki 12:18 **m** to get into his chariot and escape 599
2Ch 10:18 **m** to get into his chariot and escape 599

MANAGEMENT (1) [MANAGE]
Lk 16: 2 Give an account *of* your **m**, *3873*

MANAGER (7) [MANAGE]
Lk 8: 3 the **m** of Herod's household; *2208*
12:42 "Who then is the faithful and wise **m**, *3874*
16: 1 a rich man whose **m** was accused *3874*
16: 2 because you cannot **be m** any longer.' *3872*
16: 3 "The **m** said to himself, *3874*
16: 6 **"The m** told him, 'Take your bill, *1254+3836[S]*
16: 8 "The master commended the dishonest **m** *3874*

MANAHATH (3) [MANAHATHITES]
Ge 36:23 Alvan, **M**, Ebal, Shepho and Onam. 4969
1Ch 1:40 Alvan, **M**, Ebal, Shepho and Onam. 4969
8: 6 in Geba and were deported to **M**: 4970

MANAHATHITES (2) [MANAHATH]
1Ch 2:52 Haroeh, half the **M**, 4971
2:54 Atroth Beth Joab, half the **M**, the Zorites, 4971

MANASSEH (144) [MANASSEH'S, MANASSITES]
Ge 41:51 Joseph named his firstborn **M** and said, 4985
46:20 **M** and Ephraim were born to Joseph 4985
48: 1 So he took his two sons **M** and Ephraim 4985
48: 5 Ephraim and **M** will be mine, 4985
48:13 and **M** on his left toward Israel's right hand, 4985
48:14 even though **M** was the firstborn. 4985
48:20 'May God make you like Ephraim and **M**.' 4985
48:20 So he put Ephraim ahead of **M**. 4985
50:23 the children of Makir son of **M** were placed 4985
Nu 1:10 from **M**, Gamaliel son of Pedahzur; 4985
1:34 From the descendants of **M**: 4985
1:35 number from the tribe of **M** was 32,200. 4985
2:20 The tribe of **M** will be next to them. 4985
2:20 of the people of **M** is Gamaliel son 4985
7:54 the leader of the people of **M**, 4985
10:23 over the division of the tribe of **M**, 1201+4985
13:11 the tribe of **M** (a tribe of Joseph), Gaddi son 4985
26:28 of Joseph by their clans through **M** 4985
26:29 The descendants of **M**: 4985
26:34 These were the clans of **M**; 4985
27: 1 the son of Makir, the son of **M**, 4985
27: 1 belonged to the clans of **M** son of Joseph. 4985
32:33 the Reubenites and the half-tribe of **M** son 4985
32:39 The descendants of Makir son of **M** went 4985
32:40 the descendants of **M**, 4985
32:41 Jair, a descendant of **M**, 4985
34:14 of **M** have received their inheritance. 4985
34:23 from the tribe of **M** son of Joseph; 1201+4985
36: 1 Gilead son of Makir, the son of **M**, 4985
36:12 of the descendants of **M** son of Joseph, 4985
Dt 3:13 I gave to the half tribe of **M**. 4985
3:14 Jair, a descendant of **M**, 4985
29: 8 the Gadites and the half-tribe of **M**. 4986
33:17 such are the thousands of **M**." 4985
34: 2 the territory of Ephraim and **M**, 4985
Jos 1:12 the Gadites and the half-tribe of **M**, 4985
4:12 Gad and the half-tribe of **M** crossed over, 4985
12: 6 the half-tribe of **M** to be their possession. 4985
13: 7 the nine tribes and half of the tribe of **M**." 4985
13: 8 **The other half of M**, the Reubenites and 2257[S]
13:29 to the half-tribe of **M**, that is, to half 4985
13:29 to half the family of the descendants of **M**, 4985
13:31 for the descendants of Makir son of **M**— 4985
14: 4 Joseph had become two tribes—**M** and Ephraim. 4985
16: 4 So **M** and Ephraim, the descendants of 4985
17: 1 This was the allotment for the tribe of **M** 4985
17: 2 for the rest of the people of **M**— 4985
17: 2 the other male descendants of **M** son 4985
17: 3 the son of Makir, the son of **M**, 4985
17: 6 of the **tribe of M** received an inheritance 4985
17: 6 to the rest of the descendants of **M**. 4985
17: 7 The territory of **M** extended from Asher 4985
17: 8 (**M** had the land of Tappuah, 4985
17: 8 but Tappuah itself, on the boundary of **M**, 4985
17: 9 to Ephraim lying among the towns of **M**, 4985
17: 9 the boundary of **M** was the northern side of 4985
17:10 on the north to **M**. 4985
17:10 of **M** reached the sea and bordered Asher on 2257[S]
17:11 **M** also had Beth Shan, 4985
17:17 house of Joseph—to Ephraim and **M**— 4985
18: 7 of **M** have already received their inheritance 4985
20: 8 and Golan in Bashan in the tribe of **M**. 4985
21: 5 Ephraim, Dan and half of **M**. 4985
21: 6 Naphtali and the half-tribe of **M** in Bashan. 4985
21:25 the tribe of **M** they received Taanach 4985
21:27 from the half-tribe of **M**, 4985
22: 1 the Gadites and the half-tribe of **M** 4985
22: 7 the half-tribe of **M** Moses had given land 4985
22: 9 of **M** left the Israelites at Shiloh in Canaan 4985
22:10 the Gadites and the half-tribe of **M** built 4985
22:13 to Reuben, Gad and the half-tribe of **M**. 4985
22:15 to Reuben, Gad and the half-tribe of **M** 4985
22:21 and the half-tribe of **M** replied to the heads 4985
22:30 what Reuben, Gad and **M** had to say, 1201+4985
22:31 the priest, said to Reuben, Gad and **M**, 1201+4985
Jdg 1:27 But **M** did not drive out the people 4985
6:15 My clan is the weakest in **M**, 4985
6:35 He sent messengers throughout **M**, 4985
7:23 Asher and all **M** were called out, 4985
11:29 He crossed Gilead and **M**, 4985
12: 4 renegades from Ephraim and **M**." 4985
1Ki 4:13 of Jair son of **M** in Gilead were his, as well 4985
2Ki 10:33 and **M**), from Aroer by the Arnon Gorge 4986
20:21 And **M** his son succeeded him as king. 4985
21: 1 **M** was twelve years old when he became 4985
21: 9 **M** led them astray, 4985
21:11 "**M** king of Judah has committed these detestable sins. 4985
21:16 **M** also shed so much innocent blood 4985
21:18 **M** rested with his fathers and was buried 4985
21:20 as his father **M** had done. 4985
23:12 and the altars **M** had built in the two courts 4985
23:26 that **M** had done to provoke him to anger. 4985
24: 3 from his presence because of the sins of **M** 4985
1Ch 3:13 Ahaz his son, Hezekiah his son, **M** his son, 4985
5:18 the half-tribe of **M** had 44,760 men ready 4985
5:23 of the half-tribe of **M** were numerous; 4985
5:26 the Gadites and the half-tribe of **M** 4985
6:61 from the clans of half the tribe of **M**. 4985
6:62 the part of the tribe of **M** that is in Bashan. 4985
6:70 of **M** the Israelites gave Aner and Bileam, 4985
6:71 of the half-tribe of **M** they received Golan 4985
7:14 The descendants of **M**: 4985
7:17 Gilead son of Makir, the son of **M**. 4985
7:29 the borders of **M** were Beth Shan, 1201+4985
9: 3 and **M** who lived in Jerusalem were: 4985
12:19 of **M** defected to David when he went with 4985
12:20 these were the men of **M** who defected 4985
12:20 leaders of units of a thousand in **M**. 4985
12:31 the tribe of **M**, designated by name to come 4985
12:37 Reuben, Gad and the half-tribe of **M**, 4985
26:32 of **M** for every matter pertaining to God and 4986
27:20 over half the tribe of **M**: 4985
27:21 over the half-tribe of **M** in Gilead: 4985
2Ch 15: 9 **M** and Simeon who had settled 4985
30: 1 and also wrote letters to Ephraim and **M**, 4985
30:10 from town to town in Ephraim and **M**, 4985
30:11 **M** and Zebulun humbled themselves 4985
30:18 **M**, Issachar and Zebulun had 4985
31: 1 and Benjamin and in Ephraim and **M**. 4985
32:33 And **M** his son succeeded him as king. 4985
33: 1 **M** was twelve years old when he became 4985
33: 9 But **M** led Judah and the people 4985
33:10 The LORD spoke to **M** and his people, 4985
33:11 king of Assyria, who took **M** prisoner, 4985
33:13 Then **M** knew that the LORD is God. 4985
33:20 **M** rested with his fathers and was buried 4985
33:22 as his father **M** had done. 4985
33:22 to all the idols **M** had made. 4985
33:23 But unlike his father **M**, 4985
34: 6 In the towns of **M**, Ephraim and Simeon, 4985
34: 9 from the people of **M**, 4985
Ezr 10:30 Mattaniah, Bezalel, Binnui and **M**. 4985
10:33 Zabad, Eliphelet, Jeremai, **M** and Shimei. 4985
Ps 60: 7 Gilead is mine, and **M** is mine; 4985
80: 2 before Ephraim, Benjamin and **M**. 4985
108: 8 Gilead is mine, **M** is mine; 4985
Isa 9:21 **M** will feed on Ephraim, and Ephraim 4985
9:21 and Ephraim on **M**; 4985
Jer 15: 4 because of what **M** son of Hezekiah king 4985
Eze 48: 4 "**M** will have one portion; 4985
48: 5 it will border the territory of **M** from east 4985
Mt 1:10 Hezekiah the father of **M**, *3442*
1:10 **M** the father of Amon, *3442*
Rev 7: 6 from the tribe *of* **M** 12,000, *3442*

MANASSEH'S (6) [MANASSEH]
Ge 48:14 he put his left hand on **M** head, 4985
48:17 to move it from Ephraim's head to **M** head. 4985
Jos 17: 1 that is, for Makir, **M** firstborn. 4985
17: 5 **M** share consisted of ten tracts 4985
2Ki 21:17 As for the other events of **M** reign, 4985
2Ch 33:18 The other events of **M** reign, 4985

MANASSES (KJV) See MANASSEH

MANASSITES (3) [MANASSEH]
Dt 4:43 and Golan in Bashan, for the **M**. 4986
Jos 16: 9 within the inheritance of the **M**. 1201+4985
17:12 the **M** were not able to occupy these towns, 1201+4985

MANDRAKE (1) [MANDRAKES]
Ge 30:14 into the fields and found *some* **m plants**, 1859

MANDRAKES (5) [MANDRAKE]
Ge 30:14 "Please give me some of your son's **m**." 1859
30:15 Will you take my son's **m** too?" 1859
30:15 with you tonight in return for your son's **m**. 1859
30:16 "I have hired you with my son's **m**." 1859
SS 7:13 The **m** send out their fragrance, 1859

MANE (1)
Job 39:19 or clothe his neck with a **flowing m**? 8310

MANEH (KJV) See MINAH

MANGER (6)
Job 39: 9 Will he stay by your **m** at night? 17
Pr 14: 4 Where there are no oxen, the **m** is empty, 17
Isa 1: 3 the donkey his owner's **m**, 17
Lk 2: 7 in cloths and placed him in a **m**, *5764*
2:12 a baby wrapped in cloths and lying in a **m**." *5764*
2:16 and the baby, who was lying in the **m**. *5764*

MANGLED (1) [MANGLES]
La 3:11 the path and **m** me and left me without help. 7318

MANGLES (1) [MANGLED]
Mic 5: 8 which mauls and **m** as it goes, 3271

MANHOOD (2) [MAN]
Ps 78:51 the firstfruits of **m** in the tents of Ham. 226
105:36 the firstfruits of all their **m**. 226

MANIAC (1)
Hos 9: 7 the inspired man a **m**. 8713

MANIFESTATION (1)
1Co 12: 7 Now to each one the **m** of the Spirit is given *5748*

MANIFOLD (1)
Eph 3:10 **m** wisdom of God should be made known *4497*

MANKIND (36) [MAN]
Ge 6: 7 So the LORD said, "I will wipe **m**, 132
7:21 that swarm over the earth, and all **m**. 132
Nu 16:22 "O God, God of the spirits of all **m**, 1414
27:16 the God of the spirits of all **m**, 1414
Dt 32: 8 when he divided all **m**, 132+1201
32:26 and blot out their memory from **m**, 632
Job 12:10 every creature and the breath of all **m**. 408+1414
34:15 all **m** would perish together 1414
36:25 All **m** has seen it; men gaze on it from afar. 132
36:28 and abundant showers fall on **m**. 132
Ps 21:10 their posterity from **m**. 132+1201
33:13 the LORD looks down and sees all **m**; 132+1201
64: 9 All **m** will fear; 132
Pr 8: 4 I raise my voice to **all m**. 132+1201
8:31 in his whole world and delighting in **m**. 132+1201
30:14 the needy from among **m**. 132
Ecc 7:29 God made **m** upright, but men have gone 132

Isa 2: 9 man will be brought low and **m** humbled— 408
5:15 man will be brought low and **m** humbled, 408
38:11 no longer will I look on **m**, 132
40: 5 and all **m** together will see it. 1414
45:12 It is I who made the earth and created **m** 132
49:26 Then all **m** will know that I, the LORD, 1414
66:23 all **m** will come and bow down before me," 1414
66:24 and they will be loathsome to all **m**." 1414
Jer 25:31 on all **m** and put the wicked to the sword,' " 1414
32:20 both in Israel and among all **m**, 132
32:27 I am the LORD, the God of all **m**. 1414
Da 2:38 in your hands he has placed **m** and 10050+10120
Joel 1:12 Surely the joy of **m** is withered away. 132+1201
Mic 5: 7 do not wait for man or linger for **m**. 132+1201
Zec 2:13 Be still before the LORD, all **m**, 1414
Lk 3: 6 And all **m** will see God's salvation.' " *4922*
Rev 9:15 and year were released to kill a third *of* **m**. *476*
9:18 A third *of* **m** was killed by the three plagues *476*
9:20 The rest *of* **m** that were not killed *476*

MANNA (20)

Ex 16:31 The people of Israel called the bread **m**. 4942
16:32 omer of **m** and keep it for the generations 5647S
16:33 "Take a jar and put an omer of **m** in it. 4942
16:34 Aaron put **the m** in front of the Testimony, 2084S
16:35 The Israelites ate **m** forty years, 4942
16:35 they ate **m** until they reached the border 4942
Nu 11: 6 we never see anything but this **m**!" 4942
11: 7 The **m** was like coriander seed and looked 4942
11: 9 the **m** also came down. 4942
Dt 8: 3 to hunger and then feeding you with **m**, 4942
8:16 He gave you **m** to eat in the desert, 4942
Jos 5:12 The **m** stopped the day after they ate 4942
5:12 there was no longer any **m** for the Israelites, 4942
Ne 9:20 not withhold your **m** from their mouths, 4942
Ps 78:24 he rained down **m** for the people to eat, 4942
Jn 6:31 Our forefathers ate the **m** in the desert; *3445*
6:49 Your forefathers ate the **m** in the desert, *3445*
6:58 Your forefathers ate **m** and died, *3445*
Heb 9: 4 This ark contained the gold jar of **m**, *3445*
Rev 2:17 I will give some of the hidden **m**. *3445*

MANNED (2) [MAN]

2Ch 9:21 a fleet of trading ships **m by** Hiram's men. 6640
Eze 27:11 Men of Arvad and Helech **m** your walls 6584

MANNER (7)

Nu 15:11 is to be prepared **in this m**. 3970
Jos 6:15 around the city seven times in the same **m**, 5477
1Ki 21:26 **behaved in the vilest m** by going 4394+9493
1Co 11:27 of the Lord in an **unworthy m** will be guilty *397*
2Co 1:17 Or do I make my plans in a **worldly m** so *4922*
Php 1:27 **conduct yourselves in a m** worthy of *4488*
3Jn 1: 6 to send them on their way **in a m worthy** *545*

MANOAH (15)

Jdg 13: 2 A certain man of Zorah, named **M**, 4956
13: 8 Then **M** prayed to the LORD: 4956
13: 9 God heard **M**, and the angel 4956
13: 9 but her husband **M** was not with her. 4956
13:11 **M** got up and followed his wife. 4956
13:12 So **M** asked him, "When your words 4956
13:15 **M** said to the angel of the LORD, 4956
13:16 (**M** did not realize that it was the angel of 4956
13:17 **M** inquired of the angel of the LORD, 4956
13:19 Then **M** took a young goat, 4956
13:19 the LORD did an amazing thing while **M** 4956
13:20 **M** and his wife fell with their faces to 4956
13:21 not show himself again to **M** and his wife, 4956
13:21 **M** realized that it was the angel of 4956
16:31 and Eshtaol in the tomb of **M** his father. 4956

MANSERVANT (8) [SERVANT]

Ex 20:10 nor your **m** or maidservant, 6269
20:17 or his **m** or maidservant, his ox or donkey, 6269
21:26 "If a man hits a **m** or maidservant in the eye 6269
21:27 And if he knocks out the tooth of a **m** 6269
Lev 25: 6 for yourself, your **m** and maidservant, 6269
Dt 5:14 nor your **m** or maidservant, nor your ox, 6269
5:14 so that your **m** and maidservant may rest, 6269
5:21 his **m** or maidservant, his ox or donkey, 6269

MANSIONS (4)

Ps 49:14 far from their **princely m**. 2292
Isa 5: 9 the fine **m** left without occupants. NIH
Am 3:15 and the **m** will be demolished," 1074+8041
5:11 Therefore, though you have built stone **m**, 1074

MANSLAYER, MANSLAYER (KJV) See ACCUSED OF MURDER, WHO HAS KILLED

MANTLE (1) [MANTLED]

Ps 89:45 *you have* **covered** him **with a m** of shame. 6486

MANTLED (1) [MANTLE]

Ps 65:13 with flocks and the valleys *are* **m** 6493

MANURE (3)

Isa 25:10 as straw is trampled down in the **m**. 4523
Eze 4:15 over cow **m** instead of human excrement." 7616
Lk 14:35 for the soil nor for the **m pile**; *3161*

MANY (517)

Ge 17: 4 You will be the father of **m** nations. 2162
17: 5 for I have made you a father of **m** nations. 2162
26:14 He had **so m** flocks and herds and servants 8041
37:34 and mourned for his son **m** days. 8041
50:20 the saving of **m** lives. 8041
Ex 12:38 **M** other people went up with them, 8041
19:21 to see the LORD and **m** of them perish. 8041
Lev 11:42 or walks on all fours or on **m** feet; 8049
15:25 a discharge of blood for **m** days at 8041
25:16 When the years are **m**, you are to increase 8044
25:51 If **m** years remain, he must pay for his 8041
Nu 13:18 who live here are strong or weak, few or **m**. 8041
15:12 for as **m** as you prepare. 5031
20:15 and we lived there **m** years. 8041
21: 6 they bit the people and **m** Israelites died. 8041
22: 3 because there were so **m** people. 8041
35: 8 **Take m** towns from a tribe that has many, 8049
35: 8 Take many towns from a tribe that has **m**, 8041
Dt 1:10 so that today you are as **m** as the stars in 8044
1:46 And so you stayed in Kadesh **m** days— 8041
3: 5 there were also a great **m** unwalled villages. 2221
7: 1 and drives out before you **m** nations— 8041
11:21 and the days of your children *may be* **m** in 8049
11:21 **as m as** the days that the heavens are above 3869
15: 6 to **m** nations but will borrow from none. 8041
15: 6 over **m** nations but none will rule over you. 8041
17:17 *He must* not **take m** wives, 8049
28:12 You will lend to **m** nations but will borrow 8041
30:20 he will give you **m years** in the land 802+3427
31:17 **M** disasters and difficulties will come 8041
31:21 And when **m** disasters and difficulties come 8041
Jos 24: 3 and **gave** him **m** descendants. 8049
Jdg 7: 2 "You have too **m** men for me 8041
7: 4 "There are still too **m** men. 8041
8:30 for he had **m** wives. 8041
9:40 and **m** fell wounded in the flight— 8041
15: 8 and slaughtered **m** of them. 1524
16:30 Thus he killed **m** more when he died than 8041
1Sa 2: 5 but *she who has had* **m** sons pines away. 8041
3: 1 there were not **m** visions. 7287
14: 6 whether by **m** or by few." 8041
25:10 **M** servants are breaking away 8045
31: 1 and *m* **fell** slain on Mount Gilboa. AIT
2Sa 1: 4 **M** of them fell and died. 2221
13:34 and saw **m** people on the road west of him, 8041
14: 2 a woman who has spent **m** days grieving for 8041
19:34 **"How m more** years will I live, 3869+4537
24: 2 so that I may know **how m** there are." 5031
1Ki 7:47 because there were so **m**; 8044
8: 5 sacrificing **so m** sheep and cattle 4946+8044
10:10 Never again were **so m** spices brought 4200+8044
11: 1 Solomon loved **m** foreign women besides Pharaoh's daughter— 8041
18:25 since there are **so m** of you. 8041
22:16 **"How m** times must I make you swear 3869+4537+6330
2Ki 19:23 "With my **m** chariots I have ascended 8044
1Ch 4:27 but his brothers did not have **m** children; 8041
5:22 and **m** *others* fell slain, 8041
7: 4 for *they* **had m** wives and children. 8049
7:22 Ephraim mourned for them **m** days, 8041
8:40 *They* **had m** sons and grandsons—150 in all 8049
10: 1 and *m* **fell** slain on Mount Gilboa. AIT
21: 2 to me so that I may know **how m** there are." 5031
22: 8 and have fought **m** wars. 1524
22:15 You have **m** workmen: 4200+8044
23:11 but Jeush and Beriah *did* not **have m** sons; 8049
28: 5 and the LORD has given me **m**— 8041
2Ch 5: 6 sacrificing **so m** sheep and cattle 4946+8044
11:23 and took **m** wives for them. 2162
18: 2 Ahab slaughtered **m** sheep and cattle 4200+8044
18:15 **"How m** times must I make you swear 3869+4537+6330
21: 3 Their father had given them **m** gifts of silver 8041
24:27 the **m** prophecies about him, 8044
26:10 in the desert and dug **m** cisterns, 8041
28: 5 The Arameans defeated him and took **m** 1524
30:17 Since **m** in the crowd had 8041
30:18 Although most of the **m** people who came 8041
32:23 **M** brought offerings to Jerusalem for 8041
Ezr 3:12 But **m** of the older priests and Levites 8041
3:12 while **m** *others* shouted for joy. 8041
5:11 the temple that was built **m** years ago, 10678
10:13 But there are **m** people here and it is 8041
Ne 6:17 of Judah *were* sending **m** letters to Tobiah, 8049
6:18 For **m** in Judah were under oath to him, 8041
9:30 For **m** years you were patient with them. 8041
13:26 the **m** nations there was no king like him. 8041
Est 2: 8 **m** girls were brought to the citadel of Susa 8041
4: 3 **M** lay in sackcloth and ashes. 8041
5:11 to them about his vast wealth, his **m** sons, 8044
8:17 And **m** *people* of other nationalities 8041
10: 3 held in high esteem by his **m** fellow Jews, 8044
Job 4: 3 Think how you have instructed **m**, 8041
5:25 You will know that your children will be **m**, 8041
11:19 and **m** will court your favor. 8041
13:23 **How m** wrongs and sins have I 3869+4537
16: 2 "I have heard **m** *things* like these; 8041
23:14 and **m** such plans he still has in store. 8041
27:14 **m** his children, their fate is the sword; 8049
35: 6 your sins *are* **m**, what does that do to him? 8045
38:21 You have lived **so m** years! 5031+8041
Ps 3: 1 O LORD, how **m** *are* my foes! 8045
3: 1 How **m** rise up against me! 8041
3: 2 **M** are saying of me, "God will not deliver 8041
4: 6 **M** are asking, "Who can show us any good?" 8041
5:10 Banish them for their **m** sins, 8044
22:12 **M** bulls surround me; 8041
31:13 For I hear the slander of **m**; 8041
32:10 **M** are the woes of the wicked, 8041
34:12 and desires to see *m* good **days**, AIT
34:19 A righteous man may have **m** troubles, 8041
37:16 the wealth of **m** wicked; 8041
38:19 **M** *are* those who are my vigorous enemies; 6793
40: 3 **M** will see and fear and put their trust in 8041
40: 5 **M**, O LORD my God, 8041
40: 5 *they would be* too **m** to declare. 6793
55:18 even though **m** oppose me. 8041
56: 2 **m** are attacking me in their pride. 8041
61: 6 his years for **m generations**. 1887+1887+2256
69: 4 **m** *are* my enemies without cause, 6793
71: 7 I have become like a portent to **m**, 8041
71:20 **m** and bitter, you will restore my life again; 8041
90:15 for **as m** days as you have afflicted us, 3869
90:15 for as **m** years as we have seen trouble. NIH
104:24 How **m** *are* your works, O LORD! 8045
106: 7 they did not remember your **m** kindnesses, 8044
106:43 **M** times he delivered them, 8041
119:157 **M** are the foes who persecute me, 8041
135:10 down **m** nations and killed mighty kings— 8041
Pr 3: 2 for they will prolong your life **m years** 2256+3427+9102
4:10 and the years of your life *will be* **m**. 8049
7:26 **M** are the victims she has brought down; 8041
9:11 For through me your days *will be* **m**, 8049
10:19 When words are **m**, sin is not absent, 8044
10:21 The lips of the righteous nourish **m**, 8041
11:14 but **m** advisers make victory sure. 8044
14:20 but the rich have **m** friends. 8041
15:22 but with **m** advisers they succeed. 8044
18:24 A man of *m* **companions** may come to ruin, AIT
19: 4 Wealth brings **m** friends, 8041
19: 6 **M** curry favor with a ruler, 8041
19:21 **M** are the plans in a man's heart, 8041
20: 6 **M** a man claims to have unfailing love, 8044
24: 6 and for victory **m** advisers. 8044
28: 2 a country is rebellious, it has **m** rulers, 8041
28:27 to them receives **m** curses. 8041
29: 1 after **m** rebukes will suddenly NIH
29:22 and a hot-tempered one commits **m** sins. 8041
29:26 **M** seek an audience with a ruler, 8041
31:29 "**M** women do noble things, 8041
Ecc 5: 3 As a dream comes when there are **m** cares, 8044
5: 3 speech of a fool when there are **m** words. 8044
5: 7 and **m** words are meaningless. 2221
6: 3 a hundred children and live **m** years; 8041
7:22 **m** times you yourself have cursed others. 8041
7:29 men have gone in search of **m** schemes." 8041
10: 6 Fools are put in **m** high positions, 8041
11: 1 for after **m** days you will find it again. 8044
11: 8 However **m** years a man may live, 2221
11: 8 the days of darkness, for they will be **m**. 2221
12: 9 and set in order **m** proverbs. 2221
12:12 Of making **m** books there is no end, 2221
SS 8: 7 **M** waters cannot quench love; 8041
Isa 1:15 if *you* **offer m** prayers, I will not listen. 8049
2: 3 **M** peoples will come and say, "Come, 8041
2: 4 and will settle disputes for **m** peoples. 8041
8:15 **M** of them will stumble; 8041
10: 7 to put an end to **m** nations. 4202+5071
16:14 Moab's splendor and all her **m** people will 8041
17:12 Oh, the raging of **m** nations— 8041
22: 9 of David *had* **m** breaches in its defenses; 8045
23:16 play the harp well, sing **m** a song, 8049
24:22 up in prison and be punished after **m** days. 8044
29: 5 your **m** enemies will become like fine dust, 2162
37:24 'With my **m** chariots I have ascended 8044
41:15 new and sharp, with **m teeth**. 7092
42:20 You have seen **m** *things*, 8041
47: 9 in spite of your **m** sorceries 8044
47:12 and with your **m** sorceries, 8044
51: 2 and I blessed him and **made** him **m**. 8049
52:14 Just as there were **m** who were appalled 8041
52:15 so will he sprinkle **m** nations, 8041
53:11 by his knowledge my righteous servant will justify **m**, 8041
53:12 For he bore the sin of **m**, 8041
59:12 For our offenses *are* **m** in your sight, 8045
63: 7 the **m** good things he has done for the house 8041
63: 7 to his compassion and **m** kindnesses. 8044
66:16 and **m** *will be* those slain by the LORD. 8045
Jer 2:28 For you have **as m** gods **as** you have towns, 5031
3: 1 as a prostitute with **m** lovers— 8041
5: 6 and their backslidings **m**. 6793
11:13 You have **as m** gods **as** you have towns, 5031
11:13 to that shameful god Baal are **as m as** 5031
11:15 as she works out her evil schemes with **m**? 8041
12:10 **M** shepherds will ruin my vineyard 8041
13: 6 **M** days later the LORD said to me, 8041
13:22 it is because of your **m** sins 8044
16:16 "But now I will send for **m** fishermen," 8041
16:16 After that I will send for **m** hunters, 8041
20:10 I hear **m** whispering, "Terror on every side! 8041
22: 8 from **m** nations will pass by this city 8041
25:14 be enslaved by **m** nations and great kings; 8041
27: 7 **m** nations and great kings will subjugate 8041
28: 8 against **m** countries and great kingdoms. 8041
30:14 your guilt is so great and your sins *so* **m**. 6793

Jer 30:15 and **m** sins I have done these things to you. 6793
36:32 And **m** similar words were added to them. 8041
42: 2 as you now see, though we were once **m,** 2221
50:41 a great nation and **m** kings are being stirred 8041
51:13 You who live by **m** waters and are rich 8041
La 1: 5 because of her **m** sins. 8044
1:22 My groans are **m** and my heart is faint." 8041
Eze 3: 6 not to **m** peoples of obscure speech 8041
11: 6 *You have* killed **m** people in this city 8049
12:27 The vision he sees is for **m** years from now, 8041
16:41 on you in the sight of **m** women. 8041
17: 9 not take a strong arm or **m** people to pull it 8041
17:17 and siege works erected to destroy **m** lives. 8041
19:11 for its height and for its **m** branches. 8044
21:15 So that hearts may melt and the fallen *be* **m,** 8049
22:25 and precious things and **make m** widows 8049
26: 3 and I will bring **m** nations against you, 8041
26:10 be so **m** that they will cover you with dust. 9180
27: 3 merchant of peoples on **m** coasts, 8041
27:15 and **m** coastlands were your customers; 8041
27:16 with you because of your **m** products; 8044
27:18 of your **m** products and great wealth 8044
27:33 you satisfied **m** nations; 8041
28:18 By your **m** sins and dishonest trade 8044
32: 9 I will trouble the hearts of **m** peoples 8041
32:10 I will cause **m** peoples to be appalled at you, 8041
33:24 But we are **m;** surely the land has been 8041
37: 2 a great **m** bones on the floor of the valley, 8041
38: 6 the **m** nations with you. 8041
38: 8 After **m** days you will be called to arms. 8041
38: 8 whose people were gathered from **m** nations 8041
38: 9 You and all your troops and the **m** nations 8041
38:15 you and **m** nations with you, 8041
38:22 and on his troops and on the **m** nations 8041
38:23 in the sight of **m** nations. 8041
39:27 through them in the sight of **m** nations. 8041
47:10 The fish will be of **m** kinds— 4394+8041
Da 2:48 and lavished **m** gifts on him. 10647+10678
8:25 he will destroy **m** and take his stand against 8041
9:27 He will confirm a covenant with **m** 8041
11:12 with pride and will slaughter **m thousands,** 8052
11:14 "In those times **m** will rise against the king 8041
11:18 to the coastlands and will take **m** of them, 8041
11:26 and **m** will fall in battle. 8041
11:33 "Those who are wise will instruct **m,** 8041
11:34 and **m** who are not sincere will join them. 8041
11:39 over **m** *people* and will distribute the land at 8041
11:40 He will invade *m* **countries** and sweep AIT
11:41 **M** *countries* will fall, but Edom, 8041
11:42 He will extend his power over *m* **countries;** AIT
11:44 in a great rage to destroy and annihilate **m.** 8041
12: 3 and those who lead **m** to righteousness, 8041
12: 4 **M** will go here and there 8041
12:10 **M** will be purified, made spotless and 8041
Hos 3: 3 I told her, "You are to live with me **m** days; 8041
3: 4 the Israelites will live **m** days without king 8041
8:11 Ephraim **built m** altars for sin offerings, 8049
8:12 I wrote for them the **m** *things of* my law, 8044
8:14 Judah *has* fortified **m** towns. 8049
9: 7 Because your sins are **so m** 8044
10: 4 *They* **make m promises,** take false 1819+1821
10:13 and on your **m** warriors, 8044
12:10 **gave** them **m** visions and told parables 8049
Am 4: 9 **"M times** I struck your gardens 8049
5:12 For I know how **m** are your offenses and 8041
8: 3 **M,** many bodies—flung everywhere! 8041
8: 3 Many, **m** bodies—flung everywhere! NIH
Jnh 4:11 and **m** cattle as well. 8041
Mic 4: 2 **M** nations will come and say, "Come, 8041
4: 3 between **m** peoples and will settle disputes 8041
4:11 now **m** nations are gathered against you. 8041
4:13 and you will break to pieces **m** nations." 8041
5: 7 be in the midst of **m** peoples like dew from 8041
5: 8 in the midst of **m** peoples, 8041
Na 3: 3 **M** casualties, piles of dead, 8044
Hab 2: 8 Because you have plundered **m** nations, 8041
2:10 You have plotted the ruin of **m** peoples, 8041
3: 9 you called for **m** arrows. 8679
Zec 2:11 **"M** nations will be joined with the LORD 8041
7: 3 as I have done for **so m** years?" 3869+4537
8:20 **"M** peoples and the inhabitants NIH
8:20 the inhabitants of **m** cities will yet come, 8041
8:22 And **m** peoples and powerful nations will come to Jerusalem 8041
Mal 2: 6 and turned **m** from sin. 8041
2: 8 by your teaching have caused **m** to stumble; 8041
Mt 3: 7 But when he saw **m** of the Pharisees *4498*
6: 7 be heard because of their **m words.** *4494*
7:13 leads to destruction, and **m** enter through it. *4498*
7:22 **M** will say to me on that day, 'Lord, Lord, *4498*
7:22 and perform **m** miracles?' *4498*
8:11 that **m** will come from the east and the west, *4498*
8:16 **m** who were demon-possessed were brought *4498*
9:10 **m** tax collectors and "sinners" came and ate *4498*
10:31 you are worth more than **m** sparrows. *4498*
12:15 **M** followed him, and he healed all their sick *4498*
13: 3 he told them **m** *things* in parables, saying: *4498*
13:17 **m** prophets and righteous men longed *4498*
13:58 And he did not do **m** miracles there because *4498*
15:30 the crippled, the mute and **m** others, *4498*
15:34 **"How m** loaves do you have?" *4531*
16: 9 and **how m** basketfuls you gathered? *4531*
16:10 and **how m** basketfuls you gathered? *4531*
16:21 to Jerusalem and suffer **m** *things* at *4498*
18:21 **how m times** shall I forgive my brother *4529*
19:30 But **m** who are first will be last, *4498*
19:30 and **m** who are last will be first. *NIG*
Mt 20:28 and to give his life as a ransom for **m."** *4498*
22:14 "For **m** are invited, but few are chosen." *4498*
24: 5 For **m** will come in my name, claiming, *4498*
24: 5 'I am the Christ,' and will deceive **m.** *4498*
24:10 At that time **m** will turn away from the faith *4498*
24:11 and **m** false prophets will appear *4498*
24:11 and deceive **m** *people.* *4498*
25:21 I will put you in charge of **m** *things.* *4498*
25:23 I will put you in charge of **m** *things.* *4498*
26:28 for **m** for the forgiveness of sins. *4498*
26:60 though **m** false witnesses came forward. *4498*
27:52 of **m** holy people who had died were raised *NIG*
27:53 the holy city and appeared *to* **m** *people.* *4498*
27:55 **M** women were there, watching from a *4498*
Mk 1:34 Jesus healed **m** who had various diseases. *4498*
1:34 He also drove out **m** demons, *4498*
2: 2 So **m** gathered that there was no room left, *4498*
2:15 **m** tax collectors and "sinners" were eating *4498*
2:15 for there were **m** who followed him. *4498*
3: 8 **m** people came to him from Judea, *4498*
3:10 For he had healed **m,** *4498*
4: 2 He taught them **m** *things* by parables, *4498*
4:33 *With* **m** similar parables Jesus spoke *4498*
5: 9 Legion," he replied, "for we are **m."** *4498*
5:26 a great deal under the care *of* **m** doctors *4498*
6: 2 and **m** who heard him were amazed. *4498*
6:13 They drove out **m** demons *4498*
6:13 and anointed **m** sick people with oil *4498*
6:31 because **so m** *people* were coming and *4498*
6:33 **m** who saw them leaving recognized them *4498*
6:34 So he began teaching them **m** *things.* *4498*
6:38 **"How m** loaves do you have?" *4531*
7: 4 And they observe **m** other traditions, *4498*
7:13 And you do **m** *things* like that." *4498*
8: 5 **"How m** loaves do you have?" *4531*
8:19 for the five thousand, **how m** basketfuls *4531*
8:20 for the four thousand, **how m** basketfuls *4531*
8:31 that the Son of Man must suffer **m** *things* *4498*
9:26 so much like a corpse that **m** said, *4498*
10:31 But **m** who are first will be last, *4498*
10:45 and to give his life as a ransom for **m."** *4498*
10:48 **M** rebuked him and told him to be quiet, *4498*
11: 8 **M** *people* spread their cloaks on the road, *4498*
12: 5 He sent **m** others; some of them they beat, *4498*
12:41 **M** rich people threw in large amounts. *4498*
13: 6 **M** will come in my name, claiming, *4498*
13: 6 claiming, 'I am he,' and will deceive **m.** *4498*
14:24 which is poured out for **m,"** he said to them. *4498*
14:56 **M** testified falsely against him, *4498*
15: 3 The chief priests accused him of **m** *things.* *4498*
15: 4 See **how m** *things* they are accusing you of. *4531*
15:41 **M** other *women* who had come up with him *4498*
Lk 1: 1 **M** have undertaken to draw up an account *4498*
1:14 and **m** will rejoice because of his birth, *4498*
1:16 **M** of the people of Israel will he bring back *4498*
2:34 the falling and rising *of* **m** in Israel, *4498*
2:35 the thoughts of **m** hearts will be revealed. *4498*
3:18 And with **m** other words John exhorted *4498*
4:25 I assure you that there were **m** widows *4498*
4:27 And there were **m** in Israel with leprosy in *4498*
4:41 Moreover, demons came out of **m** *people,* *4498*
7:21 very time Jesus cured **m** who had diseases, *4498*
7:21 and gave sight *to* **m** who were blind. *4498*
7:47 I tell you, her **m** sins have been forgiven— *4498*
8: 3 Susanna; and **m** others. *4498*
8:29 **M** times it had seized him, *4498*
8:30 because **m** demons had gone into him. *4498*
9:22 "The Son of Man must suffer **m** *things* and *4498*
10:24 that **m** prophets and kings wanted *4498*
10:41 "you are worried and upset about **m** *things,* *4498*
12: 1 a crowd *of* **m thousands** had gathered, *3689*
12: 7 you are worth more than **m** sparrows. *4498*
12:19 of good things laid up for **m** years. *4498*
12:47 be beaten with **m** blows. *4498*
13:24 because **m,** I tell you, will try to enter *4498*
14:16 a great banquet and invited **m** guests. *4498*
15:17 **'How m** of my father's hired men have food *4531*
17:25 But first he must suffer **m** *things* and *4498*
18:30 to receive **m times as much** in this age and, *4491*
21: 8 For **m** will come in my name, claiming, *4498*
22:65 they said **m** other insulting *things* to him. *4498*
23: 9 He plied him with **m** questions, *2653*
Jn 2:23 at the Passover Feast, **m** *people* saw *4498*
4:39 **M** of the Samaritans from that town *4498*
4:41 of his words **m** more became believers. *4498*
6: 9 but how far will they go among **so m?"** *5537*
6:60 On hearing it, **m** of his disciples said, *4498*
6:66 From this time **m** of his disciples turned *4498*
7:31 Still, **m** in the crowd put their faith in him. *4498*
8:30 Even as he spoke, **m** put their faith in him. *4498*
10:20 **M** of them said, "He is demon-possessed *4498*
10:32 "I have shown you **m** great miracles from *4498*
10:41 and **m** *people* came to him. *4498*
10:42 And in that place **m** believed in Jesus. *4498*
11:19 and **m** Jews had come to Martha and Mary *4498*
11:45 **m** of the Jews who had come to visit Mary, *4498*
11:47 "Here is this man performing **m** miraculous signs. *4498*
11:55 **m** went up from the country to Jerusalem *4498*
12:11 on account of him **m** of the Jews were going *4498*
12:18 **M people,** because they had heard *4063*
12:24 But if it dies, it produces **m** seeds. *4498*
12:42 Yet at the same time **m** even among *4498*
14: 2 In my Father's house are **m** rooms; *4498*
19:20 **M** of the Jews read this sign, *4498*
20:30 Jesus did **m** other miraculous signs in *4498*
21:11 but even with **so m** the net was not torn. *5537*
Jn 21:25 Jesus did **m** other things as well. *4498*
Ac 1: 3 to these men and gave **m** convincing proofs *4498*
2:40 *With* **m** other words he warned them; *4498*
2:43 and **m** wonders and miraculous signs *4498*
3:24 **as m as** have spoken, *4012*
4: 4 But **m** who heard the message believed, *4498*
5:12 The apostles performed **m** miraculous signs *4498*
8: 7 With shrieks, evil spirits came out of **m,** *4498*
8: 7 and **m** paralytics and cripples were healed. *4498*
8:25 preaching the gospel in **m** Samaritan *4498*
9:13 "I have heard **m** reports about this man *4498*
9:23 After **m** days had gone by, *2653*
9:42 and **m** *people* believed in the Lord. *4498*
12:12 **m** *people* had gathered and were praying. *2653*
13:31 and for **m** days he was seen *4498*
13:43 **m** of the Jews and devout converts *4498*
14:22 "We must go through **m** hardships to enter *4498*
15:35 and **m** others taught and preached the word *4498*
16:18 She kept this up for **m** days. *4498*
17:12 **M** of the Jews believed, as did also *4498*
17:12 Greek women and **m** Greek men. *3900+4024*
18: 8 and **m** of the Corinthians who heard him *4498*
18:10 because I have **m** people in this city." *4498*
19:18 **M** of those who believed now came *4498*
20: 2 speaking **m** words of encouragement to *4498*
20: 8 There were **m** lamps in the upstairs room *2653*
21:20 **how m** thousands of Jews have believed, *4531*
25: 7 bringing **m** serious charges against him, *4498*
25:14 Since they were spending **m** days there, *4498*
26:10 On the authority of the chief priests I put **m** *4498*
26:11 **M a time** I went from one synagogue *4490*
27: 7 We made slow headway for **m** days *2653*
27:20 for **m** days and the storm continued raging, *4498*
28:10 *in* **m** *ways* and when we were ready to sail, *4498*
Ro 1:13 that I planned **m times** to come to you *4490*
4:17 "I have made you a father *of* **m** nations." *4498*
4:18 and so became the father *of* **m** nations, *4498*
5:15 if the **m** died by the trespass of the one man, *4498*
5:15 Jesus Christ, overflow to the **m!** *4498*
5:16 but the gift followed **m** trespasses *4498*
5:19 of the one man the **m** were made sinners, *4498*
5:19 the one man the **m** will be made righteous. *4498*
8:29 be the firstborn among **m** brothers. *4498*
12: 4 of us has one body with **m** members, *4498*
12: 5 so in Christ we who are **m** form one body, *4498*
15:23 I have been longing for **m** years to see you, *4498*
16: 2 for she has been a great help *to* **m** *people,* *4498*
1Co 1:26 Not **m** of you were wise *4498*
1:26 not **m** were influential; *4498*
1:26 not **m** were of noble birth. *4498*
4:15 you do not have **m** fathers, *4498*
7:28 But those who marry will face **m** troubles *NIG*
8: 5 or on earth (as indeed there are **m** "gods" *4498*
8: 5 there are many "gods" and **m** "lords"), *4498*
9:19 to win as **m** as possible. *4498*
10:17 Because there is one loaf, we, who are **m,** *4498*
10:33 seeking my own good but the good *of* **m,** *4498*
11:30 That is why **m** among you are weak *4498*
12:12 though it is made up of **m** parts; *4498*
12:12 all its parts are **m,** they form one body. *4498*
12:14 not made up of one part but of **m.** *4498*
12:20 As it is, there are **m** parts, but one body. *4498*
16: 9 and there are **m** who oppose me. *4498*
2Co 1:11 Then **m** will give thanks on our behalf for *4498*
1:11 in answer to the prayers *of* **m.** *4498*
1:20 no matter **how m** promises God has made, *4012*
2: 4 and anguish of heart and with **m** tears, *4498*
2:17 so **m,** we do not peddle the word of God *4498*
6:10 poor, yet making **m** rich; *4498*
8:22 to us in **m** *ways* that he is zealous, *4498*
9:12 also overflowing in **m** expressions of thanks *4498*
11:18 **m** are boasting in the way the world does, *4498*
12:21 be grieved over **m** who have sinned earlier *4498*
Gal 1:14 I was advancing in Judaism beyond **m** Jews *4498*
3:16 meaning **m** *people,* but "and to your seed," *4498*
Php 3:18 **m** live as enemies of the cross of Christ. *4498*
1Ti 6: 9 and into **m** foolish and harmful desires *4498*
6:10 and pierced themselves *with* **m** griefs. *4498*
6:12 in the presence *of* **m** witnesses. *4498*
2Ti 1:18 in **how m** *ways* he helped me in Ephesus. *4012*
2: 2 in the presence of **m** witnesses entrust *4498*
Tit 1:10 For there are **m** rebellious people, *4498*
Heb 1: 1 prophets **at m times** and in various ways, *4495*
2:10 In bringing **m** sons to glory, *4498*
6:14 and **give** you **m descendants."** *4437+4437*
7:23 Now there have been **m** of those priests, *4498*
9:26 to suffer **m times** since the creation of *4490*
9:28 to take away the sins of **m** *people;* *4498*
12:15 up to cause trouble and defile **m.** *4498*
Jas 1: 2 whenever you face trials of **m kinds,** *4476*
3: 1 **m** of you should presume to be teachers, *4498*
3: 2 We all stumble in **m** *ways.* *4498*
2Pe 2: 2 **M** will follow their shameful ways *4498*
1Jn 2:18 even now **m** antichrists have come. *4498*
4: 1 because **m** false prophets have gone out into *4498*
2Jn 1: 7 **M** deceivers, who do not acknowledge *4498*
Rev 5:11 I looked and heard the voice *of* **m** angels, *4498*
8:11 and **m** people died from the waters *4498*
9: 9 *of* **m** horses and chariots rushing into battle. *4498*
10:11 "You must prophesy again about **m** peoples, *4498*
17: 1 the great prostitute, who sits on **m** waters. *4498*
19:12 and on his head are **m** crowns. *4498*

MAOCH (1)

1Sa 27: 2 and went over to Achish son of **M** king of 5059

MAON (8) [MAONITES]
Jos 15:55 **M,** Carmel, Ziph, Juttah, 5063
1Sa 23:24 David and his men were in the Desert of **M,** 5063
23:25 to the rock and stayed in the Desert of **M.** 5063
23:25 into the Desert of **M** in pursuit of David. 5063
25: 1 David moved down into the Desert of **M.** 5063
25: 2 A certain man in **M,** 5063
1Ch 2:45 The son of Shammai was **M,** 5062
2:45 and **M** was the father of Beth Zur. 5062

MAONITES (1) [MAON]
Jdg 10:12 the **M** oppressed you and you cried to me 5062

MAP (1)
Jos 18: 8 As the men started on their way to **m out** 4180

MAR (KJV) See BREAK UP, CLIP OFF, DESTROYING, ENDANGER

MARA (1)
Ru 1:20 call me Naomi," she told them. "Call me **M,** 5259

MARAH (4)
Ex 15:23 When they came to **M,** 5288
15:23 (That is why the place is called **M.**) 5288
Nu 33: 8 the Desert of Etham, they camped at **M.** 5288
33: 9 They left **M** and went to Elim, 5288

MARALAH (1)
Jos 19:11 Going west it ran to **M,** 5339

MARANATHA (KJV) See COME O LORD

MARAUDERS (3) [MARAUDING]
Job 12: 6 The tents of **m** are undisturbed, 8720
15:21 when all seems well, **m** attack him. 8720
Hos 6: 9 As **m** lie in ambush for a man, 1522

MARAUDING (1) [MARAUDERS]
Zec 9: 8 I will defend my house against **m** forces. 2256+6296+8740

MARBLE (5)
1Ch 29: 2 and all kinds of fine stone and **m**— 74+8880
Est 1: 6 to silver rings on **m** pillars. 9253
1: 6 **m,** mother-of-pearl and other costly stones. 9253
SS 5:15 His legs are pillars of **m** set on bases 9253
Rev 18:12 costly wood, bronze, iron and **m;** *3454*

MARCABOTH See BETH MARCABOTH

MARCH (24) [MARCHED, MARCHES, MARCHING]
Nu 10:28 the **order of m** for the Israelite divisions 5023
20:18 if you try, *we will* **m out** and attack you 3655
Dt 20:10 When *you* **m up** to attack a city, 7928
Jos 6: 3 **M around** the city once with all 5938+6015
6: 4 **m around** the city seven times, 6015
6: 7 "Advance! **M around** the city, 6015
10: 9 After an all-night **m** from Gilgal, 6590
Jdg 5:21 **M on,** my soul; be strong! 2005
2Sa 15:22 David said to Ittai, "Go ahead, **m on."** 6296
18: 2 *I* myself *will* **surely m out** with you." 3655+3655
2Ki 3: 9 After a roundabout **m** *of* seven days, 2006
18:25 *to* **m** against this country and destroy it.' " 6590
24: 7 not **m out** from his own country again, 3655
2Ch 20:16 Tomorrow **m down** against them. 3718
25: 7 not **m** with you, for the LORD is not 995
Isa 27: 4 *I would* **m** against them in battle; 7314
36:10 *to* **m** against this country and destroy it.' " 6590
42:13 The LORD *will* **m out** like a mighty man, 3655
Jer 46: 3 both large and small, and **m out** for battle! 5602
46: 9 **M on,** O warriors— 3655
Da 11:11 of the South *will* **m out** in a rage and fight 3655
Joel 2: 7 They all **m** in line, 2143
Ob 1:13 not **m** through the gates of my people in 995
Zec 9:14 *he will* **m** in the storms of the south, 2143

MARCHED (45) [MARCH]
Ge 14: 8 Zoar) **m out** and drew up their battle lines 3655
Nu 21:23 He mustered his entire army and **m out** into 3655
21:33 and his whole army **m out** to meet them 3655
33: 3 *They* **m out** boldly in full view of all 3655
Dt 1:43 and in your arrogance *you* **m up** into 6590
3: 1 with his whole army **m out** to meet us 3655
Jos 6: 9 The armed guard **m** ahead of 2143
6:14 the second day *they* **m around** the city once 6015
6:15 they got up at daybreak and **m around** 6015
8:10 the leaders of Israel **m** before them to Ai. 6590
8:11 The entire force that was with him **m up** 6590
10: 7 So Joshua **m up** from Gilgal 6590
15:15 From there *he* **m** against the people living 6590
Jdg 5: 4 when you **m** from the land of Edom, 7575
1Sa 29: 2 As the Philistine rulers **m** with their units 6296
2Sa 2:29 All that night Abner and his men **m** through 2143
2:32 and his men **m** all night and arrived 2143
5: 6 The king and his men **m** *to* Jerusalem 2143
15:18 All his men **m past** him, 3338+6296+6584
15:18 from Gath **m** before the king. 6296
15:22 So Ittai the Gittite **m on** with all his men 6296
18: 4 the gate while all the men **m out** in units 3655
18: 6 The army **m into** the field to fight Israel, 3655
20: 7 *They* **m out** from Jerusalem 3655
1Ki 20:19 of the provincial commanders **m out** of 3655
20:27 *they* **m out** to meet them. 2143
2Ki 6:24 and **m up** and laid siege to Samaria. 6590
16: 5 of Israel **m up** to fight *against* Jerusalem 6590
17: 5 **m** *against* Samaria and laid siege to it 6590
18: 9 of Assyria **m** against Samaria and laid siege 6590
23:29 King Josiah **m out** to meet him in battle, 2143
25: 1 Nebuchadnezzar king of Babylon **m** 995
1Ch 11: 4 and all the Israelites **m** *to* Jerusalem (that is, 2143
2Ch 14: 9 Zerah the Cushite **m out** against them with 3655
24:23 the army of Aram **m** against Joash; 6590
35:20 and Josiah **m out** to meet him in battle. 3655
Job 18:14 of his tent and **m off** to the king of terrors. 7575
Ps 68: 7 O God, when you **m** through the wasteland, 7575
Isa 7: 1 of Israel **m up** to fight against Jerusalem, 6590
Jer 37: 5 Pharaoh's army *had* **m out** of Egypt, 3655
37: 7 which *has* **m out** to support you, 3655
39: 1 Nebuchadnezzar king of Babylon **m** 995
52: 4 Nebuchadnezzar king of Babylon **m** 995
Heb 11:30 people *had* **m around** them for seven days. *3240*
Rev 20: 9 *They* **m** across the breadth of the earth *326*

MARCHES (5) [MARCH]
Joel 2: 8 each **m** straight ahead. 2143
Am 5: 3 "The city that **m out** a thousand strong 3655
5: 3 the town that **m out** a hundred strong 3655
Mic 5: 5 When the Assyrian invades our land and **m** 2005
5: 6 when he invades our land and **m** 2005

MARCHING (9) [MARCH]
Ex 14: 8 who *were* **m out** boldly. 3655
14:10 and there were the Egyptians, **m** after them. 5825
Jos 6:13 **m** before the ark of the LORD and blowing 2143
1Sa 29: 2 and his men *were* **m** at the rear with Achish. 6296
2Sa 5:24 as you hear the sound of **m** in the tops of 7577
2Ki 19: 9 *was* **m out** to fight against him. 3655
1Ch 14:15 as you hear the sound of **m** in the tops of 7577
2Ch 11: 4 and turned back from **m** against Jeroboam. 2143
Isa 37: 9 *was* **m out** to fight against him. 3655

MARCUS (KJV) See MARK

MARDUK (1)
Jer 50: 2 be put to shame, **M** filled with terror. 5281

MARE (1)
SS 1: 9 to a **m** harnessed to one of the chariots 6063

MARESHAH (8)
Jos 15:44 Aczib and **M**—nine towns and their villages 5358
1Ch 2:42 who was the father of Ziph, and his son **M,** 5359
4:21 the father of Lecah, Laadah the father of **M** 5359
2Ch 11: 8 Gath, **M,** Ziph, 5358
14: 9 and came as far as **M.** 5358
14:10 in the Valley of Zephathah near **M.** 5358
20:37 Eliezer son of Dodavahu of **M** prophesied 5358
Mic 1:15 a conqueror against you who live in **M.** 5358

MARINERS (2) [MARITIME]
Eze 27:27 your **m,** seamen and shipwrights, 4876
27:29 the **m** and all the seamen will stand on 4876

MARISHES (KJV) See MARSHES

MARITAL (4) [MARRY]
Ex 21:10 food, clothing and **m rights.** 6703
Mt 5:32 except for **m unfaithfulness,** *4518*
19: 9 except for **m unfaithfulness,** *4518*
1Co 7: 3 The husband should fulfill his **m** duty *NIG*

MARITIME (1) [MARINERS]
Ge 10: 5 (From these the **m** peoples spread out 362

MARK (30) [MARKED, MARKER, MARKS]
Ge 1:14 as signs to **m** seasons and days and years, NIH
4:15 Then the LORD put a **m** on Cain so 253
1Ki 22:28 he added, **"M my words,** all you people!" 9048
2Ch 18:27 he added, **"M my words,** all you people!" 9048
Job 36:32 and commands it *to* **strike** its **m.** 7003
Isa 59: 7 ruin and destruction **m** their ways. 928
Eze 9: 4 and **put a m** on the foreheads 9338+9344
9: 6 but do not touch anyone who has the **m.** 9338
21:19 **m out** two roads *for* the sword of the king 8492
21:20 **M out** one road for the sword to come 8492
Ac 12:12 of Mary the mother of John, also called **M,** *3453*
12:25 taking with them John, also called **M.** *3453*
15:37 wanted to take John, also called **M,** *3453*
15:39 Barnabas took **M** and sailed for Cyprus, *3453*
Ro 3:16 ruin and misery **m** their ways, *NIG*
2Co 12:12 The things that **m** an apostle— *4956*
Gal 5: 2 **M my words!** *3972*
Col 4:10 as does **M,** the cousin of Barnabas. *3453*
2Th 3:17 is **the distinguishing m** in all my letters. *4956*
2Ti 3: 1 But **m** this: There will be terrible times *1182*
2Ti 4:11 Get **M** and bring him with you, *3453*
Phm 1:24 And so do **M,** Aristarchus, *3453*
1Pe 5:13 and so does my son **M.** *3453*
Rev 13:16 a **m** on his right hand or on his forehead, *5916*
13:17 or sell unless he had the **m,** *5916*
14: 9 the beast and his image and receives his **m** *5916*
14:11 anyone who receives the **m** of his name." *5916*
16: 2 the **m** of the beast and worshiped his image. *5916*
19:20 the **m** of the beast and worshiped his image. *5916*
20: 4 or his image and had not received his **m** *5916*

MARKED (10) [MARK]
Jos 18:20 the boundaries that **m** out the inheritance of NIH
Job 15:22 he *is* **m** for the sword. 7595
38: 5 Who **m off** its dimensions? 8492
Pr 8:27 when he **m out** the horizon on the face of 2980
8:29 when he **m out** the foundations of the earth. 2980
Isa 40:12 the breadth of his hand **m off** the heavens? 9419
Zec 11: 4 "Pasture the **flock** *m for* slaughter. AIT
11: 7 So I pastured the **flock** *m for* slaughter, AIT
Eph 1:13 *you were* **m** in him **with a seal,** *5381*
Heb 12: 1 with perseverance the race **m out** for us. *4618*

MARKER (2) [MARK]
Isa 44:13 with a line and makes an outline with a **m;** 8574
Eze 39:15 he will set up a **m** beside it until 7483

MARKET (5) [MARKETPLACE, MARKETPLACES]
1Ki 20:34 "You may set up your own **m areas** 2575
Am 8: 5 Sabbath be ended that *we may* **m** wheat?"— 7337
Zep 1:11 Wail, you who live in the **m district;** 4847
Jn 2:16 you turn my Father's house into a **m!"** *1866+3875*
1Co 10:25 in the **meat m** without raising questions *3425*

MARKETPLACE (8) [MARKET]
Isa 23: 3 and she became the **m** *of* the nations. 6087
Eze 27:24 In your **m** they traded with you 5326
Mt 20: 3 standing in the **m** doing nothing. *59*
Mk 7: 4 When they come from the **m** they do not eat *59*
Lk 7:32 like children sitting in the **m** and calling out *59*
Ac 16:19 and Silas and dragged them into the **m** *59*
17: 5 up some bad characters *from* the **m,** *61*
17:17 the **m** day by day with those who happened *59*

MARKETPLACES (6) [MARKET]
Mt 11:16 like children sitting in the **m** and calling out *59*
23: 7 in the **m** and to have men call them 'Rabbi.' *59*
Mk 6:56 they placed the sick in the **m.** *59*
12:38 in flowing robes and be greeted in the **m,** *59*
Lk 11:43 in the synagogues and greetings in the **m.** *59*
20:46 and love to be greeted in the **m** and *59*

MARKS (10) [MARK]
Ge 35:20 and to this day that pillar **m** Rachel's tomb. NIH
Lev 19:28 for the dead or put tattoo **m** on yourselves. 4182
1Sa 21:13 like a madman, **making m** on the doors of 9344
2Ki 23:17 "It **m** the tomb of the man of God who came NIH
Job 13:27 on all my paths *by* **putting m** on the soles 2977
26:10 *He* **m out** the horizon on the face of 2552
Ps 104:19 The moon **m off** the seasons, 6913
Isa 44:13 with chisels and **m** it with compasses. 9306
Jn 20:25 the nail **m** in his hands and put my finger *5596*
Gal 6:17 for I bear on my body the **m** of Jesus. *5116*

MAROTH (1)
Mic 1:12 Those who live in **M** writhe in pain, 5300

MARRED (2)
Isa 52:14 and his form **m** beyond human likeness— NIH
Jer 18: 4 the pot he was shaping from the clay **was m** 8845

MARRIAGE (43) [MARRY]
Ge 29:26 **give** the younger daughter **in m** 5989
Ex 2:21 **gave** his daughter Zipporah to Moses **in m.** 5989
Lev 21: 4 **related** *to* him **by m,** 1251
Dt 22:16 **gave** my daughter **in m** 851+4200+5989
23: 2 **one born of a forbidden m** 4927
Jos 15:16 **give** my daughter Acsah **in m** 851+4200+5989
15:17 **gave** his daughter Acsah to him **in m.** 851+4200+5989
Jdg 1:12 **give** my daughter Acsah **in m** 851+4200+5989
1:13 **gave** his daughter Acsah to him **in m.** 851+4200+5989
3: 6 **took** their daughters **in m** 851+4200+4374
12: 9 **gave** his daughters **away in m** 8938
21: 1 **give** his daughter **in m** 851+4200+5989
21: 7 *to* **give** them any of our daughters **in m?"** 851+4200+5989
1Sa 17:25 **give** him his daughter **in m** 5989
18:17 **give** her to you **in m;** 851+4200+5989
18:19 she **was given in m** to Adriel 851+4200+5989
18:27 Saul **gave** him his daughter Michal **in m.** 851+4200+5989
1Ki 2:21 "*Let* Abishag the Shunammite **be given in m** to your brother Adonijah." 851+4200+5989
11:19 **gave** him a sister of his own wife, Queen Tahpenes, **in m.** 851+5989
2Ki 8:27 for he was **related by m** *to* Ahab's family. 3163
14: 9 **'Give** your daughter to my son **in m.'** 851+4200+5989

1Ch 2:35 Sheshan gave his daughter in m 851+4200+5989
5:1 but when he defiled his father's m bed, 3661
2Ch 18:1 allied himself with Ahab by m. 3161
25:18 'Give your daughter to my son in m.' 851+4200+5989
Ezr 9:12 do not give your daughters in m 5989
Ne 10:30 not to give our daughters in m 5989
13:25 You are not to give your daughters in m 5989
13:25 nor are you to take their daughters in m 5951
Jer 29:6 give your daughters in m, 408+4200+5989
Da 11:17 give him a daughter in m 851+2021+5989
Mal 2:14 the wife of your m covenant. 1382
Mt 19:12 and others have renounced m because of the kingdom 1571+2335+2336
22:30 neither marry nor be given in m; 1139
24:38 marrying and giving in m, 1139
Mk 12:25 they will neither marry nor be given in m; 1139
Lk 2:36 with her husband seven years after her m, NIG
17:27 marrying and being given in m up to 1139
20:34 of this age marry and are given in m. 1140
20:35 neither marry nor be given in m, 1139
Ro 7:2 she is released from the law of m. 467
Heb 13:4 M should be honored by all, 1141
13:4 and the m bed kept pure, 3130

MARRIAGES (1) [MARRY]

Ne 13:26 because of m like these that Solomon king NIH

MARRIED (78) [MARRY]

Ge 4:19 Lamech m two women, 4374
6:2 and they m any of them they chose. 851+4374
11:29 Abram and Nahor both m. 851+4374
20:3 she is a m woman." 1249+1251
24:67 of his mother Sarah, and he m Rebekah. 4374
25:20 when he m Rebekah daughter of Bethuel 851+2257+4200+4200+4374
26:34 he m Judith daughter of Beeri the Hittite, 851+4374
28:9 so he went to Ishmael and m Mahalath, 851+4374
38:2 He m her and lay with her; 4374
Ex 2:1 of the house of Levi m a Levite woman, 4374
6:20 Amram m his father's sister Jochebed, 851+4200+4374
6:23 Aaron m Elisheba, daughter of Amminadab 851+4200+4374
6:25 Eliezer son of Aaron m one of the daughters of Putiel, 851+4200+4374
22:16 seduces a virgin who is not pledged to be m 829
Nu 5:19 and become impure while m to 9393
5:20 But if you have gone astray while m to 9393
5:29 and defiles herself while m to her husband, 9393
12:1 for he had m a Cushite, 851+4374
36:11 m their cousins on their father's side. 851+2118+4200
36:12 They m within the clans of the 851+2118+4200
Dt 20:7 pledged to a woman and not m her? 4374
22:14 saying, "I m this woman, 4374
22:23 to meet in a town a virgin pledged to be m 829
22:25 a girl pledged to be m and rapes her, 829
22:28 a virgin who is not pledged to be m 829
24:5 If a man has recently m, 851+4374
24:5 and bring happiness to the wife he has m. 4374
28:30 You will be pledged to be m to a woman, 829
Ru 1:4 They m Moabite women, 851+5951
1Sa 25:43 David had also m Ahinoam of Jezreel, 4374
2Sa 13:13 he will not keep me from being m to you." NIH
17:25 an Israelite who had m Abigail, 448+995
1Ki 3:1 of Egypt and m his daughter. 4374
4:11 (he was m to Taphath daughter 851+2118+4200
4:15 (he had m Basemath daughter of 851+4200+4374
7:8 Pharaoh's daughter, whom he had m. 4374
16:31 m Jezebel daughter of Ethbaal king of 851+4374
2Ki 8:18 for he m a daughter of Ahab. 851+2118+4200
1Ch 2:19 When Azubah died, Caleb m Ephrath, 4374
2:21 (he had m her when he was sixty years old) 4374
4:18 Bithiah, whom Mered had m. 4374
23:22 Their cousins, the sons of Kish, m them. 5951
2Ch 11:18 Rehoboam m Mahalath, 851+4374
11:20 Then he m Maacah daughter of Absalom, 4374
13:21 He m fourteen wives and had 5951
21:6 for he m a daughter of Ahab. 851+2118
Ezr 2:61 Barzillai (a man who had m a daughter 851+4374
10:10 you have m foreign women, 3782
10:14 Then let everyone in our towns who has m 3782
10:17 with all the men who had m foreign women. 3782
10:18 the following had m foreign women: 3782
10:44 All these had m foreign women, 5951
Ne 6:18 and his son Jehohanan had m the daughter 4374
7:63 Barzillai (a man who had m a daughter 851+4374
13:23 of Judah who had m women from Ashdod, 3782
Pr 30:23 an unloved woman who is m, 1249
Isa 54:6 a wife who m young, only to be rejected," AIT
62:4 and your land will be m. 1249
Hos 1:3 So he m Gomer daughter of Diblaim, 4374
Mt 1:18 His mother Mary was pledged to be m 3650
22:25 The first one m and died, 1138
22:28 since all of them were m to her?" 2400
Mk 6:17 his brother Philip's wife, whom he had m. 1138
12:20 The first one m and died 1222+3284
12:21 The second one m the widow, 3284
12:23 since the seven were m to her?" 2400
Lk 1:27 to a virgin pledged to be m to a man 3650
2:5 Mary, who was pledged to be m to him 3650
14:20 "Still another said, 'I just got m, 1138+1222
20:29 one m a woman and died childless. 1222+3284
20:31 and then the third m her, 3284
20:33 since the seven were m to her?" 1222
Ro 7:2 a m woman is bound to her husband as long 5635
1Co 7:10 To the m I give this command (not I, but 1138
7:27 Are you m? Do not seek a divorce. 1222+1313
7:33 But a m man is concerned about the affairs 1138
7:34 a m woman is concerned about the affairs 1138
7:36 They should get m. 1138

MARRIES (20) [MARRY]

Ex 21:10 If he m another woman, 4374
Lev 20:14 a man m both a woman and her mother, 4374
20:17 " 'If a man m his sister, 4374
20:21 " 'If a man m his brother's wife, 4374
21:13 " 'The woman he m must be a virgin. 4374
22:12 If a priest's daughter m anyone other than a priest, 408+2118+4200
Nu 30:6 "If she m after she makes a vow or 408+2118+2118+4200
Dt 24:1 If a man m a woman who becomes displeasing to him because 1249+2256+4374
Isa 62:5 As a young man m a maiden, 1249
Jer 3:1 she leaves him and m another man, 2118+4200
Mt 5:32 and anyone who m the divorced woman 1138
19:9 and m another woman commits adultery." 1138
Mk 10:11 and m another woman commits adultery 1138
10:12 divorces her husband and m another man, 1138
Lk 16:18 and m another woman commits adultery, 1138
16:18 and the man who m a divorced woman 1138
Ro 7:3 if she m another man while her husband is 1181
7:3 even though she m another man. 1181
1Co 7:28 and if a virgin m, she has not sinned. 1138
7:38 So then, he who m the virgin does right, 1139

MARROW (2)

Job 21:24 body well nourished, his bones rich with m. 4672
Heb 4:12 to dividing soul and spirit, joints and m; 3678

MARRY (49) [INTERMARRY, MARITAL, MARRIAGE, MARRIAGES, MARRIED, MARRIES, MARRYING]

Ge 19:14 who were pledged to m his daughters. 4374
28:1 "Do not m a Canaanite woman. 851+4374
28:6 "Do not m a Canaanite woman," 851+4374
34:21 We can m their daughters 851+4200+4374
34:21 and they can m ours. 5989
Lev 21:7 not m women defiled by prostitution 4374
21:14 He must not m a widow, a divorced woman, 4374
Nu 36:3 Now suppose they m men 851+2118+4200
36:3 added to that of the tribe they m into, 2118+4200
36:4 to that of the tribe into which they m, 2118+4200
36:6 They may m anyone they please as long as 851+2118+4200
36:6 as long as they m within the tribal clan 851+2118+4200
36:8 must m someone in her father's tribal clan, 851+2118+4200
Dt 20:7 die in battle and someone else m her." 4374
22:29 He must m the girl, for he has violated her. 851+2118+4200
22:30 A man is not to m his father's wife; 4374
24:4 to m her again after she has been defiled. 851+4200+4374
25:5 his widow must not m outside the family. 408+2118+4200
25:5 and m her and fulfill the duty of 851+4200+4374
25:7 man does not want to m his brother's wife, 4374
25:8 "I do not want to m her," 4374
Jdg 11:37 because I will never m." 1436
11:38 and wept because she would never m. 1436
14:8 when he went back to m her, 4374
Isa 62:5 so will your sons m you; 1249
Jer 16:2 "You must not m and have sons or 851+4374
29:6 M and have sons and daughters; 851+4374
Eze 44:22 not m widows or divorced women; 851+4200+4374
44:22 they may m only virgins of Israelite descent 4374
Mt 19:10 it is better not to m." 1138
22:24 his brother must m the widow 2102
22:30 the resurrection people will neither m nor 1138
Mk 12:19 the man must m the widow 3284
12:25 they will neither m nor be given 1138
Lk 20:28 the man must m the widow 3284
20:34 "The people of this age m and are given 1138
20:35 from the dead will neither m nor be given 1138
1Co 7:1 It is good for a man not to m. 721+1222
7:9 they should m, for it is better to marry than 1138
7:9 it is better to m than to burn with passion. 1138
7:28 But if you do m, you have not sinned; 1138
7:28 But those who m will face many troubles 3836+5525S
7:36 and he feels he ought to m, 1181+4048S
7:37 and who has made up his mind not to m 5498
7:38 but he who does not m her does even better. 1139
7:39 she is free to m anyone she wishes, 1138
1Ti 4:3 They forbid people to m and order them 1138
5:11 their dedication to Christ, they want to m. 1138
5:14 So I counsel younger widows to m, 1138

MARRYING (5) [MARRY]

Ezr 10:2 by m foreign women from the peoples 3782
Ne 13:27 to our God by m foreign women?" 3782
Mal 2:11 by m the daughter of a foreign god. 1249
Mt 24:38 m and giving in marriage, 1138
Lk 17:27 m and being given in marriage up to 1138

MARS' (KJV) See AREOPAGUS

MARSENA (1)

Est 1:14 Tarshish, Meres, M and Memucan, 5333

MARSH (2)

Job 8:11 Can papyrus grow tall where there is no m? 1289
40:21 hidden among the reeds in the m. 1289

MARSHAL (2) [MARSHALED]

Mic 5:1 M your troops, O city of troops, 1518
Na 2:1 brace yourselves, m all your strength! 599

MARSHALED (4) [MARSHAL]

2Ch 25:11 then m his strength and led his army to 2616
Job 6:4 God's terrors are m against me. 6885
32:14 But Job has not m his words against me, 6885
Isa 45:12 I m their starry hosts. 7422

MARSHES (2)

Jer 51:32 the m set on fire, and the soldiers terrified." 106
Eze 47:11 the swamps and m will not become fresh; 1465

MARTHA (13)

Lk 10:38 where a woman named M opened her home 3450
10:40 But M was distracted by all the preparations 3450
10:41 "M, Martha," the Lord answered, 3450
10:41 "Martha, M," the Lord answered, 3450
Jn 11:1 the village of Mary and her sister M. 3450
11:5 Jesus loved M and her sister and Lazarus. 3450
11:19 to M and Mary to comfort them in the loss 3450
11:20 When M heard that Jesus was coming, 3450
11:21 "Lord," M said to Jesus, 3450
11:24 M answered, "I know he will rise again in 3450
11:30 was still at the place where M had met him. 3450
11:39 Lord," said M, the sister of the dead man, 3450
12:2 M served, while Lazarus was 3450

MARTYR (1)

Ac 22:20 the blood of your m Stephen was shed, 3459

MARVELED (2) [MARVELOUS]

Lk 2:33 mother m at what was said about him. 1639+2513
2Th 1:10 to be m at among all those who have believed. 2513

MARVELING (1) [MARVELOUS]

Lk 9:43 While everyone was m at all that Jesus did, 2513

MARVELOUS (15) [MARVELED, MARVELING]

1Ch 16:24 his m deeds among all peoples. 7098
Job 37:5 God's voice thunders in m ways; 7098
Ps 71:17 and to this day I declare your m deeds. 7098
72:18 the God of Israel, who alone does m deeds. 7098
86:10 For you are great and do m deeds; 7098
96:3 his m deeds among all peoples. 7098
98:1 for he has done m things; 7098
118:23 and it is m in our eyes. 7098
Isa 25:1 in perfect faithfulness you have done m things, 7099
Zec 8:6 "It may seem m to the remnant 7098
8:6 but will it seem m to me?" 7098
Mt 21:42 Lord has done this, and it is m in our eyes'? 2515
Mk 12:11 Lord has done this, and it is m in our eyes'? 2515
Rev 15:1 I saw in heaven another great and m sign: 2515
15:3 "Great and m are your deeds, 2515

MARY (57) [MARY'S]

Mt 1:16 the husband of M, of whom was born Jesus, 3451
1:18 His mother M was pledged to be married 3451
1:20 not be afraid to take M home as your wife, 3451
1:24 and took M home as his wife. NIG
2:11 they saw the child with his mother M, 3451
13:55 Isn't his mother's name M, 3451
27:56 Among them were M Magdalene, 3451
27:56 M the mother of James and Joses, 3451
27:61 M Magdalene and the other Mary were sitting there opposite the tomb. 3451
27:61 and the other M were sitting there opposite 3451
28:1 M Magdalene and the other Mary went 3451
28:1 and the other M went to look at the tomb. 3451
Mk 15:40 Among them were M Magdalene, 3451
15:40 M the mother of James the younger and 3451
15:47 M Magdalene and Mary the mother 3451
15:47 Mary Magdalene and M the mother 3451
16:1 When the Sabbath was over, M Magdalene, 3451
16:1 Mary Magdalene, M the mother of James, 3451
16:9 he appeared first to M Magdalene, 3451
Lk 1:27 The virgin's name was M. 3451
1:29 M was greatly troubled at his words 1254+3836S
1:30 the angel said to her, "Do not be afraid, M, 3451
1:34 "How will this be," M asked the angel, 3451
1:38 "I am the Lord's servant," M answered. 3451
1:39 that time M got ready and hurried to a town 3451
1:46 And M said: "My soul glorifies the Lord 3451

Lk 1:56 M stayed with Elizabeth for about three 3451
2: 5 He went there to register with M, 3451
2:16 they hurried off and found M and Joseph, 3451
2:19 But M treasured up all these things 3451
2:22 and M took him to Jerusalem to present him NIG
2:34 Then Simeon blessed them and said to M, 3451
2:39 and M had done everything required by NIG
8: 2 M (called Magdalene) from whom seven demons had come out; 3451
10:39 She had a sister called M, 3451
10:42 M has chosen what is better, 3451
24:10 It was M Magdalene, Joanna, 3451
24:10 Joanna, M the mother of James, 3451
Jn 11: 1 the village *of* M and her sister Martha. 3451
11: 2 This M, whose brother Lazarus 3451
11:19 and many Jews had come to Martha and M 3451
11:20 but M stayed at home. 3451
11:28 she went back and called her sister M aside. 3451
11:29 When M heard this, she got up quickly 1697S
11:31 Jews who had been with M in the house, 899S
11:32 When M reached the place where Jesus was 3451
11:45 many of the Jews who had come to visit M, 3451
12: 3 Then M took about a pint of pure nard, 3451
19:25 his mother's sister, M the wife of Clopas, 3451
19:25 the wife of Clopas, and M Magdalene. 3451
20: 1 M Magdalene went to the tomb and saw 3451
20:11 but M stood outside the tomb crying. 3451
20:16 Jesus said to her, "M." 3451
20:18 M Magdalene went to the disciples with 3451
Ac 1:14 with the women and M the mother of Jesus, 3451
12:12 to the house *of* M the mother of John, 3451
Ro 16: 6 Greet M, who worked very hard for you. 3451

MARY'S (2) [MARY]

Mk 6: 3 Isn't this M son and the brother of James, 3451
Lk 1:41 When Elizabeth heard M greeting, 3451

MASH (1)

Isa 30:24 that work the soil will eat fodder and m, 2796

MASHAL (1)

1Ch 6:74 from the tribe of Asher they received M, 5443

MASK (1)

1Th 2: 5 nor *did we* put on a m to cover up greed— 4733

MASKIL (13)

Ps 32: T Of David. A m. 5380
42: T A m of the Sons of Korah. 5380
44: T Of the Sons of Korah. A m. 5380
45: T Of the Sons of Korah. A m. 5380
52: T A m of David. 5380
53: T A m of David. 5380
54: T A m of David. 5380
55: T A m of David. 5380
74: T A m of Asaph. 5380
78: T A m of Asaph. 5380
88: T A m of Heman the Ezrahite. 5380
89: T A m of Ethan the Ezrahite. 5380
142: T A m of David. 5380

MASONS (5)

2Ki 12:12 the m and stonecutters. 1553
22: 6 the builders and the m. 1553
1Ch 22:15 stonecutters, m and carpenters, 74+3093
2Ch 24:12 They hired m and carpenters to restore 2935
Ezr 3: 7 they gave money to the m and carpenters, 2935

MASQUERADE (1) [MASQUERADES, MASQUERADING]

2Co 11:15 his servants m as servants of righteousness. 3571

MASQUERADES (1) [MASQUERADE]

2Co 11:14 for Satan himself m as an angel of light. 3571

MASQUERADING (1) [MASQUERADE]

2Co 11:13 deceitful workmen, m as apostles of Christ. 3571

MASREKAH (2)

Ge 36:36 Samlah from M succeeded him as king. 5388
1Ch 1:47 Samlah from M succeeded him as king. 5388

MASSA (2)

Ge 25:14 Mishma, Dumah, M, 5364
1Ch 1:30 Mishma, Dumah, M, Hadad, Tema, 5364

MASSACRE (1)

Hos 1: 4 the house of Jehu for the m *at* Jezreel, 1947

MASSAH (5)

Ex 17: 7 And he called the place M and Meribah 5001
Dt 6:16 the LORD your God as you did at M. 5001
9:22 at M and at Kibroth Hattaavah. 5001
33: 8 You tested him at M; 5001
Ps 95: 8 as you did that day at M in the desert, 5001

MASSES (2) [MASSING]

Isa 5:13 and their m will be parched with thirst. 2162
Isa 5:14 and m with all their brawlers and revelers. 2162

MASSING (1) [MASSES]

Isa 13: 4 like nations m together! 665

MASSIVE (1)

Mk 13: 1 What m stones! 4534

MAST (2)

Isa 33:23 m is not held secure, the sail is not spread. 4029+9568
Eze 27: 5 a cedar from Lebanon to make a m for you. 9568

MASTER (164) [MASTER'S, MASTERED, MASTERS, MASTERS', MASTERY]

Ge 4: 7 it desires to have you, but you *must* m it." 5440
18:12 "After I am worn out and my m is old, 123
24: 9 of his m Abraham and swore an oath to him 123
24:10 of good things from his m. 123
24:12 "O LORD, God of my m Abraham, 123
24:12 and show kindness to my m Abraham. 123
24:14 that you have shown kindness to my m." 123
24:27 the LORD, the God of my m Abraham, 123
24:27 and faithfulness to my m. 123
24:35 The LORD has blessed my m abundantly, 123
24:37 And my m made me swear an oath, 123
24:39 "Then I asked my m, 123
24:42 I said, 'O LORD, God of my m Abraham, 123
24:48 the LORD, tthe God of my m Abraham, 123
24:49 and faithfulness to my m, tell me; 123
24:54 he said, "Send me on my way to my m." 123
24:56 Send me on my way so I may go to my m." 123
24:65 "He is my m," the servant answered. 123
32: 4 "This is what you are to say to my m Esau: 123
39: 2 and he lived in the house of his Egyptian m. 123
39: 3 When his m saw that the LORD was 123
39: 8 "my m does not concern himself 123
39: 9 My m has withheld nothing NIH
39:16 beside her until his m came home. 123
39:19 When his m heard the story his wife told 123
39:20 Joseph's m took him and put him in prison, 123
40: 1 of the king of Egypt offended their m. 123
44: 5 the cup my m drinks from and also uses 123
Ex 21: 4 If his m gives him a wife 123
21: 4 and her children shall belong to her m, 123
21: 5 'I love my m and my wife and children 123
21: 6 then his m must take him before the judges. 123
21: 8 the m who has selected her for himself, 123
21:32 shekels of silver to the m *of* the slave, 123
35:35 of them m craftsmen and designers. 4856+6913
Dt 23:15 do not hand him over to his m. 123
Jdg 19:11 the servant said to his m, "Come, 123
19:12 His m replied, "No. 123
19:26 to the house where her m was staying, 123
19:27 When her m got up in the morning 123
1Sa 20:38 up the arrow and returned to his m. 123
24: 6 such a thing to my m, the LORD's anointed, 123
24:10 I said, 'I will not lift my hand against my m, 123
25:14 from the desert to give our m his greetings, 123
25:17 because disaster is hanging over our m 123
25:25 I did not see the men my m sent. 123
25:26 since the LORD has kept you, my m, 123
25:26 and all who intend to harm my m be 123
25:27 which your servant has brought to my m, 123
25:28 a lasting dynasty for my m, 123
25:29 the life of my m will be bound securely in 123
25:30 for my m every good thing he promised 123
25:31 my m will not have on his conscience 123
25:31 the LORD has brought my m success, 123
26:16 because you did not guard your m, 123
30:13 My m abandoned me when I became ill 123
30:15 not kill me or hand me over to my m, 123
2Sa 2: 5 for showing this kindness to Saul your m 123
2: 7 for Saul your m is dead, 123
9:10 And Mephibosheth, grandson of your m, 123
11:11 and my m Joab and my lord's men 123
1Ki 11:23 who had fled from his m, 123
18: 8 "Go tell your m, 'Elijah is here.' " 123
18:10 where my m has not sent someone to look 123
18:11 But now you tell me to go to my m and say, 123
18:14 now you tell me to go to my m and say, 123
22:17 'These people have no m. 123
2Ki 2: 3 that the LORD is going to take your m 123
2: 5 that the LORD is going to take your m 123
2:16 Let them go and look for your m. 123
5: 1 in the sight of his m and highly regarded, 123
5: 3 "If only my m would see the prophet who is 123
5: 4 Naaman went to his m and told him what 123
5:18 When my m enters the temple of Rimmon 123
5:20 "My m was too easy on Naaman, 123
5:22 "My m sent me to say, 123
5:25 he went in and stood before his m Elisha. 123
6:22 and drink and then go back to their m." 123
6:23 and they returned to their m. 123
8:14 Hazael left Elisha and returned to his m. 123
9: 7 to destroy the house of Ahab your m, 123
9:31 Zimri, you murderer of your m?" 123
10: 9 It was I who conspired against my m 123
18:23 " 'Come now, make a bargain with my m, 123
18:27 to your m and you that my master sent me 123
18:27 that my m sent me to say these things, and 123
19: 4 whom his m, the king of Assyria, 123
19: 6 "Tell your m, 'This is what 123
1Ch 12:19 our heads if he deserts to his m Saul.") 123
2Ch 13: 6 rebelled against his m. 123
18:16 'These people have no m. 123
Job 3:19 and the slave is freed from his m. 123
Ps 12: 4 we own our lips—who is our m?" 123
105:21 He made him m of his household, 123
123: 2 of slaves look to the hand of their m, 123
Pr 27:18 he who looks after his m will be honored. 123
30:10 "Do not slander a servant to his m, 123
Isa 1: 3 The ox knows his m, 7864
19: 4 over to the power of a cruel m, 123
24: 2 for m as for servant, 123
36: 8 " 'Come now, make a bargain with my m, 123
36:12 to your m and you that my master sent me 123
36:12 that my m sent me to say these things, and 123
37: 4 whom his m, the king of Assyria, 123
37: 6 "Tell your m, 'This is what 123
Jer 22:18 They will not mourn for him: 'Alas, my m! 123
34: 5 in your honor and lament, "Alas, O m!" 123
Da 8:23 a stern-faced king, a m *of* intrigue, 1067
Hos 2:16 you will no longer call me 'my m.' 1251
Mal 1: 6 son honors his father, and a servant his m. 123
1: 6 If I am a m, where is the respect due me?" 123
Mt 10:24 nor a servant above his m. 3261
10:25 and the servant like his m. 3261
18:25 the m ordered that he and his wife 3261
18:27 The servant's m took pity on him, 3261
18:31 and went and told their m everything 3261
18:32 "Then the m called the servant in. 3261
18:34 In anger his m turned him over to the jailers 3261
23: 8 for you have only one M 1437
24:45 the m has put in charge of the servants 3261
24:46 for that servant whose m finds him doing so 3261
24:48 'My m is staying away a long time,' 3261
24:50 The m of that servant will come on a day 3261
25:19 a long time the m of those servants returned 3261
25:20 'M,' he said, 'you entrusted me 3261
25:21 "His m replied, 'Well done, 3261
25:22 'M,' he said, 'you entrusted me 3261
25:23 "His m replied, 'Well done, 3261
25:24 'M,' he said, 'I knew that you are 3261
25:26 "His m replied, 'You wicked, lazy servant! 3261
Lk 5: 5 "M, we've worked hard all night 2181
7: 2 whom his m valued highly, 899S
8:24 disciples went and woke him, saying, "M, 2181
8:24 saying, "Master, M, we're going to drown!" 2181
8:45 When they all denied it, Peter said, "M, 2181
9:33 "M, it is good for us to be here. 2181
9:49 "M," said John, "we saw a man driving out 2181
12:36 like men waiting for their m to return from 3261
12:37 servants whose m finds them watching 3261
12:38 those servants whose m finds them ready, NIG
12:42 whom the m puts in charge of his servants 3261
12:43 for that servant whom the m finds doing so 3261
12:45 'My m is taking a long time in coming,' 3261
12:46 The m of that servant will come on a day 3261
12:47 not do what his m wants will be beaten 899S
14:21 and reported this *to* his m. 3261
14:23 "Then the m told his servant, 3261
16: 3 My m is taking away my job. 3261
16: 5 'How much do you owe my m?' 3261
16: 8 "The m commended the dishonest manager 3261
17:13 "Jesus, M, have pity on us!" 2181
19:17 "Well done, my good servant!" his m replied. NIG
19:19 "His m answered, 'You take charge 4047S
19:22 "His m replied, 'I will judge you NIG
Jn 2: 8 and take it *to* the m of the banquet." 804
2: 9 and the m of the banquet tasted the water 804
13:16 no servant is greater than his m, 3261
15:20 'No servant is greater than his m.' 3261
Ro 6:14 For sin *shall* not *be* your m, 3259
14: 4 *To* his own m he stands or falls. 3261
Eph 6: 9 since you know that he who is both their M 3261
Col 4: 1 you know that you also have a M in heaven. 3261
2Ti 2:21 the M and prepared to do any good work. 1305
1Pe 3: 6 who obeyed Abraham and called him her m. 3261

MASTER'S (34) [MASTER]

Ge 24:10 servant took ten of his m camels and left, 123
24:27 the journey to the house of my m relatives." 123
24:36 My m wife Sarah has borne him a son 123
24:44 the LORD has chosen for my m son.' 123
24:48 to get the granddaughter of my m brother 123
24:51 and let her become the wife of your m son, 123
39: 7 a while his m wife took notice of Joseph 123
40: 7 in custody with him in his m house, 123
44: 8 or gold from your m house? 123
1Sa 25:41 and wash the feet of my m servants." 123
29: 4 How better could he regain his m favor than 123
29:10 along with your m servants who have come 123
2Sa 9: 9 "I have given your m grandson everything 123
9:10 that your m grandson may be provided for. 123
11: 9 to the palace with all his m servants and did 123
11:13 to sleep on his mat among his m servants; 123
12: 8 I gave your m house to you, 123
12: 8 and your m wives into your arms. 123
16: 3 "Where is your m grandson?" 123
20: 6 Take your m men and pursue him, 123
2Ki 6:32 the sound of his m footsteps behind him?" 123
10: 2 since your m sons are with you 123
10: 3 and most worthy of your m sons and set him 123
10: 3 Then fight for your m house." 123
10: 6 of your m sons and come to me in Jezreel 123
18:24 of the least of my m officials, 123
Isa 22:18 you disgrace to your m house! 123
36: 9 of the least of my m officials, 123

Mt 25:18 a hole in the ground and hid his **m** money. *3261*
25:21 Come and share your **m** happiness!' *3261*
25:23 Come and share your **m** happiness!' *3261*
Lk 12:47 "That servant who knows his **m** will *3261*
16: 5 "So he called in each one of his **m** debtors. *3261*
Jn 15:15 a servant does not know his **m** business. *3261*

MASTERBUILDER (KJV) See EXPERT BUILDER

MASTERED (2) [MASTER]

1Co 6:12 but I *will* not *be* **m** by anything. *2027*
2Pe 2:19 for a man is a slave to whatever *has* **m** him. *2487*

MASTERS (16) [MASTER]

Ex 1:11 So they put slave **m** over them 8569
1Sa 25:10 breaking away from their **m** these days. 123
Pr 25:13 he refreshes the spirit of his **m**. 123
Jer 27: 4 Give them a message for their **m** and say, 123
27: 4 "Tell this to your **m**: 123
La 1: 5 Her foes have become her **m**; 8031
Mt 6:24 "No one can serve two **m**. *3261*
Lk 16:13 "No servant can serve two **m**. *3261*
Eph 6: 5 obey your earthly **m** with respect and fear, *3261*
6: 9 And **m**, treat your slaves in the same way. *3261*
Col 3:22 Slaves, obey your earthly **m** in everything; *3261*
4: 1 **M**, provide your slaves with what is right *3261*
1Ti 6: 1 of slavery should consider their **m** worthy *1305*
6: 2 Those who have believing **m** are not *1305*
Tit 2: 9 to be subject to their **m** in everything, *1305*
1Pe 2:18 submit yourselves *to* your **m** *1305*

MASTERS' (1) [MASTER]

Mt 15:27 the crumbs that fall from their **m'** table." *3261*

MASTERY (1) [MASTER]

Ro 6: 9 death no longer **has m over** him. *3259*

MAT (15) [MATS]

2Sa 11:13 on his **m** among his master's servants; 5435
Mt 9: 2 brought to him a paralytic, lying on a **m**. *3109*
9: 6 "Get up, take your **m** and go home." *3109*
Mk 2: 4 the **m** the paralyzed man was lying on. *3187*
2: 9 or to say, 'Get up, take your **m** and walk'? *3187*
2:11 get up, take your **m** and go home." *3187*
2:12 took his **m** and walked out in full view *3187*
Lk 5:18 Some men came carrying a paralytic on a **m** *3109*
5:19 on his **m** through the tiles into the middle of *3110*
5:24 get up, take your **m** and go home. *3110*
Jn 5: 8 Pick up your **m** and walk." *3187*
5: 9 he picked up his **m** and walked. *3187*
5:10 the law forbids you to carry your **m**." *3187*
5:11 'Pick up your **m** and walk.' " *3187*
Ac 9:34 Get up and **take care of** *your* **m**." *4932+5143*

MATCH (3) [MATCHED, MATCHING]

1Ch 12:14 the least was a **m for** a hundred, 4200
Eze 31: 8 in the garden of God *could* **m** its beauty. 1948
Lk 5:36 the patch from the new *will* not **m** the old. *5244*

MATCHED (1) [MATCH]

2Co 8:11 willingness to do it may be **m** by your completion of it, *2749+2779+4048*

MATCHING (1) [MATCH]

Ezr 1:10 gold bowls 30 **m** silver bowls 410 5467

MATE (7) [MATED, MATING]

Ge 7: 2 a male and its **m**, 851
7: 2 a male and its **m**, 851
30:41 in front of the animals so they *would* **m** near 3501
Lev 19:19 " *'Do* not **m** different kinds of animals. 8061
Isa 34:15 also the falcons will gather, each with its **m**. 8295
34:16 not one will lack her **m**. 8295
Na 2:12 and strangled the prey for his **m**, 4218

MATED (1) [MATE]

Ge 30:39 they **m** in front of the branches. 3501

MATERIAL (18) [MATERIALS]

Ex 26: 4 of **blue m** along the edge of the end curtain 9418
36:11 of **blue m** along the edge of the end curtain 9418
Lev 13:48 or **knitted m** of linen or wool, any leather 6849
13:49 or leather, or woven or **knitted m**, 6849
13:51 or the woven or **knitted m**, or the leather, 6849
13:52 or the woven or **knitted m** of wool or linen, 6849
13:53 or the woven or **knitted m**, 6849
13:56 or the leather, or the woven or **knitted m**. 6849
13:57 or in the woven or **knitted m**, 6849
13:58 The clothing, or the woven or **knitted m**, 6849
13:59 woven or **knitted m**, or any leather article, 6849
14:41 inside walls of the house scraped and the **m** 6760
19:19 **woven** of two kinds of **m**. 9122
Est 1: 6 of white linen and **purple m** to silver rings 763
Pr 25: 4 and out comes **m** for the silversmith; 3998
Ro 15:27 to share with them their **m** blessings. *4920*
1Co 9:11 is it too much if we reap a **m** harvest *4920*
1Jn 3:17 If anyone has **m** possessions *3180*

MATERIALS (2) [MATERIAL]

Ex 38:21 These are the amounts of the **m** used for NIH
Ne 4:17 Those who carried **m** did their work 6023

MATHUSALA (KJV) See METHUSELAH

MATING (3) [MATE]

Ge 31:10 and saw that the male goats **m with** 6584+6590
31:12 the male goats **m with** the flock are streaked, 6584+6590
Jer 2:24 at **m time** they will find her. 2544

MATRED (2)

Ge 36:39 wife's name was Mehetabel daughter of **M**, 4765
1Ch 1:50 wife's name was Mehetabel daughter of **M**, 4765

MATRI'S (1)

1Sa 10:21 clan by clan, and **M** clan was chosen. 4767

MATRIX (KJV) See WOMB

MATS (2) [MAT]

Mk 6:55 that whole region and carried the sick on **m** *3187*
Ac 5:15 into the streets and laid them on beds and **m** *3187*

MATTAN (3)

2Ki 11:18 and idols to pieces and killed **M** the priest 5509
2Ch 23:17 the altars and idols and killed **M** the priest 5509
Jer 38: 1 Shephatiah son of **M**, 5509

MATTANAH (2)

Nu 21:18 Then they went from the desert to **M**, 5511
21:19 from **M** to Nahaliel, 5511

MATTANIAH (16)

2Ki 24:17 He made **M**, Jehoiachin's uncle, king 5514
1Ch 9:15 Galal and **M** son of Mica, the son of Zicri, 5514
25: 4 Bukkiah, **M**, Uzziel, Shubael and Jerimoth; 5515
25:16 the ninth to **M**, his sons and relatives, 12 5515
2Ch 20:14 the son of Jeiel, the son of **M**, 5514
29:13 of Asaph, Zechariah and **M**; 5515
Ezr 10:26 From the descendants of Elam: **M**, 5514
10:27 Elioenai, Eliashib, **M**, Jeremoth, 5514
10:30 Adna, Kelal, Benaiah, Maaseiah, **M**, 5514
10:37 **M**, Mattenai and Jaasu. 5514
Ne 11:17 **M** son of Mica, the son of Zabdi, the son 5514
11:22 the son of Hashabiah, the son of **M**, 5514
12: 8 Kadmiel, Sherebiah, Judah, and also **M**, 5514
12:25 **M**, Bakbukiah, Obadiah, Meshullam, 5514
12:35 the son of Shemaiah, the son of **M**, 5514
13:13 the son of **M**, their assistant, 5514

MATTATHA (1)

Lk 3:31 the son *of* **M**, the son of Nathan, *3477*

MATTATHAH (KJV) See MATTATTAH

MATTATHIAS (2)

Lk 3:25 the son **of M**, the son of Amos, *3478*
3:26 the son *of* **M**, the son of Semein, *3478*

MATTATTAH (1)

Ezr 10:33 Mattenai, **M**, Zabad, Eliphelet, Jeremai, 5523

MATTENAI (3)

Ezr 10:33 **M**, Mattattah, Zabad, Eliphelet, Jeremai, 5513
10:37 Mattaniah, **M** and Jaasu. 5513
Ne 12:19 of Joiarib's, **M**; of Jedaiah's, Uzzi; 5513

MATTER (69) [MATTERED, MATTERS]

Ge 21:11 The **m** distressed Abraham greatly 1821
21:17 **"What is the m,** Hagar? 3871+4200+4537
24: 9 and swore an oath to him concerning this **m**. 1821
37:11 but his father kept the **m** in mind. 1821
41:32 that the **m** has been firmly decided by God, 1821
Lev 4:13 though the community is unaware of the **m**, 1821
5: 4 in any **m** one might carelessly swear about 889[S]
Nu 18:32 of it you will not be guilty in **this m**; 2257[S]
Dt 3:26 "Do not speak to me anymore about this **m**. 1821
19:15 A **m** must be established by the testimony 1821
Jos 22:31 unfaithfully toward the LORD in this **m**. 5086
Jdg 18:23 **"What's the m** with you 4537
18:24 **'What's the m** with you?' " 4537
Ru 3:18 not rest until the **m** is settled today." 1821
4: 4 the **m** to your attention and suggest NIH
1Sa 17:30 and brought up the same **m**, 1821
18:23 *"Do* you think *it is a* **small** *m* to become AIT
20:23 And about the **m** you and I discussed— 1821
21: 2 "The king charged me with a *certain* **m** 1821
2Sa 15:11 knowing nothing about the **m**. 1821
2Ki 6:28 Then he asked her, **"What's the m?"** 4537
20:10 *"It is a* **simple** *m* for the shadow AIT
1Ch 26:32 of Manasseh for every **m** *pertaining to* God 1821
2Ch 8:15 to the priests or to the Levites in any **m**, 1821
19:11 over you in any **m** *concerning* the LORD, 1821
19:11 be over you in any **m** *concerning* the king, 1821
Ezr 4:22 Be careful not to neglect **this** *m*. AIT
Ezr 5:17 let the king send us his decision in **this** *m*. AIT
10: 4 Rise up; this **m** is in your hands. 1821
10:13 this **m** cannot be taken care of in a day 4856
10:14 of our God in this **m** is turned away 1821
Job 9:19 If it is **a m** of strength, he is mighty! 4200
9:19 And if it is **a m** of justice, 4200
Pr 17: 9 repeats the **m** separates close friends. 1821
17:14 so drop the **m** before a dispute breaks out. NIH
25: 2 It is the glory of God to conceal a **m**; 1821
25: 2 to search out a **m** is the glory of kings. 1821
Ecc 6: 3 yet no **m** how long he lives, NIH
7: 8 The end of a **m** is better than its beginning, 1821
8: 6 a proper time and procedure for every **m**, 2914
12:13 here is the conclusion of the **m**: 1821
Isa 43:26 *let us* **argue** *the m* together; AIT
Eze 8:17 *Is it a* **trivial** *m* for the house of Judah AIT
Da 1:20 In every **m** *of* wisdom and understanding 1821
2:15 Arioch then explained the **m** to Daniel. 10418
2:17 returned to his house and explained the **m** 10418
3:16 to defend ourselves before you in **this** *m*. AIT
7:28 "This is the end of the **m**. 10418
7:28 but I kept the **m** to myself." 10418
Mt 18:16 so that 'every **m** may be established by the *4839*
Mk 9:10 They kept the **m** to themselves, *3364*
Lk 19:17 have been trustworthy in a **very small** *m*, *AIT*
20:14 *they* **talked the m over.** *253+1368+4639*
Jn 3:25 Jew **over the m of** ceremonial washing. *4309*
Ac 18:15 **settle the m** yourselves. *3972*
Ro 4: 1 our forefather, discovered in this **m?** *NIG*
14:17 For the kingdom of God is not a **m** of eating *NIG*
1Co 4:20 For the kingdom of God is not a **m** of talk *NIG*
7:37 But the man who *has* **settled the m** *1612+2705*
2Co 1:20 no **m** how many promises God has made, *NIG*
7:11 to be innocent *in* this **m**. *4547*
8:10 about what is best for you in this **m**: *NIG*
9: 3 that our boasting about you in this **m** should *3538*
13: 1 "Every **m** must be established by the *4839*
Gal 2: 4 [This **m** arose] because some false brothers *NIG*
Php 1:18 But **what does it m?** *1142+5515*
4:15 with me in the **m** of giving and receiving, *3364*
1Th 4: 6 in this **m** no one should wrong his brother *4547*
Heb 9:10 They are only a **m** of food and drink *NIG*

MATTERED (1) [MATTER]

Jer 3: 9 Israel's immorality **m** so little to her, 2118

MATTERS (15) [MATTER]

Ex 28: 3 in such **m** that they are to make garments NIH
Ezr 7:11 in **m** *concerning* the commands and decrees 1821
Est 1:13 for the king to consult experts in *m of* **law** AIT
Ps 131: 1 I do not concern myself with **great** *m* AIT
Mal 2: 9 but have shown partiality in **m of the law."** 9368
Mt 5:25 **"Settle m** quickly with your *1639+2333*
23:23 the *more* **important m** of the law— *987*
Ac 25:20 I was at a loss how to investigate **such** *m*; *AIT*
Ro 14: 1 without passing judgment *on* **disputable** *m*. *AIT*
1Co 6: 4 if you have disputes about **such m**, *1053*[S]
7: 1 Now for **the m** you wrote about: *4005*
1Ti 4:15 Be diligent in **these** *m*; *AIT*
Heb 2:17 to represent them in **m** related to God, *3836*
2Pe 2:12 But these men blaspheme in **m** they do *4005*
3:16 speaking in them of **these** *m*. *AIT*

MATTHAN (2)

Mt 1:15 Eleazar the father of **M**, *3474*
1:15 **M** the father of Jacob, *3474*

MATTHAT (2)

Lk 3:24 the son *of* **M**, the son of Levi, *3415*
3:29 the son of Jorim, the son *of* **M**, *3415*

MATTHEW (6) [MATTHEW'S]

Mt 9: 9 he saw a man named **M** sitting at the tax *3414*
9: 9 and **M** got up and followed him. *NIG*
10: 3 Thomas and **M** the tax collector; *3414*
Mk 3:18 **M**, Thomas, James son of Alphaeus, *3414*
Lk 6:15 **M**, Thomas, James son of Alphaeus, *3414*
Ac 1:13 Philip and Thomas, Bartholomew and **M**; *3414*

MATTHEW'S (1) [MATTHEW]

Mt 9:10 While Jesus was having dinner at **M** house, *NIG*

MATTHIAS (2)

Ac 1:23 Barsabbas (also known as Justus) and **M**. *3416*
1:26 Then they cast lots, and the lot fell to **M**; *3416*

MATTITHIAH (8)

1Ch 9:31 A Levite named **M**, 5524
15:18 Jehiel, Unni, Eliab, Benaiah, Maaseiah, **M**, 5525
15:21 and **M**, Eliphelehu, Mikneiah, 5525
16: 5 then Jeiel, Shemiramoth, Jehiel, **M**, Eliab, 5524
25: 3 Zeri, Jeshaiah, Shimei, Hashabiah and **M**, 5525
25:21 the fourteenth to **M**, 5525
Ezr 10:43 From the descendants of Nebo: Jeiel, **M**, 5524
Ne 8: 4 Beside him on his right stood **M**, Shema, 5524

MATTOCKS (2)

1Sa 13:20 plowshares, **m**, axes and sickles sharpened. 908
13:21 a shekel for sharpening plowshares and **m**, 908

MATURE (7) [MATURITY, PREMATURELY]
Lk 8:14 riches and pleasures, and *they do* not **m.** *5461*
1Co 2: 6 speak a message of wisdom among the **m,** *5455*
Eph 4:13 of the Son of God and become **m,** *467+5455*
Php 3:15 All of us who are **m** should take such a view *5455*
Col 4:12 in all the will of God, **m** and fully assured. *5455*
Heb 5:14 But solid food is *for* the **m,** *5455*
Jas 1: 4 so that you may be **m** and complete, *5455*

MATURITY (1) [MATURE]
Heb 6: 1 go on to **m,** not laying again the foundation *5456*

MAULED (3) [MAULS]
1Ki 13:26 *which has* **m** him and killed him, 8689
13:28 The lion had neither eaten the body nor **m** 8689
2Ki 2:24 of the woods and **m** forty-two of the youths. 1324

MAULS (1) [MAULED]
Mic 5: 8 which **m** and mangles as it goes, 8252

MAW (KJV) See INNER PARTS

MAXIMS (1)
Job 13:12 Your **m** are proverbs of ashes; 2355

MAY (1231) See Index of Articles Etc.

MAYBE (3)
1Ki 18: 5 **M** we can find some grass to keep 218
18:27 **M** he is sleeping and must be awakened." 218
Jnh 1: 6 **M** he will take notice of us, 218

MAZZAROTH (KJV) See CONSTELLATIONS

ME (4015) [I] See Index of Articles Etc.

ME JARKON (1)
Jos 19:46 **M** and Rakkon, with the area facing Joppa. 4770

ME-ZAHAB (2)
Ge 36:39 daughter of Matred, the daughter of **M.** 4771
1Ch 1:50 daughter of Matred, the daughter of **M.** 4771

MEADOW (2) [MEADOWS]
Isa 44: 4 They will spring up like grass in a **m,** NIH
Hos 4:16 pasture them like lambs in a **m?** 5303

MEADOWS (3) [MEADOW]
Ps 65:13 The **m** are covered with flocks and 4120
Isa 30:23 that day your cattle will graze in broad **m.** 4120
Jer 25:37 The peaceful **m** will be laid waste because 5661

MEAH (KJV) See HUNDRED

MEAL (25) [MEALTIME]
Ge 19: 3 He prepared a **m** for them, 5492
31:54 and invited his relatives to a **m.** 430+4312
37:25 As they sat down to eat their **m,** 4312
Nu 15:20 the first of your **ground m** and present it as 6881
15:21 the LORD from the first of your **ground m.** 6881
1Sa 20:27 the son of Jesse come to the **m,** 4312
2Sa 12: 4 of his own sheep or cattle to prepare a **m** for NIH
1Ki 4:22 of fine flour and sixty cors of **m,** 7854
17:12 a few sticks to take home and make a **m** 2084^S
2Ki 4: 8 who urged him to **stay for a m.** 430+4312
Ne 10:37 to the priests, the first of our **ground m,** 6881
Job 33:20 and his soul loathes the choicest **m.** 4407
Pr 15:17 a **m** *of* vegetables where there is love than 786
Isa 44:16 over it he prepares his **m,** 1414
Jer 16: 5 a house where there is a **funeral m;** 5301
Eze 44:30 your **ground m** so that a blessing may rest 6881
Lk 11:38 that Jesus did not first wash before the **m,** *756*
Jn 13: 2 The **evening m** was being served, *1270*
13: 4 so he got up from the **m,** *1270*
13:28 no one **at the m** understood why Jesus said this *367+3836*
Ac 10:10 and while the **m** was being prepared, *NIG*
16:34 his house and **set a m before** them; *4192+5544*
1Co 10:27 If some unbeliever invites you to a **m** *NIG*
10:30 If I take part in the **m** with thankfulness, *NIG*
Heb 12:16 for a single **m** sold his inheritance rights as *1111*

MEALTIME (1) [MEAL]
Ru 2:14 At **m** Boaz said to her, "Come 431+2021+6961

MEAN (33) [MEANING, MEANINGLESS, MEANS, MEANT]
Ge 33: 8 "What do you **m by** all these droves I met?" 4200
Ex 12:26 'What does this ceremony **m to** you?' 4200
13:14 **'What** does this **m?'** 4537
Jos 4: 6 **'What** do these stones **m?'** 4537
4:21 **'What** do these stones **m?'** 4537
1Sa 1: 8 Don't I **m more** to you than ten sons?" 3202
25: 3 a Calebite, was surly and **m** in his dealings. 8273
2Sa 5:24 because **that will m** the LORD has gone out 255
17: 3 of the man you seek will **m** the return of all; NIH
19: 6 and their men **m** nothing **to** you. 4200
1Ch 14:15 **because that will m** God has gone out 3954
Job 6:26 *Do you* **m** to correct what I say, 3108
Isa 3:15 What do you **m by** crushing my people 4200
Eze 17:12 **what** these things **m?'** 4537
18: 2 **"What do you** people **m** 4013+4200+4537
37:18 'Won't you tell us what you **m by** this?' 4200
Da 5:26 "This is what these words **m:** 10600
Mt 12: 7 If you had known what these words **m,** *1639*
Jn 7:36 What *did* he **m** when he said, *1639*
7:47 "You **m** he has deceived you also?" *NIG*
16:17 "What *does* he **m** by saying, *1639*
16:18 "What *does* he **m** by 'a little while'? *1639*
Ac 2:12 "What *does* this **m?"** *1639+2527*
17:20 and we want to know what they **m."** *1639+2527*
1Co 1:12 What *I* **m** is this: One of you says, *3306*
7:29 What *I* **m,** brothers, is that the time is short. *5774*
10:19 *Do I* **m** then that a sacrifice offered to *5774*
10:29 the other man's conscience, *I* **m,** not yours. *3306*
15:31 **I m that,** brothers—**just as surely** *3755*
Gal 2:17 **does that m that** Christ promotes sin? *727*
3:17 What *I* **m** is this: The law, introduced *3306*
Eph 4: 9 (What *does* "he ascended" **m** except that he *1639*
Php 1:22 this will **m** fruitful labor for me. *NIG*

MEANING (27) [MEAN]
Ge 21:29 **"What is the m** *of* these seven ewe 2179+4537
40: 5 and each dream had a **m** *of* its own. 7355
41:11 and each dream had a **m** *of* its own. 7355
Dt 6:20 **"What is the m of** the stipulations, decrees 4537
1Sa 4:14 **"What is the m** *of* this uproar?" 4537
1Ki 1:41 **"What's the m of** all the noise in the city?" 4508
Ne 8: 8 making it clear and giving the **m** so that 8507
Job 7:16 Let me alone; my days have **no m.** 2039
Ecc 6: 4 It comes **without m,** it departs in darkness, 928+2021+2039
6:11 The more the words, the **less** the **m,** 2039+8049
8:17 man cannot **discover** *its* **m.** 5162
Da 2:45 **This is the m** *of* the vision of the rock cut out of a mountain, 10168+10353+10619
4:19 do not let the dream or its **m** alarm you." 10600
4:19 your enemies and its **m** to your adversaries! 10600
7:16 and asked him the **true m** of all this. 10327
7:19 to **know the true m** of the fourth beast, 10326
8:16 **tell** this man **the m** of the vision." 1067
Lk 8:11 "This is the **m** of the parable: *NIG*
18:34 Its **m** was hidden from them, *4839*
20:17 **what is the m of** that which is written: *5515*
Ac 10:17 While Peter was wondering about the **m** of *1639*
1Co 4: 6 you may learn from us the **m** of the saying, *NIG*
5:10 not at all **m** the people of this world *NIG*
14:10 yet none of them is **without m.** *936*
14:11 not **grasp the m** of what someone is saying, *1539+3836+3857*
Gal 3:16 no say "and to seeds," **m** many people, but *6055*
3:16 but "and to your seed," **m** one person, *6055*

MEANINGLESS (38) [MEAN]
Job 27:12 Why then this **m talk?** 2038+2039
Ecc 1: 2 **"M!** Meaningless!" says the Teacher. "Utterly meaningless! 2039
1: 2 "Meaningless! **M!"** says the Teacher. 2039
1: 2 says the Teacher. **"Utterly m!** 2039+2039
1: 2 Everything is **m."** 2039
1:14 all of them are **m,** a chasing after the wind. 2039
2: 1 But that also proved to be **m.** 2039
2:11 everything was **m,** a chasing after the wind; 2039
2:15 I said in my heart, "This too is **m."** 2039
2:17 All of it is **m,** a chasing after the wind. 2039
2:19 This too is **m.** 2039
2:21 This too is **m** and a great misfortune. 2039
2:23 This too is **m.** 2039
2:26 This too is **m,** a chasing after the wind. 2039
3:19 Everything is **m.** 2039
4: 4 This too is **m,** a chasing after the wind. 2039
4: 7 Again I saw *something* **m** under the sun: 2039
4: 8 This too is **m**—a miserable business! 2039
4:16 This too is **m,** a chasing after the wind. 2039
5: 7 Much dreaming and many words are **m.** 2039
5:10 This too is **m.** 2039
6: 2 This is **m,** a grievous evil. 2039
6: 9 This too is **m,** a chasing after the wind. 2039
6:12 the few and **m** days he passes through like 2039
7: 6 This too is **m.** 2039
7:15 In this **m** life of mine I have seen both 2039
8:10 This too is **m.** 2039
8:14 There is something else **m** that occurs 2039
8:14 This too, I say, is **m.** 2039
9: 9 of this **m** life that God has given you under 2039
9: 9 given you under the sun—all your **m** days. 2039
11: 8 Everything to come is **m.** 2039
11:10 for youth and vigor are **m.** 2039
12: 8 **"M!** Meaningless!" says the Teacher. 2039
12: 8 "Meaningless! **M!"** says the Teacher. 2039
12: 8 says the Teacher. "Everything is **m!"** 2039
Isa 1:13 Stop bringing **m** offerings! 8736
1Ti 1: 6 from these and turned to **m talk.** *3467*

MEANS (66) [MEAN]
Ge 40:12 "This is *what* it **m,"** Joseph said to him. 7355
40:18 "This is *what* it **m,"** Joseph said. 7355
Ex 28:30 the **m of making decisions** *for* the Israelites 5477
Lev 11:43 not make yourselves unclean **by m of** them 928
Ex 25:26 acquires **sufficient m** *to* redeem it, 1896+3869
25:28 if he does not acquire the **m** to repay him, 1896
Nu 31:16 and were **the m of** turning 5034
1Sa 6: 3 but **by all m send** a guilt offering 8740+8740
2Sa 15:21 whether **it m** life or death, 4200
1Ki 22:22 **" 'By what m?'** the LORD asked. 928+4537
2Ki 5: 5 **"By all m, go,"** the king of Aram 995+2143
5:23 **"By all m,** take two talents," 3283
2Ch 18:20 **" 'By what m?'** the LORD asked. 928+4537
Pr 16:15 When a king's face brightens, it **m** life; NIH
22:27 if you lack the **m** to pay, NIH
Jer 17:11 the man who gains riches **by** unjust **m.** 928
22:16 Is that not what it **m** to know me?" NIH
Eze 44:19 the people **by m of** their garments. 928
Da 2: 3 and I want to **know what** it **m."** 3359
2:25 who can tell the king *what* his dream **m."** 10600
4:18 Now, Belteshazzar, tell me *what* it **m,** 10600
4:26 with its roots **m** that your kingdom will NIH
5: 7 and tells me *what* it **m** will be clothed 10600
5:12 and he will tell you *what* the writing **m."** 10600
5:15 to read this writing and tell me *what* it **m,** 10600
5:16 and tell me *what* it **m,** 10600
5:17 for the king and tell him *what* it **m.** 10600
Hos 11: 7 he will **by no m** exalt them. 3480+4202
Mt 1:23 Immanuel"—which **m,** "God with us." *1639+3493*
2: 6 **by no m** least among the rulers of Judah; *4027*
5:18 will by any **m** disappear from the Law *NIG*
9:13 But go and learn what *this* **m:** *1639*
13:18 then to what the parable of the sower **m:** *NIG*
23:16 swears by the temple, *it* **m** nothing; *1639*
23:18 swears by the altar, *it* **m** nothing; *1639*
27:33 Golgotha (which **m** The Place of the Skull). *1639+3306*
27:46 which **m,** "My God, my God, why have *1639*
Mk 3:17 Boanerges, which **m** Sons of Thunder); *1639*
5:41 (which **m,** "Little girl, I say to you, *1639+3493*
7:34 (which **m,** "Be opened!"). *1639*
15:22 Golgotha (which **m** The Place of the Skull). *1639+3493*
15:34 which **m,** "My God, my God, why *1639+3493*
Lk 8: 3 to support them out of their own **m.** *5639*
Jn 1:38 They said, "Rabbi" (which **m** Teacher), *3493*
8:54 "If I glorify myself, my glory **m** nothing. *1639*
9: 7 in the Pool of Siloam" (this word **m** Sent). *2257*
13:24 "Ask him which one *he* **m."** *3306*
20:16 in Aramaic, "Rabboni!" (which **m** Teacher). *3306*
Ac 4:36 apostles called Barnabas (which **m** Son of Encouragement), *1639+3493*
13: 8 (for that is what his name **m**) opposed them *3493*
Ro 6: 2 **By no m!** We died to sin; *1181+3590*
6:15 but under grace? **By no m!** *1181+3590*
7:13 become death to me? **By no m!** *1181+3590*
11: 1 Did God reject his people? **By no m!** *1181+3590*
11:12 if their transgression **m** riches for the world, *NIG*
11:12 and their loss **m** riches for the Gentiles, *NIG*
1Co 6: 7 lawsuits among you **m** you have been completely defeated already. *1639*
9:22 that **by all possible m** I might save some. *4122*
12: 8 of knowledge **by m of** the same Spirit, *2848*
2Co 8:11 **according to** *your* **m.** *1666+2400+3836*
Gal 6:15 nor uncircumcision **m** anything; *1639*
1Ti 6: 5 think that godliness is a **m to financial gain** *4516*
Heb 7: 2 First, his name **m** "king of righteousness"; *2257*
7: 2 "king of Salem" **m** "king of peace." *1639+4005*
9:12 He did not enter **by m of** the blood of goats *1328*
2Pe 3:15 that our Lord's patience **m** salvation, *NIG*

MEANT (15) [MEAN]
Jdg 13:23 "If the LORD *had* **m** to kill us, 2911
Da 5: 8 the writing or tell the king *what* it **m.** 10600
Mk 4:22 For whatever is hidden is **m to be** disclosed, *2671*
4:22 whatever is concealed is **m to be** brought *2671*
9:10 discussing what "rising from the dead" **m.** *1639*
9:32 not understand what he **m** and were afraid *NIG*
Lk 8: 9 His disciples asked him what this parable **m** *1639*
9:45 But they did not understand what this **m.** *4839*
Jn 1:30 This is the one I **m** when I said, *NIG*
6:71 *(He* **m** Judas, the son of Simon Iscariot, *3306*
7:39 By this *he* **m** the Spirit, *3306+4309*
11:13 disciples thought *he* **m** natural sleep. *3306+4309*
13:22 at a loss to know which of them *he* **m.** *3306*
16:19 Are you asking one another **what I m** *4047+4309*
1Co 6:13 The body is not **m** *for* **sexual immorality,** *AIT*

MEANWHILE (32) [WHILE]
Ge 26:26 **M,** Abimelech had come to him 2256
37:36 **M,** the Midianites sold Joseph in Egypt 2256
38:20 **M** Judah sent the young goat by his friend 2256
Nu 32:17 **M** our women and children will live 2256
Jos 10:33 **M,** Horam king of Gezer had come up 255
Ru 4: 1 **M** Boaz went up to the town gate 2256
1Sa 2:21 **M,** the boy Samuel grew up in the presence 2256
17:41 **M,** the Philistine, with his shield bearer 2256
2Sa 2: 8 **M,** Abner son of Ner, 2256
12:26 **M** Joab fought against Rabbah of 2256
13:34 **M,** Absalom had fled. 2256
16:15 **M,** Absalom and all the men of Israel came 2256
18:17 **M,** all the Israelites fled to their homes. 2256
19: 8 **M,** the Israelites had fled to their homes. 2256
1Ki 18:45 **M,** the sky grew black with clouds, 2256+3907+3907+6330+6330
20:13 **M** a prophet came to Ahab king of Israel 2180
20:23 **M,** the officials of the king 2256
2Ch 25:13 **M** the troops that Amaziah had sent back 2256
Ne 4:10 **M,** the people in Judah said, 2256

Est 9:16 **M,** the remainder of the Jews who were in 2256
Mt 27:11 **M** Jesus stood before the governor, *1254*
Lk 1:21 **M,** the people were waiting for Zechariah *2779*
8:52 **M,** all the people were wailing *1254*
12:1 **M,** when a crowd of many thousands *NIG*
15:25 "**M,** the older son was in the field. *1254*
Jn 4:31 **M** his disciples urged him, *1877+3568+3836*
12:9 **M** a large crowd of Jews found out *4036*
18:19 **M,** the high priest questioned Jesus *4036*
Ac 7:58 **M,** the witnesses laid their clothes at *2779*
9:1 **M,** Saul was still breathing out murderous threats against the Lord's disciples. *1254*
18:24 **M** a Jew named Apollos, *1254*
2Co 5:2 **M** we groan, longing to be clothed *NIG*

MEARAH (KJV) See ARAH

MEASURE (36) [IMMEASURABLY, MEASURED, MEASURELESS, MEASUREMENT, MEASUREMENTS, MEASURES, MEASURING]

Ge 15:16 not yet reached its **full m."** 8969
41:49 because it was beyond **m.** 5031
Nu 35:5 **m** three thousand feet on the east side, 4499
Dt 21:2 and judges shall go out and **m** *the* **distance** 4499
1Ki 7:23 a line of thirty cubits *to* **m around** it. 6015+6017
2Ch 4:2 a line of thirty cubits *to* **m around** it. 6015+6017
Job 11:9 Their **m** is longer than the earth 4500
Ps 60:6 and **m off** the Valley of Succoth. 4499
71:15 though I know not its **m.** 6228
108:7 and **m off** the Valley of Succoth. 4499
Isa 34:17 his hand distributes them by **m.** 7742
47:9 They will come upon you in **full m,** 9448
64:9 Do not be angry **beyond m,** O LORD; 4394+6330
64:12 and punish us **beyond m?** 4394+6330
65:7 **m** into their laps **the full payment** 4499
La 5:22 and are angry with us **beyond m.** 4394+6330
Eze 4:11 Also **m out** a sixth of a hin of water 5374
45:3 **m off** a section 25,000 4499
45:11 the homer is to be the **standard m** *for* both. 5504
Am 8:5 the **m,** boosting the price and cheating 406
Zec 2:2 He answered me, "To **m** Jerusalem, 4499
Mt 7:2 you will be judged, and with the **m** you use, *3586*
23:32 then, the **m** of the sin of your forefathers! *3586*
Mk 4:24 "With the **m** you use, *3586*
Lk 6:38 A good **m,** pressed down, *3586*
6:38 For *with* the **m** you use, *3586*
Jn 17:13 so that they may have the full **m** of my joy *NIG*
Ro 12:3 with the **m** of faith God has given you. *3586*
15:29 I will come in the **full m** of the blessing *4445*
2Co 10:12 *When* they **m** themselves by themselves *3582*
Eph 3:19 be filled to the **m** of all the fullness of God. *NIG*
4:13 to the whole **m** of the fullness of Christ. *3586*
2Pe 1:8 you possess these qualities in increasing **m,** *NIG*
Rev 11:1 "Go and **m** the temple of God and the altar, *3582*
11:2 But exclude the outer court; *do* not **m** it, *3582*
21:15 with me had a measuring rod of gold to **m** *3582*

MEASURED (48) [MEASURE]

Ex 16:18 And when *they* **m** it by the omer, 4499
2Sa 8:2 on the ground and **m them off** with a length 4499
1Ki 6:25 The second cherub also **m** ten cubits, NIH
7:31 with its basework it **m** a cubit and a half. NIH
Job 28:25 and **m out** the waters, 928+4500+9419
Isa 40:12 Who *has* **m** the waters in the hollow 4499
Jer 31:37 "Only if the heavens above *can* **be m** and 4499
Eze 40:5 *He* **m** the wall; 4499
40:6 He climbed its steps and **m** the threshold of 4499
40:8 Then *he* **m** the portico of the gateway; 4499
40:11 Then *he* **m** the width of the entrance to 4499
40:13 Then *he* **m** the gateway from the top of 4499
40:14 *He* **m** *along* the faces of 6913
40:19 Then *he* **m** the distance from the inside of 4499
40:20 Then *he* **m** the length and width of 4499
40:23 *He* **m** from one gate to the opposite one; 4499
40:24 *He* **m** its jambs and its portico, 4499
40:27 and *he* **m** from this gate to the outer gate on 4499
40:28 and *he* **m** the south gate; 4499
40:32 and *he* **m** the gateway; 4499
40:35 he brought me to the north gate and **m** it. 4499
40:47 Then *he* **m** the court: 4499
40:48 the portico of the temple and **m** the jambs of 4499
41:1 to the outer sanctuary and **m** the jambs; 4499
41:2 *He* also **m** the outer sanctuary; 4499
41:3 into the inner sanctuary and **m** the jambs of 4499
41:4 And *he* **m** the length of the inner sanctuary; 4499
41:5 Then *he* **m** the wall of the temple; 4499
41:13 Then *he* **m** the temple; 4499
41:15 Then *he* **m** the length of the building facing 4499
42:15 by the east gate and **m** the area all around: 4499
42:16 *He* **m** the east side with the measuring rod; 4499
42:17 *He* **m** the north side; 4499
42:18 *He* **m** the south side; 4499
42:19 Then he turned to the west side and **m;** 4499
42:20 So *he* **m** the area on all four sides. 4499
45:14 The prescribed portion of oil, **m** by the bath, NIH
47:3 *he* **m off** a thousand cubits and then led me 4499
47:4 *He* **m off** another thousand cubits 4499
47:4 *He* **m off** another thousand and led me 4499
47:5 *He* **m off** another thousand, 4499
Hos 1:10 which cannot **be m** or counted. 4499
Am 7:17 Your land will be **m** and divided up, 2475
Mt 7:2 the measure you use, *it will be* **m** to you. *3582*
Mk 4:24 *it will be* **m** to you—and even more. *3582*

Lk 6:38 the measure you use, *it will be* **m** to you." *520*
Rev 21:16 *He* **m** the city with the rod and found it to *3582*
21:17 *He* **m** its wall and it was 144 cubits thick, *3582*

MEASURELESS (2) [MEASURE]

1Ki 4:29 a breadth of understanding **as m as** the sand 3869
Jer 33:22 and as **m** as the sand on the seashore.' 4202+4499

MEASUREMENT (2) [MEASURE]

Eze 40:14 The **m** was up to the portico facing NIH
Rev 21:17 by man's **m,** which the angel was using. *3586*

MEASUREMENTS (13) [MEASURE]

1Ch 23:29 and all **m of quantity** and size. 5374
Eze 40:10 the three had the same **m,** 4500
40:10 on each side had the same **m.** 4500
40:21 and its portico had the same **m** as those of 4500
40:22 the same **m** as those of the gate facing east. 4500
40:24 and they had the same **m** as the others. 4500
40:28 it had the same **m** as the others. 4500
40:29 and its portico had the same **m** as the others. 4500
40:32 it had the same **m** as the others. 4500
40:33 and its portico had the same **m** as the others. 4500
40:35 It had the same **m** as the others, 4500
43:13 "These are the **m** *of* the altar in long cubits, 4500
48:16 and will have these **m:** 4500

MEASURES (9) [MEASURE]

Dt 25:14 not have **two differing m** in your house— 406+406+2256
25:15 accurate and honest weights and **m,** 406
Ru 3:15 **poured into** it six **m** of barley 4499
3:17 "He gave me these six **m** of barley, saying, NIH
Pr 20:10 Differing weights and **differing m** 406+406+2256
Isa 44:13 The carpenter **m** *with* a line and makes 5742
Eze 48:33 "On the south side, which **m** 4,500 cubits, 4500
Hag 2:16 When anyone came to a heap of twenty **m,** NIH
2:16 anyone went to a wine vat to draw fifty **m,** 7053

MEASURING (26) [MEASURE]

Lev 19:35 not use dishonest **standards** when **m** length, 5477
1Ki 7:10 some **m** ten cubits and some eight. NIH
7:23 **m** ten cubits from rim to rim NIH
7:38 each holding forty baths and **m** four cubits NIH
2Ki 21:13 the **m line** *used against* Samaria and 7742
2Ch 3:15 each with a capital on top **m** five cubits. NIH
4:2 **m** ten cubits from rim to rim NIH
Job 38:5 Who stretched a **m line** across it? 7742
Isa 28:17 I will make justice the **m line** 7742
34:11 God will stretch out over Edom the **m line** 7742
Jer 31:39 The **m** line will stretch from there straight to 4500
La 2:8 a **m line** and did not withhold his hand 7742
Eze 40:3 the gateway with a linen cord and a **m** rod 4500
40:5 The length of the **m** rod in the man's hand 4500
40:5 it was one **m rod** thick and one rod high. 7866
42:15 When he had finished **m** what was inside 4500
42:16 He measured the east side with the **m** rod; 4500
42:17 it was five hundred cubits by the **m** rod. 4500
42:18 it was five hundred cubits by the **m** rod. 4500
42:19 it was five hundred cubits by the **m** rod. 4500
47:3 As the man went eastward with a **m line** 7742
Zec 1:16 And the **m line** will be stretched out 7742
2:1 before me was a man with a **m** line 4500
5:6 He replied, "It is a **m basket."** 406
Rev 11:1 a reed like a **m rod** and was told, *4811*
21:15 The angel who talked with me had a **m** rod *3586*

MEAT (91) [MEATS]

Ge 9:4 not eat **m** that has its lifeblood still in it. 1414
Ex 12:8 to eat the **m** roasted over the fire, 1414
12:9 Do not eat **the m** raw or cooked in water, 5647[S]
12:46 take none of the **m** outside the house. 1414
16:3 There we sat around pots of **m** and ate all 1414
16:8 that it was the LORD when he gives you **m** 1414
16:12 Tell them, 'At twilight you will eat **m,** 1414
21:28 and its **m** must not be eaten. 1414
22:31 the **m** of an animal torn by wild beasts; 1414
27:3 sprinkling bowls, **m forks** and firepans. 4657
29:31 the ram for the ordination and cook the **m** in 1414
29:32 and his sons are to eat the **m** *of* the ram and 1414
29:34 And if any of the **m** *of* the ordination ram 1414
38:3 sprinkling bowls, **m forks** and firepans. 4657
Lev 6:28 The clay pot the **m** is cooked in must NIH
7:15 The **m** *of* his fellowship offering 1414
7:17 Any **m** *of* the sacrifice left over till 1414
7:18 If any **m** *of* the fellowship offering is eaten 1414
7:19 " '**M** that touches anything ceremonially unclean must not be eaten; 1414
7:19 As for other **m,** anyone ceremonially clean 1414
7:20 But if anyone who is unclean eats any **m** of 1414
7:21 the **m** *of* the fellowship offering belonging 1414
8:31 the **m** at the entrance to the Tent of Meeting 1414
8:32 burn up the rest of the **m** and the bread. 1414
11:8 not eat their **m** or touch their carcasses; 1414
11:11 you must not eat their **m** 1414
19:26 " 'Do not eat any **m** with the blood still in it. NIH
Nu 4:14 **m forks,** shovels and sprinkling bowls. 4657
11:4 "If only we had **m** to eat! 1414
11:13 Where can I get **m** for all these people? 1414
11:13 'Give us **m** to eat!' 1414
11:18 when you will eat **m.** 1414
11:18 "If only we had **m** to eat! 1414
11:18 LORD will give you **m,** and you will eat it. 1414

Nu 11:21 'I will give them **m** to eat for a whole month 1414
11:33 while the **m** was still between their teeth 1414
18:18 Their **m** is to be yours, 1414
Dt 12:15 of your towns and eat as much of the **m** 1414
12:20 and you crave **m** and say, 1414
12:20 "I would like *some* **m,"** 1414
12:23 and you must not eat the life with the **m.** 1414
12:27 both the **m** and the blood. 1414
12:27 but you may eat the **m.** 1414
14:8 not to eat their **m** or touch their carcasses. 1414
16:4 of the **m** you sacrifice on the evening of 1414
Jdg 6:19 Putting the **m** in a basket and its broth in 1414
6:20 "Take the **m** and the unleavened bread, 1414
6:21 the angel of the LORD touched the **m** and 1414
6:21 consuming the **m** and the bread. 1414
1Sa 1:4 he would give **portions of the m** 4950
2:13 and while the **m** was being boiled, 1414
2:15 "Give the priest *some* **m** to roast; 1414
2:15 he won't accept boiled **m** from you, 1414
9:23 "Bring the **piece of m** I gave you, 4950
14:33 the LORD by eating **m** that has blood NIH
14:34 Do not sin against the LORD by eating **m** NIH
25:11 the **m** I have slaughtered for my shearers, 3186
1Ki 17:6 and **m** in the morning and bread and meat in 1414
17:6 and meat in the morning and bread and **m** in 1414
19:21 to cook the **m** and gave it to the people, 1414
2Ch 4:16 shovels, **m forks** and all related articles, 4657
Job 31:31 'Who has not had his fill of Job's **m?'—** 1414
Ps 78:20 Can he supply **m** for his people?" 8638
78:27 He rained **m** down on them like dust, 8638
Pr 9:2 She has prepared her **m** and mixed her wine 3181
23:20 or gorge themselves on **m,** 1414
Isa 22:13 eating of **m** and drinking of wine! 1414
44:16 he roasts his **m** and eats his fill. 7507
44:19 I roasted **m** and I ate. 1414
65:4 and whose pots hold broth of **unclean m;** 7002
Jer 7:21 and eat the **m** yourselves! 1414
11:15 Can consecrated **m** avert 1414
Eze 4:14 No unclean **m** has ever entered my mouth." 1414
11:3 city is a cooking pot, and we are the **m.'** 1414
11:7 The bodies you have thrown there are the **m** 1414
11:11 nor will you be the **m** in it; 1414
24:4 Put into it the **pieces of m,** 5984
24:10 Cook the **m** well, mixing in the spices; 1414
33:25 Since you eat **m** with the blood still in it NIH
Da 10:3 no **m** or wine touched my lips; 1414
Hos 8:13 sacrifices given to me and they eat the **m,** 1414
Mic 3:3 who chop them up like **m** for the pan, NIH
Hag 2:12 If a person carries consecrated **m** in the fold 1414
Zec 11:16 but will eat the **m** *of* the choice sheep, 1414
Ac 15:20 **m of strangled animals** and from blood. *4465*
15:29 blood, *from* the **m of strangled animals** *4465*
21:25 blood, *from* the **m of strangled animals** *4465*
Ro 14:6 He who eats **m,** eats to the Lord, *NIG*
14:21 to eat **m** or drink wine or to do anything else *3200*
1Co 8:13 I will never eat **m** again, so that I will not *3200*
10:25 in the **m market** without raising questions *3425*

MEATS (1) [MEAT]

Isa 25:6 the best of **m** and the finest of wines. 4683

MEBUNNAI (1)

2Sa 23:27 Abiezer from Anathoth, **M** the Hushathite, 4446

MECHERATHITE (KJV) See MEKERATHITE

MECONAH (1)

Ne 11:28 in Ziklag, in **M** and its settlements, 4828

MEDAD (2)

Nu 11:26 two men, whose names were Eldad and **M,** 4773
11:27 and **M** are prophesying in the camp." 4773

MEDAN (2)

Ge 25:2 She bore him Zimran, Jokshan, **M,** Midian, 4527
1Ch 1:32 Zimran, Jokshan, **M,** Midian, 4527

MEDDLER (1) [MEDDLES]

1Pe 4:15 any other kind of criminal, or even as a **m.** *258*

MEDDLES (1) [MEDDLER]

Pr 26:17 a passer-by *who* **m** in a quarrel not his own. 6297

MEDE (3) [MEDIA]

Da 5:31 and Darius the **M** took over the kingdom, 10404
9:1 (a **M** by descent), who was made ruler over 4512
11:1 And in the first year of Darius the **M,** 4513

MEDEBA (5)

Nu 21:30 which extends to **M."** 4772
Jos 13:9 and included the whole plateau of **M** as far 4772
13:16 and the whole plateau past **M** 4772
1Ch 19:7 who came and camped near **M,** 4772
Isa 15:2 Moab wails over Nebo and **M.** 4772

MEDES (10) [MEDIA]

2Ki 17:6 the Habor River and in the towns of the **M.** 4512
18:11 on the Habor River and in towns of the **M.** 4512

Isa 13:17 See, I will stir up against them the M, 4512
Jer 51:11 LORD has stirred up the kings of the M, 4512
51:28 battle against her—the kings of the M, 4512
Da 5:28 and given to the M and Persians." 10404
6: 8 in accordance with the laws of the M 10404
6:12 in accordance with the laws of the M 10404
6:15 to the law of the M and Persians no decree 10404
Ac 2: 9 Parthians, M and Elamites; *3597*

MEDIA (8) [MEDE, MEDES, MEDIAN]

Ezr 6: 2 in the province of M, and this was written 10404
Est 1: 3 The military leaders of Persia and M, 4512
1:14 of Persia and M who had special access to 4512
1:19 be written in the laws of Persia and M, 4512
10: 2 of the annals of the kings of M and Persia? 4512
Isa 21: 2 M, lay siege! 4512
Jer 25:25 all the kings of Zimri, Elam and M; 4512
Da 8:20 that you saw represents the kings of M 4512

MEDIAN (1) [MEDIA]

Est 1:18 This very day the Persian and M women of 4512

MEDIATE (1) [MEDIATOR]

1Sa 2:25 God *may* m *for* him; 7136

MEDIATOR (7) [MEDIATE]

Job 33:23 "Yet if there is an angel on his side as a m, 4885
Gal 3:19 The law was put into effect through angels by a m. *3542*
3:20 A m, however, does represent just one *3542*
1Ti 2: 5 there is one God and one m between God *3542*
Heb 8: 6 as the covenant *of* which he is m is superior *3542*
9:15 Christ is the m of a new covenant, *3542*
12:24 to Jesus the m of a new covenant, *3542*

MEDICINE (1)

Pr 17:22 A cheerful heart is good m, 1565

MEDITATE (14) [MEDITATED, MEDITATES, MEDITATION]

Ge 24:63 He went out to the field one evening to m, 8452
Jos 1: 8 m on it day and night, 2047
Ps 48: 9 O God, *we* m *on* your unfailing love. 1948
77:12 *I will* m on all your works 2047
119:15 *I* m on your precepts 8488
119:23 your servant *will* m on your decrees. 8488
119:27 then *I will* m on your wonders. 8488
119:48 which I love, and *I* m on your decrees. 8488
119:78 but I *will* m on your precepts. 8488
119:97 I m *on* it all day long. 8491
119:99 for I m *on* your statutes. 8491
119:148 that I *may* m on your promises. 8488
143: 5 *I* m on all your works 2047
145: 5 and *I will* m *on* your wonderful works. 8488

MEDITATED (1) [MEDITATE]

Ps 39: 3 My heart grew hot within me, and as I m, 2052

MEDITATES (1) [MEDITATE]

Ps 1: 2 and on his law *he* m day and night. 2047

MEDITATION (2) [MEDITATE]

Ps 19:14 the m *of* my heart be pleasing in your sight, 2053
104:34 May my m be pleasing to him, 8490

MEDIUM (4) [MEDIUMS]

Lev 20:27 " 'A man or woman who is a m or spiritist 200
Dt 18:11 *who is a* m or spiritist or who consults 200+8626
1Sa 28: 7 "Find me a woman who is a m, 200+1266
1Ch 10:13 and even consulted a m for guidance, 200

MEDIUMS (10) [MEDIUM]

Lev 19:31 " 'Do not turn to m or seek out spiritists, 200
20: 6 the person who turns to m and spiritists 200
1Sa 28: 3 Saul had expelled the m and spiritists from 200
28: 9 He has cut off the m and spiritists from 200
2Ki 21: 6 and consulted m and spiritists. 200
23:24 Josiah got rid of the m and spiritists, 200
2Ch 33: 6 and consulted m and spiritists. 200
Isa 8:19 When men tell you to consult m 200
19: 3 the m and the spiritists. 200
Jer 27: 9 your m or your sorcerers who tell you, 6726

MEEK (3) [MEEKLY, MEEKNESS]

Ps 37:11 But the m will inherit the land 6705
Zep 3:12 I will leave within you the m and humble, 6714
Mt 5: 5 Blessed are the m, for they will inherit *4558*

MEEKLY (1) [MEEK]

1Ki 21:27 He lay in sackcloth and went around m. 351

MEEKNESS (1) [MEEK]

2Co 10: 1 By the m and gentleness of Christ, *4559*

MEET (145) [MEETING, MEETINGS, MEETS, MET]

Ge 14:17 the king of Sodom came out to m him 7925
18: 2 to m them and bowed low to the ground. 7925
19: 1 up to m them and bowed down with his face 7925
19: 6 to m them and shut the door behind him NIH
24:17 The servant hurried to m her and said, 7925
24:65 that man in the field coming to m us?" 7925
29:13 his sister's son, he hurried to m him. 7925
30:16 Leah went out to m him. 7925
32: 6 and now he is coming to m you, 7925
32:19 the same thing to Esau when you m him. 5162
33: 4 But Esau ran to m Jacob and embraced him; 7925
46:29 and went to Goshen to m his father Israel. 7925
Ex 4:14 He is already on his way to m you, 7925
4:27 "Go into the desert to m Moses." 7925
5:14 "Why didn't *you* m your quota 3983
5:20 and Aaron waiting to m them, 7925
7:15 Wait on the bank of the Nile to m him, 7925
18: 7 So Moses went out to m his father-in-law 7925
19:17 the people out of the camp to m *with* God, 7925
25:22 *I will* m with you and give you all my 3585
29:42 There *I will* m you and speak to you; 3585
29:43 there also *I will* m with the Israelites, 3585
30: 6 where *I will* m with you. 3585
30:36 where *I will* m with you. 3585
Nu 14:35 *They will* m their end in this desert; 9462
17: 4 where *I* m with you. 3585
21:33 and his whole army marched out to m them 7925
22:36 he went out to m him at the Moabite town 7925
23: 3 the LORD will come to m *with* me. 7925
23:15 "Stay here beside your offering while I m 7936
31:13 of the community went to m them outside 7925
Dt 2:32 and all his army came out to m us in battle 7925
3: 1 with his whole army marched out to m us 7925
22:23 *to* m in a town a virgin pledged to 5162
22:25 out in the country a man *happens to* m a girl 5162
22:28 If a man *happens to* m a virgin who is 5162
23: 4 For *they did* not come to m you with bread 7709
Jos 8:14 in the morning to m Israel in battle at 7925
9:11 go and m them and say to them, 7925
Jdg 4:18 Jael went out to m Sisera and said to him, 7925
4:22 and Jael went out to m him. 7925
6:35 so that they too went up to m them. 7925
11:31 the door of my house to m me when I return 7925
11:34 who should come out to m him 7925
20:31 to m them and were drawn away from 7925
1Sa 4: 2 Philistines deployed their forces to m Israel, 7925
10: 2 *you will* m two men near Rachel's tomb, 5162
10: 3 up to God at Bethel *will* m you there. 5162
10: 5 *you will* m a procession of prophets 7003
15:12 Samuel got up and went to m Saul, 7925
17: 2 of Elah and drew up their battle line to m 7925
17:48 toward the battle line to m him. 7925
17:55 As Saul watched David going out to m 7925
18: 6 from all the towns of Israel to m King Saul 7925
21: 2 I have told them to m me at a certain place. NIH
23:28 of David and went to m the Philistines. 7925
25:32 who has sent you today to m me. 7925
25:34 if you had not come quickly to m me, 7925
30:21 They came out to m David and the people 7925
2Sa 6:20 Michal daughter of Saul came out to m him 7925
10: 5 he sent messengers to m the men, 7925
10:17 to m David and fought against him. 7925
15:32 Hushai the Arkite was there to m him, 7925
16: 1 steward of Mephibosheth, waiting to m him. 7925
18: 9 Absalom happened to m David's men. 4200+7156
19:15 to go out and m the king and bring him 7925
19:16 with the men of Judah to m King David. 7925
19:20 to come down and m my lord the king." 7925
19:24 also went down to m the king. 7925
19:25 When he came from Jerusalem to m 7925
20: 8 Amasa came to m them. 4200+7156
1Ki 2: 8 When he came down to m me *at* the Jordan, 7925
2:19 the king stood up to m her, 7925
18:16 So Obadiah went to m Ahab and told him, 7925
18:16 and Ahab went to m Elijah. 7925
18:19 the people from all over Israel to m me NIH
20: 9 but this demand I cannot m.' " 6913
20:27 they marched out to m them. 7925
21:18 "Go down to m Ahab king of Israel, 7925
2Ki 1: 3 "Go up and m the messengers of the king 7925
1: 6 "A man came to m us," they replied. 7925
1: 7 of man was it who came to m you 7925
2:15 And they went to m him and bowed to 7925
4:26 Run to m her and ask her, 7925
4:29 If *you* m anyone, do not greet him, 5162
4:31 Gehazi went back to m Elisha and told him, 7925
5:21 he got down from the chariot to m him. 7925
5:26 down from his chariot to m you? 7925
6: 1 the place where we m with you is too small 3782
8: 8 a gift with you and go to m the man of God. 7925
8: 9 Hazael went to m Elisha, 7925
9:17 "Send him to m them and ask, 7925
9:18 The horseman rode off to m Jehu and said, 7925
9:21 each in his own chariot, to m Jehu. 7925
10:15 who *was on his way* to m him. 7925
14: 8 "Come, m *me* face to face." 8011
16:10 to Damascus to m Tiglath-Pileser king 7925
23:29 Josiah marched out to m him in battle, 7925
1Ch 12:17 David went out to m them and said 4200+7156
14: 8 about it and went out to m them. 4200+7156
19: 5 he sent messengers to m them, 7925
19:17 David formed his lines to m the Arameans 7925
2Ch 14:10 Asa went out to m him, 4200+7156
15: 2 He went out to m Asa and said to him, 4200+7156
19: 2 went out to m him and said to the king, 448+7156
22: 7 he went out with Joram to m Jehu son 448
25:17 "Come, m *me* face to face." 8011
28: 9 to m the army when it returned to 4200+7156
2Ch 35:20 Josiah marched out to m him in battle. 7925
Ne 4: 9 a guard day and night to m this threat. 4946+7156
6: 2 *let us* m together in one of the villages on 3585
6:10 He said, "*Let us* m in the house of God, 3585
Ps 42: 2 When can I go and m with God? 7156+8011
79: 8 *may* your mercy come quickly to m us, 7709
85:10 Love and faithfulness m together; 7008
Pr 7:10 Then out came a woman to m him, 7925
7:15 So I came out to m you; 7925
8: 2 where the paths m, she takes her stand; 1075
17:12 Better *to* m a bear robbed of her cubs than 7008
Isa 7: 3 to m Ahaz at the end of the aqueduct of 7925
14: 9 The grave below is all astir to m you 7925
34:14 Desert creatures *will* m with hyenas, 7008
41: 1 *let us* m together at the place of judgment. 7928
66:17 *they will* m *their* end together," 6066
Jer 41: 6 went out from Mizpah to m them. 7925
Am 4:12 prepare to m your God, O Israel." 7925
5:19 as though a man fled from a lion only *to* m 7003
9:10 'Disaster will not overtake or m us.' 7709
Zec 2: 3 and another angel came to m him 7925
Mt 8:34 Then the whole town went out to m Jesus. *5637*
25: 1 and went out to m the bridegroom. *5637*
25: 6 Come out to m him!' *561*
Mk 5: 2 from the tombs *to* m him. *5636*
14:13 a man carrying a jar of water *will* m you. *560*
Lk 22:10 a man carrying a jar of water *will* m you. *5267*
Jn 11:20 *she* went out to m him, *5636*
12:13 and went out to m him, shouting, *5637*
12:18 went out to m him. *5636*
Ac 2:46 Every day they continued to m together in *NIG*
5:12 And all the believers *used to* m together *1639*
28:15 of Appius and the Three Taverns to m us. *561*
28:23 They arranged to m Paul on a certain day, *NIG*
1Co 11:34 that when *you* m together it may not result *5302*
Php 4:19 And my God *will* m all your needs *4444*
1Th 4:17 up together with them in the clouds to m *561*

MEETING (158) [MEET]

Ex 27:21 In the Tent of M, outside the curtain 4595
28:43 enter the Tent of M or approach the altar 4595
29: 4 to the Tent of M and wash them with water. 4595
29:10 the bull to the front of the Tent of M, 4595
29:11 at the entrance to the Tent of M. 4595
29:30 and comes to the Tent of M to minister in 4595
29:32 At the entrance to the Tent of M, 4595
29:42 at the entrance to the Tent of M before 4595
29:44 "So I will consecrate the Tent of M and 4595
30:16 and use it for the service of the Tent of M. 4595
30:18 between the Tent of M and the altar, 4595
30:20 Whenever they enter the Tent of M, 4595
30:26 Then use it to anoint the Tent of M, 4595
30:36 in front of the Testimony in the Tent of M, 4595
31: 7 the Tent of M, the ark of the Testimony 4595
33: 7 calling it the "tent of m." 4595
33: 7 to the tent of m outside the camp. 4595
35:21 the LORD for the work on the Tent of M, 4595
38: 8 at the entrance to the Tent of M. 4595
38:30 the bases for the entrance to the Tent of M, 4595
39:32 the Tent of M, was completed. 4595
39:40 for the tabernacle, the Tent of M; 4595
40: 2 the tabernacle, the Tent of M. 4595
40: 6 the tabernacle, the Tent of M; 4595
40: 7 place the basin between the Tent of M and 4595
40:12 to the Tent of M and wash them with water. 4595
40:22 Moses placed the table in the Tent of M on 4595
40:24 of M opposite the table on the south side of 4595
40:26 the gold altar in the Tent of M in front of 4595
40:29 the tabernacle, the Tent of M, 4595
40:30 He placed the basin between the Tent of M 4595
40:32 the Tent of M or approached the altar, 4595
40:34 Then the cloud covered the Tent of M, 4595
40:35 the Tent of M because the cloud had settled 4595
Lev 1: 1 and spoke to him from the Tent of M. 4595
1: 3 the entrance to the Tent of M so that it will 4595
1: 5 on all sides at the entrance to the Tent of M. 4595
3: 2 at the entrance to the Tent of M. 4595
3: 8 and slaughter it in front of the Tent of M. 4595
3:13 and slaughter it in front of the Tent of M. 4595
4: 4 the bull at the entrance to the Tent of M 4595
4: 5 and carry it into the Tent of M. 4595
4: 7 that is before the LORD in the Tent of M. 4595
4: 7 at the entrance to the Tent of M. 4595
4:14 and present it before the Tent of M. 4595
4:16 of the bull's blood into the Tent of M. 4595
4:18 that is before the LORD in the Tent of M. 4595
4:18 at the entrance to the Tent of M. 4595
6:16 to eat it in the courtyard of the Tent of M. 4595
6:26 in the courtyard of the Tent of M. 4595
6:30 into the Tent of M to make atonement in 4595
8: 3 at the entrance to the Tent of M." 4595
8: 4 at the entrance to the Tent of M. 4595
8:31 the Tent of M and eat it there with the bread 4595
8:33 Do not leave the entrance to the Tent of M 4595
8:35 the entrance to the Tent of M day and night 4595
9: 5 to the front of the Tent of M, 4595
9:23 and Aaron then went into the Tent of M. 4595
10: 7 Do not leave the entrance to the Tent of M 4595
10: 9 into the Tent of M, or you will die. 4595
12: 6 to the priest at the entrance to the Tent of M 4595
14:11 at the entrance to the Tent of M. 4595
14:23 the priest at the entrance to the Tent of M, 4595
15:14 to the Tent of M and give them to the priest. 4595
15:29 the priest at the entrance to the Tent of M. 4595
16: 7 at the entrance to the Tent of M. 4595
16:16 He is to do the same for the Tent of M, 4595

Lev 16:17 the Tent of M from the time Aaron goes in 4595
16:20 the Tent of M and the altar, 4595
16:23 of M and take off the linen garments he put 4595
16:33 for the Tent of M and the altar, 4595
17: 4 the entrance to the Tent of M to present it as 4595
17: 5 to the Tent of M and sacrifice them 4595
17: 6 the LORD at the entrance to the Tent of M 4595
17: 9 not bring it to the entrance to the Tent of M 4595
19:21 a ram to the entrance to the Tent of M for 4595
24: 3 of the Testimony in the Tent of M, 4595
Nu 1: 1 of M in the Desert of Sinai on the first day 4595
2: 2 around the Tent of M some distance from it, 4595
2:17 Then the Tent of M and the camp of 4595
3: 7 for the whole community at the Tent of M 4595
3: 8 of all the furnishings of the Tent of M, 4595
3:25 of M the Gershonites were responsible for 4595
3:25 the curtain at the entrance to the Tent of M, 4595
3:38 in front of the Tent of M. 4595
4: 3 to serve in the work in the Tent of M. 4595
4: 4 of the Kohathites in the Tent of M: 4595
4:15 that are in the Tent of M. 4595
4:23 to serve in the work at the Tent of M. 4595
4:25 curtains of the tabernacle, the Tent of M, 4595
4:25 for the entrance to the Tent of M, 4595
4:28 of the Gershonite clans at the Tent of M. 4595
4:30 to serve in the work at the Tent of M. 4595
4:31 as they perform service at the Tent of M: 4595
4:33 of M under the direction of Ithamar son 4595
4:35 to serve in the work in the Tent of M, 4595
4:37 who served in the Tent of M. 4595
4:39 to serve in the work at the Tent of M, 4595
4:41 who served at the Tent of M. 4595
4:43 to serve in the work at the Tent of M, 4595
4:47 of serving and carrying the Tent of M 4595
6:10 the priest at the entrance to the Tent of M. 4595
6:13 be brought to the entrance to the Tent of M. 4595
6:18 " 'Then at the entrance to the Tent of M, 4595
7: 5 be used in the work at the Tent of M. 4595
7:89 the Tent of M to speak with the LORD, 4595
8: 9 to the front of the Tent of M and assemble 4595
8:15 to come to do their work at the Tent of M. 4595
8:19 and his sons to do the work at the Tent of M 4595
8:22 to do their work at the Tent of M under 4595
8:24 to take part in the work at the Tent of M, 4595
8:26 in performing their duties at the Tent of M, 4595
10: 3 before you at the entrance to the Tent of M. 4595
11:16 Have them come to the Tent of M, 4595
12: 4 "Come out to the Tent of M, 4595
14:10 the LORD appeared at the Tent of M to all 4595
16:18 and Aaron at the entrance to the Tent of M. 4595
16:19 to them at the entrance to the Tent of M, 4595
16:42 and turned toward the Tent of M, 4595
16:43 to the front of the Tent of M, 4595
16:50 to Moses at the entrance to the Tent of M, 4595
17: 4 in the Tent of M in front of the Testimony, 4595
18: 4 be responsible for the care of the Tent of M 4595
18: 6 the LORD to do the work at the Tent of M. 4595
18:21 while serving at the Tent of M. 4595
18:22 not go near the Tent of M, 4595
18:23 at the Tent of M and bear the responsibility 4595
18:31 for your work at the Tent of M. 4595
19: 4 toward the front of the Tent of M. 4595
20: 6 to the Tent of M and fell facedown, 4595
25: 6 at the entrance to the Tent of M. 4595
27: 2 to the Tent of M and stood before Moses, 4595
31:54 Tent of M as a memorial for the Israelites 4595
Dt 31:14 and present yourselves at the Tent of M, 4595
31:14 and presented themselves at the Tent of M. 4595
Jos 18: 1 at Shiloh and set up the Tent of M there. 4595
19:51 at the entrance to the Tent of M. 4595
22:32 to Canaan from their m with the Reubenites NIH
1Sa 2:22 at the entrance to the Tent of M. 4595
20:35 to the field for his m *with* David. 4595
1Ki 8: 4 the Tent of M and all the sacred furnishings 4595
2Ki 4:38 company of the prophets *was* m with him, 3782
1Ch 6:32 music before the tabernacle, the Tent of M, 4595
9:21 at the entrance to the Tent of M. 4595
23:32 for the Tent of M, for the Holy Place and, 4595
2Ch 1: 3 for God's Tent of M was there, 4595
1: 6 of M and offered a thousand burnt offerings 4595
1:13 from before the Tent of M. 4595
5: 5 the Tent of M and all the sacred furnishings 4595
Ne 5: 7 I called together a large m to deal with them 7737
La 2: 6 he has destroyed his place of m. 4595
Jn 11:47 the Pharisees called a m of the Sanhedrin. *5251*
Ac 4:31 the place where they were m was shaken. *5251*
17:19 and brought him to a m of the Areopagus, *740*
17:22 then stood up in the m of the Areopagus *740*
20: 8 in the upstairs room where we were m. *5251*
Heb 10:25 Let us not give up m together, *2191*
Jas 2: 2 Suppose a man comes into your m wearing *5252*

MEETINGS (1) [MEET]

1Co 11:17 for *your* m do more harm than good. *5302*

MEETS (7) [MEET]

Ge 32:17 "When my brother Esau m you and asks, 7008
Nu 35:19 when he m him, he shall put him to death. 7003
35:21 the murderer to death when he m him. 7003
Ro 16: 5 Greet also the church that m at their house. *NIG*
1Co 16:19 and so does the church that m at their house. *NIG*
Phm 1: 2 and to the church that m in your home: *2848*
Heb 7:26 Such a high priest m our need— *4560*

MEGIDDO (12)

Jos 12:21 the king of Taanach one the king of M one 4459
17:11 Endor, Taanach and M, 4459
Jdg 1:27 or M and their surrounding settlements, 4459
5:19 at Taanach by the waters of M, 4459
1Ki 4:12 and M, and in all of Beth Shan next 4459
9:15 and Hazor, M and Gezer. 4459
2Ki 9:27 but he escaped to M and died there. 4459
23:29 but Neco faced him and killed him at M. 4459
23:30 from M to Jerusalem and buried him 4459
1Ch 7:29 M and Dor, together with their villages. 4459
2Ch 35:22 but went to fight him on the plain of M. 4459
Zec 12:11 of Hadad Rimmon in the plain of M. 4461

MEGIDDON (KJV) See MEGIDDO

MEHETABEL (3)

Ge 36:39 his wife's name was M daughter of Matred, 4541
1Ch 1:50 his wife's name was M daughter of Matred, 4541
Ne 6:10 the son of M, who was shut in at his home. 4541

MEHIDA (2)

Ezr 2:52 Bazluth, M, Harsha, 4694
Ne 7:54 Bazluth, M, Harsha, 4694

MEHIR (1)

1Ch 4:11 Shuhah's brother, was the father of M, 4698

MEHOLAH (1)

1Sa 18:19 she was given in marriage to Adriel of M. 4716

MEHOLATHITE (1)

2Sa 21: 8 to Adriel son of Barzillai the M. 4716

MEHUJAEL (2)

Ge 4:18 and Irad was the father of M, 4686
4:18 and M was the father of Methushael, 4686

MEHUMAN (1)

Est 1:10 M, Biztha, Harbona, Bigtha, Abagtha, 4540

MEHUNIM (KJV) See MEUNIM

MEHUNIMS (KJV) See MEUNITES

MEKERATHITE (1)

1Ch 11:36 Hepher the M, Ahijah the Pelonite, 4841

MEKONAH (KJV) See MECONAH

MELAH See TEL MELAH

MELATIAH (1)

Ne 3: 7 M of Gibeon and Jadon of Meronoth— 4882

MELCHI (KJV) See MELKI

MELCHI-SHUA (KJV) See MALKI-SHUA

MELCHIAH (KJV) See MALKIJAH

MELCHISEDEC (KJV) See MELCHIZEDEK

MELCHIZEDEK (10)

Ge 14:18 Then M king of Salem brought out bread 4900
Ps 110: 4 You are a priest forever, in the order of M." 4900
Heb 5: 6 You are a priest forever, in the order *of* M." *3519*
5:10 by God to be high priest in the order *of* M. *3519*
6:20 a high priest forever, in the order *of* M. *3519*
7: 1 This M was king of Salem and priest *3519*
7:10 because when M met Abraham, *3519*
7:11 one in the order *of* M, *3519*
7:15 if another priest like M appears, *3519*
7:17 You are a priest forever, in the order *of* M." *3519*

MELEA (1)

Lk 3:31 the son *of* M, the son of Menna, *3507*

MELECH (2)

1Ch 8:35 Pithon, M, Tarea and Ahaz. 4890
9:41 Pithon, M, Tahrea and Ahaz. 4890

MELICU (KJV) See MALLUCH

MELITA (KJV) See MALTA

MELKI (2)

Lk 3:24 the son *of* M, the son of Jannai, *3518*
3:28 the son *of* M, the son of Addi, *3518*

MELODIOUS (1) [MELODY]

Ps 81: 2 play the m harp and lyre. 5834

MELODY (1) [MELODIOUS]

Ps 92: 3 ten-stringed lyre and the m of the harp. 2053

MELON (1) [MELONS]

Jer 10: 5 Like a scarecrow in a m patch, 5252

MELONS (2) [MELON]

Nu 11: 5 the cucumbers, m, leeks, onions and garlic. 19
Isa 1: 8 like a hut in a field of m, 5252

MELT (15) [MELTED, MELTING, MELTS]

Ex 15:15 the people of Canaan *will* m away; 4570
Jos 14: 8 made the hearts of the people m with fear. 4998
2Sa 17:10 *will* m with fear, for all Israel knows 5022+5022
Ps 97: 5 mountains m like wax before the LORD, 5022
Isa 13: 7 every man's heart *will* m. 5022
14:31 M away, all you Philistines! 4570
19: 1 the hearts of the Egyptians m within them. 5022
Eze 21: 7 Every heart *will* m and every hand go limp; 5022
21:15 that hearts *may* m and the fallen be many, 4570
22:20 into a furnace to m it with a fiery blast, 5988
22:20 and put you inside the city and m you. 5988
Mic 1: 4 The mountains m beneath him and 5022
Na 1: 5 before him and the hills m away. 4570
2:10 Hearts m, knees give way, bodies tremble, 5022
2Pe 3:12 and the elements *will* m in the heat. *5494*

MELTED (11) [MELT]

Ex 16:21 and when the sun grew hot, *it* m away. 5022
Jos 2:11 our hearts m and everyone's courage failed 5022
5: 1 their hearts m and they no longer had 5022
7: 5 of the people m and became like water. 5022
Job 24:19 heat and drought snatch away the m snow, 4784
Ps 22:14 *it has* m away within me. 5022
107:26 in their peril their courage m away. 4570
Eze 22:21 and *you will* be m inside her. 5988
22:22 As silver is m in a furnace, 2247
22:22 so *you will* be m inside her, 5988
24:11 so its impurities *may* be m 5988

MELTING (5) [MELT]

Jos 2: 9 this country *are* m in fear because of you. 4570
2:24 all the people *are* m in fear because of us." 4570
1Sa 14:16 Benjamin saw the army m away 2143+2256+4570
Job 6:16 by thawing ice and swollen with m snow, NIH
Ps 58: 8 Like a slug m away as it moves along, 9468

MELTS (4) [MELT]

Ps 46: 6 he lifts his voice, the earth m. 4570
68: 2 as wax m before the fire, 5022
147:18 He sends his word and m them; 4998
Am 9: 5 he who touches the earth and *it* m, 4570

MELZAR (KJV) See GUARD

MEMBER (8) [MEMBERS]

Lev 4:27 a m of the community sins unintentionally 5883
25:47 to the alien living among you or to a m *of* 6830
Eze 17:13 a m *of* the royal family and made a treaty 4946
Mk 15:43 a prominent m of the Council, *1085*
Lk 23:50 a man named Joseph, a m of the Council, *1085*
Jn 3: 1 Nicodemus, a m of the Jewish ruling council. *NIG*
Ac 17:34 Dionysius, a m of the Areopagus, *741*
Ro 12: 5 each m belongs to all the others. *2848+3517+3836*

MEMBERS (25) [MEMBER]

Ge 36: 6 and sons and daughters and all the m 5883
46:27 the m of Jacob's family, 5883
50: 8 besides all *the m of* Joseph's household AIT
Lev 25:45 and m *of* their clans born in your country, 1201
Nu 16: 2 *who* had been appointed *m* of the council. AIT
2Sa 9:12 the m *of* Ziba's household were servants 4632
2Ch 21:13 *m of* your father's house, AIT
Mic 7: 6 the m *of* his own household. 408
Mt 10:25 how much more the m of his household! *3865*
10:36 will be the m of his own household.' *3865*
Ac 5:17 who were m of the party of the Sadducees, *NIG*
6: 9 from m of the Synagogue of the Freedmen *5516S*
16:15 and the m of her household were baptized, *3875*
Ro 7:23 law at work in the m of my body, *3517*
7:23 of the law of sin at work within my m. *3517*
12: 4 as each of us has one body with many m, *3517*
12: 4 these m do not all have the same function, *3517*
1Co 6:15 that your bodies are m of Christ himself? *3517*
6:15 then take the m of Christ and unite them *3517*
12:24 But God has combined the m of the body *NIG*
Eph 2:19 and m of God's household, *3858*
3: 6 m together of one body, and sharers *5362*
4:25 for we are all m of one body. *3517*
5:30 for we are m of his body. *3517*
Col 3:15 as m of one body you were called to peace. *NIG*

MEMORABLE (1) [MEMORY]

Eze 39:13 day I am glorified will be a m day for them, 9005

MEMORANDUM (1)
Ezr 6: 2 and this was written on it: **M:** 10176

MEMORIAL (19) [MEMORY]
Ex 28:12 the shoulder pieces of the ephod as **m** stones 2355
28:12 on his shoulders as a **m** before the LORD. 2355
28:29 as a continuing **m** before the LORD. 2355
30:16 be a **m** for the Israelites before the LORD, 2355
39: 7 the shoulder pieces of the ephod as **m** stones 2355
Lev 2: 2 and burn this as a **m portion** on the altar, 260
2: 9 the **m portion** from the grain offering 260
2:16 the **m portion** of the crushed grain and 260
5:12 a handful of it as a **m portion** and burn it on 260
6:15 and burn the **m portion** on the altar as 260
24: 7 a **m portion** to represent the bread and to be 260
Nu 5:26 as a **m offering** and burn it on the altar; 260
10:10 be a **m** for you before your God. 2355
31:54 the Tent of Meeting as a **m** for the Israelites 2355
Jos 4: 7 to be a **m** to the people of Israel forever." 2355
Isa 56: 5 within my temple and its walls a **m** and 3338
66: 3 and *whoever* **burns m** incense, 2349
Zec 6:14 Jedaiah and Hen son of Zephaniah as a **m** in 2355
Ac 10: 4 to the poor have come up as a **m offering** *3649*

MEMORIES (1) [MEMORY]
1Th 3: 6 that you always have pleasant **m** of us and *3644*

MEMORY (16) [MEMORABLE, MEMORIAL, MEMORIES]
Ex 17:14 because I will completely blot out the **m** 2352
Dt 25:19 you shall blot out the **m** *of* Amalek from 2352
32:26 and blot out their **m** from mankind, 2352
2Sa 18:18 "I have no son to **carry on the m** 2349
Est 9:28 nor should the **m** *of* them die out 2352
Job 18:17 The **m** *of* him perishes from the earth; 2352
Ps 9: 6 even the **m** *of* them has perished. 2352
34:16 to cut off the **m** *of* them from the earth. 2352
45:17 *I will* **perpetuate** your **m** 2349+9005
109:15 that he may cut off the **m** *of* them from 2352
Pr 10: 7 The **m** *of* the righteous will be a blessing, 2352
Ecc 9: 5 and even the **m** *of* them is forgotten. 2352
Isa 26:14 you wiped out all **m** of them. 2352
Mt 26:13 she has done will also be told, in **m** of her." *3649*
Mk 14: 9 she has done will also be told, in **m** of her." *3649*
2Pe 1:13 to refresh your **m** as long as I live in the tent *5704*

MEMPHIS (8)
Isa 19:13 the leaders of **M** are deceived; 5862
Jer 2:16 of **M** and Tahpanhes have shaved the crown 5862
44: 1 in Migdol, Tahpanhes and **M—** 5862
46:14 proclaim it also in **M** and Tahpanhes: 5862
46:19 for **M** will be laid waste and lie in ruins 5862
Eze 30:13 the idols and put an end to the images in **M.** 5862
30:16 **M** will be in constant distress. 5862
Hos 9: 6 and **M** will bury them. 5132

MEMUCAN (3)
Est 1:14 Admatha, Tarshish, Meres, Marsena and **M,** 4925
1:16 Then **M** replied in the presence of the king 4925
1:21 so the king did as **M** proposed. 4925

MEN (1819) [MAN]
Ge 4:26 At that time *m* **began** to call on the name of AIT
6: 1 When **m** began to increase in number on 132
6: 2 that the daughters of **m** were beautiful, 132
6: 4 the sons of God went to the daughters of **m** 132
6: 4 They were the heroes of old, **m** *of* renown. 408
6: 7 **m** and animals, and creatures that move 132
7:23 **m** and animals and the creatures that move 132
11: 2 As **m** moved eastward, 4392[S]
11: 5 and the tower that the **m** were building. 132+1201
12:20 Pharaoh gave orders about Abram to his **m,** 408
13:11 The two **m** parted company: 408
13:13 Now the **m** *of* Sodom were wicked 408
14:10 *of the m* **fell** into them and the rest fled AIT
14:14 the 318 **trained m** born in his household 2849
14:15 During the night Abram divided his **m** 6269
14:24 but what my **m** have eaten and the share 5853
14:24 that belongs to the **m** who went with me— 408
18: 2 up and saw three **m** standing nearby. 408
18:16 When the **m** got up to leave, 408
18:22 The **m** turned away and went 408
19: 4 all the **m** from every part of the city 408
19: 5 "Where are the **m** who came to you tonight? 408
19: 8 But don't do anything to these **m,** 408
19:10 But the **m** inside reached out 408
19:11 the **m** who were at the door of the house, 408
19:12 The two **m** said to Lot, 408
19:16 the **m** grasped his hand and the hands 408
21:27 and the two **m** made a treaty. 2157[S]
21:31 because the two **m** swore an oath there. 2157[S]
24:32 water for him and his **m** to wash their feet. 408
24:54 and the **m** who were with him ate and drank 408
24:59 and Abraham's servant and his **m.** 408
26: 7 **m** *of* that place asked him about his wife, 408
26: 7 "The **m** *of* this place might kill me 408
26:10 the **m** might well have slept with your wife, 6639
26:31 Early the next morning *the m* **swore an oath** AIT
32: 6 and four hundred **m** are with him." 408
32:28 with God and with **m** and have overcome." 408
33: 1 coming with his four hundred **m;** 408
33:15 let me leave some of my **m** with you." 6639
Ge 34:21 "These **m** are friendly toward us," they said. 408
34:22 But the **m** will consent to live with us 408
34:24 the *m who* **went out** *of* the city gate agreed AIT
38:12 to the *m who were* **shearing** his sheep, AIT
38:21 He asked the **m** *who lived* there, 408
38:22 Besides, the **m** *who lived* there said, 408
40: 5 each of the two **m—** 2157[S]
41: 8 so he sent for all the magicians and **wise** *m* AIT
41:43 and *m* **shouted** before him, "Make way!" AIT
42:11 Your servants are **honest** *m,* not spies." AIT
42:19 If you are **honest** *m,* AIT
42:31 But we said to him, 'We are **honest** *m;* AIT
42:33 how I will know whether you are **honest** *m:* AIT
42:34 that you are not spies but **honest** *m.* AIT
43:15 the **m** took the gifts and double the amount 408
43:16 "Take these **m** to my house, 408
43:17 as Joseph told him and took the **m** 408
43:18 the **m** were frightened when they were taken 408
43:24 The steward took the **m** into Joseph's house, 408
43:33 The **m** had been seated before him in NIH
44: 3 the **m** were sent on their way 408
44: 4 "Go after those **m** at once, 408
46:32 The **m** are shepherds; 408
49: 6 for they have killed **m** in their anger 408
Ex 4:19 all the **m** who wanted to kill you are dead." 408
5: 9 for the **m** so that they keep working 408
7:11 then summoned **wise** *m* and sorcerers, and AIT
8:17 gnats came upon **m** and animals. 132
8:18 And the gnats were on **m** and animals. 132
9: 7 Pharaoh sent **m** to investigate and found that NIH
9: 9 on **m** and animals throughout the land." 132
9:10 festering boils broke out on **m** and animals. 132
9:22 on **m** and animals and on everything 132
9:25 both **m** and animals; 132
10:11 Have only the **m** go; 1505
11: 2 Tell the people that **m** and women alike are 408
12:12 both **m** and animals— 132
12:37 There were about six hundred thousand **m** 1505
17: 9 *of* our **m** and go out to fight the Amalekites. 408
18:21 But select capable **m** from all the people— 408
18:21 *m who* **fear** God, trustworthy men AIT
18:21 trustworthy **m** who hate dishonest gain— 408
18:25 He chose capable **m** from all Israel 408
21:18 "If **m** quarrel and one hits the other with 408
21:22 "If **m** who are fighting hit 408
23:17 "Three times a year all the **m** are to appear 2344
24: 5 Then he sent **young** Israelite **m,** 5853
28: 3 Tell all the **skilled** *m* to whom I have given AIT
34:23 Three times a year all your **m** are to appear 2344
35:22 All who were willing, **m** and women alike, 408
35:29 All the Israelite **m** and women who 408
36: 8 the **skilled** *m* among the workmen made AIT
38:26 a total of 603,550 **m.** NIH
Nu 1: 3 to number by their divisions all the **m** NIH
1: 5 the names of the **m** who are to assist you: 408
1:16 These **were** the *m* **appointed** *from* AIT
1:17 Aaron took these **m** whose names had been given, 408
1:18 the **m** twenty years old or more were listed NIH
1:20 All the **m** twenty years old or more 2351
1:22 All the **m** twenty years old or more 2351
1:24 All the **m** twenty years old or more NIH
1:26 All the **m** twenty years old or more NIH
1:28 All the **m** twenty years old or more NIH
1:30 All the **m** twenty years old or more NIH
1:32 All the **m** twenty years old or more NIH
1:34 All the **m** twenty years old or more NIH
1:36 All the **m** twenty years old or more NIH
1:38 All the **m** twenty years old or more NIH
1:40 All the **m** twenty years old or more NIH
1:42 All the **m** twenty years old or more NIH
1:44 the *m* **counted** by Moses and Aaron and AIT
2: 9 All the *m* **assigned** to the camp of Judah, AIT
2:16 All the *m* **assigned** to the camp of Reuben, AIT
2:24 All the *m* **assigned** to the camp of Ephraim, AIT
2:31 All the *m* **assigned** to the camp AIT
4: 3 Count all the **m** from thirty to fifty years NIH
4:23 Count all the **m** from thirty to fifty years NIH
4:30 Count all the **m** from thirty to fifty years NIH
4:35 All the **m** from thirty to fifty years NIH
4:39 All the **m** from thirty to fifty years NIH
4:43 All the **m** from thirty to fifty years NIH
4:47 All the **m** from thirty to fifty years NIH
8:24 **M** twenty-five years old or more shall come NIH
11:21 "Here I am among six hundred thousand **m** 6639
11:26 However, two **m,** whose names were Eldad 408
13: 2 "Send *some* **m** to explore the land 408
13:16 the names of the **m** Moses sent to explore 408
13:31 But the **m** who had gone up with him said, 408
14:22 not one of the **m** who saw my glory and 408
14:36 the **m** Moses had sent to explore the land, 408
14:37 these **m** responsible for spreading 408
14:38 Of the **m** who went to explore the land, 408
16: 2 With them were 250 Israelite **m,** 408
16:14 Will you gouge out the eyes of these **m?** 408
16:26 from the tents of these wicked **m!** 408
16:29 If **these** *m* die a natural death AIT
16:29 happens to **m,** then the LORD has not sent me. 132
16:30 that these **m** have treated the LORD 408
16:32 and all Korah's **m** and all their possessions. 132
16:35 and consumed the 250 **m** who were offering 408
16:38 the censers of the **m** who sinned at the cost 465[S]
22: 9 "Who are these **m** with you?" 408
22:20 "Since these **m** have come to summon you, 408
22:35 "Go with the **m,** 408
25: 1 the **m** began to indulge in sexual immorality 6639
25: 5 to death those of your **m** who have joined 408
Ex 26: 4 "Take a census of the *m* twenty years **old** AIT
26:10 when the fire devoured the 250 **m.** 408
26:14 clans of Simeon; there were 22,200 **m.** NIH
26:51 of the **m** *of* Israel was 601,730. 1201
31: 3 "Arm some of your **m** to go to war against 408
31: 4 Send into battle a **thousand** *m* from each of AIT
31: 5 So twelve thousand *m* **armed** *for* battle, AIT
31:42 from that of the fighting **m—** 408
32:11 the **m** twenty years old or more who came 408
34:17 the **m** who are to assign the land for you as 408
34:29 These are **the m** the LORD commanded 889[S]
36: 3 Now suppose they marry **m** 1201
Dt 1:13 understanding and respected **m** from each 408
1:15 So I took the **leading** *m of* your tribes, AIT
1:15 wise and respected **m,** and appointed them 408
1:22 "Let us send **m** ahead to spy out the land 408
2:14 of fighting **m** had perished from the camp, 408
2:16 when the last of these fighting **m** among 408
2:34 **m,** women and children. 5493
3: 6 **m,** women and children. 5493
3:18 But all your able-bodied **m,** 1201
5:23 all the **leading m** *of* your tribes 8031
7:14 *m* or women will be childless, nor any of your livestock **without young.** AIT
13:13 that wicked **m** have arisen among you 408
16:16 Three times a year all your **m** must appear 2344
19:17 the two **m** involved in 408
20:13 put to the sword all the **m** *in* it. 2344
21:21 the **m** *of* his town shall stone him to death. 408
22:21 and there the **m** *of* her town shall stone her 408
23:10 If one of your **m** is unclean because of 408
25: 1 When **m** have a dispute, 408
25:11 If **two m** are fighting and the wife of one of them comes to rescue 278+408+2256+3481
29:10 your leaders and **chief m,** 8657
29:10 and all the other **m** *of* Israel, 408
31:12 Assemble the people—**m,** women and 408
32:25 **Young m** and young women will perish, 1033
32:25 infants and gray-haired **m.** 408
33: 6 nor his **m** be few." 5493
Jos 1:14 but all your **fighting m,** fully armed, 1475+2657
2: 3 "Bring out the **m** who came to you 408
2: 4 But the woman had taken the two **m** 408
2: 4 She said, "Yes, the **m** came to me, 408
2: 5 to close the city gate, the **m** left. 408
2: 7 So the **m** set out in pursuit of the spies on 408
2:14 the **m** assured her. 408
2:17 The **m** said to her, "This oath you made us 408
2:23 Then the two **m** started back. 408
3:12 choose twelve **m** from the tribes of Israel, 408
4: 2 "Choose twelve **m** from among the people, 408
4: 4 the twelve **m** he had appointed from 408
4:12 The **m** *of* Reuben, Gad and the half-tribe 1201
5: 4 all the **m** of military age— 2351
5: 6 until all the **m** who were *of* military age 408
6: 2 along with its king and its **fighting m.** 1475+2657
6: 3 around the city once with all the **armed m.** 408
6:13 The **armed** *m* went ahead of them and AIT
6:21 **m** and women, young and old, cattle, 408
6:22 Joshua said to the two **m** who had spied out 408
6:23 the **young m** who had done the spying went 5853
6:25 the **m** Joshua had sent as spies to Jericho— 4855[S]
7: 2 Now Joshua sent **m** from Jericho to Ai, 408
7: 2 So the **m** went up and spied out Ai. 408
7: 3 Send two or three thousand **m** to take it 408
7: 3 for only a few **m** are there." 2156[S]
7: 4 So about three thousand **m** went up; 408
7: 4 but they were routed by the **m** *of* Ai, 408
8: 3 his **best fighting m** and sent them out 1475+2657
8: 5 and when the **m** come out against us, NIH
8:10 the next morning Joshua mustered his **m,** 6639
8:12 Joshua had taken about five thousand **m** 408
8:14 he and all the **m** *of* the city hurried out early 408
8:16 All the **m** of Ai were called to pursue them, 6639
8:19 the *m* **in** *the* **ambush** rose quickly AIT
8:20 The **m** *of* Ai looked back and saw 408
8:21 they turned around and attacked the **m** 408
8:22 **The m of the ambush** also came out 465[S]
8:24 When Israel had finished killing all the **m** 3782
8:25 Twelve thousand **m** and women fell 408
9: 5 The **m** put worn and patched sandals NIH
9: 6 to him and the **m** *of* Israel, "We have come 408
9: 7 The **m** *of* Israel said to the Hivites, 408
9:14 The **m** of Israel sampled their provisions 408
10: 2 and all its **m** were good fighters. 408
10: 7 including all the **best fighting m.** 1475+2657
10:18 and post *some* **m** there to guard it. 408
10:24 he summoned all the **m** *of* Israel and said to 408
14: 6 **m** *of* Judah approached Joshua at Gilgal, 1201
18: 4 Appoint three **m** from each tribe. 408
18: 8 As the **m** started on their way to map out 408
18: 9 So the **m** left and went through the land. 408
22:14 With him they sent ten of the **chief** *m,* AIT
Jdg 1: 3 Then the **m** of Judah said to NIH
1: 4 and they struck down ten thousand **m** 408
1: 8 The **m** *of* Judah attacked Jerusalem also 1201
1: 9 the **m** *of* Judah went down to fight against 1201
1:16 of Palms with the **m** *of* Judah to live among 1201
1:17 Then the **m** of Judah went with NIH
1:18 The **m** of Judah also took Gaza, NIH
1:19 The LORD was with the **m** of Judah. NIH
1:23 **sent** *m* **to spy out** Bethel AIT
3:18 on their way the **m** who had carried it. 6639
4: 6 take with you ten thousand **m** of Naphtali 408
4:10 Ten thousand **m** followed him, 408
4:13 and all the **m** with him, 6639
4:14 followed by ten thousand **m.** 408

Jdg 5:13 m who were left came down to the nobles; 8586
6: 5 It was impossible to count the m 2157S
6:27 of his family and the m of the town, 408
6:28 the morning when the m of the town got up, 408
6:30 The m of the town demanded of Joash, 408
7: 1 and all his m camped at the spring of Harod. 6639
7: 2 "You have too many m for me 6639
7: 3 So twenty-two thousand m left, 6639
7: 4 "There are still too many m. 6639
7: 5 So Gideon took the m down to the water. 6639
7: 6 Three hundred m lapped with their hands 408
7: 7 "With the three hundred m 408
7: 7 Let all the other m go, 6639
7:16 the three hundred m into three companies, 408
7:19 the hundred m with him reached the edge of 408
7:22 the LORD caused the m throughout 408
7:24 So all the m of Ephraim were called out 408
8: 4 Gideon and his three hundred m, 408
8: 5 He said to the m of Succoth, 408
8: 8 but they answered as the m of Succoth had. 408
8: 9 So he said to the m of Peniel, 408
8:10 with a force of about fifteen thousand m, all NIH
8:15 Gideon came and said to the m of Succoth, 408
8:15 to your exhausted m?' " 408
8:16 of the town and taught the m of Succoth 408
8:17 down the tower of Peniel and killed the m 408
8:18 "What kind of m did you kill at Tabor?" 408
8:18 "M like you," they answered, 2157S
9: 9 by which both gods and m are honored, 408
9:13 which cheers both gods and m, 408
9:25 of Shechem set m on the hilltops to ambush NIH
9:28 Serve the m of Hamor, Shechem's father! 408
9:32 and your m should come and lie in wait in 6639
9:33 When Gaal and his m come out against you, 6639
9:36 the shadows of the mountains for m." 408
9:38 Aren't these the m you ridiculed? 6639
9:43 So he took his m, 6639
9:48 he and all his m went up Mount Zalmon. 6639
9:48 He ordered the m with him, "Quick! 6639
9:49 So all the m cut branches 6639
9:49 about a thousand m and women, also died. 408
9:51 to which all the m and women— 408
9:57 God also made the m of Shechem pay 408
11:20 He mustered all his m and encamped 6639
11:21 gave Sihon and all his m into Israel's hands, 6639
12: 1 The m of Ephraim called out their forces, 408
12: 4 then called together the m of Gilead 408
12: 5 the m of Gilead asked him, 408
14:18 Before sunset on the seventh day the m of 408
14:19 struck down thirty of their m, 408
15:10 The m of Judah asked, 408
15:11 Then three thousand m from Judah went 408
15:15 and struck down a thousand m. 408
15:16 With a donkey's jawbone I have killed a thousand m." 408
16: 9 With m hidden in the room, 2021S
16:12 Then, with m hidden in the room, 2021S
16:27 temple was crowded with m and women; 408
16:27 on the roof were about three thousand m 408
18: 2 These m represented all their clans. 408
18: 2 The m entered the hill country of Ephraim NIH
18: 7 So the five m left and came to Laish, 408
18:11 six hundred m from the clan of the Danites, 408
18:14 Then the five m who had spied out the land 408
18:17 The five m who had spied out the land went 408
18:17 and the six hundred armed m stood at 408
18:18 When these m went into Micah's house AIT
18:22 the m who lived near Micah 408
18:23 that you called out your m to fight?" NIH
18:25 or some hot-tempered m will attack you, 408
19:16 (the m of the place were Benjamites), 408
19:22 of the wicked m of the city surrounded 408
19:25 But the m would not listen to him. 408
20: 5 the night the m of Gibeah came after me 1251
20:10 We'll take ten m out of every hundred 408
20:11 the m of Israel got together and united 408
20:12 The tribes of Israel sent m throughout 408
20:13 Now surrender those wicked m of Gibeah 408
20:15 in addition to seven hundred chosen m 408
20:16 Among all these soldiers there were seven hundred chosen m who were left-handed, 408
20:17 all of them fighting m. 408
20:20 The m of Israel went out to fight 408
20:22 But the m of Israel encouraged one another 408
20:31 that about thirty m fell in the open field and 408
20:33 All the m of Israel moved from their places 408
20:34 Then ten thousand of Israel's finest m made 408
20:36 m of Israel had given way before Benjamin, 408
20:37 m who had been in ambush AIT
20:38 The m of Israel had arranged with 408
20:39 then the m of Israel would turn in the battle. 408
20:39 to inflict casualties on the m of Israel 408
20:41 Then the m of Israel turned on them, 408
20:41 and the m of Benjamin were terrified, 408
20:42 And the m of Israel who came out of NIH
20:45 the Israelites cut down five thousand m 408
20:47 But six hundred m turned and fled into 408
20:48 The m of Israel went back to Benjamin 408
21: 1 The m of Israel had taken an oath 408
21:10 assembly sent twelve thousand fighting m 408
21:16 for the m who are left? AIT
Ru 2: 9 Watch the field where the m are harvesting, AIT
2: 9 I have told the m not to touch you. 5853
2: 9 from the water jars the m have filled." 5853
2:15 Boaz gave orders to his m, 5853
3:10 You have not run after the younger m, 1033
1Sa 2:12 Eli's sons were wicked m; 1201

1Sa 2:17 This sin of the young m was very great in 5853
2:26 and in favor with the LORD and with m. 408
4: 4 So the people sent m to Shiloh, NIH
4: 9 Be m, or you will be subject to 408
4: 9 Be m, and fight!" 408
5: 7 the m of Ashdod saw what was happening, 408
6:19 down some of the m of Beth Shemesh, 408
6:20 and the m of Beth Shemesh asked, 408
7: 1 So the m of Kiriath Jearim came and took 408
7:11 The m of Israel rushed out of Mizpah 408
8:22 Then Samuel said to the m of Israel, 408
10: 2 you will meet two m near Rachel's tomb, 408
10: 3 Three m going up to God 408
10:26 valiant m whose hearts God had touched. AIT
11: 1 And all the m of Jabesh said to him, 408
11: 5 to him what the m of Jabesh had said. 408
11: 8 When Saul mustered them at Bezek, the m 1201
11: 8 and the m of Judah thirty thousand. 408
11: 9 "Say to the m of Jabesh Gilead, 408
11: 9 and reported this to the m of Jabesh, 408
11:11 The next day Saul separated his m 6639
11:12 Bring these m to us and we will put them 408
13: 2 Saul chose three thousand m from Israel; AIT
13: 2 of the m he sent back to their homes. 6639
13: 6 When the m of Israel saw that their situation 408
13: 8 and Saul's m began to scatter. 6639
13:11 "When I saw that the m were scattering, 6639
13:15 and Saul counted the m who were with him. 6639
13:16 and the m with them were staying in Gibeah 6639
14: 2 With him were about six hundred m, 408
14: 8 over toward the m and let them see us. 408
14:12 The m of the outpost shouted to Jonathan 408
14:14 and his armor-bearer killed some twenty m 408
14:17 Then Saul said to the m who were with him, 6639
14:20 Then Saul and all his m assembled and went 6639
14:24 the m of Israel were in distress that day, 408
14:28 That is why the m are faint." 6639
14:30 if the m had eaten today some of 6639
14:33 the m are sinning against the LORD 6639
14:34 he said, "Go out among the m and tell them, 6639
14:39 But not one of the m said a word. 6639
14:40 "Do what seems best to you," the m replied. 6639
14:41 and the m were cleared. 6639
14:45 the m said to Saul, "Should Jonathan die— 6639
14:45 So the m rescued Jonathan, 6639
15: 3 put to death m and women, 408
15: 4 the m and mustered them at Telaim— 6639
15: 4 and ten thousand m from Judah. 408
17:19 They are with Saul and all the m of Israel in 408
17:26 David asked the m standing near him, 408
17:28 heard him speaking with the m, 408
17:30 and the m answered him as before. 6639
17:52 the m of Israel and Judah surged forward 408
18: 6 When the m were returning home 4392S
18:13 and gave him command over a thousand m, AIT
18:27 David and his m went out 408
19:11 Saul sent m to David's house to watch it 4855
19:14 When Saul sent the m to capture David, 4855
19:15 Then Saul sent the m back to see David 4855
19:16 But when the m entered, 4855
19:20 so he sent m to capture him. 4855
19:20 upon Saul's m and they also prophesied. 4855
19:21 Saul was told about it, and he sent more m, 4855
19:21 Saul sent m a third time, 4855
21: 2 As for my m, I have told them 5853
21: 4 the m have kept themselves from women." 5853
22: 2 About four hundred m were with him. 408
22: 6 that David and his m had been discovered. 408
22: 7 Saul said to them, "Listen, m of Benjamin! 1229
22:18 That day he killed eighty-five m who wore 408
22:19 with its m and women, its children and 408
23: 3 But David's m said to him, 408
23: 5 So David and his m went to Keilah, 408
23: 8 down to Keilah to besiege David and his m. 408
23:12 of Keilah surrender me and my m to Saul?" 408
23:13 So David and his m, about six hundred 408
23:24 Now David and his m were in the Desert 408
23:25 Saul and his m began the search, 408
23:26 and David and his m were on the other side, 408
23:26 in on David and his m to capture them, 408
24: 2 So Saul took three thousand chosen m 408
24: 2 and set out to look for David and his m near 408
24: 3 David and his m were far back in the cave. 408
24: 4 The m said, "This is the day 408
24: 6 He said to his m, 408
24: 7 With these words David rebuked his m 408
24: 9 "Why do you listen when m say, 132
24:22 and his m went up to the stronghold. 408
25: 5 So he sent ten young m and said to them, 5853
25: 8 be favorable toward my young m, 5853
25: 9 When David's m arrived, 5853
25:11 to m coming from who knows where?" 408
25:12 David's m turned around and went back. 5853
25:13 David said to his m, "Put on your swords!" 408
25:13 About four hundred m went up with David, 408
25:15 Yet these m were very good to us. 408
25:20 there were David and his m descending 408
25:25 I did not see the m my master sent. 5853
25:27 be given to the m who follow you. 5853
26: 2 with his three thousand chosen m of Israel, 408
26:16 you and your m deserve to die, 917
26:19 If, however, m have done it, 132+1201+2021
26:22 of your young m come over and get it. 5853
27: 2 the six hundred m with him left and went 408
27: 3 and his m settled in Gath with Achish. 408
27: 8 Now David and his m went up and raided 408
28: 1 that you and your m will accompany me in 408

1Sa 28: 8 at night he and two m went to the woman. 408
28:23 But his m joined the woman in urging him, 6269
28:25 Then she set it before Saul and his m, 6269
29: 2 David and his m were marching at the rear 408
29: 4 by taking the heads of our own m? 408
29:11 and his m got up early in the morning 408
30: 1 and his m reached Ziklag on the third day. 408
30: 3 When David and his m came to Ziklag, 408
30: 4 So David and his m wept aloud 6639
30: 6 because the m were talking of stoning him; 6639
30: 9 David and the six hundred m with him came 408
30:10 for two hundred m were too exhausted 408
30:10 and four hundred m continued the pursuit. 408
30:17 except four hundred young m who rode off 408
30:20 and his m drove them ahead of NIH
30:21 two hundred m who had been too exhausted 408
30:21 As David and his m approached, 6639
30:22 But all the evil m and troublemakers 408
30:31 where David and his m had roamed. 408
31: 6 and all his m died together that same day. 408
31:12 all their valiant m journeyed through 408
2Sa 1: 4 He said, "The m fled from the battle. 6639
1:11 the m with him took hold of their clothes 408
1:15 Then David called one of his m and said, 5853
1:18 that the m of Judah be taught this lament of 1201
2: 3 David also took the m who were with him, 408
2: 4 Then the m of Judah came to Hebron 408
2: 4 When David was told that it was the m 408
2: 5 to the m of Jabesh Gilead to say to them, 408
2:12 together with the m of Ish-Bosheth son 6269
2:13 Joab son of Zeruiah and David's m went out 6269
2:14 the young m get up and fight hand to hand 5853
2:15 twelve m for Benjamin and Ish-Bosheth son NIH
2:17 and the m of Israel were defeated 408
2:17 of Israel were defeated by David's m. 6269
2:21 the young m and strip him of his weapons." 5853
2:25 the m of Benjamin rallied behind Abner. 1201
2:26 How long before you order your m 6639
2:27 the m would have continued the pursuit 6639
2:28 and all the m came to a halt; 6639
2:29 that night Abner and his m marched through 408
2:30 and assembled all his m. 6639
2:30 nineteen of David's m were found missing. 6269
2:31 But David's m had killed three hundred 6269
2:32 and his m marched all night and arrived 408
3:20 When Abner, who had twenty m with him, 408
3:20 David prepared a feast for him and his m. 408
3:22 Just then David's m and Joab returned from 6269
3:34 You fell as one falls before wicked m." 1201
3:38 Then the king said to his m, 6269
4: 2 Saul's son had two m who were leaders 408
4:11 when wicked m have killed 408
4:12 So David gave an order to his m, 5853
5: 6 The king and his m marched to Jerusalem 408
5:21 and David and his m carried them off. 408
6: 1 brought together out of Israel chosen m, AIT
6: 2 and all his m set out from Baalah of Judah 6639
6:19 both m and women. 408
7: 9 the names of the greatest m of the earth. AIT
7:14 I will punish him with the rod of m, 408
7:14 with floggings inflicted by m. 132+1201
7:26 Then m will say, 'The LORD Almighty NIH
10: 2 When David's m came to the land of 6269
10: 3 by sending m to you to express sympathy? 6269
10: 4 So Hanun seized David's m, 6269
10: 5 he sent messengers to meet the m, 408
10: 6 as the king of Maacah with a thousand m, 408
10: 6 and also twelve thousand m from Tob. 408
10: 7 with the entire army of fighting m. 1475
10: 8 of Zobah and Rehob and the m of Tob 408
10:10 He put the rest of the m under the command 6639
11: 1 David sent Joab out with the king's m and 6269
11:11 and my lord's m are camped in 6269
11:17 When the m of the city came out and fought 408
11:17 some of the m in David's army fell; 6269
11:23 "The m overpowered us and came out 408
11:24 and some of the king's m died. 6269
12: 1 "There were two m in a certain town, 408
13:28 Absalom ordered his m, "Listen! 5853
13:29 So Absalom's m did to Amnon 5853
13:34 "I see m in the direction of Horonaim, 408
15: 1 a chariot and horses and with fifty m to run 408
15: 6 and so he stole the hearts of the m of Israel. 408
15:11 Two hundred m from Jerusalem 408
15:13 hearts of the m of Israel are with Absalom." 408
15:18 All his m marched past him, 6269
15:22 on with all his m and the families that were 408
16: 2 the bread and fruit are for the m to eat, 5853
16:13 So David and his m continued along 408
16:15 and all the m of Israel came to Jerusalem, 6639
16:18 and by all the m of Israel— 408
17: 1 "I would choose twelve thousand m 408
17: 8 You know your father and his m; 408
17:12 nor any of his m will be left alive. 408
17:14 Absalom and all the m of Israel said, 408
17:20 When Absalom's m came to the woman at 6269
17:20 The m searched but found no one, NIH
17:21 After the m had gone, 4392S
17:24 the Jordan with all the m of Israel. 408
18: 1 David mustered the m who were with him 6639
18: 3 But the m said, "You must not go out; 6639
18: 4 the gate while all the m marched out in units 6639
18: 7 of Israel was defeated by David's m, and 6269
18: 7 that day were great—twenty thousand m. NIH
18: 9 Absalom happened to meet David's m. 6269
18:10 When one of the m saw this, he told Joab, 408
18:28 the m who lifted their hands against my lord 408

2Sa 19: 3 The **m** stole into the city that day 6639
19: 3 that day as **m** steal in who are ashamed 6639
19: 5 "Today you have humiliated all your **m,** 6269
19: 6 the commanders and their **m** mean nothing 6269
19: 7 Now go out and encourage your **m.** 6269
19: 8 When the **m** were told, 6639
19:14 over the hearts of all the **m** *of* Judah as 408
19:14 "Return, you and all your **m.**" 6269
19:15 the **m** of Judah had come to Gilgal to go out NIH
19:16 with the **m** *of* Judah to meet King David. 408
19:35 *m* and women **singers?** AIT
19:41 Soon all the **m** *of* Israel were coming to 408
19:41 "Why did our brothers, the **m** *of* Judah, 408
19:41 together with all his **m?**" 408
19:42 the **m** *of* Judah answered the men of Israel, 408
19:42 the men of Judah answered the **m** *of* Israel, 408
19:43 the **m** *of* Israel answered the men of Judah, 408
19:43 the men of Israel answered the **m** *of* Judah, 408
19:43 But the **m** *of* Judah responded 408
19:43 even more harshly than the **m** *of* Israel. 408
20: 2 So all the **m** *of* Israel deserted David 408
20: 2 But the **m** *of* Judah stayed by their king all 408
20: 4 "Summon the **m** *of* Judah to come to me 408
20: 6 Take your master's **m** and pursue him, 6269
20: 7 So Joab's **m** and the Kerethites 408
20:11 of Joab's **m** stood beside Amasa and said, 5853
20:13 all the **m** went on with Joab 408
20:22 and his **m** dispersed from the city, NIH
21:15 with his **m** to fight against the Philistines, 6269
21:17 Then David's **m** swore to him, saying, 408
21:22 they fell at the hands of David and his **m.** 6269
22: 3 from **violent** *m* you save me. AIT
22:49 from violent *m* you rescued me. 408
23: 3 'When one rules over **m** in righteousness, 132
23: 6 **evil m** are all to be cast aside like thorns, 1175
23: 8 These are the names of David's **mighty m:** 1475
23: 8 he raised his spear against eight hundred **m,** NIH
23: 9 As one of the three **mighty m,** 1475
23: 9 Then the **m** *of* Israel retreated, 408
23:13 of the thirty **chief** *m* came down to David at AIT
23:16 So the three **mighty m** broke through 1475
23:17 of **m** who went at the risk of their lives?" 408
23:17 the exploits of the three **mighty m.** 1475
23:18 He raised his spear against three hundred **m,** NIH
23:20 He struck down two of Moab's **best m.** 738
23:22 too was as famous as the three **mighty m.** 1475
24: 2 to Beersheba and enroll the **fighting m,** 6639
24: 4 the king to enroll the **fighting m** *of* Israel. 6639
24: 9 Joab reported the number of the **fighting m** 6639
24: 9 In Israel there were eight hundred thousand
able-bodied **m** who could handle a sword, 408
24:10 after he had counted the **fighting m,** 6639
24:14 but do not let me fall into the hands of **m.**" 132
24:20 the king and his **m** coming toward him, 6269
1Ki 1: 5 with fifty **m** to run ahead of him. 408
1: 9 all the **m** *of* Judah who were royal officials, 408
1:53 Then King Solomon sent **m,** NIH
2:32 of my father David he attacked two **m** 408
2:32 were **better** *m* and more upright than he. AIT
4:30 the wisdom of all the **m** *of* the East, 1201
4:34 *M* of all nations **came** to listen to AIT
5: 6 My **m** will work with yours, 6269
5: 6 for your **m** whatever wages you set. 6269
5: 9 My **m** will haul them down from Lebanon 6269
5:13 from all Israel—thirty thousand **m.** 408
5:18 the **m of Gebal** cut and prepared the timber 1490
8: 2 All the **m** *of* Israel came together 408
8:39 (for you alone know the hearts of all **m**) 132+1201
8:42 for *m* **will hear** *of* your great name AIT
9:22 they were his fighting **m,** 408
9:23 550 officials supervising the **m** who did 6639
9:27 And Hiram sent his **m—** 6269
9:27 to serve in the fleet with Solomon's **m.** 6269
10: 8 How happy your **m** must be! 408
11:15 had struck down all the **m** in Edom. 2351
11:16 until they had destroyed all the **m** in Edom. 2351
11:18 Then taking **m** from Paran with them, 408
11:24 He gathered **m** around him and became 408
12: 8 and consulted the **young m** who had grown 3529
12:10 The **young m** who had grown up 3529
12:14 he followed the advice of the **young m** 3529
12:21 a hundred and eighty thousand fighting **m—** 1033
20:10 in Samaria to give each of my **m** a handful." 6639
20:12 and he ordered his **m:** "Prepare to attack." 6269
20:15 of the provincial commanders, 232 **m.** NIH
20:17 "**M** are advancing from Samaria." 408
20:33 The **m** took this as a good sign 408
22: 6 about four hundred **m—** 408
22:49 "Let my **m** sail with your men," 6269
22:49 "Let my men sail with your **m,**" 6269
2Ki 1: 6 in Israel that you are sending **m** NIH
1: 9 a captain with his *company of* **fifty** *m.* AIT
1:10 and consume you and your **fifty** *m!*" AIT
1:10 and consumed the captain and his **m.** 2822[S]
1:11 to Elijah another captain with his **fifty** *m.* AIT
1:12 and consume you and your **fifty** *m!*" AIT
1:12 and consumed him and his **fifty** *m.* AIT
1:13 king sent a third captain with his **fifty** *m.* AIT
1:13 for my life and the lives of these **fifty** *m,* AIT
1:14 the first two captains and *all* their **m.** 2822[S]
2: 7 Fifty **m** of the company of 408
2:16 "we your servants have fifty able **m.** 408
2:17 And they sent fifty **m,** 408
2:19 The **m** *of* the city said to Elisha, "Look, 408
3:25 but **m armed with slings** surrounded it 7847
4:38 cook some stew for **these m.**" 1201+2021+5566[S]
4:40 The stew was poured out for the **m,** 408

2Ki 4:43 "How can I set this before a hundred **m?**" 408
5:22 'Two **young m** from the company of 5853
5:24 He sent the **m** away and they left. 408
6:13 "so I can send **m** and capture him." NIH
6:20 open the eyes of **these** *m* so they can see." AIT
6:22 "Would you kill **m** you have captured 889[S]
7: 3 Now there were four **m** with leprosy at 408
7: 8 The *m who* **had leprosy** reached the edge of AIT
7:13 "*Have some m* **take** five of the horses AIT
8:12 kill their **young m** with the sword, 1033
10: 6 were with the **leading** *m of* the city, AIT
10: 7 **these m** took the princes 2157[S]
10:11 as well as all his **chief** *m,* AIT
10:14 of Beth Eked—forty-two **m.** 408
10:24 Now Jehu had posted eighty **m** outside 408
10:24 "If one of you lets any of the **m** I am placing 408
11: 9 Each one took his **m—** 408
12:11 to the *m* **appointed** to supervise the work on AIT
14:19 but they sent **m** after him to Lachish NIH
15:25 Taking fifty **m** of Gilead with him, 408
16: 6 for Aram by driving out the **m of Judah.** 3374
17:30 The **m** *from* Babylon made Succoth Benoth, 408
17:30 the **m** *from* Cuthah made Nergal, 408
17:30 and the **m** *from* Hamath made Ashima; 408
18:27 and not to the **m** sitting on the wall— 408
19:35 a hundred and eighty-five thousand **m** in NIH
20:14 "What did those **m** say, 408
22: 5 to the *m* **appointed** to supervise the work on AIT
22: 5 And *have these m* **pay** the workers AIT
23: 2 the LORD with the **m** *of* Judah, the people 408
23:17 The **m** *of* the city said, 408
24:14 all the officers and **fighting m,** 1475+2657
24:15 his officials and the **leading m** *of* the land. 380
24:16 of seven thousand fighting **m,** 408
25:19 of the fighting **m** and five royal advisers. 408
25:19 the land and sixty of his **m** who were found 6639
25:23 the army officers and their **m** heard that 408
25:23 the son of the Maacathite, and their **m.** 408
25:24 an oath to reassure them and their **m.** 408
25:25 came with ten **m** and assassinated Gedaliah 408
25:25 and also the **m of Judah** and 3374
1Ch 4:12 These were the **m** *of* Recah. 408
4:22 the **m** *of* Cozeba, and Joash and Saraph, 408
4:38 The **m** listed above by name were leaders 465[S]
4:41 **The m** whose names were listed came in 465[S]
5:18 **m** ready for military service— NIH
5:18 able-bodied **m** who could handle shield 408
5:24 They were brave warriors, famous **m,** 408
6:31 These are **the m** David put in charge of 889[S]
6:33 Here are the *m who* **served,** AIT
7: 2 of Tola listed as **fighting m** 1475+2657
7: 4 had 36,000 **m ready for battle,** 1522+4878+7372
7: 5 The relatives who were **fighting m** 1475+2657
7: 7 Their genealogical record listed 22,034
fighting m. 1475+2657
7: 9 of families and 20,200 **fighting m.** 1475+2657
7:11 **fighting m** ready to go out to war. 1475+2657
7:21 and Elead were killed by the native-born **m** 408
7:40 heads of families, **choice** *m,* AIT
7:40 The number of **m** ready for battle, 408
9: 9 All these **m** were heads of their families. 408
9:13 They were **able m,** responsible for 1475+2657
10:12 all their valiant **m** went and took the bodies 408
11:10 These were the chiefs of David's **mighty m** 1475
11:11 this is the list of David's **mighty m:** 1475
11:11 against three hundred *m,* whom he **killed** AIT
11:12 one of the three **mighty m.** 1475
11:19 the blood of these **m** who went at the risk 408
11:19 the exploits of the three **mighty m.** 1475
11:20 against three hundred *m, whom* he **killed,** AIT
11:22 He struck down two of Moab's **best m.** 738
11:24 too was as famous as the three **mighty m.** 1475
11:26 The **mighty m** were: 1475+2657
12: 1 These were the *m who* **came** to David AIT
12:16 *m* from Judah also **came** AIT
12:19 *m* of Manasseh **defected** AIT
12:19 (*He and his m did* not **help** the Philistines AIT
12:20 *m* of Manasseh *who* **defected** AIT
12:22 Day after day *m* **came** to help David, AIT
12:23 the **m** armed for battle who came to David 8031
12:24 **m** *of* Judah, carrying shield and spear— 1201
12:25 **m** of Simeon, warriors ready for battle— 1201
12:26 **m** of Levi—4,600, 1201
12:27 leader of the family of Aaron, with 3,700 **m,** NIH
12:29 **m** of Benjamin, Saul's kinsmen— 1201
12:30 **m** of Ephraim, brave warriors, famous 1201
12:31 **m** of half the tribe of Manasseh, designated NIH
12:32 **m** of Issachar, who understood the times 1201
12:33 **m** of Zebulun, experienced soldiers NIH
12:34 **m** of Naphtali—1,000 NIH
12:34 **m** carrying shields and spears; NIH
12:35 **m of Dan,** ready for battle—28,600; 1974
12:36 **m** of Asher, experienced soldiers prepared NIH
12:37 **m of Reuben,** Gad and the half-tribe 8018
12:38 All these were fighting **m** who volunteered 408
12:39 *The m* **spent** three days there with David, AIT
14:11 David and *his m* **went up** to Baal Perazim, AIT
17: 8 the names of the **greatest** *m* of the earth. AIT
17:17 as though I were the most exalted of **m,** 132
17:24 Then **m** will say, 'The LORD Almighty, NIH
19: 2 When David's **m** came to Hanun in the land 6269
19: 3 by sending **m** to you to express sympathy? NIH
19: 3 Haven't his **m** come to you to explore 6269
19: 4 So Hanun seized David's **m,** shaved them, 6269
19: 5 someone came and told David about the **m,** 408
19: 8 with the entire army of **fighting m.** 1475
19:11 He put the rest of the **m** under the command 6639

1Ch 20: 8 they fell at the hands of David and his **m.** 6269
21: 5 Joab reported the number of the **fighting m** 6639
21: 5 In all Israel there were one million one
hundred thousand **m** who could handle 408
21:13 but do not let me fall into the hands of **m.**" 132
21:14 and seventy thousand **m** of Israel fell dead. 408
21:17 "Was it not I who ordered the **fighting m** to 6639
22:15 as well as **m** skilled in every kind of work 3972[S]
23: 3 number of **m** was thirty-eight thousand. 1505
25: 1 the list of the **m** who performed this service: 408
25: 6 All **these** *m* were under the supervision AIT
26: 6 because they were **very capable m.** 1475+2657
26: 7 and Semakiah were also **able m.** 1201+2657
26: 8 and their relatives were capable **m** with 408
26: 9 who were **able m—**18 in all. 1201+2657
26:12 through their chief **m,** 1505
26:30 seventeen hundred **able m—** 1201+2657
26:31 **capable m** among the Hebronites 1475+2657
26:32 were **able m** and heads of families, 1201+2657
27: 1 Each division consisted of 24,000 **m.** NIH
27: 2 There were 24,000 **m** in his division. NIH
27: 4 There were 24,000 **m** in his division. NIH
27: 5 and there were 24,000 **m** in his division. NIH
27: 7 There were 24,000 **m** in his division. NIH
27: 8 There were 24,000 **m** in his division. NIH
27: 9 There were 24,000 **m** in his division. NIH
27:10 There were 24,000 **m** in his division. NIH
27:11 There were 24,000 **m** in his division. NIH
27:12 There were 24,000 **m** in his division. NIH
27:13 There were 24,000 **m** in his division. NIH
27:14 There were 24,000 **m** in his division. NIH
27:15 There were 24,000 **m** in his division. NIH
27:23 the number of the **m** twenty years old NIH
27:24 Joab son of Zeruiah began to count the **m** NIH
28: 1 the **mighty m** and all the brave warriors. 1475
29:24 All the officers and **mighty m,** 1475
2Ch 2: 2 He conscripted seventy thousand **m** 408
2: 8 for I know that your **m** are skilled 6269
2: 8 My **m** will work with yours 6269
5: 3 the **m** *of* Israel came together to the king at 408
6:18 will God really dwell on earth with **m?** 132
6:30 (for you alone know the hearts of **m**), 132+1201
8: 9 they were his fighting **m,** 408
8:10 and fifty officials supervising the **m.** 6639
8:18 **m** who knew the sea. 6269
8:18 These, with Solomon's **m,** 6269
9: 7 How happy your **m** must be! 408
9:10 (The **m** *of* Hiram and the men 6269
9:10 the **m** *of* Solomon brought gold from Ophir; 6269
9:21 of trading ships manned by Hiram's **m.** 6269
10: 8 and consulted the **young m** who had grown 3529
10:10 The **young m** who had grown up 3529
10:14 he followed the advice of the **young m** 3529
11: 1 a hundred and eighty thousand fighting **m—** 1033
13: 3 of four hundred thousand able fighting **m,** 1475
13:12 **M** *of* Israel, do not fight against 1201
13:15 and the **m** *of* Judah raised the battle cry. 408
13:17 and his **m** inflicted heavy losses on them, 6639
13:17 among Israel's able **m.** 408
13:18 The **m** *of* Israel were subdued on 1201
13:18 and the **m** *of* Judah were victorious 1201
14: 8 of three hundred thousand **m** from Judah, NIH
14: 8 All these were **brave fighting m.** 1475+2657
14:13 The **m** of Judah carried off a large amount NIH
16: 6 Then King Asa brought all the **m** of Judah, NIH
17:13 **experienced fighting m** 408+1475+2657+4878
17:14 with 300,000 **fighting m;** 1475+2657
17:17 *m* **armed** *with* bows and shields; AIT
17:18 with 180,000 *m* **armed** *for* battle. AIT
17:19 These were the *m who* **served** the king, AIT
18: 5 together the prophets—four hundred **m—** 408
20: 2 *Some m* **came** and told Jehoshaphat, AIT
20:10 "But now here are **m** *from* Ammon, 1201
20:13 All the **m** of Judah, NIH
20:21 Jehoshaphat appointed *m to* **sing** to AIT
20:22 the LORD set ambushes against the **m** 1201
20:23 The *m of* Ammon and Moab rose up 1201
20:23 up against the **m** *from* Mount Seir to destroy 3782
20:23 After they finished slaughtering the **m** 3782
20:24 When the **m** of Judah came to the place NIH
20:25 and his **m** went to carry off their plunder, 6639
20:27 all the **m** *of* Judah 408
21:13 **m** who were better than you. 2021[S]
22: 9 and *his m* **captured** him AIT
23: 5 the other **m** are to be in the courtyards of 6639
23: 6 but all the other **m** are to guard what 6639
23: 8 The Levites and all the **m** of Judah did just NIH
23: 8 Each one took his **m—** 408
23:10 He stationed all the **m,** 6639
24:12 the *m who* **carried out** the work required for AIT
24:13 The *m* **in charge** *of* the work were diligent, AIT
24:24 Aramean army had come with only a few **m,** 408
25: 5 there were three hundred thousand **m** ready 1033
25: 6 a hundred thousand **fighting m** from 1475+2657
25:11 where he killed ten thousand **m** *of* Seir. 1201
25:12 also captured ten thousand *m* **alive,** AIT
25:27 but they sent **m** after him to Lachish NIH
26:12 over the **fighting m** was 2,600. 1475+2657
26:13 an army of 307,500 *m* **trained** *for* war, AIT
26:15 by **skillful m** for use on the towers and 3110
28:10 **make** the **m** and women of Judah and
Jerusalem your **slaves.** 3899+6269
28:15 The **m** designated by name took 408
30:11 Nevertheless, *some* **m** of Asher, 408
31: 6 The **m** *of* Israel and Judah who lived in 1201
31:19 **m** were designated by name 408
32: 4 A large **force of m** assembled, 6639

2Ch 32:21 the **fighting m** and the leaders and 1475+2657
34:10 to the *m* **appointed** to supervise the work on AIT
34:10 **These m** paid the workers who 2021+4856+6913^S
34:12 The **m** did the work faithfully. 408
34:30 the LORD with the **m** *of* Judah, the people 408
35:25 *m* and women **singers** commemorate Josiah AIT
36:17 who killed their **young m** with the sword in 1033
Ezr 2:2 The list of the **m** *of* the people of Israel: 408
2:21 the **m** *of* Bethlehem 123 1201
2:65 they also had 200 *m* and women **singers.** AIT
4:9 and officials over the **m from Tripolis,** 10305
4:11 the **m** *of* Trans-Euphrates: 10050
4:21 Now issue an order to these **m** to stop work, 10131
5:4 of the **m** constructing this building?" 10131
6:8 of these **m** are to be fully paid out of 10131
7:28 and gathered **leading** *m* from Israel to go AIT
8:3 and with him were registered 150 **m;** 2351
8:4 and with him 200 **m;** 2351
8:5 and with him 300 **m;** 2351
8:6 Ebed son of Jonathan, and with him 50 **m;** 2351
8:7 and with him 70 **m;** 2351
8:8 and with him 80 **m;** 2351
8:9 Obadiah son of Jehiel, and with him 218 **m;** 2351
8:10 and with him 160 **m;** 2351
8:11 and with him 28 **m;** 2351
8:12 and with him 110 **m;** 2351
8:13 Jeuel and Shemaiah, and with them 60 **m;** 2351
8:14 Uthai and Zaccur, and with them 70 **m.** 2351
8:16 *who were m of* **learning,** AIT
8:18 and Sherebiah's sons and brothers, **18** *m;* AIT
8:19 and his brothers and nephews, **20** *m.* AIT
10:1 **m,** women and children— 408
10:9 the **m** *of* Judah and Benjamin had gathered 408
10:16 priest selected **m** who were family heads, 408
10:17 the **m** who had married foreign women. 408
Ne 1:2 came from Judah with *some other* **m,** 408
2:12 I set out during the night with a few **m.** 408
3:2 The **m** *of* Jericho built the adjoining 408
3:5 repaired by the **m of Tekoa,** 9542
3:7 repairs were made by **m** *from* Gibeon 408
3:27 the **m of Tekoa** repaired another section, 9542
4:7 the Ammonites and the **m of Ashdod** heard 847
4:16 half of my **m** did the work, 5853
4:21 the work with half **the m** holding spears, 4392^S
4:23 nor my brothers nor my **m** nor the guards 5853
5:1 the **m** and their wives raised a great outcry 6639
5:10 and my brothers and my **m** are also lending 5853
5:16 All my **m** were assembled there for 5853
6:10 because *m are* **coming** to kill you— AIT
7:2 and feared God more than **most** *m* do. AIT
7:7 The list of the **m** *of* Israel: 408
7:26 the **m** *of* Bethlehem and Netophah 188 408
7:67 they also had 245 *m* and women **singers.** AIT
8:2 up of **m** and women and all who were able 408
8:3 the Water Gate in the presence of the **m,** 408
11:2 the **m** who volunteered to live in Jerusalem. 408
11:6 in Jerusalem totaled 468 able **m.** 408
11:8 Gabbai and Sallai—928 **m.** NIH
11:12 for the temple—822 **m;** NIH
11:13 who were heads of families—242 **m;** NIH
11:14 who were **able m**—128 1475+2657
11:19 at the gates—172 **m.** NIH
12:44 that time **m** were appointed to be in charge 408
13:13 *these m* **were considered** trustworthy. AIT
13:15 In those days I saw *m* in Judah **treading** winepresses on the Sabbath AIT
13:16 **M from Tyre** who lived in Jerusalem 7660
13:19 I stationed some of my own **m** at the gates 5853
13:23 I saw **m of Judah** who had married women 3374
13:25 beat some of the **m** and pulled out their hair. 408
Est 1:13 with the **wise m** who understood the times AIT
3:9 for the *m who* **carry out** this business." AIT
9:6 Jews killed and destroyed five hundred **m.** 408
9:12 and destroyed five hundred **m** and 408
9:15 they put to death in Susa three hundred **m,** 408
Job 4:13 when deep sleep falls on **m,** 408
7:20 what have I done to you, O watcher of **m?** 132
11:3 Will your idle talk reduce **m** to silence? 5493
11:11 Surely he recognizes deceitful **m;** 5493
12:5 *M* **at ease** have contempt for misfortune as AIT
12:19 and overthrows *m* **long established.** AIT
13:9 as you might deceive **m?** 632
14:12 the heavens are no more, **m** will not awake NIH
15:10 *m even* **older** than your father. AIT
15:18 what **wise** *m* have declared, AIT
16:10 *M* **open** their mouths to jeer at me; AIT
16:11 to **evil m** and thrown me into the clutches 6397
17:8 **Upright** *m* are appalled at this; AIT
17:12 These **m** turn night into day; NIH
18:20 *M of the* **west** are appalled at his fate; AIT
18:20 *m of the* **east** are seized with horror. AIT
21:28 the tents where **wicked** *m* lived?' AIT
21:33 all **m** follow after him, 132
22:6 you stripped **m** of their clothing, NIH
22:15 to the old path that evil **m** have trod? 5493
22:29 When *m are* **brought low** and you say, AIT
24:2 *M* **move** boundary stones; AIT
24:16 In the dark, *m* **break into** houses, AIT
24:20 **evil** *m* are no longer remembered AIT
28:4 far from **m** he dangles and sways. 632
29:8 the **young m** saw me and stepped aside and 5853
29:8 and stepped aside and the **old m** rose 3813
29:9 the **chief m** refrained from speaking 8569
29:21 "*M* **listened** to me expectantly, AIT
30:1 "But now they mock me, *m* **younger** than I, AIT
30:5 They were banished from their **fellow m,** 1569
31:10 and may **other** *m* sleep with her. AIT
Job 31:31 if the **m** *of* my household have never said, 5493
31:33 if I have concealed my sin as **m** do, 132
32:1 So these three **m** stopped answering Job, 408
32:5 that the three **m** had nothing more to say, 408
33:15 when deep sleep falls on **m** as they slumber 408
33:27 Then he comes to **m** and says, 'I sinned, 408
34:2 "Hear my words, you **wise** *m;* AIT
34:2 listen to me, you *m of* **learning.** AIT
34:8 he associates with wicked **m.** 408
34:10 "So listen to me, you **m** *of* understanding. 408
34:21 "His eyes are on the ways of **m;** 408
34:23 God has no need to examine **m** further, 408
34:34 "**M** *of* understanding declare, 408
34:34 wise **m** who hear me say to me, 1505
35:8 and your righteousness only the sons of **m.** 132
35:9 "*M* **cry out** under a load of oppression; AIT
35:12 when *m* **cry out** because of the arrogance of AIT
36:5 "God is mighty, but does not despise **m;** NIH
36:8 But if *m* **are bound** in chains, AIT
36:24 which **m** have praised in song. 408
36:25 **m** gaze on it from afar. 632
37:7 that all **m** he has made may know his work, 408
37:13 He brings the clouds to punish **m,** NIH
37:24 Therefore, **m** revere him, 408
Ps 4:2 **m,** will you turn my glory into shame? 408+1201
5:6 and deceitful **m** the LORD abhors. 408
9:20 let the nations know they are but **m.** 632
11:4 He observes the sons of **m;** 132
11:7 **upright** *m* will see his face. AIT
12:1 faithful have vanished from among **m.** 132+1201
12:8 when what is vile is honored among **m.** 132+1201
14:2 of **m** to see if there are any who understand, 132
14:4 those who devour my people as *m* **eat** bread AIT
17:4 As for the deeds of **m**— 132
17:14 by your hand save me from such **m,** 5493
17:14 from **m** of this world whose reward is 5493
18:48 from violent **m** you rescued me. 408
22:6 scorned by **m** and despised by the people. 132
22:16 a band of **evil m** has encircled me, AIT
26:4 I do not sit with deceitful **m,** 5493
26:9 my life with bloodthirsty **m,** 408
27:2 When **evil** *m* advance against me AIT
31:19 you bestow in the sight of **m** on those 132+1201
31:20 from the intrigues of **m;** 408
36:7 high and **low among m** find refuge in the shadow of your wings. 132+1201
37:1 not fret because of **evil** *m* or be envious AIT
37:7 do not fret when **m** succeed in their ways, 408
37:9 For **evil** *m* will be cut off, AIT
39:11 You rebuke and discipline **m** for their sin; 408
42:3 while **m** say to me all day long, NIH
43:1 rescue me from deceitful and wicked **m.** 408
45:2 You are the most excellent of **m** 132+1201
45:12 **m** of wealth will seek your favor. 6639
49:10 For all can see that **wise** *m* die; AIT
49:18 and *m* **praise** you when you prosper— AIT
53:2 of **m** to see if there are any who understand, 132
53:4 those who devour my people as *m* **eat** bread AIT
54:3 **ruthless** *m* seek my life— AIT
54:3 **m** without regard for God. 4392^S
55:19 *m* **who** never change their ways AIT
55:23 bloodthirsty and deceitful **m** will not live 408
56:1 O God, for **m** hotly pursue me; 632
57:4 **m** whose teeth are spears and arrows, 132+1201
58:1 Do you judge uprightly among **m?** 132+1201
58:11 Then **m** will say, "Surely the righteous 132
59:T When Saul had sent **m** to watch David's NIH
59:2 and save me from bloodthirsty **m.** 408
59:3 **Fierce** *m* conspire against me for no offense AIT
62:9 **Lowborn m** are but a breath, 132+1201
65:2 to you all **m** will come. 1414
66:12 You let **m** ride over our heads; 632
68:12 in the camps *m* **divide** the plunder. AIT
68:18 you received gifts from **m,** 132
71:4 from the grasp of evil and **cruel** *m.* AIT
74:5 They behaved like *m* **wielding** axes to cut AIT
75:1 *m* **tell** *of* your wonderful deeds. AIT
76:5 **Valiant m** lie plundered, 52+4213
76:10 your wrath against **m** brings you praise, 132
78:9 The **m** *of* Ephraim, though armed 1201
78:25 **M** ate the bread of angels; 408
78:31 cutting down the **young m** *of* Israel. 1033
78:60 the tent he had set up among **m.** 132
78:63 Fire consumed their **young m,** 1033
82:7 But you will die like mere **m;** 132
83:16 with shame so that *m will* **seek** your name, AIT
86:14 a band of **ruthless** *m* seeks my life— AIT
86:14 **m** without regard for you. 4392^S
89:47 For what futility you have created all **m!** 132+1201
90:3 You turn **m** back to dust, saying, 632
90:3 saying, "Return to dust, O sons of **m."** 132
90:5 You sweep **m** away in the sleep of death; 4392^S
101:3 The deeds of **faithless** *m* I hate; AIT
101:4 *M of* **perverse** heart shall be far from me; AIT
107:8 and his wonderful deeds for **m,** 132+1201
107:15 and his wonderful deeds for **m,** 132+1201
107:21 and his wonderful deeds for **m,** 132+1201
107:27 They reeled and staggered like **drunken m;** 8893
107:31 and his wonderful deeds for **m.** 132+1201
109:2 and **deceitful** *m* have opened their mouths AIT
115:4 silver and gold, made by the hands of **m.** 132
116:11 And in my dismay I said, "All **m** are liars." 132
119:86 help me, for *m* **persecute** me without cause. AIT
119:113 I hate **double-minded** *m,* but I love your law. AIT
119:134 Redeem me from the oppression of **m,** 132
124:2 not been on our side when **m** attacked us, 132
Ps 126:1 we were like *m who* **dreamed.** AIT
135:8 the firstborn of **m** and animals. 132
135:15 silver and gold, made by the hands of **m.** 132
139:19 Away from me, you bloodthirsty **m!** 408
140:1 Rescue me, O LORD, from evil **m;** 132
140:1 protect me from **m** *of* violence, 408
140:4 protect me from **m** *of* violence who plan 408
140:5 **Proud** *m* have hidden a snare for me; AIT
140:11 may disaster hunt down **m** *of* violence. 408
141:4 in wicked deeds with **m** who are evildoers; 408
142:3 where I walk *m have* **hidden** a snare AIT
145:12 that **all m** may know of your mighty acts 132+1201+2021
146:3 in **mortal m,** who cannot save. 132+1201
148:12 **young m** and maidens, 1033
148:12 **old** *m* and children. AIT
Pr 1:18 **These** *m* lie in wait for their own blood; AIT
2:12 save you from the ways of **wicked** *m,* AIT
2:12 from **m** whose words are perverse, 408
2:20 the ways of **good** *m* and keep to the paths of AIT
4:14 the wicked or walk in the way of **evil** *m.* AIT
6:30 *M do* **not despise** a thief if he steals AIT
7:7 I noticed among the **young m,** 1201
8:4 "To you, O **m,** I call out; 408
10:14 **Wise** *m* store up knowledge, AIT
11:16 but **ruthless** *m* gain only wealth. AIT
11:20 The LORD detests *m of* **perverse** heart AIT
12:7 **Wicked** *m* are overthrown and are no more, AIT
12:8 but *m with* **warped** minds are despised. AIT
12:12 The wicked desire the plunder of **evil** *m,* AIT
12:22 but he delights in *m who* **are** truthful. AIT
14:19 **Evil** *m* will bow down in the presence of AIT
15:11 how much more the hearts of **m!** 132+1201
20:29 The glory of **young m** is their strength, 1033
22:29 he will not serve before **obscure** *m.* AIT
23:28 and multiplies the unfaithful among **m.** 132
24:1 Do not envy wicked **m,** 408
24:9 and **m** detest a mocker. 132
24:19 not fret because of **evil** *m* or be envious of AIT
25:1 copied by the **m** *of* Hezekiah king of Judah: 408
25:6 and do not claim a place among **great** *m;* AIT
26:16 than seven *m who* **answer** discreetly. AIT
28:5 Evil **m** do not understand justice, 408
28:12 the wicked rise to power, **m** go into hiding. 132
29:8 but **wise m** turn away anger. AIT
29:10 Bloodthirsty **m** hate a man of integrity 408
30:2 "I am the most ignorant of **m;** 408
Ecc 1:11 There is no remembrance of *m* **of old,** AIT
1:13 a heavy burden God has laid on **m!** 132+1201
2:3 to see what was worthwhile for **m** 132+1201
2:8 I acquired *m* and women **singers,** AIT
3:10 seen the burden God has laid on **m.** 132+1201
3:11 He has also set eternity in the hearts of **m;** 4392^S
3:12 that there is nothing better for **m** than to 4392
3:14 God does it so that *m will* **revere** him. AIT
3:18 I also thought, "As for **m,** 132+1201
6:1 and it weighs heavily on **m:** 132
7:29 **m** have gone in search of many schemes." 2156^S
8:12 that it will go better with **God-fearing** *m,* AIT
8:14 **righteous** *m* who get what the wicked AIT
8:14 and **wicked** *m* who get what the righteous AIT
9:3 The hearts of **m,** moreover, 132+1201
9:12 a snare, so **m** are trapped by evil times 132+1201
12:3 and the strong **m** stoop, 408
12:4 when *m* **rise up** at the sound of birds, AIT
12:5 when *m are* **afraid** of heights and AIT
SS 2:3 the forest is my lover among the **young m.** 1201
Isa 2:11 be humbled and the pride of **m** brought low; 408
2:17 be brought low and the pride of **m** humbled; 408
2:19 *M will* **flee** to caves in the rocks and AIT
2:20 In that day **m** will throw away to the rodents 132
3:25 Your **m** will fall by the sword, 5493
5:3 "Now you dwellers in Jerusalem and **m** 408
5:7 the **m** *of* Judah are the garden of his delight. 408
5:13 their **m of rank** will die of hunger 3883
7:13 Is it not enough to try the patience of **m?** 408
7:24 *M will* **go** there with bow and arrow, AIT
8:14 a stone that causes **m** to stumble and a rock NIH
8:19 When *m* **tell** you to consult mediums AIT
9:3 as *m* **rejoice** when dividing the plunder. AIT
9:15 the elders and **prominent** *m* are the head, AIT
9:17 will take not pleasure in the **young m,** 1033
10:14 as **m** gather abandoned eggs, NIH
11:15 into seven streams so that *m can* **cross over** AIT
13:18 Their bows will strike down the **young m;** 5853
15:4 Therefore the **armed m** *of* Moab cry out, AIT
16:7 and grieve for the **m** *of* Kir Hareseth. 861
17:7 In that day **m** will look to their Maker 132
19:11 "I am one of the **wise m,** AIT
19:12 Where are your **wise** *m* now? AIT
29:13 of me is made up only of rules taught by **m.** 408
30:30 The LORD will cause **m** to hear NIH
31:3 But the Egyptians are **m** and not God; 132
31:8 before the sword and their **young m** will 1033
33:4 like a swarm of locusts *m* **pounce** on it. AIT
33:7 Look, their **brave m** cry aloud in the streets; 737
36:12 and not to the **m** sitting on the wall— 408
37:36 a hundred and eighty-five thousand **m** in NIH
38:16 Lord, by such things *m* **live;** AIT
39:3 "What did those **m** say, 408
40:6 "All **m** are like grass, 1414
40:30 and **young m** stumble and fall; 1033
43:4 I will give **m** in exchange for you, 132
44:11 craftsmen are nothing but **m.** 132
45:6 *m may* **know** there is none besides me. AIT
51:7 Do not fear the reproach of **m** or be terrified 632
51:12 Who are you that you fear mortal **m,** 632

Isa 51:12 the sons of **m,** who are but grass, 132
51:17 to its dregs the goblet that makes **m** stagger. NIH
53: 3 He was despised and rejected by **m,** 408
53: 3 from whom **m** hide their faces he was despised, NIH
57: 1 devout **m** are taken away, 408
59:10 feeling our way like **m** without eyes. NIH
59:19 *m will* **fear** the name of the LORD, AIT
60:11 so that **m** may bring you the wealth of NIH
65: 8 and *m* **say,** 'Don't destroy it, there is AIT
66:16 upon all **m,** and many will be those slain by 1414
Jer 2:16 the **m** *of* Memphis and Tahpanhes 1201
2:34 On your clothes *m* **find** the lifeblood of AIT
3:16 "*m will* no longer **say,** AIT
4: 3 the LORD says to the **m** *of* Judah and 408
4: 4 you **m** *of* Judah and people of Jerusalem, 408
4:17 They surround her like *m* **guarding** a field, AIT
5:26 "Among my people are **wicked** *m* who lie AIT
5:26 in wait like **m who snare birds and** 3687
5:26 and like those who set traps to catch **m.** 408
6:11 and on the **young m** gathered together; 1033
6:23 like **m** in battle formation to attack you, 408
8: 4 " 'When *m* **fall down,** do they not get up? AIT
8:10 Therefore I will give their wives to **other** *m* AIT
9:21 and the **young m** from the public squares. 1033
9:22 " 'The dead bodies of **m** will lie like refuse 132
10: 7 Among all the **wise** *m of* the nations and AIT
11:21 the LORD says about the **m** 408
11:22 Their **young m** will die by the sword, 1033
11:23 because I will bring disaster on the **m** 408
12: 5 with **m** on foot and they have worn you out, NIH
15: 8 against the mothers of their **young m;** 1033
16: 3 and the **m** who are their fathers: 3528[S]
16:14 *m will* no longer **say,** AIT
16:20 Do **m** make their own gods? 132
17:25 by the **m** *of* Judah and those living 408
18:21 let their **m** be put to death, 408
18:21 their **young m** slain by the sword in battle. 1033
21: 6 both **m** and animals— 132
26:22 along with *some* other **m.** 408
31:13 **young m** and old as well. 1033
31:27 the house of Judah with the offspring of **m** 132
32:19 Your eyes are open to all the ways of **m** 132+1201
32:32 the **m** *of* Judah and the people of Jerusalem. 408
32:43 without **m** or animals, 132
33: 5 of the **m** I will slay in my anger and wrath. 132
33:10 without **m** or animals." 132
33:10 inhabited by neither **m** nor animals, 132
33:12 desolate and without **m** or animals— 132
34:18 The **m** who have violated my covenant 408
35: 5 of wine and some cups before the **m** *of* 1201
35:13 the **m** *of* Judah and the people of Jerusalem, 408
36:29 and cut off both **m** and animals from it?" 132
37:10 and only wounded **m** were left in their tents, 408
38: 9 these **m** have acted wickedly 408
38:10 "Take thirty **m** from here with you 408
38:11 the **m** with him and went to a room under 408
40: 7 the army officers and their **m** who were still 408
40: 7 the land and had put him in charge of the **m,** 408
40: 8 the son of the Maacathite, and their **m.** 408
40: 9 took an oath to reassure them and their **m.** 408
41: 1 came with ten **m** to Gedaliah son of Ahikam 408
41: 2 and the ten **m** who were with him got up 408
41: 5 eighty **m** who had shaved off their beards, 408
41: 7 the **m** who were with him slaughtered them 408
41: 9 the bodies of the **m** he had killed along 408
41:12 they took all their **m** and went 408
41:15 of his **m** escaped from Johanan and fled to 408
43: 2 and all the arrogant **m** said to Jeremiah, 408
43: 6 They also led away all the **m,** 1505
44: 7 by cutting off from Judah the **m** 408
44:15 Then all the **m** who knew 408
44:20 both **m** and women, 1505
46: 9 **m** of Cush and Put who carry shields, NIH
46: 9 **m of Lydia** who draw the bow. 4276
46:22 like *m who* **cut down** trees. AIT
48: 2 in Heshbon *m will* **plot** her downfall: AIT
48:12 "when I will send *m who* **pour** from jars, AIT
48:14 'We are warriors, **m** valiant in battle'? 408
48:15 her finest **young m** will go down in 1033
48:31 I moan for the **m** *of* Kir Hareseth. 408
48:36 like a flute for the **m** *of* Kir Hareseth. 408
49:15 among the nations, despised among **m.** 132
49:26 Surely, her **young m** will fall in the streets; 1033
49:29 *M will* **shout** to them, AIT
50: 3 both **m** and animals will flee away. 132
50:30 her **young m** will fall in the streets; 1033
50:35 and against her officials and **wise** *m!* AIT
50:42 like **m** in battle formation to attack you, 408
51: 3 Do not spare her **young m;** 1033
51:14 I will surely fill you with **m,** 132
51:57 I will make her officials and **wise** *m* drunk, AIT
52:25 the officer in charge of the fighting **m,** 408
52:25 the land and sixty of his **m** who were found 6639
La 1:15 an army against me to crush my **young m.** 1033
1:18 My **young m** and maidens have gone 1033
2:12 as they faint like **wounded** *m* in the streets AIT
2:21 my **young m** and maidens have fallen by 1033
3:31 For *m are* not **cast off** *by* the Lord forever. AIT
3:33 or grief to the children of **m.** 408
4:14 through the streets like *m who* are **blind.** AIT
4:15 You are unclean!" *m* **cry** to them. AIT
4:18 *M* **stalked** us *at* every step, AIT
5:13 **Young m** toil at the millstones; 1033
5:14 the **young m** have stopped their music. 1033
Eze 8:16 were about twenty-five **m.** 408
9: 2 And I saw six **m** coming from the direction 408
Eze 9: 6 Slaughter **old** *m,* young men and maidens, AIT
9: 6 Slaughter old men, **young m** and maidens, 1033
11: 1 the entrance to the gate were twenty-five **m,** 408
11: 2 these are the **m** who are plotting evil 408
14: 3 these **m** have set up idols in their hearts 408
14:13 upon it and kill its **m** and their animals, 132
14:14 if these three **m**—Noah, Daniel and Job 408
14:16 even if these three **m** were in it, 408
14:17 and I kill its **m** and their animals, 132
14:18 even if these three **m** were in it, 408
14:19 killing its **m** and their animals, 132
14:21 to kill its **m** and their animals! 132
17:13 He also carried away the **leading m** *of* 380
19: 3 to tear the prey and he devoured **m.** 132
19: 6 to tear the prey and he devoured **m.** 132
21:31 I will hand you over to brutal **m,** 408
21:31 *m* **skilled** *in* destruction. AIT
22: 9 In you are slanderous **m** bent 408
22:12 In you *m* **accept** bribes to shed blood; AIT
22:20 As **m** gather silver, copper, iron, NIH
23: 6 all of them handsome **young m,** 1033
23: 8 when during her youth *m* **slept with** her, AIT
23:12 mounted horsemen, all handsome **young m.** 1033
23:14 She saw **m** portrayed on a wall, 408
23:23 the **m** of Pekod and Shoa and Koa, NIH
23:23 handsome **young m,** all of them governors 1033
23:23 chariot officers and **m of high rank,** 7924
23:40 even sent messengers for **m** who came 408
23:42 the desert along with **m** from the rabble, 408
23:44 As *m* **sleep with** a prostitute, AIT
23:45 But righteous **m** will sentence them to 408
25:13 and kill its **m** and their animals. 132
26:10 when he enters your gates as *m* **enter** AIT
26:17 O city of renown, **peopled** *by m of* the sea! AIT
27: 8 **M** *of* Sidon and Arvad were your oarsmen; 3782
27: 8 your **skilled** *m,* O Tyre, AIT
27:10 " '**M** of Persia, Lydia and Put served NIH
27:11 **M** *of* Arvad and Helech manned your walls 1201
27:11 **m of Gammad** were in your towers. 1689
27:14 " '**M** of Beth Togarmah exchanged work horses, NIH
27:15 " 'The **m** *of* Rhodes traded with you, 1201
29: 8 a sword against you and kill your **m** 132
30:12 of the Nile and sell the land to **evil** *m;* AIT
30:17 The **young m** *of* Heliopolis 1033
31:14 for the earth below, among **mortal m,** 132+1201
32:12 to fall by the swords of **mighty m—** 1475
33: 2 the people of the land choose one of their **m** 408
36:11 I will increase the number of **m** and animals 132
36:13 Because people say to you, "You devour **m** 132
36:14 therefore you will no longer devour **m** 132
39:14 " '**M** will be regularly employed to cleanse 408
39:18 You will eat the flesh of **mighty m** and 1475
39:20 **mighty m** and soldiers of every kind,' 1475
Da 1: 4 **young m** without any physical defect, 3529
1:10 the other **young m** your age? 3529
1:13 that of the **young m** who eat the royal food, 3529
1:15 of the **young m** who ate the royal food. 3529
1:17 these four **young m** God gave knowledge 3529
2:11 and they do not live among **m.**" 10125
2:12 the execution of all the **wise** *m of* Babylon. AIT
2:13 decree was issued to put the **wise** *m* to death AIT
2:13 *m were sent to* **look for** Daniel AIT
2:14 had gone out to put to death the **wise** *m* AIT
2:18 not be executed with the rest of the **wise** *m* AIT
2:24 king had appointed to execute the **wise** *m* AIT
2:24 "Do not execute the **wise** *m of* Babylon. AIT
2:30 I have greater wisdom than other **living** *m,* AIT
2:48 and placed him in charge of all its **wise** *m.* AIT
3: 4 **m of every language:** 10392
3: 7 nations and **m of every language** fell down 10392
3:13 So these **m** were brought before the king, 10131
3:21 So these **m,** wearing their robes, trousers, 10131
3:23 and these three **m,** firmly tied, fell into 10131
3:24 "Weren't there three **m** that we tied up 10131
3:25 I see four **m** walking around in the fire, 10131
4: 1 **m of every language,** 10392
4: 6 the **wise** *m of* Babylon be brought before me AIT
4:17 of **m** and gives them to anyone he wishes 10050
4:17 and sets over them the lowliest of **m.'** 10050
4:18 of the **wise** *m in* my kingdom can interpret it AIT
4:25 of **m** and gives them to anyone he wishes. 10050
4:32 of **m** and gives them to anyone he wishes." 10050
5: 7 to be brought and said to these **wise** *m* AIT
5: 8 Then all the king's **wise** *m* came in, AIT
5:15 The **wise** *m* and enchanters were brought AIT
5:19 and **m of every language** dreaded 10392
5:21 of **m** and sets over them anyone he wishes. 10050
6: 5 Finally these **m** said, 10131
6:11 Then these **m** went as a group 10131
6:15 the **m** went as a group to the king and said 10131
6:24 the **m** who had falsely accused Daniel were brought in and thrown into the lions' 10131
6:25 and **m of every language** throughout 10392
7:14 and **m of every language** worshiped him. 10392
8:24 the **mighty** *m* and the holy people. AIT
9: 7 the **m** *of* Judah and people of Jerusalem 408
10: 7 the **m** with me did not see it, 408
11:14 The violent **m** among your own people 1201
Hos 4:14 the *m* **themselves** consort with harlots AIT
6: 8 Gilead is a city of **wicked m,** 224+7188
13: 1 When Ephraim spoke, **m** trembled; NIH
14: 7 *M will* **dwell** again in his shade. AIT
Joel 2:28 your **old** *m* will dream dreams, AIT
2:28 your **young m** will see visions. 1033
2:29 Even on my **servants,** both **m** and women, 6269
3: 9 Let all the fighting **m** draw near and attack. 408
Am 2:11 and Nazirites from among your **young m.** 1033
4:10 I killed your **young m** with the sword, 1033
6: 1 *you* **notable** *m of* the foremost nation, AIT
6: 9 If ten **m** are left in one house, 408
8:12 *M will* **stagger** from sea to sea and wander AIT
8:13 and **strong young m** will faint because 1033
Ob 1: 8 "will I not destroy the **wise** *m* of Edom, AIT
1: 8 *m of* **understanding** in the mountains AIT
Jnh 1:13 the **m** did their best to row back to land. 408
1:16 At this the **m** greatly feared the LORD, 408
Mic 2: 4 In that day *m will* **ridicule** you; AIT
2: 8 like *m* **returning** *from* battle. AIT
5: 5 even eight leaders of **m.** 132
6:12 Her **rich** *m* are violent; AIT
7: 2 All **m** lie in wait to shed blood; 4392[S]
Na 3:10 and all her **great** *m* were put in chains. AIT
Hab 1:11 **guilty** *m,* whose own strength is their god." AIT
1:14 You have made **m** like fish in the sea, 132
Zep 1: 3 "I will sweep away both **m** and animals; 132
1:17 the people and they will walk like **blind** *m,* AIT
3: 4 they are treacherous **m.** 408
Hag 1:11 on **m** and cattle, and on the labor 132
Zec 2: 4 of the great number of **m** and livestock in it. 132
3: 8 who are **m** symbolic of things to come: 408
4:10 *M will* **rejoice** when they see AIT
7: 2 together with their **m,** to entreat the LORD 408
8: 4 *m* and women **of ripe old age** AIT
8:23 "In those days ten **m** from all languages 408
9: 1 the eyes of **m** and all the tribes of Israel are 132
9:17 Grain will make the **young m** thrive, 1033
10: 1 He gives showers of rain to **m,** 2157[S]
10: 5 like **mighty m** trampling the muddy streets 1475
10: 7 Ephraimites will become like **mighty m,** 1475
14:13 that day **m** will be stricken by the LORD 2157[S]
Mal 2: 7 from his mouth *m should* **seek** instruction— AIT
3: 3 LORD will have *m who will* **bring** offerings AIT
Mt 4:19 "and I will make you fishers *of* **m.**" *476*
5:13 except to be thrown out and trampled by **m.** *476*
5:16 let your light shine before **m,** *476*
6: 1 to do your 'acts of righteousness' before **m,** *476*
6: 2 to be honored by **m.** *476*
6: 5 and on the street corners to be seen *by* **m.** *476*
6:14 if you forgive **m** when they sin against you, *476*
6:15 But if you do not forgive **m** their sins, *476*
6:16 to show **m** they are fasting. *476*
6:18 not be obvious *to* **m** that you are fasting, *476*
8:27 The **m** were amazed and asked, *476*
8:28 two **demon-possessed** *m* coming from *AIT*
8:33 to the **demon-possessed** *m.* *AIT*
9: 2 *Some m* **brought** to him a paralytic, *AIT*
9: 8 who had given such authority *to* **m.** *476*
9:17 Neither *do m* **pour** new wine *AIT*
9:27 two **blind** *m* followed him, calling out, *AIT*
9:28 the **blind** *m* came to him, *AIT*
10:17 "Be on your guard against **m;** *476*
10:22 **All** *m* will hate you because of me, *AIT*
10:32 "Whoever acknowledges me before **m,** *476*
10:33 But whoever disowns me before **m,** *476*
11:12 and **forceful** *m* lay hold of it. *AIT*
12:31 and blasphemy will be forgiven **m,** *476*
12:36 that **m** will have to give account on the day *476*
12:41 The **m** of Nineveh will stand up at *467*
13:17 and **righteous** *m* longed to see what you see *AIT*
14:21 about five thousand **m,** *467*
14:35 when the **m** of that place recognized Jesus, *467*
15: 9 their teachings are but rules taught *by* **m.'** " *476*
16:23 but the things *of* **m.**" *476*
17:22 to be betrayed into the hands *of* **m.** *476*
19:12 others were made that way by **m;** *476*
20: 1 to hire **m to work** in his vineyard. *2239*
20:12 '**These** *m* who were hired last worked only one hour,' *AIT*
20:30 Two **blind** *m* were sitting by the roadside, *AIT*
21:25 Was it from heaven, or from **m?**" *476*
21:26 But if we say, 'From **m'**— *476*
22:16 You aren't swayed by **m,** *4029*
23: 5 "Everything they do is done for **m** to see: *476*
23: 7 and to have **m** call them 'Rabbi.' *476*
23:19 *You* **blind** *m!* Which is greater: *AIT*
23:34 and **wise** *m* and teachers. *AIT*
24:40 **Two** *m* will be in the field; *AIT*
26:40 "Could you **m** not keep watch with me *NIG*
26:50 Then the *m* **stepped forward,** *AIT*
26:62 that **these** *m* are bringing against you?" *AIT*
28: 4 that they shook and became like **dead** *m.* *AIT*
Mk 1:17 "and I will make you fishers *of* **m.**" *476*
1:20 the boat with the **hired m** and followed him. *3638*
2: 3 Some *m* **came,** bringing to him a paralytic, *AIT*
3:28 all the sins and blasphemies of **m** will be forgiven them. *476+3836+3836+5626*
5:35 *some m* **came** from the house of Jairus, *AIT*
6:21 and the **leading** *m* of Galilee. *AIT*
6:44 of the **m** who had eaten was five thousand. *467*
7: 7 their teachings are but rules taught by **m.'** *476*
7: 8 and are holding on to the traditions *of* **m.**" *476*
8: 9 About **four thousand** *m* were present. *AIT*
8:33 the things of God, but the things *of* **m.**" *476*
9:31 to be betrayed into the hands *of* **m.** *476*
11:30 was it from heaven, or from **m?** *476*
11:32 But if we say, 'From **m'.**" *476*
12:14 You aren't swayed by **m,** *4029[S]*
12:40 **Such** *m* will be punished most severely." *AIT*
13:13 **All** *m* will hate you because of me, *AIT*
13:26 that time *m will* **see** the Son of Man coming *AIT*
14:46 **The m** seized Jesus and arrested him. *1254+3836[S]*
14:60 that **these** *m* are bringing against you?" *AIT*
Lk 2:14 peace to **m** on whom his favor rests." *476*

Lk 2:52 and in favor with God and **m.** 476
5:10 from now on you will catch **m."** 476
5:18 Some **m** came carrying a paralytic on a mat 467
6:22 Blessed are you when **m** hate you, 476
6:26 Woe to you when all **m** speak well of you, 476
7:10 Then **the** *m* **who** had been sent returned to AIT
7:20 When the **m** came to Jesus, they said, 467
7:41 "Two **m** owed money to a certain NIG
9:14 (About five thousand **m** were there.) 467
9:30 Two **m,** Moses and Elijah, 467
9:32 they saw his glory and the two **m** standing 467
9:33 As **the m** were leaving Jesus, 899^S
9:44 to be betrayed into the hands *of* **m."** 476
11:31 the **m** of this generation and condemn them; 467
11:32 The **m** of Nineveh will stand up at 467
11:44 which **m** walk over without knowing it." 476
12:8 whoever acknowledges me before **m,** 476
12:9 before **m** will be disowned before the angels 476
12:36 like **m** waiting for their master to return 476
14:24 *of* those **m** who were invited will get a taste 467
14:31 with ten **thousand** *m* to oppose AIT
15:17 of my father's **hired m** have food to spare, 3634
15:19 make me like one *of* your **hired m.'** 3634
16:15 who justify yourselves in the eyes *of* **m,** 476
16:15 among **m** is detestable in God's sight. 476
17:12 ten **m** who had leprosy met him. 467
17:23 *M will* **tell** you, 'There he is!' AIT
18:2 neither feared God nor cared about **m.** 476
18:4 though I don't fear God or care about **m,** 476
18:10 "Two **m** went up to the temple to pray, 476
18:11 'God, I thank you that I am not like other **m** 476
18:27 "What is impossible with **m** is possible 476
20:4 was it from heaven, or from **m?"** 476
20:6 But if we say, 'From **m,'** 476
20:47 **Such** *m* will be punished most severely." AIT
21:17 **All** *m* will hate you because of me. AIT
21:26 **M** will faint from terror, 476
22:63 The **m** who were guarding Jesus began mocking and beating him. 467
23:31 if *m* **do** these things when the tree is green, AIT
23:32 Two **other** *m,* both criminals, AIT
24:4 suddenly two **m** in clothes that gleamed 467
24:5 but the *m* **said** to them, AIT
24:7 be delivered into the hands *of* sinful **m,** 476
Jn 1:4 and that life was the light *of* **m.** 476
1:7 so that through him **all** *m* might believe. AIT
2:14 the temple courts he found **m** selling cattle, 3836^S
2:24 for he knew **all** *m.* AIT
3:19 into the world, but **m** loved darkness instead 476
5:41 "I do not accept praise from **m,** 476
6:10 and the **m** sat down, about five thousand 467
8:17 that the testimony *of* two **m** is valid. 476
12:32 will draw **all** *m* to myself." AIT
12:43 *from* **m** more than praise from God. 476
13:35 By this **all** *m* will know AIT
16:9 because *m do* not **believe** in me; AIT
18:8 you are looking for me, then let **these** *m* go. AIT
Ac 1:3 showed himself *to* **these m** and gave 4005^S
1:10 when suddenly two **m** dressed in white 467
1:11 **"M** of Galilee," they said, 467
1:21 to choose one *of* the **m** who have been 467
1:23 So they proposed **two** *m:* AIT
2:7 not all **these** *m* who are speaking Galileans? AIT
2:15 **These** *m* are not drunk, as you suppose. AIT
2:17 your **young m** will see visions, 3734
2:17 your old *m* will dream **dreams.** AIT
2:18 Even on my servants, both **m** and women, NIG
2:22 **"M** of Israel, listen to this: 467
2:23 and you, with the help *of* **wicked** *m,* AIT
3:12 **"M** of Israel, why does this surprise you? 467
4:4 number *of* **m** grew to about five thousand. 467
4:6 and the **other** *m* of the high priest's family. AIT
4:12 under heaven given to **m** by which we must 476
4:13 that they were unschooled, ordinary **m,** 476
4:13 and they took note that these **m** had been NIG
4:16 "What are we going to do with these **m?"** 476
4:17 we must warn **these** *m* to speak no longer AIT
5:4 You have not lied *to* **m** but to God." 476
5:6 Then the **young** *m* came forward, AIT
5:9 *of the m* **who** buried your husband are at AIT
5:10 Then the **young m** came in and, 3734
5:14 more and more **m** and women believed in 467
5:25 The **m** you put in jail are standing in 467
5:29 "We must obey God rather than **m!** 476
5:34 up in the Sanhedrin and ordered that the **m** 476
5:35 Then he addressed them: **"M** of Israel, 467
5:35 what you intend to do to these **m.** 467
5:36 and about four hundred **m** rallied to him. 467
5:38 Leave these **m** alone! 476
5:39 you will not be able to stop **these m;** 899^S
6:3 choose seven **m** from among you 467
6:6 They presented **these** *m* to the apostles, AIT
6:9 *m* began *to* **argue with** Stephen, AIT
6:11 they secretly persuaded some **m** to say, 467
7:26 He tried to reconcile them by saying, **'M,** 467
7:48 the Most High does not live in houses **made by m.** 5935
8:2 Godly **m** buried Stephen 467
8:3 he dragged off **m** and women and put them 467
8:12 they were baptized, both **m** and women. 467
9:2 whether **m** or women, 467
9:7 The **m** traveling with Saul 467
9:38 they sent two **m** to him and urged him, 467
10:5 Now send **m** to Joppa to bring back 467
10:17 the **m** sent by Cornelius found out 467
10:19 "Simon, three **m** are looking for you. 467
10:21 Peter went down and said to the **m,** 467
Ac 10:22 **The m** replied, "We have come 1254+3836^S
10:23 Then Peter invited **the m** into the house to 899^S
10:35 but accepts **m** from every nation NIG
11:3 into the house of uncircumcised **m** and ate 467
11:11 "Right then three **m** who had been sent 467
11:20 however, **m** from Cyprus and Cyrene, 467
13:16 **"M** of Israel and you Gentiles who worship 467
13:50 of high standing and the **leading** *m* of AIT
14:15 **"M,** why are you doing this? 467
14:15 We too are only **m,** human like you. 476
15:1 **Some** *m* came down from Judea to Antioch AIT
15:17 that the remnant *of* **m** may seek the Lord, 476
15:22 of their own **m** and send them to Antioch 467
15:22 *two* **m** who were leaders among 467
15:25 to choose some **m** and send them to you 467
15:26 **m** who have risked their lives for the name 476
15:30 **The m** were sent off and went down 3525+3836^S
16:17 "These **m** are servants of the Most High God 476
16:20 "These **m** are Jews, 476
16:35 with the order: "Release those **m."** 476
17:6 **"These** *m* who have caused trouble all over AIT
17:12 Greek women and many Greek **m.** 467
17:15 **The** *m* **who** escorted Paul brought him AIT
17:22 and said: **"M** of Athens! 467
17:25 because he himself gives **all** *m* life AIT
17:26 From one man he made every nation *of* **m,** 476
17:27 God did this so that **m** would seek him NIG
17:31 *to* **all** *m* by raising him from the dead." AIT
17:34 A few **m** became followers of Paul 467
19:7 There were about twelve **m** in all. 467
19:25 **"M,** you know we receive a good income 467
19:35 **"M** of Ephesus, doesn't all the world know 467
19:37 You have brought these **m** here, 467
20:5 **These** *m* went on ahead and waited for us AIT
20:26 that I am innocent of the blood *of* **all** *m.* AIT
20:30 Even from your own number **m** will arise 467
21:23 There are four **m** with us who have made 467
21:24 Take **these** *m,* join in their purification rites AIT
21:26 the **m** and purified himself along with them. 467
21:28 **"M** of Israel, help us! 467
21:28 the man who teaches **all** *m* everywhere AIT
22:4 both **m** and women and throwing them 467
22:15 to all **m** of what you have seen and heard. 476
22:19 '**these** *m* know that I went AIT
23:13 More than **forty** *m* were involved AIT
24:15 and I have the same hope in God as **these** *m,* AIT
25:23 the high ranking officers and the leading **m** 467
27:10 **"M,** I can see that our voyage is going to 467
27:17 When the **m** had hoisted it aboard, NIG
27:21 the **m** had gone a long time without food, NIG
27:21 **"M,** you should have taken my advice not 467
27:25 So keep up your courage, **m,** 467
27:31 "Unless **these** *m* stay with the ship, AIT
28:15 At the sight of **these** *m* Paul thanked God AIT
Ro 1:18 and wickedness *of* **m** who suppress 476
1:20 so that **m** are without excuse. 899^S
1:27 the **m** also abandoned natural relations 781
1:27 **M** committed indecent acts with other men, 781
1:27 Men committed indecent acts with other **m,** 781
2:29 Such a man's praise is not from **m,** 476
5:12 and in this way death came to all **m,** 476
5:18 of one trespass was condemnation for all **m,** 476
5:18 that brings life for all **m.** 476
7:1 for I am speaking *to m who* **know** the law— AIT
9:33 a stone that **causes m to stumble** 4682
11:32 For God has bound **all** *m* over AIT
14:18 to God and approved *by* **m.** 476
1Co 2:11 For who *among* **m** knows the thoughts of 476
3:3 Are you not acting like mere **m?** 476
3:4 "I follow Apollos," are you not mere **m?** 476
3:21 So then, no more boasting about **m!** 476
4:1 **m** ought to regard us as servants of Christ 476
4:9 like *m* **condemned to die** in the arena. AIT
4:9 to angels as well as *to* **m.** 476
6:4 appoint as judges even **m** of little account 4047^S
7:7 I wish that all **m** were as I am. 476
7:23 do not become slaves *of* **m.** 476
9:22 I have become all things *to* **all** *m* so that AIT
12:6 the same God works all of them in **all** *m.* AIT
13:1 If I speak in the tongues *of* **m** and of angels, 476
14:2 in a tongue does not speak *to* **m** but to God. 476
14:3 But everyone who prophesies speaks *to* **m** 476
14:21 "Through *m of* **strange tongues** and AIT
15:19 we are to be pitied more than all **m.** 476
15:39 **M** have one kind of flesh, 476
16:3 of introduction to **the m** you approve 4005^S
16:13 *be* **m of courage;** be strong. 437
16:18 **Such** *m* deserve recognition. AIT
2Co 2:17 like **m** sent from God. NIG
3:9 If the ministry that condemns **m** is glorious, NIG
5:11 we try to persuade **m.** 476
8:21 of the Lord but also in the eyes *of* **m.** 476
8:24 Therefore show **these** *m* the proof AIT
9:13 *m will* **praise** God for the obedience AIT
11:13 For **such** *m* are false apostles, AIT
12:17 through any *of* **the m** I sent you? 4005^S
Gal 1:1 sent not from **m** nor by man, 476
1:10 Am I now trying to win the approval of **m,** 476
1:10 Or am I trying to please **m?** 476
1:10 If I were still trying to please **m,** 476
2:6 those **m** added nothing to my message. 1506^S
2:12 Before **certain** *m* came from James, AIT
Eph 2:11 (that done in the body by the hands of **m**)— NIG
3:5 not made known *to* **m** in other generations 476+3836+3836+5626
4:8 in his train and gave gifts *to* **m."** 476
4:14 and by the cunning and craftiness *of* **m** 476
Eph 6:7 as if you were serving the Lord, not **m,** 476
Php 2:29 and honor **m like him,** 5525
3:2 **those** *m* **who** do evil, AIT
Col 2:11 **not** with a circumcision **done by the hands of m** 942
3:23 as working for the Lord, not *for* **m,** 476
1Th 2:4 as **m** approved by God to be entrusted with NIG
2:4 We are not trying to please **m** but God, 476
2:6 We were not looking for praise from **m,** 476
2:13 you accepted it not as the word *of* **m,** 476
2:15 They displease God and are hostile *to* all **m** 476
4:6 The Lord will punish **m** for all such sins, NIG
4:13 or to grieve like the **rest** *of m,* AIT
2Th 3:2 be delivered from wicked and evil **m,** 476
1Ti 1:3 so that you may command **certain** *m* not AIT
2:4 who wants all **m** to be saved and to come to 476
2:5 and one mediator between God and **m,** 476
2:6 who gave himself as a ransom for **all** *m*— AIT
2:8 I want **m** everywhere to lift up holy hands 467
3:8 likewise, are to be **m** worthy of respect, NIG
4:10 who is the Savior *of* all **m,** 476
5:1 Treat **younger** *m* as brothers, AIT
5:24 The sins of some **m** are obvious, 476
6:5 and constant friction between **m** 476
6:9 and harmful desires that plunge **m** into ruin 476
2Ti 2:2 *to* reliable **m** who will also be qualified 476
3:8 so also **these** *m* oppose the truth— AIT
3:8 **m** of depraved minds, who, 476
3:9 as in the case *of* **those** *m,* AIT
3:13 while evil **m** and impostors will go 476
4:3 *m will* not **put up with** sound doctrine. AIT
Tit 2:2 Teach the **older** *m* to be temperate, AIT
2:6 the **young** *m* to be self-controlled. AIT
2:11 that brings salvation has appeared *to* all **m.** 476
3:2 and to show true humility toward all **m.** 476
Heb 2:11 Both the one who makes **m** holy NIG
5:1 among **m** and is appointed to represent them 476
6:16 **M** swear by someone greater than themselves, 476
7:8 the tenth is collected by **m** who die; 476
7:28 as high priests **m** who are weak; 476
8:4 for there are already **m who** offer 3836^S
12:3 from **sinful** *m,* so that you will AIT
12:14 to live in peace with **all** *m* and to be holy; AIT
12:23 You have come to God, the judge *of* **all** *m,* AIT
12:23 to the spirits *of* **righteous** *m* made perfect, AIT
13:17 over you as **m** who must give an account. NIG
Jas 3:9 and with it we curse **m,** 476
5:6 and murdered **innocent** *m,* AIT
1Pe 1:24 For, "All **m** are like grass, 4922
2:4 by **m** but chosen by God and precious 476
2:8 "A stone that **causes m to stumble** and 4682
2:13 to every authority instituted **among m:** 474
2:15 the ignorant talk *of* foolish **m.** 476
2:16 Live as **free** *m,* but do not use your freedom AIT
4:6 so that they might be judged according to **m** 476
5:5 **Young** *m,* in the same way be submissive AIT
2Pe 1:21 but **m** spoke from God as they were carried 476
2:7 by the filthy lives *of* **lawless** *m* AIT
2:9 to rescue **godly** *m* from trials and to hold AIT
2:10 these **m** are not afraid to slander celestial NIG
2:12 But **these** *m* blaspheme in matters they do AIT
2:17 **These** *m* are springs without water AIT
3:7 of judgment and destruction *of* ungodly **m.** 476
3:17 be carried away by the error *of* **lawless** *m* AIT
1Jn 2:13 I write to you, **young m,** 3734
2:14 I write to you, **young m,** 3734
3Jn 1:8 to **such** *m* so that we may work together for AIT
Jude 1:4 certain **m** whose condemnation was written 476
1:4 They are **godless** *m,* AIT
1:10 Yet **these** *m* speak abusively AIT
1:12 **These** *m* are blemishes at your love feasts, AIT
1:14 prophesied *about* **these** *m:* AIT
1:16 **These** *m* are grumblers and faultfinders; AIT
1:19 These are **the** *m* **who** divide you, AIT
Rev 2:2 I know that you cannot tolerate **wicked** *m,* AIT
5:9 with your blood you purchased **m** for God NIG
6:4 the earth and to make **m** slay each other. NIG
9:6 During those days **m** will seek death, 476
11:6 **These** *m* have power to shut up the sky so AIT
11:9 *m* from every people, tribe, language and nation *will* **gaze on** AIT
13:4 *M* **worshiped** the dragon AIT
13:13 from heaven to earth in full view *of* **m.** 476
14:4 among **m** and offered as firstfruits to God 476
16:10 *M* **gnawed** their tongues in agony AIT
16:21 about a hundred pounds each fell upon **m.** 476
18:13 and bodies and souls *of* **m.** 476
18:23 Your merchants were the world's **great** *m.* AIT
19:18 and **mighty** *m,* of horses and their riders, AIT
21:3 "Now the dwelling of God is with **m,** 476

MEN'S (14) [MAN]

Ge 44:1 "Fill the **m** sacks with as much food 408
Ex 30:32 on **m** bodies and do not make any oil with 132
Dt 22:5 A woman must not wear **m** clothing, 1505
1Sa 21:5 The **m** things are holy even on missions 5853
2Ki 19:18 wood and stone, fashioned by **m** hands. 132
2Ch 32:19 the work of **m** hands. 132
Mt 23:4 and put them on **m** shoulders, 476
23:13 You shut the kingdom of heaven in **m** faces. 476
23:27 but on the inside are full *of* **dead m** bones AIT
Mk 7:21 For from within, out of **m** hearts, 476
Ro 2:16 on the day when God will judge **m** secrets 476
1Co 2:5 that your faith might not rest on **m** wisdom, 476
4:5 and will expose the motives of **m** hearts. NIG

2Co 5:19 not counting **m** sins against them. 899S

MENAHEM (7) [MENAHEM'S]
2Ki 15:14 Then **M** son of Gadi went from Tirzah up 4968
15:16 At that time **M**, starting out from Tirzah, 4968
15:17 **M** son of Gadi became king of Israel, 4968
15:19 and **M** gave him a thousand talents of silver 4968
15:20 **M** exacted this money from Israel. 4968
15:22 **M** rested with his fathers. 4968
15:23 Pekahiah son of **M** became king of Israel 4968

MENAHEM'S (1) [MENAHEM]
2Ki 15:21 As for the other events of **M** reign, 4968

MENAN (KJV) See MENNA

MENCHILDREN (KJV) See MEN

MEND (2) [MENDED]
Ps 60: 2 **m** its fractures, for it is quaking. 8324
Ecc 3: 7 a time to tear and a time to **m**, 9529

MENDED (1) [MEND]
Jos 9: 4 and old wineskins, cracked and **m.** 7674

MENE (3)
Da 5:25 **M**, MENE, TEKEL, PARSIN 10428
5:25 MENE, **M**, TEKEL, PARSIN 10428
5:26 "This is what these words mean: **M**: 10428

MENPLEASERS (KJV) See WIN FAVOR

MENSTEALERS (KJV) See SLAVE TRADERS

MENNA (1)
Lk 3:31 the son *of* **M**, the son of Mattatha, 3527

MENSERVANTS (16) [SERVANT]
Ge 12:16 **m** and maidservants, and camels. 6269
24:35 silver and gold, **m** and maidservants, 6269
30:43 and maidservants and **m**, 6269
32: 5 sheep and goats, **m** and maidservants. 6269
Ex 21: 7 she is not to go free as **m** do. 6269
Dt 12:12 your **m** and maidservants, 6269
12:18 your **m** and maidservants, 6269
16:11 your **m** and maidservants, 6269
16:14 your **m** and maidservants, and the Levites, 6269
1Sa 8:16 Your **m** and maidservants and the best 6269
2Ki 5:26 flocks, herds, or **m** and maidservants? 6269
Ezr 2:65 besides their 7,337 **m** and maidservants; 6269
Ne 7:67 besides their 7,337 **m** and maidservants; 6269
Job 31:13 to my **m** and maidservants when they had 6269
Isa 14: 2 of Israel will possess the nations as **m** 6269
Lk 12:45 the **m** and maidservants and to eat and drink 4090

MENSTRUAL (1)
Isa 30:22 you will throw them away like a **m cloth** 1865

MENTION (11) [MENTIONED, MENTIONING]
Ge 40:14 **m** me to Pharaoh and get me out 2349
Job 28:18 Coral and jasper *are* not **worthy of m;** 2349
Isa 49: 1 from my birth *he has* **made m of** my name. 2349
Jer 19: 5 something I did not command or **m**, 1819
20: 9 not **m** him or speak any more in his name," 2349
23:36 not **m** 'the oracle of the LORD' again, 2349
Eze 16:56 You would not even **m** your sister Sodom in 928+7023+9019
Am 6:10 *We must* not **m** the name of the LORD." 2349
Jn 5:34 but *I* **m** it that you may be saved. 3306
Eph 5:12 even *to* **m** what the disobedient do in secret. 3306
Phm 1:19 not *to* **m** that you owe me your very self. 3306

MENTIONED (4) [MENTION]
Ru 4: 1 kinsman-redeemer *he had* **m** came along, 1819
1Sa 4:18 When he **m** the ark of God, 2349
Isa 14:20 of the wicked *will* never be **m** again. 7924
19:17 to whom Judah *is* **m** will be terrified, 2349

MENTIONING (1) [MENTION]
1Th 1: 2 for all of you, **m** you in our prayers. 3644+4472

MEON See BAAL MEON, BETH MEON

MEONENIM (KJV) See SOOTHSAYER'S

MEONOTHAI (2)
1Ch 4:13 The sons of Othniel: Hathath and **M.** 5065
4:14 **M** was the father of Ophrah. 5065

MEPHAATH (4)
Jos 13:18 Jahaz, Kedemoth, **M**, 4789
21:37 and **M**, together with their pasturelands— 4789
1Ch 6:79 and **M**, together with their pasturelands; 4789
Jer 48:21 to Holon, Jahzah and **M**, 4789

MEPHIBOSHETH (16) [MERIB-BAAL]
2Sa 4: 4 His name was **M.**) 5136
9: 6 When **M** son of Jonathan, the son of Saul, 5136
9: 6 David said, "**M!**" 5136
9: 8 **M** bowed down and said, NIH
9:10 And **M**, grandson of your master, 5136
9:11 So **M** ate at David's table like one of 5136
9:12 **M** had a young son named Mica, 5136
9:12 of Ziba's household were servants of **M.** 5136
9:13 And **M** lived in Jerusalem, 5136
16: 1 the steward of **M**, waiting to meet him. 5136
16: 4 "All that belonged to **M** is now yours." 5136
19:24 **M**, Saul's grandson, also went down 5136
19:25 "Why didn't you go with me, **M?**" 5136
19:30 **M** said to the king, 5136
21: 7 The king spared **M** son of Jonathan, 5136
21: 8 But the king took Armoni and **M**, 5136

MERAB (4)
1Sa 14:49 The name of his older daughter was **M**, 5266
18:17 "Here is my older daughter **M.** 5266
18:19 So when the time came for **M**, 5266
2Sa 21: 8 with the five sons of Saul's daughter **M**, 5266

MERAIAH (1)
Ne 12:12 of Seraiah's family, **M;** 5316

MERAIOTH (6)
1Ch 6: 6 Zerahiah the father of **M**, 5318
6: 7 **M** the father of Amariah, 5318
6:52 **M** his son, Amariah his son, Ahitub his son, 5318
9:11 the son of **M**, the son of Ahitub, 5318
Ezr 7: 3 the son of Azariah, the son of **M**, 5318
Ne 11:11 the son of **M**, the son of Ahitub, 5318

MERARI (21) [MERARITE, MERARITES]
Ge 46:11 The sons of Levi: Gershon, Kohath and **M.** 5356
Ex 6:16 Gershon, Kohath and **M.** 5356
6:19 The sons of **M** were Mahli and Mushi. 5356
Nu 3:17 Gershon, Kohath and **M.** 5356
3:33 To **M** belonged the clans of the Mahlites 5356
26:57 through **M**, the Merarite clan. 5356
Jos 21: 7 The descendants of **M**, clan by clan, 5356
1Ch 6: 1 The sons of Levi: Gershon, Kohath and **M.** 5356
6:16 The sons of Levi: Gershon, Kohath and **M.** 5356
6:19 The sons of **M**: Mahli and Mushi. 5356
6:29 The descendants of **M**: 5356
6:47 the son of Mushi, the son of **M**, 5356
6:63 The descendants of **M**, clan by clan, 5356
15: 6 of **M**, Asaiah the leader and 220 relatives; 5356
23: 6 Gershon, Kohath and **M.** 5356
23:21 The sons of **M**: Mahli and Mushi. 5356
24:26 The sons of **M**: Mahli and Mushi. 5356
24:27 The sons of **M**: from Jaaziah: 5356
26:19 descendants of Korah and **M.** 5356
2Ch 34:12 Levites descended from **M**, 5356
Ezr 8:19 with Jeshaiah from the descendants of **M**, 5356

MERARITE (10) [MERARI]
Nu 3:20 The **M** clans: Mahli and Mushi. 1201+5356
3:33 these were the **M** clans. 5356
3:35 the families of the **M** clans was Zuriel son 5356
4:33 service of the **M** clans as they work at 1201+5356
4:45 This was the total of those in the **M** 1201+5356
26:57 through Merari, the **M** clan. 5357
Jos 21:34 The **M** clans (the rest of the Levites) 1201+5356
21:40 All the towns allotted to the **M** clans, 1201+5356
1Ch 9:14 the son of Hashabiah, a **M;** 1201+5356
26:10 Hosah the **M** had sons: 1201+5356

MERARITES (9) [MERARI]
Nu 3:36 The **M** were appointed to take care of 1201+5356
4:29 "Count the **M** by their clans and 1201+5356
4:42 The **M** were counted by their clans 1201+5356
7: 8 four carts and eight oxen to the **M**, 1201+5356
10:17 the Gershonites and **M**, who carried it, 1201+5356
1Ch 6:44 the **M**, at his left hand: 1201+5356
6:77 The **M** (the rest of the Levites) 1201+5356
15:17 and from their brothers the **M**, 1201+5356
2Ch 29:12 the **M**, Kish son of Abdi and Azariah 1201+5356

MERATHAIM (1)
Jer 50:21 the land of **M** and those who live in Pekod. 5361

MERCENARIES (1)
Jer 46:21 The **m** in her ranks are like fattened calves. 8502

MERCHANDISE (12)
Ne 10:31 the neighboring peoples bring **m** or grain 5229
13:16 in fish and all kinds of **m** and selling them 4836
Isa 45:14 "The products of Egypt and the **m** *of* Cush, 6087
Eze 26:12 and loot your **m;** 8219
27:12 iron, tin and lead for your **m.** 6442
27:14 war horses and mules for your **m.** 6442
27:16 fine linen, coral and rubies for your **m.** 6442
27:19 and Greeks from Uzal bought your **m;** 6442
27:22 for your **m** they exchanged the finest 6442
Eze 27:27 Your wealth, **m** and wares, your mariners, 6442
27:33 When your **m** went out on the seas, 6442
Mk 11:16 and would not allow anyone to carry **m** 5007

MERCHANT (5) [MERCHANTS]
Pr 31:14 She is like the **m** ships, 6086
SS 3: 6 from all the spices of the **m?** 8217
Eze 27: 3 **m** *of* peoples on many coasts, 8217
Hos 12: 7 The **m** uses dishonest scales; 4047
Mt 13:45 kingdom of heaven is like a **m** looking 476+1867

MERCHANTMEN (KJV) See MERCHANTS

MERCHANTS (28) [MERCHANT]
Ge 23:16 to the weight current among the **m.** 6086
37:28 So when the Midianite **m** came by, 6086
1Ki 10:15 the revenues from **m** and traders and 408+9365
10:28 the royal **m** purchased them from Kue. 6086
2Ch 1:16 the royal **m** purchased them from Kue. 6086
9:14 the revenues brought in by **m** 408+9365
Ne 3:31 the house of the temple servants and the **m**, 8217
3:32 the goldsmiths and **m** made repairs. 8217
13:20 the **m** and sellers of all kinds of goods spent 8217
Job 6:19 the **traveling m** *of* Sheba look in hope. 2142
41: 6 Will they divide him up among the **m?** 4051
Ps 107:23 *they were* **m** on the mighty waters. 4856+6913
Pr 31:24 and supplies the **m** with sashes. 4051
Isa 23: 2 you people of the island and you **m** 6086
23: 8 whose **m** are princes, 6086
Eze 16:29 Babylonia, a land of **m**, 4047
17: 4 and carried it away to a land of **m**, 4047
27:22 **m** *of* Sheba and Raamah traded with you; 8217
27:23 Canneh and Eden and **m** *of* Sheba, 8217
27:27 your **m** and all your soldiers, 5114+6842
27:36 The **m** among the nations hiss at you; 6086
38:13 Sheba and Dedan and the **m** *of* Tarshish 6086
Na 3:16 the number of your **m** till they are more than 8217
Zep 1:11 all your **m** will be wiped out, 4047+6639
Rev 18: 3 and the **m** of the earth grew rich 1867
18:11 "The **m** of the earth will weep and mourn 1867
18:15 The **m** who sold these things 1867
18:23 Your **m** were the world's great men. 1867

MERCIFUL (22) [MERCY]
Ge 19:16 for the LORD was **m** to them. 2799
Dt 4:31 For the LORD your God is a **m** God; 8157
1Ki 20:31 that the kings of the house of Israel are **m.** 2876
Ne 9:31 for you are a gracious and **m** God. 8157
Ps 4: 1 *be* **m** *to* me and hear my prayer. 2858
6: 2 *Be* **m** *to* me, LORD, for I am faint; 2858
26:11 redeem me and *be* **m** *to* me. 2858
27: 7 *be* **m** *to* me and answer me. 2858
30:10 Hear, O LORD, and *be* **m** *to* me; 2858
31: 9 *Be* **m** *to* me, O LORD, for I am in distress; 2858
56: 1 *Be* **m** *to* me, O God, 2858
77: 9 Has God forgotten *to be* **m?** 2858
78:38 Yet he was **m;** he forgave their iniquities 8157
Jer 3:12 'I will frown on you no longer, for I am **m**,' 2883
Da 9: 9 The Lord our God is **m** and forgiving, 8171
Mt 5: 7 Blessed are the **m**, for they will be shown mercy. 1798
Lk 1:54 remembering to be **m** 1799
6:36 Be **m**, just as your Father is merciful. 3881
6:36 Be merciful, just as your Father is **m.** 3881
Heb 2:17 a **m** and faithful high priest in service 1798
Jas 2:13 be shown to anyone who has not been **m.** 1799
Jude 1:22 **Be m** to those who doubt; 1796

MERCILESS (1) [MERCY]
Pr 17:11 a **m** official will be sent against him. 426

MERCILESSLY (1) [MERCY]
Isa 30:14 shattered *so* **m** that among its pieces 2798+4202

MERCURIUS (KJV) See HERMES

MERCY (129) [MERCIFUL, MERCILESS, MERCILESSLY]
Ge 43:14 And may God Almighty grant you **m** before 8171
Ex 33:19 *I will* **have m** *on* whom I will have mercy, 2858
33:19 I will have mercy on whom *I will* **have m**, 2858
Dt 7: 2 and **show** them no **m.** 2858
13:17 he will show you **m**, 8171
Jos 11:20 exterminating them without **m**, 9382
2Sa 24:14 for his **m** is great; 8171
1Ki 8:28 and his **plea for m**, 9382
8:50 and cause their conquerors *to* **show** them **m;** 8163
1Ch 21:13 for his **m** is very great; 8171
2Ch 6:19 and his **plea for m**, 9382
Ne 9:31 But in your great **m** you did not put an end 8171
13:22 **show m** to me according to your great love. 2571
Est 4: 8 the king's presence to **beg for m** and plead 2858
Job 9:15 **plead** with my Judge **for m.** 2858
27:22 against him without **m** as he flees headlong 2798
41: 3 Will he keep **begging** you **for m?** 9384
Ps 5: 7 But I, by your great **m**, 2876
6: 9 The LORD has heard my **cry for m;** 9382
9:13 **Have m** and lift me up from the gates 2858
25: 6 O LORD, your **great m** and love, 8171
28: 2 Hear my **cry for m** as I call to you 7754+9384
28: 6 for he has heard my **cry for m.** 7754+9384

Ps 30: 8 to the Lord *I* **cried for m:** 2858
31:22 you heard my **cry for m** when I called 7754+9384
40:11 Do not withhold your **m** from me, 8171
41: 4 I said, "O LORD, **have m** *on* me; 2858
41:10 But you, O LORD, **have m** *on* me; 2858
51: 1 **Have m** *on* me, O God, 2858
57: 1 **Have m** *on* me, O God, have mercy on me, 2858
57: 1 Have mercy on me, O God, **have m** *on* me, 2858
59: 5 **show** no **m** *to* wicked traitors. 2858
69:16 in your great **m** turn to me. 8171
79: 8 may your **m** come quickly to meet us, 8171
86: 3 **Have m** *on* me, O Lord, 2858
86: 6 listen to my **cry for m.** 7754+9384
86:16 Turn to me and **have m** *on* me; 2858
116: 1 he heard my **cry for m.** 9384
119:132 Turn to me and **have m** *on* me, 2858
123: 2 till *he* **shows** us *his* **m.** 2858
123: 3 **Have m** *on* us, O LORD, have mercy on us, 2858
123: 3 Have mercy on us, O LORD, **have m** *on* us, 2858
130: 2 your ears be attentive to my **cry for m.** 7754+9384
140: 6 Hear, O LORD, my **cry for m.** 7754+9384
142: 1 **lift up** my voice to the LORD **for m.** 2858
143: 1 hear my prayer, listen to my **cry for m;** 9384
Pr 6:34 *he will* **show** no **m** when he takes revenge. 2798
18:23 A poor man pleads for **m,** 9384
21:10 his neighbor **gets** no **m** from him. 2858
28:13 and renounces them **finds m.** 8163
Isa 13:18 *they will* **have** no **m** *on* infants 8163
47: 6 and you showed them no **m.** 8171
55: 7 and *he will* **have m** *on* him, and to our God, 8163
63: 9 In his love and **m** he redeemed them; 2799
Jer 6:23 they are cruel and **show** no **m.** 8163
13:14 I will allow no pity or **m** or compassion 2571
21: 7 *he will* **show** them no **m** or pity 2571
50:42 they are cruel and without **m.** 8163
Da 2:18 He urged them to plead for **m** from the God 10664
9:18 but because of your great **m.** 8171
Hos 6: 6 For I desire **m,** not sacrifice, 2876
Am 5:15 the LORD God Almighty *will* **have m** *on* 2858
Mic 6: 8 and to love **m** and to walk humbly 2876
7:18 but delight to show **m.** 2876
7:20 and show **m** to Abraham, 2876
Hab 1:17 destroying nations without **m?** 2798
3: 2 in wrath remember **m.** 8163
Zec 1:12 how long *will* you withhold **m** 8163
1:16 'I will return to Jerusalem with **m,** 8171
7: 9 show **m** and compassion to one another. 2876
Mt 5: 7 for they *will be* **shown m.** *1796*
9:13 'I desire **m,** not sacrifice.' *1799*
9:27 calling out, **"Have m on** us, Son of David!" *1796*
12: 7 'I desire **m,** not sacrifice,' *1799*
15:22 "Lord, Son of David, **have m on** me! *1796*
17:15 "Lord, **have m on** my son," he said. *1796*
18:33 Shouldn't you *have* **had m on** your fellow *1796*
20:30 "Lord, Son of David, **have m on** us!" *1796*
20:31 "Lord, Son of David, **have m on** us!" *1796*
23:23 justice, **m** and faithfulness. *1799*
Mk 5:19 and how *he has* **had m on** you." *1796*
10:47 "Jesus, Son of David, **have m on** me!" *1796*
10:48 "Son of David, **have m on** me!" *1796*
Lk 1:50 His **m** extends to those who fear him, *1799*
1:58 that the Lord had shown her great **m,** *1799*
1:72 to show **m** to our fathers and *1799*
1:78 because of the **tender m** of our God, *1799+5073*
10:37 "The one who had **m** on him." *1799*
18:13 'God, *have* **m** on me, a sinner.' *2661*
18:38 "Jesus, Son of David, **have m on** me!" *1796*
18:39 "Son of David, **have m on** me!" *1796*
Ro 9:15 *"I will* **have m on** whom I have mercy, *1796*
9:15 "I will have mercy on whom *I have* **m,** *1796*
9:16 not, therefore, depend on man's desire or effort, but on God's **m.** *1796*
9:18 Therefore God **has m on** whom he wants *1796*
9:18 on whom he wants to have **m,** *NIG*
9:23 of his glory known to the objects *of* his **m,** *1799*
11:30 to God *have* now **received m** as a result *1796*
11:31 in order that they too *may* now **receive m** as *1799*
11:31 now receive mercy *as a result of* God's **m** *1799*
11:32 to disobedience so that *he may* **have m on** *1796*
12: 1 I urge you, brothers, in view of God's **m,** *3880*
12: 8 if it is **showing m,** let him do it cheerfully. *1796*
15: 9 that the Gentiles may glorify God for his **m,** *1799*
1Co 7:25 as one who by the Lord's **m** is trustworthy. *1796*
2Co 4: 1 through God's **m** *we* have this ministry, *1796*
Gal 6:16 Peace and **m** to all who follow this rule, *1799*
Eph 2: 4 God, who is rich in **m,** *1799*
Php 2:27 But God **had m on** him, *1796*
1Ti 1: 2 Grace, **m** and peace from God the Father *1799*
1:13 *I was* **shown m** because I acted in ignorance *1796*
1:16 for that very reason *I was* **shown m** so that *1796*
2Ti 1: 2 Grace, **m** and peace from God the Father *1799*
1:16 May the Lord show **m** to the household *1799*
1:18 May the Lord grant that he will find **m** from *1799*
Tit 3: 5 but because of his **m.** *1799*
Heb 4:16 so that we may receive **m** and find grace *1799*
10:28 rejected the law of Moses died without **m** *3880*
Jas 2:13 because judgment **without m** will be shown *447*
2:13 **M** triumphs over judgment! *1799*
3:17 submissive, full *of* **m** and good fruit, *1799*
5:11 The Lord is full of compassion and **m.** *3881*
1Pe 1: 3 In his great **m** he has given us new birth into *1799*
2:10 once you *had* not **received m,** *1796*
2:10 but now *you have* **received m.** *1796*
2Jn 1: 3 **m** and peace from God the Father and *1799*
Jude 1: 2 **M,** peace and love be yours in abundance. *1799*
1:21 the **m** of our Lord Jesus Christ to bring you *1799*
1:23 **to** others **show m,** mixed with fear— *1796*

MERCYSEAT (KJV) See PLACE OF ATONEMENT

MERE (20) [MERELY]

2Ki 8:13 "How could your servant, a **m** dog, NIH
Job 12: 4 a **m** laughingstock, though righteous NIH
41: 9 the **m** sight of him is overpowering. 1685
Ps 39: 5 You have made my days a **m** handbreadth; NIH
39: 6 Man is a **m** phantom as he goes to and fro: 421
82: 7 But you will die like **m** men; NIH
Pr 14:23 but **m talk** leads only to poverty. 1821+8557
29:19 A servant cannot be corrected by **m** words; NIH
Isa 3: 4 **m children** will govern them. 9500
50: 2 By a **m** rebuke I dry up the sea, NIH
57:13 a **m breath** will blow them away. 2039
65:20 at a hundred will be thought a *m* **youth;** AIT
Jn 7:24 Stop judging by **m** appearances, *NIG*
10:33 "but for blasphemy, because you, a **m** man, *NIG*
Ro 2: 3 So when you, a **m** man, *NIG*
1Co 3: 1 but as worldly—**m** infants in Christ. *NIG*
3: 3 Are you not acting like **m** men? *NIG*
3: 4 "I follow Apollos," are you not **m** men? *NIG*
Tit 1:10 **m talkers** and deceivers, *3468*
Jude 1:19 who **follow m natural instincts** and *6035*

MERED (2) [MERED'S]

1Ch 4:17 Jether, **M,** Epher and Jalon. 5279
4:18 whom **M** had married. 5279

MERED'S (1) [MERED]

1Ch 4:17 One of **M** wives gave birth to Miriam, NIH

MERELY (8) [MERE]

Jdg 15:11 "**I m** did to them what they did to me." NIH
1Sa 14:43 *"I* **m tasted** a little honey with the end 3247+3247
Est 7: 4 If we had **m** been sold as male NIH
Job 30:20 I stand up, but *you m* **look** at me. AIT
Ro 2:28 nor is circumcision **m** outward and physical. *NIG*
1Co 9: 8 Do I say this **m** from a human point *NIG*
15:32 in Ephesus for **m** human reasons, *NIG*
Jas 1:22 Do not **m** listen to the word, *3667*

MEREMOTH (6) [MEREMOTH'S]

Ezr 8:33 the sacred articles into the hands of **M** son 5329
10:36 Vaniah, **M,** Eliashib, 5329
Ne 3: 4 **M** son of Uriah, the son of Hakkoz, 5329
3:21 Next to him, **M** son of Uriah, 5329
10: 5 Harim, **M,** Obadiah, 5329
12: 3 Shecaniah, Rehum, **M,** 5329

MEREMOTH'S (1) [MEREMOTH]

Ne 12:15 of Harim's, Adna; of **M,** Helkai; 5329

MERES (1)

Est 1:14 Carshena, Shethar, Admatha, Tarshish, **M,** 5332

MERIB-BAAL (2) [MEPHIBOSHETH]

1Ch 8:34 **M,** who was the father of Micah. 5311
9:40 **M,** who was the father of Micah. 5311

MERIBAH (7) [MERIBAH KADESH]

Ex 17: 7 and **M** because the Israelites quarreled and 5313
Nu 20:13 These were the waters of **M,** 5313
20:24 against my command at the waters of **M.** 5313
Dt 33: 8 you contended with him at the waters of **M.** 5313
Ps 81: 7 I tested you at the waters of **M.** 5313
95: 8 do not harden your hearts as you did at **M,** 5313
106:32 the waters of **M** they angered the LORD, 5313

MERIBAH KADESH (4) [MERIBAH]

Nu 27:14 (These were the waters of **M,** 5315
Dt 32:51 the Israelites at the waters of **M** *in* 5315
Eze 47:19 as far as the waters of **M,** 5315
48:28 from Tamar to the waters of **M,** 5315

MERODACH (KJV) See MARDUK

MERODACH-BALADAN (2)

2Ki 20:12 At that time **M** son of Baladan king 5282
Isa 39: 1 At that time **M** son of Baladan king 5282

MEROM (2)

Jos 11: 5 at the Waters of **M,** 5295
11: 7 against them suddenly at the Waters of **M** 5295

MERON See SHIMRON MERON

MERONOTH (1) [MERONOTHITE]

Ne 3: 7 Melatiah of Gibeon and Jadon of **M**— 5331

MERONOTHITE (1) [MERONOTH]

1Ch 27:30 the **M** was in charge of the donkeys. 5331

MEROZ (1)

Jdg 5:23 'Curse **M,**' said the angel of the LORD. 5292

MERRIMENT (1) [MERRY]

Isa 32:13 mourn for all houses of **m** and for this city 5375

MERRY (4) [MERRIMENT, MERRYMAKERS]

Job 21:12 *they* **make m** to the sound of the flute. 8523
Ecc 10:19 and wine **makes** life **m,** 8523
Jer 15:17 never **made m** with them; 6600
Lk 12:19 Take life easy; eat, drink and *be* **m."'** *2370*

MERRYMAKERS (1) [MERRY]

Isa 24: 7 the vine withers; all the **m** groan. 4213+8524

MESECH (KJV) See MESHECH

MESH (1)

Job 18: 8 into a net and he wanders into its **m.** 8422

MESHA (4)

Ge 10:30 where they lived stretched from **M** 5392
2Ki 3: 4 Now **M** king of Moab raised sheep, 4795
1Ch 2:42 **M** his firstborn, who was the father of Ziph, 4796
8: 9 By his wife Hodesh he had Jobab, Zibia, **M,** 4791

MESHACH (14)

Da 1: 7 to Mishael, **M;** and to Azariah, Abednego. 4794
2:49 **M** and Abednego administrators over 10415
3:12 Shadrach, **M** and Abednego— 10415
3:13 Nebuchadnezzar summoned Shadrach, **M** and Abednego. 10415
3:14 "Is it true, Shadrach, **M** and Abednego, 10415
3:16 **M** and Abednego replied to the king, 10415
3:19 **M** and Abednego, and his attitude 10415
3:20 **M** and Abednego and throw them into 10415
3:22 the soldiers who took up Shadrach, **M** 10415
3:26 "Shadrach, **M** and Abednego, 10415
3:26 **M** and Abednego came out of the fire, 10415
3:28 to the God of Shadrach, **M** and Abednego, 10415
3:29 **M** and Abednego be cut into pieces 10415
3:30 **M** and Abednego in the province 10415

MESHECH (10)

Ge 10: 2 Magog, Madai, Javan, Tubal, **M** and Tiras. 5434
10:23 The sons of Aram: Uz, Hul, Gether and **M.** 5434
1Ch 1: 5 Magog, Madai, Javan, Tubal, **M** and Tiras. 5434
1:17 The sons of Aram: Uz, Hul, Gether and **M.** 5434
Ps 120: 5 Woe to me that I dwell in **M,** 5434
Eze 27:13 " 'Greece, Tubal and **M** traded with you, 5434
32:26 "**M** and Tubal are there, 5434
38: 2 the chief prince of **M** and Tubal; 5434
38: 3 O Gog, chief prince of **M** and Tubal. 5434
39: 1 O Gog, chief prince of **M** and Tubal. 5434

MESHELEMIAH (4)

1Ch 9:21 of **M** was the gatekeeper at the entrance to 5452
26: 1 **M** son of Kore, one of the sons of Asaph. 5453
26: 2 **M** had sons: Zechariah the firstborn, 5453
26: 9 **M** had sons and relatives, 5453

MESHEZABEL (3)

Ne 3: 4 the son of **M,** made repairs, 5430
10:21 **M,** Zadok, Jaddua, 5430
11:24 Pethahiah son of **M,** 5430

MESHILLEMITH (1)

1Ch 9:12 the son of Meshullam, the son of **M,** 5454

MESHILLEMOTH (2)

2Ch 28:12 of Jehohanan, Berekiah son of **M,** 5451
Ne 11:13 the son of **M,** the son of Immer, 5451

MESHOBAB (1)

1Ch 4:34 **M,** Jamlech, Joshah son of Amaziah, 5411

MESHULLAM (25)

2Ki 22: 3 the son of **M,** to the temple of the LORD. 5450
1Ch 3:19 The sons of Zerubbabel: **M** and Hananiah. 5450
5:13 Michael, **M,** Sheba, Jorai, Jacan, 5450
8:17 Zebadiah, **M,** Hizki, Heber, 5450
9: 7 Sallu son of **M,** the son of Hodaviah, 5450
9: 8 and **M** son of Shephatiah, the son of Reuel, 5450
9:11 the son of **M,** the son of Zadok, 5450
9:12 the son of **M,** the son of Meshillemith, 5450
2Ch 34:12 and Zechariah and **M,** 5450
Ezr 8:16 Jarib, Elnathan, Nathan, Zechariah and **M,** 5450
10:15 supported by **M** and Shabbethai the Levite, 5450
10:29 From the descendants of Bani: **M,** Malluch, 5450
Ne 3: 4 Next to him **M** son of Berekiah, 5450
3: 6 of Paseah and **M** son of Besodeiah. 5450
3:30 Next to them, **M** son 5450
6:18 the daughter of **M** son of Berekiah. 5450
8: 4 Hashum, Hashbaddanah, Zechariah and **M.** 5450
10: 7 **M,** Abijah, Mijamin, 5450
10:20 Magpiash, **M,** Hezir, 5450
11: 7 Sallu son of **M,** the son of Joed, 5450
11:11 the son of **M,** the son of Zadok, 5450
12:13 of Ezra's, **M;** of Amariah's, Jehohanan; 5450
12:16 of Iddo's, Zechariah; of Ginnethon's, **M;** 5450

Ne 12:25 Mattaniah, Bakbukiah, Obadiah, **M**, 5450
12:33 along with Azariah, Ezra, **M**, 5450

MESHULLEMETH (1)

2Ki 21:19 His mother's name was **M** daughter 5455

MESOBAITE (KJV) See MEZOBAITE

MESOPOTAMIA (2)

Ac 2: 9 residents of **M**, Judea and Cappadocia, *3544*
7: 2 Abraham while he was still in **M**, *3544*

MESS (KJV) See GIFT, PORTION

MESSAGE (118) [MESSENGER, MESSENGERS]

Ge 32: 5 Now I am sending *this* **m** to my lord, 5583
38:25 she **sent a m** to her father-in-law. 8938
50:17 When their **m came** to him, Joseph wept. 1819
Nu 22:10 king of Moab, **sent** me *this* **m**: 8938
23: 5 The LORD put a **m** in Balaam's mouth 1821
23: 5 "Go back to Balak and **give** him this **m**." 1819
23:16 The LORD met with Balaam and put a **m** 1821
23:16 "Go back to Balak and **give** him this **m**." 1819
Dt 18:21 a **m** has not been spoken by the LORD?" 1821
18:22 that is a **m** the LORD has not spoken. 1821
Jos 2: 3 So the king of Jericho **sent** *this* **m** to Rahab: 8938
5:14 "What **m** *does* my Lord *have* 1819
Jdg 3:19 "I have a secret **m** for you, O king." 1821
3:20 "I have a **m** *from* God for you." 1821
11:28 to the **m** Jephthah sent him. 1821
1Sa 9:27 so that I may give you a **m** *from* God." 1821
15: 1 so listen now to the **m** *from* the LORD. 1821
25: 9 they gave Nabal this **m** in David's name. 1821
2Sa 17:16 Now **send a m** immediately and tell David, 8938
19:11 King David sent this **m** to Zadok 606
1Ki 5: 2 Solomon sent back this **m** to Hiram: 606
5: 7 When Hiram heard Solomon's **m**, 1821
5: 8 *"I have* **received** *the* **m** you sent me 9048
13:32 For the **m** he declared by the word of 1821
20:10 Then Ben-Hadad sent another **m** to Ahab: 606
20:12 Ben-Hadad heard this **m** while he and 1821
2Ki 3: 7 He also sent this **m** to Jehoshaphat king 606
5: 8 he sent him *this* **m**: 606
9: 5 "I have a **m** for you, commander," he said. 1821
10: 5 the elders and the guardians sent this **m** 606
14: 9 in Lebanon sent a **m** to a cedar in Lebanon, 606
18:14 of Judah sent this **m** to the king of Assyria 606
19:20 Isaiah son of Amoz sent a **m** to Hezekiah: 606
2Ch 2: 3 Solomon sent this **m** to Hiram king of Tyre: 606
25:18 in Lebanon sent a **m** to a cedar in Lebanon, 606
32: 9 with *this* **m** for Hezekiah king of Judah and 606
Ezr 4:14 *we are* **sending** *this* **m** to inform the king, 10714
Ne 6: 2 Sanballat and Geshem sent me *this* **m**: 606
6: 4 Four times they sent me the same **m**, 1821
6: 5 to me with the same **m**, 1821
Pr 26: 6 or drinking violence is the sending of a **m** 1821
Isa 9: 8 The Lord has sent a **m** against Jacob; 1821
28: 9 To whom is he explaining his **m**? 9019
28:19 of this **m** will bring sheer terror. 9019
30:12 "Because you have rejected this **m**, 1821
37:21 Isaiah son of Amoz sent a **m** to Hezekiah: 606
53: 1 Who has believed our **m** and to whom has 9019
Jer 3:12 Go, proclaim this **m** toward the north: 1821
7: 2 and there proclaim this **m**: 1821
18: 2 and there I will give you my **m**." 1821
22: 1 the king of Judah and proclaim this **m** there: 1821
23:21 yet they have run with their **m**; NIH
27: 4 **Give** them **a m** for their masters and say, 7422
27:12 *I* **gave the** same **m** to Zedekiah king of Judah. 465+1819+1821+2021+2021+3972
29:28 He has sent this **m** to us in Babylon: 606
29:31 "Send this **m** to all the exiles: 606
37: 3 to Jeremiah the prophet with *this* **m**: 606
44:16 not listen to the **m** you have spoken to us in 1821
46: 2 This is the **m** against the army NIH
46:13 This is the **m** the LORD spoke to Jeremiah 1821
49:14 I have heard a **m** from the LORD: 9019
51:59 This is the **m** Jeremiah gave to 1821
Eze 33:30 'Come and hear the **m** that has come from 1821
Da 9:23 consider the **m** and understand the vision: 1821
10: 1 Its **m** was true and it concerned a great war. 1821
10: 1 The understanding of the **m** came to him in 1821
Am 7:10 Then Amaziah the priest of Bethel sent a **m** 606
Ob 1: 1 We have heard a **m** from the LORD: 9019
Jnh 3: 2 and proclaim to it the **m** I give you." 7952
Hag 1:12 the voice of the LORD their God and the **m** 1821
1:13 gave this **m** *of* the LORD to the people: 4857
Mt 10: 7 As you go, preach **this m**: *4022*
13:19 the **m** about the kingdom and does *3364*
27:19 his wife **sent** him this **m**: *690*
Mk 1: 7 And this *was his* **m**: *3062*
Lk 4:32 because his **m** had authority. *3364*
Jn 12:38 who has believed our **m** and to whom has *198*
17:20 in me through their **m**, *3364*
Ac 2:41 Those who accepted his **m** were baptized, *3364*
4: 4 But many who heard the **m** believed, *3364*
5:20 tell the people the full **m** of this new life." *4839*
10:36 You know the **m** God sent to the people *3364*
10:44 Holy Spirit came on all who heard the **m**. *3364*
11:14 He *will* **bring** you **a m** through which *3281+4839*
11:19 telling the **m** only to Jews. *3364*
13:15 if you have a **m** of encouragement for *3364*
13:26 to us that this **m** of salvation has been sent. *3364*
14: 3 the **m** of his grace by enabling them *3364*
15: 7 the Gentiles might hear from my lips the **m** *3364*
15:31 and were glad for its **encouraging m**. *4155*
16:14 to respond to Paul's **m**. *3281*
17:11 for they received the **m** with great eagerness *3364*
19:31 sent him a **m** begging him not to venture *NIG*
Ro 10:16 "Lord, who has believed our **m**?" *198*
10:17 faith comes from hearing the **m**, *198*
10:17 the **m** is heard through the word of Christ. *198*
1Co 1:18 For the **m** of the cross is foolishness *3364*
2: 4 My **m** and my preaching were not with wise *3364*
2: 6 speak a **m** of wisdom among the mature, *NIG*
12: 8 through the Spirit the **m** of wisdom, *3364*
12: 8 to another the **m** of knowledge by means of *3364*
2Co 1:18 our **m** to you is not "Yes" and "No." *3364*
5:19 And he has committed to us the **m** *3364*
Gal 2: 6 those men added nothing to my **m**. *NIG*
Col 4: 3 too, that God may open a door for our **m**, *3364*
1Th 1: 6 the **m** with the joy given by the Holy Spirit. *3364*
1: 8 The Lord's **m** rang out from you not only *3364*
2Th 3: 1 that the **m** of the Lord may spread rapidly *3364*
1Ti 4:14 was given you through a **prophetic m** *4735*
2Ti 4:15 because he strongly opposed our **m**. *3364*
4:17 through me the **m** might be fully proclaimed *3060*
Tit 1: 9 to the trustworthy **m** as it has been taught, *3364*
Heb 2: 2 For if the **m** spoken by angels was binding, *3364*
4: 2 the **m** they heard was of no value to them, *3364*
1Pe 2: 8 They stumble because they disobey the **m**— *3364*
1Jn 1: 5 the **m** we have heard from him and declare *32*
2: 7 This old command is the **m** you have heard. *3364*
3:11 This is the **m** you heard from the beginning: *32*

MESSENGER (39) [MESSAGE]

1Sa 23:27 a **m** came to Saul, saying, "Come quickly! 4855
2Sa 11:19 He instructed the **m**: 4855
11:22 The **m** set out, and when he arrived 4855
11:23 **m** said to David, "The men overpowered 4855
11:25 David told the **m**, "Say this to Joab: 4855
15:13 A **m** came and told David, 5583
1Ki 19: 2 So Jezebel sent a **m** to Elijah to say, 4855
22:13 The **m** who had gone to summon Micaiah 4855
2Ki 5:10 Elisha sent a **m** to say to him, "Go, 4855
6:32 The king sent a **m** ahead, 4855
6:32 Look, when the **m** comes, 4855
6:33 the **m** came down to him. 4855
9:18 "The **m** has reached them, 4855
10: 8 When the **m** arrived, he told Jehu, 4855
2Ch 18:12 The **m** who had gone to summon Micaiah 4855
Job 1:14 a **m** came to Job and said, 4855
1:16 **another m** came and said, 2296[S]
1:17 **another m** came and said, 2296
1:18 yet **another m** came and said, 2296[S]
Pr 13:17 A wicked **m** falls into trouble, 4855
16:14 A king's wrath is a **m** *of* death, 4855
25:13 is a trustworthy **m** to those who send him; 7495
Ecc 5: 6 And do not protest to the [temple] **m**, 4855
Isa 41:27 I gave to Jerusalem a **m of good tidings**. 1413
42:19 and deaf like the **m** I send? 4855
Jer 51:31 and **m** follows messenger to announce to 5583
51:31 and messenger follows **m** to announce to 5583[S]
Da 4:13 and there before me was a **m**, a holy one, 10541
4:23 "You, O king, saw a **m**, a holy one, 10541
Hag 1:13 Then Haggai, the LORD's **m**, 4855
Mal 2: 7 he is the **m** *of* the LORD Almighty. 4855
3: 1 "See, I will send my **m**, who will prepare 4855
3: 1 the **m** *of* the covenant, whom you desire, 4855
Mt 11:10 " 'I will send my **m** ahead of you, *34*
Mk 1: 2 "I will send my **m** ahead of you, *34*
Lk 7:27 " 'I will send my **m** ahead of you, *34*
Jn 13:16 nor is a **m** greater than the one who sent him. *693*
2Co 12: 7 thorn in my flesh, a **m** of Satan, to torment me. *34*
Php 2:25 who is also your **m**, *693*

MESSENGERS (72) [MESSAGE]

Ge 32: 3 Jacob sent **m** ahead of him 4855
32: 6 When the **m** returned to Jacob, they said, 4855
Nu 20:14 Moses sent **m** from Kadesh to the king 4855
21:21 Israel sent **m** to say to Sihon king of 4855
22: 5 sent **m** to summon Balaam son of Beor, 4855
24:12 "Did I not tell the **m** you sent me, 4855
Dt 2:26 From the desert of Kedemoth I sent **m** 4855
Jos 7:22 So Joshua sent **m**, and they ran to the tent, 4855
Jdg 6:35 He sent **m** throughout Manasseh, 4855
7:24 Gideon sent **m** throughout the hill country 4855
9:31 Under cover he sent **m** to Abimelech, 4855
11:12 Then Jephthah sent **m** to the Ammonite king 4855
11:13 of the Ammonites answered Jephthah's **m**, 4855
11:14 Jephthah sent back **m** to the Ammonite king 4855
11:17 Then Israel sent **m** to the king of Edom, 4855
11:19 Israel sent **m** to Sihon king of the Amorites, 4855
1Sa 6:21 they sent **m** to the people of Kiriath Jearim, 4855
11: 3 "Give us seven days so we can send **m** 4855
11: 4 When the **m** came to Gibeah of Saul 4855
11: 7 and sent the pieces by **m** throughout Israel, 4855
11: 9 They told the **m** who had come, 4855
11: 9 the **m** went and reported this to the men 4855
16:19 Then Saul sent **m** to Jesse and said, 4855
25:14 "David sent **m** from the desert 4855
25:42 went with David's **m** and became his wife. 4855
31: 9 and they sent **m** throughout the land of NIH
2Sa 2: 5 he sent **m** to the men of Jabesh Gilead 4855
3:12 Abner sent **m** on his behalf to say to David, 4855
3:14 David sent **m** to Ish-Bosheth son of Saul, 4855
3:26 Joab then left David and sent **m** after Abner, 4855
5:11 Now Hiram king of Tyre sent **m** to David, 4855
10: 5 he sent **m** to meet the men, NIH
11: 4 Then David sent **m** to get her. 4855
12:27 Joab then sent **m** to David, saying, 4855
15:10 Then Absalom sent **secret m** throughout 8078
1Ki 20: 2 He sent **m** into the city to Ahab king 4855
20: 5 The **m** came again and said, 4855
20: 9 So he replied to Ben-Hadad's **m**, 4855
2Ki 1: 2 So he sent **m**, saying to them, 4855
1: 3 the **m** *of* the king of Samaria and ask them, 4855
1: 5 When the **m** returned to the king, 4855
1:16 that you have sent **m** to consult Baal-Zebub, 4855
7:15 So the **m** returned and reported to the king. 4855
14: 8 Then Amaziah sent **m** to Jehoash son 4855
16: 7 Ahaz sent **m** to say to Tiglath-Pileser king 4855
19: 9 he again sent **m** to Hezekiah with this word: 4855
19:14 Hezekiah received the letter from the **m** 4855
19:23 By your **m** you have heaped insults on 4855
20:13 Hezekiah received **the m** and showed 2157[S]
1Ch 10: 9 and **sent m** throughout the land of 8938
14: 1 Now Hiram king of Tyre sent **m** to David, 4855
19: 5 he sent **m** to meet them, NIH
19:16 they sent **m** and had Arameans brought 4855
2Ch 35:21 But Neco sent **m** to him, saying, 4855
36:15 to them through his **m** again and again, 4855
36:16 But they mocked God's **m**, 4855
Ne 6: 3 so I sent **m** to them with this reply: 4855
Job 33:22 and his life to the **m of death**. 4637
Ps 104: 4 He makes winds his **m**, 4855
Isa 18: 2 Go, swift **m**, to a people tall and 4855
37: 9 he sent **m** to Hezekiah with this word: 4855
37:14 Hezekiah received the letter from the **m** 4855
37:24 By your **m** you have heaped insults on 6269
44:26 and fulfills the predictions of his **m**, 4855
Eze 23:16 after them and sent **m** to them in Chaldea. 4855
23:40 "They even sent **m** for men who came 4855
30: 9 that day **m** will go out from me in ships 4855
Da 4:17 " 'The decision is announced by **m**, 10541
Na 2:13 voices of your **m** will no longer be heard." 4855
Lk 7:22 So he replied *to* **the m**, *899*[S]
7:24 After John's **m** left, Jesus began to speak to *34*
9:52 And he sent **m** on ahead, *34*

MESSIAH (2) [CHRIST]

Jn 1:41 "We have found the **M**" (that is, the Christ). *3549*
4:25 "I know that **M**" (called Christ) "is coming. *3549*

MESSIAS (KJV) See MESSIAH

MET (55) [MEET]

Ge 32: 1 and the angels of God **m** him. 7003
33: 8 by all these droves *I* **m**?" 7008
38: 2 There Judah **m** the daughter of 8011
Ex 3:18 the God of the Hebrews, *has* **m** with us. 7936
4:24 the LORD **m** [Moses] and was about 7008
4:27 So *he* **m** Moses at the mountain of God 7008
5: 3 "The God of the Hebrews *has* **m** with us. 7925
18: 8 about all the hardships they *had* **m** along 5162
Nu 23: 4 God **m** with him, and Balaam said, 7936
23:16 The LORD **m** with Balaam and put 7936
Dt 25:18 *they* **m** you on your journey 7936
1Sa 9:11 they **m** some girls coming out 5162
10:10 a procession of prophets **m** him; 7925
16: 4 of the town trembled when *they* **m** him. 7925
18:30 David **m with** more **success** than the rest 8505
21: 1 Ahimelech trembled when *he* **m** him, 7925
25:20 descending toward her and *she* **m** them. 7008
2Sa 2:13 and David's men went out and **m** them at 7008
1Ki 11:29 and Ahijah the prophet of Shiloh **m** him on 5162
13:24 a lion **m** him on the road and killed him, 5162
18: 7 Obadiah was walking along, Elijah **m** him. 7925
2Ki 9:21 *They* **m** him at the plot of ground 5162
10:13 he **m** some relatives of Ahaziah king 5162
12:12 **m** all *the other* **expenses** 3655
Ne 13: 2 not **m** the Israelites with food and water 7709
Job 2:11 **m** together **by agreement** 3585
Ps 74: 4 Your foes roared in the **place where** you **m** 4595
Jer 41: 6 When he **m** them, he said, 7008
Mt 8:28 men coming from the tombs **m** him. *5636*
27:32 *they* **m** a man from Cyrene, named Simon, *2351*
28: 9 Suddenly Jesus **m** them. *5636*
28:12 *When* the chief priests *had* **m** with the elders *5251*
Lk 8:27 he was **m** by a demon-possessed man from *5636*
9:37 a large crowd **m** him. *5267*
17:12 ten men who had leprosy **m** him. *560*
22:66 **m together**, and Jesus was led before them. *5251*
Jn 4:51 his servants **m** him with the news *5636*
11:30 at the place where Martha *had* **m** him. *5636*
18: 2 Jesus *had* often **m** there with his disciples. *5251*
Ac 1: 6 So *when* they **m together**, they asked him, *5302*
4: 5 and teachers of the law **m** in Jerusalem. *5251*
4:27 Indeed Herod and Pontius Pilate **m together** *5251*
8:27 and on his way he **m** an Ethiopian eunuch, *NIG*
10:25 Cornelius **m** him and fell at his feet *5267*
11:26 for a whole year Barnabas and Saul **m** with *5251*
13: 6 There *they* **m** a Jewish sorcerer *2351*
15: 6 and elders **m** to consider this question. *5251*
16:16 we *were* **m** by a slave girl who had a spirit *5636*
16:40 where *they* **m with** the brothers *3972*
18: 2 There *he* **m** a Jew named Aquila, *2351*
20:14 When *he* **m** us at Assos, *5202*
Ro 8: 4 of the law *might be* **fully m** in us, *4444*
Col 2: 1 and for all who *have* not **m** me **personally**. *1877+3836+3972+4725+4922*

Heb 7: 1 He **m** Abraham returning from the defeat of *5267*
7:10 because when Melchizedek **m** Abraham, *5267*

METAL (12) [METALS, METALWORKER]

Lev 19: 4 not turn to idols or make gods of **cast m** 5011
1Ki 7:23 He made the Sea of **cast m,** 4607
7:33 rims, spokes and hubs were all of **cast m.** 4607
14: 9 other gods, **idols made of m;** 5011
2Ch 4: 2 He made the Sea of **cast m,** 4607
Ps 106:19 a calf and worshiped an **idol cast from m.** 5011
Isa 48: 5 and **m god** ordained them.' 5822
Eze 1: 4 of the fire looked like **glowing m,** 3133
1:27 his waist up he looked like **glowing m,** 3133
8: 2 as bright as **glowing m.** 3133
Da 11: 8 their **m images** and their valuable articles 5816
Na 2: 3 The **m** *on* the chariots flashes on 7110

METALS (1) [METAL]

Jer 6:27 a **tester of m** and my people the ore, 1031

METALWORKER (1) [METAL, WORK]

2Ti 4:14 Alexander the **m** did me a great deal *5906*

METE (1)

Ps 58: 2 and your hands **m out** violence on the earth. 7142

METEYARD (KJV) See MEASURING LENGTH

METHEG AMMAH (1)

2Sa 8: 1 and he took **M** from the control of 5497

METHOD (1) [METHODS]

Ru 4: 7 This was the **m of legalizing transactions** 9496

METHODS (1) [METHOD]

Isa 32: 7 The scoundrel's **m** are wicked, 3998

METHUSAEL (KJV) See METHUSHAEL

METHUSELAH (7)

Ge 5:21 he became the father of **M.** 5500
5:22 And after he became the father of **M,** 5500
5:25 When **M** had lived 187 years, 5500
5:26 **M** lived 782 years and had other sons 5500
5:27 Altogether, **M** lived 969 years, 5500
1Ch 1: 3 Enoch, **M,** Lamech, Noah. 5500
Lk 3:37 the son *of* **M,** son of Enoch, *3417*

METHUSHAEL (2)

Ge 4:18 and Mehujael was the father of **M,** 5499
4:18 and **M** was the father of Lamech. 5499

MEUNIM (2)

Ezr 2:50 Asnah, **M,** Nephussim, 5064
Ne 7:52 Besai, **M,** Nephussim, 5064

MEUNITES (3)

1Ch 4:41 and also the **M** who were there 5064
2Ch 20: 1 of the **M** came to make war on Jehoshaphat. 5064
26: 7 in Gur Baal and against the **M.** 5064

MEZAHAB (KJV) See ME-ZAHAB

MEZOBAITE (1)

1Ch 11:47 Eliel, Obed and Jaasiel the **M.** 5168

MIAMIN (KJV) See MIJAMIN

MIBHAR (1)

1Ch 11:38 Joel the brother of Nathan, **M** son of Hagri, 4437

MIBSAM (3)

Ge 25:13 the firstborn of Ishmael, Kedar, Adbeel, **M,** 4452
1Ch 1:29 the firstborn of Ishmael, Kedar, Adbeel, **M,** 4452
4:25 **M** his son and Mishma his son. 4452

MIBZAR (2)

Ge 36:42 Kenaz, Teman, **M,** 4449
1Ch 1:53 Kenaz, Teman, **M,** 4449

MICA (5)

2Sa 9:12 Mephibosheth had a young son named **M,** 4775
1Ch 9:15 Heresh, Galal and Mattaniah son of **M,** 4775
Ne 10:11 **M,** Rehob, Hashabiah, 4775
11:17 of **M,** the son of Zabdi, the son of Asaph, 4777
11:22 the son of Mattaniah, the son of **M.** 4775

MICAH (25) [MICAH'S]

Jdg 17: 1 Now a man named **M** from the hill country 4781
17: 5 Now this man **M** had a shrine, 4777
17: 9 **M** asked him, "Where are you from?" 4777
17:10 Then **M** said to him, "Live with me 4777
17:12 Then **M** installed the Levite, 4777
17:13 And **M** said, "Now I know that 4777
18: 2 of Ephraim and came to the house of **M,** 4777
18: 4 He told them what **M** had done for him, 4777
18:22 near **M** were called together and overtook 4777
18:23 the Danites turned and said to **M,** 4777
18:26 So the Danites went their way, and **M,** 4777
18:27 Then they took what **M** had made, 4777
18:31 to use the idols **M** had made, 4777
1Ch 5: 5 **M** his son, Reaiah his son, Baal his son, 4777
8:34 Merib-Baal, who was the father of **M.** 4777
8:35 The sons of **M:** Pithon, Melech, 4777
9:40 Merib-Baal, who was the father of **M.** 4777
9:41 The sons of **M:** Pithon, Melech, 4777
23:20 **M** the first and Isshiah the second. 4777
24:24 **M;** from the sons of Micah: Shamir. 4777
24:24 from the sons of **M:** Shamir. 4777
24:25 The brother of **M:** Isshiah; 4777
2Ch 34:20 Ahikam son of Shaphan, Abdon son of **M,** 4777
Jer 26:18 "**M** of Moresheth prophesied in the days 4777
Mic 1: 1 The word of the LORD that came to **M** of Moresheth 4777

MICAH'S (7) [MICAH]

Jdg 17: 4 And they were put in **M** house. 4781
17: 8 to **M** house in the hill country of Ephraim. 4777
18: 3 When they were near **M** house, 4777
18:13 of Ephraim and came to **M** house. 4777
18:15 to the house of the young Levite at **M** place 4777
18:18 into **M** house and took the carved image, 4777
18:22 they had gone some distance from **M** house, 4777

MICAIAH (28)

1Ki 22: 8 He is **M** son of Imlah." 4781
22: 9 "Bring **M** son of Imlah at once." 4781
22:13 to summon **M** said to him, 4781
22:14 But **M** said, "As surely as the LORD lives, 4781
22:15 When he arrived, the king asked him, "**M,** 4781
22:17 **M** answered, "I saw all Israel scattered NIH
22:19 **M** continued, "Therefore hear the word of NIH
22:24 of Kenaanah went up and slapped **M** in 4781
22:25 **M** replied, "You will find out on 4781
22:26 "Take **M** and send him back to Amon 4781
22:28 **M** declared, "If you ever return safely, 4781
2Ki 22:12 Ahikam son of Shaphan, Acbor son of **M,** 4779
2Ch 17: 7 and **M** to teach in the towns of Judah. 4780
18: 7 He is **M** son of Imlah." 4781
18: 8 "Bring **M** son of Imlah at once." 4781
18:12 to summon **M** said to him, 4781
18:13 But **M** said, "As surely as the LORD lives, 4781
18:14 When he arrived, the king asked him, "**M,** 4777
18:16 **M** answered, "I saw all Israel scattered NIH
18:18 **M** continued, "Therefore hear the word of NIH
18:23 of Kenaanah went up and slapped **M** in 4781
18:24 **M** replied, "You will find out on 4781
18:25 "Take **M** and send him back to Amon 4781
18:27 **M** declared, "If you ever return safely, 4781
Ne 12:35 the son of Mattaniah, the son of **M,** 4779
12:41 Eliakim, Maaseiah, Miniamin, **M,** Elioenai, 4779
Jer 36:11 When **M** son of Gemariah, 4781
36:13 **M** told them everything he had heard Baruch read to the people 4781

MICE (KJV) See RATS

MICHA (KJV) See MICA

MICHAEL (15)

Nu 13:13 from the tribe of Asher, Sethur son of **M;** 4776
1Ch 5:13 Their relatives, by families, were: **M,** 4776
5:14 the son of **M,** the son of Jeshishai, 4776
6:40 the son of **M,** the son of Baaseiah, 4776
7: 3 **M,** Obadiah, Joel and Isshiah. 4776
8:16 **M,** Ishpah and Joha were the sons 4776
12:20 Adnah, Jozabad, Jediael, **M,** Jozabad, 4776
27:18 Omri son of **M;** 4776
2Ch 21: 2 Zechariah, Azariahu, **M** and Shephatiah. 4776
Ezr 8: 8 Zebadiah son of **M,** and with him 80 men; 4776
Da 10:13 Then **M,** one of the chief princes, 4776
10:21 No one supports me against them except **M,** 4776
12: 1 "At that time **M,** the great prince 4776
Jude 1: 9 But even the archangel **M,** *3640*
Rev 12: 7 **M** and his angels fought against the dragon, *3640*

MICHAH (KJV) See MICAH

MICHAIAH (KJV) See MICAIAH

MICHAL (18)

1Sa 14:49 and that of the younger was **M.** 4783
18:20 Saul's daughter **M** was in love with David, 4783
18:27 Saul gave him his daughter **M** in marriage. 4783
18:28 and that his daughter **M** loved David, 4783
19:11 But **M,** David's wife, warned him, 4783
19:12 So **M** let David down through a window, 4783
19:13 Then **M** took an idol and laid it on the bed, 4783
19:14 Saul sent the men to capture David, **M** said, NIH
19:17 Saul said to **M,** "Why did you deceive me 4783
19:17 **M** told him, "He said to me, 4783
25:44 But Saul had given his daughter **M,** 4783
2Sa 3:13 unless you bring **M** daughter of Saul 4783
3:14 demanding, "Give me my wife **M,** 4783
6:16 **M** daughter of Saul watched from 4783
6:20 **M** daughter of Saul came out to meet him 4783
6:21 David said to **M,** "It was before 4783
6:23 And **M** daughter of Saul had no children to 4783
1Ch 15:29 **M** daughter of Saul watched from 4783

MICHMAS, MICHMASH (Anglicized, KJV) See MICMASH

MICHMETHAH (KJV) See MICMETHATH

MICHRI (KJV) See MICRI

MICMASH (11)

1Sa 13: 2 two thousand were with him at **M** and in 4825
13: 5 They went up and camped at **M,** 4825
13:11 that the Philistines were assembling at **M,** 4825
13:16 while the Philistines camped at **M.** 4825
13:23 of Philistines had gone out to the pass at **M.** 4825
14: 5 One cliff stood to the north toward **M,** 4825
14:31 down the Philistines from **M** to Aijalon, 4825
Ezr 2:27 of **M** 122 4820
Ne 7:31 of **M** 122 4820
11:31 of the Benjamites from Geba lived in **M,** 4825
Isa 10:28 they store supplies at **M.** 4825

MICMETHATH (2)

Jos 16: 6 From **M** on the north it curved eastward 4826
17: 7 from Asher to **M** east of Shechem. 4826

MICRI (1)

1Ch 9: 8 Elah son of Uzzi, the son of **M;** 4840

MIDAIR (4) [AIR]

2Sa 18: 9 He was left hanging **in m,** 824+1068+1068+2021+2021+2256+9028
Rev 8:13 heard an eagle that was flying in **m** call out *3547*
14: 6 Then I saw another angel flying in **m,** *3547*
19:17 in a loud voice to all the birds flying in **m,** *3547*

MIDDAY (7) [DAY]

Dt 28:29 At **m** you will grope about like a blind man 7416
1Ki 18:29 **M** passed, and they continued their frantic prophesying until 7416
Ps 91: 6 nor the plague that destroys *at* **m.** 7416
SS 1: 7 and where you rest your sheep at **m.** 7416
Isa 59:10 At **m** we stumble as if it were twilight, 7416
Jer 15: 8 At **m** I will bring a destroyer against 7416
Zep 2: 4 At **m** Ashdod will be emptied 7416

MIDDIN (1)

Jos 15:61 In the desert: Beth Arabah, **M,** Secacah, 4516

MIDDLE (49) [AMID, MIDST]

Ge 2: 9 the **m** *of* the garden were the tree of life and 9348
3: 3 not eat fruit from the tree that is in the **m** *of* 9348
6:16 and make lower, **m** and upper decks. 9108
Ex 26:28 from end to end at the **m** *of* the frames. 9348
36:33 that it extended from end to end at the **m** *of* 9348
Nu 2:17 the camp of the Levites will set out in the **m** 9348
Dt 3:16 the Arnon Gorge (the **m** *of* the gorge being 9348
11: 6 the **m** *of* all Israel and swallowed them up 7931
13:16 of the town into the **m** *of* the public square 9348
Jos 3:17 on dry ground in the **m** *of* the Jordan, 9348
4: 3 from the **m** *of* the Jordan from right where 9348
4: 5 the ark of the LORD your God into the **m** 9348
4: 8 They took twelve stones from the **m** *of* 9348
4: 9 the twelve stones that had been in the **m** *of* 9348
4:10 in the **m** *of* the Jordan until everything 9348
8:22 so that they were caught in the **m,** 9348
10:13 in the **m** of the sky and delayed going down 2942
12: 2 from the **m** *of* the gorge— 9348
13: 9 and from the town in the **m** *of* the gorge, 9348
13:16 and from the town in the **m** *of* the gorge, 9348
Jdg 7:19 the camp at the beginning of the **m** watch, 9399
16: 3 But Samson lay there only until the **m** *of* 2942
Ru 3: 8 In the **m** *of* the night something startled 2942
2Sa 10: 4 cut off their garments in the **m** at 2942
20:12 Amasa lay wallowing in his blood in the **m** 9348
23:12 But Shammah took his stand in the **m** *of* 9348
1Ki 3:20 up in the **m** *of* the night and took my son 9348
6: 6 the **m** floor six cubits and 9399
6: 8 to the **m** *level* and from there to the third. 9399
6:27 and their wings touched each other in the **m** 9348
8:64 the **m** *part of* the courtyard in front of 9348
2Ki 20: 4 Before Isaiah had left the **m** court, 9399
1Ch 11:14 they took their stand in the **m** *of* the field. 9348
19: 4 cut off their garments in the **m** at 2942
2Ch 7: 7 the **m** *part of* the courtyard in front of 9348
Job 34:20 They die in an instant, in the **m** *of* the night; 2940
Jer 39: 3 and took seats in the **m** Gate: 9348
Eze 15: 4 the fire burns both ends and chars the **m,** 9348
37: 1 the Spirit of the LORD and set me in the **m** 9348
41: 7 to the top floor through the **m** *floor.* 9399
42: 5 on the lower and **m** *floors of* the building. 9399
42: 6 on the lower and **m** *floors.* 9399
Da 4:10 there before me stood a tree in the **m** *of* 10135
9:27 *In* the **m** *of* the 'seven' he will put an end 2942
Mk 6:47 the boat was in the **m** of the lake, *3545*
Lk 5:19 through the tiles into the **m** of the crowd, *3545*

Lk 22:55 But when they had kindled a fire in the **m** of *3545*
Jn 19:18 one on each side and Jesus in the **m.** *3545*
Rev 22: 2 down the **m** of the great street of the city. *3545*

MIDIAN (35) [MIDIAN'S, MIDIANITE, MIDIANITES]

Ge 25: 2 She bore him Zimran, Jokshan, Medan, **M,** 4518
25: 4 The sons of **M** were Ephah, Epher, Hanoch, 4518
36:35 who defeated **M** in the country of Moab, 4518
Ex 2:15 from Pharaoh and went to live in **M,** 824+4518
2:16 Now a priest of **M** had seven daughters, 4518
3: 1 Jethro his father-in-law, the priest of **M,** 4518
4:19 Now the LORD had said to Moses in **M,** 4518
18: 1 the priest of **M** and father-in-law of Moses, 4518
Nu 22: 4 The Moabites said to the elders of **M,** 4518
22: 7 The elders of Moab and **M** left, 4518
31: 7 They fought against **M,** 4518
31: 8 the five kings of **M.** 4518
Jdg 6: 2 Because the power of **M** was so oppressive, 4518
6: 6 **M** so impoverished the Israelites 4518
6: 7 cried to the LORD because of **M,** 4518
6:13 and put us into the hand of **M."** 4518
7: 1 of **M** was north of them in the valley near 4518
7: 2 for me to deliver **M** into their hands. 4518
7: 8 the camp of **M** lay below him in the valley. 4518
8: 1 when you went to fight **M?"** 4518
8: 5 Zebah and Zalmunna, the kings of **M."** 4518
8:12 Zebah and Zalmunna, the two kings of **M,** 4518
8:22 you have saved us out of the hand of **M."** 4518
8:26 the purple garments worn by the kings of **M** 4518
8:28 Thus **M** was subdued before the Israelites 4518
9:17 to rescue you from the hand of **M** 4518
1Ki 11:18 They set out from **M** and went to Paran. 4518
1Ch 1:32 Zimran, Jokshan, Medan, **M,** 4518
1:33 The sons of **M:** Ephah, Epher, Hanoch, 4518
1:46 who defeated **M** in the country of Moab, 4518
Ps 83: 9 Do to them as you did to **M,** 4518
Isa 10:26 he struck down **M** at the rock of Oreb; 4518
60: 6 young camels of **M** and Ephah. 4518
Hab 3: 7 the dwellings of **M** in anguish. 824+4518
Ac 7:29 When Moses heard this, he fled to **M,** *1178+3409*

MIDIAN'S (2) [MIDIAN]

Jdg 6:14 and save Israel out of **M** hand. 4518
Isa 9: 4 For as in the day of **M** defeat, 4518

MIDIANITE (14) [MIDIAN]

Ge 37:28 So when the **M** merchants came by, 4520
Nu 10:29 Moses said to Hobab son of Reuel the **M,** 4520
25: 6 a **M** *woman* right before the eyes of Moses 4520
25:14 with the **M** *woman* was Zimri son of Salu, 4520
25:15 the name of the **M** woman who was put 4520
25:15 a tribal chief of a **M** family. 4518
25:18 the daughter of a **M** leader, 4518
31: 9 the **M** women and children and took all 4518
31: 9 and children and took all **the M** herds, 4392[S]
Jos 13:21 Moses had defeated him and the **M** chiefs, 4518
Jdg 7:13 bread came tumbling into the **M** camp. 4518
7:15 The LORD has given the **M** camp 4518
7:25 They also captured two of the **M** leaders, 4518
8: 3 God gave Oreb and Zeeb, the **M** leaders, 4518

MIDIANITES (17) [MIDIAN]

Ge 37:36 the **M** sold Joseph in Egypt to Potiphar, 4520
Nu 25:17 "Treat the **M** as enemies and kill them, 4520
31: 2 "Take vengeance on the **M** for 4520
31: 3 of your men to go to war against the **M** and 4518
31:10 the towns where **the M** had settled, 4392[S]
Jdg 6: 1 into the hands of the **M.** 4518
6: 3 the Israelites planted their crops, the **M,** 4518
6:11 in a winepress to keep it from the **M.** 4518
6:16 you will strike down all the **M** together." 4518
6:33 Now all the **M,** Amalekites and other 4518
7: 7 that lapped I will save you and give the **M** 4518
7:12 The **M,** the Amalekites and all 4518
7:14 the **M** and the whole camp into his hands." 4518
7:21 all the **M** ran, crying out as they fled. 4722[S]
7:23 and they pursued the **M.** 4518
7:24 down against the **M** and seize the waters of 4518
7:25 They pursued the **M** and brought the heads 4518

MIDIANITISH (KJV) See MIDIANITES

MIDNIGHT (9) [NIGHT]

Ex 11: 4 'About **m** I will go throughout Egypt. 2940+4326
12:29 At **m** the LORD struck down all 2021+2942+4326
Ps 119:62 *At* **m** I rise to give you thanks 2940+4326
Mt 25: 6 *"At* **m** the cry rang out: *3545+3816*
Mk 13:35 whether in the evening, or **at m,** *3543*
Lk 11: 5 and he goes to him *at* **m** and says, 'Friend, *3543*
Ac 16:25 About **m** Paul and Silas were praying *3543*
20: 7 kept on talking until **m.** *3543*
27:27 when about **m** the sailors sensed *3545+3816+3836*

MIDST (23) [MIDDLE]

Lev 16:16 among them in the **m** *of* their uncleanness. 9348
Nu 16:47 and ran into the **m** *of* the assembly. 9348
Job 20:22 In the **m** *of* his plenty, 4848
Ps 57: 4 I am in the **m** *of* lions; 9348
102:24 O my God, in the **m** *of* my days; 2942
110: 2 you will rule in the **m** *of* your enemies. 7931
116:19 in your **m,** O Jerusalem. 9348
135: 9 He sent his signs and wonders into your **m,** 9348
136:14 and brought Israel through the **m** *of* it, 9348
138: 7 Though I walk in the **m** *of* trouble, 7931
Pr 5:14 to the brink of utter ruin in the **m** *of* 9348
Isa 66:17 following the one in the **m** *of* those who eat 9348
Jer 9: 6 You live in the **m** *of* deception; 9348
48:45 a blaze from the **m** *of* Sihon; 1068
La 1: 3 overtaken her **in the m of** her distress. 1068
1:15 Lord has rejected all the warriors in my **m;** 7931
Eze 5:10 in your **m** fathers will eat their children, 9348
22: 3 on herself doom by shedding blood in her **m** 9348
22:13 and at the blood you have shed in your **m.** 9348
24: 7 " 'For the blood she shed is in her **m:** 9348
Am 5:17 for I will pass through your **m,"** 7931
Mic 5: 7 be in the **m** *of* many peoples like dew from 7931
5: 8 in the **m** *of* many peoples, 7931

MIDWIFE (2) [MIDWIVES]

Ge 35:17 the **m** said to her, "Don't be afraid, 3528
38:28 so the **m** took a scarlet thread and tied it 3528

MIDWIVES (7) [MIDWIFE]

Ex 1:15 The king of Egypt said to the Hebrew **m,** 3528
1:17 The **m,** however, feared God and did 3528
1:18 of Egypt summoned the **m** and asked them, 3528
1:19 The **m** answered Pharaoh, 3528
1:19 and give birth before the **m** arrive." 3528
1:20 the **m** and the people increased and became 3528
1:21 And because the **m** feared God, 3528

MIGDAL EDER (1) [EDER]

Ge 35:21 and pitched his tent beyond **M.** 4468

MIGDAL EL (1)

Jos 19:38 **M,** Horem, Beth Anath 4466

MIGDAL GAD (1) [GAD]

Jos 15:37 Zenan, Hadashah, **M,** 4467

MIGDOL (6)

Ex 14: 2 between **M** and the sea. 4465
Nu 33: 7 and camped near **M.** 4465
Jer 44: 1 in **M,** Tahpanhes and Memphis— 4465
46:14 and proclaim it in **M;** 4465
Eze 29:10 and a desolate waste from **M** to Aswan, 4465
30: 6 From **M** to Aswan they will fall by 4465

MIGHT (190) [ALMIGHTY, MIGHTIER, MIGHTIEST, MIGHTILY, MIGHTY]

Ge 17:18 only Ishmael *m* **live** under your blessing!" AIT
26: 7 "The men of this place **m** kill me on account 7153
26: 9 "Because I thought I **m** lose my life 7153
26:10 men **m well have** slept with your wife, 3869+5071
42: 4 he was afraid that harm *m* **come** to him. AIT
49: 3 "Reuben, you are my firstborn, my **m,** 3946
Ex 9:16 that *I m* **show** you my power and AIT
9:16 and that my name *m be* **proclaimed** in all AIT
13:17 they **m** change their minds and return 7153
16:34 that it **m** be kept. NIH
29:46 of Egypt so that I *m* **dwell** among them. AIT
33: 3 a stiff-necked people and *I m* **destroy** you AIT
33: 5 even for a moment, *I m* **destroy** you. AIT
Lev 5: 4 in any matter one *m* **carelessly** swear about AIT
Dt 4:35 so that *you m* **know** that the LORD is God; AIT
5:29 so that *it m* **go well** with them AIT
6:24 that we **m** always prosper and be kept alive, NIH
8:16 to test you so that in the end *it m* **go well** AIT
19: 6 avenger of blood *m* **pursue** him in a rage, AIT
29: 6 I did this so that *you m* **know** that I am AIT
Jos 4:24 the peoples of the earth *m* **know** that the hand of the LORD is powerful AIT
4:24 and so that *you m* always **fear** AIT
11:20 *m* **destroy** them **totally,** AIT
22:24 that some day your descendants *m* **say** AIT
22:25 *m* **cause** ours **to stop** fearing the LORD. AIT
Jdg 9:24 *m be* **avenged** on their brother Abimelech AIT
14: 6 with his bare hands as *he m have* **torn** AIT
16:30 Then he pushed with all his **m,** 3946
18: 1 a place of their own where they *m* **settle,** AIT
Ru 2:22 in someone else's field you *m be* **harmed."** AIT
4: 6 because *I m* **endanger** my own estate. AIT
1Sa 18:27 *m become* the king's **son-in-law.** AIT
27:11 "They **m** inform on us and say, 7153
2Sa 6: 5 of Israel were celebrating with all their **m** 6437
6:14 danced before the LORD with all his **m,** 6437
1Ki 2:22 *You m* as well **request** the kingdom AIT
19: 4 sat down under it and prayed that he *m* **die.** AIT
2Ki 23:33 in the land of Hamath so that he *m* not **reign** AIT
1Ch 13: 8 with all their **m** before God, 6437
2Ch 6:41 you and the ark of your **m.** 6437
20: 6 Power and **m** are in your hand, 1476
23:19 in any way unclean *m* **enter.** AIT
25:20 that he *m* **hand** them **over** to [Jehoash], AIT
Ezr 8:17 so that they *m* **bring** attendants to us for AIT
8:21 that we *m* **humble ourselves** before our God AIT
Est 8:11 that *m* **attack** them and their women AIT
10: 2 And all his acts of power and **m,** 1476
Job 3:12 and breasts that *I m be* **nursed?** AIT
6: 8 "Oh, that I *m* **have** my request, AIT
9:32 not a man like me that *I m* **answer** him, AIT
9:32 that *we m* **confront** each other in court. AIT
13: 9 as you *m* **deceive** men? AIT
Job 30:21 with the **m** *of* your hand you attack me. 6797
34:36 that Job *m* **be tested** to the utmost AIT
38:13 that *it m* **take** the earth by the edges AIT
Ps 21:13 we will sing and praise your **m.** 1476
54: 1 vindicate me by your **m.** 1476
59:11 In your **m** make them wander about, 2657
68:18 that you, O LORD God, *m* **dwell** there. AIT
71:18 your **m** to all who are to come. 1476
78:61 He sent [the ark of] his **m** into captivity, 6437
80: 2 Awaken your **m;** come and save us. 1476
105:45 that *they m* **keep** his precepts AIT
119:11 in my heart that *I m* not **sin** against you. AIT
119:71 be afflicted so that *I m* **learn** your decrees. AIT
119:101 so that *I m* **obey** your word. AIT
125: 3 the righteous *m* **use** their hands **to do** evil. AIT
132: 8 you and the ark of your **m.** 6437
145:11 of your kingdom and speak of your **m,** 1476
Ecc 9:10 do it with all your **m,** for in the grave, 3946
Isa 6:10 Otherwise *they m* **see** with their eyes, AIT
44:12 he forges it with the **m** *of* his arm. 3946
47: 7 or reflect on **what m happen.** 344
51:10 the sea so that the redeemed *m* **cross over?** AIT
63:15 Where are your zeal and your **m?** 1476
Jer 9: 2 so that *I m* **leave** my people and go away AIT
16:21 this time I will teach them my power and **m.** 1476
49:35 the mainstay of their **m.** 1476
Eze 20:26 *m* **fill** them **with horror** AIT
36: 5 so that they **m** plunder its pastureland.' NIH
Da 2:16 so that he *m* **interpret** the dream for him. AIT
2:18 so that he and his friends *m* not *be* **executed** AIT
2:37 and power and **m** and glory; 10773
5: 2 and his concubines *m* **drink** from them. AIT
6: 2 to them so that the king *m* not **suffer loss.** AIT
6:17 so that Daniel's situation *m* not *be* **changed.** AIT
11:17 the **m** *of* his entire kingdom and will make 9549
Joel 3: 3 they sold girls for wine that *they m* **drink.** AIT
3: 6 *you m* **send** them **far** from their homeland. AIT
Mic 3: 8 and with justice and **m,** 1476
Zec 4: 6 'Not by **m** nor by power, but by my Spirit,' 2657
Mt 12:14 and plotted how *they m* **kill** Jesus. *AIT*
13:15 Otherwise *they m* **see** with their eyes, *AIT*
15: 5 'Whatever help you **m** otherwise have received from me *NIG*
26:56 writings of the prophets *m be* **fulfilled."** *AIT*
Mk 3: 6 with the Herodians how *they m* **kill** Jesus. *AIT*
3:14 that *they m* **be** with him and *AIT*
3:14 be with him and that *he m* **send** them **out** *AIT*
4:12 otherwise they *m* **turn** and be forgiven!' " *AIT*
7:11 **help** *you m* otherwise *have* **received** *AIT*
14:35 and prayed that if possible the hour *m* **pass** *AIT*
16: 1 so that *they m* go to **anoint** Jesus' body. *AIT*
Lk 1:29 what kind of greeting this *m* **be.** *AIT*
3:15 if John *m possibly* **be** the Christ. *AIT*
6:11 to discuss with one another what they **m** do *323*
11:54 waiting to catch him in something he **m say.** *1666+3836+5125*
20:20 so that *they m* **hand** him **over** to the power *AIT*
22: 4 with them how *he m* **betray** Jesus. *AIT*
22:23 among themselves which of them *it m* **be** *AIT*
Jn 1: 7 so that through him all men *m* **believe.** *AIT*
1:31 with water was that *he m be* **revealed** *AIT*
9: 3 the work of God *m be* **displayed** in his life. *AIT*
11:57 so that *they m* **arrest** him. *AIT*
17: 2 over all people that *he m* **give** eternal life *AIT*
19:24 the scripture *m be* **fulfilled** which said, *AIT*
Ac 5:15 so that at least Peter's shadow *m* **fall on** *AIT*
5:31 *that he m* **give** repentance and forgiveness *AIT*
7:46 that *he m* **provide** a dwelling place for *AIT*
8:15 for them that *they m* **receive** the Holy Spirit, *AIT*
9: 2 *he m* **take** them as prisoners to Jerusalem. *AIT*
15: 7 that the Gentiles *m* **hear** from my lips *AIT*
27: 3 to go to his friends *so* they *m* **provide** *AIT*
28:27 Otherwise *they m* **see** with their eyes, *AIT*
Ro 1:13 in order that *I m* **have** a harvest among you, *AIT*
3: 7 Someone **m** argue, "If my falsehood enhances God's truthfulness *NIG*
4:11 that righteousness *m be* **credited** to them. *AIT*
5: 7 for a good man someone *m* possibly **dare** to die. *AIT*
5:20 so that the trespass *m* **increase.** *AIT*
5:21 so also grace *m* **reign** through righteousness *AIT*
6: 6 that the body of sin *m be* **done away with,** *AIT*
7: 4 that you *m* **belong** to another, *AIT*
7: 4 in order that *we m* **bear fruit** to God. *AIT*
7:13 But in order that sin *m be* **recognized** as sin, *AIT*
7:13 commandment sin *m* **become** utterly sinful. *AIT*
8: 4 requirements of the law *m be* **fully met** in us, *AIT*
8:29 that he *m* **be** the firstborn among many *AIT*
9:11 that God's purpose in election *m* **stand:** *AIT*
9:17 that *I m* **display** my power in you and *AIT*
9:17 in you and that my name *m be* **proclaimed** *AIT*
14: 9 and returned to life so that *he m* **be** the **Lord** *AIT*
15: 4 of the Scriptures *we m* **have** hope. *AIT*
15:16 Gentiles *m* **become** an offering acceptable *AIT*
16:26 that all nations **m** believe and obey him— *NIG*
1Co 2: 5 that your faith *m* not **rest** on men's wisdom, *AIT*
4: 8 so that we *m be* **kings with** you! *AIT*
9:22 that by all possible means *I m* **save** some. *AIT*
2Co 1: 9 that *we m* not **rely** on ourselves but on God, *AIT*
1:15 so that *you m* **benefit** twice. *AIT*
2:11 in order that Satan *m* not **outwit** us. *AIT*
5:21 that in him we *m* **become** the righteousness *AIT*
8: 9 you through his poverty *m become* **rich.** *AIT*
8:13 Our desire is not that others **m** be relieved *NIG*
8:13 but that there **m** be equality. *NIG*
11: 2 *I m* **present** you as a pure virgin to him. *AIT*
Gal 1:16 so that *I m* **preach** him among the Gentiles, *AIT*

Gal 2: 5 the truth of the gospel *m* **remain** with you. *AIT*
2:19 the law I died to the law so that *I m* **live** *AIT*
3:14 that the blessing given to Abraham *m* **come** *AIT*
3:14 so that by faith *we m* **receive** the promise of *AIT*
3:22 *m be* **given** to those who believe. *AIT*
3:24 to lead us to Christ that *we m be* **justified** *AIT*
4: 5 that *we m* **receive** the full rights of sons. *AIT*
Eph 1:12 *m* **be** for the praise of his glory. *AIT*
2: 7 in order that in the coming ages *he m* **show** *AIT*
Col 1:11 with all power according to his glorious **m** *3197*
1:18 that in everything he *m* **have** the supremacy. *AIT*
1Th 3: 5 the tempter **m** have tempted you *NIG*
3: 5 and our efforts *m have* **been** useless. *AIT*
2Th 2:14 that you **m** share in the glory *NIG*
1Ti 1:16 Christ Jesus *m* **display** his unlimited patience as an example *AIT*
6:16 To him be honor and **m** forever. *3197*
2Ti 4:17 the message *m be* **fully** proclaimed *AIT*
4:17 and all the Gentiles *m* **hear** it. *AIT*
Tit 1: 5 that *you m* **straighten out** what was left unfinished *AIT*
3: 7 *we m* **become** heirs having the hope *AIT*
Phm 1:15 a little while was that *you m* **have** him **back** *AIT*
Heb 2: 9 so that by the grace of God *he m* **taste** death *AIT*
2:14 by his death *he m* **destroy** him who holds *AIT*
2:17 in order that *he m* **become** a merciful *AIT*
2:17 that *he m* **make atonement for** the sins of *AIT*
7: 9 **One m even say** that Levi, *2229+3306+6055*
11:35 so that *they m* **gain** a better resurrection. *AIT*
Jas 1:18 that we **m be** a kind of firstfruits of all *AIT*
1Pe 2:24 **m** die to sins and **live** for righteousness *AIT*
4: 6 so that *they m be* **judged** according to men *AIT*
1Jn 3: 5 so that *he m* **take away** our sins. *AIT*
4: 9 and only Son into the world that *we m* **live** *AIT*
Rev 12: 4 so that *he m* **devour** her child *AIT*
12: 6 *she m be* **taken care of** for 1,260 days. *AIT*
12:14 that *she m* **fly** to the place prepared for her *AIT*

MIGHTIER (2) [MIGHT]

Ps 93: 4 **M** than the thunder of the great waters, NIH
93: 4 **m** than the breakers of the sea— 129

MIGHTIEST (1) [MIGHT]

Da 11:39 He will attack the **m fortresses** with 4448+5057

MIGHTILY (1) [MIGHT]

Jer 25:30 from his holy dwelling and **roar m** 8613+8613

MIGHTY (187) [MIGHT]

Ge 10: 8 who grew to be a **m warrior** on the earth. 1475
10: 9 He was a **m** hunter before the LORD; 1475
10: 9 Like Nimrod, a **m** hunter before the LORD." 1475
23: 6 You are a **m** prince among us. 466
49:24 because of the hand of the **M One** *of* Jacob, 51
Ex 3:19 unless a **m** hand compels him. 2617
6: 1 Because of my **m** hand he will let them go; 2617
6: 1 of my **m** hand he will drive them out 2617
6: 6 with an outstretched arm and with **m** acts 1524
7: 4 on Egypt and with **m** acts of judgment 1524
13: 3 LORD brought you out of it with a **m** hand. 2620
13: 9 out of Egypt with his **m** hand. 2617
13:14 'With a **m** hand the LORD brought us out 2620
13:16 of Egypt with his **m** hand." 2620
15:10 They sank like lead in the **m** waters. 129
32:11 of Egypt with great power and a **m** hand? 2617
Dt 3:24 the deeds and **m works** you do? 1476
4:34 by a **m** hand and an outstretched arm, 2617
5:15 with a **m** hand and an outstretched arm. 2617
6:21 out of Egypt with a **m** hand. 2617
7: 8 a **m** hand and redeemed you from the land 2617
7:19 the **m** hand and outstretched arm, 2617
9:26 and brought out of Egypt with a **m** hand. 2617
10:17 the great God, **m** and awesome, 1475
11: 2 his majesty, his **m** hand, his outstretched 2617
26: 8 with a **m** hand and an outstretched arm, 2617
34:12 For no one has ever shown the **m** power 2617
Jos 22:22 "The **M One,** God, the LORD! 446
22:22 The **M One,** God, the LORD! 446
Jdg 5:13 of the LORD came to me with the **m.** 1475
5:22 galloping, galloping go his **m** steeds. 52
5:23 to help the LORD against the **m.'** 1475
6:12 "The LORD is with you, **m** warrior." 2657
11: 1 Jephthah the Gileadite was a **m warrior.** 1475+2657
1Sa 4: 8 from the hand of these **m** gods? 129
14:52 and whenever Saul saw a **m** or brave man, 1475
2Sa 1:19 How the **m** have fallen! 1475
1:21 For there the shield of the **m** was defiled, 1475
1:22 from the flesh of the **m,** 1475
1:25 "How the **m** have fallen in battle! 1475
1:27 "How the **m** have fallen! 1475
20: 7 the **m warriors** went out under the command of Abishai. 1475
23: 8 These are the names of David's **m men:** 1475
23: 9 As one of the three **m men,** 1475
23:16 So the three **m men** broke through 1475
23:17 Such were the exploits of the three **m men.** 1475
23:22 he too was as famous as the three **m men.** 1475
1Ki 8:42 of your great name and your **m** hand 2617
2Ki 17:36 with **m** power and outstretched arm, 1524
1Ch 1:10 who grew to be a **m warrior** on earth. 1475
11:10 These were the chiefs of David's **m men—** 1475
11:11 this is the list of David's **m men:** 1475
11:12 the Ahohite, one of the three **m men.** 1475
1Ch 11:19 Such were the exploits of the three **m men.** 1475
11:24 he too was as famous as the three **m men.** 1475
11:26 The **m men** were: 1475+2657
12: 4 a **m man** among the Thirty, 1475
27: 6 This was the Benaiah who was a **m man** 1475
28: 1 the **m men** and all the brave warriors. 1475
29:24 All the officers and **m men,** 1475
2Ch 6:32 of your great name and your **m** hand 2617
14:11 to help the powerless against the **m.** 8041
16: 8 Libyans a **m** army with great numbers 4200+8044
Ne 1:10 by your great strength and your **m** hand. 2617
9:11 like a stone into **m** waters. 6434
9:32 O our God, the great, **m** and awesome God, 1475
Job 1:19 when suddenly a **m** wind swept in from 1524
9:19 If it is a matter of strength, he is **m!** 579
12:21 on nobles and disarms the **m.** 693
24:22 But God drags away the **m** by his power; 52
34:17 Will you condemn the just and **m** *One?* 3888
34:20 the **m** are removed without human hand. 52
34:24 Without inquiry he shatters the **m** and sets 3888
36: 5 "God is **m,** but does not despise men; 3888
36: 5 he is **m,** and firm in his purpose. 3888
36:19 or even all your **m** efforts sustain you 3946
37: 6 and to the rain shower, 'Be a **m** downpour.' 6437
41:25 When he rises up, the **m** are terrified; 446
Ps 24: 8 The LORD strong and **m,** 1475
24: 8 the LORD **m** *in* battle. 1475
29: 1 Ascribe to the LORD, O **m** *ones,* 446+1201
29: 3 the LORD thunders over the **m** waters. 8041
32: 6 the **m** waters rise, they will not reach him. 8041
36: 6 Your righteousness is like the **m** mountains, 446
45: 3 Gird your sword upon your side, O **m** *one;* 1475
50: 1 The **M One,** God, the LORD, 446
52: 1 Why do you boast of evil, you **m man?** 1475
62: 7 he is my **m** rock, my refuge. 6437
68:33 who thunders with **m** voice. 6437
71:16 I will come and proclaim your **m acts,** 1476
77:12 and consider all your **m deeds.** 6613
77:15 With your **m** arm you redeemed your people, NIH
77:19 your way through the **m** waters, 8041
80:10 the **m** cedars with its branches. 446
89: 8 You are **m,** O LORD, 2886
93: 4 the LORD on high is **m.** 129
99: 4 The King is **m,** he loves justice— 6437
103:20 you **m** *ones* who do his bidding, 1475+3946
106: 2 Who can proclaim the **m acts** *of* 1476
106: 8 to make his **m power** known. 1476
107:23 they were merchants on the **m** waters. 8041
110: 2 The LORD will extend your **m** scepter 6437
112: 2 His children will be **m** in the land; 1475
118:15 The LORD's right hand has done **m things!** 2657
118:16 the LORD's right hand has done **m things!"** 2657
132: 2 and made a vow to the **M One** *of* Jacob." 51
132: 5 a dwelling for the **M One** *of* Jacob." 51
135:10 down many nations and killed **m** kings— 6786
136:12 with a **m** hand and outstretched arm; 2617
136:18 killed **m** kings—His love endures forever. 129
144: 7 and rescue me from the **m** waters, 8041
145: 4 they will tell of your **m acts.** 1476
145:12 that all men may know of your **m acts** and 1476
147: 5 Great is our Lord and **m** *in* power; 8041
150: 1 praise him in his **m** heavens. 6437
Pr 7:26 her slain are a **m** throng. 6786
21:22 of the **m** and pulls down the stronghold 1475
30:30 **m** among beasts, who retreats 1475
SS 8: 6 It burns like blazing fire, like a **m flame.** 8928
Isa 1:24 the LORD Almighty, the **M One** *of* Israel, 51
1:31 The **m** *man* will become tinder and his work 2891
8: 7 to bring against them the **m** floodwaters of 6786
9: 6 **M** God, Everlasting Father, Prince of Peace. 1475
10:13 like a **m** *one* I subdued their kings. 52
10:21 remnant of Jacob will return to the **M** God. 1475
10:34 Lebanon will fall before the **M One.** 129
22:17 O you **m man.** 1505
33:21 There the LORD will be our **M One.** 129
33:21 no **m** ship will sail them. 129
40:26 Because of his great power and **m** strength, 579
42:13 The LORD will march out like a **m man,** 1475
43:16 a path through the **m** waters, 6434
49:26 your Redeemer, the **M One** *of* Jacob." 51
56:11 They are dogs with **m** appetites; 6434
60:16 your Redeemer, the **M One** *of* Jacob. 51
60:22 the smallest a **m** nation. 6786
62: 8 by his right hand and by his **m** arm: 6437
63: 1 speaking in righteousness, **m** to save." 8041
Jer 5:16 all of them are **m warriors.** 1475
10: 6 you are great, and your name is **m** in power. 1524
11:16 But with the roar of a **m** storm he will set it 1524
20:11 But the LORD is with me like a **m** warrior; 1475
21: 5 a **m** arm in anger and fury and great wrath. 2617
25:32 a **m** storm is rising from the ends of 1524
32:19 and **m** are your deeds. 8041
32:21 by a **m** hand and an outstretched arm and 2617
48:17 say, 'How broken is the **m** scepter, 6437
Eze 7:24 I will put an end to the pride of the **m,** 6434
17:17 with his **m** army and great horde will be 1524
20:33 with a **m** hand and an outstretched arm and 2617
20:34 with a **m** hand and an outstretched arm and 2617
32:12 to fall by the swords of **m men—** 1475
32:18 both her and the daughters of **m** nations, 129
32:21 the grave the **m** leaders will say of Egypt 446
38:15 a great horde, a **m** army. 8041
39:18 of **m men** and drink the blood of the princes 1475
39:20 **m men** and soldiers of every kind,' 1475
Da 2:10 No king, however great and **m,** 10718
4: 3 how **m** his wonders! 10768
4:30 by my **m** power and for the glory 10278
Da 8:24 the **m** *men* and the holy people. 6786
9:15 a **m** hand and who made for yourself a name 2617
11: 3 Then a **m** king will appear, 1475
Hos 8:10 under the oppression of the **m** king. 8569
Joel 2: 2 the mountains a large and **m** army comes, 6786
2: 5 like a **m** army drawn up for battle. 6786
2:11 and **m** are those who obey his command. 6786
Zep 3:17 your God is with you, he is **m** to save. 1475
Zec 4: 7 "What are you, O **m** mountain? 1524
10: 5 Together they will be like **m men** trampling 1475
10: 7 The Ephraimites will become like **m men,** 1475
Mt 26:64 the right hand *of* the **M** *One* and coming on *1539*
Mk 14:62 the right hand *of* the **M** *One* and coming on *1539*
Lk 1:49 the **M** *One* has done great things for me— *1543*
1:51 He has performed **m deeds** with his arm; *3197*
22:69 be seated at the right hand *of* the **m** God." *1539*
Ac 13:17 in Egypt, with **m** power he led them out of *5734*
Eph 1:19 power is like the working *of* his **m** strength, *2709*
6:10 be strong in the Lord and in his **m** power. *2709*
1Pe 5: 6 therefore, under God's **m** hand, *3193*
Rev 5: 2 I saw a **m** angel proclaiming in a loud voice, *2708*
6:15 the princes, the generals, the rich, the **m,** *2708*
10: 1 Then I saw another **m** angel coming down *2708*
18: 2 With a **m** voice he shouted: "Fallen! *2708*
18: 8 for **m** is the Lord God who judges her. *2708*
18:21 Then a **m** angel picked up a boulder the size *2708*
19:18 and **m** *men,* of horses and their riders, *2708*

MIGRATION (1)

Jer 8: 7 and the thrush observe the time of their **m.** 995

MIGRON (2)

1Sa 14: 2 of Gibeah under a pomegranate tree in **M.** 4491
Isa 10:28 They enter Aiath; they pass through **M;** 4491

MIJAMIN (4)

1Ch 24: 9 the fifth to Malkijah, the sixth to **M,** 4785
Ezr 10:25 Ramiah, Izziah, Malkijah, **M,** Eleazar, 4785
Ne 10: 7 Meshullam, Abijah, **M,** 4785
12: 5 **M,** Moadiah, Bilgah, 4785

MIKLOTH (4)

1Ch 8:32 and **M,** who was the father of Shimeah. 5235
9:37 Gedor, Ahio, Zechariah and **M.** 5235
9:38 **M** was the father of Shimeam. 5235
27: 4 **M** was the leader of his division. 5235

MIKNEIAH (2)

1Ch 15:18 **M,** Obed-Edom and Jeiel, the gatekeepers. 5240
15:21 Eliphelehu, **M,** Obed-Edom, 5240

MIKTAM (6)

Ps 16: T A **m** of David. 4846
56: T "A Dove on Distant Oaks." Of David. A **m.** 4846
57: T "Do Not Destroy." Of David. A **m.** 4846
58: T "Do Not Destroy." Of David. A **m.** 4846
59: T "Do Not Destroy." Of David. A **m.** 4846
60: T "The Lily of the Covenant." A **m** of David. 4846

MILALAI (1)

Ne 12:36 Shemaiah, Azarel, **M,** Gilalai, Maai, 4912

MILCAH (11)

Ge 11:29 and the name of Nahor's wife was **M;** 4894
11:29 the father of both **M** and Iscah. 4894
22:20 "**M** is also a mother; 4894
22:23 **M** bore these eight sons 4894
24:15 She was the daughter of Bethuel son of **M,** 4894
24:24 Bethuel, the son that **M** bore to Nahor." 4894
24:47 whom **M** bore to him.' 4894
Nu 26:33 Noah, Hoglah, **M** and Tirzah.) 4894
27: 1 Noah, Hoglah, **M** and Tirzah. 4894
36:11 Mahlah, Tirzah, Hoglah, **M** and Noah— 4894
Jos 17: 3 Noah, Hoglah, **M** and Tirzah. 4894

MILCH (KJV) See COWS THAT HAVE CALVED, FEMALE

MILDEW (30)

Lev 13:47 "If any clothing is contaminated with **m—** 7669
13:49 it is a **spreading m** and must be shown to 7669
13:50 The priest is to examine the **m** and isolate 5596
13:51 and if the **m** has spread in the clothing, 5596
13:51 it is a destructive **m;** the article is unclean. 7669
13:52 because the **m** is destructive; 7669
13:53 the **m** has not spread in the clothing, 5596
13:55 and if the **m** has not changed its appearance, 5596
13:55 the **m** has affected one side or the other. 7076
13:56 the **m** has faded after the article has been 5596
13:57 and whatever has the **m** must be burned 5596
13:58 that has been washed and is rid of the **m,** 5596
13:59 concerning contamination by **m** in woolen 7669
14:34 I put a **spreading m** in a house in that land, 5596+7669
14:35 'I have seen something that looks like **m** 5596
14:36 before he goes in to examine the **m,** 5596
14:37 He is to examine the **m** on the walls, 5596
14:39 If the **m** has spread on the walls, 5596
14:43 "If the **m** reappears in the house after 5596
14:44 if the **m** has spread in the house, 5596

Lev 14:44 it is a destructive **m;** the house is unclean. 7669
14:48 the priest comes to examine it and the **m** has 5596
14:48 because the **m** is gone. 5596
14:55 for **m** *in* clothing or in a house, 7669
14:57 **infectious skin diseases and m.** 7669
Dt 28:22 with blight and **m,** 3766
1Ki 8:37 or blight or **m,** locusts or grasshoppers, 3766
2Ch 6:28 or blight or **m,** locusts or grasshoppers, 3766
Am 4:9 I struck them with blight and **m.** 3766
Hag 2:17 **m** and hail, yet you did not turn to me,' 3766

MILE (1) [MILES]

Mt 5:41 If someone forces you to go one **m,** *3627*

MILES (4) [MILE]

Mt 5:41 to go one mile, go with him two **m.** *NIG*
Lk 24:13 about **seven m** from Jerusalem. *2008+5084*
Jn 6:19 they had rowed **three or three and a half m,** *1633+2445+4297+5084+5558*
11:18 Bethany was less than **two m** from *1278+5084*

MILETUS (3)

Ac 20:15 and on the following day arrived at **M.** *3626*
20:17 From **M,** Paul sent to Ephesus for the elders *3626*
2Ti 4:20 and I left Trophimus sick in **M.** *3626*

MILITARY (16)

Jos 5:4 all the men of **m age—** 4878
5:6 of **m age** when they left Egypt had died, 4878
2Sa 5:2 **led** Israel **on** their **m campaigns.** 995+2256+3655
20:8 Joab was wearing his **m tunic,** 4230+4496
1Ki 22:45 the things he achieved and *his* **m exploits,** 4309
2Ki 14:28 all he did, and his **m** achievements, 4309
18:20 You say you have strategy and **m** strength— 4878
1Ch 5:18 men **ready for m service—** 3655+7372
11:2 **led** Israel **on** their **m campaigns.** 995+2256+3655
2Ch 25:5 there were three hundred thousand men **ready for m service,** 3655+7372
32:3 he consulted with his officials and **m staff** 1475
32:6 He appointed **m** officers over the people 4878
33:14 He stationed **m** commanders in all 2657
Est 1:3 The **m leaders** *of* Persia and Media, 2657
Isa 36:5 You say you have strategy and **m** strength— 4878
Mk 6:21 *for* his high officials and **m commanders** *5941*

MILK (48)

Ge 18:8 then brought some curds and **m** and the calf 2692
49:12 his teeth whiter than **m.** 2692
Ex 3:8 a land flowing with **m** and honey— 2692
3:17 a land flowing with **m** and honey.' 2692
13:5 a land flowing with **m** and honey— 2692
23:19 Do not cook a young goat in its mother's **m.** 2692
33:3 up to the land flowing with **m** and honey. 2692
34:26 Do not cook a young goat in its mother's **m.** 2692
Lev 20:24 a land flowing with **m** and honey." 2692
Nu 13:27 and it does flow with **m** and honey! 2692
14:8 a land flowing with **m** and honey, 2692
16:13 up out of a land flowing with **m** and honey 2692
16:14 with **m** and honey or given us an inheritance 2692
Dt 6:3 in a land flowing with **m** and honey, 2692
11:9 a land flowing with **m** and honey. 2692
14:21 Do not cook a young goat in its mother's **m.** 2692
26:9 a land flowing with **m** and honey; 2692
26:15 a land flowing with **m** and honey." 2692
27:3 a land flowing with **m** and honey, 2692
31:20 into the land flowing with **m** and honey, 2692
32:14 with curds and **m** *from* herd and flock and 2692
Jos 5:6 a land flowing with **m** and honey. 2692
Jdg 4:19 She opened a skin of **m,** gave him a drink, 2692
5:25 He asked for water, and she gave him **m;** 2692
5:25 for nobles she brought him **curdled m.** 2772
2Sa 17:29 from cows' **m** for David and his people NIH
Job 10:10 not pour me out like **m** and curdle me 2692
Pr 27:27 of goats' **m** to feed you and your family and 2692
30:33 For as churning the **m** produces butter, 2692
SS 4:11 **m** and honey are under your tongue. 2692
5:1 I have drunk my wine and my **m.** 2692
5:12 washed in **m,** mounted like jewels. 2692
Isa 7:22 of the abundance of the **m** they give, 2692
28:9 To children weaned from their **m,** 2692
55:1 and **m** without money and without cost. 2692
60:16 You will drink the **m** *of* nations and 2692
Jer 11:5 a land flowing with **m** and honey'— 2692
32:22 a land flowing with **m** and honey. 2692
La 4:7 and whiter than **m,** 2692
Eze 20:6 a land flowing with **m** and honey, 2692
20:15 a land flowing with **m** and honey, 2692
25:4 they will eat your fruit and drink your **m.** 2692
Joel 3:18 and the hills will flow with **m;** 2692
1Co 3:2 I gave you **m,** not solid food, *1128*
9:7 a flock and does not drink of the **m?** *1128*
Heb 5:12 You need **m,** not solid food! *1128*
5:13 Anyone who lives on **m,** being still an infant *1128*
1Pe 2:2 Like newborn babies, crave pure spiritual **m** *1128*

MILL (3) [HANDMILL]

Ex 11:5 who is at her **hand m,** 8160
Joel 1:18 The herds **m about** because they have no 1003
Mt 24:41 women will be grinding with a **hand m;** *3685*

MILLET (1)

Eze 4:9 beans and lentils, **m** and spelt; 1893

MILLION (3)

1Ch 21:5 In all Israel there were *one* **m** one hundred thousand men who could handle 547+547
22:14 talents of gold, a **m** talents of silver, 547+547
Rev 9:16 mounted troops was **two hundred m.** *1490+3689*

MILLO See BETH MILLO

MILLSTONE (8) [STONE]

Jdg 9:53 a woman dropped an upper **m** on his head 7115
2Sa 11:21 Didn't a woman throw an upper **m** on him 7115
Job 41:24 His chest is hard as rock, hard as a lower **m.** 7115
Mt 18:6 better for him to have a **large m** hung *3685+3948*
Mk 9:42 to be thrown into the sea with a large **m** tied *3685*
Lk 17:2 to be thrown into the sea with a **m** tied *3345+3683*
Rev 18:21 a large **m** and threw it into the sea, and said: *3684*
18:22 *of* a **m** will never be heard in you again. *3685*

MILLSTONES (4) [STONE]

Dt 24:6 Do not take a **pair of m—** 8160
Isa 47:2 Take **m** and grind flour; take off your veil. 8160
Jer 25:10 the sound of **m** and the light of the lamp. 8160
La 5:13 Young men toil at the **m;** 3218

MINA (5) [MINAS]

Eze 45:12 Twenty shekels plus twenty-five shekels plus fifteen shekels equal one **m.** 4949
Lk 19:16 'Sir, your **m** has earned ten more.' *3641*
19:18 'Sir, your **m** has earned five more.' *3641*
19:20 'Sir, here is your **m;** *3641*
19:24 'Take his **m** away from him and give it to *3641*

MINAS (6) [MINA]

1Ki 10:17 with three **m** of gold in each shield. 4949
Ezr 2:69 5,000 **m** of silver and 100 priestly garments. 4949
Ne 7:71 drachmas of gold and 2,200 **m** of silver. 4949
7:72 2,000 **m** of silver and 67 garments for 4949
Lk 19:13 of his servants and gave them ten **m.** *3641*
19:24 and give it to the one who has ten **m.'** *3641*

MINCING (1)

Isa 3:16 **tripping along with m steps,** 2143+2256+3262

MIND (121) [DOUBLE-MINDED, LIKE-MINDED, MINDED, MINDFUL, MINDS]

Ge 37:11 his father **kept** the matter **in m.** 9068
41:8 In the morning his **m** was troubled, 8120
45:20 Never **m** about your belongings, 2571
Ex 16:29 **Bear in m** that the LORD has given you 8011
Nu 23:19 that *he should* **change** *his* **m.** 5714
Dt 28:28 blindness and confusion of **m.** 4222
28:65 the LORD will give you an anxious **m,** 4213
29:4 a **m** that understands or eyes that see or ears 4213
1Sa 2:35 according to what is in my heart and **m.** 5883
14:7 "Do all that you have in **m,"** 4222
15:29 of Israel does not lie or **change** *his* **m;** 5714
15:29 that *he should* **change** *his* **m."** 5714
2Sa 7:3 "Whatever you have in **m,** 4222
19:19 May the king put it out of his **m.** 4213
1Ki 10:2 with him about all that she had on her **m.** 4222
2Ki 10:30 to the house of Ahab all I had in **m** to do, 4222
24:1 But then *he* **changed** *his* **m** and rebelled 8740
1Ch 12:38 the rest of the Israelites were also of one **m** 4213
17:2 "Whatever you have in **m,** do it, 4222
28:9 and with a willing **m,** 5883
28:12 that the Spirit had put in his **m** for the courts NIH
2Ch 7:11 in **m** to do in the temple of the LORD and 4213
9:1 with him about all she had on her **m.** 4222
30:12 to give them unity of **m** to carry out what 4213
Ne 5:7 I pondered them in my **m** and then accused 4213
Job 10:13 and I know that this was **in** your **m:** 6640
12:3 But I have a **m** as well as you; 4222
38:36 or gave understanding to the **m?** 8498
Ps 26:2 and try me, examine my heart and my **m;** 4213
64:6 Surely the **m** and heart *of* man are cunning. 7931
83:5 *With one* **m** they plot together; 4213
110:4 LORD has sworn and *will* not **change** *his* **m:** 5714
Pr 23:33 and your **m** imagine confusing things. 4213
Ecc 2:3 my **m** still guiding me with wisdom. 4213
2:23 even at night his **m** does not rest. 4213
7:25 So I turned my **m** to understand, 4213
8:9 as I applied my **m** to everything done under 4213
8:16 When I applied my **m** to know wisdom and 4213
Isa 10:7 this is not what he **has in m;** 3108+4222
26:3 in perfect peace him whose **m** is steadfast, 3671
32:4 The **m** *of* the rash will know 4222
32:6 fool speaks folly, his **m** is busy with evil: 4213
40:13 Who has understood the **m** *of* the LORD, 8120
46:8 "Remember this, **fix** it **in m,** take it to heart, 899
65:17 nor will they come to **m.** 4213
Jer 7:31 nor did it enter my **m.** 4213
11:20 and test the heart and **m,** 4000
17:10 the heart and examine the **m,** 4000
19:5 nor did it enter my **m.** 4213
20:12 the righteous and probe the heart and **m,** 4000
32:35 nor did it enter my **m,** 4213
La 3:21 Yet this I **call to m** and 448+4213+8740
Eze 11:5 But I know what is going through your **m.** 8120
20:32 But what you have in **m** will never happen. 8120
21:24 you people *have* **brought to m** your guilt 2349
38:10 On that day thoughts will come into your **m** 4222
Da 2:1 his **m** was troubled and he could not sleep. 8120
2:28 and the visions that passed through your **m** 10646
2:29 O king, your **m** turned to things to come, 10669
2:30 that you may understand what went through your **m.** 10381+10669
4:5 that passed through my **m** terrified me. 10646
4:16 Let his **m** be changed from that of a man 10381
4:16 let him be given the **m** *of* an animal, 10381
5:12 keen **m** and knowledge and understanding, 10658
5:21 from people and given the **m** of an animal; 10381
7:1 through his **m** as he was lying on his bed. 10646
7:15 that passed through my **m** disturbed me. 10646
10:12 that you set your **m** to gain understanding 4213
Mt 1:19 *he* **had in m** to divorce her quietly. *1089*
16:23 *you do* not **have in m** the things of God, *5858*
21:29 but later *he* **changed** *his* **m** and went. *3564*
22:37 and with all your soul and with all your **m.'** *1379*
Mk 3:21 they said, *"He* **is out of** *his* **m."** *2014*
5:15 sitting there, dressed and **in** *his* **right m;** *5404*
8:33 *"You do* not **have in m** the things of God, *5858*
12:30 with all your **m** and with all your strength.' *1379*
Lk 8:35 dressed and **in** *his* **right m;** *5404*
10:27 with all your strength and with all your **m';** *1379*
21:14 But **make up** your **m** not to worry beforehand *1877+2840+3836+5502*
Jn 6:6 *already had* **in m** what he was going to do. *3857*
15:18 **keep in m** that it hated me first. *1182*
Ac 4:32 All the believers were one in heart and **m.** *6034*
12:15 *"You're* **out of** *your* **m,"** they told her. *3419*
26:24 *"You are* **out of** *your* **m,** Paul!" *3419*
Ro 1:28 he gave them over to a depraved **m,** *3808*
7:23 the law *of* my **m** and making me a prisoner *3808*
7:25 I myself *in* my **m** am a slave to God's law, *3808*
8:6 The **m** of sinful man is death, *5859*
8:6 **m** controlled by the Spirit is life and peace; *5859*
8:7 the sinful **m** is hostile to God. *5859*
8:27 knows the **m** of the Spirit, *5859*
11:34 "Who has known the **m** of the Lord? *3808*
12:2 be transformed by the renewing *of* your **m.** *3808*
14:5 be fully convinced in his own **m.** *3808*
14:13 **make up** *your* **m** not to put any stumbling *3212*
1Co 1:10 and that you may be perfectly united in **m** *3808*
2:9 no **m** has conceived what God has prepared *2840*
2:16 "For who has known the **m** of the Lord *3808*
2:16 But we have the **m** of Christ. *3808*
7:37 in his own **m,** who is under no compulsion *2840*
7:37 and who has made up his **m** not to marry *2840*
14:14 my spirit prays, but my **m** is unfruitful. *3808*
14:15 but I will also pray *with* my **m;** *3808*
14:15 but I will also sing *with* my **m.** *3808*
14:23 not say that *you are* **out of** *your* **m?** *3419*
2Co 2:1 So *I* **made up** my **m** that I would not make *3212*
2:13 I still had no peace *of* **m,** *4460*
5:13 If *we are* **out of** *our* **m,** it is for the sake of God; *2014*
5:13 if *we are* **in** *our* **right m,** it is for you. *5404*
11:23 (I am **out of** *my* **m** to talk like this.) *4196*
13:11 listen to my appeal, *be of* one **m,** *5858*
Eph 6:18 With this in **m,** be alert and always keep on *NIG*
Php 3:19 Their **m** is on earthly things. *5858*
Col 2:18 and his unspiritual **m** puffs him up *3808*
1Th 4:11 *to* **m** your own **business** and to work *4556*
2Th 1:11 With this in **m,** we constantly pray for you, *NIG*
1Ti 6:5 constant friction between men of corrupt **m,** *3808*
Heb 7:21 Lord has sworn and *will* not **change** his **m:** *3564*
12:17 He could bring about no **change of m,** *3567*
2Pe 3:15 **Bear in m** that our Lord's patience means salvation, *2451*
Rev 17:9 "This calls for a **m** with wisdom. *3808*

MINDED (1) [MIND]

1Pe 4:7 Therefore *be* **clear m** and self-controlled *5404*

MINDFUL (3) [MIND]

Ps 8:4 what is man that *you are* **m** *of* him, 2349
Lk 1:48 for *he has been* **m of** the humble state *2098*
Heb 2:6 "What is man that *you* **are m** of him, *3630*

MINDS (35) [MIND]

Ex 13:17 they might **change** *their* **m** and return 5714
14:5 and his officials changed their **m** about them 4222
Dt 11:18 these words of mine in your hearts and **m;** 5883
Job 17:4 You have closed their **m** to understanding; 4213
Ps 7:9 who searches **m** and hearts, 4000
73:7 the evil conceits of their **m** know no limits. 4222
Pr 12:8 but men with warped **m** are despised. 4213
Isa 44:18 their **m** closed so they cannot understand. 4213
Jer 3:16 It will never enter their **m** or be remembered 4213
14:14 idolatries and the delusions of their own **m.** 4213
23:16 They speak visions from their own **m,** 4213
23:26 the delusions of their own **m?** 4213
31:33 "I will put my law in their **m** and write it 7931
34:11 But afterward *they* **changed** *their* **m** 8740
Lk 24:38 and why do doubts rise in your **m?** *2840*
24:45 Then he opened their **m** so they could *3808*
Ac 14:2 and poisoned their **m** against the brothers. *6034*
15:24 troubling your **m** by what they said. *6034*
28:6 **changed** *their* **m** and said he was a god. *3554*
Ro 8:5 to the sinful nature *have their* **m set on** what *5858*
8:5 with the Spirit have their **m** set on what *NIG*
16:18 and flattery they deceive the **m** of naive *2840*
2Co 3:14 But their **m** were made dull, *3784*
4:4 of this age has blinded the **m** of unbelievers, *3784*
11:3 your **m** may somehow be led astray *3784*

Eph 4:23 to be made new in the attitude *of* your **m;** *3808*
Php 4: 7 will guard your hearts and your **m** *3784*
Col 1:21 *in* your **m** because of your evil behavior. *1379*
3: 2 **Set** *your* **m on** things above, not on *5858*
2Ti 3: 8 men of depraved **m,** who, *3808*
Tit 1:15 both their **m** and consciences are corrupted. *3808*
Heb 8:10 I will put my laws in their **m** and write them *1379*
10:16 and I will write them on their **m."** *1379*
1Pe 1:13 Therefore, prepare your **m** for action; *1379*
Rev 2:23 that I am he who searches hearts and **m,** *3752*

MINE (77) [I]

Ge 13: 8 or between your herdsmen and **m,** 3276
24: 8 you will be released from this oath of **m.** 3276
29:15 "Just because you are a relative of **m,** 3276
31:37 Put it here in front of your relatives and **m,** 3276
31:43 All you see is **m.** 3276+4200
31:43 about these daughters of **m,** 3276
37: 7 while your sheaves gathered around **m** 3276
48: 5 to you here will be reckoned as **m;** 3276+4200
48: 5 Ephraim and Manasseh will be **m,** 3276+4200
48: 5 just as Reuben and Simeon are **m.** NIH
Ex 10: 1 these miraculous signs of **m** among them 3276
19: 5 Although the whole earth is **m,** 3276+4200
22: 9 about which somebody says, 'This is **m,'** 2085
Lev 25:23 the land is **m** and you are but aliens 3276+4200
Nu 3:12 The Levites are **m,** 3276+4200
3:13 for all the firstborn are **m.** 3276+4200
3:13 They are to be **m.** 3276+4200
3:45 The Levites are to be **m.** 3276+4200
8:14 and the Levites will be **m.** 3276+4200
8:17 whether man or animal, is **m.** 3276+4200
Dt 11:18 Fix these words of **m** in your hearts 3276
32:35 It is **m** to avenge; I will repay. 3276+4200
1Sa 22:23 the man who is seeking your life is seeking **m** also. 3276
2Sa 14:30 "Look, Joab's field is next to **m,** 3276
1Ki 2:15 he said, "the kingdom was **m.** 3276+4200
3:22 The dead one is yours; the living one is **m."** 3276
3:23 Your son is dead and **m** is alive.' " 3276
8:59 And may these words of **m,** 3276
20: 3 'Your silver and gold are **m,** 3276+4200
20: 3 best of your wives and children are **m.** 3276+4200
Job 7:15 rather than this body of **m.** 3276
15: 6 Your own mouth condemns you, not **m;** 638
28: 1 "There is a **m** for silver and a place 4604
Ps 50:10 for every animal of the forest is **m,** 3276+4200
50:11 and the creatures of the field are **m.** 3276+6643
50:12 for the world is **m,** and all that is in it. 3276+4200
59: 3 against me for no offense or sin of **m,** 3276
60: 7 Gilead is **m,** and Manasseh is mine; 3276+4200
60: 7 Gilead is mine, and Manasseh is **m;** 3276+4200
108: 8 Gilead is **m,** Manasseh is mine; 3276+4200
108: 8 Gilead is mine, Manasseh is **m;** 3276+4200
Pr 8:14 Counsel and sound judgment are **m;** 3276+4200
Ecc 7:15 In this meaningless life of **m** I have seen 3276
SS 2:16 My lover is **m** and I am his; 3276+4200
6: 3 I am my lover's and my lover is **m;** 3276+4200
8:12 my own vineyard is **m** to give; 3276+4200+8611
Isa 30: 1 who carry out plans that are not **m,** 4946+5761
43: 1 by name; you are **m.** 3276+4200
Jer 44:28 in Egypt will know whose word will stand—**m** or theirs. 4946+5761
Eze 16: 8 and you became **m.** 3276+4200
23: 4 They were **m** and gave birth to sons 3276+4200
23: 5 in prostitution while she was still **m;** 3276+9393
29: 3 You say, "The Nile is **m;** 3276+4200
29: 9 " 'Because you said, "The Nile is **m;** 3276+4200
Mic 7: 1 What misery is **m!** 3276+4200
Hag 2: 8 'The silver is **m** and the gold is mine,' 3276+4200
2: 8 'The silver is mine and the gold is **m,'** 3276+4200
Mal 3:17 "They will be **m,"** 3276+4200
Mt 7:24 everyone who hears these words *of* **m** *1609*
7:26 But everyone who hears these words *of* **m** *1609*
20:21 of these two sons *of* **m** may sit at your right *1609*
25:40 for one of the least of these brothers *of* **m,** *1609*
Lk 11: 6 a friend *of* **m** on a journey has come to me, *1609*
15:24 this son *of* **m** was dead and is alive again; *1609*
19:27 *of* **m** who did not want me to be king *1609*
22:21 of him who is going to betray me is with **m** *1609*
Jn 3:29 That joy is **m,** and it is now complete. *1847*
12:30 "This voice was for your benefit, not **m.** *1609*
16:14 from what *is* **m** and making it known *1847*
16:15 All that belongs to the Father is **m.** *1847*
16:15 from what *is* **m** and make it known to you. *1847*
17:10 All I have is yours, and all you have is **m.** *1847*
Ac 20:34 hands of **m** have supplied my own needs *NIG*
Ro 12:19 "It is **m** to avenge; I will repay," *1609*
1Co 5:12 **What business is it of m** to judge *1609+5515*
2Co 11:10 of Achaia will stop this boasting of **m.** *1609+1650*
Heb 10:30 we know him who said, "It is **m** to avenge; *1609*

MINGLE (1) [MINGLED]

Ps 102: 9 For I eat ashes as my food and **m** my drink 5007

MINGLED (2) [MINGLE]

Ezr 9: 2 and *have* **m** the holy race with the peoples 6843
Ps 106:35 but *they* **m** with the nations 6843

MINIAMIN (2) [MINIAMIN'S]

2Ch 31:15 Eden, **M,** Jeshua, Shemaiah, 4975
Ne 12:41 Eliakim, Maaseiah, **M,** Micaiah, Elioenai, 4975

MINIAMIN'S (1) [MINIAMIN]

Ne 12:17 of **M** and of Moadiah's, Piltai; 4975

MINISH, MINISHED (KJV) See DECREASED, REDUCE

MINISTER (40) [MINISTERED, MINISTERING, MINISTERS, MINISTRY]

Ex 28:43 or approach the altar to **m** in the Holy Place, 9250
29:30 and comes to the Tent of Meeting to **m** in 9250
30:20 to **m** by presenting an offering made to 9250
Nu 16: 9 and to stand before the community and **m** 9250
18: 2 when you and your sons **m** before the Tent NIH
Dt 10: 8 the LORD to **m** and to pronounce blessings 9250
18: 5 and **m** in the LORD's name always. 9250
18: 7 *he may* **m** in the name of the LORD his God 9250
21: 5 the LORD your God has chosen them to **m** 9250
1Sa 2:30 and your father's house *would* **m** 2143
2:35 *he will* **m** before my anointed one always. 2143
1Ch 15: 2 the LORD and to **m** *before* him forever." 9250
16: 4 He appointed some of the Levites *to* **m** 9250
16:37 of the LORD to **m** there regularly, 9250
16:38 and his sixty-eight associates to **m** NIH
23:13 to **m** *before* him and to pronounce blessings 9250
2Ch 29:11 to **m** before him and to burn incense." 9250
31: 2 and fellowship offerings, to **m,** 9250
Ps 101: 6 he whose walk is blameless *will* **m** *to* me. 9250
134: 1 the LORD who **m** by night in the house of 6641
135: 2 you who **m** in the house of the LORD, 6641
Jer 33:22 the Levites *who* **m** *before* me as countless as 9250
Eze 40:46 near to the LORD to **m** *before* him." 9250
42:14 behind the garments in which *they* **m,** 9250
43:19 who come near to **m** *before* me, 9250
44:15 are to come near to **m** *before* me; 9250
44:16 they alone are to come near my table to **m** 9250
44:27 into the inner court of the sanctuary to **m** in 9250
45: 4 *who* **m** *in* the sanctuary and who draw near 9250
45: 4 and who draw near to **m** *before* the LORD. 9250
46:24 where *those who* **m** *at* the temple will cook 9250
Joel 1: 9 *those who* **m** *before* the LORD. 9250
1:13 wail, *you who* **m** *before* the altar. 9250
1:13 *you who* **m** *before* my God; 9250
2:17 Let the priests, *who* **m** *before* the LORD, 9250
Ro 15:16 be a **m** of Christ Jesus to the Gentiles with *3313*
Col 1: 7 who is a faithful **m** of Christ on our behalf, *1356*
4: 7 a faithful **m** and fellow servant in the Lord. *1356*
1Ti 4: 6 you will be a good **m** of Christ Jesus, *1356*
Heb 13:10 We have an altar from which those who **m** *3302*

MINISTERED (3) [MINISTER]

1Sa 2:11 but the boy **m** before the LORD under Eli 9250
3: 1 The boy Samuel **m** before the LORD 9250
1Ch 6:32 *They* **m** with music before the tabernacle, 9250

MINISTERING (23) [MINISTER]

Ex 35:19 the woven garments worn for **m** in 9250
39: 1 woven garments for **m** in the sanctuary. 9250
39:26 the hem of the robe to be worn for **m,** 9250
39:41 and the woven garments worn for **m** in 9250
Nu 3:31 the articles of the sanctuary used in **m,** 9250
4:12 are to take all the articles used for **m** 9250+9251
4:14 on it all the utensils used *for* **m** at the altar, 9250
Dt 17:12 or for the priest who stands **m** there *to* 9250
Jdg 20:28 the son of Aaron, **m** before it.) 6641
1Sa 2:18 But Samuel *was* **m** before the LORD— 9250
1Ch 9:13 responsible for **m** *in* the house of God. 6275
24: 3 for their appointed order of **m.** 6275
24:19 of **m** when they entered the temple of 6275
26:12 for **m** in the temple of the LORD, 9250
Ezr 2:63 a priest **m** with the Urim and Thummim. 6641
Ne 7:65 be a priest **m** with the Urim and Thummim. 6641
10:36 to the priests **m** there. 9250
10:39 and where the **m** priests, 9250
12:44 for Judah was pleased with the **m** priests 6641
Jer 33:21 the Levites who are priests **m** *before* me— 9250
Eze 44:17 not wear any woolen garment while **m** at 9250
44:19 to take off the clothes they *have been* **m** in 9250
Heb 1:14 Are not all angels **m** spirits sent *3312*

MINISTERS (9) [MINISTER]

Ex 28:35 Aaron must wear it when *he* **m.** 9250
2Ki 10:19 of Baal, all his **m** and all his priests. 6268
10:19 in order to destroy the **m** *of* Baal. 6268
10:21 and all the **m** *of* Baal came; 6268
10:22 "Bring robes for all the **m** *of* Baal." 6268
10:23 Jehu said to the **m** *of* Baal, 6268
10:23 only **m** *of* Baal." 6268
Isa 61: 6 you will be named **m** *of* our God. 9250
2Co 3: 6 He has made us competent as **m** of a new covenant— *1356*

MINISTRATION (KJV) See DISTRIBUTION, MINISTRY, SERVICE

MINISTRY (24) [MINISTER]

1Ch 25: 1 and Jeduthun for the **m** of prophesying, 6275
25: 6 for the **m** *at* the house of God. 6275
Lk 3:23 about thirty years old when he began his **m.** *NIG*
Ac 1:17 of our number and shared *in* this **m."** *1355*
1:25 to take over this apostolic **m,** *1355*
6: 2 to neglect the **m** of the word of God in order *NIG*
6: 4 to prayer and the **m** of the word." *1355*
8:21 You have no part or share in this **m,** *3364*
21:19 among the Gentiles through his **m.** *1355*
Ro 11:13 to the Gentiles, I make much of my **m** *1355*
2Co 3: 3 the result of our **m,** written not with ink *1354*
3: 7 Now if the **m** that brought death, *1355*
3: 8 the **m** of the Spirit be even more glorious? *1355*
3: 9 If the **m** that condemns men is glorious, *1355*
3: 9 how much more glorious is the **m** *1355*
4: 1 since through God's mercy we have this **m,** *1355*
5:18 to himself through Christ and gave us the **m** *1355*
6: 3 so that our **m** will not be discredited. *1355*
Gal 2: 8 in the **m of** Peter as **an apostle** to the Jews *692*
2: 8 at work in my **m** as an apostle to the Gentiles *NIG*
2Ti 4: 5 discharge all the duties of your **m.** *1355*
4:11 because he is helpful to me in my **m.** *1355*
Heb 8: 6 But the **m** Jesus has received is as superior *3311*
9: 6 into the outer room to carry on their **m.** *3301*

MINNI (1)

Jer 51:27 Ararat, **M** and Ashkenaz. 4973

MINNITH (2)

Jdg 11:33 from Aroer to the vicinity of **M,** 4976
Eze 27:17 they exchanged wheat from **M** 4976

MINSTREL (KJV) See HARPIST

MINT (2)

Mt 23:23 You give a tenth of your **spices—m,** *2455*
Lk 11:42 because you give God a tenth of your **m,** *2455*

MINUS (1)

2Co 11:24 from the Jews the forty lashes **m** one. *4123*

MIPHKAD (KJV) See INSPECTION GATE

MIRACLE (5) [MIRACLES, MIRACULOUS, MIRACULOUSLY]

Ex 7: 9 'Perform a **m,'** then say to Aaron, 4603
Mk 9:39 "No one who does a **m** in my name can in *1539*
Lk 23: 8 he hoped to see him perform some **m.** *4956*
Jn 7:21 Jesus said to them, "I did one **m,** *2240*
Ac 4:16 knows they have done an outstanding **m,** *4956*

MIRACLES (37) [MIRACLE]

1Ch 16:12 Remember the wonders he has done, his **m,** 4603
Ne 9:17 the **m** you performed among them. 7098
Job 5: 9 **m** that cannot be counted. 7098
9:10 **m** that cannot be counted. 7098
Ps 77:11 yes, I will remember your **m** of long ago. 7099
77:14 You are the God who performs **m;** 7099
78:12 He did **m** in the sight of their fathers in 7099
105: 5 Remember the wonders he has done, his **m,** 4603
106: 7 they gave no thought to your **m;** 7098
106:22 **m** in the land of Ham and awesome deeds 7098
Mt 7:22 and perform many **m?'** *1539*
11:20 *of* his **m** had been performed, *1539*
11:21 If the **m** that were performed *1539*
11:23 If the **m** that were performed *1539*
13:58 not do many **m** there because of their lack *1539*
24:24 and perform great signs and **m** to deceive *5469*
Mk 6: 2 that he even does **m!** *1539*
6: 5 He could not do any **m** there, *1539*
13:22 and perform signs and **m** to deceive *5469*
Lk 10:13 For if the **m** that were performed *1539*
19:37 in loud voices for all the **m** they had seen: *1539*
Jn 7: 3 so that your disciples may see the **m** you do. *2240*
10:25 **m** I do in my Father's name speak for me, *2240*
10:32 "I have shown you many great **m** from *2240*
10:38 believe the **m,** that you may know *2240*
14:11 on the evidence of the **m** themselves. *2240*
15:24 But now they have seen these **m,** *2240*
Ac 2:22 a man accredited by God to you *by* **m,** *1539*
8:13 astonished by the great signs and **m** he saw. *1539*
19:11 God did extraordinary **m** through Paul, *1539*
Ro 15:19 by the power *of* signs and **m,** *5469*
1Co 12:28 third teachers, then **workers of m,** *1539*
12:29 Do all **work m?** *1539*
2Co 12:12 that mark an apostle—signs, wonders and **m** *1539*
Gal 3: 5 Does God give you his Spirit and work **m** *1539*
2Th 2: 9 displayed in all kinds of counterfeit **m,** *1539*
Heb 2: 4 by signs, wonders and various **m,** *1539*

MIRACULOUS (61) [MIRACLE]

Ex 4: 8 or pay attention to the first **m sign,** 253
4:17 in your hand so you can perform **m signs** 253
4:28 the **m signs** he had commanded him 253
7: 3 though I multiply my **m signs** and wonders 253
8:23 This **m sign** will occur tomorrow.' " 253
10: 1 so that I may perform these **m signs** *of* mine 253
Nu 14:11 the **m signs** I have performed among them? 253
14:22 and the **m signs** I performed in Egypt and in 253
Dt 4:34 by testings, by **m signs** and wonders, by war, 253
6:22 Before our eyes the LORD sent **m signs** 253
7:19 the **m signs** and wonders, 253
13: 1 among you and announces to you a **m sign** 253
26: 8 with great terror and with **m signs** 253
29: 3 those **m signs** and great wonders. 253
34:11 who did all those **m signs** and wonders 253
2Ch 32:24 who answered him and gave him a **m sign.** 4603

2Ch 32:31 the **m sign** that had occurred in the land, 4603
Ne 9:10 You sent **m signs** and wonders 253
Ps 74: 9 We are given no **m signs;** 253
78:43 the day he displayed his **m signs** in Egypt, 253
105:27 They performed his **m signs** among them, 253
Jer 32:20 You performed **m signs** and wonders 253
Da 4: 2 to tell you about the **m signs** and wonders 10084
Mt 12:38 we want to see a **m sign** from you." *4956*
12:39 and adulterous generation asks for a **m sign!** *4956*
13:54 get this wisdom and these **m powers?"** *1539*
14: 2 That is why **m powers** are at work in him." *1539*
16: 4 adulterous generation looks for a **m sign,** *4956*
Mk 6:14 that is why **m powers** are at work in him." *1539*
8:12 Why does this generation ask for a **m sign?** *4956*
Lk 11:29 It asks for a **m sign,** but none will be given *4956*
Jn 2:11 This, the first *of* his **m signs,** *4956*
2:18 "What **m sign** can you show us *4956*
2:23 many people saw the **m signs** he was doing *4956*
3: 2 the **m signs** you are doing if God were not *4956*
4:48 "Unless you people see **m signs** *4956*
4:54 the second **m sign** that Jesus performed, *4956*
6: 2 the **m signs** he had performed on the sick. *4956*
6:14 the people saw the **m sign** that Jesus did, *4956*
6:26 not because you saw **m signs** but *4956*
6:30 "What **m sign** then will you give *4956*
7:31 will he do more **m signs** than this man?" *4956*
9:16 "How can a sinner do such **m signs?"** *4956*
10:41 "Though John never performed a **m sign,** *4956*
11:47 Here is this man performing many **m signs.** *4956*
12:18 that he had given this **m sign,** *4956*
12:37 Even after Jesus had done all these **m signs** *4956*
20:30 Jesus did many other **m signs** in the *4956*
Ac 2:43 and many wonders and **m signs** were done *4956*
4:30 and perform **m signs** and wonders through *4956*
5:12 The apostles performed many **m signs** *4956*
6: 8 did great wonders and **m signs** among *4956*
7:36 did wonders and **m signs** in Egypt, *4956*
8: 6 and saw the **m signs** he did, *4956*
14: 3 of his grace by enabling them to do **m signs** *4956*
15:12 the **m signs** and wonders God had done *4956*
1Co 1:22 Jews demand **m signs** and Greeks look *4956*
12:10 to another **m powers,** *1539+1920*
Rev 13:13 And he performed great and **m signs,** *4956*
16:14 of demons performing **m signs,** *4956*
19:20 the **m signs** on his behalf. *4956*

MIRACULOUSLY (1) [MIRACLE]
Ac 4:22 For the man who was **m** healed was *4956*

MIRE (4) [MIRY]
Ps 40: 2 out of the mud and **m;** 3431
69:14 Rescue me from the **m,** do not let me sink; 3226
Isa 57:20 whose waves cast up **m** and mud. 8347
Mic 7:10 be trampled underfoot like **m** *in* the streets. 3226

MIRIAM (13)
Ex 15:20 Then **M** the prophetess, Aaron's sister, 5319
15:21 **M** sang to them: "Sing to the LORD, 5319
Nu 12: 1 **M** and Aaron began to talk against Moses 5319
12: 4 the LORD said to Moses, Aaron and **M,** 5319
12: 5 to the Tent and summoned Aaron and **M.** 5319
12:10 there stood **M**—leprous, like snow. 5319
12:15 So **M** was confined outside the camp 5319
20: 1 There **M** died and was buried. 5319
26:59 Moses and their sister **M.** 5319
Dt 24: 9 to **M** along the way after you came out 5319
1Ch 4:17 One of Mered's wives gave birth to **M,** 5319
6: 3 of Amram: Aaron, Moses and **M.** 5319
Mic 6: 4 sent Moses to lead you, also Aaron and **M.** 5319

MIRMAH (1)
1Ch 8:10 Jeuz, Sakia and **M.** These were his sons, 5328

MIRROR (3) [MIRRORS]
Job 37:18 hard as a **m** *of* cast bronze? 8023
1Co 13:12 we see but a poor **reflection** as in a **m;** *2269*
Jas 1:23 like a man who looks at his face in a **m** *2269*

MIRRORS (2) [MIRROR]
Ex 38: 8 from the **m** *of* the women who served at 5262
Isa 3:23 and **m,** and the linen garments and tiaras 1663

MIRTH (1)
Job 20: 5 that the **m** *of* the wicked is brief, 8265

MIRY (2) [MIRE]
Ps 69: 2 I sink in the **m** depths, 3431
140:10 into **m pits,** never to rise. 4549

MISCARRIED (1) [MISCARRY]
Ge 31:38 Your sheep and goats *have* not **m,** 8897

MISCARRY (3) [MISCARRIED]
Ex 23:26 and none will **m** or be barren in your land. 8897
Job 21:10 their cows calve and *do* not **m.** 8897
Hos 9:14 Give them wombs *that* **m** and breasts 8897

MISCHIEF, MISCHIEFS (KJV) See ASSAULT, CALAMITY, EVIL, HARM, MALICE, MISERY, PUNISHMENT, RUIN, SCHEMES, SERIOUS INJURY, TROUBLE

MISDEEDS (2)
Ps 99: 8 though you punished their **m.** 6613
Ro 8:13 but if by the Spirit you put to death the **m** of *4552*

MISDEMEANOR (1)
Ac 18:14 a complaint about some **m** or serious crime, *93*

MISERABLE (5) [MISERY]
Nu 21: 5 And we detest this **m** food!" 7848
Jdg 11:35 You *have* **made** me **m** and wretched, 4156+4156
Job 16: 2 **m** comforters are you all! 6662
Ecc 4: 8 This too is meaningless—a **m** business! 8273
Gal 4: 9 to those weak and **m** principles? *4777*

MISERY (24) [MISERABLE]
Ge 16:11 for the LORD has heard of your **m.** 6715
29:32 "It is because the LORD has seen my **m.** 6715
44:29 bring my gray head down to the grave in **m.** 8288
44:34 Do not let me see the **m** that would come 8273
Ex 3: 7 "I have indeed seen the **m** *of* my people 6715
3:17 to bring you up out of your **m** *in* Egypt into 6715
4:31 about them and had seen their **m,** 6715
Nu 23:21 no **m** observed in Israel. 6662
Dt 26: 7 the LORD heard our voice and saw our **m,** 6715
Jdg 10:16 And he could bear Israel's **m** no longer. 6662
1Sa 1:11 if you will only look upon your servant's **m** 6715
Job 3:20 "Why is light given to *those in* **m,** 6664
6: 2 and all my **m** be placed on the scales! 2095
7: 3 and nights of **m** have been assigned to me. 6662
9:18 but would overwhelm me with **m.** 4936
20:22 the full force of **m** will come upon him. 6664
Ps 44:24 and forget our **m** and oppression? 6715
94:20 one that brings on **m** by its decrees? 6662
Pr 31: 7 and remember their **m** no more. 6662
Ecc 8: 6 though a man's **m** weighs heavily upon him. 8288
Hos 5:15 in their **m** they will earnestly seek me." 7639
Mic 7: 1 **What m** is mine! 518
Ro 3:16 ruin and **m** mark their ways, *5416*
Jas 5: 1 because of the **m** that is coming upon you. *5416*

MISFORTUNE (10)
Nu 23:21 "No **m** is seen in Jacob, 224
Ru 1:21 the Almighty *has* **brought m** upon me." 8317
1Ch 7:23 because there had been **m** in his family. 8288
Job 12: 5 Men at ease have contempt for **m** as the fate 7085
31:29 "If I have rejoiced at my enemy's **m** or 7085
Pr 13:21 **M** pursues the sinner, 8288
Ecc 2:21 This too is meaningless and a great **m.** 8288
5:14 or wealth lost through *some* **m,** 6721+8273
Isa 65:23 in vain or bear children doomed to **m;** 988
Ob 1:12 down on your brother in the day of his **m,** 5798

MISHAEL (8)
Ex 6:22 The sons of Uzziel were **M,** 4792
Lev 10: 4 Moses summoned **M** and Elzaphan, 4792
Ne 8: 4 and on his left were Pedaiah, **M,** Malkijah, 4792
Da 1: 6 Daniel, Hananiah, **M** and Azariah. 4792
1: 7 to **M,** Meshach; and to Azariah, Abednego. 4792
1:11 Hananiah, **M** and Azariah, 4792
1:19 Hananiah, **M** and Azariah; 4792
2:17 to his friends Hananiah, **M** and Azariah. 10414

MISHAL (2)
Jos 19:26 Allammelech, Amad and **M.** 5398
21:30 from the tribe of Asher, **M,** Abdon, 5398

MISHAM (1)
1Ch 8:12 The sons of Elpaal: Eber, **M,** 5471

MISHEAL (KJV) See MISHAL

MISHMA (4)
Ge 25:14 **M,** Dumah, Massa, 5462
1Ch 1:30 **M,** Dumah, Massa, Hadad, Tema, 5462
4:25 Mibsam his son and **M** his son. 5462
4:26 The descendants of **M:** 5462

MISHMANNAH (1)
1Ch 12:10 **M** the fourth, Jeremiah the fifth, 5459

MISHPAT See EN MISHPAT

MISHRAITES (1)
1Ch 2:53 the Ithrites, Puthites, Shumathites and **M.** 5490

MISLEAD (5) [MISLEADING, MISLEADS, MISLED]
2Ki 4:16 "Don't **m** your servant, O man of God!" 3941
2Ch 32:15 not let Hezekiah deceive you and **m** you 6077
Isa 9:16 Those who guide this people **m** them, 9494
36:18 "*Do* not **let** Hezekiah **m** you when he says, 6077
47:10 and knowledge **m** you when you say 8740

MISLEADING (4) [MISLEAD]
2Ki 18:32 for *he is* **m** you when he says, 6077
2Ch 32:11 *he is* **m** you, to let you die of hunger and 6077
La 2:14 The oracles they gave you were false and **m.** 4505
Da 2: 9 You have conspired to tell me **m** and 10343

MISLEADS (2) [MISLEAD]
Isa 44:20 He feeds on ashes, a deluded heart **m** him; 5742
Rev 2:20 By her teaching *she* **m** my servants *4414*

MISLED (2) [MISLEAD]
Jer 38:22 " *'They* **m** you and overcame you— 6077
1Co 15:33 *Do* not **be m:** "Bad company corrupts *4414*

MISPAR (1)
Ezr 2: 2 Bilshan, **M,** Bigvai, Rehum and Baanah): 5032

MISPERETH (1)
Ne 7: 7 Nahamani, Mordecai, Bilshan, **M,** Bigvai, 5033

MISREPHOTH MAIM (2)
Jos 11: 8 the way to Greater Sidon, to **M,** and 5387
13: 6 from Lebanon to **M,** 5387

MISS (2) [MISSED, MISSES, MISSING]
Jdg 20:16 could sling a stone at a hair and not **m.** 2627
Pr 19: 2 nor to be hasty and **m the way.** 2627

MISSED (3) [MISS]
1Sa 20:18 *You will* **be m,** because your seat will be 7212
Jer 3:16 *it will* not *be* **m,** nor will another one be 7212
46:17 *he has* **m** his opportunity.' 6296

MISSES (2) [MISS]
1Sa 20: 6 If your father **m** me **at all,** tell him, 7212+7212
Heb 12:15 See to it that no one **m** the grace of God and *5728*

MISSING (13) [MISS]
Nu 31:49 and not one *is* **m.** 7212
Jdg 21: 3 Why *should* one tribe *be* **m** 7212
1Sa 25: 7 at Carmel nothing of theirs *was* **m.** 7212
25:15 in the fields near them nothing *was* **m.** 7212
25:21 in the desert so that nothing of his *was* **m.** 7212
30:19 Nothing *was* **m:** young or old, 6372
2Sa 2:30 nineteen of David's men **were found m.** 7212
1Ki 20:39 If *he is* **m,** it will be your life for his 7212+7212
2Ki 10:19 See that no one *is* **m,** 7212
Job 5:24 of your property and **find** nothing **m.** 2627
Isa 34:16 None of these *will be* **m,** 6372
40:26 not one of them *is* **m.** 6372
Jer 23: 4 nor *will any* **be m,"** declares the LORD. 7212

MISSION (6) [MISSIONS]
Jos 22: 3 the **m** the LORD your God gave you. 5466
1Sa 15:18 And he sent you on a **m,** saying, 2006
15:20 "I went on the **m** the LORD assigned me. 2006
21: 2 'No one is to know anything about your **m** 889+1821+8938
Isa 48:15 and he will succeed in his **m.** 2006
Ac 12:25 Barnabas and Saul had finished their **m,** *1355*

MISSIONS (1) [MISSION]
1Sa 21: 5 The men's things are holy even on **m** 2006

MIST (5) [MISTS]
Isa 44:22 your sins like the **morning m.** 6727
Hos 6: 4 Your love is like the morning **m,** 6727
13: 3 Therefore they will be like the morning **m,** 6727
Ac 13:11 Immediately **m** and darkness came *944*
Jas 4:14 You are a **m** that appears for a little while *874*

MISTAKE (5) [MISTAKEN]
Ge 43:12 Perhaps it was a **m.** 5405
Lev 22:14 " 'If anyone eats a sacred offering by **m,** 8705
Jdg 9:36 **m** the shadows of the mountains **for** 3869+8011
Ecc 5: 6 "My vow was a **m."** 8705
Jer 42:20 that *you* **made a fatal m** when 928+5883+9494

MISTAKEN (1) [MISTAKE]
Mk 12:27 *You are* badly **m!"** *4414*

MISTREAT (9) [MISTREATED, MISTREATING]
Ge 31:50 If *you* **m** my daughters or if you take any 6700
Ex 22:21 "*Do* not **m** an alien or oppress him, 3561
Lev 19:33 lives with you in your land, *do* not **m** him. 3561
1Sa 25: 7 *we did* not **m** them, 4007
25:15 They *did* not **m** *us,* 4007
Jer 38:19 over to them and *they will* **m** me." 6618
Eze 22:29 and **m** the alien, denying the justice. 6943
Lk 6:28 pray for those who **m** you. *2092*
Ac 14: 5 *to* **m** them and stone them. *5614*

MISTREATED (12) [MISTREAT]
Ge 15:13 be enslaved and **m** four hundred years. 6700
16: 6 Then Sarai **m** Hagar; so she fled from her. 6700

Nu 20:15 The Egyptians **m** us and our fathers, 8317
Dt 26: 6 But the Egyptians **m** us and made us suffer, 8317
Jer 13:22 torn off and your body **m.** 2803
Eze 22: 7 in you they have oppressed the alien and **m** 3561
Mt 22: 6 **m** them and killed them. *5614*
Ac 7: 6 be enslaved and **m** four hundred years. *2808*
7:24 of them *being* **m** by an Egyptian, *92*
Heb 11:25 He chose *to be* **m along with** the people *5156*
11:37 destitute, persecuted and **m**— *2807*
13: 3 and those who *are* **m** as if you yourselves *2807*

MISTREATING (1) [MISTREAT]

Ac 7:27 "But the man who *was* **m** the other *92*

MISTRESS (8)

Ge 16: 4 she began to despise her **m.** 1485
16: 8 "I'm running away from my **m** Sarai," 1485
16: 9 "Go back to your **m** and submit to her." 1485
2Ki 5: 3 She said to her **m,** "If only my master 1485
Ps 123: 2 eyes of a maid look to the hand of her **m,** 1485
Pr 30:23 and a maidservant who displaces her **m.** 1485
Isa 24: 2 for master as for servant, for **m** as for maid, 1485
Na 3: 4 alluring, the **m** *of* sorceries, 1266

MISTS (1) [MIST]

2Pe 2:17 without water and **m** driven by a storm. *3920*

MISUNDERSTAND (1)

Dt 32:27 lest the adversary **m** and say, 5795

MISUSE (3) [MISUSES]

Ex 20: 7 "You shall not **m** the name of the LORD your God, 2021+4200+5951+8736
Dt 5:11 "You shall not **m** the name of the LORD your God, 2021+4200+5951+8736
Ps 139:20 adversaries **m** your name. 2021+4200+5951+8736

MISUSES (2) [MISUSE]

Ex 20: 7 the LORD will not hold anyone guiltless who **m** his name. 2021+4200+5951+8736
Dt 5:11 the LORD will not hold anyone guiltless *who* **m** his name. 2021+4200+5951+8736

MITE, MITES (KJV) See PENNY, SMALL COPPER COINS

MITHCAH (2)

Nu 33:28 They left Terah and camped at **M.** 5520
33:29 They left **M** and camped at Hashmonah. 5520

MITHNITE (1)

1Ch 11:43 Hanan son of Maacah, Joshaphat the **M,** 5512

MITHREDATH (2)

Ezr 1: 8 of Persia had them brought by **M** 5521
4: 7 of Persia, Bishlam, **M,** Tabeel and the rest 5521

MITRE (KJV) See TURBAN

MITYLENE (1)

Ac 20:14 we took him aboard and went on to **M.** *3639*

MIX (1) [MIXED, MIXES, MIXING, MIXTURE, WELL-MIXED]

Rev 18: 6 **M** her a double portion from her own cup. *3042*

MIXED (53) [MIX]

Ex 29: 2 make bread, and cakes **m** with oil, 1176
29:40 of an ephah of fine flour **m** with a quarter of 1176
Lev 2: 4 cakes made without yeast and **m** with oil, 1176
2: 5 it is to be made of fine flour **m** with oil, 1176
7:10 whether **m** with oil or dry, 1176
7:12 of bread made without yeast and **m** with oil, 1176
7:12 and cakes of fine flour well-kneaded and **m** 1176
9: 4 together with a grain offering **m** with oil. 1176
14:10 with three-tenths of an ephah of fine flour **m** 1176
14:21 of fine flour **m** with oil for a grain offering, 1176
23:13 of two-tenths of an ephah of fine flour **m** 1176
Nu 6:15 cakes made of fine flour **m** with oil, 1176
7:13 each filled with fine flour **m** with oil as 1176
7:19 each filled with fine flour **m** with oil as 1176
7:25 each filled with fine flour **m** with oil as 1176
7:31 each filled with fine flour **m** with oil as 1176
7:37 each filled with fine flour **m** with oil as 1176
7:43 each filled with fine flour **m** with oil as 1176
7:49 each filled with fine flour **m** with oil as 1176
7:55 each filled with fine flour **m** with oil as 1176
7:61 each filled with fine flour **m** with oil as 1176
7:67 each filled with fine flour **m** with oil as 1176
7:73 each filled with fine flour **m** with oil as 1176
7:79 each filled with fine flour **m** with oil as 1176
8: 8 with its grain offering of fine flour **m** 1176
15: 4 of an ephah of fine flour **m** with a quarter of 1176
15: 6 of an ephah of fine flour **m** with a third of 1176
15: 9 of an ephah of fine flour **m** with half a hin 1176
28: 5 of an ephah of fine flour **m** with a quarter of 1176
28: 9 of two-tenths of an ephah of fine flour **m** 1176
Nu 28:12 of three-tenths of an ephah of fine flour **m** 1176
28:12 of two-tenths of an ephah of fine flour **m** 1176
28:13 a tenth of an ephah of fine flour **m** with oil. 1176
28:20 of three-tenths of an ephah of fine flour **m** 1176
28:28 of three-tenths of an ephah of fine flour **m** 1176
29: 3 of three-tenths of an ephah of fine flour **m** 1176
29: 9 of three-tenths of an ephah of fine flour **m** 1176
29:14 of three-tenths of an ephah of fine flour **m** 1176
Ps 75: 8 a cup full of foaming wine **m with spices;** 5008
Pr 9: 2 She has prepared her meat and **m** her wine; 5007
9: 5 eat my food and drink the wine *I have* **m.** 5007
23:30 who go to sample **bowls of m wine.** 4932
Isa 65:11 a table for Fortune and fill **bowls of m wine** 4932
Da 2:41 even as you saw iron **m** with clay. 10569
2:43 just as you saw the iron **m** with baked clay, 10569
Mt 13:33 a woman took and **m** into a large amount *1606*
27:34 offered Jesus wine to drink, **m** with gall; *3502*
Mk 15:23 Then they offered him wine **m with myrrh,** *5046*
Lk 13: 1 the Galileans whose blood Pilate *had* **m** *3502*
13:21 It is like yeast that a woman took and **m** into *1606*
Jude 1:23 to others show mercy, **m** with fear— *NIG*
Rev 8: 7 and there came hail and fire **m** with blood, *3502*
15: 2 And I saw what looked like a sea of glass **m** *3502*

MIXES (2) [MIX]

Da 2:43 any more than iron **m** with clay. 10569
Hos 7: 8 "Ephraim **m** with the nations; 1176

MIXING (4) [MIX]

1Ch 9:30 the priests **took care of m** the spices. 5351+8379
23:29 the baking and the **m,** 8057
Isa 5:22 and champions at **m** drinks, 5007
Eze 24:10 Cook the meat well, **m in** the spices; 8379

MIXTURE (2) [MIX]

Da 2:43 will be a **m** and will not remain united, 10569
Jn 19:39 Nicodemus brought a **m** of myrrh and aloes, *3623*

MIZAR (1)

Ps 42: 6 the heights of Hermon—from Mount **M.** 5204

MIZPAH (43) [RAMATH MIZPAH]

Ge 31:49 It was also called **M,** because he said, 5207
Jos 11: 3 below Hermon in the region of **M.** 5207
11: 8 and to the Valley of **M** on the east, 5207
15:38 Dilean, **M,** Joktheel, 5206
18:26 **M,** Kephirah, Mozah, 5206
Jdg 10:17 the Israelites assembled and camped at **M.** 5207
11:11 all his words before the LORD in **M.** 5207
11:29 passed through **M** *of* Gilead, 5206
11:34 When Jephthah returned to his home in **M,** 5207
20: 1 and assembled before the LORD in **M.** 5207
20: 3 that the Israelites had gone up to **M.**) 5207
21: 1 The men of Israel had taken an oath at **M:** 5207
21: 5 before the LORD at **M** should certainly 5207
21: 8 to assemble before the LORD at **M?"** 5207
1Sa 7: 5 at **M** and I will intercede with the LORD 5207
7: 6 When they had assembled at **M,** 5207
7: 6 And Samuel was leader of Israel at **M.** 5207
7: 7 that Israel had assembled at **M,** 5207
7:11 of Israel rushed out of **M** and pursued 5207
7:12 a stone and set it up between **M** and Shen. 5207
7:16 on a circuit from Bethel to Gilgal to **M,** 5207
10:17 the people of Israel to the LORD at **M** 5207
22: 3 From there David went to **M** *in* Moab 5206
1Ki 15:22 up Geba in Benjamin, and also **M.** 5207
2Ki 25:23 they came to Gedaliah at **M**— 5207
25:25 the Babylonians who were with him at **M.** 5207
2Ch 16: 6 With them he built up Geba and **M.** 5207
Ne 3: 7 by men from Gibeon and **M**— 5207
3:15 ruler of the district of **M.** 5207
3:19 Next to him, Ezer son of Jeshua, ruler of **M,** 5207
Jer 40: 6 to Gedaliah son of Ahikam at **M** and stayed 5207
40: 8 they came to Gedaliah at **M**— 5207
40:10 I myself will stay at **M** to represent you 5207
40:12 to Gedaliah at **M,** 5207
40:13 in the open country came to Gedaliah at **M** 5207
40:15 of Kareah said privately to Gedaliah in **M,** 5207
41: 1 to Gedaliah son of Ahikam at **M.** 5207
41: 3 the Jews who were with Gedaliah at **M,** 5207
41: 6 Ishmael son of Nethaniah went out from **M** 5207
41:10 all the rest of the people who were in **M**— 5207
41:14 at **M** turned and went over to Johanan son 5207
41:16 from **M** whom he had recovered 5207
Hos 5: 1 You have been a snare at **M,** 5207

MIZPAR (KJV) See MISPAR

MIZPEH (KJV) See MIZPAH

MIZRAIM (4) [ABEL MIZRAIM]

Ge 10: 6 Cush, **M,** Put and Canaan. 5213
10:13 **M** was the father of the Ludites, Anamites, 5213
1Ch 1: 8 sons of Ham: Cush, **M,** Put and Canaan. 5213
1:11 **M** was the father of the Ludites, Anamites, 5213

MIZZAH (3)

Ge 36:13 Nahath, Zerah, Shammah and **M.** 4645
36:17 Chiefs Nahath, Zerah, Shammah and **M.** 4645
1Ch 1:37 Nahath, Zerah, Shammah and **M.** 4645

MNASON (1)

Ac 21:16 and brought us to the home of **M,** *3643*

MOAB (152) [MOAB'S, MOABITE, MOABITES, MOABITESS]

Ge 19:37 and she named him **M;** 4565
36:35 who defeated Midian in the country of **M,** 4565
Ex 15:15 leaders of **M** will be seized with trembling, 4566
Nu 21:11 the desert that faces **M** toward the sunrise. 4566
21:13 The Arnon is the border of **M,** 4566
21:13 between **M** and the Amorites. 4566
21:15 the site of Ar and lie along the border of **M.** 4566
21:20 and from Bamoth to the valley in **M** 4566+8441
21:26 against the former king of **M** and had taken 4566
21:28 It consumed Ar of **M,** 4566
21:29 Woe to you, O **M!** 4566
22: 1 of **M** and camped along the Jordan across 4566
22: 3 and **M** was terrified because there were 4566
22: 3 **M** was filled with dread because of 4566
22: 4 who was king of **M** at that time, 4566
22: 7 The elders of **M** and Midian left, 4566
22:10 "Balak son of Zippor, king of **M,** 4566
22:21 and went with the princes of **M.** 4566
23: 6 with all the princes of **M.** 4566
23: 7 the king of **M** from the eastern mountains. 4566
23:17 with the princes of **M.** 4566
24:17 He will crush the foreheads of **M,** 4566
26: 3 So on the plains of **M** by the Jordan across 4566
26:63 of **M** by the Jordan across from Jericho. 4566
31:12 at their camp on the plains of **M,** 4566
33:44 Iye Abarim on the border of **M.** 4566
33:48 of Abarim and camped on the plains of **M** 4566
33:49 There on the plains of **M** they camped 4566
33:50 On the plains of **M** by the Jordan across 4566
35: 1 On the plains of **M** by the Jordan across 4566
36:13 of **M** by the Jordan across from Jericho. 4566
Dt 1: 5 East of the Jordan in the territory of **M,** 4566
2: 8 and traveled along the desert road of **M.** 4566
2:18 "Today you are to pass by the region of **M** 4566
29: 1 to make with the Israelites in **M,** 824+4566
32:49 the Abarim Range to Mount Nebo in **M,** 824+4566
34: 1 from the plains of **M** to the top of Pisgah, 4566
34: 5 the servant of the LORD died there in **M,** 824+4566
34: 6 He buried him in **M,** 824+4566
34: 8 for Moses in the plains of **M** thirty days, 4566
Jos 13:32 in the plains of **M** across the Jordan east 4566
24: 9 When Balak son of Zippor, the king of **M,** 4566
Jdg 3:12 the LORD gave Eglon king of **M** power 4566
3:14 to Eglon king of **M** for eighteen years. 4566
3:15 with tribute to Eglon king of **M.** 4566
3:17 the tribute to Eglon king of **M,** 4566
3:28 "for the LORD has given **M,** your enemy, 4566
3:28 of the fords of the Jordan that led to **M,** 4566
3:30 That day **M** was made subject to Israel, 4566
10: 6 the gods of Sidon, the gods of **M,** 4566
11:15 the land of **M** or the land of the Ammonites. 4566
11:17 They sent also to the king of **M,** 4566
11:18 skirted the lands of Edom and **M,** 4566
11:18 along the eastern side of the country of **M,** 4566
11:18 They did not enter the territory of **M,** 4566
11:25 Balak son of Zippor, king of **M?** 4566
Ru 1: 1 went to live for a while in the country of **M.** 4566
1: 2 And they went to **M** and lived there. 4566+8441
1: 6 **M** that the LORD had come to the aid 4566+8441
1:22 So Naomi returned from **M** 4566+8441
2: 6 the Moabitess who came back from **M** 4566+8441
4: 3 "Naomi, who has come back from **M,** 4566+8441
1Sa 12: 9 of the Philistines and the king of **M,** 4566
14:47 **M,** the Ammonites, Edom, 4566
22: 3 From there David went to Mizpah in **M** 4566
22: 3 in Moab and said to the king of **M,** 4566
22: 4 So he left them with the king of **M,** 4566
2Sa 8:12 and **M,** the Ammonites and the Philistines, 4566
1Ki 11: 7 for Chemosh the detestable god of **M,** 4566
2Ki 1: 1 Ahab's death, **M** rebelled against Israel. 4566
3: 4 Now Mesha king of **M** raised sheep, 4566
3: 5 of **M** rebelled against the king of Israel. 4566
3: 7 "The king of **M** has rebelled against me. 4566
3: 7 Will you go with me to fight against **M?"** 4566
3:10 to hand us over to **M?"** 4566
3:13 to hand us over to **M."** 4566
3:18 he will also hand **M** over to you. 4566
3:23 Now to the plunder, **M!"** 4566
3:26 the king of **M** saw that the battle had gone 4566
23:13 for Chemosh the vile god of **M,** 4566
1Ch 1:46 who defeated Midian in the country of **M,** 4566
4:22 who ruled in **M** and Jashubi Lehem. 4566
8: 8 Sons were born to Shaharaim in **M** 4566+8441
18:11 and **M,** the Ammonites and the Philistines, 4566
2Ch 20:10 men from Ammon, **M** and Mount Seir, 4566
20:22 against the men of Ammon and **M** 4566
20:23 The men of Ammon and **M** rose up against 4566
Ne 13:23 from Ashdod, Ammon and **M.** 4567
Ps 60: 8 **M** is my washbasin, 4566
83: 6 of **M** and the Hagrites, 4566
108: 9 **M** is my washbasin, 4566
Isa 11:14 They will lay hands on Edom and **M,** 4566
15: 1 An oracle concerning **M:** 4566
15: 1 Ar in **M** is ruined, destroyed in a night! 4566
15: 1 Kir in **M** is ruined, destroyed in a night! 4566
15: 2 **M** wails over Nebo and Medeba. 4566
15: 4 Therefore the armed men of **M** cry out, 4566
15: 5 My heart cries out over **M;** 4566
15: 8 Their outcry echoes along the border of **M;** 4566
15: 9 fugitives of **M** and upon those who remain 4566

Isa 16: 2 the women of **M** at the fords of the Arnon. 4566
16: 7 they wail together for **M.** 4566
16:11 My heart laments for **M** like a harp, 4566
16:12 When **M** appears at her high place, 4566
16:13 LORD has already spoken concerning **M.** 4566
25:10 but **M** will be trampled under him 4566
Jer 9:26 **M** and all who live in the desert 4566
25:21 Edom, **M** and Ammon; 4566
27: 3 Then send word to the kings of Edom, **M,** 4566
40:11 When all the Jews in **M,** Ammon, 4566
48: 1 Concerning **M:** This is what the LORD Almighty, 4566
48: 2 **M** will be praised no more; 4566
48: 4 **M** will be broken; 4566
48: 9 Put salt on **M,** for she will be laid waste; 4566
48:11 "**M** has been at rest from youth, 4566
48:13 Then **M** will be ashamed of Chemosh, 4566
48:15 **M** will be destroyed and her towns invaded; 4566
48:16 "The fall of **M** is at hand; 4566
48:18 for he who destroys **M** will come up 4566
48:20 **M** is disgraced, for she is shattered. 4566
48:20 by the Arnon that **M** is destroyed. 4566
48:24 to all the towns of **M,** far and near. 824+4566
48:26 Let **M** wallow in her vomit; 4566
48:28 you who live in **M.** 4566
48:31 Therefore I wail over **M,** 4566
48:31 for all **M** I cry out, 4566
48:33 from the orchards and fields of **M.** 4566
48:35 In **M** I will put an end 4566
48:36 "So my heart laments for **M** like a flute; 4566
48:38 On all the roofs in **M** and in 4566
48:38 for I have broken **M** like a jar 4566
48:39 How **M** turns her back in shame! 4566
48:39 **M** has become an object of ridicule, 4566
48:40 spreading its wings over **M.** 4566
48:42 **M** will be destroyed as a nation 4566
48:43 O people of **M,**" declares the LORD. 4566
48:44 bring upon **M** the year of her punishment," 4566
48:45 it burns the foreheads of **M,** 4566
48:46 Woe to you, O **M!** 4566
48:47 "Yet I will restore the fortunes of **M** in days 4566
48:47 Here ends the judgment on **M.** 4566
Eze 25: 8 'Because **M** and Seir said, "Look, 4566
25: 9 flank of **M,** beginning at its frontier towns 4566
25:10 I will give **M** along with the Ammonites to 2023S
25:11 and I will inflict punishment on **M.** 4566
Da 11:41 **M** and the leaders of Ammon will 4566
Am 2: 1 "For three sins of **M,** even for four, 4566
2: 2 I will send fire upon **M** that will consume 4566
2: 2 **M** will go down in great tumult 4566
Mic 6: 5 remember what Balak king of **M** counseled 4566
Zep 2: 8 of **M** and the taunts of the Ammonites, 4566
2: 9 "surely **M** will become like Sodom, 4566

MOAB'S (7) [MOAB]

2Sa 23:20 He struck down two of **M** best men. 4566
1Ch 11:22 He struck down two of **M** best men. 4566
Isa 16: 6 We have heard of **M** pride— 4566
16:14 by contract would count them, **M** splendor 4566
Jer 48:25 **M** horn is cut off; 4566
48:29 "We have heard of **M** pride— 4566
48:41 In that day the hearts of **M** warriors will be 4566

MOABITE (12) [MOAB]

Nu 22: 8 So the **M** princes stayed with him. 4566
22:14 the **M** princes returned to Balak and said, 4566
22:36 he went out to meet him at the **M** town on 4566
25: 1 in sexual immorality with **M** women, 4566
Dt 23: 3 or **M** or any of his descendants may enter 4567
Ru 1: 4 They married **M** *women,* 4567
2Ki 13:20 Now **M** raiders used to enter 4566
24: 2 **M** and Ammonite raiders against him. 4566
1Ch 11:46 the sons of Elnaam, Ithmah the **M,** 4567
2Ch 24:26 and Jehozabad, son of Shimrith a **M** *woman.* 4567
Ne 13: 1 that no Ammonite or **M** should ever 4567
Isa 16: 4 Let the **M** fugitives stay with you; 4566

MOABITES (18) [MOAB]

Ge 19:37 he is the father of the **M** of today. 4566
Nu 22: 4 The **M** said to the elders of Midian, 4566
Dt 2: 9 not harass the **M** or provoke them to war, 4566
2:11 but the **M** called them Emites. 4567
2:29 who live in Seir, and the **M,** who live in Ar, 4567
Jdg 3:29 struck down about ten thousand **M,** 408+4566
2Sa 8: 2 David also defeated the **M.** 4566
8: 2 So the **M** became subject to David 4566
1Ki 11: 1 **M,** Ammonites, Edomites, 4567
11:33 Chemosh the god of the **M,** 4566
2Ki 3:21 the **M** had heard that the kings had come 4566
3:22 To the **M** across the way, 4566
3:24 But when the **M** came to the camp of Israel, 4566
3:24 the land and slaughtered the **M.** 4566
1Ch 18: 2 David also defeated the **M,** 4566
2Ch 20: 1 the **M** and Ammonites with some of 1201+4566
Ezr 9: 1 Ammonites, **M,** Egyptians and Amorites. 4567
Isa 16: 7 Therefore the **M** wail, 4566

MOABITESS (6) [MOAB]

Ru 1:22 from Moab accompanied by Ruth the **M,** 4567
2: 2 And Ruth the **M** said to Naomi, 4567
2: 6 "She is the **M** who came back from Moab 4567
2:21 Then Ruth the **M** said, "He even said to me, 4567
4: 5 the land from Naomi and from Ruth the **M,** 4567
4:10 I have also acquired Ruth the **M,** 4567

MOABITISH (KJV) See MOABITESS

MOADIAH (1) [MOADIAH'S]

Ne 12: 5 Mijamin, **M,** Bilgah, 5050

MOADIAH'S (1) [MOADIAH]

Ne 12:17 of Miniamin's and of **M,** Piltai; 4598

MOAN (6) [MOANED, MOANING]

Ps 90: 9 we finish our years with a **m.** 2049
Isa 59:11 *we* **m mournfully** like doves. 2047+2047
Jer 48:31 *I* **m** for the men of Kir Hareseth. 2047
Joel 1:18 How the cattle **m!** 634
Mic 1: 8 I will howl like a jackal and **m** like an owl. 65
Na 2: 7 Its slave girls **m** like doves and beat 5628

MOANED (1) [MOAN]

Isa 38:14 *I* **m** like a mourning dove. 2047

MOANING (2) [MOAN]

Jer 31:18 "I have surely heard Ephraim's **m:** 5653
Eze 7:16 **m** like doves of the valleys, 2159

MOB (6)

Eze 16:40 They will bring a **m** against you, 7736
23:46 Bring a **m** against them and give them over 7736
23:47 The **m** will stone them and cut them down 7736
Jn 7:49 But this **m** that knows nothing of the law— *4063*
Ac 17: 5 **formed a m** and started a riot in the city. *4062*
21:35 the violence *of* the **m** was so great he had to *4063*

MOBILIZED (3)

Jdg 20:15 the Benjamites **m** twenty-six thousand 7212
2Ki 3: 6 from Samaria and **m** all Israel. 7212
6:24 Ben-Hadad king of Aram **m** his entire army 7695

MOCK (19) [MOCKED, MOCKER, MOCKERS, MOCKERY, MOCKING, MOCKS]

Job 11: 3 Will no one rebuke you when *you* **m?** 4352
21: 3 and after I have spoken, **m** *on.* 4352
22:19 the innocent **m** them, saying, 4352
30: 1 "But now they **m** me, men younger than I, 8471
30: 9 "And now their sons **m** me **in song;** 5593
Ps 22: 7 All who see me **m** me; 4352
69:12 Those who sit at the gate **m** me, 8488
74:10 How long *will* the enemy **m** you, O God? 3070
74:22 remember how fools **m** you all day long. 3075
80: 6 and our enemies **m** us. 4352
119:51 The arrogant **m** me without restraint, 4329
Pr 1:26 *I will* **m** when calamity overtakes you— 4352
14: 9 Fools **m** *at* making amends for sin, 4329
Isa 52: 5 and those who rule them **m,**" 2147
La 3:14 they **m** me **in song** all day long. 5593
3:63 **m** me **in their songs.** 4947
Eze 22: 5 and those who are far away *will* **m** you, 7840
Mk 10:34 who *will* **m** him and spit on him, *1850*
Lk 18:32 They *will* **m** *him,* insult him, spit on him, *1850*

MOCKED (16) [MOCK]

2Ch 36:16 But *they* **m** God's messengers, 4351
Ne 2:19 *they* **m** and ridiculed us. 4352
Ps 35:16 Like the ungodly *they* **maliciously m;** 4352+4352
74:18 Remember how the enemy *has* **m** you, 3070
89:50 Lord, how your servant has been **m,** 3075
89:51 the taunts with which your enemies *have* **m,** 3070
89:51 with which *they have* **m** every step 3070
Mt 20:19 over to the Gentiles to *be* **m** and flogged *1850*
27:29 and knelt in front of him and **m** him. *1850*
27:31 After *they had* **m** him, *1850*
27:41 of the law and the elders **m** him. *1850*
Mk 15:20 And when *they had* **m** him, *1850*
15:31 of the law **m** him among themselves. *1850*
Lk 23:11 Herod and his soldiers ridiculed and **m** him. *1850*
23:36 The soldiers also came up and **m** him. *1850*
Gal 6: 7 Do not be deceived: God cannot *be* **m.** *3682*

MOCKER (12) [MOCK]

Pr 9: 7 "Whoever corrects a **m** invites insult; 4370
9: 8 Do not rebuke a **m** or he will hate you; 4370
9:12 if *you are a* **m,** you alone will suffer." 4329
13: 1 but a **m** does not listen to rebuke. 4370
14: 6 The **m** seeks wisdom and finds none, 4370
15:12 A **m** resents correction; 4370
19:25 a **m,** and the simple will learn prudence; 4370
20: 1 Wine is a **m** and beer a brawler; 4370
21:11 When a **m** is punished, the simple gain wisdom; 4370
21:24 proud and arrogant man—"**M**" is his name; 4370
22:10 Drive out the **m,** and out goes strife; 4370
24: 9 and men detest a **m.** 4370

MOCKERS (8) [MOCK]

Job 17: 2 Surely **m** surround me; 2253
Ps 1: 1 in the way of sinners or sit in the seat of **m.** 4370
Pr 1:22 How long will **m** delight in mockery 4370
3:34 He mocks **proud m** but gives grace to 4370
19:29 Penalties are prepared for **m,** 4370
29: 8 **M** stir up a city, 408+4371
Isa 29:20 the **m** will disappear, and all who have 4370
Hos 7: 5 and he joins hands with the **m.** 4372

MOCKERY (3) [MOCK]

Pr 1:22 How long will mockers delight in **m** 4371
Jer 10:15 They are worthless, the objects of **m;** 9511
51:18 They are worthless, the objects of **m;** 9511

MOCKING (6) [MOCK]

Ge 21: 9 the Egyptian had borne to Abraham *was* **m,** 7464
Isa 28:22 Now stop *your* **m,** or your chains will 4329
50: 6 I did not hide my face from **m** and spitting. 4009
57: 4 Whom *are you* **m?** 6695
Zep 2:10 and **m** the people of the LORD Almighty. 1540
Lk 22:63 The men who were guarding Jesus *began* **m** *1850*

MOCKS (8) [MOCK]

2Ki 19:21 of Zion despises you and **m** you. 4352
Job 9:23 *he* **m** the despair of the innocent. 4352
Pr 3:34 He **m** proud mockers but gives grace to 4329
17: 5 *He who* **m** the poor shows contempt 4352
19:28 A corrupt witness **m** *at* justice, 4329
30:17 "The eye *that* **m** a father, 4352
Isa 37:22 Daughter of Zion despises and **m** you. 4352
Jer 20: 7 I am ridiculed all day long; everyone **m** me. 4352

MODEL (3) [MODELS]

Eze 28:12 " 'You were the **m** *of* perfection, 3159
1Th 1: 7 And so you became a **m** to all the believers *5596*
2Th 3: 9 but in order to make ourselves a **m** for you *5596*

MODELS (2) [MODEL]

1Sa 6: 5 Make **m** *of* the tumors and of the rats 7512
6:11 the chest containing the gold rats and the **m** 7512

MODERATION (KJV) See GENTLENESS

MODESTLY (1) [MODESTY]

1Ti 2: 9 I also want women to dress **m,** *2950+3177*

MODESTY (1) [MODESTLY]

1Co 12:23 parts that are unpresentable are treated with special **m,** *2362*

MOISTEN (1) [MOISTURE]

Eze 46:14 of an ephah with a third of a hin of oil to **m** 8272

MOISTURE (3) [MOISTEN]

Job 36:28 the clouds **pour down** *their* **m** 5688
37:11 He loads the clouds with **m;** 8188
Lk 8: 6 the plants withered because they had no **m.** *2657*

MOLADAH (4)

Jos 15:26 Amam, Shema, **M,** 4579
19: 2 It included: Beersheba (or Sheba), **M,** 4579
1Ch 4:28 They lived in Beersheba, **M,** Hazar Shual, 4579
Ne 11:26 in Jeshua, in **M,** in Beth Pelet, 4579

MOLDED (1) [MOLDS]

Job 10: 9 Remember that *you* **m** me like clay. 6913

MOLDING (10) [MOLDS]

Ex 25:11 and make a gold **m** around it. 2425
25:24 with pure gold and make a gold **m** around it. 2425
25:25 a rim a handbreadth wide and put a gold **m** 2425
30: 3 and make a gold **m** around it. 2425
30: 4 for the altar below the **m—** 2425
37: 2 and made a gold **m** around it. 2425
37:11 with pure gold and made a gold **m** around it. 2425
37:12 a rim a handbreadth wide and put a gold **m** 2425
37:26 and made a gold **m** around it. 2425
37:27 They made two gold rings below the **m—** 2425

MOLDS (3) [MOLDED, MOLDING, MOLDY]

1Ki 7:37 They were all **cast in** the same **m** 4607
7:46 The king had them cast in clay **m** in 5043
2Ch 4:17 The king had them cast in clay **m** in 6295

MOLDY (2) [MOLDS]

Jos 9: 5 of their food supply was dry and **m.** 5926
9:12 But now see how dry and **m** it is. 5926

MOLE, MOLES (KJV) See CHAMELEON, RODENTS

MOLECH (16)

Lev 18:21 of your children to be sacrificed to **M,** 4891
20: 2 of his children to **M** must be put to death. 4891
20: 3 for by giving his children to **M,** 4891
20: 4 of his children to **M** and they fail to put him 4891
20: 5 in prostituting themselves to **M.** 4891
1Ki 11: 5 **M** the detestable god of the Ammonites. 4904
11: 7 for **M** the detestable god of the Ammonites. 4891
11:33 and **M** the god of the Ammonites, 4904
2Ki 23:10 or daughter in the fire to **M.** 4891
23:13 and for **M** the detestable god of the people 4904

Isa 57: 9 You went to **M** with olive oil 4891
Jer 32:35 to sacrifice their sons and daughters to **M,** 4891
49: 1 Why then has **M** taken possession of Gad? 4903
49: 3 for **M** will go into exile, 4903
Zep 1: 5 by the LORD and who also swear by **M,** 4903
Ac 7:43 You have lifted up the shrine *of* **M** and *3661*

MOLEST (2) [MOLESTS]

Ge 26:29 not **m** you but always treated you well 5595
Est 7: 8 even **m** the queen while she is with me in 3899

MOLESTS (1) [MOLEST]

Ge 26:11 "Anyone *who* **m** this man or his wife shall 5595

MOLID (1)

1Ch 2:29 who bore him Ahban and **M.** 4582

MOLLIFIED (KJV) See SOOTHED

MOLOCH (KJV) See MOLECH

MOLTEN (KJV) See IDOL CAST IN THE SHAPE

MOMENT (31) [MOMENT'S, MOMENTARY]

Ex 33: 5 If I were to go with you even for a **m,** 8092
Nu 4:20 even for a **m,** or they will die." 1180
Ezr 9: 8 "But now, for a brief **m,** 8092
Job 7:18 and test him every **m?** 8092
20: 5 the joy of the godless lasts but a **m.** 8092
Ps 2:12 for his wrath can flare up **in a m.** 3869+5071
30: 5 For his anger lasts only a **m,** 8092
Pr 12:19 but a lying tongue lasts *only a* **m.** 8088
Isa 47: 9 Both of these will overtake you **in a m,** 8092
54: 7 "For a brief **m** I abandoned you, 8092
54: 8 of anger I hid my face from you *for a* **m,** 8092
66: 8 a day or a nation be brought forth in a **m?** 7193
66: 9 *Do I* **bring to the m of birth** 8689
Jer 4:20 tents are destroyed, my shelter **in a m.** 8092
La 4: 6 which was overthrown **in a m** without 4017+8092
Eze 26:16 trembling every **m,** appalled at you. 8092
32:10 of them will tremble every **m** for his life. 8092
Mt 3:16 At that **m** heaven was opened, *NIG*
9:22 And the woman was healed from that **m.** *6052*
17:18 and he was healed from that **m.** *6052*
27:51 At that **m** the curtain of the temple was torn *NIG*
Mk 9:39 **in the next m** say anything bad about me *5444*
Lk 2:38 Coming up to them *at* that very **m,** *6052*
6:49 **The m** the torrent struck that house, *2317*
Jn 18:27 and **at that m** a rooster began to crow. *2311*
Ac 5:10 **At that m** she fell down at his feet *4202*
16:18 *At* that **m** the spirit left her. *6052*
22:13 And *at* that very **m** I was able to see him. *6052*
1Co 4:13 Up to **this m** we have become the scum of *785*
Gal 2: 5 We did not give in to them for a **m,** *6052*
Rev 12: 4 might devour her child **the m** it was born. *4020*

MOMENT'S (1) [MOMENT]

Job 10:20 Turn away from me so I can have a **m** joy 5071

MOMENTARY (1) [MOMENT]

2Co 4:17 For our light and **m** troubles are achieving *4194*

MONEY (123)

Ge 17:12 in your household or bought with **m** from 4084
17:13 in your household or bought with your **m,** 4084
17:23 in his household or bought with his **m,** 4084
42:35 they and their father saw the **m** pouches, 4084
47:14 Joseph collected all the **m** that was to 4084
47:15 When the **m** of the people of Egypt and 4084
47:15 Our **m** is used up." 4084
47:16 for your livestock, since your **m** is gone." 4084
47:18 the fact that since our **m** is gone 4084
Ex 21:11 without any payment *of* **m.** 4084
21:35 to sell the live one and divide both the **m** 4084
22:15 **m paid for** *the* **hire** covers the loss. 8510
22:25 "If you lend **m** to one of my people 4084
30:16 Receive the atonement **m** from the Israelites 4084
Lev 22:11 But if a priest buys a slave with **m,** 4084
25:37 not lend him **m** at interest or sell him food 4084
Nu 3:48 Give the **m** for the redemption of 4084
3:49 the redemption **m** from those who exceeded 4084
3:51 the redemption **m** to Aaron and his sons, 4084
Dt 18: 8 though he has received **m from** the **sale** 4928
23:19 whether on **m** or food or anything else 4084
2Ki 5:26 Is this the time to take **m,** 4084
12: 4 the **m** that is brought as sacred offerings to 4084
12: 4 the **m** *collected in* the census, 4084
12: 4 the **m** *received from* personal vows and 4084
12: 4 and the **m** brought voluntarily to the temple. 4084
12: 5 Let every priest receive the **m** from one of NIH
12: 7 Take no more **m** from your treasurers, 4084
12: 8 not collect any more **m** from the people and 4084
12: 9 into the chest all the **m** that was brought to 4084
12:10 that there was a large amount of **m** in 4084
12:10 the **m** that had been brought into the temple 4084
12:11 the **m** to the men appointed to supervise 4084
12:13 The **m** brought into the temple was 4084
12:15 from those to whom they gave the **m** to pay 4084
12:16 The **m** *from* the guilt offerings 4084
2Ki 15:20 Menahem exacted this **m** from Israel. 4084
22: 4 the high priest and have him get ready the **m** 4084
22: 7 not account for the **m** entrusted to them, 4084
22: 9 "Your officials have paid out the **m** that was 4084
2Ch 24: 5 of Judah and collect the **m** due annually 4084
24:11 that there was a large amount of **m,** 4084
24:11 and collected a great amount of **m.** 4084
24:14 the rest of the **m** to the king and Jehoiada, 4084
34: 9 the **m** that had been brought into the temple 4084
34:11 also gave **m** to the carpenters and builders NIH
34:14 the **m** that had been taken into the temple of 4084
34:17 the **m** that was in the temple of the LORD 4084
Ezr 3: 7 they gave **m** to the masons and carpenters, 4084
7:17 With this **m** be sure to buy bulls, 10362
Ne 5: 4 "We have had to borrow **m** to pay 4084
5:10 and my men are also lending the people **m** 4084
5:11 the hundredth part of the **m,** grain, 4084
Est 3:11 "Keep the **m,"** the king said to Haman, 4084
4: 7 the exact amount of **m** Haman had promised 4084
Ps 15: 5 who lends his **m** without usury and does 4084
Pr 7:20 with **m** and will not be home till full moon." 4084
13:11 Dishonest **m** dwindles away, 2104
13:11 but he who gathers **m** little by little NIH
17:16 Of what use is **m** in the hand of a fool, 4697
Ecc 5:10 Whoever loves **m** never has money enough; 4084
5:10 Whoever loves money never has **m** enough; 4084
7:12 Wisdom is a shelter as **m** is a shelter, 4084
10:19 but **m** is the answer for everything. 4084
Isa 52: 3 and without **m** you will be redeemed." 4084
55: 1 and you who have no **m,** come, buy and eat! 4084
55: 1 and milk without **m** and without cost. 4084
55: 2 Why spend **m** on what is not bread, 4084
Mic 3:11 and her prophets tell fortunes for **m.** 4084
Mt 6:24 You cannot serve both God and **M.** *3440*
20:15 to do what I want with my own **m?** *3836*
21:12 He overturned the tables *of* the **m changers** *3142*
25:15 To one he gave five **talents of m,** *5419*
25:16 and put his **m** to work and gained five more. *899*[S]
25:18 a hole in the ground and hid his master's **m.** *736*
25:27 you should have put my **m** on deposit with *736*
26: 9 at a high price and the **m** given to the poor." *NIG*
27: 5 Judas threw the **m** into the temple and left. *736*
27: 6 into the treasury, since it is **blood m."** *135+5507*
27: 7 to use **the m** to buy the potter's field as *899*[S]
28:12 they gave the soldiers a large sum of **m,** *736*
28:15 the **m** and did as they were instructed. *736*
Mk 6: 8 no bread, no bag, no **m** in your belts. *5910*
11:15 He overturned the tables *of* the **m changers** *3142*
12:41 and watched the crowd putting their **m** into *5910*
14: 5 a year's wages and the **m** given to the poor. *NIG*
14:11 to hear this and promised to give him **m.** *736*
Lk 3:14 He replied, "Don't **extort m** and *1398*
7:41 "Two men **owed m to** a certain *1639+5971*
7:42 Neither of them had the **m** to pay him back, *NIG*
9: 3 no staff, no bag, no bread, no **m,** *736*
14:28 to see if he has enough **m** to complete it? *NIG*
16:13 You cannot serve both God and **M."** *3440*
16:14 The Pharisees, *who* **loved m,** *5639+5795*
19:13 'Put this **m** to work,' he said, *NIG*
19:15 the servants to whom he had given the **m,** *736*
19:23 Why then didn't you put my **m** on deposit, *736*
22: 5 and agreed to give him **m.** *736*
Jn 2:14 and others sitting at tables **exchanging m.** *3048*
2:15 the **m changers** and overturned their tables. *3142*
12: 5 **the m** given to the poor? It was **worth a year's wages."** *1324+5559*
12: 6 was a thief; as **keeper of the m bag,** *1186+2400*
13:29 Since Judas had charge of the **m,** *1186*
Ac 3: 3 he asked them for **m.** *1797+3284*
4:34 brought the **m** from the sales *5507*
4:37 sold a field he owned and brought the **m** *5975*
5: 2 he kept back part *of* the **m** for himself, *5507*
5: 3 for yourself some *of* the **m** you received for *5507*
5: 4 it was sold, wasn't the **m** at your disposal? *NIG*
7:16 at Shechem for a certain sum *of* **m.** *736*
8:18 he offered them **m** *5975*
8:20 "May your **m** perish with you, *736*
8:20 you could buy the gift of God with **m!** *5975*
16:16 She earned a great deal of **m** for her owners *2238*
16:19 that their hope *of* **making m** was gone, *2238*
1Co 16: 2 each one of you should set aside a **sum of m** *2564*
1Ti 3: 3 not quarrelsome, **not a lover of m.** *921*
6:10 the **love of m** is a root of all kinds of evil. *5794*
6:10 Some people, eager for **m,** have wandered *NIG*
2Ti 3: 2 **lovers of m,** boastful, proud, abusive, *5795*
Heb 13: 5 Keep your lives **free from the love of m** *921*
Jas 4:13 carry on business and **make m."** *3045*
1Pe 5: 2 not **greedy for m,** but eager to serve; *154*

MONEYLENDER (2) [LEND]

Ex 22:25 do not be like a **m;** charge him no interest. 5957
Lk 7:41 "Two men owed money to a certain **m.** *1250*

MONITOR (1)

Lev 11:30 the **m lizard,** the wall lizard, 3947

MONSTER (6)

Job 7:12 Am I the sea, or the **m of the deep,** 9490
Ps 74:13 you broke the heads of the **m** in the waters. 9490
Isa 27: 1 he will slay the **m** of the sea. 9490
51: 9 who pierced that **m** through? 9490
Eze 29: 3 you great **m** lying among your streams. 9490
32: 2 you are like a **m** in the seas thrashing about 9490

[SEA] MONSTERS (KJV) See JACKALS

MONTH (211) [MONTHLY, MONTHS, MONTHS']

Ge 7:11 on the seventeenth day of the second **m**— 2544
8: 4 and on the seventeenth day of the seventh **m** 2544
8: 5 to recede until the tenth **m,** 2544
8: 5 and on the first day of the tenth **m** the tops 2544
8:13 of the first **m** of Noah's six hundred 2544
8:14 the second **m** the earth was completely dry. 2544
29:14 stayed with him for a **whole m,** 2544+3427
Ex 12: 2 "This **m** is to be for you the first month, 2544
12: 2 "This month is to be for you the first **m,** 2544
12: 2 the first **m** *of* your year. 2544
12: 3 that on the tenth day of this **m** each man is 2544
12: 6 of them until the fourteenth day of the **m,** 2544
12:18 In the first **m** you are to eat bread made 2544
13: 4 Today, in the **m** *of* Abib, you are leaving. 2544
13: 5 you are to observe this ceremony in this **m:** 2544
16: 1 of the second **m** after they had come out 2544
19: 1 the third **m** after the Israelites left Egypt— 2544
23:15 at the appointed time in the **m** *of* Abib, 2544
23:15 for in **that m** you came out of Egypt. 2257[S]
34:18 at the appointed time in the **m** *of* Abib, 2544
34:18 for in that **m** you came out of Egypt. 2544
40: 2 on the first day of the first **m.** 2544
40:17 up on the first day of the first **m** in 2544
Lev 16:29 of the seventh **m** you must deny yourselves 2544
23: 5 on the fourteenth day of the first **m.** 2544
23: 6 On the fifteenth day of that **m** 2544
23:24 the seventh **m** you are to have a day of rest, 2544
23:27 "The tenth day of this seventh **m** is the Day 2544
23:32 of the **m** until the following evening you are 2544
23:34 'On the fifteenth day of the seventh **m** 2544
23:39 of the seventh **m,** after you have gathered 2544
23:41 celebrate it in the seventh **m.** 2544
25: 9 on the tenth day of the seventh **m;** 2544
27: 6 a person between *one* **m** and five years, 2544
Nu 1: 1 of Sinai on the first day of the second **m** of 2544
1:18 on the first day of the second **m.** 2544
3:15 Count every male a **m** old or more." 2544
3:22 The number of all the males a **m** old 2544
3:28 of all the males a **m** old or more was 8,600. 2544
3:34 The number of all the males a **m** old 2544
3:39 including every male a **m** old or more, 2544
3:40 the firstborn Israelite males who are a **m** old 2544
3:43 The total number of firstborn males a **m** old 2544
9: 1 to Moses in the Desert of Sinai in the first **m** 2544
9: 3 at twilight on the fourteenth day of this **m,** 2544
9: 5 on the fourteenth day of the first **m.** 2544
9:11 on the fourteenth day of the second **m** 2544
9:22 or a **m** or a year, the Israelites would remain 2544
10:11 On the twentieth day of the second **m** of 2544
11:20 but *for* a whole **m**—until it comes out of 2544
11:21 give them meat to eat *for* a whole **m!'** 2544
18:16 When they are a **m** old, 2544
20: 1 In the first **m** the whole Israelite community 2544
26:62 a **m** old or more numbered 23,000. 2544
28:11 " 'On the first of every **m,** 2544
28:16 of the first **m** the LORD's Passover is to 2544
28:17 On the fifteenth day of this **m** there is to be 2544
29: 1 " 'On the first day of the seventh **m** hold 2544
29: 7 " 'On the tenth day of this seventh **m** hold 2544
29:12 " 'On the fifteenth day of the seventh **m,** 2544
33: 3 on the fifteenth day of the first **m,** 2544
33:38 where he died on the first day of the fifth **m** 2544
Dt 1: 3 on the first day of the eleventh **m,** 2544
16: 1 the **m** *of* Abib and celebrate the Passover of 2544
16: 1 the **m** *of* Abib he brought you out of Egypt 2544
21:13 her father and mother *for* a full **m,** 3732
Jos 4:19 the tenth day of the first **m** the people went 2544
5:10 the evening of the fourteenth day of the **m,** 2544
1Sa 20:27 But the next day, the second day of the **m,** 2544
20:34 on that second day of the **m** he did not eat, 2544
1Ki 4: 7 Each one had to provide supplies for one **m** 2544
4:27 The district officers, each in his **m,** 2544
5:14 to Lebanon in shifts of ten thousand a **m,** 2544
5:14 so that they spent one **m** in Lebanon 2544
6: 1 in the **m** *of* Ziv, the second month, 2544
6: 1 in the month of Ziv, the second **m,** 2544
6:37 in the fourth year, in the **m** *of* Ziv. 3732
6:38 In the eleventh year in the **m** *of* Bul, 3732
6:38 the eighth **m,** the temple was finished 2544
8: 2 the time of the festival in the **m** *of* Ethanim, 3732
8: 2 in the month of Ethanim, the seventh **m.** 2544
12:32 on the fifteenth day of the eighth **m,** 2544
12:33 On the fifteenth day of the eighth **m,** 2544
12:33 a **m** of his own choosing, 2544
2Ki 15:13 and he reigned in Samaria **one m.** 3427+3732
25: 1 on the tenth day of the tenth **m,** 2544
25: 3 the ninth day of the [fourth] **m** the famine in 2544
25: 8 On the seventh day of the fifth **m,** 2544
25:25 In the seventh **m,** however, 2544
25:27 on the twenty-seventh day of the twelfth **m.** 2544
1Ch 12:15 who crossed the Jordan in the first **m** 2544
27: 1 that were on duty **m** by month throughout 2544
27: 1 that were on duty month by **m** throughout 2544
27: 2 the first division, for the first **m,** 2544
27: 3 of all the army officers for the first **m.** 2544
27: 4 of the division for the second **m** was Dodai 2544
27: 5 The third army commander, for the third **m,** 2544
27: 7 The fourth, for the fourth **m,** 2544
27: 8 The fifth, for the fifth **m,** 2544
27: 9 The sixth, for the sixth **m,** 2544
27:10 The seventh, for the seventh **m,** 2544

1Ch 27:11 The eighth, for the eighth **m,** 2544
27:12 The ninth, for the ninth **m,** 2544
27:13 The tenth, for the tenth **m,** 2544
27:14 The eleventh, for the eleventh **m,** 2544
27:15 The twelfth, for the twelfth **m,** 2544
2Ch 3: 2 the second **m** in the fourth year of his reign. 2544
5: 3 at the time of the festival in the seventh **m.** 2544
7:10 of the seventh **m** he sent the people 2544
15:10 They assembled at Jerusalem in the third **m** 2544
29: 3 In the first **m** of the first year of his reign, 2544
29:17 on the first day of the first **m,** 2544
29:17 and by the eighth day of the **m** they reached 2544
29:17 finishing on the sixteenth day of the first **m.** 2544
30: 2 to celebrate the Passover in the second **m.** 2544
30:13 of Unleavened Bread in the second **m.** 2544
30:15 on the fourteenth day of the second **m.** 2544
31: 7 They began doing this in the third **m** 2544
31: 7 and finished in the seventh **m.** 2544
35: 1 on the fourteenth day of the first **m.** 2544
Ezr 3: 1 When the seventh **m** came and 2544
3: 6 On the first day of the seventh **m** they began 2544
3: 8 In the second **m** of the second year 2544
6:15 on the third day of the **m** Adar, 10333
6:19 On the fourteenth day of the first **m,** 2544
7: 8 the fifth **m** of the seventh year of the king. 2544
7: 9 from Babylon on the first day of the first **m,** 2544
7: 9 in Jerusalem on the first day of the fifth **m,** 2544
8:31 the first **m** we set out from the Ahava Canal 2544
10: 9 And on the twentieth day of the ninth **m,** 2544
10:16 of the tenth **m** they sat down to investigate 2544
10:17 of the first **m** they finished dealing with all 2544
Ne 1: 1 In the **m** *of* Kislev in the twentieth year, 2544
2: 1 In the **m** *of* Nisan in the twentieth year 2544
7:73 When the seventh **m** came and 2544
8: 2 So on the first day of the seventh **m** Ezra 2544
8:13 On the second day of the **m,** NIH
8:14 in booths during the feast of the seventh **m** 2544
9: 1 On the twenty-fourth day of the same **m,** 2544
Est 2:16 in the royal residence in the tenth **m,** 2544
2:16 the **m** *of* Tebeth, in the seventh year 2544
3: 7 in the first **m,** the month of Nisan, 2544
3: 7 the **m** *of* Nisan, they cast the pur 2544
3: 7 of Haman to select a day and **m.** 2544
3: 7 lot fell on the twelfth **m,** the month of Adar. 2544
3: 7 lot fell on the twelfth month, the **m** *of* Adar. 2544
3:12 Then on the thirteenth day of the first **m** 2544
3:13 the thirteenth day of the twelfth **m,** 2544
3:13 the **m** *of* Adar, and to plunder their goods. 2544
8: 9 on the twenty-third day of the third **m,** 2544
8: 9 of the third month, the **m** *of* Sivan. 2544
8:12 the thirteenth day of the twelfth **m,** 2544
8:12 the twelfth month, the **m** *of* Adar. 2544
9: 1 On the thirteenth day of the twelfth **m,** 2544
9: 1 the twelfth month, the **m** *of* Adar, 2544
9:15 on the fourteenth day of the **m** *of* Adar, 2544
9:17 on the thirteenth day of the **m** *of* Adar, 2544
9:19 the **m** *of* Adar as a day of joy and feasting, 2544
9:21 the fourteenth and fifteenth days of the **m** 2544
9:22 the **m** when their sorrow was turned into joy 2544
Isa 47:13 those stargazers who make predictions **m** NIH
47:13 by **m,** let them save you 2544
Jer 1: 3 down to the fifth **m** of the eleventh year 2544
28: 1 In the fifth **m** of that same year, 2544
28:17 In the seventh **m** of that same year, 2544
36: 9 In the ninth **m** of the fifth year 2544
36:22 It was the ninth **m** and the king was sitting 2544
39: 1 in the tenth **m,** Nebuchadnezzar king of 2544
39: 2 of the fourth **m** of Zedekiah's eleventh year, 2544
41: 1 In the seventh **m** Ishmael son of Nethaniah, 2544
52: 4 on the tenth day of the tenth **m,** 2544
52: 6 By the ninth day of the fourth **m** the famine 2544
52:12 On the tenth day of the fifth **m,** 2544
52:31 on the twenty-fifth day of the twelfth **m.** 2544
Eze 1: 1 in the fourth **m** on the fifth day, 2544
1: 2 On the fifth of the **m**— 2544
8: 1 in the sixth **m** on the fifth day, 2544
20: 1 in the fifth **m** on the tenth day, 2544
24: 1 in the tenth **m** on the tenth day, 2544
26: 1 on the first day of the **m,** 2544
29: 1 in the tenth **m** on the twelfth day, 2544
29:17 in the first **m** on the first day, 2544
30:20 in the first **m** on the seventh day, 2544
31: 1 in the third **m** on the first day, 2544
32: 1 in the twelfth **m** on the first day, 2544
32:17 on the fifteenth day of the **m,** 2544
33:21 in the tenth **m** on the fifth day, 2544
40: 1 on the tenth of the **m,** in the fourteenth year 2544
45:18 In the first **m** on the first day you are to take 2544
45:20 to do the same on the seventh day of the **m** 2544
45:21 the first **m** on the fourteenth day you are 2544
45:25 in the seventh **m** on the fifteenth day, 2544
47:12 Every **m** they will bear, 2544
Da 10: 4 On the twenty-fourth day of the first **m,** 2544
Hag 1: 1 on the first day of the sixth **m,** 2544
1:15 on the twenty-fourth day of the sixth **m** in 2544
2: 1 On the twenty-first day of the seventh **m,** 2544
2:10 On the twenty-fourth day of the ninth **m,** NIH
2:18 from this twenty-fourth day of the ninth **m,** NIH
2:20 on the twenty-fourth day of the **m:** 2544
Zec 1: 1 the eighth **m** of the second year of Darius, 2544
1: 7 On the twenty-fourth day of the eleventh **m,** 2544
1: 7 the eleventh month, the **m** *of* Shebat, 2544
7: 1 on the fourth day of the ninth **m,** 2544
7: 1 the ninth month, the **m** of Kislev. NIH
7: 3 "Should I mourn and fast in the fifth **m,** 2544
11: 8 In one **m** I got rid of the three shepherds. 3732
Lk 1:26 In the sixth **m,** God sent the angel Gabriel *3604*
Lk 1:36 who was said to be barren is in her sixth **m.** *3604*
Rev 9:15 and **m** and year were released to kill a third *3604*
22: 2 yielding its fruit every **m.** *3604*

MONTHLY (11) [MONTH]

Lev 12: 2 she is unclean during her **m period.** 1864+5614
15:19 **impurity of her m period** 5614
15:24 with her and her **m flow** touches him, 5614
15:25 at a time other than her **m period** or has 5614
15:26 as is her bed during her **m period,** 5614
15:33 for a *woman* in her **m period,** 1865+5614
18:19 during the uncleanness of her **m period.** 5614
20:18 lies with a woman during her **m period** 1865
Nu 28:14 This is the **m** burnt offering to 928+2544+2544
29: 6 to the **m** and daily burnt offerings 2544
Eze 36:17 like a **woman's m uncleanness** 2021+3240+5614

MONTHS (52) [MONTH]

Ge 38:24 About three **m** later Judah was told, 2544
Ex 2: 2 she hid him *for* three **m.** 3732
Jdg 11:37 "Give me two **m** to roam the hills and weep 2544
11:38 And he let her go *for* two **m.** 2544
11:39 After the two **m,** she returned to her father 2544
19: 2 After she had been there four **m,** 2544
20:47 where they stayed four **m.** 2544
1Sa 6: 1 in Philistine territory seven **m,** 2544
27: 7 in Philistine territory a year and four **m.** 2544
2Sa 2:11 of Judah was seven years and six **m.** 2544
5: 5 over Judah seven years and six **m,** 2544
6:11 of Obed-Edom the Gittite *for* three **m,** 2544
24: 8 at the end of nine **m** and twenty days. 2544
24:13 Or three **m** of fleeing from your enemies 2544
1Ki 5:14 in Lebanon and two **m** at home. 2544
11:16 and all the Israelites stayed there *for* six **m,** 2544
2Ki 15: 8 and he reigned six **m.** 2544
23:31 and he reigned in Jerusalem three **m.** 2544
24: 8 and he reigned in Jerusalem three **m.** 2544
1Ch 3: 4 where he reigned seven years and six **m.** 2544
13:14 of Obed-Edom in his house *for* three **m,** 2544
21:12 three **m** of being swept away 2544
2Ch 36: 2 and he reigned in Jerusalem three **m.** 2544
36: 9 and he reigned in Jerusalem three **m** 2544
Est 2:12 she had to complete twelve **m** 2544
2:12 six **m** with oil of myrrh and six 2544
Job 3: 6 of the year nor be entered in any of the **m.** 3732
7: 3 so I have been allotted **m** *of* futility, 3732
14: 5 you have decreed the number of his **m** 2544
21:21 behind when his allotted **m** come to an end? 2544
29: 2 "How I long for the **m** gone by, 3732
39: 2 Do you count the **m** till they bear? 3732
Eze 39:12 " '*For* seven **m** the house of Israel will 2544
39:14 of the seven **m** they will begin their search. 2544
Da 4:29 Twelve **m** later, as the king was walking on 10333
Am 4: 7 when the harvest was still three **m** away. 2544
Zec 7: 5 and mourned in the fifth and seventh **m** for NIH
8:19 seventh and tenth **m** will become joyful NIH
Mk 6:37 take **eight m of a man's wages!** *1324+1357*
Lk 1:24 and *for* five **m** remained in seclusion. *3604*
1:56 *for* about three **m** and then returned home. *3604*
Jn 4:35 **'Four m** more and then the harvest'? *5485*
Ac 7:20 *For* three **m** he was cared for *3604*
19: 8 and spoke boldly there for three **m,** *3604*
20: 3 where he stayed three **m.** *3604*
28:11 After three **m** we put out to sea in a ship *3604*
Gal 4:10 You are observing special days and **m** *3604*
Heb 11:23 By faith Moses' parents hid him *for* **three m** after he was born, *5564*
Rev 9: 5 but only to torture them *for* five **m.** *3604*
9:10 to torment people *for* five **m.** *3604*
11: 2 They will trample on the holy city *for* 42 **m.** *3604*
13: 5 to exercise his authority *for* forty-two **m.** *3604*

MONTHS' (1) [MONTH]

Jn 6: 7 **Eight m wages** would not buy enough *1324+1357*

MONUMENT (4)

1Sa 15:12 There he has set up a **m** in his own honor 3338
2Sa 18:18 **erected** it in the King's Valley **as a m** 5893
18:18 and it is called Absalom's **M** to this day. 3338
Isa 19:19 and a **m** to the LORD at its border. 5167

MOON (61) [MOONS]

Ge 37: 9 the sun and **m** and eleven stars were bowing 3734
Nu 10:10 your appointed feasts and **New M festivals**— 2544+8031
28:14 to be made at each **new m** *during* the year. 2544
Dt 4:19 the sun, the **m** and the stars— 3734
17: 3 or to the sun or the **m** or the stars of the sky, 3734
33:14 and the finest the **m** can yield; 3732
Jos 10:12 "O sun, stand still over Gibeon, O **m,** 3734
10:13 So the sun stood still, and the **m** stopped, 3734
1Sa 20: 5 "Look, tomorrow is the **New M festival,** 2544
20:18 "Tomorrow is the **New M festival.** 2544
20:24 and when the **New M festival** came, 2544
2Ki 4:23 "It's not the **New M** or the Sabbath." 2544
23: 5 burned incense to Baal, to the sun and **m,** 3734
1Ch 23:31 on Sabbaths and at **New M festivals** and 2544
Ezr 3: 5 the **New M** sacrifices and the sacrifices 2544
Ne 10:33 **New M festivals** and appointed feasts; 2544
Job 25: 5 the **m** is not bright and the stars are not pure 3734
26: 9 He covers the face of the **full m,** 4057
31:26 in its radiance or the **m** moving in splendor, 3734
Ps 8: 3 the **m** and the stars, which you have set in 3734
72: 5 as long as the **m,** through all generations. 3734
Ps 72: 7 prosperity will abound till the **m** is no more. 3734
74:16 you established the sun and **m.** 4401
81: 3 Sound the ram's horn at the **New M,** 2544
81: 3 and when the **m** is **full,** 4057
89:37 it will be established forever like the **m,** 3734
104:19 The **m** marks off the seasons, 3734
121: 6 nor the **m** by night. 3734
136: 9 the **m** and stars to govern the night; 3734
148: 3 Praise him, sun and **m,** praise him, 3734
Pr 7:20 and will not be home till **full m."** 3427+4057
Ecc 12: 2 the light and the **m** and the stars grow dark, 3734
SS 6:10 fair as the **m,** bright as the sun, 4244
Isa 1:14 Your **New M festivals** and your appointed 2544
13:10 and the **m** will not give its light. 3734
24:23 The **m** will be abashed, the sun ashamed; 4244
30:26 The **m** will shine like the sun, 4244
60:19 nor will the brightness of the **m** shine 3734
60:20 and your **m** will wane no more; 3734
66:23 From *one* **New M** to another and 2544
Jer 8: 2 They will be exposed to the sun and the **m** 3734
31:35 the **m** and stars to shine by night, who stirs 3734
Eze 32: 7 and the **m** will not give its light. 3734
46: 1 on the day of the **New M** it is to be opened. 2544
46: 6 of the **New M** he is to offer a young bull, 2544
Hos 5: 7 their **New M festivals** will devour them 2544
Joel 2:10 the sun and **m** are darkened, 3734
2:31 be turned to darkness and the **m** to blood 3734
3:15 The sun and **m** will be darkened, 3734
Am 8: 5 the **New M** be over that we may sell grain, 2544
Hab 3:11 and **m** stood still in the heavens at the glint 3734
Mt 24:29 and the **m** will not give its light; *4943*
Mk 13:24 and the **m** will not give its light; *4943*
Lk 21:25 "There will be signs in the sun, **m** and stars. *4943*
Ac 2:20 be turned to darkness and the **m** to blood *4943*
1Co 15:41 the **m** another and the stars another; *4943*
Col 2:16 a **New M celebration** or a Sabbath day. *3741*
Rev 6:12 the whole **m** turned blood red, *4943*
8:12 a third *of* the **m,** and a third of the stars, *4943*
12: 1 with the sun, with the **m** under her feet and *4943*
21:23 not need the sun or the **m** to shine on it, *4943*

MOONS (7) [MOON]

2Ch 2: 4 and **New M** and at the appointed feasts of 2544
8:13 **New M** and the three annual feasts— 2544
31: 3 **New M** and appointed feasts as written in 2544
Isa 1:13 **New M,** Sabbaths and convocations— 2544
Eze 45:17 the **New M** and the Sabbaths— 2544
46: 3 On the Sabbaths and **New M** the people of 2544
Hos 2:11 her yearly festivals, her **New M,** 2544

MORAL (1)

Jas 1:21 get rid of all **m filth** and the evil that is *4864*

MORASTHITE (KJV) See MORESHETH

MORDECAI (53) [MORDECAI'S]

Ezr 2: 2 Nehemiah, Seraiah, Reelaiah, **M,** Bilshan, 5283
Ne 7: 7 Nahamani, **M,** Bilshan, Mispereth, Bigvai, 5283
Est 2: 5 named **M** son of Jair, the son of Shimei, 5283
2: 7 **M** had a cousin named Hadassah, NIH
2: 7 and **M** had taken her as his own daughter 5283
2:10 because **M** had forbidden her to do so. 5283
2:15 for Esther (the girl **M** had adopted, 5283
2:19 **M** was sitting at the king's gate. 5283
2:20 and nationality just as **M** had told her to do, 5283
2:21 the time **M** was sitting at the king's gate, 5283
2:22 But **M** found out about the plot 5283
2:22 reported it to the king, giving credit to **M.** 5283
3: 2 **M** would not kneel down or pay him honor. 5283
3: 3 royal officials at the king's gate asked **M,** 5283
3: 5 When Haman saw that **M** would not kneel 5283
3: 6 he scorned the idea of killing only **M.** 5283
4: 1 When **M** learned of all that had been done, 5283
4: 4 and eunuchs came and told her about **M,** NIH
4: 5 to find out what was troubling **M** and why. 5283
4: 6 to **M** in the open square of the city in front 5283
4: 7 **M** told him everything that had happened 5283
4: 9 and reported to Esther what **M** had said. 5283
4:10 Then she instructed him to say to **M,** 5283
4:12 When Esther's words were reported to **M,** 5283
4:15 Then Esther sent this reply to **M:** 5283
4:17 So **M** went away and carried out all 5283
5: 9 But when he saw **M** at the king's gate 5283
5: 9 he was filled with rage against **M.** 5283
5:13 that Jew **M** sitting at the king's gate." 5283
5:14 the king in the morning to have **M** hanged 5283
6: 2 that **M** had exposed Bigthana and Teresh, 5283
6: 3 and recognition has **M** received for this?" 5283
6: 4 to speak to the king about hanging **M** on 5283
6:10 and do just as you have suggested for **M** 5283
6:11 He robed **M,** and led him on horseback 5283
6:12 Afterward **M** returned to the king's gate. 5283
6:13 and his wife Zeresh said to him, "Since **M,** 5283
7: 9 He had it made for **M,** 5283
7:10 on the gallows he had prepared for **M.** 5283
8: 1 And **M** came into the presence of the king, 5283
8: 2 and presented it to **M.** 5283
8: 7 to Queen Esther and to **M** the Jew, 5283
8:10 **M** wrote in the name of King Xerxes, NIH
8:15 **M** left the king's presence wearing royal 5283
9: 3 because fear of **M** had seized them. 5283
9: 4 **M** was prominent in the palace; 5283
9:20 **M** recorded these events, 5283
9:23 doing what **M** had written to them. 5283

Est 9:29 daughter of Abihail, along with **M** the Jew, 5283
9:30 And **M** sent letters to all the Jews in NIH
9:31 as **M** the Jew and Queen Esther had decreed 5283
10: 2 with a full account of the greatness of **M** 5283
10: 3 **M** the Jew was second in rank 5283

MORDECAI'S (5) [MORDECAI]

Est 2:20 for she continued to follow **M** instructions 5283
3: 4 about it to see whether **M** behavior would 5283
3: 6 Yet having learned who **M** people were, 5283
3: 6 for a way to destroy all **M** people, 5283
8: 9 They wrote out all **M** orders to the Jews, 5283

MORE (584)

Ge 3: 1 Now the serpent was **m** crafty **than** any of 4946
4:13 "My punishment is **m** than I can bear. 1524
5:24 he **was no m,** because God took him away. 401
7:20 to a depth of **m than** twenty feet. 4946
8:10 He waited seven **m** days and again sent 337+6388
8:12 He waited seven **m** days and sent 337+6388
18:32 but let me speak just **once m.** 7193
24:20 ran back to the well to **draw** *m* **water,** AIT
29:30 and he loved Rachel **m than** Leah. 4946
37: 3 Now Israel loved Joseph **m than** any 4946
37: 4 that their father loved him **m than** any 4946
37: 5 they hated him **all the m.** 3578+6388
37: 8 And they hated him **all the m** because 3578+6388
38:26 "She is **m** righteous **than** I, 4946
42:13 and one **is no m."** 401
42:32 One **is no m,** and the youngest is now 401
42:36 Joseph **is no m** and Simeon is no more, 401
42:36 Joseph is no more and Simeon **is no m,** 401
43: 2 "Go back and buy us a little **m** food." NIH
44:25 'Go back and buy a **little m** food.' 5071
Ex 1:10 or *they will become even m* **numerous** and, AIT
1:12 But the **m** they were oppressed, 889+3869
1:12 the **m** they multiplied and spread; 4027
1:20 and became even **m** numerous. 4394
5:10 'I will not give you any **m** straw. NIH
9:29 and there will be no **m** hail, 6388
10:17 Now forgive my sin **once m** and 421+2021+7193
11: 1 "I will bring one **m** plague on Pharaoh and 6388
28:27 Make two **m** gold rings and attach them to NIH
30:14 those twenty years old or **m,** 2025+5087
30:15 not *to* **give m** than a half shekel and 8049
36: 5 "The people are bringing **m** than enough 8049
36: 6 the people were restrained from bringing **m,** NIH
36: 7 what they already had *was m than* enough 3855
38:26 twenty years old or **m,** a total of 603,550 men. 2025+5087
39:20 Then they made two **m** gold rings NIH
Lev 13: 3 the sore appears to be **m than** skin deep, 4946
13: 4 to be **m than** skin deep and the hair in it has 4946
13:20 and if it appears to be **m than** skin deep and 4946
13:21 it is not **m than** skin deep and has faded, 4946
13:25 and it appears to be **m than** skin deep, 4946
13:26 in the spot and if it is not **m than** skin deep 4946
13:30 and if it appears to be **m than** skin deep and 4946
13:31 it does not seem to be **m than** skin deep 4946
13:32 not appear to be **m than** skin deep, 4946
13:34 and appears to be no **m than** skin deep, 4946
27: 7 If it is a person sixty years old or **m,** 2025+5087
Nu 1: 3 in Israel twenty years old or **m** who 2025+5087
1:18 men twenty years old or **m** were listed 2025+5087
1:20 men twenty years old or **m** who were 2025+5087
1:22 men twenty years old or **m** who were 2025+5087
1:24 men twenty years old or **m** who were 2025+5087
1:26 men twenty years old or **m** who were 2025+5087
1:28 men twenty years old or **m** who were 2025+5087
1:30 men twenty years old or **m** who were 2025+5087
1:32 men twenty years old or **m** who were 2025+5087
1:34 men twenty years old or **m** who were 2025+5087
1:36 men twenty years old or **m** who were 2025+5087
1:38 men twenty years old or **m** who were 2025+5087
1:40 men twenty years old or **m** who were 2025+5087
1:42 men twenty years old or **m** who were 2025+5087
1:45 twenty years old or **m** who were able 2025+5087
3:15 Count every male a month old or **m."** 2025+5087
3:22 or **m** who were counted was 7,500. 2025+5087
3:28 males a month old or **m** was 8,600. 2025+5087
3:34 or **m** who were counted was 6,200. 2025+5087
3:39 every male a month old or **m,** 2025+5087
3:40 or **m** and make a list of their names. 2025+5087
3:43 of firstborn males a month old or **m,** 2025+5087
8:24 Men twenty-five years old or **m** shall 2025+5087
12: 3 **m** humble **than** anyone else 4946
14:29 or **m** who was counted in the census 2025+5087
22:15 **m** numerous and more distinguished than NIH
22:15 more numerous and **m** distinguished **than** 4946
26: 2 all those twenty years old or **m** who 2025+5087
26: 4 of the men twenty years old or **m,** 2025+5087
26:62 a month old or **m** numbered 23,000. 2025+5087
32:11 men twenty years old or **m** who came 2025+5087
32:14 **making** the LORD even **m** angry with 3578
Dt 3:11 and was **m than thirteen feet** long 564+9596
5:22 and he added **nothing** *m.* AIT
7: 7 you were **m** numerous **than** other peoples, 4946
7:14 be blessed **m than** any other people; 4946
9:14 and **m** numerous **than** they." 4946
17:16 or make the people return to Egypt to **get m** 8049
19: 9 then you are to set aside three **m** cities. 3578+6388
25: 3 he must not give him **m** *than* forty lashes. 3578
25: 3 If he is flogged **m** than that, 3578+8041
30: 5 *He will* **make** you **m prosperous** and numerous than your fathers. 3512
Dt 31:27 **how much m** will you rebel after I die! 677+2256+3954
33:11 strike his foes **till** they rise **no m."** 4946
Jos 10:11 and **m** of them died from the hailstones 8041
19: 9 Judah's portion was **m** than they needed. 8041
22:33 And they talked **no** *m* about going to war AIT
Jdg 2:19 to ways **even m** corrupt **than** those 4946
6:39 Let me make just **one m** request. 7193
6:39 Allow me **one m** test with the fleece. 7193
7:12 Their camels could no **m** be counted than NIH
15: 2 Isn't her younger sister **m** attractive? 4946
16:18 "Come back **once m;** 7193
16:28 O God, please strengthen me just **once m,** 7193
16:30 he killed **m** when he died **than** while 4946
20:45 as Gidom and struck down two thousand **m.** 408[S]
Ru 1:11 Am I going to have **any m** sons, 6388
1:13 It is **m** bitter for me than for you, 4394
1Sa 1: 8 Don't I **mean m** to you than ten sons?" 3202
2: 5 but those who were hungry hunger **no m.** 2532
2:29 Why do you honor your sons **m than** me 4946
14:19 tumult in the Philistine camp **increased m and more.** 2143+2143+2256+8041
14:19 tumult in the Philistine camp **increased more and m.** 2143+2143+2256+8041
18: 8 What **m** can he get but the kingdom?" 6388
18:29 Saul *became* still **m** afraid of him, 3578
18:30 David met with **m** success **than** the rest 4946
19: 8 **Once m** war broke out, 3578
19:21 Saul was told about it, and he sent **m** men, 337
21: 5 **How much m so** today!" 677+3954
23: 3 **How much m,** then, if we go to Keilah 677
24:17 "You are **m** righteous **than** I," he said. 4946
2Sa 1:26 **m** wonderful **than** that of women. 4946
4:11 **How much m**—when wicked men have killed an innocent man in his 677
5:10 And he **became m and more powerful,** 1524+2143+2143+2256
5:10 And he **became more and m powerful,** 1524+2143+2143+2256
5:13 David took **m** concubines and wives 6388
5:13 and **m** sons and daughters were born to him. 6388
5:22 **Once m** the Philistines came up 3578+6388
6:22 I will become even **m** undignified **than** this, 4946
7:20 "What **m** can David say to you? 3578+6388
11:12 David said to him, "Stay here one **m** day, 1685
12: 8 *I would have* **given** you **even m.** 2179+2179+2256+3578+3869+3869
13:15 he hated her **m** than he had loved her. 1524
16:11 **How much m,** then, this Benjamite! 677+3954
18: 8 and the forest claimed **m** lives that day than 8049
19:28 to make **any m** appeals to the king?" 6388
19:29 The king said to him, "Why say **m?** 6388
19:34 **"How many m** years will I live, 3869+1537
19:43 of Judah responded **even m** harshly **than** 4946
20: 6 son of Bicri will do us **m** harm **than** Absalom did. 4946
1Ki 1:47 'May your God make Solomon's name **m** famous **than** yours 4946
2:32 were better men and **m** upright **than** he. 4946
8:65 for seven days and seven days **m,** NIH
13:33 but **once m** appointed priests for 8740
14: 9 You have done **m** evil **than** all who lived 4946
14:22 stirred up his jealous anger **m than** their fathers had done. 4946
16:25 of the LORD and sinned **m than** all those 4946
16:30 **m** evil in the eyes of the LORD **than** 4946
16:33 Ahab also made an Asherah pole and did **m** 3578
2Ki 2:12 And Elisha saw him no **m.** 6388
3: 9 the army had **no** *m* water for themselves or AIT
4:35 the bed and stretched out upon him once **m.** NIH
5:13 **How much m,** then, when he tells you, 677
6:16 with us are **m** than those who are 8041
12: 7 Take **no** *m* money from your treasurers, AIT
12: 8 not collect any **m** money from the people NIH
19:30 **Once m** a remnant of the house 3578
21: 9 so that they did **m** evil **than** the nations 4946
21:11 He has done **m** evil than 3972
25:16 was **m than** could be weighed. 4202
1Ch 4: 9 Jabez was **m** honorable **than** his brothers. 4946
11: 9 And David **became m and more powerful,** 1524+2143+2143+2256
11: 9 And David **became more and m powerful,** 1524+2143+2143+2256
14: 3 In Jerusalem David took **m** wives 6388
14: 3 the father of **m** sons and daughters. 6388
14:13 **Once m** the Philistines raided the valley; 3578+6388
17:18 "What **m** can David say to you 3578+6388
22: 3 and **m** bronze than could be weighed. 4200+8044
22: 4 He also provided **m** cedar logs **than** 401+4200
23: 3 thirty years old or **m** were counted, 2025+5087
23:24 twenty years old or **m** who served 2025+5087
23:27 those twenty years old or **m.** 2025+4200+5087
2Ch 7: 9 and the festival for seven days **m.** NIH
9:12 he gave her **m than** she had brought to him. 963+4200+4946
11:21 of Absalom **m than** any of his other wives 4946
15:19 There was **no** *m* war until AIT
17:12 became **m and more powerful;** 1541+2025+2143+2256+4200+5087+6330
17:12 became **more and m powerful;** 1541+2025+2143+2256+4200+5087+6330
20:25 **m** *than* they could take away. 401+4200
25: 5 mustered those twenty years old or **m** 2025+5087
25: 9 The LORD can give you much **m than** that. 4946
28:22 even **m** unfaithful to the LORD. 3578
29:17 For eight **m** days they consecrated NIH
2Ch 29:34 **m** conscientious in consecrating themselves **than** the priests 4946
30:23 to celebrate the festival seven **m** days; 337
31:16 or **m** whose names were in 2025+5087
31:17 to the Levites twenty years old or **m,** 2025+5087
33: 9 so that they did **m** evil **than** the nations 4946
36:14 **m and more unfaithful,** 5085+5086+8049
36:14 **more and m unfaithful,** 5085+5086+8049
Ezr 4:13 **no** *m* taxes, tribute or duty will be paid, AIT
Ne 5:12 we will not demand anything **m** from them. NIH
7: 2 and feared God **m than** most men do. 4946
13:18 Now you *are* **stirring up m** wrath 3578
Est 2:17 Esther **m than** to any of the other women, 4946
2:17 his favor and approval **m than** any of 4946
9: 4 **became m and more powerful.** 1524+2143+2256
9: 4 **became more and m powerful.** 1524+2143+2256
Job 3: 5 and deep shadow claim it once **m;** NIH
3:21 for it **m than** for hidden treasure, 4946
4:17 'Can a mortal be **m** righteous **than** God? 4946
4:17 Can a man be **m** pure **than** his Maker? 4946
4:19 **how much m** those who live in houses of clay, 677
4:19 are crushed **m readily than** a moth! 4200+7156
7: 8 you will look for me, but I will **be no m.** 401
7:10 his place will know him no **m.** 6388
7:21 you will search for me, but I will **be no m."** 401
8:12 they wither **m quickly than** grass. 4200+7156
8:22 and the tents of the wicked will **be no m."** 401
9:34 so that his terror would frighten me no *m.* AIT
11:12 a witless man can **no m** become wise **than** 2256
14:10 he breathes his last and is **no m.** 361
14:12 till the heavens are **no m,** 1194
20: 8 **no** *m* to be found, AIT
20: 9 his place will look on him no **m.** 6388
23:12 of his mouth **m than** my daily bread. 4946
27:19 He lies down wealthy, but *will* **do so no m;** 665
29:22 After I had spoken, *they* spoke no **m;** 9101
32: 5 that the three men had **nothing** *m* to say, AIT
32:15 "They are dismayed and have no **m** to say; 6388
34:31 'I am guilty but will offend no *m.* AIT
35:11 who teaches **m** to us **than** to the beasts of 4946
36: 2 that there is **m** to be said in God's behalf. 6388
40: 5 twice, but *I will* say no **m."** 3578
42:12 the latter part of Job's life **m than** the first. 4946
Ps 10:18 who is of the earth, may terrify no **m.** 3578+6388
12: 1 Help, LORD, for the godly *are* **no m;** 1698
19:10 They are **m** precious **than** gold, 4946
37:10 A little while, and the wicked will **be no m;** 401
37:36 but he soon passed away and **was no m;** 401
39:13 before I depart and **am no m."** 401
40:12 *They are* **m** than the hairs of my head, 6793
55:21 his words are **m** soothing **than** oil, 4946
59:13 consume them till they **are no m.** 401
69:31 This will please the LORD **m than** an ox, 4946
69:31 **m** than a bull with its horns and hoofs. NIH
71:14 *I will* praise you **m and more.** 3578+3972+6584
71:14 *I will* praise you **more and m.** 3578+3972+6584
72: 7 till the moon is **no m.** 1172
75: 4 '**Boast no** *m,*' and to the wicked, AIT
76: 4 **m** majestic **than** mountains rich with game. 4946
78:29 They ate till they had **m than** enough, 4394
83: 4 the name of Israel be remembered no **m."** 6388
87: 2 of Zion **m than** all the dwellings of Jacob. 4946
88: 5 whom you remember no **m,** 6388
89: 7 is **m** awesome **than** all who surround him. 6584
103:16 and its place remembers it no **m.** 6388
104:35 from the earth and the wicked be no **m.** 6388
116: 7 *Be* at rest **once m,** O my soul, 8740
119:72 **m** precious to me **than** thousands of pieces 4946
119:99 I have **m** insight **than** all my teachers, 4946
119:100 I have **m** understanding **than** the elders, 4946
119:127 I love your commands **m than** gold, 4946
119:127 **m than** pure gold, 4946
120: 3 What will he do to you, and what **m besides** 3578
130: 6 My soul waits for the Lord **m than** 4946
130: 6 **m** than watchmen wait for the morning. NIH
Pr 3:14 for she is **m** profitable **than** silver 4946
3:15 She is **m** precious **than** rubies; 4946
8:11 for wisdom is **m** precious **than** rubies, 4946
11:24 One man gives freely, yet gains **even m;** 6388
11:31 **how much m** the ungodly and the sinner! 677+3954
12: 7 Wicked men are overthrown and **are no m,** 401
15:11 **how much m** the hearts of men! 677+3954
17:10 of discernment **m than** a hundred lashes 4946
18:19 An offended brother is **m** unyielding **than** 4946
19: 7 **how much m** do his friends avoid him! 677+3954
21: 3 **m** acceptable to the LORD **than** 4946
21:26 All day long *he* **craves for m,** 203+9294
21:27 **how much m so** when brought with evil intent! 677+3954
22: 1 good name is **m** desirable **than** great riches; 4946
25: 1 These are **m** proverbs of Solomon, 1685
26:12 There is **m** hope for a fool **than** 4946
28:23 in the end gain **m** favor **than** he who has 4946
29:20 There is **m** hope **for** a fool than for him. 4200
31: 7 and remember their misery no **m.** 6388
31:10 She is worth far **m than** rubies. 4946
Ecc 1: 8 things are wearisome, **m than** one can say. 4202
1:16 in wisdom **m than** anyone who has ruled 6584
1:18 the **m** knowledge, the more grief. 3578
1:18 the more knowledge, the **m** grief. 3578
2: 7 also owned **m** herds and flocks than anyone 2221
2:12 **What m** can the king's successor do than what has already been done? 3954+4537
6: 5 it has **m** rest **than** does that man— 4946
6:11 The **m** the words, the less the meaning, 2221

Ecc 7:19 Wisdom makes one wise man **m** powerful **than** ten rulers 4946
7:26 I find **m** bitter **than** death the woman who is 4946
9:17 words of the wise are **m** to be heeded **than** 4946
10:10 *m* **strength** is needed but skill will bring AIT
SS 1:2 for your love is **m** delightful **than** wine. 4946
1:4 we will praise your love **m than** wine. 4946
4:10 **much m** pleasing is your love **than** 4946
Isa 1:11 *"I* **have m than enough** *of* burnt offerings, 8425
5:4 What **m** could have been done 6388
9:1 be **no** *m* gloom for those who were AIT
13:12 **m** rare **than** the gold of Ophir. 4946
15:9 but I will bring **still m** upon Dimon— 3578
19:7 will blow away and **be no m.** 401
23:12 He said, "No **m** *of* your reveling, 3578+6388
25:2 the foreigners' stronghold a city **no m;** 4946
26:14 They are now dead, they live **no** *m;* AIT
29:14 **once m** I will astound these people 3578
29:19 **Once m** the humble will rejoice in 3578
30:10 They say to the seers, **"See** no *m* **visions!"** AIT
30:10 **"Give** us no *m* **visions** AIT
30:19 *you will* **weep** no *m.* AIT
30:20 your teachers will be hidden no **m;** 6388
32:10 **In little m than** a year you who feel 3427+6584
33:19 You will see those arrogant people **no** *m,* AIT
37:31 **Once m** a remnant of the house 3578
43:25 and remembers your sins **no** *m.* AIT
47:1 No **m** will you be called tender or delicate. 3578
47:5 no **m** will you be called queen of kingdoms. 3578
49:20 **give** us **m space** to live in.' 5602
54:1 because **m** are the children of the desolate 8041
54:4 remember no **m** the reproach of your 6388
60:19 The sun will no **m** be your light by day, 6388
60:20 and your moon will wane **no** *m;* AIT
65:19 and of crying will be heard in it no **m.** 6388
Jer 2:31 we will come to you no **m'?** 6388
3:11 "Faithless Israel is **m** righteous **than** unfaithful Judah. 4946
7:26 and did **m** evil **than** their forefathers.' 4946
7:32 in Topheth until **there is no** *m* room. AIT
10:20 My sons are gone from me and **are no m;** 401
11:19 that his name be remembered no **m."** 6388
15:8 I will make their widows **m** numerous **than** 4946
16:12 you have behaved **m** wickedly **than** your fathers. 4946
19:11 in Topheth until **there is no** *m* room. AIT
20:9 "I will not mention him or speak **any m** 6388
22:15 a king *to* **have m and more** cedar? 3013
22:15 a king *to* **have more and m** cedar? 3013
25:27 and fall to rise **no** *m* because of the sword AIT
31:12 and *they will* sorrow no **m.** 3578+6388
31:15 because her children **are no m."** 401
31:34 and will remember their sins no **m."** 6388
32:43 **Once m** fields will be bought in this land 2256
33:10 there will be heard **once m** 6388
38:27 So *they* **said no m** to him, 3087
46:23 They are **m** numerous **than** locusts, 4946
48:2 Moab will be praised no **m;** 6388
49:10 and he *will* **be no m.** 401
51:64 'So will Babylon sink to rise **no** *m* because AIT
52:20 was **m than** could be weighed. 4202
La 2:9 the law **is no m,** and her prophets no longer 401
4:7 their bodies **m** ruddy **than** rubies, 4946
5:7 Our fathers sinned and **are no m,** 401
Eze 5:6 against my laws and decrees **m than** 4946
5:7 You have been **m** unruly **than** the nations 4946
5:16 *I will* **bring m and more** famine upon you 3578
5:16 *I will* **bring more and m** famine upon you 3578
8:6 that are **even m** detestable." 1524
8:13 that are **even m** detestable." 1524
8:15 that are **even m** detestable than this." 1524
12:24 For there will be no **m** false visions 6388
16:47 in all your ways you soon became **m** depraved **than** they. 4946
16:51 *You have* **done m** detestable things than they, 8049
16:52 Because your sins were **m** vile **than** theirs, 4946
16:52 they appear **m** righteous **than** you. 4946
21:32 you will be remembered **no** *m;* AIT
23:11 she was **m** depraved **than** her sister. 4946
23:19 Yet *she became* **m and more** promiscuous 8049
23:19 Yet *she became* **more and m** promiscuous 8049
26:13 the music of your harps will be heard no **m.** 6388
26:21 to a horrible end and you *will* **be no m.** 401
27:36 to a horrible end and will be no **m.' "** 6330+6409
28:19 to a horrible end and will be no **m.' "** 6330+6409
32:19 *'Are you* **m favored** than others? 5838
33:32 to them you are **nothing m than** one who sings love songs 3869
36:11 and will make you prosper **m than** before. 4946
42:5 **m** space from them **than** 4946
Da 2:7 **Once m** they replied, 10766
2:43 **any m than** iron mixes with clay. 10168+10195+10341
5:9 King Belshazzar became **even m** terrified 10678
5:9 and his face grew **m** pale. NIH
7:20 that looked **m** imposing **than** the others 10427
11:2 Three **m** kings will appear in Persia, 6388
11:19 will stumble and fall, to be seen **no** *m.* AIT
Hos 4:7 *The* **m** the priests increased, 3869
4:7 *the* **m** they sinned against me; 4027
10:1 As his fruit increased, *he* **built m** altars; 8049
11:2 But the **m** I called Israel, the further they NIH
13:2 Now they sin **m and more;** 3578
13:2 Now they sin **more and m;** 3578
14:8 O Ephraim, what **m** have I to do with idols? 6388
Am 4:4 go to Gilgal and sin **yet m.** 8049
Jnh 3:4 "Forty **m** days and Nineveh will 6388
4:11 But Nineveh has **m** than a hundred and twenty thousand people who cannot 2221
Na 1:12 I will afflict you no **m.** 6388
1:15 No **m** will the wicked invade you; 3578+6388
3:16 till they are **m than** the stars of the sky, 4946
Hab 1:13 up those **m** righteous **than** themselves? 4946
Hag 2:6 while I will once **m** shake the heavens and 6388
Zec 13:2 and they will be remembered no **m,"** 6388
Mt 2:18 because they are **no m."** *4024*
3:11 will come one who is **m powerful** than I, *2708*
5:47 what are you doing **m** than others? *4356*
6:25 Is not life **m** *important than* food, *4498*
6:25 and the body **m** important than clothes? *NIG*
6:26 *Are* you not much **m valuable than** they? *1422*
6:30 will he not much **m** clothe you, *3437*
7:11 how much **m** will your Father *3437*
10:15 be **m bearable** for Sodom and Gomorrah on *445*
10:25 how much **m** the members of his household! *3437*
10:31 you *are* **worth m than** many sparrows. *1422*
10:37 or mother **m than** me is not worthy of me; *5642*
10:37 or daughter **m than** me is not worthy of me; *5642*
11:9 Yes, I tell you, and **m than** a prophet. *4358*
11:22 it will be **m bearable** for Tyre and Sidon on *445*
11:24 that it will be **m bearable** for Sodom on *445*
12:12 **How much m** valuable is a man than a sheep! *4531*
12:45 seven other spirits **m wicked than** itself, *4505*
13:12 Whoever has will be given **m,** *NIG*
20:10 they expected to receive **m.** *4498*
21:36 **m** *than* the first time, *4498*
22:4 "Then he sent **some m** servants and said, *257*
22:46 to ask him **any m** questions. *4033*
23:23 the *m* **important matters** of the law— *AIT*
25:16 to work and gained five **m.** *257*
25:17 the one with the two talents gained two **m.** *257*
25:20 See, I have gained five **m.'** *257*
25:22 see, I have gained two **m.'** *257*
25:29 For everyone who has will be given **m,** *NIG*
26:44 So he left them and went away **once m** *4099*
26:53 at my disposal **m** *than* twelve legions *4498*
26:65 Why do we need **any m** witnesses? *2285*
Mk 1:7 After me will come one **m powerful than** I, *2708*
4:24 measured to you—**and even m.** *2779+4707+5148*
4:25 Whoever has will be given **m;** *NIG*
5:3 and no one could bind him **any m,** *4033*
5:35 "Why bother the teacher **any m?"** *2285*
7:36 But the **m** he did so, *4012*
7:36 the **m** they kept talking about it. *3437+4358*
8:25 **Once m** Jesus put his hands on *1663+4099*
10:26 The disciples were **even m** amazed, *4360*
10:48 but he **shouted all the m,** "Son of David, *3189+3437+4498*
12:33 is **m important than** all burnt offerings *4358*
12:34 on no one dared ask him any **m** questions. *NIG*
12:43 this poor widow has put **m** into *4498*
14:5 It could have been sold for **m than** *2062*
14:39 **Once m** he went away and prayed *4099*
14:63 "Why do we need **any m** witnesses?" *2285*
Lk 3:13 "Don't collect any **m** *than* you are required *4123+4498*
3:16 But one **m powerful than** I will come, *2708*
5:15 Yet the news about him spread **all the m,** *3437*
7:26 Yes, I tell you, and **m than** a prophet. *4358*
7:42 Now which of them will love him **m?"** *4498*
8:8 a hundred times **m** than was sown." *NIG*
8:18 Whoever has will be given **m;** *NIG*
8:49 **"Don't** bother the teacher **any m."** *3600*
10:12 be **m bearable** on that day for Sodom than *445*
10:14 be **m bearable** for Tyre and Sidon at *445*
11:13 how much **m** will your Father *3437*
11:26 seven other spirits **m wicked than** itself, *4505*
12:4 the body and after that can do no **m.** *4358*
12:7 *you are* **worth m than** many sparrows. *1422*
12:23 Life is **m** *than* food, *4498*
12:23 and the body **m** than clothes. *NIG*
12:24 how much **m** valuable you are **than** birds! *3437*
12:28 how much **m** will he clothe you, *3437*
12:48 how **much m** will be asked. *4358*
13:4 do you think they were **m** guilty than all *NIG*
13:8 'leave it alone for one **m** year, *NIG*
14:8 **a person m distinguished than** you *1952*
15:7 there will be **m** rejoicing in heaven over one sinner who repents **than** *2445*
16:8 For the people of this world are *m* **shrewd** *AIT*
18:39 but he shouted **all the m,** "Son of David, have mercy on me!" *3437+4498*
19:16 'Sir, your mina *has* **earned** ten **m.'** *4664*
19:18 'Sir, your mina has earned five **m.'** *3641*[S]
19:26 to everyone who has, **m** will be given, *NIG*
20:40 **no** one dared to ask him **any m** questions. *4033*
21:3 "this poor widow has put in **m** *than* all *4498*
22:44 being in anguish, he prayed *m* **earnestly,** *AIT*
22:51 But Jesus answered, **"No m** of this!" *1572*
22:71 "Why do we need **any m** testimony? *2285*
24:21 **And what is m,** it is the third day since *247+1145+2779+4047+4246+5250*
Jn 2:3 "They have no **m** wine." *NIG*
4:1 and baptizing **m** disciples than John, *4498*
4:3 he left Judea and went back **once m** *4099*
4:35 'Four months **m** and then the harvest'? *2285*
4:41 of his words many **m** became believers. *4498*
4:46 **Once m** he visited Cana in Galilee, *4099*
7:31 he do **m** miraculous signs *than* this man?" *4498*
8:21 **Once m** Jesus said to them, *4099*
11:6 he stayed where he was two **m** days. *NIG*
11:38 Jesus, **once m** deeply moved, *4099*
Jn 12:43 praise from men **m** than praise from God. *3437*
15:2 so that it will be even **m** fruitful. *4498*
16:12 "I have much **m** to say to you, *2285*
16:12 **m** than you can now bear. *NIG*
16:16 "In a little while you will see me **no m,** *4033*
16:17 'In a little while you will see me **no m,** *4024*
16:19 'In a little while you will see me **no m,** *4024*
17:14 world **any m than** I am of the world. *2777+4024*
19:4 **Once m** Pilate came out and said to *2779+4099*
19:8 he was even **m** afraid, *3437*
21:15 do you truly love me **m** *than* these?" *4498*
Ac 5:14 **m and more** men and women believed in *3437*
5:14 **more and m** men and women believed in *3437*
7:31 As he went over *to* **look m closely,** *2917*
9:22 Yet Saul grew **m** and more powerful *3437*
9:22 and **m** powerful and baffled the Jews living *NIG*
17:11 Bereans were **of m noble character than** *2302*
18:20 When they asked him to spend **m** time *4498*
18:26 to him the way of God **m adequately.** *209*
20:35 'It is **m** blessed to give than to receive.' " *3437*
23:13 **M than** forty men were involved *4498*
23:15 pretext of wanting *m* **accurate** information *AIT*
23:20 pretext of wanting *m* **accurate** information *AIT*
23:21 because **m than** forty of them are waiting *4498*
24:11 that no **m than** twelve days ago I went up *4498*
Ro 3:5 **brings out** God's righteousness **m clearly,** *5319*
5:9 how much **m** shall we be saved *3437*
5:10 how much **m,** having been reconciled, *3437*
5:15 how much **m** did God's grace and the gift *3437*
5:17 much **m** will those who receive God's abundant provision of grace *3437*
5:20 sin increased, grace **increased all the m,** *5668*
8:34 **m than that,** who was raised to life— *3437*
8:37 in all these things *we are* **m than conquerors** through him *5664*
11:24 how much **m** readily will these, *3437*
12:3 of yourself **m** highly **than** you ought, *4123*
14:5 One man considers one day **m** sacred **than** another; *4123*
15:23 now that there is **no m** place for me to work *3600*
1Co 3:21 So then, no **m** boasting about men! *NIG*
6:3 **How much m** the things of this life! *3615*
9:12 shouldn't we have it **all the m?** *3437*
11:17 for your meetings do **m** harm than good. *NIG*
14:18 that I speak in tongues **m than** all of you. *3437*
15:6 to **m than** five hundred of the brothers at *2062*
15:15 **M than that,** we are then found to *2779*
15:19 we are to be **pitied m than** all men. *1795*
2Co 3:8 of the Spirit be even **m** glorious? *3437*
3:9 how much **m** glorious is the ministry *3437*
4:15 grace that *is* **reaching m and more** people may cause thanksgiving *1328+3836+4429+4498*
4:15 grace that *is* **reaching more and m** people may cause thanksgiving *1328+3836+4429+4498*
8:19 **What is m,** he was chosen by the churches *247+1254+2779+3667+4024*
8:22 zealous, and now **even m** so because *4498+5080*[S]
11:23 I am **m.** I have worked much harder, *5642*
11:23 been in prison **m frequently,** *4359*
11:23 been flogged **m severely,** *5649*
12:6 no one will think **m** of me **than** is warranted *5642*
12:9 Therefore I will boast **all the m** gladly *3437*
12:15 If I love you **m,** will you love me less? *4359*
Gal 4:27 because **m** are the children of the desolate *4498*
Eph 3:20 to do immeasurably **m than** all we ask *5642*
4:19 with a continual lust for **m.** *NIG*
Php 1:9 that your love may abound **m** and more *3437*
1:9 and **m** in knowledge and depth of insight, *3437*
1:14 to speak the word of God **m** courageously *4359*
1:24 but it is **m necessary** for you that I remain *338*
2:12 but now much **m** in my absence— *3437*
2:28 I am **all the m eager** to send him, *5081*
3:4 to put confidence in the flesh, I have **m:** *3437*
3:8 **What is m,** I consider everything *247+3529*
4:18 I have received full payment and even **m;** *4355*
1Th 4:1 to **do this m and more.** *3437+4355*
4:1 to **do this more and m.** *3437+4355*
4:10 to **do so m and more.** *3437+4355*
4:10 to **do so more and m.** *3437+4355*
2Th 1:3 because your faith *is* **growing m and more,** *5647*
1:3 because your faith *is* **growing more and m,** *5647*
2Ti 2:16 it will become **m and more** ungodly. *2093+4498*
2:16 it will become **more and m** ungodly. *2093+4498*
Phm 1:21 knowing that you will do even **m than** I ask *5642*
1:22 And **one thing m:** Prepare a guest room *275*
Heb 2:1 We must pay **m careful** attention, *4359*
7:15 And what we have said is even **m** clear *4358*
8:12 and will remember their sins no **m."** *2285*
9:11 the greater and *m* **perfect** tabernacle that is *AIT*
9:14 How much **m,** then, will the blood *3437*
10:17 and lawless acts I will remember no **m."** *2285*
10:25 **all the m** as you see the Day approaching. *3437+5537*
10:29 How much **m severely** do you think *5937*
11:32 And what **m** shall I say? *2285*
12:9 How much **m** should we submit to *3437*
12:26 "Once **m** I will shake not only the earth but *2285*
12:27 The words "once **m"** indicate the removing *2285*
Jas 3:1 that we who teach will be judged **m** strictly. *3505*
4:6 But he gives us **m** grace. *3505*
2Pe 1:10 be **all the m** eager to make your calling *3437*
1:19 the word of the prophets made *m* **certain,** *AIT*
2:11 although they are stronger and **m** powerful, *3505*
Rev 2:19 and that you are now doing **m** *than* you did *4498*
10:6 and said, "There will be **no m** delay! *4033*
10:8 from heaven spoke to me **once m:** *4099*
18:11 because no one buys their cargoes **any m—** *4033*

Rev 21: 4 There will be no **m** death or mourning *2285*
22: 5 There will be no **m** night. *2285*

MOREH (3)

Ge 12: 6 the site of the great tree of **M** at Shechem. 4622
Dt 11:30 near the great trees of **M,** 4622
Jdg 7: 1 of them in the valley near the hill of **M.** 4622

MOREOVER (33)

Ge 31:20 **M,** Jacob deceived Laban the Aramean by 2256
Ex 6: 5 **M,** I have heard the groaning of 1685+2256
31: 6 **M,** I have appointed Oholiab son 2256
Nu 16:14 **M,** you haven't brought us into 677
Dt 7:20 **M,** the LORD your God will send 1685+2256
17:16 **m,** must not acquire great numbers 8370
2Sa 8: 3 **M,** David fought Hadadezer son of Rehob, 2256
11:17 **m,** Uriah the Hittite died. 1685+2256
11:24 **M,** your servant Uriah the Hittite is dead." 1685+2256
1Ki 1:46 **M,** Solomon has taken his seat on 1685+2256
3:13 **M,** I will give you what you have 1685+2256
16: 7 **M,** the word of the LORD came 1685+2256
2Ki 21:16 **M,** Manasseh also shed so much innocent 1685
1Ch 18: 3 **M,** David fought Hadadezer king of Zobah, 2256
Ezr 1: 7 **M,** King Cyrus brought out the articles 2256
6: 8 **M,** I hereby decree what you are to do 10221
7:15 **M,** you are to take with you the silver 10221
Ne 5:14 **M,** from the twentieth year 1685
6: 6 **M,** according to these reports you are about 2256
6:19 **M,** they kept reporting to me 1685
10:37 "**M,** we will bring to the storerooms of 2256
13:23 **M,** in those days I saw men 1685
Ecc 5:19 **M,** when God gives any man wealth 1685
9: 3 The hearts of men, **m,** 1685+2256
9:12 **M,** no man knows when his hour 1685+3954
Jer 12: 4 **M,** the people are saying, 3954
21:11 "**M,** say to the royal house of Judah, 2256
La 4:17 **M,** our eyes failed, looking in vain for help; 6388
Da 2:49 **M,** at Daniel's request the king 10221
Lk 4:41 **M,** demons came out of many people, *1254*
Jn 5:22 **M,** the Father judges no one, *1142*
Php 4:15 **M,** as you Philippians know, *1254*
Heb 12: 9 **M,** we have all had human fathers who disciplined us *1663*

MORESHETH (2) [MORESHETH GATH]

Jer 26:18 "Micah **of M** prophesied in the days 4629
Mic 1: 1 to Micah **of M** during the reigns of Jotham, 4629

MORESHETH GATH (1) [MORESHETH]

Mic 1:14 Therefore you will give parting gifts to **M.** 4628

MORIAH (2)

Ge 22: 2 whom you love, and go to the region of **M.** 5317
2Ch 3: 1 of the LORD in Jerusalem on Mount **M,** 5317

MORNING (218) [MORNING'S, MORNINGS]

Ge 1: 5 And there was evening, and there was **m**— 1332
1: 8 And there was evening, and there was **m**— 1332
1:13 And there was evening, and there was **m**— 1332
1:19 And there was evening, and there was **m**— 1332
1:23 And there was evening, and there was **m**— 1332
1:31 And there was evening, and there was **m**— 1332
19: 2 and then go on your way **early in the m.**" 8899
19:27 the next **m** Abraham got up and returned to 1332
20: 8 the next **m** Abimelech summoned all his officials, 1332
21:14 Early the next **m** Abraham took some food 1332
22: 3 Early the next **m** Abraham got up 1332
24:54 When they got up the next **m,** he said, 1332
26:31 Early the next **m** the men swore an oath 1332
28:18 Early the next **m** Jacob took 1332
29:25 When **m** came, there was Leah! 1332
31:55 the next **m** Laban kissed his grandchildren 1332
40: 6 When Joseph came to them the next **m,** 1332
41: 8 In the **m** his mind was troubled, 1332
44: 3 As **m** dawned, the men were sent 1332
49:27 in the **m** he devours the prey, 1332
Ex 7:15 Go to Pharaoh in the **m** as he goes out to 1332
8:20 "Get up early in the **m** and confront Pharaoh 1332
9:13 "Get up early in the **m,** 1332
10:13 *By* **m** the wind had brought the locusts; 1332
12:10 Do not leave any of it till **m;** 1332
12:10 if some is left till **m,** you must burn it. 1332
12:22 the door of his house until **m.** 1332
16: 7 the **m** you will see the glory of the LORD, 1332
16: 8 and all the bread you want in the **m,** 1332
16:12 and in the **m** you will be filled with bread. 1332
16:13 in the **m** there was a layer of dew around 1332
16:19 "No one is to keep any of it until **m.**" 1332
16:20 they kept part of it until **m,** 1332
16:21 **Each m** everyone gathered as much as he needed, 928+928+1332+1332+2021+2021
16:23 Save whatever is left and keep it until **m.**' " 1332
16:24 So they saved it until **m,** 1332
18:13 they stood around him from **m** till evening. 1332
18:14 around you from **m** till evening?" 1332
19:16 On the **m** of the third day there was thunder 1332
23:18 not be kept until **m.** 1332
24: 4 He got up early the next **m** and built an altar 1332
27:21 before the LORD from evening till **m.** 1332
29:34 or any bread is left over till **m,** 1332
29:39 Offer one in the **m** and the other at twilight. 1332
29:41 and its drink offering as in the **m**— 1332
30: 7 Aaron must burn fragrant incense on the altar **every m** 928+928+1332+1332+2021+2021
34: 2 Be ready in the **m,** and then come up 1332
34: 4 the **m,** as the LORD had commanded him; 1332
34:25 from the Passover Feast remain until **m.** 1332
36: 3 to bring freewill offerings **m** after morning. 1332
36: 3 to bring freewill offerings morning after **m.** 1332
Lev 6: 9 the altar hearth throughout the night, till **m,** 1332
6:12 **Every m** the priest is to add firewood 928+928+1332+1332+2021+2021
6:20 half of it in the **m** and half in the evening. 1332
7:15 he must leave none of it till **m.** 1332
22:30 leave none of it till **m.** 1332
24: 3 before the LORD from evening till **m,** 1332
Nu 9:12 not leave any of it till **m** or break any 1332
9:15 till **m** the cloud above the tabernacle looked 1332
9:21 the cloud stayed only from evening till **m,** 1332
9:21 and when it lifted in the **m,** they set out. 1332
14:40 Early the next **m** they went up toward 1332
16: 5 the **m** the LORD will show who belongs 1332
22:13 The next **m** Balaam got up and said 1332
22:21 Balaam got up in the **m,** 1332
22:41 The next **m** Balak took Balaam up 1332
28: 4 Prepare one lamb in the **m** and the other 1332
28: 8 that you prepare in the **m.** 1332
28:23 in addition to the regular **m** burnt offering. 1332
Dt 16: 4 the evening of the first day remain until **m.** 1332
16: 7 Then in the **m** return to your tents. 1332
28:67 In the **m** you will say, 1332
28:67 and in the evening, "If only it were **m!**"— 1332
Jos 3: 1 in the **m** Joshua and all the Israelites set out 1332
6:12 the next **m** and the priests took up the ark of 1332
7:14 " 'In the **m,** present yourselves tribe 1332
7:16 the next **m** Joshua had Israel come forward 1332
8:10 Early the next **m** Joshua mustered his men, 1332
8:14 of the city hurried out **early in the m** 8899
Jdg 6:28 In the **m** when the men of the town got up, 1332
6:31 for him shall be put to death by **m!** 1332
7: 1 **Early in the m,** Jerub-Baal (that is, 8899
9:33 In the **m** at sunrise, advance against the city. 1332
19: 8 On the **m** of the fifth day, 1332
19: 9 **Early** tomorrow **m** *you can* **get up** 8899
19:27 in the **m** and opened the door of the house 1332
20:19 The next **m** the Israelites got up 1332
Ru 2: 7 the field and has worked steadily from **m** till 1332
3:13 and in the **m** if he wants to redeem, good; 1332
3:13 Lie here until **m.**" 1332
3:14 So she lay at his feet until **m,** 1332
1Sa 1:19 the next **m** they arose and worshiped before 1332
3:15 down until **m** and then opened the doors of 1332
5: 4 But the following **m** when they rose, 1332
9:19 the **m** I will let you go and will tell you all 1332
15:12 the **m** Samuel got up and went to meet Saul, 1332
17:16 the Philistine came forward *every* **m** 8899
17:20 the **m** David left the flock with a shepherd, 1332
19: 2 Be on your guard tomorrow **m;** 1332
19:11 to watch it and to kill him in the **m.** 1332
20:35 In the **m** Jonathan went out to the field 1332
25:22 if by **m** I leave alive one male 1332
25:37 Then in the **m,** when Nabal was sober, 1332
29:10 and leave in the **m** as soon as it is light." 1332
29:11 and his men got up early in the **m** to go back 1332
2Sa 2:27 the pursuit of their brothers until **m.**" 1332
11:14 In the **m** David wrote a letter to Joab 1332
13: 4 look so haggard **m** after morning? 1332
13: 4 look so haggard morning after **m?** 1332
23: 4 of **m** at sunrise on a cloudless morning, 1332
23: 4 of morning at sunrise on a cloudless **m,** 1332
24:11 Before David got up the next **m,** 1332
24:15 a plague on Israel from that **m** till the end 1332
1Ki 3:21 The next **m,** I got up to nurse my son— 1332
3:21 I looked at him closely in the **m light,** 1332
17: 6 in the **m** and bread and meat in the evening, 1332
18:26 on the name of Baal from **m** till noon. 1332
2Ki 3:20 The next **m,** about the time for offering 1332
3:22 When they got up early in the **m,** 1332
6:15 up and went out **early the next m,** 8899
10: 8 at the entrance of the city gate until **m.**" 1332
10: 9 The next **m** Jehu went out. 1332
16:15 offer the **m** burnt offering and 1332
19:35 When the people got up the next **m**— 1332
1Ch 9:27 had charge of the key for opening it **each m.** 1332+1332+2021+2021+4200+4200
16:40 of burnt offering regularly, **m** and evening, 1332
23:30 They were also to stand **every m** to thank and praise 928+928+1332+1332+2021+2021
2Ch 2: 4 and for making burnt offerings every **m** 1332
13:11 **Every m** and evening they present burnt offerings 928+928+1332+1332+2021+2021
20:20 in the **m** they left for the Desert of Tekoa. 1332
29:20 **Early the next m** King Hezekiah gathered 8899
31: 3 the **m** and evening burnt offerings and for 1332
Ezr 3: 3 both the **m** and evening sacrifices. 1332
Est 2:14 the **m** return to another part of the harem to 1332
5:14 the king in the **m** to have Mordecai hanged 1332
Job 1: 5 in the **m** he would sacrifice a burnt offering 1332
3: 9 May its **m** stars become dark; 5974
7:18 that you examine him every **m** 1332
11:17 and darkness will become like **m.** 1332
24:17 For all of them, deep darkness is their **m;** 1332
38: 7 while the **m** stars sang together and all 1332
38:12 "Have you ever given orders to the **m,** 1332
Ps 5: 3 *In* the **m,** O LORD, you hear my voice; 1332
5: 3 the **m** I lay my requests before you and wait 1332
22: T To [the tune of] "The Doe of the **M.**" 8840
30: 5 but rejoicing comes in the **m.** 1332
49:14 The upright will rule over them in the **m;** 1332
55:17 Evening, **m** and noon I cry out in distress, 1332
59:16 in the **m** I will sing of your love; 1332
65: 8 where **m** dawns and evening fades you call 1332
73:14 I have been punished every **m.** 1332
88:13 in the **m** my prayer comes before you. 1332
90: 5 they are like the new grass of the **m**— 1332
90: 6 though in the **m** it springs up new, 1332
90:14 Satisfy us in the **m** with your unfailing love, 1332
92: 2 in the **m** and your faithfulness at night, 1332
101: 8 Every **m** I will put to silence all the wicked 1332
130: 6 for the **m,** more than watchmen wait for 1332
130: 6 more than watchmen wait for the **m.** 1332
143: 8 the **m** bring me word of your unfailing love, 1332
Pr 7:18 Come, let's drink deep of love till **m;** 1332
27:14 a man loudly blesses his neighbor in the **m,** 1332
Ecc 10:16 a servant and whose princes feast in the **m.** 1332
11: 6 Sow your seed in the **m,** 1332
Isa 5:11 Woe to those who rise early in the **m** to run 1332
14:12 you have fallen from heaven, O **m star,** 2122
17:11 and on the **m** when you plant them, 1332
17:14 Before the **m,** they are gone! 1332
21:12 The watchman replies, "**M** is coming, 1332
26: 9 in the **m** my spirit longs for you. 1332
26:19 Your dew is like the dew of the **m;** 245
28:19 **m** after morning, by day and by night, 1332
28:19 morning after **m,** by day and by night, 1332
33: 2 Be our strength every **m,** 1332
37:36 When the people got up the next **m**— 1332
44:22 your sins like the **m mist.** 6727
50: 4 He wakens me **m** by morning, 1332
50: 4 He wakens me morning by **m,** 1332
Jer 20:16 May he hear wailing in the **m,** 1332
21:12 " 'Administer justice every **m;** 1332
La 3:23 They are new every **m;** 1332
Eze 12: 8 the **m** the word of the LORD came to me: 1332
24:18 So I spoke to the people in the **m,** 1332
24:18 The next **m** I did as I had been commanded. 1332
33:22 before the man came to me in the **m.** 1332
46:13 **m** by morning you shall provide it. 1332
46:13 morning by **m** you shall provide it. 1332
46:14 with it **m** by morning a grain offering, 1332
46:14 with it morning by **m** a grain offering, 1332
46:15 and the oil shall be provided **m** by morning 1332
46:15 and the oil shall be provided morning by **m** 1332
Hos 6: 4 Your love is like the **m** mist, 1332
7: 6 in the **m** it blazes like a flaming fire. 1332
13: 3 Therefore they will be like the **m** mist, 1332
Am 4: 4 Bring your sacrifices every **m,** 1332
Zep 3: 3 who leave nothing for the **m.** 1332
3: 5 **M** by morning he dispenses his justice, 1332
3: 5 Morning by **m** he dispenses his justice, 1332
Mt 16: 3 and **in the m,** 'Today it will be stormy, *4745*
20: 1 landowner who went out **early in the m** *275+4745*
21:18 **Early in the m,** as he was on his way *4745*
27: 1 **Early in the m,** all the chief priests and *4746*
Mk 1:35 Very **early in the m,** while it was still dark, *4745*
11:20 **In the m,** as they went along, *4745*
15: 1 **Very early in the m,** the chief priests *2317+4745*
Lk 6:13 When **m** came, he called his disciples *2465*
21:38 all the people **came early in the m** *3983*
24: 1 **very early in the m,** the women took *960+3986*
24:22 They went to the tomb **early this m** *3984*
Jn 18:28 By now it was **early m,** *4745*
21: 4 **Early in the m,** Jesus stood on the shore, *1181+4746*
Ac 2:15 It's only **nine in the m!** *2465+3836+5569+6052*
12:18 **In the m,** there was no small commotion among the soldiers *1181+2465*
23:12 **The next m** the Jews formed a conspiracy *1181+2465*
28:23 From **m** till evening he explained *4745*
2Pe 1:19 until the day dawns and the **m star** rises *5892*
Rev 2:28 I will also give him the **m** star. *4748*
22:16 and the bright **M** Star." *4748*

MORNING'S (2) [MORNING]

Lev 9:17 the altar in addition to the **m** burnt offering. 1332
Mic 2: 1 At **m** light they carry it out because it is 1332

MORNINGS (2) [MORNING]

Da 8:14 "It will take 2,300 evenings and **m;** 1332
8:26 and **m** that has been given you is true, 1332

MORROW (KJV) See FOLLOWING DAY, MORNING, NEXT DAY, TOMORROW

MORSELS (2)

Pr 18: 8 The words of a gossip are like **choice m;** 4269
26:22 The words of a gossip are like **choice m;** 4269

MORTAL (19) [MORTALLY, MORTALS]

Ge 6: 3 not contend with man forever, for he is **m;** 1414
Dt 5:26 For what **m man** has ever heard the voice of 1414
Job 4:17 'Can a **m** be more righteous than God? 632
9: 2 But how can a **m** be righteous before God? 632
10: 4 Do you see as a **m** sees? 632
10: 5 like those of a **m** or your years like those of 632
Ps 17: 9 from my **m** enemies who surround me. 928+5883
42:10 My bones suffer **m agony** 8358
56: 4 What can **m man** do to me? 1414
146: 3 not put your trust in princes, in **m men,** 132+1201

Isa 51:12 Who are you that you fear **m** men, 4637
Eze 31:14 for the earth below, among **m men,** 132+1201
Ro 1:23 to look like **m** man and birds and animals 5778
6:12 not let sin reign in your **m** body so 2570
8:11 the dead will also give life *to* your **m** bodies 2570
1Co 15:53 and the **m** with immortality. 2570
15:54 and the **m** with immortality, 2570
2Co 4:11 that his life may be revealed in our **m** body. 2570
5:4 what *is* **m** may be swallowed up by life. 2570

MORTALITY (KJV) See MORTAL

MORTALLY (1) [MORTAL]

Eze 30:24 before him like a **m wounded man.** 2728

MORTALS (1) [MORTAL]

Isa 31:8 a sword, not *of* **m,** will devour them. 132

MORTAR (6)

Ge 11:3 used brick instead of stone, and tar for **m.** 2817
Ex 1:14 in brick and **m** and with all kinds of work in 2817
Nu 11:8 ground it in a handmill or crushed it in a **m.** 4521
Pr 27:22 Though you grind a fool in a **m,** 4847
Isa 41:25 He treads on rulers as if they were **m,** 2817
Na 3:14 Work the clay, tread the **m,** 2817

MORTER (KJV) See CLAY, MORTAR, PLASTER, WHITEWASH

MORTGAGING (1)

Ne 5:3 Others were saying, "We *are* **m** our fields, 6842

MORTIFY (KJV) See PUT TO DEATH

MOSAIC (1)

Est 1:6 and silver on a **m pavement** *of* porphyry, 8367

MOSERAH (1)

Dt 10:6 from the wells of the Jaakanites to **M.** 4594

MOSEROTH (2)

Nu 33:30 They left Hashmonah and camped at **M.** 5035
33:31 They left **M** and camped at Bene Jaakan. 5035

MOSES (828) [MOSES']

Ex 2:10 She named him **M,** saying, "I drew him out 5407
2:11 One day, after **M** had grown up, 5407
2:14 Then **M** was afraid and thought, 5407
2:15 Pharaoh heard of this, he tried to kill **M,** 5407
2:15 but **M** fled from Pharaoh and went to live 5407
2:17 but **M** got up and came to their rescue 5407
2:21 **M** agreed to stay with the man, 5407
2:21 who gave his daughter Zipporah to **M** 5407
2:22 and **M** named him Gershom, saying, NIH
3:1 Now **M** was tending the flock 5407
3:2 **M** saw that though the bush was NIH
3:3 So **M** thought, "I will go over 5407
3:4 called to him from within the bush, **"M!** 5407
3:4 from within the bush, "Moses! **M!"** 5407
3:4 And **M** said, "Here I am." NIH
3:6 At this, **M** hid his face, 5407
3:11 But **M** said to God, "Who am I, 5407
3:13 **M** said to God, "Suppose I go 5407
3:14 God said to **M,** "I AM WHO I AM. 5407
3:15 God also said to **M,** "Say to the Israelites, 5407
4:1 **M** answered, "What if they do not believe 5407
4:3 **M** threw it on the ground and it became 5407
4:4 So **M** reached out and took hold of 5407
4:6 So **M** put his hand into his cloak, NIH
4:7 So **M** put his hand back into his cloak, NIH
4:10 **M** said to the LORD, "O Lord, 5407
4:13 But **M** said, "O Lord, please send someone NIH
4:14 Then the LORD's anger burned against **M** 5407
4:18 Then **M** went back to Jethro 5407
4:19 Now the LORD had said to **M** in Midian, 5407
4:20 So **M** took his wife and sons, 5407
4:21 The LORD said to **M,** "When you return 5407
4:24 the LORD met **[M]** and was about to kill 2084[S]
4:27 "Go into the desert to meet **M."** 5407
4:27 So he met **M** at the mountain of God 2084[S]
4:28 Then **M** told Aaron everything 5407
4:29 **M** and Aaron brought together all the elders 5407
4:30 the LORD had said to **M.** 5407
5:1 Afterward **M** and Aaron went to Pharaoh 5407
5:4 But the king of Egypt said, **"M** and Aaron, 5407
5:20 they found **M** and Aaron waiting 5407
5:22 **M** returned to the LORD and said, 5407
6:1 the LORD said to **M,** "Now you will see 5407
6:2 God also said to **M,** "I am the LORD. 5407
6:9 **M** reported this to the Israelites, 5407
6:10 Then the LORD said to **M,** 5407
6:12 But **M** said to the LORD, 5407
6:13 the LORD spoke to **M** and Aaron about 5407
6:20 Jochebed, who bore him Aaron and **M.** 5407
6:26 It was this same Aaron and **M** to whom 5407
6:27 It was the same **M** and Aaron. 5407
6:28 when the LORD spoke to **M** in Egypt, 5407
6:30 But **M** said to the LORD, "Since I speak 5407
7:1 Then the LORD said to **M,** "See, 5407

Ex 7:6 **M** and Aaron did just as the LORD 5407
7:7 **M** was eighty years old and Aaron 5407
7:8 The LORD said to **M** and Aaron, 5407
7:10 So **M** and Aaron went to Pharaoh 5407
7:14 Then the LORD said to **M,** 5407
7:19 The LORD said to **M,** "Tell Aaron, 5407
7:20 **M** and Aaron did just as the LORD 5407
7:22 he would not listen to **M and Aaron,** 2157[S]
8:1 Then the LORD said to **M,** "Go to Pharaoh 5407
8:5 Then the LORD said to **M,** "Tell Aaron, 5407
8:8 Pharaoh summoned **M** and Aaron and said, 5407
8:9 **M** said to Pharaoh, "I leave to you 5407
8:10 **M** replied, "It will be as you say, NIH
8:12 After **M** and Aaron left Pharaoh, 5407
8:12 **M** cried out to the LORD about the frogs 5407
8:13 And the LORD did what **M** asked. 5407
8:15 and would not listen to **M and Aaron,** 2157[S]
8:16 Then the LORD said to **M,** "Tell Aaron, 5407
8:20 Then the LORD said to **M,** "Get up early 5407
8:25 Pharaoh summoned **M** and Aaron and said, 5407
8:26 But **M** said, "That would not be right. 5407
8:29 **M** answered, "As soon as I leave you, 5407
8:30 **M** left Pharaoh and prayed to the LORD, 5407
8:31 and the LORD did what **M** asked: 5407
9:1 Then the LORD said to **M,** "Go to Pharaoh 5407
9:8 Then the LORD said to **M** and Aaron, 5407
9:8 a furnace and have **M** toss it into the air in 5407
9:10 **M** tossed it into the air, 5407
9:11 The magicians could not stand before **M** 5407
9:12 and he would not listen to **M and Aaron,** 2157[S]
9:12 just as the LORD had said to **M.** 5407
9:13 Then the LORD said to **M,** "Get up early 5407
9:22 Then the LORD said to **M,** "Stretch out 5407
9:23 **M** stretched out his staff toward the sky, 5407
9:27 Then Pharaoh summoned **M** and Aaron. 5407
9:29 **M** replied, "When I have gone out of 5407
9:33 **M** left Pharaoh and went out of the city. 5407
9:35 just as the LORD had said through **M.** 5407
10:1 Then the LORD said to **M,** "Go to Pharaoh 5407
10:3 So **M** and Aaron went to Pharaoh and said 5407
10:6 Then **M** turned and left Pharaoh. NIH
10:8 Then **M** and Aaron were brought back 5407
10:9 **M** answered, "We will go with our young 5407
10:11 Then **M and Aaron** were driven out 4392[S]
10:12 And the LORD said to **M,** "Stretch out 5407
10:13 So **M** stretched out his staff over Egypt, 5407
10:16 Pharaoh quickly summoned **M** and Aaron 5407
10:18 **M** then left Pharaoh and prayed to the LORD NIH
10:21 Then the LORD said to **M,** "Stretch out 5407
10:22 So **M** stretched out his hand toward the sky, 5407
10:24 Then Pharaoh summoned **M** and said, "Go, 5407
10:25 But **M** said, "You must allow us 5407
10:28 Pharaoh said to **M,** "Get out of my sight! 2257[S]
10:29 "Just as you say," **M** replied, 5407
11:1 Now the LORD had said to **M,** 5407
11:3 and **M** himself was highly regarded 5407
11:4 So **M** said, "This is what the LORD says: 5407
11:8 Then **M,** hot with anger, left Pharaoh. NIH
11:9 The LORD had said to **M,** "Pharaoh will 5407
11:10 **M** and Aaron performed all these wonders 5407
12:1 The LORD said to **M** and Aaron in Egypt, 5407
12:21 Then **M** summoned all the elders of Israel 5407
12:28 the LORD commanded **M** and Aaron. 5407
12:31 the night Pharaoh summoned **M** and Aaron 5407
12:35 The Israelites did as **M** instructed and asked 5407
12:43 The LORD said to **M** and Aaron, 5407
12:50 the LORD had commanded **M** and Aaron. 5407
13:1 The LORD said to **M,** 5407
13:3 Then **M** said to the people, "Commemorate 5407
13:19 **M** took the bones of Joseph with him 5407
14:1 Then the LORD said to **M,** 5407
14:11 They said to **M,** "Was it because 5407
14:13 **M** answered the people, "Do not be afraid. 5407
14:15 Then the LORD said to **M,** "Why are you 5407
14:21 Then **M** stretched out his hand over the sea, 5407
14:26 Then the LORD said to **M,** "Stretch out 5407
14:27 **M** stretched out his hand over the sea, 5407
14:31 put their trust in him and in **M** his servant. 5407
15:1 Then **M** and the Israelites sang this song to 5407
15:22 Then **M** led Israel from the Red Sea 5407
15:24 So the people grumbled against **M,** saying, 5407
15:25 Then **M** cried out to the LORD, NIH
16:2 the whole community grumbled against **M** 5407
16:4 Then the LORD said to **M,** "I will rain down 5407
16:6 So **M** and Aaron said to all the Israelites, 5407
16:8 **M** also said, "You will know that it was 5407
16:9 Then **M** told Aaron, "Say to the entire 5407
16:11 The LORD said to **M,** 5407
16:15 **M** said to them, "It is the bread the LORD 5407
16:19 Then **M** said to them, "No one is to keep 5407
16:20 some of them paid no attention to **M;** 5407
16:20 So **M** was angry with them. 5407
16:22 and reported this to **M.** 5407
16:24 until morning, as **M** commanded, and it did 5407
16:25 "Eat it today," **M** said, 5407
16:28 Then the LORD said to **M,** 5407
16:32 **M** said, "This is what the LORD 5407
16:33 So **M** said to Aaron, "Take a jar 5407
16:34 As the LORD commanded **M,** 5407
17:2 So they quarreled with **M** and said, 5407
17:2 **M** replied, "Why do you quarrel with me? 5407
17:3 and they grumbled against **M.** 5407
17:4 Then **M** cried out to the LORD, 5407
17:5 The LORD answered **M,** "Walk on ahead 5407
17:6 So **M** did this in the sight of the elders 5407
17:9 **M** said to Joshua, "Choose some of our men 5407
17:10 fought the Amalekites as **M** had ordered, 5407

Ex 17:10 and **M,** Aaron and Hur went to the top of 5407
17:11 As long as **M** held up his hands, 5407
17:14 Then the LORD said to **M,** "Write this 5407
17:15 **M** built an altar and called it The LORD is my Banner. 5407
18:1 the priest of Midian and father-in-law of **M,** 5407
18:1 heard of everything God had done for **M** 5407
18:2 After **M** had sent away his wife Zipporah, 5407
18:3 One son was named Gershom, for **M** said, NIH
18:7 So **M** went out to meet his father-in-law 5407
18:8 **M** told his father-in-law about everything 5407
18:13 The next day **M** took his seat to serve 5407
18:14 that **M** was doing for the people, 5407
18:15 **M** answered him, "Because 5407
18:24 **M** listened to his father-in-law 5407
18:26 The difficult cases they brought to **M,** 5407
18:27 Then **M** sent his father-in-law on his way, 5407
19:3 Then **M** went up to God, 5407
19:7 So **M** went back and summoned the elders 5407
19:8 **M** brought their answer back to the LORD. 5407
19:9 The LORD said to **M,** "I am going to come 5407
19:9 Then **M** told the LORD what the people 5407
19:10 And the LORD said to **M,** "Go to the people 5407
19:14 After **M** had gone down the mountain to 5407
19:17 Then **M** led the people out of the camp 5407
19:19 Then **M** spoke and the voice of God 5407
19:20 of Mount Sinai and called **M** to the top of 5407
19:20 So **M** went up 5407
19:23 **M** said to the LORD, "The people cannot 5407
19:25 **M** went down to the people and told them. 5407
20:19 and said to **M,** "Speak to us yourself 5407
20:20 **M** said to the people, "Do not be afraid. 5407
20:21 while **M** approached the thick darkness 5407
20:22 LORD said to **M,** "Tell the Israelites this: 5407
24:1 Then he said to **M,** "Come up to the LORD, 5407
24:2 but **M** alone is to approach the LORD; 5407
24:3 When **M** went and told the people all 5407
24:4 **M** then wrote down everything 5407
24:6 **M** took half of the blood and put it 5407
24:8 **M** then took the blood, 5407
24:9 **M** and Aaron, Nadab and Abihu, 5407
24:12 The LORD said to **M,** "Come up to me 5407
24:13 Then **M** set out with Joshua his aide, 5407
24:13 and **M** went up on the mountain of God. 5407
24:15 When **M** went up on the mountain, 5407
24:16 on the seventh day the LORD called to **M** 5407
24:18 Then **M** entered the cloud as he went on up 5407
25:1 The LORD said to **M,** 5407
30:11 Then the LORD said to **M,** 5407
30:17 Then the LORD said to **M,** 5407
30:22 Then the LORD said to **M,** 5407
30:34 LORD said to **M,** "Take fragrant spices— 5407
31:1 Then the LORD said to **M,** 5407
31:12 Then the LORD said to **M,** 5407
31:18 When the LORD finished speaking to **M** 5407
32:1 that **M** was so long in coming down from 5407
32:1 As for this fellow **M** who brought us up out 5407
32:7 Then the LORD said to **M,** "Go down, 5407
32:9 the LORD said to **M,** 5407
32:11 **M** sought the favor of the LORD his God. 5407
32:15 **M** turned and went down the mountain with 5407
32:17 noise of the people shouting, he said to **M,** 5407
32:18 **M** replied: "It is not the sound of victory, NIH
32:19 When **M** approached the camp and saw 5407
32:23 As for this fellow **M** who brought us up out 5407
32:25 **M** saw that the people were running wild 5407
32:28 The Levites did as **M** commanded, 5407
32:29 Then **M** said, "You have been set apart to 5407
32:30 The next day **M** said to the people, 5407
32:31 So **M** went back to the LORD and said, 5407
32:33 LORD replied to **M,** "Whoever has sinned 5407
33:1 Then the LORD said to **M,** "Leave this 5407
33:5 For the LORD had said to **M,** 5407
33:7 Now **M** used to take a tent 5407
33:8 And whenever **M** went out to the tent, 5407
33:8 watching **M** until he entered the tent. 5407
33:9 As **M** went into the tent, 5407
33:9 while the LORD spoke with **M.** 5407
33:11 The LORD would speak to **M** face to face, 5407
33:11 Then **M** would return to the camp, NIH
33:12 **M** said to the LORD, "You have been telling 5407
33:15 Then **M** said to him, "If your Presence NIH
33:17 And the LORD said to **M,** "I will do 5407
33:18 Then **M** said, "Now show me your glory." NIH
34:1 The LORD said to **M,** "Chisel out two 5407
34:4 So **M** chiseled out two stone tablets like 5407
34:6 And he passed in front of **M,** proclaiming, 2257[S]
34:8 **M** bowed to the ground at once 5407
34:27 Then the LORD said to **M,** "Write down 5407
34:28 **M** was there with the LORD forty days NIH
34:29 When **M** came down from Mount Sinai 5407
34:30 When Aaron and all the Israelites saw **M,** 5407
34:31 But **M** called to them; 5407
34:33 When **M** finished speaking to them, 5407
34:35 Then **M** would put the veil back 5407
35:1 **M** assembled the whole Israelite community 5407
35:4 **M** said to the whole Israelite community, 5407
35:29 through **M** had commanded them to do. 5407
35:30 Then **M** said to the Israelites, "See, 5407
36:2 Then **M** summoned Bezalel and Oholiab 5407
36:3 They received from **M** all the offerings 5407
36:5 and said to **M,** "The people are bringing 5407
36:6 Then **M** gave an order and they sent 5407
38:22 made everything the LORD commanded **M;** 5407
39:1 as the LORD commanded **M.** 5407
39:5 as the LORD commanded **M.** 5407
39:7 as the LORD commanded **M.** 5407

Ex	39:21	as the LORD commanded **M.**	5407
	39:26	as the LORD commanded **M.**	5407
	39:29	as the LORD commanded **M.**	5407
	39:31	as the LORD commanded **M.**	5407
	39:32	as the LORD commanded **M.**	5407
	39:33	Then they brought the tabernacle to **M:**	5407
	39:42	as the LORD had commanded **M.**	5407
	39:43	**M** inspected the work and saw	5407
	39:43	So **M** blessed them.	5407
	40: 1	Then the LORD said to **M:**	5407
	40:16	**M** did everything just as the LORD	5407
	40:18	When **M** set up the tabernacle,	5407
	40:22	**M** placed the table in the Tent of Meeting	NIH
	40:26	**M** placed the gold altar in the Tent	NIH
	40:31	and **M** and Aaron and his sons used it	5407
	40:32	as the LORD commanded **M.**	5407
	40:33	Then **M** set up the courtyard around	NIH
	40:33	And so **M** finished the work.	5407
	40:35	**M** could not enter the Tent of Meeting	5407
Lev	1: 1	The LORD called to **M** and spoke to him	5407
	4: 1	The LORD said to **M,**	5407
	5:14	The LORD said to **M:**	5407
	6: 1	The LORD said to **M:**	5407
	6: 8	The LORD said to **M:**	5407
	6:19	The LORD also said to **M,**	5407
	6:24	The LORD said to **M,**	5407
	7:22	The LORD said to **M,**	5407
	7:28	The LORD said to **M,**	5407
	7:38	which the LORD gave **M** on Mount Sinai	5407
	8: 1	The LORD said to **M,**	5407
	8: 4	**M** did as the LORD commanded him,	5407
	8: 5	**M** said to the assembly, "This is what	5407
	8: 6	Then **M** brought Aaron and his sons	5407
	8: 9	as the LORD commanded **M.**	5407
	8:10	Then **M** took the anointing oil and anointed	5407
	8:13	as the LORD commanded **M.**	5407
	8:15	**M** slaughtered the bull and took some of	5407
	8:16	**M** also took all the fat around	5407
	8:17	as the LORD commanded **M.**	5407
	8:19	Then **M** slaughtered the ram and sprinkled	5407
	8:21	as the LORD commanded **M.**	5407
	8:23	**M** slaughtered the ram and took some	5407
	8:24	**M** also brought Aaron's sons forward	5407
	8:28	Then **M** took them from their hands	5407
	8:29	as the LORD commanded **M.**	5407
	8:30	Then **M** took some of the anointing oil	5407
	8:31	**M** then said to Aaron and his sons,	5407
	8:36	the LORD commanded through **M.**	5407
	9: 1	On the eighth day **M** summoned Aaron	5407
	9: 5	the things **M** commanded to the front of	5407
	9: 6	Then **M** said, "This is what	5407
	9: 7	**M** said to Aaron, "Come to the altar	5407
	9:10	as the LORD commanded **M;**	5407
	9:21	as a wave offering, as **M** commanded.	5407
	9:23	**M** and Aaron then went into the Tent	5407
	10: 3	**M** then said to Aaron, "This is what	5407
	10: 4	**M** summoned Mishael and Elzaphan,	5407
	10: 5	outside the camp, as **M** ordered.	5407
	10: 6	Then **M** said to Aaron and his sons Eleazar	5407
	10: 7	So they did as **M** said.	5407
	10:11	the LORD has given them through **M."**	5407
	10:12	**M** said to Aaron and his remaining sons,	5407
	10:16	When **M** inquired about the goat of	5407
	10:19	Aaron replied to **M,** "Today they sacrificed	5407
	10:20	When **M** heard this, he was satisfied.	5407
	11: 1	The LORD said to **M** and Aaron,	5407
	12: 1	The LORD said to **M,**	5407
	13: 1	The LORD said to **M** and Aaron,	5407
	14: 1	The LORD said to **M,**	5407
	14:33	The LORD said to **M** and Aaron,	5407
	15: 1	The LORD said to **M** and Aaron,	5407
	16: 1	The LORD spoke to **M** after the death of	5407
	16: 2	The LORD said to **M:**	5407
	16:34	it was done, as the LORD commanded **M.**	5407
	17: 1	The LORD said to **M,**	5407
	18: 1	The LORD said to **M,**	5407
	19: 1	The LORD said to **M,**	5407
	20: 1	The LORD said to **M,**	5407
	21: 1	The LORD said to **M,** "Speak to the priests,	5407
	21:16	The LORD said to **M,**	5407
	21:24	So **M** told this to Aaron and his sons and	5407
	22: 1	The LORD said to **M,**	5407
	22:17	The LORD said to **M,**	5407
	22:26	The LORD said to **M,**	5407
	23: 1	The LORD said to **M,**	5407
	23: 9	The LORD said to **M,**	5407
	23:23	The LORD said to **M,**	5407
	23:26	The LORD said to **M,**	5407
	23:33	The LORD said to **M,**	5407
	23:44	So **M** announced to the Israelites	5407
	24: 1	The LORD said to **M,**	5407
	24:11	so they brought him to **M.**	5407
	24:13	Then the LORD said to **M:**	5407
	24:23	Then **M** spoke to the Israelites,	5407
	24:23	as the LORD commanded **M.**	5407
	25: 1	The LORD said to **M** on Mount Sinai,	5407
	26:46	and the Israelites through **M.**	5407
	27: 1	The LORD said to **M,**	5407
	27:34	These are the commands the LORD gave **M** on Mount Sinai	5407
Nu	1: 1	to **M** in the Tent of Meeting in the Desert	5407
	1:17	**M** and Aaron took these men whose names had been given,	5407
	1:19	as the LORD commanded **M.**	5407
	1:44	by **M** and Aaron and the twelve leaders	5407
	1:48	The LORD had said to **M:**	5407
	1:54	as the LORD commanded **M.**	5407
Nu	2: 1	The LORD said to **M** and Aaron:	5407
	2:33	as the LORD commanded **M.**	5407
	2:34	the LORD commanded **M;**	5407
	3: 1	the account of the family of Aaron and **M** at	5407
	3: 1	the LORD talked with **M** on Mount Sinai.	5407
	3: 5	The LORD said to **M,**	5407
	3:11	The LORD also said to **M,**	5407
	3:14	The LORD said to **M** in the Desert	5407
	3:16	So **M** counted them,	5407
	3:38	**M** and Aaron and his sons were to camp to	5407
	3:39	at the LORD's command by **M** and Aaron	5407
	3:40	The LORD said to **M,** "Count all the	5407
	3:42	**M** counted all the firstborn of the Israelites,	5407
	3:44	The LORD also said to **M,**	5407
	3:49	So **M** collected the redemption money	5407
	3:51	**M** gave the redemption money to Aaron	5407
	4: 1	The LORD said to **M** and Aaron:	5407
	4:17	The LORD said to **M** and Aaron,	5407
	4:21	The LORD said to **M,**	5407
	4:34	**M,** Aaron and the leaders of the community	5407
	4:37	**M** and Aaron counted them according to	5407
	4:37	to the LORD's command through **M.**	5407
	4:41	**M** and Aaron counted them according to	5407
	4:45	**M** and Aaron counted them according to	5407
	4:45	to the LORD's command through **M.**	5407
	4:46	So **M,** Aaron and the leaders	5407
	4:49	At the LORD's command through **M,**	5407
	4:49	as the LORD commanded **M.**	5407
	5: 1	The LORD said to **M,**	5407
	5: 4	as the LORD had instructed **M.**	5407
	5: 5	The LORD said to **M,**	5407
	5:11	Then the LORD said to **M,**	5407
	6: 1	The LORD said to **M,**	5407
	6:22	The LORD said to **M,**	5407
	7: 1	When **M** finished setting up the tabernacle,	5407
	7: 4	The LORD said to **M,**	5407
	7: 6	So **M** took the carts and oxen	5407
	7: 9	But **M** did not give any to the Kohathites,	NIH
	7:11	For the LORD had said to **M,**	5407
	7:89	When **M** entered the Tent of Meeting	5407
	8: 1	The LORD said to **M,**	5407
	8: 3	just as the LORD commanded **M.**	5407
	8: 4	like the pattern the LORD had shown **M.**	5407
	8: 5	The LORD said to **M:**	5407
	8:20	**M,** Aaron and the whole Israelite community did with the	5407
	8:20	as the LORD commanded **M.**	5407
	8:22	as the LORD commanded **M.**	5407
	8:23	The LORD said to **M,**	5407
	9: 1	The LORD spoke to **M** in the Desert	5407
	9: 4	So **M** told the Israelites to celebrate	5407
	9: 5	as the LORD commanded **M.**	5407
	9: 6	they came to **M** and Aaron that same day	5407
	9: 7	and said to **M,** "We have become unclean	2257S
	9: 8	**M** answered them, "Wait until I find out	5407
	9: 9	Then the LORD said to **M,**	5407
	9:23	with his command through **M.**	5407
	10: 1	The LORD said to **M:**	5407
	10:13	at the LORD's command through **M.**	5407
	10:29	Now **M** said to Hobab son of Reuel	5407
	10:31	But **M** said, "Please do not leave us.	NIH
	10:35	Whenever the ark set out, **M** said, "Rise up,	5407
	11: 2	When the people cried out to **M,**	5407
	11:10	**M** heard the people of every family wailing,	5407
	11:10	and **M** was troubled.	5407
	11:16	The LORD said to **M:** "Bring me seventy	5407
	11:21	But **M** said, "Here I am among	5407
	11:23	The LORD answered **M,** "Is the LORD's arm	5407
	11:24	So **M** went out and told the people what	5407
	11:27	A young man ran and told **M,**	5407
	11:28	spoke up and said, "**M,** my lord,	5407
	11:29	**M** replied, "Are you jealous for my sake?	5407
	11:30	Then **M** and the elders of Israel returned to	5407
	12: 1	and Aaron began to talk against **M** because	5407
	12: 2	"Has the LORD spoken only through **M?"**	5407
	12: 3	(Now **M** was a very humble man,	5407
	12: 4	At once the LORD said to **M,**	5407
	12: 7	But this is not true of my servant **M;**	5407
	12: 8	not afraid to speak against my servant **M?"**	5407
	12:11	and he said to **M,** "Please, my lord,	5407
	12:13	So **M** cried out to the LORD, "O God,	5407
	12:14	The LORD replied to **M,** "If her father	5407
	13: 1	The LORD said to **M,**	5407
	13: 3	at the LORD's command **M** sent them out	5407
	13:16	the names of the men **M** sent to explore	5407
	13:16	(**M** gave Hoshea son of Nun the name Joshua.)	5407
	13:17	When **M** sent them to explore Canaan,	5407
	13:26	They came back to **M** and Aaron and	5407
	13:27	They gave **M** this account:	2257S
	13:30	Then Caleb silenced the people before **M**	5407
	14: 2	All the Israelites grumbled against **M**	5407
	14: 5	Then **M** and Aaron fell facedown in front of	5407
	14:11	The LORD said to **M,** "How long will these	5407
	14:13	**M** said to the LORD, "Then the Egyptians	5407
	14:26	The LORD said to **M** and Aaron:	5407
	14:36	So the men **M** had sent to explore the land,	5407
	14:39	When **M** reported this to all the Israelites,	5407
	14:41	But **M** said, "Why are you disobeying	5407
	14:44	though neither **M** nor the ark of the LORD's	5407
	15: 1	The LORD said to **M,**	5407
	15:17	The LORD said to **M,**	5407
	15:22	of these commands the LORD gave **M—**	5407
	15:33	to **M** and Aaron and the whole assembly,	5407
	15:35	the LORD said to **M,** "The man must die.	5407
	15:36	as the LORD commanded **M.**	5407
	15:37	The LORD said to **M,**	5407
Nu	16: 2	and rose up against **M.**	5407
	16: 3	as a group to oppose **M** and Aaron and said	5407
	16: 4	When **M** heard this, he fell facedown.	5407
	16: 8	**M** also said to Korah, "Now listen,	5407
	16:12	Then **M** summoned Dathan and Abiram,	5407
	16:15	Then **M** became very angry and said to	5407
	16:16	**M** said to Korah, "You and all your	5407
	16:18	and stood with **M** and Aaron at the entrance	5407
	16:20	The LORD said to **M** and Aaron,	5407
	16:22	**M** and Aaron fell facedown and cried out,	NIH
	16:23	Then the LORD said to **M,**	5407
	16:25	**M** got up and went to Dathan and Abiram,	5407
	16:28	Then **M** said, "This is how you will know	5407
	16:36	The LORD said to **M,**	5407
	16:40	as the LORD directed him through **M.**	5407
	16:41	community grumbled against **M** and Aaron.	5407
	16:42	to **M** and Aaron and turned toward the Tent	5407
	16:43	Then **M** and Aaron went to the front of	5407
	16:44	and the LORD said to **M,**	5407
	16:46	Then **M** said to Aaron, "Take your censer	5407
	16:47	So Aaron did as **M** said,	5407
	16:50	Then Aaron returned to **M** at the entrance to	5407
	17: 1	The LORD said to **M,**	5407
	17: 6	So **M** spoke to the Israelites,	5407
	17: 7	**M** placed the staffs before the LORD in	5407
	17: 8	The next day **M** entered the Tent of	5407
	17: 9	Then **M** brought out all the staffs from	5407
	17:10	The LORD said to **M,** "Put back Aaron's	5407
	17:11	**M** did just as the LORD commanded him.	5407
	17:12	The Israelites said to **M,** "We will die!	5407
	18:25	The LORD said to **M,**	5407
	19: 1	The LORD said to **M** and Aaron:	5407
	20: 2	and the people gathered in opposition to **M**	5407
	20: 3	They quarreled with **M** and said,	5407
	20: 6	**M** and Aaron went from the assembly to	5407
	20: 7	The LORD said to **M,**	5407
	20: 9	So **M** took the staff from the LORD's	5407
	20:10	in front of the rock and **M** said to them,	NIH
	20:11	Then **M** raised his arm and struck	5407
	20:12	But the LORD said to **M** and Aaron,	5407
	20:14	**M** sent messengers from Kadesh to the king	5407
	20:23	the LORD said to **M** and Aaron,	5407
	20:27	**M** did as the LORD commanded:	5407
	20:28	**M** removed Aaron's garments and put them	5407
	20:28	Then **M** and Eleazar came down from	5407
	21: 5	they spoke against God and against **M,**	5407
	21: 7	The people came to **M** and said,	5407
	21: 7	So **M** prayed for the people.	5407
	21: 8	The LORD said to **M,** "Make a snake	5407
	21: 9	So **M** made a bronze snake and put it up on	5407
	21:16	the well where the LORD said to **M,**	5407
	21:32	After **M** had sent spies to Jazer,	5407
	21:34	The LORD said to **M,** "Do not be afraid	5407
	25: 4	The LORD said to **M,** "Take all the leaders	5407
	25: 5	So **M** said to Israel's judges,	5407
	25: 6	of **M** and the whole assembly of Israel	5407
	25:10	The LORD said to **M,**	5407
	25:16	The LORD said to **M,**	5407
	26: 1	After the plague the LORD said to **M**	5407
	26: 3	**M** and Eleazar the priest spoke with them	5407
	26: 4	as the LORD commanded **M."**	5407
	26: 9	against **M** and Aaron and were	5407
	26:52	The LORD said to **M,**	5407
	26:59	**M** and their sister Miriam.	5407
	26:63	the ones counted by **M** and Eleazar	5407
	26:64	of them was among those counted by **M**	5407
	27: 2	to the Tent of Meeting and stood before **M,**	5407
	27: 5	So **M** brought their case before the LORD	5407
	27:11	as the LORD commanded **M.' "**	5407
	27:12	the LORD said to **M,** "Go up this mountain	5407
	27:15	**M** said to the LORD,	5407
	27:18	So the LORD said to **M,** "Take Joshua	5407
	27:22	**M** did as the LORD commanded him.	5407
	27:23	as the LORD instructed through **M.**	5407
	28: 1	The LORD said to **M,**	5407
	29:40	**M** told the Israelites all that the LORD	5407
	30: 1	**M** said to the heads of the tribes of Israel:	5407
	30:16	the regulations the LORD gave **M**	5407
	31: 1	The LORD said to **M,**	5407
	31: 3	So **M** said to the people, "Arm some of your	5407
	31: 6	**M** sent them into battle,	5407
	31: 7	as the LORD commanded **M,**	5407
	31:12	and plunder to **M** and Eleazar the priest and	5407
	31:13	**M,** Eleazar the priest and all the leaders of	5407
	31:14	**M** was angry with the officers of the army	5407
	31:21	of the law that the LORD gave **M:**	5407
	31:25	The LORD said to **M,**	5407
	31:31	So **M** and Eleazar the priest did as	5407
	31:31	the priest did as the LORD commanded **M.**	5407
	31:41	**M** gave the tribute to Eleazar the priest as	5407
	31:41	as the LORD commanded **M.**	5407
	31:42	which **M** set apart from that of	5407
	31:47	**M** selected one out of every fifty persons	5407
	31:48	commanders of hundreds—went to **M**	5407
	31:51	**M** and Eleazar the priest accepted	5407
	31:52	of hundreds that **M** and Eleazar presented	NIH
	31:54	**M** and Eleazar the priest accepted the gold	5407
	32: 2	So they came to **M** and Eleazar the priest	5407
	32: 6	**M** said to the Gadites and Reubenites,	5407
	32:20	Then **M** said to them, "If you will do this—	5407
	32:25	The Gadites and Reubenites said to **M,**	5407
	32:28	Then **M** gave orders about them to Eleazar	5407
	32:33	Then **M** gave to the Gadites,	5407
	32:40	So **M** gave Gilead to the Makirites,	5407
	33: 1	by divisions under the leadership of **M**	5407
	33: 2	At the LORD's command **M** recorded	5407
	33:50	across from Jericho the LORD said to **M,**	5407

Nu 34: 1 The LORD said to **M,** 5407
34:13 **M** commanded the Israelites: 5407
34:16 The LORD said to **M,** 5407
35: 1 the LORD said to **M,** 5407
35: 9 Then the LORD said to **M:** 5407
36: 1 came and spoke before **M** and the leaders, 5407
36: 5 the LORD's command **M** gave this order 5407
36:10 as the LORD commanded **M.** 5407
36:13 and regulations the LORD gave through **M** 5407
Dt 1: 1 These are the words **M** spoke to all Israel in 5407
1: 3 **M** proclaimed to the Israelites all that 5407
1: 5 **M** began to expound this law, saying: 5407
4:41 **M** set aside three cities east of the Jordan, 5407
4:44 This is the law **M** set before the Israelites. 5407
4:45 and laws **M** gave them when they came out 5407
4:46 and was defeated by **M** and the Israelites 5407
5: 1 **M** summoned all Israel and said: 5407
27: 1 **M** and the elders of Israel commanded 5407
27: 9 Then **M** and the priests, who are Levites, 5407
27:11 On the same day **M** commanded the people: 5407
29: 1 of the covenant the LORD commanded **M** 5407
29: 2 **M** summoned all the Israelites and said 5407
31: 1 Then **M** went out and spoke these words 5407
31: 7 Then **M** summoned Joshua and said to him 5407
31: 9 So **M** wrote down this law and gave it to 5407
31:10 Then **M** commanded them: 5407
31:14 The LORD said to **M,** "Now the day of your 5407
31:14 So **M** and Joshua came and presented 5407
31:16 And the LORD said to **M:** 5407
31:22 So **M** wrote down this song that day 5407
31:24 After **M** finished writing in a book 5407
31:30 And **M** recited the words of this song 5407
32:44 **M** came with Joshua son of Nun 5407
32:45 When **M** finished reciting all these words 5407
32:48 On that same day the LORD told **M,** 5407
33: 1 that **M** the man of God pronounced on 5407
33: 4 the law that **M** gave us, 5407
34: 1 Then **M** climbed Mount Nebo from 5407
34: 5 And **M** the servant of the LORD died there 5407
34: 7 **M** was a hundred and twenty years old 5407
34: 8 The Israelites grieved for **M** in the plains 5407
34: 9 of wisdom because **M** had laid his hands 5407
34: 9 the LORD had commanded **M.** 5407
34:10 no prophet has risen in Israel like **M,** 5407
34:12 or performed the awesome deeds that **M** did 5407
Jos 1: 1 the death of **M** the servant of the LORD, 5407
1: 2 "**M** my servant is dead. 5407
1: 3 as I promised **M.** 5407
1: 5 As I was with **M,** so I will be with you; 5407
1: 7 to obey all the law my servant **M** gave you; 5407
1:13 that **M** the servant of the LORD gave you: 5407
1:14 the land that **M** gave you east of the Jordan, 5407
1:15 which **M** the servant of the LORD gave you 5407
1:17 Just as we fully obeyed **M,** 5407
1:17 be with you as he was with **M.** 5407
3: 7 that I am with you as I was with **M.** 5407
4:10 just as **M** had directed Joshua. 5407
4:12 as **M** had directed them. 5407
4:14 just as they had revered **M.** 5407
8:31 as **M** the servant of the LORD had 5407
8:31 written in the Book of the Law of **M**— 5407
8:32 Joshua copied on stones the law of **M,** 5407
8:33 as **M** the servant of the LORD 5407
8:35 not a word of all that **M** had commanded 5407
9:24 LORD your God had commanded his servant **M** to give you 5407
11:12 as **M** the servant of the LORD 5407
11:15 As the LORD commanded his servant **M,** 5407
11:15 so **M** commanded Joshua, and Joshua did it; 5407
11:15 of all that the LORD commanded **M.** 5407
11:20 as the LORD had commanded **M.** 5407
11:23 just as the LORD had directed **M,** 5407
12: 6 **M,** the servant of the LORD, 5407
12: 6 And **M** the servant of the LORD gave 5407
13: 8 the inheritance that **M** had given them east 5407
13:12 **M** had defeated them and taken 5407
13:15 This is what **M** had given to the tribe 5407
13:21 **M** had defeated him and the Midianite 5407
13:24 This is what **M** had given to the tribe 5407
13:29 This is what **M** had given to the half-tribe 5407
13:32 the inheritance **M** had given when he was in 5407
13:33 tribe of Levi, **M** had given no inheritance; 5407
14: 2 as the LORD had commanded through **M.** 5407
14: 3 **M** had granted the two-and-a-half tribes their inheritance east of the Jordan 5407
14: 5 just as the LORD had commanded **M.** 5407
14: 6 to **M** the man of God at Kadesh Barnea 5407
14: 7 I was forty years old when **M** the servant of 5407
14: 9 So on that day **M** swore to me, 5407
14:10 since the time he said this to **M,** 5407
14:11 as strong today as the day **M** sent me out; 5407
17: 4 "The LORD commanded **M** to give us 5407
18: 7 **M** the servant of the LORD gave it 5407
20: 2 as I instructed you through **M,** 5407
21: 2 through **M** that you give us towns to live in, 5407
21: 8 as the LORD had commanded through **M.** 5407
22: 2 "You have done all that **M** the servant of 5407
22: 4 to your homes in the land that **M** the servant 5407
22: 5 that **M** the servant of the LORD gave you: 5407
22: 7 of Manasseh **M** had given land in Bashan, 5407
22: 9 the command of the LORD through **M.** 5407
23: 6 that is written in the Book of the Law of **M,** 5407
24: 5 " 'Then I sent **M** and Aaron, 5407
Jdg 1:20 As **M** had promised, Hebron was given 5407
3: 4 he had given their forefathers through **M.** 5407
18:30 Gershom, the son of **M,** and his sons 5407
1Sa 12: 6 the LORD who appointed **M** and Aaron 5407
1Sa 12: 8 and the LORD sent **M** and Aaron, 5407
1Ki 2: 3 as written in the Law of **M,** 5407
8: 9 the two stone tablets that **M** had placed in it 5407
8:53 just as you declared through your servant **M** 5407
8:56 promises he gave through his servant **M.** 5407
2Ki 14: 6 of **M** where the LORD commanded: 5407
18: 4 into pieces the bronze snake **M** had made, 5407
18: 6 the commands the LORD had given **M.** 5407
18:12 all that **M** the servant of the LORD 5407
21: 8 that my servant **M** gave them." 5407
23:25 in accordance with all the Law of **M.** 5407
1Ch 6: 3 of Amram: Aaron, **M** and Miriam. 5407
6:49 that **M** the servant of God had commanded. 5407
15:15 as **M** had commanded in accordance with 5407
21:29 which **M** had made in the desert, 5407
22:13 and laws that the LORD gave **M** for Israel. 5407
23:13 The sons of Amram: Aaron and **M.** 5407
23:14 of **M** the man of God were counted as part 5407
23:15 The sons of **M:** Gershom and Eliezer. 5407
26:24 a descendant of Gershom son of **M,** 5407
2Ch 1: 3 which **M** the LORD's servant had made in 5407
5:10 the two tablets that **M** had placed in it 5407
8:13 by **M** for Sabbaths, New Moons and 5407
23:18 of the LORD as written in the Law of **M,** 5407
24: 6 by **M** the servant of the LORD and by 5407
24: 9 to the LORD the tax that **M** the servant 5407
25: 4 written in the Law, in the Book of **M,** 5407
30:16 as prescribed in the Law of **M** the man 5407
33: 8 decrees and ordinances given through **M."** 5407
34:14 the LORD that had been given through **M.** 5407
35: 6 the LORD commanded through **M."** 5407
35:12 as is written in the Book of **M.** 5407
Ezr 3: 2 with what is written in the Law of **M** 5407
6:18 to what is written in the Book of **M.** 10441
7: 6 a teacher well versed in the Law of **M,** 5407
Ne 1: 7 decrees and laws you gave your servant **M.** 5407
1: 8 the instruction you gave your servant **M,** 5407
8: 1 to bring out the Book of the Law of **M,** 5407
8:14 the LORD had commanded through **M,** 5407
9:14 decrees and laws through your servant **M.** 5407
10:29 of God given through **M** the servant of God 5407
13: 1 On that day the Book of **M** was read aloud 5407
Ps 77:20 like a flock by the hand of **M** and Aaron. 5407
90: T A prayer of **M** the man of God. 5407
99: 6 **M** and Aaron were among his priests, 5407
103: 7 He made known his ways to **M,** 5407
105:26 He sent **M** his servant, and Aaron, 5407
106:16 In the camp they grew envious of **M** and 5407
106:23 had not **M,** his chosen one, stood in 5407
106:32 and trouble came to **M** because of them; 5407
Isa 63:11 the days of **M** and his people— 5407
Jer 15: 1 if **M** and Samuel were to stand before me, 5407
Da 9:11 sworn judgments written in the Law of **M,** 5407
9:13 Just as it is written in the Law of **M,** 5407
Mic 6: 4 I sent **M** to lead you, 5407
Mal 4: 4 "Remember the law of my servant **M,** 5407
Mt 8: 4 the priest and offer the gift **M** commanded, *3707*
17: 3 Just then there appeared before them **M** *3707*
17: 4 one for you, one *for* **M** and one for Elijah." *3707*
19: 7 "did **M** command that a man give his wife *3707*
19: 8 "**M** permitted you to divorce your wives *3707*
22:24 "**M** told us that if a man dies *3707*
Mk 1:44 and offer the sacrifices that **M** commanded *3707*
7:10 For **M** said, 'Honor your father *3707*
9: 4 there appeared before them Elijah and **M,** *3707*
9: 5 one for you, one *for* **M** and one for Elijah." *3707*
10: 3 "What did **M** command you?" he replied. *3707*
10: 4 "**M** permitted a man to write a certificate *3707*
10: 5 that **M** wrote you this law," *NIG*
12:19 "**M** wrote for us that if a man's brother dies *3707*
12:26 have you not read in the book *of* **M,** *3707*
Lk 2:22 to the Law *of* **M** had been completed, *3707*
5:14 and offer the sacrifices that **M** commanded *3707*
9:30 Two men, **M** and Elijah, *3707*
9:33 one for you, one *for* **M** and one for Elijah." *3707*
16:29 'They have **M** and the Prophets; *3707*
16:31 'If they do not listen to **M** and the Prophets, *3707*
20:28 "**M** wrote for us that if a man's brother dies *3707*
20:37 even **M** showed that the dead rise, *3707*
24:27 And beginning with **M** and all the Prophets, *3707*
24:44 that is written about me in the Law *of* **M,** *3707*
Jn 1:17 For the law was given through **M;** *3707*
1:45 "We have found the one **M** wrote about in *3707*
3:14 Just as **M** lifted up the snake in the desert, *3707*
5:45 Your accuser is **M,** on whom your hopes are *3707*
5:46 If you believed **M,** you would believe me, *3707*
6:32 it is not **M** who has given you the bread *3707*
7:19 Has not **M** given you the law? *3707*
7:22 because **M** gave you circumcision *3707*
7:22 (though actually it did not come from **M,** *3707*
7:23 the Sabbath so that the law *of* **M** may not *3707*
8: 5 In the Law **M** commanded us to stone such *3707*
9:28 We are disciples *of* **M!** *3707*
9:29 We know that God spoke *to* **M,** *3707*
Ac 3:22 For **M** said, 'The Lord your God will raise *3707*
6:11 of blasphemy against **M** and against God." *3707*
6:14 and change the customs **M** handed down *3707*
7:20 "At that time **M** was born, *3707*
7:22 **M** was educated in all the wisdom of *3707*
7:23 "When **M** was forty years old, *899*[S]
7:25 **M** thought that his own people would realize *NIG*
7:26 The next day **M** came upon two Israelites *NIG*
7:27 the other pushed **M** aside and said, *899*[S]
7:29 When **M** heard this, he fled to Midian, *3707*
7:30 an angel appeared *to* **M** in the flames of *899*[S]
7:32 **M** trembled with fear and did not dare *3707*
7:35 the same **M** whom they had rejected with *3707*
Ac 7:37 "This is that **M** who told the Israelites, *3707*
7:40 for this fellow **M** who led us out of Egypt— *3707*
7:44 It had been made as God directed **M,** *3707*
13:39 not be justified from by the law *of* **M.** *3707*
15: 1 *according to* the custom taught *by* **M,** *3707*
15: 5 and required to obey the law *of* **M."** *3707*
15:21 For **M** has been preached in every city from *3707*
21:21 among the Gentiles to turn away from **M,** *3707*
26:22 the prophets and **M** said would happen— *3707*
28:23 from the Law *of* **M** and from the Prophets. *3707*
Ro 5:14 from the time of Adam to the time *of* **M,** *3707*
9:15 For he says *to* **M,** "I will have mercy on *3707*
10: 5 **M** describes in this way the righteousness *3707*
10:19 **M** says, "I will make you envious *3707*
1Co 9: 9 For it is written in the Law *of* **M:** *3707*
10: 2 They were all baptized into **M** in the cloud *3707*
2Co 3: 7 not look steadily at the face *of* **M** because *3707*
3:13 We are not like **M,** who would put a veil *3707*
3:15 Even to this day when **M** is read, *3707*
2Ti 3: 8 Just as Jannes and Jambres opposed **M,** *3707*
Heb 3: 2 just as **M** was faithful in all God's house. *3707*
3: 3 found worthy of greater honor than **M,** *3707*
3: 5 **M** was faithful as a servant in all God's *3707*
3:16 Were they not all those **M** led out of Egypt? *3707*
7:14 to that tribe **M** said nothing about priests. *3707*
8: 5 This is why **M** was warned when he was *3707*
9:19 **M** had proclaimed every commandment *3707*
10:28 rejected the law *of* **M** died without mercy *3707*
11:24 By faith **M,** when he had grown up, *3707*
12:21 The sight was so terrifying that **M** said, *3707*
Jude 1: 9 with the devil about the body *of* **M,** *3707*
Rev 15: 3 and sang the song *of* **M** the servant of God *3707*

MOSES' (19) [MOSES]

Ex 4:25 and touched [**M'**] feet with it. 2257[S]
17:12 When **M'** hands grew tired, 5407
18: 5 Jethro, **M'** father-in-law, together with 5407
18: 5 together with **M'** sons and wife, 2257[S]
18:12 Then Jethro, **M'** father-in-law, 5407
18:12 of Israel to eat bread with **M'** father-in-law 5407
18:17 **M'** father-in-law replied, "What you are 5407
35:20 Then the whole Israelite community withdrew from **M'** presence, 5407
38:21 recorded at **M'** command by the Levites 5407
Lev 8:29 **M'** share of the ordination ram— 4200+5407
Nu 10:29 of Reuel the Midianite, **M'** father-in-law, 5407
11:28 who had been **M'** aide since youth, 5407
Jos 1: 1 to Joshua son of Nun, **M'** aide: 5407
Jdg 1:16 The descendants of **M'** father-in-law, 5407
4:11 **M'** brother-in-law, and pitched his tent by 5407
Ps 106:33 and rash words came from **M'** lips. 2257[S]
Isa 63:12 arm of power to be at **M'** right hand, 5407
Mt 23: 2 of the law and the Pharisees sit in **M'** seat. *3707*
Heb 11:23 By faith **M'** parents hid him *3707*

MOST (187) [FOREMOST, INMOST, INNERMOST, SOUTHERNMOST, TOPMOST]

Ge 14:18 He was priest of God **M High,** 6610
14:19 "Blessed be Abram by God **M High,** 6610
14:20 And blessed be God **M High,** 6610
14:22 God **M High,** Creator of heaven and earth, 6610
34:19 the **m** honored *of* all his father's household, 4946
Ex 26:33 Holy Place from the **M Holy Place.** 7731+7731
26:34 the Testimony in the **M Holy Place.** 7731+7731
29:37 Then the altar will be **m holy,** 7731+7731
30:10 It is **m holy** to the LORD." 7731+7731
30:29 so they will be **m holy,** 7731+7731
30:36 It shall be **m holy** to you. 7731+7731
40:10 the altar, and it will be **m holy.** 7731+7731
Lev 2: 3 it is a **m holy** *part* of the offerings 7731+7731
2:10 it is a **m holy** *part* of the offerings 7731+7731
6:17 the guilt offering, it is **m holy.** 7731+7731
6:25 offering is slaughtered; it is **m holy.** 7731+7731
6:29 priest's family may eat it; it is **m holy.** 7731+7731
7: 1 guilt offering, which is **m holy:** 7731+7731
7: 6 in a holy place; it is **m holy.** 7731+7731
10:12 beside the altar, for it is **m holy.** 7731+7731
10:17 It is **m holy;** it was given to you 7731+7731
14:13 belongs to the priest; it is **m holy.** 7731+7731
16: 2 into the **M Holy Place** behind the curtain 7731
16:16 for the **M Holy Place** because of 7731
16:17 in to make atonement in the **M Holy Place** 7731
16:20 making atonement for the **M Holy Place,** 7731
16:23 on before he entered the **M Holy Place,** 7731
16:27 into the **M Holy Place** to make atonement, 7731
16:33 make atonement for the **M Holy Place** 5219+7731
21:22 may eat the **m holy** food of his God, 7731+7731
24: 9 a **m holy** part of their regular share of 7731+7731
27:28 so devoted is **m holy** to the LORD. 7731+7731
Nu 4: 4 the care of the **m holy things.** 7731+7731
4:19 they come near the **m holy things,** 7731+7731
18: 9 of the **m holy offerings** that is kept 7731+7731
18: 9 they bring me as **m holy offerings,** 7731+7731
18:10 Eat it as something **m holy;** 7731+7731
24:16 who has knowledge from the **M High,** 6610
Dt 28:54 Even the **m** gentle and sensitive man 4394
28:56 The **m** gentle and sensitive woman NIH
30: 4 to the **m distant land** *under* the heavens, 7895
30: 9 Then the LORD your God *will make* you **m** prosperous 3855
32: 8 **M High** gave the nations their inheritance, 6610
33:24 "**M blessed** of sons *is* Asher; AIT
Jdg 5:24 "**M** blessed *of* women be Jael, 4946
5:24 **m** blessed *of* tent-dwelling women. 4946

1Sa 20:41 but David wept *the* m. 1540
2Sa 22:14 the voice of the **M High** resounded. 6610
23: 1 oracle of the man exalted by the **M High,** 6583
1Ki 3: 4 for that was the **m important** high place, 1524
6:16 inner sanctuary, the **M Holy Place.** 7731+7731
7:50 innermost room, the **M Holy Place,** 7731+7731
8: 6 of the temple, the **M Holy Place,** 7731+7731
11:11 **m certainly tear** the kingdom **away** 7973+7973
2Ki 10: 3 and **m** worthy *of* your master's sons 4946
1Ch 6:49 that was done in the **M Holy Place,** 7731+7731
12:29 3,000, **m** *of* whom had remained loyal 5270
16:25 great is the LORD and **m** worthy of praise; 4394
17:17 though I were the **m exalted** *of* men, 5092+9366
23:13 to consecrate the **m holy things,** 7731+7731
2Ch 3: 8 He built the **M Holy Place,** 7731+7731
3:10 In the **M Holy** Place he made a pair 7731+7731
4:22 the inner doors to the **M Holy Place** 7731+7731
5: 7 of the temple, the **M Holy Place,** 7731+7731
28:19 *had been* **m unfaithful** to the LORD. 5085+5086
30:18 Although **m** *of* the many people who came 5270
Ezr 2:63 of the **m sacred** *food* until there was 7731+7731
Ne 7: 2 and feared God more than **m** *men* do. 8041
7:65 not to eat any of the **m sacred food** 7731+7731
Est 6: 9 to one of the king's **m noble** princes. 7312
Ps 7: 8 according to my integrity, O **M High.** 6604
7:10 My shield is God **M High,** 6583
7:17 to the name of the LORD **M High.** 6610
9: 2 I will sing praise to your name, O **M High.** 6610
18:13 the voice of the **M High** resounded. 6610
21: 7 the unfailing love of the **M High** he will not be shaken. 6610
28: 2 my hands toward your **M Holy Place.** 1808+7731
45: 2 *You are the* **m excellent** of men 3636
46: 4 the holy place where the **M High** dwells. 6610
47: 2 How awesome is the LORD **M High,** 6610
48: 1 Great is the LORD, and **m** worthy of praise, 4394
50:14 fulfill your vows to the **M High,** 6610
57: 2 I cry out to God **M High,** to God, 6610
73:11 Does the **M High** have knowledge?" 6610
77:10 the years of the right hand of the **M High."** 6610
78:17 rebelling in the desert against the **M High.** 6610
78:35 that God **M High** was their Redeemer. 6610
78:56 to the test and rebelled against the **M High;** 6610
82: 6 you are all sons of the **M High.'** 6610
83:18 you alone are the **M High** over all the earth. 6610
87: 5 and the **M High** himself will establish her." 6610
89:27 the **m exalted** of the kings of the earth. 6609
91: 1 of the **M High** will rest in the shadow of 6610
91: 9 If you make the **M High** your dwelling— 6610
92: 1 and make music to your name, O **M High,** 6610
96: 4 great is the LORD and **m** worthy of praise; 4394
97: 9 O LORD, are the **M High** over all the earth; 6610
107:11 and despised the counsel of the **M High.** 6610
145: 3 Great is the LORD and **m** worthy of praise; 4394
Pr 30: 2 "I am the **m ignorant** of men; 4946
Ecc 7:24 it is far off and **m profound**— 6678+6678
SS 1: 8 you do not know, *m* **beautiful** of women, AIT
5: 9 *m* **beautiful** of women? AIT
6: 1 *m* **beautiful** of women? AIT
Isa 14:14 I will make myself like the **M High."** 6610
Jer 3:19 **m beautiful** inheritance of any nation. 7382+7382
9:17 send for the *m* **skillful** *of them.* AIT
18:13 A **m** horrible thing has been done 4394
La 1:20 for *I have been* **m rebellious.** 5286+5286
3:35 to deny a man his rights before the **M High,** 6610
3:38 the **M High** that both calamities and good 6610
Eze 7:24 I will bring the *m* **wicked** *of* the nations AIT
16: 7 became the **m beautiful of jewels.** 6344+6344
20: 6 the **m beautiful** of all lands. 7382
20:15 **m beautiful** of all lands— 7382
28: 7 the *m* **ruthless** *of* nations; AIT
30:11 the *m* **ruthless** *of* nations— AIT
31:12 and the *m* **ruthless** *of* foreign nations cut it AIT
32:12 the *m* **ruthless** *of* all nations. AIT
41: 4 "This is the **M Holy Place."** 7731+7731
41:21 the front of the **M Holy Place** was similar. 7731
41:23 and the **M Holy Place** had double doors. 7731
42:13 will eat the **m holy offerings.** 7731+7731
42:13 they will put the **m holy offerings**— 7731+7731
43:12 on top of the mountain will be **m holy.** 7731+7731
44:13 holy things or my **m holy offerings;** 7731+7731
45: 3 the sanctuary, the **M Holy Place.** 7731+7731
48:12 portion of the land, a **m holy** portion, 7731+7731
Da 3:26 servants of the **M High** God, come out! 10546
4: 2 that the **M High** God has performed for me. 10546
4:17 **M High** is sovereign over the kingdoms 10546
4:24 this is the decree the **M High** has issued 10546
4:25 **M High** is sovereign over the kingdoms 10546
4:32 **M High** is sovereign over the kingdoms 10546
4:34 Then I praised the **M High;** 10546
5:18 the **M High** God gave your father Nebuchadnezzar sovereignty 10546
5:21 that the **M High** God is sovereign over 10546
7:18 But the saints of the **M High** will receive 10548
7:19 from all the others and **m** terrifying, 10339
7:22 in favor of the saints of the **M High,** 10548
7:25 against the **M High** and oppress his saints 10546
7:27 the people of the **M High.** 10548
9:24 prophecy and to anoint the **m holy.** 7731+7731
Hos 7:16 They do not turn to the **M High;** 6583
11: 7 Even if they call to the **M High,** 6583
Mic 7: 4 the **m** upright worse than a thorn hedge. NIH
Mt 11:20 to denounce the cities in which **m** of his *4498*
23: 6 the **m important seats** in the synagogues; *4751*
24:12 the love *of* **m** will grow cold, *4498*
Mk 5: 7 Jesus, Son *of* the **M High** God? *5736*
12:28 which is the **m important?"** *4755*
12:29 "The **m important** *one,"* answered Jesus, *4755*
12:39 the **m important seats** in the synagogues *4751*
12:40 Such men will be punished **m severely."** *4358*
Lk 1: 3 account for you, **m excellent** Theophilus, *3196*
1:32 and will be called the Son *of* the **M High.** *5736*
1:35 power *of* the **M High** will overshadow you. *5736*
1:76 will be called a prophet *of* the **M High;** *5736*
6:35 and you will be sons *of* the **M High,** *5736*
8:28 Jesus, Son *of* the **M High** God? *5736*
11:43 because you love the **m important seats** in *4751*
20:46 the **m important seats** in the synagogues *4751*
20:47 Such men will be punished **m severely."** *4358*
Ac 7:48 the **M High** does not live in houses made *5736*
16:17 These men are servants *of* the **M High** God, *5736*
19:32 **M** of the *people* did not even know *3836+4498*
20:38 What grieved them **m** was his statement *3436*
24: 3 **m excellent** Felix, we acknowledge this *3196*
26:25 "I am not insane, **m excellent** Festus," *3196*
1Co 10: 5 God was not pleased with **m** of them; *4498*
12:31 I will show you the **m excellent** way. *2848+5651*
14:27 two—or at the **m** three—should speak, *4498*
15: 6 **m** of whom are still living, *4498*
2Co 8: 2 Out of the **m** severe trial, *4498*
9: 2 and your enthusiasm has stirred **m** *of them* *4498*
Eph 5:16 **making the m of** every opportunity, *1973*
Php 1:14 Because of my chains, **m** of the brothers *4498*
Col 4: 5 toward outsiders; **make the m of** every **opportunity.** *1973+2789+3836*
1Th 3:10 Night and day we pray **m earnestly** *5655*
Heb 7: 1 of Salem and priest of God **M High.** *5736*
9: 3 a room called the **M Holy Place,** *41+41*
9: 8 that the way into the **M** Holy Place had not *NIG*
9:12 but he entered the **M** Holy Place once *NIG*
9:25 the **M** Holy Place every year with blood *NIG*
10:19 the **M** Holy Place by the blood of Jesus, *NIG*
13:11 the blood of animals into the **M** Holy Place *NIG*
Jude 1:20 build yourselves up *in* your *m* **holy** faith *AIT*

MOTE (KJV) See SPECK OF SAWDUST

MOTH (7)

Job 4:19 who are crushed more readily than a **m!** 6931
Ps 39:11 you consume their wealth like a **m**— 6931
Isa 51: 8 For the **m** will eat them up like a garment; 6931
Hos 5:12 I am like a **m** to Ephraim, 6931
Mt 6:19 where **m** and rust destroy, *4962*
6:20 where **m** and rust do not destroy, *4962*
Lk 12:33 no thief comes near and no **m** destroys. *4962*

MOTH'S (1) [MOTHS]

Job 27:18 The house he builds is like a **m cocoon,** 6931

MOTHEATEN (KJV) See MOTHS

MOTHER (237) [GRANDMOTHER, GRANDMOTHER'S, MOTHER-IN-LAW, MOTHER'S, MOTHERS, MOTHERS']

Ge 2:24 a man will leave his father and **m** and 562
3:20 she would become the **m** *of* all the living. 562
17:16 I will bless her so that she will be the **m** NIH
20:12 daughter of my father though not of my **m;** 562
21:21 his **m** got a wife for him from Egypt. 562
22:20 "Milcah is also a **m;** NIH
24:53 gave costly gifts to her brother and to her **m.** 562
24:55 But her brother and her **m** replied, 562
24:67 brought her into the tent of his **m** Sarah, 562
27:11 Jacob said to Rebekah his **m,** 562
27:13 His **m** said to him, "My son, 562
27:14 and got them and brought them to his **m,** 562
27:29 may the sons of your **m** bow down to you. 562
28: 5 who was the **m** *of* Jacob and Esau. 562
28: 7 and that Jacob had obeyed his father and **m** 562
30:14 which he brought to his **m** Leah. 562
37:10 Will your **m** and I and your brothers 562
Ex 2: 8 And the girl went and got the baby's **m.** 562
20:12 "Honor your father and your **m,** 562
21:15 "Anyone who attacks his father or his **m** must be put to death. 562
21:17 "Anyone who curses his father or **m** must be put to death. 562
Lev 18: 7 by having sexual relations with your **m.** 562
18: 7 She is your **m;** do not have relations with 562
19: 3 Each of you must respect his **m** and father, 562
20: 9 " 'If anyone curses his father or **m,** 562
20: 9 He has cursed his father or his **m,** 562
20:14 a man marries both a woman and her **m,** 562
20:17 the daughter of either his father or his **m,** 562
20:19 the sister of either your **m** or your father, for 562
21: 2 such as his **m** or father, his son or daughter, 562
21:11 even for his father or **m,** 562
22:27 it is to remain with its **m** for seven days. 562
24:10 Now the son of an Israelite **m** and 851
Nu 6: 7 his own father or **m** or brother or sister dies, 562
Dt 5:16 "Honor your father and your **m,** 562
21:13 in your house and mourned her father and **m** 562
21:18 not obey his father and **m** and will not listen 562
21:19 and his **m** shall take hold of him and bring him 562
22: 6 the **m** is sitting on the young or on the eggs, 562
22: 6 do not take the **m** with the young. 562
22: 7 but be sure to let the **m** go, 562
22:15 then the girl's father and **m** shall bring proof 562
27:16 the man who dishonors his father or his **m."** 562
27:22 of his father or the daughter of his **m."** 562
33: 9 He said of his father and **m,** 562
Jos 2:13 you will spare the lives of my father and **m,** 562
2:18 unless you have brought your father and **m,** 562
6:23 and **m** and brothers and all who belonged 562
Jdg 5: 7 Deborah, arose, arose a **m** in Israel. 562
5:28 "Through the window peered Sisera's **m;** 562
8:19 my brothers, the sons of my own **m.** 562
11: 1 his **m** was a prostitute. 851
14: 2 he returned, he said to his father and **m,** 562
14: 3 His father and **m** replied, 562
14: 5 to Timnah together with his father and **m.** 562
14: 6 his father nor his **m** what he had done. 562
14:16 even explained it to my father or **m,"** 562
17: 2 said to his **m,** "The eleven hundred shekels 562
17: 2 Then his **m** said, "The LORD bless you, 562
17: 3 eleven hundred shekels of silver to his **m,** 562
17: 4 So he returned the silver to his **m,** 562
Ru 2:11 and **m** and your homeland and came to live 562
1Sa 2:19 Each year his **m** made him a little robe 562
15:33 so will your **m** be childless among women." 562
20:30 and to the shame of the **m** *who bore* you? 562
22: 3 "Would you let my father and **m** come 562
2Sa 17:25 of Nahash and sister of Zeruiah the **m** 562
19:37 near the tomb of my father and **m.** 562
20:19 You are trying to destroy a city that is a **m** 562
1Ki 1: 5 Now Adonijah, whose **m** was Haggith, NIH
1:11 Nathan asked Bathsheba, Solomon's **m,** 562
2:13 went to Bathsheba, Solomon's **m.** 562
2:19 He had a throne brought for the king's **m,** 562
2:20 The king replied, "Make it, my **m;** 562
2:22 King Solomon answered his **m,** 562
3:27 Do not kill him; she is his **m."** 562
7:14 whose **m** was a widow from the tribe 851
11:26 and his **m** was a widow named Zeruah. 562
15:13 Maacah from her **position as queen m,** 1485
17:23 He gave him to his **m** and said, "Look, 562
19:20 "Let me kiss my father and **m** good-by," 562
22:52 and **m** and in the ways of Jeroboam son 562
2Ki 3: 2 but not as his father and **m** had done. 562
3:13 of your father and the prophets of your **m."** 562
4:19 "Carry him to his **m."** 562
4:20 lifted him up and carried him to his **m,** 562
4:30 But the child's **m** said, 562
9:22 and witchcraft of your **m** Jezebel abound?" 562
10:13 the families of the king and of the **queen m.** 1485
11: 1 When Athaliah the **m** *of* Ahaziah saw 562
24:12 Jehoiachin king of Judah, his **m,** 562
24:15 from Jerusalem to Babylon the king's **m,** 562
1Ch 2:17 Abigail *was the* **m** *of* Amasa, 3528
2:26 she was the **m** *of* Onam. 562
2:46 Caleb's concubine Ephah *was the* **m** 3528
2:48 Caleb's concubine Maacah *was the* **m** 3528
4: 9 His **m** had named him Jabez, saying, 562
2Ch 2:14 whose **m** was from Dan 851
15:16 Maacah from her **position as queen m,** 1485
22: 3 for his **m** encouraged him in doing wrong. 562
22:10 When Athaliah the **m** *of* Ahaziah saw 562
Est 2: 7 up because she had neither father nor **m.** 562
2: 7 when her father and **m** died. 562
Job 17:14 and to the worm, 'My **m**' or 'My sister,' 562
Ps 27:10 Though my father and **m** forsake me, 562
35:14 in grief as though weeping for my **m.** 562
51: 5 sinful from the time my **m** conceived me. 562
109:14 may the sin of his **m** never be blotted out. 562
113: 9 the barren woman in her home as a happy **m** 562
131: 2 like a weaned child with its **m,** 562
Pr 4: 3 still tender, and an only child of my **m,** 562
10: 1 but a foolish son grief to his **m.** 562
15:20 but a foolish man despises his **m.** 562
19:26 drives out his **m** is a son who brings shame 562
20:20 If a man curses his father or **m,** 562
23:22 and do not despise your **m** when she is old. 562
23:25 May your father and **m** be glad; 562
28:24 He who robs his father or **m** and says, 562
29:15 but a child left to himself disgraces his **m.** 562
30:17 that scorns obedience to a **m,** 562
31: 1 an oracle his **m** taught him: 562
SS 3:11 with which his **m** crowned him on the day 562
6: 9 is unique, the only daughter of her **m,** 562
8: 5 there your **m** conceived you, 562
Isa 8: 4 how to say 'My father' or 'My **m,'** 562
45:10 to his **m,** 'What have you brought to birth?' 851
49:15 "Can a **m** forget the baby at her breast 851
50: 1 your transgressions your **m** was sent away. 562
66:13 **m** comforts her child, so will I comfort you; 562
Jer 13:18 Say to the king and to the **queen m,** 1485
15: 9 The **m** *of* seven will grow faint 3528
15:10 Alas, my **m,** that you gave me birth, 562
16: 7 not even for a father or a **m**— 562
20:14 May the day my **m** bore me not be blessed! 562
20:17 with my **m** as my grave, 562
22:26 and the **m** who gave you birth 562
29: 2 after King Jehoiachin and the **queen m,** 1485
50:12 your **m** will be greatly ashamed; 562
Eze 16: 3 your father was an Amorite and your **m** 562
16:44 "Like **m,** like daughter." 562
16:45 You are a true daughter of your **m,** 562
16:45 Your **m** was a Hittite and your father 562
19: 2 a lioness was your **m** among the lions! 562
19:10 " 'Your **m** was like a vine 562
22: 7 In you they have treated father and **m** 562
23: 2 daughters of the same **m.** 562
44:25 if the dead person was his father or **m,** 562
Hos 2: 2 "Rebuke your **m,** rebuke her, 562
2: 5 Their **m** has been unfaithful and 562
4: 5 So I will destroy your **m**— 562
Mic 7: 6 a daughter rises up against her **m,** 562

Zec 13: 3 if anyone still prophesies, his father and **m**, 562
Mt 1: 3 Perez and Zerah, **whose m was** Tamar, *1666*
1: 5 Boaz, **whose m was** Rahab, *1666*
1: 5 Obed, **whose m was** Ruth, *1666*
1: 6 Solomon, **whose m** had been Uriah's wife, *1666*
1: 18 His **m** Mary was pledged to be married *3613*
2: 11 they saw the child with his **m** Mary, *3613*
2: 13 the child and his **m** and escape to Egypt. *3613*
2: 14 the child and his **m** during the night and left *3613*
2: 20 take the child and his **m** and go to the land *3613*
2: 21 and his **m** and went to the land of Israel. *3613*
10: 35 a daughter against her **m**, *3613*
10: 37 or **m** more than me is not worthy of me; *3613*
12: 46 his **m** and brothers stood outside, *3613*
12: 47 "Your **m** and brothers are standing outside, *3613*
12: 48 He replied to him, "Who is my **m**, *3613*
12: 49 he said, "Here are my **m** and my brothers. *3613*
12: 50 in heaven is my brother and sister and **m**." *3613*
14: 8 Prompted by her **m**, she said, *3613*
14: 11 who carried it *to* her **m**. *3613*
15: 4 God said, 'Honor your father and **m**' *3613*
15: 4 curses his father or **m** must be put to death.' *3613*
15: 5 that if a man says *to* his father or **m**, *3613*
19: 5 a man will leave his father and **m** and *3613*
19: 19 honor your father and **m**,' *3613*
19: 29 or sisters or father or **m** or children or fields *3613*
20: 20 Then the **m** of Zebedee's sons came to Jesus *3613*
27: 56 Mary the **m** of James and Joses, *3613*
27: 56 and the **m** of Zebedee's sons. *3613*
Mk 3: 31 Then Jesus' **m** and brothers arrived. *3613*
3: 32 "Your **m** and brothers are outside looking *3613*
3: 33 "Who are my **m** and my brothers?" *3613*
3: 34 "Here are my **m** and my brothers! *3613*
3: 35 God's will is my brother and sister and **m**." *3613*
5: 40 and **m** and the disciples who were with him, *3613*
6: 24 She went out and said *to* her **m**, *3613*
6: 28 and she gave it *to* her **m**. *3613*
7: 10 'Honor your father and your **m**,' and, *3613*
7: 10 'Anyone who curses his father or **m** must *3613*
7: 11 you say that if a man says to his father or **m**: *3613*
7: 12 let him do anything *for* his father or **m**. *3613*
10: 7 a man will leave his father and **m** and *3613*
10: 19 do not defraud, honor your father and **m**.' " *3613*
10: 29 or sisters or **m** or father or children or fields *3613*
15: 40 the **m** of James the younger and of Joses, *3613*
15: 47 the **m** of Joses saw where he was laid. *3836*
16: 1 Mary Magdalene, Mary the **m** of James, *3836*
Lk 1: 43 that the **m** of my Lord should come to me? *3613*
1: 60 but his **m** spoke up and said, *3613*
2: 33 and **m** marveled at what was said about him. *3613*
2: 34 blessed them and said to Mary, his **m**: *3613*
2: 48 His **m** said to him, "Son, why have you *3613*
2: 51 his **m** treasured all these things in her heart. *3613*
7: 12 only son *of* his **m**, and she was a widow. *3613*
7: 15 and Jesus gave him back *to* his **m**. *3613*
8: 19 Jesus' **m** and brothers came to see him, *3613*
8: 20 "Your **m** and brothers are standing outside, *3613*
8: 21 He replied, "My **m** and brothers are *3613*
8: 51 and the child's father and **m**. *3613*
11: 27 the **m** who gave you birth and nursed you." *3120*
12: 53 **m** against daughter and daughter against *3613*
12: 53 against daughter and daughter against **m**, *3613*
14: 26 and does not hate his father and **m**, his wife *3613*
18: 20 honor your father and **m**.' " *3613*
24: 10 Joanna, Mary the **m** of James, *3836*
Jn 2: 1 Jesus' **m** was there, *3613*
2: 3 Jesus' **m** said to him, "They have no more *3613*
2: 5 His **m** said to the servants, *3613*
2: 12 down to Capernaum with his **m** and brothers *3613*
6: 42 whose father and **m** we know? *3613*
19: 25 Near the cross of Jesus stood his **m**, *3613*
19: 26 When Jesus saw his **m** there, *3613*
19: 26 he said *to* his **m**, "Dear woman, here is your son," *3613*
19: 27 "Here is your **m**." *3613*
Ac 1: 14 with the women and Mary the **m** of Jesus, *3613*
12: 12 he went to the house of Mary the **m** of John, *3613*
16: 1 whose **m** was a Jewess and a believer, *1222*
Ro 16: 13 Greet Rufus, chosen in the Lord, and his **m**, *3613*
16: 13 and his mother, who has been a **m** to me, *NIG*
Gal 4: 26 that is above is free, and she is our **m**. *3613*
Eph 5: 31 a man will leave his father and **m** and *3613*
6: 2 "Honor your father and **m**"— *3613*
1Th 2: 7 like a **m** caring for her little children. *5577*
2Ti 1: 5 Lois and in your **m** Eunice and, *3613*
Heb 7: 3 Without father or **m**, without genealogy, *298*
Rev 17: 5 BABYLON THE GREAT THE **M** OF PROSTITUTES *3613*

MOTHER'S (64) [MOTHER]

Ge 24: 28 The girl ran and told her **m** household 562
24: 67 and Isaac was comforted after his **m** death. 562
28: 2 to the house of your **m** father Bethuel. 562
28: 2 the daughters of Laban, your **m** brother. 562
29: 10 his **m** brother, and Laban's sheep, 562
43: 29 brother Benjamin, his own **m** son, he asked, 562
44: 20 and he is the only one of his **m** sons left, 562
Ex 23: 19 "Do not cook a young goat in its **m** milk. 562
34: 26 "Do not cook a young goat in its **m** milk." 562
Lev 18: 9 your father's daughter or your **m** daughter, 562
18: 13 not have sexual relations with your **m** sister, 562
18: 13 because she is your **m** close relative. 562
24: 11 (His **m** name was Shelomith, 562
Nu 12: 12 a stillborn infant coming from its **m** womb 562
Dt 14: 21 Do not cook a young goat in its **m** milk. 562
Jdg 9: 1 to his **m** brothers in Shechem and said 562
9: 1 and said to them and to all his **m** clan, 562
Ru 1: 8 "Go back, each of you, to your **m** home. 562
1Ki 14: 21 His **m** name was Naamah; 562
14: 31 His **m** name was Naamah; 562
15: 2 His **m** name was Maacah daughter 562
22: 42 His **m** name was Azubah daughter of Shilhi. 562
2Ki 8: 26 His **m** name was Athaliah, 562
12: 1 His **m** name was Zibiah; 562
14: 2 His **m** name was Jehoaddin; 562
15: 2 His **m** name was Jecoliah; 562
15: 33 His **m** name was Jerusha daughter of Zadok. 562
18: 2 His **m** name was Abijah daughter 562
21: 1 His **m** name was Hephzibah. 562
21: 19 His **m** name was Meshullemeth daughter 562
22: 1 His **m** name was Jedidah daughter 562
23: 31 His **m** name was Hamutal daughter 562
23: 36 His **m** name was Zebidah daughter 562
24: 8 His **m** name was Nehushta daughter 562
24: 18 His **m** name was Hamutal daughter 562
2Ch 12: 13 His **m** name was Naamah; 562
13: 2 His **m** name was Maacah, 562
20: 31 His **m** name was Azubah daughter of Shilhi. 562
22: 2 His **m** name was Athaliah, 562
24: 1 His **m** name was Zibiah; 562
25: 1 His **m** name was Jehoaddin; 562
26: 3 His **m** name was Jecoliah; 562
27: 1 His **m** name was Jerusha daughter of Zadok. 562
29: 1 His **m** name was Abijah daughter 562
Job 1: 21 "Naked I came from my **m** womb, 562
Ps 22: 9 in you even at my **m** breast. 562
22: 10 from my **m** womb you have been my God. 562
50: 20 and slander your own **m** son. 562
69: 8 an alien to my own **m** sons; 562
71: 6 you brought me forth from my **m** womb. 562
139: 13 you knit me together in my **m** womb. 562
Pr 1: 8 and do not forsake your **m** teaching. 562
6: 20 and do not forsake your **m** teaching. 562
Ecc 5: 15 Naked a man comes from his **m** womb, 562
11: 5 or how the body is formed in a **m** womb, 4849S
SS 1: 6 My **m** sons were angry with me 562
3: 4 till I had brought him to my **m** house, 562
8: 1 who was nursed at my **m** breasts! 562
8: 2 and bring you to my **m** house— 562
Isa 50: 1 "Where is your **m** certificate of divorce 562
Jer 52: 1 His **m** name was Hamutal daughter 562
Mt 13: 55 Isn't his **m** name Mary, *3613*
Jn 3: 4 a second time into his **m** womb to be born!" *3613*
19: 25 his **m** sister, Mary the wife of Clopas, *3613*

MOTHER-IN-LAW (18) [MOTHER]

Dt 27: 23 "Cursed is the man who sleeps with his **m**." 3165
Ru 1: 14 Then Orpah kissed her **m** good-by, 2792
2: 11 about what you have done for your **m** since 2792
2: 18 and her **m** saw how much she had gathered. 2792
2: 19 Her **m** asked her, "Where did you glean 2792
2: 19 Then Ruth told her **m** about the one 2792
2: 23 And she lived with her **m**. 2792
3: 1 One day Naomi her **m** said to her, 2792
3: 6 and did everything her **m** told her to do. 2792
3: 16 When Ruth came to her **m**, Naomi asked, 2792
3: 17 'Don't go back to your **m** empty-handed.' " 2792
Mic 7: 6 a daughter-in-law against her **m**— 2792
Mt 8: 14 he saw Peter's **m** lying in bed with a fever. *4289*
10: 35 a daughter-in-law against her **m**— *4289*
Mk 1: 30 Simon's **m** was in bed with a fever, *4289*
Lk 4: 38 Simon's **m** was suffering from a high fever, *4289*
12: 53 **m** against daughter-in-law *4289*
12: 53 and daughter-in-law against **m**." *4289*

MOTHER-OF-PEARL (1) [PEARL]

Est 1: 6 marble, **m** and other costly stones. 1993

MOTHERS (17) [MOTHER]

Ge 32: 11 and also the **m** with their children. 562
Ex 22: 30 Let them stay with their **m** for seven days, 562
Job 31: 15 the same one form us both within our **m**? 8167
Pr 30: 11 and do not bless their **m**; 562
Isa 49: 23 and their queens your **nursing m**. 4787
Jer 15: 8 against the **m** *of* their young men; 562
16: 3 and about the women who are their **m** and 562
31: 8 **expectant m** and women in labor; 2226
La 2: 12 They say to their **m**, "Where is bread 562
5: 3 and fatherless, our **m** like widows. 562
Hos 10: 14 of battle, when **m** were dashed to the ground 562
Mt 24: 19 for pregnant women and **nursing m!** *2558*
Mk 10: 30 brothers, sisters, **m**, children and fields— *3613*
13: 17 for pregnant women and **nursing m!** *2558*
Lk 21: 23 for pregnant women and **nursing m!** *2558*
1Ti 1: 9 *for those who* kill their fathers or **m**, *3618*
5: 2 older women as **m**, and younger women as *3613*

MOTHERS' (1) [MOTHER]

La 2: 12 as their lives ebb away in their **m'** arms. 562

MOTHS (3) [MOTH'S]

Job 13: 28 like a garment eaten by **m**. 6931
Isa 50: 9 the **m** will eat them up. 6931
Jas 5: 2 and **m have eaten** your clothes. *1181+4963*

MOTIONED (7) [MOTIONS]

Jn 13: 24 Simon Peter **m** to this disciple and said, *3748*
Ac 12: 17 Peter **m** with his hand for them to be quiet *2939*
13: 16 Standing up, Paul **m** with his hand and said: *2939*
19: 33 He **m** for silence in order to make a defense *2939*
21: 40 Paul stood on the steps and **m** to the crowd. *2939+3836+5931*
24: 10 *When* the governor **m** for him to speak, *3748*
26: 1 Paul **m with** his hand and began his defense *1753*

MOTIONS (1) [MOTIONED]

Pr 6: 13 signals with his feet and **m** with his fingers, 3721

MOTIVE (1) [MOTIVES]

1Ch 28: 9 understands every **m** *behind* the thoughts. 3671

MOTIVES (5) [MOTIVE]

Pr 16: 2 but **m** are weighed by the LORD. 8120
1Co 4: 5 and will expose the **m** of men's hearts. *1087*
Php 1: 18 whether *from* **false m** or true, *4733*
1Th 2: 3 not spring from error or impure **m**, *NIG*
Jas 4: 3 because you ask with wrong **m**, *NIG*

MOUND (5) [MOUNDS]

SS 7: 2 Your waist is a **m** *of* wheat encircled 6894
Jer 26: 18 the temple hill a **m** *overgrown with* thickets. 1195
49: 2 it will become a **m** *of* ruins, 9424
Eze 16: 24 a **m** for yourself and made a lofty shrine 1461
Mic 3: 12 the temple hill a **m** overgrown with thickets. 1195

MOUNDS (3) [MOUND]

Jos 11: 13 not burn any of the cities built on their **m**— 9424
Eze 16: 31 When you built your **m** at the head 1461
16: 39 down your **m** and destroy your lofty shrines. 1461

MOUNT (146) [MOUNTAIN, MOUNTAINS, MOUNTAINSIDE, MOUNTAINTOP, MOUNTAINTOPS, MOUNTED, MOUNTINGS, MOUNTS]

Ex 19: 11 the LORD will come down on **M** Sinai in 2215
19: 18 **M** Sinai was covered with smoke, 2215
19: 20 of **M** Sinai and called Moses to the top of 2215
19: 23 "The people cannot come up **M** Sinai, 2215
24: 16 the glory of the LORD settled on **M** Sinai. 2215
28: 11 Then **m** the stones in gold filigree settings 6913
28: 17 Then **m** four rows of precious stones 4848+4853
28: 20 **M** them in gold filigree settings. 2118+4853
31: 18 finished speaking to Moses on **M** Sinai, 2215
33: 6 So the Israelites stripped off their ornaments at **M** Horeb. 2215
34: 2 and then come up on **M** Sinai. 2215
34: 4 the first ones and went up **M** Sinai early in 2215
34: 29 down from **M** Sinai with the two tablets of 2215
34: 32 the LORD had given him on **M** Sinai. 2215
Lev 7: 38 which the LORD gave Moses on **M** Sinai 2215
25: 1 The LORD said to Moses on **M** Sinai, 2215
26: 46 that the LORD established on **M** Sinai 2215
27: 34 the LORD gave Moses on **M** Sinai for 2215
Nu 3: 1 the LORD talked with Moses on **M** Sinai. 2215
20: 22 from Kadesh and came to **M** Hor. 2215
20: 23 At **M** Hor, near the border of Edom, 2215
20: 25 and take them up **M** Hor. 2215
20: 27 They went up **M** Hor in the sight of 2215
21: 4 from **M** Hor along the route to the Red Sea, 2215
28: 6 at **M** Sinai as a pleasing aroma, 2215
33: 23 and camped at **M** Shepher. 2215
33: 24 They left **M** Shepher and camped 2215
33: 37 They left Kadesh and camped at **M** Hor, 2215
33: 38 the priest went up **M** Hor, 2215
33: 39 when he died on **M** Hor. 2215
33: 41 They left **M** Hor and camped at Zalmonah. 2215
34: 7 run a line from the Great Sea to **M** Hor 2215
34: 8 and from **M** Hor to Lebo Hamath. 2215
Dt 1: 2 to Kadesh Barnea by the **M** Seir road.) 2215
3: 8 from the Arnon Gorge as far as **M** Hermon. 2215
4: 48 on the rim of the Arnon Gorge to **M** Siyon 2215
11: 29 to proclaim on **M** Gerizim the blessings, 2215
11: 29 and on **M** Ebal the curses. 2215
27: 4 set up these stones on **M** Ebal, 2215
27: 12 these tribes shall stand on **M** Gerizim 2215
27: 13 And these tribes shall stand on **M** Ebal 2215
32: 49 into the Abarim Range to **M** Nebo in Moab, 2215
32: 50 on **M** Hor and was gathered to his people. 2215
33: 2 he shone forth from **M** Paran. 2215
34: 1 Then Moses climbed **M** Nebo from 2215
Jos 8: 30 Then Joshua built on **M** Ebal an altar to 2215
8: 33 of the people stood in front of **M** Gerizim 2215
8: 33 and half of them in front of **M** Ebal, 2215
11: 17 from **M** Halak, which rises toward Seir, 2215
11: 17 in the Valley of Lebanon below **M** Hermon. 2215
12: 1 from the Arnon Gorge to **M** Hermon, 2215
12: 5 He ruled over **M** Hermon, Salecah, 2215
12: 7 in the Valley of Lebanon to **M** Halak, 2215
13: 5 the east, from Baal Gad below **M** Hermon 2215
13: 11 all of **M** Hermon and all Bashan as far 2215
15: 9 of **M** Ephron and went down toward Baalah 2215
15: 10 it curved westward from Baalah to **M** Seir, 2215
15: 10 ran along the northern slope of **M** Jearim 2215
15: 11 along to **M** Baalah and reached Jabneel. 2215
24: 30 hill country of Ephraim, north of **M** Gaash. 2215
Jdg 1: 35 also to hold out in **M** Heres, 2215
2: 9 hill country of Ephraim, north of **M** Gaash. 2215
3: 3 from **M** Baal Hermon to Lebo Hamath. 2215
4: 6 and Zebulun and lead the way to **M** Tabor. 2215
4: 12 of Abinoam had gone up to **M** Tabor, 2215
4: 14 So Barak went down **M** Tabor, 2215
7: 3 may turn back and leave **M** Gilead.' " 2215

Jdg 9: 7 the top of **M** Gerizim and shouted to them, 2215
9:48 he and all his men went up **M** Zalmon. 2215
1Sa 31: 1 and many fell slain on **M** Gilboa. 2215
31: 8 and his three sons fallen on **M** Gilboa. 2215
2Sa 1: 6 "I happened to be on **M** Gilboa," 2215
15:30 But David continued up the **M** *of* Olives, 5090
1Ki 18:19 over Israel to meet me on **M** Carmel. 2215
18:20 and assembled the prophets on **M** Carmel. 2215
2Ki 2:25 on to **M** Carmel and from there returned 2215
4:25 and came to the man of God at **M** Carmel. 2215
19:31 and out of **M** Zion a band of survivors. 2215
1Ch 5:23 that is, to Senir (**M** Hermon). 2215
10: 1 and many fell slain on **M** Gilboa. 2215
10: 8 and his sons fallen on **M** Gilboa. 2215
2Ch 3: 1 of the LORD in Jerusalem on **M** Moriah, 2215
13: 4 Abijah stood on **M** Zemaraim, 2215
20:10 and **M** Seir, whose territory you would 2215
20:22 and **M** Seir who were invading Judah, 2215
20:23 from **M** Seir to destroy and annihilate them. 2215
Ne 2:14 not enough room for my **m** to get through; 989
9:13 "You came down on **M** Sinai; 2215
Ps 42: 6 of Hermon—from **M** Mizar. 2215
48: 2 the utmost heights of Zaphon is **M** Zion, 2215
48:11 **M** Zion rejoices, the villages 2215
74: 2 **M** Zion, where you dwelt. 2215
78:68 **M** Zion, which he loved. 2215
89: 9 when its waves **m up,** you still them. 5951
125: 1 who trust in the LORD are like **M** Zion, 2215
133: 3 the dew of Hermon were falling on **M** Zion. 2215
SS 4: 1 a flock of goats descending from **M** Gilead. 2215
7: 5 Your head crowns you like **M** Carmel. NIH
Isa 4: 5 the LORD will create over all of **M** Zion 2215
8:18 the LORD Almighty, who dwells on **M** Zion. 2215
10:12 against **M** Zion and Jerusalem, 2215
10:32 they will shake their fist at the **m** *of* 2215
14:13 I will sit enthroned on the **m** *of* assembly, 2215
16: 1 to the **m** *of* the Daughter of Zion. 2215
18: 7 the gifts will be brought to **M** Zion, 2215
24:23 the LORD Almighty will reign on **M** Zion 2215
28:21 at **M** Perazim, he will rouse himself as in 2215
29: 8 of all the nations that fight against **M** Zion. 2215
31: 4 to do battle on **M** Zion and on its heights. 2215
37:32 and out of **M** Zion a band of survivors. 2215
Jer 46: 4 Harness the horses, **m the steeds!** 6590
La 5:18 for **M** Zion, which lies desolate, 2215
Eze 28:14 You were on the holy **m** *of* God; 2215
28:16 I drove you in disgrace from the **m** *of* God, 2215
35: 2 set your face against **M** Seir; 2215
35: 3 I am against you, **M** Seir, 2215
35: 7 I will make **M** Seir a desolate waste 2215
35:15 You will be desolate, O **M** Seir, 2215
Hos 14: 3 *we will* not **m** war-horses. 8206
Joel 2:32 for on **M** Zion and in Jerusalem there will 2215
Am 4: 1 you cows of Bashan on **M** Samaria, 2215
6: 1 and to you who feel secure on **M** Samaria, 2215
Ob 1:17 But on **M** Zion will be deliverance; 2215
1:21 Deliverers will go up on **M** Zion to govern 2215
Mic 4: 7 The LORD will rule over them in **M** Zion 2215
Hab 3: 3 the Holy One from **M** Paran. 2215
Zec 14: 4 On that day his feet will stand on the **M** 2215
14: 4 and the **M** *of* Olives will be split in two 2215
Mt 21: 1 and came to Bethphage on the **M** of Olives, *4001*
24: 3 As Jesus was sitting on the **M** of Olives, *4001*
26:30 they went out to the **M** of Olives. *4001*
Mk 11: 1 to Bethphage and Bethany at the **M** *4001*
13: 3 on the **M** of Olives opposite the temple, *4001*
14:26 they went out to the **M** of Olives. *4001*
Lk 19:29 at the hill called the **M of Olives,** *1777*
19:37 where the road goes down the **M** of Olives, *4001*
21:37 on the hill called the **M of Olives,** *1777*
22:39 Jesus went out as usual to the **M** of Olives, *4001*
Jn 8: 1 But Jesus went to the **M** of Olives. *4001*
Ac 1:12 from the hill called the **M of Olives,** *1779*
7:30 a burning bush in the desert near **M** Sinai. *4001*
7:38 the angel who spoke to him on **M** Sinai, and *4001*
Gal 4:24 from **M** Sinai and bears children who are to *4001*
4:25 Hagar stands for **M** Sinai in Arabia and *4001*
Heb 12:22 But you have come to **M** Zion, *4001*
Rev 14: 1 standing on **M** Zion, and with him 144,000 *4001*

MOUNTAIN (154) [MOUNT]

Ge 22:14 the **m** *of* the LORD it will be provided." 2215
Ex 3: 1 and came to Horeb, the **m** *of* God. 2215
3:12 you will worship God on this **m.**" 2215
4:27 So he met Moses at the **m** *of* God 2215
15:17 on the **m** *of* your inheritance— 2215
18: 5 where he was camped near the **m** *of* God. 2215
19: 2 in the desert in front of the **m.** 2215
19: 3 LORD called to him from the **m** and said, 2215
19:12 for the people around the **m** and tell them, NIH
19:12 'Be careful that you do not go up the **m** 2215
19:12 Whoever touches the **m** shall surely be put 2215
19:13 a long blast may they go up to the **m.**" 2215
19:14 Moses had gone down the **m** to the people, 2215
19:16 with a thick cloud over the **m,** 2215
19:17 and they stood at the foot of the **m.** 2215
19:18 the whole **m** trembled violently, 2215
19:20 and called Moses to the top of the **m.** 2215
19:23 'Put limits around the **m** and set it apart 2215
20:18 and heard the trumpet and saw the **m** 2215
24: 4 and built an altar at the foot of the **m** and set 2215
24:12 "Come up to me on the **m** and stay here, 2215
24:13 and Moses went up on the **m** *of* God. 2215
24:15 When Moses went up on the **m,** 2215
24:16 For six days the cloud covered **the m,** 2084S
24:17 like a consuming fire on top of the **m.** 2215
Ex 24:18 the cloud as he went on up the **m.** 2215
24:18 on the **m** forty days and forty nights. 2215
25:40 to the pattern shown you on the **m.** 2215
26:30 according to the plan shown you on the **m.** 2215
27: 8 be made just as you were shown on the **m.** 2215
32: 1 so long in coming down from the **m,** 2215
32:15 and went down the **m** with the two tablets of 2215
32:19 breaking them to pieces at the foot of the **m.** 2215
34: 2 to me there on top of the **m.** 2215
34: 3 with you or be seen anywhere on the **m;** 2215
34: 3 and herds may graze in front of the **m.**" 2215
Nu 10:33 So they set out from the **m** *of* the LORD 2215
20:28 And Aaron died there on top of the **m.** 2215
20:28 Moses and Eleazar came down from the **m,** 2215
27:12 "Go up this **m** *in* the Abarim range and see 2215
Dt 1: 6 "You have stayed long enough at this **m.** 2215
4:11 the foot of the **m** while it blazed with fire to 2215
5: 4 to you face to face out of the fire on the **m.** 2215
5: 5 of the fire and did not go up the **m.**) 2215
5:22 on the **m** from out of the fire, the cloud and 2215
5:23 while the **m** was ablaze with fire, 2215
9: 9 up on the **m** to receive the tablets of stone, 2215
9: 9 on the **m** forty days and forty nights; 2215
9:10 the LORD proclaimed to you on the **m** out 2215
9:15 from the **m** while it was ablaze with fire. 2215
9:21 into a stream that flowed down the **m.** 2215
10: 1 the first ones and come up to me on the **m.** 2215
10: 3 and I went up on the **m** with the two tablets 2215
10: 4 he had proclaimed to you on the **m,** 2215
10: 5 Then I came back down the **m** and put 2215
10:10 I had stayed on the **m** forty days and nights, 2215
14: 5 the ibex, the antelope and the **m sheep.** 2378
32:50 on the **m** that you have climbed you will die 2215
33: 2 from the south, from his **m slopes.** 850
33:19 They will summon peoples to the **m** 2215
Jos 10:40 the western foothills and the **m slopes,** 844
12: 8 the **m slopes,** the desert and the Negev— 844
13: 6 "As for all the inhabitants of the **m regions** 2215
Jdg 6: 2 shelters for themselves in **m clefts,** 2215
1Sa 23:26 Saul was going along one side of the **m,** 2215
25:20 she came riding her donkey into a **m** ravine, 2215
1Ki 19: 8 until he reached Horeb, the **m** *of* God. 2215
19:11 "Go out and stand on the **m** in the presence 2215
2Ki 2:16 down on some **m** or in some valley." 2215
4:27 When she reached the man of God at the **m,** 2215
Job 14:18 "But as a **m** erodes and crumbles and as 2215
24: 8 They are drenched by **m** rains and hug 2215
39: 1 "Do you know when the **m** goats give birth? 6152
Ps 11: 1 "Flee like a bird to your **m.** 2215
30: 7 you made my **m** stand firm; 2215
43: 3 let them bring me to your holy **m,** 2215
48: 1 in the city of our God, his holy **m.** 2215
68:16 at the **m** where God chooses to reign, 2215
87: 1 He has set his foundation on the holy **m;** 2215
95: 4 and the **m** peaks belong to him. 2215
99: 9 and worship at his holy **m,** 2215
SS 4: 6 to the **m** *of* myrrh and to the hill of incense. 2215
4: 8 and the **m haunts** *of* the leopards. 2215
Isa 2: 2 the **m** *of* the LORD's temple will be established 2215
2: 3 "Come, let us go up to the **m** *of* the LORD, 2215
11: 9 harm nor destroy on all my holy **m,** 2215
14:13 on the utmost heights of the **sacred m.** 7600
18: 6 the **m** birds of prey and to the wild animals; 2215
25: 6 On this **m** the LORD Almighty will prepare 2215
25: 7 On this **m** he will destroy the shroud 2215
25:10 The hand of the LORD will rest on this **m;** 2215
27:13 the LORD on the holy **m** in Jerusalem. 2215
30:25 streams of water will flow on every high **m** 2215
30:29 go up with flutes to the **m** *of* the LORD. 2215
33:16 whose refuge will be the **m** fortress. 6152
40: 4 every **m** and hill made low; 2215
40: 9 good tidings to Zion, go up on a high **m.** 2215
56: 7 to my holy **m** and give them joy 2215
57:13 the land and possess my holy **m.**" 2215
65:11 the LORD and forget my holy **m,** 2215
65:25 nor destroy on all my holy **m,**" 2215
66:20 to my holy **m** in Jerusalem as an offering to 2215
Jer 16:16 on every **m** and hill and from the crevices of 2215
17: 3 My **m** in the land and your wealth 2215
31:23 O righteous dwelling, O sacred **m.**' 2215
50: 6 They wandered over **m** and hill 2215
51:25 "I am against you, O destroying **m,** 2215
51:25 and make you a burned-out **m.** 2215
Eze 11:23 within the city and stopped above the **m** east 2215
17:22 and plant it on a high and lofty **m.** 2215
17:23 On the **m** heights of Israel I will plant it; 2215
18: 6 the **m shrines** or look to the idols of the 2215
18:11 "He eats at the **m shrines.** 2215
18:15 the **m shrines** or look to the idols of the 2215
20:40 For on my holy **m,** the high mountain of 2215
20:40 on my holy mountain, the high **m** *of* Israel, 2215
22: 9 in you are those who eat at the **m shrines** 2215
34:14 and the **m** heights of Israel will 2215
40: 2 of Israel and set me on a very high **m,** 2215
43:12 the surrounding area on top of the **m** will 2215
Da 2:35 that struck the statue became a huge **m** 10296
2:45 vision of the rock cut out of a **m,** but not 10296
11:45 between the seas at the beautiful holy **m.** 2215
Mic 4: 1 the **m** *of* the LORD's temple will be established 2215
4: 2 "Come, let us go up to the **m** *of* the LORD, 2215
7:12 from sea to sea and from **m** to mountain. 2215
7:12 from sea to sea and from mountain to **m.** 2215
Zec 4: 7 "What are you, O mighty **m?** 2215
8: 3 and the **m** *of* the LORD Almighty will 2215
8: 3 will be called the Holy **M.**" 2215
Zec 14: 4 the **m** moving north and half moving south. 2215
14: 5 You will flee by my **m** valley, 2215
Mt 4: 8 to a very high **m** and showed him all *4001*
17: 1 and led them up a high **m** by themselves. *4001*
17: 9 As they were coming down the **m,** *4001*
17:20 you can say *to* this **m,** 'Move from here *4001*
21:21 but also you can say *to* this **m,** 'Go, *4001*
28:16 to the **m** where Jesus had told them to go. *4001*
Mk 9: 2 with him and led them up a high **m,** *4001*
9: 9 As they were coming down the **m,** *4001*
11:23 if anyone says *to* this **m,** 'Go, *4001*
Lk 3: 5 every **m** and hill made low. *4001*
9:28 and James with him and went up onto a **m** *4001*
9:37 when they came down from the **m,** *4001*
Jn 4:20 Our fathers worshiped on this **m,** *4001*
4:21 the Father neither on this **m** nor *4001*
6:15 withdrew again to a **m** by himself. *4001*
Heb 8: 5 to the pattern shown you on the **m.**" *4001*
12:18 a **m** that can be touched and that is burning *4001*
12:20 "If even an animal touches the **m,** *4001*
2Pe 1:18 when we were with him on the sacred **m.** *4001*
Rev 6:14 and every **m** and island was removed *4001*
8: 8 and something like a huge **m,** all ablaze, *4001*
21:10 in the Spirit to a **m** great and high, *4001*

MOUNTAINS (154) [MOUNT]

Ge 7:19 and all the high **m** under the entire heavens 2215
7:20 the **m** to a depth of more than twenty feet. 2215
8: 4 the ark came to rest on the **m** *of* Ararat. 2215
8: 5 the tops of the **m** became visible. 2215
19:17 Flee to the **m** or you will be swept away!" 2215
19:19 But I can't flee to the **m;** 2215
19:30 and settled in the **m,** 2215
22: 2 on one of the **m** I will tell you about." 2215
49:26 the blessings of the ancient **m,** 2215
Ex 32:12 to kill them in the **m** and to wipe them off 2215
Nu 23: 7 the king of Moab from the eastern **m.** 2215
33:47 and camped in the **m** *of* Abarim, 2215
33:48 the **m** *of* Abarim and camped on the plains 2215
Dt 1: 7 in the **m,** in the western foothills, 2215
11:11 of is a land of **m** and valleys that drinks rain 2215
11:30 As you know, these **m** are across the Jordan, NIH
12: 2 the places on the high **m** and on the hills 2215
32:22 and set afire the foundations of the **m.** 2215
33:15 with the choicest gifts of the ancient **m** and 2215
Jos 11: 2 to the northern kings who were in the **m,** in 2215
11:16 the western foothills, the Arabah and the **m** 2215
Jdg 3: 3 in the Lebanon **m** from Mount Baal Hermon 2215
5: 5 The **m** quaked before the LORD, 2215
9:36 coming down from the tops of the **m!**" 2215
9:36 "You mistake the shadows of the **m** 2215
1Sa 26:20 as one hunts a partridge in the **m.**" 2215
2Sa 1:21 "O **m** of Gilboa, may you have neither 2215
1Ki 19:11 a great and powerful wind tore the **m** apart 2215
2Ki 19:23 I have ascended the heights of the **m,** 2215
1Ch 12: 8 and they were as swift as gazelles in the **m.** 2215
Job 9: 5 He moves **m** without their knowing it 2215
28: 9 and lays bare the roots of the **m.** 2215
Ps 18: 7 and the foundations of the **m** shook; 2215
36: 6 Your righteousness is like the mighty **m,** 2215
46: 2 though the earth give way and the **m** fall 2215
46: 3 and the **m** quake with their surging. 2215
50:11 I know every bird in the **m,** 2215
65: 6 who formed the **m** by your power, 2215
68:15 The **m** *of* Bashan are majestic mountains; 2215
68:15 The mountains of Bashan are majestic **m;** 2215
68:15 rugged are the **m** *of* Bashan. 2215
68:16 Why gaze in envy, O rugged **m,** 2215
72: 3 The **m** will bring prosperity to the people, 2215
76: 4 more majestic than **m** *rich with* game. 2215
80:10 The **m** were covered with its shade, 2215
83:14 the forest or a flame sets the **m** ablaze, 2215
90: 2 the **m** were born or you brought forth 2215
97: 5 The **m** melt like wax before the LORD, 2215
98: 8 let the **m** sing together for joy; 2215
104: 6 the waters stood above the **m.** 2215
104: 8 they flowed over the **m,** 2215
104:10 it flows between the **m.** 2215
104:13 He waters the **m** from his upper chambers; 2215
104:18 The high **m** belong to the wild goats; 2215
104:32 who touches the **m,** and they smoke. 2215
114: 4 the **m** skipped like rams, 2215
114: 6 you **m,** that you skipped 2215
125: 2 As the **m** surround Jerusalem, 2215
144: 5 touch the **m,** so that they smoke. 2215
148: 9 you **m** and all hills, fruit trees and all cedars, 2215
Pr 8:25 before the **m** were settled in place, 2215
SS 2: 8 Here he comes, leaping across the **m,** 2215
8:14 or like a young stag on the spice-laden **m.** 2215
Isa 2: 2 be established as chief among the **m;** 2215
2:14 for all the towering **m** and all the high hills, 2215
5:25 The **m** shake, and the dead bodies are 2215
13: 4 Listen, a noise on the **m,** 2215
14:25 on my **m** I will trample him down. 2215
18: 3 when a banner is raised on the **m,** 2215
22: 5 down walls and of crying out to the **m.** 2215
34: 3 the **m** will be soaked with their blood. 2215
37:24 I have ascended the heights of the **m,** 2215
40:12 or weighed the **m** on the scales and the hills 2215
41:15 You will thresh the **m** and crush them, 2215
42:15 I will lay waste the **m** and hills and dry 2215
44:23 Burst into song, you **m,** 2215
45: 2 I will go before you and will level the **m;** 2065
49:11 I will turn all my **m** into roads, 2215
49:13 burst into song, O **m!** 2215
52: 7 How beautiful on the **m** are the feet 2215

Isa 54:10 the m be shaken and the hills be removed, 2215
55:12 m and hills will burst into song before you, 2215
64: 1 that the m would tremble before you! 2215
64: 3 and the m trembled before you. 2215
65: 7 "Because they burned sacrifices on the m 2215
65: 9 from Judah those who will possess my m; 2215
Jer 3:23 on the hills and m is a deception; 2215
4:24 I looked at the m, and they were quaking; 2215
9:10 I will weep and wail for the m and take up 2215
46:18 who is like Tabor among the m, 2215
50: 6 and caused them to roam on the m. 2215
La 4:19 they chased us over the m and lay in wait 2215
Eze 6: 2 set your face against the m of Israel; 2215
6: 3 'O m of Israel, hear the word 2215
6: 3 the m and hills, to the ravines and valleys: 2215
7: 7 there is panic, not joy, upon the m. 2215
7:16 and escape will be in the m, 2215
19: 9 so his roar was heard no longer on the m 2215
31:12 Its boughs fell on the m and in all 2215
32: 5 the m and fill the valleys with your remains. 2215
32: 6 your flowing blood all the way to the m, 2215
33:28 and the m of Israel will become desolate so 2215
34: 6 My sheep wandered over all the m and 2215
34:13 I will pasture them on the m of Israel, 2215
34:14 in a rich pasture on the m of Israel. 2215
35: 8 I will fill your m with the slain; 2215
35:12 you have said against the m of Israel. 2215
36: 1 prophesy to the m of Israel and say, 2215
36: 1 'O m of Israel, hear the word of 2215
36: 4 O m of Israel, hear the word of 2215
36: 4 the m and hills, to the ravines and valleys, 2215
36: 6 the land of Israel and say to the m and hills, 2215
36: 8 " 'But you, O m of Israel, will produce 2215
37:22 in the land, on the m of Israel. 2215
38: 8 from many nations to the m of Israel, 2215
38:20 The m will be overturned, 2215
38:21 a sword against Gog on all my m, 2215
39: 2 the far north and send you against the m 2215
39: 4 On the m of Israel you will fall, 2215
39:17 the great sacrifice on the m of Israel. 2215
Hos 10: 8 Then they will say to the m, "Cover us!" 2215
Joel 2: 2 Like dawn spreading across the m a large 2215
3:18 "In that day the m will drip new wine, 2215
Am 3: 9 "Assemble yourselves on the m of Samaria; 2215
4:13 He who forms the m, creates the wind, 2215
9:13 New wine will drip from the m and flow 2215
Ob 1: 8 men of understanding in the m of Esau? 2215
1: 9 and everyone in Esau's m will be cut down 2215
1:19 from the Negev will occupy the m of Esau, 2215
1:21 up on Mount Zion to govern the m of Esau. 2215
Jnh 2: 6 To the roots of the m I sank down; 2215
Mic 1: 4 The m melt beneath him and 2215
4: 1 be established as chief among the m; 2215
6: 1 "Stand up, plead your case before the m; 2215
6: 2 Hear, O m, the LORD's accusation; 2215
Na 1: 5 m quake before him and the hills melt away. 2215
1:15 Look, there on the m, the feet of one who 2215
3:18 on the m with no one to gather them. 2215
Hab 3: 6 The ancient m crumbled and 2215
3:10 the m saw you and writhed. 2215
Hag 1: 8 into the m and bring down timber and build 2215
1:11 for a drought on the fields and the m, 2215
Zec 6: 1 between two m—mountains of bronze! 2215
6: 1 between two mountains—m of bronze! 2215
Mal 1: 3 and I have turned his m into a wasteland 2215
Mt 24:16 let those who are in Judea flee to the m. 4001
Mk 13:14 let those who are in Judea flee to the m. 4001
Lk 21:21 let those who are in Judea flee to the m. 4001
23:30 " 'they will say to the m, "Fall on us!" 4001
1Co 13: 2 and if I have a faith that can move m, 4001
Heb 11:38 They wandered in deserts and m, 4001
Rev 6:15 in caves and among the rocks of the m. 4001
6:16 They called to the m and the rocks, 4001
16:20 Every island fled away and the m could not 4001

MOUNTAINSIDE (9) [MOUNT]

SS 2:14 in the hiding places on the m, 4533
Mt 5: 1 he went up on a m and sat down. 4001
8: 1 When he came down from the m, 4001
14:23 he went up on a m by himself to pray. 4001
15:29 Then he went up on a m and sat down. 4001
Mk 3:13 on a m and called to him those he wanted, 4001
6:46 he went up on a m to pray. 4001
Lk 6:12 of those days Jesus went out to a m to pray, 4001
Jn 6: 3 up on a m and sat down with his disciples. 4001

MOUNTAINTOP (1) [MOUNT]

Isa 30:17 till you are left like a flagstaff on a m, 2215+8031

MOUNTAINTOPS (4) [MOUNT]

Isa 42:11 let them shout from the m. 2215+8031
Eze 6:13 on every high hill and on all the m, 2215+8031
Hos 4:13 They sacrifice on the m and burn 2215+8031
Joel 2: 5 that of chariots they leap over the m, 2215+8031

MOUNTED (18) [MOUNT]

Ge 24:61 and her maids got ready and m their camels 8206
Ex 25: 7 and onyx stones and other gems to be m on 4853
35: 9 and onyx stones and other gems to be m on 4854
35:27 to be m on the ephod and breastpiece. 4854
39: 6 They m the onyx stones 6913
39:10 they m four rows of precious stones on it. 4848
39:13 They were m in gold filigree settings. 6015
2Sa 13:29 m their mules and fled. 8206
2Sa 22:11 He m the cherubim and flew; 8206
1Ki 13:13 the donkey for him, he m it 8206
Est 8:10 and sent them by m couriers, 928+2021+6061
Ps 18:10 He m the cherubim and flew; 8206
107:26 They m up to the heavens and went down 6590
SS 5:12 washed in milk, m like jewels. 3782+4859+6584
Eze 23: 6 young men, and m horsemen. 6061+8206
23:12 m horsemen, all handsome young 6061+8206
23:23 men of high rank, all m on horses. 8206
Rev 9:16 of the m troops was two hundred million. 2690

MOUNTINGS (1) [MOUNT]

Eze 28:13 Your settings and m were made of gold; 5920

MOUNTS (2) [MOUNT]

Ne 2:12 There were no m with me except 989
Ac 23:24 Provide m for Paul so that he may 3229

MOURN (56) [MOURNED, MOURNERS, MOURNFUL, MOURNFULLY, MOURNING, MOURNS]

Ge 23: 2 and Abraham went to m for Sarah and 6199
Ex 33: 4 to m and no one put on any ornaments. 61
Lev 10: 6 may m for those the LORD has destroyed 1134
1Sa 16: 1 "How long will you m for Saul, 61
1Ki 13:29 to his own city to m for him and bury him. 6199
14:13 All Israel will m for him and bury him. 6199
Ezr 10: 6 to m over the unfaithfulness of the exiles. 61
Ne 8: 9 Do not m or weep." 61
Job 5:11 and those who m are lifted to safety. 7722
Ecc 3: 4 a time to m and a time to dance, 6199
Isa 3:26 The gates of Zion will lament and m; 61
29: 2 she will m and lament, 9302
32:13 yes, m for all houses of merriment and NIH
61: 2 to comfort all who m, 63
66:10 all you who m over her. 61
Jer 4:28 Therefore the earth will m and the heavens 61
6:26 m with bitter wailing as for an only son, 65+6913
8:21 I m, and horror grips me. 7722
15: 5 Who will m for you? 5653
16: 5 do not go to m or show sympathy, 6199
16: 7 to comfort those who m for the dead— 65
22:10 not weep for the dead [king] or m his loss; 5653
22:18 "They will not m for him: 6199
22:18 They will not m for him: 'Alas, my master! 6199
48:17 M for her, all who live around her, 5653
49: 3 Put on sackcloth and m; 6199
La 1: 4 The roads to Zion m, for no one comes 63
Eze 7:27 The king will m, the prince will be clothed 61
24:17 Groan quietly; do not m for the dead. 65
24:23 not m or weep but will waste away because 6199
27:32 As they wail and m over you, 5951+7806
Hos 10: 5 Its people will m over it, 61
Joel 1: 8 M like a virgin in sackcloth grieving for 458
1:13 Put on sackcloth, O priests, and m; 6199
Am 8: 8 and all who live in it m? 61
9: 5 and all who live in it m— 61
Na 3: 7 who will m for her?' 5653
Zec 7: 3 "Should I m and fast in the fifth month, 1134
12:10 and they will m for him as one mourns for 6199
12:12 The land will m, each clan by itself, 6199
Mt 5: 4 Blessed are those who m, 4291
9:15 of the bridegroom m while he is with them? 4291
11:17 we sang a dirge, and you did not m.' 3164
24:30 and all the nations of the earth will m. 3164
Lk 6:25 for you will m and weep. 4291
Jn 11:31 to the tomb to m there. 3081
16:20 and m while the world rejoices. 2577
Ro 12:15 m with those who mourn. 3081
12:15 mourn with those who m. 3081
1Co 7:30 those who m, as if they did not; 3081
Jas 4: 9 Grieve, m and wail. 4291
Rev 1: 7 the peoples of the earth will m because 3164
18: 7 I am not a widow, and I will never m. 3972+4292
18: 9 they will weep and m over her. 3164
18:11 of the earth will weep and m over her 4291
18:15 They will weep and m 4291

MOURNED (25) [MOURN]

Ge 37:34 on sackcloth and m for his son many days. 61
50: 3 And the Egyptians m for him seventy days. 1134
Nu 14:39 to all the Israelites, they m bitterly. 61
20:29 of Israel m for him thirty days. 1134
Dt 21:13 in your house and m her father and mother 1134
1Sa 6:19 The people m because of the heavy blow 61
7: 2 and all the people of Israel m and sought 5629
15:35 though Samuel m for him. 61
25: 1 and all Israel assembled and m for him; 6199
28: 3 and all Israel had m for him and buried him 6199
2Sa 1:12 They m and wept and fasted till evening 6199
11:26 that her husband was dead, she m for him. 6199
13:37 But King David m for his son every day. 61
1Ki 13:30 and they m over him and said, "Oh, 6199
14:18 They buried him, and all Israel m for him, 6199
1Ch 7:22 Their father Ephraim m for them many 61
2Ch 35:24 and all Judah and Jerusalem m for him. 61
Ne 1: 4 For some days I m and fasted and prayed 61
Jer 16: 4 They will not be m or buried but will be 6199
16: 6 They will not be buried or m, 6199
25:33 They will not be m or gathered up 6199
Da 10: 2 At that time I, Daniel, m for three weeks. 61
Zec 7: 5 and m in the fifth and seventh months for 6199
Lk 23:27 including women who m and wailed 3164
Ac 8: 2 Godly men buried Stephen and m deeply for him. 3157+3489+4472

MOURNERS (8) [MOURN]

Job 29:25 I was like one who comforts m. 63
Ecc 12: 5 to his eternal home and m go about 6199
Isa 57:19 creating praise on the lips of the m in Israel. 63
Eze 24:17 or eat the customary food [of m]." 408[S]
24:22 or eat the customary food [of m]. 408[S]
Hos 9: 4 be to them like the bread of m; 230
Am 5:16 summoned to weep and the m to wail. 3359+5631
Mal 3:14 about like m before the LORD Almighty? 7726

MOURNFUL (1) [MOURN]

Mic 2: 4 they will taunt you with this m song: 5631

MOURNFULLY (1) [MOURN]

Isa 59:11 we moan m like doves. 2047+2047

MOURNING (48) [MOURN]

Ge 27:41 "The days of m for my father are near; 65
37:35 "in m will I go down to the grave 63
50: 4 When the days of m had passed, 1143
50:10 a seven-day period of m for his father. 65
50:11 the Canaanites who lived there saw the m at 65
50:11 a solemn ceremony of m." 65
Dt 26:14 of the sacred portion while I was in m, 627
34: 8 until the time of weeping and m was over. 65
2Sa 3:31 and put on sackcloth and walk in m in front 6199
11:27 After the time of m was over, 65
14: 2 "Pretend you are in m. 61
14: 2 Dress in m clothes, 65
19: 1 "The king is weeping and m for Absalom." 61
19: 2 the victory that day was turned into m, 65
Est 4: 3 there was great m among the Jews, 65
9:22 and their m into a day of celebration. 65
Job 30:31 My harp is tuned to m, 65
Ps 35:14 about m as though for my friend or brother. NIH
38: 6 all day long I go about m. 7722
42: 9 Why must I go about m, 7722
43: 2 Why must I go about m, 7722
Ecc 7: 2 to go to a house of m than to go to a house 65
7: 4 The heart of the wise is in the house of m, 65
Isa 38:14 I moaned like a m dove. NIH
61: 3 the oil of gladness instead of m, 65
Jer 31:13 I will turn their m into gladness; 65
31:15 in Ramah, m and great weeping, 5631
47: 5 Gaza will shave her head in m; 995+7947
48:38 in the public squares there is nothing but m, 5027
La 2: 5 He has multiplied m and lamentation for 9302
5:15 our dancing has turned to m. 65
Eze 2:10 of it were written words of lament and m 2049
8:14 and I saw women sitting there, m 1134
27:31 with anguish of soul and with bitter m. 5027
31:15 the grave I covered the deep springs with m 61
Joel 1: 9 The priests are in m, 61
2:12 with fasting and weeping and m." 5027
Am 8:10 into m and all your singing into weeping. 65
8:10 that time like m for an only son and the end 65
Mic 1:11 Beth Ezel is in m; 5027
1:16 in m for the children in whom you delight; NIH
Mt 2:18 weeping and great m, Rachel weeping for 3851
Mk 16:10 with him and who were m and weeping. 4291
Lk 8:52 all the people were wailing and m for her. 3164
Jas 4: 9 Change your laughter to m and your joy 4292
Rev 18: 8 death, m and famine. 4292
18:19 and with weeping and m cry out: " 'Woe! 4291
21: 4 There will be no more death or m or crying 4292

MOURNS (5) [MOURN]

Job 14:22 of his own body and m only for himself." 61
Isa 33: 9 The land m and wastes away, 61
Jer 14: 2 "Judah m, her cities languish; 61
Hos 4: 3 Because of this the land m, 61
Zec 12:10 mourn for him as one m for an only child, 5027

MOUSE (KJV) See RAT

MOUTH (270) [MOUTHS]

Ge 4:11 opened its m to receive your brother's blood 7023
29: 2 The stone over the m of the well was large. 7023
29: 3 the stone away from the well's m and water 7023
29: 3 the stone to its place over the m of the well. 7023
29: 8 the stone has been rolled away from the m 7023
29:10 over and rolled the stone away from the m 7023
42:27 and he saw his silver in the m of his sack. 7023
43:21 in the m of his sack. 7023
44: 1 put each man's silver in the m of his sack. 7023
44: 2 in the m of the youngest one's sack, 7023
Ex 4:11 "Who gave man his m? 7023
4:15 to him and put words in his m; 7023
4:16 as if he were your m and as if you were God 7023
Nu 16:30 the earth opens its m and swallows them, 7023
16:32 the earth opened its m and swallowed them, 7023
22:28 Then the LORD opened the donkey's m, 7023
22:38 I must speak only what God puts in my m." 7023
23: 5 The LORD put a message in Balaam's m 7023
23:12 not speak what the LORD puts in my m?" 7023
23:16 with Balaam and put a message in his m 7023
26:10 The earth opened its m and swallowed them 7023
Dt 8: 3 but on every word that comes from the m of the LORD. 7023

Dt 11: 6 the earth opened its **m** right in the middle 7023
18:18 I will put my words in his **m**, 7023
23:23 to the LORD your God with your own **m**. 7023
30:14 it is in your **m** and in your heart 7023
32: 1 hear, O earth, the words of my **m**. 7023
Jos 1: 8 of the Law depart from your **m**; 7023
10:18 "Roll large rocks up to the **m** *of* the cave, 7023
10:22 "Open the **m** *of* the cave 7023
10:27 the **m** *of* the cave they placed large rocks, 7023
15: 5 the Salt Sea as far as the **m** *of* the Jordan. 7895
15: 5 the bay of the sea at the **m** *of* the Jordan, 7895
18:19 at the **m** *of* the Jordan in the south. 7895
1Sa 1:12 Eli observed her **m**. 7023
2: 1 My **m** boasts over my enemies, 7023
2: 3 or let your **m** speak such arrogance, 7023
14:26 yet no one put his hand to his **m**, 7023
14:27 He raised his hand to his **m**, 7023
17:35 struck it and rescued the sheep from its **m**. 7023
2Sa 1:16 Your own **m** testified against you 7023
14: 3 And Joab put the words in her **m**. 7023
14:19 and who put all these words into the **m** 7023
22: 9 consuming fire came from his **m**, 7023
1Ki 8:15 promised with his own **m** to my father David. 7023
8:24 with your **m** you have promised and 7023
17:24 that the word of the LORD from your **m** is 7023
19:13 and went out and stood at the **m** *of* the cave. 7339
2Ki 4:34 **m** to mouth, eyes to eyes, hands to hands. 7023
4:34 mouth to **m**, eyes to eyes, hands to hands. 7023
19:28 hook in your nose and my bit in your **m**, 8557
2Ch 6: 4 promised with his **m** to my father David. 7023
6:15 with your **m** you have promised and 7023
Est 7: 8 As soon as the word left the king's **m**, 7023
Job 3: 1 Job opened his **m** and cursed the day 7023
5:15 the needy from the sword in their **m**; 7023
5:16 poor have hope, and injustice shuts its **m**. 7023
6:30 Can my **m** not discern malice? 2674
8:21 yet fill your **m** with laughter and your lips 7023
9:20 I were innocent, my **m** would condemn me; 7023
15: 5 Your sin prompts your **m**; 7023
15: 6 Your own **m** condemns you, not mine; 7023
15:13 and pour out such words from your **m**? 7023
15:30 the breath of God's **m** will carry him away. 7023
16: 5 But my **m** would encourage you; 7023
19:16 though I beg him with my own **m**. 7023
20:12 in his **m** and he hides it under his tongue, 7023
20:13 to let it go and keeps it in his **m**, 2674
21: 5 clap your hand over your **m**. 7023
22:22 Accept instruction from his **m** and lay 7023
23: 4 before him and fill my **m** with arguments. 7023
23:12 of his **m** more than my daily bread. 7023
26: 4 And whose spirit spoke from your **m**? NIH
31:30 not allowed my **m** to sin by invoking a curse 2674
33: 2 I am about to open my **m**; 7023
35:16 So Job opens his **m** with empty talk; 7023
37: 2 to the rumbling that comes from his **m**. 7023
40: 4 I put my hand over my **m**. 7023
40:23 the Jordan should surge against his **m**. 7023
41:14 Who dares open the doors of his **m**, 7156
41:19 Firebrands stream from his **m**; 7023
41:21 and flames dart from his **m**. 7023
Ps 5: 9 Not a word from their **m** can be trusted; 7023
10: 7 His **m** is full of curses and lies and threats; 7023
17: 3 I have resolved that my **m** will not sin. 7023
18: 8 consuming fire came from his **m**, 7023
19:14 May the words of my **m** and the meditation 7023
22:15 and my tongue sticks to the **roof of** my **m**; 4918
22:21 Rescue me from the **m** *of* the lions; 7023
33: 6 their starry host by the breath of his **m**. 7023
36: 3 words of his **m** are wicked and deceitful; 7023
37:30 The **m** *of* the righteous man utters wisdom, 7023
38:13 like a mute, who cannot open his **m**; 7023
38:14 whose **m** can offer no reply. 7023
39: 1 I will put a muzzle on my **m** as long as 7023
39: 9 I was silent; I would not open my **m**, 7023
40: 3 He put a new song in my **m**, 7023
49: 3 My **m** will speak words of wisdom; 7023
50:19 You use your **m** for evil 7023
51:15 and my **m** will declare your praise. 7023
54: 2 listen to the words of my **m**. 7023
63: 5 with singing lips my **m** will praise you. 7023
66:14 vows my lips promised and my **m** spoke 7023
66:17 I cried out to him with my **m**; 7023
69:15 up or the pit close its **m** over me. 7023
71: 8 My **m** is filled with your praise, 7023
71:15 My **m** will tell of your righteousness, 7023
78: 1 listen to the words of my **m**. 7023
78: 2 I will open my **m** in parables, 7023
81:10 Open wide your **m** and I will fill it. 7023
89: 1 with my **m** I will make your faithfulness known through all generations. 7023
109:30 With my **m** I will greatly extol the LORD; 7023
119:13 the laws that come from your **m**. 7023
119:43 Do not snatch the word of truth from my **m**, 7023
119:72 The law from your **m** is more precious 7023
119:88 and I will obey the statutes of your **m**. 7023
119:103 sweeter than honey to my **m**! 7023
119:108 O LORD, the willing praise of my **m**, 7023
119:131 I open my **m** and pant, 7023
137: 6 the **roof of** my **m** if I do not remember you, 2674
138: 4 when they hear the words of your **m**. 7023
141: 3 Set a guard over my **m**, O LORD; 7023
141: 7 so our bones have been scattered at the **m** 7023
145:21 My **m** will speak in praise of the LORD. 7023
Pr 2: 6 and from his **m** come knowledge 7023
4:24 Put away perversity from your **m**; 7023
6: 2 ensnared by the words of your **m**, 7023
6:12 who goes about with a corrupt **m**, 7023
8: 7 My **m** speaks what is true, 2674
8: 8 All the words of my **m** are just; 7023
10: 6 violence overwhelms the **m** *of* the wicked. 7023
10:11 The **m** *of* the righteous is a fountain of life, 7023
10:11 violence overwhelms the **m** *of* the wicked. 7023
10:14 but the **m** *of* a fool invites ruin. 7023
10:31 **m** *of* the righteous brings forth wisdom, 7023
10:32 the **m** *of* the wicked only what is perverse. 7023
11: 9 With his **m** the godless destroys his neighbor, 7023
11:11 but by the **m** *of* the wicked it is destroyed. 7023
15: 2 but the **m** *of* the fool gushes folly. 7023
15:14 but the **m** *of* a fool feeds on folly. 7023
15:28 but the **m** *of* the wicked gushes evil. 7023
16:10 and his **m** should not betray justice. 7023
16:23 A wise man's heart guides his **m**, 7023
18: 4 The words of a man's **m** are deep waters, 7023
18: 6 and his **m** invites a beating. 7023
18: 7 A fool's **m** is his undoing, 7023
18:20 the fruit of his **m** a man's stomach is filled; 7023
19:24 he will not even bring it back to his **m**! 7023
19:28 and the **m** *of* the wicked gulps down evil. 7023
20:17 but he ends up with a **m** full of gravel. 7023
21:23 He who guards his **m** and tongue 7023
22:14 The **m** *of* an adulteress is a deep pit; 7023
26: 7 hang limp is a proverb in the **m** *of* a fool. 7023
26: 9 a drunkard's hand is a proverb in the **m** *of* 7023
26:15 he is too lazy to bring it back to his **m**. 7023
26:28 and a flattering **m** works ruin. 7023
27: 2 and not your own **m**; 7023
30:20 She eats and wipes her **m** and says, 7023
30:32 clap your hand over your **m**! 7023
Ecc 5: 2 Do not be quick with your **m**, 7023
5: 6 Do not let your **m** lead you into sin. 7023
6: 7 All man's efforts are for his **m**, 7023
10:12 Words from a wise man's **m** are gracious, 7023
SS 1: 2 Let him kiss me with the kisses of his **m**— 7023
4: 3 your **m** is lovely. 4498
5:16 His **m** is sweetness itself; 2674
7: 9 and your **m** like the best wine. 2674
Isa 1:20 For the **m** *of* the LORD has spoken. 7023
5:14 and opens its **m** without limit; 7023
6: 7 With it he touched my **m** and said, "See, 7023
9:12 the west have devoured Israel with open **m**. 7023
9:17 every **m** speaks vileness. 7023
10:14 or opened its **m** to chirp.' " 7023
11: 4 the earth with the rod of his **m**; 7023
19: 7 at the **m** *of* the river. 7023
29:13 "These people come near to me with their **m** 7023
34:16 For it is his **m** that has given the order, 7023
37:29 hook in your nose and my bit in your **m**, 8557
40: 5 For the **m** *of* the LORD has spoken." 7023
45:23 my **m** has uttered in all integrity a word 7023
48: 3 my **m** announced them 7023
49: 2 He made my **m** like a sharpened sword, 7023
51:16 in your **m** and covered you with the shadow 7023
53: 7 and afflicted; yet he did not open his **m**; 7023
53: 7 so he did not open his **m**. 7023
53: 9 nor was any deceit in his **m**. 7023
55:11 so is my word that goes out from my **m**: 7023
58:14 The **m** *of* the LORD has spoken. 7023
59:21 and my words that I have put in your **m** will 7023
59:21 in your mouth will not depart from your **m**, 7023
62: 2 you will be called by a new name that the **m** 7023
Jer 1: 9 and touched my **m** and said to me, 7023
1: 9 "Now, I have put my words in your **m**. 7023
5:14 I will make my words in your **m** a fire 7023
9: 8 With his **m** each speaks cordially 7023
9:20 open your ears to the words of his **m**. 7023
23:16 not from the **m** *of* the LORD. 7023
48:28 Be like a dove that makes its nest at the **m** 7023
La 3:38 the **m** *of* the Most High that both calamities 7023
4: 4 infant's tongue sticks to the **roof** of its **m**; 2674
Eze 2: 8 open your **m** and eat what I give you." 7023
3: 2 I opened my **m**, and he gave me the scroll 7023
3: 3 and it tasted as sweet as honey in my **m**. 7023
3:26 the **roof** of your **m** so that you will be silent 2674
3:27 I will open your **m** and you shall say 7023
4:14 No unclean meat has ever entered my **m**." 7023
16:63 be ashamed and never again open your **m** 7023
24:27 At that time your **m** will be opened; 7023
29:21 and I will open your **m** among them. 7023
33:22 and he opened my **m** before the man came 7023
33:22 So my **m** was opened and I was no longer 7023
Da 6:17 A stone was brought and placed over the **m** 10588
7: 5 it had three ribs in its **m** between its teeth. 10588
7: 8 of a man and a **m** that spoke boastfully. 10588
7:20 that had eyes and a **m** that spoke boastfully. 10588
10:16 and I opened my **m** and began to speak. 7023
Hos 6: 5 I killed you with the words of my **m**; 7023
Am 3:12 the lion's **m** only two leg bones or a piece 7023
Na 3:12 the figs fall into the **m** *of* the eater. 7023
Zec 5: 8 and pushed the lead cover down over its **m**. 7023
Mal 2: 6 in his **m** and nothing false was found 7023
2: 7 from his **m** men should seek instruction— 7023
Mt 4: 4 but on every word that comes from the **m** *5125*
12:34 of the overflow of the heart the **m** speaks. *5125*
13:35 "I will open my **m** in parables, *5125*
15:11 a man's **m** does not make him 'unclean,' *5125*
15:11 but what comes out of his **m**, *5125*
15:17 the **m** goes into the stomach and then out of *5125*
15:18 the things that come out of the **m** come from *5125*
17:27 open its **m** and you will find *5125*
Mk 9:18 *He* **foams at the m**, gnashes his teeth and *930*
9:20 and rolled around, **foaming at the m**. *930*
Lk 1:64 Immediately his **m** was opened *5125*
6:45 of the overflow of his heart his **m** speaks. *5125*
9:39 into convulsions so that he **foams at the m**. *931*
Ac 1:16 through the **m** of David concerning Judas, *5125*
4:25 You spoke by the Holy Spirit *through* the **m** *5125*
8:32 so he did not open his **m**. *5125*
11: 8 or unclean has ever entered my **m**.' *5125*
15:27 by word of **m** what we are writing. *NIG*
22:14 and to hear words from his **m**. *5125*
23: 2 near Paul to strike him on the **m**. *5125*
Ro 3:19 so that every **m** may be silenced and *5125*
10: 8 it is in your **m** and in your heart," that is, *5125*
10: 9 That if you confess with your **m**, *5125*
10:10 *with* your **m** that you confess and are saved. *5125*
15: 6 and **m** you may glorify the God and Father *5125*
Eph 6:19 that whenever I open my **m**, *5125*
2Th 2: 8 with the breath *of* his **m** and destroy by *5125*
2:15 whether by **word of m** or by letter. *3364*
2Ti 4:17 And I was delivered from the lion's **m**. *5125*
Jas 3:10 Out of the same **m** come praise and cursing. *5125*
1Pe 2:22 and no deceit was found in his **m**." *5125*
2Pe 2:18 **m** empty, boastful **words** *5779*
Rev 1:16 of his **m** came a sharp double-edged sword. *5125*
2:16 against them with the sword *of* my **m**. *5125*
3:16 I am about to spit you out of my **m**. *5125*
10: 9 but in your **m** it will be as sweet as honey." *5125*
10:10 It tasted as sweet as honey in my **m**, *5125*
12:15 Then from his **m** the serpent spewed water *5125*
12:16 by opening its **m** and swallowing the river *5125*
12:16 that the dragon had spewed out of his **m**. *5125*
13: 2 but had feet like those of a bear and a **m** like *5125*
13: 5 a **m** to utter proud words and blasphemies *5125*
13: 6 He opened his **m** to blaspheme God, *5125*
16:13 they came out of the **m** of the dragon, *5125*
16:13 the dragon, out of the **m** of the beast and out *5125*
16:13 the mouth of the beast and out of the **m** of *5125*
19:15 of his **m** comes a sharp sword with which *5125*
19:21 sword that came out of the **m** of the rider *5125*

MOUTHS (52) [MOUTH]

Ge 43:12 that was put back into the **m** *of* your sacks. 7023
44: 8 of Canaan the silver we found inside the **m** 7023
Jdg 7: 6 with their hands to their **m**. 7023
1Ki 19:18 and all whose **m** have not kissed him." 7023
22:22 " 'I will go out and be a lying spirit in the **m** 7023
22:23 a lying spirit in the **m** *of* all these prophets 7023
2Ch 18:21 a lying spirit in the **m** *of* all his prophets,' 7023
18:22 the LORD has put a lying spirit in the **m** 7023
Ne 9:20 not withhold your manna from their **m**, 7023
Job 16:10 Men open their **m** to jeer at me; 7023
29: 9 and covered their **m** with their hands; 7023
29:10 their tongues stuck to the **roof of** their **m**. 2674
Ps 17:10 and their **m** speak with arrogance. 7023
22:13 lions tearing their prey open their **m** wide 7023
58: 6 Break the teeth in their **m**, O God; 7023
59: 7 See what they spew from their **m**— 7023
59:12 For the sins of their **m**, 7023
62: 4 With their **m** they bless, 7023
63:11 while the **m** *of* liars will be silenced. 7023
73: 9 Their **m** lay claim to heaven, 7023
78:30 even while it was still in their **m**, 7023
78:36 then they would flatter him with their **m**, 7023
107:42 but all the wicked shut their **m**. 7023
109: 2 and deceitful men have opened their **m** 7023
115: 5 They have **m**, but cannot speak, eyes, 7023
126: 2 Our **m** were filled with laughter, 7023
135:16 They have **m**, but cannot speak, eyes, 7023
135:17 nor is there breath in their **m**. 7023
144: 8 whose **m** are full of lies, 7023
144:11 the hands of foreigners whose **m** are full 7023
149: 6 May the praise of God be in their **m** and 1744
Isa 52:15 and kings will shut their **m** because of him. 7023
59:21 or from the **m** *of* your children, 7023
59:21 the **m** *of* their descendants from this time 7023
La 2:16 All your enemies open their **m** wide 7023
3:46 "All our enemies have opened their **m** wide 7023
Eze 33:31 With their **m** they express devotion, 7023
34:10 I will rescue my flock from their **m**, 7023
Da 6:22 and he shut the **m** *of* the lions. 10588
Mic 7:16 on their **m** and their ears will become deaf. 7023
Zep 3:13 nor will deceit be found in their **m**. 7023
Zec 9: 7 I will take the blood from their **m**, 7023
14:12 and their tongues will rot in their **m**. 7023
Ro 3:14 "Their **m** are full of cursing and bitterness." *5125*
Eph 4:29 of your **m**, but only what is helpful *5125*
Heb 11:33 who shut the **m** of lions, *5125*
Jas 3: 3 into the **m** of horses to make them obey us, *5125*
Rev 9:17 and out of their **m** came fire, *5125*
9:18 smoke and sulfur that came out of their **m**. *5125*
9:19 The power of the horses was in their **m** and *5125*
11: 5 from their **m** and devours their enemies. *5125*
14: 5 No lie was found in their **m**; *5125*

MOVABLE (7) [MOVE]

1Ki 7:27 He also made ten **m stands** of bronze; 4807
2Ki 16:17 and removed the basins from the **m stands**. 4807
25:13 the **m stands** and the bronze Sea 4807
25:16 the Sea and the **m stands**, 4807
Jer 27:19 the **m stands** and the other furnishings 4807
52:17 the **m stands** and the bronze Sea 4807
52:20 and the **m stands**, which King Solomon 4807

MOVE (50) [MOVABLE, MOVED, MOVEMENTS, MOVES, MOVING]

Ge 1:24 **creatures that m** along the ground, 8254

Ge 1:25 the **creatures that m** *along* the ground 8254
1:26 the creatures that m along the ground." 8253
1:30 of the air and all the **creatures that m** on 8253
6: 7 **creatures that m along the ground,** 8254
7: 8 of birds and of all creatures *that* **m** along 8253
7:23 and animals and the **creatures that m** along 8254
8:17 all the creatures that m along the ground— 8253
8:19 All the animals and all the **creatures that m** 8254
26:16 Abimelech said to Isaac, **"M** away from us; 2143
33:14 while I **m along** slowly at the pace of 5633
48:17 so he took hold of his father's hand to **m** it 6073
Ex 14:15 Tell the Israelites *to* **m on.** 5825
Lev 5: 2 **creatures that m along the ground—** 9238
11:29 the animals that **m about** on the ground, 9237
11:31 Of all those *that* **m along** the ground, 9238
26:10 *to* **m** it **out** to make room for the new. 3655
Nu 1:51 Whenever the tabernacle *is to* **m,** 5825
4: 5 When the camp *is to* **m,** 5825
4:15 and when the camp *is ready to* **m,** 5825
12:15 not **m on** till she was brought back. 5825
16:24 **'M away** from the tents of Korah, 6590
16:26 **"M back** from the tents of these wicked 6073
Dt 19:14 not **m** your neighbor's boundary stone set 6047
Jos 3: 3 *to* **m out** from your positions and follow it. 5825
Jdg 16: 2 *They* **made no m** during the night, saying, 3087
2Sa 5:24 in the tops of the balsam trees, **m quickly,** 3077
15:14 or *he will* **m quickly** to overtake us 4554
1Ch 14:15 **m out** to battle, because that will mean 3655
Job 24: 2 *Men* **m** boundary stones; 5952
Ps 69:34 the seas and all *that* **m** in them, 8253
Pr 22:28 *Do* not **m** an ancient boundary stone set up 6047
23:10 *Do* not **m** an ancient boundary stone 6047
30:29 four *that* **m** with stately bearing: 2143
Isa 46: 7 From that spot *it* cannot **m.** 4631
Jer 31:24 and *those who* **m about** with their flocks. 5825
Eze 36:27 in you and **m** you to follow my decrees and 6913
Hos 2:18 the birds of the air and the **creatures that m** 8254
5:10 like *those who* **m** boundary stones. 6047
Zec 12: 3 All *who try to* **m** it will injure themselves. 6673
Mt 17:20 **'M** from here to there' and it will move. *3553*
17:20 'Move from here to there' and *it will* **m.** *3553*
23: 4 not willing to lift a finger *to* **m** them. *3075*
Lk 10: 7 *Do* not **m around** from house to house. *3553*
14:10 'Friend, **m** up to a better place.' *4646*
Ac 17:28 in him *we* live and **m** and have our being.' *3075*
27:41 The bow stuck fast and **would not m,** *810+3531*
1Co 13: 2 and if I have a faith that can **m** mountains, *3496*
15:58 brothers, stand firm. Let **nothing m** you. *293*
2Co 11:26 I have been constantly **on the m.** *3845*

MOVEABLE (KJV) See CROOKED

MOVED (77) [MOVE]

Ge 7:21 living thing that **m** on the earth perished— 8253
11: 2 As men **m** eastward, they found a plain 5825
13:18 So Abram **m** *his* **tents** and went to live near 182
19: 9 and **m forward** to break down the door. 5602
20: 1 Now Abraham **m on** from there into 5825
26:17 So Isaac **m** away from there and encamped 2143
26:22 *He* **m on** from there and dug another well, 6980
35:16 Then *they* **m on** from Bethel. 5825
35:21 Israel **m on** again and pitched his tent 5825
36: 6 and **m** to a land some distance 2143
37:17 *"They have* **m** on from here," 5825
43:30 **Deeply m** at the sight of his brother, 4023+8171
Ex 14:19 also **m** from in front and stood behind them, 5825
35:21 and whose heart **m** him came and brought 5951
Nu 14:44 of the LORD's covenant **m** from the camp. 4631
16:27 So *they* **m away** from the tents of Korah, 6590
21:10 The Israelites **m on** and camped at Oboth. 5825
21:12 From there *they* **m on** and camped in 5825
22:26 Then the angel of the LORD **m on ahead** 6296
Jos 5: 6 The Israelites *had* **m about** in 2143
8: 3 and the whole army **m out** to attack Ai. 7756
10: 5 They **m up** with all their troops and took 6590
10:29 with him **m on** from Makkedah to Libnah 6296
10:31 Then Joshua and all Israel with him **m on** 6296
10:34 and all Israel with him **m on** from Lachish 6296
14:10 while Israel **m about** in the desert. 2143
Jdg 9:26 of Ebed **m** with his brothers into Shechem, 995
20:33 All the men of Israel **m** from their places 7756
1Sa 5: 8 the ark of the god of Israel **m** *to* Gath." 6015
5: 8 So *they* **m** the ark of the God of Israel. 6015
5: 9 But after *they had* **m** it, 6015
14:23 and the battle **m on beyond** Beth Aven. 6296
15: 6 the Kenites **m away** from the Amalekites. 6073
17:48 As the Philistine **m** closer to attack him, 2143
25: 1 David **m down** into the Desert of Maon. 3718
2Sa 7: 7 Wherever *I have* **m** with all the Israelites, 2143
15:23 and all the people **m on** toward the desert. 6296
2Ki 16: 6 then **m into** Elath and have lived there 995
1Ch 13: 7 *They* **m** the ark of God from 8206
16:30 firmly established; *it* cannot **be m.** 4572
17: 5 *I have* **m** from one tent site to another, 2118
17: 6 Wherever *I have* **m** with all the Israelites, 2143
19: 7 from their towns and **m out** for battle. 995
2Ch 33:13 the LORD **was m by** his **entreaty** 6983
33:19 how God **was m by** his **entreaty,** 6983
36:22 the LORD **m** the heart of Cyrus king 6424
Ezr 1: 1 the LORD **m** the heart of Cyrus king 6424
1: 5 everyone whose heart God *had* **m—** 6424
Ne 2:14 Then *I* **m on** toward the Fountain Gate and 6296
Est 2: 9 and **m** her and her maids into the best place 9101
Job 14:18 and as a rock *is* **m** from its place, 6980
18: 4 Or *must* the rocks *be* **m** from their place? 6980
Ps 93: 1 world is firmly established; *it* cannot **be m.** 4572
96:10 world is firmly established, *it* cannot **be m;** 4572
104: 5 on its foundations; *it can* never **be m.** 4572
Isa 33:20 a tent *that will* not *be* **m;** 7585
Eze 1: 9 they did not turn as they **m.** 2143
1:13 Fire **m back and forth** among the creatures; 2143
1:17 As they **m,** they would go in any one of 2143
1:19 When the living creatures **m,** 2143
1:19 the wheels beside them **m;** 2143
1:21 When the creatures **m,** they also moved; 2143
1:21 When the creatures moved, *they* also **m;** 2143
1:24 When the creatures **m,** 2143
9: 3 and **m** to the threshold of the temple. NIH
10: 4 above the cherubim and **m** to the threshold NIH
10:11 As they **m,** they would go in any one of 2143
10:16 When the cherubim **m,** 2143
10:16 the wheels beside them **m;** 2143
Mt 13:53 *he* **m on** from there. *3558*
Lk 2:27 **M** by the Spirit, he went into the temple *NIG*
Jn 11:33 *he was* **deeply m** in spirit and troubled. *1839*
11:38 Jesus, once more **deeply m,** *1839*
11:54 Therefore Jesus no longer **m about** publicly *4344*
Ac 9:28 **m about freely** in Jerusalem, *1660+1744+2779*
27: 8 We **m along** the coast with difficulty *4162*
Col 1:23 not **m** from the hope held out in the gospel. *3560*

MOVEMENTS (1) [MOVE]

2Sa 3:25 he came to deceive you and observe your **m** 2256+4569+4604

MOVER (KJV) See STIRRING UP

MOVES (22) [MOVE]

Ge 1:28 the air and over every living creature that **m** 8253
6:20 and of every kind of **creature that m** *along* 8254
7:14 every creature that **m** along the ground 8253
8:19 everything *that* **m** on the earth— 8253
9: 2 *that* **m along** the ground, and upon all 8253
9: 3 Everything that lives and **m** will be food 8254
Lev 11:41 that **m about** on the ground is detestable; 9237
11:42 You are not to eat any creature that **m about** 9237
11:42 whether *it* **m** on its belly or walks 2143
11:44 by any creature that **m about** on the ground. 8253
11:46 that **m** in the water and every creature 8253
11:46 every creature that **m about** on the ground. 9237
20:25 or anything that **m along** the ground— 8253
Dt 4:18 like any **creature that m** along the ground 8253
18: 6 If a Levite **m** from one of your towns 995
23:14 the LORD your God **m about** in your camp 2143
27:17 man *who* **m** his neighbor's boundary stone." 6047
Job 9: 5 He **m** mountains without their knowing it 6980
Ps 58: 8 Like a slug melting away *as it* **m along,** 2143
102:14 her very dust **m** *them* **to pity.** 2858
Isa 41: 3 He pursues them and **m on** unscathed, 6296
Eze 38:20 every creature that **m** along the ground, 8253

MOVING (9) [MOVE]

Ge 1:21 and **m** thing with which the water teems, 8253
13: 5 Now Lot, who *was* **m** about with Abram, 2143
1Sa 1:13 her lips *were* **m** but her voice was not heard. 5675
12:12 the Ammonites *was* **m** against you, you said 995
23:13 **m from place to place.** 889+928+2143+2143
2Sa 7: 6 *I have been* **m from place to place** 2143
Job 31:26 in its radiance or the moon **m** in splendor, 2143
Zec 14: 4 with half of the mountain **m** north 4631
14: 4 and half **m** south. NIH

MOWED (1) [MOWN]

Jas 5: 4 workmen who **m** your fields are crying out *286*

MOWN (1) [MOWED]

Ps 72: 6 He will be like rain falling on a **m field,** 1600

MOZA (5)

1Ch 2:46 the mother of Haran, **M** and Gazez. 4605
8:36 and Zimri was the father of **M.** 4605
8:37 **M** was the father of Binea; 4605
9:42 and Zimri was the father of **M.** 4605
9:43 **M** was the father of Binea; 4605

MOZAH (1)

Jos 18:26 Mizpah, Kephirah, **M,** 5173

MUCH (196)

Ge 20: 8 they were **very m** afraid. 4394
30:26 You know **how m** work I've done for you." 889
41:49 it was **so m** that he stopped keeping records 6330
43:34 Benjamin's portion *was* five times **as m as** anyone else's. 4946+8049
44: 1 "Fill the men's sacks with **as m** food **as** 889+3869
Ex 1: 9 "the Israelites have become **m too numerous** for us. 2256+6786+8041
16: 5 and that is to be **twice as m** as they gather 5467
16:16 Each one is to gather **as m as** he needs 4200+7023
16:17 some gathered **m,** some little. 8049
16:18 he *who* **gathered m** did not have too much, 8049
16:18 he who gathered much *did* not **have too m,** 6369
16:18 Each one gathered **as m as** he needed. 4200+7023
16:21 Each morning everyone gathered **as m as** he needed, 3869+7023
16:22 On the sixth day, they gathered **twice as m** 5467
Ex 30:23 **half as m** (that is, 250 shekels) 4734
Nu 16:15 not taken so **m** as a donkey from them, NIH
Dt 3:19 livestock (I know you have **m** livestock) 8041
12:15 of your towns and eat as **m** *of* the meat 3972
12:20 then you may eat as **m** *of* it as you want. 3972
12:21 and in your own towns you may eat as **m** 3972
15:18 these six years has been worth **twice as m** 5467
28:38 You will sow **m** seed in the field 8041
31:27 **how m more** will you rebel after I die! 677+2256+3954
Jos 10: 2 and his people were **very m** alarmed at this, 4394
Jdg 5:15 of Reuben there was **m** searching of heart. 1524
5:16 of Reuben there was **m** searching of heart. 1524
Ru 2:18 mother-in-law saw **how m** she had gathered. 889
1Sa 1:10 Hannah **wept m** and prayed to 1134+1134
14:30 **How m better** it would have been if 677+3954
15:22 and sacrifices **as m as** in obeying the voice 3869
16:21 Saul liked him **very m,** 4394
21: 5 **How m more so** today!" 677+3954
21:12 and was **very m** afraid of Achish king 4394
23: 3 **How m more,** then, if we go to Keilah 677
2Sa 4:11 **How m more—**when wicked men have killed an innocent man 677
16:11 **How m more,** then, this Benjamite! 677+3954
1Ki 8:27 **How m less** this temple I have built! 677+3954
10:12 **So m** almugwood has never been imported 4027
12:28 "It is too **m** for you to go up to Jerusalem. 8041
19: 7 for the journey is too **m** for you." 8041
2Ki 5:13 **How m more,** then, when he tells you, 677
5:17 as **m** earth as a pair of mules can carry, NIH
10:18 Jehu will serve him **m.** 2221
21: 6 *He* did **m** evil in the eyes of the LORD, 8049
21:16 so **m** innocent blood that he filled Jerusalem 2221
1Ch 22: 8 'You have shed **m** blood 4200+8044
22: 8 because you have shed **m** blood on the earth 8041
2Ch 4:18 that Solomon made amounted to so **m** 4200+8044
6:18 **How m less** this temple I have built! 677+3954
14:14 since there was **m** booty there. 8041
20:25 There was **so m** plunder that it took 8041
24:24 into their hands a **m** larger army. 4394
25: 9 "The LORD can give you **m** more than that." 2221
26:10 because he had **m** livestock in the foothills 8041
32:15 **How m less** will your god deliver you 677+3954+4202
33: 6 He did **m** evil in the eyes of the LORD, 8049
33:14 he also made it **m** higher. 4394
Ezr 3:13 because the people made **so m** noise. 1524
Ne 2: 2 I was very **m** afraid, 2221
2:10 they were very **m** disturbed 1524
4:10 there is **so m** rubble that we cannot rebuild 2221
Job 4:19 **how m more** those who live in houses of clay, 677
7:17 "What is man that *you* **make so m of** him, 1540
7:17 that you give him so **m** attention, NIH
15:16 **how m less** man, who is vile and 677+3954
25: 6 **how m less** man, who is but a maggot— 677+3954
35:14 **How m less,** then, will he listen 677+3954
42:10 and gave him twice as **m** as he had before. 3972
Ps 19:10 more precious than gold, than **m** pure gold; 8041
36: 2 in his own eyes *he* **flatters** himself *too m* AIT
119:107 I have suffered **m;** 4394+6330
123: 3 for we have endured **m** contempt. 8041
123: 4 We have endured **m** ridicule from the proud 8041
123: 4 **m** contempt from the arrogant. NIH
Pr 11:31 **how m more** the ungodly and the sinner! 677+3954
15:11 **how m more** the hearts of men! 677+3954
16: 8 a little with righteousness than **m** gain 8044
16:16 **How m** better to get wisdom than gold, 4537
17: 7 **how m worse** lying lips to a ruler! 677+3954
19: 7 **how m more** do his friends avoid him! 677+3954
19:10 **how m worse** for a slave to rule over princes! 677+3954
20:19 so avoid a *man who* **talks too m.** 7331+8557
21:27 **how m more so** when brought with evil intent! 677+3954
23:20 Do not join *those who* **drink too m** wine 6010
25:16 **too m** *of* it, and you will vomit. 8425
25:17 **too m** *of* you, and he will hate you. 8425
25:27 It is not good to eat **too m** honey, 8049
30: 9 *I may* **have too m** and disown you and say, 8425
Ecc 1:16 I have experienced **m** *of* wisdom 2221
1:18 For with **m** wisdom comes much sorrow; 8044
1:18 For with much wisdom comes **m** sorrow; 8044
5: 7 **M** dreaming and many words are meaningless. 8044
5:12 whether he eats little or **m,** 2221
9:18 but one sinner destroys **m** good. 2221
12:12 and **m** study wearies the body. 2221
SS 4:10 **m more** pleasing is your love **than** wine, 4946
Jer 2:36 Why do you go about **so m,** 4394
49: 9 steal only **as m as** they **wanted?** 1896
Eze 14:21 **How m worse** will it be when I send 677+3954
15: 5 **how m less** can it be made 677+3954
23:32 for it holds **so m.** 5268
38:13 and goods and to seize **m** plunder?"' 1524
46: 5 is to be **as m as** he **pleases,** 3338+5522
46: 7 and with the lambs **as m as** he wants to give, 889+3869
46:11 with the lambs **as m as** one **pleases,** 3338+5522
Ob 1: 5 **as m as** they **wanted?** 1896
1:12 nor **boast so m** in the day of their trouble. 1540+3870+7023
Hag 1: 6 You have planted **m,** but have harvested 2221
1: 9 "You expected **m,** but see, it turned out 2221
Zec 9:12 that I will restore **twice as m** to you. 5467
Mal 3:10 and pour out **so m** blessing **that** you 6330

Mt 6:26 Are you not **m** more valuable than they? *3437*
6:30 will he not **m** more clothe you, *4498*
7:11 **how m** more will your Father in heaven *4531*
10:25 **how m** more the members of his household! *4531*
12:12 **How m more** valuable is a man than a sheep! *4531*
13: 5 where it did not have **m** soil. *4498*
14: 6 danced for them and pleased Herod so **m** *NIG*
19:29 a hundred times as **m** and will inherit eternal life. *NIG*
23:15 you make him **twice as m** a son of hell *1486*
Mk 4: 5 where it did not have **m** soil. *4498*
4:33 **as m as** they could understand. *2777*
5:19 and tell them **how m** the Lord has done *4012*
5:20 **how m** Jesus had done for him. *4012*
6:37 that **m** on bread and give it to them to eat?" *NIG*
9:12 of Man must suffer **m** and be rejected? *4498*
9:26 The boy **looked so m like** a corpse *1181+6059*
10:30 will fail to receive a hundred times as **m** *NIG*
Lk 7:47 have been forgiven—for she loved **m.** *4498*
8:39 "Return home and tell **how m** God has done *4012*
8:39 told all over town **how m** Jesus had done *4012*
11: 8 up and give him **as m as** he needs. *4012*
11:13 **how m** more will your Father in heaven give the Holy Spirit *4531*
12:24 **how m** more valuable you are than birds! *4531*
12:28 **how m** more will he clothe you, *4531*
12:48 From everyone who has been given **m,** *4498*
12:48 given much, **m** will be demanded; *4498*
12:48 the one who has been entrusted with **m,** *4498*
12:48 **m more** will be asked. *4358*
16: 5 **'How m** do you owe my master?' *4531*
16: 7 'And **how m** do you owe?' *4531*
16:10 with very little can also be trusted with **m,** *4498*
16:10 also be dishonest with **m.** *4498*
18:30 to receive **many times as m** in this age and, *4491*
Jn 2:10 after the guests *have* **had too m to drink;** *3499*
6:11 to those who were seated **as m as** *4012*
8:26 "I have **m** to say in judgment of you. *4498*
14:30 I will not speak with you **m** longer, *4498*
15: 5 and I in him, he will bear **m** fruit; *4498*
15: 8 my Father's glory, that you bear **m** fruit, *4498*
16:12 "I have **m** more to say to you, *4498*
Ac 2:13 *"They have* **had too m** wine." *1639+3551*
4:33 and **m** grace was upon them all. *3489*
9:16 I will show him **how m** he must suffer *4012*
15: 7 After **m** discussion, Peter got up *4498*
15:32 said **m** to encourage and strengthen *4498*
27: 9 **M** time had been lost, *2653*
27:38 **eaten as m as** *they* **wanted,** *3170*
Ro 3: 2 **M** in every way! *4498*
5: 9 **how m** more shall we be saved *4498*
5:10 **how m** more, having been reconciled, *4498*
5:15 **how m** more did God's grace and the gift *4498*
5:17 **how m** more will those who receive God's abundant provision *4498*
11:12 **how m** greater riches will their fullness bring! *4531*
11:13 *I* **make m of** my ministry *1519*
11:24 **how m** more readily will these, *4531*
1Co 2: 3 weakness and fear, and with **m** trembling. *4498*
6: 3 **How m more** the things of this life! *3615*
7: 2 But since there is so **m** immorality, *NIG*
9:11 is it too **m** if we reap a material harvest *3489*
2Co 2: 5 not so **m** grieved me as he has grieved all *NIG*
3: 9 how **m** more glorious is the ministry *4498*
3:11 **m** greater is the glory of that which lasts! *4498*
8: 3 they gave **as m as** they **were able,** *1539+2848*
8:15 "He who gathered **m** did not have too much, *4498*
8:15 He who gathered much *did* **not have too m,** *4429*
8:17 with **m enthusiasm** and on his own initiative. *AIT*
10: 7 that we belong to Christ just as **m** as he. *NIG*
11:23 I have worked **m harder,** *4359*
Gal 3: 4 Have you suffered **so m** for nothing— *5537*
Php 2:12 but now **m** more in my absence— *4498*
Col 2: 1 to know **how m** I am struggling for you and *2462*
1Th 2: 8 We loved you **so m** that we were delighted *4048*
1Ti 3: 8 sincere, not indulging *in* **m** wine, *4498*
Tit 2: 3 not to be slanderers or addicted *to* **m** wine, *4498*
Heb 1: 4 So he became **as m** superior to the angels as *5537*
5:11 We have **m** to say about this, *4498*
9:14 **How m** more, then, will the blood of Christ, *4531*
10:29 **How m** more severely do you think *4531*
12: 9 How **m** more should we submit to *4498*
12:25 how **m** less will we, if we turn away *4498*
2Jn 1:12 I have **m** to write to you, *4498*
3Jn 1:13 I have **m** to write you, *4498*
Rev 8: 3 He was given **m** incense to offer, *4498*
12:11 not love their lives **so m as** to shrink *948*
18: 7 Give her **as m** torture and grief as the glory *5537*

MUD (15) [MUDDIED, MUDDY, MUDDYING]

2Sa 22:43 and trampled them like **m** *in* the streets. 3226
Job 30:19 He throws me into the **m,** 2817
41:30 a trail in the **m** like a threshing sledge. 3226
Ps 18:42 I poured them out like **m** *in* the streets. 3226
40: 2 out of the **m** and mire; 3226
Isa 10: 6 to trample them down like **m** *in* the streets. 2817
57:20 whose waves cast up mire and **m.** 3226
Jer 38: 6 it had no water in it, only **m,** 3226
38: 6 and Jeremiah sank down into the **m.** 3226
38:22 Your feet are sunk in the **m;** 1288
Jn 9: 6 made some **m** with the saliva, *4384*
9:11 "The man they call Jesus made some **m** *4384*
9:14 on which Jesus had made the **m** and opened *4384*
9:15 "He put **m** on my eyes," the man replied, *4384*
2Pe 2:22 goes back to her wallowing *in* the **m.**" *1079*

MUDDIED (3) [MUD]

Pr 25:26 Like a **m** spring or a polluted well is 8346
Eze 32:13 the foot of man or **m** *by* the hoofs of cattle. 1931
34:19 and drink **what** you have **m** *with* your feet? 5343

MUDDY (2) [MUD]

Eze 34:18 *Must you* also **m** the rest with your feet? 8346
Zec 10: 5 be like mighty men trampling the **m** streets 3226

MUDDYING (1) [MUD]

Eze 32: 2 the water with your feet and **m** the streams. 8346

MUFFLERS (KJV) See VEILS

MULBERRY (1)

Lk 17: 6 you can say *to* this **m tree,** 'Be uprooted *5189*

MULE (7) [MULES]

2Sa 18: 9 He was riding his **m,** 7234
18: 9 and as the **m** went under the thick branches 7234
18: 9 while the **m** he was riding kept on going. 7234
1Ki 1:33 on my own **m** and take him down to Gihon. 7235
1:38 down and put Solomon on King David's **m** 7235
1:44 and they have put him on the king's **m,** 7235
Ps 32: 9 Do not be like the horse or the **m,** 7234

MULES (11) [MULE]

2Sa 13:29 mounted their **m** and fled. 7234
1Ki 10:25 weapons and spices, and horses and **m.** 7234
18: 5 and **m** alive so we will not have to kill any 7234
2Ki 5:17 as much earth as a pair of **m** can carry, 7234
1Ch 12:40 on donkeys, camels, **m** and oxen. 7234
2Ch 9:24 weapons and spices, and horses and **m.** 7234
Ezr 2:66 They had 736 horses, 245 **m,** 7234
Ne 7:68 There were 736 horses, 245 **m,** NIH
Isa 66:20 and on **m** and camels," says the LORD. 7234
Eze 27:14 war horses and **m** for your merchandise. 7234
Zec 14:15 similar plague will strike the horses and **m,** 7234

MULTICOLORED (1) [COLORED]

Eze 27:24 embroidered work and **m** rugs 1394

MULTIPLIED (7) [MULTIPLY]

Ex 1: 7 but the Israelites were fruitful and **m** greatly 9237
1:12 the more *they* **m** and spread; 8049
11: 9 so that my wonders *may be* **m** in Egypt." 8049
Dt 8:13 and gold increase and all you have *is* **m,** 8049
Jdg 16:24 who laid waste our land and **m** our slain." 8049
Ps 25:17 The troubles of my heart *have* **m;** 8143
La 2: 5 *He has* **m** mourning and lamentation for 8049

MULTIPLIES (6) [MULTIPLY]

Job 34:37 among us and **m** his words against God." 8049
35:16 without knowledge *he* **m** words." 3892
Pr 23:28 and **m** the unfaithful among men. 3578
27: 6 but an enemy **m** kisses. 6984
Ecc 10:14 and the fool **m** words. 8049
Hos 12: 1 he pursues the east wind all day and **m** lies 8049

MULTIPLY (12) [MULTIPLIED, MULTIPLIES, MULTIPLYING]

Ge 8:17 so *they can* **m** on the earth and be fruitful 9237
9: 7 **m** on the earth and increase upon it." 9237
Ex 7: 3 and though *I* **m** my miraculous signs 8049
Lev 26:21 *I will* **m** your afflictions seven times over, 3578
Dt 7:22 or the wild animals *will* **m** around you. 8049
2Sa 24: 3 *"May* the LORD your God **m** the troops 3578
1Ch 21: 3 *"May* the LORD **m** his troops 3578
Job 9:17 a storm and **m** my wounds for no reason. 8049
Jer 46:11 But you **m** remedies in vain; 8049
Eze 36:10 *I will* **m the number** *of* people upon you, 8049
Na 3:15 **M** like grasshoppers, multiply like locusts! 3877
3:15 Multiply like grasshoppers, **m** like locusts! 3877

MULTIPLYING (1) [MULTIPLY]

Mk 4: 8 grew and produced a crop, **m** thirty, sixty, *5770*

MULTITUDE (10) [MULTITUDES]

Ps 42: 4 how I used to go with the **m,** 6107
Isa 1:11 "The **m** *of* your sacrifices— 8044
13: 4 like that of a great **m!** 6639
31: 1 who trust in the **m** *of* their chariots and in 8041
Da 10: 6 and his voice like the sound of a **m.** 2162
Jas 5:20 from death and cover over a **m** of sins. *4436*
1Pe 4: 8 because love covers over a **m** of sins. *4436*
Rev 7: 9 and there before me was a great **m** *4063*
19: 1 the roar *of* a great **m** in heaven shouting: *4063*
19: 6 Then I heard what sounded like a great **m,** *4063*

MULTITUDES (5) [MULTITUDE]

Ne 9: 6 and the **m** *of* heaven worship you. 7372
Da 12: 2 **M** who sleep in the dust of the earth will awake: 8041
Joel 3:14 **M,** multitudes in the valley of decision! 2162
3:14 Multitudes, **m** in the valley of decision! 2162
Rev 17:15 where the prostitute sits, are peoples, **m,** *4063*

MUMBLE (1)

Isa 29: 4 your speech *will* **m** out of the dust. 8820

MUNITION (KJV) See FORTRESS

MUPPIM (1)

Ge 46:21 Naaman, Ehi, Rosh, **M,** Huppim and Ard. 5137

MURDER (32) [MURDERED, MURDERER, MURDERERS, MURDERING, MURDEROUS, MURDERS]

Ex 20:13 *"You shall* not **m.** 8357
Nu 35:12 so that a *person* **accused of m** may not die 8357
35:25 the *one* **accused of m** from the avenger 8357
35:27 the accused without being **guilty of m.** 1947
Dt 5:17 *"You shall* not **m.** 8357
Jos 21:13 (a city of refuge for *one* **accused of m),** 8357
21:21 (a city of refuge for *one* **accused of m),** 8357
21:27 (a city of refuge for *one* **accused of m)** and 8357
21:32 (a city of refuge for *one* **accused of m),** 8357
21:38 (a city of refuge for *one* **accused of m),** 8357
Jdg 9:24 who had helped him **m** his brothers. 2222
2Sa 3:37 the king had no part in *the* **m** *of* Abner son 4637
Ps 94: 6 *they* **m** the fatherless. 8357
Pr 28:17 A man tormented by the **guilt of m** 1947+5883
Isa 33:15 who stops his ears against plots of **m** 1947
Jer 7: 9 " 'Will you steal and **m,** 8357
Hos 4: 2 There is only cursing, lying and **m,** 8357
6: 9 *they* **m** on the road to Shechem, 8357
Mt 5:21 *'Do* not **m,** and anyone who murders will *5839*
15:19 For out of the heart come evil thoughts, **m,** *5840*
19:18 Jesus replied, " *'Do* not **m,** *5839*
Mk 7:21 sexual immorality, theft, **m,** adultery, *5840*
10:19 You know the commandments: *'Do* not **m,** *5839*
15: 7 the insurrectionists who had committed **m** *5840*
Lk 18:20 'Do not commit adultery, *do* not **m,** *5839*
23:19 for an insurrection in the city, and for **m.)** *5840*
23:25 into prison for insurrection and **m,** *5840*
Ro 1:29 They are full of envy, **m,** strife, *5840*
13: 9 *"Do* not **m,"** "Do not steal," *5839*
Jas 2:11 also said, *"Do* not **m."** *5839*
2:11 not commit adultery but *do* **commit m,** *5839*
1Jn 3:12 And why *did he* **m** him? *5377*

MURDERED (18) [MURDER]

Jdg 9: 5 and on one stone **m** his seventy brothers, 2222
9:18 **m** his seventy sons on a single stone, 2222
20: 4 So the Levite, the husband of the **m** woman, 8357
2Sa 3:30 (Joab and his brother Abishai **m** Abner *2222*
1Ki 16:16 against the king and **m** him, 5782
21:19 not **m** a man and seized his property?' 8357
2Ki 11: 2 who *were about to* **be m.** 4637
12:21 The officials *who* **m** him were Jozabad son 5782
14: 5 the officials *who had* **m** his father the king. 5782
2Ch 21:13 *You have* also **m** your own brothers, 2222
22:11 *about to* **be m** and put him and his nurse in 4637
25: 3 the officials who *had* **m** his father the king. 5782
Pr 22:13 or, *"I will* **be m** in the streets!" 8357
Mt 23:31 descendants *of* those who **m** the prophets. *5839*
23:35 whom *you* **m** between the temple and *5839*
Ac 7:52 And now you have betrayed and **m** him— *5838*
Jas 5: 6 *You have* condemned and **m** innocent men, *5839*
1Jn 3:12 to the evil one and **m** his brother. *5377*

MURDERER (20) [MURDER]

Nu 35:16 an iron object so that he dies, he *is a* **m;** 8357
35:16 the **m** shall be put to death. 8357
35:17 strikes someone so that he dies, he *is a* **m;** 8357
35:17 the **m** shall be put to death. 8357
35:18 hits someone so that he dies, he *is a* **m;** 8357
35:18 the **m** shall be put to death. 8357
35:19 avenger of blood shall put the **m** to death; 8357
35:21 shall be put to death; he *is a* **m.** 8357
35:21 avenger of blood shall put the **m** to death 8357
35:30 be put to death as a **m** only on the testimony 8357
35:31 not accept a ransom for the life of a **m,** 8357
2Ki 6:32 how this **m** is sending someone 1201+8357
9:31 Zimri, you **m** *of* your master?" 2222
Job 24:14 the **m** rises up and kills the poor and needy; 8357
Jn 8:44 He was a **m** from the beginning, *475*
Ac 3:14 and asked that a **m** be released to you. *467+5838*
28: 4 "This man must be a **m;** *5838*
1Pe 4:15 as a **m** or thief or any other kind of criminal, *5838*
1Jn 3:15 Anyone who hates his brother is a **m,** *475*
3:15 you know that no **m** has eternal life in him. *475*

MURDERERS (6) [MURDER]

Isa 1:21 used to dwell in her—but now **m!** 8357
Jer 4:31 I am fainting; my life is given over to **m.**" 2222
Mt 22: 7 and destroyed those **m** and burned their city. *5838*
1Ti 1: 9 who kill their fathers or mothers, *for* **m,** *439*
Rev 21: 8 cowardly, the unbelieving, the vile, the **m,** *5838*
22:15 the sexually immoral, the **m,** *5838*

MURDERING (2) [MURDER]

Jdg 9:56 to his father by **m** his seventy brothers. 2222
2Ch 24:25 His officials conspired against him for **m** 1947

MURDEROUS (1) [MURDER]

Ac 9: 1 Saul was still breathing out **m** threats *5840*

MURDERS (4) [MURDER]

Dt 22:26 who attacks and **m** his neighbor, 5883+8357
Ps 10: 8 from ambush *he* **m** the innocent, 2222
Mt 5:21 anyone who **m** will be subject to judgment.' *5839*
Rev 9:21 Nor did they repent of their **m**, *5840*

MURMUR, MURMURED, MURMURERS, MURMURING, MURMURINGS (KJV) See COMPLAIN, COMPLAINED, GRUMBLE, GRUMBLED, GRUMBLERS, GRUMBLING, MUTTER, MUTTERED, WHISPERING

MURRAIN (KJV) See PLAGUE

MUSCLES (1)

Job 40:16 what power in the **m** *of* his belly! 9235

MUSED (2)

Ps 77: 3 *I* **m**, and my spirit grew faint. 8488
77: 6 My heart **m** and my spirit inquired: 8488

MUSHI (8) [MUSHITE, MUSHITES]

Ex 6:19 The sons of Merari were Mahli and **M.** 4633
Nu 3:20 The Merarite clans: Mahli and **M.** 4633
1Ch 6:19 The sons of Merari: Mahli and **M.** 4633
6:47 the son of **M,** the son of Merari, 4633
23:21 The sons of Merari: Mahli and **M.** 4633
23:23 The sons of **M:** Mahli, Eder and Jerimoth— 4633
24:26 The sons of Merari: Mahli and **M.** 4633
24:30 the sons of **M:** Mahli, Eder and Jerimoth. 4633

MUSHITE (1) [MUSHI]

Nu 26:58 the **M** clan, the Korahite clan. 4634

MUSHITES (1) [MUSHI]

Nu 3:33 the clans of the Mahlites and the **M;** 4634

MUSIC (90) [MUSICAL, MUSICIAN, MUSICIANS]

Ge 31:27 and singing to the **m of tambourines** 9512
Jdg 5: 3 *I will* **make m** to the LORD, 2376
1Ch 6:31 of the **m** *in* the house of the LORD after 8877
6:32 They ministered with **m** before the 8877
25: 6 the supervision of their fathers for the **m** of 8877
25: 7 all of them trained and skilled in **m** for 8877
Ne 12:27 of thanksgiving and with the **m** *of* cymbals, 8877
Job 21:12 They sing to the **m of tambourine** and harp 9512
Ps 4: T For the **director of m.** With stringed 5904
5: T For the **director of m.** For flutes. 5904
6: T For the **director of m.** With stringed 5904
8: T For the **director of m.** According to gittith. 5904
9: T For the **director of m.** 5904
11: T For the **director of m.** Of David. 5904
12: T For the **director of m.** According to 5904
13: T For the **director of m.** A psalm of David. 5904
14: T For the **director of m.** Of David. 5904
18: T For the **director of m.** Of David the servant 5904
19: T For the **director of m.** A psalm of David. 5904
20: T For the **director of m.** A psalm of David. 5904
21: T For the **director of m.** A psalm of David. 5904
22: T For the **director of m.** 5904
27: 6 I will sing and **make m** to the LORD. 2376
31: T For the **director of m.** A psalm of David. 5904
33: 2 **make m** to him on the ten-stringed lyre. 2376
36: T For the **director of m.** Of David the servant 5904
39: T For the **director of m.** For Jeduthun. 5904
40: T For the **director of m.** Of David. A psalm. 5904
41: T For the **director of m.** A psalm of David. 5904
42: T For the **director of m.** A maskil of 5904
44: T For the **director of m.** Of the Sons of Korah 5904
45: T For the **director of m.** 5904
45: 8 the **m of the strings** makes you glad. 4944
46: T For the **director of m.** Of the Sons of Korah 5904
47: T For the **director of m.** Of the Sons of Korah 5904
49: T For the **director of m.** Of the Sons of Korah 5904
51: T For the **director of m.** A psalm of David. 5904
52: T For the **director of m.** A maskil of David. 5904
53: T For the **director of m.** According to 5904
54: T For the **director of m.** With stringed 5904
55: T For the **director of m.** With stringed 5904
56: T For the **director of m.** 5904
57: T For the **director of m.** 5904
57: 7 I will sing and **make m.** 2376
58: T For the **director of m.** 5904
59: T For the **director of m.** 5904
60: T For the **director of m.** 5904
61: T For the **director of m.** With stringed 5904
62: T For the **director of m.** For Jeduthun. 5904
64: T For the **director of m.** A psalm of David. 5904
65: T For the **director of m.** A psalm of David. 5904
66: T For the **director of m.** A song. A psalm. 5904
67: T For the **director of m.** With stringed 5904
68: T For the **director of m.** Of David. A psalm. 5904
69: T For the **director of m.** 5904
70: T For the **director of m.** Of David. A petition. 5904
75: T For the **director of m.** 5904
76: T For the **director of m.** With stringed 5904
77: T For the **director of m.** For Jeduthun. 5904
Ps 80: T For the **director of m.** 5904
81: T For the **director of m.** According to gittith. 5904
81: 2 Begin the **m,** strike the tambourine, 2379
84: T For the **director of m.** According to gittith. 5904
85: T For the **director of m.** Of the Sons of Korah 5904
87: 7 As *they* **make m** they will sing, 2727
88: T of the Sons of Korah. For the **director of m.** 5904
92: 1 It is good to praise the LORD and **make m** 2376
92: 3 to the **m** of the ten-stringed lyre and NIH
95: 2 and extol him with **m and song.** 2369
98: 4 burst into jubilant song with **m;** 2376
98: 5 **make m** to the LORD with the harp, 2376
108: 1 I will sing and **make m** *with* all my soul. 2376
109: T For the **director of m.** Of David. A psalm. 5904
139: T For the **director of m.** Of David. A psalm. 5904
140: T For the **director of m.** A psalm of David. 5904
144: 9 the ten-stringed lyre *I will* **make m** to you, 2376
147: 7 **make m** to our God on the harp. 2376
149: 3 and **make m** to him with tambourine 2376
Isa 30:32 be to the **m of tambourines** and harps, 9512
La 5:14 the young men have stopped their **m.** 5593
Eze 26:13 the **m** *of* your harps will be heard no more. 7754
Da 3: 5 zither, lyre, harp, pipes and all kinds of **m,** 10233
3: 7 flute, zither, lyre, harp and all kinds of **m,** 10233
3:10 of **m** must fall down and worship the image 10233
3:15 zither, lyre, harp, pipes and all kinds of **m,** 10233
Am 5:23 I will not listen to the **m** *of* your harps. 2379
Hab 3:19 For the **director of m.** On my stringed 5904
Lk 15:25 he heard **m** and dancing. *5246*
Eph 5:19 Sing and **make m** in your heart to the Lord, *6010*
Rev 18:22 The **m** of harpists and musicians, *5889*

MUSICAL (7) [MUSIC]

1Ch 15:16 accompanied by **m** instruments: 8877
23: 5 with the *m* **instruments** I have provided for AIT
2Ch 7: 6 with the LORD's **m** instruments, 8877
23:13 with **m** instruments were leading 8877
34:12 in playing **m** instruments— 8877
Ne 12:36 with **m** instruments *[prescribed by]* David 8877
Am 6: 5 like David and improvise on **m** instruments. 8877

MUSICIAN (1) [MUSIC]

1Ch 6:33 Heman, the **m,** the son of Joel, 8876

MUSICIANS (8) [MUSIC]

1Ki 10:12 and to make harps and lyres for the **m.** 8876
1Ch 9:33 Those who *were* **m,** heads of Levite families 8876
15:19 The **m** Heman, Asaph and Ethan were 8876
2Ch 5:12 All the Levites who *were* **m—** 8876
9:11 and to make harps and lyres for the **m.** 8876
35:15 The **m,** the descendants of Asaph, 8876
Ps 68:25 In front are the singers, after them the **m;** 5594
Rev 18:22 The music of harpists and **m,** *3676*

MUSICK (KJV) See MUSICAL

MUST (786)

Ge 2:17 but *you m* not **eat** from the tree of AIT
3: 1 '*You m* not **eat** from any tree in AIT
3: 3 '*You m* not **eat** fruit from the tree that is in AIT
3: 3 and *you m* not **touch** it, or you will die.' " AIT
3:17 '*You m* not **eat** of it,' AIT
3:22 *m* not be allowed *to* **reach out** AIT
4: 7 it desires to have you, but you *m* **master** it." AIT
9: 4 "But *you m* not **eat** meat that has its lifeblood still in it. AIT
17: 9 "As for you, *you m* **keep** my covenant, AIT
17:12 who is eight days old *m* **be circumcised,** AIT
17:13 *they* **m be circumcised.** 4576+4576
24:37 '*You m* not **get** a wife for my son from AIT
30:16 "*You m* **sleep with** me," she said. AIT
33:13 that the children are tender and that I **m** care NIH
42:20 *you m* **bring** your youngest brother to me, AIT
42:22 *m* **give an accounting** for his blood." AIT
43:11 their father Israel said to them, "If it **m be,** 4027
43:12 for *you m* **return** the silver AIT
50:25 *m* **carry** my bones **up** from this place." AIT
Ex 1:10 *we m* **deal shrewdly** with them AIT
1:22 "Every boy that is born *you m* **throw** into AIT
2:14 "What I did *m have* **become known."** AIT
5:18 *you m* **produce** your full quota of bricks." AIT
8:27 *We m* **take** a three-day journey into AIT
8:28 but *you* **m** not go **very far.** 8178+8178
10:25 "You *m* **allow** us to have sacrifices AIT
10:26 Our livestock too *m* **go** with us; AIT
12: 4 they *m* **share** one with their nearest neighbor, AIT
12: 5 The animals you choose *m* **be** year-old AIT
12: 6 the community of Israel *m* **slaughter** them AIT
12:10 if some is left till morning, *you m* **burn** it. AIT
12:15 the seventh *m* **be cut off** from Israel. AIT
12:19 in it *m* **be cut off** from the community AIT
12:20 *you m* **eat** unleavened bread." AIT
12:46 "*It m* **be eaten** inside one house; AIT
12:47 whole community of Israel *m* **celebrate** it. AIT
12:48 *m have* all the males in his household **circumcised;** AIT
13:10 *You m* **keep** this ordinance at the appointed AIT
13:19 *m* **carry** my bones **up** with you AIT
18:19 You *m* **be** the people's representative AIT
19:22 *m* **consecrate themselves,** AIT
19:24 *m* not **force** *their* **way through** AIT
21: 6 his master *m* **take** him before the judges. AIT
21: 8 *m* **let** her **be redeemed.** AIT
21: 9 *he m* **grant** her the rights of a daughter. AIT
Ex 21:10 *he m* not **deprive** the first one *of* her food, AIT
21:15 or his mother **m be put to death.** 4637+4637
21:16 when he is caught **m be put to death.** 4637+4637
21:17 or his mother **m be put to death.** 4637+4637
21:19 however, *he m* **pay** the injured man *for* AIT
21:20 *he* **m be punished,** 5933+5933
21:22 the offender **m be fined** whatever 6740+6740
21:26 *m* **let** the servant **go** free AIT
21:27 *m* **let** the servant **go** free AIT
21:28 **m be stoned to death,** 6232+6232
21:28 and its meat *m* not **be eaten.** AIT
21:29 the bull *m* **be stoned** and the owner AIT
21:29 *m* **be put to death.** AIT
21:32 the owner *m* **pay** thirty shekels of silver to AIT
21:32 and the bull *m* **be stoned.** AIT
21:34 *m* **pay for the loss;** AIT
21:34 *he m* **pay** its owner, AIT
21:36 the owner **m pay,** animal for animal, 8966+8966
22: 1 *he m* **pay back** five head of cattle for the ox AIT
22: 3 **m certainly make restitution,** 8966+8966
22: 3 *he m* **be sold** to pay for his theft. AIT
22: 4 *he m* **pay back** double. AIT
22: 5 *he m* **make restitution** *from* the best AIT
22: 6 one who started the fire **m make restitution.** 8966+8966
22: 7 the thief, if he is caught, *m* **pay back** double. AIT
22: 8 of the house *m* **appear** before the judges AIT
22: 9 the judges declare guilty *m* **pay back** double AIT
22:12 *he m* **make restitution** to the owner. AIT
22:14 *he* **m make restitution.** 8966+8966
22:16 *he* **m pay the bride-price,** 4555+4555
22:17 *he m still* **pay** the bride-price for virgins. AIT
22:19 with an animal **m be put to death.** 4637+4637
22:20 god other than the LORD *m* **be destroyed.** AIT
22:29 "*You m* **give** me the firstborn of your sons. AIT
23:18 of my festival offerings *m* not *be* **kept** AIT
23:24 *You* **m demolish** them 2238+2238
24: 2 the others *m* not **come near.** AIT
26:24 At these two corners *they m* **be** double from AIT
28:35 Aaron *m* **wear** *it* when he ministers. AIT
28:43 his sons *m* **wear** *them* whenever they enter AIT
29:34 *It m* not **be eaten,** because it is sacred. AIT
30: 7 "Aaron *m* **burn** fragrant incense on AIT
30: 8 *He m* **burn** incense again when he lights AIT
30:10 This annual **atonement** *m be* **made** with AIT
30:12 each one *m* **pay** the LORD a ransom AIT
30:33 on anyone other than a priest *m* **be cut off** AIT
30:38 like it to enjoy its fragrance *m* **be cut off** AIT
31:13 '*You m* **observe** my Sabbaths. AIT
31:14 work on that day **m be put to death;** 4637+4637
31:14 on that day *m* **be cut off** from his people. AIT
31:15 Sabbath day **m be put to death.** 4637+4637
33:23 but my face *m* not **be seen."** AIT
34:21 the plowing season and harvest *you m* **rest.** AIT
35: 2 any work on it *m* **be put to death.** AIT
Lev 1: 3 *He m* **present** it at the entrance to the Tent AIT
2:11 to the LORD *m* **be made** without yeast, AIT
3:17 *You m* not **eat** any fat or any blood.' " AIT
4: 3 *he m* **bring** to the LORD a young bull AIT
4:12 *he m* **take** outside the camp to AIT
4:14 the assembly *m* **bring** a young bull as AIT
4:23 *he m* **bring** as his offering a male goat AIT
4:28 *he m* **bring** as his offering for AIT
5: 5 *he m* **confess** in what way he has sinned AIT
5: 6 *he m* **bring** to the LORD a female lamb AIT
5: 9 of the blood *m* **be drained out** at the base of AIT
5:11 *He m* not **put** oil or incense on it, AIT
5:16 *He m* **make restitution** *for* what he has failed to do AIT
6: 4 *he m* **return** what he has stolen or taken AIT
6: 5 *He m* **make restitution** in full, AIT
6: 6 And as a penalty *he m* **bring** to the priest, AIT
6: 9 and the fire *m* **be kept burning** on the altar. AIT
6:12 The fire on the altar *m* **be kept burning;** AIT
6:12 *it m* not **go out.** AIT
6:13 The fire *m* **be kept burning** on the altar AIT
6:13 *it m* not **go out.** AIT
6:17 *It m* not **be baked** *with* yeast; AIT
6:23 *it m* not **be eaten."** AIT
6:27 *you m* **wash** it in a holy place. AIT
6:28 the meat is cooked in *m* **be broken;** AIT
6:30 in the Holy Place *m* not **be eaten;** AIT
6:30 *it m* **be burned.** AIT
7: 6 but *it m* **be eaten** in a holy place; AIT
7:15 of thanksgiving *m* **be eaten** on AIT
7:15 *he m* **leave** none of it till morning. AIT
7:17 over till the third day *m* **be burned up.** AIT
7:19 touches anything ceremonially unclean *m* not **be eaten;** AIT
7:19 *it m* **be burned up.** AIT
7:20 that person *m* **be cut off** from his people. AIT
7:21 that person *m* **be cut off** from his people.' " AIT
7:24 but *you* **m** not **eat** it. 430+430
7:25 *m* **be cut off** from his people. AIT
7:26 *you m* not **eat** the blood of any bird AIT
7:27 that person *m* **be cut off** from his people.' " AIT
8:35 *You m* **stay** at the entrance to the Tent AIT
10: 8 You *m* **distinguish** between the holy and AIT
10:11 and you *m* **teach** the Israelites all AIT
10:15 and the breast that was waved *m be* **brought** AIT
11: 4 but *you m* not **eat** them. AIT
11: 8 *You m* not **eat** their meat or touch AIT
11:11 *you m* not **eat** their meat AIT
11:11 and *you m* **detest** their carcasses. AIT
11:25 *m* **wash** his clothes, AIT
11:28 picks up their carcasses *m* **wash** his clothes, AIT

Lev 11:33 and *you m* **break** the pot. AIT
11:35 an oven or cooking pot *m* **be broken up.** AIT
11:40 of the carcass *m* **wash** his clothes, AIT
11:40 up the carcass *m* **wash** his clothes, AIT
11:47 You *m* **distinguish** between the unclean and AIT
12: 4 Then the woman *m* **wait** thirty-three days to AIT
12: 4 *She m* not **touch** anything sacred or go to AIT
12: 5 Then *she m* **wait** sixty-six days to AIT
13: 2 *he m* **be brought** to Aaron the priest or to AIT
13: 6 The man *m* **wash** his clothes, AIT
13: 7 *he m* **appear** before the priest again. AIT
13: 9 *he m* **be brought** to the priest. AIT
13:16 *he m* **go** to the priest. AIT
13:19 *he m* **present himself** to the priest. AIT
13:33 *he m* **be shaved** except for the diseased area AIT
13:34 *He m* **wash** his clothes, and he will be clean. AIT
13:45 *m* **wear** torn clothes, let his hair be unkempt, AIT
13:46 *He m* **live** alone; AIT
13:46 he **m** live outside the camp. NIH
13:49 it is a spreading mildew and *m* **be shown** *to* AIT
13:52 *He m* **burn up** the clothing, AIT
13:52 the article *m* **be burned up.** AIT
13:57 and whatever has the mildew *m be* **burned** AIT
13:58 *m* **be washed** again, and it will be clean." AIT
14: 8 to be cleansed *m* **wash** his clothes, AIT
14: 8 *he m* **stay** outside his tent for seven days. AIT
14: 9 the seventh day *he m* **shave off** all his hair; AIT
14: 9 *he m* **shave** his head, his beard, AIT
14: 9 *He m* **wash** his clothes and bathe himself AIT
14:10 the eighth day *he m* **bring** two male lambs AIT
14:21 *he m* **take** one male lamb as a guilt offering AIT
14:23 "On the eighth day *he m* **bring** them AIT
14:35 the owner of the house *m* **go** and tell AIT
14:41 *m* **have** all the inside walls of the house **scraped** AIT
14:45 It *m be* **torn down—** AIT
14:47 or eats in the house *m* **wash** his clothes. AIT
15: 5 who touches his bed *m* **wash** his clothes AIT
15: 6 on *m* **wash** his clothes and bathe with water, AIT
15: 7 *m* **wash** his clothes and bathe with water, AIT
15: 8 that person *m* **wash** his clothes and bathe AIT
15:10 *m* **wash** his clothes and bathe with water, AIT
15:11 with water *m* **wash** his clothes and bathe AIT
15:12 that the man touches *m* **be broken,** AIT
15:13 *he m* **wash** his clothes and bathe himself AIT
15:14 On the eighth day *he m* **take** two doves AIT
15:16 *he m* **bathe** his whole body with water, AIT
15:17 has semen on it *m* **be washed** with water, AIT
15:18 *both m* **bathe** with water, AIT
15:21 touches her bed *m* **wash** his clothes AIT
15:22 on *m* **wash** his clothes and bathe with water, AIT
15:27 *he m* **wash** his clothes and bathe with water, AIT
15:28 *she m* **count off** seven days, AIT
15:29 On the eighth day *she m* **take** two doves AIT
15:31 *m* **keep** the Israelites **separate** AIT
16: 4 so *he m* **bathe** himself with water AIT
16:26 the goat as a scapegoat *m* **wash** his clothes AIT
16:27 *m be* **taken** outside the camp; AIT
16:28 man who burns them *m* **wash** his clothes AIT
16:29 the seventh month *you m* **deny** yourselves AIT
16:31 and *you m* **deny** yourselves; AIT
17: 4 he has shed blood and *m* **be cut off** AIT
17: 5 *They m* **bring** them to the priest, that is, AIT
17: 7 *They m* no longer **offer** any AIT
17: 9 that man *m* **be cut off** from his people. AIT
17:13 be eaten *m* **drain out** the blood and cover it AIT
17:14 *"You m* not **eat** the blood of any creature, AIT
17:14 anyone who eats it *m* **be cut off."** AIT
17:15 or torn by wild animals *m* **wash** his clothes AIT
18: 3 *You m* not **do** as they do in Egypt, AIT
18: 3 and *you m* not **do** as they do in the land AIT
18: 4 *You m* **obey** my laws and be careful AIT
18:21 *you m* not **profane** the name of your God. AIT
18:23 A woman *m* not **present** *herself* to AIT
18:26 But you *m* **keep** my decrees and my laws. AIT
18:26 the aliens living among you *m* not **do** any AIT
18:29 such persons *m* **be cut off** AIT
19: 3 of *you m* **respect** his mother and father, AIT
19: 3 and *you m* **observe** my Sabbaths. AIT
19: 6 over until the third day *m* **be burned up.** AIT
19: 8 that person *m* **be cut off** from his people. AIT
19:20 *there m* **be** due punishment. AIT
19:21 *m* **bring** a ram to the entrance to the Tent AIT
19:23 *it m* not **be eaten.** AIT
19:34 The alien living with you *m be* **treated** AIT
20: 2 children to Molech **m be put to death.** 4637+4637
20: 9 or mother, **m be put to death.** 4637+4637
20:10 and the adulteress **m be put to death.** 4637+4637
20:11 and the woman **m be put to death;** 4637+4637
20:12 both of them **m be put to death.** 4637+4637
20:13 *They* **m be put to death;** 4637+4637
20:14 Both he and they *m be* **burned** in the fire, AIT
20:15 with an animal, *he* **m be put to death,** 4637+4637
20:15 and *you m* **kill** the animal. AIT
20:16 *They* **m be put to death;** 4637+4637
20:17 *They m* **be cut off** before the eyes AIT
20:18 of them *m* **be cut off** from their people. AIT
20:23 *You m* not **live** according to the customs of AIT
20:25 *m* therefore **make a distinction** AIT
20:27 among you **m be put to death.** 4637+4637
21: 1 *m* not **make himself ceremonially unclean** AIT
21: 4 *m* not **make himself unclean** AIT
21: 5 " 'Priests **m** not **shave** their heads 7942+7947
21: 6 *They m* **be** holy to their God and must AIT
21: 6 and *m* not **profane** the name of their God. AIT
21: 7 " '*They m* not **marry** women defiled AIT
21: 9 *she m* **be burned** in the fire. AIT
Lev 21:10 *m* not *let* his hair *become* **unkempt** AIT
21:11 *He m* not **enter** a place where there is AIT
21:11 *m* not **make himself unclean,** AIT
21:13 " 'The woman he marries **m** be a virgin. NIH
21:14 *He m* not **marry** a widow, a divorced woman, AIT
21:21 *he m* not **come near** to offer the food AIT
21:23 *he m* not **go** near the curtain or approach AIT
22: 3 that person *m* **be cut off** from my presence. AIT
22: 6 *He m* not **eat** any of the sacred offerings AIT
22: 8 *He m* not **eat** anything found dead or torn AIT
22:14 *he m* **make restitution** to the priest *for* AIT
22:15 The priests *m* not **desecrate** AIT
22:19 you **m** present a male without defect from NIH
22:21 *it m* **be** without defect or blemish to AIT
22:24 *You m* not **offer** to the LORD AIT
22:24 *You m* not **do** this in your own land, AIT
22:25 and you **m** not accept such animals from NIH
22:30 *It m* **be eaten** that same day; AIT
22:32 *I m* **be acknowledged as holy** AIT
23: 6 for seven days *you m* **eat** bread made AIT
23:12 *you m* **sacrifice** as a burnt offering to AIT
23:14 *You m* not **eat** any bread, AIT
23:29 not deny himself on that day *m* **be cut off** AIT
23:32 and *you m* **deny** yourselves. AIT
24: 4 before the LORD *m be* **tended** continually. AIT
24:16 **m be put to death.** 4637+4637
24:16 The entire assembly **m stone** him. 8083+8083
24:16 *he* **m be put to death.** 4637
24:17 *he* **m be put to death.** 4637+4637
24:18 of someone's animal *m* **make restitution—** AIT
24:19 whatever he has done *m* **be done** to him: AIT
24:21 an animal *m* **make restitution,** AIT
24:21 *m* **be put to death.** AIT
25: 2 the land itself **m observe a sabbath** to 8697+8701
25:23 " 'The land *m* not **be sold** permanently, AIT
25:24 *you m* **provide** *for* the redemption of AIT
25:34 to their towns *m* not **be sold;** AIT
25:37 *You m* not **lend** him money at interest AIT
25:42 *they* **m** not **be sold** as slaves. 4835+4929
25:46 but *you m* not **rule** over your fellow AIT
25:51 *he m* **pay** *for* his redemption a larger share AIT
25:53 you **m** see to it that his owner does not rule NIH
27:10 *He m* not **exchange** it or substitute a good AIT
27:11 the animal *m be* **presented** to the priest, AIT
27:13 *he m* **add** a fifth to its value. AIT
27:15 *he m* **add** a fifth to its value, AIT
27:19 *he m* **add** a fifth to its value, AIT
27:23 and the man *m* **pay** its value on that day AIT
27:29 *he* **m be put to death.** 4637+4637
27:31 *he m* **add** a fifth of the value to it. AIT
27:33 *He m* not **pick out** the good from the bad AIT
Nu 1:49 *"You m* not **count** the tribe of Levi AIT
3:10 *m* **be put to death."** AIT
4:15 But *they m* not **touch** the holy things AIT
4:20 But the Kohathites *m* not **go in** to look at AIT
5: 7 and *m* **confess** the sin he has committed. AIT
5: 7 *m* **make full restitution** AIT
5: 8 the restitution belongs to the LORD and **m** NIH
5:15 *He m* also **take** an offering of a tenth of AIT
5:15 *He m* not **pour** oil on it or put incense on it, AIT
6: 3 *he m* **abstain** from wine AIT
6: 3 and *m* not **drink** vinegar made from wine or AIT
6: 3 *He m* not **drink** grape juice or eat grapes AIT
6: 4 *he m* not **eat** anything that comes from AIT
6: 5 *He m* **be** holy until the period AIT
6: 5 *m let* the hair of his head **grow long.** AIT
6: 6 to the LORD *he m* not **go** near a dead body. AIT
6: 7 *m* not **make himself ceremonially unclean** AIT
6: 9 *he m* **shave** his head on the day AIT
6:10 on the eighth day *he m* **bring** two doves AIT
6:12 *He m* **dedicate** *himself* to the LORD for AIT
6:12 for the period of his separation and *m* **bring** AIT
6:18 the Nazirite *m* **shave off** the hair AIT
6:21 *He m* **fulfill** the vow he has made, AIT
8:25 *they m* **retire** from their regular service AIT
8:26 but *they themselves m* not **do** the work. AIT
9:12 *They m* not **leave** any of it till morning AIT
9:12 they **m** follow all the regulations. NIH
9:13 that person *m* **be cut off** from his people AIT
9:14 to celebrate the LORD's Passover *m* **do** so AIT
9:14 You *m* **have** the same regulations for AIT
15:13 Everyone who is native-born *m* **do** these AIT
15:14 *he m* **do** exactly as you do. AIT
15:27 *he m* **bring** a year-old female goat for AIT
15:30 that person *m* **be cut off** from his people. AIT
15:31 **m surely be cut off;** his guilt remains 4162+4162
15:35 said to Moses, "The man **m die.** 4637+4637
15:35 The whole assembly *m* **stone** him outside AIT
17: 3 for there **m** be one staff for the head NIH
18: 3 but *they m* not **go near** the furnishings of AIT
18: 7 *m* **be put to death."** AIT
18:10 You *m* **regard it as** holy. AIT
18:15 But *you* **m redeem** every firstborn son 7009+7009
18:16 *you m* **redeem** them at the redemption price AIT
18:17 *you m* not **redeem** the firstborn of an ox, AIT
18:22 now on the Israelites *m* not **go near** the Tent AIT
18:26 as your inheritance, *you m* **present** a tenth AIT
18:28 From these tithes *you m* **give** AIT
18:29 *You m* **present** as the LORD's portion AIT
19: 7 the priest *m* **wash** his clothes AIT
19: 8 man who burns it *m* also **wash** his clothes AIT
19:10 of the heifer *m* also **wash** his clothes, AIT
19:12 He *m* **purify** himself with the water on AIT
19:13 That person *m* **be cut off** from Israel. AIT
19:18 He **m** also sprinkle anyone who has touched NIH
19:19 person being cleansed *m* **wash** his clothes AIT
Nu 19:20 he *m* **be cut off** from the community, AIT
19:21 of cleansing *m* also **wash** his clothes, AIT
20:10 *m we* **bring** you water **out** of this rock? AIT
22:12 *m* not **put a curse on** those people, AIT
22:38 *I m* **speak** only what God puts AIT
23:12 **"M** *I* not speak what the LORD puts 9068
23:26 "Did I not tell you *I m* **do** whatever AIT
24:13 and *I m* **say** only what the LORD says'? AIT
25: 5 "Each of *you m* **put to death** those AIT
27: 7 *You* **m certainly give** them property 5989+5989
29: 7 *You m* **deny** yourselves and do no work. AIT
30: 2 *he m* not **break** his word AIT
30: 2 but *m* **do** everything he said. AIT
31:19 touched anyone who was killed *m* **stay** outside the camp AIT
31:19 and seventh days you *m* **purify yourselves** AIT
31:23 that can withstand fire *m be* **put** through AIT
31:23 But *it m* also **be purified** with the water AIT
31:23 whatever cannot withstand fire *m be* **put** AIT
32:30 *m* **accept** *their* **possession** AIT
35: 7 In all *you m* **give** the Levites forty-eight AIT
35:24 the assembly *m* **judge** between him and AIT
35:25 The assembly *m* **protect** the one accused AIT
35:25 *He m* **stay** there until the death of AIT
35:28 The accused *m* **stay** in his city of refuge AIT
35:31 *He* **m** surely **be put to death.** 4637+4637
36: 8 in any Israelite tribe *m* **marry** someone AIT
Dt 3:18 *m* **cross over** ahead of your brother AIT
7: 2 then *you* **m destroy** them **totally.** 3049+3049
7:16 *You m* **destroy** all the peoples AIT
12: 1 and laws *you m be* **careful** to follow in AIT
12: 4 *You m* not **worship** the LORD your God AIT
12: 5 To that place *you m* **go;** AIT
12:16 But *you m* not **eat** the blood; AIT
12:17 *You* **m** not eat in your own towns the tithe 3523
12:23 and *you m* not **eat** the life with the meat. AIT
12:24 *You m* not **eat** the blood; AIT
12:27 The blood of your sacrifices *m* **be poured** AIT
12:31 *You m* not **worship** the LORD your God AIT
13: 3 *you m* not **listen** to the words of AIT
13: 4 It is the LORD your God *you m* **follow,** AIT
13: 4 and him *you m* **revere.** AIT
13: 5 prophet or dreamer *m* **be put to death,** AIT
13: 5 *You m* **purge** the evil from among you. AIT
13: 9 *You* **m certainly put** him to death. 2222+2222
13: 9 Your hand *m* **be** the first in putting him AIT
13:14 then *you m* **inquire,** AIT
13:15 *you* **m certainly put** to the sword 5782+5782
15: 1 of every seven years *you m* **cancel debts.** AIT
15: 3 you *m* **cancel** *any* **debt** your brother owes AIT
15:12 in the seventh year *you m* **let** him **go** free. AIT
15:21 *you m* not **sacrifice** it to the LORD AIT
15:23 But *you m* not **eat** the blood; AIT
16: 5 *You* **m** not sacrifice the Passover 3523
16: 6 There *you m* **sacrifice** the Passover in AIT
16:16 Three times a year all your men *m* **appear** AIT
16:17 Each of you **m** bring a gift in proportion to NIH
17: 4 then *you m* **investigate** it thoroughly. AIT
17: 7 of the witnesses *m* **be** the first in putting him AIT
17: 7 *You m* **purge** the evil from among you. AIT
17:10 *You m* **act** according to the decisions AIT
17:12 *m be* **put to death.** AIT
17:12 *You m* **purge** the evil from Israel. AIT
17:15 He **m** be from among your own brothers. NIH
17:16 *m* not **acquire great numbers** AIT
17:17 *He m* not **take many** wives, AIT
17:17 *m* not **accumulate large amounts** AIT
18:13 *You m* **be** blameless before the LORD AIT
18:15 *You m* **listen** to him. AIT
18:20 name of other gods, *m be* **put to death."** AIT
19:13 *You m* **purge** from Israel the guilt AIT
19:15 A matter *m be* **established** by the testimony AIT
19:17 in the dispute *m* **stand** in the presence of AIT
19:18 *m* **make** *a* thorough **investigation,** AIT
19:19 *You m* **purge** the evil from among you. AIT
21:14 *You* **m** not **sell** her or treat her as a slave, 928+2021+4084+4835+4835
21:16 *he* **m** not give the rights of the firstborn to 3523
21:17 *He m* **acknowledge** the son AIT
21:21 *You m* **purge** the evil from among you. AIT
21:23 *m* not **leave** his body on the tree **overnight.** AIT
21:23 *You m* not **desecrate** the land AIT
22: 5 A woman *m* not **wear** men's clothing, AIT
22:19 *he* **m** not divorce her as long as he lives. 3523
22:21 *You m* **purge** the evil from among you. AIT
22:22 with her and the woman *m* **die.** AIT
22:22 *You m* **purge** the evil from Israel. AIT
22:24 *You m* **purge** the evil from among you. AIT
22:29 He *m* **marry** the girl, for he has violated her. AIT
22:30 *m* not **dishonor** his father's **bed.** AIT
23:14 Your camp *m* **be** holy, AIT
23:18 *You m* not **bring** the earnings of AIT
23:23 Whatever your lips utter *you m* **be sure** AIT
23:25 but *you m* not **put** a sickle to his AIT
24: 5 *he m* not **be sent** to war AIT
24: 7 the kidnapper *m* **die.** AIT
24: 7 *You m* **purge** the evil from among you. AIT
24: 8 You *m* **follow** carefully what I have commanded them. AIT
25: 3 *m* not **give** him more than forty **lashes.** AIT
25: 5 his widow *m* not **marry** outside the family. AIT
25:15 You *m* **have** accurate and honest weights AIT
31: 5 and *you m* **do** to them all that I have AIT
31: 7 for you *m* **go** with this people into the land AIT
31: 7 *you m* **divide** it *among* them **as** their **inheritance.** AIT
31:13 *m* **hear** it and learn to fear the LORD AIT

Jos 1:14 *m* **cross over** ahead of your brothers. AIT
6:19 to the LORD and *m* **go into** his treasury." AIT
20:5 *they m* not **surrender** the one accused, AIT
23:7 *You m* not **serve** them or bow down to them. AIT
Jdg 3:24 *"He m be* **relieving himself** AIT
6:30 *He m* **die,** because he has broken AIT
13:13 "Your wife *m* **do** all that I have told her. AIT
13:14 *She m* not **eat** anything that comes from AIT
13:14 *She m* **do** everything I have commanded her." AIT
14:3 *M* you **go** to the uncircumcised Philistines AIT
14:13 you *m* **give** me thirty linen garments AIT
15:18 *M I* now **die** of thirst and fall into the hands AIT
21:17 The Benjamite survivors **m** have heirs," NIH
1Sa 5:7 of the god of Israel *m* not **stay** here with us, AIT
9:13 because he *m* **bless** the sacrifice; AIT
10:8 but *you m* **wait** seven days until I come AIT
14:39 if it lies with my son Jonathan, *he* **m die."** 4637+4637
14:43 And now *m* **I die?"** AIT
20:3 'Jonathan *m* not **know** this or he will AIT
20:22 the arrows are beyond you,' then *you m* **go,** AIT
20:26 "Something **m** have happened to David NIH
20:31 bring him to me, for he **m die!"** 1201+4638
21:15 *M* this man **come** into my house?" AIT
28:1 *"You* **m understand** that you 3359+3359
29:4 *He m* not **go** with us into battle, AIT
29:9 *'He m* not **go up** with us into battle.' AIT
30:23 *you m* not **do** that with what AIT
2Sa 2:26 *"M* the sword **devour** forever? AIT
12:6 *He m* **pay** *for* that lamb four times over, AIT
14:14 cannot be recovered, so *we* **m die.** 4637+4637
14:24 the king said, *"He m* **go** to his own house; AIT
14:24 *he m* not **see** my face." AIT
15:14 *We m* **flee,** or none of us will escape AIT
15:14 *We m* leave **immediately,** AIT
18:3 But the men said, *"You m* not **go out;** AIT
18:20 but *you m* not **do so** today, AIT
18:25 "If he is alone, he **m** have good news." NIH
18:26 *m be* **bringing good news,** AIT
1Ki 1:42 *m be* **bringing good news."** AIT
8:61 But your hearts *m* **be** fully committed to AIT
10:8 How happy your men **m** be! NIH
11:2 *"You m* not **intermarry** with them, AIT
13:9 *'You m* not **eat** bread or drink water AIT
13:17 *'You m* not **eat** bread or drink water there AIT
18:27 Maybe he is sleeping and *m be* **awakened."** AIT
20:22 and see what *m be* **done,** AIT
20:25 You *m* also **raise** an army like the one AIT
20:39 or *you m* **pay** a talent of silver.' AIT
22:16 How many times *m I* **make you swear** AIT
2Ki 3:23 "Those kings **m have fought** 2991+2991
11:8 approaches your ranks *m* **be put to death.** AIT
11:15 *m* not **be put to death** in the temple AIT
17:36 is the one *you m* **worship.** AIT
17:37 *You m* always *be* **careful** to keep AIT
18:22 *"You m* **worship** before this altar AIT
2Ch 2:9 *m be* large and **magnificent.** AIT
8:11 "My wife *m* not **live** in the palace AIT
9:7 How happy your men **m** be! NIH
18:15 How many times *m* **I make you swear** AIT
19:9 *"You m* **serve** faithfully and wholeheartedly AIT
23:7 who enters the temple *m* **be put to death.** AIT
25:7 from Israel *m* not **march** with you, for AIT
28:13 *"You m* not **bring** those prisoners here," AIT
32:12 *'You m* **worship** before one altar AIT
Ezr 6:9 *m* **be** given them daily without fail, AIT
7:26 the law of the king *m* surely **be** punished AIT
10:12 We *m* **do** as you say. AIT
Ne 5:2 for us to eat and stay alive, *we m* **get** grain." AIT
13:27 *M we* **hear** now that you too are doing AIT
Est 1:15 what *m be* **done** to Queen Vashti?" AIT
Job 2:6 but *you m* **spare** his life." AIT
10:6 that *you m* **search out** my faults and probe AIT
17:2 my eyes *m* **dwell** *on* their hostility. AIT
18:4 *m* the rocks *be* **moved** from their place? AIT
20:10 His children *m* **make amends** *to* the poor; AIT
20:10 his own hands *m* **give back** his wealth. AIT
20:18 What he toiled for *he m* **give back** uneaten; AIT
24:1 Why *m* those who know him **look** in vain AIT
32:16 *M I* **wait,** now that they are silent, AIT
32:20 *I m* **speak** and find relief; AIT
32:20 *I m* **open** my lips and reply. AIT
34:33 You *m* **decide,** not I; AIT
35:14 that your case is before him and *you m* **wait** AIT
41:11 Who has a claim against me that *I m* **pay?** AIT
Ps 13:2 How long *m I* **wrestle** *with* my thoughts AIT
32:9 but *m be* **controlled** by bit and bridle AIT
42:9 Why *m I* **go about** mourning, AIT
43:2 Why *m I* **go about** mourning, AIT
69:10 When I weep and fast, I *m* **endure** scorn; AIT
119:84 **How long m** your servant **wait?** 3427+3869+4537
Pr 6:31 Yet if he is caught, *he m* **pay** sevenfold, AIT
19:19 A hot-tempered man *m* **pay** the penalty; AIT
Ecc 2:16 Like the fool, the wise man too *m* **die!** AIT
2:18 because *I m* **leave** them to the one who AIT
2:21 and then *he m* **leave** all he owns to someone AIT
SS 5:3 *m I* **put** it on again? AIT
5:3 *m I* **soil** them again? AIT
Isa 24:6 its people *m* **bear** *their* **guilt.** AIT
28:28 Grain *m* **be ground** to make bread; AIT
36:7 *"You m* **worship** before this altar"? AIT
38:10 "In the prime of my life *m I* **go** through AIT
Jer 1:7 *You m* **go** to everyone I send you to AIT
2:25 I love foreign gods, and *I m* **go** after them.' AIT
4:21 How long *m I* **see** the battle standard AIT
6:6 This city *m* **be punished;** AIT
Jer 9:19 *We m* **leave** our land because our houses AIT
10:5 *they* **m be carried** because they cannot walk. 5951+5951
10:19 "This is my sickness, and *I m* **endure** it." AIT
15:19 but you *m* not **turn** to them. AIT
16:2 *"You m* not **marry** and have sons or daughters AIT
23:36 But *you m* not **mention** 'the oracle of AIT
23:38 though I told you that *you m* not **claim,** AIT
25:28 *You* **m drink** it! 9272+9272
26:8 seized him and said, *"You* **m die!** 4637+4637
32:31 and wrath that I *m* **remove** it from my sight. AIT
34:14 *you m* **free** any fellow Hebrew who has sold himself AIT
34:14 *you m* **let** him **go** free.' AIT
35:6 nor your descendants *m* ever **drink** wine. AIT
35:7 Also *you m* never **build** houses, AIT
35:7 *you m* never **have** any of these things, AIT
35:7 but *m* always **live** in tents. AIT
35:11 *we m* **go** *to* Jerusalem to escape AIT
35:15 of *you m* **turn** from your wicked ways AIT
36:16 *"We* **m report** all these words to the king." 5583+5583
43:2 *'You m* not **go** *to* Egypt to settle there.' AIT
49:12 who do not deserve to drink the cup **m drink** it, 9272+9272
49:12 You will not go unpunished, but **m drink** it. 9272+9272
51:49 "Babylon *m* **fall** because of Israel's slain, AIT
La 5:4 We **m** buy the water we drink; NIH
Eze 2:7 *You m* **speak** my words to them, AIT
8:17 *M they* also **fill** the land *with* violence AIT
23:35 and thrust me behind your back, you *m* **bear** AIT
34:18 *M you* also **trample** the rest of your pasture AIT
34:18 *M you* also **muddy** the rest with your feet? AIT
34:19 *M* my flock **feed on** what you have trampled AIT
44:2 *It m* not **be opened;** AIT
44:10 after their idols *m* **bear** the consequences AIT
44:12 with uplifted hand that *they m* **bear** AIT
44:13 *they m* **bear** the shame AIT
44:17 they *m* not **wear** any woolen garment AIT
44:18 *They m* not **wear** anything that makes AIT
44:20 " *'They m* not **shave** their heads AIT
44:22 *They m* not **marry** widows AIT
44:25 " 'A priest *m* not **defile** *himself* by going AIT
44:26 After he is cleansed, *he m* **wait** seven days. AIT
44:31 The priests *m* not **eat** anything, AIT
46:18 The prince *m* not **take** any of the inheritance AIT
48:14 *They m* not **sell** or exchange any of it. AIT
48:14 *m* not **pass into other hands,** AIT
Da 3:5 *you m* **fall down** and worship the image AIT
3:10 pipes and all kinds of music *m* **fall down** AIT
6:26 *people* **m** fear and reverence the God of 10201
11:36 what has been determined *m* **take place.** AIT
Hos 3:3 *you m* not *be a* **prostitute** AIT
10:2 and now *they m* **bear** *their* **guilt.** AIT
10:11 I will drive Ephraim, Judah *m* **plow,** AIT
10:11 and Jacob *m* **break up the ground.** AIT
12:6 But you *m* **return** to your God; AIT
13:16 The people of Samaria *m* **bear** *their* **guilt,** AIT
Am 6:10 *We m* not **mention** the name of the LORD." AIT
Mic 4:10 for now *you m* **leave** the city to camp in AIT
Hab 1:2 How long, O LORD, *m I* **call for help,** AIT
2:6 How long **m** this go on?' NIH
Zec 13:3 will say to him, *'You m* **die,** AIT
Mt 5:31 'Anyone who divorces his wife *m* **give** her *AIT*
15:4 or mother *m be* **put to death.'** *AIT*
16:21 to his disciples that he **m** go to Jerusalem *1256*
16:21 and that he **m** be killed and on the third day *NIG*
16:24 *he m* **deny** himself and take up his cross *AIT*
17:10 of the law say that Elijah **m** come first?" *1256*
18:7 Such things **m** come, but woe to the man *340*
19:16 what good thing *m I* **do** to get eternal life?" *AIT*
20:26 great among you *m* **be** your servant, *AIT*
20:27 whoever wants to be first *m* **be** your slave— *AIT*
22:24 his brother **m** marry the widow *NIG*
23:3 So *you m* **obey** them and do everything *AIT*
24:6 Such things **m** happen, but the end *1256*
24:44 So you also *m* **be** ready, *AIT*
26:54 that say *it* **m** happen in this way?" *1256*
Mk 7:10 or mother *m be* **put to death.'** *AIT*
8:31 that the Son of Man **m** suffer many things *1256*
8:31 and that he **m** be killed and *NIG*
8:34 *he m* **deny** himself and take up his cross *AIT*
9:11 of the law say that Elijah **m** come first?" *1256*
9:12 of Man **m** suffer much and be rejected? *NIG*
9:35 *he m* **be** the very last, and the servant of all." *AIT*
10:17 "what *m I* **do** to inherit eternal life?" *AIT*
10:43 to become great among you *m* **be** *AIT*
10:44 whoever wants to be first *m* **be** slave of all. *AIT*
12:19 the man *m* **marry** the widow *AIT*
13:7 Such things **m** happen, but the end *1256*
13:9 *"You m be* **on your guard.** *AIT*
13:10 the gospel **m** first be preached to all nations. *1256*
14:49 But the Scriptures *m be* **fulfilled."** *AIT*
Lk 4:43 "I **m** preach the good news of the kingdom *1256*
5:38 new wine **m be poured** into new wineskins. *1064*
9:22 "The Son of Man **m** suffer many things and *1256*
9:22 and he **m** be killed and on the third day *NIG*
9:23 after me, *he m* **deny** himself and take *AIT*
10:25 "what *m I* **do** to inherit eternal life?" *AIT*
12:40 You also *m* **be** ready, *AIT*
13:33 I **m** keep going today and tomorrow and *1256*
14:18 and I **m** go and see it. *340+2400*
17:25 But first he **m** suffer many things and *1256*
18:18 what *m I* **do** to inherit eternal life?" *AIT*
19:5 I **m** stay at your house today." *1256*
Lk 20:28 the man *m* **marry** the widow *AIT*
21:9 These things **m** happen first, but the end *1256*
22:37 and I tell you that this **m** be fulfilled in me. *1256*
24:7 Son of Man **m** be delivered into the hands *1256*
24:44 Everything **m** be fulfilled that is written *1256*
Jn 3:7 'You **m** be born again.' *1256*
3:14 so the Son of Man **m** be lifted up, *1256*
3:30 He **m** become greater; I must become less. *1256*
3:30 He must become greater; I **m** become less. *NIG*
4:20 where we **m** worship is in Jerusalem." *1256*
4:24 and his worshipers **m** worship in spirit and *1256*
6:28 "What *m we* **do** to do the works God *AIT*
9:4 we **m** do the work of him who sent me. *1256*
10:16 I **m** bring them also. *1256*
12:26 Whoever serves me *m* **follow** me; *AIT*
12:34 'The Son of Man **m** be lifted up'? *1256*
13:34 so you *m* **love** one another. *AIT*
14:31 but the world *m* **learn** that I love the Father *AIT*
15:4 *it m* **remain** in the vine. *AIT*
15:27 And you also *m* **testify,** *AIT*
19:7 and according to that law *he* **m** die, *4053*
21:22 You *m* **follow** me." *AIT*
Ac 1:22 one of these *m* **become** a witness with us *AIT*
3:21 He **m** remain in heaven until the time comes *1256*
3:22 *you m* **listen** to everything he tells you. *AIT*
4:12 under heaven given to men by which we **m** *1256*
4:17 *we m* **warn** these men to speak no longer *AIT*
5:29 "We **m** obey God rather than men! *1256*
9:6 and you will be told what you **m** do." *1256*
9:16 I will show him how much he **m** suffer *1256*
12:15 they said, *"It* **m be** his angel." *AIT*
14:22 "We **m** go through many hardships to enter *1256*
15:5 "The Gentiles **m** be circumcised *1256*
16:30 "Sirs, what **m** I do to be saved?" *1256*
19:21 he said, "I **m** visit Rome also." *1256*
19:39 *it* **m be settled** in a legal assembly. *2147*
20:21 to both Jews and Greeks that they **m** turn *NIG*
20:35 that by this kind of hard work *we* **m** help *1256*
23:11 so you **m** also testify in Rome." *1256*
27:24 You **m** stand trial before Caesar; *1256*
27:26 we **m** run aground on some island." *1256*
28:4 "This man **m** be a murderer; *4122*
Ro 12:9 Love **m** be sincere. *NIG*
13:1 Everyone *m* **submit** *himself* to the governing *AIT*
14:3 *m* **not look down on** him who does not, *AIT*
14:3 *m* not **condemn** the man who does, *AIT*
1Co 4:2 have been given a trust *m* **prove** faithful. *AIT*
5:11 that *you m* not **associate with** anyone who *AIT*
7:10 A wife *m* not **separate** from her husband. *AIT*
7:11 *she m* **remain** unmarried or else *AIT*
7:11 And a husband *m* not **divorce** his wife. *AIT*
7:12 *he m* not **divorce** her. *AIT*
7:13 *she m* not **divorce** him. *AIT*
7:39 but he **m** belong to the Lord. *NIG*
9:6 only I and Barnabas who **m** work for *2026+2400*
14:26 All of these *m be* **done** for the strengthening *AIT*
14:27 one at a time, and someone *m* **interpret.** *AIT*
14:34 but *m be* **in submission,** as the Law says. *AIT*
15:25 For he **m** reign until he has put all his *1256*
15:53 For the perishable **m** clothe itself with *1256*
2Co 5:10 For we **m** all appear before the judgment *1256*
11:30 If *I* **m** boast, I will boast of the things that *1256*
12:1 *I* **m** go on boasting. *1256*
13:1 "Every matter *m be* **established** by *AIT*
Gal 6:6 in the word *m* **share** all good things with *AIT*
Eph 4:17 you *m* no longer **live** as the Gentiles do, *AIT*
4:25 Therefore each of you *m* **put off** falsehood *AIT*
4:28 He who has been stealing *m* **steal** no longer, *AIT*
4:28 but *m* **work,** doing something useful *AIT*
5:3 *m* not *be* even **a hint of** sexual immorality, *AIT*
5:33 also *m* **love** his wife as he loves himself, *AIT*
5:33 and the wife *m* **respect** her husband. *AIT*
Col 3:8 But now you *m* **rid** *yourselves* **of** all such *AIT*
1Ti 2:12 authority over a man; *she m* **be** silent. *AIT*
3:2 Now the overseer **m** be above reproach, *1256*
3:4 *m* **manage** his own family well **and see that** his children obey him *AIT*
3:6 He **m** not be a recent convert, *NIG*
3:7 He **m** also have a good reputation *1256*
3:9 They **m** keep hold of the deep truths of *NIG*
3:10 They *m* first **be tested;** *AIT*
3:12 A deacon *m* **be** the husband of but one wife *AIT*
3:12 of but one wife and *m* **manage** his children *AIT*
2Ti 2:19 *m* **turn away from** wickedness." *AIT*
2:24 And the Lord's servant **m** not quarrel; *1256*
2:24 instead, *he m be* kind to everyone, *AIT*
2:25 Those who oppose him *he m* gently **instruct** *AIT*
Tit 1:6 An elder **m** be blameless, *NIG*
1:7 *he* **m** be blameless— *1256*
1:8 Rather he **m** be hospitable, *NIG*
1:9 He **m** hold firmly to the trustworthy message *NIG*
1:11 They **m** be silenced, because they are *1256*
2:1 You *m* **teach** what is in accord with sound *AIT*
3:14 Our people *m* **learn** to devote themselves *AIT*
Heb 2:1 We **m** pay more careful attention, therefore, *1256*
4:13 of him to whom we **m** give account. *NIG*
5:4 he **m** be called by God, just as Aaron was. *NIG*
7:12 there **m** also be a change of the law. *340*
11:6 to him **m** believe that he exists and *1256*
12:20 touches the mountain, *it m be* **stoned."** *AIT*
13:17 over you as men *who m* **give** an account. *AIT*
Jas 1:4 Perseverance *m* **finish** its work so *AIT*
1:6 when he asks, *he m* **believe** and not doubt, *AIT*
1Pe 3:10 and see good days *m* **keep** his tongue *AIT*
3:11 *He m* **turn** from evil and do good; *AIT*
3:11 *he m* **seek** peace and pursue it. *AIT*
5:2 not *because* you **m,** but because you are *339*

2Pe 1:20 you **m** understand that no prophecy *NIG*
3: 3 *you m* **understand** that in the last days *AIT*
1Jn 2: 6 Whoever claims to live in him **m** walk *4053*
4:21 Whoever loves God *m* also **love** his brother. *AIT*
Rev 1: 1 show his servants what **m** soon take place. *1256*
4: 1 and I will show you what **m** take place *1256*
10:11 "You **m** prophesy again *1256*
11: 5 how anyone who wants to harm them **m** die. *1256*
17:10 he **m** remain for a little while. *1256*
20: 3 After that, he **m** be set free for a short time. *1256*
22: 6 the things that **m** soon take place." *1256*

MUSTACHE (1)
2Sa 19:24 not taken care of his feet or trimmed his **m** 8559

MUSTARD (5)
Mt 13:31 "The kingdom of heaven is like a **m** seed, *4983*
17:20 if you have faith as small as a **m** seed, *4983*
Mk 4:31 It is like a **m** seed, which is the smallest *4983*
Lk 13:19 It is like a **m** seed, which a man took *4983*
17: 6 "If you have faith as small as a **m** seed, *4983*

MUSTER (4) [MUSTERED, MUSTERING]
1Sa 14:17 "**M** *the* **forces** and see who has left us." 7212
2Sa 12:28 Now **m** the rest of the troops and besiege 665
Da 11:13 the king of the North *will* **m** another army, 6641
Am 2:14 the strong *will* not **m** their strength, 599

MUSTERED (16) [MUSTER]
Nu 21:23 He **m** his entire army and marched out into 665
Jos 8:10 Early the next morning Joshua **m** his men, 7212
Jdg 11:20 He **m** all his men and encamped at Jahaz 665
20:17 **m** four hundred thousand swordsmen, 7212
1Sa 11: 8 When Saul **m** them at Bezek, 7212
15: 4 So Saul summoned the men and **m** them 7212
2Sa 12:29 So David **m** the entire army and went 665
18: 1 David **m** the men who were with him 7212
1Ki 12:21 *he* **m** the whole house of Judah and the tribe 7735
20: 1 Ben-Hadad king of Aram **m** his entire army. 7695
20:26 next spring Ben-Hadad **m** the Arameans 7212
20:27 Israelites *were* also **m** and given provisions, 7212
1Ch 19: 7 the Ammonites **were m** from their towns 665
2Ch 11: 1 *he* **m** the house of Judah and Benjamin— 7735
25: 5 *He* then **m** those twenty years old or more 7212
26:11 to their numbers as **m** by Jeiel the secretary 7213

MUSTERING (1) [MUSTER]
Isa 13: 4 LORD Almighty *is* **m** an army for war. 7212

MUTE (13)
Ex 4:11 Who makes him deaf or **m?** 522
Ps 38:13 like a **m**, who cannot open his mouth; 522
Isa 35: 6 and the **m** tongue shout for joy. 522
56:10 they are all **m** dogs, they cannot bark; 522
Mt 9:33 the **man who had been m** spoke. *3273*
12:22 blind and **m**, and Jesus healed him, *3273*
15:30 the crippled, the **m** and many others, *3273*
15:31 when they saw the **m** speaking, *3273*
Mk 7:37 even makes the deaf hear and the **m** speak." *228*
9:25 "*You* deaf and **m** spirit," he said, *228*
Lk 11:14 Jesus was driving out a demon that was **m**. *3273*
11:14 the **man who had been m** spoke, *3273*
1Co 12: 2 and led astray to **m** idols. *936*

MUTILATORS (1)
Php 3: 2 those men who do evil, those **m** of the flesh. *2961*

MUTTER (3) [MUTTERED, MUTTERS]
Isa 8:19 who whisper and **m**, 2047
La 3:62 what my enemies whisper and **m** 2053
Lk 19: 7 All the people saw this and *began to* **m**, *1339*

MUTTERED (1) [MUTTER]
Lk 15: 2 the Pharisees and the teachers of the law **m**, *1339*

MUTTERS (1) [MUTTER]
Isa 59: 3 and your tongue **m** wicked things. 2047

MUTUAL (2) [MUTUALLY]
Ro 14:19 do what leads to peace and to **m** edification. *253*
1Co 7: 5 not deprive each other except by **m consent** *5247*

MUTUALLY (1) [MUTUAL]
Ro 1:12 *be* **m encouraged** by each other's faith. *5220*

MUZZLE (4)
Dt 25: 4 *Do* not **m** an ox while it is treading out 2888
Ps 39: 1 I will put a **m** on my mouth as long as 4727
1Co 9: 9 "*Do* not **m** an ox while it is treading out *3055*
1Ti 5:18 "*Do* not **m** the ox while it is treading out *5821*

MY (4597) [I] See Index of Articles Etc.

MYRA (1)
Ac 27: 5 we landed at **M** in Lycia. *3688*

MYRIADS (1)
Dt 33: 2 with **m** *of* holy ones from the south, 8047

MYRRH (18)
Ge 37:25 balm and **m**, and they were on their way 4320
43:11 and a little honey, some spices and **m**, 4320
Ex 30:23 500 shekels of liquid **m**, 5255
Est 2:12 of **m** and six with perfumes and cosmetics. 5255
Ps 45: 8 All your robes are fragrant with **m** and aloes 5255
Pr 7:17 I have perfumed my bed with **m**, 5255
SS 1:13 a sachet of **m** resting between my breasts. 5255
3: 6 with **m** and incense made from all the spices 5255
4: 6 I will go to the mountain of **m** and to the hill 5255
4:14 with **m** and aloes and all the finest spices. 5255
5: 1 I have gathered my **m** with my spice. 5255
5: 5 and my hands dripped with **m**, 5255
5: 5 my fingers with flowing **m**, 5255
5:13 His lips are like lilies dripping with **m**. 5255
Mt 2:11 with gifts of gold and of incense and of **m**. *5043*
Mk 15:23 Then they offered him wine **mixed with m**, *5046*
Jn 19:39 Nicodemus brought a mixture *of* **m** *5043*
Rev 18:13 **m** and frankincense, of wine and olive oil, *3693*

MYRTLE (5) [MYRTLES]
Isa 41:19 and the acacia, the **m** and the olive. 2072
55:13 and instead of briers the **m** will grow. 2072
Zec 1: 8 He was standing among the **m trees** in 2072
1:10 man standing among the **m trees** explained, 2072
1:11 who was standing among the **m trees**, 2072

MYRTLES (1) [MYRTLE]
Ne 8:15 and from **m**, palms and shade trees, 2072

MYSELF (153) [I, SELF] See Index of Articles Etc.

MYSIA (2)
Ac 16: 7 When they came to the border of **M**, *3695*
16: 8 they passed by **M** and went down to Troas. *3695*

MYSTERIES (6) [MYSTERY]
Job 11: 7 "Can you fathom the **m** *of* God? 2984
Da 2:28 but there is a God in heaven who reveals **m**. 10661
2:29 the revealer of **m** showed you what is going 10661
2:47 and the Lord of kings and a revealer of **m**, 10661
1Co 13: 2 the gift of prophecy and can fathom all **m** *3696*
14: 2 he utters **m** with his spirit. *3696*

MYSTERY (25) [MYSTERIES]
Da 2:18 from the God of heaven concerning this **m**, 10661
2:19 the night the **m** was revealed to Daniel in 10661
2:27 to the king the **m** he has asked about, 10661
2:30 As for me, this **m** has been revealed to me, 10661
2:47 for you were able to reveal this **m**." 10661
4: 9 and no **m** is too difficult for you. 10661
Ro 11:25 I do not want you to be ignorant of this **m**, *3696*
16:25 the revelation *of* the **m** hidden for long ages *3696*
1Co 15:51 Listen, I tell you a **m**: *3696*
Eph 1: 9 And he made known to us the **m** of his will *3696*
3: 3 the **m** made known to me by revelation, *3696*
3: 4 be able to understand my insight into the **m** *3696*
3: 6 This **m** is that through the gospel *NIG*
3: 9 to everyone the administration *of* this **m**, *3696*
5:32 This is a profound **m**— *3696*
6:19 so that I will fearlessly make known the **m** *3696*
Col 1:26 the **m** that has been kept hidden for ages *3696*
1:27 the Gentiles the glorious riches *of* this **m**, *3696*
2: 2 in order that they may know the **m** of God, *3696*
4: 3 so that we may proclaim the **m** of Christ, *3696*
1Ti 3:16 the **m** of godliness is great: *3696*
Rev 1:20 The **m** of the seven stars that you saw *3696*
10: 7 the **m** of God will be accomplished, *3696*
17: 5 **M** BABYLON THE GREAT THE MOTHER OF PROSTITUTES *3696*
17: 7 I will explain to you the **m** of the woman *3696*

MYTHS (4)
1Ti 1: 4 nor to devote themselves *to* **m** *3680*
4: 7 to do with godless **m** and old wives' tales; *3680*
2Ti 4: 4 from the truth and turn aside to **m**. *3680*
Tit 1:14 and will pay no attention *to* Jewish **m** or to *3680*

N

NAAM (1)
1Ch 4:15 Iru, Elah and **N**. 5839

NAAMAH (5)
Ge 4:22 Tubal-Cain's sister was **N**. 5841
Jos 15:41 Beth Dagon, **N** and Makkedah— 5842
1Ki 14:21 His mother's name was **N**; 5841
14:31 His mother's name was **N**; 5841
2Ch 12:13 His mother's name was **N**; 5841

NAAMAN (20) [NAAMAN'S, NAAMITE]
Ge 46:21 Bela, Beker, Ashbel, Gera, **N**, Ehi, Rosh, 5845
Nu 26:40 of Bela through Ard and **N** were: 5845
26:40 through **N**, the Naamite clan. 5845
2Ki 5: 1 Now **N** was commander of the army of 5845
5: 4 **N** went to his master and told him what NIH
5: 5 So **N** left, taking with him ten talents NIH
5: 6 "With this letter I am sending my servant **N** 5845
5: 9 So **N** went with his horses and chariots 5845
5:11 But **N** went away angry and said, 5845
5:15 Then **N** and all his attendants went back to 2085[S]
5:16 And even though **N** urged him, he refused. NIH
5:17 "If you will not," said **N**, "please let me, 5845
5:19 After **N** had traveled some distance, NIH
5:20 "My master was too easy on **N**, 5845
5:21 So Gehazi hurried after **N**. 5845
5:21 When **N** saw him running toward him, 5845
5:23 "By all means, take two talents," said **N**. 5845
1Ch 8: 4 Abishua, **N**, Ahoah, 5845
8: 7 **N**, Ahijah, and Gera, who deported them 5845
Lk 4:27 was cleansed—only **N** the Syrian." *3722*

NAAMAN'S (3) [NAAMAN]
2Ki 5: 2 and she served **N** wife. 5845
5:13 **N** servants went to him and said, 2257[S]
5:27 **N** leprosy will cling to you and 5845

NAAMATHITE (4)
Job 2:11 Bildad the Shuhite and Zophar the **N**, 5847
11: 1 Then Zophar the **N** replied: 5847
20: 1 Then Zophar the **N** replied: 5847
42: 9 the Shuhite and Zophar the **N** did what 5847

NAAMITE (1) [NAAMAN]
Nu 26:40 through Naaman, the **N** clan. 5844

NAARAH (4)
Jos 16: 7 down from Janoah to Ataroth and **N**, 5857
1Ch 4: 5 of Tekoa had two wives, Helah and **N**. 5856
4: 6 **N** bore him Ahuzzam, Hepher, 5856
4: 6 These were the descendants of **N**. 5856

NAARAI (1)
1Ch 11:37 Hezro the Carmelite, **N** son of Ezbai, 5858

NAARAN (1)
1Ch 7:28 **N** to the east, 5860

NAARATH (KJV) See NAARAH

NAASHON, NAASSON (KJV) See NAHSHON

NABAL (18) [NABAL'S]
1Sa 25: 3 His name was **N** and his wife's name 5573
25: 4 he heard that **N** was shearing sheep. 5573
25: 5 to **N** at Carmel and greet him in my name. 5573
25: 9 they gave **N** this message in David's name. 5573
25:10 **N** answered David's servants, 5573
25:19 But she did not tell her husband **N**. 5573
25:25 pay no attention to that wicked man **N**. 5573
25:26 to harm my master be like **N**. 5573
25:34 belonging to **N** would have been left alive 5573
25:36 When Abigail went to **N**, 5573
25:37 Then in the morning, when **N** was sober, 5573
25:38 the LORD struck **N** and he died. 5573
25:39 When David heard that **N** was dead, 5573
25:39 against **N** for treating me with contempt. 5573
27: 3 and Abigail of Carmel, the widow of **N**. 5573
30: 5 Abigail, the widow of **N** of Carmel. 5573
2Sa 2: 2 Abigail, the widow of **N** of Carmel. 5573
3: 3 Kileab the son of Abigail the widow of **N** 5573

NABAL'S (2) [NABAL]
1Sa 25:14 One of the servants told **N** wife Abigail: 5573
25:39 and has brought **N** wrongdoing down 5573

NABOTH (17) [NABOTH'S]
1Ki 21: 1 a vineyard belonging to **N** the Jezreelite. 5559
21: 2 Ahab said to **N**, "Let me have your vineyard 5559
21: 3 But **N** replied, "The LORD forbid 5559
21: 4 because **N** the Jezreelite had said, 5559
21: 6 "Because I said to **N** the Jezreelite, 5559
21: 7 the vineyard of **N** the Jezreelite." 5559
21: 9 of fasting and seat **N** in a prominent place 5559
21:12 and seated **N** in a prominent place among 5559
21:13 and brought charges against **N** before 5559
21:13 "**N** has cursed both God and the king." 5559
21:14 "**N** has been stoned and is dead." 5559
21:15 as Jezebel heard that **N** had been stoned 5559
21:15 up and take possession of the vineyard of **N** 5559
21:16 When Ahab heard that **N** was dead, 5559
2Ki 9:21 at the plot of ground that had belonged to **N** 5559
9:25 the field that belonged to **N** the Jezreelite. 5559
9:26 the blood of **N** and the blood of his sons, 5559

NABOTH'S (5) [NABOTH]
1Ki 21: 8 to the elders and nobles who lived in N city 5559
21:11 and nobles who lived in N city did 2257[S]
21:16 down to take possession of N vineyard. 5559
21:18 He is now in N vineyard, 5559
21:19 In the place where dogs licked up N blood, 5559

NACHON'S (KJV) See NACON

NACHOR (KJV) See NAHOR

NACON (1)
2Sa 6: 6 they came to the threshing floor of N, 5789

NADAB (20) [NADAB'S]
Ex 6:23 and she bore him N and Abihu, 5606
24: 1 you and Aaron, N and Abihu, 5606
24: 9 Moses and Aaron, N and Abihu, 5606
28: 1 along with his sons N and Abihu, 5606
Lev 10: 1 Aaron's sons N and Abihu took their censers, 5606
Nu 3: 2 of Aaron were N the firstborn and Abihu, 5606
3: 4 N and Abihu, however, fell dead 5606
26:60 Aaron was the father of N and Abihu, 5606
26:61 But N and Abihu died when they made 5606
1Ki 14:20 And N his son succeeded him as king. 5606
15:25 N son of Jeroboam became king of Israel in 5606
15:27 while N and all Israel were besieging it. 5606
15:28 Baasha killed N in the third year 2084[S]
1Ch 2:28 The sons of Shammai: N and Abishur. 5606
2:30 The sons of N: Seled and Appaim. 5606
6: 3 N, Abihu, Eleazar and Ithamar. 5606
8:30 followed by Zur, Kish, Baal, Ner, N, 5606
9:36 followed by Zur, Kish, Baal, Ner, N, 5606
24: 1 The sons of Aaron were N, Abihu, 5606
24: 2 N and Abihu died before their father did, 5606

NADAB'S (1) [NADAB]
1Ki 15:31 As for the other events of N reign, 5606

NAGGAI (1)
Lk 3:25 the son of Esli, the son *of* N, *3710*

NAGGING (1)
Jdg 16:16 With such n she prodded him day after day 7439

NAHALAL (2)
Jos 19:15 Included were Kattath, N, Shimron, 5634
21:35 and N, together with their pasturelands— 5634

NAHALIEL (2)
Nu 21:19 from Mattanah to N, 5712
21:19 from N to Bamoth, 5712

NAHALOL (1)
Jdg 1:30 in Kitron or N, who remained among them; 5636

NAHAM (1)
1Ch 4:19 The sons of Hodiah's wife, the sister of N: 5715

NAHAMANI (1)
Ne 7: 7 Raamiah, N, Mordecai, Bilshan, Mispereth, 5720

NAHARAI (2)
2Sa 23:37 N the Beerothite, the armor-bearer 5726
1Ch 11:39 N the Berothite, the armor-bearer 5726

NAHARAIM See ARAM NAHARAIM

NAHASH (8) [IR NAHASH]
1Sa 11: 1 N the Ammonite went up 5731
11: 2 But N the Ammonite replied, 5731
12:12 that N king of the Ammonites was moving 5731
2Sa 10: 2 "I will show kindness to Hanun son of N, 5731
17:25 the daughter of N and sister of Zeruiah 5731
17:27 of N from Rabbah of the Ammonites, 5731
1Ch 19: 1 N king of the Ammonites died, 5731
19: 2 "I will show kindness to Hanun son of N, 5731

NAHATH (5)
Ge 36:13 N, Zerah, Shammah and Mizzah. 5740
36:17 Chiefs N, Zerah, Shammah and Mizzah. 5740
1Ch 1:37 N, Zerah, Shammah and Mizzah. 5740
6:26 Elkanah his son, Zophai his son, N his son, 5740
2Ch 31:13 Jehiel, Azaziah, N, Asahel, Jerimoth, 5740

NAHBI (1)
Nu 13:14 N son of Vophsi; 5696

NAHOR (17) [NAHOR'S]
Ge 11:22 he became the father of N. 5701
11:23 And after he became the father of N, 5701
11:24 When N had lived 29 years, 5701
11:25 N lived 119 years and had other sons 5701
11:26 the father of Abram, N and Haran. 5701
11:27 the father of Abram, N and Haran. 5701
11:29 Abram and N both married. 5701
22:20 she has borne sons to your brother N: 5701
22:23 to Abraham's brother N. 5701
24:10 and made his way to the town of N. 5701
24:15 who was the wife of Abraham's brother N. 5701
24:24 the son that Milcah bore to N." 5701
24:47 'The daughter of Bethuel son of N, 5701
31:53 the God of Abraham and the God of N, 5701
Jos 24: 2 the father of Abraham and N, 5701
1Ch 1:26 Serug, N, Terah 5701
Lk 3:34 the son of Terah, the son *of* N, *3732*

NAHOR'S (2) [NAHOR]
Ge 11:29 and the name of N wife was Milcah; 5701
29: 5 "Do you know Laban, N grandson?" 5701

NAHSHON (13)
Ex 6:23 daughter of Amminadab and sister of N, 5732
Nu 1: 7 from Judah, N son of Amminadab; 5732
2: 3 The leader of the people of Judah is N son 5732
7:12 on the first day was N son of Amminadab 5732
7:17 the offering of N son of Amminadab. 5732
10:14 N son of Amminadab was in command. 5732
Ru 4:20 Amminadab the father of N, 5732
4:20 N the father of Salmon, 5732
1Ch 2:10 and Amminadab the father of N, 5732
2:11 N was the father of Salmon, 5732
Mt 1: 4 Amminadab the father of N, *3709*
1: 4 N the father of Salmon, *3709*
Lk 3:32 the son of Salmon, the son *of* N, *3709*

NAHUM (2)
Na 1: 1 The book of the vision of N the Elkoshite. 5699
Lk 3:25 the son of Amos, the son *of* N, *3725*

NAIL (1) [NAILING, NAILS]
Jn 20:25 the n marks in his hands and put my finger *2464*

NAILING (2) [NAIL]
Ac 2:23 put him to death by n him **to the cross.** *4699*
Col 2:14 he took it away, n it to the cross. *4669*

NAILS (8) [NAIL]
Dt 21:12 and have her shave her head, trim her n 7632
1Ch 22: 3 to make n for the doors of the gateways and 5021
2Ch 3: 9 The gold n weighed fifty shekels. 5021
Ecc 12:11 collected sayings like firmly embedded n 5383
Isa 41: 7 *He* n **down** the idol so it will not topple. 928+2616+5021
Jer 10: 4 they fasten it with hammer and n so it will 5021
Da 4:33 an eagle and his n like the claws of a bird. 10303
Jn 20:25 and put my finger where the n were, *2464*

NAIN (1)
Lk 7:11 Jesus went to a town called N, *3723*

NAIOTH (6)
1Sa 19:18 he and Samuel went to N and stayed there. 5766
19:19 "David is in N at Ramah"; 5766
19:22 "Over in N at Ramah," they said. 5766
19:23 So Saul went to N at Ramah. 5766
19:23 along prophesying until he came to N. 5766
20: 1 from N at Ramah and went to Jonathan 5766

NAIVE (1)
Ro 16:18 they deceive the minds *of* n *people.* *179*

NAKED (32) [NAKEDNESS]
Ge 2:25 The man and his wife were both n, 6873
3: 7 and they realized they were n; 6567
3:10 and I was afraid because I was n; so I hid." 6567
3:11 he said, "Who told you that you were n? 6567
2Ch 28:15 the plunder they clothed all who were n. 5122
Job 1:21 "N I came from my mother's womb, 6873
1:21 and n I will depart. 6873
22: 6 of their clothing, leaving them n. 6873
24: 7 Lacking clothes, they spend the night n; 6873
24:10 Lacking clothes, they go about n; 6873
26: 6 Death is n before God; 6873
Ecc 5:15 N a man comes from his mother's womb, 6873
Isa 58: 7 when you see the n, to clothe him, 6873
La 4:21 you will be drunk and **stripped n.** 6867
Eze 16: 7 you who were n and bare. 6567
16:22 when you were n and bare, 6567
16:39 and take your fine jewelry and leave you n 6567
18: 7 the hungry and provides clothing for the n. 6567
18:16 the hungry and provides clothing for the n. 6567
23:10 They stripped her n, took away her sons 6872
23:29 They will leave you n and bare, 6567
Hos 2: 3 Otherwise I will strip her n and make her 6873
Am 2:16 bravest warriors will flee n on that day," 6873
Mic 1: 8 I will go about barefoot and n. 6873
Hab 2:15 so that he can gaze on their **n bodies.** 5067
Mk 14:52 he fled n, leaving his garment behind. *1218*
Ac 19:16 a beating that they ran out of the house n *1218*
2Co 5: 3 when we are clothed, we will not be found n *1218*
11:27 I have been cold and n. *1218*
Rev 3:17 pitiful, poor, blind and n. *1218*
16:15 not go n and be shamefully exposed." *1218*
17:16 They will bring her to ruin and leave her n; *1218*

NAKEDNESS (17) [NAKED]
Ge 9:22 the father of Canaan, saw his father's n 6872
9:23 in backward and covered their father's n. 6872
9:23 so that they would not see their father's n. 6872
Ex 20:26 lest your n be exposed on it.' 6872
Dt 28:48 in n and dire poverty, 6567
Isa 47: 3 Your n will be exposed and your shame 6872
57: 8 and you looked on their n. 3338
La 1: 8 for they have seen her n; 6872
Eze 16: 8 over you and covered your n. 6872
16:36 and exposed your n in your promiscuity 6872
16:37 and they will see all your n. 6872
23:18 and exposed her n, 6872
Hos 2: 9 intended to cover her n. 6872
Mic 1:11 Pass on in n and shame, 6880
Na 3: 5 I will show the nations your n and 5113
Ro 8:35 or hardship or persecution or famine or n *1219*
Rev 3:18 so you can cover your shameful n; *1219*

NAME (764) [NAME'S, NAMED, NAMELESS, NAMELY, NAMES]
Ge 2:11 The n *of* the first is the Pishon; 9005
2:13 The n *of* the second river is the Gihon; 9005
2:14 The n *of* the third river is the Tigris; 9005
2:19 to the man to see what *he would* n them; 7924
2:19 called each living creature, that was its n. 9005
4:21 His brother's n was Jubal; 9005
4:26 men began to call on the n *of* the LORD. 9005
11: 4 that we may make a n for ourselves and not 9005
11:29 The n *of* Abram's wife was Sarai, 9005
11:29 and the n *of* Nahor's wife was Milcah; 9005
12: 2 I will make your n great, 9005
12: 8 and called on the n *of* the LORD. 9005
13: 4 There Abram called on the n *of* the LORD 9005
16:11 *You shall* n him Ishmael, 7924+9005
16:13 She gave this n to the LORD who spoke 9005
16:15 the n Ishmael *to* the son she had borne. 9005
17: 5 your n will be Abraham, 9005
17:15 her n will be Sarah. 9005
21: 3 the n Isaac to the son Sarah bore him. 9005
21:33 and there he called upon the n *of* 9005
22:24 His concubine, whose n was Reumah, 9005
25: 1 whose n was Keturah. 9005
26:25 Isaac built an altar there and called on the n 9005
26:33 the n *of* the town has been Beersheba. 9005
29:16 the n *of* the older was Leah, 9005
29:16 and the n *of* the younger was Rachel. 9005
30:28 He added, **"N** your wages, 5918
31:53 So Jacob took an oath **in the n** of the Fear 928
32:27 The man asked him, "What is your n?" 9005
32:28 man said, "Your n will no longer be Jacob, 9005
32:29 Jacob said, "Please tell me your n." 9005
32:29 But he replied, "Why do you ask my n?" 9005
35:10 God said to him, "Your n is Jacob, 9005
35:10 your n will be Israel." 9005
36:39 and his wife's n was Mehetabel daughter 9005
36:40 by n, according to their clans and regions: 9005
38: 6 his firstborn, and her n was Tamar. 9005
38:30 came out and he was given the n Zerah. 9005
41:45 gave Joseph the n Zaphenath-Paneah 9005
48:16 May they be called by my n and the names 9005
48:20 "In your n will Israel pronounce this blessing: NIH
Ex 3:13 and they ask me, 'What is his n?' 9005
3:15 This is my n forever, 9005
3:15 **n by which** I *am to be* **remembered** 2352
5:23 since I went to Pharaoh to speak in your n, 9005
6: 3 but by my n the LORD I did not make 9005
9:16 and that my n might be proclaimed in all 9005
15: 3 LORD is a warrior; the LORD is his n. 9005
20: 7 not misuse the n *of* the LORD your God, 9005
20: 7 hold anyone guiltless who misuses his n. 9005
20:24 Wherever I cause my n to be honored, 9005
23:21 since my N is in him. 9005
28:21 each engraved like a seal with the n *of* one 9005
33:12 'I know you by n and you have found favor 9005
33:17 with you and I know you by n." 9005
33:19 and I will proclaim my n, the LORD, 9005
34: 5 with him and proclaimed his n, 9005
34:14 whose n is Jealous, is a jealous God. 9005
39:14 a seal with the n of one of the twelve tribes. 9005
Lev 18:21 you must not profane the n *of* your God. 9005
19:12 not swear falsely by my n and so profane 9005
19:12 and so profane the n *of* your God. 9005
20: 3 and profaned my holy n. 9005
21: 6 and must not profane the n *of* their God. 9005
22: 2 so they will not profane my holy n. 9005
22:32 Do not profane my holy n. 9005
24:11 the Israelite woman blasphemed the N with 9005
24:11 (His mother's n was Shelomith, 9005
24:16 anyone who blasphemes the n *of* the LORD 9005
24:16 when he blasphemes the N, 9005
Nu 1: 2 listing every man by n, one by one. 9005
1:18 or more were listed by n, 9005
1:20 to serve in the army were listed by n, 9005
1:22 in the army were counted and listed by n, 9005
1:24 to serve in the army were listed by n, 9005
1:26 to serve in the army were listed by n, 9005
1:28 to serve in the army were listed by n, 9005
1:30 to serve in the army were listed by n, 9005
1:32 to serve in the army were listed by n, 9005
1:34 to serve in the army were listed by n, 9005
1:36 to serve in the army were listed by n, 9005

Nu 1:38 to serve in the army were listed by **n**, 9005
1:40 to serve in the army were listed by **n**, 9005
1:42 to serve in the army were listed by **n**, 9005
3:43 listed by **n**, was 22,273. 9005
6:27 "So they will put my **n** on the Israelites, 9005
13:16 **gave** Hoshea son of Nun *the* **n** Joshua.) 7924
17: 2 Write the **n** *of* each man on his staff. 9005
17: 3 On the staff of Levi write Aaron's **n**, 9005
25:14 The **n** *of* the Israelite who was killed with 9005
25:15 the **n** *of* the Midianite woman who was put 9005
26:59 the **n** *of* Amram's wife was Jochebed, 9005
27: 4 Why should our father's **n** disappear 9005
Dt 5:11 not misuse the **n** *of* the LORD your God, 9005
5:11 hold anyone guiltless who misuses his **n**. 9005
6:13 serve him only and take your oaths in his **n**. 9005
9:14 that I may destroy them and blot out their **n** 9005
10: 8 and to pronounce blessings in his **n**, 9005
10:20 to him and take your oaths in his **n**. 9005
12: 5 among all your tribes to put his **N** there 9005
12:11 as a dwelling for his **N**— 9005
12:21 to put his **N** is too far away from you, 9005
14:23 as a dwelling for his **N**, 9005
14:24 the LORD will choose to put his **N** is 9005
16: 2 as a dwelling for his **N**. 9005
16: 6 as a dwelling for his **N**. 9005
16:11 as a dwelling for his **N**— 9005
18: 5 and minister in the LORD's **n** always. 9005
18: 7 in the **n** *of* the LORD his God 9005
18:19 that the prophet speaks in my **n**, 9005
18:20 to speak in my **n** anything I have 9005
18:20 prophet who speaks in the **n** *of* other gods, 9005
18:22 in the **n** *of* the LORD does not take place 9005
21: 5 the **n** *of* the LORD and to decide all cases 9005
22:14 and slanders her and gives her a bad **n**, 9005
22:19 has given an Israelite virgin a bad **n**. 9005
25: 6 The first son she bears shall carry on the **n** 9005
25: 6 of the dead brother so that his **n** will not 9005
25: 7 to carry on his brother's **n** in Israel. 9005
26: 2 as a dwelling for his **N** 9005
28:10 that you are called by the **n** *of* the LORD, 9005
28:58 do not revere this glorious and awesome **n** 9005
29:20 and the LORD will blot out his **n** from 9005
32: 3 I will proclaim the **n** *of* the LORD. 9005
Jos 7: 9 and wipe out our **n** from the earth. 9005
7: 9 then will you do for your own great **n**?" 9005
21: 9 they allotted the following towns by **n** 9005
22:34 **gave** the altar *this* **n**: A Witness Between Us 7924
Jdg 1:26 which is its **n** to this day. 9005
13: 6 and he didn't tell me his **n**. 9005
13:17 "What is your **n**, 9005
13:18 He replied, "Why do you ask my **n**? 9005
16: 4 in the Valley of Sorek whose **n** was Delilah. 9005
Ru 1: 2 The man's **n** was Elimelech, 9005
1: 2 his wife's **n** Naomi, 9005
2: 1 a man of standing, whose **n** was Boaz. 9005
2:19 "The **n** *of* the man I worked 9005
4: 5 in order to maintain the **n** *of* the dead 9005
4:10 in order to maintain the **n** *of* the dead 9005
4:10 so that his **n** will not disappear from 9005
1Sa 1: 1 whose **n** was Elkanah son of Jeroham, 9005
8: 2 The **n** *of* his firstborn was Joel and 9005
8: 2 and the **n** *of* his second was Abijah, 9005
9: 1 whose **n** was Kish son of Abiel, 9005
12:22 For the sake of his great **n** the LORD will 9005
14:49 The **n** *of* his older daughter was Merab, 9005
14:50 His wife's **n** was Ahinoam daughter 9005
14:50 The **n** *of* the commander of Saul's army 9005
17:45 but I come against you in the **n** *of* the LORD 9005
18:30 and his **n** became well known. 9005
20:42 with each other in the **n** *of* the LORD, 9005
24:21 or wipe out my **n** from my father's family." 9005
25: 3 His **n** was Nabal 9005
25: 3 and his wife's **n** was Abigail. 9005
25: 5 to Nabal at Carmel and greet him in my **n**. 9005
25: 9 they gave Nabal this message in David's **n**. 9005
25:25 He is just like his **n**— 9005
25:25 his **n** is Fool, and folly goes with him. 9005
28: 8 he said, "and bring up for me the one *I* **n**." 606
2Sa 4: 4 His **n** was Mephibosheth.) 9005
6: 2 which is called by the **N**, 9005
6: 2 the **n** *of* the LORD Almighty, 9005
6:18 in the **n** *of* the LORD Almighty. 9005
7: 9 Now I will make your **n** great, 9005
7:13 the one who will build a house for my **N**, 9005
7:23 and to make a **n** for himself, 9005
7:26 so that your **n** will be great forever. 9005
12:25 the prophet *to* **n** him Jedidiah. 7924+9005
14: 7 leaving my husband neither **n** nor 9005
14:27 The daughter's **n** was Tamar, 9005
16: 5 His **n** was Shimei son of Gera, 9005
18:18 to carry on the memory of my **n**." 9005
22:50 I will sing praises to your **n**. 9005
1Ki 1:47 'May your God make Solomon's **n** more famous than yours 9005
3: 2 a temple had not yet been built for the **N** *of* 9005
5: 3 a temple for the **N** *of* the LORD his God 9005
5: 5 a temple for the **N** *of* the LORD my God, 9005
5: 5 the temple for my **N**.' 9005
8:16 to have a temple built for my **N** to be there, 9005
8:17 to build a temple for the **N** *of* the LORD, 9005
8:18 in your heart to build a temple for my **N**, 9005
8:19 the temple for my **N**.' 9005
8:20 I have built the temple for the **N** *of* the LORD 9005
8:29 'My **N** shall be there,' 9005
8:33 they turn back to you and confess your **n**, 9005
8:35 and confess your **n** and turn from their sin 9005
8:41 from a distant land because of your **n**— 9005
1Ki 8:42 of your great **n** and your mighty hand 9005
8:43 of the earth may know your **n** and fear you, 9005
8:43 that this house I have built bears your **N**. 9005
8:44 and the temple I have built for your **N**, 9005
8:48 and the temple I have built for your **N**; 9005
9: 3 by putting my **N** there forever. 9005
9: 7 and will reject this temple I have consecrated for my **N**. 9005
9:13 a **n** they have to this day. NIH
10: 1 and his relation to the **n** *of* the LORD, 9005
11:36 the city where I chose to put my **N**. 9005
14:21 the tribes of Israel in which to put his **N**. 9005
14:21 His mother's **n** was Naamah; 9005
14:31 His mother's **n** was Naamah; 9005
15: 2 His mother's **n** was Maacah daughter 9005
15:10 His grandmother's **n** was Maacah daughter 9005
16:24 the **n** *of* the former owner of the hill. 9005
18:24 Then you call on the **n** *of* your god, 9005
18:24 and I will call on the **n** *of* the LORD. 9005
18:25 Call on the **n** *of* your god, 9005
18:26 on the **n** *of* Baal from morning till noon. 9005
18:31 saying, "Your **n** shall be Israel." 9005
18:32 With the stones he built an altar in the **n** *of* 9005
21: 8 So she wrote letters in Ahab's **n**, 9005
22:16 to tell me nothing but the truth in the **n** *of* 9005
22:42 His mother's **n** was Azubah daughter 9005
2Ki 2:24 and called down a curse on them in the **n** 9005
5:11 and call on the **n** *of* the LORD his God, 9005
8:26 His mother's **n** was Athaliah, 9005
12: 1 His mother's **n** was Zibiah; 9005
14: 2 His mother's **n** was Jehoaddin; 9005
14: 7 calling it Joktheel, the **n** it has to this day. 9005
14:27 not said he would blot out the **n** *of* Israel 9005
15: 2 His mother's **n** was Jecoliah; 9005
15:33 His mother's **n** was Jerusha daughter 9005
18: 2 His mother's **n** was Abijah daughter 9005
21: 1 His mother's **n** was Hephzibah. 9005
21: 4 "In Jerusalem I will put my **N**." 9005
21: 7 I will put my **N** forever. 9005
21:19 His mother's **n** was Meshullemeth daughter 9005
22: 1 His mother's **n** was Jedidah daughter 9005
23:27 'There shall my **N** be.' " 9005
23:31 His mother's **n** was Hamutal daughter 9005
23:34 and changed Eliakim's **n** to Jehoiakim. 9005
23:36 His mother's **n** was Zebidah daughter 9005
24: 8 His mother's **n** was Nehushta daughter 9005
24:17 in his place and changed his **n** to Zedekiah. 9005
24:18 His mother's **n** was Hamutal daughter 9005
1Ch 1:50 and his wife's **n** was Mehetabel daughter 9005
2:26 whose **n** was Atarah; 9005
4:38 The men listed above by **n** were leaders 9005
7:15 His sister's **n** was Maacah. 9005
8:29 His wife's **n** was Maacah, 9005
9:35 His wife's **n** was Maacah, 9005
12:31 by **n** to come and make David king— 9005
13: 6 the ark that is called by the **N**. 9005
16: 2 the people in the **n** *of* the LORD. 9005
16: 8 Give thanks to the LORD; call on his **n**; 9005
16:10 Glory in his holy **n**; 9005
16:29 ascribe to the LORD the glory due his **n**. 9005
16:35 that we may give thanks to your holy **n**, 9005
16:41 and designated by **n** to give thanks to 9005
17: 8 Now I will make your **n** like the names of 9005
17:21 and to make a **n** for yourself, 9005
17:24 and that your **n** will be great forever. 9005
21:19 to the word that Gad had spoken in the **n** *of* 9005
22: 7 a house for the **N** *of* the LORD my God. 9005
22: 8 You are not to build a house for my **N**, 9005
22: 9 His **n** will be Solomon, 9005
22:10 the one who will build a house for my **N**. 9005
22:19 that will be built for the **N** *of* the LORD." 9005
23:13 and to pronounce blessings in his **n** forever. 9005
28: 3 'You are not to build a house for my **N**, 9005
29:13 and praise your glorious **n**. 9005
29:16 for building you a temple for your Holy **N**, 9005
2Ch 2: 1 for the **N** *of* the LORD and a royal palace 9005
2: 4 Now I am about to build a temple for the **N** 9005
6: 5 to have a temple built for my **N** to be there, 9005
6: 6 But now I have chosen Jerusalem for my **N** 9005
6: 7 to build a temple for the **N** *of* the LORD, 9005
6: 8 in your heart to build a temple for my **N**, 9005
6: 9 who will build the temple for my **N**.' 9005
6:10 and I have built the temple for the **N** *of* 9005
6:20 which you said you would put your **N** there. 9005
6:24 when they turn back and confess your **n**, 9005
6:26 and confess your **n** and turn from their sin 9005
6:32 from a distant land because of your great **n** 9005
6:33 of the earth may know your **n** and fear you, 9005
6:33 that this house I have built bears your **N**. 9005
6:34 and the temple I have built for your **N**, 9005
6:38 toward the temple I have built for your **N**; 9005
7:14 if my people, who are called by my **n**, 9005
7:16 so that my **N** may be there forever. 9005
7:20 and will reject this temple I have consecrated for my **N**. 9005
12:13 the tribes of Israel in which to put his **N**. 9005
12:13 His mother's **n** was Naamah; 9005
13: 2 His mother's **n** was Maacah, 9005
14:11 and in your **n** we have come 9005
18:15 to tell me nothing but the truth in the **n** *of* 9005
20: 8 and have built in it a sanctuary for your **N**, 9005
20: 9 that bears your **N** and will cry out to you 9005
20:31 His mother's **n** was Azubah daughter 9005
22: 2 His mother's **n** was Athaliah, 9005
24: 1 His mother's **n** was Zibiah; 9005
25: 1 His mother's **n** was Jehoaddin; 9005
26: 3 His mother's **n** was Jecoliah; 9005
2Ch 27: 1 His mother's **n** was Jerusha daughter 9005
28:15 The men designated by **n** took 9005
29: 1 His mother's **n** was Abijah daughter 9005
31:19 by **n** to distribute portions to every male 9005
33: 4 "My **N** will remain in Jerusalem forever." 9005
33: 7 I will put my **N** forever. 9005
33:18 the words the seers spoke to him in the **n** 9005
36: 4 and Jerusalem and changed Eliakim's **n** 9005
36:13 who had made him take an oath in God's **n**. NIH
Ezr 2:61 the Gileadite and was called by that **n**). 9005
5: 1 the Jews in Judah and Jerusalem in the **n** *of* 10721
6:12 who has caused his **N** to dwell there, 10721
8:20 All were registered by **n**. 9005
10:16 and all of them designated by **n**. 9005
Ne 1: 9 chosen as a dwelling for my **N**.' 9005
1:11 who delight in revering your **n**. 9005
6:13 they would give me a bad **n** to discredit me. 9005
7:63 the Gileadite and was called by that **n**). 9005
9: 5 "Blessed be your glorious **n**, 9005
9:10 You made a **n** for yourself, 9005
13:25 I made them take an oath in God's **n** NIH
Est 2:14 with her and summoned her by **n**. 9005
3:12 in the **n** *of* King Xerxes himself and sealed 9005
8: 8 Now write another decree in the king's **n** 9005
8: 8 in the king's **n** and sealed with his ring can 9005
8:10 Mordecai wrote in the **n** *of* King Xerxes, 9005
Job 1: 1 of Uz there lived a man whose **n** was Job. 9005
1:21 may the **n** *of* the LORD be praised." 9005
18:17 he has no **n** in the land. 9005
Ps 5:11 those who love your **n** may rejoice in you. 9005
7:17 to the **n** *of* the LORD Most High. 9005
8: 1 how majestic is your **n** in all the earth! 9005
8: 9 how majestic is your **n** in all the earth! 9005
9: 2 I will sing praise to your **n**, O Most High. 9005
9: 5 you have blotted out their **n** for ever 9005
9:10 Those who know your **n** will trust in you, 9005
18:49 I will sing praises to your **n**. 9005
20: 1 may the **n** *of* the God of Jacob protect you. 9005
20: 5 up our banners in the **n** *of* our God. 9005
20: 7 we trust in the **n** *of* the LORD our God. 9005
22:22 I will declare your **n** to my brothers; 9005
25:11 For the sake of your **n**, O LORD, 9005
29: 2 Ascribe to the LORD the glory due his **n**; 9005
30: 4 praise his holy **n**. 2352
31: 3 for the sake of your **n** lead and guide me. 9005
33:21 for we trust in his holy **n**. 9005
34: 3 let us exalt his **n** together. 9005
41: 5 "When will he die and his **n** perish?" 9005
44: 5 through your **n** we trample our foes. 9005
44: 8 and we will praise your **n** forever. 9005
44:20 the **n** *of* our God or spread out our hands to 9005
48:10 Like your **n**, O God, your praise reaches 9005
52: 9 in your **n** I will hope, 9005
52: 9 for your **n** is good. NIH
54: 1 Save me, O God, by your **n**; 9005
54: 6 I will praise your **n**, O LORD, 9005
61: 5 the heritage of those who fear your **n**. 9005
61: 8 to your **n** and fulfill my vows day after day. 9005
63: 4 and in your **n** I will lift up my hands. 9005
63:11 all who swear by **God's n** will praise him, 2257S
66: 2 Sing the glory of his **n**; 9005
66: 4 they sing praise to your **n**." 9005
68: 4 Sing to God, sing praise to his **n**, 9005
68: 4 his **n** is the LORD— 9005
69:30 I will praise God's **n** in song 9005
69:36 and those who love his **n** will dwell there. 9005
72:17 May his **n** endure forever; 9005
72:19 Praise be to his glorious **n** forever; 9005
74: 7 they defiled the dwelling place of your **N**. 9005
74:10 Will the foe revile your **n** forever? 9005
74:18 how foolish people have reviled your **n**. 9005
74:21 may the poor and needy praise your **n**. 9005
75: 1 O God, we give thanks, for your **N** is near; 9005
76: 1 his **n** is great in Israel. 9005
79: 6 on the kingdoms that do not call on your **n**; 9005
79: 9 O God our Savior, for the glory of your **n**; 9005
80:18 revive us, and we will call on your **n**. 9005
83: 4 the **n** *of* Israel be remembered no more." 9005
83:16 with shame so that men will seek your **n**, 9005
83:18 whose **n** is the LORD— 9005
86: 9 they will bring glory to your **n**. 9005
86:11 that I may fear your **n**. 9005
86:12 I will glorify your **n** forever. 9005
89:12 Tabor and Hermon sing for joy at your **n**. 9005
89:16 They rejoice in your **n** all day long; 9005
89:24 and through my **n** his horn will be exalted. 9005
91:14 for he acknowledges my **n**. 9005
92: 1 the LORD and make music to your **n**, 9005
96: 2 Sing to the LORD, praise his **n**; 9005
96: 8 Ascribe to the LORD the glory due his **n**; 9005
97:12 and praise his holy **n**. 2352
99: 3 Let them praise your great and awesome **n** 9005
99: 6 among those who called on his **n**; 9005
100: 4 give thanks to him and praise his **n**. 9005
102: 8 against me **use** my **n as a curse**. 928+8678
102:15 The nations will fear the **n** *of* the LORD, 9005
102:21 So the **n** *of* the LORD will be declared 9005
103: 1 all my inmost being, praise his holy **n**. 9005
105: 1 Give thanks to the LORD, call on his **n**; 9005
105: 3 Glory in his holy **n**; 9005
106:47 to your holy **n** and glory in your praise. 9005
111: 9 holy and awesome is his **n**. 9005
113: 1 praise the **n** *of* the LORD. 9005
113: 2 Let the **n** *of* the LORD be praised, 9005
113: 3 the **n** *of* the LORD is to be praised. 9005
115: 1 not to us but to your **n** be the glory, 9005
116: 4 Then I called on the **n** *of* the LORD: 9005

Ps 116:13 up of salvation and call on the **n** *of* the LORD 9005
116:17 and call on the **n** *of* the LORD. 9005
118:10 but in the **n** *of* the LORD I cut them off. 9005
118:11 but in the **n** *of* the LORD I cut them off. 9005
118:12 in the **n** *of* the LORD I cut them off. 9005
118:26 Blessed is he who comes in the **n** *of* 9005
119:55 In the night I remember your **n,** O LORD, 9005
119:132 as you always do to those who love your **n.** 9005
122: 4 to praise the **n** *of* the LORD according to 9005
124: 8 Our help is in the **n** *of* the LORD, 9005
129: 8 we bless you in the **n** *of* the LORD." 9005
135: 1 Praise the **n** *of* the LORD; 9005
135: 3 sing praise to his **n,** for that is pleasant. 9005
135:13 Your **n,** O LORD, endures forever, 9005
138: 2 and will praise your **n** for your love 9005
138: 2 above all things your **n** and your word. 9005
139:20 your adversaries misuse your **n.** NIH
140:13 Surely the righteous will praise your **n** and 9005
142: 7 that I may praise your **n.** 9005
145: 1 I will praise your **n** for ever and ever. 9005
145: 2 and extol your **n** for ever and ever. 9005
145:21 Let every creature praise his holy **n** for ever 9005
147: 4 of the stars and calls them each *by* **n.** 9005
148: 5 Let them praise the **n** *of* the LORD, 9005
148:13 Let them praise the **n** *of* the LORD, 9005
148:13 for his **n** alone is exalted; 9005
149: 3 Let them praise his **n** with dancing 9005
Pr 3: 4 and a good **n** in the sight of God and man. 8507
10: 7 but the **n** *of* the wicked will rot. 9005
18:10 The **n** *of* the LORD is a strong tower; 9005
21:24 "Mocker" is his **n;** 9005
22: 1 good **n** is more desirable than great riches; 9005
30: 4 What is his **n,** and the name of his son? 9005
30: 4 What is his name, and the **n** *of* his son? 9005
30: 9 and so dishonor the **n** *of* my God. 9005
Ecc 6: 4 and in darkness its **n** is shrouded. 9005
7: 1 A good **n** is better than fine perfume, 9005
SS 1: 3 your **n** is like perfume poured out. 9005
Isa 4: 1 only let us be called by your **n.** 9005
8: 3 **"N** him Maher-Shalal-Hash-Baz. 7924+9005
12: 4 "Give thanks to the LORD, call on his **n;** 9005
12: 4 and proclaim that his **n** is exalted. 9005
14:22 from Babylon her **n** and survivors, 9005
18: 7 the place of the **N** *of* the LORD Almighty. 9005
24:15 exalt the **n** *of* the LORD, 9005
25: 1 I will exalt you and praise your **n,** 9005
26: 8 your **n** and renown are the desire 9005
26:13 but your **n** alone do we honor. 9005
29:23 they will keep my **n** holy; 9005
30:27 See, the **N** *of* the LORD comes from afar, 9005
40:26 and calls them each by **n.** 9005
41:25 one from the rising sun who calls on my **n.** 9005
42: 8 "I am the LORD; that is my **n!** 9005
43: 1 I have summoned you by **n;** you are mine. 9005
43: 7 everyone who is called by my **n,** 9005
44: 5 another will call himself by the **n** *of* Jacob; 9005
44: 5 'The LORD's,' and will take the **n** Israel. 9005
45: 3 the God of Israel, who summons you by **n.** 9005
45: 4 by **n** and bestow on you a title of honor, 9005
47: 4 the LORD Almighty is his **n—** 9005
48: 1 by the **n** *of* Israel and come from the line 9005
48: 1 in the **n** *of* the LORD and invoke the God 9005
48: 2 the LORD Almighty is his **n:** 9005
48:19 their **n** would never be cut off 9005
49: 1 from my birth he has made mention of my **n** 9005
50:10 in the **n** *of* the LORD and rely on his God. 9005
51:15 the LORD Almighty is his **n.** 9005
52: 5 all day long my **n** is constantly blasphemed. 9005
52: 6 Therefore my people will know my **n;** 9005
54: 5 the LORD Almighty is his **n—** 9005
56: 5 and a **n** better than sons and daughters; 9005
56: 5 I will give them an everlasting **n** that will 9005
56: 6 to love the **n** *of* the LORD, 9005
57:15 he who lives forever, whose **n** is holy: 9005
59:19 men will fear the **n** *of* the LORD, 9005
62: 2 be called by a new **n** that the mouth of 9005
62: 4 or **n** your land Desolate. 606
63:14 to make for yourself a glorious **n.** 9005
63:16 our Redeemer from of old is your **n.** 9005
63:19 they have not been called by your **n.** 9005
64: 2 to make your **n** known to your enemies 9005
64: 7 on your **n** or strives to lay hold of you; 9005
65: 1 To a nation that did not call on my **n,** 9005
65:15 You will leave your **n** to my chosen ones as 9005
65:15 but to his servants he will give another **n.** 9005
66: 5 and exclude you because of my **n,** 9005
66:22 "so will your **n** and descendants endure. 9005
Jer 3:17 in Jerusalem to honor the **n** *of* the LORD. 9005
7:10 which bears my **N,** and say, 9005
7:11 Has this house, which bears my **N,** 9005
7:12 where I first made a dwelling for my **N,** 9005
7:14 now do to the house that bears my **N,** 9005
7:30 that bears my **N** and have defiled it. 9005
10: 6 and your **n** is mighty in power. 9005
10:16 the LORD Almighty is his **n.** 9005
10:25 on the peoples who do not call on your **n.** 9005
11:19 that his **n** be remembered no more." 9005
11:21 'Do not prophesy in the **n** *of* the LORD 9005
12:16 the ways of my people and swear by my **n,** 9005
14: 7 do something for the sake of your **n.** 9005
14: 9 and we bear your **n;** do not forsake us! 9005
14:14 prophets are prophesying lies in my **n.** 9005
14:15 the prophets who are prophesying in my **n:** 9005
14:21 For the sake of your **n** do not despise us; 9005
15:16 for I bear your **n,** O LORD God Almighty. 9005
16:21 Then they will know that my **n** is the LORD. 9005
20: 3 "The LORD's **n** *for* you is not Pashhur, 7924+9005
Jer 20: 9 or speak any more in his **n,"** 9005
23: 6 This is the **n** by which he will be called: 9005
23:25 "I have heard what the prophets say who prophesy lies in my **n.** 9005
23:27 dreams they tell one another will make my people forget my **n,** 9005
23:27 just as their fathers forgot my **n** 9005
25:29 on the city that bears my **N,** 9005
26: 9 Why do you prophesy in the LORD's **n** 9005
26:16 to us in the **n** *of* the LORD our God." 9005
26:20 prophesied in the **n** *of* the LORD; 9005
27:15 'They are prophesying lies in my **n.** 9005
29: 9 They are prophesying lies to you in my **n.** 9005
29:21 who are prophesying lies to you in my **n:** 9005
29:23 and in my **n** have spoken lies, 9005
29:25 You sent letters in your own **n** to all 9005
31:35 the LORD Almighty is his **n:** 9005
32:18 whose **n** is the LORD Almighty, 9005
32:34 in the house that bears my **N** and defiled it. 9005
33: 2 the LORD is his **n:** 9005
33:16 This is **the n** *by which* it will be called: 889^S
34:15 before me in the house that bears my **N.** 9005
34:16 around and profaned my **n;** 9005
37:13 whose **n** was Irijah son of Shelemiah, 9005
44:16 the message you have spoken to us in the **n** 9005
44:26 'I swear by my great **n,'** says the LORD, 9005
44:26 in Egypt will ever again invoke my **n** 9005
46:18 whose **n** is the LORD Almighty, 9005
48:15 whose **n** is the LORD Almighty. 9005
50:34 the LORD Almighty is his **n.** 9005
51:19 the LORD Almighty is his **n.** 9005
51:57 whose **n** is the LORD Almighty. 9005
52: 1 His mother's **n** was Hamutal daughter 9005
La 3:55 I called on your **n,** O LORD, 9005
Eze 20: 9 the sake of my **n** I did what would keep it 9005
20:14 the sake of my **n** I did what would keep it 9005
20:22 the sake of my **n** I did what would keep it 9005
20:39 to me and no longer profane my holy **n** 9005
36:20 the nations they profaned my holy **n,** 9005
36:21 I had concern for my holy **n,** 9005
36:22 but for the sake of my holy **n,** 9005
36:23 I will show the holiness of my great **n,** 9005
36:23 **the n** you have profaned among them. 889^S
39: 7 " 'I will make known my holy **n** 9005
39: 7 I will no longer let my holy **n** be profaned, 9005
39:25 and I will be zealous for my holy **n.** 9005
43: 7 Israel will never again defile my holy **n—** 9005
43: 8 they defiled my holy **n** 9005
48: 1 "These are the tribes, listed by **n:** 9005
48:35 the **n** *of* the city from that time on will be: 9005
Da 1: 7 to Daniel, the **n** Belteshazzar; NIH
2:20 be to the **n** of God for ever and ever; 10721
4: 8 after the **n** *of* my god, 10721
9: 6 who spoke in your **n** to our kings, 9005
9:15 and who made for yourself a **n** that endures 9005
9:18 the desolation of the city that bears your **N.** 9005
9:19 your city and your people bear your **N."** 9005
12: 1 everyone whose **n** is found written in NIH
Hos 12: 5 the LORD is his **n of renown!** 2352
Joel 2:26 the **n** *of* the LORD your God, 9005
2:32 on the **n** *of* the LORD will be saved; 9005
Am 2: 7 the same girl and so profane my holy **n.** 9005
4:13 the LORD God Almighty is his **n.** 9005
5: 8 the LORD is his **n—** 9005
5:27 whose **n** is God Almighty. 9005
6:10 not mention the **n** *of* the LORD." 9005
9: 6 the LORD is his **n.** 9005
9:12 of Edom and all the nations that bear my **n,"** 9005
Mic 4: 5 the nations may walk in the **n** *of* their gods; 9005
4: 5 in the **n** *of* the LORD our God for ever 9005
5: 4 of the **n** *of* the LORD his God. 9005
6: 9 and to fear your **n** is wisdom— 9005
Na 1:14 no descendants to bear your **n.** 9005
Zep 3: 9 all of them may call on the **n** *of* the LORD 9005
3:12 who trust in the **n** *of* the LORD. 9005
Zec 5: 4 of him who swears falsely by my **n.** 9005
6:12 'Here is the man whose **n** is the Branch, 9005
10:12 in the LORD and in his **n** they will walk," 9005
13: 3 you have told lies in the LORD's **n.'** 9005
13: 9 call on my **n** and I will answer them; 9005
14: 9 and his **n** the only name. 9005
14: 9 and his name the only **n.** NIH
Mal 1: 6 O priests, who show contempt for my **n.** 9005
1: 6 'How have we shown contempt for your **n?'** 9005
1:11 My **n** will be great among the nations, 9005
1:11 and pure offerings will be brought to my **n,** 9005
1:11 my **n** will be great among the nations," 9005
1:14 my **n** is to be feared among the nations. 9005
2: 2 if you do not set your heart to honor my **n,"** 9005
2: 5 and stood in awe of my **n.** 9005
3:16 the LORD and honored his **n.** 9005
4: 2 But for you who revere my **n,** 9005
Mt 1:21 and you are to give him the **n** Jesus, *3950*
1:25 And he gave him the **n** Jesus. *3950*
6: 9 in heaven, hallowed be your **n,** *3950*
7:22 Lord, did we not prophesy *in* your **n,** *3950*
7:22 and *in* your **n** drive out demons *3950*
12:21 *In* his **n** the nations will put their hope." *3950*
13:55 Isn't his mother's **n** Mary, *3306*
18: 5 a little child like this in my **n** welcomes me. *3950*
18:20 where two or three come together in my **n,** *3950*
21: 9 "Blessed is he who comes in the **n** of *3950*
23:39 'Blessed is he who comes in the **n** of *3950*
24: 5 For many will come in my **n,** claiming, *3950*
26: 3 high priest, whose **n** *was* Caiaphas, *3306*
28:19 baptizing them in the **n** of the Father and of *3950*
Mk 3:16 Simon (to whom he gave the **n** Peter); *3950*
Mk 3:17 **n** Boanerges, which means Sons of Thunder *3950*
5: 9 Then Jesus asked him, "What is your **n?"** *3950*
5: 9 "My **n** is Legion," he replied, *3950*
6:14 for Jesus' **n** had become well known. *3950*
9:37 in my **n** welcomes me; *3950*
9:38 a man driving out demons in your **n** *3950*
9:39 "No one who does a miracle in my **n** can in *3950*
9:41 a cup of water in my **n** because you belong *3950*
11: 9 "Blessed is he who comes in the **n** of *3950*
13: 6 Many will come in my **n,** claiming, *3950*
16:17 In my **n** they will drive out demons; *3950*
Lk 1:13 and you are to give him the **n** John. *3950*
1:27 The virgin's **n** was Mary. *3950*
1:31 and you are to give him the **n** Jesus. *3950*
1:49 done great things for me—holy is his **n.** *3950*
1:59 *to* **n** him after his father Zechariah, *2813+3836+3950*
1:61 among your relatives who has that **n."** *3950*
1:62 to find out what he would like *to* **n** *2813*
1:63 "His **n** is John." *3950*
2:21 Jesus, the **n** the angel had given him *NIG*
5:27 *by* the **n** of Levi sitting at his tax booth. *3950*
6:22 and insult you and reject your **n** as evil, *3950*
8:30 Jesus asked him, "What is your **n?"** *3950*
9:48 in my **n** welcomes me; *3950*
9:49 a man driving out demons in your **n** *3950*
10:17 even the demons submit to us in your **n."** *3950*
11: 2 " 'Father, hallowed be your **n,** *3950*
13:35 'Blessed is he who comes in the **n** of *3950*
19: 2 A man was there *by* the **n** of Zacchaeus; *3950*
19:38 "Blessed is the king who comes in the **n** of *3950*
21: 8 For many will come in my **n,** claiming, *3950*
21:12 and all on account of my **n.** *3950*
24:47 be preached in his **n** to all nations, *3950*
Jn 1: 6 who was sent from God; his **n** was John. *3950*
1:12 to those who believed in his **n,** *3950*
2:23 and believed in his **n.** *3950*
3:18 because he has not believed in the **n** *3950*
5:43 I have come in my Father's **n,** *3950*
5:43 but if someone else comes in his own **n,** *3950*
10: 3 He calls his own sheep by **n** *3950*
10:25 The miracles I do in my Father's **n** speak *3950*
12:13 "Blessed is he who comes in the **n** of *3950*
12:28 Father, glorify your **n!"** *3950*
14:13 And I will do whatever you ask in my **n,** *3950*
14:14 You may ask me for anything in my **n,** *3950*
14:26 whom the Father will send in my **n,** *3950*
15:16 Then the Father will give you whatever you ask in my **n.** *3950*
15:21 will treat you this way because of my **n,** *3950*
16:23 my Father will give you whatever you ask in my **n.** *3950*
16:24 not asked for anything in my **n.** *3950*
16:26 In that day you will ask in my **n.** *3950*
17:11 protect them by the power of your **n—** *3950*
17:11 **the n** you gave me— *4005^S*
17:12 and kept them safe by that **n** you gave me. *3950*
18:10 (The servant's **n** was Malchus.) *3950*
20:31 by believing you may have life in his **n.** *3950*
Ac 2:21 everyone who calls on the **n** of the Lord *3950*
2:38 in the **n** of Jesus Christ for the forgiveness *3950*
3: 6 In the **n** of Jesus Christ of Nazareth, walk." *3950*
3:16 By faith *in* the **n** of Jesus, *3950*
3:16 It is Jesus' **n** and the faith that comes *3950*
4: 7 or what **n** did you do this?" *3950*
4:10 It is by the **n** of Jesus Christ of Nazareth, *3950*
4:12 for there is no other **n** under heaven given *3950*
4:17 to speak no longer to anyone in this **n."** *3950*
4:18 not to speak or teach at all in the **n** of Jesus. *3950*
4:30 through the **n** of your holy servant Jesus." *3950*
5:28 not to teach in this **n,"** *3950*
5:40 not to speak in the **n** of Jesus, *3950*
5:41 of suffering disgrace for the **N.** *3950*
8:12 of God and the **n** of Jesus Christ, *3950*
8:16 they had simply been baptized into the **n** of *3950*
9:14 to arrest all who call on your **n."** *3950*
9:15 to carry my **n** before the Gentiles *3950*
9:16 how much he must suffer for my **n."** *3950*
9:21 among those who call on this **n?** *3950*
9:27 preached fearlessly in the **n** of Jesus. *3950*
9:28 speaking boldly in the **n** of the Lord. *3950*
10:43 forgiveness of sins through his **n."** *3950*
10:48 So he ordered that they be baptized in the **n** *3950*
13: 8 (for that is what his **n** means) opposed them *3950*
15:17 and all the Gentiles who bear my **n,** *3950*
15:26 men who have risked their lives for the **n** *3950*
16:18 "In the **n** of Jesus Christ I command you *3950*
19: 5 they were baptized into the **n** of the Lord *3950*
19:13 *to* **invoke the n** of the Lord Jesus *3950+3951*
19:13 They would say, "In the **n** of Jesus, *NIG*
19:17 **n** of the Lord Jesus was held in high honor. *3950*
19:27 that our trade *will* **lose** its **good n,** *591+1650+2262*
21:13 in Jerusalem for the **n** of the Lord Jesus." *3950*
22:16 wash your sins away, calling on his **n.'** *3950*
26: 9 to do all that was possible to oppose the **n** *3950*
Ro 2:24 "God's **n** is blasphemed among *3950*
9:17 in you and that my **n** might be proclaimed *3950*
10:13 on the **n** of the Lord will be saved." *3950*
15: 9 I will sing hymns *to* your **n."** *3950*
1Co 1: 2 with all those everywhere who call on the **n** *3950*
1:10 brothers, in the **n** of our Lord Jesus Christ, *3950*
1:13 Were you baptized into the **n** of Paul? *3950*
1:15 that you were baptized into my **n.** *3950*
5: 4 the **n** of our Lord Jesus and I am with you *3950*
6:11 in the **n** of the Lord Jesus Christ and by *3950*
Eph 3:15 in heaven and on earth **derives** *its* **n.** *3951*
5:20 in the **n** of our Lord Jesus Christ. *3950*

Php 2: 9 gave him the **n** that is above every name, 3950
2: 9 the name that is above every **n**, 3950
2:10 at the **n** of Jesus every knee should bow, 3950
Col 3:17 do it all in the **n** of the Lord Jesus, 3950
2Th 1:12 the **n** of our Lord Jesus may be glorified 3950
3: 6 In the **n** of the Lord Jesus Christ, 3950
1Ti 6: 1 so that God's **n** and our teaching may not 3950
2Ti 2:19 "Everyone who confesses the **n** of the Lord 3950
Heb 1: 4 the **n** he has inherited is superior to theirs. 3950
2:12 "I will declare your **n** to my brothers; 3950
7: 2 First, his **n** means "king of righteousness"; *NIG*
13:15 the fruit of lips that confess his **n.** 3950
Jas 2: 7 not the ones who are slandering the noble **n** 3950
5:10 take the prophets who spoke in the **n** of 3950
5:14 over him and anoint him with oil in the **n** of 3950
1Pe 4:14 you are insulted because of the **n** of Christ, 3950
4:16 but praise God that you bear that **n.** 3950
1Jn 2:12 have been forgiven on account of his **n.** 3950
3:23 to believe *in* the **n** of his Son, Jesus Christ, 3950
5:13 to you who believe in the **n** of the Son 3950
3Jn 1: 7 for the sake of the **N** that they went out, 3950
1:14 Greet the friends there by **n.** 3950
Rev 2: 3 and have endured hardships for my **n,** 3950
2:13 Yet you remain true to my **n.** 3950
2:17 a white stone with a new **n** written on it, 3950
3: 5 I will never blot out his **n** from the book 3950
3: 5 will acknowledge his **n** before my Father 3950
3: 8 and have not denied my **n.** 3950
3:12 the **n** of my God and the name of the city 3950
3:12 of my God and the **n** of the city of my God, 3950
3:12 and I will also write on him my new **n.** 3950
8:11 the **n** of the star is Wormwood. 3950
9:11 whose **n** in Hebrew is Abaddon, 3950
11:18 and those who reverence your **n,** both small 3950
13: 1 and on each head a blasphemous **n.** 3950
13: 6 and to slander his **n** and his dwelling place 3950
13:17 which is the **n** of the beast or the number 3950
13:17 of the beast or the number *of* his **n.** 3950
14: 1 who had his **n** and his Father's name written 3950
14: 1 and his Father's **n** written on their foreheads 3950
14:11 for anyone who receives the mark *of* his **n."** 3950
15: 2 and over the number *of* his **n.** 3950
15: 4 O Lord, and bring glory to your **n?** 3950
16: 9 by the intense heat and they cursed the **n** 3950
19:12 a **n** written on him that no one knows 3950
19:13 and his **n** is the Word of God. 3950
19:16 and on his thigh he has this **n** written: 3950
20:15 If anyone's **n** was not found written in *NIG*
22: 4 and his **n** will be on their foreheads. 3950

NAME'S (8) [NAME]

Ps 23: 3 in paths of righteousness for his **n** sake. 9005
79: 9 and forgive our sins for your **n** sake. 9005
106: 8 Yet he saved them for his **n** sake, 9005
109:21 deal well with me for your **n** sake; 9005
143:11 your **n** sake, O LORD, preserve my life; 9005
Isa 48: 9 For my own **n** sake I delay my wrath; 9005
Eze 20:44 when I deal with you for my **n** sake and not 9005
Ro 1: 5 Through him and for his **n** sake, 3950

NAMED (161) [NAME]

Ge 3:20 Adam **n** his wife Eve, 7924+9005
4:17 and *he* **n** it after his son Enoch. 7924+9005
4:19 one **n** Adah and the other Zillah. 9005
4:25 she gave birth to a son and **n** him Seth, 7924+9005
4:26 Seth also had a son, and *he* **n** him Enosh. 7924+9005
5: 3 and *he* **n** him Seth. 7924+9005
5:29 *He* **n** him Noah and said, 7924+9005
10:25 One was **n** Peleg, because in his time 9005
10:25 his brother was **n** Joktan. 9005
16: 1 she had an Egyptian maidservant **n** Hagar; 9005
19:37 and *she* **n** him Moab; 7924+9005
19:38 and *she* **n** him Ben-Ammi; 7924+9005
23:16 and weighed out for him the price *he had* **n** 1819
24:29 Now Rebekah had a brother **n** Laban, 9005
25:25 so *they* **n** him Esau. 7924+9005
25:26 so he *was* **n** Jacob. 7924+9005
26:20 So *he* **n** the well Esek, 7924+9005
26:21 so *he* **n** it Sitnah. 7924+9005
26:22 *He* **n** it Rehoboth, saying, 7924+9005
27:36 Esau said, *"Isn't* he rightly **n** Jacob? 7924+9005
29:32 *She* **n** him Reuben, for she said, 7924+9005
29:33 So *she* **n** him Simeon. 7924+9005
29:34 So he *was* **n** Levi. 7924+9005
29:35 So *she* **n** him Judah. 7924+9005
30: 6 Because of this *she* **n** him Dan. 7924+9005
30: 8 So *she* **n** him Naphtali. 7924+9005
30:11 So *she* **n** him Gad. 7924+9005
30:13 So *she* **n** him Asher. 7924+9005
30:18 So *she* **n** him Issachar. 7924+9005
30:20 So *she* **n** him Zebulun. 7924+9005
30:21 birth to a daughter and **n** her Dinah. 7924+9005
30:24 *She* **n** him Joseph, and said, 7924+9005
32: 2 So *he* **n** that place Mahanaim. 7924+9005
35: 8 So it *was* **n** Allon Bacuth. 7924+9005
35:10 So *he* **n** him Israel. 7924+9005
35:18 *she* **n** her son Ben-Oni. 7924+9005
35:18 But his father **n** him Benjamin. 7924
36:12 also had a concubine **n** Timna, NIH
36:32 His city was **n** Dinhabah. 9005
36:35 His city was **n** Avith. 9005
36:39 His city was **n** Pau, 9005
38: 1 to stay with a man of Adullam **n** Hirah. 9005
38: 2 the daughter of a Canaanite man **n** Shua. 9005
Ge 38: 3 who *was* **n** Er. 7924+9005
38: 4 gave birth to a son and **n** him Onan. 7924+9005
38: 5 to still another son and **n** him Shelah. 7924+9005
38:29 And he *was* **n** Perez. 7924+9005
41:51 Joseph **n** his firstborn Manasseh and 7924+9005
41:52 The second son *he* **n** Ephraim and 7924+9005
Ex 2:10 *She* **n** him Moses, saying, 7924+9005
2:22 and Moses **n** him Gershom, saying, 7924+9005
18: 3 One son was **n** Gershom, for Moses said, 9005
18: 4 and the other was **n** Eliezer, 9005
Nu 11:34 the place *was* **n** Kibroth Hattaavah, 7924+9005
21: 3 so the place *was* **n** Hormah. 7924+9005
26:46 (Asher had a daughter **n** Serah.) 9005
Dt 3:14 it *was* **n** after him, 7924+9005
Jos 2: 1 of a prostitute **n** Rahab and stayed there. 9005
19:47 They settled in Leshem and **n** it Dan 7924
Jdg 8:31 a son, whom *he* **n** Abimelech. 8492+9005
13: 2 A certain man of Zorah, **n** Manoah, 9005
13:24 to a boy and **n** him Samson. 7924+9005
17: 1 Now a man **n** Micah from the hill country 9005
18:29 *They* **n** it Dan after their forefather Dan, 7924+9005
Ru 1: 4 one **n** Orpah and the other Ruth. 9005
4:17 And *they* **n** him Obed. 7924+9005
1Sa 1:20 *She* **n** him Samuel, saying, 7924+9005
4:21 *She* **n** the boy Ichabod, saying, 7924
7:12 *He* **n** it Ebenezer, saying, 7924+9005
9: 2 He had a son **n** Saul, 9005
17: 4 A champion **n** Goliath, 9005
17:12 David was the son of an Ephrathite **n** Jesse, 9005
2Sa 3: 7 a concubine **n** Rizpah daughter of Aiah. 9005
4: 2 One was **n** Baanah and the other Recab; 9005
9: 2 a servant of Saul's household **n** Ziba. 9005
9:12 Mephibosheth had a young son **n** Mica, 9005
12:24 and *they* **n** him Solomon. 7924+9005
12:28 and it *will* **be n** after me." 7924+9005
13: 3 Now Amnon had a friend **n** Jonadab son 9005
17:25 Amasa was the son of a man **n** Jether, 9005
18:18 *He* **n** the pillar after himself, 7924+9005
20: 1 Now a troublemaker **n** Sheba son of Bicri, 9005
20:21 A man **n** Sheba son of Bicri, 9005
1Ki 7:21 to the south *he* **n** Jakin and the one to 7924+9005
11:20 of Tahpenes bore him a son **n** Genubath, NIH
11:26 and his mother was a widow **n** Zeruah. 9005
13: 2 'A son **n** Josiah will be born to the house 9005
2Ki 17:34 whom *he* **n** Israel. 8492+9005
23:11 the room of an official **n** Nathan-Melech. NIH
1Ch 1:19 One was **n** Peleg, because in his time 9005
1:19 his brother was **n** Joktan. 9005
1:43 whose city was **n** Dinhabah. 9005
1:46 His city was **n** Avith. 9005
1:50 His city was **n** Pau, 9005
2:29 Abishur's wife was **n** Abihail, 9005
2:34 He had an Egyptian servant **n** Jarha. 9005
4: 3 Their sister was **n** Hazzelelponi. 9005
4: 9 His mother *had* **n** him Jabez, saying, 7924+9005
6:65 the *previously* **n** towns. 928+7924+9005
7:15 Another descendant was **n** Zelophehad, 9005
7:16 to a son and **n** him Peresh. 7924+9005
7:16 His brother was **n** Sheresh, 9005
7:23 *He* **n** him Beriah, 7924+9005
9:31 A Levite **n** Mattithiah, NIH
2Ch 3:17 The one to the south *he* **n** Jakin and 7924+9005
28: 9 a prophet of the LORD **n** Oded was there, 9005
Ezr 5:14 to a man **n** Sheshbazzar, 10721
Ne 9: 7 of the Chaldeans and **n** him Abraham. 8492+9005
13:13 and a Levite **n** Pedaiah in charge of NIH
Est 2: 5 **n** Mordecai son of Jair, the son of Shimei, 9005
2: 7 Mordecai had a cousin **n** Hadassah, NIH
Job 42:14 The first daughter *he* **n** Jemimah, 7924+9005
Ps 49:11 *they had* **n** lands after themselves. 7924+9005
Ecc 6:10 Whatever exists *has* already **been n,** 7924+9005
Isa 61: 6 you *will* **be n** ministers of our God. 606
Eze 23: 4 The older was **n** Oholah, 9005
48:31 the city will be **n** after the tribes of Israel. 9005
Mt 9: 9 he saw a man **n** Matthew sitting at *3306*
27:32 they met a man from Cyrene, **n** Simon, *3950*
27:57 a rich man from Arimathea, **n** Joseph, *3950*
Mk 5:22 Then one of the synagogue rulers, **n** Jairus, *3950*
Lk 1: 5 of Judea there was a priest **n** Zechariah, *3950*
1:27 to be married to a man **n** Joseph, *3950*
2:21 he *was* **n** Jesus, the name the angel *2813+3950*
6:14 Simon (whom *he* **n** Peter), *3951*
8:41 Then a man **n** Jairus, *3950*
10:38 where a woman **n** Martha opened her home *3950*
16:20 At his gate was laid a beggar **n** Lazarus, *3950*
23:50 Now there was a man **n** Joseph, *3950*
24:18 One of them, **n** Cleopas, asked him, *3950*
Jn 3: 1 a man of the Pharisees **n** Nicodemus, *899+3950*
11: 1 Now a man **n** Lazarus was sick. *NIG*
11:49 Then one of them, **n** Caiaphas, *NIG*
Ac 5: 1 Now a man **n** Ananias, *3950*
5:34 But a Pharisee **n** Gamaliel, *3950*
7:58 at the feet *of* a young man **n** Saul. *2813*
8: 9 a man **n** Simon had practiced sorcery in *3950*
9:10 a disciple **n** Ananias. *3950*
9:11 and ask for a man from Tarsus **n** Saul, *3950*
9:12 a vision he has seen a man **n** Ananias come *3950*
9:33 There he found a man **n** Aeneas, *3950*
9:36 a disciple **n** Tabitha *3950*
9:43 for some time with a tanner **n** Simon. *5516*
10: 1 At Caesarea there was a man **n** Cornelius, *3950*
10: 5 a man **n** Simon who is called Peter. *NIG*
11:28 One of them, **n** Agabus, *3950*
12:13 and a servant girl **n** Rhoda came to answer *3950*
13: 6 and false prophet **n** Bar-Jesus, *3950*
16: 1 where a disciple **n** Timothy lived, *3950*
Ac 16:14 of those listening was a woman **n** Lydia, *3950*
17:34 also a woman **n** Damaris, *3950*
18: 2 There he met a Jew **n** Aquila, *3950*
18:24 Meanwhile a Jew **n** Apollos, *3950*
19:24 A silversmith **n** Demetrius, *3950*
20: 9 in a window was a young man **n** Eutychus, *3950*
21:10 prophet **n** Agabus came down from Judea. *3950*
22:12 "A man **n** Ananias came to see me. *NIG*
24: 1 of the elders and a lawyer **n** Tertullus, *NIG*
25:19 about a dead man **n** Jesus who Paul claimed was alive. *NIG*
27: 1 over *to* a centurion **n** Julius, *3950*
Rev 6: 8 Its rider was **n** Death, *899+3950*

NAMELESS (1) [NAME]

Job 30: 8 A base and **n** brood, 1172+9005

NAMELY (1) [NAME]

Col 2: 2 that they may know the mystery of God, **n,** *NIG*

NAMES (79) [NAME]

Ge 2:20 So the man gave **n** to all the livestock, 9005
25:13 These are the **n** *of* the sons of Ishmael, 9005
25:16 the **n** of the twelve tribal rulers according 9005
26:18 the same **n** his father had given them. 9005
36:10 These are the **n** *of* Esau's sons: 9005
46: 8 These are the **n** *of* the sons of Israel (Jacob 9005
48: 6 be reckoned under the **n** *of* their brothers. 9005
48:16 May they be called by my name and the **n** 9005
Ex 1: 1 the **n** *of* the sons of Israel who went 9005
1:15 whose **n** were Shiphrah and Puah, 9005
6:16 These were the **n** *of* the sons of Levi 9005
23:13 Do not invoke the **n** *of* other gods; 9005
28: 9 and engrave on them the **n** *of* the sons 9005
28:10 six **n** on one stone and the remaining six on 9005
28:11 the **n** *of* the sons of Israel on the two stones 9005
28:12 the **n** on his shoulders as a memorial before 9005
28:21 one for each of the **n** *of* the sons of Israel, 9005
28:29 the **n** of the sons of Israel over his heart on 9005
39: 6 and engraved them like a seal with the **n** *of* 9005
39:14 one for each of the **n** *of* the sons of Israel, 9005
Nu 1: 5 the **n** *of* the men who are to assist you: 9005
1:17 Aaron took these men whose **n** had been given, 9005
3: 2 The **n** *of* the sons of Aaron were Nadab 9005
3: 3 Those were the **n** *of* Aaron's sons, 9005
3:17 These were the **n** *of* the sons of Levi: 9005
3:18 These were the **n** *of* the Gershonite clans: 9005
3:40 or more and make a list of their **n.** 9005
11:26 two men, whose **n** were Eldad and Medad, 9005
13: 4 These are their **n:** 9005
13:16 the **n** *of* the men Moses sent to explore 9005
26:33 whose **n** were Mahlah, Noah, Hoglah, 9005
26:53 as an inheritance based on the number of **n.** 9005
26:55 be according to the **n** *for* its ancestral tribe. 9005
27: 1 The **n** *of* the daughters were Mahlah, 9005
32:38 and Baal Meon (these **n** were changed) 9005
32:38 They gave **n** to the cities they rebuilt. 9005
34:17 the **n** *of* the men who are to assign the land 9005
34:19 These are their **n:** 9005
Dt 7:24 and you will wipe out their **n** from 9005
12: 3 the idols of their gods and wipe out their **n** 9005
Jos 17: 3 whose **n** were Mahlah, Noah, Hoglah, 9005
23: 7 do not invoke the **n** *of* their gods or swear 9005
Jdg 8:14 the young man wrote down for him the **n** of NIH
Ru 1: 2 **n** *of* his two sons were Mahlon and Kilion. 9005
2Sa 5:14 the **n** *of* the children born to him there: 9005
7: 9 like the **n** *of* the greatest men of the earth. 9005
23: 8 These are the **n** *of* David's mighty men: 9005
1Ki 4: 8 These are their **n:** 9005
1Ch 4:41 The men whose **n** were listed came in 9005
6:17 These are the **n** *of* the sons of Gershon: 9005
8:38 Azel had six sons, and these were their **n:** 9005
9:44 Azel had six sons, and these were their **n:** 9005
14: 4 the **n** *of* the children born to him there: 9005
17: 8 like the **n** *of* the greatest men of the earth. 9005
23:24 under their **n** and counted individually, 9005
24: 6 recorded their **n** in the presence of the king NIH
2Ch 31:16 **n** *were* **in the genealogical records—** 3509
Ezr 5: 4 "What are the **n** *of* the men constructing 10721
5:10 We also asked them their **n,** 10721
5:10 the **n** *of* their leaders for your information. 10721
8:13 the last ones, whose **n** were Eliphelet, 9005
Ps 16: 4 of blood or take up their **n** on my lips. 9005
109:13 their **n** blotted out from the next generation. 9005
Da 1: 7 The chief official gave them new **n:** 9005
Hos 2:17 the **n** *of* the Baals from her lips; 9005
2:17 no longer will their **n** be invoked. 9005
Zep 1: 4 the **n** *of* the pagan and the idolatrous 9005
Zec 13: 2 I will banish the **n** *of* the idols from 9005
Mt 10: 2 These are the **n** of the twelve apostles: *3950*
Lk 10:20 rejoice that your **n** are written in heaven." *3950*
Ac 18:15 about words and **n** and your own law— *3950*
Php 4: 3 whose **n** are in the book of life. *3950*
Heb 12:23 whose **n** are written in heaven. *NIG*
Rev 13: 8 all whose **n** have not been written in *3950*
17: 3 with blasphemous **n** and had seven heads *3950*
17: 8 of the earth whose **n** have not been written *3950*
21:12 the **n** of the twelve tribes of Israel. *3950*
21:14 on them were the **n** of the twelve apostles *3950*
21:27 but only those whose **n** are written in *NIG*

NAOMI (26) [NAOMI'S]

Ru 1: 2 Elimelech, his wife's name **N,** 5843

Ru 1: 5 and N was left without her two sons 851+2021S
1: 6 N and her daughters-in-law prepared 2085S
1: 8 Then N said to her two daughters-in-law, 5843
1:11 But N said, "Return home, my daughters. 5843
1:15 said N, "your sister-in-law is going back NIH
1:18 When N realized that Ruth was determined NIH
1:19 "Can this be N?" 5843
1:20 "Don't call me N," she told them. 5843
1:21 Why call me N? The LORD has afflicted me 5843
1:22 So N returned from Moab accompanied 5843
2: 1 N had a relative on her husband's side, 5843
2: 2 And Ruth the Moabitess said to N, 5843
2: 2 N said to her, "Go ahead, my daughter." NIH
2: 6 who came back from Moab with N. 5843
2:20 N said to her daughter-in-law. 5843
2:22 N said to Ruth her daughter-in-law, 5843
3: 1 One day N her mother-in-law said to her, 5843
3:16 Ruth came to her mother-in-law, N asked, NIH
3:18 Then N said, "Wait, my daughter, NIH
4: 3 Then he said to the kinsman-redeemer, "N, 5843
4: 5 "On the day you buy the land from N and 5843
4: 9 that I have bought from N all the property 5843
4:14 The women said to N: 5843
4:16 Then N took the child, 5843
4:17 women living there said, "N has a son." 5843

NAOMI'S (1) [NAOMI]

Ru 1: 3 Now Elimelech, N husband, died, 5843

NAPHISH (3)

Ge 25:15 Hadad, Tema, Jetur, N and Kedemah. 5874
1Ch 1:31 N and Kedemah. These were the sons of Ishmael. 5874
5:19 against the Hagrites, Jetur, N and Nodab. 5874

NAPHOTH (1) [NAPHOTH DOR]

Jos 17:11 (the third in the list is N). 5868

NAPHOTH DOR (3) [NAPHOTH]

Jos 11: 2 in the western foothills and in N on 5869
12:23 the king of Dor (in N) one 5869
1Ki 4:11 Ben-Abinadab—in N (he was married 5869

NAPHTALI (53) [NAPHTALITES]

Ge 30: 8 So she named him N. 5889
35:25 of Rachel's maidservant Bilhah: Dan and N. 5889
46:24 The sons of N: 5889
49:21 "N is a doe set free 5889
Ex 1: 4 Dan and N; Gad and Asher. 5889
Nu 1:15 from N, Ahira son of Enan." 5889
1:42 From the descendants of N: 5889
1:43 number from the tribe of N was 53,400. 5889
2:29 The tribe of N will be next. 5889
2:29 The leader of the people of N is Ahira son 5889
7:78 the leader of the people of N, 5889
10:27 over the division of the tribe of N. 1201+5889
13:14 from the tribe of N, Nahbi son of Vophsi; 5889
26:48 The descendants of N by their clans were: 5889
26:50 These were the clans of N; 5889
34:28 the leader from the tribe of N." 1201+5889
Dt 27:13 Reuben, Gad, Asher, Zebulun, Dan and N. 5889
33:23 About N he said: 5889
33:23 "N is abounding with the favor of 5889
34: 2 all of N, the territory of Ephraim 5889
Jos 19:32 The sixth lot came out for N, clan by 1201+5889
19:39 the inheritance of the tribe of N, 1201+5889
20: 7 in Galilee in the hill country of N, 5889
21: 6 N and the half-tribe of Manasseh 5889
21:32 of N, Kedesh in Galilee (a city of refuge 5889
Jdg 1:33 Neither did N drive out those living 5889
4: 6 of Abinoam from Kedesh in N and said 5889
4: 6 take with you ten thousand men of N 1201+5889
4:10 where he summoned Zebulun and N. 5889
5:18 so did N on the heights of the field. 5889
6:35 and also into Asher, Zebulun and N, 5889
7:23 Israelites from N, Asher 5889
1Ki 4:15 in N (he had married Basemath daughter 5889
7:14 the tribe of N and whose father was a man 5889
15:20 and all Kinnereth in addition to N. 824+5889
2Ki 15:29 including all the land of N, 5889
1Ch 2: 2 Dan, Joseph, Benjamin, N, Gad and Asher. 5889
6:62 of Issachar, Asher and N, and from the part 5889
6:76 from the tribe of N they received Kedesh 5889
7:13 The sons of N: 5889
12:34 men of N—1,000 officers, 5889
12:40 and N came bringing food on donkeys, 5889
27:19 Ishmaiah son of Obadiah; over N: 5889
2Ch 16: 4 Abel Maim and all the store cities of N. 5889
34: 6 as far as N, and in the ruins around them, 5889
Ps 68:27 and there the princes of Zebulun and of N. 5889
Isa 9: 1 of N, but in the future he will honor Galilee 5889
Eze 48: 3 "N will have one portion; 5889
48: 4 it will border the territory of N from east 5889
48:34 the gate of Asher and the gate of N. 5889
Mt 4:13 by the lake in the area of Zebulun and N— *3750*
4:15 "Land of Zebulun and land *of* N, the way *3750*
Rev 7: 6 from the tribe *of* N 12,000, *3750*

NAPHTALITES (1) [NAPHTALI]

Jdg 1:33 but the N too lived among the Canaanite NIH

NAPHTUHITES (2)

Ge 10:13 Anamites, Lehabites, N, 5888
1Ch 1:11 Anamites, Lehabites, N, 5888

NAPKIN (KJV) See BURIAL CLOTH, CLOTH

NARCISSUS (1)

Ro 16:11 in the household *of* N who are in the Lord. *3727*

NARD (4)

SS 4:13 with henna and n, 5948
4:14 n and saffron, calamus and cinnamon, 5948
Mk 14: 3 very expensive perfume, *made of* pure n. *3726*
Jn 12: 3 Then Mary took about a pint *of* pure n, *3726*

NARROW (12) [NARROWER]

Nu 22:24 the angel of the LORD stood in a n path 5469
22:26 a n place where there was no room to turn, 7639
1Ki 6: 4 He made n clerestory windows in 357
Pr 23:27 a deep pit and a wayward wife is a n well. 7639
Isa 28:20 the blanket *too* n to wrap around you. 7639
Eze 40:16 by n parapet openings all around, as was 357
40:25 and its portico had n openings all around, NIH
41:16 as well as the thresholds and the n windows 357
41:26 of the portico were n windows 357
Mt 7:13 "Enter through the n gate. *5101*
7:14 the gate and n the road that leads to life, *2567*
Lk 13:24 to enter through the n door, *5101*

NARROWER (1) [NARROW]

Eze 42: 5 Now the upper rooms were n, 7900

NATHAN (43)

2Sa 5:14 Shammua, Shobab, N, Solomon, 5990
7: 2 he said to N the prophet, "Here I am, 5990
7: 3 N replied to the king, "Whatever you have 5990
7: 4 the word of the LORD came to N, saying: 5990
7:17 N reported to David all the words 5990
12: 1 The LORD sent N to David. 5990
12: 5 with anger against the man and said to N, 5990
12: 7 Then N said to David, "You are the man! 5990
12:13 Then David said to N, "I have sinned 5990
12:13 sinned against the LORD." N replied, 5990
12:15 After N had gone home, 5990
12:25 he sent word through N the prophet 5990
23:36 Igal son of N from Zobah, the son of Hagri, 5990
1Ki 1: 8 Benaiah son of Jehoiada, N the prophet, 5990
1:10 not invite N the prophet or Benaiah or 5990
1:11 Then N asked Bathsheba, Solomon's 5990
1:22 N the prophet arrived. 5990
1:23 they told the king, "N the prophet is here." 5990
1:24 N said, "Have you, my lord the king, 5990
1:32 N the prophet and Benaiah son 5990
1:34 There have Zadok the priest and N 5990
1:38 So Zadok the priest, N the prophet, 5990
1:44 N the prophet, Benaiah son of Jehoiada, 5990
1:45 and N the prophet have anointed him king 5990
4: 5 Azariah son of N— 5990
4: 5 Zabud son of N— 5990
1Ch 2:36 Attai was the father of N, 5990
2:36 N the father of Zabad, 5990
3: 5 Shammua, Shobab, N and Solomon. 5990
11:38 Joel the brother of N, Mibhar son of Hagri, 5990
14: 4 Shammua, Shobab, N, Solomon, 5990
17: 1 he said to N the prophet, "Here I am, 5990
17: 2 N replied to David, "Whatever you have 5990
17: 3 That night the word of God came to N, 5990
17:15 N reported to David all the words 5990
29:29 of N the prophet and the records of Gad 5990
2Ch 9:29 not written in the records of N the prophet, 5990
29:25 and Gad the king's seer and N the prophet; 5990
Ezr 8:16 Shemaiah, Elnathan, Jarib, Elnathan, N, 5990
10:39 Shelemiah, N, Adaiah, 5990
Ps 51: T When the prophet N came to him 5990
Zec 12:12 the clan of the house of N and their wives, 5990
Lk 3:31 the son of Mattatha, the son *of* N, *3718*

NATHAN-MELECH (1)

2Ki 23:11 near the room of an official named N. 5994

NATHANAEL (6)

Jn 1:45 Philip found N and told him, *3720*
1:46 anything good come from there?" N asked. *3720*
1:47 When Jesus saw N approaching, *3720*
1:48 "How do you know me?" N asked. *3720*
1:49 Then N declared, "Rabbi, you are the Son *3720*
21: 2 N from Cana in Galilee, *3720*

NATION (155) [NATIONAL, NATIONALITIES, NATIONALITY, NATIONS, NATIONS']

Ge 12: 2 into a great n and I will bless you; 1580
15:14 But I will punish the n they serve as slaves, 1580
17:20 and I will make him into a great n. 1580
18:18 surely become a great and powerful n, 1580
20: 4 "Lord, will you destroy an innocent n? 1580
21:13 the son of the maidservant into a n also, 1580
21:18 for I will make him into a great n." 1580
35:11 A n and a community of nations will come 1580
46: 3 for I will make you into a great n there. 1580
Ex 9:24 the land of Egypt since it had become a n. 1580
19: 6 for me a kingdom of priests and a holy n.' 1580
23:27 into confusion every n you encounter. 6639
32:10 Then I will make you into a great n." 1580
33:13 Remember that this n is your people." 1580
34:10 before done in any n in all the world. 1580
Nu 14:12 into a n greater and stronger than they." 1580
Dt 4: 6 "Surely this great n is a wise 1580
4: 7 What other n is so great as 1580
4: 8 And what other n is so great as 1580
4:34 for himself one n out of another nation, 1580
4:34 for himself one nation out of another n, 1580
9:14 And I will make you into a n stronger 1580
26: 5 and lived there and became a great n, 1580
28:32 and daughters will be given to another n, 6639
28:36 the king you set over you to a n unknown 1580
28:49 The LORD will bring a n against you 1580
28:49 n whose language you will not understand, 1580
28:50 a fierce-looking n without respect for 1580
32:21 by a n that has no understanding. 1580
32:28 They are a n without sense, 1580
Jos 3:17 the whole n had completed the crossing 1580
4: 1 When the whole n had finished crossing 1580
5: 8 after the whole n had been circumcised, 1580
10:13 till the n avenged itself on its enemies, 1580
Jdg 2:20 "Because this n has violated the covenant 1580
2Sa 7:23 the one n on earth that God went out 1580
1Ki 5: 7 a wise son to rule over this great n." 6639
18:10 not a n or kingdom where my master has 1580
18:10 a n or kingdom claimed you were not there, 1580
2Ki 18:33 the god of any n ever delivered his land 1580
1Ch 16:20 they wandered from n to nation, 1580
16:20 they wandered from nation to n, 1580
17:21 the one n on earth whose God went out 1580
2Ch 15: 6 *One* n was being crushed by another 1580
32:15 of any n or kingdom has been able 1580
Job 34:29 Yet he is over man and n alike, 1580
Ps 33:12 Blessed is the n whose God is the LORD, 1580
43: 1 and plead my cause against an ungodly n; 1580
83: 4 they say, "let us destroy them as a n, 1580
105:13 they wandered from n to nation, 1580
105:13 they wandered from nation to n, 1580
106: 5 the joy of your n and join your inheritance 1580
147:20 He has done this for no other n; 1580
Pr 11:14 For lack of guidance a n falls, 6639
14:34 Righteousness exalts a n, 1580
Isa 1: 4 Ah, sinful n, a people loaded with guilt, 1580
2: 4 N will not take up sword against nation, 1580
2: 4 Nation will not take up sword against n, 1580
9: 3 the n and increased their joy; 1580
10: 6 I send him against a godless n, 1580
14:32 be given to the envoys of that n? 1580
18: 2 an aggressive n *of* strange speech, 1580
18: 7 an aggressive n *of* strange speech, 1580
26: 2 the gates that the righteous n may enter, 1580
26: 2 the n that keeps faith. NIH
26:15 You have enlarged the n, O LORD; 1580
26:15 you have enlarged the n. 1580
30: 6 the humps of camels, to that unprofitable n, 6639
36:18 the god of any n ever delivered his land 1580
49: 7 and abhorred by the n, to the servant 1580
51: 4 "Listen to me, my people; hear me, my n: 4211
58: 2 as if they were a n that does what is right 1580
60:12 For the n or kingdom that will 1580
60:22 the smallest a mighty n. 1580
65: 1 To a n that did not call on my name, I said, 1580
66: 8 a day or a n be brought forth in a moment? 1580
Jer 2:11 Has a n ever changed its gods? 1580
3:19 the most beautiful inheritance of *any* n.' 1580
5: 9 "Should I not avenge myself on such a n 1580
5:15 "I am bringing a distant n against you— 1580
5:15 an ancient and enduring n, 1580
5:29 "Should I not avenge myself on such a n 1580
6:22 a great n is being stirred up from the ends 1580
7:28 'This is the n that has not obeyed 1580
8: 3 the survivors of this evil n will prefer death 5476
9: 9 "Should I not avenge myself on such a n 1580
12:17 But if any n does not listen, 1580
18: 7 that a n or kingdom is to be uprooted, 1580
18: 8 and if that n I warned repents of its evil, 1580
18: 9 And if at another time I announce that a n 1580
19:11 I will smash this n and this city just 6639
25:12 I will punish the king of Babylon and his n, 1580
25:32 Disaster is spreading from n to nation; 1580
25:32 Disaster is spreading from nation to n; 1580
27: 8 any n or kingdom will not serve 1580
27: 8 I will punish that n with the sword, 1580
27:11 if any n will bow its neck under the yoke of 1580
27:11 I will let that n remain in its own land to 2257S
27:13 the LORD has threatened any n that will 1580
28:15 you have persuaded this n to trust in lies. 6639
31:36 of Israel ever cease to be a n before me." 1580
33:24 and no longer regard them as a n. 1580
48: 2 'Come, let us put an end to that n.' 1580
48:42 be destroyed as a n because she defied 6639
49:31 "Arise and attack a n at ease, 1580
49:31 "a n that has neither gates nor bars; NIH
49:36 to the four winds, and there will not be a n 1580
50: 3 A n from the north will attack her 1580
50:41 a great n and many kings are being stirred 1580
La 4:17 from our towers we watched for a n 1580
Eze 2: 3 a rebellious n that has rebelled against me; 1580
36:13 "You devour men and deprive your n 1580
36:14 or make your n childless, 1580
36:15 the scorn of the peoples or cause your n 1580

Eze 37:22 I will make them one **n** in the land, 1580
Da 3:29 Therefore I decree that the people of any **n** 10040
8:22 that will emerge from his **n** but will 1580
Joel 1:6 A **n** has invaded my land, 1580
3:8 sell them to the Sabeans, a **n** far away." 1580
Am 6:1 you notable men of the foremost **n**, 1580
6:14 "I will stir up a **n** against you, 1580
Mic 4:3 **N** will not take up sword against nation, 1580
4:3 Nation will not take up sword against **n**, 1580
4:7 those driven away a strong **n**. 1580
Hab 3:16 of calamity to come on the **n** invading us. 6639
Zep 2:1 gather together, O shameful **n**, 1580
2:9 of my **n** will inherit their land." 1580
Hag 2:14 with this people and this **n** in my sight,' 1580
Mal 3:9 under a curse—the whole **n** of you— 1580
Mt 24:7 **N** will rise against nation, *1620*
24:7 Nation will rise against **n**, *1620*
Mk 13:8 **N** will rise against nation, *1620*
13:8 Nation will rise against **n**, *1620*
Lk 7:5 because he loves our **n** *1620*
21:10 "**N** will rise against nation, *1620*
21:10 "Nation will rise against **n**, *1620*
23:2 "We have found this man subverting our **n**. *1620*
Jn 11:48 and take away both our place and our **n**." *1620*
11:50 the people than that the whole **n** perish." *1620*
11:51 that Jesus would die for the Jewish **n**, *1620*
11:52 for that **n** but also for the scattered children *1620*
Ac 2:5 from every **n** under heaven. *1620*
7:7 I will punish the **n** they serve as slaves,' *1620*
10:35 but accepts men from every **n** who fear him *1620*
17:26 From one man he made every **n** of men, *1620*
24:2 has brought about reforms *in* this **n**. *1620*
24:10 of years you have been a judge *over* this **n**; *1620*
Ro 10:19 envious by those who are not a **n**; *1620*
10:19 angry by a **n** that has no understanding." *1620*
1Pe 2:9 a holy **n**, a people belonging to God, *1620*
Rev 5:9 and language and people and **n**. *1620*
7:9 from every **n**, tribe, people and language, *1620*
11:9 language and **n** will gaze on their bodies *1620*
13:7 people, language and **n**. *1620*
14:6 to every **n**, tribe, language and people. *1620*

NATIONAL (1) [NATION]

2Ki 17:29 **each n group** made its own gods in 1580+1580

NATIONALITIES (2) [NATION]

Est 8:17 And many people of **other n** became Jews 824+2021+6639
9:2 the people of all the other **n** were afraid 6639

NATIONALITY (5) [NATION]

Est 2:10 not revealed her **n** and family background, 6639
2:20 and **n** just as Mordecai had told her to do, 6639
3:14 and made known to the people of every **n** NIH
8:11 kill and annihilate any armed force of any **n** 6639
8:13 of every **n** so that the Jews would be ready 6639

NATIONS (559) [NATION]

Ge 10:5 by their clans within their **n**, 1580
10:20 in their territories and **n**. 1580
10:31 in their territories and **n**. 1580
10:32 to their lines of descent, within their **n**. 1580
10:32 From these the **n** spread out over the earth 1580
17:4 You will be the father of many **n**. 1580
17:5 for I have made you a father of many **n**. 1580
17:6 I will make **n** of you, 1580
17:16 so that she will be the mother of **n**; 1580
18:18 all **n** *on* earth will be blessed through him. 1580
22:18 through your offspring all **n** *on* earth will 1580
25:23 "Two **n** are in your womb, 1580
26:4 through your offspring all **n** *on* earth will 1580
27:29 May **n** serve you and peoples bow down 6639
35:11 and a community of **n** will come from you, 1580
48:19 his descendants will become a group of **n**." 1580
49:10 and the obedience of the **n** is his. 6639
Ex 15:14 The **n** will hear and tremble; 6639
19:5 then out of all **n** you will be my treasured 6639
34:24 I will drive out **n** before you 1580
Lev 18:24 because this is how the **n** that I am going 1580
18:28 it will vomit you out as it vomited out the **n** 1580
20:23 the customs of the **n** I am going to drive out 1580
20:24 who has set you apart from the **n**. 6639
20:26 and I have set you apart from the **n** to 6639
25:44 and female slaves are to come from the **n** 1580
26:33 among the **n** and will draw out my sword 1580
26:38 You will perish among the **n**; 1580
26:45 in the sight of the **n** to be their God. 1580
Nu 14:15 the **n** who have heard this report 1580
23:9 not consider themselves one of the **n**. 1580
24:8 They devour hostile **n** 1580
24:20 "Amalek was first among the **n**, 1580
Dt 2:25 to put the terror and fear of you on all the **n** 6639
4:6 and understanding to the **n**, 6639
4:19 to all the **n** under heaven. 6639
4:27 the **n** to which the LORD will drive you. 1580
4:38 before you **n** greater and stronger than you 1580
7:1 and drives out before you many **n**— 1580
7:1 seven **n** larger and stronger than you— 1580
7:17 "These **n** are stronger than we are. 1580
7:22 The LORD your God will drive out those **n** 1580
8:20 the **n** the LORD destroyed before you, 1580
9:1 the Jordan to go in and dispossess **n** greater 1580
9:4 on account of the wickedness of these **n** 1580
9:5 on account of the wickedness of these **n**, 1580
Dt 10:15 their descendants, above all the **n**, 6639
11:23 then the LORD will drive out all these **n** 1580
11:23 and you will dispossess **n** larger 1580
12:2 **n** you are dispossessing worship their gods. 1580
12:29 before you the **n** you are about to invade 1580
12:30 saying, "How do these **n** serve their gods? 1580
15:6 lend to many **n** but will borrow from none. 1580
15:6 over many **n** but none will rule over you. 1580
17:14 a king over us like all the **n** around us," 1580
18:9 the detestable ways of the **n** there. 1580
18:12 the LORD your God will drive out **those n** 4392[S]
18:14 The **n** you will dispossess listen 1580
19:1 the **n** whose land he is giving you, 1580
20:15 and do not belong to the **n** nearby. 1580
20:16 the **n** the LORD your God is giving you as 6639
26:19 and honor high above all the **n** he has made 1580
28:1 above all the **n** *on* earth. 1580
28:12 You will lend to many **n** but will borrow 1580
28:37 an object of scorn and ridicule to all the **n** 6639
28:64 the LORD will scatter you among all **n**, 6639
28:65 Among those **n** you will find no repose, 1580
29:18 to go and worship the gods of those **n**; 1580
29:24 All the **n** will ask: 1580
30:1 LORD your God disperses you among the **n**, 1580
30:3 on you and gather you again from all the **n** 6639
31:3 He will destroy these **n** before you, 1580
32:8 the Most High gave the **n** their inheritance, 1580
32:43 Rejoice, O **n**, with his people, 1580
33:17 With them he will gore the **n**, 6639
Jos 23:3 to all these **n** for your sake; 1580
23:4 for your tribes all the land of the **n** 1580
23:4 the **n** I conquered— 1580
23:7 Do not associate with these **n** that remain 1580
23:9 before you great and powerful **n**; 1580
23:12 with the survivors of these **n** that remain 1580
23:13 LORD your God will no longer drive out
these **n** before you. 1580
24:17 among all the **n** through which we traveled. 6639
24:18 the LORD drove out before us all the **n**, 6639
Jdg 2:21 before them any of the **n** Joshua left 1580
2:23 The LORD had allowed those **n** to remain; 1580
3:1 These are the **n** the LORD left 1580
1Sa 8:5 such as all the other **n** have." 1580
8:20 Then we will be like all the other **n**, 1580
2Sa 7:23 and awesome wonders by driving out **n** 1580
8:11 and gold from all the **n** he had subdued: 1580
22:44 you have preserved me as the head of **n**. 1580
22:48 who puts the **n** under me, 6639
22:50 I will praise you, O LORD, among the **n**; 1580
1Ki 4:31 his fame spread to all the surrounding **n**. 1580
4:34 Men of all **n** came to listen 6639
8:53 For you singled them out from all the **n** *of* 6639
11:2 from **n** about which the LORD had told 1580
14:24 of the **n** the LORD had driven out before 1580
2Ki 16:3 of the **n** the LORD had driven out before 1580
17:8 of the **n** the LORD had driven out 1580
17:11 as the **n** whom the LORD had driven out 1580
17:15 They imitated the **n** around them although 1580
17:33 of the **n** from which they had been brought. 1580
19:12 Did the gods of the **n** that were destroyed 1580
19:17 the Assyrian kings have laid waste these **n** 1580
21:2 following the detestable practices of the **n** 1580
21:9 the **n** the LORD had destroyed before 1580
1Ch 14:17 and the LORD made all the **n** fear him. 1580
16:8 among the **n** what he has done. 6639
16:24 Declare his glory among the **n**, 1580
16:26 For all the gods of the **n** are idols, 6639
16:28 Ascribe to the LORD, O families of **n**, 6639
16:31 let them say among the **n**, 1580
16:35 gather us and deliver us from the **n**, 1580
17:21 by driving out **n** from before your people, 1580
18:11 and gold he had taken from all these **n**: 1580
22:5 and splendor in the sight of all the **n**. 824
2Ch 20:6 You rule over all the kingdoms of the **n**. 1580
28:3 of the **n** the LORD had driven out before 1580
32:13 of those **n** ever able to deliver their land 824+1580
32:14 Who of all the gods of these **n** 1580
32:23 then on he was highly regarded by all the **n**. 1580
33:2 following the detestable practices of the **n** 1580
33:9 the **n** the LORD had destroyed before 1580
36:14 practices of the **n** and defiling the temple of 1580
Ne 1:8 I will scatter you among the **n**, 6639
5:17 to us from the surrounding **n**. 1580
6:6 "It is reported among the **n**— 1580
6:16 all the surrounding **n** were afraid 1580
9:22 "You gave them kingdoms and **n**, 6639
13:26 the many **n** there was no king like him. 1580
Job 12:23 He makes **n** great, and destroys them; 1580
12:23 he enlarges **n**, and disperses them. 1580
36:31 the way he governs the **n** and provides food 6639
Ps 2:1 Why do the **n** conspire and the peoples plot 1580
2:8 and I will make the **n** your inheritance, 1580
9:5 You have rebuked the **n** and destroyed 1580
9:11 proclaim among the **n** what he has done. 6639
9:15 **n** have fallen into the pit they have dug; 1580
9:17 all the **n** that forget God. 1580
9:19 let the **n** be judged in your presence. 1580
9:20 let the **n** know they are but men. 1580
10:16 the **n** will perish from his land. 1580
18:43 you have made me the head of **n**; 1580
18:47 who subdues **n** under me, 6639
18:49 Therefore I will praise you among the **n**, 1580
22:27 and all the families of the **n** will bow down 1580
22:28 to the LORD and he rules over the **n**. 1580
33:10 The LORD foils the plans of the **n**; 1580
44:2 With your hand you drove out the **n** 1580
44:11 and have scattered us among the **n**. 1580
Ps 44:14 You have made us a byword among the **n**; 1580
45:5 let the **n** fall beneath your feet. 6639
45:17 the **n** will praise you for ever and ever. 6639
46:6 **N** are in uproar, kingdoms fall; 1580
46:10 I will be exalted among the **n**, 1580
47:1 Clap your hands, all you **n**; 6639
47:3 He subdued **n** under us, 6639
47:8 God reigns over the **n**; 1580
47:9 The nobles of the **n** assemble as the people 6639
56:7 in your anger, O God, bring down the **n**. 6639
57:9 I will praise you, O Lord, among the **n**; 6639
59:5 rouse yourself to punish all the **n**; 1580
59:8 you scoff at all those **n**. 1580
65:7 and the turmoil of the **n**. 4211
66:7 his eyes watch the **n**— 1580
67:2 your salvation among all **n**. 1580
67:4 May the **n** be glad and sing for joy, 4211
67:4 the peoples justly and guide the **n** of 4211
68:30 the herd of bulls among the calves of the **n**. 6639
68:30 Scatter the **n** who delight in war. 6639
72:11 down to him and all **n** will serve him. 1580
72:17 All **n** will be blessed through him, 1580
78:55 He drove out **n** before them 1580
79:1 the **n** have invaded your inheritance; 1580
79:6 on the **n** that do not acknowledge you, 1580
79:10 Why should the **n** say, 1580
79:10 make known among the **n** that you avenge 1580
80:8 you drove out the **n** and planted it. 1580
82:8 for all the **n** are your inheritance. 1580
86:9 All the **n** you have made will come 1580
89:50 I bear in my heart the taunts of all the **n**, 6639
94:10 Does he who disciplines **n** not punish? 1580
96:3 Declare his glory among the **n**, 1580
96:5 For all the gods of the **n** are idols, 6639
96:7 Ascribe to the LORD, O families of **n**, 6639
96:10 Say among the **n**, "The LORD reigns." 1580
98:2 and revealed his righteousness to the **n**. 1580
99:1 The LORD reigns, let the **n** tremble; 6639
99:2 he is exalted over all the **n**. 6639
102:15 The **n** will fear the name of the LORD, 1580
105:1 among the **n** what he has done. 6639
105:44 the lands of the **n**, and they fell heir 1580
106:27 the **n** and scatter them throughout the lands. 1580
106:35 with the **n** and adopted their customs. 1580
106:41 He handed them over to the **n**, 1580
106:47 and gather us from the **n**, 1580
108:3 I will praise you, O LORD, among the **n**; 6639
110:6 He will judge the **n**, 1580
111:6 giving them the lands of other **n**. 1580
113:4 The LORD is exalted over all the **n**, 1580
115:2 Why do the **n** say, "Where is their God?" 1580
117:1 Praise the LORD, all you **n**; 1580
118:10 All the **n** surrounded me, 1580
126:2 Then it was said among the **n**, 1580
135:10 down many **n** and killed mighty kings 1580
135:15 The idols of the **n** are silver and gold, 1580
148:11 kings of the earth and all **n**, 4211
149:7 on the **n** and punishment on the peoples, 1580
Pr 24:24 and **n** denounce him. 4211
Isa 2:2 and all **n** will stream to it. 1580
2:4 He will judge between the **n** 1580
5:26 He lifts up a banner for the distant **n**, 1580
8:9 Raise the war cry, you **n**, and be shattered! 6639
10:7 to put an end to many **n**. 1580
10:13 I removed the boundaries of **n**, 6639
10:14 my hand reached for the wealth of the **n**; 6639
11:10 the **n** will rally to him, 1580
11:12 He will raise a banner for the **n** and gather 1580
12:4 among the **n** what he has done, 6639
13:4 like **n** massing together! 1580
14:2 **N** will take them and bring them 6639
14:2 of Israel will possess **the n** as menservants 4392[S]
14:6 in fury subdued **n** with relentless aggression 1580
14:9 all those who were kings over the **n**. 1580
14:12 you who once laid low the **n**! 1580
14:18 All the kings of the **n** lie in state, 1580
14:26 this is the hand stretched out over all **n**. 1580
16:8 The rulers of the **n** have trampled down 1580
17:12 Oh, the raging of many **n**— 6639
23:3 and she became the marketplace of the **n**. 1580
24:13 So will it be on the earth and among the **n**, 6639
25:3 cities of ruthless **n** will revere you. 1580
25:7 the sheet that covers all **n**; 1580
29:7 hordes of all the **n** that fight against Ariel, 1580
29:8 of all the **n** that fight against Mount Zion. 1580
30:28 He shakes the **n** in the sieve of destruction; 1580
33:3 when you rise up, the **n** scatter. 1580
33:4 O **n**, is harvested as by young locusts; NIH
34:1 Come near, you **n**, and listen; 1580
34:2 The LORD is angry with all **n**; 1580
37:12 Did the gods of the **n** that were destroyed 1580
40:15 Surely the **n** are like a drop in a bucket; 1580
40:17 Before him all the **n** are as nothing; 1580
41:1 Let the **n** renew their strength! 4211
41:2 He hands **n** over to him and subdues kings 1580
42:1 on him and he will bring justice to the **n**. 1580
43:9 All the **n** gather together and 1580
45:1 of to subdue **n** before him and to strip kings 1580
45:20 assemble, you fugitives from the **n**. 1580
49:1 hear this, you distant **n**: 4211
51:4 my justice will become a light to the **n**. 6639
51:5 and my arm will bring justice to the **n**. 6639
52:10 bare his holy arm in the sight of all the **n**, 1580
52:15 so will he sprinkle many **n**, 1580
54:3 your descendants will dispossess **n** 1580
55:5 Surely you will summon **n** you know not, 1580
55:5 **n** that do not know you will hasten to you, 1580

Isa 56: 7 be called a house of prayer for all **n**." 6639
60: 3 **N** will come to your light, 1580
60: 5 to you the riches of the **n** will come. 1580
60: 11 that men may bring you the wealth of the **n** 1580
60: 16 the milk of **n** and be nursed at royal breasts. 1580
61: 6 You will feed on the wealth of **n**, 1580
61: 9 be known among the **n** and their offspring 1580
61: 11 and praise spring up before all **n**. 1580
62: 2 The **n** will see your righteousness, 1580
62: 10 Raise a banner for the **n**. 6639
63: 3 from the **n** no one was with me. 6639
63: 6 I trampled the **n** in my anger; 6639
64: 2 to your enemies and cause the **n** to quake 1580
66: 12 and the wealth of **n** like a flooding stream; 1580
66: 18 about to come and gather all **n** and tongues, 1580
66: 19 of those who survive to the **n**— 1580
66: 19 They will proclaim my glory among the **n**. 1580
66: 20 the **n**, to my holy mountain in Jerusalem as 1580
Jer 1: 5 I appointed you as a prophet to the **n**." 1580
1: 10 today I appoint you over **n** and kingdoms 1580
3: 17 and all **n** will gather in Jerusalem to honor 1580
4: 2 then the **n** will be blessed by him and 1580
4: 7 a destroyer of **n** has set out. 1580
4: 16 "Tell this to the **n**, proclaim it to Jerusalem: 1580
6: 18 Therefore hear, O **n**; observe, 1580
9: 16 I will scatter them among **n** 1580
9: 26 For all these **n** are really uncircumcised, 1580
10: 2 the ways of the **n** or be terrified by signs in 1580
10: 2 though the **n** are terrified by them. 1580
10: 7 O King of the **n**? 1580
10: 7 Among all the wise men of the **n** and 1580
10: 10 the **n** cannot endure his wrath. 1580
10: 25 on the **n** that do not acknowledge you, 1580
14: 22 of the worthless idols of the **n** bring rain? 1580
16: 19 the **n** will come from the ends of the earth 1580
18: 13 "Inquire among the **n**: 1580
22: 8 "People from many **n** will pass by this city 1580
25: 9 and against all the surrounding **n**. 1580
25: 11 and these **n** will serve the king 1580
25: 13 by Jeremiah against all the **n**. 1580
25: 14 be enslaved by many **n** and great kings; 1580
25: 15 the wine of my wrath and make all the **n** 1580
25: 17 from the LORD's hand and made all the **n** 1580
25: 31 the LORD will bring charges against the **n**; 1580
26: 6 of cursing among all the **n** *of* the earth.' " 1580
27: 7 All **n** will serve him and his son 1580
27: 7 then many **n** and great kings will subjugate 1580
28: 11 the neck of all the **n** within two years.' " 1580
28: 14 an iron yoke on the necks of all these **n** 1580
29: 14 I will gather you from all the **n** and places 1580
29: 18 among all the **n** where I drive them. 1580
30: 11 'Though I completely destroy all the **n** 1580
31: 7 shout for the foremost of the **n**. 1580
31: 10 "Hear the word of the LORD, O **n**; 1580
33: 9 and honor before all **n** *on* earth that hear 1580
36: 2 the other **n** from the time I began speaking 1580
43: 5 to live in the land of Judah from all the **n** 1580
44: 8 of cursing and reproach among all the **n** 1580
46: 1 to Jeremiah the prophet concerning the **n**: 1580
46: 12 The **n** will hear of your shame; 1580
46: 28 "Though I completely destroy all the **n** 1580
49: 14 An envoy was sent to the **n** to say, 1580
49: 15 "Now I will make you small among the **n**, 1580
50: 2 and proclaim among the **n**, lift up a banner 1580
50: 9 against Babylon an alliance of great **n** from 1580
50: 12 She will be the least of the **n**— 1580
50: 23 How desolate is Babylon among the **n**! 1580
50: 46 its cry will resound among the **n**. 1580
51: 7 The **n** drank her wine; 1580
51: 20 with you I shatter **n**, 1580
51: 27 Blow the trumpet among the **n**! 1580
51: 27 Prepare the **n** for battle against her; 1580
51: 28 Prepare the **n** for battle against her— 1580
51: 41 a horror Babylon will be among the **n**! 1580
51: 44 The **n** will no longer stream to him. 1580
La 1: 1 who once was great among the **n**! 1580
1: 3 She dwells among the **n**; 1580
1: 10 she saw **pagan n** enter her sanctuary— 1580
2: 9 and her princes are exiled among the **n**, 1580
3: 45 and refuse among the **n**. 6639
4: 15 people among the **n** say, 1580
4: 20 under his shadow we would live among the **n**. 1580
Eze 4: 13 of Israel will eat defiled food among the **n** 1580
5: 5 which I have set in the center of the **n**, 1580
5: 6 and decrees more than the **n** and countries 1580
5: 7 You have been more unruly than the **n** 1580
5: 7 even conformed to the standards of the **n** 1580
5: 8 punishment on you in the sight of the **n**. 1580
5: 14 and a reproach among the **n** around you, 1580
5: 15 the **n** around you when I inflict punishment 1580
6: 8 among the lands and **n**. 1580
6: 9 the **n** where they have been carried captive, 1580
7: 24 the most wicked of the **n** to take possession 1580
11: 12 to the standards of the **n** around you." 1580
11: 16 Although I sent them far away among the **n** 1580
11: 17 the **n** and bring you back from the countries 6639
12: 15 among the **n** and scatter them through 1580
12: 16 so that in the **n** where they go 1580
16: 14 among the **n** on account of your beauty, 1580
19: 4 The **n** heard about him, 1580
19: 8 Then the **n** came against him, 1580
20: 9 in the eyes of the **n** they lived among and 1580
20: 14 from being profaned in the eyes of the **n** 1580
20: 22 from being profaned in the eyes of the **n** 1580
20: 23 that I would disperse them among the **n** 1580
20: 32 " 'You say, "We want to be like the **n**, 1580
Eze 20: 34 I will bring you from the **n** and gather you 6639
20: 35 I will bring you into the desert of the **n** 6639
20: 41 the **n** and gather you from the countries 6639
20: 41 among you in the sight of the **n**. 1580
22: 4 of scorn to the **n** and a laughingstock to all 1580
22: 15 the **n** and scatter you through the countries; 1580
22: 16 you have been defiled in the eyes of the **n**, 1580
23: 30 the **n** and defiled yourself with their idols. 1580
25: 7 and give you as plunder to the **n**. 1580
25: 7 from the **n** and exterminate you from 6639
25: 8 of Judah has become like all the other **n**," 1580
25: 10 not be remembered among the **n**; 1580
26: 2 The gate to the **n** is broken, 6639
26: 3 and I will bring many **n** against you, 1580
26: 5 She will become plunder for the **n**, 1580
27: 33 you satisfied many **n**; 6639
27: 36 The merchants among the **n** hiss at you; 6639
28: 7 the most ruthless of **n**; 1580
28: 19 the **n** who knew you are appalled at you; 6639
28: 25 from the **n** where they have been scattered, 6639
28: 25 among them in the sight of the **n**. 1580
29: 12 the Egyptians among the **n** and scatter them 1580
29: 13 from the **n** where they were scattered. 6639
29: 15 never again exalt itself above the other **n**. 1580
29: 15 that it will never again rule over the **n**. 1580
30: 3 a day of clouds, a time of doom for the **n**. 1580
30: 11 He and his army—the most ruthless of **n**— 1580
30: 23 the Egyptians among the **n** and scatter them 1580
30: 26 the Egyptians among the **n** and scatter them 1580
31: 6 all the great **n** lived in its shade. 1580
31: 11 I handed it over to the ruler of the **n**, 1580
31: 12 the most ruthless of foreign **n** cut it down 1580
31: 12 All the **n** *of* the earth came out from 6639
31: 16 I made the **n** tremble at the sound of its fall 1580
31: 17 its allies among the **n**, 1580
32: 2 " 'You are like a lion among the **n**; 1580
32: 9 about your destruction among the **n**, 1580
32: 12 the most ruthless of all **n**. 1580
32: 16 The daughters of the **n** will chant it; 1580
32: 18 both her and the daughters of mighty **n**, 1580
34: 13 the **n** and gather them from the countries, 6639
34: 28 They will no longer be plundered by the **n**, 1580
34: 29 in the land or bear the scorn of the **n**. 1580
35: 10 "These two **n** and countries will be ours 1580
36: 3 the possession of the rest of the **n** and 1580
36: 4 by the rest of the **n** around you— 1580
36: 5 against the rest of the **n**, 1580
36: 6 you have suffered the scorn of the **n**. 1580
36: 7 that the **n** around you will also suffer scorn. 1580
36: 15 will I make you hear the taunts of the **n**, 1580
36: 19 I dispersed them among the **n**, 1580
36: 20 among the **n** they profaned my holy name, 1580
36: 21 the house of Israel profaned among the **n** 1580
36: 22 which you have profaned among the **n** 1580
36: 23 which has been profaned among the **n**, 1580
36: 23 Then the **n** will know that I am the LORD, 1580
36: 24 " 'For I will take you out of the **n**; 1580
36: 30 among the **n** because of famine. 1580
36: 36 the **n** around you that remain will know 1580
37: 21 I will take the Israelites out of the **n** 1580
37: 22 and they will never again be two **n** 1580
37: 28 Then the **n** will know that I the LORD 1580
38: 6 the many **n** with you. 6639
38: 8 whose people were gathered from many **n** 6639
38: 8 They had been brought out from the **n**, 6639
38: 9 the many **n** with you will go up, advancing 6639
38: 12 and the people gathered from the **n**, 1580
38: 15 you and many **n** with you, 6639
38: 16 so that the **n** may know me 1580
38: 22 on his troops and on the many **n** with him. 6639
38: 23 make myself known in the sight of many **n**. 1580
39: 4 you and all your troops and the **n** with you. 6639
39: 7 and the **n** will know that I the LORD am 1580
39: 21 "I will display my glory among the **n**, 1580
39: 21 the **n** will see the punishment I inflict and 1580
39: 23 And the **n** will know that the people 1580
39: 27 When I have brought them back from the **n** 6639
39: 27 through them in the sight of many **n**. 1580
39: 28 though I sent them into exile among the **n**, 1580
Da 3: 4 O peoples, **n** and men of every language: 10040
3: 7 **n** and men of every language fell down 10040
4: 1 **n** and men of every language, 10040
5: 19 and **n** and men of every language dreaded 10040
6: 25 **n** and men of every language throughout 10040
7: 14 all peoples, **n** and men of every language 10040
12: 1 not happened from the beginning of **n** 1580
Hos 7: 8 "Ephraim mixes with the **n**; 6639
8: 8 she is among the **n** like a worthless thing. 1580
8: 10 they have sold themselves among the **n**, 1580
9: 1 do not be jubilant like the other **n**. 6639
9: 17 they will be wanderers among the **n**. 1580
10: 10 **n** will be gathered against them to put them 6639
Joel 2: 6 At the sight of them, **n** are in anguish; 6639
2: 17 a byword among the **n**. 1580
2: 19 an object of scorn to the **n**. 1580
3: 2 I will gather all **n** and bring them down to 1580
3: 2 for they scattered my people among the **n** 1580
3: 9 Proclaim this among the **n**: 1580
3: 11 Come quickly, all you **n** from every side, 1580
3: 12 "Let the **n** be roused; 1580
3: 12 for there I will sit to judge all the **n** 1580
Am 9: 9 of Israel among all the **n** as grain is shaken 1580
9: 12 of Edom and all the **n** that bear my name," 1580
Ob 1: 1 An envoy was sent to the **n** to say, "Rise, 1580
1: 2 I will make you small among the **n**; 1580
1: 15 "The day of the LORD is near for all **n**. 1580
1: 16 so all the **n** will drink continually; 1580
Mic 4: 2 Many **n** will come and say, "Come, 1580
4: 3 and will settle disputes for strong **n** far 1580
4: 5 the **n** may walk in the name of their gods; 6639
4: 11 But now many **n** are gathered against you. 1580
4: 13 and you will break to pieces many **n**." 6639
5: 8 The remnant of Jacob will be among the **n**, 1580
5: 15 in anger and wrath upon the **n** that have 1580
6: 16 you will bear the scorn of the **n**." 6639
7: 16 **N** will see and be ashamed, 1580
Na 3: 4 who enslaved **n** by her prostitution 1580
3: 5 I will show the **n** your nakedness and 1580
Hab 1: 5 "Look at the **n** and watch— 1580
1: 17 destroying **n** without mercy? 1580
2: 5 to himself all the **n** and takes captive all 1580
2: 8 Because you have plundered many **n**, 1580
2: 13 that the **n** exhaust themselves for nothing? 4211
3: 6 he looked, and made the **n** tremble. 1580
3: 12 the earth and in anger you threshed the **n**. 1580
Zep 2: 11 The **n** on every shore will worship him, 1580
3: 6 "I have cut off **n**; their strongholds 1580
3: 8 I have decided to assemble the **n**, 1580
Hag 2: 7 I will shake all **n**, 1580
2: 7 and the desired of all **n** will come, 1580
Zec 1: 15 I am very angry with the **n** that feel secure. 1580
1: 21 of the **n** who lifted up their horns against 1580
2: 8 against the **n** that have plundered you— 1580
2: 11 "Many **n** will be joined with the LORD in 1580
7: 14 with a whirlwind among all the **n**, 1580
8: 13 an object of cursing among the **n**, 1580
8: 22 and powerful **n** will come to Jerusalem 1580
8: 23 and **n** will take firm hold of one Jew by 1580
9: 10 He will proclaim peace to the **n**. 1580
11: 10 the covenant I had made with all the **n**. 6639
12: 3 the **n** *of* the earth are gathered against her, 1580
12: 3 an immovable rock for all the **n**. 6639
12: 4 but I will blind all the horses of the **n**. 6639
12: 9 to destroy all the **n** that attack Jerusalem. 1580
14: 2 I will gather all the **n** to Jerusalem to fight 1580
14: 3 and fight against those **n**, 1580
14: 12 with which the LORD will strike all the **n** 6639
14: 14 of all the surrounding **n** will be collected— 1580
14: 16 the **n** that have attacked Jerusalem will go 1580
14: 18 on them the plague he inflicts on the **n** 1580
14: 19 the punishment of all the **n** that do not go 1580
Mal 1: 11 My name will be great among the **n**, 1580
1: 11 my name will be great among the **n**," 1580
1: 14 "and my name is to be feared among the **n**. 1580
3: 12 "Then all the **n** will call you blessed, 1580
Mt 12: 18 and he will proclaim justice *to* the **n**. *1620*
12: 21 In his name the **n** will put their hope." *1620*
24: 9 you will be hated by all **n** because of me. *1620*
24: 14 in the whole world as a testimony *to* all **n**, *1620*
24: 30 and all the **n** of the earth will mourn. *5876*
25: 32 All the **n** will be gathered before him, *1620*
28: 19 Therefore go and make disciples of all **n**, *1620*
Mk 11: 17 be called a house of prayer *for* all **n**'? *1620*
13: 10 the gospel must first be preached to all **n**. *1620*
Lk 21: 24 and will be taken as prisoners to all the **n**. *1620*
21: 25 **n** will be in anguish and perplexity at *1620*
24: 47 be preached in his name to all **n**, *1620*
Ac 4: 25 " 'Why do the **n** rage and the peoples plot *1620*
7: 45 *from* the **n** God drove out before them. *1620*
13: 19 he overthrew seven **n** in Canaan *1620*
14: 16 In the past, he let all **n** go their own way. *1620*
Ro 4: 17 "I have made you a father *of* many **n**." *1620*
4: 18 and so became the father *of* many **n**, *1620*
15: 12 one who will arise to rule over the **n**; *1620*
16: 26 so that all **n** might believe and obey him— *1620*
Gal 3: 8 "All **n** will be blessed through you." *1620*
1Ti 3: 16 was preached among the **n**, *1620*
Jas 1: 1 To the twelve tribes scattered among the **n**: *NIG*
Rev 2: 26 I will give authority over the **n**— *1620*
10: 11 many peoples, **n**, languages and kings." *1620*
11: 18 The **n** were angry; *1620*
12: 5 who will rule all the **n** with an iron scepter. *1620*
14: 8 the **n** drink the maddening wine *1620*
15: 4 All **n** will come and worship before you, *1620*
16: 19 and the cities *of* the **n** collapsed. *1620*
17: 15 are peoples, multitudes, **n** and languages. *1620*
18: 3 the **n** have drunk the maddening wine *1620*
18: 23 your magic spell all the **n** were led astray. *1620*
19: 15 with which to strike down the **n**. *1620*
20: 3 to keep him from deceiving the **n** anymore *1620*
20: 8 the **n** in the four corners of the earth— *1620*
21: 24 The **n** will walk by its light, *1620*
21: 26 and honor *of* the **n** will be brought into it. *1620*
22: 2 of the tree are for the healing *of* the **n**. *1620*

NATIONS' (1) [NATION]

Jer 51: 58 the **n'** labor is only fuel for the flames." 4211

NATIVE (13) [NATIVES]

Ge 24: 7 of my father's household and my **n** land 4580
31: 13 at once and go back to your **n** land.' " 4580
Nu 22: 5 near the River, in his **n** land. 1201+6639
Ps 37: 35 like a green tree in its **n soil,** 275
Isa 13: 14 each will flee to his **n land.** 824
Jer 22: 10 nor see his **n** land again. 4580
46: 16 to our own people and our **n** lands, 4580
Am 7: 11 away from their **n land.'** " 141
7: 17 away from their **n land.'** " 141
Jn 8: 44 When he lies, he speaks **his n language,** *1666+2625+3836*
Ac 2: 8 each of us hears them in his own **n** language? *1164+1877+4005*

Ac 18: 2 a Jew named Aquila, a **n** of Pontus, *1169*
18:24 a Jew named Apollos, a **n** of Alexandria, *1169*

NATIVE-BORN (15) [BEAR]
Ex 12:19 whether he is an alien or **n.** 275+824+2021
12:49 to the **n** and to the alien living among you." 275
Lev 16:29 whether **n** or an alien living among you— 275
17:15 " 'Anyone, whether **n** or alien, 275
18:26 The **n** and the aliens living 275
19:34 with you must be treated as one of your **n.** 275
23:42 All **n** Israelites are to live in booths 275
24:16 Whether an alien or **n,** 275
24:22 the same law for the alien and the **n.** 275
Nu 9:14 for the alien and the **n.'** " 275+824
15:13 " 'Everyone who is **n** must do these things 275
15:29 whether he is a **n** Israelite or an alien. 275
15:30 whether **n** or alien, blasphemes the LORD, 275
1Ch 7:21 Ezer and Elead were killed by the **n** men 824+928+2021+3528
Eze 47:22 You are to consider them as **n** Israelites; 275

NATIVES (1) [NATIVE]
Eze 23:15 Babylonian chariot officers, **n** of Chaldea. 4580

NATIVITY (KJV) See ANCESTRY, BIRTH, HOMELAND, NATIVE

NATURAL (15) [NATURE]
Nu 16:29 If these men die a **n** death 132+2021+3869+3972
19:16 or *someone who has* **died a n death,** 4637
19:18 or someone *who has* **died a n death.** 4637
Jn 1:13 children born not of **n descent,** *135*
11:13 but his disciples thought he meant **n sleep.** *3122+3836+3836+5678*
Ro 1:26 Even their women exchanged **n** relations *5879*
1:27 also abandoned **n** relations with women *5879*
6:19 because you are weak *in* your **n selves.** *4922*
9: 8 not the **n** children who are God's children, *4922*
11:21 if God did not spare the **n** branches, *2848+5882*
11:24 the **n** branches, be grafted into their *2848+5882*
1Co 15:44 it is sown a **n** body, it is raised a spiritual *6035*
15:44 If there is a **n** body, there is also a spiritual *6035*
15:46 The spiritual did not come first, but the **n,** *6035*
Jude 1:19 who **follow mere n instincts** *6035*

NATURE (39) [NATURAL]
Ro 1: 3 to his **human n** was a descendant of David, *4922*
1:20 his eternal power and **divine n—** *2522*
2:14 do *by* **n** things required by the law, *5882*
7: 5 when we were controlled by the **sinful n,** *4922*
7:18 that is, in my **sinful n.** *4922*
7:25 *in* the **sinful n** a slave to the law of sin. *4922*
8: 3 in that it was weakened by the **sinful n,** *4922*
8: 4 to the **sinful n** but according to the Spirit. *4922*
8: 5 the **sinful n** have their minds set on what *4922*
8: 5 minds set on what that **n** desires; *4922*
8: 8 controlled by the **sinful n** cannot please God *4922*
8: 9 are controlled not by the **sinful n** but by *4922*
8:12 but it is not *to* the **sinful n,** *4922*
8:13 For if you live according to the **sinful n,** *4922*
11:24 of an olive tree that is wild by **n,** *5882*
11:24 and contrary to **n** were grafted into *5882*
13:14 how to gratify the desires *of* the **sinful n.** *4922*
1Co 5: 5 so that the **sinful n** may be destroyed *4922*
11:14 Does not the very **n** of things teach you that *5882*
Gal 4: 8 you were slaves to those who *by* **n** are *5882*
5:13 to indulge the **sinful n;** *4922*
5:16 not gratify the desires *of* the **sinful n.** *4922*
5:17 For the **sinful n** desires what is contrary to *4922*
5:17 the Spirit what is contrary to the **sinful n.** *4922*
5:19 The acts *of* the **sinful n** are obvious: *4922*
5:24 to Christ Jesus have crucified the **sinful n** *4922*
6: 8 The one who sows to please his **sinful n,** *4922*
6: 8 from that **n** will reap destruction; *4922*
Eph 2: 3 *of* our **sinful n** and following its desires *4922*
2: 3 we were *by* **n** objects of wrath. *5882*
Php 2: 6 being in very **n** God, *3671*
2: 7 taking the very **n** of a servant, *3671*
Col 2:11 in the putting off *of* the **sinful n,** *4922*
2:13 in the uncircumcision *of* your **sinful n,** *4922*
3: 5 whatever belongs to your earthly **n:** *3517*
Heb 6:17 the unchanging **n** of his purpose very clear *NIG*
2Pe 1: 4 in the divine **n** and escape the corruption in *5882*
2:10 *of* the **sinful n** and despise authority. *4922*
2:18 to the lustful desires *of* **sinful human n,** *4922*

NAUGHT (1)
Isa 40:23 He brings princes to **n** and reduces 401

NAUGHTINESS, NAUGHTY (KJV) See EVIL, MALICIOUS, POOR, SCOUNDREL, WICKED

NAUM (KJV) See NAHUM

NAVEL (1)
SS 7: 2 Your **n** is a rounded goblet 9219

NAVES (KJV) See HUB

NAVY (KJV) See FLEET, SHIPS

NAY (KJV) See NO

NAZARENE (4) [NAZARETH]
Mt 2:23 "He will be called a **N.**" *3717*
Mk 14:67 "You also were with that **N,** Jesus," *3716*
16: 6 "You are looking for Jesus the **N,** *3716*
Ac 24: 5 He is a ringleader of the **N** sect *3717*

NAZARETH (27) [NAZARETH]
Mt 2:23 and he went and lived in a town called **N.** *3714*
4:13 Leaving **N,** he went and lived *3714*
21:11 the prophet from **N** in Galilee." *3714*
26:71 "This fellow was with Jesus **of N.**" *3717*
Mk 1: 9 At that time Jesus came from **N** in Galilee *3714*
1:24 "What do you want with us, Jesus **of N?** *3716*
10:47 When he heard that it was Jesus **of N,** *3716*
Lk 1:26 God sent the angel Gabriel to **N,** *3714*
2: 4 So Joseph also went up from the town of **N** *3714*
2:39 to Galilee to their own town *of* **N.** *3714*
2:51 to **N** with them and was obedient to them. *3714*
4:16 He went to **N,** where he had been *3714*
4:34 What do you want with us, Jesus **of N?** *3716*
18:37 told him, "Jesus **of N** is passing by." *3717*
24:19 "About Jesus **of N,**" they replied. *3716*
Jn 1:45 Jesus of **N,** the son of Joseph." *3714*
1:46 "**N!** Can anything good come from there?" *3714*
18: 5 "Jesus **of N,**" they replied. *3717*
18: 7 And they said, "Jesus **of N.**" *3717*
19:19 JESUS **OF N,** THE KING OF THE JEWS. *3717*
Ac 2:22 Jesus **of N** was a man accredited by God *3717*
3: 6 In the name of Jesus Christ **of N,** walk." *3717*
4:10 It is by the name of Jesus Christ **of N,** *3717*
6:14 that this Jesus **of N** will destroy this place *3717*
10:38 Jesus of **N** with the Holy Spirit and power, *3714*
22: 8 I am Jesus **of N,** whom you are persecuting, *3717*
26: 9 to oppose the name of Jesus **of N.** *3717*

NAZARITE (KJV) See NAZIRITE

NAZIRITE (11) [NAZIRITES]
Nu 6: 2 a vow of separation to the LORD as a **N,** 5693
6: 4 As long as he is a **N,** 5694
6:13 " 'Now this is the law for the **N** when 5687
6:18 **N** must shave off the hair that he dedicated. 5687
6:19 **N** has shaved off the hair of his dedication, 5687
6:20 After that, the **N** may drink wine. 5687
6:21 the **N** who vows his offering to the LORD 5687
6:21 according to the law of the **N.'** " 5694
Jdg 13: 5 because the boy is to be a **N,** 5687
13: 7 the boy will be a **N** *of* God from birth until 5687
16:17 "because I have been a **N** *set apart to* God 5687

NAZIRITES (2) [NAZIRITE]
Am 2:11 up prophets from among your sons and **N** 5687
2:12 "But you made the **N** drink wine and 5687

NEAH (1)
Jos 19:13 at Rimmon and turned toward **N.** 5828

NEAPOLIS (1)
Ac 16:11 and the next day on to **N.** *3735*

NEAR (300) [NEARBY, NEARED, NEARER, NEAREST, NEARLY, NEARSIGHTED]
Ge 13:12 of the plain and pitched his tents **n** Sodom. 6330
13:18 and went to live **n** the great trees of Mamre 928
14: 6 as far as El Paran **n** the desert. 6584
14:13 Now Abram was living **n** the great trees 928
16: 7 angel of the LORD found Hagar **n** a spring 6584
18: 1 to Abraham **n** the great trees of Mamre 928
18: 8 he stood **n** them under a tree. 6584
19:20 Look, here is a town **n** *enough* to run to, 7940
20: 4 Now Abimelech *had* not **gone n** her, 7928
23:17 Ephron's field in Machpelah **n** Mamre 4200+7156
23:19 the field of Machpelah **n** Mamre 6584+7156
24:11 the camels kneel down **n** the well outside 448
24:30 and found him standing by the camels **n** 6584
25: 9 in the cave of Machpelah **n** Mamre, 6584+7156
25:11 who then lived **n** Beer Lahai Roi. 6640
25:18 to Shur, **n** the border of Egypt, 6584
27:21 "**Come n** so I can touch you, my son, 5602
27:41 of mourning for my father *are* **n;** 7928
29: 2 with three flocks of sheep lying **n** it 6584
30:41 of the animals so they would mate **n** 928
32:32 of Jacob's hip was touched **n** the tendon. 928
35:27 **n** Kiriath Arba (that is, Hebron), NIH
37:12 to graze their father's flocks **n** Shechem, 928
37:13 your brothers are grazing the flocks **n** 928
37:17 after his brothers and found them **n** Dothan. 928
45:10 in the region of Goshen and be **n** me— 7940
47:29 When the time **drew n** for Israel to die, 7928
49:22 a fruitful vine **n** a spring, 6584
49:30 **n** Mamre in Canaan, 6584+7156
50:10 **n** the Jordan, they lamented loudly 928+6298
50:11 That is why that place **n** the Jordan 928+6298
50:13 field of Machpelah, **n** Mamre, 6584+7156
Ex 14: 2 and encamp **n** Pi Hahiroth, 4200+7156
14: 9 as they camped by the sea **n** Pi Hahiroth, 6584
14:20 so neither **went n** the other all night long. 7928
15:27 and they camped there **n** the water. 6584
18: 5 where he was camped **n** the mountain NIH
24: 2 the others *must* not **come n.** 5602
33:21 a place **n** me where you may stand on 907
34:30 and they were afraid *to* **come n** him. 5602
34:32 Afterward all the Israelites **came n** him, 5602
40:29 the altar of burnt offering **n** the entrance to NIH
Lev 3: 4 kidneys with the fat on them **n** the loins, 6584
3:10 kidneys with the fat on them **n** the loins, 6584
3:15 kidneys with the fat on them **n** the loins, 6584
4: 9 kidneys with the fat on them **n** the loins, 6584
7: 4 kidneys with the fat on them **n** the loins, 6584
9: 5 the entire assembly **came n** and stood 7928
21:17 a defect *may* **come n** to offer the food 7928
21:18 No man who has any defect *may* **come n:** 7928
21:21 the priest who has any defect *is to* **come n** 5602
21:21 not **come n** to offer the food of his God. 5602
21:23 not go **n** the curtain or approach the altar, 448
22: 3 and yet **comes n** the sacred offerings that 7928
Nu 1:51 Anyone else who **goes n** it shall be put 7929
4:19 when they **come n** the most holy things, 5602
6: 6 the LORD he must not go **n** a dead body. 6584
8:19 when they **go n** the sanctuary." 5602
13:29 and the Canaanites live **n** the sea and along 6584
16: 5 *he will* **have** that person **come n** 7928
16: 5 man he chooses *he will* **cause to come n** 7928
16: 9 the Israelite community and **brought** you **n** 7928
16:10 **brought** you and all your fellow Levites **n** 7928
17:13 Anyone who **even comes n** the tabernacle of the LORD will die. 7929+7929
18: 3 not **go n** the furnishings of the sanctuary or 7928
18: 4 and no *one* else *may* **come n** where you are. 7928
18: 7 Anyone else who **comes n** the sanctuary 7929
18:22 From now on the Israelites *must* not **go n** 7928
20:23 At Mount Hor, **n** the border of Edom, 6584
22: 5 who was at Pethor, **n** the River, 6584
24:17 I behold him, but not **n.** 7940
33: 7 and camped **n** Migdol. 4200+7156
33:47 in the mountains of Abarim, **n** Nebo. 4200+7156
Dt 3:29 So we stayed in the valley **n** Beth Peor. 4578
4: 7 as to have their gods **n** them the way 7940
4: 7 the way the LORD our God is **n** us NIH
4:11 *You* **came n** and stood at the foot of 7928
4:46 in the valley **n** Beth Peor east of the Jordan, 4578
5:27 **Go n** and listen to all that 7928
11:30 **n** the great trees of Moreh, 725
13: 7 whether **n** or far, 7940
15: 9 the year for canceling debts, *is* **n,"** 7928
22: 2 the brother does not live **n** you or if you do 7940
30:14 No, the word is very **n** you; 7940
31:14 "Now the day of your death *is* **n.** 7928
32:35 of disaster is **n** and their doom rushes 7940
Jos 3: 4 between you and the ark; *do* not **go n** it." 7928
5:13 Now when Joshua was **n** Jericho, 928
7: 2 which is **n** Beth Aven to the east of Bethel, 6640
9: 7 "But perhaps you live **n** us. 928+7931
9:16 that they were neighbors, living **n** them. 928+7931
9:22 while actually you live **n** us? 928+7931
10: 1 of peace with Israel and were living **n** 928+7931
12: 9 the king of Ai (**n** Bethel) one 4946+7396
13:25 as far as Aroer, **n** Rabbah; 6584+7156
19:11 and extended to the ravine **n** Jokneam. 6584+7156
22:10 When they came to **Geliloth** *n* the Jordan AIT
22:11 of Canaan at **Geliloth** *n* the Jordan on AIT
24:26 up there under the oak **n** the holy place of 928
Jdg 1:16 of the Desert of Judah in the **Negev** *n* Arad. AIT
3:19 the idols **n** Gilgal he himself turned back 907
4:11 by the great tree in Zaanannim **n** Kedesh. 907
7: 1 of Midian was north of them in the valley **n** 4946
7:22 as the border of Abel Meholah **n** Tabbath. 6584
9:34 and took up concealed positions **n** Shechem 6584
15: 9 spreading out **n** Lehi. 928
18: 3 When they were **n** Micah's house, 6640
18:12 up camp **n** Kiriath Jearim in Judah. 928
18:22 the men who lived **n** Micah 6640
18:28 The city was in a valley **n** Beth Rehob. 4200
19:11 When they were **n** Jebus and 6640
20:19 the Israelites got up and pitched camp **n** 6584
20:24 Then the Israelites **drew n** to Benjamin 7928
20:34 that the Benjamites did not realize how **n** 5595
20:36 on the ambush they had set **n** Gibeah. 448
Ru 3:12 Although it is true that I *am* **n of kin,** 1457
1Sa 4:19 pregnant and **n the time of delivery.** 3528
7:10 the Philistines **drew n** to engage Israel 5602
10: 2 you will meet two men **n** Rachel's tomb, 6640
10:20 **brought** all the tribes of Israel **n,** 7928
17:26 David asked the men standing **n** him, 6640
24: 2 for David and his men **n** the Crags 6584+7156
25:15 time we were out in the fields **n** them 907+2143
25:16 the time we were herding our sheep **n** them. 6640
26: 7 in the ground **n** his **head.** 5265
26:11 the spear and water jug that are **n** his **head,** 5265
26:12 the spear and water jug **n** Saul's **head,** 5265
26:16 and water jug that were **n** his **head?"** 5265
2Sa 2:24 **n** Giah on the way to the wasteland 6584+7156
13:23 at Baal Hazor **n** the border of Ephraim, 6640
19:37 that I may die in my own town **n** the tomb 6640
23:15 a drink of water from the well **n** the gate 928
23:16 from the well **n** the gate of Bethlehem 928
24: 5 crossing the Jordan, they camped **n** Aroer, 928
1Ki 1: 9 at the Stone of Zoheleth **n** En Rogel. 725
2: 1 When the time **drew n** for David to die, 7928
8:46 to his own land, far away or **n;** 7940
8:59 be **n** to the LORD our God day and night, 7940
9:26 which is **n** Elath in Edom, 907
16:15 The army was encamped **n** Gibbethon, 6584

2Ki 9:27 in his chariot on the way up to Gur **n** 907
11:11 **n** the altar and the temple, 4200
15: 7 with his fathers and was buried **n** them in 6640
23:11 They were in the court **n** the room of 448
23:12 on the **roof** *n* the upper room of Ahaz, AIT
25: 4 between the two walls **n** the king's garden, 6584
1Ch 8:32 They too lived **n** their relatives 5584
9:38 They too lived **n** their relatives 5584
11:17 a drink of water from the well **n** the gate 928
11:18 from the well **n** the gate of Bethlehem 928
19: 7 who came and camped **n** Medeba, 4200+7156
2Ch 6:36 to a land far away or **n;** 7940
14:10 in the Valley of Zephathah **n** Mareshah. 4200
21:16 of the Arabs who lived **n** the Cushites. 3338+6584
23:10 **n** the altar and the temple, 4200
26: 6 then rebuilt towns **n** Ashdod and elsewhere 928
26:23 and was buried **n** them in a field for burial 6640
Ne 3:25 the upper palace **n** the court of the guard. 4200
4:12 Then the Jews who lived **n** them came 725
7: 3 some at their posts and some **n** their own 5584
Est 2:11 and forth **n** the courtyard of the harem 4200+7156
9:20 the provinces of King Xerxes, **n** and far, 7940
Job 17:12 the face of darkness they say, 'Light is **n.'** 7940
33:22 His soul **draws n** to the pit, 7928
Ps 10: 8 He lies in **wait** *n* the villages; AIT
22:11 for trouble is **n** and there is no one to help. 7940
65: 4 Blessed are those you choose and **bring n** 7928
69:18 **Come n** and rescue me; 7928
73:28 But as for me, it is good to be **n** God. 7932
75: 1 we give thanks, for your Name is **n;** 7940
84: 3 a place **n** your altar, O LORD Almighty, 907
85: 9 his salvation is **n** those who fear him, 7940
88: 3 of trouble and my life **draws n** the grave. 5595
91: 7 but *it will* not **come n** you. 5602
91:10 no disaster *will* **come n** your tent. 7928
107:18 They loathed all food and **drew n** the gates 5595
119:150 Those who devise wicked schemes *are* **n,** 7928
119:151 Yet you are **n,** O LORD, 7940
145:18 The LORD is **n** to all who call on him, 7940
Pr 3:29 who lives trustfully **n** you. 907
5: 8 *do* not **go n** the door of her house, 7928
7: 8 He was going down the street **n** her corner, 725
Ecc 5: 1 **Go n** to listen rather than to offer 7928
Isa 11: 8 The infant will play **n** the hole of the cobra, 6584
13: 6 Wail, for the day of the LORD is **n;** 7940
29:13 "These people **come n** to me 5602
33:13 you *who* are **n,** acknowledge my power! 7940
34: 1 **Come n,** you nations, and listen; 7928
46:13 **bringing** my righteousness **n,** 7928
48:16 **"Come n** me and listen to this: 7928
50: 8 He who vindicates me is **n.** 7940
51: 5 My righteousness *draws* **n** speedily, 7940
54:14 *it will* not **come n** you. 7928
55: 6 call on him while he is **n.** 7940
57:19 Peace, peace, to those far and **n,"** 7940
58: 2 and seem eager for God to **come n** them. 7932
65: 5 don't **come n** me, 5602
Jer 5: 6 a leopard will lie in wait **n** their towns 6584
19: 2 **n** the entrance of the Potsherd Gate. NIH
25:26 **n** and far, one after the other— 7940
30:21 *I will* **bring** him **n** and he will come close 7928
41:12 They caught up with him **n** the great pool 448
41:17 stopping at Geruth Kimham **n** Bethlehem 725
48:24 to all the towns of Moab, far and **n.** 7940
52: 7 between the two walls **n** the king's garden, 6584
La 1:16 **No** *one is* **n** to comfort me, 8178
3:57 *You* **came n** when I called you, 7928
4:18 Our end *was* **n,** our days were numbered, 7928
Eze 3:15 to the exiles who lived at Tel Abib **n** 448
6:12 and he *that* is **n** will fall by the sword, 7940
7: 7 The time has come, the day is **n;** 7940
12:23 'The days *are* **n** when every vision will 7928
22: 5 Those who are **n** and those who are far 7940
30: 3 day is **n,** the day of the LORD is near— 7940
30: 3 the day is near, the day of the LORD is **n—** 7940
40:40 **n** the steps at the entrance to 4200
40:46 who are the only Levites who may **draw n** 7929
42:14 on other clothes before *they* **go n** the places 7928
43:19 who **come n** to minister before me, 7940
44:13 *to* **come n** to serve me as priests or come 5602
44:13 as priests or **come n** any of my holy things 5602
44:15 *are to* **come n** to minister before me; 7928
44:16 *to* **come n** my table to minister before me 7928
44:25 not defile himself by going **n** a dead 448
45: 4 in the sanctuary and who **draw n** to minister 7929
Da 5: 5 **n** the lampstand in the royal palace. 10378+10619
6:20 When he **came n** the den, 10638
8:17 he came **n** the place where I was standing, 725
9: 7 of Jerusalem and all Israel, both **n** and far, 7940
Joel 1:15 For the day of the LORD is **n;** 7940
3: 9 *Let* all the fighting men **draw n** and attack. 5602
3:14 of the LORD is **n** in the valley of decision. 7940
Am 6: 3 You put off the evil day and **bring n** a reign 5602
Ob 1:15 "The day of the LORD is **n** for all nations. 7940
Zep 1: 7 for the day of the LORD is **n.** 7940
1:14 "The great day of the LORD is **n—** 7940
1:14 **n** and coming quickly. 7940
3: 2 *she does* not **draw n** to her God. 7928
Mal 3: 5 "So *I will* **come n** to you for judgment. 7928
Mt 3: 2 "Repent, for the kingdom of heaven *is* **n."** *1581*
4:17 "Repent, for the kingdom of heaven *is* **n."** *1581*
10: 7 'The kingdom of heaven *is* **n.'** *1581*
24:32 you know that summer is **n.** *1584*
24:33 you know that it is **n,** right at the door. *1584*
26:18 My appointed time is **n.** *1584*
26:45 Look, the hour *is* **n,** *1581*
Mk 1:15 "The kingdom of God *is* **n.** *1581*
13:28 you know that summer is **n.** *1584*
13:29 you know that it is **n,** right at the door. *1584*
14:47 *of* those **standing n** drew his sword *4225*
14:70 those **standing n** said to Peter, *4225*
15:35 When some *of* those **standing n** heard this, *4225*
Lk 8:19 but they were not able *to* **get n** him *5344*
10: 9 'The kingdom of God *is* **n** you.' *1581*
10:11 be sure of this: The kingdom of God *is* **n.'** *1581*
12:33 no thief **comes n** and no moth destroys. *1581*
15:25 When *he* came **n** the house, *1581*
18:40 *When* he **came n,** Jesus asked him, *1581*
19:11 because he was **n** Jerusalem and *1584*
19:37 *When* he **came n** the place where *1581*
21: 8 claiming, 'I am he,' and, 'The time *is* **n.'** *1581*
21:20 you will know that its desolation *is* **n.** *1581*
21:28 because your redemption *is* **drawing n."** *1581*
21:30 for yourselves and know that summer is **n.** *1584*
21:31 you know that the kingdom of God is **n.** *1584*
Jn 3:23 John also was baptizing at Aenon **n** Salim, *1584*
4: 5 **n** the plot of ground Jacob had given *4446*
5: 2 Now there is in Jerusalem **n** the Sheep Gate *2093*
6: 4 The Jewish Passover Feast was **n.** *1584*
6:23 Then some boats from Tiberias landed **n** *1584*
7: 2 the Jewish Feast of Tabernacles was **n,** *1584*
8:20 in the temple area **n** the place where *1877*
11:54 Instead he withdrew to a region **n** *1584*
19:20 the place where Jesus was crucified was **n** *1584*
19:25 **N** the cross of Jesus stood his mother, *4123*
Ac 2:10 Egypt and the parts of Libya **n** Cyrene; *2848*
7:17 "As the time **drew n** for God *1581*
7:30 a burning bush in the desert **n** Mount Sinai. *NIG*
8:29 "Go to that chariot and **stay n** it." *3140*
9:38 Lydda was **n** Joppa; *1584*
22: 6 "About noon *as* I came **n** Damascus, *1581*
23: 2 Ananias ordered those **standing n** Paul *4225*
23: 4 Those who *were* **standing n** Paul said, *4225*
23:11 The following night the Lord **stood n** Paul *2392*
27: 8 **n** the town of Lasea. *1584*
Ro 10: 8 "The word is **n** you; *1584*
1Co 8: 8 But food *does* not **bring** us **n** to God; *4225*
Eph 2:13 in Christ Jesus you who once were far away have been brought **n** *1584*
2:17 and peace to those who were **n.** *1584*
Php 4: 5 The Lord is **n.** *1584*
Heb 7:19 by which *we* **draw n** to God. *1581*
10: 1 make perfect those who **draw n** to worship. *4665*
10:22 *let us* **draw n** to God with a sincere heart *4665*
11:22 By faith Joseph, *when his* **end was n,** *5462*
Jas 4: 8 **Come n** to God and he will come near *1581*
4: 8 near to God and *he will* **come n** to you. *1581*
5: 8 because the Lord's coming *is* **n.** *1581*
1Pe 4: 7 The end of all things *is* **n.** *1581*
Rev 1: 3 because the time is **n.** *1584*
22:10 because the time is **n.** *1584*

NEARBY (16) [NEAR]

Ge 18: 2 up and saw three men standing **n.** 6584
21:16 Then she went off and sat down **n,** 4946+5584
21:16 as she sat there **n,** she began to sob. 4946+5584
Dt 20:15 and do not belong to the nations **n.** 2178
Job 1:14 and the donkeys were grazing **n,** 3338+6584
40:20 and all the wild animals play **n.** 9004
Pr 27:10 better a neighbor **n** than a brother far away. 7940
Jer 23:23 "Am I only a God **n,"** declares the LORD, 4946+7940
Mk 1:38 go somewhere else—to the **n** villages— *2400*
5:11 herd of pigs was feeding on the **n** hillside. *1695*
Lk 2: 8 shepherds living out in the fields **n,** *899+3836*
Jn 2: 6 **N** stood six stone water jars, *1695*
18:22 one of the officials **n** struck him in the face. *4225*
19:26 and the disciple whom he loved **standing n,** *4225*
19:42 of Preparation and since the tomb was **n,** *1584*
Ac 28: 7 There was an estate **n** that belonged to Publius, *3836+4309+5536*

NEARED (2) [NEAR]

Jdg 19:14 sun set as *they* **n** Gibeah in Benjamin. 725+2143
Ac 9: 3 As he **n** Damascus on his journey, *1181+1581*

NEARER (2) [NEAR]

Ru 3:12 there is a kinsman-redeemer **n** than I. 7940
Ro 13:11 because our salvation is **n** now than *1584*

NEAREST (7) [NEAR]

Ex 12: 4 they must share one with their **n** neighbor, 7940
Lev 25:25 his **n** relative is to come 7940
Nu 27:11 give his inheritance to the **n** relative 7940
Dt 21: 3 the elders of the town **n** the body shall take 7940
21: 6 the town **n** the body shall wash their hands 7940
Jer 32: 7 **as n relative** it is your right and **duty** 1460
Eze 42: 8 the row on the side **n** the sanctuary 6584+7156

NEARIAH (3)

1Ch 3:22 Hattush, Igal, Bariah, **N** and Shaphat— 5859
3:23 The sons of **N:** 5859
4:42 **N,** Rephaiah and Uzziel, the sons of Ishi, 5859

NEARLY (7) [NEAR]

Jdg 19: 9 Spend the night here; the day *is* **n over.** 2837
Ps 73: 2 I had **n** lost my foothold. 401+3869
Mk 4:37 so that it was **n** swamped. *2453*
Lk 24:29 for it is **n** evening; the day is almost over." *4639*
Ac 21:27 When the seven days were **n** over, *3516*
Ro 13:12 night *is* **n over;** the day is almost here. *4621*
Heb 9:22 that **n** everything be cleansed with blood, *5385*

NEARSIGHTED (1) [NEAR, SEE]

2Pe 1: 9 does not have them, he is **n** and blind, *3697*

NEBAI (1)

Ne 10:19 Hariph, Anathoth, **N,** 5763

NEBAIOTH (5)

Ge 25:13 **N** the firstborn of Ishmael, Kedar, Adbeel, 5568
28: 9 the sister of **N** and daughter of Ishmael son 5568
36: 3 of Ishmael and sister of **N.** 5568
1Ch 1:29 **N** the firstborn of Ishmael, Kedar, Adbeel, 5568
Isa 60: 7 the rams of **N** will serve you; 5568

NEBAJOTH (KJV) See NEBAIOTH

NEBALLAT (1)

Ne 11:34 in Hadid, Zeboim and **N,** 5579

NEBAT (25)

1Ki 11:26 Jeroboam son of **N** rebelled against 5565
12: 2 son of **N** heard this (he was still in Egypt, 5565
12:15 to Jeroboam son of **N** through Ahijah 5565
15: 1 of the reign of Jeroboam son of **N,** 5565
16: 3 like that of Jeroboam son of **N.** 5565
16:26 in all the ways of Jeroboam son of **N** and 5565
16:31 to commit the sins of Jeroboam son of **N,** 5565
21:22 like that of Jeroboam son of **N** and that 5565
22:52 and in the ways of Jeroboam son of **N,** 5565
2Ki 3: 3 he clung to the sins of Jeroboam son of **N,** 5565
9: 9 of Jeroboam son of **N** and like the house 5565
10:29 from the sins of Jeroboam son of **N,** 5565
13: 2 the sins of Jeroboam son of **N,** 5565
13:11 from any of the sins of Jeroboam son of **N,** 5565
14:24 from any of the sins of Jeroboam son of **N,** 5565
15: 9 from the sins of Jeroboam son of **N.** 5565
15:18 from the sins of Jeroboam son of **N,** 5565
15:24 from the sins of Jeroboam son of **N,** 5565
15:28 from the sins of Jeroboam son of **N,** 5565
17:21 they made Jeroboam son of **N** their king. 5565
23:15 the high place made by Jeroboam son of **N,** 5565
2Ch 9:29 the seer concerning Jeroboam son of **N?** 5565
10: 2 son of **N** heard this (he was in Egypt, 5565
10:15 to Jeroboam son of **N** through Ahijah 5565
13: 6 Yet Jeroboam son of **N,** 5565

NEBO (13) [NEBO-SARSEKIM]

Nu 32: 3 Heshbon, Elealeh, Sebam, **N** and Beon— 5549
32:38 as well as **N** and Baal Meon 5549
33:47 in the mountains of Abarim, near **N.** 5549
Dt 32:49 "Go up into the Abarim Range to Mount **N** 5549
34: 1 Then Moses climbed Mount **N** from 5549
1Ch 5: 8 in the area from Aroer to **N** and Baal Meon. 5549
Ezr 2:29 of **N** 52 5549
10:43 From the descendants of **N:** 5551
Ne 7:33 of the other **N** 52 5549
Isa 15: 2 Moab wails over **N** and Medeba. 5549
46: 1 Bel bows down, **N** stoops low; 5550
Jer 48: 1 "Woe to **N,** for it will be ruined. 5549
48:22 to Dibon, **N** and Beth Diblathaim, 5549

NEBO-SARSEKIM (1) [NEBO]

Jer 39: 3 Nergal-Sharezer of Samgar, **N** 5552

NEBUCHADNEZZAR (89) [NEBUCHADNEZZAR'S]

2Ki 24: 1 **N** king of Babylon invaded the land, 5556
24: 1 and rebelled against **N.** 2257[S]
24:10 the officers of **N** king of Babylon advanced 5556
24:11 and **N** himself came up to the city 5556
24:13 **N** removed all the treasures from NIH
24:15 **N** took Jehoiachin captive to Babylon. NIH
25: 1 **N** king of Babylon marched 5556
25: 8 the nineteenth year of **N** king of Babylon, 5556
25:22 **N** king of Babylon appointed Gedaliah son 5556
1Ch 6:15 and Jerusalem into exile by the hand of **N.** 5556
2Ch 36: 6 **N** king of Babylon attacked him 5556
36: 7 **N** also took to Babylon articles from 5556
36:10 King **N** sent for him and brought him 5556
36:13 He also rebelled against King **N,** 5556
36:17 God handed all of them over to **N.** 2257[S]
Ezr 1: 7 which **N** had carried away from Jerusalem 5556
2: 1 whom **N** king of Babylon had taken captive 5556
5:12 he handed them over to **N** the Chaldean, 10453
5:14 which **N** had taken from the temple 10453
6: 5 which **N** took from the temple in Jerusalem 10453
Ne 7: 6 the captivity of the exiles whom **N** king 5556
Est 2: 6 from Jerusalem by **N** king of Babylon, 5556
Jer 21: 2 because **N** king of Babylon is attacking us. 5557
21: 7 to **N** king of Babylon and to 5557
22:25 to **N** king of Babylon and to 5557
24: 1 from Jerusalem to Babylon by **N** king 5557
25: 1 the first year of **N** king of Babylon. 5557
25: 9 and my servant **N** king of Babylon," 5557
27: 6 over to my servant **N** king of Babylon; 5556
27: 8 or kingdom will not serve **N** king 5556
27:20 which **N** king of Babylon did not take away 5556
28: 3 that **N** king of Babylon removed from here 5556
28:11 the yoke of **N** king of Babylon off the neck 5556

Jer 28:14 to make them serve N king of Babylon, 5556
29: 1 the other people N had carried into exile 5556
29: 3 of Judah sent to King N in Babylon. 5556
29:21 "I will hand them over to N king 5557
32: 1 which was the eighteenth year of **N.** 5557
32:28 the Babylonians and to N king of Babylon, 5557
34: 1 While N king of Babylon and all his army 5557
35:11 when N king of Babylon invaded this land, 5557
37: 1 of Judah by N king of Babylon; 5557
39: 1 N king of Babylon marched 5557
39: 5 They captured him and took him to N king 5557
39:11 Now N king of Babylon 5557
43:10 for my servant N king of Babylon, 5557
44:30 of Judah over to N king of Babylon, 5557
46: 2 the Euphrates River by N king of Babylon 5557
46:13 the prophet about the coming of N king 5557
46:26 to N king of Babylon and his officers. 5557
49:28 which N king of Babylon attacked: 5557
49:30 "N king of Babylon has plotted 5557
50:17 to crush his bones was N king of Babylon." 5557
51:34 "N king of Babylon has devoured us, 5557
52: 4 N king of Babylon marched 5557
52:12 the nineteenth year of N king of Babylon, 5557
52:28 This is the number of the people N carried 5557
Eze 26: 7 to bring against Tyre N king of Babylon, 5557
29:18 N king of Babylon drove his army in 5557
29:19 to give Egypt to N king of Babylon, 5557
30:10 of Egypt by the hand of N king of Babylon. 5557
Da 1: 1 N king of Babylon came to Jerusalem 5556
1:18 the chief official presented them to **N.** 5556
2: 1 the second year of his reign, N had dreams; 5556
2:28 He has shown King N what will happen 10453
2:46 Then King N fell prostrate before Daniel 10453
3: 1 King N made an image of gold, 10453
3: 3 of the image that King N had set up, 10453
3: 5 the image of gold that King N has set up. 10453
3: 7 the image of gold that King N had set up. 10453
3: 9 They said to King **N,** "O king, live forever! 10453
3:13 Furious with rage, N summoned Shadrach, 10453
3:14 and N said to them, 10453
3:16 "O **N,** we do not need to defend ourselves 10453
3:19 Then N was furious with Shadrach, 10453
3:24 Then King N leaped to his feet 10453
3:26 N then approached the opening of 10453
3:28 Then N said, "Praise be to the God 10453
4: 1 King **N,** To the peoples, 10453
4: 4 I, **N,** was at home in my palace, 10453
4:18 "This is the dream that I, King **N,** had. 10453
4:28 All this happened to King **N.** 10453
4:31 "This is what is decreed for you, King **N:** 10453
4:33 about N was fulfilled. 10453
4:34 At the end of that time, I, **N,** 10453
4:37 **N,** praise and exalt and glorify the King 10453
5: 2 that N his father had taken from the temple 10453
5:11 King N your father— 10453
5:18 the Most High God gave your father N sovereignty 10453

NEBUCHADNEZZAR'S (1) [NEBUCHADNEZZAR]
Jer 52:29 in N eighteenth year, 832 people 4200+5557

NEBUSHAZBAN (1)
Jer 39:13 N a chief officer, 5558

NEBUZARADAN (16)
2Ki 25: 8 N commander of the imperial guard, 5555
25:11 N the commander of the guard carried 5555
25:20 N the commander took them all 5555
Jer 39: 9 N commander of the imperial guard carried 5555
39:10 But N the commander of the guard left 5555
39:11 about Jeremiah through N commander of 5555
39:13 So N the commander of the guard, 5555
40: 1 from the LORD after N commander of 5555
40: 5 before Jeremiah turned to go, N added, NIH
41:10 over whom N commander of the imperial 5555
43: 6 the king's daughters whom N commander 5555
52:12 N commander of the imperial guard, 5555
52:15 N the commander of the guard carried 5555
52:16 But N left behind the rest of 5555
52:26 N the commander took them all 5555
52:30 by N the commander of the imperial guard. 5555

NECESSARY (8) [NECESSITIES]
Ac 1:21 Therefore *it is* n to choose one of *1256*
Ro 13: 5 it is **n** to submit to the authorities, *340*
2Co 9: 5 So I thought it **n** to urge the brothers *338*
Php 1:24 but it is **more n** for you that I remain in *338*
2:25 But I think it is **n** to send back *338*
Heb 8: 3 and so *it was* **n for** this one also *338*
9:16 it is **n** to prove the death of the one who *340*
9:23 It was **n,** then, for the copies of *340*

NECESSITIES (1) [NECESSARY]
Tit 3:14 they may provide for **daily n** and not live unproductive lives. *338+5970*

NECHO (KJV) See NECO

NECK (51) [NECKS, STIFF-NECKED]
Ge 27:16 the smooth part of his **n** with the goatskins. 7418
27:40 you will throw his yoke from off your **n."** 7418
33: 4 he threw his arms around his **n** 7418
41:42 and put a gold chain around his **n.** 7418
49: 8 be on the **n** *of* your enemies; 6902
Ex 13:13 but if you do not redeem it, **break** its **n.** 6904
34:20 but if you do not redeem it, **break** its **n.** 6904
Lev 5: 8 He is to wring its head from its **n,** 6902
Dt 21: 4 the valley *they are to* **break** the heifer's **n.** 6904
21: 6 the heifer whose **n was broken** in the valley, 6904
28:48 on your **n** until he has destroyed you. 7418
Jdg 5:30 highly embroidered garments for my **n—** 7418
1Sa 4:18 His **n** was broken and he died, 5154
Job 16:12 he seized me by the **n** and crushed me. 6902
30:18 he binds me like the **n** *of* my garment. 7023
39:19 the horse his strength or clothe his **n** with 7418
41:22 Strength resides in his **n;** 7418
Ps 69: 1 for the waters have come up to my **n.** 5883
75: 5 do not speak with outstretched **n.' "** 7418
105:18 his **n** was put in irons, 5883
Pr 1: 9 and a chain to adorn your **n.** 1738
3: 3 bind them around your **n,** 1738
3:22 an ornament to grace your **n.** 1738
6:21 fasten them around your **n.** 1738
SS 1:10 your **n** with strings of jewels. 7418
4: 4 Your **n** is like the tower of David, 7418
7: 4 Your **n** is like an ivory tower. 7418
Isa 8: 8 passing through it and reaching up to the **n.** 7418
10:27 their yoke from your **n;** 7418
30:28 rising up to the **n.** 7418
48: 4 the sinews of your **n** were iron, 6902
52: 2 Free yourself from the chains on your **n,** 7418
66: 3 like *one who* **breaks** a dog's **n;** 6904
Jer 27: 2 of straps and crossbars and put it on your **n.** 7418
27: 8 of Babylon or bow its **n** under his yoke, 7418
27:11 if any nation will bow its **n** under the yoke 7418
27:12 "Bow your **n** under the yoke of the king 7418
28:10 the **n** *of* the prophet Jeremiah and broke it, 7418
28:11 the **n** *of* all the nations within two years.' " 7418
28:12 the yoke off the **n** *of* the prophet Jeremiah, 7418
La 1:14 They have come upon my **n** and 7418
Eze 16:11 and a necklace around your **n,** 1744
Da 5: 7 and have a gold chain placed around his **n,** 10611
5:16 a gold chain placed around your **n,** 10611
5:29 a gold chain was placed around his **n,** 10611
Hos 10:11 so I will put a yoke on her fair **n.** 7418
11: 4 I lifted the yoke from their **n** and bent down 4305
Na 1:13 from your **n** and tear your shackles away." NIH
Mt 18: 6 to have a large millstone hung around his **n** *5549*
Mk 9:42 with a large millstone tied around his **n.** *5549*
Lk 17: 2 a millstone tied around his **n** than for him *5549*

NECK-IRONS (1) [IRON]
Jer 29:26 like a prophet into the stocks and **n.** 7485

NECKLACE (3) [NECKLACES]
Ps 73: 6 Therefore pride is their **n;** 6735
SS 4: 9 with one jewel of your **n.** 7454
Eze 16:11 on your arms and a **n** around your neck, 8054

NECKLACES (2) [NECKLACE]
Nu 31:50 bracelets, signet rings, earrings and **n—** 3921
Isa 3:18 the bangles and headbands and **crescent n,** 8448

NECKS (9) [NECK]
Jos 10:24 and put your feet on the **n** *of* these kings." 7418
10:24 and placed their feet on their **n.** 7418
Jdg 8:21 and took the ornaments off their camels' **n.** 7418
8:26 or the chains that were on their camels' **n.** 7418
Isa 3:16 walking along with outstretched **n,** 1744
Jer 28:14 an iron yoke on the **n** *of* all these nations 7418
30: 8 'I will break the yoke off their **n** 7418
Eze 21:29 on the **n** *of* the wicked who are to be slain, 7418
Ac 15:10 the **n** of the disciples a yoke that neither we *5549*

NECO (10)
2Ki 23:29 Pharaoh N king of Egypt went up to 5785
23:29 N faced him and killed him at Megiddo. 2257S
23:33 Pharaoh N put him in chains at Riblah in 5785
23:34 Pharaoh N made Eliakim son of Josiah king 5785
23:35 Jehoiakim paid Pharaoh N the silver NIH
2Ch 35:20 N king of Egypt went up to fight 5786
35:21 But N sent messengers to him, saying, NIH
35:22 He would not listen to what N had said 5786
36: 4 But N took Eliakim's brother Jehoahaz 5786
Jer 46: 2 the army of Pharaoh N king of Egypt, 5786

NECROMANCER (KJV) See CONSULTS THE DEAD

NECTAR (1)
SS 8: 2 the **n** *of* my pomegranates. 6747

NEDABIAH (1)
1Ch 3:18 Shenazzar, Jekamiah, Hoshama and N. 5608

NEED (77) [NEEDED, NEEDING, NEEDLESS, NEEDS, NEEDY]
Ge 33:11 has been gracious to me and I have **all** I *n."* AIT
Ex 14:14 the LORD will fight for you; *you n only to be* **still.** AIT
Lev 13:36 priest *does* not *n to* **look** for yellow hair; AIT
Jdg 19:19 We don't **n** anything." 4728
19:20 "Let me supply whatever you **n.** 4728
1Ki 8:59 according to each day's **n,** 1821
2Ki 22: 7 But they *n* not **account for** the money AIT
1Ch 23:26 the Levites no *longer n* to **carry** AIT
2Ch 2:16 that you **n** and will float them in rafts 7664
35:15 at each gate *did* not *n to* **leave** their posts, AIT
Job 5:21 and *n* not **fear** when destruction comes. AIT
5:22 and *n* not **fear** the beasts of the earth. AIT
34:23 God *has* no *n to* **examine** men further, AIT
Ps 50: 9 *I have* no *n of* a bull from your stall or 4374
79: 8 for *we are* **in** desperate **n.** 1937
116: 6 *when I was* **in great n,** he saved me. 1937
142: 6 Listen to my cry, for *I am* **in** desperate **n;** 1937
Pr 24: 6 for waging war you **n** guidance, NIH
Jer 2:24 that pursue her *n* not **tire** *themselves;* AIT
Eze 39:10 *They will* not *n to* **gather** wood from AIT
Da 3:16 we *do* not **n** to defend ourselves before you 10287
Hos 7: 4 like an oven whose fire the baker **n not** stir 8697
Mt 3:14 saying, "I **n** to be baptized by you, *2400+5970*
6: 8 for your Father knows what *you* **n** *2400+5970*
6:32 your heavenly Father that *you* **n** them. *5974*
9:12 "It is not the healthy **who n** a doctor, *2400+5970*
14:16 Jesus replied, *"They do* not **n** to go away. *2400+5970*
26:65 Why *do we* **n** any more witnesses? *2400+5970*
Mk 2:17 "It is not the healthy who **n** a doctor, *2400+5970*
2:25 his companions were hungry and in **n?** *2400+5970*
14:63 "Why *do we* **n** any more witnesses?" *2400+5970*
Lk 5:31 "It is not the healthy who **n** a doctor, *2400+5970*
12:30 and your Father knows that *you* **n** them. *5974*
15: 7 persons who *do* not **n** to repent. *2400+5970*
15:14 and he began *to be in* **n.** *5728*
22:71 "Why *do we* **n** any more testimony? *2400+5970*
Jn 2:25 *He did* not **n** man's testimony about man, *2400+5970*
16:30 *you do* not even **n** to have anyone ask you questions. *2400+5970*
Ac 2:45 they gave to anyone as he had **n.** *5970*
4:35 it was distributed to anyone as he had **n.** *5970*
10: 2 **gave** generously **to** those **in n** *1797+4472*
27:34 You **n** it to survive. *NIG*
Ro 12:13 Share with God's people who are in **n.** *5970*
16: 2 to give her any help *she may* **n** from you, *5974*
1Co 12:21 say to the hand, *"I* don't **n** you!" *2400+5970*
12:21 say to the feet, *"I* don't **n** you!" *2400+5970*
12:24 our presentable parts **n** no special treatment, *2400+5970*
2Co 3: 1 Or *do we* **n,** like some people, *5974*
8:14 your plenty will supply what they **n,** *5729*
8:14 in turn their plenty will supply what you **n.** *5729*
9: 1 There is **no n** for me to write to you *4356*
9: 8 having all that you **n,** *894*
Eph 4:28 to share with those in **n.** *2400+5970*
Php 4:11 I am not saying this because I am in **n,** *5730*
4:12 I know what it is *to be in* **n,** *5427*
4:16 and again when I was in **n.** *5970*
1Th 1: 8 *we do* not **n** to say anything about it, *2400+5970*
4: 9 brotherly love *we do* not **n** to write *2400+5970*
5: 1 times and dates *we do* not **n** to write *2400+5970*
1Ti 5: 3 to those widows who are really in **n.** *NIG*
5: 5 in **n** and left all alone puts her hope in God *NIG*
5:16 that the church can help those widows who are really in **n.** *NIG*
2Ti 2:15 workman who **does not n to be ashamed** *454*
Tit 3:13 see that they **have everything** they **n.** *3309+3594*
Heb 4:16 and find grace to help us in our **time of n.** *2322*
5:12 *you* **n** someone to teach you *2400+5970*
5:12 *You* **n** milk, not solid food! *1181+2400+5970*
7:11 why was there still **n** for another priest *5970*
7:26 Such a high priest **meets** our **n—** *4560*
7:27 not **n** to offer sacrifices day after day, *340+2400*
10:36 *You* **n** to persevere so that *2400+5970*
2Pe 1: 3 His divine power has given us everything we **n** for life and godliness *NIG*
1Jn 2:27 and *you do* not **n** anyone to teach you. *2400+5970*
3:17 sees his brother in **n** but has no pity *2400+5970*
Rev 3:17 I have acquired wealth and *do* not **n** *2400+5970*
21:23 The city *does* not **n** the sun or the moon to shine on it, *2400+5970*
22: 5 not **n** the light of a lamp or the light of *2400+5970*

NEEDED (16) [NEED]
Ex 12: 4 **determine** the **amount** *of* lamb **n** 4082
16:18 Each one gathered as much as he **n.** 430
16:21 everyone gathered as much as he **n,** 430
Jos 19: 9 Judah's portion was more than they **n.** NIH
Ezr 6: 9 Whatever is **n—**young bulls, 10288
7:20 And anything else **n** *for* the temple 10289
Ecc 10:10 more strength *is* **n** but skill will bring success. 1504
Mt 25:36 I **n clothes** and you clothed me, *1218*
25:43 I **n clothes** and you did not clothe me, *1218*
Lk 9:11 and healed those who **n** healing. *2400+5970*
10:42 but only one thing is **n.** *5970*
Jn 13:29 to buy what *was* **n** for the Feast, *2400+5970*
Ac 17:25 *as if he* **n** anything, *4656*
28:10 they furnished us with the supplies we **n.** *5970*
2Co 11: 9 And when I was with you and **n** something, *5728*
11: 9 from Macedonia supplied what I **n.** *5729*

NEEDING (2) [NEED]
Mt 25:38 or **n clothes** and clothe you? *1218*
25:44 a stranger or **n clothes** or sick or in prison, *1218*

NEEDLE (3)

Mt 19:24 through the eye *of* a **n** than for a rich man *4827*
Mk 10:25 through the eye *of* a **n** than for a rich man *4827*
Lk 18:25 through the eye *of* a **n** than for a rich man *1017*

NEEDLESS (2) [NEED]

1Sa 25:31 the staggering burden of **n** bloodshed or 2855
Pr 23:29 Who has **n** bruises? 2855

NEEDS (25) [NEED]

Ex 16:16 'Each one is to gather as much as he **n.** 430
Nu 4:26 to do all that *n to* **be done** with these things. AIT
Dt 15: 8 and freely lend him whatever he **n.** 2893+4728
Pr 12:10 righteous man cares for the **n** *of* his animal, 5883
Isa 58:10 and satisfy the **n** *of* the oppressed, 5883
58:11 he will satisfy your **n** in a sun-scorched land 5883
Jer 5: 7 *I* **supplied all** their **n,** 8425
Mt 21: 3 tell him that the Lord **n** them, *2400+5970*
27:55 from Galilee to care for his **n.** *NIG*
Mk 11: 3 'The Lord **n** it and will send it back *2400+5970*
15:41 followed him and **cared for** his **n.** *1354*
Lk 11: 8 up and give him as much as *he* **n.** *5974*
19:31 tell him, 'The Lord **n** it.' " *2400+5970*
19:34 They replied, "The Lord **n** it." *2400+5970*
Jn 13:10 "A person who has had a bath **n** only *2400+5970*
Ac 20:34 hands of mine have supplied my own **n** and *5970*
20:34 and the **n** of my companions. *NIG*
24:23 permit his friends to **take care of** his **n.** *5676*
27: 3 so they might provide **for** his **n.** *2149*
Ro 12: 8 if it is contributing to the **n** of others, *NIG*
2Co 9:12 not only supplying the **n** of God's people *5729*
Eph 4:29 for building others up according to their **n,** *5970*
Php 2:25 whom you sent to take care *of* my **n.** *5970*
4:19 And my God will meet all your **n** according *5970*
Jas 2:16 but does nothing about his physical **n,** *2201*

NEEDY (55) [NEED]

Ex 22:25 of my people among you who is **n,** do not 6714
Dt 15: 9 not show ill will toward your **n** brother 36
15:11 and toward the poor and **n** in your land. 36
24:14 of a hired man who is poor and **n,** 36
1Sa 2: 8 the poor from the dust and lifts the **n** from 36
Job 5:15 the **n** from the sword in their mouth; 36
24: 4 the **n** from the path and force all the poor of 36
24:14 murderer rises up and kills the poor and **n;** 36
29:16 I was a father to the **n;** 36
31:19 or a **n** *man* without a garment, 36
34:28 so that he heard the cry of the **n.** 6714
Ps 9:18 But the **n** will not always be forgotten, 36
12: 5 of the weak and the groaning of the **n,** 36
35:10 the poor and **n** from those who rob them." 36
37:14 the bow to bring down the poor and **n,** 36
40:17 Yet I am poor and **n;** 36
69:33 The LORD hears the **n** and does 36
70: 5 Yet I am poor and **n;** 36
72: 4 the people and save the children of the **n;** 36
72:12 For he will deliver the **n** who cry out, 36
72:13 on the weak and the **n** and save the needy 36
72:13 on the weak and the needy and save the **n** 36
74:21 may the poor and **n** praise your name. 36
82: 4 Rescue the weak and **n;** 36
86: 1 and answer me, for I am poor and **n.** 36
107:41 But he lifted the **n** out of their affliction 36
109:16 the poor and the **n** and the brokenhearted. 36
109:22 For I am poor and **n,** 36
109:31 For he stands at the right hand of the **n** *one,* 36
113: 7 the poor from the dust and lifts the **n** from 36
140:12 for the poor and upholds the cause of the **n.** 36
Pr 14:21 but blessed is he who is kind to the **n.** 6705
14:31 but whoever is kind to the **n** honors God. 36
22:22 and do not crush the **n** in court, 6714
30:14 the **n** from among mankind. 36
31: 9 defend the rights of the poor and **n."** 36
31:20 to the poor and extends her hands to the **n.** 36
Isa 11: 4 but with righteousness he will judge the **n,** 1924
14:30 and the **n** will lie down in safety. 36
25: 4 a refuge for the **n** in his distress, 36
29:19 **n** will rejoice in the Holy One of Israel. 36+132
32: 7 even when the plea of the **n** is just. 36
41:17 "The poor and **n** search for water, 36
Jer 20:13 He rescues the life of the **n** from the hands 36
22:16 He defended the cause of the poor and **n,** 36
Eze 16:49 they did not help the poor and **n.** 36
18:12 He oppresses the poor and **n.** 36
22:29 they oppress the poor and **n** and mistreat 36
Am 2: 6 and the **n** for a pair of sandals. 36
4: 1 and crush the **n** and say to your husbands, 36
8: 4 you who trample the **n** and do away with 36
8: 6 with silver and the **n** for a pair of sandals, 36
Mt 6: 2 "So when *you* **give to the n,** *1797+4472*
6: 3 But *when* you **give to the n,** *1797+4472*
Ac 4:34 There were no **n** persons among them. *1890*

NEESINGS (KJV) See SNORTING

NEGEV (38) [RAMOTH NEGEV]

Ge 12: 9 Abram set out and continued toward the **N.** 5582
13: 1 So Abram went up from Egypt to the **N,** 5582
13: 3 From the **N** he went from place to place 5582
20: 1 the **N** and lived between Kadesh and Shur. 5582
24:62 for he was living in the **N.** 824+5582
Nu 13:17 through the **N** and on into the hill country. 5582
13:22 up through the **N** and came to Hebron, 5582
13:29 The Amalekites live in the **N;** 824+5582
21: 1 who lived in the **N,** 5582
33:40 who lived in the **N** of Canaan, 5582
Dt 1: 7 in the **N** and along the coast, 5582
34: 3 the **N** and the whole region from the Valley 5582
Jos 10:40 including the hill country, the **N,** 5582
11:16 the hill country, all the **N,** 5582
12: 8 the mountain slopes, the desert and the **N—** 5582
15:19 Since you have given me land in the **N,** 5582
15:21 the **N** toward the boundary of Edom were: 5582
19: 8 as far as Baalath Beer (Ramah in the **N**). 5582
Jdg 1: 9 the **N** and the western foothills. 5582
1:15 Since you have given me land in the **N,** 5582
1:16 of the Desert of Judah in the **N** *near* Arad. 5582
1Sa 27:10 the **N** *of* Judah" or "Against the Negev 5582
27:10 the **N** *of* Jerahmeel" or "Against the Negev 5582
27:10 the Negev of Jerahmeel" or "Against the **N** 5582
30: 1 Amalekites had raided the **N** and Ziklag. 5582
30:14 We raided the **N** *of* the Kerethites and 5582
30:14 the territory belonging to Judah and the **N** 5582
2Sa 24: 7 they went on to Beersheba in the **N** 5582
2Ch 28:18 in the foothills and in the **N** of Judah. 5582
Ps 126: 4 O LORD, like streams in the **N.** 5582
Isa 30: 6 An oracle concerning the animals of the **N:** 5582
Jer 13:19 The cities in the **N** will be shut up, 5582
17:26 from the hill country and the **N,** 5582
32:44 of the western foothills and of the **N,** 5582
33:13 of the western foothills and of the **N,** 5582
Ob 1:19 the **N** will occupy the mountains of Esau, 5582
1:20 the towns of the **N.** 5582
Zec 7: 7 **N** and the western foothills were settled?' " 5582

NEGLECT (9) [NEGLECTED, NEGLECTING, NEGLIGENT]

Dt 12:19 not *to* **n** the Levites as long as you live 6440
14:27 *do* not **n** the Levites living in your towns, 6440
Ezr 4:22 Be careful not to **n** this matter. 10522+10712
Ne 10:39 *"We will* not **n** the house of our God." 6440
Est 6:10 not **n** anything you have recommended." 5877
Ps 119:16 *I will* not **n** your word. 8894
Lk 11:42 but *you* **n** justice and the love of God. *4216*
Ac 6: 2 for us *to* **n** the ministry of the word of God *2901*
1Ti 4:14 *Do* not **n** your gift, *288*

NEGLECTED (3) [NEGLECT]

Ne 13:11 **is the house of God n?"** 6440
SS 1: 6 my own vineyard *I have* **n.** 4202+5757
Mt 23:23 But *you* **have n** the more important matters *918*

NEGLECTING (1) [NEGLECT]

Mt 23:23 without **n** the former. *918*

NEGLIGENT (2) [NEGLECT]

2Ch 29:11 My sons, *do* not *be* **n** now, 8922
Da 6: 4 and neither corrupt nor **n.** 10712

NEHELAMITE (3)

Jer 29:24 Tell Shemaiah the **N,** 5713
29:31 the LORD says about Shemaiah the **N:** 5713
29:32 I will surely punish Shemaiah the **N** 5713

NEHEMIAH (9)

Ezr 2: 2 **N,** Seraiah, Reelaiah, Mordecai, Bilshan, 5718
Ne 1: 1 The words of **N** son of Hacaliah: 5718
3:16 Beyond him, **N** son of Azbuk, 5718
7: 7 Jeshua, **N,** Azariah, Raamiah, Nahamani, 5718
8: 9 Then **N** the governor, 5718
8:10 **N** said, "Go and enjoy choice food NIH
10: 1 **N** the governor, the son of Hacaliah. 5718
12:26 in the days of **N** the governor and of Ezra 5718
12:47 So in the days of Zerubbabel and of **N,** 5718

NEHUM (1)

Ne 7: 7 Mispereth, Bigvai, **N** and Baanah): 5700

NEHUSHTA (1)

2Ki 24: 8 His mother's name was **N** daughter 5735

NEHUSHTAN (1)

2Ki 18: 4 (It was called **N.**) 5736

NEIEL (1)

Jos 19:27 and went north to Beth Emek and **N,** 5832

NEIGH (1) [NEIGHING, NEIGHINGS]

Jer 50:11 a heifer threshing grain and **n** like stallions, 7412

NEIGHBOR (81) [NEIGHBOR'S, NEIGHBORING, NEIGHBORS, NEIGHBORS']

Ex 3:22 to ask her **n** and any woman living 8907
12: 4 they must share one with their nearest **n,** 8907
20:16 not give false testimony against your **n.** 8276
20:17 or anything that belongs to your **n."** 8276
22: 7 "If a man gives his **n** silver or goods 8276
22: 9 guilty must pay back double to his **n.** 8276
22:10 or any other animal to his **n** for safekeeping 8276
22:11 of an oath before the LORD that **the n** did 2257S
22:12 But if the animal was stolen from **the n,** 2257S
22:14 from his **n** and it is injured or dies while 8276
32:27 each killing his brother and friend and **n.'** " 7940
Lev 6: 2 unfaithful to the LORD by deceiving his **n** 6660
19:13 " 'Do not defraud your **n** or rob him. 8276
19:15 but judge your **n** fairly. 6660
19:17 Rebuke your **n** frankly so you will 6660
19:18 but love your **n** as yourself. 8276
20:10 with the wife of his **n—** 8276
24:19 If anyone injures his **n,** 6660
Dt 4:42 if he had unintentionally killed his **n** 8276
5:20 not give false testimony against your **n.** 8276
5:21 or anything that belongs to your **n."** 8276
19: 4 one who kills his **n** unintentionally, 8276
19: 5 a man may go into the forest with his **n** 8276
19: 5 the head may fly off and hit his **n** 8276
19: 6 to **his n** without malice aforethought. 2257S
19:11 a man hates his **N** and lies in wait for him, 8276
22:26 of someone who attacks and murders his **n,** 8276
24:10 you make a loan of any kind to your **n,** 8276
27:24 the man who kills his **n** secretly." 8276
Jos 20: 5 because he killed his **n** unintentionally and 8276
1Ki 8:31 "When a man wrongs his **n** and is required 8276
2Ch 6:22 "When a man wrongs his **n** and is required 8276
Ps 12: 2 Everyone lies to his **n;** 8276
15: 3 who does his **n** no wrong and casts no slur 8276
101: 5 Whoever slanders his **n** in secret, 8276
Pr 3:28 Do not say to your **n,** "Come back later; 8276
3:29 Do not plot harm against your **n,** 8276
6: 1 if you have put up security for your **n,** 8276
6: 3 press your plea with your **n!** 8276
11: 9 With his mouth the godless destroys his **n,** 8276
11:12 A man who lacks judgment derides his **n,** 8276
14:21 He who despises his **n** sins, 8276
16:29 A violent man entices his **n** and leads him 8276
17:18 in pledge and puts up security for his **n.** 8276
21:10 his **n** gets no mercy from him. 8276
24:28 Do not testify against your **n** without cause, 8276
25: 8 in the end if your **n** puts you to shame? 8276
25: 9 If you argue your case with a **n,** 8276
25:18 who gives false testimony against his **n.** 8276
26:19 is a man who deceives his **n** and says, 8276
27:10 better a **n** nearby than a brother far away. 8907
27:14 If a man loudly blesses his **n** early in 8276
29: 5 Whoever flatters his **n** is spreading a net 8276
Ecc 4: 4 from man's envy of his **n.** 8276
Isa 3: 5 man against man, **n** against neighbor. 408S
3: 5 man against man, neighbor against **n.** 8276
19: 2 **n** against neighbor, city against city, 408S
19: 2 neighbor against **n,** city against city, 8276
Jer 9: 8 to his **n,** but in his heart he sets a trap 8276
31:34 No longer will a man teach his **n,** 8276
Mic 7: 5 Do not trust a **n;** 8276
Zec 3:10 of you will invite his **n** to sit under his vine 8276
8:10 for I had turned every man against his **n.** 8276
8:17 do not plot evil against your **n,** 8276
11: 6 "I will hand everyone over to his **n** 8276
Mt 5:43 'Love your **n** and hate your enemy.' *4446*
19:19 and 'love your **n** as yourself.' " *4446*
22:39 second is like it: 'Love your **n** as yourself.' *4446*
Mk 12:31 second is this: 'Love your **n** as yourself.' *4446*
12:33 and to love your **n** as yourself is more *4446*
Lk 10:27 and, 'Love your **n** as yourself.' " *4446*
10:29 so he asked Jesus, "And who is my **n?"** *4446*
10:36 "Which of these three do you think was a **n** *4446*
Ro 13: 9 "Love your **n** as yourself." *4446*
13:10 Love does no harm *to* its **n.** *4446*
15: 2 Each of us should please his **n** for his good, *4446*
Gal 5:14 "Love your **n** as yourself." *4446*
Eph 4:25 and speak truthfully to his **n,** *4446*
Heb 8:11 No longer will a man teach his **n,** *4489*
Jas 2: 8 "Love your **n** as yourself," *4446*
4:12 But you—who are you to judge your **n?** *4446*

NEIGHBOR'S (20) [NEIGHBOR]

Ex 20:17 "You shall not covet your **n** house. 8276
20:17 You shall not covet your **n** wife, 8276
22: 7 and they are stolen from the **n** house, 408
22:26 If you take your **n** cloak as a pledge, 8276
Lev 18:20 not have sexual relations with your **n** wife 6660
19:16 not do anything that endangers your **n** life. 8276
Dt 5:21 "You shall not covet your **n** wife. 8276
5:21 not set your desire on your **n** house or land, 8276
19:14 Do not move your **n** boundary stone set up 8276
23:24 If you enter your **n** vineyard, 8276
23:25 If you enter your **n** grainfield, 8276
27:17 the man who moves his **n** boundary stone." 8276
Job 31: 9 or if I have lurked at my **n** door, 8276
Pr 6: 3 since you have fallen into your **n** hands: 8276
25:17 Seldom set foot in your **n** house— 8276
Eze 18: 6 not defile his **n** wife or lie with a woman 8276
18:11 He defiles his **n** wife. 8276
18:15 He does not defile his **n** wife. 8276
22:11 a detestable offense with his **n** wife, 8276
33:26 and each of you defiles his **n** wife. 8276

NEIGHBORING (10) [NEIGHBOR]

Dt 1: 7 go to all the **n peoples** in the Arabah, 8907
21: 2 the distance from the body to the **n** towns. 6017
1Sa 7:14 and Israel delivered the **n territory** from 1473
Ezr 9: 1 themselves separate from the **n** peoples 824
Ne 9:30 so you handed them over to the **n** peoples. 824
10:28 from the **n** peoples for the sake of the Law 824
10:31 the **n** peoples bring merchandise or grain 824
Ps 76:11 let all the **n** *lands* bring gifts to the One to 6017

Jer 49:18 along with their **n** towns," says the LORD, 8907
50:40 with their **n** towns," declares the LORD, 8907

NEIGHBORS (33) [NEIGHBOR]

Ex 11: 2 that men and women alike are to ask their **n** 8276
Jos 9:16 the Israelites heard that they were **n**, 7940
1Sa 15:28 and has given it to one of your **n**— 8276
28:17 and given it to one of your **n**— 8276
2Ki 4: 3 around and ask all your **n** for empty jars. 8907
1Ch 12:40 Also, their **n** from as far away as Issachar, 7940
Ezr 1: 6 All their **n** assisted them with articles 6017
6:21 the unclean practices of their Gentile **n** 824
Ps 28: 3 who speak cordially with their **n** 8276
31:11 I am the utter contempt of my **n**; 8907
38:11 my **n** stay far away. 7940
44:13 You have made us a reproach to our **n**, 8907
79: 4 We are objects of reproach to our **n**, 8907
79:12 Pay back into the laps of our **n** seven times 8907
80: 6 a source of contention to our **n**, 8907
89:41 he has become the scorn of his **n**. 8907
Pr 14:20 The poor are shunned even by their **n**, 8276
Jer 6:21 **n** and friends will perish." 8907
12:14 "As for all my wicked **n** who seize 8907
49:10 His children, relatives and **n** will perish, 8907
La 1:17 for Jacob that his **n** become his foes; 6017
Eze 16:26 your lustful **n**, and provoked me to anger 8907
16:57 by the daughters of Edom and all her **n** and 6017
22:12 and make unjust gain from your **n** 8276
28:24 people of Israel have malicious **n** who are painful briers 6017
28:26 on all their **n** who maligned them. 6017
Hab 2:15 "Woe to him who gives drink to his **n**, 8276
Lk 1:58 Her **n** and relatives heard that *4341*
1:65 The **n** were all filled with awe, *4340*
14:12 your brothers or relatives, or your rich **n**; *1150*
15: 6 he calls his friends and **n** together and says, *1150*
15: 9 and **n** together and says, 'Rejoice with me; *1150*
Jn 9: 8 His **n** and those who had formerly seen him begging asked, *1150*

NEIGHBORS' (1) [NEIGHBOR]

Jer 29:23 committed adultery with their **n'** wives and 8276

NEIGHING (2) [NEIGH]

Jer 5: 8 each **n** for another man's wife. 7412
8:16 at the **n** *of* their stallions 5177+7754

NEIGHINGS (1) [NEIGH]

Jer 13:27 your adulteries and **lustful n**, 5177

NEITHER (117) [NOR]

Ex 4:10 **n** in the past nor since you have spoken 1685
10: 6 something **n** your fathers 4202
13:22 **N** the pillar of cloud by day nor the pillar 4202
14:20 so **n** went near the other all night long. 2296+4202
20:10 On it you shall not do any work, **n** you, NIH
Nu 14:44 though **n** Moses nor the ark of the LORD's 4202
23:25 "**N** curse them at all nor bless them at all!" 1685+4202
Dt 2:37 **n** the land along the course of the Jabbok NIH
5:14 On it you shall not do any work, **n** you, NIH
8: 3 which **n** you nor your fathers had known, 4202
13: 6 and worship other gods" (gods that **n** you 4202
28:64 which **n** you nor your fathers have known. 4202
Jos 5:14 "**N**," he replied, "but as commander of 4202
8:22 leaving them **n** survivors nor fugitives. 1194
Jdg 1:30 **N** did Zebulun drive out the Canaanites 4202
1:33 **N** did Naphtali drive out those living 4202
2:10 who knew **n** the LORD nor what he had done 4202
6: 4 **n** sheep nor cattle nor donkeys. 2256
11:34 Except for her he had **n** son nor daughter. 401
14: 6 But he told **n** his father 4202
1Sa 5: 5 That is why to this day **n** the priests 4202
20:31 **n** you nor your kingdom will 4202
2Sa 1:21 may you have **n** dew nor rain, 440
2:19 turning **n** to the right nor to the left 4202
14: 7 leaving my husband **n** name nor descendant 1194
17:12 **N** he nor any of his men will be left alive. 4202
1Ki 3:26 said, "**N** I nor you shall have him. 1685+4202
13:28 The lion had **n** eaten the body nor mauled 4202
17: 1 there will be **n** dew nor rain in 561
2Ki 3:17 You will see **n** wind nor rain, 4202
17:34 They **n** worship the LORD nor adhere to 401
18:12 They **n** listened to the commands 4202
23:25 **N** before nor after Josiah was there a king like him 2256+4202
2Ch 36:17 spared **n** young man nor young woman, 4202
Ne 4:23 **N** I nor my brothers nor my men nor 401
5:14 **n** I nor my brothers ate the food allotted to 4202
Est 2: 7 up because she had **n** father nor mother. 401
5: 9 the king's gate and observed that he **n** rose 4202
Job 28:17 **N** gold nor crystal can compare with it, 4202
Ps 121: 4 he who watches over Israel will **n** slumber 4202
Pr 27:20 and **n** are the eyes of man. 4202
30: 8 give me **n** poverty nor riches, 440
Ecc 4: 8 he had **n** son nor brother. 401
7:16 Do not be overrighteous, **n** be overwise 440+2256
9:10 **there is n** working nor planning 401
Isa 5: 6 **n** pruned nor cultivated, 4202
11: 9 They will **n** harm nor destroy 4202
23: 4 "I have **n** been in labor nor given birth; 4202
23: 4 I have **n** reared sons nor brought 2256
30: 5 who bring **n** help nor advantage, 4202
48: 8 You have **n** heard nor understood; 1685+4202
Isa 49:10 They will **n** hunger nor thirst, 4202
55: 8 **n** are your ways my ways," 2256+4202
57:11 and have **n** remembered me 4202
65:25 They will **n** harm nor destroy 4202
Jer 9:16 that **n** they nor their fathers have known, 4202
13:23 **N** can you do good who are accustomed 1685
15:10 I have **n** lent nor borrowed, 4202
16:13 a land **n** you nor your fathers have known, 4202
19: 4 in it to gods that **n** they nor their fathers nor 4202
22:26 where **n** of you was born, 4202
33:10 inhabited by **n** men nor animals, 401+4946
35: 6 **N** you nor your descendants must ever drink 4202
35: 8 **N** we nor our wives nor our sons 1194
37: 2 **N** he nor his attendants nor the people 2256+4202
38:16 I will **n** kill you nor hand you over 561
44: 3 and by worshiping other gods that **n** they 4202
49:31 "a nation that has **n** gates nor bars; 4202
51:62 so that **n** man nor animal will live in it; 1194
Eze 14:20 they could save **n** son nor daughter. 561
43: 7 **n** they nor their kings— NIH
Da 3:12 They **n** serve your gods nor worship 10379
6: 4 because he was trustworthy and **n** corrupt NIH
11:24 and will achieve what **n** his fathers 4202
Am 7:14 "I was **n** a prophet nor a prophet's son, 4202
Zep 1: 6 and **n** seek the LORD nor inquire of him. 4202
1:18 **N** their silver nor their gold will be 1685+4202
Mt 5:15 **N** do people light a lamp and put it under *4028*
9:17 **N** do men pour new wine *4028*
11:18 For John came **n** eating nor drinking, *3612*
21:27 "**N** will I tell you by what authority *4028*
22:30 At the resurrection people will **n** marry nor *4046*
Mk 11:33 "**N** will I tell you by what authority *4028*
12:25 they will **n** marry nor be given in marriage; *4046*
Lk 7:33 For John the Baptist came **n** eating bread *3590*
7:42 **N** of them had the money to pay him back, *3590*
14:35 It is fit **n** for the soil nor for *4046*
18: 2 a judge who **n** feared God nor cared *3590*
20: 8 "**N** will I tell you by what authority *4028*
20:35 the resurrection from the dead will **n** marry *4046*
23:15 **N** has Herod, for he sent him back to us; *4028*
Jn 4:21 when you will worship the Father **n** *4046*
6:24 that **n** Jesus nor his disciples were there, *4024*
8:11 **n** do I condemn you," Jesus declared. *4028*
9: 3 "**N** this man nor his parents sinned," *4046*
12:40 so they can **n** see with their eyes, *3590*
14:17 because it **n** sees him nor knows him. *4024*
15: 4 **N** can you bear fruit unless you remain *4028*
Ac 15:10 the necks of the disciples a yoke that **n** we *4046*
19:37 though they have **n** robbed temples *4046*
23: 8 and that there are **n** angels nor spirits, *3612*
27:20 When **n** sun nor stars appeared *3612*
Ro 1:21 they **n** glorified him as God *4024*
8:38 For I am convinced that **n** death nor life, *4046*
8:38 **n** angels nor demons, *4046*
8:38 **n** the present nor the future, *4046*
8:39 **n** height nor depth, nor anything else *4046*
1Co 3: 7 So **n** he who plants nor he who waters *4046*
6: 9 **N** the sexually immoral nor idolaters *4046*
11: 9 **n** was man created for woman, 2779+4024
2Co 10:15 **N** do we go beyond our limits by boasting *4024*
Gal 3:28 There is **n** Jew nor Greek, slave nor free, *4024*
5: 6 For in Christ Jesus **n** circumcision *4046*
6:15 **N** circumcision nor uncircumcision means anything; *4046*
Jas 3:12 **N** can a salt spring produce fresh water. *4046*
Rev 3:15 that you are **n** cold nor hot. *4046*
3:16 you are lukewarm—**n** hot nor cold— *4046*

NEKEB See ADAMI NEKEB

NEKODA (4)

Ezr 2:48 Rezin, **N**, Gazzam, 5928
2:60 Tobiah and **N** 652 5928
Ne 7:50 Reaiah, Rezin, **N**, 5928
7:62 Tobiah and **N** 642 5928

NEMUEL (3) [NEMUELITE]

Nu 26: 9 and the sons of Eliab were **N**, 5803
26:12 through **N**, the Nemuelite clan; 5803
1Ch 4:24 **N**, Jamin, Jarib, Zerah and Shaul; 5803

NEMUELITE (1) [NEMUEL]

Nu 26:12 through Nemuel, the **N** clan; 5804

NEPHEG (4)

Ex 6:21 The sons of Izhar were Korah, **N** and Zicri. 5863
2Sa 5:15 Ibhar, Elishua, **N**, Japhia, 5863
1Ch 3: 7 Nogah, **N**, Japhia, 5863
14: 6 Nogah, **N**, Japhia, 5863

NEPHEW (2) [NEPHEWS]

Ge 12: 5 He took his wife Sarai, his **n** Lot, 278+1201
14:12 They also carried off Abram's **n** Lot 278+1201

NEPHEWS (1) [NEPHEW]

Ezr 8:19 and his brothers and **n**, 20 men. 1201+2157

NEPHILIM (3)

Ge 6: 4 The **N** were on the earth in those days— 5872
Nu 13:33 the **N** there (the descendants of Anak come 5872
13:33 descendants of Anak come from the **N**). 5872

NEPHISH (KJV) See NAPHISH

NEPHISHESIM (KJV) See NEPHUSSIM

NEPHTHALIM, NEPTHALIM (KJV) See NAPHTALI

NEPHTOAH (2)

Jos 15: 9 toward the spring of the waters of **N**, 5886
18:15 at the spring of the waters of **N**. 5886

NEPHUSSIM (2)

Ezr 2:50 Asnah, Meunim, **N**, 5866
Ne 7:52 Besai, Meunim, **N**, 5867

NER (18)

1Sa 14:50 of Saul's army was Abner son of **N**, 5945
14:50 and **N** was Saul's uncle. NIH
14:51 and Abner's father **N** were sons of Abiel. 5945
26: 5 He saw where Saul and Abner son of **N**, 5945
26:14 to the army and to Abner son of **N**, 5945
2Sa 2: 8 Meanwhile, Abner son of **N**, 5945
2:12 Abner son of **N**, together with the men 5945
3:23 he was told that Abner son of **N** had come 5945
3:25 You know Abner son of **N**; 5945
3:28 concerning the blood of Abner son of **N**. 5945
3:37 in the murder of Abner son of **N**. 5945
1Ki 2: 5 Abner son of **N** and Amasa son of Jether. 5945
2:32 Both of them—Abner son of **N**, 5945
1Ch 8:30 followed by Zur, Kish, Baal, **N**, Nadab, 5945
8:33 **N** was the father of Kish, 5945
9:36 followed by Zur, Kish, Baal, **N**, Nadab, 5945
9:39 **N** was the father of Kish, 5945
26:28 Abner son of **N** and Joab son of Zeruiah, 5945

NEREUS (1)

Ro 16:15 Greet Philologus, Julia, **N** and his sister, *3759*

NERGAL (1)

2Ki 17:30 the men from Cuthah made **N**, 5946

NERGAL-SHAREZER (3)

Jer 39: 3 **N** *of* Samgar, Nebo-Sarsekim 5947
39: 3 **N** a high official and all the other officials 5947
39:13 **N** a high official and all the other officers 5947

NERI (1)

Lk 3:27 the son of Shealtiel, the son *of* **N**, *3760*

NERIAH (10)

Jer 32:12 and I gave this deed to Baruch son of **N**, 5949
32:16 of purchase to Baruch son of **N**, I prayed to 5949
36: 4 So Jeremiah called Baruch son of **N**, 5949
36: 8 Baruch son of **N** did everything Jeremiah 5949
36:14 So Baruch son of **N** went to them with 5950
36:32 and gave it to the scribe Baruch son of **N**, 5950
43: 3 of **N** is inciting you against us to hand us 5949
43: 6 Jeremiah the prophet and Baruch son of **N**. 5950
45: 1 of **N** in the fourth year of Jehoiakim son 5949
51:59 to the staff officer Seraiah son of **N**, 5949

NEST (17) [NESTED, NESTING, NESTS]

Nu 24:21 your **n** is set in a rock; 7860
Dt 22: 6 you come across a bird's **n** beside the road, 7860
32:11 that stirs up its **n** and hovers over its young, 7860
Job 39:27 at your command and build his **n** on high? 7860
Ps 84: 3 and the swallow a **n** for herself, 7860
104:12 The birds of the air **n** by the waters; 8905
Pr 27: 8 that strays from its **n** is a man who strays 7860
Isa 10:14 As one reaches into a **n**, 7860
11: 8 young child put his hand into the viper's **n**. 4402
16: 2 Like fluttering birds pushed from the **n**, 7860
34:11 the great owl and the raven *will* **n** there. 8905
34:15 The owl *will* **n** there and lay eggs, 7873
Jer 48:28 like a dove *that* **makes** *its* **n** at the mouth of 7873
49:16 you build your **n** as high as the eagle's, 7860
Eze 17:23 Birds of every kind *will* **n** in it; 8905
Ob 1: 4 the eagle and make your **n** among the stars, 7860
Hab 2: 9 by unjust gain to set his **n** on high, 7860

NESTED (1) [NEST]

Eze 31: 6 All the birds of the air **n** in its boughs, 7873

NESTING (1) [NEST]

Da 4:21 and *having* **n places** in its branches for 10709

NESTLED (1)

Jer 22:23 *who are* **n** in cedar buildings, 7873

NESTS (4) [NEST]

Ps 104:17 There the birds **make** *their* **n**; 7873
Isa 60: 8 like doves to their **n**? 748
Mt 8:20 birds of the air have **n**, but the Son of Man *2943*
Lk 9:58 birds of the air have **n**, but the Son of Man *2943*

NET (33) [DRAGNET, FISHNETS, NETS]

Job 18: 8 His feet thrust him into a **n** and he wanders 8407
19: 6 that God has wronged me and drawn his **n** 5178
Ps 9:15 in the **n** they have hidden. 8407
10: 9 the helpless and drags them off in his **n.** 8407
35: 7 Since they hid their **n** for me without cause 8407
35: 8 may the **n** they hid entangle them, 8407
57: 6 They spread a **n** for my feet— 8407
140: 5 they have spread out the cords of their **n** 8407
Pr 1:17 to spread a **n** in full view of all the birds! 8407
29: 5 is spreading a **n** for his feet. 8407
Ecc 9:12 As fish are caught in a cruel **n,** 5182
Isa 51:20 like antelope caught in a **n.** 4821
La 1:13 a **n** for my feet and turned me back. 8407
Eze 12:13 I will spread my **n** for him, 8407
17:20 I will spread my **n** for him, 8407
19: 8 They spread their **n** for him, 8407
32: 3 a great throng of people I will cast my **n** 8407
32: 3 and they will haul you up in my **n.** 3052
Hos 5: 1 a **n** spread out on Tabor. 8407
7:12 they go, I will throw my **n** over them; 8407
Mic 7: 2 each hunts his brother with a **n.** 3052
Hab 1:15 he catches them in his **n,** 3052
1:16 to his **n** and burns incense to his dragnet, 3052
1:16 for by **his n** he lives in luxury and enjoys 2156[S]
1:17 Is he to keep on emptying his **n,** 3052
Mt 4:18 They were casting a **n** into the lake, *312*
13:47 of heaven is like a **n** that was let down into *4880*
Mk 1:16 and his brother Andrew **casting a n** into *311*
Jn 21: 6 "Throw your **n** on the right side of the boat *1473*
21: 6 they were unable to haul **the n** in because of *899[S]*
21: 8 towing the **n** full of fish, *1473*
21:11 aboard and dragged the **n** ashore. *1473*
21:11 but even with so many the **n** was not torn. *1473*

NETAIM (1)

1Ch 4:23 the potters who lived at **N** and Gederah; 5751

NETHANEL (14)

Nu 1: 8 from Issachar, **N** son of Zuar; 5991
2: 5 of the people of Issachar is **N** son of Zuar. 5991
7:18 On the second day **N** son of Zuar, 5991
7:23 This was the offering of **N** son of Zuar. 5991
10:15 **N** son of Zuar was over the division of 5991
1Ch 2:14 the fourth **N,** the fifth Raddai, 5991
15:24 Shebaniah, Joshaphat, **N,** Amasai, 5991
24: 6 The scribe Shemaiah son of **N,** a Levite, 5991
26: 4 Joah the third, Sacar the fourth, **N** the fifth, 5991
2Ch 17: 7 **N** and Micaiah to teach in the towns 5991
35: 9 Conaniah along with Shemaiah and **N,** 5991
Ezr 10:22 Elioenai, Maaseiah, Ishmael, **N,** 5991
Ne 12:21 of Hilkiah's, Hashabiah; of Jedaiah's, **N.** 5991
12:36 Gilalai, Maai, **N,** Judah and Hanani— 5991

NETHANIAH (20)

2Ki 25:23 Ishmael son of **N,** Johanan son of Kareah, 5992
25:25 Ishmael son of **N,** the son of Elishama, 5992
1Ch 25: 2 Zaccur, Joseph, **N** and Asarelah. 5992
25:12 the fifth to **N,** his sons and relatives, 12 5993
2Ch 17: 8 Shemaiah, **N,** Zebadiah, Asahel, 5993
Jer 36:14 all the officials sent Jehudi son of **N,** 5993
40: 8 Ishmael son of **N,** 5993
40:14 the Ammonites has sent Ishmael son of **N** 5992
40:15 "Let me go and kill Ishmael son of **N,** 5992
41: 1 In the seventh month Ishmael son of **N,** 5992
41: 2 of **N** and the ten men who were 5992
41: 6 of **N** went out from Mizpah to meet them, 5992
41: 7 Ishmael son of **N** and the men who were 5992
41: 9 Ishmael son of **N** filled it with the dead. 5993
41:10 Ishmael son of **N** took them captive 5992
41:11 crimes Ishmael son of **N** had committed, 5992
41:12 and went to fight Ishmael son of **N.** 5992
41:15 Ishmael son of **N** and eight of his men 5992
41:16 of **N** after he had assassinated Gedaliah son 5992
41:18 of **N** had killed Gedaliah son of Ahikam, 5992

NETHER, NETHERMOST (KJV) See BELOW, FOOT, LOWER, LOWEST

NETHINIMS (KJV) See TEMPLE SERVANTS

NETOPHAH (2)

Ezr 2:22 of **N** 56 5756
Ne 7:26 the men of Bethlehem and **N** 188 5756

NETOPHATHITE (8) [NETOPHATHITES]

2Sa 23:28 Zalmon the Ahohite, Maharai the **N,** 5743
23:29 Heled son of Baanah the **N,** 5743
2Ki 25:23 Seraiah son of Tanhumeth the **N,** 5743
1Ch 11:30 Maharai the **N,** Heled son of Baanah 5743
11:30 Heled son of Baanah the **N,** 5743
27:13 for the tenth month, was Maharai the **N,** 5743
27:15 for the twelfth month, was Heldai the **N,** 5743
Jer 40: 8 the sons of Ephai the **N,** 5743

NETOPHATHITES (3) [NETOPHATHITE]

1Ch 2:54 Bethlehem, the **N,** Atroth Beth Joab, 5743
9:16 who lived in the villages of the **N.** 5743
Ne 12:28 from the villages of the **N,** 5743

NETS (11) [NET]

Ps 141:10 Let the wicked fall into their own **n,** 4821
Isa 19: 8 those who throw **n** on the water will pine 4823
Eze 47:10 will be places for spreading **n.** 3052
Mt 4:20 At once they left their **n** and followed him. *1473*
4:21 with their father Zebedee, preparing their **n.** *1473*
Mk 1:18 At once they left their **n** and followed him. *1473*
1:19 in a boat, preparing their **n.** *1473*
Lk 5: 2 who were washing their **n.** *1473*
5: 4 and let down the **n** for a catch." *1473*
5: 5 because you say so, I will let down the **n.**" *1473*
5: 6 a large number of fish that their **n** began *1473*

NETTLES (1)

Isa 34:13 **n** and brambles her strongholds. 7853

NETWORK (16)

Ex 27: 4 Make a grating for it, a bronze **n,** 5126+8407
27: 4 at each of the four corners of the **n.** 8407
38: 4 a bronze **n,** to be under its ledge, 5126+8407
1Ki 7:17 A **n** of interwoven chains 5126+8422+8422
7:18 in two rows encircling each **n** to decorate 8422
7:20 above the bowl-shaped part next to the **n,** 8422
7:41 the two sets of **n** decorating 8422
7:42 two sets of **n** (two rows of pomegranates 8422
7:42 of pomegranates for each **n,** decorating 8422
2Ki 25:17 a **n** and pomegranates of bronze all around. 8422
25:17 The other pillar, with its **n,** was similar. 8422
2Ch 4:12 the two sets of **n** decorating 8422
4:13 two sets of **n** (two rows of pomegranates 8422
4:13 of pomegranates for each **n,** decorating 8422
Jer 52:22 a **n** and pomegranates of bronze all around. 8422
52:23 above the surrounding **n** was a hundred. 8422

NETWORKS (KJV) See GRATING

NEVER (343)

Ge 8:21 "**N** again will I curse the ground because 4202
8:21 **n** again will I destroy all living creatures, 4202
8:22 day and night will **n** cease." 4202
9:11 **N** again will all life be cut off by the waters 4202
9:11 **n** again will there be a flood to destroy 4202
9:15 **N** again will the waters become a flood 4202
14:23 so that you will **n** be able to say, 4202
19: 8 I have two daughters who have **n** slept with 4202
21:10 for that slave woman's son will **n** share in 4202
41:19 I had **n** seen such ugly cows in all the land 4202
45:20 **N** mind about your belongings, 440+6524
48:11 "I **n** expected to see your face again, 4202
Ex 4:10 "O Lord, I have **n** been eloquent, 4202
10:14 **N** before had there been such a plague 4202
10:29 "I will **n** appear before you again." 4202
14:13 The Egyptians you see today you will **n** see again. 4202+6330+6409
34:10 Before all your people I will do wonders **n** 4202
Lev 27:20 it can **n** be redeemed. 4202+6388
Nu 11: 6 we **n** see anything but this manna!" 401
19: 2 or blemish and that has **n** been under 4202
31:18 for yourselves every girl who has **n** slept 4202
31:35 women who had **n** slept with a man. 4202
Dt 8:16 something your fathers had **n** known, 4202
9: 7 and **n** forget how you provoked 440
13:16 a ruin forever, **n** to be rebuilt. 4202+6388
19:20 and **n** again will such an evil thing be done 4202
21: 3 that has **n** been worked and has never worn 4202
21: 3 that has never been worked and has **n** worn 4202
22:29 He can **n** divorce her as long as he lives. 4202
28:13 always be at the top, **n** at the bottom. 4202
28:66 **n** sure of your life. 4202
28:68 a journey I said you should **n** make again. 4202
29:20 LORD will **n** be willing to forgive him; 4202
31: 6 he will **n** leave you nor forsake you." 4202
31: 8 he will **n** leave you nor forsake you. 4202
Jos 1: 5 I will **n** leave you nor forsake you. 4202
3: 4 since you have **n** been this way before. 4202
9:23 You will **n** cease to serve as woodcutters 4202
10:14 There has **n** been a day like it before or 4202
Jdg 1:28 but **n** drove them out completely. 4202
2: 1 'I will **n** break my covenant with you, 4200+4202+6409
11:37 because I will **n marry.**" 1436
11:38 and wept because she would **n marry.** 1436
16:11 with new ropes that have **n** been used, 4202
19:30 "Such a thing has **n** been seen or done, 4202
21:12 young women who had **n** slept with a man, 4202
1Sa 2:32 in your family line there will **n** be an old man. 2021+3427+3972+4202
3:14 'The guilt of Eli's house will **n** be atoned for 561+6330+6409
6: 7 that have calved and have **n** been yoked. 4202
14:45 about this great deliverance in Israel? **N!** 2721
20: 2 "**N!**" Jonathan replied. "You are not 2721
20: 9 "**N!**" Jonathan said. "If I had the least 2721
2Sa 3:29 May Joab's house **n** be without someone 440
7:15 my love will **n** be taken away from him, 4202
12:10 the sword will **n** depart from your house, 4202+6330+6409
13:22 Absalom **n** said a word to Amnon, 4202
21:17 "**N** again will you go out with us to battle, 4202
1Ki 1: 6 (His father had **n** interfered with him by asking, 3427+4202+4946
2: 4 with all their heart and soul, you will **n** fail 4202
3:12 that there will **n** have been anyone like you, 4200+4202+7156
8:25 'You shall **n** fail to have a man to sit before 4202
8:57 may he **n** leave us nor forsake us. 440
9: 5 'You shall **n** fail to have a man on 4202
10:10 **N** again were so many spices brought in 4202
10:12 So much almugwood has **n** been imported 4202
21:25 (There was **n** a man like Ahab, 4202
22: 8 because he **n** prophesies anything good 4202
22:18 that he **n** prophesies anything good 4202
22:48 but they **n** set sail— 4202
2Ki 1:16 you will **n** leave the bed you are lying on. 4202
2:21 **N** again will it cause death or make 4202
5:17 servant will **n** again make burnt offerings 4202
1Ch 17:13 I will **n** take my love away from him, 4202
2Ch 6:16 'You shall **n** fail to have a man to sit 4202
7:18 'You shall **n** fail to have a man to rule 4202
9: 9 There had **n** been such spices as those 4202
18: 7 because he **n** prophesies anything good 401
18:17 that he **n** prophesies anything good 4202
Ne 5:18 I **n** demanded the food allotted to 4202
Est 1:19 that Vashti is **n** again to enter the presence 4202
9:28 of Purim should **n** cease to be celebrated by 4202
Job 3:16 like an infant who **n** saw the light of day? 4202
7: 7 my eyes will **n** see happiness again. 4202
7:10 He will **n** come to his house again; 4202
7:19 Will you **n** look away from me, 4202
8:18 'I **n** saw you.' 4202
10:19 If only I had **n** come into being, 4202
16: 3 Will your long-winded speeches **n** end? NIH
16:18 may my cry **n** be laid to rest! 440
19:22 Will you **n** get enough of my flesh? 4202
21:10 Their bulls **n** fail to breed; 4202
21:25 **n** having enjoyed anything good. 4202
21:29 Have you **n** questioned those who travel? 4202
27: 5 I will **n** admit you are in the right; 561+2721
27: 6 my righteousness and **n** let go of it; 4202
27:14 his offspring will **n** have enough to eat. 4202
30:17 my gnawing pains **n** rest. 4202
30:27 The churning inside me **n** stops; 4202
31:31 if the men of my household have **n** said, 4202
35:15 that his anger **n** punishes and he does 401
41: 8 the struggle and **n** do it again! 440
Ps 9:10 have **n** forsaken those who seek you. 4202
10: 6 I'll always be happy and **n** have trouble." 4202
10:11 he covers his face and **n** sees." 1153+4200+5905
14: 4 Will evildoers **n** learn— 4202
15: 5 He who does these things will **n** be shaken. 4200+4202+6409
28: 5 he will tear them down and **n** build them 4202
30: 6 I felt secure, I said, "I will **n** be shaken." 1153+4200+6409
31: 1 let me **n** be put to shame; 440+4200+6409
34: 5 their faces are **n** covered with shame. 440
37:25 yet I have **n** seen the righteous forsaken 4202
41: 8 he will **n** get up from the place 3578+4202
49:19 who will **n** see the light [of life]. 4202+5905+6330
53: 4 Will the evildoers **n** learn— 4202
55:11 threats and lies **n** leave its streets. 4202
55:19 men who **n** change their ways 401
55:22 he will **n** let the righteous fall. 4200+4202+6409
62: 2 he is my fortress, I will **n** be shaken. 4202+8041
71: 1 let me **n** be put to shame. 440+4200+6409
77: 7 Will he **n** show his favor again? 4202
89:28 and my covenant with him *will* **n fail.** 586
94:14 he will **n** forsake his inheritance. 4202
95:11 "They shall **n** enter my rest." 561
102:27 and your years will **n** end. 4202
104: 5 it can **n** be moved. 1153+2256+6329+6409
104: 9 **n** again will they cover the earth. 1153
109:14 may the sin of his mother **n** be blotted out. 440
109:16 For he **n** thought of doing a kindness, 4202
112: 6 Surely he will **n** be shaken; 4200+4202+6409
119:93 I will **n** forget your precepts, 4200+4202+6409
140:10 into miry pits, **n** to rise. 1153
148: 6 he gave a decree that will **n** pass away. 4202
Pr 3: 3 Let love and faithfulness **n** leave you; 440
5:17 **n** to be shared with strangers. 401
6:33 and his shame will **n** be wiped away; 4202
7:11 her feet **n** stay at home; 4202
10:30 righteous will **n** be uprooted, 1153+4200+6409
17:13 evil will **n** leave his house. 4202
21:17 whoever loves wine and oil will **n** be rich. 4202
25:10 and you will **n** lose your bad reputation. 4202
27:20 Death and Destruction are **n** satisfied, 4202
30:15 "There are three things that are **n** satisfied, 4202
30:15 four that **n** say, 'Enough!': 4202
30:16 which is **n** satisfied with water, and fire, 4202
30:16 and fire, which **n** says, 'Enough!' 4202
Ecc 1: 7 flow into the sea, yet the sea **is n** full. 401
1: 8 The eye **n** has enough of seeing, 4202
5:10 Whoever loves money **n** has money enough; 4202
5:10 whoever loves wealth is **n** satisfied 4202
6: 5 Though it **n** saw the sun or knew anything, 4202
6: 7 yet his appetite is **n** satisfied. 4202
7:20 on earth who does what is right and **n** sins. 4202
9: 6 **n** again will they have a part in anything that happens 401+4200+6409
SS 7: 2 a rounded goblet that **n** lacks blended wine. 440
Isa 6: 9 " 'Be ever hearing, but **n** understanding; 440
6: 9 be ever seeing, but **n** perceiving.' 440
13:20 She will **n** be inhabited or lived 4200+4202+5905
14:20 of the wicked will **n** be mentioned again. 4202
24:20 that it falls—**n** to rise again. 4202
25: 2 it will **n** be rebuilt. 4200+4202+6409
28:16 the one who trusts will **n** be dismayed. 4202
33:20 its stakes will **n** be pulled up, 1153+4200+5905
43:17 and they lay there, **n** to rise again, 1153
45:17 you will **n** be put to shame or disgraced, 4202

Isa 47: 8 I will **n** be a widow or suffer the loss 4202
48:19 their name would **n** be cut off 4202
51: 6 my righteousness will **n** fail. 4202
51:22 you will **n** drink again. 3578+4202
54: 1 O barren woman, you who **n** bore a child; 4202
54: 1 shout for joy, you who were **n** in labor; 4202
54: 9 the waters of Noah would **n** again cover 4946
54: 9 **n** to rebuke you again. 4946
56:11 they **n** have enough. 4202
58:11 like a spring whose waters **n** fail. 4202
60:11 they will **n** be shut, day or night, 4202
60:20 Your sun will **n** set again, 4202
62: 6 they will **n** be silent day or night. 4202+9458
62: 8 "**N** again will I give your grain as food 561
62: 8 and **n** again will foreigners drink 561
65:20 "**N** again will there be in it 4202
Jer 3:16 It will **n** enter their minds or 4202
5:12 we will **n** see sword or famine. 4202
15:17 I **n** sat in the company of revelers, 4202
15:17 **n** made merry with them; NIH
17: 8 a year of drought and **n** fails to bear fruit." 4202
20:11 their dishonor will **n** be forgotten. 4202+6409
22:10 because he will **n** return 4202+6388
22:11 "He will **n** return. 4202+6388
22:27 You will **n** come back to the land you long 4202
31:40 city will **n** again be uprooted 4200+4202+6409
32:35 though I **n** commanded, 4202
32:40 I will **n** stop doing good to them, 4202
32:40 so that they will **n** turn away from me. 1194
33:17 'David will **n** fail to have a man to sit on 4202
35: 7 Also you must **n** build houses, 4202
35: 7 you must **n** have any of these things, 4202
35:19 'Jonadab son of Recab will **n** fail to have a man to serve me.' 2021+3427+3972+4202
42:18 you will **n** see this place again.' 4202
50:39 It will **n** again be inhabited or 4200+4202+5905
La 3:22 for his compassions **n** fail. 4202
Eze 4:14 I have **n** defiled myself. 4202
4:14 now I have **n** eaten anything found dead 4202
5: 9 I will do to you what I have **n** done before 4202
5: 9 before and will **n** do again. 4202
16:48 and her daughters **n** did what you 561
16:63 be ashamed and **n** again open your mouth 4202
20:32 But what you have in mind will **n** happen. 4202
26:14 You will **n** be rebuilt, 4202+6388
26:21 but you will **n** again be found, 4200+4202+6409
29:15 of kingdoms and will **n** again exalt itself 4202
29:15 that it will **n** *again* rule over the nations. 1194
36:12 you will **n** again deprive them 4202
37:22 and they will **n** again be two nations or 4202
43: 7 of Israel will **n** again defile my holy name— 4202
Da 2:44 God of heaven will set up a kingdom that will **n** be destroyed, 10378+10379+10550
6: 5 "We will **n** find any basis for charges 10379
6:26 his dominion will **n end.** 10002+10509+10527
7:14 his kingdom is one that will **n** be destroyed. 10379
Hos 14: 3 We will **n** again say 'Our gods' 4202
Joel 2: 2 as **n** was of old nor ever will be in ages 4202
2:19 **n** again will I make you an object of scorn 4202
2:26 **n again** will my people be shamed. 4200+4202+6409
2:27 **n again** will my people be shamed. 4200+4202+6409
3:17 **n** again will foreigners invade her. 4202
Am 5: 2 **n** to rise again, deserted in her own land, 4202
8: 7 "I will **n** forget anything they have done. 561+4200+5905
8:14 they will fall, **n** to rise again." 4202
9:15 **n** again to be uprooted from 4202
Ob 1:16 and drink and be as if they had **n** been. 4202
Na 3: 1 full of plunder, **n** without victims! 4202
Hab 1: 4 and justice **n** prevails. 4200+4202+5905
2: 5 he is arrogant and **n** at rest. 4202
2: 5 as the grave and like death is **n** satisfied, 4202
Zep 3:11 **N** again will you be haughty 4202
3:15 **n** again will you fear any harm. 4202
Hag 1: 6 You eat, but **n** have enough. 401
1: 6 You drink, but **n** have your fill. 401
Zec 9: 8 **N** again will an oppressor overrun my people, 4202
14:11 **n** again will it be destroyed. 4202
Mt 7:23 'I **n** knew you. Away from me, *4030*
13:14 be ever hearing but **n** understanding; *3590+4024*
13:14 will be ever seeing but **n** perceiving. *3590+4024*
16:22 and began to rebuke him. "**N,** Lord!" *2664*
16:22 "This shall **n** happen to you!" *3590+4024*
18: 3 will **n** enter the kingdom of heaven. *3590+4024*
21:16 "Yes," replied Jesus, "have you **n** read, *4030*
21:19 "May you **n** bear fruit again!" *3600*
21:42 "Have you **n** read in the Scriptures: *4030*
24:21 **n** to be equaled **again.** *3590+4024*
24:35 but my words will **n** pass away. *3590+4024*
26:33 if all fall away on account of you, I **n** will." *4030*
26:35 I will **n** disown you." *3590+4024*
Mk 2:12 "We have **n** seen anything like this!" *4030*
2:25 "Have you **n** read what David did when he *4030*
3:29 whoever blasphemes against the Holy Spirit will **n** be forgiven; *172+1650+3836+4024*
4:12 but **n** perceiving, and ever hearing *3590*
4:12 and ever hearing but **n** understanding; *3590*
9:25 come out of him and **n** enter him **again."** *3600*
9:43 where the fire **n goes out.** *812*
10:15 like a little child will **n** enter it." *3590+4024*
13:19 and **n** to be equaled again. *3590+4024*
13:31 but my words will **n** pass away. *3590+4024*
14:31 I will **n** disown you." *3590+4024*
Lk 1:15 He is **n** to take wine or other *3590+4024*
1:33 his kingdom will **n** end." *4024*
2:37 She **n** left the temple but worshiped night *4024*
6: 3 "Have you **n** read what David did when he *4028*
15:29 for you and **n** disobeyed your orders. *4030*
15:29 Yet you **n** gave me even a young goat *4030*
18:17 like a little child will **n** enter it." *3590+4024*
20:16 they said, **"May this n** be!" *3590*
21:33 but my words will **n** pass away. *3590+4024*
23:29 the wombs that **n** bore and the breasts *4024*
23:29 and the breasts that **n** nursed!' *4024*
Jn 4:14 whoever drinks the water I give him will **n** thirst. *172+1650+3590+3836+4024*
4:48 Jesus told him, "you will **n** believe." *3590+4024*
5:37 You have **n** heard his voice *4046+4799*
6:35 He who comes to me will **n** go hungry, *3590+4024*
6:35 and he who believes in me will **n** be thirsty. *3590+4024+4799*
6:37 comes to me I will **n** drive away. *3590+4024*
8:12 Whoever follows me will **n** walk *3590+4024*
8:33 and have **n** been slaves of anyone. *4799*
8:51 he will **n** see death." *172+1650+3590+3836+4024*
8:52 he will **n** taste death. *172+1650+3590+3836+4024*
10: 5 But they will **n** follow a stranger; *3590+4024*
10:28 they shall **n** perish; *173+1650+3590+3836+4024*
10:41 "Though John **n** performed a miraculous *4029*
11:26 whoever lives and believes in me will **n** die. *172+1650+3590+3836+4024*
13: 8 said Peter, "you shall **n** wash my feet." *172+1650+3836+4024*
Ac 5:42 they **n** stopped teaching and proclaiming *4024*
6:13 "This fellow **n** stops speaking *4024*
10:14 "I have **n** eaten anything impure *4030*
13:10 Will you **n** stop perverting the right ways *4024*
13:34 **n** to decay, is stated in these words: *3516+3600*
13:41 in your days that you would **n** believe, *3590+4024*
14: 8 lame from birth and had **n** walked. *4030*
20:31 for three years I **n** stopped warning each *4024*
20:38 they would **n** see his face **again.** *4033*
28:26 be ever hearing but **n** understanding; *3590+4024*
28:26 will be ever seeing but **n** perceiving." *3590+4024*
Ro 4: 8 man whose sin the Lord will **n** count *3590+4024*
9:33 and the one who trusts in him will **n** be put *4024*
10:11 "Anyone who trusts in him will **n** be put *4024*
12:11 **N** be lacking in zeal, *3590*
1Co 6:15 and unite them with a prostitute? **N!** *1181+3590*
8:13 causes my brother to fall into sin, I will **n** eat meat **again,** *172+1650+3590+3836+4024*
13: 8 Love **n** fails. *4030*
2Co 12:13 except that I was **n** a burden to you? *4024*
Gal 4:30 the slave woman's son will **n** share in *3590+4024*
6:14 **May** I **n** boast except in the cross *1181+3590*
1Th 2: 5 You know we **n** used flattery, *4046+4537*
2Th 3:13 you, brothers, **n** tire of doing what is right. *3590*
2Ti 3: 7 always learning but **n** able to acknowledge *3595*
Heb 1:12 and your years will **n** end." *4024*
3:11 'They shall **n** enter my rest.' " *1623*
3:18 that they would **n** enter his rest if not *3590*
4: 3 'They shall **n** enter my rest.' " *1623*
4: 5 "They shall **n** enter my rest." *1623*
9: 7 only once a year and **n** without blood, *4024*
9:17 it **n** takes effect while the one who made it *3607*
10: 1 For this reason it can **n,** *4030*
10:11 which can **n** take away sins. *4030*
13: 5 God has said, "**N** will I leave you; *3590+4024*
13: 5 **n** will I forsake you." *3590+4024*
Jas 3: 2 If anyone is **n** at fault in what he says, *4024*
1Pe 1: 4 into an inheritance that **can n perish,** spoil *915*
2: 6 trusts in him will **n** be put to shame." *3590+4024*
5: 4 the crown of glory that will **n fade away.** *277*
2Pe 1:10 For if you do these things, you will **n** fall, *3590+4024+4537*
1:21 For prophecy **n** had its origin in the will of man, *4024+4537*
2:14 eyes full of adultery, they **n stop** sinning; *188*
Rev 3: 5 I will **n** blot out his name from the book of life, *3590+4024*
3:12 **N** again will he leave it. *3590+4024*
4: 8 Day and night they **n** stop saying: *4024*
7:16 **N again** will they hunger; *2285+4024*
7:16 **n again** will they thirst. *2285+4028*
18: 7 I am not a widow, and I will **n** mourn. *3590+4024*
18:14 **n** to be recovered.' *3590+4024+4033*
18:21 **n** to be found again. *3590+4024*
18:22 will **n** be heard in you again. *3590+4024*
18:22 millstone will **n** be heard in you again. *3590+4024*
18:23 of a lamp will **n** shine in you again. *3590+4024*
18:23 voice of bridegroom and bride will **n** *3590+4024*

NEVER-FAILING (1)

Am 5:24 righteousness like a **n** stream! 419

NEVERTHELESS (34)

Ge 48:19 **N,** his younger brother will 219+2256
Ex 16:27 **N,** some of the people went out on 2256
Nu 14:21 **N,** as surely as I live and as surely as 219+2256
14:44 **N,** in their presumption they went up 2256
Dt 12:15 **N,** you may slaughter your animals in any 8370
Jdg 11: 8 The elders of Gilead said to him, "**N,** 4027+4200
1Sa 29: 9 **n,** the Philistine commanders have said, 421
2Sa 5: 7 **N,** David captured the fortress of Zion, 2256
1Ki 8:19 **N,** you are not the one to build the temple, 8370
11: 2 **N,** Solomon held fast to them in love. NIH
11:12 **N,** for the sake of David your father, 421
15: 4 **N,** for David's sake the LORD his God gave him a lamp in Jerusalem 3954
2Ki 3: 3 **N** he clung to the sins of Jeroboam son 8370
8:19 **N,** for the sake of his servant David, 2256
17:29 **N,** each national group made its own gods 2256
23:26 **N,** the LORD did not turn away from 421
1Ch 11: 5 **N,** David captured the fortress of Zion, 2256
2Ch 6: 9 **N,** you are not the one to build the temple, 8370
21: 7 **N,** because of the covenant the LORD 2256
30:11 **N,** some men of Asher, 421
Est 5:10 **N,** Haman restrained himself 2256
Job 17: 9 **N,** the righteous will hold to their ways, 2256
Isa 9: 1 **N,** there will be no more gloom 3954
Jer 28: 7 **N,** listen to what I have to say 421
33: 6 " '**N,** I will bring health and healing to it; 2180
Da 5:17 **N,** I will read the writing for the king 10124
Ac 5:14 **N,** more and more men and women believed *1254*
27:26 **N,** we must run aground on some island." *1254*
Ro 5:14 **N,** death reigned from the time of Adam to *247*
1Co 7:17 **N,** each one should retain the place *1623+3590*
10: 5 **N,** God was not pleased with most of them; *247*
2Ti 2:19 **N,** God's solid foundation stands firm, *3530*
Rev 2:14 **N,** I have a few things against you: *247*
2:20 **N,** I have this against you: *247*

NEW (192) [ANEW, NEWLY]

Ge 27:28 an abundance of grain and **n wine.** 9408
27:37 I have sustained him with grain and **n wine.** 9408
45:22 To each of them he gave **n** clothing, 2722
Ex 1: 8 Then a **n** king, who did not know about 2543
Lev 2:14 offer crushed heads of **n grain** roasted in 4152
14:42 to replace these and take **n** clay and plaster 337
23:14 or roasted or **n grain,** 4152
23:16 and then present an offering of **n** grain to 2543
26:10 to move it out to make room for the **n.** 2543
Nu 10:10 feasts and **N Moon festivals—** 2544+8031
16:30 LORD brings about **something totally n,** 1375
18:12 and all the finest **n wine** and grain they give 9408
28:14 to be made at each **n moon** *during* the year. 2544
28:26 to the LORD an offering of **n** grain during 2543
Dt 7:13 your grain, **n wine** and oil— 9408
11:14 gather in your grain, **n wine** and oil. 9408
12:17 the tithe of your grain and **n wine** and oil, 9408
14:23 Eat the tithe of your grain, **n wine** and oil, 9408
18: 4 firstfruits of your grain, **n wine** and oil, 9408
20: 5 "Has anyone built a **n** house and 2543
22: 8 When you build a **n** house, 2543
28:51 They will leave you no grain, **n wine** or oil, 9408
32: 2 like showers on **n grass,** 2013
33:28 in a land of grain and **n wine,** 9408
Jos 9:13 And these wineskins that we filled were **n,** 2543
Jdg 5: 8 When they chose **n** gods, 2543
15:13 with two **n** ropes and led him up from 2543
16:11 "If anyone ties me securely with **n** ropes 2543
16:12 So Delilah took **n** ropes and tied him 2543
1Sa 6: 7 "Now then, get a **n** cart ready, 2543
20: 5 "Look, tomorrow is the **N Moon festival,** 2544
20:18 "Tomorrow is the **N Moon festival.** 2544
20:24 and when the **N Moon festival** came, 2544
2Sa 6: 3 on a **n** cart and brought it from the house 2543
6: 3 were guiding the **n** cart 2543
21:16 and who was armed with a **n** [sword], 2543
1Ki 11:29 wearing a **n** cloak. 2543
11:30 of the **n** cloak he was wearing and tore it 2543
2Ki 2:20 "Bring me a **n** bowl," he said, 2543
4:23 "It's not the **N Moon** or the Sabbath." 2544
4:42 along with *some* **heads of n grain.** 4152
16:14 the **n** altar and the temple of the LORD— NIH
16:14 and put it on the north side of the **n** altar. NIH
16:15 "On the large **n** altar, NIH
18:32 a land of grain and **n wine,** 9408
1Ch 13: 7 of God from Abinadab's house on a **n** cart, 2543
23:31 on Sabbaths and at **N Moon festivals** and 2544
2Ch 2: 4 and **N Moons** and at the appointed feasts of 2544
8:13 **N Moons** and the three annual feasts— 2544
20: 5 the LORD in the front of the **n** courtyard 2543
31: 3 **N Moons** and appointed feasts as written in 2544
31: 5 of their grain, **n wine,** oil and honey and all 9408
32:28 the harvest of grain, **n wine** and oil; 9408
Ezr 3: 5 the **N Moon** sacrifices and the sacrifices 2544
9: 9 He has granted us **n life** to rebuild 4695
Ne 5:11 grain, **n wine** and oil." 9408
10:33 **N Moon festivals** and appointed feasts; 2544
10:37 of the fruit of all our trees and of our **n wine** 9408
10:39 **n wine** and oil to the storerooms where 9408
13: 5 **n wine** and oil prescribed for the Levites, 9408
13:12 **n wine** and oil into the storerooms. 9408
Job 10:17 *You* **bring n** witnesses against me 2542
14: 7 and its **n shoots** will not fail. 3438
29:20 the bow *ever* **n** in my hand.' 2736
32:19 like **n** wineskins ready to burst. 2543
Ps 4: 7 when their grain and **n wine** abound. 9408
33: 3 Sing to him a **n** song; 2543
40: 3 He put a **n** song in my mouth, 2543
81: 3 Sound the ram's horn at the **N Moon,** 2544
90: 5 they are like the **n** grass of the morning— 2736
90: 6 though in the morning it springs up **n,** 2736
96: 1 Sing to the LORD a **n** song; 2543
98: 1 Sing to the LORD a **n** song, 2543
144: 9 I will sing a **n** song to you, O God; 2543
149: 1 Sing to the LORD a **n** song, 2543
Pr 3:10 and your vats will brim over with **n wine.** 9408
27:25 the hay is removed and **n growth** appears 2013
Ecc 1: 9 there is nothing **n** under the sun. 2543
1:10 This is something **n**"? 2543
SS 6:11 of nut trees to look at the **n growth** *in* 4
7:13 at our door is every delicacy, both **n** and old 2543
Isa 1:13 **N Moons,** Sabbaths and convocations— 2544

Isa 1:14 Your **N Moon festivals** and your appointed 2544
24: 7 The **n wine** dries up and the vine withers; 9408
36:17 a land of grain and **n wine,** 9408
41:15 **n** and sharp, with many teeth. 2543
42: 9 and **n** *things* I declare; 2543
42:10 Sing to the LORD a **n** song, 2543
43:19 See, I am doing a **n** *thing!* 2543
48: 6 "From now on I will tell you of **n** *things,* 2543
62: 2 be called by a **n** name that the mouth of 2543
62: 8 the **n wine** for which you have toiled; 9408
65:17 I will create **n** heavens and a new earth. 2543
65:17 I will create new heavens and a **n** earth. 2543
66:22 "As the **n** heavens and the new earth 2543
66:22 and the **n** earth that I make will endure 2543
66:23 From *one* **N Moon** to another and 2544
Jer 8:10 to other men and their fields to **n owners.** 3769
26:10 of the **N** Gate of the LORD's house. 2543
31:12 the grain, the **n wine** and the oil, 9408
31:22 The LORD will create a **n** *thing* 2543
31:31 a **n** covenant with the house of Israel and 2543
36:10 at the entrance of the **N** Gate of the temple, 2543
La 3:23 *They* are **n** every morning; 2543
Eze 11:19 an undivided heart and put a **n** spirit 2543
17: 9 All its **n** growth will wither. 3273
18:31 and get a **n** heart and a new spirit. 2543
18:31 and get a new heart and a **n** spirit. 2543
36:26 a **n** heart and put a new spirit in you; 2543
36:26 a new heart and put a **n** spirit in you; 2543
45:17 the **N Moons** and the Sabbaths— 2544
46: 1 on the day of the **N Moon** it is to be opened. 2544
46: 3 On the Sabbaths and **N Moons** the people of 2544
46: 6 of the **N Moon** he is to offer a young bull, 2544
Da 1: 7 The chief official gave them **n** names: NIH
Hos 2: 8 the grain, the **n wine** and oil, 9408
2: 9 and my **n wine** when it is ready. 9408
2:11 her yearly festivals, her **N Moons,** 2544
2:22 to the grain, the **n wine** and oil, 9408
4:11 to prostitution, to old wine and **n,** 9408
5: 7 their **N Moon festivals** will devour them 2544
7:14 grain and **n wine** but turn away from me. 9408
9: 2 the **n wine** will fail them. 9408
Joel 1: 5 wail because of the **n wine,** 6747
1:10 the **n wine** is dried up, the oil fails. 9408
2:19 "I am sending you grain, **n wine** and oil, 9408
2:24 the vats will overflow with **n wine** and oil. 9408
3:18 "In that day the mountains will drip **n wine,** 6747
Am 8: 5 the **N Moon** be over that we may sell grain, 2544
9:13 **N wine** will drip from the mountains 6747
Zep 1:10 wailing from the **N Quarter,** 5467
3: 5 and every **n day** he does not fail, 240
Hag 1:11 on the grain, the **n wine,** 9408
Zec 9:17 and **n wine** the young women. 9408
Mt 9:17 Neither do men pour **n** wine *3742*
9:17 No, they pour **n** wine into new wineskins, *3742*
9:17 No, they pour new wine into **n** wineskins, *2785*
13:52 of his storeroom **n** treasures as well as old." *2785*
27:60 in his own **n** tomb that he had cut out of *2785*
Mk 1:27 A **n** teaching—and with authority! *2785*
2:21 the **n** *piece* will pull away from the old, *2785*
2:22 no one pours **n** wine into old wineskins. *3742*
2:22 No, he pours **n** wine into new wineskins." *3742*
2:22 No, he pours new wine into **n** wineskins." *2785*
16:17 they will speak *in* **n** tongues; *2785*
Lk 5:36 from a **n** garment and sews it on an old one. *2785*
5:36 If he does, he will have torn the **n** garment, *2785*
5:36 the patch from the **n** will not match the old. *2785*
5:37 no one pours **n** wine into old wineskins. *3742*
5:37 If he does, the **n** wine will burst the skins, *3742*
5:38 **n** wine must be poured into new wineskins. *3742*
5:38 new wine must be poured into **n** wineskins. *2785*
5:39 no one after drinking old wine wants the **n,** *3742*
22:20 "This cup is the **n** covenant in my blood, *2785*
Jn 13:34 **n** command I give you: Love one another. *2785*
19:41 and in the garden a **n** tomb, *2785*
Ac 5:20 the people the full message of this **n** life." *NIG*
17:19 "May we know what this **n** teaching is *2785*
Ro 6: 4 we too may live a **n** life. *2786*
7: 6 from the law so that we serve in the **n way** *2786*
1Co 5: 7 that you may be a **n** batch without yeast— *3742*
11:25 "This cup is the **n** covenant in my blood; *2785*
2Co 3: 6 competent as ministers *of* a **n** covenant— *2785*
5:17 if anyone is in Christ, he is a **n** creation; *2785*
5:17 the old has gone, the **n** has come! *2785*
Gal 6:15 what counts is a **n** creation. *2785*
Eph 2:15 to create in himself one **n** man out of *2785*
4:23 *to be* **made n** in the attitude of your minds; *391*
4:24 and to put on the **n** self, *2785*
Col 2:16 a **N Moon celebration** or a Sabbath day. *3741*
3:10 and have put on the **n** self, *3742*
Heb 8: 8 a **n** covenant with the house of Israel and *2785*
8:13 By calling this covenant **"n,"** *2785*
9:10 until the time *of* **the n order.** *1481*
9:15 the mediator *of* a **n** covenant, *2785*
10:20 a **n** and living way opened for us through *4710*
12:24 to Jesus the mediator *of* a **n** covenant, *3742*
1Pe 1: 3 In his great mercy he *has* **given** us **n birth** *335*
2Pe 3:13 to a **n** heaven and a new earth, *2785*
3:13 to a new heaven and a **n** earth, *2785*
1Jn 2: 7 I am not writing you a **n** command but *2785*
2: 8 Yet I am writing you a **n** command; *2785*
2Jn 1: 5 a **n** command but one we have had from *2785*
Rev 2:17 a white stone with a **n** name written on it, *2785*
3:12 the **n** Jerusalem, which is coming down out *2785*
3:12 and I will also write on him my **n** name. *2785*
5: 9 And they sang a **n** song: *2785*
14: 3 And they sang a **n** song before the throne *2785*
21: 1 Then I saw a **n** heaven and a new earth, *2785*
Rev 21: 1 Then I saw a new heaven and a **n** earth, *2785*
21: 2 I saw the Holy City, the **n** Jerusalem, *2785*
21: 5 "I am making everything **n!"** *2785*

NEWBORN (3) [BEAR]

Jer 14: 5 Even the doe in the field deserts *her* **n** *fawn* 3528
Ac 7:19 by forcing them to throw out their **n babies** *1100*
1Pe 2: 2 Like **n** babies, crave pure spiritual milk, *786*

NEWLY (1) [NEW]

Jdg 6:28 second bull sacrificed on the **n built** altar! 1215

NEWS (79)

Ge 29:13 As soon as Laban heard the **n** *about* Jacob, 9051
45:16 When the **n** reached Pharaoh's palace 7754
1Sa 4:17 The *man who* **brought the n** replied, 1413
4:19 the **n** that the ark of God had been captured 9019
13: 4 So all Israel heard the **n:** 606
31: 9 to **proclaim the n** in the temple of their 1413
2Sa 4: 4 when the **n** *about* Saul and Jonathan came 9019
4:10 and thought he was **bringing good n,** 1413
4:10 **reward** I gave him **for** his **n!** 1415
18:19 "Let me run and **take the n** *to* the king that 1413
18:20 "You are not the one to take the **n** today," 1415
18:20 *"You may* **take the n** another time, 1413
18:22 You don't have any **n** that will bring you 1415
18:25 "If he is alone, he must have **good n."** 1415
18:26 "He *must be* **bringing good n,** too." 1413
18:27 "He comes with good **n."** 1415
18:31 "My lord the king, **hear** *the* **good n!** 1413
1Ki 1:42 like you *must be* **bringing** good **n."** 1413
2:28 When the **n** reached Joab, 9019
14: 6 I have been sent to you with **bad n.** 7997
2Ki 7: 9 a day of **good n** and we are keeping it 1415
7:11 The gatekeepers **shouted the n,** 7924
9:15 of the city to go and **tell the n** in Jezreel." 5583
1Ch 10: 9 to **proclaim the n** among their idols 1413
Ps 112: 7 He will have no fear of bad **n;** 9019
Pr 15:30 and good **n** gives health to the bones. 9019
25:25 a weary soul is good **n** from a distant land. 9019
Isa 52: 7 the feet of *those who* **bring good n,** 1413
61: 1 to **preach good n** *to* the poor. 1413
Jer 20:15 who **brought** my father **the n,** 1413
49:23 for they have heard bad **n.** 9019
Eze 21: 7 'Because of the **n** that is coming. 9019
24:26 a fugitive will come to tell you the **n.** 265+2245
Jnh 3: 6 When the **n** reached the king of Nineveh, 1821
Na 1:15 the feet of *one who* **brings good n,** 1413
3:19 who hears the **n** *about* you claps his hands 9051
Mt 4:23 preaching the **good n** of the kingdom, *2295*
4:24 **N** about him spread all over Syria, *198*
9:26 **N** of this spread through all that region. *5773*
9:31 But they went out and **spread the n about** *1424*
9:35 preaching the **good n** of the kingdom *2295*
11: 5 **the good n is preached** to the poor. *2294*
Mk 1:14 proclaiming the **good n** of God. *2295*
1:15 Repent and believe the **good n!"** *2295*
1:28 **N** about him spread quickly over *198*
1:45 and began to talk freely, spreading the **n.** *3364*
16:15 into all the world and preach the **good n** *2295*
Lk 1:19 and to **tell** you this **good n.** *2294*
2:10 *I* **bring** you **good n** of great joy that will be *2294*
3:18 and **preached the good n** to them. *2294*
4:14 and **n** about him spread through *5773*
4:18 *to* **preach good n** to the poor. *2294*
4:37 And the **n** about him spread throughout *2491*
4:43 "I must **preach the good n** of the kingdom *2294*
5:15 Yet the **n** about him spread all the more, *3364*
7:17 This **n** about Jesus spread throughout Judea *3364*
7:22 **the good n** *is* **preached** to the poor. *2294*
8: 1 **proclaiming the good n** of the kingdom *2294*
16:16 **the good n** of the kingdom of God *is being* **preached,** *2294*
Jn 4:51 his servants met him **with the n** *3306*
20:18 went to the disciples **with the n:** *33*
Ac 5:42 **proclaiming the good n** that Jesus is the *2294*
8:12 *as he* **preached the good n** of the kingdom *2294*
8:35 **told** him **the good n about** about Jesus. *2294*
10:36 **telling the good n** of peace *2294*
11:20 **telling** them **the good n about** *2294*
11:22 **N** of this reached the ears of the church *3364*
13:32 *"We* **tell** you **the good n:** *2294*
14: 7 where they continued *to* **preach the good n.** *2294*
14:15 We are **bringing** you **good n,** *2294*
14:21 *They* **preached the good n** in that city *2294*
15: 3 This **n** made all the brothers very glad. *NIG*
17:18 because Paul *was* **preaching the good n** *2294*
21:31 **n** reached the commander of the Roman *5762*
Ro 10:15 the feet *of* those who **bring** good **n!"** *2294*
10:16 not all the Israelites accepted the **good n.** *2295*
Php 2:19 that I also may be cheered *when I* **receive n** *1182*
Col 4: 7 Tychicus will tell you all the **n** about me. *NIG*
1Th 3: 6 and *has* **brought good n about** your faith *2294*

NEXT (187)

Ge 17:21 to you by this time **n** year." 337
18:10 surely return to you about this time **n year,** 2645
18:14 to you at the appointed time **n year** 2645
19:27 Early the **n** morning Abraham got up NIH
19:34 The **n day** the older daughter said to 4740
20: 8 **n** morning Abimelech summoned all his officials, NIH
21:14 the **n** morning Abraham took some food NIH
22: 3 Early the **n** morning Abraham got up NIH
Ge 24:54 When they got up the **n** morning, he said, NIH
26:31 Early the **n** morning the men swore an oath NIH
28:18 Early the **n** morning Jacob took NIH
31:55 **n** morning Laban kissed his grandchildren NIH
33: 2 Leah and her children **n,** 340
33: 7 **N,** Leah and her children came 1685
40: 6 When Joseph came to them the **n** morning, NIH
45: 6 the **n** five years there will not be plowing 6388
Ex 2:13 The **n** day he went out and saw 9108
9: 6 And the **n day** the LORD did it: 4740
18:13 The **n day** Moses took his seat to serve 4740
24: 4 up early the **n** morning and built an altar at NIH
25:33 three on the **n** branch, 285
28:26 the breastpiece on the inside edge **n to** 448+6298
32: 6 So the **n day** the people rose early 4740
32:30 The **n day** Moses said to the people, 4740
37:19 three on the **n** branch and the same 285
38: 9 **N** they made the courtyard. 2256
39:19 the breastpiece on the inside edge **n to** 448+6298
Lev 6:10 with linen undergarments **n to** his body, 6584
7:16 over may be eaten on the **n day.** 4740
16: 4 with linen undergarments **n to** his body; 6584
19: 6 on the day you sacrifice it or on the **n day;** 4740
27:18 that remain until the **n** Year of Jubilee, NIH
Nu 2: 5 The tribe of Issachar will camp **n to** them. 6584
2: 7 The tribe of Zebulun will be **n.** NIH
2:12 The tribe of Simeon will camp **n to** them. 6584
2:14 The tribe of Gad will be **n.** 2256
2:20 The tribe of Manasseh will be **n to** them. 6584
2:22 The tribe of Benjamin will be **n.** 2256
2:27 The tribe of Asher will camp **n to** them. 6584
2:29 The tribe of Naphtali will be **n.** 2256
10:18 divisions of the camp of Reuben went **n,** 2256
10:22 divisions of the camp of Ephraim went **n,** 2256
11:32 All that day and night and all the **n** day 4740
14:40 Early the **n** morning they went up toward NIH
16:41 The **n day** the whole Israelite community grumbled against Moses 4740
17: 8 The **n day** Moses entered the Tent of 4740
22: 5 and have settled **n to** me. 4578+4946
22:13 The **n** morning Balaam got up and said NIH
22:41 The **n** morning Balak took Balaam up NIH
Dt 3: 1 **N** we turned and went up along the road 2256
Jos 6:12 up early the **n** morning and the priests took NIH
7:16 **n** morning Joshua had Israel come forward NIH
8:10 the **n** morning Joshua mustered his men, NIH
Jdg 6:38 Gideon rose early the **n day;** 4740
9:10 **"N,** the trees said to the fig tree, 2256
9:42 The **n day** the people of Shechem went out 4740
9:50 **N** Abimelech went to Thebez 2256
11:18 **"N** they traveled through the desert, 2256
20:19 The **n** morning the Israelites got up NIH
21: 4 Early the **n day** the people built an altar 4740
Ru 4: 4 and I am **n in line."** 339
1Sa 1:19 the **n** morning they arose and worshiped NIH
5: 3 the people of Ashdod rose early the **n day,** 4740
11:11 The **n day** Saul separated his men 4740
18:10 The **n day** an evil spirit from God 4740
20:25 and Abner sat **n to** Saul, 4946+7396
20:27 But the **n day,** the second day of the month, 4740
30:17 from dusk until the evening of the **n day,** 4740
31: 8 The **n day,** when the Philistines came 4740
2Sa 11:12 in Jerusalem that day and the **n.** 4740
14:30 "Look, Joab's field is **n to** mine, 448+3338
23: 9 **N to** him was Eleazar son of Dodai 339
23:11 **N to** him was Shammah son of Agee 339
24:11 Before David got up the **n** morning, NIH
1Ki 1: 6 also very handsome and was born **n after** 339
3:21 The **n** morning, I got up to nurse my son— NIH
4:12 and Megiddo, and in all of Beth Shan **n to** 725
7:20 the bowl-shaped part **n to** the network, 4200+6298
17: 1 in the **n** *few* years except at my word." 465[S]
20:22 because **n** spring the king of Aram NIH
20:26 The **n** spring Ben-Hadad mustered NIH
2Ki 3:20 The **n** morning, about the time for offering NIH
4:16 "About this time **n year,"** Elisha said, 2645+6961
4:17 and the **n year** about that same time 2645+6961
6:15 up and went out **early the n morning,** 8899
6:29 The **n** day I said to her, 337
8:15 But the **n day** he took a thick cloth, 4740
10: 9 The **n** morning Jehu went out. NIH
19:35 When the people got up the **n** morning— NIH
23: 4 the priests **n in rank** and the doorkeepers 5467
25:18 Zephaniah the priest **n in rank** and 5467
1Ch 5:11 The Gadites lived **n to** them in Bashan, 4200+5584
10: 8 The **n day,** when the Philistines came 4740
11:12 **N to** him was Eleazar son of Dodai 339
15:18 and with them their brothers **n in rank:** 5467
29:21 The **n** day they made sacrifices to the LORD 4740
2Ch 17:15 **n,** Jehohanan the commander, 3338+6584
17:16 **n,** Amasiah son of Zicri, 3338+6584
17:18 **n,** Jehozabad, with 180,000 men 3338+6584
29:20 **Early the n morning** King Hezekiah gathered the city officials 8899
29:22 **n** they slaughtered the rams 2256
31:12 and his brother Shimei was **n in rank.** 5467
Ne 3: 2 Zaccur son of Imri built **n to** them. 3338+6584
3: 4 son of Hakkoz, repaired the **n section.** 3338+6584
3: 4 **N to** him Meshullam son of Berekiah, 3338+6584
3: 4 and **n to** him Zadok son of Baana 3338+6584
3: 5 The **n section** was repaired by the men 3338+6584
3: 7 **N to** them, repairs were made by men 3338+6584
3: 8 repaired the **n section;** 3338+6584
3: 8 made repairs **n to** that. 3338+6584
3: 9 repaired the **n section.** 3338+6584
3:10 of Hashabneiah made repairs **n to** him. 3338+6584
3:12 the **n section** with the help of his 3338+6584

Ne 3:17 **N to** him, the repairs were made by 339
3:18 **N to** him, the repairs were made 339
3:19 **N to** him, Ezer son of Jeshua, 3338+6584
3:20 **N to** him, Baruch son 339
3:21 **N to** him, Meremoth son of Uriah, 339
3:22 The repairs **n to** him were made by 339
3:23 and **n to** them, Azariah son of Maaseiah, 339
3:24 **N to** him, Binnui son 339
3:25 **N to** him, Pedaiah son 339
3:27 **N to** them, the men 339
3:29 **N to** them, Zadok son 339
3:29 **N to** him, Shemaiah son of Shecaniah, 339
3:30 **N to** him, Hananiah son of Shelemiah, 339
3:30 **N to** them, Meshullam son 339
3:31 **N to** him, Malkijah, one of the goldsmiths, 339
Job 41:16 to the **n** that no air can pass between. 285
Ps 48:13 you may tell of them to the **n** generation. 340
71:18 your power to the **n** generation, NIH
78:4 the **n** generation the praiseworthy deeds of 340
78:6 so the **n** generation would know them, 340
109:13 names blotted out from the **n** generation. 337
Isa 37:36 When the people got up the **n** morning— NIH
Jer 20:3 The **n day,** when Pashhur released him 4740
35:4 It was **n to** the room of the officials, 725
51:46 one rumor comes this year, another the **n,** 339
52:24 Zephaniah the priest **n in rank** and 5467
Eze 24:18 The **n** morning I did as I had been NIH
40:7 And the threshold of the gate **n to** 725+4946
42:8 While the row of rooms on the side **n to** 4200
43:8 When they placed their threshold **n to** 907
48:1 the northern border of Damascus **n to** 448+3338
Da 2:39 **N,** a third kingdom, one of bronze, 10221
6:7 to any god or man during the **n** thirty days, NIH
6:12 during the **n** thirty days anyone who prays NIH
Joel 1:3 and their children to the **n** generation. 337
Jnh 4:7 at dawn the **n day** God provided a worm, 4740
Mt 27:62 The **n day,** the one after Preparation Day, *2069*
Mk 9:39 in my name can **in the n moment** say anything bad about me, *5444*
11:12 The **n day** as they were leaving Bethany, *2069*
Lk 9:37 The **n** day, when they came down from *2009*
10:35 The **n day** he took out two silver coins *892*
13:9 If it bears fruit **n** year, fine! *1650+3516+3836*
13:33 and tomorrow and the **n day—** *2400*
Jn 1:29 The **n day** John saw Jesus coming *2069*
1:35 The **n day** John was there again with two *2069*
1:43 **n day** Jesus decided to leave for Galilee. *2069*
6:22 The **n day** the crowd that had stayed on *2069*
12:12 The **n day** the great crowd that had come *2069*
13:23 was reclining **n** to him. *1877*
19:31 and the **n** day was to be a special Sabbath. *1697*
Ac 4:3 they put them in jail until the **n day.** *892*
4:5 The **n day** the rulers, elders and *892*
7:26 The **n** day Moses came upon two *2079*
10:23 The **n day** Peter started out with them, *2069*
13:42 about these things on the **n** Sabbath. *3568*
13:44 *On* the **n** Sabbath almost the whole city *2262*
14:20 The **n day** he and Barnabas left for Derbe. *2069*
16:11 and the **n day** on to Neapolis. *2079*
18:7 the synagogue and went **n door** to *5327*
20:7 because he intended to leave the **n day,** *2069*
20:15 The **n day** we set sail from there *2079*
21:1 The **n day** we went to Rhodes and *2009*
21:8 Leaving the **n day,** *2069*
21:18 The **n day** Paul and the rest of us went *2079*
21:26 The **n day** Paul took the men *2400*
22:30 The **n day,** since the commander wanted *2069*
23:12 **The n morning** the Jews formed *1181+2465*
23:32 The **n day** they let the cavalry go on *2069*
25:6 and the **n day** he convened the court *2069*
25:17 the court the **n** day and ordered the man to *2009*
25:23 The **n day** Agrippa and Bernice came *2069*
27:3 The **n** day we landed at Sidon; *2283*
27:18 from the storm that the **n** day they began *2009*
28:13 **The n day** the south wind came *1651+2465+3552*

NEZIAH (2)

Ezr 2:54 **N** and Hatipha 5909
Ne 7:56 **N** and Hatipha 5909

NEZIB (1)

Jos 15:43 Iphtah, Ashnah, **N,** 5908

NIBHAZ (1)

2Ki 17:31 the Avvites made **N** and Tartak, 5563

NIBSHAN (1)

Jos 15:62 **N,** the City of Salt and En Gedi— 5581

NICANOR (1)

Ac 6:5 also Philip, Procorus, **N,** Timon, Parmenas, *3770*

NICODEMUS (6)

Jn 3:1 there was a man of the Pharisees named **N,** *3773*
3:4 man be born when he is old?" **N** asked. *3773*
3:9 "How can this be?" **N** asked. *3773*
7:50 **N,** who had gone to Jesus earlier *3773*
19:39 He was accompanied by **N,** *3773*
19:39 **N** brought a mixture of myrrh and aloes, *NIG*

NICOLAITANS (2)

Rev 2:6 You hate the practices *of* the **N,** *3774*
Rev 2:15 to the teaching *of* the **N.** *3774*

NICOLAS (1)

Ac 6:5 and **N** from Antioch, a convert to Judaism. *3775*

NICOPOLIS (1)

Tit 3:12 do your best to come to me at **N,** *3776*

NIGER (1)

Ac 13:1 Barnabas, Simeon called **N,** *3769*

NIGH (KJV) See NEAR

NIGHT (314) [ALL-NIGHT, MIDNIGHT, NIGHTFALL, NIGHTS, NIGHTTIME, OVERNIGHT]

Ge 1:5 and the darkness he called **"n."** 4326
1:14 of the sky to separate the day from the **n,** 4326
1:16 the day and the lesser light to govern the **n.** 4326
1:18 to govern the day and the **n,** 4326
8:22 day and **n** will never cease." 4326
14:15 *During the* **n** Abram divided his men 4326
19:2 You can wash your feet and **spend the n** 4328
19:2 *"we will* **spend the n** in the square." 4328
19:33 That **n** they got their father to drink wine, 4326
19:34 **"Last n** I lay with my father. 621
19:35 So they got their father to drink wine that **n** 4326
20:3 in a dream one **n** and said to him, "You are 4326
24:23 for us to **spend the n?"** 4328
24:25 as well as room for you to **spend the n."** 4328
24:54 and drank and **spent the n** there. 4328
26:24 That **n** the LORD appeared to him 4326
28:11 *he* **stopped for the n** because 4328
30:16 So he slept with her that **n.** 4326
31:24 to Laban the Aramean in a dream at **n** 4326
31:29 **last n** the God of your father said to me, 621
31:39 for whatever was stolen by day or **n.** 4326
31:40 in the daytime and the cold at **n,** 4326
31:42 and **last n** he rebuked you." 621
31:54 After they had eaten, *they* **spent the n** there. 4328
32:13 He spent the **n** there, 4326
32:21 but he himself spent the **n** in the camp. 4326
32:22 That **n** Jacob got up 4326
40:5 had a dream the same **n,** 4326
41:11 Each of us had a dream the same **n.** 4326
42:27 **place where they stopped for the n** 4869
43:21 **place where we stopped for the n** 4869
46:2 And God spoke to Israel in a vision at **n** 4326
Ex 10:13 across the land all that day and all that **n.** 4326
12:8 That same **n** they are to eat 4326
12:12 "On that same **n** I will pass through Egypt 4326
12:30 and all the Egyptians got up *during* the **n,** 4326
12:31 the **n** Pharaoh summoned Moses and Aaron 4326
12:42 Because the LORD kept vigil that **n** 4325
12:42 on this **n** all the Israelites are to keep vigil 4326
13:21 *by* **n** in a pillar of fire to give them light, 4326
13:21 so that they could travel by day or **n.** 4326
13:22 the pillar of fire *by* **n** left its place in front 4326
14:20 the **n** the cloud brought darkness to 4326
14:20 so neither went near the other all **n** long. 4326
14:21 that **n** the LORD drove the sea back with 4326
14:24 During the **last watch of the n** 874+1332
40:38 and fire was in the cloud *by* **n,** 4326
Lev 6:9 on the altar hearth throughout the **n,** 4326
8:35 of Meeting day and **n** for seven days 4326
Nu 9:16 and *at* **n** it looked like fire. 4326
9:21 Whether by day or *by* **n,** 4326
11:9 When the dew settled on the camp *at* **n,** 4326
11:32 All that day and **n** and all the next day 4326
14:1 That **n** all the people of the community 4326
14:14 of cloud by day and a pillar of fire *by* **n.** 4326
22:8 "Spend the **n** here," Balaam said to them, 4326
22:20 That **n** God came to Balaam and said, 4326
Dt 1:33 in fire *by* **n** and in a cloud by day, 4326
16:1 of Abib he brought you out of Egypt *by* **n.** 4326
28:66 filled with dread both **n** and day, 4326
Jos 1:8 meditate on it day and **n,** 4326
2:8 Before the spies lay down for the **n,** NIH
6:11 to camp and **spent the n** there. 4328
8:3 and sent them out *at* **n** 4326
8:9 but Joshua spent that **n** with the people. 4326
8:13 That **n** Joshua went into the valley. 4326
Jdg 6:25 That same **n** the LORD said to him, 4326
6:27 he did it *at* **n** rather than in the daytime. 4326
6:40 That **n** God did so. 4326
7:9 During that **n** the LORD said to Gideon, 4326
9:32 the **n** you and your men should come 4326
9:34 and all his troops set out *by* **n** and took 4326
16:1 **went in to spend the n with** her. 448+995
16:2 and lay in wait for him all **n** at the city gate. 4326
16:2 They made no move during the **n,** saying, 4326
16:3 until the middle of the **n.** 4326
18:2 where *they* **spent the n.** 4328
19:7 so *he* **stayed** there *that* **n.** 2256+3782+4328
19:9 **Spend the n** here; the day is nearly over. 4328
19:10 But, unwilling to **stay** another **n,** 4328
19:11 at this city of the Jebusites and **spend the n.** 4328
19:13 to reach Gibeah or Ramah and **spend the n** 4328
19:15 There they stopped to **spend the n.** 4328
19:15 no one took them into his home **for the n.** 4328
19:20 Only don't **spend the n** in the square." 4328
19:25 and abused her throughout the **n,** 4326
20:4 to Gibeah in Benjamin to **spend the n.** 4328
Jdg 20:5 the **n** the men of Gibeah came after me 4326
Ru 3:8 In the middle of the **n** something startled 4326
3:13 Stay here *for* the **n,** 4326
1Sa 3:2 One **n** Eli, whose eyes were becoming 3427
11:11 during the **last watch of the n** 874+1332+2021
14:34 So everyone brought his ox that **n** 4326
14:36 after the Philistines *by* **n** and plunder them 4326
15:11 and he cried out to the LORD all that **n.** 4326
15:16 the LORD said to me **last n."** 2021+4326
19:10 That **n** David made good his escape. 4326
19:24 He lay that way all that day and **n.** 4326
25:16 **N** and day they were a wall around us all 4326
26:7 David and Abishai went to the army *by* **n,** 4326
28:8 *at* **n** he and two men went to the woman. 4326
28:20 for he had eaten nothing all that day and **n.** 4326
28:25 That same **n** they got up and left. 4326
31:12 through the **n** to Beth Shan. 4326
2Sa 2:29 that **n** Abner and his men marched through 4326
2:32 and his men marched all **n** and arrived 4326
4:7 they traveled all **n** by way of the Arabah. 4326
7:4 That **n** the word of the LORD came 4326
17:8 *he will* not **spend the n** with the troops. 4328
17:16 not spend the **n** at the fords in the desert; 4328
21:10 by day or the wild animals *by* **n.** 4326
1Ki 3:5 to Solomon *during* the **n** in a dream, 4326
3:19 *"During* the **n** this woman's son died 4326
3:20 up in the middle of the **n** and took my son 4326
8:29 be open toward this temple **n** and day, 4326
8:59 be near to the LORD our God day and **n,** 4326
19:9 There he went into a cave and **spent the n.** 4328
2Ki 6:14 They went *by* **n** and surrounded the city. 4326
7:12 up *in* the **n** and said to his officers, 4326
8:21 but he rose up and broke through *by* **n;** 4326
19:35 That **n** the angel of the LORD went out 4326
25:4 the whole army fled *at* **n** through the gate 4326
1Ch 9:27 *They would* **spend the n** stationed around 4328
9:33 for the work day and **n.** 4326
17:3 That **n** the word of God came to Nathan, 4326
2Ch 1:7 That **n** God appeared to Solomon and said 4326
6:20 be open toward this temple day and **n,** 4326
7:12 the LORD appeared to him at **n** and said: 4326
21:9 but he rose up and broke through *by* **n.** 4326
Ne 1:6 before you day and **n** for your servants, 4326
2:12 I set out *during* the **n** with a few men. 4326
2:13 *By* **n** I went out through the Valley Gate 4326
2:15 so I went up the valley *by* **n,** 4326
4:9 to our God and posted a guard day and **n** 4326
4:22 **stay** inside Jerusalem **at n,** 4328
4:22 as guards *by* **n** and workmen by day." 4326
6:10 *by* **n** they are coming to kill you." 4326
9:12 *by* **n** with a pillar of fire to give them light 4326
9:19 by **n** to shine on the way they were to take. 4326
13:20 of goods **spent the n** outside Jerusalem. 4328
13:21 "Why *do* you **spend the n** by the wall? 4328
Est 4:16 Do not eat or drink for three days, **n** or day. 4326
6:1 That **n** the king could not sleep; 4326
Job 3:3 and the **n** it was said, 'A boy is born!' 4326
3:6 That **n**—may thick darkness seize it; 4326
3:7 May that **n** be barren; 4326
4:13 Amid disquieting dreams in the **n,** 4326
5:14 at noon they grope as *in* the **n.** 4326
7:4 The **n** drags on, and I toss till dawn. 6847
10:22 to the land of **deepest n,** 694+4017+6547
17:12 These men turn **n** into day; 4326
20:8 banished like a vision of the **n.** 4326
24:7 Lacking clothes, *they* **spend the n** naked; 4328
24:14 in the **n** he steals forth like a thief. 4326
27:20 a tempest snatches him away *in* the **n.** 4326
29:19 the dew *will* **lie all n** on my branches. 4328
30:3 in desolate wastelands *at* **n.** 621
30:17 **N** pierces my bones; 4326
31:32 but no stranger *had to* **spend the n** in 4328
33:15 In a dream, in a vision of the **n,** 4326
34:20 in the middle of the **n;** 4326
34:25 *in* the **n** and they are crushed. 4326
35:10 who gives songs in the **n,** 4326
36:20 Do not long for the **n,** 4326
39:9 **stay** by your manger **at n?** 4328
39:28 He dwells on a cliff and **stays** there **at n;** 4328
Ps 1:2 and on his law he meditates day and **n.** 4326
6:6 all **n** long I flood my bed with weeping 4326
16:7 even *at* **n** my heart instructs me. 4326
17:3 you probe my heart and examine me *at* **n,** 4326
19:2 **n** after night they display knowledge. 4326
19:2 night after **n** they display knowledge. 4326
22:2 but you do not answer, *by* **n,** 4326
30:5 weeping may remain for a **n,** 6847
32:4 day and **n** your hand was heavy upon me; 4326
42:3 My tears have been my food day and **n,** 4326
42:8 at **n** his song is with me— 4326
55:10 Day and **n** they prowl about on its walls; 4326
63:6 I think of you through the **watches of the n.** 874
74:16 The day is yours, and yours also the **n;** 4326
77:2 *at* **n** I stretched out untiring hands 4326
77:6 I remembered my songs in the **n.** 4326
78:14 by day and with light from the fire all **n.** 4326
88:1 day and **n** I cry out before you. 4326
90:4 or like a watch in the **n.** 4326
91:5 You will not fear the terror of **n,** 4326
92:2 in the morning and your faithfulness at **n,** 4326
104:20 You bring darkness, it becomes **n,** 4326
105:39 and a fire to give light at **n.** 4326
119:55 In the **n** I remember your name, O LORD, 4326
119:148 through the **watches of the n,** 874
121:6 nor the moon by **n.** 4326
134:1 the LORD who minister by **n** in the house 4326
136:9 the moon and stars to govern the **n;** 4326

Ps 139:11 and the light become **n** around me," 4326
139:12 the **n** will shine like the day, 4326
Pr 7: 9 as the dark of **n** set in. 4326
31:18 and her lamp does not go out at **n.** 4326
Ecc 2:23 even at **n** his mind does not rest. 4326
8:16 his eyes not seeing sleep day or **n**— 4326
SS 3: 1 **All n long** on my bed I looked 928+2021+4326
3: 8 prepared for the terrors of the **n.** 4326
5: 2 my hair with the dampness of the **n.**" 4326
7:11 *let us* **spend the n** in the villages. 4328
Isa 4: 5 by day and a glow of flaming fire *by* **n;** 4326
5:11 up late at **n** till they are inflamed with wine. 5974
15: 1 Ar in Moab is ruined, destroyed in a **n!** 4325
15: 1 Kir in Moab is ruined, destroyed in a **n!** 4325
16: 3 Make your shadow like **n**—at high noon. 4325
21: 8 every **n** I stay at my post. 4326
21:11 "Watchman, what is left of the **n?** 4326
21:11 Watchman, what is left of the **n?**" 4325
21:12 "Morning is coming, but also the **n.** 4326
26: 9 My soul yearns for you in the **n;** 4326
27: 3 and **n** so that no one may harm it. 4326
28:19 morning after morning, by day and by **n,** 4326
29: 7 with a vision in the **n**— 4326
30:29 And you will sing as on the **n** you celebrate 4325
34:10 It will not be quenched **n** and day; 4326
34:14 the **n creatures** will also repose and find 4327
38:12 day and **n** you made an end of me. 4326
38:13 day and **n** you made an end of me. 4326
58:10 and your **n** will become like the noonday. 696
60:11 they will never be shut, day or **n,** 4326
62: 6 they will never be silent day or **n.** 4326
Jer 6: 5 at **n** and destroy her fortresses!" 4326
9: 1 I would weep day and **n** for the slain 4326
14: 8 like a traveler *who* **stays only a n?** 4328+5742
14:17 with tears **n** and day without ceasing; 4326
16:13 there you will serve other gods day and **n,** 4326
31:35 and stars to shine *by* **n,** who stirs up the sea 4326
33:20 with the day and my covenant with the **n,** 4326
33:20 the night, so that day and **n** no longer come 4326
33:25 not established my covenant with day and **n** 4326
36:30 to the heat by day and the frost by **n.** 4326
39: 4 the city *at* **n** by way of the king's garden, 4326
49: 9 If thieves came during the **n,** 4326
52: 7 They left the city *at* **n** through the gate 4326
La 1: 2 Bitterly she weeps at **n,** 4326
2:18 let your tears flow like a river day and **n;** 4326
2:19 Arise, cry out in the **n,** 4326
2:19 as the **watches of the n** begin; 874
Da 2:19 the **n** the mystery was revealed to Daniel in 10391
5:30 That very **n** Belshazzar, 10391
6:18 to his palace and **spent the n** without eating 10102
7: 2 Daniel said: "In my vision at **n** I looked, 10391
7: 7 "After that, in my vision at **n** I looked, 10391
7:13 "In my vision at **n** I looked, 10391
Hos 4: 5 You stumble day and **n,** 4326
7: 6 Their passion smolders all **n;** 4326
Joel 1:13 Come, **spend the n** in sackcloth, 4328
Am 5: 8 into **n,** who calls for the waters of the sea 4326
Ob 1: 5 "If thieves came to you, if robbers in the **n** 4326
Mic 3: 6 Therefore **n** will come over you, 4326
Zec 1: 8 During the **n** I had a vision— 4326
Mt 2:14 took the child and his mother *during the* **n** *3816*
14:25 the fourth watch *of* the **n** Jesus went out *3816*
21:17 where *he* **spent the n.** *887*
24:43 of the house had known *at* what **time of n** *5871*
26:31 "This very **n** you will all fall away *3816*
26:34 "this very **n,** before the rooster crows, *3816*
28:13 'His disciples came *during* the **n** *3816*
Mk 4:27 **N** and day, whether he sleeps or gets up, *3816*
5: 5 **N** and day among the tombs *1328+3816+4246*
6:48 the fourth watch *of* the **n** he went out *3816*
Lk 2: 8 keeping watch over their flocks *at* **n.** *3816*
2:37 She never left the temple but worshiped **n** *3816*
5: 5 we've worked hard all **n** *3816*
6:12 and **spent the n** praying to God. *1381+1639*
12:20 This very **n** your life will be demanded *3816*
12:38 in the second or third **watch of the n.** *5871*
17:34 *on* that **n** two people will be in one bed; *3816*
18: 7 who cry out to him day and **n?** *3816*
21:37 each evening *he* went out to **spend the n** *887*
Jn 3: 2 He came to Jesus *at* **n** and said, "Rabbi, *3816*
9: 4 **N** is coming, when no one can work. *3816*
11:10 It is when he walks by **n** that he stumbles, *3816*
13:30 he went out. And it was **n.** *3816*
19:39 the man who earlier had visited Jesus *at* **n.** *3816*
21: 3 but that **n** they caught nothing. *3816*
Ac 5:19 the **n** an angel of the Lord opened the doors *3816*
9:24 Day and **n** they kept close watch on *3816*
9:25 *by* **n** and lowered him in a basket through *3816*
12: 6 The **n** before Herod was to bring him *3816*
16: 9 During the **n** Paul had a vision of a man *3816*
16:33 At that hour *of* the **n** the jailer took them *3816*
17:10 As soon as it was **n,** *3816*
18: 9 One **n** the Lord spoke to Paul in a vision: *3816*
20:31 of you **n** and day with tears. *3816*
23:11 The following **n** the Lord stood near Paul *3816*
23:31 the **n** and brought him as far as Antipatris. *3816*
26: 7 as they earnestly serve God day and **n.** *3816*
27:23 **Last n** an angel of the God *3816+3836+4047*
27:27 the fourteenth **n** we were still being driven *3816*
Ro 13:12 The **n** is nearly over; the day is almost here. *3816*
1Co 11:23 The Lord Jesus, on the **n** he was betrayed, *3816*
2Co 11:25 I spent **a n and a day** in the open sea, *3819*
1Th 2: 9 we worked **n** and day in order not to be *3816*
3:10 **N** and day we pray most earnestly *3816*
5: 2 of the Lord will come like a thief in the **n.** *3816*
5: 5 not belong to the **n** or to the darkness. *3816*
1Th 5: 7 For those who sleep, sleep *at* **n,** *3816*
5: 7 and those who get drunk, get drunk *at* **n.** *3816*
2Th 3: 8 On the contrary, we worked **n** and day, *3816*
1Ti 5: 5 in God and continues **n** and day to pray and *3816*
2Ti 1: 3 as **n** and day I constantly remember you *3816*
Rev 4: 8 Day and **n** they never stop saying: *3816*
7:15 the throne of God and serve him day and **n** *3816*
8:12 and also a third of the **n.** *3816*
12:10 before our God day and **n,** *3816*
14:11 or **n** for those who worship the beast *3816*
20:10 They will be tormented day and **n** for ever *3816*
21:25 for there will be no **n** there. *3816*
22: 5 There will be no more **n.** *3816*

NIGHTFALL (2) [NIGHT]

2Sa 19: 7 not a man will be left with you *by* **n.** 2021+4326
2Ch 35:14 and the fat portions until **n.** 4326

NIGHTS (20) [NIGHT]

Ge 7: 4 on the earth for forty days and forty **n,** 4326
7:12 rain fell on the earth forty days and forty **n.** 4326
Ex 24:18 on the mountain forty days and forty **n.** 4326
34:28 with the LORD forty days and forty **n** 4326
Dt 9: 9 on the mountain forty days and forty **n;** 4326
9:11 At the end of the forty days and forty **n,** 4326
9:18 the LORD for forty days and forty **n;** 4326
9:25 the LORD those forty days and forty **n** 4326
10:10 on the mountain forty days and **n,** 4326
1Sa 30:12 for three days and three **n.** 4326
2Sa 12:16 into his house and **spent the n** lying on 4328
1Ki 19: 8 and forty **n** until he reached Horeb, 4326
Job 2:13 with him for seven days and seven **n.** 4326
7: 3 and **n** *of* misery have been assigned to me. 4326
Isa 65: 4 and **spend** *their* **n** keeping secret vigil; 4328
Jnh 1:17 inside the fish three days and three **n.** 4326
Mt 4: 2 After fasting forty days and forty **n,** *3816*
12:40 For as Jonah was three days and three **n** in *3816*
12:40 of Man will be three days and three **n** in *3816*
2Co 6: 5 in hard work, **sleepless n** and hunger; *71*

NIGHTTIME (1) [NIGHT]

Zec 14: 7 a unique day, without daytime or **n**— 4326

NILE (32)

Ge 41: 1 He was standing by the **N,** 3284
41: 3 up out of the **N** and stood beside those on 3284
41:17 I was standing on the bank of the **N,** 3284
Ex 1:22 that is born you must throw into the **N,** 3284
2: 3 among the reeds along the bank of the **N.** 3284
2: 5 went down to the **N** to bathe, 3284
4: 9 take some water from the **N** and pour it on 3284
7:15 Wait on the bank of the **N** to meet him, 3284
7:17 in my hand I will strike the water of the **N,** 3284
7:18 The fish in the **N** will die, 3284
7:20 and struck the water of the **N,** 3284
7:21 The fish in the **N** died, 3284
7:24 And all the Egyptians dug along the **N** 3284
7:25 after the LORD struck the **N.** 3284
8: 3 The **N** will teem with frogs. 3284
8: 9 except for those that remain in the **N.**" 3284
8:11 they will remain only in the **N.**" 3284
17: 5 the staff with which you struck the **N,** 3284
Isa 19: 7 also the plants along the **N,** 3284
19: 7 along the **N** will become parched, 3284
19: 8 all who cast hooks into the **N;** 3284
23: 3 harvest of the **N** was the revenue of Tyre, 3284
23:10 Till your land as along the **N,** 3284
Jer 46: 7 "Who is this that rises like the **N,** 3284
46: 8 Egypt rises like the **N,** 3284
Eze 29: 3 You say, "The **N** is mine; 3284
29: 9 " 'Because you said, "The **N** is mine; 3284
30:12 I will dry up the **streams of the N** and sell 3284
Am 8: 8 The whole land will rise like the **N;** 3284
9: 5 the whole land rises like the **N,** 3284
Na 3: 8 situated on the **N,** with water around her? 3284
Zec 10:11 and all the depths of the **N** will dry up. 3284

NIMRAH (1) [BETH NIMRAH]

Nu 32: 3 Dibon, Jazer, **N,** Heshbon, Elealeh, Sebam, 5809

NIMRIM (2)

Isa 15: 6 of **N** are dried up and the grass is withered; 5810
Jer 48:34 for even the waters of **N** are dried up. 5810

NIMROD (4)

Ge 10: 8 Cush was the father of **N,** 5808
10: 9 "Like **N,** a mighty hunter before the LORD." 5808
1Ch 1:10 Cush was the father of **N,** 5808
Mic 5: 6 the land of **N** with drawn sword. 5808

NIMSHI (5)

1Ki 19:16 Also, anoint Jehu son of **N** king over Israel, 5811
2Ki 9: 2 Jehu son of Jehoshaphat, the son of **N.** 5811
9:14 So Jehu son of Jehoshaphat, the son of **N,** 5811
9:20 The driving is like that of Jehu son of **N**— 5811
2Ch 22: 7 with Joram to meet Jehu son of **N,** 5811

NINE (17) [NINTH]

Nu 29:26 " 'On the fifth day prepare **n** bulls, 9596
34:13 that it be given to the **n** and a half tribes, 9596
Jos 13: 7 an inheritance among the **n** tribes and half 9596
Jos 15:44 **n** towns and their villages. 9596
15:54 **n** towns and their villages. 9596
21:16 **n** towns from these two tribes. 9596
Jdg 4: 3 Because he had **n** hundred iron chariots 9596
4:13 Sisera gathered together his **n** hundred iron chariots 9596
1Sa 17: 4 He was **over n feet** tall. 564+2256+2455+9252
2Sa 24: 8 at the end of **n** months and twenty days. 9596
2Ki 17: 1 and he reigned **n** years. 9596
1Ch 3: 8 Elishama, Eliada and Eliphelet—**n** in all. 9596
Ne 11: 1 while the remaining **n** were to stay 9596
Da 3: 1 ninety feet high and **n feet** wide, 10039+10747
Lk 17:17 Where are the other **n?** *1933*
Ac 2:15 only **n in the morning!** *2465+3836+5569+6052*
23:23 to go to Caesarea at **n** tonight. *5569+6052*

NINE-AND-A-HALF (1)

Jos 14: 2 by lot to the **n** tribes, 2256+2942+9596

NINETEEN (2) [NINETEENTH]

Jos 19:38 There were **n** towns and their villages. 6926+9596
2Sa 2:30 **n** of David's men were found missing. 6925+9596

NINETEENTH (4) [NINETEEN]

2Ki 25: 8 in the **n** year of Nebuchadnezzar king 6926+9596
1Ch 24:16 the **n** to Pethahiah, 6925+9596
25:26 the **n** to Mallothi, his sons and 6925+9596
Jer 52:12 in the **n** year of Nebuchadnezzar king 6926+9596

NINETY (6) [90]

Ge 17:17 Will Sarah bear a child at the age of **n?**" 9596
Ezr 6: 3 be **n feet** high and ninety feet wide, 10039+10749
6: 3 be ninety feet high and **n feet** wide, 10039+10749
Eze 41:12 and its length was **n** cubits. 9596
Da 3: 1 **n feet** high and nine feet wide, 10039+10749
Ac 27:28 and found it was **n feet deep.** *1278+3976*

NINETY-EIGHT (1) [98]

1Sa 4:15 who was **n** years old 2256+9046+9596

NINETY-NINE (6)

Ge 17: 1 When Abram was **n** years old, 2256+9596+9596
17:24 Abraham was **n** years old 2256+9596+9596
Mt 18:12 leave the **n** on the hills and go to look for the one that wandered off? *1916+1933*
18:13 than about the **n** that did not wander *1916+1933*
Lk 15: 4 Does he not leave the **n** in the open *1916+1933*
15: 7 than over **n** righteous persons who do not need to repent. *1916+1933*

NINETY-SIX (2)

Ezr 8:35 bulls for all Israel, **n** rams, 2256+9252+9596
Jer 52:23 **n** pomegranates on the sides; 2256+9252+9596

NINEVEH (22) [NINEVITES]

Ge 10:11 where he built **N,** Rehoboth Ir, 5770
10:12 which is between **N** and Calah; 5770
2Ki 19:36 He returned to **N** and stayed there. 5770
Isa 37:37 He returned to **N** and stayed there. 5770
Jnh 1: 2 to the great city of **N** and preach against it, 5770
3: 2 "Go to the great city of **N** and proclaim 5770
3: 3 the word of the LORD and went to **N.** 5770
3: 3 Now **N** was a very important city— 5770
3: 4 Forty more days and **N** will be overturned. 5770
3: 6 When the news reached the king of **N,** 5770
3: 7 Then he issued a proclamation in **N:** 5770
4:11 But **N** has more than a hundred 5770
Na 1: 1 An oracle concerning **N.** 5770
1: 8 he will make an end of **[N];** 2023+5226[S]
1:11 [O **N,**] has one come forth who plots evil NIH
1:14 a command concerning you, **[N]:** NIH
2: 1 An attacker advances against you, **[N].** NIH
2: 8 **N** is like a pool, and its water is draining 5770
3: 7 '**N** is in ruins—who will mourn for her?' 5770
Zep 2:13 leaving **N** utterly desolate and dry as 5770
Mt 12:41 The men of **N** will stand up at the judgment *3780*
Lk 11:32 The men of **N** will stand up at the judgment *3780*

NINEVITES (2) [NINEVEH]

Jnh 3: 5 The **N** believed God. 408+5770
Lk 11:30 For as Jonah was a sign *to* the **N,** *3780*

NINTH (30) [NINE]

Lev 23:32 From the evening of the **n** day of the month 9596
25:22 until the harvest of the **n** year comes in. 9595
Nu 7:60 On the **n** day Abidan son of Gideoni, 9595
2Ki 17: 6 In the **n** year of Hoshea, 9595
18:10 which was the **n** year of Hoshea king 9596
25: 1 So in the **n** year of Zedekiah's reign, 9595
25: 3 the **n** day of the [fourth] month the famine 9596
1Ch 12:12 Johanan the eighth, Elzabad the **n,** 9595
24:11 the **n** to Jeshua, the tenth to Shecaniah, 9595
25:16 the **n** to Mattaniah, 9595
27:12 The **n,** for the ninth month, 9595
27:12 The ninth, for the **n** month, 9595
Ezr 10: 9 And on the twentieth day of the **n** month, 9595
Jer 36: 9 In the **n** month of the fifth year 9595
36:22 It was the **n** month and the king was sitting 9595
39: 1 In the **n** year of Zedekiah king of Judah, 9595
39: 2 And on the **n** day of the fourth month 9596

Jer 52: 4 So in the **n** year of Zedekiah's reign, 9595
52: 6 the **n** day of the fourth month the famine in 9596
Eze 24: 1 In the **n** year, in the tenth month on 9595
Hag 2:10 On the twenty-fourth day of the **n** month, 9595
2:18 from this twenty-fourth day of the **n** month, 9595
Zec 7: 1 on the fourth day of the **n** month, 9595
Mt 20: 5 about the sixth hour and the **n** hour and did *1888*
27:45 the **n** hour darkness came over all the land. *1888*
27:46 the **n** hour Jesus cried out in a loud voice, *1888*
Mk 15:33 over the whole land until the **n** hour. *1888*
15:34 the **n** hour Jesus cried out in a loud voice, *1888*
Lk 23:44 over the whole land until the **n** hour, *1888*
Rev 21:20 the **n** topaz, the tenth chrysoprase, *1888*

NISAN (2)

Ne 2: 1 In the month of **N** in the twentieth year 5772
Est 3: 7 the month of **N**, they cast the pur 5772

NISROCH (2)

2Ki 19:37 in the temple of his god **N**, 5827
Isa 37:38 in the temple of his god **N**, 5827

NITRE (KJV) See SODA

NO (1735) [NAUGHT, NONE, NOR, NOT, NOTHING]

Ge 2: 5 **n** shrub of the field had **yet** appeared 3270
2: 5 **n** plant of the field had **yet** appeared 3270+3972
2: 5 on the earth and **there was n** man to work 401
2:20 But for Adam **n** suitable helper was found. 4202
2:25 and they felt **n** shame. 4202
4:12 it will **n** longer yield its crops for you. 4202
4:15 that **n** one who found him would kill him. 1194
5:24 he **was n more,** because God took him away. 401
8: 9 the dove could find **n** place to set its feet 4202
11:30 Now Sarai was barren; she had **n** children. 401
15: 3 "You have given me **n** children; 4202
16: 1 Abram's wife, had borne him **n** children. 4202
17: 5 **N** longer will you be called Abram; 4202
17:15 you are **n** *longer* to call her Sarai; 4202
19: 2 **"N,"** they answered, "we will spend 4202
19: 7 and said, **"N,** my friends. NIH
19:18 But Lot said to them, **"N,** my lords, please! 440
19:31 **there is n** man around here to lie with us, 401
20:11 **'There is** surely **n** fear of God in this place, 401
23:11 **"N,** my lord," he said. 4202
24:16 **n** man had ever lain with her. 4202
26:22 and **n** one quarreled over it. 4202
26:29 that you will do us **n** harm, 561
27: 1 so weak *that* he could **n** *longer* see, 4946
27:45 When your brother *is* **n longer** angry 8740
31:50 even though **n** one is with us, 401
32:28 "Your name will **n** longer be Jacob, 4202
33:10 **"N,** please!" said Jacob. 440
34:19 lost **n** time in doing what they said, 4202
35: 5 around them so that **n** one pursued them. 4202
35:10 but you will **n** longer be called Jacob; 4202
37:24 cistern was empty; **there was n** water in it. 401
37:35 **"N,"** he said, "in mourning will I go down 3954
39: 9 **N** one is greater in this house than I am. 401
39:23 The warden paid **n** attention to anything 401
40: 8 "but **there is n** one to interpret them." 401
41: 8 but **n** one could interpret them for him. 401
41:15 "I had a dream, and **n** one can interpret it. 401
41:21 **n** one could tell that they had done so; 4202
41:39 **there is n** one so discerning and wise as you 401
41:44 but without your word **n** one will lift hand 4202
42:10 **"N,** my lord," they answered. 4202
42:12 **"N!"** he said to them. 4202
42:13 and one **is n more."** 401
42:32 One **is n more,** 401
42:36 Joseph **is n more** and Simeon is no more, 401
42:36 Joseph is no more and Simeon **is n more,** 401
44:34 if the boy is not with me? **N!** NIH
45: 1 Then Joseph could **n** *longer* control himself 4202
45: 1 So there was **n** one with Joseph 4202
47: 4 and your servants' flocks have **n** pasture. 401
47:13 **There was n** food, however, 401
48:18 Joseph said to him, **"N,** my father, 4027+4202
49: 4 you will **n** *longer* excel, 440
Ex 2: 3 But when she could hide him **n** longer, 4202
2:12 and that and seeing **n** one, 401
5: 7 "You are **n** longer to supply the people 4202
5: 9 that they keep working and pay **n** attention 440
5:16 Your servants are given **n** straw, 401
8:10 so that you may know **there is n** *one* like 401
8:22 **n** swarms of flies will be there, 1194
9: 4 so that **n** animal belonging to 3972+4202+4946
9:14 you may know that **there is n** *one* like me 401
9:29 and there will be **n** more hail, 4202
9:33 the rain **n** longer poured down on the land. 4202
10:11 **N!** Have only the men go; 4027+4202
10:23 **N** one could see anyone else 4202
12:13 **N** destructive plague will touch you 4202
12:16 Do **n** work at all on these days, 4202
12:19 For seven days **n** yeast is to be found 4202
12:43 **"N** foreigner is to eat of it. 3972+4202
12:48 **N** uncircumcised male may eat of it. 3972+4202
14:11 because **there were n** graves in Egypt 401+1172
16:19 **"N** one is to keep any of it until morning." 440
16:20 some of them paid **n** attention to Moses; 4202
16:29 **n** one is to go out." 440
17: 1 **there was n** water for the people to drink. 401
Ex 20: 3 "You shall have **n** other gods before me. 4202
21: 8 He has **n** right to sell her to foreigners, 4202
21:22 but there is **n** serious injury, 4202
22:10 or is taken away while **n** one is looking, 401
22:11 and **n** restitution is required. 4202
22:25 charge him **n** interest. 4202
23:15 **N** one is to appear before me empty-handed 4202
29:33 But **n** one else may eat them, 4202
30:12 Then **n** plague will come on them 4202
33: 4 to mourn and **n** one put on any ornaments. 4202
33:20 for **n** one may see me and live." 4202
34: 3 **N** one is to come with you or 4202
34:20 **N** one is to appear before me empty-handed 4202
34:24 and **n** one will covet your land 4202
36: 6 **"N** man or woman is to make anything else 440
Lev 13:21 **there is n** white hair in it and it is 401
13:26 and **there is n** white hair in the spot and 401
13:31 and **there is n** black hair in it, 401
13:32 and there is **n** yellow hair in it and it does 4202
13:34 and appears to **be n** more than skin deep, 401
16:17 **N** one is to be in the Tent of Meeting 3972+4202
17: 7 They must **n** longer offer any 4202
18: 6 " **'N** one is to approach any close relative 4202
20:14 so that **n** wickedness will be among you. 4202
21: 3 on him since she has **n** husband— 4202
21:18 **N** man who has any defect may come 3972+4202
21:18 **n** man who is blind or lame, NIH
21:19 **n** man with a crippled foot or hand, NIH
21:21 **N** descendant of Aaron the priest who 3972+4202
22:10 " **'N** one outside a priest's family may eat 4202
22:13 yet has **n** children, 401
22:13 **N** unauthorized person, however, 3972+4202
23: 7 assembly and do **n** regular work. 3972+4202
23: 8 and do **n** regular work.' " 3972+4202
23:21 assembly and do **n** regular work. 3972+4202
23:25 Do **n** regular work, 3972+4202
23:28 Do **n** work on that day, 3972+4202
23:31 You shall do **n** work at all. 4202
23:35 do **n** regular work. 3972+4202
23:36 do **n** regular work. 3972+4202
25:26 a man has **n** one to redeem it for him 4202
26: 6 down and **n** one will make you afraid. 401
26:13 **so that** you would **n** longer be slaves 4946
26:17 even when **n** one is pursuing you. 401
26:31 and I will take **n** delight in 4202
26:36 even though **n** one is pursuing them. 401
26:37 even though **n** one is pursuing them. 401
27:26 " **'N** one, however, may dedicate 4202
27:29 " **'N** person devoted to destruction 3972+4202
Nu 3: 4 They had **n** sons; 4202
5: 8 But if that person has **n** close relative 401
5:13 (since **there is n** witness against her 401
5:19 "If **n** other man has slept with you 4202
6: 5 of his vow of separation **n** razor may 4202
8:19 so that **n** plague will strike the Israelites 4202
8:25 and work **n** longer. 4202
10:30 He answered, **"N,** I will not go; 4202
11: 5 the fish we ate in Egypt **at n cost—** 2855
11:32 **N** one gathered **less than** 5070
14:23 **N** one who has treated me 4202
16:14 **N,** we will not come!" 4202
16:40 the Israelites that **n** one except a descendant 4202
18: 4 **n** one else may come near where you are. 4202
18:20 "You will have **n** inheritance in their land, 4202
18:23 They will receive **n** inheritance among 4202
18:24 'They will have **n** inheritance among 4202
20: 2 Now there was **n** water for the community, 4202
20: 5 It has **n** grain or figs, 4202
20: 5 And **there is n** water to drink!" 401
21: 5 **There is n** bread! 401
21: 5 **There is n** water! 401
21:35 leaving them **n** survivors. 1194
22:26 in a narrow place where **there was n** room 401
22:30 **"N,"** he said. 4202
23:21 **"N** misfortune is seen in Jacob, 4202
23:21 **n** misery observed in Israel. 4202
23:23 There is **n** sorcery against Jacob, 4202
23:23 **n** divination against Israel. 4202
26:33 (Zelophehad son of Hepher had **n** sons; 4202
26:62 because they received **n** inheritance 4202
27: 3 but he died for his own sin and left **n** sons. 4202
27: 4 from his clan because he had **n** son? 401
27: 8 'If a man dies and leaves **n** son, 401
27: 9 If he has **n** daughter, 401
27:10 If he has **n** brothers, 401
27:11 If his father had **n** brothers, 401
28:18 assembly and do **n** regular work. 3972+4202
28:25 assembly and do **n** regular work. 3972+4202
28:26 assembly and do **n** regular work. 3972+4202
29: 1 assembly and do **n** regular work. 3972+4202
29: 7 must deny yourselves and do **n** work. 3972+4202
29:12 assembly and do **n** regular work. 3972+4202
29:35 an assembly and do **n** regular work. 3972+4202
33:14 where there was **n** water for the people 4202
35:30 But **n** one is to be put to death on 4202
36: 7 **N** inheritance in Israel is to pass from tribe 4202
36: 9 **N** inheritance may pass from tribe to tribe, 4202
Dt 1:45 but he paid **n** attention to your weeping 4202
2:34 We left **n** survivors. 4202
3: 3 We struck them down, leaving **n** survivors. 1194
4:12 the sound of words but saw **n** form; 401
4:15 You saw **n** form of any kind the day 4202
4:35 besides him **there is n** other. 401
4:39 **There is n** other. 401
5: 7 "You shall have **n** other gods before me. 4202
7: 2 Make **n** treaty with them, 4202
7: 2 and show them **n** mercy. 4202
Dt 7:24 **N** one will be able to stand up against you; 4202
9: 4 **N,** it is on account of the wickedness NIH
9: 9 I ate **n** bread and drank no water. 4202
9: 9 I ate no bread and drank **n** water. 4202
9:18 I ate **n** bread and drank no water, 4202
9:18 I ate no bread and drank **n** water, 4202
10: 9 the Levites have **n** share or inheritance 4202
10:17 who shows **n** partiality 4202
10:17 and accepts **n** bribes. 4202
11:17 and the ground will yield **n** produce, 4202
11:25 **N** man will be able to stand against you. 4202
12:12 who have **n** allotment or inheritance 401
13: 8 Show him **n** pity. 4202
13:11 and **n** *one* among you will do such 4202
14:27 for they have **n** allotment or inheritance 401
14:29 so that the Levites (who have **n** allotment 401
15: 4 there should be **n** poor among you, 4202
16: 4 Let **n** yeast be found in your possession 4202
16: 8 to the LORD your God and do **n** work. 4202
16:16 **N** man should appear before 4202
17: 6 but **n** one shall be put to death on 4202
18: 1 are to have **n** allotment or inheritance 4202
18: 2 They shall have **n** inheritance 4202
18:10 Let **n** one be found among you who 4202
19:13 Show him **n** pity. 4202
19:21 Show **n** pity: life for life, 4202
22:20 and **n** proof of the girl's virginity can 4202
22:26 she has committed **n** sin deserving death. 401
22:27 **there was n** one to rescue her. 401
23: 1 **N** one who has been emasculated 4202
23: 2 **N** one born of a forbidden marriage nor any 4202
23: 3 **N** Ammonite or Moabite or any 4202
23:17 **N** Israelite man or woman is to become 4202
25:12 you shall cut off her hand. Show her **n** pity. 4202
25:18 they had **n** fear of God. 4202
28:26 **there will be n** one to frighten them away. 401
28:29 with **n** one to rescue you. 401
28:31 and **n** one will rescue them. 401
28:51 They will leave you **n** grain, 4202
28:54 among you *will* **have n compassion** 6524+8317
28:65 Among those nations you will find **n** repose, 4202
28:65 **n** resting place for the sole of your foot. 4202
28:68 but **n** one will buy you. 401
29: 6 You ate **n** bread and drank no wine 4202
29: 6 and drank **n** wine or other fermented drink. 4202
29:18 Make sure there is **n** man or woman, 7153
29:18 make sure there is **n** root among you 7153
29:23 **n** vegetation growing on it. 3972+4202
30:14 **N,** the word is very near you; 3954
31: 2 and twenty years old and I am **n** longer able 4202
32: 4 A faithful God who does **n** wrong, 401
32: 5 their shame they are **n** *longer* his children, 4202
32:12 **n** foreign god was with him. 401
32:21 They made me jealous by what is **n** god 4202
32:21 by a nation that has **n understanding.** 5572
32:28 **there is n** discernment in them. 401
32:36 and **n** one is left, 700
32:39 **There is n** god besides me. 401
32:39 and **n** one can deliver out of my hand. 401
33: 9 'I have **n** regard for them.' 4202
33:11 **till** they rise **n more."** 4946
33:26 **"There is n** *one* like the God of Jeshurun, 401
34: 6 to this day **n** one knows where his grave is. 4202
34:10 **n** prophet has risen in Israel like Moses, 4202
34:12 For **n** one has ever shown NIH
Jos 1: 5 **N** one will be able to stand up 4202
4:18 **N sooner** had they set their feet on the dry ground **than** 3869
5: 1 and they **n** longer had the courage to face 4202
5:12 there was **n** longer any manna for 4202
6: 1 **N** one went out and no one came in. 401
6: 1 No one went out and **n** one came in. 401
8:20 but they had **n** chance to escape 4202
8:31 on which **n** iron tool had been used. 4202
10:21 **n** one uttered a word against the Israelites. 4202
10:28 He left **n** survivors. 4202
10:30 He left **n** survivors there. 4202
10:33 until **n** survivors were left. 1194
10:37 They left **n** survivors. 4202
10:39 They left **n** survivors. 4202
10:40 He left **n** survivors. 4202
11: 8 until **n** survivors were left. 1194
11:22 **N** Anakites were left in Israelite territory; 4202
13:14 to the tribe of Levi he gave **n** inheritance, 4202
13:33 Moses had given **n** inheritance; 4202
14: 4 The Levites received **n** share of the land 4202
17: 3 had **n** sons but only daughters, 4202
22:24 **"N!** We did it for fear that some day 4202
22:25 You have **n** share in the LORD.' 401
22:27 'You have **n** share in the LORD.' 401
22:33 And they talked **n** *more* about going to war 4202
23: 9 to this day **n** one has been able 4202
23:13 LORD your God will **n** longer drive out these nations before you. 4202
24:21 But the people said to Joshua, **"N!** 4202
Jdg 2:14 whom they were **n** longer able to resist. 4202
2:21 I will **n** longer drive out before them any of 4202
3:28 they allowed **n** one to cross over. 4202
4:20 'Is anyone here?' say **'N.'** " 401
5:19 but they carried off **n** silver, no plunder. 4202
5:19 but they carried off no silver, **n** plunder. NIH
7:12 Their camels could **n** more be counted than 401
8:33 **N sooner** had Gideon died **than** 889+3869
10: 6 the LORD and **n** *longer* served him, 4202
10:13 so I will **n** longer save you. 4202
10:16 **bear** Israel's misery **n longer.** 7918
11:28 paid **n** attention to the message Jephthah 4202

Jdg 12: 5 you an Ephraimite?" If he replied, "**N,**" 4202
13: 4 Now see to it that you drink **n** wine 440
13: 5 **N** razor may be used on his head, 4202
13: 7 drink **n** wine or other fermented drink 440
16: 2 *They* **made n move** during the night, saying, 3087
16:17 "**N** razor has ever been used on my head," 4202
17: 6 In those days Israel had **n** king; 401
18: 1 In those days Israel had **n** king. 401
18: 7 from the Sidonians and had **n** relationship 401
18:28 **There was n** one to rescue them 401
18:28 and had **n** relationship with anyone else. 401
19: 1 In those days Israel had **n** king. 401
19:12 His master replied, "**N.** NIH
19:15 but **n** one took them into his home for 401
19:18 **N** one has taken me into his house. 401
19:23 "**N,** my friends, don't be so vile. 440
19:28 But **there was n** answer. 401
20: 8 **N,** not one of us will return to his house. NIH
21: 8 that **n** one from Jabesh Gilead had come to 4202
21:25 In those days Israel had **n** king; 401
Ru 1:13 **N,** my daughters. 440
4: 4 For **n** one has the right to do it except you, 401
1Sa 1:11 and **n** razor will ever be used on his head." 4202
1:18 and her face was **n** longer downcast. 4202
2: 2 "**There is n** one holy like the LORD; 401
2: 2 **there is n** *one* besides you; 401
2: 2 **there is n** Rock like our God. 401
2: 5 but those who were hungry hunger **n more.** 2532
2:12 they had **n** regard for the LORD. 4202
2:16 the servant would then answer, "**N,** 4202
2:24 **N,** my sons; it is not a good report 440
8:19 refused to listen to Samuel. "**N!**" 4202
9: 7 We have **n** gift to take to the man of God. 401
10:19 And you have said, '**N,** set a king over us.' 4202
10:24 **There is n** *one* like him among all 401
10:27 They despised him and brought him **n** gifts. 4202
11: 3 if **n** one comes to rescue us, 401
11:11 so that **n** two of them were left together. 4202
11:13 "**N** one shall be put to death today, 4202
12:12 '**N,** we want a king to rule over us'— 4202
12:21 They can do you **n** good, 4202
14: 3 **N** one was aware that Jonathan had left. 4202
14:26 yet **n** one put his hand to his mouth, 401
17:32 "Let **n** one lose heart on account 440
18:25 'The king wants **n** other price for 401
19: 5 like David by killing him **for n reason?"** 2855
20:21 you are safe; **there is n** danger. 401
21: 1 Why is **n** one with you?" 401
21: 2 '**N** one is to know anything 440
21: 6 since there was **n** bread there except 4202
21: 9 **there is n** sword here but that one." 401
22: 8 **N** one tells me when my son makes 401
25:17 a wicked man that **n** one can talk to him." 4946
25:18 Abigail **lost n time.** 4554
25:25 May my lord pay **n** attention to 440
25:28 Let **n** wrongdoing be found in you as long 4202
26:12 **N** one saw or knew about it, 401
27: 4 he **n** longer searched for him. 4202
28:15 He **n** longer answers me, 4202
29: 3 I have found **n** fault in him." 4202
29: 6 I have found **n** fault in you, 4202
30: 4 until they had **n** strength left to weep. 401
30:23 David replied, "**N,** my brothers, 4202
2Sa 1:21 **n longer** rubbed with oil. 1172
2:28 they **n** longer pursued Israel, 4202
3:22 Abner **was n** *longer* with David in Hebron, 401
3:37 and all Israel knew that the king had **n** part 4202
6:23 of Saul had **n** children to the day 4202
7:10 of their own and **n** longer be disturbed. 4202
7:22 **There is n** *one* like you, 401
7:22 and **there is n** God but you, 401
9: 3 "Is there **n** one still left of the house of Saul 700
12: 6 he did such a thing and had **n** pity." 4202
13:16 "**N!**" she said to him. 440
13:25 "**N,** my son," the king replied. 440
14: 6 and **n** one was there to separate them. 401
14:19 **n** one can turn to the right or to the left 561
14:25 to the sole of his foot there was **n** blemish 4202
15: 3 but **there is n** representative of the king 401
16:18 Hushai said to Absalom, "**N,** 4202
17:19 **N** one knew anything about it. 4202
17:20 The men searched but found **n** *one,* 4202
17:22 **n** one was left who had not crossed 4202
18:18 "I have **n** son to carry on the memory 401
20: 1 "We have **n** share in David, 401
20: 1 **n** part in Jesse's son! 4202
21: 4 "We have **n** right to demand silver or gold 401
21: 5 and have **n** place anywhere in Israel, 4946
22:42 but **there was n** one to save them— 401
24:24 But the king replied to Araunah, "**N,** 4202
1Ki 1: 4 the king had **n** intimate relations with her. 4202
2:30 But he answered, "**N,** I will die here." 4202
3:13 that in your lifetime you will have **n** equal 4202
3:18 **there was n** one in the house but the two 401
3:22 The other woman said, "**N!** 4202
3:22 But the first one insisted, "**N!** 4202
3:23 while that one says, '**N!** 4202
5: 4 and **there is n** adversary or disaster. 401
5: 6 You know that we have **n** one so skilled 401
6: 7 the quarry were used, and **n** hammer, chisel 4202
6:18 **n** stone was to be seen. 401
8:23 of Israel, **there is n** God like you in heaven 401
8:35 the heavens are shut up and there is **n** rain 4202
8:46 for **there is n** one who does not sin— 401
8:60 the LORD is God and that **there is n** other. 401
15:22 **n** *one* was exempt— 401
17: 7 because there had been **n** rain in the land. 4202
1Ki 18:26 But **there was n** response; no one answered. 401
18:26 But there was no response; **n** one answered. 401
18:29 But **there was n** response, no one answered, 401
18:29 But there was no response, **n** one answered, 401
18:29 no one answered, **n** *one* paid attention. 401
19: 4 I am **n** better than my ancestors." 4202
21:15 He **is n** *longer* alive, but dead." 401
22: 1 For three years **there was n** war 401
22:17 'These people have **n** master. 4202
22:47 **There was** then **n** king in Edom; 401
2Ki 1: 3 'Is it because **there is n** God in Israel 401+1172
1: 6 Is it because **there is n** God in Israel 401+1172
1:16 Is it because **there is n** God in Israel 401+1172
1:17 Because Ahaziah had **n** son, 4202
2:12 And Elisha saw him **n** more. 4202
2:16 "**N,**" Elisha replied, "do not send them." NIH
3: 9 the army had **n** *more* water for themselves 4202
3:11 "**Is there n** prophet of the LORD here, 401
3:13 "**N,**" the king of Israel answered, 440
4:14 she has **n** son and her husband is old." 401
4:16 "**N,** my lord," she objected. 440
4:31 but **there was n** sound or response. 401
4:39 though **n** one knew what they were. 4202
5:15 that **there is n** God in all the world except 401
9:10 and **n** one will bury her.' " 401
9:37 so that **n** one will be able to say, 4202
10:11 leaving him **n** survivor. 1194
10:14 He left **n** survivor. 4202
10:19 See that **n** one is missing, 440
10:19 to come will **n** longer live." 4202
10:23 "Look around and see **that n** servants of 7153
10:25 let **n** one escape." 440
12: 7 Take **n** *more* money from your treasurers, 440
14:26 **there was n** one to help them. 401
15:20 and stayed in the land **n** longer. 4202
17: 4 and he **n** longer paid tribute to the king 4202
18: 5 There was **n** one like him among all 4202
19: 3 to the point of birth and **there is n** strength 401
23:10 so **n** one could use it to sacrifice his son 1194
25: 3 that there was **n** food for the people to eat. 4202
1Ch 2:34 Sheshan had **n** sons—only daughters. 4202
15: 2 "**N** *one* but the Levites may carry the ark 4202
16:21 He allowed **n** man to oppress them; 4202
16:22 do my prophets **n** harm." 440
17: 9 of their own and **n** longer be disturbed. 4202
17:20 "**There is n** *one* like you, O LORD, 401
17:20 O LORD, and **there is n** God but you, 401
21:24 But King David replied to Araunah, "**N,** 4202
23:17 Eliezer had **n** other sons, 4202
23:26 the Levites **n** longer need to carry 401
24: 2 and they had **n** sons; 4202
24:28 From Mahli: Eleazar, who had **n** sons. 4202
29:25 as **n** king over Israel ever had before. 4202
2Ch 1:12 as **n** king who was before you ever had 4202
6:14 of Israel, **there is n** God like you in heaven 401
6:26 the heavens are shut up and there is **n** rain 4202
6:36 for **there is n** one who does not sin— 401
7:13 I shut up the heavens so that there is **n** rain, 4202
14: 6 **N** *one* was at war with him 401
14:11 **there is n** *one* like you to help the powerless 401
15:19 There was **n** *more* war until 4202
18:16 'These people have **n** master. 4202
19: 7 with the LORD our God **there is n** injustice 401
20: 6 and **n** *one* can withstand you. 401
20:12 For we have **n** power to face this vast army 401
20:24 **n** *one* had escaped. 401
21:19 His people made **n** fire in his honor, 4202
21:20 He passed away, to **n** *one's* regret, 4202
22: 9 So **there was n** *one* in the house 401
23: 6 **N** one is to enter the temple of 440
23:19 the LORD's temple so that **n** one who was 4202
32:15 for **n** god of any nation 3972+4202
33:10 but they paid **n** attention. 4202
36:16 against his people and **there was n** remedy. 401
Ezr 3:13 **N** one could distinguish the sound of 401
4: 3 "You have **n** part with us in building 4202
4:13 **n** *more* taxes, tribute or duty will be paid, 10379
7:24 that you have **n** authority to impose taxes, 10379
8:15 I found **n** Levites there. 4202
9:14 leaving us **n** remnant or survivor? 401
10: 6 he ate **n** food and drank no water, 4202
10: 6 he ate no food and drank **n** water, 4202
Ne 2:12 **There were n** mounts with me except 401
2:17 and we will **n** longer be in disgrace." 4202
2:20 you have **n** share in Jerusalem or any claim 401
9:30 Yet they paid **n** attention, 4202
13: 1 that **n** Ammonite or Moabite should ever 4202
13:19 the gates so that **n** load could be brought in 4202
13:21 From that time on they **n** *longer* came on 4202
13:26 the many nations there was **n** king like him. 4202
Est 1:18 be **n end** *of* disrespect and discord. 1896+3869
4: 2 because **n** one clothed in sackcloth 401
5:13 But all this gives me **n** satisfaction as long 401
7: 4 **n** such distress would justify disturbing 401
8: 8 for **n** document written in the king's name 401
9: 2 **N** one could stand against them, 4202
Job 1: 8 **There is n** one on earth like him; 401
2: 3 **There is n** one on earth like him; 401
2:13 **N** one said a word to him, 401
3: 4 may **n** light shine upon it. 440
3: 7 may **n** shout of joy be heard in it. 440
3:18 they **n** *longer* hear the slave driver's shout. 4202
3:26 I have **n** peace, no quietness; 4202
3:26 I have no peace, **n** quietness; 4202
3:26 I have **n** rest, but only turmoil." 4202
4:18 If God places **n** trust in his servants, 4202
5:12 so that their hands achieve **n** success. 4202
Job 5:19 in seven **n** harm will befall you. 4202
6: 3 **n wonder** my words have been impetuous. 4027+6584
6:21 Now you too have proved to be of **n** help; 4202
7: 8 eye that now sees me will see me **n** *longer;* 4202
7: 8 you will look for me, but I will **be n more.** 401
7:10 his place will know him **n** more. 4202
7:16 Let me alone; my days have **n meaning.** 2039
7:21 you will search for me, but I will **be n more."** 401
8:11 where there is **n** marsh? 4202
8:22 and the tents of the wicked will **be n more."** 401
9:17 and multiply my wounds **for n reason.** 2855
9:21 I have **n** concern for myself; 4202
9:34 so that his terror would frighten me **n** *more.* 440
10: 7 that **n** one can rescue me from your hand? 401
10:21 before I go to the place of **n** return, 4202
11: 3 Will **n** one rebuke you when you mock? 401
11:12 witless man can **n more** become wise **than** 2256
11:14 the sin that is in your hand and allow **n** evil 440
11:19 with **n** one to make you afraid, 401
12:25 They grope in darkness with **n** light; 4202
13:16 for **n** godless man would dare come 4202
14: 4 bring what is pure from the impure? **N** one! 4202
14:10 he breathes his last and is **n more.** 361
14:12 till the heavens are **n more,** 1194
15: 3 with speeches that have **n** value? 4202
15:15 If God places **n** trust in his holy ones, 4202
15:19 the land was given when **n** alien passed 4202
15:28 and houses where **n** one lives, 4202
15:29 He will **n** *longer* be rich and his wealth will 4202
16:22 before I go on the journey of **n** return. 4202
18:17 he has **n** name in the land. 4202
18:19 He has **n** offspring or descendants 4202
18:19 **n** survivor where once he lived. 401
19: 7 I get **n** response; 4202
19: 7 though I call for help, **there is n** justice. 401
20: 8 **n** *more* to be found, 4202
20: 9 his place will look on him **n** more. 4202
20:20 he will have **n** respite from his craving; 4202
21:14 We have **n** desire to know your ways. 4202
21:29 Have you paid **n** regard to their accounts— 4202
22: 6 from your brothers **for n reason;** 2855
22: 7 You gave **n** water to the weary 4202
23: 6 **N,** he would not press charges against me. 4202
23: 9 I catch **n** glimpse of him. 4202
24:12 But God charges **n** one with wrongdoing. 4202
24:15 he thinks, '**N** eye will see me,' 4202
24:18 so that **n** one goes to the vineyards. 4202
24:20 evil men are **n** longer remembered 4202
24:21 and to the widow show **n** kindness. 4202
24:22 they have **n** assurance of life. 4202
27: 4 and my tongue will utter **n** deceit. 561
27:19 but will do so **n** more; 4202
28: 7 **N** bird of prey knows that hidden path, 4202
28: 7 **n** falcon's eye has seen it. 4202
28: 8 and **n** lion prowls there. 4202
29:22 After I had spoken, they spoke **n** more; 4202
30:24 "Surely **n** one lays a hand on a broken man 4202
31:32 but **n** stranger had to spend the night in 4202
32: 3 they had found **n** way to refute Job, 4202
32:15 "They are dismayed and have **n** more 4202
32:16 now that they stand there with **n** reply? 4202
32:21 I will show partiality to **n** one, 440
33: 7 **N** fear of me should alarm you, 4202
34:19 who shows **n** partiality to princes and does 4202
34:22 **There is n** dark place, no deep shadow, 401
34:22 There is no dark place, **n** deep shadow, 401
34:23 God has **n** need to examine men further, 4202
34:27 and had **n** regard for any of his ways. 4202
34:31 'I am guilty but will offend **n** *more.* 4202
35:10 But **n** one says, 'Where is God my Maker, 4202
35:13 the Almighty pays **n** attention to it. 4202
36:18 Be careful **that n** one entices you by riches; 7153
37:21 Now **n** one can look at the sun, 4202
38:11 'This far you may come and **n** farther; 4202
38:26 to water a land where **n** man lives, 4202
38:26 a desert with **n** one in it, 4202
40: 5 I spoke once, but I have **n** answer— 4202
40: 5 twice, but I will say **n** more." 4202
41:10 **N** one is fierce enough to rouse him. 4202
41:16 to the next that **n** air can pass between. 4202
41:26 The sword that reaches him has **n** effect, 1172
42: 2 **n** plan of yours can be thwarted. 4202
Ps 6: 5 **N** *one* remembers you when he is dead. 401
7: 2 rip me to pieces with **n** one to rescue me. 401
10: 4 in all his thoughts **there is n** room for God. 401
10:18 **in order that** man, who is of the earth, may terrify **n** more. 1153
12: 1 Help, LORD, for the godly *are* **n more;** 1698
14: 1 The fool says in his heart, "**There is n** God." 401
14: 1 **there is n** one who does good. 401
14: 3 **there is n** one who does good, not even one. 401
15: 3 and has **n** slander on his tongue, 4202
15: 3 who does his neighbor **n** wrong 4202
15: 3 and casts **n** slur on his fellowman, 4202
16: 2 apart from you I have **n** good thing." 1153
18:41 but **there was n** one to save them— 401
19: 3 **There is n** speech or language 401
22:11 for trouble is near and **there is n** one to help. 401
23: 4 I will fear **n** evil, for you are with me; 4202
25: 3 **N** one whose hope is in you will ever 4202
28: 5 Since they show **n** regard for the works of 4202
32: 2 against him and in whose spirit is **n** deceit. 401
32: 9 which have **n** understanding but must 401
33:16 **N** king is saved by the size of his army; 401
33:16 **n** warrior escapes by his great strength. 4202

Ps 34:10 who seek the LORD lack **n** good thing. 3972+4202
34:22 **n** one will be condemned who takes refuge 4202
36: 1 **There is n** fear of God before his eyes. 401
37:10 and the wicked will **be n more;** 401
37:36 but he soon passed away and **was n more;** 401
38: 3 of your wrath **there is n** health in my body; 401
38: 3 my bones have **n** soundness because 401
38: 7 **there is n** health in my body. 401
38:14 whose mouth can offer **n** reply. 401
39:13 before I depart and **am n more."** 401
40: 5 for us **n** one can recount to you; 401
44: 9 you **n** longer go out with our armies. 4202
49: 7 **N** man can redeem the life of another 4202
49: 8 **n** payment *is* ever **enough—** 2532
50: 9 I have **n** need of a bull from your stall or 4202
53: 1 The fool says in his heart, **"There is n** God." 401
53: 1 **there is n** one who does good. 401
53: 3 **there is n** one who does good, not even one. 401
55:19 and have **n** fear of God. 4202
56: 7 **On n account** let them escape; 224+6584
58: 2 **N,** in your heart you devise injustice, 677
59: 3 against me for **n** offense or sin of mine, 4202
59: 4 I have done **n** wrong, 1172
59: 5 show **n** mercy to wicked traitors. 440
59:13 consume them till they **are n more.** 401
60:10 and **n** *longer* go out with our armies? 4202
63: 1 and weary land where there is **n** water. 1172
69: 2 where **there is n** foothold. 401
69:25 let there be **n** one to dwell in their tents. 440
71:11 for **n** one will rescue him." 401
72: 7 till the moon is **n more.** 1172
72:12 the afflicted who have **n** one to help. 401
73: 4 They have **n** struggles; 401
73: 7 of their minds **know n limits.** 6296
74: 9 We are given **n** miraculous signs; 4202
74: 9 **n** prophets are left, 401
75: 4 'Boast **n** *more,'* and to the wicked, 440
75: 6 **N** *one* from the east or the west or from 4202
78:63 and their maidens had **n** wedding songs; 4202
79: 3 and **there is n** one to bury the dead. 401
81: 9 You shall have **n** foreign god among you; 4202
83: 4 the name of Israel be remembered **n** more." 4202
84:11 **n** good thing does he withhold 4202
86: 8 **n** deeds can compare with yours. 401
88: 5 whom you remember **n** more, 4202
89:22 **N** enemy will subject him to tribute; 4202
89:22 **n** wicked man will oppress him. 4202
91:10 then **n** harm will befall you, 4202
91:10 **n** disaster will come near your tent. 4202
92:15 and there is **n** wickedness in him." 4202
94: 7 the God of Jacob pays **n** heed." 4202
101: 3 I will set before my eyes **n** vile thing. 4202
101: 7 **N** one who practices deceit will dwell 4202
101: 7 **n** one who speaks falsely will stand 4202
103:16 and its place remembers it **n** more. 4202
104:35 from the earth and the wicked **be n** more. 401
105:14 He allowed **n** one to oppress them; 4202
105:15 do my prophets **n** harm." 440
105:37 and from among their tribes **n** one faltered. 401
106: 7 they gave **n** thought to your miracles; 4202
107: 4 finding **n** way to a city 4202
107:12 they stumbled, and **there was n** one to help. 401
108:11 and **n** *longer* go out with our armies? 4202
109:12 May **n** one extend kindness to him 440
109:17 he found **n** pleasure in blessing— 4202
112: 7 He will have **n** fear of bad news; 4202
112: 8 His heart is secure, he will have **n** fear; 4202
119:133 let **n** sin rule over me. 440
132: 4 I will allow **n** sleep to my eyes, 561
132: 4 **n** slumber to my eyelids, NIH
142: 4 **n** one is concerned for me. 401
142: 4 I **have n** refuge; no one cares for my life. 6+4946
142: 4 I have no refuge; **n** one cares for my life. 401
143: 2 for **n** one living is righteous before you. 4202
144:14 **There will be n** breaching of walls, 401
144:14 **n** going into captivity, 401
144:14 **n** cry of distress in our streets. 401
145: 3 his greatness **n** *one* can fathom. 401
147: 5 his understanding has **n** limit. 401
147:20 He has done this for **n** other nation; 4202
Pr 1:24 when I called and **n** one gave heed 401
3:25 Have **n** fear of sudden disaster or of 440
3:30 Do not accuse a man **for n reason—** 2855
3:30 when he has done you **n** harm. 4202
5: 6 She gives **n** thought to the way of life; 7153
6: 4 Allow **n** sleep to your eyes, 440
6: 4 **n** slumber to your eyelids. NIH
6: 7 It has **n** commander, no overseer or ruler, 401
6: 7 It has no commander, **n** overseer or ruler, NIH
6:29 **n** one who touches her will go unpunished. 4202
6:34 and he will show **n** mercy 4202
8:24 When **there were n** oceans, I was given birth 401
8:24 when **there were n** springs abounding 401
10: 2 Ill-gotten treasures are of **n** value, 4202
10:22 and he adds **n** trouble to it. 4202
11:22 a beautiful woman *who* **shows n** discretion. 6073
12: 7 are overthrown and **are n more,** 401
12: 9 to be somebody and **have n** food. 2894
12:21 **N** harm befalls the righteous, 3972+4202
13: 8 but a poor man hears **n** threat. 4202
14: 4 Where **there are n** oxen, 401
14:10 and **n** one else can share its joy. 4202
17:16 since he has **n** desire to get wisdom? 401
17:21 there is **n** joy for the father of a fool. 4202
18: 2 A fool finds **n** pleasure in understanding 4202
20:14 "It's **n good,** it's no good!" 8273
20:14 "It's no good, it's **n good!"** 8273
Pr 21:10 his neighbor gets **n** mercy from him. 4202
21:30 **There is n** wisdom, no insight, 401
21:30 There is no wisdom, **n** insight, 401
21:30 **n** plan that can succeed against the LORD. 401
24:20 for the evil man has **n** future hope, 4202
28: 1 wicked man flees though **n** one pursues, 401
28: 3 like a driving rain that leaves **n** crops. 401
28:17 let **n** one support him. 440
29: 7 but the wicked have **n** such concern. 4202
29: 9 and **there is n** peace. 401
29:18 Where **there is n** revelation, 401
30:27 locusts have **n** king, 401
31: 7 and remember their misery **n** more. 4202
31:21 it snows, she has **n** fear for her household; 4202
Ecc 1:11 **There is n** remembrance of men of old, 401
2:10 I refused my heart **n** pleasure. 3972+4202+4946
3:19 man has **n** advantage over the animal. 401
4: 1 and they have **n** comforter; 401
4: 1 and they have **n** comforter. 401
4: 8 **There was n** end to his toil, 401
4:10 But pity the man who falls and has **n** one 401
4:13 an old but foolish king who **n** longer knows 4202
4:16 **There was n** end to all the people who were 401
5: 4 He has **n** pleasure in fools; fulfill your vow. 401
5:12 of a rich man permits him **n** sleep. 401
6: 3 yet **n** matter how long he lives, NIH
6:10 **n** man can contend with one who is stronger 4202
8: 5 to **n** harm, and the wise heart will know 4202
8: 7 Since **n** man knows the future, 401
8: 8 **N** man has power over the wind 401
8: 8 **n** *one* has power over the day of his death. 401
8: 8 As **n** *one* is discharged in time of war, 401
8:17 **N** one can comprehend what goes on under 4202
9: 1 but **n** man knows whether love or hate awaits 401
9: 5 they have **n** further reward, 401
9:12 **n** man knows when his hour will come: 4202
9:16 and his words are **n** *longer* heeded. 401
10:11 **there is n** profit for the charmer. 401
10:14 **N** one knows what is coming— 4202
12: 1 "I find **n** pleasure in them"— 401
12: 5 along and desire **n longer** *is* **stirred.** 7296
12:12 Of making many books **there is n** end, 401
SS 1: 3 **N wonder** the maidens love you! 4027+6584
4: 7 **there is n** flaw in you. 401
8: 1 and **n** one would despise me. 4202
Isa 1: 6 the top of your head **there is n** soundness— 401
1:11 I have **n** pleasure in the blood of bulls 4202
1:31 with **n** one to quench the fire." 401
2: 7 **there is n** end to their treasures. 401
2: 7 **there is n** end to their chariots. 401
3: 7 "I have **n** remedy. 4202
3: 7 I have **n** food or clothing in my house; 401
5: 8 and join field to field till **n** space is left 700
5:12 but they have **n** regard for the deeds of 4202
5:12 **n** respect for the work of his hands. 4202
5:29 and carry it off with **n** one to rescue. 401
7:25 you will **n** *longer* go there for fear of 4202
8:20 they have **n** light of dawn. 401
9: 1 be **n** *more* gloom for those who were 4202
9: 7 and peace **there will be n** end. 401
9:17 Therefore the Lord will take **n** pleasure in 4202
9:19 **n** one will spare his brother. 4202
10:20 will **n** longer rely on him who struck them 4202
13:17 not care for silver and have **n** delight 4202
13:18 they will have **n** mercy on infants 4202
13:20 **n** Arab will pitch his tent there, 4202
13:20 **n** shepherd will rest his flocks there. 4202
14: 8 **n** woodsman comes to cut us down." 4202
16:10 **n** one sings or shouts in the vineyards; 4202
16:10 **n** one treads out wine at the presses, 4202
16:12 it is to **n** avail. 4202
17: 1 Damascus *will* **n longer be** a city 4946+6073
17: 2 with **n** one to make them afraid. 401
17: 8 and they will have **n** regard for 4202
19: 7 will blow away and **be n more.** 401
22:22 what he opens **n** one can shut, 401
22:22 and what he shuts **n** one can open. 401
23:10 for you **n** longer have a harbor. 401
23:12 He said, **"N** more of your reveling, 4202
23:12 even there you will find **n** rest." 4202
23:13 this people that is now **of n account!** 4202
24: 9 **N** *longer* do they drink wine with a song; 4202
25: 2 the foreigners' stronghold a city **n more;** 4946
26:14 They are now dead, they live **n** *more,* 1153
26:21 she will conceal her slain **n** longer. 4202
27: 3 and night **so that n** one may harm it. 7153
27: 9 **n** Asherah poles or incense altars will 4202
27:11 so their Maker has **n** compassion on them, 4202
27:11 and their Creator shows them **n** favor. 4202
29:22 **"N** longer will Jacob be ashamed; 4202
29:22 **n** longer will their faces grow pale. 4202
30:10 "See **n** more visions!" 4202
30:10 "Give us **n** more visions of what is right! 4202
30:16 You said, **'N,** we will flee on horses.' 4202
30:19 you will weep **n** more. 4202
30:20 your teachers will be hidden **n** more; 4202
32: 3 of those who see will **n** longer be closed, 4202
32: 5 **N** longer will the fool be called noble nor 4202
33: 8 **n** travelers *are* on the roads. 8697
33: 8 **n** one is respected. 4202
33:19 You will see those arrogant people **n** *more,* 4202
33:21 **N** galley with oars will ride them, 1153
33:21 **n** mighty ship will sail them. 4202
33:24 **N** one living in Zion will say, "I am ill"; 1153
34:10 **n** one will ever pass through it again. 401
35: 9 **N** lion will be there, 4202
37: 3 to the point of birth and **there is n** strength 401
Isa 38:11 **n** longer will I look on mankind, 4202
40:24 **N sooner** are they planted, 677+1153
40:24 **n sooner** are they sown, 677+1153
40:24 **n sooner** do they take root in the ground, 677+1153
40:28 and his understanding **n** one can fathom. 401
41:26 **N** one told of this, no one foretold it, 401
41:26 No one told of this, **n** one foretold it, 401
41:26 **n** one heard any words from you. 401
41:28 I look but **there is n** one— 401
41:28 **n** one among them to give counsel, 401
41:28 **n** one to give answer when I ask them. NIH
42:20 but have paid **n** attention; 4202
42:22 with **n** one to rescue them; 401
42:22 with **n** one to say, "Send them back." 401
43:10 Before me **n** god was formed, 4202
43:11 and apart from me **there is n** savior. 401
43:13 **N** one can deliver out of my hand. 401
43:25 and remembers your sins **n** *more.* 4202
44: 6 apart from me **there is n** God. 401
44: 8 **N,** there is no other Rock; I know not one." NIH
44: 8 No, **there is n** other Rock; I know not one." 401
44:12 he drinks **n** water and grows faint. 4202
44:19 **N** one stops to think, 4202
44:19 **n** one has the knowledge or understanding 4202
45: 5 I am the LORD, and **there is n** other; 401
45: 5 apart from me **there is n** God. 401
45: 6 I am the LORD, and **there is n** other. 401
45: 9 Does your work say, 'He has **n** hands'? 401
45:14 and **there is n** other; there is no other god.' 401
45:14 there is **n** other god.' " 700
45:18 "I am the LORD, and **there is n** other. 401
45:21 And **there is n** God apart from me, 401
45:22 for I am God, and **there is n** other. 401
46: 9 I am God, and **there is n** other; 401
47: 1 **N** more will you be called tender 4202
47: 3 I will take vengeance; I will spare **n** one." 4202
47: 5 **n** more will you be called queen 4202
47: 6 and you showed them **n** mercy. 4202
47:10 **'N** one sees me.' 401
47:14 **Here are n** coals to warm anyone; 401
47:14 here is **n** fire to sit by. NIH
48:22 **"There is n** peace," says the LORD, 401
49: 4 But I said, "I have labored to **n purpose;** 8198
49:15 at her breast and have **n** compassion on 4946
50: 2 When I came, why **was there n** one? 401
50: 2 I called, why **was there n** one to answer? 401
50:10 who has **n** light, 401
52:11 Touch **n** unclean thing! 440
53: 2 He had **n** beauty or majesty to attract us 4202
53: 9 though he had done **n** violence, 4202
54: 4 of your youth and remember **n** more 4202
54:17 **n** weapon forged against you will prevail, 3972+4202
55: 1 you who have **n** money, come, buy and eat! 401
56: 3 Let **n** foreigner who has bound himself to 440
57: 1 and **n** one ponders it in his heart; 401
57: 1 and **n** one understands that 401
57:21 **"There is n** peace," says my God, 401
59: 4 **N** one calls for justice; 401
59: 4 **n** one pleads his case with integrity. 401
59: 8 **there is n** justice in their paths. 401
59: 8 **n** one who walks in them will know peace. 4202
59:15 and was displeased that **there was n** justice. 401
59:16 He saw that **there was n** one, 401
59:16 he was appalled that **there was n** one 401
60:15 with **n** one traveling through, 401
60:18 **N** longer will violence be heard 4202
60:19 The sun will **n** more be your light by day, 4202
60:20 and your moon will wane **n** *more;* 4202
62: 4 **N** longer will they call you Deserted, 4202
62: 6 give yourselves **n** rest, 440
62: 7 and give him **n** rest 440
62:12 the City **N** Longer Deserted. 4202
63: 3 from the nations **n** one was with me. 401
63: 5 I looked, but **there was n** one to help, 401
63: 5 I was appalled that **n** one gave support; 401
64: 4 Since ancient times **n** one has heard, 4202
64: 4 **n** ear has perceived, 4202
64: 4 **n** eye has seen any God besides you, 4202
64: 7 **N** one calls on your name or strives 401
65:19 and of crying will be heard in it **n** more. 4202
65:22 **N** *longer* will they build houses 4202
66: 4 For when I called, **n** one answered, 401
66: 4 when I spoke, **n** one listened. 4202
66: 8 **n sooner** is Zion in labor **than** 1685
Jer 2: 6 where **n** one travels and no one lives?' 4202
2: 6 where no one travels and **n** one lives?' 4202
2:19 the LORD your God and have **n** awe 4202
2:25 But you said, 'It's **n** use! 4202
2:31 we will come to you **n** more'? 4202
3: 3 and **n** spring rains have fallen. 4202
3: 8 that her unfaithful sister Judah had **n** fear; 4202
3:12 'I will frown on you **n** *longer,* 4202
3:16 "men will **n** longer say, 4202
3:17 **N** longer will they follow the stubbornness 4202
4: 1 of my sight and **n** *longer* go astray, 4202
4: 4 burn with **n** one to quench it. 401
4:22 they have **n** understanding. 4202
4:25 I looked, and **there were n** people; 401
4:29 **n** one lives in them. 401
5: 3 You struck them, but they felt **n** pain; 4202
5:12 **N** harm will come to us; 4202
5:28 Their evil deeds **have n limit;** 6296
6: 8 so **n** one can live in it." 4202
6:10 they find **n** pleasure in it. 4202
6:14 peace,' they say, when **there is n** peace. 401

Jer 6:15 **N,** they have no shame at all; 1685
6:15 No, they have **n** shame at all; 4202
6:23 they are cruel and show **n** mercy. 4202
7:32 when people will **n** longer call it Topheth 4202
7:32 in Topheth until **there is n** *more* room. 401
7:33 **there will be n** one to frighten them away. 401
8:6 **N** one repents of his wickedness, saying, 4202
8:11 peace," they say, when **there is n** peace. 401
8:12 **N,** they have no shame at all; 1685
8:12 No, they have **n** shame at all; 4202
8:13 **There will be n** grapes on the vine. 401
8:13 **There will be n** figs on the tree, 401
8:15 We hoped for peace but **n** good has come, 401
8:19 **Is** her King **n** *longer* there?" 401
8:22 **Is there n** balm in Gilead? 401
8:22 **Is there n** physician there? 401
8:22 Why then is there **n** healing for the wound 4202
9:5 and **n** one speaks the truth. 4202
9:11 the towns of Judah so **n** one can live there." 1172
9:12 like a desert that **n** one can cross? 1172+4946
9:22 with **n** one to gather them.' " 401
10:5 they can do **n** harm 4202
10:6 **N** *one* is like you, O LORD; 401+4946
10:7 **there is n** *one* like you. 401+4946
10:14 they have **n** breath in them. 4202
10:20 My sons are gone from me and **are n more;** 401
10:20 **n** *one* is left now to pitch my tent or to set 401
11:19 that his name be remembered **n** more." 4202
12:11 because **there is n** one who cares. 401
12:12 **n** one will be safe. 4202
13:14 I will allow **n** pity or mercy or compassion 4202
13:19 and **there will be n** one to open them. 401
14:3 they go to the cisterns but find **n** water. 4202
14:4 because there is **n** rain in the land; 4202
14:5 because there is **n** grass. 4202
14:15 '**N** sword or famine will touch this land.' 4202
14:16 **There will be n** one to bury them 401
14:19 We hoped for peace but **n** good has come, 401
14:22 **N,** it is you, O LORD our God. 4202
15:6 *I* **can n longer** show compassion. 4206
16:6 and **n** one will cut himself 4202
16:7 **N** one will offer food 4202
16:13 for I will show you **n** favor.' 4202
16:14 "when men will **n** longer say, 4202
16:19 worthless idols that did them **n** good. 401
17:6 in a salt land where **n** one lives. 4202
17:8 It has **n** worries in a year of drought 4202
17:24 and bring **n** load through the gates 1194
18:12 But they will reply, '*It's* **n use.** 3286
18:18 and pay **n** attention to anything he says." 440
19:6 people will **n** longer call this place Topheth 4202
19:11 in Topheth until **there is n** *more* room. 401
21:7 he will show them **n** mercy or pity 4202
21:12 burn with **n** one to quench it. 401
22:3 Do **n** wrong or violence to the alien, 440
22:28 broken pot, an object **n** *one* wants? 401
23:4 and they will **n** longer be afraid or terrified, 4202
23:7 "when people will **n** longer say, 4202
23:14 so that **n** one turns from his wickedness. 1194
23:17 '**N** harm will come to you.' 4202
25:27 and vomit, and fall to rise **n** *more* because 4202
25:35 the leaders of the flock **n** place to escape. 4946
29:32 He will have **n** one left among this people, 4202
30:8 **n** longer will foreigners enslave them. 4202
30:10 and **n** one will make him afraid. 401
30:13 **There is n** one to plead your cause, 401
30:13 **n** remedy for your sore, no healing for you. NIH
30:13 no remedy for your sore, **n** healing for you. NIH
30:15 your pain that has **n cure?** 631
30:17 Zion for whom **n** one cares.' 401
31:12 and they will sorrow **n** more. 4202
31:15 because her children **are n more."** 401
31:29 "In those days people will **n** longer say, 4202
31:34 **N** longer will a man teach his neighbor, 4202
31:34 and will remember their sins **n** more." 4202
33:20 so that day and night **n** longer come 1194
33:21 can be broken and David will **n** *longer* have 4946
33:24 and **n** longer regard them as a nation. 4946
34:9 **n** one was to hold a fellow Jew in bondage. 1194
34:10 and female slaves and **n** longer hold them 1194
34:22 the towns of Judah so **n** one can live there." 401
36:24 who heard all these words showed **n** fear, 4202
36:30 He will have **n** one to sit on the throne 4202
38:6 it had **n** water in it, only mud, 401
38:9 to death when **there is n** longer any bread in 401
38:27 So *they* **said n more** to him, 3087
38:27 for **n** one had heard his conversation with 4202
40:15 and **n** one will know it. 4202
42:14 '**N,** we will go and live in Egypt, 4202
44:17 and were well off and suffered **n** harm. 4202
44:22 LORD could **n** longer endure your wicked 4202
44:26 'that **n** one from Judah living anywhere 561
45:3 with groaning and find **n** rest.' " 4202
46:11 **there is n** healing for you. 401
46:27 and **n** one will make him afraid. 401
48:2 Moab will be praised **n** more; 4202
48:9 with **n** one to live in them. 401+4946
48:33 **n** one treads them with shouts of joy. 4202
48:38 like a jar that **n** *one* wants," 401
49:1 "Has Israel **n** sons? 401
49:1 Has she **n** heirs? 401
49:5 and **n** one will gather the fugitives. 401
49:7 **"Is there n** longer wisdom in Teman? 401
49:10 and he *will* **be n more.** 401
49:18 says the LORD, "so **n** one will live there; 4202
49:18 **n** man will dwell in it. 4202
49:33 **N** one will live there; 4202

Jer 49:33 **n** man will dwell in it." 4202
50:3 **N** one will live in it; 4202
50:14 Spare **n** arrows, for she has sinned against 440
50:26 and leave her **n** remnant. 440
50:29 Encamp all around her; let **n** one escape. 440
50:32 and fall and **n** one will help her up; 401
50:40 "so **n** one will live there; 4202
50:40 **n** man will dwell in it. 4202
51:17 they have **n** breath in them. 4202
51:26 **N** rock will be taken from you for 4202
51:29 of Babylon so that **n** one will live there. 401
51:37 a place where **n** one lives. 401+4946
51:43 a land where **n** one lives, 3972+4202
51:43 through which **n** man travels. 4202
51:44 The nations will **n** longer stream to him. 4202
51:64 'So will Babylon sink to rise **n** *more* 4202
52:6 that there was **n** food for the people to eat. 4202
La 1:3 she finds **n** resting place. 4202
1:4 for **n** one comes to her appointed feasts. 1172
1:6 like deer that find **n** pasture; 4202
1:7 **there was n** one to help her. 401
1:16 **N** *one is* **near** to comfort me, 8178
1:16 **n** one to restore my spirit. NIH
1:17 but **there is n** one to comfort her. 401
1:21 but **there is n** one to comfort me. 401
2:9 the law **is n more,** 401
2:9 and her prophets **n** *longer* find visions from 4202
2:18 give yourself **n** relief, your eyes no rest. 440
2:18 give yourself no relief, your eyes **n** rest. 440
2:22 of the LORD's anger **n** *one* escaped 4202
3:44 a cloud so that **n** prayer can get through. 4946
4:4 but **n** one gives it to them. 401
4:14 that **n** one dares to touch their garments. 4202
4:15 "They can stay here **n** longer." 4202
4:16 he **n** longer watches over them. 4202
4:16 The priests are shown **n** honor, 4202
4:16 the elders **n** favor. 4202
5:5 we are weary and find **n** rest. 4202
5:7 Our fathers sinned and **are n more,** 401
5:12 elders are shown **n** respect. 4202
Eze 4:14 **N** unclean meat has ever entered my mouth. 4202
7:11 **n** wealth, nothing of value. 4202
7:14 **n** one will go into battle, 401
12:23 and they will **n** longer quote it in Israel.' 4202
12:24 For there will be **n** more false visions 4202
13:10 saying, "Peace," when **there is n** peace, 401
13:16 of peace for her when **there was n** peace, 401
13:21 they will **n** longer fall prey to your power. 4202
13:22 when I had brought them **n** grief, 4202
13:23 therefore you will **n** longer see false visions 4202
14:11 Then the people of Israel will **n** longer stray 4202
14:15 so that **n** one can pass through it because of 1172
16:5 **N** one looked on you with pity 4202
16:34 **n** one runs after you for your favors. 4202
16:41 and you will **n** longer pay your lovers. 4202
16:42 I will be calm and **n** longer angry. 4202
17:17 and great horde will be of **n** help to him 4202
18:3 you will **n** longer quote this proverb 561
18:17 and takes **n** usury or excessive interest. 4202
18:32 I take **n** pleasure in the death of anyone, 4202
19:9 so his roar was heard **n** longer on 4202
19:14 **N** strong branch is left on it fit for 4202
20:39 to me and **n** longer profane my holy name 4202
21:32 you will be remembered **n** *more;* 4202
22:24 that has had **n** rain or showers in the day 4202
22:26 they teach that there is **n** difference 4202
24:27 you will speak with him and will **n** longer 4202
26:13 music of your harps will be heard **n** more. 4202
26:19 like cities **n** *longer* inhabited, 4202
26:21 to a horrible end and you *will* **be n more.** 401
27:36 to a horrible end and *will* **be n** more.' " 401
28:3 Is **n** secret hidden from you? 4202
28:19 to a horrible end and *will* **be n** more.' " 401
28:24 " '**N** longer will the people 4202
29:11 **N** foot of man or animal will pass 4202
29:11 **n** one will live there for forty years. 4202
29:16 Egypt will **n** longer be a source 4202
29:18 Yet he and his army got **n** reward from 4202
30:13 **N** longer will there be a prince in Egypt, 4202
31:8 **n** tree in the garden of God 3972+4202
31:14 Therefore **n** other trees by 4202
31:14 **N** other trees so well-watered are ever 4202
32:13 from beside abundant waters **n** longer to 4202
33:11 I take **n** pleasure in the death of the wicked, 561
33:15 and does **n** evil, he will surely live; 1194
33:22 and I was **n** longer silent. 4202
33:28 so that **n** one will cross them. 401
34:5 because there was **n** shepherd, 1172
34:6 and **n** one searched or looked for them. 401
34:10 shepherds can **n** longer feed themselves. 4202
34:10 and it will **n** *longer* be food for them. 4202
34:22 and they will **n** longer be plundered. 4202
34:28 They will **n** longer be plundered by 4202
34:28 and **n** one will make them afraid. 401
34:29 and they will **n** longer be victims of famine 4202
36:14 therefore you will **n** longer devour men 4202
36:15 **N** longer will I make you hear the taunts of 4202
36:15 and **n** longer will you suffer the scorn of 4202
36:30 so that you will **n** longer suffer disgrace 4202
37:8 but **there was n** breath in them. 401
37:23 They will **n** longer defile themselves 4202
39:7 I will **n** longer let my holy name 4202
39:26 in safety in their land with **n** one 401
39:29 I will **n** longer hide my face from them, 4202
42:6 The rooms on the third floor had **n** pillars, 401
44:2 **n** one may enter through it. 4202
44:9 **N** foreigner uncircumcised in heart 3972+4202

Eze 44:21 **N** priest is to drink wine when he 3972+4202
44:28 You are to give them **n** possession in Israel; 4202
45:8 my princes will **n** longer oppress my people 4202
46:9 **N** one is to return through the gate 4202
47:5 a river that **n** one could cross. 4202
Da 2:10 **N** king, however great and mighty, 10353+10379
2:11 **N** one can reveal it to the king except 10379
2:27 Daniel replied, **"N** wise man, enchanter, 10379
3:12 who pay **n** attention to you, O king. 10379
3:27 and there was **n** smell of fire on them. 10379
3:29 for **n** other god can save in this way." 10379
4:9 **n** mystery is too difficult for you. 10353+10379
4:35 **N** one can hold back his hand or say 10379
6:4 They could find **n** corruption in him, 10379
6:13 pays **n** attention to you, O king, 10379
6:15 Medes and Persians **n** decree or 10353+10379
6:23 **n** wound was found on him, 10353+10379
8:4 **N** animal could stand against him, 3972+4202
10:3 I ate **n** choice food; 4202
10:3 **n** meat or wine touched my lips; 4202
10:3 and I used **n** lotions at all until 4202
10:8 I had **n** strength left, 4202
10:21 (**N** one supports me 401
11:16 **n** one will be able to stand against him. 401
11:19 to be seen **n** *more.* 4202
11:27 but to **n** avail, 4202
11:37 He will show **n** regard for the gods 4202
11:45 and **n** one will help him. 401
Hos 1:6 for I will **n** longer show love to the house 4202
2:10 **n** one will take her out of my hands. 4202
2:16 you will **n** longer call me 'my master.' 4202
2:17 **n** longer will their names be invoked. 4202
4:1 **"There is n** faithfulness, no love, 401
4:1 "There is no faithfulness, **n** love, 401
4:1 **n** acknowledgment of God in the land. 401
4:4 "But let **n** man bring a charge, 440
4:4 let **n** man accuse another, 440
5:14 with **n** one to rescue them. 401
8:7 stalk has **n** head; it will produce no flour. 401
8:7 stalk has no head; it will produce **n** flour. 1172
9:11 **n** birth, no pregnancy, no conception. 4946
9:11 no birth, **n** pregnancy, no conception. 4946
9:11 no birth, no pregnancy, **n** conception. 4946
9:15 I will **n** longer love them; 4202
9:16 their root is withered, they yield **n** fruit. 1153
10:3 "We have **n** king because we did not revere 401
11:7 he will **by n means** exalt them. 3480+4202
13:4 You shall acknowledge **n** God but me, 4202
13:4 **n** Savior except me. 401
13:14 "I *will* **have n** compassion, 4946+6259+6524
Joel 1:18 about because they have **n** pasture; 401
2:10 and the stars **n longer shine.** 665+5586
2:27 and that **there is n** other; 401
3:15 and the stars **n longer shine.** 665+5586
Am 3:4 in the thicket when he has **n** prey? 401
3:5 on the ground where **n** snare has been set? 401
5:2 with **n** one to lift her up." 401
5:6 and Bethel will have **n** one to quench it. 401
5:22 I will have **n** regard for them. 4202
6:10 and he says, **"N,"** then he will say, "Hush! 700
7:8 I will spare them **n** longer. 4202
8:2 I will spare them **n** longer. 4202
Ob 1:18 There will be **n** survivors from the house 4202
Mic 2:3 You will **n** *longer* walk proudly, 4202
2:5 Therefore you will have **n** one in 4202
3:7 because **there is n** answer from God." 401
3:11 **N** disaster will come upon us." 4202
4:4 and **n** one will make them afraid, 401
4:9 have you **n** king? 401
5:8 and **n** one can rescue. 401
5:12 and you will **n** longer cast spells. 4202
5:13 you will **n** longer bow down to the work 4202
7:1 **there is n** cluster of grapes to eat, 401
7:5 put **n** confidence in a friend. 440
Na 1:12 I will afflict you **n** more. 4202
1:14 "You will have **n** descendants 4202
1:15 **N** more will the wicked invade you; 4202
2:8 they cry, but **n** one turns back. 401
2:13 *I will* **leave** you **n** prey on the earth. 4162
2:13 of your messengers will **n** longer be heard." 4202
3:17 and **n** one knows where. 4202
3:18 the mountains with **n** one to gather them. 401
Hab 1:14 like sea creatures that have **n** ruler. 4202
2:19 **there is n** breath in it. 401+3972
3:17 not bud and **there are n** grapes on the vines, 401
3:17 and the fields produce **n** food, 4202
3:17 though **there are n** sheep in the pen 1615
3:17 in the pen and **n** cattle in the stalls, 401
Zep 3:2 She obeys **n** one, she accepts no correction. 4202
3:2 She obeys no one, she accepts **n** correction. 4202
3:5 he does **n** wrong. 4202
3:5 yet the unrighteous know **n** shame. 4202
3:6 with **n** one passing through. 1172
3:6 **n** one will be left—no one at all. 401+4946
3:6 **n** one at all. 1172+4946
3:13 The remnant of Israel will do **n** wrong; 4202
3:13 they will speak **n** lies, 4202
3:13 down and **n** one will make them afraid." 401
Hag 2:12 The priests answered, **"N."** 4202
Zec 1:21 so that **n** one could raise his head, 4202
4:5 **"N,** my lord," I replied. 4202
4:13 **"N,** my lord," I said. 4202
7:14 behind them that **n** one could come or go. 4946
8:10 that time there were **n** wages for man 4202
8:10 **N** one could go about his business safely 401
8:14 upon you and showed **n** pity 4202
11:6 For I will **n** longer have pity on the people 4202

Zec 13: 2 and they will be remembered **n** more," 4202
14: 6 On that day there will be **n** light, 4202
14: 6 **n** cold or frost. NIH
14:17 they will have **n** rain. 4202
14:18 they will have **n** rain. 4202
14:21 that day there will **n** longer be a Canaanite 4202
Mal 1:10 I will accept **n** offering from your hands. 4202
2:13 and wail because he **n** longer pays attention 401
Mt 1:25 But he had **n** union with her 4024
2: 6 are **by n means** least among the rulers 4027
2:18 because they are **n more."** 4024
5:13 **n** longer good for **anything,** 4029
5:37 be 'Yes,' and your **'N,'** 'No'; 4024
5:37 be 'Yes,' and your 'No,' **'N';** 4024
6: 1 you will have **n** reward from your Father 4024
6:24 **"N one** can serve two masters. 4029
7: 3 in your brother's eye and pay **n** attention to 4024
8:20 Son of Man has **n** place to lay his head." 4024
8:28 They were so violent that **n** one could pass 3590
9:16 **"N one** sews a patch of unshrunk cloth on 4029
9:17 **N,** they pour new wine into new wineskins, 247
9:30 "See that **n one** knows about this." 3594
10:10 take **n** bag for the journey, or extra tunic, 3590
11: 8 **N,** those who wear fine clothes are NIG
11:23 **N,** you will go down to the depths. 3590
11:27 **N one** knows the Son except the Father, 4029
11:27 **and n** one knows the Father except the Son 4028
12:19 **n** one will hear his voice in the streets. 4028
13: 6 and they withered because they had **n** root. 3590
13:21 he has **n** root, he lasts only a short time. 4024
13:29 " **'N,'** he answered, 'because 4024
16: 8 among yourselves about having **n** bread? 4024
17: 8 they saw **n one** except Jesus. 4029
19: 6 So they are **n longer** two, but one. 4033
20: 7 **n one** has hired us,' they answered. 4029
22: 5 "But they **paid n attention** and went off— 288
22:16 you pay **n** attention to who they are. 4024
22:23 who say there is **n** resurrection, 3590
22:25 and since he had **n** children, 3590
22:46 **N one** could say a word in reply, 4029
22:46 and from that day on **n** one dared 4028
24: 4 "Watch out that **n** one deceives you. 3590
24:17 Let **n** one on the roof of his house go down 3590
24:18 Let **n** one in the field go back 3590
24:22 **n** one would survive, 4024
24:36 **"N one** knows about that day or hour, 4029
25: 9 " **'N,'** they replied, 'there may not 3607
27:12 he gave **n** answer. 4029
27:14 But Jesus made **n** reply, 4024
Mk 1:45 Jesus could **n longer** enter a town openly 3600
2: 2 that there was **n** room left, 3600
2:21 **"N one** sews a patch of unshrunk cloth on 4029
2:22 **n one** pours new wine into old wineskins. 4029
2:22 **N,** he pours new wine into new wineskins." 247
3:27 **n one** can enter a strong man's house 4029
4: 6 and they withered because they had **n** root, 3590
4:17 But since they have **n** root, 4024
4:40 Do you **still** have **n** faith?" 4037
5: 3 and **n one** could bind him any more, 4029
5: 4 **N one** was strong enough to subdue him. 4029
6: 8 **n** bread, no bag, no money in your belts. 3590
6: 8 no bread, **n** bag, no money in your belts. 3590
6: 8 no bread, no bag, **n** money in your belts. 3590
7:12 then you **n longer** let him do anything 4033
8:12 **n** sign will be given to it." 1623
8:16 "It is because we have **n** bread." 4024
8:17 about having **n** bread? 4024
9: 8 they **n longer** saw anyone 4033
9:39 **"N one** who does a miracle in my name can 4029
10: 8 So they are **n longer** two, but one. 4033
10:18 **"N one** is good—except God alone. 4029
10:29 **"n one** who has left home or brothers 4029
11: 2 which **n one** has ever ridden. 476+4029
11:14 "May **n one ever** eat fruit from you again." 3594
12:14 you pay **n** attention to who they are; 4024
12:18 Sadducees, who say there is **n** resurrection, 3590
12:19 and leaves a wife but **n** children, 3590
12:21 but he also died, leaving **n** child. 3590
12:31 There is **n** commandment greater than these. 4024
12:32 that God is one and there is **n** other 4024
12:34 on **n one** dared ask him any more questions. 4029
13: 5 "Watch out that **n** one deceives you. 3590
13:15 Let **n** one on the roof of his house go down 3590
13:16 Let **n** one in the field go back 3590
13:20 **n** one would survive. 4024
13:32 **"N one knows** about that day or hour, 4029
14:61 and gave **n** answer. 4024
15: 5 But Jesus **still** made **n** reply, 4033
Lk 1: 7 But they had **n** children, 4024
1:60 but his mother spoke up and said, **"N!** 4049
1:61 "There is **n one** among your relatives who 4029
2: 7 there was **n** room for them in the inn. 4024
4:24 **"n** prophet is accepted in his hometown. 4029
5:36 **"N one** tears a patch from a new garment 4029
5:37 **n one** pours new wine into old wineskins. 4029
5:38 **N,** new wine must be poured 247
5:39 And **n** one after drinking old wine wants 4029
6:41 in your brother's eye and pay **n** attention to 4024
6:43 **"N** good tree bears bad fruit, 4024
7:25 **N,** those who wear expensive clothes NIG
7:28 of women there is **n one** greater than John; 4029
8: 6 because they had **n** moisture. 3590
8:13 but they have **n** root. 4024
8:16 **"N one** lights a lamp and hides it in a jar 4029
8:43 but **n one** could heal her. 4024+4029
9: 3 **n** staff, no bag, no bread, no money, 3612
9: 3 no staff, **n** bag, no bread, no money, 3612
Lk 9: 3 no staff, no bag, **n** bread, no money, 3612
9: 3 no staff, no bag, no bread, **n** money, 3612
9: 3 no bag, no bread, no money, **n** extra tunic. 3612
9:36 told **n one** at that time what they had seen. 4029
9:58 Son of Man has **n** place to lay his head." 4024
9:62 **"N one who** puts his hand to the plow 4029
10:15 **N,** you will go down to the depths. 3590
10:22 **N one** knows who the Son is except 4029
10:22 and **n** one knows who the Father is except NIG
11:33 **"N one** lights a lamp and puts it in a place 4029
11:36 full of light, and **n** part of it dark, 3590
12: 4 the body and after that can do **n** more. 3590
12:17 I have **n place** to store my crops.' 4024+4544
12:24 they have **n** storeroom or barn; 4024
12:33 **n** thief comes near and no moth destroys. 4024
12:33 no thief comes near **and n** moth destroys. 4028
12:51 **N,** I tell you, but division. 4049
13: 3 I tell you, **n!** 4049
13: 5 I tell you, **n!** 4049
13:33 surely **n** prophet can die outside Jerusalem! 4024
15:16 but **n one** gave him anything. 4029
15:19 I am **n longer** worthy to 4033
15:21 I am **n longer** worthy to 4033
16:13 **"N** servant can serve two masters. 4029
16:30 " **'N,** father Abraham,' he said, 4049
17:18 Was **n** one found to return and give praise 4024
17:31 On that day **n** one who is on the roof 3590
17:31 **n** one in the field should go back 3590
18:19 **"N one** is good—except God alone. 4029
18:29 **"n one** who has left home or wife 4029
19:30 which **n one** has ever ridden. 4029
20:27 who say there is **n** resurrection, 3590
20:28 and leaves a wife but **n children,** 866
20:31 the seven died, leaving **n** children 4024
20:36 and they can **n** longer die; 4028
20:40 **n** one dared to ask him **any more** 4033
22: 6 **when n** crowd **was present.** 868
22:51 But Jesus answered, **"N more** of this!" 1572
23: 4 "I find **n** basis for a charge 4029
23: 9 but Jesus gave him **n** answer. 4029
23:14 in your presence and have found **n** basis 4029
23:22 in him **n** grounds for the death penalty. 4029
23:53 one in which **n one** had yet been laid. 4029
Jn 1:18 **N one** has ever seen God, 4029
1:21 He answered, **"N."** 4024
2: 3 "They have **n** more wine." 4024
3: 2 For **n one** could perform 4029
3: 3 **n** one can see the kingdom of God unless 4024
3: 5 **n** one can enter the kingdom of God unless 4024
3:13 **N one** has ever gone into heaven except 4029
3:32 but **n one** accepts his testimony. 4029
4:17 "I have **n** husband," she replied. 4024
4:17 when you say you have **n** husband. 4024
4:27 But **n one** asked, "What do you want?" 4029
4:42 "We **n longer** believe just because 4033
4:44 a prophet has **n** honor in his own country.) 4024
5: 7 "I have **n** one to help me into the pool 4024
5:13 The man who was healed had **n** idea who it was, 4024
5:22 Moreover, the Father judges **n one,** 4029
5:44 yet make **n** effort to obtain the praise 4024
6:44 **"N one** can come to me unless 4029
6:46 **N** one has seen the Father except 4024
6:53 you have **n** life in you. 4024
6:65 "This is why I told you that **n one** can come 4029
6:66 and **n longer** followed him. 4033
7: 4 **N one who** wants to become 4029
7:12 **"N,** he deceives the people." 4024
7:13 But **n one** would say anything publicly 4029
7:27 **n one** will know where he is from." 4029
7:30 but **n one** laid a hand on him, 4029
7:44 but **n one** laid a hand on him. 4029
7:46 **"N one ever** spoke the way this man does," 4030
7:49 **N!** But this mob NIG
8:10 Has **n one** condemned you?" 4029
8:11 **"N one,** sir," she said, 4029
8:14 But you have **n** idea where I come from or 4024
8:15 I pass judgment on **n one.** 4024+4029
8:20 Yet **n one** seized him, 4029
8:35 a slave has **n** permanent place in the family, 4024
8:37 because you have **n** room for my word. 4024
8:44 for there is **n** truth in him. 4024
9: 4 Night is coming, when **n one** can work. 4029
9: 9 Others said, **"N,** he only looks like him." 4049
10:18 **N one** takes it from me, 4029
10:28 **n** one can snatch them out of my hand. 4024
10:29 **n one** can snatch them out 4029
11: 4 **N,** it is for God's glory so 247
11:10 for he has **n** light." 4024
11:54 Therefore Jesus **n longer** moved 4033
12:27 **N,** it was for this very reason I came 247
12:46 that **n** one who believes in me should stay 3590
13: 8 **"N,"** said Peter, "you shall never wash my feet." 3590
13: 8 you have **n** part with me." 4024
13:16 **n** servant is greater than his master, 4024
13:28 but **n one** at the meal understood why 4029
14: 6 **N one** comes to the Father except 4029
14:30 He has **n** hold on me, 4024+4029
15: 2 cuts off every branch in me that bears **n** fruit 3590
15: 4 **N** branch can bear fruit by itself; 4024
15:13 Greater love has **n one** than this, 4029
15:15 I **n longer** call you servants, 4033
15:20 **'N** servant is greater than his master.' 4024
15:22 however, they have **n** excuse for their sin. 4024
15:24 not done among them what **n one** else did, 4029
16:10 where you can see me **n longer;** 4033
Jn 16:16 "In a little while you will see me **n more,** 4033
16:17 'In a little while you will see me **n more,** 4024
16:19 'In a little while you will see me **n more,** 4024
16:22 and **n one** will take away your joy. 4029
16:23 that day you will **n** longer ask me anything. 4024
16:25 when I will **n longer** use this kind 4033
16:27 **N,** the Father himself loves you 1142
17:11 I will remain in the world **n longer,** 4033
18:31 "But we have **n** right to execute anyone," 4024
18:38 "I find **n** basis for a charge against him. 4029
18:40 They shouted back, **"N,** not him! NIG
19: 4 that I find **n** basis for a charge against him." 4029
19: 6 I find **n** basis for a charge against him." 4024
19: 9 but Jesus gave him **n** answer. 4024
19:11 "You would have **n** power over me 4024+4029
19:12 you are **n** friend of Caesar. 4024
19:15 "We have **n** king but Caesar," 4024
19:41 in which **n one** had ever been laid. 4029
21: 5 **"N,"** they answered. 4024
Ac 1:20 let there be **n** one to dwell in it,' and, 3590
2:16 **N,** this is what was spoken by 247
4:12 Salvation is found in **n one** else, 4024+4029
4:12 for there is **n** other name under heaven 4028
4:17 we must warn these men to speak **n longer** 3600
4:32 **N** one claimed that any of his possessions 4028
4:34 There were **n** needy persons among them. 4028
5:13 **N one** else dared join them, 4029
5:23 we opened them, we found **n one** inside." 4029
7: 5 He gave him **n** inheritance here, 4024
7: 5 though at that time Abraham had **n** child. 4024
7:20 and he was **n ordinary** child. 842
8:21 You have **n** part or share in this ministry, 4024
11:12 to have **n** hesitation about going with them. 3594
11:18 *they had* **n** further **objections** 2483
12: 9 but he had **n** idea that what 4024
12:18 there was **n** small commotion among 4024
13:25 **N,** but he is coming after me, NIG
13:28 Though they found **n** proper ground for 3594
15: 9 He made **n** distinction between us 4029
15:11 **N!** We believe it is through the grace 247
16:37 to get rid of us quietly? **N!** 4024
18:10 and **n one** is going to attack and harm you, 4029
18:17 But Gallio showed **n** concern **whatever.** 4029
19: 2 **"N,** we have not even heard that there is 247
19:24 in **n** little business for the craftsmen. 4024
19:26 that man-made gods are **n** gods **at all.** 4024
19:40 since there is **n** reason for it." 3594
21:24 Then everybody will know there is **n truth** 4029
21:39 a citizen of **n** ordinary city. 4024
23: 8 that there is **n** resurrection, 3590
23:29 but there was **n** charge against him 3594
24:11 that **n** more than twelve days ago I went up 4024
24:18 There was **n** crowd with me, 4024
25:11 **n one** has the right to hand me over to them. 4029
28: 5 into the fire and suffered **n** ill effects. 4029
Ro 2: 1 You, therefore, have **n excuse,** 406
2:29 **N,** a man is a Jew if he is one inwardly; 247
3:10 "There is **n** one righteous, not even one; 4024
3:11 there is **n** one who understands, 4024
3:11 **n** one who seeks God. 4024
3:12 there is **n** one who does good, 4024
3:18 "There is **n** fear of God before their eyes." 4024
3:20 **n one** will be declared righteous 4024+4246
3:22 There is **n** difference, 4024
3:27 **N,** but on that of faith. 4049
4:14 faith *has* **n value** and the promise is 3033
4:15 there is **n** law there is no transgression. 4024
4:15 there is no law there is **n** transgression. 4028
5:13 not taken into account when there is **n** law. 3590
6: 2 **By n means!** We died to sin; 1181+3590
6: 6 that we should **n longer** be slaves to sin— 3600
6: 9 death **n longer** has mastery over him. 4033
6:15 but under grace? **By n means!** 1181+3590
7:13 become death to me? **By n means!** 1181+3590
7:17 As it is, it is **n longer** I myself who do it, 4033
7:19 **n,** the evil I do not want to do— 247
7:20 it is **n longer** I who do it, 4033
8: 1 now **n** condemnation for those who are 4029
8:24 But hope that is seen is **n** hope at all. 4024
8:37 **N,** in all these things we are more than conquerors through him 247
10:12 For there is **n** difference between Jew 4024
10:19 by a nation that has **n understanding."** 852
11: 1 God reject his people? **By n means!** 1181+3590
11: 6 if by grace, then it is **n longer** by works; 4033
11: 6 if it were, grace would **n longer** be grace. 4033
13: 1 for there is **n** authority except 4024
13: 3 rulers hold **n** terror for those who do right, 4024
13: 8 Let **n** debt remain outstanding, 3594
13:10 Love does **n** harm to its neighbor. 4024
14:14 I am fully convinced that **n** food is unclean 4029
14:15 you are **n longer** acting in love. 4033
15:23 But now that there is **n more** place for me 3600
1Co 1:10 be **n** divisions among you and that you may 3590
1:15 so **n** one can say that you were baptized 3590
1:29 so that **n** one may boast before him. 3590
2: 7 **N,** we speak of God's secret wisdom, 247
2: 9 However, as it is written: **"N** eye has seen, 4024
2: 9 "No eye has seen, **n** ear has heard, 4024
2: 9 **n** mind has conceived what God has prepared for those who love him"— 4024
2:11 In the same way **n one** knows the thoughts 4029
3:11 For **n one** can lay any foundation other than 4029
3:21 So then, **n** more boasting about men! 3594
7:25 I have **n** command from the Lord, 4024
7:37 who is under **n** compulsion but has control 3590
8: 4 the world and that there is **n** God but one. 4029

1Co 8: 8 we are **n** worse if we do not eat, *4046*
8: 8 **and n** better if we do. *4046*
9: 19 I am **free and belong to n man,** *1666+1801+4246*
9: 27 **N,** I beat my body and make it my slave so *247*
10: 13 **N** temptation has seized you except what is common to man. *4024*
10: 20 **N,** but the sacrifices of pagans are offered *NIG*
11: 16 we have **n** other practice— *4024*
11: 17 In the following directives I have **n** praise *4024*
11: 19 **N** doubt there have to be differences *NIG*
12: 3 that **n one** who is speaking by the Spirit *4029*
12: 3 "Jesus be cursed," and **n one** can say, *4029*
12: 24 presentable parts need **n** special treatment. *4024*
12: 25 that there should be **n** division in the body, *3590*
13: 5 it keeps **n** record of wrongs. *4024*
14: 2 Indeed, **n one** understands him; *4029*
14: 28 If there is **n** interpreter, *3590*
15: 10 **N,** I worked harder than all of them— *247*
15: 12 of you say that there is **n** resurrection of *4024*
15: 13 If there is **n** resurrection of the dead, *4024*
15: 29 Now if there is **n** resurrection, *NIG*
16: 2 I come **n** collections will have to be made. *3590*
16: 11 **N** one, then, should refuse to accept him. *3590*
2Co 1: 17 "Yes, yes" and **"N,** no"? *4024*
1: 17 "Yes, yes" and "No, **n"?** *4024*
1: 18 our message to you is not "Yes" and **"N."** *4024*
1: 19 was not "Yes" and **"N,"** *4024*
1: 20 **n** matter how many promises God has made, *NIG*
2: 13 I still had **n** peace of mind, *4024*
3: 10 For what was glorious has **n** glory now *4024*
5: 15 that those who live should **n longer** live *3600*
5: 16 on we regard **n one** from a worldly point *4029*
5: 16 we do so **n longer.** *4033*
5: 21 God made him who had **n** sin to be sin *3590*
6: 3 We put **n** stumbling block in anyone's path, *3594*
6: 17 Touch **n** unclean thing, *3590*
7: 2 We have wronged **n one,** *4029*
7: 2 we have corrupted **n one,** *4029*
7: 2 we have exploited **n one.** *4029*
7: 4 in all our troubles my joy **knows n bounds.** *5668*
7: 5 this body of ours had **n** rest, *4029*
7: 10 that leads to salvation and leaves **n regret,** *294*
9: 1 There is **n need** for me to write to you *4356*
11: 14 **n** wonder, for Satan himself masquerades *4024*
11: 16 I repeat: Let **n** one take me for a fool. *3590*
12: 6 so **n** one will think more *3590*
Gal 1: 7 which is really **n** gospel **at all.** *4024*
1: 20 that what I am writing you is **n** lie. *4024*
2: 6 whatever they were makes **n** difference *4029*
2: 16 because by observing the law **n** one will *4024*
2: 20 with Christ and I **n longer** live, *4033*
3: 11 Clearly **n one** is justified before God by *4029*
3: 15 Just as **n one** can set aside or add to *4029*
3: 18 then it **n longer** depends on a promise; *4033*
3: 25 we are **n longer** under the supervision of *4033*
4: 1 he is **n** different from a slave, *4029*
4: 7 So you are **n longer** a slave, but a son; *4033*
4: 12 You have done me **n** wrong. *4029*
4: 17 but for **n** good. *4024*
4: 27 O barren woman, who bears **n** children; *4024*
4: 27 you who have **n** labor pains; *4024*
5: 2 **n** value to you **at all.** *4029*
5: 10 in the Lord that you will take **n** other view. *4029*
5: 23 Against such things there is **n** law. *4024*
6: 17 Finally, let **n one** cause me trouble, *3594*
Eph 2: 9 not by works, so that **n** one can boast. *3590*
2: 19 you are **n longer** foreigners and aliens, *4033*
4: 14 Then we will **n longer** be infants, *3600*
4: 17 you must **n longer** live as the Gentiles do, *3600*
4: 28 He who has been stealing must steal **n longer,** *3600*
5: 5 **N** immoral, impure or greedy person *4024+4246*
5: 6 Let **n one** deceive you with empty words, *3594*
5: 29 After all, **n one** ever hated his own body, *4029*
6: 9 and there is **n** favoritism with him. *4024*
Php 1: 20 and hope that I will in **n way** be ashamed, *4029*
2: 20 I have **n one** else like him, *4029*
3: 1 It is **n** trouble for me to write *4024*
3: 3 and who put **n** confidence in the flesh— *4024*
4: 10 but *you* **had n opportunity** to show it. *177*
Col 2: 4 so that **n one** may deceive you *3594*
2: 8 that **n** one takes you captive through hollow *3590*
3: 11 Here there is **n** Greek or Jew, *4024*
3: 25 and there is **n** favoritism. *4024*
1Th 3: 1 So when we could stand it **n longer,** *3600*
3: 3 **n one** would be unsettled by these trials. *3594*
3: 5 when I could stand it **n longer,** *3600*
4: 6 this matter **n** one should wrong his brother *3590*
4: 13 who have **n** hope. *3590*
1Ti 5: 7 **n** one may be **open to blame.** *455*
5: 9 **N** widow may be put on the list of widows *3590*
5: 14 the enemy **n** opportunity for slander. *3594*
6: 16 whom **n one** has seen or can see. *4029*
2Ti 2: 4 **N one** serving as a soldier gets involved *4029*
2: 14 it is of **n** value, *4029*
4: 16 **n one** came to my support, *4029*
Tit 1: 14 and will pay **n** attention to Jewish myths or *3590*
2: 5 so that **n** one will malign the word of God. *3590*
2: 12 It teaches us to **say "N" to** ungodliness *766*
3: 2 to slander **n one,** *3594*
Phm 1: 16 **n longer** as a slave, *4033*
Heb 4: 2 message they heard was of **n** value to them, *4024*
4: 11 so that **n** one will fall *3590*
5: 4 **N** one takes this honor upon himself; *4024*
6: 13 there was **n one** greater for him to swear by, *4029*
7: 13 and **n one** from that tribe has ever served at *4029*
8: 7 **n** place would have been sought *4024*
Heb 8: 11 **N longer** will a man teach his neighbor, *3590+4024*
8: 12 and will remember their sins **n** more." *3590+4024*
9: 22 of blood there is **n** forgiveness. *4024*
10: 2 and would **n longer** have felt guilty *3594*
10: 17 lawless acts I will remember **n** more." *3590+4024*
10: 18 there is **n longer** any sacrifice for sin. *4033*
10: 26 **n** sacrifice for sins is left, *4033*
11: 23 because they saw *he was* **n ordinary** child, *842*
12: 11 **N** discipline seems pleasant at the time, *4024*
12: 14 without holiness **n one** will see the Lord. *4029*
12: 15 to it that **n** one misses the grace of God and *3590*
12: 15 that **n** bitter root grows up to cause trouble *3590*
12: 16 See that **n** one is sexually immoral, *3590*
12: 17 He could bring about **n** change of mind, *4024*
12: 19 that **n** further word be spoken to them, *3590*
13: 9 which are of **n** value to those who eat them. *4024*
13: 10 at the tabernacle have **n** right to eat. *4024*
13: 17 for that would be of **n advantage** to you. *269*
Jas 1: 13 When tempted, **n one** should say, *3594*
2: 14 a man claims to have faith but has **n** deeds? *3590*
3: 8 but **n** man can tame the tongue. *4029*
5: 12 Let your "Yes" be yes, and your **"N,"** no, *4024*
5: 12 Let your "Yes" be yes, and your "No," **n,** *4024*
1Pe 2: 22 "He committed **n** sin, *4024*
2: 22 **and n** deceit was found in his mouth." *4028*
2: 23 when he suffered, he made **n** threats. *4024*
2Pe 1: 20 that **n** prophecy of Scripture came about by *4024*
1Jn 1: 5 in him there is **n** darkness at all. *4024*
1: 10 a liar and his word has **n** place in our lives. *4024*
2: 21 because **n** lie comes from the truth. *4024+4246*
2: 23 **N** one who denies the Son has the Father; *4028+4246*
3: 5 And in him is **n** sin. *4024*
3: 6 **N one** who lives in him keeps on sinning. *4024+4246*
3: 6 **N one** who continues to sin has *4024+4246*
3: 9 **N one** who is born of God will continue to sin, *4024+4246*
3: 15 that **n** murderer has eternal life in him. *4024+4246*
3: 17 sees his brother in need but **has n pity** *3091+3836+5073*
4: 12 **N one** has ever seen God; *4029*
4: 18 There is **n** fear in love. *4024*
3Jn 1: 4 I have **n** greater joy than to hear *4024*
1: 7 receiving **n** help from the pagans. *3594*
Rev 3: 7 What he opens **n one** can shut, *4029*
3: 7 and what he shuts **n one** can open. *4029*
3: 8 an open door that **n one** can shut. *4029*
3: 11 so that **n one** will take your crown. *3594*
5: 3 But **n one** in heaven or on earth or under *4029*
5: 4 because **n one** was found who was worthy *4029*
7: 9 a great multitude that **n one** could count, *4029*
10: 6 and said, "There will be **n more** delay! *4033*
13: 17 that **n** one could buy or sell unless he had *3590*
14: 3 **N one** could learn the song except *4029*
14: 5 **N** lie was found in their mouths; *4024*
14: 11 There is **n** rest day or night *4024*
15: 8 and **n one** could enter the temple until *4029*
16: 18 **N** earthquake like it has ever occurred *4024*
18: 11 **n one** buys their cargoes any more— *4029*
18: 22 **N** workman of any trade will ever be found *4024*
19: 12 on him that **n one** knows but he himself. *4029*
20: 6 The second death has **n** power over them, *4024*
20: 11 and there was **n** place for them. *4024*
21: 1 and there was **n** longer any sea. *4024*
21: 4 There will be **n** more death or mourning *4024*
21: 25 On **n** day will its gates ever be shut, *4024*
21: 25 **ever** be shut, for there will be **n** *3590+4024*
22: 3 **N** longer will there be any curse. *4024*
22: 5 There will be **n** more night. *4024*

NO [THE CITY] (KJV) See THEBES

NOADIAH (2)

Ezr 8: 33 of Jeshua and N son of Binnui. 5676
Ne 6: 14 remember also the prophetess N and 5676

NOAH (54) [NOAH'S]

Ge 5: 29 He named him N and said, 5695
5: 30 After N was born, Lamech lived 595 years 5695
5: 32 After N was 500 years old, 5695
6: 8 N found favor in the eyes of the LORD. 5695
6: 9 This is the account of **N.** 5695
6: 9 N was a righteous man, 5695
6: 10 N had three sons: Shem, Ham and Japheth. 5695
6: 13 So God said to **N,** "I am going to put an end 5695
6: 22 N did everything just as God commanded 5695
7: 1 The LORD then said to **N,** 5695
7: 5 N did all that the LORD commanded him. 5695
7: 6 N was six hundred years old when 5695
7: 7 And N and his sons and his wife 5695
7: 9 came to N and entered the ark, 5695
7: 9 as God had commanded **N.** 5695
7: 13 On that very day N and his sons, Shem, 5695
7: 15 in them came to N and entered the ark. 5695
7: 16 as God had commanded **N.** 2257[S]
7: 23 Only N was left, and those with him 5695
8: 1 But God remembered N and all the wild 5695
8: 6 After forty days N opened the window 5695
8: 9 so it returned to N in the ark. 2257[S]
8: 11 Then N knew that the water had receded 5695
8: 13 N then removed the covering from the ark 5695
8: 15 Then God said to **N,** 5695
8: 18 So N came out, together with his sons 5695
Ge 8: 20 Then N built an altar to the LORD and, 5695
9: 1 Then God blessed N and his sons, 5695
9: 8 God said to N and to his sons with him: 5695
9: 17 So God said to **N,** "This is the sign 5695
9: 18 of N who came out of the ark were Shem, 5695
9: 19 These were the three sons of **N,** 5695
9: 20 **N,** a man of the soil, 5695
9: 24 When N awoke from his wine 5695
9: 28 After the flood N lived 350 years. 5695
9: 29 Altogether, N lived 950 years, 5695
Nu 26: 33 whose names were Mahlah, **N,** Hoglah, 5829
27: 1 **N,** Hoglah, Milcah and Tirzah. 5829
36: 11 Mahlah, Tirzah, Hoglah, Milcah and **N**— 5829
Jos 17: 3 whose names were Mahlah, **N,** Hoglah, 5829
1Ch 1: 3 Enoch, Methuselah, Lamech, **N.** 5695
1: 4 The sons of **N:** Shem, Ham and Japheth. 5695
Isa 54: 9 "To me this is like the days of **N,** 5695
54: 9 the waters of N would never again cover 5695
Eze 14: 14 these three men—**N,** Daniel and Job— 5695
14: 20 declares the Sovereign LORD, even if **N,** 5695
Mt 24: 37 As it was in the days *of* **N,** *3820*
24: 38 up to the day N entered the ark; *3820*
Lk 3: 36 the son *of* **N,** the son of Lamech, *3820*
17: 26 "Just as it was in the days *of* **N,** *3820*
17: 27 in marriage up to the day N entered the ark. *3820*
Heb 11: 7 By faith **N,** when warned about things not *3820*
1Pe 3: 20 the days *of* N while the ark was being built. *3820*
2Pe 2: 5 but protected **N,** a preacher of righteousness *3820*

NOAH'S (4) [NOAH]

Ge 7: 11 In the six hundredth year of N life, 5695
8: 13 first month of N six hundred and first year, NIH
10: 1 Ham and Japheth, N sons, 5695
10: 32 These are the clans of N sons, 5695

NOB (6)

1Sa 21: 1 David went to **N,** to Ahimelech the priest. 5546
22: 9 to Ahimelech son of Ahitub at **N.** 5546
22: 11 who were the priests at **N,** 5546
22: 19 He also put to the sword **N,** 5546
Ne 11: 32 in Anathoth, N and Ananiah, 5546
Isa 10: 32 This day they will halt at **N;** 5546

NOBAH (3)

Nu 32: 42 And N captured Kenath 5561
32: 42 and called it N after himself. 5562
Jdg 8: 11 the nomads east of N and Jogbehah and fell 5562

NOBILITY (2) [NOBLE]

Est 1: 18 Median **women of the n** who have heard 8576
Da 1: 3 from the royal family and the **n**— 7312

NOBLE (21) [NOBILITY, NOBLEMAN, NOBLES, NOBLEST]

Ru 3: 11 that you are a woman of **n character.** 2657
Est 6: 9 to one of the king's **most n** princes. 7312
Ps 45: 1 a **n** theme as I recite my verses for the king; 3202
Pr 12: 4 wife of **n character** is her husband's crown, 2657
31: 10 A wife of **n character** who can find? 2657
31: 29 "Many women do **n** *things,* 2657
Ecc 10: 17 of **n** birth and whose princes eat at 2985
Isa 32: 5 No longer will the fool be called **n** nor 5618
32: 8 But the **n** *man* makes noble plans, 5618
32: 8 But the noble man makes **n** plans, 5619
32: 8 and by *n deeds* he stands. 5619
Lk 8: 15 on good soil stands for those with a **n** *2819*
19: 12 "A man *of* **n birth** went to a distant country *2302*
Ac 17: 11 Bereans were **of more n character than** *2302*
Ro 9: 21 for **n** purposes and some for common use? *5507*
1Co 1: 26 not many were **of n birth.** *2302*
Php 4: 8 brothers, whatever is true, whatever is **n,** *4948*
1Ti 3: 1 being an overseer, he desires a **n** task. *2819*
2Ti 2: 20 for **n purposes** and some for ignoble. *5507*
2: 21 he will be an instrument for **n purposes,** *5507*
Jas 2: 7 not the ones who are slandering the **n** name *2819*

NOBLEMAN (1) [NOBLE]

Pr 25: 7 than for him to humiliate you before a **n.** 5618

NOBLES (60) [NOBLE]

Nu 21: 18 that the **n** *of* the people sank— 5618
21: 18 the **n** with scepters and staffs." NIH
Jdg 5: 13 men who were left came down to the **n;** 129
5: 25 for **n** she brought him curdled milk. 129
2Sa 10: 3 the Ammonite **n** said to Hanun their lord, 8569
1Ki 21: 8 and sent them to the elders and **n** who lived 2985
21: 11 and **n** who lived in Naboth's city did 2985
2Ki 24: 12 his **n** and his officials all surrendered 8569
1Ch 19: 3 the Ammonite **n** said to Hanun, 8569
2Ch 23: 20 of hundreds, the **n,** the rulers of the people 129
Ne 2: 16 or **n** or officials or any others who would 2985
3: 5 but their **n** would not put their shoulders to 129
4: 14 I stood up and said to the **n,** 2985
4: 19 Then I said to the **n,** 2985
5: 7 and then accused the **n** and officials. 2985
5: 12 and made **the n and officials** take an oath 4392[S]
6: 17 the **n** *of* Judah were sending many letters 2985
7: 5 into my heart to assemble the **n,** 2985
10: 29 all these now join their brothers the **n,** 129
13: 17 I rebuked the **n** *of* Judah and said to them, 2985
Est 1: 3 of his reign he gave a banquet for all his **n** 8569
1: 3 and the **n** *of* the provinces were present. 8569

Est 1:11 to display her beauty to the people and **n**, 8569
1:14 and Memucan, the seven **n** *of* Persia 8569
1:16 in the presence of the king and the **n**, 8569
1:16 also against all the **n** and the peoples of all 8569
1:18 to all the king's **n** in the same way. 8569
1:21 and his **n** were pleased with this advice, 8569
2:18 Esther's banquet, for all his **n** and officials. 8569
3:1 of honor higher than that of all the other **n**. 8569
3:12 of the various provinces and the **n** *of* 8569
5:11 how he had elevated him above the other **n** 8569
8:9 and **n** *of* the 127 provinces stretching 8569
9:3 And all the **n** *of* the provinces, the satraps, 8569
Job 12:21 He pours contempt on **n** and disarms 5618
29:10 the voices of the **n** were hushed, 5592
34:18 and to **n**, 'You are wicked,' 5618
Ps 47:9 The **n** *of* the nations assemble as 5618
83:11 Make their **n** like Oreb and Zeeb, 5618
107:40 who pours contempt on **n** made them 5618
149:8 their **n** with shackles of iron, 3877
Pr 8:16 and all **n** who rule on earth. 5618
Isa 5:14 into it will descend their **n** and masses 2077
13:2 beckon to them to enter the gates of the **n**. 5618
34:12 Her **n** will have nothing there to be called 2985
Jer 14:3 The **n** send their servants for water; 129
27:20 with all the **n** *of* Judah and Jerusalem— 2985
39:6 before his eyes and also killed all the **n** 2985
Eze 17:12 and carried off her king and her **n**, 8569
Da 4:36 My advisers and **n** sought me out, 10652
5:1 for a thousand of his **n** and drank wine 10652
5:2 so that the king and his **n**, 10652
5:3 and the king and his **n**, 10652
5:9 His **n** were baffled. 10652
5:10 hearing the voices of the king and his **n**, 10652
5:23 and you and your **n**, 10652
6:17 and with the rings of his **n**, 10652
Jnh 3:7 "By the decree of the king and his **n**: 1524
Na 3:10 Lots were cast for her **n**, 3877
3:18 your **n** lie down to rest. 129

NOBLEST (1) [NOBLE]
SS 3:7 by sixty warriors, the **n** *of* Israel, 1475+4946

NOBODY (7)
Pr 12:9 Better *to* **be a n** and yet have a servant 7829
Ecc 9:15 But **n** remembered that poor man. 132+4202
Jn 9:32 **N** has ever heard of opening the eyes *4024+5516*
1Co 6:5 that there is **n** among you wise enough *4029*
10:24 **N** should seek his own good, *3594*
2Co 11:10 **n** in the regions of Achaia will stop this *4024*
1Th 5:15 that **n** pays back wrong for wrong, *3590+5516*

NOCTURNAL (1)
Dt 23:10 unclean because of a **n** emission, 4326

NOD (1)
Ge 4:16 and lived in the land of **N**, 5655

NODAB (1)
1Ch 5:19 against the Hagrites, Jetur, Naphish and **N**. 5656

NOE (KJV) See NOAH

NOGAH (2)
1Ch 3:7 **N**, Nepheg, Japhia, 5587
14:6 **N**, Nepheg, Japhia, 5587

NOHAH (1)
1Ch 8:2 **N** the fourth and Rapha the fifth. 5666

NOISE (20) [NOISY]
Ex 32:17 Joshua heard the **n** *of* the people shouting, 7754
1Ki 1:41 the meaning of all the **n** *in* the city?" 2159+7754
1:45 That's the **n** you hear 7754
2Ki 11:13 the **n** *made by* the guards and the people, 7754
2Ch 23:12 the **n** *of* the people running and cheering 7754
Ezr 3:13 because the people **made** so much **n**. 8131+9558
Isa 13:4 Listen, a **n** on the mountains, 2162
14:11 along with the **n** *of* your harps; 2166
24:8 the **n** *of* the revelers has stopped, 8623
29:6 with thunder and earthquake and great **n**, 7754
66:6 hear that **n** from the temple! 7754
Jer 46:17 'Pharaoh king of Egypt is only a **loud n**; 8623
47:3 at the **n** of enemy chariots and the rumble 8323
50:22 The **n** *of* battle is in the land, 7754
50:22 the **n** of great destruction! NIH
Eze 23:42 "The **n** *of* a carefree crowd was around her; 7754
26:10 Your walls will tremble at the **n** *of* 7754
37:7 And as I was prophesying, there was a **n**, 7754
Joel 2:5 With a **n** like that of chariots they leap over 7754
Am 5:23 Away with the **n** *of* your songs! 2162

NOISED (KJV) See HEARD, SPREAD, TALKING

NOISOME (KJV) See DEADLY, UGLY, WILD

NOISY (7) [NOISE]
Ps 64:2 from that **n crowd** *of* evildoers. 8095
Pr 1:21 at the head of the **n** streets she cries out, 2159
Isa 32:14 the **n** city deserted; 2162
Jer 48:45 the skulls of the **n boasters**. 1201+8623
51:55 he will silence her **n din**. 1524+7754
Eze 26:13 I will put an end to your **n** songs, 2162
Mt 9:23 and saw the flute players and the **n** crowd, *2572*

NOMAD (1) [NOMADS]
Jer 3:2 sat like a **n** in the desert. 6862

NOMADS (2) [NOMAD]
Jdg 8:11 the **n** east of Nobah and Jogbehah 185+928+8905
Jer 35:7 a long time in the land where you *are* **n**.' 1591

NON (KJV) See NUN

NON-GREEKS (1)
Ro 1:14 I am obligated both to Greeks and **n**, *975*

NONE (111) [NO]
Ge 23:6 **N** of us will refuse you his tomb 408+4202
28:17 This *is* **n** other than the house of God; 401
39:11 **n** of the household servants was inside. 401+408
41:24 but **n** could explain it to me." 401
Ex 12:46 take **n** of the meat outside the house. 4202
16:27 but they found **n**. 4202
23:26 **n** will miscarry or be barren in your land. 4202
Lev 7:15 he must leave **n** of it till morning. 4202
17:12 "**N** of you may eat blood, 3972+4202+5883
21:17 **n** of your descendants who has a defect 408+4202
22:30 leave **n** of it till morning. 4202
Nu 30:5 **n** *of* her vows or the pledges 3972+4202
30:12 then **n** of the vows or pledges that 3972+4202
Dt 7:14 **n** of your men or women will be childless, 4202
13:17 **N** of those condemned things shall 4202+4399
15:6 to many nations but will borrow from **n**. 4202
15:6 over many nations but **n** will rule over you. 4202
28:12 to many nations but will borrow from **n**. 4202
28:31 but you will eat **n** of it. 4202
Jdg 20:8 saying, "**N** *of* us will go home. 408+4202
21:9 they found that **n** of the people 401+408
1Sa 1:2 Peninnah had children, but Hannah had **n**. 401
3:19 he let **n** of his words fall to the ground. 3972+4202
14:24 So **n** *of* the troops tasted food. 3972+4202
21:9 David said, "**There is n** like it; 401
22:8 **N** of you is concerned about me or tells me 401
30:2 They killed **n** of them, 4202
30:17 and **n** of them got away, 408+4202
2Sa 15:14 or **n** of us will escape from Absalom. 4202
2Ki 6:12 "**N** of us, my lord the king," 4202
2Ch 1:12 and **n** after you will have." 4202
35:18 and **n** *of* the kings of Israel had ever 3972+4202
Job 29:12 and the fatherless who had **n** to assist him. 4202
32:12 **n** of you has answered his arguments. NIH
33:13 that he answers **n** *of* man's words? 3972+4202
Ps 50:22 with **n** to rescue: 401
69:20 I looked for sympathy, but **there was n**, 401
69:20 for comforters, but I found **n**. 4202
74:9 and **n** of us knows how long this will be. 4202
86:8 Among the gods **there is n** like you, O Lord; 401
Pr 2:19 **N** who go to her return or 3972+4202
8:8 **n** of them is crooked or perverse. 401
14:6 The mocker seeks wisdom and *finds* **n**, 401
Isa 30:15 but you would have **n** of it. 4202
34:16 **N** of these will be missing, 285+4202
41:17 but **there is n**; 401
45:6 men may know there is **n** besides me. 700
45:21 **there is n** but me. 401
46:9 I am God, and there is **n** like me. 700
47:8 'I am, and there is **n** besides me. 700
47:10 'I am, and there is **n** besides me.' 700
51:18 the sons she bore **there was n** to guide her; 401
51:18 the sons she reared **there was n** to take her 401
59:11 We look for justice, but find **n**; 401
Jer 22:30 for **n** of his offspring will prosper, 4202
22:30 of his offspring will prosper, **n** will sit on 408[S]
30:7 **N will be** like it. 401+4946
44:14 **N** of the remnant of Judah who have gone 4202
44:14 **n** will return except a few fugitives." 4202
50:20 but **there will be n**, 401
50:20 but **n** will be found, 4202
La 1:2 Among all her lovers **there is n** 401
1:9 **there was n** to comfort her. 401
5:8 and **there is n** to free us from their hands. 401
Eze 7:11 **n** of the people will be left, 4202
7:11 of the people will be left, **n** of that crowd— 4202
7:25 they will seek peace, but **there will be n**. 401
12:28 **N** *of* my words will be delayed any 3972+4202
16:34 for you give payment and **n** is given to you. 4202
18:11 (though the father has done **n** *of* them) 3972+4202
18:22 **N** *of* the offenses he has committed 3972+4202
18:24 **N** *of* the righteous things he has done 3972+4202
22:30 but I found **n**. 4202
33:13 **n** *of* the righteous things he has done 3972+4202
33:16 **N** *of* the sins he has committed will 3972+4202
46:18 that **n** of my people will be separated 408+4202
Da 1:19 and he found **n** equal to Daniel, 3972+4202+4946
4:18 for **n** *of* the wise men in my 10353+10379
8:4 and **n** could rescue from his power. 401
8:7 and **n** could rescue the ram from his power. 4202
12:10 **N** *of* the wicked will understand, 3972+4202
Hos 7:7 and **n** of them calls on me. 401
Am 4:7 another had **n** and dried up. 4202
9:1 Not one will get away, **n** will escape. 4202
Mic 7:1 **n** of the early figs that I crave. NIH
Zep 2:5 "I will destroy you, and **n** will be left." 401+4946
2:15 "I am, and there is **n** besides me." 700
Mt 12:39 But **n** will be given it except the sign of the prophet Jonah. *4024+4956[S]*
16:4 **n** will be given it except the sign of Jonah." *4024+4956[S]*
Mk 12:22 In fact, **n** of the seven left any children. *4024*
Lk 3:11 with him who has **n**, *3590*
11:29 **n** will be given it except the sign of Jonah. *4024+4956[S]*
21:15 that **n** of your adversaries will be able *570+4024*
Jn 6:39 I shall lose **n** of all that he has given me, *3590*
16:5 yet **n** of you asks me, *4029*
17:12 **N** has been lost except the one doomed *4029*
21:12 **N** of the disciples dared ask him, *4029*
Ac 20:25 that **n** of you among whom I have gone *4246*
26:26 that **n** of this has escaped his notice, *4024+4029*
28:21 **and n** of the brothers who have come *4046+5516*
Ro 14:7 For **n** of us lives to himself alone and none *4029*
14:7 of us lives to himself alone and **n** of us dies *4029*
1Co 2:8 **N** of the rulers of this age understood it, *4029*
7:29 who have wives should live as if they had **n**; *3590*
14:10 yet **n** of them is without meaning. *4029*
Gal 1:19 I saw **n** of the other apostles— *4024*
Heb 3:12 brothers, **that n** of you has a sinful, *3607+5516*
3:13 so that **n** of you may be hardened *3590+5516*
4:1 let us be careful **that n** of you be found to have fallen short *3607+5516*
11:39 yet **n** of them received what had been *4024*
1Jn 2:19 that **n** *of them* belonged to us. *4024+4246*

NONSENSE (3)
Job 21:34 "So how can you console me with your **n**? 2039
Isa 44:25 the learning of the wise and **turns** it **into n**, 6118
Lk 24:11 because their words seemed to them like **n**. *3333*

NOON (16) [AFTERNOON, NOONDAY]
Ge 43:16 they are to eat with me at **n**." 7416
43:25 gifts for Joseph's arrival at **n**, 7416
1Ki 18:26 on the name of Baal from morning till **n**. 7416
18:27 At **n** Elijah began to taunt them. 7416
20:16 They set out at **n** while Ben-Hadad and 7416
2Ki 4:20 the boy sat on her lap until **n**, 7416
Ne 8:3 from daybreak till **n** as he faced the square 2021+3427+4734
Job 5:14 at **n** they grope as in the night. 7416
Ps 55:17 morning and **n** I cry out in distress, 7416
Isa 16:3 Make your shadow like night—at **high n**. 7416
Jer 6:4 Arise, let us attack at **n**! 7416
20:16 a battle cry at **n**. 7416
Am 8:9 at **n** and darken the earth in broad daylight. 7416
Ac 10:9 About **n** the following day as they *1761+6052*
22:6 "About **n** as I came near Damascus, *3540*
26:13 About **n**, O king, as I was on the road, *2465+3545*

NOONDAY (4) [NOON]
2Sa 4:5 of the day while he was taking his **n** rest. 7416
Job 11:17 Life will be brighter than **n**, 7416
Ps 37:6 the justice of your cause like the **n sun**. 7416
Isa 58:10 and your night will become like the **n**. 7416

NOOSE (2)
Job 18:10 A **n** is hidden *for* him on the ground; 2475
Pr 7:22 like a deer stepping into a **n** 4591+6577

NOPHAH (1)
Nu 21:30 We have demolished them as far as **N**, 5871

NOR (328) [NEITHER, NO]
Ge 31:38 **n** have I eaten rams from your flocks. 2256+4202
49:10 **n** the ruler's staff from between his feet, 2256
Ex 4:10 neither in the past **n** since you have spoken 1685
10:6 something neither your fathers **n** 2256
10:14 **n** will there ever be again. 2256+4202
13:7 **n** shall any yeast be seen anywhere 2256+4202
13:22 the pillar of cloud by day **n** the pillar of fire 2256
20:10 neither you, **n** your son or daughter, 2256
20:10 **n** your manservant or maidservant, NIH
20:10 nor your manservant or maidservant, **n** 2256
20:10 **n** the alien within your gates. 2256
Lev 17:12 **n** may an alien living 2256+4202
21:12 **n** leave the sanctuary of his God 2256+4202
22:10 **n** may the guest of a priest 4202
26:20 **n** will the trees of the land yield their 2256+4202
Nu 14:44 though neither Moses **n** the ark of 2256
16:15 **n** have I wronged any of them." 2256+4202
18:20 **n** will you have any share among them 2256+4202
23:19 that he should lie, **n** a son of man, 2256
23:25 Neither curse them at all **n** bless them 1685+4202
Dt 2:37 the land along the course of the Jabbok **n** 2256
5:14 neither you, **n** your son or daughter, 2256
5:14 **n** your manservant or maidservant, 2256
5:14 or maidservant, **n** your ox, your donkey 2256
5:14 **n** the alien within your gates, 2256
7:14 **n** any of your livestock without young. 2256
8:3 which neither you **n** your fathers 2256+4202
13:6 that neither you **n** your fathers have known, 2256
18:16 the LORD our God **n** see this great fire 2256+4202
21:7 **n** did our eyes see it done. 2256+4202
22:5 **n** a man wear women's clothing, 2256+4202
23:2 No one born of a forbidden marriage **n** any 4202
24:16 **n** children put to death for their fathers 2256+4202

Dt 26:13 **n** have I forgotten any of them. 2256+4202
26:14 **n** have I removed any of it 2256+4202
26:14 **n** have I offered any of it to the dead. 2256+4202
28:51 **n** any calves of your herds or lambs NIH
28:64 neither you **n** your fathers have known. 2256
29: 5 **n** did the sandals on your feet. 2256+4202
30:13 **N** is it beyond the sea, 2256+4202
31: 6 he will never leave you **n** forsake you. 2256+4202
31: 8 he will never leave you **n** forsake you. 2256+4202
33: 6 **n** his men be few." 2256
34: 7 were not weak **n** his strength gone. 2256+4202
Jos 1: 5 I will never leave you **n** forsake you. 2256+4202
8:22 leaving them neither survivors **n** fugitives. 2256
Jdg 1:29 **N** did Ephraim drive out 2256+4202
1:31 **N** did Asher drive out those living in Acco 4202
2:10 LORD **n** what he had done for Israel. 1685+2256
6: 4 neither sheep **n** cattle nor donkeys. 2256
6: 4 neither sheep nor cattle **n** donkeys. 2256
8:23 **n** will my son rule over you. 2256+4202
11:34 for her he had neither son **n** daughter. 196
13:14 **n** drink any wine or other fermented 440+2256
13:14 or other fermented drink **n** eat 440+2256
13:23 **n** shown us all these things or 2256+4202
14: 6 But he told neither his father **n** 2256
1Sa 5: 5 to this day neither the priests of Dagon **n** 2256
12:21 **n** can they rescue you, 2256+4202
16: 9 "**N** has the LORD chosen this one." 1685+4202
20:31 neither you **n** your kingdom will 2256
26:12 **n** did anyone wake up. 401+2256
2Sa 1:21 may you have neither dew **n** rain, 440+2256
1:21 **n** fields that yield offerings 2256
2:19 to the right **n** to the left as he pursued him. 2256
2:28 **n** did they fight anymore. 2256+4202
14: 7 leaving my husband neither name **n** 2256
17:12 Neither he **n** any of his men will 2256
21: 4 **n** do we have the right to put anyone 401+2256
1Ki 3:11 **n** have asked for the death of your enemies 2256+4202
3:12 **n** will there ever be. 2256+4202
3:26 other said, "Neither I **n** you shall have him. 1685
8:57 may he never leave us **n** forsake us. 440+2256
11:33 **n** done what is right in my eyes, NIH
11:33 **n** kept my statutes and laws as David, 2256
13: 8 **n** would I eat bread or drink water 2256+4202
13:16 **n** can I eat bread or drink water with 2256+4202
13:28 The lion had neither eaten the body **n** 2256+4202
17: 1 there will be neither dew **n** rain in 2256
2Ki 3:17 You will see neither wind **n** rain, 2256+4202
14: 6 **n** children put to death for their fathers 2256+4202
17:34 neither worship the LORD **n** adhere 401+2256
18:12 neither listened to the commands **n** 2256+4202
23:22 **n** throughout the days of the kings of Israel 2256
23:25 Neither before **n** after Josiah was there 2256+4202
2Ch 1:11 **n** for the death of your enemies, 2256
6: 5 **n** have I chosen anyone to be the leader over my people 2256+4202
25: 4 **n** children put to death for their fathers 2256+4202
36:17 spared neither young man **n** young woman, 2256
Ne 4:23 Neither I **n** my brothers nor my men nor 2256
4:23 nor my brothers **n** my men nor the guards 2256
4:23 nor my brothers nor my men **n** the guards 2256
5:14 neither I **n** my brothers ate the food allotted 2256
9:19 **n** the pillar of fire by night to shine on 2256
9:21 their clothes did not wear out **n** 2256+4202
13:25 in marriage to their sons, **n** are you 561
Est 2: 7 up because she had neither father **n** mother. 2256
5: 9 and observed that he neither rose **n** 2256+4202
9:28 **n** should the memory of them die out 2256+4202
Job 3: 6 the year **n** be entered in any of the months. 440
5: 6 **n** does trouble sprout from the ground. 2256+4202
15:29 **n** will his possessions spread over the land. 2256+4202
28:15 **n** can its price be weighed in silver. 2256+4202
28:17 Neither gold **n** crystal can compare with it, 2256
28:17 **n** can it be had for jewels of gold. 2256
32:21 **n** will I flatter any man; 2256+4202
33: 7 **n** should my hand be heavy upon you. 2256+4202
41:26 **n** does the spear or the dart or the javelin. NIH
Ps 1: 5 **n** sinners in the assembly of the righteous. 2256
9:18 **n** the hope of the afflicted ever perish. NIH
16:10 **n** will you let your Holy One see decay. 4202
25: 2 **n** let my enemies triumph over me. 440
26: 4 **n** do I consort with hypocrites; 2256+4202
36:11 **n** the hand of the wicked drive me 440+2256
44: 3 **n** did their arm bring them victory; 2256+4202
89:33 **n** will I ever betray my faithfulness. 2256+4202
91: 5 **n** the arrow that flies by day, NIH
91: 6 **n** the pestilence that stalks in the darkness, NIH
91: 6 **n** the plague that destroys at midday. NIH
103: 9 **n** will he harbor his anger forever; 2256+4202
115: 7 **n** can they utter a sound with their throats. 4202
121: 4 who watches over Israel will neither slumber **n** sleep. 2256+4202
121: 6 **n** the moon by night. 2256
129: 7 **n** the one who gathers fill his arms. 2256
135:17 **n** is there breath in their mouths. 401+677
147:10 **n** his delight in the legs of a man; 4202
Pr 19: 2 **n** to be hasty and miss the way. 2256
25:27 **n** is it honorable to seek one's own honor. 2256
30: 3 **n** have I knowledge of the Holy One. 2256
30: 8 give me neither poverty **n** riches, 2256
Ecc 1: 8 **n** the ear its fill of hearing. 2256+4202
4: 8 he had neither son **n** brother. 2256
9:10 there is neither working **n** planning 2256
9:10 nor planning **n** knowledge nor wisdom. 2256
9:10 nor planning nor knowledge **n** wisdom. 2256
9:11 **n** does food come to the wise 1685+2256+4202

Isa 2: 4 **n** will they train for war anymore. 2256+4202
5: 6 neither pruned **n** cultivated, 2256+4202
9:13 **n** have they sought the LORD 2256+4202
9:17 **n** will he pity the fatherless and 2256+4202
11: 9 They will neither harm **n** destroy 2256+4202
11:13 **n** Judah hostile toward Ephraim. 2256+4202
13:18 on infants **n** will they look with compassion 4202
22: 2 **n** did they die in battle. 2256+4202
23: 4 neither been in labor **n** given birth; 2256+4202
23: 4 I have neither reared sons **n** brought 4202
28:27 **n** is a cartwheel rolled over cummin; 2256
30: 5 who bring neither help **n** advantage, 2256+4202
32: 5 fool be called noble **n** the scoundrel 2256+4202
33:20 **n** any of its ropes broken. 1153+2256
35: 9 **n** will any ferocious beast get up on it; 1153+2256
40:16 **n** its animals enough for burnt offerings 401+2256
43:10 **n** will there be one after me. 2256+4202
43:23 **n** honored me with your sacrifices. 2256+4202
43:23 **n** wearied you with demands for 2256+4202
48: 8 You have neither heard **n** understood; 1685+4202
48:19 cut off **n** destroyed from before me." 2256+4202
49:10 They will neither hunger **n** thirst, 2256+4202
49:10 **n** will the desert heat or the sun beat 2256+4202
51:14 **n** will they lack bread. 2256+4202
53: 9 **n** was any deceit in his mouth. 2256+4202
54:10 you will not be shaken **n** my covenant 2256+4202
57:11 have neither remembered me **n** pondered 4202
57:16 **n** will I always be angry, 2256+4202
59: 1 **n** his ear too dull to hear. 2256+4202
60:18 **n** ruin or destruction within your borders, NIH
60:19 **n** will the brightness of the moon 2256+4202
65:17 **n** will they come to mind. 2256+4202
65:25 They will neither harm **n** destroy 2256+4202
66:24 **n** will their fire be quenched, 2256+4202
Jer 3:16 **n** will another one be made. 2256+4202
7:16 this people **n** offer any plea or petition 440+2256
7:31 **n** did it enter my mind. 2256+4202
9:16 among nations that neither they **n** 2256
10: 5 they can do no harm **n** 401+1685+2256
11:14 this people **n** offer any plea or petition 440+2256
15:10 I have neither lent **n** borrowed, 2256+4202
16: 7 **n** will anyone give them a drink NIH
16:13 of this land into a land neither you **n** 2256
16:17 **n** is their sin concealed from my eyes. 2256+4202
18:18 **n** will counsel from the wise, 2256
18:18 **n** the word from the prophets. 2256
19: 4 in it to gods that neither they **n** their fathers 2256
19: 4 to gods that neither they nor their fathers **n** 2256
19: 5 **n** did it enter my mind. 2256+4202
22:10 because he will never return **n** 2256
23: 4 **n** will any be missing," 2256+4202
29:32 **n** will he see the good things I will do 2256+4202
32:35 **n** did it enter my mind, 2256+4202
33:10 by neither men **n** animals, 401+2256+4946
33:18 **n** will the priests, 2256+4202
35: 6 'Neither you **n** your descendants must ever drink wine. 2256
35: 8 Neither we **n** our wives nor our sons NIH
35: 8 Neither we nor our wives **n** our sons NIH
36:24 **n** did they tear their clothes. 2256+4202
37: 2 Neither he **n** his attendants nor the people 2256
37: 2 Neither he nor his attendants **n** the people 2256
38:16 I will neither kill you **n** hand you over 561+2256
44: 3 that neither they **n** you NIH
44: 3 nor you **n** your fathers ever knew. 2256
44:10 **n** have they followed my law and 2256+4202
46: 6 swift cannot flee **n** the strong escape. 440+2256
49:31 a nation that has neither gates **n** bars; 2256+4202
51: 3 **n** let him put on his armor. 440+2256
51:26 **n** any stone for a foundation, 2256
51:62 so that neither man **n** animal will live in it; 2256
La 4:12 **n** did any of the world's people, 2256
Eze 7:12 not the buyer rejoice **n** the seller grieve, 440+2256
11:11 **n** will you be the meat in it; 2256
13: 9 **n** will they enter the land of Israel. 2256+4202
14:11 **n** will they defile themselves anymore 2256+4202
14:20 they could save neither son **n** daughter. 561
16: 4 **n** were you washed with water 2256+4202
16: 4 **n** were you rubbed with salt or 2256+4202
16:16 **n** should they ever occur. 2256+4202
18:20 **n** will the father share the guilt of the son. 2256+4202
20: 8 **n** did they forsake the idols of Egypt. 2256+4202
24:14 I will not have pity, **n** will I relent. 2256+4202
31: 8 **n** could the pine trees equal its boughs, 4202
31: 8 **n** could the plane trees compare 2256+4202
34:28 **n** will wild animals devour them. 2256+4202
43: 7 neither they **n** their kings— 2256
47:12 **n** will their fruit fail. 2256+4202
Da 2:44 **n** will it be left to another people. 10221+10379
3:12 neither serve your gods **n** worship 10221+10379
3:27 **n** was a hair of their heads singed; 10221+10379
6: 4 and neither corrupt **n** negligent. 10221
6:22 **N** have I ever done any wrong before you, 10059+10221+10379
11: 4 **n** will it have the power he exercised, 2256+4202
11:24 and will achieve what neither his fathers **n** 2256
11:37 **n** will he regard any god, 2256+4202
Hos 4:14 **n** your daughters-in-law 2256
9: 4 **n** will their sacrifices please him. 2256+4202
11: 9 **n** will I turn and devastate Ephraim. 4202
Joel 2: 2 never was of old **n** ever will be in ages 2256+4202
Am 7:14 neither a prophet **n** a prophet's son, 2256+4202
Ob 1:12 **n** rejoice over the people of Judah in 440+2256
1:12 **n** boast so much in the day of their trouble. 440+2256
1:13 **n** look down on them in their calamity in 440

Ob 1:13 **n** seize their wealth in the day 440+2256
1:14 **n** hand over their survivors in the day 440+2256
Mic 4: 3 **n** will they train for war anymore. 2256+4202
Zep 1: 6 the LORD and neither seek the LORD **n** 2256+4202
1:18 Neither their silver **n** their gold will be able 1685
3: 7 **n** all my punishments come upon her. NIH
3:13 **n** will deceit be found in their mouths. 2256+4202
Zec 4: 6 'Not by might **n** by power, 2256+4202
Mt 10:24 **n** a servant above his master. *4028*
11:18 For John came neither eating **n** drinking, *3612*
22:30 the resurrection people will neither marry **n** *4046*
23:10 **N** are you to be called 'teacher,' *3593*
23:13 **n** will you let those enter who are trying to. *4028*
24:36 not even the angels in heaven, **n** the Son, *4028*
Mk 12:25 they will neither marry **n** be given *4046*
13:32 not even the angels in heaven, **n** the Son, *4028*
Lk 6:43 **n** does a bad tree bear good fruit. *4028*
7:33 the Baptist came neither eating bread **n** *3612*
14:35 for the soil **n** for the manure pile; *4046*
16:26 **n** can anyone cross over from there to us.' *3593*
17:21 **n** will people say, *4028*
18: 2 judge who neither feared God **n** cared *2779+3590*
20:35 from the dead will neither marry **n** be given *4046*
Jn 1:13 **n** of human decision or a husband's will, *4028*
1:25 **n** Elijah, nor the Prophet?" *4028*
1:25 nor Elijah, **n** the Prophet?" *4028*
4:21 the Father neither on this mountain **n** *4046*
5:37 You have never heard his voice **n** *4046*
5:38 **n** does his word dwell in you, *2779+4024*
6:24 that neither Jesus **n** his disciples were there, *4028*
9: 3 "Neither this man **n** his parents sinned," *4046*
12:40 **n** understand with their hearts, nor turn— *2779*
12:40 nor understand with their hearts, **n** turn— *2779*
13:16 **n** is a messenger greater than *4028*
14:17 because it neither sees him **n** knows him. *4028*
Ac 2:27 **n** will you let your Holy One see decay. *4028*
2:31 **n** did his body see decay. *4046*
15:10 that neither we **n** our fathers have been able *4046*
19:37 though they have neither robbed temples **n** *4046*
23: 8 and that there are neither angels **n** spirits, *3612*
24:18 **n** was I involved in any disturbance. *4028*
27:20 When neither sun **n** stars appeared *3612*
Ro 1:21 they neither glorified him as God **n** *2445*
2:28 **n** is circumcision merely outward *4028*
8: 7 not submit to God's law, **n** can it do so. *4028*
8:38 I am convinced that neither death **n** life, *4046*
8:38 neither angels **n** demons, *4046*
8:38 neither the present **n** the future, *4046*
8:38 the present nor the future, **n** any powers, *4046*
8:39 neither height **n** depth, *4046*
8:39 **n** anything else in all creation, *4046*
9: 7 **N** because they are his descendants are they all Abraham's children. *4028*
1Co 3: 7 So neither he who plants **n** he who waters *4046*
6: 9 Neither the sexually immoral **n** idolaters *4046*
6: 9 the sexually immoral nor idolaters **n** *4046*
6: 9 nor adulterers **n** male prostitutes *4046*
6: 9 nor adulterers nor male prostitutes **n** *4046*
6:10 **n** thieves nor the greedy nor drunkards *4046*
6:10 nor thieves **n** the greedy nor drunkards *4046*
6:10 nor the greedy **n** drunkards nor slanderers *4024*
6:10 nor the greedy nor drunkards **n** slanderers *4024*
6:10 nor drunkards nor slanderers **n** swindlers *4024*
11:11 **n** is man independent of woman. *4046*
11:16 **n** do the churches of God. *4028*
15:50 **n** does the perishable inherit *4028*
2Co 4: 2 **n** do we distort the word of God. *3593*
Gal 1: 1 sent not from men **n** by man, *4028*
1:12 **n** was I taught it; *4046*
1:17 **n** did I go up to Jerusalem *4028*
3:28 There is neither Jew **n** Greek, *4028*
3:28 slave **n** free, male nor female, *4028*
3:28 slave nor free, male **n** female, *2779*
5: 6 For in Christ Jesus neither circumcision **n** *4046*
6:15 Neither circumcision **n** *4046*
Eph 5: 4 **N** should there be obscenity, *2779*
1Th 2: 3 **n** are we trying to trick you. *4028*
2: 5 **n** did we put on a mask to cover up greed— *4046*
2Th 3: 8 **n** did we eat anyone's food without paying *4028*
1Ti 1: 4 **n** to devote themselves to myths *3593*
6:17 to be arrogant **n** to put their hope in wealth, *3593*
Heb 9:25 **N** did he enter heaven to offer himself *4028*
10: 8 **n** were you pleased with them" *4028*
Jas 1:13 **n** does he tempt **anyone;** *1254+4029*
1Jn 3:10 **n** is anyone who does not love his brother. *2779*
Rev 3:15 that you are neither cold **n** hot. *4046*
3:16 you are lukewarm—neither hot **n** cold— *4046*
7:16 **n** any scorching heat. *4028*
9:21 **N** did they repent of their murders, *2779+4024*
21:27 **n** will anyone who does what is shameful *2779+4024*

NORMALLY (1) [ABNORMALLY]

2Ki 11: 7 that **n** go off Sabbath duty are all to guard NIH

NORTH (150) [NORTHERN, NORTHWARD]

Ge 13:14 where you are and look **n** and south, 2025+7600
14:15 as far as Hobah, **n** of Damascus. 4946+8520
28:14 to the **n** and to the south. 7600
Ex 26:20 the **n** side of the tabernacle, 7600
26:35 the table outside the curtain on the **n** side of 7600
27:11 The **n** side shall also be 7600
36:25 the **n** side of the tabernacle, 7600
38:11 The **n** side was also a hundred cubits long 7600
40:22 the Tent of Meeting on the **n** side of 2025+7600

Lev 1:11 to slaughter it at the **n** side of the altar 2025+7600
Nu 2:25 On the **n** will be the divisions of the camp 7600
3:35 camp on the **n** side of the tabernacle. 2025+7600
34: 9 This will be your boundary on the **n.** 7600
35: 5 on the west and three thousand on the **n,** 7600
Dt 2: 3 hill country long enough; now turn **n.** 2025+7600
3:12 and the Gadites the territory **n** of Aroer by NIH
3:27 the top of Pisgah and look west and **n** 2025+7600
Jos 8:11 They set up camp **n** of Ai, 7600
8:13 all those in the camp to the **n** of the city and 7600
13: 3 of Egypt to the territory of Ekron on the **n,** 7600
15: 6 up to Beth Hoglah and continued **n** 4946+7600
15: 7 of Achor and turned **n** to Gilgal, 2025+7600
16: 6 the **n** it curved eastward to Taanath Shiloh, 7600
17:10 on the **n** to Manasseh. 7600
17:10 and bordered Asher on the **n** and Issachar 7600
18: 5 the house of Joseph in its territory on the **n.** 7600
18:12 On the **n** side their boundary began at 7600
18:16 **n** of the Valley of Rephaim. 2025+7600
18:17 It then curved **n,** went to En Shemesh, 4946+7600
19:14 the **n** to Hannathon and ended at the Valley 7600
19:27 and went **n** to Beth Emek and Neiel, 2025+7600
24:30 of Ephraim, **n** of Mount Gaash. 4946+7600
Jdg 2: 9 of Ephraim, **n** of Mount Gaash. 4946+7600
7: 1 Midian was **n** of them in the valley 4946+7600
21:19 to the **n** of Bethel, 4946+7600
1Sa 14: 5 One cliff stood to the **n** toward Micmash, 7600
1Ki 7:21 and the one to the **n** Boaz. 8522
7:25 stood on twelve bulls, three facing **n,** 2025+7600
7:39 of the temple and five on the **n.** 4946+8520
2Ki 11:11 the temple, from the south side to the **n** side 8522
16:14 put it on the **n** side of the new altar. 2025+7600
1Ch 9:24 east, west, **n** and south. 2025+7600
26:14 and the lot for the **N** Gate fell to him. 7600
26:17 four a day on the **n,** 2025+7600
2Ch 3:17 one to the south and one to the **n.** 8520
3:17 and the *one to the* **n** Boaz. 8522
4: 4 stood on twelve bulls, three facing **n,** 2025+7600
4: 6 on the south side and five on the **n.** 8520
4: 7 five on the south side and five on the **n.** 8520
4: 8 five on the south side and five on the **n.** 8520
23:10 the temple, from the south side to the **n** side 8522
Job 23: 9 he is at work in the **n,** I do not see him; 8520
37:22 Out of the **n** he comes in golden splendor; 7600
Ps 89:12 You created the **n** and the south; 7600
107: 3 from east and west, from **n** and south. 7600
Pr 25:23 As a **n** wind brings rain, 7600
Ecc 1: 6 wind blows to the south and turns to the **n;** 7600
11: 3 Whether a tree falls to the south or to the **n,** 7600
SS 4:16 Awake, **n wind,** and come, south wind! 7600
Isa 14:31 A cloud of smoke comes from the **n,** 7600
41:25 "I have stirred up one from the **n,** 7600
43: 6 I will say to the **n,** 'Give them up!' 7600
49:12 some from the **n,** some from the west, 7600
Jer 1:13 tilting away from the **n,"** I answered. 2025+7600
1:14 "From the **n** disaster will be poured out 7600
3:12 Go, proclaim this message toward the **n:** 7600
4: 6 For I am bringing disaster from the **n,** 7600
6: 1 For disaster looms out of the **n,** 7600
6:22 an army is coming from the land of the **n;** 7600
10:22 a great commotion from the land of the **n!** 7600
13:20 and see those who are coming from the **n.** 7600
15:12 "Can a man break iron—iron from the **n—** 7600
16:15 the land of the **n** and out of all the countries 7600
23: 8 the land of the **n** and out of all the 2025+7600
25: 9 the **n** and my servant Nebuchadnezzar king 7600
25:26 of the **n,** near and far, one after the other— 7600
31: 8 of the **n** and gather them from the ends of 7600
46: 6 the **n** by the River Euphrates they stumble 7600
46:10 in the land of the **n** by the River Euphrates. 7600
46:20 a gadfly is coming against her from the **n.** 7600
46:24 handed over to the people of the **n."** 7600
47: 2 "See how the waters are rising in the **n;** 7600
50: 3 the **n** will attack her and lay waste her land. 7600
50: 9 of great nations from the land of the **n.** 7600
50: 9 and from **the n** she will be captured. 9004[S]
50:41 An army is coming from the **n;** 7600
51:48 for out of the **n** destroyers will attack her," 7600
Eze 1: 4 and I saw a windstorm coming out of the **n** 7600
8: 3 to the **n** gate of the inner court, 2025+7600
8: 5 "Son of man, look toward the **n."** 2025+7600
8: 5 and in the entrance **n** of the gate of 4946+7600
8:14 entrance to the **n** gate of the house of 2025+7600
9: 2 of the upper gate, which faces **n,** 2025+7600
16:46 to the **n** *of* you with her daughters; 8520
20:47 from south to **n** will be scorched by it. 7600
21: 4 against everyone from south to **n.** 7600
26: 7 From the **n** I am going to bring 7600
32:30 of the **n** and all the Sidonians are there; 7600
38: 6 from the far **n** with all its troops— 7600
38:15 You will come from your place in the far **n,** 7600
39: 2 from the far **n** and send you against 7600
40:19 on the east side as well as on the **n.** 7600
40:20 the length and width of the gate facing **n,** 7600
40:23 a gate to the inner court facing the **n** gate, 7600
40:35 Then he brought me to the **n** gate 7600
40:40 to the **n** gateway were two tables, 2025+7600
40:44 at the side of the **n** gate and facing south, 7600
40:44 at the side of the south gate and facing **n.** 7600
40:46 and the room facing **n** is for 7600
41:11 one on the **n** and another on the south; 7600
42: 1 and opposite the outer wall on the **n** *side.* 7600
42: 2 The building whose door faced **n** was 7600
42: 4 Their doors were on the **n.** 7600
42:11 These were like the rooms on the **n;** 7600
42:11 Similar to the doorways on the **n** NIH
42:13 "The **n** and south rooms facing 7600
Eze 42:17 He measured the **n** side; 7600
44: 4 the man brought me by way of the **n** gate to 7600
46: 9 whoever enters by the **n** gate to worship is 7600
46: 9 the south gate is to go out the **n** gate. 2025+7600
46:19 the gate to the sacred rooms facing **n,** 2025+7600
47: 2 **n** gate and led me around the outside 2025+7600
47:15 **n** side it will run from the Great Sea 2025+7600
47:17 with the border of Hamath to the **n.** 7600
47:17 This will be the **n** boundary. 7600
48:10 It will be 25,000 cubits long on the **n** *side,* 7600
48:16 the **n** side 4,500 cubits, the south side 4,500 7600
48:17 for the city will be 250 cubits on the **n,** 7600
48:30 Beginning on the **n** side, which is 4,500 7600
48:31 on the **n** *side* will be the gate of Reuben, 7600
Da 8: 4 toward the west and the **n** and the south. 7600
11: 6 to the king of the **N** to make an alliance, 7600
11: 7 of the king of the **N** and enter his fortress; 7600
11: 8 he will leave the king of the **N** alone. 7600
11: 9 the **N** will invade the realm of the king of NIH
11:11 a rage and fight against the king of the **N,** 7600
11:13 the king of the **N** will muster another army, 7600
11:15 Then the king of the **N** will come and build 7600
11:28 of the **N** will return to his own country NIH
11:40 the king of the **N** will storm out against him 7600
11:44 from the east and the **n** will alarm him, 7600
Am 8:12 from sea to sea and wander from **n** to east, 7600
Zep 2:13 He will stretch out his hand against the **n** 7600
Zec 2: 6 Flee from the land of the **n,"** 7600
6: 6 is going toward the **n** country, 7600
6: 8 the **n** country have given my Spirit rest in 7600
6: 8 in the land of the **n."** 7600
14: 4 with half of the mountain moving **n** 2025+7600
Lk 13:29 People will come from east and west and **n** *1080*
Rev 21:13 three gates on the east, three on the **n,** *1080*

NORTHEASTER (1) [EAST]

Ac 27:14 called **the "n,"** swept down from the island *2350*

NORTHERN (18) [NORTH]

Nu 34: 7 " 'For your **n** boundary, 7600
Jos 11: 2 **n** kings who were in the mountains, 4946+7600
15: 5 The **n** boundary started from the bay 2025+7600
15: 8 at the **n** end of the Valley of Rephaim. 2025+7600
15:10 the **n** slope of Mount Jearim 2025+4946+7600
15:11 It went to the **n** slope of Ekron, 2025+7600
17: 9 boundary of Manasseh was the **n** *side* 4946+7600
18:12 the **n** slope of Jericho and headed west 4946+7600
18:18 to the **n** slope of Beth Arabah and 2025+7600
18:19 to the **n** slope of Beth Hoglah and 2025+7600
18:19 and came out at the **n** bay 2025+7600
Job 26: 7 spreads out the **n** [skies] over empty space; 7600
Jer 1:15 the peoples of the **n** kingdoms," 2025+7600
3:18 a **n** land to the land I gave your forefathers 7600
Eze 47:17 along the **n** border of Damascus, 7600
48: 1 **n** frontier, Dan will have one portion; 2025+7600
48: 1 and the **n** border of Damascus next 2025+7600
Joel 2:20 "I will drive the **n** *army* far from you, 7603

NORTHWARD (1) [NORTH]

Eze 42: 1 Then the man led me **n** into the outer court 2006+2021+7600

NORTHWEST (1) [WEST]

Ac 27:12 facing both southwest and **n.** *6008*

NOSE (13) [NOSES]

Ge 24:22 the man took out a gold **n ring** weighing 5690
24:30 As soon as he had seen the **n ring,** 5690
24:47 in her **n** and the bracelets on her arms, 678
2Ki 19:28 I will put my hook in your **n** and my bit 678
2Ch 33:11 put a hook in his **n,** NIH
Job 40:24 or trap him and pierce his **n?** 678
41: 2 a cord through his **n** or pierce his jaw with 678
Pr 30:33 and as twisting the **n** produces blood, 678
SS 7: 4 Your **n** is like the tower 678
Isa 3:21 the signet rings and **n** rings, 678
37:29 I will put my hook in your **n** and my bit 678
Eze 8:17 Look at them putting the branch to their **n!** 678
16:12 and I put a ring on your **n,** 678

NOSES (2) [NOSE]

Ps 115: 6 but cannot hear, **n,** but they cannot smell; 678
Eze 23:25 They will cut off your **n** and your ears, 678

NOSTRILS (16)

Ge 2: 7 and breathed into his **n** the breath of life, 678
7:22 that had the breath of life in its **n** died. 678
Ex 15: 8 By the blast of your **n** the waters piled up. 678
Nu 11:20 comes out of your **n** and you loathe it— 678
2Sa 10: 6 they had become a stench in David's **n,** NIH
16:21 made yourself a stench in your father's **n,** NIH
22: 9 Smoke rose from his **n;** 678
22:16 at the blast of breath from his **n.** 678
1Ch 19: 6 they had become a stench in David's **n,** NIH
Job 27: 3 the breath of God in my **n,** 678
41:20 from his **n** as from a boiling pot over a fire 5705
Ps 18: 8 Smoke rose from his **n;** 678
18:15 at the blast of breath from your **n.** 678
Isa 2:22 who has but a breath in his **n.** 678
65: 5 Such people are smoke in my **n,** 678
Am 4:10 I filled your **n** with the stench 678

NOT (5888) [AREN'T, CAN'T, COULDN'T, DIDN'T, DOESN'T, DON'T, HASN'T, HAVEN'T, ISN'T, NO, SHOULDN'T, WASN'T, WEREN'T, WON'T, WOULDN'T]

See Index of Articles Etc.

NOTABLE (1) [NOTE]

Am 6: 1 *you* **n** *men of* the foremost nation, 5918

NOTE (13) [ANNOTATIONS, NOTABLE, NOTES]

Ru 3: 4 **n** the place where he is lying. 3359
2Sa 3:36 All the people **took n** and were pleased; 5795
Job 11:11 and when he sees evil, *does he* not **take n?** 1067
34:25 Because *he* **takes n of** their deeds, 5795
Ps 106:44 But *he* **took n** of their distress 8011
Pr 21:12 The Righteous One **takes n** of the house of 8505
23: 1 **n well** what is before you, 1067+1067
Jer 31:21 **Take n** of the highway, 4213+8883
Eze 20:37 **take n** *of* you as you **pass** 6296
Ac 4:13 and *they* **took n** that these men had been *2105*
Php 3:17 and **take n of** those who live according to *5023*
2Th 3:14 **take special n** of him. *4957*
Jas 1:19 My dear brothers, **take n of** this: *3857*

NOTES (1) [NOTE]

1Co 14: 7 unless there is a distinction *in* the **n?** *5782*

NOTHING (342) [NO, THING]

Ge 11: 6 then **n** they plan to do will be impossible for them. 3972+4202
14:23 I will accept **n** belonging to you, 561+3972+4946
14:24 I will accept **n** but what my men have eaten 1187
18:27 though I am **n** but dust and ashes, NIH
24:50 we can say **n** to you one way or the other. 4202
29:15 should you work for me **for n?** 2855
31:33 but he found **n.** 4202
31:34 through everything in the tent but found **n.** 4202
39: 9 My master has withheld **n** 4202+4399
40:15 and even here I have done **n** 4202+4399
47:18 there is **n** left for our lord except our bodies 4202
Ex 10:15 **N** green remained on tree or plant in 3972+4202
12:20 Eat **n** made with yeast. 3972+4202
13: 3 Eat **n** containing yeast. 4202
13: 7 **n** with yeast in it is to be seen among you, 4202
22: 3 but if he has **n,** he must be sold to pay 401
23: 7 **Have n to do** with a false charge and do 8178
Lev 14:36 **n** in the house will be pronounced unclean. 3972+4202
27:28 But **n** that a man owns and devotes to 3972+4202
Nu 20:19 to pass through on foot—**n** else." 401
23:11 but *you have* **done n but bless** them!" 1385+1385
30: 4 about her vow or pledge but **says n** to her, 3087
30: 7 her husband hears about it but **says n** to her, 3087
30:11 and her husband hears about it but **says n** 3087
30:14 if her husband **says n** to her *about* it 3087+3087
30:14 He confirms them by **saying n** to her 3087
Dt 5:22 and he added **n** *more.* 4202
8: 9 not be scarce and you will lack **n;** 3972+4202
15: 9 toward your needy brother and give him **n.** 4202
22:26 Do **n** to the girl; 1821+4202
28:33 and you will have **n but** cruel oppression 8370
29:23 **n** planted, nothing sprouting, 4202
29:23 nothing planted, **n** sprouting, 4202
Jos 11:15 he left **n** undone of all that 1821+4202
Jdg 7:14 "This can **be n** other than the sword 401+1194
18: 7 land lacked **n,** they were prosperous. 401+1821
18:10 a land that lacks **n whatever."** 401+1821+3972
1Sa 3:18 hiding **n** from him. 4202
4: 7 **N** like this has happened before. 4202
14: 6 **N** can hinder the LORD from saving, 401
20:26 Saul said **n** that day, for he thought, 4202+4399
20:39 (The boy knew **n** of all this; 4202
22:15 for your servant knows **n** at all 4202
25: 7 the whole time they were at Carmel **n** 4202+4399
25:15 in the fields near them **n** was missing. 4202+4399
25:21 the desert so that **n** of his was missing. 4202+4399
25:36 So she told him **n** until daybreak. 1524+1821+2256+4202+7785
28:20 he had eaten **n** all that day and night. 4202+4312
29: 7 do **n** to displease the Philistine rulers." 4202
30:19 **N** was missing: young or old, 4202
2Sa 12: 3 poor man had **n** except one little ewe lamb he had bought. 401+3972
15:11 knowing **n** about the matter. 3972+4202
18:13 and **n** is hidden from the king— 1821+3972+4202
19: 6 commanders and their men mean **n** to you. 401
19:10 So why *do* you **say n** *about* bringing 3087
19:28 my grandfather's descendants deserved **n** 4202
24:24 burnt offerings that **cost** me **n."** 2855
1Ki 4:27 They saw to it that **n** was lacking. 1821+4202
6: 6 the temple so that **n** would be inserted into 1194
8: 9 **There was n** in the ark except 401
10: 3 **n** was too hard for the king to explain 1821+4202
10:20 **N** like it had ever been made 4202
10:21 **N** was made of silver, 401
11:22 **"N,"** Hadad replied, "but do let me go!" 4202
18:21 But the people said **n.** 1821+4202
18:43 **"There is n** there," he said. 401+4399
22: 3 and yet we *are* **doing n** to retake it from 3120
22:16 to tell me **n** but the truth in the name of 4202
22:27 Put this fellow in prison and give him **n but** 4316

2Ki 4: 2 "Your servant has **n** there at all," she said, 401
4:41 And there was **n** harmful in the pot. 1821+4202
9:35 they found **n** except her skull, 4202
13: 7 **N** had been left of the army 4202
18:36 remained silent and said **n** in reply, 1821+4202
20:13 There was **n** in his palace or 1821+4202
20:15 "There is **n** among my treasures that 1821+4202
20:17 **N** will be left, says the LORD. 1821+4202
1Ch 21:24 sacrifice a burnt offering that **costs** me **n."** 2855
2Ch 5:10 **There was n** in the ark except 401
9: 2 **n** was too hard for him to explain 1821+4202
9:11 **N** like them had ever been seen in Judah.) 4202
9:19 **N** like it had ever been made 4202
9:20 **N** was made of silver, 401
18:15 to tell me **n** but the truth in the name of 4202
18:26 Put this fellow in prison and give him **n but** 4316
30:26 of David king of Israel there had been **n** 4202
Ezr 4:16 be left with **n** in Trans-Euphrates. 10269+10379
Ne 2: 2 This can be **n** but sadness of heart." 401
2:16 as yet I had said **n** to the Jews or the priests 4202
5: 8 because they could find **n** to say. 4202
6: 8 **"N** like what you are saying is happening; 4202
8:10 send some to those who have **n** prepared. 401
9:21 they lacked **n,** their clothes did 4202
Est 2:15 she asked for **n** other than what Hegai, 1821+4202
6: 3 **"N** has been done for him," 1821+4202
Job 1: 9 "Does Job fear God **for n?"** Satan replied. 2855
5:24 of your property and find **n** missing. 4202
8: 9 we were born only yesterday and know **n,** 4202
15:18 hiding **n** received from their fathers 4202
15:31 for he will get **n** in return. 8736
19:20 I am **n but skin** and bones; 1414+2256+6425
20:21 **N** is left for him to devour; 401
21:34 **N** is left of your answers but falsehood!" NIH
24: 7 they have **n** to cover themselves in the cold. 401
24:16 they want **n** to do with the light. 4202
24:25 and reduce my words to **n?"** 440
26: 7 he suspends the earth over **n.** 1172+4537
32: 5 he saw that the three men had **n** *more* to say, 401
33:21 His flesh wastes away **to n,** 4946+8024
34: 9 a man **n** when he tries to please God.' 4202
37: 4 When his voice resounds, he holds **n** back. 4202
39:22 He laughs at fear, afraid of **n;** 4202
41:33 **N** on earth is his equal— 401
Ps 10: 6 He says to himself, **"N** will shake me; 1153
17: 3 though you test me, you will find **n;** 1153
19: 6 **n** is hidden from its heat. 401
34: 9 for those who fear him lack **n.** 401
35:11 they question me on things I know **n** about. 4202
39: 5 the span of my years **is** as **n** before you. 401
44:12 gaining **n** from their sale. 4202
49:17 for he will take **n** with him when he dies, 2021+3972+4202
53: 5 where there was **n** to dread. 4202
62: 9 if weighed on a balance, they are **n;** NIH
73:25 And earth has **n** I desire besides you. 4202
82: 5 "They know **n,** they understand nothing. 4202
82: 5 "They know nothing, they understand **n.** 4202
101: 4 I will have **n** to do with evil. 4202
112:10 the longings of the wicked *will* **come to n.** 6
119: 3 They do **n** wrong; they walk in his ways. 4202
119:165 and **n** can make them stumble. 401
139:22 I have **n but** hatred for them; 9417
146: 4 on that very day their plans **come to n.** 6
Pr 3:15 **n** you desire can compare with her. 3972+4202
8:11 **n** you desire can compare with her. 3972+4202
10:28 but the hopes of the wicked **come to n.** 6
11: 7 all he expected from his power **comes to n.** 6
13: 4 The sluggard craves and *gets* **n,** 401
13: 7 One man pretends to be rich, yet *has* **n;** 401+3972
20: 4 so at harvest time he looks but finds **n.** 401
24: 7 in the assembly at the gate he has **n** to say. 4202
24:12 If you say, "But we knew **n** about this," 4202
28:27 He who gives to the poor will lack **n,** 401
30:20 and says, 'I've done **n** wrong.' 4202
30:30 who retreats before **n;** 3972+4202
31:11 in her and lacks **n** of value. 4202
Ecc 1: 9 **there is n** new under the sun. 401+3972
2:10 I denied myself **n** my eyes desired; 3972+4202
2:11 **n** was gained under the sun. 401
2:24 A man can do **n** better than to eat and drink 401
3:12 I know that **there is n** better for men than to 401
3:14 **n** can be added to it and nothing taken 401
3:14 nothing can be added to it and **n** taken 401
3:22 So I saw that **there is n** better for a man 401
5:14 he has a son **there is n** left for him. 401+4399
5:15 He takes **n** from his labor that he can carry in his hand. 4202+4399
6: 2 so that he lacks **n** his heart desires, 401+3972
8:15 because **n** is better for a man under 401
9: 5 but the dead know **n;** 401+4399
Isa 10: 4 **N** will remain but to cringe among 1194
15: 6 the vegetation is gone and **n** green is left. 4202
17:11 yet the harvest *will be as* **n** in the day 5610
19: 3 **bring** their plans **to n;** 1182
19:11 The officials of Zoan are **n but** fools; 421
19:15 There is **n** Egypt can do— 4202+5126
29:11 For you this whole vision is **n but** 3869
29:16 the pot say of the potter, "He knows **n"?** 4202
34:12 Her nobles will have **n** there to be called 401
36:21 remained silent and said **n** in reply, 1821+4202
39: 2 There was **n** in his palace or 1821+4202
39: 4 "There is **n** among my treasures that 1821+4202
39: 6 **N** will be left, says the LORD. 1821+4202
40:17 Before him all the nations are as **n;** 401
40:17 by him as worthless and less than **n.** 700
40:23 and reduces the rulers of this world to **n.** 9332

Isa 41:11 those who oppose you will be as **n** 401
41:12 against you will be as **n at all.** 401+700+2256
41:24 But you are less than **n** 401
41:29 Their deeds **amount to n;** 700
42:20 your ears are open, but you hear **n."** 4202
44: 9 All who make idols are **n,** 9332
44:10 which can profit him **n?** 1194
44:11 craftsmen are **n but** men. 4946
44:18 They know **n,** they understand nothing; 4202
44:18 They know nothing, they understand **n;** 4202
49: 4 I have spent my strength in vain and for **n.** 9332
52: 3 "You were sold **for n,** 2855
52: 5 my people have been taken away **for n,** 2855
53: 2 **n** in his appearance 4202
54:14 you will have **n** to fear. 4202
Jer 5:12 they said, "He will do **n!** 4202
10:24 not in your anger, lest *you* **reduce** me **to n.** 5070
12:13 they will wear themselves out but gain **n.** 4202
16:19 "Our fathers possessed **n but** false gods, 421
22:13 making his countrymen work **for n,** 2855
30:14 they care **n** for you. 4202
32:17 **N** is too hard for you. 1821+3972+4202
32:30 and Judah have done **n but** evil in my sight 421
32:30 of Israel have done **n but** provoke me 421
38: 5 "The king can do **n** to oppose you." 401+1821
39:10 of the poor people, who owned **n;** 401+4399
42: 4 the LORD says and will keep **n** back 1821+4202
44:18 *have* **had n** and have been perishing 2893+3972
48:30 "and her boasts accomplish **n.** 4027+4202
48:38 the public squares there is **n but** mourning, 3972
50: 2 keep **n** back, but say, 440
51:58 exhaust themselves **for n,** 928+1896+8198
La 1:12 "Is it **n** to you, all you who pass by? 4202
Eze 7:11 no wealth, **n** of value. 4202
12:22 days go by and every vision **comes to n'?** 6
13: 3 and have seen **n!** 1194
14:23 know that I have done **n** in it without cause, 889+3972+4202
33:32 to them you are **n more than** one who sings love songs 3869
Da 1:12 Give us **n but** vegetables to eat and water 4946
4:35 the peoples of the earth are regarded as **n.** 10379
9:12 the whole heaven **n** has ever been done 4202
9:26 be cut off and will have **n.** 401
Joel 2: 3 a desert waste—**n** escapes them. 4202
Am 3: 4 in his den when he has caught **n?** 1194
3: 5 up from the earth when there is **n** to catch? 4202
3: 7 Surely the Sovereign LORD does **n** 1821+4202
5: 5 and Bethel will be reduced to **n."** 224
Mic 6:14 You will store up but save **n,** 4202
Na 2:11 and the cubs, with **n** to fear? 401
3:19 **N** can heal your wound; your injury is fatal. 401
Hab 2:13 exhaust themselves **for n?** 928+1896+8198
Zep 1:12 'The LORD will do **n,** either good or bad.' 4202
3: 3 who leave **n** for the morning. 4202
Hag 2: 3 Does it not seem to you like **n?** 401
Mal 2: 6 in his mouth and **n** false was found 4202
Mt 9:33 **"N** like this has **ever** been seen *4030*
10:26 There is **n** concealed that will not *4029*
15:32 with me three days and have **n** to eat. *4024+5515*
17:20 **N** will be impossible for you." *4029*
20: 3 in the marketplace **doing n.** *734*
20: 6 standing here all day long **doing n?'** *734*
21:19 up to it but found **n** on it except leaves. *4029*
23:16 anyone swears by the temple, it means **n;** *4029*
23:18 'If anyone swears by the altar, it means **n;** *4029*
24:39 and they knew **n** about what would happen *4024*
25:42 For I was hungry and you gave me **n** to eat, *4024*
25:42 I was thirsty and you gave me **n** to drink, *4024*
Mk 6: 8 "Take **n** for the journey except a staff— *3594*
7:15 **N** outside a man can make him 'unclean' *4029*
7:18 Don't you see that **n** that enters a man *4024+4246*
8: 1 Since they had **n** to eat, *3590+5515*
8: 2 with me three days and have **n** to eat. *4024+5515*
11:13 When he reached it, he found **n but** leaves, *4029*
14:51 **wearing n** but a linen garment, *1218+2093+4314*
16: 8 They said **n** to anyone, *4029*
Lk 1:37 For **n** is impossible with God." *4024+4246+4839*
4: 2 He ate **n** during those days, *4029*
8:17 there is **n** hidden that will not be disclosed, *4024*
8:17 **and n** concealed that will not be known *4028*
9: 3 He told them: "Take **n** for the journey— *3594*
10:19 **n** will harm you. *3590+4024+4029*
11: 6 and I have **n** to set before him.' *4024*
12: 2 There is **n** concealed that will not be *4029*
14: 6 And they had **n** to say. *4024*
19:26 but as for the one who has **n,** *3590*
22:35 **"N,"** they answered. *4029*
23:15 he has done **n** to deserve death. *4029*
23:41 But this man has done **n** wrong." *4029*
Jn 1: 3 without him **n** was made *1651+4028*
1:47 in whom there is **n** false." *4024*
4:11 "you have **n** to draw with and the well *4046*
4:32 "I have food to eat that you know **n** about." *4024*
5:19 the Son can do **n** by himself; *4024+4029*
5:30 By myself I can do **n;** *4024+4029*
6:12 Let **n** be wasted." *3590+5516*
6:63 The Spirit gives life; the flesh counts for **n.** *4024+4029*
7:18 there is **n false** about him. *94+4024*
7:49 But this mob that knows **n** of the law— *3590*
8:28 that I do **n** on my own but speak just what *4029*
8:54 "If I glorify myself, my glory means **n.** *4029*
9:33 If this man were not from God, he could do **n."** *4024+4029*
10:13 because he is a hired hand and cares **n** for *4024*
11:49 spoke up, "You know **n at all!** *4024+4029*

Jn 15: 5 apart from me you can do **n.** *4024+4029*
18:20 I said **n** in secret. *4029*
21: 3 but that night they caught **n.** *4029*
Ac 4:14 there was **n** they could say. *4029*
5:36 and it all came to **n.** *4029*
7:18 another king, who knew **n** about Joseph, *4024*
8:24 so that **n** you have said may happen to me." *3594*
9: 8 when he opened his eyes he could see **n.** *4029*
11: 8 **N** impure or unclean has **ever** *4030*
17:21 who lived there spent their time doing **n** *4029*
20:24 I consider my life worth **n** to me, *3364+4029*
23: 9 "We find **n** wrong with this man," *4029*
25: 8 "I have done **n** wrong against the law *4046+5516*
25:25 I found he had done **n** deserving of death, *3594*
25:26 But I have **n** definite to write *4024+5516*
26:22 I am saying **n** beyond what the prophets *4029*
28: 6 a long time and seeing **n** unusual happen *3594*
28:17 although I have done **n** against our people *4029*
Ro 7:18 I know that **n** good lives in me, that is, *4024*
13: 4 for he does not bear the sword *for* **n.** *1632*
1Co 2: 2 For I resolved to know **n** while I was *4024+5516*
2: 6 rulers of this age, who *are* **coming to n.** *2934*
4: 5 judge **n** before the appointed time; *3590+5516*
7:19 Circumcision is **n** and uncircumcision is *4029*
7:19 and uncircumcision is **n.** *4029*
8: 4 that an idol is **n** at all in the world and *4029*
11:22 of God and humiliate those who have **n?** *3590*
13: 2 but have not love, I am **n.** *4029*
13: 3 but have not love, I gain **n.** *4029*
15:58 Let **n move** you. *293*
16:10 that he has **n to fear** while he is with you, *925*
2Co 6:10 having **n,** and yet possessing everything. *3594*
10:10 and his speaking **amounts to n."** *2024*
12: 1 Although there is **n** to be gained, *4024*
12:11 even though I am **n.** *4029*
Gal 2: 6 those men added **n** to my message. *4029*
2:21 gained through the law, Christ died **for n!"** *1562*
3: 4 Have you suffered so much **for n—** *1632*
3: 4 if it really was **for n?** *1632*
6: 3 anyone thinks he is something when he is **n,** *3594*
Eph 5:11 Have **n** to do with the fruitless deeds *3590*
Php 2: 3 Do **n** out of selfish ambition *3594*
2: 7 but **made** himself **n,** taking the very nature *3033*
2:16 of Christ that I did not run or labor for **n.** *3031*
1Ti 3:10 and then if there is **n against them,** *441*
4: 4 and **n** is to be rejected if it is received *4029*
4: 7 *Have* **n to do with** godless myths *4148*
5:21 and to do **n** out of favoritism. *3594*
6: 4 he is conceited and understands **n.** *3594*
6: 7 For we brought **n** into the world, *4029*
6: 7 **and** we can take **n** out of it. *4028+5516*
2Ti 3: 5 **Have n to do with** them. *706*
Tit 1:15 and do not believe, **n** is pure. *4029*
2: 8 be ashamed because they have **n** bad to say *3594*
3:10 After that, *have* **n to do with** him. *4148*
Heb 2: 8 God left **n** that is not subject to him. *4029*
4:13 **N** in all creation is hidden *4024*
7:14 to that tribe Moses said **n** about priests. *4029*
7:19 (for the law made **n** perfect), *4029*
8: 7 For if there had been **n wrong with** *289*
Jas 2:16 but does **n** about his physical needs, *3590*
1Pe 3: 7 so that **n** will hinder your prayers. *3590*
1Jn 2:10 and there is **n** in him to make him stumble. *4024*
3Jn 1: 9 will have **n** to do with us. *4024*
Rev 21:27 **N** impure will **ever** enter it, *3590*

NOTICE (15) [NOTICED, NOTICING]

Ge 39: 7 his master's wife **took n** of Joseph 5951+6524
Dt 21:11 if *you* **n** among the captives a beautiful 8011
Ru 2:10 such favor in your eyes that you **n** me— 5795
2:19 Blessed be the *man who* **took n** *of* you!" 5795
2Sa 9: 8 that *you should* **n** a dead dog like me?" 7155
2Ki 3:14 I would not look at you or even **n** you. 8011
Job 35:15 not **take** the least **n** of wickedness. 3359
Eze 38:14 *will you* not **take n** *of* it? 3359
Hos 7: 9 but he *does* not **n.** 3359
Jnh 1: 6 Maybe he *will* **take n** of us, 6951
Mk 15:26 The **written n** of the charge against him *2107*
Lk 23:38 There was a **written n** above him, *2107*
Jn 19:19 Pilate **had a n prepared** and fastened *1211+5518*
Ac 21:26 to the temple *to* **give n of** the date when *1334*
26:26 that none of this *has* **escaped** his **n,** *3291*

NOTICED (9) [NOTICE]

Ge 31: 2 And Jacob **n** *that* Laban's attitude 8011
2Sa 12:19 David **n** that his servants were whispering 8011
1Ki 21:29 *Have you* **n** how Ahab has humbled himself 8011
Pr 7: 7 *I* **n** among the young men, 1067
Isa 58: 3 and *you have* not **n?'** 3359
Jer 33:24 not **n** that these people are saying, 8011
Mt 22:11 *he* **n** a man there who was not wearing *3972*
Lk 14: 7 *When he* **n** how the guests picked the places *2091*
Jn 11:31 **n** how quickly she got up and went out, *3972*

NOTICING (2) [NOTICE]

Mk 12:28 **N** that Jesus had given them a good answer, *3972*
Lk 11:38 **n** that Jesus did not first wash before *3972*

NOTIONS (2)

Job 15: 2 "Would a wise man answer with empty **n** 1981
Col 2:18 unspiritual mind puffs him up *with* **idle n.** *1632*

NOTORIOUS (1)

Mt 27:16 At that time they had a **n** prisoner, *2168*

NOTWITHSTANDING (KJV) See BUT, HOWEVER, NEVERTHELESS, YET

NOUGHT (KJV) See CRUMBLES, FAILS, FOILS, FRUSTRATED, IDOLATRIES, IGNORED, LO DEBAR, NO REASON, NONE, NOTHING, NULLIFY, PITTANCE, REJECTED, RIDICULED, RUIN, THWARTED, USELESS, VANISHED, WORTHLESS

NOURISH (2) [NOURISHED, NOURISHING, NOURISHMENT, WELL-NOURISHED]

Pr 10:21 The lips of the righteous n many, 8286
27:27 and your family and to n your servant girls. 2644

NOURISHED (4) [NOURISH]

Dt 32:13 *He* n him *with* honey from the rock, 3567
Job 21:24 his body well n, his bones rich with 2692+4848
Eze 31: 4 waters n it, deep springs made it grow tall; 1540
Da 1:15 looked healthier and better n than any 1374+1414

NOURISHING (1) [NOURISH]

Ro 11:17 the others and now share in the n sap from *4404*

NOURISHMENT (1) [NOURISH]

Pr 3: 8 This will bring health to your body and n 9198

NOVICE (KJV) See RECENT CONVERT

NOW (1208)

Ge 1: 2 N the earth was formless and empty, 2256
2: 8 N the LORD God had planted a garden in 2256
2:19 N the LORD God had formed out of 2256
2:23 "This is n bone of my bones and flesh 7193
3: 1 N the serpent was more crafty than any of 2256
3:22 "The man has n become like one of us, 6964
4: 2 N Abel kept flocks, 2256
4: 8 N Cain said to his brother Abel, 2256
4:11 N you are under a curse and driven from 6964
6:11 N the earth was corrupt in God's sight 2256
7: 4 Seven days from n I will send rain on 6388
8: 2 N the springs of the deep and 2256
9: 3 I n give you everything. NIH
9: 9 "I n establish my covenant with you and 2180
11: 1 N the whole world had one language and 2256
11:30 N Sarai was barren; she had no children. 2256
12:10 N there was a famine in the land, 2256
12:19 N then, here is your wife. 6964
13: 5 N Lot, who was moving about with Abram, 2256
13:13 N the men of Sodom were wicked 2256
14:10 N the Valley of Siddim was full of tar pits, 2256
14:13 N Abram was living near the great trees 2256
16: 1 N Sarai, Abram's wife, 2256
16: 5 and n that she knows she is pregnant, 2256
16:11 "You are n with child and you will have 2180
16:13 "I have n seen the One who sees me." 2151
17: 8 where you are n an alien, NIH
18: 5 n that you have come to your servant." 3954
18:10 N Sarah was listening at the entrance to 2256
18:12 *will* I *n* have this pleasure?" AIT
18:13 n that I am old?' 2256
18:27 "N that I have been so bold as to speak to 2180
18:31 "N that I have been so bold as to speak to 2180
19: 9 and n he wants to play the judge! 6964
20: 1 N Abraham moved on from there into 2256
20: 4 N Abimelech had not gone near her, 2256
20: 7 N return the man's wife, 6964
21: 1 N the LORD was gracious to Sarah 2256
21:23 N swear to me here before God 6964
22:12 N I know that you fear God, 6964
24: 1 Abraham was n old and well advanced 2256
24:29 N Rebekah had a brother named Laban, 2256
24:49 N if you will show kindness 6964
24:56 n that the LORD has granted success 2256
24:62 N Isaac had come from Beer Lahai Roi, 2256
26: 1 N there was a famine in the land— 2256
26:22 "N the LORD has given us room 6964
26:29 And n you are blessed by the LORD." 6964
27: 2 "I am n an old man and don't know the day 2180
27: 3 N then, get your weapons— 6964
27: 5 N Rebekah was listening as Isaac spoke 2256
27: 8 N, my son, listen carefully 6964
27:36 and n he's taken my blessing!" 6964
27:43 N then, my son, do what I say: 6964
28: 4 of the land where you n live as an alien, NIH
28: 6 N Esau learned that Isaac had blessed Jacob 2256
29:16 N Laban had two daughters; 2256
29:32 Surely my husband will love me n." 6964
29:34 when she gave birth to a son she said, "N 6964
30:30 But n, when may I do something 6964
31:13 N leave this land at once and go back 6964
31:30 N you have gone off because you longed 6964
31:32 N Jacob did not know 2256
31:34 N Rachel had taken the household gods 2256
31:37 N that you have searched 3954
31:38 "I have been with you for twenty years n. 2296
Ge 31:44 Come n, let's make a covenant, you and I, 6964
32: 4 with Laban and have remained there till n. 6964
32: 5 N I am sending this message to my lord, 2256
32: 6 and n he is coming to meet you, 1685
32:10 but n I have become two groups. 6964
33:10 n that you have received me favorably. 2256
34: 1 N Dinah, the daughter Leah had borne 2256
34: 7 N Jacob's sons had come in from the fields 2256
35: 8 N Deborah, Rebekah's nurse, 2256
37: 3 N Israel loved Joseph more than any 2256
37:12 N his brothers had gone 2256
37:20 "Come n, let's kill him and throw him 6964
37:24 N the cistern was empty; 2256
37:30 Where *can* I turn *n?"* AIT
38:14 though Shelah had n grown up, 2256
38:16 "Come n, let me sleep with you." 5528
38:24 and as a result she is n pregnant." 2180
39: 1 N Joseph had been taken down to Egypt. 2256
39: 6 N Joseph was well-built and handsome, 2256
40:20 N the third day was Pharaoh's birthday, 2256
41:12 N a young Hebrew was there with us, 2256
41:33 "And n let Pharaoh look for a discerning 6964
42: 6 N Joseph was the governor of the land, 2256
42:13 The youngest is n with our father, 2021+3427
42:22 N we must give an accounting 2180
42:32 and the youngest is n with our father 2021+3427
42:36 and n you want to take Benjamin. 2256
43: 1 N the famine was still severe in the land. 2256
43:18 N the men were frightened 2256
44: 1 N Joseph gave these instructions to 2256
44:16 We are n my lord's slaves— 2180
44:30 "So n, if the boy is not with us 6964
44:33 "N then, please let your servant remain here 6964
45: 5 And n, do not be distressed and do not 6964
45: 6 For two years n there has been famine 2296+3954
45: 9 N hurry back to my father and say to him, 2256
46:28 N Jacob sent Judah ahead of him to Joseph 2256
46:30 Israel said to Joseph, "N I am ready to die, 2021+7193
47: 1 the land of Canaan and are n in Goshen." 2180
47: 4 So n, please let your servants settle 6964
47:23 "N *that* I have bought you 2176
47:27 N the Israelites settled in Egypt in 2256
48: 5 "N then, your two sons born to you 6964
48:10 N Israel's eyes were failing because 2256
48:11 and n God has allowed me 2180
50: 5 N let me go up and bury my father; 6964
50:17 N please forgive the sins of the servants of 6964
50:20 to accomplish what is n being done, 2021+2021+2296+3427
Ex 1: 6 N Joseph and all his brothers and all 2256
2: 1 N a man of the house of Levi married 2256
2:16 N a priest of Midian had seven daughters, 2256
3: 1 N Moses was tending the flock 2256
3: 9 n the cry of the Israelites has reached me, 6964
3:10 So n, go. 6964
4: 7 "N put it back into your cloak," he said. 2256
4:12 N go; I will help you speak 6964
4:19 N the LORD had said to Moses in Midian, 2256
5: 3 N let us take a three-day journey into 5528
5: 5 the people of the land are n numerous, 6964
5:18 N get to work. 6964
6: 1 "N you will see what I will do to Pharaoh: 6964
6:13 N the LORD spoke to Moses and Aaron 2256
6:28 N when the LORD spoke to Moses 2256
7:16 But until n you have not listened. 3907
8:28 N pray for me." NIH
9:15 *by* n I could have stretched out my hand 6964
9:18 from the day it was founded till n. 6964
9:19 Give an order n to bring your livestock 6964
10: 6 the day they settled in this land till n.' " 2021+2021+2296+3427
10:17 N forgive my sin once more and pray to 6964
11: 1 N the LORD had said to Moses, 2256
12:40 N the length of time the Israelite people 2256
18: 1 N Jethro, the priest of Midian 2256
18:11 N I know that the LORD is greater than all 6964
18:19 Listen n to me and I will give you some 6964
19: 5 N if you obey me fully and keep my 6964
32:10 N leave me alone so that my anger may 6964
32:30 But n I will go up to the LORD; 6964
32:32 But n, please forgive their sin— 6964
32:34 N go, lead the people to the place I spoke 6964
33: 5 N take off your ornaments 6964
33: 7 N Moses used to take a tent 2256
33:18 Then Moses said, "N show me your glory." 5528
Lev 17: 5 the LORD the sacrifices they *are n* making AIT
24:10 N the son of an Israelite mother and 2256
Nu 6:13 " 'N this is the law for the Nazirite when 2256
10:29 N Moses said to Hobab son of Reuel 2256
11: 1 N the people complained 2256
11: 6 But n we have lost our appetite; 6964
11:15 put me to death right n— 5528
11:18 N the LORD will give you meat, 2256
11:23 You will n see whether or 6964
11:31 N a wind went out from the LORD 2256
12: 3 (N Moses was a very humble man, 2256
14:17 "N may the Lord's strength be displayed, 2256+6964
14:19 from the time they left Egypt until n." 2178
15:22 " 'N if you unintentionally fail to keep any 2256
16: 8 Moses also said to Korah, "N listen, 5528
16:10 but n you are trying to get 2256
16:13 And n you also want to lord it over us? 3954
18:22 From n on the Israelites must not go near 6388
20: 2 N there was no water for the community, 2256
20:16 "N we are here at Kadesh, 2180
Nu 22: 2 N Balak son of Zippor saw all 2256
22: 6 N come and put a curse on these people, 6964
22:11 N come and put a curse on them for me. 6964
22:19 N stay here tonight as the others did, 6964
22:29 I would kill you right n." 6964
22:33 I would certainly have killed you by n, 6964
22:34 N if you are displeased, I will go back." 6964
22:38 "Well, I have come to you n," 6964
23:23 It will n be said of Jacob and of Israel, 2021+3869+6961
24: 1 N when Balaam saw that it pleased 2256
24:11 N leave at once and go home! 6964
24:14 N I am going back to my people, but come, 6964
24:17 but not n; I behold him, but not near. 6964
31:17 N kill all the boys. 6964
36: 3 N suppose they marry men 2256
Dt 2: 3 this hill country long enough; n turn north. NIH
2:13 "N get up and cross the Zered Valley." 6964
2:16 N when the last of these fighting men 2256
2:24 "Set out n and cross the Arnon Gorge. 7756
2:30 as he has n done. 2021+2021+2296+3427
2:31 N begin to conquer and possess his land." NIH
4: 1 Hear n, O Israel, the decrees and laws I am 6964
4:20 as you n are. 2021+2021+2296+3427
4:32 Ask n about the former days, 5528
5:25 But n, why should we die? 6964
7:19 the same to all the peoples you n fear. NIH
9: 1 You are n about to cross the Jordan 2021+3427
10: 5 and they are there n. NIH
10:10 N I had stayed on the mountain forty days 2256
10:12 And n, O Israel, what does 6964
10:22 and n the LORD your God has made you 6964
22:17 N he has slandered her and said, 2180
26:10 n I bring the firstfruits of the soil that you, 6964
27: 9 You have n become the people of the LORD your God. 2021+2021+2296+3427
29:28 another land, as it is n." 2021+2021+2296+3427
30:11 N what I am commanding you today is 3954
30:19 N choose life, so that you 2256
31: 2 I am n a hundred and twenty years old 2021+3427
31:14 "N the day of your death is near. 2176
31:19 "N write down for yourselves this song 6964
32:37 He will say: "N where are their gods, NIH
32:39 "See n that I myself am He! 6964
34: 9 N Joshua son of Nun was filled with 2256
Jos 1: 2 N then, you and all these people, 6964
1:11 Three days from n you will cross 928+6388
2:12 N then, please swear to me by the LORD 6964
2:16 N she had said to them, 2256
3:12 N then, choose twelve men from the tribes 6964
3:15 N the Jordan is at flood stage all 2256
4:10 N the priests who carried 2256
5: 1 N when all the Amorite kings west of 2256
5: 4 N this is why he did so: 2256
5:13 N when Joshua was near Jericho, 2256
5:14 of the army of the LORD I have n come." 6964
6: 1 N Jericho was tightly shut up because of 2256
7: 2 N Joshua sent men from Jericho to Ai, 2256
7: 8 n that Israel has been routed 339
9: 1 N when all the kings west of 2256
9:12 But n see how dry and moldy it is. 6964
9:19 and we cannot touch them n. 6964
9:23 You are n under a curse: 6964
9:25 We are n in your hands. 6964
10: 1 N Adoni-Zedek king of Jerusalem heard 2256
10:16 N the five kings had fled and hidden in 2256
14: 1 N these are the areas the Israelites received 2256
14: 6 N the men of Judah approached Joshua 2256
14:10 "N then, just as the LORD promised, 6964
14:11 I'm just as vigorous to go out to battle n 6964
14:12 N give me this hill country that 6964
17: 3 N Zelophehad son of Hepher, 2256
21: 1 N the family heads of 2256
22: 3 For a long time n— 2296
22: 4 N that the LORD your God has given your brothers rest 6964
22:16 an altar in rebellion against him n? 2021+3427
22:18 you n turning away from the LORD? 2021+3427
22:31 N you have rescued the Israelites from 255
23: 8 as you have until n. 2021+2021+2296+3427
23:14 "N I am about to go the way of all 2021+3427
24:14 "N fear the LORD and serve him 6964
24:23 "N then," said Joshua, 6964
Jdg 1: 7 N God has paid me back for what I did NIH
1:22 N the house of Joseph attacked Bethel, 2256
2: 3 N therefore I tell you that I will 1685
3:16 N Ehud had made a double-edged sword 2256
4:11 N Heber the Kenite had left 2256
6:13 But n the LORD has abandoned us 6964
6:17 "If n I have found favor in your eyes, 5528
6:33 N all the Midianites, 2256
7: 3 announce n to the people, 6964
7: 8 N the camp of Midian lay below him in 2256
8: 1 N the Ephraimites asked Gideon, 2256
8:10 N Zebah and Zalmunna were in Karkor 2256
9:16 "N if you have acted honorably and 6964
9:26 N Gaal son of Ebed moved 2256
9:32 N then, during the night you 6964
9:35 N Gaal son of Ebed had gone out 2256
9:38 "Where is your big talk n, you who said, 686
10:15 but please rescue us n." 2021+2021+2296+3427
11: 7 Why do you come to me n, 6964
11: 8 "Nevertheless, we are turning to you n; 6964
11:13 N give it back peaceably." 6964
11:23 "N since the LORD, the God of Israel, 6964
11:36 n that the LORD has avenged you 339
12: 3 N why have you come up today 2256

Jdg 13: 4 N see to it that you drink no wine 6964
13: 7 N then, drink no wine 6964
13:23 or n told us this." 2021+3869+6961
14: 2 n get her for me as my wife." 6964
14:10 N his father went down to see the woman. 2256
15:18 Must I n die of thirst and fall into the hands 6964
16:10 Come n, tell me how you can be tied." 5528+6964
16:13 Delilah then said to Samson, "Until n, 2178
16:23 N the rulers of the Philistines assembled 2256
16:27 N the temple was crowded with men 2256
17: 1 N a man named Micah from 2256
17: 5 N this man Micah had a shrine, 2256
17:13 "N I know that the LORD will be good 6964
18:14 N you know what to do." 6964
19: 1 N a Levite who lived in a remote area in 2256
19: 9 said, "N look, it's almost evening. 5528
19:18 to Bethlehem in Judah and n I am going to 2256
19:24 I will bring them out to you n, 5528
20: 7 N, all you Israelites, speak up 2180
20: 9 But n this is what we'll do to Gibeah: 6964
20:13 N surrender those wicked men of Gibeah 6964
20:36 N the men of Israel had given way 2256
21: 6 N the Israelites grieved for their brothers, 2256
Ru 1: 3 N Elimelech, Naomi's husband, died, 2256
2: 1 N Naomi had a relative 2256
2: 7 from morning till n, 6964
3:11 And n, my daughter, don't be afraid. 6964
4: 7 (N in earlier times in Israel, 2256
1Sa 1: 9 N Eli the priest was sitting on a chair by 2256
1:28 So n I give him to the LORD. 1685
2:13 N it was the practice of the priests with 2256
2:16 "No, hand it over n; 6964
2:22 N Eli, who was very old, 2256
2:27 N a man of God came to Eli and said 2256
2:30 n the LORD declares: 'Far be it from me! 6964
3: 7 N Samuel did not yet know the LORD: 2256
4: 1 N the Israelites went out to fight against 2256
6: 7 "N then, get a new cart ready, 2256
6:13 N the people of Beth 2256
8: 5 n appoint a king to lead us, 6964
8: 9 N listen to them; 6964
9: 3 N the donkeys belonging 2256
9: 6 Let's go there n. 6964
9:12 "He's ahead of you. Hurry n; 6964
9:13 those who are invited will eat. Go up n; 6964
9:15 N the day before Saul came, 2256
10: 2 And n your father has stopped thinking 2180
10:14 N Saul's uncle asked him and his servant, 2256
10:19 But you have n rejected your God, 2021+3427
10:19 So n present yourselves before the LORD 6964
12: 2 N you have a king as your leader. 6964
12: 7 N then, stand here, because I am going 6964
12:10 n deliver us from the hands of our enemies, 6964
12:13 N here is the king you have chosen, 6964
12:16 "N then, stand still and see this great thing 6964
12:17 Is it not wheat harvest n? 2021+3427
13: 4 and n Israel has become a stench to 1685
13:12 'N the Philistines will come down 6964
13:14 But n your kingdom will not endure; 6964
13:23 N a detachment of Philistines had gone out 2256
14:24 N the men of Israel were in distress 2256
14:43 And n must I die?" 2180
15: 1 so listen n to the message from the LORD. 6964
15: 3 N go, attack the Amalekites 6964
15:25 N I beg you, 6964
16:14 N the Spirit of the LORD had departed 2256
17: 1 N the Philistines gathered their forces 2256
17:12 N David was the son of 2256
17:17 N Jesse said to his son David, 2256
17:25 N the Israelites had been saying, 2256
17:29 "N what have I done?" 6964
18:20 N Saul's daughter Michal was in love 2256
18:21 "N you have a second opportunity 2021+3427
18:22 n become his son-in-law.'" 6964
20:31 N send and bring him to me, 6964
21: 3 N then, what do you have on hand? 6964
21: 7 N one of Saul's servants was there that day, 2256
22: 6 N Saul heard that David 2256
22:12 Saul said, "Listen n, son of Ahitub." 5528
23: 6 (N Abiathar son of Ahimelech had brought 2256
23:20 N, O king, come down 6964
23:24 N David and his men were in the Desert 2256
24:11 N understand and recognize that I am NIH
24:18 You have just n told me of 2021+3427
24:21 N swear to me by the LORD that you will 6964
25: 1 N Samuel died, and all Israel assembled 2256
25: 7 "'N I hear that it is sheep-shearing time. 6964
25:17 N think it over and see what you can do, 6964
25:26 "N since the LORD has kept you, 6964
26: 8 N let me pin him to the ground 6964
26:11 N get the spear and water jug that are 6964
26:19 N let my lord the king listen 6964
26:19 They have n driven me from my share 2021+3427
26:20 N do not let my blood fall to the ground far 6964
27: 8 N David and his men went up and raided 2256
28: 3 N Samuel was dead, 2256
28:16 n that the LORD has turned away 2256
28:22 N please listen to your servant 6964
29: 3 and from the day he left Saul until n, 2021+2021+2296+3427
29: 6 From the day you came to me until n, 2021+2021+2296+3427
29: 8 from the day I came to you until n? 2021+2021+2296+3427
29:10 N get up early, 6964
30: 1 N the Amalekites had raided the Negev 2256
31: 1 N the Philistines fought against Israel; 2256
2Sa 2: 6 May the LORD n show you kindness 6964
2: 7 N then, be strong and brave, 6964
2:18 N Asahel was as fleet-footed as 2256
3: 7 N Saul had had a concubine 2256
3: 8 Yet n you accuse me of 2021+3427
3:18 N do it! 6964
3:24 N he is gone! 2256
3:27 N when Abner returned to Hebron, 2256
4: 2 N Saul's son had two men who were leaders 2256
4: 5 N Recab and Baanah, 2256
4:11 not n demand his blood from your hand 6964
5:11 N Hiram king of Tyre sent messengers 2256
5:18 N the Philistines had come and spread out 2256
6:12 N King David was told, 2256
7: 8 "N then, tell my servant David, 6964
7: 9 N I will make your name great, 2256
7:25 "And n, LORD God, 6964
7:29 N be pleased to bless the house 6964
9: 2 N there was a servant 2256
9:10 (N Ziba had fifteen sons 2256
12: 4 "N a traveler came to the rich man, 2256
12:10 N, therefore, the sword will never depart 6964
12:21 but n that the child is dead, 889+3869
12:23 But n that he is dead, why should I fast? 6964
12:28 N muster the rest of the troops and besiege 6964
13: 3 N Amnon had a friend named Jonadab son 2256
13:20 Be quiet n, my sister; he is your brother. 6964
13:34 N the man standing watch looked up 2256
14: 7 N the whole clan has risen up 2180
14:15 "And n I have come to say this to my lord 6964
14:17 "And n your servant says, 2256
14:32 N then, I want to see the king's face, 6964
15:31 N David had been told, 2256
15:34 but n I will be your servant,' 6964
16: 4 that belonged to Mephibosheth is n yours." 2180
16:23 N in those days 2256
17: 9 Even n, he is hidden in a cave 6964
17:16 N send a message immediately 6964
18: 3 be better n for you to give us support from 6964
18: 9 N Absalom happened to meet David's men. 2256
18:19 N Ahimaaz son of Zadok said, 2256
19: 7 N go out and encourage your men. 6964
19: 7 upon you from your youth till n." 6964
19: 9 But n he has fled the country because 6964
19:13 if from n on you are not the commander 2021+3427+3972
19:15 N the men of Judah had come to Gilgal 2256
19:30 n that my lord the king has arrived 339
19:32 N Barzillai was a very old man, 2256
19:35 I am n eighty years old. 2021+3427
20: 1 N a troublemaker named Sheba son 2256
20: 6 to Abishai, "N Sheba son of Bicri 6964
21: 2 (N the Gibeonites were not a part of Israel 2256
24:10 N, O LORD, I beg you, 6964
24:13 N then, think it over and decide 6964
1Ki 1: 5 N Adonijah, whose mother was Haggith, 2256
1:12 N then, let me advise you 6964
1:18 But n Adonijah has become king, and you, 6964
1:25 Right n they are eating and drinking 2180
2: 5 "N you yourself know what Joab son 1685+2256
2: 9 But n, do not consider him innocent. 6964
2:13 N Adonijah, the son of Haggith, 2256
2:16 N I have one request to make of you. 6964
2:24 And n, as surely as the LORD lives— 6964
2:26 but I will not put you to death n, 2021+2021+2296+3427
2:44 N the LORD will repay you 2256
2:46 The kingdom was n firmly established 2256
3: 7 "N, O LORD my God, 6964
3:16 N two prostitutes came to the king 255
5: 4 But n the LORD my God has given me rest 6964
8:20 I have succeeded David my father and n 2256
8:25 "N LORD, God of Israel, 6964
8:26 And n, O God of Israel, 6964
9: 8 And though this temple is *n* imposing, AIT
9:14 N Hiram had sent to the king 120 talents 2256
11:28 N Jeroboam was a man of standing, 2256
12: 4 but n lighten the harsh labor and 6964
12:26 "The kingdom will n likely revert to 6964
13: 2 the high places who n make offerings here, NIH
13:11 N there was a certain old prophet living 2256
14: 4 N Ahijah could not see; 2256
14:14 Yes, even n. 6964
15:19 N break your treaty with Baasha king NIH
17: 1 N Elijah the Tishbite, 2256
17:24 "N I know that you are a man of God 2296+6964
18: 2 N the famine was severe in Samaria, 2256
18:11 n you tell me to go to my master and say, 6964
18:14 n you tell me to go to my master and say, 6964
18:19 N summon the people from all over Israel 6964
19: 1 N Ahab told Jezebel everything Elijah had done 2256
19:10 and n they are trying to kill me too." 2256
19:14 and n they are trying to kill me too." 2256
20: 1 N Ben-Hadad king of Aram 2256
20:17 N Ben-Hadad had dispatched scouts, 2256
21:18 He is n in Naboth's vineyard, 2180
22:11 N Zedekiah son of Kenaanah 2256
22:23 "So n the LORD has put a lying spirit in 6964
22:31 N the king of Aram 2256
22:48 N Jehoshaphat built a fleet of trading ships NIH
2Ki 1: 2 N Ahaziah had fallen through the lattice 2256
1:14 But n have respect for my life!" 6964
2:14 "Where n is the LORD, 677
3: 4 N Mesha king of Moab raised sheep, 2256
3:15 But n bring me a harpist." 6964
3:21 N all the Moabites had heard that 2256
2Ki 3:23 N to the plunder, Moab!" 6964
4: 1 But n his creditor is coming 2256
4:13 N what can be done for you? NIH
5: 1 N Naaman was commander of the army of 2256
5: 2 N bands from Aram had gone out 2256
5:15 "N I know that there is no God in all 2180
5:15 Please accept n a gift from your servant." 6964
6: 8 N the king of Aram was at war with Israel. 2256
6:32 N Elisha was sitting in his house, 2256
7: 3 N there were four men with leprosy at 2256
7:17 N the king had put the officer 2256
8: 1 N Elisha had said to the woman 2256
8: 6 from the day she left the country until n." 6964
9:14 (N Joram and all Israel had been defending 2256
9:26 N then, pick him up and throw him on 6964
10: 1 N there were in Samaria seventy sons of 2256
10: 6 N the royal princes, seventy of them, 2256
10:19 N summon all the prophets of Baal, 6964
10:24 N Jehu had posted eighty men outside 2256
13:14 N Elisha was suffering from the illness 2256
13:19 But n you will defeat it only three times." 6964
13:20 N Moabite raiders used to enter 2256
14:10 You have indeed defeated Edom and n 2256
18:21 Look n, you are depending on Egypt, 6964
18:23 "'Come n, make a bargain with my master, 5528+6964
19: 9 N Sennacherib received a report 2256
19:19 N, O LORD our God, 6964
19:25 n I have brought it to pass, 6964
20: 5 On the third day from n you will go up to NIH
20: 8 of the LORD on the third day from n?" NIH
24:20 N Zedekiah rebelled against the king 2256
1Ch 9: 2 N the first to resettle on their own property 2256
10: 1 N the Philistines fought against Israel; 2256
14: 1 N Hiram king of Tyre sent messengers 2256
14: 9 N the Philistines had come and raided 2256
15:27 N David was clothed in a robe of fine linen, 2256
17: 7 "N then, tell my servant David, 6964
17: 8 N I will make your name like the names of 2256
17:23 "And n, LORD, let the promise you have made concerning your servant 6964
17:27 N you have been pleased to bless the house 6964
21: 8 N, I beg you, take away the guilt 6964
21:12 N then, decide how I should answer 6964
22:11 "N, my son, the LORD be with you, 6964
22:16 N begin the work, NIH
22:19 N devote your heart and soul to seeking 6964
28: 8 "So n I charge you in the sight of all Israel 6964
28:10 Consider n, for the LORD has chosen you 6964
29: 3 of my God *I n give* my personal treasures AIT
29: 5 N, who is willing to consecrate 2256
29:13 N, our God, we give you thanks, 6964
29:17 And n I have seen with joy 6964
2Ch 1: 4 N David had brought up the ark of God 66
1: 9 N, LORD God, let your promise 6964
2: 4 N I am about to build a temple for 2180
2:15 "N let my lord send his servants the wheat 6964
6: 6 But n I have chosen Jerusalem 2256
6:10 I have succeeded David my father and n 2256
6:13 N he had made a bronze platform, 3954
6:16 "N LORD, God of Israel, 6964
6:17 And n, O LORD, God of Israel, 6964
6:40 "N, my God, may your eyes be open 6964
6:41 "N arise, O LORD God, 6964
7:15 N my eyes will be open 6964
7:21 And though this temple is n so imposing, NIH
10: 4 but n lighten the harsh labor and 6964
12: 5 therefore, I n abandon you to Shishak.'" 677
13: 8 "And n you plan to resist the kingdom of 6964
13:13 N Jeroboam had sent troops around to 2256
16: 3 N break your treaty with Baasha king NIH
16: 9 and from n on you will be at war." 6964
18: 1 N Jehoshaphat had great wealth and honor, 2256
18:10 N Zedekiah son of Kenaanah 2256
18:22 "So n the LORD has put a lying spirit in 6964
18:30 N the king of Aram 2256
19: 7 N let the fear of the LORD be upon you. 6964
20:10 "But n here are men from Ammon, 6964
21:14 n the LORD is about to strike your people, 2180
23: 4 N this is what you are to do: NIH
24: 5 Do it n." 4554
24: 7 N the sons of that wicked woman Athaliah 3954
24:15 N Jehoiada was old and full of years, 2256
25:19 and n you are arrogant and proud. 6964
28:10 And n you intend to make the men 6964
28:11 N listen to me! 6964
29: 5 Consecrate yourselves n and consecrate 6964
29:10 N I intend to make a covenant with 6964
29:11 My sons, do not be negligent n, 6964
29:19 They are n in front of the LORD's altar." 2180
29:31 "You have n dedicated yourselves to 6964
32:15 N do not let Hezekiah deceive you 6964
34:28 N I will gather you to your fathers, 2180
35: 3 N serve the LORD your God 6964
Ezr 1: 4 where survivors *may n be* living are AIT
2: 1 N these are the people of 2256
4:14 N since we are under obligation to 10363
4:21 N issue an order to these men to stop work, 10363
5: 1 N Haggai the prophet and Zechariah 10221
5:17 N if it pleases the king, 10363
6: 6 N then, Tattenai, governor 10363
7:13 N I decree that any of the Israelites 10364
7:21 N I, King Artaxerxes, order all 10221
9: 7 From the days of our forefathers until n, 2021+2021+2296+3427
9: 8 "But n, for a brief moment, 6964
9:10 n, O our God, what can we say after this? 6964

Ezr 10: 3 N let us make a covenant before our God 6964
10:11 N make confession to the LORD, 6964
Ne 5: 1 N the men and their wives raised 2256
5: 8 N you are selling your brothers, 1685+2256
6: 7 N this report will get back to the king; 6964
6: 9 "N strengthen my hands." 6964
7: 4 N the city was large and spacious, 2256
8:12 because they n understood the words NIH
9:32 "N therefore, O our God, the great, 6964
10:29 all these n join their brothers the nobles, NIH
11: 1 N the leaders of the people settled 2256
11: 3 in Jerusalem (n some Israelites, 2256
13:18 N you are stirring up more wrath 2256
13:27 Must we hear n that you too are doing NIH
Est 2: 5 N there was in the citadel of Susa a Jew of NIH
2:17 N the king was attracted 2256
5: 6 "N what is your petition? NIH
6: 4 N Haman had just entered the outer court 2256
6: 6 N Haman thought to himself, 2256
8: 8 N write another decree in the king's name 2256
9: 1 but n the tables were turned and 2256
9:12 N what is your petition? 2256
Job 3:13 For n I would be lying down in peace; 6964
3:14 who built for themselves places n lying NIH
4: 5 But n trouble comes to you, 6964
4: 7 "Consider n: Who, being innocent, 5528
6:13 n that success has been driven from me? NIH
6:21 N you too have proved to be of no help; 6964
6:28 "But n be so kind as to look at me. 2256
7: 8 eye *that n* sees me will see me no longer; AIT
8: 6 even n he will rouse himself on your behalf 6964
9:35 but as it n stands with me, I cannot. NIH
10: 8 Will you n turn and destroy me? 3480
10: 9 Will you n turn me to dust again? 2256
13: 6 Hear n my argument; 5528
13:18 N that I have prepared my case, 2180
16:19 Even n my witness is in heaven; 6964
19: 3 Ten times n you have reproached me; 2296
21:28 'Where n is the great man's house, NIH
30: 1 "But n they mock me, men younger than I, 6964
30: 9 "And n their sons mock me in song; 6964
30:11 N that God has unstrung my bow 3954
30:16 "And n my life ebbs away; 6964
31:35 I sign n my defense— 2176
32: 4 N Elihu had waited before speaking to Job 2256
32:16 Must I wait, n that they are silent, 3954
32:16 n that they stand there with no reply? 3954
33: 1 "But n, Job, listen to my words; 5528
33:14 n one way, now another— NIH
33:14 now one way, n another— 2256
33:21 and his bones, once hidden, n stick out. NIH
36:17 But n you are laden with the judgment due 2256
37:21 N no one can look at the sun, 6964
42: 4 'Listen n, and I will speak; 5528
42: 5 of you but n my eyes have seen you. 6964
42: 8 So n take seven bulls and seven rams 6964
Ps 12: 5 I will n arise," says the LORD. 6964
17:11 they n surround me, with eyes alert, 6964
20: 6 N I know that the LORD saves his anointed; 6964
37:25 I was young and n I am old, 1685
39: 7 "But n, Lord, what do I look for? 6964
44: 9 But n you have rejected and humbled us; 677
52: 7 "Here n is the man who did 2180
60: 1 you have been angry—n restore us! NIH
113: 2 both n and forevermore. 6964
115:18 both n and forevermore. 6964
119:67 but n I obey your word. 6964
121: 8 over your coming and going both n 6964
125: 2 so the LORD surrounds his people both n 6964
131: 3 in the LORD both n and forevermore. 6964
Pr 3:28 when you *n* have it with you. AIT
5: 7 N then, my sons, listen to me; 6964
7:12 n in the street, 7193
7:12 n in the squares, at every corner she lurks.) 7193
7:24 N then, my sons, listen to me; 6964
8:32 "N then, my sons, listen to me; 6964
Ecc 2: 1 I thought in my heart, "Come n, 5528
9: 7 for it is n that God favors what you do. 3893
9:15 N there lived in that city a man poor 2256
12:13 N all has been heard; NIH
SS 3: 2 I will get up n and go about the city, 5528
Isa 1:18 "Come n, let us reason together," 5528
1:21 in her—but n murderers! 6964
3: 1 See n, the Lord, the LORD Almighty, 3954
5: 3 "N you dwellers in Jerusalem and men 6964
5: 5 N I will tell you what I am going to do 6964
7: 2 N the house of David was told, 2256
7:13 Isaiah said, "Hear n, you house of David! 5528
14: 8 "N that you have been laid low, 255+4946
16:14 But n the LORD says: 6964
19:12 Where are your wise men n? 686
22: 1 What troubles you n, 686
23:12 O Virgin Daughter of Sidon, *n* crushed! AIT
23:13 this people *that is n* of no account! AIT
26:14 *They are n* dead, they live no more; AIT
28:22 N stop your mocking, 6964
30: 8 Go n, write it on a tablet for them, 6964
33:10 "N will I arise," says the LORD. 6964
33:10 "N will I be exalted; 6964
33:10 will I be exalted; n will I be lifted up. 6964
36: 6 Look n, you are depending on Egypt, NIH
36: 8 " 'Come n, make a bargain with my master, 5528+6964
37: 9 N Sennacherib received a report 2256
37:20 N, O LORD our God, 6964
37:26 n I have brought it to pass, 6964
38:11 or be with *those who n* dwell in this world. AIT
Isa 42:14 But n, like a woman in childbirth, I cry out, NIH
43: 1 But n, this is what the LORD says— 6964
43:19 N it springs up; do you not perceive it? 6964
44: 1 "But n listen, O Jacob, my servant, Israel, 6964
47: 8 "N then, listen, you wanton creature, 6964
48: 6 "From n on I will tell you of new things, 6964
48: 7 They are created n, and not long ago; 6964
48:16 And n the Sovereign LORD has sent me, 6964
49: 5 And n the LORD says— 6964
49:19 n you will be too small for your people, 6964
50:11 But n, all you who light fires 2176
52: 5 "And n what do I have here?" 6964
54: 9 So n I have sworn not to be angry with you, NIH
63:18 but n our enemies have trampled NIH
Jer 1: 9 "N, I have put my words in your mouth. 2180
2:18 N why go to Egypt to drink water from 6964
3: 1 would you n return to me?" 2256
4:12 N I pronounce my judgments 6964
5:19 so n you will serve foreigners in a land NIH
7:12 " 'Go n to the place in Shiloh 5528
7:14 what I did to Shiloh *I will n* do to AIT
7:25 the time your forefathers left Egypt until n, 2021+2021+2296+3427
9:17 the LORD Almighty says: "Consider n! 2256
9:20 N, O women, hear the word of the LORD; 3954
10:20 no one is left n to pitch my tent or to set 6388
13: 4 and go n to Perath and hide it there in 7756
13: 6 "Go n to Perath and get the belt I told you 7756
13: 7 but n it was ruined and completely useless. 2180
14:10 he will n remember their wickedness 6964
16:16 "But n I will send for many fishermen," 2180
17:15 Let it n be fulfilled!" 5528
18:11 "N therefore say to the people of Judah 6964
21: 2 "Inquire n of the LORD for us 5528
25: 5 They said, "Turn n, each of you, 5528
25:30 "N prophesy all these words against them 2256
26:13 N reform your ways and your actions 6964
26:20 (N Uriah son of Shemaiah 2256
27: 6 N I will hand all your countries over 6964
27:16 to the prophets who say, 'Very soon n 6964
32: 3 N Zedekiah king of Judah NIH
32:24 What you said has happened, as you n see. 2180
32:31 From the day it was built until n, 2021+2021+2296+3427
34:16 But n you have turned around 2256
34:17 So I n proclaim 'freedom' for you, 2180
36: 2 the reign of Josiah till n. 2021+2021+2296+3427
37: 4 N Jeremiah was free to come and go among 2256
37:20 But n, my lord the king, please listen. 6964
39:11 N Nebuchadnezzar king of Babylon 2256
40: 3 And n the LORD has brought it about; 2256
41: 9 N the cistern where he threw all the bodies 2256
42: 2 For as you n see, NIH
42: 2 n only a few are left. NIH
42:11 whom you n fear. NIH
42:22 So n, be sure of this: 6964
44: 7 "N this is what the LORD God Almighty, 6964
44:23 as you n see." 2021+2021+2296+3427
49:15 "N I will make you small among 2180
51: 7 therefore they *have n* gone mad. AIT
52: 3 N Zedekiah rebelled against the king 2256
La 1: 1 among the provinces *has n* become a slave. AIT
4: 2 are n considered as pots of clay, NIH
4: 5 Those nurtured in purple n lie on ash heaps. NIH
4: 8 But n they are blacker than soot; NIH
4:14 N they grope through the streets NIH
Eze 3: 4 Son of man, go n to the house of Israel 995+2143
3:11 Go n to your countrymen in exile 995+2143
4: 1 "N, son of man, take a clay tablet, 2256
4:14 From my youth until n 6964
5: 1 "N, son of man, take a sharp sword 2256
7: 3 The end is n upon you 6964
8: 8 "Son of man, n dig into the wall." 5528
9: 3 N the glory of the God of Israel went up 2256
10: 3 N the cherubim were standing on 2256
11:13 N as I was prophesying, 2256
12:27 for many years *from n,* AIT
13: 2 of Israel who *are n* prophesying. AIT
13:17 "N, son of man, set your face against 2256
16:49 " 'N this was the sin of your sister Sodom: 2180
16:57 you are n scorned by the daughters 6961
17: 7 The vine n sent out its roots toward him 2180
19: 6 for he was n a strong lion. NIH
19:13 N it is planted in the desert, 6964
23:43 'N let them use her as a prostitute, 6964
24: 6 to the pot n encrusted, NIH
24:13 " 'N your impurity is lewdness. 928
26: 2 n that she lies in ruins I will prosper,' NIH
26:18 N the coastlands tremble on the day 6964
27:34 N you are shattered by the sea in the depths 6961
33:22 N the evening before the man arrived, 2256
36:35 *n* fortified and inhabited." AIT
38: 8 and n all of them live in safety. 2256
39:25 I will n bring Jacob back from captivity 6964
42: 5 N the upper rooms were narrower, 2256
43: 9 N let them put away from me 6964
47: 5 but n it was a river that I could not cross, NIH
Da 1: 9 N God had caused the official 2256
2:36 and n we will interpret it to the king. 10221
3:15 N when you hear the sound of the horn, 10363
4:18 N, Belteshazzar, tell me what it means, 10221
4:37 N I, Nebuchadnezzar, praise and exalt 10363
5:16 N I have heard that you are able 10221
6: 3 N Daniel so distinguished himself among 10008
6: 8 N, O king, issue the decree and put it 10363
6:10 N when Daniel learned that 10221
9:15 "N, O Lord our God, 6964
Da 9:17 "N, our God, hear the prayers and petitions 6964
9:22 I have n come to give you insight 6964
10:11 for I have n been sent to you." 6964
10:14 N I have come to explain 2256
10:19 Be strong n; be strong." 2256
11: 2 "N then, I tell you the truth: 6964
Hos 2: 7 for then I was better off than n.' 6964
2:10 So n I will expose her lewdness before 6964
2:14 "Therefore I am n going to allure her; 2180
5: 3 Ephraim, you have n turned to prostitution; 6964
5: 7 N their New Moon festivals will devour 6964
7:11 n calling to Egypt, now turning to Assyria. NIH
7:11 now calling to Egypt, n turning to Assyria. NIH
8: 8 n she is among the nations like 6964
8:10 I will n gather them together. 6964
8:13 N he will remember their wickedness 6964
10: 2 and n they must bear their guilt. 6964
13: 2 N they sin more and more; 6964
Joel 2:12 "Even n," declares the LORD, 6964
3: 4 "N what have you against me, 1685+2256
Am 2:13 "N then, I will crush you as a cart crushes 2180
7:16 N then, hear the word of the LORD. 6964
Jnh 3: 3 N Nineveh was a very important city— 2256
4: 3 N, O LORD, take away my life, 6964
Mic 4: 9 Why do you n cry aloud— 6964
4:10 for n you must leave the city to camp in 6964
4:11 n many nations are gathered against you. 6964
7: 4 N is the time of their confusion. 6964
7:10 even n she will be trampled underfoot 6964
Na 1:13 N I will break their yoke from your neck 6964
2:11 Where n is the lions' den, NIH
Hab 2:16 N it is your turn! 1685
Hag 1: 5 N this is what the LORD Almighty says: 6964
2: 3 How does it look to you n? 6964
2: 4 But n be strong, O Zerubbabel,' 6964
2:15 " 'N give careful thought to this 6964
2:19 Until n, the vine and the fig tree, NIH
Zec 1: 5 Where are your forefathers n? NIH
3: 3 N Joshua was dressed in filthy clothes 2256
8: 9 "You who n hear these words spoken 465+928+2021+2021+3427
8:11 But n I will not deal with the remnant 6964
8:15 "so n I have determined to do good again to Jerusalem 465+928+2021+2021+3427
9: 8 for n I am keeping watch. 6964
9:12 n I announce that I will restore twice 2021+3427
Mal 1: 9 "N implore God to be gracious to us. 6964
2: 1 n this admonition is for you, O priests. 6964
3:15 But n we call the arrogant blessed. 6964
Mt 3:15 Jesus replied, "Let it be so n; *785*
5: 1 N when he saw the crowds, *1254*
11:12 From the days of John the Baptist until n, *785*
12:41 and n one greater than Jonah is here. *2627*
12:42 and n one greater than Solomon is here. *2627*
14: 3 N Herod had arrested John and bound him *1142*
19:16 N a man came up to Jesus and asked, *2779*
20:17 N as Jesus was going up to Jerusalem, *2779*
22:25 N there were seven brothers among us. *1254*
22:28 N then, at the resurrection, *4036*
24:21 from the beginning of the world until n— *3814*
24:32 "N learn this lesson from the fig tree: *1254*
26:29 not drink of this fruit of the vine from n on *785*
26:48 N the betrayer had arranged a signal *1254*
26:65 Look, n you have heard the blasphemy. *3814*
26:69 N Peter was sitting out in the courtyard, *1254*
27:15 N it was the governor's custom at the Feast *1254*
27:42 Let him come down n from the cross, *3814*
27:43 Let God rescue him n if he wants him, *3814*
27:49 The rest said, "N leave him alone. *NIG*
28: 7 N I have told you." *2627*
Mk 2: 6 N some teachers of the law were sitting *1254*
2:18 N John's disciples and the Pharisees *2779*
6:25 "I want you to give me right n the head *1994*
12:20 N there were seven brothers. *NIG*
12:26 N about the dead rising— *1254*
13:19 until n—and never to be equaled again. *3814*
13:28 "N learn this lesson from the fig tree: *1254*
14: 1 N the Passover and the Feast *1254*
14:44 N the betrayer had arranged a signal *1254*
15: 6 N it was the custom at the Feast to release *1254*
15:32 come down n from the cross, *3814*
15:36 "N leave him alone. *NIG*
Lk 1:20 And n you will be silent and not able *2627*
1:48 From n on all generations will call me blessed, *3814*
2:25 N there was a man in Jerusalem *2779*
2:29 you n dismiss your servant in peace. *3814*
3:23 N Jesus himself was about thirty years old *2779*
4:38 N Simon's mother-in-law was suffering *1254*
5:10 from n on you will catch men." *3814+3836*
6:21 Blessed are you who hunger n, *3814*
6:21 Blessed are you who weep n, *3814*
6:25 Woe to you who are well fed n, *3814*
6:25 Woe to you who laugh n, *3814*
7:36 N one of the Pharisees invited Jesus *1254*
7:42 N which of them will love him more?" *4036*
8:19 N Jesus' mother and brothers came *1254*
8:40 N when Jesus returned, *1254*
9: 7 N Herod the tetrarch heard about all *1254*
11:19 N if I drive out demons by Beelzebub, *1254*
11:31 and n one greater than Solomon is here. *2627*
11:32 and n one greater than Jonah is here. *2627*
11:39 Then the Lord said to him, "N then, *3814*
12:52 From n on there will be five *3814+3836*
13: 1 N there were some present at *1254*
13: 7 three years n I've been coming to look *608+4005*
14:17 'Come, for everything is n ready.' *2453*

Lk 15: 1 **N** the tax collectors and "sinners" *1254*
16: 3 'What shall I do **n**? *NIG*
16:25 but **n** he is comforted here and you are *3814*
17: 7 'Come along **n** and sit down to eat'? *2311*
17:11 **N** on his way to Jerusalem, *1181+2779*
19: 8 Here and *n I* **give** half of my possessions *AIT*
19:42 but **n** it is hidden from your eyes. *3814*
20:29 **N** there were seven brothers. *4036*
20:33 **N then,** at the resurrection whose wife will she be, *4036*
22: 1 **N** the Feast of Unleavened Bread, *1254*
22:36 "But **n** if you have a purse, take it, *3814*
22:69 But from **n on,** *3814+3836*
23:44 It was **n** about the sixth hour, *2453*
23:50 **N** there was a man named Joseph, *2779*
24:13 **N** that same day two of them were going to *2779*
Jn 1:19 **N** this was John's testimony when the Jews *2779*
1:24 **N** some Pharisees who had been sent *2779*
2: 8 "**N** draw some out and take it to the master *3814*
2:10 but you have saved the best till **n**." *785*
2:23 **N** while he was in Jerusalem at *1254*
3: 1 **N** there was a man of the Pharisees *1254*
3:23 **N** John also was baptizing at Aenon *1254*
3:29 That joy is mine, and *it is n* **complete.** *AIT*
4: 4 **N** he had to go through Samaria. *1254*
4:18 the man you **n** have is not your husband. *3814*
4:23 Yet a time is coming and has **n** come when *3814*
4:36 **Even n** the reaper draws his wages, *2453*
4:36 even **n** he harvests the crop for eternal life, *NIG*
4:42 **n** we have heard for ourselves, *1142*
4:44 (**N** Jesus himself had pointed out that *1142*
5: 2 **N** there is in Jerusalem near the Sheep Gate *1254*
5:25 and has **n** come when the dead will hear *3814*
6:17 **By n** it was dark, *2453*
6:34 they said, "**from n on** give us this bread." *4121*
6:42 can he **n** say, 'I came down from heaven'?" *3814*
7:11 **N** at the Feast the Jews were watching *4036*
7:23 **N** if a child can be circumcised on *NIG*
8: 5 **N** what do you say?" *4036*
8:11 "Go **n** and leave your life of sin." *608+3814+3836*
8:35 **N** a slave has no permanent place in *1254*
8:42 for I came from God and *n am* **here.** *AIT*
8:52 At this the Jews exclaimed, "**N** we know *3814*
9:14 **N** the day on which Jesus had made *1254*
9:15 "and I washed, and *n I* **see.**" *AIT*
9:19 How is it that **n** he can see? *785*
9:21 But how he can see **n,** *3814*
9:25 I was blind but **n** I see!" *785*
9:30 The man answered, "**N** that is remarkable! *1142*
9:37 Jesus said, "You have **n** seen him; *2779*
9:41 but **n** that you claim you can see, *3814*
11: 1 **N** a man named Lazarus was sick. *1254*
11: 2 whose brother Lazarus **n** lay sick, *NIG*
11:22 But I know that even **n** *3814*
11:30 **N** Jesus had not yet entered the village, *1254*
12:17 **N** the crowd that was with him *4036*
12:20 **N** there were some Greeks *1254*
12:27 "**N** my heart is troubled, *3814*
12:31 **N** is the time for judgment on this world; *3814*
12:31 **n** the prince of this world will *3814*
13: 1 he **n** showed them the full extent *NIG*
13: 7 "You do not realize **n** what I am doing, *785*
13:14 **N** that I, your Lord and Teacher, *4036*
13:17 **N** that you know these things, *NIG*
13:19 "I am telling you **n** before it happens, *608+785*
13:31 "**N** is the Son of Man glorified *3814*
13:33 and just as I told the Jews, so I tell you **n**: *785*
13:36 "Where I am going, you cannot follow **n,** *3814*
13:37 "Lord, why can't I follow you **n**? *785*
14: 7 From **n on,** you do know him *785*
14:29 I have told you **n** before it happens, *3814*
14:31 "**Come n**; let us leave. *1586*
15: 9 **N** remain in my love. *NIG*
15:22 **N,** however, they have no excuse *3814*
15:24 But **n** they have seen these miracles, *3814*
16: 5 "**N** I am going to him who sent me, *3814*
16:11 prince of this world *n stands* **condemned.** *AIT*
16:12 more than you can **n** bear. *785*
16:22 So with you: **N** is your time of grief, *3814*
16:24 Until **n** you have not asked for anything *785*
16:28 **n** I am leaving the world and going back to *4099*
16:29 "**N** you are speaking clearly and *3814*
16:30 **N** we can see that you know all things and *3814*
17: 3 **N** this is eternal life: *1254*
17: 5 And **n,** Father, glorify me in your presence *3814*
17: 7 **N** they know that everything you have given me comes from you. *3814*
17:13 "I am coming to you **n,** *3814*
18: 2 **N** Judas, who betrayed him, *1254*
18:28 **By n** it was early morning, *1254*
18:36 But **n** my kingdom is from another place." *3814*
18:40 **N** Barabbas had taken part in a rebellion. *1254*
19:28 Later, knowing that all was **n** completed, *2453*
19:31 **N** it was the day of Preparation, *4036*
19:38 **N** Joseph was a disciple of Jesus, *NIG*
20:24 **N** Thomas (called Didymus), *1254*
21:14 This was **n** the third time Jesus appeared *2453*
Ac 2: 5 **N** there were staying in Jerusalem *1254*
2:33 and has poured out what you **n** see *NIG*
3: 2 **N** a man crippled from birth *2779*
3:17 "**N,** brothers, I know that you acted *3814*
4:29 **N,** Lord, consider their threats *3814*
5: 1 **N** a man named Ananias, *1254*
6: 8 **N** Stephen, a man full of God's grace *1254*
7: 4 God sent him to this land where you are **n** *3814*
7:34 **N** come, I will send you back to Egypt.' *3814*
7:52 **n** you have betrayed and murdered him— *3814*
Ac 8: 9 **N** for some time a man named Simon *1254*
8:26 **N** an angel of the Lord said to Philip, *1254*
9: 6 "**N** get up and go into the city, *247*
10: 5 **N** send men to Joppa to bring back *3814*
10:33 **N** we are all here in the presence of God *3814*
10:34 "*I n* **realize** how true it is that God does *AIT*
11:19 **N** those who had been scattered by *4036*
12:11 "**N** I know without a doubt that *3814*
12:20 they **n** joined together and sought *NIG*
13:11 **N** the hand of the Lord is against you. *3814*
13:31 They are **n** his witnesses to our people. *3814*
13:46 we **n** turn to the Gentiles. *2627*
14:26 to the grace of God for the work they had **n** *NIG*
15:10 **N** then, why do you try to test God *3814*
16:36 **N** you can leave. *3814*
16:37 And **n** do they want to get rid of us quietly? *3814*
17: 6 over the world have **n** come here, *2779*
17:11 **N** the Bereans were of more noble character *1254*
17:23 **N** what you worship as something unknown *4036*
17:30 but **n** he commands all people everywhere to repent. *3814+3836*
18: 6 From **n on** I will go to the Gentiles." *3814*
19:18 Many of those who believed **n** came *NIG*
20:22 "And **n,** compelled by the Spirit, *3814*
20:25 "**N** I know that none of you *3814*
20:32 "**N** I commit you to God and to the word of his grace, *3814+3836*
22: 1 listen **n** to my defense." *3815*
22:16 And **n** what are you waiting for? *3814*
23:15 **N** then, you and the Sanhedrin petition *3814*
23:21 They are ready **n,** *3814*
24:13 the charges they are **n** making against me. *3815*
24:25 "That's enough **for n!** *2400+3814+3836*
25:10 "I am **n** standing before Caesar's court, *NIG*
26: 6 And **n** it is because of my hope *3814*
26:16 '**N** get up and stand on your feet. *247*
27: 9 because **by n** it was after the Fast. *2453*
27:22 But **n** I urge you to keep up your courage, *3814+3836*
27:34 **N** I urge you to take some food. *1475*
Ro 1:10 that **n at last** by God's will the way may be opened *2453+4537*
1:13 been prevented from doing so until **n**) *1306*
2: 2 **N** we know that God's judgment *1254*
2:15 and their thoughts **n** accusing, *NIG*
2:15 **n** even defending them.) *NIG*
2:17 **N** you, if you call yourself a Jew; *1254*
3:19 **N** we know that whatever the law says, *1254*
3:21 But **n** a righteousness from God, *3815*
4: 4 **N** when a man works, *1254*
5: 2 by faith into this grace in which *we n* **stand.** *AIT*
5: 9 Since we have **n** been justified *3814*
5:11 whom we have **n** received reconciliation. *3814*
6: 8 **N** if we died with Christ, *1254*
6:19 so **n** offer them in slavery *3814*
6:21 from the things you are **n** ashamed of? *3814*
6:22 But **n** that you have been set free from sin *3815*
7: 6 But **n,** by dying to what once bound us, *3815*
7:20 **N** if I do what I do not want to do, *1254*
8: 1 there is **n** no condemnation for those *3814*
8:17 **N** if we are children, then we are heirs— *1254*
11:17 the others and **n** share in the nourishing sap *NIG*
11:30 to God have **n** received mercy as a result *3814*
11:31 so they too have **n** become disobedient *3814*
11:31 in order that they too may **n** receive mercy *3814*
13:11 because our salvation is nearer **n** than *3814*
15:23 But **n** that there is no more place for me *3815*
15:25 **N,** however, I am on my way to Jerusalem *3815*
16:25 **N** to him who is able to establish you *1254*
16:26 but **n** revealed and made known through *3814*
1Co 4: 2 **N** it is required that those who have been *3370*
4: 6 **N,** brothers, I have applied these things *1254*
5:11 But **n** I am writing you that you must *3814*
7: 1 **N** for the matters you wrote about: *1254*
7: 8 **N** to the unmarried and the widows I say: *1254*
7:25 **N** about virgins: I have no command from *1254*
7:29 **n on** those who have wives should live as if they had none; *3370+3836*
8: 1 **N** about food sacrificed to idols: *1254*
10: 6 **N** these things occurred as examples *1254*
11: 3 **N** I want you to realize that the head *1254*
12: 1 **N** about spiritual gifts, brothers, *1254*
12: 7 **N** to each one the manifestation of *1254*
12:14 **N** the body is not made up of one part but *2779*
12:27 **N** you are the body of Christ, *1254*
12:31 **n** I will show you the most excellent way. *2285*
13:12 **N** we see but a poor reflection as in *785*
13:12 **N** I know in part; *785*
13:13 **n** these three remain: faith, hope and love. *3815*
14: 6 **N,** brothers, if I come to you and speak *3814*
15: 1 **N,** brothers, I want to remind you of *1254*
15:27 **N** when it says that "everything" has been *1254*
15:29 **N if** there is no resurrection, *2075*
16: 1 **N** about the collection for God's people: *1254*
16: 7 to see you **n** and make only a passing visit; *785*
16:12 **N** about our brother Apollos: *1254*
16:12 He was quite unwilling to go **n,** *3814*
2Co 1:12 **N** this is our boast: *1142*
1:21 **N** it is God who makes both us *1254*
2: 7 **N** instead, you ought to forgive *6063*
2:12 **N** when I went to Troas to preach *1254*
3: 7 **N** if the ministry that brought death, *1254*
3:10 For what was glorious *has* no **glory** *n* *AIT*
3:17 **N** the Lord is the Spirit, *1254*
5: 1 **N** we know that if the earthly tent we live *1142*
5: 5 **N** it is God who has made us *1254*
5:16 So from **n on** we regard no one from *3814+3836*
2Co 6: 2 I tell you, **n** is the time of God's favor, *3814*
6: 2 **n** is the day of salvation. *3814*
7: 9 yet **n** I am happy, *3814*
8: 1 **And n,** brothers, we want you to know *1254*
8:11 **N** finish the work, *3815*
8:22 and **n** even more so because *3815*
9:10 **N** he who supplies seed to the sower *1254*
12:14 **N** I am ready to visit you for the third time, *2627*
13: 2 I **n** repeat it while absent: *3814*
13: 7 **N** we pray to God that you will *1254*
Gal 1: 9 As we have already said, so **n** I say again: *785*
1:10 Am I **n** trying to win the approval of men, *785*
1:23 "The man who formerly persecuted us is **n** *3814*
3: 3 are you **n** trying to attain your goal *3814*
3:25 **N that** faith has come, *1254*
4: 9 But **n** that you know God— *3814*
4:16 Have I **n** become your enemy *NIG*
4:20 be with you **n** and change my tone, *785*
4:25 **N** Hagar stands for Mount Sinai in Arabia *1254*
4:28 **N** you, brothers, like Isaac, *1254*
4:29 It is the same **n.** *3814*
Eph 2: 2 the spirit who is **n** at work in those who *3814*
2:13 But **n** in Christ Jesus you who once were far away have been brought near *3815*
3: 5 to men in other generations as it has **n** *3814*
3:10 His intent was that **n,** through the church, *3814*
3:20 **N** to him who is able to do immeasurably *1254*
5: 8 but **n** you are light in the Lord. *3814*
5:24 **N** as the church submits to Christ, *247*
Php 1: 5 in the gospel from the first day until **n,** *3814*
1:12 **N** I want you to know, brothers, *1254*
1:20 so that **n** as always Christ will be exalted *3814*
1:30 and **n** hear that I still have. *3814*
2:12 but **n** much more in my absence— *3814*
3: 7 to my profit *I n* **consider** loss for the sake *AIT*
3:18 before and **n** say again even with tears, *3814*
4:18 I am amply supplied, **n** that I have received *NIG*
Col 1:22 But **n** he has reconciled you *3815*
1:24 **N** I rejoice in what was suffered for you, *3814*
1:26 but is **n** disclosed to the saints. *3814*
3: 3 your life *is n* **hidden** with Christ in God. *AIT*
3: 8 But **n** you must rid yourselves *3815*
1Th 3: 6 But Timothy has **just n** come to us *785*
3: 8 For **n** we really live, *3814*
3:11 **N** may our God and Father himself *1254*
4: 1 **N** we ask you and urge you in *NIG*
4: 9 **N** about brotherly love we do not need *1254*
5: 1 **N,** brothers, about times and dates we do *1254*
5:12 **N** we ask you, brothers, *1254*
2Th 2: 6 And **n** you know what is holding him back, *3814*
2: 7 the one who **n** holds it back will continue *785*
3:16 **N** may the Lord of peace himself give you *1254*
1Ti 1:17 **N** to the King eternal, immortal, invisible, *1254*
3: 2 **N** the overseer must be above reproach, *4036*
2Ti 1: 5 I am persuaded, **n** lives in you also. *NIG*
1:10 but it has **n** been revealed through *3814*
4: 8 **N** there is in store for me the crown *3370*
Phm 1: 9 and **n** also a prisoner of Christ Jesus— *3815*
1:11 but **n** he has become useful both to you and *3815*
Heb 2: 9 **n** crowned with glory and honor *NIG*
4: 3 **N** we who have believed enter that rest, *1142*
7: 5 **N** the law requires the descendants *2779*
7:23 **N** there have been many of those priests, *3525*
9: 1 **N** the first covenant had regulations *4036*
9: 5 we cannot discuss these things in detail **n.** *3814*
9:15 *n that he has* **died** as a ransom *AIT*
9:24 **n** to appear for us in God's presence. *3814*
9:26 But **n** he has appeared once for all at *3815*
11: 1 **N** faith is being sure of what we hope for *1254*
12:26 but **n** he has promised, *3814*
Jas 4:13 **N** listen, you who say, *3814*
5: 1 **N** listen, you rich people, *3814*
1Pe 1: 6 though **n** for a little while you may have *785*
1: 8 and even though you do not see him **n,** *785*
1:12 when they spoke of the things that have **n** *3814*
1:22 *N that you have* **purified** yourselves *AIT*
2: 3 **n that** you have tasted that *1623*
2: 7 **N** to you who believe, *4036*
2:10 but **n** you are the people of God; *3814*
2:10 but **n** you have received mercy. *3814*
2:25 but **n** you have returned to the Shepherd *3814*
3:21 and this water symbolizes baptism that **n** *3814*
4: 6 even to those who are **n** dead, *NIG*
2Pe 1:12 firmly established in the truth *you* **n have.** *4205*
3: 1 this is **n** my second letter to you. *2453*
3:18 To him be glory both **n** and forever! *3814*
1Jn 2:18 even **n** many antichrists have come. *3814*
2:28 **And n,** dear children, continue in him, *3814*
3: 2 Dear friends, **n** we are children of God, *3814*
4: 3 and even **n** is already in the world. *3814*
2Jn 1: 5 **And n,** dear lady, I am not writing you *3814*
Jude 1:25 before all ages, **n** and forevermore! *3814*
Rev 1:19 what **is n** and what will take place later. *1639*
2:19 and that you are **n** doing more than you did *2274*
2:24 **N** I say to the rest of you in Thyatira, *1254*
11: 7 **N** when they have finished their testimony, *2779*
12:10 "**N** have come the salvation and the power *785*
14:13 the dead who die in the Lord from **n on.**" *785*
17: 8 beast, which you saw, once was, *n* **is** not, *AIT*
17: 8 because he once was, *n* **is** not, *AIT*
17:11 The beast who once was, and *n* **is** not, *AIT*
21: 3 "**N** the dwelling of God is with men, *2627*

NOWHERE (6)

Job 42:15 **N** in all the land were there found women 4202
Pr 19: 7 they are **n** to be found. 4202

Isa 59:15 Truth is **n to be found,** 6372
Jer 25:35 The shepherds *will* **have n** to flee, 6+4946
Mt 27:24 Pilate saw that *he* **was getting n,** *4029+6067*
Jn 12:19 "See, *this is* **getting** us **n.** *4024+4029+6067*

NOWHERE (Anglicized) See also NO PLACE

NUBIANS (1)

Da 11:43 with the Libyans and **N** in submission. 3934

NUGGETS (2)

Job 22:24 and assign your **n** to the dust, 1309
28: 6 and its dust contains **n of gold.** 2298

NULLIFIED (1) [ANNULLED, NULLIFY]

Nu 30:12 Her husband *has* **n** them, 7296

NULLIFIES (3) [NULLIFY]

Nu 30: 8 *he* **n** the vow that obligates her or 7296
30:12 But if her husband **n** them when 7296+7296
30:15 *he* **n** them some time after he hears 7296+7296

NULLIFY (6) [NULLIFIED, NULLIFIES]

Nu 30:13 Her husband may confirm or **n** any vow she makes 7296
Mt 15: 6 Thus *you* **n** the word of God for the sake *218*
Mk 7:13 Thus *you* **n** the word of God *218*
Ro 3: 3 of faith **n** God's faithfulness? *2934*
3:31 *Do we,* then, **n** the law by this faith? *2934*
1Co 1:28 to **n** the things that are, *2934*

NUMBER (164) [NUMBERED, NUMBERING, NUMBERLESS, NUMBERS, NUMEROUS]

Ge 1:22 and **increase in n** and fill the water in 8049
1:28 "Be fruitful and **increase in n;** 8049
6: 1 When men began to **increase in n** on 8045
8:17 and be fruitful and **increase in n** upon it." 8049
9: 1 "Be fruitful and **increase in n** and fill 8049
9: 7 As for you, be fruitful and **increase in n;** 8049
18:28 **n** of the righteous is five **less than** 2893
26:24 I will bless you and *will* **increase the n** 8049
34:30 We are few in **n,** 5031
35:11 be fruitful and **increase in n.** 8049
42:16 Send one of **your** *n* to get your brother; AIT
47:12 according to the **n** *of* their children. 7023
47:27 were fruitful and **increased** greatly **in n.** 8049
Ex 5: 8 to make the same **n** *of* bricks as before; 5504
5:19 *to* **reduce the n** *of* bricks required of you 1757
12: 4 into account the **n** *of* people there are. 4831
30:12 on them when *you* **n** them. 7212
Lev 25:15 the basis of the **n** *of* years since the Jubilee. 5031
25:15 of the **n** *of* years left for harvesting crops. 5031
25:16 really selling you is the **n** *of* crops. 5031
25:50 on the rate paid to a hired man for that **n** 5031
26:22 **make** you *so* **few in n** that your roads 5070
27:18 according to the **n** *of* years that remain 7023
Nu 1: 3 and Aaron *are to* **n** by their divisions all 7212
1:21 The **n** from the tribe of Reuben was 46,500. 7212
1:23 The **n** from the tribe of Simeon was 59,300. 7212
1:25 The **n** from the tribe of Gad was 45,650. 7212
1:27 The **n** from the tribe of Judah was 74,600. 7212
1:29 **n** from the tribe of Issachar was 54,400. 7212
1:31 **n** from the tribe of Zebulun was 57,400. 7212
1:33 **n** from the tribe of Ephraim was 40,500. 7212
1:35 **n** from the tribe of Manasseh was 32,200. 7212
1:37 **n** from the tribe of Benjamin was 35,400. 7212
1:39 The **n** from the tribe of Dan was 62,700. 7212
1:41 The **n** from the tribe of Asher was 41,500. 7212
1:43 **n** from the tribe of Naphtali was 53,400. 7212
1:46 The total **n** was 603,550. 7212
2: 9 according to their divisions, **n** 186,400. NIH
2:16 according to their divisions, **n** 151,450. NIH
2:24 according to their divisions, **n** 108,100. NIH
2:31 to the camp of Dan **n** 157,600. NIH
2:32 by their divisions, **n** 603,550. 7212
3:22 The **n** *of* all the males a month old 5031
3:28 The **n** *of* all the males a month old 5031
3:34 The **n** *of* all the males a month old 5031
3:39 The total **n** *of* Levites counted at 7212
3:43 The total **n** *of* firstborn males a month old 7212
3:46 the 273 firstborn Israelites who **exceed** the **n** 6369
3:49 from those *who* **exceeded** the **n** redeemed 6369
7:87 The **total** *n of* animals for the burnt offering AIT
7:88 The **total** *n of* animals for the sacrifice of AIT
23:10 of Jacob or **n** the fourth part of Israel? 5031
26:51 total **n** *of* the men of Israel was 601,730. 7212
26:53 as an inheritance based on the **n** *of* names. 5031
26:54 to receive its inheritance according to the **n** 7023
29:18 according to the **n** specified. 5031
29:21 according to the **n** specified. 5031
29:24 according to the **n** specified. 5031
29:27 according to the **n** specified. 5031
29:30 according to the **n** specified. 5031
29:33 according to the **n** specified. 5031
29:37 according to the **n** specified. 5031
Dt 25: 2 with the **n** of lashes his crime deserves, 5031
28:62 will be left but **few in n,** 5071+5493
28:63 to make you prosper and **increase in n,** 8049
32: 8 the peoples according to the **n** *of* the sons 5031

Jos 4: 5 to the **n** *of* the tribes of the Israelites, 5031
4: 8 to the **n** *of* the tribes of the Israelites, as 5031
11: 4 with all their troops and a large **n** of horses 8041
1Sa 6: 4 according to the **n** *of* the Philistine rulers, 5031
6:18 And the **n** *of* the gold rats was according to 5031
6:18 to the **n** of Philistine towns belonging to NIH
9:22 who were invited—about thirty in **n.** NIH
18:27 and **presented the full n** to the king so 4848
23:13 David and his men, about six hundred in **n,** NIH
2Sa 12: 2 The rich man had a very **large n** *of* sheep 2221
24: 9 Joab reported the **n** *of* the fighting men 5031+5152
1Ki 3: 8 a great people, too numerous to count or **n.** 4948
1Ch 7:40 The **n** *of* men ready for battle, 5031
16:19 When they were but few in **n,** few indeed, 5031
21: 5 Joab reported the **n** *of* the fighting men 5031+5152
22:16 and iron—craftsmen beyond **n.** 5031
23: 3 the total **n** of men was thirty-eight thousand. 5031
23:31 before the LORD regularly in the *proper* **n** 5031
24: 4 A **larger n** of leaders were found 8041
27:23 not take the **n** *of* the men twenty years old 5031
27:24 and the **n** was not entered in the book of 5031
2Ch 14:13 a great **n** of Cushites fell that they could NIH
26:12 The total **n** *of* family leaders over 5031
29:32 The **n** *of* burnt offerings 5031
30:24 A **great n** of priests consecrated 4200+8044
Ezr 3: 4 the required **n** of burnt offerings prescribed 5031
8:34 Everything was accounted for by **n** 5031
Est 9:11 The **n** *of* those slain in the citadel 5031
Job 1: 3 and had a large **n** of servants. 8041
14: 5 you have decreed the **n** *of* his months 5031
36:26 The **n** *of* his years is past finding out. 5031
Ps 39: 4 my life's end and the **n** *of* my days; 4500
40:12 For troubles without **n** surround me; 5031
90:12 Teach us to **n** our days aright, 4948
104:25 teeming with creatures beyond **n**— 5031
105:12 When they were but few in **n,** few indeed, 5031
105:34 grasshoppers without **n;** 5031
147: 4 the **n** of the stars and calls them each 5031
SS 6: 8 and virgins beyond **n;** 5031
Jer 2:32 Yet my people have forgotten me, days without **n.** 5031
23: 3 they will be fruitful and **increase in n.** 8049
29: 6 **Increase in n** there; do not decrease. 8049
52:23 the **total** *n* of pomegranates above AIT
52:28 the **n** of the people Nebuchadnezzar carried NIH
Eze 4: 4 to bear their sin for the **n** *of* days you lie 5031
4: 5 the same **n** *of* days as the years of their sin. 5031
36:10 and *I will* **multiply the n** *of* people 8049
36:11 *I will* **increase the n** *of* men and animals 8049
47: 7 a great **n** of trees on each side of the river. 8041
Joel 1: 6 powerful and without **n;** 5031
2:11 his forces are **beyond n,** 4394+8041
Na 3: 3 piles of dead, bodies without **n,** 7897
3:16 *You have* **increased** *the* **n** *of* your merchants 8049
Zec 2: 4 a city without walls because of the **great n** 8044
Mt 14:21 **n** of those who ate was about five thousand, *NIG*
15:38 The **n** of those who ate was four thousand, *NIG*
Mk 5:13 The herd, about two thousand in **n,** *NIG*
6:44 The **n** of the men who had eaten was five thousand. *NIG*
Lk 5: 6 a large **n** of fish that their nets began *4436*
6:17 and a great **n** of people from all over Judea, *4436*
23:27 A large **n** of people followed him, *4436*
Jn 5: 3 a **great n** of disabled people used to lie— *4436*
7:50 and who was one of **their own n,** *899*
21: 6 the net in because of the **large n** of fish. *4436*
Ac 1:17 of our **n** and shared in this ministry." *2935*
2:41 about three thousand were added to their **n** *NIG*
2:47 Lord added **to their n** daily those who were being saved. *899+2093+3836*
4: 4 the **n** of men grew to about five thousand. *750*
5:14 in the Lord and were added to their **n.** *4436*
6: 1 when the **n** of disciples was increasing, *NIG*
6: 7 The **n** of disciples in Jerusalem increased *750*
6: 7 and a large **n** of priests became obedient to *4063*
7:17 **n** of our people in Egypt greatly increased. *NIG*
11:21 and a great **n** of people believed and turned *750*
11:24 and a **great n** *of* people were brought to *2653*
14: 1 a great **n** of Jews and Gentiles believed. *4436*
14:21 in that city and won a **large n** *of* disciples. *2653*
17: 4 as did a large **n** of God-fearing Greeks and *4436*
17:12 as did also a **n** of prominent Greek women *NIG*
17:34 a woman named Damaris, and a **n** of others. *NIG*
19:19 A **n** who had practiced sorcery brought *2653*
20:30 from your own **n** men will arise and distort *NIG*
21:10 After we had been there a **n** of days, *4498*
24:10 "I know that for a **n** of years you have been *4498*
Ro 9:27 the **n** of the Israelites be like the sand by *750*
11:25 the **full n** of the Gentiles has come in. *4445*
1Co 11:30 and a **n** *of* you have fallen asleep. *2653*
2Ti 4: 3 they will gather around them a great **n** *NIG*
Rev 6:11 until the **n** of their fellow servants *NIG*
7: 4 I heard the **n** of those who were sealed: *750*
9:16 The **n** of the mounted troops was two hundred million. *750*
9:16 I heard their **n.** *750*
13:17 the name of the beast or the **n** of his name. *750*
13:18 let him calculate the **n** of the beast, *750*
13:18 the number of the beast, for it is man's **n.** *750*
13:18 His **n** is 666. *750*
15: 2 and his image and over the **n** of his name. *750*
20: 8 **In n** they are like the sand on the seashore. *750+3836+4005*

NUMBERED (34) [NUMBER]

Ge 46:26 **n** sixty-six persons. 3972
Ex 1: 5 The descendants of Jacob **n** seventy in all; 2118
Nu 4:48 **n** 8,580. 7212
25: 9 but those who died in the plague **n** 24,000. 2118
26: 7 Reuben; those **n** were 43,730. 7212
26:18 Gad; those **n** were 40,500. 7212
26:22 Judah; those **n** were 76,500. 7212
26:25 Issachar; those **n** were 64,300. 7212
26:27 Zebulun; those **n** were 60,500. 7212
26:34 Manasseh; those **n** were 52,700. 7212
26:37 Ephraim; those **n** were 32,500. 7212
26:41 Benjamin; those **n** were 45,600. 7212
26:43 Shuhamite clans; and those **n** were 64,400. 7212
26:47 Asher; those **n** were 53,400. 7212
26:50 Naphtali; those **n** were 45,400. 7212
26:62 Levites a month old or more **n** 23,000. 7212
1Sa 11: 8 the men of Israel **n** three hundred thousand 2118
13:15 They **n** about six hundred. NIH
1Ki 4:32 and his songs **n** a thousand and five. 2118
1Ch 7: 2 in their genealogy **n** 22,600. NIH
9: 6 The people from Judah **n** 690. NIH
9: 9 as listed in their genealogy, **n** 956. NIH
9:13 who were heads of families, **n** 1,760. NIH
9:22 to be gatekeepers at the thresholds **n** 212. NIH
25: 7 skilled in music for the LORD—they **n** 288. 5031
Ezr 2:64 The whole company **n** 42,360, 285+3869
Ne 7:66 The whole company **n** 42,360, 285+3869
Job 25: 3 Can his forces be **n?** 5031
Isa 53:12 and **was n** with the transgressors. 4948
La 4:18 Our end was near, our days *were* **n,** 4848
Da 5:26 God *has* **n** the days of your reign 10431
Mt 10:30 even the very hairs of your head are all **n.** *749*
Lk 12: 7 the very hairs of your head *are* all **n.** *749*
22:37 'And *he was* **n** with the transgressors'; *3357*

NUMBERING (4) [NUMBER]

1Ch 21: 6 not include Levi and Benjamin *in the* **n,** 7212
27:24 Wrath came on Israel on account of this **n,** NIH
Ac 1:15 the believers (a group **n about** a hundred and twenty) *6059*
Rev 5:11 angels, **n** thousands upon thousands, *750+1639*

NUMBERLESS (1) [NUMBER]

Isa 48:19 your children like its **n grains;** 5054

NUMBERS (43) [NUMBER]

Ge 17: 2 and you and *will* greatly **increase** your **n."** 8049
17:20 and *will* greatly **increase** his **n.** 8049
28: 3 and make you fruitful and **increase** your **n** 8049
48: 4 and *will* **increase** your **n.** 8049
Ex 10:14 in every area of the country *in* **great n.** 3878+4394
Lev 26: 9 and make you fruitful and **increase** your **n,** 8049
Nu 2: 4 His division **n** 74,600. 7212
2: 6 His division **n** 54,400. 7212
2: 8 His division **n** 57,400. 7212
2:11 His division **n** 46,500. 7212
2:13 His division **n** 59,300. 7212
2:15 His division **n** 45,650. 7212
2:19 His division **n** 40,500. 7212
2:21 His division **n** 32,200. 7212
2:23 His division **n** 35,400. 7212
2:26 His division **n** 62,700. 7212
2:28 His division **n** 41,500. 7212
2:30 His division **n** 53,400. 7212
Dt 1:10 The LORD your God *has* **increased** your **n** 8049
7:13 and bless you and **increase** your **n.** 8049
13:17 on you, and **increase** your **n,** 8049
17:16 not **acquire great n** *of* horses for himself 8049
1Ki 1:19 He has sacrificed **great n** of cattle, 8044
1:25 down and sacrificed **great n** of cattle, 8044
1Ch 12:23 These are the **n** *of* the men armed 5031
22: 4 Tyrians had brought **large n** of them 4200+8044
2Ch 15: 9 for **large n** had come over to him 4200+8044
16: 8 Libyans a mighty army with **great n** 2221+4394
26:11 to their **n** as mustered by Jeiel the secretary 5031
30: 5 It had not been celebrated **in large n** 4200+8044
32: 5 made **large n** of weapons and shields. 4200+8044
32:29 acquired **great n** of flocks and herds, 4200+8044
Ps 107:38 and *their* **n** greatly **increased,** 8049
107:39 Then *their* **n decreased,** 5070
Jer 3:16 *your* **n** *have* **increased greatly** 2256+7238+8049
30:19 *I will* **add to their n,** 8049
Eze 37:26 I will establish them and **increase** their **n,** 8049
47: 9 There will be large **n** *of* fish, 8041
Ac 9:31 *it* **grew in n,** living in the fear of the Lord. *4437*
11:26 the church and taught great **n of people.** *4063*
16: 5 in the faith and grew daily *in* **n.** *750*
19:26 and led astray **large n** *of* people here *2653*
28:23 and came in even **larger** *n* to the place *AIT*

NUMEROUS (45) [NUMBER]

Ge 16:10 that they will be too **n** to count." 8044
22:17 and **make** your descendants as **n** as 8049+8049
26: 4 *I will* **make** your descendants as **n** as 8049
Ex 1: 7 and *became* exceedingly **n,** 6793
1: 9 Israelites have become **much too n** for us. 2256+6786+8041
1:10 or *they will become even more* **n** and, 8049
1:20 and *became* even more **n.** 6793
5: 5 "Look, the people of the land are now **n,** 8041
23:29 and the wild animals too **n** for you. 8041
32:13 *'I will* **make** your descendants as **n** as 8049
Nu 22:15 more **n** and more distinguished than 8041
Dt 2:10 a people strong and **n,** 8041
2:21 They were a people strong and **n,** 8041

Dt 7: 7 you *were* more **n** than other peoples, 8045
9: 14 a nation stronger and more **n** than they." 8041
10: 22 the LORD your God has made you as **n** as 8044
26: 5 and became a great nation, powerful and **n.** 8041
28: 62 as **n** as the stars in the sky will be left 4200+8044
30: 5 more prosperous and **n** than your fathers. 8049
Jos 11: 4 as **n** as the sand on the seashore. 8044
17: 14 We are a **n** people and 8041
17: 15 "If you are so **n,**" Joshua answered, 8041
17: 17 "You are **n** and very powerful. 8041
1Sa 13: 5 soldiers as **n** as the sand on the seashore. 8044
2Sa 17: 11 as **n** as the sand on the seashore— 8044
1Ki 3: 8 a great people, too **n** to count or number. 8044
4: 20 of Judah and Israel were as **n** as the sand on 8041
1Ch 4: 27 so their entire clan *did* not *become* as **n** as 8049
5: 23 of the half-tribe of Manasseh *were* **n;** 8049
23: 17 but the sons of Rehabiah *were* very **n.** 8049
27: 23 the LORD had promised to **make** Israel as **n** 8049
2Ch 1: 9 over a people who are as **n** as the dust of 8041
Ne 5: 2 "We and our sons and daughters are **n;** 8041
9: 23 **made** their sons as **n** as the stars in the sky, 8049
Job 29: 18 my days as **n** as the grains of sand. 8049
Ps 38: 19 those who hate me without reason *are* **n.** 8045
105: 24 *he* **made** them too **n** for their foes, 6793
Jer 15: 8 I *will make* their widows more **n** than 6793
46: 23 *They are* more **n** than locusts, 8045
Eze 36: 11 and they will be fruitful and *become* **n.** 8049
36: 37 *I will* **make** their people as **n** as sheep, 8049
36: 38 as **n** as the flocks for offerings at Jerusalem NIH
Na 1: 12 "Although they have allies and are **n,** 8041
Zec 10: 8 *they will be* as **n** as before. 8049
Heb 11: 12 *as* **n** as the stars in the sky and as countless *4436*

NUN (30)

Ex 33: 11 but his young aide Joshua son of **N** did 5673
Nu 11: 28 Joshua son of **N,** 5673
13: 8 Hoshea son of **N;** 5673
13: 16 (Moses gave Hoshea son of **N** the name Joshua.) 5673
14: 6 Joshua son of **N** and Caleb son of 5673
14: 30 son of Jephunneh and Joshua son of **N.** 5673
14: 38 of **N** and Caleb son of Jephunneh survived. 5673
26: 65 son of Jephunneh and Joshua son of **N.** 5673
27: 18 "Take Joshua son of **N,** 5673
32: 12 the Kenizzite and Joshua son of **N** 5673
32: 28 to Eleazar the priest and Joshua son of **N** 5673
34: 17 Eleazar the priest and Joshua son of **N.** 5673
Dt 1: 38 But your assistant, Joshua son of **N,** 5673
31: 23 gave this command to Joshua son of **N:** 5673
32: 44 of **N** and spoke all the words of this song 5673
34: 9 of **N** was filled with the spirit of wisdom 5673
Jos 1: 1 the LORD said to Joshua son of **N,** 5673
2: 1 of **N** secretly sent two spies from Shittim. 5673
2: 23 to Joshua son of **N** and told him everything 5673
6: 6 of **N** called the priests and said to them, 5673
14: 1 of **N** and the heads of the tribal clans 5673
17: 4 Joshua son of **N,** and the leaders and said, 5673
19: 49 the Israelites gave Joshua son of **N** 5673
19: 51 Joshua son of **N** and the heads of 5673
21: 1 Joshua son of **N,** 5673
24: 29 After these things, Joshua son of **N,** 5673
Jdg 2: 8 Joshua son of **N,** the servant of the LORD, 5673
1Ki 16: 34 of the LORD spoken by Joshua son of **N.** 5673
1Ch 7: 27 **N** his son and Joshua his son. 5673
Ne 8: 17 the days of Joshua son of **N** until that day, 5673

NURSE (14) [NURSED, NURSING]

Ge 21: 7 to Abraham that Sarah *would* **n** children? 3567
24: 59 along with her **n** and Abraham's servant 4787
35: 8 Now Deborah, Rebekah's **n,** 4787
Ex 2: 7 the Hebrew women *to* **n** the baby for you?" 3567
2: 9 "Take this baby and **n** him for me, 3567
Nu 11: 12 as a **n** carries an infant, 587
2Sa 4: 4 His **n** picked him up and fled, 587
1Ki 3: 21 The next morning, I got up to **n** my son— 3567
2Ki 11: 2 She put him and his **n** in a bedroom 4787
11: 3 remained hidden with **his n** at the temple 2023S
2Ch 22: 11 about to be murdered and put him and his **n** 4787
Isa 66: 11 For *you will* **n** and be satisfied 3567
66: 12 *you will* **n** and be carried on her arm 3567
La 4: 3 jackals offer their breasts *to* **n** their young, 3567

NURSED (8) [NURSE]

Ex 2: 9 So the woman took the baby and **n** him. 3567
1Sa 1: 23 the woman stayed at home and **n** her son 3567
Job 3: 12 and breasts that *I might be* **n?** 3567
SS 8: 1 *who* was **n** *at* my mother's breasts! 3437
Isa 60: 16 and *be* **n** at royal breasts. 3567
Mk 6: 19 So Herodias **n a grudge against** John *1923*
Lk 11: 27 the mother who gave you birth and **n** you." *2558*
23: 29 and the breasts that never **n!'** *5555*

NURSING (6) [NURSE]

Ge 33: 13 the ewes and cows *that are* **n** *their* **young.** 6402
Isa 49: 23 and their queens your **n mothers.** 4787
Joel 2: 16 gather the children, *those* **n** *at* the breast. 3437
Mt 24: 19 for pregnant women and **n mothers!** *2558*
Mk 13: 17 for pregnant women and **n mothers!** *2558*
Lk 21: 23 for pregnant women and **n mothers!** *2558*

NURTURED (1) [WELL-NURTURED]

La 4: 5 Those **n** in purple now lie on ash heaps. 587

NUT (1) [NUTS]

SS 6: 11 I went down to the grove of **n trees** to look 100

NUTS (1) [NUT]

Ge 43: 11 *some* **pistachio n** and almonds. 1063

NYMPHA (1)

Col 4: 15 and to **N** and the church in her house. *3809*

O

O (978) [OH] See Index of Articles Etc.

OAK (14) [OAKS]

Ge 35: 4 Jacob buried them under the **o** at Shechem. 461
35: 8 and was buried under the **o** below Bethel. 473
Jos 24: 26 a large stone and set it up there under the **o** 464
Jdg 6: 11 the LORD came and sat down under the **o** 461
6: 19 and offered them to him under the **o.** 461
2Sa 18: 9 under the thick branches of a large **o,** 461
18: 10 "I just saw Absalom hanging in an **o tree.**" 461
18: 14 while Absalom was still alive in the **o tree.** 461
1Ki 13: 14 He found him sitting under an **o tree** 461
Isa 1: 30 You will be like an **o** with fading leaves, 461
6: 13 But as the terebinth and **o** leave stumps 473
44: 14 or perhaps took a cypress or **o.** 473
Eze 6: 13 and every leafy **o**— 461
Hos 4: 13 under **o,** poplar and terebinth, 473

OAKS (9) [OAK]

Ps 29: 9 The voice of the LORD twists the **o** 381
56: T To [the tune of] "A Dove on Distant **O.**" 381
Isa 1: 29 the **sacred o** in which you have delighted; 381
2: 13 tall and lofty, and all the **o** *of* Bashan, 473
57: 5 the **o** and under every spreading tree; 381
61: 3 They will be called **o** *of* righteousness, 381
Eze 27: 6 Of **o** from Bashan they made your oars; 473
Am 2: 9 as the cedars and strong as the **o.** 473
Zec 11: 2 Wail, **o** *of* Bashan; 473

OARS (4) [OARSMEN]

Isa 33: 21 No galley with **o** will ride them, 8868
Eze 27: 6 Of oaks from Bashan they made your **o;** 5415
27: 29 the **o** will abandon their ships; 5414
Mk 6: 48 He saw the disciples straining at the **o,** *1785*

OARSMEN (2) [OARS]

Eze 27: 8 Men of Sidon and Arvad were your **o;** 8763
27: 26 Your **o** take you out to the high seas. 8763

OATH (128) [OATHS]

Ge 14: 22 *I have* **raised** my hand to the LORD, God Most High, Creator of heaven and earth, **and** *have* **taken an o** 8123
21: 31 because the two men **swore an o** there. 8678
24: 7 who spoke to me and **promised** me **on o,** 8678
24: 8 you will be released from this **o** *of* mine. 8652
24: 9 of his master Abraham and **swore an o** 8678
24: 37 my master **made** me **swear an o,** 8678
24: 41 be released from my **o** even if they refuse 460
24: 41 you will be released from my **o.'** 460
25: 33 So *he* **swore an o** to him, 8678
26: 3 the **o** I swore to your father Abraham. 8652
26: 31 Early the next morning *the men* **swore an o** 8678
31: 53 So Jacob **took an o** in the name of the Fear 8678
50: 5 'My father **made** me **swear an o** 8678
50: 24 to the land *he* **promised on o** to Abraham, 8678
50: 25 Joseph **made** the sons of Israel **swear an o** 8678
Ex 13: 11 as *he* **promised on o** to you 8678
13: 19 **made** the sons of Israel **swear an o.** 8678+8678
22: 11 the taking of an **o** *before* the LORD that 8652
33: 1 up to the land *I* **promised on o** to Abraham, 8678
Lev 5: 4 " 'Or if a person thoughtlessly **takes an o** 8678
Nu 5: 19 priest *shall* **put** the woman **under o** 8678
5: 21 priest *is to* **put** the woman under this curse *of* the **o**— 8652+8678
11: 12 to the land *you* **promised on o** 8678
14: 16 into the land *he* **promised** them **on o;** 8678
14: 23 the land *I* **promised on o** 8678
30: 2 or **takes an o** to obligate himself 8652+8678
30: 10 or obligates herself by a pledge under **o** 8652
32: 10 that day and *he* **swore** *this* **o:** 8678
32: 11 the land *I* **promised on o** to Abraham, Isaac 8678
Dt 4: 31 **confirmed** to them **by o.** 8678
6: 18 the good land that the LORD **promised on o** 8678
6: 23 give us the land that *he* **promised on o** 8678
7: 8 and kept the **o** he swore to your forefathers 8652
8: 1 the land that the LORD **promised on o** 8678
13: 17 as *he* **promised on o** to your forefathers, 8678
19: 8 as *he* **promised on o** to your forefathers, 8678
26: 15 as *you* **promised on o** to our forefathers, 8678
28: 9 as *he* **promised** you **on o,** 8678
29: 12 with you this day and sealing with an **o,** 460
29: 14 I am making this covenant, with its **o,** 460
29: 19 a person hears the words of this **o,** 460
31: 20 land *I* **promised on o** to their forefathers, 8678
31: 21 into the land *I* **promised** them **on o.**" 8678
31: 23 into the land *I* **promised** them **on o,** 8678
34: 4 the land *I* **promised on o** to Abraham, 8678
Jos 2: 17 "This **o** you made us swear will not 8652
2: 20 be released from the **o** you made us swear." 8652
6: 22 in accordance with *your* **o** to her." 8678
6: 26 Joshua **pronounced** *this* **solemn o:** 8678
9: 15 the leaders of the assembly **ratified** it **by o.** 8678
9: 18 the leaders of the assembly *had* **sworn an o** 8678
9: 19 "We *have* **given** them *our* **o** by the LORD, 8678
9: 20 not fall on us for breaking the **o** we swore 8652
Jdg 21: 1 men of Israel *had* **taken an o** at Mizpah: 8678
21: 5 a solemn **o** that anyone who failed 8652
21: 7 since we *have* **taken an o** by the LORD not 8678
21: 18 since *we* Israelites *have* **taken** *this* **o:** 8678
1Sa 14: 24 **bound** the people **under an o,** 457
14: 26 because they feared the **o.** 8652
14: 27 **bound** the people **with the o,** 8678
14: 28 **bound** the army **under a strict o,** 8678+8678
19: 6 Saul listened to Jonathan and **took** *this* **o:** 8678
20: 3 But David **took an o** and said, 8678
20: 17 And Jonathan had David reaffirm his **o** out 8678
24: 22 So David **gave** *his* **o** to Saul. 8678
2Sa 3: 9 the LORD **promised** him **on o** 8678
3: 35 but David **took an o,** saying, 8678
19: 23 And the king **promised** him **on o.** 8678
21: 7 of the **o** *before* the LORD between David 8652
1Ki 1: 29 The king then **took an o:** 8678
2: 43 not keep your **o** *to* the LORD and obey 8652
8: 31 and is required to **take an o** and he comes 457
8: 31 an oath and he comes and **swears the o** 457
2Ki 11: 4 a covenant with them and **put** them **under o** 8678
25: 24 Gedaliah **took an o** to reassure them 8678
1Ch 16: 16 the **o** he **swore** to Isaac. 8652
2Ch 6: 22 and is required to **take an o** and he comes 457
6: 22 an oath and he comes and **swears the o** 457
15: 14 *They* **took an o** to the LORD 8678
15: 15 All Judah rejoiced about the **o** 8652
36: 13 **made** him **take an o** 8678
Ezr 10: 5 **put** the leading priests and Levites and all Israel **under o** 8678
10: 5 And *they* **took the o.** 8678
Ne 5: 12 **made** the nobles and officials **take an o** 8678
6: 18 many in Judah were **under o** to him, 1251+8652
10: 29 and bind themselves with a curse and an **o** 8652
13: 25 **made** them **take an o** 8678
Ps 15: 4 who keeps *his* **o** even when it hurts, 8678
95: 11 So *I* **declared on o** in my anger, 8678
105: 9 the **o** he swore to Isaac. 8652
119: 106 *I have* **taken an o** and confirmed it, 8678
132: 2 He **swore an o** to the LORD and made 8678
132: 11 The LORD **swore an o** to David, 8678
132: 11 a sure **o** that he will not revoke: NIH
Pr 29: 24 *he is* **put under o** and dare not testify. 460+9048
Ecc 8: 2 because you took an **o** *before* God. 8652
Isa 65: 16 he *who* **takes an o** in the land will swear by 8678
Jer 11: 5 the **o** I swore to your forefathers, 8652
38: 16 But King Zedekiah **swore** *this* **o** secretly 8678
40: 9 **took an o** to reassure them and their men. 8678
Eze 16: 8 *I* **gave** you *my* **solemn o** 8678
16: 59 because you have despised my **o** 460
17: 13 putting him under **o.** 460
17: 16 whose **o** he despised 460
17: 18 the **o** by breaking the covenant. 460
17: 19 down on his head my **o** that he despised 460
Mic 7: 20 as *you* **pledged on o** to our fathers 8678
Mt 5: 33 *'Do* not **break** *your* **o,** *2155*
14: 7 with an **o** to give her whatever she asked. *3992*
23: 16 *he is* **bound by his o.'** *4053*
23: 18 *he is* **bound by his o.'** *4053*
26: 63 "*I* **charge** you **under o** by the living God: *2019*
26: 72 He denied it again, with an **o:** *3992*
Mk 6: 23 **promised** her **with an o,** *3923*
Lk 1: 73 the **o** he swore to our father Abraham: *3992*
Ac 2: 30 and knew that God had promised him *on* **o** *3992*
23: 12 **bound** themselves **with an o** *354*
23: 14 "*We have* **taken a solemn o** not *353+354*
23: 21 They *have* **taken an o** not to eat or drink *354*
Heb 3: 11 So *I* **declared on o** in my anger, *3923*
4: 3 "So *I* **declared on o** in my anger, *3923*
6: 16 the **o** confirms what is said and puts an end *3992*
6: 17 he confirmed it *with* an **o.** *3992*
7: 20 And it was not without an **o!** *3993*
7: 20 Others became priests without any **o,** *3993*
7: 21 a priest with an **o** when God said to him: *3993*
7: 22 Because of this **o,** Jesus has become *NIG*
7: 28 but the **o,** which came after the law, *3993*

OATHS (8) [OATH]

Dt 6: 13 serve him only and **take** *your* **o** in his name. 8678
10: 20 to him and **take** *your* **o** in his name. 8678
Ecc 9: 2 as it is with those *who* **take o,** 8678
Isa 48: 1 you who **take o** in the name of the LORD 8678
Hos 10: 4 **take** false **o** and make agreements; 457
Mt 5: 33 but keep the **o** you have made to the Lord.' *3992*
14: 9 but because of his **o** and his dinner guests, *3992*
Mk 6: 26 but because of his **o** and his dinner guests, *3992*

OBADIAH (22)

1Ki 18: 3 and Ahab had summoned **O,** 6282
18: 3 (**O** was a devout believer in the LORD. 6282

1Ki 18: 4 O had taken a hundred prophets 6282
18: 5 Ahab had said to O, 6282
18: 6 Ahab going in one direction and O 6282
18: 7 As O was walking along, Elijah met him. 6282
18: 7 O recognized him, bowed down to NIH
18: 9 "What have I done wrong," asked O, NIH
18:16 So O went to meet Ahab and told him, 6282
1Ch 3:21 of Arnan, of O and of Shecaniah. 6281
7: 3 Michael, O, Joel and Isshiah. 6281
8:38 Bokeru, Ishmael, Sheariah, O and Hanan. 6281
9:16 O son of Shemaiah, the son of Galal, 6281
9:44 Bokeru, Ishmael, Sheariah, O and Hanan. 6281
12: 9 O the second in command, Eliab the third, 6281
27:19 Ishmaiah son of O; 6282
2Ch 17: 7 O, Zechariah, Nethanel and Micaiah 6281
34:12 to direct them were Jahath and O, 6282
Ezr 8: 9 O son of Jehiel, and with him 218 men; 6281
Ne 10: 5 Harim, Meremoth, O, 6281
12:25 Mattaniah, Bakbukiah, O, Meshullam, 6281
Ob 1: 1 The vision of O. 6281

OBAL (2)

Ge 10:28 O, Abimael, Sheba, 6382
1Ch 1:22 O, Abimael, Sheba, 6382

OBED (13)

Ru 4:17 And they named him O. 6381
4:21 Boaz the father of O, 6381
4:22 O the father of Jesse, 6381
1Ch 2:12 the father of O and Obed the father of Jesse. 6381
2:12 the father of Obed and O the father of Jesse. 6381
2:37 Ephlal the father of O, 6381
2:38 O the father of Jehu, 6381
11:47 Eliel, O and Jaasiel the Mezobaite. 6381
26: 7 Othni, Rephael, O and Elzabad; 6381
2Ch 23: 1 Azariah son of O, Maaseiah son of Adaiah, 6381
Mt 1: 5 Boaz the father of O, *2725*
1: 5 O the father of Jesse, *2725*
Lk 3:32 the son of O, the son of Boaz, *2725*

OBED-EDOM (19)

2Sa 6:10 he took it aside to the house of O 6273
6:11 the house of O the Gittite for three months, 6273
6:12 the household of O and everything he has, 6273
6:12 up the ark of God from the house of O to 6273
1Ch 13:13 he took it aside to the house of O 6273
13:14 of God remained with the family of O 6273
15:18 Mikneiah, O and Jeiel, the gatekeepers. 6273
15:21 O, Jeiel and Azaziah were to play the harps, 6273
15:24 O and Jehiah were also to be doorkeepers 6273
15:25 of the LORD from the house of O, 6273
16: 5 Mattithiah, Eliab, Benaiah, O and Jeiel. 6273
16:38 He also left O and his sixty-eight associates 6273
16:38 O son of Jeduthun, and also Hosah, 6273
26: 4 O also had sons: 6273
26: 5 (For God had blessed O.) 2257S
26: 8 All these were descendants of O; 6273
26: 8 descendants of O, 62 in all. 6273
26:15 The lot for the South Gate fell to O, 6273
2Ch 25:24 of God that had been in the care of O, 6273

OBEDIENCE (17) [OBEY]

Ge 49:10 and the o of the nations is his. 3682
Jdg 2:17 the way of o to the LORD's commands. 9048
1Ch 21:19 up in o to the word that Gad had spoken in 928
2Ch 31:21 in the service of God's temple and in o to 928
Pr 30:17 that scorns o to a mother, 3682
Lk 23:56 on the Sabbath in o to the commandment. *2848*
Ac 21:24 that you yourself are living in o to the law. *5875*
Ro 1: 5 the Gentiles to the o that comes from faith. *5633*
5:19 through the o of the one man the many will *5633*
6:16 or to o, which leads to righteousness? *5633*
16:19 Everyone has heard about your o, *5633*
2Co 9:13 for the o that accompanies your confession *5717*
10: 6 once your o is complete. *5633*
Phm 1:21 Confident of your o, I write to you, *5633*
Heb 5: 8 he learned o from what he suffered *5633*
1Pe 1: 2 for o to Jesus Christ and sprinkling *5633*
2Jn 1: 6 that we walk in o to his commands. *2848*

OBEDIENT (10) [OBEY]

Dt 30:17 if your heart turns away and you are not o, 9048
Isa 1:19 If you are willing and o, 9048
Lk 2:51 to Nazareth with them and was o to them. *5718*
Ac 6: 7 and a large number of priests became o to *5634*
2Co 2: 9 to see if you would stand the test and be o *5675*
7:15 when he remembers that you were all o, *5633*
10: 5 every thought to make it o to Christ. *5633*
Php 2: 8 he humbled himself and became o *5675*
Tit 3: 1 and authorities, to be o, to be ready *4272*
1Pe 1:14 As o children, do not conform to *5633*

OBEY (165) [OBEDIENCE, OBEDIENT, OBEYED, OBEYING, OBEYS]

Ex 5: 2 the LORD, that I should o him and let Israel go? 928+7754+9048
12:24 "O these instructions as a lasting ordinance 9068
19: 5 if you o me fully and keep my covenant, 928+7754+9048+9048
24: 7 "We will do everything the LORD has said; we will o." 9048
34:11 O what I command you today. 9068
Lev 18: 4 You must o my laws and be careful 6913
25:18 and be careful to o my laws, 6913
26: 3 and are careful to o my commands, 6913
Nu 15:39 that you may o them and 6913
15:40 to o all my commands and will 6913
27:20 the whole Israelite community will o him. 9048
Dt 4:30 to the LORD your God and o him. 928+7754+9048
5:27 We will listen and o." 6913
6: 3 and be careful to o so that it may go well 6913
6:24 to o all these decrees and to fear the LORD 6913
6:25 if we are careful to o all this law before 6913
9:23 You did not trust him or o him. 928+7754+9048
11:13 So if you faithfully o all 9048+9048
11:27 the blessing if you o the commands of 9048
11:32 be sure that you o all the decrees 6913
12:28 to o all these regulations I am giving you, 9048
13: 4 Keep his commands and o him; 928+7754+9048
13:18 you o the LORD your God, 928+7754+9048
15: 5 if only you fully o the LORD your God 928+7754+9048+9048
21:18 does not o his father and mother 928+7754+9048
21:20 He will not o us. 928+7754+9048
26:17 and that you will o him. 928+7754+9048
27:10 O the LORD your God 928+7754+9048
28: 1 If you fully o the LORD your God 928+7754+9048+9048
28: 2 and accompany you if you o 928+7754+9048
28:15 you do not o the LORD your God 928+7754+9048
28:45 not o the LORD your God and 928+7754+9048
28:62 not o the LORD your God. 928+7754+9048
30: 2 to the LORD your God and o him 928+7754+9048
30: 8 You will again o the LORD 928+7754+9048
30:10 if you o the LORD your God 928+7754+9048
30:12 and proclaim it to us so we may o it?" 6913
30:13 and proclaim it to us so we may o it?" 6913
30:14 and in your heart so you may o it. 6913
32:46 to o carefully all the words of this law. 6913
Jos 1: 7 Be careful to o all the words of this 6913
1:17 we fully obeyed Moses, so we will o you. 9048
1:18 and does not o your words, 9048
22: 5 to walk in all his ways, to o his commands, 9068
23: 6 to o all that is written in the Book of 6913
24:24 the LORD our God and o him." 928+7754+9048
Jdg 3: 4 the Israelites to see whether they would o 9048
1Sa 12:14 If you fear the LORD and serve and o him 928+7754+9048
12:15 But if you do not o the LORD, 928+7754+9048
15:19 Why did you not o the LORD? 928+7754+9048
15:20 "But I did o the LORD," Saul said 928+7754+9048
15:22 To o is better than sacrifice, 9048
28:18 Because you did not o the LORD 928+7754+9048
2Sa 22:45 as soon as they hear me, they o me. 9048
1Ki 2:42 'What you say is good. I will o.' 9048
2:43 not keep your oath to the LORD and o NIH
3:14 if you walk in my ways and o my statutes 9068
6:12 and keep all my commands and o them, 928+2143
8:61 to live by his decrees and o his commands, 9068
2Ki 10: 6 "If you are on my side and will o me, 4200+7754+9048
17:13 that I commanded your fathers to o and NIH
1Ch 28:21 the people will o your every command." 4200
2Ch 14: 4 and to o his laws and commands. 6913
34:31 and to o the words of the covenant written 6913
Ezr 7:26 Whoever does not o the law of your God 10522
Ne 1: 5 who love him and o his commands, 9068
1: 9 if you return to me and o my commands, 2256+6913+9068
9:16 and did not o your commands. 9048
10:29 the servant of God and to o carefully all 6913
Est 3: 8 of all other people and who do not o 6913
Job 36:11 If they o and serve him, 9048
Ps 18:44 As soon as they hear me, they o me; 9048
103:18 and remember to o his precepts. 6913
103:20 who o his word. 928+7754+9048
106:25 They grumbled in their tents and did not o 928+7754+9048
119: 8 I will o your decrees; 9068
119:17 I will o your word. 9068
119:34 and I will keep your law and o it 9068
119:44 I will always o your law, 9068
119:56 I o your precepts. 5915
119:57 I have promised to o your words. 9068
119:60 and not delay to o your commands. 9068
119:67 but now I o your word. 9068
119:88 and I will o the statutes of your mouth. 9068
119:100 for I o your precepts. 5915
119:101 so that I might o your word. 9068
119:129 therefore I o them. 5915
119:134 that I may o your precepts. 9068
119:145 O LORD, and I will o your decrees. 5915
119:158 for they do not o your word. 9068
119:167 I o your statutes, for I love them greatly. 9068
119:168 I o your precepts and your statutes, 9068
Pr 5:13 I would not o my teachers or 928+7754+9048
Ecc 8: 2 O the king's command, I say, 9068
Isa 42:24 they did not o his law. 9048
Jer 7:23 O me, and I will be your God 928+7754+9048
11: 3 'Cursed is the man who does not o 9048
11: 4 'O me and do everything I command you, 928+7754+9048
11: 7 again and again, saying, "O me." 928+7754+9048
17:24 But if you are careful to o me, 9048+9048
17:27 not o me to keep the Sabbath day holy by 9048
18:10 in my sight and does not o me, 928+7754+9048
22: 5 But if you do not o these commands, 9048
26:13 and o the LORD your God. 928+7754+9048
32:23 but they did not o you or follow your law; 928+7754+9048
35:13 not learn a lesson and o my words?' 9048
35:14 because they o their forefather's command. 9048
38:20 "O the LORD by doing what I tell you. 928+7754+9048
40: 3 sinned against the LORD and did not o him. 928+7754+9048
42: 6 we will o the LORD our God, 928+7754+9048
42: 6 for we will o the LORD our God." 928+7754+9048
Da 7:27 and all rulers will worship and o him.' 10725
9: 4 with all who love him and o his commands, 9068
9:11 turned away, refusing to o you. 928+7754+9048
Joel 2:11 and mighty are those who o his command. 6913
Zec 6:15 This will happen if you diligently o the LORD your God." 928+7754+9048+9048
Mt 8:27 Even the winds and the waves o him!" *5634*
19:17 want to enter life, o the commandments." *5498*
23: 3 So you must o them *5498*
28:20 to o everything I have commanded you. *5498*
Mk 1:27 to evil spirits and they o him." *5634*
4:41 Even the wind and the waves o him!" *5634*
Lk 8:25 the winds and the water, and they o him." *5634*
11:28 who hear the word of God and o it." *5875*
17: 6 and it will o you. *5634*
Jn 14:15 you love me, you will o what I command. *5498*
14:23 he will o my teaching. *5498*
14:24 not love me will not o my teaching. *5498*
15:10 If you o my commands, *5498*
15:20 they will o yours also. *5498*
Ac 4:19 in God's sight to o you rather than God. *201*
5:29 "We must o God rather than men! *4272*
5:32 whom God has given to those who o him." *4272*
7:39 "But our fathers refused to o him. *1181+5675*
15: 5 be circumcised and required to o the law *5498*
16: 4 and elders in Jerusalem for the people to o. *5875*
Ro 2:13 but it is those who o the law who will *4475*
6:12 so that you o its evil desires. *5634*
6:16 to o him as slaves, you are slaves to the one *5633*
6:16 you are slaves to the one whom you o— *5634*
15:18 the Gentiles to o God by what I have said *5633*
16:26 that all nations might believe and o him— *5633*
Gal 5: 3 be circumcised that he is obligated to o *4472*
6:13 even those who are circumcised o the law, *5875*
Eph 6: 1 Children, o your parents in the Lord, *5634*
6: 5 o your earthly masters with respect *5634*
6: 5 just as you would o Christ. *NIG*
6: 6 O them not only to win their favor *NIG*
Col 3:20 Children, o your parents in everything, *5634*
3:22 o your earthly masters in everything; *5634*
2Th 1: 8 and do not o the gospel of our Lord Jesus. *5634*
3:14 If anyone does not o our instruction *5634*
1Ti 3: 4 his children o him with proper respect. *2400+5717*
Heb 5: 9 source of eternal salvation for all who o him *5634*
13:17 O your leaders and submit to their *4275*
13:17 O them so that their work will be a joy, *NIG*
Jas 3: 3 the mouths of horses to make them o us, *4275*
1Pe 4:17 for those who do not o the gospel of God? *578*
1Jn 2: 3 to know him if we o his commands. *5498*
3:22 because we o his commands *5498*
3:24 Those who o his commands live in him, *5498*
5: 3 This is love for God: to o his commands. *5498*
Rev 3: 3 what you have received and heard; o it, *5498*
12:17 those who o God's commandments *5498*
14:12 of the saints who o God's commandments *5498*

OBEYED (48) [OBEY]

Ge 22:18 because you have o me." 928+7754+9048
26: 5 Abraham o me and kept my requirements, 928+7754+9048
28: 7 and that Jacob had o his father and mother 9048
Nu 9:19 the Israelites o the LORD's order and did 9068
9:23 They o the LORD's order, 9068
Dt 26:14 I have o the LORD my God; 928+7754+9048
Jos 1:17 Just as we fully o Moses, so we will obey 9048
5: 6 since they had not o the LORD, 928+7754+9048
22: 2 and you have o me 928+7754+9048
1Sa 28:21 your maidservant has o you. 928+7754+9048
1Ki 12:24 So they o the word of the LORD 9048
20:36 Because you have not o the LORD 928+7754+9048
2Ki 18:12 because they had not o the LORD 928+7754+9048
22:13 against us because our fathers have not o 9048
1Ch 29:23 He prospered and all Israel o him. 9048
2Ch 11: 4 So they o the words of the LORD 9048
Ne 1: 7 We have not o the commands, 9068
Est 1:15 She has not o the command of King Xerxes 6913
Ps 119: 4 laid down precepts that are to be fully o. 9068
119:136 for your law is not o. 9068
Jer 3:13 and have not o me,' " declares the LORD. 928+7754+9048
3:25 from our youth till this day we have not o the LORD our God." 928+7754+9048
7:28 the nation that has not o the LORD its God 928+7754+9048
9:13 they have not o me or followed 928+7754+9048
22:21 you have not o me. 928+7754+9048
34:17 You have not o me; 9048
35: 8 We have o everything our forefather Jonadab son of Recab 928+7754+9048
35:10 have fully o everything our forefather Jonadab commanded us. 2256+6913+9048
35:14 yet you have not o me. 9048
35:16 but these people have not o me.' 9048
35:18 'You have o the command 9048
42:21 not o the LORD your God 928+7754+9048
44:23 and have not o the LORD 928+7754+9048
Eze 20:24 not o my laws but had rejected my decrees 6913
Da 9:10 we have not o the LORD our God 928+7754+9048

Da 9:14 yet *we have* not o him. 928+7754+9048
Hos 9:17 because *they have* not o him; 9048
Jnh 3:3 Jonah o the word of the LORD and 3869+7756
Mic 5:15 upon the nations that *have* not o me." 9048
Hag 1:12 and the whole remnant of the people o 9048
Jn 15:10 just as I *have* o my Father's commands *5498*
15:20 If *they* o my teaching, *5498*
17:6 to me and *they have* o your word. *5498*
Ac 7:53 into effect through angels but *have* not o it." *5875*
Ro 6:17 *you* wholeheartedly o the form of teaching *5634*
Php 2:12 my dear friends, as *you have* always o— *5634*
Heb 11:8 o and went, even though he did not know *5634*
1Pe 3:6 who o Abraham and called him her master. *5634*

OBEYING (6) [OBEY]
Dt 8:20 so you will be destroyed for not o 928+7754+9048
1Sa 15:22 and sacrifices as much as *in* o the voice of 9048
Ps 119:5 my ways were steadfast *in* o your decrees! 9068
Jer 16:12 of his evil heart instead of o me. 9048
Gal 5:7 in on you and kept you from o the truth? *4275*
1Pe 1:22 Now that you have purified yourselves by o *5633*

OBEYS (12) [OBEY]
Lev 18:5 for the man who o them will live by them. 6913
Ne 9:29 by which a man will live if *he* o them. 6913
Pr 19:16 *He who* o instructions guards his life, 9068
Ecc 8:5 *Whoever* o his command will come 9068
Isa 50:10 the LORD and o the word of his servant? 9048
Eze 20:11 for the man *who* o them will live by them. 6913
20:13 the man who o them will live by them— 6913
20:21 the man who o them will live by them— 6913
Zep 3:2 *She* o no one, she accepts no correction. 928+7754+9048
Jn 14:21 Whoever has my commands and o them, *5498*
Ro 2:27 and yet o the law will condemn you who, *5464*
1Jn 2:5 But if anyone o his word, *5498*

OBIL (1)
1Ch 27:30 O the Ishmaelite was in charge of the camels 201

OBEISANCE (KJV) See BOWED

OBJECT (35) [OBJECTED, OBJECTION, OBJECTIONS, OBJECTS]
Nu 35:16 " 'If a man strikes someone with an iron o 3998
35:18 Or if anyone has a wooden o *in* his hand 3998
Dt 28:37 an **o of scorn** and ridicule to all the nations 5442
1Ki 9:7 and an **o of ridicule** among all peoples. 9110
2Ch 7:20 and an **o of ridicule** among all peoples. 9110
29:8 he has made them an **o of dread** and horror 2317
30:7 so that he made them an **o of horror,** 9014
Ps 109:25 I am an **o of scorn** to my accusers; 3075
Jer 18:16 an **o** of lasting **scorn;** 9241
19:8 and make it an **o of scorn;** 9240
22:28 broken pot, an o no one wants? 3998
24:9 an **o of ridicule** and cursing, 9110
25:9 and make them an **o of horror** and scorn, 9014
25:18 and an **o of horror** and scorn and cursing, 9014
26:6 an **o of cursing** among all the nations of 7839
29:18 of the earth and an **o of cursing** and horror, 460
42:18 You will be an **o of cursing** and horror, 460
44:8 an **o of cursing** and reproach among all 7839
44:12 They will become an **o of cursing** 460
44:22 your land became an **o of cursing** and 7839
48:26 let her be an **o of ridicule.** 8468
48:27 Was not Israel the **o of** your **ridicule?** 8468
48:39 Moab has become an **o of ridicule,** 8468
48:39 an **o of horror** to all those around her." 4745
49:13 an **o of horror,** of reproach and of cursing; 2997
49:17 "Edom will become an **o of horror;** 9014
51:37 a haunt of jackals, an **o of horror** and scorn, 9014
Eze 5:15 a warning and an **o of horror** to the nations 5457
22:4 Therefore I will make you an **o of scorn** to 3075
24:21 the o *of* your affection. 4720
36:3 and an **o** of people's **malicious talk** 4383+6584+6590+8557
Da 9:16 and your people an **o of scorn** to all those 3075
Joel 2:17 never make your inheritance an **o of scorn,** 3075
2:19 never again will I make you an **o of scorn** 3075
Zec 8:13 As you have been an **o of cursing** among 7839

OBJECTED (4) [OBJECT]
2Ki 4:16 "No, my lord," *she* o. 606
Jn 12:4 Judas Iscariot, who was later to betray him, o, *3306*
18:31 no right to execute anyone," the Jews o. *3306*
Ac 28:19 But *when* the Jews o, *515*

OBJECTION (1) [OBJECT]
Ac 10:29 I came **without raising any o.** *395*

OBJECTIONS (1) [OBJECT]
Ac 11:18 *they had* **no** further o and praised God, *2483*

OBJECTS (14) [OBJECT]
1Sa 6:8 the gold o you are sending back to him as 3998
6:15 with the chest containing the gold o, 3998
1Ki 7:45 All these o that Huram made 3998
2Ki 12:18 of Judah took all the **sacred** o dedicated 7731
2Ch 4:16 All the o that Huram-Abi made NIH
24:7 of God and had used even its **sacred** o for 7731
24:14 also dishes and other o *of* gold and silver. 3998
Ps 79:4 We are **o of reproach** to our neighbors, 3075
Jer 10:15 They are worthless, the o *of* mockery; 5126
51:18 They are worthless, the o *of* mockery; 5126
Ac 17:23 and looked carefully at your **o of worship,** *4934*
Ro 9:22 with great patience the o of his wrath— *5007*
9:23 of his glory known to the o of his mercy, *5007*
Eph 2:3 Like the rest, we were by nature o of wrath. *5451*

OBLATION, OBLATIONS (KJV) See GIFTS, OFFERING, OFFERINGS, PORTION, SACRIFICE

OBLIGATE (1) [OBLIGATED, OBLIGATES, OBLIGATION, OBLIGATIONS]
Nu 30:2 or takes an oath to o himself by a pledge, 673

OBLIGATED (6) [OBLIGATE]
Nu 30:4 by which *she* o herself will stand. 673
30:5 by which *she* o herself will stand; 673
30:7 by which *she* o herself will stand. 673
30:11 by which *she* o herself will stand. 673
Ro 1:14 I am o both to Greeks and non-Greeks, *4050*
Gal 5:3 circumcised that he is o to obey the whole *4050*

OBLIGATES (5) [OBLIGATE]
Nu 30:3 to the LORD or o *herself* by a pledge 673
30:6 a rash promise by which *she* o herself 673
30:8 the vow that o her or the rash promise 6584
30:8 or the rash promise by which *she* o herself, 673
30:10 with her husband makes a vow or o herself 673

OBLIGATION (5) [OBLIGATE]
Nu 30:9 "Any vow or o **taken** by a widow 673
32:22 and be **free from** your o to the LORD and 5929
Ezr 4:14 since *we are* **under** o *to* the palace 10419+10420
Ro 4:4 not credited to him as a gift, but as an o. *4052*
8:12 Therefore, brothers, *we* **have an o**— *1639+4050*

OBLIGATIONS (2) [OBLIGATE]
Nu 3:8 the o *of* the Israelites by doing the work of 5466
1Ki 9:25 **fulfilled** the temple o. 8966

OBLIVION (1)
Ps 88:12 or your righteous deeds in the land of o? 5964

OBOTH (4)
Nu 21:10 The Israelites moved on and camped at O. 95
21:11 Then they set out from O and camped 95
33:43 They left Punon and camped at O. 95
33:44 They left O and camped at Iye Abarim, 95

OBSCENITY (1)
Eph 5:4 Nor should there be o, *157*

OBSCURE (4) [OBSCURES]
Pr 22:29 he will not serve before o *men.* 3126
Isa 33:19 those people of an o speech, 4946+6680+9048
Eze 3:5 a people of o speech and difficult language, 6680
3:6 of o speech and difficult language, 6680

OBSCURES (1) [OBSCURE]
Job 42:3 *that* o my counsel without knowledge?' 6623

OBSERVANCE (2) [OBSERVE]
Ex 13:9 This o will be for you like a sign NIH
Ezr 7:10 the study and o *of* the Law of the LORD, 6913

OBSERVATION (1) [OBSERVE]
Lk 17:20 not come with your **careful** o, *4191*

OBSERVE (47) [OBSERVANCE, OBSERVATION, OBSERVED, OBSERVER, OBSERVES, OBSERVING]
Ex 1:16 and o them on the delivery stool, 8011
12:25 as he promised, o this ceremony. 9068
13:5 *you are to* o this ceremony in this month: 6268
31:13 *'You must* o my Sabbaths. 9068
31:14 " 'O the Sabbath, because it is holy to you. 9068
31:16 The Israelites *are to* o the Sabbath, 9068
Lev 19:3 and *you must* o my Sabbaths. 9068
19:30 " 'O my Sabbaths and have reverence 9068
23:32 *to* o your **sabbath."** 8697+8701
25:2 the land itself **must** o **a sabbath** 8697+8701
26:2 " 'O my Sabbaths and have reverence 9068
Dt 4:6 O them carefully, for this will show your wisdom 6913
5:12 "O the Sabbath day by keeping it holy, 9068
5:15 commanded you to o the Sabbath day. 6913
6:1 to teach you to o in the land 6913
8:6 O the commands of the LORD your God, 9068
8:11 failing *to* o his commands, 9068
10:13 to o the LORD's commands and decrees 9068
11:8 O therefore all the commands I am giving 9068
11:22 If *you* **carefully** o all these commands 9068+9068
12:14 and there o everything I command you. 6913
16:1 O the month of Abib and celebrate 9068
26:16 carefully o them with all your heart and 6913
28:45 the LORD your God and o the commands 9068
2Sa 3:25 to deceive you and o your movements 3359
1Ki 2:3 and o what the LORD your God requires: 9068
9:4 and do all I command and o my decrees 9068
9:6 from me and *do* not o the commands 9068
2Ki 17:13 O my commands and decrees, 9068
1Ch 22:13 if you are careful to o the decrees and laws 6913
2Ch 7:17 and o my decrees and laws, 9068
Est 9:19 o the fourteenth of the month of Adar as 6913
9:22 to o the days as days of feasting and joy 6913
9:27 without fail o these two days every year, 6913
Ps 37:37 Consider the blameless, o the upright; 8011
91:8 *You will* only o with your eyes and see 5564
105:45 keep his precepts and o his laws. 5915
Ecc 8:16 to know wisdom and to o man's labor 8011
Jer 2:10 send to Kedar and o closely; 1067
6:18 o, O witnesses, what will happen to them. 3359
6:27 that *you may* o and test their ways. 3359
8:7 and the thrush o the time of their migration. 9068
Eze 45:21 on the fourteenth day you *are to* o 2118
Mk 7:4 And *they* o many other traditions, *3195*
7:9 of God in order to o your own traditions! *5498*
Ro 2:25 Circumcision has value if *you* o the law, *4556*
Gal 3:5 among you because you o the law, *2240*

OBSERVED (14) [OBSERVE]
Ge 50:10 and there Joseph o a seven-day period 6913
Nu 23:21 no misery o in Israel. 8011
1Sa 1:12 Eli o her mouth. 9068
1Ki 8:65 So Solomon o the festival at that time, 6913
11:34 whom I chose and who o my commands 9068
2Ki 23:22 *had* any such Passover **been o.** 6913
2Ch 7:8 So Solomon o the festival at that time 6913
35:17 the Passover at that time and o the Feast NIH
35:18 not **been o** like this in Israel since the days 6913
Est 5:9 at the king's gate and o that he neither rose NIH
9:28 and o in every generation by every family, 6913
Job 4:8 As *I have* o, those who plow evil 8011
Pr 24:32 I applied my heart to what *I* o and learned 2600
Mic 6:16 *You have* o the statutes of Omri and all 9068

OBSERVER (1) [OBSERVE]
Ac 22:12 He was a devout **o of the law** and *2848+3795*

OBSERVES (1) [OBSERVE]
Ps 11:4 He o the sons of men; 2600

OBSERVING (12) [OBSERVE]
1Sa 20:29 because our family is o a sacrifice in NIH
2Ch 13:11 We *are* o the requirements of the LORD 9068
Lk 1:6 o all the Lord's commandments *1877+4513*
Ro 3:20 be declared righteous in his sight by o *2240*
3:27 On that *of* o the law? *2240*
3:28 that a man is justified by faith apart from o *2240*
Gal 2:16 that a man is not justified by o the law, *2240*
2:16 be justified by faith in Christ and not by o *2240*
2:16 by o the law no one will be justified. *2240*
3:2 Did you receive the Spirit by o the law, *2240*
3:10 All who rely on o the law are under a curse, *2240*
4:10 *You are* o special days and months *4190*

OBSESSION (1)
Ac 26:11 *In my* o against them, *1841+4360*

OBSOLETE (2)
Heb 8:13 *he has* **made** the first one **o;** *4096*
8:13 what is o and aging will soon disappear. *4096*

OBSTACLE (1) [OBSTACLES]
Ro 14:13 not to put any stumbling block or o *4998*

OBSTACLES (3) [OBSTACLE]
Isa 57:14 the o out of the way of my people." 4842
Jer 6:21 "I will put o before this people. 4842
Ro 16:17 and put o in your way that are contrary to *4998*

OBSTINATE (7)
Dt 2:30 and his heart o in order to give him 599
Isa 30:1 "Woe to the o children," 6253
65:2 to an o people, who walk in ways 6253
Eze 2:4 to whom I am sending you are o 7156+7997
3:7 house of Israel is hardened and o. 4213+7997
Ac 19:9 But some of them *became* o; *5020*
Ro 10:21 to a disobedient and o people." *515*

OBTAIN (6) [OBTAINED, OBTAINS]
Nu 27:21 *who will* **o decisions** for him by inquiring of 8626
Ezr 7:16 with all the silver and gold *you may* o from 10708
Pr 20:18 if you wage war, o guidance. NIH
Jn 5:44 **make** no **effort to** o the praise that comes *2426*
Ro 11:7 so earnestly *it did* not o, *2209*
2Ti 2:10 that they too *may* o the salvation that is *5593*

OBTAINED (6) [OBTAIN]
Ex 38:25 The **silver** *o from* those of the community AIT
Ac 22:5 *I* even o letters from them to their brothers *1312*
27:13 they thought they *had* o what they wanted; *3195*
Ro 9:30 who did not pursue righteousness, *have* o it, *2898*

Php 3:12 Not that *I have* already **o** all this, *3284*
Heb 9:12 *having* **o** eternal redemption. *2351*

OBTAINS (1) [OBTAIN]
Pr 12:2 A good man **o** favor from the LORD, 7049

OBVIOUS (4)
Mt 6:18 *be* **o** to men that you are fasting, but only *5743*
Gal 5:19 The acts of the sinful nature are **o:** *5745*
1Ti 5:24 The sins of some men are **o,** *4593*
5:25 In the same way, good deeds are **o,** *4593*

OCCASION (9) [OCCASIONS]
Jdg 14:4 who was seeking an **o** to confront 9301
1Sa 9:24 because it was set aside for you for this **o,** 4595
2Ch 13:18 The men of Israel were subdued on that **o,** 6961
Ezr 7:20 that you *may* **have o** to supply, 10484
10:9 greatly distressed by the **o** and because of 1821
Ne 8:4 on a high wooden platform built for the **o.** 1821
Lk 10:25 **On one o** an expert in the law stood *2627+2779*
Ac 1:4 **On one o,** while he was eating with them, *2779*
2Co 9:11 so that you can be generous on **every** *o,* *AIT*

OCCASIONED (KJV) See RESPONSIBLE

OCCASIONS (2) [OCCASION]
Zec 8:19 and **glad o** and happy festivals for Judah. 8525
Eph 6:18 the Spirit on all **o** with all kinds of prayers *2789*

OCCUPANTS (1) [OCCUPY]
Isa 5:9 the fine mansions left without **o.** 3782

OCCUPATION (2)
Ge 46:33 'What is your **o?**' 5126
47:3 "What is your **o?**" 5126

OCCUPIED (12) [OCCUPY]
Ge 36:43 to their settlements in the land they **o.** 299
Nu 21:25 the cities of the Amorites and **o** them, 3782
Jos 19:47 took it, put it to the sword and **o** it. 3769
Jdg 11:26 For three hundred years Israel **o** Heshbon, 3782
1Sa 17:3 The Philistines **o** one hill and 448+6641
31:7 And the Philistines came and **o** them. 3782
1Ch 5:9 To the east *they* **o** the land up to the edge 3782
5:10 *they* **o** the dwellings of the Hagrites 3782
5:22 And *they* **o** the land until the exile. 3782
10:7 And the Philistines came and **o** them. 3782
2Ch 28:18 They captured and **o** Beth Shemesh, 3782
Ecc 5:20 God **keeps** him **o** with gladness of heart. 6701

OCCUPY (8) [OCCUPANTS, OCCUPIED]
Jos 1:15 you may go back and **o** your own land, 3769
17:12 Manassites were not able to **o** these towns, 3769
Ne 2:8 and for the residence *I will* **o?**" 448+995
Ecc 10:6 while the rich **o** the low ones. 3782
Jer 49:16 *who* **o** the heights of the hill, 9530
Ob 1:19 the Negev *will* **o** the mountains of Esau, 3769
1:19 *They will* **o** the fields of Ephraim 3769
Zec 9:6 Foreigners *will* **o** Ashdod, 3782

OCCUR (3) [OCCURRED, OCCURS]
Ex 8:23 This miraculous sign *will* **o** tomorrow.' " 2118
Eze 16:16 nor *should they ever* **o.** 2118
1Co 5:1 a kind that does not **o** even among pagans: *NIG*

OCCURRED (3) [OCCUR]
2Ch 32:31 the miraculous sign that *had* **o** in the land, 2118
1Co 10:6 Now these things **o** as examples to keep us *1181*
Rev 16:18 like it *has* ever **o** since man has been *1181*

OCCURS (2) [OCCUR]
Ecc 8:14 There is something else meaningless that **o** 6913
2Th 2:3 until the rebellion **o** and the man of *2262*

OCEAN (2) [OCEANS]
Ps 148:7 you great sea creatures and all **o depths,** 9333
Eze 26:19 and when I bring the **o depths** over you 9333

OCEANS (1) [OCEAN]
Pr 8:24 When there were no **o,** I was given birth, 9333

OCRAN (5)
Nu 1:13 from Asher, Pagiel son of **O;** 6581
2:27 of the people of Asher is Pagiel son of **O.** 6581
7:72 On the eleventh day Pagiel son of **O,** 6581
7:77 This was the offering of Pagiel son of **O.** 6581
10:26 Pagiel son of **O** was over the division of 6581

ODD (KJV) See ADDITIONAL

ODED (3)
2Ch 15:1 of God came upon Azariah son of **O.** 6389
15:8 and the prophecy of Azariah son of **O** 6389
28:9 prophet of the LORD named **O** was there, 6389

ODIOUS (1)
1Sa 27:12 *"He has become* **so o** to his people, 944+944

ODOR (1)
Jn 11:39 "by this time *there is* **a bad o,** *3853*

ODOUR (KJV) See AROMA

OF (25210) See Index of Articles Etc.

OFF (437) [OFFSET, OFFSHOOTS, OFFSPRING]
Ge 9:11 Never again *will* all life **be cut o** by 4162
14:12 They also carried **o** Abram's nephew Lot 2143
17:14 *will* **be cut o** from his people; 4162
21:14 on her shoulders and then **sent** her **o** with 8938
21:16 Then *she* **went o** and sat down nearby, 2143
22:19 and *they* **set o** together for Beersheba. 2143
27:40 **throw** his yoke from **o** 7293
31:26 and *you've* **carried o** my daughters 5627
31:27 Why *did you* **run o** secretly 1368
31:30 Now *you have* **gone o** because 2143+2143
34:29 *They* **carried o** all their wealth 8647
37:14 *he* **sent** him **o** from the Valley of Hebron. 8938
38:14 *she* **took o** her widow's clothes, 6073
38:19 *she* **took o** her veil and put 6073
40:15 **was forcibly carried o** 1704+1704
40:19 Pharaoh will lift **o** your head 4946+6584
Ex 3:5 **"Take o** your sandals, 5970
4:25 **cut o** her son's foreskin 4162
9:15 with a plague that would have wiped you **o** 4946
12:15 the seventh *must* **be cut o** from Israel. 4162
12:19 in it *must* **be cut o** from the community 4162
14:25 **made** the wheels of their chariots **come o** 6073
23:4 or donkey **wandering o,** 9494
30:33 a priest *must* **be cut o** from his people.' " 4162
30:38 like it to enjoy its fragrance *must* **be cut o** 4162
31:14 on that day *must* **be cut o** from his people. 4162
32:2 **"Take o** the gold earrings that your wives, 7293
32:3 So all the people **took o** their earrings 7293
32:12 and to wipe them **o** the face 4946+6584
32:24 'Whoever has any gold jewelry, **take it o.'** 7293
33:5 Now **take o** your ornaments 3718+4946+6584
33:6 So the Israelites **stripped o** their ornaments 5911
Lev 1:15 **wring o** the head and burn it on the altar; 4916
3:9 entire fat tail **cut o** close to the backbone, 6073
6:11 Then *he is to* **take o** these clothes and put 7320
7:20 that person *must* **be cut o** from his people. 4162
7:21 to the LORD, that person *must* **be cut o** 4162
7:25 the LORD *must* **be cut o** from his people. 4162
7:27 that person *must* **be cut o** 4162
14:8 **shave o** all his hair and bathe with water; 1662
14:9 seventh day *he must* **shave o** all his hair; 1662
14:41 the material that *is* **scraped o** dumped into 7894
15:13 *he is to* **count o** seven days 6218
15:28 *she must* **count o** seven days, 6218
16:23 to go into the Tent of Meeting and **take o** 7320
17:4 he has shed blood and *must* **be cut o** 4162
17:9 that man *must* **be cut o** from his people. 4162
17:10 and *will* **cut** him **o** from his people. 4162
17:14 anyone who eats it *must* **be cut o."** 4162
18:29 such persons *must* **be cut o** 4162
19:8 that person *must* **be cut o** from his people. 4162
19:27 the hair at the sides of your head or **clip o** 8845
20:3 and *I will* **cut** him **o** from his people; 4162
20:5 and *will* **cut o** from their people both him 4162
20:6 and *I will* **cut** him **o** from his people. 4162
20:17 *They must* **be cut o** before the eyes 4162
20:18 of them *must* **be cut o** from their people. 4162
21:5 not shave their heads or **shave o** the edges 1662
22:3 to the LORD, that person *must* **be cut o** 4162
23:15 **count o** seven full weeks. 6218
23:16 **Count o** fifty days up to the day after 6218
23:29 not deny himself on that day *must* **be cut o** 4162
25:8 **" 'Count o** seven sabbaths of years— 6218
26:26 When I **cut o** your supply of bread, 8689
Nu 4:18 the Kohathite tribal clans *are* not **cut o** 4162
5:23 and then **wash** them **o** into the bitter water. 4681
6:18 the Nazirite *must* **shave o** the hair 1662
6:19 " 'After the Nazirite *has* **shaved o** the hair 1662
9:13 that person *must* **be cut o** from his people 4162
11:18 We were **better o** in Egypt!" 3202
13:23 *they* **cut o** a branch bearing a single cluster 4162
13:24 of grapes the Israelites **cut o** there. 4162
15:30 that person *must* **be cut o** from his people. 4162
15:31 **must surely be cut o;** 4162+4162
19:13 That person *must* **be cut o** from Israel. 4162
19:20 he *must* **be cut o** from the community, 4162
22:23 she turned **o** the road into a field. 4946
23:3 Then *he* **went o** *to* a barren height. 2143
Dt 2:35 the towns we had captured *we* **carried o** 1024
3:7 from their cities *we* **carried o** for ourselves. 1024
12:29 The LORD your God *will* **cut o** 4162
15:16 and your family and *is* **well o** with you, 3201
16:9 **Count o** seven weeks from 6218
19:5 the head *may* **fly o** and hit his neighbor 5970
25:9 **take o** one of his sandals, 2740
25:12 *you shall* **cut o** her hand. 7915
25:18 and **cut o** all who were lagging behind; 2386
28:40 because the olives *will* **drop o.** 5970
29:26 *They* **went o** and worshiped other gods 2143
Jos 3:13 its waters flowing downstream *will* **be cut o** 4162
3:16 (the Salt Sea) **was** completely **cut o.** 4162
4:7 that the flow of the Jordan **was cut o** before 4162
4:7 the waters of the Jordan **were cut o.** 4162
5:15 **"Take o** your sandals, 5970
8:2 except that *you may* **carry o** their plunder 1024
8:9 Then Joshua **sent** them **o,** 8938
8:27 But Israel *did* **carry o** for themselves 1024
11:14 The Israelites **carried o** for themselves all 1024
15:18 When *she* **got o** her donkey, 4946+6584+7563
Jdg 1:6 and **cut o** his thumbs and big toes. 7915
1:7 and big toes **cut o** have picked up scraps 7915
1:14 When *she* **got o** her donkey, 4946+6584+7563
5:19 but *they* **carried o** no silver, no plunder. 4374
8:21 the ornaments **o** their camels' necks. 928
9:48 He took an ax and **cut o** some branches, 4162
16:12 he snapped the ropes **o** his arms 4946+6584
16:19 *to* **shave o** the seven braids of his hair, 1662
21:6 "Today one tribe *is* **cut o** from Israel," 1548
21:23 each man caught one and **carried** her **o** to 5951
Ru 4:7 one party **took o** his sandal and gave it to 8990
1Sa 2:33 not **cut o** from my altar will be spared only 4162
4:18 Eli fell backward **o** his chair by the 4946+6584
5:4 and hands *had* **been broken o** and 4162
17:34 a lion or a bear came and **carried o** a sheep 5951
17:39 So he **took** them **o.** 6073
17:46 I'll strike you down and **cut o** your head. 6073
17:51 *he* **cut o** his head with the sword. 4162
18:4 Jonathan **took o** the robe he was wearing 7320
19:24 He **stripped o** his robes and also prophesied 7320
20:15 and *do* not ever **cut o** your kindness 4162
20:15 even when the LORD *has* **cut o** every one 4162
23:5 the Philistines and **carried o** their livestock. 5627
23:28 Saul **broke o** his pursuit of David 4946+8740
24:4 Then David crept up unnoticed and **cut o** 4162
24:5 for *having* **cut o** a corner of his robe. 4162
24:11 I **cut o** the corner of your robe but did 4162
24:21 that *you will* not **cut o** my descendants 4162
25:23 she quickly **got o** her donkey 3718+4946+6584
28:9 *He has* **cut o** the mediums and spiritists 4162
30:2 **carried** them **o** as they went on their way. 5627
30:17 except four hundred young men who **rode o** 8206
31:9 *They* **cut o** his head 4162
31:9 and **stripped o** his armor, 7320
2Sa 2:15 stood up and *were* **counted o—** 928+5031+6296
4:7 *they* **cut o** his head. 6073
4:12 *They* **cut o** their hands and feet and hung 7915
5:6 the blind and the lame *can* **ward** you **o."** 6073
5:21 and David and his men **carried** them **o.** 5951
7:9 and *I have* **cut o** all your enemies from 4162
8:2 and **measured** them **o** with a length of cord. 4499
10:4 **shaved o** half of each man's beard, 1662
10:4 **cut o** their garments in the middle at 4162
11:1 at the time when kings **go o to war,** 3655
14:16 the hand of the man *who is trying to* **cut o** 9012
16:9 Let me go over and **cut o** his head." 6073
18:21 down before Joab and **ran o.** 8132
20:22 and *they* **cut o** the head of Sheba son 4162
1Ki 2:39 two of Shimei's slaves **ran o** to Achish son 1368
5:14 *He* **sent** them **o** to Lebanon in shifts 8938
6:16 *He* **partitioned o** twenty cubits at the rear 1215
9:6 and decrees I have given you and **go o** 2143
9:7 then *I will* **cut o** Israel from 4162
14:10 *I will* **cut o** from Jeroboam 4162
14:14 over Israel who *will* **cut o** the family 4162
14:26 *He* **carried o** the treasures of the temple of 4374
16:11 *he* **killed o** Baasha's whole family. 5782
18:4 While Jezebel *was* **killing o** the LORD's 4162
18:42 So Ahab **went o** to eat and drink, 6590
18:45 a heavy rain came on and Ahab **rode o** 8206
20:11 not boast like *one who* **takes** *it* **o.' "** 7337
21:21 I will consume your descendants and **cut o** 4162
2Ki 1:3 that you *are* **going o** to consult Baal-Zebub, 2143
5:12 So he turned and **went o** in a rage. 2143
6:32 to **cut o** my head? 6073
7:8 gold and clothes, and **went o** and hid them. 2143
9:8 *I will* **cut o** from Ahab every last male 4162
9:18 The horseman **rode o** to meet Jehu and said, 2143
11:7 *that* normally **go o** Sabbath **duty** are all 3655
11:9 and *those who were* **going o duty—** 3655
17:26 which *are* **killing** them **o,** 4637
18:16 of Judah **stripped o** the gold 7915
20:17 *will* **be carried o** to Babylon. 5951
23:34 But he took Jehoahaz and **carried** him **o** 995
1Ch 17:8 and *I have* **cut o** all your enemies from 4162
19:4 **cut o** their garments in the middle at 4162
20:1 at the time when kings **go o** to war, 3655
2Ch 7:19 and commands I have given you and **go o** 2143
12:9 *he* **carried o** the treasures of the temple of 4374
14:13 The men of Judah **carried o** a large amount 5951
14:15 the herdsmen and **carried o** droves of sheep 8647
20:25 and his men went to **carry o** their plunder, 1024
21:17 invaded it and **carried o** all the goods found 8647
23:8 and *those who were* **going o duty—** 3655
25:13 and **carried o** great quantities of plunder. 1024
32:3 and military staff about **blocking o** 6258
36:4 and **carried** him **o** to Egypt. 995
Ne 4:23 nor the guards with me **took o** our clothes; 7320
Est 8:2 The king **took o** his signet ring, 6073
Job 1:15 the Sabeans attacked and **carried** them **o.** 4374
1:17 down on your camels and **carried** them **o.** 4374
6:9 to let loose his hand and **cut** me **o!** 1298
9:7 *he* **seals o** the light of the stars. 1237+3159
12:18 *He* **takes o** the shackles put on by kings 7337
18:14 from the security of his tent and **marched o** 7575
20:28 A flood *will* **carry o** his house, 1655
22:16 They **were carried o** before their time, 7855
24:24 *they* **are cut o** like heads of grain. 4909
27:8 the godless when *he is* **cut o,** 1298

Job 27:21 east wind **carries** him **o**, and he is gone; 5951
30:11 *they* **throw o** restraint in my presence. 8938
31:22 *let* it **be broken o** at the joint. 8689
36:7 He does not take his eyes **o** the righteous; 4946
38:5 Who **marked o** its dimensions? 8492
41:13 Who *can* **strip o** his outer coat? 1655
Ps 2:3 they say, "and **throw o** their fetters." 8959
10:1 O LORD, do you stand **far o?** 928+8158
10:9 he catches the helpless and **drags** them **o** 5432
12:3 *May* the LORD **cut o** all flattering lips 4162
22:19 But you, O LORD, *be* not **far o;** 8178
31:22 *"I* **am cut o** from your sight!" 1746
34:16 to **cut o** the memory of them from 4162
37:9 For evil men *will* **be cut o,** 4162
37:22 but those he curses *will* **be cut o.** 4162
37:28 the offspring of the wicked *will* **be cut o;** 4162
37:34 when the wicked **are cut o,** you will see it. 4162
37:38 the future of the wicked *will* **be cut o.** 4162
60:6 and **measure o** the Valley of Succoth. 4499
75:10 *I will* **cut o** the horns of all the wicked, 1548
88:5 who **are cut o** from your care. 1615
101:8 I *will* **cut o** every evildoer from the city 4162
104:19 The moon **marks o** the seasons, 6913
108:7 and **measure o** the Valley of Succoth. 4499
109:13 May his descendants **be cut o,** 4162
109:15 that *he may* **cut o** the memory of them from 4162
109:23 *I* **am shaken o** like a locust. 5850
118:10 in the name of the LORD *I* **cut** them **o.** 4577
118:11 in the name of the LORD *I* **cut** them **o.** 4577
118:12 in the name of the LORD *I* **cut** them **o.** 4577
Pr 2:22 the wicked *will* **be cut o** from the land, 4162
20:14 **o** *he* **goes** and boasts about his purchase. 261
23:5 for they will surely sprout wings and **fly o** 6414
23:18 and your hope *will* not **be cut o.** 4162
24:14 and your hope *will* not **be cut o.** 4162
26:6 Like **cutting o** one's feet 7894
29:18 the people **cast o restraint;** 7277
Ecc 6:3 that a stillborn child is **better o** than he. 3202
7:24 it is **far o** and most profound— 8158
9:4 even a live dog is **better o** than a dead lion! 3202
11:10 banish anxiety from your heart and **cast o** 6296
SS 5:3 *I have* **taken o** my robe— 7320
Isa 5:29 as they seize their prey and **carry** it **o** 7117
7:20 and *to* **take o** your beards also. 6200
8:4 the plunder of Samaria *will* **be carried o** by 5951
9:14 So the LORD *will* **cut o** from Israel 4162
10:33 *will* **lop o** the boughs with great power. 6188
11:13 and Judah's enemies *will* **be cut o;** 4162
14:22 *"I will* **cut o** from Babylon her name 4162
15:2 and every beard **cut o.** 1757
18:5 *he will* **cut o** the shoots 4162
20:2 **"Take o** the sackcloth from your body and 7337
22:25 *it will* **be sheared o** and will fall, 1548
27:11 *they* **are broken o** and women come 8689
30:11 Leave this way, **get o** this path, 5742
30:16 You said, *'We will* **ride o** on swift horses.' 8206
32:11 **Strip o** *your* **clothes,** 2256+6910+7320
33:23 and even the lame *will* **carry o** plunder. 1024
38:12 and *he has* **cut** me **o** from the loom; 1298
39:6 *will* **be carried o** to Babylon. 5951
40:12 or with the breadth of his hand **marked o** 9419
45:16 *they will* **go o** into disgrace together. 2143
46:2 *they* themselves **go o** into captivity. 2143
47:2 **take o** your veil. 1655
47:11 **ward o with a ransom;** 4105
48:9 so as not *to* **cut** you **o.** 4162
48:19 their name *would* never **be cut o** 4162
52:2 **Shake o** your dust; 5850
53:8 For *he* **was cut o** from the land of the living; 1615
56:5 an everlasting name that *will* not **be cut o.** 4162
57:13 **carry** all of them **o,** 5951
Jer 2:20 "Long ago *you* **broke o** your yoke 8689
2:20 and **tore o** your bonds; 5998
5:5 But with one accord they too *had* **broken o** 8689
5:5 the yoke and **torn o** the bonds. 5998
5:10 **Strip o** her branches, 6073
7:29 **Cut o** your hair and throw it away; 1605
9:21 *it has* **cut o** the children from the streets 4162
11:19 *let us* **cut** him **o** from the land of 4162
12:3 **Drag** them **o** like sheep to be butchered! 5998
13:22 that your skirts *have* **been torn o** 1655
20:5 as plunder and **carry** it **o** to Babylon. 995
22:24 *I would* still **pull** you **o.** 5998
28:10 the yoke **o** the neck of the prophet 4946+6584
28:11 Babylon **o** the neck of all the nations 4946+6584
28:12 the yoke **o** the neck of the prophet 4946+6584
30:8 'I will break the yoke **o** their necks 4946+6584
30:8 and *will* **tear o** their bonds; 5998
36:23 the king **cut** them **o** with a scribe's knife 7973
36:29 and **cut o** both men and animals from it?" 8697
41:5 eighty men *who had* **shaved o** their beards, 1662
44:7 on yourselves by **cutting o** from Judah 4162
44:17 and were **well o** and suffered no harm. 3202
47:4 to **cut o** all survivors who could help Tyre 4162
48:25 Moab's horn **is cut o;** 1548
48:37 and every beard **cut o;** 1757
49:29 *be* **carried o** with all their goods 5951
50:16 **Cut o** from Babylon the sower, 4162
51:13 the time for you to be **cut o.** 1299
51:25 roll you **o** the cliffs, 4946
La 2:3 In fierce anger *he has* **cut o** every horn 1548
2:14 to **ward o** your captivity. 8740
3:31 For *men are* not **cast o** *by* the Lord forever. 2396
3:54 and I thought *I was about to* **be cut o.** 1615
4:9 the sword are **better o** than those who die 3202
Eze 4:16 "Son of man, I *will* **cut o** the supply of food 8689
5:16 upon you and **cut o** your supply of food. 8689
Eze 13:21 *I will* **tear o** your veils 7973
14:8 *I will* **cut** him **o** from my people. 4162
14:13 *to* **cut o** its food supply and send famine 8689
17:4 *he* **broke o** its topmost shoot 7786
17:12 and **carried o** her king and her nobles, 4374
17:22 *I will* **break o** a tender sprig 7786
21:3 from its scabbard and **cut o** from you both 4162
21:4 Because *I am going to* **cut o** the righteous 4162
21:19 Make a signpost where the road **branches o** 8031
21:26 **Take o** the turban, remove the crown. 6073
23:25 *They will* **cut o** your noses and your ears, 6073
25:7 *I will* **cut** you **o** from the nations 4162
25:16 against the Philistines, and *I will* **cut o** 4162
26:16 and **take o** their embroidered garments. 7320
29:19 and *he will* **carry o** its wealth. 5951
30:15 and **cut o** the hordes of Thebes. 4162
32:20 *let* her *be* **dragged o** with all her hordes. 5432
35:7 and **cut o** from it all who come and go. 4162
37:11 we **are cut o.'** 1615
38:13 to **carry o** silver and gold, 5951
44:19 *they are to* **take o** 7320
45:3 **measure o** a section 25,000 4499
46:18 driving them **o** their property. 4946
47:3 *he* **measured o** a thousand cubits and 4499
47:4 *He* **measured o** another thousand cubits 4499
47:4 *He* **measured o** another thousand and 4499
47:5 *He* **measured o** another thousand, 4499
Da 1:2 These *he* **carried o** *to* the temple of his god 995
4:14 'Cut down the tree and **trim o** its branches; 10635
4:14 **strip o** its leaves and scatter its fruit. 10499
7:4 until its wings **were torn o** and it was lifted 10440
8:8 of his power his large horn **was broken o,** 8689
8:22 *that* **was broken o** represent four kingdoms 8689
9:26 the Anointed One *will* **be cut o** 4162
11:8 and **carry** them **o** *to* Egypt. 928+995+2021+8660
11:12 When the army **is carried o,** 5951
Hos 2:7 for then I was **better o** than now.' 3202
5:14 *I will* **carry** them **o,** 5951
Joel 1:7 *It has* **stripped o** their **bark** 3106+3106
1:9 and drink offerings *are* **cut o** from 4162
1:16 the food **been cut o** before our very eyes— 4162
3:5 and **carried o** my finest treasures 995
Am 3:14 the horns of the altar *will* **be cut o** and fall 1548
6:2 Are *they* **better o** than your two kingdoms? 3202
6:3 *You* **put o** the evil day and bring near 5612
Ob 1:11 while strangers **carried o** his wealth 8647
Jnh 3:6 **took o** his royal robes, 6296
Mic 2:8 You strip **o** the rich robe 4578+4946
3:3 **strip o** their skin and break their bones 7320
Na 1:12 *they will* **be cut o** and pass away. 1605
Zep 1:3 of rubble when *I* **cut o** man from the face 4162
1:4 *I will* **cut o** from this place every remnant 4162
3:6 *"I have* **cut o** nations; 4162
3:7 Then her dwelling *would* not **be cut o,** 4162
Zec 3:4 **"Take o** his filthy clothes." 6073
9:6 *I will* **cut o** the pride of the Philistines. 4162
11:16 **tearing o** their hoofs. 7293
Mal 2:3 and you *will* **be carried o** with it. 5951
2:12 *may* the LORD **cut** him **o** from the tents 4162
Mt 5:30 **cut** it **o** and throw it away. *1716*
8:33 Those tending the pigs **ran o,** *5771*
10:14 **shake** the dust **o** your feet when you leave *1759*
12:29 and **carry o** his possessions *773*
18:8 **cut** it **o** and throw it away. *1716*
18:12 and go to look for the one that **wandered o?** *4414*
18:13 about the ninety-nine that *did* not **wander o.** *4414*
18:30 he **went o** and had the man thrown *599*
22:5 "But *they* paid no attention and **went o—** *599*
25:18 the one talent **went o,** *599*
26:51 **cutting o** his ear. *904*
27:31 *they* **took o** the robe *1694*
Mk 1:35 left the house and **went o** to a solitary place, *599*
3:27 and **carry o** his possessions *1395*
5:14 **ran o** and reported this in the town *5771*
6:11 **shake** the dust **o** your feet when you leave, *1759*
9:43 If your hand causes you to sin, **cut** it **o.** *644*
9:45 And if your foot causes you to sin, **cut** it **o.** *644*
14:47 **cutting o** his ear. *904*
15:20 *they* **took o** the purple robe *1694*
Lk 2:16 *they* **hurried o** and found Mary and *2262+5067*
8:34 *they* **ran o** and reported this in the town *5771*
9:5 **shake** the dust **o** your feet *701*
10:11 that sticks to our feet *we* **wipe o against** *669*
12:58 or *he may* **drag** you **o** to the judge, *2955*
14:32 the other is still a **long way o** and will ask *4522*
15:13 **set o** for a distant country *623*
15:20 "But while he was still a **long way o,** *3426*
17:23 *Do* not **go running o after** them. *599+1503+3593*
18:7 *Will he keep* **putting** them **o?** *3428*
22:50 **cutting o** his right ear. *904*
23:1 the whole assembly rose and led him **o** *NIG*
Jn 6:17 where they got into a boat and **set o** across *2262*
11:44 **"Take o** the grave clothes and let him go." *3395*
13:4 **took o** his outer clothing, *5502*
15:2 *He* **cuts o** every branch in me *149*
18:10 **cutting o** his right ear. *644*
18:26 of the man whose ear Peter *had* **cut o,** *644*
21:7 (for he had **taken it o**) and jumped into *1218*
Ac 2:39 and for all who are **far o—** *1650+3426*
3:23 *will be* **completely cut o from** among *2017*
7:33 the Lord said to him, **'Take o** your sandals; *3395*
8:3 *he* **dragged o** men and women and put them *5359*
9:30 down to Caesarea and **sent** him **o** to Tarsus. *1990*
12:7 and the chains **fell o** Peter's wrists. *1738*
13:3 on them and **sent** them **o.** *668*
15:30 The men *were* **sent o** and went down *668*
15:33 *they were* **sent o** by the brothers with *668*
Ac 18:18 *he had* his hair **cut o** at Cenchrea because of *3025*
20:15 from there and arrived **o** Kios. *513*
22:23 and **throwing o** their cloaks *4849*
27:5 When we had sailed across the open sea **o** *2848*
27:7 and had difficulty arriving **o** Cnidus. *2848*
28:5 But Paul **shook** the snake **o** into the fire *701*
Ro 9:3 that I myself were cursed and **cut o from** *608*
11:17 some of the branches *have been* **broken o,** *1709*
11:19 "Branches *were* **broken o** so that I could *1709*
11:20 *they were* **broken o** because of unbelief, *1709*
11:22 Otherwise, you also *will be* **cut o.** *1716*
1Co 11:6 *she should have* her hair **cut o;** *3025*
11:6 a woman *to have her* hair cut or **shaved o,** *3834*
Eph 4:22 *to* **put o** your old self, *700*
4:25 of you *must* **put o** falsehood *700*
Col 2:11 in the **putting o** of the sinful nature, *589*
3:9 *since you have* **taken o** your old self *588*
Heb 12:1 *let us* **throw o** everything that hinders and *700*
Jas 2:25 and **sent** them **o** in a different direction? *1675*
2Pe 2:15 the straight way and **wandered o** to follow *4414*
2:20 **worse o** at the end **than** they were *5937*
Rev 12:17 the woman and **went o** to make war against *599*
18:10 they will stand **far o** and cry: " 'Woe! *608+3427*
18:15 from her will stand **far o,** *608+3427*
18:17 will stand **far o.** *608+3427*

OFFAL (6)

Ex 29:14 and its hide and its **o** outside the camp. 7302
Lev 4:11 the inner parts and **o—** 7302
8:17 and its flesh and its **o** he burned up outside 7302
16:27 their hides, flesh and **o** are to be burned up. 7302
Nu 19:5 its hide, flesh, blood and **o.** 7302
Mal 2:3 the **o** *from* your festival sacrifices, 7302

OFFEND (3) [OFFENDED, OFFENDER, OFFENDERS, OFFENSE, OFFENSES, OFFENSIVE]

Job 34:31 'I am guilty but *will* **o** no more. 2472
Mt 17:27 "But so that *we may* not **o** them, *4997*
Jn 6:61 Jesus said to them, *"Does* this **o** you? *4997*

OFFENDED (3) [OFFEND]

Ge 40:1 of the king of Egypt **o** their master, 2627
Pr 18:19 An **o** brother is more unyielding than 7321
Mt 15:12 the Pharisees *were* **o** when they heard this?" *4997*

OFFENDER (1) [OFFEND]

Ex 21:22 **the o** must be fined whatever 2257S

OFFENDERS (1) [OFFEND]

1Co 6:9 nor male prostitutes nor **homosexual o** *780*

OFFENSE (15) [OFFEND]

Ge 20:16 This is to **cover the o** against you 4064+6524
Dt 19:15 of any crime or **o** he may have committed. 2633
21:22 guilty of a **capital o** is put to death 4638+5477
1Sa 25:28 Please forgive your servant's **o,** 7322
2Sa 3:8 of an **o** *involving* this woman! 6411
Job 10:14 and would not let my **o** go unpunished. 6411
13:23 Show me my **o** and my sin. 7322
Ps 59:3 Fierce men conspire against me *for* no **o** 7322
Pr 17:9 He who covers over an **o** promotes love, 7322
19:11 it is to his glory to overlook an **o.** 7322
Jer 24:9 I will make them abhorrent and an **o** to all 8288
Eze 22:11 a **detestable o** with his neighbor's wife, 9359
Mt 13:57 And *they* **took o** at him. *4997*
Mk 6:3 And *they* **took o** at him. *4997*
Gal 5:11 the **o** of the cross has been abolished. *4998*

OFFENSE (Anglicized) See also STENCH

OFFENSES (18) [OFFEND]

Nu 18:1 to bear the **responsibility for o** *against* 6411
18:1 to bear the **responsibility for o** *against* 6411
18:23 the **responsibility for o** *against* it. 6411
1Ki 8:50 the **o** they have committed against you, 7322
Job 7:21 not pardon my **o** and forgive my sins? 7322
14:17 My **o** will be sealed up in a bag; 7322
Isa 43:24 with your sins and wearied me with your **o.** 6411
44:22 I have swept away your **o** like a cloud, 7322
59:12 For our **o** are many in your sight, 7322
59:12 Our **o** are ever with us, 7322
Eze 18:22 the **o** he has committed will be remembered 7322
18:28 the **o** he has committed and turns away 7322
18:30 Turn away from all your **o;** 7322
18:31 of all the **o** you have committed, 7322
33:10 "Our **o** and sins weigh us down, 7322
37:23 and vile images or with any of their **o,** 7322
39:24 according to their uncleanness and their **o,** 7322
Am 5:12 For I know how many are your **o** and 7322

OFFENSIVE (3) [OFFEND]

Job 19:17 My breath *is* **o** to my wife; 2320
Ps 139:24 See if there is any **o** way in me, 6778
Jer 6:10 The word of the LORD is **o** to them; 3075

OFFER (126) [OFFERED, OFFERING, OFFERINGS, OFFERS]

Ex 3:18 *to* **o sacrifices** to the LORD our God.' 2284

Ex 5: 3 to o sacrifices to the LORD our God, 2284
8: 8 and I will let your people go to o sacrifices 2284
8:26 The sacrifices we o the LORD 2284
8:26 And if we o sacrifices that are detestable 2284
8:27 to o sacrifices to the LORD our God, 2284
8:28 to o sacrifices to the LORD your God in 2284
8:29 by not letting the people go to o sacrifices 2284
23:18 not o the blood of a sacrifice to me along 2284
29:38 to o on the altar regularly each day: 6913
29:39 O one in the morning and the other 6913
29:40 With the first lamb o a tenth of an ephah NIH
30: 9 Do not o on this altar any other incense 6590
34:25 not o the blood of a sacrifice to me along 8821
Lev 1: 3 he is to o a male without defect. 7928
1:10 he is to o a male without defect. 7928
1:14 he is to o a dove or a young pigeon. 7928
2:14 o crushed heads of new grain roasted in 7928
3: 6 he is to o a male or female without defect. 7928
5: 8 who shall first o the one for 7928
5:10 then o the other as a burnt offering in 6913
7:12 with this thank offering he is to o cakes 7928
12: 7 He shall o them before the LORD 7928
14:12 the male lambs and o it as a guilt offering, 7928
14:20 and o it on the altar, 6590
16: 6 to o the bull for his own sin offering 7928
17: 7 They must no longer o any of their 2284
21: 8 because they o up the food of your God. 7928
21:17 a defect may come near to o the food 7928
21:21 not come near to o the food of his God. 7928
22:22 Do not o to the LORD the blind, 7928
22:24 You must not o to the LORD an animal 7928
22:25 from the hand of a foreigner and o them as 7928
Nu 6:11 The priest is to o one as a sin offering and 6913
15: 7 O it as an aroma pleasing to the LORD. 7928
15:24 the whole community is to o a young bull 6913
Dt 12:14 O them only at the place the LORD 6590
20:10 make its people an o of peace. 7924
27: 6 with fieldstones and o burnt offerings on it 6590
28:68 There you will o yourselves for sale 4835
33:19 and there o sacrifices of righteousness; 2284
Jos 22:23 from the LORD and to o burnt offerings 6590
Jdg 5: 2 the people willingly o themselves— 5605
6:26 o the second bull as a burnt offering." 6590
13:16 o it to the LORD." 6590
16:23 the rulers of the Philistines assembled to o 2284
21:13 an o of peace to the Benjamites at the rock 7924
1Sa 1:21 with all his family to o the annual sacrifice 2284
2:19 with her husband to o the annual sacrifice. 2284
10: 4 They will greet you and o you two loaves 5989
13:12 to o the burnt offering." 6590
2Sa 7:27 found courage to o you this prayer. 7137+9525
24:22 take whatever pleases him and o it up. 6590
1Ki 3: 4 The king went to Gibeon to o sacrifices, 2284
12:27 to o sacrifices at the temple of the LORD 6913
22:43 and the people continued to o sacrifices 2284
2Ki 12: 3 to o sacrifices and burn incense there. 2284
14: 4 to o sacrifices and burn incense there. 2284
15: 4 to o sacrifices and burn incense there. 2284
15:35 to o sacrifices and burn incense there. 2284
16:15 o the morning burnt offering and 7787
17:36 down and to him o sacrifices. 2284
1Ch 23:13 to o sacrifices before the LORD, 7787
2Ch 11:16 to Jerusalem to o sacrifices to the LORD, 2284
29:21 to o these on the altar of the LORD. 6590
31: 2 to o burnt offerings NIH
35:12 of the families of the people to o to 7928
Ezr 3: 6 to o burnt offerings to the LORD, 6590
6:10 so that they may o sacrifices pleasing to 10638
Ne 4: 2 Will they o sacrifices? 2284
Ps 4: 5 O right sacrifices and trust in the LORD. 2284
38:14 whose mouth can o no reply. 928
66:15 I will o bulls and goats. 6913
Ecc 5: 1 near to listen rather than to o the sacrifice 5989
9: 2 who o sacrifices and those who do not. 2284
Isa 1:15 if you o many prayers, I will not listen. 8049
57: 7 there you went up to o your sacrifices. 2284
Jer 7:16 for this people nor o any plea or petition 5951
11:14 "Do not pray for this people nor o any plea 5951
14:12 though they o burnt offerings 6590
16: 7 No one will o food to comfort 7271
33:18 before me continually to o burnt offerings, 6590
46:10 will o sacrifice in the land of the north by NIH
La 3:30 Let him o his cheek 5989
4: 3 jackals o their breasts to nurse their young, 2740
Eze 20:31 When you o your gifts— 5951
43:22 the second day you are to o a male goat 7928
43:23 to o a young bull and a ram from the flock, 7928
43:24 You are to o them before the LORD, 7928
44:15 before me to o sacrifices of fat and blood, 7928
44:27 he is to o a sin offering for himself, 7928
45:13 " 'This is the special gift you are to o: 8123
46: 6 of the New Moon he is to o a young bull, NIH
46:12 He shall o his burnt offering 6913
48: 9 "The special portion you are to o to 8123
Hos 8:13 They o sacrifices given to me and they eat 2284
13: 2 "They o human sacrifice and kiss 2284
14: 2 that we may o the fruit of our lips. 8966
Mic 6: 7 Shall I o my firstborn for my transgression, 5989
Hag 2:14 and whatever they o there is defiled. 7928
Mal 1:13 crippled or diseased animals and o them 995
Mt 5:24 then come and o your gift. 4712
8: 4 the priest and o the gift Moses commanded, 4712
Mk 1:44 and o the sacrifices that Moses commanded 4712
Lk 2:24 to o a sacrifice in keeping with what is said 1443
5:14 and o the sacrifices that Moses commanded 4712
Ac 14:13 the crowd wanted to o sacrifices to them. 2604
24:26 that Paul would o him a bribe. 1443
Ro 6:13 Do not o the parts of your body to sin, 4225
6:13 but rather o yourselves to God, 4225
6:13 and o the parts of your body to him NIG
6:16 that when you o yourselves to someone 4225
6:19 as you used to o the parts of your body 4225
6:19 so now o them in slavery 4225
12: 1 to o your bodies as living sacrifices, 4225
1Co 9:18 that in preaching the gospel I may o it free 5502
Heb 5: 1 to o gifts and sacrifices for sins. 4712
5: 3 This is why he has to o sacrifices 4712
7:27 not need to o sacrifices day after day, 429
8: 3 Every high priest is appointed to o 4712
8: 3 for this one also to have something to o. 4712
8: 4 for there are already men who o 4712
9:25 Nor did he enter heaven to o himself again 4712
13:15 let us continually o to God a sacrifice 429
1Pe 4: 9 O hospitality to one another NIG
Rev 8: 3 He was given much incense to o, 1443

OFFERED (90) [OFFER]

Ge 31:54 He o a sacrifice there in the hill country 2284
46: 1 he o sacrifices to the God 2284
Ex 24: 5 and they o burnt offerings 6590
40:29 o on it burnt offerings and grain offerings, 6590
Lev 2:12 to be o on the altar as a pleasing aroma. 6590
7: 3 All its fat shall be o: 7928
7:15 be eaten on the day it is o; 7933
7:18 It will not be credited to the one who o it, 7928
9:15 o it for a sin offering 2627
9:16 He brought the burnt offering and o it in 6913
10: 1 they o unauthorized fire before the LORD, 7928
Nu 16:47 but Aaron o the incense 5989
18:15 that is o to the LORD is yours. 7928
23: 2 of them o a bull and a ram on each altar. 6590
23: 4 on each altar I have o a bull and a ram." 6590
23:14 and there he built seven altars and o a bull 6590
23:30 and o a bull and a ram on each altar. 6590
Dt 26:14 nor have I o any of it to the dead. 5989
Jos 8:31 On it they o to the LORD burnt offerings 6590
Jdg 2: 5 There they o sacrifices to the LORD. 2284
6:19 he brought them out and o them to him 5602
Ru 2:14 he o her some roasted grain. 7381
1Sa 2:13 with the people that whenever anyone o 2284
6:15 of Beth Shemesh o burnt offerings 6590
7: 9 and o it up as a whole burnt offering to 6590
13: 9 And Saul o up the burnt offering. 6590
2Sa 15:24 and Abiathar o sacrifices until all 6590
1Ki 3: 3 that he o sacrifices and burned incense on 2284
3: 4 and Solomon o a thousand burnt offerings 6590
8:62 the king and all Israel with him o sacrifices 2284
8:63 Solomon o a sacrifice 2284
8:64 and there he o burnt offerings, 6913
11: 8 who burned incense and o sacrifices 2284
12:32 and o sacrifices on the altar. 6590
12:33 he o sacrifices on the altar he had built 6590
20:34 from your father," Ben-Hadad o. 606
2Ki 3:27 and o him as a sacrifice on the city wall. 6590
16: 4 He o sacrifices and burned incense at 2284
16:13 He o up his burnt offering 7787
1Ch 21:28 he o sacrifices there. 2284
2Ch 1: 6 and o a thousand burnt offerings on it. 6590
6:40 and your ears attentive to the prayers o AIT
7: 4 the people o sacrifices before the LORD. 2284
7: 5 And King Solomon o a sacrifice 2284
7: 7 and there he o burnt offerings and the fat of 6913
7:15 and my ears attentive to the prayers o AIT
28: 4 He o sacrifices and burned incense at 2284
28:23 He o sacrifices to the gods of Damascus, 2284
30:22 and o fellowship offerings and praised 2284
33:22 Amon worshiped and o sacrifices to all 2284
Ezr 6:17 the dedication of this house of God they o 10638
Ne 12:43 And on that day they o great sacrifices, 2284
Job 26: 3 What advice you have o to one 3619
31:27 o them a kiss of homage, 4200+5975+7023
Ps 51:19 then bulls will be o on your altar. 6590
106:28 and ate sacrifices o to lifeless gods, AIT
Isa 50: 6 I o my back to those who beat me, 5989
57: 6 and o grain offerings. 6590
Eze 6:13 places where they o fragrant incense 5989
16:18 and you o my oil and incense before them. 5989
16:19 you o as fragrant incense before them. 5989
20:28 there they o their sacrifices, 2284
44: 7 while you o me food, 7928
Jnh 1:16 and they o a sacrifice to the LORD 2284
Mt 26:27 gave thanks and o it to them, saying, 1443
27:34 There they o Jesus wine to drink, 1443
27:48 o it to Jesus to drink. 4540
Mk 14:23 gave thanks and o it to them, 1443
15:23 Then they o him wine mixed with myrrh, 1443
15:36 o it to Jesus to drink. 4540
Lk 23:36 They o him wine vinegar 4712
Ac 8:18 he o them money 4712
Ro 11:16 the part of the dough o as firstfruits is holy, NIG
1Co 9:13 at the altar share in what is o on the altar? NIG
10:19 sacrifice o to an idol is anything, 1628
10:20 sacrifices of pagans are o to demons, 2604
10:28 "This has been o in sacrifice," 2638
Heb 5: 7 he o up prayers and petitions 4712
6:18 to take hold of the hope o to us may 4618
7:27 for their sins once for all when he o himself. 429
9: 7 which he o for himself and for the sins 4712
9: 9 that the gifts and sacrifices being o were 4712
9:14 the eternal Spirit o himself unblemished 4712
10: 2 would they not have stopped being o? 4712
10:12 But when this priest had o 4712
11: 4 By faith Abel o God a better sacrifice 4712
Heb 11:17 when God tested him, o Isaac as a sacrifice. 4712
Jas 2:21 for what he did when he o his son Isaac on 429
5:15 And the prayer o in faith will make NIG
Rev 14: 4 from among men and o as firstfruits to God NIG

OFFERING (689) [OFFER]

Ge 4: 3 the fruits of the soil as an o to the LORD. 4966
4: 4 LORD looked with favor on Abel and his o, 4966
4: 5 but on Cain and his o he did not look 4966
22: 2 Sacrifice him there as a burnt o on one of 6592
22: 3 he had cut enough wood for the burnt o, 6592
22: 6 the burnt o and placed it on his son Isaac, 6592
22: 7 "but where is the lamb for the burnt o?" 6592
22: 8 the lamb for the burnt o, 6592
22:13 and sacrificed it as a burnt o instead 6592
35:14 and he poured out a drink o on it; 5821
Ex 18:12 brought a burnt o and other sacrifices 6592
25: 2 "Tell the Israelites to bring me an o. 9556
25: 2 You are to receive the o for me 9556
29:14 It is a sin o. 2633
29:18 It is a burnt o to the LORD, 6592
29:18 o made to the LORD by fire. 852
29:24 before the LORD as a wave o. 9485
29:25 along with the burnt o for a pleasing aroma 6592
29:25 o made to the LORD by fire. 852
29:26 wave it before the LORD as a wave o, 9485
29:36 Sacrifice a bull each day as a sin o 2633
29:40 and a quarter of a hin of wine as a drink o. 5821
29:41 the same grain o and its drink offering as in 4966
29:41 the same grain offering and its drink o as in 5821
29:41 o made to the LORD by fire. 852
29:42 the generations to come this burnt o is to 6592
30: 9 or any burnt o or grain offering, 6592
30: 9 or any burnt offering or grain o, 4966
30: 9 and do not pour a drink o on it. 5821
30:10 be made with the blood of the atoning sin o 2633
30:13 This half shekel is an o to the LORD. 9556
30:14 are to give an o to the LORD. 9556
30:15 the o to the LORD to atone for your lives. 9556
30:20 o made to the LORD by fire, 852
30:28 the altar of burnt o and all its utensils, 6592
31: 9 the altar of burnt o and all its utensils, 6592
35: 5 take an o for the LORD. 9556
35: 5 the LORD an o of gold, silver and bronze; 9556
35:16 the altar of burnt o with its bronze grating, 6592
35:21 and brought an o to the LORD for 9556
35:22 They all presented their gold as a wave o to 9485
35:24 an o of silver or bronze brought it as 9556
35:24 or bronze brought it as an o to the LORD, 9556
36: 6 or woman is to make anything else as an o 9556
38: 1 the altar of burnt o of acacia wood, 6592
38:24 from the wave o used for all the work on 9485
38:29 The bronze from the wave o was 70 talents 9485
40: 6 the altar of burnt o in front of the entrance 6592
40:10 the altar of burnt o and all its utensils; 6592
40:29 He set the altar of burnt o near the entrance 6592
Lev 1: 2 any of you brings an o to the LORD, 7933
1: 2 the LORD, bring as your o an animal from 7933
1: 3 " 'If the o is a burnt offering from the herd, 7933
1: 3 " 'If the offering is a burnt o from the herd, 6592
1: 4 to lay his hand on the head of the burnt o, 6592
1: 6 to skin the burnt o and cut it into pieces. 6592
1: 9 It is a burnt o, an offering made by fire, 6592
1: 9 It is a burnt offering, an o made by fire, 852
1:10 the o is a burnt offering from the flock, 7933
1:10 the offering is a burnt o from the flock, 6592
1:13 It is a burnt o, an offering made by fire, 6592
1:13 It is a burnt offering, an o made by fire, 852
1:14 " 'If the o to the LORD is a burnt offering 7933
1:14 " 'If the offering to the LORD is a burnt o 6592
1:17 It is a burnt o, an offering made by fire, 6592
1:17 It is a burnt offering, an o made by fire, 852
2: 1 " 'When someone brings a grain o to 4966
2: 1 his o is to be of fine flour. 7933
2: 2 an o made by fire, 852
2: 3 the grain o belongs to Aaron and his sons; 4966
2: 4 " 'If you bring a grain o baked in an oven, 4966
2: 5 If your grain o is prepared on a griddle, 4966
2: 6 it is a grain o. 4966
2: 7 If your grain o is cooked in a pan, 4966
2: 8 Bring the grain o made of these things to 4966
2: 9 from the grain o and burn it on the altar as 4966
2: 9 burn it on the altar as an o made by fire, 852
2:10 the grain o belongs to Aaron and his sons; 4966
2:11 " 'Every grain o you bring to the LORD 4966
2:11 o made to the LORD by fire. 852
2:12 You may bring them to the LORD as an o 7933
2:14 " 'If you bring a grain o of firstfruits to 4966
2:15 Put oil and incense on it; it is a grain o. 4966
2:16 o made to the LORD by fire. 852
3: 1 " 'If someone's o is a fellowship offering, 7933
3: 1 " 'If someone's offering is a fellowship o, 2285
3: 2 of his o and slaughter it at the entrance to 7933
3: 3 From the fellowship o he is to bring 2285
3: 5 of the burnt o that is on the burning wood, 6592
3: 5 as an o made by fire, 852
3: 6 an animal from the flock as a fellowship o 2285
3: 8 on the head of his o and slaughter it in front 7933
3: 9 From the fellowship o he is to bring 2285
3:11 o made to the LORD by fire. 852
3:12 " 'If his o is a goat, 7933
3:14 o to the LORD by fire: 852
3:16 an o made by fire, a pleasing aroma. 852
4: 3 a young bull without defect as a sin o for 2633
4: 7 of the altar of burnt o at the entrance to 6592
4: 8 the fat from the bull of the sin o— 2633

Lev 4:10	from the ox sacrificed as a **fellowship o.**	8968
4:10	burn them on the altar of **burnt o.**	6592
4:14	a young bull as a **sin o** and present it before	2633
4:18	of the altar of **burnt o** at the entrance to	6592
4:20	as he did with the bull for the **sin o.**	2633
4:21	This is the **sin o** *for* the community.	2633
4:23	as his **o** a male goat without defect.	7933
4:24	the place where the **burnt o** is slaughtered	6592
4:24	It is a **sin o.**	2633
4:25	of the **sin o** with his finger and put it on	2633
4:25	the altar of **burnt o** and pour out the rest of	6592
4:26	as he burned the fat of the fellowship **o.**	2285
4:28	as his **o** for the sin he committed	7933
4:29	of the **sin o** and slaughter it at the place of	2633
4:29	and slaughter it at the place of the **burnt o.**	6592
4:30	the altar of **burnt o** and pour out the rest of	6592
4:31	as the fat is removed from the fellowship **o,**	2285
4:32	" 'If he brings a lamb as his **sin o,**	7933
4:33	on its head and slaughter it for a **sin o** at	2633
4:33	the place where the **burnt o** is slaughtered.	6592
4:34	of the **sin o** with his finger and put it on	2633
4:34	the altar of **burnt o** and pour out the rest of	6592
4:35	from the lamb of the fellowship **o,**	2285
5: 6	or goat from the flock as a **sin o;**	2633
5: 7	a **sin o** and the other for a burnt offering.	2633
5: 7	a sin offering and the other for a **burnt o.**	6592
5: 8	who shall first offer the one for the **sin o.**	2633
5: 9	of the blood of the **sin o** against the side of	2633
5: 9	It is a **sin o.**	2633
5:10	the other as a **burnt o** in the prescribed way	6592
5:11	he is to bring as an **o** for his sin a tenth of	7933
5:11	a tenth of an ephah of fine flour for a **sin o.**	2633
5:11	because it is a **sin o.**	2633
5:12	It is a **sin o.**	2633
5:13	The rest of the **o** will belong to the priest,	NIH
5:13	as in the case of the **grain o.' "**	4966
5:15	It is a **guilt o.**	871
5:16	for him with the ram as a **guilt o,**	871
5:18	to bring to the priest as a **guilt o** a ram	871
5:19	It is a **guilt o;**	871
6: 5	on the day he presents his **guilt o.**	873
6: 6	that is, to the LORD, his **guilt o,**	871
6: 9	'These are the regulations for the **burnt o:**	6592
6: 9	The **burnt o** is to remain on the altar hearth	6592
6:10	and shall remove the ashes of the **burnt o**	6592
6:12	to add firewood and arrange the **burnt o** on	6592
6:14	" 'These are the regulations for the **grain o:**	4966
6:15	together with all the incense on the **grain o,**	4966
6:17	Like the **sin o** and the guilt offering,	2633
6:17	Like the sin offering and the **guilt o,**	871
6:20	the **o** Aaron and his sons are to bring to	7933
6:20	an ephah of fine flour as a regular **grain o,**	4966
6:21	and present the **grain o** broken in pieces as	4966
6:23	Every **grain o** *of* a priest shall	4966
6:25	'These are the regulations for the **sin o:**	2633
6:25	The **sin o** is to be slaughtered before	2633
6:25	in the place the **burnt o** is slaughtered;	6592
6:30	But any **sin o** whose blood is brought into	2633
7: 1	for the **guilt o,** which is most holy:	871
7: 2	The **guilt o** is to be slaughtered in	871
7: 2	the place where the **burnt o** is slaughtered,	6592
7: 5	**o made** to the LORD **by fire.**	852
7: 5	It is a **guilt o.**	871
7: 7	" 'The same law applies to both the **sin o**	2633
7: 7	to both the sin offering and the **guilt o:**	871
7: 8	a **burnt o** *for* anyone may keep its hide	6592
7: 9	Every **grain o** baked in an oven or cooked	4966
7:10	and every **grain o,**	4966
7:11	for the fellowship **o** a person may present	2285
7:12	along with this thank **o** he is to offer cakes	2285
7:13	with his fellowship **o** *of* thanksgiving he is	2285
7:13	an **o** with cakes of bread made with yeast.	7933
7:14	He is to bring one of each kind as an **o,**	7933
7:15	of his fellowship **o** *of* thanksgiving must	2285
7:16	his **o** is the result of a vow or is	7933
7:16	the result of a vow or is a freewill **o,**	2285
7:18	If any meat of the fellowship **o** is eaten on	2285
7:20	the fellowship **o** belonging to the LORD,	2285
7:21	the fellowship **o** belonging to the LORD,	2285
7:25	of an animal from which an **o by fire** may	852
7:29	'Anyone who brings a fellowship **o** to	2285
7:30	**o made** *to* the LORD **by fire;**	852
7:30	the breast before the LORD as a **wave o.**	9485
7:33	the **fellowship o** shall have the right thigh	8968
7:37	then, are the regulations for the **burnt o,**	6592
7:37	the **grain o,** the sin offering,	4966
7:37	the grain offering, the **sin o,**	2633
7:37	the sin offering, the **guilt o,**	871
7:37	the **ordination o** and the fellowship	4854
7:37	and the fellowship **o,**	2285
8: 2	the anointing oil, the bull for the **sin o,**	2633
8:14	He then presented the bull for the **sin o,**	2633
8:18	He then presented the ram for the **burnt** *o,*	AIT
8:21	the whole ram on the altar as a **burnt o,**	6592
8:21	**o made** to the LORD **by fire,**	852
8:27	before the LORD as a **wave o.**	9485
8:28	of the **burnt o** as an ordination offering,	6592
8:28	of the burnt offering as an **ordination o,**	4854
8:28	**o made** to the LORD **by fire.**	852
8:29	waved it before the LORD as a **wave o,**	9485
9: 2	"Take a bull calf for your **sin o** and a ram	2633
9: 2	and a ram for your **burnt o,**	6592
9: 3	'Take a male goat for a **sin o,**	2633
9: 3	and without defect—for a **burnt o,**	6592
9: 4	a ram for a **fellowship o** to sacrifice before	8968
9: 4	together with a **grain o** mixed with oil.	4966
9: 7	"Come to the altar and sacrifice your **sin o**	2633
Lev 9: 7	and your **burnt o** and make atonement	6592
9: 7	sacrifice the **o** that is *for* the people	7933
9: 8	the altar and slaughtered the calf as a **sin o**	2633
9:10	and the covering of the liver from the **sin o,**	2633
9:12	Then he slaughtered the **burnt o.**	6592
9:13	They handed him the **burnt o** piece	6592
9:14	and burned them on top of the **burnt o** on	6592
9:15	then brought the **o** *that* was *for* the people.	7933
9:15	for the people's **sin o** and slaughtered it	2633
9:15	**offered it for a sin o** as he did	2627
9:16	He brought the **burnt o** and offered it in	6592
9:17	He also brought the **grain o,**	4966
9:17	in addition to the morning's **burnt o.**	6592
9:18	the ram as the fellowship **o** for the people.	2285
9:21	before the LORD as a **wave o,**	9485
9:22	And having sacrificed the **sin o,**	2633
9:22	the **burnt o** and the fellowship offering,	6592
9:22	the burnt offering and the **fellowship o,**	8968
9:24	the LORD and consumed the **burnt o** and	6592
10:12	"Take the **grain o** left over from	4966
10:15	be waved before the LORD as a **wave o.**	9485
10:16	the **sin o** and found that it had been burned	2633
10:17	"Why didn't you eat the **sin o** in	2633
10:19	"Today they sacrificed their **sin o**	2633
10:19	and their **burnt o** before the LORD,	6592
10:19	if I had eaten the **sin o** today?"	2633
12: 6	a **burnt o** and a young pigeon or a dove for	6592
12: 6	and a young pigeon or a dove for a **sin o.**	2633
12: 8	a **burnt o** and the other for a sin offering.	6592
12: 8	a burnt offering and the other for a **sin o.**	2633
14:10	of fine flour mixed with oil for a **grain o,**	4966
14:12	of the male lambs and offer it as a **guilt o,**	871
14:12	before the LORD as a **wave o.**	9485
14:13	the lamb in the holy place where the **sin o**	2633
14:13	and the **burnt o** are slaughtered.	6592
14:13	Like the **sin o,** the guilt offering belongs to	2633
14:13	the **guilt o** belongs to the priest;	871
14:14	to take some of the blood of the **guilt o**	871
14:17	on top of the blood of the **guilt o.**	871
14:19	the **sin o** and make atonement for the one to	2633
14:19	the priest shall slaughter the **burnt o**	6592
14:20	together with the **grain o,**	4966
14:21	a **guilt o** to be waved to make atonement	871
14:21	of fine flour mixed with oil for a **grain o,**	4966
14:22	a **sin o** and the other for a burnt offering.	2633
14:22	a sin offering and the other for a **burnt o.**	6592
14:24	to take the lamb for the **guilt o,**	871
14:24	wave them before the LORD as a **wave o.**	9485
14:25	He shall slaughter the lamb for the **guilt o**	871
14:28	the blood of the **guilt o**—	871
14:31	as a **sin o** and the other as a burnt offering,	2633
14:31	as a sin offering and the other as a **burnt o,**	6592
14:31	together with the **grain o.**	4966
15:15	a **sin o** and the other for a burnt offering.	2633
15:15	a sin offering and the other for a **burnt o.**	6592
15:30	The priest is to sacrifice one for a **sin o** and	2633
15:30	a sin offering and the other for a **burnt o.**	6592
16: 3	with a young bull for a **sin o** and a ram for	2633
16: 3	for a sin offering and a ram for a **burnt o.**	6592
16: 5	to take two male goats for a **sin o** and a ram	2633
16: 5	for a sin offering and a ram for a **burnt o.**	6592
16: 6	"Aaron is to offer the bull for his own **sin o**	2633
16: 9	to the LORD and sacrifice it for a **sin o.**	2633
16:11	for his own **sin o** to make atonement	2633
16:11	he is to slaughter the bull for his own **sin o.**	2633
16:15	the **sin o** for the people and take its blood	2633
16:24	and sacrifice the **burnt o** *for* himself and	6592
16:24	for himself and the **burnt o** *for* the people,	6592
16:25	also burn the fat of the **sin o** on the altar.	2633
17: 4	the Tent of Meeting to present it as an **o** to	7933
17: 8	among them who offers a **burnt o**	6592
19: 5	" 'When you sacrifice a fellowship **o** to	2285
19:21	Tent of Meeting for a **guilt o** to the LORD.	871
19:22	the **guilt o** the priest is to make atonement	871
19:24	an **o of praise** to the LORD.	2136
22:10	a priest's family may eat the **sacred o,**	7731
22:14	" 'If anyone eats a **sacred o** by mistake,	7731
22:14	for the **o** and add a fifth of the value to it.	7731
22:18	presents a gift for a **burnt o** to the LORD,	6592
22:18	either to fulfill a vow or as a **freewill o,**	5607
22:21	from the herd or flock a fellowship **o** to	2285
22:21	to fulfill a special vow or as a **freewill o,**	5607
22:22	**o made** to the LORD **by fire.**	852
22:23	present as a **freewill o** an ox or a sheep	5607
22:27	**o made** to the LORD **by fire.**	852+7933
22:29	"When you sacrifice a thank **o** to	2285
23: 8	**o made** to the LORD **by fire.**	852
23:12	a **burnt o** to the LORD a lamb a year old	6592
23:13	with its **grain o** *of* two-tenths of an ephah	4966
23:13	**o made** to the LORD **by fire,**	852
23:13	and its **drink o** *of* a quarter of a hin of wine.	5821
23:14	the very day you bring this **o** *to* your God.	7933
23:15	the sheaf of the **wave o,**	9485
23:16	present an **o** of new **grain** to the LORD.	4966
23:17	as a **wave o** of firstfruits to the LORD.	9485
23:18	They will be a **burnt o** to the LORD,	6592
23:18	an **o made by fire,**	852
23:19	Then sacrifice one male goat for a **sin o**	2633
23:19	each a year old, for a fellowship **o.**	2285
23:20	before the LORD as a **wave o,**	9485
23:20	a **sacred o** to the LORD for the priest.	7731
23:25	**o made** to the LORD **by fire.' "**	852
23:27	**o made** to the LORD **by fire.**	852
23:36	**o made** to the LORD **by fire.**	852
24: 7	**o made** to the LORD **by fire.**	852
27: 9	that is acceptable as an **o** to the LORD,	7933
27:11	not acceptable as an **o** to the LORD—	7933
Nu 3: 4	when they **made an o** *with* unauthorized fire	7928
4:16	the regular **grain o** and the anointing oil.	4966
5:15	an **o** *of* a tenth of an ephah of barley flour	7933
5:15	because it is a **grain o** *for* jealousy,	4966
5:15	a reminder **o** to draw attention to guilt.	4966
5:18	and place in her hands the reminder **o,**	4966
5:18	the **grain o** *for* jealousy,	4966
5:25	from her hands the **grain o** *for* jealousy,	4966
5:26	then to take a handful of the **grain o** as	4966
5:26	as a **memorial o** and burn it on the altar;	260
6:11	as a **sin o** and the other as a burnt offering	2633
6:11	as a sin offering and the other as a **burnt o**	6592
6:12	a year-old male lamb as a **guilt o.**	871
6:14	without defect for a **burnt o,**	6592
6:14	without defect for a **sin o,**	2633
6:14	a ram without defect for a **fellowship o,**	8968
6:16	before the LORD and make the **sin o** and	2633
6:16	and make the sin offering and the **burnt o.**	6592
6:17	and is to sacrifice the ram as a fellowship **o**	2285
6:17	together with its **grain o** and drink offering.	4966
6:17	together with its grain offering and **drink o.**	5821
6:18	under the sacrifice of the **fellowship o.**	8968
6:20	before the LORD as a **wave o;**	9485
6:21	the Nazirite who vows his **o** to the LORD	7933
7:11	"Each day one leader is to bring his **o** for	7933
7:12	The one who brought his **o** on	7933
7:13	His **o** was one silver plate weighing	7933
7:13	with fine flour mixed with oil as a **grain o;**	4966
7:15	one male lamb a year old, for a **burnt o;**	6592
7:16	one male goat for a **sin o;**	2633
7:17	to be sacrificed as a **fellowship o.**	8968
7:17	the **o** *of* Nahshon son of Amminadab.	7933
7:18	the leader of Issachar, **brought** his **o.**	7928
7:19	**o** he brought was one silver plate weighing	7933
7:19	with fine flour mixed with oil as a **grain o;**	4966
7:21	one male lamb a year old, for a **burnt o;**	6592
7:22	one male goat for a **sin o;**	2633
7:23	to be sacrificed as a **fellowship o.**	8968
7:23	This was the **o** *of* Nethanel son of Zuar.	7933
7:24	of the people of Zebulun, brought his **o.**	NIH
7:25	His **o** was one silver plate weighing	7933
7:25	with fine flour mixed with oil as a **grain o;**	4966
7:27	one male lamb a year old, for a **burnt o;**	6592
7:28	one male goat for a **sin o;**	2633
7:29	to be sacrificed as a **fellowship o.**	8968
7:29	This was the **o** *of* Eliab son of Helon.	7933
7:30	of the people of Reuben, brought his **o.**	NIH
7:31	His **o** was one silver plate weighing	7933
7:31	with fine flour mixed with oil as a **grain o;**	4966
7:33	one male lamb a year old, for a **burnt o;**	6592
7:34	one male goat for a **sin o;**	2633
7:35	to be sacrificed as a **fellowship o.**	8968
7:35	This was the **o** *of* Elizur son of Shedeur.	7933
7:36	of the people of Simeon, brought his **o.**	NIH
7:37	His **o** was one silver plate weighing	7933
7:37	with fine flour mixed with oil as a **grain o;**	4966
7:39	one male lamb a year old, for a **burnt o;**	6592
7:40	one male goat for a **sin o;**	2633
7:41	to be sacrificed as a **fellowship o.**	8968
7:41	the **o** *of* Shelumiel son of Zurishaddai.	7933
7:42	of the people of Gad, brought his **o.**	NIH
7:43	His **o** was one silver plate weighing	7933
7:43	with fine flour mixed with oil as a **grain o;**	4966
7:45	one male lamb a year old, for a **burnt o;**	6592
7:46	one male goat for a **sin o;**	2633
7:47	to be sacrificed as a **fellowship o.**	8968
7:47	This was the **o** *of* Eliasaph son of Deuel.	7933
7:48	of the people of Ephraim, brought his **o.**	NIH
7:49	His **o** was one silver plate weighing	7933
7:49	with fine flour mixed with oil as a **grain o;**	4966
7:51	one male lamb a year old, for a **burnt o;**	6592
7:52	one male goat for a **sin o;**	2633
7:53	to be sacrificed as a **fellowship o.**	8968
7:53	the **o** *of* Elishama son of Ammihud.	7933
7:54	of the people of Manasseh, brought his **o.**	NIH
7:55	His **o** was one silver plate weighing	7933
7:55	with fine flour mixed with oil as a **grain o;**	4966
7:57	one male lamb a year old, for a **burnt o;**	6592
7:58	one male goat for a **sin o;**	2633
7:59	to be sacrificed as a **fellowship o.**	8968
7:59	the **o** *of* Gamaliel son of Pedahzur.	7933
7:60	of the people of Benjamin, brought his **o.**	NIH
7:61	His **o** was one silver plate weighing	7933
7:61	with fine flour mixed with oil as a **grain o;**	4966
7:63	one male lamb a year old, for a **burnt o;**	6592
7:64	one male goat for a **sin o;**	2633
7:65	to be sacrificed as a **fellowship o.**	8968
7:65	This was the **o** *of* Abidan son of Gideoni.	7933
7:66	of the people of Dan, brought his **o.**	NIH
7:67	His **o** was one silver plate weighing	7933
7:67	with fine flour mixed with oil as a **grain o;**	4966
7:69	one male lamb a year old, for a **burnt o;**	6592
7:70	one male goat for a **sin o;**	2633
7:71	to be sacrificed as a **fellowship o.**	8968
7:71	the **o** *of* Ahiezer son of Ammishaddai.	7933
7:72	of the people of Asher, brought his **o.**	NIH
7:73	His **o** was one silver plate weighing	7933
7:73	with fine flour mixed with oil as a **grain o;**	4966
7:75	one male lamb a year old, for a **burnt o;**	6592
7:76	one male goat for a **sin o;**	2633
7:77	to be sacrificed as a **fellowship o.**	8968
7:77	This was the **o** *of* Pagiel son of Ocran.	7933
7:78	of the people of Naphtali, brought his **o.**	NIH
7:79	His **o** was one silver plate weighing	7933
7:79	with fine flour mixed with oil as a **grain o;**	4966
7:81	one male lamb a year old, for a **burnt o;**	6592
7:82	one male goat for a **sin o;**	2633

Nu 7:83 to be sacrificed as a **fellowship o.** 8968
7:83 This was the **o** *of* Ahira son of Enan. 7933
7:87 for the **burnt o** came to twelve young bulls, 6592
7:87 together with their **grain o.** 4966
7:87 Twelve male goats were used for the **sin o.** 2633
7:88 for the sacrifice of the **fellowship o** came 8968
8: 8 with its **grain o** *of* fine flour mixed 4966
8: 8 to take a second young bull for a **sin o.** 2633
8:11 the LORD as a **wave o** from the Israelites, 9485
8:12 for a **sin o** to the LORD and the other for 2633
8:12 to the LORD and the other for a **burnt o,** 6592
8:13 and then present them as a **wave o** to 9485
8:15 and presented them as a **wave o,** 9485
8:21 Then Aaron presented them as a **wave o** 9485
9: 7 the LORD's **o** with the other Israelites at 7933
9:13 because he did not present the LORD's **o** 7933
15: 4 then the one who brings his **o** shall present 7933
15: 4 the LORD a **grain o** *of* a tenth of an ephah 4966
15: 5 With each lamb for the **burnt o** or 6592
15: 5 a quarter of a hin of wine as a **drink o.** 5821
15: 6 a ram prepare a **grain o** *of* two-tenths of 4966
15: 7 and a third of a hin of wine as a **drink o.** 5821
15: 8 a young bull as a **burnt o** or sacrifice, 6592
15: 8 for a special vow or a **fellowship o** to 8968
15: 9 bring with the bull a **grain o** *of* three-tenths 4966
15:10 Also bring half a hin of wine as a **drink o.** 5821
15:10 It will be an **o made by fire,** 852
15:13 an **o made by fire** as an aroma pleasing to 852
15:14 an **o made by fire** as an aroma pleasing to 852
15:19 present a portion as an **o** to the LORD. 9556
15:20 of your ground meal and present it as an **o** 9556
15:21 to give this **o** to the LORD from the first 9556
15:24 for a **burnt o** as an aroma pleasing to 6592
15:24 along with its prescribed **grain o** 4966
15:24 and **drink o,** and a male goat for 5821
15:24 and a male goat for a **sin o.** 2633
15:25 to the LORD for their wrong an **o** made 7933
15:25 an offering made by fire and a **sin o.** 2633
15:27 a year-old female goat for a **sin o.** 2633
16:15 "Do not accept their **o.** 4966
16:35 and consumed the 250 men *who were* **o** 7928
18:17 and burn their fat as an **o made by fire,** 852
18:18 of the **wave o** and the right thigh are yours. 9485
18:24 the Israelites present as an **o** to the LORD. 9556
18:26 a tenth of that tithe as the LORD's **o.** 9556
18:27 Your **o** will be reckoned to you as grain 9556
18:28 In this way you also will present an **o** *to* 9556
19:17 from the burned **purification o** into a jar 2633
23: 3 "Stay here beside your **o** while I go aside. 6592
23: 6 and found him standing beside his **o,** 6592
23:15 "Stay here beside your **o** while I meet 6592
23:17 and found him standing beside his **o,** 6592
26:61 and Abihu died when they **made an o** 7928
28: 3 the **o made by fire** that you are to present to 852
28: 3 as a regular **burnt o** each day. 6592
28: 5 with a **grain o** of a tenth of an ephah 4966
28: 6 This is the regular **burnt o** instituted 6592
28: 6 **o made** to the LORD **by fire.** 852
28: 7 The accompanying **drink o** is to be a 5821
28: 7 the **drink o** to the LORD at the sanctuary. 5821
28: 8 the same kind of **grain o** and drink offering 4966
28: 8 **drink o** that you prepare in the morning. 5821
28: 8 This is an **o made by fire,** 852
28: 9 make an **o** of two lambs a year old NIH
28: 9 with its **drink o** and a grain offering 5821
28: 9 and a **grain o** of two-tenths of an ephah 4966
28:10 This is the **burnt o** *for* every Sabbath, 6592
28:10 the regular **burnt o** and its drink offering. 6592
28:10 to the regular burnt offering and its **drink o.** 5821
28:11 the LORD a **burnt o** of two young bulls, 6592
28:12 to be a **grain o** of three-tenths of an ephah 4966
28:12 with the ram, a **grain o** of two-tenths of 4966
28:13 a **grain o** of a tenth of an ephah 4966
28:13 This is for a **burnt o,** a pleasing aroma, 6592
28:13 **o made** to the LORD **by fire.** 852
28:14 With each bull there is to be a **drink o** 5821
28:14 This is the monthly **burnt o** to be made 6592
28:15 the regular **burnt o** with its drink offering, 6592
28:15 the regular burnt offering with its **drink o,** 5821
28:15 to be presented to the LORD as a **sin o.** 2633
28:19 Present to the LORD an **o made by fire,** 852
28:19 a **burnt o** of two young bulls, 6592
28:20 a **grain o** of three-tenths of an ephah 4966
28:22 as a **sin o** to make atonement for you. 2633
28:23 in addition to the regular morning **burnt o.** 6592
28:24 the **o made by fire** every day for seven days 852
28:24 the regular **burnt o** and its drink offering. 6592
28:24 to the regular burnt offering and its **drink o.** 5821
28:26 to the LORD an **o** of new **grain** during 4966
28:27 Present a **burnt o** of two young bulls, 6592
28:28 to be a **grain o** of three-tenths of an ephah 4966
28:31 the regular **burnt o** and its grain offering. 6592
28:31 to the regular burnt offering and its **grain o.** 4966
29: 2 prepare a **burnt o** of one young bull, 6592
29: 3 the bull prepare a **grain o** of three-tenths of 4966
29: 5 as a **sin o** to make atonement for you. 2633
29: 8 to the LORD a **burnt o** of one young bull, 6592
29: 9 the bull prepare a **grain o** of three-tenths of 4966
29:11 Include one male goat as a **sin o,** 2633
29:11 in addition to the **sin o** *for* atonement and 2633
29:11 the regular **burnt o** with its grain offering, 6592
29:11 the regular burnt offering with its **grain o,** 4966
29:13 an **o made by fire** as an aroma pleasing to 852
29:13 a **burnt o** of thirteen young bulls, 6592
29:14 of the thirteen bulls prepare a **grain o** 4966
29:16 Include one male goat as a **sin o,** 2633
29:16 the regular **burnt o** with its grain offering 6592

Nu 29:16 the regular burnt offering with its **grain o** 4966
29:16 with its grain offering and **drink o.** 5821
29:19 Include one male goat as a **sin o,** 2633
29:19 the regular **burnt o** with its grain offering, 6592
29:19 the regular burnt offering with its **grain o,** 4966
29:22 Include one male goat as a **sin o,** 2633
29:22 the regular **burnt o** with its grain offering 6592
29:22 the regular burnt offering with its **grain o** 4966
29:22 with its grain offering and **drink o.** 5821
29:25 Include one male goat as a **sin o,** 2633
29:25 the regular **burnt o** with its grain offering 6592
29:25 the regular burnt offering with its **grain o** 4966
29:25 with its grain offering and **drink o.** 5821
29:28 Include one male goat as a **sin o,** 2633
29:28 the regular **burnt o** with its grain offering 6592
29:28 the regular burnt offering with its **grain o** 4966
29:28 with its grain offering and **drink o.** 5821
29:31 Include one male goat as a **sin o,** 2633
29:31 the regular **burnt o** with its grain offering 6592
29:31 the regular burnt offering with its **grain o** 4966
29:31 with its grain offering and **drink o.** 5821
29:34 Include one male goat as a **sin o,** 2633
29:34 the regular **burnt o** with its grain offering 6592
29:34 the regular burnt offering with its **grain o** 4966
29:34 with its grain offering and **drink o.** 5821
29:36 an **o made by fire** as an aroma pleasing to 852
29:36 a **burnt o** of one bull, 6592
29:38 Include one male goat as a **sin o,** 2633
29:38 the regular **burnt o** with its grain offering 6592
29:38 the regular burnt offering with its **grain o** 4966
29:38 with its grain offering and **drink o.** 5821
31:50 So we have brought as an **o** *to* the LORD 7933
Dt 2:26 to Sihon king of Heshbon **o** peace 1821
13:16 a **whole burnt o** to the LORD your God. 4003
16:10 a **freewill o** in proportion to the blessings 5607
24:10 to get *what* he is **o as a pledge.** 6287
Jdg 6:18 until I come back and bring my **o** and set it 4966
6:26 offer the second bull as a **burnt o."** 6592
11:31 and I will sacrifice it as a **burnt o."** 6592
13:16 But if you prepare a **burnt o,** 6592
13:19 together with the **grain o,** 4966
13:23 he would not have accepted a **burnt o** 6592
13:23 and **grain o** from our hands, 4966
1Sa 2:17 for they were treating the LORD's **o** 4966
2:29 and **o** that I prescribed *for* my dwelling? 4966
2:29 of every **o** *made* by my people Israel?' 4966
3:14 be atoned for by sacrifice or **o.'** " 4966
6: 3 but by all means send a **guilt o** to him. 871
6: 4 "What **guilt o** should we send to him?" 871
6: 8 to him as a **guilt o.** 871
6:14 and sacrificed the cows as a **burnt o** to 6592
6:17 the Philistines sent as a **guilt o** to the LORD 871
7: 9 and offered it up as a whole **burnt o** to 6592
7:10 While Samuel was sacrificing the **burnt o,** 6592
13: 9 the **burnt o** and the fellowship offerings." 6592
13: 9 And Saul offered up the **burnt o.** 6592
13:10 Just as he finished making the **o,** 6592
13:12 So I felt compelled to offer the **burnt o."** 6592
26:19 then may he accept an **o.** 4966
2Sa 15:12 While Absalom *was* **o** sacrifices, 2284
24:22 Here are oxen for the **burnt o,** 6592
1Ki 13: 1 by the altar to **make** *an* **o.** 7787
18:33 and pour it on the **o** and on the wood." 6592
2Ki 3:20 about the time for **o** the sacrifice, 6590
10:25 as Jehu had finished making the **burnt o,** 6592
16:13 up his **burnt o** and grain offering, 6592
16:13 up his burnt offering and **grain o,** 4966
16:13 poured out his **drink o,** 5821
16:15 offer the morning **burnt o** and 6592
16:15 and the evening **grain o,** 4966
16:15 the king's **burnt o** and his grain offering, 6592
16:15 the king's burnt offering and his **grain o,** 4966
16:15 the **burnt o** *of* all the people of the land, 6592
16:15 and their **grain o** and their drink offering. 4966
16:15 and their grain offering and their **drink o.** 5821
1Ch 6:49 on the altar of **burnt o** and on the altar 6592
9:31 the responsibility for baking the **o bread.** 2503
16:29 Bring an **o** and come before him; 4966
16:40 on the altar of **burnt o** regularly, 6592
21:23 and the wheat for the **grain o.** 4966
21:24 sacrifice a **burnt o** that costs me nothing." 6592
21:26 from heaven on the altar of **burnt o.** 6592
21:29 and the altar of **burnt o** were at that time on 6592
22: 1 and also the altar of **burnt o** for Israel." 6592
2Ch 7: 1 from heaven and consumed the **burnt o** and 6592
29:18 the altar of **burnt o** with all its utensils, 6592
29:21 and seven male goats as a **sin o** for 2633
29:23 The goats for the **sin o** were brought before 2633
29:24 **presented** their blood on the altar **for a sin o** to atone for all Israel, 2627
29:24 because the king had ordered the **burnt o** 6592
29:24 the burnt offering and the **sin o** 2633
29:27 the order to sacrifice the **burnt o** on 6592
29:27 As the **o** began, singing to the LORD began 6592
29:28 the sacrifice of the **burnt o** was completed. 6592
35:16 of the Passover and the **o** *of* burnt offerings 6590
Ezr 6:17 as a **sin o** for all Israel, twelve male goats, 10260
8:25 the **o** *of* silver and gold and the articles that 9556
8:28 and gold are a **freewill o** to the LORD, 5607
8:35 seventy-seven male lambs and, as a **sin o,** 2633
8:35 All this was a **burnt o** to the LORD. 6592
10:19 a ram from the flock as a **guilt o.)** 871
Job 1: 5 in the morning he would sacrifice a **burnt o** 6592
42: 8 to my servant Job and sacrifice a **burnt o** 6592
Ps 40: 6 Sacrifice and **o** you did not desire, 4966
54: 6 I will sacrifice a **freewill o** to you; 5607
66:15 I will sacrifice fat animals to you and an **o** 7792

Ps 96: 8 bring an **o** and come into his courts. 4966
116:17 I will sacrifice a thank **o** to you and call on 2285
Isa 40:20 to **present** *such* **an o** selects wood that will 9556
53:10 the LORD makes his life a **guilt o,** 871
65: 3 **o sacrifices** in gardens and burning incense 2284
66: 3 *whoever* **makes** a grain **o** is 6590
66:20 to my holy mountain in Jerusalem as an **o** 4966
Eze 16:25 **o** your **body** with increasing promiscuity 906+7316+8079
43:19 to give a young bull as a **sin o** to the priests, 2633
43:21 the **sin o** and burn it in the designated part 2633
43:22 a male goat without defect for a **sin o,** 2633
43:24 on them and sacrifice them as a **burnt o** to 6592
43:25 to provide a male goat daily for a **sin o;** 2633
44:27 he is to offer a **sin o** for himself, 2633
45:19 of the **sin o** and put it on the doorposts of 2633
45:22 a **sin o** for himself and for all the people of 2633
45:23 and seven rams without defect as a **burnt o** 6592
45:23 and a male goat for a **sin o.** 2633
45:24 as a **grain o** an ephah for each bull and 4966
46: 2 The priests are to sacrifice his **burnt o** 6592
46: 4 The **burnt o** the prince brings to 6592
46: 5 The **grain o** given with the ram is to be 4966
46: 5 the **grain o** with the lambs is to be as much 4966
46: 7 He is to provide as a **grain o** one ephah 4966
46:11 the **grain o** is to be an ephah with a bull, 4966
46:12 When the prince provides a **freewill o** to 5607
46:12 a **burnt o** or fellowship offerings— 6592
46:12 He shall offer his **burnt o** 6592
46:13 without defect for a **burnt o** to the LORD; 6592
46:14 with it morning by morning a **grain o,** 4966
46:14 The presenting of this **grain o** to 4966
46:15 the lamb and the **grain o** and the oil shall 4966
46:15 by morning for a regular **burnt o.** 6592
46:20 where the priests will cook the **guilt o** and 871
46:20 and the **sin o** and bake the grain offering, 2633
46:20 and the sin offering and bake the **grain o,** 4966
Da 2:46 that an **o** and incense be presented to him. 10432
9:27 he will put an end to sacrifice and **o.** 4966
Am 4: 5 Burn leavened bread as a **thank o** and brag 9343
Mal 1: 8 *Try* **o** them to your governor! 7928
1:10 "and I will accept no **o** from your hands. 4966
Mt 5:23 if *you are* **o** your gift at the altar *4712*
Jn 16: 2 anyone who kills you will think *he is* **o** *4712*
Ac 10: 4 to the poor have come up as a **memorial o** *3649*
21:26 the **o** *would be* **made** for each of them. *4712+4714*
Ro 8: 3 in the likeness of sinful man to be a **sin o.** *281*
15:16 the Gentiles might become an **o** acceptable *4714*
2Co 8:19 to accompany us as we carry the **o,** *5921*
Eph 5: 2 for us as a fragrant **o** and sacrifice to God. *4714*
Php 2:17 *I am being* **poured out like a drink o** *5064*
4:18 They are a fragrant **o,** an acceptable *2602*
2Ti 4: 6 *I am* already *being* **poured out like a drink o,** *5064*
Heb 10: 5 "Sacrifice and **o** you did not desire, *4714*
13:11 into the Most Holy Place as a **sin o,** *281*
1Pe 2: 5 **o** spiritual sacrifices acceptable to God *429*

OFFERINGS (377) [OFFER]

Ge 8:20 he sacrificed **burnt o** on it. 6592
Ex 10:25 to have sacrifices and **burnt o** to present to 6592
20:24 on it your **burnt o** and fellowship offerings, 6592
20:24 and **fellowship o,** your sheep and goats 8968
22:29 "Do not hold back **o** from your granaries NIH
23:18 "The fat of my **festival o** must not 2504
24: 5 and they offered **burnt o** 6592
24: 5 and sacrificed young bulls as fellowship **o** 2285
25: 3 the **o** you are to receive from them: 9556
25:29 and bowls *for the* **pouring out of o.** 5818
29:28 to the LORD from their fellowship **o.** 2285
29:33 eat **these o** by which atonement was made 4392S
32: 6 the people rose early and sacrificed **burnt o** 6592
32: 6 and presented **fellowship o.** 8968
35:29 to the LORD **freewill o** for all the work 5607
36: 3 the **o** the Israelites had brought to carry out 9556
36: 3 to bring **freewill o** morning 5607
37:16 pitchers for the **pouring out of drink o.** 5818
40:29 offered on it **burnt o** and grain offerings, 6592
40:29 offered on it burnt offerings and **grain o,** 4966
Lev 2: 3 **o made** *to* the LORD **by fire.** 852
2:10 **o made** *to* the LORD **by fire.** 852
2:13 Season all your **grain o** with salt. 4966
2:13 of your God out of your **grain o;** 4966
2:13 add salt to all your **o.** 7933
4:35 **o made** *to* the LORD **by fire.** 852
5:12 **o made** *to* the LORD **by fire.** 852
6:12 and burn the fat of the **fellowship o** on it. 8968
6:17 **o made** *to* me **by fire.** 852
6:18 **o made** *to* the LORD **by fire** 852
7:14 the blood of the **fellowship o.** 8968
7:32 to give the right thigh of your fellowship **o** 2285
7:34 From the fellowship **o** of the Israelites, 2285
7:35 **o made** *to* the LORD **by fire** 852
7:38 the Israelites to bring their **o** to the LORD, 7933
8:31 the bread from the basket of **ordination o,** 4854
10:12 **o made** *to* the LORD **by fire** 852
10:13 **o made** *to* the LORD **by fire;** 852
10:14 as your share of the Israelites' fellowship **o.** 2285
10:15 with the fat portions of the **o made by fire,** 852
14:11 both the one to be cleansed and **his o** before 4392S
14:32 and who cannot afford the regular **o** NIH
16:27 The bull and the goat for the **sin o,** 2633
17: 5 and sacrifice them as fellowship **o.** 2285
21: 6 **o made** *to* the LORD **by fire,** 852
21:21 **o made** *to* the LORD **by fire.** 852
22: 2 the **sacred o** the Israelites consecrate to me, 7731

Lev 22: 3 the **sacred o** that the Israelites consecrate to 7731
22: 4 not eat the **sacred o** until he is cleansed. 7731
22: 6 of the **sacred o** unless he has bathed himself 7731
22: 7 and after that he may eat the **sacred o,** 7731
22:15 The priests must not desecrate the **sacred o** 7731
22:16 by allowing them to eat the **sacred o** and 7731
23:18 with their **grain o** and drink offerings— 4966
23:18 with their grain offerings and **drink o—** 5821
23:36 **o made** to the LORD **by fire,** 852
23:37 **o made** to the LORD **by fire—** 852
23:37 the **burnt o** and grain offerings, 6592
23:37 the burnt offerings and **grain o,** 4966
23:37 and **drink o** required for each day. 5821
23:38 These **o** are in addition to those for NIH
23:38 the **freewill o** you give to the LORD.) 5607
24: 9 **o made** *to* the LORD **by fire."** 852
26:31 in the pleasing aroma of your **o.** NIH
Nu 4: 7 dishes and bowls, and the jars for **drink o;** 5821
6:14 There he is to present his **o** to the LORD: 7933
6:15 with their **grain o** and drink offerings, and 4966
6:15 with their grain offerings and **drink o,** and 5821
7: 2 of those who were counted, **made o.** 7928
7:10 the leaders brought their **o** 7933
7:84 **o** of the Israelite leaders **for the dedication** 2853
7:88 These were the **o for the dedication** *of* 2853
10:10 over your **burnt o** and fellowship offerings, 6592
10:10 over your burnt offerings and **fellowship o,** 2285
15: 3 the LORD **o made by fire,** from the herd or 852
15: 3 whether **burnt o** or sacrifices, 6592
15: 3 or **freewill o** or festival offerings— 5607
15: 3 or freewill offerings or **festival o—** 4595
18: 8 in charge of the **o** *presented to* me; 9556
18: 8 all the **holy o** the Israelites give me I give 7731
18: 9 **most holy o** that is kept from the fire. 7731+7731
18: 9 the gifts they bring me as **most holy o,** 7731+7731
18: 9 whether grain or sin or **guilt o,** 871
18:11 the gifts of all the **wave o** *of* the Israelites. 9485
18:19 from the **holy o** the Israelites present to 7731
18:32 not defile the **holy o** *of* the Israelites, 7731
28: 2 the appointed time the food for my **o** made 7933
28:31 Prepare these together with their **drink o,** 5821
29: 6 and daily **burnt o** with their grain offerings 6592
29: 6 and daily burnt offerings with their **grain o** 4966
29: 6 with their grain offerings and **drink o** 5821
29: 6 **o made** to the LORD **by fire—** 852
29:11 and their **drink o.** 5821
29:18 prepare their **grain o** and drink offerings 4966
29:18 prepare their grain offerings and **drink o** 5821
29:19 and their **drink o.** 5821
29:21 prepare their **grain o** and drink offerings 4966
29:21 prepare their grain offerings and **drink o** 5821
29:24 prepare their **grain o** and drink offerings 4966
29:24 prepare their grain offerings and **drink o** 5821
29:27 prepare their **grain o** and drink offerings 4966
29:27 prepare their grain offerings and **drink o** 5821
29:30 prepare their **grain o** and drink offerings 4966
29:30 prepare their grain offerings and **drink o** 5821
29:33 prepare their **grain o** and drink offerings 4966
29:33 prepare their grain offerings and **drink o** 5821
29:37 prepare their **grain o** and drink offerings 4966
29:37 prepare their grain offerings and **drink o** 5821
29:39 and your **freewill o,** prepare these for 5607
29:39 your **burnt o,** grain offerings, 6592
29:39 your burnt offerings, **grain o,** 4966
29:39 **drink o** and fellowship offerings.' " 5821
29:39 drink offerings and **fellowship o.' "** 8968
Dt 12: 6 there bring your **burnt o** and sacrifices, 6592
12: 6 vowed to give and your **freewill o,** 5607
12:11 your **burnt o** and sacrifices, 6592
12:13 not to sacrifice your **burnt o** anywhere you please. 6592
12:17 or your **freewill o** or special gifts. 5607
12:27 Present your **burnt o** on the altar of 6592
18: 1 **o made** *to* the LORD **by fire,** 852
27: 6 with fieldstones and offer **burnt o** on it to 6592
27: 7 Sacrifice **fellowship o** there, 8968
32:38 and drank the wine of their **drink o?** 5816
33:10 and **whole burnt o** on your altar. 4003
Jos 8:31 On it they offered to the LORD **burnt o** 6592
8:31 and sacrificed **fellowship o.** 8968
13:14 since the **o made by fire** *to* the LORD, 852
22:23 and to offer **burnt o** and grain offerings, 6592
22:23 and to offer burnt offerings and **grain o,** 4966
22:23 or to sacrifice fellowship **o** on it, 2285
22:26 but not for **burnt o** or sacrifices.' 6592
22:27 at his sanctuary with our **burnt o,** 6592
22:27 sacrifices and **fellowship o.** 8968
22:28 not for **burnt o** and sacrifices, 6592
22:29 by building an altar for **burnt o,** 6592
22:29 **grain o** and sacrifices, 4966
Jdg 20:26 until evening and presented **burnt o** 6592
20:26 and **fellowship o** to the LORD. 8968
21: 4 an altar and presented **burnt o** and 6592
21: 4 burnt offerings and **fellowship o.** 8968
1Sa 2:28 the **o made with fire** *by* the Israelites. 852
6:15 people of Beth Shemesh offered **burnt o** 6592
10: 8 down to you to sacrifice **burnt o** 6592
10: 8 to sacrifice burnt offerings and fellowship **o,** 2285
11:15 There they sacrificed fellowship **o** before 2285
13: 9 the burnt offering and the **fellowship o."** 8968
15:22 "Does the LORD delight in **burnt o** 6592
2Sa 1:21 neither dew nor rain, nor fields that yield **o** 9556
6:17 and David sacrificed **burnt o** 6592
6:17 and **fellowship o** before the LORD. 8968
6:18 the **burnt o** and fellowship offerings, 6592
6:18 the burnt offerings and **fellowship o,** 8968
24:24 **burnt o** that cost me nothing." 6592
2Sa 24:25 to the LORD there and sacrificed **burnt o** 6592
24:25 sacrificed burnt offerings and **fellowship o.** 8968
1Ki 3: 4 and Solomon offered a thousand **burnt o** 6592
3:15 the Lord's covenant and sacrificed **burnt o** 6592
3:15 sacrificed burnt offerings and **fellowship o.** 8968
8:63 Solomon offered a sacrifice of fellowship **o** 2285
8:64 and there he offered **burnt o,** 6592
8:64 **grain o** and the fat of 4966
8:64 and the fat of the **fellowship o,** 8968
8:64 to hold the **burnt o,** 6592
8:64 the **grain o** and the fat of 4966
8:64 and the fat of the **fellowship o.** 8968
9:25 a year Solomon sacrificed **burnt o** 6592
9:25 and **fellowship o** on the altar he had built 8968
10: 5 and the **burnt o** he made at the temple of 6592
12:33 and went up to the altar to **make o.** 7787
13: 2 of the high places who now **make o** here, 7787
2Ki 5:17 your servant will never again make **burnt o** 6592
10:24 in to make sacrifices and **burnt o.** 6592
12: 4 that is brought as **sacred o** to the temple of 7731
12:16 from the **guilt o** and sin offerings was 871
12:16 and **sin o** was not brought into the temple of 2633
16:12 he approached it and **presented o** on it. 6590
16:13 the blood of his **fellowship o** on the altar. 8968
16:15 on the altar all the blood of the **burnt o** 6592
1Ch 6:49 the *ones who* **presented o** on the altar 7787
16: 1 and they presented **burnt o** and 6592
16: 1 and **fellowship o** before God. 8968
16: 2 the **burnt o** and fellowship offerings, 6592
16: 2 the burnt offerings and **fellowship o,** 8968
16:40 to present **burnt o** to the LORD on 6592
21:23 Look, I will give the oxen for the **burnt o,** 6592
21:26 to the LORD there and sacrificed **burnt o** 6592
21:26 sacrificed burnt offerings and **fellowship o.** 8968
23:29 the flour for the **grain o,** 4966
23:31 and whenever **burnt o** were presented to 6592
29:21 the LORD and presented **burnt o** to him: 6592
29:21 together with their **drink o,** 5821
2Ch 1: 6 of Meeting and offered a thousand **burnt o** 6592
2: 4 and for making **burnt o** every morning 6592
4: 6 to be used for the **burnt o** were rinsed, 6592
7: 7 and there he offered **burnt o** and the fat of 6592
7: 7 and the fat of the **fellowship o,** 8968
7: 7 could not hold the **burnt o,** 6592
7: 7 the **grain o** and the fat portions. 4966
8:12 Solomon sacrificed **burnt o** to the LORD, 6592
8:13 to the daily requirement for **o** commanded 6590
9: 4 and the **burnt o** he made at the temple of 6592
13:11 and evening they present **burnt o** 6592
23:18 the **burnt o** *of* the LORD as written in 6592
24:14 articles for the service and for the **burnt o,** 6592
24:14 **burnt o** were presented continually in 6592
29: 7 not burn incense or present any **burnt o** at 6592
29:29 When the **o** were finished, 6590
29:31 and **thank o** to the temple of the LORD." 9343
29:31 assembly brought sacrifices and **thank o,** 9343
29:31 all whose hearts were willing brought **burnt o.** 6592
29:32 The number of **burnt o** the assembly 6592
29:32 all of them for **burnt o** to the LORD. 6592
29:34 were too few to skin all the **burnt o;** 6592
29:35 There were **burnt o** in abundance, 6592
29:35 of the **fellowship o** and the drink offerings 8968
29:35 of the fellowship offerings and the **drink o** 5821
29:35 that accompanied the **burnt o.** 6592
30:15 and brought **burnt o** to the temple of 6592
30:22 and offered fellowship **o** and praised 2285
31: 2 to offer **burnt o** and fellowship offerings, 6592
31: 2 to offer burnt offerings and **fellowship o,** 8968
31: 3 the morning and evening **burnt o** and for 6592
31: 3 and for the **burnt o** on the Sabbaths, 6592
31:14 in charge of the **freewill o** *given to* God, 5607
32:23 Many brought **o** to Jerusalem for 4966
33:16 of the LORD and sacrificed fellowship **o** 2285
33:16 fellowship offerings and **thank o** on it, 9343
35: 7 and goats for the **Passover o,** and 7175
35: 8 the priests twenty-six hundred **Passover o** 7175
35: 9 provided five thousand **Passover o** 7175
35:12 They set aside the **burnt o** to give them to 6592
35:13 and boiled the **holy o** in pots, 7731
35:14 were sacrificing the **burnt o** and 6592
35:16 the Passover and the offering of **burnt o** on 6592
Ezr 1: 4 and with **freewill o** for the temple of God 5607
1: 6 in addition to all the **freewill o.** 5605
2:68 the heads of the families **gave freewill o** 5605
3: 2 the God of Israel to sacrifice **burnt o** on it, 6592
3: 3 and sacrificed **burnt o** on it to the LORD, 6592
3: 4 the required number of **burnt o** prescribed 6592
3: 5 they presented the regular **burnt o,** 6592
3: 5 those **brought as freewill o** 5605+5607
3: 6 to offer **burnt o** to the LORD, 6592
6: 9 young bulls, rams, male lambs for **burnt o** 10545
7:16 as the **freewill o** *of* the people and priests 10461
7:17 with their **grain o** and drink offerings, 10432
7:17 with their grain offerings and **drink o,** 10483
8:35 from captivity sacrificed **burnt o** to 6592
Ne 10:33 for the regular **grain o** and burnt offerings; 4966
10:33 for the regular grain offerings and **burnt o;** 6592
10:33 for the **o** on the Sabbaths, NIH
10:33 for the **holy o;** for the sin offerings 7731
10:33 for **sin o** to make atonement for Israel; 2633
10:37 first of our ground meal, of our [grain] **o,** 9556
13: 5 the **grain o** and incense and temple articles, 4966
13: 9 with the **grain o** and the incense. 4966
Ps 20: 3 and accept your **burnt o.** 6592
40: 6 **burnt o** and sin offerings you did not 6592
40: 6 burnt offerings and **sin o** you did not require 2631
Ps 50: 8 for your sacrifices or your **burnt o,** 6592
50:14 Sacrifice **thank o** to God, 9343
50:23 He who sacrifices **thank o** honors me, 9343
51:16 you do not take pleasure in **burnt o.** 6592
51:19 whole **burnt o** to delight you; 6592
56:12 I will present my **thank o** to you. 9343
66:13 with **burnt o** and fulfill my vows to you— 6592
107:22 Let them sacrifice thank **o** and tell 2285
Pr 7:14 "I have fellowship **o** at home; 2285
Isa 1:11 "I have more than enough of **burnt o,** 6592
1:13 Stop bringing meaningless **o!** 4966
19:21 with sacrifices and **grain o;** 4966
40:16 nor its animals enough for **burnt o.** 6592
43:23 not brought me sheep for **burnt o,** 6592
43:23 with **grain o** nor wearied you with demands 4966
56: 7 Their **burnt o** and sacrifices will 6592
57: 6 to them you have poured out **drink o** 5821
57: 6 and offered **grain o.** 4966
60: 7 *they will be* accepted *as* **o** *on* my altar, 6590
66:20 as the Israelites bring their **grain o,** 4966
Jer 6:20 Your **burnt o** are not acceptable; 6592
7:18 They pour out **drink o** to other gods 5821
7:21 add your **burnt o** to your other sacrifices 6592
7:22 about **burnt o** and sacrifices, 6592
14:12 though they offer **burnt o** 6592
14:12 and **grain o,** I will not accept them. 4966
17:26 bringing **burnt o** and sacrifices, 6592
17:26 **grain o,** incense and thank offerings to 4966
17:26 and **thank o** to the house of the LORD. 9343
19: 5 to burn their sons in the fire as **o** to Baal— 6592
19:13 and poured out **drink o** to other gods." 5821
32:29 and by pouring out **drink o** to other gods. 5821
33:11 of those who bring **thank o** to the house of 9343
33:18 before me continually to offer **burnt o,** 6592
33:18 to burn **grain o** and to present sacrifices.' " 4966
41: 5 bringing **grain o** and incense with them to 4966
44:17 and will pour out **drink o** to her just as we 5821
44:18 of Heaven and pouring out **drink o** to her, 5821
44:19 of Heaven and poured out **drink o** to her, 5821
44:19 like her image and pouring out **drink o** 5821
44:25 to burn incense and pour out **drink o** to 5821
48:35 to *those who* **make o** *on* the high places 6590
52:19 **bowls used for drink o—** 4984
Eze 20:28 made **o** that provoked me to anger, 7933
20:28 and poured out their **drink o.** 5821
20:40 There I will require your **o** 9556
36:38 as numerous as the flocks for **o** 7731
40:38 where the **burnt o** were washed. 6592
40:39 on which the **burnt o,** 6592
40:39 **sin o** and guilt offerings were slaughtered. 2633
40:39 and **guilt o** were slaughtered. 871
40:42 of dressed stone for the **burnt o,** 6592
40:42 the utensils for slaughtering the **burnt o** 6592
40:43 The tables were for the flesh of the **o.** 7933
42:13 the LORD will eat the **most holy o.** 7731+7731
42:13 There they will put the **most holy o—** 7731+7731
42:13 the **grain o,** the sin offerings and 4966
42:13 the **sin o** and the guilt offerings— 2633
42:13 the sin offerings and the **guilt o—** 871
43:18 for sacrificing **burnt o** and sprinkling blood 6592
43:27 the priests are to present your **burnt o** 6592
43:27 and **fellowship o** on the altar. 8968
44:11 the **burnt o** and sacrifices for the people 6592
44:13 of my holy things or my **most holy o;** 7731+7731
44:29 They will eat the **grain o,** 4966
44:29 the **sin o** and the guilt offerings; 2633
44:29 the sin offerings and the **guilt o;** 871
45:15 These will be used for the **grain o,** 4966
45:15 **burnt o** and fellowship offerings 6592
45:15 and **fellowship o** to make atonement for 8968
45:17 to provide the **burnt o,** grain offerings 6592
45:17 **grain o** and drink offerings at the festivals, 4966
45:17 grain offerings and **drink o** at the festivals, 5821
45:17 He will provide the **sin o,** grain offerings, 2633
45:17 He will provide the sin offerings, **grain o,** 4966
45:17 **burnt o** and fellowship offerings 6592
45:17 and **fellowship o** to make atonement for 8968
45:25 he is to make the same provision for **sin o,** 2633
45:25 **burnt o,** grain offerings and oil. 6592
45:25 burnt offerings, **grain o** and oil. 4966
46: 2 and his **fellowship o.** 8968
46:12 whether a burnt offering or **fellowship o—** 8968
46:12 or his **fellowship o** as he does on 8968
Hos 4:13 the mountaintops and **burn o** on the hills, 7787
6: 6 and acknowledgment of God rather than **burnt o.** 6592
8:11 Ephraim built many altars for **sin o,** 2627
9: 4 not pour out **wine o** to the LORD, 3516
Joel 1: 9 **Grain o** and drink offerings are cut off 4966
1: 9 Grain offerings and **drink o** are cut off from 5821
1:13 the **grain o** and drink offerings are withheld 4966
1:13 the grain offerings and **drink o** are withheld 5821
2:14 **grain o** and drink offerings for 4966
2:14 and **drink o** for the LORD your God. 5821
Am 4: 5 and brag about your **freewill o—** 5607
5:22 you bring me **burnt o** and grain offerings, 6592
5:22 you bring me burnt offerings and **grain o,** 4966
5:22 Though you bring choice **fellowship o,** 8968
5:25 and **o** forty years in the desert, 4966
Mic 6: 6 Shall I come before him with **burnt o,** 6592
Zep 3:10 my scattered people, will bring me **o.** 4966
Mal 1: 9 With **such o** from your hands, 2296S
1:11 and pure **o** will be brought to my name, 4966
2:12 he brings **o** to the LORD Almighty. 4966
2:13 to your **o** or accepts them with pleasure 4966
3: 3 the LORD will have men who will bring **o** 4966
3: 4 and the **o** *of* Judah and Jerusalem will 4966

Mal 3: 8 "In tithes and **o**." 9556
Mk 12:33 yourself is more important than all **burnt o** *3906*
12:41 the **place where the o were put** *1126*
Jn 8:20 the **place where the o were put.** *1126*
Ac 7:42 and **o** forty years in the desert, *5376*
24:17 for the poor and to present **o**. *4714*
Heb 10: 6 with **burnt o** and sin offerings you were *3906*
10: 6 with burnt offerings and **sin o** you were *281+4309*
10: 8 First he said, "Sacrifices and **o**, *4714*
10: 8 **burnt o** and sin offerings you did *3906*
10: 8 offerings and **sin o** you did not desire, *281+4309*
11: 4 when God spoke well of his **o**. *1565*

OFFERS (14) [OFFER]

Lev 3: 1 and he **o** an animal from the herd, 7928
3: 6 " 'If he **o** an animal from the flock as 7933
3: 7 If he **o** a lamb, 7928
3:14 From what he **o** he is to make this offering 7933
6:26 The priest who **o** it shall eat it; 2627
7: 8 The priest who **o** a burnt offering 7928
7: 9 on a griddle belongs to the priest who **o** it, 7928
7:12 *he* **o** it as an expression of thankfulness, 7928
7:16 sacrifice shall be eaten on the day *he* **o** it, 7928
7:33 of Aaron who **o** the blood and the fat of 7928
17: 8 or any alien living among them who **o** 6590
Dt 33:10 *He* **o** incense before you 8492
Isa 66: 3 and *whoever* **o** a lamb, 2284
Heb 10:11 again and again *he* **o** the same sacrifices, *4712*

OFFICE (7) [OFFICER, OFFICERS, OFFICIAL, OFFICIALS, OFFICIATE]

Dt 17: 9 and to the **judge** who is **in o** 9149
19:17 and the **judges** who are **in o** 9149
26: 3 and say to the priest **in o** at the time, 2118
1Sa 2:36 to some **priestly o** so I can have food 3914
Ne 13:29 because they defiled the **priestly o** and 3914
Isa 22:19 I will depose you from your **o**, 5163
Heb 7:23 death prevented them from continuing **in o**; *NIG*

OFFICER (34) [OFFICE]

1Sa 29: 3 who was an **o** *of* Saul king of Israel? 6269
2Ki 3:11 An **o** *of* the king of Israel answered, 6269
7: 2 The **o** on whose arm the king was leaning 8957
7:17 the **o** on whose arm he leaned in charge of 8957
7:19 The **o** had said to the man of God, "Look, 8957
9:25 Jehu said to Bidkar, his **chariot o**, 8957
18:17 his chief **o** and his field commander with 6247
18:24 How can you repulse one **o** *of* the least 7068
25:19 he took the **o** in charge of the fighting men 6247
25:19 the secretary who was **chief o** 2021+7372+8569
1Ch 26:24 was the **o** in charge of the treasuries. 5592
2Ch 24:11 and the **o** *of* the chief priest would come 7224
26:11 by Jeiel the secretary and Maaseiah the **o** 8853
28: 7 Azrikam the **o in charge** *of* the palace, 5592
Ezr 4: 8 Rehum the **commanding o** and 10116+10302
4: 9 Rehum the **commanding o** and 10116+10302
4:17 To Rehum the **commanding o**, 10116+10302
Ne 11: 9 Joel son of Zicri was their **chief o**, 7224
11:14 Their **chief o** was Zabdiel son 7224
11:22 The **chief o** *of* the Levites 7224
Isa 33:18 "Where is that **chief o?** 6221
33:18 Where is the **o in charge** *of* the towers?" 6221
36: 9 then can you repulse one **o** *of* the least 7068
Jer 20: 1 the chief **o** in the temple of the LORD, 7224
39: 3 Nebo-Sarsekim a chief **o**, 6247
39:13 Nebushazban a chief **o**, 6247
51:59 to the staff **o** Seraiah son of Neriah, 8569
52:25 he took the **o** in charge of the fighting men, 6247
52:25 the secretary who was **chief o** 2021+7372+8569
Da 2:15 He asked the king's **o**, 10718
Mt 5:25 and the judge may hand you over *to* the **o**, *5677*
Lk 12:58 and the judge turn you over *to* the **o**, *4551*
12:58 and the **o** throw you into prison. *4551*
2Ti 2: 4 he wants to please his **commanding o.** *5133*

OFFICERS (88) [OFFICE]

Ex 14: 7 with **o** over all of them. 8957
15: 4 of Pharaoh's **o** are drowned in the Red Sea. 8957
Nu 31:14 Moses was angry with the **o** *of* the army— 7212
31:48 **o** who were over the units of the army— 7212
Dt 20: 5 The **o** shall say to the army: 8853
20: 8 Then the **o** shall add, "Is any man afraid 8853
20: 9 the **o** have finished speaking to the army, 8853
Jos 1:10 So Joshua ordered the **o** *of* the people: 8853
3: 2 After three days the **o** went throughout 8853
1Sa 18: 5 and Saul's **o** as well. 6269
18:30 with more success than the rest of Saul's **o**, 6269
2Sa 8: 7 to the **o** *of* Hadadezer and brought them 6269
1Ki 4: 5 in charge of the **district o;** 5893
4:27 The **district o**, each in his month, 5893
9:22 his government officials, his **o**, 8569
20:14 'The **young o** *of* the provincial commanders 5853
20:15 the **young o** *of* the provincial commanders, 5853
20:17 The **young o** *of* the provincial commanders 5853
20:19 The **young o** *of* the provincial commanders 5853
20:24 and replace them with *other* **o**. 7068
2Ki 6: 8 After conferring with his **o**, he said, 6269
6:11 He summoned his **o** and demanded 6269
6:12 my lord the king," said one of his **o**, 6269
7:12 up in the night and said to his **o**, 6269
7:13 One of his **o** answered, 6269
9: 5 he found the army **o** sitting together. 8569
9:11 When Jehu went out to his **fellow o**, 123+6269
10:25 he ordered the guards and **o**: 8957
2Ki 10:25 and **o** threw the bodies out and then entered 8957
11:14 The **o** and the trumpeters were beside 8569
15:25 One of his **chief o**, Pekah son of Remaliah, 8957
24:10 At that time the **o** *of* Nebuchadnezzar king 6269
24:11 up to the city while his **o** were besieging it. 6269
24:14 all the **o** and fighting men, 8569
25:23 When all the army **o** and their men heard 8569
25:26 together with the army **o**, 8569
1Ch 11:11 a Hacmonite, was chief of the **o;** 8957
12:28 with 22 **o** from his family; 8569
12:34 1,000 **o**, together with 37,000 8569
13: 1 David conferred with each of his **o**, 5592
18: 7 David took the gold shields carried by the **o** 6269
27: 1 and commanders of hundreds, and their **o**, 8853
27: 3 of Perez and chief of all the army **o** for 8569
27:16 The **o** over the tribes of Israel: 5592
27:22 These were the **o** *over* the tribes of Israel. 8569
28: 1 the **o** *over* the tribes, 8569
29: 6 the **o** *of* the tribes of Israel, 8569
29:24 All the **o** and mighty men, 8569
2Ch 8:18 ships commanded by his own **o**, 6269
21: 9 So Jehoram went there with his **o** 8569
23:13 The **o** and the trumpeters were beside 8569
32: 6 He appointed military **o** over the people 8569
32: 9 he sent his **o** to Jerusalem 6269
32:16 Sennacherib's **o** spoke further against 6269
32:21 the fighting men and the leaders and **o** in 8569
35:23 Archers shot King Josiah, and he told his **o**, 6269
Ne 2: 9 The king had also sent army **o** and cavalry 8569
4:16 The **o** posted themselves behind all 8569
Est 2:21 of the king's **o** who guarded the doorway, 6247
6: 2 of the king's **o** who guarded the doorway, 6247
Isa 21: 5 Get up, you **o**, oil the shields! 8569
Jer 26:21 and all his **o** and officials heard his words, 1475
38:17 the **o** *of* the king of Babylon, your life will 8569
38:18 the **o** *of* the king of Babylon, this city will 8569
39:13 and all the other **o** *of* the king of Babylon 8042
40: 7 the army **o** and their men who were still in 8569
40:13 the army **o** still in the open country came 8569
41: 1 and had been one of the king's **o**, 8042
41:11 of Kareah and all the army **o** who were 8569
41:13 of Kareah and the army **o** who were 8569
41:16 the army **o** who were with him led away all 8569
42: 1 Then all the army **o**, 8569
42: 8 of Kareah and all the army **o** who were 8569
43: 4 the army **o** and all the people disobeyed 8569
43: 5 and all the army **o** led away all the remnant 8569
46:26 of Babylon and his **o**. 6269
51:57 her governors, **o** and warriors as well; 6036
Eze 23:15 of them looked like Babylonian **chariot o**, 8957
23:23 **chariot o** and men of high rank, 8957
Lk 22: 4 and the **o of the temple guard** *5130*
22:52 the **o of** the temple **guard,** *5130*
Ac 5:22 the **o** did not find them there. *5677*
5:26 the captain went with his **o** and brought *5677*
16:35 the magistrates sent their **o** to the jailer *4812*
16:37 But Paul said to **the o:** *899S*
16:38 The **o** reported this to the magistrates, *4812*
21:32 at once took some **o** and soldiers and ran *1672*
25:23 the **high ranking o** and the leading men *5941*

OFFICIAL (23) [OFFICE]

2Ki 8: 6 Then he assigned an **o** to her case and said 6247
23:11 the room of an **o** named Nathan-Melech. 6247
25: 8 an **o** *of* the king of Babylon, 6269
1Ch 9:11 the **o in charge** *of* the house of God; 5592
2Ch 13: 6 an **o** *of* Solomon son of David, 6269
31:13 and Azariah the **o in charge** *of* the temple 5592
Ne 2:10 and Tobiah the Ammonite **o** heard 6269
2:19 Tobiah the Ammonite **o** and Geshem 6269
Pr 17:11 a merciless **o** will be sent against him. 4855
Ecc 5: 8 for *one* **o** is eyed by a higher one, 1469
Jer 38: 7 a Cushite, an **o** in the royal palace, 6247
39: 3 a chief officer, Nergal-Sharezer a high **o** 4454
39:13 a high **o** and all the other officers of 4454
Da 1: 7 The chief **o** gave them new names: 6247
1: 8 and he asked the chief **o** for permission not 6247
1: 9 Now God had caused the **o** to show favor 6247
1:10 but the **o** told Daniel, "I am afraid of 6247
1:11 the guard whom the chief **o** had appointed 6247
1:18 the chief **o** presented them to 6247
Jn 4:46 a certain **royal o** whose son lay sick *997*
4:49 The **royal o** said, "Sir, come down before *997*
Ac 8:27 an **important o** in charge of all the treasury *1541*
28: 7 Publius, the **chief o** of the island. *4755*

OFFICIALS (226) [OFFICE]

Ge 12:15 And when Pharaoh's **o** saw her, 8569
20: 8 Abimelech summoned all his **o**, 6269
37:36 Potiphar, *one of* Pharaoh's **o**, 6247
39: 1 an Egyptian who was one of Pharaoh's **o**, 6247
40: 2 Pharaoh was angry with his two **o**, 6247
40: 7 So he asked Pharaoh's **o** who were 6247
40:20 and he gave a feast for all his **o**. 6269
40:20 and the chief baker in the presence of his **o:** 6269
41:37 to Pharaoh and to all his **o**. 6269
45:16 Pharaoh and all his **o** were pleased. 6269
50: 7 All Pharaoh's **o** accompanied him— 6269
Ex 5:21 a stench to Pharaoh and his **o** and have put 6269
7:10 down in front of Pharaoh and his **o**, 6269
7:20 and his **o** and struck the water of the Nile, 6269
8: 3 the houses of your **o** and on your people, 6269
8: 4 up on you and your people and all your **o**.' " 6269
8: 9 to pray for you and your **o** and your people 6269
8:11 your **o** and your people; 6269
Ex 8:21 of flies on you and your **o**, 6269
8:24 and into the houses of his **o**, 6269
8:29 the flies will leave Pharaoh and his **o** 6269
8:31 The flies left Pharaoh and his **o** 6269
9:14 and against your **o** and your people, 6269
9:20 Those **o** *of* Pharaoh who feared the word of 6269
9:30 But I know that you and your **o** still do 6269
9:34 He and his **o** hardened their hearts. 6269
10: 1 and the hearts of his **o** so 6269
10: 6 of all your **o** and all the Egyptians— 6269
10: 7 Pharaoh's **o** said to him, 6269
11: 3 by Pharaoh's **o** and by the people.) 6269
11: 8 All these **o** *of* yours will come to me, 6269
12:30 and all his **o** and all the Egyptians got up 6269
14: 5 and his **o** changed their minds about them 6269
18:21 and appoint them as **o** over thousands, 8569
18:25 **o** *over* thousands, hundreds, 8569
Nu 11:16 to you as leaders and **o** *among* the people. 8853
26: 9 the community **o** who rebelled 7951
Dt 1:15 of fifties and of tens and as tribal **o**. 8853
16:18 and **o** for each of your tribes in every town 8853
29: 2 to all his **o** and to all his land. 6269
29:10 and chief men, your elders and **o**, 8853
31:28 the elders of your tribes and all your **o**, 8853
34:11 and to all his **o** and to his whole land. 6269
Jos 8:33 with their elders, **o** and judges, 8853
23: 2 their elders, leaders, judges and **o**— 8853
24: 1 leaders, judges and **o** *of* Israel, 8853
Jdg 8: 6 But the **o** *of* Succoth said, 8569
8:14 for him the names of the seventy-seven **o** 8569
1Sa 8:15 and of your vintage and give it to his **o** 6247
22: 6 with all his **o** standing around him. 6269
22: 9 who was standing with Saul's **o**, said, 6269
22:17 But the king's **o** were not willing to raise 6269
2Sa 13:24 Will the king and his **o** please join me?" 6269
15:14 Then David said to all his **o** who were 6269
15:15 The king's **o** answered him, 6269
16: 6 He pelted David and all the king's **o** 6269
16:11 David then said to Abishai and all his **o**, 6269
1Ki 1: 9 and all the men of Judah who were royal **o**, 6269
1:47 the royal **o** have come to congratulate 6269
4: 2 And these were his **chief o:** 8569
9:22 his **government o**, his officers, his captains, 6269
9:23 They were also the chief **o** in charge 5893
9:23 550 **o** supervising the men who did 8097
10: 5 the seating of his **o**, 6269
10: 8 How happy your **o**, 6269
11:17 some Edomite **o** who had served his father. 408
11:26 He was one of Solomon's **o**, 6269
15:18 to his **o** and sent them to Ben-Hadad son 6269
16: 9 Zimri, one of his **o**, 6269
20: 6 to send my **o** to search your palace and 6269
20: 6 and the houses of your **o**. 6269
20:23 the **o** *of* the king of Aram advised him, 6269
20:31 His **o** said to him, "Look, 6269
22: 3 The king of Israel had said to his **o**, 6269
22: 9 king of Israel called one of his **o** and said, 6247
2Ki 10: 1 to the **o** *of* Jezreel, to the elders 8569
12:20 His **o** conspired against him 6269
12:21 The **o** who murdered him were Jozabad son 6269
14: 5 the **o** who had murdered his father the king. 6269
18:24 of the least *of* my master's **o**, 6269
19: 5 When King Hezekiah's **o** came to Isaiah, 6269
21:23 Amon's **o** conspired against him 6269
22: 9 "Your **o** have paid out the money that was 6269
24:12 his nobles and his **o** all surrendered to him. 6247
24:15 his **o** and the leading men of the land. 6247
25:24 "Do not be afraid of the Babylonian **o**," 6269
1Ch 18:17 and David's sons were **chief o** at 8037
23: 4 of the LORD and six thousand *are to be* **o** 8853
24: 5 for there were **o** *of* the sanctuary 8569
24: 5 and **o** *of* God among the descendants of 8569
24: 6 in the presence of the king and of the **o:** 8569
26:29 as **o** and judges over Israel. 8853
27:31 the **o in charge** *of* King David's property. 8569
28: 1 the **o** *of* Israel to assemble at Jerusalem: 8569
28: 1 of hundreds, and the **o in charge** *of* all 8569
28: 1 together with the **palace o**, 6247
28:21 The **o** and all the people will obey 8569
29: 6 and the **o in charge** *of* the king's work 8569
2Ch 8:10 They were also King Solomon's chief **o**— 5893
8:10 two hundred and fifty **o** supervising 8097
9: 4 the seating of his **o**, 6269
9: 7 How happy your **o**, 6269
17: 7 of his reign he sent his **o** Ben-Hail, 8569
18: 8 king of Israel called one of his **o** and said, 6247
19:11 and the Levites *will* **serve as o** before you. 8853
24:10 All the **o** and all the people brought 8569
24:11 by the Levites to the king's **o** and they saw 7213
24:17 the **o** *of* Judah came and paid homage to 8569
24:25 His **o** conspired against him for murdering 6269
25: 3 the **o** who had murdered his father the king. 6269
26:11 Hananiah, one of the royal **o**. 8569
28:14 and plunder in the presence of the **o** and all 8569
29:20 the city **o** together and went up to 8569
29:30 and his **o** ordered the Levites to praise 8569
30: 2 The king and his **o** and the whole assembly 8569
30: 6 from the king and from his **o**, which read: 8569
30:12 the king and his **o** had ordered, 8569
30:24 the **o** provided them with a thousand bulls 8569
31: 8 When Hezekiah and his **o** came and saw 8569
32: 3 he consulted with his **o** and military staff 8569
33:24 Amon's **o** conspired against him 6269
34:16 "Your **o** are doing everything 6269
35: 8 His **o** also contributed voluntarily to 8569
36:18 and the treasures of the king and his **o**. 8569
Ezr 4: 9 judges and **o** over the men from Tripolis, 10062

Ezr 5: 6 the o of Trans-Euphrates, 10061
6: 6 their fellow o of that province, 10061
7:28 and all the king's powerful o. 8569
8:20 a body that David and the o had established 8569
8:25 the articles that the king, his advisers, his o 8569
9: 2 And the leaders and o have led the way 6036
10: 8 in accordance with the decision of the o 8569
10:14 Let our o act for the whole assembly. 8569
Ne 2:16 The o did not know where I had gone 6036
2:16 or nobles or o or any others who would 6036
4:14 the o and the rest of the people, 6036
4:19 the o and the rest of the people, 6036
5: 7 and then accused the nobles and o. 6036
5:12 the priests and made **the nobles and o** take 4392[S]
5:17 and fifty Jews and o ate at my table, 6036
7: 5 the o and the common people 6036
9:10 against all his o and all the people 6269
12:40 so did I, together with half the o, 6036
13:11 So I rebuked the o and asked them, 6036
Est 1: 3 a banquet for all his nobles and o. 6269
2:18 Esther's banquet, for all his nobles and o. 6269
2:23 the two o were hanged on a gallows. 2157[S]
3: 2 the royal o at the king's gate knelt down 6269
3: 3 royal o at the king's gate asked Mordecai, 6269
4:11 "All the king's o and the people of 6269
5:11 above the other nobles and o. 6269
Pr 17:26 or to flog o for their integrity. 5618
29:12 all his o become wicked. 9250
Isa 3: 4 I will make boys their o; 8569
19:11 The o *of* Zoan are nothing but fools; 8569
19:13 The o *of* Zoan have become fools, 8569
30: 4 Though *they* have o in Zoan 8569
36: 9 of the least of my master's o, 6269
37: 5 When King Hezekiah's o came to Isaiah, 6269
Jer 1:18 against the kings of Judah, its o, 8569
2:26 they, their kings and their o, 8569
4: 9 "the king and the o will lose heart, 8569
8: 1 the bones of the kings and o *of* Judah, 8569
17:25 through the gates of this city with their o. 8569
17:25 and their o will come riding in chariots and 8569
21: 7 his o and the people 6269
22: 2 you, your o and your people who come 6269
22: 4 accompanied by their o and their people. 6269
24: 1 of Jehoiakim king of Judah and the o, 8569
24: 8 his o and the survivors from Jerusalem, 8569
25:18 and o, to make them a ruin and an object 8569
25:19 his attendants, his o and all his people, 8569
26:10 the o *of* Judah heard about these things, 8569
26:11 the priests and the prophets said to the o 8569
26:12 Then Jeremiah said to all the o and all 8569
26:16 the o and all the people said to the priests 8569
26:21 and all his officers and o heard his words, 8569
29: 2 the **court** o and the leaders of Judah 6247
32:32 they, their kings and o, 8569
34:10 So all the o and people who entered 8569
34:19 the **court** o, the priests and all the people 6247
34:21 of Judah and his o over 8569
35: 4 It was next to the room of the o, 8569
36:12 where all the o were sitting: 8569
36:12 and all the other o. 8569
36:14 all the o sent Jehudi son of Nethaniah, 8569
36:19 Then the o said to Baruch, 8569
36:21 the king and all the o standing beside him. 8569
37:14 and brought him to the o. 8569
37:18 against you or your o or this people, 6269
38: 4 Then the o said to the king, 8569
38:22 king of Judah will be brought out to the o *of* 8569
38:25 If the o hear that I talked with you, 8569
38:27 All the o did come to Jeremiah 8569
39: 3 Then all the o *of* the king of Babylon came 8569
39: 3 and all the other o *of* the king of Babylon. 8569
41:16 and **court** o he had brought from Gibeon. 6247
44:17 and our o did in the towns of Judah and in 8569
44:21 your kings and your o and the people of 8569
48: 7 together with his priests and o. 8569
49: 3 together with his priests and o. 8569
49:38 in Elam and destroy her king and o," 8569
50:35 and against her o and wise men! 8569
51:23 with you I shatter governors and o. 6036
51:28 their governors and all their o, 6036
51:57 I will make her o and wise men drunk, 8569
52:10 he also killed all the o *of* Judah. 8569
Eze 22:27 Her o within her are like wolves 8569
Da 1: 3 Ashpenaz, chief of his **court** o, 6247
3: 2 magistrates and all the other provincial o 10716
3: 3 and all the other provincial o assembled for 10716
Am 1:15 he and his o together," says the LORD. 8569
2: 3 I will destroy her ruler and kill all her o 8569
Na 3:17 your o like swarms of locusts that settle in 3261
Zep 3: 3 Her o are roaring lions, 8569
Mt 20:25 their **high** o exercise authority over them. *3489*
Mk 6:21 *for* his **high** o and military commanders and *3491*
10:42 their **high** o exercise authority over them. *3489*
Jn 18: 3 a detachment of soldiers and some o from *5677*
18:12 and the Jewish o arrested Jesus. *5677*
18:18 and o stood around a fire they had made *5677*
18:22 one *of* the o nearby struck him in the face. *5677*
19: 6 as the chief priests and their o saw him, *5677*
Ac 17: 6 and some other brothers before the **city** o, *4485*
17: 8 and the **city** o were thrown into turmoil. *4485*
19:31 Even some *of* the **o of the province,** *825*

OFFICIATE (1) [OFFICE]

2Ki 17:32 of their own people *to* o for them *as* priests 6913

OFFSCOURING (KJV) See SCUM

OFFSET (1) [OFF]

1Ki 6: 6 He made **o ledges** around the outside of 4492

OFFSHOOTS (1) [OFF, SHOOT]

Isa 22:24 its offspring and o—all its lesser vessels, 7617

OFFSPRING (61) [OFF]

Ge 3:15 and between your o and hers; 2446
12: 7 "To your o I will give this land." 2446
13:15 I will give to you and your o forever. 2446
13:16 I will make your o like the dust of 2446
13:16 then your o could be counted. 2446
15: 5 Then he said to him, "So shall your o be." 2446
17:12 those who are not your o. 2446
21:12 through Isaac that your o will be reckoned. 2446
21:13 because he is your o." 2446
22:18 your o all nations on earth will be blessed, 2446
24: 7 saying, 'To your o I will give this land'— 2446
24:60 may your o possess the gates 2446
26: 4 your o all nations on earth will be blessed, 2446
28:14 be blessed through you and your o. 2446
38: 8 to her as a brother-in-law to produce o 2446
38: 9 But Onan knew that the o would not be his; 2446
38: 9 to keep from producing o for his brother. 2446
46: 6 and Jacob and all his o went to Egypt. 2446
46: 7 and granddaughters—all his o. 2446
Ex 13: 2 The **first** o *of* every womb among 7081
13:12 to the LORD the **first** o *of* every womb. 7081
13:15 the **first** male o *of* every womb 7081
34:19 "The **first** o *of* every womb belongs to me, 7081
Lev 21:15 he will not defile his o among his people. 2446
Nu 3:12 the **first male** o of every Israelite woman. 1147+7081+8167
8:16 **first male** o from every Israelite woman. 1147
18:15 The **first** o *of* every womb, 7081
18:19 before the LORD for both you and your o." 2446
Ru 4:12 Through the o the LORD gives you 2446
2Sa 4: 8 the king against Saul and his o." 2446
7:12 I will raise up your o to succeed you, 2446
1Ch 17:11 I will raise up your o to succeed you, 2446
Job 18:19 He has no o or descendants 5769
21: 8 their o before their eyes. 7368
27:14 his o will never have enough to eat. 7368
Ps 37:28 but the o *of* the wicked will be cut off; 2446
Isa 9:20 Each will feed on the flesh of his own o: 2446
14:20 The o *of* the wicked will never 2446
14:22 her o and descendants," 5769
22:24 its o and offshoots—all its lesser vessels, 7368
44: 3 I will pour out my Spirit on your o, 2446
53:10 he will see his o and prolong his days, 2446
57: 3 you o *of* adulterers and prostitutes! 2446
57: 4 a brood of rebels, the o *of* liars? 2446
61: 9 the nations and their o among the peoples. 7368
Jer 22:30 for none of his o will prosper, 2446
31:27 of Judah with the o *of* men and of animals. 2446
La 2:20 Should women eat their o, 7262
Hos 9:16 I will slay their cherished o." 1061
Mal 2:15 Because he was seeking godly o. 2446
Ac 3:25 'Through your o all peoples on earth will *5065*
17:28 'We are his o.' *1169*
17:29 "Therefore since we are God's o, *1169*
Ro 4:13 that Abraham and his o received *5065*
4:16 may be guaranteed *to* all Abraham's o— *5065*
4:18 "So shall your o be." *5065*
9: 7 "It is through Isaac that your o will *5065*
9: 8 children of the promise who are regarded as Abraham's o. *5065*
Heb 11:18 "It is through Isaac that your o will *5065*
Rev 12:17 to make war against the rest *of* her o— *5065*
22:16 I am the Root and the O of David, *1169*

OFTEN (24)

1Sa 18:30 and **as o as** they did, 1896+4946
2Ki 4: 9 that this man who o comes our way is 9458
Job 21:17 "Yet **how** o is the lamp of the wicked 3869+4537
21:17 How o does calamity come upon them, NIH
21:18 How o are they like straw before the wind, NIH
Ps 78:40 **How** o they rebelled against him in 3869+4537
Isa 28:19 **As o as** it comes it will carry you away; 1896+4946
Jer 31:20 I o speak against him, I still remember 1896+4946
Mt 17:15 He o falls into the fire or into the water. *4490*
23:37 **how** o I have longed to gather your children *4529*
Mk 5: 4 For he had o been chained hand and foot, *4490*
9:22 "It has o thrown him into fire or water *4490*
Lk 5:16 But Jesus o **withdrew** to lonely places *AIT*
5:33 "John's disciples o fast and pray, *4781*
13:34 **how** o I have longed to gather your children *4529*
Jn 18: 2 Jesus had o met there with his disciples. *4490*
Ro 15:22 This is why I have o been hindered *4498*
2Co 8:22 with them our brother who has o proved *4490*
11:27 I have labored and toiled and have o gone *4490*
11:27 and thirst and have o gone without food; *4490*
Php 3:18 as I have o told you before and *4490*
2Ti 1:16 because he o refreshed me and was *4490*
Heb 6: 7 in the rain o falling on it and that produces *4490*
Rev 11: 6 with every kind of plague **as o as** they want. *4006*

OG (20) [OG'S]

Nu 21:33 and O king of Bashan and his whole army 6384
32:33 of the Amorites and the kingdom of O king 6384
Dt 1: 4 and at Edrei had defeated O king of Bashan, 6384
3: 1 and O king of Bashan with his whole army 6384
3: 3 also gave into our hands O king of Bashan 6384
3:11 (Only O king of Bashan was left of 6384
3:13 all of Bashan, the kingdom of O, 6384
4:47 and the land of O king of Bashan, 6384
29: 7 of Heshbon and O king of Bashan came out 6384
31: 4 to them what he did to Sihon and O, 6384
Jos 2:10 and what you did to Sihon and O, 6384
9:10 and O king of Bashan, 6384
12: 4 And the territory of O king of Bashan, 6384
13:12 the whole kingdom of O in Bashan, 6384
13:30 the entire realm of O king of Bashan— 6384
13:31 and Edrei (the royal cities of O in Bashan). 6384
1Ki 4:19 of the Amorites and the country of O king 6384
Ne 9:22 of Heshbon and the country of O king 6384
Ps 135:11 O king of Bashan and all the kings 6384
136:20 and O king of Bashan— 6384

OG'S (2) [OG]

Dt 3: 4 O kingdom in Bashan. 6384
3:10 towns of O kingdom in Bashan. 6384

OH (37) [O] See Index of Articles Etc.

OHAD (2)

Ge 46:10 The sons of Simeon: Jemuel, Jamin, O, 176
Ex 6:15 The sons of Simeon were Jemuel, Jamin, O, 176

OHEL (1)

1Ch 3:20 There were also five others: Hashubah, O, 186

OHOLAH (5)

Eze 23: 4 The older was named O, 188
23: 4 O is Samaria, and Oholibah is Jerusalem. 188
23: 5 "O engaged in prostitution 188
23:36 will you judge O and Oholibah? 188
23:44 with those lewd women, O and Oholibah. 188

OHOLIAB (5)

Ex 31: 6 I have appointed O son of Ahisamach, 190
35:34 And he has given both him and O son 190
36: 1 O and every skilled person to whom 190
36: 2 and O and every skilled person to whom 190
38:23 with him was O son of Ahisamach, of 190

OHOLIBAH (6)

Eze 23: 4 and her sister was O. 191
23: 4 Oholah is Samaria, and O is Jerusalem. 191
23:11 "Her sister O saw this, 191
23:22 O, this is what the Sovereign LORD says: 191
23:36 will you judge Oholah and O? 191
23:44 with those lewd women, Oholah and O. 191

OHOLIBAMAH (8)

Ge 36: 2 of Elon the Hittite, and O daughter of Anah 192
36: 5 and O bore Jeush, 192
36:14 The sons of Esau's wife O daughter 192
36:18 The sons of Esau's wife O: 192
36:18 from Esau's wife O daughter of Anah. 192
36:25 Dishon and O daughter of Anah. 192
36:41 O, Elah, Pinon, 192
1Ch 1:52 O, Elah, Pinon, 192

OIL (211) [OILS]

Ge 28:18 and set it up as a pillar and poured o on top 9043
35:14 he also poured o on it. 9043
Ex 25: 6 **olive** o for the light; 9043
25: 6 the anointing o and for the fragrant incense; 9043
27:20 to bring you clear o *of* pressed olives for 9043
29: 2 make bread, and cakes mixed with o, 9043
29: 2 and wafers spread with o. 9043
29: 7 Take the anointing o and anoint him 9043
29:21 and some of the anointing o and sprinkle it 9043
29:23 and a cake made with o, and a wafer. 9043
29:40 a quarter of a hin of o *from* pressed olives, 9043
30:24 and a hin of olive o. 9043
30:25 Make these into a sacred anointing o, 9043
30:25 It will be the sacred anointing o. 9043
30:31 'This is to be my sacred anointing o for 9043
30:32 on men's bodies and do not make any o NIH
31:11 and the anointing o and fragrant incense for 9043
35: 8 **olive** o for the light; 9043
35: 8 the anointing o and for the fragrant incense; 9043
35:14 lamps and o *for* the light; 9043
35:15 the anointing o and the fragrant incense; 9043
35:28 They also brought spices and **olive** o for 9043
35:28 the anointing o and for the fragrant incense. 9043
37:29 They also made the sacred anointing o and 9043
39:37 and the o *for* the light; 9043
39:38 the anointing o, the fragrant incense, 9043
40: 9 the anointing o and anoint the tabernacle 9043
Lev 2: 1 He is to pour o on it, 9043
2: 2 a handful of the fine flour and o, 9043
2: 4 without yeast and mixed with o, 9043
2: 4 without yeast and spread with o. 9043
2: 5 it is to be made of fine flour mixed with o, 9043
2: 6 Crumble it and pour o on it; 9043
2: 7 it is to be made of fine flour and o. 9043
2:15 Put o and incense on it; 9043
2:16 of the crushed grain and the o, 9043

Lev 5:11 He must not put **o** or incense on it, 9043
6:15 to take a handful of fine flour and **o**, 9043
6:21 Prepare it with **o** on a griddle; 9043
7:10 whether mixed with **o** or dry, 9043
7:12 without yeast and mixed with **o**, 9043
7:12 without yeast and spread with **o**, 9043
7:12 and mixed with **o**. 9043
8:2 their garments, the anointing **o**, 9043
8:10 the anointing **o** and anointed the tabernacle 9043
8:11 of **the o** on the altar seven times, 5647S
8:12 of the anointing **o** on Aaron's head 9043
8:26 and one made with **o**, and a wafer; 9043
8:30 the anointing **o** and some of the blood from 9043
9:4 with a grain offering mixed with **o**. 9043
10:7 the LORD's anointing **o** is on you." 9043
14:10 of an ephah of fine flour mixed with **o** for 9043
14:10 and one log of **o**. 9043
14:12 along with the log of **o**; 9043
14:15 priest shall then take some of the log of **o**, 9043
14:16 dip his right forefinger into the **o** 9043
14:17 The priest is to put some of the **o** remaining 9043
14:18 of the **o** in his palm the priest shall put on 9043
14:21 of an ephah of fine flour mixed with **o** for 9043
14:21 a log of **o**, 9043
14:24 together with the log of **o**, 9043
14:26 of the **o** into the palm of his own left hand, 9043
14:27 of the **o** from his palm seven times before 9043
14:28 Some of the **o** in his palm he is to put on 9043
14:29 of the **o** in his palm the priest shall put on 9043
21:10 the anointing **o** poured on his head 9043
21:12 by the anointing **o** *of* his God. 9043
23:13 of an ephah of fine flour mixed with **o**— 9043
24:2 to bring you clear **o** *of* pressed olives for 9043
Nu 4:9 and all its jars for the **o** used to supply it. 9043
4:16 is to have charge of the **o** *for* the light, 9043
4:16 and the anointing **o**. 9043
5:15 He must not pour **o** on it or put incense 9043
6:15 cakes made of fine flour mixed with **o**, 9043
6:15 and wafers spread with **o**. 9043
7:13 each filled with fine flour mixed with **o** as 9043
7:19 each filled with fine flour mixed with **o** as 9043
7:25 each filled with fine flour mixed with **o** as 9043
7:31 each filled with fine flour mixed with **o** as 9043
7:37 each filled with fine flour mixed with **o** as 9043
7:43 each filled with fine flour mixed with **o** as 9043
7:49 each filled with fine flour mixed with **o** as 9043
7:55 each filled with fine flour mixed with **o** as 9043
7:61 each filled with fine flour mixed with **o** as 9043
7:67 each filled with fine flour mixed with **o** as 9043
7:73 each filled with fine flour mixed with **o** as 9043
7:79 each filled with fine flour mixed with **o** as 9043
8:8 of fine flour mixed with **o**; 9043
11:8 like something made with **olive o**. 9043
15:4 with a quarter of a hin of **o**. 9043
15:6 with a third of a hin of **o**, 9043
15:9 of fine flour mixed with half a hin of **o**. 9043
18:12 "I give you all the finest **olive o** and all 3658
28:5 a quarter of a hin of **o** *from* pressed olives. 9043
28:9 of an ephah of fine flour mixed with **o**; 9043
28:12 of an ephah of fine flour mixed with **o**; 9043
28:12 of an ephah of fine flour mixed with **o**; 9043
28:13 of an ephah of fine flour mixed with **o**; 9043
28:20 of an ephah of fine flour mixed with **o**; 9043
28:28 of an ephah of fine flour mixed with **o**; 9043
29:3 of an ephah of fine flour mixed with **o**; 9043
29:9 of an ephah of fine flour mixed with **o**; 9043
29:14 of an ephah of fine flour mixed with **o**; 9043
35:25 who was anointed with the holy **o**. 9043
Dt 7:13 your grain, new wine and **o**— 3658
8:8 pomegranates, olive **o** and honey; 9043
11:14 gather in your grain, new wine and **o**. 3658
12:17 the tithe of your grain and new wine and **o**, 3658
14:23 Eat the tithe of your grain, new wine and **o**, 3658
18:4 new wine and **o**, 3658
28:40 but you will not use the **o**, 9043
28:51 firstfruits of your grain, new wine or **o**, 3658
32:13 and with **o** from the flinty crag, 9043
33:24 and let him bathe his feet in **o**. 9043
Jdg 9:9 'Should I give up my **o**, 2016
1Sa 10:1 a flask of **o** and poured it on Saul's head 9043
16:1 Fill your horn with **o** and be on your way; 9043
16:13 of **o** and anointed him in the presence 9043
2Sa 1:21 no longer rubbed with **o**. 9043
1Ki 1:39 Zadok the priest took the horn of **o** from 9043
5:11 twenty thousand baths of pressed olive **o**. 9043
17:12 only a handful of flour in a jar and a little **o** 9043
17:14 be used up and the jug of **o** will not run dry 9043
17:16 up and the jug of **o** did not run dry, 9043
2Ki 4:2 she said, "except a little **o**." 9043
4:4 **Pour o** into all the jars, and as each is filled, NIH
4:6 Then the **o** stopped flowing. 9043
4:7 "Go, sell the **o** and pay your debts. 9043
9:1 of **o** with you and go to Ramoth Gilead. 9043
9:3 the **o** on his head and declare, 'This is what 9043
9:6 the prophet poured the **o** on Jehu's head 9043
20:13 silver, the gold, the spices and the fine **o**— 9043
1Ch 9:29 as well as the flour and wine, and the **o**, 9043
12:40 raisin cakes, wine, **o**, cattle and sheep, 9043
27:28 in charge of the supplies of **olive o**. 9043
2Ch 2:10 and twenty thousand baths of **olive o**." 9043
2:15 and the **olive o** and wine he promised, 9043
11:11 with supplies of food, **olive o** and wine. 9043
31:5 grain, new wine, **o** and honey and all that 3658
32:28 harvest of grain, new wine and **o**; 3658
Ezr 3:7 and **o** to the people of Sidon and Tyre, 9043
6:9 and wheat, salt, wine and **o**, 10442
7:22 a hundred baths of **olive o**, 10442
Ne 5:11 grain, new wine and **o**." 3658
10:37 of all our trees and of our new wine and **o**. 3658
10:39 and **o** to the storerooms where the articles 3658
13:5 new wine and **o** prescribed for the Levites, 3658
13:12 new wine and **o** into the storerooms. 3658
Est 2:12 with **o** *of* myrrh and six with perfumes 9043
Job 29:6 poured out for me streams of **olive o**. 9043
Ps 23:5 You anoint my head with **o**; 9043
45:7 by anointing you with the **o** *of* joy. 9043
55:21 his words are more soothing than **o**, 9043
89:20 with my sacred **o** I have anointed him. 9043
104:15 **o** to make his face shine, 9043
109:18 into his bones like **o**. 9043
133:2 It is like precious **o** poured on the head, 9043
141:5 it is **o** *on* my head. 9043
Pr 5:3 and her speech is smoother than **o**; 9043
21:17 whoever loves wine and **o** will never 9043
21:20 of the wise are stores of choice food and **o**, 9043
27:16 like restraining the wind or grasping **o** with 9043
Ecc 9:8 and always anoint your head with **o**. 9043
Isa 1:6 cleansed or bandaged or soothed with **o**. 9043
21:5 Get up, you officers, **o** the shields! 5417
39:2 the silver, the gold, the spices, the fine **o**, 9043
57:9 with **olive o** and increased your perfumes. 9043
61:3 the **o** *of* gladness instead of mourning, 9043
Jer 31:12 the grain, the new wine and the **o**, 3658
40:10 the wine, summer fruit and **o**, 9043
41:8 We have wheat and barley, **o** and honey, 9043
Eze 16:13 fine flour, honey and **olive o**. 9043
16:18 you offered my **o** and incense before them. 9043
16:19 **olive o** and honey I gave you to eat— 9043
23:41 on which you had placed the incense and **o** 9043
27:17 honey, **o** and balm for your wares. 9043
32:14 and make her streams flow like **o**, 9043
45:14 The prescribed portion of **o**, 9043
45:24 along with a hin of **o** for each ephah. 9043
45:25 burnt offerings, grain offerings and **o**. 9043
46:5 along with a hin of **o** for each ephah. 9043
46:7 along with a hin of **o** with each ephah. 9043
46:11 along with a hin of **o** for each ephah. 9043
46:14 a third of a hin of **o** to moisten the flour. 9043
46:15 and the grain offering and the **o** shall 9043
Hos 2:5 my **o** and my drink.' 9043
2:8 the new wine and **o**, 3658
2:22 the new wine and **o**, 3658
12:1 with Assyria and sends **olive o** to Egypt. 9043
Joel 1:10 the new wine is dried up, the **o** fails. 3658
2:19 "I am sending you grain, new wine and **o**, 3658
2:24 with new wine and **o**. 3658
Mic 6:7 with ten thousand rivers of **o**? 9043
6:15 you will press olives but not use the **o** 9043
Hag 1:11 the **o** and whatever the ground produces, 3658
2:12 some wine, **o** or other food, 9043
Zec 4:12 the two gold pipes that pour out **golden** *o*?" AIT
Mt 6:17 **put o on** your head and wash your face, *230*
25:3 but did not take any **o** with them. *1778*
25:4 took **o** in jars along with their lamps. *1778*
25:8 'Give us some of your **o**; *1778*
25:9 go to those who sell **o** and buy some *NIG*
25:10 while they were on their way to buy the **o**, *NIG*
Mk 6:13 and anointed many sick people *with* **o** *1778*
Lk 7:46 You did not put **o** on my head, *1778*
10:34 pouring on **o** and wine. *1778*
16:6 " 'Eight hundred gallons *of* **olive o**,' *1778*
Heb 1:9 by anointing you with the **o** of joy." *1778*
Jas 5:14 over him and anoint him *with* **o** in the name *1778*
Rev 6:6 and do not damage the **o** and the wine!" *1778*
18:13 of wine and **olive o**, of fine flour and wheat; *1778*

OILS (1) [OIL]

Ps 92:10 fine **o** have been poured upon me. 9043

OINTMENT (1) [OINTMENTS]

Job 41:31 and stirs up the sea like a **pot of o**. 5350

OINTMENTS (1) [OINTMENT]

Eze 16:9 and washed the blood from you and put **o** 9043

OLD (325) [OLDER, OLDEST]

Ge 5:32 After Noah was 500 years **o**, 1201
6:4 They were the heroes of **o**, men of renown. 6409
7:6 Noah was six hundred years **o** when 1201
11:10 when Shem was 100 years **o**, 1201
12:4 Abram was seventy-five years **o** 1201
15:9 a goat and a ram, each **three years o**, 8992
15:15 in peace and be buried at a good **o age**. 8484
16:16 Abram was eighty-six years **o** 1201
17:1 When Abram was ninety-nine years **o**, 1201
17:12 among you who is eight days **o** must 1201
17:17 a son be born to a *man* a hundred years **o**? 1201
17:24 Abraham was ninety-nine years **o** 1201
18:11 Abraham and Sarah were already **o** 2418
18:12 "After I am worn out and my master *is* **o**, 2416
18:13 I really have a child, now that I *am* **o**?' 2416
19:4 both young and **o**—surrounded the house. 2418
19:11 the house, young and **o**, with blindness so 1524
19:31 "Our father *is* **o**, 2416
21:2 and bore a son to Abraham in his **o age**, 2421
21:4 When his son Isaac was eight days **o**, 1201
21:5 Abraham was a hundred years **o** 1201
21:7 Yet I have borne him a son in his **o age**." 2421
23:1 to be a hundred and twenty-seven **years** *o*. AIT
24:1 Abraham *was* now **o** and well advanced 2416
24:36 Sarah had borne him a son in her **o age**, 2420
Ge 25:8 a good **o age**, an old man and full of years; 8484
25:8 an **o** *man* and full of years; 2418
25:20 and Isaac was forty years **o** 1201
25:26 Isaac was sixty years **o** 1201
26:34 When Esau was forty years **o**, 1201
27:1 When Isaac *was* **o** and his eyes were 2416
27:2 *I am* now *an* **o** *man* and don't know the day 2416
35:29 gathered to his people, **o** and full of years. 2418
37:3 he had been born to him in his **o age**; 2421
41:46 Joseph was thirty years **o** when he entered 1201
44:20 a young son born to him in his **o age**. 2421
47:8 Pharaoh asked him, "How **o** are you?" 2644+3427+9102
48:10 Israel's eyes were failing because of **o age**, 2419
Ex 7:7 Moses was eighty years **o** and Aaron 1201
10:9 "We will go with our young and **o**, 2418
29:38 two lambs a year **o**. 1201
30:14 those twenty years **o** or more, 1201
38:26 twenty years **o** or more, a total of 603,550 1201
Lev 9:3 *both* a year **o** and without defect— 1201
14:10 and one ewe lamb a year **o**, 1426
23:12 the LORD a lamb a year **o** without defect, 1201
23:18 each a year **o** and without defect, 1201
23:19 each a year **o**, for a fellowship offering. 1201
25:22 the **o** crop and will continue to eat from it 3824
27:7 If it is a person sixty years **o** or more, 1201
Nu 1:3 the men in Israel twenty years **o** or more 1201
1:18 the men twenty years **o** or more were listed 1201
1:20 All the men twenty years **o** or more 1201
1:22 All the men twenty years **o** or more 1201
1:24 All the men twenty years **o** or more 1201
1:26 All the men twenty years **o** or more 1201
1:28 All the men twenty years **o** or more 1201
1:30 All the men twenty years **o** or more 1201
1:32 All the men twenty years **o** or more 1201
1:34 All the men twenty years **o** or more 1201
1:36 All the men twenty years **o** or more 1201
1:38 All the men twenty years **o** or more 1201
1:40 All the men twenty years **o** or more 1201
1:42 All the men twenty years **o** or more 1201
1:45 All the Israelites twenty years **o** or more 1201
3:15 Count every male a month **o** or more." 1201
3:22 The number of all the males a month **o** 1201
3:28 the males a month **o** or more was 8,600. 1201
3:34 The number of all the males a month **o** 1201
3:39 including every male a month **o** or more, 1201
3:40 a month **o** or more and make a list 1201
3:43 of firstborn males a month **o** or more, 1201
7:15 one ram and one male lamb a year **o**, 1201
7:17 and five male lambs a year **o**, 1201
7:21 one ram and one male lamb a year **o**, 1201
7:23 and five male lambs a year **o**, 1201
7:27 one ram and one male lamb a year **o**, 1201
7:29 and five male lambs a year **o**, 1201
7:33 one ram and one male lamb a year **o**, 1201
7:35 and five male lambs a year **o**, 1201
7:39 one ram and one male lamb a year **o**, 1201
7:41 and five male lambs a year **o**, 1201
7:45 one ram and one male lamb a year **o**, 1201
7:47 and five male lambs a year **o**, 1201
7:51 one ram and one male lamb a year **o**, 1201
7:53 and five male lambs a year **o**, 1201
7:57 one ram and one male lamb a year **o**, 1201
7:59 and five male lambs a year **o**, 1201
7:63 one ram and one male lamb a year **o**, 1201
7:65 and five male lambs a year **o**, 1201
7:69 one ram and one male lamb a year **o**, 1201
7:71 and five male lambs a year **o**, 1201
7:75 one ram and one male lamb a year **o**, 1201
7:77 and five male lambs a year **o**, 1201
7:81 one ram and one male lamb a year **o**, 1201
7:83 and five male lambs a year **o**, 1201
7:87 and twelve male lambs a year **o**, 1201
7:88 and sixty male lambs a year **o**. 1201
8:24 Men twenty-five years **o** or more 1201
14:29 every one of you twenty years **o** or more 1201
18:16 When they are a month **o**, 1201
26:2 all those twenty years **o** or more 1201
26:4 a census of the *men* twenty years **o** or more, 1201
26:62 a month **o** or more numbered 23,000. 1201
28:3 two lambs a year **o** without defect, 1201
28:9 make an offering of two lambs a year **o** 1201
28:11 one ram and seven male lambs a year **o**, 1201
28:19 one ram and seven male lambs a year **o**, 1201
28:27 one ram and seven male lambs a year **o** as 1201
29:2 one ram and seven male lambs a year **o**, 1201
29:8 one ram and seven male lambs a year **o**, 1201
29:13 two rams and fourteen male lambs a year **o**, 1201
29:17 two rams and fourteen male lambs a year **o**, 1201
29:20 two rams and fourteen male lambs a year **o**, 1201
29:23 two rams and fourteen male lambs a year **o**, 1201
29:26 two rams and fourteen male lambs a year **o**, 1201
29:29 two rams and fourteen male lambs a year **o**, 1201
29:32 two rams and fourteen male lambs a year **o**, 1201
29:36 one ram and seven male lambs a year **o**, 1201
32:11 the men twenty years **o** or more who came 1201
33:39 and twenty-three years **o** when he died 1201
Dt 28:50 without respect for the **o** or pity for 2418
31:2 and twenty years **o** and I am no longer able 1201
32:7 Remember the days **of o**; 6409
34:7 Moses was a hundred and twenty years **o** 1201
Jos 6:21 men and women, young and **o**, cattle, 2418
9:4 with worn-out sacks and **o** wineskins, 1165
9:5 on their feet and wore **o** clothes. 1165
13:1 Joshua *was* **o** and well advanced in years, 2416
13:1 the LORD said to him, "You *are* **very o**, 928+995+2021+2416+3427

Dt 14: 7 I was forty years o when Moses the servant 1201
14:10 So here I am today, eighty-five years o! 1201
23: 1 by then o and well advanced in years, 2416
23: 2 "I *am* o and well advanced in years. 2416
Jdg 6:25 the one seven years o. NIH
8:32 at a good o age and was buried in the tomb 8484
19:16 an o man from the hill country of Ephraim, 2418
19:17 the o man asked, "Where are you going? 2418
19:20 welcome at my house," the o man said. 2418
19:22 they shouted to the o man who owned 2418
Ru 1:12 *I am* too o to have another husband. 2416
4:15 and sustain you in your o age. 8484
1Sa 2:22 Now Eli, *who was* very o, 2416
2:31 not be an o *man* in your family line 2418
2:32 family line there will never be an o *man.* 2418
4:15 who was ninety-eight years o 1201
4:18 for he was an o man and heavy. 2418
5: 9 both young and o, 1524
8: 1 When Samuel grew o, 2416
8: 5 They said to him, "You *are* o, 2416
12: 2 As for me, *I am* o and gray, 2416
13: 1 Saul was [thirty] years o when he became 1201
17:12 in Saul's time he *was* o and well advanced 2416
24:13 As the o saying goes, 'From evildoers come 7719
28:14 "An o man wearing a robe is coming up," 2418
30: 2 both young and o. 1524
30:19 Nothing was missing: young or o, 1524
2Sa 2:10 Ish-Bosheth son of Saul was forty years o 1201
4: 4 He was five years o when the news 1201
5: 4 David was thirty years o when he became 1201
19:32 Now Barzillai *was* a very o *man,* 2416
19:35 I am now eighty years o. 1201
1Ki 1: 1 When King David *was* o and well advanced 2416
11: 4 As Solomon grew o, his wives turned his 2420
13:11 Now there was a certain o prophet living 2418
13:18 The o prophet answered, NIH
13:20 to the o prophet who had brought him back. NIH
13:25 in the city where the o prophet lived. 2418
14:21 He was forty-one years o when he became 1201
15:23 In his o age, however, his feet became 2420
22:42 Jehoshaphat was thirty-five years o 1201
2Ki 3:21 so every man, young and o, 2025+2256+5087
4:14 she has no son and her husband *is* o." 2416
8:17 He was thirty-two years o when he became 1201
8:26 Ahaziah was twenty-two years o 1201
11:21 Joash was seven years o when he began 1201
14: 2 He was twenty-five years o when he became 1201
14:21 Azariah, who was sixteen years o, 1201
15: 2 He was sixteen years o when he became 1201
15:33 He was twenty-five years o when he became 1201
16: 2 Ahaz was twenty years o when he became 1201
18: 2 He was twenty-five years o when he became 1201
19:25 In days of o I planned it; 7710
21: 1 Manasseh was twelve years o 1201
21:19 Amon was twenty-two years o 1201
22: 1 Josiah was eight years o when he became 1201
23:31 Jehoahaz was twenty-three years o 1201
23:36 Jehoiakim was twenty-five years o 1201
24: 8 Jehoiachin was eighteen years o 1201
24:18 Zedekiah was twenty-one years o 1201
1Ch 2:21 married her when he was sixty years o), 1201
23: 1 When David *was* o and full of years, 2416
23: 3 The Levites thirty years o or more 1201
23:24 that is, the workers twenty years o 1201
23:27 from *those* twenty years o or more. 1201
25: 8 Young and o alike, 1524
26:13 young and o alike. 1524
27:23 the number of the men twenty years o 1201
29:28 He died at a good o age, 8484
2Ch 3: 3 the cubit of the o standard). 8037
12:13 He was forty-one years o when he became 1201
20:31 He was thirty-five years o when he became 1201
21: 5 Jehoram was thirty-two years o 1201
21:20 Jehoram was thirty-two years o 1201
22: 2 Ahaziah was twenty-two years o 1201
24: 1 Joash was seven years o when he became 1201
24:15 Now Jehoiada *was* o and full of years, 2416
25: 1 Amaziah was twenty-five years o 1201
25: 5 then mustered those twenty years o or more 1201
26: 1 Uzziah, who was sixteen years o, 1201
26: 3 Uzziah was sixteen years o when he became 1201
27: 1 Jotham was twenty-five years o 1201
27: 8 He was twenty-five years o when he became 1201
28: 1 Ahaz was twenty years o when he became 1201
29: 1 Hezekiah was twenty-five years o 1201
31:15 o and young alike. 1524
31:16 they distributed to the males three years o 1201
31:17 and likewise to the Levites twenty years o 1201
33: 1 Manasseh was twelve years o 1201
33:21 Amon was twenty-two years o 1201
34: 1 Josiah was eight years o when he became 1201
36: 2 Jehoahaz was twenty-three years o 1201
36: 5 Jehoiakim was twenty-five years o 1201
36: 9 Jehoiachin was eighteen years o 1201
36:11 Zedekiah was twenty-one years o 1201
36:17 o *man* or aged. 2418
Est 3:13 young and o, women and little children— 2418
Job 14: 8 Its roots *may* grow o in the ground 2416
20: 4 you know how it has been from of o, 6329
21: 7 growing o and increasing in power? 6980
22:15 to the o path that evil men have trod? 6409
29: 8 and stepped aside and the o men rose 3813
32: 6 "I am young in years, and you are o; 3813
32: 9 It is not only the o who are wise, 8041
42:17 And so he died, o and full of years. 2418
Ps 25: 6 for they are from of o. 6409
37:25 I was young and now *I am* o, 2416
71: 9 Do not cast me away when I am o; 2420
71:18 Even when I am o and gray, 2420
74: 2 Remember the people you purchased of o, 7710
74:12 But you, O God, are my king from of o; 7710
78: 2 I will utter hidden things, things from of o— 7710
92:14 They will still bear fruit in o age, 8484
148:12 o *men* and children. 2418
Pr 8:22 before his deeds of o; 255
20:29 gray hair the splendor of the o. 2418
22: 6 and when *he is* o he will not turn from it. 2416
23:22 do not despise your mother when *she is* o. 2416
Ecc 1:11 There is no remembrance of *men* of o, 8037
4:13 an o but foolish king who no longer knows 2418
7:10 "Why were the o days better than these?" 8037
SS 7:13 every delicacy, both new and o, 3824
Isa 1:26 I will restore your judges as in days of o, 8037
3: 5 The young will rise up against the o, 2418
20: 4 young and o, with buttocks bared— 2418
22:11 the two walls for the water of the O Pool, 3824
23: 7 city of revelry, the o, old city, 3427+4946+7710
23: 7 Is this your city of revelry, the old, o city, 7712
37:26 In days of o I planned it; 7710
46: 4 Even to your o age and gray hairs I am he, 2420
48: 8 from of o your ear has not been open. 255
51: 9 as in days gone by, as in generations of o. 6409
63: 9 up and carried them all the days of o. 6409
63:11 Then his people recalled the days of o, 6409
63:16 our Redeemer from of o is your name. 6409
63:19 We are yours from of o; 6409
65:20 or an o *man* who does not live out his years; 2418
Jer 6:11 and the o, those weighed down with years. 2418
30:20 Their children will be as in days of o, 7710
31:13 young men and o as well. 2418
38:11 He took some o rags and worn-out clothes 1170
38:12 "Put these o rags and worn-out clothes 1170
51:22 with you I shatter o *man* and youth, 2418
52: 1 Zedekiah was twenty-one years o 1201
La 1: 7 the treasures that were hers in days of o. 7710
2:21 and o lie together in the dust of the streets; 2418
3: 4 made my skin and my flesh grow o 1162
5:21 renew our days as of o 7710
Eze 9: 6 Slaughter o *men,* young men and maidens, 2418
16: 8 and saw that you were o *enough for* love, 6961
Hos 4:11 to o wine and new, 3516
Joel 2: 2 as never was of o nor ever will be in ages 6409
2:28 your o *men* will dream dreams, 2418
Mic 5: 2 whose origins are from of o, 7710
6: 6 with calves a year o? 1201
Zec 8: 4 and women of ripe o age will sit in 2418
Mt 2:16 and its vicinity who were two years o and *1453*
9:16 a patch of unshrunk cloth on an o garment, *4094*
9:17 Neither do men pour new wine into o
wineskins. *4094*
13:52 his storeroom new treasures as well as o." *4094*
Mk 2:21 a patch of unshrunk cloth on an o garment. *4094*
2:21 the new piece will pull away from the o, *4094*
2:22 no one pours new wine into o wineskins. *4094*
5:42 around (she was twelve years o). *NIG*
Lk 1:18 I am an o man and my wife is well along *4566*
1:36 to have a child in her o age, *1179*
2:36 She *was* very o; *1877+2465+4581*
2:42 When he was twelve years o, *2291*
3:23 Now Jesus himself was about thirty years o *2291*
5:36 a new garment and sews it on an o one. *4094*
5:36 patch from the new will not match the o. *4094*
5:37 no one pours new wine into o wineskins. *4094*
5:39 And no one after drinking o wine wants *4094*
5:39 for he says, 'The o is better.' " *4094*
Jn 3: 4 "How can a man be born when he is o?" *1173*
8:57 "You are not yet fifty years o," *2291*
21:18 *you are* o you will stretch out your hands, *1180*
Ac 2:17 your o men will dream dreams. *4565*
4:22 miraculously healed was over forty years o. *NIG*
7:23 "When Moses was forty years o, *5989*
Ro 4:19 since he was about a hundred years o— *1670*
6: 6 For we know that our o self was crucified *4094*
7: 6 and not in the o way of the written code. *4095*
1Co 5: 7 of the o yeast that you may be a new batch *4094*
5: 8 not with the o yeast, *4094*
2Co 3:14 when the o covenant is read. *4094*
5:17 the o has gone, the new has come! *792*
Eph 4:22 to put off your o self, *4094*
Col 3: 9 since you have taken off your o self *4094*
1Ti 4: 7 with godless myths and o wives' tales; *1212*
Phm 1: 9 an o man and now also a prisoner *4566*
Heb 8: 6 he is mediator is superior to the o one, *NIG*
1Jn 2: 7 a new command but an o one, *4094*
2: 7 This o command is the message you have *4094*
Rev 21: 4 for the o order of things has passed away." *4755*

OLDER (32) [OLD]

Ge 10:21 whose o brother was Japheth; 1524
19:31 One day the o *daughter* said to the younger, 1142
19:33 the o *daughter* went in and lay with him. 1142
19:34 The next day the o *daughter* said to 1142
19:37 The o *daughter* had a son, 1142
25:23 and the o will serve the younger." 8041
27: 1 he called for Esau his o son and said 1524
27:15 the best clothes of Esau her o son, 1524
27:42 Rebekah was told what her o son Esau had
said, 1524
29:16 the name of the o was Leah, 1524
29:26 in marriage before the o *one.* 1142
Ex 2:10 When the child grew o, 1540
1Sa 14:49 The name of his o daughter was Merab, 1142
18:17 "Here is my o daughter Merab. 1524
1Ki 2:22 after all, he is my o brother— 1524+4946
2Ch 22: 1 had killed all the o sons. 8037
Ezr 3: 8 of age and o to supervise the building 2025+5087
3:12 the o priests and Levites and family heads, 2418
Job 15:10 *men even* o than your father. 3427+3888
32: 4 because they were o than he. 2418+3427+4200
Eze 16:46 Your o sister was Samaria, 1524
16:61 both those *who* are o than you 1524
23: 4 The o was named Oholah, 1524
Lk 15:25 "Meanwhile, the o son was in the field. *4565*
15:28 "The o brother became angry and refused *NIG*
Jn 8: 9 the o *ones* first, until only Jesus was left, *4565*
Ro 9:12 "The o will serve the younger." *3505*
1Ti 5: 1 Do not rebuke an o man harshly, *4565*
5: 2 o *women* as mothers, and younger women *4565*
Tit 2: 2 Teach the o *men* to be temperate, *4566*
2: 3 teach the o *women* to be reverent in *4567*
1Pe 5: 5 be submissive *to* those who are o. *4565*

OLDEST (9) [OLD]

Ge 44:12 with the o and ending with the youngest. 1524
Jdg 8:20 Turning to Jether, his o *son,* he said, 1147
1Sa 17:13 Jesse's three o sons had followed Saul to 1524
17:14 The three o followed Saul, 1524
17:28 When Eliab, David's o brother, 1524
1Ch 24:31 the o brother were treated the same as those 8031
Job 1:13 and drinking wine at the o brother's house, 1147
1:18 and drinking wine at the o brother's house, 1147
Heb 12:16 inheritance rights as the o son. *4757*

OLDNESS (KJV) See OLD WAY

OLIVE (62) [OLIVES]

Ge 8:11 in its beak was a freshly plucked o leaf! 2339
Ex 23:11 with your vineyard and your o grove. 2339
25: 6 o oil for the light; 9043
30:24 and a hin of o oil. 2339
35: 8 o oil for the light; 9043
35:28 also brought spices and o oil for the light 9043
Nu 11: 8 it tasted like something made with o oil. 9043
18:12 the finest o oil and all the finest new wine 3658
Dt 6:11 vineyards and o groves you did not plant— 2339
8: 8 pomegranates, o oil and honey; 2339
28:40 You will have o trees throughout 2339
Jos 24:13 from vineyards and o groves that you did 2339
Jdg 9: 8 They said to the o tree, 'Be our king.' 2339
9: 9 "But the o tree answered, 2339
15: 5 together with the vineyards and o groves. 2339
1Sa 8:14 and vineyards and o groves and give them 2339
1Ki 5:11 to twenty thousand baths of pressed o oil. 4184
6:23 a pair of cherubim of o wood, 9043
6:31 of o wood with five-sided jambs. 9043
6:32 the two o wood doors he carved cherubim, 9043
6:33 of o wood for the entrance to the main hall. 9043
2Ki 5:26 or to accept clothes, o groves, vineyards, 2339
18:32 a land of o trees and honey. 2339+3658
1Ch 27:28 in charge of the o and sycamore-fig trees in 2339
27:28 in charge of the supplies of o oil. 9043
2Ch 2:10 and twenty thousand baths of o oil." 9043
2:15 and the o oil and wine he promised, 9043
11:11 with supplies of food, o oil and wine. 9043
Ezr 7:22 a hundred baths of o oil, 10442
Ne 5:11 vineyards, o groves and houses, 2339
8:15 from o and wild olive trees, and 2339
8:15 and wild o trees, and from myrtles, palms 9043
9:25 o groves and fruit trees in abundance. 2339
Job 15:33 like an o tree shedding its blossoms. 2339
29: 6 poured out for me streams of o oil. 9043
Ps 52: 8 an o tree flourishing in the house of God; 2339
128: 3 be like o shoots around your table. 2339
Isa 17: 6 as when an o tree is beaten, 2339
24:13 as when an o tree is beaten, 2339
41:19 the myrtle and the o. 6770+9043
57: 9 with o oil and increased your perfumes. 9043
Jer 11:16 The LORD called you a thriving o tree 2339
Eze 16:13 Your food was fine flour, honey and o oil. 9043
16:19 o oil and honey I gave you to eat— 9043
Hos 12: 1 with Assyria and sends o oil to Egypt. 9043
14: 6 His splendor will be like an o tree, 2339
Am 4: 9 Locusts devoured your fig and o trees, 2339
Hab 3:17 o crop fails and the fields produce no food, 2339
Hag 2:19 the pomegranate and the o tree have 2339
Zec 4: 3 Also there are two o trees by it, 2339
4:11 "What are these two o trees on the right and 2339
4:12 "What are these two o branches beside 2339
Lk 16: 6 " 'Eight hundred gallons *of* o oil,' *1778*
Jn 18: 1 On the other side there was an o grove, *NIG*
18:26 "Didn't I see you with him in the o grove?" *NIG*
Ro 11:17 and you, *though* a wild o shoot, *66*
11:17 in the nourishing sap *from* the o root, *1777*
11:24 cut out of an o tree that is wild *66*
11:24 grafted into a cultivated o tree, *2814*
11:24 be grafted into their own o tree! *1777*
Rev 11: 4 the two o trees and the two lampstands *1777*
18:13 of wine and o oil, of fine flour and wheat; *1778*

OLIVES (25) [OLIVE]

Ex 27:20 to bring you clear oil of pressed o for 2339
29:40 a quarter of a hin of oil from pressed o, 4184
Lev 24: 2 to bring you clear oil of pressed o for 2339
Nu 28: 5 a quarter of a hin of oil from pressed o. 4184
Dt 24:20 When you beat the o from your trees, 2339
28:40 because the o will drop off. 2339
2Sa 15:30 But David continued up the Mount of O, 2339

Job 24:11 *They* **crush** o among the terraces; 7414
Isa 17: 6 or three o on the topmost branches, 1737
Mic 6:15 you will press o but not use the oil 2339
Zec 14: 4 his feet will stand on the Mount of **O,** 2339
14: 4 of **O** will be split in two from east to west, 2339
Mt 21: 1 and came to Bethphage on the Mount *of* **O,** *1777*
24: 3 As Jesus was sitting on the Mount *of* **O,** *1777*
26:30 they went out to the Mount *of* **O.** *1777*
Mk 11: 1 and Bethany at the Mount *of* **O,** *1777*
13: 3 on the Mount *of* **O** opposite the temple, *1777*
14:26 they went out to the Mount *of* **O.** *1777*
Lk 19:29 at the hill called the **Mount of O,** *1777*
19:37 where the road goes down the Mount *of* **O,** *1777*
21:37 the night on the hill called the **Mount of O,** *1777*
22:39 Jesus went out as usual to the Mount *of* **O,** *1777*
Jn 8: 1 But Jesus went to the Mount *of* **O.** *1777*
Ac 1:12 from the hill called the **Mount of O,** *1779*
Jas 3:12 My brothers, can a fig tree bear **o,** *1777*

OLIVET (KJV) See OLIVES

OLYMPAS (1)

Ro 16:15 and **O** and all the saints with them. *3912*

OMAR (3)

Ge 36:11 Teman, **O,** Zepho, Gatam and Kenaz. 223
36:15 Chiefs Teman, **O,** Zepho, Kenaz, 223
1Ch 1:36 Teman, **O,** Zepho, Gatam and Kenaz; 223

OMEGA (3)

Rev 1: 8 "I am the Alpha and the **O,"** *6042*
21: 6 I am the Alpha and the **O,** *6042*
22:13 I am the Alpha and the **O,** *6042*

OMEN (2) [OMENS]

Eze 21:21 to **seek an o:** he will cast lots 7876+7877
21:23 It will seem like a false **o** 7876

OMENS (1) [OMEN]

Dt 18:10 **interprets o,** engages in witchcraft, 5727

OMER (5) [OMERS]

Ex 16:16 Take an **o** for each person you have 6685
16:18 And when they measured it by the **o,** 6685
16:32 'Take an **o** of manna and keep it for 6685
16:33 "Take a jar and put an **o** *of* manna in it. 6685
16:36 (An **o** is one tenth of an ephah.) 6685

OMERS (1) [OMER]

Ex 16:22 two **o** for each person— 6685

OMIT (1)

Jer 26: 2 everything I command you, *do* not **o** a word. 1757

OMNIPOTENT (KJV) See ALMIGHTY

OMRI (15) [OMRI'S]

1Ki 16:16 and murdered him, they proclaimed **O,** 6687
16:17 Then **O** and all the Israelites 6687
16:21 and the other half supported **O.** 6687
16:22 So Tibni died and **O** became king. 6687
16:23 **O** became king of Israel, 6687
16:25 But **O** did evil in the eyes of the LORD 6687
16:28 **O** rested with his fathers and was buried 6687
16:29 Ahab son of **O** became king of Israel, 6687
16:30 Ahab son of **O** did more evil in the eyes of 6687
2Ki 8:26 a granddaughter of **O** king of Israel. 6687
1Ch 7: 8 Zemirah, Joash, Eliezer, Elioenai, **O,** 6687
9: 4 the son of **O,** the son of Imri, 6687
27:18 **O** son of Michael; 6687
2Ch 22: 2 a granddaughter of **O.** 6687
Mic 6:16 You have observed the statutes of **O** and all 6687

OMRI'S (2) [OMRI]

1Ki 16:22 But **O** followers proved stronger than those 6687
16:27 As for the other events of **O** reign, 6687

ON (4 of 4658) For ON as a Preposition, See Index of Articles Etc. (See Introduction, p. xi)

Ge 41:45 Asenath daughter of Potiphera, priest of **O,** 228
41:50 Asenath daughter of Potiphera, priest of **O.** 228
46:20 Asenath daughter of Potiphera, priest of **O.** 228
Nu 16: 1 and **O** son of Peleth—became insolent 227

ONAM (4)

Ge 36:23 Alvan, Manahath, Ebal, Shepho and **O.** 231
1Ch 1:40 Alvan, Manahath, Ebal, Shepho and **O.** 231
2:26 she was the mother of **O.** 231
2:28 The sons of **O:** Shammai and Jada. 231

ONAN (7)

Ge 38: 4 and gave birth to a son and named him **O.** 232
38: 8 Then Judah said to **O,** 232
38: 9 **O** knew that the offspring would not be his; 232
46:12 The sons of Judah: Er, **O,** Shelah, 232
46:12 Perez and Zerah (but Er and **O** had died in 232
Nu 26:19 Er and **O** were sons of Judah, 232
1Ch 2: 3 The sons of Judah: Er, **O** and Shelah. 232

ONCE (179) [ONE]

Ge 18:29 **O again** he spoke to him, 3578+6388
18:32 but let me speak just **o more.** 7193
25:29 **O** when Jacob was cooking some stew, NIH
27:43 Flee **at o** to my brother Laban in Haran. 7756
28: 2 Go **at o** to Paddan Aram, 7756
31:10 "In breeding season *I o* **had** a dream AIT
31:13 Now leave this land **at o** and go back 7756
40:21 *he o again* **put** the cup into Pharaoh's hand, AIT
41:10 Pharaoh *was o* **angry** with his servants, AIT
43: 8 the boy along with me and we will go **at o,** 7756
43:13 also and go back to the man **at o.** 7756
44: 4 "Go after those men **at o,** 7756
Ex 10:17 Now forgive my sin **o more** and 421+2021+7193
12:21 **"Go at o** and select the animals 5432
30:10 **O** a year Aaron shall make atonement 285
34: 8 to the ground **at o** and worshiped. 4554
Lev 16:34 Atonement is to be made **o** a year for all 285
Nu 12: 4 **At o** the LORD said to Moses, 7328
16:21 so I can put an end to them **at o."** 3869+8092
16:45 so I can put an end to them **at o."** 3869+8092
24:11 Now **leave at o** and go home! 1368
Dt 7:22 be allowed to eliminate them **all at o,** 4554
9:12 LORD told me, "Go down from here **at o,** 4554
9:18 Then **o again** I fell prostrate 2021+3869+8037
Jos 6: 3 the city **o** with all the armed men. 285+7193
6:11 around the city, circling it **o.** 285+7193
6:14 the city **o** and returned to the camp. 285+7193
Jdg 2:23 not drive them out **at o** by giving them into 4554
3:12 **O again** the Israelites did evil in the eyes of 3578
4: 1 the Israelites **o again** did evil in the eyes of 3578
16:18 "Come back **o more;** 7193
16:28 O God, please strengthen me just **o more,** 7193
20:15 **At o** the Benjamites mobilized twenty-six thousand swordsmen 928+2021+2021+2085+3427
1Sa 1: 9 **O** when they had finished eating NIH
10: 7 **O** these signs are fulfilled, 3954
14:33 "Roll a large stone over here **at o."** 2021+3427
15:17 you were **o** small in your own eyes, NIH
19: 8 **O more** war broke out, 3578
23: 4 **O again** David inquired of the LORD, 3578+6388
28:24 which she butchered **at o.** 4554
2Sa 3:21 "Let me go **at o** and assemble all Israel 7756
5:22 **O more** the Philistines came up 3578+6388
17:21 "Set out and cross the river **at o;** 4559
21:15 **O again** there was a battle between 6388
1Ki 10:22 **O** every three years it returned, 285
13:33 but **o more** appointed priests for 8740
17: 9 "Go **at o** to Zarephath of Sidon 7756
19: 5 **All at o** an angel touched him and 2180+2296
22: 9 **"Bring** Micaiah son of Imlah **at o."** 4554
2Ki 1:11 'Come down **at o!'** " 4559
4:35 the bed and stretched out upon him **o** more. NIH
7: 9 *Let's* **go at o** and report this to 995+2143+2256
13:21 **O** while some Israelites were burying 2118
19:30 **O more** a remnant of the house 3578
1Ch 14:13 **O more** the Philistines raided the 3578+6388
2Ch 9:21 **O** every three years it returned, 285
18: 8 **"Bring** Micaiah son of Imlah **at o."** 4554
24: 5 But the Levites *did* not **act at o.** 4554
Ne 13:20 **O** or twice the merchants and sellers 7193
Est 5: 5 **"Bring** Haman **at o,"** the king said, 4554
6:10 **"Go at o,"** the king commanded Haman. 4554
8: 9 **At o** the royal secretaries were summoned— 928+2021+2021+2085+6961
Job 3: 5 and deep shadow claim it **o** more; NIH
14:20 You overpower him **o for all,** 4200+5905
18:19 no survivor where **o** he lived. NIH
33:21 and his bones, *o* **hidden,** now stick out. AIT
40: 5 I spoke **o,** but I have no answer— 285
Ps 55:14 with whom *I o* **enjoyed sweet** fellowship AIT
71:21 and comfort me **o again.** 6015
89:19 **O** you spoke in a vision, 255
89:35 **O for all,** I have sworn 285
116: 7 *Be* at rest **o more,** O my soul, 8740
Pr 7:22 **All at o** he followed her like an ox going 7328
12:16 A fool shows his annoyance **at o,** 928+2021+3427
Ecc 9:14 There was **o** a small city with only NIH
Isa 1:21 She **o** was full of justice; NIH
7:25 for all the hills *o* **cultivated** by the hoe, AIT
14: 1 **o again** he will choose Israel 6388
14:12 *you who o* **laid low** the nations! AIT
16: 8 *which o* **reached** Jazer and spread toward AIT
29:14 **o more** I will astound these people 3578
29:19 **O more** the humble will rejoice in 3578
35: 7 In the haunts where jackals **o** lay, NIH
37:31 **O more** a remnant of the house 3578
Jer 12:16 even as *they o* **taught** my people to swear AIT
31:23 in its towns will **o again** use these words: 6388
32:43 **O more** fields will be bought in this land 2256
33:10 there will be heard **o more** 6388
42: 2 as you now see, though we were **o** many, 4946
La 1: 1 deserted lies the city, **o** so full of people! NIH
1: 1 who **o** was great among the nations! NIH
4: 2 **o** worth their weight in gold, NIH
4: 5 Those *who o* **ate** delicacies are destitute in AIT
Eze 31: 3 Consider Assyria, **o** a cedar in Lebanon, NIH
36:37 **O** again I will yield to the plea of the house 2296
42:14 **O** the priests enter the holy precincts, 928
Da 2: 7 **O more** they replied, 10766
2:25 Arioch took Daniel to the king **at o** 10097
Hag 2: 6 while I will **o** more shake the heavens and 285
Zec 8: 4 **"O again** men and women of ripe old age 6388
8:21 *'Let us* **go at o** to entreat the LORD 2143+2143
Mt 4:20 **At o** they left their nets and followed him. *2311*
13:20 the word and **at o** receives it with joy. *2317*
13:47 **"O again,** the kingdom of heaven is like *4099*
21: 2 and **at o** you will find a donkey tied there, *2311*
25:16 went **at o** and put his money to work *2311*
26:44 So he left them and went away **o more** *4099*
26:49 Going **at o** to Jesus, Judas said, *2311*
26:53 and he will **at o** put at my disposal *785*
Mk 1:12 **At o** the Spirit sent him out into the desert, *2317*
1:18 **At o** they left their nets and followed him. *2317*
1:43 Jesus sent him away **at o** with *2317*
2:13 **O** again Jesus went out beside the lake. *2779*
4:16 the word and **at o** receive it with joy. *2317+4020*
5:30 **At o** Jesus realized that power had gone out *2317*
6:25 **At o** the girl hurried in to the king with *2317*
8:25 **O more** Jesus put his hands on *1663+4099*
14:39 **O more** he went away and prayed *4099*
14:45 Going **at o** to Jesus, Judas said, "Rabbi!" *2317*
Lk 1: 8 **O** when Zechariah's division was on *1181+1254*
4:39 She got up **at o** and began to wait on them. *4202*
8:55 Her spirit returned, and **at o** she stood up. *4202*
9:18 **O** when Jesus was praying in private *1181+2779*
13:25 **O** the owner of the house gets up *323+608+4005*
17:20 **O,** having been asked by the Pharisees *1254*
19: 6 down **at o** and welcomed him gladly. *5067*
19:11 of God was going to appear **at o.** *4202*
24:33 and returned **at o** to Jerusalem. *899+3836+6052*
Jn 4: 3 he left Judea and went back **o more** *4099*
4:46 **O more** he visited Cana in Galilee, *4099*
5: 9 **At o** the man was cured; *2311*
6:24 **O** the crowd realized that neither Jesus *4021*
8:21 **O more** Jesus said to them, *4099*
11:38 Jesus, **o more** deeply moved, *4099*
13:32 and will glorify him **at o.** *2317*
19: 4 **O more** Pilate came out and said *2779+4099*
Ac 9:20 **At o** he began to preach in the synagogues *2311*
9:38 and urged him, "Please come **at o!"** *3590+3890*
16:10 we got ready **at o** to leave for Macedonia, *2311*
16:16 **O** when we were going to the place *1181+1254*
16:26 **At o** all the prison doors flew open, *4202*
21:32 He **at o** took some officers and soldiers *1994*
23:30 I sent him to you **at o.** *1994*
28: 1 **O** safely on shore, *5538*
Ro 6:10 he died to sin **o for all;** *2384*
7: 6 But now, by dying to what **o** bound us, *NIG*
7: 9 **O** I was alive apart from law; *4537*
2Co 5:16 Though *we o* **regarded** Christ in this way, *AIT*
10: 6 **o** your obedience is complete. *4020*
11:25 **o** I was stoned, three times I was *562*
Gal 1:23 now preaching the faith he **o** tried *4537*
Eph 2:13 in Christ Jesus you who **o** were far away have been brought near *4537*
5: 8 For you were **o** darkness, *4537*
Col 1:21 **O** you were alienated from God *4537*
3: 7 in the life you **o** lived. *4021*
1Ti 1:13 Even though I was **o** a blasphemer and *4728*
1:18 with the prophecies **o made** about you, *4575*
Tit 3:10 Warn a divisive person **o,** *1651*
Heb 5: 9 and, *o* **made perfect,** he became the source *AIT*
6: 4 for those who have **o** been enlightened, *562*
7:27 He sacrificed for their sins **o for all** *2384*
9: 7 the inner room, and that only **o** a year, *562*
9:12 the Most Holy Place **o for all** *2384*
9:26 now he has appeared **o for all** at the end *562*
9:27 Just as man is destined to die **o,** *562*
9:28 so Christ was sacrificed **o** to take away *562*
10: 2 would have been cleansed **o for all,** *562*
10:10 sacrifice of the body of Jesus Christ **o for all.** *2384*
12:26 **"O** more I will shake not only the earth but *562*
12:27 The words **"o more"** indicate the removing *562*
1Pe 2:10 **O** you were not a people, *4537*
2:10 **o** you had not received mercy, *NIG*
3:18 For Christ died for sins **o for all,** *562*
Jude 1: 3 that was **o for all** entrusted to the saints. *562*
Rev 4: 2 **At o** I was in the Spirit, *2311*
10: 8 from heaven spoke to me **o more:** *4099*
17: 8 The beast, which you saw, *o* **was,** *AIT*
17: 8 because *he o* **was,** now is not, *AIT*
17:11 The beast who *o* **was,** and now is not, *AIT*

ONE (2485) [ONCE, ONE'S, ONE-TENTH, ONE-THIRD, ONES, ONESELF]

Ge 1: 9 under the sky be gathered to **o** place, 285
2:21 he took **o** of the man's ribs and closed up 285
2:24 and they will become **o** flesh. 285
3:22 "The man has now become like **o** of us, 285
4:15 so that no **o** who found him would kill him. 3972
4:19 **o** named Adah and the other Zillah. 285
8:19 the ark, **o kind after another.** 2157+4200+5476
10:25 **O** was named Peleg, because in his time 285
11: 1 Now the whole world had **o** language and 285
11: 6 "If as **o** people speaking 285
14:13 *O* who had escaped **came** and reported AIT
15: 2 the **o who will inherit** my estate is Eliezer 1201+5479
16:13 "I have now seen the *O who* **sees** me." AIT
19:17 *o of them* **said,** "Flee for your lives! AIT
19:31 **O day** the older daughter said to 2256
20: 3 a dream **o** night and said to him, "You are 2021
21:15 she put the boy under **o** *of* the bushes. 285
22: 2 Sacrifice him there as a burnt offering on **o** 285
24: 2 the *o* **in charge** of all that he had, AIT
24:14 let her be the **o** you have chosen NIH
24:44 let her be the **o** the LORD has chosen 851
24:50 we can say nothing to you **o way** or 8273S

Ge 24:63 He went out to the field **o** evening NIH
25:23 *o* **people** will be stronger than the other, AIT
26:10 **O** *of* the men might well have slept 285
26:21 but they quarreled over *that* **o** also; 2023
26:22 and no *o* **quarreled** over it. AIT
27:38 "Do you have only **o** blessing, my father? 285
27:45 Why should I lose both of you in **o** day?" 285
28:11 Taking **o** *of* the stones there, 4946
29:26 in marriage before the **older** *o*. AIT
29:27 then we will give you **the younger** *o* also, 2296S
29:33 he gave me **this** *o* too." AIT
30:31 "But if you will do this *o* **thing** for me, AIT
31:50 even though no **o** is with us, 408
32:8 "If Esau comes and attacks **o** group, 285
32:17 He instructed the **o in the lead:** 8037
33:13 If they are driven hard just **o** day, 285
34:15 to you on **o condition** only: 2296S
34:16 among you and become **o** people with you. 285
34:22 with us as **o** people only on the condition 285
35:5 around them so that no *o* **pursued** them. AIT
37:20 and throw him into **o** *of* these cisterns 285
37:36 *o of* Pharaoh's **officials,** AIT
38:28 *o of them* **put out** his hand; AIT
38:28 "**This** *o* came out first." AIT
39:1 Egyptian who was **o** of Pharaoh's officials, NIH
39:9 No **o** is greater in this house than I am. 5647
39:11 **O** day he went into the house to attend 2296
40:8 "but there is no *o to* **interpret** them." AIT
41:8 but no *o could* **interpret** them for him. AIT
41:15 "I had a dream, and no *o can* **interpret** it. AIT
41:21 no *o could* **tell** that they had done so; AIT
41:25 "The dreams of Pharaoh are **o and the same.** 285
41:26 it is **o and the same** dream. 285
41:38 **o** in whom is the spirit of God?" 2257
41:39 there is no *o so* **discerning** and wise as you. AIT
41:44 but without your word no **o** will lift hand 408
42:6 the *o who* **sold grain** to all its people. AIT
42:11 We are all the sons of **o** man. 285
42:13 the sons of **o** man, 285
42:13 and **o** is no more." 285
42:16 Send **o** of your number to get your brother; 285
42:19 let **o** *of* your brothers stay here in prison, 285
42:21 They said to **o** another, 408
42:27 for the night **o** of them opened his sack 285
42:32 We were twelve brothers, sons of **o** father. 5646
42:32 **O** is no more, 285
42:33 Leave **o** *of* your brothers here with me, 285
42:38 and he is the **only o** left. 963+2257+4200
43:29 the **o** you told me about?" 889
44:2 Then put my cup, the silver **o,** 1483S
44:16 and the **o** who was found to have the cup." 2257
44:20 he is the only **o** of his mother's sons left, 2257
44:28 **O** *of them* went away from me, and I said, 285
44:29 If you take **this** *o* from me too AIT
45:1 So there was no **o** with Joseph 408
45:4 **the o** you sold into Egypt! 889S
47:20 The Egyptians, **o and all,** 408
47:21 from *o* **end** *of* Egypt to the other. AIT
48:18 "No, my father, **this** *o* is the firstborn; AIT
48:22 And to you, as **o** *who* is over your brothers, 285
49:16 for his people as **o** *of* the tribes of Israel. 285
49:24 of the hand of the **Mighty O** *of* Jacob, 51
Ex 2:6 "This is **o** *of* the Hebrew babies," she said. 4946
2:7 and get **o** *of* the Hebrew women to nurse 4946
2:11 **O** day, after Moses had grown up, 2021
2:11 a Hebrew, **o** *of* his own people. 4946
2:12 this way and that and seeing no **o,** 408
2:13 He asked the **o in the wrong,** 8401
6:25 son of Aaron married **o** *of* the daughters 4946
7:12 **Each** *o* threw down his staff and it became AIT
8:10 so that you may know **there is no** *o* like AIT
9:6 not **o** animal belonging to the Israelites died. 285
9:7 and found that not even **o** of the animals of 285
9:14 so you may know that **there is no** *o* like me AIT
10:23 No **o** could see anyone else 408
11:1 "I will bring **o** more plague on Pharaoh and 285
12:3 **o** for each household. 8445S
12:4 they must share **o** with their nearest NIH
12:16 and **another** *o* on the seventh day. AIT
12:22 Not **o** *of* you shall go out the door 408
12:46 "It must be eaten inside **o** house; 285
12:48 then he may take part like *o* **born** *in* AIT
14:20 the cloud brought darkness to the **o** side NIH
14:28 Not **o** of them survived. 285
16:16 '**Each** *o* is to gather as much as he needs. AIT
16:18 **Each** *o* gathered as much as he needed. AIT
16:19 "No **o** is to keep any of it until morning." 408
16:29 no **o** is to go out." 408
16:36 (An omer is *o* **tenth** *of* an ephah.) AIT
17:12 **o** on one side, one on the other— 285
17:12 one on *o* **side,** one on the other— AIT
17:12 one on one side, **o** on the other— 285
18:3 **O** son was named Gershom, for Moses said, 285
21:10 he must not deprive the first **o** of her food, NIH
21:18 "If men quarrel and **o** hits the other with 408
21:19 *o who* **struck the blow** AIT
21:33 "If a man uncovers a pit or digs **o** and fails 1014S
21:35 to sell the live **o** and divide both the money 8802S
22:6 *o who* **started** the fire must make restitution. AIT
22:9 *o* **whom** the judges declare guilty must pay back double to his neighbor. AIT
22:10 or is taken away *while* no *o is* **looking,** AIT
22:25 "If you lend money to **o** of my people NIH
23:15 "No *o is to* **appear** before me empty-handed AIT
24:3 they responded with **o** voice, 285

Ex 25:12 with two rings on **o** side and two rings on 285
25:19 Make **o** cherub on one end and 285
25:19 on **o** end and the second cherub on 2296
25:19 the cherubim **of o piece with** the cover, 4946
25:31 buds and blossoms shall be **of o piece with** 4946
25:32 three on **o** side and three on the other. 285
25:33 and blossoms are to be on **o** branch, 285
25:35 **O** bud shall be under the first pair NIH
25:36 and branches shall all be of **o** *piece* with 285
26:4 along the edge of the end curtain in **o** set, 285
26:5 on **o** curtain and fifty loops on 285
26:9 five of the curtains together **into o set** 963+4200
26:10 the edge of the end curtain in **o** set and also 285
26:19 **o** under each projection. NIH
26:26 for the frames on **o** side of the tabernacle, 285
27:2 that the horns and the altar are **of o piece,** 4946
27:14 to be on **o** side of the entrance, 2021
28:8 **of o piece with** the ephod and made 4946
28:10 six names on **o** stone and the remaining six 285
28:21 **o** for each of the names of the sons NIH
28:21 with the name of **o** of the twelve tribes. NIH
29:15 "Take **o** of the rams, 285
29:33 But no *o* else *may* **eat** them, AIT
29:39 Offer **o** in the morning and the other 285
30:2 its horns **of o piece with** it. 4946
30:12 **each** *o* must pay the LORD a ransom AIT
30:13 Each *o* who **crosses over** AIT
32:27 through the camp from *o* **end** to the other, AIT
33:4 to mourn and no **o** put on any ornaments. 408
33:20 for no **o** may see me and live." 132
34:3 No **o** is to come with you or 408
34:20 "No *o is to* **appear** before me empty-handed AIT
34:24 and no **o** will covet your land when you go 408
36:11 along the edge of the end curtain in **o** set, 285
36:12 They also made fifty loops on **o** curtain 285
36:16 into *o* **set** and the other six into another set. AIT
36:17 the edge of the end curtain in **o** set and also 2021
36:24 **o** under each projection. NIH
36:31 for the frames on **o** side of the tabernacle, 285
37:3 with two rings on **o** side and two rings on 285
37:8 He made **o** cherub on one end and 285
37:8 on **o** end and the second cherub on 2296
37:8 the two ends he made them **of o piece with** 4946
37:17 buds and blossoms were **of o piece with** it. 4946
37:18 three on **o** side and three on the other. 285
37:19 with buds and blossoms were on **o** branch, 285
37:21 **O** bud was under the first pair NIH
37:22 and the branches were all **of o piece with** 4946
37:24 and all its accessories from *o* **talent** AIT
37:25 its horns **of o piece with** it. 4946
38:2 that the horns and the altar were **of o piece,** 4946
38:14 Curtains fifteen cubits long were on **o** side 2021
38:26 *o* **beka** per person, AIT
38:27 **o** talent for each base. NIH
39:5 **of o piece with** the ephod and made 4946
39:14 **o** for each of the names of the sons NIH
39:14 with the name of **o** of the twelve tribes. NIH
Lev 5:4 in any matter **o** might carelessly swear about 132
5:7 **o** for a sin offering and the other for 285
5:8 who shall first offer **the o** for 889S
5:15 **o** without defect and of the proper value NIH
5:18 **o** without defect and of the proper value. NIH
6:6 **o** without defect and of the proper value. NIH
7:14 He is to bring **o** of each kind as an offering, 285
7:18 to the *o who* **offered** it, for it is impure; AIT
8:26 and **o** made with oil, and a wafer; 285
9:15 for a sin offering as he did with the **first** *o*. AIT
11:25 Whoever picks up **o** *of* their carcasses 4946
11:32 When **o** of them dies and falls 3972
11:33 If **o** *of* them falls into a clay pot, 4946
11:35 Anything that **o** *of* their carcasses falls 4946
11:36 but anyone who touches **o** NIH
12:8 **o** for a burnt offering and the other for 285
13:2 the priest or to **o** of his sons who is a priest. 285
13:55 the mildew has affected **o** side or the other. 2257S
14:4 be brought for the *o to* **be cleansed.** AIT
14:5 that **o** of the birds be killed over fresh water 285
14:7 the *o to* **be cleansed** of the infections AIT
14:10 and **o** ewe lamb a year old, 285
14:10 and **o** log of oil. 285
14:11 both the **o** to be cleansed and his offerings 408
14:12 to take **o** of the male lambs and offer it as 285
14:14 of the right ear of the *o to* **be cleansed,** AIT
14:17 of the right ear of the *o to* **be cleansed,** AIT
14:18 the *o to* **be cleansed** and make atonement AIT
14:19 the *o to* **be cleansed** from his uncleanness. AIT
14:21 he must take **o** male lamb as 285
14:22 **o** for a sin offering and the other for 285
14:25 of the right ear of the *o to* **be cleansed,** AIT
14:28 of the right ear of the *o to* **be cleansed,** AIT
14:29 on the head of the *o to* **be cleansed,** AIT
14:31 **o** as a sin offering and the other as 285
14:31 on behalf of the *o to* **be cleansed."** AIT
14:50 He shall kill **o** of the birds over fresh water 285
15:15 the **o** for a sin offering and the other for 285
15:30 The priest is to sacrifice **o** for a sin offering 285
16:8 **o** lot for the LORD and the other for 285
16:17 No **o** is to be in the Tent of Meeting from 132
18:6 " 'No **o** is to approach any close relative 408
18:22 not lie with a man as **o** lies with a woman; NIH
19:11 " 'Do not deceive **o** another. 408
19:18 not seek revenge or bear a grudge against **o** 1201S
19:34 be treated as **o** *of* your native-born. 4946
20:4 that man gives **o** *of* his children to Molech 4946
20:13 " 'If a man lies with a man as **o** lies with NIH
21:10 the **o** among his brothers who has had NIH
22:6 The **o** who touches any such thing will 5883

Lev 22:10 " 'No **o** outside a priest's family may eat 3972
23:18 **o** young bull and two rams. 285
23:19 Then sacrifice **o** male goat for 285
25:10 **each** *o* of you is to return to his family AIT
25:14 " 'If you sell land to **o** of your countrymen NIH
25:25 " 'If **o** of your countrymen becomes poor NIH
25:26 a man has no *o to* **redeem** it *for* him AIT
25:35 " 'If **o** of your countrymen becomes poor NIH
25:39 " 'If **o** of your countrymen becomes poor NIH
25:47 and **o** of your countrymen becomes poor NIH
25:48 **O** of his relatives may redeem him: 285
26:6 *o will* **make** you **afraid.** AIT
26:17 even when no *o is* **pursuing** you. AIT
26:26 be able to bake your bread in **o** oven, 285
26:36 even though no *o is* **pursuing** them. AIT
26:37 over **o** another as though fleeing from 408
26:37 even though no *o is* **pursuing** them. AIT
27:6 a person between *o* **month** and five years, AIT
27:10 not exchange it or substitute a good **o** for 2257
27:10 for a **bad** *o*, or a bad one for a good one; AIT
27:10 or a **bad** *o* for a good one; AIT
27:10 or a bad one for a **good** *o;* AIT
27:10 if he should substitute *o* **animal** AIT
27:11 **o** that is not acceptable as an offering to 5626
27:24 **the o** whose land it was. 2257
27:26 " 'No **o,** however, may dedicate 408
27:27 If it is **o of** the unclean animals, 928S
Nu 1:2 every man by name, **o by one.** 1653+4200+4392
1:2 every man by name, **one by o.** 1653+4200+4392
1:4 **O** man from each tribe, 408
1:18 were listed by name, **o by one,** 1653+4200+4392
1:18 were listed by name, **one by o,** 1653+4200+4392
1:20 were listed by name, **o by one,** 1653+4200+4392
1:20 were listed by name, **one by o,** 1653+4200+4392
1:22 and listed by name, **o by one,** 1653+4200+4392
1:22 and listed by name, **one by o,** 1653+4200+4392
1:44 each **o** representing his family. 285
3:47 collect five shekels for **each o,** 1653
5:7 add **o fifth** to it and give it all to 2797
6:11 The priest is to offer **o** as a sin offering and 285
7:11 "Each day **o** leader is to bring his offering 285
7:12 The *o who* **brought** his offering on AIT
7:13 His offering was **o** silver plate weighing 285
7:13 **o** silver sprinkling bowl weighing seventy 285
7:14 **o** gold dish weighing ten shekels, filled 285
7:15 **o** young bull, one ram and one male lamb 285
7:15 **o** ram and one male lamb a year old, 285
7:15 one ram and **o** male lamb a year old, 285
7:16 **o** male goat for a sin offering; 285
7:19 **o** silver plate weighing weighing 285
7:19 **o** silver sprinkling bowl weighing seventy 285
7:20 **o** gold dish weighing ten shekels, filled 285
7:21 **o** young bull, one ram and one male lamb 285
7:21 **o** ram and one male lamb a year old, 285
7:21 one ram and **o** male lamb a year old, 285
7:22 **o** male goat for a sin offering; 285
7:25 His offering was **o** silver plate weighing 285
7:25 **o** silver sprinkling bowl weighing seventy 285
7:26 **o** gold dish weighing ten shekels, filled 285
7:27 **o** young bull, one ram and one male lamb 285
7:27 **o** ram and one male lamb a year old, 285
7:27 one ram and **o** male lamb a year old, 285
7:28 **o** male goat for a sin offering; 285
7:31 His offering was **o** silver plate weighing 285
7:31 **o** silver sprinkling bowl weighing seventy 285
7:32 **o** gold dish weighing ten shekels, filled 285
7:33 **o** young bull, one ram and one male lamb 285
7:33 **o** ram and one male lamb a year old, 285
7:33 one ram and **o** male lamb a year old, 285
7:34 **o** male goat for a sin offering; 285
7:37 His offering was **o** silver plate weighing 285
7:37 **o** silver sprinkling bowl weighing seventy 285
7:38 **o** gold dish weighing ten shekels, filled 285
7:39 **o** young bull, one ram and one male lamb 285
7:39 **o** ram and one male lamb a year old, 285
7:39 one ram and **o** male lamb a year old, 285
7:40 **o** male goat for a sin offering; 285
7:43 His offering was **o** silver plate weighing 285
7:43 **o** silver sprinkling bowl weighing seventy 285
7:44 **o** gold dish weighing ten shekels, filled 285
7:45 **o** young bull, one ram and one male lamb 285
7:45 **o** ram and one male lamb a year old, 285
7:45 one ram and **o** male lamb a year old, 285
7:46 **o** male goat for a sin offering; 285
7:49 His offering was **o** silver plate weighing 285
7:49 **o** silver sprinkling bowl weighing seventy 285
7:50 **o** gold dish weighing ten shekels, filled 285
7:51 **o** young bull, one ram and one male lamb 285
7:51 **o** ram and one male lamb a year old, 285
7:51 one ram and **o** male lamb a year old, 285
7:52 **o** male goat for a sin offering; 285
7:55 His offering was **o** silver plate weighing 285
7:55 **o** silver sprinkling bowl weighing seventy 285
7:56 **o** gold dish weighing ten shekels, filled 285
7:57 **o** young bull, one ram and one male lamb 285
7:57 **o** ram and one male lamb a year old, 285
7:57 one ram and **o** male lamb a year old, 285
7:58 **o** male goat for a sin offering; 285
7:61 His offering was **o** silver plate weighing 285
7:61 **o** silver sprinkling bowl weighing seventy 285
7:62 **o** gold dish weighing ten shekels, filled 285
7:63 **o** young bull, one ram and one male lamb 285
7:63 **o** ram and one male lamb a year old, 285
7:63 one ram and **o** male lamb a year old, 285
7:64 **o** male goat for a sin offering; 285
7:67 His offering was **o** silver plate weighing 285
7:67 **o** silver sprinkling bowl weighing seventy 285

Nu 7:68 **o** gold dish weighing ten shekels, filled 285
7:69 **o** young bull, one ram and one male lamb 285
7:69 **o** ram and one male lamb a year old, 285
7:69 one ram and **o** male lamb a year old, 285
7:70 **o** male goat for a sin offering; 285
7:73 His offering was **o** silver plate weighing 285
7:73 **o** silver sprinkling bowl weighing seventy 285
7:74 **o** gold dish weighing ten shekels, filled 285
7:75 **o** young bull, one ram and one male lamb 285
7:75 **o** ram and one male lamb a year old, 285
7:75 one ram and **o** male lamb a year old, 285
7:76 **o** male goat for a sin offering; 285
7:79 His offering was **o** silver plate weighing 285
7:79 **o** silver sprinkling bowl weighing seventy 285
7:80 **o** gold dish weighing ten shekels, filled 285
7:81 **o** young bull, one ram and one male lamb 285
7:81 **o** ram and one male lamb a year old, 285
7:81 one ram and **o** male lamb a year old, 285
7:82 **o** male goat for a sin offering; 285
8:12 the **o** for a sin offering to the LORD and 285
10:4 If only **o** is sounded, the leaders— 285
11:19 You will not eat it for just **o** day, 285
11:32 No **o** gathered less than ten homers. 2021
13:2 From each ancestral tribe send **o** 285
14:15 you put these people to death all at **o time,** 285
14:22 not **o** *of* the men who saw my glory and 3972
14:23 not *o* of them *will ever* **see** the land AIT
14:23 No **o** who has treated me with contempt 3972
14:29 **every** *o of* you twenty years old AIT
14:30 Not **o** of you will enter the land I swore NIH
14:34 **o** year for each of the forty days 2021
15:4 the *o who* **brings** his offering shall present AIT
15:12 Do this for **each o,** 285
15:27 " 'But if just **o** person sins unintentionally, 285
15:28 the **o** who erred by sinning unintentionally, 5883
15:29 **O and the same** law applies 285
16:3 whole community is holy, **every** *o of* them, AIT
16:7 be the **o** who is holy. 2085
16:22 when only **o** man sins?" 285
16:40 no **o** except a descendant of Aaron 408+2424[S]
17:2 **o** from the leader of each 4751[S]
17:3 for there must be **o** staff for the head 285
17:6 **o** for the leader of each 285
18:4 and no *o* else *may* **come near** AIT
22:32 because your path *is a* **reckless** *o* AIT
23:9 not consider themselves *o* **of** the nations. AIT
24:3 the oracle of **o** whose eye sees clearly, 1505
24:4 the oracle of *o who* **hears** the words of God, AIT
24:15 the oracle of **o** whose eye sees clearly, 1505
24:16 the oracle of *o who* **hears** the words of God, AIT
26:54 and to a smaller group a smaller **o**; 5709[S]
26:64 Not **o** of them was among those counted 408
26:65 and not **o** of them was left except Caleb son 408
27:17 *o* who *will* **lead** them **out** AIT
28:4 Prepare **o** lamb in the morning and 285
28:11 **o** ram and seven male lambs a year old, 285
28:15 **o** male goat is to be presented to 285
28:19 **o** ram and seven male lambs a year old, 285
28:22 Include **o** male goat as a sin offering 285
28:27 **o** ram and seven male lambs a year old as 285
28:30 Include **o** male goat to make atonement 285
29:2 prepare a burnt offering of **o** young bull, 285
29:2 **o** ram and seven male lambs a year old, 285
29:5 Include **o** male goat as a sin offering 285
29:8 a burnt offering of **o** young bull, 285
29:8 **o** ram and seven male lambs a year old, 285
29:11 Include **o** male goat as a sin offering, 285
29:16 Include **o** male goat as a sin offering, 285
29:19 Include **o** male goat as a sin offering, 285
29:22 Include **o** male goat as a sin offering, 285
29:25 Include **o** male goat as a sin offering, 285
29:28 Include **o** male goat as a sin offering, 285
29:31 Include **o** male goat as a sin offering, 285
29:34 Include **o** male goat as a sin offering, 285
29:36 a burnt offering of **o** bull, 285
29:36 **o** ram and seven male lambs a year old, 285
29:38 Include **o** male goat as a sin offering, 285
31:28 for the LORD **o** out of every five hundred, 285
31:30 select **o** out of every fifty, whether persons, 285
31:47 Moses selected **o** out of every fifty persons 285
31:49 and not **o** is missing. 408
32:11 **not o** of the men twenty years old 561
32:12 not **o** except Caleb son of Jephunneh NIH
33:54 and to a smaller group a smaller **o.** 5709[S]
34:18 And appoint **o** leader from each tribe 285
35:8 but few from **o** that has few," 2021
35:25 the *o* **accused of murder** from the avenger AIT
35:30 But no **o** is to be put to death on 5883
35:30 to death on the testimony of only **o** witness. 285
35:33 except by the blood of the *o who* **shed** it. AIT
Dt 1:16 between brother Israelites or between **o** 408
1:23 **o** man from each tribe. 285
1:41 So **every** *o* of you put on his weapons, AIT
2:36 not **o** town was too strong for us. NIH
3:4 not **o** of the sixty cities that we did not take 7953[S]
4:32 ask from *o* **end** *of* the heavens to the other. AIT
4:34 for himself **o** nation out of another nation, NIH
4:42 into **o** of these cities and save his life. 285
6:4 The LORD our God, the LORD is **o.** 285
7:24 No **o** will be able to stand up against you; 408
9:3 the *o who* **goes across** ahead of you like AIT
12:14 the LORD will choose in **o** *of* your tribes, 285
13:1 *o who* **foretells by dreams,** AIT
13:7 from **o** end of the land to the other), NIH
13:11 and **no** *o* among you will do such AIT
13:12 If you hear it said about **o** *of* the towns 285
17:2 a man or woman living among you in **o** *of* 285
Dt 17:6 no *o shall* **be put to death** on the testimony AIT
17:6 to death on the testimony of only **o** witness. 285
17:15 **o** who is not a brother Israelite. 408
18:6 from **o** *of* your towns anywhere in Israel 285
18:10 *Let* no **o be found** among you who AIT
19:4 *o* who **kills** his neighbor unintentionally, AIT
19:5 That man may flee to **o** *of* these cities 285
19:11 and then flees to **o** *of* these cities, 285
19:15 **O** witness is not enough to convict 285
20:4 For the LORD your God *is* the *o who* **goes** AIT
21:15 and he loves **o** but not the other, 285
22:27 there was no *o to* **rescue** her. AIT
23:1 *o who has* **been emasculated** AIT
23:2 **o born of a forbidden marriage** 4927
23:10 If *o* of your men **is** unclean because of AIT
24:5 For **o** year he is to be free to stay at home 285
24:6 not even the **upper o—** 8207
24:7 If a man is caught kidnapping **o** 4946
24:14 a brother Israelite or an alien living in **o** NIH
25:5 If brothers are living together and **o** 285
25:9 take off **o** of his sandals, NIH
25:11 of **o** of them comes to rescue her husband 285
25:13 differing weights in your bag—**o** heavy, NIH
25:13 one heavy, **o** light. NIH
25:14 differing measures in your house—**o** large, NIH
25:14 one large, **o** small. NIH
28:7 from **o** direction but flee from you in seven. 285
28:25 at them from **o** direction but flee from them 285
28:26 no *o to* **frighten** them **away.** AIT
28:29 with no *o to* **rescue** you. AIT
28:31 and no *o will* **rescue** them. AIT
28:55 to **o** of them any of the flesh of his children 285
28:64 from **o** end of the earth to the other. NIH
28:68 but no *o will* **buy** you. AIT
32:22 *o that* **burns** to the realm of death below. AIT
32:30 How could **o** *man* chase a thousand, 285
32:36 and no **o** is left, slave or free. NIH
32:39 and no *o can* **deliver** out of my hand. AIT
33:12 and the *o* the LORD **loves** rests AIT
33:26 **"There is no** *o* like the God of Jeshurun, AIT
34:6 to this day no **o** knows where his grave is. 408
34:12 For no **o** has ever shown the mighty power NIH
Jos 1:5 No **o** will be able to stand up 408
3:12 **o** from each tribe. 285
4:2 **o** from each tribe, 285
4:4 **o** from each tribe, 285
6:1 No *o* **went out** and no one came in. AIT
6:1 No one went out and no *o* **came in.** AIT
8:24 and when **every** *o of* them had been put to AIT
10:2 like **o** *of* the royal cities; 285
10:8 **o** of them will be able to withstand you." 408
10:21 no **o** uttered a word against the Israelites. 408
10:42 in **o** campaign, because the LORD, 285
11:19 not **o** city made a treaty of peace with NIH
12:4 **o** *of* the last of the Rephaites, 4946
12:9 the king of Jericho **o** the king of Ai 285
12:9 the king of Ai (near Bethel) **o** 285
12:10 king of Jerusalem **o** the king of Hebron one 285
12:10 king of Jerusalem one the king of Hebron **o** 285
12:11 king of Jarmuth **o** the king of Lachish one 285
12:11 king of Jarmuth one the king of Lachish **o** 285
12:12 the king of Eglon **o** the king of Gezer one 285
12:12 the king of Eglon one the king of Gezer **o** 285
12:13 the king of Debir **o** the king of Geder one 285
12:13 the king of Debir one the king of Geder **o** 285
12:14 the king of Hormah **o** the king of Arad one 285
12:14 the king of Hormah one the king of Arad **o** 285
12:15 king of Libnah **o** the king of Adullam one 285
12:15 king of Libnah one the king of Adullam **o** 285
12:16 king of Makkedah **o** the king of Bethel one 285
12:16 king of Makkedah one the king of Bethel **o** 285
12:17 king of Tappuah **o** the king of Hepher one 285
12:17 king of Tappuah one the king of Hepher **o** 285
12:18 king of Aphek **o** the king of Lasharon one 285
12:18 king of Aphek one the king of Lasharon **o** 285
12:19 the king of Madon **o** the king of Hazor one 285
12:19 the king of Madon one the king of Hazor **o** 285
12:20 the king of Shimron Meron **o** 285
12:20 the king of Acshaph **o** 285
12:21 king of Taanach **o** the king of Megiddo one 285
12:21 king of Taanach one the king of Megiddo **o** 285
12:22 the king of Kedesh **o** the king of Jokneam 285
12:22 the king of Jokneam in Carmel **o** 285
12:23 the king of Dor (in Naphoth Dor) **o** 285
12:23 the king of Goyim in Gilgal **o** 285
12:24 the king of Tirzah **o** thirty-one kings in all. 285
13:12 and Edrei and had survived as **o** *of* the last 4946
15:18 **O day** when she came to Othniel, 2118+2256
17:14 "Why have you given us only **o** allotment 285
17:14 and **o** portion for an inheritance? 285
17:17 You will have not only **o** allotment 285
20:4 "When he flees to **o** of these cities, 285
20:5 they must not surrender the *o* **accused,** AIT
21:13 (a city of refuge for *o* **accused of murder),** AIT
21:21 (a city of refuge for *o* **accused of murder)** AIT
21:27 for *o* **accused of murder)** and Be Eshtarah, AIT
21:32 (a city of refuge for *o* **accused of murder),** AIT
21:38 (a city of refuge for *o* **accused of murder),** AIT
21:44 Not **o** of their enemies withstood them; 408
21:45 Not **o** of all the LORD's good promises to 1821[S]
21:45 **every** *o* was fulfilled. AIT
22:14 **o** for each of the tribes of Israel, 285
22:20 not the only **o** who died for his sin.' " 408
22:22 "The **Mighty O,** God, the LORD! 446
22:22 The **Mighty O,** God, the LORD! 446
23:9 to this day no **o** has been able 408
23:10 **O** of you routs a thousand, 285
Jos 23:14 with all your heart and soul that not **o** of all 285
23:14 not **o** has failed. 285
Jdg 1:14 **O day** when she came to Othniel, 2118+2256
3:28 they allowed no **o** to cross over. 408
5:5 the **O** of Sinai, before the LORD, 2296
6:25 the **o** seven years old. 7228[S]
6:39 Let me make just **o more** request. 7193
6:39 Allow me **o more** test with the fleece. 7193
7:4 If I say, **'This** *o* shall go with you,' AIT
7:4 but if I say, **'This** *o* shall not go with you,' AIT
8:18 *"each* **o** with the bearing of a prince." 285
8:24 And he said, *"I do* **have** *o* **request,** AIT
9:2 over you, or just **o** man?' 285
9:5 on **o** stone murdered his seventy brothers, 285
9:8 **O** day the trees went out to anoint a king NIH
11:37 But grant me **this** *o* request," she said. AIT
13:11 "Are you the **o** who talked to my wife?" 408
14:3 She's the **right** *o* for me." AIT
16:1 **O day** Samson went to Gaza, 2256
16:5 **Each** *o* of us will give you eleven hundred shekels of silver." AIT
16:24 the *o who* **laid waste** our land AIT
16:28 with **o** *blow* get revenge on the Philistines 285
16:29 his right hand on the **o** and his left hand on 285
17:5 and some idols and installed **o** of his sons 285
17:11 young man was to him like **o** of his sons. 285
18:14 "Do you know that **o** of these houses has NIH
18:19 priest rather than just **o** man's household?" 285
18:28 There was no *o to* **rescue** them AIT
19:13 and spend the night in **o** *of* those places." 285
19:15 no **o** took them into his home for the night. 408
19:18 No **o** has taken me into his house. 408
20:1 as **o** man and assembled before the LORD 285
20:6 into pieces and sent *o* **piece** to each region AIT
20:8 All the people rose as **o** man, saying, 285
20:8 No, not **o** of us will return to his house. 408
20:11 of Israel got together and united as **o** man 285
20:22 men of Israel encouraged **o another** 2021+6639
20:31 the **o** leading to Bethel and the other 285
21:1 "Not **o** of us will give his daughter 408
21:3 Why should **o** tribe be missing 285
21:6 "Today **o** tribe is cut off from Israel," 285
21:8 "Which **o** of the tribes of Israel failed 285
21:8 that no **o** from Jabesh Gilead had come to 408
21:23 each man caught **o** and carried her off to 889[S]
Ru 1:4 **o** named Orpah and the other Ruth. 285
2:13 the standing of **o** *of* your servant girls." 285
2:19 the **o** at whose place she had been working. 2257
2:20 he is **o** *of* our kinsman-redeemers." 4946
3:1 **O day** Naomi her mother-in-law said to her, 2256
4:4 For no **o has the right to do it** except you, AIT
4:7 **o party** took off his sandal and gave it to 408[S]
1Sa 1:2 **o** was called Hannah and 285
2:2 "There is no *o* **holy** like the LORD; AIT
2:2 **there is no** *o* besides you; AIT
2:9 "It is not by strength that **o** prevails; 408
2:20 the place of the *o* she **prayed for** and gave AIT
2:33 **Every** *o* of you that I do not cut off AIT
2:35 before my **anointed** *o* always. AIT
3:2 **O** night Eli, whose eyes were becoming 2085
6:17 **o** *each* for Ashdod, Gaza, Ashkelon, 285
9:3 "Take **o** of the servants with you and go 285
9:23 **the o** I told you to lay aside." 889[S]
10:3 **O** will be carrying three young goats, 285
10:24 **There is no** *o* like him among all AIT
11:2 that I gouge out the right eye of **every** *o* AIT
11:3 if no *o* comes *to* **rescue** us, AIT
11:7 and they turned out as **o** man. 285
11:13 "No **o** shall be put to death today, 408
12:13 **the o** you asked for; 889[S]
13:17 **O** turned toward Ophrah in the vicinity 285
14:1 **O** day Jonathan son of Saul said to 2021
14:3 No **o** was aware that Jonathan had left. 2021+6639[S]
14:4 **o** was called Bozez, and the other Seneh. 285
14:5 **O** cliff stood to the north toward Micmash, 285
14:26 yet no *o* **put** his hand to his mouth, AIT
14:28 Then **o** of the soldiers told him, 408
14:36 and let us not leave **o** of them alive." 408
14:39 But not **o** of the men said a word. 3972
15:1 the **o** the LORD sent to anoint you king NIH
15:28 and has given it to **o** of your neighbors— NIH
15:28 one of your neighbors—to **o** better than you. 2021
16:1 I have chosen **o** *of* his sons to be king." 928
16:3 You are to anoint for me **the o** I indicate." 889[S]
16:8 "The LORD has not chosen **this** *o* either." AIT
16:9 "Nor has the LORD chosen **this** *o.*" AIT
16:12 "Rise and anoint him; he is the **o."** 2296
16:18 **O** of the servants answered, 285
16:21 and David became **o** of his armor-bearers. NIH
17:3 The Philistines occupied **o** hill and 2296
17:32 "Let no **o** lose heart on account 132
17:36 this uncircumcised Philistine will be like **o** 285
18:1 Jonathan **became o** in spirit **with** David, 8003
20:15 even when the LORD has cut off **every** *o* AIT
21:1 Why is no **o** with you?" 408
21:2 'No **o** is to know anything 408
21:7 **o** of Saul's servants was there that day, 408
21:9 there is no sword here but *that* **o."** 2023
21:11 the **o** they sing about in their dances: NIH
22:8 No *o* **tells** me when my son makes AIT
23:26 Saul was going along **o** side of 2296
25:14 **O** of the servants told Nabal's wife Abigail: 285
25:17 a wicked man that no *o can* **talk** to him." AIT
25:22 if by morning I leave alive *o* **male** AIT
25:34 not *o* **male** belonging to Nabal AIT
26:8 to the ground with **o** thrust of my spear; 285

1Sa 26:12 No *o* **saw** or knew about it, AIT
26:20 as *o* **hunts** a partridge in the mountains." AIT
26:22 "Let **o** of your young men come over 285
27: 1 "**O** of these days I will be destroyed by 285
27: 5 let a place be assigned to me in **o** *of* 285
28: 7 "There is **o** in Endor," they said. 200+1266S
28: 8 he said, "and bring up for me **the o** I name." 889S
28:17 and given it to **o** of your neighbors— NIH
30: 6 each **o** was bitter in spirit because 408
2Sa 1:15 Then David called **o** of his men and said, 285
2: 1 "Shall I go up to **o** *of* the towns of Judah?" 285
2:13 **O group** sat down on one side of the pool 465S
2:13 down on *o* **side** of the pool and one group AIT
2:13 down on one side of the pool and **o group** 465S
2:21 take on **o** of the young men and strip him 285
3:13 But I demand **o** thing of you: 285
3:34 You fell as *o* **falls** before wicked men." AIT
4: 2 **O** was named Baanah and the other Recab; 285
5: 2 *o who* **led** Israel **on** their **military campaigns.** AIT
7: 5 the **o** to build me a house to dwell in? NIH
7:13 the **o** who will build a house for my Name, NIH
7:22 **There is no** *o* like you, AIT
7:23 the **o** nation on earth that God went out 285
9: 3 "Is there no **o** still left of the house of Saul 408
9:11 So Mephibosheth ate at David's table like **o** 285
11: 2 **O** evening David got up from his bed 2021
11:12 David said to him, "Stay here **o** more day, 2021
11:25 the sword devours **o** as well as another. 2297
12: 1 **o** rich and the other poor. 285
12: 3 poor man had nothing except **o** little ewe 285
12: 4 from taking **o** *of* his own sheep or cattle 4946
12: 4 and prepared it for the **o** who had come 408
12:11 and give them to **o who is close** *to* you, 8276
13:13 You would be like **o** *of* the wicked fools 285
13:30 not **o** of them is left." 285
14: 6 and no *o was there to* **separate** AIT
14: 6 **O** struck the other and killed him. 285
14: 7 the *o who* **struck** his brother **down,** AIT
14:11 "not **o** hair of your son's head will fall to 4946
14:19 no **o** can turn to the right or to the left 838
15: 2 "Your servant is from **o** *of* the tribes 285
16:18 "No, **the o** chosen by the LORD, 889S
16:23 like that of **o** who inquires of God. 408
17:19 No *o* **knew** anything **about** it. AIT
17:20 The men searched but found **no** *o,* AIT
17:22 no **o** was left who had not crossed 285
18:10 When **o** of the men saw this, he told Joab, 285
18:20 "You are not the **o** to take the news today," 408
18:27 that the **first** *o* runs like Ahimaaz son AIT
19: 9 he *is the o who* **rescued** us from the hand of AIT
19:14 of Judah as though they were **o** man. 285
20:11 **O** of Joab's men stood beside Amasa 408
20:21 Hand over **this o** man, 963+4200
21: 6 the LORD's **chosen** *o.*" AIT
21:16 **o** of the descendants of Rapha, NIH
21:18 **o** of the descendants of Rapha. NIH
22:42 but there was no *o to* **save** them— AIT
23: 3 *'When o* **rules** over men *in* righteousness, AIT
23: 8 whom he killed in **o** encounter. 285
23: 9 As **o** of the three mighty men, NIH
24:12 Choose **o** of them for me to carry out 285
24:13 how I should answer the *o who* **sent** me." AIT
24:17 *I am the o who has* **sinned** and done wrong. AIT
1Ki 2:16 Now I have **o** request to make of you. 285
2:20 "I have **o** small request to make of you," 285
3:17 **O** of them said, "My lord, 285
3:18 there was no **o** in the house but the two 2424S
3:22 The **living** *o* is my son; AIT
3:22 the **dead** *o* is yours." AIT
3:22 But **the first o** insisted, "No! 2296S
3:22 **dead** *o* is yours; the living one is mine." AIT
3:22 dead one is yours; the **living** *o* is mine." AIT
3:23 The king said, "**This** *o* says, AIT
3:23 while **that** *o* says, 'No! AIT
3:25 Cut the living child in two and give half to **o** 285
4: 7 Each **o** had to provide supplies 285
4: 7 to provide supplies for **o** month in the year. NIH
5: 6 You know that we have no **o** so skilled 408
5:14 so that they spent **o** month in Lebanon NIH
6:24 **O** wing of the first cherub was five cubits long, NIH
6:27 The wing of **o** cherub touched one wall, 285
6:27 The wing of one cherub touched **o** wall, 2021
6:36 and **o** course of trimmed cedar beams. NIH
7:12 and **o** course of trimmed cedar beams, NIH
7:21 to the south he named Jakin and the **o** to 6647S
7:24 in two rows in **o piece with** the Sea. 3669
7:31 that had a circular frame **o** cubit deep. NIH
7:34 **o** on each corner, projecting from the stand. 4190S
7:38 **o** basin to go on each of the ten stands. 285
8:19 you *are not the o to* **build** the temple, AIT
8:19 he *is the o who will* **build** the temple AIT
8:38 **each** *o* aware of the afflictions AIT
8:46 for there is no **o** who does not sin— 132
8:56 Not **o** word has failed of all 285
10:20 **o** at either end of each step. NIH
11:11 and give it to **o** of your subordinates. NIH
11:13 but will give him **o** tribe for the sake 285
11:26 He was **o** of Solomon's officials, NIH
11:32 he will have **o** tribe. 285
11:36 I will give **o** tribe to his son so 285
11:38 the **o** I built for David and will give Israel NIH
12:24 Go home, **every** *o* of you, AIT
12:29 **O** he set up in Bethel, and the other in Dan. 285
12:30 even as far as Dan to worship the **o** there. 285
14: 2 the **o** who told me I would be king 2085
1Ki 14:10 up the house of Jeroboam as *o* **burns** dung, AIT
14:13 the only **o** belonging to Jeroboam who will 2296
14:13 because he is the only **o** in the house NIH
15:22 **no** *o* was exempt— AIT
16: 9 Zimri, **o** of his officials, NIH
18: 6 Ahab going in **o** direction and Obadiah 285
18:22 the **only o** of the LORD's prophets left, 963+4200
18:23 Let them choose **o** for themselves, 285
18:25 "Choose **o** of the bulls and prepare it first, 285
18:26 But there was no response; no *o* **answered.** AIT
18:29 But there was no response, no *o* **answered,** AIT
18:29 no one answered, **no** *o* paid attention. AIT
18:31 **o for each** *of* the tribes descended 3869+5031
19: 2 not make your life like that of **o** of them." 285
19:10 I am the **only o** left, 963+4200
19:14 I am the **only o** left, 963+4200
20:11 *'O who* **puts on** *his* **armor** should not AIT
20:11 not boast like *o who* **takes** *it* **off.'** " AIT
20:20 and **each** *o* struck down his opponent. AIT
20:25 also raise an army like the **o** you lost— 2657S
20:29 on the Aramean foot soldiers in **o** day. 285
20:35 By the word of the LORD **o** of the sons of 285
20:41 and the king of Israel recognized him as **o** 4946
22: 8 "There is still **o** man through whom 285
22: 9 So the king of Israel called **o** of his officials 285
22:13 to him, "Look, *as* **no o** the other prophets 285
22:17 Let **each** *o* go home in peace.' " AIT
22:20 "**O** suggested this, and another that. 2296
2Ki 4: 4 as each is filled, **put it to o side."** 5825
4: 6 she said to her son, "Bring me another **o."** 3998S
4: 8 **O** day Elisha went to Shunem. 2021
4:11 **O** day when Elisha came, 2021
4:18 and **o** day he went out to his father, 2021
4:22 "Please send me **o** of the servants and 285
4:39 **O** of them went out into the fields 285
4:39 though no *o* **knew** what they were. AIT
5:18 forgive your servant for **this** *o* thing: AIT
6: 3 Then **o** of them said, 285
6: 5 As **o** of them was cutting down a tree, 285
6:12 my lord the king," said **o** of his officers, 285
7: 6 so that they said to **o** another, "Look, 408
7: 8 of the camp and entered **o** of the tents. 285
7:13 **O** of his officers answered, 285
8:26 and he reigned in Jerusalem **o** year. 285
9:10 and no *o will* **bury** her.' " AIT
9:11 *o* of them **asked** him, AIT
9:37 so that no *o will be able to* **say,** AIT
10:19 See that no **o** is missing, 408
10:21 not **o** stayed away. 408
10:21 until it was full from *o* **end** to the other. AIT
10:24 "If **o** of you lets any of the men NIH
10:25 let no **o** escape." 408
11: 9 **Each** *o* took his men— AIT
12: 5 Let every priest receive the money from **o** NIH
12: 9 on the right side as **o** enters the temple of 408
14: 7 the *o who* **defeated** ten thousand Edomites AIT
14:22 the *o who* **rebuilt** Elath and restored it AIT
14:25 the *o who* **restored** the boundaries of Israel AIT
14:26 there was no *o to* **help** them. AIT
15:13 and he reigned in Samaria **o month.** 3427+3732
15:25 **O** of his chief officers, NIH
17:27 "Have **o** of the priests you took captive 285
17:28 So **o** of the priests who had been exiled 285
17:36 is the **o** you must worship. 2257
18: 5 *There* **was** no *o* like him among all the kings AIT
18:22 isn't he **the o** whose high places 889S
18:24 How can you repulse **o** officer of the least 285
18:31 Then **every** *o* of you will eat AIT
19:22 Against the **Holy** *O of* Israel! AIT
19:37 **O day,** while he was worshiping in 2118+2256
21:13 I will wipe out Jerusalem as *o* **wipes** a dish, AIT
23:10 so no **o** could use it to sacrifice his son 408
25:17 of **o** pillar was four and a half feet high NIH
1Ch 1:19 **O** was named Peleg, because in his time 285
4:17 **O** of Mered's wives gave birth to Miriam, NIH
5:21 took *o* **hundred** thousand people captive, AIT
11: 2 *o who* **led** Israel **on** their **military campaigns.** AIT
11:11 whom he killed in **o** encounter. 285
11:12 **o** of the three mighty men. 2085
12:38 the rest of the Israelites were also of **o** mind 285
15: 2 "**No** *o* but the Levites may carry the ark AIT
16:20 from **o** kingdom to another. NIH
17: 4 not the **o** to build me a house to dwell in. NIH
17: 5 I have moved from **o** tent site to another, NIH
17: 5 from **o** dwelling place to another. NIH
17:11 **o** *of* your own sons, 4946
17:12 *the o who will* **build** a house for me, AIT
17:20 "**There is no** *o* like you, O LORD, AIT
17:21 the **o** nation on earth whose God went out 285
20: 4 **o** *of* the descendants of the Rephaites, 4946
21: 5 In all Israel there were *o* **million** one hundred thousand men who could handle AIT
21: 5 one million *o* **hundred** thousand men who AIT
21:10 Choose **o** of them for me to carry out 285
21:12 how I should answer the *o who* **sent** me." AIT
21:17 I am the **o** who has sinned and done wrong. 2085
22:10 He *is the o who will* **build** a house AIT
23:11 as **o** family with one assignment. NIH
23:11 as one family with **o** assignment. 285
24: 6 **o** family being taken from Eleazar and 285
24: 6 from Eleazar and then **o** from Ithamar. 285
26: 1 **o** *of* the sons of Asaph. 4946
28: 6 the **o** who will build my house 2085
29: 1 the **o** whom God has chosen, 285
2Ch 3:11 **O** wing of the first cherub was five cubits 285
3:12 Similarly **o** wing of the second cherub NIH
2Ch 3:17 **o** to the south and one to the north. 285
3:17 one to the south and **o** to the north. 285
3:17 The *o to the* **south** he named Jakin and AIT
3:17 and the *o to the* **north** Boaz. AIT
4: 3 in two rows in **o piece with** the Sea. 4609
5:13 joined in unison, as with **o** voice, 285
6: 9 you are not *the o to* **build** the temple, AIT
6: 9 he is *the o who will* **build** the temple AIT
6:29 **each** *o* aware of his afflictions and pains, AIT
6:36 for there is no **o** who does not sin— 132
6:42 do not reject your **anointed** *o.* AIT
9:19 **o** at either end of each step. NIH
11: 4 Go home, **every** *o* of you, AIT
14: 6 **No** *o* was at war with him AIT
14:11 **there is no** *o* like you to help the powerless AIT
15: 6 *O* **nation** was being crushed by another AIT
15: 6 by another and *o* **city** by another, AIT
18: 7 "There is still **o** man through whom 285
18: 8 So the king of Israel called **o** of his officials 285
18:12 to him, "Look, *as* **o** man the other prophets 285
18:16 Let **each** *o* go home in peace.' " AIT
18:19 "**O** suggested this, and another that. 2296
20: 6 and **no** *o* can withstand you. AIT
20:23 they helped to destroy **o** another. 408
20:24 **no** *o* had escaped. AIT
22: 2 and he reigned in Jerusalem **o** year. 285
22: 9 So **there was no** *o* in the house AIT
23: 6 No *o is to* **enter** the temple of AIT
23: 8 **Each** *o* took his men— AIT
23:19 *o who* was in any way **unclean** AIT
26: 2 the **o** who rebuilt Elath and restored it NIH
26:11 **o** *of* the royal officials. 4946
28: 6 In **o** day Pekah son of Remaliah killed 285
32: 5 He built another wall outside that **o** NIH
32:12 before **o** altar and burn sacrifices on it'? 285
Ezr 3: 1 the people assembled as **o** man 285
3:13 No **o** could distinguish the sound of 2021+6639S
5:11 the temple that was built many years ago, **o** 10204
6: 4 with three courses of large stones and **o** 10248
6:17 **o** for each of the tribes of Israel. NIH
9:11 with their impurity from *o* **end** to the other. AIT
9:15 though because of it **not** *o* of us can stand AIT
10: 2 **o** *of* the descendants of Elam, said to Ezra, 4946
10:16 **o** from each family division, NIH
Ne 1: 2 Hanani, **o** of my brothers, 285
2:12 with me except the **o** I was riding on. 989S
3: 8 **o** of the goldsmiths, repaired the next NIH
3: 8 and Hananiah, **o** *of* the perfume-makers, 1201S
3:31 Next to him, Malkijah, **o** *of* the goldsmiths, 1201S
4:17 with **o** hand and held a weapon in the other, 285
5:18 Each day **o** ox, six choice sheep 285
6: 2 let us meet together in **o** of the villages on NIH
6:10 **O day** I went to the house of Shemaiah son 2256
6:11 Or should **o** like me go into the temple 4769
8: 1 all the people assembled as **o** man in 285
8:16 the square by the Water Gate and the **o** *by* 8148S
11: 1 of the people cast lots to bring **o** out 285
11:22 Uzzi was **o** *of* Asaph's descendants, 4946
11:24 **o** *of* the descendants of Zerah son of Judah, 4946
12:24 **o section** responding to the other, AIT
12:31 **O** was to proceed on top of the wall to NIH
13:24 **o of the other peoples,** 2256+6639+6639
13:28 **O** *of* the sons of Joiada son of Eliashib 4946
Est 1: 7 *each* **o** different from the other, 3998S
4: 2 because no *o* **clothed** in sackcloth AIT
4: 5 **o** *of* the king's eunuchs assigned 4946
4:11 the king has but **o** law: 285
6: 8 **o** with a royal crest placed on its head. 889S
6: 9 the robe and horse be entrusted to **o** of 408
7: 9 **o** of the eunuchs attending the king, said, 285
9: 2 No **o** could stand against them, 408
9:22 of food to **o** another and gifts to the poor. 408
Job 1: 6 **O** day the angels came to present 2021
1: 8 There is no **o** on earth like him; NIH
1:13 **O** day when Job's sons 2021
1:15 the **only o** who has escaped to tell you! 963+4200
1:16 the **only o** who has escaped to tell you! 963+4200
1:17 the **only o** who has escaped to tell you! 963+4200
1:19 the **only o** who has escaped to tell you! 963+4200
2: 3 There is no **o** on earth like him; NIH
2:13 No *o* **said** a word to him, AIT
6:10 I had not denied the words of the **Holy O.** 7705
9: 3 Though *o* **wished** to dispute with him, AIT
9: 3 not answer him **o** *time* out of a thousand. 285
10: 7 that no *o can* **rescue** me from your hand? AIT
11: 3 *Will* no *o* **rebuke** you when you mock? AIT
11:19 with no *o* to **make** you **afraid,** AIT
14: 3 Do you fix your eye on **such** *a o?* AIT
14: 4 bring what is pure from the impure? No **o!** 285
15:14 that he could be pure, or *o* **born** *of* woman, AIT
15:28 and houses where no *o* **lives,** AIT
18:21 such is the place of *o who* **knows** not God." AIT
21:23 *O* **man** dies in full vigor, AIT
22:30 *o who* is not **innocent,** AIT
24:12 But God charges no **o** with wrongdoing. NIH
24:18 so that no *o* **goes** to the vineyards. AIT
25: 4 How can *o* **born** *of* woman be pure? AIT
26: 3 What advice you have offered to **o** NIH
29:25 I was like *o who* **comforts** mourners. AIT
30:24 "Surely no *o* **lays** a hand on a broken man AIT
31:15 Did not the **same o** form us both within our mothers? 285
32:12 But not *o* of you *has* **proved** Job **wrong;** AIT
32:21 I will show partiality to no **o,** 408
33:14 now **o way,** now another— 285+928
33:23 **o** out of a thousand, 285
34:17 Will you condemn the just and **mighty** *O?* AIT

Job 34:18 Is he not the *O* who **says** to kings, AIT
35:10 But no *o* **says,** 'Where is God my Maker, AIT
36: 4 *o* **perfect** *in* knowledge is with you. AIT
36:18 Be careful that no *o* **entices** you by riches; AIT
37:21 Now no *o* **can look** *at* the sun, AIT
38:26 a desert with no **o** in it, 132
40: 2 *"Will* the *o* who **contends** with AIT
41:10 No *o* is **fierce** *enough* to rouse him. AIT
41:17 They are joined fast to *o* another; 408
41:32 *o would* **think** the deep had white hair. AIT
42:11 and **each** *o* gave him a piece of silver and AIT
Ps 2: 2 the LORD and against his **Anointed** *O*. AIT
2: 4 The *O* **enthroned** in heaven laughs; AIT
6: 5 **No** *o* remembers you when he is dead. AIT
7: 2 to pieces with no *o to* **rescue** me. AIT
14: 1 there is no *o* who **does** good. AIT
14: 3 there is no *o* who **does** good, not even one. AIT
14: 3 there is no one who does good, not even **o.** 285
16:10 nor will you let your **Holy** *O* see decay. AIT
18:41 but there was no *o to* **save** them— AIT
19: 6 It rises at *o* **end** *of* the heavens AIT
22: 3 Yet you are enthroned as the **Holy O;** 7705
22:11 trouble is near and there is no *o to* **help.** AIT
22:24 the suffering of the **afflicted** *o;* AIT
25: 3 No **o** whose hope is in you will ever be put 3972
27: 4 **O** *thing* I ask of the LORD, 285
28: 8 a fortress of salvation for his **anointed** *o*. AIT
34:20 not **o** of them will be broken. 285
34:22 no **o** will be condemned who takes refuge 3972
39: 9 for you are the *o* who *has* **done** this. AIT
40: 5 for us no *o can* **recount** to you; AIT
41: 6 Whenever *o* **comes** to see me, AIT
45: 3 upon your side, O **mighty** *o;* AIT
50: 1 The **Mighty O,** God, the LORD, 446
53: 1 there is no *o* who **does** good. AIT
53: 3 there is no *o* who **does** good, not even one. AIT
53: 3 there is no one who does good, not even **o.** 285
54: 4 the Lord is the *o* who **sustains** me. AIT
62:11 **O** *thing* God has spoken, 285
68: 8 before God, the **O** *of* Sinai, before God, 2296
69:25 let there be no *o to* **dwell** in their tents. AIT
71:11 for no *o will* **rescue** him." AIT
71:22 O **Holy O** *of* Israel. 7705
72:12 the afflicted who have no *o to* **help.** AIT
73:20 As a dream when *o* **awakes,** AIT
75: 6 **No** *o* from the east or the west or from AIT
75: 7 He brings **o** down, he exalts another. 2296
76: 5 not *o of* the warriors can lift his hands. 3972
76:11 bring gifts to the *O* to be **feared.** AIT
78:41 they vexed the **Holy O** *of* Israel. 7705
79: 3 and there is no *o to* **bury** the dead. AIT
83: 5 *With o* **mind** they plot together; AIT
84: 9 look with favor on your **anointed** *o*. AIT
84:10 Better is *o* **day** in your courts than AIT
87: 4 and will say, **'This** *o* was born in Zion.' " AIT
87: 5 *"This* **o** and that one were born in her, 408
87: 5 "This one and *that* **o** were born in her, 408
87: 6 **"This** *o* was born in Zion." AIT
89: 3 "I have made a covenant with my **chosen** *o*, AIT
89:10 You crushed Rahab like *o of* the **slain;** AIT
89:18 our king to the **Holy O** *of* Israel. 7705
89:38 very angry with your **anointed** *o*. AIT
89:51 mocked every step of your **anointed** *o*. AIT
94:20 *o that* **brings on** misery by its decrees? AIT
101: 7 No *o* who **practices** deceit will dwell AIT
101: 7 no *o* who **speaks** falsely will stand AIT
105:13 from *o* **kingdom** to another. AIT
105:14 He allowed no **o** to oppress them; 132
106:11 not **o** of them survived. 285
106:23 had not Moses, his **chosen** *o*, AIT
107:12 they stumbled, and there was no *o to* **help.** AIT
109:12 *May* no *o* **extend** kindness to him AIT
109:31 he stands at the right hand of the **needy** *o*, AIT
113: 5 *O* who sits enthroned *on* **high,** AIT
119:14 in following your statutes as **o** rejoices NIH
119:42 then I will answer the *o* who **taunts** me, AIT
119:162 in your promise like *o* who **finds** great spoil. AIT
129: 7 nor the *o* who **gathers** fill his arms. AIT
132: 2 and made a vow to the **Mighty O** *of* Jacob: 51
132: 5 a dwelling for the **Mighty O** *of* Jacob." 51
132:10 do not reject your **anointed** *o*. AIT
132:11 **"O** *of* your own descendants I will place 4946
132:17 and set up a lamp for my **anointed** *o*. AIT
136:23 to the *O* who **remembered** us AIT
137: 3 they said, "Sing us *o of* the songs of Zion!" 4946
139:16 in your book before **o** of them came to be. 285
141: 7 "As *o* **plows** and breaks up the earth, AIT
142: 4 no *o* is **concerned** for me. AIT
142: 4 I have no refuge; no *o* **cares for** my life. AIT
143: 2 for no **o** living is righteous before you. 3972
144:10 to the *O* who **gives** victory to kings, AIT
145: 3 his greatness **no** *o* can fathom. AIT
145: 4 *O* **generation** will commend your works AIT
Pr 1:24 when I called and no *o* **gave heed** AIT
5: 9 to others and your years to *o* who is **cruel,** AIT
6:29 no **o** who touches her will go unpunished. 3972
9:10 knowledge of the **Holy O** is understanding. 7705
11:24 *O man* **gives freely,** yet gains even more; AIT
13: 7 *O man* **pretends to be rich,** AIT
14: 1 the **foolish** *o* tears hers down. AIT
14:10 and no *o* **else** can share its joy. AIT
16:32 controls his temper than *o* who **takes** a city. AIT
17: 2 the inheritance as **o** *of* the brothers. 928+9348
17: 8 A bribe is a charm to the **o who gives** it; 1251
17:25 and bitterness to the *o* who **bore** him. AIT
18: 9 *O* who is **slack** in his work is brother AIT
Pr 18: 9 is brother to **o who destroys.** 1251+5422
19:23 Then *o* **rests** content, untouched by trouble. AIT
20:16 *o* who **puts up security** for a stranger. AIT
21:12 The **Righteous O** takes note of the house of 7404
22:24 do not associate with **o** easily angered, 408
23:34 be like *o* **sleeping** on the high seas, AIT
25:20 Like *o* who **takes away** a garment on AIT
25:20 is *o* who **sings** songs to a heavy heart. AIT
26:17 Like *o* who **seizes** a dog by the ears is AIT
27:13 Take the garment of **o** who puts up security 2257
27:17 so *o* **man** sharpens another. AIT
28: 1 The wicked man flees though no *o* **pursues,** AIT
28:17 *let* no *o* **support** him. AIT
28:19 the *o* who **chases** fantasies will have his fill AIT
28:20 *o* **eager** to get rich will not go unpunished. AIT
29: 4 but *o* who *is* **greedy** *for* bribes tears it down. 408
29: 6 but a **righteous** *o* can sing and be glad. AIT
29:22 and a **hot-tempered** *o* commits many sins. AIT
30: 3 nor have I knowledge of the **Holy O.** 7705
Ecc 1: 8 things are wearisome, more than **o** can say. 408
1:10 Is there anything of which *o can* **say,** AIT
2:18 to the **o** who comes after me. 132
2:26 to hand it over to the *o* who **pleases** God. AIT
3:19 As **o** dies, so dies the other. 2296
4: 6 Better *o* **handful** with tranquillity AIT
4: 9 Two are better than **o,** 285
4:10 If **o** falls down, his friend can help him up! 285
4:10 But pity the man who falls and has no **o** 9108
4:11 But how can **o** keep warm *alone?* 285
4:12 Though **o** may be overpowered, 285
5: 8 for *o* **official** is eyed by a higher one, AIT
5: 8 for one official is eyed by a higher **o,** 1469[S]
6:10 with *o* **who** is stronger than he. AIT
7:14 God has made the **o** as well as the other. 2296
7:18 It is good to grasp the **o** and not let go of 2296
7:19 Wisdom makes **o** wise man more powerful than ten rulers 2021
7:27 "Adding *o thing* to another to discover 285
7:28 I found **o** [upright] man among a thousand, 285
7:28 but not **o** [upright] woman among them all. NIH
8: 8 **no** *o* has power over the day of his death. AIT
8: 8 As **no** *o* is discharged in time of war, AIT
8:17 No **o** can comprehend what goes on under 132
9:18 but **o** sinner destroys much good. 285
10:14 No **o** knows what is coming— 132
12:11 given by **o** Shepherd. 285
SS 1: 9 to a mare harnessed to **o** of the chariots NIH
2:10 "Arise, my darling, my **beautiful** *o*, AIT
2:13 my **beautiful** *o*, come with me." AIT
3: 1 for **the o** my heart loves; 8611[S]
3: 2 I will search for **the o** my heart loves. 8611[S]
3: 3 "Have you seen **the o** my heart loves?" 8611[S]
3: 4 when I found **the o** my heart loves. 8611[S]
3: 4 to the room of the *o* who **conceived** me. AIT
4: 2 Each has its twin; not **o** of them is alone. NIH
4: 9 you have stolen my heart with **o** glance 285
4: 9 with **o** jewel of your necklace. 285
5: 2 my darling, my dove, my **flawless** *o*. AIT
6: 6 Each has its twin, not *o* **of** them is alone. AIT
6: 9 my **perfect** *o*, is unique, AIT
6: 9 the favorite of the *o* who **bore** her. AIT
8: 1 and no *o would* **despise** me. AIT
8: 7 If **o** were to give all the wealth of his house 408
8:10 in his eyes like *o* **bringing** contentment. AIT
Isa 1: 4 the **Holy O** *of* Israel and turned their backs 7705
1:24 the **Mighty O** *of* Israel, declares: 51
1:31 with no *o to* **quench** *the* **fire."** AIT
3: 6 A man will seize *o of* his **brothers** AIT
4: 1 seven women will take hold of **o** man and 285
5: 1 for the **o** I **love** a song about his vineyard: AIT
5: 1 My **loved o** had a vineyard on 3351
5:19 let the plan of the **Holy O** *of* Israel come, 7705
5:24 and spurned the word of the **Holy O** 7705
5:27 Not *o of* them grows **tired** or stumbles, AIT
5:27 not *o* **slumbers** or sleeps; AIT
5:29 and carry it off with no *o to* **rescue.** AIT
5:30 And if *o* **looks** at the land, AIT
6: 3 And they were calling to **o** another: 2296
6: 6 Then **o** of the seraphs flew to me with 285
8:13 The LORD Almighty is the **o** you are 2257
8:13 he is the **o** you are to fear, NIH
8:13 he is the *o* you are to **dread,** AIT
9:19 no **o** will spare his brother. 408
10:13 like a **mighty** *o* I subdued their kings. AIT
10:14 As *o* **reaches** into a **nest,** AIT
10:14 not *o* **flapped** a wing, AIT
10:17 their **Holy O** a flame; 7705
10:20 rely on the LORD, the **Holy O** *of* Israel. 7705
10:34 Lebanon will fall before the **Mighty O.** 129
12: 6 great is the **Holy O** *of* Israel among you." 7705
16: 5 **o** from the house of David— NIH
16: 5 *o* who *in* **judging** seeks justice and speeds AIT
16:10 no *o* **sings** or shouts in the vineyards; AIT
16:10 no *o* **treads out** wine at the presses, AIT
17: 2 with no *o to* **make** them **afraid.** AIT
17: 7 and turn their eyes to the **Holy O** *of* Israel. 7705
19:11 "I am *o of* the wise men, 1201
19:18 **O** of them will be called the City 285
21:16 "Within *o* **year,** as a servant bound AIT
22:11 but you did not look to the *O* who **made** it, AIT
22:11 for the *O* who **planned** it long ago. AIT
22:22 what he opens no *o can* **shut,** AIT
22:22 and what he shuts no *o can* **open.** AIT
24:16 "Glory to the **Righteous O."** 7404
26: 7 O **upright** *O*, you make the way of AIT
27: 3 and night so that no *o may* **harm** it. AIT
27:12 O Israelites, will be gathered up **o** by one. 285
Isa 27:12 O Israelites, will be gathered up one by **o.** 285
28: 2 the Lord has *o* who is **powerful** and strong. AIT
28:16 the *o* who **trusts** will never be dismayed. AIT
28:28 *o does* not **go on threshing** AIT
29:19 the needy will rejoice in the **Holy O** 7705
29:23 the holiness of the **Holy O** *of* Jacob, 7705
30:11 and stop confronting us with the **Holy O** 7705
30:12 this is what the **Holy O** *of* Israel says: 7705
30:15 the **Holy O** *of* Israel, says: 7705
30:17 A thousand will flee at the threat of **o;** 285
31: 1 but do not look to the **Holy O** *of* Israel, 7705
31: 7 that day **every** *o of* you will reject the idols AIT
33: 8 no **o** is respected. 632
33:18 Where is the *o* who **took** *the* **revenue?** AIT
33:21 There the LORD will be our **Mighty O.** 129
33:24 No **o living** in Zion will say, "I am ill"; 8907
34:10 no *o will* ever **pass** through it again. AIT
34:16 not **o** will lack her mate. 851
36: 7 isn't he **the o** whose high places 889[S]
36: 9 then can you repulse **o** officer of the least 285
36:16 Then **every** *o of* you will eat AIT
37:23 Against the **Holy O** *of* Israel! 7705
37:38 **O day,** while he was worshiping in 2118+2256
40: 3 A voice of *o* **calling:** AIT
40:25 says the **Holy O.** 7705
40:26 who brings out the starry host **o by one,** 928+5031
40:26 who brings out the starry host **one by o,** 928+5031
40:26 not **o** of them is missing. 408
40:28 and his understanding no **o** can fathom. NIH
41: 2 "Who has stirred up **o** from the east, NIH
41:14 your Redeemer, the **Holy O** *of* Israel. 7705
41:16 in the LORD and glory in the **Holy O** 7705
41:20 that the **Holy O** *of* Israel has created it. 7705
41:25 "I have stirred up **o** from the north, NIH
41:25 **o** from the rising sun who calls NIH
41:26 No *o* **told** *of* this, no one foretold it, AIT
41:26 No one told of this, no *o* **foretold** it, AIT
41:26 no *o* **heard** any words from you. AIT
41:28 I look but there is no **o—** 408
41:28 no **o** among them **to give counsel,** 3446
41:28 no *o to* **give** answer when I ask them. AIT
42: 1 my **chosen** *o* in whom I delight; AIT
42:19 Who is blind like the *o* **committed** to me, AIT
42:22 with no *o to* **rescue** them; AIT
42:22 with no *o to* **say,** "Send them back." AIT
43: 3 the **Holy O** *of* Israel, your Savior; 7705
43:10 nor *will there* **be** *o* after me. AIT
43:13 No *o can* **deliver** out of my hand. AIT
43:14 your Redeemer, the **Holy O** *of* Israel: 7705
43:15 I am the LORD, your **Holy O,** 7705
44: 5 **O** will say, 'I belong to the LORD'; 2296
44: 8 No, there is no other Rock; I know not **o."** NIH
44:19 No **o** stops to think, 2257
44:19 no **o** has the knowledge or understanding NIH
45:11 the **Holy O** *of* Israel, and its Maker: 7705
46: 7 Though *o* **cries out** to it, it does not answer; AIT
47: 3 I will take vengeance; I will spare no **o."** 132
47: 4 is the **Holy O** *of* Israel. 7705
47:10 'No *o* **sees** me.' AIT
47:15 there is not *o that can* **save** you. AIT
48:17 your Redeemer, the **Holy O** *of* Israel: 7705
49: 7 the Redeemer and **Holy O** *of* Israel— 7705
49: 7 the **Holy O** *of* Israel, who has chosen you." 7731
49:26 your Redeemer, the **Mighty O** *of* Jacob." 51
50: 2 When I came, why was there no **o**? 408
50: 2 I called, why was there no *o to* **answer?** AIT
50: 4 to listen like **o** being **taught.** 4341
51: 2 When I called him he was but **o,** 285
51:21 Therefore hear this, you **afflicted** *o*, AIT
53: 3 Like *o* from whom men **hide** their faces AIT
54: 5 the **Holy O** *of* Israel is your Redeemer; 7705
55: 5 the **Holy O** *of* Israel, 7705
56:12 "Come," each **o** cries, "let me get wine! NIH
57: 1 and no **o** ponders it in his heart; 408
57: 1 and no *o* **understands** that AIT
57:15 For this is what the high and lofty *O* **says**— AIT
59: 4 No *o* **calls** for justice; AIT
59: 4 no *o* **pleads** *his* **case** with integrity. AIT
59: 5 and when **o** is broken, an adder is hatched. 2021
59: 8 no **o** who walks in them will know peace. 3972
59:16 He saw that there was no **o,** 408
59:16 that there was no *o to* **intervene;** AIT
60: 9 the **Holy O** of Israel, 7705
60:14 Zion of the **Holy O** *of* **Israel.** 7705
60:15 with no *o* **traveling through,** AIT
60:16 your Redeemer, the **Mighty O** *of* Jacob. 51
63: 2 like those of *o* **treading** the winepress? AIT
63: 3 from the nations no **o** was with me. 408
63: 5 I looked, but there was no *o to* **help,** AIT
63: 5 I was appalled that no *o* **gave support;** AIT
64: 4 Since ancient times no *o has* **heard,** AIT
64: 6 of us have become like **o** who is unclean, 2021
64: 7 No *o* **calls** on your name or strives AIT
66: 2 **"This** is *the o* I esteem: AIT
66: 3 like *o* who **kills** a man, and whoever offers AIT
66: 3 like *o* who **breaks** a dog's **neck;** AIT
66: 3 like **o** who presents pig's blood, NIH
66: 3 like *o* who **worships** an idol. AIT
66: 4 For when I called, no *o* **answered,** AIT
66: 4 when I spoke, no *o* **listened.** AIT
66:17 the **o** in the midst of those who eat the flesh 285
66:23 From *o* **New Moon** to another and AIT
66:23 to another and from *o* **Sabbath** to another, AIT
Jer 1: 1 *o of* the priests at Anathoth in the territory 4946
2: 6 where no **o** travels and no one lives?' 408
2: 6 where no one travels and no **o** lives?' 132
3:14 **o** from a town and two from a clan— 285

Jer 3:16 nor *will* another *o* **be made.** AIT
4: 4 burn with no *o to* **quench** it. AIT
4:29 no *o* lives in them. 408
4:30 What are you doing, O **devastated** *o?* AIT
4:31 *o* **bearing** *her* **first child—** AIT
5: 1 but *o* **person** who deals honestly and seeks AIT
5: 5 But **with o accord** they too had broken off 3481
6: 8 so no *o* **can live in** *it.*" AIT
6: 9 like *o* **gathering grapes."** AIT
7:19 But am I the **o** they are provoking? NIH
7:33 be no *o to* **frighten** them **away.** AIT
8: 6 No **o** repents of his wickedness, saying, 408
9: 3 They go from *o* **sin** to another; AIT
9: 5 and no *o* **speaks** the truth. AIT
9:11 of Judah so no *o can* **live** there." AIT
9:12 like a desert that no *o can* **cross?** AIT
9:20 teach **o** another a lament. 851
9:22 with no *o to* **gather** them.' " AIT
10: 6 **No** *o* is like you, O LORD; AIT
10: 7 **there is no** *o* like you. AIT
10:20 **no** *o* is left now to pitch my tent or to set AIT
12: 7 the *o* I **love** into the hands of her enemies. AIT
12:11 because there is no **o** who cares. 408
12:12 of the LORD will devour from *o* **end** *of* AIT
12:12 no **o** will be safe. 1414+3972[S]
13:14 I will smash them **o** against the other, 408
13:19 and there will be no *o to* **open** them. AIT
14:16 be no *o to* **bury** them or their wives, AIT
14:22 for you are the *o who* **does** all this. AIT
16: 6 and no *o will* **cut himself** AIT
16: 7 No *o will* **offer food** AIT
17: 5 "Cursed is the **o** who trusts in man, 1505
17: 6 in a salt land where no *o* **lives.** AIT
17:14 for you are the *o* I **praise.** AIT
18:11 So turn from your evil ways, **each** *o* of you, AIT
19: 9 and they will eat **o** another's flesh during 408
21:12 *o who has* **been robbed,** AIT
21:12 burn with no *o to* **quench** it. AIT
22: 3 *o who has* **been robbed.** AIT
22: 8 by this city and will ask **o** another, 408
22:28 broken pot, an object **no** *o* wants? AIT
23:14 so that no **o** turns from his wickedness. 408
23:27 dreams they tell **o** another will make my
people forget my name, 408
23:28 the **o** who has my word speak it faithfully. 2257
23:30 from **o** another words supposedly from me. 408
24: 2 **O** basket had very good figs, 285
25:26 near and far, **o** after the other— 408
25:33 from *o* **end** *of* the earth to the other. AIT
28: 9 as **o** truly sent by the LORD only 2021+5566[S]
29:32 He will have no **o** left among this people, 408
30:10 and no *o will* **make** him **afraid.** AIT
30:13 There is no *o to* **plead** your cause, AIT
30:17 Zion for whom no *o* **cares.'** AIT
30:21 Their leader will be *o of* their own; 4946
33:13 under the hand of the *o who* **counts** them,' AIT
33:26 and will not choose **o** *of* his sons to rule 4946
34: 9 no **o** was to hold a fellow Jew in bondage. 408
34:22 of Judah so no *o can* **live** there." AIT
35: 2 to come to *o of* the side rooms of the house 285
36:30 He will have no *o to* **sit** on the throne AIT
38:27 for no *o had* **heard** his conversation with AIT
40:15 and no **o** will know it. 408
41: 1 who was of royal blood and had been **o** of NIH
41: 2 killing the **o** whom the king 2257
41: 9 the **o** King Asa had made as part 2085
42:17 not *o* of them **will** survive or escape AIT
44:26 'that no *o from* Judah living anywhere 408
46:12 *O* **warrior** will stumble over another; AIT
46:18 "*o will* **come** who is like Tabor among AIT
46:27 and no *o will* **make** him **afraid.** AIT
48: 9 with no *o to* **live** in them. AIT
48:11 not poured from *o* **jar** to another— AIT
48:33 no *o* **treads** them with shouts of joy. AIT
48:38 like a jar that **no** *o* wants," AIT
49: 5 **"Every** *o* of you will be driven away, AIT
49: 5 and no *o will* **gather** the fugitives. AIT
49:18 says the LORD, "so no **o** will live there; 408
49:19 Who *is the* **chosen** *o* I will appoint for this? AIT
49:33 No **o** will live there; 408
50: 3 No *o will* **live** in it; AIT
50:29 Encamp all around her; let no *o* **escape.** AIT
50:29 the **Holy O** *of* Israel. 7705
50:31 "See, I am against you, O **arrogant** *o,*" AIT
50:32 The **arrogant** *o* will stumble and fall AIT
50:32 and no *o will* **help** her **up;** AIT
50:40 "so no **o** will live there; 408
50:44 Who *is* the **chosen** *o* I will appoint for this? AIT
51: 5 of guilt before the **Holy O** *of* Israel. 7705
51:29 of Babylon so that no *o will* **live** there. AIT
51:31 *O* **courier** follows another AIT
51:37 a place where no *o* **lives.** AIT
51:43 a land where no **o** lives, 408
51:46 *o* **rumor** comes this year, another the next, AIT
52:22 on top of the **o** pillar was five cubits high NIH
La 1: 4 for no *o* **comes** *to* her appointed feasts. AIT
1: 7 there was no *o to* **help** her. AIT
1:16 **No** *o is* **near** to comfort me, AIT
1:16 no *o to* **restore** my spirit. AIT
1:17 but there is no *o to* **comfort** her. AIT
1:21 but there is no *o to* **comfort** me. AIT
2:22 the day of the LORD's anger **no** *o* escaped AIT
3:25 to the **o** who seeks him; 5883
3:30 to *o who would* **strike** him, AIT
4: 4 but no *o* **gives** it to them. AIT
4:14 that no *o* **dares** to touch their garments. AIT
Eze 1: 9 and their wings touched **o** another. 851
Eze 1: 9 **Each** *o* went straight ahead; AIT
1:11 *o* **touching** the wing of another creature on AIT
1:12 **Each** *o* went straight ahead. AIT
1:17 in any **o** of the four directions NIH
1:23 expanse their wings were stretched out **o** 851
1:28 and I heard the voice of *o* **speaking.** AIT
4: 8 so that you cannot turn from **o** side to 3870[S]
7:13 not **o** of them will preserve his life. 408
7:14 no *o will* **go** into battle, AIT
10: 7 Then **o** of the cherubim reached out 2021+4131[S]
10: 9 **o** beside each of the cherubim; 285
10:11 in any **o** of the four directions NIH
10:14 **O** face was that of a cherub, 285
10:22 **Each** *o* went straight ahead. AIT
14:10 be as guilty as the *o who* **consults** him. AIT
14:15 so that no *o can* **pass through** it because of AIT
16: 5 *o* **looked** on you **with pity** AIT
16:34 *o* **runs after** you **for your favors.** AIT
18: 4 The soul who sins is the **o** who will die. 2085
18:20 The soul who sins is the **o** who will die. 2085
18:30 **each** *o* according to his ways, AIT
19: 3 She brought up **o** of her cubs, 285
19:14 Fire spread **from** *o of* its main branches AIT
20:39 Go and serve your idols, **every** *o* of you! AIT
21:20 Mark out *o* **road** for the sword to come AIT
22:11 In you *o* **man** commits a detestable offense AIT
23:43 I said about the *o* **worn out** *by* adultery, AIT
24:16 with *o* **blow** I am about to take away AIT
29:11 no *o will* **live** there for forty years. AIT
30:22 the good arm as well as the **broken** *o,* AIT
33: 2 a land, and the people of the land choose **o** 285
33: 6 and the sword comes and takes the life of **o** NIH
33:24 'Abraham was only **o** *man,* 285
33:28 so that no *o will* **cross** them. AIT
33:32 nothing more than **o** who sings love songs NIH
34: 6 and no *o* **searched** or looked for them. AIT
34:17 I will judge between *o* **sheep** and another, AIT
34:22 I will judge between *o* **sheep** and another. AIT
34:23 I will place over them **o** shepherd, 285
34:28 and not *o will* **make** them **afraid.** AIT
37:17 into **o** stick so that they will become one 285
37:17 into one stick so that they will become **o** 285
37:19 and they will become **o** in my hand.' 285
37:22 I will make them **o** nation in the land, 285
37:22 There will be **o** king over all of them 285
37:24 and they will all have **o** shepherd. 285
38:17 Are you not the **o** I spoke of in former days 2085
39: 7 that I the LORD am the **Holy O** in Israel. 7705
39:15 the land and *o of them* **sees** a human bone, AIT
39:26 with no *o to* **make** them **afraid.** AIT
40: 5 it was **o** measuring rod thick 285
40: 5 and **o** rod high. 285
40: 6 it was **o** rod deep. 285
40: 7 The alcoves for the guards were **o** rod long 285
40: 7 and **o** rod wide, 285
40: 7 the temple was **o** rod deep. 285
40:12 of each alcove was a wall **o** cubit high, 285
40:13 from the top of the rear wall of **o** alcove to 2021
40:13 of one alcove to the top of the **opposite** *o;* AIT
40:13 from *o* **parapet opening** to AIT
40:13 from one parapet opening to the opposite **o.** 7339[S]
40:23 from **o** gate to the opposite one; NIH
40:23 from one gate to the **opposite** *o;* AIT
40:41 So there were four tables on *o* **side** of AIT
40:44 **o** at the side of the north gate 285
41: 6 **o** above another, thirty on each level. 7521[S]
41: 7 that the rooms widened as **o** went upward. NIH
41:11 **o** on the north and another on the south; 285
41:19 toward the palm tree on **o** side and the face NIH
41:21 and the **o** at the front of NIH
42: 9 on the east side as **o** enters them from 2257
42:12 by which *o* **enters** the rooms. AIT
43:13 with a rim of **o** span around the edge. 285
44: 1 the *o* **facing** east, and it was shut. AIT
44: 2 no **o** may enter through it. 408
44: 3 the *only* **o** who may sit inside the gateway 2085
45: 7 to the eastern border parallel to **o** *of* 285
45:12 Twenty shekels plus twenty-five shekels
plus fifteen shekels equal **o** mina. 2021
45:14 of ten baths or **o** homer, NIH
45:15 Also **o** sheep is to be taken 285
46: 7 He is to provide as a grain offering *o* **ephah** AIT
46: 7 *o* **ephah** with the ram, AIT
46: 9 No *o is to* **return** through the gate AIT
46:11 and with the lambs as much as **o** pleases, 2257
46:16 from his inheritance to **o** of his sons, it will 408
46:17 to **o** of his servants, the servant may keep it 285
47: 5 a river that no *o could* **cross.** AIT
48: 1 Dan will have **o** *portion;* 285
48: 2 "Asher will have **o** *portion;* 285
48: 3 "Naphtali will have **o** *portion;* 285
48: 4 "Manasseh will have **o** *portion;* 285
48: 5 "Ephraim will have **o** *portion;* 285
48: 6 "Reuben will have **o** *portion;* 285
48: 7 "Judah will have **o** *portion;* 285
48: 8 and its length from east to west will equal **o** 285
48:23 Benjamin will have **o** *portion;* 285
48:24 "Simeon will have **o** *portion;* 285
48:25 "Issachar will have **o** *portion;* 285
48:26 "Zebulun will have **o** *portion;* 285
48:27 "Gad will have **o** *portion;* 285
Da 2: 9 there is just **o** penalty for you. 10248
2:11 No **o** can reveal it to the king except 10025
2:39 Next, a third kingdom, **o** of bronze, 10023
4:13 a **holy** *o,* coming down from heaven. AIT
4:23 "You, O king, saw a messenger, a **holy** *o,* AIT
4:35 No **o** can hold back his hand or say to him: 10168
Da 5:13 **o** *of* the exiles my father the king brought 10427
6: 2 **o** of whom was Daniel. 10248
6:13 "Daniel, who is **o** *of* the exiles from Judah, 10427
7: 5 It was raised up on **o** of its sides, 10248
7: 6 **o** that looked like a leopard. NIH
7: 8 a **little** *o,* which came up among them; AIT
7:13 and there before me was **o** like a son NIH
7:14 and his kingdom is *o* **that** will never AIT
7:16 I approached **o** of those standing there 10248
8: 1 *o that had* already **appeared** AIT
8: 3 **O** of the horns was longer than the other 285
8: 9 Out of **o** of them came another horn, 285
8:13 Then I heard a **holy** *o* speaking, AIT
8:13 and another **holy** *o* said to him, AIT
8:15 before me stood **o** who looked like a man. NIH
8:22 *o that* **was broken off** AIT
9:25 and rebuild Jerusalem until the **Anointed** *O,* AIT
9:26 the **Anointed** *O* will be cut off AIT
9:27 a covenant with many for **o** 'seven.' 285
10: 7 was the **only** *o* who saw the vision; 963+4200
10:13 Then Michael, **o** *of* the chief princes, 285
10:16 *o* who looked like a man **touched** AIT
10:16 I said to the *o* **standing** before me, AIT
10:18 *o* who looked like a man **touched** AIT
10:21 (No **o** supports me against them except 285
11: 5 but **o** *of* his commanders will become 4946
11: 6 and her father and the *o who* **supported** her. AIT
11: 7 *"O* from her family line *will* **arise** AIT
11:16 no *o will be able to* **stand** against AIT
11:37 or for the *o* **desired** *by* women, AIT
11:45 and no *o will* **help** him. AIT
12: 5 **o** on this bank of the river and one on 285
12: 5 of the river and **o** on the opposite bank. 285
12: 6 *O of them* **said** to the man clothed in linen, AIT
12:12 Blessed is the *o who* **waits for** and reaches AIT
Hos 1:11 and they will appoint **o** leader 285
2: 1 and of your sisters, 'My **loved** *o.'* AIT
2: 8 the *o who* **gave** her the grain, the new wine AIT
2:10 no **o** will take her out of my hands. 408
2:23 to the **o** I called 'Not my loved one.' NIH
2:23 to the one I called 'Not my **loved** *o.'* AIT
5:14 with no *o to* **rescue** them. AIT
9:12 I will bereave them of **every** *o.* AIT
11: 9 the **Holy O** among you. 7705
11:12 even against the faithful **Holy O.** 7705
Am 1: 1 **o** of the shepherds of Tekoa— NIH
1: 5 in the Valley of Aven and the *o who* **holds** AIT
1: 8 of Ashdod and the *o who* **holds** the scepter AIT
4: 7 I sent rain on **o** town, 285
4: 7 **O** field had rain; 285
5: 2 with no *o to* **lift** her **up."** AIT
5: 6 and Bethel will have no *o to* **quench** it. AIT
5:10 you hate the *o who* **reproves** in court AIT
6: 9 If ten men are left in **o** house, 285
6:12 *Does o* **plow** there with oxen? AIT
9: 1 Not **o** will get away, none will 2157+4200[S]
9:13 and the planter by the *o* **treading** grapes. AIT
Ob 1:11 you were like **o** of them. 285
Mic 2: 5 no *o* in the assembly of the LORD *to* **divide** AIT
2:13 **O** who breaks open the way will go up 2021
3: 5 if **o** feeds them, they proclaim 'peace'; 2021
4: 4 and no *o will* **make** them **afraid,** AIT
5: 2 of you will come for me *o who will* **be** ruler AIT
5: 8 and no *o can* **rescue.** AIT
6: 9 "Heed the rod and the *O* **who** appointed it. AIT
7: 1 I am like *o who* **gathers** summer fruit at AIT
7: 2 not **o** upright man remains. NIH
Na 1:11 *has o* **come forth** who plots evil against AIT
1:15 *o who* **brings good news,** AIT
2: 8 they cry, but no *o* **turns back.** AIT
3:17 and no *o* **knows** where. AIT
3:18 on the mountains with no *o to* **gather** them. AIT
Hab 1:12 My God, my **Holy O,** we will not die. 7705
3: 3 the **Holy O** from Mount Paran. 7705
3:13 to save your **anointed** *o.* AIT
Zep 2:11 **every** *o* in its own land. AIT
3: 2 She obeys no **o,** she accepts no correction. NIH
3: 6 with no *o* **passing through.** AIT
3: 6 no *o will be* **left—**no one at all. AIT
3: 6 no **o** at all. 408
3:13 and no *o will* **make** them **afraid."** AIT
Hag 2:13 with a dead body touches **o** *of* these things, 3972
2:15 how things were before **o** stone was laid NIH
Zec 1:21 so that no **o** could raise his head, 408
3: 9 There are seven eyes on that **o** stone, 285
4: 3 **o** on the right of the bowl and the other 285
5: 3 for according to what it says on *o* **side,** AIT
6: 6 The **o** with the black horses is going toward 2023
6: 6 the **o** with the white horses toward NIH
6: 6 and the **o** with the dappled horses toward NIH
7: 9 show mercy and compassion to **o** another. 408
7:14 behind them that no *o could* **come** or go. AIT
8:10 No **o** could go about his business safely 2021
8:21 the inhabitants of **o** city will go to another 285
8:23 and nations will take firm hold of **o** Jew by 408
11: 7 Then I took two staffs and called **o** Favor 285
11: 8 In **o** month I got rid of the three shepherds. 285
11: 9 Let those who are left eat **o** another's flesh." 851
12:10 **the** *o* they have pierced, 889[S]
12:10 and they will mourn for him as **o** mourns NIH
12:10 and grieve bitterly for him as *o* **grieves** for AIT
14: 9 On that day there will be **o** LORD, 285
Mal 1:10 that **o** of you would shut the temple doors, 4769
2:10 Have we not all **o** Father? 285
2:10 Did not **o** God create us? 285
2:10 by breaking faith with **o** another? 408
2:15 Has not [the LORD] made them **o?** 285

Mal 2:15 And why **o?** Because he was seeking godly 285
Mt 2: 2 "Where is **the** *o* **who** has been born king of the Jews? *AIT*
3: 3 "A voice *of o* **calling** in the desert, *AIT*
3:11 will come **o who** is more powerful than I, *3836*
5:19 Anyone who breaks **o** of the least *1651*
5:29 for you to lose **o** part of your body than *1651*
5:30 for you to lose **o** part of your body than *1651*
5:36 for you cannot make even **o** hair white *1651*
5:37 beyond this comes from the **evil** *o*. *AIT*
5:41 If someone forces you to go **o** mile, *1651*
5:42 Give *to* **the** *o* **who** asks you, *AIT*
5:42 and do not turn away from **the** *o* **who** wants *AIT*
6:13 but deliver us from the **evil** *o*.' *AIT*
6:24 "**No o** can serve two masters. *4029*
6:24 Either he will hate the **o** and love the other, *1651*
6:24 or he will be devoted to the **o** and despise *1651*
6:29 in all his splendor was dressed like **o** *1651*
7:29 because he taught as **o who had** authority, *2400*
8: 9 I tell **this o,** 'Go,' and he goes; *4047*
8: 9 and **that o,** 'Come,' and he comes. *257*
8:28 They were so violent that no **o** could pass *5516*
9:16 "**No o** sews a patch of unshrunk cloth on *4029*
9:30 "See that **no o** knows about this." *3594*
10:23 When you are persecuted in **o** place, *NIG*
10:28 **the** *O* **who** can destroy both soul and body *AIT*
10:29 not **o** of them will fall to the ground apart *1651*
10:40 he who receives me receives **the** *o* **who** sent me. *AIT*
10:42 a cup of cold water to **o** of these little ones *1651*
11: 3 "Are you **the** *o* **who** was to come, *AIT*
11:10 This is the **o** about whom it is written: *NIG*
11:27 **No o** knows the Son except the Father, *4029*
11:27 and no **o** knows the Father except the Son *5516*
12: 6 that **o greater than** the temple is here. *3505*
12:18 **the o** I love, in whom I delight; *3836*
12:19 no **o** will hear his voice in the streets. *5516*
12:41 and now *o* **greater** *than* Jonah is here. *AIT*
12:42 and now *o* **greater** *than* Solomon is here. *AIT*
13:19 the **evil** *o* comes and snatches away *AIT*
13:20 **The** *o* **who** received the seed that fell *AIT*
13:22 **The** *o* **who** received the seed that fell *AIT*
13:23 But **the** *o* **who** received the seed that fell *AIT*
13:37 "**The** *o* **who** sowed the good seed is the Son *AIT*
13:38 The weeds are the sons *of* the **evil** *o*, *AIT*
13:46 When he found **o** of great value, *1651*
16:14 still others, Jeremiah or **o** of the prophets." *1651*
17: 4 **o** for you, one for Moses and one *1651*
17: 4 **o** for Moses and one for Elijah." *1651*
17: 4 one for Moses and **o** for Elijah." *1651*
17: 8 they saw **no o** except Jesus. *4029*
18: 6 But if anyone causes **o** of these little ones *1651*
18: 9 with **o eye** than to have two eyes and *3669*
18:10 not look down on **o** of these little ones. *1651*
18:12 and **o** of them wanders away, *1651*
18:12 and go to look for the *o* **that** wandered off? *AIT*
18:13 he is happier about **that o sheep** than about *899*[S]
18:16 take **o** or two others along, *1651*
18:28 when that servant went out, he found **o** *1651*
19: 5 and the two will become **o** flesh'? *1651*
19: 6 So they are no longer two, but **o.** *1651*
19:12 **The** *o* **who** can accept this should accept it." *AIT*
19:17 "There is only **O** who is good. *1651*
20: 7 **no o** has hired us,' they answered, *4029*
20:10 **each o** of them also received a denarius. *324+3836*
20:12 who were hired last worked only **o** hour,' *1651*
20:13 "But he answered **o** of them, 'Friend, *1651*
20:21 that **o** of these two sons of mine may sit *NIG*
21:24 "I will also ask you **o** question. *1651*
21:35 they beat **o**, killed another, *4005*
22: 5 **o** to his field, another to his business. *4005*
22:25 The **first** *o* married and died, *AIT*
22:35 **O** of them, an expert in the law, *1651*
22:46 **No o** could say a word in reply, *4029*
22:46 and from that day on no **o** dared *5516*
23: 8 for you have only **o** Master *1651*
23: 9 for you have **o** Father, and he is in heaven. *1651*
23:10 for you have **o** Teacher, the Christ. *1651*
23:15 and when he becomes **o,** *NIG*
23:21 by it and by **the** *o* **who** dwells in it. *AIT*
23:22 by God's throne and by **the** *o* **who** sits on it. *AIT*
24: 2 not *o* **stone** here will be left on **another;** *AIT*
24: 2 every **o** will be thrown down." *NIG*
24: 4 "Watch out that no **o** deceives you. *5516*
24:17 Let no **o** on the roof of his house go down *3836*
24:18 Let no **o** in the field go back *3836*
24:22 no **o** would survive, *4246+4922*
24:31 from **o** end of the heavens to the other. *NIG*
24:36 "**No o** knows about that day or hour, *4029*
24:40 **o** will be taken and the other left. *1651*
24:41 **o** will be taken and the other left. *1651*
25:15 *To* **o** he gave five talents of money, *4005*
25:15 and to another **o** talent, *1651*
25:17 **the** *o* with the two talents gained two more. *AIT*
25:18 the **o** talent went off, *1651*
25:24 man who had received the **o** talent came. *1651*
25:28 and give it *to* **the** *o* **who** has the ten talents. *AIT*
25:32 the people **o** from **another** as *253*
25:40 *for* **o** of the least of these brothers of mine, *1651*
25:45 whatever you did not do *for* **o** of the least *1651*
26:14 Then **o** of the Twelve— *1651*
26:14 **the** *o* called Judas Iscariot— *AIT*
26:21 **o** of you will betray me." *1651*
26:22 began to say to him **o after the other,** *1651+1667*
26:23 "**The** *o* **who** has dipped his hand into *AIT*
26:25 Then Judas, **the** *o* **who** would betray him, *AIT*
26:40 not keep watch with me *for* **o** hour?" *1651*
Mt 26:47 Judas, **o** of the Twelve, arrived. *1651*
26:48 "The **o** I kiss is the man; arrest him." *4005*
26:51 **o** of Jesus' companions reached *1651*
26:64 the right hand *of* the **Mighty** *O* and coming *AIT*
26:73 "Surely you are **o** of them, *NIG*
27:17 "**Which** *o* do you want me to release to you: *AIT*
27:38 **o** on his right and one on his left. *1651*
27:38 one on his right and **o** on his left. *1651*
27:48 Immediately **o** of them ran and got *1651*
27:62 The next day, **the o** after Preparation Day, *4015*
Mk 1: 3 "a voice *of o* **calling** in the desert, *AIT*
1: 7 After me will come **o** more powerful than I, *3836*
1:22 he taught them as *o who* **had** authority, *AIT*
1:24 the **Holy** *O* of God!" *AIT*
2:21 "**No o** sews a patch of unshrunk cloth on *4029*
2:22 **no o** pours new wine into old wineskins. *4029*
2:23 **O Sabbath** Jesus was going *1877+3836+4879*
3:27 **no o** can enter a strong man's house *4029*
5: 3 and **no o** could bind him any more, *4029*
5: 4 **No o** was strong enough to subdue him. *4029*
5:22 Then **o** of the synagogue rulers, *1651*
6:15 like **o** of the prophets of long ago." *1651*
8:14 for **o** loaf they had with them in the boat. *1651*
8:16 They discussed this with **o another** *253*
8:28 and still others, **o** of the prophets." *1651*
9: 5 Let us put up three shelters—**o** for you, *1651*
9: 5 **o** for Moses and one for Elijah." *1651*
9: 5 one for Moses and **o** for Elijah." *1651*
9:37 Whoever welcomes **o** of these little children *1651*
9:37 not welcome me but **the** *o* **who** sent me." *AIT*
9:38 because he was not **o** of us." *NIG*
9:39 "**No o** who does a miracle in my name can *4029*
9:42 "And if anyone causes **o** of these little ones *1651*
9:47 to enter the kingdom of God with **o eye** than *3669*
10: 8 and the two will become **o** flesh.' *1651*
10: 8 So they are no longer two, but **o.** *1651*
10:18 "**No o** is good—except God alone. *4029*
10:21 "**O** *thing* you lack," he said. *1651*
10:29 "**no o** who has left home or brothers *4029*
10:37 "Let **o** of us sit at your right and the other *1651*
11: 2 which **no o** has ever ridden. *476+4029*
11:14 "May **no o** ever eat fruit from you again." *3594*
11:29 Jesus replied, "I will ask you **o** question. *1651*
12: 5 He sent still another, and **that** *o* they killed. *AIT*
12: 6 "He had **o** left to send, a son, *1651*
12: 7 "But the tenants said to **o another,** *1571*
12:20 The **first** *o* married and died *AIT*
12:21 The second **o** married the widow, *NIG*
12:28 **O** of the teachers of the law came *1651*
12:29 "The **most important** *o*," answered Jesus, *AIT*
12:29 O Israel, the Lord our God, the Lord is **o.** *1651*
12:32 in saying that God is **o** and there is no other *1651*
12:34 on **no o** dared ask him any more questions. *4029*
13: 1 **o** of his disciples said to him, "Look, *1651*
13: 2 "**Not o** stone here will be left on another; *3590+4024*
13: 2 every **o** will be thrown down." *NIG*
13: 5 "Watch out that no **o** deceives you. *5516*
13:15 Let no **o** on the roof of his house go down *3836*
13:16 Let no **o** in the field go back *3836*
13:20 no **o** would survive. *4246+4922*
13:32 "**No o** knows about that day or hour, *4029*
13:34 and tells the **o at the door** to keep watch. *2601*
14: 4 to **o another,** "Why this waste *1571*
14:10 Then Judas Iscariot, **o** of the Twelve, *1651*
14:18 **o** of you will betray me— *1651*
14:18 **o** who is eating with me." *NIG*
14:19 and **o** by one they said to him, *1651*
14:19 and one by **o** they said to him, *1651*
14:20 "It is **o** of the Twelve," he replied, *1651*
14:20 "**o** who dips bread into the bowl with me. *NIG*
14:37 Could you not keep watch *for* **o** hour? *1651*
14:43 Judas, **o** of the Twelve, appeared. *1651*
14:44 "**The o** I kiss is the man; *323+4005*
14:47 Then **o** of those standing *1651+5516*
14:61 the Christ, the Son *of* the **Blessed** *O*?" *AIT*
14:62 the right hand *of* the **Mighty O** and coming *1539*
14:66 **o** of the servant girls of the high priest *1651*
14:69 "This fellow is **o** of them." *NIG*
14:70 "Surely you are **o** of them, *NIG*
15:12 with the **o** you call the king of the Jews?" *4005*
15:27 **o** on his right and one on his left. *1651*
15:27 one on his right and **o** on his left. *1651*
15:36 **O** *man* ran, filled a sponge *5516*
Lk 1:35 the **holy** *o* to be born will be called the Son *AIT*
1:49 **Mighty** *O* has done great things for me— *AIT*
1:61 "There is **no o** among your relatives *4029*
2:15 the shepherds said to **o another,** *253*
3: 4 "A voice *of o* **calling** in the desert, *AIT*
3:11 **the** *o* **who** has food should do the same." *AIT*
3:16 But **o** more powerful than I will come, *3836*
4:27 yet **not o** of them was cleansed— *4029*
4:34 the **Holy** *O* of God!" *AIT*
4:40 and laying his hands on each **o,** *1651*
5: 1 **O day** as Jesus was standing by the *1181+1254*
5: 3 He got into **o** of the boats, *1651*
5: 3 **the o** belonging to Simon, *4005*
5:12 While Jesus was in **o** of the towns, *1651*
5:17 **O** day as he was teaching, *1651*
5:36 "**No o** tears a patch from a new garment *4029*
5:36 a new garment and sews it on an old **o.** *2668*[S]
5:37 **no o** pours new wine into old wineskins. *4029*
5:39 **no o** after drinking old wine wants the new, *4029*
6: 1 **O Sabbath** Jesus was going through *1877+4879*
6:11 with **o another** what they might do to Jesus. *253*
6:12 **O** of those days Jesus went out to *NIG*
6:29 If someone strikes you on **o** cheek, *NIG*
Lk 6:49 But **the** *o* **who** hears my words and does *AIT*
7: 8 I tell **this** *o*, 'Go,' and he goes; *AIT*
7: 8 and **that o,** 'Come,' and he comes. *257*
7:19 "Are you **the** *o* **who** was to come, *AIT*
7:20 'Are you **the** *o* **who** was to come, *AIT*
7:27 **This** is the **o** about whom it is written: *4047*
7:28 of women there is **no o** greater than John; *4029*
7:28 yet **the** *o* **who** is least in the kingdom *AIT*
7:36 Now **o** of the Pharisees invited Jesus *5516*
7:41 **O** owed him five hundred denarii, *1651*
7:43 the *o* **who** had the bigger debt canceled." *AIT*
8: 1 **from o** town and village **to another,** *2848*
8:16 "**No o** lights a lamp and hides it in a jar *4029*
8:22 **O** day Jesus said to his disciples, *1651*
8:25 and amazement they asked **o another,** *253*
8:43 but **no o** could heal her. *4024+4029*
9: 8 and still others that **o** of the prophets *5516*
9:19 and still others, that **o** of the prophets *5516*
9:33 Let us put up three shelters—**o** for you, *1651*
9:33 **o** for Moses and one for Elijah." *1651*
9:33 one for Moses and **o** for Elijah." *1651*
9:36 told **no o** at that time what they had seen. *4029*
9:48 whoever welcomes me welcomes **the** *o* **who** sent me. *AIT*
9:49 because he **is not o of us."** *199+1609+3552*
9:62 "**No o who** puts his hand to the plow *4029*
10:22 **No o** knows who the Son is except *4029*
10:22 and no **o** knows who the Father is except *NIG*
10:25 **On o occasion** an expert in the law *2627+2779*
10:37 "**The** *o* **who** had mercy on him." *AIT*
10:42 but only **o** *thing* is needed. *1651*
11: 1 **O day** Jesus was praying in a certain *1181+2779*
11: 1 he finished, **o** of his disciples said to him, *5516*
11: 5 "**Suppose o** of you has a friend, *5515*
11: 7 "Then **the o** inside answers, *1697*
11:31 and now *o* **greater** *than* Solomon is here. *AIT*
11:32 and now *o* **greater** *than* Jonah is here. *AIT*
11:33 "**No o** lights a lamp and puts it in a place *4029*
11:40 Did not **the** *o* **who** made the outside make *AIT*
11:45 **O** of the experts in the law answered him, *5516*
11:46 and you yourselves will not lift **o** finger *1651*
12: 1 so that they were trampling on **o another,** *253*
12: 6 Yet **not o** of them is forgotten by God. *1651*
12:27 in all his splendor was dressed like **o** *1651*
12:48 But **the** *o* **who** does not know *AIT*
12:48 the *o* **who** has been entrusted with much, *AIT*
12:52 on there will be five in **o** family divided *1651*
13: 8 'leave it alone for **o** more year, *NIG*
13:10 On a Sabbath Jesus was teaching in **o** of *1651*
14: 1 **O** Sabbath, when Jesus went to eat in *NIG*
14: 5 "If **o** of you has a son or an ox that falls *5515*
14:15 When **o** of those at the table *5516*
14:24 I tell you, **not o** of those men *4029*
14:28 "**Suppose o** of you wants to build a tower. *5515*
14:31 to oppose **the** *o* **coming against him** *AIT*
15: 4 "**Suppose o** of you has a hundred sheep *476+5515*
15: 4 of you has a hundred sheep and loses **o** *1651*
15: 7 in heaven over **o** sinner who repents than *1651*
15: 8 a woman has ten silver coins and loses **o.** *1651*
15:10 of God over **o** sinner who repents." *1651*
15:12 The **younger** *o* said to his father, 'Father, *AIT*
15:16 but **no o** gave him anything. *4029*
15:19 make me like **o** of your hired men.' *1651*
15:26 So he called **o** of the servants *1651*
16: 5 he called in each **o** of his master's debtors. *1651*
16:13 Either he will hate the **o** and love the other, *1651*
16:13 or he will be devoted to **the o** and despise *1651*
17: 2 for him to cause **o** of these little ones to sin. *1651*
17: 7 "**Suppose o** of you had a servant plowing *5515*
17:15 **O** of them, when he saw he was healed, *1651*
17:18 *Was* no *o* **found** to return and give praise *AIT*
17:22 when you will long to see **o** of the days of *1651*
17:24 and lights up the sky from **o** end to *NIG*
17:31 On that day no *o* **who** is on the roof *AIT*
17:31 no **o** in the field should go back *3836*
17:34 on that night two people will be in **o** bed; *1651*
17:34 **o** will be taken and the other left. *1651*
17:35 **o** will be taken and the other left." *1651*
18:10 **o** a Pharisee and the other a tax collector. *1651*
18:19 "**No o** is good—except God alone. *4029*
18:22 he said to him, "You still lack **o** *thing*. *1651*
18:29 "**no o** who has left home or wife or brothers *4029*
19:16 "The **first** *o* came and said, 'Sir, *AIT*
19:24 and give it *to* **the** *o* **who** has ten minas.' *AIT*
19:26 but as for **the** *o* **who** has nothing, *AIT*
19:30 which **no o** has ever ridden. *4029*
19:44 They will not leave **o** stone on another, *NIG*
20: 1 **O** day as he was teaching the people in *1651*
20:11 but **that** *o* also they beat *AIT*
20:29 The **first** *o* married a woman *AIT*
20:40 no *o* **dared** to ask him any more questions. *AIT*
21: 6 the time will come when not **o** stone will *NIG*
21: 6 every **o** of them will be thrown down." *NIG*
22: 3 called Iscariot, **o** of the Twelve. *1639*
22:26 **the** *o* **who** rules like the one who serves. *AIT*
22:26 the one who rules like **the** *o* **who** serves. *AIT*
22:27 **the** *o* **who** is at the table or *AIT*
22:27 one who is at the table or **the** *o* **who** serves? *AIT*
22:27 Is it not **the** *o* **who** is at the table? *AIT*
22:27 But I am among you as **o who** serves. *3836*
22:29 just as my Father conferred **o** on me, *NIG*
22:36 sell your cloak and buy **o.** *NIG*
22:47 **o** of the Twelve, was leading them. *1651*
22:50 And **o** of them struck the servant of *1651+5516*
22:58 "You also are **o** of them." *NIG*
23:14 *o* **who** *was* **inciting** the people **to rebellion.** *AIT*
23:18 **With o voice** they cried out, *4101*

Lk 23:25 **the** *o* they asked for, *AIT*
23:33 **o** on his right, the other on his left. *3525+4005*
23:35 if he is the Christ of God, the **Chosen** *O*." *AIT*
23:39 **O** of the criminals who hung there hurled insults at him: *1651*
23:53 **o in which** no one had yet been laid. *4023*
23:53 one in which **no o** had yet been laid. *4029*
24:18 **O** of them, named Cleopas, asked him, *1651*
24:21 that he was **the** *o* **who** was going *AIT*
Jn 1:14 the glory of the **O and Only,** *3666*
1:16 of his grace we have all received **o** blessing *NIG*
1:18 **No o** has ever seen God, *4029*
1:18 but God the **O and Only,** *3666*
1:23 the voice *of o* **calling** in the desert, *AIT*
1:26 "but among you stands **o** you do not know. *4005*
1:27 He is **the** *o* **who** comes after me, *AIT*
1:30 This is the **o** I meant when I said, *4005*
1:33 except that **the** *o* who sent me to baptize *AIT*
1:40 Simon Peter's brother, was **o** of *1651*
1:45 "We have found the **o** Moses wrote about *4005*
3: 2 For **no o** could perform *4029*
3: 3 no *o* **can** see the kingdom of God *AIT*
3: 5 no *o* **can** enter the kingdom of God *AIT*
3:13 **No o** has ever gone into heaven except *4029*
3:13 into heaven except **the** *o* **who** came *AIT*
3:16 the world that he gave his **o and only** Son, *3666*
3:18 in the name of God's **o and only** Son. *3666*
3:26 the **o** you testified about— *4005*
3:31 "**The** *o* **who** comes from above is above all; *AIT*
3:31 **the** *o* **who** is from the earth belongs to *AIT*
3:31 and speaks as **o** from the earth. *NIG*
3:31 **The** *o* **who** comes from heaven is above all. *AIT*
3:32 but **no o** accepts his testimony. *4029*
3:34 the *o* **whom** God has sent speaks the words *AIT*
4:27 But **no o** asked, "What do you want?" *4029*
4:37 Thus the saying '**O** sows and another reaps' *257*
5: 5 **O** who was there had been an invalid *5516*
5: 7 "I have **no o** to help me into the pool when *476*[S]
5:22 Moreover, the Father judges **no o,** *4029*
5:38 for you do not believe **the o** he sent. *4005*
5:44 if you accept praise from **o another,** *253*
6: 7 not buy enough bread for **each o** to have *1667*
6:22 that only **o** boat had been there, *257+1651+4024*
6:29 to believe in **the o** he has sent." *4005*
6:44 "**No o** can come to me unless *4029*
6:46 No **o** has seen the Father except *5516*
6:46 the Father except **the** *o* **who** is from God; *AIT*
6:57 so **the** *o* **who** feeds on me will live because *AIT*
6:65 "This is why I told you that **no o** can come *4029*
6:69 and know that you are the **Holy** *O* of God." *AIT*
6:70 Yet **o** of you is a devil!" *1651*
6:71 who, though **o** of the Twelve, *1651*
7: 4 **No o who** wants to become *4029*
7:13 But **no o** would say anything publicly *4029*
7:18 for the honor *of* **the** *o* **who** sent him is a man *AIT*
7:19 Yet **not o** of you keeps the law. *4029*
7:21 Jesus said to them, "I did **o** miracle, *1651*
7:27 **no o** will know where he is from." *4029*
7:30 but **no o** laid a hand on him, *4029*
7:33 and then I go to **the** *o* **who** sent me. *AIT*
7:35 The Jews said to **o another,** *1571*
7:44 but **no o** laid a hand on him. *4029*
7:46 "**No o ever** spoke the way this man does," *4030*
7:50 and who was **o** of their own number, *1651*
8: 7 "If any **o** of you is without sin, *3836*
8: 9 to go away **o at a time,** *1651+1651+2848*
8:10 Has **no o** condemned you?" *4029*
8:11 "**No o,** sir," she said. *4029*
8:15 I pass judgment on **no o.** *4024+4029*
8:18 I am **o who** testifies for myself; *3836*
8:20 Yet **no o** seized him, *4029*
8:24 not believe that I am [the **o** I claim to be] *NIG*
8:28 you will know that I am [the **o** I claim to be] *NIG*
8:29 **The** *o* **who** sent me is with me; *AIT*
8:50 there is **o who** seeks it, and he is the judge. *3836*
8:54 is **the** *o* **who** glorifies me. *AIT*
9: 4 Night is coming, when **no o** can work. *4029*
9:19 "Is this *the* **o** you say was born blind? *4005*
9:25 **O** *thing* I do know. *1651*
9:37 in fact, he is **the** *o* speaking with you." *AIT*
10:16 there shall be **o** flock and one shepherd. *1651*
10:16 there shall be one flock and **o** shepherd. *1651*
10:18 **No o** takes it from me, *4029*
10:28 no **o** can snatch them out of my hand. *5516*
10:29 **no o** can snatch them out *4029*
10:30 I and the Father are **o."** *1651*
10:36 what about the *o* **whom** the Father set apart *AIT*
11: 2 was **the** same *o* **who** poured perfume on *AIT*
11: 3 "Lord, *the o* you love is sick." *4005*
11:49 Then **o** of them, named Caiaphas, *1651+5516*
11:50 for you that **o** man die for the people than *1651*
11:52 bring them together and **make** them **o.** *1650+1651*
11:56 in the temple area they asked **o another,** *253*
12: 4 But **o** of his disciples, Judas Iscariot, *1651*
12:19 So the Pharisees said to **o another,** "See, *1571*
12:26 My Father will honor **the o** who serves me. *899*[S]
12:44 but in **the** *o* **who** sent me. *AIT*
12:45 he looks at me, he sees **the** *o* **who** sent me. *AIT*
12:46 so that no **o** who believes in me should stay *4246*
12:48 a judge for **the** *o* **who** rejects me and does *AIT*
13:10 you are clean, though not **every** *o* of you." *AIT*
13:11 that was why he said not **every** *o* was clean. *AIT*
13:14 you also should wash **o another's** feet. *253*
13:16 messenger greater than **the** *o* **who** sent him. *AIT*
13:20 accepts me accepts **the** *o* **who** sent me." *AIT*
13:21 **o** of you is going to betray me." *1651*
13:22 His disciples stared at **o another,** *253*
Jn 13:23 **O** of them, the disciple whom Jesus loved, *1651*
13:24 "Ask him which **o** he means." *4005*
13:26 "It is **the o** to whom I will give this piece *1697*
13:28 but **no o** at the meal understood *4029*
13:34 new command I give you: Love **o another.** *253*
13:34 so you must love **o another.** *253*
13:35 if you love **o another."** *253*
14: 6 **No o** comes to the Father except through me *4029*
14:21 he is **the** *o* **who** loves me. *AIT*
15:13 Greater love has **no o** than this, *4029*
15:21 for they do not know **the** *O* **who** sent me. *AIT*
15:24 not done among them what **no o** else did, *4029*
16:17 Some of his disciples said to **o another,** *253*
16:19 "Are you asking **o another** what I meant *253*
16:22 and **no o** will take away your joy. *4029*
17:11 so that they may be **o** as we are one. *1651*
17:11 so that they may be one as we are **o.** *NIG*
17:12 except the **o** doomed to destruction *5626*[S]
17:15 but that you protect them from the **evil** *o.* *AIT*
17:21 that all of them may be **o,** *1651*
17:22 that they may be **o** as we are one: *1651*
17:22 that they may be one as we are **o:** *1651*
18: 9 "I have not lost **o** of those you gave me." *4029*
18:14 Caiaphas was **the** *o* **who** had advised *AIT*
18:14 that it would be good if **o** man died for *1651*
18:17 "You are not **o** of his disciples, are you?" *NIG*
18:22 **o** of the officials nearby struck him in *1651*
18:25 "You are not **o** of his disciples, are you?" *NIG*
18:26 **O** of the high priest's servants, *1651*
18:39 to release to you **o** prisoner at the time of *1651*
19:11 Therefore **the** *o* **who** handed me over *AIT*
19:18 **o on each side** and Jesus in the middle. *1949+1949+2779*
19:23 **o** for each of them, *3538*[S]
19:23 woven in **o** piece from top to bottom. *NIG*
19:24 "Let's not tear it," they said to **o another.** *253*
19:34 **o** of the soldiers pierced Jesus' side with *1651*
19:36 "Not **o** of his bones will be broken," *NIG*
19:37 on *the* **o** they have pierced." *4005*
19:41 in which **no o** had ever been laid. *4029*
20: 2 **the o** Jesus loved, and said, *4005*
20:12 **o** at the head and the other at the foot. *1651*
20:24 Thomas (called Didymus), **o** of the Twelve, *1651*
21:20 the *o* **who** had leaned back against Jesus at *AIT*
21:25 If every **o** of them were written down, *1651*
Ac 1: 4 **On o occasion,** while he was eating *2779*
1:17 he was *o* of our **number** and shared *AIT*
1:20 let there be no **o** to dwell in it,' and, *3836*
1:21 Therefore it is necessary to choose **o** of *1651*
1:22 For **o** of these must become a witness *1651*
2: 1 they were all together **in o place.** *899+2093+3836*
2: 6 because each **o** heard them speaking *1651*
2:12 they asked **o another,** *257+257+4639*
2:27 nor will you let your **Holy** *O* see decay. *AIT*
2:30 that he would place **o** of his descendants *1651*
2:38 "Repent and be baptized, **every o** of you, *1667*
3: 1 **O** day Peter and John were going up to *NIG*
3:14 You disowned the **Holy** and **Righteous** *O* *AIT*
4:12 Salvation is found in **no o** else, *4024+4029*
4:26 the Lord and against his **Anointed O.'** *5986*
4:32 All the believers were **o** in heart and mind. *1651*
4:32 No **o** claimed that any of their possessions *1651*
5:13 **No o** else dared join them, *4029*
5:23 we opened them, we found **no o** inside." *4029*
7:24 He saw **o** of them being mistreated by *5516*
7:52 the coming *of* the **Righteous** *O.* *AIT*
10: 3 **O** day at about three in the afternoon he had *NIG*
10: 7 devout soldier who *was o of* his **attendants.** *AIT*
10:21 "I'm **the o** you're looking for. *4005*
10:42 he is **the** *o* **whom** God appointed as judge *AIT*
11:28 **O** of them, named Agabus, *1651*
12:10 they had walked *the length of* **o** street, *1651*
13:25 I am not that **o.** *NIG*
13:35 " 'You will not let your **Holy** *O* see decay.' *AIT*
13:37 But **the o whom** God raised from the dead *4005*
16:14 **O** of those listening was *5516*
17: 7 that there is another king, **o** called Jesus." *NIG*
17:26 From **o** *man* he made every nation of men, *1651*
17:27 though he is not far from each **o** of us. *1651*
18: 9 **O** night the Lord spoke to Paul in a vision: *NIG*
18:10 and **no o** is going to attack and harm you, *4029*
19: 4 the people to believe in **the** *o* coming *AIT*
19:15 **[O** day] the evil spirit answered them, *NIG*
19:29 and rushed **as o man** into the theater. *3924*
19:32 Some were shouting *o* **thing,** some another. *AIT*
21: 8 **o of** the Seven. *1639+1666*
21:16 from Cyprus and **o** of the early disciples. *NIG*
21:34 Some in the crowd shouted **o** *thing* *5516*
22:14 to know his will and to see the **Righteous** *O* *AIT*
22:19 **from o** synagogue **to another** *2848*
23:17 Paul called **o** of the centurions and said, *1651*
24:21 unless it was this **o** *thing* I shouted *1651*
25:11 **no o** has the right to hand me over to them. *4029*
26:11 **from o synagogue to another** *2848+4246+5252*
26:12 "On **o of these journeys** I was going *4005*[S]
26:31 and while talking with **o another,** they said, *253*
27:22 because **not o** of you will be lost; *4029*
27:34 **Not o** of you will lose a single hair *4029*
Ro 1:24 of their bodies with **o another.** *899*
1:27 and were inflamed with lust for **o another.** *253*
2:27 **The** *o* **who** is not circumcised physically *AIT*
2:28 not a Jew if he is only **o** outwardly, *NIG*
2:29 No, a man is a Jew if he is **o** inwardly; *NIG*
3:10 "There is no *o* **righteous,** not even one; *AIT*
3:10 "There is no one righteous, not even **o;** *1651*
3:11 there is no **o who** understands, *3836*
3:11 no **o who** seeks God. *3836*
Ro 3:12 there is no **o who** does good, not even one." *3836*
3:12 there is no one who does good, not even **o."** *1651*
3:20 Therefore **no o** will be declared righteous *4024+4246*
3:26 and the *o* **who justifies** those who have faith *AIT*
3:30 since there is only **o** God, *1651*
5:12 just as sin entered the world through **o** man, *1651*
5:14 who was a pattern *of* **the** *o* to come. *AIT*
5:15 the many died by the trespass *of* the **o** *man,* *1651*
5:15 that came by the grace *of* the **o** man, *1651*
5:16 not like the result of the **o** *man's* sin: *1651*
5:16 The judgment followed **o** sin *1651*
5:17 For if, by the trespass *of* the **o** *man,* *1651*
5:17 death reigned through that **o** *man,* *1651*
5:17 in life through the **o** *man,* *1651*
5:18 the result of **o** trespass was condemnation *1651*
5:18 of **o** act of righteousness was justification *1651*
5:19 *of* the **o** man the many were made sinners, *1651*
5:19 the **o** *man* the many will be made righteous. *1651*
6:16 you are slaves *to* **the o whom** you obey— *4005*
8:20 but by the will of **the** *o* **who** subjected it, *AIT*
9:10 but Rebekah's children had **o** and the same father, *1651+1666*
9:19 **O** of you will say to me: *NIG*
9:25 and I will call her 'my **loved** *o*' who is *AIT*
9:25 not my **loved** *o,*" *AIT*
9:33 and **the** *o* **who** trusts in him will never be put to shame." *AIT*
10:14 on **the o** they have not believed in? *4005*
10:14 in the **o** of whom they have not heard? *NIG*
11: 3 I am the **only** *o* **left,** *AIT*
11:30 Just as you who were **at o time** disobedient *4537*
12: 3 the grace given me I say *to* **every** *o* of you: *AIT*
12: 4 of us has **o** body with many members, *1651*
12: 5 so in Christ we who are many form **o** body, *1651*
12:10 Be devoted to **o another** in brotherly love. *253*
12:10 Honor **o another** above yourselves. *253*
12:16 Live in harmony with **o another.** *253*
13: 3 Do you want to be free from fear of **the** *o* *AIT*
13: 8 the continuing debt to love **o another,** *253*
13: 9 are summed up in this **o** rule: *3836*
14: 2 **O** *man's* faith allows him to eat everything, *4005*
14: 5 **O** *man* considers one day more sacred than *4005*
14: 5 One man considers **o** day more sacred than *NIG*
14: 5 **Each** *o* should be fully convinced *AIT*
14: 6 He who regards **o** day as special, *3836*
14:13 let us stop passing judgment on **o another.** *253*
14:14 As **o** who is in the Lord Jesus, *NIG*
15: 6 with **o** heart and mouth you may glorify *1651*
15: 7 Accept **o another,** then, *253*
15:12 **o who** will arise to rule over the nations; *3836*
15:14 and competent to instruct **o another.** *253*
16:16 Greet **o another** with a holy kiss. *253*
1Co 1:10 that all of you agree with **o** another so *NIG*
1:12 **O** of you says, "I follow Paul"; *1667*
1:15 so no **o** can say that you were baptized *5516*
1:29 so that no **o** may boast before him. *4246+4922*
2:11 In the same way **no o** knows the thoughts *4029*
3: 4 For when **o** says, "I follow Paul," *5516*
3: 8 and the man who waters have **o** purpose, *1651*
3:10 But **each** *o* should be careful how he builds. *AIT*
3:11 For **no o** can lay any foundation other than *4029*
3:11 any foundation other than **the** *o* already laid, *AIT*
3:15 but only as **o** escaping through the flames. *NIG*
3:18 If **any o** of you thinks he is wise by *5516*
4: 6 you will not take pride in **o** *man* over *1651+3836*
5: 3 on **the** *o* **who** did this, *AIT*
6: 6 **o** brother goes to law against another— *NIG*
6:16 with a prostitute is **o** with her in body? *1651*
6:16 it is said, "The two will become **o** flesh." *1651*
6:17 with the Lord is **o** with him in spirit. *1651*
7: 7 **o** has this gift, another has that. *3525+3836*
7:17 **each** *o* should retain the place in life that *AIT*
7:20 **Each** *o* should remain in the situation *AIT*
7:25 the Lord, but I give a judgment as **o** who by *NIG*
8: 4 in the world and that there is no God but **o.** *1651*
8: 6 yet for us there is but **o** God, the Father, *1651*
8: 6 and there is but **o** Lord, Jesus Christ, *1651*
9:20 under the law I became like **o** under the law *NIG*
9:21 To those not having the law I became like **o** *NIG*
9:24 but only **o** gets the prize? *1651*
10: 8 and *in* **o** day twenty-three thousand *1651*
10:17 Because there is **o** loaf, we, who are many, *1651*
10:17 we, who are many, are **o** body, *1651*
10:17 for we all partake of the **o** loaf. *1651*
11:21 **O** remains hungry, another gets drunk. *3525+4005*
12: 3 that **no o** who is speaking by the Spirit *4029*
12: 3 and **no o** can say, "Jesus is Lord," except *4029*
12: 7 Now *to* **each** *o* the manifestation of *AIT*
12: 8 *To* **o** there is given through the Spirit *4005*
12: 9 to another gifts of healing by that **o** Spirit, *1651*
12:11 the work of **o** and the same Spirit, *1651*
12:11 and he gives them *to* **each** *o,* *AIT*
12:12 all its parts are many, they form **o** body. *1651*
12:13 For we were all baptized by **o** Spirit *1651*
12:13 by one Spirit into **o** body— *1651*
12:13 and we were all given the **o** Spirit to drink. *1651*
12:14 Now the body is not made up of **o** part but *1651*
12:18 every **o** of them, *1651*
12:19 If they were all **o** part, *1651*
12:20 As it is, there are many parts, but **o** body. *1651*
12:26 If **o** part suffers, every part suffers with it; *1651*
12:26 if **o** part is honored, *1651*
12:27 and **each** *o* of you is a part of it. *3517*[S]
14: 2 Indeed, **no o** understands him; *4029*
14: 5 like **every** *o* of you to speak in tongues, *AIT*
14: 5 who prophesies is greater than **o who** speaks *3836*

1Co 14:16 how can **o who** finds himself *3836*
14:27 should speak, **o at a time,** *324+3538*
15: 8 as *to* **o** abnormally born. *3836*
15:39 Men have **o** kind of flesh, *NIG*
15:40 of the heavenly bodies is **o** kind, *NIG*
15:41 The sun has **o** kind of splendor, *NIG*
16: 2 **each** *o* of you should set aside a sum *AIT*
16:11 No **o,** then, should refuse to accept him. *5516*
16:20 Greet **o another** with a holy kiss. *253*
2Co 2:16 **To the o** we are the smell of death; *3525+4005*
4:14 that **the** *o* **who** raised the Lord Jesus from *AIT*
5:10 that **each** *o* may receive what is due him for *AIT*
5:14 we are convinced that **o** died for all, *1651*
5:16 on we regard **no o** from a worldly point *4029*
7: 2 We have wronged **no o,** *4029*
7: 2 we have corrupted **no o,** *4029*
7: 2 we have exploited **no o.** *4029*
7:12 not on account of **the** *o* **who** did the wrong *AIT*
8:12 gift is acceptable according to what *o* **has,** *AIT*
9: 5 not as **o grudgingly given.** *4432*
10:18 **the** *o* **who** commends himself who is approved, *AIT*
10:18 but **the** *o* **whom** the Lord commends. *AIT*
11: 2 I promised you *to* **o** husband, to Christ, *1651*
11: 4 a different spirit from **the o** you received, *4005*
11: 4 a different gospel from **the o** you accepted, *4005*
11:16 I repeat: Let no **o** take me for a fool. *5515*
11:24 from the Jews the forty lashes minus **o.** *1651*
12: 6 so no **o** will think more of me than is *5516*
13:11 listen to my appeal, be of **o** mind, *899+3836*
13:12 Greet **o another** with a holy kiss. *253*
Gal 1: 6 so quickly deserting **the** *o* **who** called you *AIT*
1: 8 a gospel other than **the** *o* we preached *AIT*
2:16 by observing the law no **o** will be justified. *4246+4922*
3: 2 I would like to learn **just o** *thing* from *3668+4047*
3:11 Clearly **no o** is justified before God by *4029*
3:15 Just as **no o** can set aside or add to *4029*
3:16 but "and to your seed," meaning **o** *person,* *1651*
3:20 however, does not represent just **o** *party;* *1651*
3:20 but God is **o.** *1651*
3:28 for you are all **o** in Christ Jesus. *1651*
4:22 **o** by the slave woman and the other by *1651*
4:24 **O** covenant is from Mount Sinai *1651*
5: 8 not come from **the** *o* **who** calls you. *AIT*
5:10 **The** *o* **who** is throwing you *AIT*
5:13 rather, serve **o another** in love. *253*
6: 4 **Each** *o* should test his own actions. *AIT*
6: 5 for **each** *o* should carry his own load. *AIT*
6: 8 **The** *o* **who** sows to please his sinful nature, *AIT*
6: 8 **the** *o* **who** sows to please the Spirit, *AIT*
6:17 Finally, let **no o** cause me trouble, *3594*
Eph 1: 6 in **the O** he loves. *3836*
1:10 **bring** all things in heaven and on earth **together under o head,** *368*
1:21 in the present age but also in **the** *o* to come. *AIT*
2: 3 All of us also lived among them **at o time,** *4537*
2: 9 not by works, so that no **o** can boast. *5516*
2:14 who has made the two **o** and has destroyed *1651*
2:15 to create in himself **o** new man out of *1651*
2:16 and in this **o** body to reconcile both of them *1651*
2:18 both have access to the Father by **o** Spirit. *1651*
3: 6 **members together of o body,** *5362*
4: 2 be patient, bearing with **o another** in love. *253*
4: 4 There is **o** body and one Spirit— *1651*
4: 4 There is one body and **o** Spirit— *1651*
4: 4 to **o** hope when you were called— *1651*
4: 5 **o** Lord, one faith, one baptism; *1651*
4: 5 one Lord, **o** faith, one baptism; *1651*
4: 5 one Lord, one faith, **o** baptism; *1651*
4: 6 **o** God and Father of all, *1651*
4: 7 But to each **o** of us grace has been given *1651*
4:10 He who descended is **the very** *o* who ascended higher than all *899*
4:25 for we are all members *of* **o body.** *253*
4:32 Be kind and compassionate to **o another,** *253*
5: 6 Let **no o** deceive you with empty words, *3594*
5:19 Speak *to* **o another** with psalms, *4932*
5:21 to **o another** out of reverence for Christ. *253*
5:29 After all, **no o** ever hated his own body, *4029*
5:31 and the two will become **o** flesh." *1651*
5:33 each **o** of you also must love his wife *1651*
6:16 the flaming arrows *of* **the evil o.** *4505*
Php 1:27 I will know that you stand firm in **o** spirit, *1651*
1:27 contending as **o** man for the faith of *1651*
2: 2 being **o** in spirit and purpose. *1651*
2:20 I have **no o** else like him, *4029*
3:13 But **o** *thing* I do. *1651*
4:15 **not o** church shared with me in the matter *4029*
Col 2: 4 I tell you this so that **no o** may deceive you *3594*
2: 8 that no **o** takes you captive through hollow *5516*
3:13 and forgive whatever grievances you may have against **o** another. *5516*
3:15 as members of **o** body you were called *1651*
3:16 and admonish **o another** with all wisdom, *4932*
4: 9 who is **o** of you. *NIG*
4:12 who is **o of** you and a servant *1666*
1Th 3: 3 that **no o** would be unsettled by these trials. *3594*
4: 6 in this matter no **o** should wrong his brother *NIG*
5:11 Therefore encourage **o another** *253*
5:24 **The** *o* **who** calls you is faithful *AIT*
2Th 1: 3 and the love every **o** of you has *1651*
2: 7 but **the** *o* **who** now holds it back *AIT*
2: 8 And then the **lawless** *o* will be revealed, *AIT*
2: 9 *of* **the lawless o** will be in accordance *4005*[S]
3: 3 and protect you from the **evil** *o.* *AIT*
1Ti 1: 8 that the law is good if **o** uses it properly. *5516*
1Ti 2: 5 For there is **o** God and one mediator *1651*
2: 5 and **o** mediator between God and men, *1651*
2:14 And Adam was not the **o** deceived; *NIG*
3: 2 the husband *of* but **o** wife, temperate, *1651*
3:12 *of* but **o** wife and must manage his children *1651*
5: 7 too, so that no **o** may be open to blame. *NIG*
6:16 whom **no o** has seen or can see. *4029*
2Ti 2: 4 **No o** serving as a soldier gets involved *4029*
2:15 to present yourself to God as **o** approved, *NIG*
4:16 **no o** came to my support, *4029*
Tit 1: 6 the husband *of* but **o** wife, *1651*
1: 8 **o who loves what is good,** *5787*
1:12 Even **o** of their own prophets has said, *5516*
2: 5 so that no **o** will malign the word of God. *NIG*
3: 2 to slander **no o,** to be peaceable *3594*
3: 3 **At o time** we too were foolish, disobedient, *4537*
3: 3 being hated and hating **o another.** *253*
Phm 1:22 And **o thing more:** *275*
Heb 2:11 Both **the** *o* **who** makes men holy *AIT*
3: 2 He was faithful *to* **the** *o* **who** appointed him, *AIT*
3:13 But encourage **o another** daily, *4932*
4:11 so that no **o** will fall *5516*
4:15 *o who has been* **tempted** *AIT*
5: 4 No **o** takes this honor upon himself; *5516*
5: 7 to **the** *o* **who** could save him from death, *AIT*
6:13 there was **no o** greater for him to swear by, *4029*
7: 8 **In the o case,** the tenth is collected *3525+6045*
7: 9 **O might even say** that Levi, *2229+3306+6055*
7:11 **o** in the order of Melchizedek, *NIG*
7:13 and **no o** from that tribe has ever served at *4029*
7:16 *o* **who** has become a priest not on the basis *AIT*
7:26 *o* **who** is holy, blameless, pure, *AIT*
8: 3 for **this** *o* also to have something to offer. *AIT*
8: 6 is superior to the old **o,** *NIG*
8:13 he has made the **first** *o* obsolete; *AIT*
9:16 to prove the death *of* **the** *o* **who** made it, *AIT*
9:17 while **the** *o* **who** made it is living. *AIT*
9:24 that was only a copy *of* **the true** *o;* *AIT*
10:12 for all time **o** sacrifice for sins, *1651*
10:14 *by* **o** sacrifice he has made perfect forever those who are being made holy. *1651*
10:24 how we may spur **o another** on toward love *253*
10:25 but let us encourage **o** another— *NIG*
10:38 But my **righteous** *o* will live by faith. *AIT*
11: 5 he was commended as **o** who pleased God. *NIG*
11:12 And so from this **o** *man,* *1651*
11:16 for a better country—a **heavenly** *o.* *AIT*
11:17 about to sacrifice his **o and only son,** *3666*
12:14 without holiness **no o** will see the Lord. *4029*
12:15 to it that no **o** misses the grace of God and *5516*
12:16 See that no **o** is sexually immoral, *5516*
Jas 1:10 But **the** *o* **who** is rich should take pride *AIT*
1:13 When tempted, **no o** should say, *3594*
1:14 but **each** *o* is tempted when, *AIT*
2:10 at just **o** *point* is guilty of breaking all of it. *1651*
2:16 If **o** of you says to him, "Go, *5516*
2:19 You believe that there is **o** God. *1651*
4:11 Brothers, do not slander **o another.** *253*
4:12 There is only **o** Lawgiver and Judge, *1651*
4:12 **the** *o* **who** is able to save and destroy. *AIT*
5:13 **Is any** *o* of you in trouble? *AIT*
5:14 **Is any o** of you sick? *5516*
5:19 if **o** of you should wander from the truth *5516*
1Pe 1:22 love **o another** deeply, from the heart. *253*
2: 6 and **the** *o* **who** trusts in him will never be put to shame." *AIT*
3: 8 all of you, live in harmony with **o** another; *NIG*
4: 9 to **o another** without grumbling. *253*
4:10 **Each** *o* should use whatever gift he has received *AIT*
4:11 as **o** speaking the very words of God. *NIG*
5: 1 a witness of Christ's sufferings and **o who** *3836*
5: 5 with humility *toward* **o another,** *253*
5:14 Greet **o another** with a kiss of love. *253*
2Pe 3: 8 But do not forget this **o** *thing,* dear friends: *1651*
1Jn 1: 7 we have fellowship with **o another,** *253*
2: 1 **o who speaks** to the Father **in** *our* **defense** *4156*
2: 1 Jesus Christ, the **Righteous** *O.* *AIT*
2: 7 a new command but an old **o,** *1953*[S]
2:13 because you have overcome the **evil** *o.* *AIT*
2:14 and you have overcome the **evil** *o.* *AIT*
2:20 you have an anointing from the **Holy O,** *41*
2:23 No **o who** denies the Son has the Father; *3836*
3: 6 **No o** who lives in him keeps on sinning. *4024+4246*
3: 6 **No o** who continues to sin has *4024+4246*
3: 9 **No o** who is born of God will continue to sin, *4024+4246*
3:11 We should love **o another.** *253*
3:12 to the **evil** *o* and murdered his brother. *AIT*
3:23 and to love **o another** as he commanded us. *253*
4: 4 because **the** *o* **who** is in you is greater than *AIT*
4: 4 in you is greater than **the** *o* **who** is in *AIT*
4: 7 Dear friends, let us love **o another,** *253*
4: 9 He sent his **o and only** Son into the world *3666*
4:11 we also ought to love **o another.** *253*
4:12 **No o** has ever seen God; *4029*
4:12 but if we love **o another,** *253*
4:18 **The** *o* **who** fears is not made perfect in love. *AIT*
5: 6 This is **the** *o* **who** came by water and blood *AIT*
5:18 **the** *o* **who** was born of God keeps him safe, *AIT*
5:18 and the **evil** *o* cannot harm him. *AIT*
5:19 under the control of the **evil** *o.* *AIT*
2Jn 1: 5 a new command but **o** we have had from *4005*
1: 5 I ask that we love **o another.** *253*
Rev 1: 3 Blessed is **the** *o* **who** reads the words *AIT*
1:18 I am the **Living** *O;* I was dead, and behold *AIT*
Rev 3: 7 What he opens **no o** can shut, *4029*
3: 7 and what he shuts **no o** can open. *4029*
3: 8 before you an open door that **no o** can shut. *4029*
3:11 so that no **o** will take your crown. *3594*
3:15 I wish you were either **o** or the other! *6037*[S]
4: 3 And **the** *o* **who** sat there had the appearance *AIT*
5: 3 But **no o** in heaven or on earth or under *4029*
5: 4 because **no o** was found who was worthy *4029*
5: 5 **o** of the elders said to me, "Do not weep! *1651*
5: 8 **Each** *o* had a harp *AIT*
6: 1 Then I heard **o** of the four living creatures *1651*
6: 4 Then another horse came out, a **fiery red** *o.* *AIT*
7: 9 a great multitude that **no o** could count, *4029*
7:13 Then **o** of the elders asked me, *1651*
11:17 **the** *O* **who** is and who was, *AIT*
13: 3 **O** of the heads of the beast seemed *1651*
13:17 so that no **o** could buy or sell unless he had *5516*
14: 3 **No o** could learn the song except *4029*
14:14 **seated** on the cloud *was o* *AIT*
15: 7 Then **o** of the four living creatures gave to *1651*
15: 8 and **no o** could enter the temple until *4029*
16: 5 the **Holy** *O,* because you have so judged; *AIT*
17: 1 **O** of the seven angels who had *1651*
17:10 Five have fallen, **o** is, the other has not yet *1651*
17:12 but who *for* **o** hour will receive authority *1651*
17:13 They have **o** purpose and will give their *1651*
18: 8 in **o** day her plagues will overtake her: *1651*
18:10 *In* **o** hour your doom has come!' *1651*
18:11 **no o** buys their cargoes any more— *4029*
18:17 *In* **o** hour such great wealth has been brought to ruin!' *1651*
18:19 *In* **o** hour she has been brought to ruin! *1651*
19:12 on him that **no o** knows but he himself. *4029*
21: 9 **O** of the seven angels who had the *1651*
22: 8 am **the** *o* **who** heard and saw these things. *AIT*

ONE'S (8) [ONE]

Ge 44: 2 in the mouth of the **youngest** *o* sack, AIT
Lev 17:11 the blood that makes atonement for **o** life. 2021
2Ch 21:20 He passed away, to **no** *o* regret, AIT
Ps 127: 4 of a warrior are sons born in **o** youth. 2021
Pr 25:27 nor is it honorable to seek **o own** honor. 4392
26: 6 Like cutting off **o** feet NIH
27: 9 and the pleasantness of **o** friend springs 2084
Isa 58: 5 Is it only for bowing **o** head like a reed and 2257

ONE-TENTH (5) [ONE, TEN]

Nu 28:21 and with each of the seven lambs, **o.** 6928
28:29 and with each of the seven lambs, **o.** 6928
29: 4 and with each of the seven lambs, **o.** 285+6928
29:10 and with each of the seven lambs, **o.** 6928
29:15 and with each of the fourteen lambs, **o.** 6928

ONE-THIRD (1) [ONE, THREE]

Zec 13: 8 yet **o** will be left in it. 8958

ONES (83) [ONE]

Ge 30:42 to Laban and the **strong** *o* to Jacob. AIT
31: 8 'The **speckled** *o* will be your wages,' AIT
31: 8 'The **streaked** *o* will be your wages,' AIT
Ex 6:27 They *were* the *o who* **spoke** to Pharaoh king AIT
18:26 but the simple **o** they decided themselves. 1821[S]
34: 1 two stone tablets like the **first** *o,* AIT
34: 4 the **first** *o* and went up Mount Sinai early AIT
Lev 11: 2 these are the **o** you may eat: 2651[S]
Nu 16:27 children and **little o** at the entrances 3251
26:63 the *o* **counted** *by* Moses and Eleazar AIT
31:16 the **o** who followed Balaam's advice NIH
Dt 1:39 And the **little o** that you said would 3251
10: 1 like the **first** *o* and come up to me on AIT
10: 3 two stone tablets like the **first** *o,* AIT
11: 2 that your children *were* not *the o* who **saw** AIT
33: 2 with myriads of **holy o** from the south, 7731
33: 3 all the **holy** *o* are in your hand. AIT
Jos 5: 7 and these were the **o** Joshua circumcised. NIH
2Ki 23:13 **the o** Solomon king of Israel had built 889[S]
1Ch 6:49 *o who* **presented offerings** AIT
16:13 O sons of Jacob, his **chosen** *o.* AIT
16:22 "Do not touch my **anointed** *o;* AIT
2Ch 20:13 and children and **little o,** 3251
31:18 They included all the **little o,** the wives, 3251
Ezr 8:13 the **last** *o,* whose names were Eliphelet, AIT
Job 5: 1 To which of the **holy** *o* will you turn? AIT
15:15 If God places no trust in his **holy** *o,* AIT
21:11 their **little o** dance about. 3529
39:30 His **young o** feast on blood, 711
Ps 16: 3 the **glorious** *o* in whom is all my delight. AIT
29: 1 Ascribe to the LORD, O **mighty** *o,* AIT
37:28 and will not forsake his **faithful** *o.* AIT
50: 5 "Gather to me my **consecrated** *o,* AIT
72: 2 your **afflicted** *o* with justice. AIT
88:18 taken my companions and **loved** *o* from me; AIT
89: 5 in the assembly of the **holy** *o.* AIT
89: 7 of the **holy** *o* God is greatly feared; AIT
94: 8 you **senseless** *o* among the people; AIT
97:10 of his **faithful** *o* and delivers them from AIT
103:20 you **mighty** *o* who do his bidding, AIT
105: 6 O sons of Jacob, his **chosen** *o,* AIT
105:15 "Do not touch my **anointed** *o;* AIT
105:43 his **chosen** *o* with shouts of joy; AIT
106: 5 I may enjoy the prosperity of your **chosen** *o,* AIT
Pr 1:22 "How long will you **simple** *o* love your simple ways? AIT
2: 8 and protects the way of his **faithful** *o.* AIT

Ecc 10: 6 while the rich occupy the **low** *o.* AIT
Isa 1: 27 her **penitent** *o* with righteousness. AIT
10: 33 the **tall** *o* will be brought low. AIT
13: 3 I have commanded my **holy** *o;* AIT
49: 13 have compassion on his **afflicted** *o.* AIT
65: 15 You will leave your name to my **chosen** *o* AIT
65: 22 my **chosen** *o* will long enjoy the works AIT
Jer 24: 3 "The good **o** are very good, 9300^{S}
24: 3 the **poor** *o* are so bad they cannot be eaten." AIT
48: 4 her **little** *o* will cry out. AIT
Da 4: 17 the **holy** *o* declare the verdict, AIT
7: 24 different from the **earlier** *o;* AIT
Hos 13: 16 their **little o** will be dashed to 6407
Zec 1: 10 "They are **the o** the LORD has sent to go 889^{S}
13: 7 I will turn my hand against the **little o.** 7592
14: 5 and all the **holy** *o* with him. AIT
Mt 10: 42 of cold water to one *of* these **little** *o* *AIT*
18: 6 of these **little** *o* who believe in me *AIT*
18: 10 not look down on one *of* these **little** *o.* *AIT*
18: 14 that any *of* these **little** *o* should be lost. *AIT*
19: 18 **"Which** *o?"* the man inquired. *AIT*
20: 8 beginning with the **last** *o* hired and going *AIT*
25: 3 The **foolish** *o* took their lamps but did *AIT*
25: 8 The **foolish** *o* said to the wise, *AIT*
Mk 9: 42 *of* these **little** *o* who believe in me *AIT*
Lk 8: 12 Those along the path are **the** *o* **who** hear, *AIT*
8: 13 on the rock are **the** *o* **who** receive the word *AIT*
12: 18 down my barns and build **bigger** *o,* *AIT*
16: 15 "You are **the** *o* **who** justify yourselves in *AIT*
17: 2 for him to cause one *of* these **little** *o* *AIT*
18: 7 God bring about justice *for* his **chosen** *o,* *AIT*
Jn 8: 9 the **older** *o* first, until only Jesus was left, *AIT*
Ro 1: 26 Even their women exchanged natural
relations for **unnatural o.** *3836+4123+5882*
1Th 3: 13 with all his **holy** *o.* *AIT*
Jas 2: 6 not the **o** who are dragging you into court? *NIG*
2: 7 the **o** who are slandering the noble name *NIG*
Jude 1: 14 thousands upon thousands of his **holy o** *41*

ONESELF (1) [ONE, SELF]

Jas 1: 27 to keep **o** from being polluted by the world. *1571*

ONESIMUS (2)

Col 4: 9 He is coming with **O,** *3946*
Phm 1: 10 I appeal to you for my son **O,** *3946*

ONESIPHORUS (2)

2Ti 1: 16 the Lord show mercy to the household *of* **O,** *3947*
4: 19 and Aquila and the household *of* **O.** *3947*

ONIONS (1)

Nu 11: 5 the cucumbers, melons, leeks, **o** and garlic. 1294

ONLY (496)

Ge 6: 5 thoughts of his heart was **o** evil all the time. 8370
7: 23 **O** Noah was left, and those with him 421
17: 18 **If o** Ishmael might live under your blessing! 4273
18: 29 "What if **o** forty are found there?" NIH
18: 30 What if **o** thirty can be found there?" NIH
18: 31 what if **o** twenty can be found there?" NIH
18: 32 What if **o** ten can be found there?" NIH
21: 26 and I heard about it **o** today." 1194+4202
22: 2 Then God said, "Take your son, your **o son,** 3495
22: 12 not withheld from me your son, your **o**
son." 3495
22: 16 and have not withheld your son, your **o son,** 3495
24: 8 **O** do not take my son back there." 8370
27: 38 "Do you have **o** one blessing, my father? 2085^{S}
29: 20 like **o a few** days to him because of his love 285
31: 15 **Not o** has he sold us, 3954
32: 10 I had **o** my staff when I crossed this Jordan, 3954
34: 12 **O** give me the girl as my wife." 2256
34: 15 to you on one condition **o:** 421
34: 22 **But** the men will consent to live with us as
one people **o** on the condition 421
41: 40 **O** with respect to the throne will I 8370
42: 38 is dead and he is the **o one** left. 963+2257+4200
44: 17 **O** the man who was found to have 2085^{S}
44: 20 he is the **o** one of his mother's sons left, 963+4200
44: 26 **O if** our youngest brother is 561
47: 26 It was **o** the land of the priests that did 8370
50: 8 **O** their children and their flocks 8370
Ex 8: 11 they will remain **o** in the Nile." 8370
8: 29 **O** be sure that Pharaoh does 8370
9: 26 The **o** place it did not hail was the land 8370
10: 11 Have **o** the men go; NIH
10: 24 **o** leave your flocks and herds behind." 8370
14: 14 you *need o to be* **still."** AIT
16: 3 **"If o** we had died by the LORD's hand 4769+5989
18: 18 **o wear** *yourselves* **out.** 5570+5570
19: 13 **O** when the ram's horn sounds NIH
21: 4 and **o** the man shall go free. 928+1727+2257
22: 27 his cloak is the **o** covering he has 963+4200
Lev 11: 4 " 'There are some that **o** chew the cud NIH
11: 4 that only chew the cud or **o** have NIH
13: 6 it is **o** a rash. NIH
13: 23 it is **o** a scar from the boil, NIH
13: 28 it is **o** a scar from the burn. 3954
21: 14 **but o** a virgin from his own people, 561+3954
25: 12 eat **o** what is taken directly from the fields. NIH
25: 52 If **o a few** years remain until the Year 5071
Nu 3: 4 so **o** Eleazar and Ithamar served as priests NIH
9: 20 over the tabernacle **o a few** days; 5031
9: 21 the cloud stayed **o** from evening NIH
Nu 10: 4 If **o** one is sounded, the leaders— NIH
11: 4 **"If o** we had meat to eat! 4769
11: 18 **"If o** we had meat to eat! 4769
12: 2 the LORD spoken **o** through Moses?" 421+8370
14: 2 **"If o** we had died in Egypt! 4273
14: 3 to this land **o** to let us fall by the sword? NIH
14: 9 **O** do not rebel against the LORD. 421
14: 38 **o** Joshua son of Nun and Caleb son 2256
16: 22 the entire assembly when **o** one man sins?" NIH
16: 29 and experience **o** what usually happens NIH
17: 8 had not **o** sprouted but had budded, NIH
18: 7 But **o** you and your sons may serve NIH
20: 3 **"If o** we had died when our brothers 4273
20: 19 We **o** want to pass through on foot— 8370
21: 24 but **o** as far as the Ammonites, NIH
22: 20 go with them, but do **o** what I tell you." 421
22: 35 but speak **o** what I tell you." 700
22: 38 I must speak **o** what God puts NIH
23: 13 you will see **o** a part but not all of them. 700
24: 13 and I must say **o** what the LORD says'? NIH
26: 33 he had **o** daughters, 561+3954
35: 28 **o** after the death of the high priest 2256
35: 30 a murderer **o** on the testimony of witnesses. NIH
35: 30 to death on the testimony of **o** one witness. NIH
Dt 2: 28 **O** let us pass through on foot— 8370
3: 11 (**O** Og king of Bashan was left of 8370
4: 9 **O** be careful, and watch yourselves closely 8370
4: 12 but saw no form; there was **o** a voice. 2314
4: 27 and **o a few** of you will survive among 5031+5493
6: 13 serve him **o** and take your oaths NIH
12: 14 Offer them **o** at the place 561+3954
15: 5 if **o** you fully obey the LORD your God 8370
17: 6 to death on the testimony of **o** one witness. NIH
22: 9 if you do, not **o** the crops you plant but also NIH
22: 25 **o** the man who has done this shall die. 963+4200
28: 67 **"If o** it were evening!" 4769+5989
28: 67 in the evening, **"If o** it were morning!" 4769+5989
29: 14 covenant, with its oath, not **o** with you 963+4200
32: 29 **If o** they were wise 4273
32: 52 you will see the land **o** from a distance; NIH
Jos 1: 17 **O** may the LORD your God be with you 8370
1: 18 **O** be strong and courageous!" 8370
6: 17 **O** Rahab the prostitute and all who are 8370
7: 3 for **o a few** men are there." 5071
7: 7 **If o** we had been content to stay on 4273
11: 22 **o** in Gaza, Gath and Ashdod did any
survive. 8370
14: 4 of the land but **o** towns to live in, 561
17: 3 had no sons but **o** daughters, 561
17: 14 "Why have you given us **o** one allotment NIH
17: 17 You will have not **o** one allotment NIH
22: 20 not the **o** one who died for his sin.' " 285
Jdg 3: 2 (he did this **o** to teach warfare to 8370
6: 37 If there is dew **o** on the fleece and all 963+4200
6: 40 **O** the fleece was dry; 963+4200
8: 20 because he was **o** a boy and was afraid. 6388
9: 29 **If o** this people were under my command!
4769+5989
11: 34 She was an **o child.** 3495
15: 13 "We will **o** tie you up and hand you over 3954
16: 3 But Samson lay there **o** until the middle of NIH
19: 20 **O** don't spend the night in the square." 8370
1Sa 1: 11 if *you will* **o look** upon your servant's 8011+8011
1: 23 **o** may the LORD make good his word." 421
2: 15 accept boiled meat from you, but **o** raw." 561
2: 33 not cut off from my altar will be spared **o** NIH
5: 4 **o** his body remained. 8370
7: 3 to the LORD and serve him **o,** 963+4200
7: 4 and served the LORD **o.** 963+4200
11: 2 a treaty with you **o** on the condition NIH
13: 22 **o** Saul and his son Jonathan had them. 2256
17: 28 you came down **o** to watch the battle." 3954
17: 33 you are **o** a boy, and he has been a fighting 3954
17: 42 David over and saw that he was **o** a boy, NIH
18: 8 he thought, "but me with **o** thousands. NIH
18: 17 **o** serve me bravely and fight the battles of 421
18: 23 I'm **o** a poor man and little known." NIH
20: 3 there is **o** a step between me and death." 3954
20: 39 **o** Jonathan and David knew.) 421
2Sa 13: 25 we would **o** be a burden to you." 4202^{S}
13: 32 **o** Amnon is dead. 963+4200
13: 33 **O** Amnon is dead." 963+4200
14: 7 the **o** burning coal I have left, NIH
15: 4 **"If o** I were appointed judge in the land! 4769
15: 20 You came **o** yesterday. NIH
17: 2 I would strike down **o** the king 963+4200
18: 33 **If o** I had died instead of you— 4769+5989
23: 10 **but o** to strip the dead. 421
1Ki 3: 7 But I am **o** a little child and do not know NIH
4: 19 He was the **o** governor over the district. 285
6: 7 **o** blocks dressed at the quarry were used, NIH
8: 25 if **o** your sons are careful in all they do 8370
11: 17 But Hadad, still **o** a boy, NIH
12: 20 **O** the tribe of Judah remained loyal to the
house of David. 963+2314+4200
14: 8 doing **o** what was right in my eyes. 8370
14: 13 the **o** one belonging to Jeroboam who 963+4200
14: 13 because he is the **o** one in the house NIH
16: 31 He **not o** considered it trivial to commit 2022
17: 12 **o** a handful of flour in a jar and a little 561+3954
18: 22 the **o one** of the LORD's prophets left, 963+4200
19: 10 I am the **o one** left, 963+4200
19: 14 I am the **o one** left, 963+4200
22: 14 I can tell him **o** what the LORD tells me." 3954
22: 18 anything good about me, **but o** bad?" 561+3954
2Ki 3: 10 the LORD called us three kings together **o** NIH
3: 25 **O** Kir Hareseth was left with its stones 6330
2Ki 5: 3 **"If o** my master would see 332
7: 10 **o** tethered horses and donkeys, 561+3954
7: 13 yes, they will **o** be like all these NIH
10: 23 **o** ministers of Baal." 561+3954
13: 19 But now you will defeat it **o** three times." NIH
17: 18 **O** the tribe of Judah was left, 4202+8370
18: 20 **but** you speak **o** empty words. 421
18: 27 "Was it **o** to your master and you NIH
19: 18 they were not gods but **o** wood and stone, 561
21: 8 if **o** they will be careful to do everything 8370
24: 14 **O** the poorest people of the land were 2314+4202
1Ch 2: 34 Sheshan had no sons—**o** daughters. 561+3954
7: 15 who had **o** daughters. NIH
23: 22 he had **o** daughters. 561+3954
29: 14 and we have given you **o** what comes NIH
2Ch 6: 16 if **o** your sons are careful in all they do 8370
16: 12 **but o** from the physicians. 3954
18: 13 I can tell him **o** what my God says." 3954
18: 17 about me, but **o** bad?" 561
20: 24 they saw **o** dead bodies lying on 2256
24: 24 Aramean army had come with **o a few** men, 5203
32: 8 With him is **o** the arm of flesh, NIH
33: 8 if **o** they will be careful to do everything 8370
33: 17 **but o** to the LORD their God. 8370
Ezr 10: 15 **O** Jonathan son of Asahel and Jahzeiah son 421
Ne 5: 8 **o** for them to be sold back to us!" 2256
Est 1: 16 not **o** against the king but also against 963+4200
3: 6 scorned the idea of killing **o** Mordecai. 963+4200
4: 2 But he went **o** as far as the king's gate, NIH
4: 11 The **o exception** to this is for the king 963+4200
5: 12 "I'm the **o** person Queen Esther invited 561+3954
Job 1: 15 the **o one** who has escaped to tell you!" 963+4200
1: 16 the **o one** who has escaped to tell you!" 963+4200
1: 17 the **o one** who has escaped to tell you!" 963+4200
1: 19 the **o one** who has escaped to tell you!" 963+4200
3: 26 I have no rest, but **o** turmoil." NIH
6: 2 **"If o** my anguish could be weighed 4273
6: 20 they arrive there, **o** to be disappointed. 2256
8: 9 for we were born **o** yesterday NIH
9: 15 I could **o** plead with my Judge for mercy. NIH
9: 33 **If o** there were someone to arbitrate 4273
10: 19 **If o** I had never come into being, 889+3869
11: 16 recalling it **o** as waters gone by. NIH
13: 5 **If o** you would be altogether silent! 4769+5989
13: 20 **"O** grant me these two things, O God, 421
14: 13 **"If o** you would hide me in the grave 4769+5989
14: 13 If **o** you would set me a time and NIH
14: 22 of his own body and mourns **o** for himself." NIH
16: 22 **"O** a few years will pass before I go on 3954
17: 13 If the **o** home I hope for is the grave, NIH
19: 20 I have escaped with **o** the skin of my teeth. NIH
23: 3 **If o** I knew where to find him; 4769+5989
23: 3 if **o** I could go to his dwelling! NIH
25: 6 a son of man, who is **o** a worm!" NIH
28: 22 **'O** a rumor of it has reached our ears.' NIH
32: 9 It is not **o** the old who are wise, NIH
32: 9 not only the old who are wise, not **o** NIH
35: 8 Your wickedness affects **o** a man NIH
35: 8 and your righteousness **o** the sons of men. NIH
Ps 25: 15 for **o** he will release my feet from the snare. NIH
30: 5 For his anger lasts **o** a moment, NIH
37: 8 it leads **o** to evil. 421
39: 6 He bustles about, **but o** in vain; 421
51: 4 Against you, and you **o,** have I sinned 963+4200
62: 9 together they are **o** a breath. 4946
91: 8 You will **o** observe with your eyes and see 8370
139: 19 **If o** you would slay the wicked, O God! 561
Pr 1: 18 they waylay **o** themselves! NIH
4: 3 still tender, and an **o child** of my mother, 3495
4: 26 for your feet and take **o** ways that are firm. 3972
10: 32 the mouth of the wicked **o** what is perverse. NIH
11: 16 but ruthless men gain **o** wealth. NIH
11: 23 The desire of the righteous ends **o** in good, 421
11: 23 but the hope of the wicked **o** in wrath. NIH
11: 29 on his family will inherit **o** wind, NIH
12: 19 but a lying tongue lasts *o a* **moment.** AIT
13: 10 Pride **o** breeds quarrels, 8370
14: 23 but mere talk leads **o** to poverty. 421
17: 11 An evil man is bent **o** on rebellion; 421
20: 25 to dedicate something rashly **and** *o* later AIT
26: 19 "I was **o** joking!" 2022+4202
30: 8 but give me **o** my daily bread. NIH
Ecc 7: 29 This **o** have I found: 963+4200
9: 14 a small city with **o a few** people in it. 5071
12: 9 **Not o** was the Teacher wise, 3463
SS 6: 9 is unique, the **o** daughter of her mother, 285
8: 1 **If o** you were to me like a brother, 4769+5989
Isa 1: 6 **o** wounds and welts and open sores, NIH
4: 1 **o** let us be called by your name. 8370
5: 2 but it yielded **o** bad fruit. NIH
5: 4 why did it yield **o** bad? NIH
5: 10 A ten-acre vineyard will produce **o** a bath NIH
5: 10 a homer of seed **o** an ephah of grain." NIH
7: 8 and the head of Damascus is **o** Rezin. NIH
7: 9 the head of Samaria is **o** Remaliah's son. NIH
7: 23 there will be **o** briers and thorns. NIH
8: 22 the earth and see **o** distress and darkness NIH
10: 22 **o** a remnant will return. NIH
16: 12 she **o** wears herself out; 3954
27: 4 **If o** there were briers 4769+5989
29: 13 of me is *made up o of* rules taught by men. AIT
30: 5 **but o** shame and disgrace." 3954
35: 9 But **o** the redeemed will walk there, NIH
36: 5 But you speak **o** empty words. NIH
36: 12 "Was it **o** to your master and you NIH
37: 19 they were not gods but **o** wood and stone, 561
47: 13 you have received *has o* **worn** *you* **out!** AIT

Isa 48:18 If o you had paid attention 4273
54: 6 wife who married young, o to be rejected," 3954
56: 3 "I am o a dry tree." 2176
58: 5 o a day for a man to humble himself? NIH
58: 5 Is it o for bowing one's head like a reed NIH
Jer 1: 6 I am o a child." 3954
1: 7 "Do not say, 'I am o a child.' NIH
3:10 but o in pretense," declares the LORD. 561
3:13 O acknowledge your guilt— 421
5: 4 I thought, "These are o the poor; 421
6:26 mourn with bitter wailing as for an o son, 3495
8:15 for a time of healing but there was o terror. NIH
9:25 I will punish all who are circumcised o NIH
10:24 Correct me, LORD, but o with justice— 421
14: 8 like a traveler *who* stays o a night? 4328+5742
14:19 for a time of healing but there is o terror. NIH
22:17 your heart are set o on dishonest gain, 561+3954
23:23 "Am I o a God nearby," NIH
27:10 *o serve to* remove you far AIT
28: 9 the LORD o if his prediction comes true." 928
30:11 I will discipline you but o with justice; NIH
31:36 "O if these decrees vanish from my sight," 561
31:37 "O if the heavens above can be measured 561
34: 7 These were the o fortified cities left NIH
37:10 and o wounded men were left in their tents, NIH
38: 6 it had no water in it, o mud, 561+3954
42: 2 now o a few are left. 5071
46:17 'Pharaoh king of Egypt is o a loud noise; NIH
46:28 I will discipline you but o with justice; NIH
49: 9 not steal o as much as they wanted? NIH
51:58 the nations' labor is o fuel for the flames." NIH
La 1:20 inside, there is o death. 3869
5: 4 our wood can be had o at a price. NIH
Eze 14:14 were in it, they could save o themselves NIH
14:20 They would save o themselves NIH
16:47 You not o walked in their ways 2256
17:14 surviving o by keeping his treaty. NIH
33:24 'Abraham was o one man, NIH
34: 2 the shepherds of Israel who *o* take care of AIT
40:46 who are the o Levites who may draw near 4946
43: 8 with o a wall between me and them, NIH
44: 3 The prince himself is the *o* one who may sit AIT
44:22 they may marry o virgins 561+3954
44:28 to be the o inheritance the priests have. NIH
46:17 His inheritance belongs to his sons o; 421
Da 4:19 if o the dream applied to your enemies NIH
10: 7 Daniel, was the o one who saw the vision; 963+4200
11:23 with o a few people he will rise to power. 5071
11:24 overthrow of fortresses—but o for a time. NIH
Hos 4: 2 There is o cursing, lying and murder, NIH
Am 3: 2 "You o have I chosen of all the families of 8370
3:12 the lion's mouth o two leg bones or a piece NIH
5: 3 a thousand strong for Israel will have o NIH
5: 3 a hundred strong will have o ten left." NIH
5:19 as though a man fled from a lion o to meet 2256
5:19 and rested his hand on the wall o to have 2256
8:10 like mourning for an o son and the end of it 3495
Ob 1: 5 not steal o as much as they wanted? NIH
Hab 2:13 that the people's labor is o fuel for the fire, NIH
Zep 1: 3 The wicked will have o heaps of rubble NIH
Hag 1: 6 o to put them in a purse with holes in it." NIH
2:16 there were o ten. NIH
2:16 there were o twenty. NIH
Zec 1:15 I was o a little angry, 5071
12:10 for him as one mourns for an o child, 3495
14: 9 and his name the o name. 285
Mt 4:10 the Lord your God, and serve him o.' " *3668*
5:47 And if you greet o your brothers, *3668*
6:18 but o to your Father, who is unseen; *NIG*
7:14 and o a few find it. *NIG*
7:21 but o he who does the will *NIG*
9:21 She said to herself, "If I o touch his cloak, *3668*
12: 4 but o for the priests. *3668*
12:24 they said, "It is o by Beelzebub, *1623+3590*
13:21 since he has no root, he lasts o a short time. *4672*
13:57 "O in his hometown and in his own house is a prophet without honor." *1623+3590*
14:17 "We have here o five loaves of bread and two fish, *1623+3590+4024*
15:24 "I was sent o to the lost sheep of Israel." *1623+3590+4024*
19:11 but o those to whom it has been given. *NIG*
19:17 "There is o One who is good. *NIG*
20:12 who were hired last worked o one hour,' *NIG*
21:21 o can you do what was done to the fig tree, *3668*
23: 8 for you have o one Master *NIG*
24:36 nor the Son, but o the Father. *1623+3590*
Mk 2:26 which is lawful o for priests to eat. *1623+3590*
4:17 they have no root, they last o a short time. *4672*
6: 4 to them, "O in his hometown, *1623+3590+4024*
9:29 "This kind can come out o by prayer." *1623+3590*
12:42 worth o a fraction of a penny. *NIG*
13:32 nor the Son, but o the Father. *1623+3590*
14: 1 Unleavened Bread were o two days away, *NIG*
Lk 4: 8 Worship the Lord your God and serve him o *3668*
4:27 o Naaman the Syrian." *1623+3590*
6: 4 he ate what is lawful o for priests to eat. *1623+3590+3668*
7:12 o son of his mother, and she was a widow. *3666*
8:42 because his o daughter, *1639+3666*
9:13 "We have o five loaves of bread *2445+4024+4498*
9:38 for he is my o *child*. *3666*
10:42 but o one thing is needed. *NIG*
13:23 are o a few people going to be saved?" *NIG*
17:10 we have o done our duty.' " *NIG*
19:42 and said, "If you, even you, had o known *NIG*
Lk 24:18 "Are you o a visitor to Jerusalem and do *3668*
Jn 1: 8 he came o as a witness to the light. *247*
1:14 the glory of the One and O, *3666*
1:18 but God the One and O, *3666*
3:16 the world that he gave his one and o Son, *3666*
3:18 in the name of God's one and o Son. *3666*
3:27 A man can receive o what is given him *1651+4028*
5:18 not o was he breaking the Sabbath, *3668*
5:19 he can do o what he sees his Father doing, *1569+3590*
5:30 I judge o as I hear, *NIG*
5:44 the praise that comes from the o God? *3668*
6: 6 He asked this o to test him, *NIG*
6:22 that o one boat had been there, *1623+3590*
6:46 o he has seen the Father. *NIG*
7:33 "I am with you for o a short time, *2285*
8: 9 the older ones first, until o Jesus was left, *3668*
8:41 "The o Father we have is God himself." *1651*
9: 9 Others said, "No, he o looks like him." *247*
10:10 thief comes o to steal and kill *1623+3590+4024*
10:17 lay down my life—o to take it up again. *2671*
11:52 and not o for that nation but also for *3667*
12: 9 o because of him but also to see Lazarus, *3667*
12:16 O after Jesus was glorified did they realize *247*
12:24 it remains o a single seed. *3668*
12:44 he does not believe in me o, *NIG*
13:10 "A person who has had a bath needs o to wash his feet; *1623+3590+4024*
13:33 I will be with you o a little longer. *NIG*
16:13 he will speak o what he hears, *247*
17: 3 that they may know you, the o true God, *3668*
21:23 he o said, "If I want him to remain alive *247*
Ac 2:15 It's o nine in the morning! *NIG*
5:39 you will o find yourselves fighting *3607*
10:26 he said, "I am o a man myself." *NIG*
11:19 telling the message o to Jews. *3668*
14:15 We too are o men, human like you. *NIG*
18:25 though he knew o the baptism of John. *3668*
19:27 not o that our trade will lose its good name, *3667*
20:23 I o know that in every city *4440*
20:24 if o I may finish the race and complete *6055*
21:13 I am ready not o to be bound, *3667*
26:29 that not o you but all who are listening *3667*
27:22 o the ship will be destroyed. *4440*
Ro 1:32 they not o continue to do these very things *3667*
2:28 not a Jew if he is o one outwardly, *NIG*
3:29 Is God the God of Jews o? *3668*
3:30 since there is o one God, *NIG*
4: 9 Is this blessedness o for the circumcised, *NIG*
4:12 not o are circumcised but who also walk in *3667*
4:16 not o to those who are of the law but also *3668*
5: 3 Not o so, but we also rejoice *3668*
5:11 Not o is this so, but we also rejoice *3668*
7: 1 a man o as long as he lives? *2093+4012+5989*
8:23 Not o so, but we ourselves, *3668*
9:10 Not o that, but Rebekah's children had one *3667*
9:24 o from the Jews but also from the Gentiles? *3668*
9:27 o the remnant will be saved. *NIG*
11: 3 I am the o *one* left, *3668*
13: 5 not o because of possible punishment but *3667*
14: 2 whose faith is weak, eats o vegetables. *NIG*
16: 4 Not o I but all the churches of the Gentiles *3668*
16:27 *to* the o wise God be glory forever *3668*
1Co 3: 5 O servants, through whom you came *NIG*
3: 7 but o God, who makes things grow. *247*
3:15 but o as one escaping through the flames. *NIG*
4:19 and then I will find out not o how these *NIG*
9: 6 Or is it o I and Barnabas who must work *3668*
9:24 but o one gets the prize? *NIG*
13: 1 I am o a resounding gong or *NIG*
14:36 Or are you the o *people* it has reached? *3668*
15:19 If o for this life we have hope in Christ, *3667*
16: 7 to see you now and make o a passing visit; *NIG*
2Co 3:14 because o in Christ is it taken away. *NIG*
7: 7 and not o by his coming but also by *3667*
7: 8 but o for a little while— *NIG*
8:10 Last year you were the first not o to give *3667*
8:17 For Titus not o welcomed our appeal, *NIG*
8:21 not o in the eyes of the Lord but also in *3667*
9:12 not o supplying the needs of God's people *3667*
10: 7 You are looking o on the surface of things. *NIG*
13: 8 but o for the truth. *247*
Gal 1:19 o James, the Lord's brother. *1623+3590*
1:23 They o heard the report: *3667*
5: 6 The o thing that counts is faith expressing itself through love. *247*
6:12 The o reason they do this is to avoid *3667*
Eph 1:21 not o in the present age but also in the one *3668*
4:29 but o what is helpful for building others up *1623*
6: 6 not o to win their favor when their eye is *NIG*
Php 1:27 whether I come and see you or o hear *NIG*
1:29 on behalf of Christ not o to believe on him, *3668*
2: 4 Each of you should look not o to your own *3590*
2:12 not o in my presence, *3590*
2:27 and not on him o but also on me, *3668*
3:16 O let us live up to what we have already *4440*
4:15 of giving and receiving, except you o; *3668*
Col 3:22 and do it, not o when their eye is on you *NIG*
4:11 the o Jews among my fellow workers for *3668*
1Th 1: 8 from you not o in Macedonia and Achaia— *3667*
2: 8 to share with you not o the gospel of God *3668*
1Ti 1:17 immortal, invisible, the o God, *3668*
5:13 And not o do they become idlers, *3667*
5:23 Stop drinking o water, *5621*
6:15 God, the blessed and o Ruler, *3668*
2Ti 2:14 and o ruins those who listen. *NIG*
2:20 a large house there are articles not o of gold *3667*
2Ti 4: 8 and not o to me, *3667*
4:11 O Luke is with me. *3668*
Heb 9: 7 o the high priest entered the inner room, *3668*
9: 7 and that o once a year, *NIG*
9:10 They are o a matter of food and drink *3667*
9:17 will is in force o when somebody has died; *NIG*
9:24 a man-made sanctuary that was o a copy of *NIG*
10: 1 The law is o a shadow of the good things *NIG*
10:27 but o a fearful expectation of judgment and *NIG*
11:13 they o saw them and welcomed them from *247*
11:17 about to sacrifice his one and o son, *3666*
11:40 for us so that o together with us would they *NIG*
12:26 "Once more I will shake not o the earth but *3668*
13:22 for I have written you o a short letter. *NIG*
Jas 4:12 There is o one Lawgiver and Judge, *NIG*
1Pe 2:18 o to those who are good and considerate, *3667*
3:20 In it o a few people, eight in all, *NIG*
2Pe 2:12 born o to be caught and destroyed, *NIG*
1Jn 2: 2 and not o for ours but also for the sins of *3667*
4: 9 He sent his one and o Son into the world *3666*
5: 5 O he who believes that Jesus is the Son of God. *1623+3590*
5: 6 He did not come by water o, *3667*
2Jn 1: 1 not I o, but also all who know the truth— *3668*
Jude 1: 4 and deny Jesus Christ our o Sovereign *3668*
1:12 shepherds who feed o themselves. *NIG*
1:25 *to* the o God our Savior be glory, *3668*
Rev 2:17 known o to him who receives it. *1623+3590+4029*
2:25 O hold on to what you have until I come. *4440*
9: 4 but o those people who did not have *1623+3590*
9: 5 but o to torture them for five months. *247*
21:27 but o those whose names are written *1623+3590*

ONO (5)

1Ch 8:12 Misham, Shemed (who built O and Lod 229
Ezr 2:33 of Lod, Hadid and O 725 229
Ne 6: 2 in one of the villages on the plain of O." 229
7:37 of Lod, Hadid and O 721 229
11:35 in Lod and O, and in the Valley of the 229

ONTO (9) [ON]

Ge 49: 4 for *you* went up *o* your father's bed, AIT
49: 4 o my couch and defiled it. NIH
Ex 8: 3 and your bedroom and o your bed, 6584
Nu 19: 6 and scarlet wool and throw them o 448+9348
Jdg 8:25 a ring from his plunder o it. 2025
1Ki 22:35 The blood from his wound ran o the floor 448
Est 9:25 the Jews should come back o his own head, 6584
Jnh 2:10 and it vomited Jonah o dry land. 448
Lk 9:28 with him and went up o a mountain to pray. *1650*

ONWARD (KJV) See SET OUT

ONYCHA (1)

Ex 30:34 gum resin, o and galbanum— 8829

ONYX (11)

Ge 2:12 aromatic resin and o are also there.) 74+8732
Ex 25: 7 and o stones and other gems to be mounted 8732
28: 9 "Take two o stones and engrave on them 8732
28:20 an o and a jasper. 8732
35: 9 and o stones and other gems to be mounted 8732
35:27 The leaders brought o stones 8732
39: 6 the o stones in gold filigree settings 8732
39:13 an o and a jasper. 8732
1Ch 29: 2 as well as o for the settings, turquoise, 74+8732
Job 28:16 with precious o or sapphires. 8732
Eze 28:13 topaz and emerald, chrysolite, o and jasper, 8732

OOZING (1)

1Sa 14:26 they saw the honey o out, 2144

OPEN (164) [OPENED, OPENHANDED, OPENING, OPENINGS, OPENLY, OPENS]

Ge 25:27 a man of the o country, 8441
25:29 Esau came in from the o country, 8441
27: 3 to the o country to hunt some wild game 8441
27: 5 When Esau left for the o country 8441
34:10 the land is o *to* you. 4200+7156
Lev 1:17 *He shall* tear it o by the wings, 9117
14: 7 he is to release the live bird in the o fields. 7156
14:53 the live bird in the o fields outside 7156
17: 5 now making in the o fields. 7156
25:31 to be considered as o country. 8441
Nu 19:15 and every o container without a lid fastened 7337
19:16 o who touches someone who has been killed 8441
Dt 20:11 If they accept and o their gates, 7337
28:12 The LORD *will* o the heavens, 7337
Jos 8:17 They left the city o and went in pursuit 7337
10:22 "O the mouth of the cave 7337
Jdg 3:25 when he *did* not o the doors of the room, 7337
20:31 that about thirty men fell in the o field and 8441
2Sa 10: 8 by themselves in the o country. 8441
11:11 my lord's men are camped in the o fields. 7156
11:23 and came out against us in the o, 8441
1Ki 6:18 carved with gourds and o flowers. 7080
6:29 palm trees and o flowers. 7080
6:32 palm trees and o flowers, 7080
6:35 and o flowers on them and overlaid them 7080
8:29 be o toward this temple night and day, 7337
8:52 "May your eyes be o to your servant's plea 7337
2Ki 6:17 "O LORD, o his eyes so he may see." 7337

2Ki 6:20 o the eyes of these men so they can see." 7219
7:2 *if* the LORD *should* o the floodgates of 6913
7:19 *if* the LORD *should* o the floodgates of 6913
8:12 and **rip** o their pregnant women." 1324
9:3 Then o the door and run; don't delay!" 7337
13:17 "O the east window," he said, 7337
15:16 because *they* refused *to* o their gates. 7337
15:16 and **ripped** o all the pregnant women. 1324
19:16 o your eyes, O LORD, and see; 7219
1Ch 19:9 by themselves in the o **country.** 8441
2Ch 6:20 May your eyes be o toward this temple day 7337
6:40 may your eyes be o and your ears attentive 7337
7:15 be o and my ears attentive to 7337
Ne 1:6 let your ear be attentive and your eyes o 7337
Est 4:6 to Mordecai in the o **square** *of* the city 8148
Job 11:5 that *he would* o his lips against you 7337
16:10 *Men* o their mouths to jeer at me; 7196
31:32 for my door *was always* o to the traveler— 7337
32:20 *I must* o my lips and reply. 7337
33:2 *I am about to* o my mouth; 7337
41:14 Who *dares* o the doors of his mouth, 7337
Ps 5:9 Their throat is an o grave; 7337
22:13 Roaring lions tearing their prey o their mouths **wide** against me. 7198
38:9 All my longings lie o before you, O Lord; NIH
38:13 like a mute, *who* cannot o his mouth; 7337
39:9 I was silent; *I would* not o my mouth, 7337
51:15 O Lord, o my lips, 7337
60:2 You have shaken the land and **torn** it o; 7204
74:13 It was you *who* **split** o the sea 7297
78:2 *I will* o my mouth in parables, 7337
81:10 O **wide** your mouth and I will fill it. 8143
104:28 *when you* o your hand, 7337
118:19 O for me the gates of righteousness; 7337
119:18 O my eyes that I may see wonderful things 1655
119:131 *I* o my mouth and pant, 7196
119:148 My eyes **stay** o *through* the watches of 7709
145:16 You o your hand and satisfy the desires 7337
Pr 8:6 I o my lips to speak what is right. 5157
15:11 and Destruction lie o before the LORD— NIH
27:5 Better is o rebuke than hidden love. 1655
SS 5:2 My lover is knocking: "O to me, my sister, 7337
5:5 I arose to o for my lover, 7337
Isa 1:6 only wounds and welts and o sores, 3269
9:12 west have devoured Israel with o mouth. 3972
22:22 and what he shuts no *one can* o. 7337
26:2 O the gates that the righteous nation may 7337
37:17 o your eyes, O LORD, and see; 7219
42:7 to o eyes that are blind, 7219
42:20 your ears *are* o, but you hear nothing." 7219
45:1 to o doors before him so that gates will not 7337
45:8 *Let* the earth o **wide,** 7337
48:8 from of old your ear *has* not *been* o. 7337
53:7 and afflicted, yet *he did* not o his mouth; 7337
53:7 is silent, so *he did* not o his mouth. 7337
60:11 Your gates *will* always *stand* o, 7337
63:13 Like a horse in o **country,** 4497
Jer 5:16 Their quivers are like an o grave; 7337
9:20 o your ears **to** the words of his mouth. 4374
9:22 of men will lie like refuse on the o field, 7156
13:19 and there will be no *one to* o them. 7337
17:16 What passes my lips is o **before** you. 5790+7156
32:19 Your eyes *are* o to all the ways of men; 7219
40:7 in the o **country** heard that the king 8441
40:13 the o **country** came to Gedaliah at Mizpah 8441
50:26 **Break** o her granaries; 7337
La 2:16 All your enemies o their mouths **wide** 7198
Eze 2:8 o your mouth and eat what I give you." 7198
3:27 *I will* o your mouth and you shall say 7337
16:5 you were thrown out into the o field, 7156
16:63 be ashamed and never again o your mouth 7341
21:24 by your o rebellion, revealing your sins 1655
26:2 and its doors *have* **swung** o to me; 6015
29:5 You will fall on the o field and not 7156
29:7 and *you* **tore** o their shoulders; 1324
29:21 and *I will* o your mouth among them. 5989+7341
32:4 on the land and hurl you on the o field. 7156
37:12 *I am going to* o your graves and bring you 7337
37:13 when I o your graves and bring you up 7337
39:5 You will fall in the o field, 8441
41:9 The o **area** between the side rooms of 4965
41:11 the o **area,** one on the north and another on 4965
41:11 the o **area** was five cubits wide all around. 4965
45:2 with 50 cubits around it for o **land.** 4494
Da 9:18 o your eyes and see the desolation of 7219
Hos 13:8 will attack them and **rip** them o. 4213+6033+7973
13:16 their pregnant women **ripped** o." 1324
Joel 1:19 the o pastures and flames have burned 4497
1:20 up and fire has devoured the o pastures. 4497
2:22 for the o pastures are becoming green. 4497
Am 1:13 Because he **ripped** o the pregnant women 1324
Mic 2:13 One *who* **breaks** o the way will go up 7287
4:10 the city to camp in the o **field.** 8441
Na 2:6 The river gates *are* **thrown** o and 7337
3:13 your land *are* **wide** o to your enemies; 7337+7337
Zec 11:1 O your doors, O Lebanon, 7337
Mal 3:10 not **throw** o the floodgates of heaven 7337
Mt 13:35 "*I will* o my mouth in parables, 487
17:27 o its mouth and you will find a four-drachma coin. 487
25:11 'O the door for us!' 487
27:52 The tombs **broke** o and the bodies 487
Mk 1:10 he saw heaven *being* **torn** o and 5387
4:22 to be brought out into the o. 5745
Lk 8:17 not be known or brought out into the o. 5745
12:36 and knocks *they can* immediately o 487
13:25 'Sir, o the door for us.' 487
Lk 15:4 in the o **country** and go after the lost sheep 2245
Jn 1:51 "I tell you the truth, you shall see heaven o, 487
4:35 o **your eyes** and look at the fields! 2048+4057
9:26 How *did he* o your eyes?" 487
10:21 Can a demon o the eyes of the blind?" 487
Ac 1:18 there he fell headlong, his body burst o 3545
7:56 "I see heaven o and the Son 1380
8:32 so *he did* not o his mouth. 487
16:26 At once all the prison doors **flew** o, 487
16:27 and when he saw the prison doors o, 487
19:38 the **courts are** o and there are proconsuls. 61+72
26:18 *to* o their eyes and turn them 487
27:5 When we had sailed across the o **sea** off 4283
Ro 3:13 "Their throats are o graves; 487
2Co 6:13 o **wide** *your* hearts also. 4425
11:25 I spent a night and a day in the o **sea,** 1113
Eph 6:19 that whenever I o my mouth, 489
Col 4:3 too, that God *may* o a door for our message, 487
1Ti 5:7 **no** one may be o **to blame.** 455
Tit 1:6 a man whose children believe and are not o NIG
Rev 3:7 and what he shuts no one can o. 487
3:8 before you an o door that no one can shut. 487
4:1 before me was a door **standing** o in heaven. 487
5:2 "Who is worthy *to* break the seals and o 487
5:3 the earth could o the scroll or even look 487
5:4 *to* o the scroll or look inside. 487
5:5 *to* o the scroll and its seven seals." 487
5:9 to take the scroll and *to* o its seals, 487
10:2 *which* **lay** o in his hand. 487
10:8 "Go, take the scroll that *lies* o in the hand 487
19:11 I saw heaven **standing** o and there 487

OPENED (109) [OPEN]

Ge 3:5 that when you eat of it your eyes *will* **be** o, 7219
3:7 Then the eyes of both of them **were** o, 7219
4:11 which o its mouth to receive your brother's 7198
7:11 and the floodgates of the heavens **were** o. 7337
8:6 After forty days Noah o the window 7337
21:19 Then God o her eyes and she saw a well 7219
29:31 *he* o her womb, but Rachel was barren. 7337
30:22 he listened to her and o her womb. 7337
41:56 Joseph o the storehouses and sold grain to 7337
42:27 the night one of them o his sack to get feed 7337
43:21 for the night *we* o our sacks and each 7337
44:11 his sack to the ground and o it. 7337
Ex 2:6 *She* o it and saw the baby. 7337
Nu 16:32 the earth o its mouth and swallowed them, 7337
22:28 Then the LORD o the donkey's mouth, 7337
22:31 Then the LORD o Balaam's eyes, 1655
24:4 who falls prostrate, and whose eyes *are* o: 1655
24:16 who falls prostrate, and whose eyes *are* o: 1655
26:10 The earth o its mouth and swallowed them 7337
Dt 11:6 the earth o its mouth right in the middle 7198
Jdg 4:19 *She* o a skin of milk, gave him a drink, 7337
15:19 Then God o **up** the hollow place in Lehi, 1324
19:27 and o the door of the house and stepped out 7337
1Sa 3:15 down until morning and then o the doors of 7337
2Ki 4:35 boy sneezed seven times and o his eyes. 7219
6:17 Then the LORD o the servant's eyes, 7219
6:20 the LORD o their eyes and they looked, 7219
9:10 Then *he* o the door and ran. 7337
13:17 he said, and *he* o it. 7337
2Ch 29:3 he o the doors of the temple of the LORD 7337
Ne 7:3 "The gates of Jerusalem *are* not *to* **be** o 7337
8:5 Ezra o the book. 7337
8:5 and as *he* o it, the people all stood up. 7337
13:19 I ordered the doors to be shut and not o 7337
Job 3:1 Job o his mouth and cursed the day 7337
Ps 74:15 It was you *who* o **up** springs and streams; 1324
78:23 above and o the doors of the heavens; 7337
105:41 *He* o the rock, and water gushed out; 7337
106:17 The earth o **up** and swallowed Dathan; 7337
109:2 and deceitful men *have* o their mouths 7337
SS 5:6 I o for my lover, but my lover had left; 7337
7:12 if their blossoms *have* o, 7337
Isa 10:14 or o its mouth to chirp.' " 7198
24:18 The floodgates of the heavens **are** o, 7337
35:5 Then *will* the eyes of the blind **be** o and 7219
50:5 The Sovereign LORD *has* o my ears, 7337
57:8 you climbed into it and o it **wide;** 8143
Jer 50:25 The LORD *has* o his arsenal 7337
La 3:46 "All our enemies *have* o their mouths **wide** 7198
Eze 1:1 heavens **were** o and I saw visions of God. 7337
3:2 So *I* o my mouth, and he gave me the scroll 7337
24:27 At that time your mouth *will* **be** o; 7337
33:22 and *he* o my mouth before the man came 7337
33:22 my mouth **was** o and I was no longer silent. 7337
44:2 *It must* not **be** o; 7337
46:1 on the day of the New Moon *it is to* **be** o. 7337
46:12 the gate facing east *is to be* o for him. 7337
Da 6:10 to his upstairs room where the windows o 10602
7:10 court was seated, and the books **were** o. 10602
10:16 and *I* o my mouth and began to speak. 7337
Zec 13:1 a fountain will be o to the house of David 7337
Mt 2:11 Then they o their treasures 487
3:16 At that moment heaven *was* o, 487
7:7 knock and the door *will be* o to you. 487
7:8 to him who knocks, the door *will be* o. 487
Mk 7:34 (which means, *"Be* **o!"**). 1380
7:35 At this, the man's ears *were* o, 487
8:25 Then *his* **eyes** *were* o, his sight was restored, 1332
Lk 1:64 Immediately his mouth *was* o 487
3:21 And as he was praying, heaven *was* o 487
10:38 a woman named Martha o her **home to** him. 5685
11:9 knock and the door *will be* o to you. 487
11:10 to him who knocks, the door *will be* o. 487
Lk 24:31 their eyes *were* o and they recognized him, 1380
24:32 while he talked with us on the road and o 1380
24:45 Then *he* o their minds so they could 1380
Jn 9:10 "How then *were* your eyes o?" 487
9:14 and o the man's eyes was a Sabbath. 487
9:17 It was your eyes *he* o." 487
9:21 But how he can see now, or who o his eyes, 487
9:30 yet *he* o my eyes. 487
11:37 "Could not he who o the eyes of the blind 487
Ac 5:19 the night an angel of the Lord o the doors 487
5:23 *when we* o them, we found no one inside." 487
9:8 but *when he* o his eyes he could see nothing. 487
9:40 She o her eyes, and seeing Peter she sat up. 487
10:11 He saw heaven o and something like 487
12:10 It o for them by itself, and they went through 487
12:16 and *when* they o the door and saw him, 487
14:27 through them and how *he had* o the door 487
16:14 The Lord o her heart to respond 1380
Ro 1:10 **way** *may be* o **for** me to come to you. 2338
1Co 16:9 a great door for effective work *has* o to me, 487
2Co 2:12 and found that the Lord *had* o a door for me, 487
6:11 Corinthians, and o **wide** our hearts to you. 4425
Heb 10:20 and living way o for us through the curtain, 1590
Rev 6:1 as the Lamb o the first of the seven seals. 487
6:3 When the Lamb o the second seal, 487
6:5 When the Lamb o the third seal, 487
6:7 When the Lamb o the fourth seal, 487
6:9 When *he* o the fifth seal, 487
6:12 I watched as *he* o the sixth seal. 487
8:1 When *he* o the seventh seal, 487
9:2 When *he* o the Abyss, 487
11:19 Then God's temple in heaven *was* o, 487
13:6 *He* o his mouth to blaspheme God, 487
15:5 the tabernacle of the Testimony, *was* o. 487
20:12 before the throne, and books *were* o. 487
20:12 Another book *was* o, which is the book of life. 487

OPENHANDED (2) [OPEN, HAND]

Dt 15:8 Rather *be* o and freely lend him whatever he needs. 906+3338+7337+7337
15:11 *be* o toward your brothers 906+3338+7337+7337

OPENING (18) [OPEN]

Ex 28:32 with an o *for* the head in its center. 7023
28:32 be a woven edge like a collar around this o, 7023
39:23 with an o in the center of the robe like 7023
39:23 the center of the robe like the o *of* a collar, 7023
39:23 and a band around this o, 7023
2Sa 17:19 the o *of* the well and scattered grain over it. 7156
1Ki 7:31 inside of the stand there was an o that had 7023
7:31 This o was round, 7023
7:31 Around its o there was engraving. 7023
1Ch 9:27 of the **key for** o it each morning. 5158
Eze 40:13 from *one* **parapet** o to the opposite one. 7339
Da 3:26 Nebuchadnezzar then approached the o *of* 10776
Hos 13:13 does not come to the o **of the womb.** 1201+5402
Mk 2:4 *they* **made an** o **in** the roof above Jesus and, 689
Jn 9:32 Nobody has ever heard of o the eyes of 487
Ac 9:25 and lowered him in a basket through an o NIG
12:14 so overjoyed she ran back without o it 487
Rev 12:16 the earth helped the woman by o its mouth 487

OPENINGS (8) [OPEN]

Eze 40:16 by narrow **parapet** o all around, as was 2707
40:16 the o all around faced inward. 2707
40:22 Its o, its portico and its palm tree 2707
40:25 and its portico had narrow o all around, 2707
40:25 like the o of the others. 2707
40:29 and its portico had o all around. 2707
40:33 and its portico had o all around. 2707
40:36 and it had o all around. 2707

OPENLY (4) [OPEN]

Eze 23:18 *she* **carried on** her prostitution o 1655
Mk 1:45 Jesus could no longer enter a town o 5747
Jn 18:20 "I have spoken o to the world," 4244
Ac 19:18 came and o **confessed** their evil deeds. 334+2018

OPENS (10) [OPEN]

Nu 16:30 the earth o its mouth and swallows them, 7198
Job 27:19 *when he* o his eyes, all is gone. 7219
35:16 So Job o his mouth *with* empty talk; 7198
Pr 18:16 A gift o **the way** for the giver 8143
31:20 *She* o her arms to the poor 7298
Isa 5:14 and o its mouth without limit; 7196
22:22 what *he* o no one can shut, 7337
Jn 10:3 The watchman o the gate for him, 487
Rev 3:7 What he o no one can shut, 487
3:20 If anyone hears my voice and o the door, 487

OPERATION (KJV) See DONE, POWER, WORK

OPHEL (5)

2Ch 27:3 on the wall at the **hill of O.** 6755
33:14 and encircling the **hill of O;** 6755
Ne 3:26 living on the **hill of O** made repairs up to 6755
3:27 the great projecting tower to the wall of **O.** 6755
11:21 The temple servants live on the **hill of O,** 6755

OPHIR (12)
Ge 10:29 O, Havilah and Jobab. 234
1Ki 9:28 to O and brought back 420 talents of gold, 234
10:11 (Hiram's ships brought gold from O; 234
22:48 to go to O for gold, but they never set sail— 234
1Ch 1:23 O, Havilah and Jobab. 234
29: 4 three thousand talents of gold (gold of O) 234
2Ch 8:18 sailed to O and brought back four hundred 234
9:10 the men of Solomon brought gold from O; 234
Job 22:24 your gold of O to the rocks in the ravines, 234
28:16 It cannot be bought with the gold of O, 234
Ps 45: 9 the royal bride in gold of O. 234
Isa 13:12 more rare than the gold of O. 234

OPHNI (1)
Jos 18:24 Kephar Ammoni, O and Geba— 6756

OPHRAH (8) [BETH OPHRAH]
Jos 18:23 Avvim, Parah, O, 6764
Jdg 6:11 under the oak in O that belonged to Joash 6764
6:24 To this day it stands in O *of* the Abiezrites. 6764
8:27 which he placed in O, his town. 6764
8:32 of his father Joash in O *of* the Abiezrites. 6764
9: 5 He went to his father's home in O and 6764
1Sa 13:17 One turned toward O in the vicinity 6764
1Ch 4:14 Meonothai was the father of O. 6763

OPINION (2) [OPINIONS]
2Sa 17: 6 If not, give us your o." 1819
Mt 22:17 Tell us then, what *is* your o? *1506*

OPINIONS (2) [OPINION]
1Ki 18:21 "How long will you waver between two o? 6191
Pr 18: 2 but delights in airing his own o. 4213

OPPONENT (3) [OPPOSE]
2Sa 2:16 Then each man grabbed his o by the head 8276
1Ki 20:20 and each one struck down his o. 408
Job 16: 9 my o fastens on me his piercing eyes. 7640

OPPONENT'S (1) [OPPOSE]
2Sa 2:16 and thrust his dagger into his o side, 8276

OPPONENTS (2) [OPPOSE]
Pr 18:18 and keeps strong *o* apart. AIT
Lk 13:17 all his o were humiliated, *512*

OPPORTUNE (2) [OPPORTUNITY]
Mk 6:21 Finally the o time came. *2322*
Lk 4:13 he left him until an o time. *2789*

OPPORTUNITY (17) [OPPORTUNE]
1Sa 18:21 a second *o* to become my son-in-law." AIT
Jer 46:17 he has missed his o.' 4595
Mt 26:16 From then on Judas watched for an o *2321*
Mk 14:11 So he watched for an o to hand him over. *2323*
Lk 22: 6 and watched for an o to hand Jesus over *2321*
Ac 25:16 and has had an o to defend himself *5536*
Ro 7: 8 the o afforded by the commandment, *929*
7:11 the o afforded by the commandment, *929*
1Co 16:12 but he will go when *he* has the o. *2320*
2Co 5:12 but are giving you an o to take pride in us, *929*
11:12 the ground from under those who want an o *929*
Gal 6:10 Therefore, as we have o, let us do good *2789*
Eph 5:16 making the most of every o, *2789*
Php 4:10 but *you* had no o to show it. *177*
Col 4: 5 make the most of every o. *1973+2789+3836*
1Ti 5:14 and to give the enemy no o for slander. *929*
Heb 11:15 they would have had o to return. *2789*

OPPOSE (28) [OPPONENT, OPPONENT'S, OPPONENTS, OPPOSED, OPPOSES, OPPOSING, OPPOSITE, OPPOSITION]
Ex 23:22 and *will* o those who oppose you. 7444
23:22 and will oppose *those who* o you. 7675
Nu 16: 3 as a group to o Moses and Aaron and said 6584
22:22 of the LORD stood in the road to o him. 8477
22:32 to o you because your path is a reckless one 8477
22:34 you were standing in the road to o me. 7925
Jdg 20:25 came out from Gibeah to o them, 7925
1Sa 2:10 *those who* o the LORD will be shattered. 8189
Job 11:10 who *can* o him? 8740
23: 6 *Would he* o me with great power? 6643+8189
23:13 "But he stands alone, and who *can* o him? 8740
Ps 55:18 even though many o me. 6643
109: 6 Appoint an evil man to o him; 6584
Isa 41:11 those who o you will be as nothing 8190
Jer 38: 5 "The king can do nothing to o you." 907
51: 2 they will o her on every side in the day 6584
Da 11:30 of the western coastlands *will* o him, 928+995
Lk 11:53 teachers of the law began *to* o him fiercely *1923*
14:31 with ten thousand men *to* o the one coming *5636*
Ac 11:17 who was I to think that I could o God?" *3266*
26: 9 that I ought to do all that was possible to o *1885*
1Co 16: 9 and there are many who o me. *512*
Php 1:28 in any way by those who o you. *512*
2Th 2: 4 He will o and will exalt himself *512*
2Ti 2:25 Those who o him he must gently instruct, *507*
3: 8 so also these men o the truth— *468*
Tit 1: 9 and refute those who o it. *515*
2: 8 that those who o you may be ashamed *1666+1885*

OPPOSED (11) [OPPOSE]
Ex 15: 7 down *those who* o you. 7756
2Ch 13: 7 and o Rehoboam son of Solomon 599+6584
Ezr 10:15 and Shabbethai the Levite, o this. 6584+6641
Jer 50:24 and captured because *you* o the LORD. 1741
Ac 13: 8 (for that is what his name means) o them *468*
18: 6 *when* the Jews o Paul and became abusive, *530*
Gal 2:11 *I* o him to his face, *468*
3:21 therefore, o to the promises of God? *2848*
Col 2:14 was against us and that stood o to us; *1639+5641*
2Ti 3: 8 Just as Jannes and Jambres o Moses, *468*
4:15 because *he* strongly o our message. *468*

OPPOSES (5) [OPPOSE]
Mk 3:26 And if Satan o himself and is divided, *482+2093*
Lk 23: 2 *He* o payment of taxes to Caesar and claims *3266*
Jn 19:12 Anyone who claims to be a king o Caesar." *515*
Jas 4: 6 "God o the proud but gives grace to the humble." *530*
1Pe 5: 5 "God o the proud but gives grace to the humble." *530*

OPPOSING (3) [OPPOSE]
2Ch 35:21 God has told me to hurry; so stop o God, 4946
1Ti 6:20 from godless chatter and the o ideas *509*
Jas 5: 6 innocent men, *who were* not o you. *530*

OPPOSITE (49) [OPPOSE]
Ge 15:10 and arranged the halves o each other; 7925
Ex 14: 2 directly o Baal Zephon. 4200+5790+7156
14: 9 near Pi Hahiroth, o Baal Zephon. 4200+7156
26: 5 with the loops o each other. 7691
26:35 the tabernacle and put the lampstand o it on 5790
30: 4 two on o sides— 7396+7521
36:12 with the loops o each other. 7691
37:27 two on o sides— 7396+7521
40:24 of Meeting o the table on the south side of 5790
Dt 1: 1 o Suph, between Paran and Tophel, Laban, 4578
34: 6 in the valley o Beth Peor, 4578
Jos 3:16 So the people crossed over o Jericho. 5584
1Sa 20:25 o Jonathan, and Abner sat next to Saul, 7756
2Sa 16:13 along the hillside o him, 4200+6645
1Ki 20:27 The Israelites camped o them 5584
20:29 For seven days they camped o each other, 5790
21:10 But seat two scoundrels o him 5584
21:13 Then two scoundrels came and sat o him 5584
1Ch 19:17 and formed his battle lines o them. 448
2Ch 7: 6 O the Levites, the priests blew their trumpets 5584
Ne 3:10 of Harumaph made repairs o his house, 5584
3:16 made repairs up to a point o the tombs 5584
3:25 Palal son of Uzai worked o the angle 4946+5584
3:26 to a point o the Water Gate toward the east 5584
3:29 of Immer made repairs o his house. 5584
3:30 made repairs o his living quarters. 5584
3:31 and the merchants, o the Inspection Gate, 5584
12: 9 stood o them in the services. 4200+5584
12:24 who stood o them to give praise 4200+5584
12:38 proceeded in the o direction. 4578
Eze 16:34 in your prostitution you are the o of others; 2201
16:34 You are the very o, for you give payment 2201
40:13 of one alcove to the top of the o *one;* 2257S
40:13 from one parapet opening to the o one. 5584
40:22 with its portico o them. 4200+7156
40:23 He measured from one gate to the o *one;* 9133S
40:26 with its portico o them; 4200+7156
42: 1 to the rooms o the temple courtyard 5584
42: 1 the temple courtyard and o the outer wall 5584
42: 3 from the inner court and in the section o 5584
42:10 temple courtyard and o the outer wall, 448+7156
46: 9 but each is to go out the o gate. 5790
47:20 be the boundary to a point o Lebo Hamath. 5790
Da 12: 5 this bank of the river and one on the o bank. 2178
Mt 27:61 and the other Mary were sitting there o *595*
Mk 12:41 Jesus sat down o the place where *2978*
13: 3 on the Mount of Olives o the temple, *2978*
Jn 6:22 the crowd that had stayed on the o shore of *4305*
Ac 27: 7 we sailed to the lee of Crete, o Salmone. *2848*

OPPOSITION (7) [OPPOSE]
Nu 16:19 Korah had gathered all his followers in o to 6584
16:42 when the assembly gathered in o to Moses 6584
20: 2 people gathered in o to Moses and Aaron. 6584
Jdg 9:25 In o to him these citizens of Shechem 4200
Ac 6: 9 O arose, however, from members of *482*
1Th 2: 2 to tell you his gospel in spite of strong o. *74*
Heb 12: 3 Consider him who endured such o *517*

OPPRESS (28) [OPPRESSED, OPPRESSES, OPPRESSING, OPPRESSION, OPPRESSIVE, OPPRESSOR, OPPRESSORS]
Ex 1:11 over them to o them with forced labor, 6700
22:21 "Do not mistreat an alien or o him, 4315
23: 9 "*Do* not o an alien; 4315
Dt 23:16 *Do* not o him. 3561
2Sa 7:10 Wicked people *will* not o them anymore, 6700
1Ch 16:21 He allowed no man to o them; 6943
17: 9 Wicked people *will* not o them anymore, 1162
Job 10: 3 Does it please you *to* o me, 6943
37:23 and great righteousness, *he does* not o. 6700
Ps 89:22 no wicked man *will* o him. 6700
94: 5 *they* o your inheritance. 6700
105:14 He allowed no one to o them; 6943
119:122 *let* not the arrogant o me. 6943
Isa 3: 5 People *will* o each other— 5601
3:12 Youths o my people, 5601
Jer 7: 6 if *you do* not o the alien, 6943
30:20 I will punish all *who* o them. 4315
Eze 18: 7 *He does* not o anyone, 3561
18:16 not o anyone or require a pledge for a loan. 3561
22:29 *they* o the poor and needy and mistreat 3561
45: 8 my princes *will* no longer o my people 3561
Da 7:25 against the Most High and o his saints 10106
Am 4: 1 you *women who* o the poor and crush 6943
5:12 *You* o the righteous and take bribes 7674
6:14 *that will* o you all the way 4315
Zec 7:10 *Do* not o the widow or the fatherless, 6943
11: 6 *They will* o the land, 4198
Mal 3: 5 who o the widows and the fatherless, NIH

OPPRESSED (47) [OPPRESS]
Ex 1:12 But the more they *were* o, 6700
Dt 28:29 day after day you will be o and robbed, 6943
Jdg 2:18 on them as they groaned under *those who* o 4315
4: 3 and *had* cruelly o the Israelites 4315
10: 8 For eighteen years they o all the Israelites NIH
10:12 the Maonites o you and you cried to me 4315
1Sa 10:18 of Egypt and all the kingdoms that o you.' 4315
12: 3 Whom *have I* o? 8368
12: 4 "You have not cheated or o us," 8368
2Ki 13:22 Hazael king of Aram o Israel throughout 4315
2Ch 16:10 At the same time Asa brutally o some of 8368
Ne 9:27 over to their enemies, *who* o them. 7674
9:27 when they were o they cried out to you. 7650
Job 20:19 *he has* o the poor and left them destitute; 8368
Ps 9: 9 The LORD is a refuge for the o, 1916
10:18 defending the fatherless and the o, 1916
42: 9 go about mourning, o by the enemy?" 4316
43: 2 go about mourning, o by the enemy? 4316
74:21 Do not let the o retreat in disgrace; 1916
82: 3 maintain the rights of the poor and o. 8133
103: 6 and justice for all the o. 6943
106:42 Their enemies o them and subjected them 4315
129: 1 *They have* greatly o me from my youth— 7675
129: 2 *they have* greatly o me from my youth, 7675
146: 7 of the o and gives food to the hungry. 6943
Pr 15:15 All the days of the o are wretched, 6714
16:19 and among the o than to share plunder with 6705
31: 5 and deprive all the o of their rights. 1201+6715
Ecc 4: 1 I saw the tears of the o— 6943
5: 8 If you see the poor o in a district, 6945
Isa 1:17 Seek justice, encourage the o. 2787
10: 2 and withhold justice from the o 6714
26: 6 the feet of the o, the footsteps of the poor. 6714
52: 4 lately, Assyria *has* o them. 6943
53: 7 He was o and afflicted, 5601
58: 6 to set the o free and break every yoke? 8368
58:10 the hungry and satisfy the needs of the o, 6700
Jer 50:33 "The people of Israel *are* o, 6943
Eze 22: 7 *they have* o the alien and 928+2021+6913+6945
Da 4:27 your wickedness by being kind to the o. 10559
Hos 5:11 Ephraim *is* o, trampled in judgment, 6943
Am 2: 7 of the ground and deny justice to the o. 6705
Zep 3:19 At that time I will deal with all *who* o you; 6700
Zec 10: 2 the people wander like sheep o for lack of 6700
11: 7 particularly the o *of* the flock. 6714
Lk 4:18 sight for the blind, to release the o, *2575*
Ac 7:19 and o our forefathers by forcing them *2808*

OPPRESSES (4) [OPPRESS]
Pr 14:31 *He who* o the poor shows contempt 6943
22:16 *He who* o the poor to increase his wealth 6943
28: 3 A ruler *who* o the poor is like a driving rain 6943
Eze 18:12 *He* o the poor and needy. 3561

OPPRESSING (3) [OPPRESS]
Ex 3: 9 the way the Egyptians *are* o them. 4315
Nu 10: 9 against an enemy who *is* o you, 7675
2Ki 13: 4 how severely the king of Aram *was* o 4315+4316

OPPRESSION (20) [OPPRESS]
Dt 26: 7 and saw our misery, toil and o. 4316
28:33 but cruel o all your days. 6943
Job 35: 9 "Men cry out under a load of o; 6935
Ps 12: 5 Because of the o *of* the weak and 8719
44:24 and forget our misery and o? 4316
72:14 He will rescue them from o and violence, 9412
73: 8 in their arrogance they threaten o. 6945
107:39 and they were humbled by o, 6808
119:134 Redeem me from the o *of* men, 6945
Ecc 4: 1 the o that was taking place under the sun: 6935
Isa 30:12 relied on o and depended on deceit, 6945
53: 8 By o and judgment he was taken away. 6808
58: 9 "If you do away with the yoke of o, NIH
59:13 fomenting o and revolt, 6945
Jer 6: 6 it is filled with o. 6945
22:17 on shedding innocent blood and on o 6945
Eze 45: 9 up your violence and o and do what is just 8719
Hos 8:10 They will begin to waste away under the o 5362
Am 3: 9 within her and the o among her people." 6935
Ac 7:34 I have indeed seen the o of my people *2810*

OPPRESSIVE (3) [OPPRESS]

Jdg 6: 2 Because the power of Midian *was so* **o**, 6451
Ps 73:16 I tried to understand all this, it was **o** to me 6662
Isa 10: 1 to those who issue **o** decrees, 6662

OPPRESSOR (14) [OPPRESS]

Ps 72: 4 he will crush the **o**. 6943
78:42 the day he redeemed them from the **o**, 7640
Pr 29:13 and the **o** have this in common: 408+9412
Isa 9: 4 the rod of their **o**. 5601
14: 4 How the **o** has come to an end! 5601
16: 4 The **o** will come to an end, 5160
51:13 because of the wrath of the **o**, 7439
51:13 For where is the wrath of the **o**? 7439
Jer 21:12 of his **o** the one who has been robbed, 6943
22: 3 of his **o** the one who has been robbed. 6934
25:38 because of the sword of the **o** and because 3561
46:16 away from the sword of the **o**.' 3561
50:16 the **o** let everyone return to his own people, 3561
Zec 9: 8 Never again will an **o** overrun my people, 5601

OPPRESSORS (9) [OPPRESS]

Jdg 6: 9 of Egypt and from the hand of all your **o**. 4315
Ps 27:11 lead me in a straight path because of my **o**. 8806
119:121 do not leave me to my **o**. 6943
Ecc 4: 1 power was on the side of their **o**— 6943
Isa 14: 2 of their captors and rule over their **o**. 5601
19:20 to the LORD because of their **o**, 4315
49:26 I will make your **o** eat their own flesh; 3561
60:14 sons of your **o** will come bowing before you 6700
Zep 3: 1 Woe to the city of **o**, rebellious and defiled! 3561

OPTIONS (2)

2Sa 24:12 I am giving you **three** *o*. AIT
1Ch 21:10 I am giving you **three** *o*. AIT

OR (1970)

Ge 3: 3 and you must not touch it, **o** you will die.' " 7153
13: 8 **o** between your herdsmen and mine, 2256
14:23 not even a thread **o** the thong of a sandal, 2256
17:12 including those born in your household **o** 2256
17:13 *Whether* born in your household **o** bought 2256
17:23 in his household **o** bought with his money, 2256
17:27 in his household **o** bought from a foreigner, 2256
19:12 sons-in-law, sons **o** daughters, 2256
19:12 **o** anyone else in the city who belongs 2256
19:15 **o** you will be swept away when 7153
19:17 the mountains **o** you will be swept away!" 7153
19:33 of it when she lay down **o** when she got up. 2256
19:35 of it when she lay down **o** when she got up. 2256
21:23 with me **o** my children or my descendants. 2256
21:23 with me or my children **o** my descendants. 2256
24:21 to learn whether **o** not 561
24:50 we can say nothing to you one way **o** 196
24:55 "Let the girl remain with us ten days **o** so; 196
26:11 "Anyone who molests this man **o** his wife 2256
27:21 whether you really are my son Esau **o** 561
30: 1 "Give me children, **o** I'll die!" 401+561+2256
30:32 from them every speckled **o** spotted sheep, 2256
30:32 and every spotted **o** speckled goat. 2256
30:33 in my possession that is not speckled **o** 2256
30:33 **o** any lamb that is not dark-colored, 2256
30:35 the male goats that were streaked **o** spotted, 2256
30:35 the speckled **o** spotted female goats 2256
30:39 And they bore young that were streaked **o** NIH
30:39 that were streaked or speckled **o** spotted. 2256
31:10 the flock were streaked, speckled **o** spotted. 2256
31:12 the flock are streaked, speckled **o** spotted, 2256
31:24 to say anything to Jacob, either good **o** bad. 6330
31:29 to say anything to Jacob, either good **o** bad. 6330
31:39 from me for whatever was stolen by day **o** 2256
31:43 **o** about the children they have borne? 196
31:50 If you mistreat my daughters **o** if 2256
38:23 **o** we will become a laughingstock. 7153
39:10 he refused to go to bed with her **o** even be NIH
41:44 without your word no one will lift hand **o** 2256
44: 8 So why would we steal silver **o** gold 196
44:19 'Do you have a father **o** a brother?' 196
Ex 1:10 we must deal shrewdly with them **o** 7153
4: 1 "What if they do not believe me **o** listen 2256
4: 8 "If they do not believe you **o** pay attention 2256
4: 9 But if they do not believe these two signs **o** 2256
4:11 Who makes him deaf **o** mute? 196
4:11 Who gives him sight **o** makes him blind? 196
5: 3 **o** he may strike us with plagues or with 7153
5: 3 or he may strike us with plagues **o** with 196
5:14 of bricks yesterday **o** today, 1685
9:14 **o** this time I will send the full force 3954
10:15 Nothing green remained on tree **o** plant 2256
10:23 No one could see anyone else **o** 2256
11: 6 worse than there has ever been **o** ever will 2256
11: 7 not a dog will bark at any man **o** animal.' 2256
12: 5 and you may take them from the sheep **o** 2256
12: 9 Do not eat the meat raw **o** cooked in water, 2256
12:19 whether he is an alien **o** native-born. 2256
13: 2 whether man **o** animal." 2256
13:21 so that they could travel by day **o** night. 2256
16:24 and it did not stink **o** get maggots in it. 2256
17: 7 "Is the LORD among us **o** not?" 561
19:12 that you do not go up the mountain **o** touch 2256
19:13 surely be stoned **o** shot with arrows; 196
19:13 Whether man **o** animal, 561
19:22 **o** the LORD will break out against them." 7153
19:24 **o** he will break out against them." 7153
Ex 20: 4 the form of anything in heaven above **o** on 2256
20: 4 on the earth beneath **o** in the waters below. 2256
20: 5 not bow down to them **o** worship them; 2256
20:10 neither you, nor your son **o** daughter, 2256
20:10 nor your manservant **o** maidservant, 2256
20:17 **o** his manservant or maidservant, 2256
20:17 or his manservant **o** maidservant, 2256
20:17 his ox **o** donkey, 2256
20:17 **o** anything that belongs to your neighbor." 2256
20:19 do not have God speak to us **o** we will die." 7153
20:23 do not make for yourselves gods of silver **o** 2256
21: 4 a wife and she bears him sons **o** daughters, 196
21: 6 the door **o** the doorpost and pierce his ear 196
21:15 "Anyone who attacks his father **o** his mother 2256
21:16 and either sells him **o** still has him 2256
21:17 "Anyone who curses his father **o** his mother 2256
21:18 a stone **o** with his fist and he does not die 196
21:20 a man beats his male **o** female slave with 196
21:21 if the slave gets up after a day **o** two, 196
21:26 "If a man hits a manservant **o** maidservant 196
21:27 the tooth of a manservant **o** maidservant, 196
21:28 "If a bull gores a man **o** a woman to death, 196
21:29 not kept it penned up and it kills a man **o** 196
21:31 also applies if the bull gores a son **o** 196
21:32 If the bull gores a male **o** female slave, 196
21:33 a man uncovers a pit **o** digs one and fails 196
21:33 or digs one and fails to cover it and an ox **o** 196
22: 1 an ox **o** a sheep and slaughters it or sells it, 196
22: 1 an ox or a sheep and slaughters it **o** sells it, 196
22: 4 whether ox **o** donkey or sheep— 6330
22: 4 whether ox or donkey **o** sheep— 6330
22: 5 "If a man grazes his livestock in a field **o** 196
22: 5 from the best of his own field **o** vineyard. 2256
22: 6 of grain **o** standing grain or the whole field, 196
22: 6 of grain or standing grain **o** the whole field, 196
22: 7 "If a man gives his neighbor silver **o** goods 196
22: 9 **o** any other lost property NIH
22:10 a sheep **o** any other animal to his neighbor 2256
22:10 and it dies **o** is injured or is taken away 196
22:10 for safekeeping and it dies or is injured **o** 196
22:14 and it is injured **o** dies while the owner is 196
22:21 "Do not mistreat an alien **o** oppress him, 2256
22:22 not take advantage of a widow **o** an orphan. 2256
22:28 "Do not blaspheme God **o** curse the ruler 2256
22:29 from your granaries **o** your vats. 2256
23: 4 "If you come across your enemy's ox **o** 196
23: 7 and do not put an innocent **o** honest person 2256
23:24 down before their gods **o** worship them 2256
23:24 or worship them **o** follow their practices. 2256
23:26 and none will miscarry **o** be barren 2256
23:32 a covenant with them **o** with their gods. 2256
23:33 **o** they will cause you to sin against me, 7153
28:43 of Meeting **o** approach the altar to minister 196
29:34 the ordination ram **o** any bread is left over 2256
30: 9 not offer on this altar any other incense **o** 2256
30: 9 or any burnt offering **o** grain offering, 2256
30:14 those twenty years old **o** more, 2256
34: 3 come with you **o** be seen anywhere on 1685+2256
34:12 **o** they will be a snare among you. 7153
34:19 whether from herd **o** flock. 2256
34:28 and forty nights without eating bread **o** 2256
35:23 purple **o** scarlet yarn or fine linen, 2256
35:23 purple or scarlet yarn **o** fine linen, 2256
35:23 or scarlet yarn or fine linen, **o** goat hair, 2256
35:23 ram skins dyed red **o** hides 2256
35:24 of silver **o** bronze brought it as an offering 2256
35:25 blue, purple **o** scarlet yarn or fine linen. NIH
35:25 blue, purple or scarlet yarn **o** fine linen. 2256
36: 6 "No man **o** woman is to make anything else 2256
38:26 twenty years old **o** more, a total of 603,550 2256
40:32 the Tent of Meeting **o** approached the altar, 2256
Lev 1: 2 an animal from **either** the herd **o** the flock. 2256
1:10 from **either** the sheep **o** the goats, 196
1:14 he is to offer a dove **o** a young pigeon. 196
2: 4 **o** wafers made without yeast and spread 2256
2:11 for you are not to burn any yeast **o** honey in 2256
3: 1 whether male **o** female, 561
3: 3 that covers the inner parts **o** is connected 2256
3: 6 to offer a male **o** female without defect. 196
3: 9 that covers the inner parts **o** is connected 2256
3:14 that covers the inner parts **o** is connected 2256
3:17 You must not eat any fat **o** any blood.' " 2256
4: 8 that covers the inner parts **o** is connected 2256
5: 1 to testify regarding something he has seen **o** 196
5: 2 " '**O** if a person touches anything
ceremonially unclean— 196
5: 2 the carcasses of unclean wild animals **o** 196
5: 2 of unclean livestock **o** of unclean creatures 196
5: 3 " '**O** if he touches human uncleanness— 196
5: 4 " '**O** if a person thoughtlessly takes an oath 196
5: 4 **whether** good **o** evil— 196
5: 6 to the LORD a female lamb **o** goat from 196
5: 7 to bring two doves **o** two young pigeons to 196
5:11 he cannot afford two doves **o** two young 196
5:11 He must not put oil **o** incense on it, 2256
6: 2 about something entrusted to him **o** left 196
6: 2 to him or left in his care **o** stolen, 196
6: 2 **o** if he cheats him, 196
6: 3 **o** if he finds lost property and lies about it, 196
6: 3 **o** if he swears falsely, 2256
6: 3 **o** if he commits any such sin NIH
6: 4 he must return what he has stolen **o** taken 196
6: 4 **o** what was entrusted to him, 196
6: 4 **o** the lost property he found, 196
6: 5 **o** whatever it was he swore falsely about. 196
7: 9 Every grain offering baked in an oven **o** 2256
7: 9 or cooked in a pan **o** on a griddle belongs 2256
Lev 7:10 **whether** mixed with oil **o** 2256
7:16 the result of a vow **o** is a freewill offering, 196
7:21 **whether** human uncleanness **o** 196
7:21 or an unclean animal **o** any unclean, 196
7:23 'Do not eat any of the fat of cattle, sheep **o** 2256
7:24 The fat of an animal found dead **o** torn 2256
7:26 you must not eat the blood of any bird **o** 2256
10: 6 **o** you will die and the LORD will 2256+4202
10: 7 to the Tent of Meeting **o** you will die, 7153
10: 9 "You and your sons are not to drink wine **o** 2256
10: 9 the Tent of Meeting, **o** you will die. 2256+4202
11: 4 " 'There are some that only chew the cud **o** 2256
11: 8 not eat their meat **o** touch their carcasses; 2256
11:10 in the seas **o** streams that do not have fins 2256
11:10 **whether** among all the swarming things **o** 2256
11:22 katydid, cricket **o** grasshopper. 2256
11:26 a split hoof not completely divided **o** 2256
11:32 **whether** it is made of wood, cloth, hide **o** 196
11:35 an oven **o** cooking pot must be broken up. 2256
11:36 A spring, however, **o** a cistern 2256
11:42 **whether** it moves on its belly **o** 2256
11:42 or walks on all fours **o** on many feet; 6330
11:43 by means of them **o** be made unclean 2256
12: 4 She must not touch anything sacred **o** go to 2256
12: 6 of her purification for a son **o** daughter are 196
12: 6 a young pigeon **o** a dove for a sin offering. 196
12: 7 for the woman who gives birth to a boy **o** 196
12: 8 to bring two doves **o** two young pigeons, 196
13: 2 "When anyone has a swelling **o** a rash or 196
13: 2 "When anyone has a swelling or a rash **o** 196
13: 2 he must be brought to Aaron the priest **o** 196
13:19 a white swelling **o** reddish-white spot 196
13:24 and a reddish-white **o** white spot appears in 196
13:29 "If a man **o** woman has a sore on the head 196
13:29 a man or woman has a sore on the head **o** 196
13:30 an infectious disease of the head **o** chin. 196
13:38 "When a man **o** woman has white spots on 196
13:42 a reddish-white sore on his bald head **o** 196
13:42 on his head **o** forehead. 196
13:43 on his head **o** forehead is reddish-white like 196
13:47 any woolen **o** linen clothing, 196
13:48 any woven **o** knitted material of linen 196
13:48 any woven or knitted material of linen **o** 2256
13:48 any leather **o** anything made of leather— 196
13:49 **o** leather, or woven or knitted material, 196
13:49 or leather, **o** woven or knitted material, 196
13:49 or leather, or woven **o** knitted material, 196
13:49 **o** any leather article, is greenish or reddish, 196
13:49 or any leather article, is greenish **o** reddish, 196
13:51 **o** the woven or knitted material, 196
13:51 or the woven **o** knitted material, 196
13:51 **o** the leather, whatever its use, 196
13:52 **o** the woven or knitted material of wool 196
13:52 or the woven **o** knitted material of wool 196
13:52 or the woven or knitted material of wool **o** 196
13:52 **o** any leather article that has 196
13:53 **o** the woven or knitted material, 196
13:53 or the woven **o** knitted material, 196
13:53 **o** the leather article, 196
13:55 **whether** the mildew has affected one side **o** 196
13:56 the contaminated part out of the clothing, **o** 196
13:56 **o** the woven or knitted material. 196
13:56 or the woven **o** knitted material. 196
13:57 **o** in the woven or knitted material, 196
13:57 or in the woven **o** knitted material, 196
13:57 **o** in the leather article, it is spreading, 196
13:58 **o** the woven or knitted material, 196
13:58 or the woven **o** knitted material, 196
13:58 **o** any leather article that has been washed 196
13:59 by mildew in woolen **o** linen clothing, 196
13:59 woven **o** knitted material, 196
13:59 **o** any leather article, 196
13:59 for pronouncing them clean **o** unclean. 196
14:22 and two doves **o** two young pigeons, 196
14:30 Then he shall sacrifice the doves **o** 196
14:37 and if it has greenish **o** reddish depressions 196
14:47 Anyone who sleeps **o** eats in 2256
14:55 for mildew in clothing **o** in a house, 2256
14:56 and for a swelling, a rash **o** a bright spot, 2256
14:57 to determine when something is clean **o** 2256
15: 3 **Whether** it continues flowing from his
body **o** is blocked, 196
15:14 On the eighth day he must take two doves **o** 196
15:17 Any clothing **o** leather that has semen 2256
15:23 the bed **o** anything she was sitting on, 196
15:25 a time other than her monthly period **o** has 196
15:29 the eighth day she must take two doves **o** 196
15:33 for a man **o** a woman with a discharge, 2256
16: 2 on the ark, **o** else he will die, 2256
16:29 **whether** native-born **o** an alien living 2256
17: 3 a lamb **o** a goat in the camp or outside of it 196
17: 3 a lamb or a goat in the camp **o** outside of it 196
17: 8 'Any Israelite **o** any alien living 2256
17: 8 among them who offers a burnt offering **o** 196
17:10 " 'Any Israelite **o** any alien living 2256
17:13 " 'Any Israelite **o** any alien living 2256
17:13 among you who hunts any animal **o** bird 196
17:15 " 'Anyone, whether native-born **o** alien, 2256
17:15 who eats anything found dead **o** torn 2256
18: 9 **either** your father's daughter **o** 196
18: 9 **whether** she was born in the same home **o** 196
18:10 with your son's daughter **o** 196
18:17 **either** her son's daughter **o** 2256
19: 4 not turn to idols **o** make gods of cast metal 2256
19: 6 the day you sacrifice it **o** on the next day; 2256
19: 9 not reap to the very edges of your field **o** 2256
19:10 over your vineyard a second time **o** pick up 2256

Lev	19:13	" 'Do not defraud your neighbor **o** rob him.	2256
	19:14	the deaf **o** put a stumbling block in front of	2256
	19:15	not show partiality to the poor **o** favoritism	2256
	19:18	" 'Do not seek revenge **o** bear a grudge	2256
	19:20	not been ransomed **o** given her freedom,	196
	19:26	" 'Do not practice divination **o** sorcery.	2256
	19:27	the hair at the sides of your head **o** clip off	2256
	19:28	the dead **o** put tattoo marks on yourselves.	2256
	19:29	**o** the land will turn to prostitution and	2256+4202
	19:31	not turn to mediums **o** seek out spiritists,	2256
	19:35	when measuring length, weight **o** quantity.	2256
	20: 2	'Any Israelite **o** any alien living	2256
	20: 9	" 'If anyone curses his father **o** mother,	2256
	20: 9	He has cursed his father **o** his mother,	2256
	20:17	daughter of **either** his father **o** his mother,	196
	20:19	of **either** your mother **o** your father, for	2256
	20:25	not defile yourselves by any animal **o** bird	2256
	20:25	or bird **o** anything that moves along	2256
	20:27	" 'A man **o** woman who is a medium	196
	20:27	" 'A man or woman who is a medium **o**	196
	21: 2	such as his mother **o** father,	2256
	21: 2	his son **o** daughter, his brother,	2256
	21: 3	**o** an unmarried sister who is dependent	2256
	21: 5	not shave their heads **o** shave off the edges	2256
	21: 5	the edges of their beards **o** cut their bodies.	2256
	21: 7	not marry women defiled by prostitution **o**	2256
	21:10	must not let his hair become unkempt **o**	2256
	21:11	even for his father **o** mother,	2256
	21:12	the sanctuary of his God **o** desecrate it,	2256
	21:14	**o** a woman defiled by prostitution,	2256
	21:18	no man who is blind **o** lame,	196
	21:18	disfigured **o** deformed;	196
	21:19	no man with a crippled foot **o** hand,	196
	21:20	**o** who is hunchbacked or dwarfed,	196
	21:20	or who is hunchbacked **o** dwarfed,	196
	21:20	**o** who has any eye defect,	196
	21:20	**o** who has festering or running sores	196
	21:20	or who has festering **o** running sores	196
	21:20	or who has festering or running sores **o**	196
	21:23	not go near the curtain **o** approach the altar,	2256
	22: 4	of Aaron has an infectious skin disease **o**	196
	22: 4	a corpse **o** by anyone who has an emission	196
	22: 5	**o** if he touches any crawling thing	196
	22: 5	**o** any person who makes him unclean,	196
	22: 8	He must not eat anything found dead **o** torn	2256
	22:10	of a priest **o** his hired worker eat it.	2256
	22:11	**o** if a slave is born in his household,	2256
	22:13	if a priest's daughter becomes a widow **o**	2256
	22:18	**either** an Israelite **o** an alien living	2256
	22:18	**either** to fulfill a vow **o** as a freewill	2256
	22:19	sheep **o** goats in order that it may	2256
	22:21	from the herd **o** flock a fellowship offering	196
	22:21	to the LORD to fulfill a special vow **o** as	196
	22:21	without defect **o** blemish to be acceptable.	4202
	22:22	the injured **o** the maimed,	196
	22:22	**o** anything with warts or festering	196
	22:22	with warts **o** festering or running sores.	196
	22:22	with warts or festering **o** running sores.	196
	22:23	an ox **o** a sheep that is deformed or stunted,	2256
	22:23	an ox or a sheep that is deformed **o** stunted,	2256
	22:24	are bruised, crushed, torn **o** cut.	2256
	22:27	a lamb **o** a goat is born,	196
	22:28	not slaughter a cow **o** a sheep and its young	196
	23:14	**o** roasted or new grain,	2256
	23:14	or roasted **o** new grain,	2256
	23:22	not reap to the very edges of your field **o**	2256
	24:16	Whether an alien **o** native-born,	3869
	25: 4	not sow your fields **o** prune your vineyards.	2256
	25: 5	Do not reap what grows of itself **o** harvest	2256
	25:11	not reap what grows of itself **o** harvest	2256
	25:14	of your countrymen **o** buy any from him,	196
	25:20	if we do not plant **o** harvest our crops?"	2256
	25:35	help him as you would an alien **o**	2256
	25:37	You must not lend him money at interest **o**	2256
	25:40	as a hired worker **o** a temporary resident	NIH
	25:47	" 'If an alien **o** a temporary resident	2256
	25:47	the alien living among you **o** to a member	196
	25:49	An uncle **o** a cousin or any blood relative	196
	25:49	An uncle or a cousin **o** any blood relative	196
	25:49	**O** if he prospers, he may redeem himself.	196
	26: 1	" 'Do not make idols **o** set up an image or	2256
	26: 1	or set up an image **o** a sacred stone	2256
	26:44	I will not reject them **o** abhor them so as	2256
	27: 7	If it is a person sixty years old **o** more,	2256
	27:10	not exchange it **o** substitute a good one for	2256
	27:10	**o** a bad one for a good one;	196
	27:12	who will judge its quality as good **o** bad	2256
	27:14	the priest will judge its quality as good **o**	2256
	27:20	**o** if he has sold it to someone else,	2256
	27:26	whether an ox **o** a sheep, it is the LORD's.	561
	27:28	whether man **o** animal or family land—	2256
	27:28	whether man or animal **o** family land—	2256
	27:28	may be sold **o** redeemed;	2256
	27:30	from the soil **o** fruit from the trees, belongs	4946
	27:33	from the bad **o** make any substitution.	2256
Nu	1: 3	the men in Israel twenty years old **o** more	2256
	1:18	and the men twenty years old **o** more	2256
	1:20	All the men twenty years old **o** more	2256
	1:22	All the men twenty years old **o** more	2256
	1:24	All the men twenty years old **o** more	2256
	1:26	All the men twenty years old **o** more	2256
	1:28	All the men twenty years old **o** more	2256
	1:30	All the men twenty years old **o** more	2256
	1:32	All the men twenty years old **o** more	2256
	1:34	All the men twenty years old **o** more	2256
	1:36	All the men twenty years old **o** more	2256
	1:38	All the men twenty years old **o** more	2256
Nu	1:40	All the men twenty years old **o** more	2256
	1:42	All the men twenty years old **o** more	2256
	1:45	All the Israelites twenty years old **o** more	2256
	1:49	not count the tribe of Levi **o** include them	2256
	3:13	whether man **o** animal.	6330
	3:15	Count every male a month old **o** more."	2256
	3:22	number of all the males a month old **o** more	2256
	3:28	number of all the males a month old **o** more	2256
	3:34	number of all the males a month old **o** more	2256
	3:39	including every male a month old **o** more,	2256
	3:40	a month old **o** more and make a list	2256
	3:43	of firstborn males a month old **o** more,	2256
	4:15	But they must not touch the holy things **o**	2256
	4:20	even for a moment, **o** they will die."	2256
	4:27	whether carrying **o** doing other work,	2256
	5: 2	an infectious skin disease **o** a discharge	2256
	5: 2	**o** who is ceremonially unclean because of	2256
	5: 6	a man **o** woman wrongs another in any way	196
	5:14	**o** if he is jealous and suspects her even	196
	5:15	He must not pour oil on it **o** put incense	2256
	5:30	**o** when feelings of jealousy come over	196
	6: 2	'If a man **o** woman wants to make	196
	6: 3	from wine **o** from other fermented drink.	2256
	6: 3	not drink grape juice **o** eat grapes or raisins.	2256
	6: 3	not drink grape juice or eat **grapes o raisins.**	2256+3313+4300+6694
	6: 4	not even the seeds **o** skins.	2256
	6: 7	Even if his own father **o** mother or brother	2256
	6: 7	Even if his own father or mother **o** brother	NIH
	6: 7	or mother or brother **o** sister dies,	2256
	6:10	the eighth day he must bring two doves **o**	196
	8:17	whether man **o** animal, is mine.	2256
	8:24	Men twenty-five years old **o** more	2256
	9:10	of you **o** your descendants are unclean	196
	9:10	of a dead body **o** are away on a journey,	196
	9:12	They must not leave any of it till morning **o**	2256
	9:21	Whether by day **o** by night,	2256
	9:22	over the tabernacle for two days **o** a month	196
	9:22	the tabernacle for two days or a month **o**	196
	11: 8	then ground it in a handmill **o** crushed it in	196
	11: 8	They cooked it in a pot **o** made it	2256
	11:19	**o** two days, or five, ten or twenty days,	2256
	11:19	or two days, **o** five, ten or twenty days,	2256
	11:19	or two days, or five, ten **o** twenty days,	2256
	11:23	You will now see whether **o** not	561
	13:18	the people who live there are strong **o** weak,	2022
	13:18	or weak, few **o** many.	561
	13:19	Is it good **o** bad?	561
	13:19	Are they unwalled **o** fortified?	561
	13:20	Is it fertile **o** poor?	561
	13:20	Are there trees on it **o** not?	561
	14: 2	**O** in this desert!	196
	14:29	every one of you twenty years old **o** more	2256
	15: 3	from the herd **o** the flock,	196
	15: 3	**whether** burnt offerings **o** sacrifices,	196
	15: 3	for special vows **o** freewill offerings	196
	15: 3	or freewill offerings **o** festival offerings—	196
	15: 5	With each lamb for the burnt offering **o**	196
	15: 8	a young bull as a burnt offering **o** sacrifice,	196
	15: 8	for a special vow **o** a fellowship offering to	196
	15:11	Each bull **o** ram, each lamb or young goat,	196
	15:11	Each bull or ram, each lamb **o** young goat,	196
	15:14	whenever an alien **o** anyone else living	196
	15:29	**whether** he is a native-born Israelite **o**	2256
	15:30	**whether** native-born **o** alien,	2256
	16:14	into a land flowing with milk and honey **o**	2256
	16:26	**o** you will be swept away because	7153
	16:40	**o** he would become like Korah	2256+4202
	18: 3	the furnishings of the sanctuary **o** the altar,	2256
	18: 3	**o** both they and you will die.	2256+4202
	18: 9	**whether** grain **o** sin or guilt offerings,	2256
	18: 9	whether grain or sin **o** guilt offerings,	2256
	18:17	a sheep **o** a goat; they are holy.	196
	18:22	**o** they will bear the consequences	NIH
	18:27	as grain from the threshing floor **o** juice	2256
	18:30	of the threshing floor **o** the winepress.	2256
	19: 2	to bring you a red heifer without defect **o**	401
	19:16	with a sword **o** someone who has died	196
	19:16	**o** anyone who touches a human bone or	196
	19:16	who touches a human bone **o** a grave,	196
	19:18	a human bone **o** a grave	196
	19:18	or a grave **o** someone who has been killed	196
	19:18	someone who has been killed **o** someone	196
	20: 5	It has no grain **o** figs,	2256
	20: 5	grapevines **o** pomegranates.	2256
	20:17	not go through any field **o** vineyard,	2256
	20:17	**o** drink water from any well.	2256
	20:17	the right **o** to the left until we have passed	2256
	20:19	we **o** our livestock drink any of your water,	2256
	21:22	not turn aside into any field **o** vineyard,	2256
	21:22	**o** drink water from any well.	4202
	22:18	not do anything great **o** small to go beyond	196
	22:26	**either** to the right **o** to the left.	2256
	23:10	of Jacob **o** number the fourth part of Israel?	2256
	24:13	good **o** bad, to go beyond the command of	196
	26: 2	all those twenty years old **o** more	2256
	26: 4	a census of the men twenty years old **o** more	2256
	26:62	a month old **o** more numbered 23,000.	2256
	30: 2	When a man makes a vow to the LORD **o**	196
	30: 3	a vow to the LORD **o** obligates herself by	2256
	30: 4	and her father hears about her vow **o** pledge	2256
	30: 5	none of her vows **o** the pledges	2256
	30: 6	after she makes a vow **o** after her lips utter	196
	30: 7	then her vows **o** the pledges	2256
	30: 8	he nullifies the vow that obligates her **o**	2256
	30: 9	"Any vow **o** obligation taken by a widow	NIH
	30: 9	a widow **o** divorced woman will be binding	2256
Nu	30:10	a vow **o** obligates herself by a pledge	196
	30:11	then all her vows **o** the pledges	2256
	30:12	then none of the vows **o** pledges that came	2256
	30:13	Her husband may confirm **o** nullify	2256
	30:13	or nullify any vow she makes **o** any sworn	2256
	30:14	then he confirms all her vows **o** the pledges	196
	31:19	"All of you who have killed anyone **o**	2256
	31:20	goat hair **o** wood."	2256
	31:28	cattle, donkeys, **sheep o goats.**	7366
	31:30	donkeys, **sheep, goats o** other animals.	7366
	32:11	the men twenty years old **o** more who came	2256
	35:17	**O** if anyone has a stone in his hand	2256
	35:18	**O** if anyone has a wooden object	196
	35:20	with malice aforethought shoves another **o**	196
	35:21	**o** if in hostility he hits him with his fist so	196
	35:22	without hostility someone suddenly shoves another **o** throws something	196
	35:23	**o**, without seeing him, drops a stone	196
Dt	1:16	**whether** the case is between brother Israelites **o** between	2256
	2: 9	not harass the Moabites **o** provoke them	2256
	2:19	do not harass them **o** provoke them to war,	2256
	2:27	not turn aside to the right **o** to the left.	2256
	3:24	in heaven **o** on earth who can do the deeds	2256
	4: 9	not forget the things your eyes have seen **o**	2256
	4:16	**whether** formed like a man **o** a woman,	196
	4:17	**o** like any animal on earth or any bird	NIH
	4:17	on earth **o** any bird that flies in the air,	NIH
	4:18	**o** like any creature that moves along	NIH
	4:18	the ground **o** any fish in the waters below.	NIH
	4:28	which cannot see **o** hear or eat or smell.	2256
	4:28	which cannot see or hear **o** eat or smell.	2256
	4:28	which cannot see or hear or eat **o** smell.	2256
	4:31	he will not abandon **o** destroy you or forget	2256
	4:31	he will not abandon or destroy you **o** forget	2256
	4:32	**o** has anything like it ever been heard of?	196
	4:34	**o** by great and awesome deeds,	2256
	5: 8	the form of anything in heaven above **o** on	2256
	5: 8	on the earth beneath **o** in the waters below.	2256
	5: 9	not bow down to them **o** worship them;	2256
	5:14	neither you, nor your son **o** daughter,	2256
	5:14	nor your manservant **o** maidservant,	2256
	5:14	your donkey **o** any of your animals,	2256
	5:21	on your neighbor's house **o** land,	NIH
	5:21	his manservant **o** maidservant,	2256
	5:21	his ox **o** donkey,	2256
	5:21	**o** anything that belongs to your neighbor."	2256
	5:32	do not turn aside to the right **o** to the left.	2256
	7: 3	Do not give your daughters to their sons **o**	2256
	7:14	of your men **o** women will be childless,	2256
	7:22	**o** the wild animals will multiply	7153
	7:25	**o** you will be ensnared by it,	7153
	7:26	a detestable thing into your house **o** you,	2256
	8: 2	to know what was in your heart, whether **o**	561
	9: 5	It is not because of your righteousness **o**	2256
	9:23	You did not trust him **o** obey him.	2256
	10: 9	That is why the Levites have no share **o**	2256
	11:16	**o** you will be enticed to turn away	7153
	12:12	who have no allotment **o** inheritance	2256
	12:15	as if it were gazelle **o** deer,	2256
	12:17	**o** the firstborn of your herds and flocks,	2256
	12:17	**o** whatever you have vowed to give,	2256
	12:17	**o** your freewill offerings or special gifts.	2256
	12:17	or your freewill offerings **o** special gifts.	2256
	12:22	Eat them as you would gazelle **o** deer.	2256
	12:32	do not add to it **o** take away from it.	2256
	13: 1	If a prophet, **o** one who foretells by dreams,	196
	13: 1	and announces to you a miraculous sign **o**	196
	13: 2	and if the sign **o** wonder	2256
	13: 3	not listen to the words of that prophet **o**	196
	13: 5	That prophet **o** dreamer must be put	196
	13: 6	**o** your son or daughter,	196
	13: 6	or your son **o** daughter,	196
	13: 6	**o** the wife you love,	196
	13: 6	**o** your closest friend secretly entices you,	196
	13: 7	**whether** near **o** far,	196
	13: 8	do not yield to him **o** listen to him.	2256
	13: 8	Do not spare him **o** shield him.	2256
	14: 1	Do not cut yourselves **o** shave the front	2256
	14: 7	of those that chew the cud **o** that have	2256
	14: 7	the rabbit **o** the coney.	2256
	14: 8	not to eat their meat **o** touch their carcasses.	2256
	14:21	**o** you may sell it to a foreigner,	196
	14:26	cattle, sheep, wine **o** other fermented drink,	2256
	14:26	fermented drink, **o** anything you wish.	2256
	14:27	for they have no allotment **o** inheritance	2256
	14:29	that the Levites (who have no allotment **o**	2256
	15: 2	from his fellow Israelite **o** brother,	2256
	15: 7	do not be hardhearted **o** tightfisted	2256
	15:12	If a fellow Hebrew, a man **o** a woman,	196
	15:21	If an animal has a defect, is lame **o** blind,	196
	15:21	is lame or blind, **o** has any serious flaw,	NIH
	15:22	as if it were gazelle **o** deer.	2256
	16: 2	an animal from your flock **o** herd at	2256
	16:19	Do not pervert justice **o** show partiality.	4202
	17: 1	an ox **o** a sheep that has any defect or flaw	2256
	17: 1	an ox or a sheep that has any defect **o** flaw	NIH
	17: 2	a man **o** woman living among you in one of	196
	17: 3	down to them **o** to the sun or the moon or	2256
	17: 3	the sun **o** the moon or the stars of the sky,	196
	17: 3	the sun or the moon **o** the stars of the sky,	196
	17: 5	take the man **o** woman who has done this	196
	17: 6	of two **o** three witnesses a man shall be put	196
	17: 8	whether bloodshed, lawsuits **o** assaults—	1068
	17:11	to the right **o** to the left.	2256
	17:12	for the judge **o** for the priest	196
	17:16	for himself **o** make the people return	2256

Dt	17:17	**o** his heart will be led astray.	2256+4202
	17:20	turn from the law to the right **o** to the left.	2256
	18: 1	are to have no allotment **o** inheritance	2256
	18: 3	the people who sacrifice a bull **o** a sheep:	561
	18:10	among you who sacrifices his son **o**	2256
	18:10	who practices divination **o** sorcery,	2256
	18:11	**o** casts spells, or who is a medium	2256
	18:11	**o** who is a medium or spiritist	2256
	18:11	a medium **o** spiritist or who consults	2256
	18:11	a medium or spiritist **o** who consults	2256
	18:14	to those who practice sorcery **o** divination.	2256
	18:16	great fire anymore, **o** we will die."	2256+4202
	18:20	**o** a prophet who speaks in the name	2256
	18:22	does not take place **o** come true,	2256
	19:15	to convict a man accused of any crime **o**	2256
	19:15	by the testimony of two **o** three witnesses.	196
	20: 3	Do not be fainthearted **o** afraid;	2256
	20: 3	do not be terrified **o** give way to panic	2256
	20: 5	Let him go home, **o** he may die in battle	7153
	20: 6	Let him go home, **o** he may die in battle	7153
	20: 7	Let him go home, **o** he may die in battle	7153
	20: 8	"Is any man afraid **o** fainthearted?	2256
	21: 4	a valley that has not been plowed **o** planted	2256
	21:14	You must not sell her **o** treat her as a slave,	4202
	22: 1	you see your brother's ox **o** sheep straying,	196
	22: 2	near you **o** if you do not know who he is,	2256
	22: 3	if you find your brother's donkey **o** his	2256
	22: 3	or his cloak **o** anything he loses.	2256
	22: 4	If you see your brother's donkey **o** his ox	196
	22: 6	**either** in a tree **o** on the ground,	196
	22: 6	and the mother is sitting on the young **o** on	196
	23: 1	emasculated by crushing **o** cutting may	2256
	23: 3	No Ammonite **o** Moabite or any of his	2256
	23: 3	No Ammonite or Moabite **o** any of his	NIH
	23:17	No Israelite man **o** woman is to become	2256
	23:18	of a female prostitute **o** of a male prostitute	2256
	23:19	whether on money **o** food or anything else	NIH
	23:19	whether on money or food **o** anything else	NIH
	24: 3	**o** if he dies,	196
	24: 5	to war **o** have any other duty laid on him.	2256
	24: 7	and treats him as a slave **o** sells him,	2256
	24:14	**whether** he is a brother Israelite **o**	196
	24:17	Do not deprive the alien **o** the fatherless	NIH
	24:17	**o** take the cloak of the widow as a pledge.	2256
	27:15	"Cursed is the man who carves an image **o**	2256
	27:16	the man who dishonors his father **o**	2256
	27:19	the fatherless **o** the widow."	2256
	27:22	of his father **o** the daughter of his mother."	196
	28:14	to the right **o** to the left,	2256
	28:36	to a nation unknown to you **o** your fathers.	2256
	28:39	but you will not drink the wine **o** gather	2256
	28:50	without respect for the old **o** pity for	2256
	28:51	leave you no grain, new wine **o** oil,	2256
	28:51	nor any calves of your herds **o** lambs	2256
	28:54	on his own brother **o** the wife he loves	2256
	28:54	the wife he loves **o** his surviving children,	2256
	28:56	the husband she loves and her own son **o**	2256
	29: 4	not given you a mind that understands **o**	2256
	29: 4	a mind that understands or eyes that see **o**	2256
	29: 6	and drank no wine **o** other fermented drink.	2256
	29:18	Make sure there is no man **o** woman,	196
	29:18	or woman, clan **o** tribe among you today	196
	30:11	difficult for you **o** beyond your reach.	2256
	31: 6	not be afraid **o** terrified because of them,	2256
	32:30	**o** two put ten thousand to flight,	2256
	32:36	and no one is left, slave **o** free.	2256
	33: 9	He did not recognize his brothers **o**	2256
	33:20	tearing at arm **o** head.	677
	34:12	shown the mighty power **o** performed	2256
Jos	1: 7	do not turn from it to the right **o** to the left,	2256
	5:13	"Are you for us **o** for our enemies?"	561
	7: 3	Send two **o** three thousand men to take it	196
	8:17	Not a man remained in Ai **o** Bethel who did	2256
	10:14	There has never been a day like it before **o**	2256
	15:36	Adithaim and Gederah (**o** Gederothaim)—	2256
	19: 2	It included: Beersheba (**o** Sheba), Moladah,	2256
	20: 9	Any of the Israelites **o** any alien living	2256
	22:19	against the LORD **o** against us by building	2256
	22:22	If this has been in rebellion **o** disobedience	2256
	22:23	**o** to sacrifice fellowship offerings on it,	2256
	22:26	but not for burnt offerings **o** sacrifices.'	2256
	22:28	**o** to our descendants, we will answer:	2256
	23: 6	without turning aside to the right **o** to	2256
	23: 7	not invoke the names of their gods **o** swear	2256
	23: 7	You must not serve them **o** bow down	2256
	24:15	**o** the gods of the Amorites,	561
Jdg	1:27	the people of Beth Shan **o** Taanach or Dor	2256
	1:27	the people of Beth Shan or Taanach **o** Dor	2256
	1:27	of Beth Shan or Taanach or Dor **o** Ibleam	2256
	1:27	or Taanach or Dor or Ibleam **o** Megiddo	2256
	1:30	the Canaanites living in Kitron **o** Nahalol,	2256
	1:31	in Acco **o** Sidon or Ahlab or Aczib	2256
	1:31	or Sidon **o** Ahlab or Aczib or Helbah	2256
	1:31	or Ahlab **o** Aczib or Helbah or Aphek	2256
	1:31	or Aczib **o** Helbah or Aphek or Rehob,	2256
	1:31	or Sidon or Ahlab or Aczib or Helbah **o**	2256
	1:31	or Ahlab or Aczib or Helbah or Aphek **o**	2256
	1:33	in Beth Shemesh **o** Beth Anath;	2256
	5: 8	and not a shield **o** spear was seen	2256
	5:30	a girl **o** two for each man,	NIH
	8:26	the kings of Midian **o** the chains that were	2256
	9: 2	of Jerub-Baal's sons rule over you, **o**	561
	11:15	not take the land of Moab **o** the land of	2256
	11:25	Did he ever quarrel with Israel **o** fight	561
	13: 4	Now see to it that you drink no wine **o** other	2256
	13: 7	drink no wine **o** other fermented drink	2256
	13:14	nor drink any wine **o** other fermented drink	2256
Jdg	13:23	nor shown us all these things **o** now told	2256
	14: 3	among your relatives **o** among all your	2256
	14:15	**o** we will burn you	7153
	14:16	"I haven't even explained it to my father **o**	2256
	18:25	**o** some hot-tempered men will attack you,	7153
	19:13	to reach Gibeah **o** Ramah and spend	196
	19:30	"Such a thing has never been seen **o** done,	2256
	20:28	to battle with Benjamin our brother, **o**	561
	21:22	When their fathers **o** brothers complain	196
Ru	1:16	"Don't urge me to leave you **o** to turn back	NIH
	3:10	the younger men, whether rich **o** poor.	561+2256
	4:10	among his family **o** from the town records.	2256
1Sa	1:15	I have not been drinking wine **o** beer;	2256
	2: 3	"Do not keep talking so proudly **o** let	NIH
	2:14	He would plunge it into the pan **o** kettle	196
	2:14	into the pan or kettle **o** caldron or pot,	196
	2:14	into the pan or kettle or caldron **o** pot,	196
	3:14	be atoned for by sacrifice **o** offering.' "	2256
	4: 9	**o** you will be subject to the Hebrews,	7153
	4:20	she did not respond **o** pay any attention.	2256
	5:11	**o** it will kill us and our people."	2256+4202
	6:12	they did not turn to the right **o** to the left.	2256
	9: 5	**o** my father will stop thinking about	7153
	12: 4	"You have not cheated **o** oppressed us,"	2256
	13:19	the Hebrews will make swords **o** spears!"	196
	13:22	with Saul and Jonathan had a sword **o** spear	2256
	14: 6	**whether** by many **o** by few."	196
	14:52	whenever Saul saw a mighty **o** brave man,	2256
	15:29	He who is the Glory of Israel does not lie **o**	2256
	16: 7	not consider his appearance **o** his height,	2256
	17:34	a lion **o** a bear came and carried off a sheep	2256
	17:47	by sword **o** spear that the LORD saves;	2256
	18:18	and what is my family **o** my father's clan	NIH
	20: 2	great **o** small, without confiding in me.	196
	20: 3	'Jonathan must not know this **o** he will	7153
	20:27	either yesterday **o** today?"	1685
	21: 3	**o** whatever you can find."	196
	21: 8	"Don't you have a spear **o** a sword here?	196
	21: 8	I haven't brought my sword **o** any	1685+2256
	22: 2	All those who were in distress **o** in debt	2256
	22: 2	in distress or in debt **o** discontented	2256
	22: 8	of you is concerned about me **o** tells me	2256
	22:15	Let not the king accuse your servant **o** any	NIH
	24: 6	**o** lift my hand against him;	NIH
	24:11	not guilty of wrongdoing **o** rebellion.	2256
	24:21	that you will not cut off my descendants **o**	561
	25:31	of needless bloodshed **o** of having avenged	2256
	26:10	**o** he will go into battle and perish.	196
	26:12	No one saw **o** knew about it,	2256
	27: 9	he did not leave a man **o** woman alive,	2256
	27:10	the Negev of Judah" **o** "Against the Negev	2256
	27:10	of Jerahmeel" **o** "Against the Negev of	2256
	27:11	He did not leave a man **o** woman alive to	2256
	28: 6	not answer him by dreams **o** Urim	1685
	28: 6	by dreams or Urim **o** prophets.	1685
	28:15	either by prophets **o** by dreams.	1685
	28:18	Because you did not obey the LORD **o**	2256
	29: 4	**o** he will turn against us during	2256+4202
	30:12	not eaten any food **o** drunk any water	2256
	30:15	not kill me **o** hand me over to my master,	2256
	30:19	Nothing was missing: young **o** old,	2256
	30:19	young or old, boy **o** girl,	2256
	30:19	plunder **o** anything else they had taken.	2256
	31: 4	**o** these uncircumcised fellows will come	7153
2Sa	2:21	"Turn aside to the right **o** to the left;	196
	3:29	without someone who has a running sore **o**	2256
	3:29	a running sore or leprosy **o** who leans on	2256
	3:29	leans on a crutch **o** who falls by the sword	2256
	3:29	or who falls by the sword **o** who lacks food.	2256
	3:35	so severely, if I taste bread **o** anything else	196
	6:21	who chose me rather than your father **o**	2256
	12: 4	of his own sheep **o** cattle to prepare a meal	2256
	13:22	either good **o** bad;	2256
	14:19	the right **o** to the left from anything my lord	2256
	15: 4	Then everyone who has a complaint **o**	2256
	15:14	**o** none of us will escape from Absalom.	3954
	15:14	**o** he will move quickly to overtake us	7153
	15:21	whether it means life **o** death,	561
	17: 9	he is hidden in a cave **o** some other place.	196
	17:16	**o** the king and all the people with him will	7153
	19:24	of his feet **o** trimmed his mustache	2256
	19:24	trimmed his mustache **o** washed his clothes	2256
	20: 6	**o** he will find fortified cities and escape	7153
	20:20	be it from me to swallow up **o** destroy!	561+2256
	21: 4	"We have no right to demand silver **o** gold	2256
	21: 4	silver or gold from Saul **o** his family,	2256
	21:10	the birds of the air touch them by day **o**	2256
	23: 7	a tool of iron **o** the shaft of a spear;	2256
	24:13	**O** three months of fleeing	561
	24:13	**O** three days of plague in your land?	561
1Ki	1:10	not invite Nathan the prophet **o** Benaiah or	2256
	1:10	Nathan the prophet or Benaiah **o** the special	2256
	1:10	or the special guard **o** his brother Solomon.	2256
	3: 8	too numerous to count **o** number.	2256
	3:11	and not for long life **o** wealth for yourself,	2256
	5: 4	and there is no adversary **o** disaster.	2256
	6: 7	chisel **o** any other iron tool was heard at	NIH
	8: 5	and cattle that they could not be recorded **o**	2256
	8:23	there is no God like you in heaven above **o**	2256
	8:37	"When famine **o** plague comes to the land,	NIH
	8:37	**o** blight or mildew, locusts or grasshoppers,	NIH
	8:37	or blight **o** mildew, locusts or grasshoppers,	NIH
	8:37	or blight or mildew, locusts **o** grasshoppers,	NIH
	8:37	**o** when an enemy besieges them in any	NIH
	8:37	whatever disaster **o** disease may come,	NIH
	8:38	and when a prayer **o** plea is made by any	NIH
	8:46	to his own land, far away **o** near;	196
1Ki	9: 6	"But if you **o** your sons turn away from me	2256
	10:12	never been imported **o** seen since that day.)	2256
	13: 8	nor would I eat bread **o** drink water here.	2256
	13: 9	not eat bread **o** drink water or return by	2256
	13: 9	'You must not eat bread or drink water **o**	2256
	13:16	nor can I eat bread **o** drink water with you	2256
	13:17	'You must not eat bread **o** drink water there	2256
	13:17	not eat bread or drink water there **o** return	4202
	13:22	in the place where he told you not to eat **o**	2256
	14:10	in Israel—slave **o** free.	2256
	15:17	to prevent anyone from leaving **o** entering	2256
	16:11	whether relative **o** friend.	2256
	18:10	a nation **o** kingdom where my master has	2256
	18:10	a nation **o** kingdom claimed you were	2256
	18:27	Perhaps he is deep in thought, **o** busy,	2256+3954
	18:27	in thought, or busy, **o** traveling.	2256+3954
	20: 8	to him **o** agree to his demands."	2256
	20:39	**o** you must pay a talent of silver.'	196
	21: 2	a better vineyard **o**, if you prefer, I will pay	NIH
	21: 6	**o** if you prefer, I will give you another	196
	21:21	in Israel—slave **o** free.	2256
	22: 6	against Ramoth Gilead, **o** shall I refrain?"	561
	22:15	against Ramoth Gilead, **o** shall I refrain?"	561
	22:31	"Do not fight with anyone, small **o** great,	NIH
2Ki	2:16	down on some mountain **o** in some valley."	196
	2:21	Never again will it cause death **o** make	2256
	3: 9	for themselves **o** for the animals with them.	2256
	3:14	I would not look at you **o even** notice you.	2256
	4:13	Can we speak on your behalf to the king **o**	196
	4:23	"It's not the New Moon **o** the Sabbath."	2256
	4:31	but there was no sound **o** response.	2256
	5:26	**o** to accept clothes, olive groves, vineyards,	2256
	5:26	herds, **o** menservants and maidservants?	2256
	6:22	with your own sword **o** bow?	2256
	9: 8	in Israel—slave **o** free.	2256
	9:32	Two **o** three eunuchs looked down at him.	NIH
	12:13	trumpets **o** any other articles of gold	NIH
	12:13	or any other articles of gold **o** silver for	2256
	13:19	"You should have struck the ground five **o**	196
	13:23	to destroy them **o** banish them	2256
	14:26	whether slave **o** free, was suffering;	700+2256
	17:35	not worship any other gods **o** bow down	2256
	17:35	serve them **o** sacrifice to them.	2256
	18: 5	**either** before him **o** after him.	2256
	19:13	**o** of Hena or Ivvah?"	NIH
	19:13	or of Hena **o** Ivvah?"	2256
	19:32	not enter this city **o** shoot an arrow here.	2256
	19:32	with shield **o** build a siege ramp against it.	2256
	20: 9	**o** shall it go back ten steps?"	561
	20:13	There was nothing in his palace **o**	2256
	22: 2	not turning aside to the right **o** to the left.	2256
	23:10	so no one could use it to sacrifice his son **o**	2256
	25:15	all that were made of pure gold **o** silver.	2256
1Ch	10: 4	**o** these uncircumcised fellows will come	7153
	12: 2	with bows and were able to shoot arrows **o**	2256
	12: 2	to sling stones right-handed **o** left-handed;	2256
	21:12	**o** three days of the sword of the LORD—	561+2256
	21:24	**o** sacrifice a burnt offering	2256
	22:13	Do not be afraid **o** discouraged.	2256
	23: 3	The Levites thirty years old **o** more	2256
	23:24	the workers twenty years old **o** more	2256
	23:26	the tabernacle **o** any of the articles used	2256
	23:27	from those twenty years old **o** more.	2256
	27:23	the number of the men twenty years old **o**	2256
	28:20	Do not be afraid **o** discouraged,	2256
	28:20	not fail you **o** forsake you until all the work	2256
2Ch	1:11	for wealth, riches **o** honor, nor for the death	2256
	5: 6	and cattle that they could not be recorded **o**	2256
	6:14	there is no God like you in heaven **o**	2256
	6:28	"When famine **o** plague comes to the land,	NIH
	6:28	**o** blight or mildew, locusts or grasshoppers,	NIH
	6:28	or blight **o** mildew, locusts or grasshoppers,	2256
	6:28	or blight or mildew, locusts **o** grasshoppers,	2256
	6:28	**o** when enemies besiege them in any	NIH
	6:28	whatever disaster **o** disease may come,	2256
	6:29	and when a prayer **o** plea is made by any	NIH
	6:36	to a land far away **o** near;	196
	7:13	**o** command locusts to devour the land	2256
	7:13	the land **o** send a plague among my people,	2256
	8:15	to the priests **o** to the Levites in any matter,	2256
	15:13	whether small **o** great, man or woman.	6330
	15:13	whether small or great, man **o** woman.	6330
	16: 1	to prevent anyone from leaving **o** entering	2256
	18: 5	against Ramoth Gilead, **o** shall I refrain?"	561
	18:14	against Ramoth Gilead, **o** shall I refrain?"	561
	18:30	"Do not fight with anyone, small **o** great,	NIH
	19: 7	the LORD our God there is no injustice **o**	2256
	19: 7	or partiality **o** bribery."	2256
	19:10	whether bloodshed **o** other concerns of	1068
	19:10	commands, decrees **o** ordinances—	2256
	20: 9	**whether** the sword of judgment, **o**	2256
	20: 9	or plague **o** famine,	2256
	20:15	'Do not be afraid **o** discouraged because	2256
	21:12	of your father Jehoshaphat **o** of Asa king	2256
	25: 5	He then mustered those twenty years old **o**	2256
	25: 8	God has the power to help **o** to overthrow."	2256
	28:13	"**o** we will be guilty before the LORD.	3954
	29: 7	They did not burn incense **o** present any	2256
	31: 2	to their duties as priests **o** Levites—	2256
	31:16	to the males three years old **o** more	2256
	31:17	to the Levites twenty years old **o** more,	2256
	31:19	around their towns **o** in any other towns,	NIH
	32: 7	be afraid **o** discouraged because of the king	2256
	32:15	of any nation **o** kingdom has been able	2256
	32:15	from my hand **o** the hand of my fathers.	2256
	34: 2	not turning aside to the right **o** to the left.	2256
	35:21	who is with me, **o** he will destroy you."	440+2256

2Ch 36:17 nor young woman, old man **o** aged. 2256
Ezr 4:13 no more taxes, tribute **o** duty will be paid, 10221
6:12 overthrow any king **o** people who lifts 10221
6:12 a hand to change this decree **o** to destroy NIH
7:24 tribute **o** duty on any of the priests, Levites, 10221
7:24 temple servants **o** other workers 10221
7:26 confiscation of property, **o** imprisonment. 10221
9:12 to their sons **o** take their daughters 2256
9:14 leaving us no remnant **o** survivor? 2256
10:13 be taken care of in a day **o** two, 2256
Ne 2:16 where I had gone **o** what I was doing, 2256
2:16 the Jews **o** the priests or nobles or officials 2256
2:16 the Jews or the priests **o** nobles or officials 2256
2:16 the Jews or the priests or nobles **o** officials 2256
2:16 or nobles or officials **o** any others 2256
2:20 you have no share in Jerusalem **o** any claim 2256
2:20 in Jerusalem or any claim **o** historic right 2256
4:5 not cover up their guilt **o** blot out their sins 2256
4:11 "Before they know it **o** see us, 2256
6:11 **O** should one like me go into the temple 2256
8:9 Do not mourn **o** weep." 2256
9:18 **o** when they committed awful blasphemies. 2256
9:31 not put an end to them **o** abandon them, 2256
9:34 not pay attention to your commands **o** 2256
9:35 not serve you **o** turn from their evil ways. 2256
10:30 in marriage to the peoples around us **o** 2256
10:31 neighboring peoples bring merchandise **o** 2256
10:31 not buy from them on the Sabbath **o** 2256
13:1 that no Ammonite **o** Moabite should ever 2256
13:20 Once **o** twice the merchants and sellers 2256
13:24 the language of Ashdod **o** the language 2256
13:25 in marriage for your sons **o** for yourselves. 2256
Est 3:2 But Mordecai would not kneel down **o** 2256
3:5 that Mordecai would not kneel down **o** 2256
4:11 that for any man **o** woman who approaches 2256
4:16 Do not eat **o** drink for three days, 2256
4:16 not eat or drink for three days, night **o** day. 2256
8:11 of any nationality **o** province 2256
Job 3:16 **O** why was I not hidden in the ground like 196
6:5 **o** an ox bellow when it has fodder? 561
6:6 **o** is there flavor in the white of an egg? 561
7:2 **o** a hired man waiting eagerly 2256
7:12 Am I the sea, **o** the monster of the deep, 561
7:19 **o** let me alone even for an instant? 4202
8:20 a blameless man **o** strengthen the hands 2256
10:5 a mortal **o** your years like those of a man, 561
10:19 **o** had been carried straight from the womb NIH
12:7 **o** the birds of the air, and they will tell you; 2256
12:8 **o** speak to the earth, 196
12:8 **o** let the fish of the sea inform you. 2256
13:22 **o** let me speak, and you reply. 196
14:11 from the sea **o** a riverbed becomes parched 2256
14:12 not awake **o** be roused from their sleep. 2256
15:2 **o** fill his belly with the hot east wind? 2256
15:14 **o** one born of woman, 2256
17:14 'My mother' **o** 'My sister,' 2256
18:4 **O** must the rocks be moved from their place 2256
18:19 He has no offspring **o** descendants 2256
19:24 **o** engraved in rock forever! NIH
24:13 not know its ways **o** stay in its paths. 2256
28:16 with precious onyx **o** sapphires. 2256
31:5 in falsehood **o** my foot has hurried 2256
31:7 **o** if my hands have been defiled, 2256
31:9 **o** if I have lurked at my neighbor's door, 2256
31:16 "If I have denied the desires of the poor **o** 2256
31:19 **o** a needy man without a garment, 2256
31:24 "If I have put my trust in gold **o** said 2256
31:26 if I have regarded the sun in its radiance **o** 2256
31:29 at my enemy's misfortune **o** gloated over 2256
31:39 without payment **o** broken the spirit 2256
33:19 **O** a man may be chastened on a bed of pain 2256
35:7 **o** what does he receive from your hand? 196
36:19 Would your wealth **o** even all your mighty 2256
36:23 **o** said to him, 'You have done wrong'? 2256
37:13 **o** to water his earth and show his love. 561
38:6 **o** who laid its cornerstone— 196
38:12 **o** shown the dawn its place, NIH
38:16 of the sea **o** walked in the recesses of 2256
38:22 the snow **o** seen the storehouses of the hail, 2256
38:24 **o** the place where the east winds are NIH
38:32 **o** lead out the Bear with its cubs? 2256
38:36 **o** gave understanding to the mind? 196
38:40 when they crouch in their dens **o** lie in wait NIH
39:17 God did not endow her with wisdom **o** 2256+4202
39:19 the horse his strength **o** clothe his neck 2022
40:24 **o** trap him and pierce his nose? NIH
41:1 with a fishhook **o** tie down his tongue with 2256
41:2 a cord through his nose **o** pierce his jaw 2256
41:5 a pet of him like a bird **o** put him on a leash 2256
41:7 Can you fill his hide with harpoons **o** 2256
41:26 nor does the spear **o** the dart or the javelin. NIH
41:26 nor does the spear or the dart **o** the javelin. 2256
Ps 1:1 of the wicked **o** stand in the way of sinners 2256
1:1 way of sinners **o** sit in the seat of mockers. 2256
6:1 **o** discipline me in your wrath. 2256
7:2 **o** they will tear me like a lion and rip me 7153
7:4 **o** without cause have robbed my foe— 2256
13:3 **o** I will sleep in death; 7153
16:4 I will not pour out their libations of blood **o** 2256
19:3 There is no speech **o** language 2256
22:24 not despised **o** disdained the suffering of 2256
24:4 who does not lift up his soul to an idol **o** 2256
27:9 Do not reject me **o** forsake me, 2256
32:9 Do not be like the horse **o** the mule, NIH
32:9 be controlled by bit and bridle **o** they will NIH
35:14 about mourning as though for my friend **o** NIH
35:25 **o** say, "We have swallowed him up." 440
Ps 36:2 to detect **o** hate his sin. NIH
37:1 not fret because of evil men **o** be envious 440
37:25 the righteous forsaken **o** their children 2256
37:33 not leave them in their power **o** let them 2256
38:1 **o** discipline me in your wrath. 2256
38:16 "Do not let them gloat **o** exalt themselves NIH
44:17 though we had not forgotten you **o** been 2256
44:20 If we had forgotten the name of our God **o** 2256
49:7 the life of another **o** give to God a ransom 4202
50:8 for your sacrifices **o** your burnt offerings, 2256
50:9 from your stall **o** of goats from your pens, NIH
50:13 Do I eat the flesh of bulls **o** drink the blood 2256
50:16 "What right have you to recite my laws **o** 2256
50:22 **o** I will tear you to pieces, 7153
51:11 from your presence **o** take your Holy Spirit 2256
51:16 **o** I would bring it; 2256
58:9 whether they be green **o** dry— 4017
59:3 against me for no offense **o** sin of mine, 2256
59:11 **O** Lord our shield, **o** my people will forget. 7153
62:10 in extortion **o** take pride in stolen goods; 2256
66:20 not rejected my prayer **o** withheld his love 2256
69:15 Do not let the floodwaters engulf me **o** 2256
69:15 **o** the pit close its mouth over me. 2256
75:6 No one from the east **o** the west or from 2256
75:6 the west **o** from the desert can exalt a man. 2256
78:22 for they did not believe in God **o** trust 2256
83:14 As fire consumes the forest **o** a flame sets 2256
88:12 **o** your righteous deeds in the land 2256
89:34 I will not violate my covenant **o** alter 2256
89:48 **o** save himself from the power of the grave? NIH
90:2 Before the mountains were born **o** you 2256
90:4 **o** like a watch in the night. 2256
90:10 **o** eighty, if we have the strength; 2256
103:10 not treat us as our sins deserve **o** repay us 2256
106:2 of the LORD **o** fully declare his praise? NIH
109:12 May no one extend kindness to him **o** 2256
131:1 with great matters **o** things too wonderful 2256
132:3 not enter my house **o** go to my bed— 561
140:8 **o** they will become proud. NIH
143:7 Do not hide your face from me **o** I will be 2256
Pr 2:19 to her return **o** attain the paths of life. 2256
3:25 Have no fear of sudden disaster **o** of the ruin 2256
3:31 Do not envy a violent man **o** choose any 2256
4:5 not forget my words **o** swerve from them. 2256
4:14 on the path of the wicked **o** walk in the way 2256
4:27 Do not swerve to the right **o** the left; 2256
5:13 I would not obey my teachers **o** listen 2256
6:7 It has no commander, no overseer **o** ruler, 2256
6:25 Do not lust in your heart after her beauty **o** 2256
7:25 not let your heart turn to her ways **o** stray NIH
8:8 none of them is crooked **o** perverse. 2256
8:26 before he made the earth **o** its fields or any 2256
8:26 before he made the earth or its fields **o** any 2256
9:8 Do not rebuke a mocker **o** he will hate you; 7153
17:26 **o** to flog officials for their integrity. NIH
18:5 It is not good to be partial to the wicked **o** NIH
20:13 Do not love sleep **o** you will grow poor; 7153
20:20 If a man curses his father **o** mother, 2256
22:1 to be esteemed is better than silver **o** gold. 2256
22:13 **o**, "I will be murdered in the streets!" NIH
22:25 **o** you may learn his ways 7153
22:26 not be a man who strikes hands in pledge **o** NIH
23:10 Do not move an ancient boundary stone **o** 2256
23:20 not join those who drink too much wine **o** NIH
24:18 **o** the LORD will see and disapprove 7153
24:19 not fret because of evil men **o** be envious of 440
24:28 **o** use your lips to deceive. 2256
25:10 **o** he who hears it may shame you 7153
25:12 Like an earring of gold **o** an ornament 2256
25:18 Like a club **o** a sword or a sharp arrow is 2256
25:18 Like a club or a sword **o** a sharp arrow is 2256
25:19 Like a bad tooth **o** a lame foot is reliance 2256
25:20 **o** like vinegar poured on soda, NIH
25:26 Like a muddied spring **o** a polluted well is 2256
26:1 Like snow in summer **o** rain in harvest, 2256
26:2 a fluttering sparrow **o** a darting swallow, NIH
26:4 **o** you will be like him yourself. 7153
26:5 **o** he will be wise in his own eyes. 7153
26:6 Like cutting off one's feet **o** drinking NIH
26:10 is he who hires a fool **o** any passer-by. 2256
26:18 Like a madman shooting firebrands **o** 2256
27:16 like restraining the wind **o** grasping oil with 2256
28:15 Like a roaring lion **o** a charging bear is 2256
28:24 He who robs his father **o** mother and says, 2256
30:6 **o** he will rebuke you and prove you a liar. 7153
30:9 **O** I may become poor and steal, 7153
30:10 **o** he will curse you, and you will pay for it. 7153
30:32 **o** if you have planned evil, 2256
Ecc 2:19 be a wise man **o** a fool? 196
2:25 who can eat **o** find enjoyment? 2256
4:14 **o** he may have been born in poverty 1685+3954
5:12 whether he eats little **o** much, 2256
5:14 **o** wealth lost through some misfortune, 2256
6:5 it never saw the sun **o** knew anything, 2256
7:21 **o** you may hear your servant cursing you— 889+4202
8:16 his eyes not seeing sleep day **o** night— 2256
9:1 but no man knows whether love **o** 1685
9:11 The race is not to the swift **o** the battle to 2256
9:11 to the wise **o** wealth to the brilliant 1685+2256
9:11 brilliant **o** favor to the learned; 1685+2256
9:12 **o** birds are taken in a snare, 2256
10:20 **o** curse the rich in your bedroom, 2256
11:3 a tree falls to the south **o** to the north, 561
11:5 **o** how the body is formed in NIH
11:6 which will succeed, whether this **o** that, 196
11:6 **o** whether both will do equally well. 2256
Ecc 12:6 **o** the golden bowl is broken; 2256
12:6 **o** the wheel broken at the well, 2256
12:14 whether it is good **o** evil. 2256
SS 2:7 not arouse **o** awaken love until it so desires. 2256
2:9 My lover is like a gazelle **o** a young stag. 196
2:17 and be like a gazelle **o** like a young stag on 196
3:5 not arouse **o** awaken love until it so desires. 2256
6:11 to see if the vines had budded **o** NIH
8:4 not arouse **o** awaken love until it so desires. 2256
8:14 and be like a gazelle **o** like a young stag on 196
Isa 1:6 cleansed **o** bandaged or soothed with oil. 2256
1:6 cleansed or bandaged **o** soothed with oil. 2256
3:7 I have no food **o** clothing in my house; 2256
5:27 Not one of them grows tired **o** stumbles, 2256
5:27 not one slumbers **o** sleeps; 2256
7:11 **whether** in the deepest depths **o** in the 196
8:4 Before the boy knows how to say 'My father' **o** 'My mother' 2256
10:4 among the captives **o** fall among the slain. 2256
10:14 **o** opened its mouth to chirp.' " 2256
10:15 **o** the saw boast against him who uses it? 561
10:15 **o** a club brandish him who is not wood! NIH
11:3 **o** decide by what he hears with his ears; 2256
13:20 She will never be inhabited **o** lived in 2256
16:10 no one sings **o** shouts in the vineyards; 4202
17:6 leaving two **o** three olives on NIH
17:6 four **o** five on the fruitful boughs," NIH
19:15 head **o** tail, palm branch or reed. 2256
19:15 head or tail, palm branch **o** reed. 2256
21:7 riders on donkeys **o** riders on camels, NIH
22:11 **o** have regard for the One who planned it 2256
23:1 and left without house **o** harbor. NIH
23:18 they will not be stored up **o** hoarded. 2256
24:13 **o** as when gleanings are left after NIH
27:5 **O else** let them come to me for refuge; 196
27:9 no Asherah poles **o** incense altars will 2256
28:22 **o** your chains will become heavier; 7153
29:12 **O** if you give the scroll 2256
30:14 a hearth **o** scooping water out of a cistern." 2256
30:21 Whether you turn to the right **o** to the left, 2256
31:1 **o** seek help from the LORD. 2256
31:4 not frightened by their shouts **o** disturbed 2256
37:13 **o** of Hena or Ivvah?" NIH
37:13 or of Hena **o** Ivvah?" 2256
37:33 not enter this city **o** shoot an arrow here. 2256
37:33 with shield **o** build a siege ramp against it. 2256
38:11 no longer will I look on mankind, **o** be NIH
38:14 I cried like a swift **o** thrush, NIH
39:2 There was nothing in his palace **o** 2256
40:12 **o** with the breadth of his hand marked off 2256
40:12 **o** weighed the mountains on the scales and 2256
40:13 **o** instructed him as his counselor? 2256
40:14 that taught him knowledge **o** showed him 2256
40:25 **O** who is my equal?" 2256
40:28 He will not grow tired **o** weary, 2256
41:22 **O** declare to us the things to come, 196
41:23 Do something, whether good **o** bad, 2256
41:26 so we could know, **o** beforehand, 2256
42:2 He will not shout **o** cry out, 2256
42:2 **o** raise his voice in the streets. 2256
42:4 he will not falter **o** be discouraged 2256
42:8 not give my glory to another **o** my praise 2256
42:22 all of them trapped in pits **o** hidden away 2256
42:23 to this **o** pay close attention in time NIH
43:24 **o** lavished on me the fat of your sacrifices. 2256
44:14 **o** perhaps took a cypress or oak. 2256
44:14 or perhaps took a cypress **o** oak. 2256
44:14 **o** planted a pine, and the rain made it grow. NIH
44:19 no one has the knowledge **o** understanding 2256
44:20 he cannot save himself, **o** say, 2256
45:10 **o** to his mother, 2256
45:11 about my children, **o** give me orders about 2256
45:13 but not for a price **o** reward, 2256
45:17 you will never be put to shame **o** disgraced, 2256
46:5 "To whom will you compare me **o** 2256
47:1 No more will you be called tender **o** 2256
47:7 But you did not consider these things **o** 4202
47:8 be a widow **o** suffer the loss of children.' 2256
48:1 but not in truth **o** righteousness— 2256
49:10 the desert heat **o** the sun beat upon them. 2256
49:24 **o** captives rescued from the fierce? 2256
50:1 **O** to which of my creditors did I sell you? 196
51:7 not fear the reproach of men **o** be terrified 2256
52:12 you will not leave in haste **o** go in flight; 2256
53:2 He had no beauty **o** majesty to attract us 2256
56:12 like today, **o** even far better." NIH
58:13 as you please **o** speaking idle words, 2256
59:21 **o** from the mouths of your children, 2256
59:21 **o** from the mouths of their descendants 2256
60:11 they will never be shut, day **o** night, 2256
60:12 For the nation **o** kingdom that will 2256
60:18 nor ruin **o** destruction within your borders, 2256
62:4 **o** name your land Desolate. 2256
62:6 they will never be silent day **o** night. 2256
63:16 not know us **o** Israel acknowledge us; 2256
64:7 on your name **o** strives to lay hold of you; NIH
65:20 **o** an old man who does not live out 2256
65:22 **o** plant and others eat. 4202
65:23 not toil in vain **o** bear children doomed 2256
66:8 be born in a day **o** a nation be brought forth 561
66:19 not heard of my fame **o** seen my glory. 2256
Jer 1:17 **o** I will terrify you before them. 7153
2:31 a desert to Israel **o** a land of great darkness? 561
3:16 never enter their minds **o** be remembered; 2256
4:4 **o** my wrath will break out and burn like fire 7153
4:11 but not to winnow **o** cleanse; 2256
5:12 we will never see sword **o** famine. 2256

Isa 6: 8 o I will turn away from you 7153
6:20 What do I care about incense from Sheba o 2256
6:25 not go out to the fields o walk on the roads, 2256
7: 6 the fatherless o the widow and do 2256
7:16 not pray for this people nor offer any plea o 2256
7:24 But they did not listen o pay attention; 2256
7:26 they did not listen to me o pay attention. 2256
7:28 not obeyed the LORD its God o responded 2256
7:32 people will no longer call it Topheth o 2256
8: 2 They will not be gathered up o buried, 2256
9:13 not obeyed me o followed my law. 2256
9:23 o the strong man boast of his strength 2256
9:23 o the rich man boast of his riches, 440
10: 2 "Do not learn the ways of the nations o 2256
10:20 now to pitch my tent o to set up my shelter. 2256
11: 8 But they did not listen o pay attention; 2256
11:14 not pray for this people nor offer any plea o 2256
11:21 the LORD o you will die by our hands' 2256+4202
13:14 I will allow no pity o mercy or compassion 2256
13:14 I will allow no pity or mercy o compassion 2256
13:23 Can the Ethiopian change his skin o 2256
14:13 not see the sword o suffer famine. 2256
14:14 not sent them o appointed them or spoken 2256
14:14 not sent them or appointed them o spoken 2256
14:15 'No sword o famine will touch this land.' 2256
14:16 be no one to bury them o their wives, 2256
14:16 their sons o their daughters. 2256
15:12 from the north—o bronze? 2256
16: 2 and have sons o daughters in this place." 2256
16: 4 They will not be mourned o buried but will 2256
16: 5 do not go to mourn o show sympathy, 2256
16: 6 They will not be buried o mourned, 2256
16: 6 and no one will cut himself o 2256
16: 7 not even for a father o a mother— 2256
17:21 the Sabbath day o bring it through the gates 2256
17:22 a load out of your houses o do any work on 2256
17:23 Yet they did not listen o pay attention; 2256
17:23 not listen o respond to discipline. 2256
18: 7 that a nation o kingdom is to be uprooted, 2256
18: 9 if at another time I announce that a nation o 2256
18:23 not forgive their crimes o blot out their sins 2256
19: 5 something I did not command o mention, 2256
19: 6 Topheth o the Valley of Ben Hinnom, 2256
20: 4 who will carry them away to Babylon o 2256
20: 9 "I will not mention him o speak any more 2256
21: 7 he will show them no mercy o pity 2256
21: 7 no mercy or pity o compassion.' 2256
21: 9 will die by the sword, famine o plague. 2256
21:12 o my wrath will break out and burn like fire 7153
22: 3 Do no wrong o violence to the alien, 440
22: 3 the fatherless o the widow, 2256
22:10 for the dead [king] o mourn his loss; 2256
22:30 on the throne of David o rule anymore 2256
23: 4 and they will no longer be afraid o terrified, 2256
23:18 of the LORD to see o to hear his word? 2256
23:32 yet I did not send o appoint them. 2256
23:33 "When these people, o a prophet or a priest, 196
23:33 "When these people, or a prophet o a priest, 196
23:34 a prophet o a priest or anyone else claims, 2256
23:34 a prophet or a priest o anyone else claims, 2256
23:35 of you keeps on saying to his friend o 2256
23:35 o 'What has the LORD spoken?' 2256
23:37 o 'What has the LORD spoken?' 2256
24: 8 **whether** they remain in this land o 2256
25: 4 you have not listened o paid any attention. 2256
25:33 not be mourned o gathered up or buried, 2256
25:33 They will not be mourned or gathered up o 2256
26:19 "Did Hezekiah king of Judah o anyone else 2256
27: 8 any nation o kingdom will 2256
27: 8 of Babylon o bow its neck under his yoke, 2256
27: 9 of dreams, your mediums o your sorcerers 2256
31:34 o a man his brother, saying, 2256
31:40 The city will never again be uprooted o 2256
32:23 they did not obey you o follow your law; 2256
32:33 and again, they would not listen o respond NIH
32:43 without men o animals, 2256
33:10 without men o animals." 2256
33:12 desolate and without men o animals— 2256
34:14 did not listen to me o pay attention to me. 2256
35: 7 sow seed o plant vineyards; 2256
35: 9 o built houses to live in or had vineyards, 2256
35: 9 or built houses to live in o had vineyards, 2256
35: 9 to live in or had vineyards, fields o crops. 2256
35:15 But you have not paid attention o listened 2256
36:23 Whenever Jehudi had read three o 2256
37:18 against you o your officials or this people, 2256
37:18 against you or your officials o this people, 2256
37:19 of Babylon will not attack you o this land'? 2256
37:20 o I will die there." 2256+4202
38: 2 will die by the sword, famine o plague, 2256
38:24 o you may die. 2256+4202
38:25 not hide it from us o we will kill you,' 2256+4202
40: 5 o go anywhere else you please." 196
42: 6 Whether it is favorable o unfavorable, 561+2256
42:14 not see war o hear the trumpet or be hungry 2256
42:14 not see war or hear the trumpet o be hungry 2256
42:17 not one of them will survive o escape 2256
43: 3 so they may kill us o carry us into exile 2256
44: 5 But they did not listen o pay attention; 2256
44: 5 they did not turn from their wickedness o NIH
44:10 not humbled themselves o shown reverence, 2256
44:12 by the sword o die from famine. NIH
44:12 they will die by sword o famine. 2256
44:14 in Egypt will escape o survive to return to 2256
44:23 the LORD and have not obeyed him o 2256
44:23 not obeyed him o followed his law o 2256
44:23 or followed his law or his decrees o 2256

Jer 44:26 will ever again invoke my name o swear, NIH
44:28 whose word will stand—mine o theirs. 2256
50:39 It will never again be inhabited o lived in 2256
51:46 Do not lose heart o be afraid 2256
52:19 all that were made of pure gold o silver. 2256
La 2:22 of the LORD's anger no one escaped o 2256
3: 8 Even when I call out o cry for help, 2256
3:33 For he does not willingly bring affliction o 2256
3:63 Sitting o standing, they mock me 2256
Eze 1:13 like burning coals of fire o like torches. NIH
2: 5 And whether they listen o fail to listen— 2256
2: 6 do not be afraid of them o their words. 2256
2: 6 not be afraid of what they say o terrified 2256
2: 7 whether they listen o fail to listen, 2256
3: 9 not be afraid of them o terrified by them, 2256
3:11 whether they listen o fail to listen." 2256
3:18 not warn him o speak out to dissuade him 2256
3:19 and he does not turn from his wickedness o 2256
4:14 I have never eaten anything found dead o 2256
5: 7 not followed my decrees o kept my laws. 2256
5:11 not look on you with pity o spare you. 2256
5:12 the plague o perish by famine inside you; 2256
7: 4 not look on you with pity o spare you; 2256
7: 9 not look on you with pity o spare you; 2256
7:19 not satisfy their hunger o fill their stomachs 2256
8:18 not look on them with pity o spare them. 2256
9: 5 without showing pity o compassion. 2256
9:10 not look on them with pity o spare them, 2256
11:12 not followed my decrees o kept my laws 2256
12:24 For there will be no more false visions o 2256
13: 9 of my people o be listed in the records of 2256
13:23 see false visions o practice divination. 2256
14: 7 " 'When any Israelite o any alien living 2256
14:15 "O if I send wild beasts through NIH
14:16 they could not save their own sons o 2256
14:17 "O if I bring a sword against that country 196
14:18 they could not save their own sons o 2256
14:19 "O if I send a plague into that land 196
16: 4 nor were you rubbed with salt o wrapped 2256
16: 5 on you with pity o had compassion enough NIH
17: 9 a strong arm o many people to pull it up by 2256
18: 6 the mountain shrines o look to the idols of 2256
18: 6 He does not defile his neighbor's wife o lie 2256
18: 8 not lend at usury o take excessive interest. 2256
18:10 who sheds blood o does any of these other 2256
18:15 "He does not eat at the mountain shrines o 2256
18:16 not oppress anyone o require a pledge for 4202
18:17 and takes no usury o excessive interest. 2256
20:17 not destroy them o put an end to them in 2256
20:18 not follow the statutes of your fathers o 2256
20:18 or keep their laws o defile yourselves 2256
20:28 and they saw any high hill o any leafy tree, 2256
22:14 Will your courage endure o your hands 561
22:24 that has had no rain o showers in the day 4202
23:27 with longing o remember Egypt anymore. 2256
24:16 do not lament o weep or shed any tears. 2256
24:16 do not lament or weep o shed any tears. 2256
24:17 not cover the lower part of your face o eat 2256
24:22 not cover the lower part of your face o eat 2256
24:23 not mourn o weep but will waste away 2256
26:20 and you will not return o take your place in 2256
29: 5 and not be gathered o picked up. 2256
29:11 of man o animal will pass through it; 2256
30:21 It has not been bound up for healing o put NIH
32:13 be stirred by the foot of man o muddied by 2256
34: 4 not strengthened the weak o healed the sick 2256
34: 4 or healed the sick o bound up the injured. 2256
34: 4 not brought back the strays o searched for 2256
34: 6 and no one searched o looked for them. 2256
34:29 in the land o bear the scorn of the nations. 2256
36:14 therefore you will no longer devour men o 2256
36:15 of the peoples o cause your nation to fall, 2256
37:22 and they will never again be two nations o 2256
37:23 with their idols and vile images o with any 2256
39:10 to gather wood from the fields o cut it from 2256
44:13 near to serve me as priests o come near any 2256
44:13 or come near any of my holy things o NIH
44:17 at the gates of the inner court o inside 2256
44:20 " 'They must not shave their heads o 2256
44:22 not marry widows o divorced women; 2256
44:22 of Israelite descent o widows of priests. 2256
44:25 if the dead person was his father o mother, 2256
44:25 son o daughter, brother or unmarried sister, 2256
44:25 son or daughter, brother o unmarried sister, 2256
44:31 not eat anything, bird o animal, found dead 2256
44:31 found dead o torn by wild animals. 2256
45:14 of ten baths o one homer, NIH
45:20 for anyone who sins unintentionally o 2256
46:12 **whether** a burnt offering o fellowship 196
46:12 He shall offer his burnt offering o his 2256
48:14 They must not sell o exchange any of it. 2256
Da 2:10 of any magician o enchanter or astrologer. 10221
2:10 of any magician or enchanter o astrologer. 10221
2:27 magician o diviner can explain to the king NIH
3:14 that you do not serve my gods o worship 10221
3:18 that we will not serve your gods o worship 10221
3:28 to give up their lives rather than serve o 10221
3:29 of any nation o language who say anything 10221
4:19 not let the dream o its meaning alarm you." 10221
4:35 No one can hold back his hand o say 10221
5: 8 but they could not read the writing o tell 10221
5:23 which cannot see o hear or understand. 10221
5:23 which cannot see or hear o understand. 10221
6: 7 that anyone who prays to any god o man 10221
6:12 to any god o man except to you, 10221
6:13 O king, o to the decree you put in writing. 10221
6:15 of the Medes and Persians no decree o edict 10221

Da 9:10 we have not obeyed the LORD our God o NIH
10: 3 no meat o wine touched my lips; 2256
11:17 but his plans will not succeed o help him. 2256
11:20 yet not in anger o in battle. 2256
11:33 they will fall by the sword o be burned or 2256
11:33 or be burned o captured or plundered. NIH
11:33 or be burned or captured o plundered. 2256
11:37 the gods of his fathers o for the one desired 2256
Hos 1: 7 not by bow, sword o battle, 2256
1: 7 sword or battle, o by horses and horsemen, NIH
1:10 which cannot be measured o counted. 2256
3: 3 be a prostitute o be intimate with any man, 2256
3: 4 without king o prince, 2256
3: 4 without sacrifice o sacred stones, 2256
3: 4 without ephod o idol. 2256
7:10 not return to the LORD his God o search 2256
12: 8 not find in me any iniquity o sin." 889
Joel 1: 2 ever happened in your days o in 561+2256
Am 3:12 from the lion's mouth only two leg bones o 196
5: 6 o he will sweep through the house 7153
8:11 not a famine of food o a thirst for water, 2256
8:14 o say, 'As surely as your god lives, O Dan,' 2256
8:14 o, 'As surely as the god of Beersheba 2256
9:10 'Disaster will not overtake o meet us.' 2256
Jnh 3: 7 Do not let any man o beast, herd or flock, 2256
3: 7 Do not let any man or beast, herd o flock, 2256
3: 7 do not let them eat o drink. 2256
4:10 though you did not tend it o make it grow. 2256
Mic 5: 7 not wait for man o linger for mankind. 2256
Hab 1: 2 O cry out to you, "Violence!" NIH
2:18 O an image that teaches lies? 2256
2:19 O to lifeless stone, 'Wake up!' NIH
Zep 1:12 either good o bad.' 2256
Hag 2:12 and that fold touches some bread o stew, 2256
2:12 some wine, oil o other food, 2256
Zec 1: 4 But they would not listen o pay attention 2256
7:10 Do not oppress the widow o the fatherless, 2256
7:10 the alien o the poor. 2256
7:12 as flint and would not listen to the law o to 2256
7:14 behind them that no one could come o go. 2256
8:10 that time there were no wages for man o 2256
11:16 o seek the young, or heal the injured, 4202
11:16 o heal the injured, or feed the healthy, 2256
11:16 or heal the injured, o feed the healthy, 4202
14: 6 no cold o frost. 2256
14: 7 a unique day, without daytime o nighttime 2256
Mal 1: 8 When you sacrifice crippled o diseased 2256
1:13 crippled o diseased animals and offer them 2256
2:13 to your offerings o accepts them 2256
2:17 o "Where is the God of justice?" 196
3: 2 be like a refiner's fire o a launderer's soap. 2256
4: 1 "Not a root o a branch will be left to them. 2256
4: 6 **o else** I will come and strike the land with 7153
Mt 5:17 that I have come to abolish the Law o *2445*
5:25 o he may hand you over to the judge, *3607*
5:35 o by the earth, for it is his footstool; *3612*
5:35 o by Jerusalem, for it is the city of *3612*
5:36 for you cannot make even one hair white o *2445*
6:24 o he will be devoted to the one and despise *2445*
6:25 what you will eat o drink; *2445*
6:25 o about your body, what you will wear. *3593*
6:26 not sow o reap or store away in barns, *4028*
6:26 not sow or reap o store away in barns, *4028*
6:28 They do not labor o spin. *4028*
6:31 o 'What shall we drink?' *2445*
6:31 o 'What shall we wear?' *2445*
7: 1 Do not judge, o you too will be judged *2671+3590*
7:10 O if he asks for a fish, will give him a snake *2445*
7:16 o figs from thistles? *2445*
9: 5 to say, 'Your sins are forgiven,' o to say, *2445*
10: 5 not go among the Gentiles o enter any town *2779*
10: 9 not take along any gold o silver or copper *3593*
10: 9 not take along any gold or silver o copper *3593*
10:10 o extra tunic, or sandals or a staff; *3593*
10:10 or extra tunic, o sandals or a staff; *3593*
10:10 or extra tunic, or sandals o a staff; *3593*
10:11 "Whatever town o village you enter, *2445*
10:14 not welcome you o listen to your words, *3593*
10:14 when you leave that home o town. *2445*
10:19 do not worry about what to say o how *2445*
10:26 o hidden that will not be made known. *2779*
10:37 "Anyone who loves his father o mother *2445*
10:37 anyone who loves his son o daughter *2445*
11: 3 o should we expect someone else?" *2445*
12: 5 O haven't you read in the Law that on *2445*
12:19 He will not quarrel o cry out; *4028*
12:25 and every city o household divided *2445*
12:29 "O again, how can anyone enter *2445*
12:32 either in this age o in the age to come. *4046*
12:33 o make a tree bad and its fruit will be bad, *2445*
13: 8 sixty o thirty times what was sown. *NIG*
13:13 they do not hear o understand. *4028*
13:21 When trouble o persecution comes because *2445*
13:23 sixty o thirty times what was sown." *1254+4005*
15: 4 and 'Anyone who curses his father o *2445*
15: 5 that if a man says to his father o mother, *2445*
15:32 o they may collapse on the way." *3607*
16:10 O the seven loaves for the four thousand, *4028*
16:14 Jeremiah o one of the prophets." *2445*
16:26 O what can a man give in exchange *2445*
17:15 He often falls into the fire o into the water. *2779*
17:25 from their own sons o from others?" *2445*
18: 8 If your hand o your foot causes you to sin, *2445*
18: 8 for you to enter life maimed o crippled than *2445*
18: 8 to have two hands o two feet and be thrown *2445*
18:16 take one o two others along, *2445*
18:16 by the testimony of two o three witnesses.' *2445*

Mt 18:17 as you would a pagan o a tax collector. 2779
18:20 two o three come together in my name, 2445
19:29 And everyone who has left houses o 2445
19:29 or brothers o sisters or father or mother 2445
19:29 or sisters o father or mother or children 2445
19:29 or sisters or father o mother or children 2445
19:29 or sisters or father or mother o children 2445
19:29 or children o fields for my sake will receive 2445
20:15 O are you envious because I am generous?' 2445
20:23 but to sit at my right o left is not for me 2779
21:25 Was it from heaven, o from men?" 2445
22:17 Is it right to pay taxes to Caesar o not?" 2445
22:29 because you do not know the Scriptures o 3593
23:17 o the temple that makes the gold sacred? 2445
23:19 gift, o the altar that makes the gift sacred? 2445
24:20 not take place in winter o on the Sabbath. 3593
24:23 o, 'There he is!' 2445
24:26 o, 'Here he is, in the inner rooms,' NIG
24:36 "No one knows about that day o hour, 2779
25:13 you do not know the day o the hour. 4028
25:37 o thirsty and give you something to drink? 2445
25:38 o needing clothes and clothe you? 2445
25:39 When did we see you sick o in prison 2445
25:44 when did we see you hungry o thirsty or 2445
25:44 or thirsty o a stranger or needing clothes 2445
25:44 or a stranger o needing clothes or sick or 2445
25:44 or a stranger or needing clothes o sick or 2445
25:44 or needing clothes or sick o in prison, 2445
26: 5 "o there may be a riot among the people." 2671+3590
27:17 Barabbas, o Jesus who is called Christ?" 2445
Mk 2: 9 o to say, 'Get up, take your mat and walk'? 2445
3: 4 to do good o to do evil, 2445
3: 4 to save life o to kill?" 2445
4: 8 sixty, o even a hundred times." NIG
4:17 When trouble o persecution comes because 2445
4:20 thirty, sixty o even a hundred times 2779
4:21 in a lamp to put it under a bowl o a bed? 2445
4:27 Night and day, whether he sleeps o gets up, 2779
4:30 o what parable shall we use to describe it? 2445
6:11 if any place will not welcome you o listen 3593
6:56 into villages, towns o countryside— 2445
7:10 'Anyone who curses his father o mother 2445
7:11 that if a man says to his father o mother: 2445
7:12 for his father o mother. 2445
8:17 Do you still not see o understand? 4028
8:37 O what can a man give in exchange NIG
9:22 "It has often thrown him into fire o water 2779
10:29 "no one who has left home o brothers 2445
10:29 who has left home or brothers o sisters 2445
10:29 or sisters o mother or father or children 2445
10:29 or sisters or mother o father or children 2445
10:29 or sisters or mother or father o children 2445
10:29 mother or father or children o fields for me 2445
10:38 the cup I drink o be baptized with 2445
10:40 but to sit at my right o left is not for me 2445
11:30 was it from heaven, o from men? 2445
12:14 Is it right to pay taxes to Caesar o not? 2445
12:15 Should we pay o shouldn't we?" 2445
12:24 because you do not know the Scriptures o 3593
13:15 on the roof of his house go down o enter 3593
13:21 o, 'Look, there he is!' NIG
13:32 "No one knows about that day o hour, 2445
13:35 whether in the evening, o at midnight, 2445
13:35 or at midnight, o when the rooster crows, 2445
13:35 or when the rooster crows, o at dawn. 2445
14: 2 they said, "o the people may riot." 3607
14:68 "I don't know o understand 4046
Lk 1:15 to take wine o other fermented drink, 2779
2:24 "a pair of doves o two young pigeons." 2445
5:23 to say, 'Your sins are forgiven,' o to say, 2445
6: 9 to do good o to do evil, 2445
6: 9 to save life o to destroy it?" 2445
6:44 o grapes from briers. 4028
7:19 o should we expect someone else?" 2445
7:20 o should we expect someone else?' " 2445
8:16 "No one lights a lamp and hides it in a jar o 2445
8:17 not be known o brought out into the open. 2779
8:27 not worn clothes o lived in a house, 2779+4024
9:25 and yet lose o forfeit his very self? 2445
10: 4 Do not take a purse o bag or sandals; 3590
10: 4 Do not take a purse or bag o sandals; 3590
11:12 O if he asks for an egg, 2445
11:33 o under a bowl. 4028
12: 2 o hidden that will not be made known. 2779
12:11 about how you will defend yourselves o 2445
12:14 who appointed me a judge o an arbiter 2445
12:22 o about your body, what you will wear. 3593
12:24 They do not sow o reap, 4028
12:24 they have no storeroom o barn; 4028
12:27 They do not labor o spin. 4028
12:29 not set your heart on what you will eat o 2779
12:38 if he comes in the second o third watch of 2779
12:41 to us, o to everyone?" 2445
12:47 and does not get ready o does 2445
12:58 o he may drag you off to the judge, 3607
13: 4 O those eighteen who died when the tower 2445
13:15 on the Sabbath untie his ox o donkey from 2445
13:25 'I don't know you o where you come from.' NIG
13:27 'I don't know you o where you come from. NIG
14: 3 "Is it lawful to heal on the Sabbath o not?" 2445
14: 5 "If one of you has a son o an ox that falls 2445
14:12 "When you give a luncheon o dinner, 2445
14:12 your brothers o relatives, 3593
14:12 o your rich neighbors; 3593
14:31 "O suppose a king is about to go to war 2445
15: 8 "O suppose a woman has ten silver coins 2445
Lk 16:13 o he will be devoted to the one and despise 2445
17: 7 a servant plowing o looking after the sheep. 2445
17:21 'Here it is,' o 'There it is,' 2445
17:23 o 'Here he is!' 2445
18: 4 though I don't fear God o care about men, 4028
18:11 o even like this tax collector. 2445
18:29 "no one who has left home o wife 2445
18:29 or wife o brothers or parents or children for 2445
18:29 or wife or brothers o parents or children for 2445
18:29 or wife or brothers or parents o children for 2445
20: 4 was it from heaven, o from men?" 2445
20:22 Is it right for us to pay taxes to Caesar o 2445
21:15 of your adversaries will be able to resist o 2445
21:34 o your hearts will be weighed down 3607
22:27 at the table o the one who serves? 2445
22:35 bag o sandals, did you lack anything?" 2779
Jn 1:13 nor of human decision o a husband's will, 4028
3: 8 but you cannot tell where it comes from o 2779
4:27 o "Why are you talking with her?" 2445
5:14 Stop sinning o something worse may happen to you." 2671+3590
6:19 they had rowed **three o three and a half miles,** 1633+2445+4297+5084+5558
7:17 from God o whether I speak on my own. 2445
7:48 of the rulers o of the Pharisees believed 2445
8:14 But you have no idea where I come from o 2445
8:19 "You do not know me o my Father," 4046
9: 2 "Rabbi, who sinned, this man o his parents, 2445
9:21 he can see now, o who opened his eyes, 2445
9:25 "**Whether** he is a sinner **o not,** 1623
13:29 o to give something to the poor. 2445
14:11 **o at least** believe on the evidence of the miracles 1254+1623+3590
16: 3 because they have not known the Father o 4028
18:20 "I always taught in synagogues o at 2779
18:34 "o did others talk to you about me?" 2445
19:10 either to free you o to crucify you?" 2779
Ac 1: 7 to know the times o dates the Father has set 2445
3: 6 Peter said, "Silver o gold I do not have, 2779
3:12 at us as if by our own power o godliness 2445
4: 7 By what power o what name did you do this 2445
4:18 to speak o teach at all in the name of Jesus. 3593
4:34 from time to time those who owned lands o 2445
5:38 their purpose o activity is of human origin, 2445
6:10 not stand up against his wisdom o the Spirit 2779
7:49 O where will my resting place be? 2445
8:21 You have no part o share in this ministry, 4028
8:34 himself o someone else?" 2445
9: 2 whether men o women, 2779
9: 9 and did not eat o drink anything. 4028
10:14 "I have never eaten anything impure o 2779
10:28 to associate with a Gentile o visit him. 2445
10:28 that I should not call any man impure o 2445
11: 8 Nothing impure o unclean has ever entered my mouth.' 2445
16:21 for us Romans to accept o practice." 4028
17:29 not think that the divine being is like gold o 2445
17:29 is like gold or silver o stone— 2445
18:14 about some misdemeanor o serious crime, 2445
20:33 I have not coveted anyone's silver o gold 2445
20:33 anyone's silver or gold o clothing. 2445
21:21 not to circumcise their children o live 3593
23: 9 if a spirit o an angel has spoken to him?" 2445
23:12 not to eat o drink until they had killed Paul. 3612
23:21 They have taken an oath not to eat o drink 3612
23:29 that deserved death o imprisonment. 2445
24:12 o stirring up a crowd in the synagogues 2445
24:12 the synagogues o anywhere else in the city. 4046
24:20 O these who are here should state what crime they found in me 2445
25: 6 After spending eight o ten days with them, 2445
25: 8 the law of the Jews o against the temple or 4046
25: 8 the law of the Jews or against the temple o 4046
26:29 Paul replied, "Short time o long— 2779
26:31 not doing anything that deserves death o 2445
27:44 The rest were to get there on planks o 1254
28: 6 The people expected him to swell up o 2445
28:17 against our people o against the customs 2445
28:21 from there has reported o said anything bad 2445
Ro 2: 4 O do you show contempt for the riches 2445
3: 1 o what value is there in circumcision? 2445
4: 9 o also for the uncircumcised? 2445
4:10 Was it after he was circumcised, o before? 2445
6: 3 O don't you know that all 2445
6:16 which leads to death, o to obedience, 2445
8:35 Shall trouble o hardship or persecution 2445
8:35 Shall trouble or hardship o persecution 2445
8:35 or hardship or persecution o famine or 2445
8:35 or famine o nakedness or danger or sword? 2445
8:35 or famine or nakedness o danger or sword? 2445
8:35 or famine or nakedness or danger o sword? 2445
9:11 before the twins were born o had done 3593
9:11 or had done anything good o bad— 2445
9:16 therefore, depend on man's desire o effort, 4028
10: 7 "o 'Who will descend into the deep?' " 2445
11:34 O who has been his counselor?" 2445
14: 4 To his own master he stands o falls. 2445
14: 8 So, whether we live o die, 5445
14:10 O why do you look down on your brother? 2445
14:13 not to put any stumbling block o obstacle 2445
14:21 It is better not to eat meat o drink wine or 3593
14:21 not to eat meat or drink wine o to do 3593
1Co 2: 1 with eloquence o superior wisdom 2445
2: 6 not the wisdom of this age o of the rulers 4028
3:12 silver, costly stones, wood, hay o straw, NIG
3:22 whether Paul o Apollos or Cephas or 1664
3:22 or Apollos o Cephas or the world or life 1664
1Co 3:22 or Cephas o the world or life or death or 1664
3:22 or the world o life or death or the present or 1664
3:22 or the world or life o death or the present or 1664
3:22 or the world or life or death o the present or 1664
3:22 or life or death or the present o the future— 1664
4: 3 I care very little if I am judged by you o 2445
4:21 o in love and with a gentle spirit? 2445
5:10 o the greedy and swindlers, or idolaters. 2445
5:10 or the greedy and swindlers, o idolaters. 2445
5:11 a brother but is sexually immoral o greedy, 2445
5:11 an idolater o a slanderer, 2445
5:11 a drunkard o a swindler. 2445
7:11 she must remain unmarried o else 2445
7:15 A believing man o woman is not bound 2445
7:16 O, how do you know, husband, 2445
7:34 An unmarried woman o virgin is concerned 2779
8: 5 whether in heaven o on earth 1664
9: 6 O is it only I and Barnabas who must work 2445
10:19 o that an idol is anything? 2445
10:31 So whether you eat o drink or whatever 1664
10:31 you eat or drink o whatever you do, 1664
10:32 Greeks o the church of God— 2779
11: 4 Every man who prays o prophesies 2445
11: 5 And every woman who prays o prophesies 2445
11: 6 a woman to have her hair cut o shaved off, 2445
11:22 O do you despise the church of God 2445
11:27 whoever eats the bread o drinks the cup of 2445
12: 2 **somehow o other** you were influenced 323+6055
12:13 whether Jews o Greeks, slave or free— 1664
12:13 whether Jews or Greeks, slave o free— 1664
13: 1 a resounding gong o a clanging cymbal. 2445
14: 6 unless I bring you some revelation o 2445
14: 6 or knowledge o prophecy or word 2445
14: 6 or prophecy o word of instruction? 2445
14: 7 such as the flute o harp, 1664
14:23 not understand o some unbelievers come 2445
14:24 But if an unbeliever o someone who does 2445
14:26 o a word of instruction, a revelation, NIG
14:26 a revelation, a tongue o an interpretation. NIG
14:27 o at the most three—should speak, 2445
14:29 Two o three prophets should speak, 2445
14:36 O are you the only people it has reached? 2445
14:37 If anybody thinks he is a prophet o 2445
15:11 Whether, then, it was I o they, 1664
15:37 perhaps of wheat o of something else. 2445
16: 6 o even spend the winter, 2445
2Co 1:13 not write you anything you cannot read o 2445
1:17 O do I make my plans in a worldly manner 2445
3: 1 O do we need, like some people, 2445
3: 1 of recommendation to you o from you? 2445
5: 9 whether we are at home in the body o away 1664
5:10 whether good o bad. 1664
6:14 O what fellowship can light have 2445
7: 3 a place in our hearts that we would live o 2779
7:12 on account of the one who did the wrong o 4028
9: 7 not reluctantly o under compulsion, 2445
10:12 not dare to classify o compare ourselves 2445
11: 4 o if you receive a different spirit from 2445
11: 4 o a different gospel from the one 2445
11:20 you put up with anyone who enslaves you o NIG
11:20 or exploits you o takes advantage of you NIG
11:20 advantage of you o pushes himself forward NIG
11:20 forward o slaps you in the face. NIG
12: 2 the body o out of the body I do not know— 1664
12: 3 in the body o apart from the body I do not 1664
12: 6 of me than is warranted by what I do o say. 2445
13: 1 by the testimony of two o three witnesses." 2779
13: 2 not spare those who sinned earlier o any of 2779
Gal 1: 8 if we o an angel from heaven should preach 2445
1:10 to win the approval of men, o of God? 2445
1:10 O am I trying to please men? 2445
2: 2 that I was running o had run my race 2445
3: 2 o by believing what you heard? 2445
3: 5 o because you believe what you heard? 2445
3:15 Just as no one can set aside o add to 2445
4: 9 o rather are known by God— 1254
4:14 you did not treat me with contempt o scorn. 4028
5:15 watch out o you will be destroyed 3590
6: 1 watch yourself, o you also may be tempted. 3590
Eph 3:20 to do immeasurably more than all we ask o 2445
5: 3 o of any kind of impurity, or of greed, 2445
5: 3 or of any kind of impurity, o of greed, NIG
5: 4 foolish talk o coarse joking 2445
5: 5 No immoral, impure o greedy person— 2445
5:27 without stain o wrinkle 2445
5:27 or wrinkle o any other blemish, 2445
6: 8 whether he is slave o free. NIG
Php 1: 7 for whether I am in chains o defending 2779
1:18 whether from false motives o true, 1664
1:20 whether by life o by death. 1664
1:27 whether I come and see you o only hear 1664
2: 3 Do nothing out of selfish ambition o 3593
2:14 Do everything without complaining o 2779
2:16 the day of Christ that I did not run o labor 4028
3:12 o have already been made perfect, 2445
4: 8 if anything is excellent o praiseworthy— 2779
4: 9 Whatever you have learned o received 2779
4: 9 learned or received o heard from me, or 2779
4: 9 o seen in me—put it into practice. 2779
4:12 whether well fed o hungry, 2779
4:12 whether living in plenty o in want. 2779
Col 1:16 and invisible, whether thrones o powers 1664
1:16 whether thrones or powers o rulers 1664
1:16 thrones or powers or rulers o authorities; 1664
1:20 whether things on earth o things in heaven, 1664
2:16 not let anyone judge you by what you eat o 2779
2:16 o with regard to a religious festival, 2445

Col 2:16 a New Moon celebration o a Sabbath day. 2445
3:11 Here there is no Greek o Jew, 2779
3:11 circumcised o uncircumcised, barbarian, 2779
3:11 slave o free, but Christ is all, and is in all. NIG
3:17 whatever you do, whether in word o deed, 2445
3:21 o they will become discouraged. 2671+3590
1Th 2: 3 not spring from error o impure motives, 4028
2: 6 not from you o anyone else. 4046
2:19 o the crown in which we will glory in 2445
4: 6 no one should wrong his brother o take 2779
4:13 o to grieve like the rest of men, NIG
5: 5 not belong to the night o to the darkness. 4028
5:10 whether we are awake o asleep, 1664
2Th 2: 2 not to become easily unsettled o alarmed 3593
2: 2 report o letter supposed to have come 3612
2: 4 over everything that is called God o 2445
2:15 whether by word of mouth o by letter. 1664
1Ti 1: 7 about o what they so confidently affirm. 3612
1: 9 for those who kill their fathers o mothers, 2779
2: 8 without anger o disputing. 2779
2: 9 not with braided hair o gold or pearls 2779
2: 9 or gold o pearls or expensive clothes, 2445
2: 9 not with braided hair or gold or pearls o 2445
2:12 a woman to teach o to have authority over 4028
3: 6 o he may become conceited and 2671+3590
5: 4 if a widow has children o grandchildren, 2445
5:19 an elder unless it is brought by two o 2445
6:14 to keep this command without spot o blame NIG
6:16 whom no one has seen o can see. 4028
2Ti 1: 8 o ashamed of me his prisoner. 3593
Tit 1:14 pay no attention to Jewish myths o to the 2779
2: 3 to be slanderers o addicted to much wine, 3593
3:12 soon as I send Artemas o Tychicus to you, 2445
Phm 1:18 If he has done you any wrong o owes you 2445
Heb 1: 5 O again, "I will be his Father, 2779
7: 3 Without father o mother, NIG
7: 3 without beginning of days o end of life, 3612
8:11 o a man his brother, saying, 2779
10:28 on the testimony of two o three witnesses. 2445
12:16 o is godless like Esau, 2445
12:19 to a trumpet blast o to such 2779
Jas 2: 3 "You stand there" o "Sit on the floor 2445
2:15 a brother o sister is without clothes 2445
3: 4 O take ships as an example. 2779
3:12 o a grapevine bear figs? 2445
3:14 do not boast about it o deny the truth. 2779
4: 5 O do you think Scripture says 2445
4:11 Anyone who speaks against his brother o 2445
4:13 "Today o tomorrow we will go to this or 2445
4:13 we will go to this o that city, 3836+3840
4:15 we will live and do this o that." 2445
5: 9 brothers, o you will be judged. 2671+3590
5:12 by heaven o by earth or by anything else. 3612
5:12 by heaven or by earth o by anything else. 3612
5:12 no, o you will be condemned. 2671+3590
1Pe 1: 4 an inheritance that can never perish, spoil o 2779
1:18 with perishable things such as silver o gold 2445
1:19 a lamb without blemish o defect. 2779
2:14 o to governors, who are sent by him 1664
3: 9 not repay evil with evil o insult with insult, 2445
4:15 be as a murderer o thief or any other kind 2445
4:15 be as a murderer or thief o any other kind 2445
4:15 o even as a meddler. 2445
1Jn 2:15 Do not love the world o anything in the world. 3593+3836
3: 6 to sin has either seen him o known him. 4028
3:18 with words o tongue but with actions and 3593
2Jn 1:10 do not take him into your house o 2779
Rev 3:15 I wish you were either one o the other! 2445
5: 3 But no one in heaven o on earth or under 4028
5: 3 But no one in heaven or on earth o under 4028
5: 3 under the earth could open the scroll o even 4046
5: 4 to open the scroll o look inside. 4046
7: 1 from blowing on the land o on the sea or 3612
7: 1 on the land or on the sea o on any tree. 3612
7: 3 "Do not harm the land o the sea or the trees 3612
7: 3 "Do not harm the land or the sea o the trees 3612
9: 4 to harm the grass of the earth o any plant 4028
9: 4 grass of the earth or any plant o tree, 4028
9:20 idols that cannot see o hear or walk. 4046
9:20 idols that cannot see or hear o walk. 4046
9:21 their sexual immorality o their thefts. 4046
12: 9 ancient serpent called the devil, o Satan, 2779
13:16 a mark on his right hand o on his forehead, 2445
13:17 that no one could buy o sell unless he had 2445
13:17 of the beast o the number of his name. 2445
14: 9 and receives his mark on the forehead o on 2445
14:11 There is no rest day o night 2779
14:11 o for anyone who receives the mark 2779
20: 2 who is the devil, o Satan, 2779
20: 4 not worshiped the beast o his image 4028
20: 4 not received his mark on their foreheads o 2779
21: 4 There will be no more death o mourning 4046
21: 4 no more death or mourning o crying 4046
21: 4 no more death or mourning or crying o pain, 4046
21:23 not need the sun o the moon to shine on it, 4028
21:27 will anyone who does what is shameful o 2779
22: 5 not need the light of a lamp o the light of 2779

ORACLE (44) [ORACLES]

Nu 23: 7 Then Balaam uttered his o: 5442
23:18 Then he uttered his o: 5442
24: 3 and he uttered his o: 5442
24: 3 "The o of Balaam son of Beor, 5536
24: 3 the o of one whose eye sees clearly, 5536
24: 4 the o of one who hears the words of God, 5536
24:15 Then he uttered his o: 5442
24:15 "The o of Balaam son of Beor, 5536
24:15 the o of one whose eye sees clearly, 5536
24:16 the o of one who hears the words of God, 5536
24:20 Balaam saw Amalek and uttered his o: 5442
24:21 Then he saw the Kenites and uttered his o: 5442
24:23 Then he uttered his o: 5442
2Sa 23: 1 "The o of David son of Jesse, 5536
23: 1 the o of the man exalted by the Most High, 5536
Ps 36: 1 An o is within my heart concerning 5536
Pr 16:10 The lips of a king speak as an o, 7877
30: 1 The sayings of Agur son of Jakeh—an o: 5363
31: 1 an o his mother taught him: 5363
Isa 13: 1 An o concerning Babylon that Isaiah son 5363
14:28 This o came in the year King Ahaz died: 5363
15: 1 An o concerning Moab: 5363
17: 1 An o concerning Damascus: 5363
19: 1 An o concerning Egypt: 5363
21: 1 An o concerning the Desert by the Sea: 5363
21:11 An o concerning Dumah: 5363
21:13 An o concerning Arabia: 5363
22: 1 An o concerning the Valley of Vision: 5363
23: 1 An o concerning Tyre: 5363
30: 6 An o concerning the animals of the Negev: 5363
Jer 23:33 ask you, 'What is the o of the LORD?' 5363
23:33 say to them, 'What o?' 5363
23:34 'This is the o of the LORD,' 5363
23:36 not mention 'the o of the LORD' again, 5363
23:36 every man's own word becomes his o 5363
23:38 'This is the o of the LORD,' 5363
23:38 'This is the o of the LORD,' 5363
23:38 'This is the o of the LORD.' 5363
Eze 12:10 This o concerns the prince in Jerusalem 5363
Na 1: 1 An o concerning Nineveh. 5363
Hab 1: 1 The o that Habakkuk the prophet received. 5363
Zec 9: 1 An O The word of the LORD is against 5363
12: 1 An O This is the word of the LORD 5363
Mal 1: 1 An o: The word of the 5363

ORACLES (1) [ORACLE]

La 2:14 The o they gave you were false 5363

ORCHARD (1) [ORCHARDS]

SS 4:13 an o of pomegranates with choice fruits, 7236

ORCHARDS (2) [ORCHARD]

Isa 16:10 and gladness are taken away from the o; 4149
Jer 48:33 and gladness are gone from the o and fields 4149

ORDAIN (3) [ORDAINED, ORDINATION]

Ex 28:41 and his sons, anoint and o them. 906+3338+4848
29: 9 In this way you shall o Aaron and his 3338+4848
29:35 taking seven days to o them. 3338+4848

ORDAINED (14) [ORDAIN]

Ex 29:29 so that they can be anointed and o in them. 906+3338+4848
Lev 16:32 and o to succeed his father as high priest 906+3338+4848
21:10 and who has been o to wear 906+3338+4848
Nu 3: 3 who were o to serve as priests. 3338+4848
2Ki 19:25 Long ago I o it. 6913
Ps 8: 2 of children and infants you have o praise 3569
65: 9 for so you have o it. 3922
111: 9 he o his covenant forever— 7422
139:16 All the days o for me were written 3670
Isa 37:26 Long ago I o it. 6913
48: 5 my wooden image and metal god o them.' 7422
Eze 28:14 guardian cherub, for so I o you. 5989
Hab 1:12 O Rock, you have o them to punish. 3569
Mt 21:16 and infants you have o praise'?" 2936

ORDER (148) [ORDERED, ORDERLY, ORDERS]

Ge 25:13 listed in the o of their birth: 9352
38:20 the Adullamite in o to get his pledge back 4200
43:33 before him in the o of their ages, from 3869
Ex 1:22 Pharaoh gave this o to all his people: 7422
5: 6 That same day Pharaoh gave this o to 7422
9:19 Give an o now to bring your livestock 8938
28:10 in the o of their birth— 3869
36: 6 Then Moses gave an o and 7422
Lev 13:54 he shall o that the contaminated article 7422
14: 4 the priest shall o that two live clean birds 7422
14: 5 Then the priest shall o that one of the birds 7422
14:36 The priest is to o the house to be emptied 7422
14:40 he is to o that the contaminated stones 7422
22:19 sheep or goats in o that it may be accepted 4200
Nu 2:17 They will set out in the same o 4027
9:19 the Israelites obeyed the LORD's o 5466
9:23 They obeyed the LORD's o, 5466
10:28 the o of march for the Israelite divisions 5023
36: 5 LORD's command Moses gave this o 7422
Dt 2:30 and his heart obstinate in o to give him 5100
8: 2 and to test you in o to know what was 4200
29:12 You are standing here in o to enter into 4200
Jos 10:27 At sunset Joshua gave the o 7422
Jdg 7: 2 In o that Israel may not boast against me 7153
9:24 God did this in o that the crime 4200
Ru 4: 5 in o to maintain the name of the dead 4200
4:10 in o to maintain the name of the dead 4200
1Sa 1: 6 her rival kept provoking her in o to 6288
15:21 in o to sacrifice them to the LORD 4200
2Sa 2:26 How long before you o your men 606
4:12 So David gave an o to his men, 7422
13:28 Have not I given you this o? 7422
14: 8 and I will issue an o in your behalf." 7422
14:29 for Joab in o to send him to the king, 4200
17:14 the good advice of Ahithophel in o to 6288
17:23 put his house in o and then hanged himself. 7422
19:29 I o you and Ziba to divide the fields." 606
1Ki 2:46 Then the king gave the o to Benaiah son 7422
3:25 He then gave an o: 606
15:22 Then King Asa issued an o to all Judah— 9048
2Ki 10:19 But Jehu was acting deceptively in o to 5100
17:27 Then the king of Assyria gave this o: 7422
20: 1 Put your house in o, 7422
23:21 The king gave this o to all the people: 7422
23:35 In o to do so, 4200
24: 3 in o to remove them from his presence 4200
1Ch 15:14 Levites consecrated themselves in o to 4200
24: 3 for their appointed o of ministering. 7213
24:19 This was their appointed o of ministering 7213
2Ch 11:22 in o to make him king. 3954
24:21 by o of the king they stoned him to death 5184
29:27 Hezekiah gave the o to sacrifice 606
31: 5 As soon as the o went out, 1821
32:18 and make them afraid in o to capture 5100
35:20 set the temple in o, 3922
36:22 in o to fulfill the word of the LORD 4200
Ezr 1: 1 in o to fulfill the word of the LORD 4200
4:19 I issued an o and a search was made, 10302
4:21 Now issue an o to these men to stop work, 10302
4:21 that this city will not be rebuilt until I so o. 10002+10302+10682
6: 1 King Darius then issued an o, 10302
6:21 of their Gentile neighbors in o to seek 4200
7:21 o all the treasurers of Trans-Euphrates to provide 10302+10682
Ne 5: 2 in o for us to eat and stay alive, 2256
9:17 in their rebellion appointed a leader in o to 4200
9:26 who had admonished them in o to 4200
13:22 and go and guard the gates in o to keep 4200
Est 1:11 in o to display her beauty to the people 4200
2: 8 the king's o and edict had been proclaimed, 1821
3:13 with the o to destroy, kill and annihilate all NIH
4: 3 to which the edict and o of the king came, 2017
8: 5 an o be written overruling the dispatches 4180
Job 25: 2 he establishes o in the heights of heaven. 8934
Ps 10:18 in o that man, who is of the earth, may terrify no more. 1153
59: T to watch David's house in o to kill him. 4200
110: 4 a priest forever, in the o of Melchizedek." 1826
Pr 28: 2 and knowledge maintains o. 4026
Ecc 12: 9 and set in o many proverbs. 9545
Isa 23:11 He has given an o concerning Phoenicia 7422
34:16 For it is his mouth that has given the o, 7422
38: 1 Put your house in o, 7422
Jer 34:22 I am going to give the o, 7422
Eze 3:18 to dissuade him from his evil ways in o to 4200
13:18 of various lengths for their heads in o to 4200
39:12 be burying them in o to cleanse the land. 5100
Da 6:16 So the king gave the o, 10042
11:17 in marriage in o to overthrow the kingdom, 4200
Am 1:13 the pregnant women of Gilead in o to 5100
Zec 13: 4 a prophet's garment of hair in o to deceive. 5100
Mt 12:44 swept clean and put in o. 3175
27:64 So give the o for the tomb to 3027
Mk 7: 9 setting aside the commands of God in o to 2671
Lk 4:29 in o to throw him down the cliff. 6063
8:31 not to o them to go into the Abyss. 2199
11:25 it finds the house swept clean and put in o. 3175
19:15 in o to find out what they had gained 2671
Jn 8: 6 in o to have a basis for accusing him. 2671
17:26 to make you known in o that 2671
Ac 6: 2 of the word of God in o to wait on tables. AIT
9:24 on the city gates in o to kill him. 3968
16:35 the jailer with the o: "Release those men." 3306
17: 5 in o to bring them out AIT
19:33 in o to make a defense AIT
20:30 the truth in o to draw away disciples 3836
22:24 that he be flogged and questioned in o to 2671
24: 4 But in o not to weary you further, 2671
Ro 1:13 until now) in o that I might have a harvest 2671
4:11 in o that righteousness might be credited 1650+3836
6: 4 through baptism into death in o that, 2671
7: 4 in o that we might bear fruit to God. 2671
7:13 But in o that sin might be recognized 2671
8: 4 in o that the righteous requirements of 2671
8:17 we share in his sufferings in o that we may 2671
9:11 in o that God's purpose in election might 2671
11:31 now become disobedient in o that 2671
15: 7 in o to bring praise to God. 1650
2Co 1:23 as my witness that it was in o to spare you AIT
2:11 in o that Satan might not outwit us. 2671
8:19 which we administer in o to honor 4639
9: 3 But I am sending the brothers in o that 2671
11: 7 Was it a sin for me to lower myself in o to 2671
11:12 on doing what I am doing in o to cut 2671
11:32 guarded in o to arrest me. AIT
Gal 3:14 He redeemed us in o that the blessing 2671
Eph 1:12 in o that we, who were the first 1650+3836
1:18 heart may be enlightened in o that 1650+3836
2: 7 in o that in the coming ages he might show 2671
4:10 in o to fill the whole universe.) 2671
Php 2:16 in o that I may boast on the day of Christ AIT
Col 1:10 o that you may live a life worthy AIT
2: 2 in o that they may know the mystery 1650
1Th 2: 9 and day in o not to be a burden to anyone 4639

1Th 4: 1 we instructed you how to live in o to *2671*
2Th 3: 9 but in o to make ourselves a model for you *2671*
3:14 in o that he may feel ashamed. *2671*
1Ti 4: 3 and o them to abstain from certain foods, *NIG*
Tit 3:14 in o that they may provide *2671*
Phm 1: 8 be bold and o you to do what you ought *2199*
Heb 2:17 in o that he might become a merciful *2671*
5: 6 a priest forever, in the o of Melchizedek." *5423*
5:10 to be high priest in the o of Melchizedek. *5423*
6:11 in o to make your hope sure. *4639*
6:20 high priest forever, in the o of Melchizedek. *5423*
7:11 one in the o of Melchizedek, *5423*
7:11 not in the o of Aaron? *5423*
7:17 a priest forever, in the o of Melchizedek." *5423*
9:10 until the time *of* the new o. *1481*
Rev 21: 4 for the old o of things has passed away." *NIG*

ORDERED (94) [ORDER]

Ex 17:10 the Amalekites as Moses *had* o, 606
Lev 10: 5 outside the camp, as Moses o. 1819
Nu 34:13 The LORD *has* o that it be given to 7422
36: 2 he o you to give the inheritance 7422
Jos 1:10 So Joshua o the officers of the people: 7422
6: 7 And *he* o the people, "Advance! 606
8:29 Joshua o them to take his body from 7422
Jdg 3:28 *he* o, "for the LORD has given Moab, 606
9:48 *He* o the men with him, "Quick! 606
1Sa 18:22 Then Saul o his attendants: 7422
20:29 in the town and my brother *has* o me to 7422
22:17 Then the king o the guards at his side: 606
22:18 The king then o Doeg, 606
2Sa 1:18 and o that the men of Judah 606
13:28 Absalom o his men, "Listen! 7422
13:29 to Amnon what Absalom *had* o. 7422
1Ki 2:29 Then Solomon o Benaiah son of Jehoiada, 8938
12:24 as the LORD had o, 1821
17: 4 and *I have* o the ravens to feed you there." 7422
18:34 "Do it a third time," *he* o, 606
20:12 and *he* o his men: "Prepare to attack." 606
22:26 The king of Israel then o, 606
22:31 *had* o his thirty-two chariot commanders, 7422
2Ki 6:13 "Go, find out where he is," the king o, 606
9:17 "Get a horseman," Joram o. 606
9:21 "Hitch up my chariot," Joram o. 606
10: 8 Then Jehu o, "Put them in two piles at 606
10:14 "Take them alive!" *he* o. 606
10:25 he o the guards and officers: 606
11: 9 a hundred did just as Jehoiada the priest o. 7422
11:15 the priest o the commanders of units of 7422
16:16 Uriah the priest did just as King Ahaz *had* o. 7422
17:15 although the LORD *had* o them, 7422
23: 4 The king o Hilkiah the high priest, 7422
1Ch 21:17 not I *who* o the fighting men to be counted? 606
21:18 the angel of the LORD o Gad to tell David 606
22:17 Then David o all the leaders of Israel 7422
2Ch 8:14 the man of God had o. 5184
18:25 The king of Israel then o, 606
18:30 king of Aram *had* o his chariot commanders 7422
23: 8 of Judah did just as Jehoiada the priest o. 7422
23:18 with rejoicing and singing, as David had o. 3338
29:15 as the king had o, 5184
29:24 because the king *had* o the burnt offering 606
29:30 and his officials o the Levites to praise 606
30:12 what the king and his officials had o, 5184
31: 4 *He* o the people living in Jerusalem to give 606
35:10 in their divisions as the king had o. 5184
35:16 as King Josiah had o. 5184
Ezr 2:63 The governor o them not to eat any of 606
Ne 7:65 o them not to eat any of the most sacred 606
13:19 *I* o the doors to be shut and not opened 606
Est 4: 5 to attend her, and o him to find out 7422
6: 1 so *he* o the book of the chronicles, 606
6: 5 "Bring him in," the king o. 606
Jer 35:14 son of Recab o his sons not to drink wine 7422
35:18 and have done everything *he* o.' 7422
38:27 the king *had* o him to say. 7422
47: 7 when *he has* o it to attack Ashkelon and 3585
Da 1: 3 Then the king o Ashpenaz, 606
2:12 so angry and furious that *he* o the execution 10042
2:46 and paid him honor and o that an offering 10042
3:19 *He* o the furnace heated seven times 10558
Mt 14: 9 *he* o that her request be granted *3027*
18:25 the master o that he and his wife *3027*
27:58 and Pilate o that it be given to him. *3027*
Lk 5:14 Then Jesus o him, "Don't tell anyone, *4133*
8:56 but he o them not to tell anyone *4133*
14:21 the house became angry and o his servant, *3306*
14:22 'what *you* o has been done, *2199*
18:40 Jesus stopped and o the man to be brought *3027*
Ac 4:15 So *they* o them to withdraw from *3027*
5:34 up in the Sanhedrin and o that the men *3027*
5:40 Then *they* o them not to speak in the name *4133*
10:48 So *he* o that they be baptized in the name *4705*
12:19 he cross-examined the guards and o that *3027*
16:22 and the magistrates o them to be stripped *3027*
16:36 "The magistrates *have* o that you and Silas *690*
18: 2 Claudius *had* o all the Jews to leave Rome. *1411*
21:33 up and arrested him and o him to be bound *3027*
21:34 *he* o that Paul be taken into the barracks. *3027*
22:24 the commander o Paul to be taken into *3027*
22:30 and o the chief priests and all the Sanhedrin *3027*
23: 2 the high priest Ananias o those standing *2199*
23:10 *He* o the troops to go down *3027*
23:23 *he* called two of his centurions and o them, *3306*
23:30 *I* also o his accusers to present *4133*
23:35 Then *he* o that Paul be kept under guard *3027*
Ac 24:23 *He* o the centurion to keep Paul under guard *1411*
25: 6 and o that Paul be brought before him. *3027*
25:17 but convened the court the next day and o *3027*
25:21 *I* o him held until I could send him *3027*
27:43 *He* o those who could swim *3027*
Rev 13:14 *He* o them to set up an image in honor of *3306*

ORDERLY (3) [ORDER]

Lk 1: 3 also to me to write an o account for you, *2759*
1Co 14:40 be done in a fitting and o way. *2848+5423*
Col 2: 5 in spirit and delight to see how o you are *5423*

ORDERS (50) [ORDER]

Ge 12:20 Pharaoh gave o about Abram *to* his men, 7422
26:11 So Abimelech gave o *to* all the people: 7422
41:40 and all my people are to submit to your o. 7023
42:25 Joseph gave o to fill their bags with grain, 7422
Nu 32:28 Then Moses gave o about them *to* Eleazar 7422
Dt 2: 4 Give the people *these* o: 7422
Jos 3: 3 giving o *to* the people: 7422
8: 4 with these o: "Listen carefully. 7422
8: 8 See to it; you *have my* o." 7422
Ru 2:15 Boaz gave o *to* his men, 7422
2Sa 3:15 So Ish-Bosheth gave o 8938
18: 5 And all the troops heard the king giving o 7422
1Ki 2:25 So King Solomon gave o to Benaiah son 8938
5: 6 "So give o that cedars of Lebanon be cut 7422
2Ki 16:15 King Ahaz then gave *these* o *to* Uriah 7422
22:12 He gave *these* o *to* Hilkiah the priest, 7422
1Ch 14:12 and David gave o to burn them in the fire. 606
22: 2 So David gave o to assemble 606
2Ch 2: 1 Solomon gave o to build a temple for 606
19: 9 *He* gave them *these* o: 7422
31:11 Hezekiah gave o to prepare storerooms in 606
34:20 He gave *these* o *to* Hilkiah, 7422
Ezr 8:36 the king's o to the royal satraps and to 2017
Ne 11:23 The singers were under the king's o, 5184
13: 9 *I* gave o to purify the rooms, 606
Est 3:12 the language of each people all Haman's o 7422
8: 9 They wrote out all Mordecai's o to 7422
8: 9 These o were written in the script NIH
9:25 *he* issued written o that 606
Job 38:12 *"Have you* ever given o *to* the morning, 7422
Isa 45:11 or give me o about the work of my hands? 7422
Jer 37:21 King Zedekiah then gave o *for* Jeremiah to 7422
39:11 of Babylon *had* given *these* o 7422
Da 5: 2 *he* gave o to bring in the gold 10042
6:23 and gave o to lift Daniel out of the den. 10042
Mt 2:16 and he gave o to kill all the boys *690*
8:18 *he* gave o to cross to the other side of *3027*
Mk 1:27 *He* even gives o to evil spirits *2199*
3:12 But *he* gave them strict o not *2203*
5:43 *He* gave strict o not to let anyone know *1403*
6:17 For Herod himself *had* given o *690*
6:27 an executioner with o to bring John's head. *2199*
9: 9 Jesus gave them o not to tell *1403*
Lk 4:36 With authority and power *he* gives o *2199*
15:29 for you and never disobeyed your o. *1953*
Jn 11:57 the chief priests and Pharisees had given o *1953*
Ac 5:28 *"We* gave you strict o not to teach *4132+4133*
8:38 And *he* gave o to stop the chariot. *3027*
16:24 Upon receiving such o, *4132*
23:31 So the soldiers, carrying out their o, *1411*

ORDINANCE (29) [ORDINANCES]

Ex 12:14 to the LORD—a lasting o. 2978
12:17 as a lasting o for the generations to come. 2978
12:24 as a lasting o for you and your descendants. 2976
13:10 You must keep this o at the appointed time 2978
27:21 to be a lasting o among the Israelites for 2978
28:43 a lasting o for Aaron and his descendants. 2978
29: 9 The priesthood is theirs by a lasting o. 2978
30:21 a lasting o for Aaron and his descendants 2976
Lev 3:17 " 'This is a lasting o for the generations 2978
10: 9 a lasting o for the generations to come. 2978
16:29 "This is to be a lasting o for you: 2978
16:31 it is a lasting o. 2978
16:34 "This is to be a lasting o for you: 2978
17: 7 a lasting o for them and for the generations 2978
23:14 This is to be a lasting o for the generations 2978
23:21 This is to be a lasting o for the generations 2978
23:31 This is to be a lasting o for the generations 2978
23:41 This is to be a lasting o for the generations 2978
24: 3 This is to be a lasting o for the generations 2978
Nu 10: 8 to be a lasting o for you and the generations 2978
15:15 a lasting o for the generations to come. 2978
18:23 a lasting o for the generations to come. 2978
19:10 be a lasting o both for the Israelites and for 2978
19:21 This is a lasting o for them. 2978
1Sa 30:25 David made this a statute and o for Israel 5477
2Ch 2: 4 This is a lasting o for Israel. NIH
8:14 In keeping with the o *of* his father David, 5477
Ps 81: 4 an o of the God of Jacob. 5477
Eze 46:14 grain offering to the LORD is a lasting o. 2978

ORDINANCES (7) [ORDINANCE]

2Ki 17:34 nor adhere to the decrees and o, 5477
17:37 be careful to keep the decrees and o, 5477
2Ch 19:10 commands, decrees or o— 5477
33: 8 decrees and o given through Moses." 5477
Ne 9:29 They sinned against your o, 5477
Ps 19: 9 The o *of* the LORD are sure 5477
Eze 44:24 as judges and decide it according to my o. 5477

ORDINARY (8)

1Sa 21: 4 "I don't have any o bread on hand; 2687
Isa 8: 1 a large scroll and write on it with an o pen: 632
Ac 4:13 that they were unschooled, o men, *2626*
7:20 and he was no o child. *842*
21:39 a citizen of no o city. *817*
Gal 4:23 His son by the slave woman was born in the o way; *2848+4922*
4:29 the son born in the o way persecuted *2848+4922*
Heb 11:23 because they saw *he was* no o child, *842*

ORDINATION (13) [ORDAIN]

Ex 29:22 (This is the ram for the o.) 4854
29:26 the breast of the ram for Aaron's o, 4854
29:27 "Consecrate those parts of the o ram 4854
29:31 "Take the ram for the o and cook the meat 4854
29:33 by which atonement was made for their o 906+3338+4848
29:34 of the meat of the o ram or any bread is left 4854
Lev 7:37 the o offering and the fellowship offering, 4854
8:22 the ram for the o, 4854
8:28 of the burnt offering as an o offering, 4854
8:29 Moses' share of the o ram— 4854
8:31 the bread from the basket of o offerings, 4854
8:33 until the days of your o are completed, 4854
8:33 for your o will last seven days. 906+3338+4848

ORE (3)

Job 28: 2 and copper is smelted from o. 74
28: 3 he searches the farthest recesses for o in 74
Jer 6:27 a tester of metals and my people the o, 4450

OREB (7)

Jdg 7:25 of the Midianite leaders, O and Zeeb. 6855
7:25 They killed O at the rock of Oreb, 6855
7:25 They killed Oreb at the rock of O, 6855
7:25 the Midianites and brought the heads of O 6855
8: 3 God gave O and Zeeb, 6855
Ps 83:11 Make their nobles like O and Zeeb, 6855
Isa 10:26 he struck down Midian at the rock of O; 6855

OREN (1)

1Ch 2:25 Ram his firstborn, Bunah, O, 816

ORGAN (KJV) See FLUTE

ORGIES (3)

Ro 13:13 not *in* o and drunkenness, *3269*
Gal 5:21 drunkenness, o, and the like. *3269*
1Pe 4: 3 living in debauchery, lust, drunkenness, o, *3269*

ORIGIN (3) [ORIGINAL, ORIGINATE, ORIGINS]

Est 6:13 is of Jewish o, you cannot stand 2446
Ac 5:38 if their purpose or activity is of human o, *NIG*
2Pe 1:21 For prophecy never *had its* o in the will *5770*

ORIGINAL (1) [ORIGIN]

2Ch 24:13 the temple of God according to its o design 5504

ORIGINATE (1) [ORIGIN]

1Co 14:36 *Did* the word of God o with you? *2002*

ORIGINS (1) [ORIGIN]

Mic 5: 2 whose o are from of old, 4606

ORION (3)

Job 9: 9 He is the Maker of the Bear and O, 4068
38:31 Can you loose the cords of O? 4068
Am 5: 8 the Pleiades and O, who turns blackness 4068

ORNAMENT (2) [ORNAMENTED, ORNAMENTS]

Pr 3:22 an o to grace your neck. 2834
25:12 or an o *of* fine gold is a wise man's rebuke 2717

ORNAMENTED (5) [ORNAMENT]

Ge 37: 3 and he made a richly o robe for him. 7168
37:23 the richly o robe he was wearing— 7168
37:32 They took the o robe back to their father 7168
2Sa 13:18 She was wearing a richly o robe, 7168
13:19 and tore the o robe she was wearing. 7168

ORNAMENTS (10) [ORNAMENT]

Ex 33: 4 to mourn and no one put on any o. 6344
33: 5 Now take off your o and I will decide what 6344
33: 6 So the Israelites stripped off their o 6344
35:22 brooches, earrings, rings and o. 3921
Jdg 8:21 and took the o off their camels' necks. 8448
8:26 not counting the o, 8448
2Sa 1:24 who adorned your garments with o *of* gold. 6344
Isa 3:16 with o jingling on their ankles. 6576
49:18 "you will wear them all as o; 6344
Jer 2:32 a bride her wedding o? 8005

ORPAH (2)
Ru 1: 4 one named **O** and the other Ruth. 6905
1:14 Then **O** kissed her mother-in-law good-by, 6905

ORPHAN (1) [ORPHAN'S, ORPHANS]
Ex 22:22 "Do not take advantage of a widow or an **o**. 3846

ORPHAN'S (1) [ORPHAN]
Job 24: 3 They drive away the **o** donkey and take 3846

ORPHANS (4) [ORPHAN]
Jer 49:11 Leave your **o**; I will protect their lives. 3846
La 5: 3 We have become **o** and fatherless, 3846
Jn 14:18 I will not leave you as **o**; *4003*
Jas 1:27 to look after **o** and widows in their distress *4003*

OSEE (KJV) See HOSEA

OSHEA (KJV) See JOSHUA

OSPRAY (KJV) See BLACK VULTURE

OSPREY (2)
Lev 11:18 the white owl, the desert owl, the **o**, 8164
Dt 14:17 the desert owl, the **o**, the cormorant, 8168

OSSIFRAGE (KJV) See VULTURE

OSTRICH (1) [OSTRICHES]
Job 39:13 "The wings of the **o** flap joyfully, 8266

OSTRICHES (1) [OSTRICH]
La 4: 3 but my people have become heartless like **o** 3612

OTHER (730) [OTHER'S, OTHERS, OTHERWISE]
Ge 4:19 one named Adah and the **o** Zillah. 9108
5: 4 Adam lived 800 years and had **o** sons NIH
5: 7 Seth lived 807 years and had **o** sons NIH
5:10 Enosh lived 815 years and had **o** sons NIH
5:13 Kenan lived 840 years and had **o** sons NIH
5:16 Mahalalel lived 830 years and had **o** sons NIH
5:19 Jared lived 800 years and had **o** sons NIH
5:22 walked with God 300 years and had **o** sons NIH
5:26 Methuselah lived 782 years and had **o** sons NIH
5:30 Lamech lived 595 years and had **o** sons NIH
9:23 Their faces were **turned the o way** so 345
11: 3 They said to each **o**, "Come, 8276S
11: 7 so they will not understand each **o**." 8276S
11:11 Shem lived 500 years and had **o** sons NIH
11:13 Arphaxad lived 403 years and had **o** sons NIH
11:15 Shelah lived 403 years and had **o** sons NIH
11:17 Eber lived 430 years and had **o** sons NIH
11:19 Peleg lived 209 years and had **o** sons NIH
11:21 Reu lived 207 years and had **o** sons NIH
11:23 Serug lived 200 years and had **o** sons NIH
11:25 Nahor lived 119 years and had **o** sons NIH
14:16 together with the women and the **o** people. NIH
15:10 and arranged the halves opposite each **o**; 8276S
24:50 to you one way or **the o.** 3202S
25:22 The babies **jostled each o** within her, 8368
25:23 one people will be stronger than the **o**, 4211S
26:31 the men swore an oath to each **o**. 278S
28:17 This is none **o than** the house of God; 561+3954
29:19 that I give her to you than to *some* **o** man. 337
31:49 and me when we are away from each **o**. 8276S
34:23 and all their *o* **animals** become ours? AIT
36: 6 as his livestock and all his *o* **animals** AIT
37: 3 of his *o* **sons**, because he had been born AIT
37:19 they said to each **o**. 278S
41: 3 After them, seven **o** cows, ugly and gaunt, 337
41: 6 seven **o** heads of grain sprouted— NIH
41:13 and **the o man** was hanged." 2257S
41:19 After them, seven **o** cows came up— 337
41:23 After them, seven **o** heads sprouted— NIH
41:54 There was famine in all the **o** lands, NIH
42: 1 "Why *do you just keep* **looking at each o?"** 8011
42:28 and they turned to each **o** trembling 278S
43:14 the man so that he will let your **o** brother 337
43:33 and they looked at each **o** in astonishment. 8276S
45:23 and bread and *o* **provisions** for his journey. AIT
47:21 from one end of Egypt to the **o**. 7895S
47:24 The *o* **four-fifths** you may keep as seed for AIT
Ex 12:38 Many **o people** went up with them, 6850
14: 7 along with all the **o** chariots of Egypt, NIH
14:20 to the one side and light to the **o** side; NIH
14:20 so neither went near the **o** all night long. 2296S
16: 5 as much as they gather *on* the **o days."** 3427+3427
16:15 the Israelites saw it, they said to each **o**, 278S
17:12 one on one side, one on the **o**— 2296S
18: 4 and the **o** was named Eliezer, 285S
18: 7 They greeted each **o** and then went into 8276S
18:11 that the LORD is greater than all **o** gods, 2021S
18:12 brought a burnt offering and **o** sacrifices NIH
20: 3 "You shall have no **o** gods before me. 337
21:18 "If men quarrel and one hits the **o** with 8276S
21:19 if the **o** gets up and walks around outside NIH
22: 8 on the **o** *man's* property. 8276S
22: 9 or **any** *o* lost property AIT
Ex 22:10 a sheep or **any** *o* animal to his neighbor AIT
22:11 not lay hands on the **o** *person's* property. 8276S
22:20 "Whoever sacrifices to any god **o than** the LORD 963+1194+4200
23:13 Do not invoke the names of **o** gods; 337
24: 6 and the **o** half he sprinkled on the altar. 1947S
25: 7 and onyx stones and *o* **gems** to be mounted AIT
25:12 on one side and two rings on the **o**. 9108
25:19 and the second cherub on the **o**; 7896S
25:20 The cherubim are to face each **o**, 278S
25:32 three on one side and three on the **o**. 9108
26: 3 and do the same with the **o** five. 3749S
26: 4 the same with the end curtain in the **o** set. 9108
26: 5 on the end curtain of the **o** set, 9108
26: 5 with the loops opposite each **o**. 295S
26: 9 into one set and the **o** six into another set. 3749S
26:10 the edge of the end curtain in the **o** set. 9108
26:17 with two projections set parallel to each **o**. 295S
26:20 For the **o** side, 9108
26:27 five for those on the **o** side, 9108
27:15 to be on the **o** side, 9108
27:19 All the **o** articles used in the service of NIH
28:10 and the remaining six on the **o**. 9108
28:25 the **o** ends of the chains to the two settings, 9109S
28:26 the **o** two corners of the breastpiece on the NIH
29:17 putting them with the head and the *o* **pieces.** AIT
29:19 "Take the **o** ram, 9108
29:39 in the morning and the **o** at twilight. 9108
29:41 Sacrifice the **o** lamb at twilight with 9108
30: 9 Do not offer on this altar any **o** incense 2424
30:33 **anyone o than a priest** must be cut off 2424
31: 7 and all the **o** furnishings of the tent— NIH
32:27 through the camp from one end to the **o**, 9133S
33:16 and your people from all the **o** people on NIH
34:14 Do not worship *any* **o** god, for the LORD, 337
35: 9 and onyx stones and **o** gems to be mounted NIH
35:27 and **o** gems to be mounted on the ephod NIH
36:10 and did the same with the **o** five. 3749S
36:11 with the end curtain in the **o** set. 9108
36:12 on the end curtain of the **o** set, 9108
36:12 with the loops opposite each **o**. 285S
36:16 into one set and the **o** six into another set. 3749S
36:17 the edge of the end curtain in the **o** set. 9108
36:22 with two projections set parallel to each **o**. 285S
36:25 For the **o** side, 9108
36:32 five for those on the **o** side, 9108
37: 3 on one side and two rings on the **o**. 9108
37: 8 and the second cherub on the **o**; 2296S
37: 9 The cherubim faced each **o**, 278S
37:18 three on one side and three on the **o**. 9108
38:15 the **o** side of the entrance to the courtyard, 9108
39:18 the **o** ends of the chains to the two settings, 9109S
39:19 the **o** two corners of the breastpiece on the NIH
Lev 5: 7 a sin offering and the **o** for a burnt offering. 285S
5:10 then offer the **o** as a burnt offering in 9108
7:19 As for **o** meat, anyone ceremonially clean 2021S
7:24 be used for any **o** purpose, NIH
8:22 He then presented the **o** ram, 9108
10: 9 or **o** fermented drink whenever you go into NIH
11:10 or among all the **o** living creatures in NIH
11:23 But all **o** winged creatures NIH
12: 8 a burnt offering and the **o** for a sin offering. 285S
13:55 the mildew has affected one side or the **o**. 1478S
14:22 a sin offering and the **o** for a burnt offering. 285S
14:31 a sin offering and the **o** as a burnt offering, 285S
14:42 to take **o** stones to replace these 337
15:15 a sin offering and the **o** for a burnt offering. 285S
15:25 at a time **o than** her monthly period or has 4202
15:30 a sin offering and the **o** for a burnt offering. 285S
16: 8 for the LORD and the **o** for the scapegoat. 285S
22:12 daughter marries **anyone o than a priest,** 2424
24:20 he has injured the **o**, so he is to be injured. 132S
25:14 do not take advantage of each **o**. 278S
25:17 Do not take advantage of each **o**, 6660S
Nu 1:49 in the census of the **o** Israelites. NIH
2:33 not counted along with the **o** Israelites, NIH
4:27 whether carrying or doing **o** work, 3972S
5:19 "If no **o** man has slept with you NIH
5:20 with a man **o than** your husband"— 1187+4946
6: 3 from wine and **o** fermented drink and must NIH
6: 3 from wine or from **o** fermented drink. NIH
6:11 the **o** as a burnt offering to make atonement 285S
8: 6 the Levites from among the **o** Israelites NIH
8:12 the LORD and the **o** for a burnt offering, 285S
8:14 the Levites apart from the **o** Israelites, NIH
9: 7 with the **o** Israelites at the appointed time?" NIH
11: 4 with them *began to* **crave o food,** 203+9294
11:34 the people who *had* **craved o food.** 203
14: 4 And they said to each **o**, 278S
22:15 Then Balak sent **o** princes, 6388
24: 1 he did not resort to sorcery as **at o times,** 928+7193+7193
26:62 not counted along with the **o** Israelites NIH
28: 4 Prepare one lamb in the morning and the **o** 9108
31:30 cattle, donkeys, sheep, goats or **o** animals. 3972S
32:19 inheritance with them **on the o side of the** Jordan, 2134+2256+4946+6298
35: 3 flocks and all their *o* **livestock.** AIT
35: 6 In addition, give them forty-two **o** towns. NIH
35:15 and any *o* **people living** among them, AIT
36: 3 from **o** Israelite tribes; 285S
Dt 4: 7 What **o** nation is so great as NIH
4: 8 And what **o** nation is so great as NIH
4:32 from one end of the heavens to the **o**. 7895+9028S
4:33 Has any **o** people heard the voice NIH
4:35 besides him there is no **o**. 6388
4:39 There is no **o**. 6388
Dt 5: 7 "You shall have no **o** gods before me. 337
6:14 Do not follow **o** gods, 337
7: 4 from following me to serve **o** gods, 337
7: 7 you were more numerous than **o** peoples, 3972S
7:14 be blessed more than any **o** people; 2021S
8:19 the LORD your God and follow **o** gods 337
11:16 and worship **o** gods and bow down to them. 337
11:28 by following **o** gods, 337
13: 2 "Let us follow **o** gods" (gods you have 337
13: 6 and worship **o** gods" (gods that neither you 337
13: 7 one end of the land to **the o**), 824+2021+7895S
13:13 and worship **o** gods" (gods you have 337
14:26 cattle, sheep, wine or **o** fermented drink, 2021S
17: 3 to my command has worshiped **o** gods, 337
18:20 prophet who speaks in the name of **o** gods, 337
21:15 and he loves one but not the **o**, 285S
24: 5 not be sent to war or have any **o** duty laid NIH
28:14 following **o** gods and serving them. 337
28:36 There you will worship **o** gods, 337
28:64 from one end of the earth to the **o**. 7895S
28:64 There you will worship **o** gods— 337
29: 6 and drank no wine or **o** fermented drink. NIH
29:10 and all the **o** men of Israel, NIH
29:26 and worshiped **o** gods and bowed down 337
30:17 to bow down to **o** gods and worship them, 337
31:18 of all their wickedness in turning to **o** gods. 337
31:20 they will turn to **o** gods and worship them, 337
Jos 4:11 and the priests **came to the o side** 6296
7: 7 to stay on the **o side** *of* the Jordan! 6298
7: 9 and the **o** people of the country will hear 3972S
13: 8 **The o half of Manasseh,** the Reubenites 2257S
17: 2 the **o** male descendants of Manasseh son NIH
21: 1 the heads of the **o** tribal families of Israel NIH
22: 4 of the LORD gave you on the **o side** *of* 6298
22: 7 the **o** half of the tribe Joshua gave land on NIH
22:19 **o than** the altar of the LORD our God. 1187+4946
22:29 **o than** the altar of the LORD our God 963+4200+4946
23:16 and serve **o** gods and bow down to them, 337
24: 2 beyond the River and worshiped **o** gods. 337
24:16 to forsake the LORD to serve **o** gods! 337
Jdg 2:17 but prostituted themselves to **o** gods 337
2:19 following **o** gods and serving 337
4:11 Heber the Kenite had left the **o** Kenites, NIH
6: 3 and **o** eastern peoples invaded the country. NIH
6:29 They asked each **o**, "Who did this?" 8276S
6:33 and **o** eastern peoples joined forces NIH
7: 7 Let all the **o** men go, NIH
7:12 and all the **o** eastern peoples had settled in NIH
7:14 be nothing **o than** the sword of Gideon son 561
7:22 throughout the camp to turn on each **o** 8276S
10:13 you have forsaken me and served **o** gods, 337
10:18 of the people of Gilead said to each **o**, 8276S
11:18 and camped on the **o side** *of* the Arnon. 6298
13: 4 or **o** fermented drink and that you do NIH
13: 7 drink no wine or **o** fermented drink and do NIH
13:10 The man who appeared to me the **o** day!" NIH
13:14 nor drink any wine or **o** fermented drink NIH
16: 7 I'll become as weak as any **o** man." 2021S
16:11 I'll become as weak as any **o** man." 2021S
16:13 I'll become as weak as any **o** man." 2021S
16:17 I would become as weak as any **o** man." 2021S
16:29 on the one and his left hand on the **o**, 285S
17: 8 that town in search of **some o place** to stay. 889S
18:14 **o** household gods, a carved image and NIH
18:17 the **o** household gods and the cast idol NIH
18:18 the **o** household gods and the cast idol, NIH
18:20 the **o** household gods and the carved image NIH
20:31 the one leading to Bethel and the **o** 285S
Ru 1: 4 one named Orpah and the **o** Ruth. 9108
4: 7 and gave it to the **o**. 8276S
1Sa 1: 2 one was called Hannah and the **o** Peninnah. 9108
3:10 calling as at the **o** times, "Samuel! 7193S
8: 5 such as all the **o** nations have." NIH
8: 8 forsaking me and serving **o** gods, 337
8:20 Then we will be like all the **o** nations, NIH
10:11 they asked each **o**, "What is this 8276S
12:19 for we have added to all our **o** sins the evil NIH
14: 1 over to the Philistine outpost on the **o side."** 6298
14: 4 one was called Bozez, and the **o** Seneh. 285S
14: 5 the **o** to the south toward Geba. 285S
14:20 striking each **o** with their swords. 8276S
17:10 Give me a man and let us fight **each o."** 3480
17:21 up their lines **facing each o.** 5120+7925
18:25 king wants no **o** price for the bride **than** 3954
20:41 they kissed each **o** and wept together— 8276S
20:42 we have sworn friendship with **each o** 5646+9109
21: 8 haven't brought my sword or any *o* **weapon,** AIT
23:26 and David and his men were on the **o** side, 2296S
26:13 Then David crossed over to the **o side** 6298
26:19 and have said, 'Go, serve **o** gods.' 337
28: 8 Saul disguised himself, putting on **o** clothes, 337
30:20 ahead of the **o** livestock, 2085S
30:31 to those in all the *o* **places** where David AIT
2Sa 2:13 of the pool and one group on the *o* **side.** AIT
4: 2 One was named Baanah and the **o** Recab; 9108
12: 1 one rich and the **o** poor. 285S
14: 6 They got into a fight with **each o** in 2157+9109S
14: 6 One struck the **o** and killed him. 285S
17: 9 now, he is hidden in a cave or **some o** place. 285S
19: 9 the people *were* all **arguing with each o,** 1906
1Ki 3:22 The **o** woman said, "No! 337
3:25 and give half to one and half to the **o**." 285S
3:26 **o** said, "Neither I nor you shall have him. 2296S
4:28 for the chariot horses and the **o** horses. NIH
4:31 He was wiser than any **o** man, 2021S
6: 7 chisel or any **o** iron tool was heard at NIH

1Ki 6:24 and the **o** wing five cubits— 9108
6:27 the wing of the **o** touched the other wall, 9108
6:27 the wing of the other touched the **o** wall, 9108
6:27 and their wings touched each **o** in 4053[S]
7:4 in sets of three, **facing each o.** 448+4691+4691
7:5 in sets of three, **facing each o.** 448+4691+4691
8:60 the LORD is God and that there is no **o.** 6388
9:6 to serve **o** gods and worship them, 337
9:9 and have embraced **o** gods, 337
10:20 ever been made for any **o** kingdom. NIH
10:23 in riches and wisdom than all the **o** kings of NIH
11:4 his wives turned his heart after **o** gods, 337
11:10 forbidden Solomon to follow **o** gods, 337
11:41 As for the **o** events of Solomon's reign— 3856
12:29 One he set up in Bethel, and the **o** in Dan. 285[S]
14:9 You have made for yourself **o** gods, 337
14:19 The **o** events of Jeroboam's reign, 3856
14:29 As for the **o** events of Rehoboam's reign, 3856
15:7 As for the **o** events of Abijah's reign, 3856
15:23 As for all the **o** events of Asa's reign, 3856
15:31 As for the **o** events of Nadab's reign, 3856
16:5 As for the **o** events of Baasha's reign, 3856
16:14 As for the **o** events of Elah's reign, 3856
16:20 As for the **o** events of Zimri's reign, 3856
16:21 and the **o** half supported Omri. NIH
16:27 As for the **o** events of Omri's reign, 3856
18:23 I will prepare the **o** bull and put it on 285[S]
20:24 and replace them with *o* **officers.** AIT
20:29 seven days they camped opposite **each o,** 465
22:12 All the **o** prophets were prophesying NIH
22:13 the **o** prophets are predicting success for NIH
22:39 As for the **o** events of Ahab's reign, 3856
22:45 As for the **o** events of Jehoshaphat's reign, 3856
2Ki 1:18 As for *all* the **o** events of Ahaziah's reign, 3856
3:13 "What do we have to do with **each o?** 3870[S]
3:17 your cattle and your **o** animals will drink. NIH
3:23 and slaughtered each **o.** 8276[S]
5:17 and sacrifices to *any o* god but the LORD. 337
7:3 They said to each **o,** "Why stay here 8276[S]
7:9 they said to each **o,** "We're not doing right. 8276[S]
8:23 As for the **o** events of Jehoram's reign, 3856
10:21 until it was full from one end to the **o.** 7023[S]
10:34 As for the **o** events of Jehu's reign, 3856
11:7 and you who are in the **o** two companies NIH
12:7 the priest and the **o** priests and asked them, NIH
12:12 **met** all *the o* **expenses** of restoring AIT
12:13 trumpets or any **o** articles of gold or silver NIH
12:19 As for the **o** events of the reign of Joash, 3856
13:8 for the **o** events of the reign of Jehoahaz, 3856
13:12 As for the **o** events of the reign of Jehoash, 3856
14:11 Amaziah king of Judah **faced each o** 7156+8011
14:15 As for the **o** events of the reign of Jehoash, 3856
14:18 As for the **o** events of Amaziah's reign, 3856
14:28 As for the **o** events of Jeroboam's reign, 3856
15:6 As for the **o** events of Azariah's reign, 3856
15:11 The **o** events of Zechariah's reign 3856
15:15 The **o** events of Shallum's reign, 3856
15:21 As for the **o** events of Menahem's reign, 3856
15:26 The **o** events of Pekahiah's reign, 3856
15:31 As for the **o** events of Pekah's reign, 3856
15:36 As for the **o** events of Jotham's reign, 3856
16:19 As for the **o** events of the reign of Ahaz, 3856
17:7 They worshiped **o** gods 337
17:35 "Do not worship *any o* gods or bow down 337
17:37 Do not worship **o** gods. 337
17:38 and do not worship **o** gods. 337
20:20 As for the **o** events of Hezekiah's reign, 3856
21:17 As for the **o** events of Manasseh's reign, 3856
21:25 As for the **o** events of Amon's reign, 3856
22:17 to **o** gods and provoked me to anger by all 337
23:24 and all the **o** detestable things seen in Judah NIH
23:28 As for the **o** events of Josiah's reign, 3856
24:5 As for the **o** events of Jehoiakim's reign, 3856
25:17 The **o** pillar, with its network, was similar. 9108
25:28 the **o** kings who were with him in Babylon. NIH
1Ch 6:48 to all the **o** duties of the tabernacle, NIH
9:29 of the furnishings and all the **o** articles of NIH
9:33 and **were exempt from** *o* **duties** because AIT
12:16 **O** Benjamites and some men from Judah NIH
16:42 and for the playing of the **o** instruments NIH
23:17 Eliezer had no **o** sons, 337
23:28 the performance of *o* **duties** *at* the house AIT
26:26 and by the **o** army commanders. NIH
26:28 the **o** dedicated things were in the care NIH
29:21 and **o** sacrifices in abundance for all Israel. NIH
29:30 and the kingdoms of all the **o** lands. NIH
2Ch 2:5 because our God is greater than all **o** gods. 2021[S]
3:11 while its **o** wing, also five cubits long, 337
3:11 touched the wing of the **o** cherub. 337
3:12 and touched the **o** temple wall, NIH
3:12 and its **o** wing, also five cubits long, 337
5:13 cymbals and **o** instruments, NIH
7:19 to serve **o** gods and worship them, 337
7:22 and have embraced **o** gods, 337
9:19 ever been made for any **o** kingdom. NIH
9:22 in riches and wisdom than all the **o** kings of NIH
9:28 from Egypt and from all **o** countries. 2021[S]
9:29 As for the **o** events of Solomon's reign, 8637
11:21 of Absalom more than any of his **o** wives NIH
12:8 and serving the kings of **o** lands." 2021[S]
13:9 of your own as the peoples of **o** lands do? 2021[S]
13:22 The **o** events of Abijah's reign, 3856
18:11 All the **o** prophets were prophesying NIH
18:12 the **o** prophets are predicting success for NIH
19:10 whether bloodshed or **o** concerns of NIH
20:2 from the **o side** of the Sea. 6298
20:34 The **o** events of Jehoshaphat's reign, 3856
2Ch 23:5 the **o** men are to be in the courtyards of NIH
23:6 but all the **o** men are to guard what NIH
24:14 also dishes and **o** objects of gold and silver. NIH
25:21 Amaziah king of Judah **faced each o** 7156+8011
25:26 As for the **o** events of Amaziah's reign, 3856
26:17 the priest with eighty **o** courageous priests NIH
26:20 the chief priest and all the **o** priests looked NIH
26:22 The **o** events of Uzziah's reign, 3856
27:7 The **o** events in Jotham's reign, 3856
27:7 and the **o** things he did, NIH
28:25 to burn sacrifices to **o** gods and provoked 337
28:26 The **o** events of his reign and all his ways, 3856
29:34 and until **o** priests had been consecrated, 2021[S]
31:19 around their towns or in **any** *o* towns, AIT
32:13 to all the peoples of the **o** lands? NIH
32:17 as the gods of the peoples of the **o** lands did NIH
32:19 as they did about the gods of the **o** peoples NIH
32:32 The **o** events of Hezekiah's reign 3856
33:18 The **o** events of Manasseh's reign, 3856
34:25 to **o** gods and provoked me to anger by all 337
35:24 in the **o** chariot he had and brought him 5467
35:26 The **o** events of Josiah's reign and his acts 3856
36:8 The **o** events of Jehoiakim's reign, 3856
Ezr 1:10 matching silver bowls 410 **o** articles 1,000 337
2:31 of the **o** Elam 1,254 337
2:70 along with some of the **o** people, NIH
4:10 and the **o** people whom the great 10692
7:24 temple servants or **o** workers at this house NIH
9:11 with their impurity from one end to the **o.** 7023[S]
10:25 And among the **o** Israelites: NIH
Ne 1:2 came from Judah with *some o* **men,** AIT
3:18 ruler of the **o** half-district of Keilah. NIH
4:16 while the **o** half were equipped with spears, NIH
4:17 with one hand and held a weapon in the **o,** 285[S]
4:19 and we are widely separated from each **o** 278[S]
7:33 of the **o** Nebo 52 337
7:34 of the **o** Elam 1,254 337
9:36 and the **o** good things it produces. NIH
11:4 while **o** people from both Judah NIH
12:24 one section responding to the **o,** 5464[S]
12:47 also set aside the portion for the **o** Levites, NIH
13:15 grapes, figs and **all** *o kinds of* loads. AIT
13:24 **one of the o peoples,** 2256+6639+6639
Est 1:6 mother-of-pearl and **o** costly stones. NIH
1:7 each one different from the **o,** 3998[S]
2:15 she asked for nothing **o than** what 561+3954
2:17 to Esther more than to any of the **o** women, NIH
2:17 approval more than any of the **o** virgins. NIH
3:1 higher than that of all the **o** nobles. 889+907[S]
3:8 from those of all **o** people and who do NIH
5:11 above the **o** nobles and officials. NIH
8:17 of **o nationalities** became Jews 824+2021+6639
9:2 the **o** nationalities were afraid of them. NIH
9:19 a day for giving presents to each **o.** 8276[S]
Job 8:19 and from the soil **o** plants grow. 337
9:32 that we might confront **each o** in court. 3481
31:10 and may *o men* sleep with her. 337
Ps 16:4 of those will increase who run after **o gods.** 337
19:6 the heavens and makes its circuit to the **o;** 7895[S]
64:5 They encourage **each o** in evil plans, 4564[S]
82:7 you will fall like *every o* ruler." 285[S]
85:10 righteousness and peace **kiss** *each o.* AIT
111:6 giving them the lands of **o** nations. NIH
147:20 He has done this for no **o** nation; 3972[S]
Ecc 2:7 and had **o** slaves who were born NIH
3:19 As one dies, so dies **the o.** 2296[S]
7:14 God has made the one as well as **the o.** 2296[S]
7:18 to grasp the one and not let go of **the o.** 2296[S]
Isa 3:5 People *will* **oppress each o—** 5601
13:8 They will look aghast at each **o,** 8276[S]
26:13 **o** lords besides you have ruled over us, NIH
34:14 and wild goats will bleat to **each o;** 8276[S]
41:6 each helps the **o** and says to his brother, 8276[S]
44:8 No, there is no **o** Rock; I know not one." NIH
45:5 I am the LORD, and there is no **o;** 6388
45:6 I am the LORD, and there is no **o.** 6388
45:14 'Surely God is with you, and there is no **o;** 6388
45:14 there is no **o** god.' " NIH
45:18 "I am the LORD, and there is no **o.** 6388
45:22 for I am God, and there is no **o.** 6388
46:9 I am God, and there is no **o;** 6388
50:8 Let us face **each o!** 3480
58:4 and *in* **striking** *each o* with wicked fists. AIT
66:17 of pigs and rats and **o** abominable things— 2021[S]
Jer 1:16 in burning incense to **o** gods and 337
7:5 and deal with each **o** justly, 8276[S]
7:6 not follow **o** gods to your own harm, 337
7:9 and follow **o** gods you have not known, 337
7:18 They pour out drink offerings to **o** gods 337
7:21 to your **o** sacrifices and eat NIH
8:10 Therefore I will give their wives to **o** *men* 337
11:10 They have followed **o** gods to serve them. 337
12:9 that **o** birds of prey surround and attack? 2021[S]
12:12 from one end of the land to the **o;** 7895[S]
13:10 of their hearts and go after **o** gods to serve 337
13:14 I will smash them one against the **o,** 278[S]
16:11 'and followed **o** gods and served 337
16:13 there you will serve **o** gods day and night, 337
17:19 stand also at all the **o** gates of Jerusalem. NIH
19:13 and poured out drink offerings to **o** gods.' " 337
22:9 and have worshiped and served **o** gods.' " 337
24:2 the **o** basket had very poor figs, 285[S]
25:6 Do not follow **o** gods to serve 337
25:26 near and far, one after the **o—** 278[S]
25:33 one end of the earth to **the o.** 824+2021+7895[S]
26:22 along with some **o** men. NIH
27:19 the movable stands and the **o** furnishings 3856
Jer 28:4 and all the **o** exiles from Judah who went NIH
29:1 the **o** people Nebuchadnezzar had carried NIH
29:25 and to all the **o** priests. NIH
32:29 by pouring out drink offerings to **o** gods. 337
34:7 against Jerusalem and the **o** cities of Judah 3972[S]
35:15 do not follow **o** gods to serve them. 337
36:2 Judah and all the **o** nations from NIH
36:12 and all the **o** officials. NIH
36:16 they looked at each **o** in fear and said 8276[S]
39:3 a high official and all the **o** officials of 8642
39:13 and all the **o** officers of the king of Babylon NIH
40:11 and all the **o** countries heard that the king NIH
44:3 and by worshiping **o** gods that neither they 337
44:5 or stop burning incense to **o** gods. 337
44:8 burning incense to **o** gods in Egypt, 337
44:15 burning incense to **o** gods, along with all 337
46:16 they will fall over each **o.** 8276[S]
52:22 The **o** pillar, with its pomegranates, 9108
52:32 the **o** kings who were with him in Babylon. NIH
Eze 1:23 wings were stretched out one toward the **o,** 295[S]
3:13 the living creatures brushing against each **o** 295[S]
4:8 that you cannot turn from one side to the **o** 7396[S]
4:17 They will be appalled at the sight of each **o** 278[S]
16:23 In addition to all your **o** wickedness, NIH
16:43 to all your **o** detestable practices? NIH
18:10 or does any of these **o** things 278[S]
25:8 of Judah has become like all the **o** nations," NIH
29:15 exalt itself above the **o** nations. NIH
31:14 Therefore no **o** trees by the waters are ever 3972[S]
31:14 No **o** trees so well-watered are ever 3972[S]
32:27 **o** uncircumcised warriors who have fallen, NIH
33:30 saying to each **o,** 'Come and hear 285[S]
40:40 on the **o** side of the steps were two tables. 337
40:41 of the gateway and four on the **o—** 7024[S]
40:42 the burnt offerings and the **o** sacrifices. NIH
41:19 of a lion toward the palm tree on the **o.** 7024[S]
42:14 They are to put on **o** clothes before they go 337
44:7 to all your **o** detestable practices, NIH
44:19 and put on **o** clothes, 337
48:14 of the land and *must* not **pass into o hands,** 6296
Da 1:10 the **o** young men your age? NIH
2:30 I have greater wisdom than **o** living men, 10353[S]
3:2 and all the **o** provincial officials to come to NIH
3:3 and all the **o** provincial officials assembled NIH
3:21 trousers, turbans and **o** clothes, NIH
3:29 for no **o** god can save in this way." 10025
7:12 (The **o** beasts had been stripped 10692
7:20 the **o** horn that came up, before which three 10023
7:23 It will be different from all the **o** kingdoms NIH
8:3 of the horns was longer than the **o** but grew 9108
11:27 will sit at the same table and **lie** *to each o,* AIT
Hos 3:1 though they turn to **o** gods and 337
9:1 do not be jubilant like the **o** nations. NIH
Joel 1:4 young locusts have left **o** locusts have eaten. 2021[S]
2:8 They do not jostle each **o;** 278[S]
2:25 the **o** locusts and the locust swarm— NIH
2:27 the LORD your God, and that there is no **o;** 6388
Jnh 1:7 Then the sailors said to each **o,** "Come, 8276[S]
Hag 2:12 some wine, oil or **o** food, 3972[S]
Zec 4:3 the right of the bowl and **the o** on its left." 285[S]
5:3 and according to what it says on **the o,** 2296[S]
7:10 In your hearts do not think evil of each **o.'** 278[S]
8:16 Speak the truth to each **o,** 8276[S]
11:7 and called one Favor and **the o** Union, 285[S]
14:13 and they will attack each **o.** 8276[S]
Mal 3:16 the LORD talked with each **o,** 8276[S]
Mt 4:21 he saw two **o** brothers, 257
5:39 turn to him the **o** also. 257
6:24 Either he will hate the one and love the **o,** 2283
6:24 be devoted to the one and despise the **o.** 2283
8:18 he gave orders to cross to the **o side** of 4305
8:28 at the **o side** in the region of the Gadarenes, 4305
12:13 completely restored, just as sound as the **o.** 257
12:45 seven **o** spirits more wicked than itself, 2283
13:7 **O** seed fell among thorns, 257+1254
13:8 Still **o** seed fell on good soil, 257
14:22 and go on ahead of him to the **o side,** 4305
18:31 the **o** servants saw what had happened, NIG
19:1 into the region of Judea **to the o side** of 4305
20:21 and **the o** at your left in your kingdom." 1651[S]
21:30 "Then the father went to the **o** son and said 2283
21:36 Then he sent **o** servants to them, 257
21:38 the tenants saw the son, they said to **each o,** 1571
21:41 "and he will rent the vineyard *to* **o** tenants, 257
24:10 the faith and will betray and hate **each o,** 253
24:31 from one end of the heavens to the **o.** 216[S]
24:40 one will be taken and **the o** left. 1651[S]
24:41 one will be taken and **the o** left. 1651[S]
25:20 the five talents brought the **o** five. 257
26:22 began to say to him **one after the o,** 1651+1667
26:35 And all the **o** disciples said the same. NIG
27:61 and the **o** Mary were sitting there opposite 257
28:1 and the **o** Mary went to look at the tomb. 257
Mk 1:27 so amazed that they asked **each o,** 1571
4:7 **O** seed fell among thorns, 257
4:8 Still **o** seed fell on good soil. 257
4:19 of wealth and the desires for **o** *things* come 3370
4:35 "Let us go over to the **o side."** 4305
4:36 There were also **o** boats with him. 257
4:41 They were terrified and asked **each o,** 253
5:21 over by boat to the **o side** of the lake, 4305
7:4 And they observe many **o** traditions, 257
8:13 into the boat and crossed to the **o side.** 4305
9:14 When they came to the **o** disciples, NIG
9:50 and be at peace with **each o."** 253
10:26 even more amazed, and said to **each o,** 1571
10:37 of us sit at your right and **the o** at your left 1651[S]

Mk 12:32 in saying that God is one and there is no o *257*
15:41 Many o *women* who had come up with him *257*
16: 3 they asked each o, "Who will roll away *1571*
Lk 1:15 to take wine or o fermented drink, *NIG*
3:18 And with many o words John exhorted *2283*
3:19 and all the o evil things he had done, *NIG*
4:36 the people were amazed and said to each o, *253*
4:43 of the kingdom of God *to* the o towns also, *2283*
5: 7 So they signaled their partners in the o boat *2283*
6:29 on one cheek, turn to him the o also. *257*
7:32 the marketplace and calling out *to* each o: *253*
7:41 five hundred denarii, and the o fifty. *2283*
7:49 The o guests began to say *NIG*
8: 7 O seed fell among thorns, *2283*
8: 8 Still o seed fell on good soil. *2283*
8:22 "Let's go over to the o side of the lake." *4305*
10:31 *he* passed by on the o side. *524*
10:32 passed by on the o side. *524*
11:26 seven o spirits more wicked than itself, *2283*
11:42 rue and all o kinds of garden herbs, *NIG*
12:52 in one family divided against each o, *NIG*
13: 2 were worse sinners than all the o Galileans *NIG*
14:32 he will send a delegation while the o is still *899[S]*
16:13 Either he will hate the one and love the o, *2283*
16:13 be devoted to the one and despise the o. *2283*
17:17 Where are the o nine? *NIG*
17:24 and lights up the sky from one end to the o. *NIG*
17:34 one will be taken and the o left. *2283*
17:35 one will be taken and the o left." *2283*
18:10 one a Pharisee and the o a tax collector. *2283*
18:11 I thank you that I am not like o men— *3370*
18:14 "I tell you that this man, rather than the o, *1697*
22:65 they said many o insulting *things* to him. *2283*
23:32 Two o *men,* both criminals, *2283*
23:33 one on his right, the o on his left. *1254+4005*
23:40 But the o criminal rebuked him. *2283*
24:14 They were talking with each o *253*
24:15 and discussed these things with each o, *NIG*
24:32 They asked each o, "Were not our hearts *253*
Jn 1:28 This all happened at Bethany on the o side *4305*
3:26 that man who was with you on the o side of *4305*
4:33 Then his disciples said to each o, *253*
6:25 When they found him on the o side of *4305*
8:18 my o witness is the Father, who sent me." *NIG*
10: 1 but climbs in by some o way, *249*
10:16 I have o sheep that are not of this sheep pen. *257*
15:12 Love each o as I have loved you. *253*
15:17 This is my command: Love each o. *253*
18: 1 On the o side there was an olive grove, *3963[S]*
18:16 The o disciple, who was known to *257*
19:32 and then those *of* the o. *257*
20: 2 to Simon Peter and the o disciple, *257*
20: 3 and the o disciple started for the tomb. *257*
20: 4 but the o disciple outran Peter and reached *257*
20: 8 Finally the o disciple, *257*
20:12 one at the head and the o at the foot. *1651[S]*
20:25 So the o disciples told him, *257*
20:30 Jesus did many o miraculous signs in *257*
21: 2 and two o disciples were together. *257*
21: 8 The o disciples followed in the boat, *257*
21:25 Jesus did many o *things* as well. *257*
Ac 2: 4 *in* o tongues as the Spirit enabled them. *2283*
2:37 and said to Peter and the o apostles, *3370*
2:40 *With* many o words he warned them; *2283*
4: 6 and the o *men* of the high priest's family. *4012*
4:12 for there is no o name under heaven given *2283*
5:29 Peter and the o apostles replied: *NIG*
7:26 why do you want to hurt each o?' *253*
7:27 the o pushed Moses aside and said, *4446*
9:39 and showing him the robes and o clothing *NIG*
15: 2 along with some o believers, *257*
16:25 and the o prisoners were listening to them. *NIG*
17: 6 they dragged Jason and some o brothers *NIG*
21: 6 After saying good-by to each o, *253*
27: 1 and some o prisoners were handed over to *2283*
28: 4 they said to each o, *253*
Ro 1:13 just as I have had among the o Gentiles. *3370*
1:27 Men committed indecent acts with o men, *NIG*
2: 1 for at whatever point you judge the o, *2283*
9: 8 In o words, it is not the natural *1639+4047*
13: 9 whatever o commandment there may be, *2283*
1Co 3:11 For no one can lay any foundation o than *257*
6:18 o sins a man commits are outside his body, *NIG*
7: 5 Do not deprive each o except by mutual *253*
9: 5 as do the o apostles and the Lord's brothers *3370*
10:29 the o *man's* conscience, I mean, not yours. *2283*
11:16 we have no o practice—nor do the churches *NIG*
11:33 come together to eat, wait for each o. *253*
12: 2 somehow or o you were influenced *323+6055*
12:25 parts should have equal concern for each o. *253*
14:17 but the o *man* is not edified. *2283*
2Co 2:16 to the o, the fragrance of life. *1254+4005*
11: 4 a Jesus o than the Jesus we preached, *257*
11: 8 I robbed o churches by receiving support *257*
12:13 How were you inferior to the o churches, *3370*
Gal 1: 8 from heaven should preach a gospel o than *4123*
1: 9 to you a gospel o than what you accepted, *4123*
1:19 I saw none of the o apostles— *2283*
2:13 The o Jews joined him in his hypocrisy, *3370*
4:22 one by the slave woman and the o by *1651[S]*
5:10 in the Lord that you will take no o view. *257*
5:15 If you keep on biting and devouring each o, *253*
5:15 or you will be destroyed by each o. *253*
5:17 They are in conflict *with* each o, *253*
5:26 provoking and envying each o. *253*
Eph 3: 5 not made known to men *in* o generations *2283*
4:32 to one another, forgiving each o, just as *4932*
Eph 5:27 without stain or wrinkle or any o blemish, *5516*
Php 4: 2 with Syntyche to agree with each o in *NIG*
Col 3: 9 Do not lie to each o, *253*
3:13 Bear with each o and forgive whatever *253*
1Th 3:12 for each o and for everyone else, *253*
4: 9 taught by God to love each o. *253*
4:18 encourage each o with these words. *253*
5:11 and build each o up, *1651+1651+3836*
5:13 Live in peace with each o. *4932*
5:15 to be kind to each o and to everyone else. *253*
2Th 1: 3 of you has for each o is increasing. *253*
Heb 7: 8 but in the o case, *1254+1695*
7:27 Unlike the o high priests, *NIG*
10:33 at o times you stood side by side *1254+4047*
13: 1 Keep on loving each o as brothers. *5789*
Jas 5: 9 Don't grumble against each o, brothers, *253*
5:16 Therefore confess your sins *to* each o *253*
5:16 for each o so that you may be healed. *253*
1Pe 4: 8 Above all, love each o deeply, *4932*
4:15 not be as a murderer or thief or any o kind *NIG*
2Pe 3:16 as they do the o Scriptures, *3370*
Rev 2:24 not impose any o burden on you): *257*
3:15 I wish you were either one or the o! *2412[S]*
4: 4 the throne were twenty-four o thrones, *NIG*
6: 4 from the earth and to make men slay each o. *253*
8:13 about to be sounded by the o three angels!" *3370*
9:12 two o woes are yet to come. *2285*
11:10 and will celebrate by sending each o gifts, *253*
17:10 one is, the o has not yet come; *257*

OTHER'S (2) [OTHER]

Ro 1:12 be mutually encouraged by each o faith. *253*
Gal 6: 2 Carry each o burdens, *253*

OTHERS (177) [OTHER]

Ge 32:19 and all the *o who* followed the herds: AIT
42: 4 Joseph's brother, with the o, 278[S]
50:14 with his brothers and all the *o who had* gone AIT
Ex 24: 2 the o must not come near. 2156[S]
35:34 of the tribe of Dan, the ability to teach o. NIH
Lev 6:11 he is to take off these clothes and put on o, 337
Nu 1:47 were not counted along with the o. 4392[S]
22:19 Now stay here tonight as the o did, NIH
Jdg 7: 8 over the provisions and trumpets of the o. 6639[S]
1Sa 5: 5 nor any *o* who enter Dagon's temple AIT
8:12 o to plow his ground and reap his harvest, NIH
8:12 and still o to make weapons of war NIH
9: 2 a head taller than any of the o. 6639[S]
10:23 a head taller than any of the o. 6639[S]
1Ch 3:20 There were also five o: NIH
5:22 and many *o* fell slain, AIT
9:29 O were assigned to take care of 2157+4946[S]
2Ch 32:22 of Assyria and from the hand of all o. NIH
Ezr 3:12 while many *o* shouted for joy. AIT
Ne 2:16 or nobles or officials or *any* o who would 3856
5: 3 O were saying, "We are mortgaging 889[S]
5: 4 Still o were saying, "We have had to borrow 889[S]
5: 5 and our vineyards belong to o." 337
8: 3 women and o who could understand. 2021[S]
Job 24:24 and gathered up like all *o;* AIT
31: 8 then may o eat what I have sown, 337
34:24 the mighty and sets up o in their place. 337
Ps 49:10 and leave their wealth to o. 337
52: 7 and grew strong by destroying o!" 2257[S]
105:44 and they fell heir to what o had toiled for— 4211[S]
107:23 *O* went out *on* the sea in ships; AIT
Pr 5: 9 to o and your years to one who is cruel, 337
10:17 whoever ignores correction leads o astray. NIH
11:25 he who refreshes o will himself NIH
Ecc 5: 8 and over them both are o higher still. 1469[S]
6: 8 how to conduct himself before o? 2645[S]
7:22 many times you yourself have cursed o. 337
8: 9 when a man lords it over o to his own hurt. 132[S]
SS 5: 9 How is your beloved better than o, 1856[S]
5: 9 How is your beloved better than o, 1856[S]
Isa 43: 9 so that *o may* hear and say, "It is true." AIT
56: 8 "I will gather *still* o to them 6388
65:22 No longer will they build houses and o live 337
65:22 or plant and o eat. 337
Jer 6:12 Their houses will be turned over to o, 337
41: 8 and did not kill them with the o. 278[S]
41:10 along with all the o who were left there, 6639[S]
50:15 do to her as she has done to o. NIH
Eze 9: 5 As I listened, he said to the o, 465[S]
16:34 you are the opposite of o; 851+2021[S]
32:19 'Are you more favored than o? 4769[S]
39:14 *o will* bury those that remain on AIT
40:24 the same measurements as the o. NIH
40:25 like the openings of the o. 465[S]
40:28 it had the same measurements as the o. 465[S]
40:29 the same measurements as the o. 465[S]
40:32 it had the same measurements as the o. 465[S]
40:33 the same measurements as the o. 465[S]
40:35 It had the same measurements as the o. 465[S]
44: 8 you put *o* in charge of my sanctuary. AIT
Da 2:40 so it will crush and break all the o. 10036[S]
7: 3 each different from the o, 10154[S]
7:19 which was different from all the o 10214[S]
7:20 that looked more imposing than the o and 10246
11: 2 who will be far richer than all *the o.* AIT
11: 4 his empire will be uprooted and given to o. 337
12: 2 o to shame and everlasting contempt. 465[S]
12: 5 looked, and there before me stood two o, 337
Mt 5:19 commandments and teaches o to do the same *476*
5:47 what are you doing more than o? *NIG*
7: 2 For in the same way you judge o, *NIG*
7:12 *to* o what you would have them do to you, *899*
11:16 in the marketplaces and calling out *to* o: *2283*
15:30 the crippled, the mute and many o, *2283*
16:14 "Some say John the Baptist; o say Elijah; *257*
16:14 still o, Jeremiah or one of the prophets." *2283*
17:25 from their own sons or from o?" *259*
17:26 "From o," Peter answered. *259*
18:16 he will not listen, take one or two o along, *NIG*
19:12 o were made that way by men; *4015*
19:12 and o have renounced marriage because of *4015*
20: 3 and saw o standing in the marketplace *257*
20: 6 and found *still* o standing around. *257*
21: 8 while o cut branches from the trees *257*
23:34 o you will flog in your synagogues *NIG*
25:11 "Later the o also came. *3370*
26:67 O slapped him *1254+3836*
27:42 "He saved o," they said, "but he can't save *257*
Mk 4:10 the Twelve and the *o* around him asked him *AIT*
4:16 O, like seed sown on rocky places, *4047*
4:18 Still o, like seed sown among thorns, *257*
4:20 O, like seed sown on good soil, *1697*
6:15 O said, "He is Elijah." *257*
6:15 And still o claimed, "He is a prophet, *257*
8:28 "Some say John the Baptist; o say Elijah; *257*
8:28 and still o, one of the prophets." *257*
11: 8 o spread branches they had cut in the fields. *257*
12: 5 He sent many o; *257*
12: 5 some of them they beat, o they killed. *1254+4005*
12: 9 and give the vineyard *to* o. *257*
12:43 into the treasury than all the o. *NIG*
14:31 And all the o said the same. *NIG*
15:31 "He saved o," they said, "but he can't save *257*
Lk 5:29 of tax collectors and o were eating *257*
6:31 Do *to* o as you would have them do to you. *899*
8: 3 Susanna; and many o. *2283*
8:10 but *to* o I speak in parables, so that, *3370*
9: 8 o that Elijah had appeared, *5516*
9: 8 and *still* o that one of the prophets *257*
9:19 "Some say John the Baptist; o say Elijah; *257*
9:19 and *still* o, that one of the prophets *257*
10: 1 the Lord appointed seventy-two o *2283*
11:16 O tested him by asking for a sign *2283*
11:49 they will kill and o they will persecute.' *2779*
13: 4 the o living in Jerusalem? *476*
20:16 and give the vineyard *to* o." *257*
21: 3 poor widow has put in more than all the o. *NIG*
23:35 said, "He saved o; let him save himself *257*
24: 9 to the Eleven and *to* all the o. *3370*
24:10 o with them who told this to the apostles. *3370*
Jn 2:14 and o sitting at tables exchanging money. *3836*
4:38 O have done the hard work, *257*
7:12 O replied, "No, he deceives the people." *257+1254*
7:41 O said, "He is the Christ." *257*
7:41 Still o asked, "How can the Christ *1254+3836*
9: 9 O said, "No, he only looks like him." *257*
9:16 But o asked, "How can a sinner do such *257*
10:21 But o said, "These are not the sayings of *257*
12:29 o said an angel had spoken to him. *257*
18:34 "or did o talk to you about me?" *257*
19:18 they crucified him, and with him two o— *257*
Ac 14: 4 with the Jews, o with the apostles. *1254+3836*
15:35 and many o taught and preached the word *2283*
16:32 the word of the Lord to him and to all the o *NIG*
17: 9 Then they made Jason and the o post bond *3370*
17:18 O remarked, "He seems to be *1254+3836*
17:32 some of them sneered, but o said, *3836*
17:34 woman named Damaris, and a number of o. *2283*
20: 6 and five days later joined the o at Troas, *899*
23: 6 Sadducees and the o Pharisees, *2283*
28:24 but o would not believe. *3836*
Ro 2:21 who teach o, do you not teach yourself? *2283*
11: 7 The o were hardened, *3370*
11:17 the o and now share in the nourishing sap *899*
12: 5 and each member belongs to all the o. *253*
12: 8 if it is contributing to the needs of o, *NIG*
1Co 9: 2 Even though I may not be an apostle *to* o, *257*
9:12 If o have this right of support from you, *257*
9:27 so that after I have preached *to* o, *257*
10:24 seek his own good, but the good *of* o. *2283*
12:28 those able to help o, *NIG*
14:19 to instruct o than ten thousand words in *257*
14:29 the o should weigh carefully what is said. *257*
2Co 8: 8 by comparing it with the earnestness *of* o. *2283*
8:13 Our desire is not that o might be relieved *257*
10:15 by boasting of work done by o. *259*
13: 2 who sinned earlier or any of the o, *3370*
Eph 4:29 for building o up according to their needs, *NIG*
Php 1:15 but o out of goodwill. *5516*
2: 3 in humility consider o better than yourselves. *253*
2: 4 but also to the interests *of* o. *2283*
3:17 Join with o in following my example, *1181+5213*
1Th 5: 6 So then, let us not be like o, *3370*
1Ti 5:20 so that the o may take warning. *3370*
5:22 and do not share in the sins of o. *259*
5:24 the sins of o trail behind them. *5516*
2Ti 2: 2 also be qualified to teach o. *2283*
Tit 1: 9 that he can encourage o by sound doctrine *NIG*
Heb 7:20 O became priests without any oath, *3525+3836*
11:35 O were tortured and refused to be released, *257*
11:36 while still o were chained and put in prison. *NIG*
13:16 not forget to do good and to share with o, *NIG*
1Pe 4:10 Each one should use whatever gift he has received to serve o, *1571*
2Pe 2: 5 a preacher of righteousness, and seven o; *NIG*
Jude 1:16 they boast about themselves and flatter o *NIG*
1:23 snatch o from the fire and save them; *1254+4005*

Jude 1:23 to o show mercy, mixed with fear— *4005*

OTHERWISE (27) [OTHER]

Ge 45:11 O you and your household 7153
Ex 12:33 "For o," they said, "we will all die!" 3954
Dt 8:12 O, when you eat and are satisfied, 7153
9:28 O, the country from which you brought us will say, 7153
19: 6 O, the avenger of blood might pursue him 7153
20:18 O, they will teach you to follow 889+4202+5100
24:15 O he may cry to the LORD against you, 2256+4202
Jos 6:18 O you will make the camp of Israel liable 2256
1Sa 13:19 "O the Hebrews will make swords 7153
25:34 O, as surely as the LORD, 219
2Sa 12:28 O I will take the city, 7153
1Ki 1:21 O, as soon as my lord the king is laid to rest 2256
2Ki 2:10 it will be yours—o not." 401+561
2Ch 19:10 o his wrath will come on you 2256
Pr 30: 9 O, I may have too much and disown you 7153
Isa 6:10 O they might see with their eyes, 7153
Hos 2: 3 O I will strip her naked and make her 7153
Mt 13:15 O they might see with their eyes, *3607*
15: 5 'Whatever help you might o have received *NIG*
27:64 O, his disciples may come and steal *3607*
Mk 4:12 o they might turn and be forgiven!' " *3607*
7:11 'Whatever help you might o have received *NIG*
Ac 28:27 O they might see with their eyes, *3607*
Ro 11:22 O, you also will be cut off. *2075*
1Co 7:14 O your children would be unclean, *726+2075*
15: 2 O, you have believed in vain. *1623+1760+3590*
Rev 2:16 O, I will soon come to you *1254+1623+3590*

OTHNI (1)

1Ch 26: 7 O, Rephael, Obed and Elzabad; 6978

OTHNIEL (10)

Jos 15:17 O son of Kenaz, Caleb's brother, took it; 6979
15:18 One day when she came to O, NIH
Jdg 1:13 O son of Kenaz, Caleb's younger brother, 6979
1:14 One day when she came to O, NIH
3: 9 O son of Kenaz, Caleb's younger brother, 6979
3:10 of Aram into the hands of O, 2257[S]
3:11 until O son of Kenaz died. 6979
1Ch 4:13 The sons of Kenaz: O and Seraiah. 6979
4:13 The sons of O: Hathath and Meonothai. 6979
27:15 from the family of O. 6979

OUCHES (KJV) See FILIGREE

OUGHT (40)

Ge 26:28 '*There o to* be a sworn agreement AIT
Mal 2: 7 lips of a priest *o to* preserve knowledge, AIT
Jn 7: 3 "*You o to* leave here and go to Judea, *AIT*
Ac 19:36 you o to be quiet and not do anything rash. *1256*
24:19 who o to be here before you *1256*
25:10 where I o to be tried. *1256*
25:24 shouting that he o not to live any longer. *1256*
26: 9 "I too was convinced that *I* o to do all *1256*
Ro 1:28 to do what o not to be done. *2763*
8:26 We do not know what we o to pray for, *1256*
12: 3 of yourself more highly than *you* o, *1256*
15: 1 We who are strong o to bear with *4053*
1Co 4: 1 men *o to* regard us as servants of Christ *AIT*
7:36 along in years and he feels *he* o to marry, *4053*
8: 2 not yet know as *he* o to know. *1256*
9:10 *they* o to do so in the hope of sharing in *4053*
11: 7 A man o not to cover his head, *4053*
11:10 the woman o to have a sign of authority *4053*
11:28 A man *o to* examine himself before he eats *AIT*
15:34 Come back to your senses as you o, *1469*
2Co 2: 3 by those who o to make me rejoice. *1256*
2: 7 *o to* forgive and comfort *AIT*
12:11 I o to have been commended by you, *4053*
Eph 5:28 husbands o to love their wives *4053*
2Th 1: 3 *We* o always to thank God for you, *4053*
2:13 But we o always to thank God for you, *4053*
3: 7 For you yourselves know how *you* o *1256*
1Ti 3:15 how people o to conduct themselves *1256*
5:13 saying things *they* o not to. *1256*
Tit 1:11 by teaching things they o not to teach— *1256*
Phm 1: 8 you to do what you o to do, *465+3836*
Heb 5:12 *though* by this time *you* o to be teachers, *4053*
Jas 1: 9 in humble circumstances *o to* take pride *AIT*
4:15 Instead, you *o to* say, *AIT*
4:17 the good *he o to* do and doesn't do it, *AIT*
2Pe 3:11 what kind of people o you to be? *1256*
3:11 You o to live holy and godly lives *NIG*
1Jn 3:16 we o to lay down our lives for our brothers. *4053*
4:11 we also o to love one another. *4053*
3Jn 1: 8 We o therefore to show hospitality *4053*

OUR (1200) [WE] See Index of Articles Etc.

OURS (20) [WE] See Index of Articles Etc.

OURSELVES (45) [SELF, WE] See Index of Articles Etc.

OUSTED (1)

Isa 22:19 and you *will be* o from your position. 2238

OUT (2407) [OUTER] See Index of Articles Etc.

OUTBREAK (1)

1Sa 5: 9 both young and old, with an o of tumors. 8609

OUTBURSTS (1)

2Co 12:20 jealousy, o of anger, factions, slander, *2596*

OUTCAST (1) [CAST]

Jer 30:17 'because you are called an o, 5615

OUTCOME (6)

Isa 41:22 and know their final o. 344
Da 11:29 but this time the o will be different 3869+4202
12: 8 "My lord, what will the o *of* all this be?" 344
Mt 26:58 and sat down with the guards to see the o. *5465*
Heb 13: 7 Consider the o of their way of life *1676*
1Pe 4:17 and if it begins with us, what will the o be *5465*

OUTCRY (8)

Ge 18:20 "The o *against* Sodom and Gomorrah is 2411
18:21 if what they have done is as bad as the o 7591
19:13 The o to the LORD *against* its people is 7591
1Sa 4:14 Eli heard the o and asked, 7591+7754
5:12 and the o *of* the city went up to heaven. 8784
Ne 5: 1 the men and their wives raised a great o 7591
5: 6 When I heard their o and these charges, 2411
Isa 15: 8 Their o echoes along the border of Moab; 2411

OUTDOOR (1)

Pr 24:27 Finish your o work 928+2021+2575

OUTGOINGS (KJV) See CAME OUT, DAWNS, ENDED, ENDING, FADES, FARTHEST LIMITS

OUTER (49) [OUT]

Nu 4:25 the o covering of hides of 2025+4200+4946+5087
2Sa 18:24 between the inner and o gates, 9109[S]
20:15 and it stood against the o fortifications. 2658
1Ki 6:29 in both the inner and o *rooms,* 2667
6:30 both the inner and o *rooms* 2667
7: 9 with a saw on their inner and o *faces.* 2575
2Ch 6:13 in the center of the o court. 6478
33:14 Afterward he rebuilt the o wall of the City 2667
Est 6: 4 Now Haman had just entered the o court of 2667
Job 26:14 these are but the o fringe *of* his works; 7896
41:13 Who can strip off his o coat? 7156
Eze 10: 5 be heard as far away as the o court, 2667
40:17 Then he brought me into the o court. 2667
40:20 leading into the o court. 2667
40:27 to the o gate on the south side; NIH
40:31 Its portico faced the o court; 2667
40:34 Its portico faced the o court; 2667
40:37 Its portico faced the o court; 2667
41: 1 to the o sanctuary and measured the jambs; 2121
41: 2 He also measured the o sanctuary; NIH
41: 4 across the end of the o sanctuary. 2121
41: 9 The o wall of the side rooms 2575
41:15 The o sanctuary, the inner sanctuary and 2121
41:17 around the inner and o sanctuary 2667
41:20 on the wall of the o sanctuary. 2121
41:21 o sanctuary had a rectangular doorframe, 2121
41:23 Both the o sanctuary and 2121
41:25 of the o sanctuary were carved cherubim 2121
42: 1 the man led me northward into the o court 2667
42: 1 and opposite the o wall on the north side. 1230
42: 3 the pavement of the o court, 2667
42: 7 an o wall parallel to the rooms 2021+2575+4200
42: 7 to the rooms and the o court; 2667
42: 8 to the o court was fifty cubits long, 2667
42: 9 as one enters them from the o court. 2667
42:10 along the length of the wall of the o court, NIH
42:10 and opposite the o wall, 1230
42:14 not to go into the o court until they leave 2667
44: 1 the man brought me back to the o gate of 2667
44:19 When they go out into the o court where 2667
46:20 the o court and consecrating the people." 2667
46:21 then brought me to the o court and led me 2667
46:22 of the o court were enclosed courts, NIH
47: 2 around the outside to the o gate facing east, 2575
Jn 13: 4 took off his o clothing, *2668*
21: 7 he wrapped his o garment around him *2087*
Ac 12:13 Peter knocked at the o entrance, *2598+4784*
Heb 9: 6 the priests entered regularly into the o room *4755*
Rev 11: 2 But exclude the o court; *2033*

OUTLANDISH (KJV) See FOREIGN

OUTLAW (1)

Pr 24:15 like an o against a righteous man's house, 8401

OUTLET (1)

2Ch 32:30 It was Hezekiah who blocked the upper o 4604

OUTLINE (1)

Isa 44:13 with a line and makes an o with a marker; 9306

OUTLIVED (2) [LIVE]

Jos 24:31 lifetime of Joshua and of the elders who o him 339+799+3427
Jdg 2: 7 lifetime of Joshua and of the elders who o him 339+799+3427

OUTLYING (2)

1Ch 5:16 in Bashan and its o villages, 1426
27:25 of the storehouses in the o districts, 8441

OUTMOST (KJV) See DISTANT, END, TOPMOST

OUTNUMBER (2) [NUMBER]

Ps 69: 4 o the hairs of my head; 4946+8045
139:18 *they would* o the grains of sand. 4946+8049

OUTPOST (8) [OUTPOSTS]

1Sa 10: 5 where there is a Philistine o. 5907
13: 3 Jonathan attacked the Philistine o at Geba, 5907
13: 4 "Saul has attacked the Philistine o, 5907
14: 1 over to the Philistine o on the other side." 5163
14: 4 to cross to reach the Philistine o was a cliff; 5163
14: 6 to the o *of* those uncircumcised fellows. 5163
14:11 showed themselves to the Philistine o. 5163
14:12 The men of the o shouted to Jonathan 5165

OUTPOSTS (2) [OUTPOST]

Jdg 7:11 Purah his servant went down to the o 2821+7895
1Sa 14:15 and those in the o and raiding parties 5163

OUTPOURED (3) [POUR]

Ps 79:10 the nations that you avenge the o blood 9161
Eze 20:33 and an outstretched arm and with o wrath. 9161
20:34 and an outstretched arm and with o wrath. 9161

OUTPOURING (1) [POUR]

Eze 9: 8 in this o *of* your wrath on Jerusalem?" 9161

OUTRAGEOUS (1) [RAGE]

Jer 29:23 For they have done o things in Israel; 5576

OUTRAN (2) [RUN]

2Sa 18:23 by way of the plain and o the Cushite. 6296
Jn 20: 4 the other disciple o Peter and reached *4708+5441*

OUTSIDE (130) [OUTSIDERS]

Ge 9:22 and told his two brothers o. 928+2021+2575
15: 5 He took him o and said, 2025+2575
19: 6 Lot went o to meet them and 2025+7339
24:11 the camels kneel down near the well o 2575+4946
Ex 12:46 take none of the meat o the house. 2025+2575
21:19 gets up and walks around o 928+2021+2575
26:35 the table o the curtain on the north 2575+4946
27:21 o the curtain that is in front of 2575+4946
29:14 bull's flesh and its hide and its offal o 2575+4946
33: 7 to take a tent and pitch it o 2575+4946
33: 7 to the tent of meeting o the camp. 2575+4946
40:22 on the north side of the tabernacle o 2575+4946
Lev 4:12 he must take o the camp to 2575+4946
4:21 Then he shall take the bull o the camp 2575+4946
6:11 carry the ashes o the camp to a place 2575+4946
8:17 its flesh and its offal he burned up o 2575+4946
9:11 and the hide he burned up o the camp. 2575+4946
10: 4 carry your cousins o the camp, 2575+4946
10: 5 still in their tunics, o the camp, 2575+4946
13:46 he must live o the camp. 2575+4946
14: 3 to go o the camp and examine him. 2575+4946
14: 8 he must stay o his tent for seven days. 2575+4946
14:40 and thrown into an unclean place o 2575+4946
14:41 into an unclean place o the town. 2575+4946
14:53 the live bird in the open fields o 2575+4946
16:27 must be taken o the camp; 2575+4946
17: 3 a lamb or a goat in the camp or o of it 2575+4946
22:10 " 'No one o a priest's family may eat 2424
24: 3 O the curtain of the Testimony in the 2575+4946
24:14 "Take the blasphemer o the camp. 2575+4946
24:23 the blasphemer o the camp and stoned 2575+4946
Nu 5: 3 send them o the camp so they will 2575+4946
5: 4 they sent them o the camp. 2575+4946
12:14 Confine her o the camp for seven days 2575+4946
12:15 So Miriam was confined o the camp 2575+4946
15:35 The whole assembly must stone him o 2575+4946
15:36 So the assembly took him o the camp 2575+4946
19: 3 be taken o the camp and slaughtered 2575+4946
19: 9 a ceremonially clean place o the camp. 2575+4946
31:13 the community went to meet them o 2575+4946
31:19 anyone who was killed must stay o 2575+4946
35: 5 O the town, measure three thousand 2575+4946
35:26 " 'But if the accused ever goes o the 3655+3655
35:27 avenger of blood finds him o the city, 2575+4946
Dt 23:10 he is to go o the camp and stay there. 2575+4946
23:12 a place o the camp where you can go 2575+4946
24:11 Stay o and let the man 2575
25: 5 his widow must not marry o the family. 2021+2025+2424+2575
Jos 2:19 If anyone goes o your house into the 1946+4946
6:23 and put them in a place o the camp 2575+4946
Jdg 12: 9 in marriage to those o his *clan,* 2575
12: 9 as wives from o his *clan.* 2575

Jdg 19:23 The owner of the house **went o** and said 3655
19:25 the man took his concubine and sent her **o** 2575
1Sa 9:26 he and Samuel went **o** together. 2025+2575
1Ki 6:6 the **o** of the temple so that nothing 2025+2575
7:9 from the **o** to the great courtyard and 2575
8:8 but not from **o** the Holy Place; 2025+2575
21:13 took him **o** the city and stoned him 2575+4946
2Ki 10:24 Jehu had posted eighty men **o** 928+2021+2575
16:18 the royal entryway **o** the temple of 2025+2667
23:4 burned them **o** Jerusalem in the fields 2575+4946
23:6 to the Kidron Valley **o** Jerusalem 2575+4946
25:1 He encamped **o** the city 6584
2Ch 5:9 but not from **o** the Holy Place; 2025+2575
24:8 a chest was made and placed **o**, 2025+2575
32:3 the water from the springs **o** the city, 2575+4946
32:5 He built another wall **o** that one 2025+2575
Ezr 10:13 so we cannot stand **o.** 928+2021+2575
Ne 11:16 who had charge of the **o** work of the house 2667
13:20 of goods spent the night **o** Jerusalem. 2575+4946
Job 31:34 that I kept silent and would not go **o** 7339
Pr 22:13 sluggard says, "There is a lion **o**! 928+2021+2575
SS 8:1 Then, if I found you **o**, I would kiss you, 928+2021+2575
Jer 21:4 and the Babylonians who are **o** 2575+4946
22:19 and thrown **o** the gates of Jerusalem." 2134+4946
52:4 They camped **o** the city 6584
La 1:20 **O**, the sword bereaves; 2575+4946
Eze 5:12 by the sword **o** your **walls;** 6017
7:15 **O** is the sword, inside are plague 928+2021+2575
40:19 inside of the lower gateway to the **o** of 2575+4946
40:40 By the **o** wall of the portico of 2025+2575+4946
40:44 **O** the inner gate, within the 2025+2575+4946
41:17 the **o** of the entrance to the inner sanctuary 2575
43:21 designated part of the temple area **o** 2575+4946
46:2 to enter from the **o** through the portico of 2575
47:2 around the **o** to the outer gate facing east, 2575
Mt 8:12 subjects of the kingdom will be thrown **o**, *2035*
9:25 After the crowd *had been* **put o**, *1675*
12:46 his mother and brothers stood **o**, *2032*
12:47 "Your mother and brothers are standing **o**, *2032*
22:13 'Tie him hand and foot, and **throw** him **o**, *1675*
23:25 You clean the **o** of the cup and dish, *2033*
23:26 and then the **o** also will be clean. *1760*
23:27 which look beautiful **on the o** but on the *2033*
23:28 **on the o** you appear to people as righteous *2033*
25:30 And throw that worthless servant **o**, *2035*
26:75 And he went **o** and wept bitterly. *2032*
Mk 1:45 a town openly but stayed **o** in lonely places. *2032*
2:2 not even **o** the door, *4639*
3:31 Standing **o**, they sent someone in *2032*
3:32 "Your mother and brothers are **o** looking *2032*
4:11 But to those on the **o** everything is said *2032*
7:15 Nothing **o** a man can make him 'unclean' *2033*
7:18 a man **from the o** can make him 'unclean'? *2033*
8:23 the blind man by the hand and led him **o** *2032*
11:4 They went and found a colt **o** in the street, *2032*
Lk 1:10 the assembled worshipers were praying **o.** *2032*
8:20 "Your mother and brothers are standing **o**, *2032*
11:39 you Pharisees clean the **o** of the cup *2033*
11:40 Did not the one who made the **o** make the *2033*
13:25 you will stand **o** knocking and pleading, *2032*
13:33 for surely no prophet can die **o** Jerusalem! *2032*
22:62 And he went **o** and wept bitterly. *2032*
Jn 18:16 but Peter had to wait **o** at the door. *2032*
20:11 but Mary stood **o** the tomb crying. *2032*
Ac 5:34 that the men be put **o** for a little while. *2032*
7:21 *When* he *was* **placed o**, *1758*
14:13 whose temple was **just o** the city, *4574*
14:19 They stoned Paul and dragged him **o** *2032*
16:13 On the Sabbath we went **o** the city gate to *2032*
1Co 5:12 What business is it of mine to judge those **o** *2032*
5:13 God will judge those **o.** *2032*
6:18 other sins a man commits are **o** his body, *1760*
2Co 7:5 conflicts on the **o**, fears within. *2033*
Heb 13:11 but the bodies are burned **o** the camp. *2032*
13:12 And so Jesus also suffered **o** the city gate *2032*
13:13 Let us, then, go to him **o** the camp, *2032*
Rev 14:20 They were trampled in the winepress **o** *2033*
22:15 **O** are the dogs, those who practice magic *2032*

OUTSIDERS (3) [OUTSIDE]

Col 4:5 Be wise in the way you act toward **o**; *2032+3836*
1Th 4:12 daily life may win the respect of **o** *2032+3836*
1Ti 3:7 also have a good reputation with **o**, *2033*

OUTSKIRTS (4)

Nu 11:1 and consumed some of the **o** *of* the camp. 7895
Jos 18:15 at the **o** *of* Kiriath Jearim on the west, 7895
1Sa 14:2 Saul was staying on the **o** *of* Gibeah under 7895
1Ch 4:39 and they went to the **o** *of* Gedor to the east 4427

OUTSPREAD (1) [SPREAD]

Isa 8:8 Its **o** wings will cover the breadth 5742

OUTSTANDING (6)

1Ch 7:40 choice men, brave warriors and **o** leaders. 8031
SS 5:10 **o** among ten thousand. 1838
Da 5:14 insight, intelligence and **o** wisdom. 10339
Ac 4:16 Everybody living in Jerusalem knows they have done an **o** miracle, *1196*
Ro 13:8 *Let* no **debt remain o**, except *4053*
16:7 They are **o** among the apostles, *2168*

OUTSTRETCHED (19) [STRETCH]

Ex 6:6 an **o** arm and with mighty acts of judgment. 5742
Dt 4:34 by war, by a mighty hand and an **o** arm, 5742
5:15 of there with a mighty hand and an **o** arm. 5742
7:19 the mighty hand and **o** arm, 5742
9:29 by your great power and your **o** arm." 5742
11:2 his majesty, his mighty hand, his **o** arm; 5742
26:8 of Egypt with a mighty hand and an **o** arm, 5742
1Ki 8:42 and your mighty hand and your **o** arm— 5742
2Ki 17:36 of Egypt with mighty power and **o** arm, 5742
2Ch 6:32 and your mighty hand and your **o** arm— 5742
Ps 75:5 do not speak with **o** neck.' " 6981
136:12 with a mighty hand and **o** arm; 5742
Isa 3:16 walking along with **o** necks, 5742
Jer 21:5 with an **o** hand and a mighty arm in anger 5742
27:5 and **o** arm I made the earth and its people 5742
32:17 the earth by your great power and **o** arm. 5742
32:21 by a mighty hand and an **o** arm and 5742
Eze 20:33 over you with a mighty hand and an **o** arm 5742
20:34 and an **o** arm and with outpoured wrath. 5742

OUTWARD (3) [OUTWARDLY]

1Sa 16:7 Man looks at the **o appearance,** 6524
Ro 2:28 nor is circumcision merely **o** and physical. *1877+3836+5745*
1Pe 3:3 beauty should not come **from o** adornment, *2033*

OUTWARDLY (4) [OUTWARD]

Ro 2:28 is not a Jew if he is only one **o**, *1877+3836+5745*
2Co 4:16 Though **o** we are wasting away, *476+2032+3836*
Gal 6:12 make a good impression **o** are trying *1877+4922*
Heb 9:13 sanctify them so that they are **o** clean. *4922*

OUTWEIGH (1) [WEIGH]

Job 6:3 *It would* surely **o** the sand of the seas 3877+4946

OUTWEIGHS (2) [WEIGH]

Ecc 10:1 so a little folly **o** wisdom and honor. 3701+4946
2Co 4:17 an eternal weight of glory **that far o them all.** *983+1650+2848+5651+5651*

OUTWENT (KJV) See AHEAD

OUTWIT (1) [OUTWITTED]

2Co 2:11 in order that Satan *might* not **o** *us.* *4430*

OUTWITTED (1) [OUTWIT]

Mt 2:16 When Herod realized that *he had been* **o** by *1850*

OVEN (8) [OVENS]

Lev 2:4 in an **o**, it is to consist of fine flour: 9486
7:9 Every grain offering baked in an **o** 9486
11:35 an **o** or cooking pot must be broken up. 9486
26:26 be able to bake your bread in one **o**, 9486
La 5:10 Our skin is hot as an **o**, 9486
Hos 7:4 an **o** whose fire the baker need not stir from 9486
7:6 Their hearts are like an **o**; 9486
7:7 All of them are hot as an **o**; 9486

OVENS (3) [OVEN]

Ex 8:3 and into your **o** and kneading troughs. 9486
Ne 3:11 another section and the Tower of the **O.** 9486
12:38 past the Tower of the **O** to the Broad Wall, 9486

OVER (1169)

Ge 1:2 darkness was **o** the surface of the deep, 6584
1:2 the Spirit of God was hovering **o** the waters. 6584+7156
1:26 and let them rule **o** the fish of the sea and 928
1:26 **o** the livestock, over all the earth, 928
1:26 over the livestock, **o** all the earth, 928
1:26 and **o** all the creatures that move along 928
1:28 Rule **o** the fish of the sea and the birds of 928
1:28 and **o** every living creature that moves on 928
3:16 and he will rule **o** you." 928
4:15 he will suffer vengeance **seven** *times o.*" AIT
7:21 all the creatures that swarm **o** the earth, 6584
8:1 and he sent a wind **o** the earth, 6584
8:9 because there was water **o** all the surface of 6584
9:14 Whenever I bring clouds **o** the earth and 6584
9:19 *the people who were* **scattered** *o* the earth. AIT
10:32 the nations spread out **o** the earth after 928
11:4 for ourselves and not be scattered **o** the face 6584
11:8 the LORD scattered them from there **o** 6584+7156
11:9 From there the LORD scattered them **o** 6584
15:12 a thick and dreadful darkness came **o** him. 6584
19:23 the sun had risen **o** the land. 6584
19:31 as is the custom **all** *o* the earth. AIT
22:5 the donkey while I and the boy go **o** there. 6330
22:13 He **went o** and took the ram 2143
23:2 to mourn for Sarah and to **weep** *o* her. AIT
26:21 but they quarreled **o** that one also; 6584
26:22 and no one quarreled **o** it. 6584
27:29 Be lord **o** your brothers, 4200
27:37 "I have made him lord **o** you 4200
28:15 and *will* **watch o** you wherever you go, 9068
28:20 "If God will be with me and *will* **watch o** 9068
29:2 The stone **o** the mouth of the well 6584
29:3 the stone to its place **o** the mouth of 6584
29:10 he **went o** and rolled the stone away from 5602
Ge 30:31 on tending your flocks and **watching o** 9068
32:23 *he* **sent o** all his possessions. 6296
35:20 **O** her tomb Jacob set up a pillar, 6584
37:8 "Do you intend to reign **o** us? 6584
38:16 *he* **went o** to her by the roadside and said, 5742
41:34 Let Pharaoh appoint commissioners **o** 6584
41:56 famine had spread **o** the whole country 6584+7156
42:30 "The man who is **lord** *o* the whole AIT
42:33 the man who is **lord** *o* the land said to us, AIT
45:15 he kissed all his brothers and wept **o** them. 6584
47:18 When that year *was* **o**, 9462
48:22 And to you, as one who is **o** your brothers, 6584
49:22 whose branches climb **o** a wall. 6584
50:1 and wept **o** him and kissed him. 6584
Ex 1:11 So they put slave masters **o** them 6584
2:14 "Who made you ruler and judge **o** us? 6584
3:3 "*I will* **go o** and see this strange sight— 6073
3:4 the LORD saw that *he had* **gone o** to look, 6073
3:16 **watched o** you **and** *have* **seen** 7212+7212
5:12 So the people scattered all **o** Egypt 928
7:19 and stretch out your hand **o** the waters 6584
7:19 **o** the streams and canals, 6584
7:19 **o** the ponds and all the reservoirs'— 6584
8:5 'Stretch out your hand with your staff **o** 6584
8:6 So Aaron stretched out his hand **o** 6584
9:9 It will become fine dust **o** the whole land 6584
9:22 the sky so that hail will fall all **o** Egypt— 928
10:12 "Stretch out your hand **o** Egypt so 6584
10:12 over Egypt so that locusts will swarm **o** 6584
10:13 So Moses stretched out his staff **o** Egypt, 6584
10:21 so that darkness will spread **o** Egypt— 6584
12:8 to eat the meat **roasted** *o* the fire, AIT
12:9 but **roast** it *o* the fire— AIT
12:13 *I will* **pass o** you. 7173
12:23 and sides of the doorframe and *will* **pass o** 7173
12:27 who **passed o** the houses of the Israelites 7173
13:12 *to* **give o** to the LORD the first offspring 6296
14:7 with officers **o** all of them. 6584
14:16 Raise your staff and stretch out your hand **o** 6584
14:21 Moses stretched out his hand **o** the sea, 6584
14:26 "Stretch out your hand **o** the sea so that 6584
14:26 the sea so that the waters may flow back **o** 6584
14:27 Moses stretched out his hand **o** the sea, 6584
15:19 the waters of the sea back **o** them, 6584
18:21 and appoint them as officials **o** thousands, 6584
18:25 **officials** *o* thousands, hundreds, AIT
19:16 with a thick cloud **o** the mountain, 6584
23:31 *I will* **hand o** to you the people 928+3338+5989
25:22 between the two cherubim that are **o** the ark 6584
26:7 of goat hair for the tent **o** the tabernacle— 6584
26:12 that *is* **left o** is to hang down at the rear 6369
26:13 what is left will hang **o** the sides of 6584
26:14 and **o** that a covering of hides of sea cows. 2025+4200+4946+5087
28:29 the names of the sons of Israel **o** his heart 6584
28:30 be **o** Aaron's heart whenever he enters 6584
28:30 the Israelites **o** his heart before the LORD. 6584
29:34 the ordination ram or any bread *is* **left o** 3855
30:6 before the atonement cover that is **o** 6584
30:13 Each *one* who **crosses o** 6296
30:14 All who **cross o**, 6296
34:33 he put a veil **o** his face. 6584
34:35 the veil back **o** his face until he went in 6584
36:14 of goat hair for the tent **o** the tabernacle— 6584
36:19 and **o** that a covering of hides of sea cows. 2025+4200+4946+5087
38:26 from everyone who *had* **crossed o** 6296
40:19 Then he spread the tent **o** the tabernacle 6584
40:19 over the tabernacle and put the covering **o** 6584
40:20 to the ark and put the atonement cover **o** it. 6584
40:38 of the LORD was **o** the tabernacle by day, 6584
Lev 7:16 but anything **left o** may be eaten on 3855
7:17 the sacrifice **left o** till the third day must 3855
10:12 "Take the grain offering **left o** from 3855
12:4 until the days of her purification *are* **o.** 4848
12:6 purification for a son or daughter *are* **o**, 4848
13:12 the disease **breaks out all o** his skin 7255+7255
14:5 that one of the birds be killed **o** fresh water 6584
14:6 of the bird that was killed **o** the fresh water. 6584
14:50 He shall kill one of the birds **o** fresh water 6584
16:2 in the cloud **o** the atonement cover. 6584
16:21 the head of the live goat and confess **o** it all 6584
19:6 anything **left o** until the third day must 3855
19:10 **go o** your vineyard **a second time** 6618
25:43 Do not rule **o** them ruthlessly, 928
25:46 not rule **o** your fellow Israelites ruthlessly. 928
25:53 to it that his owner *does* not **rule o** 8097
26:17 those who hate you will rule **o** you, 928
26:18 for your sins seven times **o.** 3578
26:21 I will multiply your afflictions **seven** *times o* AIT
26:24 afflict you for your sins **seven** *times o.* AIT
26:28 punish you for your sins **seven** *times o.* AIT
26:37 They will stumble **o** one another as 928
Nu 1:50 **o** all its furnishings 6584
3:32 He was **appointed** *o* those who were AIT
4:6 cloth of solid blue **o** that 2025+4200+4946+5087
4:7 **"O** the table of the Presence they are 6584
4:8 **O** these they are to spread a scarlet cloth, 6584
4:11 **"O** the gold altar they are to spread 6584
4:13 the bronze altar and spread a purple cloth **o** 6584
4:14 **O** it they are to spread a covering of hides 6584
5:14 if feelings of jealousy come **o** her husband 6584
5:30 or when feelings of jealousy come **o** a man 6584
6:5 of his separation to the LORD *is* **o**; 4848
6:13 when the period of his separation *is* **o.** 4848
9:18 long as the cloud stayed **o** the tabernacle, 6584
9:19 When the cloud remained **o** the tabernacle 6584

Nu 9:20 the cloud was **o** the tabernacle only 6584
9:22 Whether the cloud stayed **o** the tabernacle 6584
10:10 the trumpets **o** your burnt offerings 6584
10:15 Nethanel son of Zuar was **o** the division of 6584
10:16 and Eliab son of Helon was **o** the division 6584
10:19 of Zurishaddai was **o** the division of 6584
10:20 of Deuel was **o** the division of the tribe 6584
10:23 of Pedahzur was **o** the division of the tribe 6584
10:24 of Gideoni was **o** the division of the tribe 6584
10:26 Pagiel son of Ocran was **o** the division of 6584
10:27 and Ahira son of Enan was **o** the division 6584
10:34 The cloud of the LORD was **o** them 6584
14:14 that your cloud stays **o** them, 6584
16:13 And now you also want to lord it **o** us? 6584
16:33 the earth closed **o** them, 6584
19:17 into a jar and pour fresh water **o** them. 6584
21:3 **gave** the Canaanites **o** *to* them. 5989
21:24 put him to the sword and **took o** his land 3769
21:34 for *I have* **handed** him **o** *to* you, 928+3338+5989
23:15 while I meet with him **o there."** 3907
27:7 **turn** their father's inheritance **o** 6296
27:8 **turn** his inheritance **o** to his daughter. 6296
27:16 appoint a man **o** this community 6584
31:48 officers who were **o** the units of the army— 4200
32:7 the Israelites from **going o** into the land 6296
32:8 from Kadesh Barnea to **look o** the land. 8011
32:21 of you *will* **go** armed **o** the Jordan before 6296
32:27 *will* **cross o** to fight before the LORD, 6296
32:29 **cross o** the Jordan with you before 6296
32:30 But if *they do* not **cross o** with you armed, 6296
32:32 We *will* **cross o** before the LORD 6296
34:4 Then it will go to Hazar Addar and **o** 6296
Dt 1:13 and I will set them **o** you." 928+8031
1:15 appointed them to have authority **o** you— 6584
2:7 *He has* **watched o** your journey 3359
2:31 **deliver** Sihon and his country **o** 5989
2:33 the LORD our God **delivered** him **o** to us 5989
3:2 for *I have* **handed** him **o** *to* you 928+3338+5989
3:12 Of the land that *we* **took o** at that time, 3769
3:18 *must* **cross o** ahead of your brother 6296
3:20 and they too *have* **taken o** the land that 3769
3:21 **o** there where you *are* **going.** 6296
3:25 *Let me* **go o** and see the good land beyond 6296
4:22 *about to* **cross o** and take possession of 6296
6:18 and you may go in and **take o** the good land 3769
7:2 the LORD your God *has* **delivered** them **o** 5989
7:16 the peoples the LORD your God **gives o** 5989
7:23 the LORD your God *will* **deliver** them **o** 5989
11:8 in and **take o** the land that you are crossing 3769
11:10 The land you are entering to **take o** is not 3769
11:31 *you have* **taken** it **o** and are living there, 3769
15:6 You will rule **o** many nations 928
15:6 over many nations but none will rule **o** you. 928
17:14 a king **o** us like all the nations around us," 6584
17:15 be sure to appoint **o** you the king 6584
17:15 Do not place a foreigner **o** you, 6584
17:20 **reign** a long time **o** his kingdom 6584
19:12 **hand** him **o** *to* the avenger of blood to die. 928+3338+5989
20:9 they shall appoint commanders **o** it. 928+8031
21:6 the body shall wash their hands **o** 6584
23:15 *do* not **hand** him **o** to his master. 6037
24:20 not **go o the branches a second time.** 339+6994
24:21 not **go o the vines again.** 339+6618
27:3 of this law when you *have* **crossed o** to 6296
28:23 The sky **o** your head will be bronze, 6584
28:36 the king you set **o** you to a nation unknown 6584
28:42 of locusts *will* **take o** all your trees and 3769
31:3 The LORD your God himself *will* **cross o** 6296
31:3 Joshua also *will* **cross o** ahead of you, 6296
31:15 the cloud stood **o** the entrance to the Tent. 6584
32:11 that stirs up its nest and hovers **o** its young, 6584
33:2 from Sinai and dawned **o** them from Seir; 4200
33:5 He was king **o** Jeshurun when the leaders 928
33:9 but *he* **watched o** your word 9068
34:4 but *you will* not **cross o** into it." 6296
34:8 the time of weeping and mourning *was* **o.** 9462
Jos 1:14 *must* **cross o** ahead of your brothers. 6296
2:1 "Go, **look o** the land," he said, 8011
3:1 where they camped before **crossing o.** 6296
3:16 So the people **crossed o** opposite Jericho. 6296
4:3 and *to* **carry** them **o** with you and put them 6296
4:5 **"Go o** before the ark of the LORD 6296
4:8 and *they* **carried** them **o** with them 6296
4:10 The people hurried **o,** 6296
4:12 and the half-tribe of Manasseh **crossed o,** 6296
4:13 for battle **crossed o** before the LORD to 6296
4:23 before you until you *had* **crossed o.** 6296
4:23 up before us until we *had* **crossed o.** 6296
5:1 before the Israelites until we *had* **crossed o,** 6296
7:26 **O** Achan they heaped up a large pile 6584
8:29 And they raised a large pile of rocks **o** it, 6584
10:12 the LORD **gave** the Amorites **o** to Israel, 5989
10:12 "O sun, stand still **o** Gibeon, O moon, 928
10:12 O moon, **o** the Valley of Aijalon." 928
10:32 The LORD **handed** Lachish **o** *to* Israel, 928+3338+5989
11:6 *I will* **hand** all of them **o** *to* Israel, 5989
12:1 and whose territory *they* **took o** east of 3769
12:3 He also ruled **o** the eastern Arabah from NIH
12:5 He ruled **o** Mount Hermon, Salecah, 928
13:1 still very large areas of land to *be* **taken o.** 3769
13:12 Moses had defeated them and **taken o** 3769
15:3 continued on to Zin and **went o** to the south 6590
16:2 **crossed o** to the territory of the Arkites 6296
21:44 **handed** all their enemies **o** 928+3338+5989
22:19 **come o** to the LORD's land, 6296
Jos 24:7 the sea **o** them and covered them. 6584
Jdg 2:14 In his anger against Israel the LORD **handed** them **o** 928+3338+5989
3:12 gave Eglon king of Moab power **o** Israel. 6584
3:22 and the fat closed in **o** it. 1237
3:28 they allowed no one to **cross o.** 6296
4:9 the LORD *will* **hand** Sisera **o** *to* a woman." 928+3338+4835
4:18 and *she* **put** a covering **o** him. 4059
6:33 and **crossed o** the Jordan and camped in 6296
7:8 *who* **took o** the provisions and trumpets of 4374
8:22 The Israelites said to Gideon, "Rule **o** us— 928
8:23 Gideon told them, "I will not rule **o** you, 928
8:23 nor will my son rule **o** you. 928
8:23 The LORD will rule **o** you." 928
9:2 of Jerub-Baal's sons rule **o** you, 928
9:9 to hold sway **o** the trees?' 6584
9:11 to hold sway **o** the trees?' 6584
9:13 to hold sway **o** the trees?' 6584
9:15 'If you really want to anoint me king **o** you, 6584
9:18 king **o** the citizens of Shechem 6584
9:45 he destroyed the city and **scattered** salt *o* it. AIT
9:49 against the stronghold and set it on fire **o** 6584
11:8 the Ammonites, and you will be our head **o** 4200
11:11 head and commander **o** them. 6584
11:21 Israel **took o** all the land of 3769
11:23 what right have you *to* **take** it **o?** 3769
11:32 Jephthah went **o** to fight the Ammonites, 448
12:1 **crossed o** to Zaphon and said to Jephthah, 6296
12:1 We're going to burn down your house **o** 6584
12:3 I took my life in my hands and crossed **o** 448
12:3 the LORD **gave** me the **victory** *o* them. AIT
12:5 *"Let me* **cross o,"** 6296
14:4 for at that time they were ruling **o** Israel.) 928
15:11 that the Philistines are rulers **o** us? 928
15:12 to tie you up and **hand** you **o** 928+3338+5989
15:13 only tie you up and **hand** you **o** 928+3338+5989
18:9 Don't hesitate to go there and **take** it **o.** 3769
19:9 Spend the night here; the day *is* **nearly o.** 2837
Ru 2:14 Boaz said to her, "Come **o here.** 2151
2:14 She ate all she wanted and **had some left o.** 3855
2:18 and gave her what *she* **had left o** 3855
3:7 *he* **went o** to lie down at the far end of 995
3:9 "Spread the corner of your garment **o** me, 6584
4:1 **"Come o** here, my friend, and sit down." 6073
4:1 So *he* **went o** and sat down. 6073
1Sa 1:28 For his whole life he *will* **be given o** to 8626
2:1 My mouth boasts **o** my enemies, 6584
2:16 "No, **hand** it **o** now; 5989
4:14 The man hurried **o** to Eli, 995
7:15 Samuel *continued as* **judge** *o* Israel all AIT
8:9 the king who will reign **o** them will do." 6584
8:11 "This is what the king who will reign **o** 6584
8:19 "We want a king **o** us. 6584
9:16 Anoint him leader **o** my people Israel; 6584
10:1 "Has not the LORD anointed you leader **o** 6584
10:19 And you have said, 'No, set a king **o** us.' 6584
11:12 'Shall Saul reign **o** us?' 6584
12:1 to me and have set a king **o** you. 6584
12:12 'No, we want a king to rule **o** us'— 6584
12:13 see, the LORD has set a king **o** you. 6584
12:14 and if both you and the king who reigns **o** 6584
13:1 and he reigned **o** Israel [forty-]two years. 6584
13:13 he would have established your kingdom **o** 448
14:1 *let's* **go o** to the Philistine outpost on 6296
14:6 *let's* **go o** to the outpost 6296
14:8 we *will* **cross o** toward the men 6296
14:21 up with them to their camp **went o** to 2118+6017
14:33 "Roll a large stone **o** here at once." 448
14:40 "You stand **o there;** 285+4200+6298
14:40 I and Jonathan my son will stand **o here."** 285+4200+6298
14:47 After Saul had assumed rule **o** Israel, 6584
15:1 to anoint you king **o** his people Israel; 6584
15:17 The LORD anointed you king **o** Israel. 6584
15:26 LORD has rejected you as king **o** Israel!" 6584
15:35 that he had made Saul king **o** Israel. 6584
16:1 since I have rejected him as king **o** Israel? 6584
17:4 He was **o nine feet** tall. 564+2256+2455+9252
17:39 fastened on his sword **o** the tunic and 4946+6584
17:42 He **looked** David **o** and saw 5564
17:46 day the LORD *will* **hand** you **o** 928+3338+6037
17:50 So David triumphed **o** the Philistine with 4946
17:51 David ran and stood **o** him. 448
18:13 and gave him **command** *o* a thousand men, AIT
19:22 **"O** in Naioth at Ramah," they said. NIH
20:8 Why **hand** me **o** to your father?" 995
23:7 "God *has* **handed** him **o** *to* me, 928+3338+5796
23:17 You will be king **o** Israel, 6584
23:20 responsible for **handing** him **o** *to* 928+3338+6037
25:17 Now **think it o** and see what you can do, 3359
25:17 because disaster is hanging **o** our master 448
25:21 all *my* **watching o** this fellow's property in 9068
25:30 and has appointed him leader **o** Israel, 6584
26:13 Then David **crossed o** *to* the other side 6296
26:22 of your young men **come o** and get it. 6296
27:2 and **went o** to Achish son of Maoch king 6296
28:19 The LORD *will* **hand o** both Israel 928+3338+5989
28:19 LORD *will* also **hand o** the army 928+3338+5989
29:3 He has already been with me for **o a year,** 196+2296+2296+3427+9102
30:15 or **hand** me **o** *to* my master, 928+3338+6037
30:16 scattered **o** the countryside, eating, 6584+7156
30:23 and **handed o** *to* us the forces 928+3338+5989
2Sa 1:9 he said to me, 'Stand **o** me and kill me! 6584
1:10 "So I stood **o** him and killed him, 6584
2:4 anointed David king **o** the house of Judah. 6584
2Sa 2:7 the house of Judah has anointed me king **o** 6584
2:8 of Saul and **brought** him **o** *to* Mahanaim. 6296
2:9 He made him king **o** Gilead, 448
2:9 Ashuri and Jezreel, and also **o** Ephraim, 6584
2:10 when he became king **o** Israel, 6584
2:11 David was king in Hebron **o** the house of 6584
3:8 *I* haven't **handed** you **o** *to* David. 928+3338+5162
3:10 establish David's throne **o** Israel and Judah 6584
3:12 I will help you **bring** all Israel **o** to you." 6015
3:21 you may rule **o** all that your heart desires." 928
3:34 And all the people wept **o** him again. 6584
5:2 In the past, while Saul was king **o** us, 6584
5:3 and they anointed David king **o** Israel. 6584
5:5 In Hebron he reigned **o** Judah seven years 6584
5:5 and in Jerusalem he reigned **o** all Israel 6584
5:12 the LORD had established him as king **o** 6584
5:17 that David had been anointed king **o** Israel, 6584
5:19 *Will you* **hand** them **o** *to* me?" 928+3338+5989
5:19 **surely hand** the Philistines **o** *to* you." 928+3338+5989+5989
6:21 when he appointed me ruler **o** 6584
7:8 and from following the flock to be ruler **o** 6584
7:11 since the time I appointed leaders **o** 6584
7:12 When your days *are* **o** and you rest 4848
7:26 'The LORD Almighty is God **o** Israel!' 6584
8:10 on his victory in battle **o** Hadadezer, 928
8:15 David reigned **o** all Israel, 6584
8:16 Joab son of Zeruiah was **o** the army; 6584
8:18 of Jehoiada was **o** the Kerethites NIH
11:27 After the time of mourning *was* **o,** 6296
12:6 He must pay for that lamb **four** *times o,* AIT
12:7 'I anointed you king **o** Israel, 6584
14:7 **'Hand o** the one who struck his brother 5989
16:8 LORD *has* **handed** the kingdom **o** 928+3338+5989
16:9 *Let me* **go o** and cut off his head." 6296
17:16 **cross o without fail,** or the king 6296+6296
17:19 His wife took a covering and spread it out **o** 6584
17:19 of the well and scattered grain **o** it. 6584
17:20 *"They* **crossed o** the brook." 6296
17:25 Absalom had appointed Amasa **o** the army 6584
18:1 and appointed **o** them commanders 6584
18:8 The battle spread out **o** the whole 6584+7156
18:17 and piled up a large heap of rocks **o** him. 6584
18:33 up to the **room o** the gateway and wept. 6608
19:10 whom we anointed to **rule o** us, 6584
19:14 *He* **won o** the hearts of all the men of Judah 5742
19:18 **take** the king's household **o** 6296
19:22 not know that today I am king **o** Israel?" 6584
19:33 **"Cross o** with me and stay with me 6296
19:36 Your servant *will* **cross o** the Jordan with 6296
19:37 *Let him* **cross o** with my lord the king. 6296
19:38 "Kimham *shall* **cross o** with me, 6296
19:39 and then the king **crossed o.** 6296
19:40 When the king **crossed o** to Gilgal, 6296
19:40 the troops of Israel *had* **taken** the king **o.** 6296
20:8 and strapped **o** it at his waist was a belt 6584
20:12 the road into a field and threw a garment **o** 6584
20:21 **Hand o** this one man, 5989
20:23 Joab was **o** Israel's entire army; 448
20:23 of Jehoiada was **o** the Kerethites 6584
21:9 *He* **handed** them **o** *to* the Gibeonites, 928+3338+5989
23:3 'When one rules **o** men in righteousness, 928
24:3 the troops a hundred **times** *o,* AIT
24:13 **think** *it* **o** and decide how I should answer 3359
1Ki 1:1 even when *they* **put** covers **o** him. 4059
1:34 and Nathan the prophet anoint him king **o** 6584
1:35 I have appointed him ruler **o** Israel 6584
2:11 He had reigned forty years **o** Israel— 6584
2:35 of Jehoiada **o** the army in Joab's position 6584
4:1 So King Solomon ruled **o** all Israel. 6584
4:7 also had twelve district governors **o** 6584
4:19 He was the only governor **o** the district. 928
4:21 And Solomon ruled **o** all the kingdoms 928
4:24 For he ruled **o** all the kingdoms west of 928
5:7 a wise son to **rule o** this great nation." 6584
6:1 the fourth year of Solomon's reign **o** Israel, 6584
6:35 with gold hammered evenly **o** the carvings. 6584
8:7 The cherubim spread their wings **o** 448
8:46 with them and **give** them **o** to the enemy, 5989
9:5 I will establish your royal throne **o** 6584
11:37 you will rule **o** all that your heart desires; 928
11:37 you will be king **o** Israel. 6584
11:42 in Jerusalem **o** all Israel forty years. 6584
12:17 Rehoboam still ruled **o** them. 6584
12:20 to the assembly and made him king **o** 6584
13:26 The LORD *has* **given** him **o** to the lion, 5989
13:30 and they mourned **o** him and said, "Oh, 6584
14:2 the one who told me I would be king **o** 6584
14:7 among the people and made you a leader **o** 6584
14:14 for himself a king **o** Israel who will cut off 6584
14:17 as she stepped **o** the threshold of the house, 928
15:25 and he reigned **o** Israel two years. 6584
16:16 king **o** Israel that very day there in 6584
16:29 in Samaria **o** Israel twenty-two years. 6584
18:9 **handing** your servant **o** 928+3338+5989
18:19 the people from **all o** Israel to meet me 3972
19:6 a cake of bread **baked o hot coals,** 8363
19:13 *he* **pulled** his cloak **o** his face 4286
19:15 you get there, anoint Hazael king **o** Aram. 6584
19:16 anoint Jehu son of Nimshi king **o** Israel, 6584
20:38 with his headband down **o** his eyes. 6584
21:7 "Is this how you act as king **o** Israel? 6584
22:51 and he reigned **o** Israel two years. 6584
2Ki 2:8 the two of them **crossed o** on dry ground. 6296
2:14 and he **crossed o.** 6296
3:10 to **hand** us **o** *to* Moab?" 928+3338+5989

2Ki 3:13 to **hand** us **o** *to* Moab." 928+3338+5989
3:18 *he will* also **hand** Moab **o** *to* you. 928+3338+5989
4:27 Gehazi **came o** to push her away, 5602
4:43 'They will eat and **have** *some* **left o.'** " 3855
4:44 and they ate and **had** *some* **left o,** 3855
5:11 wave his hand **o** the spot and cure me 448
7:4 So *let's* **go o** to the camp of the Arameans 2143
8:15 in water and spread it **o** the king's face, 6584
9:3 I anoint you king **o** Israel.' 448
9:6 'I anoint you king **o** the LORD's people 448
9:12 I anoint you king **o** Israel.' " 448
10:36 The time that Jehu reigned **o** Israel 6584
12:7 but **hand** it **o** for repairing the temple." 5989
13:14 went down to see him and wept **o** 6584+7156
13:17 the arrow of victory **o** Aram!" 928
17:24 *They* **took o** Samaria and lived in its towns. 3769
19:10 'Jerusalem *will* not **be handed o** *to* the king of Assyria.' 928+3338+5989
19:15 you alone are God **o** all the kingdoms 4200
21:13 I will stretch out **o** Jerusalem 6584
21:14 **hand** them **o** *to* their enemies. 928+3338+5989
23:6 and scattered the dust **o** the graves of 6584
25:11 and those who *had* **gone o** to the king 5877
25:22 be **o** the people he had left behind in Judah. 6584
1Ch 5:20 **handed** the Hagrites and all their allies **o** *to* them, 928+3338+5989
10:14 and **turned** the kingdom **o** to David son 6015
11:3 and they anointed David king **o** Israel, 6584
11:10 to extend it **o** the whole land, as 6584
12:23 **turn** Saul's kingdom **o** *to* him, 6015
12:38 to make David king **o** all Israel. 6584
14:2 the LORD had established him as king **o** 6584
14:8 that David had been anointed king **o** 6584
14:10 *Will you* **hand** them **o** *to* me?" 928+3338+5989
14:10 "Go, *I will* **hand** them **o** *to* you." 928+3338+5989
17:7 to be ruler **o** my people Israel. 6584
17:10 since the time I appointed leaders **o** 6584
17:11 When your days *are* **o** and you go to be 4848
17:14 I will set him **o** my house 928
17:24 'The LORD Almighty, the **God** *o* Israel, AIT
18:10 on his victory in battle **o** Hadadezer, 928
18:14 David reigned **o** all Israel, 6584
18:15 Joab son of Zeruiah was **o** the army; 6584
18:17 of Jehoiada was **o** the Kerethites 6584
21:3 multiply his troops a hundred **times** *o.* AIT
21:16 with a drawn sword in his hand extended **o** 6584
22:10 the throne of his kingdom **o** Israel forever.' 6584
22:12 when he puts you in command **o** Israel, 6584
22:18 **handed** the inhabitants of the land **o** *to* me, 928+3338+5989
23:1 he made his son Solomon king **o** Israel. 6584
26:29 as officials and judges **o** Israel. 6584
27:6 a mighty man among the Thirty and was **o** 6584
27:16 The officers **o** the tribes of Israel: 6584
27:16 of Israel: **o** the Reubenites: 4200
27:16 of Zicri; **o** the Simeonites: 4200
27:17 **o** Levi: Hashabiah son of Kemuel; 4200
27:17 Hashabiah son of Kemuel; **o** Aaron: 4200
27:18 **o** Judah: Elihu, a brother of David; 4200
27:18 a brother of David; **o** Issachar: 4200
27:19 **o** Zebulun: Ishmaiah son of Obadiah; 4200
27:19 of Obadiah; **o** Naphtali: 4200
27:20 **o** the Ephraimites: Hoshea son of Azaziah; 4200
27:20 **o** half the tribe of Manasseh: 4200
27:21 **o** the half-tribe of Manasseh in Gilead: 4200
27:21 of Zechariah; **o** Benjamin: 4200
27:22 **o** Dan: Azarel son of Jeroham. 4200
27:22 These were the **officers** *o* the tribes AIT
28:1 the **officers** *o* the tribes, AIT
28:4 from my whole family to be king **o** 6584
28:4 to make me king **o** all Israel. 6584
28:5 the throne of the kingdom of the LORD **o** 6584
29:3 **o and above** everything I have provided 2025+4200+5087
29:11 you are exalted as head **o** all. 4200
29:25 on him royal splendor such as no king **o** 6584
29:26 David son of Jesse was king **o** all Israel. 6584
29:27 He ruled **o** Israel forty years— 6584
2Ch 1:1 son of David established himself firmly **o** 6584
1:9 for you have made me king **o** a people 6584
1:11 and knowledge to govern my people **o** 6584
1:13 And he reigned **o** Israel. 6584
2:2 and thirty-six hundred as foremen **o** them. 6584
2:18 3,600 foremen **o** them to keep NIH
5:8 The cherubim spread their wings **o** 6584
6:5 nor have I chosen anyone to be the leader **o** 6584
6:36 with them and **give** them **o** to the enemy, 5989
7:18 to have a man to rule **o** Israel.' 928
9:8 he has made you king **o** them, 6584
9:26 He ruled **o** all the kings from the River to 6584
9:30 in Jerusalem **o** all Israel forty years. 6584
10:17 Rehoboam still ruled **o** them. 6584
15:9 for large numbers *had* **come o** to him 5877
19:11 the chief priest will be **o** you in any matter 6584
19:11 be **o** you in any matter concerning the king, NIH
20:6 You rule **o** all the kingdoms of the nations. 928
20:27 to rejoice **o** their enemies. 4946
20:31 So Jehoshaphat reigned **o** Judah. 6584
21:4 When Jehoram established himself firmly **o** 6584
25:20 that he *might* **hand** them **o** to 928+3338+5989
26:12 The total number of family leaders **o** 4200
28:5 Therefore the LORD his God **handed** him **o** 928+3338+5989
31:10 and this great amount *is* **left o.**" 3855
32:6 He appointed military officers **o** the people 6584
34:4 he broke to pieces and scattered **o** 6584+7156
34:12 **O** them to direct them were Jahath 6584
2Ch 35:13 They roasted the Passover animals **o** 928
36:4 king **o** Judah and Jerusalem 6584
36:10 Zedekiah, king **o** Judah and Jerusalem. 6584
36:17 **handed** all of them **o** 928+3338+5989
Ezr 4:9 and officials **o** the men from Tripolis, NIH
4:20 Jerusalem has had powerful kings ruling **o** 10089
5:1 God of Israel, who was **o** them. 10542
5:5 of their God was watching **o** the elders of 10542
5:12 *he* **handed** them **o** *to* Nebuchadnezzar 10089+10311+10314
10:6 to mourn **o** the unfaithfulness of the exiles. 6584
Ne 3:15 **roofing** it **o** and putting its doors and bolts 3233
4:4 **Give** them **o** as plunder in a land 5989
4:12 near them came and told us ten **times** *o,* AIT
4:14 After *I* **looked things o,** 8011
5:15 Their assistants also **lorded it o** 8948
9:22 *They* **took o** the country of Sihon king 3769
9:24 **handed** the Canaanites **o** *to* them. 928+3338+5989
9:27 So *you* **handed** them **o** *to* their enemies, 928+3338+5989
9:28 of their enemies so that they ruled **o** them. 928
9:30 so *you* **handed** them **o** *to* 928+3338+5989
9:37 to the kings you have placed **o** us. 6584
9:37 They rule **o** our bodies and our cattle 6584
11:9 of Hassenuah was **o** the Second District of 6584
12:39 **o** the Gate of Ephraim, 4946+6584
13:19 and not opened until the Sabbath was **o.** 339
13:26 and God made him king **o** all Israel, 6584
Est 1:1 the Xerxes who **ruled o** 127 provinces 4887
1:5 When these days *were* **o,** 4848
1:22 that every man should be ruler **o** 928
8:2 Esther appointed him **o** Haman's estate. 6584
9:1 the upper hand **o** those who hated them. 928
Job 3:5 may a cloud settle **o** it; 6584
8:4 *he* **gave** them **o** to the penalty of their sin. 8938
8:16 spreading its shoots **o** the garden; 6584
10:12 in your providence **watched o** my spirit. 9068
10:20 *Are* not my few days *almost* **o**? 2532
14:17 you will cover **o** my sin. 6584
15:29 nor will his possessions spread **o** the land. 4200
16:11 God *has* **turned** me **o** to evil men 6037
16:15 "I have sewed sackcloth **o** my skin 6584
18:15 burning sulfur is scattered **o** his dwelling. 6584
20:25 Terrors will come **o** him; 6584
21:5 clap your hand **o** your mouth. 6584
21:32 and watch is kept **o** his tomb. 6584
26:7 He spreads out the northern [skies] **o** empty 6584
26:7 he suspends the earth **o** nothing. 6584
26:9 spreading his clouds **o** it. 6584
29:2 for the days when God **watched o** me, 9068
31:25 if *I have* **rejoiced** *o* my great wealth, AIT
31:29 or **gloated** *o* the trouble that came to him— AIT
34:13 Who appointed him **o** the earth? 2025
34:19 does not favor the rich **o** the poor, 4200+7156
34:29 Yet he is **o** man and nation alike, 6584
37:12 around **o** the face of the whole earth 6584
38:24 the east winds are scattered **o** the earth? 6584
38:33 Can you set up [God's] dominion **o** the earth 928
38:37 Who *can* **tip o** the water jars of the heavens 8886
40:4 I put my hand **o** my mouth. 4344
41:20 from his nostrils as from a boiling pot **o** NIH
41:34 he is king **o** all that are proud." 6584
42:11 They comforted and consoled him **o** all 6584
Ps 1:6 LORD **watches o** the way of the righteous, 3359
5:11 Spread your protection **o** them, 6584
7:7 Rule **o** them from on high; 6584
8:6 You made him ruler **o** the works 928
13:2 How long will my enemy triumph **o** me? 6584
19:13 may they not rule **o** me. 928
22:17 people stare and gloat **o** me. 928
22:28 to the LORD and he rules **o** the nations. 928
25:2 nor let my enemies triumph **o** me. 4200
27:12 *Do* not **turn** me **o** to the desire of my foes, 5989
29:3 The voice of the LORD is **o** the waters; 6584
29:3 the LORD thunders **o** the mighty waters. 6584
29:10 The LORD sits enthroned **o** the flood; 4200
30:1 and did not let my enemies gloat **o** me. 4200
31:8 *You have* not **handed** me **o** *to* the enemy 928+3338+6037
32:8 I will counsel you and watch **o** you. 6584
35:19 not those gloat **o** me who are my enemies 4200
35:24 do not let them gloat **o** me. 4200
35:26 May all *who* **gloat** *o* my distress be put AIT
35:26 may all who exalt themselves **o** me 6584
38:16 not let them gloat or exalt themselves **o** me 6584
41:11 for my enemy does not triumph **o** me. 6584
42:7 all your waves and breakers have swept **o** 6584
44:7 but you give us victory **o** our enemies, 4946
44:19 and covered us **o** with deep darkness. 6584
47:2 the great King **o** all the earth! 6584
47:8 God reigns **o** the nations; 6584
49:14 The upright will rule **o** them in 928
57:5 let your glory be **o** all the earth. 6584
57:11 let your glory be **o** all the earth. 6584
59:10 before me and will let me gloat **o** 928
59:13 to the ends of the earth that God rules **o** 928
60:8 **o** Philistia I shout in triumph." 6584
63:10 *be* **given o** *to* the sword and 3338+5599+6584
66:12 You let men ride **o** our heads; 4200
68:34 whose majesty is **o** Israel, 6584
69:15 up or the pit close its mouth **o** me. 6584
74:19 *Do* not **hand o** the life of your dove 5989
78:48 *He* **gave o** their cattle to the hail, 6037
78:50 not spare them from death but **gave** them **o** 6037
78:62 *He* **gave** his people **o** to the sword; 6037
80:14 **Watch o** this vine, 7212
81:12 So *I* **gave** them **o** to their stubborn hearts 8938
Ps 83:18 you alone are the Most High **o** all the earth. 6584
88:16 Your wrath has swept **o** me; 6584
89:9 You rule **o** the surging sea; 928
89:25 I will set his hand **o** the sea, 928
89:25 his right hand **o** the rivers. 928
97:9 are the Most High **o** all the earth; 6584
99:2 he is exalted **o** all the nations. 6584
103:16 the wind blows **o** it and it is gone, 928
103:19 and his kingdom rules **o** all. 928
104:8 *they* **flowed o** the mountains, 6590
105:21 ruler **o** all he possessed, 928
106:41 *He* **handed** them **o** *to* the nations, 928+3338+5989
106:41 and their foes ruled **o** them. 928
108:5 and let your glory be **o** all the earth. 6584
108:9 **o** Philistia I shout in triumph." 6584
113:4 The LORD is exalted **o** all the nations, 6584
118:18 but *he has* not **given** me **o** to death. 5989
119:133 let no sin rule **o** me. 928
121:3 *he who* **watches o** you will not slumber; 9068
121:4 *he who* **watches o** Israel will neither slumber nor sleep. 9068
121:5 The LORD **watches o** you— 9068
121:7 *he will* **watch o** your life; 9068
121:8 the LORD *will* **watch o** your coming 9068
124:4 the torrent would have swept **o** us, 6584
125:3 The scepter of the wicked will not remain **o** 6584
127:1 Unless the LORD **watches o** the city, 9068
129:2 but they have not gained the victory **o** me. 4200
141:3 Set a guard **o** my mouth, O LORD; 4200
141:3 keep watch **o** the door of my lips. 6584
141:8 *do* not **give** me **o to death.** 6867
145:20 The LORD **watches o** all who love him, 9068
146:9 The LORD **watches o** the alien 9068
Pr 1:27 disaster **sweeps o** you like a whirlwind, 910
3:10 and your vats *will* **brim o** *with* new wine. 7287
4:6 love her, and *she will* **watch o** you. 5915
6:22 when you sleep, they will watch **o** you; 6584
10:12 but love covers **o** all wrongs. 6584
17:2 wise servant will rule **o** a disgraceful son, 928
17:5 whoever gloats **o** disaster will 4200
17:9 *He who* **covers o** an offense promotes love, 4059
19:10 much worse for a slave to rule **o** princes! 928
20:26 he drives the threshing wheel **o** them. 6584
22:7 The rich rule **o** the poor, 928
22:12 eyes of the LORD **keep watch o** knowledge, 5915
23:30 Those who linger **o** wine, 6584
26:23 of glaze **o** earthenware are fervent lips with 6584
28:15 or a charging bear is a wicked man ruling **o** 6584
30:32 clap your hand **o** your mouth! 4200
31:27 *She* **watches o** the affairs of her household 7595
Ecc 1:12 the Teacher, was king **o** Israel in Jerusalem. 6584
1:16 in wisdom more than anyone who has **ruled o** Jerusalem before me: 6584
2:19 Yet he will have control **o** all the work 928
2:20 to despair **o** all my toilsome labor under 6584
2:26 to **hand** it **o** to the one who pleases God. 5989
3:19 man has no advantage **o** the animal. 4946
5:8 **o** them both are others **higher** 6584
6:6 if he lives a thousand years **twice o** but fails 7193
6:8 What advantage has a wise man **o** a fool? 4946
8:8 No man has power **o** the wind to contain it; 928
8:8 so no one has power **o** the day of his death. 928
8:9 a man **lords it o** others to his own hurt. 8948
SS 2:4 and his banner **o** me is love. 6584
2:8 bounding **o** the hills. 6584
2:11 The winter is past; the rains *are* **o** and gone. 2736
7:9 **flowing gently** *o* lips and teeth. AIT
8:6 Place me like a seal **o** your heart, 6584
Isa 3:12 women rule **o** them. 928
4:5 the LORD will create **o** all of Mount Zion 6584
4:5 and **o** those who assemble there a cloud 6584
4:5 **o** all the glory will be a canopy. 6584
5:30 that day they will roar **o** it like the roaring 6584
7:6 and make the son of Tabeel king **o** it." 928+9348
8:6 of Shiloah and rejoices **o** Rezin and the son 907
8:7 overflow all its channels, run **o** all its banks 6584
8:8 into Judah, **swirling o** it, passing through it 8851
9:7 He will reign on David's throne and **o** 6584
10:26 and he will raise his staff **o** the waters, 6584
10:29 *They* **go o** the pass, and say, 6296
11:15 a scorching wind he will sweep his hand **o** 6584
11:15 into seven streams so that *men can* **cross o** 2005
14:2 of their captors and rule **o** their oppressors. 928
14:8 the cedars of Lebanon exult **o** you and say, 4200
14:9 all *those who* were **kings** *o* the nations. AIT
14:26 this is the hand stretched out **o** all nations. 6584
15:2 Moab wails **o** Nebo and Medeba. 6584
15:5 My heart cries out **o** Moab; 4200
15:7 and stored up they carry away **o** the Ravine 6584
16:9 The shouts of joy **o** your ripened fruit and 6584
16:9 and **o** your harvests have been stilled. 6584
18:2 by sea in papyrus boats **o** the water. 6584+7156
19:4 *I will* **hand** the Egyptians **o** to the power 6127
19:4 and a fierce king will rule **o** them," 928
22:4 Do not try to console me **o** the destruction 6584
22:21 and **hand** your authority **o** 928+3338+5989
23:6 **Cross o** to Tarshish; 6296
23:11 The LORD has stretched out his hand **o** 6584
23:12 "Up, **cross o** *to* Cyprus; 6296
26:13 other lords besides you *have* **ruled o** us, 1249
27:3 **watch o** it; I water it continually. 5915
28:27 nor is a cartwheel rolled **o** cummin; 6584
28:28 **drives** the wheels of his threshing cart **o** 2169
29:10 The LORD has brought **o** you 6584
31:4 "As a lion growls, a great lion **o** his prey— 6584
31:5 *he will* **'pass o'** it and will rescue it." 7173
34:2 *he will* **give** them **o** to slaughter. 5989

Isa 34:11 God will stretch out **o** Edom 6584
37:10 'Jerusalem *will* not **be handed o** *to* the king of Assyria.' 928+3338+5989
37:16 you alone are God **o** all the kingdoms of 4200
41: 2 *He* **hands** nations **o** *to* him 5989
42:13 and will triumph **o** his enemies. 6584
42:24 Who **handed** Jacob **o** to become loot, 5989
43: 2 *they will* not **sweep o** you. 8851
44:16 **o** it he prepares his meal, 6584
44:18 their eyes *are* **plastered o** so they cannot 3220
44:19 I even baked bread **o** its coals, 6584
45:14 *they will* **come o** to you and will be yours; 6296
45:14 **coming o** to you in chains. 6296
51:10 the sea so that the redeemed *might* **cross o?** 6296
51:23 'Fall prostrate that *we may* **walk o** you.' 6296
51:23 like a street to *be* **walked o.**" 6296
60: 2 and thick darkness is **o** the peoples, NIH
60: 2 upon you and his glory appears **o** you. 6584
62: 5 as a bridegroom rejoices **o** his bride, 6584
62: 5 so will your God rejoice **o** you. 6584
63:19 but you have not ruled **o** them, 928
65:19 I will rejoice **o** Jerusalem and take delight 928
66:10 all you who mourn **o** her. 6584
66:13 and you will be comforted **o** Jerusalem." 928
Jer 1:10 today I appoint you **o** nations 6584
2:10 **Cross o** *to* the coasts of Kittim and look, 6296
4:31 my life is **given o** *to* murderers." 4200
6: 1 Raise the signal **o** Beth Hakkerem! 6584
6: 9 pass your hand **o** the branches again, 6584
6:12 Their houses *will* **be turned o** to others, 6015
6:17 I appointed watchmen **o** you and said, 6584
6:21 Fathers and sons alike will stumble **o** them; 928
9:18 Let them come quickly and wail **o** us 6584
12:12 **O** all the barren heights in 6584
13:21 sets **o** you those you cultivated as your 6584
13:26 I will pull up your skirts **o** your face 6584
18:21 So **give** their children **o** to famine; 5989
18:21 **hand** them **o** to the power of the sword. 5599
20: 4 *I will* **hand** all Judah **o** *to* the king 928+3338+5989
20: 5 *I will* **hand o** *to* their enemies all 928+3338+5989
20:10 then we will prevail **o** him 4200
21: 7 *I will* **hand o** Zedekiah king of 928+3338+5989
22:25 *I will* **hand** you **o** *to* those who 928+3338+5989
23: 4 I will place shepherds **o** 6584
24: 6 My eyes *will* **watch o** them for their good, 6584+8492
26:24 so he *was* not **handed o** *to* the people to be put to death. 928+3338+5989
27: 6 **hand** all your countries **o** 928+3338+5989
28:14 I will even give him control **o** the wild animals.' " NIH
29:21 "I *will* **hand** them **o** *to* 928+3338+5989
30:15 Why do you cry out **o** your wound, 6584
31:10 and *will* **watch o** his flock like 9068
31:28 Just as I watched **o** them to uproot and tear 6584
31:28 I will watch **o** them to build and to plant," 6584
32: 3 *to* **hand** this city **o** *to* the king of Babylon, 928+3338+5989
32: 4 but *will* **certainly be handed o** *to* the king of Babylon, 928+3338+5989+5989
32:24 the city *will* **be handed o** *to* 928+3338+5989
32:25 the city *will* **be handed o** *to* 928+3338+5989
32:28 *to* **hand** this city **o** *to* the Babylonians and 928+3338+5989
32:36 *it will* **be handed o** *to* the king 928+3338+5989
32:43 *it has* **been handed o** *to* the Babylonians.' 928+3338+5989
33:26 to rule **o** the descendants of Abraham, 448
34: 2 *to* **hand** this city **o** *to* the king of Babylon, 928+3338+5989
34: 3 surely be captured and **handed o** 928+3338+5989
34:20 *I will* **hand o** *to* their enemies 928+3338+5989
34:21 **hand** Zedekiah king of Judah and his officials **o** *to* their enemies 928+3338+5989
35: 4 which was **o** that of Maaseiah son 4946+5087
37:17 *you will* **be handed o** *to* the king 928+3338+5989
38: 2 or plague, but whoever **goes o** to 3655
38: 3 'This city *will* **certainly be handed o** *to* the army 928+3338+5989+5989
38:16 neither kill you nor **hand** you **o** 928+3338+5989
38:18 this city *will* **be handed o** *to* 928+3338+5989
38:19 "I am afraid of the Jews who *have* **gone o** to 5877
38:19 for the Babylonians *may* **hand** me **o** *to* them 928+3338+5989
38:20 "*They will* not **hand** you **o,**" 5989
39: 9 along with those who *had* **gone o** to him, 5877
39:14 *They* **turned** him **o** to Gedaliah son 5989
39:17 *you will* not **be handed o** *to* those you fear. 928+3338+5989
40: 5 whom the king of Babylon has appointed **o** 928
40: 7 as governor **o** the land and had put him 928
40:10 and live in the towns *you have* **taken o.**" 9530
40:11 the son of Shaphan, as governor **o** them, 6584
41: 2 of Babylon had appointed as governor **o** 928
41:10 *o* whom Nebuzaradan commander of the imperial guard *had* **appointed** AIT
41:10 and set out to **cross o** to the Ammonites. 6296
41:14 and **went o** to Johanan son of Kareah. 2143
41:18 of Babylon had appointed as governor **o** 928
42:10 and not uproot you, for I am grieved **o** 448
43: 3 to **hand** us **o** *to* the Babylonians, 928+3338+5989
43:10 and I will set his throne **o** these stones 4946+5087
44:27 For I am watching **o** them for harm, 6584
44:30 **hand** Pharaoh Hophra king of Egypt **o** *to* his enemies 928+3338+5989
44:30 **handed** Zedekiah king of Judah **o** *to* Nebuchadnezzar 928+3338+5989
Jer 46:12 One warrior will stumble **o** another; 928
46:16 they will fall **o** each other. 448
46:24 **handed o** *to* the people of the north." 928+3338+5989
46:26 *I will* **hand** them **o** *to* those who 928+3338+5989
48: 5 anguished **cries** *o* the destruction AIT
48:31 Therefore I wail **o** Moab, 6584
48:40 spreading its wings **o** Moab. 448
49:22 spreading its wings **o** Bozrah. 6584
50: 6 They wandered **o** mountain and hill 4946
51: 8 Wail **o** her! 6584
51:14 and they will shout in triumph **o** you. 6584
51:42 The sea will rise **o** Babylon; 6584
51:48 that is in them will shout for joy **o** Babylon, 6584
52:15 of the craftsmen and those who *had* **gone o** 5877
La 1:14 *He has* **handed** me **o** *to* those 928+3338+5989
2: 7 *He has* **handed o** *to* the enemy 928+3338+6037
2:17 he has let the enemy gloat **o** you, 6584
3:54 the waters closed **o** my head, 6584
3:65 Put a **veil** *o* their hearts, AIT
4:16 he no longer **watches o** them. 5564
4:19 they chased us **o** the mountains and lay 6584
5: 2 Our inheritance *has* **been turned o** to aliens 2200
5: 8 Slaves rule **o** us, 928
5:18 with jackals prowling **o** it. 928
Eze 1:25 the expanse **o** their heads as they stood 6584
1:26 the expanse **o** their heads was what looked 6584
4:15 "I will let you bake your bread **o** 6584
7:21 *I will* **hand** it all **o** as plunder 928+3338+5989
8:10 and I saw portrayed **all o** 6017+6017+6584
9: 4 and lament **o** all the detestable things 6584
10: 1 above the expanse that was **o** the heads of 6584
10: 2 the cherubim and scatter them **o** the city." 6584
10:18 the LORD departed from **o** the threshold 6584
11: 9 and **hand** you **o** *to* foreigners 928+3338+5989
16: 8 I spread the corner of my garment **o** you 6584
16:27 *I* **gave** you **o** to the greed of your enemies, 5989
16:39 *I will* **hand** you **o** *to* your lovers, 928+3338+5989
20:25 I also **gave** them **o** *to* statutes that were 5989
20:33 I will rule **o** you with a mighty hand and 6584
21:31 *I will* **hand** you **o** *to* brutal men, 928+3338+5989
23: 9 *I* **handed** her **o** *to* her lovers, 928+3338+5989
23:24 *I will* **turn** you **o** to them for punishment, 5989
23:28 *about to* **hand** you **o** *to* those you hate, 928+3338+5989
23:46 Bring a mob against them and **give** them **o** 5989
25: 3 **o** my sanctuary when it was desecrated and 448
25: 3 when it was desecrated and **o** the land 448
25: 3 and **o** the people of Judah when they went 448
26:19 and when I bring the ocean depths **o** you 6584
27:30 and cry bitterly **o** you; 6584
27:31 They will weep **o** you with anguish of soul 448
27:32 As they wail and mourn **o** you, 448
29:15 that it will never again rule **o** the nations. 928
31:11 *I* **handed** it **o** to the ruler of the nations, 5989
32: 3 a great throng of people I will cast my net **o** 6584
32: 8 in the heavens I will darken **o** you; 6584
32: 8 I will bring darkness **o** your land, 6584
34: 6 My sheep wandered **o** all the mountains 928
34: 6 They were scattered **o** the whole earth, 6584+7156
34:23 I will place **o** them one shepherd, 6584
35: 5 **delivered** the Israelites **o** 5599
35: 6 *I will* **give** you **o** to bloodshed 6913
35:12 and *have been* **given o** to us to devour." 5989
37:22 There will be one king **o** all of them 4200
37:24 " 'My servant David will be king **o** them, 6584
39:23 **handed** them **o** *to* their enemies, 928+3338+5989
Da 1:11 the chief official had appointed **o** Daniel, 6584
2:38 he has made you ruler **o** them all. 10089
2:39 one of bronze, will rule **o** the whole earth. 10089
2:48 He made him ruler **o** the entire province 10542
2:49 Meshach and Abednego administrators **o** 10168
3:12 there are some Jews whom you have set **o** 10542
4:17 the Most High is sovereign **o** the kingdoms 10089
4:17 and sets **o** them the lowliest of men.' 10542
4:25 the Most High is sovereign **o** the kingdoms 10089
4:32 the Most High is sovereign **o** the kingdoms 10089
5:21 that the Most High God is sovereign **o** 10089
5:21 of men and sets **o** them anyone he wishes. 10542
5:31 and Darius the Mede **took o** the kingdom, 10618
6: 2 with three administrators **o** them, 10427+10543
6: 3 that the king planned to set him **o** 10542
6:17 and placed **o** the mouth of the den, 10542
7:25 The saints *will* **be handed o** *to* him for a time, 10089+10311+10314
7:27 *will* **be handed o** to the saints, 10314
8:12 and the daily sacrifice **were given o** to it. 5989
9: 1 who was made ruler **o** the Babylonian 6584
10: 3 at all until the three weeks *were* **o.** 4848
11: 6 In those days she *will* **be handed o,** 5989
11:39 He will make them rulers **o** many people 928
11:42 He will extend his power **o** many countries; 928
Hos 7: 8 Ephraim is a flat cake not **turned o.** 2200
7:12 When they go, I will throw my net **o** them; 6584
8: 1 An eagle is **o** the house of the LORD 6584
9: 6 Their treasures of silver *will be* **taken o** 3769
9: 8 *is* the **watchman** *o* Ephraim, AIT
10: 5 Its people will mourn **o** it, 6584
10: 5 those who had rejoiced **o** its splendor, 6584
11: 5 to Egypt and will not Assyria **rule o** them 4889
11: 8 How *can I* **hand** you **o,** Israel? 4481
Joel 2: 5 of chariots they leap **o** the mountaintops, 6584
Am 5: 8 and pours them out **o** the face of the land— 6584
6: 6 but you do not grieve **o** the ruin of Joseph. 6584
8: 5 the New Moon **be o** that we may sell grain, 6296
9: 6 and pours them out **o** the face of the land— 6584
Ob 1:12 nor rejoice **o** the people of Judah in the day 4200
Ob 1:14 nor **hand o** their survivors in the day 6037
Jnh 2: 3 all your waves and breakers swept **o** me. 6584
4: 6 grow up **o** Jonah to give shade 4200+4946+6584
Mic 3: 6 Therefore night will come **o** you, 4200
4: 7 The LORD will rule **o** them 6584
4:11 let our eyes gloat **o** Zion!" 928
5: 2 for me one who will be ruler **o** Israel, 928
5: 9 Your hand will be lifted up in triumph **o** 6584
6:16 Therefore I *will* **give** you **o** to ruin 5989
7: 8 Do not gloat **o** me, my enemy! 4200
Na 3: 3 people stumbling **o** the corpses— 928
3: 5 "I will lift your skirts **o** your face." 6584
Zep 3:17 he will rejoice **o** you with singing." 6584
Zec 1:16 the measuring line will be stretched out **o** 6584
5: 3 the curse that is going out **o** the whole land; 6584+7156
5: 8 and pushed the lead cover down **o** 448
9:14 Then the LORD will appear **o** them; 6584
11: 6 "I *will* **hand** everyone **o** *to* his neighbor 928+3338+5162
11:16 a shepherd **o** the land who will not care for 928
12: 4 "I will keep a watchful eye **o** the house 6584
14: 9 The LORD will be king **o** the whole earth. 6584
Mt 2: 9 of them until it stopped **o** the place where *2062*
4:24 News about him spread **all o** Syria, *1650+3910*
5:25 or he *may* **hand** you **o** to the judge, *4140*
5:25 the judge may hand you **o** to the officer, *NIG*
8:24 so that the waves **swept o** the boat. *2821*
9: 1 **crossed o** and came to his own town. *1385*
9:31 the news about him **all o** that region. *3910*
10:17 *they will* **hand** you **o** to the local councils *4140*
14:20 of broken pieces that *were* **left o.** *4355*
14:34 *When they had* **crossed o,** *1385*
15:37 of broken pieces that *were* **left o.** *4355*
18:15 *you have* **won** your brother **o.** *3045*
18:34 In anger his master **turned** him **o** to *4140*
20:19 and *will* **turn** him **o** to the Gentiles to *4140*
20:25 the rulers of the Gentiles **lord it o** them, *2894*
20:25 and their high officials **exercise authority o** *2980*
23:15 *You* **travel o** land and sea to win *4310*
24: 9 *be* **handed o** to be persecuted and put *4140*
26: 2 of Man *will be* **handed o** to be crucified." *4140*
26:15 to give me if I **hand** him **o** to you?" *4140*
26:16 for an opportunity to **hand** him **o.** *4140*
26:36 "Sit here while I **go o** there and pray." *599*
27: 2 led him away and **handed** him **o** to Pilate, *4140*
27:18 envy that *they had* **handed** Jesus **o** to him. *4140*
27:26 and **handed** him **o** to be crucified. *4140*
27:36 sitting down, *they* **kept watch o** him there. *5498*
27:45 the ninth hour darkness came **o** all the land. *2093*
Mk 1:28 News about him spread quickly **o** the whole *1650*
4:35 "*Let us* **go o** to the other side." *1451*
4:37 and the waves broke **o** the boat, *1650*
5:21 *When* Jesus *had* again **crossed o** by boat to *1385*
6: 7 and gave them **authority o** evil spirits. *2026*
6:53 *When they had* **crossed o,** *1385*
8: 8 of broken pieces *that were* **left o.** *4354*
10:33 and *will* **hand** him **o** to the Gentiles, *4140*
10:42 as rulers of the Gentiles **lord it o** them, *2894*
10:42 and their high officials **exercise authority o** *2980*
11: 7 the colt to Jesus and **threw** their cloaks **o** it, *2095*
13: 9 You *will be* **handed o** to the local councils *4140*
14:11 for an opportunity *to* **hand** him **o.** *4140*
15: 1 led him away and **handed** him **o** to Pilate. *4140*
15:10 the chief priests *had* **handed** Jesus **o** to him. *4140*
15:15 and **handed** him **o** to be crucified. *4140*
15:33 At the sixth hour darkness came **o** *2093*
16: 1 *When* the Sabbath **was o,** Mary Magdalene, *1335*
Lk 1:33 he will reign **o** the house of Jacob forever; *2093*
2: 8 keeping watch **o** their flocks at night. *2093*
2:43 *After* the Feast *was* **o,** *5457*
4:39 So he bent **o** her and rebuked the fever, *2062*
6:17 and a great number of people from **all o** *4246*
6:38 shaken together and **running o,** *5658*
8:22 "*Let's* **go o** to the other side of the lake." *1451*
8:39 the man went away and told **all o** town *2848+3910*
9:17 of broken pieces that *were* **left o.** *4355*
11:44 which men walk **o** without knowing it." *2062*
12:58 and the judge **turn** you **o** to the officer, *4140*
13:11 She was **bent o** and could not straighten up *5174*
15: 7 in heaven **o** one sinner who repents than *2093*
15: 7 over one sinner who repents than **o** *2093*
15:10 in the presence of the angels of God **o** *2093*
16:26 nor can anyone **cross o** from there to us.' *1385*
18:32 *He will be* **handed o** to the Gentiles. *4140*
19:27 who did not want me to be king **o** them— *2093*
19:41 and saw the city, he wept **o** it *2093*
20:14 *they* **talked the matter o.** *253+1368+4639*
20:20 so that *they might* **hand** him **o** to the power *4140*
22: 6 for an opportunity to **hand** Jesus **o** to them *4140*
22:25 "The kings of the Gentiles **lord it o** them; *3259*
22:25 and those who **exercise authority o** *2027*
23: 5 up the people all **o** Judea by his teaching. *2848*
23:44 and darkness came **o** the whole land until *2093*
24:12 **Bending o,** he saw the strips of linen lying *4160*
24:20 our rulers **handed** him **o** to be sentenced *4140*
24:29 the day *is* **almost o.**" *3111*
Jn 3:25 and a certain Jew **o the matter of** *4309*
5:24 *he has* **crossed o** from death to life. *3553*
6:12 "Gather the pieces *that are* **left o.** *4355*
6:13 the pieces of the five barley loaves **left o** *4355*
12:11 of him many of the Jews *were* **going o** *5632*
17: 2 For you granted him **authority o** all people *2026*
18:30 "*we* would not *have* **handed** him **o** to you." *4140*
18:35 and your chief priests who **handed** you **o** *4140*
19:11 "You would have no power **o** me if it were *2848*
19:11 one who **handed** me **o** to you is guilty of *4140*

Jn 19:16 Finally Pilate **handed** him o to them to 4140
20: 5 He **bent** o and looked in at the strips 4160
20:11 *she* **bent** o **to look** into the tomb 4160
Ac 1: 3 to them o **a period** of forty days and spoke 1328
1:25 *to* **take** o this apostolic ministry, 3284
2:23 This man *was* **handed** o to you 1692
3:13 You **handed** him o to be killed, 4140
4:22 man who was miraculously healed was o 4498
6: 3 **turn** this responsibility o **to** 2770
7:10 so he made him ruler o Egypt 2093
7:27 'Who made you ruler and judge o us? 2093
7:31 *As* he **went** o to look more closely, 4665
7:42 But God turned away and **gave** them o to 4140
9:42 This became known all o Joppa, 2848
11:28 that a severe famine would spread o 2093
12: 4 **handing** him o to be guarded by four 4140
13:11 Immediately mist and darkness came o 2093
14:19 and Iconium and **won** the crowd o. 4275
16: 9 **"Come** o to Macedonia and help us." 1329
17: 6 "These men who have caused trouble all *o* **the world** have now come AIT
19:13 to invoke the name of the Lord Jesus o 2093
20:15 The day after that *we* **crossed** o to Samos, 4125
20:28 **Keep watch** o yourselves and all the flock 4668
21: 2 We found a ship **crossing** o to Phoenicia, 1385
21:11 Coming o to us, he took Paul's belt, NIG
21:11 *will* **hand** him o **to** the Gentiles. 1650+4140+5931
21:27 When the seven days *were* nearly o, 5334
23:33 the letter to the governor and **handed** Paul o 4225
24: 5 up riots among the Jews all o the world. 2848
24:10 a judge *o* **this nation;** AIT
25:11 no one has the right *to* **hand** me o to them. 5919
25:16 not the Roman custom *to* **hand** o any man 5919
25:21 When Paul made his appeal *to be* **held** o 5498
27: 1 and some other prisoners *were* **handed** o to 4140
28:17 *I* was arrested in Jerusalem and **handed** o to 4140
Ro 1: 8 your faith is being reported all o the world. 1877
1:24 Therefore God **gave** them o in the sinful 4140
1:26 of this, God **gave** them o to shameful lusts. 4140
1:28 he **gave** them o to a depraved mind, 4140
4:25 He *was* **delivered** o to death for our sins 4140
5:14 even o those who did not sin by breaking 2093
6: 9 death no longer **has mastery** o him. 3259
7: 1 the law *has* **authority** o a man only as long 3259
9: 5 who is God o all, forever praised! 2093
9:32 *They* **stumbled** o the "stumbling stone." 4684
11:18 *do* not **boast** o those branches. 2878
11:32 God *has* **bound** all men o to disobedience 5168
13:12 night *is* **nearly** o; the day is almost here. 4621
15:12 one who will arise *to* **rule** o the nations; 806
16:19 so I am full of joy o you; 2093
1Co 4: 6 not take pride in one man o **against** 2848
5: 5 **hand** this man o to Satan, 4140
7:37 under no compulsion but has control o 4309
10: 5 their bodies were scattered o the desert. 1877
15:24 when *he* **hands** o the kingdom to God 4140
15:31 *I* **glory** o you in Christ Jesus our Lord. 2400+3018
2Co 1: 5 For just as the sufferings of Christ **flow** o 4355
1:24 Not that *we* **lord it** o your faith, 3259
3:13 who would put a veil o his face to keep 2093
4:11 we who are alive *are* always *being* **given** o 4140
12:21 *be* **grieved** o many who have sinned earlier 4291
Gal 4: 9 to be enslaved by them **all o again?** 540+4099
4:17 Those people are zealous to win you o, NIG
Eph 1:22 and appointed him to be head o everything 5642
4: 6 who is o all and through all and in all. 2093
4:19 they *have* **given** themselves o to sensuality 4140
Col 1: 6 **All** o the world this gospel is bearing fruit 4246
1:15 the firstborn *o* **all creation.** AIT
2:10 the head *o* **every power** and authority. AIT
2:15 **triumphing** o them by the cross. 2581
3:14 And o all these virtues put on love, 2093
1Th 5:12 who *are* o you in the Lord 4613
2Th 2: 4 He will oppose and will exalt himself o 2093
1Ti 1:20 whom *I have* **handed** o to Satan to be taught 4140
2:12 a woman to teach or *to* **have authority** o 883
5: 9 be put on the list of widows unless she is o NIG
2Ti 3: 6 and **gain control** o weak-willed women, 170
Heb 3: 6 Christ is faithful as a son o God's house. 2093
5:12 the elementary truths of God's word all o NIG
6: 6 **crucifying** the Son of God **all o again** 416
10:21 we have a great priest o the house of God, 2093
13:17 They keep watch o you 5642
Jas 2:13 Mercy **triumphs** o judgment! 2878
5:14 of the church to pray o him and anoint him 2093
5:20 from death and **cover** o a multitude of sins. 2821
1Pe 3: 1 *be* **won** o without words by the behavior 3045
4: 8 because love **covers** o a multitude of sins. 2821
5: 3 not **lording it** o those entrusted to you, 2894
2Pe 2: 3 condemnation has long been hanging o NIG
Rev 2:26 I will give authority o the nations— 2093
6: 8 They were given power o a fourth of 2093
7:15 on the throne will spread his tent o them. 2093
9:11 as king o them the angel of the Abyss, 2093
11:10 The inhabitants of the earth will gloat o 2093
13: 7 And he was given authority o every tribe, 2093
14:16 on the cloud swung his sickle o the earth, 2093
15: 2 those who had been victorious o the beast 1666
15: 2 the beast and his image and o the number 1666
16: 9 who had control o these plagues, 2093
17:18 the great city that rules o the kings of 2093
18: 9 they will weep and mourn o her. 2093
18:11 of the earth will weep and mourn o her 2093
18:20 Rejoice o her, O heaven! 2093
20: 3 and locked and sealed it o him, 2062
20: 6 The second death has no power o them, 2093
20: 7 When the thousand years *are* o, 5464

OVERAWED (1) [AWE]

Ps 49:16 *Do* not *be* o when a man grows rich, when 3707

OVERBEARING (1)

Tit 1: 7 not o, not quick-tempered, 881

OVERBOARD (4)

Jnh 1:15 they took Jonah and threw him **o**, 448+2021+3542
Ac 27:18 began to **throw the cargo o.** 1678
27:19 *they* **threw** the ship's tackle o 4849
27:43 to **jump** o first and get to land. 681

OVERCAME (5) [OVERCOME]

Ex 17:13 So Joshua o the Amalekite army with 2765
Jer 38:22 " 'They misled you and o you— 3523
Hos 12: 4 He struggled with the angel and o him; 3523
Rev 3:21 just as I o and sat down with my Father 3771
12:11 They o him by the blood of the Lamb and 3771

OVERCAST (1)

Mt 16: 3 for the sky is red and o.' 5145

OVERCHARGE (KJV) See PUT IT TOO SEVERELY

OVERCOME (25) [OVERCAME, OVERCOMES]

Ge 32:28 with God and with men and *have* o." 3523
1Sa 4:19 but **was** o *by* her labor pains. 2200
17: 9 but if I o him and kill him, 3523
Ps 13: 4 *"I have* o him," 3523
39:10 I *am* o by the blow of your hand. 3983
116: 3 *I was* o *by* trouble and sorrow. 5162
Jer 1:19 against you but *will* not o you, 3523
15:20 against you but *will* not o you, 3523
23: 9 like a man o *by* wine, 6296
Da 10:16 "I *am* o *with* anguish because of the vision, 2200
Zec 9:15 They will destroy and o *with* slingstones. 3899
Mt 16:18 and the gates of Hades *will* not o it. 2996
Mk 9:24 help me o my unbelief!" NIG
Lk 8:37 because *they were* o with fear. 5309
10:19 and scorpions and to o all the power of 2093
Jn 16:33 I *have* o the world." 3771
Ro 12:21 *Do* not *be* o by evil, 3771
12:21 but o evil with good. 3771
1Ti 5:11 **sensual desires** o **their dedication to** 2952
2Pe 2:20 and are again entangled in it and **o**, 2487
1Jn 2:13 because *you have* o the evil one. 3771
2:14 and *you have* o the evil one. 3771
4: 4 are from God and *have* o them, 3771
5: 4 This is the victory that *has* o the world, 3771
Rev 17:14 the Lamb *will* o them because he is Lord 3771

OVERCOMES (10) [OVERCOME]

1Jn 5: 4 for everyone born of God o the world. 3771
5: 5 Who is it that o the world? 3771
Rev 2: 7 *To* him who **o**, I will give the right to eat 3771
2:11 He who o will not be hurt at all by 3771
2:17 *To* him who **o**, I will give some of 3771
2:26 To him who o and does my will to the end, 3771
3: 5 He who o will, like them, be dressed in 3771
3:12 Him who o I will make a pillar in 3771
3:21 To him who **o**, I will give the right to sit 3771
21: 7 He who o will inherit all this, 3771

OVERDRIVE (KJV) See DRIVEN HARD

OVERFED (1) [FEED]

Eze 16:49 her daughters were arrogant, **o** and 4312+8430

OVERFLOW (21) [OVERFLOWING, OVERFLOWS]

Job 6:15 as the streams *that* o 6296
Ps 65:11 and your carts o *with* abundance. 8319
65:12 The grasslands of the desert **o;** 8319
119:171 *May* my lips o *with* praise, 5580
Pr 5:16 *Should* your springs o in the streets, 7046
Isa 8: 7 *It will* o all its channels, 6584+6590
28:17 the lie, and water *will* o your hiding place. 8851
Jer 9:18 till our eyes o *with* tears and water streams 3718
14:17 " '*Let* my eyes o *with* tears night and day 3718
47: 2 *They will* o the land and everything in it, 8851
La 1:16 "This is why I weep and my eyes o 3718
Joel 2:24 the vats *will* o *with* new wine and oil. 8796
3:13 for the winepress is full and the vats **o—** 8796
Zec 1:17 'My towns *will* again o with prosperity, 7046
Mt 12:34 out of the o of the heart the mouth speaks. 4354
Lk 6:45 out of the o of his heart his mouth speaks. 4354
Ro 5:15 of the one man, Jesus Christ, o to the many! 4355
15:13 so that you *may* o with hope by the power 4355
2Co 4:15 thanksgiving *to* o to the glory of God. 4355
Php 1:26 in Christ Jesus *will* o on account of me. 4355
1Th 3:12 and o for each other and for everyone else, 4355

OVERFLOWING (8) [OVERFLOW]

1Ch 12:15 the first month when it *was* o all its banks, 4848
Pr 3:10 then your barns will be filled *to* **o**, 8426
Isa 66:11 and delight in her o abundance." 2329
Jer 13:17 my eyes will weep bitterly, o *with* tears, 3718
47: 2 they will become an o torrent. 8851
2Co 8: 2 of the most severe trial, their o joy 4353
9:12 but is also o in many expressions of thanks 4355
Col 2: 7 and o with thankfulness. 4355

OVERFLOWS (2) [OVERFLOW]

Ps 23: 5 You anoint my head with oil; my cup **o.** 8122
2Co 1: 5 so also through Christ our comfort **o.** 4355

OVERGROWN (3) [GROW]

Isa 32:13 a land o *with* thorns and briers— 6590
Jer 26:18 the temple hill a **mound** *o with* thickets.' AIT
Mic 3:12 the temple hill a mound o with thickets. NIH

OVERHANG (1) [HANG]

Eze 41:25 and there was a wooden o on the front of 6264

OVERHANGING (3) [HANG]

1Ki 7: 6 in front of that were pillars and an o **roof.** 6264
Isa 2:21 the rocks and to the o crags from dread of 6186
57: 5 in the ravines and under the o crags. 6186

OVERHANGS (1) [HANG]

Eze 41:26 The side rooms of the temple also had **o.** 6264

OVERHEAD (1)

Isa 31: 5 Like birds **hovering o,** 6414

OVERHEARD (2) [HEAR]

Ge 27: 6 *I* o your father say to your brother Esau, 9048
1Sa 17:31 What David said **was** o and reported 9048

OVERJOYED (5) [JOY]

Da 6:23 The king *was* o and gave orders 10293+10678
Mt 2:10 When they saw the star, *they were* **o.** 3489+5379+5897+5915
Jn 20:20 The disciples *were* o when they saw 5897
Ac 12:14 so o she ran back without opening it 5915
1Pe 4:13 *you may be* o when his glory is revealed. 22+5897

OVERLAID (33) [OVERLAY]

Ex 26:32 on four posts of acacia wood o *with* gold 7596
26:37 and five posts of acacia wood o *with* gold. 7596
36:34 *They* o the frames *with* gold 7596
36:34 *They* also o the crossbars *with* gold. 7596
36:36 of acacia wood for it and o them *with* gold. 7596
36:38 *They* o the tops of the posts and their bands 7596
37: 2 *He* o it *with* pure gold, both inside and out, 7596
37: 4 of acacia wood and o them *with* gold. 7596
37:11 Then *they* o it *with* pure gold and made 7596
37:15 of acacia wood and *were* o *with* gold. 7596
37:26 *They* o the top and all the sides and 7596
37:28 of acacia wood and o them *with* gold. 7596
38: 2 and *they* o the altar *with* bronze. 7596
38: 6 of acacia wood and o them *with* bronze. 7596
38:17 and their tops were o *with* silver; 7599
38:19 and their tops were o *with* silver. 7599
1Ki 6:20 *He* o the inside with pure gold, 7596
6:20 and *he* also o the altar of cedar. 7596
6:21 which *was* o *with* gold. 7596
6:22 So *he* o the whole interior *with* gold. 7596
6:22 *He* also o *with* gold the altar that belonged 7596
6:28 *He* o the cherubim *with* gold. 7596
6:32 and o the cherubim and palm trees 7596
6:35 and o them *with* gold hammered evenly 7596
10:18 a great throne inlaid with ivory and o 7596
2Ch 3: 4 *He* o the inside *with* pure gold. 7596
3: 7 *He* o the ceiling beams, doorframes, 2902
3: 8 *He* o the inside with six hundred talents 2902
3: 9 *He* also o the upper parts *with* gold. 2902
3:10 a pair of sculptured cherubim and o them 7596
4: 9 and o the doors *with* bronze. 7596
9:17 a great throne inlaid with ivory and o 7596
Isa 30:22 Then you will defile your idols o 7599

OVERLAY (13) [OVERLAID, OVERLAYING, OVERLAYS]

Ex 25:11 **O** it *with* pure gold, both inside and out, 7596
25:13 of acacia wood and o them *with* gold. 7596
25:24 **O** it *with* pure gold and make 7596
25:28 o them *with* gold and carry the table. 7596
26:29 **O** the frames *with* gold and make gold rings 7596
26:29 Also o the crossbars *with* gold. 7596
27: 2 and o the altar *with* bronze. 7596
27: 6 of acacia wood for the altar and o them 7596
30: 3 **O** the top and all the sides and the horns 7596
30: 5 Make the poles of acacia wood and o them 7596
38:28 *to* o the tops of the posts, 7596
Nu 16:38 Hammer the censers into sheets to o 7599
16:39 he had them hammered out to o the altar, 7599

OVERLAYING (1) [OVERLAY]

1Ch 29: 4 for the o *of* the walls of the buildings, 3212

OVERLAYS (1) [OVERLAY]

Isa 40:19 and a goldsmith o it with gold 8392

OVERLIVED (KJV) See OUTLIVED

OVERLOOK (3) [OVERLOOKED, OVERLOOKING, OVERLOOKS]

Dt 9:27 O the stubbornness of this people, 440+7155
24:19 in your field and *you* o a sheaf, 8894
Pr 19:11 it is to his glory *to* o an offense. 6296

OVERLOOKED (2) [OVERLOOK]

Ac 6: 1 because their widows *were being* o in *4145*
17:30 In the past God o such ignorance, *5666*

OVERLOOKING (3) [OVERLOOK]

Nu 23:28 to the top of Peor, o the wasteland. 9207
Jos 8:14 Israel in battle at a certain place o 4200+7156
1Sa 13:18 and the third toward the borderland o 9207

OVERLOOKS (3) [OVERLOOK]

Nu 21:20 where the top of Pisgah o the wasteland. 9207
2Ch 20:24 the men of Judah came to the **place that** o 5205
Pr 12:16 but a prudent man o an insult. 4059

OVERMUCH (KJV) See EXCESSIVE

OVERNIGHT (5) [NIGHT]

Lev 19:13 *Do* not **hold back** the wages of a hired man o. 1332+4328+6330
Dt 21:23 *you must* not **leave** his body on the tree o. 4328
Isa 10:29 and say, "We will **camp** o at Geba." 4869
Jnh 4:10 It sprang up o and died overnight. 1201+4326
4:10 It sprang up overnight and died o. 1201+4326

OVERPASS (KJV) See NO LIMIT

OVERPAST (KJV) See PASSED BY

OVERPLUS (KJV) See BALANCE

OVERPOWER (9) [POWER]

Ge 32:25 When the man saw that *he could* not o him, 3523
43:18 He wants to attack us and o us and seize us 5877
Jdg 16: 5 of his great strength and how *we can* o him 3523
2Ki 16: 5 but they could not o him. 4309
Est 9: 1 of the Jews had hoped to o them, 8948
Job 14:20 *You* o him once for all, and he is gone; 9548
Isa 7: 1 but they could not o it. 4309+6584
Ob 1: 7 your friends will deceive and o you; 3523
Rev 11: 7 and o and kill them. *3771*

OVERPOWERED (8) [POWER]

Jdg 3:10 hands of Othniel, who o him. 3338+6451+6584
2Sa 11:23 "The men o us and came out against us in 1504
1Ki 20:21 king of Israel advanced and o the horses 5782
2Ki 10:32 Hazael o the Israelites throughout 5782
Ecc 4:12 Though one *may be* o, two can defend 9548
Jer 20: 7 *you* o me and prevailed. 2616
Da 6:24 the lions o them and crushed all their bones 10715
Ac 19:16 jumped on them and o them all. *2894*

OVERPOWERING (1) [POWER]

Job 41: 9 the mere sight of him *is* o. 3214

OVERPOWERS (1) [POWER]

Lk 11:22 when someone stronger attacks and o him, *3771*

OVERRAN (1) [RUN]

Jdg 20:43 and easily o them in the vicinity of Gibeah 2005

OVERRIGHTEOUS (1) [RIGHTEOUS]

Ecc 7:16 Do not be o, neither be overwise— 2221+7404

OVERRULED (2) [OVERRULING]

2Sa 24: 4 o Joab and the army commanders; 448+2616
1Ch 21: 4 The king's word, however, o Joab; 2616+6584

OVERRULING (1) [OVERRULED]

Est 8: 5 be written o the dispatches that Haman son 8740

OVERRUN (4) [RUN]

Isa 34:13 Thorns *will* o her citadels, 6590
Hos 9: 6 and thorns will o their tents. 928
Am 3:11 "An enemy will o the land; 6017
Zec 9: 8 an oppressor o my people, 6296

OVERSEER (5) [OVERSEERS, OVERSIGHT]

Pr 6: 7 It has no commander, no o or ruler, 8853
1Ti 3: 1 If anyone sets his heart on being an o, *2175*
3: 2 Now the o must be above reproach, *2176*
Tit 1: 7 Since an o is entrusted with God's work, *2176*
1Pe 2:25 to the Shepherd and O of your souls. *2176*

OVERSEERS (3) [OVERSEER]

Ac 20:28 of which the Holy Spirit has made you o. *2176*
Php 1: 1 together with the o and deacons: *2176*
1Pe 5: 2 that is under your care, **serving as o**— *2174*

OVERSHADOW (1) [OVERSHADOWED, OVERSHADOWING]

Lk 1:35 the power of the Most High *will* o you. *2173*

OVERSHADOWED (1) [OVERSHADOW]

1Ki 8: 7 the ark and o the ark and its carrying poles. 6114

OVERSHADOWING (4) [OVERSHADOW]

Ex 25:20 o the cover with them. 6114
37: 9 o the cover with them. 6114
Eze 31: 3 with beautiful branches o the forest; 7511
Heb 9: 5 o the atonement cover. *2944*

OVERSIGHT (1) [OVERSEER]

2Ch 23:18 Then Jehoiada placed the o *of* the temple 7213

OVERSPREAD (KJV) See SCATTERED

OVERSTEP (1) [STEP]

Pr 8:29 so the waters *would* not o his command, 6296

OVERTAKE (27) [OVERTAKEN, OVERTAKES, OVERTAKING, OVERTOOK]

Ge 19:19 this disaster *will* o me, and I'll die. 1815
Ex 15: 9 'I will pursue, *I will* o them. 5952
Dt 19: 6 o him if the distance is too great, 5952
28:15 upon you and o you: 5952
28:45 and o you until you are destroyed, 5952
1Sa 30: 8 *Will I* o them?" 5952
30: 8 *"You will* **certainly** o them and 5952+5952
2Sa 15:14 *to* o us and bring ruin upon us and 5952
2Ki 7: 9 punishment *will* o *us.* 5162
Job 20:22 distress will o him; 4200
27:20 Terrors o him like a flood; 5952
Ps 7: 5 then let my enemy pursue and o me; 5952
35: 8 *may* ruin o them by surprise— 995
69:24 *let* your fierce anger o them. 5952
Pr 6:15 Therefore disaster *will* o him in an instant; 995
10:24 What the wicked dreads *will* o him; 995
Ecc 2:15 "The fate of the fool *will* o me also. 7936
Isa 35:10 Gladness and joy *will* o them, 5952
47: 9 Both of these *will* o you in a moment, 995
51:11 Gladness and joy *will* o them, 5952
Jer 42:16 then the sword you fear *will* o you there, 5952
Hos 10: 9 *Did* not war o the evildoers in Gibeah? 5952
Am 9:10 'Disaster *will* not o or meet us.' 5602
Mic 2: 6 disgrace *will* not o us." 6047
Zec 1: 6 the prophets, o your forefathers? 5952
Rev 12:15 to o the woman and sweep her away with *3958*
18: 8 in one day her plagues *will* o her: *2457*

OVERTAKEN (4) [OVERTAKE]

Ps 9: 6 Endless ruin *has* o the enemy, 9462
40:12 my sins *have* o me, and I cannot see. 5952
La 1: 3 All who pursue her *have* o her in the midst 5952
Am 9:13 "when the reaper *will* **be** o by the plowman 5602

OVERTAKES (6) [OVERTAKE]

Pr 1:26 I will mock when calamity o you— 995
1:27 when calamity o you like a storm, 995
3:25 or of the ruin that o the wicked, 995
Ecc 2:14 to realize that the same fate o them both. 7936
9: 3 The same destiny o all. 4200
Jn 12:35 before darkness o you. *2898*

OVERTAKING (1) [OVERTAKE]

1Ch 21:12 with their swords o you, 5952

OVERTHREW (9) [OVERTHROW]

Ge 19:25 Thus *he* o those cities and the entire plain, 2200
19:29 that o the cities where Lot had lived. 2200
Dt 29:23 which the LORD o in fierce anger. 2200
Isa 14:17 *who* o its cities and 2238
Jer 20:16 like the towns the LORD o without pity. 2200
50:40 As God o Sodom and Gomorrah along 4550
Am 4:11 *"I* o some of you as I overthrew Sodom 2200
4:11 "I overthrew some of you as I o Sodom 4550
Ac 13:19 *he* o seven nations in Canaan *2747*

OVERTHROW (15) [OVERTHREW, OVERTHROWN, OVERTHROWS]

Ge 19:21 I *will* not o the town you speak of. 2200
2Sa 10: 3 to explore the city and spy it out and o it?" 2200
2Ki 3:19 *You will* o every fortified city 5782
1Ch 19: 3 and spy out the country and o it?" 2200
2Ch 25: 8 God *will* o you before the enemy, 4173
25: 8 for God has the power to help or to o." 4173
Ezr 6:12 o any king or people who lifts a hand 10400
Jer 1:10 to destroy and o, to build and to plant." 2238
31:28 and to o, destroy and bring disaster, 2238
45: 4 I *will* o what I have built 2238
Da 11:17 in marriage in order to o the kingdom, 8845
11:24 He will plot the o *of* fortresses— 4742
Hag 2:22 *I will* o chariots and their drivers; 2200
Zec 10: 5 they will fight and o the horsemen. 3312
2Th 2: 8 the Lord Jesus *will* o with the breath *359*

OVERTHROWN (9) [OVERTHROW]

Nu 21:30 "But *we have* o them; 3721
Pr 12: 7 Wicked men *are* o and are no more, 2200
Isa 1: 7 laid waste as when o *by* strangers. 4550
13:19 be o *by* God like Sodom and Gomorrah. 4550
Jer 18:23 Let them be o before you; 4173
49:18 As Sodom and Gomorrah were o, 4550
La 2:17 *He has* o you without pity, 2238
4: 6 which **was** o in a moment without 2200
Eze 32:12 and all her hordes *will* **be** o. 9012

OVERTHROWS (4) [OVERTHROW]

Job 12:19 and o men long established. 6156
34:25 *he* o them in the night and they are crushed. 2200
Pr 13: 6 but wickedness o the sinner. 6156
Isa 44:25 *who* o the learning of the wise and 294+8740

OVERTOOK (10) [OVERTAKE]

Ge 31:25 hill country of Gilead when Laban o him, 5952
Ex 14: 9 the Israelites and o them as they camped by 5952
Jdg 18:22 near Micah were called together and o 1815
1Sa 31: 3 and when the archers o him, 5162
2Ki 25: 5 the king and o him in the plains of Jericho. 5952
1Ch 10: 3 and when the archers o him, 5162
Ps 18:37 I pursued my enemies and o them; 5952
Jer 2: 3 and disaster o them,' " 448+995
39: 5 and o Zedekiah in the plains of Jericho. 5952
52: 8 and o him in the plains of Jericho. 5952

OVERTURN (1) [OVERTURNED, OVERTURNS]

Hag 2:22 *I will* o royal thrones and shatter 2200

OVERTURNED (6) [OVERTURN]

Jdg 7:13 struck the tent with such force that the tent o 2025+2200+4200+5087
Eze 38:20 The mountains *will* **be** o, 2238
Jnh 3: 4 "Forty more days and Nineveh *will* **be** o." 2200
Mt 21:12 *He* o the tables of the money changers and *2951*
Mk 11:15 *He* o the tables of the money changers and *2951*
Jn 2:15 of the money changers and o their tables. *418*

OVERTURNS (1) [OVERTURN]

Job 9: 5 without their knowing it and o them 2200

OVERWEENING (3)

Pr 21:24 he behaves with **o pride.** 2295+6301
Isa 16: 6 her o pride and conceit, 4394
Jer 48:29 her o pride and conceit, 4394

OVERWHELM (7) [OVERWHELMED, OVERWHELMING, OVERWHELMS]

Job 3: 5 *may* blackness o its light. 1286
9:18 but *would* o me *with* misery. 8425
15:24 *they* o him, like a king poised to attack, 9548
30:15 Terrors o me; my dignity is driven away 2200
Pr 1:27 when distress and trouble o you. 995+6584
SS 6: 5 Turn your eyes from me; they o me. 8104
Hab 2:17 to Lebanon *will* o you, 4059

OVERWHELMED (18) [OVERWHELM]

Dt 11: 4 how *he* o them *with* the waters of 7429
2Sa 22: 5 the torrents of destruction o me. 1286
1Ki 10: 5 she *was* o. 928+2118+4202+6388+8120
2Ch 9: 4 she *was* o. 928+2118+4202+6388+8120
Ps 14: 5 There they are, **o with dread,** 7064+7065
18: 4 the torrents of destruction o me. 1286
38: 4 My guilt *has* o me like a burden 6296+8031
53: 5 There they were, **o with dread,** 7064+7065
55: 5 horror *has* o me. 4059
65: 3 *When* we *were* o *by* sins, 1504
88: 7 *you have* o me *with* all your waves. 6700
Eze 3:15 among them for seven days—o. 9037
Da 10: 7 but such terror o them that they fled 3877+6584
Mt 26:38 "My soul is **o with sorrow** to the point *4337*
Mk 7:37 *People were* **o with amazement.** *1742+5669*
9:15 *they were* **o with wonder** and ran *1701*
14:34 "My soul is **o with sorrow** to the point *4337*
2Co 2: 7 that he *will* not *be* o by excessive sorrow. *2927*

OVERWHELMING (6) [OVERWHELM]

Pr 27: 4 Anger is cruel and fury o, 8852
Isa 10:22 Destruction has been decreed, o and righteous. 8851
28:15 When an o scourge sweeps by, 8851
28:18 When the o scourge sweeps by, 8851
Da 11:22 an o army will be swept away before him; 8852
Na 1: 8 but with an o flood he will make an end 6296

OVERWHELMS (2) [OVERWHELM]

Pr 10: 6 but violence o the mouth of the wicked. 4059
10:11 but violence o the mouth of the wicked. 4059

OVERWICKED (1) [WICKED]

Ecc 7:17 *Do* not *be* o, and do not be a fool— 2221+8399

OVERWISE (1) [WISE]

Ecc 7:16 Do not be overrighteous, neither *be* **o**— 2681+3463

OWE (8) [OWED, OWES]

Mt 18:28 'Pay back what *you* **o** me!' *4053*
Lk 16: 5 'How much *do you* **o** my master?' *4053*
16: 7 'And how much *do* you **o?'** *4053*
Ro 13: 7 Give everyone what *you* **o** him: *4051*
13: 7 If you **o** taxes, pay taxes; *NIG*
15:27 and indeed *they* **o** it to them. *1639+4050*
15:27 *they* **o** it to the Jews to share *4053*
Phm 1:19 to mention that *you* **o** me your very self. *4695*

OWED (5) [OWE]

Mt 18:24 *who* **o** him ten thousand talents was brought *4050*
18:28 one of his fellow servants who **o** him *4053*
18:34 until he should pay back all he **o.** *4053*
Lk 7:41 "Two men **o money** to a certain *1639+5971*
7:41 One **o** him five hundred denarii, *4053*

OWES (2) [OWE]

Dt 15: 3 must cancel any debt your brother **o** you. 2118
Phm 1:18 has done you any wrong or **o** you anything, *4053*

OWL (22) [OWLS]

Lev 11:16 the **horned o,** the screech owl, 1426+3613
11:16 the **screech o,** the gull, any kind of hawk, 9379
11:17 the **little o,** the cormorant, the great owl, 3927
11:17 the little owl, the cormorant, the **great o,** 3568
11:18 the **white o,** the desert owl, the osprey, 9492
11:18 the white owl, the **desert o,** the osprey, 7684
Dt 14:15 the **horned o,** the screech owl, 1426+3613
14:15 the **screech o,** the gull, any kind of hawk, 9379
14:16 the **little o,** the great owl, the white owl, 3927
14:16 the little owl, the **great o,** the white owl, 3568
14:16 the little owl, the great owl, the **white o,** 9492
14:17 the **desert o,** the osprey, the cormorant, 7684
Ps 102: 6 I am like a desert **o,** 7684
102: 6 like an **o** *among* the ruins. 3927
Isa 34:11 **desert o** and screech owl will possess it; 7684
34:11 The desert owl and **screech o** will possess it 7887
34:11 the **great o** and the raven will nest there. 3568
34:15 The **o** will nest there and lay eggs, 7889
Jer 50:39 and there the **o** will dwell. 1426+3613
Mic 1: 8 like a jackal and moan like an **o.** 1426+3613
Zep 2:14 The **desert o** and the screech owl will roost 7684
2:14 and the **screech o** will roost on her columns. 7887

OWLS (5) [OWL]

Job 30:29 brother of jackals, a companion of **o.** 1426+3613
Isa 13:21 there the **o** will dwell, 1426+3613
14:23 into a place for **o** and into swampland; 7887
34:13 a haunt for jackals, a home for **o.** 1426+3613
43:20 the jackals and the **o,** 1426+3613

OWN (653) [OWNED, OWNER, OWNER'S, OWNERS, OWNERSHIP, OWNING, OWNS]

Ge 1:27 So God created man in **his o** image, 2257
5: 3 he had a son in **his o** likeness, 2257
5: 3 in **his o** image; and he named him Seth. 2257
10: 5 each with **its o** language.) 2257
15: 4 but a son coming from **your o** body will 3870
15:13 be strangers in a country not **their o,** 2157+4200
24: 4 but will go to my country and **my o** relatives 3276
24:38 go to my father's family and to **my o** clan, 3276
24:40 a wife for my son from **my o** clan and 3276
29:14 "You are **my o** flesh and blood." 3276
30:25 so I can go back to **my o** homeland. 3276
30:30 may I do something for **my o** household?" 3276
30:43 and *came to* **o** large flocks, 2118+4200
37:27 he is our brother, **our o** flesh and blood." 5646
40: 5 and each dream had a meaning of **its o.** 2257
41:11 and each dream had a meaning of **its o.** 2257
43:29 **his o** mother's son, he asked, 2257
46: 4 And Joseph's **o** hand will close your eyes." 2257
46:32 and herds and everything they **o.'** 4200
47: 1 and herds and everything they **o,** 4200
47: 6 put them in charge of **my o** livestock." 3276+4200
Ex 1:21 he gave them families of their **o.** NIH
2:11 where **his o** people were and watched them 2257
2:11 one of **his o** people. 2257
4:18 "Let me go back to **my o** people in Egypt 3276
5: 7 let them go and gather **their o** straw. 2157+4200
5:11 get **your o** straw wherever you can find it, 4013+4200
5:16 but the fault is with **your o** people." 3870
6: 7 I will take you as **my o** people, 3276+4200
18:27 and Jethro returned to **his o** country. 2257
22: 5 from the best of **his o** field or vineyard. 2084
32:13 to whom you swore by **your o self:** 3870
32:29 you were against **your o** sons and brothers, 2257
Lev 7:30 With **his o** hands he is to bring 2257
14:15 pour it in the palm of **his o** left hand, 2021+3913[S]
14:26 oil into the palm of **his o** left hand, 2021+3913[S]
16: 6 for **his o** sin offering to make atonement 2257
16:11 for **his o** sin offering to make atonement 2257
16:11 to slaughter the bull for **his o** sin offering. 2257
20: 9 and his blood will be on **his o** head. 2257
20:11 their blood will be on **their o** heads. 4392
20:12 their blood will be on **their o** heads. 4392
20:13 their blood will be on **their o** heads. 4392
Lev 20:16 their blood will be on **their o** heads. 4392
20:26 from the nations to be **my o.** 3276+4200
20:27 their blood will be on **their o** heads.' " 4392
21:14 but only a virgin from **his o** people, 2257
22:24 You must not do this in **your o** land, 4013
25:10 his family property and each to **his o** clan. 2257
25:13 to return to **his o** property. 2257
25:27 he can then go back to **his o** property. 2257
25:41 and he will go back to **his o** clan and to 2257
Nu 1:52 in **his o** camp under his own standard. 2084
1:52 in his own camp under **his o** standard. 2257
2:17 each in **his o** place under his standard. 2257
5:10 Each man's sacred gifts are **his o,** 2257+4200
6: 7 Even if **his o** father or mother or brother 2257
8:16 I have taken them as **my o** in place of 3276
10: 9 When you go into battle in **your o** land 4013
10:30 to **my o** land and my own people." 3276
10:30 to my own land and **my o** people." 3276
11:15 and do not let me face **my o** ruin." 3276
13:33 like grasshoppers in **our o** eyes, 5646
15:39 after the lusts of **your o** hearts and eyes. 4013
17: 9 and each man took **his o** staff. 2084
22:13 "Go back to **your o** country, 4013
22:30 "Am I not **your o** donkey, 3870
24:13 I could not do anything of **my o** accord, 3276
24:25 and Balak went **his o** way. 2257
27: 3 but he died for **his o** sin and left no sons. 2257
35:28 may he return to **his o** property. 2257
35:32 and live on **his o** land before the death of 2021[S]
Dt 2: 5 the hill country of Seir as his **o.** 3772
3:21 "You have seen with **your o** eyes all that 3870
3:27 Look at the land with **your o** eyes, 3870
4: 3 with **your o** eyes what the LORD did 4013
7:19 You saw with **your o** eyes the great trials, 3870
9:26 **your o** inheritance that you redeemed 3870
10:13 giving you today for **your o** good? 3870+4200
10:21 wonders you saw with **your o** eyes. 3870
11: 7 But it was **your o** eyes 4013
12:12 or inheritance of **their o.** 2257
12:17 You must not eat in **your o** towns the tithe 3870
12:21 and in **your o** towns you may eat as much 3870
13: 6 If your **very o brother,** 278+562+1201+3870
14:27 or inheritance of their **o.** NIH
14:29 or inheritance of their **o**) and the aliens, NIH
15:22 You are to eat it in **your o** towns. 3870
17:15 He must be from among **your o** brothers. 3870
18:15 like me from among **your o** brothers. 3870
23:23 the LORD your God with **your o** mouth. 3870
24:16 each is to die for **his o** sin. 2257
28:54 on **his o** brother or the wife he loves 2257
28:56 the husband she loves and **her o** son 2023
29: 3 With **your o** eyes you saw those great trials, 3870
29:19 **persist in** going **my o way."** 4213+9244
32:49 the Israelites as their **o** possession. NIH
33: 7 With **his o** hands he defends his cause. 2257
33: 9 or acknowledge **his o** children, 2257
Jos 1:11 the land the LORD your God is giving you for your **o.'** " 3769
1:15 you may go back and occupy your **o** land, 3772
2:19 his blood will be on **his o** head; 2257
6:18 **bring about** *your o* **destruction** AIT
7: 9 then will you do for **your o** great name?" 3870
7:11 with **their o** possessions. 2157
20: 6 Then he may go back to **his o** home in 2257
21: 3 and pasturelands out of **their o** inheritance: 4392
22: 9 in Canaan to return to Gilead, **their o** land, 4392
22:23 If we have built **our o** altar to turn away 5646
24: 7 You saw with **your o** eyes what I did to 4013
24:12 not do it with **your o** sword and bow. 3870
24:28 each to **his o** inheritance. 2257
Jdg 2: 6 each to **his o** inheritance. 2257
3: 6 and gave **their o** daughters to their sons, 2157
7: 2 against me that **her o** strength has saved her, 3276
7: 7 each to **his o** place." 2257
8:19 the sons of **my o** mother. 3276
8:30 He had seventy sons of **his o,** 2257+3655+3751
11:19 through your country to **our o** place.' 3276
18: 1 the Danites was seeking a place of **their o** 2257
21:24 each to **his o** inheritance. 2257
Ru 4: 6 because I might endanger **my o** estate. 3276
1Sa 5:11 let it go back to **its o** place, 2257
6: 9 If it goes up to **its o** territory, 2257
8:16 and donkeys he will take for **his o** use. 2257
10:25 each to **his o** home. 2257
12:22 LORD was pleased to make you **his o.** 2257+4200
13:14 after **his o** heart and appointed him leader 2257
14:46 and they withdrew to **their o** land. 4392
15:12 a monument in **his o** honor and has turned 2257
15:17 you were once small in **your o** eyes, 3870
17:38 Then Saul dressed David in **his o** tunic. 2257
17:54 he put the Philistine's weapons in **his o** tent. 2257
20:30 of Jesse to **your o** shame and to the shame 3870
24:10 This day you have seen with **your o** eyes 3870
25: 8 Ask **your o** servants and they will tell you. 3870
25:26 from avenging yourself with **your o** hands, 3870
25:33 and from avenging myself with **my o** hands. 3276
25:39 Nabal's wrongdoing down on **his o** head." 2257
28: 3 and buried him in **his o** town of Ramah. 2257
29: 4 by taking the heads of **our o** men? 2156[S]
31: 4 so Saul took **his o** sword and fell on it. 2021[S]
2Sa 1:16 "Your blood be on **your o** head. 3870
1:16 **Your o** mouth testified against you 3870
3: 6 **strengthening his o position** in the house 2616
4:11 in **his o** house and on his own bed— 2257
4:11 in his own house and on **his o** bed— 2257
5: 1 "We are **your o** flesh and blood. 3870
6:22 and I will be humiliated in **my o** eyes. 3276
2Sa 7:10 so that they can have a home of **their o** 2257
7:12 who will come from **your o** body, 3870
7:22 as we have heard with **our o** ears. 5646
7:24 as **your very o** forever, 3870+4200
12: 4 of **his o** sheep or cattle to prepare a meal for 2257
12: 9 the sword and took his wife to be **your o.** 3870
12:10 wife of Uriah the Hittite to be **your o.'** 3870+4200
12:11 'Out of **your o** household I am going 3870
12:20 Then he went to **his o** house, 2257
14:24 the king said, "He must go to **his o** house; 2257
14:24 to **his o** house and did not see the face of 2257
16:11 "My son, who is of **my o** flesh, 3276
19:12 You are my brothers, **my o** flesh and blood. 3276
19:13 'Are you not **my o** flesh and blood? 3276
19:37 that I may die in **my o** town near the tomb 3276
23:21 and killed him with **his o** spear. 2257
1Ki 1:12 how you can save **your o** life and the life 3871
1:33 set Solomon my son on **my o** mule 3276+4200
2:34 he was buried on **his o** land in the desert. 2257
2:37 your blood will be on **your o** head." 3870
4:25 each man under **his o** vine and fig tree. 2257
8:15 **his o** hand has fulfilled what he promised 2257
8:15 with **his o** mouth to my father David. 2257
8:19 who is **your o** flesh and blood— 3870
8:32 down on **his o** head what he has done. 2257
8:38 of **his o** heart, and spreading out his hands 2257
8:43 as do **your o** people Israel, 3870
8:46 who takes them captive to **his o** land, 367+2021[S]
8:53 of the world to be **your o** inheritance, 3870+4200
9:15 **his o** palace, the supporting terraces, 2257
10: 6 in **my o** country about your achievements 3276
10: 7 until I came and saw with **my o** eyes. 3276
10:13 with her retinue to **her o** country. 2023
11:19 that he gave him a sister of **his o** wife, 2257
11:20 with **Pharaoh's** *o* children. AIT
11:21 that I may return to **my o** country." 3276
11:22 to go back to **your o** country?" 3870
11:38 Look after **your o** house, O David!" 3870
12:33 a month of **his o** choosing, 2257+4213+4946
13:29 to **his o** city to mourn for him and bury him. 2021+2021+2418+5566[S]
13:30 Then he laid the body in **his o** tomb, 2257
15:18 LORD's temple and of **his o** palace. 2021+4889[S]
20:34 "You may set up **your o** market areas 3870+4200
2Ki 2:12 of **his o** clothes and tore them apart. 2257
3:27 they withdrew and returned to **their o** land. 2021[S]
4:13 "I have a home among **my o** people." 3276
6:22 with **your o** sword or bow? 3870
7: 2 "You will see it with **your o** eyes," 3870
7:19 "You will see it with **your o** eyes, 3870
8:20 against Judah and set up **its o** king. 2157
9:21 each in **his o** chariot, to meet Jehu. 2257
13: 5 So the Israelites lived in **their o** homes 2157
14: 6 each is to die for **his o** sins." 2257
14:10 for trouble and cause **your o** downfall and 911
15:19 to gain his support and strengthen **his o** hold 2257
17:29 each national group made **its o** gods in 2257
17:32 also appointed all sorts of **their o** people 4392
17:33 also served **their o** gods in accordance with 2157
18:27 who, like you, will have to eat **their o** filth 2157
18:27 and drink **their o** urine?" 2157
18:31 from **his o** vine and fig tree and drink water 2257
18:31 and drink water from **his o** cistern, 2257
18:32 and take you to a land like **your o,** 4013
19: 7 he will return to **his o** country, 2257
20:18 **your o flesh and blood,** 3655+3870+4946
21: 6 He sacrificed **his o** son in the fire, 2257
23:30 to Jerusalem and buried him in **his o** tomb. 2257
24: 7 not march out from **his o** country again, 2257
1Ch 9: 2 Now the first to resettle on **their o** property 4392
9: 2 in **their o** towns were some Israelites, 2157
10: 4 so Saul took **his o** sword and fell on it. 2021[S]
11: 1 "We are **your o** flesh and blood. 3870
11:23 and killed him with **his o** spear. 2257
12:30 brave warriors, famous in **their o** clans— 4392
16:43 all the people left, each for **his o** home, 2257
17: 9 that *they can* **have a home** *of their o* AIT
17:11 one of **your o** sons, 3870
17:20 as we have heard with **our o** ears. 5646
17:22 You made your people Israel **your very o** forever, 3870+4200
2Ch 6: 9 who is **your o** flesh and blood— 3870
6:23 down on **his o** head what he has done. 2257
6:33 as do **your o** people Israel, 3870
7:11 of the LORD and in **his o** palace, 2257
8: 1 the temple of the LORD and **his o** palace, 2257
8:18 ships commanded by **his o** officers, 2257
9: 5 in **my o** country about your achievements 3276
9: 6 until I came and saw with **my o** eyes. 3276
9:12 with her retinue to **her o** country. 2023
10:16 Look after **your o** house, O David!" 3870
11:15 And he appointed **his o** priests for 2257+4200
13: 9 of **your o** as the peoples of other lands do? 4013
16: 2 LORD's temple and of **his o** palace 2021+4889[S]
21: 8 against Judah and set up **its o** king. 2157
21:13 You have also murdered **your o** brothers, 3870
25: 4 each is to die for **his o** sins." 2257
25:14 He set them up as **his o** gods, 2257+4200
25:15 not save **their o** people from your hand?" 4392
25:19 for trouble and cause **your o** downfall and 911
29: 8 as you can see with **your o** eyes. 4013
31: 1 to **their o** towns and to their own property. 2157
31: 1 to their own towns and to **their o** property. 2257
31: 3 The king contributed from **his o** possessions 2257
32:21 So he withdrew to **his o** land in disgrace. 2257
35: 7 all from the **king's** *o* possessions. AIT
Ezr 2: 1 each to **his o** town, 2257

Ezr 2:70 the temple servants settled in **their o** towns, 2157
Ne 3:28 each in front of **his o** house. 2257
4:4 Turn their insults back on **their o** heads. 4392
4:15 each to **his o** work. 2257
5:7 from **your o** countrymen!" 2257
7:3 and some near **their o** houses." 2257
7:6 each to **his o** town, 2257
7:73 settled in **their o** towns. 2157
8:16 on **their o** roofs, 2257
11:1 to stay in **their o** towns. 2021[S]
11:3 each on **his o** property in the various towns, 2257
13:10 the service had gone back to **their o** fields. 2084
13:19 I stationed some of **my o** men at the gates so 3276
13:30 and assigned them duties, each to **his o** task. 2257
Est 1:8 was allowed to **drink in his o way,** 9276
1:22 to each province in **its o** script and 2023
1:22 and to each people in **its o** language, 2257
1:22 be ruler over **his o** household. 2257
2:7 as **his o** daughter when her father 2257+4200
3:12 and sealed with **his o** ring. 2021+4889[S]
8:9 to the Jews in **their o** script and language. 4392
9:25 the Jews should come back onto **his o** head, 2257
Job 2:4 "A man will give all he has for **his o** life. 2257
9:21 I despise **my o** life. 3276
14:22 of **his o** body and mourns only for himself." 2257
15:6 **Your o** mouth condemns you, not mine; 3870
15:6 **your o** lips testify against you. 3870
18:7 **his o** schemes throw him down. 2257
19:16 though I beg him with **my o** mouth. 3276
19:17 I am loathsome to **my o** brothers. 3276
19:27 I myself will see him with **my o** eyes— 3276
20:7 he will perish forever, like **his o** dung; 2257
20:10 **his o** hands must give back his wealth. 2257
21:16 But their prosperity is not in **their o** hands, 4392
21:20 Let **his o** eyes see his destruction; 2257
29:18 "I thought, 'I will die in **my o** house, 3276
32:1 because he was righteous in **his o** eyes. 2257
40:14 to you that **your o** right hand can save you 3870
Ps 7:16 his violence comes down on **his o** head. 2257
12:4 we **o** our lips—who is our master?" 907
35:21 With **our o** eyes we have seen it." 5646
36:2 in **his o** eyes he flatters himself too much 2257
37:15 But their swords will pierce **their o** hearts, 4392
40:15 be appalled at **their o** shame. 4392
50:20 and slander **your o** mother's son. 3870
64:8 He will turn **their o** tongues against them 4392
69:8 an alien to **my o** mother's sons; 3276
81:12 to follow **their o** devices. 2157
132:11 "One of **your o** descendants I will place 3870
135:4 the LORD has chosen Jacob to be **his o** 2257+4200
141:10 Let the wicked fall into **their o** nets, 2257
Pr 1:18 These men lie in wait for **their o** blood; 4392
3:5 and lean not on **your o** understanding; 3870
3:7 Do not be wise in **your o** eyes; 3870
5:15 Drink water from **your o** cistern, 3870
5:15 running water from **your o** well. 3870
5:23 led astray by **his o** great folly. 2257
11:5 down by **their o** wickedness. 2257
14:1 but with **her o** hands the foolish one tears 2023
14:10 Each heart knows **its o** bitterness, 2257+5883
16:4 LORD works out everything for **his o** ends 2084
18:2 but delights in airing **his o** opinions. 2257
19:3 **A man's** *o* folly ruins his life, AIT
19:8 He who gets wisdom loves **his o** soul; 2257
20:24 How then can anyone understand **his o** way? 2257
25:27 nor is it honorable to seek **one's o** honor. 4392
26:5 or he will be wise in **his o** eyes. 2257
26:12 Do you see a man wise in **his o** eyes? 2257
26:16 The sluggard is wiser in **his o** eyes than 2257
26:17 who meddles in a quarrel not **his o.** 2257+4200
27:2 and not **your o** mouth; 3870
27:2 someone else, and not **your o** lips. 3870
28:10 along an evil path will fall into **his o** trap, 2257
28:11 A rich man may be wise in **his o** eyes, 2257
29:6 An evil man is snared by his **o** sin, NIH
29:24 accomplice of a thief is **his o** enemy; 2257+5883
30:12 in **their o** eyes and yet are not cleansed 2257
Ecc 8:9 man lords it over others to **his o** hurt. 2257+4200
10:12 but a fool is consumed by **his o** lips. 5647
SS 1:6 **my o** vineyard I have neglected. 3276+4200+8611
8:12 But **my o** vineyard is mine to give; 3276
Isa 4:1 "We will eat **our o** food 5646
4:1 and provide **our o** clothes; 5646
5:17 Then sheep will graze as in **their o** pasture; 4392
5:21 in **their o** eyes and clever in their own sight. 2157
5:21 in their own eyes and clever in **their o** sight. 2157
9:20 on the flesh of **his o** offspring: 2257
13:14 each will return to **his o** people, 2257
14:1 and will settle them in **their o** land. 4392
14:2 and bring them to **their o** place. 4392
14:18 each in **his o** tomb. 2257
30:20 with **your o** eyes you will see them. 3870
36:12 who, like you, will have to eat **their o** filth 2157
36:12 and drink **their o** urine?" 2157
36:16 from **his o** vine and fig tree and drink water 2257
36:16 and drink water from **his o** cistern, 2257
36:17 and take you to a land like **your o—** 4013
37:7 he will return to **his o** country, 2257
39:7 **your o flesh and blood** 3655+3870+4946
43:25 for **my o** sake, 3276
44:9 they are ignorant, to *their o* **shame.** AIT
45:12 **My o** hands stretched out the heavens; 3276
48:9 For **my o** name's sake I delay my wrath; 3276
48:11 For **my o** sake, for my own sake, I do this. 3276
48:11 For my own sake, for **my o** sake, I do this. 3276
48:13 **My o** hand laid the foundations of the earth, 3276

Isa 49:26 I will make your oppressors eat **their o** flesh 4392
49:26 they will be drunk on **their o** blood, 4392
52:8 they will see it with **their o** eyes. NIH
53:6 each of us has turned to **his o** way; 2257
56:11 they all turn to **their o** way, 4392
56:11 each seeks **his o** gain. 2257
58:7 to turn away from **your o** flesh and blood? 3870
58:13 and if you honor it by not going **your o** way 3870
59:16 so **his o** arm worked salvation for him, 2257
59:16 and **his o** righteousness sustained him. 2257
63:5 so **my o** arm worked salvation for me, 3276
63:5 and **my o** wrath sustained me. 3276
65:2 pursuing **their o** imaginations— 2157
66:3 They have chosen **their o** ways, 2157
Jer 2:13 and have dug **their o** cisterns, 2157+4200
3:15 I will give you shepherds after **my o** heart, 3276
4:18 **"Your o** conduct and actions have brought this upon you. 3871
5:19 and served foreign gods in **your o** land, 4013
5:19 in a land not **your o.'** 4013+4200
5:31 the priests rule by **their o** authority, 2157
6:3 each tending **his o** portion." 2257
7:6 not follow other gods to **your o** harm, 4013+4200
7:19 harming themselves, to **their o** shame? 2157+7156
8:6 Each pursues **his o** course like 4392
10:23 O LORD, that a man's life is not **his o;** 2257
12:6 Your brothers, **your o** family— 3870
12:15 to **his o** inheritance and his own country. 2257
12:15 to his own inheritance and **his o** country. 2257
14:14 and the delusions of **their o** minds. 4392
16:20 Do men make **their o** gods? 2257+4200
17:4 Through **your o** fault you will lose 3870
18:12 We will continue with **our o** plans; 5646
20:4 with **your o** eyes you will see them fall by 3870
23:8 Then they will live in **their o** land." 4392
23:16 They speak visions from **their o** minds, 4392
23:26 the delusions of **their o** minds? 4392
23:31 the prophets who wag **their o** tongues and 4392
23:36 *every* **man's** *o* word becomes his oracle AIT
26:11 You have heard it with **your o** ears!" 4013
27:11 that nation remain in **its o** land to till it and 2257
29:25 You sent letters in **your o** name to all 3870
30:21 Their leader will be one of **their o;** 5647
31:17 "Your children will return to **their o** land. 4392
31:30 Instead, everyone will die for **his o** sin; 2257
31:30 **his o** teeth will be set on edge. 2257
32:4 to face and see him with **his o** eyes. 2257
32:39 for **their o** good and the good 2157+4200
34:3 the king of Babylon with **your o** eyes, 3870
37:7 will go back to **its o** land, to Egypt. 2257
39:14 So he remained among **his o** people. 2021[S]
46:16 to **our o** people and our native lands, 5646
50:6 and hill and forgot **their o** resting place. 4392
50:16 to **his o** people, 2257
50:16 let everyone flee to **his o** land. 2257
50:19 to **his o** pasture and he will graze on Carmel 2084
51:9 let us leave her and each go to **his o** land, 2257
La 4:10 With their o hands compassionate women NIH
4:10 With their own hands compassionate women have cooked **their o** children, 2177
Eze 7:27 and by **their o** standards I will judge them. 2157
8:12 each at the shrine of **his o** idol? 2257
9:10 on **their o** heads what they have done." 4392
11:21 down on **their o** heads what they have done, 4392
13:2 of **their o** imagination: 4392
13:3 foolish prophets who follow **their o** spirit 4392
13:17 prophesy out of **their o** imagination. 2177
13:18 of my people but preserve **your o?** 4032
14:16 not save their **o** sons or daughters. NIH
14:18 not save their **o** sons or daughters. NIH
16:32 You prefer strangers to **your o** husband! 2023
18:13 to death and his blood will be on **his o** head. 2257
18:18 But his father will die for **his o** sin, 2257
22:11 violates his sister, **his o** father's daughter. 2257
22:31 down on **their o** heads all they have done, 4392
28:25 Then they will live in **their o** land, 4392
33:4 his blood will be on **his o** head. 2257
33:5 his blood will be on **his o** head. 2257
33:20 of you according to **his o** ways." 2257
34:13 and I will bring them into **their o** land. 4392
36:5 in their hearts they made my land **their o** possession 2157+4200
36:17 people of Israel were living in **their o** land, 4392
36:24 and bring you back into **your o** land. 4013
37:14 and I will settle you in **your o** land. 4013
37:21 and bring them back into **their o** land. 4392
39:28 I will gather them to **their o** land, 4392
46:18 inheritance out of **his o** property, 2257
Da 3:28 or worship any god except **their o** God. 10203
6:17 and the king sealed it with **his o** signet ring 10192
8:24 but not by **his o** power. 2257
11:5 and will rule **his o** kingdom 2257
11:9 of the South but will retreat to **his o** country. 2257
11:14 among **your o** people will rebel 3870
11:19 of **his o** country but will stumble and fall, 2257
11:28 of the North will return to **his o** country 2257
11:28 against it and then return to **his o** country. 2257
Hos 8:4 for themselves to *their o* **destruction.** AIT
10:13 you have depended on **your o** strength 3870
14:3 to what **our o** hands have made, 5646
Joel 3:4 on **your o** heads what you have done. 4013
3:7 on **your o** heads what you have done. 4013
Am 5:2 never to rise again, deserted in **her o** land, 2023
6:13 not take Karnaim by **our o** strength?" 5646
9:15 I will plant Israel in **their o** land, 4392
Ob 1:15 your deeds will return upon **your o** head. 3870
Jnh 1:5 and each cried out to **his o** god. 2257

Mic 4:4 under **his** *o* vine and under his own fig tree, AIT
4:4 under his own vine and under **his** *o* fig tree, AIT
7:6 the members of **his** *o* household. AIT
Hab 1:6 to seize dwelling places not **their o.** 2257+4200
1:7 to themselves and promote **their o** honor. 2257
1:11 guilty men, whose **o** strength is their god." 2257
2:10 shaming **your o** house 3870
2:18 For he who makes it trusts in **his o** creation; 2257
3:14 With **his o** spear you pierced his head 2257
Zep 2:11 every one in **its o** land. 2257
Hag 1:9 while each of you is busy with **his o** house. 2257
Zec 11:5 **Their o** shepherds do not spare them. 2157
13:3 **his o** parents will stab him. 2084
Mal 1:5 You will see it with **your o** eyes and say, 4013
Mt 6:34 Each day has enough trouble *of* **its o.** *899*
7:3 to the plank in **your o** eye? *5050*
7:4 the time there is a plank in **your o** eye? *5148*
7:5 first take the plank out *of* **your o** eye, *5148*
8:22 and let the dead bury **their o** dead." *1571*
9:1 crossed over and came to **his o** town. *2625*
10:36 members of his **o** household.' *899*
13:57 in his **o** house is a prophet without honor." *NIG*
17:25 from **their o** sons or from others?" *899*
20:15 to do what I want with **my o** money? *1847*
27:31 they took off the robe and put **his o** clothes *899*
27:60 in **his o** new tomb that he had cut out of *899*
Mk 4:34 But when he was alone *with* **his o** disciples, *2625*
6:4 in **his o** house is a prophet without honor." *899*
7:9 in order to observe **your o** traditions! *5148*
15:20 purple robe and put **his o** clothes on him. *899*
Lk 2:3 And everyone went to **his o** town to register. *1571*
2:35 And a sword will pierce your **o** soul too." *899*
2:39 they returned to Galilee to **their o** town *1571*
6:41 to the plank in **your o** eye? *2625*
6:42 to see the plank in your **o** eye? *NIG*
6:44 Each tree is recognized by **its o** fruit. *2625*
8:3 to support them out of **their o** means. *899*
9:60 "Let the dead bury **their o** dead, *1571*
10:34 Then he put the man on **his o** donkey, *2625*
11:21 fully armed, guards *his* **o** house, *1571*
14:26 yes, even **his o** life— *1571*
16:8 with **their o** kind than are the people of *1571*
16:12 who will give you property *of* **your o?** *5629*
18:9 of **their o** righteousness and looked down *1571*
19:22 'I will judge you by **your o** words, *5148*
22:71 We have heard it from **his o** lips." *899*
Jn 1:11 He came to that which was **his o,** *2625*
1:11 but *his* **o** did not receive him. *2625*
4:44 a prophet has no honor in **his o** country.) *2625*
5:18 but he was even calling God **his o** Father, *2625*
5:43 but if someone else comes in **his o** name, *2625*
7:5 even **his o** brothers did not believe in him. *899*
7:16 Jesus answered, "My teaching is not **my o.** *1847*
7:17 from God or whether I speak on **my o.** *1831*
7:18 on **his o** does so to gain honor for himself, *1571*
7:28 I am not here on **my o,** *1831*
7:50 and who was one of **their o number,** *899*
7:53 Then each went to **his o** home. *899*
8:13 "Here you are, appearing as **your o** witness; *4932*
8:14 "Even if I testify on **my o** behalf, *1831*
8:17 In **your o** Law it is written that *5629*
8:28 to be] and that I do nothing on **my o** *1831*
8:41 the things **your o** father does." *5148*
8:42 I have not come on **my o;** but he sent me. *1831*
10:3 He calls **his o** sheep by name *2625*
10:4 When he has brought out all **his o,** *2625*
10:18 but I lay it down of **my o accord.** *1831*
10:36 the Father set apart as his very **o** and sent *NIG*
11:51 He did not say this on **his o,** *1571*
12:49 For I did not speak of **my o accord,** *1831*
13:1 Having loved **his o** who were in the world, *2625*
14:10 The words I say to you are not just **my o.** *1831*
14:24 These words you hear are not **my o;** *1847*
15:19 it would love you as **its o.** *2625*
16:13 He will not speak on **his o;** *1571*
16:32 each to **his o home.** *2625+3836*
18:31 and judge him by **your o** law." *5148*
18:34 "Is that **your o** idea," Jesus asked, *4932*
19:17 Carrying **his o** cross, *1571*
Ac 1:7 the Father has set by **his o** authority, *2625*
2:6 in **his o** language. *2625*
2:8 of us hears them *in* **his o** native language? *2625*
2:11 the wonders of God *in* **our o** tongues!" *2466*
3:12 Why do you stare at us as if by **our o** power *2625*
3:22 like me from among **your o** people; *5148*
4:23 Peter and John went back to **their o** *people* *2625*
4:32 that any of his possessions was **his o,** *2625*
5:31 to **his o** right hand as Prince and Savior *899*
7:6 be strangers in a country **not their o,** *259*
7:21 and brought him up as **her o** son. *1571*
7:25 that his **o people** would realize *81*
7:37 a prophet like me from your **o people.'** *81*
13:22 of Jesse a man after **my o** heart; *1609*
13:36 *in* **his o** generation, he fell asleep; *2625*
14:16 In the past, he let all nations go **their o** way. *899*
15:22 of **their o** men and send them to Antioch *899*
17:28 As some of **your o** poets have said, *2848+5148*
18:6 "Your blood be on **your o** heads! *5148*
18:15 words and names and **your o** law— *2848+5148*
20:28 which he bought with **his o** blood. *2625*
20:30 Even from your **o** number men will arise *899*
20:34 of mine have supplied **my o** needs and *1609*
21:11 tied **his o** hands and feet with it and said, *1571*
25:19 of dispute with him about **their o** religion *2625*
26:4 the beginning of my life in **my o** country, *1609*
26:17 from **your o** people and from the Gentiles. *3836*
26:23 would proclaim light *to* **his o** people and to *3836*

Ac 27:10 and to our o lives also." *1609*
27:19 ship's tackle overboard with *their* o hands. *901*
28:19 to bring against my o people. *3836*
28:30 Paul stayed there in his o rented house *2625*
Ro 5:8 God demonstrates his o love for us in this: *1571*
8:3 God did by sending his o Son in the likeness *1571*
8:20 not by its o choice, *1776*
8:32 He who did not spare his o Son, *2625*
9:3 my brothers, those *of* my o race, *1609*
10:3 from God and sought to establish their o, *2625*
11:14 that I may somehow arouse my o people *1609*
11:24 be grafted into *their* o olive tree! *2625*
14:4 *To* his o master he stands or falls. *2625*
14:5 be fully convinced in his o mind. *2625*
16:18 our Lord Christ, but their o appetites. *1571*
1Co 3:8 be rewarded according to his o labor. *2625*
4:12 We work hard *with* our o hands. *2625*
6:18 who sins sexually sins against his o body. *2625*
6:19 You are not your o; *4932*
7:2 each man should have his o wife, *1571*
7:2 and each woman her o husband. *2625*
7:7 But each man has his o gift from God; *2625*
7:35 I am saying this for your o good, *899*
7:37 in his o mind, who is under no compulsion *899*
7:37 over his o will, and who has made *2625*
9:7 Who serves as a soldier *at* his o expense? *2625*
10:24 Nobody should seek his o good, *1571*
10:33 not seeking my o good but the good *1831*
14:35 they should ask their o husbands at home; *2625*
15:23 But each in his o turn: *2625*
15:38 to each kind of seed he gives its o body. *2625*
16:21 I, Paul, write this greeting *in* my o hand. *1847*
2Co 7:13 In addition to our o encouragement, *1609*
8:3 Entirely on their o, *882*
8:17 and on *his* o initiative. *882*
11:26 in danger from my o countrymen, *NIG*
Gal 1:14 in Judaism beyond many Jews of my o age *5312*
6:4 Each one should test his o actions. *1571*
6:5 for each one should carry his o load. *2625*
6:11 as I write to you *with* my o hand! *1847*
Eph 4:28 doing something useful *with* his o hands, *2625*
5:28 love their wives as their o bodies. *1571*
5:29 After all, no one ever hated his o body, *1571*
Php 2:4 not only to your o interests, *4932*
2:21 For everyone looks out for his o interests, *1571*
3:9 a righteousness of my o that comes from *1847*
Col 4:18 I, Paul, write this greeting *in* my o hand. *1847*
1Th 2:11 of you as a father deals with his o children, *1571*
2:14 You suffered from your o countrymen *2625*
4:4 of you should learn to control his o body in *1571*
4:11 to mind your o business and to work *2625+3836*
4:15 According to the Lord's o word, *NIG*
2Th 3:17 I, Paul, write this greeting *in* my o hand, *1847*
1Ti 3:4 He must manage his o family well and see *2625*
3:5 not know how to manage his o family, *2625*
5:4 into practice by caring for their o family *2625*
6:15 which God will bring about *in* his o time— *2625*
2Ti 1:9 but because of his o purpose and grace. *2625*
4:3 Instead, to suit their o desires, *2625*
Tit 1:12 Even one of their o prophets has said, *2625*
2:14 for himself a people that are his very o, *4342*
Phm 1:19 I, Paul, am writing this *with* my o hand. *1847*
Heb 4:10 also rests from his o work, *899*
5:3 to offer sacrifices for his o sins, *899*
7:27 first for his o sins, *2625*
9:12 Most Holy Place once for all by his o blood, *2625*
9:25 every year with blood that is not his o. *259*
11:14 looking for a country of their o. *4258*
13:12 the people holy through his o blood. *2625*
Jas 1:14 by his o evil desire, he is dragged away *2625*
1Pe 3:5 They were submissive *to* their o husbands, *2625*
2Pe 1:3 of him who called us *by* his o glory *2625*
1:20 about by the prophet's o interpretation. *2625*
3:3 scoffing and following their o evil desires. *2625*
3:16 to their o destruction. *2625*
1Jn 3:12 Because his o actions were evil *899*
Jude 1:6 of authority but abandoned their o home— *2625*
1:8 these dreamers pollute their o bodies, *NIG*
1:16 they follow their o evil desires; *1571*
1:16 and flatter others for their o advantage. *NIG*
1:18 scoffers who will follow their o ungodly desires." *1571*
Rev 18:6 Mix her a double portion from her o cup. *3836*

OWNED (12) [OWN]

Ge 25:5 Abraham left everything he o to Isaac. 4200
31:1 "Jacob has taken everything our father o 4200
39:4 entrusted to his care everything he o. 3780+4200
39:5 of his household and of all that he o, 3780+4200
Nu 16:33 with everything they o; 4200
Jdg 19:22 they shouted to the old man who o 1251
1Ki 17:17 of the woman who o the house became ill. 1266
Job 1:3 and he o seven thousand sheep, 2118+5238
Ecc 2:7 I also o more herds and flocks than 2118+5238
Jer 39:10 of the poor people, who o nothing; 4200
Ac 4:34 from time to time those who o lands *3230+5639*
4:37 sold a field he o and brought the money *5639*

OWNER (36) [OWN]

Ex 21:28 But the o *of* the bull will not be held 1251
21:29 habit of goring and the o has been warned 1251
21:29 the bull must be stoned and the o also must 1251
21:32 the o must pay thirty shekels of silver to NIH
21:34 the o *of* the pit must pay for the loss; 1251
21:34 he must pay its o, 1251
21:36 yet the o did not keep it penned up, 1251
21:36 the o must pay, animal for animal, NIH
22:8 the o *of* the house must appear before 1251
22:11 The o is to accept this, 1251
22:12 he must make restitution to the o. 1251
22:14 and it is injured or dies while the o is 1251
22:15 But if the o is with the animal, 1251
Lev 6:5 and give it all to the o on the day 2257+4200
14:35 the o *of* the house must go and tell 2257+4200
25:53 that his o does not rule over him ruthlessly. NIH
27:13 If the o wishes to redeem the animal, NIH
Jdg 19:23 The o *of* the house went outside and said 1251
1Ki 16:24 the name of the former o *of* the hill. 123
Ecc 5:11 And what benefit are they to the o except 1251
5:13 wealth hoarded to the harm of its o, 1251
Mt 13:52 like the o of a house who brings out *476+3867*
20:8 the o of the vineyard said to his foreman, *3261*
21:40 when the o of the vineyard comes, *3261*
24:43 the o of the house had known at what time *3867*
Mk 12:9 "What then will the o of the vineyard do? *3261*
13:35 when the o of the house will come back— *3261*
14:14 Say *to* the o of the house he enters, *3867*
Lk 12:39 the o of the house had known at what hour *3867*
13:25 Once the o of the house gets up and closes *3867*
14:21 Then the o of the house became angry *3867*
20:13 o of the vineyard said, 'What shall I do? *3261*
20:15 then will the o of the vineyard do to them? *3261*
22:11 *to* the o of the house, 'The Teacher asks: *3867*
Ac 21:11 the o of this belt and will hand him over *467+4005*
27:11 of the pilot and of the o of the ship. *3729*

OWNER'S (2) [OWN]

Isa 1:3 the donkey his o manger, 1251
Mt 13:27 "The o servants came to him and said, 'Sir, *3867*

OWNERS (4) [OWN]

Jer 8:10 to other men and their fields to new o. 3769
Lk 19:33 its o asked them, "Why are you untying *3261*
Ac 16:16 She earned a great deal of money *for* her o *3261*
16:19 When the o of the slave girl realized *3261*

OWNERSHIP (1) [OWN]

2Co 1:22 set his seal of o on us, and put his Spirit in *5381*

OWNING (1) [OWN]

Job 22:8 o land—an honored man, living on it. 4200

OWNS (9) [OWN]

Ge 24:36 and he has given him everything he o. 4200
32:17 who o all these animals in front of you?' 4200
38:25 "I am pregnant by the man who o these," 4200
39:8 everything he o he has entrusted 3780+4200
Lev 27:28 " 'But nothing that a man o and devotes to 4200
Ecc 2:21 and then he must leave *all* he o 2750
Mt 18:12 If a man o a hundred sheep, *1181*
Jn 10:12 hired hand is not the shepherd who o *1639+2625*
Gal 4:1 *although he* o the whole estate. *1639+3261*

OX (53) [OXEN]

Ex 20:17 his o or donkey, or anything that belongs to 8802
21:33 to cover it and an o or a donkey falls into it, 8802
22:1 an o or a sheep and slaughters it or sells it, 8802
22:1 for the o and four sheep for the sheep. 8802
22:4 whether o or donkey or sheep— 8802
22:9 In all cases of illegal possession of an o, 8802
22:10 "If a man gives a donkey, an o, 8802
23:4 "If you come across your enemy's o 8802
23:12 that your o and your donkey may rest and 8802
Lev 4:10 the fat is removed from the o sacrificed as 8802
9:4 an o and a ram for a fellowship offering 8802
9:18 the o and the ram as the fellowship offering 8802
9:19 But the fat portions of the o and the ram— 8802
17:3 Any Israelite who sacrifices an o, 8802
22:23 an o or a sheep that is deformed or stunted, 8802
27:26 whether an o or a sheep, it is the LORD's. 8802
Nu 7:3 an o from each leader and a cart 8802
18:17 you must not redeem the firstborn of an o, 8802
22:4 as an o licks up the grass of the field." 8802
23:22 they have the strength of a wild o. 8028
24:8 they have the strength of a wild o. 8028
Dt 5:14 or maidservant, nor your o, your donkey 8802
5:21 his o or donkey, or anything that belongs to 8802
14:4 These are the animals you may eat: the o, 8802
17:1 an o or a sheep that has any defect or flaw 8802
22:1 you see your brother's o or sheep straying, 8802
22:4 or his o fallen on the road, 8802
22:10 with an o and a donkey yoked together. 8802
25:4 Do not muzzle an o while it is treading out 8802
28:31 Your o will be slaughtered 8802
33:17 his horns are the horns of a wild o. 8028
1Sa 12:3 Whose o have I taken? 8802
14:34 So everyone brought his o that night 8802
2Sa 24:22 and here are threshing sledges and o yokes 1330
Ne 5:18 Each day one o, six choice sheep 8802
Job 6:5 or an o bellow when it has fodder? 8802
24:3 and take the widow's o in pledge. 8802
39:9 "Will the wild o consent to serve you? 8028
40:15 and which feeds on grass like an o. 1330
Ps 29:6 Sirion like a young wild o. 8028
69:31 This will please the LORD more than an o, 8802
92:10 like that of a wild o; 8028
Pr 7:22 All at once he followed her like an o going 8802
14:4 but from the strength of an o comes 8802
Isa 1:3 The o knows his master, 8802
11:7 and the lion will eat straw like the o. 1330
65:25 and the lion will eat straw like the o, 1330
Eze 1:10 and on the left the face of an o; 8802
Lk 13:15 of you on the Sabbath untie his o or donkey *1091*
14:5 "If one of you has a son or an o that falls *1091*
1Co 9:9 "Do not muzzle an o while it is treading out *1091*
1Ti 5:18 "Do not muzzle the o while it is treading out *1091*
Rev 4:7 the second was like an o, *3675*

OXEN (44) [OX]

Ge 49:6 and hamstrung o as they pleased. 8802
Nu 7:3 the LORD six covered carts and twelve o— 1330
7:6 and o and gave them to the Levites. 1330
7:7 He gave two carts and four o to 1330
7:8 and he gave four carts and eight o to 1330
7:17 and two o, five rams, five male goats 1330
7:23 and two o, five rams, five male goats 1330
7:29 and two o, five rams, five male goats 1330
7:35 and two o, five rams, five male goats 1330
7:41 and two o, five rams, five male goats 1330
7:47 and two o, five rams, five male goats 1330
7:53 and two o, five rams, five male goats 1330
7:59 and two o, five rams, five male goats 1330
7:65 and two o, five rams, five male goats 1330
7:71 and two o, five rams, five male goats 1330
7:77 and two o, five rams, five male goats 1330
7:83 and two o, five rams, five male goats 1330
7:88 fellowship offering came to twenty-four o, 7228
Dt 15:19 Do not put the firstborn of your o to work, 8802
1Sa 11:5 behind his o, and he asked, 1330
11:7 He took a pair of o, cut them into pieces, 1330
11:7 the o *of* anyone who does not follow Saul 1330
2Sa 6:6 because the o stumbled. 1330
24:22 Here are o for the burnt offering, 1330
24:24 and the o and paid fifty shekels of silver 1330
1Ki 19:19 He was plowing with twelve yoke of o, 7538
19:20 Elisha then left his o and ran after Elijah. 1330
19:21 took his yoke of o and slaughtered them. 1330
1Ch 12:40 on donkeys, camels, mules and o. 1330
13:9 because the o stumbled. 1330
21:23 I will give the o for the burnt offerings, 1330
Job 1:3 of o and five hundred donkeys, 1330
1:14 "The o were plowing and 1330
42:12 a thousand yoke of o and a thousand 1330
Ps 22:21 save me from the horns of the wild o. 8028
144:14 our o will draw heavy loads. 476
Pr 14:4 Where there are no o, the manger is empty, 546
Isa 30:24 The o and donkeys that work 546
34:7 And the wild o will fall with them, 8028
Jer 51:23 with you I shatter farmer and o, 7538
Am 6:12 Does one plow there with o? 1330
Mt 22:4 o and fattened cattle have been *5436*
Lk 14:19 'I have just bought five yoke *of* o, *1091*
1Co 9:9 Is it *about* o that God is concerned? *1091*

OXGOAD (1)

Jdg 3:31 six hundred Philistines with an o. 1330+4913

OZEM (2)

1Ch 2:15 the sixth O and the seventh David. 730
2:25 Bunah, Oren, O and Ahijah. 730

OZIAS (KJV) See UZZIAH

OZNI (1) [OZNITE]

Nu 26:16 through O, the Oznite clan; 269

OZNITE (1) [OZNI]

Nu 26:16 through Ozni, the O clan; 270

P

PAARAI (1)

2Sa 23:35 Hezro the Carmelite, P the Arbite, 7197

PACE (1)

Ge 33:14 at the p *of* the droves before me and that of 8079

PACES (KJV) See STEPS

PACIFIES (1) [PEACE]

Pr 21:14 bribe concealed in the cloak p great wrath. NIH

PACIFY (1) [PEACE]

Ge 32:20 *"I will* p him with these gifts 4105+7156

PACK (2) [PACKED]

Jer 46:19 P your belongings for exile, 6913
Eze 12:3 p your belongings for exile and in 6913

PACKED (3) [PACK]
Jos 9:12 of ours was warm *when we* **p** it at home on 7472
Eze 12: 4 bring out your belongings **p** *for* exile. 3998
12: 7 the day I brought out my things **p** *for* exile. 3998

PACT (1)
Isa 57: 8 *you* **made a p** with those whose beds you love, 4162

PAD (1)
Jer 38:12 worn-out clothes under your arms to **p** 4946+9393

PADAN (KJV) See PADDAN

PADANARAM (KJV) See PADDAN ARAM

PADDAN (1) [PADDAN ARAM]
Ge 48: 7 As I was returning from **P,** 7019

PADDAN ARAM (10) [ARAM, PADDAN]
Ge 25:20 of Bethuel the Aramean from **P** 7020
28: 2 Go at once to **P,** 7020
28: 5 and he went to **P,** 7020
28: 6 and had sent him to **P** to take a wife 7020
28: 7 and mother and had gone to **P.** 7020
31:18 the goods he had accumulated in **P,** 7020
33:18 After Jacob came from **P,** 7020
35: 9 After Jacob returned from **P,** 7020
35:26 who were born to him in **P.** 7020
46:15 the sons Leah bore to Jacob in **P,** 7020

PADON (2)
Ezr 2:44 Keros, Siaha, **P,** 7013
Ne 7:47 Keros, Sia, **P,** 7013

PAGAN (8) [PAGANS]
2Ki 23: 5 He did away with the **p priests** appointed 4024
Isa 57: 8 doorposts you have put your **p symbols.** 2355
La 1:10 she saw **p nations** enter her sanctuary— 1580
Am 7:17 and you yourself will die in a **p** country. 3238
Zep 1: 4 of the **p** and the idolatrous priests— 4024
Mt 18:17 to the church, treat him as you would a **p** or *1618*
Lk 12:30 For the **p** world runs after all such things, *1620*
1Co 10: 7 and got up to **indulge in p revelry."** *4089*

PAGANS (10) [PAGAN]
Isa 2: 6 the Philistines and clasp hands with **p.** 3529+5799
Mt 5:47 Do not even **p** do that? *1618*
6: 7 you pray, do not keep on babbling like **p,** *1618*
6:32 For the **p** run after all these things, *1620*
1Co 5: 1 of a kind that does not occur even among **p:** *1620*
10:20 the sacrifices of **p** are offered to demons, *1620*
12: 2 You know that when you were **p,** *1620*
1Pe 2:12 Live such good lives among the **p** that, *1620*
4: 3 in the past doing what **p** choose to do— *1620*
3Jn 1: 7 receiving no help from the **p.** *1618*

PAGIEL (5)
Nu 1:13 from Asher, **P** son of Ocran; 7005
2:27 The leader of the people of Asher is **P** son 7005
7:72 On the eleventh day **P** son of Ocran, 7005
7:77 This was the offering of **P** son of Ocran. 7005
10:26 **P** son of Ocran was over the division of 7005

PAHATH-MOAB (6)
Ezr 2: 6 of **P** (through the line of Jeshua 7075
8: 4 of the descendants of **P,** Eliehoenai son 7075
10:30 From the descendants of **P:** 7075
Ne 3:11 of **P** repaired another section and 7075
7:11 of **P** (through the line of Jeshua 7075
10:14 The leaders of the people: Parosh, **P,** Elam, 7075

PAID (51) [PAY]
Ge 30:33 check on the **wages** you *have p* me. AIT
31:15 but he has used up **what** was **p** *for* us. 4084
39:23 The warden **p** no **attention** *to* anything 8011
Ex 16:20 some of them **p** no **attention** to Moses; 9048
22:15 **money p for** *the* **hire** covers the loss. 8510
Lev 25:50 **based on the rate p** to a hired man 3427+3869
25:51 a larger share of the price **p** *for* him. 5239
Dt 1:45 but he **p** no **attention** to your weeping 9048
Jdg 1: 7 God *has* **p** me **back** *for* what I did to them." 8966
11:28 **p** no **attention** to the message Jephthah 9048
1Sa 25:21 *He has* **p** me **back** evil for good. 8740
2Sa 24:24 and the oxen and **p** fifty shekels of silver 928
1Ki 18:29 no one answered, no one **p attention.** 7993
2Ki 12:11 *With it they* **p** those who worked on 3655
12:14 it *was* **p** to the workmen, 5989
17: 3 and *had* **p** him tribute. 8740
17: 4 and *he* no *longer* **p** tribute to the king 6590
22: 9 "Your officials *have* **p out** the money 5988
23:35 Jehoiakim **p** Pharaoh Neco the silver 5989
1Ch 21:25 David **p** Araunah six hundred shekels 5486+5989
2Ch 24:17 officials of Judah came and **p homage** to 2556
25: 9 "But what about the hundred talents *I* **p** 5989
27: 5 the Ammonites **p** him a hundred talents 5989
33:10 but *they* **p** no **attention.** 7992
34:10 These men **p** the workers who repaired 5989
34:17 *They have* **p out** the money that was in 5988
Ezr 4:13 no more taxes, tribute or duty *will be* **p,** 10498
4:20 and taxes, tribute and duty **were p** to them. 10314
6: 4 The costs *are to* **be p** by the royal treasury. 10314
6: 8 to be fully **p** out of the royal treasury, 10314
Ne 9:30 Yet *they* **p** no **attention,** 263
Est 3: 2 at the king's gate knelt down and **p honor** 2556
Job 15:32 Before his time *he will* **be p in full,** 4848
21:29 *Have you* **p** no **regard** *to* their accounts— 5795
Isa 3:11 They *will* **be p back** for what their hands 6913
40: 2 that her sin *has* **been p for,** 8355
42:20 but *have* **p** no **attention;** 9068
48:18 only *you had* **p attention** to my commands, 7992
Jer 25: 4 you have not listened or **p any attention.** 265+4200+5742+9048
35:15 *you have* not **p attention** or listened to 265+5742
37: 2 nor the people of the land **p** *any* **attention** 9048
Eze 27:15 *they* **p** you *with* ivory tusks and ebony. 868+8740
Da 2:46 before Daniel and **p** him **honor** and ordered 10504
Zec 11:12 So *they* **p** me thirty pieces of silver. 8510+9202
Mt 5:26 not get out until *you have* **p** the last penny. *625*
22: 5 "But they **p no attention** and went off— *288*
Mk 15:19 *they* **p homage** to him. *4686*
Lk 12:59 not get out until *you have* **p** the last penny." *625*
Ac 8: 6 *they* all **p close attention** to what he said. *4668*
Heb 7: 9 **p the tenth** through Abraham, *1282*
2Pe 2:13 They will be **p** back with harm for the harm *3635*

PAIN (40) [PAINFUL, PAINS]
Ge 3:16 with **p** you will give birth to children. 6776
6: 6 and his heart **was filled with p.** 6772
34:25 while all of them were *still* **in p,** 3872
1Ch 4: 9 saying, "I gave birth to him **in p."** 6778
4:10 from harm so that I will be free from **p."** 6778
2Ch 21:19 and he died in great **p.** 9377
Job 6:10 my joy in unrelenting **p—** 2660
14:22 *He* **feels** but *the* **p** of his own body 3872
16: 6 "Yet if I speak, my **p** is not relieved; 3873
33:19 Or a man may be chastened on a bed of **p** 4799
Ps 38: 7 My back is filled with **searing p;** 7828
38:17 and my **p** is ever with me. 4799
48: 6 **p** like that of a woman in labor. 2659
69:26 and talk about the **p** *of* those you hurt. 4799
69:29 I *am* **in p** and distress; 3872
Ecc 2:23 All his days his work is **p** and grief; 4799
Isa 13: 8 **p** and anguish will grip them; 7496
17:11 in the day of disease and incurable **p.** 3873
21: 3 At this my body is racked with **p,** 2714
26:17 to give birth writhes and cries out in her **p,** 2477
26:18 We were with child, *we* **writhed in p,** 2655
Jer 4:19 *I* **writhe in p.** 2655
5: 3 You struck them, but *they* **felt** no **p;** 2655
6:24 **p** like that of a woman in labor. 2659
13:21 Will not **p** grip you like that of a woman 2477
15:18 Why is my **p** unending and my wound 3873
22:23 **p** like that of a woman in labor! 2659
30:15 your **p** that has no cure? 4799
45: 3 The LORD has added sorrow to my **p;** 4799
49:24 anguish and **p** have seized her, 2477
49:24 **p** like that of a woman in labor. NIH
50:43 **p** like that of a woman in labor. 2659
51: 8 Get balm for her **p;** 4799
Mic 1:12 Those who live in Maroth **writhe in p,** 2655
4: 9 **p** seizes you like that of a woman in labor? 2659
Mt 4:24 those suffering **severe p,** *992*
Jn 16:21 to a child has **p** because her time has come; *3383*
1Pe 2:19 up under the **p** of unjust suffering *3383*
Rev 12: 2 She was pregnant and cried out *in* **p** *989*
21: 4 no more death or mourning or crying or **p,** *4506*

PAINFUL (10) [PAIN]
Ge 3:17 through **p toil** you will eat of it all 6779
5:29 "He will comfort us in the labor and **p toil** 6779
Dt 28:35 and legs with **p** boils that cannot be cured, 8273
Job 2: 7 the LORD and afflicted Job with **p** sores 8273
6:25 How **p** *are* honest words! 5344
Eze 28:24 have malicious neighbors *who are* **p** briers 4421
2Co 2: 1 that I would not make another **p** visit *1877+3383*
Heb 12:11 discipline seems pleasant at the time, but **p.** *3383*
1Pe 4:12 be surprised *at* the **p** trial you are suffering, *4796*
Rev 16: 2 and ugly and **p** sores broke out on *4505*

PAINS (16) [PAIN]
Ge 3:16 I will greatly increase your **p** in childbearing 6779
1Sa 4:19 but was overcome by her **labor p.** 7496
1Ch 22:14 "I have **taken great p** to provide for 928+6715
2Ch 6:29 each one aware of his afflictions and **p,** 4799
Job 30:17 my **gnawing p** never rest. 6908
39: 3 their **labor p** are ended. 2477
Isa 66: 7 before the **p** come upon her, 2477
Hos 13:13 **P** *as of* a woman in childbirth come 2477
Mt 24: 8 All these are the beginning *of* **birth p.** *6047*
Mk 13: 8 These are the beginning *of* **birth p.** *6047*
Ro 8:22 has been groaning as **in the p of childbirth** *5349*
2Co 8:21 For *we are* **taking p** to do what is right, *4629*
Gal 4:19 *I am* again **in the p of childbirth** *6048*
4:27 you who **have** no **labor p;** *6048*
1Th 5: 3 as **labor p** on a pregnant woman, *6047*
Rev 16:11 cursed the God of heaven because of their **p** *4506*

PAINT (1) [PAINTED]
Jer 4:30 Why shade your eyes with **p?** 7037

PAINTED (2) [PAINT]
2Ki 9:30 *she* **p** her eyes, 928+2021+7037+8531
Eze 23:40 **p** your eyes and put on your jewelry. 3949

PAIR (17) [PAIRS]
Ex 25:35 be under the first **p** *of* branches extending 9109
25:35 a second bud under the second **p,** 9109
25:35 and a third bud under the third **p—** 9109
37:21 under the first **p** *of* branches extending 9109
37:21 a second bud under the second **p,** 9109
37:21 and a third bud under the third **p—** 9109
Dt 24: 6 Do not take a **p of millstones—** 8160
Jdg 15: 4 He then fastened a torch to every **p** *of* tails, 9109
1Sa 11: 7 He took a **p** *of* oxen, cut them into pieces, 7538
1Ki 6:23 In the inner sanctuary he made a **p** 9109
19:19 and he himself was driving the twelfth **p.** NIH
2Ki 5:17 as much earth as a **p** *of* mules can carry, 7538
2Ch 3:10 In the Most Holy Place he made a **p** 9109
Am 2: 6 and the needy for a **p** *of* **sandals.** AIT
8: 6 and the needy for a **p** *of* **sandals,** AIT
Lk 2:24 "a **p** of doves or two young pigeons." *2414*
Rev 6: 5 Its rider was holding a **p of scales** *2433*

PAIRS (3) [PAIR]
Ge 7: 8 **P** of clean and unclean animals, 9109+9109
7:15 **P** of all creatures that have the breath 9109+9109
Jdg 15: 4 and tied them tail to tail in **p.** NIH

PALACE (166) [PALACES, PALATIAL]
Ge 12:15 and she was taken into his **p.** 1074
41:40 You shall be in charge of my **p,** 1074
45:16 When the news reached Pharaoh's **p** 1074
47:14 and he brought it to Pharaoh's **p.** 1074
Ex 7:23 Instead, he turned and went into his **p,** 1074
8: 3 up into your **p** and your bedroom 1074
8:24 of flies poured into Pharaoh's **p** and into 1074
Nu 22:18 if Balak gave me his **p** filled with silver 1074
24:13 if Balak gave me his **p** filled with silver 1074
Jdg 3:20 in the upper room of his **summer p** and 5249
2Sa 5: 8 "The 'blind and lame' will not enter the **p."** 1074
5:11 and they built a **p** for David. 1074
7: 1 in his **p** and the LORD had given him rest 1074
7: 2 "Here I am, living in a **p** *of* cedar, 1074
11: 2 walked around on the roof of the **p.** 1074+4889
11: 8 So Uriah left the **p,** 1074+4889
11: 9 the **p** with all his master's servants 1074+4889
13: 7 David sent word to Tamar at the **p:** 1074
15:16 he left ten concubines to take care of the **p.** 1074
15:35 anything you hear in the king's **p.** 1074
16:21 whom he left to take care of the **p.** 1074
19:11 be the last to bring the king back to his **p,** 1074
20: 3 When David returned to his **p** in Jerusalem, 1074
20: 3 the **p** and put them in a house under guard. 1074
1Ki 3: 1 of David until he finished building his **p** 1074
4: 6 Ahishar—in charge of the **p;** 1074
7: 1 to complete the construction of his **p.** 1074
7: 2 He built the **P** *of* the Forest of Lebanon 1074
7: 8 And the **p** in which he was to live, 1074
7: 8 a **p** like this hall for Pharaoh's daughter, 1074
9: 1 the temple of the LORD and the royal **p,** 1074
9:10 the temple of the LORD and the royal **p—** 1074
9:15 his own **p,** the supporting terraces, 1074
9:24 of David to the **p** Solomon had built 1074
10: 4 of Solomon and the **p** he had built, 1074
10:12 of the LORD and for the royal **p,** 1074
10:17 The king put them in the **P** *of* the Forest 1074
10:21 household articles in the **P** *of* the Forest 1074
11:20 whom Tahpenes brought up in the royal **p.** 1074
14:26 the LORD and the treasures of the royal **p.** 1074
14:27 on duty at the entrance to the royal **p.** 1074
15:18 of the LORD's temple and of his own **p.** 1074
16: 9 the man in charge of the **p** at Tirzah. 1074
16:18 the citadel of the royal **p** and set the palace 1074
16:18 the citadel of the royal palace and set the **p** 1074
18: 3 who was in charge of his **p.** 1074
20: 6 to send my officials to search your **p** and 1074
20:43 the king of Israel went to his **p** in Samaria. 1074
21: 1 close to the **p** of Ahab king of Samaria. 2121
21: 2 since it is close to my **p.** 1074
22:39 the **p** he built and inlaid with ivory, 1074
2Ki 7: 9 at once and report this to the royal **p."** 1074
7:11 and it was reported within the **p.** 1074+4889
10: 5 So the **p** administrator, the city governor, 1074
11: 5 a third of you guarding the royal **p,** 1074
11:16 where the horses enter the **p grounds,** 1074+4889
11:19 of the LORD and went into the **p,** 1074+4889
11:20 with the sword at the **p.** 1074+4889
12:18 of the LORD and of the royal **p,** 1074
14:14 and in the treasuries of the royal **p.** 1074
15: 5 the **p** and governed the people of the land. 1074
15:25 in the citadel of the royal **p** at Samaria. 1074
16: 8 in the treasuries of the royal **p** and sent it as 1074
18:15 and in the treasuries of the royal **p.** 1074
18:18 Eliakim son of Hilkiah the **p** administrator, 1074
18:37 Eliakim son of Hilkiah the **p** administrator, 1074
19: 2 He sent Eliakim the **p** administrator, 1074
20:13 There was nothing in his **p** or 1074
20:15 "What did they see in your **p?"** 1074
20:15 "They saw everything in my **p,"** 1074
20:17 surely come when everything in your **p,** 1074
20:18 and they will become eunuchs in the **p** *of* 2121
21:18 and was buried in his **p** garden, 1074
21:23 and assassinated the king in his **p.** 1074
24:13 of the LORD and from the royal **p,** 1074
25: 9 the royal **p** and all the houses of Jerusalem. 1074
1Ch 14: 1 stonemasons and carpenters to build a **p** 1074
17: 1 After David was settled in his **p,** 1074

2Ki 17: 1 "Here I am, living in a **p** *of* cedar, 1074
28: 1 together with the **p officials,** 6247
2Ch 2: 1 for the Name of the LORD and a royal **p** 1074
2: 3 when you sent him cedar to build a **p** 1074
2: 12 for the LORD and a **p** for himself. 1074+4895
7: 11 the temple of the LORD and the royal **p,** 1074
7: 11 the temple of the LORD and in his own **p,** 1074
8: 1 the temple of the LORD and his own **p,** 1074
8: 11 from the City of David to the **p** he had built 1074
8: 11 not live in the **p** *of* David king of Israel, 1074
9: 3 as well as the **p** he had built, 1074
9: 11 of the LORD and for the royal **p,** 1074
9: 16 The king put them in the **P** *of* the Forest 1074
9: 20 household articles in the **P** *of* the Forest 1074
12: 9 the LORD and the treasures of the royal **p.** 1074
12: 10 on duty at the entrance to the royal **p.** 1074
16: 2 of his own **p** and sent it to Ben-Hadad king 1074
19: 1 of Judah returned safely to his **p** 1074
21: 17 the goods found in the king's **p,** 1074
23: 5 a third of you at the royal **p** and a third at 1074
23: 15 of the Horse Gate on the **p grounds,** 1074+4889
23: 20 the **p** through the Upper Gate and 1074+4889
25: 24 with the **p** treasures and the hostages, 1074+4889
26: 21 **p** and governed the people of the land. 1074+4889
28: 7 Azrikam the officer in charge of the **p,** 1074
28: 21 the LORD and from the royal **p** and from 1074
33: 20 with his fathers and was buried in his **p.** 1074
33: 24 against him and assassinated him in his **p.** 1074
Ezr 4: 14 Now since we are under obligation to the **p** 10206
Ne 3: 25 the tower projecting from the upper **p** 1074+4889
Est 1: 5 in the enclosed garden of the king's **p,** 1131
1: 9 the women in the royal **p** of King Xerxes. 1074
2: 8 also was taken to the king's **p** and entrusted 1074
2: 9 the king's **p** and moved her and her maids 1074
2: 13 with her from the harem to the king's **p.** 1074
5: 1 and stood in the inner court of the **p,** 1074+4889
6: 4 court of the **p** to speak to the king 1074+4889
7: 7 and went out into the **p** garden. 1131
7: 8 Just as the king returned from the **p** garden 1131
9: 4 Mordecai was prominent in the **p;** 1074+4889
Ps 45: 15 they enter the **p** *of* the king. 2121
144: 12 be like pillars carved to adorn a **p.** 2121
Isa 22: 8 to the weapons in the **P** *of* the Forest; 1074
22: 15 to Shebna, who is in charge of the **p:** 1074
36: 3 Eliakim son of Hilkiah the **p** administrator, 1074
36: 22 Eliakim son of Hilkiah the **p** administrator, 1074
37: 2 He sent Eliakim the **p** administrator, 1074
39: 2 There was nothing in his **p** or 1074
39: 4 "What did they see in your **p?"** 1074
39: 4 "They saw everything in my **p,"** 1074
39: 6 surely come when everything in your **p,** 1074
39: 7 and they will become eunuchs in the **p** *of* 2121
Jer 22: 1 "Go down to the **p** *of* the king of Judah 1074
22: 4 through the gates of this **p,** 1074
22: 5 by myself that this **p** will become a ruin.' " 1074
22: 6 the LORD says about the **p** *of* the king 1074
22: 13 "Woe to him who builds his **p** 1074
22: 14 a great **p** with spacious upper rooms.' 1074
26: 10 from the royal **p** to the house of the LORD 1074
27: 18 the **p** *of* the king of Judah and in Jerusalem 1074
27: 21 in the house of the LORD and in the **p** *of* 1074
30: 18 and the **p** will stand in its proper place. 810
32: 2 in the courtyard of the guard in the royal **p** 1074
36: 12 down to the secretary's room in the royal **p,** 1074
37: 17 for him and had him brought to the **p,** 1074
38: 7 a Cushite, an official in the royal **p,** 1074
38: 8 Ebed-Melech went out of the **p** and 1074+4889
38: 11 to a room under the treasury in the **p.** 1074+4889
38: 22 All the women left in the **p** *of* the king 1074
39: 8 The Babylonians set fire to the royal **p** and 1074
43: 9 the entrance to Pharaoh's **p** in Tahpanhes. 1074
52: 13 the royal **p** and all the houses of Jerusalem. 1074
Da 1: 4 and qualified to serve in the king's **p.** 2121
4: 4 I, Nebuchadnezzar, was at home in my **p,** 10206
4: 29 on the roof of the royal **p** of Babylon, 10206
5: 5 near the lampstand in the royal **p.** 10206
6: 18 to his **p** and spent the night without eating 10206
Am 9: 6 he who builds his **lofty p** in the heavens 5092
Na 2: 6 and the **p** collapses. 2121
Mt 26: 3 the elders of the people assembled in the **p** *885*
Mk 15: 16 The soldiers led Jesus away into the **p** *885*
Jn 18: 28 from Caiaphas to **p of the Roman governor** *4550*
18: 28 the Jews did not enter the **p;** *4550*
18: 33 Pilate then went back inside the **p,** *4550*
19: 9 and he went back inside the **p.** *4550*
Ac 7: 10 he made him ruler over Egypt and all his **p.** *3875*
23: 35 that Paul be kept under guard in Herod's **p.** *4550*
Php 1: 13 the whole **p guard** and to everyone else *4550*

PALACES (10) [PALACE]

2Ch 36: 19 the **p** and destroyed everything 810
Ps 45: 8 from **p** *adorned with* ivory the music of 2121
Pr 30: 28 yet it is found in kings' **p.** 2121
Isa 13: 22 jackals in her luxurious **p.** 2121
Jer 33: 4 about the houses in this city and the royal **p** 1074
La 2: 5 up all her **p** and destroyed her strongholds. 810
2: 7 over to the enemy the walls of her **p;** 810
Hos 8: 14 Israel has forgotten his Maker and built **p;** 2121
Mt 11: 8 those who wear fine clothes are in kings' **p.** *3875*
Lk 7: 25 and indulge in luxury are in **p.** *994*

PALAL (1)

Ne 3: 25 and **P** son of Uzai worked opposite 7138

PALATIAL (2) [PALACE]

1Ch 29: 1 because this **p structure** is not for man but 1072
29: 19 the **p structure** for which I have provided." 1072

PALE (10)

Isa 29: 22 no longer *will* their faces **grow p.** 2578
Jer 30: 6 every face turned **deathly p?** 3766
Da 5: 6 His **face** turned **p** and he was so frightened 10228
5: 9 and his **face** grew more **p.** 10228
5: 10 Don't **look so p!** 10228+10731
7: 28 and my **face** turned **p,** 10228
10: 8 my face turned **deathly p** 5422
Joel 2: 6 every face **turns p.** 6999+7695
Na 2: 10 bodies tremble, every face **grows p.** 6999+7695
Rev 6: 8 and there before me was a **p** horse! *5952*

PALESTINA, PALESTINE (KJV) See PHILISTIA, PHILISTINE

PALLU (5) [PALLUITE]

Ge 46: 9 Hanoch, **P,** Hezron and Carmi. 7112
Ex 6: 14 of Israel were Hanoch and **P,** 7112
Nu 26: 5 through **P,** the Palluite clan; 7112
26: 8 The son of **P** was Eliab, 7112
1Ch 5: 3 Hanoch, **P,** Hezron and Carmi. 7112

PALLUITE (1) [PALLU]

Nu 26: 5 through Pallu, the **P** clan; 7101

PALM (39) [PALMS]

Ex 15: 27 twelve springs and seventy **p trees,** 9469
Lev 14: 15 **p of** his own left **hand,** 4090
14: 16 dip his right forefinger into the oil in his **p,** 4090
14: 17 to put some of the oil remaining in his **p** on 4090
14: 18 in his **p** the priest shall put on the head of 4090
14: 26 **p of** his own left **hand,** 4090
14: 27 from his **p** seven times before the LORD. 4090
14: 28 Some of the oil in his **p** he is to put on 4090
14: 29 in his **p** the priest shall put on the head of 4090
23: 40 and **p** fronds, leafy branches and poplars, 9469
Nu 33: 9 twelve springs and seventy **p trees,** 9469
Jdg 4: 5 under the **P** *of* Deborah between Ramah 9472
1Ki 6: 29 **p trees** and open flowers. 9474
6: 32 **p trees** and open flowers, 9474
6: 32 the cherubim and **p trees** with beaten gold. 9474
6: 35 **p trees** and open flowers on them 9474
7: 36 and **p trees** on the surfaces of the supports 9474
2Ch 3: 5 **p tree** and chain **designs.** 9474
Ps 92: 12 The righteous will flourish like a **p tree,** 9469
SS 7: 7 Your stature is like that of the **p,** 9469
7: 8 I said, "I will climb the **p tree;** 9469
Isa 9: 14 both **p branch** and reed in a single day; 4093
19: 15 head or tail, **p branch** or reed. 4093
Eze 40: 16 walls were decorated with **p trees.** 9474
40: 22 its portico and its **p tree decorations** had 9474
40: 26 it had **p tree decorations** on the faces of 9474
40: 31 **p trees** decorated its jambs, 9474
40: 34 **p trees** decorated the jambs on either side, 9474
40: 37 **p trees** decorated the jambs on either side, 9474
41: 18 were carved cherubim and **p trees.** 9474
41: 18 **P trees** alternated with cherubim. 9474
41: 19 the **p tree** on one side and the face of a lion 9474
41: 19 and the face of a lion toward the **p tree** on 9474
41: 20 and **p trees** were carved on the wall of 9474
41: 25 and **p trees** like those carved on the walls, 9474
41: 26 with **p trees** carved on each side. 9474
Joel 1: 12 the pomegranate, the **p** and the apple tree— 9469
Jn 12: 13 They took **p** branches and went out *5836*
Rev 7: 9 and were holding **p branches** in their hands. *5836*

PALMERWORM (KJV) See LOCUST SWARM

PALMS (6) [PALM]

Dt 34: 3 the City of **P,** as far as Zoar. 9469
Jdg 1: 16 the City of **P** with the men of Judah to live 9469
3: 13 and they took possession of the City of **P.** 9469
2Ch 28: 15 the City of **P,** and returned to Samaria. 9469
Ne 8: 15 **p** and shade trees, to make booths"— 9469
Isa 49: 16 I have engraved you on the **p of** my **hands;** 4090

PALSY (KJV) See PARALYZED, PARALYTIC

PALTI (1)

Nu 13: 9 **P** son of Raphu; 7120

PALTIEL (3)

Nu 34: 26 **P** son of Azzan, the leader from the tribe 7123
1Sa 25: 44 to **P** son of Laish, who was from Gallim. 7120
2Sa 3: 15 from her husband **P** son of Laish. 7123

PALTITE (1)

2Sa 23: 26 Helez the **P,** Ira son of Ikkesh from Tekoa, 7121

PAMPERS (1)

Pr 29: 21 If a *man* **p** his servant from youth, 7167

PAMPHYLIA (5)

Ac 2: 10 and **P,** Egypt and the parts of Libya *4103*
13: 13 and his companions sailed to Perga *in* **P,** *4103*
14: 24 going through Pisidia, they came into **P,** *4103*
15: 38 because he had deserted them in **P** and had *4103*
27: 5 the open sea off the coast of Cilicia and **P,** *4103*

PAN (6) [PANS]

Lev 2: 7 If your grain offering is cooked in a **p,** 5306
7: 9 or cooked in a **p** or on a griddle belongs to 5306
1Sa 2: 14 He would plunge it into the **p** or kettle 3963
2Sa 13: 9 she took the **p** and served him the bread, 5389
Eze 4: 3 Then take an iron **p,** 4679
Mic 3: 3 who chop them up like meat for the **p,** 6105

PANELED (2) [PANELING, PANELS]

2Ch 3: 5 *He* **p** the main hall *with* pine and covered it 2902
Hag 1: 4 to be living in your **p** houses, 6211

PANELING (2) [PANELED]

1Ki 6: 15 **p** them from the floor of the temple to 6770+7596
Ps 74: 6 the **carved p** with their axes and hatchets. 7334

PANELS (9) [PANELED]

1Ki 7: 28 They had **side p** attached to uprights. 4995
7: 29 On the **p** between the uprights were lions, 4995
7: 31 The **p** *of* the stands were square, not round. 4995
7: 32 The four wheels were under the **p,** 4995
7: 35 The supports and **p** were attached to the top 4995
7: 36 the surfaces of the supports and on the **p,** 4995
2Ki 16: 17 the **side p** and removed the basins from 4995
SS 8: 9 we will enclose her with **p** *of* cedar. 4283
Jer 22: 14 **p** it with cedar and decorates it in red. 6211

PANGS (2)

Isa 21: 3 **p** seize me, like those of a woman in labor; 7496
Jer 22: 23 you will groan when **p** come upon you, 2477

PANIC (11)

Dt 20: 3 be terrified or **give way to p** before them. 6907
1Sa 5: 9 throwing it into a great **p.** 4539
5: 11 For death had filled the city with **p;** 4539
7: 10 **threw** them **into** *such* **a p** 2169
14: 15 Then **p** struck the whole army— 3010
14: 15 It was a **p** *sent by* God. 3010
Isa 31: 9 battle standard their commanders *will* **p,"** 3169
Jer 49: 24 to flee and **p** has gripped her; 8185
Eze 7: 7 there is **p,** not joy, upon the mountains. 4539
Zec 12: 4 On that day I will strike every horse with **p** 9451
14: 13 be stricken by the LORD with great **p.** 4539

PANNAG (KJV) See CONFECTIONS

PANS (2) [PAN]

2Ch 35: 13 caldrons and **p** and served them quickly 7505
Ezr 1: 9 silver dishes 1,000 silver **p** 29 4709

PANT (5) [PANTS]

Job 5: 5 and the thirsty **p** *after* his wealth. 8634
Ps 119: 131 I open my mouth and **p,** 8634
Isa 42: 14 I cry out, I gasp and **p.** 8634
Jer 14: 6 the barren heights and **p** like jackals; 8120+8634
Joel 1: 20 Even the wild animals **p** for you; 6864

PANTED, PANTETH (KJV) See FALTERS, PANT, PANTS, POUNDS

PANTS (2) [PANT]

Ps 42: 1 As the deer **p** for streams of water, 6864
42: 1 so my soul **p** for you, O God. 6864

PAPER (1)

2Jn 1: 12 but I do not want to use **p** and ink. *5925*

PAPHOS (2)

Ac 13: 6 the whole island until they came to **P.** *4265*
13: 13 From **P,** Paul and his companions sailed *4265*

PARAMOURS (KJV) See LOVERS

PAPYRUS (5)

Ex 2: 3 a **p** basket for him and coated it with tar 1687
Job 8: 11 Can **p** grow tall where there is no marsh? 1687
9: 26 They skim past like boats of **p,** 15
Isa 18: 2 which sends envoys by sea in **p** boats over 1687
35: 7 grass and reeds and **p** will grow. 1687

PARABLE (32) [PARABLES]

Eze 17: 2 an allegory and tell the house of Israel a **p.** 5442
24: 3 Tell this rebellious house a **p** and say 5442
Mt 13: 18 then to what the **p** of the sower means: *4130*
13: 24 Jesus told them another **p:** *4130*
13: 31 He told them another **p:** *4130*
13: 33 He told them still another **p:** *4130*
13: 34 not say anything to them without using a **p.** *4130*
13: 36 to us the **p** of the weeds in the field." *4130*

Mt 15:15 Peter said, "Explain the **p** to us." *4130*
21:33 "Listen to another **p:** *4130*
Mk 4:13 "Don't you understand this **p?** *4130*
4:13 How then will you understand any **p?** *4130*
4:30 or what **p** shall we use to describe it? *4130*
4:34 not say anything to them without using a **p.** *4130*
7:17 his disciples asked him about this **p.** *4130*
12:12 because they knew he had spoken the **p** *4130*
Lk 5:36 He told them this **p:** *4130*
6:39 He also told them this **p:** *4130*
8:4 he told this **p:** *4130*
8:9 His disciples asked him what this **p** meant. *4130*
8:11 "This is the meaning of the **p:** *4130*
12:16 And he told them this **p:** *4130*
12:41 "Lord, are you telling this **p** to us, *4130*
13:6 Then he told this **p:** *4130*
14:7 he told them this **p:** *4130*
15:3 Then Jesus told them this **p:** *4130*
18:1 Then Jesus told his disciples a **p** *4130*
18:9 Jesus told this **p:** *4130*
19:11 he went on to tell them a **p,** *4130*
20:9 He went on to tell the people this **p:** *4130*
20:19 because they knew he had spoken this **p** *4130*
21:29 He told them this **p:** *4130*

PARABLES (19) [PARABLE]

Ps 78:2 I will open my mouth in **p,** 5442
Pr 1:6 for understanding proverbs and **p,** 4886
Eze 20:49 'Isn't he just telling **p?'** " 5442
Hos 12:10 gave them many visions and **told p** 1948
Mt 13:3 he told them many things in **p,** saying: *4130*
13:10 "Why do you speak to the people in **p?"** *4130*
13:13 This is why I speak to them in **p:** *4130*
13:34 spoke all these things to the crowd in **p;** *4130*
13:35 "I will open my mouth in **p,** *4130*
13:53 When Jesus had finished these **p,** *4130*
21:45 and the Pharisees heard Jesus' **p,** *4130*
22:1 Jesus spoke to them again in **p,** saying: *4130*
Mk 3:23 Jesus called them and spoke to them in **p:** *4130*
4:2 He taught them many things by **p,** *4130*
4:10 around him asked him *about* the **p.** *4130*
4:11 on the outside everything is said in **p** *4130*
4:33 *With* many similar **p** Jesus spoke the word *4130*
12:1 He then began to speak to them in **p:** *4130*
Lk 8:10 but to others I speak in **p,** so that, *4130*

PARADE (1)

Isa 3:9 *they* **p** their sin like Sodom; 5583

PARADISE (3)

Lk 23:43 today you will be with me in **p."** *4137*
2Co 12:4 was caught up to **p.** *4137*
Rev 2:7 the tree of life, which is in the **p** of God. *4137*

PARAH (1)

Jos 18:23 Avvim, **P,** Ophrah, 7240

PARALLEL (5)

Ex 26:17 with two projections **set p** to each other. 8917
36:22 with two projections **set p** to each other. 8917
Eze 42:7 an outer wall **p to** the rooms and 4200+6645
42:12 beginning of the passageway that was **p** 928+7156
45:7 the western to the eastern border **p to** 4200+6645

PARALYTIC (9) [PARALYZED]

Mt 9:2 Some men brought to him a **p,** *4166*
9:2 he said *to* the **p,** "Take heart, son; *4166*
9:6 Then he said *to* the **p,** "Get up, *4166*
Mk 2:3 Some men came, bringing to him a **p,** *4166*
2:5 said *to* the **p,** "Son, your sins are forgiven." *4166*
2:9 to say *to* the **p,** 'Your sins are forgiven,' *4166*
2:10 He said *to* the **p,** *4166*
Lk 5:18 Some men came carrying a **p** on a mat *4168*
Ac 9:33 a **p** who had been bedridden for eight years. *4168*

PARALYTICS (1) [PARALYZED]

Ac 8:7 and many **p** and cripples were healed. *4168*

PARALYZED (6) [PARALYTIC, PARALYTICS]

Hab 1:4 Therefore the law *is* **p,** 7028
Mt 4:24 those having seizures, and the **p,** *4166*
8:6 at home **p** and in terrible suffering." *4166*
Mk 2:4 lowered the mat the **p** *man* was lying on. *4166*
Lk 5:24 He said *to* the **p** *man,* "I tell you, get up, *4168*
Jn 5:3 the blind, the lame, the **p.** *3831*

PARAN (10)

Ge 21:21 While he was living in the Desert of **P,** 7000
Nu 10:12 the cloud came to rest in the Desert of **P.** 7000
12:16 and encamped in the Desert of **P.** 7000
13:3 sent them out from the Desert of **P.** 7000
13:26 at Kadesh in the Desert of **P.** 7000
Dt 1:1 opposite Suph, between **P** and Tophel, 7000
33:2 he shone forth from Mount **P.** 7000
1Ki 11:18 They set out from Midian and went to **P.** 7000
11:18 Then taking men from **P** with them, 7000
Hab 3:3 the Holy One from Mount **P.** 7000

PARAPET (3)

Dt 22:8 make a **p** around your roof so that you may 5111
Eze 40:13 from *one* **p opening** to the opposite one. 7339
40:16 by narrow **p openings** all around, as was 2707

PARBAR (KJV) See COURT

PARCEL (2) [PARCELED]

Ps 60:6 "In triumph *I will* **p out** Shechem 2745
108:7 "In triumph *I will* **p out** Shechem 2745

PARCELED (1) [PARCEL]

Da 11:4 and **p out** toward the four winds of heaven. 2936

PARCHED (18)

Job 14:11 the sea or a riverbed *becomes* **p** and dry, 2990
30:3 the **p land** in desolate wastelands at night. 7480
Ps 69:3 calling for help; my throat *is* **p.** 3081
107:35 and the **p** ground into flowing springs; 7480
143:6 my soul thirsts for you like a **p** land. 6546
Isa 5:13 and their masses will be **p** *with* thirst. 7457
19:5 and the riverbed *will be* **p** and dry. 2990
19:7 sown field along the Nile *will become* **p,** 3312
35:1 The desert and the **p land** will be glad; 7480
41:17 their tongues *are* **p** with thirst. 5980
41:18 and the **p** ground into springs. 7480
Jer 12:4 How long *will* the land *lie* **p** 62
12:11 a wasteland, **p** and desolate before me; 62
17:6 He will dwell in the **p places** of the desert, 3083
23:10 the curse the land *lies* **p** and the pastures 62
48:18 from your glory and sit on the **p ground,** 7533
Hos 2:3 turn her into a **p** land, 7480
Joel 2:20 pushing it into a **p** and barren land, 7480

PARCHMENTS (1)

2Ti 4:13 and my scrolls, especially the **p.** *3521*

PARDON (4) [PARDONED, PARDONS]

2Ch 30:18 the LORD, who is good, **p** everyone 4105
Job 7:21 not **p** my offenses and forgive my sins? 5951
Isa 55:7 and to our God, for he will freely **p.** 6142
Joel 3:21 which I have not pardoned, *I will* **p."** 5927

PARDONED (2) [PARDON]

Nu 14:19 as *you have* **p** them from the time they left 5951
Joel 3:21 Their bloodguilt, which *I have* not **p,** 5927

PARDONS (1) [PARDON]

Mic 7:18 *who* **p** sin and forgives the transgression of 5951

PARENTS (29) [GRANDPARENTS]

Dt 22:17 Then her **p** shall display the cloth before NIH
Jdg 14:4 (His **p** did not know that this was 3+562+2256
14:9 When he rejoined his **p,** 3+562+2256
Pr 17:6 and **p** are the pride of their children. 3
19:14 Houses and wealth are inherited from **p,** 3
Zec 13:3 his own **p** will stab him. 3+562+2256
Mt 10:21 against their **p** and have them put to death. *1204*
Mk 13:12 against their **p** and have them put to death. *1204*
Lk 2:27 When the **p** brought in the child Jesus to do *1204*
2:41 Every year his **p** went to Jerusalem for *1204*
2:43 while **his p** were returning home, *899*[S]
2:48 When his **p** saw him, they were astonished. *NIG*
8:56 Her **p** were astonished, *1204*
18:29 or **p** or children for the sake of the kingdom *1204*
21:16 You will be betrayed even by **p,** brothers, *1204*
Jn 9:2 this man or his **p,** that he was born blind?" *1204*
9:3 "Neither this man nor his **p** sinned," *1204*
9:18 until they sent for the man's **p.** *1204*
9:20 "We know he is our son," the **p** answered, *1204*
9:22 His **p** said this because they were afraid of *1204*
9:23 That was why his **p** said, "He is of age; *1204*
Ro 1:30 ways of doing evil; they disobey their **p;** *1204*
2Co 12:14 not have to save up *for* their **p,** *1204*
12:14 but **p** for their children. *1204*
Eph 6:1 Children, obey your **p** in the Lord, *1204*
Col 3:20 Children, obey your **p** in everything, *1204*
1Ti 5:4 and so repaying their **p and grandparents,** *4591*
2Ti 3:2 abusive, disobedient *to* their **p,** ungrateful, *1204*
Heb 11:23 By faith Moses' **p** hid him for three months *4252*

PARKS (1)

Ecc 2:5 I made gardens and **p** and planted all kinds 7236

PARMASHTA (1)

Est 9:9 **P,** Arisai, Aridai and Vaizatha, 7269

PARMENAS (1)

Ac 6:5 also Philip, Procorus, Nicanor, Timon, **P,** *4226*

PARNACH (1)

Nu 34:25 of **P,** the leader from the tribe of Zebulun; 7270

PAROSH (6)

Ezr 2:3 the descendants of **P** 2,172 7283
8:3 of the descendants of **P,** Zechariah, 7283
10:25 From the descendants of **P:** 7283
Ne 3:25 Pedaiah son of **P** 7283
Ne 7:8 the descendants of **P** 2,172 7283
10:14 **P,** Pahath-Moab, Elam, Zattu, Bani, 7283

PARSHANDATHA (1)

Est 9:7 They also killed **P,** Dalphon, Aspatha, 7309

PARSIN (1)

Da 5:25 that was written: MENE, MENE, TEKEL, **P** 10593

PART (97) [APART, PARTED, PARTING, PARTITIONED, PARTLY, PARTS]

Ge 13:9 *Let's* **p company.** 7233
19:4 from **every p** of the city of Sodom— 7895
27:16 also covered his hands and the **smooth** *p* AIT
47:6 and your brothers in the **best** *p of* the land. AIT
47:11 gave them property in the **best** *p of* the land, AIT
Ex 12:48 *may* **take p** like one born in the land. 6913+7928
16:20 they kept **p** *of* it until morning, 4946
35:24 for any **p** *of* the work brought it. 4856
Lev 2:3 it is a **most holy** *p* of the offerings made to AIT
2:10 it is a **most holy** *p* of the offerings made to AIT
7:29 to bring **p** *of* it as his sacrifice to 4946
13:45 cover the **lower p of** his **face** 8559
13:56 he is to tear **the contaminated p** out of 2257[S]
24:9 a most holy **p** *of* their regular share of 4946
27:16 " 'If a man dedicates to the LORD **p** 4946
27:22 which is not **p** *of* his family land, 4946
Nu 8:24 shall come to **take p** in the work at 7371+7372
18:9 the **p** *of* the most holy offerings that is kept 4946
18:9 **that p** belongs to you and your sons. 2085[S]
18:29 the LORD's portion the best and holiest **p** 4946
18:30 'When you present the best **p,** 4946
18:32 By presenting the best **p** *of* it you will not 4946
22:41 and from there he saw **p** *of* the people. 7895
23:10 of Jacob or number the **fourth p** *of* Israel? 8065
23:13 you will see only a **p** but not all of them. 7895
31:27 the soldiers who **took p in** the battle 3655+4200
31:29 to Eleazar the priest as the LORD's **p.** 9556
31:41 to Eleazar the priest as the LORD's **p,** 9556
36:3 so **p** *of* the inheritance allotted to us will 4946
Dt 2:9 for I will not give you any **p** of their land. 3772
23:13 As **p** *of* your equipment have something 6584
Jos 2:15 house she lived in was **p of** the city wall. 928
1Sa 30:12 **p** *of* a cake of pressed figs and two cakes 7115
2Sa 3:37 Israel knew that the king **had** no **p in** 2118+4946
4:2 Beeroth is considered **p of** Benjamin, 6584
4:6 They went into the **inner p** *of* the house as 9348
20:1 no share in David, no **p** in Jesse's son! 5709
21:2 (Now the Gibeonites were not a **p** *of* Israel 4946
23:5 arranged and secured in **every** *p?* AIT
1Ki 7:5 they were **in the front p** in sets of three, 4578
7:20 the **bowl-shaped p** next to the network, 1061
8:64 the **middle** *p of* the courtyard in front of AIT
12:16 what **p** in Jesse's son? 5709
1Ch 6:62 from the **p** of the tribe of Manasseh that is NIH
21:12 of the LORD ravaging every **p** *of* Israel.' 1473
23:14 of God were counted **as p of** the tribe 6584
2Ch 7:7 the **middle** *p of* the courtyard in front of AIT
10:16 what **p** in Jesse's son? 5709
25:13 *to* **take p** in the war raided Judean 2143+6640
Ezr 4:3 "You **have** no **p** with us in building 4200
Ne 5:11 the **hundredth** *p of* the money, grain, AIT
Est 2:14 and in the morning return to **another p** *of* 9108
Job 42:12 The LORD blessed the **latter p of** Job's **life** 344
Ps 141:4 to **take p in** wicked deeds 6618
144:5 **P** your heavens, O LORD, 5742
Ecc 9:6 a **p** in anything that happens under the sun. 2750
Jer 41:9 as **p** of his defense against Baasha king NIH
Eze 24:17 do not cover the **lower p of** your **face** 8559
24:22 not cover the **lower p** of your **face** 8559
43:21 the **designated p** *of* the temple area outside 5152
48:1 of Damascus next to Hamath will be **p** NIH
Da 6:26 in every **p** *of* my kingdom people must fear 10717
8:23 "In the **latter p** *of* their reign, 344
Zec 14:18 not go up and **take p,** 995
Mt 5:29 for you to lose one **p of** your **body** than *3517*
5:30 for you to lose one **p of** your **body** than *3517*
23:30 not *have* **taken p** with them in shedding the blood of the prophets.' *1639+3128*
Lk 11:36 full of light, and no **p** of it dark, *3538*
20:35 worthy of **taking p** in that age and in *5593*
Jn 13:8 you have no **p** with me." *3538*
18:40 Barabbas **had taken p in a rebellion.** *1639+3334*
Ac 5:2 he kept back **p** of the money for himself, *608*
8:21 You have no **p** or share in this ministry, *3535*
Ro 11:16 If the **p** of the dough offered *NIG*
11:25 a hardening in **p** until the full number *608+3538*
1Co 10:21 you cannot **have** a **p** in both the Lord's *3576*
10:30 If I **take p** in the meal with thankfulness, *3576*
12:14 Now the body is not made up of one **p** but *3517*
12:15 it would not for that reason cease to be **p of** *1666*
12:16 it would not for that reason cease to be **p of** *1666*
12:19 If they were all one **p,** *3517*
12:26 If one **p** suffers, every part suffers with it; *3517*
12:26 If one part suffers, every **p** suffers with it; *3517*
12:26 if one **p** is honored, every part rejoices *3517*
12:26 every **p** rejoices with it. *3517*
12:27 and each one of you is a **p** of it. *3538*
13:9 For we know in **p** and we prophesy in part, *3538*
13:9 For we know in part and we prophesy in **p,** *3538*
13:12 Now I know in **p;** then I shall know fully, *3538*
2Co 1:14 as you have understood us **in p,** *608+3538*
8:6 to completion this act of grace on your **p.** *NIG*
Eph 4:16 as each **p** does its work. *3538*

Heb 9:11 that is to say, not a p of this creation. AIT
Jas 3: 5 the tongue is a small p of the body, 3517
Rev 13:10 and faithfulness on the p of the saints. AIT
14:12 endurance on the p of the saints who obey God's commandments AIT
20: 6 Blessed and holy are those who have p in 3538

PARTAKE (1)

1Co 10:17 are one body, for we all p of the one loaf. 3576

PARTED (7) [PART]

Ge 13:11 The two men p company: 7233
13:14 The LORD said to Abram after Lot had p 7233
2Sa 1:23 and in death they were not p. 7233
22:10 He p the heavens and came down; 5742
Job 41:17 they cling together and cannot be p. 7233
Ps 18: 9 He p the heavens and came down; 5742
Ac 15:39 such a sharp disagreement that they p company. 253+608+714

PARTHIANS (1)

Ac 2: 9 P, Medes and Elamites; 4222

PARTIAL (1) [PARTIALITY]

Pr 18: 5 It is not good to be p to the wicked or 5951+7156

PARTIALITY (15) [PARTIAL]

Lev 19:15 do not show p to the poor or favoritism to the great, 5951+7156
Dt 1:17 Do not show p in judging; 5795+7156
10:17 shows no p and accepts no bribes. 5951+7156
16:19 Do not pervert justice or show p. 5795+7156
2Ch 19: 7 no injustice or p or bribery." 5365+7156
Job 13: 8 Will you show him p? 5951+7156
13:10 rebuke you if you secretly showed p. 5951+7156
32:21 I will show p to no one, 5951+7156
34:19 who shows no p to princes and does 5951+7156
Ps 82: 2 the unjust and show p to the wicked? 5951+7156
Pr 24:23 To show p in judging is not good: 5795+7156
28:21 To show p is not good— 5795+7156
Mal 2: 9 not followed my ways but have shown p in matters of the law." 5951+7156
Lk 20:21 and that you do not show p but teach 3284+4725
1Ti 5:21 to keep these instructions without p, 4622

PARTICIPANTS (1) [PARTICIPATE]

1Co 10:20 and I do not want you to be p with demons. 3128

PARTICIPATE (4) [PARTICIPANTS, PARTICIPATION]

Eze 45:16 of the land will p in this special gift 448+2118
1Co 10:18 Do not those who eat the sacrifices p in the altar? 1639+3128
1Pe 4:13 rejoice that you p in the sufferings of Christ, 3125
2Pe 1: 4 you may p in the divine nature 1181+3128

PARTICIPATION (2) [PARTICIPATE]

1Co 10:16 for which we give thanks a p in the blood 3126
10:16 not the bread that we break a p in the body 3126

PARTICULARLY (2)

Zec 11: 7 p the oppressed of the flock. 4027+4200
Heb 13:19 I p urge you to pray so that I may 4359

PARTIES (5) [PARTY]

Ex 18:16 I decide between the p and 408+2084+2256+8276
22: 9 both p are to bring their cases before AIT
1Sa 13:17 Raiding p went out from 8845
14:15 and those in the outposts and raiding p— 8845
Job 1:17 "The Chaldeans formed three raiding p 8031

PARTING (1) [PART]

Mic 1:14 Therefore you will give p gifts 8933

PARTITIONED (1) [PART]

1Ki 6:16 He p off twenty cubits at the rear of the 1215

PARTLY (8) [PART]

Da 2:33 its feet p of iron and partly of baked clay. 10427
2:33 its feet partly of iron and p of baked clay. 10427
2:41 that the feet and toes were p of baked clay 10427
2:41 of baked clay and p of iron, so this will be 10427
2:42 As the toes were p iron and partly clay, 10427
2:42 As the toes were partly iron and p clay, 10427
2:42 so this kingdom will be p strong 10427+10636
2:42 be partly strong and p brittle. 10427

PARTNER (6) [PARTNERS, PARTNERSHIP]

Pr 2:17 who has left the p of her youth and ignored 476
28:24 he is p to him who destroys. 2492
Mal 2:14 though she is your p, 2500
2Co 8:23 he is my p and fellow worker among you; 3128
Phm 1:17 So if you consider me a p, 3128
1Pe 3: 7 and treat them with respect as the weaker p 5007

PARTNERS (3) [PARTNER]

Lk 5: 7 So they signaled their p in the other boat 3581
5:10 the sons of Zebedee, Simon's p. 3128
Eph 5: 7 Therefore do not be p with them. 5212

PARTNERSHIP (1) [PARTNER]

Php 1: 5 of your p in the gospel from the first day 3126

PARTRIDGE (2)

1Sa 26:20 as one hunts a p in the mountains." 7926
Jer 17:11 Like a p that hatches eggs it did not lay is 7926

PARTS (50) [PART]

Ex 12: 9 head, legs and inner p. 7931
29:13 Then take all the fat around the inner p, 7931
29:17 the ram into pieces and wash the inner p 7931
29:22 the fat tail, the fat around the inner p, 7931
29:27 "Consecrate those p of the ordination ram NIH
Lev 1: 9 to wash the inner p and the legs with water, 7931
1:13 to wash the inner p and the legs with water, 7931
3: 3 that covers the inner p or is connected 7931
3: 9 that covers the inner p or is connected 7931
3:14 that covers the inner p or is connected 7931
4: 8 that covers the inner p or is connected 7931
4:11 the inner p and offal— 7931
7: 3 and the fat that covers the inner p, 7931
8:16 also took all the fat around the inner p, 7931
8:21 He washed the inner p and the legs 7931
8:25 the fat tail, all the fat around the inner p, 7931
9:14 the inner p and the legs and burned them 7931
Dt 18: 3 the shoulder, the jowls and the inner p. 7687
19: 3 Build roads to them and divide into three p 1473
25:11 and seizes him by his private p, 4434
Jos 18: 5 You are to divide the land into seven p. 2750
18: 6 of the seven p of the land, 2750
18: 9 town by town, in seven p, 2750
Jdg 19:29 into twelve p and sent them into all 5984
1Sa 2:29 on the choice p of every offering made 8040
2Ki 19:23 I have reached its remotest p, 4869
1Ch 28:11 its buildings, its storerooms, its upper p, 6608
2Ch 3: 9 He also overlaid the upper p with gold. 6608
Est 1:22 He sent dispatches to all p of the kingdom, 4519
Job 18:13 It eats away p of his skin; 963
Ps 51: 6 Surely you desire truth in the inner p; 3219
Pr 18: 8 they go down to a man's inmost p. 1061+2540
26:22 they go down to a man's inmost p. 1061+2540
Da 4:22 and your dominion extends to distant p of 10509
Ac 2:10 Egypt and the p of Libya near Cyrene; 3538
Ro 6:13 Do not offer the p of your body to sin, 3517
6:13 the p of your body to him as instruments 3517
6:19 Just as you used to offer the p of your body 3517
1Co 12:12 though it is made up of many p; 3517
12:12 all its p are many, they form one body. 3517
12:18 in fact God has arranged the p in the body, 3517
12:20 As it is, there are many p, but one body. 3517
12:22 those p of the body that seem to 3517
12:23 and the p that we think are less honorable we treat with special honor. 3836+4047+5393S
12:23 And the p that are unpresentable are treated NIG
12:24 our presentable p need no special treatment. NIG
12:24 and has given greater honor to the p NIG
12:25 but that its p should have equal concern 3517
Jas 3: 6 a world of evil among the p of the body. 3517
Rev 16:19 The great city split into three p, 3538

PARTY (8) [PARTIES]

Ru 4: 7 one p took off his sandal and gave it to 408S
1Sa 30: 8 "Shall I pursue this raiding p? 1522
30:15 "Can you lead me down to this raiding p?" 1522
Pr 19:18 do not be a willing p to his death. 5883+5951
Ac 5:17 members of the p of the Pharisees 146
15: 5 to the p of the Pharisees stood up and said, 146
2Co 7:12 who did the wrong or of the injured p, AIT
Gal 3:20 however, does not represent just one p; AIT

PARUAH (1)

1Ki 4:17 Jehoshaphat son of P—in Issachar; 7245

PARVAIM (1)

2Ch 3: 6 And the gold he used was gold of P. 7246

PAS DAMMIM (2)

2Sa 23: 9 the Philistines gathered [at P] 9004S
1Ch 11:13 He was with David at P when 7169

PASACH (1)

1Ch 7:33 P, Bimhal and Ashvath. 7179

PASEAH (4)

1Ch 4:12 P and Tehinnah the father of Ir Nahash. 7176
Ezr 2:49 Uzza, P, Besai, 7176
Ne 3: 6 of P and Meshullam son of Besodeiah. 7176
7:51 Gazzam, Uzza, P, 7176

PASHHUR (13)

1Ch 9:12 the son of P, the son of Malkijah; 7319
Ezr 2:38 of P 1,247 7319
10:22 From the descendants of P: 7319
Ne 7:41 of P 1,247 7319
10: 3 P, Amariah, Malkijah, 7319
11:12 the son of Zechariah, the son of P, 7319
Jer 20: 1 When the priest P son of Immer, 7319
20: 3 when P released him from the stocks, 7319
20: 3 "The LORD's name for you is not P, 7319
20: 6 P, and all who live in your house will go 7319
21: 1 when King Zedekiah sent to him P son 7319
38: 1 Gedaliah son of P, 7319
38: 1 and P son of Malkijah heard what Jeremiah 7319

PASS (115) [PASSED, PASSER-BY, PASSES, PASSING]

Ge 18: 3 my lord, do not p your servant by. 6296
Ex 12:12 that same night I will p through Egypt 6296
12:13 I will p over you. 7173
12:23 of the doorframe and will p over 7173
15:16 until your people p by, O LORD, 6296
15:16 until the people you bought p by. 6296
33:19 cause all my goodness to p in front of you, 6296
Lev 26: 6 the sword will not p through your country. 6296
Nu 20:17 Please let us p through your country. 6296
20:18 "You may not p through here; 6296
20:19 We only want to p through on foot— 6296
20:20 "You may not p through." 6296
21:22 "Let us p through your country. 6296
21:23 not let Israel p through his territory. 6296
34: 4 cross south of Scorpion P, 5090
36: 7 No inheritance in Israel is to p from tribe 6015
36: 9 No inheritance may p from tribe to tribe, 6015
Dt 2: 4 'You are about to p through the territory 6296
2:18 "Today you are to p by the region of Moab 6296
2:27 "Let us p through your country. 6296
2:28 Only let us p through on foot— 6296
2:30 of Heshbon refused to let us p through. 6296
Jos 3: 6 the covenant and p on ahead of the people." 6296
15: 3 crossed south of Scorpion P, 5090
15: 7 which faces the P of Adummim south of 5090
18:17 which faces the P of Adummim, 5090
Jdg 1:36 the Amorites was from Scorpion P to Sela 5090
8:13 then returned from the battle by the P 5090
11:19 'Let us p through your country 6296
11:20 not trust Israel to p through his territory. 6296
1Sa 13:23 of Philistines had gone out to the p 5044
14: 4 of the p that Jonathan intended to cross 5045
16: 8 Then Jesse called Abinadab and had him p 6296
16: 9 Jesse then had Shammah p by, 6296
16:10 had seven of his sons p before Samuel, 6296
1Ki 9: 8 all who p by will be appalled and will scoff 6296
19:11 for the LORD is about to p by." 6296
2Ki 19:25 now I have brought it to p, 995
1Ch 28: 8 p it on as an inheritance 5706
2Ch 7:21 all who p by will be appalled and say, 6296
20:16 They will be climbing up by the P of Ziz, 5090
Job 16:22 "Only a few years will p before I go on 910
19: 8 He has blocked my way so I cannot p; 6296
34:20 the people are shaken and they p away; 6296
41:16 to the next that no air can p between. 995
Ps 80:12 so that all who p by pick its grapes? 2006+6296
84: 6 As they p through the Valley of Baca, 6296
89:41 All who p by have plundered him; 2006+6296
90: 9 All our days p away under your wrath; 7155
90:10 for they quickly p, and we fly away. 1577
105:19 till what he foretold came to p, 995
129: 8 May those who p by not say, 6296
141:10 while I p by in safety. 6296
148: 6 he gave a decree that will never p away. 6296
Pr 9:15 calling out to those who p by, 2006+6296
Isa 10:28 They enter Aiath; they p through Migron; 6296
10:29 They go over the p, and say, 5045
31: 5 he will 'p over' it and will rescue it." 7173
34:10 no one will ever p through it again. 6296
37:26 now I have brought it to p, 995
43: 2 When you p through the waters, 6296
43: 2 and when you p through the rivers, NIH
48: 3 then suddenly I acted, and they came to p. 995
62:10 P through, pass through the gates! 6296
62:10 Pass through, p through the gates! 6296
Jer 2:35 I will p judgment on you because you say, 9149
6: 9 p your hand over the branches again, 8740
18:16 all who p by will be appalled 6296
19: 8 all who p by will be appalled and will scoff 6296
22: 8 from many nations will p by this city 6296
33:13 flocks will again p under the hand of 6296
49:17 all who p by will be appalled and will scoff 6296
50:13 All who p Babylon will be horrified 6296
La 1:12 Is it nothing to you, all you who p by? 2006+6296
2:15 All who p your way clap their hands at you; 6296
Eze 5:14 in the sight of all who p by. 6296
14:15 so that no one can p through it because of 6296
14:17 'Let the sword p throughout the land,' 6296
20:37 take note of you as you p 6296
29:11 of man or animal will p through it; 6296
36:34 in the sight of all who p through it. 6296
48:14 the land and must not p into other hands, 6296
Da 4:16 till seven times p by for him. 10268
4:23 until seven times p by for him.' 10268
4:25 Seven times will p by for you 10268
4:32 Seven times will p by for you 10268
7:14 everlasting dominion that will not p away, 10528
Am 5:17 for I will p through your midst," 6296
Mic 1:11 P on in nakedness and shame, 6296
2: 8 the rich robe from those who p by without 6296
2:13 Their king will p through before them, 6296
Na 1:12 they will be cut off and p away. 6296
Zep 2:15 All who p by her scoff and shake their fists. 6296
Zec 10:11 They will p through the sea of trouble; 6296
10:11 and Egypt's scepter will p away. 6073

Mt 8:28 They were so violent that no one could **p** *4216*
24:34 this generation *will* certainly not **p away** *4216*
24:35 Heaven and earth *will* **p away,** *4216*
24:35 but my words *will* never **p away.** *4216*
Mk 6:48 He was about *to* **p by** them, *4216*
13:30 this generation *will* certainly not **p away** *4216*
13:31 Heaven and earth *will* **p away,** *4216*
13:31 but my words *will* never **p away.** *4216*
14:35 and prayed that if possible the hour *might* **p** *4216*
Lk 21:32 this generation *will* certainly not **p away** *4216*
21:33 Heaven and earth *will* **p away,** *4216*
21:33 but my words *will* never **p away.** *4216*
Jn 8:15 I **p judgment on** no one. *3212*
Ac 7:38 and he received living words *to* **p on** to us. *1443*
Ro 2: 1 you who **p judgment on** someone else, *3212*
2: 1 you who **p judgment** do the same things. *3212*
2: 3 **p judgment on** them and yet do *3212*
1Co 13: 8 where there is knowledge, *it will* **p away.** *2934*
Jas 1:10 because *he will* **p away** like a wild flower. *4216*
1Jn 2:17 The world and its desires **p away,** *4135*

PASSAGE (4) [PASSAGEWAY]

Ac 8:32 The eunuch was reading this **p** of Scripture: *4343*
8:35 with that very **p** of Scripture and told him *NIG*
Ro 11: 2 the Scripture says in the **p** about Elijah— *NIG*
Heb 4: 5 And again in **the p above** he says, *4047*

PASSAGEWAY (3) [PASSAGE]

Eze 42: 4 of the rooms was an inner **p** ten cubits wide 4544
42:11 with a **p** in front of them. 2006
42:12 the beginning of the **p** that was parallel to 2006

PASSED (78) [PASS]

Ge 15:17 a blazing torch appeared and **p** between 6296
32:31 The sun rose above him as *he* **p** Peniel, 6296
41: 1 When two full years had **p,** 7891
50: 4 When the days of mourning *had* **p,** 6296
Ex 7:25 Seven days **p** after the LORD struck 4848
12:27 who **p over** the houses of the Israelites 7173
33:22 with my hand until I *have* **p by.** 6296
34: 6 And he **p** in front of Moses, proclaiming, 6296
Lev 25:30 not redeemed before a full year *has* **p,** 4848
Nu 14: 7 "The land *we* **p** through 6296
20:17 until *we have* **p through** your territory." 6296
21:22 the king's highway until *we have* **p through** 6296
33: 8 They left Pi Hahiroth and **p** through the sea 6296
Dt 2:14 Thirty-eight years **p** from the time NIH
29:16 and how *we* **p** through the countries on 6296
Jos 3:17 while all Israel **p by** until the whole nation 6296
15: 4 *It* then **p along** to Azmon and joined 6296
15:11 **p along** *to* Mount Baalah 6296
18:12 **p** the northern slope of Jericho 6590
23: 1 After a long time *had* **p** and 2118
Jdg 3:26 He **p by** the idols and escaped to Seirah. 6296
9:25 to ambush and rob everyone who **p** by, 6296
11:18 **p** along the eastern side of the country 995
11:29 **p through** Mizpah of Gilead, 6296
1Sa 9: 4 So *he* **p** through the hill country of Ephraim 6296
9: 4 *he* **p** through the territory of Benjamin, 6296
2Sa 15:23 wept aloud as all the people **p by.** 6296
20:14 Sheba **p** through all the tribes of Israel 6296
1Ki 13:25 Some people *who* **p by** saw the body thrown 6296
18:29 Midday **p,** and they continued their frantic 6296
20:39 As the king **p by,** the prophet called out 6296
2Ch 21:20 *He* **p away,** to no one's regret, 2143
Ne 9:11 so that *they* **p** through it on dry ground, 6296
12:37 and **p** above the house of David to NIH
Est 4:11 But thirty days have **p** since I was called NIH
Job 14:13 and conceal me till your anger *has* **p!** 8740
15:19 the land was given when no alien **p** 6296
17:11 My days *have* **p,** my plans are shattered, 6296
Ps 37:36 but *he soon* **p away** and was no more; 6296
57: 1 of your wings until the disaster *has* **p.** 6296
66: 6 *they* **p** through the waters on foot— 6296
SS 3: 4 Scarcely *had I* **p** them when I found 6296
Isa 26:20 for a little while until his wrath *has* **p by.** 6296
La 4:21 But to you also the cup *will be* **p;** 6296
Eze 16: 6 " 'Then *I* **p** by and saw you kicking about 6296
16: 8 " 'Later *I* **p** by, and when I looked at you 6296
16:15 lavished your favors on anyone *who* **p by** 6296
16:25 promiscuity to anyone *who* **p by.** 6296
Da 2:28 and the **visions** *that p through* your mind AIT
4: 5 images and **visions** *that p through* my mind AIT
7: 1 and **visions** *p through* his mind AIT
7:15 and the **visions** *that p through* my mind AIT
Mt 27:39 Those who **p by** hurled insults at him, *4182*
Mk 9:30 *They* left that place and **p** through Galilee. *4182*
15:29 Those who **p by** hurled insults at him, *4182*
Lk 10:31 **p by on the other side.** *524*
10:32 **p by on the other side.** *524*
Ac 5:15 on some of them *as he* **p by.** *2262*
7:30 **"After** forty years **had p,** *4444*
12:10 *They* **p** the first and second guards *1451*
16: 8 *they* **p by** Mysia and went down to Troas. *4216*
17: 1 *When they had* **p through** Amphipolis *1476*
24:27 *When* two years *had* **p,** *4444*
27: 4 and **p to the lee of** Cyprus *5709*
27:16 **p to the lee of** a small island called Cauda, *5720*
27:17 **p** ropes **under** the ship itself **to hold it together.** *5690*
1Co 5: 3 *I have* already **p judgment on** the one *3212*
10: 1 under the cloud and that *they* all **p through** *1451*
11: 2 just as *I* **p** them **on** to you. *4140*
11:23 from the Lord what *I* also **p on** to you: *4140*
15: 3 For what I received *I* **p on** to you as *4140*
2Th 2:15 and hold to the teachings we **p on** to you, *4142*
Heb 11:29 By faith the people **p through** the Red Sea *1329*
2Pe 2:21 the sacred command *that was* **p on** to them. *4140*
1Jn 3:14 We know that *we have* **p** from death to life, *3553*
Rev 11:14 The second woe *has* **p;** *599*
21: 1 first heaven and the first earth *had* **p away,** *599*
21: 4 for the old order of things *has* **p away."** *599*

PASSER-BY (2) [PASS]

Pr 26:10 at random is he who hires a fool or any **p.** 6296
26:17 by the ears is a **p** who meddles in a quarrel 6296

PASSES (5) [PASS]

Ex 33:22 When my glory **p by,** 6296
Lev 27:32 that **p** under the shepherd's rod— 6296
Job 9:11 When *he* **p** me, I cannot see him; 6296
Ecc 6:12 the few and meaningless days *he* **p through** 6913
Jer 17:16 **What p** my lips is open before you. 4604

PASSING (20) [PASS]

Jos 16: 6 **p by** it to Janoah on the east. 6296
19:27 **p** Cabul on the left. 3655
19:33 **p** Adami Nekeb and Jabneel to Lakkum NIH
2Ki 6: 9 "Beware of **p** that place, 6296
6:26 As the king of Israel was **p by** on the wall, 6296
Ps 78:39 a **p** breeze that does not return. 2143
Isa 8: 8 **p through** it and reaching up to the neck. 6296
Zep 3: 6 with no *one* **p through.** 6296
Mk 15:21 was **p by** on his way in from the country, *4135*
Lk 18:37 They told him, "Jesus of Nazareth *is* **p by."** *4216*
19: 1 Jesus entered Jericho and *was* **p through.** *1451*
Jn 1:36 When he saw Jesus **p by,** he said, "Look, *4344*
Ac 19:21 **p through** Macedonia and Achaia, *1451*
21: 3 After sighting Cyprus and **p** to the south *2901*
Ro 14: 1 without **p judgment** on disputable matters. *1360*
14:13 *let us* stop **p judgment on** one another. *3212*
15:24 *while* **p through** and to have you assist me *1388*
1Co 7:31 this world in its present form *is* **p away.** *4135*
16: 7 to see you now and make only a **p** visit; *4227*
1Jn 2: 8 because the darkness *is* **p** and the true light *4135*

PASSION (2) [PASSIONATE, PASSIONS]

Hos 7: 6 Their **p** smolders all night; 678
1Co 7: 9 for it is better to marry than *to* **burn with p.** *4792*

PASSIONATE (1) [PASSION]

1Th 4: 5 not in **p** lust like the heathen, who do *2123*

PASSIONS (4) [PASSION]

Ro 7: 5 the sinful **p** aroused by the law were *4077*
Gal 5:24 the sinful nature with its **p** and desires. *4077*
Tit 2:12 to say "No" to ungodliness and worldly **p,** *2123*
3: 3 deceived and enslaved by all kinds of **p** *2123*

PASSOVER (77)

Ex 12:11 Eat it in haste; it is the LORD's **P.** 7175
12:21 for your families and slaughter the **P lamb.** 7175
12:27 'It is the **P** sacrifice to the LORD, 7175
12:43 "These are the regulations for the **P:** 7175
12:48 to celebrate the LORD's **P** must have all 7175
34:25 of the sacrifice from the **P** Feast remain 7175
Lev 23: 5 The LORD's **P** begins at twilight on 7175
Nu 9: 2 "Have the Israelites celebrate the **P** at 7175
9: 4 Moses told the Israelites to celebrate the **P,** 7175
9: 6 But some of them could not celebrate the **P** 7175
9:10 they may still celebrate the LORD's **P.** 7175
9:12 When they celebrate the **P,** 7175
9:13 not on a journey fails to celebrate the **P,** 7175
9:14 the LORD's **P** must do so in accordance 7175
28:16 of the first month the LORD's **P** is to 7175
33: 3 the day after the **P.** 7175
Dt 16: 1 the month of Abib and celebrate the **P** of 7175
16: 2 as the **P** to the LORD your God an animal 7175
16: 5 You must not sacrifice the **P** in any town 7175
16: 6 There you must sacrifice the **P** in 7175
Jos 5:10 the Israelites celebrated the **P.** 7175
5:11 The day after the **P,** that very day, 7175
2Ki 23:21 "Celebrate the **P** to the LORD your God, 7175
23:22 had any such **P** been observed. 7175
23:23 this **P** was celebrated to the LORD 7175
2Ch 30: 1 in Jerusalem and celebrate the **P** to 7175
30: 2 in Jerusalem decided to celebrate the **P** in 7175
30: 5 to come to Jerusalem and celebrate the **P** to 7175
30:15 the **P lamb** on the fourteenth day of 7175
30:17 to kill the **P lambs** for all those who were 7175
30:18 not purified themselves, yet they ate the **P,** 7175
35: 1 Josiah celebrated the **P** to the LORD 7175
35: 1 and the **P lamb** was slaughtered on 7175
35: 6 Slaughter the **P lambs,** 7175
35: 7 and goats for the **P offerings,** and 7175
35: 8 the priests twenty-six hundred **P offerings** 7175
35: 9 provided five thousand **P offerings** 7175
35:11 The **P lambs** were slaughtered, 7175
35:13 the **P animals** over the fire as prescribed, 7175
35:16 for the celebration of the **P** and the offering 7175
35:17 the **P** at that time and observed the Feast 7175
35:18 The **P** had not been observed like this 7175
35:18 of Israel had ever celebrated such a **P** 7175
35:19 This **P** was celebrated in 7175
Ezr 6:19 the exiles celebrated the **P.** 7175
6:20 The Levites slaughtered the **P lamb** for all 7175
Eze 45:21 to observe the **P,** a feast lasting seven days, 7175
Mt 26: 2 the **P** is two days away— *4247*
26:17 to make preparations for you to eat the **P?"** *4247*
26:18 the **P** with my disciples at your house.' " *4247*
26:19 and prepared the **P.** *4247*
Mk 14: 1 the **P** and the Feast of Unleavened Bread *4247*
14:12 it was customary to sacrifice the **P lamb,** *4247*
14:12 make preparations for you to eat the **P?"** *4247*
14:14 where I may eat the **P** with my disciples?' *4247*
14:16 So they prepared the **P.** *4247*
Lk 2:41 to Jerusalem for the Feast *of* the **P.** *4247*
22: 1 Feast of Unleavened Bread, called the **P,** *4247*
22: 7 on which the **P lamb** had to be sacrificed. *4247*
22: 8 and make preparations for us to eat the **P."** *4247*
22:11 where I may eat the **P** with my disciples?' *4247*
22:13 So they prepared the **P.** *4247*
22:15 desired to eat this **P** with you before I suffer *4247*
Jn 2:13 When it was almost time for the Jewish **P,** *4247*
2:23 while he was in Jerusalem at the **P** Feast, *4247*
4:45 in Jerusalem at the **P Feast,** *2038*
6: 4 The Jewish **P** Feast was near. *4247*
11:55 When it was almost time for the Jewish **P,** *4247*
11:55 for their ceremonial cleansing before the **P.** *4247*
12: 1 Six days before the **P,** *4247*
13: 1 It was just before the **P** Feast. *4247*
18:28 they wanted to be able to eat the **P.** *4247*
18:39 to you one prisoner at the time of the **P.** *4247*
19:14 It was the day of Preparation *of* **P** Week, *4247*
Ac 12: 4 to bring him out for public trial after the **P.** *4247*
1Co 5: 7 Christ, our **P lamb,** has been sacrificed. *4247*
Heb 11:28 By faith he kept the **P** and the sprinkling *4247*

PAST (48)

Ge 18:11 and Sarah was **p** the age of childbearing, 2532
31:52 not **go p** this heap to your side to harm you 6296
31:52 that you *will* not **go p** this heap and pillar 6296
Ex 4:10 neither in the **p** nor since you have 8997+9453
Dt 2: 8 **p** our brothers the descendants of Esau, 907+4946
32: 7 consider the **generations long p.** 1887+1887+2256+9102
Jos 13:16 and the whole plateau **p** Medeba 6584
15: 3 Then *it* **ran p** Hezron up to Addar 6296
1Sa 15:32 "Surely the bitterness of death *is* **p."** 6073
2Sa 5: 2 **In the p,** while Saul was king over us, 919+1685+1685+8997
15:18 All his men **marched p** him, 3338+6296+6584
15:34 I was your father's servant in the **p,** 255
1Ch 11: 2 **In the p,** even while Saul was king, 8997+9453
Ne 12:38 **p** the Tower of the Ovens to 4946+6584
Job 4:15 A spirit **glided p** my face, 2736
9:26 *They* **skim p** like boats of papyrus, 2736
36:26 The number of his years is **p** finding out. 4202
Pr 24:30 *I* went **p** the field of the sluggard, 6584
24:30 **p** the vineyard of the man who lacks 6584
Ecc 3:15 and God will call the **p** to account. 8103
SS 2:11 winter *is* **p;** the rains are over and gone. 6296
Isa 9: 1 the **p** he humbled the land of Zebulun 6961+8037
43:18 do not dwell on the **p.** 7719
43:26 **Review the p** *for* me, 2349
45:21 who declared it from the **distant p?** 255
65:16 the **p** troubles will be forgotten and hidden 8037
Jer 8:20 "The harvest *is* **p,** the summer has ended, 6296
21: 2 perform wonders for us **as in times p** 3869+3972
31: 3 the LORD appeared to us in the **p,** saying: 8158
46:26 Egypt will be inhabited as in times **p,"** 7710
Eze 36:11 I will settle people on you as *in the* **p** 7712
47:15 the Hethlon road **p** Lebo Hamath to Zedad, NIH
Hab 1:11 *they* **sweep p** like the wind and go on— 2736
Zec 7: 5 and seventh months for the **p** seventy years, NIH
8:11 of this people as I did in the **p,"** 3427+8037
Ac 14:16 In the **p,** he let all nations go their own way. *1155+4233*
17:30 *In* the **p** God overlooked such ignorance, *5989*
20:16 *to* **sail p** Ephesus to avoid spending time *4179*
Ro 15: 4 For everything that *was* **written in the p** *4592*
16:25 of the mystery hidden for long ages **p,** *NIG*
Eph 3: 9 which *for* **ages p** was kept hidden in God, *172*
Heb 1: 1 **In the p** God spoke to our forefathers *4093*
11:11 even though he was **p** age— *4123*
1Pe 3: 5 For this is the way the holy women **of the p** *4537*
4: 3 in the **p** doing what pagans choose to do— *4216*
2Pe 1: 9 that he has been cleansed from his **p** sins. *4093*
3: 2 to recall the words **spoken in the p** by *4625*
Rev 9:12 The first woe *is* **p;** *599*

PASTOR (KJV) See SHEPHERD

PASTORS (1)

Eph 4:11 and some to be **p** and teachers, *4478*

PASTURE (41) [PASTURED, PASTURELAND, PASTURELANDS, PASTURES]

Ge 29: 7 Water the sheep and take them back to **p."** 8286
47: 4 and your servants' flocks have no **p.** 5337
2Sa 7: 8 from the **p** and from following the flock to 5659
1Ch 4:39 of the valley in search of **p** for their flocks. 5337
4:40 They found rich, good **p,** 5337
4:41 because there was **p** for their flocks. 5337
17: 7 I took you from the **p** and from following 5659
Job 24: 2 *they* **p** flocks they have stolen. 8286
39: 8 for his **p** and searches for any green thing. 5337
Ps 37: 3 dwell in the land and **enjoy** safe **p.** 8286
74: 1 against the sheep of your **p?** 5338

Ps 79:13 Then we your people, the sheep of your **p**, 5338
95: 7 and we are the people of his **p**, 5338
100: 3 we are his people, the sheep of his **p**. 5338
Isa 5:17 Then sheep will graze as in their own **p**; 1824
14:30 The poorest of the poor *will* **find p**, 8286
32:14 the delight of donkeys, a **p** *for* flocks, 5337
49: 9 "They will feed beside the roads and find **p** 5338
65:10 Sharon will become a **p** *for* flocks, 5659
Jer 14: 6 their eyesight fails for lack of **p**." 6912
23: 1 and scattering the sheep of my **p**!" 5338
23: 3 and will bring them back to their **p**, 5659
25:36 for the LORD is destroying their **p**. 5338
49:20 he will completely destroy their **p** because 5659
50: 7 sinned against the LORD, their true **p**, 5659
50:19 to his own **p** and he will graze on Carmel 5659
50:45 he will completely destroy their **p** because 5659
La 1: 6 Her princes are like deer that find no **p**; 5337
Eze 25: 5 I will turn Rabbah into a **p** *for* camels 5659
34:13 *I will* **p** them on the mountains of Israel, 8286
34:14 I will tend them in a good **p**, 5337
34:14 in a rich **p** on the mountains of Israel. 5337
34:18 not enough for you to feed on the good **p**? 5337
34:18 Must you also trample the rest of your **p** 5337
34:31 You my sheep, the sheep of my **p**, 5338
Hos 4:16 then *can* the LORD **p** them like lambs in 8286
Joel 1:18 herds mill about because they have no **p**; 5337
Mic 2:12 like a flock in its **p**; 1824
Zep 2: 7 there *they will* **find p**. 8286
Zec 11: 4 "**P** the flock marked for slaughter. 8286
Jn 10: 9 He will come in and go out, and find **p**. *3786*

PASTURE-FED (1) [FEED]
1Ki 4:23 of **p** cattle and a hundred sheep and goats, 8297

PASTURED (2) [PASTURE]
Zec 11: 7 So *I* **p** the flock marked for slaughter, 8286
11: 7 and *I* **p** the flock. 8286

PASTURELAND (8) [PASTURE]
Lev 25:34 But the **p** *belonging to* their towns 4494+8441
Nu 35: 5 They will have this area as **p** *for* the towns. 4494
Jos 21:11 Hebron), with its surrounding **p**, 4494
Jer 49:19 up from Jordan's thickets to a rich **p**, 5659
50:44 up from Jordan's thickets to a rich **p**, 5659
Eze 36: 5 so that they might plunder its **p**.' 4494
48:15 use of the city, for houses and for **p**. 4494
48:17 The **p** for the city will be 250 cubits on 4494

PASTURELANDS (43) [PASTURE]
Nu 35: 2 And give them **p** around the towns. 4494
35: 3 Then they will have towns to live in and **p** 4494
35: 4 "The **p** around the towns that you give 4494
35: 7 together with their **p**. 4494
Jos 14: 4 with **p** for their flocks and herds. 4494
21: 2 with **p** for our livestock." 4494
21: 3 the Levites the following towns and **p** out 4494
21: 8 to the Levites these towns and their **p**, 4494
21:16 together with their **p**—nine towns 4494
21:18 together with their **p**—four towns. 4494
21:19 were thirteen, together with their **p**. 4494
21:22 together with their **p**—four towns. 4494
21:24 together with their **p**—four towns. 4494
21:25 together with their **p**—two towns. 4494
21:26 All these ten towns and their **p** were given 4494
21:27 and Be Eshtarah, together with their **p**— 4494
21:29 together with their **p**—four towns; 4494
21:31 together with their **p**—four towns; 4494
21:32 together with their **p**—three towns. 4494
21:33 together with their **p**. 4494
21:35 together with their **p**—four towns; 4494
21:37 together with their **p**—four towns; 4494
21:39 together with their **p**—four towns in all. 4494
21:41 together with their **p**. 4494
21:42 Each of these towns had **p** surrounding it; 4494
1Ch 5:16 the **p** *of* Sharon as far as they extended. 4494
6:55 in Judah with its surrounding **p**. 4494
6:59 together with their **p**. 4494
6:60 together with their **p**. 4494
6:64 the Levites these towns and their **p**. 4494
6:69 together with their **p**. 4494
6:70 together with their **p**, 4494
6:71 and also Ashtaroth, together with their **p**; 4494
6:73 Ramoth and Anem, together with their **p**; 4494
6:75 Hukok and Rehob, together with their **p**; 4494
6:76 together with their **p**. 4494
6:77 Rimmono and Tabor, together with their **p**; 4494
6:79 together with their **p**; 4494
6:81 Heshbon and Jazer, together with their **p**. 4494
13: 2 with them in their towns and **p**, 4494
2Ch 11:14 even abandoned their **p** and property, 4494
Ps 83:12 "Let us take possession of the **p** *of* God." 5661
Mic 7:14 by itself in a forest, in **fertile p**. 4149

PASTURES (10) [PASTURE]
Ps 23: 2 He makes me lie down in green **p**, 5661
Jer 9:10 up a lament concerning the desert **p**. 5661
23:10 the curse the land lies parched and the **p** *in* 5661
33:12 be **p** *for* shepherds to rest their flocks. 5659
Eze 45:15 of two hundred from the well-watered **p** NIH
Joel 1:19 the open **p** and flames have burned up all 5661
1:20 up and fire has devoured the open **p**. 5661
2:22 for the open **p** are becoming green. 5661
Am 1: 2 the **p** *of* the shepherds dry up, 5661
Zec 11: 3 their **rich p** are destroyed! 168

PATARA (1)
Ac 21: 1 to Rhodes and from there to **P**. *4249*

PATCH (6) [PATCHED]
Jer 10: 5 Like a scarecrow in a **melon p**, 5252
Mt 9:16 a **p** of unshrunk cloth on an old garment, *2099*
9:16 for the **p** will pull away from the garment, *NIG*
Mk 2:21 a **p** of unshrunk cloth on an old garment. *2099*
Lk 5:36 a **p** from a new garment and sews it on *2099*
5:36 the **p** from the new will not match the old. *2099*

PATCHED (1) [PATCH]
Jos 9: 5 The men put worn and **p** sandals 3229

PATH (61) [BYPATHS, PATHS]
Ge 49:17 a viper along the **p**, 784
Nu 22:24 the angel of the LORD stood in a **narrow p** 5469
22:32 because your **p** is a reckless one before me. 2006
2Sa 22:37 You broaden the **p** beneath me, 7576
Ne 9:19 not cease to guide them on their **p**, 2006
Job 18:10 a trap lies in his **p**. 5985
22:15 to the old **p** that evil men have trod? 784
24: 4 from the **p** and force all the poor of the land 2006
28: 7 No bird of prey knows that **hidden p**, 5985
28:26 when he made a decree for the rain and a **p** 2006
29: 6 when my **p** was drenched with cream and 2141
31: 7 if my steps have turned from the **p**, 2006
38:25 and a **p** for the thunderstorm, 2006
Ps 16:11 You have made known to me the **p** *of* life; 784
18:36 You broaden the **p** beneath me, 7576
27:11 in a straight **p** because of my oppressors. 784
35: 6 may their **p** be dark and slippery, 2006
44:18 our feet had not strayed from your **p**. 784
57: 6 They dug a pit **in** my **p**— 4200+7156
77:19 Your **p** led through the sea, 2006
78:50 He prepared a **p** for his anger; 5985
119:32 I run in the **p** *of* your commands, 2006
119:35 Direct me in the **p** *of* your commands, 5985
119:101 I have kept my feet from every evil **p** so 784
119:104 therefore I hate every wrong **p**. 784
119:105 a lamp to my feet and a light for my **p**. 5986
119:128 I hate every wrong **p**. 784
140: 5 and have set traps for me along my **p**. 5047
142: 3 In the **p** where I walk men have hidden 784
Pr 2: 9 right and just and fair—every good **p**. 5047
4:14 not set foot on the **p** *of* the wicked or walk 784
4:18 The **p** *of* the righteous is like 784
5: 8 Keep to a **p** far from her, 2006
12:28 along that **p** is immortality. 5986
15:10 discipline awaits him who leaves the **p**; 784
15:19 but the **p** *of* the upright is a highway. 784
15:24 The **p** *of* life leads upward for the wise 784
16:29 and leads him down a **p** that is not good. 2006
21:16 from the **p** *of* understanding comes to rest 2006
23:19 and keep your heart on the right **p**. 2006
28:10 along an evil **p** will fall into his own trap, 2006
Ecc 11: 5 As you do not know the **p** *of* the wind, 2006
Isa 3:12 they turn you from the **p**. 784+2006
26: 7 The **p** of the righteous is level; 784
30:11 Leave this way, get off this **p**, 784
40:14 or showed him the **p** *of* understanding? 2006
41: 3 by a **p** his feet have not traveled before. 784
43:16 a **p** through the mighty waters, 5986
Jer 23:12 "Therefore their **p** will become slippery; 2006
31: 9 on a level **p** where they will not stumble, 2006
La 3:11 he dragged me from the **p** and mangled me 2006
Hos 2: 6 Therefore I will block her **p** 2006
13: 7 like a leopard I will lurk by the **p**. 2006
Mt 13: 4 some fell along the **p**, *3847*
13:19 This is the seed sown along the **p**. *3847*
Mk 4: 4 some fell along the **p**, *3847*
4:15 Some people are like seed along the **p**, *3847*
Lk 1:79 to guide our feet into the **p** of peace." *3847*
8: 5 some fell along the **p**; *3847*
8:12 Those along the **p** are the ones who hear, *3847*
2Co 6: 3 We put no stumbling block in anyone's **p**, *NIG*

PATHRUSITES (2)
Ge 10:14 **P**, Casluhites (from whom the Philistines 7357
1Ch 1:12 **P**, Casluhites (from whom the Philistines 7357

PATHS (41) [PATH]
Jdg 5: 6 travelers took to winding **p**. 784
Job 13:27 on all my **p** by putting marks on the soles 784
19: 8 he has shrouded my **p** in darkness. 5986
24:13 who do not know its ways or stay in its **p**. 5986
33:11 he keeps close watch on all my **p**.' 784
38:20 Do you know the **p** *to* their dwellings? 5986
Ps 8: 8 all that swim the **p** *of* the seas. 784
17: 5 My steps have held to your **p**; 5047
23: 3 in **p** *of* righteousness for his name's sake. 5047
25: 4 O LORD, teach me your **p**; 2006
Pr 1:15 do not set foot on their **p**; 5986
2:13 the straight **p** to walk in dark ways, 784
2:15 whose **p** are crooked and who are devious 784
2:18 to death and her **p** to the spirits of the dead. 5047
2:19 return or attain the **p** of life. 784
2:20 and keep to the **p** *of* the righteous. 784
3: 6 and he will make your **p** straight. 784
3:17 and all her **p** are peace. 5986
4:11 of wisdom and lead you along straight **p**. 5047
4:26 Make level **p** *for* your feet 5047
5: 6 her **p** are crooked, but she knows it not. 5047
5:21 and he examines all his **p**. 5047
7:25 to her ways or stray into her **p**. 5986
8: 2 where the **p** meet, she takes her stand; 5986
8:20 along the **p** *of* justice, 5986
10: 9 he who takes crooked **p** will be found out. 2006
22: 5 the **p** *of* the wicked lie thorns and snares, 2006
Isa 2: 3 so that we may walk in his **p**." 784
42:16 along unfamiliar **p** I will guide them; 5986
59: 8 there is no justice in their **p**. 5047
Jer 6:16 ask for the ancient **p**, 5986
18:15 in their ways and in the ancient **p**. 8666
La 3: 9 he has made my **p** crooked. 5986
Hos 9: 8 yet snares await him on all his **p**, 2006
Mic 4: 2 so that we may walk in his **p**." 784
Mt 3: 3 make straight **p** for him.' " *5561*
Mk 1: 3 make straight **p** for him.' " *5561*
Lk 3: 4 make straight **p** for him. *5561*
Ac 2:28 You have made known to me the **p** of life; *3847*
Ro 11:33 and his **p** beyond tracing out! *3847*
Heb 12:13 "Make level **p** for your feet," *5579*

PATIENCE (17) [PATIENT]
Pr 19:11 A man's wisdom **gives** him **p**; 678+799
25:15 Through **p** a ruler can be persuaded, 678+802
Ecc 7: 8 and **p** is better than pride. 800+8120
Isa 7:13 Is it not enough *to* **try** *the* **p** *of* men? 4206
7:13 *Will you* **try** *the* **p** *of* my God also? 4206
Ro 2: 4 the riches *of* his kindness, tolerance and **p**, *3429*
9:22 bore with great **p** the objects of his wrath— *3429*
2Co 6: 6 understanding, **p** and kindness; *3429*
Gal 5:22 the fruit of the Spirit is love, joy, peace, **p**, *3429*
Col 1:11 that you may have great endurance and **p**, *3429*
3:12 kindness, humility, gentleness and **p**. *3429*
1Ti 1:16 Christ Jesus might display his unlimited **p** *3429*
2Ti 3:10 my way of life, my purpose, faith, **p**, love, *3429*
4: 2 with **great p** and careful instruction. *3429+4246*
Heb 6:12 and **p** inherit what has been promised. *3429*
Jas 5:10 as an example *of* **p** in the face of suffering, *3429*
2Pe 3:15 in mind that our Lord's **p** means salvation, *3429*

PATIENT (19) [PATIENCE, PATIENTLY]
Ne 9:30 For many years *you were* **p** with them. 5432
Job 6:11 What prospects, that I *should be* **p**? 799
Pr 14:29 A **p** *man* has great understanding, 678+800
15:18 but a **p** *man* calms a quarrel. 678+800
16:32 Better a **p** *man* than a warrior, 678+800
Mt 18:26 '*Be* **p** with me,' he begged, *3428*
18:29 '*Be* **p** with me, and I will pay you back.' *3428*
Ro 12:12 Be joyful in hope, **p** in affliction, *5702*
1Co 13: 4 Love *is* **p**, love is kind. *3428*
2Co 1: 6 which produces in you **p endurance** of *5705*
Eph 4: 2 be **p**, bearing with one another in love. *3429*
1Th 5:14 help the weak, *be* **p** with everyone. *3428*
Jas 5: 7 *Be* **p**, then, brothers, until *3428*
5: 7 to yield its valuable crop and how **p** he is *3428*
5: 8 You too, *be* **p** and stand firm, *3428*
2Pe 3: 9 *He is* **p** with you, *3428*
Rev 1: 9 the suffering and kingdom and **p endurance** *5705*
13:10 for **p endurance** and faithfulness on the part *5705*
14:12 This calls for **p endurance** on the part of *5705*

PATIENTLY (9) [PATIENT]
Ps 37: 7 before the LORD and **wait p** for him; 2565
40: 1 *I* **waited p for** the LORD; 7747+7747
Isa 38:13 *I* **waited p** till dawn, 8750
Hab 3:16 Yet *I will* **wait p** for the day of calamity 5663
Ac 26: 3 Therefore, I beg you to listen to me **p**. *3430*
Ro 8:25 we wait for it **p**. *1328+5705*
Heb 6:15 And so *after* **waiting p**, *3428*
1Pe 3:20 when God waited **p** in the days of Noah *3429*
Rev 3:10 you have kept my command **to endure p**, *5705*

PATMOS (1)
Rev 1: 9 was on the island of **P** because of the word *4253*

PATRIARCH (2) [PATRIARCHS]
Ac 2:29 that the **p** David died and was buried, *4256*
Heb 7: 4 Even the **p** Abraham gave him a tenth of *4256*

PATRIARCHS (6) [PATRIARCH]
Jn 7:22 did not come from Moses, but from the **p**), *4252*
Ac 7: 8 Jacob became the father of the twelve **p**. *4256*
7: 9 "Because the **p** were jealous of Joseph, *4256*
Ro 9: 5 Theirs are the **p**, from them is traced *4252*
11:28 they are loved on account of the **p**, *4252*
15: 8 to confirm the promises *made to* the **p** *4252*

PATROBAS (1)
Ro 16:14 Greet Asyncritus, Phlegon, Hermes, **P**, *4259*

PATTERN (9)
Ex 25: 9 like the **p** I will show you. 9322
25:40 to the **p** shown you on the mountain. 9322
Nu 8: 4 The lampstand was made exactly like the **p** 5260
Ac 7:44 according to the **p** he had seen. *5596*
Ro 5:14 who was a **p** of the one to come. *5596*
12: 2 *Do* not **conform** *any longer* **to the p of** *5372*
Php 3:17 according to the **p** we gave you. *5596*
2Ti 1:13 keep as the **p** of sound teaching, *5721*
Heb 8: 5 to the **p** shown you on the mountain." *5596*

PAU (2)

Ge 36:39 His city was named P, 7185
1Ch 1:50 His city was named P, 7185

PAUL (202) [PAUL'S, SAUL]

Ac 13: 9 Then Saul, who was also called P, 4263
13:13 P and his companions sailed to Perga 4263
13:16 P motioned with his hand and said: 4263
13:42 As P and Barnabas were leaving 899S
13:43 and devout converts to Judaism followed P 4263
13:45 abusively against what P was saying. 4263
13:46 P and Barnabas answered them boldly: 4263
13:50 persecution against P and Barnabas, 4263
14: 1 At Iconium P and Barnabas went as usual 899S
14: 3 So P and Barnabas spent considerable time there, NIG
14: 9 He listened to P as he was speaking. 4263
14: 9 P looked directly at him, 4005S
14:11 When the crowd saw what P had done, 4263
14:12 and P they called Hermes because he was 4263
14:14 the apostles Barnabas and P heard of this, 4263
14:19 They stoned P and dragged him outside 4263
14:23 P and Barnabas appointed elders for them NIG
15: 2 This brought P and Barnabas into sharp 4263
15: 2 So P and Barnabas were appointed, 4263
15:12 as they listened to Barnabas and P telling 4263
15:22 send them to Antioch with P and Barnabas. 4263
15:25 with our dear friends Barnabas and P— 4263
15:35 But P and Barnabas remained in Antioch, 4263
15:36 Some time later P said to Barnabas, 4263
15:38 but P did not think it wise to take him, 4263
15:40 but P chose Silas and left, 4263
16: 3 P wanted to take him along on the journey, 4263
16: 6 P and his companions traveled throughout NIG
16: 9 During the night P had a vision of a man 4263
16:10 After P had seen the vision, NIG
16:17 This girl followed P and the rest of us, 4263
16:18 Finally P became so troubled 4263
16:19 they seized P and Silas and dragged them 4263
16:22 in the attack against P and Silas, 899S
16:25 About midnight P and Silas were praying 4263
16:28 But P shouted, "Don't harm yourself! 4263
16:29 in and fell trembling before P and Silas. 4263
16:36 The jailer told P, "The magistrates 4263
16:37 But P said to the officers: 4263
16:38 that P and Silas were Roman citizens, NIG
16:40 After P and Silas came out of the prison, NIG
17: 2 P went into the synagogue, 4263
17: 4 of the Jews were persuaded and joined P 4263
17: 5 to Jason's house in search of P and Silas 899S
17:10 brothers sent P and Silas away to Berea. 4263
17:11 to see if what P said was true. 4047S
17:13 that P was preaching the word of God 4263
17:14 The brothers immediately sent P to 4263
17:15 The men who escorted P brought him 4263
17:16 While P was waiting for them in Athens, 4263
17:18 because P was preaching the good news NIG
17:22 P then stood up in the meeting of 4263
17:33 At that, P left the Council. 4263
17:34 A few men became followers of P 899S
18: 1 this, P left Athens and went to Corinth. NIG
18: 2 P went to see them, NIG
18: 5 P devoted himself exclusively 4263
18: 6 the Jews opposed P and became abusive, NIG
18: 7 Then P left the synagogue NIG
18: 9 One night the Lord spoke to P in a vision: 4263
18:11 So P stayed for a year and a half, NIG
18:12 a united attack on P and brought him 4263
18:14 Just as P was about to speak, 4263
18:18 P stayed on in Corinth for some time. 4263
18:19 where P left Priscilla and Aquila. NIG
18:23 P set out from there and traveled NIG
19: 1 P took the road through the interior 4263
19: 3 So P asked, "Then what baptism did you receive?" NIG
19: 4 P said, "John's baptism was a baptism 4263
19: 6 When P placed his hands on them, 4263
19: 8 P entered the synagogue and spoke NIG
19: 9 So P left them. NIG
19:11 God did extraordinary miracles through P, 4263
19:13 "In the name of Jesus, whom P preaches, 4263
19:15 and I know about P, but who are you?" 4263
19:21 P decided to go to Jerusalem, 4263
19:26 and hear how this fellow P has convinced 4263
19:30 P wanted to appear before the crowd, 4263
19:31 of P, sent him a message begging him not 899S
20: 1 P sent for the disciples and, 4263
20: 7 P spoke to the people and, 4263
20: 9 into a deep sleep as P talked on and on. 4263
20:10 P went down, threw himself on 4263
20:13 where we were going to take P aboard. 4263
20:16 P had decided to sail past Ephesus 4263
20:17 P sent to Ephesus for the elders of NIG
21: 4 Through the Spirit they urged P not to go 4263
21:12 we and the people there pleaded with P not 899S
21:13 Then P answered, "Why are you weeping 4263
21:18 The next day P and the rest of us went 4263
21:19 P greeted them and reported NIG
21:20 Then they said to P: 899S
21:26 The next day P took the men 4263
21:27 the province of Asia saw P at the temple. 899S
21:29 in the city with P and assumed 899S
21:29 and assumed that P had brought him into 4263
21:30 Seizing P, they dragged him from the 4263
21:32 and his soldiers, they stopped beating P. 4263
Ac 21:34 that P be taken into the barracks. 899S
21:35 When P reached the steps, NIG
21:37 As the soldiers were about to take P into 4263
21:39 P answered, "I am a Jew, 4263
21:40 P stood on the steps and motioned to 4263
22: 2 they became very quiet. Then P said: NIG
22:22 The crowd listened to P until he said this. 899S
22:24 the commander ordered P to be taken into 899S
22:25 P said to the centurion standing there, 4263
22:27 The commander went to P and asked, NIG
22:28 "But I was born a citizen," P replied. 4263
22:29 when he realized that he had put P, 899S
22:30 to find out exactly why P was being accused NIG
22:30 Then he brought P and had him stand 4263
23: 1 P looked straight at the Sanhedrin and said, 4263
23: 2 near P to strike him on the mouth. 899S
23: 3 Then P said to him, "God will strike you, 4263
23: 4 Those who were standing near P said, NIG
23: 5 P replied, "Brothers, I did not realize 4263
23: 6 Then P, knowing that some of them 4263
23:10 the commander was afraid P would be torn 4263
23:11 The following night the Lord stood near P 899S
23:12 not to eat or drink until they had killed P. 4263
23:14 not to eat anything until we have killed P. 4263
23:16 he went into the barracks and told P. 4263
23:17 P called one of the centurions and said, 4263
23:18 The centurion said, "P, the prisoner, 4263
23:20 to bring P before the Sanhedrin tomorrow 4263
23:24 Provide mounts for P so that he may 4263
23:31 took P with them during the night 4263
23:33 to the governor and handed P over to him. 4263
23:35 Then he ordered that P be kept under guard 899S
24: 1 and they brought their charges against P 4263
24: 2 When P was called in, 899S
24:10 for him to speak, P replied: 4263
24:23 the centurion to keep P under guard but 899S
24:24 for P and listened to him as he spoke 4263
24:25 As P discoursed on righteousness, 899S
24:26 that P would offer him a bribe, 4263
24:27 he left P in prison. 4263
25: 2 and presented the charges against P. 4263
25: 3 to have P transferred to Jerusalem, 899S
25: 4 "P is being held at Caesarea, 4263
25: 6 and ordered that P be brought before him. 4263
25: 7 When P appeared, the Jews who had come 899S
25: 8 Then P made his defense: 4263
25: 9 wishing to do the Jews a favor, said to P, 4263
25:10 P answered: "I am now standing before 4263
25:19 about a dead man named Jesus who P claimed was alive. 4263
25:21 When P made his appeal to be held over 4263
25:23 P was brought in. 4263
26: 1 Then Agrippa said to P, 4263
26: 1 So P motioned with his hand 4263
26:24 "You are out of your mind, P!" 4263
26:25 most excellent Festus," P replied. 4263
26:28 Then Agrippa said to P, "Do you think 4263
26:29 P replied, "Short time or long— 4263
27: 1 P and some other prisoners were handed 4263
27: 3 and Julius, in kindness to P, 4263
27: 9 So P warned them, 4263
27:11 instead of listening to what P said, 4263
27:21 P stood up before them and said: 4263
27:24 and said, 'Do not be afraid, P. 4263
27:31 P said to the centurion and the soldiers, 4263
27:33 Just before dawn P urged them all to eat. 4263
28: 3 P gathered a pile of brushwood and, 4263
28: 5 P shook the snake off into the fire 3525+3836S
28: 8 P went in to see him and, after prayer, 4263
28:15 At the sight of these men P thanked God 4263
28:16 P was allowed to live by himself, 4263
28:17 When they had assembled, P said to them: NIG
28:23 They arranged to meet P on a certain day, 899S
28:25 after P had made this final statement: 4263
28:30 For two whole years P stayed there NIG
Ro 1: 1 P, a servant of Christ Jesus, 4263
1Co 1: 1 P, called to be an apostle of Christ Jesus 4263
1:12 One of you says, "I follow P"; 4263
1:13 Was P crucified for you? 4263
1:13 Were you baptized into the name of P? 4263
3: 4 For when one says, "I follow P," 4263
3: 5 And what is P? Only servants, 4263
3:22 whether P or Apollos or Cephas or 4263
16:21 I, P, write this greeting in my own hand. 4263
2Co 1: 1 P, an apostle of Christ Jesus by the will 4263
10: 1 I, P, who am "timid" when face to face 4263
Gal 1: 1 P, an apostle—sent not from men nor by man, but by Jesus Christ 4263
5: 2 P, tell you that if you let yourselves 4263
Eph 1: 1 P, an apostle of Christ Jesus by the will 4263
3: 1 For this reason I, P, the prisoner of Christ 4263
Php 1: 1 P and Timothy, servants of Christ Jesus, 4263
Col 1: 1 P, an apostle of Christ Jesus by the will 4263
1:23 and of which I, P, have become a servant. 4263
4:18 I, P, write this greeting in my own hand. 4263
1Th 1: 1 P, Silas and Timothy, 4263
2:18 certainly I, P, did, again and again— 4263
2Th 1: 1 P, Silas and Timothy, 4263
3:17 I, P, write this greeting in my own hand, 4263
1Ti 1: 1 P, an apostle of Christ Jesus by the command of God our Savior 4263
2Ti 1: 1 P, an apostle of Christ Jesus by the will of 4263
Tit 1: 1 P, a servant of God and an apostle of Jesus 4263
Phm 1: 1 P, a prisoner of Christ Jesus, 4263
1: 9 I then, as P—an old man and now also a 4263
1:19 I, P, am writing this with my own hand. 4263
2Pe 3:15 as our dear brother P also wrote you with 4263

PAUL'S (7) [PAUL]

Ac 16:14 opened her heart to respond to P message. 4263
19:29 P traveling companions from Macedonia, 4263
21:11 Coming over to us, he took P belt, 4263
23:16 when the son of P sister heard of this plot, 4263
25:14 Festus discussed P case with the king. 4263
26:24 At this point Festus interrupted P defense. 899S
27:43 But the centurion wanted to spare P life 4263

PAULUS (1) [SERGIUS]

Ac 13: 7 an attendant of the proconsul, Sergius P. 4263

PAVEMENT (9)

Ex 24:10 Under his feet was something like a p made 4246
2Ch 7: 3 on the p with their faces to the ground, 8367
Est 1: 6 and silver on a mosaic p of porphyry, 8367
Jer 43: 9 and bury them in clay in the brick p at 4861
Eze 40:17 a p that had been constructed all around 8367
40:17 there were thirty rooms along the p. 8367
40:18 this was the lower p. 8367
42: 3 and in the section opposite the p of 8367
Jn 19:13 at a place known as the Stone P 3346

PAVILION (2)

Job 36:29 how he thunders from his p? 6109
Ps 19: 5 like a bridegroom coming forth from his p, 2903

PAW (2) [PAWS]

1Sa 17:37 The LORD who delivered me from the p 3338
17:37 and the p of the bear will deliver me from 3338

PAWS (2) [PAW]

Lev 11:27 that walk on their p are unclean for you; 4090
Job 39:21 He p fiercely, rejoicing in his strength, 2916

PAY (140) [PAID, PAYING, PAYMENT, PAYS, REPAID, REPAY, REPAYING, REPAYMENT, REPAYS]

Ge 23:13 I will p the price of the field. 5989
30:28 "Name your wages, and I will p them." 5989
34:12 and I'll p whatever you ask me. 5989
43:28 And they bowed low to p him honor. 2556
Ex 2: 9 nurse him for me, and I will p you." 5989+8510
4: 8 or p attention to the first miraculous sign, 9048
5: 9 that they keep working and p no attention 9120
15:26 if you p attention to his commands 263
21:19 however, he must p the injured man for 5989
21:32 the owner must p thirty shekels of silver to 5989
21:34 the owner of the pit must p for the loss; 8966
21:34 he must p its owner, 4084+8740
21:36 the owner must p, animal for animal, 8966+8966
22: 1 he must p back five head of cattle for 8966
22: 3 he must be sold to p for his theft. NIH
22: 4 he must p back double. 8966
22: 7 if he is caught, must p back double. 8966
22: 9 judges declare guilty must p back double 8966
22:13 not be required to p for the torn animal. 8966
22:15 the borrower will not have to p. 8966
22:16 he must p the bride-price, 4555+4555
22:17 he must still p the bride-price 4084+9202
23:21 P attention to him and listen 9068
30:12 each one must p the LORD a ransom 5989
Lev 25:51 he must p for his redemption a larger share 8740
25:52 that and p for his redemption accordingly. 8740
26:41 and they p for their sin, 8355
26:43 They will p for their sins 8355
27: 8 If anyone making the vow is too poor to p 4575
27:23 and the man must p its value on that day 5989
Nu 20:19 any of your water, we will p for it. 4836+5989
Dt 2: 6 p them in silver for the food you eat 8690
7:12 If you p attention to these laws 9048
22:29 he shall p the girl's father fifty shekels 5989
23:18 of the LORD your God to p any vow, NIH
23:21 do not be slow to p it, 8966
24:15 P him his wages each day before sunset, 5989
28:13 If you p attention to the commands of 9048
Jdg 9:57 made the men of Shechem p for 928+8031+8740
1Sa 4:20 But she did not respond or p any attention. 8883
6: 5 and p honor to Israel's god. 5989
25:25 May my lord p no attention to 8492
2Sa 1: 2 he fell to the ground to p him honor. 2556
9: 6 he bowed down to p him honor. 2556
12: 6 He must p for that lamb four times over, 8966
14: 4 with her face to the ground to p him honor, 2556
14:22 with his face to the ground to p him honor, 2556
1Ki 2:23 so severely, if Adonijah does not p with 928
5: 6 and I will p you for your men whatever 5989
20:39 or you must p a talent of silver.' 9202
21: 2 I will p you whatever it is worth." 4084+5989
2Ki 4: 7 "Go, sell the oil and p your debts. 8966
9:26 and I will surely make you p for it 8966
12:15 to whom they gave the money to p 5989
18:14 I will p whatever you demand of me." 5951
22: 5 And have these men p the workers 5989
Ne 5: 4 "We have had to borrow money to p 4200
9:34 they did not p attention to your commands 7992
Est 3: 2 not kneel down or p him honor. 2556
3: 5 not kneel down or p him honor, 2556
4: 7 of money Haman had promised to p into 9202
Job 6:22 p a ransom for me from your wealth, 8815
33: 1 p attention to everything I say. 263
33:31 "P attention, Job, and listen to me; 7992

Job 41:11 a claim against me that *I must* **p?** 8966
Ps 79:12 **P back** into the laps of our neighbors 8740
94: 2 **p back** to the proud what they deserve. 8740
Pr 4: 1 **p attention** and gain understanding. 7992
4:20 My son, **p attention** to what I say; 7992
5: 1 My son, **p attention** to my wisdom, 7992
6:31 Yet if he is caught, *he must* **p** sevenfold, 8966
7:24 **p attention** to what I say. 7992
13:13 He who scorns instruction *will* **p for it,** 2472
19:19 A hot-tempered man *must* **p** the penalty; 5951
20:22 *"I'll* **p** you **back** *for* this wrong!" 8966
22:17 **P attention** and listen to the sayings of 265+5742
22:27 if you lack the means to **p,** 8966
24:29 *I'll* **p** that man **back** *for* what he did." 8740
30:10 and *you will* **p for it.** 870
Ecc 7:21 not **p** attention to every word people say, 5989
Isa 28:23 **p attention** and hear what I say. 7992
34: 1 **p attention,** *you* peoples! 7992
42:23 or **p close attention** in time 2256+7992+9048
65: 6 not keep silent but *will* **p back in full;** 8966
65: 6 *I will* **p** it **back** into their laps— 8966
Jer 7:24 But they did not listen or **p attention;** 265+5742
7:26 they did not listen to me or **p attention.** 265+5742
11: 8 But they did not listen or **p attention;** 265+5742
13:15 Hear and **p attention,** do not be arrogant, 263
17:23 Yet they did not listen or **p attention;** 265+5742
18:18 and **p** no **attention** to anything he says." 7992
34:14 not listen to me or **p attention** to me. 265+5742
44: 5 But they did not listen or **p attention;** 265+5742
51: 6 he *will* **p** her what she deserves. 8966
La 3:64 **P** them **back** what they deserve, O LORD, 8740
Eze 16:41 and *you will* no longer **p** your lovers. 924+5989
29:19 and plunder the land as **p** for his army. 8510
40: 4 and **p** attention to everything I am going 8492
Da 3:12 who **p** no attention to you, O king. 10682
Hos 2:12 which she said were her **p** from her lovers; 921
5: 1 **P attention,** *you* Israelites! 7992
12:12 and to **p** for her he tended sheep. NIH
Zec 1: 4 But they would not listen or **p attention** 7992
7:11 "But they refused to **p attention;** 7992
11:12 "If you think it best, give me my **p;** 8510
Mt 7: 3 and **p** no **attention to** the plank *2917*
17:24 "Doesn't your teacher **p** the temple tax?" *5464*
18:25 Since he was not able *to* **p,** *625*
18:26 he begged, 'and *I will* **p back** everything.' *625*
18:28 **'P back** what you owe me!' *625*
18:29 and *I will* **p** you **back.'** *625*
18:30 the man thrown into prison until *he could* **p** *625*
18:34 until *he should* **p back** all he owed. *625*
20: 2 He agreed to **p** them a denarius for the day *NIG*
20: 4 and *I will* **p** you whatever is right.' *1443*
20: 8 'Call the workers and **p** them their wages, *625*
20:14 Take your **p** and go. *NIG*
22:16 **p** no **attention to who they are.** *476+1063+4725*
22:17 Is it right *to* **p** taxes to Caesar or not?" *1443*
Mk 12:14 **p** no **attention to who they are;** *476+1063+4725*
12:14 Is it right *to* **p** taxes to Caesar or not? *1443*
12:15 *Should we* **p** or shouldn't we?" *1443*
Lk 3:14 be content *with* your **p."** *4072*
6:41 and **p** no **attention to** the plank *2917*
7:42 of them had the money *to* **p** him **back,** *625*
19: 8 *I will* **p back** four times the amount." *625*
20:22 Is it right for us *to* **p** taxes to Caesar *1443*
Ac 21:24 their purification rites and **p** their **expenses,** *1251*
22:28 **p** a big price **for** my citizenship." *3227*
25:13 at Caesarea *to* **p** *their* **respects to** Festus. *832*
Ro 13: 6 This is also why *you* **p** taxes, *5464*
13: 7 If you owe taxes, **p** taxes; *NIG*
Gal 5:10 you into confusion *will* **p** the penalty, *1002*
2Th 1: 6 *He will* **p back** trouble on those who *500*
Tit 1:14 and *will* **p** no **attention** to Jewish myths *4668*
Phm 1:19 I *will* **p** it **back**—not to mention that you owe *702*
Heb 2: 1 **p** more careful **attention,** therefore, **to** *4668*
Jas 5: 4 The wages *you* **failed to p** *691*
2Pe 1:19 and you will do well to **p attention** to it, *4668*
Rev 18: 6 **p** her **back double** for what she has done. *1486+1488*

PAYING (9) [PAY]

Ex 21: 2 he shall go free, **without p anything.** 2855
21:30 *by* **p** whatever is demanded. 5989
2Sa 24:24 *I* **insist on p** you **for** it. 928+4697+7864+7864
1Ch 21:24 "No, *I* **insist on p** the full price. 7864+7864
Jer 22:13 not **p** them *for* their labor. 5989
Joel 3: 4 If you *are* **p** me **back,** 1694
Jnh 1: 3 After **p** the fare, he went aboard 5989
Mt 22:19 Show me the coin used for **p** the tax." *NIG*
2Th 3: 8 did we eat anyone's food **without p for it.** *1562*

PAYMENT (15) [PAY]

Ge 31:39 And *you* **demanded p** from me 1335
47:14 Egypt and Canaan **in p for** the grain 928
Ex 21:11 is to go free, **without any p** of money. 401+2855
21:30 However, if **p** is demanded of him, 4111
Lev 22:16 and so bring upon them guilt **requiring p.** 873
Dt 15: 2 not **require p** *from* his fellow Israelite 5601
15: 3 *You may* **require p** *from* a foreigner, 5601
Job 31:39 without **p** or broken the spirit of its tenants, 4084
Ps 49: 8 the ransom for a life is costly, no **p** is ever enough— NIH
109:20 May this be the LORD's **p** *to* my accusers, 7190
Isa 65: 7 *will* **measure** into their laps **the full p** 4499
Eze 16:31 because you scorned **p.** 924
16:34 for you give **p** and none is given to you. 924
Lk 23: 2 He opposes **p** of taxes to Caesar and claims *1443*
Php 4:18 *I have* **received** full **p** and even more; *600*

PAYS (9) [PAY]

Ge 50:15 and **p** us **back** *for* all the wrongs 8740+8740
Job 35:13 the Almighty **p** no **attention** *to* it. 8800
Ps 31:23 but the proud *he* **p back** in full. 8966
94: 7 the God of Jacob **p** no **heed."** 1067
Pr 17: 4 a liar **p attention** to a malicious tongue. 263
17:13 If a *man* **p back** evil for good, 8740
Da 6:13 **p** no attention to you, O king, 10682
Mal 2:13 and wail because *he* no longer **p attention** 7155
1Th 5:15 that nobody **p back** wrong for wrong, *625*

PAZZEZ See BETH PAZZEZ

PEACE (250) [PACIFIES, PACIFY, PEACE-LOVING, PEACEABLE, PEACEABLY, PEACEFUL, PEACEFULLY, PEACEMAKERS, PEACETIME]

Ge 15:15 will go to your fathers in **p** and be buried at 8934
26:29 and sent you away in **p.** 8934
26:31 and they left him in **p.** 8934
44:17 The rest of you, go back to your father in **p.** 8934
Lev 26: 6 " 'I will grant **p** in the land, 8934
Nu 6:26 turn his face toward you and give you **p."** ' 8934
25:12 I am making my covenant of **p** with him. 8934
Dt 2:26 to Sihon king of Heshbon offering **p** 8934
20:10 make its people an offer of **p.** 8934
20:12 If they refuse *to* **make p** and they engage 8966
Jos 9:15 Then Joshua made a treaty of **p** with them 8934
10: 1 **made a treaty of p** with Israel 8966
10: 4 "because *it has* **made p** with Joshua and 8966
11:19 **made a treaty of p** with the Israelites, 8966
Jdg 3:11 So the land **had p** for forty years, 9200
3:30 and the land **had p** for eighty years. 9200
5:31 Then the land **had p** forty years. 9200
6:23 But the LORD said to him, **"P!** 8934
6:24 and called it The LORD is **P.** 8934
8:28 the land **enjoyed p** forty years. 9200
18: 6 The priest answered them, "Go in **p.** 8934
21:13 Then the whole assembly sent an offer of **p** 8934
1Sa 1:17 Eli answered, "Go in **p,** 8934
7:14 And there was **p** between Israel and 8934
16: 4 They asked, "Do you come **in p?"** 8934
16: 5 Samuel replied, "Yes, **in p;** 8934
20:42 Jonathan said to David, "Go in **p,** 8934
25:35 "Go home in **p.** 8934
29: 7 Turn back and go in **p;** 8934
2Sa 3:21 David sent Abner away, and he went in **p.** 8934
3:22 and he had gone in **p.** 8934
3:23 and that he had gone in **p.** 8934
10:19 *they* **made p** with the Israelites 8966
15: 9 The king said to him, "Go in **p."** 8934
15:27 Go back to the city in **p,** 8934
1Ki 2: 6 his gray head go down to the grave in **p.** 8934
2:33 may there be the LORD's **p** forever." 8934
4:24 and had **p** on all sides. 8934
20:18 He said, "If they have come out for **p,** 8934
22:17 Let each one go home in **p.'** " 8934
22:44 Jehoshaphat *was* also **at p** with the king 8966
2Ki 5:19 "Go in **p,"** Elisha said. 8934
9:17 'Do you **come in p?'** " 8934
9:18 'Do you **come in p?'** " 8934
9:18 "What do you have to do with **p?"** 8934
9:19 'Do you **come in p?'** " 8934
9:19 "What do you have to do with **p?** 8934
9:22 "Have you **come in p,** Jehu?" 8934
9:22 "How can there be **p,"** Jehu replied, 8934
9:31 she asked, "Have you **come in p,** Zimri, 8934
18:31 Make **p** with me and come out to me. 1388
20:19 not be **p** and security in my lifetime?" 8934
22:20 and you will be buried in **p.** 8934
1Ch 12:17 "If you have come to me in **p,** to help me, 8934
19:19 *they* **made p** with David and became subject 8966
22: 9 a son who will be a man of **p and rest,** 4957
22: 9 and I will grant Israel **p** and quiet 8934
2Ch 14: 1 and in his days the country *was* **at p** 9200
14: 5 and the kingdom *was* **at p** under him. 9200
14: 6 since the land *was* **at p.** 9200
18:16 Let each one go home in **p.'** " 8934
20:30 And the kingdom of Jehoshaphat *was* **at p,** 9200
34:28 and you will be buried in **p.** 8934
Job 3:13 For now I would be lying down **in p;** 9200
3:26 *I* **have** no **p,** no quietness; 8922
5:23 the wild animals *will be* **at p** with you. 8966
21:13 in prosperity and go down to the grave in **p.** 8092
22:21 "Submit to God and *be* **at p** with him; 8966
Ps 4: 8 I will lie down and sleep in **p,** 8934
7: 4 if I have done evil to *him who is* **at p** 8966
29:11 the LORD blesses his people with **p.** 8934
34:14 seek **p** and pursue it. 8934
37:11 the land and enjoy great **p.** 8934
37:37 there is a future for the man of **p.** 8934
85: 8 he promises **p** to his people, his saints— 8934
85:10 righteousness and **p** kiss each other. 8934
119:165 Great **p** have they who love your law, 8934
120: 6 among those who hate **p.** 8934
120: 7 I am a man of **p;** 8934
122: 6 Pray for the **p** *of* Jerusalem: 8934
122: 7 May there be **p** within your walls and 8934
122: 8 I will say, **"P** be within you." 8934
125: 5 **P** be upon Israel. 8934
128: 6 **P** be upon Israel. 8934
147:14 He grants **p** to your borders 8934
Pr 3:17 and all her paths are **p.** 8934
12:20 but joy for those who promote **p.** 8934
14:30 A heart **at p** gives life to the body, 5341
16: 7 **makes** even his enemies **live at p** with him. 8966
17: 1 Better a dry crust with **p and quiet** than 8932
29: 9 the fool rages and scoffs, and there is no **p.** 5739
29:17 and *he will* **give** you **p;** 5663
Ecc 3: 8 a time for war and a time for **p.** 8934
Isa 9: 6 Everlasting Father, Prince of **P.** 8934
9: 7 of his government and **p** there will 8934
14: 7 All the lands are at rest and **at p;** 9200
26: 3 You will keep in **perfect p** him whose mind is steadfast, 8934+8934
26:12 LORD, you establish **p** for us; 8934
27: 5 let them make **p** with me, yes, 8934
27: 5 yes, let them make **p** with me." 8934
32:17 The fruit of righteousness will be **p;** 8934
33: 7 the envoys of **p** weep bitterly. 8934
36:16 Make **p** with me and come out to me. 1388
39: 8 be **p** and security in my lifetime." 8934
48:18 your **p** would have been like a river, 8934
48:22 "There is no **p,"** says the LORD, 8934
52: 7 who proclaim **p,** who bring good tidings, 8934
53: 5 the punishment that brought us **p** was 8934
54:10 not be shaken nor my covenant of **p** 8934
54:13 and great will be your children's **p.** 8934
55:12 in joy and be led forth in **p;** 8934
57: 2 Those who walk uprightly enter into **p;** 8934
57:19 **P,** peace, to those far and near," 8934
57:19 Peace, **p,** to those far and near," 8934
57:21 "There is no **p,"** says my God, 8934
59: 8 The way of **p** they do not know; 8934
59: 8 no one who walks in them will know **p.** 8934
60:17 I will make **p** your governor 8934
66:12 "I will extend **p** to her like a river, 8934
Jer 4:10 'You will have **p,'** 8934
6:14 **'P,** peace,' they say, when there is no peace. 8934
6:14 **p,'** they say, when there is no peace. 8934
6:14 peace,' they say, when there is no **p.** 8934
8:11 **"P,** peace," they say, when there is no peace 8934
8:11 "Peace, **p,"** they say, when there is no peace 8934
8:11 peace," they say, when there is no **p.** 8934
8:15 We hoped for **p** but no good has come, 8934
14:13 I will give you lasting **p** in this place.' " 8934
14:19 We hoped for **p** but no good has come, 8934
23:17 You will have **p.'** 8934
28: 9 But the prophet who prophesies **p** will 8934
29: 7 seek the **p and prosperity** *of* the city 8934
30: 5 of fear are heard—terror, not **p.** 8934
30:10 Jacob will again **have p** and security, 9200
33: 6 and will let them enjoy abundant **p** 8934
33: 9 at the abundant prosperity and **p** I provide 8934
46:27 Jacob will again **have p** and security, 9200
La 3:17 I have been deprived of **p;** 8934
Eze 7:25 When terror comes, they will seek **p,** 8934
13:10 they lead my people astray, saying, **"P,"** 8934
13:10 "Peace," when there is no **p,** and because, 8934
13:16 to Jerusalem and saw visions of **p** for her 8934
13:16 of peace for her when there was no **p,** 8934
34:25 a covenant of **p** with them and rid the land 8934
37:26 I will make a covenant of **p** with them; 8934
Da 10:19 O man highly esteemed," he said. **"P!** 8934
Mic 3: 5 if one feeds them, they proclaim **'p';** 8934
5: 5 And he will be their **p.** 8934
Na 1:15 brings good news, who proclaims **p!** 8934
Hag 2: 9 'And in this place I will grant **p,'** 8934
Zec 1:11 and found the whole world at rest and **in p."** 9200
8:19 Therefore love truth and **p."** 8934
9:10 He will proclaim **p** to the nations. 8934
Mal 2: 5 a covenant of life and **p,** 8934
2: 6 He walked with me in **p** and uprightness, 8934
Mt 10:13 let your **p** rest on it; *1645*
10:13 if it is not, let your **p** return to you. *1645*
10:34 not suppose that I have come to bring **p** to *1645*
10:34 I did not come to bring **p,** but a sword. *1645*
Mk 5:34 Go in **p** and be freed from your suffering." *1645*
9:50 and **be at p** with each other." *1644*
Lk 1:79 to guide our feet into the path *of* **p."** *1645*
2:14 on earth **p** to men on whom his favor rests." *1645*
2:29 you now dismiss your servant in **p.** *1645*
7:50 "Your faith has saved you; go in **p."** *1645*
8:48 your faith has healed you. Go in **p."** *1645*
10: 5 first say, **'P** to this house.' *1645*
10: 6 If a man *of* **p** is there, *1645*
10: 6 your **p** will rest on him; *1645*
12:51 Do you think I came to bring **p** on earth? *1645*
14:32 a long way off and will ask for terms of **p.** *1645*
19:38 **"P** in heaven and glory in the highest!" *1645*
19:42 on this day what would bring you **p—** *1645*
24:36 **"P be with** you." *1645*
Jn 14:27 **P** I leave with you; my peace I give you. *1645*
14:27 Peace I leave with you; my **p** I give you. *1645*
16:33 so that in me you may have **p.** *1645*
20:19 **"P be with** you!" *1645*
20:21 Again Jesus said, **"P be with** you! *1645*
20:26 **"P be with** you!" *1645*
Ac 9:31 Galilee and Samaria enjoyed a time of **p.** *1645*
10:36 the good news of **p** through Jesus Christ, *1645*
12:20 they asked for **p,** *1645*
15:33 the brothers with **the blessing of p** to return *1645*
16:36 Now you can leave. Go in **p."** *1645*
24: 2 "We have enjoyed a long period *of* **p** *1645*
Ro 1: 7 and **p** to you from God our Father and from *1645*
2:10 honor and **p** for everyone who does good: *1645*
3:17 and the way *of* **p** they do not know." *1645*
5: 1 we have **p** with God through our Lord *1645*
8: 6 mind controlled by the Spirit is life and **p;** *1645*

Ro 12:18 **live at p** with everyone. *1644*
14:17 righteousness, **p** and joy in the Holy Spirit, *1645*
14:19 to **p** and to mutual edification. *1645*
15:13 the God of hope fill you with all joy and **p** *1645*
15:33 The God *of* **p** be with you all. Amen. *1645*
16:20 The God *of* **p** will soon crush Satan under your feet. *1645*
1Co 1: 3 Grace and **p** to you from God our Father *1645*
7:15 God has called us to live in **p**. *1645*
14:33 For God is not a God of disorder but *of* **p**. *1645*
16:11 on his way in **p** so that he may return *1645*
2Co 1: 2 Grace and **p** to you from God our Father *1645*
2:13 I still had no **p** of mind, *457*
13:11 be of one mind, **live in p**. *1644*
13:11 the God *of* love and **p** will be with you. *1645*
Gal 1: 3 Grace and **p** to you from God our Father *1645*
5:22 But the fruit of the Spirit is love, joy, **p**, *1645*
6:16 **P** and mercy to all who follow this rule, *1645*
Eph 1: 2 Grace and **p** to you from God our Father *1645*
2:14 For he himself is our **p**, *1645*
2:15 of the two, thus making **p**, *1645*
2:17 and preached **p** to you who were far away *1645*
2:17 to you who were far away and **p** *1645*
4: 3 of the Spirit through the bond *of* **p**. *1645*
6:15 that comes from the gospel *of* **p**. *1645*
6:23 **P** to the brothers, *1645*
Php 1: 2 Grace and **p** to you from God our Father *1645*
4: 7 And the **p** of God, which transcends all *1645*
4: 9 And the God *of* **p** will be with you. *1645*
Col 1: 2 Grace and **p** to you from God our Father. *1645*
1:20 *by* **making p** through his blood, *1647*
3:15 Let the **p** of Christ rule in your hearts, *1645*
3:15 members of one body you were called to **p**. *4005S*
1Th 1: 1 Grace and **p** to you. *1645*
5: 3 While people are saying, "**P** and safety," *1645*
5:13 **Live in p** with each other. *1644*
5:23 May God himself, the God *of* **p**, *1645*
2Th 1: 2 Grace and **p** to you from God the Father *1645*
3:16 the Lord *of* **p** himself give you peace *1645*
3:16 of peace himself give you **p** at all times and *1645*
1Ti 1: 2 Grace, mercy and **p** from God the Father *1645*
2Ti 1: 2 Grace, mercy and **p** from God the Father *1645*
2:22 and pursue righteousness, faith, love and **p**, *1645*
Tit 1: 4 Grace and **p** from God the Father *1645*
Phm 1: 3 Grace to you and **p** from God our Father *1645*
Heb 7: 2 "king of Salem" means "king *of* **p**." *1645*
12:11 it produces a harvest of righteousness and **p** *1646*
12:14 Make every effort to live in **p** with all men *1645*
13:20 May the God *of* **p**, *1645*
Jas 3:18 Peacemakers who sow in **p** raise a harvest *1645*
1Pe 1: 2 Grace and **p** be yours in abundance. *1645*
3:11 he must seek **p** and pursue it. *1645*
5:14 **P** to all of you who are in Christ. *1645*
2Pe 1: 2 Grace and **p** be yours in abundance through *1645*
3:14 blameless and at **p** with him. *1645*
2Jn 1: 3 mercy and **p** from God the Father and *1645*
3Jn 1:14 **P** to you. *1645*
Jude 1: 2 Mercy, **p** and love be yours in abundance. *1645*
Rev 1: 4 Grace and **p** to you from him who is, *1645*
6: 4 Its rider was given power to take **p** from *1645*

PEACE-LOVING (1) [PEACE, LOVE]
Jas 3:17 then **p**, considerate, submissive, *1646*

PEACEABLE (1) [PEACE]
Tit 3: 2 to be **p** and considerate, *285*

PEACEABLY (2) [PEACE]
Jdg 11:13 Now give it back **p**." 928+8934
Ps 35:20 They do not speak **p**, 8934

PEACEFUL (9) [PEACE]
Jdg 18:27 against a **p** and unsuspecting people. 9200
2Sa 20:19 We are the **p** and faithful in Israel. 8966
1Ki 5:12 There were **p relations** between Hiram 8934
1Ch 4:40 and the land was spacious, **p** and quiet. 9200
Isa 32:18 My people will live in **p** dwelling places, 8934
33:20 your eyes will see Jerusalem, a **p** abode, 8633
Jer 25:37 The **p** meadows will be laid waste because 8934
Eze 38:11 I will attack a **p** and unsuspecting people— 9200
1Ti 2: 2 that we may live **p** and quiet lives *2475*

PEACEFULLY (3) [PEACE]
1Ki 2:13 Bathsheba asked him, "Do you come **p**?" 8934
2:13 He answered, "Yes, **p**." 8934
Jer 34: 5 you will die **p**. 928+8934

PEACEMAKERS (2) [PEACE]
Mt 5: 9 Blessed are the **p**, for they will be called sons of God. *1648*
Jas 3:18 **P** who sow in peace raise a harvest *1645+4472*

PEACETIME (1) [PEACE]
1Ki 2: 5 shedding their blood in **p** as if in battle, 8934

PEACOCKS (KJV) See BABOON, OSTRICH

PEAKS (2)
Nu 23: 9 From the rocky **p** I see them, 8031
Ps 95: 4 and the mountain **p** belong to him. 9361

PEAL (1) [PEALS]
Rev 14: 2 and like a loud **p of thunder**. *1103*

PEALS (5) [PEAL]
Rev 4: 5 rumblings and **p of thunder**. *1103*
8: 5 and there came **p of thunder**, rumblings, *1103*
11:19 rumblings, **p of thunder**, *1103*
16:18 **p of thunder** and a severe earthquake. *1103*
19: 6 the roar of rushing waters and like loud **p** *5889*

PEARL (1) [MOTHER-OF-PEARL, PEARLS]
Rev 21:21 each gate made of a single **p**. *3449*

PEARLS (7) [PEARL]
Mt 7: 6 do not throw your **p** to pigs. *3449*
13:45 like a merchant looking for fine **p**. *3449*
1Ti 2: 9 or gold or **p** or expensive clothes, *3449*
Rev 17: 4 precious stones and **p**. *3449*
18:12 silver, precious stones and **p**; *3449*
18:16 precious stones and **p**! *3449*
21:21 The twelve gates were twelve **p**, *3449*

PEBBLE (1) [PEBBLES]
Am 9: 9 and not a **p** will reach the ground. 7656

PEBBLES (1) [PEBBLE]
Ps 147:17 He hurls down his hail like **p**. 7326

PECKED (1)
Pr 30:17 *will be* **p out** *by* the ravens of the valley, 5941

PEDAHEL (1)
Nu 34:28 **P** son of Ammihud, 7010

PEDAHZUR (5)
Nu 1:10 from Manasseh, Gamaliel son of **P**; 7011
2:20 of Manasseh is Gamaliel son of **P**. 7011
7:54 On the eighth day Gamaliel son of **P**, 7011
7:59 This was the offering of Gamaliel son of **P**. 7011
10:23 Gamaliel son of **P** was over the division of 7011

PEDAIAH (8)
2Ki 23:36 mother's name was Zebidah daughter of **P**; 7015
1Ch 3:18 **P**, Shenazzar, Jekamiah, 7015
3:19 The sons of **P**: Zerubbabel and Shimei. 7015
27:20 of Manasseh: Joel son of **P**; 7016
Ne 3:25 **P** son of Parosh 7015
8: 4 and on his left were **P**, Mishael, Malkijah, 7015
11: 7 the son of **P**, the son of Kolaiah, 7015
13:13 Levite named **P** in charge of the storerooms 7015

PEDDLE (1)
2Co 2:17 we do not **p** the word of God **for profit**. *2836*

PEDESTAL (1)
Am 5:26 the **p** *of* your idols, the star of your god— 3962

PEELED (1) [PEELING, PEELS]
Ge 30:38 the **p** branches in all the watering troughs, 7202

PEELING (1) [PEELED]
Ge 30:37 on them *by* **p** *the bark* and exposing 7202

PEELS (1) [PEELED]
Job 30:30 My skin grows black and **p**; 4946+6584

PEERED (1) [PEERING]
Jdg 5:28 "Through the window **p** Sisera's mother; 9207

PEERING (1) [PEERED]
SS 2: 9 **p** through the lattice. 7438

PEG (7) [PEGS]
Jdg 4:21 up a tent **p** and a hammer and went quietly 3845
4:21 the **p** through his temple into the ground, 3845
4:22 with the **tent p** through his temple— 3845
5:26 Her hand reached for the **tent p**, 3845
Isa 22:23 I will drive him like a **p** into a firm place; 3845
22:25 **p** driven into the firm place will give way; 3845
Zec 10: 4 the cornerstone, from him the **tent p**, 3845

PEGS (8) [PEG]
Ex 27:19 including all the **tent p** *for* it and those for 3845
35:18 the **tent p** *for* the tabernacle and for 3845
38:20 All the **tent p** of the tabernacle and of 3845
38:31 and those for its entrance and all the **tent p** 3845
39:40 the ropes and **tent p** *for* the courtyard; 3845
Nu 3:37 **tent p** and ropes. 3845
4:32 **tent p**, ropes, all their equipment 3845
Eze 15: 3 Do they make **p** from it to hang things on? 3845

PEKAH (11) [PEKAH'S]
2Ki 15:25 **P** son of Remaliah, conspired against him. 7220
15:25 So **P** killed Pekahiah and succeeded him NIH
15:27 **P** son of Remaliah became king of Israel 7220
15:29 In the time of **P** king of Israel, 7220
15:30 of Elah conspired against **P** son 7220
15:32 the second year of **P** son of Remaliah king 7220
15:37 and **P** son of Remaliah against Judah.) 7220
16: 1 the seventeenth year of **P** son of Remaliah, 7220
16: 5 of Aram and **P** son of Remaliah king 7220
2Ch 28: 6 In one day **P** son of Remaliah killed 7220
Isa 7: 1 of Aram and **P** son of Remaliah king 7220

PEKAH'S (1) [PEKAH]
2Ki 15:31 As for the other events of **P** reign, 7220

PEKAHIAH (5) [PEKAHIAH'S]
2Ki 15:22 And **P** his son succeeded him as king. 7222
15:23 **P** son of Menahem became king of Israel 7222
15:24 **P** did evil in the eyes of the LORD. NIH
15:25 of Gilead with him, he assassinated **P**, 2084S
15:25 Pekah killed **P** and succeeded him as king. 2084S

PEKAHIAH'S (1) [PEKAHIAH]
2Ki 15:26 The other events of **P** reign, and all he did, 7222

PEKOD (2)
Jer 50:21 of Merathaim and those who live in **P**. 7216
Eze 23:23 the men of **P** and Shoa and Koa, 7216

PELAIAH (3)
1Ch 3:24 Hodaviah, Eliashib, **P**, Akkub, Johanan, 7126
Ne 8: 7 Kelita, Azariah, Jozabad, Hanan and **P**— 7102
10:10 Shebaniah, Hodiah, Kelita, **P**, Hanan, 7102

PELALIAH (1)
Ne 11:12 Adaiah son of Jeroham, the son of **P**, 7139

PELATIAH (5)
1Ch 3:21 **P** and Jeshaiah, and the sons of Rephaiah, 7124
4:42 five hundred of these Simeonites, led by **P**, 7124
Ne 10:22 **P**, Hanan, Anaiah, 7124
Eze 11: 1 son of Azzur and **P** son of Benaiah, 7125
11:13 **P** son of Benaiah died. 7125

PELEG (8)
Ge 10:25 One was named **P**, because in his time 7105
11:16 he became the father of **P**. 7105
11:17 And after he became the father of **P**, 7105
11:18 When **P** had lived 30 years, 7105
11:19 **P** lived 209 years and had other sons 7105
1Ch 1:19 One was named **P**, because in his time 7105
1:25 Eber, **P**, Reu, 7105
Lk 3:35 the son *of* **P**, the son of Eber, *5744*

PELET (2) [BETH PELET]
1Ch 2:47 Regem, Jotham, Geshan, **P**, 7118
12: 3 Jeziel and **P** the sons of Azmaveth; 7118

PELETH (2) [PELETHITES]
Nu 16: 1 sons of Eliab, and On son of **P**— 7150
1Ch 2:33 The sons of Jonathan: **P** and Zaza. 7150

PELETHITES (7) [PELETH]
2Sa 8:18 of Jehoiada was over the Kerethites and **P**; 7152
15:18 along with all the Kerethites and **P**; 7152
20: 7 and **P** and all the mighty warriors went out 7152
20:23 of Jehoiada was over the Kerethites and **P**; 7152
1Ki 1:38 and the **P** went down and put Solomon 7152
1:44 the Kerethites and the **P**, 7152
1Ch 18:17 of Jehoiada was over the Kerethites and **P**; 7152

PELICAN (KJV) See DESERT OWL

PELONITE (3)
1Ch 11:27 Shammoth the Harorite, Helez the **P**, 7113
11:36 Hepher the Mekerathite, Ahijah the **P**, 7113
27:10 for the seventh month, was Helez the **P**, 7113

PELT (1) [PELTED]
Na 3: 6 *I will* **p** you *with* filth, 8959

PELTED (1) [PELT]
2Sa 16: 6 *He* **p** David and all the king's officials 6232

PELUSIUM (2)
Eze 30:15 I will pour out my wrath on **P**, 6096
30:16 **P** will writhe in agony. 6096

PEN (11) [PENNED, PENS, PENT-UP]
1Sa 6: 7 take their calves away and **p** them **up**. 1074+2025
Ps 45: 1 my tongue is the **p** *of* a skillful writer. 6485
Isa 8: 1 and write on it with an ordinary **p**: 3032
Jer 8: 8 when actually the lying **p** *of* 6485
Mic 2:12 I will bring them together like sheep in a **p**, 1312
Hab 3:17 though there are no sheep in the **p** 4813
Mt 5:18 not the **least stroke of a p**, *3037*
Lk 16:17 **least stroke of a p** to drop out of the Law. *3037*
Jn 10: 1 who does not enter the sheep **p** by the gate, *885*

Jn 10:16 other sheep that are not of this sheep p. 885
3Jn 1:13 but I do not want to do so with p and ink. 2812

PENALTIES (1) [PENALTY]

Pr 19:29 P are prepared for mockers, 9150

PENALTY (11) [PENALTIES]

Lev 5: 6 as a p for the sin he has committed, 871
5: 7 or two young pigeons to the LORD as a p 871
5:15 to the LORD as a p a ram from the flock, 871
6: 6 And as a p he must bring to the priest, 871
Job 8: 4 he gave them over to the p of their sin. 7322
Pr 19:19 A hot-tempered man must pay the p; 6741
Eze 23:49 You will suffer the p for your lewdness 2365
Da 2: 9 there is just one p *for* you. 10186
Lk 23:22 no grounds for the death p. *165+2505*
Ro 1:27 and received in themselves the due p *521*
Gal 5:10 into confusion will pay the p, *3210*

PENCE (KJV) See DENARII, A YEAR'S WAGES, COINS

PENDANTS (1)

Jdg 8:26 the p and the purple garments worn by 5755

PENETRATES (1)

Heb 4:12 it p even to dividing soul and spirit, *1459*

PENIEL (6)

Ge 32:30 So Jacob called the place P, saying, 7161
32:31 The sun rose above him as he passed P, 7159
Jdg 8: 8 to P and made the same request of them, 7159
8: 9 So he said to the men of P, 7159
8:17 also pulled down the tower of P and killed 7159
1Ki 12:25 From there he went out and built up P. 7159

PENINNAH (3)

1Sa 1: 2 one was called Hannah and the other P. 7166
1: 2 P had children, but Hannah had none. 7166
1: 4 his wife P and to all her sons and daughters. 7166

PENITENT (1) [REPENT]

Isa 1:27 her p *ones* with righteousness. 8740

PENNED (3) [PEN]

Ex 21:29 but *has* not kept it p up and it kills a man 9068
21:36 yet the owner *did* not keep it p up, 9068
1Sa 6:10 and p up their calves. 928+1074+2021+3973

PENNIES (1) [PENNY]

Lk 12: 6 Are not five sparrows sold *for* two p? *837*

PENNY (4) [PENNIES]

Mt 5:26 not get out until you have paid the last p. *3119*
10:29 Are not two sparrows sold *for* a p? *837*
Mk 12:42 worth only a fraction of a p. *3119*
Lk 12:59 not get out until you have paid the last p." *3321*

PENNYWORTH (KJV) See EIGHT MONTHS' WAGES

PENS (8) [PEN]

Nu 32:16 to build p here for our livestock and 1556+7366
32:24 and p for your flocks, 1556
32:36 and built p *for* their flocks. 1556
1Sa 24: 3 He came to the sheep p along the way; 1556
2Ch 32:28 and p for the flocks. 774
Ps 50: 9 from your stall or of goats from your p, 4813
78:70 and took him from the sheep p; 4813
Zep 2: 6 will be a place for shepherds and sheep p. 1556

PENT-UP (1) [PEN]

Isa 59:19 For he will come like a p flood that 7639

PENTECOST (3)

Ac 2: 1 When the day *of* P came, *4300*
20:16 if possible, by the day *of* P. *4300*
1Co 16: 8 But I will stay on at Ephesus until P, *4300*

PENUEL (2)

1Ch 4: 4 P was the father of Gedor, 7158
8:25 Iphdeiah and P were the sons of Shashak. 7158

PEOPLE (2213) [PEOPLE'S, PEOPLED, PEOPLES]

Ge 6: 9 blameless among the p of his time, 1887
6:12 the p on earth had corrupted their ways. 1414
6:13 "I am going to put an end to all p, 1414
9:19 from them came *the p who were* scattered AIT
11: 6 "If as one p speaking the same language 6639
12: 1 your p and your father's household and go 4580
12: 5 and the p they had acquired in Haran, 5883
14:16 together with the women and the other p. 6639
14:21 the p and keep the goods for yourself." 5883
17:14 will be cut off from his p; 6638
18:24 if there are fifty righteous *p* in the city? AIT
18:24 for the sake of the fifty righteous *p* AIT
18:26 I find fifty righteous *p* in the city of Sodom, AIT
18:28 the whole city because of five *p?"* AIT
19:13 against its p is so great that he has sent us 4392^S
23: 7 and bowed down before the p *of* the land, 6639
23:10 the Hittite was sitting among his p 1201+3147^S
23:11 give it to you in the presence of my p. 1201+6639
23:12 Again Abraham bowed down before the p 6639
25: 8 and he was gathered to his p. 6638
25:17 and he was gathered to his p. 6638
25:23 *one* p will be stronger than the other, 4211
26:11 So Abimelech gave orders to all the p: 6639
29:22 So Laban brought together all the p *of* 408
32: 7 and distress Jacob divided the p who were 6639
34:16 We'll settle among you and become one p 6639
34:22 with us as one p only on the condition 6639
34:30 the *p* living in this land. AIT
35: 6 and all the p with him came to Luz 6639
35:29 and died and was gathered to his p, 6638
41:40 and all my p are to submit to your orders. 6639
41:55 the p cried to Pharaoh for food. 6639
42: 6 the one who sold grain to all its p. 6639
47:15 of the p of Egypt and Canaan was gone, NIH
47:21 and Joseph reduced the p to servitude, 6639
47:23 Joseph said to the p, 6639
48:19 He too will become a p, 6639
49:16 "Dan will provide justice for his p as one of 6639
49:29 "I am about to be gathered to my p. 6638
49:33 breathed his last and was gathered to his p. 6638
Ex 1: 9 "Look," he said to his p, 6639
1:20 to the midwives and the p increased 6639
1:22 Then Pharaoh gave this order to all his p: 6639
2:11 to where his own p were and watched them 278
2:11 a Hebrew, one of his own p. 278
3: 7 "I have indeed seen the misery of my p 6639
3:10 I am sending you to Pharaoh to bring my p 6639
3:12 When you have brought the p out of Egypt, 6639
3:21 Egyptians favorably disposed toward this p, 6639
4:16 He will speak to the p for you, 6639
4:18 "Let me go back to my own p in Egypt 278
4:21 so that he will not let the p go. 6639
4:30 He also performed the signs before the p, 6639
5: 1 'Let my p go, so that they may hold a 6639
5: 4 why are you taking the p away 6639
5: 5 the p *of* the land are now numerous, 6639
5: 6 and foremen in charge of the p: 6639
5: 7 the p with straw for making bricks; 6639
5:10 and the foremen went out and said to the p, 6639
5:12 So the p scattered all over Egypt 6639
5:16 but the fault is with your own p." 6639
5:22 why have you brought trouble upon this p? 6639
5:23 he has brought trouble upon this p, 6639
5:23 and you have not rescued your p at all." 6639
6: 7 I will take you as my own p, 6639
7: 4 bring out my divisions, my p the Israelites. 6639
7:14 he refuses to let the p go. 6639
7:16 Let my p go, so that they may worship me 6639
8: 1 Let my p go, so that they may worship me. 6639
8: 3 the houses of your officials and on your p, 6639
8: 4 on you and your p and all your officials.' " 6639
8: 8 to take the frogs away from me and my p, 6639
8: 8 and I will let your p go to offer sacrifices to 6639
8: 9 and your p that you and your houses may 6639
8:11 your officials and your p; 6639
8:20 Let my p go, so that they may worship me. 6639
8:21 If you do not let my p go, 6639
8:21 on your p and into your houses. 6639
8:22 land of Goshen, where my p live; 6639
8:23 I will make a distinction between my p 6639
8:23 between my people and your p. 6639
8:29 and his officials and his p. 6639
8:29 by not letting the p go to offer sacrifices to 6639
8:31 and his officials and his p; 6639
8:32 and would not let the p go. 6639
9: 1 Let my p go, so that they may worship me. 6639
9: 7 and he would not let the p go. 6639
9:13 Let my p go, so that they may worship me, 6639
9:14 and against your officials and your p, 6639
9:15 and struck you and your p with a plague 6639
9:17 You still set yourself against my p and will 6639
9:27 and I and my p are in the wrong. 6639
10: 3 Let my p go, so that they may worship me. 6639
10: 7 Let the p go, so that they may worship the 408
11: 2 Tell the p that men and women alike are 6639
11: 3 (The LORD made the Egyptians favorably disposed toward the p, 6639
11: 3 by Pharaoh's officials and by the p.) 6639
11: 8 'Go, you and all the p who follow you!' 6639
12: 4 into account the number of p there are. 5883
12: 6 when all the p *of* the community 7736
12:27 Then the p bowed down and worshiped. 6639
12:31 Leave my p, you and the Israelites! 6639
12:33 the p to hurry and leave the country. 6639
12:34 So the p took their dough before 6639
12:36 The LORD had made the Egyptians favorably disposed toward the p, 6639
12:38 Many other p went up with them, 6850
12:40 the length of time the Israelite *p* lived AIT
13: 3 Then Moses said to the p, 6639
13:17 When Pharaoh let the p go, 6639
13:18 So God led the p around by the desert road 6639
13:22 by night left its place in front of the p. 6639
14: 5 king of Egypt was told that the p had fled, 6639
14:13 Moses answered the p, "Do not be afraid. 6639
14:31 the p feared the LORD and put their trust 6639
15:13 you will lead the p you have redeemed. 6639
Ex 15:14 anguish will grip the p *of* Philistia. 3782
15:15 the p *of* Canaan will melt away; 3782
15:16 until your p pass by, O LORD, 6639
15:16 O LORD, until the p you bought pass by. 6639
15:24 So the p grumbled against Moses, saying, 6639
16: 4 The p are to go out each day 6639
16:27 some of the p went out on the seventh day 6639
16:30 So the p rested on the seventh day. 6639
16:31 The p *of* Israel called the bread manna. 1074
17: 1 but there was no water for the p to drink. 6639
17: 3 But the p were thirsty for water there, 6639
17: 4 "What am I to do with these p? 6639
17: 5 "Walk on ahead of the p. 6639
17: 6 and water will come out of it for the p 6639
18: 1 for Moses and for his p Israel, 6639
18:10 and who rescued the p from the hand of 6639
18:13 to serve as judge for the p, 6639
18:14 that Moses was doing for the p, 6639
18:14 "What is this you are doing for the p? 6639
18:14 while all these p stand around you 6639
18:15 the p come to me to seek God's will. 6639
18:18 You and these p who come to you 6639
18:21 But select capable men from all the p— 6639
18:22 Have them serve as judges for the p 6639
18:23 and all these p will go home satisfied." 6639
18:25 and made them leaders of the p, 6639
18:26 They served as judges for the p at all times. 6639
19: 3 and what you are to tell the p *of* Israel: 1201
19: 7 of the p and set before them all the words 6639
19: 8 The p all responded together, 6639
19: 9 that the p will hear me speaking with you 6639
19: 9 Moses told the LORD what the p had said. 6639
19:10 "Go to the p and consecrate them today 6639
19:11 on Mount Sinai in the sight of all the p. 6639
19:12 the p around the mountain and tell them, 6639
19:14 down the mountain to the p, 6639
19:15 Then he said to the p, 6639
19:17 the p out of the camp to meet with God, 6639
19:21 the p so they do not force their way through 6639
19:23 "The p cannot come up Mount Sinai, 6639
19:24 and the p must not force their way through 6639
19:25 Moses went down to the p and told them. 6639
20:18 When the p saw the thunder and lightning 6639
20:20 Moses said to the p, "Do not be afraid. 6639
20:21 The p remained at a distance, 6639
22:25 of my p among you who is needy, do not 6639
22:28 or curse the ruler of your p. 6639
22:31 "You are to be my holy p. 408
23: 6 "Do not deny justice to your poor *p* AIT
23:11 Then the poor among your p may get food 6639
23:31 I will hand over to you the *p who* live in AIT
24: 2 And the p may not come up with him." 6639
24: 3 the p all the LORD's words and laws, 6639
24: 7 of the Covenant and read it to the p. 6639
24: 8 sprinkled it on the p and said, 6639
30:33 a priest must be cut off from his p.' " 6638
30:38 be cut off from his p." 6638
31:14 on that day must be cut off from his p. 6638
32: 1 When the p saw that Moses was so long 6639
32: 3 So all the p took off their earrings 6639
32: 6 So the next day the p rose early 6639
32: 7 "Go down, because your p, 6639
32: 9 "I have seen these p," 6639
32: 9 "and they are a stiff-necked p. 6639
32:11 against your p, whom you brought out 6639
32:12 relent and do not bring disaster on your p. 6639
32:14 on his p the disaster he had threatened. 6639
32:17 Joshua heard the noise of the p shouting, 6639
32:21 "What did these p do to you, 6639
32:22 "You know how prone these p are to evil. 6639
32:25 Moses saw that the p were running wild 6639
32:28 that day about three thousand of the p died. 6639
32:30 The next day Moses said to the p, 6639
32:31 what a great sin these p have committed! 6639
32:34 Now go, lead the p to the place I spoke of, 6639
32:35 And the LORD struck the p with a plague 6639
33: 1 you and the p you brought up out of Egypt, 6639
33: 3 a stiff-necked p and I might destroy you on 6639
33: 4 When the p heard these distressing words, 6639
33: 5 'You are a stiff-necked p. 6639
33: 8 all the p rose and stood at the entrances 6639
33:10 the p saw the pillar of cloud standing at 6639
33:12 "You have been telling me, 'Lead these p,' 6639
33:13 Remember that this nation is your p." 6639
33:16 and with your p unless you go with us? 6639
33:16 What else will distinguish me and your p 6639
33:16 and your people from all the other p on 6639
34: 9 Although this is a stiff-necked p, 6639
34:10 Before all your p I will do wonders never 6639
34:10 The p you live among will see 6639
36: 3 And the p continued to bring freewill 2156^S
36: 5 "The p are bringing more than enough 6639
36: 6 the p were restrained from bringing more, 6639
Lev 4: 3 bringing guilt on the p, 6639
6: 3 if he commits any such sin that p may do— 132
7:20 that person must be cut off from his p. 6638
7:21 that person must be cut off from his p.' " 6638
7:25 to the LORD must be cut off from his p. 6638
7:27 that person must be cut off from his p.' " 6638
9: 7 make atonement for yourself and the p; 6639
9: 7 for the p and make atonement for them, 6639
9:15 then brought the offering that was for the p. 6639
9:18 the ram as the fellowship offering for the p. 6639
9:22 Then Aaron lifted his hands toward the p 6639
9:23 When they came out, they blessed the p; 6639
9:23 glory of the LORD appeared to all the p. 6639
9:24 And when all the p saw it, 6639

Lev 10: 3 in the sight of all the **p** I will be honored.' " 6639
16:15 the sin offering for the **p** and take its blood 6639
16:24 for himself and the burnt offering for the **p**, 6639
16:24 make atonement for himself and for the **p**. 6639
16:33 the priests and all the **p** *of* the community. 6639
17: 4 and must be cut off from his **p**. 6638
17: 9 that man must be cut off from his **p**. 6638
17:10 and will cut him off from his **p**. 6638
18:27 by the **p** who lived *in* the land before you, 408
18:29 such persons must be cut off from their **p**. 6638
19: 8 that person must be cut off from his **p**. 6638
19:16 about spreading slander among your **p**. 6638
19:18 or bear a grudge against one of your **p**, 6639
20: 2 The **p** *of* the community are to stone him. 6639
20: 3 that man and I will cut him off from his **p**; 6639
20: 4 If the **p** *of* the community close their eyes 6639
20: 5 and his family and will cut off from their **p** 6639
20: 6 and I will cut him off from his **p**. 6639
20:17 be cut off before the eyes of their **p**. 1201+6639
20:18 Both of them must be cut off from their **p**. 6639
21: 1 for any of his **p** who die, 6638
21: 4 not make himself unclean for **p** related 6638
21:14 but only a virgin from his own **p**, 6638
21:15 not defile his offspring among his **p**. 6638
23:29 on that day must be cut off from his **p**. 6638
23:30 among his **p** anyone who does any work on 6639
26:12 be your God, and you will be my **p**. 6639
Nu 1:18 The **p** indicated their ancestry by their clans NIH
2: 3 of the **p** *of* Judah is Nahshon son 1201
2: 5 the **p** *of* Issachar is Nethanel son of Zuar. 1201
2: 7 The leader of the **p** *of* Zebulun is Eliab son 1201
2:10 The leader of the **p** *of* Reuben is Elizur son 1201
2:12 of the **p** *of* Simeon is Shelumiel son 1201
2:14 The leader of the **p** *of* Gad is Eliasaph son 1201
2:18 of the **p** *of* Ephraim is Elishama son 1201
2:20 of the **p** *of* Manasseh is Gamaliel son 1201
2:22 of the **p** *of* Benjamin is Abidan son 1201
2:25 The leader of the **p** *of* Dan is Ahiezer son 1201
2:27 The leader of the **p** *of* Asher is Pagiel son 1201
2:29 of the **p** *of* Naphtali is Ahira son of Enan. 1201
5:21 "may the LORD cause your **p** to curse 6639
5:27 and she will become accursed among her **p**. 6639
7:24 the leader of the **p** *of* Zebulun, 1201
7:30 the leader of the **p** *of* Reuben, 1201
7:36 the leader of the **p** *of* Simeon, 1201
7:42 the leader of the **p** *of* Gad, 1201
7:48 the leader of the **p** *of* Ephraim, 1201
7:54 the leader of the **p** *of* Manasseh, 1201
7:60 the leader of the **p** *of* Benjamin, 1201
7:66 the leader of the **p** *of* Dan, 1201
7:72 the leader of the **p** *of* Asher, 1201
7:78 the leader of the **p** *of* Naphtali, 1201
9:13 that person must be cut off from his **p** 6638
10:30 to my own land and my own **p**." 4580
11: 1 the **p** complained about their hardships in 6639
11: 2 When the **p** cried out to Moses, 6639
11: 8 The **p** went around gathering it, 6639
11:10 Moses heard the **p** of every family wailing, 6639
11:11 that you put the burden of all these **p** 6639
11:12 Did I conceive all these **p**? 6639
11:13 Where can I get meat for all these **p**? 6639
11:14 I cannot carry all these **p** by myself; 6639
11:16 to you as leaders and officials among the **p**. 6639
11:17 the burden of the **p** so that you will 6639
11:18 "Tell the **p**: 'Consecrate yourselves 6639
11:24 and told the **p** what the LORD had said. 6639
11:29 that all the LORD's **p** were prophets and 6639
11:32 and all the next day the **p** went out 6639
11:33 of the LORD burned against the **p**, 6639
11:34 the **p** who had craved other food. 6639
11:35 the **p** traveled to Hazeroth and stayed there. 6639
12:15 and the **p** did not move on 6639
12:16 the **p** left Hazeroth and encamped in 6639
13:18 and whether the **p** who live there are strong 6639
13:28 But the **p** who live there are powerful, 6639
13:30 Caleb silenced the **p** before Moses and said, 6639
13:31 "We can't attack those **p**; 6639
13:32 All the **p** we saw there are of great size. 6639
14: 1 the **p** of the community raised their voices 6639
14: 9 And do not be afraid of the **p** *of* the land, 6639
14:11 "How long will these **p** treat me 6639
14:13 By your power you brought these **p** up 6639
14:14 are with these **p** and that you, O LORD, 6639
14:15 If you put these **p** to death all at one time, 6639
14:16 'The LORD was not able to bring these **p** 6639
14:19 forgive the sin of these **p**, 6639
15:26 because all the **p** were involved in 6639
15:30 and that person must be cut off from his **p**. 6639
16:41 "You have killed the LORD's **p**," 6639
16:47 among the **p**, but Aaron offered the incense 6639
16:49 But 14,700 *p* **died** from the plague, AIT
19:18 the furnishings and the **p** who were there. 5883
20: 2 and the **p** gathered in opposition to Moses NIH
20:24 "Aaron will be gathered to his **p**. 6638
20:26 for Aaron will be gathered to his **p**; NIH
21: 2 "If you will deliver these **p** into our hands, 6639
21: 4 But the **p** grew impatient on the way; 6639
21: 6 they bit the **p** and many Israelites died. 6639
21: 7 The **p** came to Moses and said, 6639
21: 7 So Moses prayed for the **p**. 6639
21:16 the **p** together and I will give them water." 6639
21:18 that the nobles of the **p** sank— 6639
21:29 You are destroyed, O **p** *of* Chemosh! 6639
22: 3 because there were so many **p**. 6639
22: 5 Balak said: "A **p** has come out of Egypt; 6639
22: 6 Now come and put a curse on these **p**, 6639
22:11 'A **p** that has come out of Egypt covers 6639
Nu 22:12 You must not put a curse on those **p**, 6639
22:17 Come and put a curse on these **p** for me." 6639
22:41 and from there he saw part of the **p**. 6639
23: 9 I see a **p** who live apart and do 6639
23:24 The **p** rise like a lioness; 6639
24:14 Now I am going back to my **p**, but come, 6639
24:14 let me warn you of what this **p** will do 6639
24:14 of what this people will do to your **p** 6639
25: 2 **p** ate and bowed down before these gods. 6639
25: 4 "Take all the leaders of these **p**, 6639
27:13 you too will be gathered to your **p**, 6638
27:17 so the LORD's **p** will not be like sheep 6337
31: 2 After that, you will be gathered to your **p**." 6638
31: 3 So Moses said to the **p**, 6639
31:11 including the **p** and animals, 132
31:16 so that a plague struck the LORD's **p**. 6337
31:26 of the community are to count all the **p** 132
31:40 16,000 **p**, of which the tribute for the LORD 132
31:46 and 16,000 **p**. 132
32: 4 the land the LORD subdued before the **p** 6337
32:15 he will again leave all this **p** in the desert, 6639
33:14 where there was no water for the **p** to drink. 6639
35:15 and any *other* **p** **living** among them, 9369
Dt 1:28 'The **p** are stronger and taller than we are; 6639
2: 4 Give the **p** these orders: 6639
2:10 a **p** strong and numerous, 6639
2:16 these fighting men among the **p** had died, 6639
2:21 They were a **p** strong and numerous, 6639
3:28 for he will lead this **p** across 6639
4: 6 a wise and understanding **p**." 6639
4:10 the **p** before me to hear my words so 6639
4:20 out of Egypt, to be the **p** *of* his inheritance, 6639
4:33 Has any other **p** heard the voice 6639
5:28 "I have heard what this **p** said to you. 6639
7: 6 you are a **p** holy to the LORD your God. 6639
7: 6 on the face of the earth to be his **p**, 6639
7:14 You will be blessed more than any other **p**; 6639
9: 2 The **p** are strong and tall—Anakites! 6639
9: 6 for you are a stiff necked **p**. 6639
9:12 because your **p** whom you brought out 6639
9:13 the LORD said to me, "I have seen this **p**, 6639
9:13 and they are a stiff-necked **p** indeed! 6639
9:26 do not destroy your **p**, 6639
9:27 Overlook the stubbornness of this **p**, 6639
9:29 But they are your **p**, 6639
10:11 "and lead the **p** on their way, 6639
13: 9 and then the hands of all the **p**. 6639
13:13 and have led the **p** *of* their town astray, 3782
13:15 both its **p** and its livestock. 889+928+3972[S]
14: 2 you are a **p** holy to the LORD your God. 6639
14:21 you are a **p** holy to the LORD your God. 6639
15:11 There will always be **poor** *p* in the land. AIT
16:18 and they shall judge the **p** fairly. 6639
17: 7 and then the hands of all the **p**. 6639
17:13 All the **p** will hear and be afraid, 6639
17:16 the **p** return to Egypt to get more of them, 6639
18: 3 from the **p** who sacrifice a bull or a sheep: 6639
19:20 The **rest** *of the p* will hear of this and AIT
20:10 make its **p** an offer of peace. NIH
20:11 the **p** in it shall be subject to forced labor 6639
20:19 Are the trees of the field **p**? 132
21: 8 Accept this atonement for your **p** Israel, 6639
21: 8 and do not hold your **p** guilty of the blood 6639
26: 5 and he went down into Egypt with a few **p** 5493
26:15 and bless your **p** Israel and 6639
26:18 declared this day that you are his **p**, 6639
26:19 be a **p** holy to the LORD your God, 6639
27: 1 and the elders of Israel commanded the **p**: 6639
27: 9 now become the **p** of the LORD your God. 6639
27:11 On the same day Moses commanded the **p**: 6639
27:12 on Mount Gerizim to bless the **p**: 6639
27:14 to all the **p** *of* Israel in a loud voice: 408
27:15 Then all the **p** shall say, "Amen!" 6639
27:16 Then all the **p** shall say, "Amen!" 6639
27:17 Then all the **p** shall say, "Amen!" 6639
27:18 Then all the **p** shall say, "Amen!" 6639
27:19 Then all the **p** shall say, "Amen!" 6639
27:20 Then all the **p** shall say, "Amen!" 6639
27:21 Then all the **p** shall say, "Amen!" 6639
27:22 Then all the **p** shall say, "Amen!" 6639
27:23 Then all the **p** shall say, "Amen!" 6639
27:24 Then all the **p** shall say, "Amen!" 6639
27:25 Then all the **p** shall say, "Amen!" 6639
27:26 Then all the **p** shall say, "Amen!" 6639
28: 9 LORD will establish you as his holy **p**, 6639
28:33 A **p** that you do not know will eat what 6639
29:13 to confirm you this day as his **p**, 6639
29:25 because this **p** abandoned the covenant of NIH
31: 7 for you must go with this **p** into the land 6639
31:12 Assemble the **p**—men, women 6639
31:16 and these **p** will soon prostitute themselves 6639
32: 6 O foolish and unwise **p**? 6639
32: 9 For the LORD's portion is his **p**, 6639
32:21 by those who are not a **p**; 6639
32:36 The LORD will judge his **p** 6639
32:43 Rejoice, O nations, with his **p**, 6639
32:43 and make atonement for his land and **p**. 6639
32:44 of this song in the hearing of the **p**. 6639
32:50 and be gathered to your **p**, 6638
32:50 on Mount Hor and was gathered to his **p**. 6639
32:52 the land I am giving to the **p** *of* Israel." 1201
33: 3 Surely it is you who love the **p**; 6639
33: 5 when the leaders of the **p** assembled, 6639
33: 7 the cry of Judah; bring him to his **p**. 6639
33:21 When the heads of the **p** assembled, 6639
33:29 Who is like you, a **p** saved by the LORD? 6639
Jos 1: 2 Now then, you and all these **p**, 6639
Jos 1: 6 because you will lead these **p** to inherit 6639
1:10 So Joshua ordered the officers of the **p**: 6639
1:11 "Go through the camp and tell the **p**, 6639
2:24 all the **p** are melting in fear because of us." 3782
3: 3 giving orders to the **p**: 6639
3: 5 Joshua told the **p**, "Consecrate yourselves, 6639
3: 6 of the covenant and pass on ahead of the **p**." 6639
3:14 when the **p** broke camp to cross the Jordan, 6639
3:16 So the **p** crossed over opposite Jericho. 6639
4: 2 "Choose twelve men from among the **p**, 6639
4: 7 to be a memorial to the **p** *of* Israel forever." 1201
4:10 until everything the LORD had commanded
Joshua was done by the **p**, 6639
4:10 The **p** hurried over, 6639
4:11 to the other side while the **p** watched. 6639
4:19 the **p** went up from the Jordan and camped 6639
5: 5 the **p** that came out had been circumcised, 6639
5: 5 the **p** born in the desert during the journey 6639
6: 5 have all the **p** give a loud shout; 6639
6: 5 the city will collapse and the **p** will go up, 6639
6: 7 And he ordered the **p**, "Advance! 6639
6: 8 When Joshua had spoken to the **p**, 6639
6:10 But Joshua had commanded the **p**, 6639
6:11 Then the **p** returned to camp and spent NIH
6:16 Joshua commanded the **p**, "Shout! 6639
6:20 When the trumpets sounded, the **p** shouted, 6639
6:20 when the **p** gave a loud shout, 6639
7: 3 "Not all the **p** will have to go up against Ai. 6639
7: 3 to take it and do not weary all the **p**, 6639
7: 5 the hearts of the **p** melted and 6639
7: 7 why did you ever bring this **p** across 6639
7: 9 and the other **p** *of* the country will hear 3782
7:13 "Go, consecrate the **p**. 6639
8: 1 his **p**, his city and his land 6639
8: 9 but Joshua spent that night with the **p**. 6639
8:25 all the **p** *of* Ai. 408
8:33 of the **p** stood in front of Mount Gerizim 2257[S]
8:33 when he gave instructions to bless the **p** 6639
9: 3 when the **p** *of* Gibeon 3782
10: 1 the **p** *of* Gibeon had made a treaty of peace 3782
10: 2 *p were* very much **alarmed** AIT
11:14 but all the **p** they put to the sword 132
12: 5 the border of the **p of Geshur** and Maacah, 1771
13:11 territory of the **p of Geshur** and Maacah, 1771
13:13 not drive out the **p of Geshur** and Maacah, 1771
14: 8 up with me made the hearts of the **p** melt 6639
15:12 These are the boundaries around the **p** 1201
15:15 against the *p* **living in** Debir AIT
15:63 the Jebusites live there with the **p** *of* Judah. 1201
16:10 to this day the Canaanites live among the **p** NIH
17: 2 So this allotment was for the rest of the **p** 1201
17: 7 to include the *p* **living at** En Tappuah. AIT
17:11 Ibleam and the **p** *of* Dor, Endor, 3782
17:14 The **p** *of* Joseph said to Joshua, 1201
17:14 We are a numerous **p** and 6639
17:16 The **p** *of* Joseph replied, 1201
18:14 Kiriath Jearim), a town of the **p** *of* Judah. 1201
24: 2 Joshua said to all the **p**, 6639
24:16 Then the **p** answered, 6639
24:19 Joshua said to the **p**, 6639
24:21 But the **p** said to Joshua, "No! 6639
24:24 And the **p** said to Joshua, 6639
24:25 that day Joshua made a covenant for the **p**, 6639
24:27 he said to all the **p**. 6639
24:28 Then Joshua sent the **p** away, 6639
Jdg 1:11 against the *p* **living in** Debir AIT
1:16 with the men of Judah to live among the **p** 6639
1:19 but they were unable to drive the **p** from 3782
1:27 *the* **p** *of* Beth Shan or Taanach or Dor 3782
1:32 because of this the **p of Asher** lived among 896
2: 2 a covenant with the **p** *of* this land, 3782
2: 4 the **p** wept aloud, 6639
2: 7 The **p** served the LORD throughout 6639
2:19 *the* **p** **returned** *to* ways AIT
5: 2 when the **p** willingly offer themselves— 6639
5: 9 with the willing volunteers among the **p**. 6639
5:11 "Then the **p** *of* the LORD went down to 6639
5:13 the **p** *of* the LORD came to me with 6639
5:14 with the **p** who followed you. 6639
5:18 The **p** of Zebulun risked their very lives; 6639
5:23 'Curse its **p** bitterly, 3782
7: 3 announce now to the **p**, 6639
9:29 If only this **p** were under my command! 6639
9:36 **p** are coming down from the tops of 6639
9:37 "Look, **p** are coming down from the center 6639
9:42 The next day the **p** of Shechem went out to 6639
9:43 When he saw the **p** coming out of the city, 6639
9:45 until he had captured it and killed its **p**. 6639
9:49 and set it on fire over **the p** inside. 2157[S]
9:49 So all the **p** *in* the tower of Shechem, 408
9:51 all the **p** *of* the city—fled. 1251
10:18 of the **p** of Gilead said to each other, 6639
11:11 and the **p** made him head and commander 6639
11:23 the Amorites out before his **p** Israel, 6639
12: 2 and my **p** were engaged in a great struggle 6639
14: 3 among your relatives or among all our **p**? 6638
14:16 You've given my **p** a riddle, 1201+6639
14:17 in turn explained the riddle to her **p**. 1201+6639
16: 2 The **p of Gaza** were told, "Samson is here!" 6484
16:24 When the **p** saw him, they praised their god, 6639
16:30 the temple on the rulers and all the **p** in it. 6639
18: 7 where they saw that the **p** were living 6639
18:10 an unsuspecting **p** and a spacious land 6639
18:20 and went along with the **p**. 6639
18:27 against a peaceful and unsuspecting **p**. 6639
19:12 whose **p** are not Israelites. 2179[S]
20: 2 The leaders of all the **p** *of* the tribes 6639

Jos 20: 2 in the assembly of the **p** *of* God, 6639
20: 8 All the **p** rose as one man, saying, 6639
20:26 Then the Israelites, all the **p,** 6639
21: 2 The **p** went to Bethel, 6639
21: 4 Early the next day the **p** built an altar 6639
21: 9 For when they counted the **p,** 6639
21: 9 of the **p** *of* Jabesh Gilead were there. 3782
21:12 They found among the *p* **living in** Jabesh AIT
21:15 The **p** grieved for Benjamin, 6639
Ru 1: 6 the aid of his **p** by providing food for them, 6639
1:10 "We will go back with you to your **p."** 6639
1:15 "your sister-in-law is going back to her **p** 6639
1:16 Your **p** will be my people 6639
1:16 be my **p** and your God my God. 6639
2:11 to live with a **p** you did not know before. 6639
4: 4 and in the presence of the elders of my **p.** 6639
4: 9 Boaz announced to the elders and all the **p,** 6639
1Sa 2:13 with the **p** that whenever anyone offered 6639
2:23 the **p** about these wicked deeds of yours. 6639
2:24 that I hear spreading among the LORD's **p.** 6639
2:29 of every offering made by my **p** Israel?' 6639
4: 4 So the **p** sent men to Shiloh, 6639
5: 3 the **p of Ashdod** rose early the next day, 847
5: 6 upon the **p of Ashdod** and its vicinity; 847
5: 9 He afflicted the **p** *of* the city, 408
5:10 the **p of Ekron** cried out, 6834
5:10 of Israel around to us to kill us and our **p."** 6639
5:11 or it will kill us and our **p."** 6639
6:13 Now the **p** of Beth Shemesh were NIH
6:14 The **p** chopped up the wood of the cart NIH
6:15 On that day the **p** of Beth Shemesh 408
6:19 The **p** mourned because of the heavy blow 6639
6:21 Then they sent messengers to the **p** 3782
7: 2 and all the **p** *of* Israel mourned and sought 1074
8: 7 "Listen to all that the **p** are saying to you; 6639
8:10 the LORD to the **p** who were asking him 6639
8:19 But the **p** refused to listen to Samuel. 6639
8:21 When Samuel heard all that the **p** said, 6639
9:12 for the **p** have a sacrifice at the high place. 6639
9:13 The **p** will not begin eating until he comes, 6639
9:16 Anoint him leader over my **p** Israel; 6639
9:16 he will deliver my **p** from the hand of 6639
9:16 I have looked upon my **p,** 6639
9:17 he will govern my **p."** 6639
10:17 the **p** of Israel to the LORD at Mizpah 6639
10:23 among the **p** he was a head taller than any 6639
10:24 Samuel said to all the **p,** 6639
10:24 There is no one like him among all the **p."** 6639
10:24 Then the **p** shouted, "Long live the king!" 6639
10:25 Samuel explained to the **p** the regulations 6639
10:25 Then Samuel dismissed the **p,** 6639
11: 4 of Saul and reported these terms to the **p,** 6639
11: 5 and he asked, "What is wrong with the **p?** 6639
11: 7 Then the terror of the LORD fell on the **p,** 6639
11:12 The **p** then said to Samuel, 6639
11:14 Then Samuel said to the **p,** "Come, 6639
11:15 the **p** went to Gilgal and confirmed Saul 6639
12: 6 Then Samuel said to the **p,** 6639
12:18 So all the **p** stood in awe of the LORD and 6639
12:19 The **p** all said to Samuel, 6639
12:22 the LORD will not reject his **p,** 6639
13: 4 **p** were summoned to join Saul at Gilgal. 6639
13:14 and appointed him leader of his **p,** 6639
14:24 Saul had bound the **p** under an oath, 6639
14:27 not heard that his father had bound the **p** 6639
15: 1 to anoint you king over his **p** Israel; 6639
15: 8 and all his **p** he totally destroyed with 6639
15:18 'Go and completely destroy those **wicked p,** 2629
15:24 I was afraid of the **p** and so I gave in 6639
15:30 before the elders of my **p** and before Israel; 6639
18: 5 This pleased all the **p,** and Saul's officers 6639
19:24 This is why *p* **say,** "Is Saul also among AIT
23: 5 the Philistines and saved the **p** *of* Keilah. 3782
27:12 "He has become so odious to his **p,** 6639
30:21 They came out to meet David and the **p** 6639
31: 9 the temple of their idols and among their **p.** 6639
31:11 When the **p** *of* Jabesh Gilead heard of what 3782
2Sa 3:18 'By my servant David I will rescue my **p** Israel 6639
3:31 David said to Joab and all the **p** with him, 6639
3:32 All the **p** wept also. 6639
3:34 And all the **p** wept over him again. 6639
3:36 All the **p** took note and were pleased; 6639
3:37 on that day all the **p** and all Israel knew that 6639
4: 3 because the **p of Beeroth** fled to Gittaim 943
5: 2 'You will shepherd my **p** Israel, 6639
5:12 for the sake of his **p** Israel. 6639
6:18 the **p** in the name of the LORD Almighty. 6639
6:19 And all the **p** went to their homes. 6639
6:21 appointed me ruler over the LORD's **p** Israel 6639
7: 7 I commanded to shepherd my **p** Israel, 6639
7: 8 the flock to be ruler over my **p** Israel. 6639
7:10 a place for my **p** Israel and will plant them 6639
7:10 Wicked **p** will not oppress them anymore, 1201
7:11 I appointed leaders over my **p** Israel. 6639
7:23 And who is like your **p** Israel— 6639
7:23 on earth that God went out to redeem as a **p** 6639
7:23 and their gods from before your **p,** 6639
7:24 You have established your **p** Israel 6639
8:15 doing what was just and right for all his **p.** 6639
10:12 Be strong and let us fight bravely for our **p** 6639
12:31 and brought out the **p** who were there, 6639
13:34 and saw many **p** on the road west of him, 6639
14:13 a thing like this against the **p** *of* God? 6639
14:15 because the **p** have made me afraid. 6639
15:17 king set out, with all the **p** following him, 6639
15:23 wept aloud as all the **p** passed by. 6639

2Sa 15:23 and all the **p** moved on toward the desert. 6639
15:24 until all the **p** had finished leaving the city. 6639
15:30 All the **p** with him covered their heads too 6639
15:32 where *p used to* **worship** God, AIT
16:14 The king and all the **p** with him arrived 6639
16:18 the one chosen by the LORD, by these **p,** 6639
17: 2 and then all the **p** with him will flee. 6639
17: 3 and bring all the **p** back to you. 6639
17: 3 all the **p** will be unharmed." 6639
17:16 over without fail, or the king and all the **p** 6639
17:22 and all the **p** with him set out and crossed 6639
17:29 from cows' milk for David and his **p** to eat. 6639
17:29 "The **p** have become hungry and tired 6639
19: 9 the **p** were all arguing with each other, 6639
19:39 So all the **p** crossed the Jordan, 6639
20:22 Then the woman went to all the **p** 6639
22:44 from the attacks of my **p;** 6639
22:44 **P** I did not know are subject to me, 6639
24:15 and seventy thousand of the **p** from Dan 6639
24:16 to the angel who was afflicting the **p,** 6639
24:17 the angel who was striking down the **p,** 6639
24:21 that the plague on the **p** may be stopped." 6639
1Ki 1:39 the trumpet and all the **p** shouted, 6639
1:40 And all the **p** went up after him, 6639
3: 2 The **p,** however, were still sacrificing at 6639
3: 8 among the **p** you have chosen, 6639
3: 8 the people you have chosen, a great **p,** 6639
3: 9 a discerning heart to govern your **p** and 6639
3: 9 For who is able to govern this great **p** 6639
4:20 The **p** of Judah and Israel were NIH
6:13 and will not abandon my **p** Israel." 6639
8:16 the day I brought my **p** Israel out of Egypt, 6639
8:16 I have chosen David to rule my **p** Israel.' 6639
8:30 and of your **p** Israel when they pray 6639
8:33 "When your **p** Israel have been defeated by 6639
8:34 the sin of your **p** Israel and bring them back 6639
8:35 because your **p** have sinned against you, NIH
8:36 the sin of your servants, your **p** Israel. 6639
8:36 the land you gave your **p** for an inheritance. 6639
8:38 or plea is made by any of your **p** Israel— 6639
8:41 not belong to your **p** Israel but has come 6639
8:43 as do your own **p** Israel, 6639
8:44 your **p** go to war against their enemies, 6639
8:50 And forgive your **p,** who have sinned 6639
8:51 for they are your **p** and your inheritance, 6639
8:52 and to the plea of your **p** Israel, 6639
8:56 who has given rest to his **p** Israel just 6639
8:59 of his servant and the cause of his **p** Israel 6639
8:65 **p** from Lebo Hamath to the Wadi of Egypt. NIH
8:66 On the following day he sent the **p** away. 6639
8:66 for his servant David and his **p** Israel. 6639
9: 9 *P will* **answer,** 'Because they have forsaken AIT
9:20 All the **p** left from the Amorites, Hittites, 6639
12: 5 So the **p** went away. 6639
12: 6 would you advise me to answer these **p?"** 6639
12: 7 "If today you will be a servant to these **p** 6639
12: 9 How should we answer these **p** who say 6639
12:10 "Tell these **p** who have said to you, 6639
12:12 and all the **p** returned to Rehoboam, 6639
12:13 The king answered the **p** harshly. 6639
12:15 So the king did not listen to the **p,** 6639
12:23 and to the rest of the **p,** 6639
12:27 If these **p** go up to offer sacrifices at 6639
12:28 He said to **the p,** 2157[S]
12:30 the **p** went even as far as Dan to worship 6639
12:31 and appointed priests from all sorts of **p,** 6639
13:25 *Some* **p** who passed by saw the body 408
13:33 for the high places from all sorts of **p.** 6639
14: 2 told me I would be king over this **p.** 6639
14: 7 from among the **p** and made you a leader 6639
14: 7 and made you a leader over my **p** Israel. 6639
14:24 the **p** engaged in all the detestable practices NIH
16: 2 and made you leader of my **p** Israel, 6639
16: 2 of Jeroboam and caused my **p** Israel to sin 6639
16:21 the **p** *of* Israel were split into two factions; 6639
18:19 Now summon the **p** from all over Israel NIH
18:21 Elijah went before the **p** and said, 6639
18:21 But the **p** said nothing. 6639
18:24 all the **p** said, "What you say is good." 6639
18:30 Elijah said to all the **p,** "Come here to me." 6639
18:37 answer me, so these **p** will know that you, 6639
18:39 When all the **p** saw this, 6639
19:21 to cook the meat and gave it to the **p,** 6639
20: 8 The elders and the **p** all answered, 6639
20:42 your **p** for his people.' " 6639
20:42 your people for his **p.' "** 6639
21: 9 in a prominent place among the **p.** 6639
21:12 in a prominent place among the **p.** 6639
21:13 against Naboth before the **p,** 6639
22: 4 "I am as you are, my **p** as your people, 6639
22: 4 "I am as you are, my people as your **p,** 6639
22:17 **'These** *p* have no master. AIT
22:28 he added, "Mark my words, all you **p!"** 6639
22:43 and the **p** continued to offer sacrifices 6639
2Ki 3: 7 "I am as you are, my **p** as your people, 6639
3: 7 "I am as you are, my people as your **p,** 6639
4:13 "I have a home among my own **p."** 6638
4:41 "Serve it to the **p** to eat." 6639
4:42 "Give it to the **p** to eat," Elisha said. 6639
4:43 Elisha answered, "Give it to the **p** to eat. 6639
6:18 "Strike these **p** with blindness." 1580
6:30 As he went along the wall, the **p** looked, 6639
7:16 the **p** went out and plundered the camp of 6639
7:17 and the **p** trampled him in the gateway, 6639
7:20 for the **p** trampled him in the gateway, 6639
9: 6 I anoint you king over the LORD's **p** Israel. 6639
10: 9 He stood before all the **p** and said, 6639

2Ki 10:18 Then Jehu brought all the **p** together 6639
10:27 and **p** *have* **used** it for a latrine to this day. AIT
11:12 and the **p** clapped their hands and shouted, NIH
11:13 the noise made by the guards and the **p,** 6639
11:13 to the **p** at the temple of the LORD. 6639
11:14 and all the **p** *of* the land were rejoicing 6639
11:17 between the LORD and the king and **p** 6639
11:17 that they would be the LORD's **p.** 6639
11:17 a covenant between the king and the **p.** 6639
11:18 the **p** *of* the land went to the temple of Baal 6639
11:19 the guards and all the **p** *of* the land, 6639
11:20 and all the **p** *of* the land rejoiced. 6639
12: 3 the **p** continued to offer sacrifices 6639
12: 8 not collect any more money from the **p** and 6639
14: 4 the **p** continued to offer sacrifices 6639
14:21 Then all the **p** *of* Judah took Azariah, 6639
15: 4 the **p** continued to offer sacrifices 6639
15: 5 the palace and governed the **p** *of* the land. 6639
15:10 He attacked him in front of the **p,** 6639
15:29 and deported **the p** to Assyria. 4392[S]
15:35 the **p** continued to offer sacrifices 6639
16:15 the burnt offering of all the **p** *of* the land, 6639
17:20 the LORD rejected all the **p** *of* Israel; 2446
17:23 So the **p** of Israel were taken NIH
17:24 of Assyria brought **p** from Babylon, NIH
17:25 among them and they killed some of **the p.** 2157[S]
17:26 "The **p** you deported and resettled in 1580
17:26 **the p** do not know what he requires." 4392[S]
17:27 and teach **the p** what the god of the land 4392[S]
17:29 in the shrines the **p of Samaria** had made at 9085
17:32 **all sorts** *of* their own **p** to officiate AIT
17:41 while these **p** were worshiping the LORD, 1580
18:26 to us in Hebrew in the hearing of the **p** on 6639
18:36 **p** remained silent and said nothing in reply, 6639
19:12 and the **p** *of* Eden who were in Tel Assar? 1201
19:26 Their **p,** drained of power, 3782
19:35 When *the p* **got up** the next morning— AIT
20: 5 tell Hezekiah, the leader of my **p,** 6639
21: 9 But *the p did* not **listen.** AIT
21:24 the **p** *of* the land killed all who had plotted 6639
22: 4 the doorkeepers have collected from the **p.** 6639
22:13 of the LORD for me and for the **p** and 6639
22:16 to bring disaster on this place and its **p,** 3782
22:19 against this place and its **p,** 3782
23: 2 the **p** *of* Jerusalem, the priests and 3782
23: 2 all the **p** from the least to the greatest. 6639
23: 3 the **p** pledged themselves to the covenant. 6639
23: 6 over the graves of the **common p.** 1201+6639
23:13 and for Molech the detestable god of the **p** 1201
23:21 The king gave this order to all the **p:** 6639
23:30 And the **p** *of* the land took Jehoahaz son 6639
23:35 and exacted the silver and gold from the **p** 6639
24:14 Only the poorest **p** *of* the land were left. 6639
25: 3 so severe that there was no food for the **p** 6639
25:11 into exile the **p** who remained in the city, 6639
25:12 behind some of the **poorest** *p of* the land AIT
25:19 in charge of conscripting the **p** *of* the land 6639
25:22 to be over the **p** he had left behind in Judah. 6639
25:26 all the **p** from the least to the greatest, 6639
1Ch 2:10 the leader of the **p** *of* Judah. 1201
4:14 because *its p* **were** craftsmen. AIT
4:27 not become as numerous as the **p** *of* Judah. 1201
5:21 took one hundred thousand **p** captive, 132+5883
5:23 The **p** *of* the half-tribe of Manasseh 1201
9: 1 The **p** of Judah were taken captive NIH
9: 6 The **p from Judah** numbered 690. 278+2157
9: 9 The **p from Benjamin,** 278+2157
10: 9 the news among their idols and their **p.** 6639
11: 2 'You will shepherd my **p** Israel, 6639
13: 4 because it seemed right to all the **p.** 6639
14: 2 for the sake of his **p** Israel. 6639
16: 2 he blessed the **p** in the name of the LORD. 6639
16:36 Then all the **p** said "Amen" and "Praise 6639
16:43 Then all the **p** left, each for his own home, 6639
17: 6 whom I commanded to shepherd my **p,** 6639
17: 7 to be ruler over my **p** Israel. 6639
17: 9 a place for my **p** Israel and will plant them 6639
17: 9 Wicked **p** will not oppress them anymore, 1201
17:10 I appointed leaders over my **p** Israel. 6639
17:21 And who is like your **p** Israel— 6639
17:21 on earth whose God went out to redeem a **p** 6639
17:21 by driving out nations from before your **p,** 6639
17:22 You made your **p** Israel your very own forever, 6639
18:14 doing what was just and right for all his **p.** 6639
19:13 Be strong and let us fight bravely for our **p** 6639
20: 3 and brought out the **p** who were there, 6639
21:15 to the angel who was destroying the **p,** NIH
21:17 but do not let this plague remain on your **p."** 6639
21:22 that the plague on the **p** may be stopped. 6639
22:18 land is subject to the LORD and to his **p.** 6639
23:25 has granted rest to his **p** and has come 6639
28: 2 "Listen to me, my brothers and my **p.** 6639
28:21 the **p** will obey your every command." 6639
29: 9 The **p** rejoiced at the willing response 6639
29:14 "But who am I, and who are my **p,** 6639
29:17 willingly your **p** who are here have given 6639
29:18 in the hearts of your **p** forever, 6639
2Ch 1: 9 over a **p** who are as numerous as the dust of 6639
1:10 and knowledge, that I may lead this **p,** 6639
1:10 for who is able to govern this great **p** 6639
1:11 for wisdom and knowledge to govern my **p** 6639
2:11 "Because the LORD loves his **p,** 6639
2:18 foremen over them to keep the **p** working. 6639
6: 5 'Since the day I brought my **p** out of Egypt, 6639
6: 5 to be the leader over my **p** Israel. 6639
6: 6 I have chosen David to rule my **p** Israel.' 6639

2Ch 6:11 that he made with the **p** of Israel." 1201
6:21 and of your **p** Israel when they pray 6639
6:24 "When your **p** Israel have been defeated by 6639
6:25 the sin of your **p** Israel and bring them back 6639
6:26 because your **p** have sinned against you, NIH
6:27 the sin of your servants, your **p** Israel. 6639
6:27 the land you gave your **p** for an inheritance. 6639
6:29 or plea is made by any of your **p** Israel— 6639
6:32 not belong to your **p** Israel but has come 6639
6:33 as do your own **p** Israel, 6639
6:34 your **p** go to war against their enemies, 6639
6:39 And forgive your **p**, who have sinned 6639
7:4 the **p** offered sacrifices before the LORD. 6639
7:5 the king and all the **p** dedicated the temple 6639
7:8 **p** from Lebo Hamath to the Wadi of Egypt. NIH
7:10 of the seventh month he sent the **p** 6639
7:10 for David and Solomon and for his **p** Israel. 6639
7:13 the land or send a plague among my **p**, 6639
7:14 if my **p**, who are called by my name, 6639
7:22 *P will* **answer,** 'Because they have forsaken AIT
8:7 All the **p** left from the Hittites, Amorites, 6639
10:5 So the **p** went away. 6639
10:6 advise me to answer these **p**?" 6639
10:7 to these **p** and please them and give them 6639
10:9 How should we answer these **p** who say 6639
10:10 "Tell the **p** who have said to you, 6639
10:12 and all the **p** returned to Rehoboam, 6639
10:15 So the king did not listen to the **p**, 6639
15:9 *p* from Ephraim, Manasseh and Simeon *who had* **settled** AIT
16:10 Asa brutally oppressed some of the **p**. 6639
17:9 to all the towns of Judah and taught the **p**. 6639
18:2 for him and the **p** with him and urged him 6639
18:3 "I am as you are, and my **p** as your people; 6639
18:3 "I am as you are, and my people as your **p**; 6639
18:16 **'These** *p* have no master. AIT
18:27 he added, "Mark my words, all you **p**!" 6639
19:4 the **p** from Beersheba to the hill country 6639
20:4 The **p** of Judah came together to seek help NIH
20:7 before your **p** Israel and give it forever to 6639
20:18 and all the **p** *of* Judah and Jerusalem fell 3782
20:20 "Listen to me, Judah and **p** *of* Jerusalem! 3782
20:21 After consulting the **p**, 6639
20:33 and the **p** still had not set their hearts on 6639
21:11 of Judah and had caused the **p** *of* Jerusalem 3782
21:13 the **p** *of* Jerusalem to prostitute themselves, 3782
21:14 now the LORD is about to strike your **p**, 6639
21:19 His **p** made no fire in his honor, 6639
22:1 The **p** *of* Jerusalem made Ahaziah, 3782
23:12 the noise of the **p** running and cheering 6639
23:13 and all the **p** *of* the land were rejoicing 6639
23:16 then made a covenant that he and the **p** and 6639
23:16 and the king would be the LORD's **p**. 6639
23:17 All the **p** went to the temple of Baal 6639
23:20 the rulers of the **p** and all the people of 6639
23:20 the rulers of the people and all the **p** *of* 6639
23:21 and all the **p** *of* the land rejoiced. 6639
24:10 the **p** brought their contributions gladly, 6639
24:19 Although the LORD sent prophets to **the p** 2157[S]
24:20 He stood before the **p** and said, 6639
24:23 and killed all the leaders of the **p**. 6639
25:5 the **p** of Judah together and assigned them NIH
25:7 not with any of the **p** *of* Ephraim. 1201
25:13 They killed three thousand **p** 2157[S]
25:14 he brought back the gods of the **p** *of* Seir. 1201
25:15 not save their own **p** from your hand?" 6639
26:1 Then all the **p** *of* Judah took Uzziah, 6639
26:10 He had **p** working his fields and vineyards 438
26:21 the palace and governed the **p** *of* the land. 6639
26:23 for *p* **said,** "He had leprosy." AIT
27:2 The **p**, however, continued their corrupt 6639
28:5 and took **many** of his *p* as prisoners AIT
29:36 the **p** rejoiced at what God had brought 6639
29:36 at what God had brought about for his **p**, 6639
30:3 and the **p** had not assembled in Jerusalem. 6639
30:5 the **p** to come to Jerusalem and celebrate NIH
30:6 "**P** *of* Israel, return to the LORD, 1201
30:10 but the **p** scorned and ridiculed them. NIH
30:12 Also in Judah the hand of God was on the **p** NIH
30:13 of **p** assembled in Jerusalem to celebrate 6639
30:18 Although most of the many **p** who came 6639
30:20 LORD heard Hezekiah and healed the **p**. 6639
30:27 and the Levites stood to bless the **p**, 6639
31:4 He ordered the **p** living in Jerusalem 6639
31:8 the LORD and blessed his **p** Israel. 6639
31:10 the **p** began to bring their contributions to NIH
31:10 because the LORD has blessed his **p**, 6639
32:6 over the **p** and assembled them before him 6639
32:8 And the **p** gained confidence 6639
32:9 for Hezekiah king of Judah and for all the **p** NIH
32:14 to save his **p** from me? 6639
32:15 to deliver his **p** from my hand or the hand 6639
32:17 of the other lands did not rescue their **p** 6639
32:17 so the god of Hezekiah will not rescue his **p** 6639
32:18 in Hebrew to the **p** *of* Jerusalem who were 6639
32:22 So the LORD saved Hezekiah and the **p** 3782
32:26 as did the **p** *of* Jerusalem; 3782
32:33 and the **p** *of* Jerusalem honored him 3782
33:9 But Manasseh led Judah and the **p** 3782
33:10 The LORD spoke to Manasseh and his **p**, 6639
33:17 The **p**, however, continued to sacrifice at 6639
33:25 the **p** *of* the land killed all who had plotted 6639
34:9 the doorkeepers had collected from the **p** NIH
34:9 from all the **p** of Judah and Benjamin and NIH
34:24 to bring disaster on this place and its **p**— 3782
34:27 against this place and its **p**, 3782
34:30 the **p** *of* Jerusalem, the priests and 3782

2Ch 34:30 all the **p** from the least to the greatest. 6639
34:32 the **p** *of* Jerusalem did this in accordance 3782
35:3 the LORD your God and his **p** Israel. 6639
35:5 of your fellow countrymen, the **lay p**. 1201+6639
35:7 for all the **lay p** who were there 1201+6639
35:8 also contributed voluntarily to the **p** and 6639
35:12 families of the **p** to offer to the LORD, 1201+6639
35:13 and served them quickly to all the **p**. 1201+6639
35:18 and Israel who were there with the **p** 3782
36:1 And the **p** *of* the land took Jehoahaz son 6639
36:14 the **p** became more and more unfaithful, 6639
36:15 on his **p** and on his dwelling place. 6639
36:16 of the LORD was aroused against his **p** 6639
36:23 Anyone of his **p** among you— 6639
Ezr 1:3 Anyone of his **p** among you— 6639
1:4 the **p** of any place where survivors may 408
2:1 the **p** *of* the province who came up from 1201
2:2 The list of the men of the **p** *of* Israel: 6639
2:70 along with some of the other **p**, 6639
3:1 the **p** assembled as one man in Jerusalem. 6639
3:7 and oil to the **p of Sidon** and Tyre, 7479
3:11 And all the **p** gave a great shout of praise to 6639
3:13 because the **p** made so much noise. 6639
4:4 the **p** *of* Judah and make them afraid to go 6639
4:6 they lodged an accusation against the **p** 3782
4:10 and the other **p** whom the great and 10040
5:8 The **p** are building it with large stones NIH
5:12 and deported the **p** to Babylon. 10553
6:12 or **p** who lifts a hand to change this decree 10553
6:16 Then the **p** *of* Israel— 10120
7:16 the **p** and priests for the temple of their God 10553
7:25 and judges to administer justice to all the **p** 10553
8:15 I checked among the **p** and the priests, 6639
8:36 who then gave assistance to the **p** and to 6639
9:1 "The **p** of Israel, including the priests 6639
10:9 all the **p** were sitting in the square before 6639
10:13 But there are many **p** here and it is 6639
Ne 1:6 for your servants, the **p** *of* Israel. 1201
1:9 if your **exiled** *p* are at the farthest horizon, AIT
1:10 "They are your servants and your **p**, 6639
4:6 for the **p** worked with all their heart. 6639
4:10 Meanwhile, the **p** in Judah said, NIH
4:13 the **p** behind the lowest points of the wall at 6639
4:14 the officials and the rest of the **p**, 6639
4:16 behind all the **p** *of* Judah 1074
4:19 the officials and the rest of the **p**, 6639
4:22 At that time I also said to the **p**, 6639
5:10 and my men are also lending **the p** money 2157[S]
5:13 And the **p** did as they had promised. 6639
5:15 on the **p** and took forty shekels of silver 6639
5:15 Their assistants also lorded it over the **p**. 6639
5:18 the demands were heavy on these **p**. 6639
5:19 O my God, for all I have done for these **p**. 6639
7:4 but there were few **p** in it, 6639
7:5 the **common p** for registration by families. 6639
7:6 These are the **p** *of* the province who came 1201
7:72 by the rest of the **p** was 20,000 6639
7:73 along with certain of the **p** and the rest of 6639
8:1 the **p** assembled as one man in the square 6639
8:3 the **p** listened attentively to the Book of 6639
8:5 All the **p** could see him 6639
8:5 and as he opened it, the **p** all stood up. 6639
8:6 all the **p** lifted their hands and responded, 6639
8:7 instructed the **p** in the Law while 6639
8:7 in the Law while the **p** were standing there. 6639
8:8 **p** could understand what was being read. NIH
8:9 the Levites who were instructing the **p** said 6639
8:9 the **p** had been weeping as they listened to 6639
8:11 The Levites calmed all the **p**, saying, 6639
8:12 Then all the **p** went away to eat and drink, 6639
8:16 the **p** went out and brought back branches 6639
9:10 against all his officials and all the **p** 6639
9:32 upon our fathers and all your **p**, 6639
10:14 The leaders of the **p**: 6639
10:28 "The rest of the **p**—priests, Levites, 6639
10:34 "We—the priests, the Levites and the **p**— 6639
10:39 The **p** *of* Israel, including the Levites, 1201
11:1 the leaders of the **p** settled in Jerusalem, 6639
11:1 the **p** cast lots to bring one out of every ten 6639
11:2 The **p** commended all the men 6639
11:4 while other **p** from both Judah 1201
11:24 in all affairs relating to the **p**. 6639
11:25 of the **p** *of* Judah lived in Kiriath Arba 1201
12:30 they purified the **p**, the gates and the wall. 6639
12:38 together with half the **p**— 6639
13:1 was read aloud in the hearing of the **p** 6639
13:3 When **the p** heard this law, 4392[S]
13:16 in Jerusalem on the Sabbath to the **p** 1201
Est 1:5 for all the **p** from the least to the greatest, 6639
1:11 to display her beauty to the **p** and nobles, 6639
1:22 to **each p** in its own language, 2256+6639+6639
3:6 having learned who Mordecai's **p** were, 6639
3:6 for a way to destroy all Mordecai's **p**, 6639
3:8 a certain **p** dispersed and scattered among 6639
3:8 from those of all other **p** and who do 6639
3:11 "and do with the **p** as you please." 6639
3:12 and in the language of **each p** 2256+6639+6639
3:14 in every province and made known to the **p** 6639
4:8 for mercy and plead with him for her **p**. 6639
4:11 and the **p** *of* the royal provinces know that 6639
7:3 And spare my **p**—this is my request. 6639
7:4 and my **p** have been sold for destruction 6639
8:6 can I bear to see disaster fall on my **p**? 6639
8:9 and the language of **each p** 2256+6639+6639
8:13 in every province and made known to the **p** NIH
8:17 and celebrating. And **many** *p* AIT
9:2 because the **p** of all the other nationalities NIH

Est 10:3 because he worked for the good of his **p** 6639
Job 1:3 He was the greatest man among all the **p** *of* 1201
12:2 "Doubtless you are the **p**, 6639
17:6 a man in whose face **p** spit. NIH
18:19 or descendants among his **p**, 6639
28:4 Far from where *p* **dwell** he cuts a shaft, AIT
34:20 the **p** are shaken and they pass away; 6639
34:30 from laying snares for the **p**. 6639
36:20 to drag **p** away from their homes. 6639
Ps 3:8 May your blessing be on your **p**. 6639
12:7 and protect us from such **p** forever. 1887
14:4 those who devour my **p** as men eat bread 6639
14:7 the LORD restores the fortunes of his **p**, 6639
18:43 delivered me from the attacks of the **p**; 6639
18:43 **p** I did not know are subject to me. 6639
22:6 scorned by men and despised by the **p**. 6639
22:17 **p** stare and gloat over me. 2156[S]
22:31 They will proclaim his righteousness to a **p** 6639
28:8 The LORD is the strength of **his p**, 4564[S]
28:9 Save your **p** and bless your inheritance; 6639
29:11 The LORD gives strength to his **p**; 6639
29:11 the LORD blesses his **p** with peace. 6639
33:8 let all the **p** *of* the world revere him. 3782
33:12 the **p** he chose for his inheritance. 6639
35:18 among throngs of **p** I will praise you. 6639
44:12 You sold your **p** for a pittance, 6639
45:10 Forget your **p** and your father's house. 6639
47:9 of the nations assemble as the **p** *of* the God 6639
50:4 and the earth, that he may judge his **p**: 6639
50:7 O my **p**, and I will speak, O Israel, 6639
53:4 those who devour my **p** as men eat bread 6639
53:6 When God restores the fortunes of his **p**, 6639
59:11 O Lord our shield, or my **p** will forget. 6639
60:3 You have shown your **p** desperate times; 6639
62:8 Trust in him at all times, O **p**; 6639
65:9 with water to provide **the p** with grain, 4392[S]
68:7 When you went out before your **p**, O God, 6639
68:10 Your **p** settled in it, and from your bounty, 2653
68:35 of Israel gives power and strength to his **p**. 6639
69:11 **p** make sport of me. 2157[S]
69:33 and does not despise his **captive** *p*. AIT
69:35 Then *p will* **settle** there and possess it; AIT
72:2 He will judge your **p** in righteousness, 6639
72:3 mountains will bring prosperity to the **p**, 6639
72:4 He will defend the afflicted among the **p** 6639
72:15 *May p* ever **pray** for him and bless him AIT
73:10 Therefore their **p** turn to them and drink 6639
74:2 Remember the **p** you purchased of old, 6337
74:18 how foolish **p** have reviled your name. 6639
74:19 the lives of your **afflicted** *p* forever. AIT
75:3 When the earth and all its **p** quake, 3782
77:15 With your mighty arm you redeemed your **p** 6639
77:20 You led your **p** like a flock by the hand 6639
78:1 O my **p**, hear my teaching; 6639
78:20 Can he supply meat for his **p**?" 6639
78:24 he rained down manna for **the p** to eat, 2157[S]
78:52 But he brought his **p** out like a flock; 6639
78:62 He gave his **p** over to the sword; 6639
78:71 to be the shepherd of his **p** Jacob, 6639
79:13 Then we your **p**, the sheep of your pasture, 6639
80:4 against the prayers of your **p**? 6639
80:16 at your rebuke your *p* **perish.** AIT
81:8 O my **p**, and I will warn you— 6639
81:11 "But my **p** would not listen to me; 6639
81:13 "If my **p** would but listen to me, 6639
83:3 With cunning they conspire against your **p**; 6639
83:7 Philistia, with the **p** *of* Tyre. 3782
85:2 of your **p** and covered all their sins. 6639
85:6 that your **p** may rejoice in you? 6639
85:8 he promises peace to his **p**, his saints— 6639
89:19 to your **faithful** *p* you said: AIT
89:19 a young man from among the **p**. 6639
94:5 They crush your **p**, O LORD; 6639
94:8 you senseless ones among the **p**; 6639
94:14 For the LORD will not reject his **p**; 6639
95:7 for he is our God and we are the **p** 6639
95:10 I said, "They are a **p** *whose* hearts go astray, 6639
100:3 we are his **p**, the sheep of his pasture. 6639
102:18 a **p** not yet created may praise the LORD: 6639
103:7 his deeds to the **p** *of* Israel: 1201
105:24 The LORD made his **p** very fruitful; 6639
105:25 whose hearts he turned to hate his **p**, 6639
105:43 He brought out his **p** with rejoicing, 6639
106:4 O LORD, when you show favor to your **p**, 6639
106:40 Therefore the LORD was angry with his **p** 6639
106:48 Let all the **p** say, "Amen!" 6639
107:32 Let them exalt him in the assembly of the **p** 6639
111:6 He has shown his **p** the power of his works, 6639
111:9 He provided redemption for his **p**; 6639
113:8 with the princes of their **p**. 6639
114:1 house of Jacob from a **p** *of* foreign tongue, 6639
116:14 to the LORD in the presence of all his **p**. 6639
116:18 to the LORD in the presence of all his **p**, 6639
125:2 so the LORD surrounds his **p** both now 6639
135:12 an inheritance to his **p** Israel. 6639
135:14 For the LORD will vindicate his **p** 6639
136:16 to him who led his **p** through the desert, 6639
144:15 Blessed are the **p** of whom this is true; 6639
144:15 blessed are the **p** whose God is the LORD. 6639
147:13 the bars of your gates and blesses your **p** 1201
148:14 He has raised up for his **p** a horn, 6639
148:14 of Israel, the **p** close to his heart. 6639
149:2 let the **p** *of* Zion be glad in their King. 1201
149:4 For the LORD takes delight in his **p**; 6639
Pr 11:26 **P** curse the man who hoards grain, 4211
14:34 but sin is a disgrace to any **p**. 4211
28:15 a wicked man ruling over a helpless **p**. 6639

Pr 28:28 the wicked rise to power, **p** go into hiding; 132
29: 2 When the righteous thrive, the **p** rejoice; 6639
29: 2 when the wicked rule, the **p** groan. 6639
29:18 the **p** cast off restraint; 6639
Ecc 4:16 There was no end to all the **p** who were 6639
7:21 Do not pay attention to every word *p* **say,** AIT
8:11 **p** are filled with schemes to do wrong. 132+1201
9:14 a small city with only a few **p** in it. 408
12: 9 but also he imparted knowledge to the **p.** 6639
SS 6:12 among the royal chariots of my **p.** 6639
Isa 1: 3 my **p** do not understand." 6639
1: 4 Ah, sinful nation, a **p** loaded with guilt, 6639
1:10 to the law of our God, you **p** *of* Gomorrah! 6639
2: 6 You have abandoned your **p,** 6639
3: 5 **P** will oppress each other— 6639
3: 7 do not make me the leader of the **p."** 6639
3:12 Youths oppress my **p,** 6639
3:12 O my **p,** your guides lead you astray; 6639
3:13 he rises to judge the **p.** 6639
3:14 against the elders and leaders of his **p:** 6639
3:15 by crushing my **p** and grinding the faces of 6639
5:13 Therefore my **p** will go into exile for lack 6639
5:25 the LORD's anger burns against his **p;** 6639
6: 5 and I live among a **p** *of* unclean lips, 6639
6: 9 He said, "Go and tell this **p:** 6639
6:10 Make the heart of this **p** calloused; 6639
7: 2 the hearts of Ahaz and his **p** were shaken, 6639
7: 8 be too shattered to be a **p.** 6639
7:17 on your **p** and on the house of your father 6639
8: 6 "Because this **p** has rejected the gently 6639
8:11 warning me not to follow the way of this **p.** 6639
8:12 that these **p** call conspiracy; 6639
8:14 And for the **p** *of* Jerusalem he will be a trap 3782
8:19 should not a **p** inquire of their God? 6639
9: 2 The **p** walking in darkness have seen 6639
9: 3 they rejoice before you as **p** rejoice at NIH
9: 9 All the **p** will know it— 6639
9:13 But the **p** have not returned 6639
9:16 Those who guide this **p** mislead them, 6639
9:19 the land will be scorched and the **p** will 6639
10: 2 from the oppressed of my **p,** 6639
10: 6 I dispatch him against a **p** who anger me, 6639
10:22 Though your **p,** O Israel, 6639
10:24 "O my **p** who live in Zion, 6639
10:31 the **p** *of* Gebim take cover. 3782
11:11 to reclaim the remnant that is left of his **p** 6639
11:12 he will assemble the **scattered** *p of* Judah AIT
11:14 together they will plunder the **p** *to* the east. 1201
11:16 be a highway for the remnant of his **p** 6639
12: 6 Shout aloud and sing for joy, **p** *of* Zion, 3782
13:14 each will return to his own **p,** 6639
14:20 destroyed your land and killed your **p.** 6639
14:25 His yoke will be taken from **my p,** 2157[S]
14:32 and in her his afflicted **p** will find refuge." 6639
16:14 Moab's splendor and all her many **p** will 2162
18: 2 to a **p** tall and smooth-skinned, 1580
18: 2 to a **p** feared far and wide, 6639
18: 3 All you **p** *of* the world, 3782
18: 7 from a **p** tall and smooth-skinned, from 6639
18: 7 from a **p** feared far and wide, 6639
19:25 saying, "Blessed be Egypt my **p,** 6639
20: 6 the *p who* **live** *on* this coast will say, AIT
21:10 O my **p,** crushed on the threshing floor, 1201
22: 4 to console me over the destruction
of my **p."** 1426+6639
23: 2 you **p** *of* the island and you merchants 3782
23: 6 wail, you **p** *of* the island. 3782
23:13 this **p** that is now of no account! 6639
24: 2 it will be the same for priest as for **p,** 6639
24: 5 The earth is defiled by its **p;** 3782
24: 6 its **p** must bear their guilt. 3782
24:17 O **p** *of* the earth. 3782
25: 8 the disgrace of his **p** from all the earth. 6639
26: 9 the **p** *of* the world learn righteousness. 3782
26:11 Let them see your zeal for your **p** and 6639
26:18 we have not given birth to **p** *of* the world. 3782
26:20 my **p,** enter your rooms and shut the doors 6639
26:21 of his dwelling to punish the **p** *of* the earth 3782
27:11 For this is a **p** without understanding; 6639
28: 5 a beautiful wreath for the remnant of his **p.** 6639
28:11 strange tongues God will speak to this **p,** 6639
28:14 you scoffers who rule this **p** in Jerusalem. 6639
29:13 "These **p** come near to me with their mouth 6639
29:14 Therefore once more I will astound these **p** 6639
30: 5 to shame because of a **p** useless to them, 6639
30: 9 These are rebellious **p,** deceitful children, 6639
30:19 O **p** of Zion, who live in Jerusalem, 6639
30:26 of his **p** and heals the wounds he inflicted. 6639
30:29 when **p** go up with flutes to the mountain 2021[S]
32:13 and for the land of my **p,** a land overgrown 6639
32:18 My **p** will live in peaceful dwelling places, 6639
33:19 You will see those arrogant **p** no more, 6639
33:19 those **p** *of* an obscure speech, 6639
34: 5 the **p** I have totally destroyed. 6639
36:11 to us in Hebrew in the hearing of the **p** on 6639
36:21 *p remained* **silent** and said nothing in reply, AIT
37:12 and the **p** *of* Eden who were in Tel Assar? 1201
37:27 Their **p,** drained of power, 3782
37:36 When *the p* **got up** the next morning— AIT
40: 1 Comfort, comfort my **p,** says your God. 6639
40: 7 Surely the **p** are grass. 6639
40:22 and its **p** are like grasshoppers. 3782
41:20 so that **p** may see and know, 3481[S]
42: 5 who gives breath to its **p,** 6639
42: 6 to be a covenant for the **p** and a light for 6639
42:11 Let the **p** *of* Sela sing for joy; 3782
42:22 But this is a **p** plundered and looted, 6639
Isa 43: 4 and **p** in exchange for your life. 4211
43:20 to give drink to my **p,** my chosen, 6639
43:21 the **p** I formed for myself 6639
44: 7 since I established my ancient **p,** 6639
47: 6 with my **p** and desecrated my inheritance; 6639
49: 8 to be a covenant for the **p,** 6639
49:13 For the LORD comforts his **p** 6639
49:19 now you will be too small for your **p,** 3782
51: 4 "Listen to me, my **p;** 6639
51: 7 you **p** who have my law in your hearts: 6639
51:16 and who say to Zion, 'You are my **p.'** " 6639
51:22 your God, who defends his **p:** 6639
52: 4 "At first my **p** went down to Egypt to live; 6639
52: 5 my **p** have been taken away for nothing, 6639
52: 6 Therefore my **p** will know my name; 6639
52: 9 for the LORD has comforted his **p,** 6639
53: 8 the transgression of my **p** he was stricken. 6639
56: 3 surely exclude me from his **p."** 6639
57:14 the obstacles out of the way of my **p."** 6639
58: 1 to my **p** their rebellion and to the house 6639
58:12 *Your p will* **rebuild** the ancient ruins AIT
60:21 Then will all your **p** be righteous 6639
61: 7 Instead of their shame my **p** will receive NIH
61: 9 that they are a **p** the LORD has blessed." 2446
62:10 Prepare the way for the **p.** 6639
62:12 They will be called the Holy **P,** 6639
63: 8 He said, "Surely they are my **p,** 6639
63:11 Then *his p* **recalled** the days of old, AIT
63:11 the days of Moses and his **p—** 6639
63:14 This is how you guided your **p** to make 6639
63:18 while your **p** possessed your holy place, 6639
64: 9 we pray, for we are all your **p.** 6639
65: 2 to an obstinate **p,** who walk in ways 6639
65: 3 a **p** who continually provoke me 6639
65: 5 **Such** *p* are smoke in my nostrils, AIT
65: 9 my **chosen** *p* will inherit them, AIT
65:10 for my **p** who seek me. 6639
65:18 to be a delight and its **p** a joy. 6639
65:19 over Jerusalem and take delight in my **p;** 6639
65:22 days of a tree, so will be the days of my **p;** 6639
65:23 for they will be a **p** blessed by the LORD, 2446
Jer 1: 3 when the **p** of Jerusalem went into exile. NIH
1:16 I will pronounce my judgments on **my p** 4392[S]
1:18 its priests and the **p** *of* the land. 6639
2:11 But my **p** have exchanged their Glory 6639
2:13 "My **p** have committed two sins: 6639
2:30 "In vain I punished your **p;** 1201
2:31 Why do my **p** say, 'We are free to roam; 6639
2:32 Yet my **p** have forgotten me, 6639
3:14 "Return, faithless **p,"** declares the LORD, 1201
3:21 the weeping and pleading of the **p** *of* Israel, 1201
3:22 faithless **p;** I will cure you of backsliding." 1201
4: 4 you men of Judah and **p** *of* Jerusalem, 3782
4:10 how completely you have deceived this **p** 6639
4:11 that time this **p** and Jerusalem will be told, 6639
4:11 in the desert blows toward my **p,** 1426+6639
4:22 "My **p** are fools; they do not know me. 6639
4:25 I looked, and there were no **p;** 132
5:10 for **these** *p* do not belong to the LORD. AIT
5:14 "Because **the p** have spoken these words, 4013[S]
5:14 a fire and these **p** the wood it consumes. 6639
5:15 a **p** whose language you do not know, 1580
5:19 And when *the p* **ask,** 'Why has the LORD AIT
5:21 you foolish and senseless **p,** 6639
5:23 these **p** have stubborn and rebellious hearts; 6639
5:26 "Among my **p** are wicked men who lie 6639
5:31 and my **p** love it this way. 6639
6: 1 "Flee for safety, **p** *of* Benjamin! 1201
6:14 of my **p** as though it were not serious. 6639
6:19 I am bringing disaster on this **p,** 6639
6:21 "I will put obstacles before this **p.** 6639
6:26 **p,** put on sackcloth and roll in ashes; 1426+6639
6:27 a tester of metals and my **p** the ore, 6639
7: 2 " 'Hear the word of the LORD, all you **p** NIH
7:12 because of the wickedness of my **p** Israel. 6639
7:15 all your brothers, the **p** *of* Ephraim.' 2446
7:16 for this **p** nor offer any plea or petition 6639
7:23 I will be your God and you will be my **p.** 6639
7:30 " 'The **p** *of* Judah have done evil 1201
7:32 when **p** will no longer call it Topheth or NIH
7:33 the carcasses of this **p** will become food for 6639
8: 1 and the bones of the **p** *of* Jerusalem will 3782
8: 5 Why then have these **p** turned away? 6639
8: 7 But my **p** do not know the requirements of 6639
8:11 of my **p** as though it were not serious. 1426+6639
8:19 the cry of my **p** from a land far away: 1426+6639
8:21 Since my **p** are crushed, I am crushed; 1426+6639
8:22 no healing for the wound of my **p?** 1426+6639
9: 1 and night for the slain of my **p.** 1426+6639
9: 2 so that I might leave my **p** and go away 6639
9: 2 a crowd of **unfaithful** *p.* AIT
9: 7 because of the sin of my **p?** 1426+6639
9:15 "See, I will make this **p** eat bitter food 6639
11: 2 to the **p** *of* Judah and to those who live 408
11: 4 you will be my **p,** and I will be your God. 6639
11: 9 among the **p** *of* Judah and those who live 408
11:12 and the **p** *of* Jerusalem will go and cry out 3782
11:14 "Do not pray for this **p** nor offer any plea 6639
12: 4 Moreover, *the p are* **saying,** AIT
12:14 the inheritance I gave my **p** Israel, 6639
12:16 the ways of my **p** and swear by my name, 6639
12:16 they once taught my **p** to swear by Baal— 6639
12:16 then they will be established among my **p.** 6639
13:10 These wicked **p,** who refuse to listen 6639
13:11 'to be my **p** for my renown and praise 6639
14:10 This is what the LORD says about this **p:** 6639
14:11 "Do not pray for the well-being of this **p.** 6639
Jer 14:16 And the **p** they are prophesying to will 6639
14:17 for my virgin daughter—my **p—** 6639
15: 1 my heart would not go out to this **p.** 6639
15: 7 and destruction on my **p,** 6639
15:19 Let **this** *p* turn to you, AIT
15:20 I will make you a wall to this **p,** 6639
16: 5 my love and my pity from this **p,"** 6639
16:10 "When you tell these **p** all this 6639
17:19 "Go and stand at the gate of the **p,** 1201+6639
17:20 and all **p** of Judah and everyone living NIH
17:26 *P will* **come** from the towns of Judah and AIT
18:11 "Now therefore say to the **p** *of* Judah 408
18:15 Yet my **p** have forgotten me; 6639
19: 1 Take along some of the elders of the **p** and 6639
19: 3 O kings of Judah and **p** *of* Jerusalem. 3782
19: 6 *p will* no longer **call** this place Topheth AIT
19:14 the LORD's temple and said to all the **p,** 6639
21: 7 the **p** in this city who survive the plague, 6639
21: 8 "Furthermore, tell the **p,** 6639
22: 2 and your **p** who come through these gates. 6639
22: 4 accompanied by their officials and their **p.** 6639
22: 8 **"P** from many nations will pass by this city NIH
23: 2 says to the shepherds who tend my **p:** 6639
23: 7 *p will* no longer **say,** AIT
23:13 by Baal and led my **p** Israel astray. 6639
23:14 the **p** *of* Jerusalem are like Gomorrah." 3782
23:22 to my **p** and would have turned them 6639
23:27 will make my **p** forget my name, 6639
23:32 "They tell them and lead my **p** astray 6639
23:32 They do not benefit these **p** in the least," 6639
23:33 "When these **p,** or a prophet or a priest, 6639
24: 7 They will be my **p,** and I will be their God, 6639
25: 1 to Jeremiah concerning all the **p** *of* Judah 6639
25: 2 to all the **p** *of* Judah and to all those living 6639
25:19 his attendants, his officials and all his **p,** 6639
25:20 and all the **foreign p** there; 6850
25:20 Gaza, Ekron, and the *p* **left** *at* Ashdod); AIT
25:24 and all the kings of the **foreign p** who live 6850
26: 2 to all the **p** of the towns of Judah who come NIH
26: 7 the **p** heard Jeremiah speak these words in 6639
26: 8 as Jeremiah finished telling all the **p** 6639
26: 8 the prophets and all the **p** seized him 6639
26: 9 And all the **p** crowded around Jeremiah in 6639
26:11 to the officials and all the **p,** 6639
26:12 to all the officials and all the **p:** 6639
26:16 the officials and all the **p** said to the priests 6639
26:17 and said to the entire assembly of **p,** 6639
26:18 He told all the **p** *of* Judah, 6639
26:23 the burial place of the **common p.)** 1201+6639
26:24 not handed over to the **p** to be put to death. 6639
27: 5 the earth and its **p** and the animals that are 132
27:12 serve him and his **p,** and you will live. 6639
27:13 Why will you and your **p** die by the sword, 6639
27:16 Then I said to the priests and all these **p,** 6639
28: 1 in the presence of the priests and all the **p:** 6639
28: 5 the priests and all the **p** who were standing 6639
28: 7 and in the hearing of all the **p:** 6639
28:11 and he said before all the **p,** "This is what 6639
29: 1 the other **p** Nebuchadnezzar had carried 6639
29:16 on David's throne and all the **p** who remain 6639
29:25 in your own name to all the **p** in Jerusalem, 6639
29:32 He will have no one left among this **p,** 6639
29:32 the good things I will do for my **p,** 6639
30: 3 'when I will bring my **p** Israel 6639
30:22 you will be my **p,** and I will be your God. 6639
31: 1 and they will be my **p."** 6639
31: 2 "The **p** who survive the sword 6639
31: 7 save your **p,** the remnant of Israel.' 6639
31:14 and my **p** will be filled with my bounty," 6639
31:23 *p* in the land of Judah and in its towns *will*
once again **use** these words: AIT
31:24 *P will* **live** together in Judah AIT
31:29 *p will* no longer **say,** 'The fathers have eaten AIT
31:33 I will be their God, and they will be my **p.** 6639
32:21 You brought your **p** Israel out of Egypt 6639
32:29 *p* **provoked** me to **anger** by burning AIT
32:30 "The **p** *of* Israel have done nothing but 1201
32:30 indeed, the **p** *of* Israel have done nothing 1201
32:32 The **p** *of* Israel and Judah has provoked 1201
32:32 the men of Judah and the **p** *of* Jerusalem. 3782
32:38 They will be my **p,** and I will be their God. 6639
32:42 all this great calamity on this **p,** 6639
33: 6 I will heal **my p** and will let them enjoy 4392[S]
33:24 not noticed that these **p** are saying, 6639
33:24 So they despise my **p** and no longer regard 6639
34: 5 As **p** made a funeral fire in honor NIH
34: 8 the **p** in Jerusalem to proclaim freedom for 6639
34:10 So all the officials and **p** who entered 6639
34:19 the **p** *of* the land who walked between 6639
35:13 the men of Judah and the **p** *of* Jerusalem, 3782
35:16 but these **p** have not obeyed me.' 6639
36: 3 Perhaps when the **p** *of* Judah hear 1074
36: 6 and read to the **p** from the scroll the words 6639
36: 6 to **all** *the p of* Judah who come in AIT
36: 7 against this **p** by the LORD are great." 6639
36: 9 the **p** in Jerusalem and those who had come 6639
36:10 the **p** at the LORD's temple the words 6639
36:13 Baruch read to the **p** from the scroll, 6639
36:14 from which you have read to the **p** 6639
36:31 the **p** *of* Judah every disaster I pronounced 408
37: 2 nor the **p** *of* the land paid any attention to 6639
37: 4 to come and go among the **p,** 6639
37:12 of the property among the **p** there. 6639
37:18 against you or your officials or this **p,** 6639
38: 1 Jeremiah was telling all the **p** when he said, 6639
38: 4 as well as all the **p,** 6639
38: 4 This man is not seeking the good of these **p** 6639

Jer 39: 8 to the royal palace and the houses of the **p** 6639
39: 9 to Babylon the **p** who remained in the city, 6639
39: 9 gone over to him, and the rest of the **p.** 6639
39:10 in the land of Judah some of the poor **p,** 6639
39:14 So he remained among his own **p.** 6639
40: 3 because *you p* **sinned** against the LORD AIT
40: 5 and live with him among the **p,** 6639
40: 6 with him among the **p** who were left behind 6639
41:10 the rest of the **p** who were in Mizpah— 6639
41:13 When all the **p** Ishmael had with him 6639
41:14 All the **p** Ishmael had taken captive 6639
42: 1 and all the **p** from the least to the greatest 6639
42: 8 and all the **p** from the least to the greatest. 6639
43: 1 When Jeremiah finished telling the **p** all 6639
43: 4 the army officers and all the **p** disobeyed 6639
44:15 all the **p** living in Lower and Upper Egypt, 6639
44:20 Then Jeremiah said to all the **p,** 6639
44:21 your kings and your officials and the **p** *of* 6639
44:24 Then Jeremiah said to all the **p,** 6639
44:24 **"Hear** the word of the LORD, all *you p* AIT
45: 5 For I will bring disaster on all **p,** 1414
46: 8 I will destroy cities and their **p.'** 3782
46:16 to our own **p** and our native lands, 6639
46:24 handed over to the **p** *of* the north." 6639
47: 2 The **p** will cry out; 132
48:43 O **p** *of* Moab," declares the LORD. 3782
48:46 The **p** *of* Chemosh are destroyed; 6639
49: 1 Why do his **p** live in its towns? 6639
49:28 attack Kedar and destroy the **p** *of* the East. 1201
49:31 neither gates nor bars; its *p* **live** alone. AIT
50: 4 "the **p** *of* Israel and the people of Judah 1201
50: 4 and the **p** *of* Judah together will go in tears 1201
50: 6 "My **p** have been lost sheep; 6639
50:16 let everyone return to his own **p,** 6639
50:33 "The **p** *of* Israel are oppressed, 1201
50:33 and the **p** *of* Judah as well. 1201
51: 1 against Babylon and the **p** *of* Leb Kamai. 3782
51:12 his decree against the **p** *of* Babylon. 3782
51:38 Her *p* all **roar** like young lions, AIT
51:45 "Come out of her, my **p!** 6639
51:64 And *her p will* **fall.'"** AIT
52: 6 so severe that there was no food for the **p** 6639
52:15 of the poorest **p** and those who remained in 6639
52:16 the rest of the **poorest** *p of* the land to work AIT
52:25 in charge of conscripting the **p** *of* the land 6639
52:28 of the **p** Nebuchadnezzar carried into exile: 6639
52:29 832 **p** from Jerusalem; 5883
52:30 There were 4,600 **p** in all. 5883
La 1: 1 deserted lies the city, once so full of **p!** 6639
1: 7 When her **p** fell into enemy hands, 6639
1:11 All her **p** groan as they search for bread; 6639
1:21 *"P have* **heard** my groaning, AIT
2:11 because my **p** are destroyed, 1426+6639
2:18 The hearts of **the p** cry out to the Lord. 4392^S
3:14 I became the laughingstock of all my **p;** 6639
3:48 because my **p** are destroyed. 1426+6639
4: 3 but my **p** have become heartless 1426+6639
4: 6 The punishment of my **p** is greater 1426+6639
4:10 when my **p** were destroyed. 1426+6639
4:12 nor did any of the world's **p,** 3782
4:15 *p* among the nations **say,** AIT
Eze 2: 4 **p** to whom I am sending you are obstinate 1201
3: 5 not being sent to a **p** *of* obscure speech 6639
3:25 so that you cannot go out among **the p.** 4392^S
4:12 bake it in the sight of **the p,** 2157^S
4:13 the **p** *of* Israel will eat defiled food among 1201
4:16 *The p will* **eat** rationed food in anxiety AIT
5:12 A **third** *of your p* will die of the plague AIT
6: 4 and I will slay your **p** in front of your idols. 2728
6: 7 Your *p will* **fall** slain among you, AIT
6:13 when their *p* lie **slain** among their idols AIT
7:11 none of **the p** will be left, 2157^S
7:27 the hands of the **p** *of* the land will tremble. 6639
11: 1 leaders of the **p.** 6639
11: 6 You have **killed** many *p* in this city AIT
11:15 of whom the **p** *of* Jerusalem have said, 3782
11:20 They will be my **p,** and I will be their God. 6639
12: 2 you are living among a rebellious **p.** 1074
12: 2 for they are a rebellious **p.** 1074
12:19 Say to the **p** *of* the land: 6639
12:24 or flattering divinations among the **p** 1074
13: 9 They will not belong to the council of my **p** 6639
13:10 " 'Because they lead my **p** astray, saying, 6639
13:12 the wall collapses, will **p** not ask you, NIH
13:17 the daughters of your **p** who prophesy out 6639
13:18 for their heads in order to ensnare **p.** 5883
13:18 the lives of my **p** but preserve your own? 6639
13:19 among my **p** for a few handfuls of barley 6639
13:19 By lying to my **p,** who listen to lies, 6639
13:20 with which you ensnare **p** like birds 5883
13:20 I will set free the **p** that you ensnare 5883
13:21 I will tear off your veils and save my **p** 6639
13:23 I will save my **p** from your hands. 6639
14: 5 I will do this to recapture the hearts of the **p** 1074
14: 8 I will cut him off from my **p.** 6639
14: 9 and destroy him from among my **p** Israel. 6639
14:11 **p** *of* Israel will no longer stray from me, 1074
14:11 They will be my **p,** and I will be their God, 6639
15: 6 so will I treat the *p* **living in** Jerusalem. AIT
17: 9 not take a strong arm or many **p** to pull it 6639
18: 2 "What do you **p** mean by quoting this 917^S
18:18 and did what was wrong among his **p.** 6638
20:13 " 'Yet the **p** *of* Israel rebelled against me in 1074
20:27 speak to the **p** *of* Israel and say to them, 1074
21: 5 Then all **p** will know that I the LORD 1414
21:12 son of man, for it is against my **p;** 6639
21:12 to the sword along with my **p.** 6639
Eze 21:24 'Because **you** *p* have brought to mind AIT
22:25 they devour **p,** take treasures 5883
22:27 and kill **p** to make unjust gain. 5883
22:29 The **p** *of* the land practice extortion 6639
23:24 and wagons and with a throng of **p;** 6639
24:18 So I spoke to the **p** in the morning, 6639
24:19 Then the **p** asked me, 6639
25: 3 the **p** *of* Judah when they went into exile, 1074
25: 4 therefore I am going to give you to the **p** *of* 1201
25:10 with the Ammonites to the **p** *of* the East as 1201
25:14 the hand of my **p** Israel, and they will deal 6639
26:11 he will kill your **p** with the sword, 6639
26:20 to the **p** *of* long ago. 6639
28:24 " 'No longer will the **p** 1074
28:25 When I gather the **p** *of* Israel from 1074
29:16 of confidence for the **p** *of* Israel but will be 1074
30: 5 and the **p** *of* the covenant land will fall by 1201
32: 3 a great throng of **p** I will cast my net 6639
33: 2 the **p** *of* the land choose one of their men 6639
33: 3 and blows the trumpet to warn the **p,** 6639
33: 6 not blow the trumpet to warn the **p** and 6639
33:24 the *p* **living in** those ruins in the land AIT
33:31 My **p** come to you, as they usually do, 6639
34:27 *the p will* **be** secure in their land. AIT
34:30 are my **p,** declares the Sovereign LORD. 6639
34:31 the sheep of my pasture, are **p,** 132
36: 8 and fruit for my **p** Israel, 6639
36:10 I will multiply the number of **p** upon you, 132
36:11 *I will* **settle** *p* **on** you as in the past AIT
36:12 I will cause **p,** my people Israel, 132
36:12 I will cause people, my **p** Israel, 6639
36:13 Because *p* **say** to you, AIT
36:17 **p** *of* Israel were living in their own land, 1074
36:20 'These are the LORD's **p,** 6639
36:28 you will be my **p,** and I will be your God. 6639
36:37 I will make their **p** as numerous as sheep, 132
36:38 the ruined cities be filled with flocks of **p.** 132
37:12 O my **p,** I am going to open your graves 6639
37:13 my **p,** will know that I am the LORD, 6639
37:23 They will be my **p,** and I will be their God. 6639
37:27 I will be their God, and they will be my **p.** 6639
38: 8 whose *p* **were gathered** from many nations AIT
38:11 I will attack a peaceful and unsuspecting **p** 3782
38:12 the resettled ruins and the **p** gathered from 6639
38:14 when my **p** Israel are living in safety, 6639
38:16 against my **p** Israel like a cloud that covers 6639
38:20 the **p** on the face of the earth will tremble 132
39: 7 my holy name among my **p** Israel. 6639
39:13 All the **p** *of* the land will bury them, 6639
39:23 the **p** *of* Israel went into exile for their sin, 1074
39:25 and will have compassion on all the **p** 1074
42:14 near the places that are for the **p."** 6639
43:10 describe the temple to the **p** *of* Israel, 1074
44:11 the burnt offerings and sacrifices for the **p** 6639
44:11 and stand before **the p** and serve them. 2157^S
44:19 into the outer court where the **p** are, 6639
44:19 that they do not consecrate the **p** by means 6639
44:23 They are to teach my **p** the difference 6639
45: 8 my princes will no longer oppress my **p** 6639
45: 9 Stop dispossessing my **p,** 6639
45:15 to make atonement for **the p,** 2157^S
45:16 All the **p** *of* the land will participate 6639
45:22 a sin offering for himself and for all the **p** 6639
46: 3 On the Sabbaths and New Moons the **p** *of* 6639
46: 9 the **p** *of* the land come before the LORD 6639
46:18 not take any of the inheritance of the **p,** 6639
46:18 so that none of my **p** will be separated 6639
46:20 into the outer court and consecrating the **p."** 6639
46:24 will cook the sacrifices of the **p."** 6639
Da 2:43 so the **p** will be a mixture and will 10050+10240
2:44 nor will it be left to another **p.** 10553
3:29 Therefore I decree that the **p** *of* any nation 10553
4:25 from **p** and will live with the wild animals; 10050
4:32 from **p** and will live with the wild animals; 10050
4:33 He was driven away from **p** and ate grass 10050
5:21 driven away from **p** and given the mind of
an animal; 10050+10120
6:26 of my kingdom *p* **must** fear and reverence AIT
7:27 the **p** *of* the Most High. 10553
8:24 the mighty men and the holy **p.** 6639
9: 6 and to all the **p** *of* the land. 6639
9: 7 of Judah and **p** *of* Jerusalem and all Israel, 3782
9:15 who brought your **p** out of Egypt with 6639
9:16 and your **p** an object of scorn to all those 6639
9:19 your city and your **p** bear your Name." 6639
9:20 of my **p** Israel and making my request to 6639
9:24 "Seventy 'sevens' are decreed for your **p** 6639
9:26 The **p** *of* the ruler who will come will 6639
10:14 to you what will happen to your **p** in 6639
11:14 among your own **p** will rebel in fulfillment 6639
11:21 the kingdom when its **p** feel secure, NIH
11:23 and with only a few **p** he will rise to power. 1580
11:32 the **p** who know their God will firmly resist
him. 6639
11:39 over **many** *p* and will distribute the land at AIT
12: 1 the great prince who protects your **p,** 1201+6639
12: 1 But at that time your **p—** 6639
12: 7 of the holy **p** has been finally broken, 6639
Hos 1: 9 "Call him Lo-Ammi, for you are not my **p,** 6639
1:10 'You are not my **p,'** they will be called 6639
1:11 The **p** *of* Judah and the people of Israel 1201
1:11 and the **p** *of* Israel will be reunited, 1201
2: 1 "Say of your brothers, 'My **p,'** 6639
2:23 I will say to those called 'Not my **p,'** 6639
2:23 'You are my **p'**; and they will say, 6639
4: 4 for your **p** are like those who bring charges 6639
4: 6 my **p** are destroyed from lack of knowledge 6639
Hos 4: 8 of my **p** and relish their wickedness. 6639
4: 9 And it will be: Like **p,** like priests. 6639
4:12 of my **p.** They consult a wooden idol 6639
4:14 a **p** without understanding will come 6639
5:12 like rot to the **p** *of* Judah. 1074
6:11 I would restore the fortunes of my **p,** 6639
8: 1 because the **p** have broken my covenant NIH
9: 2 and winepresses will not feed **the p;** 4392^S
10: 5 The **p who live in** Samaria fear for 8907
10: 5 Its **p** will mourn over it, 6639
10:14 the roar of battle will rise against your **p,** so 6639
11: 7 My **p** are determined to turn from me. 6639
12:11 *Its p* **are** worthless! AIT
13: 2 It is said of **these** *p,* AIT
13:16 The **p** of Samaria must bear their guilt, NIH
Joel 2:16 Gather the **p,** consecrate the assembly; 6639
2:17 Let them say, "Spare your **p,** O LORD. 6639
2:18 for his land and take pity on his **p.** 6639
2:23 Be glad, O **p** *of* Zion, 1201
2:26 never again will my **p** be shamed. 6639
2:27 never again will my **p** be shamed. 6639
2:28 I will pour out my Spirit on all **p.** 1414
3: 2 my **p** Israel, for they scattered my people 6639
3: 2 for they scattered **my p** among the nations 889^S
3: 3 for my **p** and traded boys for prostitutes; 6639
3: 6 You sold the **p** *of* Judah and Jerusalem to 1201
3: 8 I will sell your sons and daughters to the **p** 1201
3:16 But the LORD will be a refuge for his **p,** 6639
3:16 a stronghold for the **p** *of* Israel. 1201
3:19 because of violence done to the **p** *of* Judah, 1201
Am 1: 5 The **p** *of* Aram will go into exile to Kir," 6639
2:11 Is this not true, **p** *of* Israel?" 1201
3: 1 spoken against you, O **p** *of* Israel— 1201
3: 6 do not the **p** tremble? 6639
3: 9 and the oppression among her **p."** NIH
4: 8 **P** staggered from town to town for water
8993+9109^S
6: 1 to whom the **p** *of* Israel come! 1074
7: 8 a plumb line among my **p** Israel; 6639
7:15 'Go, prophesy to my **p** Israel.' 6639
8: 2 "The time is ripe for my **p** Israel; 6639
9: 1 Bring them down on the heads of all **the p;** 4392^S
9:10 All the sinners among my **p** will die by 6639
9:14 I will bring back my exiled **p** Israel; 6639
Ob 1:12 nor rejoice over the **p** *of* Judah in the day 1201
1:13 not march through the gates of my **p** in 6639
1:19 **P** from the Negev will occupy NIH
1:19 and **p** from the foothills will possess NIH
Jnh 1: 8 From what **p** are you?" 6639
4:11 hundred and twenty thousand **p** who cannot
tell their right hand from their left, 132
Mic 1: 9 It has reached the very gate of my **p,** 6639
2: 3 "I am planning disaster against this **p,** 5476
2: 8 Lately my **p** have risen up like an enemy. 6639
2: 9 women of my **p** from their pleasant homes. 6639
2:11 he would be just the prophet for this **p!** 6639
2:12 the place will throng with **p.** 132
3: 2 from **my p** and the flesh from their bones; 2157^S
3: 5 "As for the prophets who lead my **p** astray, 6639
6: 2 For the LORD has a case against his **p;** 6639
6: 3 "My **p,** what have I done to you? 6639
6: 5 My **p,** remember what Balak king 6639
6:12 her **p** are liars and their tongues speak 3782
6:16 over to ruin and your **p** to derision; 3782
7:12 In that day *p will* **come** to you from Assyria AIT
7:14 Shepherd your **p** with your staff, 6639
Na 3: 3 *p* **stumbling** over the corpses— AIT
3:18 Your **p** are scattered on the mountains 6639
Hab 1: 6 that ruthless and impetuous **p,** 1580
1: 7 They are a feared and **dreaded** *p;* AIT
3:13 You came out to deliver your **p,** 6639
Zep 1:17 on the **p** and they will walk like blind men, 132
2: 5 to you who live by the sea, O Kerethite **p;** 1580
2: 8 who insulted my **p** and made threats 6639
2: 9 The remnant of my **p** will plunder them; 6639
2:10 insulting and mocking the **p** *of* the LORD 6639
3:10 my scattered **p,** will bring me offerings. 1426
Hag 1: 2 "These **p** say, 'The time has not yet come 6639
1:12 and the whole remnant of the **p** obeyed 6639
1:12 And the **p** feared the LORD. 6639
1:13 gave this message of the LORD to the **p:** 6639
1:14 the spirit of the whole remnant of the **p.** 6639
2: 2 the high priest, and to the remnant of the **p.** 6639
2: 4 Be strong, all you **p** *of* the land,' 6639
2:14 with this **p** and this nation in my sight,' 6639
Zec 1: 3 Therefore tell the **p:** 2157^S
1:21 against the land of Judah to scatter **its p."** 2023^S
2:11 in that day and will become my **p.** 6639
5: 6 the iniquity of **the p** throughout the land." 4392
7: 2 The **p** of Bethel had sent Sharezer NIH
7: 5 "Ask all the **p** *of* the land and the priests, 6639
8: 6 to the remnant of this **p** at that time, 6639
8: 7 "I will save my **p** from the countries of 6639
8: 8 they will be my **p,** and I will be faithful 6639
8:11 not deal with the remnant of this **p** as I did 6639
8:12 as an inheritance to the remnant of this **p.** 6639
9: 8 an oppressor overrun **my p,** 2157^S
9:16 on that day as the flock of his **p.** 6639
10: 2 Therefore *the p* **wander** like sheep oppressed AIT
11: 6 For I will no longer have pity on the **p** *of* 3782
12: 5 'The **p** *of* Jerusalem are strong, 3782
13: 9 I will say, 'They are my **p,'** 6639
14: 2 rest of the **p** will not be taken from the city. 6639
14:18 the Egyptian **p** do not go up and take part, 5476
Mal 1: 4 a **p** always under the wrath of the LORD. 6639
2: 9 be despised and humiliated before all the **p,** 6639
Mt 1:21 because he will save his **p** from their sins." *3295*

Mt	2: 6	be the shepherd of my **p** Israel.' "	*3295*
	3: 5	**P** went out to him from Jerusalem	*NIG*
	4:16	**p** living in darkness have seen a great light;	*3295*
	4:23	and sickness among the **p.**	*3295*
	4:24	and **p** brought to him all who were ill	*NIG*
	5:11	"Blessed are you when *p* **insult** you,	*AIT*
	5:15	Neither *do p* **light** a lamp and put it under	*AIT*
	5:21	that it was said *to* the **p long ago,**	*792*
	5:33	that it was said *to* the **p long ago,**	*792*
	7:16	*Do p* **pick** grapes from thornbushes,	*AIT*
	12:23	All the **p** were astonished and said,	*4063*
	12:27	by whom do your **p** drive them out?	*3836+5626*
	13: 2	while all the **p** stood on the shore.	*4063*
	13:10	"Why do you speak *to* **the p** in parables?"	*899S*
	13:54	he began teaching **the p** in their synagogue,	*899S*
	14: 5	but he was afraid of the **p,**	*4063*
	14:19	he directed the **p** to sit down on the grass.	*4063*
	14:19	and the disciples gave them *to* the **p.**	*4063*
	14:35	*P* **brought** all their sick to him	*AIT*
	15: 8	" 'These **p** honor me with their lips,	*3295*
	15:31	The **p** were amazed when they saw	*4063*
	15:32	"I have compassion for these **p;**	*4063*
	15:36	and they in turn *to* the **p.**	*4063*
	16:13	"Who do **p** say the Son of Man is?"	*476*
	18: 7	the world because of the things that cause **p**	*NIG*
	21:23	and the elders *of* the **p** came to him.	*3295*
	21:26	we are afraid of the **p,**	*4063*
	21:43	and given *to* a **p** who will produce its fruit.	*1620*
	21:46	of the crowd because the **p** held that he was	*NIG*
	22:10	and gathered all the **p** they could find,	*NIG*
	22:30	*p will* neither **marry** nor *be* **given in marriage;**	*AIT*
	23:28	on the outside you appear *to* **p** as righteous	*476*
	24:11	and deceive **many** *p.*	*AIT*
	24:38	*p* **were** eating and drinking,	*AIT*
	25:32	and he will separate **the p** one from another	*899S*
	26: 3	the elders *of* the **p** assembled in the palace	*3295*
	26: 5	"or there may be a riot among the **p."**	*3295*
	26:47	the chief priests and the elders *of* the **p.**	*3295*
	26:71	another girl saw him and said *to* **the p** there,	*AIT*
	27: 1	and the elders *of* the **p** came to the decision	*3295*
	27: 9	the price set on him by the **p** *of* **Israel,**	*2702+5626*
	27:25	All the **p** answered,	*3295*
	27:52	*of* many **holy p** who had died were raised	*41*
	27:53	into the holy city and appeared *to* **many** *p.*	*AIT*
	27:64	the **p** that he has been raised from the dead.	*3295*
Mk	1: 5	the **p of Jerusalem** went out to him.	*2643*
	1:22	The *p were* **amazed** at his teaching,	*AIT*
	1:27	The *p were* all so **amazed** that they asked	*AIT*
	1:32	That evening after sunset the *p* **brought**	*AIT*
	1:45	Yet the *p* still **came** to him from everywhere.	*AIT*
	2: 1	the *p* **heard** that he had come home.	*AIT*
	2:18	*Some p* **came** and asked Jesus,	*AIT*
	3: 8	many **p** came to him from Judea,	*4436*
	3: 9	to keep the *p* from **crowding** him.	*AIT*
	4: 1	while all the **p** were along the shore at	*4063*
	4:15	**Some** *p* are like seed along the path,	*AIT*
	5:14	the *p* **went out** to see what had happened.	*AIT*
	5:16	had seen it told **the p** what had happened	*899S*
	5:17	Then the *p* **began** to plead with Jesus	*AIT*
	5:20	And **all** the *p* were amazed.	*AIT*
	5:31	"You see the **p** crowding against you,"	*4063*
	5:38	with **p** crying and wailing loudly.	*NIG*
	6: 5	except lay his hands on a few **sick** *p*	*AIT*
	6:12	and preached that *p should* **repent.**	*AIT*
	6:13	and anointed many **sick** *p* with oil	*AIT*
	6:31	because **so many** *p* were coming and going	*AIT*
	6:36	Send **the p** away so they can go to	*899S*
	6:39	to have **all** the *p* sit down in groups on	*AIT*
	6:41	to his disciples to set before **the p.**	*899S*
	6:54	of the boat, *p* **recognized** Jesus.	*AIT*
	7: 6	" 'These **p** honor me with their lips,	*3295*
	7:32	There *some p* **brought** to him a man	*AIT*
	7:37	*P were* **overwhelmed with amazement.**	*AIT*
	8: 2	"I have compassion for these **p;**	*4063*
	8: 6	to his disciples to set before the **p,**	*4063*
	8: 8	The *p* **ate** and were satisfied.	*AIT*
	8:22	and *some p* **brought** a blind man	*AIT*
	8:24	He looked up and said, "I see **p;**	*476*
	8:27	"Who do **p** say I am?"	*476*
	9:15	As soon as all the **p** saw Jesus,	*4063*
	10: 1	Again crowds of **p** came to him,	*NIG*
	10:13	*P were* **bringing** little children to Jesus	*AIT*
	11: 5	**some** *p* standing there asked,	*AIT*
	11: 6	and the *p* **let** them **go.**	*AIT*
	11: 8	**Many** *p* spread their cloaks on the road,	*AIT*
	11:32	(They feared the **p,**	*4063*
	12:41	Many **rich** *p* threw in large amounts.	*AIT*
	14: 2	they said, "or the **p** may riot."	*3295*
	15: 6	to release a prisoner whom the *p* **requested.**	*AIT*
	16:18	they will place their hands on **sick** *p,*	*AIT*
Lk	1:16	Many *of* the **p** of Israel will he bring back	*5626*
	1:17	to make ready a **p** prepared for the Lord."	*3295*
	1:21	the **p** were waiting for Zechariah	*3295*
	1:25	and taken away my disgrace among the **p."**	*476*
	1:65	of Judea *p were* **talking about**	*AIT*
	1:68	he has come and has redeemed his **p.**	*3295*
	1:77	to give his **p** the knowledge of salvation	*3295*
	2:10	of great joy that will be *for* all the **p.**	*3295*
	2:31	you have prepared in the sight *of* all **p,**	*3295*
	2:32	the Gentiles and for glory *to* your **p** Israel."	*3295*
	3:14	and don't accuse **p** falsely—	*NIG*
	3:15	The **p** were waiting expectantly	*3295*
	3:18	with many other words John exhorted the **p**	*3295*
	3:21	When all the **p** were being baptized,	*3295*
	4:28	**All** the *p* in the synagogue were furious	*AIT*
	4:31	and on the Sabbath began to teach **the p.**	*899S*
Lk	4:36	**All** the *p* were amazed and said	*AIT*
	4:40	When the sun was setting, **the p** brought	*899S*
	4:41	Moreover, demons came out of **many** *p,*	*AIT*
	4:42	The **p** were looking for him and	*4063*
	5: 1	the **p** crowding around him and listening to	*4063*
	5: 3	he sat down and taught the **p** from the boat.	*4063*
	5:15	so that **crowds of p** came to hear him and	*4063*
	6:17	a great number *of* **p** from all over Judea,	*3295*
	6:19	and the **p** all tried to touch him,	*4063*
	6:44	*P do* not **pick** figs from thornbushes,	*AIT*
	7: 1	saying all this in the hearing *of* the **p,**	*3295*
	7:16	"God has come to help his **p."**	*3295*
	7:29	(All the **p,** even the tax collectors,	*3295*
	7:31	can I compare the **p** of this generation?	*476*
	8: 4	and **p** were coming to Jesus from town	*3836*
	8:35	the *p* **went out** to see what had happened.	*AIT*
	8:36	Those who had seen it told **the p** how	*899S*
	8:37	all the **p** of the region of the Gerasenes	*4436*
	8:45	**p** are crowding and pressing against you."	*4063*
	8:47	In the presence *of* all the **p,**	*3295*
	8:52	**all** the *p* were wailing and mourning	*AIT*
	9: 5	If **p** do not welcome you,	*4012*
	9: 6	the gospel and healing **p** everywhere.	*NIG*
	9:16	to the disciples to set before the **p.**	*4063*
	9:53	*p* there *did* not **welcome**	*AIT*
	11:40	*You* **foolish** *p!*	*AIT*
	11:46	because you load **p** down	*476*
	13:14	the synagogue ruler said *to* the **p,**	*4063*
	13:17	but the **p** were delighted with all	*4063*
	13:23	"Lord, are only a few **p** going to be saved?"	*3836*
	13:29	*P will* **come** from east and west and north	*AIT*
	13:32	'I will drive out demons and **heal p**	*699+2617*
	16: 4	*p will* **welcome** me into their houses.'	*AIT*
	16: 8	For the **p** of this world are more shrewd	*5626*
	16: 8	with their own kind than are the **p** of	*5626*
	17: 1	that **cause p to sin** are bound to come,	*4998*
	17:21	nor *will p* **say,**	*AIT*
	17:27	*P were* **eating,** drinking, marrying and	*AIT*
	17:28	*P were* **eating** and drinking,	*AIT*
	17:34	on that night **two** *p* will be in one bed;	*AIT*
	18:15	*P were* also **bringing** babies to Jesus	*AIT*
	18:43	all the **p** saw it, they also praised God.	*3295*
	19: 7	**All** *the p* saw this and began to mutter,	*AIT*
	19:11	near Jerusalem and **the p** thought that	*899S*
	19:36	*p* **spread** their cloaks on the road.	*AIT*
	19:47	and the leaders *among* the **p** were trying	*3295*
	19:48	because all the **p** hung on his words.	*3295*
	20: 1	the **p** in the temple courts and preaching	*3295*
	20: 6	we say, 'From men,' all the **p** will stone us,	*3295*
	20: 9	He went on to tell the **p** this parable:	*3295*
	20:16	*When* the *p* **heard** this, they said,	*AIT*
	20:19	But they were afraid of the **p.**	*3295*
	20:34	"The **p** of this age marry and are given	*5626*
	20:45	While all the **p** were listening,	*3295*
	21: 4	All **these** *p* gave their gifts out	*AIT*
	21:23	in the land and wrath *against* this **p.**	*3295*
	21:38	the **p** came early in the morning to hear him	*3295*
	22: 2	for they were afraid of the **p.**	*3295*
	22:66	the council of the elders *of* the **p,**	*3295*
	23: 5	up the **p** all over Judea by his teaching.	*3295*
	23:13	the rulers and the **p,**	*3295*
	23:14	as one who was inciting the **p** to rebellion.	*3295*
	23:27	A large number *of* **p** followed him,	*3295*
	23:35	The **p** stood watching,	*3295*
	23:48	When all the **p** who had gathered	*4063*
	24:19	in word and deed before God and all the **p.**	*3295*
Jn	2:23	at the Passover Feast, **many** *p* saw	*AIT*
	3:11	but still *you p do* not **accept** our testimony.	*AIT*
	3:23	*p were constantly* **coming**	*AIT*
	4:28	to the town and said *to* the **p,**	*476*
	4:48	"Unless *you p* **see** miraculous signs	*AIT*
	5: 3	a great number *of* **disabled** *p* used to lie—	*AIT*
	6: 2	and a great **crowd of p** followed him	*4063*
	6: 5	shall we buy bread for **these** *p* to eat?"	*AIT*
	6:10	Jesus said, "Have the **p** sit down."	*476*
	6:14	After the **p** saw the miraculous sign	*476*
	6:23	the place where the **p** had eaten the bread	*NIG*
	7:12	Others replied, "No, he deceives the **p."**	*4063*
	7:25	of the **p** *of* **Jerusalem** began to ask,	*2643*
	7:35	**p live scattered among** the Greeks,	*1402+3836*
	7:40	On hearing his words, some of the **p** said,	*4063*
	7:43	Thus the **p** were divided because of Jesus.	*4063*
	8: 2	where all the **p** gathered around him,	*3295*
	8:12	When Jesus spoke again *to* **the p,** he said,	*899S*
	10:41	and **many** *p* came to him.	*AIT*
	11:42	for the benefit of the **p** standing here,	*4063*
	11:50	for the **p** than that the whole nation perish."	*3295*
	12:18	**Many p,** because they had heard	*4063*
	17: 2	For you granted him authority over all **p**	*4922*
	18:14	be good if one man died for the **p.**	*3295*
	18:35	"It was your **p** and your chief priests	*1620*
Ac	2:17	God says, I will pour out my Spirit on all **p.**	*4922*
	2:37	*When* the *p* **heard** this,	*AIT*
	2:47	and enjoying the favor of all the **p.**	*3295*
	3: 9	the **p** saw him walking and praising God,	*3295*
	3:11	all the **p** were astonished and came running	*3295*
	3:22	a prophet like me from among your own **p;**	*81*
	3:23	be completely cut off from among his **p.'**	*3295*
	4: 1	while they were speaking to the **p.**	*3295*
	4: 2	because the apostles were teaching the **p**	*3295*
	4: 8	"Rulers and elders *of* the **p!**	*3295*
	4:10	you and all the **p** of Israel:	*3295*
	4:17	from spreading any further among the **p,**	*3295*
	4:21	because all the **p** were praising God	*3295*
	4:23	Peter and John went back to **their own** *p*	*AIT*
	4:27	the Gentiles and the **p** of Israel in this city	*3295*
	5:12	miraculous signs and wonders among the **p.**	*3295*
Ac	5:13	though they were highly regarded by the **p.**	*3295*
	5:15	**p** brought the sick into the streets	*NIG*
	5:20	tell the **p** the full message of this new life."	*3295*
	5:21	and began to teach the **p.**	*NIG*
	5:25	in the temple courts teaching the **p."**	*3295*
	5:26	they feared that the **p** would stone them.	*3295*
	5:34	who was honored *by* all the **p,**	*3295*
	5:37	of the census and led a band of **p** in revolt.	*3295*
	6: 8	and miraculous signs among the **p.**	*3295*
	6:12	So they stirred up the **p** and the elders and	*3295*
	7: 3	'Leave your country and your **p,'** God said,	*5149*
	7:17	number of our **p** in Egypt greatly increased.	*3295*
	7:19	with our **p** and oppressed our forefathers	*1169*
	7:25	Moses thought that his **own p** would realize	*81*
	7:34	I have indeed seen the oppression *of* my **p**	*3295*
	7:37	a prophet like me from your **own p.'**	*81*
	7:51	"You **stiff-necked** *p,* with uncircumcised	*AIT*
	8: 9	in the city and amazed all the **p** of Samaria.	*1620*
	8:10	and **all** the *p,* both high and low,	*AIT*
	9:15	and their kings and before the **p** of Israel.	*5626*
	9:42	and **many** *p* believed in the Lord.	*AIT*
	10:22	who is respected by all the Jewish **p.**	*1620*
	10:27	inside and found a large gathering of **p.**	*NIG*
	10:36	You know the message God sent *to* the **p**	*5626*
	10:41	He was not seen *by* all the **p,**	*3295*
	10:42	He commanded us to preach *to* the **p** and	*3295*
	10:47	"Can anyone keep **these** *p* from	*AIT*
	11:21	a great number of **p** believed and turned to	*NIG*
	11:24	and a great **number of p** were brought to	*4063*
	11:26	the church and taught great **numbers of p.**	*4063*
	12:11	the Jewish **p** were anticipating."	*3295*
	12:12	**many** *p* had gathered and were praying.	*AIT*
	12:20	He had been quarreling *with* the **p of Tyre**	*5601*
	12:21	and delivered a public address to **the p.**	*899S*
	13:15	a message of encouragement for the **p,**	*3295*
	13:17	God *of* the **p** of Israel chose our fathers;	*3295*
	13:17	the **p** prosper during their stay in Egypt,	*3295*
	13:19	in Canaan and gave their land to his **p**	*NIG*
	13:21	Then the *p* **asked for** a king,	*AIT*
	13:24	and baptism *to* all the **p** of Israel.	*3295*
	13:27	**The p** of Jerusalem and their rulers did	*3836*
	13:31	They are now his witnesses to our **p.**	*3295*
	13:42	the *p* **invited** them to speak further	*AIT*
	14: 4	The **p** of the city were divided;	*4436*
	15:14	by taking from the Gentiles a **p** for himself.	*3295*
	15:31	The *p* **read** it and were glad	*AIT*
	16: 4	and elders in Jerusalem *for* **the p** to obey.	*899S*
	17:30	but now he commands all **p** everywhere	*476*
	18:10	because I have many **p** in this city."	*3295*
	18:13	the **p** to worship God in ways contrary to	*476*
	19: 4	He told the **p** to believe in the one coming	*3295*
	19:26	and led astray large numbers of **p** here	*4063*
	19:29	*p* seized Gaius and Aristarchus, Paul's traveling companions from Macedonia, and **rushed** as one man	*AIT*
	19:32	**Most** of the *p* did not even know why	*AIT*
	19:33	in order to make a defense *before* the **p.**	*1322*
	20: 2	many words of encouragement to **the p,**	*899S*
	20: 7	Paul spoke to **the p** and,	*899S*
	20:12	The *p* **took** the young man home alive	*AIT*
	21:12	and the **p there** pleaded with Paul not to go	*1954*
	21:28	against our **p** and our law and this place.	*3295*
	21:30	and the **p** came running from all directions.	*3295*
	21:39	Please let me speak to the **p."**	*3295*
	22: 5	to bring **these** *p* as prisoners to Jerusalem to	*AIT*
	22:24	to find out why the *p were* **shouting at** him	*AIT*
	23: 5	not speak evil about the ruler *of* your **p.' "**	*3295*
	24:17	I came to Jerusalem to bring my **p** gifts for	*1620*
	26:17	from your own **p** and from the Gentiles.	*3295*
	26:23	would proclaim light *to* his own **p** and to	*3295*
	28: 6	**The p** expected him to swell up	*1254+3836S*
	28:17	although I have done nothing against our **p**	*3295*
	28:19	to bring against my own **p.**	*1620*
	28:22	for we know that **p** everywhere are talking	*NIG*
	28:26	to this **p** and say, "You will be ever hearing	*3295*
Ro	1: 5	we received grace and apostleship to call **p**	*NIG*
	2:22	that **p** should not commit adultery,	*NIG*
	9: 4	**the p** of Israel. Theirs is the adoption as	*4015S*
	9:25	"I will call them 'my **p'** who are not	*3295*
	9:25	'my people' who are not my **p;**	*3295*
	9:26	'You are not my **p,'**	*3295*
	10:21	to a disobedient and obstinate **p."**	*3295*
	11: 1	I ask then: Did God reject his **p?**	*3295*
	11: 2	God did not reject his **p,**	*3295*
	11:14	that I may somehow arouse my own **p**	*4922*
	12:13	Share with **God's p** who are in need.	*41*
	12:16	to associate *with p* **of low position.**	*AIT*
	15:10	it says, "Rejoice, O Gentiles, with his **p."**	*3295*
	16: 2	for she has been a great help to **many** *p,*	*AIT*
	16:18	For **such** *p* are not serving our Lord Christ,	*AIT*
	16:18	they deceive the minds *of* **naive** *p.*	*AIT*
1Co	4:19	not only how these **arrogant** *p* are talking,	*AIT*
	5: 9	not to associate with **sexually immoral** *p*—	*AIT*
	5:10	**the** *p* of this world **who** are immoral,	*AIT*
	8: 7	**Some** *p* are still so accustomed to idols that	*AIT*
	10: 7	"The **p** sat down to eat and drink and got	*3295*
	10:15	I speak *to* **sensible** *p;*	*AIT*
	10:18	Consider the **p** of Israel:	*NIG*
	14:21	the lips of foreigners I will speak *to* this **p,**	*3295*
	14:36	Or are you the **only** *p* it has reached?	*AIT*
	15:29	why *are p* **baptized** for them?	*AIT*
	16: 1	Now about the collection for **God's p:**	*41*
2Co	3: 1	Or do we need, like **some** *p,*	*AIT*
	4:15	and more **p** may cause thanksgiving	*NIG*
	6:16	and they will be my **p."**	*3295*
	9:12	not only supplying the needs *of* **God's p**	*41*
	10: 2	be toward **some** *p* who think that we live by	*AIT*

2Co 10:11 Such p should realize that what we are AIT
13: 7 that p will see that we have stood the test NIG
Gal 1: 7 Evidently some p are throwing you AIT
3:16 meaning many p, but "and to your seed," AIT
4:17 Those p are zealous to win you over, AIT
6:10 let us do good to all p, AIT
Eph 2:19 but fellow citizens with God's p 41
3: 8 I am less than the least of all God's p, 41
4:12 to prepare God's p for works of service, 41
5: 3 these are improper for God's holy p. 41
Php 3: 5 of the p of Israel, of the tribe of Benjamin, 1169
Col 3:12 Therefore, as God's chosen p, AIT
1Th 5: 3 While p are saying, "Peace and safety," AIT
2Th 1:10 he comes to be glorified in his holy p and 41
3:12 Such p we command and urge in AIT
1Ti 3:15 how p ought to conduct themselves NIG
4: 3 They forbid p to marry and order them NIG
5: 7 Give the p these instructions, too, NIG
6: 9 P who want to get rich fall into temptation 3836
6:10 Some p, eager for money, AIT
2Ti 3: 2 P will be lovers of themselves, 476
Tit 1:10 For there are many rebellious p, AIT
2:14 for himself a p that are his very own, 3295
3: 1 Remind the p to be subject to rulers 899S
3:14 Our p must learn to devote themselves AIT
Heb 2:17 make atonement for the sins of the p. 3295
4: 9 then, a Sabbath-rest for the p of God; 3295
5: 3 as well as for the sins of the p. 3295
6:10 as you have helped his p and continue 41
7: 5 to collect a tenth from the p— 3295
7:11 the basis of it the law was given to the p), 3295
7:27 and then for the sins of the p. 3295
8: 8 But God found fault with the p and said: 899S
8:10 I will be their God, and they will be my p. 3295
9: 7 the sins the p had committed in ignorance. 3295
9:19 every commandment of the law to all the p, 3295
9:19 and sprinkled the scroll and all the p. 3295
9:28 to take away the sins of many p; AIT
10:30 and again, "The Lord will judge his p." 3295
11:13 All these p were still living by faith AIT
11:14 P who say such things show 3836
11:25 He chose to be mistreated along with the p 3295
11:29 By faith the p passed through the Red Sea NIG
11:30 p had marched around them for seven days. NIG
13: 2 by so doing some p have entertained angels AIT
13:12 to make the p holy through his own blood. 3295
13:24 Greet all your leaders and all God's p. 41
Jas 4: 4 You adulterous p, don't you know AIT
5: 1 Now listen, you rich p, weep and wail AIT
1Pe 2: 9 But you are a chosen p, a royal priesthood, 1169
2: 9 a holy nation, a p belonging to God, 3295
2:10 Once you were not a p, but now 3295
2:10 but now you are the p of God; 3295
3:20 In it only a few p, eight in all, 6034
2Pe 2: 1 there were also false prophets among the p, 3295
2: 5 on its ungodly p, but protected Noah, 3180
2:18 they entice p who are just escaping 3836
3:11 what kind of p ought you to be? AIT
3:16 which ignorant and unstable p distort, AIT
Jude 1: 5 that the Lord delivered his p out of Egypt, 3295
Rev 2:14 p there who hold to the teaching of Balaam, AIT
3: 4 Yet you have a few p in Sardis who have 3950
5: 9 from every tribe and language and p 3295
7: 9 from every nation, tribe, p and language, 3295
8:11 and many p died from the waters 476
9: 4 but only those p who did not have the seal 476
9:10 in their tails they had power to torment p 476
11: 9 and a half days men from every p, 3295
11:13 Seven thousand p were killed in AIT
13: 7 he was given authority over every tribe, p, 3295
14: 6 to every nation, tribe, language and p. 3295
16: 2 on the p who had the mark of the beast 476
16: 8 sun was given power to scorch p with fire. 476
18: 4 "Come out of her, my p, 3295
19:18 and the flesh of all p, free and slave, AIT
20: 9 and surrounded the camp of God's p, 41
21: 3 They will be his p, and God himself 3295
22:21 grace of the Lord Jesus be with God's p. 41

PEOPLE'S (11) [PEOPLE]

Ex 18:19 be the p representative before God 4200+6639
Lev 9:15 for the p sin offering and slaughtered it 6639
2Ch 25:15 which said, "Why do you consult this p gods, 6639
Est 1:22 in each p tongue that every man should 6639
Eze 36: 3 the object of p malicious talk and slander, 6639
Mic 2: 4 my p possession is divided up. 6639
3: 3 who eat my p flesh, strip off their skin 6639
Hab 2:13 that the p labor is only fuel for the fire, 6639
Mt 2: 4 the p chief priests and teachers of the law, 3295
13:15 For this p heart has become calloused; 3295
Ac 28:27 For this p heart has become calloused; 3295

PEOPLED (1) [PEOPLE]

Eze 26:17 O city of renown, p by men of the sea! 3782

PEOPLES (156) [PEOPLE]

Ge 10: 5 (From these the maritime p spread out 1580
12: 3 all p on earth will be blessed through you." 5476
17:16 kings of p will come from her." 6639
25:23 two p from within you will be separated; 4211
27:29 May nations serve you and p bow down 4211
28: 3 until you become a community of p. 6639
28:14 All p on earth will be blessed through you 5476
29: 1 and came to the land of the eastern p. 1201
48: 4 I will make you a community of p, 6639
Dt 1: 7 go to all the neighboring p in the Arabah, 8907
4:27 The LORD will scatter you among the p, 6639
6:14 the gods of the p around you; 6639
7: 6 of all the p on the face of the earth to 6639
7: 7 you were more numerous than other p, 6639
7: 7 for you were the fewest of all p. 6639
7:16 the p the LORD your God gives over to you. 6639
7:19 the same to all the p you now fear. 6639
13: 7 gods of the p around you, 6639
14: 2 Out of all the p on the face of the earth, 6639
28:10 the p on earth will see that you are called 6639
32: 8 he set up boundaries for the p according to 6639
33:19 They will summon p to the mountain 6639
Jos 4:24 the p of the earth might know that the hand 6639
Jdg 2:12 and worshiped various gods of the p 6639
6: 3 and other eastern p invaded the country. 1201
6:33 and other eastern p joined forces 1201
7:12 the other eastern p had settled in the valley, 1201
8:10 of the armies of the eastern p; 1201
1Sa 27: 8 (From ancient times these p had lived in AIT
1Ki 8:43 the p of the earth may know your name 6639
8:60 so that all the p of the earth may know that 6639
9: 7 and an object of ridicule among all p. 6639
9:20 and Jebusites (these p were not Israelites), 889S
1Ch 5:25 to the gods of the p of the land, 6639
16:24 his marvelous deeds among all p. 6639
2Ch 6:33 the p of the earth may know your name 6639
7:20 and an object of ridicule among all p. 6639
8: 7 and Jebusites (these p were not Israelites), 889S
13: 9 of your own as the p of other lands do? 6639
32:13 and my fathers have done to all the p of 6639
32:17 as the gods of the p of the other lands did 1580
32:19 as they did about the gods of the other p of 6639
Ezr 3: 3 Despite their fear of the p around them, 6639
4: 4 the p around them set out to discourage 6639
9: 1 separate from the neighboring p 6639
9: 2 and have mingled the holy race with the p 6639
9:11 a land polluted by the corruption of its p. 6639
9:14 the p who commit such detestable practices? 6639
10: 2 by marrying foreign women from the p 6639
10:11 Separate yourselves from the p around you 6639
Ne 9:24 to them, along with their kings and the p of 6639
9:30 you handed them over to the neighboring p. 6639
10:28 the neighboring p for the sake of the Law 6639
10:30 to give our daughters in marriage to the p 6639
10:31 the neighboring p bring merchandise 6639
13:24 language of one of the other p, 2256+6639+6639
Est 1:16 the p of all the provinces of King Xerxes. 6639
3: 8 among the p in all the provinces 6639
3:12 and the nobles of the various p. 2256+6639+6639
Ps 2: 1 Why do the nations conspire and the p plot 4211
7: 7 Let the assembled p gather around you. 4211
7: 8 let the LORD judge the p. 6639
9: 8 he will govern the p with justice. 4211
33:10 he thwarts the purposes of the p. 6639
44: 2 the p and made our fathers flourish. 4211
44:14 the p shake their heads at us. 4211
47: 3 p under our feet. 4211
49: 1 Hear this, all you p; 6639
57: 9 I will sing of you among the p. 4211
66: 8 O p, let the sound of his praise be heard; 6639
67: 3 May the p praise you, O God; 6639
67: 3 may all the p praise you. 6639
67: 4 the p justly and guide the nations of 6639
67: 5 May the p praise you, O God; 6639
67: 5 may all the p praise you. 6639
77:14 you display your power among the p. 6639
87: 6 LORD will write in the register of the p: 6639
96: 3 his marvelous deeds among all p. 6639
96:10 he will judge the p with equity. 6639
96:13 in righteousness and the p in his truth. 6639
97: 6 and all the p see his glory. 6639
98: 9 in righteousness and the p with equity. 6639
102:22 when the p and the kingdoms assemble 6639
105:20 the ruler of p set him free. 6639
106:34 the p as the LORD had commanded them, 6639
108: 3 I will sing of you among the p. 4211
117: 1 extol him, all you p. 569
144: 2 who subdues p under me. 6639
149: 7 on the nations and punishment on the p, 4211
Pr 24:24 p will curse him and nations denounce him. 6639
Isa 2: 3 Many p will come and say, "Come, 6639
2: 4 and will settle disputes for many p. 6639
11:10 of Jesse will stand as a banner for the p; 6639
14: 6 struck down p with unceasing blows, 6639
17:12 Oh, the uproar of the p— 4211
17:13 the p roar like the roar of surging waters, 4211
19:13 cornerstones of her p have led Egypt astray. 8657
25: 3 Therefore strong p will honor you; 6639
25: 6 a feast of rich food for all p, a banquet 6639
25: 7 the shroud that enfolds all p, the sheet 6639
30:28 of the p a bit that leads them astray. 6639
33: 3 At the thunder of your voice, the p flee; 6639
33:12 The p will be burned as if to lime; 6639
34: 1 pay attention, you p! 4211
37:18 Assyrian kings have laid waste all these p 824
43: 9 nations gather together and the p assemble. 4211
49:22 I will lift up my banner to the p; 6639
55: 4 See, I have made him a witness to the p, 4211
55: 4 a leader and commander of the p. 4211
60: 2 the earth and thick darkness is over the p, 4211
61: 9 the nations and their offspring among the p. 6639
Jer 1:15 I am about to summon all the p of 5476
10: 3 For the customs of the p are worthless; 6639
10:25 on the p who do not call on your name. 5476
25: 9 I will summon all the p of the north 5476
34: 1 and all his army and all the kingdoms and p 6639
Jer 51:58 the p exhaust themselves for nothing, 6639
La 1:18 Listen, all you p; look upon my suffering. 6639
Eze 3: 6 not to many p of obscure speech 6639
20:32 like the p of the world, 5476
27: 3 merchant of p on many coasts, 6639
32: 9 I will trouble the hearts of many p 6639
32:10 I will cause many p to be appalled at you, 6639
36:15 the scorn of the p or cause your nation 6639
Da 3: 4 O p, nations and men of every language: 10553
3: 7 lyre, harp and all kinds of music, all the p, 10553
4: 1 King Nebuchadnezzar, To the p, 10553
4:35 the p of the earth are regarded as nothing. 10163
4:35 with the powers of heaven and the p of 10163
5:19 all the p and nations and men 10553
6:25 Then King Darius wrote to all the p, 10553
7:14 all p, nations and men of every language 10553
Joel 2:17 Why should they say among the p, 6639
Mic 1: 2 Hear, O p, all of you, listen, 6639
4: 1 and p will stream to it. 6639
4: 3 between many p and will settle disputes 6639
5: 7 be in the midst of many p like dew from 6639
5: 8 in the midst of many p, 6639
Na 3: 4 by her prostitution and p by her witchcraft. 5476
Hab 2: 5 the nations and takes captive all the p. 6639
2: 8 the p who are left will plunder you. 6639
2:10 You have plotted the ruin of many p, 6639
Zep 3: 9 "Then will I purify the lips of the p, 6639
3:20 and praise among all the p of the earth 6639
Zec 8:20 "Many p and the inhabitants 6639
8:22 And many p and powerful nations will
come to Jerusalem 6639
10: 9 Though I scatter them among the p, 6639
12: 2 that sends all the surrounding p reeling. 6639
12: 6 and left all the surrounding p, 6639
14:17 the p of the earth do not go up to Jerusalem 5476
Ac 3:25 'Through your offspring all p on earth will 4255
4:25 " 'Why do the nations rage and the p plot 3295
Ro 15:11 and sing praises to him, all you p." 3295
Rev 1: 7 the p of the earth will mourn because 5876
10:11 "You must prophesy again about many p, 3295
17:15 where the prostitute sits, are p, multitudes, 3295

PEOR (9) [BAAL PEOR, BETH PEOR]

Nu 23:28 And Balak took Balaam to the top of P, 7186
25: 3 Israel joined in worshiping the Baal of P. 7186
25: 5 in worshiping the Baal of P." 7186
25:18 when they deceived you in the affair of P 7186
25:18 when the plague came as a result of P." 7186
31:16 from the LORD in what happened at P, 7186
Dt 4: 3 everyone who followed the Baal of P, 7186
Jos 22:17 Was not the sin of P enough for us? 7186
Ps 106:28 to the Baal of P and ate sacrifices offered 7186

PER (1)

Ex 38:26 one beka p person, 4200

PERATH (4)

Jer 13: 4 now to P and hide it there in a crevice in 7310
13: 5 So I went and hid it at P, 7310
13: 6 "Go now to P and get the belt I told you 7310
13: 7 to P and dug up the belt and took it from 7310

PERAZIM (1) [BAAL PERAZIM]

Isa 28:21 as he did at Mount P, he will rouse himself 7292

PERCEIVE (5) [PERCEIVED, PERCEIVING]

Job 9:11 when he goes by, I cannot p him. 1067
33:14 though man may not p it. 8800
Ps 139: 2 you p my thoughts from afar. 1067
Pr 24:12 does not he who weighs the heart p it? 1067
Isa 43:19 Now it springs up; do you not p it? 3359

PERCEIVED (1) [PERCEIVE]

Isa 64: 4 no one has heard, no ear has p, 263

PERCEIVING (4) [PERCEIVE]

Isa 6: 9 be ever seeing, but never p.' 3359
Mt 13:14 you will be ever seeing but never p. 3972
Mk 4:12 " 'they may be ever seeing but never p, 3972
Ac 28:26 you will be ever seeing but never p." 3972

PERCH (2) [PERCHED]

Mt 13:32 birds of the air come and p in its branches." 2942
Mk 4:32 that the birds of the air can p in its shade." 2942

PERCHED (1) [PERCH]

Lk 13:19 and the birds of the air p in its branches." 2942

PERES (1)

Da 5:28 P: Your kingdom is divided and given to 10593

PERESH (1)

1Ch 7:16 gave birth to a son and named him P. 7303

PEREZ (18) [PEREZ UZZAH, PEREZITE, RIMMON PEREZ]

Ge 38:29 And he was named P. 7289
46:12 P and Zerah (but Er and Onan had died in 7289
46:12 The sons of P: Hezron and Hamul. 7289

Nu 26:20 through P, the Perezite clan; 7289
26:21 The descendants of P were: 7289
Ru 4:12 may your family be like that of P, 7289
4:18 This, then, is the family line of P: 7289
4:18 P was the father of Hezron, 7289
1Ch 2:4 bore him P and Zerah. 7289
2:5 The sons of P: Hezron and Hamul. 7289
4:1 P, Hezron, Carmi, Hur and Shobal. 7289
9:4 a descendant of P son of Judah. 7289
27:3 He was a descendant of P and chief of all 7289
Ne 11:4 the son of Mahalalel, a descendant of P; 7289
11:6 The descendants of P who lived 7289
Mt 1:3 Judah the father of P and Zerah, *5756*
1:3 P the father of Hezron, *5756*
Lk 3:33 the son of Hezron, the son *of* P, *5756*

PEREZ UZZAH (2) [PEREZ]
2Sa 6:8 to this day that place is called P. 7290
1Ch 13:11 to this day that place is called P. 7290

PEREZITE (1) [PEREZ]
Nu 26:20 through Perez, the P clan; 7291

PERFECT (38) [PERFECTER, PERFECTING, PERFECTION, PERFECTLY]
Dt 32:4 He is the Rock, his works are p, 9459
2Sa 22:31 "As for God, his way is p; 9459
22:33 with strength and makes my way p. 9459
Job 36:4 *one* p *in* knowledge is with you. 9459
37:16 wonders of *him who* is p *in* knowledge? 9459
Ps 18:30 As for God, his way is p; 9459
18:32 with strength and makes my way p. 9459
19:7 law of the LORD is p, reviving the soul. 9459
50:2 From Zion, p *in* beauty, God shines forth. 4817
64:6 *"We have* devised *a* p plan!" 9462
SS 6:9 but my dove, my p *one*, is unique, 9447
Isa 25:1 in p faithfulness you have done marvelous things, 590
26:3 You will keep in p peace him whose mind is steadfast, 8934+8934
Eze 16:14 the splendor I had given you made your beauty p, 4003
27:3 " 'You say, O Tyre, "I am p *in* beauty." 4003
28:12 full of wisdom and p *in* beauty. 4003
Mt 5:48 Be p, therefore, as your heavenly Father is perfect. *5455*
5:48 therefore, as your heavenly Father is p. *5455*
19:21 Jesus answered, "If you want to be p, go, *5455*
Ro 12:2 his good, pleasing and p will. *5455*
2Co 12:9 for my power *is* made p in weakness." *5464*
Php 3:12 or *have* already *been* made p, *5457*
Col 1:28 that we may present everyone p in Christ. *5455*
3:14 which binds them all together in p unity. *5456*
Heb 2:10 make the author of their salvation p *5457*
5:9 and, *once* made p, he became the source *5457*
7:19 (for the law made nothing p), *5457*
7:28 *who has been* made p forever. *5457*
9:11 and *more* p tabernacle that is not man-made, *5455*
10:1 make p those who draw near to worship. *5457*
10:14 by one sacrifice *he has* made p forever those who are being made holy. *5457*
11:40 with us *would they be* made p. *5457*
12:23 to the spirits of righteous men made p, *5457*
Jas 1:17 Every good and p gift is from above, *5455*
1:25 the p law that gives freedom, and continues *5455*
3:2 he is a p man, able to keep his whole body *5455*
1Jn 4:18 But p love drives out fear, *5455*
4:18 The one who fears *is* not made p in love. *5457*

PERFECTER (1) [PERFECT]
Heb 12:2 Jesus, the author and p of our faith, *5460*

PERFECTING (1) [PERFECT]
2Co 7:1 p holiness out of reverence for God. *2200*

PERFECTION (9) [PERFECT]
Ps 119:96 To all p I see a limit; 9416
La 2:15 the city that was called the p *of* beauty, 4003
Eze 27:4 your builders brought your beauty to p. 4005
27:11 *they* brought your beauty to p. 4005
28:12 " 'You were the model of p, full of wisdom 9422
1Co 13:10 but when p comes, the imperfect disappears. *5455*
2Co 13:9 and our prayer is for your p. *2937*
13:11 Aim for p, listen to my appeal, *2936*
Heb 7:11 If p could have been attained through *5459*

PERFECTLY (2) [PERFECT]
1Co 1:10 and that you may be p united *899+2936+3836*
2Co 11:6 We have made this p clear to you *1877+4246*

PERFORM (26) [PERFORMANCE, PERFORMED, PERFORMING, PERFORMS]
Ex 3:20 the wonders that *I will* p among them. 6913
4:17 in your hand so *you can* p miraculous signs 6913
4:21 that *you* p before Pharaoh all the wonders 6913
4:28 miraculous signs he had commanded him to p. NIH
7:9 'P a miracle,' then say to Aaron, 5989
10:1 that I *may* p these miraculous signs of mine 8883
18:20 the way to live and the duties *they are to* p. 6913
Nu 3:7 *They are to* p duties for him and for 9068
4:31 as they p service at the Tent of Meeting: NIH
18:3 to be responsible to you and are to p all NIH
Jdg 16:27 men and women watching Samson p. 8471
2Sa 7:23 to make a name for himself, and to p great 6913
1Ki 8:11 the priests could not p their service because 6641
1Ch 17:21 to make a name for yourself, and to p great NIH
2Ch 5:14 the priests could not p their service because 6641
31:16 to p the daily duties of their various tasks, NIH
Isa 28:21 his strange work, and p his task, 6268
Jer 21:2 Perhaps the LORD *will* p wonders for us 6913
Eze 44:16 to minister before me and p my service. 9068
Mt 7:22 drive out demons and p many miracles?' *4472*
24:24 and p great signs and miracles to deceive *1443*
Mk 13:22 and false prophets will appear and p signs *1443*
Lk 23:8 he hoped to see him p some miracle. *1181*
Jn 3:2 For no one could p the miraculous signs *4472*
Ac 4:30 to heal and p miraculous signs and wonders *1181*
2Co 9:12 This service that *you* p is *1355+3311+3836+4047*

PERFORMANCE (1) [PERFORM]
1Ch 23:28 the p *of* other duties at the house of God. 5126

PERFORMED (35) [PERFORM]
Ex 4:30 *He* also p the signs before the people, 6913
10:2 with the Egyptians and how *I* p my signs 8492
11:10 Moses and Aaron p all these wonders 6913
Nu 14:11 in spite of all the miraculous signs *I have* p 6913
14:22 and the miraculous signs *I* p in Egypt and 6913
Dt 10:21 he is your God, who p for you those great 6913
11:3 the signs *he* p and the things he did in 6913
34:12 the mighty power or p the awesome deeds NIH
Jos 24:17 and p those great signs before our eyes. 6913
Jdg 16:25 and *he* p for them. 7464
1Sa 12:7 as to all the righteous acts p *by* the LORD 6913
2Sa 23:20 who p great exploits. NIH
1Ch 6:32 *They* p their duties according to 6641
11:22 who p great exploits. 7189
25:1 the list of the men who p this service: 4856
Ne 9:17 and failed to remember the miracles *you* p 6913
12:45 *They* p the service of their God and 9068
Ps 105:27 *They* p his miraculous signs among them, 8492
Jer 32:20 *You* p miraculous signs and wonders 8492
Da 4:2 and wonders that the Most High God *has* p 10522
Mt 11:20 in which most of his miracles *had been* p, *1181*
11:21 that *were* p in you had been performed *1181*
11:21 that were performed in you *had been* p *1181*
11:23 that *were* p in you had been performed *1181*
11:23 that were performed in you *had been* p *1181*
Lk 1:51 *He has* p mighty deeds with his arm; *4472*
10:13 that *were* p in you had been performed *1181*
10:13 that were performed in you *had been* p *1181*
Jn 2:11 Jesus p at Cana in Galilee. *4472*
4:54 the second miraculous sign that Jesus p, *4472*
6:2 the miraculous signs *he had* p on the sick. *4472*
10:41 "Though John never p a miraculous sign, *4472*
Ac 5:12 The apostles p many miraculous signs *1181*
Rev 13:13 And *he* p great and miraculous signs, *4472*
19:20 and with him the false prophet who *had* p *4472*

PERFORMING (3) [PERFORM]
Nu 8:26 in p their duties at the Tent of Meeting, 9068
Jn 11:47 "Here *is* this man p many miraculous signs. *4472*
Rev 16:14 spirits of demons p miraculous signs, *4472*

PERFORMS (5) [PERFORM]
Job 5:9 *He* p wonders that cannot be fathomed, 6913
9:10 *He* p wonders that cannot be fathomed, 6913
Ps 77:14 You are the God *who* p miracles; 6913
Da 6:27 *he* p signs and wonders in the heavens and 10522
Heb 10:11 priest stands and p his religious duties; *3310*

PERFUME (25) [PERFUME-MAKERS, PERFUMED, PERFUMER, PERFUMERS, PERFUMES]
Ex 30:33 Whoever makes p like it and whoever puts 8379
Ru 3:3 Wash and p *yourself*, and put on 6057
Pr 27:9 P and incense bring joy to the heart, 9043
Ecc 7:1 A good name is better than fine p, 9043
10:1 As dead flies give p a bad smell, 8379+9043
SS 1:3 your name is like p poured out. 9043
1:12 my p spread its fragrance. 5948
4:10 and the fragrance of your p than any spice! 9043
5:13 like beds of spice yielding p. 5349
Isa 3:20 the p bottles and charms, 5883
Mt 26:7 with an alabaster jar *of* very expensive p, *3693*
26:9 "This p could have been sold at a high price *3693*
26:12 When she poured this p on my body, *3693*
Mk 14:3 with an alabaster jar of very expensive p, *3693*
14:3 the jar and poured the p on his head. *899S*
14:4 "Why this waste *of* p? *3693*
14:8 *She* poured p on my body beforehand to prepare for my burial. *3690*
Lk 7:37 she brought an alabaster jar *of* p, *3693*
7:38 kissed them and poured p on them. *3693*
7:46 but she has poured p on my feet. *3693*
Jn 11:2 the same one who poured p on the Lord *3693*
12:3 about a pint of pure nard, an expensive p; *3693*
12:3 with the fragrance *of* the p. *3693*
12:5 "Why wasn't this p sold and the money *3693*
12:7 save this p for the day of my burial. *899S*

PERFUME-MAKERS (1) [PERFUME]
Ne 3:8 and Hananiah, one of the p, 8382

PERFUMED (2) [PERFUME]
Pr 7:17 *I have* p my bed *with* myrrh, 5678
SS 3:6 p *with* myrrh and incense made from all 7787

PERFUMER (3) [PERFUME]
Ex 30:25 a fragrant blend, the work of a p. 8379
30:35 fragrant blend of incense, the work of a p. 8379
37:29 fragrant incense—the work of a p. 8379

PERFUMERS (1) [PERFUME]
1Sa 8:13 He will take your daughters to be p 8384

PERFUMES (5) [PERFUME]
2Ch 16:14 with spices and various blended p, 5126+5351
Est 2:12 six months with oil of myrrh and six with p 1411
SS 1:3 Pleasing is the fragrance of your p; 9043
Isa 57:9 with olive oil and increased your p. 8383
Lk 23:56 they went home and prepared spices and p. *3693*

PERGA (3)
Ac 13:13 Paul and his companions sailed to P *4308*
13:14 From P they went on to Pisidian Antioch. *4308*
14:25 and when they had preached the word in P, *4308*

PERGAMOS (KJV) See PERGAMUM

PERGAMUM (2)
Rev 1:11 to Ephesus, Smyrna, P, Thyatira, Sardis, *4307*
2:12 "To the angel of the church in P write: *4307*

PERHAPS (36)
Ge 16:2 p I can build a family through her." 218
32:20 when I see him, p he will receive me." 218
43:12 P it was a mistake. 218
Ex 32:30 p I can make atonement for your sin." 218
Nu 22:6 P then I will be able to defeat them 218
22:11 P then I will be able to fight them 218
23:3 P the LORD will come to meet with me. 218
23:27 P it will please God to let you curse them 218
Jos 9:7 "But p you live near us. 218
1Sa 6:5 P he will lift his hand from you 218
9:6 P he will tell us what way to take." 218
14:6 P the LORD will act in our behalf. 218
2Sa 14:15 p he will do what his servant asks. 218
14:16 P the king will agree to deliver his servant 3954
1Ki 18:27 P he is deep in thought, or busy, 3954
20:31 P he will spare your life." 218
2Ki 2:16 P the Spirit of the LORD has picked him 7153
Job 1:5 "P my children have sinned 218
Isa 44:14 or p took a cypress or oak. NIH
47:12 P you will succeed, 218
47:12 p you will cause terror. 218
Jer 20:10 saying, "P he will be deceived; 218
21:2 P the LORD will perform wonders for us 218
26:3 P they will listen and each will turn 218
36:3 P when the people of Judah hear 218
36:7 P they will bring their petition before 218
51:8 Get balm for her pain; p she can be healed. 218
Eze 12:3 P they will understand, 218
Am 5:15 P the LORD God Almighty will have mercy on the remnant of Joseph. 218
Zep 2:3 p you will be sheltered on the day of 218
Lk 20:13 p they will respect him.' *2711*
Ac 8:22 P he will forgive you for having such *726+1623*
17:27 and p reach out for him and *726+1145+1623*
1Co 15:37 p of wheat or of something else. *1623+5593*
16:6 P I will stay with you awhile, *5593*
Phm 1:15 P the reason he was separated from you for *5440*

PERIDA (1)
Ne 7:57 the descendants of Sotai, Sophereth, P, 7263

PERIL (3)
Job 22:10 why sudden p terrifies you, 7065
Ps 107:26 in their p their courage melted away. 8288
2Co 1:10 He has delivered us from such a deadly p, *NIG*

PERIOD (28) [PERIODS]
Ge 31:35 I'm having my p." 851+2006
50:10 a seven-day p of mourning for his father. 65
Ex 2:23 During that long p, the king of Egypt died. 3427
Lev 12:2 she is unclean during her monthly p. 1864+5614
12:5 the woman will be unclean, as during her p. 5614
15:19 the impurity of her monthly p 5614
15:20 " 'Anything she lies on during her p will 5614
15:25 at a time other than her monthly p or has 5614
15:25 a discharge that continues beyond her p, 5614
15:25 just as in the days of her p. 5614
15:26 as is her bed during her monthly p, 5614
15:26 will be unclean, as during her p. 5614
15:33 for a *woman* in her monthly p, 1865+5614
18:19 during the uncleanness of her monthly p. 5614
20:18 with a woman during her monthly p 1865
25:8 of years amount to a p *of* forty-nine years. 3427
Nu 6:5 " '*During* the entire p *of* his vow 3427
6:5 be holy until the p of his separation to 3427

Nu 6: 6 Throughout the p of his separation to 3427
6: 8 the p of his separation he is consecrated to 3427
6:12 for the p of his separation and must bring 3427
6:13 when the p of his separation is over. 3427
Job 1: 5 When a p of feasting had run its course, 3427
Eze 18: 6 or lie with a woman during her p. 5614
22:10 those who violate women during their p, 5614
Da 7:12 but were allowed to live for a p of time.) 10221+10232+10530
Ac 1: 3 He appeared to them over a p of forty days 1328
24: 2 "We have enjoyed a long p of peace 4498

PERIODS (1) [PERIOD]

1Ch 9:25 and share their duties for seven-day p. 2021+3427+8679

PERISH (84) [PERISHABLE, PERISHED, PERISHES, PERISHING]

Ge 6:17 Everything on earth will p. 1588
47:19 Why should we p before your eyes— 4637
Ex 19:21 to see the LORD and many of them p. 5877
Lev 26:38 You will p among the nations; 6
Dt 4:26 that you will quickly p from the land 6+6
11:17 and you will soon p from the good land 6
28:22 which will plague you until you p. 6
32:25 Young men and young women will p, NIH
Jos 23:13 until you p from this good land, 6
23:16 and you will quickly p from 6
Jdg 5:31 "So may all your enemies p, O LORD! 6
1Sa 26:10 or he will go into battle and p. 6200
2Ki 9: 8 The whole house of Ahab will p. 6
Est 4:14 but you and your father's family will p. 6
4:16 And if I p, I perish." 6
4:16 And if I perish, I p." 6
Job 3: 3 "May the day of my birth p, 6
3:11 "Why did I not p at birth, 4637
4: 9 at the blast of his anger they p. 3983
4:20 unnoticed, they p forever. 6
6:18 they go up into the wasteland and p. 6
20: 7 he will p forever, like his own dung; 6
34:15 all mankind would p together 1588
36:12 they will p by the sword and die 6296
Ps 1: 6 but the way of the wicked will p. 6
9: 3 they stumble and p before you. 6
9:18 nor the hope of the afflicted ever p. 6
10:16 the nations will p from his land. 6
37:20 But the wicked will p: 6
41: 5 "When will he die and his name p?" 6
49:10 the senseless alike p and leave their wealth 6
49:12 he is like the beasts that p. 1950
49:20 like the beasts that p. 1950
68: 2 may the wicked p before God. 6
71:13 May my accusers p in shame; 3983
73:27 Those who are far from you will p; 6
80:16 at your rebuke your people p. 6
83:17 may they p in disgrace. 6
92: 9 O LORD, surely your enemies will p; 6
102:26 They will p, but you remain; 6
Pr 11:10 when the wicked p, there are shouts of joy. 6
19: 9 and he who pours out lies will p. 6
21:28 A false witness will p, 6
28:28 when the wicked p, the righteous thrive. 6
Isa 1:28 and those who forsake the LORD will p. 3983
29:14 the wisdom of the wise will p, 6
31: 3 both will p together. 3983
41:11 who oppose you will be as nothing and p. 6
57: 1 The righteous p, and no one ponders it 6
60:12 or kingdom that will not serve you will p; 6
Jer 6:21 neighbors and friends will p." 6
8:14 to the fortified cities and p there! 1959
8:14 For the LORD our God has doomed us to p 1959
10:11 not make the heavens and the earth, will p 10005
10:15 when their judgment comes, they will p. 6
14:15 Those same prophets will p by sword 9462
16: 4 They will p by sword and famine, 3983
27:10 I will banish you and you will p. 6
27:15 I will banish you and you will p, 6
40:15 and the remnant of Judah to p?" 6
44:12 They will all p in Egypt; 9462
44:27 in Egypt will p by sword and famine 9462
49:10 relatives and neighbors will p, 8720
51:18 when their judgment comes, they will p. 6
Eze 5:12 of your people will die of the plague or p 3983
Jnh 1: 6 will take notice of us, and we will not p." 6
3: 9 from his fierce anger so that we will not p." 6
Zec 11: 9 Let the dying die, and the perishing p. 3948
13: 8 "two-thirds will be struck down and p; 1588
Lk 13: 3 But unless you repent, you too will all p. 660
13: 5 But unless you repent, you too will all p." 660
21:18 But not a hair of your head will p. 660
Jn 3:16 that whoever believes in him shall not p 660
10:28 I give them eternal life, and they shall never p; 660
11:50 for the people than that the whole nation p." 660
Ac 8:20 "May your money p with you, 724+1639+1650
13:41 you scoffers, wonder and p, 906
Ro 2:12 the law will also p apart from the law, 660
Col 2:22 These are all destined to p with use, 5785
2Th 2:10 They p because they refused to love NIG
Heb 1:11 They will p, but you remain; 660
1Pe 1: 4 into an inheritance that can never p, spoil 915
2Pe 2:12 and like beasts they too will p. 5780+5785
3: 9 patient with you, not wanting anyone to p, 660

PERISHABLE (6) [PERISH]

1Co 15:42 The body that is sown is p, 1877+5785
15:50 nor does the p inherit the imperishable. 5785
15:53 p must clothe itself with the imperishable, 5778
15:54 When the p has been clothed with 5778
1Pe 1:18 that it was not with p things such as silver 5778
1:23 you have been born again, not of p seed, 5778

PERISHED (14) [PERISH]

Ge 7:21 Every living thing that moved on the earth p 1588
Nu 16:33 they p and were gone from the community. 6
Dt 2:14 that entire generation of fighting men had p 9462
7:20 the survivors who hide from you have p. 6
2Sa 1:27 The weapons of war have p!" 6
Job 4: 7 Who, being innocent, has ever p? 6
Ps 9: 6 even the memory of them has p. 6
83:10 who p at Endor and became like refuse on 9012
119:92 I would have p in my affliction. 6
Jer 7:28 Truth has p; it has vanished from their lips. 6
12: 4 the animals and birds have p. 6200
49: 7 Has counsel p from the prudent? 6
La 1:19 My priests and my elders p in the city 1588
Mic 4: 9 Has your counselor p, 6

PERISHES (5) [PERISH]

Job 4:11 The lion p for lack of prey, 6
8:13 so p the hope of the godless. 6
18:17 The memory of him p from the earth; 6
Pr 11: 7 When a wicked man dies, his hope p; 6
1Pe 1: 7 which p even though refined by fire— 660

PERISHING (11) [PERISH]

Job 31:19 if I have seen anyone p for lack of clothing, 6
33:18 his life from p by the sword. 6296
Pr 31: 6 Give beer to those who are p, 6
Ecc 7:15 a righteous man p in his righteousness, 6
Isa 27:13 Those who were p in Assyria 6
Jer 44:18 and have been p by sword and famine." 9462
Zec 11: 9 Let the dying die, and the p perish. 3948
1Co 1:18 the cross is foolishness to those who are p, 660
2Co 2:15 who are being saved and those who are p. 660
4: 3 it is veiled to those who are p. 660
2Th 2:10 of evil that deceives those who are p. 660

PERIZZITES (23)

Ge 13: 7 The Canaanites and P were also living in 7254
15:20 Hittites, P, Rephaites, 7254
34:30 a stench to the Canaanites and P, 7254
Ex 3: 8 Amorites, P, Hivites and Jebusites. 7254
3:17 Amorites, P, Hivites and Jebusites— 7254
23:23 P, Canaanites, Hivites and Jebusites, 7254
33: 2 Hittites, P, Hivites and Jebusites. 7254
34:11 Hittites, P, Hivites and Jebusites. 7254
Dt 7: 1 Girgashites, Amorites, Canaanites, P, 7254
20:17 the Hittites, Amorites, Canaanites, P, 7254
Jos 3:10 P, Girgashites, Amorites and Jebusites. 7254
9: 1 Canaanites, P, Hivites and Jebusites)— 7254
11: 3 Hittites, P and Jebusites in the hill country; 7254
12: 8 Canaanites, P, Hivites and Jebusites): 7254
17:15 for yourselves there in the land of the P 7254
24:11 as did also the Amorites, P, Canaanites, 7254
Jdg 1: 4 the LORD gave the Canaanites and P 7254
1: 5 putting to rout the Canaanites and P. 7254
3: 5 Amorites, P, Hivites and Jebusites. 7254
1Ki 9:20 from the Amorites, Hittites, P, Hivites 7254
2Ch 8: 7 from the Hittites, Amorites, P, Hivites 7254
Ezr 9: 1 like those of the Canaanites, Hittites, P, 7254
Ne 9: 8 Amorites, P, Jebusites and Girgashites. 7254

PERJURERS (2) [PERJURY]

Mal 3: 5 to testify against sorcerers, adulterers and p, 2021+4200+8678+9214
1Ti 1:10 for slave traders and liars and p— 2156

PERJURY (1) [PERJURERS]

Jer 7: 9 commit adultery and p, 2021+4200+8678+9214

PERMANENT (4) [PERMANENTLY]

Lev 25:34 it is their p possession. 6409
Jos 8:28 So Joshua burned Ai and made it a p heap 6409
Jn 8:35 Now a slave has no p place in the family, 3531
Heb 7:24 he has a p priesthood. 563

PERMANENTLY (2) [PERMANENT]

Lev 25:23 " 'The land must not be sold p, 4200+7552
25:30 the house in the walled city shall belong p to the buyer 2021+4200+7552

PERMISSIBLE (4) [PERMIT]

1Co 6:12 "Everything is p for me"—but not everything is beneficial. 2003
6:12 "Everything is p for me"—but I will not be mastered by anything. 2003
10:23 "Everything is p"—but not everything is beneficial. 2003
10:23 "Everything is p"—but not everything is constructive. 2003

PERMISSION (12) [PERMIT]

Jdg 11:17 'Give us p to go through your country,' AIT
1Sa 20: 6 'David earnestly asked my p to hurry 8626+8626
20:28 "David earnestly asked me for p to 8626+8626
Ne 13: 6 Some time later I asked his p 4946
Est 9:13 "give the Jews in Susa p to carry out 5989
Isa 22:16 and who gave you p to cut out a grave 4200
Da 1: 8 asked the chief official for p not to defile 1335
Mk 5:13 He gave them p, and the evil spirits came 2205
Lk 8:32 and he gave them p. 2205
Jn 19:38 With Pilate's p, he came and took 2205
Ac 21:40 Having received the commander's p, 2205
26: 1 "You have p to speak for yourself." 2205

PERMIT (4) [PERMISSIBLE, PERMISSION, PERMITS, PERMITTED, PERMITTING]

Ex 12:23 not p the destroyer to enter your houses 5989
Hos 5: 4 "Their deeds do not p them to return 5989
Ac 24:23 p his friends to take care of his needs. 3266+3594
1Ti 2:12 not p a woman to teach or to have authority 2205

PERMITS (2) [PERMIT]

Ecc 5:12 abundance of a rich man p him no sleep. 5663
1Co 16: 7 to spend some time with you, if the Lord p. 2205

PERMITTED (5) [PERMIT]

Ex 19:13 he shall not be p to live.' AIT
Dt 18:14 LORD your God has not p you to do so. 5989
Mt 19: 8 "Moses p you to divorce your wives 2205
Mk 10: 4 "Moses p a man to write a certificate 2205
2Co 12: 4 things that man is not p to tell. 2003

PERMITTING (1) [PERMIT]

Heb 6: 3 And God p, we will do so. 2205

PERPETUATE (1)

Ps 45:17 I will p your memory through all 2349+9005

PERPLEXED (5) [PERPLEXITY]

Da 4:19 (also called Belteshazzar) was greatly p 10724
Lk 9: 7 And he was p, because some were saying 1389
Ac 2:12 Amazed and p, they asked one another, 1389
2Co 4: 8 p, but not in despair; 679
Gal 4:20 because I am p about you! 679

PERPLEXITY (1) [PERPLEXED]

Lk 21:25 in anguish and p at the roaring and tossing 680

PERSECUTE (18) [PERSECUTED, PERSECUTING, PERSECUTION, PERSECUTIONS, PERSECUTOR, PERSECUTORS]

Dt 30: 7 curses on your enemies who hate and p you. 8103
Ps 9:13 O LORD, see how my enemies p me! 6715
69:26 For they p those you wound and talk about 8103
119:86 help me, for men p me without cause. 8103
119:157 Many are the foes who p me, 8103
119:161 Rulers p me without cause, 8103
Mt 5:11 p you and falsely say all kinds of evil 1503
5:44 and pray for those who p you, 1503
Lk 11:49 and others they will p.' 1503
21:12 they will lay hands on you and p you. 1503
Jn 15:20 they persecuted me, they will p you also. 1503
Ac 7:52 a prophet your fathers did not p? 1503
9: 4 "Saul, Saul, why do you p me?" 1503
12: 1 belonged to the church, intending to p them. 2808
22: 7 Why do you p me?' 1503
26:11 I even went to foreign cities to p them. 1503
26:14 'Saul, Saul, why do you p me? 1503
Ro 12:14 Bless those who p you; 1503

PERSECUTED (18) [PERSECUTE]

Mt 5:10 Blessed are those who are p because 1503
5:12 the same way they p the prophets who were 1503
10:23 When you are p in one place, 1503
24: 9 be handed over to be p and put to death, 2568
Jn 5:16 things on the Sabbath, the Jews p him. 1503
15:20 If they p me, they will persecute you also. 1503
Ac 22: 4 I p the followers of this Way to their death, 1503
1Co 4:12 when we are p, we endure it; 1503
15: 9 because I p the church of God. 1503
2Co 4: 9 p, but not abandoned; 1503
Gal 1:13 how intensely I p the church of God 1503
1:23 "The man who formerly p us is now 1503
4:29 the son born in the ordinary way p the son 1503
5:11 why am I still being p? 1503
6:12 to avoid being p for the cross of Christ. 1503
1Th 3: 4 we kept telling you that we would be p. 2567
2Ti 3:12 a godly life in Christ Jesus will be p, 1503
Heb 11:37 destitute, p and mistreated— 2567

PERSECUTING (4) [PERSECUTE]

Ac 9: 5 "I am Jesus, whom you are p," he replied. 1503
22: 8 'I am Jesus of Nazareth, whom you are p,' 1503
26:15 " 'I am Jesus, whom you are p,' 1503
Php 3: 6 as for zeal, p the church; 1503

PERSECUTION (9) [PERSECUTE]

Mt 13:21 trouble or p comes because of the word, 1501
Mk 4:17 trouble or p comes because of the word, 1501

Ac 8: 1 On that day a great **p** broke out against *1501*
11:19 Now those who had been scattered by the **p** *2568*
13:50 stirred up **p** against Paul and Barnabas, *1501*
Ro 8:35 or hardship or **p** or famine or nakedness *1501*
1Th 3: 7 and **p** we were encouraged about you *2568*
Heb 10:33 you were publicly exposed to insult and **p;** *2568*
Rev 2:10 and *you will* **suffer p** for ten days. *2400+2568*

PERSECUTIONS (5) [PERSECUTE]

Mk 10:30 and with them, **p)** and in the age to come, *1501*
2Co 12:10 in insults, in hardships, in **p,** in difficulties. *1501*
2Th 1: 4 in all the **p** and trials you are enduring. *1501*
2Ti 3:11 **p,** sufferings—what kinds of things *1501*
3:11 Iconium and Lystra, the **p** I endured. *1501*

PERSECUTOR (1) [PERSECUTE]

1Ti 1:13 a blasphemer and a **p** and a violent man, *1502*

PERSECUTORS (4) [PERSECUTE]

Ps 119:84 When will you punish my **p?** 8103
Jer 15:15 Avenge me on my **p.** 8103
17:18 Let my **p** be put to shame, 8103
20:11 so my **p** will stumble and not prevail. 8103

PERSEVERANCE (13) [PERSEVERE]

Ro 5: 3 we know that suffering produces **p;** *5705*
5: 4 **p,** character; and character, hope. *5705*
2Co 12:12 were done among you with great **p.** *5705*
2Th 1: 4 about your **p** and faith in all *5705*
3: 5 into God's love and Christ's **p.** *5705*
Heb 12: 1 let us run with **p** the race marked out for us. *5705*
Jas 1: 3 that the testing of your faith develops **p.** *5705*
1: 4 **P** must finish its work so that you may *5705*
5:11 You have heard of Job's **p** and *5705*
2Pe 1: 6 and to self-control, **p;** *5705*
1: 6 and to **p,** godliness; *5705*
Rev 2: 2 your hard work and your **p.** *5705*
2:19 your love and faith, your service and **p,** *5705*

PERSEVERE (2) [PERSEVERANCE, PERSEVERED, PERSEVERES, PERSEVERING]

1Ti 4:16 **P in** them, because if you do, *2152*
Heb 10:36 You need **to p** so that when you have done *5705*

PERSEVERED (3) [PERSEVERE]

Heb 11:27 *he* **p** because he saw him who is invisible. *2846*
Jas 5:11 we consider blessed those who *have* **p.** *5702*
Rev 2: 3 *have* **p** and have endured hardships *2400+5702*

PERSEVERES (2) [PERSEVERE]

1Co 13: 7 always trusts, always hopes, always **p.** *5702*
Jas 1:12 Blessed is the man who **p** under trial, *5702*

PERSEVERING (1) [PERSEVERE]

Lk 8:15 retain it, and by **p** produce a crop. *5705*

PERSIA (29) [PERSIAN, PERSIANS]

2Ch 36:20 until the kingdom of **P** came to power. 7273
36:22 In the first year of Cyrus king of **P,** 7273
36:22 of Cyrus king of **P** to make a proclamation 7273
36:23 "This is what Cyrus king of **P** says: 7273
Ezr 1: 1 In the first year of Cyrus king of **P,** 7273
1: 1 of Cyrus king of **P** to make a proclamation 7273
1: 2 "This is what Cyrus king of **P** says: 7273
1: 8 king of **P** had them brought by Mithredath 7273
3: 7 as authorized by Cyrus king of **P.** 7273
4: 3 Cyrus, the king of **P,** commanded us." 7273
4: 5 king of **P** and down to the reign of Darius 7273
4: 5 and down to the reign of Darius king of **P.** 7273
4: 7 And in the days of Artaxerxes king of **P,** 7273
4: 9 **P,** Erech and Babylon, 10060
4:24 of the reign of Darius king of **P.** 10594
6:14 Darius and Artaxerxes, kings of **P.** 10594
7: 1 during the reign of Artaxerxes king of **P,** 7273
9: 9 in the sight of the kings of **P:** 7273
Est 1: 3 The military leaders of **P** and Media, 7273
1:14 of **P** and Media who had special access to 7273
1:19 be written in the laws of **P** and Media, 7273
10: 2 the annals of the kings of Media and **P?** 7273
Eze 27:10 of **P,** Lydia and Put served as soldiers 7273
38: 5 **P,** Cush and Put will be with them, 7273
Da 8:20 the kings of Media and **P.** 7273
10: 1 In the third year of Cyrus king of **P,** 7273
10:13 I was detained there with the king of **P.** 7273
10:20 the prince of **P,** and when I go, the prince 7273
11: 2 Three more kings will appear in **P,** 7273

PERSIAN (4) [PERSIA]

Ne 12:22 were recorded in the reign of Darius the **P.** 7275
Est 1:18 This very day the **P** and Median women of 7273
Da 6:28 of Darius and the reign of Cyrus the **P.** 10595
10:13 **P** kingdom resisted me twenty-one days. 7273

PERSIANS (4) [PERSIA]

Da 5:28 and given to the Medes and **P.**" 10594
6: 8 with the laws of the Medes and **P,** 10594
6:12 with the laws of the Medes and **P,** 10594
6:15 law of the Medes and **P** no decree or edict 10594

PERSIS (1)

Ro 16:12 Greet my dear friend **P,** *4372*

PERSIST (5) [PERSISTED, PERSISTENCE, PERSISTS]

Dt 29:19 though *I* **p in** going my **own way."** 4213+9244
1Sa 12:25 Yet if *you* **p in doing evil,** 8317+8317
2Ki 17:34 To this day they **p** in their former practices. 6913
Isa 1: 5 Why *do you* **p** *in* rebellion? 3578
Ro 11:23 And if they *do* not **p in** unbelief, *2152*

PERSISTED (3) [PERSIST]

2Ki 2:17 *they* **p** until he was too ashamed to refuse. 7210
17:22 The Israelites **p** in all the sins of Jeroboam 2143
17:40 but **p in** their former practices. 3869+6913

PERSISTENCE (1) [PERSIST]

Ro 2: 7 who by **p** in doing good seek glory, honor *5705*

PERSISTS (1) [PERSIST]

Dt 25: 8 If *he* **p** in saying, "I do not want to marry 6641

PERSON (102) [PERSON'S, PERSONAL, PERSONALLY, PERSONS]

Ex 12: 4 in accordance with what **each** *p* will eat. AIT
16:16 an omer for each **p** you have in your tent.' " 5883
16:22 two omers for **each** *p*— AIT
23: 7 not put an innocent or **honest** *p* to death, AIT
36: 1 Oholiab and every skilled **p** to whom 408
36: 2 and Oholiab and every skilled **p** to whom 408
38:26 one beka per **p,** 1653
Lev 5: 1 " 'If a **p** sins because he does not speak up 5883
5: 2 **p** touches anything ceremonially unclean— 5883
5: 4 " 'Or if a **p** thoughtlessly takes an oath 5883
5:15 "When a **p** commits a violation 5883
5:17 a **p** sins and does what is forbidden in any 5883
7:11 for the fellowship offering a **p** may present NIH
7:18 the **p** who eats any of it will 5883
7:20 that **p** must be cut off from his people. 5883
7:21 that **p** must be cut off from his people.' " 5883
7:27 that **p** must be cut off from his people.' " 5883
13: 4 the **infected p** in isolation for seven days. 5596
13:12 it covers all the skin of the **infected p** 5596
13:13 he shall pronounce that **p** clean. 5596^{S}
13:17 priest shall pronounce the **infected p** clean; 5596
13:30 the priest shall pronounce **that p** unclean; 2257^{S}
13:31 **infected p** in isolation for seven days. 5596+5999
13:36 **the p** is unclean. 2085^{S}
13:39 **that p** is clean. 2085^{S}
13:45 *p with* such an infectious **disease** AIT
14: 2 "These are the regulations for the **diseased** *p* AIT
14: 3 If the **p** has been healed of his infectious 7665^{S}
14: 8 The *p to* **be cleansed** must wash his clothes, AIT
14:30 which **the p** can afford, 2257^{S}
15: 8 that **p** must wash his clothes and bathe NIH
17:10 that **p** who eats blood and will cut him off 5883
19: 8 that **p** must be cut off from his people. 5883
20: 6 " 'I will set my face against the **p** who turns 5883
22: 3 that **p** must be cut off from my presence. 5883
22: 5 or *any* **p** who makes him unclean, 132
22:13 No **unauthorized p,** however, 2424
27: 5 a **p** between the ages of five and twenty, NIH
27: 6 a **p** between one month and five years, NIH
27: 7 If it is a **p** sixty years old or more, NIH
27: 8 he is to present **the p** to the priest, 2257
27:24 of Jubilee the field will revert to **the p** 2257^{S}
27:29 " 'No **p** devoted to destruction may 132
Nu 5: 6 is unfaithful to the LORD, that **p** is guilty 5883
5: 7 to it and give it all to **the p** he has wronged. 889^{S}
5: 8 But if that **p** has no close relative 408
9:13 that **p** must be cut off from his people 5883
15:27 " 'But if just one **p** sins unintentionally, 5883
15:30 and that **p** must be cut off from his people. 5883
15:31 that **p** must surely be cut off; 5883
16: 5 and he will have that **p** come near him. NIH
19:13 That **p** must be cut off from Israel. 5883
19:14 the law that applies when a **p** dies in a tent: 132
19:17 "For the **unclean** *p*, put some ashes AIT
19:19 to sprinkle the **unclean** *p* on the third AIT
19:19 The **p** being cleansed must wash his clothes NIH
19:20 a **p** who is unclean does not purify himself, 408
19:22 an **unclean** *p* touches becomes unclean, AIT
35: 6 a *p who has* **killed** someone may flee. AIT
35:11 *p who has* **killed** someone accidentally may flee. AIT
35:12 so that a *p* **accused of murder** may not die AIT
35:21 that **p** shall be put to death; 5782^{S}
35:30 a **p** is to be put to death as a murderer only 5883
Dt 4:42 which *anyone* who *had* **killed a p** could flee 8357
17: 5 to your city gate and stone **that p** to death. 4392^{S}
27:25 who accepts a bribe to kill an innocent **p."** 1947^{S}
29:19 When such a **p** hears the words of this oath, 2257^{S}
Jos 20: 3 so that anyone who kills a **p** accidentally 5883
1Sa 10: 6 and you will be changed into a different **p.** 408
2Sa 3:19 Abner also spoke to the Benjamites **in p.** 265+928
6:19 to each **p** in the whole crowd of Israelites, 6639
14:14 that a **banished** *p* may not remain estranged AIT
Est 5:12 "I'm the only **p** Queen Esther invited NIH
Ps 62:12 Surely you will reward *each* **p** according 408
Pr 24:12 Will he not repay *each* **p** according 132
Jer 5: 1 but *one* **p** who deals honestly and seeks 408
Eze 44:25 not defile himself by going near a dead **p;** 132
Eze 44:25 if the dead **p** was his father or mother, NIH
Da 11:21 be succeeded by a **contemptible** *p* who has AIT
Hag 2:12 If a **p** carries consecrated meat in the fold 408
2:13 "If a *p* **defiled** *by contact with* AIT
Mt 5:39 But I tell you, Do not resist an **evil** *p.* *AIT*
10:11 search for some **worthy** *p* there and stay *AIT*
16:27 and then he will reward **each** *p* according *AIT*
Lk 7:12 a **dead** *p* was being carried out— *AIT*
14: 8 a **p more distinguished than** you *1952*
17: 1 but woe to that *p* through **whom** they come. *AIT*
Jn 12:47 "As for the **p who** hears my words but does *5516*
13:10 "A **p who** has had a bath needs only *3836*
Ro 2: 6 *to* **each** *p* according to what he has done." *AIT*
2Co 10:10 **in p** he is unimpressive *3836+3836+4242+5393*
Gal 3:16 but "and to your seed," meaning **one** *p,* *AIT*
Eph 5: 5 No immoral, impure or **greedy p—** *4431*
Col 2:18 Such a **p** goes into great detail *NIG*
1Th 2:17 for a short time **(in p,** not in thought), *4725*
Tit 3:10 Warn a divisive **p** once, *476*
Heb 7: 7 And without doubt the **lesser** *p* is blessed *AIT*
Jas 2:24 that a **p** is justified by what he does and not *476*
3: 6 It corrupts the whole **p,** *5393*
5:15 in faith will make the **sick** *p* well; *AIT*
2Jn 1: 7 **Any such p** is the deceiver and *4047*
Rev 20:13 and **each** *p* was judged according *AIT*

PERSON'S (1) [PERSON]

Ex 22:11 not lay hands on the **other** *p* property. AIT

PERSONAL (7) [PERSON]

Ge 26:26 with Ahuzzath his **p adviser** and Phicol 5335
2Sa 13:17 He called his **p servant** and said, 5853+9250
1Ki 4: 5 a priest and **p adviser** *to* the king; 8291
2Ki 12: 4 the money received from **p vows** and 5883+6886
1Ch 29: 3 now give my **p treasures** of gold and silver 6035
Est 2: 2 the king's **p attendants** proposed, 5853+9250
Ac 12:20 a **trusted p servant** of the king, *2093+3131+3836*

PERSONALLY (3) [PERSON]

Ge 43: 9 you can hold **me** *p* responsible for him. AIT
Gal 1:22 I was **p** unknown to the churches of Judea *4725*
Col 2: 1 and for all who *have* not **met** me **p.** *1877+3836+3972+4725+4922*

PERSONS (8) [PERSON]

Ge 46:26 numbered sixty-six **p.** 5883
Lev 18:29 such **p** must be cut off from their people. 5883
27: 2 a special vow to dedicate **p** to the LORD 5883
Nu 31:28 whether **p,** cattle, donkeys, sheep or goats. 132
31:30 select one out of every fifty, whether **p,** 132
31:47 Moses selected one out of every fifty **p** 132
Lk 15: 7 over ninety-nine **righteous** *p* who do *AIT*
Ac 4:34 There were no needy **p** among them. *5516*

PERSPIRE (1)

Eze 44:18 not wear anything that makes them **p.** 3472

PERSUADE (6) [PERSUADED, PERSUADING, PERSUASION, PERSUASIVE, PERSUASIVELY]

Jdg 19: 3 went to her to **p** her to return. 1819+4213+6584
2Ki 18:30 *Do* not **let** Hezekiah **p** you **to trust** 1053
Isa 36:15 *Do* not **let** Hezekiah **p** you **to trust** 1053
Ac 18: 4 **trying to p** Jews and Greeks. *4275*
26:28 *you can* **p** me to be a Christian?" *4275*
2Co 5:11 to fear the Lord, *we try to* **p** men. *4275*

PERSUADED (11) [PERSUADE]

Jdg 19: 7 man got up to go, his father-in-law **p** him, 7210
Pr 25:15 Through patience a ruler *can* **be p,** 7331
Jer 28:15 **p** this nation **to trust** in lies. 1053
Mt 27:20 the chief priests and the elders **p** the crowd *4275*
Lk 20: 6 they are **p** that John was a prophet." *4275*
Ac 5:40 His speech **p** them. *4275*
6:11 Then *they* **secretly p** some men to say, *5680*
16:15 And *she* **p** us. *4128*
17: 4 the Jews *were* **p** and joined Paul and Silas, *4275*
Ro 4:21 *being* **fully p** that God had power *4442*
2Ti 1: 5 *I am* **p,** now lives in you also. *4275*

PERSUADING (1) [PERSUADE]

Ac 18:13 "*is* **p** the people to worship God in ways *400*

PERSUASION (1) [PERSUADE]

Gal 5: 8 That kind of **p** does not come from *4282*

PERSUASIVE (2) [PERSUADE]

Pr 7:21 With **p words** she led him astray; 4375
1Co 2: 4 not with wise and **p** words, *4273*

PERSUASIVELY (1) [PERSUADE]

Ac 19: 8 arguing **p** about the kingdom of God. *4275*

PERTAINING (1)

1Ch 26:32 for every **matter** *p to* God and for the AIT

PERUDA (1)

Ezr 2:55 the descendants of Sotai, Hassophereth, **P,** 7243

PERVERSE (17) [PERVERT]

Dt 32:20 for they are a p generation, 9337
1Sa 20:30 "You son of a p and rebellious *woman!* 6390
Ps 101: 4 *Men of* p heart shall be far from me; 6836
Pr 2:12 from men whose words are p, 9337
3:32 for the LORD detests a p *man* but takes 4279
8: 8 none of them is crooked or p. 6836
8:13 evil behavior and p speech. 9337
10:31 but a p tongue will be cut out. 9337
10:32 but the mouth of the wicked only *what* is p. 9337
11:20 The LORD detests *men of* p heart 6836
16:28 A p man stirs up dissension, 9337
17:20 A *man of* p heart does not prosper; 6836
19: 1 a fool whose lips are p. 6836
28: 6 a rich man whose ways are p. 6836
28:18 but he whose ways *are* p will suddenly fall. 6835
Mt 17:17 "O unbelieving and p generation," *1406*
Lk 9:41 "O unbelieving and p generation," *1406*

PERVERSENESS (1) [PERVERT]

Pr 2:14 in doing wrong and rejoice in the p *of* evil, 9337

PERVERSION (4) [PERVERT]

Lev 18:23 to have sexual relations with it; that is a p. 9316
20:12 What they have done is a p; 9316
Ro 1:27 in themselves the due penalty *for* their p. *4415*
Jude 1: 7 to sexual immorality and p. *599+2283+3958+4922*

PERVERSITY (2) [PERVERT]

Pr 4:24 Put away p from your mouth; 6838
16:30 He who winks with his eye is plotting p; 9337

PERVERT (8) [PERVERSE, PERVERSENESS, PERVERSION, PERVERSITY, PERVERTED, PERVERTING, PERVERTS]

Ex 23: 2 *do* not p justice by siding with the crowd, 5742
Lev 19:15 *Do* not p justice; do not show partiality 6404+6913
Dt 16:19 *Do* not p justice or show partiality. 5742
Job 8: 3 *Does* God p justice? 6430
8: 3 *Does* the Almighty p what is right? 6430
34:12 that the Almighty *would* p justice. 6430
Pr 17:23 A wicked man accepts a bribe in secret to p 5742
Gal 1: 7 and are trying *to* p the gospel of Christ. *3570*

PERVERTED (4) [PERVERT]

1Sa 8: 3 and accepted bribes and p justice. 5742
Job 33:27 'I sinned, and p what was right, 6390
Jer 3:21 because *they have* p their ways 6390
Hab 1: 4 hem in the righteous, so that justice is p. 6823

PERVERTING (1) [PERVERT]

Ac 13:10 you never stop p the right ways of the Lord? *1406*

PERVERTS (1) [PERVERT]

1Ti 1:10 *for* adulterers and p, for slave traders *780*

PESTILENCE (4) [PESTILENCES]

Dt 32:24 consuming p and deadly plague; 8404
Ps 91: 3 the fowler's snare and from the deadly p. 1822
91: 6 nor the p that stalks in the darkness, 1822
Hab 3: 5 p followed his steps. 8404

PESTILENCES (1) [PESTILENCE]

Lk 21:11 famines and p in various places, *3369*

PESTILENT (KJV) See TROUBLEMAKER

PESTLE (1)

Pr 27:22 grinding him like grain with a p, 6605

PESTS (1)

Mal 3:11 I will prevent p from devouring your crops, 430

PET (1)

Job 41: 5 *Can you* make a p of him like a bird 8471

PETER (176) [CEPHAS, PETER'S, SIMON]

Mt 4:18 Simon called P and his brother Andrew. *4377*
10: 2 first, Simon (who is called P) *4377*
14:28 "Lord, if it's you," P replied, *4377*
14:29 Then P got down out of the boat, *4377*
15:15 P said, "Explain the parable to us." *4377*
16:16 Simon P answered, "You are the Christ, *4377*
16:18 I tell you that you are P, and on this rock *4377*
16:22 P took him aside and began to rebuke him. *4377*
16:23 Jesus turned and said *to* P, "Get behind me, *4377*
17: 1 After six days Jesus took with him P, *4377*
17: 4 P said to Jesus, "Lord, it is good for us *4377*
17:24 came to P and asked, "Doesn't your teacher *4377*
17:25 When P came into the house, *899S*
17:26 "From others," P answered. *NIG*
18:21 Then P came to Jesus and asked, "Lord, *4377*
19:27 P answered him, "We have left everything *4377*
26:33 P replied, "Even if all fall away on account *4377*
26:35 But P declared, "Even if I have to die *4377*
Mt 26:37 He took P and the two sons of Zebedee *4377*
26:40 watch with me for one hour?" he asked P. *4377*
26:58 But P followed him at a distance, *4377*
26:69 Now P was sitting out in the courtyard, *4377*
26:73 those standing there went up to P and said, *4377*
26:75 P remembered the word Jesus had spoken: *4377*
Mk 3:16 Simon (to whom he gave the name P); *4377*
5:37 He did not let anyone follow him except P, *4377*
8:29 P answered, "You are the Christ." *4377*
8:32 P took him aside and began to rebuke him. *4377*
8:33 and looked at his disciples, he rebuked P. *4377*
9: 2 After six days Jesus took P, James and John *4377*
9: 5 P said to Jesus, "Rabbi, it is good for us *4377*
10:28 P said to him, "We have left everything *4377*
11:21 P remembered and said to Jesus, "Rabbi, *4377*
13: 3 Mount of Olives opposite the temple, P, *4377*
14:29 P declared, "Even if all fall away, *4377*
14:31 But P insisted emphatically, *3836S*
14:33 He took P, James and John along *4377*
14:37 "Simon," he said *to* P, "are you asleep? *4377*
14:54 P followed him at a distance, *4377*
14:66 While P was below in the courtyard, *4377*
14:67 When she saw P warming himself, *4377*
14:70 those standing near said *to* P, *4377*
14:72 Then P remembered the word Jesus had *4377*
16: 7 But go, tell his disciples and P, *4377*
Lk 5: 8 When Simon P saw this, *4377*
6:14 Simon (whom he named P), *4377*
8:45 When they all denied it, P said, "Master, *4377*
8:51 not let anyone go in with him except P, *4377*
9:20 P answered, "The Christ of God." *4377*
9:28 after Jesus said this, he took P, John *4377*
9:32 P and his companions were very sleepy, *4377*
9:33 P said to him, "Master, it is good for us *4377*
12:41 P asked, "Lord, are you telling this parable *4377*
18:28 P said to him, "We have left all we had *4377*
22: 8 Jesus sent P and John, saying, *4377*
22:34 Jesus answered, "I tell you, P, *4377*
22:54 P followed at a distance. *4377*
22:55 P sat down with them. *4377*
22:58 "Man, I am not!" P replied. *4377*
22:60 P replied, "Man, I don't know what you're talking about!" *4377*
22:61 The Lord turned and looked straight at P. *4377*
22:61 Then P remembered the word the Lord had *4377*
24:12 P, however, got up and ran to the tomb. *4377*
Jn 1:42 Cephas" (which, when translated, is P). *4377*
1:44 Philip, like Andrew and P, was from *4377*
6:68 Simon P answered him, "Lord, *4377*
13: 6 He came to Simon P, who said to him, *4377*
13: 8 said P, "you shall never wash my feet." *4377*
13: 9 "Then, Lord," Simon P replied, "not just *4377*
13:24 Simon P motioned to this disciple and said, *4377*
13:36 Simon P asked him, "Lord, where are you *4377*
13:37 P asked, "Lord, why can't I follow you *4377*
18:10 Then Simon P, who had a sword, *4377*
18:11 Jesus commanded P, "Put your sword away! *4377*
18:15 Simon P and another disciple were following Jesus. *4377*
18:16 but P had to wait outside at the door. *4377*
18:16 to the girl on duty there and brought P in. *4377*
18:17 the girl at the door asked P. *4377*
18:18 P also was standing with them, *4377*
18:25 As Simon P stood warming himself, *4377*
18:26 of the man whose ear P had cut off, *4377*
18:27 Again P denied it, and at that moment *4377*
20: 2 So she came running to Simon P and *4377*
20: 3 So P and the other disciple started for *4377*
20: 4 but the other disciple outran P and reached *4377*
20: 6 Then Simon P, who was behind him, *4377*
21: 2 Simon P, Thomas (called Didymus), *4377*
21: 3 Simon P told them, and they said, *4377*
21: 7 the disciple whom Jesus loved said *to* P, *4377*
21: 7 As soon as Simon P heard him say, *4377*
21:11 Simon P climbed aboard and dragged *4377*
21:15 Jesus said *to* Simon P, "Simon son of John, *4377*
21:17 P was hurt because Jesus asked him *4377*
21:19 of death by which P would glorify God. *NIG*
21:20 P turned and saw that the disciple *4377*
21:21 When P saw him, he asked, "Lord, *4377*
Ac 1:13 Those present were P, John, James and *4377*
1:15 In those days P stood up among *4377*
1:20 said P, "it is written in the book of Psalms, *NIG*
2:14 Then P stood up with the Eleven, *4377*
2:37 they were cut to the heart and said to P and *4377*
2:38 P replied, "Repent and be baptized, *4377*
3: 1 One day P and John were going up to *4377*
3: 3 When he saw P and John about to enter, *4377*
3: 4 P looked straight at him, as did John. *4377*
3: 4 Then P said, "Look at us!" *NIG*
3: 6 Then P said, "Silver or gold I do not have, *4377*
3:11 While the beggar held on to P and John, *4377*
3:12 When P saw this, he said to them: *4377*
4: 1 up *to* P and John while they were speaking *899S*
4: 3 They seized P and John, *899S*
4: 7 They had P and John brought before them *899S*
4: 8 P, filled with the Holy Spirit, said to them: *4377*
4:13 When they saw the courage *of* P and John *4377*
4:19 P and John replied, "Judge for yourselves *4377*
4:23 P and John went back to their own people *NIG*
5: 3 Then P said, "Ananias, how is it that *4377*
5: 8 P asked her, "Tell me, is this the price *4377*
5: 9 P said to her, "How could you agree to test *4377*
5:29 P and the other apostles replied: *4377*
8:14 they sent P and John to them. *4377*
8:17 P and John placed their hands on them, *NIG*
8:20 P answered: "May your money perish with *4377*
Ac 8:25 P and John returned to Jerusalem, *3525+3836S*
9:32 As P traveled about the country, *4377*
9:34 "Aeneas," P said to him, *4377*
9:38 the disciples heard that P was in Lydda, *4377*
9:39 P went with them, and when he arrived *4377*
9:40 P sent them all out of the room; *4377*
9:40 and seeing P she sat up. *4377*
9:43 P stayed in Joppa for some time with *NIG*
10: 5 a man named Simon who is called P. *4377*
10: 9 P went up on the roof to pray. *4377*
10:13 Then a voice told him, "Get up, P. *4377*
10:14 "Surely not, Lord!" P replied. *4377*
10:17 While P was wondering about the meaning *4377*
10:18 as P was staying there. *4377*
10:19 While P was still thinking about the vision, *4377*
10:21 P went down and said to the men, *4377*
10:23 Then P invited the men into the house to *NIG*
10:23 The next day P started out with them, *NIG*
10:25 As P entered the house, *4377*
10:26 But P made him get up. *4377*
10:27 P went inside and found a large gathering *NIG*
10:32 Send to Joppa for Simon who is called P. *4377*
10:34 Then P began to speak: *4377*
10:44 While P was still speaking these words, *4377*
10:45 who had come with P were astonished *4377*
10:46 in tongues and praising God. Then P said, *4377*
10:48 Then they asked P to stay with them for *899S*
11: 2 So when P went up to Jerusalem, *4377*
11: 4 P began and explained everything *4377*
11: 7 Then I heard a voice telling me, 'Get up, P. *4377*
11:13 'Send to Joppa for Simon who is called P. *4377*
12: 3 he proceeded to seize P also. *4377*
12: 5 So P was kept in prison, *4377*
12: 6 P was sleeping between two soldiers, *4377*
12: 7 He struck P on the side and woke him up. *4377*
12: 8 And P did so. *NIG*
12: 9 P followed him out of the prison, *NIG*
12:11 Then P came to himself and said, *4377*
12:13 P knocked at the outer entrance, *899S*
12:14 "P is at the door!" *4377*
12:16 But P kept on knocking, *4377*
12:17 P motioned with his hand for them to *NIG*
12:18 the soldiers as to what had become of P. *4377*
15: 7 P got up and addressed them: *4377*
1Co 15: 5 and that he appeared *to* P, *3064*
Gal 1:18 up to Jerusalem to get acquainted with P *3064*
2: 7 just as P had been to the Jews. *4377*
2: 8 the ministry of P as an apostle to the Jews, *4377*
2: 9 P and John, those reputed to be pillars, *3064*
2:11 When P came to Antioch, *3064*
2:14 I said *to* P in front of them all, *3064*
1Pe 1: 1 P, an apostle of Jesus Christ, *4377*
2Pe 1: 1 Simon P, a servant and apostle *4377*

PETER'S (7) [PETER]

Mt 8:14 When Jesus came into P house, *4377*
8:14 he saw P mother-in-law lying in bed with *899S*
Jn 1:40 Andrew, Simon P brother, was one of *4377*
6: 8 Andrew, Simon P brother, spoke up, *4377*
Ac 5:15 that at least P shadow might fall on some *4377*
12: 7 he said, and the chains fell off P wrists. *899S*
12:14 When she recognized P voice, *4377*

PETHAHIAH (4)

1Ch 24:16 the nineteenth to P, 7342
Ezr 10:23 Shimei, Kelaiah (that is, Kelita), P, 7342
Ne 9: 5 Sherebiah, Hodiah, Shebaniah and P— 7342
11:24 P son of Meshezabel, 7342

PETHOR (2)

Nu 22: 5 who was at P, near the River, 7335
Dt 23: 4 and they hired Balaam son of Beor from P 7335

PETHUEL (1)

Joel 1: 1 of the LORD that came to Joel son of P. 7333

PETITION (18) [PETITIONED, PETITIONS]

1Ch 16: 4 to make p, to give thanks, 2349
Est 5: 6 "Now what is your p? 8629
5: 7 "My p and my request is this: 8629
5: 8 and if it pleases the king to grant my p 8629
7: 2 "Queen Esther, what is your p? 8629
7: 3 grant me my life—this is my p. 8629
9:12 Now what is your p? 8629
Ps 38: T A psalm of David. A p. 2349
70: T For the director of music. Of David. A p. 2349
Jer 7:16 for this people nor offer any plea or p 9525
11:14 for this people nor offer any plea or p 9525
36: 7 Perhaps they will bring their p before 9382
37:20 Let me bring my p before you: 9382
42: 2 "Please hear our p and pray to 9382
42: 9 to whom you sent me to present your p, 9382
Da 9: 3 and pleaded with him in prayer and p, 9384
Ac 23:15 you and the Sanhedrin p the commander *1872*
Php 4: 6 by prayer and p, with thanksgiving, *1255*

PETITIONED (2) [PETITION]

Ezr 8:23 So we fasted and p our God about this, 1335
Ac 25:24 The whole Jewish community *has* p me *1961*

PETITIONS (2) [PETITION]

Da 9:17 hear the prayers and p *of* your servant. 9384

Heb 5: 7 he offered up prayers and **p** with loud cries *2656*

PEULLETHAI (1)

1Ch 26: 5 Issachar the seventh and **P** the eighth. 7191

PHALEC (KJV) See PELEG

PHALLU (KJV) See PALLU

PHALTI, PHALTIEL (KJV) See PALTIEL

PHANTOM (1)

Ps 39: 6 Man is a mere **p** as he goes to and fro: 7513

PHANUEL (1)

Lk 2:36 the daughter *of* **P**, of the tribe of Asher. *5750*

PHARAOH (214) [PHARAOH'S]

Ge 12:15 they praised her to **P**, 7281
12:17 the LORD inflicted serious diseases on **P** 7281
12:18 So **P** summoned Abram. 7281
12:20 **P** gave orders about Abram to his men, 7281
40: 2 **P** was angry with his two officials, 7281
40:13 Within three days **P** will lift up your head 7281
40:14 to **P** and get me out of this prison. 7281
40:17 all kinds of baked goods for **P**, 7281
40:19 Within three days **P** will lift off your head 7281
41: 1 **P** had a dream: He was standing by 7281
41: 4 Then **P** woke up. 7281
41: 7 Then **P** woke up; it had been a dream. 7281
41: 8 **P** told them his dreams, 7281
41: 9 Then the chief cupbearer said to **P**, 7281
41:10 **P** was once angry with his servants, 7281
41:14 So **P** sent for Joseph, 7281
41:14 he came before **P**. 7281
41:15 **P** said to Joseph, "I had a dream, 7281
41:16 "I cannot do it," Joseph replied to **P**, 7281
41:16 "but God will give **P** the answer he desires." 7281
41:17 Then **P** said to Joseph, 7281
41:25 Then Joseph said to **P**, 7281
41:25 "The dreams of **P** are one and the same. 7281
41:25 God has revealed to **P** what he is about 7281
41:28 "It is just as I said to **P**: 7281
41:28 God has shown **P** what he is about to do. 7281
41:32 the dream was given to **P** in two forms is 7281
41:33 "And now let **P** look for a discerning and 7281
41:34 Let **P** appoint commissioners over the land 7281
41:35 store up the grain under the authority of **P**, 7281
41:37 The plan seemed good to **P** and to all 7281
41:38 So **P** asked them, "Can we find anyone like 7281
41:39 Then **P** said to Joseph, "Since God has 7281
41:41 So **P** said to Joseph, "I hereby put you 7281
41:42 Then **P** took his signet ring from his finger 7281
41:44 Then **P** said to Joseph, "I am Pharaoh, 7281
41:44 Then Pharaoh said to Joseph, "I am **P**, 7281
41:45 **P** gave Joseph the name Zaphenath-Paneah 7281
41:46 when he entered the service of **P** king 7281
41:55 the people cried to **P** for food. 7281
41:55 Then **P** told all the Egyptians, 7281
42:15 As surely as **P** lives, you will not leave 7281
42:16 If you are not, then as surely as **P** lives, 7281
44:18 though you are equal to **P** *himself.* 7281
45: 8 He made me father to **P**, 7281
45:16 **P** and all his officials were pleased. 7281
45:17 **P** said to Joseph, "Tell your brothers, 7281
45:21 as **P** had commanded, 7281
46: 5 and their wives in the carts that **P** had sent 7281
46:31 "I will go up and speak to **P** and will say 7281
46:33 When **P** calls you in and asks, 7281
47: 1 Joseph went and told **P**, "My father and 7281
47: 2 and presented them before **P**. 7281
47: 3 **P** asked the brothers, "What is your 7281
47: 3 servants are shepherds," they replied to **P**, 7281
47: 5 **P** said to Joseph, "Your father and brothers 7281
47: 7 father Jacob in and presented him before **P**. 7281
47: 7 After Jacob blessed **P**, 7281
47: 8 **P** asked him, "How old are you?" 7281
47: 9 And Jacob said to **P**, 7281
47:10 Then Jacob blessed **P** and went out 7281
47:11 the district of Rameses, as **P** directed. 7281
47:19 we with our land will be in bondage to **P**. 7281
47:20 Joseph bought all the land in Egypt for **P**. 7281
47:22 from **P** and had food enough from 7281
47:22 from the allotment **P** gave them. 7281
47:23 and your land today for **P**, 7281
47:24 give a fifth of it to **P**. 7281
47:25 we will be in bondage to **P**." 7281
47:26 that a fifth of the produce belongs to **P**. 7281
50: 4 speak to **P** for me. 7281
50: 6 **P** said, "Go up and bury your father, 7281
Ex 1:11 and Rameses as store cities for **P**. 7281
1:19 The midwives answered **P**, 7281
1:22 Then **P** gave this order to all his people: 7281
2:15 When **P** heard of this, he tried to kill Moses, 7281
2:15 but Moses fled from **P** and went to live 7281
3:10 I am sending you to **P** to bring my people 7281
3:11 to **P** and bring the Israelites out of Egypt?" 7281
4:21 before **P** all the wonders I have given you 7281
4:22 say to **P**, 'This is what the LORD says: 7281
5: 1 to **P** and said, "This is what the LORD, 7281
5: 2 **P** said, "Who is the LORD, 7281
5: 5 Then **P** said, "Look, the people of the land 7281
Ex 5: 6 That same day **P** gave this order to 7281
5:10 "This is what **P** says: 7281
5:15 Israelite foremen went and appealed to **P**: 7281
5:17 **P** said, "Lazy, that's what you are—lazy! NIH
5:20 When they left **P**, 7281
5:21 a stench to **P** and his officials and have put 7281
5:23 since I went to **P** to speak in your name, 7281
6: 1 "Now you will see what I will do to **P**: 7281
6:11 tell **P** king of Egypt to let the Israelites go 7281
6:12 why would **P** listen to me, 7281
6:13 and Aaron about the Israelites and **P** king 7281
6:27 They were the ones who spoke to **P** king 7281
6:29 Tell **P** king of Egypt everything I tell you." 7281
6:30 why would **P** listen to me?" 7281
7: 1 "See, I have made you like God to **P**, 7281
7: 2 and your brother Aaron is to tell **P** to let 7281
7: 7 when they spoke to **P**. 7281
7: 9 "When **P** says to you, 'Perform a miracle,' 7281
7: 9 and throw it down before **P**,' 7281
7:10 So Moses and Aaron went to **P** and did just 7281
7:10 Aaron threw his staff down in front of **P** 7281
7:11 **P** then summoned wise men and sorcerers, 7281
7:15 Go to **P** in the morning as he goes out to 7281
7:20 of **P** and his officials and struck the water 7281
8: 1 "Go to **P** and say to him, 'This is what 7281
8: 8 **P** summoned Moses and Aaron and said, 7281
8: 9 Moses said to **P**, 'I leave to you the honor 7281
8:10 "Tomorrow," **P** said. NIH
8:12 After Moses and Aaron left **P**, 7281
8:12 about the frogs he had brought on **P**. 7281
8:15 But when **P** saw that there was relief, 7281
8:19 The magicians said to **P**, 7281
8:20 and confront **P** as he goes to the water 7281
8:25 **P** summoned Moses and Aaron and said, 7281
8:28 **P** said, "I will let you go to offer sacrifices 7281
8:29 the flies will leave **P** and his officials 7281
8:29 be sure that **P** does not act deceitfully again 7281
8:30 Moses left **P** and prayed to the LORD, 7281
8:31 The flies left **P** and his officials 7281
8:32 also **P** hardened his heart and would not let 7281
9: 1 "Go to **P** and say to him, 7281
9: 7 **P** sent men to investigate and found that 7281
9: 8 into the air in the presence of **P**. 7281
9:10 from a furnace and stood before **P**. 7281
9:13 confront **P** and say to him, 7281
9:20 Those officials of **P** who feared the word 7281
9:27 Then **P** summoned Moses and Aaron. 7281
9:33 Then Moses left **P** and went out of the city. 7281
9:34 When **P** saw that the rain and hail 7281
10: 1 Then the LORD said to Moses, "Go to **P**, 7281
10: 3 So Moses and Aaron went to **P** and said 7281
10: 6 Then Moses turned and left **P**. 7281
10: 8 Moses and Aaron were brought back to **P**. 7281
10:10 **P** said, "The LORD be with you— NIH
10:16 **P** quickly summoned Moses and Aaron 7281
10:18 then left **P** and prayed to the LORD. 7281
10:24 Then **P** summoned Moses and said, "Go, 7281
10:28 **P** said to Moses, "Get out of my sight! 7281
11: 1 "I will bring one more plague on **P** and 7281
11: 5 from the firstborn son of **P**, 7281
11: 8 Then Moses, hot with anger, left **P**. 7281
11: 9 "**P** will refuse to listen to you— 7281
11:10 performed all these wonders before **P**, but 7281
12:29 from the firstborn of **P**, 7281
12:30 **P** and all his officials and all 7281
12:31 the night **P** summoned Moses and Aaron NIH
13:15 When **P** stubbornly refused to let us go, 7281
13:17 When **P** let the people go, 7281
14: 3 **P** will think, 'The Israelites are wandering 7281
14: 4 But I will gain glory for myself through **P** 7281
14: 5 **P** and his officials changed their minds 7281
14: 8 The LORD hardened the heart of **P** king 7281
14:10 As **P** approached, the Israelites looked up, 7281
14:17 And I will gain glory through **P** 7281
14:18 the LORD when I gain glory through **P**, 7281
14:28 of **P** that had followed the Israelites into 7281
18: 4 he saved me from the sword of **P**." 7281
18: 8 to **P** and the Egyptians for Israel's sake and 7281
18:10 from the hand of the Egyptians and of **P**, 7281
Dt 6:21 tell him: "We were slaves of **P** in Egypt, 7281
6:22 and **P** and his whole household. 7281
7: 8 from the power of **P** king of Egypt. 7281
7:18 the LORD your God did to **P** and 7281
11: 3 both to **P** king of Egypt and 7281
29: 2 that the LORD did in Egypt to **P**, 7281
34:11 to **P** and to all his officials and 7281
1Sa 2:27 when they were in Egypt under **P**? 7281
6: 6 as the Egyptians and **P** did? 7281
1Ki 3: 1 Solomon made an alliance with **P** king 7281
9:16 (**P** king of Egypt had attacked 7281
11:18 they went to Egypt, to **P** king of Egypt, 7281
11:19 **P** was so pleased with Hadad 7281
11:21 Then Hadad said to **P**, "Let me go, 7281
11:22 to your own country?" **P** asked. 7281
2Ki 17: 7 from under the power of **P** king of Egypt. 7281
18:21 Such is **P** king of Egypt to all who depend 7281
23:29 **P** Neco king of Egypt went up to 7281
23:33 **P** Neco put him in chains at Riblah in 7281
23:34 **P** Neco made Eliakim son of Josiah king 7281
23:35 Jehoiakim paid **P** Neco the silver 7281
Ne 9:10 miraculous signs and wonders against **P**, 7281
Ps 135: 9 O Egypt, against **P** and all his servants. 7281
136:15 but swept **P** and his army into the Red Sea; 7281
SS 1: 9 mare harnessed to one of the chariots of **P**. 7281
Isa 19:11 wise counselors of **P** give senseless advice. 7281
19:11 How can you say to **P**, 7281
36: 6 Such is **P** king of Egypt to all who depend 7281
Jer 25:19 **P** king of Egypt, his attendants, 7281
44:30 to hand **P** Hophra king of Egypt over 7281
46: 2 against the army of **P** Neco king of Egypt, 7281
46:17 '**P** king of Egypt is only a loud noise; 7281
46:25 on **P**, on Egypt and her gods and her kings, 7281
46:25 and on those who rely on **P**. 7281
47: 1 the Philistines before **P** attacked Gaza: 7281
Eze 17:17 **P** with his mighty army and great horde 7281
29: 2 against **P** king of Egypt and prophesy 7281
29: 3 " 'I am against you, **P** king of Egypt, 7281
30:21 I have broken the arm of **P** king of Egypt. 7281
30:22 I am against **P** king of Egypt. 7281
30:24 but I will break the arms of **P**, 7281
30:25 but the arms of **P** will fall limp. 7281
31: 2 say to **P** king of Egypt and to his hordes: 7281
31:18 " 'This is **P** and all his hordes, 7281
32: 2 take up a lament concerning **P** king of 7281
32:28 O **P**, will be broken and will lie among NIH
32:31 "**P**—he and all his army—will see them 7281
32:32 **P** and all his hordes will be laid among 7281
Ac 7:10 to gain the goodwill *of* **P** king of Egypt; *5755*
7:13 and **P** learned about Joseph's family. *5755*
Ro 9:17 For the Scripture says *to* **P**: *5755*

PHARAOH'S (56) [PHARAOH]

Ge 12:15 And when **P** officials saw her, 7281
37:36 one of **P** officials, the captain of the guard. 7281
39: 1 an Egyptian who was one of **P** officials, 7281
40: 7 So he asked **P** officials who were 7281
40:11 **P** cup was in my hand, 7281
40:11 squeezed them into **P** cup and put the cup 7281
40:13 and you will put **P** cup in his hand, 7281
40:20 Now the third day was **P** birthday, 7281
40:21 that he once again put the cup into **P** hand, 7281
41:46 And Joseph went out from **P** presence 7281
45: 2 and **P** household heard about it. 7281
45:16 When the news reached **P** palace 7281
47:14 and he brought it to **P** palace. 7281
47:20 The land became **P**, 4200+7281
47:26 of the priests that did not become **P**. 4200+7281
50: 4 Joseph said to **P** court, "If I have found 7281
50: 7 All **P** officials accompanied him— 7281
Ex 2: 5 **P** daughter went down to the Nile to bathe, 7281
2: 7 Then his sister asked **P** daughter, 7281
2: 9 **P** daughter said to her, "Take this baby 7281
2:10 to **P** daughter and he became her son. 7281
5:14 by **P** slave drivers were beaten 7281
7: 3 But I will harden **P** heart, 7281
7:13 Yet **P** heart became hard and he would 7281
7:14 "**P** heart is unyielding; 7281
7:22 and **P** heart became hard; 7281
8:19 **P** heart was hard and he would not listen, 7281
8:24 Dense swarms of flies poured into **P** palace 7281
9:12 the LORD hardened **P** heart and he would 7281
9:35 So **P** heart was hard and he would not let 7281
10: 7 **P** officials said to him, 7281
10:11 and Aaron were driven out of **P** presence. 7281
10:20 But the LORD hardened **P** heart, 7281
10:27 But the LORD hardened **P** heart, 7281
11: 3 in Egypt by **P** officials and by the people.) 7281
11:10 but the LORD hardened **P** heart, 7281
14: 4 And I will harden **P** heart, 7281
14: 9 The Egyptians—all **P** horses and chariots, 7281
14:23 and all **P** horses and chariots 7281
15: 4 **P** chariots and his army he has hurled into 7281
15: 4 of **P** officers are drowned in the Red Sea. 2257[S]
15:19 When **P** horses, chariots and horsemen 7281
1Ki 7: 8 a palace like this hall for **P** daughter, 7281
9:24 After **P** daughter had come up from 7281
11: 1 Solomon loved many foreign women
besides **P** daughter— 7281
11:20 There Genubath lived with **P** *own* children. 7281
1Ch 4:18 the children of **P** daughter Bithiah, 7281
2Ch 8:11 Solomon brought **P** daughter up from 7281
Isa 30: 2 who look for help to **P** protection, 7281
30: 3 But **P** protection will be to your shame, 7281
Jer 37: 5 **P** army had marched out of Egypt, 7281
37: 7 who sent you to inquire of me, '**P** army, 7281
37:11 from Jerusalem because of **P** army, 7281
43: 9 at the entrance to **P** palace in Tahpanhes. 7281
Ac 7:21 **P** daughter took him and brought him up *5755*
Heb 11:24 to be known as the son *of* **P** daughter. *5755*

PHARAOH-NECHO, PHARAOH-NECHOH (KJV) See PHARAOH NECO

PHARES, PHAREZ (KJV) See PEREZ

PHARISEE (12) [PHARISEE'S, PHARISEES]

Mt 23:26 Blind **P**! First clean the inside of the cup *5757*
Lk 7:39 When the **P** who had invited him saw this, *5757*
11:37 a **P** invited him to eat with him; *5757*
11:38 the **P**, noticing that Jesus did not first wash *5757*
14: 1 to eat in the house of a prominent **P**, *5757*
18:10 one a **P** and the other a tax collector. *5757*
18:11 The **P** stood up and prayed about himself: *5757*
Ac 5:34 But a **P** named Gamaliel, *5757*
23: 6 I am a **P**, the son of a Pharisee. *5757*
23: 6 I am a Pharisee, the son *of* a **P**. *5757*
26: 5 strictest sect of our religion, I lived as a **P**. *5757*
Php 3: 5 in regard to the law, a **P**; *5757*

PHARISEE'S (2) [PHARISEE]
Lk 7:36 so he went to the **P** house and reclined at *5757*
7:37 that Jesus was eating at the **P** house, *5757*

PHARISEES (84) [PHARISEE]
Mt 3: 7 many *of* the **P** and Sadducees coming to *5757*
5:20 that *of* the **P** and the teachers of the law, *5757*
9:11 When the **P** saw this, *5757*
9:14 "How is it that we and the **P** fast, *5757*
9:34 the **P** said, "It is by the prince of demons *5757*
12: 2 When the **P** saw this, they said to him, *5757*
12:14 But the **P** went out and plotted *5757*
12:24 But when the **P** heard this, they said, *5757*
12:38 the **P** and teachers of the law said to him, *5757*
15: 1 Then some **P** and teachers of the law came *5757*
15:12 "Do you know that the **P** were offended *5757*
16: 1 The **P** and Sadducees came to Jesus *5757*
16: 6 against the yeast *of* the **P** and Sadducees." *5757*
16:11 be on your guard against the yeast *of* the **P** *5757*
16:12 the teaching *of* the **P** and Sadducees. *5757*
19: 3 Some **P** came to him to test him. *5757*
21:45 and the **P** heard Jesus' parables, *5757*
22:15 the **P** went out and laid plans to trap him *5757*
22:34 silenced the Sadducees, the **P** got together. *5757*
22:41 While the **P** were gathered together, *5757*
23: 2 of the law and the **P** sit in Moses' seat. *5757*
23:13 "Woe to you, teachers of the law and **P**, *5757*
23:15 "Woe to you, teachers of the law and **P**, *5757*
23:23 "Woe to you, teachers of the law and **P**, *5757*
23:25 "Woe to you, teachers of the law and **P**, *5757*
23:27 "Woe to you, teachers of the law and **P**, *5757*
23:29 "Woe to you, teachers of the law and **P**, *5757*
27:62 the chief priests and the **P** went to Pilate. *5757*
Mk 2:16 of the law who were **P** saw him eating with *5757*
2:18 John's disciples and the **P** were fasting. *5757*
2:18 and the disciples *of* the **P** are fasting, *5757*
2:24 The **P** said to him, "Look, why are they *5757*
3: 6 Then the **P** went out and began to plot with *5757*
7: 1 The **P** and some of the teachers of the law *5757*
7: 3 (The **P** and all the Jews do not eat *5757*
7: 5 the **P** and teachers of the law asked Jesus, *5757*
8:11 The **P** came and began to question Jesus. *5757*
8:15 "Watch out for the yeast *of* the **P** and that *5757*
10: 2 Some **P** came and tested him by asking, *5757*
12:13 the **P** and Herodians to Jesus to catch him *5757*
Lk 5:17 **P** and teachers of the law, who had come *5757*
5:21 The **P** and the teachers of the law began *5757*
5:30 But the **P** and the teachers of the law *5757*
5:33 and so do the disciples *of* the **P**, *5757*
6: 2 Some *of* the **P** asked, "Why are you doing *5757*
6: 7 The **P** and the teachers of the law *5757*
7:30 But the **P** and experts in the law rejected *5757*
7:36 one *of* the **P** invited Jesus to have dinner *5757*
11:39 you **P** clean the outside of the cup *5757*
11:42 "Woe to you **P**, because you give God *5757*
11:43 "Woe to you **P**, because you love the most *5757*
11:53 the **P** and the teachers of the law began *5757*
12: 1 on your guard against the yeast *of* the **P**, *5757*
13:31 At that time some **P** came to Jesus and said *5757*
14: 3 Jesus asked the **P** and experts in the law, *5757*
15: 2 the **P** and the teachers of the law muttered, *5757*
16:14 The **P**, who loved money, *5757*
17:20 having been asked by the **P** when *5757*
19:39 Some *of* the **P** in the crowd said to Jesus, *5757*
Jn 1:24 Now some **P** who had been sent *5757*
3: 1 a man of the **P** named Nicodemus, *5757*
4: 1 The **P** heard that Jesus was gaining *5757*
7:32 The **P** heard the crowd whispering such
things about him. *5757*
7:32 and the **P** sent temple guards to arrest him. *5757*
7:45 guards went back to the chief priests and **P**, *5757*
7:47 he has deceived you also?" the **P** retorted. *5757*
7:48 "Has any of the rulers or of the **P** believed *5757*
8: 3 The teachers of the law and the **P** brought *5757*
8:13 The **P** challenged him, "Here you are, *5757*
9:13 to the **P** the man who had been blind. *5757*
9:15 Therefore the **P** also asked him *5757*
9:16 Some of the **P** said, "This man is not from
God, *5757*
9:40 Some **P** who were with him heard him *5757*
11:46 the **P** and told them what Jesus had done. *5757*
11:47 the chief priests and the **P** called a meeting *5757*
11:57 the chief priests and **P** had given orders *5757*
12:19 So the **P** said to one another, "See, *5757*
12:42 of the **P** they would not confess their faith *5757*
18: 3 from the chief priests and **P**. *5757*
Ac 15: 5 to the party *of* the **P** stood up and said, *5757*
23: 6 of them were Sadducees and the others **P**, *5757*
23: 7 a dispute broke out *between* the **P** and *5757*
23: 8 but the **P** acknowledge them all.) *5757*
23: 9 the teachers of the law who were **P** stood *5757*

PHAROSH (KJV) See PAROSH

PHARPAR (1)
2Ki 5:12 Abana and **P**, the rivers of Damascus, 7286

PHARZITES (KJV) See PEREZITE

PHASEAH (KJV) See PASEAH

PHEBE (KJV) See PHOEBE

PHENICE (KJV) See PHOENIX, PHOENICIA

PHENICIA (KJV) See PHOENICIA

PHICHOL (KJV) See PHICOL

PHICOL (3)
Ge 21:22 that time Abimelech and **P** the commander 7087
21:32 Abimelech and **P** the commander 7087
26:26 with Ahuzzath his personal adviser and **P** 7087

PHILADELPHIA (2)
Rev 1:11 Thyatira, Sardis, **P** and Laodicea." *5788*
3: 7 "To the angel of the church in **P** write: *5788*

PHILEMON (1)
Phm 1: 1 *To* **P** our dear friend and fellow worker, *5800*

PHILETUS (1)
2Ti 2:17 Among them are Hymenaeus and **P**, *5801*

PHILIP (34) [PHILIP'S]
Mt 10: 3 **P** and Bartholomew; Thomas *5805*
Mk 3:18 **P**, Bartholomew, Matthew, Thomas, *5805*
Lk 3: 1 of Galilee, his brother **P** tetrarch of Iturea *5805*
6:14 his brother Andrew, James, John, **P**, *5805*
Jn 1:43 Finding **P**, he said to him, "Follow me." *5805*
1:44 **P**, like Andrew and Peter, *5805*
1:45 **P** found Nathanael and told him, *5805*
1:46 "Come and see," said **P**. *5805*
1:48 under the fig tree before **P** called you." *5805*
6: 5 he said to **P**, "Where shall we buy bread *5805*
6: 7 **P** answered him, "Eight months' wages *5805*
12:21 They came to **P**, who was from Bethsaida *5805*
12:22 **P** went to tell Andrew; *5805*
12:22 Andrew and **P** in turn told Jesus. *5805*
14: 8 **P** said, "Lord, show us the Father and *5805*
14: 9 Jesus answered: "Don't you know me, **P**, *5805*
Ac 1:13 **P** and Thomas, Bartholomew *5805*
6: 5 also **P**, Procorus, Nicanor, Timon, *5805*
8: 5 **P** went down to a city in Samaria *5805*
8: 6 When the crowds heard **P** and saw *5805*
8:12 But when they believed **P** as he preached *5805*
8:13 And he followed **P** everywhere, *5805*
8:26 Now an angel of the Lord said to **P**, *5805*
8:29 The Spirit told **P**, "Go to that chariot *5805*
8:30 Then **P** ran up to the chariot and heard *5805*
8:30 "Do you understand what you are reading?"
P asked. *NIG*
8:31 he invited **P** to come up and sit with him. *5805*
8:34 The eunuch asked **P**, "Tell me, please, *5805*
8:35 Then **P** began with that very passage *5805*
8:38 Then both **P** and the eunuch went down *5805*
8:38 down into the water and **P** baptized him. *NIG*
8:39 Spirit of the Lord suddenly took **P** away, *5805*
8:40 **P**, however, appeared at Azotus *5805*
21: 8 and stayed at the house *of* **P** the evangelist, *5805*

PHILIP'S (2) [PHILIP]
Mt 14: 3 because of Herodias, his brother **P** wife, *5805*
Mk 6:17 his brother **P** wife, whom he had married. *5805*

PHILIPPI (6) [PHILIPPIANS]
Mt 16:13 to the region *of* Caesarea **P**, *5805*
Mk 8:27 on to the villages around Caesarea **P**. *5805*
Ac 16:12 From there we traveled to **P**, *5804*
20: 6 But we sailed from **P** after the Feast *5804*
Php 1: 1 To all the saints in Christ Jesus at **P**, *5804*
1Th 2: 2 suffered and been insulted in **P**, *5804*

PHILIPPIANS (1) [PHILIPPI]
Php 4:15 Moreover, as you **P** know, *5803*

PHILISTIA (8) [PHILISTINE]
Ex 15:14 anguish will grip the people of **P**. 7148
Ps 60: 8 over **P** I shout in triumph. 7148
83: 7 **P**, with the people of Tyre. 7148
87: 4 **P** too, and Tyre, along with Cush— 7148
108: 9 over **P** I shout in triumph." 7148
Isa 11:14 They will swoop down on the slopes of **P** 7149
Joel 3: 4 and Sidon and all you regions of **P**? 7148
Am 6: 2 and then go down to Gath in **P**. 7148

PHILISTINE (62) [PHILISTIA, PHILISTINE'S, PHILISTINES]
Ex 13:17 on the road through the **P** country, 7149
Jos 13: 3 (the territory of the five **P** rulers in Gaza, 7149
Jdg 14: 1 and saw there a young **P** woman. 7149
14: 2 "I have seen a **P** woman in Timnah; 7149
1Sa 6: 1 had been in **P** territory seven months, 7149
6: 4 according to the number of the **P** rulers, 7149
6:18 of **P** towns belonging to the five rulers— 7149
10: 5 where there is a **P** outpost. 7149
13: 3 Jonathan attacked the **P** outpost at Geba, 7149
13: 4 "Saul has attacked the **P** outpost, 7149
13:17 Raiding parties went out from the **P** camp 7149
14: 1 over to the **P** outpost on the other side." 7149
1Sa 14: 4 to cross to reach the **P** outpost was a cliff; 7149
14:11 showed themselves to the **P** outpost. 7149
14:19 the tumult in the **P** camp increased more 7149
17: 4 came out of the **P** camp. 7149
17: 8 Am I not a **P**, and are you not the servants 7149
17:10 **P** said, "This day I defy the ranks of Israel! 7149
17:16 the **P** came forward every morning 7149
17:23 Goliath, the **P** champion from Gath, 7149
17:26 be done for the man who kills this **P** 7149
17:26 Who is this uncircumcised **P** 7149
17:32 "Let no one lose heart on account of this **P**; 7149
17:33 "You are not able to go out against this **P** 7149
17:36 this uncircumcised **P** will be like one 7149
17:37 from the hand of this **P**." 7149
17:40 his sling in his hand, approached the **P**. 7149
17:41 the **P**, with his shield bearer in front of him, 7149
17:43 And the **P** cursed David by his gods. 7149
17:45 David said to the **P**, "You come against me 7149
17:46 the carcasses of the **P** army to the birds of 7149
17:48 As the **P** moved closer to attack him, 7149
17:49 and struck the **P** on the forehead. 7149
17:50 So David triumphed over the **P** with a sling 7149
17:50 a sword in his hand he struck down the **P** 7149
17:55 watched David going out to meet the **P**, 7149
17:57 as David returned from killing the **P**, 7149
18: 6 after David had killed the **P**, 7149
18:25 for the bride than a hundred **P** foreskins, 7149
18:30 The **P** commanders continued to go out 7149
19: 5 in his hands when he killed the **P**. 7149
21: 9 "The sword of Goliath the **P**, 7149
22:10 and the sword of Goliath the **P**." 7149
23: 3 if we go to Keilah against the **P** forces!" 7149
27: 7 in **P** territory a year and four months. 7149
27:11 as long as he lived in **P** territory. 7149
28: 5 When Saul saw the **P** army, he was afraid; 7149
29: 2 As the **P** rulers marched with their units 7149
29: 4 the **P** commanders were angry with him 7149
29: 7 do nothing to displease the **P** rulers." 7149
29: 9 nevertheless, the **P** commanders have said, 7149
2Sa 3:14 for the price of a hundred **P** foreskins." 7149
5:24 in front of you to strike the **P** army." 7149
21:17 he struck the **P** down and killed him. 7149
23:14 and the **P** garrison was at Bethlehem. 7149
23:16 three mighty men broke through the **P** lines, 7149
1Ki 15:27 down at Gibbethon, a **P** town, while Nadab 7149
16:15 near Gibbethon, a **P** town. 7149
1Ch 11:16 and the **P** garrison was at Bethlehem. 7149
11:18 So the Three broke through the **P** lines, 7149
14:15 in front of you to strike the **P** army." 7149
14:16 and they struck down the **P** army, 7149

PHILISTINE'S (5) [PHILISTINE]
1Sa 17:11 On hearing the **P** words, Saul and all the 7149
17:51 the **P** sword and drew it from the scabbard. 7149
17:54 the **P** head and brought it to Jerusalem, 7149
17:54 and he put the **P** weapons in his own tent. 2257^{S}
17:57 with David still holding the **P** head. 7149

PHILISTINES (210) [PHILISTINE]
Ge 10:14 Casluhites (from whom the **P** came) 7149
21:32 of his forces returned to the land of the **P**. 7149
21:34 And Abraham stayed in the land of the **P** 7149
26: 1 and Isaac went to Abimelech king of the **P** 7149
26: 8 Abimelech king of the **P** looked down 7149
26:14 and servants that the **P** envied him. 7149
26:15 the **P** stopped up, filling them with earth. 7149
26:18 the **P** had stopped up after Abraham died, 7149
Ex 23:31 from the Red Sea to the Sea of the **P**, 7149
Jos 13: 2 all the regions of the **P** and Geshurites: 7149
Jdg 3: 3 the five rulers of the **P**, 7149
3:31 who struck down six hundred **P** with 7149
10: 6 of the Ammonites and the gods of the **P**. 7149
10: 7 into the hands of the **P** and the Ammonites, 7149
10:11 the Amorites, the Ammonites, the **P**, 7149
13: 1 into the hands of the **P** for forty years. 7149
13: 5 of Israel from the hands of the **P**." 7149
14: 3 Must you go to the uncircumcised **P** to get 7149
14: 4 an occasion to confront the **P**; 7149
15: 3 a right to get even with the **P**; 7149
15: 5 in the standing grain of the **P**. 7149
15: 6 When the **P** asked, "Who did this?" 7149
15: 6 So the **P** went up and burned her 7149
15: 9 The **P** went up and camped in Judah, 7149
15:11 "Don't you realize that the **P** are rulers 7149
15:12 to tie you up and hand you over to the **P**." 7149
15:14 the **P** came toward him shouting. 7149
15:20 for twenty years in the days of the **P**. 7149
16: 5 The rulers of the **P** went to her and said, 7149
16: 8 of the **P** brought her seven fresh thongs 7149
16: 9 "Samson, the **P** are upon you!" 7149
16:12 "Samson, the **P** are upon you!" 7149
16:14 "Samson, the **P** are upon you!" 7149
16:18 she sent word to the rulers of the **P**, 7149
16:18 the rulers of the **P** returned with the silver 7149
16:20 she called, "Samson, the **P** are upon you!" 7149
16:21 Then the **P** seized him, 7149
16:23 of the **P** assembled to offer a great sacrifice 7149
16:27 all the rulers of the **P** were there, 7149
16:28 with one blow get revenge on the **P** 7149
16:30 "Let me die with the **P**!" 7149
1Sa 4: 1 Israelites went out to fight against the **P**. 7149
4: 1 camped at Ebenezer, and the **P** at Aphek. 7149
4: 2 The **P** deployed their forces to meet Israel, 7149
4: 2 Israel was defeated by the **P**, 7149
4: 3 bring defeat upon us today before the **P**? 7149

1Sa 4: 6 Hearing the uproar, the **P** asked, 7149
4: 7 the **P** were afraid. "A god has come 7149
4: 9 Be strong, **P!** Be men, or you will be subject 7149
4: 10 So the **P** fought, and the Israelites were 7149
4: 17 "Israel fled before the **P**, 7149
5: 1 After the **P** had captured the ark of God, 7149
5: 8 the rulers of the **P** and asked them, 7149
5: 11 of the **P** and said, "Send the ark of the god 7149
6: 2 the **P** called for the priests and the diviners 7149
6: 4 The **P** asked, "What guilt offering should NIH
6: 12 of the **P** followed them as far as the border 7149
6: 16 The five rulers of the **P** saw all this and 7149
6: 17 These are the gold tumors the **P** sent as 7149
6: 21 **P** have returned the ark of the LORD. 7149
7: 3 deliver you out of the hand of the **P**." 7149
7: 7 the **P** heard that Israel had assembled 7149
7: 7 the rulers of the **P** came up to attack them. 7149
7: 7 they were afraid because of the **P**. 7149
7: 8 he may rescue us from the hand of the **P**." 7149
7: 10 the **P** drew near to engage Israel in battle. 7149
7: 10 the **P** and threw them into such a panic 7149
7: 11 of Mizpah and pursued the **P**, 7149
7: 13 So the **P** were subdued and did 7149
7: 13 the hand of the LORD was against the **P**. 7149
7: 14 from Ekron to Gath that the **P** had captured 7149
7: 14 territory from the power of the **P**. 7149
9: 16 deliver my people from the hand of the **P**. 7149
12: 9 of Hazor, and into the hands of the **P** and 7149
13: 3 and the **P** heard about it. 7149
13: 4 now Israel has become a stench to the **P**." 7149
13: 5 The **P** assembled to fight Israel, 7149
13: 11 that the **P** were assembling at Micmash, 7149
13: 12 the **P** will come down against me at Gilgal, 7149
13: 16 while the **P** camped at Micmash. 7149
13: 19 because the **P** had said, 7149
13: 20 down to the **P** to have their plowshares, 7149
13: 23 a detachment of **P** had gone out to the pass 7149
14: 11 said the **P**. "The Hebrews are crawling out 7149
14: 13 The **P** fell before Jonathan, NIH
14: 20 They found the **P** in total confusion, NIH
14: 21 with the **P** and had gone up with them 7149
14: 22 of Ephraim heard that the **P** were on 7149
14: 30 Would not the slaughter of the **P** have been 7149
14: 31 after the Israelites had struck down the **P** 7149
14: 36 the **P** by night and plunder them till dawn, 7149
14: 37 "Shall I go down after the **P?** 7149
14: 46 Then Saul stopped pursuing the **P**, 7149
14: 47 Edom, the kings of Zobah, and the **P**. 7149
14: 52 of Saul there was bitter war with the **P**, 7149
17: 1 Now the **P** gathered their forces for war 7149
17: 2 and drew up their battle line to meet th· **P**. 7149
17: 3 The **P** occupied one hill and the Israelites 7149
17: 19 fighting against the **P**." 7149
17: 21 Israel and the **P** were drawing up their 7149
17: 51 When the **P** saw that their hero was dead, 7149
17: 52 and pursued the **P** to the entrance of Gath 7149
17: 53 the Israelites returned from chasing the **P**, 7149
18: 17 Let the **P** do that!" 7149
18: 21 so that the hand of the **P** may be against him 7149
18: 25 to have David fall by the hands of the **P**. 7149
18: 27 went out and killed two hundred **P**. 7149
19: 8 and David went out and fought the **P**. 7149
23: 1 the **P** are fighting against Keilah 7149
23: 2 saying, "Shall I go and attack these **P?**" 7149
23: 2 "Go, attack the **P** and save Keilah." 7149
23: 4 I am going to give the **P** into your hand." 7149
23: 5 fought the **P** and carried off their livestock. 7149
23: 5 on **the P** and saved the people of Keilah. 2157S
23: 27 The **P** are raiding the land." 7149
23: 28 pursuit of David and went to meet the **P**. 7149
24: 1 After Saul returned from pursuing the **P**, 7149
27: 1 to escape to the land of the **P**. 7149
28: 1 In those days the **P** gathered their forces 7149
28: 4 The **P** assembled and came and set 7149
28: 15 "The **P** are fighting against me, 7149
28: 19 over both Israel and you to the **P**, 7149
28: 19 also hand over the army of Israel to the **P**." 7149
29: 1 The **P** gathered all their forces at Aphek, 7149
29: 3 The commanders of the **P** asked, 7149
29: 11 to go back to the land of the **P**, 7149
29: 11 and the **P** went up to Jezreel. 7149
30: 16 from the land of the **P** and from Judah. 7149
31: 1 Now the **P** fought against Israel; 7149
31: 2 The **P** pressed hard after Saul and his sons, 7149
31: 7 And the **P** came and occupied them. 7149
31: 8 when the **P** came to strip the dead, 7149
31: 9 of the **P** to proclaim the news in the temple 7149
31: 11 of what the **P** had done to Saul, 7149
2Sa 1: 20 lest the daughters of the **P** be glad, 7149
3: 18 from the hand of the **P** and from the hand 7149
5: 17 When the **P** heard that David had been 7149
5: 18 Now the **P** had come and spread out in 7149
5: 19 "Shall I go and attack the **P?** 7149
5: 19 for I will surely hand the **P** over to you." 7149
5: 21 The **P** abandoned their idols there, NIH
5: 22 the **P** came up and spread out in the Valley 7149
5: 25 the **P** all the way from Gibeon to Gezer. 7149
8: 1 David defeated the **P** and subdued them, 7149
8: 1 Metheg Ammah from the control of the **P**. 7149
8: 12 the Ammonites and the **P**, and Amalek. 7149
19: 9 who rescued us from the hand of the **P**. 7149
21: 12 the **P** had hung them after they struck Saul 7149
21: 15 a battle between the **P** and Israel. 7149
21: 15 down with his men to fight against the **P**, 7149
21: 18 there was another battle with the **P**, at Gob. 7149
21: 19 In another battle with the **P** at Gob, 7149
23: 9 the **P** gathered [at Pas Dammim] for battle. 7149
2Sa 23: 10 struck down the **P** till his hand grew tired 7149
23: 11 When the **P** banded together at a place 7149
23: 12 He defended it and struck the **P** down, 7149
23: 13 a band of **P** was encamped in the Valley 7149
1Ki 4: 21 from the River to the land of the **P**, 7149
2Ki 8: 2 and stayed in the land of the **P** seven years. 7149
8: 3 from the land of the **P** and went to the king 7149
18: 8 he defeated the **P**, as far as Gaza 7149
1Ch 1: 12 Casluhites (from whom the **P** came) 7149
10: 1 Now the **P** fought against Israel; 7149
10: 2 The **P** pressed hard after Saul and his sons, 7149
10: 7 And the **P** came and occupied them. 7149
10: 8 when the **P** came to strip the dead, 7149
10: 9 throughout the land of the **P** to proclaim 7149
10: 11 of everything the **P** had done to Saul, 7149
11: 13 at Pas Dammim when the **P** gathered there 7149
11: 13 the troops fled from the **P**. 7149
11: 14 They defended it and struck the **P** down, 7149
11: 15 a band of **P** was encamped in the Valley 7149
12: 19 to David when he went with the **P** to fight 7149
12: 19 and his men did not help the **P** because, 7149
14: 8 When the **P** heard that David had been 7149
14: 9 Now the **P** had come and raided the Valley 7149
14: 10 "Shall I go and attack the **P?** 7149
14: 12 The **P** had abandoned their gods there, NIH
14: 13 Once more the **P** raided the valley; 7149
18: 1 David defeated the **P** and subdued them, 7149
18: 1 villages from the control of the **P**. 7149
18: 11 the Ammonites and the **P**, and Amalek. 7149
20: 4 war broke out with the **P**, at Gezer. 7149
20: 4 and the **P** were subjugated. NIH
20: 5 In another battle with the **P**, 7149
2Ch 9: 26 from the River to the land of the **P**, 7149
17: 11 Some **P** brought Jehoshaphat gifts 7149
21: 16 against Jehoram the hostility of the **P** and 7149
26: 6 the **P** and broke down the walls of Gath, 7149
26: 6 near Ashdod and elsewhere among the **P**. 7149
26: 7 God helped him against the **P** and against 7149
28: 18 the **P** had raided towns in the foothills and 7149
Ps 56: T When the **P** had seized him in Gath. 7149
Isa 2: 6 like the **P** and clasp hands with pagans. 7149
9: 12 and **P** from the west have devoured Israel 7149
14: 29 Do not rejoice, all you **P**, 7148
14: 31 Melt away, all you **P!** 7148
Jer 25: 20 to destroy all the kings of the **P** 824+7149
47: 1 to Jeremiah the prophet concerning the **P** 7149
47: 4 the day has come to destroy all the **P** and 7149
47: 4 The LORD is about to destroy the **P**, 7149
Eze 16: 27 of your enemies, the daughters of the **P**, 7149
16: 57 and the daughters of the **P**— 7149
25: 15 the **P** acted in vengeance and took revenge 7149
25: 16 about to stretch out my hand against the **P**, 7149
Am 1: 8 till the last of the **P** is dead," 7149
9: 7 the **P** from Caphtor and the Arameans 7149
Ob 1: 19 the foothills will possess the land of the **P**. 7149
Zep 2: 5 O Canaan, land of the **P**. 7149
Zec 9: 6 and I will cut off the pride of the **P**. 7149

PHILOLOGUS (1)

Ro 16: 15 Greet **P**, Julia, Nereus and his sister, *5807*

PHILOSOPHER (1) [PHILOSOPHY]

1Co 1: 20 Where is the **p** of this age? *5186*

PHILOSOPHERS (1) [PHILOSOPHY]

Ac 17: 18 *of* Epicurean and Stoic **p** began to dispute *5815*

PHILOSOPHY (1) [PHILOSOPHER, PHILOSOPHERS]

Col 2: 8 through hollow and deceptive **p**, *5814*

PHINEHAS (25)

Ex 6: 25 and she bore him **P**. 7090
Nu 25: 7 When **P** son of Eleazar, the son of Aaron, 7090
25: 11 "**P** son of Eleazar, the son of Aaron, 7090
31: 6 along with **P** son of Eleazar, the priest, 7090
Jos 22: 13 So the Israelites sent **P** son of Eleazar, 7090
22: 30 When **P** the priest and the leaders of 7090
22: 31 And **P** son of Eleazar, the priest, 7090
22: 32 Then **P** son of Eleazar, the priest, 7090
24: 33 to his son **P** in the hill country of Ephraim. 7090
Jdg 20: 28 with **P** son of Eleazar, 7090
1Sa 1: 3 where Hophni and **P**, the two sons of Eli, 7090
2: 34 Hophni and **P**, will be a sign to you— 7090
4: 4 And Eli's two sons, Hophni and **P**, 7090
4: 11 and Eli's two sons, Hophni and **P**, died. 7090
4: 17 Also your two sons, Hophni and **P**, 7090
4: 19 His daughter-in-law, the wife of **P**, 7090
14: 3 of Ichabod's brother Ahitub son of **P**, 7090
1Ch 6: 4 Eleazar was the father of **P**, 7090
6: 4 **P** the father of Abishua, 7090
6: 50 Eleazar his son, **P** his son, Abishua his son, 7090
9: 20 In earlier times **P** son of Eleazar was 7090
Ezr 7: 5 the son of **P**, the son of Eleazar, 7090
8: 2 of the descendants of **P**, Gershom; 7090
8: 33 Eleazar son of **P** was with him, 7090
Ps 106: 30 But **P** stood up and intervened, 7090

PHLEGON (1)

Ro 16: 14 Greet Asyncritus, **P**, Hermes, Patrobas, *5823*

PHOEBE (1)

Ro 16: 1 I commend to you our sister **P**, *5833*

PHOENICIA (4) [SYRIAN PHOENICIA]

Isa 23: 11 an order concerning **P** that her fortresses 4046
Ac 11: 19 with Stephen traveled as far as **P**, *5834*
15: 3 as they traveled through **P** and Samaria, *5834*
21: 2 We found a ship crossing over to **P**, *5834*

PHOENIX (1)

Ac 27: 12 hoping to reach **P** and winter there. *5837*

PHRYGIA (3)

Ac 2: 10 **P** and Pamphylia, Egypt and the parts *5867*
16: 6 throughout the region of **P** and Galatia, *5867*
18: 23 throughout the region of Galatia and **P**, *5867*

PHURAH (KJV) See PURAH

PHUT (KJV) See PUT

PHUVAH (KJV) See PUAH

PHYGELUS (1)

2Ti 1: 15 including **P** and Hermogenes. *5869*

PHYLACTERIES (1)

Mt 23: 5 They make their **p** wide and the tassels *5873*

PHYSICAL (5) [PHYSICALLY]

Da 1: 4 young men without any **p defect**, 4583
Ro 2: 28 nor is circumcision merely outward and **p**. *4922*
Col 1: 22 he has reconciled you by Christ's **p** body *4922*
1Ti 4: 8 For **p** training is of some value, *5394*
Jas 2: 16 but does nothing about his **p** needs, *5393*

PHYSICALLY (2) [PHYSICAL]

Ro 2: 27 The one who is not circumcised **p** and *1666+5882*
1Co 5: 3 I am not **p** present, I am with you in spirit. *5393*

PHYSICIAN (2) [PHYSICIANS]

Jer 8: 22 Is there no **p** there? 8324
Lk 4: 23 '**P**, heal yourself! Do here in your hometown what we have heard *2620*

PHYSICIANS (4) [PHYSICIAN]

Ge 50: 2 Then Joseph directed the **p** in his service 8324
50: 2 So the **p** embalmed him, 8324
2Ch 16: 12 help from the LORD, but only from the **p**. 8324
Job 13: 4 you *are* worthless **p**, all of you! 8324

PI HAHIROTH (4)

Ex 14: 2 to turn back and encamp near **P**, 7084
14: 9 they camped by the sea near **P**, 7084
Nu 33: 7 They left Etham, turned back to **P**, 7084
33: 8 They left **P** and passed through the sea 7084

PI-BESETH (KJV) See BUBASTIS

PICK (24) [PICKED, PICKERS, PICKS]

Lev 19: 10 over your vineyard a second time or **p up** 4377
27: 33 *He must* not **p out** the good from the bad 1329
Dt 23: 25 *you may* **p** kernels with your hands, 7786
Ru 2: 2 and **p up** the leftover grain behind anyone 4377
2: 16 the bundles and leave them for *her to* **p up**, 4377
1Ki 20: 33 as a good sign and were quick *to* **p up** 2715
2Ki 5: 7 he *is* **trying to p a quarrel** with me!" 628
9: 25 "**P** him **up** and throw him on the field 5951
9: 26 then, **p** him **up** and throw him on that plot, 5951
Ps 80: 12 so that all who pass by **p** its grapes? 768
Isa 41: 16 the wind *will* **p** them **up**, 5951
Eze 24: 5 take the **p** *of* the flock. 4436
Jnh 1: 12 "**P** me **up** and throw me into the sea," 5951
Mt 7: 16 *Do people* **p** grapes from thornbushes, *5198*
12: 1 *to* **p** some heads of grain and eat them. *5504*
Mk 2: 23 they began *to* **p** some heads of grain. *5504*
8: 19 many basketfuls of pieces *did you* **p up?**" *149*
8: 20 many basketfuls of pieces *did you* **p up?**" *149*
16: 18 *they will* **p up** snakes with their hands; *149*
Lk 6: 1 and his disciples *began to* **p** some heads *5504*
6: 44 *People do* not **p** figs from thornbushes, *5198*
Jn 5: 8 **P up** your mat and walk." *149*
5: 11 '**P up** your mat and walk.' " *149*
5: 12 "Who is this fellow who told you *to* **p** it **up** *149*

PICKED (23) [PICK]

Jdg 1: 7 and big toes cut off *have* **p up scraps** 4377
4: 21 **p up** a tent peg and a hammer 4374
1Sa 20: 38 The boy **p up** the arrow and returned 4377
2Sa 4: 4 His nurse **p** him **up** and fled, 5951
1Ki 13: 29 prophet **p up** the body of the man of God, 5951
17: 23 Elijah **p up** the child and carried him down 4374
2Ki 2: 13 *He* **p up** the cloak that had fallen 8123
2: 16 the LORD *has* **p** him **up** and set him down 5951
Eze 29: 5 the open field and not be gathered or **p up**. 7695
Na 2: 5 He summons his **p troops**, 129

Mt 14:20 and the disciples **p up** twelve basketfuls *149*
15:37 the disciples **p up** seven basketfuls *149*
27: 6 The chief priests **p up** the coins and said, *3284*
Mk 6:43 and the disciples **p up** twelve basketfuls *149*
8: 8 the disciples **p up** seven basketfuls *149*
Lk 9:17 and the disciples **p up** twelve basketfuls *149*
14: 7 the guests **p** the places of honor at the table, *1721*
Jn 5: 9 *he* **p up** his mat and walked. *149*
8:59 At this, *they* **p up** stones to stone him, *149*
10:31 Again the Jews **p up** stones to stone him, *1002*
15: 6 such branches *are* **p up,** thrown into the fire *5251*
Ac 20: 9 from the third story and *was* **p up** dead. *149*
Rev 18:21 Then a mighty angel **p up** a boulder the size *149*

PICKERS (2) [PICK]

Jer 49: 9 If **grape p** came to you, 1305
Ob 1: 5 If **grape p** came to you, 1305

PICKS (6) [PICK]

Lev 11:25 Whoever **p up** one of their carcasses 5951
11:28 Anyone *who* **p up** their carcasses must wash 5951
11:40 Anyone *who* **p up** the carcass must wash 5951
15:10 whoever **p up** those things must wash his 5951
2Sa 12:31 with saws and with iron **p** and axes, 3044
1Ch 20: 3 with saws and with iron **p** and axes. 3044

PIECE (39) [PIECES]

Ex 15:25 and the LORD showed him a **p of wood.** 6770
25:19 make the cherubim **of one p with** the cover, 4946
25:31 buds and blossoms shall be **of one p with** it. 4946
25:36 The buds and branches shall all be **of one** *p* AIT
27: 2 so that the horns and the altar are **of one p,** 4946
28: 8 **of one p with** the ephod and 4946
30: 2 its horns **of one p with** it. 4946
37: 8 at the two ends he made them **of one p with** 4946
37:17 buds and blossoms were **of one p with** it. 4946
37:22 and the branches were all **of one p with** 4946
37:25 its horns **of one p with** it. 4946
38: 2 that the horns and the altar were **of one p,** 4946
39: 5 **of one p with** the ephod and made 4946
Lev 9:13 the burnt offering **p by piece,** 4200+5984
9:13 the burnt offering **piece by p,** 4200+5984
Jdg 16: 9 as a **p of string** snaps when it comes 5861+7348
20: 6 into pieces and sent *one* **p** to each region 2023[S]
Ru 4: 3 is selling the **p** *of* land that belonged 2754
1Sa 2:36 a **p** *of* silver and a crust of bread and plead, 102
9:23 "Bring the **p of meat** I gave you, 4950
24:11 look at this **p** *of* your robe in my hand! 4053
2Sa 17:13 to the valley until not even a **p** of it can 7656
1Ki 7:24 in two rows in **one p with** the Sea. 3669
17:11 "And bring me, please, a **p** *of* bread." 7326
2Ch 4: 3 in two rows in **one p with** the Sea. 4609
Job 2: 8 a **p of broken pottery** and scraped himself 3084
41:29 A club seems to him but a **p of straw;** 7990
42:11 and each one gave him a **p of silver** and 7988
Pr 28:21 yet a man will do wrong for a **p** *of* bread. 7326
Eze 24: 6 Empty it **p** by piece without casting lots 5984
24: 6 Empty it piece by **p** without casting lots 5984
Am 3:12 the lion's mouth only two leg bones or a **p** 977
Mk 2:21 the **new** *p* will pull away from the old, *AIT*
Lk 19:20 I have kept it laid away in a **p of cloth.** *5051*
24:42 They gave him a **p** of broiled fish, *3538*
Jn 13:26 the one to whom I will give this **p of bread** *6040*
13:26 Then, dipping the **p of bread,** *6040*
19:23 woven in one **p** from top to bottom. *NIG*
Ac 5: 1 also sold a **p of property.** *3228*

PIECES (97) [PIECE]

Ge 15:17 torch appeared and passed between the **p.** 1617
33:19 For a hundred **p of silver,** 7988
37:33 Joseph *has* **surely been torn to p."** 3271+3271
44:28 *"He has* surely **been torn to p."** 3271+3271
Ex 22:13 **was torn to p by a wild animal,** 3271+3271
23:24 **break** their sacred stones **to p.** 8689+8689
28: 7 It is to have two **shoulder p** attached to two 4190
28:12 and fasten them on the **shoulder p** *of* 4190
28:25 to the **shoulder p** *of* the ephod at the front. 4190
28:27 the bottom of the **shoulder p** on the front of 4190
29:17 Cut the ram into **p** and wash the inner parts 5984
29:17 putting them with the head and the *other* **p.** 5984
32:19 **breaking** them **to p** at the foot of 8689
39: 4 They made **shoulder p** for the ephod, 4190
39: 7 Then they fastened them on the **shoulder p** 4190
39:18 to the **shoulder p** *of* the ephod at the front. 4190
39:20 the bottom of the **shoulder p** on the front of 4190
Lev 1: 6 to skin the burnt offering and cut it into **p.** 5984
1: 8 Aaron's sons the priests shall arrange the **p,** 5984
1:12 He is to cut it into **p,** 5984
6:21 and present the grain offering broken in **p** 7326
8:20 He cut the ram into **p** and burned the head, 5984
8:20 the head, the **p** and the fat. 5984
Nu 24: 8 and **break** their bones **in p;** 1751
Dt 9:17 **breaking** them **to p** before your eyes. 8689
Jos 24:32 for a hundred **p of silver** from the sons 7988
Jdg 20: 6 **cut** her **into p** and sent one piece to each 5983
1Sa 11: 7 He took a pair of oxen, **cut** them **into p,** 5983
11: 7 sent the **p** by messengers throughout Israel, NIH
1Ki 11:30 and tore it into twelve **p.** 7974
11:31 "Take ten **p** for yourself, 7974
18:23 and *let them* **cut** it **into p** and put it on 5983
18:33 **cut** the bull **into p** and laid it on the wood. 5983
2Ki 11:18 and idols **to p** and killed Mattan the priest 3512
18: 4 *He* **broke into p** the bronze snake 4198
23:12 **smashed** them **to p** and threw the rubble 8368
2Ch 25:12 down so that all **were dashed to p.** 1324
34: 4 *he* **cut to p** the incense altars that were 1548
34: 4 These *he* **broke to p** and scattered over 1990
34: 7 the idols to powder and **cut to p** all 1548
Job 4:20 and dusk *they* **are broken to p;** 4198
18: 4 You *who* **tear** yourself **to p** in your anger, 3271
26:12 by his wisdom *he* **cut** Rahab **to p.** 4730
Ps 2: 9 *you will* **dash** them **to p** like pottery." 5879
7: 2 and **rip** me **to p** with no one to rescue me. 7293
29: 5 the LORD **breaks in p** the cedars 8689
50:22 or *I will* **tear** you **to p,** 3271
119:72 to me than **thousands** *of p of* silver AIT
Isa 13:16 Their infants *will* **be dashed to p** 8187
24:12 its gate *is* **battered to p.** 4198+8625
27: 9 to be like chalk stones **crushed to p,** 5879
30:14 It will **break in p** like pottery, 8691
30:14 among its **p** not a fragment will be found 4845
51: 9 Was it not you who **cut** Rahab **to p,** 2933
Jer 5: 6 *to* **tear to p** any who venture out, 3271
23:29 like a hammer that **breaks** a rock **in p?** 7207
34:18 in two and then walked between its **p.** 1440
34:19 of the land who walked between the **p** *of* 1440
Eze 16:40 who will stone you and **hack** you **to p** 1438
23:34 you will dash it to **p** and tear your breasts. 3084
24: 4 Put into it the **p of meat,** 5984
24: 4 all the choice **p**—the leg and the shoulder. 5984
27:26 But the east wind *will* **break** you **to p** in 8689
Da 2: 5 and interpret it, I will have you cut into **p** 10197
2:35 the gold *were* **broken to p** at the same time 10182
2:40 and as iron **breaks** things **to p,** 10671
2:45 **broke** the iron, the bronze, the clay, the silver and the gold **to p.** 10182
3:29 into **p** and their houses be turned into piles 10197
Hos 5:14 I *will* **tear** them **to p** and go away; 3271
6: 1 He *has* **torn** us **to p** but he will heal us; 3271
6: 5 Therefore *I* **cut** you **in p** with my prophets, 2933
8: 6 It will be **broken in p,** that calf of Samaria. 8646
Am 6:11 the great house into **p** and the small house 8269
Mic 1: 7 All her idols *will* **be broken to p;** 4198
3: 3 **break** their bones **in p;** 7200
4:13 and *you will* **break to p** many nations." 1990
Na 3:10 Her infants **were dashed to p** at the head 8187
Zec 11:12 So they paid me **thirty** *p of* silver. AIT
11:13 the **thirty** *p of* silver and threw them into AIT
Mt 7: 6 and then turn and **tear** you **to p.** *4838*
14:20 picked up twelve basketfuls *of* **broken p** *3083*
15:37 picked up seven basketfuls *of* **broken p** *3083*
21:44 who falls on this stone *will be* **broken to p,** *5314*
24:51 *He will* **cut** him **to p** and assign him *1497*
Mk 6:43 picked up twelve basketfuls of **broken p** *3083*
8: 8 picked up seven basketfuls *of* **broken p** *3083*
8:19 many basketfuls *of* **p** did you pick up?" *3083*
8:20 many basketfuls *of* **p** did you pick up?" *3083*
Lk 9:17 picked up twelve basketfuls *of* **broken p** *3083*
12:46 *He will* **cut** him **to p** and assign him *1497*
20:18 who falls on that stone *will be* **broken to p,** *5314*
Jn 6:12 "Gather the **p** that are left over. *3083*
6:13 *with* the **p** of the five barley loaves left over *3083*
Ac 23:10 Paul *would be* **torn to p** by them. *1400*
27:41 the stern *was* **broken to p** by the pounding *3395*
27:44 The rest were to get there on planks or on **p** *5516*
Rev 2:27 *he will* **dash** them **to p** like pottery'— *5341*

PIERCE (9) [PIERCED, PIERCES, PIERCING]

Ex 21: 6 the door or the doorpost and **p** his ear with 8361
Nu 24: 8 with their arrows *they* **p** them. 4730
Job 40:24 or trap him and **p** his nose? 5918
41: 2 through his nose or **p** his jaw with a hook? 5918
Ps 37:15 But their swords *will* **p** their own hearts, 928+995
45: 5 Let your sharp arrows **p** the hearts of 928
Pr 12:18 Reckless words **p** like a sword, 4532
Eze 28: 7 and wisdom and **p** your shining splendor. 2726
Lk 2:35 And a sword *will* **p** your own soul too." *1451*

PIERCED (16) [PIERCE]

Jdg 5:26 she shattered and **p** his temple. 2737
2Ki 9:24 The arrow **p** his heart and he slumped 3655
Job 26:13 his hand **p** the gliding serpent. 2726
Ps 22:16 *they have* **p** my hands and my feet. 4125
38: 2 For your arrows *have* **p** me, 928+5737
40: 6 but my ears *you have* **p;** 4125
Isa 14:19 with *those* **p** *by* the sword, 3249
51: 9 who **p** that monster **through?** 2726
53: 5 But he **was p** for our transgressions, 2726
La 3:13 *He* **p** my heart *with* arrows from his 928+995
Hab 3:14 With his own spear *you* **p** his head 5918
Zec 12:10 They will look on me, the one *they have* **p,** 1991
Jn 19:34 one of the soldiers **p** Jesus' side with a spear *3817*
19:37 "They will look on the one *they have* **p."** *1708*
1Ti 6:10 and **p** themselves with many griefs. *4345*
Rev 1: 7 eye will see him, even those who **p** him; *1708*

PIERCES (7) [PIERCE]

2Ki 18:21 *which* **p** a man's hand and wounds him 5918
Job 16:13 Without pity, *he* **p** my kidneys and 7114
20:24 a bronze-tipped arrow **p** him. 2737
30:17 Night **p** my bones; 5941
Pr 7:23 till an arrow **p** his liver, 7114
Isa 36: 6 *which* **p** a man's hand and wounds him 5918
Jer 4:18 How *it* **p** to the heart!" 5595

PIERCING (1) [PIERCE]

Job 16: 9 my opponent **fastens** on me his **p** eyes. 4323

PIETY (3)

Job 4: 6 Should not your **p** be your confidence 3711
15: 4 even undermine **p** and hinder devotion 3711
22: 4 "Is it for your **p** that he rebukes you 3711

PIG (2) [PIG'S, PIGS]

Lev 11: 7 And the **p,** though it has a split hoof 2614
Dt 14: 8 The **p** is also unclean; although it has 2614

PIG'S (2) [PIG]

Pr 11:22 Like a gold ring in a **p** snout is 2614
Isa 66: 3 like one who presents **p** blood, 2614

PIGEON (3) [PIGEONS]

Ge 15: 9 along with a dove and a **young p."** 1578
Lev 1:14 he is to offer a dove or a young **p.** 3433
12: 6 a burnt offering and a young **p** or a dove for 3433

PIGEONS (9) [PIGEON]

Lev 5: 7 he is to bring two doves or two young **p** to 3433
5:11 cannot afford two doves or two young **p,** 3433
12: 8 she is to bring two doves or two young **p,** 3433
14:22 and two doves or two young **p,** 3433
14:30 he shall sacrifice the doves or the young **p,** 3433
15:14 or two young **p** and come before 3433
15:29 or two young **p** and bring them to the priest 3433
Nu 6:10 or two young **p** to the priest at the entrance 3433
Lk 2:24 "a pair of doves or two young **p."** *4361*

PIGS (17) [PIG]

Isa 65: 4 who eat the flesh of **p,** 2614
66:17 in the midst of those who eat the flesh of **p** 2614
Mt 7: 6 do not throw your pearls to **p.** *5956*
8:30 from them a large herd *of* **p** was feeding. *5956*
8:31 send us into the herd *of* **p."** *5956*
8:32 So they came out and went into the **p,** *5956*
8:33 Those tending the **p** ran off, *NIG*
Mk 5:11 herd *of* **p** was feeding on the nearby hillside. *5956*
5:12 "Send us among the **p;** *5956*
5:13 evil spirits came out and went into the **p.** *5956*
5:14 Those tending **the p** ran off *899[S]*
5:16 and told about the **p** as well. *5956*
Lk 8:32 A large herd *of* **p** was feeding there on *5956*
8:33 they went into the **p,** *5956*
8:34 those tending the **p** saw what had happened, *NIG*
15:15 who sent him to his fields to feed **p.** *5956*
15:16 with the pods that the **p** were eating, *5956*

PILATE (61) [PILATE'S]

Mt 27: 2 led him away and handed him over *to* **P,** *4397*
27:13 Then **P** asked him, "Don't you hear *4397*
27:17 the crowd had gathered, **P** asked them, *4397*
27:19 While **P** was sitting on the judge's seat, *899[S]*
27:22 with Jesus who is called Christ?" **P** asked. *4397*
27:23 What crime has he committed?" asked **P.** *1254+3836[S]*
27:24 When **P** saw that he was getting nowhere, *4397*
27:58 Going to **P,** he asked for Jesus' body, *4397*
27:58 and **P** ordered that it be given to him. *4397*
27:62 chief priests and the Pharisees went to **P.** *4397*
27:65 "Take a guard," **P** answered. *4397*
Mk 15: 1 led him away and handed him over *to* **P.** *4397*
15: 2 "Are you the king of the Jews?" asked **P.** *4397*
15: 4 So again **P** asked him, *4397*
15: 5 still made no reply, and **P** was amazed. *4397*
15: 8 The crowd came up and asked **P** to do *NIG*
15: 9 to you the king of the Jews?" asked **P,** *4397*
15:11 to have **P** release Barabbas instead. *NIG*
15:12 the king of the Jews?" **P** asked them. *4397*
15:14 What crime has he committed?" asked **P.** *4397*
15:15 **P** released Barabbas to them. *4397*
15:43 went boldly to **P** and asked for Jesus' body. *4397*
15:44 **P** was surprised to hear that he was already *4397*
Lk 3: 1 when Pontius **P** was governor of Judea, *4397*
13: 1 the Galileans whose blood **P** had mixed *4397*
23: 1 whole assembly rose and led him off to **P.** *4397*
23: 3 So **P** asked Jesus, "Are you the king of the Jews?" *4397*
23: 4 Then **P** announced to the chief priests and *4397*
23: 6 **P** asked if the man was a Galilean. *4397*
23:11 they sent him back *to* **P.** *4397*
23:12 That day Herod and **P** became friends— *4397*
23:13 **P** called together the chief priests, *4397*
23:20 **P** appealed to them again. *4397*
23:24 So **P** decided to grant their demand. *4397*
23:52 Going to **P,** he asked for Jesus' body. *4397*
Jn 18:29 So **P** came out to them and asked, *4397*
18:31 **P** said, "Take him yourselves *4397*
18:33 **P** then went back inside the palace, *4397*
18:35 "Am I a Jew?" **P** replied. *4397*
18:37 "You are a king, then!" said **P.** *4397*
18:38 "What is truth?" **P** asked. *4397*
19: 1 Then **P** took Jesus and had him flogged. *4397*
19: 4 Once more **P** came out and said to *4397*
19: 5 **P** said to them, "Here is the man!" *NIG*
19: 6 But **P** answered, "You take him *4397*
19: 8 When **P** heard this, he was even more afraid *4397*
19:10 "Do you refuse to speak to me?" **P** said. *4397*
19:12 From then on, **P** tried to set Jesus free, *4397*
19:13 When **P** heard this, he brought Jesus out *4397*
19:14 "Here is your king," **P** said to the Jews. *NIG*
19:15 "Shall I crucify your king?" **P** asked. *4397*

Jn 19:16 Finally **P** handed him over to them to *NIG*
19:19 **P** had a notice prepared and fastened to *4397*
19:21 The chief priests of the Jews protested *to* **P**, *4397*
19:22 **P** answered, "What I have written, *4397*
19:31 they asked **P** to have the legs broken and *4397*
19:38 Joseph of Arimathea asked **P** for the body *4397*
Ac 3:13 and you disowned him before **P**, *4397*
4:27 Indeed Herod and Pontius **P** met together *4397*
13:28 they asked **P** to have him executed. *4397*
1Ti 6:13 while testifying before Pontius **P** made *4397*

PILATE'S (1) [PILATE]

Jn 19:38 With **P** permission, he came and took *4397*

PILDASH (1)

Ge 22:22 Kesed, Hazo, **P**, Jidlaph and Bethuel." 7109

PILE (11) [PILED, PILES]

Lev 26:30 and **p** your dead bodies on the lifeless forms 5989
Jos 7:26 Over Achan they heaped up a large **p** 1643
8:29 And they raised a large **p** *of* rocks over it, 1643
Ru 3:7 to lie down at the far end of the **grain p.** 6894
Ezr 6:11 to be made a **p of rubble.** 10470
Job 8:17 around a **p of rocks** and looks for a place 1643
Jer 50:26 **p** her **up** like heaps of grain. 6148
Eze 24:5 **P wood** beneath it *for* the bones; 1883
24:9 I, too, *will* **p** the wood **high.** 1540
Lk 14:35 for the soil nor for the **manure p;** *3161*
Ac 28:3 Paul gathered a **p** of brushwood and, *4436*

PILED (8) [PILE]

Ge 31:46 So they took stones and **p** them *in* a heap, 6913
Ex 8:14 They *were* **p** *into* heaps, 7392
15:8 the blast of your nostrils the waters **p up.** 6890
Jos 3:16 *It* **p up** in a heap a great distance away, 7756
Jdg 9:49 *They* **p** them against the stronghold 8492
2Sa 18:17 a big pit in the forest and **p up** a large heap 5893
2Ch 31:6 and *they* **p** them in heaps. 5989
Rev 18:5 for her sins *are* **p up** to heaven, *3140*

PILEHA (KJV) See PILHA

PILES (9) [PILE]

2Ki 10:8 in two **p** at the entrance of the city gate 7393
19:25 fortified cities into **p of stone.** 1643+5898
Job 27:16 up silver like dust and clothes like **p** 3922
Isa 37:26 fortified cities into **p of stone.** 1643+5898
Da 2:5 and your houses turned into **p of rubble.** 10470
3:29 be turned into **p of rubble,** 10470
Hos 12:11 Their altars will be like **p of stones** on 1643
Na 3:3 Many casualties, **p** *of* dead, 3880
Hab 2:6 " 'Woe to him *who* **p up** stolen goods 8049

PILGRIMAGE (3)

Ge 47:9 years of my **p** are a hundred and thirty. 4472
47:9 not equal the years of the **p** *of* my fathers." 4472
Ps 84:5 who have set their hearts on **p.** 5019

PILGRIMS (KJV) See STRANGERS

PILHA (1)

Ne 10:24 Hallohesh, **P**, Shobek, 7116

PILLAGE (2) [PILLAGED]

Ezr 9:7 to **p** and humiliation at the hand 1023
Jer 50:11 you *who* **p** my inheritance, 9115

PILLAGED (2) [PILLAGE]

Ob 1:6 his hidden treasures **p!** 1239
Na 2:10 She is **p**, plundered, stripped! 1011

PILLAR (44) [PILLARS]

Ge 19:26 and she became a **p** *of* salt. 5907
28:18 and set it up as a **p** and poured oil on top 5167
28:22 and this stone that I have set up as a **p** will 5167
31:13 a **p** and where you made a vow to me. 5167
31:45 So Jacob took a stone and set it up as a **p.** 5167
31:51 and here is this **p** I have set up between you 5167
31:52 and this **p** is a witness, 5167
31:52 past this heap and **p** to my side to harm me. 5167
35:14 a stone **p** at the place where God had talked 5167
35:20 Over her tomb Jacob set up a **p**, 5167
35:20 and to this day that **p** marks Rachel's tomb. 5167
Ex 13:21 in a **p** *of* cloud to guide them on their way 6647
13:21 by night in a **p** *of* fire to give them light, 6647
13:22 Neither the **p** *of* cloud by day nor the pillar 6647
13:22 Neither the pillar of cloud by day nor the **p** 6647
14:19 The **p** *of* cloud also moved from in front 6647
14:24 the LORD looked down from the **p** *of* fire 6647
33:9 the **p** *of* cloud would come down and stay 6647
33:10 the people saw the **p** *of* cloud standing at 6647
Nu 12:5 the LORD came down in a **p** *of* cloud; 6647
14:14 and that you go before them in a **p** *of* cloud 6647
14:14 in a pillar of cloud by day and a **p** *of* fire 6647
Dt 31:15 the LORD appeared at the Tent in a **p** 6647
Jdg 9:6 beside the great tree at the **p** in Shechem 5164
2Sa 18:18 During his lifetime Absalom had taken a **p** 5170
18:18 He named the **p** after himself, 5170
1Ki 7:21 The **p** to the south he named Jakin and 6647
2Ki 11:14 standing by the **p**, as the custom was. 6647
23:3 by the **p** and renewed the covenant in 6647
25:17 Each **p** was twenty-seven feet high. 6647
25:17 The bronze capital on top of one **p** was four 2257S
25:17 The other **p**, with its network, was similar. 6647
2Ch 23:13 standing by his **p** at the entrance. 6647
34:31 by his **p** and renewed the covenant in 6641
Ne 9:12 By day you led them with a **p** *of* cloud, 6647
9:12 by night with a **p** *of* fire to give them light 6647
9:19 the **p** *of* cloud did not cease to guide them 6647
9:19 nor the **p** *of* fire by night to shine on 6647
Ps 99:7 He spoke to them from the **p** *of* cloud; 6647
Jer 1:18 an iron **p** and a bronze wall to stand against 6647
52:22 on top of **the one p** was five cubits high 2257S
52:22 The other **p**, with its pomegranates, 6647
1Ti 3:15 the **p** and foundation of the truth. *5146*
Rev 3:12 Him who overcomes I will make a **p** in *5146*

PILLARS (45) [PILLAR]

Ex 24:4 and set up twelve **stone p** representing 5167
Jdg 16:25 When they stood him among the **p**, 6647
16:26 "Put me where I can feel the **p** that support 6647
16:29 toward the two central **p** on which 6647
1Ki 7:6 of that were **p** and an overhanging roof. 6647
7:15 He cast two bronze **p**, 6647
7:16 of cast bronze to set on the tops of the **p;** 6647
7:17 the capitals on top of the **p**, 6647
7:18 to decorate the capitals on top of the **p.** 6647
7:19 of the **p** in the portico were in the shape 6647
7:20 On the capitals of both **p**, 6647
7:21 the **p** at the portico of the temple. 6647
7:22 And so the work on the **p** was completed. 6647
7:41 two **p;** the two bowl-shaped capitals on top 6647
7:41 bowl-shaped capitals on top of the **p;** 6647
7:41 bowl-shaped capitals on top of the **p;** 6647
7:42 the bowl-shaped capitals on top of the **p);** 6647
2Ki 25:13 The Babylonians broke up the bronze **p**, 6647
25:16 The bronze from the two **p**, 6647
1Ch 18:8 the **p** and various bronze articles. 6647
2Ch 3:15 In the front of the temple he made two **p**, 6647
3:16 and put them on top of the **p.** 6647
3:17 He erected the **p** in the front of the temple, 6647
4:12 two **p;** the two bowl-shaped capitals on top 6647
4:12 bowl-shaped capitals on top of the **p;** 6647
4:12 bowl-shaped capitals on top of the **p;** 6647
4:13 the bowl-shaped capitals on top of the **p);** 6647
Est 1:6 to silver rings on marble **p.** 6647
Job 9:6 from its place and makes its **p** tremble. 6647
26:11 The **p** *of* the heavens quake, 6647
Ps 75:3 it is I who hold its **p** firm. 6647
144:12 and our daughters will be like **p** carved 2312
Pr 9:1 she has hewn out its seven **p.** 6647
SS 5:15 His legs are **p** *of* marble set on bases 6647
Jer 27:19 the LORD Almighty says about the **p**, 6647
43:13 in Egypt he will demolish the **sacred p** 5167
52:17 The Babylonians broke up the bronze **p**, 6647
52:20 The bronze from the two **p**, 6647
52:21 Each of the **p** was eighteen cubits high 6647
Eze 26:11 and your strong **p** will fall to the ground. 5167
40:49 and there were **p** on each side of the jambs. 6647
42:6 The rooms on the third floor had no **p**, 6647
Am 9:1 "Strike the **tops of the p** so that 4117
Gal 2:9 Peter and John, those reputed to be **p**, *5146*
Rev 10:1 and his legs were like fiery **p.** *5146*

PILLED (KJV) See PEELED

PILOT (2)

Ac 27:11 the advice of the **p** and of the owner of *3237*
Jas 3:4 a very small rudder wherever the **p** wants *3995*

PILTAI (1)

Ne 12:17 of Miniamin's and of Moadiah's, **P;** 7122

PIN (6)

Jdg 16:13 and tighten it with the **p**, 3845
16:14 and tightened it with the **p.** 3845
16:14 from his sleep and pulled up the **p** and 3845
1Sa 18:11 *"I'll* **p** David to the wall." 5782
19:10 to **p** him to the wall with his spear, 5782
26:8 Now *let me* **p** him to the ground 5782

PINE (18) [PINES]

1Ki 5:8 in providing the cedar and **p** logs. 1360
5:10 with all the cedar and **p** logs he wanted, 1360
6:15 the floor of the temple with planks of **p.** 1360
6:34 He also made two **p** doors, 1360
9:11 the cedar and **p** and gold he wanted. 1360
2Ch 2:8 **p** and algum logs from Lebanon, 1360
3:5 with **p** and covered it with fine gold 1360+6770
Ps 104:17 the stork has its home in the **p trees.** 1360
Isa 14:8 the **p trees** and the cedars of Lebanon exult 1360
19:8 on the water *will* **p away.** 581
44:14 or planted a **p**, and the rain made it grow. 815
55:13 of the thornbush will grow the **p tree,** 1360
60:13 glory of Lebanon will come to you, the **p**, 1360
Eze 27:5 They made all your timbers of **p trees** 1360
31:8 nor could the **p trees** equal its boughs, 1360
Hos 14:8 I am like a green **p tree;** 1360
Na 2:3 the **spears of p** are brandished. 1360
Zec 11:2 Wail, O **p tree,** for the cedar has fallen; 1360

PINES (4) [PINE]

1Sa 2:5 but she who has had many sons **p away.** 581
2Ki 19:23 its tallest cedars, the choicest of its **p.** 1360
Isa 37:24 its tallest cedars, the choicest of its **p.** 1360
41:19 I will set **p** in the wasteland, 1360

PINIONS (2)

Dt 32:11 to catch them and carries them on its **p.** 89
Job 39:13 with the **p** and feathers *of* the stork. 89

PINON (2)

Ge 36:41 Oholibamah, Elah, **P**, 7091
1Ch 1:52 Oholibamah, Elah, **P**, 7091

PINS (KJV) See TENT PEGS

PINT (1)

Jn 12:3 Then Mary took **about a p** of pure nard, *3354*

PIPES (4)

Da 3:5 zither, lyre, harp, **p** and all kinds of music, 10507
3:10 **p** and all kinds of music must fall down 10507
3:15 zither, lyre, harp, **p** and all kinds of music, 10507
Zec 4:12 the two gold **p** that pour out golden oil?" 7574

PIRAM (1)

Jos 10:3 **P** king of Jarmuth, Japhia king of Lachish 7231

PIRATHON (2) [PIRATHONITE]

Jdg 12:13 After him, Abdon son of Hillel, **from P**, 7285
12:15 and was buried at **P** in Ephraim, 7284

PIRATHONITE (3) [PIRATHON]

2Sa 23:30 Benaiah the **P**, Hiddai from the ravines 7285
1Ch 11:31 from Gibeah in Benjamin, Benaiah the **P**, 7285
27:14 for the eleventh month, was Benaiah the **P**, 7285

PISGAH (8)

Nu 21:20 in Moab where the top of **P** overlooks 7171
23:14 to the field of Zophim on the top of **P**, 7171
Dt 3:17 below the slopes of **P.** 7171
3:27 up to the top of **P** and look west and north 7171
4:49 below the slopes of **P.** 7171
34:1 from the plains of Moab to the top of **P**, 7171
Jos 12:3 and then southward below the slopes of **P.** 7171
13:20 Beth Peor, the slopes of **P**, 7171

PISHON (1)

Ge 2:11 The name of the first is the **P;** 7093

PISIDIA (1)

Ac 14:24 After going through **P**, they came into *4407*

PISIDIAN (1)

Ac 13:14 From Perga they went on to **P** Antioch. *4408*

PISON (KJV) See PISHON

PISPAH (1)

1Ch 7:38 The sons of Jether: Jephunneh, **P** and Ara. 7183

PISS (KJV) See URINE

PISSETH (KJV) See MALE

PISTACHIO (1)

Ge 43:11 *some* **p nuts** and almonds. 1063

PIT (66) [PITS]

Ex 21:33 "If a man uncovers a **p** or digs one and fails 1014
21:34 the owner of the **p** must pay for the loss; 1014
2Sa 18:17 into a big **p** in the forest and piled up 7074
23:20 He also went down into a **p** on a snowy day 1014
1Ch 11:22 He also went down into a **p** on a snowy day 1014
Job 9:31 you would plunge me into a **slime p** so that 8846
33:18 to preserve his soul from the **p**, 8846
33:22 His soul draws near to the **p**, 8846
33:24 'Spare him from going down to the **p;** 8846
33:28 from going down to the **p**, 8846
33:30 to turn back his soul from the **p**, 8846
Ps 7:15 into the **p** he has made. 8846
9:15 into the **p** they have dug; 8846
28:1 be like those who have gone down to the **p.** 1014
30:3 you spared me from going down into the **p.** 1014
30:9 in my going down into the **p?** 8846
35:7 and without cause dug a **p** for me, 8846
35:8 may they fall into **the p**, to their ruin. 2023S
40:2 He lifted me out of the **slimy p**, 1014+8622
55:23 down the wicked into the **p** *of* corruption; 931
57:6 They dug a **p** in my path— 8864
69:15 up or the **p** close its mouth over me. 931
88:4 among those who go down to the **p;** 1014
88:6 You have put me in the lowest **p**, 1014
94:13 till a **p** is dug for the wicked. 8846
103:4 who redeems your life from the **p** and 8846

Ps 143: 7 I will be like those who go down to the **p.** 1014
Pr 1:12 like those who go down to the **p;** 1014
22:14 The mouth of an adulteress is a deep **p;** 8757
23:27 for a prostitute is a deep **p** 8757
26:27 If a man digs a **p,** he will fall into it; 8846
Ecc 10: 8 Whoever digs a **p** may fall into it; 1585
Isa 14:15 to the grave, to the depths of the **p.** 1014
14:19 those who descend to the stones of the **p.** 1014
24:17 Terror and **p** and snare await you, 7074
24:18 at the sound of terror will fall into a **p;** 7074
24:18 whoever climbs out of the **p** will be caught 7074
30:33 Its **fire p** has been made deep and wide, 4509
38:17 In your love you kept me from the **p** 8846
38:18 to the **p** cannot hope for your faithfulness. 1014
Jer 18:20 Yet they have dug a **p** for me. 8757
18:22 a **p** to capture me and have hidden snares 8757
48:43 Terror and **p** and snare await you, 7074
48:44 into a **p,** whoever climbs out of the pit will 7074
48:44 whoever climbs out of the **p** will be caught 7074
La 3:53 to end my life in a **p** and threw stones 1014
3:55 O LORD, from the depths of the **p.** 1014
Eze 19: 4 and he was trapped in their **p.** 8846
19: 8 and he was trapped in their **p.** 8846
26:20 down with those who go down to the **p,** 1014
26:20 with those who go down to the **p,** 1014
28: 8 They will bring you down to the **p,** 8846
31:14 with those who go down to the **p.** 1014
31:16 the grave with those who go down to the **p.** 1014
32:18 with those who go down to the **p.** 1014
32:23 of the **p** and her army lies around her grave. 1014
32:24 with those who go down to the **p.** 1014
32:25 with those who go down to the **p;** 1014
32:29 with those who go down to the **p.** 1014
32:30 with those who go down to the **p.** 1014
Jnh 2: 6 But you brought my life up from the **p,** 8846
Zec 9:11 your prisoners from the waterless **p.** 1014
Mt 12:11 a sheep and it falls into a **p** on the Sabbath, *1073*
15:14 leads a blind man, both will fall into a **p."** *1073*
Mk 12: 1 dug a **p for the winepress** and *5700*
Lk 6:39 Will they not both fall into a **p?** *1073*

PITCH (11) [PITCHED]

Ge 6:14 make rooms in it and coat it with **p** inside 4109
Ex 2: 3 for him and coated it with tar and **p.** 2413
33: 7 to take a tent and **p** it outside the camp 5742
Pr 20:20 his lamp will be snuffed out in **p darkness.** 854+3125
Isa 13:20 no Arab *will* **p** *his* **tent** there, 182
34: 9 Edom's streams will be turned into **p,** 2413
34: 9 her land will become blazing **p!** 2413
Jer 6: 3 *they will* **p** their tents around her, 9546
10:20 now *to* **p** my tent or to set up my shelter. 5742
Eze 25: 4 up their camps and **p** their tents 5989
Da 11:45 *He will* **p** his royal tents between the seas 5749

PITCH-DARK (1) [DARK]

Am 5:20 **p,** without a ray of brightness? 695

PITCHED (15) [PITCH]

Ge 12: 8 the hills east of Bethel and **p** his tent, 5742
13:12 of the plain and **p** *his* **tents** near Sodom. 182
26:25 There *he* **p** his tent, 5742
31:25 Jacob *had* **p** his tent in the hill country 9546
33:19 the plot of ground where *he* **p** his tent. 5742
35:21 Israel moved on again and **p** his tent 5742
Jdg 4:11 **p** his tent by the great tree in Zaanannim 5742
20:19 the Israelites got up and **p camp** 2837
1Sa 17: 1 *They* **p camp** at Ephes Dammim, 2837
2Sa 6:17 in its place inside the tent that David *had* **p** 5742
16:22 So *they* **p** a tent for Absalom on the roof, 5742
1Ch 15: 1 a place for the ark of God and **p** a tent 5742
16: 1 and set it inside the tent that David *had* **p** 5742
2Ch 1: 4 because *he had* **p** a tent for it in Jerusalem. 5742
Ps 19: 4 In the heavens *he has* **p** a tent for the sun, 8492

PITCHER (1) [PITCHERS]

Ecc 12: 6 before the **p** is shattered at the spring, 3902

PITCHERS (4) [PITCHER]

Ex 25:29 as its **p** and bowls for the pouring out 7987
37:16 its plates and dishes and bowls and its **p** for 7987
1Ch 28:17 sprinkling bowls and **p;** 7987
Mk 7: 4 such as the washing of cups, **p** and kettles.) *3829*

PITFALLS (2)

Ps 119:85 arrogant dig **p** for me, contrary to your law. 8864
La 3:47 We have suffered terror and **p,** 7074

PITHOM (1)

Ex 1:11 and they built **P** and Rameses as store cities 7351

PITHON (2)

1Ch 8:35 **P,** Melech, Tarea and Ahaz. 7094
9:41 **P,** Melech, Tahrea and Ahaz. 7094

PITIED (2) [PITY]

Ps 106:46 to be **p** by all who held them captive. 8171
1Co 15:19 we are to be **p more than** all men. *1795*

PITIFUL (1) [PITY]

Rev 3:17 you do not realize that you are wretched, **p,** *1795*

PITS (5) [PIT]

Ge 14:10 the Valley of Siddim was **full of** tar **p,** 931+931
1Sa 13: 6 among the rocks, and in **p** and cisterns. 7663
Ps 140:10 into **miry p,** never to rise. 4549
Isa 42:22 all of them trapped in **p** or hidden away 2987
Zep 2: 9 a place of weeds and salt **p,** 4838

PITTANCE (1)

Ps 44:12 You sold your people for a **p,** 2104+4202

PITY (44) [PITIED, PITIFUL]

Dt 7:16 *Do* not **look** on them **with p** 2571+6524
13: 8 **Show** him no **p.** 2571+6524
19:13 **Show** him no **p.** 2571+6524
19:21 **Show** no **p:** life for life, 2571+6524
25:12 shall cut off her hand. **Show** her no **p.** 2571+6524
28:50 respect for the old or **p** *for* the young. 2858
2Sa 12: 6 because he did such a thing and **had** no **p."** 2798
2Ch 36:15 because *he* **had p** on his people and 2798
Job 16:13 Without **p,** he pierces my kidneys 2798
19:21 **"Have p** *on* me, my friends, have pity, 2858
19:21 "Have pity on me, my friends, **have p,** 2858
Ps 72:13 *He will* **take p** on the weak and the needy 2571
102:14 her very dust **moves** *them* **to p.** 2858
109:12 to him or **take p** on his fatherless children. 2858
Ecc 4:10 But **p** the man who falls and has no one 365
Isa 9:17 nor *will he* **p** the fatherless and widows, 8163
Jer 13:14 *I will* **allow** no **p** or mercy 2798
15: 5 "Who *will* **have p** on you, O Jerusalem? 2798
16: 5 my love and my **p** from this people," 8171
20:16 the towns the LORD overthrew without **p.** 5714
21: 7 he will show them no mercy or **p** 2798
La 2: 2 Without **p** the Lord has swallowed up all 2798
2:17 He has overthrown you without **p,** 2798
2:21 you have slaughtered them without **p.** 2798
3:43 you have slain without **p.** 2798
Eze 5:11 I *will* not **look** *on* you **with p** 2571+6524
7: 4 I *will* not **look** on you **with p** 2571+6524
7: 9 I *will* not **look** on you **with p** 2571+6524
8:18 I *will* not **look** *on* them **with p** 2571+6524
9: 5 without **showing p** or compassion. 2571+6524
9:10 I *will* not **look** on them **with p** 2571+6524
16: 5 No *one* **looked** on you **with p** 2571+6524
20:17 Yet I **looked** on them **with p** 2571+6524
24:14 *I will* not **have p,** nor will I relent. 2571
Joel 2:14 He may turn and **have p** and leave behind 5714
2:18 for his land and **take p** on his people. 2798
Zec 8:14 to bring disaster upon you and **showed** no **p** 5714
11: 6 For *I will* no longer **have p** on the people 2798
Mt 18:27 The servant's master **took p** on him, *5072*
Mk 9:22 **take p** on us and help us." *5072*
Lk 10:33 and when he saw him, *he* **took p** on him. *5072*
16:24 **have p** on me and send Lazarus to dip *1796*
17:13 "Jesus, Master, **have p** on us!" *1796*
1Jn 3:17 and sees his brother in need but **has no p** *3091+3836+5073*

PLACE (792) [PLACED, PLACES, PLACING]

Ge 1: 9 under the sky be gathered to one **p,** 5226
2:21 of the man's ribs and closed up the **p** 9393
4:25 "God has granted me another child **in p of** 9393
8: 9 But the dove could find no **p to set** its feet 4955
13: 3 he went **from p to place** until he came 4200+5023
13: 3 he went **from place to p** until he came 4200+5023
13: 3 to the **p** between Bethel and Ai 5226
18:24 not spare the **p** for the sake of the fifty 5226
18:26 I will spare the whole **p** for their sake." 5226
19:13 because we are going to destroy this **p.** 5226
19:14 He said, "Hurry and get out of this **p,** 5226
19:27 up and returned to the **p** where he had stood 5226
20:11 'There is surely no fear of God in this **p,** 5226
21:31 So that **p** was called Beersheba, 5226
22: 3 he set out for the **p** God had told him about. 5226
22: 4 looked up and saw the **p** in the distance. 5226
22: 9 they reached the **p** God had told him about, 5226
22:14 that **p** The LORD Will Provide. 5226
24:31 I have prepared the house and a **p** for 5226
26: 7 the men of that **p** asked him about his wife, 5226
26: 7 of this **p** might kill me on account 5226
28:11 When he reached a certain **p,** 5226
28:16 he thought, "Surely the LORD is in this **p,** 5226
28:17 "How awesome is this **p!** 5226
28:19 He called that **p** Bethel, 5226
29: 3 Then they would return the stone to its **p** 5226
29:22 the people of the **p** and gave a feast. 5226
30: 2 "Am I **in the p of** God, 9393
30:41 Jacob *would* **p** the branches in the troughs 8492
30:42 *he would* not **p** them there. 8492
32: 2 So he named that **p** Mahanaim. 5226
32:30 So Jacob called the **p** Peniel, saying, 5226
33:17 a **p** for himself and made shelters 1074
33:17 That is why the **p** is called Succoth. 5226
35: 7 and he called the **p** El Bethel, 5226
35:13 up from him at the **p** where he had talked 5226
35:14 a stone pillar at the **p** where God had talked 5226
35:15 Jacob called the **p** where God had talked 5226
39:20 and put him in prison, the **p** where 5226
42:15 as Pharaoh lives, you will not leave **this** *p* AIT
42:27 **p where they stopped for the night** 4869
Ge 43:21 **p where we stopped for the night** 4869
43:30 Joseph hurried out and looked for a **p** NIH
44:33 as my lord's slave **in p of** the boy, 9393
49:15 When he sees how good is his **resting p** and 4957
49:30 as a burial **p** from Ephron the Hittite, 299
50:11 That is why **that p** near the Jordan 2023S
50:13 which Abraham had bought as a burial **p** 299
50:19 Am I **in** *the* **p of** God? 9393
50:25 you must carry my bones up from **this** *p."* AIT
Ex 3: 5 "Take off your sandals, for the **p** 5226
4:24 At a **lodging p** on the way, 4869
9:19 **bring** your livestock and everything you have in the field **to a p of shelter,** 6395
9:26 The only **p** it did not hail was the land 9004
10:23 No one could see anyone else or leave his **p** 9393
13:19 carry my bones up with you from **this** *p."* AIT
13:22 by night **left** *its* **p** in front of the people. 4631
14:27 and at daybreak the sea went back to its **p.** 419
15:17 the **p,** O LORD, you made for your dwelling, 4806
15:23 (That is why **the p** is called Marah.) 2023S
16:33 Then **p** it before the LORD to be kept for 5663
17: 1 **traveling from p to place** as the LORD 5023
17: 1 **traveling from place to p** as the LORD 5023
17: 7 And he called the **p** Massah and Meribah 5226
21:13 he is to flee to a **p** I will designate. 5226
23:20 and to bring you to the **p** I have prepared. 5226
25:21 **P** the cover on top of the ark and put in 5989
26:33 the curtain from the clasps and **p** the ark of 995
26:33 The curtain will separate the **Holy P** from 7731
26:33 the Holy Place from the **Most Holy P.** 7731+7731
26:34 of the Testimony in the **Most Holy P.** 7731+7731
26:35 **P** the table outside the curtain on 8492
28:29 "Whenever Aaron enters the **Holy P,** 7731
28:35 be heard when he enters the **Holy P** before 7731
28:43 the altar to minister in the **Holy P,** 7731
29:30 in the **Holy P** is to wear them seven days. 7731
29:31 and cook the meat in a sacred **p.** 5226
29:43 and the **p** will be consecrated by my glory. NIH
30:18 **P** it between the Tent of Meeting and 5989
30:36 Grind some of it to powder and **p** it in front 5989
31:11 and fragrant incense for the **Holy P.** 7731
32:34 Now go, lead the people to the **p** I spoke of, 889S
33: 1 the LORD said to Moses, "Leave this **p,** NIH
33:21 "There is a **p** near me where you may stand 5226
40: 3 **P** the ark of the Testimony in it and shield 8492
40: 5 **P** the gold altar of incense in front of 5989
40: 6 **"P** the altar of burnt offering in front of 5989
40: 7 **p** the basin between the Tent of Meeting 5989
40:18 set up the tabernacle, *he* **put** the bases **in p,** 5989
Lev 4:12 the camp to a **p** ceremonially clean, 5226
4:24 on the goat's head and slaughter it at the **p** 5226
4:29 the sin offering and slaughter it at the **p** *of* 5226
4:33 and slaughter it for a sin offering at the **p** 5226
6:10 on the altar and **p** them beside the altar. 8492
6:11 and carry the ashes outside the camp to a **p** 5226
6:16 it is to be eaten without yeast in a holy **p;** 5226
6:25 be slaughtered before the LORD in the **p** 5226
6:26 it is to be eaten in a holy **p,** 5226
6:27 you must wash it in a holy **p.** 5226
6:30 to make atonement in the **Holy P** must not 7731
7: 2 to be slaughtered in the **p** where 5226
7: 6 but it must be eaten in a holy **p;** 5226
10:13 Eat it in a holy **p,** because it is your share 5226
10:14 Eat them in a ceremonially clean **p;** 5226
10:18 its blood was not taken into the **Holy P,** 7731
13:19 and in the **p** where the boil was, 5226
14:13 to slaughter the lamb in the holy **p** where 5226
14:40 and thrown into an unclean **p** outside 5226
14:41 into an unclean **p** outside the town. 5226
14:45 and taken out of the town to an unclean **p.** 5226
15:31 for defiling my **dwelling p,** 5438
16: 2 the **Most Holy P** behind the curtain in front 7731
16:16 make atonement for the **Most Holy P** 7731
16:17 in to make atonement in the **Most Holy P** 7731
16:20 making atonement for the **Most Holy P,** 7731
16:22 on itself all their sins to a **solitary p;** 824
16:23 on before he entered the **Most Holy P,** 7731
16:24 in a holy **p** and put on his regular garments. 5226
16:27 the **Most Holy P** to make atonement, must 7731
16:33 make atonement for the **Most Holy P,** 5219+7731
21:11 not enter a **p** where there is a dead body. NIH
22:22 *Do* not **p** any of these on the altar as 5989
24: 9 who are to eat it in a holy **p,** 5226
26: 1 not **p** a carved stone in your land to bow 5989
26:11 I will put my **dwelling p** among you, 5438
Nu 2:17 each in his own **p** under his standard. 3338
3:12 from among the Israelites **in p of** 9393
3:41 the Levites for me **in p of** all the firstborn 9393
3:41 and the livestock of the Levites **in p of** all 9393
3:45 "Take the Levites **in p of** all the firstborn 9393
3:45 and the livestock of the Levites **in p of** 9393
4: 6 and **put** the poles **in p.** 8492
4: 8 and **put** its poles **in p.** 8492
4:11 and **put** its poles **in p.** 8492
4:14 *to* **p** on it all the utensils used 5989
4:14 and **put** its poles **in p.** 8492
5:18 he shall loosen her hair and **p** in her hands 5989
6:19 *to* **p** in his hands a boiled shoulder of 5989
8:16 I have taken them as my own **in p of** 9393
8:18 the Levites **in p of** all the firstborn sons 9393
10:12 **traveled from p to place** until the cloud 5023
10:12 **traveled from place to p** until the cloud 5023
10:29 "We are setting out for the **p** about which 5226
10:33 to find them a **p to rest.** 4957
11: 3 So that **p** was called Taberah, 5226
11:34 the **p** was named Kibroth Hattaavah, 5226
13:24 That **p** was called the Valley of Eshcol 5226

Nu 14:40 up to the **p** the LORD promised." 5226
17: 4 **P** them in the Tent of Meeting in front of 5663
19: 9 in a ceremonially clean **p** outside the camp. 5226
20: 5 up out of Egypt to this terrible **p**? 5226
21: 3 so the **p** was named Hormah. 5226
22:26 in a narrow **p** where there was no room 5226
23:13 to another **p** where you can see them; 5226
23:27 "Come, let me take you to another **p.** 5226
24:21 "Your **dwelling p** is secure, 4632
32:14 standing **in** the **p of** your fathers 9393
32:17 until we have brought them to their **p.** 5226
35:15 These six towns will be a **p of refuge** 5236
Dt 1:31 the way you went until you reached this **p."** 5226
2:12 from before them and settled **in** their **p,** 9393
2:21 who drove them out and settled **in** their **p.** 9393
2:22 and have lived **in** their **p** to this day. 9393
2:23 and settled **in** their **p.)** 9393
11: 5 in the desert until you arrived at this **p,** 5226
11:24 Every **p** where you set your foot will 5226
12: 5 the **p** the LORD your God will choose 5226
12: 5 To **that p** you must go; 9004[S]
12: 9 not yet reached the **resting p** and 4957
12:11 the **p** the LORD your God will choose as 5226
12:14 at the **p** the LORD will choose in one 5226
12:18 the **p** the LORD your God will choose— 5226
12:21 the **p** where the LORD your God chooses 5226
12:26 and go to the **p** the LORD will choose. 5226
13: 2 or wonder of which he has spoken **takes p,** 995
14:23 at the **p** he will choose as a dwelling 5226
14:24 But if that **p** is too distant NIH
14:24 and cannot carry your tithe (because the **p** 5226
14:25 and take the silver with you and go to the **p** 5226
15:20 at the **p** he will choose. 5226
16: 2 the **p** the LORD will choose as a dwelling 5226
16: 6 except in the **p** he will choose as a dwelling 5226
16: 7 at the **p** the LORD your God will choose. 5226
16:11 at the **p** he will choose as a dwelling 5226
16:15 the Feast to the LORD your God at the **p** 5226
16:16 at the **p** he will choose: 5226
17: 8 to the **p** the LORD your God will choose. 5226
17:10 to the decisions they give you at the **p** 5226
17:15 *Do* not **p** a foreigner over you, 5989
18: 6 and comes in all earnestness to the **p** 5226
18:22 of the LORD *does* not **take p** or come true, 2118
23:12 a **p** outside the camp where you can go 3338
26: 2 the **p** the LORD your God will choose as 5226
26: 9 to this **p** and gave us this land, 5226
26:10 **P** the basket before the LORD your God 5663
26:15 down from heaven, your holy **dwelling p,** 5061
28:65 no **resting p** for the sole of your foot. 4955
29: 7 When you reached this **p,** 5226
31:11 at the **p** he will choose, 5226
31:26 "Take this Book of the Law and **p** it beside 8492
Jos 1: 3 I will give you every **p** where you set 5226
4: 3 over with you and put them down at the **p** 4869
4:18 the waters of the Jordan returned to their **p** 5226
5: 7 So he raised up their sons **in** their **p,** 9393
5: 9 So the **p** has been called Gilgal to this day. 5226
5:15 for the **p** where you are standing is holy." 5226
6:23 and put them in a **p** outside the camp NIH
7:26 Therefore that **p** has been called the Valley 5226
8: 9 and they went to the **p of ambush** and lay 4422
8:14 at a **certain p** overlooking the Arabah. 4595
8:28 heap of ruins, a **desolate p** to this day. 9039
9:27 and for the altar of the LORD at the **p** 5226
20: 4 into their city and give him a **p** to live 5226
24:26 up there under the oak near the **holy p** *of* 5219
Jdg 2: 5 and they called that **p** Bokim. 5226
6:20 **p** them on this rock, 5663
6:37 I *will* **p** a wool fleece on the threshing floor. 3657
7: 7 Let all the other men go, each to his own **p.** 5226
9:35 soldiers came out from their **hiding p.** 4422
11:19 through your country to our own **p.'** 5226
15:17 and the **p** was called Ramath Lehi. 5226
15:19 God opened up the **hollow p** in Lehi, 4847
16: 2 So they surrounded the **p** and lay in wait NIH
17: 8 that town in search of **some other p** to stay. 889[S]
17: 9 he said, "and I'm looking for a **p** to stay." 889[S]
18: 1 of the Danites was seeking a **p** of their own 5709
18: 3 What are you doing in **this** *p?* AIT
18:12 This is why the **p** west of Kiriath Jearim 5226
18:15 the house of the young Levite at Micah's **p** 1074
19:16 (the men of the **p** were Benjamites), 5226
20:33 the Israelite ambush charged out of its **p** on 5226
21:24 the Israelites left **that p** and went home 9004[S]
Ru 1: 7 the **p** where she had been living and set out 5226
2:19 the one at whose **p** she had been working. NIH
3: 4 note the **p** where he is lying. 5226
1Sa 2:20 to **take the p of** the one she prayed for 9393
3: 2 was lying down in his usual **p.** 5226
3: 9 So Samuel went and lay down in his **p.** 5226
5: 3 and put him back in his **p.** 5226
5:11 let it go back to its own **p,** 5226
6: 2 Tell us how we should send it back to its **p."** 5226
6:21 Come down and take it up to your **p."** NIH
9:12 for the people have a sacrifice at the **high p.** 1195
9:13 before he goes up to the **high p** to eat. 1195
9:14 toward them on his way up to the **high p.** 1195
9:19 "Go up ahead of me to the **high p,** 1195
9:25 After they came down from the **high p** to 1195
10: 5 of prophets coming down from the **high p** 1195
10:13 he went to the **high p.** 1195
12: 8 of Egypt and settled them in this **p.** 5226
20:19 go to the **p** where you hid when this trouble 5226
20:25 He sat in his customary **p** by the wall, 4632
20:25 but David's **p** was empty. 5226
20:27 David's **p** was empty again. 5226
1Sa 20:37 to the **p** where Jonathan's arrow had fallen, 5226
21: 2 I have told them to meet me at a certain **p.** 5226
23:13 **moving from p to place.** 889+928+2143+2143
23:13 **moving from place to p.** 889+928+2143+2143
23:28 why they call this **P** Sela Hammahlekoth. 5226
26: 5 and went to the **p** where Saul had camped. 5226
27: 5 let a **p** be assigned to me in one of 5226
29: 4 to the **p** you assigned him. 5226
2Sa 2:16 So that **p** in Gibeon was called 5226
2:23 to the **p** where Asahel had fallen and died. 5226
5:20 So that **p** was called Baal Perazim. 5226
6: 8 and to this day that **p** is called Perez Uzzah. 5226
6:17 the LORD and set it in its **p** inside the tent 5226
7: 6 **moving from p to place** with a tent 2143
7: 6 **moving from place to p** with a tent 2143
7:10 a **p** for my people Israel and will plant them 5226
11:16 he put Uriah at a **p** where he knew 5226
15:17 and they halted at a **p** some distance away. 1074
15:25 and let me see it and his **dwelling p** again. 5659
16: 8 Saul, **in** whose **p** you have reigned. 9393
17: 9 he is hidden in a cave or some other **p.** 5226
17:25 over the army **in p of** Joab. 9393
18: 6 the battle **took p** in the forest of Ephraim. 2118
19:13 the commander of my army **in p of** Joab.' " 9393
19:28 but *you* **gave** your servant **a p** among 8883
21: 5 and *have* no **p** anywhere in Israel, 3656
21:20 In still another battle, *which* **took p** at Gath, 2118
22:20 He brought me out into a **spacious p;** 5303
23:11 When the Philistines banded together at a **p** NIH
1Ki 1:30 and he will sit on my throne **in** my **p."** 9393
1:35 and sit on my throne and reign **in** my **p.** 9393
3: 4 for that was the most important **high p,** 1195
3: 7 you have made your servant king **in p of** 9393
4:28 brought to the **proper p** 889+2118+5226+9004
5: 5 the throne **in** your **p** will build the temple 9393
5: 9 in rafts by sea to the **p** you specify. 5226
6:16 an inner sanctuary, the **Most Holy P.** 7731+7731
7:50 the innermost room, the **Most Holy P,** 7731+7731
8: 6 to its **p** in the inner sanctuary of the temple, 5226
8: 6 of the temple, the **Most Holy P,** 7731+7731
8: 7 The cherubim spread their wings over the **p** 5226
8: 8 the **Holy P** in front of the inner sanctuary, 7731
8: 8 but not from outside the Holy **P;** NIH
8:10 the priests withdrew from the **Holy P,** 7731
8:13 a **p** for you to dwell forever." 4806
8:21 I have provided a **p** there for the ark, 5226
8:29 this **p** of which you said, 'My Name 5226
8:29 the prayer your servant prays toward this **p.** 5226
8:30 when they pray toward this **p.** 5226
8:30 Hear from heaven, your dwelling **p,** 5226
8:35 toward this **p** and confess your name 5226
8:39 then hear from heaven, your dwelling **p.** 4806
8:43 then hear from heaven, your dwelling **p,** 4806
8:49 then from heaven, your dwelling **p,** 4806
11: 7 a **high p** for Chemosh the detestable god 1195
13:16 or drink water with you in this **p.** 5226
13:22 and drank water in the **p** where he told you 5226
17: 9 I have commanded a widow **in that p** 9004[S]
21: 6 I will give you another vineyard **in** its **p.'** 9393
21: 9 of fasting and seat Naboth in a **prominent p** 8031
21:12 and seated Naboth in a **prominent p** *among* 8031
21:19 the **p** where dogs licked up Naboth's blood, 5226
2Ki 2: 7 the **p** where Elijah and Elisha had stopped NIH
3:25 was left with its stones in **p,** NIH
6: 1 the **p** where we meet with you is too small 5226
6: 2 and let us build a **p** there for us to live." 5226
6: 6 When he showed him the **p,** 5226
6: 8 up my camp in such and such a **p."** 5226
6: 9 "Beware of passing that **p,** 5226
6:10 king of Israel checked on the **p** indicated by 5226
11:16 as she reached the **p** *where* the horses enter 2006
11:19 king then **took** *his* **p** on the royal throne, 3782
14:21 and made him king **in p of** 9393
17: 7 *All this* **took p** because the Israelites 2118
17:11 At every **high p** they burned incense, 1195
18:25 to attack and destroy this **p** without word 5226
21:24 and they made Josiah his son king **in** his **p.** 9393
22:16 to bring disaster on this **p** and its people, 5226
22:17 my anger will burn against this **p** and will 5226
22:19 against this **p** and its people, 5226
22:20 the disaster I am going to bring on this **p.'** " 5226
23:15 the **high p** made by Jeroboam son of Nebat, 1195
23:15 even that altar and **high p** he demolished. 1195
23:15 the **high p** and ground it to powder, 1195
23:30 and made him king **in p of** his father. 9393
23:34 of Josiah king **in p of** his father Josiah 9393
24:17 king **in** his **p** and changed his name 9393
1Ch 4:41 Then they settled **in** their **p,** 9393
6:49 all that was done in the **Most Holy P,** 7731+7731
11:13 a **p** where there was a field full of barley, NIH
13:11 and to this day that **p** is called Perez Uzzah. 5226
14:11 So that **p** was called Baal Perazim. 5226
15: 1 a **p** for the ark of God and pitched a tent 5226
15: 3 the LORD to the **p** he had prepared for it. 5226
15:12 to the **p** I have prepared for it. NIH
16:27 strength and joy in his **dwelling p.** 5226
16:39 the tabernacle of the LORD at the **high p** 1195
17: 5 from one **dwelling p** to another. 5438
17: 9 a **p** for my people Israel and will plant them 5226
20: 6 In still another battle, *which* **took p** at Gath, 2118
21:29 at that time on the **high p** at Gibeon. 1195
23:32 the Tent of Meeting, for the **Holy P** and, 7731
28: 2 to build a house as a **p of rest** for the ark of 4957
28:11 its inner rooms and the **p** *of* atonement. 1074
29:23 on the throne of the LORD as king **in p of** 9393
2Ch 1: 3 and the whole assembly went to the **high p** 1195
1: 4 to **the p** he had prepared for it, 2021[S]
2Ch 1: 8 and have made me king **in** his **p.** 9393
1:13 to Jerusalem from the **high p** at Gibeon, 1195
2: 6 except as a **p** to burn sacrifices before him? NIH
3: 1 the **p** provided by David. 5226
3: 8 He built the **Most Holy P,** 7731+7731
3:10 In the Most Holy **P** he made a pair 1074
4:22 the inner doors to the **Most Holy P** 7731+7731
5: 7 to its **p** in the inner sanctuary of the temple, 5226
5: 7 of the temple, the **Most Holy P,** 7731+7731
5: 8 The cherubim spread their wings over the **p** 5226
5: 9 but not from outside the Holy **P;** NIH
5:11 priests then withdrew from the **Holy P.** 7731
6: 2 a **p** for you to dwell forever." 4806
6:20 toward this temple day and night, this **p** 5226
6:20 the prayer your servant prays toward this **p.** 5226
6:21 when they pray toward this **p.** 5226
6:21 Hear from heaven, your dwelling **p;** 5226
6:26 toward this **p** and confess your name 5226
6:30 then hear from heaven, your dwelling **p.** 4806
6:33 then hear from heaven, your dwelling **p,** 4806
6:39 then from heaven, your dwelling **p,** 4806
6:40 to the prayers offered in this **p.** 5226
6:41 and come to your **resting p,** 5665
7:12 and have chosen this **p** for myself as 5226
7:15 to the prayers offered in this **p.** 5226
20:24 the **p that overlooks** the desert and looked 5205
22: 1 Jehoram's youngest son, king **in** his **p,** 9393
24:11 the chest and carry it back to its **p.** 5226
26: 1 made him king **in p of** his father Amaziah. 9393
29: 6 faces away from the LORD's **dwelling p** 5438
30:27 reached heaven, his holy **dwelling p.** 5061
33:25 and they made Josiah his son king **in** his **p.** 9393
34:24 to bring disaster on this **p** and its people— 5226
34:25 my anger will be poured out on this **p** 5226
34:27 against this **p** and its people, 5226
34:28 the disaster I am going to bring on this **p** 5226
35: 5 in the **holy p** with a group of Levites 7731
36: 1 and made him king in Jerusalem **in p of** 9393
36:15 on his people and on his **dwelling p.** 5061
Ezr 1: 4 the people of any **p** where survivors may 5226
4:15 a **p** of rebellion from ancient times. 10089+10135+10193[S]
4:19 and has been a **p** of rebellion 10089+10193[S]
6: 3 be rebuilt as a **p** to present sacrifices, 10087
9: 8 and giving us a **firm p** in his sanctuary, 3845
Ne 1: 9 and bring them to the **p** I have chosen as 5226
3: 1 They dedicated it and **set** its doors **in p,** 6641
3: 3 **put** its doors and bolts and bars **in p.** 6641
3: 6 **put** its doors and bolts and bars **in p.** 6641
3:13 **put** its doors and bolts and bars **in p.** 6641
3:14 **put** its doors and bolts and bars **in p.** 6641
3:15 **putting** its doors and bolts and bars **in p.** 6641
7: 1 **set** the doors **in p,** 6641
Est 2: 9 and moved her and her maids into the **best** *p* AIT
4:14 for the Jews will arise from another **p,** 5226
Job 7:10 his **p** will know him no more. 5226
8: 6 and restore you to your rightful **p.** 5661
8:17 of rocks and looks for a *p* **among** the stones. AIT
8:18 that **p** disowns it and says, NIH
9: 6 from its **p** and makes its pillars tremble. 5226
10:21 before I go to the **p** of no return, NIH
14:18 and as a rock is moved from its **p,** 5226
16: 4 if you were **in** my **p;** 9393
18: 4 Or must the rocks be moved from their **p?** 5226
18:21 such is the **p** *of* one who knows not God." 5226
20: 9 his **p** will look on him no more. 5226
27:21 it sweeps him out of his **p.** 5226
27:23 in derision and hisses him out of his **p.** 5226
28: 1 for silver and a **p** where gold is refined. 5226
30:23 to the **p** appointed for all the living. 1074
34:22 There is no **dark p,** no deep shadow, 3125
34:24 the mighty and sets up others **in** their **p.** 9393
36:16 the jaws of distress to a **spacious p** free 8144
37: 1 and leaps from its **p.** 5226
38:10 and **set** its doors and bars **in p,** 8492
38:12 or shown the dawn its **p,** 5226
38:24 to the **p** where the lightning is dispersed, NIH
38:24 or the **p** where the east winds are scattered NIH
Ps 8: 3 which *you have* **set in p,** 3922
18:19 He brought me out into a **spacious p;** 5303
24: 3 Who may stand in his holy **p?** 5226
26: 8 O LORD, the **p** where your glory dwells. 5226
28: 2 my hands toward your **Most Holy P.** 1808+7731
31: 8 but have set my feet in a **spacious p.** 5303
32: 7 You are my **hiding p;** 6260
33:14 from his dwelling **p** he watches all who live 4806
40: 2 on a rock and gave me a firm **p to stand.** 892
41: 8 he will never get up from the **p** NIH
43: 3 to the **p where** you **dwell.** 5438
45:16 sons *will* **take the p of** your fathers; 2118+9393
46: 4 the **holy** *p* where the Most High dwells. AIT
50: 1 the rising of the sun to the **p where** it **sets.** 4427
51: 6 you teach me wisdom in the **inmost p.** 6258
55: 8 I would hurry to my **p of shelter,** 5144
62: 4 to topple him from his **lofty p;** 8420
66:12 but you brought us to a **p of abundance.** 8122
69:25 May their **p** be deserted; 3227
73:18 Surely *you* **p** them on slippery ground; 8883
74: 4 Your foes roared in the **p where** you **met** 4595
74: 7 the **dwelling p** *of* your Name. 5438
74: 8 burned every **p where** God was **worshiped** 4595
76: 2 his **dwelling p** in Zion. 5104
84: 1 How lovely is your **dwelling p,** 5438
84: 3 a **p** near your altar, O LORD Almighty, NIH
84: 6 they make it a **p** of springs; NIH
88:12 Are your wonders in the *p of* **darkness,** AIT
90: 1 you have been our **dwelling p** 5061

Ps 103:16 and its **p** remembers it no more. 5226
104: 8 to the **p** you assigned for them. 5226
109: 8 may another take his **p of leadership.** 7213
113: 3 the rising of the sun to the **p where** it **sets,** 4427
132: 5 till I find a **p** for the LORD, 5226
132: 7 "Let us go to his **dwelling p;** 5438
132: 8 O LORD, and come to your **resting p,** 4957
132:11 "One of your own descendants *I will* **p** 8883
132:14 "This is my **resting p** for ever and ever; 4957
139:15 from you when I was made in the **secret p.** 6260
148: 6 *He* **set** them **in p** for ever and ever; 6641
Pr 3:19 by understanding *he* **set** the heavens **in p;** 3922
8:25 before the mountains **were settled in p,** 3190
8:27 I was there when *he* **set** the heavens **in p,** 3922
24:15 do not raid his **dwelling p;** 8070
25: 6 and do not claim a **p** among great men; 5226
Ecc 1: 7 To the **p** the streams come from, 5226
3:16 In the **p** *of* judgment—wickedness 5226
3:16 wickedness was there, in the **p** *of* justice— 5226
3:20 All go to the same **p;** 5226
4: 1 the oppression that *was* **taking p** under 6913
6: 6 Do not all go to the same **p?** 5226
8:10 and go from the holy **p** and receive praise 5226
11: 3 in the **p** where it falls, there will it lie. 5226
SS 8: 6 **P** me like a seal over your heart, 8492
Isa 3:13 The LORD **takes** *his* **p** in court; 5893
4: 6 and **hiding p** from the storm and rain. 5039
7: 7 " '*It will* not **take p,** it will not happen, 7756
7:23 in every **p** where there were 5226
11:10 and his **p of rest** will be glorious. 4957
13:13 the earth will shake from its **p** at the wrath 5226
14: 2 and bring them to their own **p.** 5226
14:21 Prepare a **p to slaughter** his sons for 4749
14:23 into a **p** *for* owls and into swampland; 4625
16:12 When Moab appears at her **high p,** 1195
18: 4 and will look on from my **dwelling p,** 4806
18: 7 **p** *of* the Name of the LORD Almighty. 5226
22:16 on the height and chiseling your **resting p** 5438
22:22 *I will* **p** on his shoulder the key to 5989
22:23 I will drive him like a peg into a firm **p;** 5226
22:25 peg driven into the firm **p** will give way; 5226
23:13 The Assyrians *have* **made** it **a p** 3569
28:12 "This is the **resting p,** let the weary rest"; 4957
28:12 and, "This is the **p of repose"**— 5276
28:15 a lie our refuge and falsehood *our* **hiding p.** 6259
28:17 and water will overflow your **hiding p.** 6260
28:25 Does he not plant wheat *in* its **p,** 8463
33:21 be like a **p** *of* broad rivers and streams. 5226
41: 1 let us meet together at the **p of judgment.** 5477
42: 9 See, the former things *have* **taken p,** 995
45: 6 to the **p of** its **setting** men may know there
is none besides me. 5115
46: 7 they set it up **in** its **p,** and there it stands. 9393
49:20 'This **p** is too small for us; 5226
51:16 I *who* **set** the heavens **in p,** 5749
54: 2 "Enlarge the **p** *of* your tent, 5226
57:15 "I live in a high and **holy** *p,* AIT
60:13 to adorn the **p** *of* my sanctuary; 5226
60:13 and I will glorify the **p** *of* my feet. 5226
60:17 and silver **in p of** iron. 9393
60:17 and iron **in p of** stones. 9393
63:18 while your people possessed your **holy p,** 7731
65:10 the Valley of Achor a **resting p** *for* herds, 8070
66: 1 Where will my resting **p** be? 5226
Jer 2:37 You will also leave **that** *p* with your hands AIT
3: 2 Is there *any p* **where** you have AIT
4: 7 He has left his **p** to lay waste your land. 5226
7: 3 and I will let you live in this **p.** 5226
7: 6 and do not shed innocent blood in this **p,** 5226
7: 7 then I will let you live in this **p,** 5226
7:12 now to the **p** in Shiloh where I first made 5226
7:14 the **p** I gave to you and your fathers. 5226
7:20 and my wrath will be poured out on this **p,** 5226
9: 2 in the desert a **lodging p** *for* travelers, so 4869
13: 7 and dug up the belt and took it from the **p** 5226
14:13 I will give you lasting peace in this **p.' "** 5226
16: 2 and have sons or daughters in this **p."** 5226
16: 9 of bride and bridegroom in this **p.** 5226
17:12 is the **p** *of* our sanctuary. 5226
19: 3 to bring a disaster on this **p** that will make 5226
19: 4 and made this a **p** of foreign gods; 5226
19: 4 and they have filled this **p** with the blood of 5226
19: 6 people will no longer call this **p** Topheth 5226
19: 7 " 'In this **p** I will ruin the plans of Judah 5226
19:12 to this **p** and to those who live here, 5226
19:13 of Judah will be defiled like this **p,** 5226
22: 3 and do not shed innocent blood in this **p.** 5226
22:11 as king of Judah but has gone from this **p:** 5226
22:12 in the **p** where they have led him captive; 5226
23: 4 *I will* **p** shepherds over them 7756
24: 5 whom I sent away from this **p** to the land of 5226
25:35 the leaders of the flock no **p to escape.** 7129
26:23 into the **burial p** *of* the common people.) 7700
27:22 and restore them to this **p.' "** 5226
28: 3 to this **p** all the articles of the LORD's house 5226
28: 4 to this **p** Jehoiachin son of Jehoiakim king 5226
28: 6 the exiles back to this **p** from Babylon. 5226
28:13 but **in** its **p** you will get a yoke of iron. 9393
29:10 to bring you back to this **p.** 5226
29:14 the **p** from which I carried you into exile." 5226
29:26 the LORD has appointed you priest **in p of** 9393
30:10 'I will surely save you out of a **distant p,** 8158
30:18 and the palace will stand in its **proper p.** 5477
32:37 to this **p** and let them live in safety. 5226
33:10 'You say about this **p,** 5226
33:12 'In this **p,** desolate and without men 5226
37: 1 he reigned **in p of** Jehoiachin son of 9393
Jer 40: 2 "The LORD your God decreed this disaster
for this **p.** 5226
42:18 you will never see this **p** again.' 5226
42:22 famine and plague in the **p** where you want 5226
44:29 to you that I will punish you in this **p,'** 5226
46:27 I will surely save you out of a **distant p,** 8158
49:33 a haunt of jackals, a **desolate p** forever. 9039
50: 6 and hill and forgot their own **resting p.** 8070
51:37 a **p** where no one lives. NIH
51:62 you have said you will destroy this **p,** 5226
La 1: 3 she finds no **resting p.** 4955
2: 6 he has destroyed his **p of meeting.** 4595
Eze 3:12 the LORD be praised in his **dwelling p!**— 5226
4: 3 **p** it as an iron wall between you and 5989
7:22 and they will desecrate my **treasured p;** 7621
12: 3 and go from where you are to another **p.** 5226
20:29 What is this **high p** you go to?' " 1195
21: 7 *It will* **surely take p,** 2118
21:30 In the **p** where you were created, 5226
25: 5 for camels and Ammon into a **resting p** 5271
26: 5 she will become a **p to spread** fishnets, 5427
26:14 and you will become a **p to spread** fishnets. 5427
26:15 and *the* **slaughter takes p** in you? 2222+2223
26:20 and you will not return or **take** *your* **p** in 3656
34:23 *I will* **p** over them one shepherd, 7756
37:27 My **dwelling p** will be with them; 5438
38:15 You will come from your **p** in the far north, 5226
39: 8 *It will* surely **take p,** 2118
39:11 that day I will give Gog a burial **p** in Israel, 5226
41: 4 said to me, "This is the **Most Holy P."** 7731+7731
41:21 the front of the **Most Holy P** was similar. 7731
41:23 and the **Most Holy P** had double doors. 7731
42:13 for the **p** is holy. 5226
43: 7 "Son of man, this is the **p** *of* my throne and 5226
43: 7 this is the place of my throne and the **p** *for* 5226
45: 3 the sanctuary, the **Most Holy P.** 7731+7731
45: 4 a **p** for their houses as well as a holy place 5226
45: 4 a place for their houses as well as a **holy p** 5219
46:19 and showed me a **p** at the western end. 5226
46:20 "This is the **p** where the priests will cook 5226
Da 2:45 the king what *will* **take p** in the future. 10201
7: 9 "As I looked, "thrones **were set in p,** 10667
8: 8 and **in** its **p** four prominent horns grew up 9393
8:11 the **p** *of* his sanctuary was brought low. 4806
8:17 he came near the **p where** I was **standing,** 6642
11: 7 from her family line will arise to take her **p.** 4030
11:36 for what has been determined *must* **take p.** 6913
Hos 1:10 In the **p** where it was said to them, 5226
5:15 to my **p** until they admit their guilt. 5226
9:13 like Tyre, planted in a **pleasant p.** 5659
Jnh 4: 5 Jonah went out and sat down at a **p** east of NIH
Mic 1: 3 The LORD is coming from his **dwelling p;** 5226
1: 5 What is Judah's **high p?** Is it not Jerusalem? 1195
1: 6 a **p** for planting vineyards. 8441
2:10 For this is not your **resting p,** 4957
2:12 the **p** will throng with people. NIH
Na 2: 5 the protective shield *is* **put in p.** 3922
2:11 the **p where** they **fed** their young, 5337
Zep 1: 4 I will cut off from this **p** every remnant 5226
2: 6 will be a **p** for shepherds and sheep pens. NIH
2: 9 a **p** *of* weeds and salt pits, 4940
Hag 2: 9 'And in this **p** I will grant peace,' 5226
Zec 3: 7 of my courts, and I will give you a **p** 4544
5:11 the basket will be set there in its **p."** 4807
6:12 and he will branch out from his **p** and build 9393
12: 6 but Jerusalem will remain intact **in** her **p.** 9393
14:10 be raised up and remain **in** its **p,** 9393
Mal 1: 7 *"You* **p** defiled food on my altar. 5602
1:11 In every **p** incense and pure offerings will 5226
Mt 1:22 All this **took p** to fulfill what the Lord *1181*
2: 9 of them until it stopped over **the p where** *4023*
2:22 that Archelaus was reigning in Judea **in p** *505*
8:20 the Son of Man has no **p** to lay his head." *4544*
10:23 When you are persecuted in one **p,** *NIG*
12: 9 Going on **from that p,** *1696*
12:15 Aware of this, Jesus withdrew **from that p.** *1696*
14:13 by boat privately to a solitary **p.** *5536*
14:15 and said, "This is a remote **p,** *5536*
14:35 when the men *of* that **p** recognized Jesus, *5536*
15:21 Leaving **that p,** Jesus withdrew to *1696*
15:33 in this **remote p** to feed such a crowd?" *2244*
19:13 *to* **p** his hands **on** them and pray for them. *2202*
21: 4 This **took p** to fulfill what was spoken *1181*
23: 6 they love the **p of honor** at banquets and *4752*
24:15 "So when you see standing in the holy **p** *5536*
24:20 that your flight *will* not **take p** in winter or *1181*
24:51 and assign him a **p** with the hypocrites, *3538*
26:36 with his disciples to a **p** called Gethsemane, *6005*
26:52 "Put your sword back in its **p,"** *5536*
26:56 But this *has* all **taken p** that the writings of *1181*
27: 7 to buy the potter's field as a **burial p** *5438*
27:33 to a **p** called Golgotha (which means *5536*
27:33 Golgotha (which means The **P** of the Skull). *5536*
28: 6 Come and see the **p** where he lay. *5536*
Mk 1:35 left the house and went off to a solitary **p,** *5536*
6:11 And if any **p** will not welcome you or listen *5536*
6:31 "Come with me by yourselves to a quiet **p** *5536*
6:32 by themselves in a boat to a solitary **p.** *5536*
6:35 "This is a remote **p,"** they said, *5536*
7:24 Jesus **left that p** and went to the vicinity *1696*
7:32 they begged him to **p** his hand **on** the man. *2202*
8: 4 in this **remote p** can anyone get enough
bread to feed them?" *2244*
9:30 They left **that p** and passed *1696*
10: 1 then left **that p** and went into the region *1696*
12:41 the **p where the offerings were put** *1126*
13:18 Pray that *this will* not **take p** in winter, *1181*
Mk 14:32 They went to a **p** called Gethsemane, *6005*
15:22 to the **p** called Golgotha (which means *5536*
15:22 Golgotha (which means The **P** of the Skull). *5536*
16: 6 See the **p** where they laid him. *5536*
16:18 *they will* **p** their hands **on** sick people, *2202*
Lk 2: 2 that took **p** while Quirinius was governor *NIG*
4: 5 to a high **p** and showed him in an instant all *4001*
4:17 he found the **p** where it is written: *5536*
4:42 At daybreak Jesus went out to a solitary **p.** *5536*
6:17 down with them and stood on a level **p.** *5536*
9:12 because we are in a remote **p** here." *5536*
9:58 the Son of Man has no **p** to lay his head." *4544*
10: 1 of him to every town and **p** where he was *5536*
10:32 when he came to the **p** and saw him, *5536*
11: 1 One day Jesus was praying in a certain **p.** *5536*
11:33 and puts it in a **p** where it will be **hidden,** *3219*
12:17 I have **no p** to store my crops.' *4024+4544*
12:46 and assign him a **p** with the unbelievers. *3538*
13:31 "Leave **this p** and go somewhere else. *1949*
14: 8 do not take the **p of honor,** *4752*
14: 9 you will have to take the least important **p.** *5536*
14:10 when you are invited, take the lowest **p,** *5536*
14:10 'Friend, move up to a better **p.'** *NIG*
16:28 so that they will not also come to this **p** *5536*
19:37 near the **p where the road goes down** *2853*
21: 7 be the sign that they are about to **take p?"** *1181*
21:28 When these things begin *to* **take p,** *1181*
22:40 On reaching the **p,** he said to them, *5536*
23:33 When they came to the **p** called the Skull, *5536*
23:48 to witness this sight saw what **took p,** *1181*
24:21 it is the third day since all this **took p.** *1181*
Jn 2: 1 On the third day a wedding **took p** at Cana *1181*
4:20 that the **p** where we must worship is *5536*
5: 9 on which this took **p** was a Sabbath, *NIG*
6:10 There was plenty of grass in that **p,** *5536*
6:23 the **p** where the people had eaten the bread *5536*
8:20 near the **p where the offerings were put.** *1126*
8:35 a slave *has* no **permanent p** in the family, *3531*
10:40 to the **p** where John had been baptizing in *5536*
10:42 And **in that p** many believed in Jesus. *1695*
11:30 at the **p** where Martha had met him. *5536*
11:32 When Mary reached **the p where** Jesus was *3963*
11:48 and take away both our **p** and our nation." *5536*
13:12 he put on his clothes and **returned to** *his* **p.**
404+4099
14: 2 I am going there to prepare a **p** for you. *5536*
14: 3 And if I go and prepare a **p** for you, *5536*
14: 4 the way to the **p** where I am going." *NIG*
18: 2 Now Judas, who betrayed him, knew the **p,** *5536*
18:36 But now my kingdom is **from another p."** *1949*
19:13 at a **p** known as the Stone Pavement *5536*
19:17 he went out to the **p** of the Skull (which *5536*
19:20 the **p** where Jesus was crucified was near *5536*
19:41 At the **p** where Jesus was crucified, *5536*
Ac 1:20 " 'May his **p** be deserted; *2068*
1:20 " 'May another take his **p of leadership.'** *2175*
2: 1 they were all together **in one p.** *899+2093+3836*
2:30 that he would **p** one of his descendants *2767*
3:11 in the **p** called Solomon's Colonnade. *NIG*
4:31 the **p** where they were meeting was shaken. *5536*
6:13 against this holy **p** and against the law. *5536*
6:14 Jesus of Nazareth will destroy this **p** and *5536*
7: 7 of that country and worship me in this **p.'** *5536*
7:33 the **p** where you are standing is holy *5536*
7:46 that he might provide a **dwelling p** for *5013*
7:49 Or where will my resting **p** be? *5536*
9:12 and **p** his hands **on** him *2202*
12:17 he said, and then he left for another **p.** *5536*
16:13 where we expected to find a **p of prayer.** *4666*
16:16 when we were going to the **p of prayer,** *4666*
18:23 and traveled **from p to place** throughout *2759*
18:23 and traveled **from place to p** throughout *2759*
21:28 against our people and our law and this **p.** *5536*
21:28 into the temple area and defiled this holy **p.** *5536*
26:18 a **p** among those who are sanctified by faith *3102*
27: 8 and came to a **p** called Fair Havens, *5536*
28:23 to the **p where** *he* was **staying.** *3825*
Ro 2:16 This will take **p** on the day when God *NIG*
9:26 that in the very **p** where it was said to them, *5536*
15:23 now that there is no more **p** for me to work *5536*
1Co 7:17 **retain the p in life** that the Lord *4344*
11:18 **In the first p,** I hear that when you come *4754*
2Co 7: 3 before that *you* **have such a p** in our hearts *1639*
Eph 5: 4 or coarse joking, which *are* **out of p,** *465+4024*
6:14 with the breastplate of righteousness **in p,** *1907*
Php 2: 9 God **exalted** him **to the highest p** *5671*
1Ti 5:24 reaching the **p** of judgment ahead of them; *NIG*
2Ti 2:18 that the resurrection *has* already **taken p,** *1181*
Phm 1:13 so that he could **take** your **p** in helping me *5642*
Heb 2: 6 there is **a p where** someone has testified: *4543*
5: 6 And he says in **another** *p,* *AIT*
8: 7 no **p** would have been sought for another. *5536*
9: 2 this was called the **Holy P.** *41*
9: 3 a room called the **Most Holy P,** *41+41*
9: 8 that the way into the Most Holy **P** had not *NIG*
9:12 but he entered the Most Holy **P** once for all *NIG*
9:25 the Most Holy **P** every year with blood *NIG*
10:19 the Most **Holy** *P* by the blood of Jesus, *AIT*
11: 8 to go to a **p** he would later receive *5536*
13:11 the blood of animals into the Most **Holy** *P* *AIT*
2Pe 1:19 as to a light shining in a dark **p,** *5536*
1Jn 1:10 be a liar and his word *has* no **p** in our lives. *1639*
Rev 1: 1 to show his servants what must soon **take p.** *1181*
1:19 what is now and what will **take p** later. *1181*
2: 5 and remove your lampstand from its **p.** *5536*
4: 1 and I will show you what must **take p** *1181*
6:14 and island was removed from its **p.** *5536*

Rev 12: 6 the desert to a **p** prepared for her by God, *5536*
12: 8 and they lost their **p** in heaven. *5536*
12:14 that she might fly to the **p** prepared for her *5536*
13: 6 to slander his name and his **dwelling p** *5008*
16:16 the **p** that in Hebrew is called Armageddon. *5536*
20:11 and there was no **p** for them. *5536*
21: 8 their **p** will be in the fiery lake *3538*
22: 6 the things that must soon **take p.**" *1181*

PLACED (87) [PLACE]

Ge 3:24 *he* **p** on the east side of the Garden 8905
22: 6 the burnt offering and **p** it on his son Isaac, 8492
28:18 the stone *he had* **p** under his head and set it 8492
30:35 and *he* **p** them in the care of his sons. 5989
30:38 Then *he* **p** the peeled branches in all 3657
50:23 of Makir son of Manasseh *were* **p at birth** 3528
50:26 *he* **was p** in a coffin in Egypt. 8492
Ex 2: 3 Then *she* **p** the child in it and put it among 8492
40:20 He took the Testimony and **p** it in the ark, 5989
40:22 Moses **p** the table in the Tent of Meeting on 5989
40:24 *He* **p** the lampstand in the Tent of Meeting 8492
40:26 Moses **p** the gold altar in the Tent 8492
40:30 *He* **p** the basin between the Tent of Meeting 8492
Lev 8: 8 *He* **p** the breastpiece on him and put 8492
8: 9 Then *he* **p** the turban on Aaron's head 8492
Nu 17: 7 Moses **p** the staffs before the LORD in 5663
Jos 10:24 So they came forward and **p** their feet 8492
10:27 the mouth of the cave *they* **p** large rocks, 8492
Jdg 7:16 *he* **p** trumpets and empty jars in the hands 5989
8:27 which *he* **p** in Ophrah, his town. 3657
1Sa 6:11 *They* **p** the ark of the LORD on the cart 8492
6:15 and **p** them on the large rock. 8492
2Sa 12:30 and it was *p* **on** David's head. AIT
15: 2 with a complaint to *be* **p** before the king for 995
1Ki 6:27 *He* **p** the cherubim inside the innermost 5989
7: 4 Its **windows** were **p high** in sets of three, 9209
7:39 *He* **p** five of the stands on the south side of 5989
7:39 *He* **p** the Sea on the south side, 5989
7:51 and *he* **p** them in the treasuries of 5989
8: 9 the two stone tablets that Moses *had* **p** *in* it 5663
10: 9 in you and **p** you on the throne of Israel. 5989
21: 8 Ahab's name, **p** his **seal** *on* them, 928+2597+3159
2Ki 12: 9 *He* **p** it beside the altar, 5989
1Ch 20: 2 and it was **p on** David's head. 6584
2Ch 4: 6 for washing and **p** five on the south side 5989
4: 7 to the specifications for them and **p** them in 5989
4: 8 He made ten tables and **p** them in 5663
4:10 *He* **p** the Sea on the south side, 5989
5: 1 *he* **p** them in the treasuries of God's temple. 5989
5:10 the two tablets that Moses *had* **p** in it 5989
6:11 There *I have* **p** the ark, 8492
6:13 and *had* **p** it in the center of the outer court. 5989
9: 8 and **p** you on his throne as king to rule for 5989
23:18 Then Jehoiada **p** the oversight of the temple 8492
24: 8 a chest was made and **p** outside, 5989
28:27 but he *was* not **p** in the tombs of the kings 995
Ezr 1: 7 from Jerusalem and *had* **p** in the temple 5989
Ne 5:15 **p a heavy burden** on the people 3877
9:37 to the kings *you have* **p** over us. 5989
Est 2: 3 Let them be **p** under the care of Hegai. NIH
6: 8 one with a royal crest **p** on its head. 5989
Job 6: 2 be weighed and all my misery *be* **p** on 5951
20: 4 ever since man *was* **p** on the earth, 8492
Ps 21: 3 and **p** a crown of pure gold on his head. 8883
Jer 24: 1 baskets of figs **p** in front of the temple of 3585
37:21 then gave orders for Jeremiah *to be* **p** in 7212
Eze 23:41 a table spread before it on which *you had* **p** 8492
32:27 whose swords *were* **p** under their heads? 5989
40:42 On them *were* **p** the utensils 5663
43: 8 When they **p** their threshold next 5989
Da 2:38 in your hands *he has* **p** mankind and 10314
2:48 **p** Daniel **in a high position** 10648
2:48 the entire province of Babylon and **p** him NIH
5: 7 and have a gold chain **p** around his neck, NIH
5:16 and have a gold chain **p** around your neck, NIH
5:29 a gold chain was **p** around his neck, NIH
6:17 A stone was brought and **p** over the mouth 10682
Mt 19:15 *When he had* **p** his hands **on** them, *2202*
21: 7 **p** their cloaks **on** them, *2202*
27:37 Above his head *they* **p** the written charge *2202*
27:60 and **p** it in his own new tomb *5502*
Mk 6:56 *they* **p** the sick in the marketplaces. *5502*
15:46 and **p** it in a tomb cut out of rock. *5502*
Lk 2: 7 She wrapped him in cloths and **p** him in *369*
23:53 in linen cloth and **p** it in a tomb cut in *5502*
Jn 3:35 the Son and *has* **p** everything in his hands. *1443*
6:27 **On** him God the Father *has* **p** *his* **seal** *5381*
Ac 7:16 and **p** in the tomb that Abraham had bought *5502*
7:21 *When he was* **p outside,** *1758*
8:17 Then Peter and John **p** their hands **on** them, *2202*
9:37 and her body was washed and **p** in *5502*
13: 3 *they* **p** their hands **on** them *2202*
19: 6 *When* Paul **p** his hands **on** them, *2202*
28: 8 **p** his hands **on** him and healed him. *2202*
Eph 1:22 And God **p** all things **under** his feet *5718*
Rev 1:17 Then *he* **p** his right hand on me and said: *5502*
3: 8 *I have* **p** before you an open door *1443*

PLACES (144) [PLACE]

Ex 10:23 in the **p where** they **lived.** 4632
Lev 14:28 to put on the same **p** he put the blood of 5226
26:30 I will destroy your **high p,** 1195
Nu 24: 5 O Jacob, your **dwelling p,** O Israel! 5438
33:52 and demolish all their **high p.** 1195
35:12 They will be **p** of refuge from the avenger, 6551
Dt 1:33 to search out **p** for you to camp and 5226
12: 2 the **p** on the high mountains and on the hills 5226
12: 3 and wipe out their names from those **p.** 5226
33:29 and you will trample down their **high p.**" 1195
Jdg 5:11 the voice of the singers at the **watering p.** 5393
19:13 and spend the night in one of those **p.**" 5226
20: 2 of Israel **took** *their* **p** in the assembly of 3656
20:33 All the men of Israel moved from their **p** 5226
1Sa 7:16 judging Israel in all those **p.** 5226
23:23 the **hiding p** he uses and come back to me 4676
30:31 and to those in all the *other* **p** where David 5226
1Ki 3: 2 however, were still sacrificing at the **high p,** 1195
3: 3 and burned incense on the **high p.** 1195
12:31 Jeroboam built shrines on **high p** 1195
12:32 at the **high p** he had made. 1195
13: 2 of the **high p** who now make offerings here, 1195
13:32 and against all the shrines on the **high p** in 1195
13:33 for the **high p** from all sorts of people. 1195
13:33 a priest he consecrated for the **high p.** 1195
14:23 They also set up for themselves **high p,** 1195
15:14 Although he did not remove the **high p,** 1195
22:43 The **high p,** however, were not removed, 1195
2Ki 6:10 so that he was on his guard **in such p.** 9004S
8:12 "You will set fire to their **fortified p,** 4448
12: 3 The **high p,** however, were not removed; 1195
14: 4 The **high p,** however, were not removed; 1195
15: 4 The **high p,** however, were not removed; 1195
15:35 The **high p,** however, were not removed; 1195
16: 4 and burned incense at the **high p,** 1195
17: 9 to fortified city they built themselves **high p** 1195
17:29 people of Samaria had made at the **high p.** 1195
17:32 as priests in the shrines at the **high p.** 1195
18: 4 He removed the **high p,** 1195
18:22 isn't he the one whose **high p** and altars 1195
21: 3 **high p** his father Hezekiah had destroyed; 1195
23: 5 to burn incense on the **high p** of the towns 1195
23: 8 of Judah and desecrated the **high p,** 1195
23: 9 of the **high p** did not serve at the altar of 1195
23:13 the **high p** that were east of Jerusalem on 1195
23:19 the **high p** that the kings of Israel had built 1195
23:20 the priests of those **high p** on the altars 1195
2Ch 8:11 because **the p** the ark of the LORD 2156S
11:15 for the **high p** and for the goat 1195
14: 3 the foreign altars and the **high p,** 1195
14: 5 the **high p** and incense altars in every town 1195
15:17 Although he did not remove the **high p** 1195
17: 6 furthermore, he removed the **high p** and 1195
20:33 The **high p,** however, were not removed, 1195
21:11 had also built **high p** on the hills of Judah 1195
28: 4 and burned incense at the **high p,** 1195
28:25 in Judah he built **high p** to burn sacrifices 1195
31: 1 the **high p** and the altars throughout Judah 1195
32:12 Hezekiah himself remove this god's **high p** 1195
33: 3 **high p** his father Hezekiah had demolished; 1195
33:17 continued to sacrifice at the **high p,** 1195
33:19 and the sites where he built **high p** and set 1195
34: 3 to purge Judah and Jerusalem of **high p,** 1195
35:10 in their **p** with the Levites in their divisions 6642
35:15 were in the **p** prescribed by David, Asaph, 5096
Ezr 3:10 **took** *their* **p** to praise the LORD, 6641
6: 5 are to be returned to their **p** in the temple 10087
Ne 3: 7 **p** under the authority of the governor NIH
4:13 of the wall at the **exposed p,** 7460
9: 2 *They* **stood in** *their* **p** and confessed 6641
12:40 then **took** *their* **p** in the house of God; 6641
Job 3:14 **p** now **lying in ruins,** 2999
4:18 If God **p** no **trust** in his servants, 586
15:15 If God **p** no **trust** in his holy ones, 586
28: 4 in **p** forgotten by the foot of man; 2021S
38:20 Can you take them to their **p?** 1473
Ps 16: 6 for me in **pleasant** *p;* AIT
74:20 haunts of violence fill the **dark p** *of* the land 4743
78:58 They angered him with their **high p;** 1195
SS 2:14 in the **hiding p** *on* the mountainside, 6260
Isa 7:25 **p where** cattle are **turned loose** 5448
15: 2 to its **high p** to weep; 1195
17: 9 will be like *p* **abandoned** *to* thickets AIT
30:28 he **p** in the jaws of the peoples a bit NIH
32:18 My people will live in peaceful **dwelling p,** 5659
32:18 in secure homes, in undisturbed **p of rest.** 4957
34:14 and find for themselves **p of rest.** 4955
36: 7 isn't he the one whose **high p** and altars 1195
40: 4 the **rugged p** a plain. 8221
42:16 before them and make the **rough p** smooth. 5112
45: 3 riches stored in **secret p,** 5041
61: 4 and restore the *p* long **devastated;** AIT
Jer 7:31 They have built the **high p** *of* Topheth in 1195
9:26 and all who live in the desert in distant **p.** 6991
17: 3 together with your **high p,** 1195
17: 6 He will dwell in the **parched p** of the desert 3083
19: 5 the **high p** *of* Baal to burn their sons in 1195
23:24 in **secret p** so that I cannot see him?" 5041
25:23 Buz and all who are in **distant p;** 6991+7899
26:10 to the house of the LORD and **took** *their* **p** 3782
29:14 I will gather you from all the nations and **p** 5226
32:35 They built **high p** *for* Baal in the Valley 1195
48:35 the **high p** and burn incense to their gods," 1195
49:10 I will uncover his **hiding p,** 5041
49:32 those who are in **distant p** 6991+7899
51:51 because foreigners have entered the **holy p** 5219
Eze 6: 3 and I will destroy your **high p.** 1195
6: 6 be laid waste and the **high p** demolished, 1195
6:13 **p** where they offered fragrant incense 5226
16:16 of your garments to make gaudy **high p,** 1195
34:12 from all the **p** where they were scattered on 5226
34:26 and the *p* **surrounding** my hill. AIT
42:14 on other clothes before they go near **the p** 889S
Eze 43: 7 lifeless idols of their kings at their **high p.** 1195
46:23 with **p for fire** built all around under 4453
47:10 be **p for spreading** nets. 5427
Da 4:21 and *having* **nesting p** in its branches for 10709
Hos 10: 8 The **high p** *of* wickedness will be destroyed 1195
Joel 3: 7 I am going to rouse them out of the **p** 5226
Am 4:13 and treads the **high p** *of* the earth— 1195
7: 9 "The **high p** *of* Isaac will be destroyed and 1195
9:11 I will repair its **broken p,** restore its ruins, 7288
Mic 1: 3 he comes down and treads the **high p** *of* 1195
Hab 1: 6 across the whole earth to seize **dwelling p** 5438
Mt 8:11 **take** *their* **p at the feast** with Abraham, *369*
12:43 it goes through arid **p** seeking rest and does *5536*
13: 5 Some fell on **rocky p,** *4378*
13:20 on **rocky p** is the man who hears the word *4378*
20:23 These **p** belong to those for whom *NIG*
24: 7 be famines and earthquakes in various **p.** *5536*
Mk 1:45 but stayed outside in lonely **p.** *5536*
4: 5 Some fell on **rocky p,** *4378*
4:16 Others, like seed sown on **rocky p,** *4378*
10:40 These **p** belong to those for whom *NIG*
12:39 in the synagogues and the **p of honor** *4752*
13: 8 There will be earthquakes in various **p,** *5536*
Lk 5:16 But Jesus often withdrew to **lonely p** *2245*
8:29 driven by the demon into **solitary p.** *2245*
11:24 it goes through arid **p** seeking rest and does *5536*
13:29 **take** *their* **p at the feast** in the kingdom *369*
14: 7 guests picked the **p of honor at the table,** *4752*
20:46 in the synagogues and the **p of honor** *4752*
21:11 famines and pestilences in various **p,** *5536*
Ac 17:26 and the **exact p** where they should live. *3999*

PLACING (4) [PLACE]

Ge 48:17 Joseph saw his father **p** his right hand 8883
2Ki 10:24 "If one of you lets any of the men I *am* **p** 995
Ezr 5: 8 with large stones and **p** the timbers in 10682
Ac 9:17 **P** his hands **on** Saul, he said, *2202*

PLAGUE (84) [PLAGUED, PLAGUES]

Ex 8: 2 I *will* **p** your whole country with frogs. 5597
9: 3 a terrible **p** on your livestock in the field— 1822
9:15 and struck you and your people with a **p** 1822
10:14 before had there been such a **p** of locusts, NIH
10:17 to take this **deadly p** away from me." 4638
11: 1 "I will bring one more **p** on Pharaoh and 5596
12:13 No destructive **p** will touch you 5598
30:12 Then no **p** will come on them 5598
32:35 the LORD **struck** the people **with a p** 5597
Lev 26:25 I will send a **p** among you, 1822
Nu 8:19 so that no **p** will strike the Israelites 5598
11:33 and he struck them with a severe **p.** 4804
14:12 strike them down with a **p** and destroy them, 1822
14:37 were struck down and died of a **p** 4487
16:46 the **p** has started." 5598
16:47 The **p** had already started among the people 5598
16:48 and the **p** stopped. 4487
16:49 But 14,700 people died from the **p,** 4487
16:50 for the **p** had stopped. 4487
25: 8 the **p** against the Israelites was stopped; 4487
25: 9 those who died in the **p** numbered 24,000. 4487
25:18 when the **p** came as a result of Peor." 4487
26: 1 After the **p** the LORD said to Moses 4487
31:16 so that a **p** struck the LORD's people. 4487
Dt 28:21 The LORD *will* **p** you *with* diseases 1815
28:22 *which will* **p** you until you perish. 8103
32:24 consuming pestilence and deadly **p;** 7776
Jos 22:17 a **p** fell on the community of the LORD! 5598
1Sa 6: 4 same **p** has struck both you and your rulers. 4487
2Sa 24:13 Or three days of **p** in your land? 1822
24:15 So the LORD sent a **p** on Israel from 1822
24:21 that the **p** on the people may be stopped." 4487
24:25 and the **p** on Israel was stopped. 4487
1Ki 8:37 "When famine or **p** comes to the land, 1822
1Ch 21:12 days of **p** in the land, 1822
21:14 So the LORD sent a **p** on Israel, 1822
21:17 not let this **p** remain on your people." 4487
21:22 that the **p** on the people may be stopped. 4487
2Ch 6:28 "When famine or **p** comes to the land, 1822
7:13 the land or send a **p** among my people, 1822
20: 9 the sword of judgment, or **p** or famine, 1822
Job 27:15 The **p** will bury those who survive him, 4638
Ps 78:50 from death but gave them over to the **p.** 1822
91: 6 nor the **p** that destroys at midday. 7776
106:29 and a **p** broke out among them. 4487
106:30 and the **p** was checked. 4487
Isa 19:22 The LORD *will* **strike** Egypt **with a p;** 5597
Jer 14:12 with the sword, famine and **p.**" 1822
21: 6 and they will die of a terrible **p.** 1822
21: 7 the people in this city who survive the **p,** 1822
21: 9 by the sword, famine or **p.** 1822
24:10 and **p** against them until they are destroyed 1822
27: 8 the sword, famine and **p,** declares the LORD, 1822
27:13 the sword, famine and **p** with which 1822
28: 8 disaster and **p** against many countries 1822
29:17 and **p** against them and I will make them 1822
29:18 famine and **p** and will make them abhorrent 1822
32:24 Because of the sword, famine and **p,** 1822
32:36 and **p** it will be handed over to the king 1822
34:17 to fall by the sword, **p** and famine. 1822
38: 2 by the sword, famine or **p,** 1822
42:17 by the sword, famine and **p;** 1822
42:22 You will die by the sword, famine and **p** in 1822
44:13 famine and **p,** as I punished Jerusalem. 1822
Eze 5:12 of your people will die of the **p** or perish 1822
5:17 **P** and bloodshed will sweep through you, 1822

Jer 6:11 by the sword, famine and **p**. 1822
6:12 He that is far away will die of the **p**, 1822
7:15 inside are **p** and famine; 1822
7:15 the city will be devoured by famine and **p**. 1822
12:16 of them from the sword, famine and **p**, so 1822
14:19 a **p** into that land and pour out my wrath 1822
14:21 sword and famine and wild beasts and **p**— 1822
28:23 a **p** upon her and make blood flow 1822
33:27 in strongholds and caves will die of a **p**. 1822
38:22 I will execute judgment upon him with **p** 1822
Hab 3:5 **P** went before him; 1822
Zec 14:12 the **p** with which the LORD will strike all 4487
14:15 A similar **p** will strike the horses 4487
14:18 on them the **p** he inflicts on the nations 4487
Rev 6:8 of the earth to kill by sword, famine and **p**, *2505*
11:6 and to strike the earth with every kind of **p** *4435*
16:21 And they cursed God on account of the **p** *4435*
16:21 because the **p** was so terrible. *4435*

PLAGUED (2) [PLAGUE]

Ps 73:5 *they* **are** not **p** by human ills. 5595
73:14 All day long I have been **p**; 5595

PLAGUES (16) [PLAGUE]

Ex 5:3 he may strike us with **p** or with the sword." 1822
9:14 the full force of my **p** against you and 4487
Dt 28:59 the LORD will send fearful **p** *on* you 4804
1Sa 4:8 the Egyptians with all kinds of **p** in 4804
Hos 13:14 Where, O death, are your **p**? 1822
Am 4:10 "I sent **p** among you as I did to Egypt. 1822
Rev 9:18 of mankind was killed by the three **p** *4435*
9:20 not killed by these **p** still did not repent of *4435*
15:1 seven angels with the seven last **p**— *4435*
15:6 the seven angels with the seven **p**. *4435*
15:8 the temple until the seven **p** of *4435*
16:9 who had control over these **p**, *4435*
18:4 so that you will not receive any of her **p**; *4435*
18:8 in one day her **p** will overtake her: *4435*
21:9 *of* the seven last **p** came and said to me, *4435*
22:18 God will add to him the **p** described *4435*

PLAIN (30) [PLAINLY, PLAINS]

Ge 11:2 they found a **p** in Shinar and settled there. 1326
13:10 Lot looked up and saw that the whole **p** *of* 3971
13:11 So Lot chose for himself the whole **p** *of* 3971
13:12 of the **p** and pitched his tents near Sodom. 3971
19:17 and don't stop anywhere in the **p**! 3971
19:25 and the entire **p**, including all those living 3971
19:28 toward all the land of the **p**, 3971
19:29 So when God destroyed the cities of the **p**, 3971
Jos 17:16 in the **p** have iron chariots, 824+6677
Jdg 1:34 not allowing them to come down into the **p**. 6677
2Sa 18:23 by way of the **p** and outran the Cushite. 3971
1Ki 7:46 in the **p** *of* the Jordan between Succoth 3971
2Ch 4:17 in the **p** *of* the Jordan between Succoth 3971
26:10 in the foothills and in the **p**. 4793
35:22 but went to fight him on the **p** *of* Megiddo. 1326
Ne 6:2 in one of the villages on the **p** *of* Ono." 1326
Isa 40:4 the rugged places a **p**. 1326
63:14 like cattle that go down to the **p**, 1326
Jer 47:5 O remnant on the **p**, 6677
Eze 3:22 "Get up and go out to the **p**, 1326
3:23 So I got up and went out to the **p**. 1326
8:4 as in the vision I had seen in the **p**. 1326
Da 3:1 the **p** *of* Dura in the province of Babylon. 10117
Hab 2:2 the revelation and **make** it **p** on tablets 930
Zec 12:11 of Hadad Rimmon in the **p** *of* Megiddo. 1326
Ro 1:19 since what may be known about God is **p** *5745*
1:19 because God *has* **made** it **p** to them. *5746*
2Co 5:11 *What we are* is **p** to God, *5746*
5:11 and I hope it *is* also **p** to your conscience. *5746*
Eph 3:9 *to* **make p to** everyone the administration *5894*

PLAINLY (8) [PLAIN]

Mt 7:23 Then *I will* **tell** them **p**, *3933*
Mk 7:35 and he began to speak **p**. *3987*
8:32 He spoke **p** about this, *4244*
Jn 3:21 so that *it may be* **seen p** *5746*
10:24 If you are the Christ, tell us **p**." *4244*
11:14 So then he told them **p**, "Lazarus is dead, *4244*
16:25 but will tell you **p** about my Father. *4244*
2Co 4:2 by **setting forth** the truth **p** we commend *5748*

PLAINS (20) [PLAIN]

Nu 22:1 the Israelites traveled to the **p** *of* Moab 6858
26:3 So on the **p** *of* Moab by the Jordan across 6858
26:63 when they counted the Israelites on the **p** 6858
31:12 at their camp on the **p** *of* Moab, 6858
33:48 of Abarim and camped on the **p** *of* Moab 6858
33:49 There on the **p** *of* Moab they camped along 6858
33:50 On the **p** *of* Moab by the Jordan across 6858
35:1 On the **p** *of* Moab by the Jordan across 6858
36:13 through Moses to the Israelites on the **p** 6858
Dt 34:1 from the **p** *of* Moab to the top of Pisgah, 6858
34:8 The Israelites grieved for Moses in the **p** 6858
Jos 4:13 over before the LORD to the **p** *of* Jericho 6858
5:10 while camped at Gilgal on the **p** *of* Jericho, 6858
13:32 in the **p** *of* Moab across the Jordan east 6858
Jdg 1:19 to drive the people from the **p**, 6677
1Ki 20:23 But if we fight them on the **p**, 4793
20:25 so we can fight Israel on the **p**. 4793
2Ki 25:5 and overtook him in the **p** *of* Jericho. 6858
Jer 39:5 and overtook Zedekiah in the **p** *of* Jericho. 6858
52:8 and overtook him in the **p** *of* Jericho. 6858

PLAITING (KJV) See BRAIDED

PLAN (31) [PLANNED, PLANNING, PLANS]

Ge 11:6 then nothing *they* **p** to do will be impossible 2372
41:37 The **p** seemed good to Pharaoh and 1821
Ex 26:30 to the **p** shown you on the mountain. 5477
Nu 33:56 I will do to you what *I* **p** to do to them.' " 1948
1Sa 18:25 Saul's **p** *was* to have David fall by 3108
2Sa 17:4 This **p** seemed good to Absalom and to all 1821
1Ch 28:18 He also gave him the **p** *for* the chariot, 9322
28:19 in all the details of the **p**." 9322
2Ch 13:8 you **p** to resist the kingdom of the LORD, 606
30:4 The **p** seemed right both to the king and to 1821
Est 8:3 an end to the evil **p** *of* Haman the Agagite, 4742
Job 42:2 no **p** of yours can be thwarted. 4659
Ps 64:6 "We have devised a perfect **p**!" 2925
140:4 protect me from men of violence who **p** 3108
Pr 14:22 But *those who* **p** what is good find love 3086
21:30 no **p** that can succeed against the LORD. 6783
Isa 5:19 let the **p** *of* the Holy One of Israel come, 6783
8:10 propose your **p**, but it will not stand, 1821
14:26 the **p** determined for the whole world; 6783
Jer 18:11 for you and devising a **p** against you. 4742
36:3 about every disaster I **p** to inflict on them, 3108
49:30 he has devised a **p** against you. 4742
Eze 43:10 Let them consider the **p**, 9422
Am 3:7 without revealing his **p** to his servants 6051
Mic 2:1 Woe to *those who* **p** iniquity, 3108
4:12 they do not understand his **p**, 6783
Mt 28:12 with the elders and **devised a p**, *3284+5206*
Ac 9:24 but Saul learned of their **p**. *2101*
27:43 and kept them from carrying out their **p**. *1088*
Ro 15:24 I **p** to do so when I go to Spain. *NIG*
Eph 1:11 having been predestined according to the **p** *4606*

PLANE (2)

Ge 30:37 and **p trees** and made white stripes on them 6895
Eze 31:8 the **p trees** compare with its branches— 6895

PLANES (KJV) See CHISELS

PLANK (6) [PLANKS]

Mt 7:3 pay no attention to the **p** in your own eye? *1512*
7:4 the time there is a **p** in your own eye? *1512*
7:5 first take the **p** out of your own eye, *1512*
Lk 6:41 pay no attention to the **p** in your own eye? *1512*
6:42 when you yourself fail to see the **p** in your *1512*
6:42 first take the **p** out of your eye, *1512*

PLANKS (3) [PLANK]

1Ki 6:9 roofing it with beams and cedar **p**. 8444
6:15 and covered the floor of the temple with **p** 7521
Ac 27:44 The rest were to get there on **p** or on pieces *4909*

PLANNED (22) [PLAN]

2Ki 19:25 In days of old *I* **p** it; 3670
Ps 40:5 The **things** you **p** for us no one can recount 4742
Pr 30:32 or if *you have* **p evil**, 2372
Isa 14:24 "Surely, as *I have* **p**, so it will be, 1948
19:12 the LORD Almighty *has* **p** against Egypt. 3619
22:11 have regard for the *One who* **p** it long ago. 3670
23:8 Who **p** this against Tyre, 3619
23:9 The LORD Almighty **p** it, 3619
25:1 marvelous things, *things* **p** long ago. 6783
37:26 In days of old *I* **p** it; 3670
46:11 what *I have* **p**, that will I do. 3670
Jer 18:8 and not inflict on it the disaster *I had* **p**. 3108
49:20 what the LORD *has* **p** against Edom, 3619+6783
50:45 the LORD *has* **p** against Babylon, 3619+6783
La 2:17 The LORD has done what *he* **p**; 2372
Da 6:3 by his exceptional qualities that the king **p** 10575
Ac 27:42 The soldiers **p** to kill the prisoners *1087+1181*
Ro 1:13 that *I* **p** many times to come to you *4729*
2Co 1:15 *I* **p** to visit you first so *1089*
1:16 I **p** to visit you on my way to Macedonia *NIG*
1:17 *When I* **p** this, did I do it lightly? *1089*
Heb 11:40 God *had* **p** something better for us so *4587*

PLANNING (4) [PLAN]

Ecc 9:10 nor **p** nor knowledge nor wisdom. 3113
Isa 19:17 of what the LORD Almighty *is* **p** 3619+6783
Jer 26:3 and not bring on them the disaster I *was* **p** 3108
Mic 2:3 "I *am* **p** disaster against this people, 3108

PLANS (41) [PLAN]

1Sa 23:10 that Saul **p** to come to Keilah and destroy 1335
2Ki 16:10 with detailed **p** for its construction. 9322
16:11 with all **the p** that King Ahaz had sent 889S
1Ch 28:2 and *I* **made p** to build it. 3922
28:11 Then David gave his son Solomon the **p** 9322
28:12 the **p** *of* all that the Spirit had put 9322
Ezr 4:5 and frustrate their **p** during the entire reign 6783
Job 5:12 He thwarts the **p** *of* the crafty, 4742
17:11 My days have passed, my **p** are shattered, 2365
23:14 and many such **p** he still has in store. 2179S
Ps 14:6 You evildoers frustrate the **p** *of* the poor, 6783
20:4 of your heart and make all your **p** succeed. 6783
33:10 The LORD foils the **p** *of* the nations; 6783
33:11 But the **p** *of* the LORD stand firm forever, 6783
64:5 They encourage each other in evil **p**, 1821
140:2 who **devise** evil **p** in their hearts and stir 3108
140:8 do not let their **p** succeed, 2373
146:4 on that very day their **p** come to nothing. 6955
Pr 12:5 The **p** *of* the righteous are just, 4742
15:22 **P** fail for lack of counsel, 4742
16:1 To man belong the **p** *of* the heart, 5119
16:3 and your **p** will succeed. 4742
16:9 In his heart a man **p** his course, 3108
19:21 Many are the **p** in a man's heart, 4742
20:18 Make **p** by seeking advice; 4742
21:5 The **p** *of* the diligent lead to profit as surely 4742
Isa 19:3 and I will bring their **p** to nothing; 6783
29:15 to great depths to hide their **p** from 6783
30:1 "to those who carry out **p** that are not mine, 6783
32:8 But the noble man **makes** noble **p**, 3619
Jer 18:12 We will continue with our own **p**; 4742
18:18 "Come, *let's* **make p** against Jeremiah; 3108+4742
19:7 " 'In this place I will ruin the **p** *of* Judah 6783
29:11 For I know the **p** I **have** for you," 3108+4742
29:11 "**p** to prosper you and not to harm you, 4742
29:11 **p** to give you hope and a future. NIH
Da 11:17 but his **p** will not succeed or help him. NIH
Hos 11:6 of their gates and put an end to their **p**. 4600
Mt 22:15 the Pharisees went out and **laid p** *3284+5206*
Jn 12:10 chief priests **made p** to kill Lazarus as well, *1086*
2Co 1:17 Or *do I* **make** *my* **p** in a worldly manner so *1086*

PLANT (59) [IMPLANTED, PLANTED, PLANTER, PLANTING, PLANTS, REPLANTED, TRANSPLANTED]

Ge 1:29 "I give you every seed-bearing **p** on 6912
1:30 I give every green **p** for food." 6912
2:5 and no **p** *of* the field had yet sprung up, 6912
9:20 proceeded *to* **p** a vineyard. 5749
47:23 here is seed for you so *you can* **p** 2445
Ex 10:15 Nothing green remained on tree or **p** in all 6912
15:17 You will bring them in and **p** them on 5749
Lev 19:19 **p** your field **with** two kinds of **seed**. 2445
19:23 " 'When you enter the land and **p** any kind 5749
25:20 if *we* do not **p** or harvest our crops?" 2445
25:22 While *you* **p** during the eighth year, 2445
26:16 *You will* **p** seed in vain, 2445
Dt 6:11 vineyards and olive groves *you did* not **p**— 5749
22:9 *Do* not **p** two kinds of **seed** in your vineyard 2445
22:9 if you do, not only the crops *you* **p** but 2445+2446
28:30 *You will* **p** a vineyard, but you will not 5749
28:39 *You will* **p** vineyards and cultivate them 5749
Jos 24:13 and olive groves that you *did* not **p**.' 5749
2Sa 7:10 for my people Israel and *will* **p** them so 5749
1Ki 4:33 He described **p life**, from the cedar of 6770
2Ki 19:29 **p** vineyards and eat their fruit. 5749
1Ch 17:9 for my people Israel and *will* **p** them so 5749
Job 8:16 like a **well-watered p** in the sunshine, 8183
14:9 and put forth shoots like a **p**. 5750
Ecc 3:2 a time to **p** and a time to uproot, 5749
11:4 Whoever watches the wind *will* not **p**; 2445
Isa 17:10 the finest plants and **p** imported vines, 2445
17:11 and on the morning when you **p** them, 2446
28:25 *Does he* not **p** wheat in its place, 8492
37:30 **p** vineyards and eat their fruit. 5749
65:21 *they will* **p** vineyards and eat their fruit. 5749
65:22 or **p** and others eat. 5749
Jer 1:10 to destroy and overthrow, to build and to **p**. 5749
24:6 *I will* **p** them and not uproot them. 5749
29:5 **p** gardens and eat what they produce. 5749
29:28 **p** gardens and eat what they produce.' " 5749
31:5 Again *you will* **p** vineyards on the hills 5749
31:5 farmers *will* **p** them and enjoy their fruit. 5749
31:27 "when *I will* **p** the house of Israel and 2445
31:28 so I will watch over them to build and to **p**," 5749
32:41 and *will* assuredly **p** them in this land 5749
35:7 sow seed or **p** vineyards; 5749
42:10 *I will* **p** you and not uproot you, 5749
Eze 16:7 I made you grow like a **p** *of* the field. 7542
17:22 from the very top of a cedar and **p** it; 5989
17:22 from its topmost shoots and **p** it on a high 9278
17:23 the mountain heights of Israel *I will* **p** it; 9278
28:26 and will build houses and **p** vineyards; 5749
Hos 2:23 *I will* **p** her for myself in the land; 2445
Am 9:14 *They will* **p** vineyards 5749
9:15 *I will* **p** Israel in their own land, 5749
Mic 6:15 You *will* **p** but not harvest; 2445
Zep 1:13 *they will* **p** vineyards but not drink 5749
Mt 15:13 "Every **p** that my heavenly Father has *5884*
Mk 4:31 the smallest seed *you* **p** in the ground. *5062*
Jn 19:29 put the sponge *on* a stalk of the **hyssop p**, *5727*
1Co 15:37 *you do* not **p** the body that will be, *5062*
Jas 1:11 with scorching heat and withers the **p**; *5965*
Rev 9:4 not to harm the grass of the earth or any **p** *5952*

PLANTED (51) [PLANT]

Ge 2:8 the LORD God *had* **p** a garden in the east, 5749
21:33 Abraham **p** a tamarisk tree in Beersheba, 5749
26:12 Isaac **p crops** in that land and 2445
Lev 11:37 a carcass falls on any seeds that *are to* **be p**, 2445
Nu 24:6 like aloes **p** *by* the LORD, 5749
Dt 11:10 where *you* **p** your seed and irrigated it 2445
20:6 *Has* anyone **p** a vineyard and not begun 5749
21:4 a valley that has not been plowed or **p** and 2445
29:23 nothing **p**, nothing sprouting, 2445
Jdg 6:3 Whenever the Israelites **p** *their* **crops**, 2445
Ps 1:3 He is like a tree **p** by streams of water, 9278
44:2 the nations and **p** our fathers; 5749
80:8 you drove out the nations and **p** it. 5749
80:15 the root your right hand *has* **p**, 5749
92:13 **p** in the house of the LORD, 9278

Ps 104:16 the cedars of Lebanon that *he* **p**. 5749
107:37 They sowed fields and **p** vineyards 5749
Ecc 2: 4 I built houses for myself and **p** vineyards. 5749
2: 5 I made gardens and parks and **p** all kinds 5749
Isa 5: 2 of stones and **p** it with the choicest vines. 5749
40:24 No sooner **are** *they* **p**, 5749
44:14 or **p** a pine, and the rain made it grow. 5749
60:21 They are the shoot I have **p**, 4760
Jer 2:21 I *had* **p** you like a choice vine of sound 5749
11:17 The LORD Almighty, who **p** you, 5749
12: 2 *You have* **p** them, and they have taken root; 5749
17: 8 a tree **p** by the water that sends out its roots 9278
18: 9 a nation or kingdom is to be built up and **p**, 5749
45: 4 and uproot what *I have* **p**, 5749
Eze 17: 4 where *he* **p** it in a city of traders. 8492
17: 5 *He* **p** it like a willow by abundant water, 8492
17: 7 toward him from the plot where it was **p** 4760
17: 8 *had* **been p** in good soil by abundant water 9278
19:10 like a vine in your vineyard **p** by the water; 9278
19:13 Now *it* **is p** in the desert, 9278
Hos 9:13 like Tyre, **p** in a pleasant place. 9278
10:13 But *you have* **p** wickedness, 3086
Am 5:11 though *you have* **p** lush vineyards, 5749
Hag 1: 6 *You have* **p** much, but have harvested little. 2445
Mt 13:31 which a man took and **p** in his field. *5062*
15:13 that my heavenly Father *has* not **p** will *5885*
21:33 There was a landowner who **p** a vineyard. *5885*
Mk 4:32 when **p**, it grows and becomes the largest *5062*
12: 1 "A man **p** a vineyard. *5885*
Lk 13: 6 "A man had a fig tree, **p** in his vineyard, *5885*
13:19 which a man took and **p** in his garden. *965*
17: 6 'Be uprooted and **p** in the sea,' *5885*
20: 9 "A man **p** a vineyard, *5885*
1Co 3: 6 I **p** the seed, Apollos watered it, *5885*
Jas 1:21 and humbly accept the word **p in** you, *1875*
Rev 10: 2 *He* **p** his right foot on the sea *5502*

PLANTER (1) [PLANT]

Am 9:13 and the **p** by the one treading grapes. 2446+5432

PLANTING (5) [PLANT]

Lev 26: 5 and the grape harvest will continue until **p**, 2446
Isa 28:24 When a farmer plows for **p**, 2445
61: 3 **p** *of* the LORD for the display of his splendor 4760
Mic 1: 6 a place for **p** vineyards. 4760
Lk 17:28 buying and selling, **p** and building. *5885*

PLANTS (30) [PLANT]

Ge 1:11 seed-bearing **p** and trees on the land 6912
1:12 **p** bearing seed according to their kinds 6912
3:18 and you will eat the **p** *of* the field. 6912
9: 3 Just as I gave you the green **p**, 6912
30:14 into the fields and found *some* **mandrake p**, 1859
Dt 32: 2 like abundant rain on **tender p**. 6912
2Ki 19:26 They are like **p** *in* the field, 6912
Job 8:19 and from the soil other **p** grow. NIH
40:21 Under the **lotus p** he lies, 7365
Ps 37: 2 like green **p** they will soon die away. 3764
104:14 and **p** for man to cultivate— 6912
144:12 in their youth will be like well-nurtured **p**, 5745
Pr 31:16 out of her earnings *she* **p** a vineyard. 5749
SS 4:13 Your **p** are an orchard of pomegranates 8945
Isa 17:10 the finest **p** and plant imported vines, 5750
19: 7 also the **p** along the Nile, 6868
37:27 They are like **p** *in* the field, 6912
Da 4:15 with the animals among the **p** *of* the earth. 10572
Zec 10: 1 and **p** of the field to everyone. 6912
Mt 13: 6 the sun came up, the **p** were scorched, *NIG*
13: 7 which grew up and choked **the p.** *899S*
13:32 the largest *of* **garden p** and becomes a tree, *3303*
Mk 4: 6 the sun came up, the **p** were scorched, *NIG*
4: 7 which grew up and choked **the p**, *899S*
4:32 and becomes the largest of all **garden p**, *3303*
Lk 8: 6 **p** withered because they had no moisture. *NIG*
8: 7 which grew up with it and choked **the p.** *899S*
1Co 3: 7 So neither he who **p** nor he who waters *5885*
3: 8 The man who **p** and the man who waters *5885*
9: 7 Who **p** a vineyard and does not eat *5885*

PLASTER (5) [PLASTERED]

Lev 14:42 to replace these and take new clay and **p** 3212
14:45 its stones, timbers and all the **p—** 6760
Dt 27: 2 up some large stones and coat them with **p.** 8487
27: 4 command you today, and coat them with **p.** 8487
Da 5: 5 a human hand appeared and wrote on the **p** 10142

PLASTERED (3) [PLASTER]

Lev 14:43 and the house scraped and **p**, 3212
14:48 not spread after the house *has* **been p**, 3212
Isa 44:18 their eyes *are* **p over** so they cannot see, 3220

PLATE (16) [PLATES, PLATTER]

Ex 28:36 "Make a **p** *of* pure gold and engrave on it 7488
39:30 They made the **p**, the sacred diadem, 7488
Lev 8: 9 on Aaron's head and set the gold **p**, 7488
Nu 7:13 His offering was one silver **p** weighing 7883
7:19 he brought was one silver **p** weighing 7883
7:25 His offering was one silver **p** weighing 7883
7:31 His offering was one silver **p** weighing 7883
7:37 His offering was one silver **p** weighing 7883
7:43 His offering was one silver **p** weighing 7883
7:49 His offering was one silver **p** weighing 7883
7:55 His offering was one silver **p** weighing 7883
Nu 7:61 His offering was one silver **p** weighing 7883
7:67 His offering was one silver **p** weighing 7883
7:73 His offering was one silver **p** weighing 7883
7:79 His offering was one silver **p** weighing 7883
7:85 Each silver **p** weighed a hundred and thirty shekels, 7883

PLATEAU (10)

Dt 3:10 We took all the towns on the **p**, 4793
4:43 in the desert **p**, for the Reubenites; 824+4793
Jos 13: 9 and included the whole **p** *of* Medeba as far 4793
13:16 and the whole **p** past Medeba 4793
13:17 to Heshbon and all its towns on the **p**, 4793
13:21 on the **p** and the entire realm of Sihon king 4793
20: 8 the desert on the **p** in the tribe of Reuben, 4793
Jer 21:13 above this valley on the rocky **p**, declares 4793
48: 8 be ruined and the **p** destroyed, 4793
48:21 Judgment has come to the **p—** 4793

PLATES (4) [PLATE]

Ex 25:29 And make its **p** and dishes of pure gold, 7883
37:16 its **p** and dishes and bowls and its pitchers 7883
Nu 4: 7 and put on it the **p**, dishes and bowls, and 7883
7:84 when it was anointed: twelve silver **p**, 7883

PLATFORM (3)

2Ch 6:13 Now he had made a bronze **p**, 3963
6:13 He stood on **the p** and then knelt down 2257S
Ne 8: 4 Ezra the scribe stood on a **high** wooden **p** 4463

PLATTED (KJV) See TWISTED

PLATTER (4) [PLATE]

Mt 14: 8 "Give me here on a **p** the head of John *4402*
14:11 His head was brought in on a **p** and given *4402*
Mk 6:25 now the head of John the Baptist on a **p**." *4402*
6:28 and brought back his head on a **p.** *4402*

PLAY (14) [PLAYED, PLAYERS, PLAYING, PLAYS]

Ge 4:21 the father of all *who* **p** the harp and flute. 9530
19: 9 and now *he wants to* **p the judge!** 9149+9149
1Sa 16:16 to search for someone who can **p** the harp. 5594
16:16 He *will* **p** when the evil spirit 928+3338+5594
16:18 who knows how *to* **p the harp.** 5594
16:23 David would take his harp and **p.** 928+3338+5594
1Ch 15:20 and Benaiah were to **p** the lyres according NIH
15:21 Jeiel and Azaziah were to **p** the harps, NIH
16: 5 They were to **p** the lyres and harps, NIH
Job 40:20 and all the wild animals **p** nearby. 8471
Ps 33: 3 **p** skillfully, and shout for joy. 5594
81: 2 **p** the melodious harp and lyre. NIH
Isa 11: 8 The infant *will* **p** near the hole of 9130
23:16 **p the harp** well, sing many a song, 5594

PLAYED (6) [PLAY]

1Sa 10: 5 flutes and harps being **p** before them, NIH
2Ch 29:28 the singers sang and the trumpeters **p.** 2955
Pr 30:32 *you have* **p the fool** and exalted yourself, 5571
Mt 11:17 " '*We* **p the flute** for you, and you did not *884*
Lk 7:32 " '*We* **p the flute** for you, and you did not *884*
1Co 14: 7 will anyone know what tune *is being* **p** *884*

PLAYERS (2) [PLAY]

Mt 9:23 the ruler's house and saw the **flute p** and *886*
Rev 18:22 **flute p** and trumpeters, *886*

PLAYING (11) [PLAY]

1Sa 18:10 while David *was* **p the harp**, 928+3338+5594
19: 9 While David *was* **p the harp**, 928+3338+5594
1Ki 1:40 **p** flutes and rejoicing greatly, 2727
2Ki 3:15 While the harpist was **p**, 5594
1Ch 15:28 and the **p** of lyres and harps. 9048
16:42 the trumpets and cymbals and for the **p** of NIH
2Ch 5:12 dressed in fine linen and **p** cymbals, NIH
34:12 skilled in **p** musical instruments— NIH
Ps 68:25 with them are the maidens **p tambourines.** 9528
Zec 8: 5 be filled with boys and girls **p** there." 8471
Rev 14: 2 like that of harpists **p** their harps. *3068*

PLAYS (2) [PLAY]

1Sa 16:17 "Find someone *who* **p** well and bring him 5594
Eze 33:32 a beautiful voice and **p an instrument** well, 5594

PLEA (25) [PLEAD, PLEADED, PLEADING, PLEADS, PLEAS]

Ge 30: 6 he has listened to my **p** and given me 7754
Nu 21: 3 The LORD listened to Israel's **p** and gave 7754
1Ki 8:28 your servant's prayer and his **p for mercy**, 9382
8:38 or **p** is made by any of your people Israel— 9382
8:45 hear from heaven their prayer and their **p**, 9382
8:49 hear their prayer and their **p**, 9382
8:52 "May your eyes be open to your servant's **p** 9382
8:52 be open to your servant's plea and to the **p** 9382
9: 3 the prayer and **p** you have made before me; 9382
2Ch 6:19 and his **p for mercy**, 9382
6:29 or **p** is made by any of your people Israel— 9382
6:35 hear from heaven their prayer and their **p**, 9382
33:13 by his entreaty and listened to his **p**; 9382
Job 13: 6 listen to the **p** *of* my lips. 8191
35:13 God does not listen to their **empty p**; 8736
Ps 17: 1 Hear, O LORD, my righteous **p**; NIH
55: 1 O God, do not ignore my **p**; 9382
102:17 he will not despise their **p**. 9525
Pr 6: 3 **press** *your* **p** *with* your neighbor! 8104
Isa 32: 7 even when the **p** *of* the needy is just. 1819
Jer 7:16 for this people nor offer any **p** or petition 8262
11:14 "Do not pray for this people nor offer any **p** 8262
La 3:56 You heard my **p**: 7754
Eze 36:37 Once again *I will* **yield to the p** of 2011
Lk 18: 3 who kept coming to him **with the p**, *3306*

PLEAD (22) [PLEA]

Jdg 6:31 *"Are you going to* **p** Baal's **cause?** 8189
1Sa 2:36 a piece of silver and a crust of bread and **p**, 606
1Ki 8:47 and repent and **p** with you in the land 2858
2Ch 6:37 and **p** with you in the land of their captivity 2858
Est 4: 8 for mercy and **p with** him for her people. 1335
Job 8: 5 But if you will look to God and **p** with 2858
9:15 **p** with my Judge **for mercy.** 2858
35: 9 *they* **p for relief** from the arm of 8775
Ps 43: 1 and **p** my cause against an ungodly nation; 8189
Isa 1:17 **p the case** *of* the widow. 8189
45:14 down before you and **p** with you, saying, 7137
Jer 5:28 not **p** the case of the fatherless to win it, 1906
7:16 *do* not **p** with me, for I will not listen to you. 7003
15:11 surely *I will* **make** your enemies **p** 7003
27:18 *let them* **p** with the LORD Almighty that 7003
30:13 There is no *one to* **p** your cause, 1906
Da 2:18 to **p** *for* mercy from the God of heaven 10114
Mic 6: 1 **p** *your* **case** *before* the mountains; 8189
Mk 5:17 Then the people began *to* **p with** Jesus *4151*
Gal 4:12 *I* **p** with you, brothers, become like me, *1289*
Php 4: 2 *I* **p with** Euodia and I plead with Syntyche *4151*
4: 2 with Euodia and *I* **p with** Syntyche to agree *4151*

PLEADED (13) [PLEA]

Ge 42:21 We saw how distressed he was when he **p** 2858
Dt 3:23 At that time *I* **p** with the LORD: 2858
2Sa 12:16 David **p** *with* God for the child. 1335
Est 8: 3 Esther again **p** with the king, 1819
Da 9: 3 So I turned to the Lord God and **p with** him 1335
Mt 8:34 *they* **p with** him to leave their region. *4151*
Mk 5:23 and **p** earnestly **with** him, *4151*
Lk 7: 4 *they* **p** earnestly **with** him, *4151*
15:28 So his father went out and **p with** him. *4151*
Ac 2:40 and *he* **p with** them, *4151*
21:12 and the people there **p with** Paul not to go *4151*
2Co 8: 4 *they* urgently **p with** us for the privilege *1289*
12: 8 Three times *I* **p with** the Lord *4151*

PLEADING (5) [PLEA]

Pr 19: 7 Though he pursues them with **p**, 609
Jer 3:21 the weeping and **p** *of* the people of Israel, 9384
38:26 'I *was* **p** with the king not to send me 5877+9382
Lk 8:41 **p with** him to come to his house *4151*
13:25 you will stand outside knocking and **p**, *3306*

PLEADS (5) [PLEA]

Job 16:21 on behalf of a man *he* **p** with God as a man 3519
16:21 he pleads with God as a man **p** for his friend. NIH
Pr 18:23 A poor man **p** *for* mercy, 1819
Isa 59: 4 no *one* **p** *his* **case** with integrity. 9149
Mic 7: 9 until *he* **p** my case and establishes my right. 8189

PLEAS (2) [PLEA]

2Ch 6:39 hear their prayer and their **p**, 9382
Isa 19:22 *he will* **respond to** their **p** and heal them. 6983

PLEASANT (20) [PLEASE]

Ge 49:15 and how **p** *is* his land, 5838
Ps 16: 6 lines have fallen for me in **p** *places;* 5833
106:24 Then they despised the **p** land; 2775
133: 1 **p** it is when brothers live together in unity! 5833
135: 3 sing praise to his name, for that is **p.** 5833
147: 1 how **p** and fitting to praise him! 5833
Pr 2:10 and knowledge *will be* **p** to your soul. 5838
3:17 Her ways are **p** ways, 5840
16:21 and **p** words promote instruction. 5518
16:24 **P** words are a honeycomb, 5840
Isa 30:10 Tell us **p** *things*, prophesy illusions. 2747
32:12 Beat your breasts for the **p** fields, 2774
Jer 12:10 they will turn my **p** field into 2775
31:26 My sleep *had been* **p** to me. 6844
Hos 4:13 poplar and terebinth, where the shade is **p.** 3202
9:13 like Tyre, planted in a **p place.** 5659
Mic 2: 9 of my people from their **p** homes. 9503
Zec 7:14 how they made the **p** land desolate.' " 2775
1Th 3: 6 that you always have **p** memories of us and *19*
Heb 12:11 No discipline seems **p** at the time, *5915*

PLEASANTNESS (1) [PLEASE]

Pr 27: 9 and the **p** *of* one's friend springs 5518

PLEASE (115) [PLEASANT, PLEASANTNESS, PLEASED, PLEASES, PLEASING, PLEASURE, PLEASURES]

Ge 19: 2 "**p** turn aside to your servant's house. 5528
19:18 But Lot said to them, "No, my lords, **p!** 5528
24:14 '**P** let down your jar that I may have 5528

Ge 24:17 “P give me a little water from your jar.” 5528
24:23 P tell me, is there room 5528
24:42 p grant success to the journey 5528
24:43 to her, “P let me drink a little water 5528
24:45 and I said to her, ‘P give me a drink.’ 5528
27:19 P sit up and eat some of my game so 5528
30:14 “P give me some of your son’s mandrakes.” 5528
30:27 “If I have found favor in your eyes, p stay. 5528
32:29 Jacob said, “P tell me your name.” 5528
33:10 “No, p!” said Jacob. 5528
33:11 P accept the present that was brought 5528
34:8 P give her to him as his wife. 5528
43:20 “P, sir,” they said, “we came down here 1065
44:18 Then Judah went up to him and said: “P, 1065
44:33 p let your servant remain here 5528
47:4 now, p let your servants settle in Goshen.” 5528
50:17 Now p forgive the sins of the servants of 5528
Ex 4:13 “O Lord, p send someone else to do it.” 5528
21:8 If *she does* not p the master 928+6524+8317
32:32 But now, p forgive their sin— 561
Nu 10:31 But Moses said, “P do not leave us. 5528
12:11 and he said to Moses, “P, my lord, do 1065+5528
12:13 “O God, p heal her!” 5528
20:17 P let us pass through your country. 5528
23:27 Perhaps *it will* p God 928+3837+6524
36:6 They may marry anyone they p as long as 928+3202+6524
Dt 12:13 not to sacrifice your burnt offerings anywhere *you* p. 8011
28:63 so *it will* p him to ruin and destroy you. 8464
Jos 2:12 p swear to me by the LORD 5528
Jdg 4:19 “P give me some water.” 5528
6:18 P do not go away until I come back 5528
10:15 but p rescue us now.” 5528
16:28 O God, p strengthen me just once more, 5528
18:5 “P inquire of God to learn whether 5528
19:6 “P stay tonight and enjoy yourself.” 5528
Ru 2:7 ‘P let me glean and gather among 5528
1Sa 9:18 “Would you p tell me where 5528
15:30 But p honor me before the elders 5528
25:8 P give your servants and your son David 5528
25:24 P let your servant speak to you; 5528
25:28 P forgive your servant’s offense, 5528
28:22 Now p listen to your servant 5528
2Sa 13:13 P speak to the king; 5528
13:24 Will the king and his officials p join me?” 5528
13:26 p let my brother Amnon come with us.” 5528
18:22 p let me run behind the Cushite.” 5528
1Ki 2:17 So he continued, “P ask King Solomon— 5528
3:26 “P, my lord, give her the living baby! 1065
17:11 “And bring me, p, a piece of bread.” 5528
20:32 Ben-Hadad says: ‘P let me live.’ ” 5528
20:37 and said, “Strike me, p.” 5528
2Ki 1:13 “p have respect for my life and the lives 5528
4:22 “P send me one of the servants and 5528
5:15 P accept now a gift from your servant.” 5528
5:17 “If you will not,” said Naaman, “p let me, 5528
5:22 P give them a talent of silver and two sets 5528
6:3 Won’t you p come with your servants? 3283+5528
18:26 “P speak to your servants in Aramaic, 5528
2Ch 10:7 to these people and p them and give them 8354
Ne 9:37 over our bodies and our cattle as they p. 8356
Est 3:11 and do with the people as you p. 928+3202+6524
Job 10:3 Does it p you to oppress me, 3202
34:9 a man nothing when he *tries to* p God.’ 8354
Ps 69:31 *This will* p the LORD more than an ox, 3512
Pr 20:23 and dishonest scales do not p him. 3202
Isa 29:11 say to him, “Read this, p,” he will answer, 5528
29:12 and say, “Read this, p,” he will answer, 5528
36:11 “P speak to your servants in Aramaic, 5528
44:28 and will accomplish all *that* I p; 2914
46:10 and I will do all *that* I p. 2914
58:3 as you p and exploit all your workers. 2914
58:13 and from doing *as* you p on my holy day, 2914
58:13 not doing *as* you p or speaking idle words, 2914
Jer 6:20 your sacrifices *do not* p me.” 6844
27:5 and I give it to anyone I p. 928+3837+6524
36:15 They said to him, “Sit down, p, 5528
37:3 “P pray to the LORD our God for us.” 5528
37:20 But now, my lord the king, p listen. 5528
40:4 go wherever you p.” 928+2256+3202+3838+6524
40:5 or go anywhere else you p.” 928+3838+6524
42:2 “P hear our petition and pray to the LORD 5528
Da 1:12 “P test your servants for ten days: 5528
Hos 9:4 nor *will* their sacrifices p him. 6844
10:10 When I p, I will punish them; 205
Jnh 1:14 p do not let us die for taking this man’s life. 5528
Mk 5:23 P come and put your hands on her so *NIG*
Lk 14:18 P excuse me.’ *2263+5148*
14:19 P excuse me.’ *2263+5148*
Jn 5:30 I seek not to p myself but him who sent me. *2525*
Ac 8:34 The eunuch asked Philip, “Tell me, p, *1289+5148*
9:38 to him and urged him, “P come at once!” *NIG*
13:15 of encouragement for the people, p speak.” *NIG*
21:39 P let me speak to the people.” *1289+5148*
Ro 8:8 by the sinful nature cannot p God. *743*
15:1 of the weak and not *to* p ourselves. *743*
15:2 of us *should* p his neighbor for his good, *743*
15:3 Christ *did* not p himself but, as it is written: *743*
1Co 7:32 how *he can* p the Lord. *743*
7:33 how *he can* p his wife— *743*
7:34 how *she can* p her husband. *743*
10:33 even as I try to p everybody in every way. *743*
2Co 5:9 So we make it our goal *to* p him, *1639+2298*
Gal 1:10 Or am I trying *to* p men? *743*
1:10 If *I were* still trying to p men, *743*
6:8 The one who sows to p his sinful nature, *NIG*
Gal 6:8 the one who sows to p the Spirit, *NIG*
Col 1:10 of the Lord and may p him in every way: *742*
1Th 2:4 *We are* not trying to p men but God, *743*
4:1 how to live in order to p God, *743*
2Ti 2:4 he wants *to* p his commanding officer. *743*
Tit 2:9 to try to p them, not to talk back to them, *2298*
Heb 11:6 without faith it is impossible *to* p God, *2297*

PLEASED (78) [PLEASE]

Ge 45:16 Pharaoh and all his officials *were* p. 928+3512+6524
49:6 and hamstrung oxen as they p. 8356
Ex 33:13 If you *are* p with *me*, 928+2834+5162+6524
33:16 that you *are* p with me and with your people 928+2834+5162+6524
33:17 I *am* p with *you* and I know you by name.” 928+2834+5162+6524
Lev 10:19 Would the LORD *have been* p if I had eaten 928+3512+6524
Nu 14:8 If the LORD *is* p with us, 2911
24:1 when Balaam saw that *it* p the LORD to bless Israel, 928+3201+6524
Dt 21:14 If *you are* not p with her, 2911
28:63 as *it* p the LORD to make you prosper 8464
33:11 and *be* p with the work of his hands. 8354
Jos 22:30 Gad and Manasseh had to say, they *were* p. 928+3512+6524
1Sa 12:22 the LORD *was* p to make you his own. 3283
16:22 for I *am* p with *him*.” 928+2834+5162+6524
18:5 *This* p all the people, 928+3512+6524
18:20 they told Saul about it, he *was* p. 928+3837+6524
18:22 ‘Look, the king *is* p with you, 2911
18:26 he *was* p to become the king’s son-in-law, 928+3837+6524
29:6 be p to have you serve with me in the army 928+3202+6524
2Sa 3:36 All the people took note and *were* p; 928+3512+6524
3:36 everything the king did p them. 928+3202+6524
7:29 *be* p to bless the house of your servant, 3283
15:26 But if he says, ‘*I am* not p with you,’ 2911
19:6 be p if Absalom were alive today 928+3838+6524
1Ki 3:10 The Lord *was* p that Solomon had asked for this. 928+3512+6524
5:7 *he was* greatly p and said, 8523
9:12 he *was* not p with them. 928+3837+6524
11:19 Pharaoh *was* so p with Hadad that he gave him a sister 928+2834+5162+6524
1Ch 17:27 Now *you have been* p to bless the house 3283
28:4 and from my father’s sons *he was* p 8354
29:17 you test the heart and *are* p with integrity. 8354
Ne 2:6 *It* p the king to send me; so I set a time. 3512
9:24 to deal with them as they p. 8356
12:44 for Judah was p with the ministering priests 8525
Est 1:21 nobles *were* p with this advice, 928+3512+6524
2:9 The girl p him and won his favor. 928+3512+6524
2:14 not return to the king unless he *was* p 2911
5:2 he *was* p with *her* and 928+2834+5951+6524
8:5 and if he is p with me, 928+3202+6524
9:5 they did what they p to those who hated 8356
Ps 40:13 *Be* p, O LORD, to save me; 8354
41:11 I know that *you are* p with me, 2911
105:22 as he p and teach his elders wisdom. 5883
Ecc 4:16 But those who came later *were* not p with 8523
Isa 42:21 *It* p the LORD for the sake of his 2911
Eze 18:23 am I not p when they turn from their ways NIH
Da 4:27 O king, *be* p to accept my advice: 10739
6:1 *It* p Darius to appoint 120 satraps to rule 10739
8:4 He did as he p and became great. 8356
Hos 8:13 but the LORD *is* not p with them. 8354
Jnh 1:14 for you, O LORD, have done as *you* p.” 2911
Mic 6:7 the LORD *be* p with thousands of rams, 8354
Mal 1:8 *Would he be* p with you? 8354
1:10 I am not p with you,” 2914
2:17 who do evil are in the eyes of the LORD, and he *is* p with them” 2911
Mt 3:17 with him *I am* well p.” *2305*
14:6 of Herodias danced for them and p Herod *743*
17:5 with him *I am* well p. *2305*
Mk 1:11 with you *I am* well p.” *2305*
6:22 *she* p Herod and his dinner guests. *743*
Lk 3:22 with you *I am* well p.” *2305*
12:32 for your Father *has been* p to give you *2305*
23:8 When Herod saw Jesus, *he was* greatly p, *5897*
Jn 5:21 Son gives life to whom *he is* p to give it. *2527*
Ac 6:5 This proposal p the whole group. *743*
12:3 When he saw that *this* p the Jews, *744+1639*
Ro 15:26 For Macedonia and Achaia *were* p to make *2305*
15:27 *They were* p to do it, *2305*
1Co 1:21 God *was* p through the foolishness *2305*
10:5 God *was* not p with most of them; *2305*
Gal 1:15 and called me by his grace, *was* p *2305*
Col 1:19 For God *was* p to have all his fullness dwell *2305*
Heb 10:6 with burnt offerings and sin offerings *you were* not p. *2305*
10:8 nor *were you* p with them” *2305*
10:38 he shrinks back, I *will* not *be* p with him.” *2305*
11:5 he was commended as one who p God. *2297*
13:16 for with such sacrifices God *is* p. *2297*
2Pe 1:17 with him I *am* well p.” *2305*

PLEASES (40) [PLEASE]

1Sa 23:20 come down whenever it p you to do so, 205
2Sa 19:27 so do whatever p you. 928+3202+6524
19:37 Do for him whatever p you.” 928+3202+6524
Mt 19:38 I will do for him whatever p you. 928+3202+6524
24:22 “Let my lord the king take whatever p him 928+3202+6524
1Ch 21:23 Let my lord the king do whatever p him. 928+3202+6524
Ezr 5:17 Now if it p the king, let him issue 10294
Ne 2:5 “If *it* p the king and if your servant 3201
2:7 I also said to him, “If *it* p the king, 3201
Est 1:19 “Therefore, if *it* p the king, 3201
2:4 the girl who p the king be queen instead of Vashti. 928+3512+6524
3:9 If *it* p the king, let a decree be issued 3201
5:4 “If *it* p the king,” replied Esther, 3201
5:8 the king regards me with favor and if *it* p 3201
7:3 O king, and if *it* p your majesty, 3201
8:5 “If it p the king,” she said, 3202
9:13 “If it p the king,” Esther answered, 3202
Job 23:13 He does whatever he p. 203
Ps 115:3 he does whatever p *him*. 2911
135:6 The LORD does whatever p *him*, 2911
Pr 15:8 but the prayer of the upright p him. 8356
21:1 like a watercourse wherever *he* p. 2911
Ecc 2:26 To the man who p him, God gives wisdom, 3202
2:26 to hand it over to the *one who* p God. 3202
7:26 The *man who* p God will escape her, 3202
8:3 for he will do whatever *he* p. 2911
11:7 and it p the eyes to see the sun. 3202
Isa 56:4 who choose what p me and hold fast 2911
Eze 46:5 is to be as much as he p, 3338+5522
46:11 with the lambs as much as one p, 3338+5522
Da 4:35 He does as he p with the powers of heaven 10605
11:3 with great power and do as he p. 8356
11:16 The invader will do as he p; 8356
11:36 “The king will do as he p. 8356
Jn 3:8 The wind blows wherever *it* p. *2527*
8:29 for I always do what p him.” *744*
Eph 5:10 and find out what p the Lord. *1639+2298*
Col 3:20 for this p the Lord. *1639+2298*
1Ti 2:3 This is good, and p God our Savior, *621*
1Jn 3:22 we obey his commands and do what p him. *744*

PLEASING (58) [PLEASE]

Ge 2:9 *that were* p to the eye and good for food. 2773
3:6 the fruit of the tree was good for food and p 9294
8:21 The LORD smelled the p aroma and said 5767
Ex 29:18 the LORD, a p aroma, an offering made to 5767
29:25 along with the burnt offering for a p aroma 5767
29:41 a p aroma, an offering made to the LORD 5767
Lev 1:9 an aroma p to the LORD. 5767
1:13 an aroma p to the LORD. 5767
1:17 an aroma p to the LORD. 5767
2:2 an aroma p to the LORD. 5767
2:9 an aroma p to the LORD. 5767
2:12 not to be offered on the altar as a p aroma. 5767
3:5 an aroma p to the LORD. 5767
3:16 an offering made by fire, a p aroma. 5767
4:31 on the altar as an aroma p to the LORD. 5767
6:15 on the altar as an aroma p to the LORD. 5767
6:21 in pieces as an aroma p to the LORD. 5767
8:21 a p aroma, an offering made to the LORD 5767
8:28 a p aroma, an offering made to the LORD 5767
17:6 of Meeting and burn the fat as an aroma p 5767
23:13 to the LORD by fire, a p aroma— 5767
23:18 an aroma p to the LORD. 5767
26:31 and I will take no delight in the p aroma 5767
Nu 15:3 as an aroma p to the LORD— 5767
15:7 Offer it as an aroma p to the LORD. 5767
15:10 an aroma p to the LORD. 5767
15:13 an offering made by fire as an aroma p to 5767
15:14 an offering made by fire as an aroma p to 5767
15:24 for a burnt offering as an aroma p to 5767
18:17 an aroma p to the LORD. 5767
28:2 as an aroma p *to* me.’ 5767
28:6 at Mount Sinai as a p aroma, 5767
28:8 an aroma p to the LORD. 5767
28:13 This is for a burnt offering, a p aroma, 5767
28:24 for seven days as an aroma p to 5767
28:27 a year old as an aroma p to the LORD. 5767
29:2 As an aroma p to the LORD, 5767
29:6 by fire—a p aroma. 5767
29:8 an aroma p to the LORD a burnt offering 5767
29:13 an offering made by fire as an aroma p to 5767
29:36 an offering made by fire as an aroma p to 5767
1Sa 29:9 “I know that you have been as p in my eyes 3202
Ezr 6:10 that they may offer sacrifices p to the God 10478
Ps 19:14 and the meditation of my heart be p 8356
104:34 *May* my meditation *be* p to him, 6844
Pr 15:26 but those of the pure are p to him. 5840
16:7 When a man’s ways *are* p *to* the LORD, 8354
22:18 for it is p when you keep them 5833
SS 1:3 P is the fragrance of your perfumes; 3202
4:10 How much more p *is* your love than wine, 3201
7:6 How beautiful you are and how p, O love, 5838
La 2:4 a foe he has slain all *who* were p *to* the eye; 4718
Ro 12:1 holy and p to God— *2298*
12:2 his good, p and perfect will. *2298*
14:18 in this way is p to God and approved *2298*
Php 4:18 an acceptable sacrifice, p to God. *2298*
1Ti 5:4 for this is p to God. *621*
Heb 13:21 and may he work in us what is p to him, *2298*

PLEASURE (34) [PLEASE]

Ge 18:12 my master is old, will I now have this p?” 6366
Job 22:3 What p would it give the Almighty 2914
Ps 5:4 You are not a God *who* takes p in evil; 2913

Ps 51:16 *you do* not **take p in** burnt offerings. 8354
51:18 In your **good p** make Zion prosper; 8356
109:17 *he* **found** no p in blessing— 2911
147:10 *His* p *is* not in the strength of the horse, 2911
Pr 10:23 A fool finds p in evil conduct, 8468
16:13 Kings take p *in* honest lips; 8356
18:2 A fool **finds** no p in understanding 2911
21:17 He who loves p will become poor; 8525
Ecc 2:1 with p to find out what is good." 8525
2:2 And what does p accomplish?" 8525
2:10 I refused my heart no p. 8525
5:4 He has no p in fools; fulfill your vow. 2914
7:4 but the heart of fools is in the house of p. 8525
12:1 "I find no p in them"— 2914
Isa 1:11 *I* **have** no p *in* the blood of bulls 2911
9:17 the Lord *will* **take** no p in the young men, 8523
Jer 6:10 *they* **find** no p in it. 2911
Eze 16:37 with whom *you* **found p,** 6844
18:23 *Do I* **take any p in** the death of the wicked? 2911+2911
18:32 For *I* **take** no p in the death of anyone, 2911
33:11 *I* **take** no p in the death of the wicked, 2911
Da 4:2 *It is* my p to tell you about the miraculous 10739
Hag 1:8 so that *I may* **take** p in it and be honored," 8354
Mal 2:13 or accepts them *with* p from your hands. 8356
Mt 11:26 Yes, Father, for this was your **good p.** *2306*
Lk 10:21 Yes, Father, for this was your **good p.** *2306*
Eph 1:5 in accordance with his p and will— *2306*
1:9 of his will according to his **good p,** *2306*
1Ti 5:6 the widow who **lives for p** is dead even *5059*
2Ti 3:4 **lovers of p** rather than lovers of God— *5798*
2Pe 2:13 of p is to carouse in broad daylight. *2454*

PLEASURES (6) [PLEASE]

Ps 16:11 with eternal p at your right hand. 5833
Lk 8:14 riches and p, and they do not mature. *2454*
Tit 3:3 by all kinds of passions and p. *2454*
Heb 11:25 the people of God rather than to enjoy the p *656*
Jas 4:3 you may spend what you get on your p. *2454*
2Pe 2:13 in their p while they feast with you. *573*

PLEDGE (32) [PLEDGED, PLEDGES]

Ge 38:17 "Will you give me something as a p 6860
38:18 He said, "What p should I give you?" 6860
38:20 in order to get his p back from the woman, 6860
Ex 22:26 **take** your neighbor's cloak **as a p,** 2471+2471
Nu 30:2 or takes an oath to obligate himself by a p, 674
30:3 to the LORD or obligates herself by a p 674
30:4 about her vow or p but says nothing to her, 674
30:4 then all her vows and every p 674
30:10 a vow or obligates herself by a p under oath 674
30:13 or any sworn p to deny herself. 674
Dt 24:10 to get *what* he is **offering as a p.** 6287
24:11 the loan bring the p out to you. 6287
24:12 to sleep with his p in your possession. 6287
24:17 **take** the cloak of the widow **as a p.** 2471
2Ch 34:32 **had** everyone in Jerusalem and Benjamin **p** 6641
Ezr 10:19 **gave** their hands **in p** to put away their 5989
Job 17:3 "Give me, O God, the p you demand. 6842
24:3 **take** the widow's ox **in p.** 2471
Pr 6:1 if *you have* **struck** hands **in p** for another, 9546
11:15 to **strike hands in p** is safe. 9364
17:18 in judgment **strikes** hands **in p** and puts 9546
20:16 **hold** it **in p** if he does it for a wayward 2471
22:26 not be a *man who* **strikes** hands **in p** or puts 9546
27:13 **hold it in p** if he does it for a wayward 2471
Eze 17:18 Because *he had* **given** his hand **in p** 5989
18:7 returns **what** he **took in p** for a loan. 2481
18:12 not return **what** he **took in p.** 2478
18:16 or **require a p for a loan.** 2471+2478
33:15 gives back **what** he **took in p for a loan,** 2478
Am 2:8 beside every altar on garments **taken in p.** 2471
1Ti 5:12 because they have broken their first **p.** *4411*
1Pe 3:21 but the p of a good conscience toward God. *2090*

PLEDGED (13) [PLEDGE]

Ge 19:14 *who were* **p to marry** his daughters. 4374
Ex 22:16 seduces a virgin *who is* not **p to be married** 829
Dt 20:7 *Has* anyone *become* **p** *to* a woman and 829
22:23 to meet in a town a virgin **p to be married** 829
22:25 meet a girl **p to be married** and rapes her, 829
22:28 to meet a virgin who *is* not **p to be married** 829
28:30 *You will be* **p** *to* a woman, 829
2Ki 23:3 the people **p** *themselves* to the covenant. 6641
1Ch 29:24 **p** their submission to King Solomon. 3338+5989
Mic 7:20 as *you* **p on oath** to our fathers 8678
Mt 1:18 His mother Mary *was* **p to be married** *3650*
Lk 1:27 to a virgin **p to be married** to a man *3650*
2:5 Mary, who *was* **p to be married** to him *3650*

PLEDGES (5) [PLEDGE]

Nu 30:5 none of her vows or the p by which she 674
30:7 then her vows or the p by which she 674
30:11 then all her vows or the p by which she 674
30:12 or p that came from her lips will stand. 674
30:14 or the p binding on her. 674

PLEIADES (3)

Job 9:9 the P and the constellations of the south. 3966
38:31 "Can you bind the beautiful **P?** 3966
Am 5:8 the P and Orion, who turns blackness 3966

PLENTIFUL (8) [PLENTY]

1Ki 10:27 as p as sycamore-fig trees in the foothills. 4200+8044
1Ch 12:40 were p supplies of flour, fig cakes, 4200+8044
2Ch 1:15 as p as sycamore-fig trees in the foothills. 4200+8044
9:27 as p as sycamore-fig trees in the foothills. 4200+8044
Isa 30:23 that comes from the land will be rich and p. 9045
Eze 36:29 and **make** it p and will not bring famine 8049
Mt 9:37 "The harvest is p but the workers are few. *4498*
Lk 10:2 He told them, "The harvest is p, *4498*

PLENTIFULLY (1) [PLENTY]

Ge 41:47 of abundance the land produced p. 4200+7859

PLENTY (21) [PLENTIFUL, PLENTIFULLY]

Ge 24:25 "We have p *of* straw and fodder, 8041
33:9 Esau said, "I already have p, my brother. 8041
34:21 the land has **p of room** for them. 3338+8146
2Ch 2:9 to provide me with p of lumber, 4200+8044
31:10 we have had enough to eat and p to spare, 4200+8044
32:4 kings of Assyria come and find p of water?" 8041
Job 20:22 In the midst of his **p,** distress will overtake 8565
Ps 17:14 their sons **have p,** and they store up wealth 8425
37:19 in days of famine *they will* **enjoy p.** 8425
Pr 27:27 You will have p *of* goats' milk to feed you 1896
Jer 44:17 At that time *we* **had p** *of* food 8425
Joel 2:26 *You will* **have p to eat,** until you are full, 430+430
Mic 2:11 'I will prophesy for you p of wine NIH
Lk 12:19 "You have p of good things laid up *4498*
Jn 3:23 because there was **p of** water, *4498*
6:10 There was p of grass in that place, *4498*
Ac 14:17 *he* **provides** you **with p** of food *1855*
2Co 8:14 your p will supply what they need, *4354*
8:14 in turn their p will supply what you need. *4354*
Php 4:12 and I know what it is *to have* **p.** *4355*
4:12 whether **living in p** or in want. *4355*

PLIED (1) [PLY]

Lk 23:9 He p him with many questions, *2089*

PLIGHT (2)

2Ki 7:13 Their p will be like that of all the Israelites NIH
Ps 59:4 Arise to help me; look on my **p!** NIH

PLOT (41) [PLOTS, PLOTTED, PLOTTING]

Ge 33:19 the p *of* ground where he pitched his tent. 2754
2Ki 9:10 dogs will devour her on the **p of ground** 2750
9:21 at the **p of ground** *that had belonged* 2754
9:26 make you pay for it on this **p of ground,** 2754
9:26 then, pick him up and throw him on that **p,** 2754
9:36 On the **p of ground** at Jezreel 2750
9:37 be like refuse on the ground in the p 2750
Ne 4:15 of their p and that God had frustrated it, 6783
Est 2:22 But Mordecai found out about the p 1821
9:25 when **the p** came to the king's attention, 2023[S]
Ps 2:1 the nations conspire and the peoples p 2047
21:11 Though *they* p evil against you 5742
31:13 against me and p to take my life. 2372
35:4 may *those who* p my ruin be turned back 3108
37:12 The wicked p against the righteous 2372
38:12 all day long *they* p deception. 2047
64:6 *They* p injustice and say, 2924
83:3 *they* p against those you cherish. 3619
83:5 With one mind *they* p together; 3619
Pr 3:29 *Do* not p harm against your neighbor, 3086
12:20 in the hearts of *those who* p evil, 3086
14:22 Do not *those who* p evil go astray? 3086
24:2 for their hearts p violence, 2047
Isa 28:25 barley *in its* **p,** and spelt in its field? 6168
Jer 11:18 Because the LORD revealed their p to me, NIH
48:2 in Heshbon *men will* p her downfall: 3108
Eze 17:7 toward him from the p *where* it was planted 6870
17:10 wither away in the p *where* it grew?' " 6870
Da 11:24 *He will* p the overthrow of fortresses— 3108
Hos 7:15 but *they* p evil against me. 3108
Mic 2:1 to *those who* p evil on their beds! 7188
Na 1:9 Whatever *they* p against 3108
Zec 8:17 *do* not p evil **against** your neighbor, 928+3108+4222
Mk 3:6 the Pharisees went out and *began to* p *1443+5206*
Jn 4:5 near the **p of ground** Jacob had given *6005*
Ac 4:25 the nations rage and the peoples p in vain? *3509*
14:5 There was a **p afoot** among the Gentiles *3995*
20:3 Because the Jews made a p against him just *2101*
23:13 More than forty men were involved in this p *5350*
23:16 the son of Paul's sister heard of this **p,** *1909*
23:30 *of* a p to be carried out against the man, *2101*

PLOTS (12) [PLOT]

Ps 36:4 Even on his bed *he* p evil; 3108
52:2 Your tongue p destruction; 3108
Pr 6:14 *who* p evil with deceit in his heart— 3086
16:27 A scoundrel p evil, 4125
24:8 *He who* p evil will be known as a schemer. 3108
Isa 33:15 who stops his ears against p *of* murder 9048
Jer 18:23 you know, O LORD, all their p to kill me. 6783
La 3:60 all their p against me. 4742
3:61 all their p against me— 4742
Da 11:25 not be able to stand because of the p devised 4742
Na 1:11 has one come forth *who* p evil against 3108
Ac 20:19 although I was severely tested by the p of *2101*

PLOTTED (17) [PLOT]

Ge 37:18 *they* p to kill him. 5792
2Sa 21:5 the man who destroyed us and p against us 1948
1Ki 15:27 of the house of Issachar p against him, 8003
16:9 of half his chariots, p against him. 8003
16:16 in the camp heard that Zimri *had* **p** *against* 8003
2Ki 21:24 the people of the land killed all who *had* p 8003
2Ch 24:21 But *they* p against him, 8003
33:25 the people of the land killed all who *had* p 8003
Ne 4:8 They all p together to come and fight 8003
Est 9:24 *had* p against the Jews to destroy them 3108
Isa 7:5 and Remaliah's son *have* p your ruin, 3619
Jer 11:19 I did not realize that *they had* p against me, 3108+4742
49:30 "Nebuchadnezzar king of Babylon *has* p against you; 3619+6783
Hab 2:10 *You have* p the ruin of many peoples, 3619
Mt 12:14 But the Pharisees went out and p *3284+5206*
26:4 and *they* p to arrest Jesus in some sly way *5205*
Jn 11:53 So from that day on *they* p to take his life. *1086*

PLOTTING (5) [PLOT]

1Sa 23:9 David learned that Saul *was* p against him, 2021+3086+8288
Ne 6:6 that you and the Jews *are* p to revolt, 3108
Ps 56:5 they are always p to harm me. 4742
Pr 16:30 He who winks with his eye *is* p perversity; 3108
Eze 11:2 these are the men who *are* p evil 3108

PLOUGH (KJV) See PLOW

PLOW (8) [PLOWED, PLOWING, PLOWMAN, PLOWMEN, PLOWS, PLOWSHARES]

Dt 22:10 *Do* not p with an ox and a donkey 3086
1Sa 8:12 others to p his ground and reap his harvest, 3086
Job 4:8 *those who* p evil and those who sow trouble 3086
Pr 20:4 A sluggard *does* not p in season; 3086
Isa 28:24 does he p continually? NIH
Hos 10:11 I will drive Ephraim, Judah *must* **p,** 3086
Am 6:12 *Does one* p there with oxen? 3086
Lk 9:62 to the p and looks back is fit for service in *770*

PLOWED (8) [PLOW]

Dt 21:4 to a valley that *has* not **been p** or planted 6268
Jdg 14:18 "If *you had* not p with my heifer, 3086
Ps 129:3 Plowmen *have* p my back 3086
Jer 26:18 " 'Zion *will* **be p** like a field, 3086
Eze 36:9 *you will* **be p** and sown, 6268
Hos 10:4 up like poisonous weeds in a p field. 9439
12:11 be like piles of stones on a p field. 9439
Mic 3:12 Zion *will* **be p** like a field, 3086

PLOWING (6) [PLOW]

Ge 45:6 for the next five years there will not be p 3045
Ex 34:21 the **p season** and harvest you must rest. 3045
1Ki 19:19 He *was* **p** *with* twelve yoke of oxen, 3086
19:21 He burned the p equipment to cook 1330
Job 1:14 "The oxen were p and the donkeys 3086
Lk 17:7 "Suppose one of you had a servant p or *769*

PLOWMAN (2) [PLOW]

Am 9:13 "when the reaper will be overtaken by the p 3086
1Co 9:10 when the p plows and the thresher threshes, *769*

PLOWMEN (1) [PLOW]

Ps 129:3 **P** have plowed my back and 3086

PLOWS (3) [PLOW]

Ps 141:7 "As *one* p and breaks up the earth, 7114
Isa 28:24 When a farmer p for planting, 3086
1Co 9:10 the plowman p and the thresher threshes, *769*

PLOWSHARES (5) [PLOW]

1Sa 13:20 down to the Philistines to have their **p,** 4739
13:21 of a shekel for sharpening p and mattocks, 4739
Isa 2:4 into p and their spears into pruning hooks. 908
Joel 3:10 Beat your p into swords 908
Mic 4:3 into p and their spears into pruning hooks. 908

PLUCK (1) [PLUCKED]

Mk 9:47 And if your eye causes you to sin, **p** it **out.** *1675*

PLUCKED (1) [PLUCK]

Ge 8:11 there in its beak was a **freshly p** olive leaf! 3273

PLUMAGE (2)

Eze 17:3 and full p of varied colors came 5681
17:7 with powerful wings and full **p.** 5681

PLUMB (8)

2Ki 21:13 and the **p line** *used against* the house 5487
Isa 28:17 and righteousness the **p line;** 5487
34:11 the measuring line of chaos and the **p line** 74

Am 7: 7 by a wall that had been built **true to p,** 643
7: 7 with a **p line** in his hand. 643
7: 8 "A **p line,"** I replied. 643
7: 8 a **p line** among my people Israel; 643
Zec 4:10 Men will rejoice when they see the **p line** 74+974

PLUNDER (105) [PLUNDERED, PLUNDERERS]

Ge 34:29 **taking as p** everything in the houses. 1024
49:27 in the evening he divides the **p."** 8965
Ex 3:22 And so *you will* **p** the Egyptians." 5911
Nu 14: 3 Our wives and children will be taken as **p.** 1020
14:31 that you said would be taken as **p,** 1020
31: 9 **took** all the Midianite herds, flocks and goods **as p.** 1024
31:11 They took all the **p** and spoils, 8965
31:12 and **p** to Moses and Eleazar the priest and 8965
31:32 The **p** remaining from the spoils that 1020
31:53 Each soldier *had* **taken p** for himself. 1024
Dt 2:35 But the livestock and the **p** *from* 8965
3: 7 and the **p** *from* their cities we carried off 8965
13:16 Gather all the **p** *of* the town into the middle 8965
13:16 and completely burn the town and all its **p** 8965
20:14 you may take these as **p** for yourselves. 8965
20:14 the **p** the LORD your God gives you 8965
Jos 7:21 in the **p** a beautiful robe from Babylonia, 8965
8: 2 that you may carry off their **p** and livestock 8965
8:27 for themselves the livestock and **p** 8965
11:14 for themselves all the **p** and livestock 8965
22: 8 and divide with your brothers the **p** 8965
Jdg 5:19 but they carried off no silver, no **p.** 1299
5:30 colorful garments as **p** for Sisera, 8965
5:30 garments for my neck—all this as **p?'** 8965
8:24 an earring from your **share of** the **p."** 8965
8:25 each man threw a ring from his **p** onto it. 8965
1Sa 14:30 of the **p** they took *from* their enemies. 8965
14:32 They pounced on the **p** and, taking sheep, 8965
14:36 after the Philistines by night and **p** them 1024
15:19 Why did you pounce on the **p** and do evil 8965
15:21 took sheep and cattle from the **p,** 8965
30:16 the great amount of **p** they had taken from 8965
30:19 **p** or anything else they had taken. 8965
30:20 saying, "This is David's **p."** 8965
30:22 not share with them the **p** we recovered. 8965
30:26 he sent some of the **p** to the elders of Judah, 8965
30:26 "Here is a present for you from the **p** *of* 8965
2Sa 3:22 and brought with them a great deal of **p.** 8965
8:12 the **p** taken from Hadadezer son of Rehob, 8965
12:30 He took a great quantity of **p** from the city 8965
2Ki 3:23 Now to the **p,** Moab!" 8965
1Ch 20: 2 He took a great quantity of **p** from the city 8965
26:27 of the **p** taken in battle they dedicated for 8965
2Ch 14:13 of Judah carried off a large amount of **p.** 8965
15:11 from the **p** they had brought back. 8965
20:25 and his men went to carry off their **p,** 8965
20:25 There was so much **p** that it took three days 8965
24:23 the **p** to their king in Damascus. 8965
25:13 and carried off great quantities of **p.** 1023
28: 8 They also took a great deal of **p,** 8965
28:14 and **p** in the presence of the officials and all 1023
28:15 the **p** they clothed all who were naked. 8965
Ne 4: 4 Give them over as **p** in a land of captivity. 1023
Est 3:13 the month of Adar, and to **p** their goods. 1024
8:11 and to **p** the property of their enemies. 1024
9:10 But they did not lay their hands on the **p.** 1023
9:15 but they did not lay their hands on the **p.** 1023
9:16 but did not lay their hands on the **p.** 1023
Ps 68:12 in the camps men divide the **p.** 8965
109:11 *may* strangers **p** the fruits of his labor. 1024
Pr 1:13 and fill our houses with **p;** 8965
12:12 The wicked desire the **p** *of* evil men, 5179
16:19 among the oppressed than to share **p** with 8965
22:23 and *will* **p** those who plunder them. 5883+7693
22:23 and will plunder *those who* **p** them. 7693
Isa 3:14 the **p** *from* the poor is in your houses. 1611
8: 4 and the **p** *of* Samaria will be carried off by 8965
9: 3 as men rejoice when dividing the **p.** 8965
10: 6 to seize loot and snatch **p,** 1020
11:14 together *they will* **p** the people to the east. 1024
17:14 the lot of *those who* **p** us. 1024
33: 4 Your **p,** O nations, is harvested as 8965
33:23 and even the lame will carry off **p.** 1020
42:22 They have become **p,** with no one 1020
49:24 Can **p** be taken from warriors, 4917
49:25 and **p** retrieved from the fierce; 4917
Jer 2:14 Why then has he become **p?** 1020
15:13 and your treasures I will give as **p,** 1020
17: 3 and all your treasures I will give away as **p,** 1020
20: 5 They will take it away *as* **p** and carry it off 1024
30:16 *Those who* **p** you will be plundered; 9116
49:32 Their camels will become **p,** 1020
50:10 all *who* **p** her will have their fill," 8964
Eze 7:21 I will hand it all over as **p** to foreigners and 1020
23:46 and give them over to terror and **p.** 1020
25: 7 and give you as **p** to the nations. 1020
26: 5 She will become **p** for the nations, 1020
26:12 *They will* **p** your wealth 8964
29:19 and **p** the land as pay for his army. 1020+1024
36: 5 so that they might **p** its pastureland.' 1020
38:12 I *will* **p** and loot and turn my hand 8964+8965
38:13 "Have you come to **p?** 8964+8965
38:13 and goods and to seize much **p?"'** 8965
39:10 And *they will* **p** those who plundered them 8964
Da 11:24 He will distribute **p,** loot and wealth 1023
Am 3:10 "who hoard **p** and loot in their fortresses." 2805
3:11 and **p** your fortresses." 1024
Na 2: 9 **P** the silver! Plunder the gold! 1024
2: 9 **P** the gold! The supply is endless, 1024
3: 1 full of lies, full of **p,** never without victims! 7294
Hab 2: 8 the peoples who are left *will* **p** you. 8964
Zep 2: 9 The remnant of my people *will* **p** them; 1024
Zec 2: 9 so that their slaves will **p** them. 8965
14: 1 day of the LORD is coming when your **p** will 8965
Heb 7: 4 Abraham gave him a tenth of the **p!** *215*

PLUNDERED (27) [PLUNDER]

Ex 12:36 so *they* **p** the Egyptians. 5911
Jdg 2:14 handed them over to raiders *who* **p** them. 9116
1Sa 14:48 from the hands of *those who had* **p** them. 9115
17:53 *they* **p** their camp. 9116
2Ki 7:16 Then the people went out and **p** the camp 1024
21:14 They will be looted and **p** by all their foes, 5468
2Ch 14:14 *They* **p** all these villages, 1024
Ps 44:10 and our adversaries *have* **p** us. 9115
76: 5 Valiant men *lie* **p,** 8964
89:41 All who pass by *have* **p** him; 9116
Isa 10:13 *I* **p** their treasures; 9115
24: 3 completely laid waste and **totally p.** 1024+1024
42:22 But this is a people **p** and looted, 1024
Jer 30:16 Those who plunder you will be **p;** 5468
50:10 So Babylonia will be **p;** 8965
50:37 *They will* **be p.** 1024
Eze 34: 8 so has been **p** and has become food for all 1020
34:22 and they will no longer be **p.** 1020
34:28 They will no longer be **p** by the nations, 1020
36: 4 that have been **p** and ridiculed by the rest of 1020
39:10 And they will plunder *those who* **p** them 8964
Da 11:33 by the sword or be burned or captured or **p.** 1023
Hos 13:15 His storehouse *will be* **p** 9115
Na 2:10 She is pillaged, **p,** stripped! 4433
Hab 2: 8 Because you *have* **p** many nations, 8964
Zep 1:13 Their wealth will be **p,** 5468
Zec 2: 8 against the nations that *have* **p** you— 8964

PLUNDERERS (2) [PLUNDER]

2Ki 17:20 and gave them into the hands of **p,** 9115
Isa 42:24 and Israel to the **p?** 1024

PLUNGE (6) [PLUNGED]

1Sa 2:14 *He would* **p** it into the pan or kettle 5782
Job 9:31 *you would* **p** me into a slime pit so that 3188
Ps 68:23 that *you may* **p** your feet in the blood 8175
Joel 2: 8 *They* **p** through defenses 5877
1Ti 6: 9 and harmful desires that **p** men into ruin *1112*
1Pe 4: 4 They think it strange that you *do* not **p with** *5340*

PLUNGED (4) [PLUNGE]

Jdg 3:21 drew the sword from his right thigh and **p** it 9546
2Sa 18:14 and **p** them into Absalom's heart 9546
20:10 and Joab **p** it into his belly, 5782
Rev 16:10 and his kingdom *was* **p into** darkness. *1181*

PLUS (2)

Eze 45:12 Twenty shekels **p** twenty-five shekels plus fifteen shekels equal one mina. NIH
45:12 Twenty shekels plus twenty-five shekels **p** fifteen shekels equal one mina. NIH

PLY (1) [PLIED]

Isa 23:17 as a prostitute and *will* **p her trade** with all 2388

POCHERETH (KJV) See POKERETH HAZZEBAIM

POCKET (1)

1Sa 25:29 as from the **p** *of* a sling. 4090

PODS (2)

2Ki 6:25 a quarter of a cab of **seed p** for five shekels. 1807
Lk 15:16 He longed to fill his stomach with the **p** *3044*

POETS (2)

Nu 21:27 That is why the **p** say: 5439
Ac 17:28 As some *of* your own **p** have said, *4475*

POINT (34) [POINTED, POINTING, POINTS]

Jdg 3:25 They waited **to the p** of embarrassment, 6330
1Sa 7:11 along the way to a **p** below Beth Car. NIH
17: 7 and its iron **p** weighed six hundred shekels. 4259
2Sa 13: 2 Amnon became frustrated **to the p of** 4200
2Ki 19: 3 to the **p of birth** and there is no strength 5402
20: 1 and was **at the p** of death. 4200
2Ch 32:24 and was **at the p** of death. 6330
Ne 3:16 made repairs up to a **p** opposite the tombs NIH
3:19 a **p** facing the ascent to the armory as far as NIH
3:26 a **p** opposite the Water Gate toward the east NIH
Job 20:25 the **gleaming p** out of his liver. 1398
Pr 9: 3 calls from the **highest p** *of* the city. 1726+5294
9:14 on a seat at the **highest p** *of* the city, 5294
Isa 37: 3 to the **p of birth** and there is no strength 5402
38: 1 and was **at the p** of death. 4200
Jer 17: 1 inscribed with a flint **p,** 7632
Eze 47:20 the boundary to a **p** opposite Lebo Hamath. NIH
Mt 4: 5 and had him stand on the **highest p** of *4762*
26:38 with sorrow **to the p** of death. *2401*
Mk 14:34 with sorrow **to the p** of death," *2401*
Lk 4: 9 and had him stand on the **highest p** of *4762*
Jn 7:25 **At that p** some of the people *4036*
Ac 26:24 **At this p** Festus interrupted Paul's defense. *1254+4047*
Ro 2: 1 for at **whatever** *p* you judge the other, *AIT*
1Co 9: 8 **from a human p of view?** *476+2848*
2Co 5:16 **from a worldly p of view.** *2848+4922*
7:11 At **every** *p* you have proved yourselves to *AIT*
Php 3:15 And if on **some p** you think differently, *5516*
1Ti 4: 6 *If you* **p** these things **out** to the brothers, *5719*
2Ti 2: 9 am suffering **even to the p of** being chained *3588*
Heb 8: 1 **The p** of what we are saying **is this:** *3049*
12: 4 you have not yet resisted **to the p of** shedding your blood. *3588*
Jas 2:10 at just **one** *p* is guilty of breaking all of it. *AIT*
Rev 2:10 Be faithful, **even to the p of** death, *948*

POINTED (1) [POINT]

Jn 4:44 (Now Jesus himself *had* **p out** that *3455*

POINTING (3) [POINT]

Isa 58: 9 *with the* **p** finger and malicious talk, 8938
Mt 12:49 **P** to his disciples, he said, *899+1753+3836+5931*
1Pe 1:11 to which the Spirit of Christ in them *was* **p** *1317*

POINTS (3) [POINT]

Ne 4:13 the people behind the lowest **p** of the wall 5226
Ac 25:19 they had some **p of dispute** with him *2427*
Ro 15:15 I have written you quite boldly on **some p,** *608+3538*

POISED (2)

Job 15:24 like a king **p** to attack, 6969
37:16 Do you know how the clouds **hang p,** 5146

POISON (10) [POISONED, POISONOUS, POISONS]

Dt 29:18 among you that produces such bitter **p.** 8032
32:32 Their grapes are filled with **p,** 8032
32:33 the deadly **p** *of* cobras. 8032
Job 6: 4 my spirit drinks in their **p;** 2779
20:16 He will suck the **p** *of* serpents; 8032
Ps 140: 3 the **p** *of* vipers is on their lips. 2779
Am 6:12 But you have turned justice into **p** and 8032
Mk 16:18 and when they drink **deadly p,** *2503+5516*
Ro 3:13 "The **p** of vipers is on their lips." *2675*
Jas 3: 8 It is a restless evil, full *of* deadly **p.** *2675*

POISONED (4) [POISON]

Jer 8:14 to perish and given us **p** water to drink, 8032
9:15 people eat bitter food and drink **p** water. 8032
23:15 make them eat bitter food and drink **p** water, 8032
Ac 14: 2 and **p** their minds against the brothers. *2808*

POISONOUS (1) [POISON]

Hos 10: 4 therefore lawsuits spring up like **p weeds** in 8032

POISONS (1) [POISON]

Pr 23:32 In the end it bites like a snake and **p** like 7301

POKERETH-HAZZEBAIM (2)

Ezr 2:57 Shephatiah, Hattil, **P** and Ami 7097
Ne 7:59 Shephatiah, Hattil, **P** and Amon 7097

POLE (20) [POLES]

Nu 13:23 of them carried it on a **p** between them, 4573
21: 8 "Make a snake and put it up on a **p;** 5812
21: 9 a bronze snake and put it up on a **p.** 5812
Dt 16:21 Do not set up any wooden **Asherah p** 895
Jdg 6:25 and cut down the **Asherah p** beside it. 895
6:26 the wood of the **Asherah p** that you cut 895
6:28 with the **Asherah p** beside it cut down and 895
6:30 and cut down the **Asherah p** beside it." 895
1Ki 15:13 she had made a repulsive **Asherah p.** 895
15:13 Asa cut the **p** down and burned it in 5145[S]
16:33 Ahab also made an **Asherah p** and did more 895
2Ki 6: 2 where each of us can get a **p;** 7771
13: 6 **Asherah p** remained standing in Samaria. 895
17:16 and an **Asherah p.** 895
21: 3 to Baal and made an **Asherah p,** 895
21: 7 the carved **Asherah p** he had made 895
23: 6 the **Asherah p** from the temple of the LORD 895
23:15 and burned the **Asherah p** also. 895
2Ch 15:16 she had made a repulsive **Asherah p.** 895
15:16 Asa cut the **p** down, broke it up and 5145[S]

POLES (56) [POLE]

Ex 25:13 Then make **p** *of* acacia wood 964
25:14 the **p** into the rings on the sides of the chest 964
25:15 The **p** are to remain in the rings of this ark; 964
25:27 to the rim to hold the **p** used in carrying 964
25:28 Make the **p** of acacia wood, 964
27: 6 Make **p** *of* acacia wood for the altar 964
27: 7 The **p** are to be inserted into the rings 964
30: 4 to hold the **p** used to carry it. 964
30: 5 the **p** of acacia wood and overlay them 964
34:13 and cut down their **Asherah p.** 895
35:12 the ark with its **p** and the atonement cover 964

Ex 35:13 with its **p** and all its articles and the bread 964
35:15 of incense with its **p**, the anointing oil and 964
35:16 its **p** and all its utensils; 964
37: 4 Then he made **p** *of* acacia wood 964
37: 5 the **p** into the rings on the sides of the ark 964
37:14 to the rim to hold the **p** used in carrying 964
37:15 The **p** for carrying the table were made 964
37:27 to hold the **p** used to carry it. 964
37:28 the **p** *of* acacia wood and overlaid them 964
38: 5 They cast bronze rings to hold the **p** for 964
38: 6 the **p** of acacia wood and overlaid them 964
38: 7 the **p** into the rings so they would be on 964
39:35 the ark of the Testimony with its **p** and 964
39:39 its **p** and all its utensils; 964
40:20 attached the **p** to the ark and put 964
Nu 4: 6 a cloth of solid blue over that and put the **p** 964
4: 8 that with hides of sea cows and put its **p** 964
4:11 that with hides of sea cows and put its **p** 964
4:14 of hides of sea cows and put its **p** in place. 964
Dt 7: 5 cut down their **Asherah p** and burn their 895
12: 3 and burn their **Asherah p** in the fire; 895
1Ki 8: 7 the ark and its **carrying p.** 964
8: 8 These **p** were so long that their ends could 964
14:15 the LORD to anger by making **Asherah p.** 895
14:23 and **Asherah p** on every high hill and 895
2Ki 17:10 They set up sacred stones and **Asherah p** 895
18: 4 and cut down the **Asherah p.** 895
23:14 down the **Asherah p** and covered the sites 895
1Ch 15:15 ark of God with the **p** on their shoulders, 4574
2Ch 5: 8 and covered the ark and its **carrying p.** 964
5: 9 These **p** were so long that their ends, 964
14: 3 and cut down the **Asherah p.** 895
17: 6 the high places and the **Asherah p** 895
19: 3 for you have rid the land of the **Asherah p** 895
24:18 and worshiped **Asherah p** and idols. 895
31: 1 and cut down the **Asherah p.** 895
33: 3 to the Baals and made **Asherah p.** 895
33:19 and set up **Asherah p** and idols 895
34: 3 **Asherah p**, carved idols and cast images. 895
34: 4 and smashed the **Asherah p**, 895
34: 7 he tore down the altars and the **Asherah p** 895
Isa 17: 8 for the **Asherah p** and the incense altars 895
27: 9 no **Asherah p** or incense altars will be left 895
Jer 17: 2 and **Asherah p** beside the spreading trees 895
Mic 5:14 uproot from among you your **Asherah p** 895

POLISH (1) [POLISHED]

Jer 46: 4 **P** your spears, put on your armor! 5347

POLISHED (9) [POLISH]

2Ch 4:16 the temple of the LORD were of **p** bronze. 5347
Ezr 8:27 darics, and two fine articles of **p** bronze, 7410
SS 5:14 like **p** ivory decorated with sapphires. 6952
Isa 49: 2 a **p** arrow and concealed me in his quiver. 1406
Eze 21: 9 " 'A sword, a sword, sharpened and **p**— 5307
21:10 **p** to flash like lightning! 5307
21:11 " 'The sword is appointed to *be* **p**, 5307
21:11 it is sharpened and **p**, 5307
21:28 **p** to consume and to flash like lightning! 5307

POLLUTE (2) [POLLUTED, POLLUTES]

Nu 35:33 " '*Do* not **p** the land where you are. 2866
Jude 1: 8 these dreamers **p** their own bodies, *3620*

POLLUTED (4) [POLLUTE]

Ezr 9:11 a land **p** by the corruption of its peoples. 5614
Pr 25:26 a **p** well is a righteous man who gives way 8845
Ac 15:20 telling them to abstain from food **p** by idols, *246*
Jas 1:27 to keep oneself **from being p** by the world. *834*

POLLUTES (1) [POLLUTE]

Nu 35:33 Bloodshed **p** the land, 2866

POLLUX (1)

Ac 28:11 the **twin gods Castor and P.** *1483*

POMEGRANATE (5) [POMEGRANATES]

1Sa 14: 2 on the outskirts of Gibeah under a **p tree** 8232
SS 4: 3 behind your veil are like the halves of a **p.** 8232
6: 7 behind your veil are like the halves of a **p.** 8232
Joel 1:12 the **p**, the palm and the apple tree— 8232
Hag 2:19 the **p** and the olive tree have 8232

POMEGRANATES (24) [POMEGRANATE]

Ex 28:33 Make **p** *of* blue, purple and scarlet yarn 8232
28:34 and the **p** are to alternate around the hem of 8232
39:24 made **p** *of* blue, purple and scarlet yarn 8232
39:25 around the hem between the **p.** 8232
39:26 and **p** alternated around the hem of the robe 8232
Nu 13:23 along with some **p** and figs. 8232
20: 5 It has no grain or figs, grapevines or **p.** 8232
Dt 8: 8 vines and fig trees, **p**, olive oil and honey; 8232
1Ki 7:18 He made **p** in two rows encircling each 8232
7:20 were the two hundred **p** in rows all around. 8232
7:42 the four hundred **p** for the two sets 8232
7:42 for the two sets of network (two rows of **p** 8232
2Ki 25:17 with a network and **p** of bronze all around. 8232
2Ch 3:16 also made a hundred **p** and attached them 8232
4:13 the four hundred **p** for the two sets 8232
4:13 for the two sets of network (two rows of **p** 8232
SS 4:13 an orchard of **p** with choice fruits, 8232
6:11 to see if the vines had budded or the **p** were 8232
7:12 and if the **p** are in bloom— 8232
8: 2 spiced wine to drink, the nectar of my **p.** 8232
Jer 52:22 with a network and **p** of bronze all around. 8232
52:22 The other pillar, with its **p**, was similar. 8232
52:23 There were ninety-six **p** on the sides; 8232
52:23 of **p** above the surrounding network was 8232

POMP (5)

Isa 8: 7 the king of Assyria with all his **p.** 3883
10:16 under his **p** a fire will be kindled like 3883
14:11 All your **p** has been brought down to 1454
21:16 all the **p** *of* Kedar will come to an end. 3883
Ac 25:23 with great **p** and entered the audience room *5752*

PONDER (4) [PONDERED, PONDERS]

Ps 64: 9 the works of God and **p** what he has done. 8505
119:95 but *I will* **p** your statutes. 1067
Isa 14:16 stare at you, *they* **p** your fate: 1067
33:18 In your thoughts *you will* **p** the former terror 2047

PONDERED (5) [PONDER]

Ne 5: 7 I **p** them in my mind and then accused 4888
Ps 111: 2 *they* **are p** by all who delight in them. 2011
Ecc 12: 9 *He* **p** and searched out and set 264
Isa 57:11 and have neither remembered me nor **p** this 8492
Lk 2:19 up all these things and **p** them in her heart. *5202*

PONDERS (1) [PONDER]

Isa 57: 1 and no one **p** it in his heart; 8492

PONDS (2)

Ex 7:19 over the **p** and all the reservoirs'— 106
8: 5 over the streams and canals and **p**, 106

PONTIUS (3)

Lk 3: 1 when **P** Pilate was governor of Judea, *4508*
Ac 4:27 and **P** Pilate met together with the Gentiles *4508*
1Ti 6:13 before **P** Pilate made the good confession, *4508*

PONTUS (3)

Ac 2: 9 Judea and Cappadocia, **P** and Asia, *4509*
18: 2 a Jew named Aquila, a native **of P**, *4507*
1Pe 1: 1 scattered throughout **P**, Galatia, *4509*

POOL (20) [POOLS]

2Sa 2:13 and met them at the **p** *of* Gibeon. 1391
2:13 down on one side of the **p** and one group 1391
4:12 and hung the bodies by the **p** in Hebron. 1391
1Ki 22:38 They washed the chariot at a **p** *in* Samaria 1391
2Ki 18:17 at the aqueduct of the Upper **P**, 1391
20:20 and how he made the **p** and the tunnel 1391
Ne 2:14 the Fountain Gate and the King's **P**, 1391
3:15 also repaired the wall of the **P** *of* Siloam, 1391
3:16 the artificial **p** and the House of the Heroes. 1391
Ps 114: 8 who turned the rock into a **p**, 106+4784
Isa 7: 3 at the end of the aqueduct of the Upper **P**, 1391
22: 9 you stored up water in the Lower **P.** 1391
22:11 the two walls for the water of the Old **P**, 1391
35: 7 The burning sand will become a **p**, 106
36: 2 at the aqueduct of the Upper **P**, 1391
Jer 41:12 They caught up with him near the great **p** 4784
Na 2: 8 Nineveh is like a **p**, 1391+4784
Jn 5: 2 in Jerusalem near the Sheep Gate a **p**, *3148*
5: 7 "I have no one to help me into the **p** when *3148*
9: 7 the **P** of Siloam" (this word means Sent). *3148*

POOLS (6) [POOL]

Dt 8: 7 a land with streams and **p** of water, 6524
Ps 84: 6 the autumn rains also cover it with **p.** 1391
107:35 He turned the desert into **p** *of* water and 106
SS 7: 4 Your eyes are the **p** of Heshbon by the gate 1391
Isa 41:18 I will turn the desert into **p** *of* water, 106
42:15 into islands and dry up the **p.** 106

POOR (177) [IMPOVERISHED, POOREST, POVERTY]

Ex 23: 3 and do not show favoritism to a **p** *man* 1924
23: 6 "Do not deny justice to your **p** *people* 36
23:11 Then the **p** *among* your people may get food 36
30:15 a half shekel and the **p** are not to give less 1924
Lev 14:21 however, he is **p** and cannot afford these, 1924
19:10 Leave them for the **p** and the alien. 6714
19:15 do not show partiality to the **p** or favoritism 1924
23:22 Leave them for the **p** and the alien. 6714
25:25 " 'If one of your countrymen *becomes* **p** 4575
25:35 " 'If one of your countrymen *becomes* **p** 4575
25:39 of your countrymen *becomes* **p** among you 4575
25:47 and one of your countrymen *becomes* **p** 4575
27: 8 If anyone making the vow *is* too **p to pay** 4575
Nu 13:20 Is it fertile or **p**? 8136
Dt 15: 4 However, there should be no **p** among you, 36
15: 7 If there is a **p** *man* among your brothers 36
15: 7 or tightfisted toward your **p** brother. 36
15:11 There will always be **p** *people* in the land. 36
15:11 and toward the **p** and needy in your land. 6714
24:12 If the man is **p**, 6714
24:14 not take advantage of a hired man who is **p** 6714
24:15 because he is **p** and is counting on it. 6714
Ru 3:10 after the younger men, whether rich or **p.** 1924
1Sa 2: 8 raises the **p** from the dust and lifts the needy 1924
18:23 I'm only a **p** man and little known." 8133
2Sa 12: 1 one rich and the other **p.** 8133
12: 3 **p** *man* had nothing except one little ewe lamb he had bought. 8133
12: 4 that belonged to the **p** man and prepared it 8133
Est 9:22 of food to one another and gifts to the **p.** 36
Job 5:16 **p** have hope, and injustice shuts its mouth. 1924
20:10 His children must make amends to the **p**; 1924
20:19 the **p** and left them destitute; 1924
24: 4 the needy from the path and force all the **p** 6714
24: 5 the **p** go about their labor of foraging food; NIH
24: 9 the infant of the **p** is seized for a debt. 6714
24:14 murderer rises up and kills the **p** and needy; 6714
29:12 because I rescued the **p** who cried for help, 6714
30:25 Has not my soul grieved for the **p**? 36
31:16 "If I have denied the desires of the **p** or let 1924
34:19 and does not favor the rich over the **p**, 1924
34:28 They caused the cry of the **p** to come 1924
Ps 14: 6 You evildoers frustrate the plans of the **p**, 6714
22:26 The **p** will eat and be satisfied; 6705
34: 6 This **p** *man* called, and the LORD heard him; 6714
35:10 You rescue the **p** from those too strong 6714
35:10 the **p** and needy from those who rob them." 6714
37:14 the bow to bring down the **p** and needy, 6714
40:17 Yet I am **p** and needy; 6714
49: 2 both low and high, rich and **p** alike: 36
68:10 O God, you provided for the **p.** 6714
69:32 The **p** will see and be glad— 6705
70: 5 Yet I am **p** and needy; 6714
74:21 may the **p** and needy praise your name. 6714
82: 3 maintain the rights of the **p** and oppressed. 6714
86: 1 and answer me, for I am **p** and needy. 6714
109:16 the **p** and the needy and the brokenhearted. 6714
109:22 For I am **p** and needy, 6714
112: 9 He has scattered abroad his gifts to the **p**, 36
113: 7 raises the **p** from the dust and lifts the needy 1924
132:15 her **p** will I satisfy with food. 36
140:12 the **p** and upholds the cause of the needy. 6714
Pr 10: 4 Lazy hands make *a man* **p**, 8133
10:15 but poverty is the ruin of the **p.** 1924
13: 7 *another* **pretends to be p**, 8133
13: 8 but a **p** *man* hears no threat. 8133
13:23 **p** *man's* field may produce abundant food, 8133
14:20 The **p** are shunned even by their neighbors, 8133
14:31 He who oppresses the **p** shows contempt 1924
17: 5 the **p** shows contempt for their Maker; 8133
18:23 A **p** *man* pleads for mercy, 8133
19: 1 a **p** *man* whose walk is blameless than 8133
19: 4 but a **p** *man's* friend deserts him. 1924
19: 7 A **p** *man* is shunned by all his relatives— 8133
19:17 He who is kind to the **p** lends to the LORD, 1924
19:22 better *to be* **p** than a liar. 8133
20:13 Do not love sleep or *you will* **grow p**; 3769
21:13 If a man shuts his ears to the cry of the **p**, 1924
21:17 He who loves pleasure will become **p**; 4728
22: 2 Rich and **p** have this in common: 8133
22: 7 The rich rule over the **p**, 8133
22: 9 for he shares his food with the **p.** 1924
22:16 who oppresses the **p** to increase his wealth 1924
22:22 Do not exploit the **p** because they are poor 1924
22:22 Do not exploit the poor because they are **p** 1924
23:21 for drunkards and gluttons *become* **p**, 3769
28: 3 A ruler who oppresses the **p** is like 1924
28: 6 a **p** *man* whose walk is blameless than 8133
28: 8 who will be kind to the **p.** 1924
28:11 but a **p** *man* who has discernment sees 1924
28:27 He who gives to the **p** will lack nothing, 8133
29: 7 The righteous care about justice for the **p**, 1924
29:13 The **p** *man* and the oppressor have this 8133
29:14 If a king judges the **p** with fairness, 1924
30: 9 Or *I may* **become p** and steal, 3769
30:14 with knives to devour the **p** from the earth, 6714
31: 9 defend the rights of the **p** and needy." 6714
31:20 to the **p** and extends her hands to the needy. 6714
Ecc 4:13 Better a **p** but wise youth than an old 5014
5: 8 If you see the **p** oppressed in a district, 8133
6: 8 What does a **p** *man* gain by knowing how 6714
9:15 there lived in that city a man **p** but wise, 5014
9:15 But nobody remembered that **p** man. 5014
9:16 But the **p** *man's* wisdom is despised, 5014
Isa 3:14 the plunder from the **p** is in your houses. 6714
3:15 and grinding the faces of the **p**?" 6714
10: 2 to deprive the **p** of their rights 1924
10:30 O Laishah! **P** Anathoth! 6714
11: 4 with justice he will give decisions for the **p** 6705
14:30 The **poorest of the p** will find pasture, 1147+1924
25: 4 You have been a refuge for the **p**, 1924
26: 6 feet of the oppressed, the footsteps of the **p.** 1924
32: 7 he makes up evil schemes to destroy the **p** 6714
40:20 A *man* **too p** *to* present such an offering 6123
41:17 "The **p** and needy search for water, 6714
58: 7 the hungry and to provide the **p** wanderer 6714
61: 1 to preach good news to the **p.** 6705
Jer 2:34 the lifeblood of the innocent **p**, 36
5: 4 I thought, "These are only the **p**; 1924
5:28 they do not defend the rights of the **p.** 36
22:16 He defended the cause of the **p** and needy, 6714
24: 2 the other basket had very **p** figs, 8273
24: 3 **p** *ones* are so bad they cannot be eaten." 8273
24: 8 " 'But like the **p** figs, 8273
29:17 and I will make them like **p** figs that are 9135
39:10 in the land of Judah some of the **p** people, 1924
Eze 16:49 they did not help the **p** and needy. 6714
18:12 He oppresses the **p** and needy. 6714
22:29 they oppress the **p** and needy and mistreat 6714
Am 2: 7 They trample on the heads of the **p** as upon 1924
4: 1 you women who oppress the **p** and crush 1924

Am 5:11 You trample on the **p** and force him 1924
5:12 you deprive the **p** of justice in the courts. 36
8: 4 and do away with the **p** *of* the land, 6714
8: 6 buying the **p** with silver and the needy for 1924
Zec 7:10 the fatherless, the alien or the **p.** 6714
Mt 5: 3 "Blessed are the **p** in spirit, *4777*
11: 5 and the good news is preached to the **p.** *4777*
19:21 go, sell your possessions and give *to* the **p,** *4777*
26: 9 a high price and the money given *to* the **p."** *4777*
26:11 The **p** you will always have with you, *4777*
Mk 10:21 sell everything you have and give *to* the **p,** *4777*
12:42 But a **p** widow came and put two very small *4777*
12:43 this **p** widow has put more into *4777*
14: 5 and the money given *to* the **p."** *4777*
14: 7 The **p** you will always have with you, *4777*
Lk 4:18 to preach good news *to* the **p.** *4777*
6:20 "Blessed are you who are **p,** *4777*
7:22 and the good news is preached to the **p.** *4777*
11:41 **give** what is inside [the dish] **to the p,** *1443+1797*
12:33 Sell your possessions and **give to the p.** *1443+1797*
14:13 But when you give a banquet, invite the **p,** *4777*
14:21 and alleys of the town and bring in the **p,** *4777*
18:22 Sell everything you have and give *to* the **p,** *4777*
19: 8 now I give half of my possessions *to* the **p,** *4777*
21: 2 He also saw a **p** widow put in two very small *4293*
21: 3 "this **p** widow has put in more than all *4777*
Jn 12: 5 and the money given *to* the **p?** *4777*
12: 6 not say this because he cared about the **p** *4777*
12: 8 You will always have the **p** among you, *4777*
13:29 or to give something *to* the **p.** *4777*
Ac 9:36 always doing good and **helping the p.** *1797+4472*
10: 4 and **gifts to the p** have come up as *1797*
10:31 and remembered your **gifts to the p.** *1797*
24:17 to bring my people **gifts for the p** and *1797*
Ro 15:26 a contribution for the **p** among the saints *4777*
1Co 13: 3 If *I* **give** all I possess **to the p** *6039*
13:12 Now we see but a **p** reflection as in *141+1877*
2Co 6:10 **p,** yet making many rich; *4777*
8: 9 yet for your sakes *he became* **p,** *4776*
9: 9 "He has scattered abroad his gifts *to* the **p;** *4288*
Gal 2:10 that we should continue to remember the **p,** *4777*
Jas 2: 2 a **p** *man* in shabby clothes also comes in. *4777*
2: 3 but say *to* the **p** *man,* *4777*
2: 5 not God chosen those who are **p** in the eyes *4777*
2: 6 But you have insulted the **p.** *4777*
Rev 3:17 pitiful, **p,** blind and naked. *4777*
13:16 small and great, rich and **p,** free and slave, *4777*

POOREST (6) [POOR]

2Ki 24:14 Only the **p** people of the land were left. 1930
25:12 behind some of the **p** *people of* the land 1930
Isa 14:30 The **p of the poor** will find pasture, 1147+1924
Jer 40: 7 and children who were the **p** *in* the land 1930
52:15 of the **p** people and those who remained in 1930
52:16 the rest of the **p** *people of* the land to work 1930

POPLAR (3) [POPLARS]

Ge 30:37 however, took fresh-cut branches from **p,** 4242
Isa 44: 4 like **p trees** by flowing streams. 6857
Hos 4:13 under oak, **p** and terebinth, 4242

POPLARS (4) [POPLAR]

Lev 23:40 and palm fronds, leafy branches and **p,** 5707+6857
Job 40:22 the **p** *by* the stream surround him. 6857
Ps 137: 2 There on the **p** we hung our harps, 6857
Isa 15: 7 over the Ravine of the **P.** 6857

POPULACE (1) [POPULATION]

2Ki 25:11 the rest of the **p** and those who had gone 2162

POPULATION (1) [POPULACE]

Pr 14:28 A large **p** is a king's glory, 6639

POPULOUS (KJV) See NUMEROUS

PORATHA (1)

Est 9: 8 **P,** Adalia, Aridatha, 7054

PORCH (2) [PORTICO, PORTICOES]

Jdg 3:23 Then Ehud went out to the **p;** 4997
Joel 2:17 weep between the **temple p** and the altar. 395

PORCIUS (1) [FESTUS]

Ac 24:27 Felix was succeeded by **P** Festus, *4517*

PORPHYRY (1)

Est 1: 6 and silver on a mosaic pavement of **p,** 985

PORT (1)

Jnh 1: 3 where he found a ship bound for **that p.** 9576[S]

PORTENT (2)

Ps 71: 7 I have become like a **p** to many, 4603
Isa 20: 3 as a sign and **p** against Egypt and Cush, 4603

PORTICO (44) [PORCH]

1Ki 6: 3 The **p** at the front of the main hall of 395
7: 6 In front of it was a **p,** 395
7:12 of the temple of the LORD with its **p.** 395
7:19 of the pillars in the **p** were in the shape 395
7:21 the pillars at the **p** *of* the temple. 395
1Ch 28:11 the plans for the **p** of the temple, 395
2Ch 3: 4 The **p** at the front of the temple 395
8:12 that he had built in front of the **p,** 395
15: 8 of the LORD that was in front of the **p** *of* 395
29: 7 the doors of the **p** and put out the lamps. 395
29:17 of the month they reached the **p** *of* 395
Eze 8:16 between the **p** and the altar, 395
40: 7 the **p** facing the temple was one rod deep. 395
40: 8 Then he measured the **p** *of* the gateway; 395
40: 9 The **p** *of* the gateway faced the temple. 395
40:14 The measurement was up to the **p** *facing* 395
40:15 to the far end of its **p** was fifty cubits. 395
40:16 openings all around, as was the **p;** 395
40:21 and its **p** had the same measurements 395
40:22 its **p** and its palm tree decorations had 395
40:22 with its **p** opposite them. 395
40:24 He measured its jambs and its **p,** 395
40:25 and its **p** had narrow openings all around, 395
40:26 with its **p** opposite them; 395
40:29 and its **p** had the same measurements as 395
40:29 and its **p** had openings all around. 395
40:31 Its **p** faced the outer court; 395
40:33 and its **p** had the same measurements as 395
40:33 and its **p** had openings all around. 395
40:34 Its **p** faced the outer court; 395
40:36 its projecting walls and its **p,** 395
40:37 Its **p** faced the outer court; 395
40:38 with a doorway was by the **p** *in* each of 395
40:39 In the **p** *of* the gateway were two tables 395
40:40 the outside wall of the **p** *of* the gateway, 395
40:48 He brought me to the **p** *of* the temple 395
40:48 and measured the jambs of the **p;** 395
40:49 The **p** was twenty cubits wide, 395
41:15 inner sanctuary and the **p** *facing* the court, 395
41:25 a wooden overhang on the front of the **p.** 395
41:26 of the **p** were narrow windows 395
44: 3 by way of the **p** *of* the gateway and go out 395
46: 2 through the **p** *of* the gateway and stand by 395
46: 8 he is to go in through the **p** *of* the gateway, 395

PORTICOES (1) [PORCH]

Eze 40:30 (The **p** of the gateways around 395

PORTION (73) [APPORTIONED, PORTIONS]

Ge 43:34 Benjamin's **p** was five times as much 5368
Lev 2: 2 and burn this as a **memorial p** on the altar, 260
2: 9 the **memorial p** from the grain offering 260
2:16 the **memorial p** of the crushed grain and 260
5:12 as a **memorial p** and burn it on the altar 260
6:15 and burn the **memorial p** on the altar as 260
7:35 the **p** of the offerings made to the LORD 5419
24: 7 as a **memorial p** to represent the bread and 260
Nu 15:19 **present a p** as an offering to the LORD. 8123
18: 8 and your sons as your **p** and regular share. 5421
18:28 the LORD's **p** to Aaron the priest. 9556
18:29 as the LORD's **p** the best and holiest part 9556
Dt 26:13 the **sacred p** and have given it to the Levite, 7731
26:14 not eaten any of **the sacred p** while I was 5647[S]
32: 9 For the LORD's **p** is his people, 2750
33:21 the leader's **p** was kept for him. 2754
Jos 15:13 Joshua gave to Caleb son of Jephunneh a **p** 2750
17:14 and one **p** for an inheritance? 2475
18: 7 however, do not get a **p** among you, 2750
19: 9 Judah's **p** was more than they needed. 2750
1Sa 1: 5 But to Hannah he gave a double **p** 4950
2Ki 2: 9 "Let me inherit a double **p** of your spirit," 7023
1Ch 16:18 of Canaan as the **p** you will inherit." 2475
2Ch 30:22 For the seven days they ate their **assigned p** 4595
31: 4 in Jerusalem to give the **p** *due* the priests 4987
Ne 12:47 also set aside the **p** for the other Levites, NIH
12:47 the **p** for the descendants of Aaron. NIH
Job 24:18 their **p** of the land is cursed, 2754
Ps 16: 5 you have assigned me my **p** and my cup; 2750
73:26 the strength of my heart and my **p** forever. 2750
105:11 of Canaan as the **p** you will inherit." 2475
119:57 You are my **p,** O LORD; 2750
142: 5 my **p** in the land of the living." 2750
Isa 17:14 This is the **p** *of* those who loot us, 2750
53:12 **Therefore** *I will* **give** him **a p** among 2745
57: 6 smooth stones of the ravines are your **p;** 2750
61: 7 my people will receive a **double p,** 5467
61: 7 and so they will inherit a **double p** 5467
Jer 6: 3 each tending his own **p."** 3338
10:16 He who is the **P** *of* Jacob is not like these, 2750
13:25 the **p** I have decreed for you," 4987
51:19 He who is the **P** *of* Jacob is not like these, 2750
La 3:24 I say to myself, "The LORD is my **p;** 2750
Eze 44:30 the **first** *p of* your ground meal so that AIT
45: 1 to present to the LORD a **p** of the land as 9556
45: 4 be the sacred **p** of the land for the priests, NIH
45: 6 cubits long, adjoining the sacred **p;** 9556
45:14 The **prescribed p** *of* oil, 2976
48: 1 Dan will have **one** *p;* AIT
48: 2 "Asher will have **one** *p;* AIT
48: 3 "Naphtali will have **one** *p;* AIT
48: 4 "Manasseh will have **one** *p;* AIT
48: 5 "Ephraim will have **one** *p;* AIT
48: 6 "Reuben will have **one** *p;* AIT
48: 7 "Judah will have **one** *p;* AIT
48: 8 **p** you are to present **as a special gift.** 9556
48: 9 "The **special p** you are to offer to the LORD 9556
Eze 48:10 This will be the sacred **p** for the priests. 9556
48:12 a special gift to them from the sacred **p** *of* 9556
48:12 a most holy **p,** bordering the territory of NIH
48:18 on the sacred **p** and running the length of it, 9556
48:20 The entire **p** will be a square, 25,000 9556
48:20 the sacred **p,** along with the property of 9556
48:21 of the area formed by the sacred **p** and 9556
48:21 cubits of the sacred **p** to the eastern border, 9556
48:21 the sacred **p** with the temple sanctuary will 9556
48:23 Benjamin will have **one** *p;* AIT
48:24 "Simeon will have **one** *p;* AIT
48:25 "Issachar will have **one** *p;* AIT
48:26 "Zebulun will have **one** *p;* AIT
48:27 "Gad will have **one** *p;* AIT
Zec 2:12 The LORD will inherit Judah as his **p** in 2750
Rev 18: 6 Mix her a **double** *p* from her own cup. *AIT*

PORTIONS (23) [PORTION]

Ge 4: 4 But Abel brought **fat p** from some of 2693
43:34 **p** were served to them from Joseph's table, 5368
Lev 8:26 on the **fat p** and on the right thigh. 2693
9:19 But the **fat p** of the ox and the ram— 2693
9:24 the burnt offering and the **fat p** on 2693
10:15 the **fat p** *of* the offerings made by fire, 2693
Jos 19:49 the land into its **allotted p,** 1473
1Sa 1: 4 he would give **p of** the **meat** 4950
2Ch 7: 7 the grain offerings and the **fat p.** 2693
31:19 to distribute **p** to every male among them 4950
35:14 the burnt offerings and the **fat p** 2693
Ne 8:12 to send **p of food** and to celebrate 4950
12:44 to bring into the storerooms the **p** *required* 4987
12:47 the daily **p** *for* the singers and gatekeepers. 4987
13:10 that the **p** *assigned to* the Levites had 4987
Pr 31:15 for her family and **p** for her servant girls. 2976
Ecc 11: 2 Give **p** to seven, yes to eight, 2750
Isa 34:17 He allots their **p;** his hand distributes them 1598
Eze 45: 7 border parallel to one of the tribal **p.** 2750
47:13 with *two* **p** for Joseph. 2475
48: 8 to west will equal one of the tribal **p;** 2750
48:21 of the tribal **p** will belong to the prince, 2750
48:29 and these will be their **p,"** 4713

PORTRAIT (3)

Mt 22:20 "Whose **p** is this? And whose inscription?" *1635*
Mk 12:16 "Whose **p** is this? And whose inscription?" *1635*
Lk 20:24 Whose **p** and inscription are on it?" *1635+2400*

PORTRAYED (4)

Eze 8:10 and I saw **p** all over the walls all kinds 2977
23:14 She saw men **p** on a wall, 2977
23:14 figures of Chaldeans **p** in red, 2980
Gal 3: 1 Before your very eyes Jesus Christ *was* clearly **p** as crucified. *4592*

PORTS (1)

Ac 27: 2 a ship from Adramyttium about to sail for **p** *NIG*

POSES (1)

Jer 29:27 who **p as a prophet** among you? 5547

POSITION (21) [POSITIONS]

Ge 40:13 up your head and restore you to your **p,** 4030
40:21 He restored the chief cupbearer to his **p,** 5482
41:13 I was restored to my **p,** 4030
Jos 8:19 in the ambush rose quickly from their **p** 5226
Jdg 7:21 each man held his **p** around the camp, 9393
9:44 *to a* **p** at the entrance to the city gate. 6641
2Sa 3: 6 **strengthening his own p** in the house of 2616
1Ki 2:35 the army **in** Joab's **p** and replaced Abiathar 9393
15:13 from her **p as queen mother,** 1485
20:22 **"Strengthen** *your* **p** and see what must 2616
2Ch 12: 1 Rehoboam's **p as king** was established 4895
15:16 Maacah from her **p as queen mother,** 1485
Est 1:19 Also let the king give her **royal p** 4895
4:14 but that you have come to **royal p** for such 4895
Isa 22:19 and you will be ousted from your **p.** 5096
Da 2:48 the king **placed** Daniel **in a high p** 10648
5:19 Because of the **high p** he gave him, 10650
Ro 12:16 willing to associate *with people* **of low p.** *5424*
Jas 1: 9 ought to take pride in his **high p.** *5737*
1:10 rich whould take pride in his **low p,** *5428*
2Pe 3:17 of lawless men and fall from your **secure p.** *5113*

POSITIONS (23) [POSITION]

Jos 3: 3 to move out from your **p** and follow it. 5226
8:13 **had** the soldiers **take up** *their* **p**— 8492
10: 5 up with all their troops and **took up p** 2837
10:31 *he* **took up p** against it and attacked it. 2837
10:34 *they* **took up p** against it and attacked it. 2837
Jdg 9:34 and **took up concealed p** near Shechem 741
20:20 to fight the Benjamites and **took up** battle **p** 6885
20:22 and again **took up** *their* **p** 6885
20:30 the third day and **took up p** against Gibeah 6885
20:33 from their places and **took up p** 6885
1Sa 17:20 as the army was going out to its **battle p,** 5120
1Ch 9:22 gatekeepers *had been* **assigned to** their **p** 3569
2Ch 7: 6 The priests took their **p,** 5466
14:10 and *they* **took up** battle **p** in the Valley 6885
20:17 **Take up** *your* **p;** stand firm and see 3656
30:16 their *regular* **p** as prescribed in the Law 6642
Ecc 10: 6 Fools are put in many **high p,** 5294
Jer 46: 4 **Take** *your* **p** with helmets on! 3656

Jer 46:14 'Take your p and get ready, 3656
50: 9 They will take up their p against her, 6885
50:14 "Take up your p around Babylon, 6885
Eze 23:24 they will take up p against you 8492
Jude 1: 6 not keep their p of authority 794

POSSESS (67) [POSSESSED, POSSESSING, POSSESSION, POSSESSIONS, POSSESSOR]

Ge 24:60 may your offspring p the gates 3769
Lev 20:24 But I said to you, "You will p their land; 3769
25:32 in the Levitical towns, which they p. 299
Nu 27:11 nearest relative in his clan, that he may p it. 3769
33:53 for I have given you the land to p. 3769
35: 2 in from the inheritance the Israelites will p. 299
35: 8 the Israelites p are to be given in proportion 299
36: 8 that every Israelite will p the inheritance 3769
Dt 2:31 Now begin to conquer and p his land." 3769
4:14 that you are crossing the Jordan to p. 3769
4:26 that you are crossing the Jordan to p. 3769
5:31 to follow in the land I am giving them to p." 3769
5:33 in the land that you will p. 3769
6: 1 that you are crossing the Jordan to p, 3769
7: 1 into the land you are entering to p 3769
8: 1 and increase and may enter and p the land 3769
9: 6 giving you this good land to p, 3769
10:11 and p the land that I swore to their fathers 3769
11: 8 that you are crossing the Jordan to p, 3769
11:29 into the land you are entering to p, 3769
12: 1 the God of your fathers, has given you to p 3769
15: 4 the LORD your God is giving you to p 3769
16:20 so that you may live and p the land 3769
19: 2 the LORD your God is giving you to p. 3769
19:14 the LORD your God is giving you to p. 3769
21: 1 the LORD your God is giving you to p, 3769
23:20 in the land you are entering to p. 3769
25:19 around you in the land he is giving you to p 3769
28:21 from the land you are entering to p. 3769
28:63 from the land you are entering to p. 3769
30:16 in the land you are entering to p. 3769
30:18 the Jordan to enter and p. 3769
31:13 the land you are crossing the Jordan to p." 3769
32:47 the land you are crossing the Jordan to p." 3769
Jos 22:19 If the land you p is defiled, 299
Jdg 11:24 whatever the LORD our God has given us, we will p. 3769
1Ch 28: 8 that you may p this good land and pass it on 3769
Ezr 7:25 wisdom of your God, which you p, 10089+10311
9:11 to p is a land polluted by the corruption 3769
Ne 9:23 that you told their fathers to enter and p. 3769
Ps 69:35 Then people will settle there and p it; 3769
Pr 8:12 I p knowledge and discretion. 5162
Isa 14: 2 of Israel will p the nations as menservants 5706
34:11 The desert owl and screech owl will p it; 3769
34:17 They will p it forever and dwell there 3769
57:13 the land and p my holy mountain." 3769
60:21 and they will p the land forever. 3769
65: 9 from Judah those who will p my mountains; 3769
Jer 11: 5 the land you p today." NIH
30: 3 to the land I gave their forefathers to p,' 3769
32: 8 Since it is your right to redeem it and p it, 3772
Eze 33:25 should you then p the land? 3769
33:26 Should you then p the land?' 3769
36:12 They will p you, and you will 3769
45: 8 will allow the house of Israel to p 5989
Da 7:18 the kingdom and will p it forever— 10277
Am 9:12 so that they may p the remnant of Edom 3769
Ob 1:17 the house of Jacob will p its inheritance. 3769
1:19 and people from the foothills will p NIH
1:19 and Benjamin will p Gilead. NIH
1:20 of Israelite exiles who are in Canaan will p NIH
1:20 in Sepharad will p the towns of the Negev. 3769
Jn 5:39 that by them you p eternal life. 2400
Ac 7: 5 and his descendants after him would p 2959
1Co 8: 1 We know that we all p knowledge. 2400
13: 3 If I give all I p to the poor 3836+5639
2Pe 1: 8 you p these qualities in increasing measure, 5639

POSSESSED (13) [POSSESS]

Ps 105:21 master of his household, ruler over all he p, 7871
Isa 63:18 a little while your people p your holy place, 3769
Jer 16:19 "Our fathers p nothing but false gods, 5706
Eze 33:24 yet he p the land. 3769
Da 7:22 the time came when they p the kingdom. 10277
Mk 1:23 then a man in their synagogue who was p NIG
3:22 "He is p by Beelzebub! 2400
5:15 p by the legion of demons, 1227
7:25 a woman whose little daughter was p by 2400
9:17 who is p by a spirit that has robbed him 2400
Lk 4:33 In the synagogue there was a man p by 2400
Jn 8:49 "I am not p by a demon," said Jesus, 2400
10:21 not the sayings of a man p by a demon. 1227

POSSESSING (1) [POSSESS]

2Co 6:10 having nothing, and yet p everything. 2988

POSSESSION (97) [POSSESS]

Ge 15: 7 to give you this land to take p of it." 3769
15: 8 how can I know that I will gain p of it?" 3769
17: 8 I will give as an everlasting p to you 299
22:17 Your descendants will take p of the cities 3769
28: 4 that you may take p of the land where you 3769
30:33 Any goat in my p that is not speckled 907
48: 4 and I will give this land as an everlasting p 299
Ex 6: 8 I will give it to you as a p. 4627
19: 5 of all nations you will be my treasured p. 6035
22: 4 "If the stolen animal is found alive in his p 3338
22: 9 In all cases of illegal p of an ox, 7322
23:30 until you have increased enough to take p 5706
Lev 14:34 which I am giving you as your p, 299
25:24 the country that you hold as a p, 299
25:28 the p of the buyer until the Year of Jubilee. 3338
25:34 it is their permanent p. 299
Nu 13:30 "We should go up and take p of the land, 3769
21:35 And they took p of his land. 3769
32: 5 be given to your servants as our p. 299
32:22 this land will be your p before the LORD. 299
32:29 give them the land of Gilead as their p. 299
32:30 they must accept their p with you 296
33:53 Take p of the land and settle in it, 3769
Dt 1: 8 Go in and take p of the land that 3769
1:21 Go up and take p of it as the LORD, 3769
1:39 I will give it to them and they will take p 3769
2: 9 to the descendants of Lot as a p." 3772
2:12 the land the LORD gave them as their p.) 3772
2:19 not give you p of any land belonging to 3772
2:19 I have given it as a p to the descendants 3772
2:24 to take p of it and engage him in battle. 3769
3:18 has given you this land to take p of it. 3769
3:20 to the p I have given you." 3772
4: 1 that you may live and may go in and take p 3769
4: 5 in the land you are entering to take p of it. 3769
4:22 to cross over and take p of that good land. 3769
4:47 They took p of his land and the land 3769
7: 6 the earth to be his people, his treasured p. 6035
9: 4 "The LORD has brought me here to take p 3769
9: 5 that you are going in to take p of their land; 3769
9:23 and take p of the land I have given you." 3769
11:11 to take p of is a land of mountains 3769
11:31 about to cross the Jordan to enter and take p 3769
14: 2 LORD has chosen you to be his treasured p. 6035
16: 4 be found in your p in all your land 4200
17:14 and have taken p of it and settled in it, 3769
24:12 not go to sleep with his pledge in your p. 928
26: 1 as an inheritance and have taken p of it 3769
26:18 his treasured p as he promised, 6035
30: 5 and you will take p of it. 3769
31: 3 and you will take p of their land. 3769
32:49 the Israelites as their own p. 299
33: 4 the p of the assembly of Jacob. 4627
Jos 1:11 the Jordan here to go in and take p of 3769
1:15 until they too have taken p of the land that 3769
12: 6 and the half-tribe of Manasseh to be their p. 3772
18: 3 before you begin to take p of the land that 3769
19:47 Danites had difficulty taking p of 3655+4946
21:12 to Caleb son of Jephunneh as his p. 299
21:43 and they took p of it and settled there. 3769
23: 5 and you will take p of their land, 3769
24: 8 and you took p of their land. 3769
Jdg 1:19 They took p of the hill country, 3769
2: 6 they went to take p of the land, 3769
3:13 and they took p of the City of Palms. 3769
3:28 taking p of the fords of the Jordan that led 4334
8: 6 hands of Zebah and Zalmunna in your p? 3338
8:15 hands of Zebah and Zalmunna in your p? 3338
1Ki 21:15 up and take p of the vineyard of Naboth 3769
21:16 down to take p of Naboth's vineyard. 3769
21:18 where he has gone to take p of it. 3769
2Ch 20:11 of the p you gave us as an inheritance. 3772
Ne 9:15 in and take p of the land you had sworn 3769
9:24 Their sons went in and took p of the land. 3769
9:25 they took p of houses filled with all kinds 3769
Ps 2: 8 the ends of the earth your p. 299
73: 9 and their tongues take p of the earth. 2143
83:12 "Let us take p of the pasturelands of God." 3769
135: 4 Israel to be his treasured p. 6035
Jer 32:23 They came in and took p of it, 3769
49: 1 Why then has Molech taken p of Gad? 3769
Eze 7:24 the most wicked of the nations to take p 3769
11:15 this land was given to us as our p.' 4627
25: 4 to give you to the people of the East as a p. 4627
25:10 the East as a p, so that the Ammonites will 4627
33:24 the land has been given to us as our p.' 4627
35:10 be ours and we will take p of them," 3769
36: 2 The ancient heights have become our p." ' 4627
36: 3 from every side so that you became the p of 4627
36: 5 their hearts they made my land their own p 4627
44:28 You are to give them no p in Israel; 299
44:28 I will be their p. 299
45: 5 as their p for towns to live in. 299
45: 8 This land will be his p in Israel. 299
Mic 2: 4 my people's p is divided up. 2750
Mal 3:17 in the day when I make up my treasured p. 6035
Eph 1:14 the redemption of those who are God's p— 4348

POSSESSIONS (38) [POSSESS]

Ge 12: 5 all the p they had accumulated and 8214
13: 6 for their p were so great that they were 8214
14:12 Abram's nephew Lot and his p, 8214
14:16 and brought back his relative Lot and his p, 8214
15:14 afterward they will come out with great p. 8214
32:23 he sent over all his p. 889[S]
36: 7 Their p were too great for them 8214
46: 6 and the p they had acquired in Canaan, 8214
Nu 16:32 and all Korah's men and all their p. 8214
Dt 12:11 the choice p you have vowed to the LORD. 4436
18: 8 from the sale of family p. 3
Jos 7:11 they have put them with their own p. 3998
Jdg 18:21 their livestock and their p in front of them, 3885
1Ki 13: 8 "Even if you were to give me half your p, 1074
2Ch 31: 3 The king contributed from his own p for 8214
35: 7 all from the king's own p. 8214
Ezr 8:21 for us and our children, with all our p. 8214
Ne 5:13 of his house and p every man who does 3330
Job 15:29 nor will his p spread over the land. 4978
Pr 12:27 but the diligent man prizes his p. 2104
Ecc 5:19 when God gives any man wealth and p, 5794
6: 2 God gives a man wealth, p and honor, 5794
Zec 9: 4 But the Lord will take away her p 3769
Mt 12:29 a strong man's house and carry off his p 5007
19:21 go, sell your p and give to the poor, 3836+5639
24:47 he will put him in charge of all his p. 5639
Mk 3:27 a strong man's house and carry off his p 5007
Lk 11:21 guards his own house, his p are safe. 5639
12:15 not consist in the abundance of his p." 5639
12:33 Sell your p and give to the poor. 5639
12:44 he will put him in charge of all his p. 5639
16: 1 was accused of wasting his p. 3836+5639
19: 8 and now I give half of my p to the poor, 5639
Ac 2:45 Selling their p and goods, 3228
4:32 that any of his p was his own, 5639
2Co 12:14 because what I want is not your p but you. 3836
Heb 10:34 that you yourselves had better and lasting p. 5638
1Jn 3:17 If anyone has material p and sees his 1050

POSSESSOR (1) [POSSESS]

Ecc 7:12 that wisdom preserves the life of its p. 1251

POSSIBLE (19) [POSSIBLY]

Ne 5: 8 "As far as p, we have bought back 1896+3869
Mt 19:26 but with God all things are p." 1543
24:24 deceive even the elect—if that were p. 1543
26:39 if it is p, may this cup be taken from me. 1543
26:42 if it is not p for this cup to be taken away 1538
Mk 9:23 "Everything is p for him who believes." 1543
10:27 all things are p with God." 1543
13:22 to deceive the elect—if that were p. 1543
14:35 and prayed that if p the hour might pass from him. 1543+1639
14:36 Father," he said, "everything is p for you. 1543
Lk 18:27 "What is impossible with men is p 1543
Ac 17:15 and Timothy to join him as soon as p. AIT
20:16 if p, by the day of Pentecost. 1543
26: 9 that I ought to do all that was p to oppose NIG
Ro 12:18 If it is p, as far as it depends on you, 1543
13: 5 not only because of p punishment but also NIG
1Co 6: 5 Is it p that there is nobody among you wise 4024
9:19 a slave to everyone, to win as many as p. NIG
9:22 so that by all p means I might save some. 4122

POSSIBLY (3) [POSSIBLE]

Ge 27:37 So what can I p do for you, my son?" AIT
Lk 3:15 in their hearts if John might p be the Christ. AIT
Ro 5: 7 a good man someone might p dare to die. 5440

POST (5) [POSTED, POSTING, POSTS]

Jos 10:18 and p some men there to guard it. 7212
Ecc 10: 4 do not leave your p; 5226
Isa 21: 6 "Go, p a lookout and have him report 6641
21: 8 every night I stay at my p. 5466
Ac 17: 9 and the others p bond and let them go. 2653

POSTED (6) [POST]

2Ki 10:24 Now Jehu had p eighty men outside 8492
11:18 Then Jehoiada the priest p guards at 8492
Ne 4: 9 to our God and p a guard day and night 6641
4:16 The officers p themselves behind all NIH
Isa 22: 7 and horsemen are p at the city gates; 8883+8883
62: 6 I have p watchmen on your walls, 7212

POSTERITY (2)

Ps 21:10 their p from mankind. 2446
22:30 P will serve him; future generations 2446

POSTING (2) [POST]

Ne 4:13 p them by families, with their swords, 6641
Mt 27:66 by putting a seal on the stone and p NIG

POSTS (42) [POST]

Ex 26:32 on four p of acacia wood overlaid 6647
26:37 Make gold hooks for this curtain and five p 6647
27:10 with twenty p and twenty bronze bases and 6647
27:10 and with silver hooks and bands on the p. 6647
27:11 with twenty p and twenty bronze bases and 6647
27:11 and with silver hooks and bands on the p. 6647
27:12 with ten p and ten bases. 6647
27:14 with three p and three bases, 6647
27:15 with three p and three bases. 6647
27:16 with four p and four bases. 6647
27:17 All the p around the courtyard are 6647
35:11 clasps, frames, crossbars, p and bases; 6647
35:17 of the courtyard with its p and bases, and 6647
36:36 They made four p of acacia wood for it 6647
36:38 and they made five p with hooks for them. 6647
36:38 the tops of the p and their bands with gold 2157[S]
38:10 with twenty p and twenty bronze bases, 6647
38:10 and with silver hooks and bands on the p. 6647
38:11 and had twenty p and twenty bronze bases, 6647
38:11 with silver hooks and bands on the p. 6647
38:12 with ten p and ten bases, 6647
38:12 with silver hooks and bands on the p. 6647

Ex 38:14 with three p and three bases, 6647
38:15 with three p and three bases. 6647
38:17 The bases for the p were bronze. 6647
38:17 The hooks and bands on the p were silver, 6647
38:17 all the p *of* the courtyard had silver bands. 6647
38:19 with four p and four bronze bases. 6647
38:28 shekels to make the hooks for the p, 6647
38:28 to overlay the tops of the p, 2157S
39:33 its clasps, frames, crossbars, p and bases; 6647
39:40 of the courtyard with its p and bases, and 6647
40:18 inserted the crossbars and set up the p. 6647
Nu 3:36 its crossbars, p, bases, all its equipment, 6647
3:37 as the p *of* the surrounding courtyard 6647
4:31 its crossbars, p and bases, 6647
4:32 as the p *of* the surrounding courtyard 6647
Jdg 16:3 together with the two p, 4647
2Ch 35:15 at each gate did not need to leave their p, 6275
Ne 7:3 at their p and some near their own houses." 5464
13:11 and stationed them at their p. 6642
SS 3:10 Its p he made of silver, its base of gold. 6647

POT (34) [POTS, POTSHERD, POTSHERDS, POTTER, POTTER'S, POTTERS, POTTERY]

Lev 6:28 The clay p the meat is cooked in must 3998
6:28 but if it is cooked in a bronze p, 3998
6:28 but if it is cooked in a bronze pot, the p is NIH
11:33 If one of them falls into a clay p, 3998
11:33 and you must break the p. 2257S
11:34 on it from such a p is unclean, 3998
11:35 an oven or cooking p must be broken up. 3968
14:5 be killed over fresh water in a clay p. 3998
14:50 of the birds over fresh water in a clay p. 3998
15:12 " 'A clay p that the man touches must 3998
Nu 11:8 They cooked it in a p or made it into cakes. 7248
Jdg 6:19 the meat in a basket and its broth in a p, 7248
1Sa 2:14 into the pan or kettle or caldron or p, 7248
2Ki 4:38 "Put on the large p and cook some stew 6105
4:39 he cut them up into the p *of* stew, 6105
4:40 "O man of God, there is death in the p!" 6105
4:41 He put it into the p and said, 6105
4:41 And there was nothing harmful in the p. 6105
Job 41:20 from his nostrils as from a boiling p over 1857
41:31 and stirs up the sea like a p of ointment. 5350
Ecc 7:6 Like the crackling of thorns under the p, 6105
Isa 29:16 Can the p say of the potter, 3671
Jer 1:13 "I see a boiling p, tilting away from 6105
18:4 But the p he was shaping from the clay 3998
18:4 so the potter formed it into another p, 3998
22:28 broken p, an object no one wants? 6775
Eze 11:3 This city is a cooking p, 6105
11:7 the meat and this city is the p, 6105
11:11 This city will not be a p for you, 6105
24:3 " 'Put on the cooking p; 6105
24:6 to the p now encrusted, 6105
24:11 the empty p on the coals till it becomes hot NIH
Mic 3:3 like flesh for the p?" 7831
Zec 14:21 Every p in Jerusalem and Judah will 6105

POTENT (1)

Isa 47:9 your many sorceries and all your p spells. 6800

POTENTATE (KJV) See RULER

POTIPHAR (4)

Ge 37:36 the Midianites sold Joseph in Egypt to P, 7035
39:1 P, an Egyptian who was one of 7035
39:4 P put him in charge of his household, NIH
39:5 The blessing of the LORD was on everything P had, 2257S

POTIPHERA (3)

Ge 41:45 and gave him Asenath daughter of P, 7036
41:50 to Joseph by Asenath daughter of P, 7036
46:20 to Joseph by Asenath daughter of P, 7036

POTS (15) [POT]

Ex 16:3 There we sat around p *of* meat and ate all 6105
27:3 its p to remove the ashes, and its shovels, 6105
38:3 its p, shovels, sprinkling bowls, 6105
1Ki 7:45 the p, shovels and sprinkling bowls. 6105
2Ki 25:14 They also took away the p, shovels, 6105
2Ch 4:11 the p and shovels and sprinkling bowls. 6105
4:16 the p, shovels, meat forks 6105
35:13 and boiled the holy offerings in p, 6105
Ps 58:9 Before your p can feel [the heat of] 6105
Isa 65:4 and whose p hold broth of unclean meat; 3998
Jer 52:18 They also took away the p, shovels, 6105
52:19 censers, sprinkling bowls, p, lampstands, 6105
La 4:2 are now considered as p *of* clay, 5574
Zec 14:20 the cooking p in the LORD's house will 6105
14:21 to sacrifice will take some of the p 2157S

POTSHERD (3) [POT]

Ps 22:15 My strength is dried up like a p, 3084
Isa 45:9 but a p among the potsherds on the ground. 3084
Jer 19:2 near the entrance of the P Gate. 3068

POTSHERDS (2) [POT]

Job 41:30 His undersides are jagged p, 3084
Isa 45:9 but a potsherd among the p *on* the ground. 3084

POTTAGE (KJV) See STEW

POTTER (12) [POT]

Isa 29:16 as if the p were thought to be like the clay! 3450
29:16 Can the pot say of the p, 3450
41:25 as if he were a p treading the clay. 3450
45:9 Does the clay say to the p, 3450
64:8 We are the clay, you are the p; 3450
Jer 18:4 so the p formed it into another pot, 3450
18:6 can I not do with you as this p does?" 3450
18:6 "Like clay in the hand of the p, 3450
19:1 "Go and buy a clay jar from a p. 3450
Zec 11:13 the LORD said to me, "Throw it to the p"— 3450
11:13 into the house of the LORD to the p. 3450
Ro 9:21 Does not the p have the right to make out *3038*

POTTER'S (6) [POT]

Jer 18:2 "Go down to the p house, 3450
18:3 So I went down to the p house, 3450
19:11 and this city just as this p jar is smashed 3450
La 4:2 as pots of clay, the work of a p hands! 3450
Mt 27:7 the p field as a burial place for foreigners. *3038*
27:10 and they used them to buy the p field, *3038*

POTTERS (1) [POT]

1Ch 4:23 the p who lived at Netaim and Gederah; 3450

POTTERY (8) [POT]

2Sa 17:28 and bowls and articles of p. 3450
Job 2:8 a piece of broken p and scraped himself 3084
Ps 2:9 you will dash them to pieces like p." 3450+3998
31:12 I have become like broken p. 3998
Isa 30:14 It will break in pieces like p, 3450+5574
Jer 25:34 you will fall and be shattered like fine p. 3998
Ro 9:21 lump of clay some p for noble purposes *5007*
Rev 2:27 he will dash them to pieces like p'— *3039+5007*

POUCH (2) [POUCHES]

Ge 42:35 in each man's sack was his p *of* silver! 7655
1Sa 17:40 put them in the p of his shepherd's bag and, 3541

POUCHES (1) [POUCH]

Ge 42:35 they and their father saw the money p, 7655

POULTICE (2)

2Ki 20:7 Then Isaiah said, "Prepare a p of figs." 1811
Isa 38:21 "Prepare a p *of* figs and apply it to the boil, 1811

POULTRY (1)

Ne 5:18 six choice sheep and *some* p were prepared 7606

POUNCE (2) [POUNCED]

1Sa 15:19 Why *did you* p on the plunder and do evil 6513
Isa 33:4 like a swarm of locusts *men* p on it. 9212

POUNCED (1) [POUNCE]

1Sa 14:32 They p on the plunder and, taking sheep, 6513

POUND (1) [POUNDED, POUNDING, POUNDS]

SS 5:4 my heart *began to* p for him. 2159

POUNDED (2) [POUND]

2Sa 22:43 *I* p and trampled them like mud in 1990
Hab 3:16 I heard and my heart p, 8074

POUNDING (3) [POUND]

Jdg 19:22 P on the door, they shouted to the old man 1985
Ps 93:3 the seas have lifted up their p waves. 1922
Ac 27:41 and the stern was broken to pieces by the p *1040*

POUNDS (5) [POUND]

Job 37:1 "At this my heart p and leaps 3006
Ps 38:10 My heart p, my strength fails me; 6086
Jer 4:19 My heart p within me, I cannot keep silent. 2159
Jn 19:39 myrrh and aloes, about seventy-five p. *1669+3354*
Rev 16:21 of about a hundred p each fell upon men. *5418*

POUR (78) [DOWNPOUR, OUTPOURED, OUTPOURING, POURED, POURING, POURS]

Ex 4:9 take some water from the Nile and p it *on* 9161
29:12 p out the rest of it at the base of the altar. 9161
30:9 and *do* not p a drink offering on it. 5818
30:32 *Do* not p it on men's bodies and do 6057
Lev 2:1 *He is to* p oil on it, 3668
2:6 Crumble it and p oil on it; 3668
4:7 The rest of the bull's blood *he shall* p out 9161
4:18 of the blood *he shall* p out at the base of 9161
4:25 the altar of burnt offering and p out the rest 9161
4:30 the altar of burnt offering and p out the rest 9161
4:34 the altar of burnt offering and p out the rest 9161
14:15 p it in the palm of his own left hand, 3668
14:26 The priest *is to* p some of the oil into 3668
Nu 5:15 *He must* not p oil on it or put incense on it, 3668
19:17 into a jar and p fresh water over them. 5989
Nu 20:8 and *it will* p out its water. 5989
28:7 P out the drink offering to the LORD at 5818
Dt 12:16 p it out on the ground like water. 9161
12:24 p it out on the ground like water. 9161
15:23 p it out on the ground like water. 9161
Jdg 6:20 and p out the broth." 9161
1Ki 18:33 and p it on the offering and on the wood." 3668
2Ki 3:11 *to* p water on the hands of Elijah." 3668
4:4 P oil into all the jars, and as each is filled, 3668
9:3 and p the oil on his head and declare, 3668
Job 3:24 my groans p out like water. 5988
10:10 *Did you* not p me out like milk and 5988
15:13 and p out such words from your mouth? 3655
16:20 *as* my eyes p out tears to God; 1940
36:28 the clouds p down *their* moisture 5688
Ps 16:4 *I will* not p out their libations of blood 5818
19:2 Day after day *they* p forth speech; 5580
42:4 as *I* p out my soul: 9161
62:8 p out your hearts to him, 9161
69:24 P out your wrath on them; 9161
79:6 P out your wrath on the nations that do not 9161
94:4 *They* p out arrogant words; 5580
104:10 He makes springs p water into the ravines; 8938
142:2 *I* p out my complaint before him; 9161
Ecc 11:3 *they* p rain upon the earth. 8197
Isa 44:3 For *I will* p water on the thirsty land, 3668
44:3 *I will* p out my Spirit on your offspring, 3668
46:6 Some p out gold from their bags 2313
Jer 6:11 "P it out on the children in the street and 9161
7:18 *They* p out drink offerings to other gods 5818
10:25 P out your wrath on the nations that do not 9161
14:16 *I will* p out on them the calamity 9161
44:17 of Heaven and *will* p out drink offerings 5818
44:25 to burn incense and p out drink offerings 5818
48:12 "when I will send *men who* p from jars, 7579
48:12 and *they will* p her out; 7579
La 2:19 p out your heart like water in the presence 9161
Eze 7:8 *I am* about to p out my wrath on you 9161
14:19 a plague into that land and p out my wrath 9161
20:8 So I said I *would* p out my wrath on them 9161
20:13 So I said *I would* p out my wrath on them 9161
20:21 So I said I *would* p out my wrath on them 9161
21:31 *I will* p out my wrath upon you 9161
22:31 So *I will* p out my wrath on them 9161
24:3 put it on and p water into it. 3668
24:7 *she did* not p it on the ground, 9161
30:15 *I will* p out my wrath on Pelusium, 9161
38:22 *I will* p down torrents of rain, 4763
39:29 for *I will* p out my Spirit on the house 9161
Hos 5:10 *I will* p out my wrath on them like 9161
9:4 not p out wine offerings to the LORD, 5818
Joel 2:28 *I will* p out my Spirit on all people. 9161
2:29 *I will* p out my Spirit in those days. 9161
Mic 1:6 *I will* p her stones into the valley 5599
Zep 3:8 the kingdoms and to p out my wrath 9161
Zec 4:12 the two gold pipes that p out golden oil?" 8197
12:10 "And *I will* p out on the house of David 8197
Mal 3:10 and p out so much blessing that you will 8197
Mt 9:17 Neither *do men* p new wine *965*
9:17 No, *they* p new wine into new wineskins, *965*
Ac 2:17 *I will* p out my Spirit on all people. *1772*
2:18 *I will* p out my Spirit in those days, *1772*
Rev 16:1 p out the seven bowls of God's wrath on *1772*

POURED (94) [POUR]

Ge 28:18 and set it up as a pillar and p oil on top 3668
35:14 and *he* p out a drink offering on it; 5818
35:14 *he* also p oil on it. 3668
Ex 8:24 swarms of flies p into Pharaoh's palace 995
9:33 and the rain no *longer* p down on the land. 5988
Lev 8:12 *He* p some of the anointing oil on Aaron's 3668
8:15 *He* p out the rest of the blood at the base of 3668
9:9 the rest of the blood *he* p out at the base of 3668
21:10 the anointing oil p on his head 3668
Dt 12:27 of your sacrifices *must* be p beside the altar 9161
Jdg 5:4 the earth shook, the heavens p, 5752
5:4 the clouds p down water. 5752
Ru 3:15 *he* p into it six measures of barley 4499
1Sa 7:6 they drew water and p it out before 9161
10:1 Then Samuel took a flask of oil and p it 3668
2Sa 21:10 till the rain p down from the heavens on 5988
23:16 instead, *he* p it out before the LORD. 5818
1Ki 13:3 and the ashes on it *will* be p out." 9161
13:5 was split apart and its ashes p out 4946+9161
2Ki 4:40 The stew *was* p out for the men, 3668
9:6 Then the prophet p the oil on Jehu's head 3668
16:13 p out his drink offering, 5818
1Ch 11:18 instead, *he* p it out before the LORD. 5818
2Ch 12:7 My wrath *will* not *be* p out on Jerusalem 5988
34:21 that is p out on us because our fathers have 5988
34:25 my anger *will be* p out on this place 5988
Job 29:6 the rock p out for me streams of olive oil. 3668
Ps 18:42 *I* p them out like mud in the streets. 8197
22:14 *I* am p out like water, 9161
68:8 the heavens p down rain, before God, 5752
77:17 The clouds p down water, 2442
79:3 *They have* p out blood like water all 9161
92:10 fine oils *have been* p *upon me.* 1176
133:2 It is like precious oil p on the head, NIH
Pr 1:23 *I would have* p out my heart to you 5580
25:20 or like vinegar p on soda, NIH
Ecc 2:19 the work into which *I have* p *my* effort 6661
SS 1:3 your name is like perfume p out. 8197
Isa 19:14 The LORD *has* p into them a spirit 5007
32:15 till the Spirit is p upon us from on high, 6867
42:25 So *he* p out on them his burning anger, 9161

Isa 53:12 because *he* **p out** his life unto death, 6867
57:6 to them *you have* **p out** drink offerings 9161
63:6 and **p** their blood on the ground." 3718
Jer 1:14 "From the north disaster *will* **be p out** 7337
7:20 and my wrath *will* **be p out** on this place, 5988
19:13 and **p out** drink offerings to other gods.'" 5818
42:18 'As my anger and wrath *have* **been p out** 5988
42:18 in Jerusalem, so *will* my wrath *be* **p out** 5988
44:6 Therefore, my fierce anger *was* **p out;** 5988
44:19 of Heaven and **p out** drink offerings to her, 5818
48:11 not **p** from one jar to another— 8197
La 2:4 *he has* **p out** his wrath like fire on the tent 9161
2:11 my heart *is* **p out** on the ground 9161
4:11 *he has* **p out** his fierce anger. 9161
Eze 16:36 Because you **p out** your wealth 9161
20:28 and **p out** their drink offerings. 5818
22:22 that I the LORD *have* **p out** my wrath 9161
23:8 and **p out** their lust upon her. 9161
24:7 *She* **p** it on the bare rock; 8492
36:18 So *I* **p out** my wrath on them 9161
Da 9:11 the servant of God, *have been* **p out** on us, 5988
9:27 the end that is decreed *is* **p out** on him." 5988
Na 1:6 His wrath *is* **p out** like fire; 5988
Zep 1:17 Their blood *will* **be p out** like dust 9161
Mt 26:7 which *she* **p** on his head as he was reclining *2972*
26:12 *When* she **p** this perfume on my body, *965*
26:28 blood of the covenant, which *is* **p out** for *1772*
Mk 14:3 *She* broke the jar and **p** the perfume **on** *2972*
14:8 **p perfume on** my body beforehand to **prepare** for my burial. *3690*
14:24 blood of the covenant, which *is* **p out** for *1772*
Lk 5:38 new wine **must be p** into new wineskins. *1064*
6:38 *will be* **p** into your lap. *1443*
7:38 kissed them and **p** perfume **on** them. *230*
7:46 but she *has* **p** perfume on my feet. *230*
22:20 in my blood, which *is* **p out** for you. *1772*
Jn 11:2 the same one who **p** perfume **on** the Lord *230*
12:3 *she* **p** it **on** Jesus' feet and wiped his feet *230*
13:5 *he* **p** water into a basin and began *965*
Ac 2:33 and *has* **p out** what you now see and hear. *1772*
10:45 of the Holy Spirit *had been* **p out** even on *1772*
Ro 5:5 because God *has* **p out** his love *1772*
Php 2:17 I am *being* **p out like a drink offering** *5064*
1Ti 1:14 *was* **p out** on me **abundantly,** *5670*
2Ti 4:6 already *being* **p out like a drink offering,** *5064*
Tit 3:6 whom *he* **p out** on us generously *1772*
Rev 14:10 which *has been* **p** full strength into the cup *3042*
16:2 The first angel went and **p out** his bowl on *1772*
16:3 The second angel **p out** his bowl on *1772*
16:4 The third angel **p out** his bowl on the rivers *1772*
16:8 The fourth angel **p out** his bowl on the sun, *1772*
16:10 The fifth angel **p out** his bowl on *1772*
16:12 The sixth angel **p out** his bowl on *1772*
16:17 The seventh angel **p out** his bowl into *1772*

POURING (10) [POUR]

Ex 25:29 and bowls *for the* **p out of offerings.** 5818
29:7 the anointing oil and anoint him *by* **p** it 3668
37:16 pitchers for the **p out of drink offerings.** 5818
1Sa 1:15 *I was* **p out** my soul to the LORD. 9161
2Ki 4:5 the jars to her and she *kept* **p.** 3668
Jer 32:29 and by **p out** drink offerings to other gods. 5818
44:18 of Heaven and **p out** drink offerings to her, 5818
44:19 like her image and **p out** drink offerings 5818
Hab 2:15 **p** it *from* the wineskin till they are drunk, 6203
Lk 10:34 bandaged his wounds, **p on** oil and wine. *2219*

POURS (16) [POUR]

Job 12:21 *He* **p** contempt on nobles and disarms 9161
41:20 Smoke **p** from his nostrils as from 3655
Ps 75:8 *he* **p** it **out,** and all the wicked of the earth 5599
102:T and **p out** his lament before the LORD. 9161
107:40 *he who* **p** contempt on nobles 9161
Pr 6:19 a false witness *who* **p out** lies and 7032
14:5 but a false witness **p out** lies. 7032
19:5 and *he who* **p out** lies will not go free. 7032
19:9 and *he who* **p out** lies will perish. 7032
Jer 6:7 As a well **p out** its water, 7981
6:7 so *she* **p out** her wickedness. 7981
Am 5:8 and **p** them **out** over the face of the land— 9161
9:6 and **p** them **out** over the face of the land— 9161
Mk 2:22 And no one **p** new wine into old wineskins." *965*
2:22 No, he **p** new wine into new wineskins." *NIG*
Lk 5:37 And no one **p** new wine into old wineskins. *965*

POURTRAY (KJV) See DRAW

POVERTY (20) [POOR]

Dt 28:48 in nakedness and dire **p,** 2896
1Sa 2:7 The LORD **sends p** and wealth; 3769
Pr 6:11 and **p** will come on you like a bandit 8203
10:15 but **p** is the ruin of the poor. 8203
11:24 another withholds unduly, but comes to **p.** 4728
13:18 He who ignores discipline comes to **p** 8203
14:23 but mere talk leads only to **p.** 4728
21:5 to profit as surely as haste leads to **p.** 4728
22:16 who gives gifts to the rich—both come to **p.** 4728
24:34 and **p** will come on you like a bandit 8203
28:19 who chases fantasies will have his fill of **p.** 8203
28:22 and is unaware that **p** awaits him. 2895
30:8 give me neither **p** nor riches, 8203
31:7 let them drink and forget their **p** 8203
Ecc 4:14 or he may have been born in **p** 8133
Mk 12:44 but she, out *of* her **p,** put in everything— *5730*
Lk 21:4 of her **p** put in all she had to live on." *5729*
2Co 8:2 their extreme **p** welled up in rich generosity. *4775*
8:9 that you *through* his **p** might become rich. *4775*
Rev 2:9 I know your afflictions and your **p**— *4775*

POWDER (7)

Ex 30:36 Grind some of it to **p** and place it in front of 1990
32:20 then he ground it to **p,** 1990
Dt 9:21 and **ground** it **to p** as fine as dust and 3221+3512
28:24 the rain of your country into dust and **p;** 85
2Ki 23:6 to **p** and scattered the dust over the graves 6760
23:15 the high place and ground it to **p,** 6760
2Ch 34:7 to **p** and cut to pieces all the incense altars 1990

POWER (276) [OVERPOWER, OVERPOWERED, OVERPOWERING, OVERPOWERS, POWERFUL, POWERFULLY, POWERLESS, POWERS]

Ge 31:29 I have the **p** to harm you; 445+3338
49:3 excelling in honor, excelling in **p.** 6435
Ex 1:8 not know about Joseph, **came to p** in Egypt. 7756
4:21 the wonders I have given you the **p** to do. 3338
9:16 that I might show you my **p** and 3946
14:31 the great **p** the LORD displayed against 3338
15:6 Your right hand, O LORD, was majestic in **p.** 3946
15:16 By the **p** *of* your arm they will be as still as 1524
32:11 of Egypt with great **p** and a mighty hand? 3946
Nu 14:13 By your **p** you brought these people up 3946
Dt 7:8 from the **p** *of* Pharaoh king of Egypt. 3338
8:17 "My **p** and the strength of my hands 3946
9:26 by your **great p** and brought out of Egypt 1542
9:29 by your great **p** and your outstretched arm." 3946
34:12 For no one has ever shown the mighty **p** 3338
Jdg 1:35 the **p** *of* the house of Joseph increased, 3338
3:12 **gave** Eglon king of Moab **p** over Israel. 2616
6:2 the **p** *of* Midian was so oppressive, 3338
6:9 I snatched you from the **p** *of* Egypt and 3338
14:6 The Spirit of the LORD **came** upon him **in p** 7502
14:19 the Spirit of the LORD **came** upon him **in p.** 7502
15:14 The Spirit of the LORD **came** upon him **in p.** 7502
1Sa 7:14 the neighboring territory from the **p** *of* 3338
10:6 Spirit of the LORD *will* **come** upon you **in p,** 7502
10:10 the Spirit of God **came** upon him **in p,** 7502
10:18 from the **p** *of* Egypt and all the kingdoms 3338
11:6 the Spirit of God **came** upon him **in p,** 7502
16:13 Spirit of the LORD **came** upon David **in p.** 7502
1Ki 18:46 The **p** *of* the LORD came upon Elijah 3338
2Ki 13:3 for a long time he kept them under the **p** 3338
13:5 and they escaped from the **p** *of* Aram. 3338
17:7 from under the **p** *of* Pharaoh king of Egypt. 3338
17:36 with mighty **p** and outstretched arm, 3946
19:26 Their people, drained of **p,** 3338
1Ch 29:11 and the **p** and the glory and the majesty and 1476
29:12 In your hands are strength and **p** to exalt 1476
29:30 together with the details of his reign and **p,** 1476
2Ch 13:20 Jeroboam did not regain **p** during the time 3946
20:6 **P** and might are in your hand, 3946
20:12 For we have no **p** to face this vast army 3946
25:8 for God has the **p** to help or to overthrow." 3946
32:7 there is a **greater p** with us than with him. 8041
36:20 until the kingdom of Persia **came to p.** 4887
Est 10:2 And all his acts of **p** and might, 9549
Job 6:13 Do I have any **p** to help myself, NIH
9:4 His wisdom is profound, his **p** is vast. 3946
10:16 again **display** *your* **awesome p** against me. 7098
12:13 "To God belong wisdom and **p;** 1476
21:7 growing old and increasing in **p?** 2657
23:6 Would he oppose me with great **p?** 3946
24:22 But God drags away the mighty by his **p;** 3946
26:12 By his **p** he churned up the sea; 3946
26:14 then can understand the thunder of his **p?"** 1476
27:11 "I will teach you about the **p** *of* God; 3338
27:22 as he flees headlong from its **p.** 3338
30:18 In his great **p** [God] becomes like clothing 3946
36:22 "God is exalted in his **p.** 3946
37:23 beyond our reach and exalted in **p;** 3946
40:16 what **p** in the muscles of his belly! 226
Ps 20:6 from his holy heaven with the saving **p** 1476
22:20 my precious life from the **p** *of* the dogs. 3338
37:17 for the **p** *of* the wicked will be broken, 2432
37:33 the LORD will not leave them in their **p** 3338
63:2 in the sanctuary and beheld your **p** 6437
65:6 who formed the mountains by your **p,** 3946
66:3 So great is your **p** that your enemies cringe 6437
66:7 He rules forever by his **p,** 1476
68:28 Summon your **p,** O God; 6437
68:34 Proclaim the **p** of God, 6437
68:34 whose **p** is in the skies. 6437
68:35 of Israel gives **p** and strength to his people. 6437
71:18 till I declare your **p** to the next generation, 2432
74:13 you who split open the sea by your **p;** 6437
77:14 you display your **p** among the peoples. 6437
78:4 his **p,** and the wonders he has done. 6449
78:26 and led forth the south wind by his **p.** 6437
78:42 They did not remember his **p**— 3338
89:13 Your arm is endued with **p;** 1476
89:48 or save himself from the **p** *of* the grave? 3338
90:11 Who knows the **p** *of* your anger? 6437
106:8 to make his **mighty p** known. 1476
106:42 and subjected them to their **p.** 3338
111:6 He has shown his people the **p** of his works, 3946
145:6 of the **p** *of* your awesome works, 6449
147:5 Great is our Lord and mighty in **p;** 3946
150:2 Praise him for his **acts of p;** 1476
Pr 3:27 when it is in your **p** to act. 445+3338
8:14 I have understanding and **p.** 1476
11:7 all he expected from his **p** comes to nothing. 226
18:21 The tongue has the **p** *of* life and death, 3338
24:5 A wise man has **great p,** 6437
28:12 the wicked **rise to p,** men go into hiding. 7756
28:28 the wicked **rise to p,** people go into hiding; 7756
30:26 of little **p,** yet they make their home in 6786
Ecc 4:1 **p** was on the side of their oppressors— 3946
8:8 No man has **p** over the wind to contain it; 8954
8:8 so no one has **p** over the day of his death. 8950
Isa 10:33 will lop off the boughs with **great p.** 5124
11:2 the Spirit of counsel and of **p,** 1476
17:3 and **royal p** from Damascus; 4930
19:4 I will hand the Egyptians over to the **p** *of* 3338
33:13 you who are near, acknowledge my **p!** 1476
37:27 Their people, drained of **p,** 3338
40:10 See, the Sovereign LORD comes with **p,** 2617
40:26 Because of his great **p** and mighty strength, 226
40:29 the weary and increases the **p** of the weak. 6800
47:14 even save themselves from the **p** *of* 3338
63:12 who sent his glorious **arm of p** to be 2432
Jer 10:6 and your name is mighty in **p.** 1476
10:12 But God made the earth by his **p;** 3946
16:21 this time I will teach them my **p** and might. 3338
18:21 hand them over to the **p** *of* the sword. 3338
23:10 an evil course and use their **p** unjustly. 1476
27:5 With my great **p** and outstretched arm 3946
32:17 the heavens and the earth by your great **p** 3946
51:15 "He made the earth by his **p;** 3946
Eze 13:21 and they will no longer fall prey to your **p.** 3338
22:6 who are in you uses his **p** to shed blood. 2432
26:17 You were a **p** on the seas, 2617
32:29 despite their **p,** they are laid with those 1476
32:30 despite the terror caused by their **p.** 1476
Da 2:20 wisdom and **p** are his. 10130
2:23 You have given me wisdom and **p,** 10130
2:37 of heaven has given you dominion and **p** 10278
4:30 by my mighty **p** and for the glory 10774
6:27 He has rescued Daniel from the **p** *of* 10311
7:14 authority, glory and **sovereign p;** 10424
7:26 and his **p** will be taken away 10717
7:27 **p** and greatness of the kingdoms under 10717
8:4 and none could rescue from his **p.** 3338
8:7 and none could rescue the ram from his **p.** 3338
8:8 at the **height of** his **p** his large horn was broken off, 6793
8:9 in **p** to the south and to the east and toward 3856
8:22 but will not have the same **p.** 3946
8:24 become very strong, but not by his own **p.** 3946
8:25 he will be destroyed, but not by human **p.** 3338
11:2 When he has **gained p** by his wealth, 2621
11:3 with great **p** and do as he pleases. 4938
11:4 nor will it have the **p** he exercised, 5445
11:5 and will rule his own kingdom with great **p.** 4938
11:6 but she will not retain her **p,** 2432+3946
11:6 and he and his **p** will not last. 2432
11:16 and will have the **p to destroy** it. 3986
11:23 with only a few people he will rise *to* **p.** 6793
11:42 He will extend his **p** over many countries; 3338
12:7 When the **p** *of* the holy people 3338
Hos 13:14 "I will ransom them from the **p** *of* the grave; 3338
Mic 2:1 because it is in their **p** to do it. 445+3338
3:8 But as for me, I am filled with **p,** 3946
7:16 deprived of all their **p.** 1476
Na 1:3 LORD is slow to anger and great in **p;** 3946
Hab 3:4 where his **p** was hidden. 6437
Hag 2:22 and shatter the **p** *of* the foreign kingdoms. 2620
Zec 4:6 'Not by might nor by **p,** but by my Spirit,' 3946
9:4 and destroy her **p** on the sea, 2657
Mt 22:29 not know the Scriptures or the **p** of God. *1539*
24:30 with **p** and great glory. *1539*
Mk 5:30 At once Jesus realized that **p** had gone out *1539*
9:1 the kingdom of God come with **p."** *1539*
12:24 not know the Scriptures or the **p** of God? *1539*
13:26 Son of Man coming in clouds with great **p** *1539*
Lk 1:17 in the spirit and **p** of Elijah, *1539*
1:35 **p** of the Most High will overshadow you. *1539*
4:14 Jesus returned to Galilee in the **p** of the Spirit, *1539*
4:36 With authority and **p** he gives orders *1539*
5:17 And the **p** of the Lord was present for him *1539*
6:19 because **p** was coming from him *1539*
8:46 I know that **p** has gone out from me." *1539*
9:1 he gave them **p** and authority *1539*
10:19 to overcome all the **p** of the enemy; *1539*
12:5 has **p** to throw you into hell. *2026*
20:20 over *to* the **p** and authority of the governor. *794*
21:27 the Son of Man coming in a cloud with **p** *1539*
24:49 the city until you have been clothed with **p** *1539*
Jn 13:3 Father had put all things **under** his **p,** *1650+5931*
17:11 protect them **by the p of** your name— *1877*
19:10 "Don't you realize I have **p** either to free *2026*
19:11 "You would have no **p** over me if it were *2026*
Ac 1:8 But you will receive **p** when the Holy Spirit comes on you; *1539*
3:12 Why do you stare at us as if *by* our own **p** *1539*
4:7 "By what **p** or what name did you do this?" *1539*
4:28 They did what your **p** and will had *5931*
4:33 *With* great **p** the apostles continued *1539*
6:8 Stephen, a man full of God's grace and **p,** *1539*
8:10 the divine **p** known as the Great Power." *1539*
8:10 the divine power known as the Great **P."** *NIG*
10:38 Jesus of Nazareth with the Holy Spirit and **p** *1539*
10:38 and healing all who *were* **under the p** of *2872*
13:17 in Egypt, with mighty **p** he led them out of *1098*
19:20 of the Lord spread widely and grew in **p.** *3197*

Ac 26:18 and from the **p** of Satan to God, *2026*
Ro 1: 4 the Spirit of holiness was declared with **p** *1539*
1:16 because it is the **p** of God for the salvation *1539*
1:20 his eternal **p** and divine nature— *1539*
4:21 that God **had p** to do what he had promised. *1543+1639*
9:17 that I might display my **p** in you and *1539*
9:22 to show his wrath and make his **p** known, *1543*
15:13 that you may overflow with hope by the **p** *1539*
15:19 by the **p** of signs and miracles, *1539*
15:19 through the **p** of the Spirit. *1539*
1Co 1:17 lest the cross of Christ be emptied of its **p.** *NIG*
1:18 but to us who are being saved it is the **p** *1539*
1:24 the **p** of God and the wisdom of God. *1539*
2: 4 but with a demonstration *of* the Spirit's **p,** *1539*
2: 5 not rest on man's wisdom, but on God's **p.** *1539*
4:19 but what **p** they have. *1539*
4:20 of God is not a matter of talk but of **p.** *1539*
5: 4 and the **p** of our Lord Jesus is present, *1539*
6:14 By his **p** God raised the Lord from *1539*
15:24 after he has destroyed all dominion, authority and **p.** *1539*
15:43 it is sown in weakness, it is raised in **p;** *1539*
15:56 and the **p** of sin is the law. *1539*
2Co 4: 7 show that this all-surpassing **p** is from God *1539*
6: 7 in truthful speech and in the **p** of God; *1539*
10: 4 they have divine **p** to demolish strongholds. *1543*
12: 9 for my **p** is made perfect in weakness." *1539*
12: 9 so that Christ's **p** may rest on me. *1539*
13: 4 yet he lives by God's **p.** *1539*
13: 4 yet by God's **p** we will live with him *1539*
Gal 4:29 the son born by the **p** of the Spirit. *NIG*
Eph 1:19 and his incomparably great **p** for us *1539*
1:19 **p** is like the working of his mighty strength, *NIG*
1:21 **p** and dominion, and every title that can *1539*
3: 7 through the working *of* his **p.** *1539*
3:16 *with* **p** through his Spirit *1539*
3:18 *may have* **p,** together with all the saints, *2015*
3:20 according to his **p** that is at work within us, *1539*
6:10 be strong in the Lord and in his mighty **p.** *3197*
Php 3:10 to know Christ and the **p** of his resurrection *1539*
3:21 the **p** that enables him to bring everything *1918*
Col 1:11 with all **p** according to his glorious might *1539*
2:10 who is the head *over* every **p** and authority. *794*
2:12 with him through your faith *in* the **p** *1918*
1Th 1: 5 not simply with words, but also with **p,** *1539*
2Th 1: 9 of the Lord and from the majesty *of* his **p** *2709*
1:11 by his **p** he may fulfill every good purpose *1539*
2: 7 secret **p** of lawlessness is already at work; *NIG*
2Ti 1: 7 give us a spirit of timidity, but a spirit *of* **p,** *1539*
1: 8 suffering for the gospel, by the **p** of God, *1539*
3: 5 a form of godliness but denying its **p.** *1539*
Heb 2:14 destroy him who holds the **p** of death— *3197*
7:16 to his ancestry but on the basis of the **p** of *1539*
1Pe 1: 5 through faith are shielded by God's **p** until *1539*
4:11 be the glory and the **p** for ever and ever. *3197*
5:11 To him be the **p** for ever and ever. Amen. *3197*
2Pe 1: 3 His divine **p** has given us everything we need for life and godliness *1539*
1:16 the **p** and coming of our Lord Jesus Christ, *1539*
Jude 1:25 be glory, majesty, **p** and authority, *3197*
Rev 1: 6 to him be glory and **p** for ever and ever! *3197*
4:11 to receive glory and honor and **p,** *1539*
5:12 the Lamb, who was slain, to receive **p** *1539*
5:13 be praise and honor and glory and **p,** *3197*
6: 4 Its rider was given **p** to take peace from *NIG*
6: 8 They were given **p** over a fourth of *2026*
7: 2 to the four angels who had been given **p** *NIG*
7:12 and honor and **p** and strength be to our God *1539*
9: 3 down upon the earth and were given **p** like *2026*
9: 5 They were not given **p** to kill them, *NIG*
9:10 in their tails they had **p** to torment people *2026*
9:19 The **p** of the horses was in their mouths and *2026*
11: 3 And I will give **p** to my two witnesses, *NIG*
11: 6 These men have **p** to shut up the sky so *2026*
11: 6 and they have **p** to turn the waters *2026*
11:17 because you have taken your great **p** *1539*
12:10 "Now have come the salvation and the **p** *1539*
13: 2 The dragon gave the beast his **p** *1539*
13: 7 He was given **p** to make war against *NIG*
13:14 the signs he was given **p** to do on behalf of *NIG*
13:15 He was given **p** to give breath to the image *NIG*
15: 8 from the glory of God and from his **p,** *1539*
16: 8 sun was given **p** to scorch people with fire *NIG*
17:13 and will give their **p** and authority to *1539*
17:17 by agreeing to give the beast their **p** to rule, *NIG*
18:10 Woe, O great city, O Babylon, city of **p!** *2708*
19: 1 and glory and **p** belong to our God, *1539*
20: 6 The second death has no **p** over them, *2026*

POWERFUL (56) [POWER]

Ge 18:18 surely become a great and **p** nation, 6786
26:16 *you have become* too **p** for us." 6793
Nu 13:28 But the people who live there are **p,** 6434
20:20 against them with a large and **p** army. 2617
22: 6 because they are too **p** for me. 6786
Dt 26: 5 a great nation, **p** and numerous. 6786
Jos 4:24 that the hand of the LORD is **p** and so 2617
17:17 "You are numerous and very **p.** 3946
23: 9 before you great and **p** nations; 6786
2Sa 5:10 *he* **became more and more p,** 1524+2143+2143+2256
22:18 He rescued me from my **p** enemy, 6434
1Ki 19:11 a great and **p** wind tore the mountains apart 2617
1Ch 11: 9 David **became more and more p,** 1524+2143+2143+2256
2Ch 17:12 Jehoshaphat became **more and more p;** 1541+2025+2143+2256+4200+5087+6330
22: 9 of Ahaziah **p** *enough* to retain the kingdom. 3946
26: 8 because *he had become* very **p.** 2616
26:13 a **p** force to support the king 3946
26:15 for he was greatly helped until *he became* **p.** 2616
26:16 But after Uzziah **became p,** 2621
27: 6 Jotham *grew* **p** because he walked 2616
Ezr 4:20 Jerusalem has had **p** kings ruling over 10768
7:28 and all the king's **p** officials. 1475
Est 9: 4 **became more and more p.** 1524+2143+2256
Job 5:15 he saves them from the clutches of the **p.** 2617
22: 8 though you were a **p** man, owning land— 2432
35: 9 they plead for relief from the arm of the **p.** 8041
Ps 18:17 He rescued me from my **p** enemy, 6434
29: 4 The voice of the LORD is **p;** 3946
Ecc 7:19 Wisdom **makes** one wise man more **p** than 6451
9:14 And a **p** king came against it, 1524
Isa 27: 1 his fierce, great and **p** sword, 2617
28: 2 See, the Lord has *one who* is **p** and strong. 2617
Jer 5:27 they have become rich and **p** 1540
32:18 O great and **p** God, 1475
Eze 17: 3 A great eagle with **p** wings, 1524
17: 7 with **p** wings and full plumage. 1524
Da 7: 7 terrifying and frightening and very **p.** 10768
11:25 with a large and very **p** army, 6786
Joel 1: 6 **p** and without number; 6786
Mic 7: 3 the **p** dictate what they desire— 1524
Zec 6: 3 the fourth dappled—*all of them* **p.** 600
6: 7 When the **p** horses went out, 600
8:22 And many peoples and **p** nations will come 6786
Mt 3:11 me will come one who is **more p** than I, *2708*
Mk 1: 7 "After me will come one **more p than** I, *2708*
Lk 3:16 But one **more p than** I will come, *2708*
24:19 **p** in word and deed before God and all *1543*
Ac 7:22 the wisdom of the Egyptians and was **p** *1543*
9:22 Yet Saul *grew* more and more **p** and baffled *1904*
2Co 13: 3 but *is* **p** among you. *1542*
2Th 1: 7 in blazing fire with his **p** angels. *1539*
2:11 a **p** delusion so that they will believe the lie *1918*
Heb 1: 3 sustaining all things by his **p** word. *1539*
11:34 and who became **p** in battle *2708*
Jas 5:16 of a righteous man *is* **p** and effective. *2710*
2Pe 2:11 although they are stronger and more **p,** *1539*

POWERFULLY (1) [POWER]

Col 1:29 his energy, which **so p** works in me. *1539+1877*

POWERLESS (9) [POWER]

Dt 28:32 **p** to lift a hand. 401+445+4200
2Ch 14:11 you to help the **p** against the mighty. 401+3946
Ne 5: 5 but we are **p,** 401+445+3338+4200
Job 26: 2 "How you have helped the **p!** 3946+4202
Jer 14: 9 like a warrior **p** to save? 3523+4202
Da 8: 7 The ram was **p** to stand against him; 3946+4202
11:15 The forces of the South will be **p** to resist; 4202
Ro 5: 6 at just the right time, when we were still **p,** *820*
8: 3 the law was **p** to do in that it was weakened *105*

POWERS (12) [POWER]

Isa 24:21 In that day the LORD will punish the **p** *in* 7372
Da 4:35 He does as he pleases with the **p** *of* heaven 10264
Mt 13:54 and these **miraculous p?"** *1539*
14: 2 That is why **miraculous p** are at work *1539*
Mk 6:14 and that is why **miraculous p** are at work *1539*
Ro 8:38 the present nor the future, nor any **p,** *1539*
1Co 12:10 to another **miraculous p,** *1539+1920*
Eph 6:12 against the **p of** this dark **world** *3179*
Col 1:16 and invisible, whether thrones or **p** or rulers *3262*
2:15 And having disarmed the **p** and authorities, *794*
Heb 6: 5 the goodness of the word of God and the **p** *1539*
1Pe 3:22 authorities and **p** in submission to him. *1539*

PRACTICALLY (1)

Ac 19:26 in Ephesus and in **p** the whole province *5385*

PRACTICE (31) [PRACTICED, PRACTICES]

Lev 19:26 " '*Do* not **p divination** or sorcery. 5727
Dt 18:11 to *those who* **p sorcery** or divination. 6726
1Sa 2:13 Now it was the **p** *of* the priests with 5477
27:11 And such was his **p** as long as he lived 5477
Ps 52: 2 like a sharpened razor, you *who* **p** deceit. 6913
119:56 **This** has been my *p:* I obey your precepts. AIT
Ecc 8: 8 wickedness will not release *those who* **p** it. 1251
Isa 2: 6 *they* **p divination** like the Philistines 6726
Jer 6:13 prophets and priests alike, all **p** deceit. 6913
8:10 prophets and priests alike, all **p** deceit. 6913
Eze 13:23 therefore you will no longer see false visions or **p divination.** 7876+7877
22:29 land **p extortion** and commit robbery; 6943+6945
33:31 but *they do* not **put** them **into p.** 6913
33:32 but *do* not **put** them **into p.** 6913
Hos 7: 1 *They* **p** deceit, thieves break into houses, 7188
Mt 7:24 words of mine and **puts** them **into p** is like *4472*
7:26 words of mine and *does* not **put** them **into p** *4472*
23: 3 for *they do* not **p** what they preach. *4472*
Lk 6:47 and hears my words and **puts** them **into p.** *4472*
6:49 not **put** them **into p** is like a man who built *4472*
8:21 who hear God's word and **put** it **into p."** *4472*
Ac 16:21 for us Romans to accept or **p."** *4472*
Ro 1:32 but also approve of those who **p** them. *4556*
3:13 their tongues **p deceit."** *1514*
Ro 12:13 God's people who are in need. **P** hospitality. *1503*
1Co 11:16 we have no other **p**—nor do the churches *5311*
Php 4: 9 or seen in me—**put** it **into p.** *4556*
1Ti 5: 4 **put** *their* **religion into p by caring for** *2355*
Jas 3:16 there you find disorder and every evil **p.** *4547*
Rev 21: 8 **those who p magic arts,** *5761*
22:15 those who **p magic arts,** *5761*

PRACTICED (10) [PRACTICE]

Lev 18:30 detestable customs that **were p** before you 6913
Jos 13:22 Balaam son of Beor, who **p divination.** 7876
2Ki 17:17 *They* **p divination** and sorcery 7876+7877
21: 6 **p sorcery** and divination, 6726
2Ch 33: 6 **p sorcery,** divination and witchcraft, 6726
Eze 18:18 because *he* **p extortion,** 6943+6945
Mt 23:23 You should have **p** the latter, *4472*
Lk 11:42 You should *have* **p** the latter *4472*
Ac 8: 9 a man named Simon *had* **p sorcery** in *3405*
19:19 A number who *had* **p** sorcery brought their scrolls together *4556*

PRACTICES (53) [PRACTICE]

Ex 23:24 or worship them or follow their **p.** 5126
Lev 18: 3 Do not follow their **p.** 2978
Dt 18:10 *who* **p divination** or sorcery, 7876+7877
18:12 and because of these **detestable p** 9359
Jdg 2:19 to give up their **evil p** and stubborn ways. 5095
1Ki 14:24 the people engaged in all the **detestable p** 9359
2Ki 17: 8 and followed the **p** *of* the nations 2978
17: 8 as well as the **p** that the kings of Israel NIH
17:19 They followed the **p** Israel had introduced. 2978
17:34 To this day they persist in their former **p.** 5477
17:40 however, but persisted in their former **p.** 5477
21: 2 following the **detestable p** *of* the nations 9359
2Ch 17: 4 his commands rather than the **p** *of* Israel. 5126
27: 2 however, continued *their* **corrupt p.** 8845
33: 2 following the **detestable p** *of* the nations 9359
36:14 following all the **detestable p** *of* the nations 9359
Ezr 6:21 the **unclean p** *of* their Gentile neighbors 3240
9: 1 peoples with their **detestable p,** 9359
9:11 By their **detestable p** they have filled it 9359
9:14 peoples who commit such **detestable p?** 9359
Ps 101: 7 No *one who* **p** deceit will dwell 6913
Isa 32: 6 He **p** ungodliness and spreads error 6913
Jer 25: 5 from your evil ways and your evil **p,** 5095
Eze 5:11 with all your vile images and **detestable p,** 9359
6: 9 and for all their **detestable p.** 9359
6:11 because of all the wicked and **detestable p** 9359
7: 3 and repay you for all your **detestable p.** 9359
7: 4 for your conduct and the **detestable p** 9359
7: 8 and repay you for all your **detestable p.** 9359
7: 9 with your conduct and the **detestable p** 9359
12:16 may acknowledge all their **detestable p.** 9359
14: 6 and renounce all your **detestable p!** 9359
16: 2 confront Jerusalem with her **detestable p** 9359
16:22 In all your **detestable p** 9359
16:43 to all your other **detestable p?** 9359
16:47 and copied their **detestable p,** 9359
16:58 of your lewdness and your **detestable p,** 9359
20: 4 Then confront them with the **detestable p** 9359
20:44 to your evil ways and your corrupt **p,** 6613
22: 2 Then confront her with all her **detestable p** 9359
23:36 confront them with their **detestable p,** 9359
36:31 for your sins and **detestable p.** 9359
43: 8 defiled my holy name by their **detestable p.** 9359
44: 6 Enough of your **detestable p,** 9359
44: 7 In addition to all your other **detestable p,** 9359
44:13 the shame of their **detestable p.** 9359
Mic 6:16 of Omri and all the **p** *of* Ahab's house, 5126
Zec 1: 4 'Turn from your evil ways and your evil **p.'** 5095
1: 6 to us what our ways and **p** deserve, 5095
Mt 5:19 in the kingdom of heaven, but whoever **p** *4472*
Col 3: 9 you have taken off your old self with its **p** *4552*
Rev 2: 6 You hate the **p** of the Nicolaitans, *2240*
22:15 and everyone who loves and **p** falsehood. *4472*

PRAETORIUM (2)

Mt 27:27 into the **P** and gathered the whole company *4550*
Mk 15:16 the palace (that is, the **P**) and called together *4550*

PRAISE (340) [PRAISED, PRAISES, PRAISEWORTHY, PRAISING]

Ge 24:27 "**P** *be to* the LORD, 1385
29:35 "This time *I will* **p** the LORD." 3344
49: 8 "Judah, your brothers *will* **p** you; 3344
Ex 15: 2 He is my God, and *I will* **p** him, 5658
18:10 He said, "**P** *be to* the LORD, 1385
Lev 19:24 an **offering** of **p** to the LORD. 2136
Dt 8:10 **p** the LORD your God for the good land 1385
10:21 He is your **p;** he is your God, 9335
26:19 He has declared that he will set you in **p,** 9335
32: 3 Oh, **p** the greatness of our God! 2035
Jos 7:19 the God of Israel, and give him the **p.** 9343
Jdg 5: 2 when the people willingly offer themselves—**p** the LORD! 1385
5: 9 **P** the LORD! 1385
Ru 4:14 "**P** *be to* the LORD, 1385
1Sa 25:32 "**P** *be to* the LORD, the God of Israel, 1385
25:39 he said, "**P** *be to* the LORD, 1385
2Sa 18:28 "**P** *be to* the LORD your God! 1385
22: 4 I call to the LORD, *who is* **worthy of p,** 2146
22:47 **P** *be to* my Rock! 1385
22:50 Therefore *I will* **p** you, O LORD, 3344
1Ki 1:48 '**P** *be to* the LORD, the God of Israel, 1385

1Ki 5: 7 "P be to the LORD today, 1385
8:15 "P be to the LORD, the God of Israel, 1385
8:56 "P be to the LORD, who has given rest 1385
10: 9 P be to the LORD your God, 1385
1Ch 16: 4 and to p the LORD, the God of Israel: 2146
16: 9 Sing to him, sing p to him; 2376
16:25 great is the LORD and most worthy of p; 2146
16:35 that we may glory in your p." 9335
16:36 P be to the LORD, the God of Israel, 1385
16:36 Then all the people said "Amen" and "P 2146
23: 5 and four thousand are to p the LORD with 2146
23:30 also to stand every morning to thank and p 2146
29:10 saying, "P be to you, O LORD, 1385
29:13 and p your glorious name. 2146
29:20 "P the LORD your God." 1385
2Ch 2:12 And Hiram added: "P be to the LORD, 1385
5:13 to give p and thanks to the LORD. 2146
5:13 they raised their voices in p to the LORD 2146
6: 4 "P be to the LORD, the God of Israel, 1385
8:14 and the Levites to lead the p and to assist 2146
9: 8 P be to the LORD your God, 1385
20:21 the LORD and to p him for the splendor 2146
20:22 As they began to sing and p, 9335
29:30 the Levites to p the LORD with the words 2146
30:21 by the LORD's instruments of p. 6437
Ezr 3:10 took their places to p the LORD, 2146
3:11 With p and thanksgiving they sang to 2146
3:11 And all the people gave a great shout of p 2146
7:27 P be to the LORD, the God of our fathers, 1385
Ne 9: 5 "Stand up and p the LORD your God, 1385
9: 5 may it be exalted above all blessing and p. 9335
12:24 who stood opposite them to give p 2146
12:46 for the songs of p and thanksgiving to God. 9335
Ps 7:17 and will sing p to the LORD Most High. 2376
8: 2 of children and infants you have ordained p 6437
9: 1 I will p you, O LORD, 3344
9: 2 I will sing p to your name, O Most High. 2376
16: 7 I will p the LORD, who counsels me; 1385
18: 3 I call to the LORD, who is worthy of p, 2146
18:46 P be to my Rock! 1385
18:49 Therefore I will p you among the nations, 3344
21:13 we will sing and p your might. 2376
22: 3 you are the p of Israel. 9335
22:22 in the congregation I will p you. 2146
22:23 You who fear the LORD, p him! 2146
22:25 the theme of my p in the great assembly; 9335
22:26 they who seek the LORD will p him— 2146
26: 7 proclaiming aloud your p and telling 9343
26:12 in the great assembly I will p the LORD. 1385
28: 6 P be to the LORD, 1385
30: 4 p his holy name. 3344
30: 9 Will the dust p you? 3344
31:21 P be to the LORD, 1385
33: 1 it is fitting for the upright to p him. 9335
33: 2 P the LORD with the harp; 3344
34: 1 his p will always be on my lips. 9335
35:18 among throngs of people I will p you. 2146
40: 3 a hymn of p to our God. 9335
41:13 P be to the LORD, the God of Israel, 1385
42: 5 for I will yet p him, 3344
42:11 for I will yet p him, 3344
43: 4 I will p you with the harp, O God, 3344
43: 5 for I will yet p him, 3344
44: 8 and we will p your name forever. 3344
45:17 the nations will p you for ever and ever. 3344
47: 7 sing to him a psalm of p. 5380
48: 1 Great is the LORD, and most worthy of p, 2146
48:10 your p reaches to the ends of the earth; 9335
49:18 and men p you when you prosper— 3344
51:15 and my mouth will declare your p. 9335
52: 9 I will p you forever 3344
52: 9 I will p you in the presence of your saints. NIH
54: 6 I will p your name, O LORD, 3344
56: 4 In God, whose word I p, in God I trust; 2146
56:10 In God, whose word I p, in the LORD, 2146
56:10 in the LORD, whose word I p— 2146
57: 9 I will p you, O Lord, among the nations; 3344
59:17 O my Strength, I sing p to you; 2376
61: 8 Then will I ever sing p to your name 2376
63: 4 I will p you as long as I live, 1385
63: 5 with singing lips my mouth will p you. 2146
63:11 all who swear by God's name will p him, 2146
64:10 let all the upright in heart p him! 2146
65: 1 P awaits you, O God, in Zion; 9335
66: 2 make his p glorious! 9335
66: 4 they sing p to you, 2376
66: 4 they sing p to your name." 2376
66: 8 P our God, O peoples, let the sound 1385
66: 8 O peoples, let the sound of his p be heard; 9335
66:17 his p was on my tongue. 8128
66:20 P be to God, 1385
67: 3 May the peoples p you, O God; 3344
67: 3 may all the peoples p you. 3344
67: 5 May the peoples p you, O God; 3344
67: 5 may all the peoples p you. 3344
68: 4 Sing to God, sing p to his name, 2376
68:19 P be to the Lord, to God our Savior, 1385
68:26 P God in the great congregation; 1385
68:26 p the LORD in the assembly of Israel. NIH
68:32 sing p to the Lord, 2376
68:35 P be to God! 1385
69:30 I will p God's name in song 2146
69:34 Let heaven and earth p him, 2146
71: 6 I will ever p you. 9335
71: 8 My mouth is filled with your p, 9335
71:14 I will p you more and more. 9335
71:22 I will p you with the harp 3344
Ps 71:22 I will sing p to you with the lyre, 2376
71:23 My lips will shout for joy when I sing p 2376
72:18 P be to the LORD God, the God of Israel, 1385
72:19 P be to his glorious name forever; 1385
74:21 may the poor and needy p your name. 2146
75: 9 I will sing p to the God of Jacob. 2376
76:10 your wrath against men brings you p, 3344
79:13 sheep of your pasture, will p you forever; 3344
79:13 to generation we will recount your p. 9335
86:12 I will p you, O Lord my God, 3344
88:10 Do those who are dead rise up and p you? 3344
89: 5 The heavens p your wonders, 3344
89:52 P be to the LORD forever! 1385
92: 1 It is good to p the LORD and make music 3344
96: 2 Sing to the LORD, p his name; 1385
96: 4 great is the LORD and most worthy of p; 2146
97:12 and p his holy name. 3344
99: 3 Let them p your great and awesome name 3344
100: 4 with thanksgiving and his courts with p; 9335
100: 4 give thanks to him and p his name. 1385
101: 1 to you, O LORD, I will sing p. 2376
102:18 a people not yet created may p the LORD: 2146
102:21 be declared in Zion and his p in Jerusalem 9335
103: 1 P the LORD, O my soul; 1385
103: 1 all my inmost being, p his holy name. NIH
103: 2 P the LORD, O my soul, 1385
103:20 P the LORD, you his angels, 1385
103:21 P the LORD, all his heavenly hosts, 1385
103:22 P the LORD, all his works everywhere 1385
103:22 P the LORD, O my soul. 1385
104: 1 P the LORD, O my soul. 1385
104:33 I will sing p to my God as long as I live. 2376
104:35 P the LORD, O my soul. 1385
104:35 P the LORD. 2146
105: 2 Sing to him, sing p to him; 2376
105:45 P the LORD. 2146
106: 1 P the LORD. 2146
106: 2 acts of the LORD or fully declare his p? 9335
106: 5 and join your inheritance in giving p. 2146
106:12 they believed his promises and sang his p. 9335
106:47 to your holy name and glory in your p. 9335
106:48 P be to the LORD, the God of Israel, 1385
106:48 P the LORD. 2146
107:32 and p him in the council of the elders. 2146
108: 3 I will p you, O LORD, 3344
109: 1 O God, whom I p, do not remain silent, 9335
109:30 in the great throng I will p him. 2146
111: 1 P the LORD. 2146
111:10 To him belongs eternal p. 9335
112: 1 P the LORD. 2146
113: 1 P the LORD. 2146
113: 1 P, O servants of the LORD, 2146
113: 1 p the name of the LORD. 2146
113: 9 P the LORD. 2146
115:17 It is not the dead who p the LORD, 2146
115:18 P the LORD. 2146
116:19 P the LORD. 2146
117: 1 P the LORD, all you nations; 2146
117: 2 P the LORD. 2146
119: 7 I will p you with an upright heart 3344
119:12 P be to you, O LORD; 1385
119:108 O LORD, the willing p of my mouth, NIH
119:164 a day I p you for your righteous laws. 2146
119:171 May my lips overflow with p, 9335
119:175 Let me live that I may p you, 2146
122: 4 to p the name of the LORD according to 3344
124: 6 P be to the LORD, 1385
134: 1 P the LORD, all you servants of the LORD 1385
134: 2 Lift up your hands in the sanctuary and p 1385
135: 1 P the LORD. 2146
135: 1 P the name of the LORD; 2146
135: 1 Praise the name of the LORD; p him, 2146
135: 3 P the LORD, for the LORD is good; 2146
135: 3 sing p to his name, for that is pleasant. 2376
135:19 O house of Israel, p the LORD; 1385
135:19 O house of Aaron, p the LORD; 1385
135:20 O house of Levi, p the LORD; 1385
135:20 you who fear him, p the LORD. 1385
135:21 P be to the LORD from Zion, 1385
135:21 P the LORD. 2146
138: 1 I will p you, O LORD, 3344
138: 1 before the "gods" I will sing your p. 2376
138: 2 and will p your name for your love 3344
138: 4 May all the kings of the earth p you, 3344
139:14 I p you because I am fearfully 3344
140:13 Surely the righteous will p your name and 3344
142: 7 that I may p your name. 3344
144: 1 P be to the LORD my Rock, 1385
145: T A psalm of p. Of David. 9335
145: 1 I will p your name for ever and ever. 1385
145: 2 Every day I will p you 1385
145: 3 Great is the LORD and most worthy of p; 2146
145:10 All you have made will p you, O LORD; 3344
145:21 My mouth will speak in p of the LORD. 9335
145:21 Let every creature p his holy name 1385
146: 1 P the LORD. 2146
146: 1 P the LORD, O my soul. 2146
146: 2 I will p the LORD all my life; 2146
146: 2 I will sing p to my God as long as I live. 2376
146:10 P the LORD. 2146
147: 1 P the LORD. 2146
147: 1 how pleasant and fitting to p him! 9335
147:12 p your God, O Zion, 2146
147:20 P the LORD. 2146
148: 1 P the LORD. 2146
148: 1 P the LORD from the heavens, 2146
148: 1 p him in the heights above. 2146
Ps 148: 2 P him, all his angels, praise him, 2146
148: 2 Praise him, all his angels, p him, 2146
148: 3 P him, sun and moon, praise him, 2146
148: 3 Praise him, sun and moon, p him, 2146
148: 4 P him, you highest heavens and you waters 2146
148: 5 Let them p the name of the LORD, 2146
148: 7 P the LORD from the earth, 2146
148:13 Let them p the name of the LORD, 2146
148:14 the p of all his saints, of Israel, 9335
148:14 P the LORD. 2146
149: 1 P the LORD. 2146
149: 1 his p in the assembly of the saints. 9335
149: 3 Let them p his name with dancing 2146
149: 6 May the p of God be in their mouths and 8128
149: 9 P the LORD. 2146
150: 1 P the LORD. 2146
150: 1 P God in his sanctuary; 2146
150: 1 p him in his mighty heavens. 2146
150: 2 P him for his acts of power; 2146
150: 2 p him for his surpassing greatness. 2146
150: 3 P him with the sounding of the trumpet, 2146
150: 3 p him with the harp and lyre, 2146
150: 4 p him with tambourine and dancing, 2146
150: 4 p him with the strings and flute, 2146
150: 5 p him with the clash of cymbals, 2146
150: 5 p him with resounding cymbals. 2146
150: 6 Let everything that has breath p the LORD. 2146
150: 6 P the LORD. 2146
Pr 27: 2 Let another p you, and 2146
27:21 but man is tested by the p he receives. 4545
28: 4 Those who forsake the law p the wicked, 2146
31:31 let her works bring her p at the city gate. 2146
Ecc 8:10 and receive p in the city where they did this. 8655
SS 1: 4 we will p your love more than wine. 2349
Isa 12: 1 "I will p you, O LORD. 3344
25: 1 I will exalt you and p your name, 3344
38:18 For the grave cannot p you, 3344
38:18 death cannot sing your p; 2146
38:19 they p you, as I am doing today; 3344
42: 8 I will not give my glory to another or my p 9335
42:10 his p from the ends of the earth, 9335
42:12 glory to the LORD and proclaim his p in the islands. 9335
43:21 for myself that they may proclaim my p. 9335
48: 9 the sake of my p I hold it back from you, 9335
57:19 creating p on the lips of the mourners 5762
60: 6 and proclaiming the p of the LORD. 9335
60:18 and your gates P. 9335
61: 3 a garment of p instead of a spirit of despair. 9335
61:11 and p spring up before all nations. 9335
62: 7 and makes her the p of the earth. 9335
62: 9 but those who harvest it will eat it and p 2146
Jer 13:11 'to be my people for my renown and p 9335
17:14 for you are the one I p. 9335
20:13 Give p to the LORD! 2146
33: 9 p and honor before all nations on earth 9335
Da 2:20 "P be to the name of God for ever 10122
2:23 I thank and p you, O God of my fathers: 10693
3:28 "P be to the God of Shadrach, 10122
4:37 p and exalt and glorify the King of heaven, 10693
Joel 2:26 and you will p the name of the LORD 2146
Hab 3: 3 the heavens and his p filled the earth. 9335
Zep 3:19 I will give them p and honor in every land 9335
3:20 and p among all the peoples of the earth 9335
Zec 11: 5 Those who sell them say, 'P the LORD, 1385
Mt 5:16 and p your Father in heaven. 1519
11:25 At that time Jesus said, "I p you, Father, 2018
21:16 and infants you have ordained p'?" 142
Lk 1:68 "P be to the Lord, 2329
5:26 Everyone was amazed and gave p to God. 1519
10:21 "I p you, Father, Lord of heaven and earth, 2018
17:18 and give p to God except this foreigner?" 1518
19:37 of disciples began joyfully to p God 140
Jn 5:41 "I do not accept p from men, 1518
5:44 How can you believe if you accept p 1518
5:44 the p that comes from the only God? 1518
12:43 for they loved p from men more than praise 1518
12:43 for they loved praise from men more than p 1518
Ac 12:23 because Herod did not give p to God, 1518
Ro 2:29 Such a man's p is not from men, 2047
15: 7 in order to bring p to God. 1518
15: 9 "Therefore I will p you among 2018
15:11 And again, "P the Lord, all you Gentiles, 140
1Co 4: 5 that time each will receive his p from God. 2047
11: 2 I p you for remembering me in everything 2046
11:17 In the following directives I have no p 2046
11:22 Shall I p you for this? 2046
2Co 1: 3 P be to the God and Father 2329
9:13 men will p God for the obedience 1519
Eph 1: 3 P be to the God and Father 2329
1: 6 to the p of his glorious grace, 2047
1:12 might be for the p of his glory. 2047
1:14 to the p of his glory. 2047
Php 1:11 to the glory and p of God. 2047
1Th 2: 6 We were not looking for p from men, 1518
Heb 13:15 to God a sacrifice of p— 139
Jas 3: 9 With the tongue we p our Lord and Father, 2328
3:10 Out of the same mouth come p and cursing. 2330
5:13 Let him sing songs of p. 6010
1Pe 1: 3 P be to the God and Father 2329
1: 7 be proved genuine and may result in p, 2047
4:16 but p God that you bear that name. 1519
Rev 5:12 and strength and honor and glory and p!" 2330
5:13 the throne and to the Lamb be p and honor 2330
7:12 P and glory and wisdom and thanks 2330
19: 5 "P our God, all you his servants, 140

PRAISED (45) [PRAISE]

Ge 12:15 *they* **p** her to Pharaoh, 2146
24:48 *I* **p** the LORD, the God of my master 1385
Jos 22:33 to hear the report and **p** God. 1385
Jdg 16:24 When the people saw him, *they* **p** their god, 2146
2Sa 14:25 In all Israel there was not a man so highly **p** 2146
1Ch 29:10 David **p** the LORD in the presence of 1385
29:20 So they all **p** the LORD, 1385
2Ch 20:19 and Korahites stood up and **p** the LORD, 2146
20:26 where *they* **p** the LORD. 1385
30:22 and offered fellowship offerings and **p** 3344
31:8 they **p** the LORD and blessed his people NIH
Ne 5:13 "Amen," and **p** the LORD. 2146
8:6 Ezra **p** the LORD, the great God; 1385
Job 1:21 may the name of the LORD be **p."** 1385
36:24 which men *have* **p in song.** 8876
Ps 113:2 Let the name of the LORD be **p,** 1385
113:3 the name of the LORD *is to* **be p.** 2146
Pr 12:8 A man is **p** according to his wisdom, 2146
31:30 a woman who fears the LORD *is to* **be p.** 2146
SS 6:9 the queens and concubines **p** her. 2146
Isa 63:7 the *deeds for which* he is to be **p,** 9335
64:11 where our fathers **p** you, 2146
Jer 48:2 Moab will be **p** no more; 9335
Eze 3:12 May the glory of the LORD **be p** in his dwelling place! 1385
Da 2:19 Then Daniel **p** the God of heaven 10122
4:34 Then *I* **p** the Most High; 10122
5:4 *they* **p** the gods of gold and silver, 10693
5:23 *You* **p** the gods of silver and gold, 10693
Mt 9:8 they were filled with awe, and *they* **p** God, *1519*
15:31 And *they* **p** the God of Israel. *1519*
Mk 2:12 This amazed everyone and they **p** God, *1519*
Lk 2:28 Simeon took him in his arms and **p** God, *2328*
4:15 and everyone **p** *him.* *1519*
7:16 They were all filled with awe and **p** God. *1519*
13:13 she straightened up and **p** God. *1519*
18:43 all the people saw it, *they* also **p** God. *142+1443*
23:47 seeing what had happened, **p** God and said, *1519*
Ac 11:18 they had no further objections and **p** God, *1519*
21:20 When they heard this, *they* **p** God. *1519*
Ro 1:25 who is forever **p.** *2329*
9:5 who is God over all, forever **p!** *2329*
2Co 8:18 along with him the brother who is **p** by all *2047*
11:31 who is *to be* **p** forever, *2329*
Gal 1:24 And *they* **p** God because of me. *1519*
1Pe 4:11 so that in all things God *may be* **p** *1519*

PRAISES (19) [PRAISE]

2Sa 22:50 *I will* **sing p** to your name. 2376
2Ch 23:13 musical instruments were leading the **p.** 2146
29:30 So *they* **sang p** with gladness 2146
31:2 to give thanks and to **sing p** at the gates of 2146
Ps 6:5 Who **p** you from the grave? 3344
9:11 **Sing p** to the LORD, enthroned in Zion; 2376
9:14 that I may declare your **p** in the gates of 9335
18:49 *I will* **sing p** to your name. 2376
35:28 and of your **p** all day long. 9335
47:6 **Sing p** *to* God, sing praises; 2376
47:6 Sing praises to God, **sing p;** 2376
47:6 **sing p** to our King, sing praises. 2376
47:6 sing praises to our King, **sing p.** 2376
147:1 How good it is *to* **sing p** *to* our God, 2376
Pr 31:28 her husband also, and *he* **p** her: 2146
Jer 31:7 Make *your* **p** heard, and say, 'O LORD, 2146
Ro 15:11 and **sing p to** him, all *you* peoples." *2046*
Heb 2:12 of the congregation *I will* **sing** your **p."** *5630*
1Pe 2:9 declare the **p** of him who called you out *746*

PRAISEWORTHY (2) [PRAISE]

Ps 78:4 we will tell the next generation the **p deeds** 9335
Php 4:8 if anything is excellent or **p—** *2047*

PRAISING (16) [PRAISE]

1Ch 25:3 the harp in thanking and **p** the LORD. 2146
2Ch 7:6 King David had made for **p** the LORD 3344
Ps 84:4 *they are* ever **p** you. 2146
Lk 1:64 and he began to speak, **p** God. *2328*
2:13 **p** God and saying, *140*
2:20 and **p** God for all the things they had heard *140*
5:25 he had been lying on and went home **p** God. *1519*
17:15 came back, **p** God in a loud voice. *1519*
18:43 and followed Jesus, **p** God. *1519*
24:53 at the temple, **p** God. *2328*
Ac 2:47 **p** God and enjoying the favor of all *140*
3:8 walking and jumping, and **p** God. *140*
3:9 all the people saw him walking and **p** God, *140*
10:46 speaking in tongues and **p** God. *3486*
1Co 14:16 If *you are* **p** God with your spirit, *2328*

PRAY (121) [PRAYED, PRAYER, PRAYERS, PRAYING, PRAYS]

Ge 20:7 and *he will* **p** for you and you will live. 7137
32:11 **I p,** from the hand of my brother Esau, 5528
Ex 8:8 "**P** to the LORD to take the frogs away 6983
8:9 the honor of setting the time *for me to* **p** 6983
8:28 Now **p** for me." 6983
8:29 *I will* **p** to the LORD, 6983
9:28 **P** to the LORD, for we have had enough 6983
10:17 Now forgive my sin once more and **p** to 6983
Nu 21:7 **P** that the LORD will take the snakes away 7137
Dt 4:7 God is near us whenever we **p** to him? 7924
1Sa 12:19 "**P** to the LORD your God 7137
12:23 against the LORD by failing to **p** for you. 7137
1Ki 8:30 and of your people Israel when *they* **p** 7137
8:35 and when *they* **p** toward this place 7137
8:44 and when *they* **p** to the LORD toward 7137
8:48 and **p** to you toward the land 7137
13:6 "Intercede with the LORD your God and **p** 7137
2Ki 19:4 **p** for the remnant that still survives." 5951+9525
1Ch 17:25 So your servant has found courage to **p** 7137
2Ch 6:21 and of your people Israel when *they* **p** 7137
6:26 and when *they* **p** toward this place 7137
6:34 and when *they* **p** to you toward this city 7137
6:38 where they were taken, and **p** toward 7137
7:14 humble themselves and **p** and seek my face 7137
Ezr 6:10 the God of heaven and **p** for the well-being 10612
Job 22:27 *You will* **p** to him, and he will hear you, 6983
42:8 My servant Job *will* **p** for you, 7137
Ps 5:2 my King and my God, for to you *I* **p.** 7137
32:6 Therefore *let* everyone who is godly **p** 7137
69:13 But I **p** to you, O LORD, 9525
72:15 *May people* ever **p** for him 7137
122:6 **P** *for* the peace of Jerusalem: 8626
Isa 16:12 she goes to her shrine to **p,** it is to no avail. 7137
37:4 **p** for the remnant that still survives." 5951+9525
45:20 *who* **p** to gods that cannot save. 7137
64:9 Oh, look upon us, **we p,** 5528
Jer 7:16 not **p** for this people nor offer any plea 7137
11:14 "*Do* not **p** for this people nor offer any plea 7137
14:11 "*Do* not **p** for the well-being of this people. 7137
29:7 **P** to the LORD for it, 7137
29:12 upon me and come and **p** to me, 7137
31:9 they will **p** as I bring them back. 9384
37:3 "Please **p** to the LORD our God for us." 7137
42:2 "Please hear our petition and **p** to 7137
42:3 **P** that the LORD your God will tell us NIH
42:4 "I *will* certainly **p** to the LORD your God 7137
42:20 '**P** to the LORD our God for us; 7137
Da 9:23 As soon as you began to **p,** 9384
Mt 5:44 and **p** for those who persecute you, *4667*
6:5 "And when *you* **p,** do not be like the hypocrites, *4667*
6:5 *to* **p** standing in the synagogues and on *4667*
6:6 But when you **p,** go into your room, *4667*
6:6 close the door and **p** to your Father, *4667*
6:7 And *when you* **p,** do not keep on babbling *4667*
6:9 "This, then, is how you *should* **p:** *4667*
14:23 up on a mountainside by himself *to* **p.** *4667*
19:13 to place his hands on them and **p for** them. *4667*
24:20 **P** that your flight will not take place *4667*
26:36 "Sit here while *I* go over there and **p."** *4667*
26:41 "Watch and **p** so that you will not fall *4667*
Mk 6:46 he went up on a mountainside *to* **p.** *4667*
13:18 **P** that this will not take place in winter, *4667*
14:32 "Sit here while *I* **p."** *4667*
14:38 Watch and **p** so that you will not fall *4667*
Lk 5:33 "John's disciples often fast and **p,** *1255+4472*
6:12 to a mountainside *to* **p,** *4667*
6:28 **p** for those who mistreat you. *4667*
9:28 and went up onto a mountain *to* **p.** *4667*
11:1 "Lord, teach us *to* **p,** *4667*
11:2 He said to them, "When *you* **p,** say: *4667*
18:1 to show them that they should always **p** and *4667*
18:10 "Two men went up to the temple *to* **p,** *4667*
21:36 and **p** that you may be able to escape all *1289*
22:40 "**P** that you will not fall into temptation." *4667*
22:46 "Get up and **p** so that you will not fall *4667*
Jn 17:9 **I p** for them. I am not praying for the world, *2263*
17:20 **I p** also for those who will believe in me *NIG*
Ac 8:22 of this wickedness and **p** to the Lord. *1289*
8:24 "**P** to the Lord for me so *1289*
10:9 Peter went up on the roof *to* **p.** *4667*
21:5 and there on the beach we knelt *to* **p.** *4667*
26:29 *I* **p** God that not only you *323+2377*
Ro 1:10 and *I* **p** that now at last by God's will *1289*
8:26 We do not know what *we* ought *to* **p for,** *4667*
15:31 **P** that I may be rescued from the *NIG*
1Co 11:13 *to* **p** to God with her head uncovered? *4667*
14:13 in a tongue *should* **p** that he may interpret *4667*
14:14 For if *I* **p** in a tongue, my spirit prays, *4667*
14:15 *I will* **p** with my spirit, *4667*
14:15 but *I will* also **p** with my mind; *4667*
2Co 13:7 Now *we* **p** to God that you will *2377*
Eph 1:18 **I p** also that the eyes of your heart may *NIG*
3:16 **I p** that out of his glorious riches *NIG*
3:17 And I **p** that you, being rooted and *NIG*
6:18 And **p** in the Spirit on all occasions *4667*
6:19 **P** also for me, that whenever I open my *NIG*
6:20 **P** that I may declare it fearlessly, *NIG*
Php 1:4 I always **p** with joy *1255+4472*
Col 1:3 when *we* **p** for you, *4667*
1:10 And we **p** this in order that you may live *NIG*
4:3 And **p** for us, too, *4667*
4:4 **P** that I may proclaim it clearly, *NIG*
1Th 3:10 Night and day *we* **p** most earnestly *1289*
5:17 **p** continually; *4667*
5:25 Brothers, **p** for us. *4667*
2Th 1:11 With this in mind, *we* constantly **p** for you, *4667*
1:12 We **p** this so that the name of our Lord Jesus *NIG*
3:1 **p** for us that the message of the Lord *4667*
3:2 And **p** that we may be delivered *NIG*
1Ti 5:5 **p** and to ask God **for help.** *1255*
Phm 1:6 **I p** that you may be active in sharing *NIG*
Heb 13:18 **P** for us. *4667*
13:19 *to* **p** so that I may be restored to you *4047+4472S*
Jas 5:13 Is any one of you in trouble? *He should* **p.** *4667*
5:14 He should call the elders of the church *to* **p** *4667*
5:16 and **p** for each other so that you may *2377*
1Pe 4:7 and self-controlled so that you can **p.** *4666*
1Jn 5:16 *he should* **p** and God will give him life. *160*
5:16 I am not saying that *he should* **p** about that. *2263*
3Jn 1:2 *I* **p** that you may enjoy good health and *2377*
Jude 1:20 most holy faith and **p** in the Holy Spirit. *4667*

PRAYED (68) [PRAY]

Ge 20:17 Then Abraham **p** to God, 7137
24:12 Then *he* **p,** "O LORD, 606
25:21 Isaac **p** to the LORD on behalf of his wife, 6983
32:9 Then Jacob **p,** "O God 606
Ex 8:30 Moses left Pharaoh and **p** to the LORD, 6983
10:18 then left Pharaoh and **p** to the LORD. 6983
Nu 11:2 he **p** to the LORD and the fire died down. 7137
21:7 So Moses **p** for the people. 7137
Dt 9:20 but at that time *I* **p** for Aaron too. 7137
9:26 *I* **p** to the LORD and said, 7137
Jdg 13:8 Then Manoah **p** to the LORD: 6983
16:28 Then Samson **p** to the LORD, 7924
1Sa 1:10 Hannah wept much and **p** to the LORD. 7137
1:27 *I* **p** for this child, 7137
2:1 Then Hannah **p** and said: 7137
2:20 the *one* she **p for** and gave to the LORD." 8629
8:6 so he **p** to the LORD. 7137
14:41 Then Saul **p** to the LORD, 606
2Sa 15:31 So David **p,** "O LORD, 606
1Ki 8:59 which *I have* **p** before the LORD, 2858
18:36 the prophet Elijah stepped forward and **p:** 606
19:4 sat down under it and **p** that he might die. 8626
2Ki 4:33 shut the door on the two of them and **p** to 7137
6:17 And Elisha **p,** "O LORD, 7137
6:18 Elisha **p** to the LORD, 7137
19:15 And Hezekiah **p** to the LORD: 7137
20:2 Hezekiah turned his face to the wall and **p** 7137
2Ch 30:18 But Hezekiah **p** for them, saying, 7137
32:24 *He* **p** to the LORD, 7137
33:13 And when *he* **p** to him, 7137
Ezr 9:6 and **p:** "O my God, 606
Ne 1:4 and fasted and **p** before the God of heaven. 7137
2:4 Then *I* **p** to the God of heaven, 7137
4:9 But *we* **p** to our God and posted a guard day 7137
6:9 [But I **p,**] "Now strengthen my hands." NIH
Job 42:10 After Job *had* **p** for his friends, 7137
Isa 37:15 And Hezekiah **p** to the LORD: 7137
37:21 Because *you have* **p** to me 7137
38:2 Hezekiah turned his face to the wall and **p** 7137
Jer 32:16 *I* **p** to the LORD: 7137
Da 6:10 a day he got down on his knees and **p,** 10612
9:4 *I* **p** to the LORD my God and confessed: 7137
Jnh 2:1 the fish Jonah **p** to the LORD his God. 7137
4:2 *He* **p** to the LORD, "O LORD, 7137
Mt 26:39 he fell with his face to the ground and **p,** *4667*
26:42 *He* went away a second time and **p,** *4667*
26:44 and went away once more and **p** *4667*
Mk 1:35 and went off to a solitary place, where *he* **p.** *4667*
14:35 he fell to the ground and **p** that if possible *4667*
14:39 Once more *he* went away and **p** *4667*
Lk 5:16 often withdrew to lonely places and **p.** *4667*
18:11 The Pharisee stood up and **p** about himself: *4667*
22:32 But I *have* **p** for you, Simon, *1289*
22:41 knelt down and **p,** *4667*
22:44 And being in anguish, *he* **p** more earnestly, *4667*
Jn 17:1 *he* looked toward heaven and **p:** *3306*
Ac 1:24 *they* **p,** "Lord, you know everyone's heart. *4667*
4:31 *After* they **p,** the place where they were *1289*
6:6 *who* **p** and laid their hands on them. *4667*
7:59 While they were stoning him, Stephen **p,** *2126*
8:15 they **p** for them that they might receive *4667*
9:40 then he got down on his knees and **p.** *4667*
10:2 to those in need and **p to** God regularly. *1289*
13:3 So *after they had* fasted and **p,** *4667*
20:36 he knelt down with all of them and **p.** *4667*
27:29 from the stern and **p for** daylight. *2377*
Jas 5:17 *He* **p earnestly** that it would not rain, *4666+4667*
5:18 Again *he* **p,** and the heavens gave rain, *4667*

PRAYER (106) [PRAY]

Ge 25:21 The LORD **answered** his **p,** 6983
Ex 9:29 I will spread out my hands in **p** to the LORD. NIH
2Sa 7:27 has found courage to **offer** you this **p.** 7137+9525
21:14 God **answered p** in behalf of the land. 6983
24:25 the LORD **answered p** in behalf of the land, 6983
1Ki 8:28 to your servant's **p** and his plea for mercy, 9525
8:28 and the **p** that your servant is praying 9525
8:29 the **p** your servant prays toward this place. 9525
8:38 and when a **p** or plea is made by any 9525
8:45 hear from heaven their **p** and their plea, 9525
8:49 hear their **p** and their plea, 9525
9:3 "I have heard the **p** and plea you have made 9525
2Ki 19:20 I have heard *your* **p** concerning Sennacherib 7137
20:5 I have heard your **p** and seen your tears; 9525
2Ch 6:19 to your servant's **p** and his plea for mercy, 9525
6:19 and the **p** that your servant is praying 9525
6:20 the **p** your servant prays toward this place. 9525
6:29 and when a **p** or plea is made by any 9525
6:35 hear from heaven their **p** and their plea, 9525
6:39 hear their **p** and their pleas, 9525
7:12 "I have heard your **p** and have chosen this 9525
30:27 for their **p** reached heaven, 9525
32:20 Isaiah son of Amoz cried out *in* **p** *to* heaven 7137
33:18 including his **p** to his God and the words 9525
33:19 His **p** and how God was moved 6983
Ezr 8:23 and *he* **answered** our **p.** 6983
Ne 1:6 to hear the **p** your servant is praying 9525
1:11 the **p** *of* this your servant and to the prayer 9525

Ne 1:11 the prayer of this your servant and to the p 9525
11:17 the director who led in thanksgiving and p; 9525
Job 16:17 free of violence and my p is pure. 9525
42: 8 and I will accept his p and not deal NIH
42: 9 and the LORD accepted Job's p. NIH
Ps 4: 1 be merciful to me and hear my p. 9525
6: 9 the LORD accepts my p. 9525
17: T A p of David. 9525
17: 1 Give ear to my p— 9525
17: 6 give ear to me and hear my p. 614
39:12 "Hear my p, O LORD, listen to my cry 9525
42: 8 a p to the God of my life. 9525
54: 2 Hear my p, O God; 9525
55: 1 Listen to my p, O God, 9525
61: 1 Hear my cry, O God; listen to my p. 9525
65: 2 O you who hear p, 9525
66:19 surely listened and heard my voice in p. 9525
66:20 not rejected my p or withheld his love 9525
84: 8 Hear my p, O LORD God Almighty; 9525
86: T A p of David. 9525
86: 6 Hear my p, O LORD; 9525
88: 2 May my p come before you; 9525
88:13 in the morning my p comes before you. 9525
90: T A p of Moses the man of God. 9525
102: T A p of an afflicted man. 9525
102: 1 Hear my p, O LORD; 9525
102:17 He will respond to the p of the destitute; 9525
109: 4 but I am a man of p. 9525
141: 2 May my p be set before you like incense; 9525
141: 5 my p is ever against the deeds of evildoers; 9525
142: T When he was in the cave. A p. 9525
143: 1 O LORD, hear my p, 9525
Pr 15: 8 but the p of the upright pleases him. 9525
15:29 from the wicked but he hears the p of 9525
Isa 1:15 When you spread out your hands in p, NIH
26:16 they could barely whisper a p. 4318+7440
38: 5 I have heard your p and seen your tears; 9525
56: 7 and give them joy in my house of p. 9525
56: 7 for my house will be called a house of p 9525
La 3: 8 I call out or cry for help, he shuts out my p. 9525
3:44 with a cloud so that no p can get through. 9525
Da 9: 3 to the Lord God and pleaded with him in p 9525
9:21 while I was still in p, Gabriel, 9525
Jnh 2: 7 and my p rose to you, to your holy temple. 9525
Hab 3: 1 A p of Habakkuk the prophet. 9525
Mt 21:13 " 'My house will be called a house of p,' 4666
21:22 you will receive whatever you ask for in p." 4666
Mk 9:29 "This kind can come out only by p." 4666
11:17 " 'My house will be called a house of p 4666
11:24 whatever you ask for in p, believe that you 4667
Lk 1:13 your p has been heard. 1255
19:46 " 'My house will be a house of p'; 4666
22:45 When he rose from p and went back to 4666
Jn 17:15 My p is not that you take them out of 2263
17:20 "My p is not for them alone. 2263
Ac 1:14 They all joined together constantly in p, 4666
2:42 to the breaking of bread and to p. 4666
3: 1 going up to the temple at the time of p— 4666
4:24 they raised their voices together in p NIG
6: 4 and will give our attention to p and 4666
10:31 God has heard your p and remembered 4666
14:23 with p and fasting, committed them to 4667
16:13 where we expected to find a place of p. 4666
16:16 when we were going to the place of p, 4666
28: 8 Paul went in to see him and, after p, 4667
Ro 10: 1 heart's desire and p to God for the Israelites 1255
12:12 patient in affliction, faithful in p. 4666
1Co 7: 5 so that you may devote yourselves to p. 4666
2Co 13: 9 and our p is for your perfection. 2377
Php 1: 9 this is my p: that your love may abound 4667
4: 6 by p and petition, with thanksgiving, 4666
Col 4: 2 Devote yourselves to p, 4666
4:12 He is always wrestling in p for you, 4666
1Ti 2: 8 to lift up holy hands in p, 4667
4: 5 it is consecrated by the word of God and p. 1950
Jas 5:15 And the p offered in faith will make 2376
5:16 The p of a righteous man is powerful 1255
1Pe 3:12 and his ears are attentive to their p, 1255

PRAYERS (32) [PRAY]

1Ki 8:54 When Solomon had finished all these p 9525
1Ch 5:20 He answered their p, 6983
2Ch 6:40 and your ears attentive to the p offered 9525
7:15 and my ears attentive to the p offered 9525
Ps 35:13 When my p returned to me unanswered, 9525
72:20 This concludes the p of David son of Jesse. 9525
80: 4 anger smolder against the p of your people? 9525
109: 7 and may his p condemn him. 9525
Pr 28: 9 even his p are detestable. 9525
Isa 1:15 even if you offer many p, I will not listen. 9525
Da 9:17 hear the p and petitions of your servant. 9525
Mk 12:40 and for a show make lengthy p. 4667
Lk 20:47 and for a show make lengthy p. 4667
Ac 10: 4 "Your p and gifts to the poor have come up 4666
Ro 1:10 in my p at all times; 4666
2Co 1:11 as you help us by your p. 1255
1:11 in answer to the p of many. NIG
9:14 in their p for you their hearts will go out 1255
Eph 1:16 remembering you in my p. 4666
6:18 on all occasions with all kinds of p 4666
Php 1: 4 In all my p for all of you, 1255
1:19 that through your p and the help given by 1255
1Th 1: 2 mentioning you in our p. 4666
1Ti 2: 1 I urge, then, first of all, that requests, p, 4666
2Ti 1: 3 and day I constantly remember you in my p. 1255
Phm 1: 4 as I remember you in my p, 4666
Phm 1:22 to be restored to you in answer to your p. 4666
Heb 5: 7 offered up p and petitions with loud cries 1255
1Pe 3: 7 so that nothing will hinder your p. 4666
Rev 5: 8 which are the p of the saints. 4666
8: 3 with the p of all the saints, 4666
8: 4 together with the p of the saints, 4666

PRAYING (36) [PRAY]

Ge 24:15 Before he had finished p, 1819
24:45 "Before I finished p in my heart, 1819
1Sa 1:12 As she kept on p to the LORD, 7137
1:13 Hannah was p in her heart, 1819
1:16 I have been p here out of my great anguish 1819
1:26 the woman who stood here beside you p to 7137
1Ki 8:28 and the prayer that your servant is p 7137
8:33 p and making supplication to you 7137
2Ch 6:19 that your servant is p in your presence. 7137
6:24 p and making supplication before you 7137
7: 1 When Solomon finished p, 7137
Ezr 10: 1 While Ezra was p and confessing, 7137
Ne 1: 6 the prayer your servant is p before you day 7137
Job 21:15 What would we gain by p to him?' 7003
Da 6:11 and found Daniel p and asking God 10114
9:20 While I was speaking and p, 7137
Mk 11:25 And when you stand p, 4667
Lk 1:10 the assembled worshipers were p outside. 4667
2:37 but worshiped night and day, fasting and p. 1255
3:21 And as he was p, heaven was opened 4667
6:12 and spent the night p to God. 4666
9:18 Once when Jesus was p in private 4667
9:29 As he was p, the appearance of his face 4667
11: 1 One day Jesus was p in a certain place. 4667
Jn 17: 9 I am not p for the world, 2263
18: 1 When he had finished p, 3306
Ac 9:11 a man from Tarsus named Saul, for he is p. 4667
10:30 "Four days ago I was in my house p 4667
11: 5 "I was in the city of Joppa p, 4667
12: 5 church was earnestly p to God for him. 1181+4666
12:12 many people had gathered and were p. 4667
16:25 p and singing hymns to God, 4667
22:17 "When I returned to Jerusalem and was p at 4667
Ro 15:30 to join me in my struggle by p to God 4666
Eph 6:18 and always keep on p for all the saints. 1255
Col 1: 9 not stopped p for you and asking God 4667

PRAYS (12) [PRAY]

1Ki 8:29 the prayer your servant p toward this place. 7137
8:42 when he comes and p toward this temple, 7137
2Ch 6:20 the prayer your servant p toward this place. 7137
6:32 when he comes and p toward this temple, 7137
Job 33:26 He p to God and finds favor with him, 6983
Isa 44:17 He p to it and says, "Save me; 7137
Da 6: 7 the decree that anyone who p 10114+10115
6:12 during the next thirty days anyone who p 10114
6:13 He still p three times a day." 10114+10115
1Co 11: 4 Every man who p or prophesies 4667
11: 5 And every woman who p or prophesies 4667
14:14 For if I pray in a tongue, my spirit p, 4667

PREACH (41) [PREACHED, PREACHER, PREACHES, PREACHING]

Isa 61: 1 the LORD has anointed me to p good news 1413
Eze 20:46 p against the south and prophesy against 5752
21: 2 set your face against Jerusalem and p 5752
Jnh 1: 2 the great city of Nineveh and p against it, 7924
Mt 4:17 From that time on Jesus began to p, 3062
10: 7 As you go, p this message: 3062+3306
11: 1 on from there to teach and p in the towns 3062
23: 3 for they do not practice what they p. 3306
Mk 1:38 so I can p there also. 3062
3:14 and that he might send them out to p 3062
16:15 "Go into all the world and p the good news 3062
Lk 4:18 because he has anointed me to p good news 2294
4:43 "I must p the good news of the kingdom 2294
9: 2 and he sent them out to p the kingdom 3062
Ac 9:20 to p in the synagogues that Jesus is the Son 3062
10:42 He commanded us to p to the people and 3062
14: 7 where they continued to p the good news. 2294
16:10 that God had called us to p the gospel 2294
20:20 to p anything that would be helpful to you 334
Ro 1:15 That is why I am so eager to p the gospel 2294
2:21 You who p against stealing, do you steal? 3062
10:15 And how can they p unless they are sent? 3062
15:20 to p the gospel where Christ was not known 2294
1Co 1:17 but to p the gospel— 2294
1:23 but we p Christ crucified: 3062
9:14 the Lord has commanded that those who p 2859
9:16 Yet when I p the gospel, I cannot boast, 2294
9:16 I cannot boast, for I am compelled to p. NIG
9:16 Woe to me if I do not p the gospel! 2294
9:17 If I p voluntarily, I have a reward; 4556S
15:11 then, it was I or they, this is what we p, 3062
2Co 2:12 Now when I went to Troas to p the gospel 2295
4: 5 For we do not p ourselves, 3062
10:16 so that we can p the gospel in the regions 2294
Gal 1: 8 from heaven should p a gospel other than 2294
1:16 so that I might p him among the Gentiles, 2294
2: 2 the gospel that I p among the Gentiles. 3062
Eph 3: 8 to p to the Gentiles the unsearchable riches 2294
Php 1:15 that some p Christ out of envy and rivalry, 3062
1:17 The former p Christ out of selfish ambition, 2859
2Ti 4: 2 P the Word; be prepared in season and 3062

PREACHED (47) [PREACH]

Dt 13: 5 he p rebellion against the LORD your God, 1819
Jer 28:16 you have p rebellion against the LORD.' " 1819
29:32 because he has p rebellion against me.' " 1819
Mt 11: 5 the good news is p to the poor. 2294
24:14 the kingdom will be p in the whole world 3062
26:13 wherever this gospel is p throughout 3062
Mk 2: 2 and he p the word to them. 3281
6:12 and p that people should repent. 3062
13:10 the gospel must first be p to all nations. 3062
14: 9 the gospel is p throughout the world, 3062
16:20 the disciples went out and p everywhere, 3062
Lk 3:18 the people and p the good news to them. 2294
7:22 the good news is p to the poor. 2294
16:16 the good news of the kingdom of God is being p, 2294
24:47 forgiveness of sins will be p in his name 3062
Ac 8: 4 Those who had been scattered p 2294
8:12 as he p the good news of the kingdom 2294
9:27 and how in Damascus he had p fearlessly 4245
10:37 in Galilee after the baptism that John p— 3062
13:24 John p repentance and baptism to all 4619
14:21 They p the good news in that city and won 2294
14:25 and when they had p the word in Perga, 3281
15:21 For Moses has been p in every city 2400+3062
15:35 and many others taught and p the word of 2294
15:36 the towns where we p the word of the Lord 2859
26:20 I p that they should repent and turn to God 550
28:31 without hindrance he p the kingdom of God 3062
1Co 1:21 of what was p to save those who believe. 3060
9:27 so that after I have p to others, 3062
15: 1 to remind you of the gospel I p to you, 2294
15: 2 if you hold firmly to the word I p to you. 2294
15:12 if it is p that Christ has been raised from 3062
2Co 1:19 who was p among you by me and Silas 3062
11: 4 a Jesus other than the Jesus we p, 3062
Gal 1: 8 a gospel other than the one we p to you, 2294
1:11 that the gospel I p is not something 2294+2295
4:13 an illness that I first p the gospel to you. 2294
Eph 2:17 and p peace to you who were far away 2294
Php 1:18 from false motives or true, Christ is p. 2859
1Th 2: 9 a burden to anyone while we p the gospel 3062
1Ti 3:16 seen by angels, was p among the nations, 3062
Heb 4: 2 For we also have had the gospel p to us, 2294
4: 6 and those who formerly had the gospel p 2294
1Pe 1:12 by those who have p the gospel to you by 2294
1:25 And this is the word that was p to you. 2294
3:19 also he went and p to the spirits in prison 3062
4: 6 For this is the reason the gospel was p even 2294

PREACHER (1) [PREACH]

2Pe 2: 5 but protected Noah, a p of righteousness, 3061

PREACHES (2) [PREACH]

Ac 19:13 "In the name of Jesus, whom Paul p, 3062
2Co 11: 4 For if someone comes to you and p 3062

PREACHING (34) [PREACH]

Ezr 6:14 the p of Haggai the prophet and Zechariah, 10452
Am 7:16 and stop p against the house of Isaac.' 5752
Mt 3: 1 John the Baptist came, p in the Desert of 3062
4:23 p the good news of the kingdom, 3062
9:35 p the good news of the kingdom 3062
12:41 for they repented at the p of Jonah, 3060
Mk 1: 4 in the desert region and p a baptism 3062
1:39 p in their synagogues 3062
Lk 3: 3 p a baptism of repentance for 3062
4:44 he kept on p in the synagogues of Judea. 3062
9: 6 from village to village, p the gospel 2294
11:32 for they repented at the p of Jonah, 3060
20: 1 in the temple courts and p the gospel, 2294
Ac 8:25 p the gospel in many Samaritan villages. 2294
8:40 p the gospel in all the towns 2294
16: 6 having been kept by the Holy Spirit from p 3281
17:13 that Paul was p the word of God at Berea, 2859
17:18 because Paul was p the good news 2294
18: 5 Paul devoted himself exclusively to p, 3364+3836
20:25 of you among whom I have gone about p 3062
Ro 1: 9 with my whole heart in p the gospel 2295
10:14 can they hear without someone p to them? 3062
1Co 2: 4 My message and my p were not with wise 3060
9:18 that in p the gospel I may offer it free 2294
9:18 and so not make use of my rights in p it. 2295
15:14 our p is useless and so is your faith. 3060
2Co 11: 7 in order to elevate you by p the gospel 2294+2295
Gal 1: 9 p to you a gospel other than what you 2294
1:23 now p the faith he once tried to destroy." 2294
2: 7 the task of p the gospel to the Gentiles, 2295
5:11 Brothers, if I am still p circumcision, 3062
1Ti 4:13 to p and to teaching. 4155
5:17 especially those whose work is p 1877+3364
Tit 1: 3 to light through the p entrusted to me by 3060

PRECEDE (1) [PRECEDED, PRECEDING]

1Th 4:15 not p those who have fallen asleep. 5777

PRECEDED (4) [PRECEDE]

2Ki 17: 2 but not like the kings of Israel who p him. 2118+4200+7156
21:11 Amorites who p him and has led Judah 4200+7156
Jer 28: 8 early times the prophets who p you 4200+7156
34: 5 the former kings who p you, 2118+4200+7156

PRECEDING (1) [PRECEDE]
Ne 5:15 the earlier governors—those **p** me— 4200+7156

PRECEPTS (27)
Dt 33:10 He teaches your **p** to Jacob and your law 5477
Ps 19: 8 The **p** *of* the LORD are right, 7218
103:18 and remember to obey his **p**. 7218
105:45 they might keep his **p** and observe his laws. 2976
111: 7 all his **p** are trustworthy. 7218
111:10 all who follow **his p** have good understanding. 2157S
119: 4 You have laid down **p** that are to be fully obeyed. 7218
119:15 I meditate on your **p** and consider 7218
119:27 Let me understand the teaching of your **p**; 7218
119:40 How I long for your **p**! 7218
119:45 for I have sought out your **p**. 7218
119:56 This has been my practice: I obey your **p**. 7218
119:63 to all who follow your **p**. 7218
119:69 I keep your **p** with all my heart. 7218
119:78 but I will meditate on your **p**. 7218
119:87 but I have not forsaken your **p**. 7218
119:93 I will never forget your **p**, 7218
119:94 I have sought out your **p**. 7218
119:100 for I obey your **p**. 7218
119:104 I gain understanding from your **p**; 7218
119:110 but I have not strayed from your **p**. 7218
119:128 and because I consider all your **p** right, 7218
119:134 that I may obey your **p**. 7218
119:141 I do not forget your **p**. 7218
119:159 See how I love your **p**; 7218
119:168 I obey your **p** and your statutes, 7218
119:173 for I have chosen your **p**. 7218

PRECINCTS (1)
Eze 42:14 Once the priests enter the **holy p**, 7731

PRECIOUS (48)
Ge 30:20 "God has presented me with a **p** gift. 3202
Ex 28:17 Then mount four rows of **p** stones on it. NIH
39:10 they mounted four rows of **p** stones on it. NIH
Dt 33:13 the LORD bless his land with the **p** dew 4458
1Sa 26:21 Because you considered my life **p** today, 3700
2Sa 12:30 and it was set with **p** stones— 3701
1Ki 10: 2 large quantities of gold, and **p** stones— 3701
10:10 large quantities of spices, and **p** stones. 3701
10:11 of almugwood and **p** stones. 3701
1Ch 20: 2 and it was set with **p** stones— 3701
29: 8 Any who had **p** stones gave them to NIH
2Ch 3: 6 He adorned the temple with **p** stones. 3701
9: 1 large quantities of gold, and **p** stones— 3701
9: 9 large quantities of spices, and **p** stones. 3701
9:10 they also brought algumwood and **p** stones. 3701
32:27 for his silver and gold and for his **p** stones, 3701
Ezr 8:27 articles of polished bronze, as **p** as gold. 2776
Job 28:16 with **p** onyx or sapphires. 3701
29:24 the light of my face *was* **p** *to them.* 4202+5877
Ps 19:10 They *are* more **p** than gold, 2773
22:20 my **p life** from the power of the dogs. 3495
35:17 my **p life** from these lions. 3495
72:14 for **p** *is* their blood in his sight. 3700
116:15 **P** in the sight of the LORD is the death 3701
119:72 The law from your mouth is more **p** 3202
133: 2 It is like **p** oil poured on the head, 3202
139:17 How **p** to me are your thoughts, O God! 3700
Pr 3:15 She is more **p** than rubies; 3701
8:11 for wisdom is more **p** than rubies, 3202
Isa 28:16 a **p** cornerstone for a sure foundation; 3701
43: 4 Since *you are* **p** and honored in my sight, 3700
54:12 and all your walls of **p** stones. 2914
La 4: 2 How the **p** sons of Zion, 3701
Eze 22:25 and **p things** and make many widows 3702
27:22 of all kinds of spices and **p** stones, 3701
28:13 every **p** stone adorned you: 3701
Da 11:38 with **p** stones and costly gifts. 3701
1Pe 1:19 but *with* the **p** blood of Christ, 5508
2: 4 by men but chosen by God and **p** to him— 1952
2: 6 a chosen and **p** cornerstone, 1952
2: 7 Now to you who believe, this stone is **p**. 5507
2Pe 1: 1 have received a faith **as p as** ours: 2700
1: 4 his very great and **p** promises, 5508
Rev 17: 4 with gold, silver, **p** stones and pearls. 5508
18:12 cargoes of gold, silver, **p** stones and pearls; 5508
18:16 with gold, silver, **p** stones and pearls! 5508
21:11 like that of a **very p** jewel, 5508
21:19 *with* every kind of **p** stone. 5508

PRECISELY (1)
Ac 11: 4 and explained everything to them **p** NIG

PREDECESSOR (1) [PREDECESSORS]
1Ch 17:13 I took it away from your **p**. 889+2118+4200+7156

PREDECESSORS (2) [PREDECESSOR]
Dt 19:14 neighbor's boundary stone set up by your **p** 8037
Ezr 4:15 may be made in the archives of your **p**. 10003

PREDESTINATE, PREDESTINATED
(KJV) See PREDESTINED

PREDESTINED (4) [DESTINE]
Ro 8:29 **p** to be conformed to the likeness of his Son 4633
8:30 And those *he* **p**, he also called; 4633
Eph 1: 5 he **p** us to be adopted as his sons 4633
1:11 *having been* **p** according to the plan 4633

PREDICTED (5) [PREDICTION]
1Sa 28:17 The LORD has done what *he* **p** 1819
Ac 7:52 They even killed those who **p** the coming 4615
11:28 stood up and through the Spirit **p** that 4955
16:16 **spirit** by **which** she **p the future.** 4460+4780
1Pe 1:11 *when he* **p** the sufferings of Christ and 4626

PREDICTING (2) [PREDICTION]
1Ki 22:13 as one man the other prophets are **p** success 1821
2Ch 18:12 as one man the other prophets are **p** success 1821

PREDICTION (1) [PREDICTED, PREDICTING, PREDICTIONS]
Jer 28: 9 sent by the LORD only if his **p** comes true." 1821

PREDICTIONS (2) [PREDICTION]
Isa 44:26 the words of his servants and fulfills the **p** 6783
47:13 those stargazers *who* **make p** month 3359

PREEMINENT (1)
Est 10: 3 **p** among the Jews, and held in high esteem 1524

PREFECTS (4)
Da 3: 2 He then summoned the satraps, **p**, 10505
3: 3 So the satraps, **p**, governors, advisers, 10505
3:27 **p**, governors and royal advisers crowded 10505
6: 7 The royal administrators, **p**, satraps, 10505

PREFER (8) [PREFERENCE]
1Ki 21: 2 a better vineyard or, if you **p**, 928+3202+6524
21: 6 or if you **p**, I will give you another vineyard 2913
Job 7:15 so that I **p** strangling and death, 1047
36:21 which *you seem to* **p** to affliction. 1047
Jer 8: 3 of this evil nation *will* **p** death to life, 1047
Eze 16:32 *You* **p** strangers to your own husband! 4374
1Co 4:21 What *do you* **p**? 2527
2Co 5: 8 and *would* **p** to be away from the body 2305+3437

PREFERENCE (1) [PREFER]
Dt 21:16 to the son of the wife he loves **in p to** 6584+7156

PREGNANCY (1) [PREGNANT]
Hos 9:11 no birth, no **p**, no conception. 1061

PREGNANT (33) [PREGNANCY]
Ge 4: 1 and *she became* **p** and gave birth to Cain. 2225
4:17 and *she became* **p** and gave birth to Enoch. 2225
16: 4 When she knew *she was* **p**, 2225
16: 5 and now that she knows *she is* **p**, 2225
19:36 of Lot's daughters *became* **p** by their father. 2225
21: 2 Sarah *became* **p** and bore a son to Abraham 2225
25:21 and his wife Rebekah *became* **p**. 2225
29:32 Leah *became* **p** and gave birth to a son. 2225
30: 5 and she *became* **p** and bore him a son. 2225
30:17 *she became* **p** and bore Jacob a fifth son. 2225
30:23 *She became* **p** and gave birth to a son 2225
38: 3 *she became* **p** and gave birth to a son, 2225
38:18 and *she became* **p** by him. 2225
38:24 and as a result *she* is now **p**." 2226
38:25 "I am **p** by the man who owns these," 2226
Ex 2: 2 and she *became* **p** and gave birth to a son. 2225
21:22 a **p** woman and she gives birth prematurely 2226
Lev 12: 2 'A woman *who becomes* **p** and gives birth 2445
1Sa 4:19 was **p** and near the time of delivery. 2226
2Sa 11: 5 and sent word to David, saying, "I am **p**." 2226
2Ki 4:17 But the woman *became* **p**, 2225
8:12 and rip open their **p** *women*." 2226
15:16 and ripped open all the **p** *women*. 2226
1Ch 7:23 and *she became* **p** and gave birth to a son. 2225
Ps 7:14 *He who is* **p** *with* evil and conceives trouble 2473
Hos 13:16 their **p women** ripped open." 2230
Am 1:13 Because he ripped open the **p women** 2226
Mt 24:19 **p women** and nursing mothers! 1143+1877+2400
Mk 13:17 **p women** and nursing mothers! 1143+1877+2400
Lk 1:24 After this his wife Elizabeth *became* **p** and 5197
21:23 **p women** and nursing mothers! 1143+1877+2400
1Th 5: 3 as labor pains *on* a **p woman**, 1143+1877+2400
Rev 12: 2 *She was* **p** and cried out in pain 1143+1877+2400

PREMATURELY (1) [MATURE]
Ex 21:22 and she **gives birth p** but there is no 3529+3655

PREPARATION (9) [PREPARE]
Nu 11:18 'Consecrate yourselves **in p for** tomorrow, 4200
Jos 7:13 'Consecrate yourselves in **p** for tomorrow; NIH
1Sa 23:22 Go and **make** further **p**. 3922
Mt 27:62 The next day, the one after **P Day**, 4187
Mk 15:42 **P Day** (that is, the day before the Sabbath). 4187
Lk 23:54 **P** Day, the Sabbath was about to begin. 4187
Jn 19:14 It was the **day of P** of Passover Week, 4187
19:31 Now it was the **day of P**, 4187
19:42 Because it was the Jewish **day of P** and 4187

PREPARATIONS (11) [PREPARE]
1Ch 22: 5 Therefore *I will* **make p** for it." 3922
22: 5 David **made** extensive **p** before his death. 3922
2Ch 35:14 *they* **made p** for themselves and for 3922
35:14 the Levites **made p** for themselves and for 3922
35:15 their fellow Levites **made** *the* **p** for them. 3922
Mt 26:17 "Where do you want *us to* **make p** for you 2286
Mk 14:12 "Where do you want *us* to go and **make p** 2286
14:15 **Make p** for us there." 2286
Lk 10:40 distracted by all the **p** that had **to be made.** 1355
22: 8 "Go and **make p** for us to eat the Passover." 2286
22:12 **Make p** there." 2286

PREPARE (95) [PREPARATION, PREPARATIONS, PREPARED, PREPARES, PREPARING]
Ge 18: 7 who hurried to **p** it. 6913
27: 4 **P** me the kind of tasty food I like 6913
27: 7 and **p** me some tasty food to eat, 6913
27: 9 so *I can* **p** some tasty food for your father, 6913
43:16 slaughter an animal and **p** dinner; 3922
Ex 12:16 **p food** for everyone **to eat—** 430
12:39 of Egypt and did not have time *to* **p** food 6913
16: 5 the sixth day *they are to* **p** what they bring 3922
19:15 "**P** *yourselves* for the third day. 2118+3922
Lev 6:21 **P** it with oil on a griddle; 6913
6:22 to succeed him as anointed priest *shall* **p** it. 6913
Nu 15: 5 **p** a quarter of a hin of wine as 6913
15: 6 a ram **p** a grain offering of two-tenths of 6913
15: 8 " 'When *you* **p** a young bull as 6913
15:12 Do this for each one, for as many as *you* **p**. 6913
23: 1 and **p** seven bulls and seven rams for me." 3922
23:29 and **p** seven bulls and seven rams for me." 3922
28: 4 **P** one lamb in the morning and the other 6913
28: 8 **P** the second lamb at twilight, 6913
28: 8 and drink offering that *you* **p** in 6913
28:20 With each bull **p** a grain offering 6913
28:23 **P** these in addition to the regular morning 6913
28:24 In this way **p** the food for the offering made 6913
28:31 **P** these together with their drink offerings, 6913
29: 2 **p** a burnt offering of one young bull, 6913
29: 3 the bull **p** a grain offering of three-tenths of NIH
29: 9 the bull **p** a grain offering of three-tenths of NIH
29:14 of the thirteen bulls **p** a grain offering NIH
29:17 " 'On the second day **p** twelve young bulls, NIH
29:18 **p** their grain offerings and drink offerings NIH
29:20 " 'On the third day **p** eleven bulls, NIH
29:21 **p** their grain offerings and drink offerings NIH
29:23 " 'On the fourth day **p** ten bulls, NIH
29:24 **p** their grain offerings and drink offerings NIH
29:26 " 'On the fifth day **p** nine bulls, NIH
29:27 **p** their grain offerings and drink offerings NIH
29:29 " 'On the sixth day **p** eight bulls, NIH
29:30 **p** their grain offerings and drink offerings NIH
29:32 " 'On the seventh day **p** seven bulls, NIH
29:33 **p** their grain offerings and drink offerings NIH
29:37 **p** their grain offerings and drink offerings NIH
29:39 **p** these for the LORD at your appointed 6913
Jdg 13:15 to stay until *we* **p** a young goat for you." 6913
13:16 But if *you* **p** a burnt offering, 6913
2Sa 12: 4 to **p** a meal for the traveler who had come 6913
13: 5 *Let her* **p** the food in my sight 6913
13: 7 of your brother Amnon and **p** some food 6913
1Ki 18:23 I *will* **p** the other bull and put it on 6913
18:25 "Choose one of the bulls and **p** it first, 6913
20:12 and he ordered his men: "**P** to attack." 8492
2Ki 20: 7 Then Isaiah said, "**P** a poultice of figs." 4374
1Ch 22: 2 to **p** dressed stone for building the house 2933
2Ch 31:11 Hezekiah gave orders to **p** storerooms in 3922
35: 4 **P** *yourselves* by families 3922
35: 6 consecrate yourselves and **p** [the lambs] 3922
Est 5: 8 to the banquet *I will* **p** for them. 6913
Job 33: 5 **p** *yourself* and confront me. 6885
Ps 23: 5 *You* **p** a table before me in the presence 6885
Isa 8: 9 **P for battle,** and be shattered! 273
8: 9 **P for battle,** and be shattered! 273
14:21 **P** a place to slaughter his sons for the sins 3922
25: 6 the LORD Almighty *will* **p** a feast 6913
38:21 "**P** a poultice of figs and apply it to 5951
40: 3 "In the desert **p** the way for the LORD; 7155
57:14 "Build up, build up, **p** the road! 7155
62:10 **P** the way for the people. 7155
Jer 6: 4 "**P** *for* battle against her! 7727
46: 3 "**P** your shields, both large and small, 6885
51:12 station the watchmen, **p** an ambush! 3922
51:27 **P** the nations for battle against her; 7727
51:28 **P** the nations for battle against her— 7727
Eze 7:23 "**P** chains, because the land is full 6913
Da 11:10 His sons *will* **p for war** and assemble 1741
Joel 3: 9 among the nations: **P** *for* war! 7727
Am 4:12 **p** to meet your God, O Israel." 3922
Mic 3: 5 *they* **p** to wage war against him. 7727
Na 1:14 *I will* **p** your grave, for you are vile." 8492
Mal 3: 1 *who will* **p** the way before me. 7155
Mt 3: 3 '**P** the way for the Lord, 2286
11:10 who *will* **p** your way before you.' 2941
26:12 she did it to **p** me **for burial.** 1946
Mk 1: 2 who *will* **p** your way"— 2941
1: 3 '**P** the way for the Lord, 2286
14: 8 **poured perfume on** my body beforehand **to p** for my burial. 3690
Lk 1:76 on before the Lord *to* **p** the way for him, 2286
3: 4 '**P** the way for the Lord, 2286
7:27 who *will* **p** your way before you.' 2941
17: 8 Would he not rather say, '**P** my supper, 2286

Lk 22: 9 “Where do you want *us to* **p** for it?” *2286*
Jn 14: 2 I am going there *to* **p** a place for you. *2286*
14: 3 And if I go and **p** a place for you, *2286*
Eph 4:12 to **p** God's people for works of service, *2938*
Phm 1:22 **P** a guest room for me, *2286*
1Pe 1:13 **p** your minds **for action;** *350+3836+4019*
Rev 16:12 to **p** the way for the kings from the East. *2286*

PREPARED (79) [PREPARE]

Ge 18: 8 and milk and the calf that *had been* **p,** 6913
19: 3 *He* **p** a meal for them, 6913
24:31 I *have* **p** the house and a place for 7155
27:14 and she **p** some tasty food, 6913
27:31 He too **p** some tasty food and brought it 6913
43:25 *They* **p** their gifts for Joseph's arrival 3922
Ex 23:20 and to bring you to the place *I have* **p.** 3922
Lev 2: 5 If your grain offering is **p** on a griddle, NIH
10:12 and eat it **p without yeast** beside the altar, 5174
Nu 15:11 *is to* **be p** in this manner. 6913
23: 4 and Balaam said, *“I have* **p** seven altars, 6885
28:24 *it is to* **be p** in addition to 6913
Jos 24: 9 the king of Moab, **p** to fight against Israel, 7756
Jdg 6: 2 the Israelites **p** shelters for themselves 6913
6:19 Gideon went in, **p** a young goat, 6913
19: 5 and *he* **p** to leave, but the girl's father said 7756
Ru 1: 6 and her daughters-in-law **p** to return home 7756
2Sa 3:20 David **p** a feast for him and his men. 6913
12: 4 and **p** it for the one who had come to him.” 6913
13:10 And Tamar took the bread *she had* **p** 6913
1Ki 5:18 of Gebal cut and **p** the timber and stone for 3922
6:19 *He* **p** the inner sanctuary within the temple 3922
18:26 So they took the bull given them and **p** it. 6913
20:12 So *they* **p** to attack the city. 8492
2Ki 6:23 So *he* **p a** great **feast** for them, 4127+4130
1Ch 12:33 experienced soldiers **p** *for* battle 6885
12:36 experienced soldiers **p** *for* battle— 6885
15: 1 *he* **p** a place for the ark of God and pitched 3922
15: 3 the ark of the LORD to the place *he had* **p** 3922
15:12 to the place *I have* **p** for it. 3922
2Ch 1: 4 from Kiriath Jearim to the place he *had* **p** 3922
29:19 *We have* **p** and consecrated all the articles 3922
Ezr 1: 5 **p** to go up and build the house of 7756
Ne 5:18 six choice sheep and some poultry **were p** 6913
8:10 and send some to those *who have* nothing **p.** 3922
Est 5: 4 come today to a banquet *I have* **p** for him.” 6913
5: 5 to the banquet Esther *had* **p.** 6913
6:14 to the banquet Esther *had* **p.** 6913
7:10 on the gallows *he had* **p** for Mordecai. 3922
Job 13:18 Now that *I have* **p** my case, 6885
Ps 7:13 *He has* **p** his deadly weapons; 3922
78:50 *He* **p** a path for his anger; 7142
Pr 9: 2 *She has* **p** her meat and mixed her wine; 3180
19:29 Penalties **are p** for mockers, 3922
SS 3: 8 **p** for the terrors of the night. NIH
Isa 30:33 Topheth *has* long **been p;** 6885
Eze 28:13 on the day you were created *they* **were p.** 3922
38: 7 *be* **p,** you and all the hordes gathered 3922
Zep 1: 7 The LORD *has* **p** a sacrifice; 3922
Mt 20:23 for whom *they have been* **p** by my Father.” *2286*
22: 2 like a king who **p** a wedding banquet *4472*
22: 4 that *I have* **p** my dinner: *2286*
25:34 the kingdom **p** for you since the creation of *2286*
25:41 into the eternal fire **p** for the devil *2286*
26:19 as Jesus had directed them and **p** *2286*
Mk 10:40 to those for whom *they have been* **p.”** *2286*
14:16 So *they* **p** the Passover. *2286*
Lk 1:17 to make ready a people **p** for the Lord.” *2941*
2:31 which *you have* **p** in the sight of all people, *2286*
12:20 Then who will get what *you have* **p** *2286*
22:13 So *they* **p** the Passover. *2286*
23:56 *they* went home and **p** spices and perfumes. *2286*
24: 1 the spices *they had* **p** and went to the tomb. *2286*
Jn 19:19 Pilate **had a notice p** and fastened to *1211+5518*
Ac 10:10 and *while* the meal *was being* **p,** *4186*
Ro 9:22 of his wrath—**p** for destruction? *2936*
9:23 whom *he* **p in advance** for glory— *4602*
1Co 2: 9 no mind has conceived what God *has* **p** *2286*
Eph 2:10 which God **p in advance** for us to do. *4602*
2Ti 2:21 to the Master and **p** to do any good work. *2286*
4: 2 *be* **p** in season and out of season; *2392*
Heb 10: 5 but a body *you* **p** for me; *2936*
11:16 for *he has* **p** a city for them. *2286*
1Pe 3:15 Always be **p** to give an answer *2289*
Rev 8: 6 the seven trumpets **p** to sound them. *2286*
9: 7 The locusts looked like horses **p** for battle. *2286*
12: 6 The woman fled into the desert to a place **p** *2286*
12:14 so that she might fly to the place **p** for her *NIG*
21: 2 **p** as a bride beautifully dressed *2286*

PREPARES (3) [PREPARE]

Ps 50:23 and *he* **p** the way so that I may show him 8492
85:13 before him and **p** the way for his steps. 8492
Isa 44:16 over it *he* **p** his meal, 430

PREPARING (9) [PREPARE]

1Ch 9:32 of **p** for every Sabbath the bread set out on 3922
Jer 18:11 *I am* **p** a disaster for you and devising a plan 3670
Eze 39:17 from all around to the sacrifice *I am* **p** 2284
39:19 At the sacrifice *I am* **p** for you, 2284
Am 7: 1 *He was* **p** swarms of locusts after 3670
Mt 4:21 with their father Zebedee, **p** their nets. *2936*
Mk 1:19 and his brother John in a boat, **p** their nets. *2936*
Lk 14:16 “A certain man *was* **p** a great banquet *4472*
Ac 25: 3 *for they were* **p** an ambush to kill him along *4472*

PRESBYTERY (KJV) See ELDERS

PRESCRIBED (23)

Lev 5:10 the other as a burnt offering in the **p way** 5477
9:16 and offered it in the **p way.** 5477
Nu 15:24 with its **p** grain offering and drink offering, 5477
1Sa 2:29 and offering that *I* **p** for my dwelling? 7422
1Ch 15:13 of him about how to do it in the **p way.”** 5477
23:31 in the proper number and in the **way p** 5477
24:19 according to the **regulations p** *for* them 5477
2Ch 4:20 to burn in front of the inner sanctuary as **p;** 5477
29:25 the **way p** *by* David and Gad the king's seer 5184
30:16 as **p** in the Law of Moses the man of God. 5477
35:13 the Passover animals over the fire as **p,** 5477
35:15 were in the places **p** *by* David, Asaph, 5184
Ezr 3: 4 required number of burnt offerings **p** 3869+5477
3:10 **as p by** David king of Israel. 3338+6584
7:23 Whatever the God of heaven has **p,** 10302+10427
Ne 12:24 as **p** *by* David the man of God. 5184
12:36 **musical** instruments *[p by]* David AIT
13: 5 new wine and oil **p** *for* the Levites, 5184
Est 2:12 of beauty treatments **p** *for* the women, 2017
9:27 in the way **p** and at the time appointed. 4181
Job 36:23 Who *has* **p** his ways for him, or said to him, 7212
Eze 45:14 The **p portion** *of* oil, 2976
Heb 8: 4 the gifts **p by** the law. *2848*

PRESENCE (202) [PRESENT]

Ge 4:14 and I will be hidden from your **p;** 7156
4:16 So Cain went out from the LORD's **p** 4200+7156
23:11 I give it to you in the **p** *of* my people. 6524
23:18 in the **p** of all the Hittites who had come to 6524
27: 7 that I may give you my blessing in the **p** *of* 7156
27:30 and Jacob had scarcely left his father's **p,** 7156
31:32 **In the p of** our relatives, 5584
31:35 my lord, that I cannot stand up in your **p;** 7156
40:20 and the chief baker in the **p** *of* his officials: 9348
41:46 And Joseph went out from Pharaoh's **p** 4200+7156
45: 1 “Have everyone leave my **p!”** 4946+6584
45: 3 because they were terrified at his **p.** 7156
47:10 and went out from his **p.** 4200+7156
Ex 7:20 He raised his staff in the **p** *of* Pharaoh 6524
9: 8 and have Moses toss it into the air in the **p** 6524
10:11 and Aaron were driven out of Pharaoh's **p.** 7156
18:12 with Moses' father-in-law in the **p** *of* God. 7156
25:30 Put the bread of the **P** on this table to be 7156
28:30 whenever he enters the **p** *of* the LORD. 4200+7156
29:11 the LORD's **p** at the entrance to the Tent 7156
33:14 “My **P** will go with you, 7156
33:15 “If your **P** does not go with us, 7156
33:19 proclaim my name, the LORD, in your **p.** 7156
34:34 whenever he entered the LORD's **p** 4200+7156
35:13 and all its articles and the bread of the **P;** 7156
35:20 Then the whole Israelite community withdrew from Moses' **p,** 4200+7156
39:36 with all its articles and the bread of the **P;** 7156
Lev 9:24 from the **p** *of* the LORD and consumed 4200+7156
10: 2 fire came out from the **p** *of* the LORD 4200+7156
19:32 “ ‘Rise in the **p** *of* the aged, 7156
22: 3 that person must be cut off from my **p.** 4200+7156
Nu 4: 7 “Over the table of the **P** they are to spread 7156
6: 9 “ ‘If someone dies suddenly **in** his **p,** 6584
6:11 because he sinned by being **in the p of** 6584
17: 9 from the LORD's **p** to all the Israelites. 4200+7156
19: 3 the camp and slaughtered in his **p.** 7156
20: 9 Moses took the staff from the LORD's **p,** 4200+7156
27:19 and commission him in their **p.** 6524
Dt 4:37 of Egypt by his **P** and his great strength, 7156
12: 7 There, in the **p** *of* the LORD your God, 7156
12:18 the **p** *of* the LORD your God at the place 7156
14:23 and flocks in the **p** *of* the LORD your God 7156
14:26 the **p** *of* the LORD your God and rejoice. 7156
15:20 and your family are to eat them in the **p** *of* 7156
18: 7 who serve there in the **p** *of* the LORD. 7156
19:17 the **p** *of* the LORD before the priests and 7156
25: 2 down and have him flogged in his **p** with 7156
25: 9 up to him in the **p** *of* the elders, 6524
27: 7 eating them and rejoicing in the **p** *of* 7156
29:10 All of you are standing today in the **p** *of* 7156
29:15 in the **p** *of* the LORD our God but also 7156
31: 7 and said to him in the **p** *of* all Israel, 6524
32:51 both of you broke faith with me in the **p** *of* 9348
Jos 8:32 There, in the **p** *of* the Israelites, 7156
10:12 Joshua said to the LORD in the **p** 6524
18: 6 to me and I will cast lots for you in the **p** *of* 7156
18: 8 at Shiloh in the **p** *of* the LORD.” 7156
18:10 then cast lots for them in Shiloh in the **p** *of* 7156
19:51 of Israel assigned by lot at Shiloh in the **p** 7156
Ru 4: 4 that you buy it **in the p of** these seated here 5584
4: 4 and **in the p of** the elders of my people. 5584
1Sa 2:21 the boy Samuel grew up **in the p of** 6640
2:28 and to wear an ephod in my **p.** 7156
6:20 “Who can stand in the **p** *of* the LORD, 7156
11:15 and confirmed Saul as king in the **p** *of* 7156
12: 3 Testify against me **in the p of** the LORD 5584
16:13 and anointed him in the **p** *of* his brothers, 7931
19:24 and also prophesied in Samuel's **p.** 7156
21: 6 the bread of the **P** that had been removed 7156
21:13 So he pretended to be insane in their **p;** 6524
26:20 to the ground far from the **p** *of* the LORD. 7156
2Sa 3:13 *Do* not **come into** my **p** 906+7156+8011
22:13 of his **p** bolts of lightning blazed forth. 5584
24: 4 left the **p** *of* the king to enroll 4200+7156
1Ki 1:28 So she came *into* the king's **p** and 4200+7156
7:48 on which was the bread of the **P;** 7156
8: 1 Then King Solomon summoned **into** his **p** 448
8:28 your servant is praying in your **p** this day. 7156
19:11 “Go out and stand on the mountain in the **p** 7156
2Ki 3:14 for the **p** *of* Jehoshaphat king of Judah, 7156
5:27 from Elisha's **p** and he was leprous, 4200+7156
13:23 to destroy them or banish them from his **p.** 7156
17:18 with Israel and removed them from his **p.** 7156
17:20 until he thrust them from his **p.** 7156
17:23 until the LORD removed them from his **p,** 7156
22:10 Shaphan read from it in the **p** *of* the king. 7156
22:19 you tore your robes and wept in my **p,** 7156
23: 3 the pillar and renewed the covenant in the **p** 7156
23:27 “I will remove Judah also from my **p** 7156
24: 3 in order to remove them from his **p** because 7156
24:20 and in the end he thrust them from his **p.** 7156
1Ch 12: 1 from the **p** *of* Saul son of Kish (they were 7156
24: 6 recorded their names in the **p** *of* the king 7156
24:31 in the **p** *of* King David and of Zadok, 7156
29:10 the LORD in the **p** *of* the whole assembly, 6524
29:22 They ate and drank with great joy in the **p** 7156
2Ch 4:19 on which was the bread of the **P;** 7156
6:19 that your servant is praying in your **p.** 7156
20: 9 we will stand in your **p** before this temple 7156
26:19 the priests in their **p** before the incense altar 7156
28:14 and plunder in the **p** *of* the officials and all 7156
34:18 Shaphan read from it in the **p** *of* the king. 7156
34:24 in the book that has been read in the **p** *of* 7156
34:27 and tore your robes and wept in my **p,** 7156
34:31 the covenant in the **p** *of* the LORD— 7156
Ezr 4:18 and translated **in** my **p.** 10621
9:15 of it not one of us can stand in your **p.”** 7156
Ne 1:11 by granting him favor in the **p** 7156
2: 1 I had not been sad in his **p** before; 7156
4: 2 and in the **p** *of* his associates and the army 7156
8: 3 before the Water Gate **in the p of** the men, 5584
Est 1:16 Then Memucan replied in the **p** *of* the king 7156
1:19 Vashti is never again to enter the **p** 4200+7156
2:23 the book of the annals in the **p** *of* the king. 7156
3: 7 the **p** *of* Haman to select a day and month. 7156
4: 8 to urge her to go **into** the king's **p** to beg 448
5: 9 nor showed fear **in** his **p,** 4946
8: 1 And Mordecai came into the **p** *of* the king, 7156
8:15 Mordecai left the king's **p** 4200+7156
Job 1:12 Satan went out from the **p** *of* the LORD. 7156
2: 7 from the **p** *of* the LORD and afflicted Job 7156
30:11 they throw off restraint in my **p.** 7156
Ps 5: 5 arrogant cannot stand **in** your **p;** 4200+5584+6524
9:19 let the nations be judged in your **p.** 7156
16:11 you will fill me with joy in your **p,** 7156
18:12 of the brightness of his **p** clouds advanced, 5584
21: 6 and made him glad with the joy of your **p.** 7156
23: 5 a table before me **in the p of** my enemies. 5584
31:20 In the shelter of your **p** you hide them from 7156
39: 1 as long as the wicked are in my **p.”** 5584
41:12 and set me in your **p** forever. 7156
51:11 from your **p** or take your Holy Spirit 4200+7156
52: 9 I will praise you **in the p of** your saints. 5584
61: 7 May he be enthroned in God's **p** forever; 7156
89:15 who walk in the light of your **p,** O LORD. 7156
90: 8 our secret sins in the light of your **p.** 7156
101: 7 no one who speaks falsely will stand **in** my **p.** 4200+5584+6524
102:28 of your servants will live in your **p;** NIH
114: 7 Tremble, O earth, at the **p** *of* the Lord, 4200+7156
114: 7 at the **p** *of* the God of Jacob, 4200+7156
116:14 to the LORD **in the p of** all his people. 2025+5584
116:18 to the LORD **in the p of** all his people, 2025+5584
139: 7 Where can I flee from your **p?** 7156
Pr 8:30 rejoicing always in his **p,** 7156
14:19 Evil men will bow down in the **p** *of* 7156
18:16 for the giver and ushers him into the **p** *of* 7156
25: 5 remove the wicked from the king's **p,** 7156
25: 6 Do not exalt yourself in the king's **p,** 7156
Ecc 8: 3 Do not be in a hurry to leave the king's **p.** 7156
Isa 3: 8 defying his glorious **p.** 6524
26:17 so were we in your **p,** O LORD. 7156
63: 9 and the angel of his **p** saved them. 7156
Jer 5:22 “Should you not tremble in my **p?** 7156
7:15 I will thrust you from my **p,** 7156
15: 1 Send them away from my **p!** 7156
23:39 surely forget you and cast you out of my **p** 7156
28: 1 of the LORD in the **p** *of* the priests and all 6524
32:12 in the **p** *of* my cousin Hanamel and of 6524
32:13 “In their **p** I gave Baruch these instructions: 6524
52: 3 and in the end he thrust them from his **p.** 7156
La 2:19 pour out your heart like water **in the p of** the Lord. 5790+7156
Eze 28: 9 in the **p** *of* those who kill you? 7156
38:20 the face of the earth will tremble at my **p.** 7156
44: 3 the gateway to eat in the **p** *of* the LORD. 7156
44:12 in the **p** *of* their idols and made the house 7156
46: 3 in the **p** *of* the LORD at the entrance to 7156
Da 4: 8 Daniel came into my **p** and I told him 10621
7:13 the Ancient of Days and was led **into** his **p.** 10621
Hos 6: 2 that we may live in his **p.** 7156
Na 1: 5 The earth trembles at his **p,** 7156
Zec 6: 5 from standing **in the p of** the Lord of 6584
Mal 3:16 in his **p** concerning those who feared 7156
Mk 7:24 yet he could not keep his **p** secret. *NIG*
Lk 1:19 I stand **in the p** of God, *1967*
8:47 **In the p** of all the people, *1967*
14:10 Then you will be honored **in the p** of *1967*
15:10 there is rejoicing **in the p** of the angels *1967*
23:14 I have examined him **in** your **p** *1967*
24:43 and he took it and ate it **in** their **p.** *1967*
Jn 8:38 what I have seen **in the** Father's **p,** *4123*

Jn 12:37 Jesus had done all these miraculous signs in their p, 1869
17:5 glorify me in your p with the glory I had 4123
20:30 Jesus did many other miraculous signs in the p of his disciples, 1967
Ac 2:28 will fill me with joy in your p.' 3552+3836+4725
10:33 Now we are all here in the p of God 1967
24:21 I shouted as I stood in their p: 1877
2Co 4:14 with Jesus and present us with you in his p. NIG
Php 2:12 not only in my p, but now much more 4242
1Th 2:19 or the crown in which we will glory in the p 1869
3:9 the joy we have in the p of our God because 1869
3:13 be blameless and holy in the p of our God 1869
2Th 1:9 and shut out from the p of the Lord and 4725
1Ti 6:12 you made your good confession in the p 1967
2Ti 2:2 things you have heard me say in the p of 1328
4:1 In the p of God and of Christ Jesus, 1967
Heb 2:12 in the p of the congregation I will sing 3545
9:24 now to appear for us in God's p. 4725
2Pe 2:11 against such beings in the p of the Lord. 4123
1Jn 3:19 and how we set our hearts at rest in his p 1869
Jude 1:24 and to present you before his glorious p 1518
Rev 14:10 tormented with burning sulfur in the p of 1967
20:11 Earth and sky fled from his p, 4725

PRESENT (153) [EVER-PRESENT, PRESENCE, PRESENTABLE, PRESENTED, PRESENTING, PRESENTS]

Ge 33:11 Please accept the p that was brought to you, 1388
Ex 10:25 to have sacrifices and burnt offerings to p 6913
22:14 or dies while the owner is not p, 6640
29:3 Put them in a basket and p them in it— 7928
34:2 P yourself to me there on top of 5893
Lev 1:3 He must p it at the entrance to the Tent 7928
2:8 p it to the priest, who shall take it to the 7928
3:1 he is to p before the LORD an animal 7928
3:7 he is to p it before the LORD. 7928
3:12 he is to p it before the LORD. 7928
4:4 to p the bull at the entrance to the Tent 995
4:14 as a sin offering and p it before the Tent 995
6:21 and p the grain offering broken in pieces as 7928
7:11 for the fellowship offering a person may p 7928
7:13 to p an offering with cakes of bread made 7928
9:2 and p them before the LORD. 7928
13:19 he must p himself to the priest. 8011
14:11 priest who pronounces him clean shall p 6641
16:7 Then he is to take the two goats and p them 6641
17:4 the Tent of Meeting to p it as an offering to 7928
18:23 A woman must not p herself to an animal 6641
21:6 Because they p the offerings made to 7928
21:21 near to p the offerings made to the LORD 7928
22:15 the sacred offerings the Israelites p to 8123
22:19 you must p a male without defect from NIH
22:23 p as a freewill offering an ox or a sheep 6913
23:8 For seven days p an offering made to 7928
23:16 p an offering of new grain to the LORD. 7928
23:18 P with this bread seven male lambs, 7928
23:25 but p an offering made to the LORD 7928
23:27 and p an offering made to the LORD 7928
23:36 For seven days p offerings made to 7928
23:36 a sacred assembly and p an offering made 7928
27:8 he is to p the person to the priest, 6641
Nu 3:6 of Levi and p them to Aaron the priest 6641
6:14 to p his offerings to the LORD: 7928
6:16 to p them before the LORD and make 7928
6:17 He is to p the basket of unleavened bread 6913
8:11 to p the Levites before the LORD as 5677
8:13 of Aaron and his sons and then p them as 5677
9:13 because he did not p the LORD's offering 7928
15:3 and you p to the LORD offerings made 6913
15:4 the one who brings his offering shall p to 7928
15:19 p a portion as an offering to the LORD. 8123
15:20 P a cake from the first of your 8123+9556
15:20 of your ground meal and p it as an offering 8123
16:17 and p it before the LORD. 7928
16:17 You and Aaron are to p your censers also." NIH
18:19 the Israelites p to the LORD I give to you 8123
18:24 the tithes that the Israelites p as an offering 8123
18:26 as your inheritance, you must p a tenth of 8123
18:28 In this way you also will p an offering to 8123
18:29 You must p as the LORD's portion 8123
18:30 'When you p the best part, 8123
28:2 'See that you p to me at the appointed time 7928
28:3 the offering made by fire that you are to p 7928
28:11 p to the LORD a burnt offering 7928
28:19 P to the LORD an offering made by fire, 7928
28:26 when you p to the LORD an offering 7928
28:27 P a burnt offering of two young bulls, 7928
29:8 P as an aroma pleasing to the LORD 7928
29:13 P an offering made by fire as 7928
29:36 P an offering made by fire as 7928
Dt 12:27 P your burnt offerings on the altar of 6913
31:14 and p yourselves at the Tent of Meeting, 3656
Jos 7:14 p yourselves tribe by tribe. 7928
1Sa 1:22 I will take him and p him before 8011
10:19 So now p yourselves before the LORD 3656
30:26 "Here is a p for you from the plunder of 1388
2Sa 14:20 Joab did this to change the p situation. 7156
1Ki 18:1 "Go and p yourself to Ahab, 8011
18:2 So Elijah went to p himself to Ahab. 8011
18:15 I will surely p myself to Ahab today." 8011
1Ch 9:18 up to the p time. 2178
16:40 to p burnt offerings to the LORD on 6590
2Ch 13:11 and evening they p burnt offerings 7787
23:18 to p the burnt offerings of the LORD 6590
29:7 not burn incense or p any burnt offerings at 6590
29:29 the king and everyone p with him knelt 5162
30:21 The Israelites who were p 5162
34:33 and he had all who were p in Israel serve 5162
35:17 The Israelites who were p celebrated 5162
Ezr 5:16 to the p it has been under construction 10363
6:3 be rebuilt as a place to p sacrifices, 10156
8:25 and all Israel p there had donated for 5162
Est 1:3 the nobles of the provinces were p. 4200+7156
Job 1:6 One day the angels came to p themselves 3656
2:1 the angels came to p themselves before 3656
2:1 and Satan also came with them to p himself 3656
23:7 There an upright man could p his case 3519
Ps 14:5 God is p in the company of the righteous. 928
56:12 I will p my thank offerings to you. 8966
72:10 kings of Sheba and Seba will p him gifts. 7928
Pr 4:9 a garland of grace on your head and p you 4481
18:17 The first to p his case seems right, NIH
Isa 40:20 to p such an offering selects wood 9556
41:21 "P your case," says the LORD. 7928
45:21 Declare what is to be, p it— 5602
Jer 33:18 and to p sacrifices.' " 6913
40:5 and a p and let him go. 5368
42:9 you sent me to p your petition, 4200+5877+7156
44:15 along with all the women who were p— 6641
Eze 43:27 the priests are to p your burnt offerings 6913
45:1 to p to the LORD a portion of the land as 8123
48:8 to west will be the portion you are to p as 8123
Hag 2:9 of this p house will be greater than 340
Mk 8:9 About four thousand men were p. 1639
10:30 as much in this p age (homes, brothers, 3814
14:4 Some of those p were saying indignantly NIG
Lk 2:22 and Mary took him to Jerusalem to p him 4225
5:17 the power of the Lord was p for him to heal 1639
12:56 don't know how to interpret this p time? NIG
13:1 Now there were some p at that time 4205
22:6 when no crowd was p. 868
Ac 1:13 Those p were Peter, John, NIG
5:38 Therefore, in the p case I advise you: 3814
21:18 and all the elders were p. 4134
23:30 to p to you their case against him. 3306
24:17 for the poor and to p offerings. NIG
25:24 "King Agrippa, and all who are p with us, 5223
Ro 3:26 to demonstrate his justice at the p time, 3814
8:18 I consider that our p sufferings 2789+3814+3836
8:22 of childbirth right up to the p time. 3814
8:38 neither the p nor the future, nor any powers, 1931
11:5 at the p time there is a remnant chosen 3814
13:11 And do this, understanding the p time. 2789
1Co 3:22 or the world or life or death or the p or 1931
5:3 Even though I am not physically p, 582
5:3 just as if I were p. 4205
5:4 and the power of our Lord Jesus is p, NIG
7:26 Because of the p crisis, 1931
7:31 this world in its p form is passing away. NIG
2Co 4:14 also raise us with Jesus and p us with you 4225
8:14 At the p time your plenty will supply what they need, 3814
10:11 we will be in our actions when we are p. 4205
11:2 that I might p you as a pure virgin to him. 4225
Gal 1:4 to rescue us from the p evil age, 1931
4:25 and corresponds to the p city of Jerusalem, 3814
Eph 1:21 in the p age but also in the one to come. 4047
5:27 and to p her to himself as a radiant church, 4225
Php 4:6 with thanksgiving, p your requests to God. 1192
Col 1:22 to p you holy in his sight, without blemish 4225
1:25 p to you the word of God in its fullness— 4444
1:28 so that we may p everyone perfect in Christ. 4225
2:5 I am p with you in spirit and delight to see 1639
1Ti 4:8 holding promise for both the p life and 3814
6:17 in this p world not to be arrogant nor 3814
2Ti 2:15 to p yourself to God as one approved, 4225
Tit 2:12 upright and godly lives in this p age, 3814
Heb 2:8 Yet at p we do not see everything subject 3814
9:9 This is an illustration for the p time, 1931
2Pe 3:7 the p heavens and earth are reserved 3814
Jude 1:24 and to p you before his glorious presence 2705

PRESENTABLE (1) [PRESENT]

1Co 12:24 while our p parts need no special treatment. 2363

PRESENTED (56) [PRESENT]

Ge 30:20 "God has p me with a precious gift. 2272
43:15 to Egypt and p themselves to Joseph. 6641
43:26 they p to him the gifts they had brought 995
47:2 of his brothers and p them before Pharaoh. 3657
47:7 in and p him before Pharaoh. 6641
Ex 29:27 and the thigh that was p. 8123+9556
32:6 and p fellowship offerings. 5602
35:22 They all p their gold as a wave offering to 5677
Lev 7:34 and the thigh that is p and have given them 9556
7:35 and his sons on the day they were p to serve 7928
8:14 He then p the bull for the sin offering, 5602
8:18 He then p the ram for the burnt offering, 7928
8:22 He then p the other ram, 7928
10:14 that was waved and the thigh that was p. 9556
10:15 The thigh that was p and the breast 9556
16:10 as the scapegoat shall be p alive before 6641
27:11 the animal must be p to the priest, 6641
Nu 6:20 that was waved and the thigh that was p. 9556
7:3 These they p before the tabernacle. 7928
7:10 its dedication and p them before the altar. 7928
8:15 the Levites and p them as a wave offering, 5677
8:21 Then Aaron p them as a wave offering 5677
16:38 for they were p before the LORD 7928
18:8 in charge of the offerings p to me; AIT
28:15 one male goat is to be p to the LORD as 6913
31:52 of hundreds that Moses and Eleazar p as 8123
Dt 31:14 and p themselves at the Tent of Meeting. 3656
Jos 24:1 and they p themselves before God. 3656
Jdg 3:17 He p the tribute to Eglon king of Moab, 7928
3:18 After Ehud had p the tribute, 7928
20:26 that day until evening and p burnt offerings 6590
21:4 an altar and p burnt offerings 6590
1Sa 18:27 and p the full number to the king so 4848
2Ki 11:12 he p him with a copy of the covenant NIH
16:12 he approached it and p offerings on it. 6590
1Ch 6:49 the ones who p offerings on the altar 7787
16:1 and they p burnt offerings 7928
23:31 and whenever burnt offerings were p to 6590
29:21 to the LORD and p burnt offerings to him: 6590
2Ch 23:11 they p him with a copy of the covenant NIH
24:14 burnt offerings were p continually in 6590
28:21 and from the princes and p them to the king 5989
29:24 p their blood on the altar for a sin offering 2627
Ezr 3:5 they p the regular burnt offerings, NIH
10:19 and for their guilt they each p a ram from NIH
Est 8:2 and p it to Mordecai. 5989
Eze 20:28 p their fragrant incense and poured out 8492
Da 1:18 the chief official p them to Nebuchadnezzar. 995
2:46 that an offering and incense be p to him. 10482
Mt 2:11 and p him with gifts of gold and of incense 4712
Mk 6:28 He p it to the girl, 1443
Ac 6:6 They p these men to the apostles, 2705
9:41 and the widows and p her to them alive. 4225
24:2 Tertullus p his case before Felix: 2989
25:2 appeared before him and p the charges 1872
Ro 3:25 God p him as a sacrifice of atonement, 4729

PRESENTING (6) [PRESENT]

Ex 30:20 the altar to minister by p an offering made 7787
35:24 Those p an offering of silver 8123
Nu 9:7 be kept from p the LORD's offering with 7928
18:32 By p the best part of it you will not 8123
Eze 46:14 The p of this grain offering to the LORD NIH
Ac 17:19 this new teaching that you are p? 3281

PRESENTS (6) [PRESENT]

Lev 6:5 on the day he p his guilt offering. NIH
22:18 p a gift for a burnt offering to the LORD, 7928
Nu 15:14 an alien or anyone else living among you p 6913
Est 9:19 a day for giving p to each other. 4950
9:22 of feasting and joy and giving p of food 4950
Isa 66:3 like one who p pig's blood, NIH

PRESERVE (24) [PRESERVED, PRESERVES]

Ge 19:32 and then lie with him and p our family line 2649
19:34 and lie with him so we can p our family line 2649
45:7 But God sent me ahead of you to p for you 8492
Job 33:18 to p his soul from the pit, 3104
Ps 36:6 O LORD, you p both man and beast. 3828
41:2 LORD will protect him and p his life; 2649
79:11 of your arm p those condemned to die. 3855
119:25 p my life according to your word. 2649
119:37 p my life according to your word. 2649
119:40 P my life in your righteousness. 2649
119:88 P my life according to your love, 2649
119:107 I have suffered much; p my life, 2649
119:149 p my life, O LORD, 2649
119:154 p my life according to your promise. 2649
119:156 p my life according to your laws. 2649
119:159 See how I love your precepts; p my life, 2649
138:7 you p my life; 2649
143:11 your name's sake, O LORD, p my life; 2649
Pr 3:21 p sound judgment and discernment, 5915
5:2 and your lips may p knowledge. 5915
Eze 7:13 not one of them will p his life. 2616
13:18 the lives of my people but p your own? 2649
Mal 2:7 the lips of a priest ought to p knowledge, 9068
Lk 17:33 and whoever loses his life will p it. 2441

PRESERVED (4) [PRESERVE]

2Sa 22:44 you have p me as the head of nations. 9068
Ps 66:9 he has p our lives and kept 928+2021+2645+8492
119:93 for by them you have p my life. 2649
Mt 9:17 into new wineskins, and both are p." 5337

PRESERVES (3) [PRESERVE]

Ps 31:23 The LORD p the faithful, 5915
119:50 Your promise p my life. 2649
Ecc 7:12 that wisdom p the life of its possessor. 2649

PRESIDENTS (KJV) See ADMINISTRATORS

PRESIDES (1)

Ps 82:1 God p in the great assembly; 5893

PRESS (12) [PRESSED, PRESSES, PRESSING, PRESSURE]

Jdg 14:17 because she continued to p him. 7439
2Sa 11:25 P the attack against the city and destroy it.' 2616
Job 23:6 No, he would not p charges against me. 8492
Ps 56:1 all day long they p their attack. 4315
Pr 6:3 p your plea with your neighbor! 8104

Hos 6: 3 *let us* **p on** to acknowledge him. 8103
Mic 6:15 you *will* **p** olives but not use the oil 2005
Ac 19:38 *They can* **p charges.** *1592*
25: 5 and **p charges against** the man there, *2989*
Php 3:12 but *I* **p on** to take hold of that *1503*
3:14 *I* **p on** toward the goal to win the prize *1503*
Rev 14:20 and blood flowed out of the **p,** *3332*

PRESSED (18) [PRESS]
Ex 27:20 to bring you clear oil of **p** olives for 4184
29:40 a quarter of a hin of oil from **p olives,** 4184
Lev 24: 2 to bring you clear oil of **p** olives for 4184
Nu 22:25 *she* **p close** to the wall, 4315
28: 5 a quarter of a hin of oil from **p olives.** 4184
Jdg 1:28 *they* **p** the Canaanites into forced labor 8492
1:35 they too were **p** into forced labor. NIH
9:45 that day Abimelech **p** *his* **attack** against 4309
1Sa 13: 6 and that their army *was* **hard p,** 5601
25:18 of raisins and two hundred **cakes of p figs,** 1811
30:12 of a **cake of p figs** and two cakes of raisins. 1811
31: 2 The Philistines **p hard after** Saul 1815
1Ki 5:11 to twenty thousand baths of **p olive** oil. 4184
1Ch 10: 2 The Philistines **p hard** after Saul 1815
Mk 5:24 A large crowd followed and **p around** him. *5315*
Lk 6:38 A good measure, **p down,** *4390*
2Co 4: 8 We are **hard p** on every side, *2567*
8:13 be relieved while you are **hard p,** *2568*

PRESSES (2) [PRESS]
Isa 16:10 no one treads out wine at the **p,** 3676
Jer 48:33 the flow of wine from the **p;** 3676

PRESSING (3) [PRESS]
Ex 5:13 The slave drivers *kept* **p** them, saying, 237
Jdg 20:45 *They kept* **p** after the Benjamites as far 1815
Lk 8:45 people are crowding and **p** against you." *632*

PRESSURE (3) [PRESS]
Ge 19: 9 *They* **kept bringing p** on Lot 4394+7210
2Co 1: 8 *We were* **under** great **p,** *976*
11:28 the **p** of my concern for all the churches. *2180*

PRESUME (1) [PRESUMES, PRESUMPTION, PRESUMPTUOUSLY]
Jas 3: 1 Not many of you should **p** to be teachers, *NIG*

PRESUMES (1) [PRESUME]
Dt 18:20 But a prophet who **p** to speak 2326

PRESUMPTION (1) [PRESUME]
Nu 14:44 *in their* **p** they went up toward 6753

PRESUMPTUOUSLY (1)
Dt 18:22 That prophet has spoken **p.** 928+2295

PRETEND (4) [PRETENDED, PRETENDING, PRETENDS, PRETENSE, PRETENSION]
2Sa 13: 5 "Go to bed and **p to be ill,"** Jonadab said. 2703
14: 2 **"P** *you are* **in mourning.** 61
1Ki 14: 5 **p to be someone else."** 5796
Pr 12: 9 yet have a servant than **p to be somebody** 3877

PRETENDED (5) [PRETEND]
Ge 42: 7 but *he* **p to be a stranger** 5796
1Sa 21:13 So *he* **p to be insane** in their presence; 3248+9101
2Sa 13: 6 So Amnon lay down and **p to be ill.** 2703
Ps 34: T he **p to be insane** before Abimelech, 3248+9101
Lk 20:20 they sent spies, *who* **p** to be honest. *5693*

PRETENDING (1) [PRETEND]
Ac 27:30 **p** they were going to lower some anchors *4733*

PRETENDS (2) [PRETEND]
Pr 13: 7 *One man* **p to be rich,** yet has nothing; 6947
13: 7 *another* **p to be poor,** yet has great wealth. 8133

PRETENSE (2) [PRETEND]
1Ki 14: 6 Why this **p?** 5796
Jer 3:10 but only in **p,"** declares the LORD. 9214

PRETENSION (1) [PRETEND]
2Co 10: 5 and every **p** that sets itself up against *5739*

PRETEXT (2)
Ac 23:15 to bring him before you **on the p of** *6055*
23:20 before the Sanhedrin tomorrow **on the p of** *6055*

PREVAIL (6) [PREVAILED, PREVAILS, PREVALENT]
2Ch 14:11 *do* not *let* man **p** against you." 6806
Isa 54:17 no weapon forged against you *will* **p,** 7503
Jer 5:22 The waves may roll, but they cannot **p;** 3523
20:10 then *we will* **p** over him 3523
20:11 so my persecutors will stumble and not **p.** 3523
Ro 3: 4 when you speak and **p** when you judge." *3771*

PREVAILED (4) [PREVAIL]
Jdg 19: 4 the girl's father, **p upon** him to stay; 928+2616
Jer 20: 7 you overpowered me and **p.** 3523
La 1:16 because the enemy *has* **p."** 1504
Lk 23:23 and their shouts **p.** *2996*

PREVAILS (3) [PREVAIL]
1Sa 2: 9 "It is not by strength that one **p;** 1504
Pr 19:21 but it is the LORD's purpose *that* **p.** 7756
Hab 1: 4 the law is paralyzed, and justice never **p.** 3655

PREVALENT (1) [PREVAIL]
Jas 1:21 rid of all moral filth and the evil that is so **p** *4353*

PREVENT (7) [PREVENTED]
2Sa 14:11 to **p** the avenger of blood **from** 4946
1Ki 15:17 to **p** anyone *from* leaving or entering 1194+5989
2Ch 16: 1 to **p** anyone *from* leaving or entering 1194+5989
Mal 3:11 *I will* **p** pests from devouring your crops, 1721
Jn 18:36 my servants would fight to **p** my arrest by *3590*
Ac 27:42 to kill the prisoners **to p** any of them *3590*
Rev 7: 1 to **p** any wind **from blowing** *3590+4463*

PREVENTED (2) [PREVENT]
Ro 1:13 to come to you (but *have been* **p from** doing *3266*
Heb 7:23 since death **p** them **from** continuing *3266*

PREVIOUS (3) [PREVIOUSLY]
Nu 6:12 The **p** days do not count, 8037
Jdg 3: 2 not had **p** battle experience): 4200+7156
Gal 1:13 For you have heard of my **p** way of life *4537*

PREVIOUSLY (6) [PREVIOUS]
1Sa 14:21 Hebrews who had **p** been with 919+3869+8997
1Ch 6:65 they allotted the *p* **named** towns. AIT
Ac 21:29 *(They had* **p seen** Trophimus the Ephesian in the city *1639+4632*
Ro 9:29 It is just as Isaiah **said p:** *4625*
Gal 3:17 not set aside the covenant **p established** *4623*
1Th 2: 2 *We had* **p suffered** and been insulted *4634*

PREY (29) [PREYS]
Ge 15:11 **birds of p** came down on the carcasses, 6514
49: 9 you return from the **p,** my son. 3272
49:27 in the morning he devours the **p,** 6331
Nu 23:24 a lion that does not rest till he devours his **p** 3272
Job 4:11 The lion perishes for lack of **p,** 3272
9:26 like eagles swooping down on their **p.** 431
24:21 *They* **p on** the barren and childless woman, 8286
28: 7 No **bird of p** knows that hidden path, 6514
38:39 the **p** for the lioness and satisfy the hunger 3272
Ps 17:12 They are like a lion hungry for **p,** 3271
22:13 Roaring lions **tearing** their **p** open their mouths wide 3271
104:21 The lions roar for their **p** and seek their food 3272
Isa 5:29 as they seize their **p** and carry it off 3272
10: 2 making widows their **p** and robbing 8965
18: 6 be left to the mountain **birds of p** and to 6514
31: 4 "As a lion growls, a great lion over his **p—** 3272
46:11 From the east I summon a **bird of p;** 6514
59:15 and whoever shuns evil **becomes** *a* **p.** 8964
Jer 12: 9 like a speckled **bird of p** that other birds 6514
12: 9 that other **birds of p** surround and attack? 6514
Eze 13:21 they will no longer fall **p** to your power. 5180
19: 3 to tear the **p** and he devoured men. 3272
19: 6 to tear the **p** and he devoured men. 3272
22:25 within her like a roaring lion tearing its **p;** 3272
22:27 within her are like wolves tearing their **p;** 3272
Am 3: 4 a lion roar in the thicket when he has no **p?** 3272
Na 2:12 and strangled the **p** for his mate, NIH
2:12 with the kill and his dens with the **p.** 3274
2:13 I will leave you no **p** on the earth. 3272

PREYS (1) [PREY]
Pr 6:26 and the adulteress **p upon** your very life. 7421

PRICE (31) [PRICED, PRICELESS]
Ge 23: 9 to sell it to me for the full **p** as a burial site 4084
23:13 I will pay the **p** *of* the field. 4084
23:16 for him the **p** he had named in the hearing 4084
34:12 Make the **p for the bride** and the gift 4558
Lev 25:16 you are to increase the **p,** 5239
25:16 you are to decrease the **p,** 5239
25:50 The **p** *for* his release is to be based on 4084
25:51 a larger share of the **p** paid for him. 4084
Nu 18:16 at the redemption **p set** *at* five shekels 6886
Dt 2:28 and water to drink for their **p** in silver. NIH
1Sa 13:21 The **p** was two thirds of a shekel NIH
18:25 king wants no other **p for** *the* **bride** than 4558
2Sa 3:14 for the **p** of a hundred Philistine foreskins." NIH
1Ch 21:22 Sell it to me at the full **p."** 4084
21:24 "No, I insist on paying the full **p.** 4084
Job 28:15 nor can its **p** be weighed in silver. 4697
28:18 the **p** *of* wisdom is beyond rubies. 5433
Pr 27:26 and the goats with the **p** *of* a field. 4697
Isa 45:13 but not for a **p** or reward, 4697
La 5: 4 our wood can be had only at a **p.** 4697
Da 11:39 and will distribute the land at a **p.** 4697
Am 8: 5 the measure, boosting the **p** and cheating 9203
Mic 3:11 her priests teach for a **p,** 4697
Zec 11:13 the handsome **p** at which they priced me! 3702
Mt 26: 9 a **high** *p* and the money given to the poor." *AIT*
27: 9 **p set on** him by the people of Israel, *5506+5507*
Ac 5: 8 the **p** you and Ananias got for the land?" *NIG*
5: 8 "Yes," she said, "that is the **p."** *NIG*
22:28 "I had to pay a big **p** for my citizenship." *3049*
1Co 6:20 you were bought *at* a **p.** *5507*
7:23 You were bought *at* a **p;** *5507*

PRICED (1) [PRICE]
Zec 11:13 the handsome price at which they **p** *me!* 3700

PRICELESS (1) [PRICE]
Ps 36: 7 How **p** is your unfailing love! 3701

PRICKS (KJV) See BARBS, GOAD

PRIDE (69) [PROUD]
Lev 26:19 I will break down your stubborn **p** and 1454
2Ki 19:22 and lifted your eyes *in* **p?** 5294
2Ch 26:16 his **p** led to his downfall. 1467+4213
32:26 Hezekiah repented of the **p** *of* his heart, 1470
Job 20: 6 Though his **p** reaches to the heavens 8480
33:17 from wrongdoing and keep him from **p,** 1575
Ps 10: 4 In his **p** the wicked does not seek him; 678+1470
31:18 with **p** and contempt they speak arrogantly 1452
47: 4 the **p** *of* Jacob, whom he loved. 1454
56: 2 many are attacking me in their **p.** 5294
59:12 let them be caught in their **p.** 1454
62:10 in extortion or **take p** in stolen goods; 2038
73: 6 Therefore **p** is their necklace; 1452
Pr 8:13 I hate **p** and arrogance, 1449
11: 2 When **p** comes, then comes disgrace, 2295
13:10 **P** only breeds quarrels, 2295
16:18 **P** goes before destruction, 1454
17: 6 and parents are the **p** *of* their children. 9514
21:24 he behaves with **overweening p.** 2295+6301
29:23 A man's **p** brings him low, 1452
Ecc 7: 8 and patience is better than **p.** 1468+8120
Isa 2:11 the arrogant man will be humbled and the **p** 8124
2:17 be brought low and the **p** *of* men humbled; 8124
4: 2 be the **p** and glory of the survivors in Israel. 1454
9: 9 who say with **p** and arrogance of heart, 1452
10:12 of Assyria for the **willful p** *of* his heart 1542+7262
13:11 and will humble the **p** *of* the ruthless. 1452
13:19 the glory of the Babylonians' **p,** 1454
16: 6 We have heard of Moab's **p—** 1454
16: 6 her overweening **p** and conceit, 1447
16: 6 her **p** and her insolence— 1454
23: 9 to bring low the **p** *of* all glory and 1454
25:11 God will bring down their **p** despite 1452
28: 1 the **p** *of* Ephraim's drunkards, 1455
28: 1 to that city, the **p** of those laid low by wine! NIH
28: 3 That wreath, the **p** *of* Ephraim's drunkards, 1455
37:23 and lifted your eyes *in* **p?** 5294
43:14 in the ships in which they took **p.** 8262
60:15 I will make you the everlasting **p** and 1454
Jer 13: 9 the same way I will ruin the **p** *of* Judah and 1454
13: 9 of Judah and the great **p** *of* Jerusalem. 1454
13:17 I will weep in secret because of your **p;** 1575
48:29 "We have heard of Moab's **p—** 1454
48:29 her overweening **p** and conceit, 1450
48:29 her overweening pride and conceit, her **p** 1454
49:16 and the **p** *of* your heart have deceived you, 2295
Eze 7:24 I will put an end to the **p** *of* the mighty, 1454
16:56 in the day of your **p,** 1454
24:21 the stronghold in which you take **p,** 1454
28: 2 " 'In *the* **p** *of* your heart you say, 1467
32:12 They will shatter the **p** *of* Egypt, 1454
Da 4:37 those who walk in **p** he is able to humble. 10136
5:20 and hardened *with* **p,** 10225
11:12 of the South *will be* **filled with p** 4222+8123
Am 6: 8 the **p** of Jacob and detest his fortresses; 1454
8: 7 The LORD has sworn by the **P** *of* Jacob: 1454
Ob 1: 3 The **p** *of* your heart has deceived you, 2295
Zep 2:10 in return for their **p,** 1454
3:11 from this city those who rejoice in their **p.** 1452
Zec 9: 6 and I will cut off the **p** *of* the Philistines. 1454
10:11 Assyria's **p** will be brought down 1454
1Co 4: 6 not **take p** in one man over against another. *5881*
2Co 5:12 but are giving you an opportunity to take **p** *3017*
5:12 so that you can answer those who **take p** *3016*
7: 4 I take great **p** in you. *3018*
8:24 of your love and the reason for our **p** *3018*
Gal 6: 4 Then *he can* take **p** in himself, *3017*
Jas 1: 9 in humble circumstances *ought to* **take p** *3016*
1:10 But the one who is rich should take **p** *NIG*

PRIEST (478) [PRIEST'S, PRIESTHOOD, PRIESTLY, PRIESTS, PRIESTS']
Ge 14:18 He was **p** of God Most High, 3913
41:45 of Potiphera, **p** of On, to be his wife. 3913
41:50 by Asenath daughter of Potiphera, **p** *of* On. 3913
46:20 by Asenath daughter of Potiphera, **p** *of* On. 3913
Ex 2:16 Now a **p** *of* Midian had seven daughters, 3913
3: 1 Now Jethro, the **p** *of* Midian, 3913
18: 1 **p** of Midian and father-in-law of Moses, 3913
28: 3 so he *may* **serve me as p.** 3912
29:30 The son who succeeds him as **p** and comes 3913
30:33 whoever puts it on **anyone other than a p** 2424
31:10 both the sacred garments for Aaron the **p** 3913

Ex 35:19 both the sacred garments for Aaron the **p** 3913
38:21 the direction of Ithamar son of Aaron, the **p.** 3913
39:41 both the sacred garments for Aaron the **p** 3913
40:13 consecrate him so *he may* **serve** me **as p.** 3912
Lev 1: 7 The sons of Aaron the **p** are to put fire on 3913
1: 9 and the **p** is to burn all of it on the altar. 3913
1:12 and the **p** shall arrange them, 3913
1:13 **p** is to bring all of it and burn it on the altar. 3913
1:15 The **p** shall bring it to the altar, 3913
1:17 then the **p** shall burn it on the wood that is 3913
2: 2 The **p** shall take a handful of the fine flour 3913
2: 8 present it to the **p,** who shall take it to 3913
2:16 The **p** shall burn the memorial portion of 3913
3:11 The **p** shall burn them on the altar as food, 3913
3:16 The **p** shall burn them on the altar as food, 3913
4: 3 " 'If the anointed **p** sins, 3913
4: 5 Then the anointed **p** shall take some of 3913
4: 7 The **p** shall then put some of the blood on 3913
4:10 Then the **p** shall burn them on the altar 3913
4:16 Then the anointed **p** is to take some of 3913
4:20 In this way the **p** will make atonement 3913
4:25 Then the **p** shall take some of the blood of 3913
4:26 In this way the **p** will make atonement for 3913
4:30 Then the **p** is to take some of the blood 3913
4:31 and the **p** shall burn it on the altar as 3913
4:31 In this way the **p** will make atonement 3913
4:34 Then the **p** shall take some of the blood of 3913
4:35 and the **p** shall burn it on the altar on top of 3913
4:35 In this way the **p** will make atonement 3913
5: 6 **p** shall make atonement for him for his sin. 3913
5: 8 He is to bring them to the **p,** 3913
5:10 The **p** shall then offer the other as 3913
5:12 He is to bring it to the **p,** 3913
5:13 the **p** will make atonement for him for any 3913
5:13 of the offering will belong to the **p,** 3913
5:16 of the value to that and give it all to the **p,** 3913
5:18 to bring to the **p** as a guilt offering a ram 3913
5:18 In this way the **p** will make atonement 3913
6: 6 And as a penalty he must bring to the **p,** 3913
6: 7 the **p** will make atonement for him before 3913
6:10 The **p** shall then put on his linen clothes, 3913
6:12 Every morning the **p** is to add firewood 3913
6:15 The **p** is to take a handful of fine flour NIH
6:22 as anointed **p** shall prepare it. 3913
6:23 of a **p** shall be burned completely; 3913
6:26 The **p** who offers it shall eat it; 3913
7: 5 The **p** shall burn them on the altar as 3913
7: 7 They belong to the **p** who makes atonement 3913
7: 8 The **p** who offers a burnt offering 3913
7: 9 on a griddle belongs to the **p** who offers it, 3913
7:14 it belongs to the **p** who sprinkles the blood 3913
7:31 The **p** shall burn the fat on the altar, 3913
7:32 of your fellowship offerings to the **p** as 3913
7:34 the **p** and his sons as their regular share 3913
12: 6 the **p** at the entrance to the Tent of Meeting 3913
12: 8 In this way the **p** will make atonement 3913
13: 2 he must be brought to Aaron the **p** or to one 3913
13: 2 the priest or to one of his sons who is a **p.** 3913
13: 3 The **p** is to examine the sore on his skin, 3913
13: 3 When the **p** examines him, 3913
13: 4 the **p** is to put the infected person 3913
13: 5 the seventh day the **p** is to examine him, 3913
13: 6 the **p** is to examine him again, and if 3913
13: 6 the **p** shall pronounce him clean; 3913
13: 7 after he has shown himself to the **p** to 3913
13: 7 he must appear before the **p** again. 3913
13: 8 The **p** is to examine him, 3913
13: 9 he must be brought to the **p.** 3913
13:10 The **p** is to examine him, 3913
13:11 and the **p** shall pronounce him unclean. 3913
13:12 so far as the **p** can see, 3913
13:13 the **p** is to examine him, 3913
13:15 When the **p** sees the raw flesh, 3913
13:16 he must go to the **p.** 3913
13:17 The **p** is to examine him, 3913
13:17 the **p** shall pronounce the infected person 3913
13:19 he must present himself to the **p.** 3913
13:20 The **p** is to examine it, 3913
13:20 the **p** shall pronounce him unclean. 3913
13:21 But if, when the **p** examines it, 3913
13:21 **p** is to put him in isolation for seven days. 3913
13:22 the **p** shall pronounce him unclean; 3913
13:23 and the **p** shall pronounce him clean. 3913
13:25 the **p** is to examine the spot, 3913
13:25 The **p** shall pronounce him unclean; 3913
13:26 the **p** examines it and there is no white hair 3913
13:26 **p** is to put him in isolation for seven days. 3913
13:27 the seventh day the **p** is to examine him, 3913
13:27 the **p** shall pronounce him unclean; 3913
13:28 and the **p** shall pronounce him clean; 3913
13:30 the **p** is to examine the sore, and 3913
13:30 the **p** shall pronounce that person unclean; 3913
13:31 if, when the **p** examines this kind of sore, 3913
13:31 then the **p** is to put the infected person 3913
13:32 On the seventh day the **p** is to examine 3913
13:33 and the **p** is to keep him in isolation 3913
13:34 the seventh day the **p** is to examine the itch, 3913
13:34 the **p** shall pronounce him clean. 3913
13:36 the **p** is to examine him, and if 3913
13:36 the **p** does not need to look for yellow hair; 3913
13:37 and the **p** shall pronounce him clean. 3913
13:39 the **p** is to examine them, and if 3913
13:43 The **p** is to examine him, 3913
13:44 The **p** shall pronounce him unclean because 3913
13:49 and must be shown to the **p.** 3913
13:50 The **p** is to examine the mildew and isolate 3913
13:53 "But if, when the **p** examines it, 3913
Lev 13:55 the **p** is to examine it, 3913
13:56 If, when the **p** examines it, 3913
14: 2 when he is brought to the **p:** 3913
14: 3 The **p** is to go outside the camp 3913
14: 4 the **p** shall order that two live clean birds 3913
14: 5 Then the **p** shall order that one of the birds 3913
14:11 **p** who pronounces him clean shall present 3913
14:12 the **p** is to take one of the male lambs 3913
14:13 the guilt offering belongs to the **p;** 3913
14:14 The **p** is to take some of the blood of 3913
14:15 The **p** shall then take some of the log of oil, 3913
14:17 The **p** is to put some of the oil remaining 3913
14:18 in his palm the **p** shall put on the head of 3913
14:19 "Then the **p** is to sacrifice the sin offering 3913
14:19 the **p** shall slaughter the burnt offering NIH
14:23 the **p** at the entrance to the Tent of Meeting, 3913
14:24 The **p** is to take the lamb for 3913
14:26 The **p** is to pour some of the oil into 3913
14:29 in his palm the **p** shall put on the head of 3913
14:31 In this way the **p** will make atonement 3913
14:35 of the house must go and tell the **p,** 3913
14:36 The **p** is to order the house to be emptied 3913
14:36 the **p** is to go in and inspect the house. 3913
14:38 the **p** shall go out the doorway of the house 3913
14:39 the seventh day the **p** shall return to inspect 3913
14:44 the **p** is to go and examine it and, if 3913
14:48 "But if the **p** comes to examine it and 3913
15:14 the Tent of Meeting and give them to the **p.** 3913
15:15 The **p** is to sacrifice them, 3913
15:29 the **p** at the entrance to the Tent of Meeting. 3913
15:30 The **p** is to sacrifice one for a sin offering 3913
16:32 The **p** who is anointed and ordained 3913
16:32 to succeed his father as **high p** is 3912
17: 5 They must bring them to the **p,** that is, 3913
17: 6 The **p** is to sprinkle the blood against 3913
19:22 the **p** is to make atonement for him before 3913
21: 1 **p** must not make himself ceremonially unclean for any of his people NIH
21:10 " 'The high **p,** the one among his brothers 3913
21:21 the **p** who has any defect is to come near 3913
22:10 the guest of a **p** or his hired worker eat it. 3913
22:11 But if a **p** buys a slave with money, 3913
22:12 daughter marries **anyone other than a p,** 2424
22:14 to the **p** for the offering and add a fifth of 3913
23:10 the **p** a sheaf of the first grain you harvest. 3913
23:11 **p** is to wave it on the day after the Sabbath. 3913
23:20 The **p** is to wave the two lambs before 3913
23:20 a sacred offering to the LORD for the **p.** 3913
27: 8 he is to present the person to the **p,** 3913
27:11 the animal must be presented to the **p,** 3913
27:12 Whatever value the **p** then sets, 3913
27:14 the **p** will judge its quality as good or bad. 3913
27:14 Whatever value the **p** then sets, 3913
27:18 the **p** will determine the value according to 3913
27:23 the **p** will determine its value up to 3913
Nu 3: 6 of Levi and present them to Aaron the **p** 3913
3:32 Levites was Eleazar son of Aaron, the **p.** 3913
4:16 "Eleazar son of Aaron, the **p,** 3913
4:28 of Ithamar son of Aaron, the **p.** 3913
4:33 of Ithamar son of Aaron, the **p."** 3913
5: 8 to the LORD and must be given to the **p,** 3913
5: 9 the Israelites bring to a **p** will belong 3913
5:10 but what he gives to the **p** will belong to 3913
5:10 to the priest will belong to **the p.'** " 2257S
5:15 then he is to take his wife to the **p.** 3913
5:16 " 'The **p** shall bring her and have her stand 3913
5:18 After the **p** has had the woman stand before 3913
5:19 Then the **p** shall put the woman under oath 3913
5:21 the **p** is to put the woman under this curse 3913
5:23 " 'The **p** is to write these curses on a scroll 3913
5:25 The **p** is to take from her hands 3913
5:26 The **p** is then to take a handful of 3913
5:30 The **p** is to have her stand before 3913
6:10 the **p** at the entrance to the Tent of Meeting. 3913
6:11 The **p** is to offer one as a sin offering and 3913
6:16 " 'The **p** is to present them before 3913
6:19 the **p** is to place in his hands 3913
6:20 The **p** shall then wave them before 3913
6:20 they are holy and belong to the **p,** 3913
7: 8 of Ithamar son of Aaron, the **p.** 3913
15:25 The **p** is to make atonement for 3913
15:28 The **p** is to make atonement before 3913
16:37 the **p,** to take the censers out of 3913
16:39 the **p** collected the bronze censers brought 3913
18:28 the LORD's portion to Aaron the **p.** 3913
19: 3 Give it to Eleazar the **p;** 3913
19: 4 Then Eleazar the **p** is to take some 3913
19: 6 The **p** is to take some cedar wood, 3913
19: 7 the **p** must wash his clothes 3913
25: 7 the **p,** saw this, he left the assembly, 3913
25:11 son of Eliezer, the son of Aaron, the **p,** 3913
26: 1 to Moses and Eleazar son of Aaron, the **p,** 3913
26: 3 Moses and Eleazar the **p** spoke with them 3913
26:63 the **p** when they counted the Israelites on 3913
26:64 the **p** when they counted the Israelites in 3913
27: 2 the **p,** the leaders and the whole assembly, 3913
27:19 Have him stand before Eleazar the **p** and 3913
27:21 He is to stand before Eleazar the **p,** 3913
27:22 and had him stand before Eleazar the **p** and 3913
31: 6 along with Phinehas son of Eleazar, the **p,** 3913
31:12 and Eleazar the **p** and the Israelite assembly 3913
31:13 Eleazar the **p** and all the leaders of 3913
31:21 the **p** said to the soldiers who had gone 3913
31:26 and Eleazar the **p** and the family heads of 3913
31:29 to Eleazar the **p** as the LORD's part. 3913
31:31 So Moses and Eleazar the **p** did as 3913
31:41 Moses gave the tribute to Eleazar the **p** as 3913
Nu 31:51 and Eleazar the **p** accepted from them 3913
31:54 Moses and Eleazar the **p** accepted the gold 3913
32: 2 the **p** and to the leaders of the community, 3913
32:28 to Eleazar the **p** and Joshua son of Nun and 3913
33:38 the LORD's command Aaron the **p** went 3913
34:17 Eleazar the **p** and Joshua son of Nun. 3913
35:25 until the death of the high **p,** 3913
35:28 of refuge until the death of the high **p;** 3913
35:28 after the death of the high **p** may he return 3913
35:32 before the death of the high **p.** 3913
Dt 10: 6 and Eleazar his son succeeded him *as* **p.** 3912
17:12 or for the **p** who stands ministering there to 3913
20: 2 the **p** shall come forward and address 3913
26: 3 and say to the **p** in office at the time, 3913
26: 4 The **p** shall take the basket from your hands 3913
Jos 14: 1 which Eleazar the **p,** Joshua son of Nun 3913
17: 4 They went to Eleazar the **p,** 3913
19:51 These are the territories that Eleazar the **p,** 3913
20: 6 until the death of the high **p** who is serving 3913
21: 1 of the Levites approached Eleazar the **p,** 3913
21: 4 of Aaron the **p** were allotted thirteen towns 3913
21:13 the **p** they gave Hebron (a city of refuge 3913
22:13 the **p,** to the land of Gilead— 3913
22:30 the **p** and the leaders of the community— 3913
22:31 And Phinehas son of Eleazar, the **p,** 3913
22:32 Then Phinehas son of Eleazar, the **p,** 3913
Jdg 17: 5 and installed one of his sons as his **p.** 3913
17:10 "Live with me and be my father and **p,** 3913
17:12 and the young man became his **p** and lived 3913
17:13 since this Levite has become my **p."** 3913
18: 4 and said, "He has hired me and I am his **p."** 3913
18: 6 The **p** answered them, "Go in peace. 3913
18:17 the **p** and the six hundred armed men stood 3913
18:18 the **p** said to them, "What are you doing?" 3913
18:19 Come with us, and be our father and **p.** 3913
18:19 as **p** rather than just one man's household?" 3913
18:20 Then the **p** was glad. 3913
18:24 "You took the gods I made, and my **p,** 3913
18:27 they took what Micah had made, and his **p,** 3913
1Sa 1: 9 the **p** was sitting on a chair by the doorpost 3913
2:11 before the LORD under Eli the **p.** 3913
2:13 the servant of the **p** would come with 3913
2:14 and the **p** would take for himself whatever 3913
2:15 the servant of the **p** would come and say to 3913
2:15 "Give the **p** some meat to roast; 3913
2:28 of all the tribes of Israel to be my **p,** 3913
2:35 I will raise up for myself a faithful **p,** 3913
14: 3 the son of Eli, the LORD's **p** in Shiloh. 3913
14:19 While Saul was talking to the **p,** 3913
14:19 So Saul said to the **p,** 3913
14:36 the **p** said, "Let us inquire of God here." 3913
21: 1 David went to Nob, to Ahimelech the **p.** 3913
21: 2 David answered Ahimelech the **p,** 3913
21: 4 But the **p** answered David, 3913
21: 6 So the **p** gave him the consecrated bread, 3913
21: 9 The **p** replied, "The sword of Goliath 3913
22:11 Then the king sent for the **p** Ahimelech son 3913
23: 9 he said to Abiathar the **p,** 3913
30: 7 Then David said to Abiathar the **p,** 3913
2Sa 15:27 The king also said to Zadok the **p,** 3913
20:26 and Ira the Jairite was David's **p.** 3913
1Ki 1: 7 of Zeruiah and with Abiathar the **p,** 3913
1: 8 But Zadok the **p,** Benaiah son of Jehoiada, 3913
1:19 the **p** and Joab the commander of the army, 3913
1:25 of the army and Abiathar the **p.** 3913
1:26 But me your servant, and Zadok the **p,** 3913
1:32 King David said, "Call in Zadok the **p,** 3913
1:34 There have Zadok the **p** and Nathan 3913
1:38 So Zadok the **p,** Nathan the prophet, 3913
1:39 Zadok the **p** took the horn of oil from 3913
1:42 Jonathan son of Abiathar the **p** arrived. 3913
1:44 The king has sent with him Zadok the **p,** 3913
1:45 and Zadok the **p** and Nathan 3913
2:22 for him and for Abiathar the **p** and Joab son 3913
2:26 To Abiathar the **p** the king said, 3913
2:35 and replaced Abiathar with Zadok the **p.** 3913
4: 2 Azariah son of Zadok—the **p;** 3913
4: 5 a **p** and personal adviser to the king; 3913
13:33 a **p** he consecrated *for* the high places. 3913
2Ki 11: 9 as Jehoiada the **p** ordered. 3913
11: 9 and came to Jehoiada the **p.** 3913
11:15 the **p** ordered the commanders of units of 3913
11:15 For the **p** had said 3913
11:18 and idols to pieces and killed Mattan the **p** 3913
11:18 Then Jehoiada the **p** posted guards at 3913
12: 2 the years Jehoiada the **p** instructed him. 3913
12: 5 Let every **p** receive the money from one of 3913
12: 7 the **p** and the other priests and asked them, 3913
12: 9 Jehoiada the **p** took a chest and bored 3913
12:10 the royal secretary and the high **p** came, 3913
16:10 and sent to Uriah the **p** a sketch of the altar, 3913
16:11 So Uriah the **p** built an altar in accordance 3913
16:15 then gave these orders to Uriah the **p:** 3913
16:16 the **p** did just as King Ahaz had ordered. 3913
22: 4 the high **p** and have him get ready 3913
22: 8 the high **p** said to Shaphan the secretary, 3913
22:10 "Hilkiah the **p** has given me a book." 3913
22:12 He gave these orders to Hilkiah the **p,** 3913
22:14 Hilkiah the **p,** Ahikam, Acbor, 3913
23: 4 The king ordered Hilkiah the high **p,** 3913
23:24 the book that Hilkiah the **p** had discovered 3913
25:18 as prisoners Seraiah the chief **p,** 3913
25:18 Zephaniah the **p** next in rank and 3913
1Ch 6:10 of Azariah (it was he who **served as p** in 3912
16:39 the **p** and his fellow priests before 3913
24: 6 Zadok the **p,** Ahimelech son of Abiathar 3913
27: 5 was Benaiah son of Jehoiada the **p.** 3913

1Ch 29:22 the LORD to be ruler and Zadok to be **p.** 3913
2Ch 13: 9 and seven rams may become a **p** 3913
15: 3 without a **p** to teach and without the law. 3913
19:11 the chief **p** will be over you in any matter 3913
22:11 and wife of the **p** Jehoiada, 3913
23: 8 of Judah did just as Jehoiada the **p** ordered. 3913
23: 8 the **p** had not released any of the divisions. 3913
23:14 the **p** sent out the commanders of units of 3913
23:14 For the **p** had said, 3913
23:17 the altars and idols and killed Mattan the **p** 3913
24: 2 the LORD all the years of Jehoiada the **p.** 3913
24: 6 the king summoned Jehoiada the chief **p** NIH
24:11 and the officer of the chief **p** would come 3913
24:20 upon Zechariah son of Jehoiada the **p.** 3913
24:25 for murdering the son of Jehoiada the **p,** 3913
26:17 the **p** with eighty other courageous priests 3913
26:20 the chief **p** and all the other priests looked 3913
31:10 and Azariah the chief **p,** 3913
34: 9 the high **p** and gave him the money 3913
34:14 Hilkiah the **p** found the Book of the Law of 3913
34:18 "Hilkiah the **p** has given me a book." 3913
Ezr 2:63 until there was a **p** ministering with 3913
7: 5 the son of Aaron the chief **p—** 3913
7:11 the **p** and teacher, a man learned in matters 3913
7:12 king of kings, To Ezra the **p,** 10347
7:21 the **p,** a teacher of the Law of the God 10347
8:33 the hands of Meremoth son of Uriah, the **p.** 3913
10:10 Then Ezra the **p** stood up and said to them, 3913
10:16 the **p** selected men who were family heads, 3913
Ne 3: 1 the high **p** and his fellow priests went 3913
3:20 of the house of Eliashib the high **p.** 3913
7:65 until there should be a **p** ministering with 3913
8: 2 the **p** brought the Law before the assembly, 3913
8: 9 Ezra the **p** and scribe, 3913
10:38 A **p** descended from Aaron is 3913
12:26 the governor and of Ezra the **p** and scribe. 3913
13: 4 Eliashib the **p** had been put in charge of 3913
13:13 I put Shelemiah the **p,** Zadok the scribe, 3913
13:28 the high **p** was son-in-law to Sanballat 3913
Ps 110: 4 "You are a **p** forever, in the order of Melchizedek." 3913
Isa 8: 2 the **p** and Zechariah son of Jeberekiah 3913
24: 2 it will be the same for **p** as for people, 3913
61:10 as a bridegroom adorns his head *like a* **p,** 3912
Jer 14:18 and **p** have gone to a land they know not.' " 3913
18:18 for the teaching of the law by the **p** will not 3913
20: 1 When the **p** Pashhur son of Immer, 3913
21: 1 and the **p** Zephaniah son of Maaseiah. 3913
23:11 "Both prophet and **p** are godless; 3913
23:33 "When these people, or a prophet or a **p,** 3913
23:34 If a prophet or a **p** or anyone else claims, 3913
29:25 to Zephaniah son of Maaseiah the **p,** 3913
29:26 'The LORD has appointed you **p** in place 3913
29:29 Zephaniah the **p,** however, 3913
37: 3 of Shelemiah with the **p** Zephaniah son 3913
52:24 as prisoners Seraiah the chief **p,** 3913
52:24 Zephaniah the **p** next in rank and 3913
La 2: 6 both king and **p.** 3913
2:20 Should **p** and prophet be killed in 3913
Eze 1: 3 word of the LORD came to Ezekiel the **p,** 3913
7:26 the teaching of the law by the **p** will be lost, 3913
44:21 No **p** is to drink wine when he enters 3913
44:25 " 'A **p** must not defile himself by going NIH
45:19 The **p** is to take some of the blood of 3913
Hos 4: 4 like those who bring charges against a **p.** 3913
Am 7:10 Then Amaziah the **p** *of* Bethel sent 3913
Hag 1: 1 and to Joshua son of Jehozadak, the high **p:** 3913
1:12 Joshua son of Jehozadak, the high **p,** 3913
1:14 of Joshua son of Jehozadak, the high **p,** 3913
2: 2 to Joshua son of Jehozadak, the high **p,** 3913
2: 4 O Joshua son of Jehozadak, the high **p.** 3913
Zec 3: 1 the high **p** standing before the angel of 3913
3: 8 O high **p** Joshua and your associates seated 3913
6:11 and set it on the head of the high **p,** 3913
6:13 And he will be a **p** on his throne. 3913
Mal 2: 7 the lips of a **p** ought to preserve knowledge, 3913
Mt 8: 4 the **p** and offer the gift Moses commanded, *2636*
26: 3 in the palace *of* the **high p,** *797*
26:51 and struck the servant *of* the **high p,** *797*
26:57 the **high p,** where the teachers of the law *797*
26:58 right up to the courtyard *of* the **high p.** *797*
26:62 Then the **high p** stood up and said to Jesus, *797*
26:63 The **high p** said to him, *797*
26:65 Then the **high p** tore his clothes and said, *797*
Mk 1:44 show yourself *to* the **p** and offer *2636*
2:26 In the days of Abiathar the **high p,** *797*
14:47 and struck the servant *of* the **high p,** *797*
14:53 They took Jesus to the **high p,** *797*
14:54 right into the courtyard *of* the **high p.** *797*
14:60 Then the **high p** stood up before them *797*
14:61 Again the **high p** asked him, *797*
14:63 The **high p** tore his clothes. *797*
14:66 of the servant girls *of* the **high p** came by. *797*
Lk 1: 5 of Judea there was a **p** named Zechariah, *2636*
1: 8 and he *was* **serving as p** before God, *2634*
5:14 show yourself *to* the **p** and offer *2636*
10:31 A **p** happened to be going down *2636*
22:50 one of them struck the servant *of* the **high p,** *797*
22:54 and took him into the house *of* the **high p.** *797*
Jn 11:49 named Caiaphas, who was **high p** that year, *797*
11:51 but as **high p** that year he prophesied *797*
18:13 Caiaphas, the **high p** that year. *797*
18:15 this disciple was known *to* the **high p,** *797*
18:16 who was known *to* the **high p,** came back, *797*
18:19 the **high p** questioned Jesus *797*
18:22 "Is this the way you answer the **high p?"** *797*
18:24 still bound, to Caiaphas the **high p.** *797*
Ac 4: 6 Annas the **high p** was there, *797*
5:17 Then the **high p** and all his associates, *797*
5:21 When the **high p** and his associates arrived, *797*
5:27 to be questioned by the **high p.** *797*
7: 1 **high p** asked him, "Are these charges true?" *797*
9: 1 He went to the **high p** *797*
14:13 The **p** of Zeus, whose temple was *2636*
19:14 Seven sons of Sceva, a Jewish **chief p,** *797*
22: 5 the **high p** and all the Council can testify. *797*
23: 2 the **high p** Ananias ordered those standing *797*
23: 4 "You dare to insult God's **high p?"** *797*
23: 5 I did not realize that he was the **high p;** *797*
24: 1 the **high p** Ananias went down to Caesarea *797*
Heb 2:17 a merciful and faithful **high p** in service *797*
3: 1 the apostle and **high p** whom we confess. *797*
4:14 since we have a great **high p** who has gone *797*
4:15 For we do not have a **high p** who is unable *797*
5: 1 Every **high p** is selected from among men *797*
5: 5 the glory of becoming a **high p.** *797*
5: 6 "You are a **p** forever, in the order of Melchizedek." *2636*
5:10 and was designated by God to be **high p** in *797*
6:20 He has become a **high p** forever, *797*
7: 1 This Melchizedek was king of Salem and **p** *2636*
7: 3 like the Son of God he remains a **p** forever. *2636*
7:11 why was there still need for another **p** *2636*
7:15 if another **p** like Melchizedek appears, *2636*
7:16 one who has become a **p** not on the basis of *NIG*
7:17 For it is declared: "You are a **p** forever, in the order of Melchizedek." *2636*
7:21 a **p** with an oath when God said to him: *NIG*
7:21 'You are a **p** forever.' " *2636*
7:26 Such a **high p** meets our need— *797*
8: 1 We do have such a **high p,** *797*
8: 3 Every **high p** is appointed to offer both gifts *797*
8: 4 If he were on earth, he would not be a **p,** *2636*
9: 7 But only the **high p** entered the inner room, *797*
9:11 When Christ came as **high p** of the good *797*
9:25 the **high p** enters the Most Holy Place *797*
10:11 Day after day every **p** stands *2636*
10:12 But when this **p** had offered for all time *NIG*
10:21 we have a great **p** over the house of God, *2636*
13:11 The **high p** carries the blood of animals into *797*

PRIEST'S (10) [PRIEST]

Lev 6:29 Any male in a **p** family may eat it; 3913
7: 6 Any male in a **p** family may eat it, 3913
21: 9 a **p** daughter defiles herself by becoming 3913
22:10 " 'No one **outside a p family** may eat 2424
22:12 If a **p** daughter marries anyone other than 3913
22:13 But if a **p** daughter becomes a widow 3913
Jn 18:10 drew it and struck the **high p** servant, *797*
18:15 he went with Jesus into the **high p** courtyard, *797*
18:26 One of the **high p** servants, *797*
Ac 4: 6 and the other men of the **high p** family. *796*

PRIESTHOOD (17) [PRIEST]

Ex 29: 9 The **p** is theirs by a lasting ordinance. 3914
40:15 to a **p** that will continue for all generations 3914
Nu 16:10 but now you are trying to get the **p** too. 3914
18: 1 the responsibility for offenses against the **p.** 3914
18: 7 I am giving you the service of the **p** as 3914
25:13 a covenant of a lasting **p,** 3914
1Ki 2:27 So Solomon removed Abiathar from the **p** 3913
Ezr 2:62 so were excluded from the **p** as unclean. 3914
Ne 7:64 so were excluded from the **p** as unclean. 3914
13:29 the priestly office and the covenant of the **p** 3914
Lk 1: 9 according to the custom *of* the **p,** *2632*
3: 2 during the **high p** of Annas and Caiaphas, *797*
Heb 7:11 through the Levitical **p** (for on the basis *2648*
7:12 For when there is a change *of* the **p,** *2648*
7:24 he has a permanent **p.** *2648*
1Pe 2: 5 into a spiritual house to be a holy **p,** *2633*
2: 9 But you are a chosen people, a royal **p,** *2633*

PRIESTLY (8) [PRIEST]

Lev 21:10 to wear the **p** garments, NIH
Jos 18: 7 **p service** *of* the LORD is their inheritance. 3914
1Sa 2:36 to some **p office** so I can have food 3914
Ezr 2:69 5,000 minas of silver and 100 **p** garments. 3913
Ne 12:12 these were the heads of the **p** families: 3913
13:29 because they defiled the **p office** and 3914
Lk 1: 5 who belonged to the **p division** of Abijah; *2389*
Ro 15:16 the Gentiles *with* the **p duty** of proclaiming *2646*

PRIESTS (422) [PRIEST]

Ge 47:22 However, he did not buy the land of the **p,** 3913
47:26 of the **p** that did not become Pharaoh's. 3913
Ex 19: 6 for me a kingdom of **p** and a holy nation.' 3913
19:22 Even the **p,** who approach the LORD, 3913
19:24 But the **p** and the people must 3913
28: 1 so they *may* **serve** me **as p.** 3912
28: 4 so they *may* **serve** me **as p.** 3912
28:41 Consecrate them so *they may* **serve** me **as p.** 3912
29: 1 so *they may* **serve** me **as p:** 3912
29:44 and his sons to **serve** me **as p.** 3912
30:30 so they *may* **serve** me **as p.** 3912
31:10 for his sons when *they* **serve as p,** 3912
35:19 for his sons when *they* **serve as p."** 3912
39:41 for his sons when **serving as p.** 3912
40:15 so *they may* **serve** me **as p.** 3912
Lev 1: 5 the **p** shall bring the blood and sprinkle it 3913
1: 8 Aaron's sons the **p** shall arrange the pieces, 3913
1:11 the **p** shall sprinkle its blood against 3913
Lev 2: 2 and take it to Aaron's sons the **p.** 3913
3: 2 Then Aaron's sons the **p** shall sprinkle 3913
7:35 presented to **serve** the LORD **as p.** 3912
16:33 the **p** and all the people of the community. 3913
21: 1 "Speak to the **p,** the sons of Aaron, 3913
21: 5 " '**P** must not shave their heads NIH
21: 7 because **p** are holy to their God. 2085[S]
22: 9 " 'The **p** are to keep my requirements so NIH
22:15 The **p** must not desecrate NIH
27:21 it will become the property of the **p.** 3913
Nu 3: 3 the anointed **p,** who were ordained to serve 3913
3: 3 who were ordained to **serve as p.** 3912
3: 4 and Ithamar **served as p** during the lifetime 3912
3:10 Appoint Aaron and his sons to serve as **p;** 3914
10: 8 "The sons of Aaron, the **p,** 3913
18: 7 and your sons may serve as **p** in connection 3914
Dt 17: 9 Go to the **p,** who are Levites, 3913
17:18 taken from that of the **p,** who are Levites. 3913
18: 1 The **p,** who are Levites— 3913
18: 3 the **p** from the people who sacrifice a bull 3913
19:17 in the presence of the LORD before the **p** 3913
21: 5 The **p,** the sons of Levi, shall step forward, 3913
24: 8 be very careful to do exactly as the **p,** 3913
27: 9 Then Moses and the **p,** who are Levites, 3913
31: 9 down this law and gave it to the **p,** 3913
Jos 3: 3 and the **p,** who are Levites, carrying it, 3913
3: 6 Joshua said to the **p,** 3913
3: 8 the **p** who carry the ark of the covenant: 3913
3:13 as the **p** who carry the ark of the LORD— 3913
3:14 the **p** carrying the ark of the covenant went 3913
3:15 as the **p** who carried the ark reached 3913
3:17 The **p** who carried the ark of the covenant 3913
4: 3 the Jordan from right where the **p** stood and 3913
4: 9 the spot where the **p** who carried the ark of 3913
4:10 Now the **p** who carried the ark 3913
4:11 the LORD and the **p** came to the other side 3913
4:16 the **p** carrying the ark of the Testimony 3913
4:17 So Joshua commanded the **p,** 3913
4:18 And the **p** came up out of the river carrying 3913
6: 4 Have seven **p** carry trumpets of rams' horns 3913
6: 4 with the **p** blowing the trumpets. 3913
6: 6 So Joshua son of Nun called the **p** and said 3913
6: 6 and have seven **p** carry trumpets in front 3913
6: 8 the seven **p** carrying the seven trumpets 3913
6: 9 ahead of the **p** who blew the trumpets, 3913
6:12 up early the next morning and the **p** took up 3913
6:13 The seven **p** carrying the seven trumpets 3913
6:16 when the **p** sounded the trumpet blast, 3913
8:33 the **p,** who were Levites. 3913
21:19 All the towns for the **p,** 3913
Jdg 18:30 and his sons were **p** for the tribe of Dan 3913
1Sa 1: 3 the two sons of Eli, were **p** of the LORD. 3913
2:13 Now it was the practice of the **p** with 3913
5: 5 That is why to this day neither the **p** 3913
6: 2 for the **p** and the diviners and said, 3913
22:11 who were the **p** at Nob, 3913
22:17 "Turn and kill the **p** *of* the LORD, 3913
22:17 not willing to raise a hand to strike the **p** *of* 3913
22:18 "You turn and strike down the **p."** 3913
22:19 the town of the **p,** with its men and women, 3913
22:21 He told David that Saul had killed the **p** *of* 3913
2Sa 8:17 and Ahimelech son of Abiathar were **p;** 3913
15:35 Won't the **p** Zadok and Abiathar be there 3913
17:15 Hushai told Zadok and Abiathar, the **p,** 3913
19:11 to Zadok and Abiathar, the **p:** 3913
20:25 Zadok and Abiathar were **p;** 3913
1Ki 4: 4 Zadok and Abiathar—**p;** 3913
8: 3 the **p** took up the ark, 3913
8: 4 The **p** and Levites carried them up, 3913
8: 6 The **p** then brought the ark of 3913
8:10 When the **p** withdrew from the Holy Place, 3913
8:11 And the **p** could not perform their service 3913
12:31 and appointed **p** from all sorts of people, 3913
12:32 And at Bethel he also installed **p** *at* 3913
13: 2 On you he will sacrifice the **p** *of* the high 3913
13:33 once more appointed **p** *for* the high places 3913
2Ki 10:11 his close friends and his **p,** 3913
10:19 all his ministers and all his **p.** 3913
12: 4 Joash said to the **p,** 3913
12: 6 of King Joash the **p** still had not repaired 3913
12: 7 the priest and the other **p** and asked them, 3913
12: 8 The **p** agreed that they would 3913
12: 9 The **p** who guarded the entrance put into 3913
12:16 it belonged to the **p.** 3913
17:27 "Have one of the **p** you took captive 3913
17:28 So one of the **p** who had been exiled 3913
17:32 to officiate for them as **p** in the shrines at 3913
19: 2 Shebna the secretary and the leading **p,** 3913
23: 2 the **p** and the prophets— 3913
23: 4 the **p** next in rank and the doorkeepers 3913
23: 5 He did away with the **pagan p** appointed by 4024
23: 8 Josiah brought all the **p** from the towns 3913
23: 8 where the **p** had burned incense. 3913
23: 9 the **p** *of* the high places did not serve at 3913
23: 9 with their fellow **p.** NIH
23:20 the **p** *of* those high places on the altars 3913
1Ch 9: 2 **p,** Levites and temple servants. 3913
9:10 Of the **p:** Jedaiah; Jehoiarib; Jakin; 3913
9:13 The **p,** who were heads of families, 278+2157[S]
9:30 of the **p** took care of mixing the spices. 3913
13: 2 also to the **p** and Levites who are with them 3913
15:11 Zadok and Abiathar the **p,** 3913
15:14 the **p** and Levites consecrated themselves 3913
15:24 the **p** were to blow trumpets before the ark 3913
16: 6 the **p** were to blow the trumpets regularly 3913
16:39 David left Zadok the priest and his fellow **p** 3913
18:16 and Ahimelech son of Abiathar were **p;** 3913

1Ch 23: 2 as well as the **p** and Levites. 3913
24: 2 so Eleazar and Ithamar **served as** *the* **p.** 3912
24: 6 and the heads of families of the **p** and of 3913
24:31 and the heads of families of the **p** and of 3913
28:13 for the divisions of the **p** and Levites, 3913
28:21 The divisions of the **p** and Levites are ready 3913
2Ch 4: 6 but the Sea was to be used by the **p** 3913
4: 9 He made the courtyard of the **p,** 3913
5: 5 The **p,** who were Levites, carried them up; 3913
5: 7 The **p** then brought the ark of 3913
5:11 The **p** then withdrew from the Holy Place. 3913
5:11 All the **p** who were there had consecrated themselves, 3913
5:12 by 120 **p** sounding trumpets. 3913
5:14 and the **p** could not perform their service 3913
6:41 May your **p,** O LORD God, 3913
7: 2 The **p** could not enter the temple of 3913
7: 6 The **p** took their positions, 3913
7: 6 the **p** blew their trumpets, 3913
8:14 the divisions of the **p** for their duties, 3913
8:14 the **p** according to each day's requirement. 3913
8:15 from the king's commands to the **p** or to 3913
11:13 The **p** and Levites from all their districts 3913
11:14 and his sons had rejected them as **p** of 3912
11:15 And he appointed his own **p** for 3913
13: 9 But didn't you drive out the **p** *of* 3913
13: 9 and make **p** of your own as the peoples 3913
13:10 The **p** who serve the LORD are sons 3913
13:12 His **p** with their trumpets will sound 3913
13:14 The **p** blew their trumpets 3913
17: 8 and the **p** Elishama and Jehoram. 3913
19: 8 **p** and heads of Israelite families 3913
23: 4 of you **p** and Levites who are going on duty 3913
23: 6 of the LORD except the **p** and Levites 3913
23:18 of the LORD in the hands of the **p,** 3913
24: 5 He called together the **p** and Levites 3913
26:17 the priest with eighty other courageous **p** of 3913
26:18 That is for the **p,** the descendants of Aaron, 3913
26:19 at the **p** in their presence before 3913
26:20 the chief priest and all the other **p** looked 3913
29: 4 He brought in the **p** and the Levites, 3913
29:16 The **p** went into the sanctuary of 3913
29:21 The king commanded the **p,** 3913
29:22 and the **p** took the blood and sprinkled it on 3913
29:24 The **p** then slaughtered the goats 3913
29:26 and the **p** with their trumpets. 3913
29:34 The **p,** however, were too few to skin all 3913
29:34 and until other **p** had been consecrated, 3913
29:34 consecrating themselves than the **p** had been 3913
30: 3 not enough **p** had consecrated themselves 3913
30:15 The **p** and the Levites were ashamed 3913
30:16 The **p** sprinkled the blood handed to them 3913
30:21 and **p** sang to the LORD every day, 3913
30:24 great number of **p** consecrated themselves. 3913
30:25 along with the **p** and Levites 3913
30:27 The **p** and the Levites stood to bless 3913
31: 2 Hezekiah assigned the **p** and Levites 3913
31: 2 each of them according to their duties as **p** 3913
31: 4 in Jerusalem to give the portion due the **p** 3913
31: 9 Hezekiah asked the **p** and Levites about 3913
31:15 in the towns of the **p,** 3913
31:15 distributing to their fellow **p** according NIH
31:17 And they distributed to the **p** enrolled 3913
31:19 As for the **p,** the descendants of Aaron, 3913
34: 5 the bones of the **p** on their altars, 3913
34:30 the **p** and the Levites— 3913
35: 2 the **p** to their duties and encouraged them 3913
35: 8 to the people and the **p** and Levites. 3913
35: 8 **p** twenty-six hundred Passover offerings 3913
35:10 the **p** stood in their places with the Levites 3913
35:11 the **p** sprinkled the blood handed to them, 3913
35:14 for themselves and for the **p,** 3913
35:14 because the **p,** the descendants of Aaron, 3913
35:14 for themselves and for the Aaronic **p.** 3913
35:18 a Passover as did Josiah, with the **p,** 3913
36:14 of the **p** and the people became more 3913
Ezr 1: 5 and the **p** and Levites— 3913
2:36 The **p:** the descendants of Jedaiah 3913
2:61 And from among the **p:** 3913
2:70 The **p,** the Levites, the singers, 3913
3: 2 and his fellow **p** and Zerubbabel son 3913
3: 8 and the rest of their brothers (the **p** and 3913
3:10 the **p** in their vestments and with trumpets, 3913
3:12 the older **p** and Levites and family heads, 3913
6: 9 as requested by the **p** in Jerusalem 10347
6:16 **p,** the Levites and the rest of the exiles— 10347
6:18 And they installed the **p** in their divisions 10347
6:20 The **p** and Levites had purified themselves 3913
6:20 for their brothers the **p** and for themselves. 3913
7: 7 Some of the Israelites, including **p,** Levites, 3913
7:13 including **p** and Levites, 10347
7:16 as the freewill offerings of the people and **p** 10347
7:24 tribute or duty on any of the **p,** Levites, 10347
8:15 I checked among the people and the **p,** 3913
8:24 Then I set apart twelve of the leading **p,** 3913
8:29 before the leading **p** and the Levites and 3913
8:30 Then the **p** and Levites received the silver 3913
9: 1 including the **p** and the Levites, 3913
9: 7 and our **p** have been subjected to the sword 3913
10: 5 the leading **p** and Levites and all Israel 3913
10:18 Among the descendants of the **p,** 3913
Ne 2:16 yet I had said nothing to the Jews or the **p** 3913
3: 1 and his fellow **p** went to work and rebuilt 3913
3:22 The repairs next to him were made by the **p** 3913
3:28 Above the Horse Gate, the **p** made repairs, 3913
5:12 Then I summoned the **p** and made 3913
7:39 The **p:** the descendants of Jedaiah 3913
Ne 7:63 And from among the **p:** 3913
7:70 50 bowls and 530 garments for **p.** 3913
7:72 minas of silver and 67 garments for **p.** 3913
7:73 The **p,** the Levites, the gatekeepers, 3913
8:13 along with the **p** and the Levites, 3913
9:32 upon our **p** and prophets, 3913
9:34 our **p** and our fathers did 3913
9:38 and our **p** are affixing their seals to it." 3913
10: 8 These were the **p.** 3913
10:28 "The rest of the people—**p,** Levites, 3913
10:34 "We—the **p,** the Levites and the people— 3913
10:36 to the **p** ministering there. 3913
10:37 to the **p,** the first of our ground meal, 3913
10:39 and where the ministering **p,** 3913
11: 3 **p,** Levites, temple servants and descendants 3913
11:10 From the **p:** Jedaiah; the son of Joiarib; 3913
11:20 with the **p** and Levites, 3913
12: 1 These were the **p** and Levites who returned 3913
12: 7 the leaders of the **p** and their associates in 3913
12:22 as well as those of the **p,** 3913
12:30 When the **p** and Levites had purified themselves ceremonially, 3913
12:35 as well as some **p** with trumpets, 3913
12:41 as well as the **p**— 3913
12:44 the portions required by the Law for the **p** 3913
12:44 with the ministering **p** and Levites. 3913
13: 5 as well as the contributions for the **p.** 3913
13:30 the **p** and the Levites of everything foreign, 3913
Job 12:19 He leads **p** away stripped 3913
Ps 78:64 their **p** were put to the sword, 3913
99: 6 Moses and Aaron were among his **p,** 3913
132: 9 May your **p** be clothed with righteousness; 3913
132:16 I will clothe her **p** with salvation, 3913
Isa 28: 7 **P** and prophets stagger from beer 3913
37: 2 and the leading **p,** all wearing sackcloth, 3913
61: 6 And you will be called **p** *of* the LORD, 3913
66:21 And I will select some of them also to be **p** 3913
Jer 1: 1 one of the **p** at Anathoth in the territory 3913
1:18 its officials, its **p** and the people of the land. 3913
2: 8 The **p** did not ask, 'Where is the LORD?' 3913
2:26 their **p** and their prophets. 3913
4: 9 the **p** will be horrified, 3913
5:31 the **p** rule by their own authority, 3913
6:13 prophets and **p** alike, all practice deceit. 3913
8: 1 the bones of the **p** and prophets, 3913
8:10 prophets and **p** alike, all practice deceit. 3913
13:13 the kings who sit on David's throne, the **p,** 3913
19: 1 of the elders of the people and of the **p** 3913
26: 7 The **p,** the prophets and all 3913
26: 8 to say, the **p,** the prophets and all 3913
26:11 the **p** and the prophets said to the officials 3913
26:16 the officials and all the people said to the **p** 3913
27:16 Then I said to the **p** and all these people, 3913
28: 1 the LORD in the presence of the **p** and all 3913
28: 5 the **p** and all the people who were standing 3913
29: 1 among the exiles and to the **p,** 3913
29:25 and to all the other **p.** 3913
31:14 I will satisfy the **p** with abundance, 3913
32:32 they, their kings and officials, their **p** 3913
33:18 nor will the **p,** who are Levites, 3913
33:21 with the Levites who are **p** ministering 3913
34:19 the **p** and all the people of the land 3913
48: 7 together with his **p** and officials. 3913
49: 3 together with his **p** and officials. 3913
La 1: 4 All her gateways are desolate, her **p** groan, 3913
1:19 My **p** and my elders perished in the city 3913
4:13 of her prophets and the iniquities of her **p,** 3913
4:16 **p** are shown no honor, the elders no favor. 3913
Eze 22:26 Her **p** do violence to my law 3913
40:45 for the **p** who have charge of the temple, 3913
40:46 for the **p** who have charge of the altar. 3913
42:13 the **p** who approach the LORD will eat 3913
42:14 Once the **p** enter the holy precincts, 3913
43:19 a young bull as a sin offering to the **p,** 3913
43:24 and the **p** are to sprinkle salt on them 3913
43:27 the **p** are to present your burnt offerings 3913
44:13 They are not to come near to **serve** me **as p** 3912
44:15 the **p,** who are Levites and descendants 3913
44:22 of Israelite descent or widows of **p.** 3913
44:24 **the p** are to serve as judges and decide it 2156S
44:28 to be the only inheritance **the p** have. 4392S
44:30 of all your special gifts will belong to the **p.** 3913
44:31 The **p** must not eat anything, 3913
45: 4 be the sacred portion of the land for the **p,** 3913
46: 2 The **p** are to sacrifice his burnt offering 3913
46:19 which belonged to the **p,** 3913
46:20 where the **p** will cook the guilt offering and 3913
48:10 This will be the sacred portion for the **p.** 3913
48:11 This will be for the consecrated **p,** 3913
48:13 "Alongside the territory of the **p,** 3913
Hos 4: 6 I also reject you as my **p;** 3912
4: 7 The more the **p** increased, 4392S
4: 9 And it will be: Like people, like **p.** 3913
5: 1 "Hear this, you **p!** 3913
6: 9 so do bands of **p;** they murder 3913
10: 5 and so will its **idolatrous p,** 4024
Joel 1: 9 The **p** are in mourning, 3913
1:13 Put on sackcloth, O **p,** and mourn; 3913
2:17 Let the **p,** who minister before the LORD, 3913
Mic 3:11 her **p** teach for a price, 3913
Zep 1: 4 of the pagan and the **idolatrous p**— 3913
3: 4 Her **p** profane the sanctuary 3913
Hag 2:11 'Ask the **p** what the law says: 3913
2:12 The **p** answered, "No." 3913
2:13 "Yes," the **p** replied, "it becomes defiled." 3913
Zec 7: 3 the **p** of the house of the LORD Almighty 3913
7: 5 "Ask all the people of the land and the **p,** 3913
Mal 1: 6 "It is you, O **p,** who show contempt for my 3913
2: 1 "And now this admonition is for you, O **p.** 3913
Mt 2: 4 the people's **chief p** and teachers of the law, *797*
12: 4 but only *for* the **p.** *2636*
12: 5 the Sabbath the **p** in the temple desecrate *2636*
16:21 **chief p** and teachers of the law, *797*
20:18 be betrayed *to* the **chief p** and the teachers *797*
21:15 the **chief p** and the teachers of the law saw *797*
21:23 the **chief p** and the elders of *797*
21:45 When the **chief p** and the Pharisees heard *797*
26: 3 Then the **chief p** and the elders of *797*
26:14 called Judas Iscariot—went to the **chief p** *797*
26:47 the **chief p** and the elders of the people. *797*
26:59 The **chief p** and the whole Sanhedrin *797*
27: 1 all the **chief p** and the elders of *797*
27: 3 the thirty silver coins *to* the **chief p** and *797*
27: 6 The **chief p** picked up the coins and said, *797*
27:12 When he was accused by the **chief p** and *797*
27:20 But the **chief p** and the elders persuaded *797*
27:41 In the same way the **chief p,** *797*
27:62 the **chief p** and the Pharisees went to Pilate. *797*
28:11 the **chief p** everything that had happened. *797*
28:12 When the chief **p** had met with the elders *NIG*
Mk 2:26 which is lawful only for **p** to eat. *2636*
8:31 **chief p** and teachers of the law, *797*
10:33 be betrayed *to* the **chief p** and teachers of *797*
11:18 The **chief p** and the teachers of *797*
11:27 the temple courts, the **chief p,** the teachers *797*
14: 1 and the **chief p** and the teachers of *797*
14:10 went to the **chief p** to betray Jesus to them. *797*
14:43 sent from the **chief p,** the teachers of the law *797*
14:53 and all the **chief p,** elders and *797*
14:55 The **chief p** and the whole Sanhedrin *797*
15: 1 Very early in the morning, the **chief p,** *797*
15: 3 The **chief p** accused him of many things. *797*
15:10 the **chief p** had handed Jesus over to him. *797*
15:11 But the **chief p** stirred up the crowd *797*
15:31 the same way the **chief p** and the teachers *797*
Lk 6: 4 he ate what is lawful only for **p** to eat. *2636*
9:22 **chief p** and teachers of the law, *797*
17:14 he said, "Go, show yourselves *to* the **p.**" *2636*
19:47 But the **chief p,** the teachers of the law and *797*
20: 1 the **chief p** and the teachers of the law, *797*
20:19 of the law and the **chief p** looked for a way *797*
22: 2 and the **chief p** and the teachers of the law *797*
22: 4 And Judas went *to* the **chief p** and *797*
22:52 Then Jesus said to the **chief p,** *797*
22:66 both the **chief p** and teachers of the law, *797*
23: 4 Then Pilate announced to the **chief p** and *797*
23:10 The **chief p** and the teachers of the law *797*
23:13 Pilate called together the **chief p,** *797*
24:20 The **chief p** and our rulers handed him over *797*
Jn 1:19 the Jews of Jerusalem sent **p** and Levites *2636*
7:32 Then the **chief p** and the Pharisees sent *797*
7:45 the temple guards went back to the **chief p** *797*
11:47 Then the **chief p** and the Pharisees called *797*
11:57 the **chief p** and Pharisees had given orders *797*
12:10 **chief p** made plans to kill Lazarus as well, *797*
18: 3 and some officials from the **chief p** *797*
18:35 and your **chief p** who handed you over *797*
19: 6 as the **chief p** and their officials saw him, *797*
19:15 the **chief p** answered. *797*
19:21 The **chief p** of the Jews protested to Pilate, *797*
Ac 4: 1 The **p** and the captain of the temple guard *2636*
4:23 that the **chief p** and elders had said to them. *797*
5:24 and the **chief p** were puzzled, *797*
6: 7 and a large number *of* **p** became obedient *2636*
9:14 from the **chief p** to arrest all who call *797*
9:21 to take them as prisoners to the **chief p?**" *797*
22:30 he released him and ordered the **chief p** *797*
23:14 They went to the **chief p** and elders *797*
25: 2 the **chief p** and Jewish leaders appeared *797*
25:15 the **chief p** and elders of the Jews *797*
26:10 On the authority of the **chief p** I put many *797*
26:12 and commission *of* the **chief p.** *797*
Heb 7: 5 of Levi who become **p** to collect a tenth *2632*
7:14 to that tribe Moses said nothing about **p.** *2636*
7:20 Others became **p** without any oath, *2636*
7:23 Now there have been many of those **p,** *2636*
7:27 Unlike the other **high p,** *797*
7:28 law appoints as **high p** men who are weak; *797*
9: 6 the **p** entered regularly into the outer room *2636*
Rev 1: 6 and has made us to be a kingdom and **p** *2636*
5:10 to be a kingdom and **p** to serve our God, *2636*
20: 6 be **p** of God and of Christ and will reign *2636*

PRIESTS' (2) [PRIEST]

Eze 41:10 the **[p']** rooms was twenty cubits wide all NIH
42:13 the temple courtyard are the **p' rooms,** 4384+7731

PRIME (3)

1Sa 2:33 your descendants will die **in the p of life.** 408
Job 29: 4 Oh, for the days when I was in my **p,** 3074
Isa 38:10 the **p** *of* my life must I go through the gates 1953

PRINCE (54) [PRINCE'S, PRINCELY, PRINCES, PRINCESS]

Ge 23: 6 You are a mighty **p** among us. 5954
49:26 on the brow of the **p** *among* his brothers. 5687
Dt 33:16 on the brow of the **p** *among* his brothers. 5687
Jdg 8:18 "each one with the bearing of a **p.**" 1201+4889
2Sa 3:38 that a **p** and a great man has fallen 8569
2Ch 11:22 to be the chief **p** among his brothers, 5592
Ezr 1: 8 who counted them out to Sheshbazzar the **p** 5954

Job 31:37 like a **p** I would approach him.)— 5592
Pr 14:28 but without subjects a **p** is ruined. 8138
Isa 9: 6 Everlasting Father, **P** *of* Peace. 8569
Eze 7:27 the **p** will be clothed with despair, 5954
12:10 This oracle concerns the **p** in Jerusalem and 5954
12:12 "The **p** among them will put his things 5954
21:25 " 'O profane and wicked **p** *of* Israel, 5954
30:13 No longer will there be a **p** in Egypt, 5954
34:24 my servant David will be **p** among them. 5954
37:25 David my servant will be their **p** forever. 5954
38: 2 the chief **p** *of* Meshech and Tubal; 5954
38: 3 O Gog, chief **p** *of* Meshech and Tubal. 5954
39: 1 O Gog, chief **p** *of* Meshech and Tubal. 5954
44: 3 The **p** himself is the only one who may sit 5954
45: 7 " 'The **p** will have the land bordering 5954
45:16 in this special gift for the use of the **p** 5954
45:17 of the **p** to provide the burnt offerings, 5954
45:22 the **p** is to provide a bull as a sin offering 5954
46: 2 The **p** is to enter from the outside through 5954
46: 4 The burnt offering the **p** brings to 5954
46: 8 When the **p** enters, he is to go in through 5954
46:10 The **p** is to be among them, 5954
46:12 When the **p** provides a freewill offering to 5954
46:16 If the **p** makes a gift from his inheritance 5954
46:17 then it will revert to the **p**. 5954
46:18 The **p** must not take any of the inheritance 5954
48:21 and the city property will belong to the **p**. 5954
48:21 of the tribal portions will belong to the **p**, 5954
48:22 the center of the area that belongs to the **p**. 5954
48:22 the **p** will lie between the border of Judah 5954
Da 8:11 It set itself up to be as great as the **P** *of* 8569
8:25 and take his stand against the **P** *of* princes. 8569
10:13 But the **p** *of* the Persian kingdom resisted 8569
10:20 the **p** *of* Persia, and when I go, the prince 8569
10:20 and when I go, the **p** *of* Greece will come; 8569
10:21 against them except Michael, your **p**. 8569
11:22 and a **p** *of* the covenant will be destroyed. 5592
12: 1 the great **p** who protects your people, 8569
Hos 3: 4 will live many days without king or **p**, 8569
Mt 9:34 "It is by the **p** of demons that he drives out 807
12:24 "It is only by Beelzebub, the **p** of demons, 807
Mk 3:22 the **p** of demons he is driving out demons." 807
Lk 11:15 the **p** of demons, he is driving out demons." 807
Jn 12:31 now the **p** of this world will be driven out. 807
14:30 for the **p** of this world is coming. 807
16:11 the **p** of this world now stands condemned. 807
Ac 5:31 God exalted him to his own right hand as **P** 795

PRINCE'S (1) [PRINCE]

SS 7: 1 beautiful your sandaled feet, O **p** daughter! 5618

PRINCELY (1) [PRINCE]

Ps 49:14 in the grave, far from their **p mansions.** 2292

PRINCES (72) [PRINCE]

Nu 21:18 the well that the **p** dug, that the nobles of 8569
22: 8 So the Moabite **p** stayed with him. 8569
22:13 up and said to Balak's **p**, 8569
22:14 the Moabite **p** returned to Balak and said, 8569
22:15 Then Balak sent other **p**, 8569
22:21 saddled his donkey and went with the **p** 8569
22:35 So Balaam went with the **p** *of* Balak. 8569
22:40 to Balaam and the **p** who were with him. 8569
23: 6 with all the **p** *of* Moab. 8569
23:17 with the **p** *of* Moab. 8569
Jos 13:21 **p** *allied with* Sihon—who lived in that 5817
Jdg 5: 2 "When the **p** in Israel take the lead, when 7278
5: 9 My heart is with Israel's **p**, 2980
5:15 The **p** of Issachar were with Deborah; 8569
1Sa 2: 8 he seats them with **p** and has them inherit 5618
2Sa 13:32 not think that they killed all the **p**; 1201+4889
2Ki 10: 6 Now the royal **p**, seventy of them, 1201
10: 7 took the **p** and slaughtered all seventy 1201+4889
10: 8 They have brought the heads of the **p**. 1201+4889
11: 2 from among the royal **p**, 1201
2Ch 21: 4 to the sword along with some of the **p** 8569
22: 8 he found the **p** *of* Judah and the sons 8569
22:11 the royal **p** who were about to be murdered 1201
28:21 from the **p** and presented them to the king 8569
Est 1: 3 of Persia and Media, the **p**, and the nobles 7312
6: 9 to one of the king's most noble **p**. 8569
Job 34:19 who shows no partiality to **p** and does 8569
Ps 45:16 you will make them **p** throughout the land. 8569
68:27 there the great throng of Judah's **p**, 8569
68:27 and there the **p** *of* Zebulun and of Naphtali. 8569
83:11 all their **p** like Zebah and Zalmunna, 5817
105:22 to instruct his **p** as he pleased 8569
113: 8 he seats them with **p**, 5618
113: 8 with the **p** *of* their people. 5618
118: 9 take refuge in the LORD than to trust in **p**. 5618
146: 3 Do not put your trust in **p**, in mortal men, 5618
148:11 you **p** and all rulers on earth, 8569
Pr 8:16 by me **p** govern, and all nobles who rule 8569
19:10 how much worse for a slave to rule over **p**! 8569
Ecc 10: 7 while **p** go on foot like slaves. 8569
10:16 a servant and whose **p** feast in the morning. 8569
10:17 and whose **p** eat at a proper time— 8569
Isa 23: 8 whose merchants are **p**, 8569
34:12 all her **p** will vanish away. 8569
40:23 He brings **p** to naught and reduces 8142
49: 7 **p** will see and bow down, 8569
La 1: 6 Her **p** are like deer that find no pasture; 8569
2: 2 and its **p** down to the ground in dishonor. 8569
2: 9 and her **p** are exiled among the nations, 8569
4: 7 Their **p** were brighter than snow 5687
La 5:12 **P** have been hung up by their hands; 8569
Eze 19: 1 up a lament concerning the **p** *of* Israel 5954
21:12 it is against all the **p** *of* Israel. 5954
22: 6 " 'See how each of the **p** *of* Israel who are 5954
22:25 There is a conspiracy of her **p** within her 5954
26:16 Then all the **p** *of* the coast will step down 5954
27:21 the **p** *of* Kedar were your customers; 5954
32:29 "Edom is there, her kings and all her **p**; 5954
32:30 "All the **p** *of* the north and all 5817
39:18 of mighty men and drink the blood of the **p** 5954
45: 8 my **p** will no longer oppress my people 5954
45: 9 You have gone far enough, O **p** *of* Israel! 5954
Da 8:25 and take his stand against the Prince of **p**. 8569
9: 6 our kings, our **p** and our fathers, 8569
9: 8 our **p** and our fathers are covered 8569
10:13 Then Michael, one of the chief **p**, 8569
Hos 7: 3 the **p** with their lies. 8569
7: 5 the **p** become inflamed with wine, 8569
8: 4 *they* **choose p** without my approval. 8606
13:10 'Give me a king and **p**'? 8569
Zep 1: 8 the **p** and the king's sons and all those clad 8569
Rev 6:15 Then the kings of the earth, the **p**, 3491

PRINCESS (1) [PRINCE]

Ps 45:13 All glorious is the **p** within 1426+4889

PRINCIPAL (1)

1Ch 9:26 But the four **p** gatekeepers, 1475

PRINCIPLE (1) [PRINCIPLES]

Ro 3:27 On what **p**? On that of observing the law? 3795

PRINCIPLES (4) [PRINCIPLE]

Gal 4: 3 in slavery under the **basic p** of the world. 5122
4: 9 to those weak and miserable **p**? 5122
Col 2: 8 and the **basic p** of this world rather than 5122
2:20 Since you died with Christ to the **basic p** 5122

PRIOR (1)

Jos 20: 9 and not be killed by the avenger of blood **p** 6330

PRISCILLA (7)

Ac 18: 2 recently come from Italy with his wife **P**, 4571
18:18 accompanied by **P** and Aquila. 4571
18:19 where Paul left **P and Aquila.** 1697S
18:26 When **P** and Aquila heard him, 4571
Ro 16: 3 Greet **P** and Aquila, 4571
1Co 16:19 Aquila and **P** greet you warmly in the Lord, 4571
2Ti 4:19 Greet **P** and Aquila and the household 4571

PRISON (74) [IMPRISON, IMPRISONED, IMPRISONMENT, IMPRISONMENTS, IMPRISONS, PRISONER, PRISONERS, PRISONS]

Ge 39:20 Joseph's master took him and put him in **p**, 1074+2021+6045
39:20 while Joseph was there in *the* **p**, 1074+2021+6045
39:21 granted him favor in the eyes of the **p** warden. 1074+2021+6045
39:22 put Joseph in charge of all those held in the **p**, 1074+2021+6045
40: 3 in the same **p** where Joseph was 1074+2021+6045
40: 5 who were being held in **p**— 1074+2021+6045
40:14 to Pharaoh and get me out of this **p**. 1074
42:16 the rest of you *will* **be kept in p**, 673
42:19 let one of your brothers stay here in **p**, 1074+5464
Jdg 16:21 they set him to grinding in the **p**. 673+1074
16:25 So they called Samson out of the **p**, 673+1074
1Ki 22:27 Put this fellow in **p** and give 1074+2021+3975
2Ki 17: 4 Shalmaneser seized him and put him in **p**. 1074+3975
25:27 he released Jehoiachin from **p** 1074+3975
25:29 So Jehoiachin put aside his **p** clothes and 3975
2Ch 16:10 so enraged that he put him in **p**. 1074+2021+4551
18:26 Put this fellow in **p** and give 1074+2021+3975
Job 11:10 and **confines** you **in p** and convenes a court, 6037
Ps 66:11 You brought us into **p** and laid burdens 5181
142: 7 Set me free from my **p**, 4993
Ecc 4:14 youth may have come from **p** to 673+1074+2021
Isa 24:22 they will be shut up in **p** and be punished 4993
42: 7 to free captives from **p** and to release from 4993
Jer 37: 4 for he had not yet been put in **p**. 1074+2021+3989
37:15 which they had made into a **p**. 1074+2021+3975
37:18 that you have put me in **p**? 1074+2021+3975
52:11 he put him in **p** till the day 1074+2021+7213
52:31 and freed him from **p** 1074+2021+3989
52:33 So Jehoiachin put aside his **p** clothes and 3975
Eze 19: 9 They put him in **p**, 5183
Mt 4:12 that John *had been* **put in p**, 4140
5:25 and you may be thrown into **p**. 5871
11: 2 John heard in **p** what Christ was doing, 1303
14: 3 and bound him and put him in **p** because 5871
14:10 and had John beheaded in the **p**. 5871
18:30 he went off and had the man thrown into **p** 5871
25:36 I was in **p** and you came to visit me.' 5871
25:39 When did we see you sick or in **p** and go 5871
25:43 I was sick and in **p** and you did not look 5871
25:44 or needing clothes or sick or in **p**, 5871
Mk 1:14 After John *was* **put in p**, 4140
6:17 and he had him bound and put in **p**. 5871
6:27 The man went, beheaded John in the **p**, 5871
Mk 15: 7 A man called Barabbas was **in p** with 1313
Lk 3:20 He locked John up in **p**. 5871
12:58 and the officer throw you into **p**. 5871
22:33 I am ready to go with you to **p** and 5871
23:19 (Barabbas had been thrown into **p** for 5871
23:25 the man who had been thrown into **p** 5871
Jn 3:24 (This was before John was put in **p**.) 5871
Ac 8: 3 and women and put them in **p**. 5871
12: 4 After arresting him, he put him in **p**, 5871
12: 5 So Peter was kept in **p**, 5871
12: 9 Peter followed him out of the **p**, NIG
12:17 how the Lord had brought him out of **p**. 5871
16:23 they were thrown into **p**, 5871
16:26 that the foundations *of* the **p** were shaken. 1303
16:26 At once all the **p** doors flew open, NIG
16:27 and when he saw the **p** doors open, 5871
16:37 and threw us into **p**. 5871
16:39 and escorted them from the **p**, NIG
16:40 After Paul and Silas came out of the **p**, 5871
20:23 that **p** and hardships are facing me. 1301
22: 4 and women and throwing them into **p**, 5871
24:27 a favor to the Jews, he left Paul **in p**. 1313
26:10 I put many of the saints in **p**, 5871
Ro 16: 7 my relatives *who have been* **in p with** me. 5257
2Co 11:23 been in **p** more frequently, 5871
Heb 10:34 You sympathized with those **in p** 1300
11:36 while still others were chained and put in **p**. 5871
13: 3 Remember those **in p** as if you were 1300
1Pe 3:19 also he went and preached to the spirits in **p** 5871
Rev 2:10 devil will put some of you in **p** to test you, 5871
20: 7 Satan will be released from his **p** 5871

PRISONER (21) [PRISON]

Ex 12:29 to the firstborn of the **p**, 8660
Jdg 15:10 "We have come to **take** Samson **p**," 673
2Ki 24:12 *he* **took** Jehoiachin **p**. 4374
2Ch 33:11 *who* **took** Manasseh **p**, 4334
Isa 22: 3 All you who were caught **were taken p** 673
Mt 27:15 custom at the Feast to release a **p** chosen by 1300
27:16 At that time they had a notorious **p**, 1300
Mk 15: 6 the custom at the Feast to release a **p** whom 1300
Jn 18:39 for me to release to you one **p** at the time of NIG
Ac 23:18 The centurion said, "Paul, the **p**, 1300
25:14 a man here whom Felix left as a **p**. 1300
25:27 For I think it is unreasonable to send on a **p** 1300
Ro 7:23 and **making** me **a p** of the law of sin at work within my members. 170
Gal 3:22 that the whole world *is* a **p** of sin, 5168
Eph 3: 1 the **p** of Christ Jesus for the sake of you 1300
4: 1 As a **p** for the Lord, then, 1300
Col 4:10 My **fellow p** Aristarchus sends you his greetings, 5257
2Ti 1: 8 or ashamed of me his **p**. 1300
Phm 1: 1 Paul, a **p** of Christ Jesus, 1300
1: 9 old man and now also a **p** of Christ Jesus— 1300
1:23 Epaphras, my **fellow p** in Christ Jesus, 5257

PRISONERS (32) [PRISON]

Ge 39:20 the place where the king's **p** were confined. 659
2Ki 25:18 the guard **took as p** Seraiah the chief priest, 4374
2Ch 28: 5 **took** many of his people **as p** 8647+8664
28:11 Send back your fellow countrymen *you have* **taken as p**, 8647+8664
28:13 "You must not bring those **p** here," 8664
28:14 So the soldiers gave up the **p** and plunder in 8664
28:15 The men designated by name took the **p**, 8664
28:17 and attacked Judah and carried away **p**, 8660
Ps 68: 6 he leads forth the **p** with singing; 659
79:11 May the groans of the **p** come before you; 659
102:20 of the **p** and release those condemned 659
107:10 **p** suffering *in* iron chains, 659
146: 7 The LORD sets **p** free, 673
Isa 24:22 They will be herded together like **p** *bound* 660
51:14 The **cowering p** will soon be set free; 7579
61: 1 and release from darkness for the **p**, 673
Jer 52:24 the guard **took as p** Seraiah the chief priest, 4374
La 3:34 To crush underfoot all **p** *in* the land, 659
Hab 1: 9 like a desert wind and gather **p** like sand. 8660
Zec 9:11 I will free your **p** from the waterless pit. 659
9:12 Return to your fortress, O **p** *of* hope; 659
Lk 4:18 to proclaim freedom *for* the **p** and recovery 171
21:24 by the sword and *will be* **taken as p** to all 170
Ac 9: 2 he might take them as **p** to Jerusalem. 1313
9:21 And hasn't he come here to take them *as* **p** 1313
16:25 and the other **p** were listening to them. 1300
16:27 because he thought the **p** had escaped. 1300
22: 5 to bring these people as **p** to Jerusalem to 1313
27: 1 Paul and some other **p** were handed over to 1304
27:42 to kill the **p** to prevent any of them 1304
Gal 3:23 *we were* **held p** by the law, 5864
Heb 13: 3 in prison as if you were their **fellow p**, 5279

PRISONS (2) [PRISON]

Isa 42:22 trapped in pits or hidden away in **p**. 1074+3975
Lk 21:12 They will deliver you to synagogues and **p**, 5871

PRIVATE (4) [PRIVATELY]

Ge 43:30 He went into his **p room** and wept there. 2540
Dt 25:11 and seizes him by his **p parts**, 4434
Mt 17:19 the disciples came to Jesus in **p** and asked, 2625
Lk 9:18 in **p** and his disciples were with him, 3668

PRIVATELY (10) [PRIVATE]

1Sa 18:22 "Speak to David **p** and say, 928+2021+4319

2Sa 3:27 as though to speak with him p. 928+2021+8952
Jer 37:17 where he asked him p, 928+2021+6260
40:15 said p to Gedaliah in Mizpah, 928+2021+6260
Mt 14:13 withdrew by boat p to a solitary place. 2625+2848
24: 3 the disciples came to him p. 2625+2848
Mk 9:28 his disciples asked him p, 2625+2848
13: 3 James, John and Andrew asked him p, 2625+2848
Lk 10:23 he turned to his disciples and said p, 2625+2848
Gal 2: 2 But I did this p to those who seemed 2625+2848

PRIVILEGE (1)
2Co 8: 4 the p of sharing in this service to the saints. 5921

PRIZE (5) [PRIZES]
1Co 9:24 but only one gets the p? 1092
9:24 Run in such a way as to **get the p.** 2898
9:27 I myself will not be disqualified for the p. NIG
Php 3:14 I press on toward the goal to win the p 1092
Col 2:18 **disqualify** you **for the p.** 2857

PRIZES (1) [PRIZE]
Pr 12:27 but the diligent man p his possessions. 3701

PROBE (5)
Dt 13:14 p and investigate it thoroughly. 2983
Job 10: 6 that you must search out my faults and p 2011
11: 7 *Can you* p the limits of the Almighty? 5162
Ps 17: 3 *you* p my heart and examine me at night, 1043
Jer 20:12 the righteous and p the heart and mind, 8011

PROBLEMS (3)
Dt 1:12 how can I bear your p and your burdens 3268
Da 5:12 explain riddles and solve **difficult p.** 10626
5:16 and to solve **difficult p.** 10626

PROCEDURE (2) [PROCEED]
Ecc 8: 5 wise heart will know the **proper** time and p. 5477
8: 6 a **proper** time and p for every matter, 5477

PROCEED (1) [PROCEDURE, PROCEEDED, PROCEEDINGS, PROCESSION]
Ne 12:31 *to* p on top of the wall to the right, 2143

PROCEEDED (8) [PROCEED]
Ge 9:20 a man of the soil, p to plant a vineyard. 2725
42:20 This *they p to* **do.** AIT
44:12 Then the steward *p to* **search,** AIT
2Ki 8: 2 The woman p to do as the man of God said. 7756
11: 1 *she* p to destroy the whole royal family. 7756
2Ch 22:10 *she* p to destroy the whole royal family of 7756
Ne 12:38 The second choir p in the opposite direction 2143
Ac 12: 3 *he* p to seize Peter also. 4707

PROCEEDINGS (1) [PROCEED]
Ac 24:22 acquainted with the Way, **adjourned the p.** 327

PROCESSION (11) [PROCEED]
1Sa 10: 5 you will meet a p *of* prophets coming 2474
10:10 a p *of* prophets met him; 2474
Ne 12:36 Ezra the scribe led **the p.** 2157[S]
Ps 42: 4 leading **the** p to the house of God, 4392[S]
68:24 Your p has come into view, O God, 2142
68:24 p *of* my God and King into the sanctuary. 2142
118:27 in the **festal** p up to the horns of the altar. 2504
SS 6:10 majestic as the stars **in p?** 1839
Isa 60:11 their kings **led in triumphal p.** 5627
1Co 4: 9 apostles on display at the end of the p, NIG
2Co 2:14 who always **leads** us **in triumphal p** 2581

PROCHORUS (KJV) See PROCORUS

PROCLAIM (85) [PROCLAIMED, PROCLAIMING, PROCLAIMS, PROCLAMATION]
Ex 33:19 and *I will* p my name, the LORD, 928+7924
Lev 23: 2 which *you are to* p as sacred assemblies. 7924
23: 4 the sacred assemblies *you are to* p 7924
23:21 On that same day *you are to* p 7924
23:37 which *you are to* p as sacred assemblies 7924
25:10 Consecrate the fiftieth year and p liberty 7924
Dt 11:29 *to* p on Mount Gerizim the blessings, 5989
30:12 to get it and p it *to* us so we may obey it?" 9048
30:13 to get it and p it *to* us so we may obey it?" 9048
32: 3 *I will* p the name of the LORD. 7924
1Sa 31: 9 to **p the news** *in* the temple of their idols 1413
2Sa 1:20 p it not in the streets of Ashkelon, 1413
1Ki 21: 9 "P a day of fasting and seat Naboth in 7924
1Ch 10: 9 Philistines to **p the news** *among* their idols 1413
16:23 p his salvation day after day. 1413
Ne 8:15 that *they should* p this word and spread it 9048
Ps 2: 7 *I will* p the decree of the LORD: 6218
9:11 p among the nations what he has done. 5583
19: 1 the skies p the work of his hands. 5583
22:31 *They will* p his righteousness to a people 5583
30: 9 *Will it* p your faithfulness? 5583
40: 9 *I* p righteousness in the great assembly; 1413
50: 6 And the heavens p his righteousness, 5583
64: 9 *they will* p the works of God 5583
68:34 P the power of God, 5989
71:16 I will come and p your mighty acts, 2349
71:16 I will p your righteousness, yours alone. NIH
92: 2 to p your love in the morning 5583
96: 2 p his salvation day after day. 1413
97: 6 The heavens p his righteousness, 5583
106: 2 Who *can* p the mighty acts of the LORD 4910
118:17 and *will* p what the LORD has done. 6218
145: 6 and *I will* p your great deeds. 6218
Isa 12: 4 and p that his name is exalted. 2349
40: 2 and p to her that her hard service has been 7924
42:12 the LORD and p his praise in the islands. 5583
43:21 for myself *that they may* p my praise. 6218
44: 7 *Let him* p it. 7924
44: 8 *Did I* not p this and foretell it long ago? 9048
48:20 Announce this with shouts of joy and p it. 9048
52: 7 *who* p peace, who bring good tidings, 9048
52: 7 who bring good tidings, *who* p salvation, 9048
61: 1 to p freedom for the captives and release 7924
61: 2 to p the year of the LORD's favor and 7924
66:19 *They will* p my glory among the nations. 5583
Jer 2: 2 "Go and p in the hearing of Jerusalem: 7924
3:12 Go, p this message toward the north: 7924
4: 5 "Announce in Judah and p in Jerusalem 9048
4:16 "Tell this to the nations, p it to Jerusalem: 9048
5:20 to the house of Jacob and p it in Judah: 9048
7: 2 and there p this message: 7924
11: 6 "P all these words in the towns of Judah 7924
19: 2 There p the words I tell you, 7924
22: 1 the king of Judah and p this message there: 1819
31:10 p it in distant coastlands: 5583
34: 8 in Jerusalem to p freedom for the slaves. 7924
34:17 So I now p 'freedom' for you, 7924
46:14 and p it in Migdol; 9048
46:14 p it also in Memphis and Tahpanhes: 9048
50: 2 "Announce and p among the nations, lift up 9048
50: 2 lift up a banner and p it; 9048
Hos 5: 9 the tribes of Israel *I* p what is certain. 3359
Joel 3: 9 P this among the nations: Prepare for war! 7924
Am 3: 9 P to the fortresses of Ashdod and to 9048
Jnh 3: 2 "Go to the great city of Nineveh and p to it 7924
Mic 3: 5 if one feeds them, *they* p 'peace'; 7924
Zec 1:14 to me said, "P this word: 7924
1:17 "P further: This is what the LORD Almighty says: 7924
9:10 *He will* p peace to the nations. 1819
Mt 10:27 what is whispered in your ear, p from 3062
12:18 and *he will* p justice to the nations. 550
Lk 4:18 He has sent me *to* p freedom for 3062
4:19 *to* p the year of the Lord's favor." 3062
9:60 but you go and p the kingdom of God." 1334
Ac 17:23 as something unknown I *am going to* p 2859
20:27 not hesitated *to* p to you the whole will 334
26:23 would p light to his own people and to 2859
1Co 11:26 *you* p the Lord's death until he comes. 2859
Col 1:28 We p him, admonishing and teaching 2859
4: 3 *so that* we *may* p the mystery of Christ, 3281
4: 4 Pray that *I may* p it **clearly,** as I should. 5746
1Jn 1: 1 this we p concerning the Word of life. NIG
1: 2 and *we* p to you the eternal life, 550
1: 3 *We* p to you what we have seen and heard, 550
Rev 14: 6 eternal **gospel to p** to those who live 2294+2295

PROCLAIMED (43) [PROCLAIM]
Ex 9:16 that my name *might be* p in all the earth. 6218
34: 5 stood there with him and p his name, 928+7924
Dt 1: 3 Moses p to the Israelites all that 1819
5:22 These are the commandments the LORD p 1819
9:10 the LORD p to you on the mountain out of 1819
10: 4 the Ten Commandments *he had* p to you on 1819
15: 2 time for canceling debts *has been* p. 7924
1Ki 16:16 p Omri, the commander of the army, **king** 4887
21:12 *They* p a fast and seated Naboth in a 7924
2Ki 10:20 assembly in honor of Baal." So *they* p it. 7924
11:12 with a copy of the covenant and p him **king.** 4887
23:16 with the word of the LORD p *by* the man 7924
24: 2 the LORD p by his servants the prophets. 1819
2Ch 20: 3 and *he* p a fast for all Judah. 7924
23:11 with a copy of the covenant and p him **king.** 4887
Ezr 8:21 There, by the Ahava Canal, *I* p a fast, 7924
Est 1:20 Then when the king's edict **is p** 9048
2: 8 the king's order and edict *had* **been p,** 9048
2:18 *He* p a holiday throughout the provinces 6913
Ps 68:11 great was the company of those *who* p it: 1413
Isa 43: 9 Which of them foretold this and p *to* us 9048
43:12 I have revealed and saved and p— 9048
Jer 23:22 *they would have* p my words *to* my people 9048
34:15 Each of you p freedom to his countrymen. 7924
34:17 not p freedom for your fellow countrymen. 7924
36: 9 before the LORD *was* p *for* all the people 7924
Da 3: 4 Then the herald loudly p, 10637
5:29 and he *was* p the third highest ruler in 10371
Jnh 3: 4 *He* p: "Forty more days and Nineveh 7924
Zec 1: 4 to whom the earlier prophets p: 7924
7: 7 the LORD p through the earlier prophets 7924
Lk 12: 3 the inner rooms *will be* p from the roofs. 3062
16:16 Law and the Prophets were p until John. NIG
Ac 8: 5 Philip went down to a city in Samaria and p 3062
8:25 *When they* had testified and p the word of 3281
13: 5 *they* p the word of God in the Jewish 2859
13:38 through Jesus the forgiveness of sins *is* p 2859
Ro 9:17 in you and that my name *might be* p in all 1334
15:19 I have fully p the gospel of Christ. NIG
1Co 2: 1 with eloquence or superior wisdom *as I* p 2859
Col 1:23 and that *has been* p to every creature 3062
2Ti 4:17 be fully p and all the Gentiles might hear it. NIG
Heb 9:19 *When* Moses *had* p every commandment of 3281

PROCLAIMING (19) [PROCLAIM]
Ex 34: 6 And he passed in front of Moses, p, 7924
1Sa 11: 7 p, "This is what will be done to the oxen 606
Est 1:22 p in each people's tongue 1819
6: 9 p before him, 'This is what is done for 7924
6:11 on horseback through the city streets, p 7924
Ps 26: 7 p aloud your praise and telling of all your 9048
92:15 p, "The LORD is upright; he is my Rock, 5583
Isa 60: 6 and incense and p the praise of the LORD. 1413
Jer 4:15 p disaster from the hills of Ephraim. 9048
20: 8 I cry out p violence and destruction. 7924
Mk 1:14 p the good news of God. 3062
Lk 8: 1 **p the good news** of the kingdom of God. 2294
Ac 4: 2 the apostles were teaching the people and p 2859
5:42 **p the good news** that Jesus is the Christ. 2294
17: 3 "This Jesus I *am* p to you is the Christ," 2859
Ro 10: 8 that is, the word of faith *we are* p: 3062
15:16 the priestly duty of p the **gospel** of God, 2295
2Th 2: 4 p himself to be God. 617
Rev 5: 2 And I saw a mighty angel p in a loud voice, 3062

PROCLAIMS (2) [PROCLAIM]
Dt 18:22 a prophet p in the name of the LORD does 1819
Na 1:15 of one who brings good news, *who* p peace! 9048

PROCLAMATION (9) [PROCLAIM]
2Ch 24: 9 A p was then issued in Judah 7754
30: 5 They decided to send a p throughout Israel, 7754
36:22 of Persia to make a p throughout his realm 7754
Ezr 1: 1 of Persia to make a p throughout his realm 7754
10: 7 A p was then issued throughout Judah 7754
Ne 6: 7 even appointed prophets to **make** *this* p 7924
Isa 62:11 The LORD *has* **made** p to the ends of 9048
Jnh 3: 7 Then *he* **issued a p** in Nineveh: 2410
Ro 16:25 to establish you by my gospel and the p 3060

PROCONSUL (5) [PROCONSULS]
Ac 13: 7 who was an attendant of the p, 478
13: 7 The p, an intelligent man, NIG
13: 8 and tried to turn the p from the faith. 478
13:12 When the p saw what had happened, 478
18:12 While Gallio was p of Achaia, 478

PROCONSULS (1) [PROCONSUL]
Ac 19:38 the courts are open and there are **p.** 478

PROCORUS (1)
Ac 6: 5 also Philip, P, Nicanor, Timon, Parmenas, 4743

PRODDED (1)
Jdg 16:16 With such nagging *she* p him day after day 552

PRODUCE (42) [PRODUCED, PRODUCES, PRODUCING, PRODUCT, PRODUCTS]
Ge 1:11 Then God said, "*Let* the land p vegetation: 2012
1:24 "*Let* the land p living creatures according 3655
3:18 *It will* p thorns and thistles for you, 7541
38: 8 to her as a brother-in-law *to* p offspring 7756
47:26 that a fifth of the p belongs to Pharaoh. NIH
Ex 5:18 yet *you must* p your full quota of bricks." 5989
8:18 But when the magicians tried to p gnats 3655
Dt 8:18 the ability to p wealth, 6913
11:17 not rain and the ground will yield no p, 3292
14:22 a tenth of all that your fields p each year. 2446+3655+9311
14:28 of that year's p and store it in your towns, 9311
16:13 after you have gathered the p NIH
26: 2 take some of the firstfruits of all that *you* p 995
26:12 a tenth of all your p in the third year, 9311
28:33 and labor p, and you will have nothing 7262
Jos 5:11 they ate some of the p *of* the land: 6289
5:12 but that year they ate of the p *of* Canaan. 9311
1Ch 27:27 Zabdi the Shiphmite was in charge of **the p** 8611[S]
Job 40:20 The hills bring him their p, 1006
Ps 78:46 their p to the locust. 3330
105:35 ate up the p *of* their soil. 7262
Pr 13:23 A poor man's field may p abundant food, NIH
Isa 5:10 A ten-acre vineyard *will* p only a bath 6913
Jer 2: 7 into a fertile land to eat its fruit and **rich p.** 3206
29: 5 plant gardens and eat *what* they p. 7262
29:28 plant gardens and eat *what* they p.' " 7262
Eze 17: 8 so that *it would* p branches, 6913
17:23 *it will* p branches and bear fruit 5951
36: 8 *will* p branches and fruit 5989
48:18 Its p will supply food for the workers of 9311
Hos 8: 7 The stalk has no head; *it will* p no flour. 6913
Hab 3:17 the olive crop fails and the fields p no food, 6913
Zec 8:12 the ground *will* p its crops, 5989
Mt 3: 8 P fruit in keeping with repentance. 4472
3:10 that *does* not p good fruit will be cut down 4472
21:43 and given to a people who will p its fruit. 4472
Mk 4:20 hear the word, accept it, and **p a crop—** 2844
Lk 3: 8 P fruit in keeping with repentance. 4472
3: 9 *that does* not p good fruit will be cut down 4472
8:15 retain it, and by persevering **p a crop.** 2844
2Ti 2:23 because you know *they* p quarrels. 1164
Jas 3:12 Neither can a salt spring p fresh water. 4472

PRODUCED (16) [PRODUCE]

Ge 1:12 The land **p** vegetation: 3655
41:47 of abundance the land **p** plentifully. 6913
41:48 the food **p** in those seven years 2118
Nu 17:8 blossomed and **p** almonds. 1694
Dt 8:17 the strength of my hands *have* **p** this wealth 6913
2Ch 31:5 oil and honey and all *that* the fields **p.** 9311
Eze 17:6 and **p** branches and put out leafy boughs. 6913
Mt 13:8 where *it* **p** a crop—a hundred, sixty or *1443*
Mk 4:8 *It* came up, grew and **p** a crop, *1443*
Lk 12:16 of a certain rich man **p a good crop.** *2369*
Ac 6:13 *They* **p** false witnesses, who testified, *2705*
Ro 7:8 **p** in me every kind of covetous desire. *2981*
7:13 *it* **p** death in me through what was good, *2981*
2Co 7:11 See what this godly sorrow *has* **p** in you: *2981*
1Th 1:3 and Father your work *p by* **faith,** *AIT*
Jas 5:18 and the earth **p** its crops. *1056*

PRODUCES (16) [PRODUCE]

Lev 25:7 Whatever the land **p** may be eaten. 9311
Dt 29:18 among you *that* **p** such bitter poison. 7238
Ne 9:36 and the other **good things** it *p.* AIT
Job 37:10 The breath of God **p** ice, 5989
Pr 30:33 For as churning the milk **p** butter, 3655
30:33 and as twisting the nose **p** blood, 3655
30:33 so stirring up anger **p** strife." 3655
Hag 1:11 the oil and whatever the ground **p,** 3655
Mt 13:23 He **p a crop,** yielding a hundred, *2844*
Mk 4:28 All by itself the soil **p grain—** *2844*
Jn 12:24 But if it dies, *it* **p** many seeds. *5770*
Ro 5:3 we know that suffering **p** perseverance; *2981*
2Co 1:6 which **p in** you patient endurance of *1919*
Heb 6:7 in the rain often falling on it and that **p** *5503*
6:8 that **p** thorns and thistles is worthless and is *1766*
12:11 *it* **p** a harvest of righteousness and peace *625*

PRODUCING (1) [PRODUCE]

Ge 38:9 to keep from **p** offspring for his brother. 5989

PRODUCT (1) [PRODUCE]

Nu 18:30 to you as the **p** *of* the threshing floor or 9311

PRODUCTS (5) [PRODUCE]

Ge 43:11 of the **best p** *of* the land in your bags 2380
Isa 45:14 **p** *of* Egypt and the merchandise of Cush, 3330
Jer 20:5 all its **p,** all its valuables and all 3330
Eze 27:16 with you because of your many **p;** 5126
27:18 of your many **p** and great wealth of goods, 5126

PROFANE (12) [PROFANED]

Lev 18:21 for *you must* not **p** the name of your God. 2725
19:12 not swear falsely by my name and so **p** 2725
21:6 and *must* not **p** the name of their God. 2725
22:2 so *they will* not **p** my holy name. 2725
22:32 *Do* not **p** my holy name. 2725
Eze 20:39 no longer **p** my holy name with your gifts 2725
21:25 " 'O **p** and wicked prince of Israel, 2729
22:26 to my law and **p** my holy things; 2725
Am 2:7 use the same girl and so **p** my holy name. 2725
Zep 3:4 Her priests **p** the sanctuary and do violence 2725
Mal 1:12 "But you **p** it by saying of the Lord's table, 2725
2:10 Why *do we* **p** the covenant of our fathers 2725

PROFANED (13) [PROFANE]

Lev 20:3 and **p** my holy name. 2725
Jer 34:16 you have turned around and **p** my name; 2725
Eze 13:19 *You have* **p** me among my people for 2725
20:9 from **being p** in the eyes of the nations 2725
20:14 from **being p** in the eyes of the nations 2725
20:22 from **being p** in the eyes of the nations 2725
22:26 so that *I* **am p** among them. 2725
36:20 among the nations *they* **p** my holy name, 2725
36:21 the house of Israel **p** among the nations 2725
36:22 of my holy name, which *you have* **p** among 2725
36:23 which *has* **been p** among the nations, 2725
36:23 the name *you have* **p** among them. 2725
39:7 *I will* no longer **let** my holy name **be p,** 2725

PROFESS (3) [PROFESSED]

1Ti 2:10 *for* women who **p** to worship God. *2040*
Heb 4:14 let us hold firmly to the faith we **p.** *3934*
10:23 Let us hold unswervingly to the hope we **p,** *3934*

PROFESSED (1) [PROFESS]

1Ti 6:21 which some *have* **p** and in doing so have *2040*

PROFIT (12) [PROFITABLE, PROFITS]

Lev 25:37 at interest or sell him food at a **p.** 5270
Job 20:18 he will not enjoy the **p** *from* his trading. 2657
35:3 Yet you ask him, 'What **p** *is it* to me, 6122
Pr 14:23 All hard work brings a **p,** 4639
21:5 The plans of the diligent lead to **p** as surely 4639
Ecc 6:11 and how does that **p** anyone? 3463
10:11 there is no **p** for the charmer. 3862
Isa 23:18 Yet her **p** and her earnings will be set apart 6087
44:10 *which can* **p** him nothing? 3603
2Co 2:17 **peddle** the word of God **for p.** *2836*
Php 3:7 to my **p** I now consider loss for the sake *3046*
Jude 1:11 they have rushed *for* **p** into Balaam's error; *3635*

PROFITABLE (3) [PROFIT]

Pr 3:14 for she is more **p** than silver 3202+6087
31:18 She sees that her trading is **p,** 3202
Tit 3:8 These things are excellent and **p** *6068*

PROFITS (3) [PROFIT]

Job 34:9 '*It* **p** a man nothing when he tries to please God.' 6122
Ecc 5:9 the king *himself* **p** from the fields. 6268
Isa 23:18 Her **p** will go to those who live before 6087

PROFLIGATE (1)

Dt 21:20 *He is a* **p** and a drunkard." 2361

PROFOUND (5)

Job 9:4 His wisdom is **p,** his power is vast. 4222
Ps 92:5 O LORD, how **p** your thoughts! 6676
Ecc 7:24 it is far off and **most p**—who can discover it? 6678+6678
Ac 24:3 we acknowledge this with **p** gratitude. *4246*
Eph 5:32 This is a **p** mystery— *3489*

PROGRESS (3) [PROGRESSED]

Ezr 5:8 *is* **making rapid p** under their direction. 10613
Php 1:25 all of you for your **p** and joy in the faith, *4620*
1Ti 4:15 so that everyone may see your **p.** *4620*

PROGRESSED (1) [PROGRESS]

2Ch 24:13 and the repairs **p** under them. 6590

PROJECT (3) [PROJECTED, PROJECTING, PROJECTION, PROJECTIONS, PROJECTS]

1Ki 5:16 supervised the **p** and directed the workmen. 4856
Ne 6:3 carrying on a great **p** and cannot go down. 4856
Eze 43:15 and four horns **p upward** from the hearth. 2025+4200+5087

PROJECTED (1) [PROJECT]

1Ki 6:3 and **p** ten cubits from the front of the temple 8145

PROJECTING (17) [PROJECT]

1Ki 7:34 one on each corner, **p from** the stand. 4946
Ne 3:25 and the tower **p** from the upper palace near 3655
3:26 toward the east and the **p** tower. 3655
3:27 from the great **p** tower to the wall of Ophel. 3655
Eze 40:7 and the **p** walls between the alcoves NIH
40:10 the faces of the **p walls** on each side had 382
40:14 along the faces of the **p walls** all around 382
40:16 The alcoves and the **p walls** inside 382
40:16 The faces of the **p walls** were decorated 382
40:21 its **p walls** and its portico had 382
40:26 on the faces of the **p walls** on each side. 382
40:29 its **p walls** and its portico had 382
40:33 its **p walls** and its portico had 382
40:36 its **p walls** and its portico, 382
40:48 and its **p walls** were three cubits wide on 4190
41:2 and the **p walls** on each side 4190
41:3 and the **p** walls on each side NIH

PROJECTION (2) [PROJECT]

Ex 26:19 for each frame, one under each **p.** 3338
36:24 for each frame, one under each **p.** 3338

PROJECTIONS (2) [PROJECT]

Ex 26:17 with two **p** set parallel to each other. 3338
36:22 with two **p** set parallel to each other. 3338

PROJECTS (2) [PROJECT]

1Ki 9:23 the chief officials in charge of Solomon's **p** 4856
Ecc 2:4 I undertook great **p:** I built houses 5126

PROLONG (5) [PROLONGED]

Dt 5:33 and prosper and **p** your days in the land 799
Ps 85:5 *Will you* **p** your anger through all 5432
Pr 3:2 for they will **p** your life many years 802
Isa 53:10 he will see his offspring and **p** his days, 799
La 4:22 *he will* not **p** your exile. 3578

PROLONGED (2) [PROLONG]

Dt 28:59 harsh and **p** disasters, and severe and 586
Isa 13:22 and her days *will* not **be p.** 5432

PROMINENT (10)

1Ki 21:9 of fasting and seat Naboth in a **p place** 8031
21:12 and seated Naboth in a **p place** *among* 8031
Est 9:4 Mordecai was **p** in the palace; 1524
Isa 9:15 the elders and **p** *men* are the head, 5951+7156
Da 8:5 a goat with a **p** horn between his eyes came 2607
8:8 in its place four **p** horns grew up toward 2607
Mk 15:43 a **p** member of the Council, *2363*
Lk 14:1 to eat in the house of a **p** Pharisee, *807*
Ac 17:4 and not a few **p** women. *4755*
17:12 *of* **p** Greek women and many Greek men. *2363*

PROMISCUITY (5) [PROMISCUOUS]

Eze 16:25 with increasing **p** to anyone who passed by. 9373
16:26 to anger with your increasing **p.** 9373
16:29 you increased your **p** to include Babylonia, 9373
16:36 and exposed your nakedness in your **p** 9373
23:29 Your lewdness and **p** 9373

PROMISCUOUS (2) [PROMISCUITY]

Dt 22:21 by *being* **p** while still in her father's house. 2388
Eze 23:19 and more **p** as she recalled the days 9373

PROMISE (66) [PROMISED, PROMISES]

Ge 47:29 and **p** that you will show me kindness NIH
Nu 23:19 *Does he* **p** and not fulfill? 1819
30:6 a **rash p** by which she obligates herself 4439
30:8 or the **rash p** by which she obligates herself, 4439
Jos 9:21 So the leaders' **p** to them *was kept.* 1819
23:14 Every **p** has been fulfilled; 1821
23:15 But just as every good **p** of the LORD 1821
2Sa 7:25 keep forever the **p** you have made 1821
1Ki 2:4 that the LORD may keep his **p** to me: 1819+1821
6:12 I will fulfill through you the **p** I gave 1821
8:20 "The LORD has kept the **p** he made: 1821
8:24 You have kept *your* **p** to your servant 1819
1Ch 17:23 let the **p** you have made 1821
2Ch 1:9 let your **p** to my father David be confirmed, 1821
6:10 "The LORD has kept the **p** he made. 1821
6:15 You have kept *your* **p** to your servant 1819
Ne 5:13 every man who does not keep this **p.** 1821
9:8 You have kept your **p** because you are 1821
10:30 "We **p** not to give our daughters NIH
Ps 77:8 Has his **p** failed for all time? 608
105:42 For he remembered his holy **p** given 1821
106:24 they did not believe his **p.** 1821
119:38 Fulfill your **p** to your servant, 614
119:41 your salvation according to your **p;** 614
119:50 Your **p** preserves my life. 614
119:58 be gracious to me according to your **p.** 614
119:76 according to your **p** to your servant. 614
119:82 My eyes fail, looking for your **p;** 614
119:116 Sustain me according to your **p;** 614
119:123 looking for your righteous **p.** 614
119:154 preserve my life according to your **p.** 614
119:162 I rejoice in your **p** like one who finds great spoil. 614
119:170 deliver me according to your **p.** 614
Jer 29:10 I will come to you and fulfill my gracious **p** 1821
33:14 'when I will fulfill the gracious **p** I made to 1821
34:4 " 'Yet hear the **p** *of* the LORD, 1821
34:5 *I* myself **make** *this* **p,** 1819+1821
Ac 2:39 The **p** is for you and your children and *2039*
7:17 the time drew near for God to fulfill his **p** *2039*
26:7 This is **the p** our twelve tribes are hoping *4005*[S]
Ro 4:13 the **p** that he would be heir of the world, *2039*
4:14 faith has no value and the **p** is worthless, *2039*
4:16 Therefore, the **p** comes by faith, *2039*
4:20 not waver through unbelief regarding the **p** *2039*
9:8 the children *of* the **p** who are regarded *2039*
9:9 For this was how the **p** was stated: *2039*
Gal 3:14 so that by faith we might receive the **p** of *2039*
3:17 by God and thus do away with the **p.** *2039*
3:18 then it no longer depends on a **p;** *2039*
3:18 gave it to Abraham through a **p.** *2039*
3:19 the Seed to whom the **p** referred had come. *2040*
3:29 and heirs according to the **p.** *2039*
4:23 was born as the result of a **p.** *2039*
4:28 you, brothers, like Isaac, are children *of* **p.** *2039*
Eph 2:12 and foreigners to the covenants *of* the **p,** *2039*
3:6 sharers together in the **p** in Christ Jesus. *2039*
6:2 which is the first commandment with a **p**— *2039*
1Ti 4:8 holding **p** for both the present life and *2039*
2Ti 1:1 to the **p** of life that is in Christ Jesus, *2039*
Heb 4:1 since the **p** of entering his rest still stands, *2039*
6:13 *When* God **made** his **p** to Abraham, *2040*
11:9 who were heirs with him *of* the same **p.** *2039*
11:11 he considered him faithful who *had* **made** the **p.** *2040*
2Pe 2:19 *They* **p** them freedom, while they *2040*
3:9 The Lord is not slow in keeping his **p,** *2039*
3:13 keeping with his **p** we are looking forward *2041*

PROMISED (133) [PROMISE]

Ge 18:19 about for Abraham what *he has* **p** him." 1819
21:1 and the LORD did for Sarah what *he had* **p.** 1819
21:2 at the very time God *had* **p** him. 1819
24:7 and who spoke to me and **p** me **on oath,** 8678
28:15 until I have done what *I have* **p** you." 1819
50:24 up out of this land to the land *he* **p on oath** 8678
Ex 3:17 And *I have* **p** to bring you up out 606
12:25 that the LORD will give you as *he* **p,** 1819
13:5 as *he* **p on oath** to you and your forefathers, 8678
32:13 I will give your descendants all this land *I* **p** them, 606
33:1 go up to the land *I* **p on oath** to Abraham, 8678
Lev 19:20 a slave girl **p** to another man but who has 3072
Nu 10:29 for the LORD *has* **p** good things to Israel." 1819
11:12 the land *you* **p on oath** to their forefathers? 8678
14:16 into the land *he* **p** them **on oath;** 8678
14:23 of them will ever see the land *I* **p on oath** 8678
14:40 "We will go up to the place the LORD **p."** 606
32:11 the land *I* **p on oath** to Abraham, Isaac 8678
32:24 but do what you have **p."** 3655+4946+7023
Dt 1:11 a thousand times and bless you as *he has* **p!** 1819
6:3 the LORD the God of your fathers, **p** you. 1819

Dt 6:18 the LORD **p on oath** to your forefathers, 8678
6:23 the land that *he* **p on oath** to our forefathers. 8678
8: 1 the LORD **p on oath** to your forefathers, 8678
9: 3 as the LORD *has* **p** you. 1819
9:28 to take them into the land *he had* **p** them, 1819
11:25 The LORD your God, as *he* **p** you, 1819
12:20 has enlarged your territory as *he* **p** you, 1819
13:17 as *he* **p on oath** to your forefathers, 8678
15: 6 your God will bless you as *he has* **p,** 1819
18: 2 LORD is their inheritance, as *he* **p** them. 1819
19: 8 as *he* **p on oath** to your forefathers, 8678
19: 8 and gives you the whole land *he* **p** them, 1819
26:15 as *you* **p on oath** to our forefathers, 8678
26:18 his treasured possession as *he* **p,** 1819
26:19 to the LORD your God, as *he* **p.** 1819
27: 3 the God of your fathers, **p** you. 1819
28: 9 as his holy people, as *he* **p** you **on oath,** 8678
29:13 as *he* **p** you and as he swore to your fathers, 1819
31:20 the land *I* **p on oath** to their forefathers, 8678
31:21 into the land *I* **p** them **on oath."** 8678
31:23 into the land *I* **p** them **on oath,** 8678
34: 4 "This is the land *I* **p on oath** to Abraham, 8678
Jos 1: 3 as *I* **p** Moses. 1819
5: 6 that he *had* **solemnly p** their fathers 8678
13:14 are their inheritance, as *he* **p** them. 1819
13:33 is their inheritance, as *he* **p** them. 1819
14:10 "Now then, just as the LORD **p,** 1819
14:12 that the LORD **p** me that day. 1819
22: 4 as *he* **p,** return to your homes in the land 1819
23: 5 as the LORD your God **p** you. 1819
23:10 LORD your God fights for you, just as *he* **p.** 1819
Jdg 1:20 As Moses *had* **p,** Hebron was given to Caleb, 1819
6:36 by my hand as *you have* **p—** 1819
11:36 Do to me just as you **p,** 3655+4946+7023
1Sa 2:30 '*I* **p** that your house and your father's 606+606
25:30 for my master every good thing *he* **p** 1819
2Sa 3: 9 for David what the LORD **p** him **on oath** 8678
3:18 For the LORD **p** David, 606
7:25 Do as *you* **p,** 1819
7:28 and *you have* **p** these good things 1819
19:23 And the king **p** him **on oath.** 8678
1Ki 2:24 and has founded a dynasty for me as *he* **p—** 1819
5:12 just as *he had* **p** him. 1819
8:15 with his own hand has fulfilled what *he* **p** 1819
8:20 the throne of Israel, just as the LORD **p,** 1819
8:24 with your mouth *you have* **p** and 1819
8:26 let your word that *you* **p** your servant David my father come true. 1819
8:56 to his people Israel just as *he* **p.** 1819
9: 5 as *I* **p** David your father when I said, 1819
2Ki 8:19 *He had* **p** to maintain a lamp for David 606
10:10 The LORD has done what *he* **p** 1819
20: 9 that the LORD will do what *he has* **p:** 1819
1Ch 11: 3 as the LORD had **p** through Samuel. 1821
11:10 over the whole land, as the LORD had **p—** 1821
17:23 house be established forever. Do as *you* **p,** 1819
17:26 *You have* **p** these good things 1819
27:23 because the LORD *had* **p** to make Israel 606
2Ch 2:15 and barley and the olive oil and wine *he* **p,** 606
6: 4 who with his hands has fulfilled what *he* **p** 1819
6:10 the throne of Israel, just as the LORD **p,** 1819
6:15 with your mouth *you have* **p** and 1819
6:17 that *you* **p** your servant David come true. 1819
6:42 the **great love** *p to* David your servant." AIT
21: 7 *He had* **p** to maintain a lamp for him 606
23: 3 the LORD **p** concerning the descendants 1819
Ne 5:12 an oath to do what they had **p.** 1821
5:13 And the people did as they had **p.** 1821
Est 4: 7 the exact amount of money Haman *had* **p** 606
Ps 66:14 vows my lips **p** and my mouth spoke 7198
119:57 *I have* **p** to obey your words. 606
Isa 38: 7 that the LORD will do what *he has* **p:** 1819
55: 3 my faithful **love** *p to* David. AIT
Jer 32:42 the prosperity I *have* **p** them. 1819
44:25 what you **p** when you said, 928+1819+7023
44:25 "Go ahead then, do **what** you **p!** 5624
Mt 14: 7 that *he* **p** with an oath to give her whatever *3933*
Mk 6:23 **p** her **with an oath,** "Whatever you ask *3923*
14:11 They were delighted to hear this and **p** *2040*
Lk 2:29 as you have **p,** you now dismiss *4839*
24:49 to send you what my Father has **p;** *2039*
Ac 1: 4 but wait for the gift my Father **p,** *2039*
2:30 a prophet and knew that God *had* **p** him *3923*
2:33 from the Father the **p** Holy Spirit *2039*
3:21 as he **p** long ago through his holy prophets. *3281*
7: 5 But God **p** him that he and his descendants *2040*
13:23 to Israel the Savior Jesus, as he **p.** *2039*
13:32 What God **p** our fathers *1181+2039*
13:34 **holy** and sure **blessings p** to David.' *4008*
18:21 But as he left, *he* **p,** "I will come back *3306*
26: 6 hope in what God has **p** our fathers *1181+2039*
Ro 1: 2 the gospel *he* **p beforehand** through his *4600*
4:21 that God had power to do what *he had* **p.** *2040*
2Co 9: 5 for the generous gift you *had* **p.** *4600*
11: 2 *I* **p** you to one husband, to Christ, *764*
Gal 3:22 that what **was p,** being given through faith *2039*
Eph 1:13 with a seal, the **p** Holy Spirit, *2039*
Tit 1: 2 **p** before the beginning of time, *2040*
Heb 6:12 and patience inherit **what has been p.** *2039+3836*
6:15 Abraham received **what was p.** *2039+3836*
6:17 to the heirs *of* **what was p,** *2039+3836*
9:15 may receive the **p** eternal inheritance— *2039*
10:23 for he who **p** is faithful. *2040*
10:36 you will receive what he **has p.** *2039*
11: 9 By faith he made his home in the **p** land *2039*
11:13 They did not receive the things **p;** *2039*
Heb 11:33 and gained **what was p;** *2039*
11:39 yet none of them received **what had been p.** *2039+3836*
12:26 but now *he has* **p,** *2040*
Jas 1:12 that God *has* **p** to those who love him. *2040*
2: 5 the kingdom *he* **p** those who love him? *2040*
2Pe 3: 4 "Where is this 'coming' he **p?** *2039*
1Jn 2:25 this is what he **p** us—even eternal life. *2039+2040*

PROMISES (23) [PROMISE]

Jos 21:45 of all the LORD's good **p** to the house 1819+1821
23:14 that not one of all the good **p** the LORD 1821
1Ki 8:25 *the* **p** *you* **made** to him when you said, 1819
8:56 has failed of all the good **p** he gave 1821
1Ch 17:19 and made known all these **great** *p.* AIT
25: 5 They were given him through the **p** *of* God 1821
2Ch 6:16 *the* **p** *you* **made** to him when you said, 1819
Ps 85: 8 *he* **p** peace to his people, his saints— 1819
106:12 they believed his **p** and sang his praise. 1821
119:140 Your **p** have been thoroughly tested, 614
119:148 that I may meditate on your **p.** 614
145:13 The LORD is faithful to all his **p** 1821
Hos 10: 4 *They* **make many p,** take false oaths 1819+1821
Ro 9: 4 the temple worship and the **p.** *2039*
15: 8 to confirm the **p** made to the patriarchs *2039*
2Co 1:20 For no matter how many **p** God has made, *2039*
7: 1 Since we have these **p,** dear friends, *2039*
Gal 3:16 The **p** were spoken to Abraham and *2039*
3:21 the law, therefore, opposed to the **p** of God? *2039*
Heb 7: 6 and blessed him who had the **p.** *2039*
8: 6 and it is founded on better **p.** *2039*
11:17 He who had received the **p** was about to *2039*
2Pe 1: 4 his very great and precious **p,** so that *2041*

PROMOTE (7) [PROMOTED, PROMOTES]

Ne 2:10 that someone had come to **p** the welfare of 1335
Pr 12:20 but joy for *those who* **p** peace. 3619
16:21 and pleasant words **p** instruction. 3578
16:23 and his lips **p** instruction. 3578
Da 5:19 those he wanted to **p,** he promoted; NIH
Hab 1: 7 a law to themselves and **p** their own honor. 3655
1Ti 1: 4 These **p** controversies rather than God's work— *4218*

PROMOTED (3) [PROMOTE]

2Ch 28:19 for *he had* **p wickedness** in Judah 7277
Da 3:30 Then the king **p** Shadrach, Meshach and 10613
5:19 those he wanted to promote, *he* **p;** 10659

PROMOTES (2) [PROMOTE]

Pr 17: 9 He who covers over an offense **p** love, 1335
Gal 2:17 does that mean that Christ **p sin?** *281+1356*

PROMPT (1) [PROMPTED, PROMPTS]

Job 20: 2 "My troubled thoughts **p** me **to answer** 8740

PROMPTED (4) [PROMPT]

Mt 14: 8 **P** by her mother, she said, *4586*
Jn 13: 2 and the devil *had* already **p** Judas Iscariot, *965+1650+2840+3836*
1Th 1: 3 your labor *p by* **love,** your endurance *AIT*
2Th 1:11 of yours and every act *p by* your **faith.** *AIT*

PROMPTS (2) [PROMPT]

Ex 25: 2 from each man whose heart **p** him **to give.** 5605
Job 15: 5 Your sin **p** your mouth; 544

PRONE (1)

Ex 32:22 "You know how **p** these people are **to** evil. 928

PRONOUNCE (30) [PRONOUNCED, PRONOUNCES, PRONOUNCING]

Ge 48:20 "In your name *will* Israel **p** *this* **blessing:** 1385
Lev 13: 3 *shall* **p** him **ceremonially unclean.** 3237
13: 6 the priest *shall* **p** him **clean;** 3197
13: 8 he *shall* **p** him **unclean;** 3237
13:11 and the priest *shall* **p** him **unclean.** 3237
13:13 *he shall* **p** that person **clean.** 3197
13:15 *he shall* **p** him **unclean.** 3237
13:17 the priest *shall* **p** the infected person **clean;** 3197
13:20 the priest *shall* **p** him **unclean.** 3237
13:22 the priest *shall* **p** him **unclean;** 3237
13:23 and the priest *shall* **p** him **clean.** 3197
13:25 The priest *shall* **p** him **unclean;** 3237
13:27 the priest *shall* **p** him **unclean;** 3237
13:28 and the priest *shall* **p** him **clean;** 3197
13:30 the priest *shall* **p** that person **unclean;** 3237
13:34 the priest *shall* **p** him **clean.** 3197
13:37 and the priest *shall* **p** him **clean.** 3197
13:44 The priest *shall* **p** him **unclean** 3237+3237
14: 7 of the infectious disease and **p** him **clean.** 3197
14:48 he *shall* **p** the house **clean,** 3197
Dt 10: 8 to minister and to **p blessings** in his name, 1385
21: 5 to minister and to **p blessings** in the name 1385
23: 4 in Aram Naharaim to **p a curse on** you. 7837
27:13 stand on Mount Ebal to **p curses:** 7839
Jdg 12: 6 because *he* could not **p** the word correctly, 1819
1Ch 23:13 to minister before him and to **p blessings** 1385
Job 9:20 I were blameless, *it would* **p** me **guilty.** 6835
Ps 109:17 He loved to **p** a curse—may it come on him; NIH
Jer 1:16 *I will* **p** my judgments *on* my people 1819
Jer 4:12 Now I **p** my judgments against them." 1819

PRONOUNCED (20) [PRONOUNCE]

Lev 13: 7 to the priest to be **p clean,** 3200
13:35 in the skin after he is **p clean,** 3200
14:36 nothing in the house *will be* **p unclean.** 3237
Dt 33: 1 of God **p** *on* the Israelites before his death. 1385
Jos 6:26 At that time Joshua **p** *this* **solemn oath:** 8678
1Ki 20:40 *"You have* **p** it yourself." 3076
2Ki 23:17 from Judah and **p** against the altar of Bethel 7924
25: 6 where sentence *was* **p on** him. 907+1819
1Ch 16:12 his miracles, and the judgments he **p,** 7023
Ps 76: 8 From heaven *you* **p** judgment, 9048
105: 5 his miracles, and the judgments he **p,** 7023
Jer 19:15 around it every disaster *I* **p** against them, 1819
26:13 not bring the disaster *he has* **p** against you. 1819
26:19 not bring the disaster *he* **p** against them? 1819
35:17 in Jerusalem every disaster *I* **p** against them. 1819
36: 7 the anger and wrath **p** against this people 1819
36:31 and the people of Judah every disaster *I* **p** 1819
39: 5 where *he* **p** sentence **on** him. 907+1819
52: 9 where *he* **p** sentence **on** him. 907+1819
Da 7:22 the Ancient of Days came and **p** judgment 10314

PRONOUNCES (1) [PRONOUNCE]

Lev 14:11 The priest who **p** him **clean** shall present 3197

PRONOUNCING (1) [PRONOUNCE]

Lev 13:59 for **p** them **clean** or unclean. 3197

PROOF (7) [PROVE]

Dt 22:14 I did not find **p** of her **virginity,"** 1436
22:15 shall bring **p that** she was **a virgin** 1436
22:17 here is the **p of** my daughter's **virginity."** 1436
22:20 and no **p** of the girl's **virginity** can be 1436
Ac 17:31 *He has* **given p** of this to all men *4218+4411*
2Co 8:24 show these men the **p** of your love *1893*
13: 3 since you are demanding **p** that Christ *1509*

PROOFS (1) [PROVE]

Ac 1: 3 to these men and gave many **convincing p** *5447*

PROPER (29) [PROPERLY]

Lev 5:15 one without defect and of the **p value** 6886
5:18 one without defect and of the **p value.** 6886
6: 6 one without defect and of the **p value.** 6886
Jdg 6:26 a **p kind** of altar to the LORD your God on 5120
2Sa 15: 3 "Look, your claims are valid and **p,** 5791
1Ki 4:28 also brought to the **p place** their quotas 889+2118+5226+9004
1Ch 23:31 before the LORD regularly in the *p* **number** AIT
Ezr 4:14 to the palace and it is not **p** for us to see 10071
Ps 104:27 to you to give them their food at the **p time.** 6961
145:15 and you give them their food at the **p time.** 6961
Ecc 5:18 Then I realized that it is good and **p** for 3637
6: 3 and does not receive **p burial,** 7690
8: 5 will know the **p** time and **procedure.** 5477
8: 6 a **p** time and **procedure** for every matter, 5477
10:17 and whose princes eat at a *p* **time—** AIT
Jer 30:18 and the palace will stand in its **p place.** 5477
Mt 3:15 it is **p** for us to do this to fulfill all righteousness." *4560*
24:45 to give them their food at **the p time?** *2789*
Lk 1:20 which will come true at their **p time."** *2789*
12:42 their food allowance at **the p time?** *2789*
Ac 13:28 Though they found no **p ground** for *162*
1Co 11:13 Is it **p** for a woman to pray to God *4560*
2Co 10:13 however, will not boast beyond **p** limits, *NIG*
Gal 6: 9 the **p** time we will reap a harvest if we do *2625*
2Th 2: 6 so that he may be revealed at the **p** time. *1571*
1Ti 2: 6 the testimony given *in* **its p** time. *2625*
3: 4 that his children obey him with **p** respect. *4246*
5: 3 Give **p** recognition to those widows *NIG*
1Pe 2:17 **Show p respect to** everyone: *5506*

PROPERLY (1) [PROPER]

1Ti 1: 8 that the law is good if one uses it **p.** *3789*

PROPERTY (65)

Ge 23: 4 Sell me *some* **p** *for* a burial site here 299
23:18 to Abraham as his **p** in the presence of all 5239
34:10 Live in it, trade in it, and **acquire p** in it." 296
34:23 Won't their livestock, their **p** 7871
47:11 and gave them **p** in the best part of the land, 299
47:27 *They* **acquired p** there and were fruitful 296
Ex 21:21 since the slave is his **p.** 4084
22: 8 has laid hands on the other man's **p.** 4856
22: 9 or any other **lost** *p* about which someone AIT
22:11 not lay hands on the other person's **p.** 4856
Lev 6: 3 or if he finds **lost p** and lies about it, or 8
6: 4 entrusted to him, or the **lost p** he found, 8
25:10 each one of you is to return to his **family p** 299
25:13 everyone is to return to his own **p.** 299
25:25 becomes poor and sells some of his **p,** 299
25:27 he can then go back to his own **p.** 299
25:28 and he can then go back to his **p.** 299
25:33 So **the p** of the Levites is redeemable— 889S
25:33 the Levites are their **p** among the Israelites. 299
25:41 and to the **p** *of* his forefathers. 299
25:45 and they will become your **p.** 299
25:46 as inherited **p** and can make them slaves 299
27:21 it will become the **p** of the priests. 299

Nu 27: 4 Give us **p** among our father's relatives." 299
27: 7 You must certainly give them **p** as 299
32:32 but the **p** we inherit will be on this side of 299
35:28 high priest may he return to his own **p**. 299+824
36: 4 and their **p** will be taken from the tribal 5709
Dt 21:16 when he wills his **p** to his sons, 889+2118+4200[S]
Ru 4: 5 maintain the name of the dead with his **p**." 5709
4: 7 for the redemption and **transfer of p** to become final, 1821+3972+9455
4: 9 that I have bought from Naomi all **the p** 889[S]
4:10 the name of the dead with his **p**, 5709
1Sa 25: 2 who had **p** there at Carmel, 5126
25:21 all my watching over this fellow's **p** in 889[S]
1Ki 21:19 not murdered a man and **seized** his **p**?' 3769
1Ch 9: 2 Now the first to resettle on their own **p** 299
27:31 the officials in charge of King David's **p**. 8214
28: 1 the **p** and livestock belonging to the king 8214
2Ch 11:14 even abandoned their pasturelands and **p**, 299
31: 1 to their own towns and to their own **p**. 299
Ezr 7:26 confiscation of **p**, or imprisonment. 10479
10: 8 within three days would forfeit all his **p**, 8214
Ne 11: 3 each on his own **p** in the various towns, 299
11:20 each on his **ancestral p**. 5709
Est 8:11 and to plunder the **p** *of* their enemies. 8965
Job 5:24 of your **p** and find nothing missing. 5659
Jer 37:12 **get** *his* **share of** *the* **p** among the people 2745
Eze 45: 6 the city as its **p** an area 5,000 cubits wide 299
45: 7 by the sacred district and the **p** *of* the city. 299
46:16 it is to be their **p** by inheritance. 299
46:18 driving them off their **p**. 299
46:18 inheritance out of his own **p**, 299
46:18 be separated from his **p**.'" 299
48:20 along with the **p** *of* the city. 299
48:21 and the city **p** will belong to the prince. 299
48:22 So the **p** *of* the Levites and the property of 299
48:22 and the **p** *of* the city will lie in the center of 299
Mt 25:14 called his servants and entrusted his **p** *3836+5639*
Lk 15:12 So he divided his **p** between them. *1050*
15:30 of yours who has squandered your **p** *1050*
16:12 not been trustworthy with someone else's **p**, *NIG*
16:12 who will give you **p** of your own? *NIG*
Ac 5: 1 his wife Sapphira, also sold a **piece of p**. *3228*
Heb 10:34 the confiscation *of* your **p**, *5639*

PROPHECIES (4) [PROPHESY]

2Ch 24:27 the many **p** about him, and the record of 5363
1Co 13: 8 But where there are **p**, they will cease; *4735*
1Th 5:20 do not treat **p** with contempt. *4735*
1Ti 1:18 in keeping with the **p** once made about you, *4735*

PROPHECY (20) [PROPHESY]

2Ki 9:25 when the LORD made this **p** about him: 5363
2Ch 9:29 in the **p** *of* Ahijah the Shilonite and in 5553
15: 8 the **p** of Azariah son of Oded the prophet, 5553
Eze 14: 9 "'And if the prophet is enticed to utter a **p**, 1821
Da 9:24 to seal up vision and **p** and to anoint 5566
Mt 13:14 In them is fulfilled the **p** of Isaiah: *4735*
1Co 12:10 to another miraculous powers, to another **p**, *4735*
13: 2 the **gift of p** and can fathom all mysteries *4735*
14: 1 spiritual gifts, especially the gift of **p**. *4736*
14: 6 or knowledge or **p** or word of instruction? *4735*
14:22 **p**, however, is for believers, *4735*
2Th 2: 2 unsettled or alarmed by some **p**, *4460*
2Pe 1:20 that no **p** of Scripture came about by *4735*
1:21 **p** never had its origin in the will of man, *4735*
Rev 1: 3 the one who reads the words *of* this **p**, *4735*
19:10 For the testimony of Jesus is the spirit *of* **p**." *4735*
22: 7 Blessed is he who keeps the words *of* the **p** *4735*
22:10 not seal up the words *of* the **p** of this book, *4735*
22:18 the words *of* the **p** of this book: *4735*
22:19 takes words away from this book *of* **p**, *4735*

PROPHESIED (36) [PROPHESY]

Nu 11:25 When the Spirit rested on them, *they* **p**, 5547
11:26 and *they* **p** in the camp. 5547
1Sa 19:20 upon Saul's men and they also **p**. 5547
19:21 and he sent more men, and they **p** too. 5547
19:21 Saul sent men a third time, and they also **p**. 5547
19:24 He stripped off his robes and also **p** 5547
1Ch 25: 2 who **p** under the king's supervision. 5547
25: 3 of their father Jeduthun, who **p**, 5547
2Ch 20:37 Eliezer son of Dodavahu of Mareshah **p** 5547
Ezr 5: 1 **p** to the Jews in Judah and Jerusalem in 10451
Ne 6:12 but that *he had* **p** against me because 1819+5553
Jer 2: 8 The prophets **p** by Baal, 5547
20: 6 to whom *you have* **p** lies.'" 5547
23:13 *They* **p** by Baal and led my people Israel 5547
23:21 I did not speak to them, yet they *have* **p**. 5547
25:13 in this book and **p** by Jeremiah against all 5547
26:11 to death because *he has* **p** against this city. 5547
26:18 "Micah of Moresheth **p** in the days 5547
26:20 from Kiriath Jearim was another man *who* **p** 5547
26:20 *he* **p** the same things against this city 5547
28: 6 the LORD fulfill the words *you have* **p** 5547
28: 8 who preceded you and me *have* **p** war, 5547
29:31 Because Shemaiah *has* **p** to you, 5547
37:19 Where are your prophets who **p** to you, 5547
Eze 13:16 those prophets of Israel who **p** to Jerusalem 5547
37: 7 So *I* **p** as I was commanded. 5547
37:10 So *I* **p** as he commanded me, 5547
38:17 At that time they **p** for years 5547
Mt 11:13 all the Prophets and the Law **p** until John. *4736*
15: 7 Isaiah was right when he **p** about you: *3306+4736*
Mk 7: 6 when *he* **p** about you hypocrites; *4736*
Lk 1:67 was filled with the Holy Spirit and **p**: *4736*
Jn 11:51 that year *he* **p** that Jesus would die for *4736*
Ac 19: 6 and they spoke in tongues and **p**. *4736*
21: 9 He had four unmarried daughters *who* **p**. *4736*
Jude 1:14 the seventh from Adam, **p** about these men: *4736*

PROPHESIES (13) [PROPHESY]

1Ki 22: 8 because *he* never **p** anything good 5547
22:18 that *he* never **p** anything good about me, 5547
2Ch 18: 7 because he never **p** anything good 5547
18:17 that *he* never **p** anything good about me, 5547
Jer 28: 9 the prophet who **p** peace will be recognized 5547
Eze 12:27 and he **p** about the distant future.' 5547
Zec 13: 3 And if anyone still **p**, his father and mother 5547
13: 3 When he **p**, his own parents will stab him. 5547
1Co 11: 4 Every man *who* prays or **p** with his head *4736*
11: 5 And every woman *who* prays or **p** *4736*
14: 3 But everyone who **p** speaks to men *4736*
14: 4 but he who **p** edifies the church. *4736*
14: 5 He who **p** is greater than one who speaks *4736*

PROPHESY (65) [PROPHECIES, PROPHECY, PROPHESIED, PROPHESIES, PROPHESYING, PROPHET, PROPHET'S, PROPHETESS, PROPHETIC, PROPHETS]

1Sa 10: 6 and *you will* **p** with them; 5547
Isa 30:10 Tell us pleasant things, **p** illusions. 2600
Jer 5:31 The prophets **p** lies, the priests rule 5547
11:21 '*Do* not **p** in the name of the LORD 5547
19:14 where the LORD had sent him to **p**, 5547
23:25 the prophets say who **p** lies in my name. 5547
23:26 *who* **p** the delusions of their own minds? 5566
23:32 I am against *those who* **p** false dreams," 5547
25:30 "Now **p** all these words against them 5547
26: 9 Why *do you* **p** in the LORD's name 5547
26:12 to **p** against this house and this city all 5547
27:10 They **p** lies to you that will only serve 5547
27:15 both you and the prophets who **p** to you.'" 5547
32: 3 saying, "Why *do you* **p** as you do? 5547
Eze 4: 7 of Jerusalem and with bared arm **p** 5547
6: 2 the mountains of Israel; **p** against them 5547
11: 4 Therefore **p** against them; 5547
11: 4 Therefore prophesy against them; **p**, 5547
13: 2 **p** against the prophets of Israel who are 5547
13: 2 to **those who p** out of their own imagination 5566
13:17 the daughters of your people who **p** out 5547
13:17 of their own imagination. **P** against them 5547
20:46 and **p** against the forest of the southland. 5547
21: 2 **P** against the land of Israel 5547
21: 9 **p** and say, 'This is what the Lord says: 5547
21:14 **p** and strike your hands together. 5547
21:28 "And you, son of man, **p** and say, 5547
25: 2 against the Ammonites and **p** against them. 5547
28:21 your face against Sidon; **p** against her 5547
29: 2 and **p** against him and against all Egypt. 5547
30: 2 "Son of man, **p** and say: 5547
34: 2 **p** against the shepherds of Israel; 5547
34: 2 **p** and say to them: 5547
35: 2 face against Mount Seir; **p** against it 5547
36: 1 **p** to the mountains of Israel and say, 5547
36: 3 Therefore **p** and say, 'This is what 5547
36: 6 Therefore **p** concerning the land of Israel 5547
37: 4 "**P** to these bones and say to them, 5547
37: 9 Then he said to me, "**P** to the breath; 5547
37: 9 **p**, son of man, and say to it, 5547
37:12 Therefore **p** and say to them: 5547
38: 2 of Meshech and Tubal; **p** against him 5547
38:14 "Therefore, son of man, **p** and say to Gog: 5547
39: 1 "Son of man, **p** against Gog and say: 5547
Joel 2:28 Your sons and daughters *will* **p**, 5547
Am 2:12 and commanded the prophets not *to* **p**. 5547
3: 8 LORD has spoken—who *can* but **p**? 5547
7:13 Don't **p** anymore at Bethel, 5547
7:15 'Go, **p** to my people Israel.' 5547
7:16 You say, "'*Do* not **p** against Israel, 5547
Mic 2: 6 "*Do* not **p**," their prophets say. 5752
2: 6 "*Do* not **p** about these things; 5752
2:11 '*I will* **p** for you plenty of wine 5752
Mt 7:22 'Lord, Lord, *did we* not **p** in your name, *4736*
26:68 and said, "**P** to us, Christ. Who hit you?" *4736*
Mk 14:65 struck him with their fists, and said, "**P**!" *4736*
Lk 22:64 They blindfolded him and demanded, "**P**! *4736*
Ac 2:17 Your sons and daughters *will* **p**, *4736*
2:18 my Spirit in those days, and *they will* **p**. *4736*
1Co 13: 9 For we know in part and *we* **p** in part, *4736*
14: 5 but I would rather *have you* **p**. *4736*
14:31 For you can all **p** in turn so *4736*
14:39 Therefore, my brothers, be eager *to* **p**, *4736*
Rev 10:11 "You must **p** again about many peoples, *4736*
11: 3 and *they will* **p** for 1,260 days, *4736*

PROPHESYING (32) [PROPHESY]

Nu 11:27 "Eldad and Medad *are* **p** in the camp." 5547
1Sa 10: 5 and they *will be* **p**. 5547
10:10 and *he* joined in their **p**. 5547
10:11 who had formerly known him saw him **p** 5547
10:13 Saul stopped **p**, he went to the high place. 5547
18:10 *He was* **p** in his house, 5547
19:20 But when they saw a group of prophets **p**, 5547
19:23 and he walked along **p** until he came 5547
1Ki 18:29 and *they continued their* **frantic p** until 5547
22:10 with all the prophets **p** before them. 5547
22:12 the other prophets *were* **p** the same thing. 5547
1Ch 25: 1 Heman and Jeduthun for the ministry of **p**, 5547
2Ch 18: 9 with all the prophets **p** before them. 5547
18:11 the other prophets *were* **p** the same thing. 5547
Jer 14:14 "The prophets *are* **p** lies in my name. 5547
14:14 They *are* **p** to you false visions, divinations, 5547
14:15 about the prophets who *are* **p** in my name: 5547
14:16 the people they *are* **p** to will be thrown out 5547
20: 1 heard Jeremiah **p** these things, 5547
23:16 not listen to what the prophets *are* **p** to you; 5547
27:14 for they *are* **p** lies to you. 5547
27:15 'They *are* **p** lies in my name. 5547
27:16 They *are* **p** lies to you. 5547
29: 9 They *are* **p** lies to you in my name. 5547
29:21 who *are* **p** lies to you in my name: 5547
Eze 11:13 as I *was* **p**, Pelatiah son of Benaiah died. 5547
13: 2 the prophets of Israel who *are now* **p**. 5547
37: 7 And as I *was* **p**, there was a noise, 5547
Am 7:12 Earn your bread there and *do your* **p** there. 5547
Ro 12: 6 If a man's gift is **p**, let him use it *4735*
1Co 14:24 comes in while everybody *is* **p**, *4736*
Rev 11: 6 not rain during the time they are **p**; *4735*

PROPHET (238) [PROPHESY]

Ge 20: 7 Now return the man's wife, for he is a **p**, 5566
Ex 7: 1 and your brother Aaron will be your **p**. 5566
Nu 12: 6 "When a **p** *of* the LORD is *among* you, 5566
Dt 13: 1 If a **p**, or one who foretells by dreams, 5566
13: 3 not listen to the words of that **p** or dreamer. 5566
13: 5 That **p** or dreamer must be put to death, 5566
18:15 a **p** like me from among your own brothers. 5566
18:18 I will raise up for them a **p** like you from 5566
18:19 to my words that the **p** speaks in my name, NIH
18:20 But a **p** who presumes to speak in my name 5566
18:20 a **p** who speaks in the name of other gods, 5566
18:22 If what a **p** proclaims in the name of 5566
18:22 That **p** has spoken presumptuously. 5566
34:10 no **p** has risen in Israel like Moses, 5566
Jdg 6: 8 he sent them a **p**, who said, "This is what 5566
1Sa 3:20 Samuel was attested as a **p** of the LORD. 5566
9: 9 the **p** of today used to be called a seer.) 5566
22: 5 But the **p** Gad said to David, 5566
2Sa 7: 2 he said to Nathan the **p**, 5566
12:25 he sent word through Nathan the **p** 5566
24:11 of the LORD had come to Gad the **p**, 5566
1Ki 1: 8 Benaiah son of Jehoiada, Nathan the **p**, 5566
1:10 not invite Nathan the **p** or Benaiah or 5566
1:22 Nathan the **p** arrived. 5566
1:23 they told the king, "Nathan the **p** is here." 5566
1:32 Nathan the **p** and Benaiah son of Jehoiada." 5566
1:34 the priest and Nathan the **p** anoint him king 5566
1:38 So Zadok the priest, Nathan the **p**, 5566
1:44 Nathan the **p**, Benaiah son of Jehoiada, 5566
1:45 and Nathan the **p** have anointed him king 5566
11:29 Ahijah the **p** of Shiloh met him on the way, 5566
13:11 there was a certain old **p** living in Bethel, 5566
13:15 So the **p** said to him, NIH
13:18 The old **p** answered, "I too am a prophet, NIH
13:18 The old prophet answered, "I too am a **p**, 5566
13:20 to the old **p** who had brought him back. 5566
13:23 the **p** who had brought him back saddled his donkey 5566
13:25 in the city where the old **p** lived. 5566
13:26 When the **p** who had brought him back 5566
13:27 The **p** said to his sons, NIH
13:29 **p** picked up the body of the man of God, 5566
14: 2 Ahijah the **p** is there— 5566
14:18 through his servant the **p** Ahijah. 5566
16: 7 through the **p** Jehu son of Hanani to Baasha 5566
16:12 against Baasha through the **p** Jehu— 5566
18:36 the **p** Elijah stepped forward and prayed: 5566
19:16 from Abel Meholah to succeed you as **p**. 5566
20:13 Meanwhile a **p** came to Ahab king of Israel 5566
20:14 The **p** replied, "This is what NIH
20:14 The **p** answered, "You will." NIH
20:22 the **p** came to the king of Israel and said, 5566
20:36 So the **p** said, "Because you have not obeyed NIH
20:37 The **p** found another man and said, NIH
20:38 the **p** went and stood by the road waiting 5566
20:39 the king passed by, **the p** called out to him, 2085[S]
20:41 Then the **p** quickly removed the headband NIH
22: 7 "Is there not a **p** of the LORD here 5566
2Ki 3:11 "Is there no **p** of the LORD here, 5566
5: 3 "If only my master would see the **p** who is 5566
5: 8 and he will know that there is a **p** in Israel." 5566
5:13 if the **p** had told you to do some great thing, 5566
5:16 The **p** answered, "As surely as the LORD NIH
6:12 "but Elisha, the **p** who is in Israel, 5566
6:16 "Don't be afraid," the **p** answered. NIH
9: 1 The **p** Elisha summoned a man from 5566
9: 4 young man, the **p**, went to Ramoth Gilead. 5566
9: 6 Then the **p** poured the oil on Jehu's head NIH
14:25 Jonah son of Amittai, the **p** from Gath Hepher. 5566
19: 2 to the **p** Isaiah son of Amoz. 5566
20: 1 The **p** Isaiah son of Amoz went to him 5566
20:11 Then the **p** Isaiah called upon the LORD, 5566
20:14 Then Isaiah the **p** went to King Hezekiah 5566
20:15 The **p** asked, "What did they see NIH
23:18 of the **p** who had come from Samaria. 5566
1Ch 17: 1 he said to Nathan the **p**, "Here I am, 5566
29:29 the records of Nathan the **p** and the records 5566
2Ch 9:29 not written in the records of Nathan the **p**, 5566
12: 5 the **p** Shemaiah came to Rehoboam and to 5566
12:15 the records of Shemaiah the **p** and of Iddo 5566
13:22 are written in the annotations of the **p** Iddo. 5566
15: 8 the prophecy of Azariah son of Oded the **p**, 5566

2Ch 18: 6 "Is there not a **p** of the LORD here 5566
21:12 Jehoram received a letter from Elijah the **p**, 5566
25:15 and he sent a **p** to him, who said, 5566
25:16 So the **p** stopped but said, 5566
26:22 are recorded by the **p** Isaiah son of Amoz. 5566
28: 9 a **p** of the LORD named Oded was there, 5566
29:25 and Gad the king's seer and Nathan the **p**; 5566
32:20 and the **p** Isaiah son of Amoz cried out 5566
32:32 in the vision of the **p** Isaiah son of Amoz in 5566
35:18 in Israel since the days of the **p** Samuel; 5566
36:12 not humble himself before Jeremiah the **p**, 5566
Ezr 5: 1 Haggai the **p** and Zechariah the prophet, 10455
5: 1 Haggai the prophet and Zechariah the **p**, 10455
6:14 under the preaching of Haggai the **p** 10455
Ps 51: T When the **p** Nathan came to him 5566
Isa 3: 2 the judge and **p**, the soothsayer and elder, 5566
37: 2 to the **p** Isaiah son of Amoz. 5566
38: 1 The **p** Isaiah son of Amoz went to him 5566
39: 3 Then Isaiah the **p** went to King Hezekiah 5566
39: 4 The **p** asked, "What did they see NIH
Jer 1: 5 I appointed you as a **p** to the nations." 5566
14:18 Both **p** and priest have gone to 5566
20: 2 he had Jeremiah the **p** beaten and put in 5566
23:11 "Both **p** and priest are godless; 5566
23:28 Let the **p** who has a dream tell his dream, 5566
23:33 "When these people, or a **p** or a priest, 5566
23:34 If a **p** or a priest or anyone else claims, 5566
23:37 This is what you keep saying to a **p**: 5566
25: 2 the **p** said to all the people of Judah and 5566
28: 1 the **p** Hananiah son of Azzur, 5566
28: 5 Then the **p** Jeremiah replied to 5566
28: 5 to the **p** Hananiah before the priests and all 5566
28: 9 But the **p** who prophesies peace will 5566
28:10 the **p** Hananiah took the yoke off the neck 5566
28:10 the neck of the **p** Jeremiah and broke it, 5566
28:11 At this, the **p** Jeremiah went on his way. 5566
28:12 Shortly after the **p** Hananiah had broken 5566
28:12 the yoke off the neck of the **p** Jeremiah, 5566
28:15 **p** Jeremiah said to Hananiah the prophet, 5566
28:15 prophet Jeremiah said to Hananiah the **p**, 5566
28:17 Hananiah the **p** died. 5566
29: 1 the text of the letter that the **p** Jeremiah sent 5566
29:26 you should put any madman *who* **acts like a p** into the stocks 5547
29:27 who **poses as a p** among you? 5547
29:29 however, read the letter to Jeremiah the **p**. 5566
32: 2 the **p** was confined in the courtyard of 5566
34: 6 the **p** told all this to Zedekiah king 5566
36: 8 everything Jeremiah the **p** told him to do; 5566
36:26 the scribe and Jeremiah the **p**. 5566
37: 2 through Jeremiah the **p**. 5566
37: 3 to Jeremiah the **p** with this message: 5566
37: 6 of the LORD came to Jeremiah the **p**: 5566
38: 9 in all they have done to Jeremiah the **p**. 5566
38:10 and lift Jeremiah the **p** out of the cistern 5566
38:14 for Jeremiah the **p** and had him brought to 5566
42: 2 Jeremiah the **p** and said to him, 5566
42: 4 "I have heard you," replied Jeremiah the **p**. 5566
43: 6 Jeremiah the **p** and Baruch son of Neriah. 5566
45: 1 the **p** told Baruch son of Neriah in 5566
46: 1 of the LORD that came to Jeremiah the **p** 5566
46:13 the LORD spoke to Jeremiah the **p** about 5566
47: 1 to Jeremiah the **p** concerning the Philistines 5566
49:34 to Jeremiah the **p** concerning Elam, 5566
50: 1 through Jeremiah the **p** concerning Babylon 5566
La 2:20 priest and **p** be killed in the sanctuary of 5566
Eze 2: 5 they will know that a **p** has been among 5566
7:26 They will try to get a vision from the **p**; 5566
14: 4 before his face and then goes to a **p**, 5566
14: 7 and then goes to a **p** to inquire of me, 5566
14: 9 if the **p** is enticed to utter a prophecy, 5566
14: 9 I the LORD have enticed that **p**, 5566
14:10 the **p** will be as guilty as the one who 5566
33:33 then they will know that a **p** has been 5566
Da 9: 2 of the LORD given to Jeremiah the **p**, 5566
Hos 9: 7 the **p** is considered a fool, 5566
9: 8 The **p**, along with my God, 5566
12:13 The LORD used a **p** to bring Israel up 5566
12:13 by a **p** he cared for him. 5566
Am 7:14 "I was neither a **p** nor a prophet's son, 5566
Mic 2:11 he would be just the **p** *for* this people! 5752
Hab 1: 1 The oracle that Habakkuk the **p** received. 5566
3: 1 A prayer of Habakkuk the **p**. 5566
Hag 1: 1 of the LORD came through the **p** Haggai 5566
1: 3 of the LORD came through the **p** Haggai: 5566
1:12 and the message of the **p** Haggai, 5566
2: 1 of the LORD came through the **p** Haggai: 5566
2:10 word of the LORD came to the **p** Haggai: 5566
Zec 1: 1 word of the LORD came to the **p** Zechariah 5566
1: 7 word of the LORD came to the **p** Zechariah 5566
13: 4 "On that day every **p** will be ashamed 5566
13: 5 He will say, 'I am not a **p**. 5566
Mal 4: 5 I will send you the **p** Elijah before 5566
Mt 1:22 the Lord had said through the **p**: *4737*
2: 5 "for this is what the **p** has written: *4737*
2:15 the Lord had said through the **p**: *4737*
2:17 through the **p** Jeremiah was fulfilled: *4737*
3: 3 he who was spoken of through the **p** Isaiah: *4737*
4:14 what was said through the **p** Isaiah: *4737*
8:17 what was spoken through the **p** Isaiah: *4737*
10:41 a **p** because he is a prophet will receive *4737*
10:41 a prophet because he is a **p** will receive *4737*
11: 9 Then what did you go out to see? A **p**? *4737*
11: 9 Yes, I tell you, and more than a **p**. *4737*
12:17 what was spoken through the **p** Isaiah: *4737*
12:39 be given it except the sign *of* the **p** Jonah. *4737*
13:35 fulfilled what was spoken through the **p**: *4737*
Mt 13:57 and in his own house is a **p** without honor." *4737*
14: 5 because they considered him a **p**. *4737*
21: 4 to fulfill what was spoken through the **p**: *4737*
21:11 the **p** from Nazareth in Galilee." *4737*
21:26 for they all hold that John was a **p**." *4737*
21:46 because the people held that he was a **p**. *4737*
24:15 spoken of through the **p** Daniel— *4737*
27: 9 by Jeremiah the **p** was fulfilled: *4737*
Mk 1: 2 It is written in Isaiah the **p**: *4737*
6: 4 and in his own house is a **p** without honor." *4737*
6:15 And still others claimed, "He is a **p**, *4737*
11:32 for everyone held that John really was a **p**.) *4737*
Lk 1:76 will be called a **p** of the Most High; *4737*
3: 4 in the book of the words of Isaiah the **p**: *4737*
4:17 The scroll *of* the **p** Isaiah was handed *4737*
4:24 "no **p** is accepted in his hometown. *4737*
4:27 with leprosy in the time of Elisha the **p**, *4737*
7:16 "A great **p** has appeared among us," *4737*
7:26 But what did you go out to see? A **p**? *4737*
7:26 Yes, I tell you, and more than a **p**. *4737*
7:39 he said to himself, "If this man were a **p**, *4737*
13:33 for surely no **p** can die outside Jerusalem! *4737*
20: 6 they are persuaded that John was a **p**." *4737*
24:19 "He was a **p**, powerful in word and *467+4737*
Jn 1:21 "Are you the **P**?" *4737*
1:23 John replied in the words of Isaiah the **p**, *4737*
1:25 nor Elijah, nor the **P**?" *4737*
4:19 the woman said, "I can see that you are a **p**. *4737*
4:44 that a **p** has no honor in his own country.) *4737*
6:14 "Surely this is the **P** who is to come into *4737*
7:40 "Surely this man is the **P**." *4737*
7:52 that a **p** does not come out of Galilee." *4737*
9:17 The man replied, "He is a **p**." *4737*
12:38 This was to fulfill the word *of* Isaiah the **p**: *4737*
Ac 2:16 No, this is what was spoken by the **p** Joel: *4737*
2:30 a **p** and knew that God had promised him *4737*
3:22 a **p** like me from among your own people; *4737*
7:37 a **p** like me from your own people.' *4737*
7:48 As the **p** says: *4737*
7:52 ever a **p** your fathers did not persecute? *4737*
8:28 reading the book of Isaiah the **p**. *4737*
8:30 and heard the man reading Isaiah the **p**. *4737*
8:34 please, who is the **p** talking about, *4737*
13: 6 and **false p** named Bar-Jesus, *6021*
13:20 until the time of Samuel the **p**. *4737*
21:10 a **p** named Agabus came down from Judea. *4737*
28:25 when he said through Isaiah the **p**: *4737*
1Co 14:37 If anybody thinks he is a **p** *4737*
Rev 16:13 and out of the mouth *of* the **false p**. *6021*
19:20 with him the **false p** who had performed *6021*
20:10 the beast and the **false p** had been thrown. *6021*

PROPHET'S (5) [PROPHESY]

Am 7:14 "I was neither a prophet nor a **p** son, 5566
Zec 13: 4 on a **p garment** *of* hair in order to deceive. 168
Mt 10:41 a prophet will receive a **p** reward, *4737*
2Pe 1:20 about by the **p** own interpretation. *NIG*
2:16 and restrained the **p** madness. *4737*

PROPHETESS (8) [PROPHESY]

Ex 15:20 Then Miriam the **p**, Aaron's sister, 5567
Jdg 4: 4 Deborah, a **p**, the wife of Lappidoth, 5567
2Ki 22:14 and Asaiah went to speak to the **p** Huldah, 5567
2Ch 34:22 with him went to speak to the **p** Huldah, 5567
Ne 6:14 remember also the **p** Noadiah and the rest 5567
Isa 8: 3 Then I went to the **p**, and she conceived 5567
Lk 2:36 There was also a **p**, Anna, *4739*
Rev 2:20 that woman Jezebel, who calls herself a **p**. *4739*

PROPHETIC (3) [PROPHESY]

Zec 13: 4 be ashamed of his **p** vision. 5547
Ro 16:26 and made known through the **p** writings by *4738*
1Ti 4:14 which was given you through a **p message** *4735*

PROPHETS (245) [PROPHESY]

Nu 11:29 I wish that all the LORD's people were **p** 5566
1Sa 10: 5 you will meet a procession of **p** coming 5566
10:10 a procession of **p** met him; 5566
10:11 the **p**, they asked each other, "What is this 5566
10:11 Is Saul also among the **p**?" 5566
10:12 "Is Saul also among the **p**?" 5566
19:20 when they saw a group of **p** prophesying, 5566
19:24 "Is Saul also among the **p**?" 5566
28: 6 not answer him by dreams or Urim or **p**. 5566
28:15 either by **p** or by dreams. 5566
1Ki 18: 4 Jezebel was killing off the LORD's **p**, 5566
18: 4 a hundred **p** and hidden them in two caves, 5566
18:13 what I did while Jezebel was killing the **p** 5566
18:13 a hundred of the LORD's **p** in two caves, 5566
18:19 the four hundred and fifty **p** *of* Baal and 5566
18:19 of Baal and the four hundred **p** *of* Asherah, 5566
18:20 throughout all Israel and assembled the **p** 5566
18:22 "I am the only one of the LORD's **p** left, 5566
18:22 but Baal has four hundred and fifty **p**. 5566
18:25 Elijah said to the **p** *of* Baal, 5566
18:40 "Seize the **p** *of* Baal. 5566
19: 1 how he had killed all the **p** with the sword. 5566
19:10 and put your **p** to death with the sword. 5566
19:14 and put your **p** to death with the sword. 5566
20:35 of the LORD one of the sons of the **p** said 5566
20:41 of Israel recognized him as one of the **p**. 5566
22: 6 So the king of Israel brought together the **p** 5566
22:10 with all the **p** prophesying before them. 5566
22:12 All the other **p** were prophesying 5566
1Ki 22:13 the other **p** are predicting success for 5566
22:22 be a lying spirit in the mouths of all his **p**,' 5566
22:23 a lying spirit in the mouths of all these **p** 5566
2Ki 2: 3 The company of the **p** at Bethel came out 5566
2: 5 The company of the **p** at Jericho went up 5566
2: 7 of the company of the **p** went and stood at 5566
2:15 The company of the **p** from Jericho, 5566
3:13 Go to the **p** *of* your father and the prophets 5566
3:13 Go to the prophets of your father and the **p** 5566
4: 1 a man from the company of the **p** cried out 5566
4:38 company of the **p** was meeting with him, 5566
5:22 the company of the **p** have just come to me 5566
6: 1 The company of the **p** said to Elisha, 5566
9: 1 from the company of the **p** and said to him, 5566
9: 7 of my servants the **p** and the blood of all 5566
10:19 Now summon all the **p** *of* Baal, 5566
17:13 and Judah through all his **p** and seers: 5566
17:13 I delivered to you through my servants the **p** 5566
17:23 had warned through all his servants the **p**. 5566
21:10 the LORD said through his servants the **p**: 5566
23: 2 people of Jerusalem, the priests and the **p**— 5566
24: 2 proclaimed by his servants the **p**. 5566
1Ch 16:22 do my **p** no harm." 5566
2Ch 18: 5 So the king of Israel brought together the **p** 5566
18: 9 with all the **p** prophesying before them. 5566
18:11 All the other **p** were prophesying 5566
18:12 the other **p** are predicting success for 5566
18:21 be a lying spirit in the mouths of all his **p**,' 5566
18:22 a lying spirit in the mouths of these **p** 5566
20:20 in his **p** and you will be successful." 5566
24:19 Although the LORD sent **p** to the people 5566
29:25 commanded by the LORD through his **p**. 5566
36:16 despised his words and scoffed at his **p** 5566
Ezr 5: 2 the **p** of God were with them, helping them. 10455
9:11 through your servants the **p** when you said: 5566
Ne 6: 7 even appointed **p** to make this proclamation 5566
6:14 and the rest of the **p** who have been trying 5566
9:26 They killed your **p**, who had admonished 5566
9:30 By your Spirit you admonished them through your **p**. 5566
9:32 upon our priests and **p**, upon our fathers 5566
Ps 74: 9 no miraculous signs; no **p** are left, 5566
105:15 do my **p** no harm." 5566
Isa 9:15 the **p** who teach lies are the tail. 5566
28: 7 and **p** stagger from beer and are befuddled 5566
29:10 He has sealed your eyes (the **p**); 5566
30:10 and to the **p**, "Give us no more visions 2602
44:25 signs of **false p** and makes fools of diviners, 967
Jer 2: 8 The **p** prophesied by Baal, 5566
2:26 their priests and their **p**. 5566
2:30 Your sword has devoured your **p** like 5566
4: 9 and the **p** will be appalled." 5566
5:13 The **p** are but wind and the word is not 5566
5:31 The **p** prophesy lies, 5566
6:13 **p** and priests alike, all practice deceit. 5566
7:25 and again I sent you my servants the **p**. 5566
8: 1 the bones of the priests and **p**, 5566
8:10 **p** and priests alike, all practice deceit. 5566
13:13 the **p** and all those living in Jerusalem. 5566
14:13 Sovereign LORD, the **p** keep telling them, 5566
14:14 "The **p** are prophesying lies in my name. 5566
14:15 the **p** who are prophesying in my name: 5566
14:15 Those same **p** will perish by sword 5566
18:18 nor the word from the **p**. 5566
23: 9 Concerning the **p**: My heart is broken 5566
23:10 The [**p**] follow an evil course 4392[S]
23:13 the **p** *of* Samaria I saw this repulsive thing: 5566
23:14 And among the **p** of Jerusalem 5566
23:15 this is what the LORD Almighty says concerning the **p**: 5566
23:15 the **p** *of* Jerusalem ungodliness has spread 5566
23:16 not listen to what the **p** are prophesying 5566
23:21 I did not send these **p**, 5566
23:25 the **p** say who prophesy lies in my name. 5566
23:26 in the hearts of these lying **p**, 5566
23:30 "I am against the **p** who steal 5566
23:31 against the **p** who wag their own tongues 5566
25: 4 the LORD has sent all his servants the **p** 5566
26: 5 to the words of my servants the **p**, 5566
26: 7 the **p** and all the people heard Jeremiah 5566
26: 8 the **p** and all the people seized him 5566
26:11 the **p** said to the officials and all the people, 5566
26:16 the people said to the priests and the **p**, 5566
27: 9 So do not listen to your **p**, your diviners, 5566
27:14 Do not listen to the words of the **p** who say 5566
27:15 both you and the **p** who prophesy to you.' " 5566
27:16 Do not listen to the **p** who say, 5566
27:18 If they are **p** and have the word of 5566
28: 8 From early times the **p** who preceded you 5566
29: 1 the priests, the **p** and all the other people 5566
29: 8 the **p** and diviners among you deceive you. 5566
29:15 LORD has raised up **p** for us in Babylon," 5566
29:19 again and again by my servants the **p**. 5566
32:32 their kings and officials, their priests and **p**, 5566
35:15 Again and again I sent all my servants the **p** 5566
37:19 Where are your **p** who prophesied to you, 5566
44: 4 Again and again I sent my servants the **p**, 5566
50:36 A sword against her **false p**! 967
La 2: 9 and her **p** no longer find visions from 5566
2:14 visions of your **p** were false and worthless; 5566
4:13 But it happened because of the sins of her **p** 5566
Eze 13: 2 the **p** *of* Israel who are now prophesying. 5566
13: 3 to the foolish **p** who follow their own spirit 5566
13: 4 Your **p**, O Israel, are like jackals 5566
13: 9 be against the **p** who see false visions 5566
13:16 those **p** *of* Israel who prophesied 5566
22:28 Her **p** whitewash these deeds for them 5566

Eze 38:17 of in former days by my servants the **p** 5566
Da 9: 6 not listened to your servants the **p**, 5566
9:10 laws he gave us through his servants the **p**. 5566
Hos 4: 5 and the **p** stumble with you. 5566
6: 5 Therefore I cut you in pieces with my **p**, 5566
12:10 I spoke to the **p**, gave them many visions 5566
Am 2:11 up **p** from among your sons and Nazirites 5566
2:12 and commanded the **p** not to prophesy. 5566
3: 7 his plan to his servants the **p**. 5566
Mic 2: 6 "Do not prophesy," their **p say.** 5752
3: 5 "As for the **p** who lead my people astray, 5566
3: 6 The sun will set for the **p**, 5566
3:11 and her **p** tell fortunes for money. 5566
Zep 3: 4 Her **p** are arrogant; 5566
Zec 1: 4 to whom the earlier **p** proclaimed: 5566
1: 5 And the **p**, do they live forever? 5566
1: 6 which I commanded my servants the **p**, 5566
7: 3 of the LORD Almighty and the **p**, 5566
7: 7 through the earlier **p** when Jerusalem 5566
7:12 by his Spirit through the earlier **p**. 5566
8: 9 by the **p** who were there when 5566
13: 2 both the **p** and the spirit of impurity from 5566
Mt 2:23 was fulfilled what was said through the **p**: *4737*
5:12 the **p** who were before you. *4737*
5:17 to abolish the Law or the **P**; *4737*
7:12 for this sums up the Law and the **P**. *4737*
7:15 "Watch out for **false p**. *6021*
11:13 the **P** and the Law prophesied until John. *4737*
13:17 many **p** and righteous men longed *4737*
16:14 and still others, Jeremiah or one *of* the **p**." *4737*
22:40 the **P** hang on these two commandments." *4737*
23:29 You build tombs *for* the **p** and decorate *4737*
23:30 with them in shedding the blood *of* the **p**.' *4737*
23:31 of those who murdered the **p**. *4737*
23:34 Therefore I am sending you **p** *4737*
23:37 you who kill the **p** and stone those sent *4737*
24:11 and many **false p** will appear *6021*
24:24 For false Christs and **false p** will appear *6021*
26:56 the writings *of* the **p** might be fulfilled." *4737*
Mk 6:15 like one *of* the **p** of long ago." *4737*
8:28 and still others, one *of* the **p**." *4737*
13:22 and **false p** will appear and perform signs *6021*
Lk 1:70 (as he said through his holy **p** of long ago), *4737*
6:23 For that is how their fathers treated the **p**. *4737*
6:26 how their fathers treated the **false p**. *6021*
9: 8 *of* the **p** of long ago had come back to life. *4737*
9:19 *of* the **p** of long ago has come back to life." *4737*
10:24 For I tell you that many **p** and kings wanted *4737*
11:47 because you build tombs *for* the **p**, *4737*
11:48 they killed **the p**, and you build their tombs. *899S*
11:49 'I will send them **p** and apostles, *4737*
11:50 for the blood of all the **p** that has been shed *4737*
13:28 and Jacob and all the **p** in the kingdom *4737*
13:34 you who kill the **p** and stone those sent *4737*
16:16 Law and the **P** were proclaimed until John. *4737*
16:29 'They have Moses and the **P**; *4737*
16:31 'If they do not listen to Moses and the **P**, *4737*
18:31 and everything that is written by the **p** *4737*
24:25 to believe all that the **p** have spoken! *4737*
24:27 And beginning with Moses and all the **P**, *4737*
24:44 the Law of Moses, the **P** and the Psalms." *4737*
Jn 1:45 and about whom the **p** also wrote— *4737*
6:45 It is written in the **P**: *4737*
8:52 Abraham died and so did the **p**, *4737*
8:53 He died, and so did the **p**. *4737*
Ac 3:18 through all the **p**, saying that his Christ *4737*
3:21 he promised long ago through his holy **p**. *4737*
3:24 "Indeed, all the **p** from Samuel on, *4737*
3:25 *of* the **p** and of the covenant God made *4737*
7:42 with what is written in the book *of* the **p**: *4737*
10:43 All the **p** testify about him *4737*
11:27 During this time some **p** came down *4737*
13: 1 In the church at Antioch there were **p** *4737*
13:15 After the reading *from* the Law and the **P**, *4737*
13:27 *of* the **p** that are read every Sabbath. *4737*
13:40 that what the **p** have said does not happen *4737*
15:15 The words *of* the **p** are in agreement *4737*
15:32 Judas and Silas, who themselves were **p**, *4737*
24:14 with the Law and that is written in the **P**, *4737*
26:22 I am saying nothing beyond what the **p** *4737*
26:27 King Agrippa, do you believe the **p**? *4737*
28:23 from the Law of Moses and from the **P**. *4737*
Ro 1: 2 through his **p** in the Holy Scriptures *4737*
3:21 to which the Law and the **P** testify. *4737*
11: 3 they have killed your **p** and torn *4737*
1Co 12:28 first of all apostles, second **p**, third teachers, *4737*
12:29 Are all apostles? Are all **p**? *4737*
14:29 Two or three **p** should speak, *4737*
14:32 *of* **p** are subject to the control of prophets. *4737*
14:32 of prophets are subject to the control *of* **p**. *4737*
Eph 2:20 on the foundation *of* the apostles and **p**, *4737*
3: 5 by the Spirit to God's holy apostles and **p**. *4737*
4:11 some to be **p**, some to be evangelists, *4737*
1Th 2:15 who killed the Lord Jesus and the **p** and *4737*
Tit 1:12 Even one of their own **p** has said, *4737*
Heb 1: 1 the **p** at many times and in various ways, *4737*
11:32 Jephthah, David, Samuel and the **p**, *4737*
Jas 5:10 the **p** who spoke in the name of the Lord. *4737*
1Pe 1:10 Concerning this salvation, the **p**, *4737*
2Pe 1:19 the word of the **p** made more certain, *4738*
2: 1 there were also **false p** among the people, *6021*
3: 2 past by the holy **p** and the command given *4737*
1Jn 4: 1 because many **false p** have gone out into *6021*
Rev 10: 7 just as he announced to his servants the **p**." *4737*
11:10 these two **p** had tormented those who live *4737*
11:18 and for rewarding your servants the **p** *4737*
16: 6 the blood of your saints and **p**, *4737*
Rev 18:20 Rejoice, saints and apostles and **p**! *4737*
18:24 In her was found the blood *of* **p** and of *4737*
22: 6 The Lord, the God of the spirits *of* the **p**, *4737*
22: 9 with you and with your brothers the **p** and *4737*

PROPITIATION (KJV) See ATONEMENT

PROPORTION (4)

Nu 35: 8 given **in p to** the inheritance of each 3869+7023
Dt 16:10 a freewill offering **in p to** the blessings the LORD your God 889+3869+5002
16:17 of you must bring a gift **in p to** the way 3869
Ro 12: 6 let him use it in **p** to his faith. *381*

PROPOSAL (2) [PROPOSE]

Ge 34:18 Their **p** seemed good to Hamor 1821
Ac 6: 5 This **p** pleased the whole group. *3364*

PROPOSE (2) [PROPOSAL, PROPOSED]

Dt 1:14 "What *you* **p** to do is good." 1819
Isa 8:10 **p** your plan, but it will not stand, 1819

PROPOSED (4) [PROPOSE]

Ezr 10:16 So the exiles did as was **p**. NIH
Est 1:21 so the king did as Memucan **p**. 1821
2: 2 Then the king's personal attendants **p**, 606
Ac 1:23 So *they* **p** two men: *2705*

PROPPED (2)

1Ki 22:35 and the king was **p up** in his chariot facing 6641
2Ch 18:34 of Israel **p** *himself* **up** in his chariot facing 6641

PROPRIETY (2)

1Ti 2: 9 dress modestly, with decency and **p**, *5408*
2:15 continue in faith, love and holiness with **p**. *5408*

PROSELYTE (KJV) See CONVERT

PROSPECT (1) [PROSPECTS]

Pr 10:28 The **p** *of* the righteous is joy, 9347

PROSPECTS (1) [PROSPECT]

Job 6:11 What **p**, that I should be patient? 7891

PROSPER (30) [PROSPERED, PROSPERITY, PROSPEROUS, PROSPERS]

Ge 32: 9 and *I will* **make** you **p**,' 3512
32:12 *'I will* **surely make** you **p** 3512+3512
Dt 5:33 and **p** and prolong your days in the land 3201
6:24 that we might always **p** and be kept alive, 3202
28:63 Just as it pleased the LORD to **make** you **p** 3512
29: 9 so that *you may* **p** *in* everything you do. 8505
1Ki 2: 3 of Moses, so that *you may* **p** in all you do 8505
2Ch 24:20 *You will* not **p**. 7503
Ezr 6:14 of the Jews continued to build and **p** under 10613
Ps 49:18 and men praise you when *you* **p**— 3512
51:18 In your good pleasure **make** Zion **p**; 3512
Pr 11:10 When the righteous **p**, the city rejoices; 3206
11:25 A generous man *will* **p**; 2014
17:20 A man of perverse heart *does* not **p**; 3202+5162
28:13 He who conceals his sins *does* not **p**, 7503
28:25 but he who trusts in the LORD *will* **p**. 2014
Isa 53:10 the will of the LORD *will* **p** in his hand. 7503
Jer 10:21 not **p** and all their flock is scattered. 8505
12: 1 Why *does* the way of the wicked **p**? 7503
22:30 a man *who will* not **p** in his lifetime, 7503
22:30 for none of his offspring *will* **p**, 7503
29: 7 because if it prospers, you too will **p**." 8934
29:11 "plans to **p** you and not to harm you, 8934
Eze 26: 2 now that she lies in ruins *I will* **p**,' 4848
36:11 past and *will* **make** you **p** more than before. 3201
Da 4: 1 May you **p** greatly! 10720
6:25 "May you **p** greatly! 10720
8:25 He *will* cause deceit *to* **p**, 7503
Mal 3:15 Certainly the evildoers **p**, 1215
Ac 13:17 *he* **made** the people **p** during their stay *5738*

PROSPERED (7) [PROSPER]

Ge 39: 2 The LORD was with Joseph and he **p**, 7503
1Ch 29:23 *He* **p** and all Israel obeyed him. 7503
2Ch 14: 7 So they built and **p**. 7503
31:21 And so *he* **p**. 7503
Da 6:28 So Daniel **p** during the reign of Darius and 10613
8:12 *It* **p** in everything it did, 7503
Hos 10: 1 as his land **p**, he adorned his sacred stones. 3202

PROSPERITY (31) [PROSPER]

Dt 28:11 The LORD will grant you abundant **p**— 3208
28:47 and gladly in the time of **p**, 3972+8044
30:15 See, I set before you today life and **p**, 3202
Job 20:21 his **p** will not endure. 3206
21:13 They spend their years in **p** and go down to 3202
21:16 But their **p** is not in their own hands, 3206
22:21 in this way **p** will come to you. 3208
36:11 they will spend the rest of their days in **p** 3202
Ps 25:13 He will spend his days in **p**, 3202
72: 3 The mountains will bring **p** to the people, 8934
Ps 72: 7 **p** will abound till the moon is no more. 8934
73: 3 For I envied the arrogant when I saw the **p** 8934
106: 5 that I may enjoy the **p** *of* your chosen ones, 3208
122: 9 I will seek your **p**. 3202
128: 2 blessings and **p** will be yours. 3202
128: 5 may you see the **p** *of* Jerusalem, 3206
Pr 3: 2 and bring you **p**. 8934
8:18 enduring wealth and **p**. 7407
13:21 but **p** is the reward of the righteous. 3202
21:21 and love finds life, **p** and honor. 7407
Ecc 6: 3 how long he lives, if he cannot enjoy his **p** 3208
6: 6 over but fails to enjoy his **p**. 3208
Isa 45: 7 I bring **p** and create disaster; 8934
Jer 17: 6 he will not see **p** when it comes. 3202
29: 7 seek the **peace and p** *of* the city 8934
32:42 the **p** I have promised them. 3208
33: 9 the abundant **p** and peace I provide for it.' 3208
39:16 against this city through disaster, not **p**. 3208
La 3:17 I have forgotten what **p** is. 3208
Da 4:27 It may be that then your **p** will continue." 10713
Zec 1:17 'My towns will again overflow with **p**, 3202

PROSPEROUS (11) [PROSPER]

Ge 30:43 In this way the man *grew* exceedingly **p** 7287
Dt 30: 5 *He will* **make** you **more p** 3512
30: 9 the LORD your God will make you most **p** 3208
30: 9 delight in you and make you **p**, 3202
Jos 1: 8 Then you *will be* **p** and successful. 7503
Jdg 18: 7 their land lacked nothing, *they were* **p**. 3769+6807
Job 8: 7 so **p** will your future be. 8436
42:10 the LORD **made** him **p again** 8654+8740
Ps 10: 5 His ways *are* always **p**; 2656
Da 4: 4 was at home in my palace, contented and **p**. 10670
Zec 7: 7 its surrounding towns were at rest and **p**, 8929

PROSPERS (6) [PROSPER]

Lev 25:26 to redeem it for him but *he* himself **p** 3338+5952
25:49 Or if he **p**, he may redeem himself. 3338+5952
Ps 1: 3 Whatever he does **p**. 7503
Pr 16:20 Whoever gives heed to instruction **p**, 3202+5162
19: 8 he who cherishes understanding **p**. 3202+5162
Jer 29: 7 Pray to the LORD for it, because if it **p**, 8934

PROSTITUTE (52) [PROSTITUTE'S, PROSTITUTED, PROSTITUTES, PROSTITUTING, PROSTITUTION]

Ge 34:31 "Should he have treated our sister like a **p**?" 2390
38:15 Judah saw her, he thought she *was a* **p**, 2390
38:21 "Where is the **shrine p** who was beside 7728
38:21 "There hasn't been any **shrine p** here." 7728
38:22 'There hasn't been any **shrine p** here.' " 7728
Ex 34:15 for when *they* **p** *themselves* to their gods 2388
34:16 and those daughters **p** *themselves* 2388
Lev 17: 7 the goat idols to whom they **p** *themselves*. 2388
19:29 degrade your daughter by **making** her **a p**, 2388
20: 6 to mediums and spiritists to **p** *himself* 2388
21: 9 by *becoming a* **p**, she disgraces her father; 2388
Nu 15:39 not **p** yourselves by going after the lusts 2388
Dt 23:17 or woman is to become a **shrine p**. 7728
23:18 not bring the earnings of a *female* **p** or of 2390
23:18 of a female prostitute or of a **male p** into 3978
31:16 and these people *will* soon **p** *themselves* 2388
Jos 2: 1 and entered the house of a **p** named Rahab 2390
6:17 Only Rahab the **p** and all who are with her 2390
6:25 But Joshua spared Rahab the **p**, 2390
Jdg 11: 1 His father was Gilead; his mother was a **p**. 2390
16: 1 Samson went to Gaza, where he saw a **p**. 2390
2Ch 21:11 **caused** the people of Jerusalem **to p themselves** 2388
21:13 **led** Judah and the people of Jerusalem **to p themselves,** 2388
Pr 6:26 for the **p** reduces you to a loaf of bread, 2390
7:10 dressed like a **p** and with crafty intent. 2390
23:27 for a **p** is a deep pit and a wayward wife is 2390
Isa 23:15 to Tyre as in the song of the **p**: 2390
23:16 walk through the city, O **p** forgotten; 2390
23:17 to her **hire as a p** and will ply her trade 924
Jer 2:20 every spreading tree you lay down as a **p**. 2390
3: 1 you have lived *as a* **p** with many lovers— 2388
3: 3 Yet you have the brazen look of a **p**; 2390
Eze 16:15 and used your fame *to become a* **p**. 2388
16:30 acting like a brazen **p**! 2390
16:31 you were unlike a **p**, 2390
16:33 Every **p** receives a fee, 2390
16:35 you **p**, hear the word of the LORD! 2390
23: 7 She gave herself as a **p** to all the elite of 9373
23:19 when *she was a* **p** in Egypt. 2388
23:43 **use** her **as a p**, for that is all she is.' 2388+9373
23:44 As men sleep with a **p**, 2390
Hos 3: 3 not *be a* **p** or be intimate with any man, 2388
9: 1 the **wages of a p** at every threshing floor. 924
Am 7:17 " 'Your wife *will become a* **p** in the city, 2388
1Co 6:15 members of Christ and unite them *with* a **p**? *4520*
6:16 that he who unites himself *with* a **p** is one *4520*
Heb 11:31 By faith the **p** Rahab, because she *4520*
Jas 2:25 the **p** considered righteous for what she did *4520*
Rev 17: 1 the punishment *of* the great **p**, *4520*
17:15 where the **p** sits, are peoples, multitudes, *4520*
17:16 and the ten horns you saw will hate the **p**. *4520*
19: 2 the great **p** who corrupted the earth *4520*

PROSTITUTE'S (1) [PROSTITUTE]

Jos 6:22 "Go into the **p** house and bring her out 2390

PROSTITUTED (5) [PROSTITUTE]

Jdg 2:17 not listen to their judges but **p** *themselves* 2388
8:27 All Israel **p** *themselves* by worshiping it 2388
8:33 the Israelites again **p** *themselves* to 2388
1Ch 5:25 the God of their fathers and **p** *themselves* 2388
Ps 106:39 by their deeds *they* **p** *themselves.* 2388

PROSTITUTES (20) [PROSTITUTE]

1Ki 3:16 Now two **p** came to the king and stood 2390
14:24 There were even *male* **shrine p** in the land; 7728
15:12 He expelled the *male* **shrine p** from the land 7728
22:38 at a pool in Samaria (where the **p** bathed), 2390
22:46 the *male* **shrine p** who remained there even 7728
2Ki 23:7 down the quarters of the *male* **shrine p,** 7728
Job 36:14 among *male* **p of the shrines.** 7728
Pr 29:3 but a companion of **p** squanders his wealth. 2390
Isa 57:3 you offspring of adulterers and **p!** 2388
Jer 5:7 and thronged to the houses of **p.** 2390
Eze 23:3 *They became* **p** in Egypt, 2388
Hos 4:14 with harlots and sacrifice with **shrine p—** 7728
Joel 3:3 for my people and traded boys for **p;** 2390
Mic 1:7 she gathered her gifts from the wages of **p,** 2390
1:7 as the wages of **p** they will again be used." 2390
Mt 21:31 and the **p** are entering the kingdom of God *4520*
21:32 but the tax collectors and the **p** did. *4520*
Lk 15:30 who has squandered your property with **p** *4520*
1Co 6:9 nor idolaters nor adulterers nor **male p** *3434*
Rev 17:5 BABYLON THE GREAT THE MOTHER OF P *4520*

PROSTITUTING (1) [PROSTITUTE]

Lev 20:5 and all who follow him in **p** *themselves* 2388

PROSTITUTION (35) [PROSTITUTE]

Ge 38:24 "Your daughter-in-law Tamar *is* **guilty of p,** 2388
Lev 19:29 or the land *will* **turn to p** and be filled 2388
21:7 not marry women defiled by **p** or divorced 2390
21:14 or a woman defiled by **p,** 2390
Jer 3:2 You have defiled the land with your **p** 2394
13:27 and lustful neighings, your shameless **p!** 2394
Eze 16:16 where *you* **carried on** *your* **p.** 2388
16:17 for yourself male idols and **engaged in p** 2388
16:20 Was your **p** not enough? 9373
16:22 and your **p** you did not remember the days 9373
16:26 You **engaged in p** with the Egyptians, 2388
16:28 *You* **engaged in p** with the Assyrians too, 2388
16:34 So in your **p** you are the opposite of others; 9373
16:41 I will put a stop to your **p,** 2388
23:3 **engaging in p** from their youth. 2388
23:5 "Oholah **engaged in p** while she was still 2388
23:8 not give up the **p** she began in Egypt, 9373
23:11 **p** she was more depraved than her sister. 9373
23:14 "But she carried her **p** still further. 9373
23:18 When she carried on her **p** openly 9373
23:27 to the lewdness and **p** you began in Egypt. 2394
23:29 and the shame of your **p** will be exposed. 2393
23:35 the consequences of your lewdness and **p."** 9373
43:7 by their **p** and the lifeless idols 2394
43:9 Now let them put away from me their **p** and 2394
Hos 4:10 *they will* **engage in p** but not increase, 2388
4:11 to **p,** to old wine and new, which take away 2394
4:12 A spirit of **p** leads them astray; 2393
4:13 Therefore your daughters **turn to p** 2388
4:14 when *they* **turn to p,** 2388
4:18 *they* **continue** *their* **p;** 2388+2388
5:3 Ephraim, *you have* now **turned to p;** 2388
5:4 A spirit of **p** is in their heart; 2393
6:10 There Ephraim is given to **p** 2394
Na 3:4 who enslaved nations by her **p** and peoples 2393

PROSTRATE (11) [PROSTRATED]

Nu 24:4 *who* **falls p,** and whose eyes are opened: 5877
24:16 *who* **falls p,** and whose eyes are opened: 5877
Dt 9:18 Then once again *I* **fell p** before the LORD 5877
9:25 *I* **lay p** before the LORD those forty days 5877
2Sa 19:18 *he* **fell p** before the king 5877
1Ki 18:39 they fell **p** and cried, "The LORD— 6584+7156
1Ch 29:20 they bowed low and **fell p** before the LORD 2556
Isa 15:3 and in the public squares they all wail, **p** 3718
51:23 **'Fall p** that we may walk over you.' 8817
Da 2:46 Then King Nebuchadnezzar fell **p** 10049+10542
8:17 I was terrified and fell **p.** 6584+7156

PROSTRATED (2) [PROSTRATE]

1Sa 24:8 and **p himself** with his face to the ground. 2556
28:14 and **p himself** with his face to the ground. 2556

PROTECT (28) [PROTECTED, PROTECTION, PROTECTIVE, PROTECTS]

Nu 35:25 The assembly *must* **p** the one accused 5911
Dt 23:14 to **p** you and to deliver your enemies 5911
2Sa 18:12 **'P** the young man Absalom for my sake.' 9068
Ezr 8:22 the king for soldiers and horsemen to **p** us 6468
Est 8:11 the right to assemble and **p** themselves; 6584+6641
9:16 also assembled *to* **p** themselves 6584+6641
Ps 12:5 *"I will* **p** them from those who 928+3829+8883
12:7 and **p** us from such people forever. 5915
20:1 *may* the name of the God of Jacob **p** you. 8435
25:21 *May* integrity and uprightness **p** me, 5915
32:7 *you will* **p** me from trouble 5915
40:11 *may* your love and your truth always **p** me. 5915
41:2 LORD *will* **p** him and preserve his life; 9068
59:1 **p** me from those who rise up against me. 8435
Ps 61:7 and faithfulness *to* **p** him. 5915
64:1 **p** my life from the threat of the enemy. 5915
69:29 *may* your salvation, O God, **p** me. 8435
91:14 *I will* **p** him, for he acknowledges my name. 8435
140:1 **p** me from men of violence, 5915
140:4 **p** me from men of violence who plan 5915
Pr 2:11 Discretion *will* **p** you, 9068
4:6 and *she will* **p** you; 9068
14:3 but the lips of the wise **p** them. 9068
Jer 49:11 Leave your orphans; I *will* **p** their **lives.** 2649
Da 11:1 I took my stand to support and **p** him.) 5057
Jn 17:11 **p** them by the power of your name— *5498*
17:15 but that *you* **p** them from the evil one. *5498*
2Th 3:3 and he *will* strengthen and **p** you from *5875*

PROTECTED (8) [PROTECT]

Jos 24:17 *He* **p** us on our entire journey and among all 9068
1Sa 30:23 *He has* **p** us and handed over to us 9068
Ezr 8:31 and *he* **p** us from enemies and bandits along 5911
Job 5:21 *You will* **be p** from the lash of the tongue, 2461
Ps 37:28 *They will* **be p** forever, 9068
Mk 6:20 because Herod feared John and **p** him, *5337*
Jn 17:12 I **p** them and kept them safe by that name *5498*
2Pe 2:5 but **p** Noah, a preacher of righteousness, *5875*

PROTECTION (9) [PROTECT]

Ge 19:8 they have come under the **p** *of* my roof." 7498
Nu 14:9 Their **p** is gone, but the LORD is with us. 7498
32:17 for **p from** the inhabitants of the land. 4946+7156
Jos 20:3 and find **p** from the avenger of blood. 5236
Ezr 9:9 and he has given us a **wall of p** in Judah 1555
Ps 5:11 **Spread** *your* **p** over them, 6114
Isa 30:2 who look for help to Pharaoh's **p,** 5057
30:3 But Pharaoh's **p** will be to your shame, 5057
Mic 1:11 its **p** is taken from you. 6644

PROTECTIVE (1) [PROTECT]

Na 2:5 the **p shield** is put in place. 6116

PROTECTS (5) [PROTECT]

Ps 34:20 *he* **p** all his bones, 9068
116:6 The LORD **p** the simplehearted; 9068
Pr 2:8 the just and **p** the way of his faithful ones. 9068
Da 12:1 the great prince who **p** your people, 6584+6641
1Co 13:7 *It* always **p,** always trusts, always hopes, *5095*

PROTEST (3) [PROTESTED]

Ecc 5:6 And *do* not **p** to the [temple] messenger, 606
Ac 13:51 So they shook the dust from their feet in **p** *NIG*
18:6 he shook out his clothes in **p** and said *NIG*

PROTESTED (2) [PROTEST]

Jn 8:41 "We are not illegitimate children," *they* **p.** *3306*
19:21 The chief priests of the Jews **p** to Pilate, *3306*

PROUD (44) [PRIDE, PROUDLY]

Dt 8:14 then your heart *will become* **p** 8123
2Ch 25:19 and now you are arrogant and **p.** 3877
32:25 But Hezekiah's heart *was* **p** and he did 1467
Job 28:8 **P beasts** do not set foot on it, 1201+8832
38:11 here is where your **p** waves halt'? 1454
39:20 striking terror with his **p** snorting? 2086
40:11 look at every **p** *man* and bring him low, 1450
40:12 look at every **p** *man* and humble him, 1450
41:34 he is king over all that are **p."** 1201+8832
Ps 31:23 but the **p** he pays back in full. 1452+6913
36:11 May the foot of the **p** not come against me, 1452
40:4 who does not look to the **p,** 8107
94:2 pay back to the **p** what they deserve. 1450
101:5 whoever has haughty eyes and a **p** heart, 8146
123:4 We have endured much ridicule from the **p,** 8633
131:1 My heart *is* not **p,** O LORD, 1467
138:6 but the **p** he knows from afar. 1469
140:5 **P** *men* have hidden a snare for me; 1450
140:8 or *they will become* **p.** 8123
Pr 3:34 He mocks **p mockers** but gives grace to 4370
15:25 The LORD tears down the **p** *man's* house 1450
16:5 The LORD detests all the **p** *of* **heart.** 1468
16:19 to share plunder with the **p.** 1450
18:12 Before his downfall a man's heart *is* **p,** 1467
21:4 Haughty eyes and a **p** heart, 8146
21:24 The **p** and arrogant man— 2294
Isa 2:12 a day in store for all the **p** and lofty, 1450
Eze 7:20 They were **p** of their beautiful jewelry 1454
28:5 of your wealth your heart *has grown* **p.** 1467
28:17 Your heart *became* **p** on account 1467
30:6 and her **p** strength will fail. 1454
30:18 there her **p** strength will come to an end. 1454
31:10 and because *it was* **p** of its height, 4222+8123
33:28 and her **p** strength will come to an end, 1454
Hos 13:6 they were satisfied, they *became* **p;** 4213+8123
Zec 10:3 and make them like a **p** horse in battle. 2086
Lk 1:51 he has scattered *those who are* **p** *5662*
Ro 12:16 *Do* not **be p,** but be willing to *3836+5734+5858*
1Co 5:2 And you are **p!** *5881*
13:4 it does not boast, *it is* not **p.** *5881*
2Ti 3:2 **p,** abusive, disobedient to their parents, *5662*
Jas 4:6 "God opposes the **p** but gives grace to *5662*
1Pe 5:5 "God opposes the **p** but gives grace to *5662*
Rev 13:5 a mouth to utter **p** words and blasphemies *3489*

PROUDLY (3) [PROUD]

1Sa 2:3 "Do not keep talking **so p** 1469+1469
Eze 31:14 by the waters *are ever to* **tower p** on high, 1467
Mic 2:3 You will no longer walk **p,** 8127

PROVE (18) [PROOF, PROOFS, PROVED, PROVES, PROVING]

Ge 44:16 How *can we* **p** *our* **innocence?** 7405
Job 6:25 But what *do* your arguments **p?** 3519
24:25 who *can* **p** me **false** and reduce my words 3941
Pr 29:25 Fear of man *will* **p to be** a snare, 5989
30:6 or he will rebuke you and **p** *you* **a liar.** 3941
Isa 43:9 in their witnesses *to* **p** *they were* **right,** 7405
Jer 17:11 and in the end *he will* **p to be** a fool. 2118
Mic 1:14 The town of Aczib will **p** deceptive to NIH
Hab 2:3 it speaks of the end and *will* not **p false.** 3941
Jn 2:18 "What miraculous sign *can you* **show** us to **p** your authority *1259*
8:46 *Can* any of you **p** me **guilty** of sin? *1794*
Ac 24:13 And they cannot **p** to you the charges *4225*
25:7 charges against him, which they could not **p.** *617*
26:20 and turn to God and **p** their repentance *NIG*
1Co 4:2 who has been given a trust *must* **p** faithful. *2351*
2Co 9:3 in this matter *should* not **p hollow,** *3033*
Gal 2:18 *I* **p that** I am a lawbreaker. *5319*
Heb 9:16 *to* **p** the death of the one who made it, *5770*

PROVED (18) [PROVE]

Dt 13:14 And if it is true and *it has* **been p** 3922
17:4 If it is true and *it has* **been p** 3922
1Ki 16:22 But Omri's followers **p stronger** *than* those 2616
Job 6:21 Now *you* too *have* **p to be** of no help; 2118
32:12 But not *one* of you *has* **p** Job **wrong;** 3519
Ps 51:4 so that *you are* **p right** when you speak 7405
105:19 till the word of the LORD **p** him **true.** 7671
Ecc 2:1 But that also **p** to be meaningless. NIH
Mt 11:19 But wisdom *is* **p right** by her actions." *1467*
Lk 7:35 But wisdom *is* **p right** by all her children." *1467*
Ro 3:4 that *you may be* **p right** when you speak *1467*
2Co 7:11 At every point *you have* **p** yourselves to *5319*
7:14 about you to Titus *has* **p to be** true as well. *1181*
8:22 with them our brother who *has* often **p** *1507*
9:13 by which you have **p** yourselves, *1509*
Php 2:22 But you know that Timothy has **p** himself, *1509*
Col 4:11 and *they have* **p** a comfort to me. *1181*
1Pe 1:7 may be **p genuine** and may result in praise, *1510*

PROVENDER (KJV) See FODDER

PROVERB (9) [PROVERBS]

Ps 49:4 I will turn my ear to a **p;** 5442
Pr 26:7 that hang limp is a **p** in the mouth of a fool. 5442
26:9 in a drunkard's hand is a **p** in the mouth of 5442
Eze 12:22 what is this **p** you have in the land of Israel: 5442
12:23 I am going to put an end to this **p,** 5442
16:44 " 'Everyone who quotes proverbs *will* **quote** *this* **p** 5439
18:2 by quoting this **p** about the land of Israel: 5442
18:3 you will no longer quote this **p** in Israel. 5442
Lk 4:23 "Surely you will quote this **p** to me: *4130*

PROVERBS (9) [PROVERB]

1Ki 4:32 He spoke three thousand **p** 5442
Job 13:12 Your maxims are **p** *of* ashes; 5442
Pr 1:1 **p** *of* Solomon son of David, king of Israel: 5442
1:6 for understanding **p** and parables, 5442
10:1 The **p** *of* Solomon: 5442
25:1 These are more **p** *of* Solomon, 5442
Ecc 12:9 and searched out and set in order many **p.** 5442
Eze 16:44 " 'Everyone who **quotes p** will quote this 5439
2Pe 2:22 Of them the **p** are true: *4231*

PROVES (1) [PROVE]

Dt 19:18 and if the witness **p** to be a liar, NIH

PROVIDE (53) [PROVIDED, PROVIDES, PROVIDING, PROVISION, PROVISIONS]

Ge 22:8 "God himself *will* **p** the lamb for 8011
22:14 called that place The LORD *Will* **P.** 8011
45:11 *I will* **p** *for* you there, 3920
49:16 "Dan *will* **p justice** *for* his people as one 1906
49:20 he *will* **p** delicacies fit for a king. 5989
50:21 I *will* **p** *for* you and your children." 3920
Ex 21:11 If *he does* not **p** her *with* these three things, 6913
27:16 **p** a curtain twenty cubits long, of blue, NIH
Lev 25:24 *you must* **p** *for* the redemption of the land. 5989
Dt 6:11 with all kinds of good things *you did* not **p,** 4848
11:15 *I will* **p** grass in the fields for your cattle, 5989
Jdg 21:7 *can we* **p** wives for those who are left, 6913
21:16 *shall we* **p** wives for the men who are left? 6913
2Sa 7:10 And *I will* **p** a place for my people Israel 8492
19:33 in Jerusalem, and *I will* **p** *for* you." 3920
1Ki 4:7 Each one had to **p supplies** *for* one month 3920
5:17 to **p a foundation** *of* dressed stone *for* 3569
1Ch 17:9 And *I will* **p** a place for my people Israel 8492
22:14 *to* **p** for the temple of the LORD 3922
2Ch 2:9 to **p** me *with* plenty of lumber, 3922
Ezr 1:4 be living *are to* **p** him with silver and gold, 5951
7:20 *you may* **p** from the royal treasury. 10498
7:21 the treasurers of Trans-Euphrates *to* **p** 10522
Ne 2:7 so that *they will* **p** me **safe-conduct** 6296

Ps 65: 9 filled with water *to* p the people with grain, 3922
Pr 27:26 the lambs will p you **with** clothing, 4200
Isa 4: 1 and p our own clothes; 4252
43:20 because *I* p water in the desert and streams 5989
50:11 all you who light fires and p *yourselves* 273
58: 7 and *to* p the poor wanderer *with* shelter— 995
61: 3 and p for those who grieve in Zion— 8492
Jer 33: 9 at the abundant prosperity and peace I p 6913
Eze 34:29 *I will* p for them a land renowned 7756
43:25 *to* p a male goat daily *for* a sin offering; 6913
43:25 *to* p a young bull and a ram from the flock, 6913
45:17 *to* p the burnt offerings, grain offerings NIH
45:17 He *will* p the sin offerings, 6913
45:22 *to* p a bull as a sin offering for himself and 6913
45:23 of the Feast *he is to* p seven bulls 6913
45:24 *He is to* p as a grain offering an ephah 6913
46: 7 *He is to* p as a grain offering one ephah 6913
46:13 " 'Every day *you are to* p a year-old lamb 6913
46:13 morning by morning *you shall* p it. 6913
46:14 also *to* p with it morning by morning 6913
Lk 12:33 **P** purses for yourselves that will *4472*
Ac 7:46 that *he might* p a dwelling place for the God *2351*
11:29 *to* p help for the brothers living in Judea. *4287*
23:24 **P** mounts for Paul so that he may *4225*
27: 3 to his friends *so* they *might* p for his needs. *5593*
1Co 10:13 also p a way out so that you can stand up *4472*
Col 4: 1 p your slaves **with** what is right and fair, *4218*
1Ti 5: 8 **p for** his relatives, and especially for *4629*
Tit 3:14 that they may p for daily necessities and *NIG*

PROVIDED (40) [PROVIDE]

Ge 22:14 the mountain of the LORD *it will* **be p."** 8011
43:24 and p fodder for their donkeys. 5989
47:12 Joseph also p his father and his brothers 3920
Ru 3: 1 where you *will be* **well p for?** 3512
1Sa 21: 4 p the men have kept themselves from 421+561
2Sa 9:10 your master's grandson *may be* **p for.** 430+2118+2256+4200+4312
15: 1 Absalom p himself with a chariot 6913
19:32 He *had* p *for* the king during his stay 3920
20: 3 *He* p *for* them, but did not lie with them. 3920
1Ki 8:21 *I have* p a place there for the ark, 8492
11:18 a house and land and p him *with* food. 606
2Ki 13: 5 The LORD p a deliverer for Israel, 5989
1Ch 22: 3 He p a large amount of iron to make nails 3922
22: 4 He also p more cedar logs than could NIH
23: 5 with the musical instruments *I have* p for 6913
29: 2 With all my resources *I have* p for 3922
29: 3 over and above everything *I have* p 3922
29:16 that *we have* p for building you a temple 3922
29:19 the palatial structure for which *I have* **p."** 3922
2Ch 2: 7 craftsmen, whom my father David **p.** 3922
3: 1 the place p *by* David. 3922
26:14 Uzziah p shields, spears, helmets, 3922
28:15 *They* p them **with clothes** and sandals, 4252
30:24 Hezekiah king of Judah p a thousand bulls 8123
30:24 the officials p them *with* a thousand bulls 8123
35: 7 Josiah p for all the lay people 8123
35: 9 p five thousand Passover offerings 8123
Ne 13: 5 and *he had* p him *with* a large room 6913
Est 2: 9 he p her with her beauty treatments and 5989
Ps 68:10 O God, *you* p for the poor. 3922
111: 9 *He* p redemption for his people; 8938
Eze 16:19 Also the food *I* p for you— 5989
46:15 and the oil *shall be* p morning by morning 6913
Jnh 1:17 the LORD p a great fish to swallow Jonah, 4948
4: 6 the LORD God p a vine and made it grow 4948
4: 7 But at dawn the next day God p a worm, 4948
4: 8 God p a scorching east wind, 4948
Ro 11:22 **p that** you continue in his kindness. *1569*
Gal 4:18 **p** the purpose is good, *NIG*
Heb 1: 3 *After he had* p purification for sins, *4472*

PROVIDENCE (1)

Job 10:12 and in your p watched over my spirit. 7213

PROVIDES (12) [PROVIDE]

Job 24: 5 the wasteland p food **for** their children. 4200
36:31 the way he governs the nations and p food 5989
38:41 Who p food for the raven 3922
Ps 111: 5 *He* p food for those who fear him; 5989
147: 9 *He* p food for the cattle and for 5989
Pr 31:15 *she* p food for her family and portions 5989
Eze 18: 7 to the hungry and p clothing *for* the naked. 4059
18:16 to the hungry and p clothing *for* the naked. 4059
46:12 When the prince p a freewill offering to 6913
Ac 14:17 *he* p you **with plenty** of food *1855*
1Ti 6:17 who richly p us **with** everything *4218*
1Pe 4:11 he should do it with the strength God **p,** *5961*

PROVIDING (5) [PROVIDE]

Ru 1: 6 to the aid of his people by p food for them, 5989
1Ki 5: 8 and will do all you want in p the cedar NIH
5: 9 And you are to grant my wish by p food 5989
Ne 13: 7 *in* p Tobiah a room in the courts of 6913
Da 4:21 p food for all, giving shelter to the beasts of NIH

PROVINCE (41) [PROVINCES, PROVINCIAL]

Ezr 2: 1 of the p who came up from the captivity of 4519
6: 2 in the citadel of Ecbatana in the p of Media, 10406
6: 6 fellow officials of **that p,** 10191+10468+10526S
7:16 and gold you may obtain from the p 10406
Ne 1: 3 in the p are in great trouble and disgrace. 4519
7: 6 of the p who came up from the captivity of 4519
Est 1:22 to **each** p in its own script and 2256+4519+4519
2: 3 the king appoint commissioners in every p 4519
3:12 They wrote out in the script of **each p** and in the language 2256+4519+4519
3:14 the edict was to be issued as law in every **p** 4519
4: 3 In every p to which the edict and order of 4519
8: 9 written in the script of **each p** 2256+4519+4519
8:11 any nationality or p that might attack them 4519
8:13 the edict was to be issued as law in every **p** 4519
8:17 In every **p** and in every city, 4519
9:28 in **every p** and in every city. 2256+4519+4519
Da 2:48 the entire p *of* Babylon and placed him 10406
2:49 and Abednego administrators over the p 10406
3: 1 on the plain of Dura in the p *of* Babylon. 10406
3:12 over the affairs of the p *of* Babylon— 10406
3:30 and Abednego in the p *of* Babylon. 10406
8: 2 in the citadel of Susa in the p *of* Elam; 4519
Ac 16: 6 from preaching the word in the **p of Asia.** *823*
19:10 in the **p of Asia** heard the word of the Lord. *823*
19:22 he stayed in the **p of Asia** a little longer. *823*
19:26 and *in* practically the whole **p of Asia.** *823*
19:27 who is worshiped throughout the **p of Asia** *823*
19:31 Even some *of* the **officials of the p,** *825*
20: 4 Trophimus **from the p of Asia.** *824*
20:16 to avoid spending time in the **p of Asia,** *823*
20:18 from the first day I came into the **p of Asia.** *823*
21:27 from the **p of Asia** saw Paul at the temple. *823*
23:34 the letter and asked what **p** he was from. *2065*
24:19 there are some Jews from the **p of Asia,** *823*
25: 1 Three days after arriving in the **p,** *2065*
27: 2 for ports along the coast of the **p of Asia,** *823*
Ro 16: 5 the first convert to Christ *in* the **p of Asia.** *823*
1Co 16:19 *in* the **p of Asia** send you greetings. *823*
2Co 1: 8 the hardships we suffered in the **p of Asia.** *823*
2Ti 1:15 in the **p of Asia** has deserted me, *823*
Rev 1: 4 To the seven churches in the **p of Asia:** *823*

PROVINCES (23) [PROVINCE]

Ezr 4:15 troublesome to kings and **p,** 10406
Est 1: 1 the Xerxes who ruled over 127 p stretching 4519
1: 3 and the nobles of the p were present. 4519
1:16 the peoples of all the p *of* King Xerxes. 4519
2:18 He proclaimed a holiday throughout the p 4519
3: 8 and scattered among the peoples in all the p 4519
3:12 the governors of the **various p** 2256+4519+4519
3:13 to all the king's p with the order to destroy, 4519
4:11 and the people of the royal p know that 4519
8: 5 to destroy the Jews in all the king's **p.** 4519
8: 9 of the 127 p stretching from India to Cush. 4519
8:12 to do this in all the p *of* King Xerxes was 4519
9: 2 in their cities in all the p *of* King Xerxes 4519
9: 3 And all the nobles of the p, the satraps, 4519
9: 4 his reputation spread throughout the **p,** 4519
9:12 in the rest of the king's **p?** 4519
9:16 of the Jews who were in the king's p 4519
9:20 the Jews throughout the p *of* King Xerxes, 4519
9:30 to all the Jews in the 127 p of the kingdom 4519
Ecc 2: 8 and the treasure of kings and **p.** 4519
La 1: 1 among the p has now become a slave. 4519
Da 11:24 When the richest p feel secure, 4519
Ac 6: 9 and Alexandria as well as the **p of Cilicia** *3070*

PROVINCIAL (7) [PROVINCE]

1Ki 20:14 of the p commanders will do it.' " 4519
20:15 the young officers of the p commanders, 4519
20:17 of the p commanders went out first. 4519
20:19 the p commanders marched out of the city 4519
Ne 11: 3 the p leaders who settled in Jerusalem 4519
Da 3: 2 magistrates and all the other p officials 10406
3: 3 and all the other p officials assembled for 10406

PROVING (3) [PROVE]

Ac 9:22 in Damascus *by* p that Jesus is the Christ. *5204*
17: 3 and p that the Christ had to suffer and rise *4192*
18:28 p from the Scriptures that Jesus was *2109*

PROVISION (4) [PROVIDE]

Ne 13:31 I also made p for contributions of wood NIH
Ps 144:13 be filled with every kind of **p.** 7049
Eze 45:25 *he is to* **make** the same p *for* sin offerings, 6913
Ro 5:17 those who receive God's **abundant p** *4353*

PROVISIONS (19) [PROVIDE]

Ge 42:25 and to give them p for their journey. 7476
45:21 and he also gave them p for their journey. 7476
45:23 and bread and *other* p for his journey. 4648
Jos 9:11 'Take p for your journey; 7476
9:14 of Israel sampled their p but did not inquire 7474
Jdg 7: 8 over the p and trumpets of the others. 7476
20:10 to get p for the army. 7476
1Sa 22:10 also gave him p and the sword of Goliath 7476
2Sa 19:42 **eaten** any of the king's **p?** 430+430
1Ki 4: 7 *who* **supplied** p *for* the king and 3920
4:22 Solomon's daily p were thirty cors 4312
4:27 **supplied** p *for* King Solomon 3920
20:27 Israelites were also mustered and **given p,** 3920
1Ch 12:39 for their families *had* **supplied** p for them. 3922
2Ch 11:23 He gave them abundant p 4648
Ps 132:15 I will bless her with abundant **p;** 7474
Pr 6: 8 yet it stores its p in summer 4312
Jer 40: 5 the commander gave him p and a present 786
Da 11:26 from the king's p will try to destroy him; 7329

PROVOCATION (1) [PROVOKE]

Pr 27: 3 but p *by* a fool is heavier than both. 4088

PROVOKE (14) [PROVOCATION, PROVOKED, PROVOKES, PROVOKING]

Dt 2: 5 *Do* not p them **to war,** 1741
2: 9 not harass the Moabites or p them *to* war, 1741
2:19 do not harass them or p them **to war,** 1741
31:29 the sight of the LORD and p him **to anger** 4087
1Ki 16: 2 to sin and to p me **to anger** by their sins. 4087
16:33 p the LORD, the God of Israel, **to anger** 4087
2Ki 23:26 Manasseh *had done to* p him **to anger** 4087+4088
Job 12: 6 and *those who* p God are secure— 8074
Isa 65: 3 a people who continually p me to my 4087
Jer 7:18 to other gods to p me **to anger.** 4087
25: 6 *do* not p me **to anger** with what your hands 4087
32:30 but p me with what their hands have made, 4087
44: 8 Why p me **to anger** with what your hands 4087
Eze 8:17 and continually p me **to anger?** 4087

PROVOKED (27) [PROVOKE]

Dt 9: 7 how *you* p the LORD your God **to anger** 7911
Jdg 2:12 *They* p the LORD **to anger** 4087
1Sa 1: 7 her rival p her till she wept and would 4087
1Ki 14: 9 you *have* p me **to anger** and thrust me 4087
14:15 because *they* p the LORD **to anger** 4087
15:30 *he* p the LORD, the God of Israel, **to anger.** 4087+4088
16:13 *they* p the LORD, the God of Israel, **to anger** 4087
16:26 *they* p the LORD, the God of Israel, **to anger** 4087
21:22 because *you have* p me **to anger** 4087+4088
22:53 and p the LORD, the God of Israel, **to anger,** 4087
2Ki 17:11 that p the LORD **to anger.** 4087
21:15 in my eyes and have p me **to anger** from 4087
22:17 to other gods and p me **to anger** by all 4087
23:19 that *had* p the LORD **to anger.** 4087
2Ch 28:25 p the LORD, the God of his fathers, **to anger.** 4087
34:25 to other gods and p me **to anger** by all 4087
Ps 106:29 *they* p the LORD **to anger** 4087
Ecc 7: 9 *Do* not *be* quickly p in your spirit, 4087
Jer 8:19 "Why *have they* p me **to anger** 4087
11:17 of Judah have done evil and p me **to anger** 4087
25: 7 "and *you have* p me with what your hands 4087
32:29 the houses where *the people* p me **to anger** 4087
32:32 The people of Israel and Judah *have* p me 4087
44: 3 They p me **to anger** by burning incense 4087
Eze 16:26 and p me **to anger** with your 4087
20:28 made offerings that p me **to anger,** 4088
Hos 12:14 But Ephraim *has* bitterly p him **to anger;** 4087

PROVOKES (1) [PROVOKE]

Eze 8: 3 where the idol that p **to jealousy** stood. 7861

PROVOKING (9) [PROVOKE]

Dt 4:25 the LORD your God and p him **to anger,** 4087
9:18 the LORD's sight and so p him **to anger.** 4087
1Sa 1: 6 her rival **kept** p her in order to irritate her. 1685+4087+4088
1Ki 16: 7 p him **to anger** by the things he did, 4087
2Ki 17:17 evil in the eyes of the LORD, **p him to anger** 4087
21: 6 evil in the eyes of the LORD, **p him to anger** 4087
2Ch 33: 6 evil in the eyes of the LORD, **p him to anger** 4087
Jer 7:19 But am I the one they *are* **p?** 4087
Gal 5:26 conceited, p and envying each other. *4614*

PROWL (4) [PROWLED, PROWLING, PROWLS]

Ps 55:10 Day and night *they* p **about** on its walls; 6015
59: 6 snarling like dogs, and p **about** the city. 6015
59:14 snarling like dogs, and p **about** the city. 6015
104:20 and all the beasts of the forest **p.** 8253

PROWLED (1) [PROWL]

Eze 19: 6 *He* p among the lions, 2143

PROWLING (1) [PROWL]

La 5:18 which lies desolate, with jackals p over it. 2143

PROWLS (2) [PROWL]

Job 28: 8 and no lion p there. 6334
1Pe 5: 8 Your enemy the devil p **around** like *4344*

PRUDENCE (5) [PRUDENT]

Pr 1: 4 for giving p to the simple, knowledge 6893
8: 5 You who are simple, gain **p;** 6893
8:12 "I, wisdom, dwell together with **p;** 6893
15: 5 but whoever heeds correction **shows p.** 6891
19:25 and the simple *will* **learn p;** 6891

PRUDENT (12) [PRUDENCE]

Pr 1: 3 and p *life,* doing what is right and just 8505
12:16 but a p *man* overlooks an insult. 6874
12:23 A p man keeps his knowledge to himself, 6874
13:16 Every p *man* acts out of knowledge, 6874
14: 8 of the p is to give thought to their ways, 6874
14:15 but a p *man* gives thought to his steps. 6874
14:18 but the p are crowned with knowledge. 6874
19:14 but a p wife is from the LORD. 8505

Pr 22: 3 A **p** *man* sees danger and takes refuge, 6874
27:12 The **p** see danger and take refuge, 6874
Jer 49: 7 Has counsel perished from the **p**? 1067
Am 5:13 the **p** *man* keeps quiet in such times, 8505

PRUNE (2) [PRUNED, PRUNES, PRUNING]
Lev 25: 3 and for six years **p** your vineyards 2377
25: 4 Do not sow your fields or **p** your vineyards. 2377

PRUNED (1) [PRUNE]
Isa 5: 6 a wasteland, neither **p** nor cultivated, 2377

PRUNES (1) [PRUNE]
Jn 15: 2 while every branch that does bear fruit *he* **p** *2748*

PRUNING (4) [PRUNE]
Isa 2: 4 and their spears into **p hooks.** 4661
18: 5 he will cut off the shoots with **p knives,** 4661
Joel 3:10 into swords and your **p hooks** into spears. 4661
Mic 4: 3 and their spears into **p hooks.** 4661

PRUNINGHOOKS (KJV) See PRUNING HOOKS

PSALM (61) [PSALMS]
1Ch 16: 7 *this* **p of thanks** to the LORD: 3344
Ps 3: T A **p** of David. When he fled from his son 4660
4: T With stringed instruments. A **p** of David. 4660
5: T For flutes. A **p** of David. 4660
6: T According to sheminith. A **p** of David. 4660
8: T According to gittith. A **p** of David. 4660
9: T "The Death of the Son." A **p** of David. 4660
12: T According to sheminith. A **p** of David. 4660
13: T For the director of music. A **p** of David. 4660
15: T A **p** of David. 4660
19: T For the director of music. A **p** of David. 4660
20: T For the director of music. A **p** of David. 4660
21: T For the director of music. A **p** of David. 4660
22: T "The Doe of the Morning." A **p** of David. 4660
23: T A **p** of David. 4660
24: T Of David. A **p.** 4660
29: T A **p** of David. 4660
30: T A **p.** A song. For the dedication of the temple. Of David. 4660
31: T For the director of music. A **p** of David. 4660
38: T A **p** of David. A petition. 4660
39: T For Jeduthun. A **p** of David. 4660
40: T For the director of music. Of David. A **p.** 4660
41: T For the director of music. A **p** of David. 4660
47: T Of the Sons of Korah. A **p.** 4660
47: 7 sing to him a **p of praise.** 5380
48: T A song. A **p** of the Sons of Korah. 4660
49: T Of the Sons of Korah. A **p.** 4660
50: T A **p** of Asaph. 4660
51: T For the director of music. A **p** of David. 4660
62: T For Jeduthun. A **p** of David. 4660
63: T A **p** of David. When he was in the Desert 4660
64: T For the director of music. A **p** of David. 4660
65: T For the director of music. A **p** of David. 4660
66: T For the director of music. A song. A **p.** 4660
67: T With stringed instruments. A **p.** 4660
68: T Of David. A **p.** 4660
73: T A **p** of Asaph. 4660
75: T "Do Not Destroy." A **p** of Asaph. 4660
76: T With stringed instruments. A **p** of Asaph. 4660
77: T For Jeduthun. Of Asaph. A **p.** 4660
79: T A **p** of Asaph. 4660
80: T Lilies of the Covenant." Of Asaph. A **p.** 4660
82: T A **p** of Asaph. 4660
83: T A song. A **p** of Asaph. 4660
84: T Of the Sons of Korah. A **p.** 4660
85: T Of the Sons of Korah. A **p.** 4660
87: T Of the Sons of Korah. A **p.** A song. 4660
88: T A **p** of the Sons of Korah. 4660
92: T A **p.** A song. For the Sabbath day. 4660
98: T A **p.** 4660
100: T A **p.** For giving thanks. 4660
101: T Of David. A **p.** 4660
108: T A song. A **p** of David. 4660
109: T For the director of music. Of David. A **p.** 4660
110: T Of David. A **p.** 4660
139: T For the director of music. Of David. A **p.** 4660
140: T For the director of music. A **p** of David. 4660
141: T A **p** of David. 4660
143: T A **p** of David. 4660
145: T A **p of praise.** Of David. 9335
Ac 13:33 As it is written in the second **P:** *6011*

PSALMS (5) [PSALM]
Lk 20:42 David himself declares in the Book *of* **P:** *6011*
24:44 Law of Moses, the Prophets and the **P."** *6011*
Ac 1:20 said Peter, "it is written in the book *of* **P,** *6011*
Eph 5:19 Speak to one another with **p,** hymns and *6011*
Col 3:16 and as you sing **p,** hymns and spiritual *6011*

PTOLEMAIS (1)
Ac 21: 7 our voyage from Tyre and landed at **P,** *4767*

PUAH (5) [PUITE]
Ge 46:13 Tola, **P,** Jashub and Shimron. 7026
Ex 1:15 whose names were Shiphrah and **P,** 7045
Nu 26:23 through **P,** the Puite clan; 7025
Jdg 10: 1 Tola son of **P,** the son of Dodo, 7025
1Ch 7: 1 Tola, **P,** Jashub and Shimron—four in all. 7025

PUBLIC (23) [PUBLICLY]
Lev 5: 1 not speak up when he hears a **p charge** 460
Dt 13:16 of the town into the middle of the **p square** 8148
2Sa 21:12 from the **p square** *at* Beth Shan, 8148
Job 29: 7 of the city and took my seat in the **p square,** 8148
Pr 1:20 she raises her voice in the **p squares;** 8148
5:16 your streams of water in the **p squares?** 8148
Isa 15: 3 the roofs and in the **p squares** they all wail, 8148
Jer 9:21 and the young men from the **p squares.** 8148
48:38 in the **p squares** there is nothing but mourning, 8148
Eze 16:24 and made a lofty shrine in every **p square.** 8148
16:31 lofty shrines in every **p square,** 8148
Am 5:16 and cries of anguish in every **p square.** 8148
Mt 1:19 **expose** her **to p disgrace,** *1258*
Lk 20:26 to trap him in what he had said there **in p.** *1883+3295+3836*
Jn 7: 4 to become **a p figure** acts in secret. *1877+4244*
Ac 5:18 the apostles and put them in the **p** jail. *1323*
12: 4 Herod intended to bring him out *for* **p** trial *3295*
12:21 sat on his throne and **delivered a p address** *1319*
18:28 he vigorously refuted the Jews *in* **p** debate, *1323*
Ro 16:23 who is the city's **director of p works,** *3874*
Col 2:15 he made a **p** spectacle of them, *4244*
1Ti 4:13 devote yourself *to* the **p reading** *342*
Heb 6: 6 **subjecting** him **to p disgrace.** *4136*

PUBLICAN (KJV) See PAGANS, TAX COLLECTOR

PUBLICK (KJV) See PUBLIC

PUBLICLY (11) [PUBLIC]
Lk 1:80 in the desert until he **appeared p** to Israel. *345*
Jn 7:10 he went also, not **p,** but in secret. *5747*
7:13 But no one would say anything **p** about him *4244*
7:26 Here he is, speaking **p,** *4244*
11:54 Therefore Jesus no longer moved about **p** *4244*
Ac 16:37 "They beat us **p** without a trial, *1323*
19: 9 they refused to believe and **p** maligned the Way. *1967+3836+4436*
19:19 scrolls together and burned them **p.** *1967+4246*
20:20 have taught you **p** and from house to house. *1323*
1Ti 5:20 Those who sin are to be rebuked **p,** *1967+4246*
Heb 10:33 Sometimes *you were* **p exposed** to insult *2518*

PUBLISH (1) [PUBLISHED]
Da 6:12 *"Did you* not **p** a decree that during 10673

PUBLISHED (2) [PUBLISH]
Est 4: 8 which *had* **been p** in Susa, 5989
Da 6:10 Daniel learned that the decree *had* **been p,** 10673

PUBLIUS (1)
Ac 28: 7 an estate nearby that belonged *to* **P,** *4511*

PUDENS (1)
2Ti 4:21 Eubulus greets you, and so do **P,** Linus, *4545*

PUFFED (1) [PUFFS]
Hab 2: 4 "See, *he is* **p up;** his desires are not upright 6752

PUFFS (2) [PUFFED]
1Co 8: 1 Knowledge **p up,** but love builds up. *5881*
Col 2:18 and his unspiritual mind **p** him **up** *5881*

PUHITES (KJV) See PUTHITES

PUITE (1) [PUAH]
Nu 26:23 through Puah, the **P** clan; 7027

PUL (2) [TIGLATH-PILESER]
2Ki 15:19 Then **P** king of Assyria invaded the land, 7040
1Ch 5:26 up the spirit of **P** king of Assyria (that is, 7040

PULL (15) [PULLED, PULLING, PULLS]
Jdg 3:22 Ehud *did* not **p** the sword **out,** 8990
Ru 2:16 **p out** some stalks for her from the bundles 8963+8963
1Ki 13: 4 so that he could not **p** it **back.** 8740
Job 41: 1 *"Can you* **p in** the leviathan with a fishhook 5432
Jer 13:26 I *will* **p up** your skirts over your face 3106
22:24 *I would* still **p** you **off.** 5998
Eze 17: 9 a strong arm or many people to **p** it **up** by 5951
26: 4 the walls of Tyre and **p down** her towers; 2238
29: 4 *I will* **p** you **out** from among your streams, 6590
Hos 7:12 *I will* **p** them **down** like birds of the air. 3718
Am 3:11 *he will* **p down** your strongholds 3718
Mt 9:16 the patch *will* **p away** from the garment, *149*
13:28 'Do you want *us* to go and **p** them **up?'** *5198*
Mk 2:21 the new piece *will* **p away** from the old, *149*
Lk 14: 5 *will you* not immediately **p** him **out?"** *413*

PULLED (20) [PULL]
Ge 19:10 the men inside reached out and **p** Lot **back** 995
37:28 his brothers **p** Joseph up out of the cistern 5432
Jdg 8:17 also **p down** the tower of Peniel and killed 5997
16:14 He awoke from his sleep and **p up** the pin 5825
1Ki 19:13 *he* **p** his cloak **over** his face and went out 4286
2Ki 23:12 *He* **p down** the altars the kings 5997
Ezr 6:11 *to* **be p** from his house and he is to be lifted 10481
9: 3 **p** hair from my head and beard and sat 5307
Ne 13:25 I beat some of the men and **p out** their **hair.** 5307
Job 4:21 **Are** not the cords of their tent **p up,** 5825
Isa 33:20 its stakes *will* never *be* **p up,** 5825
38:12 Like a shepherd's tent my house *has* **been p down** 5825
50: 6 my cheeks to *those who* **p out** my **beard;** 5307
Jer 38:13 and *they* **p** him **up** with the ropes 5432
Eze 19: 9 With hooks *they* **p** him into a cage 5989
Mt 13:40 the weeds *are* **p up** and burned in the fire, *5198*
13:48 the fishermen **p** it **up** on the shore. *328*
15:13 *will be* **p up by the roots.** *1748*
Lk 5:11 So they **p** their boats **up** on shore, *2864*
Ac 11:10 and then *it was* all **p up** to heaven again. *413*

PULLING (2) [PULL]
Mt 13:29 'because *while you are* **p** the weeds, *5198*
2Co 10: 8 for building you up rather than **p** you **down,** *2746*

PULLS (3) [PULL]
Job 20:25 *He* **p** it out of his back, 8990
Pr 21:22 of the mighty and **p down** the stronghold 3718
Hab 1:15 The wicked foe **p** all of them **up** 6590

PULSE (KJV) See VEGETABLES

PUNISH (71) [PUNISHED, PUNISHES, PUNISHING, PUNISHMENT, PUNISHMENTS]
Ge 15:14 But I *will* **p** the nation they serve 1906
Ex 32:34 when the time comes for me *to* **p,** 7212
32:34 *I will* **p** them *for* their sin." 7212
Lev 26:18 *I will* **p** you for your sins seven times over 3579
26:28 and *I* myself *will* **p** you 3579
Dt 22:18 the elders shall take the man and **p** him. 3579
1Sa 15: 2 *'I will* **p** the Amalekites 7212
2Sa 7:14 *I will* **p** him with the rod of men, 3519
Job 37:13 He brings the clouds to **p** men, 8657
Ps 59: 5 rouse yourself to **p** all the nations; 7212
89:32 *I will* **p** their sin with the rod, 7212
94:10 *Does he* who disciplines nations not **p?** 3519
119:84 When *will you* **p** my persecutors? 5477+6913
120: 4 He will **p** you with a warrior's sharp arrows NIH
Pr 17:26 It is not good *to* **p** an innocent man, 6740
23:13 if *you* **p** him with the rod, he will not die. 5782
23:14 **P** him with the rod and save his soul 5782
Isa 10:12 *"I will* **p** the king of Assyria for 7212
13:11 *I will* **p** the world *for* its evil, 7212
24:21 In that day the LORD *will* **p** the powers 7212
26:21 of his dwelling *to* **p** the people of the earth 7212
27: 1 the LORD *will* **p** with his sword, 7212
64:12 Will you keep silent and **p** us 6700
Jer 2:19 Your wickedness *will* **p** you; 3579
5: 9 *Should I* not **p** them for this?" 7212
5:29 *Should I* not **p** them for this?" 7212
6:15 be brought down when *I* **p** them," 7212
9: 9 *Should I* not **p** them for this?" 7212
9:25 *I will* **p** all who are circumcised only 7212
11:22 *'I will* **p** them. 7212
14:10 and **p** them *for* their sins." 7212
21:14 *I will* **p** you as your deeds deserve, 7212
23:34 *I will* **p** that man and his household. 7212
25:12 *I will* **p** the king of Babylon 7212
27: 8 *I will* **p** that nation with the sword, 7212
29:32 I *will* surely **p** Shemaiah the Nehelamite 7212
30:20 *I will* **p** all who oppress them. 7212
36:31 *I will* **p** him and his children 7212
44:13 *I will* **p** those who live in Egypt with 7212
44:29 to you that I *will* **p** you in this place,' 7212
49: 8 on Esau at the time *I* **p** him. 7212
50:18 "I *will* **p** the king of Babylon and his land 7212
51:44 *I will* **p** Bel in Babylon 7212
51:47 the time will surely come when *I will* **p** 7212
51:52 "when *I will* **p** her idols, 7212
La 4:22 Daughter of Edom, *he will* **p** your sin 7212
Eze 7:11 into a **rod** *to* **p** wickedness; AIT
23:24 and *they will* **p** you according 9149
25:17 on them and **p** them in my wrath. 9350
Hos 1: 4 because *I will* soon **p** the house of Jehu 7212
2:13 *I will* **p** her *for* the days she burned incense 7212
4: 9 *I will* **p** both of them *for* their ways 7212
4:14 not **p** your daughters when they turn 7212
8:13 and **p** their sins: 7212
9: 9 and **p** them *for* their sins. 7212
10:10 When I please, *I will* **p** them; 3579
12: 2 *he will* **p** Jacob according to his ways 7212
Am 3: 2 therefore *I will* **p** you *for* all your sins." 7212
3:14 "On the day I **p** Israel for her sins, 7212
Hab 1:12 O Rock, you have ordained them to **p.** 3519
Zep 1: 8 the day of the LORD's sacrifice *I will* **p** 7212
1: 9 that day *I will* **p** all who avoid stepping 7212
1:12 and **p** those who are complacent, 7212
Zec 10: 3 and *I will* **p** the leaders; 7212
Lk 23:16 I will **p** him and then release him." *4084*
Ac 4:21 They could not decide how *to* **p** them, *3134*

Ac 7: 7 I *will* **p** the nation they serve as slaves,' *3212*
2Co 10: 6 be ready *to* **p** every act of disobedience, *1688*
1Th 4: 6 The Lord will **p** men for all such sins, *1690*
2Th 1: 8 *He will* **p** those who do not know God *1443+1689*
1Pe 2: 14 by him to **p** those who do wrong and *1689*

PUNISHED (34) [PUNISH]

Ge 19: 15 you will be swept away when the city is **p."** 6411
42: 21 "Surely we are being **p** because 872
Ex 21: 20 dies as a direct result, *he* **must be p,** 5933+5933
21: 21 not *to* **be p** if the slave gets up after a day 5933
Lev 18: 25 so *I* **p** it *for* its sin, 7212
1Sa 28: 10 you *will* not *be* **p** for this." 6411+7936
1Ch 21: 7 evil in the sight of God; so *he* **p** Israel. 5782
Ezr 7: 26 must surely be **p** by death, 10170+10191+10522
9: 13 you *have* **p** us **less** than our sins have deserved 3104+4200+4752
Ps 73: 14 I have been **p** every morning. 9350
99: 8 though you **p** their misdeeds. 5933
Pr 21: 11 a mocker *is* **p,** the simple gain wisdom; 6740
Isa 24: 22 they will be shut up in prison and **be p** 7212
26: 14 *You* **p** them and brought them to ruin; 7212
57: 17 I was enraged by his sinful greed; *I* **p** him, 5782
Jer 2: 30 "In vain *I* **p** your people; 5782
6: 6 This city *must* **be p;** 7212
8: 12 they will be brought down when they are **p,** 7213
23: 12 on them in the year they are **p,"** 7213
30: 14 as an enemy would and **p** you as would 4592
44: 13 famine and plague, as *I* **p** Jerusalem. 7212
46: 21 the time for them to be **p.** 7213
50: 18 of Babylon and his land as *I* **p** the king 7212
50: 27 the time for them to be **p.** 7213
50: 31 the time for you *to be* **p.** 7212
La 3: 39 when **p for** his **sins?** 2628
Mk 12: 40 Such men *will* **be p** most severely." *3210+3284*
Lk 20: 47 Such men *will* be **p** most severely." *3210+3284*
23: 22 *I will* have him **p** and then release him." *4084*
23: 41 We are **p** justly, for we are getting what *NIG*
Ac 22: 5 people as prisoners to Jerusalem to *be* **p.** *5512*
26: 11 one synagogue to another *to have* them **p,** *5512*
2Th 1: 9 *be* **p** with everlasting destruction *1472+5514*
Heb 10: 29 a man deserves to be **p** who has trampled *5513*

PUNISHES (5) [PUNISH]

Ex 34: 7 *he* **p** the children and their children *for* 7212
Nu 14: 18 *he* **p** the children *for* the sin of the fathers to 7212
Job 34: 26 *He* **p** them for their wickedness 6215
35: 15 that his anger never **p** and he does not take 7212
Heb 12: 6 and *he* **p** everyone he accepts as a son." *3463*

PUNISHING (4) [PUNISH]

Ex 20: 5 the LORD your God, am a jealous God, **p** 7212
Dt 5: 9 the LORD your God, am a jealous God, **p** 7212
Jdg 8: 16 by **p** them with desert thorns and briers. NIH
Isa 30: 32 the LORD lays on them with his **p** rod will 4592

PUNISHMENT (56) [PUNISH]

Ge 4: 13 "My **p** is more than I can bear. 6411
Lev 19: 20 there must be **due p.** 1334
1Sa 14: 47 *he* **inflicted p** on them. 8399
2Ki 7: 9 we wait until daylight, **p** will overtake us. 6411
Job 19: 29 for wrath will bring **p** *by* the sword, 6411
21: 19 'God stores up a man's **p** for his sons.' 224
Ps 81: 15 and their **p** would last forever. 6961
91: 8 with your eyes and see the **p** *of* the wicked. 8974
149: 7 to inflict vengeance on the nations and **p** on 9349
Pr 10: 16 the income of the wicked brings them **p.** 2633
16: 22 but folly brings **p** *to* fools. 4592
Isa 53: 5 the **p** *that brought* us peace was upon him, 4592
Jer 4: 18 This is your **p.** 8288
11: 15 Can consecrated meat avert [your **p**]? NIH
11: 23 the men of Anathoth in the year of their **p.'** 7213
23: 2 not bestowed care on them, I *will* **bestow p** 7212
32: 18 but **bring** the **p** for the fathers' sins 8966
46: 25 *about to* **bring p** on Amon god of Thebes, 7212
48: 44 I will bring upon Moab the year of her **p,"** 7213
La 4: 6 The **p** *of* my people is greater than that 6411
4: 22 O Daughter of Zion, your **p** will end; 6411
5: 7 and we bear their **p.** 6411
Eze 5: 8 against you, Jerusalem, and I will inflict **p** 5477
5: 10 I will inflict **p** on you 9150
5: 15 around you when I inflict **p** on you in anger 9150
11: 9 over to foreigners and inflict **p** on you. 9150
16: 38 to the **p** *of* women who commit adultery 5477
16: 41 down your houses and inflict **p** on you in 9150
21: 25 whose time of **p** has reached its climax, 6411
21: 29 whose time of **p** has reached its climax. 6411
23: 10 and **p** was inflicted on her. 9144
23: 24 I will turn you over to them for **p,** 5477
23: 45 to the **p** *of* women who commit adultery 5477
25: 11 and I will inflict **p** on Moab. 9150
28: 22 when I inflict **p** on her 9150
28: 26 they will live in safety when I inflict **p** 9150
30: 14 set fire to Zoan and inflict **p** on Thebes. 9150
30: 19 So I will inflict **p** on Egypt, 9150
32: 27 The **p for** their **sins** rested on their bones, 6411
35: 5 the time their **p** reached its climax, 6411
39: 21 the **p** I inflict and the hand I lay upon them. 5477
Hos 9: 7 The days of **p** are coming, 7213
Zep 3: 15 The LORD has taken away your **p,** 5477
Zec 14: 19 be the **p** *of* Egypt and the punishment of all 2633
14: 19 of Egypt and the **p** *of* all the nations that do 2633
Mt 25: 46 "Then they will go away to eternal **p,** *3136*
Lk 12: 48 and does things deserving **p** will be beaten *4435*
Lk 21: 22 For this is the time *of* **p** in fulfillment of all *1689*
Ro 13: 4 **agent** of wrath **to bring p** on the wrongdoer *1690*
13: 5 not only because of possible **p** but also *3973*
2Co 2: 6 The **p** inflicted on him by the majority *2204*
Heb 2: 2 and disobedience received its just **p,** *3632*
2Pe 2: 9 *while continuing* their **p.** *3134*
1Jn 4: 18 because fear has to do with **p.** *3136*
Jude 1: 7 of those who suffer the **p** of eternal fire. *1472*
Rev 17: 1 the **p** of the great prostitute, *3210*

PUNISHMENTS (1) [PUNISH]

Zep 3: 7 nor all *my* **p come** upon her. 7212

PUNITES (KJV) See PUITES

PUNON (2)

Nu 33: 42 They left Zalmonah and camped at **P.** 7044
33: 43 They left **P** and camped at Oboth. 7044

PUR (3) [LOT]

Est 3: 7 the month of Nisan, they cast the **p** (that is, 7052
9: 24 the Jews to destroy them and had cast the **p** 7052
9: 26 days were called Purim, from the word **p.**) 7052

PURAH (2)

Jdg 7: 10 go down to the camp with your servant **P** 7242
7: 11 So he and **P** his servant went down to 7242

PURCHASE (6) [PURCHASED]

2Ki 22: 6 Also *have* them **p** timber and dressed stone 7864
2Ch 34: 11 and builders to **p** dressed stone, 7864
Pr 20: 14 then off he goes and boasts about his **p.** NIH
Jer 32: 11 I took the deed of **p—** 5239
32: 14 and unsealed copies of the deed of **p,** 5239
32: 16 of **p** to Baruch son of Neriah, I prayed to 5239

PURCHASED (6) [PURCHASE]

1Ki 10: 28 merchants **p** them from Kue. 928+4374+4697
2Ki 12: 12 They **p** timber and dressed stone for 7864
2Ch 1: 16 merchants **p** them from Kue. 928+4374+4697
Ps 74: 2 Remember the people *you* **p** of old, 7864
Rev 5: 9 and with your blood *you* **p** men for God *60*
14: 4 They *were* **p** from among men and offered *60*

PURE (108) [PUREST, PURIFICATION, PURIFIED, PURIFIER, PURIFIES, PURIFY, PURIFYING, PURITY]

Ex 25: 11 Overlay it with **p** gold, both inside and out, 3196
25: 17 "Make an atonement cover of **p** gold— 3196
25: 24 with **p** gold and make a gold molding 3196
25: 29 And make its plates and dishes of **p** gold, 3196
25: 31 a lampstand of **p** gold and hammer it out, 3196
25: 36 hammered out of **p** gold. 3196
25: 38 and trays are to be of **p** gold. 3196
25: 39 of **p** gold is to be used for the lampstand 3196
28: 14 and two braided chains of **p** gold, 3196
28: 22 breastpiece make braided chains of **p** gold, 3196
28: 36 "Make a plate of **p** gold and engrave on it 3196
30: 3 and all the sides and the horns with **p** gold, 3196
30: 34 and **p** frankincense, all in equal amounts, 2341
30: 35 It is to be salted and **p** and sacred. 3196
31: 8 the **p** gold lampstand and all its accessories, 3196
37: 2 He overlaid it with **p** gold, 3196
37: 6 He made the atonement cover of **p** gold— 3196
37: 11 Then they overlaid it with **p** gold and made 3196
37: 16 And they made from **p** gold the articles for 3196
37: 17 of **p** gold and hammered it out, base 3196
37: 22 hammered out of **p** gold. 3196
37: 23 as its wick trimmers and trays, of **p** gold. 3196
37: 24 from one talent of **p** gold. 3196
37: 26 and all the sides and the horns with **p** gold, 3196
37: 29 the sacred anointing oil and the **p,** 3196
39: 15 they made braided chains of **p** gold, 3196
39: 25 of **p** gold and attached them around 3196
39: 30 out of **p** gold and engraved on it, 3196
39: 37 the **p** gold lampstand with its row of lamps 3196
Lev 24: 4 The lamps on the **p** gold lampstand before 3196
24: 6 on the table of **p** gold before the LORD. 3196
24: 7 Along each row put some **p** incense as 2341
2Sa 22: 27 to the **p** you show yourself pure, 1405
22: 27 to the pure *you* **show yourself p,** 1405
1Ki 6: 20 He overlaid the inside with **p** gold, 6034
6: 21 the inside of the temple with **p** gold, 6034
7: 49 the lampstands of **p** gold (five on the right 6034
7: 50 the **p** gold basins, 6034
10: 21 of the Forest of Lebanon were **p** gold. 6034
2Ki 25: 15 all that were made of **p gold** or silver. 2298+2298
1Ch 28: 17 of **p** gold for the forks, sprinkling bowls 3196
2Ch 3: 4 He overlaid the inside with **p** gold. 3196
4: 20 of **p** gold with their lamps, to burn in front 6034
4: 22 the **p** gold wick trimmers, 6034
9: 17 with ivory and overlaid with **p** gold. 3196
9: 20 of the Forest of Lebanon were **p** gold. 6034
Job 4: 17 *Can* a man *be* more **p** than his Maker? 3197
8: 6 if you are **p** and upright, 2341
11: 4 'My beliefs are flawless and I am **p** 1338
14: 4 Who can bring *what* is **p** from the impure? 3196
15: 14 "What is man, that *he could be* **p,** 2342
15: 15 if even the heavens *are* not **p** in his eyes, 2348
16: 17 of violence and my prayer is **p.** 2341
25: 4 How *can* one born of woman *be* **p?** 2342
Job 25: 5 and the stars *are* not **p** in his eyes, 2348
28: 19 it cannot be bought with **p** gold. 3196
31: 24 put my trust in gold or said to **p gold,** 4188
33: 9 'I am **p** and without sin; 2341
Ps 18: 26 to the **p** you show yourself pure, 1405
18: 26 to the pure *you* **show yourself p,** 1405
19: 9 fear of the LORD is **p,** enduring forever. 3196
19: 10 than much **p gold;** 7058
21: 3 and placed a crown of **p gold** on his head. 7058
24: 4 He who has clean hands and a **p** heart, 1338
51: 10 Create in me a **p** heart, O God, 3196
73: 1 to *those who* are **p** *in* heart. 1338
73: 13 Surely in vain *have I* **kept** my heart **p;** 2342
119: 9 How *can* a young man **keep** his way **p?** 2342
119: 127 more than **p gold,** 7058
Pr 15: 26 but those of the **p** are pleasing to him. 3196
20: 9 Who can say, *"I have* **kept** my heart **p;** 2342
20: 11 by whether his conduct is **p** and right. 2341
22: 11 He who loves a **p** heart and whose speech 3196
30: 12 those who are **p** in their own eyes and 3196
SS 5: 15 pillars of marble set on bases of **p gold.** 7058
Isa 13: 12 I will make man scarcer than **p gold,** 7058
52: 11 Come out from it and *be* **p,** 1405
Jer 52: 19 all that were made of **p gold** or silver. 2298+2298
Da 2: 32 The head of the statue was made of **p** gold, 10294
Hab 1: 13 Your eyes are too **p** to look on evil; 3196
Mal 1: 11 In every place incense and **p** offerings will 3196
Mt 5: 8 Blessed are the **p** in heart, *2754*
Mk 14: 3 very expensive perfume, *made of* **p** nard. *4410*
Jn 12: 3 Then Mary took about a pint *of* **p** nard, *4410*
2Co 11: 2 I might present you as a **p** virgin to him. *54*
11: 3 from your sincere and **p** devotion to Christ. *55*
Php 1: 10 be **p** and blameless until the day of Christ, *1637*
2: 15 so that you may become blameless and **p,** *193*
4: 8 whatever is **p,** whatever is lovely, *54*
1Ti 1: 5 from a **p** heart and a good conscience and *2754*
5: 22 Keep yourself **p.** *54*
2Ti 2: 22 on the Lord out of a **p** heart. *2754*
Tit 1: 15 *To the* **p,** all things are pure, *2754*
1: 15 To the pure, all things are **p,** *2754*
1: 15 and do not believe, nothing is **p.** *2754*
2: 5 to be self-controlled and **p,** *54*
Heb 7: 26 one who is holy, blameless, **p,** *299*
10: 22 and having our bodies washed *with* **p** water. *2754*
13: 4 and the marriage bed kept **p,** *299*
Jas 1: 2 Consider it **p** joy, my brothers, *4246*
1: 27 Religion that God our Father accepts as **p** *2754*
3: 17 that comes from heaven is first of all **p;** *54*
1Pe 2: 2 Like newborn babies, crave **p** spiritual milk, *100*
1Jn 3: 3 hope in him purifies himself, just as he is **p.** *54*
Rev 14: 4 for they kept themselves **p.** *4221*
21: 18 and the city of **p** gold, as pure as glass. *2754*
21: 18 and the city of pure gold, as **p** as glass. *2754*
21: 21 The great street of the city was of **p** gold, *2754*

PUREST (1) [PURE]

SS 5: 11 His head is **p gold;** 4188+7058

PURGE (16) [PURGED]

Dt 13: 5 *You must* **p** the evil from among you. 1278
17: 7 *You must* **p** the evil from among you. 1278
17: 12 *You must* **p** the evil from Israel. 1278
19: 13 *You must* **p** from Israel the guilt 1278
19: 19 *You must* **p** the evil from among you. 1278
21: 9 So you *will* **p** from yourselves the guilt 1278
21: 21 *You must* **p** the evil from among you. 1278
22: 21 *You must* **p** the evil from among you. 1278
22: 22 *You must* **p** the evil from Israel. 1278
22: 24 *You must* **p** the evil from among you. 1278
24: 7 *You must* **p** the evil from among you. 1278
Jdg 20: 13 so that we may put them to death and **p** 1278
2Ch 34: 3 to **p** Judah and Jerusalem of high places, 3197
Pr 20: 30 and beatings **p** the inmost being. NIH
Isa 1: 25 *I will* **thoroughly p away** your dross 1342+2021+3869+7671
Eze 20: 38 *I will* **p** you of those who revolt and rebel 1405

PURGED (2) [PURGE]

2Ch 34: 5 and so *he* **p** Judah and Jerusalem. 3197
Jer 6: 29 the wicked **are** not **p out.** 5998

PURGETH (KJV) See PRUNES

PURIFICATION (10) [PURE]

Lev 12: 4 until the days of her **p** are over. 3198
12: 6 the days of her **p** for a son or daughter are 3198
Nu 19: 9 the water of cleansing; it is for **p from sin.** 2633
19: 17 put some ashes from the burned **p offering** 2633
1Ch 23: 28 the side rooms, the **p** of all sacred things 3200
Ne 12: 45 service of their God and the service of **p,** 3200
Lk 2: 22 the time *of* their **p** according to the Law *2752*
Ac 21: 24 join in their **p rites** and pay their expenses, *49*
21: 26 the date when the days *of* **p** would end and *50*
Heb 1: 3 After he had provided **p** for sins, *2752*

PURIFIED (22) [PURE]

Lev 12: 4 thirty-three days to be **p** from her bleeding. 3200
12: 5 sixty-six days to be **p** from her bleeding. 3200
Nu 8: 15 "After *you have* **p** the Levites 3197
8: 21 The Levites **p themselves** and washed 2627
31: 23 But *it must* also **be p** with the water 2627
2Sa 11: 4 (She *had* **p herself** from her uncleanness.) 7727
2Ch 29: 18 *"We have* **p** the entire temple of the LORD, 3197

2Ch 30:18 Issachar and Zebulun *had* not **p themselves,** 3197
Ezr 6:20 The priests and Levites *had* **p themselves** 3197
Ne 12:30 Levites *had* **p themselves ceremonially,** 3197
12:30 *they* **p** the people, the gates and the wall. 3197
13:30 So *I* **p** the priests and the Levites 3197
Job 1: 5 Job would send and **have** them **p.** 7727
Ps 12: 6 in a furnace of clay, **p** seven times. 2423
Eze 43:22 the altar *is to be* **p** as it was purified with 2627
43:22 the altar is to be purified as *it was* **p** with 2627
Da 11:35 refined, **p** and made spotless until the time 1405
12:10 Many *will* **be p,** made spotless and refined, 1405
Ac 15: 9 for *he* **p** their hearts by faith. *2751*
21:26 the men and **p** *himself* along with them. *49*
Heb 9:23 the copies of the heavenly things *to be* **p** *2751*
1Pe 1:22 *Now that you have* **p** yourselves by obeying *49*

PURIFIER (1) [PURE]

Mal 3: 3 He will sit as a refiner and **p** *of* silver; 3197

PURIFIES (2) [PURE]

1Jn 1: 7 his Son, **p** us from all sin. *2751*
3: 3 hope in him **p** himself, just as he is pure. *49*

PURIFY (29) [PURE]

Ge 35: 2 and **p yourselves** and change your clothes. 3197
Ex 29:36 **P** the altar by making atonement for it, 2627
Lev 8:15 on all the horns of the altar *to* **p** the altar. 2627
14:49 To **p** the house he is to take two birds 2627
14:52 *He shall* **p** the house with the bird's blood, 2627
Nu 8: 7 To **p** them, do this: Sprinkle the water 3197
8: 7 and so **p themselves.** 3197
8:21 and made atonement for them to **p** them. 3197
19:12 He *must* **p** himself with the water on 2627
19:12 not **p himself** on the third and seventh days, 2627
19:13 of anyone and fails *to* **p himself** defiles 2627
19:19 and on the seventh day *he is to* **p** him. 2627
19:20 a person who is unclean *does* not **p himself,** 2627
31:19 and seventh days you *must* **p yourselves** 2627
31:20 **P** every garment as well 2627
2Ch 29:15 they went in to **p** the temple of the LORD, 3197
29:16 into the sanctuary of the LORD to **p** it. 3197
34: 8 to **p** the land and the temple, 3197
Ne 13: 9 I gave orders *to* **p** the rooms, 3197
13:22 *to* **p themselves** and go and guard the gates 3197
Isa 66:17 "Those who consecrate and **p themselves** 3197
Eze 43:20 so **p** the altar and make atonement for it. 2627
45:18 to take a young bull without defect and **p** 2627
Zep 3: 9 "Then *will I* **p** the lips of the peoples, 1359+2200
Mal 3: 3 *he will* **p** the Levites and refine them 3197
2Co 7: 1 *let us* **p** ourselves from everything that *2751*
Tit 2:14 to redeem us from all wickedness and *to* **p** *2751*
Jas 4: 8 and **p** your hearts, you double-minded. *49*
1Jn 1: 9 and **p** us from all unrighteousness. *2751*

PURIFYING (1) [PURE]

Eze 43:23 When you have finished **p** it, 2627

PURIM (5)

Est 9:26 (Therefore these days were called **P,** 7052
9:28 of **P** should never cease to be celebrated by 7052
9:29 to confirm this second letter concerning **P.** 7052
9:31 of **P** at their designated times, 7052
9:32 about **P,** and it was written down in 7052

PURITY (5) [PURE]

Hos 8: 5 How long will they be incapable of **p?** 5931
2Co 6: 6 in **p,** understanding, patience and kindness; *55*
1Ti 4:12 in life, in love, in faith and in **p.** *48*
5: 2 younger women as sisters, with absolute **p.** *48*
1Pe 3: 2 they see the **p** and reverence of your lives. *54*

PURLOINING (KJV) See STEAL

PURPLE (51)

Ex 25: 4 **p** and scarlet yarn and fine linen; 763
26: 1 and blue, **p** and scarlet yarn, 763
26:31 **p** and scarlet yarn and finely twisted linen, 763
26:36 **p** and scarlet yarn and finely twisted linen 763
27:16 **p** and scarlet yarn and finely twisted linen 763
28: 5 and blue, **p** and scarlet yarn, and fine linen. 763
28: 6 and of blue, **p** and scarlet yarn, 763
28: 8 and with blue, **p** and scarlet yarn, 763
28:15 of gold, and of blue, **p** and scarlet yarn, 763
28:33 **p** and scarlet yarn around the hem of 763
35: 6 **p** and scarlet yarn and fine linen; 763
35:23 **p** or scarlet yarn or fine linen, or goat hair, 763
35:25 blue, **p** or scarlet yarn or fine linen. 763
35:35 **p** and scarlet yarn and fine linen, 763
36: 8 blue, **p** and scarlet yarn, 763
36:35 **p** and scarlet yarn and finely twisted linen, 763
36:37 **p** and scarlet yarn and finely twisted linen; 763
38:18 **p** and scarlet yarn and finely twisted linen 763
38:23 **p** and scarlet yarn and fine linen.) 763
39: 1 From the blue, **p** and scarlet yarn 763
39: 2 and of blue, **p** and scarlet yarn, 763
39: 3 **p** and scarlet yarn and fine linen— 763
39: 5 and with blue, **p** and scarlet yarn, 763
39: 8 of gold, and of blue, **p** and scarlet yarn, 763
39:24 **p** and scarlet yarn and finely twisted linen 763
39:29 blue, **p** and scarlet yarn— 763
Nu 4:13 the bronze altar and spread a **p** cloth over it. 763
Jdg 8:26 the pendants and the **p** garments worn by 763
2Ch 2: 7 and in **p,** crimson and blue yarn, 760
2:14 and with **p** and blue and crimson yarn 763
3:14 **p** and crimson yarn and fine linen, 763
Est 1: 6 with cords of white linen and **p material** 763
8:15 a large crown of gold and a **p** robe 763
Pr 31:22 she is clothed in fine linen and **p.** 763
SS 3:10 Its seat was upholstered with **p,** 763
Jer 10: 9 then dressed in blue and **p—** 763
La 4: 5 Those nurtured in **p** now lie on ash heaps. 9355
Eze 27: 7 of blue and **p** from the coasts of Elishah. 763
27:16 they exchanged turquoise, **p** fabric, 763
Da 5: 7 in **p** and have a gold chain placed 10066
5:16 in **p** and have a gold chain placed 10066
5:29 Daniel was clothed in **p,** 10066
Mk 15:17 They put a **p robe** on him, *4525*
15:20 the **p robe** and put his own clothes on him. *4525*
Lk 16:19 a rich man who was dressed in **p** *4525*
Jn 19: 2 They clothed him in a **p** robe *4526*
19: 5 the crown of thorns and the **p** robe, *4526*
Ac 16:14 a **dealer in p cloth** from the city *4527*
Rev 17: 4 The woman was dressed in **p** and scarlet, *4526*
18:12 fine linen, **p,** silk and scarlet cloth; *4525*
18:16 **p** and scarlet, and glittering with gold, *4526*

PURPOSE (42) [PURPOSED, PURPOSELY, PURPOSES]

Ex 9:16 But I have raised you up **for this** very **p,** 6288
Lev 7:24 may be used for any other **p,** 4856
1Ch 23: 5 the musical instruments I have provided for **that p."** 2146S
Job 36: 5 he is mighty, and firm in his **p.** 4213
Ps 57: 2 to God, who fulfills [his **p**] for me. NIH
138: 8 The LORD will fulfill [his **p**] for me; NIH
Pr 19:21 but it is the LORD's **p** that prevails. 6783
Isa 10: 7 his **p** is to destroy, 4222
46:10 I say: My **p** will stand, 6783
46:11 from a far-off land, a man to fulfill my **p.** 6783
48:14 LORD's chosen ally will carry out his **p** 2914
49: 4 But I said, "I have labored to **no p;** 8198
55:11 and **achieve** *the* **p** for which I sent it. 7503
Jer 15:11 "Surely I will deliver you for a **good** *p;* AIT
51:11 because his **p** is to destroy Babylon. 4659
51:12 The LORD *will* **carry out** *his* **p,** 2372
Lk 7:30 in the law rejected God's **p** for themselves, *1087*
Ac 2:23 to you *by* God's set **p** and foreknowledge; *1087*
5:38 For if their **p** or activity is of human origin, *1087*
13:36 "For when David had served God's **p** *1087*
Ro 8:28 who have been called according to his **p.** *4606*
9:11 that God's **p** in election might stand: *4606*
9:17 "I raised you up **for** this very **p,** *1650*
1Co 3: 8 and the man who waters have one **p,** *NIG*
2Co 5: 5 it is God who has made us **for** this very **p** *1650*
Gal 3:19 What, then, was the **p** of the law? *NIG*
4:18 provided the **p** is good, *NIG*
Eph 1:11 in conformity with the **p** of his will, *1087*
2:15 His **p** was **to** create in himself one new man *2671*
3:11 to his eternal **p** which he accomplished *4606*
6:22 I am sending him to you **for** this very **p,** *1650*
Php 2: 2 being one in spirit and **p.** *5858*
2:13 to will and to act according to his **good p.** *2306*
Col 2: 2 My **p** is **that** they may be encouraged *2671*
4: 8 **for the express p** that you may know about our circumstances *899+1650+4047*
2Th 1:11 by his power he may fulfill every good **p** *2306*
1Ti 2: 7 And **for** this **p** I was appointed a herald and *1650*
2Ti 1: 9 but because of his own **p** and grace. *4606*
3:10 my way of life, my **p,** faith, patience, love, *4606*
Heb 6:17 the unchanging nature *of* his **p** very clear *1087*
Rev 17:13 They have one **p** and will give their power *1191*
17:17 to accomplish his **p** by agreeing to give *1191*

PURPOSED (5) [PURPOSE]

Isa 14:24 and as *I have* **p,** so it will stand. 3619
14:27 For the LORD Almighty *has* **p,** 3619
Jer 49:20 what *he has* **p** against those who live in Teman: 3108+4742
50:45 what *he has* **p** against the land of the Babylonians: 3108+4742
Eph 1: 9 which *he* **p** in Christ, *4729*

PURPOSELY (1) [PURPOSE]

Jn 7: 1 **p** staying away from Judea because *2527*

PURPOSES (10) [PURPOSE]

Ps 33:10 he thwarts the **p** *of* the peoples. 4742
33:11 the **p** *of* his heart through all generations. 4742
Pr 20: 5 The **p** of a man's heart are deep waters, 6783
Jer 23:20 until he fully accomplishes the **p** 4659
30:24 until he fully accomplishes the **p** 4659
32:19 great are your **p** and mighty are your deeds. 6783
51:29 the LORD's **p** against Babylon stand— 4742
Ro 9:21 of clay some pottery for noble **p** and some *NIG*
2Ti 2:20 some are for **noble p** and some for ignoble. *5507*
2:21 he will be an instrument for **noble p,** *5507*

PURSE (6) [PURSES]

Pr 1:14 and we will share a common **p"—** 3967
7:20 He took his **p** *filled with* money and 7655
Hag 1: 6 only to put them in a **p** with holes in it." 7655
Lk 10: 4 Do not take a **p** or bag or sandals; *964*
22:35 "When I sent you without **p,** *964*
22:36 He said to them, "But now if you have a **p,** *964*

PURSES (3) [PURSE]

Pr 16:30 *he who* **p** his lips is bent on evil. 7975
Isa 3:22 and the capes and cloaks, the **p** 3038
Lk 12:33 Provide **p** for yourselves that will not wear *964*

PURSUE (51) [PURSUED, PURSUER, PURSUERS, PURSUES, PURSUING, PURSUIT]

Ex 14: 4 and *he will* **p** them. 8103
15: 9 "The enemy boasted, *'I will* **p,** 8103
Lev 26: 7 *You will* **p** your enemies, 8103
26:33 and will draw out my sword and **p** you. 339
Dt 19: 6 the avenger of blood *might* **p** him in a rage, 8103
28:45 *They will* **p** you and overtake you 8103
Jos 8: 6 *They will* **p** us until we have lured them 339+3655
8:16 All the men of Ai were called to **p** them, 8103
10:19 **P** your enemies, attack them from the rear 8103
1Sa 30: 8 *"Shall I* **p** this raiding party? 8103
30: 8 **"P** them," he answered. 8103
2Sa 20: 6 Take your master's men and **p** him, 8103
20: 7 from Jerusalem to **p** Sheba son of Bicri. 8103
20:13 the men went on with Joab to **p** Sheba son 8103
24:13 from your enemies while they **p** you? 8103
Job 19:22 Why *do you* **p** me as God does? 8103
Ps 7: 1 save and deliver me from all *who* **p** me, 8103
7: 5 then *let* my enemy **p** and overtake me; 8103
31:15 from my enemies and from *those who* **p** me. 8103
34:14 seek peace and **p** it. 8103
35: 3 and javelin against *those who* **p** me. 8103
38:20 with evil slander me when I **p** what is good. 8103
56: 1 O God, for men **hotly p** me; 8634
56: 2 My slanderers **p** me all day long; 8634
57: 3 rebuking *those who* **hotly p** me; 8634
71:11 **p** him and seize him, 8103
83:15 so **p** them with your tempest 8103
142: 6 rescue me from *those who* **p** me, 8103
Pr 15: 9 but he loves *those who* **p** righteousness. 8103
Isa 51: 1 *you who* **p** righteousness and who seek 8103
Jer 2:24 *that* **p** her need not tire themselves; 1335
9:16 and *I will* **p** them *with* the sword 339+8938
29:18 *I will* **p** them with the sword, 8103
48: 2 the sword *will* **p** you. 339+2143
49:37 *"I will* **p** them *with* the sword 339+8938
50:21 **P,** kill and completely destroy them," 339
La 1: 3 All *who* **p** her have overtaken her in 8103
3:66 **P** them in anger and destroy them from 8103
5: 5 *Those who* **p** *us* are at our heels; 8103
Eze 5: 2 For I will **p** them with drawn sword. 339
5:12 and a third I will scatter to the winds and **p** 339
12:14 and I will **p** them with drawn sword. 339
35: 6 over to bloodshed and it *will* **p** you. 8103
35: 6 bloodshed *will* **p** you. 8103
Hos 8: 3 an enemy *will* **p** him. 8103
Na 1: 8 *he will* **p** his foes into darkness. 8103
Mt 23:34 in your synagogues and **p** from town *1503*
Ro 9:30 the Gentiles, who *did* not **p** righteousness, *1503*
1Ti 6:11 and **p** righteousness, godliness, faith, love, *1503*
2Ti 2:22 and **p** righteousness, faith, love and peace, *1503*
1Pe 3:11 he must seek peace and **p** it. *1503*

PURSUED (31) [PURSUE]

Ge 31:23 *he* **p** Jacob *for* seven days and caught up 8103
35: 5 around them so that no *one* **p** them. 8103
Ex 14: 8 so that *he* **p** the Israelites, 8103
14: 9 **p** the Israelites and overtook them 8103
14:23 The Egyptians **p** them, 8103
Jos 8:16 and *they* **p** Joshua and were lured away 8103
10:10 Israel **p** them *along* the road going up 8103
11: 8 They defeated them and **p** them all the way 8103
24: 6 and the Egyptians **p** them with chariots 8103
Jdg 4:16 But Barak **p** the chariots and army as far 8103
7:23 and *they* **p** the Midianites. 8103
7:25 *They* **p** the Midianites and brought 8103
8:12 fled, but *he* **p** them and captured them, 8103
1Sa 7:11 of Israel rushed out of Mizpah and **p** 8103
17:52 and **p** the Philistines to the entrance of Gath 8103
2Sa 2:19 to the right nor to the left as he **p** him. 339+2143
2:24 But Joab and Abishai **p** Abner, 8103
2:28 they no longer **p** Israel, 8103
20:10 and his brother Abishai **p** Sheba son 8103
22:38 *"I* **p** my enemies and crushed them; 8103
2Ki 25: 5 but the Babylonian army **p** the king 8103
2Ch 13:19 Abijah **p** Jeroboam and took from him 8103
14:13 Asa and his army **p** them as far as Gerar. 8103
Ps 18:37 *I* **p** my enemies and overtook them; 8103
Jer 39: 5 But the Babylonian army **p** them 8103
52: 8 but the Babylonian army **p** King Zedekiah 8103
La 3:43 covered yourself with anger and **p** us; 8103
Am 1:11 Because he **p** his brother with a sword, 8103
Ro 9:31 *who* **p** a law of righteousness, *1503*
9:32 Because they **p** it not by faith but as if *NIG*
Rev 12:13 *he* **p** the woman who had given birth to *1503*

PURSUER (1) [PURSUE]

La 1: 6 in weakness they have fled before the **p.** 8103

PURSUERS (7) [PURSUE]

Jos 2: 7 and as soon as the **p** had gone out, 8103
2:16 "Go to the hills so the **p** will not find you. 8103
2:22 until the **p** had searched all along the road 8103
8:20 the desert had turned back against their **p.** 8103
Ne 9:11 but you hurled their **p** into the depths, 8103
Isa 30:16 Therefore your **p** will be swift! 8103

La 4:19 Our **p** were swifter than eagles in the sky; 8103

PURSUES (11) [PURSUE]

Jos 20:5 If the avenger of blood **p** him, 8103
Ps 143:3 The enemy **p** me, he crushes me to 8103
Pr 11:19 but *he who* **p** evil goes to his death. 8103
13:21 Misfortune **p** the sinner, 8103
18:1 An unfriendly man **p** selfish ends; 1335
19:7 Though *he* **p** them with pleading, 8103
21:21 *He who* **p** righteousness and love finds life, 8103
28:1 The wicked man flees though no *one* **p**, 8103
Isa 41:3 *He* **p** them and moves on unscathed, 8103
Jer 8:6 Each **p** his own course like a horse 928+8740
Hos 12:1 *he* **p** the east wind all day 8103

PURSUING (22) [PURSUE]

Ge 14:15 **p** them as far as Hobah, north of Damascus. 8103
Lev 26:17 you will flee even when no *one is* **p** you. 8103
26:36 even though no *one is* **p** them. 8103
26:37 even though no *one is* **p** them. 8103
Dt 11:4 waters of the Red Sea as they *were* **p** you, 8103
Jdg 8:5 and I *am still* **p** Zebah and Zalmunna, 8103
1Sa 14:46 Then Saul stopped **p** the Philistines, 339
24:1 After Saul returned from **p** the Philistines, 339
24:14 Whom *are* you **p**? A dead dog? 8103
25:29 though someone *is* **p** you to take your life, 8103
26:18 he added, "Why is my lord **p** his servant? 8103
2Sa 2:26 order your men to stop **p** their brothers?" 339
2:30 from **p** Abner and assembled all his men. 339
18:16 and the troops stopped **p** Israel, 8103
1Ki 22:33 the king of Israel and stopped **p** him. 339+4946
2Ch 18:32 they stopped **p** him. 339+4946
Ps 35:6 with the angel of the LORD **p** them. 8103
Isa 65:2 **p** their own imaginations— 339
Jer 2:33 How skilled you are at **p** love! 1335
Hos 5:11 trampled in judgment, intent on **p** idols. 339+2143
1Ti 3:8 and not **p dishonest gain.** *153*
Tit 1:7 not violent, not **p dishonest gain.** *153*

PURSUIT (13) [PURSUE]

Ge 14:14 in his household and **went in p** as far 8103
Jos 2:7 So the men **set out in p** of the spies *on* 8103
8:17 the city open and **went in p** *of* Israel. 8103
Jdg 4:22 Barak **came by in p** *of* Sisera, 8103
8:4 exhausted yet *keeping up the* **p,** 8103
1Sa 14:22 they joined the battle **in hot p.** 339
23:25 **went** *into* the Desert of Maon **in p** 8103
23:28 Then Saul broke off his **p** of David 8103
30:10 and four hundred men *continued the* **p.** 8103
2Sa 2:23 But Asahel refused to **give up the p;** 6073
2:27 the **p** *of* their brothers until morning." 339
17:1 and set out tonight **in p** of David. 8103
1Ki 20:20 the Arameans fled, with the Israelites **in p.** 8103

PUSH (5) [PUSHED, PUSHES, PUSHING]

Dt 15:17 and **p** it through his ear lobe into the door, 5989
Jos 23:5 *He will* **p** them **out** before you. 3769
2Ki 4:27 Gehazi came over to **p** her **away,** 2074
Ps 44:5 Through you *we* **p back** our enemies; 5590
Jer 46:15 for the LORD *will* **p** them **down.** 2074

PUSHED (7) [PUSH]

Jdg 16:30 Then *he* **p** with all his might, 5742
Ps 118:13 I *was* **p back** and about to fall, 1890+1890
Isa 16:2 Like fluttering birds **p** *from* the nest, 8938
Zec 5:8 and *he* **p** her **back** into the basket 8959
5:8 **p** the lead cover **down** over its mouth. 8959
Ac 7:27 the other **p** Moses **aside** and said, *723*
19:33 The Jews **p** Alexander **to the front,** *4582*

PUSHES (1) [PUSH]

2Co 11:20 advantage of you or **p** *himself* **forward** *2048*

PUSHES (Anglicized) See also SHOVES

PUSHING (2) [PUSH]

Joel 2:20 **p** it into a parched and barren land, 5615
Mk 3:10 with diseases *were* **p forward** to touch him. *2158*

PUT (1021) [PUTS, PUTTING]

Ge 2:8 and there *he* **p** the man he had formed. 8492
2:15 and **p** him in the Garden of Eden to work it 5663
3:12 "The woman *you* **p** here with me— 5989
3:15 And *I will* **p** enmity between you and 8883
4:15 Then the LORD **p** a mark on Cain so 8492
6:13 "I *am going to* **p** an end to all people, 995+4200+7156
6:16 **P** a door in the side of the ark 8492
10:6 Cush, Mizraim, **P** and Canaan. 7033
16:5 I **p** my servant in your arms, 5989
21:15 *she* **p** the boy under one of the bushes. 8959
24:2 "**P** your hand under my thigh. 8492
24:9 So the servant **p** his hand under the thigh 8492
24:47 "Then *I* **p** the ring in her nose and 8492
26:11 or his wife *shall* **surely be p to death.** 4637+4637
27:15 and **p** them **on** her younger son Jacob. 4252
28:11 *he* **p** it under his head and lay down 8492
30:36 Then *he* **p** a three-day journey 8492
30:40 and *did* not **p** them with Laban's animals. 8883
31:17 Then Jacob **p** his children and his wives 5951
31:34 and **p** them inside her camel's saddle 8492
Ge 31:37 **P** it here in front of your relatives 8492
32:16 *He* **p** them in the care of his servants, 5989
33:2 *He* **p** the maidservants and their children 8492
34:26 *They* **p** Hamor and his son Shechem to 2222
37:34 **p on** sackcloth and mourned 928+5516+8492
38:7 so the LORD **p** him **to death.** 4637
38:10 so *he* **p** him **to death** also. 4637
38:19 and **p on** her widow's clothes again. 4252
38:28 *one of them* **p out** his hand; 5989
39:4 Potiphar **p** him **in charge** of his household, 7212
39:5 time *he* **p** him **in charge** of his household 7212
39:20 Joseph's master took him and **p** him 5989
39:22 So the warden **p** Joseph in charge 5989
40:3 and **p** them in custody in the house of 5989
40:11 squeezed them into Pharaoh's cup and **p** 5989
40:13 and *you will* **p** Pharaoh's cup in his hand, 5989
40:15 *to deserve being* **p** in a dungeon." 8492
40:21 so that *he once again* **p** the cup 5989
41:33 and **p** him in charge of the land of Egypt. 8883
41:41 "*I hereby* **p** you in charge of the whole land 5989
41:42 from his finger and **p** it on Joseph's finger. 5989
41:42 He dressed him in robes of fine linen and **p** 8492
41:43 Thus *he* **p** him in charge of the whole land 5989
41:48 In each city *he* **p** the food grown in 5989
42:17 And *he* **p** them all in custody for three days. 665
42:25 **p** each man's silver **back** in his sack, 8740
42:37 "*You may* **p** both of my sons **to death** if 4637
43:11 **P** some of the best products of the land 4374
43:12 the silver that *was* **p back** into the mouths 8740
43:18 that *was* **p back** into our sacks the first time. 8740
43:22 We don't know who **p** our silver 8492
44:1 as they can carry, and **p** each man's silver 8492
44:2 Then **p** my cup, the silver one, 8492
47:6 **p** them in charge of my own livestock." 8492
47:29 **p** your hand under my thigh and promise 8492
48:14 and **p** it on Ephraim's head, 8883
48:14 he **p** his left hand on Manasseh's head, NIH
48:18 **p** your right hand on his head." 8492
48:20 So *he* **p** Ephraim ahead of Manasseh. 8492
Ex 1:11 So *they* **p** slave masters over them 8492
2:3 and **p** it among the reeds along the bank of 8492
3:22 which *you will* **p** on your sons 8492
4:6 "**P** your hand inside your cloak." 995
4:6 So Moses **p** his hand into his cloak, 995
4:7 "Now **p** it **back** into your cloak," he said. 8740
4:7 So Moses **p** his hand **back** into his cloak, 8740
4:15 You shall speak to him and **p** words 8492
4:20 **p** them on a donkey and started back 8206
5:21 and *have* **p** a sword in their hand to kill us." 5989
12:7 the blood and **p** it on the sides and tops of 5989
12:22 and **p** some of the blood on the top and on 5595
14:31 feared the LORD and **p** *their* **trust** in him 586
16:33 "Take a jar and **p** an omer of manna in it. 5989
16:34 Aaron **p** the manna in front of the 5663
17:2 Why *do you* **p** the LORD **to the test?"** 5814
17:12 a stone and **p** it under him and he sat on it. 8492
19:9 and *will* always **p** *their* **trust** in you." 586
19:12 **P limits** *for* the people around the mountain 1487
19:12 *shall* **surely be p to death.** 4637+4637
19:23 '**P limits around** the mountain 1487
21:12 *shall* **surely be p to death.** 4637+4637
21:14 from my altar and *p* him *to* **death.** AIT
21:15 **must be p to death.** 4637+4637
21:16 when he is caught **must be p to death.** 4637+4637
21:17 **must be p to death.** 4637+4637
21:29 and the owner also *must* **be p to death.** 4637
22:19 with an animal **must be p to death.** 4637+4637
23:7 **p** an innocent or honest person **to death,** 2222
24:6 Moses took half of the blood and **p** it 8492
25:16 Then **p** in the ark the Testimony, 5989
25:21 the cover on top of the ark and **p** in the ark 5989
25:25 a handbreadth wide and **p** a gold molding 6913
25:30 **P** the bread of the Presence on this table to 5989
26:11 Then make fifty bronze clasps and **p** them 995
26:34 **P** the atonement cover on the ark of 5989
26:35 on the north side of the tabernacle and **p** 5989
27:5 **P** it under the ledge of the altar so 5989
28:30 Also **p** the Urim and the Thummim in 5989
28:41 After *you* **p** these **clothes on** 4252
29:3 **P** them in a basket and present them in it— 5989
29:6 **P** the turban on his head and attach 8492
29:9 and **p** headbands on them. 2502
29:12 of the bull's blood and **p** it on the horns of 5989
29:20 take some of its blood and **p** it on the lobes 5989
29:24 **P** all these in the hands of Aaron 8492
30:6 **P** the altar in front of the curtain that is 5989
30:18 and **p** water in it. 5989
31:14 who desecrates it **must be p to death;** 4637+4637
31:15 **must be p to death.** 4637+4637
33:4 to mourn and no one **p** on any ornaments. 8883
33:22 *I will* **p** you in a cleft in the rock 8492
34:33 *he* **p** a veil over his face. 5989
34:35 Then Moses *would* **p** the veil **back** 8740
35:2 does any work on it *must* **be p to death.** 4637
37:12 a handbreadth wide and **p** a gold molding 6913
37:14 The rings were **p** close to the rim to hold NIH
40:5 the ark of the Testimony and **p** the curtain 8492
40:7 of Meeting and the altar and **p** water in it. 5989
40:8 up the courtyard around it and **p** the curtain 5989
40:18 **p** the bases **in place,** 5989
40:19 over the tabernacle and **p** the covering over 8492
40:20 the ark and **p** the atonement cover over it. 5989
40:28 Then *he* **p up** the curtain at the entrance to 8492
40:30 and the altar and **p** water in it for washing, 5989
40:33 the tabernacle and altar and **p up** the curtain 5989
Lev 1:7 of Aaron the priest *are to* **p** fire on the altar 5989
2:1 pour oil on it, **p** incense on it 5989
Lev 2:15 **P** oil and incense on it; 5989
4:7 The priest *shall* then **p** some of the blood 5989
4:18 *He is to* **p** some of the blood on the horns 5989
4:25 the sin offering with his finger and **p** it on 5989
4:30 of the blood with his finger and **p** it on 5989
4:34 the sin offering with his finger and **p** it on 5989
5:11 *He must* not **p** oil or incense on it, 8492
6:10 The priest *shall* then **p on** his linen clothes, 4252
6:11 to take off these clothes and **p on** others, 4252
8:7 *He* **p** the tunic on Aaron, 5989
8:7 clothed him with the robe and **p** the ephod 5989
8:8 on him and **p** the Urim and Thummim in 5989
8:13 **p** tunics **on** them, 4252
8:13 tied sashes around them and **p** headbands 2502
8:15 and with his finger *he* **p** it on all the horns 5989
8:23 the ram and took some of its blood and **p** it 5989
8:24 and **p** some of the blood on the lobes 5989
8:26 *he* **p** these on the fat portions and on 8492
8:27 *He* **p** all these in the hands of Aaron 5989
9:9 the blood and **p** it on the horns of the altar; 5989
10:1 **p** fire in them and added incense; 5989
11:32 **P** *it* in water; 995
11:38 But if water *has* **been p** on the seed and 5989
13:4 **p** the infected person **in isolation** 6037
13:11 *He is* not *to* **p** him **in isolation,** 6037
13:21 then the priest *is to* **p** him **in isolation** 6037
13:26 then the priest *is to* **p** him **in isolation** 6037
13:31 **p** the infected person **in isolation** 6037
14:14 of the blood of the guilt offering and **p** it on 5989
14:17 *to* **p** some of the oil remaining in his palm 5989
14:18 the priest *shall* **p** on the head of the one to 5989
14:25 and take some of its blood and **p** it on 5989
14:28 *to* **p** on the same places he put the blood of 5989
14:28 to put on the same places he **p** the blood of NIH
14:29 the priest *shall* **p** on the head of the one to 5989
14:34 and *I* **p** a spreading mildew in a house in 5989
16:4 *He is to* **p on** the sacred linen tunic, 4252
16:4 to tie the linen sash around him and **p on** 7571
16:13 *He is to* **p** the incense on the fire before 5989
16:18 and some of the goat's blood and **p** it on all 5989
16:21 and **p** them on the goat's head. 5989
16:23 and take off the linen garments *he* **p on** 4252
16:24 a holy place and **p on** his regular garments. 4252
16:32 *He is to* **p on** the sacred linen garments 4252
19:14 or **p** a stumbling block in front of the blind, 5989
19:20 Yet *they are* not *to* **be p to death,** 4637
19:28 the dead or **p** tattoo marks on yourselves. 5989
20:2 to Molech **must be p to death.** 4637+4637
20:4 to Molech and they fail to **p** him **to death,** 4637
20:9 *he* **must be p to death.** 4637+4637
20:10 the adulteress **must be p to death.** 4637+4637
20:11 and the woman **must be p to death;** 4637+4637
20:12 both of them **must be p to death.** 4637+4637
20:13 *They* **must be p to death;** 4637+4637
20:15 *he* **must be p to death,** 4637+4637
20:16 *he* **must be p to death;** 4637+4637
20:27 among you **must be p to death.** 4637+4637
24:7 Along each row **p** some pure incense as 5989
24:12 *They* **p** him in custody until the will of 5663
24:16 **must be p to death.** 4637+4637
24:16 *he* **must be p to death.** 4637
24:17 **must be p to death.** 4637+4637
24:21 whoever kills a man *must* **be p to death.** 4637
26:11 *I will* **p** my dwelling place among you, 5989
26:36 a windblown leaf *will* **p** them **to flight.** 8103
27:29 *he* **must be p to death.** 4637+4637
Nu 1:51 who goes near it *shall* **be p to death.** 4637
3:10 approaches the sanctuary *must* **be p to death."** 4637
3:38 *was to* **be p to death.** 4637
4:6 and **p** the poles **in place.** 8492
4:7 to spread a blue cloth and **p** on it the plates, 5989
4:8 and **p** its poles **in place.** 8492
4:10 a covering of hides of sea cows and **p** it on 5989
4:11 and **p** its poles **in place.** 8492
4:12 that with hides of sea cows and **p** them on 5989
4:14 and **p** its poles **in place.** 8492
5:15 He must not pour oil on it or **p** incense 5989
5:17 and **p** some dust from the tabernacle floor 5989
5:19 **p** the woman **under oath** 8678
5:21 **p** the woman under this curse *of* the **oath—** 8652+8678
6:18 and **p** it in the fire that is under the sacrifice 5989
6:27 "So *they will* **p** my name on the Israelites, 8492
11:11 that *you* **p** the burden of all these people 8492
11:15 **p** me **to death** right now— 2222+2222
11:17 of the Spirit that is on you and **p** the Spirit 8492
11:25 the Spirit that was on him and **p** the Spirit 5989
11:29 the LORD *would* **p** his Spirit on them!" 5989
14:15 If *you* **p** these people **to death** all at one 4637
16:7 and tomorrow **p** fire and incense in them 5989
16:17 to take his censer and **p** incense in it— 5989
16:18 **p** fire and incense in it, 5989
16:21 from this assembly so *I can* **p an end** 3983
16:45 from this assembly so *I can* **p an end** 3983
16:46 "Take your censer and **p** incense in it, 5989
17:10 "**P back** Aaron's staff in front of 8740
17:10 *This will* **p an end** *to* their grumbling 3983
18:7 near the sanctuary *must* **be p to death."** 4637
18:8 "*I* myself *have* **p** you in charge of 5989
19:9 up the ashes of the heifer and **p** them in 5663
19:17 **p** some ashes from the burned purification 4374
20:26 Remove Aaron's garments and **p** them **on** 4252
20:28 and **p** them **on** his son Eleazar. 4252
21:8 "Make a snake and **p** it **up** on a pole; 8492
21:9 So Moses made a bronze snake and **p** it **up** 8492
21:24 **p** him to the sword and took over his land 5782

Nu 22: 6 Now come and p a curse on these people, 826
22:11 Now come and p a curse on them for me. 7686
22:12 You must not p a curse on those people, 826
22:17 and p a curse on these people for me." 7686
23: 5 The LORD p a message in Balaam's mouth 8492
23:16 with Balaam and p a message in his mouth 8492
25: 5 "Each of you must p to death those 2222
25:11 that in my zeal I did not p an end to them. 3983
25:15 Midianite woman who was p to death was 5782
31:23 that can withstand fire must be p through 6296
31:23 be p through that water. 6296
35:16 the murderer shall be p to death. 4637+4637
35:17 the murderer shall be p to death. 4637+4637
35:18 the murderer shall be p to death. 4637+4637
35:19 shall p the murderer to death; 4637
35:19 he shall p him to death. 4637
35:21 that person shall be p to death; 4637+4637
35:21 shall p the murderer to death 4637
35:30 to be p to death as a murderer only on 8357
35:30 But no one is to be p to death on 4637
35:31 must surely be p to death. 4637+4637
Dt 1:41 So every one of you p on his weapons, 2520
2: 5 not even enough to p your foot on. 4534
2:25 This very day I will begin to p the terror 5989
9:28 he brought them out to p them to death in 4637
10: 2 Then you are to p them in the chest." 8492
10: 5 down the mountain and p the tablets in 8492
11:25 will p the terror and fear of you on 5989
12: 5 among all your tribes to p his Name there 8492
12: 7 in everything you have p your hand to, 5448
12:18 in everything you p your hand to. 5448
12:21 to p his Name is too far away from you, 8492
13: 5 or dreamer must be p to death, 4637
13: 9 you must certainly p him to death. 2222+2222
13:15 you must certainly p to the sword 5782+5782
14:24 the LORD will choose to p his Name is 8492
15:10 and in everything you p your hand to. 5448
15:19 p the firstborn of your oxen to work, 6268
16: 9 from the time you begin to p the sickle to NIH
17: 6 a man shall be p to death, 4637
17: 6 but no one shall be p to death on 4637
17:12 the LORD your God must be p to death. 4637
18:18 I will p my words in his mouth, 5989
18:20 of other gods, must be p to death." 4637
20:13 p to the sword all the men in it. 5782
21:13 and p aside the clothes she was wearing 6073
21:22 of a capital offense is p to death 4637
23:20 in everything you p your hand to in 5448
23:24 but do not p any in your basket. 5989
23:25 not p a sickle to his standing grain. 5677
24:16 not be p to death for their children, 4637
24:16 nor children p to death for their fathers; 4637
26: 2 and p them in a basket. 8492
28: 8 and on everything you p your hand to. 5448
28:20 in everything you p your hand to, 5448
28:48 He will p an iron yoke on your neck 5989
30: 7 The LORD your God will p all these curses 5989
32:30 or two p ten thousand to flight, 5674
32:39 I p to death and I bring to life, 4637
Jos 1:18 will be p to death. 4637
4: 3 over with you and p them down at the place 5663
4: 8 where they p them down. 5663
6:23 and p them in a place outside the camp 5663
6:24 but they p the silver and gold and 5989
7:11 they have p them with their own possessions 8492
8:24 and when every one of them had been p to 5877
9: 5 The men p worn and patched sandals NIH
10:24 "Come here and p your feet on the necks 8492
10:28 He p the city and its king to the sword 5782
10:30 and everyone in it Joshua p to the sword. 5782
10:32 and everyone in it he p to the sword, 5782
10:35 They captured it that same day and p it to 5782
10:37 They took the city and p it to the sword, 5782
10:39 and p them to the sword. 5782
11:10 captured Hazor and p its king to the sword. 5782
11:11 Everyone in it they p to the sword. 5782
11:12 and their kings and p them to the sword. 5782
11:14 but all the people they p to the sword 5782
13:22 the Israelites had p to the sword Balaam son 2222
19:47 took it, p it to the sword and occupied it. 5782
24: 7 and he p darkness between you and 8492
24: 9 for Balaam son of Beor to p a curse on you. 7837
Jdg 1: 8 They p the city to the sword and set it 5782
1:25 and they p the city to the sword but spared 5782
4:18 and she p a covering over him. 4059
6:13 now the LORD has abandoned us and p us 5989
6:31 Whoever fights for him shall be p to death 4637
9:26 and its citizens p their confidence in him. 1053
16:19 Having p him to sleep on her lap, 3822
16:26 "P me where I can feel the pillars 5663
17: 4 And they were p in Micah's house. 2118
18:10 and a spacious land that God has p 5989
19:28 the man p her on his donkey and set out 4374
20:13 so that we may p them to death and purge 4637
20:37 and p the whole city to the sword. 5782
20:48 of Israel went back to Benjamin and p all 5782
21: 5 should certainly be p to death. 4637+4637
21:10 and p to the sword those living there, 5782
Ru 3: 3 and p on your best clothes. 8492
3:15 into it six measures of barley and p it 8883
1Sa 2:25 the LORD's will to p them to death. 4637
5: 3 They took Dagon and p him back 8740
6: 8 the ark of the LORD and p it on the cart, 5989
6: 8 and in a chest beside it p the gold objects 8492
7: 4 So the Israelites p away their Baals 6073
11:12 to us and we will p them to death." 4637
11:13 "No one shall be p to death today, 4637
1Sa 14:26 yet no one p his hand to his mouth, 5952
14:45 and he was not p to death. 4637
15: 3 p to death men and women, 4637
15:33 And Samuel p Agag to death before 9119
17:38 He p a coat of armor on him 4252
17:40 p them in the pouch of his shepherd's bag 8492
17:54 and he p the Philistine's weapons 8492
19: 6 David will not be p to death." 4637
20:32 "Why should he be p to death? 4637
22:19 He also p to the sword Nob, 5782
25:13 "P on your swords!" 2520
25:13 So they p on their swords, 2520
25:13 and David p on his. 2520
26:12 the LORD had p them into a deep sleep. 5877
31:10 They p his armor in the temple of 8492
2Sa 3:31 and p on sackcloth and walk in mourning 2520
4:10 I seized him and p him to death in Ziklag. 2222
8: 2 Every two lengths of them were p to death, 4637
8: 6 He p garrisons in the Aramean kingdom 8492
8:14 He p garrisons throughout Edom, 8492
10:10 He p the rest of the men under the command 5989
11:15 "P Uriah in the front line where 2035
11:16 he p Uriah at a place where he knew 5989
12:20 p on lotions and changed his clothes, 6057
13:18 So his servant p her out and 2021+2575+3655
13:19 Tamar p ashes on her head and tore 4374
13:19 She p her hand on her head and went away, 8492
14: 3 And Joab p the words in her mouth. 8492
14: 7 so that we may p him to death for the life 4637
14: 7 They would p out the only burning coal 3882
14:19 and who p all these words into the mouth 8492
14:32 let him p me to death." 4637
15:14 to overtake us and bring ruin upon us and p 5782
17:23 p his house in order and then hanged 7422
18:13 p my life in jeopardy— 6913+9214
19:19 May the king p it out of his mind. 8492
19:21 "Shouldn't Shimei be p to death for this? 4637
19:22 Should anyone be p to death 4637
20: 3 to take care of the palace and p them in 5989
21: 1 because he p the Gibeonites to death." 4637
21: 4 the right to p anyone in Israel to death." 4637
21: 9 they were p to death during the first days 4637
23:23 David p him in charge of his bodyguard. 8492
1Ki 1: 1 even when they p covers over him. 4059
1: 5 p himself forward and said, 5951
1:38 the Pelethites went down and p Solomon 8206
1:44 and they have p him on the king's mule, 8206
1:51 that he will not p his servant to death 4637
2: 8 'I will not p you to death by the sword.' 4637
2:24 Adonijah shall be p to death today!" 4637
2:26 but I will not p you to death now, 4637
2:35 The king p Benaiah son of Jehoiada over 5989
3:20 She p him by her breast 8886
3:20 and p her dead son by my breast. 8886
5: 3 the LORD p his enemies under his feet. 5989
5: 5 'Your son whom I will p on the throne 5989
8: 6 and p it beneath the wings of the cherubim. NIH
10:17 The king p them in the Palace of the Forest 5989
10:24 to hear the wisdom God had p in his heart. 5989
11:28 he p him in charge of the whole labor force 7212
11:36 the city where I chose to p my Name. 8492
12: 4 "Your father p a heavy yoke on us, 7996
12: 4 the harsh labor and the heavy yoke he p 5989
12: 9 'Lighten the yoke your father p on us'?" 5989
12:10 'Your father p a heavy yoke on us, 3877
14:21 the tribes of Israel in which to p his Name. 8492
18: 9 over to Ahab to be p to death? 4637
18:23 and p it on the wood but not set fire to it. 8492
18:23 and p it on the wood but not set fire to it. 5989
18:42 bent down to the ground and p his face 8492
19:10 p your prophets to death with the sword. 2222
19:14 p your prophets to death with the sword. 2222
19:17 Jehu will p to death any who escape 4637
19:17 and Elisha will p to death any who escape 4637
21:27 p on sackcloth and fasted. 8492
22:23 "So now the LORD has p a lying spirit in 5989
22:27 P this fellow in prison 8492
2Ki 2:20 he said, "and p salt in it." 8492
4: 4 as each is filled, p it to one side." 5825
4:10 Let's make a small room on the roof and p 8492
4:38 "P on the large pot and cook some stew 9189
4:41 He p it into the pot and said, 8959
5:24 the servants and p them away in the house. 7212
7:17 p the officer on whose arm he leaned in charge of the gate, 7212
10: 7 They p their heads in baskets and sent them 8492
10: 8 "P them in two piles at the entrance of 8492
11: 2 She p him and his nurse in a bedroom NIH
11: 4 and p them under oath at the temple of 8678
11: 8 Anyone who approaches your ranks must be p to death. 4637
11:12 Jehoiada brought out the king's son and p 5989
11:15 "Bring her out between the ranks and p to 4637S
11:15 "She must not be p to death in the temple 4637
11:16 and there she was p to death. 4637
12: 9 The priests who guarded the entrance p into 5989
12:10 of the LORD and p it into bags. 7443
13:16 Elisha p his hands on the king's hands. 8492
14: 6 p the sons of the assassins to death, 4637
14: 6 not be p to death for their children, 4637
14: 6 nor children p to death for their fathers; 4637
16: 9 to Kir and p Rezin to death. 4637
16:14 and p it on the north side of the new altar. 5989
17: 4 and p him in prison. 673
18:23 if you can p riders on them! 5989
19: 1 he tore his clothes and p on sackcloth 4059
19: 7 to p such a spirit in him that when he hears 5989
2Ki 19:26 are dismayed and p to shame. 1017
19:28 I will p my hook in your nose and my bit 8492
19:35 of the LORD went out and p to death 5782
20: 1 P your house in order, 7422
21: 4 "In Jerusalem I will p my Name." 8492
21: 7 and p it in the temple, 8492
21: 7 I will p my Name forever. 8492
23:33 Pharaoh Neco p him in chains at Riblah in 673
25: 7 Then they p out his eyes, 6422
25:29 So Jehoiachin p aside his prison clothes and 9101
1Ch 1: 8 Cush, Mizraim, P and Canaan. 7033
2: 3 so the LORD p him to death. 4637
6:31 the men David p in charge of the music 3338+6584+6641
10:10 They p his armor in the temple 8492
10:14 So the LORD p him to death and turned 4637
11:25 David p him in charge of his bodyguard. 8492
12:15 and they p to flight everyone living in 1368
13:10 down because he had p his hand on the ark. 8938
18: 6 He p garrisons in the Aramean kingdom 8492
18:13 He p garrisons in Edom, 8492
19:11 He p the rest of the men under the command 5989
21:27 and he p his sword back into its sheath. 8740
26:32 and King David p them in charge of 7212
28:12 the Spirit had p in his mind for the courts of 2118
2Ch 3:16 He made interwoven chains and p them 5989
5: 7 and p it beneath the wings of the cherubim. NIH
6:20 you said you would p your Name there. 8492
9:16 The king p them in the Palace of the Forest 5989
9:23 to hear the wisdom God had p in his heart. 5989
10: 4 "Your father p a heavy yoke on us, 7996
10: 4 the harsh labor and the heavy yoke he p 5989
10: 9 'Lighten the yoke your father p on us'?" 5989
10:10 'Your father p a heavy yoke on us, 3877
11:11 and p commanders in them, 5989
11:12 He p shields and spears in all the cities, NIH
12:13 the tribes of Israel in which to p his Name. 8492
14: 7 he said to Judah, "and p walls around them, 6015
15:13 the God of Israel, were to be p to death, 4637
16:10 he was so enraged that he p him in prison. 5989
17: 2 the fortified cities of Judah and p garrisons 5989
18:22 "So now the LORD has p a lying spirit in 5989
18:26 P this fellow in prison 8492
21: 4 he p all his brothers to the sword along 2222
22: 9 He was brought to Jehu and p to death. 4637
22:11 to be murdered and p him and his nurse in 5989
23: 7 enters the temple must be p to death. 4637
23:11 the king's son and p the crown on him; 5989
23:14 "Bring her out between the ranks and p to 4637S
23:14 "Do not p her to death at the temple of 4637
23:15 and there they p her to death. 4637
25: 4 he did not p their sons to death, 4637
25: 4 not be p to death for their children, AIT
25: 4 nor children p to death for their fathers; AIT
28:15 All those who were weak they p on donkeys 5633
29: 7 also shut the doors of the portico and p out 3882
33: 7 the carved image he had made and p it 8492
33: 7 I will p my Name forever. 8492
33:11 p a hook in his nose, NIH
35: 3 "P the sacred ark in the temple 5989
35:24 p him in the other chariot he had 8206
36: 7 the LORD and p them in his temple there. 5989
36:22 throughout his realm and to p it in writing: NIH
Ezr 1: 1 throughout his realm and to p it in writing: NIH
7:27 who has p it into the king's heart 5989
10: 5 p the leading priests and Levites and all Israel under oath 8678
10:19 in pledge to p away their wives, 3655
Ne 2:12 I had not told anyone what my God had p 5989
3: 3 p its doors and bolts and bars in place. 6641
3: 5 but their nobles would not p their shoulders 995
3: 6 p its doors and bolts and bars in place. 6641
3:13 p its doors and bolts and bars in place. 6641
3:14 p its doors and bolts and bars in place. 6641
4:11 kill them and p an end to the work." 8697
7: 2 I p in charge of Jerusalem 7422
7: 5 So my God p it into my heart to assemble 5989
9:26 they p your law behind their backs. 8959
9:31 in your great mercy you did not p an end 6913
13: 4 Eliashib the priest had been p in charge of 5989
13: 9 then I p back into them the equipment of 8740
13:13 p Shelemiah the priest, Zadok the scribe, and a Levite named Pedaiah in charge of the storerooms 238+732+6584
Est 2: 8 to the citadel of Susa and p under the care NIH
3: 9 and I will p ten thousand talents of silver 995+4200+9202
4: 1 p on sackcloth and ashes, 4252
4: 4 for him to p on instead of his sackcloth, 4252
4:11 but one law: that he be p to death. 4637
5: 1 Esther p on her royal robes 4252
8: 3 She begged him to p an end to the evil plan 6296
9:15 they p to death in Susa three hundred men, 2222
Job 1:10 "Have you not p a hedge around him 8455
1:15 They p the servants to the sword, 5782
1:17 They p the servants to the sword, 5782
7:12 that you p me under guard? 8492
11:14 if you p away the sin that is in your hand 8178
12:18 He takes off the shackles p on by kings AIT
13:14 Why do I p myself in jeopardy 928+1414+5951+9094
14: 6 till he has p in his time like a hired man. 8354
14: 9 it will bud and p forth shoots like a plant. 6913
17: 3 Who else will p up security for me? 3338+4200+9546
29:14 p on righteousness as my clothing; 4252
30: 1 whose fathers I would have disdained to p 8883

Job 31:24 "If *I have* **p** my trust *in* gold or said 8492
31:35 **p** *his* indictment **in writing.** 4180
31:36 *I would* **p** it **on** like a crown. 6698
34:13 Who **p** him **in charge** *of* the whole world? 8492
40: 4 *I* **p** my hand over my mouth. 8492
41: 2 *Can you* **p** a cord through his nose 8492
41: 5 or **p** him **on a leash** for your girls? 8003
Ps 8: 6 *you* **p** everything under his feet: 8883
22: 4 In you our fathers **p** *their* **trust;** 1053
25: 2 Do not *let me be* **p to shame,** 1017
25: 3 in you *will* ever *be* **p to shame,** 1017
25: 3 *be* **p to shame** who are treacherous 1017
25:20 *let me* not *be* **p to shame,** 1017
31: 1 *let me* never *be* **p to shame;** 1017
31:17 *Let me* not *be* **p to shame,** O LORD, 1017
31:17 the wicked *be* **p to shame** and lie silent in 1017
33:22 O LORD, even as *we* **p** *our* **hope** in you. 3498
35: 4 be disgraced and **p to shame;** 4007
35:13 **I p on** sackcloth and humbled myself 4230
35:26 over my distress *be* **p to shame** 1017
39: 1 *I will* **p** a muzzle on my mouth as long as 9068
40: 3 *He* **p** a new song in my mouth, 5989
40: 3 Many will see and fear and **p** *their* **trust** in 1053
40:14 *be* **p to shame** and confusion; 1017
42: 5 **P** *your* **hope** in God, 3498
42:11 **P** *your* **hope** in God, 3498
43: 5 **P** *your* **hope** in God, 3498
44: 7 **p** our adversaries **to shame.** 1017
53: 5 *you* **p** them **to shame,** 1017
69: 6 *may* those who seek you not **be p to shame** 4007
69:11 when *I* **p on** sackcloth, 4230+5989
69:21 *They* **p** gall in my food 5989
70: 2 *May* those who seek my life *be* **p to shame** 1017
71: 1 *let me* never *be* **p to shame.** 1017
71:24 to harm me *have been* **p to shame** 1017
78: 7 Then *they would* **p** their trust in God 8492
78:18 *They* willfully **p** God **to the test** 5814
78:31 *he* **p to death** the sturdiest among them, 2222
78:41 Again and again *they* **p** God **to the test;** 5814
78:56 But *they* **p** God **to the test** 5814
78:64 their priests *were* **p** to the sword, 5877
78:66 *he* **p** them to everlasting shame. 5989
85: 4 and **p away** your displeasure toward us. 7296
86:17 my enemies may see it and *be* **p to shame,** 1017
88: 6 *You have* **p** me in the lowest pit, 8883
89:44 *You have* **p an end** to his splendor 8697
97: 7 All who worship images *are* **p to shame,** 1017
101: 5 him *will I* **p to silence;** 7551
101: 8 Every morning *I will* **p to silence** all 7551
105:18 his neck *was* **p** in irons, 995
106:14 in the wasteland *they* **p** God **to the test.** 5814
109:28 when they attack *they will be* **p to shame,** 1017
119: 6 Then *I would* not *be* **p to shame** 1017
119:31 *do* not **let** me **be p to shame.** 1017
119:43 for *I have* **p** *my* **hope** in your laws. 3498
119:46 before kings and *will* not **be p to shame,** 1017
119:74 for *I have* **p** *my* **hope** in your word. 3498
119:78 the arrogant *be* **p to shame** for wronging me 1017
119:80 that *I may* not *be* **p to shame.** 1017
119:81 but *I have* **p** *my* **hope** in your word. 3498
119:114 *I have* **p** *my* **hope** in your word. 3498
119:147 *I have* **p** *my* **hope** in your word. 3498
127: 5 not *be* **p to shame** when they contend 1017
130: 5 my soul waits, and in his word *I* **p** *my* **hope.** 3498
130: 7 O Israel, **p** *your* **hope** in the LORD, 3498
131: 3 **p** *your* **hope** in the LORD both now 3498
143: 8 for *I have* **p** *my* **trust** in you. 1053
146: 3 *Do* not **p** *your* **trust** in princes, 1053
147:11 who **p** *their* **hope** in his unfailing love. 3498
Pr 4:24 **P away** perversity from your mouth; 6073
6: 1 *you have* **p up security** for your neighbor, 6842
23: 2 and **p** a knife to your throat if you are given 8492
29:24 *he is* **p under oath** and dare not testify. 460+9048
Ecc 10: 6 Fools **are p** in many high positions, 5989
SS 5: 3 *must I* **p** it **on** again? 4252
Isa 5:20 *who* **p** darkness for light and light 8492
5:20 *who* **p** bitter for sweet and sweet for bitter. 8492
7:12 *I will* not **p** the LORD **to the test."** 5814
8:17 *I will* **p** *my* **trust** in him. 7747
10: 7 to **p an end** *to* many nations. 4162
11: 8 young child **p** his hand into the viper's nest. 2063
13:11 *I will* **p an end** *to* the arrogance of 8697
16:10 for *I have* **p an end** *to* the shouting. 8697
20: 5 in Egypt will be afraid and **p to shame.** 1017
22:12 to tear out your hair and **p on** sackcloth. 2520
26:11 for your people and *be* **p to shame;** 1017
30: 5 *be* **p to shame** because of a people useless 1017
31: 8 the sword and their young men *will be* **p** 2118
32:11 **p sackcloth around** your waists. 2520
36: 8 if you can **p** riders on them! 5989
37: 1 he tore his clothes and **p on** sackcloth 4059
37: 7 *to* **p** a spirit in him so that when he hears 5989
37:27 are dismayed and **p to shame.** 1017
37:29 *I will* **p** my hook in your nose and my bit 8492
37:36 of the LORD went out and **p to death** 5782
38: 1 **P** your house **in order,** 7422
38:17 *you have* **p** all my sins behind your back. 8959
41:19 *I will* **p** in the desert the cedar and 5989
42: 1 *I will* **p** my Spirit on him 5989
42: 4 In his law the islands *will* **p** *their* **hope."** 3498
44:11 *He* and his kind *will be* **p to shame;** 1017
45:16 All the makers of idols *will be* **p to shame** 1017
45:17 *you will* never *be* **p to shame** or disgraced, 1017
45:24 to him and *be* **p to shame.** 1017
49:18 *you will* **p** them **on,** like a bride. 8003
50: 7 and I know *I will* not *be* **p to shame.** 1017
51:16 *I have* **p** my words in your mouth 8492
Isa 51:23 *I will* **p** it into the hands of your tormentors, 8492
52: 1 **P on** your garments of splendor, 4252
57: 8 doorposts *you have* **p** your pagan symbols. 8492
59:17 *He* **p on** righteousness as his breastplate, 4252
59:17 *he* **p on** the garments of vengeance 4252+9432
59:21 that *I have* **p** in your mouth will not depart 8492
65:13 but you *will be* **p to shame.** 1017
65:15 the Sovereign LORD *will* **p** you **to death,** 4637
66: 5 Yet they *will be* **p to shame.** 1017
Jer 1: 9 "Now, *I have* **p** my words in your mouth. 5989
4: 1 **p** your detestable idols **out** of my sight 6073
4: 8 So **p on** sackcloth, lament and wail, 2520
4:30 Why dress yourself in scarlet and **p on** 6335
6:21 "I *will* **p** obstacles before this people. 5989
6:26 **p on** sackcloth and roll in ashes; 2520
8: 9 The wise *will be* **p to shame;** 1017
13: 1 a linen belt and **p** it around your waist, 8492
13: 2 and **p** it around my waist. 8492
15: 9 *I will* **p** the survivors to the sword 5989
17:13 all who forsake you *will be* **p to shame.** 1017
17:18 *Let* my persecutors *be* **p to shame,** 1017
18:21 let their men be **p to death,** 2222+4638
20: 2 he had Jeremiah the prophet beaten and **p** 5989
20: 4 to Babylon or **p** them to the sword. 5782
21: 7 *He will* **p** them to the sword; 5782
25:31 on all mankind and **p** the wicked to 5989
26:15 however, that if you **p** me **to death,** 4637
26:19 anyone else in Judah **p** him **to death?** 4637+4637
26:21 the king sought to **p** him **to death.** 4637
26:24 over to the people to *be* **p to death.** 4637
27: 2 a yoke out of straps and crossbars and **p** it 5989
28:14 *I will* **p** an iron yoke on the necks 5989
29:21 of Babylon, and *he will* **p** them **to death** 5782
29:26 *you should* **p** any madman who acts like 5989
31:21 "Set up road signs; **p up** guideposts. 8492
31:33 *"I will* **p** my law in their minds 5989
32:14 and **p** them in a clay jar so they will last 5989
36:20 After *they* **p** the scroll in the room 7212
37: 4 for he *had* not yet *been* **p** *in* prison. 5989
37:16 Jeremiah *was* **p** into a vaulted cell in 995
37:18 that *you have* **p** me in prison? 5989
38: 4 "This man *should* **be p to death.** 4637
38: 6 and **p** him into the cistern of Malkijah, 8959
38: 7 that *they had* **p** Jeremiah into the cistern. 5989
38:12 **"P** these old rags and worn-out clothes 8492
39: 7 Then *he* **p out** Zedekiah's eyes 6422
40: 7 and *had* **p** him **in charge** *of* the men, 7212
40:10 and **p** them in your storage jars, 8492
46: 4 Polish your spears, **p on** your armor! 4252
46: 9 men of Cush and **P** who carry shields, 7033
46:24 The Daughter of Egypt *will be* **p to shame,** 1017
48: 2 'Come, *let us* **p an end** to that nation.' 4162
48: 9 **P** salt on Moab, for she will be laid waste; 5989
48:35 In Moab *I will* **p an end** *to* those who 8697
49: 3 **P on** sackcloth and mourn; 2520
50: 2 Bel *will be* **p to shame,** 1017
50: 2 *be* **p to shame** and her idols filled 1017
51: 3 nor *let him* **p on** his armor. 6590
52:11 Then *he* **p out** Zedekiah's eyes, 6422
52:11 where *he* **p** him in prison till the day 5989
52:33 So Jehoiachin **p aside** his prison clothes and 9101
La 2:10 on their heads and **p on** sackcloth. 2520
3:65 **P** a veil over their hearts, 5989
Eze 3:20 and *I* **p** a stumbling block before him, 5989
4: 1 **p** it in front of you and draw the city 5989
4: 2 set up camps against it and **p** battering rams 8492
4: 4 on your left side and **p** the sin of the house 8492
4: 9 **p** them in a storage jar and use them 5989
7:18 *They will* **p on** sackcloth and be clothed 2520
7:24 *I will* **p an end** *to* the pride of the mighty, 8697
9: 4 and **p a mark** *on* the foreheads of 9338+9344
10: 7 and **p** it into the hands of the man in linen, 5989
11:19 I will give them an undivided heart and **p** 5989
12: 6 **P** them on your shoulder 5951
12:12 "The prince among them *will* **p** his things 5951
12:23 *I am going to* **p an end** *to* this proverb, 8697
14: 3 and **p** wicked stumbling blocks 5989
16: 9 and **p** ointments **on** you. 6057
16:10 and **p** leather **sandals on** you. 5836
16:11 *I* **p** bracelets on your arms and a necklace 5989
16:12 and *I* **p** a ring on your nose, 5989
16:18 embroidered clothes *to* **p on** them, 4059
16:41 *I will* **p a stop** to your prostitution, 8697
17: 5 the seed of your land and **p** it in fertile soil. 5989
17: 6 and **p out** leafy boughs. 8938
17:16 the king who **p** him **on** *the* **throne,** 4887
18:13 *he will* **surely be p to death** 4637+4637
19: 9 *They* **p** him in prison, 995
20:17 not destroy them or **p** an end *to* them in 6913
22:15 and *I will* **p an end** *to* your uncleanness. 9462
22:20 in my anger and my wrath and **p** you inside 5663
23:27 So *I will* **p a stop** *to* the lewdness 8697
23:31 so *I will* **p** her cup into your hand. 5989
23:40 your eyes and **p on** *your* **jewelry.** 6335+6344
23:42 the rabble, and *they* **p** bracelets on the arms 5989
23:48 *I will* **p an end** *to* lewdness in the land, 8697
24: 3 " **'P on** the cooking pot; 9189
24: 3 **p** it **on** and pour water into it. 9189
24: 4 **P** into it the pieces of meat, 665
24: 8 up wrath and take revenge *I* **p** her blood 5989
26:13 *I will* **p an end** *to* your noisy songs, 8697
26:17 *you* **p** your terror on all who lived there. 5989
27:10 and **P** served as soldiers in your army. 7033
27:31 because of you and *will* **p on** sackcloth. 2520
29: 4 But *I will* **p** hooks in your jaws and make 5989
30: 5 Cush and **P**, Lydia and all Arabia, 7033
30:10 " *'I will* **p an end** *to* the hordes of Egypt 8697
Eze 30:13 " 'I will destroy the idols and **p an end** *to* 8697
30:21 It has not been bound up for healing or **p** 8492
30:24 of Babylon and **p** my sword in his hand, 5989
30:25 when I **p** my sword into the hand of 5989
33:31 but *they do* not **p** them **into practice.** 6913
33:32 but *do* not **p** them **into practice.** 6913
36:26 a new heart and **p** a new spirit in you; 5989
36:27 And *I will* **p** my Spirit in you 5989
37: 6 *I will* **p** breath in you, 5989
37:14 *I will* **p** my Spirit in you 5989
37:26 and *I will* **p** my sanctuary among them 5989
38: 4 **p** hooks in your jaws and bring you out 5989
38: 5 Persia, Cush and **P** will be with them, 7033
42:13 There *they will* **p** the most holy offerings 5663
42:14 *to* **p on** other clothes before they go near 4252
43: 9 Now *let them* **p away** from me 8178
43:20 You are to take some of its blood and **p** it 5989
44: 8 *you* **p** others in charge of my sanctuary. 8492
44:14 Yet *I will* **p** them in charge of the duties 5989
44:19 and **p on** other clothes, 4252
45:19 the sin offering and **p** it on the doorposts of 5989
Da 1: 2 in Babylonia and **p in** the treasure house 995
2:13 to **p** the wise men **to death,** 10625
2:13 and his friends to **p** them **to death.** 10625
2:14 had gone out to **p to death** the wise men 10625
5:19 Those the king wanted to **p** to death, NIH
5:19 wanted to put to death, *he* **p to death;** 10625
6: 8 issue the decree and **p** it **in writing** 10375+10673
6: 9 Darius **p** the decree **in writing.** 10375+10673
6:13 O king, or to the decree *you* **p in writing.** 10673
9:24 to **p an end** *to* sin, to atone for wickedness, 9462
9:27 of the 'seven' *he will* **p an end** *to* sacrifice 8697
11:18 commander *will* **p an end** *to* his insolence 8697
Hos 1: 4 *I will* **p an end** *to* the kingdom of Israel. 8697
8: 1 **"P** the trumpet to your lips! NIH
10:10 *to* **p** them **in bonds** for their double sin. 673
10:11 so I *will* **p a yoke** on her fair neck. 6296
11: 6 of their gates and **p an end** to their plans. 430
Joel 1:13 **P on** sackcloth, O priests, and mourn; 2520
Am 6: 3 *You* **p off** the evil day and bring near 5612
Jnh 3: 5 from the greatest to the least, **p on** sackcloth 4252
Mic 7: 5 **p** no **confidence** in a friend. 1053
Na 2: 5 the protective shield *is* **p in place.** 3922
3: 9 **P** and Libya were among her allies. 7033
3:10 and all her great men **were p in chains.** 928+2414+8415
Zep 3:11 that day *you will* not *be* **p to shame** for all 1017
3:19 and honor in every land where they were **p** NIH
Hag 1: 6 *You* **p on clothes,** but are not warm. 4252
1: 6 only to **p** them in a purse with holes in it." NIH
Zec 3: 4 and *I will* **p** rich garments **on** you." 4252
3: 5 Then I said, **"P** a clean turban on his head." 8492
3: 5 So *they* **p** a clean turban on his head 8492
13: 4 *He will* not **p on** a prophet's garment 4252
Mt 4: 7 *'Do* not **p** the Lord your God **to the test.' "** *1733*
4:12 that John *had been* **p in prison,** *4140*
5:15 Neither do people light a lamp and **p** it *5502*
5:15 Instead they **p** it on its stand, *NIG*
6:17 **p oil on** your head and wash your face, *230*
7:26 and *does* not **p** them **into practice** is like *4472*
9:18 But come and **p** your hand **on** her, *2202*
9:25 After the crowd *had been* **p outside,** *1675*
10:21 and *have* them **p to death.** *2506*
12:18 *I will* **p** my Spirit on him, *5502*
12:21 In his name the nations *will* **p** *their* **hope."** *1827*
12:44 swept clean and **p in order.** *3175*
14: 3 and bound him and **p** him in prison because *700*
15: 4 or mother *must be* **p to death.'** *2505+5462*
17: 4 If you wish, *I will* **p up** three shelters— *4472*
17:17 How long *shall I* **p up with** you? *462*
21:33 *He* **p** a wall **around** it, *4363*
22:44 until *I* **p** your enemies under your feet." ' *5502*
23: 4 *They* tie up heavy loads and **p** them **on** *2202*
24: 9 over to be persecuted and **p to death,** *650*
24:45 the master *has* **p in charge** of the servants *2770*
24:47 *he will* **p** him **in charge** of all *2770*
25:16 **p** his money **to work** and gained five more. *2237*
25:21 *I will* **p** you **in charge** of many things. *2770*
25:23 *I will* **p** you **in charge** of many things. *2770*
25:27 you should have **p** my money on deposit *965*
25:33 *He will* **p** the sheep on his right and *2705*
26:52 **"P** your sword **back** in its place," *695*
26:53 at once **p at** my **disposal** more than twelve legions of angels? *4225*
26:59 so that *they could* **p** him **to death.** *2506*
27: 1 to the decision *to* **p** Jesus **to death.** *2506*
27: 6 against the law *to* **p** this into the treasury, *965*
27:28 and **p** a scarlet robe **on** him, *4363*
27:29 They **p** a staff in his right hand and knelt *NIG*
27:31 and **p** his own clothes **on** him. *1907*
27:48 **p** it **on** a stick, and offered it to Jesus *4363*
Mk 1:14 After John *was* **p in prison,** *4140*
4:21 in a lamp to **p** it under a bowl or a bed? *5502*
4:21 Instead, don't you **p** it on its stand? *5502*
5:23 Please come and **p** your hands **on** her so *2202*
5:40 *After* he **p** them all **out,** *1675*
6:17 and he had him bound and **p** in prison. *NIG*
7:10 or mother *must be* **p to death.'** *2505+5462*
7:33 Jesus **p** his fingers into the man's ears. *965*
8:23 on the man's eyes and **p** his hands **on** him, *2202*
8:25 Once more Jesus **p** his hands **on** *2202*
9: 5 *Let us* **p up** three shelters— *4472*
9:19 How long *shall I* **p up with** you? *462*
10:16 **p** his hands on them and blessed them. *5502*
12: 1 *He* **p** a wall **around** it, *4363*
12:36 until *I* **p** your enemies under your feet." ' *5502*
12:41 the **place where the offerings were p** *1126*

Mk 12:42 and **p** in two very small copper coins, *965*
12:43 this poor widow *has* **p** more into *965*
12:44 **p** in everything—all she had to live on." *965*
13:12 and *have* them **p to death.** *2506*
14:55 so that they could **p** him **to death,** *2506*
15:17 *They* **p** a purple robe **on** him, *1898*
15:20 and **p** his own clothes **on** him. *1907*
15:36 **p** it **on** a stick, and offered it to Jesus *4363*
Lk 4:12 *'Do not* **p** the Lord your God **to the test.'** " *1733*
5:3 and asked him *to* **p out** a little from shore. *2056*
5:4 he said to Simon, "**P out** into deep water, *2056*
6:49 and *does* not **p** them **into practice** is like *4472*
7:46 *You did* not **p** oil **on** my head, *230*
8:21 hear God's word and **p** it **into practice."** *4472*
9:33 *Let us* **p up** three shelters— *4472*
9:41 with you and **p up with** you? *462*
10:34 Then *he* **p** the man **on** his own donkey, *2097*
11:25 the house swept clean and **p in order.** *3175*
12:44 *he will* **p** him **in charge** of all *2770*
13:13 Then *he* **p** his hands **on** her, *2202*
15:22 Bring the best robe and **p** it **on** him. *1907*
15:22 **P** a ring on his finger and sandals *1443*
19:13 '**P** this money **to work,'** *4549*
19:21 not **p in** and reap what you did not sow.' *5502*
19:22 taking out what *I did* not **p in,** *5502*
19:23 then didn't *you* **p** my money on deposit, *1443*
19:35 on the colt and **p** Jesus **on** it. *2097*
21:2 He also saw a poor widow **p** *965*
21:3 "this poor widow *has* **p** in more than all *965*
21:4 of her poverty **p** in all she had to live on." *965*
21:16 and *they will* **p** some of you **to death.** *2506*
23:26 and **p** the cross **on** him and made him carry *2202*
Jn 2:11 and his disciples **p** *their* **faith** in him. *4409*
3:24 (This was before John was **p** in prison.) *965*
7:31 many in the crowd **p** *their* **faith** in him. *4409*
8:20 the **place where the offerings were p.** *1126*
8:30 as he spoke, many **p** *their* **faith** in him. *4409*
9:6 and **p** it **on** the man's eyes. *2222*
9:11 and **p** it **on** my eyes. *2222*
9:15 *"He* **p** mud **on** my eyes," the man replied, *2202*
9:22 *would be* **p out of the synagogue.** *697*
11:45 had seen what Jesus did, **p** *their* **faith** in him *4409*
12:6 he used to help himself to what *was* **p** into it. *965*
12:36 **P** *your* **trust** in the light while you have it, *4409*
12:42 *they would be* **p out of the synagogue;** *697*
13:3 the Father *had* **p** all things under his power, *1443*
13:12 *he* **p on** his clothes and returned *3284*
16:2 *They will* **p** you **out of the synagogue;** *697+4472*
18:11 "**P** your sword away! *965*
19:2 a crown of thorns and **p** it **on** his head. *2202*
19:29 **p** the sponge **on** a stalk of the hyssop plant, *4363*
20:2 we don't know where *they have* **p** him!" *5502*
20:13 "and I don't know where *they have* **p** him." *5502*
20:15 tell me where *you have* **p** him, *5502*
20:25 the nail marks in his hands and **p** my finger *965*
20:25 and **p** my hand into his side, *965*
20:27 he said to Thomas, "**P** your finger here; *5770*
20:27 Reach out your hand and **p** it into my side. *965*
Ac 2:23 **p** him **to death** by nailing him to the cross. *359*
3:2 where he *was* **p** every day to beg *5502*
4:3 *they* **p** them in jail until the next day, *5502*
4:35 and **p** it at the apostles' feet. *5502*
4:37 the money and **p** it at the apostles' feet. *5502*
5:2 the rest and **p** it at the apostles' feet. *5502*
5:18 the apostles and **p** them in the public jail. *5502*
5:25 The men *you* **p** in jail are standing in *5502*
5:33 and wanted *to* **p** them **to death.** *359*
5:34 that the men *be* **p** outside for a little while. *4472*
7:53 that was **p into effect** through angels *1408*
8:3 he dragged off men and women and **p** them *4140*
12:2 **p to death** with the sword. *359*
12:4 After arresting him, *he* **p** him in prison, *5502*
12:8 "**P on** your **clothes** and sandals." *2439*
14:23 in whom *they had* **p** *their* **trust.** *4409*
16:11 From Troas we **p out to sea** *343*
16:24 *he* **p** them in the inner cell *965*
20:10 the young man and **p** *his* **arms around** him. *5227*
21:1 we **p out to sea** and sailed straight to Cos. *343*
22:29 **p** Paul, a Roman citizen, **in chains.** *1313*
26:10 the authority of the chief priests I **p** many *2881*
26:10 and *when* they *were* **p to death,** *359*
27:2 and *we* **p out to sea.** *343*
27:4 From there we **p out to sea** again *343*
27:6 for Italy and **p** us **on board.** *899+1650+1837*
28:3 *as he* **p** it **on** the fire, a viper, *2202*
28:11 After three months *we* **p out to sea** in *343*
28:12 We **p in** at Syracuse and stayed there *2864*
Ro 6:19 **I p this in human terms** because *474+3306*
7:11 through the commandment **p** me **to death.** *650*
8:13 if by the Spirit *you* **p to death** the misdeeds *2506*
9:33 trusts in him *will* never *be* **p to shame."** *2875*
10:11 trusts in him *will* never *be* **p to shame."** *2875*
13:12 So *let us* **p aside** the deeds of darkness *700*
13:12 the deeds of darkness and **p on** the armor *1907*
14:13 up your mind not *to* **p** any stumbling block *5502*
16:17 and **p** obstacles in your way that are *NIG*
1Co 4:9 God *has* **p** us apostles **on display** *617*
5:2 with grief and *have* **p** out of your fellowship *149*
9:12 *we* **p up with** anything rather than hinder *5095*
10:27 eat whatever *is* **p before** you *4192*
13:11 *I* **p** childish ways **behind** *me.* *2934*
15:25 until *he has* **p** all his enemies under his feet. *5502*
15:27 For *he "has* **p** everything **under** his feet." *5718*
15:27 that "everything" *has been* **p under** him, *5718*
15:27 who **p** everything **under** Christ. *5718*
15:28 to him who **p** everything **under** him, *5718*
2Co 1:22 and **p** his Spirit in our hearts as a deposit, *1443*
2:5 not to **p it too severely.** *2096*
3:13 who *would* **p** a veil over his face to keep *5502*
6:3 We **p** no stumbling block in anyone's path, *1443*
8:16 who **p** into the heart of Titus the same *1443*
11:1 I hope *you will* **p up with** a little of my *462*
11:4 *you* **p up with** it easily enough. *462*
11:19 *You* gladly **p up with** fools since you are *462*
11:20 even **p up with** anyone who enslaves you *462*
Gal 2:16 *have* **p** *our* **faith** in Christ Jesus *4409*
3:19 The law *was* **p into effect** through angels *1411*
3:24 So the law was **p in charge to lead** *4080*
Eph 1:10 to be **p into effect** when the times *3873*
2:16 by which he **p to death** their hostility. *650*
4:22 *to* **p off** your old self, *700*
4:24 and *to* **p on** the new self, *1907*
4:25 each of you *must* **p off** falsehood *700*
6:11 **P on** the full armor of God so that you can *1907*
6:13 Therefore **p on** the full armor of God, *377*
Php 1:16 knowing that *I am* **p here** for the defense of *3023*
3:3 and who **p** no **confidence** in the flesh— *4275*
3:4 *to* **p confidence** in the flesh, I have more: *4275*
4:9 or seen in me—**p** it **into practice.** *4556*
Col 3:5 **P to death,** therefore, whatever belongs *3739*
3:10 and *have* **p on** the new self, *1907*
3:14 And over all these virtues **p** on love, *NIG*
1Th 2:5 **p on a mask to cover up** greed— *4733*
5:19 *Do* not **p out** the Spirit's fire; *4931*
1Ti 4:10 that *we have* **p** *our* **hope** in the living God, *1827*
5:4 **p** *their* **religion into practice by caring for** *2355*
5:9 No widow *may be* **p on the list** of widows *2899*
5:11 **not p** them **on such a list.** *4148*
6:17 to be arrogant nor *to* **p** their **hope** in wealth, *1827*
6:17 but to **p** their hope in God, *NIG*
2Ti 4:3 when *men will* not **p up with** *462*
Heb 2:8 and **p** everything **under** his feet." *5718*
2:13 And again, "I *will* **p** *my* **trust** in him." *1639+4275*
8:10 *I will* **p** my laws in their minds *1443*
9:18 the first covenant *was* not **p into effect** *1590*
10:16 *I will* **p** my laws in their hearts, *1443*
11:36 still others were chained and **p** in prison. *NIG*
11:37 *they were* **p to death** by the sword. *633+1877+5840*
Jas 3:3 When *we* **p** bits into the mouths of horses *965*
1Pe 2:6 in him *will* never *be* **p to shame."** *2875*
3:5 women of the past who **p** *their* **hope** in God *1827*
3:18 *He was* **p to death** in the body *2506*
2Pe 1:14 I know that *I will* soon **p** it **aside,** *629+1639*
Rev 2:10 the devil will **p** some of you in prison *965*
2:13 who *was* **p to death** in your city— *650*
3:18 salve *to* **p on** your eyes, so you can see. *1608*
7:3 the trees until *we* **p a seal** on the foreheads *5381*
17:17 For God *has* **p** it into their hearts *1443*

PUTEOLI (1)

Ac 28:13 and on the following day we reached **P.** *4541*

PUTHITES (1)

1Ch 2:53 the Ithrites, **P,** Shumathites and Mishraites. 7057

PUTIEL (1)

Ex 6:25 married one of the daughters of **P,** 7034

PUTS (32) [PUT]

Ex 30:33 and whoever **p** it on anyone other than 5989
Lev 16:4 with water before *he* **p** them **on.** 4252
Nu 22:38 I must speak only what God **p** in my mouth. 8492
23:12 "Must I not speak what the LORD **p** in 8492
2Sa 22:48 *who* **p** the nations under me, 3718
1Ki 20:11 *'One who* **p on** *his* **armor** should not boast 2520
1Ch 22:12 when *he* **p** you **in command** over Israel, 7422
Job 28:3 *Man* **p** an end to the darkness; 8492
Ps 33:7 *he* **p** the deep into storehouses. 5989
Pr 11:15 *He who* **p up security** *for* another will 6842
17:18 and **p up security** for his neighbor. 6842+6859
20:16 Take the garment of *one who* **p up security** 6842
21:29 wicked man **p up a bold front,** 928+6451+7156
22:26 in pledge or **p up security** *for* debts; 6842
25:8 in the end if your neighbor **p** you **to shame?** 4007
27:13 Take the garment of one *who* **p up security** 6842
Eze 14:4 in his heart and **p** a wicked stumbling block 8492
14:7 in his heart and **p** a wicked stumbling block 8492
Mt 7:24 words of mine and **p** them **into practice** is *4472*
Mk 4:29 *he* **p** the sickle to it, *690*
13:34 He leaves his house and **p** his servants *1443*
Lk 6:47 hears my words and **p** them **into practice.** *4472*
8:16 a lamp and hides it in a jar or **p** it under *5502*
8:16 Instead, *he* **p** it on a stand, *5502*
9:62 "No one who **p** his hand **to** the plow *2095*
11:33 and **p** it in a place where it will be hidden, *5502*
11:33 Instead he **p** it on its stand, *NIG*
12:42 the master **p in charge** of his servants *2770*
15:5 *he* joyfully **p** it **on** his shoulders *2202*
1Ti 5:5 in need and left all alone **p** *her* **hope** in God *1827*
Heb 6:16 the oath confirms what is said and **p** an end *NIG*
3Jn 1:10 to do so and **p** them **out** of the church. *1675*

PUTTING (28) [PUT]

Ex 29:17 **p** them with the head and the other pieces. 5989
Dt 13:9 be the first in **p** him **to death,** 4637
17:7 be the first in **p** him **to death,** 4637
20:19 do not destroy its trees by **p** an ax to them, 5616
26:6 made us suffer, **p** us *to* hard labor. 5989
Jos 11:17 struck them down, **p** them **to death.** 4637
Jdg 1:5 **p to rout** the Canaanites and Perizzites. 5782
6:19 **P** the meat in a basket and its broth in 8492
18:21 **P** their little children, their livestock 8492
1Sa 6:19 **p** seventy of them **to death** because 5782
19:13 with a garment and **p** some goats' hair *at* 8492
28:8 Saul disguised himself, **p on** other clothes, 4252
1Ki 9:3 by **p** my Name there forever. 8492
Ne 3:15 **p** its doors and bolts and bars **in place.** 6641
9:38 **p** it **in writing,** and our leaders, 4180
Job 13:27 on all my paths *by* **p marks** on the soles 2977
Eze 8:17 Look at them **p** the branch to their nose! 8938
17:13 made a treaty with him, **p** him under oath. 995
Mt 27:66 and made the tomb secure *by* **p a seal on** *5381*
Mk 12:41 and watched the crowd **p** their money into *965*
Lk 18:7 *Will he keep* **p** them **off?** *3428*
21:1 Jesus saw the rich **p** their gifts into *965*
Jn 12:11 over to Jesus and **p** *their* **faith** in him. *4409*
Ac 15:10 *by* **p on** the necks of the disciples a yoke *2202*
Col 2:11 in the **p off** of the sinful nature, *589*
1Th 5:8 **p on** faith and love as a breastplate, *1907*
Heb 2:8 In **p** everything **under** him, *5718*
2Pe 2:4 **p** them **into** gloomy dungeons to be held *4140*

PUZZLED (2)

Mk 6:20 When Herod heard John, *he was* greatly **p;** *679*
Ac 5:24 temple guard and the chief priests *were* **p,** *1389*

PYGARG (KJV) See IBEX

PYRRHUS (1)

Ac 20:4 He was accompanied by Sopater *son of* **P** *4795*

Q

QUAIL (4)

Ex 16:13 That evening **q** came and covered the camp, 8513
Nu 11:31 the LORD and drove **q** in from the sea. 8513
11:32 the people went out and gathered **q.** 8513
Ps 105:40 and he brought them **q** and satisfied them 8513

QUAKE (7) [EARTHQUAKE, EARTHQUAKES, QUAKED, QUAKING]

Job 26:11 The pillars of the heavens **q,** 8344
Ps 46:3 and the mountains **q** with their surging. 8321
75:3 *When* the earth and all its people **q,** 4570
Isa 64:2 to your enemies and *cause* the nations *to* **q** 8074
Eze 27:28 The shorelands *will* **q** when your seamen cry 8321
Na 1:5 The mountains **q** before him and 8321
Rev 16:18 so tremendous was the **q.** *4939*

QUAKED (4) [QUAKE]

Jdg 5:5 The mountains **q** before the LORD, 5688
2Sa 22:8 "The earth trembled and **q,** 8321
Ps 18:7 The earth trembled and **q,** 8321
77:18 the earth trembled and **q.** 8321

QUAKING (3) [QUAKE]

1Sa 13:7 all the troops with him *were* **q with fear.** 3006
Ps 60:2 mend its fractures, for *it is* **q.** 4572
Jer 4:24 I looked at the mountains, and *they were* **q;** 8321

QUALIFIED (3)

Da 1:4 and **q** to serve in the king's palace. 3946
Col 1:12 who *has* **q** you to share in the inheritance of *2655*
2Ti 2:2 to reliable men who will also be **q** *2653*

QUALITIES (3) [QUALITY]

Da 6:3 by his exceptional **q** that the king planned 10658
Ro 1:20 God's **invisible** *q*—his eternal power and divine nature— *AIT*
2Pe 1:8 you possess these **q** in increasing measure, *NIG*

QUALITY (5) [QUALITIES]

Lev 27:12 who *will* **judge** its **q** as good or bad. 6885
27:14 the priest *will* **judge** its **q** as good or bad. 6885
1Ki 5:17 from the quarry large blocks of **q** stone 3701
7:10 with large stones of **good q,** 3701
1Co 3:13 the fire will test **the q** of each man's work. *3961*

QUALM (1)

Jude 1:12 eating with you **without the slightest q—** *925*

QUANTITIES (9) [QUANTITY]

Ge 41:49 Joseph stored up huge **q** of grain, 2221
1Ki 10:2 large **q** *of* gold, and precious stones— 8041
10:10 large **q** of spices, and precious stones. 2221
1Ch 22:14 **q** of bronze and iron too great to NIH
29:2 all of these *in* **large q.** 4200+8044
2Ch 9:1 **large q** of gold, and precious stones— 4200+8044
9:9 large **q** of spices, and precious stones. 4200+8044
25:13 and carried off **great q** of plunder. 8041

Zec 14:14 **great q** *of* gold and silver and 4200+4394+8044

QUANTITY (7) [QUANTITIES]
Lev 19:35 when measuring length, weight or **q.** 5374
Jos 22: 8 and a **great q** *of* clothing— 2221+4394
2Sa 8: 8 King David took a **great q** of bronze. 2221+4394
12:30 took a **great q** *of* plunder from the city 2221+4394
1Ch 18: 8 David took a great **q** of bronze, 8041
20: 2 took a **great q** *of* plunder from the city 2221+4394
23:29 and all **measurements of q** and size. 5374

QUARREL (15) [QUARRELED, QUARRELING, QUARRELS, QUARRELSOME]
Ge 45:24 "Don't **q** on the way!" 8074
Ex 17: 2 Moses replied, "Why *do you* **q** with me? 8189
21:18 "If men **q** and one hits the other with 8189
Jdg 11:25 *Did he ever* **q** with Israel or fight with them? 8189+8189
2Ki 5: 7 how he *is* **trying to pick a q** with me!" 628
2Ch 35:21 "What **q** is there **between** you and me, 4200
Pr 15:18 but a patient man calms a **q.** 8190
17:14 Starting a **q** is like breaching a dam; 4506
17:19 He who loves a **q** loves sin; 5175
20: 3 but every fool *is* **quick to q.** 1679
26:17 the ears is a passer-by who meddles in a **q** 8190
26:20 without gossip a **q** dies down. 4506
Mt 12:19 *He will* not **q** or cry out; *2248*
2Ti 2:24 And the Lord's servant must not **q;** *3481*
Jas 4: 2 *You* **q** and fight. *3481*

QUARRELED (7) [QUARREL]
Ge 26:20 of Gerar **q** with Isaac's herdsmen and said, 8189
26:21 but *they* **q** over that one also; 8189
26:22 and no *one* **q** over it. 8189
Ex 17: 2 So they **q** with Moses and said, 8189
17: 7 and Meribah because the Israelites **q** and 8189
Nu 20: 3 They **q** with Moses and said, 8189
20:13 where the Israelites **q** with the LORD and 8189

QUARRELING (7) [QUARREL]
Ge 13: 7 And **q** arose between Abram's herdsmen 8190
13: 8 "Let's not have any **q** between you and me, 5312
Isa 58: 4 Your fasting ends in **q** and strife, 8190
Ac 12:20 He had been **q** with the people of Tyre *2595*
1Co 3: 3 since there is jealousy and **q** among you, *2251*
2Co 12:20 I fear that there may be **q,** jealousy, *2251*
2Ti 2:14 before God against **q about words;** *3362*

QUARRELS (8) [QUARREL]
Pr 13:10 Pride only breeds **q,** 5175
22:10 **q** and insults are ended. 1907
Isa 45: 9 "Woe to *him who* **q** with his Maker, 8189
1Co 1:11 that there are **q** among you. *2251*
1Ti 6: 4 and **q about words** that result in envy, *3363*
2Ti 2:23 because you know they produce **q.** *3480*
Tit 3: 9 and arguments and **q** about the law, *3480*
Jas 4: 1 What causes fights and **q** among you? *3480*

QUARRELSOME (7) [QUARREL]
Pr 19:13 and a **q** wife is like a constant dripping. 4506
21: 9 of the roof than share a house with a **q** wife. 4506
21:19 a desert than with a **q** and ill-tempered wife. 4506
25:24 of the roof than share a house with a **q** wife. 4506
26:21 so is a **q** man for kindling strife. 4506
27:15 A **q** wife is like a constant dripping on 4506
1Ti 3: 3 not violent but gentle, **not q,** *285*

QUARRIES (2) [QUARRY]
Jos 7: 5 as far as the **stone q** and struck them down 8696
Ecc 10: 9 *Whoever* **q** stones may be injured by them; 5825

QUARRY (3) [QUARRIES]
1Ki 5:17 *they* **removed from** the **q** large blocks 5825
6: 7 only blocks dressed at the **q** were used, 5024
Isa 51: 1 to the **q** *from which* you were hewn; 1014+5217

QUART (1) [QUARTS]
Rev 6: 6 saying, "A **q** of wheat for a day's wages, *5955*

QUARTER (13) [QUARTERS]
Ex 29:40 with a **q** *of* a hin of oil from pressed olives, 8063
29:40 and a **q** *of* a hin of wine as a drink offering. 8055
Lev 23:13 its drink offering of a **q** *of* a hin of wine. 8055
Nu 15: 4 of an ephah of fine flour mixed with a **q** *of* 8055
15: 5 a **q** *of* a hin of wine as a drink offering. 8055
28: 5 with a **q** *of* a hin of oil from pressed olives. 8055
28: 7 to be a **q** *of* a hin of fermented drink 8055
28:14 and with each lamb, a **q** *of* a hin. 8055
1Sa 9: 8 he said, "I have a **q** *of* a shekel of silver. 8063
2Ki 6:25 a **q** *of* a cab of seed pods for five shekels. 8065
Ne 9: 3 the Law of the LORD their God for a **q** *of* 8055
9: 3 and spent another **q** in confession and 8055
Zep 1:10 wailing from the **New Q,** 5467

QUARTERS (5) [QUARTER]
2Sa 19:11 has reached the king at his **q?** 1074
2Ki 23: 7 down the **q** *of* the male shrine prostitutes, 1074
Ne 3:30 made repairs opposite his **living q.** 5969
Isa 11:12 of Judah from the four **q** *of* the earth. 4053
Jer 49:36 against Elam the four winds from the four **q** 7896

QUARTS (1) [QUART]
Rev 6: 6 and three **q** of barley for a day's wages, *5955*

QUARTUS (1)
Ro 16:23 and our brother **Q** send you their greetings. *3181*

QUATERNIONS (KJV) See SQUADS OF FOUR SOLDIERS

QUEEN (53) [QUEEN'S, QUEENS]
1Ki 10: 1 When the **q** *of* Sheba heard about the fame 4893
10: 4 When the **q** *of* Sheba saw all the wisdom 4893
10:10 so many spices brought in as those the **q** 4893
10:13 gave the **q** *of* Sheba all she desired and 4893
11:19 of his own wife **Q** Tahpenes, in marriage. 1485
15:13 from her **position as q mother,** 1485
2Ki 10:13 families of the king and of the **q mother."** 1485
2Ch 9: 1 the **q** *of* Sheba heard of Solomon's fame, 4893
9: 3 the **q** *of* Sheba saw the wisdom of Solomon, 4893
9: 9 the **q** *of* Sheba gave to King Solomon. 4893
9:12 gave the **q** *of* Sheba all she desired 4893
15:16 from her **position as q mother,** 1485
Ne 2: 6 Then the king, with the **q** sitting beside him, 8712
Est 1: 9 **Q** Vashti also gave a banquet for 4893
1:11 to bring before him **Q** Vashti, 4893
1:12 **Q** Vashti refused to come. 4893
1:15 what must be done to **Q** Vashti?" 4893
1:16 **"Q** Vashti has done wrong, 4893
1:17 'King Xerxes commanded **Q** Vashti to 4893
2: 4 the girl who pleases the king *be* **q** instead 4887
2:17 crown on her head and **made** her **q** instead 4887
2:22 about the plot and told **Q** Esther, 4893
5: 2 When he saw **Q** Esther standing in 4893
5: 3 Then the king asked, "What is it, **Q** Esther? 4893
5:12 "I'm the only person **Q** Esther invited 4893
7: 1 and Haman went to dine with **Q** Esther, 4893
7: 2 **"Q** Esther, what is your petition? 4893
7: 3 Then **Q** Esther answered, 4893
7: 5 King Xerxes asked **Q** Esther, "Who is he? 4893
7: 6 Haman was terrified before the king and **q.** 4893
7: 7 stayed behind to beg **Q** Esther for his life. 4893
7: 8 even molest the **q** while she is with me 4893
8: 1 That same day King Xerxes gave **Q** Esther 4893
8: 7 to **Q** Esther and to Mordecai the Jew, 4893
9:12 The king said to **Q** Esther, 4893
9:29 So **Q** Esther, daughter of Abihail, 4893
9:31 the Jew and **Q** Esther had decreed for them, 4893
Isa 47: 5 no more will you be called **q** *of* kingdoms. 1509
47: 7 'I will continue forever—the eternal **q!'** 1509
Jer 7:18 cakes of bread for the **Q** *of* Heaven. 4906
13:18 Say to the king and to the **q mother,** 1485
29: 2 after King Jehoiachin and the **q mother,** 1485
44:17 We will burn incense to the **Q** *of* Heaven 4906
44:18 stopped burning incense to the **Q** *of* Heaven 4906
44:19 burned incense to the **Q** *of* Heaven 4906
44:25 drink offerings to the **Q** *of* Heaven.' 4906
La 1: 1 She who was **q** among the provinces has 8576
Eze 16:13 and rose to be a **q.** 4867
Da 5:10 The **q,** hearing the voices of the king 10423
Mt 12:42 The **Q** of the South will rise at the judgment *999*
Lk 11:31 The **Q** of the South will rise at the judgment *999*
Ac 8:27 Candace, **q** of the Ethiopians. *999*
Rev 18: 7 In her heart she boasts, 'I sit as **q;** *999*

QUEEN'S (2) [QUEEN]
Est 1:17 For the **q** conduct will become known to all 4893
1:18 about the **q** conduct will respond to all 4893

QUEENS (4) [QUEEN]
SS 6: 8 Sixty **q** there may be, 4893
6: 9 the **q** and concubines praised her. 4893
Isa 49:23 and their **q** your nursing mothers. 8576
Jer 44: 9 by your fathers and by the kings and **q** 851S

QUENCH (6) [QUENCHED]
Ps 104:11 the wild donkeys **q** their thirst. 8689
SS 8: 7 Many waters cannot **q** love; 3882
Isa 1:31 with no *one to* **q** *the* **fire."** 3882
Jer 4: 4 burn with no *one to* **q** it. 3882
21:12 burn with no *one to* **q** it. 3882
Am 5: 6 and Bethel will have no *one to* **q** it. 3882

QUENCHED (10) [QUENCH]
2Ki 22:17 burn against this place and *will* not *be* **q.'** 3882
2Ch 34:25 poured out on this place and *will* not *be* **q.'** 3882
Isa 34:10 *It will* not *be* **q** night and day; 3882
66:24 nor will their fire *be* **q,** 3882
Jer 7:20 and it will burn and not *be* **q.** 3882
46:10 till *it has* **q its thirst** with blood. 8115
Eze 20:47 The blazing flame *will* not *be* **q,** 3882
20:48 LORD have kindled it; *it will* not *be* **q.'"** 3882
Mk 9:48 worm does not die, and the fire *is* not **q.'** *4931*
Heb 11:34 **q** the fury of the flames, and escaped *4931*

QUESTION (24) [QUESTIONED, QUESTIONING, QUESTIONS]
Jdg 11:12 to the Ammonite king with the **q:** 606
Est 5: 8 Then I will answer the king's **q."** 1821
Job 38: 3 *I will* **q** you, and you shall answer me. 8626
40: 7 *I will* **q** you, and you shall answer me. 8626
42: 4 *I will* **q** you, and you shall answer me.' 8626
Ps 35:11 *they* **q** me on things I know nothing about. 8626
Isa 45:11 *do you* **q** me about my children, 8626
Jer 38:27 officials did come to Jeremiah and **q** him, 8626
Mt 21:24 Jesus replied, "I will also ask you one **q.** *3364*
22:23 came to him with a **q.** *2089*
22:35 an expert in the law, tested him with this **q:** *2089*
Mk 8:11 The Pharisees came and began *to* **q** Jesus. *5184*
11:29 Jesus replied, "I will ask you one **q.** *3364*
12:18 came to him with a **q.** *2089*
Lk 20: 3 He replied, "I will also ask you a **q.** *3364*
20:27 came to Jesus with a **q.** *2089*
22:23 They began *to* **q** among themselves which *5184*
Jn 8: 6 *They were* using this **q** as a trap, *3306*
18:21 Why **q** me? Ask those who heard me. *2263*
Ac 4: 7 before them and *began to* **q** them: *4785*
15: 2 to see the apostles and elders about this **q.** *2427*
15: 6 apostles and elders met to consider this **q.** *3364*
22:29 about to **q** him withdrew immediately. *458*
1Ti 3:16 **Beyond all q,** the mystery of godliness *3935*

QUESTIONED (11) [QUESTION]
Ge 43: 7 The man **q** us **closely** about ourselves 8626+8626
Jdg 8:14 a young man of Succoth and **q** him, 8626
Ezr 5: 9 *We* **q** the elders and asked them, 10689
Ne 1: 2 and *I* **q** them about the Jewish remnant 8626
Job 21:29 *Have you* never **q** those who travel? 8626
Da 1:20 about which the king **q** them, 1335
Lk 20:21 So the spies **q** him: *2089*
Jn 1:25 **q** him, "Why then do you baptize if you are *2263*
18:19 the high priest **q** Jesus about his disciples *2263*
Ac 5:27 the Sanhedrin to be **q** by the high priest. *2089*
22:24 *be* flogged and **q** in order to find out why *458*

QUESTIONING (1) [QUESTION]
Jn 8: 7 When they kept on **q** him, *2263*

QUESTIONS (18) [QUESTION]
Ge 43: 7 We simply answered his **q.** 1821
1Ki 10: 1 she came to test him with **hard q.** 2648
10: 3 Solomon answered all her **q;** 1821
2Ch 9: 1 to Jerusalem to test him with **hard q.** 2648
9: 2 Solomon answered all her **q;** 1821
Pr 18:17 till another comes forward and **q** him. 2983
Ecc 7:10 For it is not wise to ask **such q.** 2296S
Mt 22:46 no one dared *to* **ask** him any more **q.** *2089*
Mk 12:34 no one dared **ask** him any more **q.** *2089*
Lk 2:46 listening to them and **asking** them **q.** *2089*
11:53 and *to* **besiege** him **with q,** *694+4309+4498*
20:40 And no one dared to ask him any more **q.** *NIG*
23: 9 *He* plied him with many **q,** *3364*
Jn 16:30 not even need to have anyone **ask** you **q.** *2263*
Ac 18:15 since it involves **q** about words and names *2427*
23:29 I found that the accusation had to do with **q** *2427*
1Co 10:25 in the meat market without **raising q** *373*
10:27 before you without **raising q** of conscience. *373*

QUICK (15) [QUICK-TEMPERED, QUICKLY]
Ge 18: 6 **"Q,"** he said, "get three seahs of fine flour 4554
25:30 He said to Jacob, **"Q,** let me have some 5528
Ex 32: 8 *They have been* **q** to turn away 4554
Jdg 9:48 He ordered the men with him, **"Q!** 4554
1Ki 20:33 men took this as a good sign and *were* **q** 4554
Pr 6:18 feet *that are* **q** to rush into evil, 4554
20: 3 but every fool *is* **q to quarrel.** 1679
Ecc 5: 2 *Do* not *be* **q** with your mouth, 987
Da 1: 4 well informed, **q to understand,** 1067+4529
Jnh 4: 2 That is why *I was so* **q** to flee to Tarshish. 7709
Mal 3: 5 I will be **q** to testify against sorcerers, 4554
Lk 15:22 "But the father said to his servants, **'Q!** *5444*
Ac 12: 7 **"Q,** get up!" he said, *1877+5443*
22:18 and saw the Lord speaking. **'Q!'** *5067*
Jas 1:19 Everyone should be **q** to listen, *5444*

QUICK, QUICKEN (KJV) See also GIVE LIFE, LIVING

QUICK-TEMPERED (3) [QUICK, TEMPER]
Pr 14:17 A **q** *man* does foolish things, 678+7920
14:29 but a **q** *man* displays folly. 7920+8120
Tit 1: 7 not overbearing, not **q,** *3975*

QUICKLY (75) [QUICK]
Ge 19:22 But flee there **q,** because I cannot do 4554
24:18 and **q** lowered the jar to her hands 4554
24:20 So *she* **q** emptied her jar into the trough, 4554
24:46 "She **q** lowered her jar from her shoulder 4554
27:20 "How did you find it *so* **q,** my son?" 4554
41:14 and he *was* **q brought** from the dungeon. 8132
44:11 of them **q** lowered his sack to the ground 4554
45:13 And bring my father down here **q."** 4554
Ex 10:16 Pharaoh **q** summoned Moses and Aaron 4554
Dt 4:26 against you this day that you will **q** perish 4554
7: 4 against you and will **q** destroy you. 4554
9: 3 and annihilate them **q,** 4554
9:12 They have turned away **q** 4554
9:16 You had turned aside **q** from the way that 4554
Jos 2: 5 Go after them **q.** 4554
8:19 in the ambush rose **q** from their position 4559

Jos 8:19 the city and captured it and **q** set it on fire. 4554
10: 6 Come up to us **q** and save us! 4559
23:16 and you will **q** perish from the good land 4559
Jdg 2:17 they **q** turned from the way 4554
1Sa 17:48 David ran **q** toward the battle line 4554
20:38 Then he shouted, "Hurry! **Go q!** 2590
23:27 to Saul, saying, "Come **q!** 4554
25:23 *she* **q** got off her donkey and bowed down 4554
25:34 if you had not come **q** to meet me, 4554
25:42 Abigail **q** got on a donkey and, 4554
2Sa 5:24 in the tops of the balsam trees, **move q,** 3077
15:14 or *he will* **move q** to overtake us 4554
17:18 the two of them left **q** and went to the house 4559
1Ki 20:41 Then the prophet **q** removed the headband 4554
2Ki 4:22 **go** to the man of God **q** 8132
2Ch 29:36 because it was done so **q.** 928+7328
35:13 caldrons and pans and **served** them **q** to all 8132
Job 8:12 they wither **more q than** grass. 4200+7156
Ps 22:19 O my Strength, **come q** to help me. 2590
31: 2 Turn your ear to me, come **q** to my rescue; 4559
38:22 **Come q** to help me, O Lord my Savior. 2590
40:13 O LORD, **come q** to help me. 2590
69:17 answer me **q,** for I am in trouble. 4554
70: 1 O LORD, **come q** to help me. 2590
70: 5 I am poor and needy; **come q** to me, O God. 2590
71:12 **come q,** O my God, to help me. 2590
79: 8 may your mercy come **q** to meet us, 4554
81:14 **how q** would I subdue their enemies 3869+5071
90:10 for they **q** pass, and we fly away. 2673
102: 2 when I call, answer me **q.** 4554
118:12 but they died out as **q** as burning thorns; NIH
141: 1 O LORD, I call to you; **come q** to me. 2590
143: 7 Answer me **q,** O LORD; 4554
Pr 20:21 An inheritance **q gained** at the beginning 987
Ecc 4:12 A cord of three strands is not **q** broken. 928+4559
7: 9 Do not be **q** provoked in your spirit, 987
8:11 the sentence for a crime is not **q** carried out, 4559
Isa 58: 8 and your healing will **q** appear; 4559
Jer 9:18 *Let them* **come q** and wail over us 4554
48:16 her calamity *will* **come q.** 4394+4554
49:30 "Flee **q** away! Stay in deep caves, 4394
Joel 3:11 Come **q,** all you nations from every side, 6429
Zep 1:14 near and **coming q.** 4394+4554
Mt 5:25 "Settle matters **q** with your *5444*
13: 5 It sprang up **q,** because the soil was shallow. *2311*
13:21 he **q** falls away. *2317*
21:20 "How did the fig tree wither **so q?"** *4202*
28: 7 Then go **q** and tell his disciples: *5444*
Mk 1:28 about him spread **q** over the whole region *2317*
4: 5 It sprang up **q,** because the soil was shallow. *2317*
4:17 they **q** fall away. *2317*
Lk 14:21 'Go out **q** into the streets and alleys of *5441*
16: 6 sit down **q,** and make it four hundred.' *5441*
18: 8 he will see that they get justice, and **q.** *1877+5443*
Jn 11:29 she got up **q** and went to him. *5444*
11:31 noticed how **q** she got up and went out, *5441*
13:27 "What you are about to do, do **q,"** *5441*
Gal 1: 6 I am astonished that you are so **q** deserting *5441*
2Ti 4: 9 Do your best to come to me **q,** *5441*

QUIET (38) [QUIETED, QUIETLY, QUIETNESS]

Ge 25:27 while Jacob was a **q** man, 9447
34: 5 so he **kept q** *about* it until they came home. 3087
Jdg 3:19 The king said, **"Q!"** 2187
18:19 They answered him, *"Be* **q!** 3087
2Sa 13:20 *Be* **q** now, my sister; he is your brother. 3087
2Ki 11:20 And the city *was* **q,** 9200
1Ch 4:40 and the land was spacious, peaceful and **q.** 8929
22: 9 and I will grant Israel peace and **q** 9201
2Ch 23:21 And the city *was* **q,** 9200
Ne 5: 8 to us!" *They kept* **q,** 3087
Est 7: 4 *I would have kept* **q,** 3087
Job 6:24 "Teach me, and I *will be* **q;** 3087
Ps 23: 2 he leads me beside **q** waters, 4957
76: 8 and the land feared and *was* **q—** 9200
83: 1 *be* not **q,** O God, be not still. 3087
Pr 17: 1 Better a dry crust with **peace and q** than 8932
Ecc 9:17 The **q** words of the wise are more to 5739
Isa 18: 4 *"I will remain* **q** and will look on 9200
42:14 *I have been* **q** and held myself back. 3087
62: 1 for Jerusalem's sake *I will* not *remain* **q,** 9200
Am 5:13 the prudent man **keeps q** in such times, 1957
Zep 3:17 *he will* **q** you with his love, 3087
Mt 20:31 and told them to *be* **q,** *4995*
Mk 1:25 *"Be* **q!"** said Jesus sternly. *5821*
4:39 the wind and said to the waves, **"Q!** *4995*
6:31 "Come with me by yourselves to a **q** place *2245*
9:34 But *they kept* **q** because on the way *4995*
10:48 Many rebuked him and told him to *be* **q,** *4995*
Lk 4:35 *"Be* **q!"** Jesus said sternly. *5821*
18:39 rebuked him and told him to *be* **q,** *4967*
19:40 "I tell you," he replied, "if they *keep* **q,** *4995*
Ac 12:17 for them *to be* **q** and described how *4967*
19:36 you ought to be **q** and not do anything rash. *2948*
22: 2 they became very **q.** *2484*
1Co 14:28 the speaker *should keep* **q** in the church *4967*
1Th 4:11 Make it your ambition *to* **lead a q life,** *2483*
1Ti 2: 2 and **q** lives in all godliness and holiness. *2485*
1Pe 3: 4 the unfading beauty *of* a gentle and **q** spirit, *2485*

QUIETED (2) [QUIET]

Ps 131: 2 But I have stilled and **q** my soul; 1957
Ac 19:35 The city clerk **q** the crowd and said: *2948*

QUIETENED (Anglicized) See QUIETED

QUIETLY (7) [QUIET]

Jdg 4:21 a tent peg and a hammer and went **q** to him 928+2021+4319
Ru 3: 7 Ruth approached **q,** uncovered his feet and lay down. 928+2021+4319
Ps 35:20 against *those who* **live q** *in* the land. 8091
La 3:26 to wait **q** for the salvation of the LORD. 1876
Eze 24:17 Groan **q;** do not mourn for the dead. 1957
Mt 1:19 he had in mind to divorce her **q.** *3277*
Ac 16:37 And now do they want to get rid of us **q?** *3277*

QUIETNESS (4) [QUIET]

Job 3:26 I have no peace, no **q;** 9200
Isa 30:15 in **q** and trust is your strength, 9200
32:17 the effect of righteousness *will be* **q** 9200
1Ti 2:11 A woman should learn in **q** and full submission. *2484*

QUIRINIUS (1)

Lk 2: 2 the first census that took place while **Q** was governor of Syria.) *3256*

QUITE (5)

2Sa 15:11 as guests and went **q innocently,** 4200+9448
Jn 4:18 What you have just said is **q** true." *NIG*
Ro 15:15 I have written you **q boldly** *5529*
1Co 16:12 He was **q** unwilling to go now, *4122*
1Th 3: 3 You know **q** well that we were destined *NIG*

QUIVER (6) [QUIVERED, QUIVERS]

Ge 27: 3 get your weapons—your **q** and bow— 9437
Job 39:23 The **q** rattles against his side, 880
Ps 127: 5 Blessed is the man whose **q** is full of them. 880
Isa 22: 6 Elam takes up the **q,** 880
49: 2 a polished arrow and concealed me in his **q.** 880
La 3:13 He pierced my heart with arrows from his **q.** 880

QUIVERED (1) [QUIVER]

Hab 3:16 my lips **q** at the sound; 7509

QUIVERS (1) [QUIVER]

Jer 5:16 Their **q** are like an open grave; 880

QUOTA (3) [QUOTAS]

Ex 5: 8 don't reduce the **q.** NIH
5:14 "Why didn't you meet your **q** *of* bricks 2976
5:18 you must produce your **full q** *of* bricks." 9420

QUOTAS (1) [QUOTA]

1Ki 4:28 their **q** of barley and straw for the 3869+5477

QUOTE (4) [QUOTES, QUOTING]

Eze 12:23 and *they will* no longer **q** it in Israel.' 5439
16:44 " 'Everyone who quotes proverbs *will* **q** *this* **proverb** 5439
18: 3 you *will* no longer **q** this proverb in Israel. 5439
Lk 4:23 "Surely *you will* **q** this proverb to me: *3306*

QUOTES (1) [QUOTE]

Eze 16:44 " 'Everyone who **q proverbs** will quote this proverb 5439

QUOTING (1) [QUOTE]

Eze 18: 2 *by* **q** this proverb about the land of Israel: 5439

R

RAAMAH (5)

Ge 10: 7 Seba, Havilah, Sabtah, **R** and Sabteca. 8311
10: 7 The sons of **R:** Sheba and Dedan. 8311
1Ch 1: 9 Seba, Havilah, Sabta, **R** and Sabteca. 8309
1: 9 The sons of **R:** Sheba and Dedan. 8309
Eze 27:22 merchants of Sheba and **R** traded with you; 8311

RAAMIAH (1)

Ne 7: 7 Azariah, **R,** Nahamani, Mordecai, Bilshan, 8313

RAAMSES (KJV) See RAMESES

RABBAH (15)

Dt 3:11 It is still in **R** *of* the Ammonites.) 8051
Jos 13:25 as far as Aroer, near **R;** 8051
15:60 Kiriath Baal (that is, Kiriath Jearim) and **R** 8051
2Sa 11: 1 the Ammonites and besieged **R.** 8051
12:26 against **R** *of* the Ammonites and captured 8051
2Sa 12:27 against **R** and taken its water supply. 8051
12:29 the entire army and went to **R,** 8051
17:27 of Nahash from **R** *of* the Ammonites, 8051
1Ch 20: 1 the land of the Ammonites and went to **R** 8051
20: 1 Joab attacked **R** and left it in ruins. 8051
Jer 49: 2 the battle cry against **R** *of* the Ammonites; 8051
49: 3 Cry out, O inhabitants of **R!** 8051
Eze 21:20 against **R** *of* the Ammonites and another 8051
25: 5 I will turn **R** into a pasture for camels 8051
Am 1:14 I will set fire to the walls of **R** 8051

RABBATH (KJV) See RABBAH

RABBI (16) [RABBONI]

Mt 23: 7 and to have men call them **'R.'** *4806*
23: 8 "But you are not to be called **'R,'** *4806*
26:25 said, "Surely not I, **R?"** *4806*
26:49 Judas said, "Greetings, **R!"** *4806*
Mk 9: 5 Peter said to Jesus, **"R,** it is good for us *4806*
10:51 The blind man said, **"R,** I want to see." *4808*
11:21 Peter remembered and said to Jesus, **"R,** *4806*
14:45 Going at once to Jesus, Judas said, **"R!"** *4806*
Jn 1:38 They said, **"R"** (which means Teacher), *4806*
1:49 Then Nathanael declared, **"R,** *4806*
3: 2 He came to Jesus at night and said, **"R,** *4806*
3:26 They came to John and said to him, **"R,** *4806*
4:31 Meanwhile his disciples urged him, **"R,** *4806*
6:25 **"R,** when did you get here?" *4806*
9: 2 His disciples asked him, **"R,** who sinned, *4806*
11: 8 "But **R,"** they said, "a short while ago *4806*

RABBIM See BATH RABBIM

RABBIT (2)

Lev 11: 6 The **r,** though it chews the cud, 817
Dt 14: 7 not eat the camel, the **r** or the coney. 817

RABBITH (1)

Jos 19:20 **R,** Kishion, Ebez, 8056

RABBLE (2)

Nu 11: 4 The **r** with them began to crave other food, 671
Eze 23:42 the desert along with men from the **r,** 132+8044

RABBONI (1) [RABBI]

Jn 20:16 toward him and cried out in Aramaic, **"R!"** *4808*

RABMAG (KJV) See OFFICIAL

RABSARIS (KJV) See CHIEF OFFICER

RABSHAKEH (KJV) See FIELD COMMANDER

RACA (1)

Mt 5:22 Again, anyone who says to his brother, **'R,'** *4819*

RACAL (1)

1Sa 30:29 and **R;** to those in the towns of the 8218

RACE (9) [RACED]

Ezr 9: 2 mingled the holy **r** with the peoples around 2446
Ecc 9:11 The **r** is not to the swift or the battle to 5296
Ac 20:24 if only I may finish the **r** and complete *1536*
Ro 9: 3 my brothers, those *of* my own **r,** *5150*
1Co 9:24 not know that in a **r** all the runners run, *5084*
Gal 2: 2 that I was running or *had* **run** *my* **r** in vain. *5556*
5: 7 You were **running a** good **r.** *5556*
2Ti 4: 7 I have finished the **r,** I have kept the faith. *1536*
Heb 12: 1 with perseverance the **r** marked out for us. *74*

RACED (2) [RACE]

Est 8:14 The couriers, riding the royal horses, **r** out, 987
Jer 12: 5 "If *you have* **r** with men on foot 8132

RACHAB (KJV) See RAHAB

RACHAL (KJV) See RACAL

RACHEL (42) [RACHEL'S]

Ge 29: 6 here comes his daughter **R** with the sheep." 8162
29: 9 **R** came with her father's sheep, 8162
29:10 When Jacob saw **R** daughter of Laban, 8162
29:11 Jacob kissed **R** and began to weep aloud. 8162
29:12 He had told **R** that he was a relative 8162
29:16 and the name of the younger was **R.** 8162
29:17 but **R** was lovely in form, and beautiful. 8162
29:18 Jacob was in love with **R** and said, 8162
29:18 in return for your younger daughter **R."** 8162
29:20 So Jacob served seven years to get **R,** 8162
29:25 I served you for **R,** didn't I? 8162
29:28 and then Laban gave him his daughter **R** to 8162
29:29 Bilhah to his daughter **R** as her maidservant. 8162
29:30 Jacob lay with **R** also, 8162
29:30 and he loved **R** more than Leah. 8162
29:31 he opened her womb, but **R** was barren. 8162

Ge 30: 1 When **R** saw that she was 8162
30: 6 Then **R** said, "God has vindicated me; 8162
30: 8 Then **R** said, "I have had a great struggle 8162
30:14 **R** said to Leah, "Please give me some 8162
30:15 **R** said, "he can sleep with you tonight 8162
30:22 Then God remembered **R;** 8162
30:25 After **R** gave birth to Joseph, 8162
31: 4 to **R** and Leah to come out to the fields 8162
31:14 Then **R** and Leah replied, 8162
31:19 **R** stole her father's household gods. 8162
31:32 Now Jacob did not know that **R** had stolen 8162
31:34 Now **R** had taken the household gods 8162
31:35 **R** said to her father, "Don't be angry, NIH
33: 1 **R** and the two maidservants. 8162
33: 2 and **R** and Joseph in the rear. 8162
33: 7 Last of all came Joseph and **R,** 8162
35:16 **R** began to give birth 8162
35:19 So **R** died and was buried on the way 8162
35:24 The sons of **R:** Joseph and Benjamin. 8162
46:19 The sons of Jacob's wife **R:** 8162
46:22 These were the sons of **R** who were born 8162
46:25 whom Laban had given to his daughter **R—** 8162
48: 7 to my sorrow **R** died in the land of Canaan 8162
Ru 4:11 into your home like **R** and Leah, 8162
Jer 31:15 **R** weeping for her children and refusing to 8162
Mt 2:18 **R** weeping for her children and refusing to *4830*

RACHEL'S (5) [RACHEL]

Ge 30: 7 **R** servant Bilhah conceived again 8162
31:33 he entered **R** tent. 8162
35:20 and to this day that pillar marks **R** tomb. 8162
35:25 The sons of **R** maidservant Bilhah: 8162
1Sa 10: 2 you will meet two men near **R** tomb, 8162

RACKED (2)

Isa 21: 3 At this my body *is* **r with** pain, 4848
La 4: 9 **r with hunger,** they waste away for lack 1991

RADDAI (1)

1Ch 2:14 the fourth Nethanel, the fifth **R,** 8099

RADIANCE (5) [RADIANT]

Job 31:26 in *its* **r** or the moon moving in splendor, 2145
Eze 1:28 so was the **r** around him. 5586
10: 4 and the court was full of the **r** *of* the glory 5586
2Co 3:13 at it while the **r** was fading away. *NIG*
Heb 1: 3 The Son is the **r** of God's glory and *575*

RADIANT (9) [RADIANCE]

Ex 34:29 that his face *was* **r** because he had spoken 7966
34:30 Israelites saw Moses, his face *was* **r,** 7966
34:35 they saw that his face *was* **r.** 7966
Ps 19: 8 The commands of the LORD are **r,** 1338
34: 5 Those who look to him *are* **r;** 5642
SS 5:10 My lover is **r** and ruddy, 7456
Isa 60: 5 Then you will look and *be* **r,** 5642
Eze 43: 2 and the land *was* **r** with his glory. 239
Eph 5:27 and to present her to himself as a **r** church, *1902*

RAFTERS (2)

Ecc 10:18 If a man is lazy, the **r** sag; 5248
SS 1:17 beams of our house are cedar; our **r** are firs. 8112

RAFTS (2)

1Ki 5: 9 in **r** by sea to the place you specify. 1827
2Ch 2:16 that you need and will float them in **r** 8343

RAGAU (KJV) See REU

RAGE (25) [ENRAGED, OUTRAGEOUS, RAGED, RAGES, RAGING]

Dt 19: 6 avenger of blood might pursue him **in a r,** 2801+4222
2Ki 5:12 So he turned and went off in a **r.** 2779
19:27 and when you come and go and *how* you **r** 8074
19:28 Because you **r** against me 8074
2Ch 25:10 and left for home in a **great r.** 678+3034
28: 9 But you have slaughtered them in a **r** 2408
Est 5: 9 he was filled with **r** against Mordecai. 2779
7: 7 The king got up in a **r,** 2779
Job 15:13 so that you vent your **r** against God 8120
Ps 7: 6 rise up against the **r** *of* my enemies. 6301
Pr 19:12 A king's **r** is like the roar of a lion, 2408
Isa 17:12 *they* **r** like the raging sea! 2159
37:28 and when you come and go and *how* you **r** 8074
37:29 Because you **r** against me and 8074
41:11 "All who **r** against you will surely 3013
Jer 51:55 Waves [of enemies] *will* **r** like great waters; 2159
Da 3:13 Furious with **r,** Nebuchadnezzar summoned Shadrach, Meshach and Abednego. 10654
8: 6 the canal and charged at him in great **r.** 2779
11:11 of the South will march out *in a* **r** and fight 5352
11:44 in a great **r** to destroy and annihilate many. 2779
Hab 3: 8 Did you **r** against the sea when you rode 6301
Ac 4:25 the nations **r** and the peoples plot in vain? *5865*
Gal 5:20 hatred, discord, jealousy, **fits of r,** *2596*
Eph 4:31 Get rid of all bitterness, **r** and anger, *2596*
Col 3: 8 anger, **r,** malice, slander, *2596*

RAGED (5) [RAGE]

1Ki 22:35 All day long the battle **r,** 6590
2Ch 18:34 All day long the battle **r,** 6590
Isa 45:24 All who *have* **r** against him will come 3013
Jer 44: 6 *it* **r** against the towns of Judah and 1277
Am 1:11 because his anger **r** continually 3271

RAGES (4) [RAGE]

Job 40:23 When the river **r,** he is not alarmed; 6943
Ps 50: 3 and around him a **tempest r.** 4394+8548
Pr 19: 3 yet his heart **r** against the LORD. 2406
29: 9 the fool **r** and scoffs, and there is no peace. 8074

RAGING (9) [RAGE]

2Ch 26:19 While he *was* **r** at the priests 2406
Ps 124: 5 the **r** waters would have swept us away. 2327
Isa 17:12 Oh, the **r** *of* many nations— 2162
17:12 they rage like the **r** sea! 2159
30:30 down with **r** anger and consuming fire, 2408
Jnh 1:15 and the **r** sea grew calm. 2408
Lk 8:24 up and rebuked the wind and the **r** waters; *3114*
Ac 27:20 and the storm **continued r,** *2130+3900+4024*
Heb 10:27 of judgment and *of* **r** fire that will consume *2419*

RAGS (5)

Pr 23:21 and drowsiness clothes them in **r.** 7974
Isa 64: 6 and all our righteous acts are like filthy **r;** 955
Jer 38:11 He took *some* old **r** and worn-out clothes 6080
38:12 "Put these old **r** and worn-out clothes 6080
1Co 4:11 *we are* **in r,** we are brutally treated, *1217*

RAGUEL (KJV) See REUEL

RAHAB (14)

Jos 2: 1 of a prostitute named **R** and stayed there. 8147
2: 3 the king of Jericho sent this message to **R:** 8147
6:17 Only **R** the prostitute and all who are 8147
6:23 went in and brought out **R,** 8147
6:25 But Joshua spared **R** the prostitute, 8147
Job 9:13 even the cohorts of **R** cowered at his feet. 8105
26:12 by his wisdom he cut **R** to pieces. 8105
Ps 87: 4 "I will record **R** and Babylon 8105
89:10 You crushed **R** like one of the slain; 8105
Isa 30: 7 Therefore I call her **R** the Do-Nothing. 8105
51: 9 Was it not you who cut **R** to pieces, 8105
Mt 1: 5 Boaz, whose mother was **R,** *4829*
Heb 11:31 By faith the prostitute **R,** because she *4805*
Jas 2:25 even **R** the prostitute considered righteous *4805*

RAHAM (2)

1Ch 2:44 Shema was the father of **R,** 8165
2:44 and **R** the father of Jorkeam. NIH

RAHEL (KJV) See RACHEL

RAID (2) [RAIDED, RAIDERS, RAIDING]

2Sa 3:22 from a **r** and brought with them a great deal 1522
Pr 24:15 *do* not **r** his dwelling place; 8720

RAIDED (7) [RAID]

1Sa 27: 8 and his men went up and **r** the Geshurites, 7320
30: 1 the Amalekites *had* **r** the Negev and Ziklag. 7320
30:14 We **r** the Negev of the Kerethites and 7320
1Ch 14: 9 the Philistines had come and **r** the Valley 7320
14:13 Once more the Philistines **r** the valley; 7320
2Ch 25:13 in the war **r** Judean towns from Samaria 7320
28:18 the Philistines *had* **r** towns in the foothills 7320

RAIDERS (7) [RAID]

Ge 49:19 "Gad will be attacked by a **band of r,** 1522
Jdg 2:14 over to **r** who plundered them. 9115
2:16 who saved them out of the hands of these **r.** 9115
2Ki 13:20 Now Moabite **r** used to enter the country 1522
13:21 suddenly they saw a **band of r;** 1522
24: 2 Moabite and Ammonite **r** against him. 1522
2Ch 22: 1 king in his place, since the **r,** 1522

RAIDING (11) [RAID]

1Sa 13:17 **R parties** went out from the Philistine camp 8845
14:15 and those in the outposts and **r parties—** 8845
23:27 The Philistines *are* **r** the land." 7320
27:10 "Where *did you* **go r** today?" 7320
30: 8 "Shall I pursue this **r party?** 1522
30:15 "Can you lead me down to this **r party?"** 1522
2Sa 4: 2 Now Saul's son had two men who were leaders of **r bands.** 1522
2Ki 6:23 from Aram stopped **r** Israel's territory. 928+995
1Ch 12:18 and made them leaders of his **r bands.** 1522
12:21 They helped David against **r bands,** 1522
Job 1:17 "The Chaldeans formed three **r parties** 8031

RAIL (1)

Ps 102: 8 *those who* **r** *against* me use my name as 2147

RAIMENT (KJV) See CLOTHING, DRESS, GARMENT

RAIN (90) [RAINBOW, RAINED, RAINING, RAINS, RAINY]

Ge 2: 5 the LORD God *had* not **sent r** on the earth 4763
7: 4 Seven days from now I *will* **send r** on 4763
7:12 And **r** fell on the earth forty days 1773
8: 2 and the **r** had stopped falling from the sky. 1773
Ex 9:33 the **r** no longer poured down on the land. 4764
9:34 that the **r** and hail and thunder had stopped, 4764
16: 4 "I *will* **r down** bread from heaven for you. 4763
Lev 26: 4 I will send you **r** in its season, 1773
Dt 11:11 and valleys that drinks **r** from heaven. 4764
11:14 then I will send **r** *on* your land in its season, 4764
11:17 not **r** and the ground will yield no produce, 4764
28:12 to send **r** *on* your land in season and 4764
28:24 the **r** *of* your country into dust and powder; 4764
32: 2 like **r** and my words descend like dew, 4764
32: 2 like **abundant r** on tender plants. 8053
1Sa 12:17 upon the LORD to send thunder and **r.** 4764
12:18 the LORD sent thunder and **r.** 4764
2Sa 1:21 may you have neither dew nor **r,** 4764
21:10 till the **r** poured down from the heavens on 4784
22:12 the dark **r** clouds of the sky. 4784
23: 4 after **r** that brings the grass from the earth.' 4764
1Ki 8:35 the heavens are shut up and there is no **r** 4764
8:36 and send **r** on the land you gave 4764
17: 1 nor **r** in the next few years except 4764
17: 7 up because there had been no **r** in the land. 1773
17:14 not run dry until the day the LORD gives **r** 1773
18: 1 and I will send **r** on the land." 4764
18:41 for there is the sound of a heavy **r."** 1773
18:44 and go down before the **r** stops you.' " 1773
18:45 a heavy **r** came on and Ahab rode off 1773
2Ki 3:17 You will see neither wind nor **r,** 1773
2Ch 6:26 the heavens are shut up and there is no **r** 4764
6:27 and send **r** on the land you gave 4764
7:13 I shut up the heavens so that there is no **r,** 4764
Ezr 10: 9 by the occasion and because of the **r.** 1773
Job 5:10 He bestows **r** on the earth; 4764
20:23 and **r down** his blows upon him. 4763
28:26 when he made a decree for the **r** and a path 4764
29:23 and drank in my words as the **spring r.** 4919
36:27 which distill as **r** to the streams; 4764
37: 6 'Fall on the earth,' and to the **r** shower, 4764
38:25 Who cuts a channel for the **torrents of r,** 8852
38:28 Does the **r** have a father? 4764
Ps 11: 6 On the wicked *he will* **r** fiery coals 4763
18:11 the dark **r** clouds of the sky. 4784
68: 8 the heavens **poured down r,** before God, 5752
72: 6 He will be like **r** falling on a mown field, 4764
105:32 He turned their **r** into hail, 1773
135: 7 he sends lightning with the **r** and brings out 4764
147: 8 the earth with **r** and makes grass grow on 4764
Pr 16:15 his favor is like a **r** cloud **in spring.** 4919
25:14 and wind without **r** is a man who boasts 1773
25:23 As a north wind brings **r,** 1773
26: 1 Like snow in summer or **r** in harvest, 4764
28: 3 like a driving **r** that leaves no crops. 4764
Ecc 11: 3 they pour **r** upon the earth. 1773
12: 2 and the clouds return after the **r;** 1773
Isa 4: 6 and hiding place from the storm and **r.** 4764
5: 6 command the clouds not *to* **r** on it." 4763+4764
28: 2 like a **driving r** and a flooding 2443+4784
30:23 also send you **r** *for* the seed you sow in 4764
44:14 or planted a pine, and the **r** made it grow. 1773
45: 8 *"You* heavens above, **r down** righteousness; 8319
55:10 As the **r** and the snow come down 1773
Jer 10:13 with the **r** and brings out the wind 4764
14: 4 The ground is cracked because there is no **r** 1773
14:22 the worthless idols of the nations **bring r?** 1772
51:16 with the **r** and brings out the wind 4764
Eze 13:11 **R** will come in torrents, 1773
13:13 of **r** will fall with destructive fury. 1773
22:24 You are a land that *has* **had** no **r** or showers 4763
38:22 I will pour down torrents of **r,** 1773
Am 4: 7 "I also withheld **r** from you when 1773
4: 7 *I* **sent r** on one town, 4763
4: 7 One field **had r;** another had none 4763
Zec 10: 1 Ask the LORD for **r** in the springtime; 4764
10: 1 He gives showers of **r** to men, 1773
14:17 the LORD Almighty, they will have no **r.** 1773
14:18 they will have no **r.** NIH
Mt 5:45 and **sends r** on the righteous and *1101*
7:25 The **r** came down, the streams rose, *1104*
7:27 The **r** came down, the streams rose, *1104*
Lk 12:54 immediately you say, *'It's* **going to r,'** *2262+3915*
Ac 14:17 He has shown kindness by giving you **r** *5624*
Heb 6: 7 in the **r** often falling on it and that produces *5624*
Jas 5:17 He prayed earnestly that *it would* not **r,** *1101*
5:17 not **r** on the land for three and a half years. *1101*
5:18 Again he prayed, and the heavens gave **r,** *5624*
Jude 1:12 They are clouds **without r,** *536*
Rev 11: 6 not **r** during the time they are prophesying; *1101*

RAINBOW (6) [RAIN]

Ge 9:13 I have set my **r** in the clouds, 8008
9:14 the earth and the **r** appears in the clouds, 8008
9:16 Whenever the **r** appears in the clouds, 8008
Eze 1:28 Like the appearance of a **r** in the clouds on 8008
Rev 4: 3 A **r,** resembling an emerald, *2692*
10: 1 with a **r** above his head; *2692*

RAINED (5) [RAIN]

Ge 19:24 Then the LORD **r down** burning sulfur 4763
Ex 9:23 So the LORD **r** hail on the land of Egypt; 4763

Ps 78:24 *he* **r down** manna for the people to eat, 4763
78:27 *He* **r** meat **down** on them like dust, 4763
Lk 17:29 fire and sulfur **r** down from heaven *1101*

RAINING (1) [RAIN]

Ac 28: 2 a fire and welcomed us all because it was **r** *5624*

RAINS (11) [RAIN]

Dt 11:14 both autumn and **spring r,** 4919
Job 24: 8 They are drenched by mountain **r** and hug 2443
Ps 84: 6 the **autumn r** also cover it with pools. 4620
SS 2:11 The winter is past; the **r** are over and gone. 1773
Jer 3: 3 and no **spring r** have fallen. 4919
5:24 who gives autumn and spring **r** in season, 1773
Hos 6: 3 he will come to us like the **winter r,** 1773
6: 3 like the **spring r** that water the earth." 4919
Joel 2:23 for he has given you the **autumn r** 4620
2:23 both autumn and **spring r,** as before. 4919
Jas 5: 7 for the **autumn** and spring **r.** *4611*

RAINY (3) [RAIN]

Ezr 10:13 and it is the **r** season; 1773
Pr 27:15 like a constant dripping on a **r** day; 6039
Eze 1:28 of a rainbow in the clouds on a **r** day, 1773

RAISE (61) [RISE]

Ge 4:20 of those who live in tents and **r** livestock. NIH
Ex 14:16 **R** your staff and stretch out your hand over 8123
24:11 not **r** his hand against these leaders of 8938
Dt 18:15 The LORD your God *will* **r up** for you 7756
18:18 *I will* **r up** for them a prophet like you 7756
Jos 6:10 *do* not **r** your voices, 9048
Jdg 8:28 the Israelites and *did* not **r** its head again. 5951
1Sa 2:35 *I will* **r up** for myself a faithful priest, 7756
18:17 "I *will* not **r** a hand against him. 2118
22:17 not willing to **r** a hand to strike the priests 8938
2Sa 7:12 *I will* **r up** your offspring to succeed you, 7756
1Ki 14:14 "The LORD *will* **r up** for himself a king 7756
20:25 also **r** an army like the one you lost— 4948
2Ki 4:28 "Didn't I tell you, 'Don't **r** my **hopes**'?" 8922
1Ch 17:11 *I will* **r up** your offspring to succeed you, 7756
Job 38:34 *"Can you* **r** your voice to the clouds 8123
Ps 41:10 **r** me **up,** that I may repay them. 7756
Pr 8: 1 *Does* not understanding **r** her voice? 5989
8: 4 I **r** my voice to all mankind. NIH
Isa 8: 9 **R the war cry,** *you* nations, 8131
10:15 the ax **r itself** above him who swings it, 6995
10:26 and *he will* **r** his staff over the waters, 5951
11:12 *He will* **r** a banner for the nations 5951
13: 2 **R** a banner on a bare hilltop, shout to them; 5951
14:13 *I will* **r** my throne above the stars of God; 8123
24:14 They **r** their voices, they shout for joy; 5951
42: 2 or **r** his voice in the streets. 5951
42:11 *Let* the desert and its towns **r** their voices; 5951
42:13 with a shout *he will* **r the battle cry** 7658
45:13 I *will* **r up** Cyrus in my righteousness: 6424
58: 1 **R** your voice like a trumpet. 8123
58:12 and *will* **r up** the age-old foundations; 7756
62:10 **R** a banner for the nations. 8123
Jer 4: 6 **R** the signal to go to Zion! 5951
6: 1 **R** the signal over Beth Hakkerem! 5951
23: 5 *I will* **r up** to David a righteous Branch, 7756
30: 9 whom *I will* **r up** for them. 7756
Eze 26: 8 to your walls and **r** his shields against you. 7756
27:30 *They will* **r** their voice and cry bitterly 9048
Da 11:11 *who will* **r** a large army, 6641
Hos 5: 8 **R the battle cry** in Beth Aven; 8131
Mic 5: 5 *we will* **r** against him seven shepherds, 7756
Zec 1:21 so that no one *could* **r** his head, 5951
2: 9 I *will* surely **r** my hand against them so 5677
11:16 *to* **r up** a shepherd over the land who will 7756
Mt 3: 9 of these stones God can **r up** children *1586*
10: 8 Heal the sick, **r** the dead, *1586*
Lk 3: 8 of these stones God can **r up** children *1586*
Jn 2:19 and *I will* **r** it **again** in three days." *1586*
2:20 and you *are going to* **r** it in three days?" *1586*
6:39 but **r** them **up** at the last day. *482*
6:40 and I *will* **r** him **up** at the last day." *482*
6:44 and I *will* **r** him **up** at the last day. *482*
6:54 and I *will* **r** him **up** at the last day. *482*
Ac 3:22 'The Lord your God *will* **r up** for you *482*
1Co 6:14 and *he will* **r** us also. *1995*
15:15 not **r** him if in fact the dead are not raised. *1586*
2Co 4:14 also **r** us with Jesus and present us with you *1586*
Heb 11:19 Abraham reasoned that God could **r** *1586*
Jas 3:18 Peacemakers who sow in peace **r** a harvest *NIG*
5:15 the Lord *will* **r** him **up.** *1586*

RAISED (127) [RISE]

Ge 14:22 *I have* **r** my hand to the LORD, God Most High, Creator of heaven and earth, **and** *have* **taken an oath** 8123
Ex 7:20 *He* **r** his staff in the presence of Pharaoh 8123
9:16 But *I have* **r** you up for this very purpose, 6641
Nu 14: 1 the people of the community **r** their voices 2256+5951+5989
20:11 Then Moses **r** his arm and struck 8123
Jos 5: 7 So *he* **r up** their sons in their place, 7756
8:29 And *they* **r** a large pile of rocks over it, 7756
Jdg 2:16 Then the LORD **r up** judges, 7756
2:18 the LORD **r up** a judge for them, he was 7756
3: 9 he **r up** for them a deliverer, 7756
1Sa 4: 5 all Israel **r** such **a great shout** 8131+9558
14:27 *He* **r** his hand to his mouth, 8740
2Sa 12: 3 *He* **r** it, and it grew up with him 2649
23: 8 he **r** his spear against eight hundred men, 6424
23:18 He **r** his spear against three hundred men, 6424
1Ki 11:14 LORD **r up** against Solomon an adversary, 7756
11:23 And God **r up** against Solomon another 7756
14: 7 *'I* **r** you **up** from among the people 8123
2Ki 3: 4 Now Mesha king of Moab **r sheep,** 5924
19:22 Against whom *have you* **r** your voice 8123
1Ch 11:11 he **r** his spear against three hundred men, 6424
11:20 He **r** his spear against three hundred men, 6424
2Ch 5:13 they **r** their voices in praise to the LORD 8123
13:15 and the men of Judah **r the battle cry.** 8131
Ne 5: 1 the men and their wives **r** a great outcry 2118
Est 10: 2 of Mordecai to which the king *had* **r** him, 1540
Job 31:21 if *I have* **r** my hand against the fatherless, 5677
Ps 60: 4 *you have* **r** a banner to be unfurled against 5989
80:15 the son *you have* **r up** for yourself. 599
80:17 the son of man *you have* **r up** for yourself. 599
148:14 *He has* **r up** for his people a horn, 8123
Isa 2: 2 *it will* **be r** above the hills, 5951
5:25 his hand *is* **r** and he strikes them down. 5742
18: 3 when a banner *is* **r** on the mountains, 5951
23:13 *they* **r up** their siege towers, 7756
37:23 Against whom *have you* **r** your voice 8123
40: 4 Every valley *shall* **be r up,** 5951
49:11 and my highways *will be* **r up.** 8123
52:13 *be* **r** and lifted up and highly exalted. 8123
Jer 12: 6 they *have* **r a** loud **cry** against you. 7924
29:15 "The LORD *has* **r up** prophets for us 7756
La 2: 7 *they have* **r** a shout in the house of 5989
Eze 2: 2 Spirit came into me and **r** me to my feet. 6641
3:24 Spirit came into me and **r** me to my feet. 6641
41: 8 that the temple had a **r** *base* all around it, 1470
Da 4:34 Nebuchadnezzar, **r** my eyes toward heaven, 10475
7: 5 *It* **was r up** on one of its sides, 10624
8:18 Then he touched me and **r** me to my feet. 6641
Am 2:11 *I* also **r up** prophets from among your sons 7756
Mic 4: 1 it *will* **be r** above the hills, 5951
Zec 5: 7 Then the cover of lead **was r,** 5951
14:10 But Jerusalem *will be* **r up** and remain 8027
Mt 11: 5 the deaf hear, the dead *are* **r,** *1586*
16:21 be killed and on the third day *be* **r to life.** *1586*
17: 9 the Son of Man *has been* **r** from the dead." *1586*
17:23 and on the third day *he will be* **r to life."** *1586*
20:19 On the third day *he will be* **r to life!"** *1586*
27:52 holy people who had died *were* **r to life.** *1586*
27:64 the people that *he has been* **r** from the dead. *1586*
Mk 6:14 "John the Baptist *has been* **r** from the dead, *1586*
6:16 *has been* **r** from the dead!" *1586*
Lk 1:69 *He has* **r up** a horn of salvation for us in *1586*
7:22 the deaf hear, the dead *are* **r,** *1586*
9: 7 that John *had been* **r** from the dead, *1586*
9:22 be killed and on the third day *be* **r to life."** *1586*
24: 7 and on the third day *be* **r again.' "** *482*
Jn 2:22 After *he was* **r** from the dead, *1586*
12: 1 whom Jesus *had* **r** from the dead. *1586*
12: 9 whom *he had* **r** from the dead. *1586*
12:17 and **r** him from the dead continued *1586*
21:14 to his disciples *after he was* **r** from *1586*
Ac 2:14 **r** his voice and addressed the crowd: *2048*
2:24 But God **r him from the dead,** *482*
2:32 God *has* **r** this Jesus **to life,** *482*
3:15 but God **r** him from the dead. *1586*
3:26 *When* God **r up** his servant, *482*
4:10 whom you crucified but whom God **r** from *1586*
4:24 *they* **r** their voices together in prayer *149*
5:30 **r** Jesus **from the dead—** *1586*
9:21 the man who **r havoc** in Jerusalem *4514*
10:40 but God **r** him **from the dead** *1586*
13:30 But God **r** him from the dead, *1586*
13:34 The fact that God **r** him from the dead, *482*
13:37 But the one whom God **r from the dead** did *1586*
22:22 Then *they* **r** their voices and shouted, *2048*
Ro 4:24 in him who **r** Jesus our Lord from the dead. *1586*
4:25 over to death for our sins and *was* **r to life** *1586*
6: 4 just as Christ *was* **r** from the dead through *1586*
6: 9 For we know that *since* Christ *was* **r** from *1586*
7: 4 *to* him who *was* **r** from the dead, *1586*
8:11 *of* him who **r** Jesus from the dead is living *1586*
8:11 he who **r** Christ from the dead will *1586*
8:34 more than that, who *was* **r to life—** *1586*
9:17 *"I* **r** you **up** for this very purpose, *1995*
10: 9 in your heart that God **r** him from the dead, *1586*
1Co 6:14 his power God **r** the Lord **from the dead,** *1586*
15: 4 that *he was* **r** on the third day according to *1586*
15:12 if it is preached that Christ *has been* **r** from *1586*
15:13 then not even Christ *has been* **r.** *1586*
15:14 And if Christ *has* not *been* **r,** *1586*
15:15 that *he* **r** Christ **from the dead.** *1586*
15:15 not raise him if in fact the dead *are* not **r.** *1586*
15:16 For if the dead *are* not **r,** *1586*
15:16 then Christ *has* not *been* **r** either. *1586*
15:17 if Christ *has* not *been* **r,** your faith is futile; *1586*
15:20 But Christ *has* indeed *been* **r** from the dead, *1586*
15:29 If the dead *are* not **r** at all, *1586*
15:32 If the dead *are* not **r,** "Let us eat and drink, *1586*
15:35 someone may ask, "How *are* the dead **r?** *1586*
15:42 is sown is perishable, *it is* **r** imperishable; *1586*
15:43 it is sown in dishonor, *it is* **r** in glory; *1586*
15:43 it is sown in weakness, *it is* **r** in power; *1586*
15:44 sown a natural body, *it is* **r** a spiritual body. *1586*
15:52 the dead *will be* **r** imperishable, *1586*
2Co 4:14 one who **r** the Lord Jesus **from the dead** *1586*
5:15 for him who died for them and *was* **r again.** *1586*
Gal 1: 1 who **r** him from the dead— *1586*
Eph 1:20 *when* he **r** him from the dead and seated him *1586*
2: 6 And God **r** us **up with** Christ and seated us *5283*
Col 2:12 and **r** with him through your faith in *5283*
2:12 who **r** him from the dead. *1586*
3: 1 Since, then, *you have been* **r with** Christ, *5283*
1Th 1:10 whom *he* **r** from the dead— *1586*
2Ti 2: 8 Remember Jesus Christ, **r** from the dead, *1586*
Heb 11:35 received back their dead, **r to life again.** *414*
1Pe 1:21 who **r** him from the dead and glorified him, *1586*
Rev 10: 5 and on the land **r** his right hand to heaven. *149*

RAISES (8) [RISE]

1Sa 2: 6 he brings down to the grave and **r up.** 6590
2: 8 *He* **r** the poor from the dust and lifts 7756
Ps 113: 7 *He* **r** the poor from the dust and lifts 7756
Pr 1:20 *she* **r** her voice in the public squares; 5989
Isa 19:16 that the LORD Almighty **r** against them. 5677
Jn 5:21 as the Father **r** the dead and gives them life, *1586*
Ac 26: 8 consider it incredible that God **r** the dead? *1586*
2Co 1: 9 but on God, who **r** the dead. *1586*

RAISIN (2) [RAISINS]

1Ch 12:40 **r cakes,** wine, oil cattle and sheep, 7540
Hos 3: 1 to other gods and love the sacred **r** cakes." 6694

RAISING (11) [RISE]

Jdg 21: 2 **r** their voices and weeping bitterly. 5951
1Ki 15: 4 in Jerusalem by **r up** a son to succeed him 7756
Ps 55:12 if a foe *were* **r** *himself* against me, 1540
Jer 4:16 **r** a war cry against the cities of Judah. 5989
Am 7:10 "Amos *is* **r a conspiracy** against you in 8003
Hab 1: 6 I *am* **r up** the Babylonians, 7756
Ac 10:29 **without r any objection.** *395*
13:33 their children, *by* **r up** Jesus. *482*
17:31 of this to all men *by* **r** him from the dead." *482*
1Co 10:25 in the meat market without **r questions** *373*
10:27 without **r questions** of conscience. *373*

RAISINS (7) [RAISIN]

Nu 6: 3 not drink grape juice or eat **grapes or r.** 2256+3313+4300+6694
1Sa 25:18 a hundred **cakes of r** and two hundred cakes 7540
30:12 of a cake of pressed figs and two **cakes of r.** 7540
2Sa 6:19 of dates and a **cake of r** to each person in 862
16: 1 a hundred **cakes of r,** 7540
1Ch 16: 3 and a **cake of r** to each Israelite man 862
SS 2: 5 Strengthen me with **r,** 862

RAKEM (1)

1Ch 7:16 and his sons were Ulam and **R.** 8388

RAKKATH (1)

Jos 19:35 Zer, Hammath, **R,** Kinnereth, 8395

RAKKON (1)

Jos 19:46 Me Jarkon and **R,** 8378

RALLIED (4) [RALLY]

Ge 48: 2 Israel **r** *his* **strength** and sat up on the bed. 2616
Ex 32:26 And all the Levites **r** to him. 665
2Sa 2:25 Then the men of Benjamin **r** behind Abner. 7695
Ac 5:36 and about four hundred men **r** to him. *4679*

RALLY (1) [RALLIED]

Isa 11:10 the nations *will* **r** to him, 2011

RAM (101) [RAM'S, RAMS, RAMS']

Ge 15: 9 a goat and a **r,** each three years old, 380
22:13 up and there in a thicket he saw a **r** caught 380
22:13 over and took the **r** and sacrificed it as 380
Ex 25: 5 **r** skins dyed red and hides of sea cows; 380
26:14 for the tent a covering of **r** skins dyed red, 380
29:17 the **r** into pieces and wash the inner parts 380
29:18 Then burn the entire **r** on the altar. 380
29:19 "Take the other **r,** 380
29:22 "Take from this **r** the fat, the fat tail, 380
29:22 (This is the **r** *for* the ordination.) 380
29:26 the breast of the **r** for Aaron's ordination, 380
29:27 "Consecrate those parts of the ordination **r** 380
29:31 the **r** *for* the ordination and cook the meat 380
29:32 and his sons are to eat the meat of the **r** and 380
29:34 of the **ordination r** or any bread is left over 4854
35: 7 **r** skins dyed red and hides of sea cows; 380
35:23 **r** skins dyed red or hides of sea cows 380
36:19 for the tent a covering of **r** skins dyed red, 380
39:34 of **r** skins dyed red, the covering of hides 380
Lev 5:15 to bring to the LORD as a penalty a **r** from 380
5:16 for him with the **r** as a guilt offering, 380
5:18 to bring to the priest as a guilt offering a **r** 380
6: 6 his guilt offering, a **r** from the flock, 380
8:18 then presented the **r** *for* the burnt offering, 380
8:19 the **r** and sprinkled the blood against NIH
8:20 the **r** into pieces and burned the head, 380
8:21 the whole **r** on the altar as a burnt offering, 380
8:22 He then presented the other **r,** 380
8:22 the **r** *for* the ordination, 380
8:23 the **r** and took some of its blood and put it NIH
8:29 Moses' share of the ordination **r—** 380
9: 2 a bull calf for your sin offering and a **r** 380
9: 4 and a **r** for a fellowship offering to sacrifice 380
9:18 the ox and the **r** as the fellowship offering 380
9:19 But the fat portions of the ox and the **r—** 380

Lev 16: 3 with a young bull for a sin offering and a **r** 380
16: 5 a sin offering and a **r** for a burnt offering. 380
19:21 a **r** to the entrance to the Tent of Meeting 380
19:22 With the **r** *of* the guilt offering the priest is 380
Nu 5: 8 with the **r** with which atonement is made 380
6:14 a **r** without defect for a fellowship offering, 380
6:17 of unleavened bread and is to sacrifice the **r** 380
6:19 in his hands a boiled shoulder of the **r**, 380
7:15 one **r** and one male lamb a year old, 380
7:21 one **r** and one male lamb a year old, 380
7:27 one **r** and one male lamb a year old, 380
7:33 one **r** and one male lamb a year old, 380
7:39 one **r** and one male lamb a year old, 380
7:45 one **r** and one male lamb a year old, 380
7:51 one **r** and one male lamb a year old, 380
7:57 one **r** and one male lamb a year old, 380
7:63 one **r** and one male lamb a year old, 380
7:69 one **r** and one male lamb a year old, 380
7:75 one **r** and one male lamb a year old, 380
7:81 one **r** and one male lamb a year old, 380
15: 6 a **r** prepare a grain offering of two-tenths of 380
15:11 Each bull or **r**, each lamb or young goat, 380
23: 2 of them offered a bull and a **r** on each altar. 380
23: 4 on each altar I have offered a bull and a **r**." 380
23:14 and offered a bull and a **r** on each altar. 380
23:30 and offered a bull and a **r** on each altar. 380
28:11 one **r** and seven male lambs a year old, 380
28:12 with the **r**, a grain offering of two-tenths of 380
28:14 with the **r**, a third of a hin; 380
28:19 one **r** and seven male lambs a year old, 380
28:20 with the **r**, two-tenths; 380
28:27 one **r** and seven male lambs a year old as 380
28:28 with the **r**, two-tenths; 380
29: 2 one **r** and seven male lambs a year old, 380
29: 3 with the **r**, two-tenths; 380
29: 8 one **r** and seven male lambs a year old, 380
29: 9 with the **r**, two-tenths; 380
29:36 one **r** and seven male lambs a year old, 380
29:37 With the bull, the **r** and the lambs, 380
Ru 4:19 Hezron the father of **R**, 8226
4:19 **R** the father of Amminadab, 8226
1Ch 2: 9 Jerahmeel, **R** and Caleb. 8226
2:10 **R** was the father of Amminadab, 8226
2:25 **R** his firstborn, Bunah, Oren, 8226
2:27 The sons of **R** the firstborn of Jerahmeel: 8226
Ezr 10:19 for their guilt they each presented a **r** *from* 380
Job 32: 2 the Buzite, of the family of **R**, 8226
Eze 43:23 to offer a young bull and a **r** from the flock. 380
43:25 you are also to provide a young bull and a **r** 380
45:24 for each bull and an ephah for each **r**, 380
46: 4 to be six male lambs and a **r**, 380
46: 5 The grain offering given with the **r** is to be 380
46: 6 six lambs and a **r**, all without defect. 380
46: 7 one ephah with the **r**, 380
46:11 an ephah with a **r**, 380
Da 8: 3 before me was a **r** with two horns, 380
8: 4 the **r** as he charged toward the west and 380
8: 6 the two-horned **r** I had seen standing beside 380
8: 7 I saw him attack the **r** furiously, 380
8: 7 striking the **r** and shattering his two horns. 380
8: 7 The **r** was powerless to stand against him; 380
8: 7 none could rescue the **r** from his power. 380
8:20 The two-horned **r** that you saw represents 380
Mt 1: 3 Hezron the father of **R**, *730*
1: 4 **R** the father of Amminadab, *730*
Lk 3:33 the son *of* **R**, the son of Hezron, *730*

RAM'S (3) [RAM]

Ex 19:13 the **r horn** sounds a long blast may they go 3413
Ps 81: 3 Sound the **r horn** at the New Moon, 8795
98: 6 with trumpets and the blast of the **r horn**— 8795

RAMAH (34)

Jos 18:25 Gibeon, **R**, Beeroth, 8230
19: 8 as far as Baalath Beer (**R** *in* the Negev). 8230
19:29 The boundary then turned back toward **R** 8230
19:36 Adamah, **R**, Hazor, 8230
Jdg 4: 5 the Palm of Deborah between **R** and Bethel 8230
19:13 to reach Gibeah or **R** and spend the night 8230
1Sa 1:19 and then went back to their home at **R**. 8230
2:11 Then Elkanah went home to **R**, 8230
7:17 But he always went back to **R**, 8230
8: 4 and came to Samuel at **R**. 8230
15:34 Then Samuel left for **R**, 8230
16:13 Samuel then went to **R**. 8230
19:18 at **R** and told him all that Saul had done 8230
19:19 "David is in Naioth at **R**"; 8230
19:22 for **R** and went to the great cistern at Secu. 8230
19:22 "Over in Naioth at **R**," they said. 8230
19:23 So Saul went to Naioth at **R**. 8230
20: 1 Then David fled from Naioth at **R** and went 8230
25: 1 and they buried him at his home in **R**. 8230
28: 3 and buried him in his own town of **R**. 8230
1Ki 15:17 and fortified **R** to prevent anyone 8230
15:21 he stopped building **R** and withdrew 8230
15:22 and they carried away from **R** the stones 8230
2Ch 16: 1 and fortified **R** to prevent anyone 8230
16: 5 he stopped building **R** 8230
16: 6 and they carried away from **R** the stones 8230
Ezr 2:26 of **R** and Geba 621 8230
Ne 7:30 of **R** and Geba 621 8230
11:33 in Hazor, **R** and Gittaim, 8230
Isa 10:29 **R** trembles; Gibeah of Saul flees. 8230
Jer 31:15 "A voice is heard in **R**, mourning and great 8230
40: 1 of the imperial guard had released him at **R**. 8230
Hos 5: 8 Sound the trumpet in Gibeah, the horn in **R**. 8230
Mt 2:18 "A voice is heard in **R**, weeping and great *4821*

RAMATH LEHI (1) [LEHI]

Jdg 15:17 and the place was called **R**. 8257

RAMATH MIZPAH (1) [MIZPAH]

Jos 13:26 from Heshbon to **R** and Betonim, 8256

RAMATHAIM (1)

1Sa 1: 1 There was a certain man from **R**, 8259

RAMATHAIM-ZOPHIM (KJV) See RAMATHAIM, ZUPHITE

RAMATHITE (1) [RAMATH]

1Ch 27:27 the **R** was in charge of the vineyards. 8258

RAMESES (5)

Ge 47:11 the district of **R**, as Pharaoh directed. 8314
Ex 1:11 and they built Pithom and **R** as store cities 8314
12:37 The Israelites journeyed from **R** to Succoth. 8314
Nu 33: 3 The Israelites set out from **R** on 8314
33: 5 The Israelites left **R** and camped at Succoth. 8314

RAMIAH (1)

Ezr 10:25 **R**, Izziah, Malkijah, Mijamin, Eleazar, 8243

RAMOTH (7) [RAMOTH GILEAD, RAMOTH NEGEV]

Dt 4:43 **R** in Gilead, for the Gadites; 8030
Jos 20: 8 **R** in Gilead in the tribe of Gad, 8030
21:38 **R** in Gilead (a city of refuge 8030
2Ki 8:29 at **R** in his battle with Hazael king of Aram. 8230
1Ch 6:73 **R** and Anem, together with their 8030
6:80 the tribe of Gad they received **R** in Gilead, 8030
2Ch 22: 6 at **R** in his battle with Hazael king of Aram. 8230

RAMOTH GILEAD (20) [RAMOTH]

1Ki 4:13 in **R** (the settlements of Jair son of 8240
22: 3 "Don't you know that **R** belongs 8240
22: 4 with me to fight against **R**?" 8240
22: 6 "Shall I go to war against **R**, 8240
22:12 "Attack **R** and be victorious," 8240
22:15 shall we go to war against **R**, 8240
22:20 entice Ahab into attacking **R** and going 8240
22:29 Jehoshaphat king of Judah went up to **R**. 8240
2Ki 8:28 against Hazael king of Aram at **R**. 8240
9: 1 of oil with you and go to **R**. 8240
9: 4 young man, the prophet, went to **R**. 8240
9:14 and all Israel had been defending **R** 8240
2Ch 18: 2 with him and urged him to attack **R**. 8240
18: 3 "Will you go with me against **R**?" 8240
18: 5 "Shall we go to war against **R**, 8240
18:11 "Attack **R** and be victorious," 8240
18:14 shall we go to war against **R**, 8240
18:19 of Israel into attacking **R** and going 8240
18:28 Jehoshaphat king of Judah went up to **R**. 8240
22: 5 against Hazael king of Aram at **R**. 8240

RAMOTH NEGEV (1) [RAMOTH]

1Sa 30:27 who were in Bethel, **R** and Jattir; 8241

RAMP (7) [RAMPS]

2Sa 20:15 They built a **siege r** up to the city, 6149
2Ki 19:32 with shield or build a **siege r** against it. 6149
Job 19:12 they build a **siege r** against me and encamp 2006
Isa 37:33 with shield or build a **siege r** against it. 6149
Eze 4: 2 siege works against it, build a **r** up to it, 6149
21:22 to build a **r** and to erect siege works. 6149
26: 8 a **r** up to your walls and raise his shields 6149

RAMPART (1) [RAMPARTS]

Ps 91: 4 his faithfulness will be your shield and **r**. 6089

RAMPARTS (4) [RAMPART]

Ps 48:13 consider well her **r**, 2658
Isa 26: 1 God makes salvation its walls and **r**. 2658
La 2: 8 He made **r** and walls lament; 2658
Hab 2: 1 at my watch and station myself on the **r**; 5189

RAMPS (7) [RAMP]

Job 30:12 they build their **siege r** against me. 369+784
Jer 6: 6 "Cut down the trees and build **siege r** 6149
32:24 how the **siege r** are built up to take the city. 6149
33: 4 to be used against the **siege r** and the sword 6149
Eze 17:17 when **r** are built and siege works erected 6149
Da 11:15 of the North will come and build up **siege r** 6149
Hab 1:10 they build **earthen r** and capture them. 6760

RAMS (68) [RAM]

Ge 31:38 nor have I eaten **r** *from* your flocks. 380
32:14 two hundred ewes and twenty **r**, 380
Ex 29: 1 a young bull and two **r** without defect. 380
29: 3 along with the bull and the two **r**. 380
29:15 "Take one of the **r**, 380
Lev 8: 2 the two **r** and the basket containing bread 380
Lev 23:18 one young bull and two **r**. 380
Nu 7:17 five **r**, five male goats and five male lambs 380
7:23 five **r**, five male goats and five male lambs 380
7:29 five **r**, five male goats and five male lambs 380
7:35 five **r**, five male goats and five male lambs 380
7:41 five **r**, five male goats and five male lambs 380
7:47 five **r**, five male goats and five male lambs 380
7:53 five **r**, five male goats and five male lambs 380
7:59 five **r**, five male goats and five male lambs 380
7:65 five **r**, five male goats and five male lambs 380
7:71 five **r**, five male goats and five male lambs 380
7:77 five **r**, five male goats and five male lambs 380
7:83 five **r**, five male goats and five male lambs 380
7:87 twelve **r** and twelve male lambs a year old, 380
7:88 to twenty-four oxen, sixty **r**, 380
23: 1 and prepare seven bulls and seven **r** 380
23:29 and prepare seven bulls and seven **r** 380
29:13 two **r** and fourteen male lambs a year old, 380
29:14 with each of the two **r**, two-tenths; 380
29:17 two **r** and fourteen male lambs a year old, 380
29:18 With the bulls, **r** and lambs, 380
29:20 two **r** and fourteen male lambs a year old, 380
29:21 With the bulls, **r** and lambs, 380
29:23 two **r** and fourteen male lambs a year old, 380
29:24 With the bulls, **r** and lambs, 380
29:26 two **r** and fourteen male lambs a year old, 380
29:27 With the bulls, **r** and lambs, 380
29:29 two **r** and fourteen male lambs a year old, 380
29:30 With the bulls, **r** and lambs, 380
29:32 two **r** and fourteen male lambs a year old, 380
29:33 With the bulls, **r** and lambs, 380
Dt 32:14 with choice **r** of Bashan and 380
1Sa 15:22 and to heed is better than the fat of **r**. 380
2Ki 3: 4 and with the wool of a hundred thousand **r**. 380
1Ch 15:26 seven bulls and seven **r** were sacrificed. 380
29:21 a thousand **r** and a thousand male lambs, 380
2Ch 13: 9 with a young bull and seven **r** may become 380
17:11 seven thousand seven hundred **r** 380
29:21 They brought seven bulls, seven **r**, 380
29:22 the **r** and sprinkled their blood on the altar; 380
29:32 a hundred **r** and two hundred male lambs— 380
Ezr 6: 9 Whatever is needed—young bulls, **r**, 10175
6:17 two hundred **r**, four hundred male lambs 10175
7:17 to buy bulls, **r** and male lambs, 10175
8:35 twelve bulls for all Israel, ninety-six **r**, 380
Job 42: 8 So now take seven bulls and seven **r** and go 380
Ps 66:15 fat animals to you and an offering of **r**; 380
114: 4 the mountains skipped like **r**, 380
114: 6 that you skipped like **r**, you hills, 380
Isa 1:11 of **r** and the fat of fattened animals; 380
34: 6 fat from the kidneys of **r**. 380
60: 7 the **r** *of* Nebaioth will serve you; 380
Jer 51:40 like lambs to the slaughter, like **r** and goats. 380
Eze 4: 2 set up camps against it and put **battering r** 4119
21:22 where he is to set up **battering r**, 4119
21:22 to set **battering r** against the gates, 4119
26: 9 He will direct the blows of his **battering r** 7692
27:21 they did business with you in lambs, **r** 380
34:17 and between **r** and goats. 380
39:18 if they were **r** and lambs, goats and bulls— 380
45:23 to provide seven bulls and seven **r** 380
Mic 6: 7 the LORD be pleased with thousands of **r**, 380

RAMS' (2) [RAM]

Jos 6: 4 carry trumpets of **r horns** in front of the ark. 3413
1Ch 15:28 with the sounding of **r horns** and trumpets, 8795

RAN (61) [RUN]

Ge 18: 7 Then he **r** to the herd and selected a choice, 8132
24:20 **r** back to the well to draw more water, 8132
24:28 The girl **r** and told her mother's household 8132
29:12 So *she* **r** and told her father. 8132
33: 4 Esau **r** to meet Jacob and embraced him; 8132
39:12 But he left his cloak in her hand and **r** out 5674
39:15 he left his cloak beside me and **r** out of 5674
39:18 he left his cloak beside me and **r** out of 5674
Ex 4: 3 it became a snake, and *he* **r** from it. 5674
Nu 11:27 A young man **r** and told Moses, 8132
16:47 and **r** into the midst of the assembly. 8132
Jos 4:18 to their place and **r** at flood stage as before. 2143
7:22 and *they* **r** to the tent, and there it was, 8132
15: 3 Then *it* **r past** Hezron up to Addar 6296
15: 8 Then it **r up** the Valley of Ben Hinnom 6590
15:10 **r** along the northern slope of Mount Jearim 6296
17: 7 The boundary **r** southward from there 2143
18:17 and **r down** *to* the Stone of Bohan son 3718
19:11 Going west it **r** *to* Maralah, 6590
19:34 The boundary **r** west *through* Aznoth Tabor 8740
Jdg 7:21 all the Midianites **r**, crying out as they fled. 8132
9:54 So his servant **r** him **through**, and he died. 1991
1Sa 3: 5 And *he* **r** to Eli and said, "Here I am; 8132
4:12 a Benjamite **r** from the battle line and went 8132
10:23 *They* **r** and brought him out, 8132
17:22 **r** *to* the battle lines and greeted his brothers. 8132
17:24 *they* all **r** from him in great fear. 5674
17:48 David **r** quickly *toward* the battle line 8132
17:51 David **r** and stood over him. 8132
17:51 their hero was dead, *they* **turned and r**. 5674
20:36 *As* the boy **r**, he shot an arrow beyond him. 8132
2Sa 18:21 down before Joab and **r off**. 8132
18:23 Then Ahimaaz **r** by way of the plain 8132
1Ki 2:39 two of Shimei's slaves **r off** to Achish son 1368
18:35 The water **r down** around the altar and 2143
18:46 *he* **r** ahead of Ahab all the way to Jezreel. 8132
19: 3 Elijah was afraid and **r** for his life. 2143

1Ki 19:20 Elisha then left his oxen and **r** after Elijah. 8132
22:35 The blood from his wound **r** onto the floor 3668
2Ki 7: 7 the camp as it was and **r** for their lives. 5674
9:10 Then he opened the door and **r.** 5674
Jnh 1: 3 But Jonah **r away** from the LORD 1368
Mt 8:33 Those tending the pigs **r off,** *5771*
27:48 Immediately one of them **r** and got *5556*
28: 8 and **r** to tell his disciples. *5556*
Mk 5: 6 *he* **r** and fell on his knees in front of him. *5556*
5:14 the pigs **r off** and reported this in the town *5771*
6:33 and **r** on foot from all the towns *5340*
6:55 *They* **r throughout** that whole region *4366*
9:15 they were overwhelmed with wonder and **r** *4708*
10:17 a man **r up to** him and fell on his knees *4708*
15:36 One man **r,** filled a sponge *5556*
Lk 8:34 *they* **r off** and reported this in the town *5771*
15:20 he **r** to his son, threw his arms around him *5556*
19: 4 So *he* **r** ahead and climbed *4731*
24:12 Peter, however, got up and **r** to the tomb. *5556*
Ac 8:30 Then Philip **r up to** the chariot and heard *4708*
12:14 so overjoyed *she* **r** back without opening it *1661*
19:16 that *they* **r out** of the house naked *1767*
21:32 and soldiers and **r down** to the crowd. *2963*
27:41 the ship struck a sandbar and **r aground.** *2131*

RANDOM (3)

1Ki 22:34 But someone drew his bow **at r** and 4200+9448
2Ch 18:33 But someone drew his bow **at r** and 4200+9448
Pr 26:10 an archer who wounds **at r** is he who hires 3972

RANG (2) [RING]

Mt 25: 6 "At midnight the cry **r out:** *1181*
1Th 1: 8 The Lord's message **r out** from you *2010*

RANGE (5) [RANGES]

Nu 27:12 the Abarim **r** and see the land I have given NIH
Dt 32:49 into the Abarim **R** to Mount Nebo in Moab, 2215
2Ch 16: 9 For the eyes of the LORD **r** throughout 8763
Isa 32:20 **letting** your cattle and donkeys **r free.** 8079+8938
Zec 4:10 *which* **r** throughout the earth.)" 8763

RANGES (1) [RANGE]

Job 39: 8 *He* **r** the hills *for* his pasture and searches 9365

RANGING (KJV) See CHARGING

RANK (10) [RANKING, RANKS]

1Sa 18: 5 **gave** him **a high r in** the army. 6584+8492
2Ki 23: 4 the priests **next in r** and the doorkeepers 5467
25:18 Zephaniah the priest **next in r** and 5467
1Ch 15:18 and with them their brothers **next in r:** 5467
2Ch 31:12 and his brother Shimei was **next in r.** 5467
Est 10: 3 the Jew was **second in r** to King Xerxes, 5467
Isa 3: 3 the captain of fifty and **man of r,** 5951+7156
5:13 their **men of r** will die of hunger 3883
Jer 52:24 Zephaniah the priest **next in r** and 5467
Eze 23:23 chariot officers and **men of high r,** 7924

RANKING (1) [RANK]

Ac 25:23 with the **high r officers** and the leading men *5941*

RANKS (13) [RANK]

1Sa 17: 8 Goliath stood and shouted to the **r** *of* Israel, 5120
17:10 "This day I defy the **r** *of* Israel! 5120
2Ki 11: 8 Anyone who approaches your **r** must be put 8444
11:15 "Bring her out between the **r** and put to 8444
1Ch 12:38 who volunteered to serve in the **r.** 5120
2Ch 23:14 "Bring her out between the **r** and put to 8444
Job 40:19 He **r** first among the works of God, NIH
Pr 30:27 yet they advance together **in r;** 2951
Isa 14:31 and there is not a straggler in its **r.** 4596
Jer 46:21 in her **r** are like fattened calves. 7931
50:37 and chariots and all the foreigners in her **r!** 9348
Joel 2: 8 through defenses without **breaking r.** 1298
Gal 2: 4 false brothers *had* **infiltrated** *our* **r** *4207+4209*

RANSACKED (2)

Ob 1: 6 But how Esau *will* **be r,** 2924
Zec 14: 2 the city will be captured, the houses **r,** 9116

RANSOM (20) [RANSOMED, RANSOMS]

Ex 30:12 a **r** *for* his life at the time he is counted. 4111
Nu 35:31 not accept a **r** for the life of a murderer, 4111
35:32 not accept a **r** *for* anyone who has fled to 4111
Job 5:20 In famine *he will* **r** you from death, 7009
6:22 **pay a r** for me from your wealth, 8815
6:23 **r** me from the clutches of the ruthless'? 7009
33:24 I have found a **r** for him'— 4111
Ps 49: 7 of another or give to God a **r** *for* him— 4111
49: 8 the **r** *for* a life is costly, 7018
Pr 13: 8 A man's riches may **r** his life, 4111
21:18 The wicked become a **r** for the righteous, 4111
Isa 43: 3 I give Egypt for your **r,** 4111
47:11 that *you* cannot **ward off with a r;** 4105
50: 2 Was my arm too short to **r** you? 7014
Jer 31:11 the LORD *will* **r** Jacob and redeem them 7009
Hos 13:14 *"I will* **r** them from the power of 7009
Mt 20:28 and to give his life as a **r** for many." *3389*
Mk 10:45 and to give his life as a **r** for many." *3389*
1Ti 2: 6 who gave himself as a **r** for all men— *519*
Heb 9:15 a **r** to set them free from the sins committed *667*

RANSOMED (4) [RANSOM]

Lev 19:20 but *who has* not **been r** or given her freedom, 7009+7009
27:29 No person devoted to destruction *may* **be r;** 7009
Isa 35:10 and the **r** *of* the LORD will return. 7009
51:11 The **r** *of* the LORD will return. 7009

RANSOMS (1) [RANSOM]

Ps 55:18 *He* **r** me unharmed from the battle waged 7009

RAPED (5) [RAPES]

Jdg 19:25 and *they* **r** her and abused her throughout 3359
20: 5 *They* **r** my concubine, and she died. 6700
2Sa 13:14 and since he was stronger than she, *he* **r** her. 2256+6700+8886
13:32 since the day Amnon **r** his sister Tamar. 6700
Zec 14: 2 the houses ransacked, and the women **r.** 8711

RAPED (Anglicized) See also VIOLATED

RAPES (2) [RAPED]

Dt 22:25 a man happens to meet a girl pledged to be married and **r** her, 2256+2616+6640+8886
22:28 happens to meet a virgin not pledged to be married and **r** her 2256+6640+8886+9530

RAPHA (7) [BETH RAPHA]

2Sa 21:16 Ishbi-Benob, one of the descendants of **R,** 8335
21:18 one of the descendants of **R.** 8335
21:20 He also was descended from **R.** 8335
21:22 These four were descendants of **R** in Gath, 8335
1Ch 8: 2 Nohah the fourth and **R** the fifth. 8325
20: 6 He also was descended from **R.** 8325
20: 8 These were descendants of **R** in Gath, 8325

RAPHAH (1)

1Ch 8:37 **R** was his son, Eleasah his son 8334

RAPHU (1)

Nu 13: 9 from the tribe of Benjamin, Palti son of **R;** 8336

RAPID (1) [RAPIDLY]

Ezr 5: 8 with diligence and *is* **making r progress** 10613

RAPIDLY (2) [RAPID]

Ac 6: 7 of disciples in Jerusalem increased **r,** *5379*
2Th 3: 1 that the message of the Lord *may* **spread r** *5556*

RARE (4) [RARELY]

1Sa 3: 1 In those days the word of the LORD was **r;** 3701
Pr 20:15 but lips that speak knowledge are a **r** jewel. 3702
24: 4 with **r** and beautiful treasures. 3701
Isa 13:12 more **r** than the gold of Ophir. NIH

RARELY (1) [RARE]

Ro 5: 7 **Very r** will anyone die for a righteous man, *3660*

RASE (KJV) See TEAR DOWN

RASH (12) [RASHLY]

Lev 13: 2 a swelling or a **r** or a bright spot on his skin 6204
13: 6 pronounce him clean, it is only a **r.** 5030
13: 7 But if the **r** does spread in his skin 5030
13: 8 and if the **r** has spread in the skin, 5030
13:39 a **harmless r** that has broken out on the skin 993
14:56 and for a swelling, a **r** or a bright spot, 6204
Nu 30: 6 a **r promise** by which she obligates herself 4439
30: 8 **r promise** by which she obligates herself, 4439
Ps 106:33 and **r words came** from Moses' lips. 1051
Isa 32: 4 mind of the **r** will know and understand, 4554
Ac 19:36 to be quiet and not do anything **r.** *4637*
2Ti 3: 4 **r,** conceited, lovers of pleasure *4637*

RASHLY (2) [RASH]

Pr 13: 3 but he *who* **speaks r** will come to ruin. 7316+8557
20:25 a trap for a man *to* dedicate something **r** 4362

RAT (1) [RATS]

Lev 11:29 the weasel, the **r,** any kind of great lizard, 6572

RATE (1)

Lev 25:50 **based on the r paid** to a hired man 3427+3869

RATHER (69)

Ge 27:12 a curse on myself **r than** a blessing." 2256+4202
Dt 15: 8 **R** be openhanded and freely lend him 3954
Jdg 6:27 he did it at night **r than** in the daytime. 4946
18:19 as priest **r than** just one man's household?" 196
Ru 2:16 **R,** pull out some stalks for her from 1685+2256
2Sa 6:21 who chose me **r than** your father or anyone 4946
2Ki 17:39 **R,** worship the LORD your God; 561+3954
20:10 **"R,** have it go back ten steps." 3954+4202
2Ch 17: 4 and followed his commands **r than** 2256+4202
Est 6: 6 that the king *would* **r** honor than me?" 2911
Job 7:15 **r than** this body of mine. 4946
32: 2 with Job for justifying himself **r than** God. 4946
Ps 52: 3 You love evil **r than** good, 4946
52: 3 falsehood **r than** speaking the truth. 4946
84:10 *I* **would r** be a doorkeeper in the house 1047
Pr 8:10 knowledge **r than** choice gold, 4946
16:16 to choose understanding **r than** silver! 4946
Ecc 5: 1 near to listen **r than** to offer the sacrifice 4946
Jer 7:19 Are they not **r** harming themselves, 2022
22:10 **r,** weep bitterly for him who is exiled, NIH
La 3: 2 and made me walk in darkness **r than** light; 4202
Eze 16: 5 **R,** you were thrown out into the open field, 2256
18:23 **R,** am I not pleased when they turn 2022
33:11 **r** that they turn from their ways and live. 561
34: 8 for themselves **r than** for my flock, 4202
Da 3:28 to give up their lives **r than** serve 10379
Hos 6: 6 of God **r than** burnt offerings. 4946
Mt 10: 6 Go **r** to the lost sheep of Israel. *3437*
10:28 **R,** be afraid of the One who can *1254+3437*
Mk 7:15 **R,** it is what comes out of a man *247*
Lk 11:28 "Blessed **r** are those who hear the word *3528*
17: 8 Would he not **r** say, 'Prepare my supper, *247*
18:14 "I tell you that this man, **r than** the other, *4123*
Jn 14:10 **R,** it is the Father, living in me, *1254*
Ac 4:19 in God's sight to obey you **r** than God. *3437*
5:29 "We must obey God **r** than men! *3437*
Ro 1:25 and served created things **r than** *4123*
3:20 **r,** through the law we become conscious *1142*
3:31 **R,** we uphold the law. *247*
6:13 **but r** offer yourselves to God, *247*
11:11 **R,** because of their transgression, *247*
12: 3 **but r** think of yourself with sober judgment, *247*
13:14 **R,** clothe yourselves with the Lord Jesus *247*
15:21 **R,** as it is written: *247*
1Co 5: 2 Shouldn't you **r** have been filled with grief *3437*
6: 7 Why not **r** be wronged? *3437*
6: 7 Why not **r** be cheated? *3437*
9:12 with anything **r than** hinder the gospel *2671+3590*
9:15 I would **r** die than have anyone deprive me *3437*
14: 5 but I would **r** have you prophesy. *3437*
14:19 But in the church *I* **would r** speak five intelligible words *2527*
2Co 4: 2 **R,** we have renounced secret and *247*
5:12 is seen **r than** in what is in the heart. *2779+3590*
6: 4 **R,** as servants of God *247*
7:12 **but r** that before God you could see *247*
10: 8 for building you up **r than** pulling you *2779+4024*
Gal 1:12 **r,** I received it by revelation *247*
4: 9 or **r** are known by God— *3437*
5:13 **r,** serve one another in love. *247*
Eph 5: 4 which are out of place, but **r** thanksgiving. *3437*
5:11 deeds of darkness, but **r** expose them. *3437*
Col 2: 8 basic principles of this world **r than** *2779+4024*
1Ti 1: 4 These promote controversies **r** than God's work— *3437*
4: 7 **r,** train yourself to be godly. *1254*
2Ti 3: 4 lovers of pleasure **r** than lovers of God— *3437*
Tit 1: 8 **R** he must be hospitable, *247*
Heb 11:25 of God **r** than to enjoy the pleasures of sin *3437*
12:13 the lame may not be disabled, but **r** healed. *3437*
1Pe 4: 2 **but r** for the will of God. *247*

RATIFIED (1)

Jos 9:15 and the leaders of the assembly **r** it **by oath.** 8678

RATIONED (2)

Eze 4:16 The people will eat **r** food in anxiety 928+5486
4:16 in anxiety and drink **r** water in despair, 928+5374

RATS (5) [RAT]

1Sa 6: 4 "Five gold tumors and five gold **r,** 6572
6: 5 and of the **r** that are destroying the country, 6572
6:11 along with it the chest containing the gold **r** 6572
6:18 of the gold **r** was according to the number 6572
Isa 66:17 of those who eat the flesh of pigs and **r** 6572

RATTLES (1) [RATTLING]

Job 39:23 The quiver **r** against his side, 8261

RATTLING (2) [RATTLES]

Job 41:29 he laughs at the **r** *of* the lance. 8323
Eze 37: 7 a **r sound,** and the bones came together, 8323

RAVAGE (6) [RAVAGED, RAVAGES, RAVAGING]

Ge 41:30 and the famine *will* **r** the land. 3983
Jdg 6: 5 they invaded the land to **r** it. 8845
Ps 80:13 Boars from the forest **r** it and the creatures 4155
Jer 5: 6 a wolf from the desert *will* **r** them, 8720
5:10 "Go through her vineyards and **r** them, 8845
Eze 26: 8 *He will* **r** your settlements on the mainland 2222

RAVAGED (3) [RAVAGE]

Isa 6:11 and the fields ruined and **r,** 9039
Eze 26: 6 on the mainland *will* **be r** by the sword. 2222
36: 3 Because *they* **r** and hounded you 9037

RAVAGES (2) [RAVAGE]

Ps 35:17 Rescue my life from their **r,** 8738
Jer 14:18 if I go into the city, I see the **r** *of* famine. 9377

RAVAGING (1) [RAVAGE]
1Ch 21:12 with the angel of the LORD **r** every part 8845

RAVEN (6) [RAVENS]
Ge 8: 7 and sent out a **r**, and it kept flying 6854
Lev 11:15 any kind of **r**, 6854
Dt 14:14 any kind of **r**, 6854
Job 38:41 Who provides for the **r** when 6854
SS 5:11 his hair is wavy and black as a **r**. 6854
Isa 34:11 the great owl and the **r** will nest there. 6854

RAVENING (1) [RAVENOUS]
Jer 2:30 has devoured your prophets like a **r** lion. 8845

RAVENOUS (2) [RAVENING]
Ge 49:27 "Benjamin *is* a **r** wolf; 3271
Ps 57: 4 I lie among **r beasts—** 4266

RAVENS (5) [RAVEN]
1Ki 17: 4 and I have ordered the **r** to feed you there." 6854
17: 6 The **r** brought him bread and meat in 6854
Ps 147: 9 and for the young **r** when they call. 6854
Pr 30:17 will be pecked out by the **r** *of* the valley, 6854
Lk 12:24 Consider the **r**: They do not sow or reap, *3165*

RAVIN (KJV) See PREY, RAVENOUS

RAVINE (13) [RAVINES]
Jos 16: 8 the border went west to the Kanah **R** 5707
17: 9 boundary continued south to the Kanah **R.** 5707
17: 9 of Manasseh was the northern side of the **r** 5707
19:11 and extended to the **r** near Jokneam. 5707
1Sa 15: 5 of Amalek and set an ambush in the **r.** 5707
25:20 riding her donkey into a mountain **r,** 6260
30: 9 with him came to the Besor **R,** 5707
30:10 too exhausted to cross the **r.** 5707
30:21 and who were left behind at the Besor **R.** 5707
1Ki 17: 3 turn eastward and hide in the Kerith **R,** 5707
17: 5 He went to the Kerith **R,** east of the Jordan, 5707
Isa 15: 7 and stored up they carry away over the **R** 5707
Zec 1: 8 among the myrtle trees in a **r.** 5185

RAVINES (17) [RAVINE]
Nu 21:14 "...Waheb in Suphah and the **r,** 5707
21:15 the **r** that lead to the site of Ar and lie along 5707
2Sa 23:30 Hiddai from the **r** *of* Gaash, 5707
1Ch 11:32 Hurai from the **r** *of* Gaash, 5707
Job 22:24 your gold of Ophir to the rocks in the **r,** 5707
Ps 104:10 He makes springs pour water into the **r;** 5707
Isa 7:19 the steep **r** and in the crevices in the rocks, 5707
57: 5 in the **r** and under the overhanging crags. 5707
57: 6 the smooth stones of the **r** are your portion; 5707
Eze 6: 3 mountains and hills, to the **r** and valleys: 692
31:12 its branches lay broken in all the **r** *of* 692
32: 6 and the **r** will be filled with your flesh. 692
34:13 the **r** and in all the settlements in the land. 692
35: 8 and in your valleys and in all your **r.** 692
36: 4 mountains and hills, to the **r** and valleys, 692
36: 6 mountains and hills, to the **r** and valleys: 692
Joel 3:18 all the **r** *of* Judah will run with water. 692

RAVING (1)
Jn 10:20 "He is demon-possessed and **r mad.** *3419*

RAVISH (1) [RAVISHED]
Dt 28:30 but another *will* take her and **r** her. 8711

RAVISHED (3) [RAVISH]
Isa 13:16 houses will be looted and their wives **r.** 8711
Jer 3: 2 any place where *you have* not **been r?** 8711
La 5:11 Women *have been* **r** in Zion, 6700

RAW (9)
Ex 12: 9 Do not eat the meat **r** or cooked in water, 5529
Lev 13:10 the hair white and if there is **r** flesh in 2645+4695
13:14 But whenever **r** flesh appears on him, 2645
13:15 When the priest sees the **r** flesh, 2645
13:15 The **r** flesh is unclean; 2645
13:16 Should the **r** flesh change and turn white, 2645
13:24 or white spot appears in the **r flesh** *of* 4695
1Sa 2:15 boiled meat from you, but only **r."** 2645
Eze 29:18 and every shoulder **made r.** 5307

RAWBONED (1)
Ge 49:14 "Issachar is a **r** donkey lying down 1752

RAY (1) [RAYS]
Am 5:20 pitch-dark, without a **r of brightness?** 5586

RAYS (3) [RAY]
Job 3: 9 for daylight in vain and not see the **first r** 6757
41:18 his eyes are like the **r** *of* dawn. 6757
Hab 3: 4 **r** flashed from his hand, 7967

RAZOR (7)
Nu 6: 5 of separation no **r** may be used on his head. 9509
Jdg 13: 5 No **r** may be used on his head, 4623
16:17 "No **r** has ever been used on my head," 4623
1Sa 1:11 and no **r** will ever be used on his head." 4623
Ps 52: 2 it is like a sharpened **r,** 9509
Isa 7:20 In that day the Lord will use a **r** hired from 9509
Eze 5: 1 and use it as a barber's **r** to shave your head 9509

REACH (29) [REACHED, REACHES, REACHING]
Ge 3:22 be allowed *to* **r out** his hand and take also 8938
19:22 I cannot do anything until you **r** it." 995
Ex 4: 4 **"R out** your hand and take it by the tail." 8938
Dt 30:11 not too difficult for you or **beyond** your **r.** 8158
Jos 3: 8 'When you **r** the edge of the Jordan's 995+6330
10:19 the rear and don't let them **r** their cities, 448+995
Jdg 19:13 *let's try to* **r** Gibeah or Ramah and spend 7928
1Sa 10: 3 on from there until *you* **r** the great tree 995+6330
14: 4 to cross **to r** the Philistine outpost 6584
2Sa 5: 8 *to* use the water shaft *to* **r** those 'lame and 5595
15: 5 Absalom *would* **r out** his hand, 8938
Job 3:22 with gladness and rejoice when *they* **r** 5162
29:19 My roots *will* **r** to the water, 7337
37:23 The Almighty is beyond *our* **r** and exalted 5162
Ps 32: 6 mighty waters rise, *they will* not **r** him. 5595
144: 7 **R down** your hand from on high; 8938
Isa 11:11 the Lord *will* **r out** his hand a second time 3578*
59: 9 and righteousness *does* not **r** us. 5952
65:20 he *who* **fails to r** a hundred will 2627
Eze 31:14 so well-watered *are ever to* **r** such 6641
Am 9: 9 and not a pebble *will* **r** the ground. 5877
Mic 5: 4 his greatness will **r to** the ends of the earth. 6330
Lk 13:32 and on the third day *I will* **r** *my* **goal.'** *5457*
Jn 20:27 **R out** your hand and put it into my side. *5770*
Ac 17:27 and perhaps **r out for** him and find him, *6027*
20:16 for he was in a hurry *to* **r** Jerusalem, *1181+1650*
27:12 hoping *to* **r** Phoenix and winter there. *2918*
Eph 4:13 until *we* all **r** unity in the faith and in *2918*
Rev 12:14 times and half a time, out of the serpent's **r.** *NIG*

REACHED (102) [REACH]
Ge 8: 9 *He* **r out** his hand and took the dove 8938
10:19 of Canaan **r** from Sidon toward Gerar as far 2118
15:16 the Amorites has not yet **r** its full measure." NIH
18:21 as bad as the outcry that *has* **r** me. 448+995
19:10 men inside **r out** and pulled Lot back 3338+8938
19:23 By the time Lot **r** Zoar, 995+2025
22: 9 *they* **r** the place God had told him about, 448+995
22:10 Then he **r out** his hand and took the knife 8938
28:11 When *he* **r** a certain place, 7003
37:18 and before *he* **r** them, 7928
45:16 When the news **r** Pharaoh's palace 9048
46: 1 and when *he* **r** Beersheba, 995+2025
48:14 But Israel **r out** his right hand and put it 8938
50:10 *they* **r** the threshing floor of Atad, 995+6330
Ex 3: 9 now the cry of the Israelites *has* **r** me, 448+995
4: 4 So Moses **r out** and took hold of the snake 8938
16:35 they ate manna until they **r** the border 448+995
Nu 13:23 When *they* **r** the Valley of Eshcol, 995+6330
21:23 When *he* **r** Jahaz, he fought with Israel. 995+2025
Dt 1:19 and so *we* **r** Kadesh Barnea. 995+6330
1:20 *"You have* **r** the hill country of the Amorites, 995+6330
1:31 way you went until you **r** this place." 995+6330
12: 9 yet **r** the resting place and the inheritance 448+995
29: 7 When *you* **r** this place, 448+995
Jos 3:15 priests who carried the ark **r** the Jordan 995+6330
10:20 few who were left **r** their fortified cities. 448+995
15:11 along to Mount Baalah and **r** Jabneel. 3655
17:10 of Manasseh **r** the sea and bordered Asher 2118
Jdg 3:21 Ehud **r** *with* his left hand, 8938
5:26 Her hand **r** for the tent peg, 8938
7:19 the hundred men with him **r** the edge 928+995
16:29 Then Samson **r toward** 4369
19:29 When *he* **r** home, 448+995
1Sa 9: 5 When they **r** the district of Zuph, 928+995
9:16 for their cry *has* **r** me." 448+995
14:27 so *he* **r out** the end of the staff that was 8938
15:13 When Samuel **r** him, Saul said, 448+995
17:20 *He* **r** the camp as the army was going out 995
30: 1 and his men **r** Ziklag on the third day. 995
2Sa 6: 6 Uzzah **r out** and took hold of the ark 8938
19:11 throughout Israel *has* **r** the king 448+995
22:17 *"He* **r down** from on high and took hold 8938
1Ki 2:28 When the news **r** Joab, 995+6330
19: 8 and forty nights until he **r** Horeb, NIH
2Ki 4:27 *she* **r** the man of God at the mountain, 448+995
4:32 When Elisha **r** the house, 995+2025
6: 7 Then the man **r out** his hand and took it. 8938
7: 5 When *they* **r** the edge of the camp, 995+6330
7: 8 The men who had leprosy **r** the edge of 995+6330
9:18 "The messenger *has* **r** them, 995+6330
9:20 The lookout reported, *"He has* **r** them, 995+6330
11:16 So they seized her as *she* **r** the place where 995
19:23 *I have* **r** its remotest parts, 995
19:28 and your insolence *has* **r** my ears, 6590
1Ch 13: 9 Uzzah **r out** his hand to steady the ark, 8938
2Ch 23:15 So they seized her as *she* **r** the entrance 448+995
29:17 the month *they* **r** the portico of the LORD. 995
30:27 for their prayer **r** heaven, 995+4200
Ezr 9: 6 and our guilt *has* **r** to the heavens. 1540+6330
Ne 4: 6 the wall till all of it **r** half its **height,** 6330+8003
Job 28:22 'Only a rumor of it *has* **r** our ears.' 928+9048
Ps 18:16 *He* **r down** from on high and took hold 8938
Isa 10:14 so my hand **r** for the wealth of the nations; NIH
16: 8 *which once* **r** Jazer and spread toward 5595
37:24 *I have* **r** its remotest heights, 995
37:29 and because your insolence *has* **r** my ears, 6590
Jer 1: 9 Then the LORD **r out** his hand 8938
37:13 But *when* he **r** the Benjamin Gate, 928+2118
48:32 *they* **r** as far as the sea of Jazer. 5595
Eze 10: 7 Then one of the cherubim **r out** his hand to 8938
21:25 whose time of punishment has **r** its climax, NIH
21:29 whose time of punishment has **r** its climax. NIH
35: 5 the time their punishment **r** its climax, NIH
40:49 It *was* **r** by a flight of stairs, 448+6590
Da 6:24 And before *they* **r** the floor of the den, 10413
8:10 It grew until it **r** the host of the heavens, NIH
Jnh 3: 6 When the news **r** the king of Nineveh, 5595
Mic 1: 9 *It has* **r** the very gate of my people, 5595
Mt 8: 3 Jesus **r out** his hand and touched the man. *1753*
14:31 Immediately Jesus **r out** his hand *1753*
26:51 one of Jesus' companions **r for** his sword, *1753+3836+5931*
Mk 1:41 Jesus **r out** his hand and touched the man. *1753*
11:13 *When he* **r** it, he found nothing but leaves, *2093+2262*
15: 1 and the whole Sanhedrin, **r** a decision. *4472*
Lk 1:44 as the sound of your greeting **r** my ears, *1181*
5:13 Jesus **r out** his hand and touched the man. *1753*
19: 5 When Jesus **r** the spot, *2093+2262*
Jn 6:21 and immediately the boat **r** the shore *1181+2093*
11:32 When Mary **r** the place where Jesus was *2262*
20: 4 but the other disciple outran Peter and **r** *2262*
20: 8 who *had* **r** the tomb first, also went inside. *2262*
Ac 8:40 in all the towns until he **r** Caesarea. *1650+2262*
11:22 **r** the ears of the church at Jerusalem, *201+1650*
16: 4 the decisions **r by** the apostles and elders *5679*
21: 8 *we* **r** Caesarea and stayed at the house *1650+2262*
21:31 news **r** the commander of the Roman *326*
21:35 When Paul **r** the steps, *1181+2093*
27:44 In this way everyone **r** land in safety. *2093*
28:13 and on the following day *we* **r** Puteoli. *1650+2262*
1Co 14:36 Or are you the only people *it has* **r?** *2918*
Eph 1:10 the times will have **r** their fulfillment— *NIG*
Jas 5: 4 The cries of the harvesters *have* **r** the ears *1656*

REACHES (18) [REACH]
Ge 11: 4 with a tower that **r** to the heavens, 8031
Dt 25:11 and *she* **r out** and seizes him 3338+8938
2Ki 10: 2 "As soon as this letter **r** you, 448+995
2Ch 28: 9 in a rage *that* **r** to heaven. 5595
Job 20: 6 Though his pride **r** to the heavens 6590
41:26 The sword *that* **r** him has no effect, 5952
Ps 36: 5 Your love, O LORD, **r to** the heavens, 928
48:10 your praise **r to** the ends of the earth; 6584
57:10 your faithfulness **r to** the skies. 6330
71:19 Your righteousness **r to** the skies, O God, 6330
108: 4 your faithfulness **r to** the skies. 6330
Isa 10:14 As *one* **r** into a nest, 5162
15: 8 their wailing **r** as far as Eglaim, NIH
Jer 51: 9 for her judgment **r** to the skies, 5595
51:53 Even if Babylon **r** the sky 6590
Da 4:22 your greatness has grown until *it* **r** the sky, 10413
12:12 Blessed is the one who waits for and **r** 5595
2Co 10:13 a field that **r** even to you. *2391*

REACHETH (KJV) See EXTENDS, PIERCES, REACHES, TOUCHED

REACHING (11) [REACH]
Ge 28:12 with its top **r** to heaven, 5595
Ex 28:42 **r** from the waist to the thigh. 2118
1Sa 17:49 **R** into his bag and taking out a stone, 3338+8938
Ps 57:10 For great is your love, **r to** the heavens; 6330
Isa 8: 8 passing through it and **r** up to the neck. 5595
Mk 11:15 On **r** Jerusalem, Jesus entered *1650+2262*
Lk 22:37 about me *is* **r** its fulfillment." *2400*
22:40 *On* **r** the place, he said to them, *1181+2093*
2Co 4:15 grace that *is* **r more and more** people may cause thanksgiving *1328+3836+4429+4498*
1Ti 5:24 **r** the place of judgment **ahead of** them; *4575*
Rev 1:13 **a robe r down to** his **feet** *4468*

READ (77) [READER, READING, READS]
Ex 24: 7 Book of the Covenant and **r** it to the people. 7924
Dt 17:19 and *he is to* **r** it all the days of his life so 7924
31:11 *you shall* **r** this law before them 7924
Jos 8:34 Joshua **r** all the words of the law— 7924
8:35 that Joshua *did* not **r** to the whole assembly 7924
2Ki 5: 6 that he took to the king of Israel **r:** 606
5: 7 As soon as the king of Israel **r** the letter, 7924
19:14 the letter from the messengers and **r** it. 7924
22: 8 He gave it to Shaphan, *who* **r** it. 7924
22:10 And Shaphan **r** *from* it in the presence of 7924
22:16 in the book the king of Judah *has* **r.** 7924
23: 2 *He* **r** in their hearing all the words of 7924
2Ch 30: 6 the king and from his officials, which **r:** 606
34:18 And Shaphan **r** from it in the presence of 7924
34:24 the book that *has been* **r** in the presence of 7924
34:30 *He* **r** in their hearing all the words of 7924
Ezr 4:18 The letter you sent us *has* **been r** 10637
4:23 of the letter of King Artaxerxes **was r** 10637
5: 7 The report they sent him **r** as follows: 10374
Ne 8: 3 *He* **r** it **aloud** from daybreak till noon 7924
8: 8 *They* **r** from the Book of the Law of God, 7924
8: 8 people could understand what was being **r.** 5246
8:18 Ezra **r** from the Book of the Law of God. 7924
9: 3 where they were and **r** from the Book of 7924
13: 1 that day the Book of Moses **was r aloud** in 7924
Est 6: 1 to be brought in and **r** to him. 7924

Isa 29:11 give the scroll to *someone who* **can r**, 3359+6219
29:11 **"R** this, please," he will answer, "I can't; 7924
29:12 scroll to someone *who* **cannot r**, 3359+4202+6219
29:12 and say, **"R** this, please," he will answer, 7924
29:12 will answer, *"I* don't **know how to r."** 3359+6219
34:16 Look in the scroll of the LORD and **r**: 7924
37:14 the letter from the messengers and **r** it. 7924
Jer 29:29 **r** the letter to Jeremiah the prophet. 7924
36:6 on a day of fasting and **r** to the people from 7924
36:6 **R** them to all the people of Judah who come 7924
36:8 at the LORD's temple *he* **r** the words of 7924
36:10 Baruch **r** to all the people at the LORD's 7924
36:13 Micaiah told them everything he had heard Baruch **r** to the people 7924
36:14 "Bring the scroll from which *you have* **r** to 7924
36:15 "Sit down, please, and **r** it to us." 7924
36:15 So Baruch **r** it to them. 7924
36:21 the room of Elishama the secretary and **r** it 7924
36:23 Whenever Jehudi *had* **r** three 7924
51:61 see that *you* **r** all these words **aloud.** 7924
Da 5:8 but they could not **r** the writing or tell 10637
5:15 *to* **r** this writing and tell me what it means, 10637
5:16 If you can **r** this writing 10637
5:17 *I will* **r** the writing for the king 10637
Mt 12:3 "Haven't *you* **r** what David did when he *336*
12:5 Or haven't *you* **r** in the Law that on *336*
19:4 "Haven't *you* **r**," he replied, *336*
21:16 "Yes," replied Jesus, *"have you* never **r**, *336*
21:42 *"Have you* never **r** in the Scriptures: *336*
22:31 *have you* not **r** what God said to you, *336*
Mk 2:25 *"Have you* never **r** what David did when he *336*
12:10 Haven't *you* **r** this scripture: *336*
12:26 *have you* not **r** in the book of Moses, *336*
15:26 notice of the charge against him **r**: *1639+2108*
Lk 4:16 And he stood up *to* **r**. *336*
6:3 *"Have you* never **r** what David did when he *336*
10:26 "How *do you* **r** it?" *336*
23:38 a written notice above him, which **r**: *NIG*
Jn 19:19 *It* **r**: JESUS OF NAZARETH, KING OF THE JEWS *1211+1639*
19:20 Many of the Jews **r** this sign, *336*
Ac 13:27 of the prophets that *are* **r** every Sabbath. *336*
15:21 from the earliest times and *is* **r** in *336*
15:31 The *people* **r** it and were glad *336*
23:34 The governor **r** the letter *336*
2Co 1:13 not write you anything *you* cannot **r** *336*
3:2 on our hearts, known and **r** by everybody. *336*
3:14 when the old covenant *is* **r**. *342*
3:15 Even to this day when Moses *is* **r**, *336*
Col 4:16 After this letter *has been* **r** to you, *336*
4:16 also **r** in the church of the Laodiceans and *336*
4:16 that you in turn **r** the letter from Laodicea. *336*
1Th 5:27 before the Lord *to have* this letter **r** to all *336*

READER (2) [READ]

Mt 24:15 let the **r** understand— *336*
Mk 13:14 let the **r** understand— *336*

READILY (2) [READY]

Job 4:19 who are crushed **more r than** a moth! 4200+7156
Ro 11:24 how much more **r** will these, *NIG*

READINESS (2) [READY]

2Co 7:11 **r to see justice done.** *1689*
Eph 6:15 the **r** that comes from the gospel of peace. *2288*

READING (8) [READ]

Jer 51:63 When you finish **r** this scroll, 7924
Ac 8:28 on his way home was sitting in his chariot **r** *336*
8:30 up to the chariot and heard the man **r** Isaiah *336*
8:30 "Do you understand what *you are* **r?"** *336*
8:32 The eunuch was **r** this passage of Scripture: *336*
13:15 After the **r** from the Law and the Prophets, *342*
Eph 3:4 *In* **r** this, then, you will be able *336*
1Ti 4:13 devote yourself *to* the **public r** of Scripture, *342*

READS (2) [READ]

Da 5:7 "Whoever **r** this writing 10637
Rev 1:3 the one who **r** the words of this prophecy, *336*

READY (94) [ALREADY, READILY, READINESS]

Ge 24:61 Then Rebekah and her maids **got r** 7756
46:29 Joseph *had* his chariot **made r** and went 673
46:30 Israel said to Joseph, "Now *I am* **r to die,** 4637
Ex 14:6 So *he* **had** his chariot **made r** 673
17:4 *They are* almost *r to* **stone** me." AIT
19:11 and be **r** by the third day, 3922
34:2 Be **r** in the morning, 3922
Nu 4:15 and when the camp *is r to* **move,** AIT
8:11 *they may be* **r** to do the work of the LORD. 2118
32:17 But we *are* **r** to arm ourselves and go ahead 2590
Jos 1:2 **get r** to cross the Jordan River into 7756
1:11 **'Get** your supplies **r**. 3922
22:26 *'Let us* **get r** and build an altar— 6913
1Sa 6:7 "Now then, get a new cart **r**, 6913
9:26 **"Get r,** and I will send you on your way." 7756
9:26 When Saul **got r**, 7756
25:41 **r** to serve you and wash the feet NIH
2Sa 15:15 "Your servants are **r to do** whatever 2180
15:26 'I am not pleased with you,' then I am **r**; 2180
1Ki 1:5 So *he* **got** chariots and horses **r**, 6913
2Ki 22:4 high priest and **have** *him* **get r** the money 9462
1Ch 5:18 **r for military service—** 3655+7372
7:4 had 36,000 **men r for battle,** 1522+4878+7372
7:11 fighting men **r to go out** to war. 3655+7372
7:40 of men **r for battle,** 928+2021+4878+7372
12:8 **r for battle** and able 408+2021+4200+4878+7372
12:17 *r to have* you **unite** with me. AIT
12:25 Simeon, warriors **r for** battle—7,100; 4200
12:35 men of Dan, **r** *for* battle—28,600; 6885
28:21 the priests and Levites are **r** for all the work NIH
2Ch 25:5 men **r for military service,** 3655+7372
26:11 **r to go out** by divisions according 3655+7372
26:19 a censer in his hand *r* to **burn incense,** AIT
29:26 Levites **stood** *r* with David's instruments, AIT
Est 3:14 of every nationality so they would be **r** for 6969
8:13 so that the Jews would be **r** on that day 6969
Job 3:8 those *who are* **r** to rouse Leviathan. 6969
18:12 disaster *is* **r** for him when he falls. 3922
32:19 like new wineskins **r to burst.** 1324
Ps 7:13 *he* **makes r** his flaming arrows. 7188
59:4 yet *they are* **r** to attack me. 3922
119:173 May your hand be **r** to help me, NIH
Pr 21:31 The horse **is made r** for the day of battle, 3922
22:18 **have** all of them **r** on your lips. 3922
24:27 and **get** your fields **r**; 6963
Isa 30:33 it *has* **been made r** for the king. 3922
Jer 1:17 **"Get** yourself **r**! 273+5516
9:3 **make r** their tongue like a bow, **to shoot** 2005
46:14 'Take your positions and **get r**, 3922
La 2:4 his right hand *is* **r**. 5893
Eze 7:14 the trumpet and **get** everything **r**, 3922
21:11 **made r** for the hand of the slayer. 5989
38:7 **" 'Get r**; be prepared, 3922
Da 3:15 if you are **r** to fall down and worship 10577
Hos 2:9 and my new wine when it is **r**. 4595
Na 2:3 on the day they *are* **made r**; 3922
Zec 5:11 When *it is* **r**, the basket will be set there 3922
Mt 22:4 and everything *is* **r**. *2289*
22:8 'The wedding banquet is **r**, *2289*
24:44 So you also must be **r**, *2289*
25:10 The virgins who were **r** went in with him to *2289*
Mk 3:9 to *have* a small boat **r** for him, *4674*
14:15 a large upper room, furnished and **r**. *2289*
Lk 1:17 *to* **make r** a people prepared for the Lord." *2286*
1:39 that time Mary **got r** and hurried to a town *482*
9:52 a Samaritan village to **get** things **r** for him; *2286*
12:35 "Be **dressed r for service** *3836+4019+4322*
12:38 those servants whose master finds them **r**, *NIG*
12:40 You also must be **r**, because the Son of Man *2289*
12:47 and *does* not **get r** or does *2286*
14:17 'Come, for everything is now **r**.' *2289*
17:8 **get** *yourself* **r** and wait on me while I eat *4322*
22:33 I am **r** to go with you to prison and *2289*
Jn 8:37 Yet *you are* **r** to kill me, *2426*
Ac 16:10 *we* **got r** at once to leave for Macedonia, *2426*
21:13 I am **r** not only to be bound, *2290*
21:15 we **got r** and went up to Jerusalem. *2171*
23:15 We are **r** to kill him before he gets here." *2289*
23:21 They are **r** now, waiting for your consent *2289*
23:23 **"Get r** a detachment of two hundred *2286*
28:10 in many ways and *when we were r to* **sail,** AIT
1Co 3:2 not solid food, for *you were* not yet **r** for it. *1538*
3:2 Indeed, *you are* still not **r**. *1538*
14:8 who *will* **get r** for battle? *4186*
2Co 9:2 that since last year *you* in Achaia *were* **r** *4186*
9:3 but that you may be **r**, *4186*
9:5 Then it will be **r** as a generous gift, *2289*
10:6 be **r** to punish every act of disobedience, *2289*
12:14 Now I am **r** to visit you for the third time, *2290*
Tit 3:1 to be **r** to do whatever is good, *2289*
1Pe 1:5 until the coming of the salvation that is **r** to *2289*
4:5 give account *to* him who *is* **r** to judge *2290+2400*
Rev 9:15 And the four angels who *had been* **kept r** *2286*
19:7 and his bride *has* **made** herself **r**. *2286*

REAFFIRM (3) [AFFIRM]

1Sa 11:14 to Gilgal and there **r** the kingship." 2542
20:17 And Jonathan **had** David **r** his oath out 3578
2Co 2:8 therefore, *to* **r** your love for him. *3263*

REAIAH (4)

1Ch 4:2 **R** son of Shobal was the father of Jahath, 8025
5:5 Micah his son, **R** his son, Baal his son, 8025
Ezr 2:47 Giddel, Gahar, **R**, 8025
Ne 7:50 **R**, Rezin, Nekoda, 8025

REAL (3) [REALITIES, REALITY, REALLY]

Jn 6:55 For my flesh is **r** food *239*
6:55 and my blood is **r** drink. *239*
1Jn 2:27 and as that anointing is **r**, not counterfeit— *239*

REALITIES (1) [REAL]

Heb 10:1 that are coming—not the **r** themselves. *1635*

REALITY (1) [REAL]

Col 2:17 the **r**, however, is found in Christ. *5393*

REALIZE (32) [REALIZED, REALIZING]

Ge 42:23 not **r** that Joseph could understand them, 3359
Ex 10:7 *Do you* not yet **r** that Egypt is ruined?" 3359
Nu 22:34 *I did* not **r** you were standing in the road 3359
Jdg 13:16 not **r** that it was the angel of the LORD.) 3359
15:11 "Don't *you* **r** that the Philistines are rulers 3359
20:34 so heavy that the Benjamites *did* not **r** how 3359
1Sa 12:17 And *you will* **r** what an evil thing you did 2256+3359+8011
2Sa 2:26 Don't *you* **r** that this will end in bitterness? 3359
3:38 *"Do you* not **r** that a prince and 3359
Ecc 2:14 *to* **r** that the same fate overtakes them both. 3359
Jer 2:19 Consider then and **r** how evil and bitter it is 8011
11:19 not **r** that they had plotted against me, 3359
Da 2:8 you are trying to gain time, because *you* **r** 10255
Hos 7:2 not **r** that I remember all their evil deeds. 606+4200+4222
7:9 but he *does* not **r** it. 3359
11:3 but *they did* not **r** it was I who healed them. 3359
14:9 *He will* **r** these things. 1067
Jn 2:9 *He did* not **r** where it had come from, *3857*
11:50 *You do* not **r** that it is better for you *3357*
12:16 Only after Jesus was glorified *did they* **r** *3630*
13:7 "You *do* not **r** now what I am doing, *3857*
14:20 that day you *will* **r** that I am in my Father, *1182*
19:10 "Don't *you* **r** I have power either *3857*
20:14 but *she did* not **r** that it was Jesus. *3857*
21:4 but the disciples *did* not **r** that it was Jesus. *3857*
Ac 7:25 Moses thought that his own people *would* **r** *5317*
10:34 *"I now* **r** how true it is that God does *2898*
23:5 *I did* not **r** that he was the high priest; *3857*
1Co 11:3 *to* **r** that the head of every man is Christ, *3857*
2Co 10:11 Such people *should* **r** that what we are *3357*
13:5 *Do you* not **r** that Christ Jesus is in you— *2105*
Rev 3:17 But *you do* not **r** that you are wretched, *3857*

REALIZED (29) [REALIZE]

Ge 3:7 and *they* **r** they were naked; 3359
28:8 Esau then **r** how displeasing the Canaanite 8011
Ex 5:19 The Israelite foremen **r** they were in trouble 8011
Jdg 6:22 When Gideon **r** that it was the angel of 8011
13:21 Manoah **r** that it was the angel of 3359
20:41 *they* **r** that disaster had come upon them. 8011
Ru 1:18 When Naomi **r** that Ruth was determined 8011
1Sa 3:8 Eli **r** that the LORD was calling the boy. 1067
18:28 When Saul **r** that the LORD was 2256+3359+8011
2Sa 10:6 the Ammonites **r** that they had become 8011
12:19 and he **r** the child was dead. 1067
20:12 When *he* **r** that everyone who came up 8011
1Ki 3:15 and he **r** it had been a dream. 2180
1Ch 19:6 the Ammonites **r** that they had become 8011
Ne 6:12 *I* **r** that God had not sent him, 5795
6:16 lost their self-confidence, because *they* **r** 3359
Ecc 5:18 Then I **r** that it is good and proper for 8011
SS 6:12 Before *I* **r** it, my desire set me among 3359
Eze 10:20 and *I* **r** that they were cherubim. 3359
Mt 2:16 *When* Herod **r** that he had been outwitted by *3972*
Mk 5:30 At once Jesus **r that** power had gone out *2105*
Lk 1:22 *They* **r** he had seen a vision in the temple, *2105*
Jn 4:53 the father **r** that this was the exact time *1182*
6:22 on the opposite shore of the lake **r** *3972*
6:24 Once the crowd **r** that neither Jesus *3972*
Ac 4:13 and John and **r** that they were unschooled, *2898*
16:19 the owners of the slave girl **r** that their hope *3972*
19:34 But *when they* **r** he was a Jew, *2105*
22:29 *when he* **r** that he had put Paul, *2105*

REALIZING (3) [REALIZE]

Ge 38:16 Not **r** that she was his daughter-in-law, 3359
Est 7:7 **r** that the king had already decided his fate, 8011
Ro 2:4 **not r** that God's kindness leads you *51*

REALLY (44) [REAL]

Ge 3:1 He said to the woman, "Did God **r** say, 677+3954
18:13 Will I **r** have a child, now that I am old? 598+677
18:24 Will you **r** sweep it away and not spare 677
20:12 Besides, she **r** is my sister, 593
26:9 "She is **r** your wife! 421
27:21 to know whether you **r** are my son Esau 2296
27:24 "Are you **r** my son Esau?" 2296
45:12 **that** it is **r** I who am speaking to you. 3954
Lev 25:16 because what he is **r** selling you is NIH
Nu 22:37 Am I **r** not able to reward you?" 598
Jdg 6:17 give me a sign that it is **r** you talking to me. NIH
6:31 If Baal **r** is a god, NIH
9:15 If you **r** want to anoint me king over you 622+928
11:9 *will* I *r* **be** your head?" AIT
14:16 You don't **r** love me. 8370
15:3 I will **r** harm them." 3954
1Ki 8:27 "But will God **r** dwell on earth? 598
18:7 and said, "Is it **r** you, my lord Elijah?" 2296
2Ch 6:18 "But will God **r** dwell on earth with men? 598
Ecc 8:17 he cannot *r* **comprehend** it. AIT
Jer 7:5 If *you* **r change** your ways and your 3512+3512
9:26 For all these nations are **r** uncircumcised, NIH
Zec 7:5 was it **r** for me that you fasted? NIH
Mk 11:32 everyone held that John **r** was a prophet.) *3953*
Jn 4:42 that this man **r** is the Savior of the world." *242*
7:26 Have the authorities **r** concluded that he is *242*
8:31 hold to my teaching, you are **r** my disciples. *242*
13:38 "Will you **r** lay down your life for me? *NIG*
14:7 If you **r** knew me, you would know my *NIG*
Ac 9:26 not believing that he **r** was a disciple. *NIG*
12:9 what the angel was doing was **r** happening; *239*
Ro 7:7 not have known what coveting **r** was if *NIG*
1Co 4:8 How I wish that you **r** had become kings so *1145*
5:7 a new batch without yeast—as you **r** are. *NIG*
14:25 exclaiming, "God is **r** among you!" *3953*
Gal 1:7 which is **r** no gospel at all. *NIG*
3:4 if it **r** was for nothing? *1145*
Php 1:12 that what has happened to me has **r** served *3437*
1Th 3:8 For now we **r** live, *NIG*

1Ti 5: 3 to those widows who *are* r in need. *3953*
5: 5 The widow who is r in need *3953*
5:16 church can help those widows who are r *3953*
Jas 2: 8 you r keep the royal law found in Scripture, *3530*
1Jn 2:19 but they did not r belong to us. *NIG*

REALM (11) [REALMS]

Dt 32:22 one that burns to the r **of death** below. 8619
Jos 13:21 the entire r *of* Sihon king of the Amorites, 4931
13:27 the rest of the r *of* Sihon king of Heshbon 4931
13:30 the entire r *of* Og king of Bashan— 4931
2Ch 36:22 to make a proclamation throughout his r 4895
Ezr 1: 1 to make a proclamation throughout his r 4895
7:23 Why should there be wrath against the r *of* 10424
Est 1:20 proclaimed throughout all his vast **r,** 4895
2: 3 of his r to bring all these beautiful girls into 4895
Da 11: 9 Then the king of the North will invade the r 4895
Hab 2: 9 to him who builds his r by unjust gain 1074

REALMS (5) [REALM]

Eph 1: 3 who has blessed us in the **heavenly r** *2230*
1:20 at his right hand in the **heavenly r,** *2230*
2: 6 with him in the **heavenly r** in Christ Jesus, *2230*
3:10 the rulers and authorities in the **heavenly r,** *2230*
6:12 spiritual forces of evil in the **heavenly r.** *2230*

REAP (30) [REAPED, REAPER, REAPERS, REAPING, REAPS]

Lev 19: 9 " 'When you r the harvest of your land, 7917
19: 9 *do* not r *to* the very edges of your field 7917
23:10 to give you and *you* r its harvest, 7917
23:22 " 'When you r the harvest of your land, 7917
23:22 *do* not r *to* the very edges of your field 7917
25: 5 *Do* not r what grows of itself or 7907+7917
25:11 and *do* not r what grows of itself or harvest 7917
1Sa 8:12 others to plow his ground and r his harvest, 7917
2Ki 19:29 But in the third year sow and r, 7917
Job 4: 8 and those who sow trouble r it. 7917
Ps 126: 5 Those who sow in tears *will* r with songs 7917
Ecc 11: 4 whoever looks at the clouds *will* not **r.** 7917
Isa 37:30 But in the third year sow and r, 7917
Jer 12:13 They will sow wheat but r thorns; 7917
Hos 8: 7 "They sow the wind and r the whirlwind. 7917
10:12 r the fruit of unfailing love, 7917
Mt 6:26 they do not sow or r or store away in barns, *2545*
Lk 12:24 Consider the ravens: They do not sow or **r,** *2545*
19:21 not put in and r what you did not sow.' *2545*
Jn 4:38 *to* r what you have not worked for. *2545*
Ro 6:21 What benefit *did you* r at that time from *2400*
6:22 the benefit *you* r leads to holiness, *2400*
1Co 9:11 is it too much if we r a material **harvest** *2545*
2Co 9: 6 sows sparingly *will* also r sparingly, *2545*
9: 6 sows generously *will* also r generously. *2545*
Gal 6: 8 from that nature *will* r destruction; *2545*
6: 8 from the Spirit *will* r eternal life. *2545*
6: 9 for at the proper time *we will* **r a harvest** *2545*
Rev 14:15 "Take your sickle and **r,** *2545*
14:15 because the time *to* r has come, *2545*

REAPED (3) [REAP]

Ge 26:12 and the same year r a hundredfold, 5162
Hos 10:13 planted wickedness, *you have* r evil, 7917
Jn 4:38 and you *have* r **the benefits of** their labor." *1656*

REAPER (7) [REAP]

Ps 129: 7 with it the r cannot fill his hands, 7917
Isa 17: 5 a r gathers the standing grain and harvests 7907
Jer 9:22 like cut grain behind the **r,** 7917
50:16 and the r with his sickle at harvest. 9530
Am 9:13 the r will be overtaken by the plowman and 7917
Jn 4:36 Even now the r draws his wages, *2545*
4:36 the sower and the r may be glad together. *2545*

REAPERS (1) [REAP]

2Ki 4:18 who was with the **r.** 7917

REAPING (2) [REAP]

Ge 45: 6 not be plowing and **r.** 7907
Lk 19:22 and r what I did not sow? *2545*

REAPPEARS (2) [APPEAR]

Lev 13:57 But if *it* r in the clothing, 6388+8011
14:43 "If the mildew r in the house 2256+7255+8740

REAPS (4) [REAP]

Pr 11:18 he who sows righteousness r a sure reward. NIH
22: 8 He who sows wickedness r trouble, 7917
Jn 4:37 the saying 'One sows and another r' is true. *2545*
Gal 6: 7 A man r what he sows. *2545*

REAR (17) [REARED, REARING]

Ge 33: 2 and Rachel and Joseph *in* the r. 340
Ex 26:12 that is left over is to hang down at the r *of* 294
Nu 10:25 Finally, as the r **guard** for all the units, 665
Jos 6: 9 and the r **guard** followed the ark. 665
6:13 the r **guard** followed the ark of the LORD, 665
10:19 **attack** them **from the r** 2386
1Sa 29: 2 David and his men were marching at the r 340
1Ki 6:16 He partitioned off twenty cubits at the r *of* 3752
2Ch 13:13 Jeroboam had sent troops around to the **r,** 339
13:14 at both front and **r.** 294
Ps 83: 2 how your foes r their heads. 5951
Isa 52:12 the God of Israel will be your r **guard.** 665
58: 8 glory of the LORD *will be* your r **guard.** 665
Eze 40:13 from the **top of the r wall** AIT
41:15 the building facing the courtyard at the r *of* 339
Hos 9:12 Even if *they* r children, 1540
Joel 2:20 into the eastern sea and *those in the* r into 6067

REARED (6) [REAR]

Job 31:18 from my youth I r *him* as would a father, 1540
Isa 1: 2 *"I* r children and brought them up, 1540
23: 4 *I have* neither r sons nor brought 1540
51:18 the sons *she* r there was none to take her by 1540
La 2:22 those I cared for and **r,** 8049
Eze 19: 2 among the young lions and r her cubs. 8049

REARING (1) [REAR]

2Ki 10: 6 leading men of the city, *who were* r them. 1540

REASON (58) [REASONABLE, REASONED, REASONING, REASONS]

Ge 2:24 For **this** r a man will leave his father 4027
20:10 "What *was your* r for doing this?" 8011
41:32 The r the dream was given to Pharaoh 6584
1Sa 19: 5 like David by killing him **for no r?"** 2855
Job 2: 3 against him to ruin him **without any r."** 2855
9:17 a storm and multiply my wounds **for no r.** 2855
12:24 the leaders of the earth of their **r;** 4213
22: 6 from your brothers **for no r;** 2855
Ps 35:19 who hate me **without** r maliciously wink 2855
38:19 those who hate me **without** r are numerous. 9214
69: 4 Those who hate me **without** r outnumber 2855
Pr 3:30 Do not accuse a man **for no r—** 2855
Isa 1:18 "Come now, *let us* **r together,"** 3519
Mt 12:10 Looking for a r to accuse Jesus, *2671*
19: 3 to divorce his wife for any and every **r?"** *162*
19: 5 **'For this r** a man will leave his father *1915*
Mk 3: 2 Some of them were looking for a **r to** *2671*
10: 7 **'For this** r a man will leave his father *1915*
Lk 6: 7 the teachers of the law were looking for a r *NIG*
Jn 1:31 but **the r** I came baptizing with water *1328+4047*
5:18 **For this r** the Jews tried all the harder *1328+4047*
8:47 **The r** you do not hear is that you do *1328+4047*
10:17 **The r** my Father loves me is that I lay *1328+4047*
12:27 **for this very r** I came to this hour. *1328+4047*
12:39 **For this r** they could not believe, *1328+4047*
15:25 'They hated me **without r.'** *1562*
18:37 In fact, **for this r** I was born, *1650+4047*
Ac 19:40 since there is no r for it." *165*
28:20 For this r I have asked to see you and talk *162*
Ro 14: 9 For **this very r,** Christ died *1650+4047*
1Co 4:17 **For this r** I am sending to you Timothy, *1328+4047*
11:10 **For this r,** and because of the angels, *1328+4047*
12:15 not **for that** r cease to be part of the body. *4047+4123*
12:16 not **for that** r cease to be part of the body. *4047+4123*
14:13 **For this r** anyone who speaks in a tongue *1475*
2Co 2: 9 **The r** I wrote you was to see *1142+1650+4047*
8:24 of your love and the r for our pride in you, *NIG*
Gal 6:12 The only r they do this is *NIG*
Eph 1:15 **For this r,** ever since I heard *1328+4047*
3: 1 **For this r** I, Paul, *4047+5920*
3:14 **For this r** I kneel before the Father, *4047+5920*
5:31 **"For this r** a man will leave his father *505+4047*
Col 1: 9 **For this r,** since the day we heard *1328+4047*
1Th 3: 5 **For this r,** when I could stand it no longer, *1328+4047*
2Th 2:11 **For this r** God sends them *1328+4047*
1Ti 1:16 **for that very r** I was shown mercy so *1328+4047*
2Ti 1: 6 For this r I remind you to fan into flame *162*
Tit 1: 5 **The r** I left you in Crete was *4047+5920*
Phm 1:15 Perhaps **the r** he was separated from *1328+4047*
Heb 2:17 **For this r** he had to be made like *3854*
9:15 **For this r** Christ is the mediator of *1328+4047*
10: 1 For this r it can never, *NIG*
Jas 4: 5 Or do you think Scripture says **without r** *3036*
1Pe 3:15 to everyone who asks you to give the r for *3364*
4: 6 For **this is the r** the gospel was preached even to those *1650+4047*
2Pe 1: 5 **For this very r,** make every effort to add to your faith goodness; *899+4047*
1Jn 3: 1 **The r** the world does not know us is *1328+4047*
3: 8 **The r** the Son of God appeared was *1650+4047*

REASONABLE (2) [REASON]

Ac 18:14 it would be r for me to listen to you. *2848+3364*
26:25 "What I am saying is true and **r.** *5408*

REASONED (6) [REASON]

Ac 17: 2 on three Sabbath days *he* r with them from *1363*
17:17 So *he* r in the synagogue with the Jews and *1363*
18: 4 Every Sabbath *he* r in the synagogue, *1363*
18:19 He himself went into the synagogue and r *1363*
1Co 13:11 I thought like a child, *I* r like a child. *3357*
Heb 11:19 Abraham r that God could raise the dead, *3357*

REASONING (1) [REASON]

Job 32:11 while you spoke, I listened to your **r;** 9312

REASONS (3) [REASON]

1Co 15:32 in Ephesus for merely **human r,** *476*
Php 3: 4 though I myself have r for such confidence. *NIG*
3: 4 If anyone else thinks he has r *NIG*

REASSIGN (1) [ASSIGN]

Isa 49: 8 the land and to r its desolate inheritances, 5706

REASSURE (2) [ASSURE]

2Ki 25:24 an oath to r them and their men. NIH
Jer 40: 9 took an oath to r them and their men. NIH

REASSURED (1) [ASSURE]

Ge 50:21 And *he* r them and spoke kindly to them. 5714

REBA (2)

Nu 31: 8 Zur, Hur and **R—**the five kings of Midian. 8064
Jos 13:21 Evi, Rekem, Zur, Hur and **R—** 8064

REBECCA (KJV) See REBEKAH

REBEKAH (30) [REBEKAH'S]

Ge 22:23 Bethuel became the father of **R.** 8071
24:15 **R** came out with her jar on her shoulder. 8071
24:29 Now **R** had a brother named Laban, 8071
24:30 had heard **R** tell what the man said to her, 8071
24:45 I finished praying in my heart, **R** came out, 8071
24:51 Here is **R;** take her and go, 8071
24:53 of clothing and gave them to **R;** 8071
24:58 So they called **R** and asked her, 8071
24:59 So they sent their sister **R** on her way, 8071
24:60 And they blessed **R** and said to her, 8071
24:61 Then **R** and her maids got ready 8071
24:61 So the servant took **R** and left. 8071
24:64 **R** also looked up and saw Isaac. 8071
24:67 and he married **R.** 8071
25:20 when he married **R** daughter of Bethuel 8071
25:21 and his wife **R** became pregnant. 8071
25:26 Isaac was sixty years old when **R** gave birth NIH
25:28 loved Esau, but **R** loved Jacob. 8071
26: 7 of this place might kill me on account of **R,** 8071
26: 8 and saw Isaac caressing his wife **R.** 8071
26:35 They were a source of grief to Isaac and **R.** 8071
27: 5 Now **R** was listening as Isaac spoke 8071
27: 6 **R** said to her son Jacob, 8071
27:11 Jacob said to **R** his mother, 8071
27:15 Then **R** took the best clothes 8071
27:42 **R** was told what her older son Esau had said 8071
27:46 Then **R** said to Isaac, "I'm disgusted 8071
28: 5 the Aramean, the brother of **R,** 8071
29:12 a relative of her father and a son of **R.** 8071
49:31 there Isaac and his wife **R** were buried, 8071

REBEKAH'S (2) [REBEKAH]

Ge 35: 8 Now Deborah, **R** nurse, 8071
Ro 9:10 but **R** children had one and the same father, *4831*

REBEL (18) [REBELLED, REBELLING, REBELLION, REBELLIOUS, REBELS]

Ex 23:21 *Do* not r against him; 5352
Nu 14: 9 Only *do* not r against the LORD. 5277
Dt 31:27 how much more will you r after I die! NIH
Jos 22:18 " 'If you r against the LORD today, 5277
22:19 not r against the LORD or against us 5277
22:29 "Far be it from us to r against the LORD 5277
1Sa 12:14 and *do* not r against his commands, and if 5286
12:15 and if *you* r against his commands, 5286
2Ki 18:20 that *you* r against me? 5277
Job 24:13 "There are those *who* r *against* the light, 5277
Isa 1:20 but if you resist and r, 5286
36: 5 that *you* r against me? 5277
48: 8 you were called a r from birth. 7321
Eze 2: 8 *Do* not r like that rebellious house; 2118+5308
20:38 I will purge you of those who revolt and r 7321
Da 11:14 men among your own people *will* r 5951
Mt 10:21 children *will* **r against** their parents *2060*
Mk 13:12 Children *will* **r against** their parents *2060*

REBELLED (52) [REBEL]

Ge 14: 4 but in the thirteenth year *they* **r.** 5277
Nu 20:24 *both of you* r against my command at 5286
26: 9 the community officials who r 5897
26: 9 among Korah's followers when they r 5897
27:14 the community r at the waters in the Desert 5312
Dt 1:26 *you* r against the command of the LORD 5286
1:43 *You* r against the LORD's command and 5286
9:23 But *you* r against the command of 5286
1Sa 22:13 he *has* r against me and lies in wait for me, 7756
1Ki 11:26 Jeroboam son of Nebat r against the king. 3338+8123
11:27 account of how *he* r against the king: 3338+8123
2Ki 1: 1 After Ahab's death, Moab r against Israel. 7321
3: 5 of Moab r against the king of Israel. 7321
3: 7 "The king of Moab *has* r against me. 7321
8:20 Edom r against Judah and set 7321
18: 7 *He* r against the king of Assyria and did 5277
24: 1 But then he changed his mind and r 5277
24:20 Zedekiah r against the king of Babylon. 5277
2Ch 13: 6 r against his master. 5277
21: 8 Edom r against Judah and set up its own 7321

2Ch 36:13 *He* also **r** against King Nebuchadnezzar, 5277
Ne 9:26 they were disobedient and **r** against you; 5277
Ps 5:10 for *they have* **r** against you. 5286
78:40 How often *they* **r** *against* him in the desert 5286
78:56 But they put God to the test and **r** against 5286
105:28 for *had they* not **r** against his words? 5286
106:7 and *they* **r** by the sea, the Red Sea. 5286
106:33 for *they* **r** against the Spirit of God, 5286
107:11 for *they had* **r** *against* the words of God 5286
Isa 1:2 but they *have* **r** against me. 7321
43:27 your spokesmen **r** against me. 7321
63:10 Yet they **r** and grieved his Holy Spirit. 5286
66:24 the dead bodies of those who **r** against me; 7321
Jer 2:8 the leaders **r** against me. 7321
2:29 You *have* all **r** against me," 7321
3:13 *you have* **r** against the LORD your God, 7321
4:17 because *she has* **r** against me,' " 5286
52:3 Zedekiah **r** against the king of Babylon. 5277
La 1:18 yet *I* **r** *against* his command. 5286
3:42 "We have sinned and **r** and you have 5286
Eze 2:3 to a rebellious nation that *has* **r** against me; 5277
5:6 in her wickedness *she has* **r** against my laws 5286
17:15 But the king **r** against him 5277
20:8 " 'But *they* **r** against me and would 5286
20:13 people of Israel **r** against me in the desert. 5286
20:21 " 'But the children **r** against me: 5286
Da 9:5 We have been wicked and *have* **r**; 5277
9:9 even though *we have* **r** against him; 5277
Hos 7:13 because *they have* **r** against me! 7321
8:1 the people have broken my covenant and **r** 7321
13:16 because *they have* **r** against their God. 5286
Heb 3:16 Who were *they* who heard and **r**? *4176*

REBELLING (3) [REBEL]

Ne 2:19 *"Are* you **r** against the king?" 5277
Ps 78:17 **r** in the desert *against* the Most High. 5286
Ro 13:2 against the authority *is* **r against** what God *468*

REBELLION (42) [REBEL]

Ex 23:21 he will not forgive your **r**, 7322
34:7 and forgiving wickedness, **r** and sin. 7322
Lev 16:16 of the uncleanness and **r** *of* the Israelites, 7322
16:21 and confess over it all the wickedness and **r** 7322
Nu 14:18 abounding in love and forgiving sin and **r**. 7322
Dt 13:5 because he preached **r** against the LORD 6240
Jos 22:16 and build yourselves an altar in **r** 5277
22:22 If this has been in **r** or disobedience to 5278
24:19 He will not forgive your **r** and your sins. 7322
1Sa 15:23 For **r** is like the sin of divination, 5308
24:11 that I am not guilty of wrongdoing or **r**. 7322
1Ki 12:19 So Israel *has been* **in r** against the house 7321
16:20 and the **r** he carried out, 8004
2Ki 8:20 To this day Edom *has been* **in r** 7321
2Ch 10:19 So Israel *has been* **in r** against the house 7321
21:10 To this day Edom *has been* **in r** 7321
Ezr 4:15 a place of **r** from ancient times. 10083
4:19 against kings and has been a place of **r** 10438
Ne 9:17 and in their **r** appointed a leader in order 5308
Job 34:37 To his sin he adds **r**; 7322
Ps 106:43 on **r** and they wasted away in their sin. 5286
Pr 17:11 An evil man is bent only on **r**; 5308
Isa 1:5 Why do you persist in **r**? 6240
24:20 upon it is the **guilt of** its **r** that it falls— 7322
58:1 to my people their **r** and to the house 7322
59:13 **r** and treachery against the LORD, 7321
Jer 5:6 for their **r** is great 7322
28:16 you have preached **r** against the LORD.' " 6240
29:32 because he has preached **r** against me.' " 6240
33:8 and will forgive all their sins of **r** 7321
Eze 21:24 by your open **r**, revealing your sins in all 7322
Da 8:12 Because of **r**, the host [of the saints] and 7322
8:13 the **r** that causes desolation, 7322
Mt 26:55 "Am I **leading a r**, that you have come out *3334*
Mk 14:48 "Am I **leading a r**," said Jesus, *3334*
Lk 22:52 who had come for him, "Am I **leading a r**, *3334*
23:14 **who** *was* **inciting** the people **to r**. *695*
Jn 18:40 Barabbas **had taken part in a r**. *1639+3334*
2Th 2:3 until the **r** occurs and the man of lawlessness *686*
Heb 3:8 not harden your hearts as you did in the **r**, *4177*
3:15 not harden your hearts as you did in the **r**." *4177*
Jude 1:11 they have been destroyed *in* Korah's **r**. *517*

REBELLIOUS (42) [REBEL]

Nu 17:10 to be kept as a sign to the **r**. 1201+5308
Dt 9:7 you have been **r** against the LORD. 5286
9:24 You have been **r** against the LORD ever 5286
21:18 If a man has a stubborn and **r** son who does 5286
21:20 "This son of ours is stubborn and **r**. 5286
31:27 For I know how **r** and stiff-necked you are. 5308
31:27 If you have been **r** against the LORD 5286
1Sa 20:30 "You son of a perverse and **r** woman! 5280
Ezr 4:12 and are rebuilding that **r** and wicked city. 10439
4:15 that this city is a **r** city, 10439
Ps 25:7 not the sins of my youth and my **r** *ways;* 7322
66:7 let not the **r** rise up against him. 6253
68:6 but the **r** live in a sun-scorched land. 6253
68:18 from men, even from the **r**— 6253
78:8 a stubborn and **r** generation, 5286
107:17 through their **r** ways and suffered affliction 7322
Pr 24:21 my son, and do not join with the **r**, 9101
28:2 When a country is **r**, it has many rulers, 7322
Isa 30:9 These are **r** people, deceitful children, 5308
50:5 and I *have* not *been* **r**; 5286
Jer 5:23 these people have stubborn and **r** hearts; 5286
La 1:20 for *I have been* **most r**. 5286+5286

Eze 2:3 to a **r** nation that has rebelled against me; 5277
2:5 or fail to listen—for they are a **r** house— 5308
2:6 though they are a **r** house. 5308
2:7 or fail to listen, for they are **r**. 5308
2:8 Do not rebel like that **r** house; 5308
3:9 though they are a **r** house." 5308
3:26 though they are a **r** house. 5308
3:27 for they are a **r** house. 5308
12:2 you are living among a **r** people. 5308
12:2 for they are a **r** people. 5308
12:3 though they are a **r** house. 5308
12:9 did not that **r** house of Israel ask you, 5308
12:25 For in your days, you **r** house, 5308
17:12 "Say to this **r** house, 5308
24:3 Tell this **r** house a parable and say to them: 5308
44:6 Say to the **r** house of Israel, 5308
Hos 9:15 all their leaders *are* **r**. 6253
14:9 but the **r** stumble in them. 7321
Zep 3:1 to the city of oppressors, **r** and defiled! 5286
Tit 1:10 For there are many **r** *people,* *538*

REBELS (13) [REBEL]

Nu 20:10 and Moses said to them, "Listen, you **r**, 5286
Jos 1:18 Whoever **r** against your word and does 5286
1Ki 11:24 the leader of a **band of r** when David 1522
11:24 the **r** went to Damascus, NIH
Isa 1:23 Your rulers *are* **r**, companions of thieves; 6253
1:28 But **r** and sinners will both be broken, 7321
46:8 fix it in mind, take it to heart, you **r**. 7321
57:4 Are you not a brood of **r**, 7322
Jer 6:28 They are all **hardened r**, 6073+6253
Da 8:23 when **r** have become completely wicked, 7321
Hos 5:2 The **r** are deep in slaughter. 8473
Ro 13:2 he who **r against** the authority is rebelling *530*
1Ti 1:9 for the righteous but *for* lawbreakers and **r**, *538*

REBIRTH (1) [BEAR]

Tit 3:5 through the washing *of* **r** and renewal by *4098*

REBUILD (27) [BUILD]

Jos 6:26 the man who undertakes *to* **r** this city, 1215
Ezr 5:2 to work to **r** the house of God in Jerusalem. 10111
5:3 to **r** this temple and restore this structure?" 10111
5:9 to **r** this temple and restore this structure?" 10111
5:13 King Cyrus issued a decree to **r** this house 10111
5:15 And **r** the house of God on its site.' 10111
5:17 in fact issue a decree to **r** this house of God 10111
6:7 the Jews and the Jewish elders **r** this house 10111
9:9 He has granted us new life to **r** the house 8123
Ne 2:5 my fathers are buried so that *I can* **r** it." 1215
2:17 Come, *let us* **r** the wall of Jerusalem, 1215
4:10 so much rubble that we cannot **r** the wall." 1215
Ps 69:35 for God will save Zion and **r** the cities 1215
102:16 For the LORD *will* **r** Zion and appear 1215
Isa 9:10 but *we will* **r** *with* dressed stone; 1215
45:13 He *will* **r** my city and set my exiles free, 1215
58:12 *Your people will* **r** the ancient ruins 1215
60:10 "Foreigners *will* **r** your walls, 1215
61:4 *They will* **r** the ancient ruins and restore 1215
Jer 33:7 and *will* **r** them as they were before. 1215
Da 9:25 the decree to restore and **r** Jerusalem until 1215
Am 9:14 *they will* **r** the ruined cities and live 1215
Mal 1:4 *we will* **r** the ruins." 1215+2256+8740
Mt 26:61 the temple of God and **r** it in three days.' " *3868*
Ac 15:16 this I will return and **r** David's fallen tent. *488*
15:16 Its ruins *I will* **r**, and I will restore it, *488*
Gal 2:18 If *I* **r** what I destroyed, *3868+4099*

REBUILDING (6) [BUILD]

Ezr 2:68 the **r** *of* the house of God on its site. 6641
4:12 from you have gone to Jerusalem and *are* **r** 10111
5:11 the God of heaven and earth, and we *are* **r** 10111
Ne 2:18 They replied, "Let us start **r**." 1215
2:20 We his servants will start **r**, but as for you, 1215
4:1 When Sanballat heard that we *were* **r** 1215

REBUILT (42) [BUILD]

Nu 21:27 "Come to Heshbon and *let it* **be r**; 1215
32:37 And the Reubenites **r** Heshbon, 1215
32:38 They gave names to the cities *they* **r**. 1215
Dt 13:16 It is to remain a ruin forever, never *to* **be r**. 1215
Jdg 18:28 The Danites **r** the city and settled there. 1215
21:23 and **r** the towns and settled in them. 1215
1Ki 9:17 And Solomon **r** Gezer.) 1215
16:34 In Ahab's time, Hiel of Bethel **r** Jericho. 1215
2Ki 14:22 the *one who* **r** Elath and restored it to Judah 1215
15:35 Jotham **r** the Upper Gate of the temple of 1215
21:3 *He* **r** the high places his father Hezekiah
had destroyed; 1215+2256+8740
2Ch 8:2 Solomon **r** the villages tht Hiram had given 1215
8:5 *He* **r** Upper Beth Horon and Lower Beth 1215
24:13 *They* **r** the temple of God according 6641
26:2 the one *who* **r** Elath and restored it to Judah 1215
26:6 *He* then **r** towns near Ashdod and elsewhere 1215
27:3 Jotham **r** the Upper Gate of the temple of 1215
33:3 *He* **r** the high places his father Hezekiah
had demolished; 1215+2256+8740
33:14 Afterward *he* **r** the outer wall of the City 1215
Ezr 4:21 that this city *will* not **be r** until I so order. 10111
6:3 *Let* the temple **be r** as a place 10111
Ne 3:1 and his fellow priests went to work and **r** 1215
3:3 The Fish Gate *was* **r** *by* the sons 1215
3:13 They **r** it and put its doors and bolts 1215
3:14 He **r** it and put its doors and bolts and bars 1215

Ne 3:15 He **r** it, roofing it over and putting its doors 1215
4:6 So *we* **r** the wall till all 1215
6:1 of our enemies that *I had* **r** the wall and not 1215
7:1 the wall *had* **been r** and I had set the doors 1215
7:4 and the houses *had* not yet **been r**. 1215
Job 12:14 What he tears down cannot **be r**; 1215
Isa 25:2 *it will* never **be r**. 1215
44:28 he will say of Jerusalem, *"Let it* **be r**," 1215
Jer 30:18 the city *will* **be r** on her ruins, 1215
31:4 I will build you up again and *you will* **be r**, 1215
31:38 "when this city *will* **be r** for me from 1215
Eze 26:14 *You will* never **be r**, 1215
36:10 The towns will be inhabited and the ruins **r**. 1215
36:33 and the ruins *will* **be r**. 1215
36:36 the LORD *have* **r** what was destroyed 1215
Da 9:25 *It will* **be r** with streets and a trench, 1215
Zec 1:16 and there my house *will* **be r**. 1215

REBUKE (61) [REBUKED, REBUKES, REBUKING]

Lev 19:17 **R** your neighbor **frankly** 3519+3519
Dt 28:20 and **r** in everything you put your hand to, 4486
Ru 2:16 and don't **r** her." 1721
1Sa 2:25 however, did not listen to their father's **r**, 7754
2Sa 22:16 the earth laid bare at the **r** *of* the LORD, 1722
2Ki 19:3 a day of distress and **r** and disgrace, 9349
19:4 and that *he will* **r** him for the words 3519
Job 11:3 *Will* no *one* **r** you when you mock? 4007
13:10 *He would* **surely r** you 3519+3519
20:3 I hear a **r** *that* dishonors me, 4592
26:11 pillars of the heavens quake, aghast at his **r**. 1722
Ps 6:1 *do* not **r** me in your anger or discipline me 3519
18:15 foundations of the earth laid bare at your **r**, 1722
38:1 *do* not **r** me in your anger or discipline me 3519
39:11 You **r** and discipline men for their sin; 9350
50:8 *I do* not **r** you for your sacrifices 3519
50:21 *I will* **r** you and accuse you to your face. 3519
68:30 **R** the beast among the reeds, 1721
76:6 At your **r**, O God of Jacob, both horse and 1722
80:16 at your **r** your people perish. 1722
104:7 But at your **r** the waters fled, 1722
119:21 *You* **r** the arrogant, 1721
141:5 *let him* **r** me—it is oil on my head. 3519
Pr 1:23 If you had responded to my **r**, 9350
1:25 and would not accept my **r**, 9350
1:30 not accept my advice and spurned my **r**, 9350
3:11 and do not resent his **r**, 9350
9:8 *Do* not **r** a mocker or he will hate you; 3519
9:8 **r** a wise man and he will love you. 3519
13:1 but a mocker does not listen to **r**. 1722
15:31 to a life-giving **r** will be at home among 9350
17:10 A **r** impresses a man 1722
19:25 **r** a discerning man, 3519
25:12 an ornament of fine gold is a wise man's **r** 3519
27:5 Better is open **r** than hidden love. 9350
30:6 or *he will* **r** you and prove you a liar. 3519
Ecc 7:5 a wise man's **r** than to listen to the song 1722
Isa 37:3 a day of distress and **r** and disgrace, 9349
37:4 and that *he will* **r** him for the words 3519
50:2 By a mere **r** I dry up the sea, 1722
51:20 with the wrath of the LORD and the **r** 1722
54:9 never *to* **r** you again. 1721
66:15 and his **r** with flames of fire. 1722
Jer 2:19 your backsliding *will* **r** you. 3519
Eze 3:26 be silent and unable *to* **r** them, 3519
5:15 in anger and in wrath and with stinging **r**. 9350
Hos 2:2 **"R** your mother, rebuke her, 8189
2:2 "Rebuke your mother, **r** her, 8189
Zec 3:2 "The LORD **r** you, Satan! 1721
3:2 who has chosen Jerusalem, **r** you! 1721
Mal 2:3 "Because of you I *will* **r** your descendants; 1721
Mt 16:22 Peter took him aside and began *to* **r** him. *2203*
Mk 8:32 Peter took him aside and began *to* **r** him. *2203*
Lk 17:3 "If your brother sins, **r** him, *2203*
19:39 "Teacher, **r** your disciples!" *2203*
1Ti 5:1 *Do* not **r** an older man **harshly**, *2159*
2Ti 4:2 correct, **r** and encourage— *2203*
Tit 1:13 Therefore, **r** them sharply, *1794*
2:15 Encourage and **r** with all authority. *1794*
Jude 1:9 but said, "The Lord **r** you!" *2203*
Rev 3:19 Those whom I love *I* **r** and discipline. *1794*

REBUKED (32) [REBUKE]

Ge 31:42 and last night *he* **r** you." 3519
37:10 his father **r** him and said, 1721
1Sa 24:7 With these words David **r** his men and did 9117
1Ch 16:21 for their sake *he* **r** kings: 3519
Ne 13:11 So *I* **r** the officials and asked them, 8189
13:17 *I* **r** the nobles of Judah and said to them, 8189
13:25 *I* **r** them and called curses down on them. 8189
Ps 9:5 *You have* **r** the nations and destroyed 1721
105:14 for their sake *he* **r** kings: 3519
106:9 *He* **r** the Red Sea, and it dried up; 1721
Mt 8:26 *he* got up and **r** the winds and the waves, *2203*
17:18 Jesus **r** the demon, *2203*
19:13 But the disciples **r** those who brought them. *2203*
20:31 The crowd **r** them and told them to *2203*
Mk 4:39 *He* got up, **r** the wind and said to the waves, *2203*
8:33 and looked at his disciples, *he* **r** Peter. *2203*
9:25 *he* **r** the evil spirit. *2203*
10:13 but the disciples **r** them. *2203*
10:48 Many **r** him and told him to be quiet, *2203*
14:5 And *they* **r** her **harshly.** *1839*
16:14 he **r** them for their lack of faith *3943*
Lk 3:19 But *when* John **r** Herod the tetrarch because *1794*

Lk 4:39 So *he* bent over her and **r** the fever, *2203*
4:41 But he **r** them and would not allow them *2203*
8:24 up and **r** the wind and the raging waters; *2203*
9:42 But Jesus **r** the evil spirit, *2203*
9:55 But Jesus turned and **r** them, *2203*
18:15 When the disciples saw this, *they* **r** them. *2203*
18:39 Those who led the way **r** him and told him *2203*
23:40 But the other criminal **r** him. *2203*
1Ti 5:20 Those who sin *are to be* **r** publicly, *1794*
2Pe 2:16 *he was* **r** for his wrongdoing by a donkey— *1792+2400*

REBUKES (8) [REBUKE]
Job 22:4 "Is it for your piety that *he* **r** you 3519
Ps 2:5 Then *he* **r** them in his anger 1819
Pr 9:7 *whoever* **r** a wicked man incurs abuse. 3519
28:23 *He who* **r** a man will in 3519
29:1 after many **r** will suddenly be destroyed— 9350
Isa 17:13 when *he* **r** them they flee far away, 1721
Na 1:4 *He* **r** the sea and dries it up; 1721
Heb 12:5 and do not lose heart when he **r** you, *1794*

REBUKING (2) [REBUKE]
Ps 57:3 **r** those who hotly pursue me; 3070
2Ti 3:16 **r**, correcting and training in righteousness, *1791*

RECAB (13) [RECABITE, RECABITES]
2Sa 4:2 One was named Baanah and the other **R**; 8209
4:5 Now **R** and Baanah, 8209
4:6 **R** and his brother Baanah slipped away. 8209
4:9 David answered **R** and his brother Baanah, 8209
2Ki 10:15 he came upon Jehonadab son of **R**, 8209
10:23 Then Jehu and Jehonadab son of **R** went 8209
1Ch 2:55 the father of the house of **R**. 8209
Ne 3:14 by Malkijah son of **R**, 8209
Jer 35:6 Jonadab son of **R** gave us this command: 8209
35:8 Jonadab son of **R** commanded us. 8209
35:14 son of **R** ordered his sons not to drink wine 8209
35:16 of Jonadab son of **R** have carried out 8209
35:19 'Jonadab son of **R** will never fail to have 8209

RECABITE (2) [RECAB]
Jer 35:2 the **R** family and invite them to come to one 8211
35:5 the men of the **R** family and said to them, 8211

RECABITES (2) [RECAB]
Jer 35:3 the whole family of the **R**. 8211
35:18 Then Jeremiah said to the family of the **R**, 8211

RECAH (1)
1Ch 4:12 These were the men of **R**. 8212

RECALL (1) [RECALLED, RECALLING]
2Pe 3:2 I *want* you *to* **r** the words spoken in the *3630*

RECALLED (3) [RECALL]
Isa 63:11 Then *his people* **r** the days of old, 2349
Eze 23:19 and more promiscuous as she **r** the days 2349
Jn 2:22 his disciples **r** what he had said. *3630*

RECALLING (2) [RECALL]
Job 11:16 **r** it only as waters gone by. 2349
2Ti 1:4 **R** your tears, I long to see you, *3630*

RECAPTURE (1) [CAPTURE]
Eze 14:5 I will do this to **r** the hearts of the people 9530

RECAPTURED (1) [CAPTURE]
2Ki 13:25 Jehoash son of Jehoahaz **r** from Ben-Hadad son of Hazael 2256+4374+8740

RECEDE (1) [RECEDED]
Ge 8:5 The waters continued *to* **r** until the tenth 2893

RECEDED (5) [RECEDE]
Ge 8:1 and the waters **r**. 8896
8:3 The water **r** **steadily** from the earth. 2143+2256+8740+8740
8:8 to see if the water *had* **r** from the surface of 7837
8:11 Then Noah knew that the water *had* **r** from 7837
Rev 6:14 The sky **r** like a scroll, rolling up, *714*

RECEIPT OF CUSTOM (KJV) See TAX COLLECTOR'S BOOTH, TAX BOOTH

RECEIVE (104) [RECEIVED, RECEIVES, RECEIVING, RECEPTION]
Ge 4:11 to **r** your brother's blood from your hand. 4374
32:20 when I see him, perhaps *he will* **r** me." 5951+7156
Ex 25:2 *You are to* **r** the offering for me 4374
25:3 the offerings *you are to* **r** from them: 4374
30:16 **R** the atonement money from the Israelites 4374
Nu 18:23 *They will* **r** no **inheritance** among 5706+5709
18:26 'When *you* **r** from the Israelites 4374
18:28 from all the tithes *you* **r** from the Israelites. 4374
26:54 to **r** its inheritance according to the number 5989
32:19 *We will* not **r** *any* **inheritance** with them on 5706
Dt 9:9 up on the mountain to **r** the tablets of stone, 4374
19:14 in the inheritance *you* **r** in the land 5706
33:3 and from you **r** instruction, 5951
2Ki 12:5 *Let* every priest **r** the money from one of 4374
Ne 10:38 the Levites when they **r** *the* **tithes,** 6923
Job 3:12 Why were these knees *to* **r** me 7709
35:7 or what *does he* **r** from your hand? 4374
Ps 24:5 *He will* **r** blessing from the LORD 5951
27:10 the LORD *will* **r** me. 665
110:3 the dawn you will **r** the dew of your youth. 4200
Pr 11:31 If the righteous **r** *their* **due** on earth, 8966
28:10 the blameless *will* **r** a good **inheritance.** 5706
Ecc 6:3 and *does* not **r** proper burial, 2118+4200
8:10 and **r** **praise** in the city where they did this. 8655
Isa 50:11 This is what you *shall* **r** from my hand 2118+4200
61:7 Instead of their shame my people will **r** NIH
Eze 16:61 and be ashamed when you **r** your sisters, 4374
Da 2:6 *you will* **r** from me gifts and rewards 10618
7:18 But the saints of the Most High *will* **r** 10618
11:34 they fall, *they will* **r** a little **help,** 6468+6469
12:13 to **r** your allotted inheritance." NIH
Hos 14:2 "Forgive all our sins and **r** us graciously, 4374
Mt 10:41 a prophet because he is a prophet *will* **r** *3284*
10:41 because he is a righteous man *will* **r** *3284*
11:5 The blind **r** **sight,** the lame walk, *329*
19:29 for my sake *will* **r** a hundred times as much *3284*
20:10 they expected *to* **r** more. *3284*
21:22 *you will* **r** whatever you ask for *3284*
Mk 4:16 hear the word and at once **r** it with joy. *3284*
10:15 anyone who *will* not **r** the kingdom *1312*
10:30 *will* fail *to* **r** a hundred times as much *3284*
Lk 7:22 The blind **r** **sight,** the lame walk, *329*
8:13 on the rock are the ones who **r** the word *1312*
18:17 anyone who *will* not **r** the kingdom *1312*
18:30 *to* **r** many times as much in this age and, *655*
18:42 Jesus said to him, **"R** *your* **sight;** *329*
Jn 1:11 but his own *did* not **r** him. *4161*
3:27 "A man can **r** only what is given him *3284*
7:39 those who believed in him *were* later *to* **r**. *3284*
16:24 Ask and *you will* **r**, *3284*
20:22 **"R** the Holy Spirit. *3284*
Ac 1:8 But *you will* **r** power when the Holy Spirit *3284*
2:38 And *you will* **r** the gift of the Holy Spirit. *3284*
7:59 Stephen prayed, "Lord Jesus, **r** my spirit." *1312*
8:15 for them that *they might* **r** the Holy Spirit, *3284*
8:19 on whom I lay my hands *may* **r** the *3284*
19:2 *"Did you* **r** the Holy Spirit when you *3284*
19:3 "Then what **baptism** *did you* **r?"** *966*
19:25 "Men, you know we **r** a good income *1639*
20:35 'It is more blessed to give than *to* **r.'** " *3284*
22:13 'Brother Saul, **r** *your* **sight!'** *329*
26:18 so that they *may* **r** forgiveness of sins and *3284*
Ro 5:17 much more will those who **r** God's abundant provision of grace *3284*
8:15 not **r** a spirit that makes you a slave again *3284*
11:31 in order that they too *may* now **r** **mercy** as *1796*
16:2 to **r** her in the Lord in a way worthy of *4657*
1Co 3:14 *he will* **r** his reward. *3284*
4:5 that time each *will* **r** his praise from God. *1181*
4:7 What do you have that *you did* not **r**? *3284*
4:7 And if *you did* **r** it, *3284*
9:14 the gospel *should* **r** *their* **living** from *2409*
2Co 5:10 that each one *may* **r** what is due him for *3152*
6:1 not *to* **r** God's grace in vain. *1312*
6:17 Touch no unclean thing, and I *will* **r** you." *1654*
11:4 or if *you* **r** a different spirit from the *3284*
11:16 you do, then **r** me just as you would a fool, *1312*
Gal 1:12 I *did* not **r** it from any man, *4161*
3:2 *Did you* **r** the Spirit by observing the law, *3284*
3:14 by faith *we might* **r** the promise of the Spirit *3284*
4:5 that *we might* **r** the full rights of sons. *655*
Php 2:19 that I also may be cheered *when I* **r** **news** *1182*
Col 3:24 that *you will* **r** an inheritance **from** *655*
1Th 5:9 to suffer wrath but to **r** salvation *4348*
1Ti 1:16 believe on him and **r** eternal life. *NIG*
2Ti 2:5 *he does* not **r** **the victor's crown** *5110*
2:6 be the first *to* **r** **a share** of the crops. *3561*
Heb 4:16 so that *we may* **r** mercy and find grace *3284*
9:15 that those who are called *may* **r** the *3284*
10:36 *you will* **r** what he has promised. *3152*
11:8 a place he would later **r** as his inheritance, *3284*
11:13 *They did* not **r** the things promised; *3152*
11:19 *he did* **r** Isaac **back** from death. *3152*
Jas 1:7 not think *he will* **r** anything from the Lord; *3284*
1:12 *he will* **r** the crown of life *3284*
4:3 When you ask, *you do* not **r**, *3284*
1Pe 2:20 how is it to your credit if you **r a beating** *3139*
5:4 *you will* **r** the crown of glory *3152*
2Pe 1:11 and you *will* **r** a rich welcome into *2220*
1Jn 3:22 and **r** from him anything we ask, *3284*
Rev 4:11 *to* **r** glory and honor and power, *3284*
5:12 the Lamb, who was slain, *to* **r** power *3284*
13:16 to **r** a mark on his right hand or *1443*
17:12 but who for one hour *will* **r** authority *3284*
18:4 so that *you will* not **r** any of her plagues; *3284*

RECEIVED (142) [RECEIVE]
Ge 33:10 now that *you have* **r** me **favorably.** 8354
43:23 I **r** your silver." 448+995
47:22 because they **r** a regular allotment 4200
Ex 18:2 his father-in-law Jethro **r** her 4374
36:3 *They* **r** from Moses all the offerings 4374
Nu 23:20 *I have* **r** a command to bless; 4374
26:62 because they **r** no inheritance among them. 5989
32:18 until every Israelite *has* **r** his inheritance. 5706
34:14 of Manasseh *have* **r** their inheritance. 4374
34:15 and a half tribes *have* **r** their inheritance on 4374
Dt 18:8 even though he has **r** money from the sale NIH
Jos 13:8 the Reubenites and the Gadites *had* **r** 4374
14:1 the areas the Israelites **r as an inheritance** 5706
14:4 The Levites **r** no share of the land 5989
16:4 of Joseph, **r** *their* **inheritance.** 5706
17:1 who *had* **r** Gilead and Bashan because 2118+4200
17:6 of the tribe of Manasseh **r** an inheritance 5706
18:2 not *yet* **r** their inheritance. 2745
18:7 Manasseh *have already* **r** their inheritance 4374
19:9 the Simeonites **r** *their* **inheritance** within 5706
21:7 **r** twelve towns from the tribes of Reuben, 4200
21:23 Also from the tribe of Dan they **r** Eltekeh, NIH
21:25 the tribe of Manasseh they **r** Taanach NIH
1Ki 5:8 *"I have* **r** *the* **message** you sent me 9048
10:14 that Solomon **r** yearly was 666 talents, 995+4200
2Ki 12:4 the census, the **money** *r from* personal vows AIT
19:9 Now Sennacherib **r a report** that Tirhakah, 9048
19:14 Hezekiah **r** the letter from the messengers 4374
20:13 Hezekiah **r** the messengers 9048
1Ch 6:71 The Gershonites **r** the following: 4200
6:71 of the half-tribe of Manasseh they **r** Golan NIH
6:72 from the tribe of Issachar they **r** Kedesh, NIH
6:74 from the tribe of Asher they **r** Mashal, NIH
6:76 from the tribe of Naphtali they **r** Kedesh NIH
6:77 (the rest of the Levites) **r** the following: 4200
6:77 From the tribe of Zebulun they **r** Jokneam, NIH
6:78 the Jordan east of Jericho they **r** Bezer in NIH
6:80 the tribe of Gad they **r** Ramoth in Gilead, NIH
11:6 and so *he* **r** the command. 2118
12:18 So David **r** them and made them leaders 7691
2Ch 9:13 gold that Solomon **r** yearly was 666 talents, 995
21:12 Jehoram **r** a letter from Elijah the prophet, 448+995
Ezr 5:5 to Darius and his written reply *be* **r**. 10754
8:30 the priests and Levites **r** the silver and gold 7691
Est 6:3 and recognition *has* Mordecai **r** for this?" 6913
Job 15:18 hiding nothing **r from** their fathers 4946
Ps 68:18 *you* **r** gifts from men, 4374
Isa 37:9 Now Sennacherib **r a report** that Tirhakah, 9048
37:14 Hezekiah **r** the letter from the messengers 4374
39:2 Hezekiah **r** the envoys **gladly** 6584+8523
40:2 that *she has* **r** from the LORD's hand 4374
47:13 **counsel** you have *r* has only worn you out! AIT
Hab 1:1 The oracle that Habakkuk the prophet **r**. 2600
Mt 6:2 *they have* **r** their reward **in full.** *600*
6:5 *they have* **r** their reward **in full.** *600*
6:16 *they have* **r** their reward **in full.** *600*
10:8 Freely *you have* **r**, freely give. *3284*
13:20 **r the seed that fell** on the rocky places *5062*
13:22 **r the seed that fell** among the thorns *5062*
13:23 **r the seed that fell** on good soil *5062*
15:5 'Whatever help you might otherwise have **r** *NIG*
20:9 about the eleventh hour came and each **r** *3284*
20:10 But each one of them also **r** a denarius. *3284*
20:11 *When they* **r** it, they began to grumble *3284*
20:34 Immediately *they* **r** *their* **sight** *329*
25:16 The man who *had* **r** the five talents went *3284*
25:18 the man who *had* **r** the one talent went off, *3284*
25:20 The man who *had* **r** the five talents brought *3284*
25:24 the man who *had* **r** the one talent came. *3284*
25:27 that when I returned I would *have* **r** it **back** *3152*
Mk 7:11 **help** *you might* otherwise *have* **r** *6067*
10:52 Immediately *he* **r** *his* **sight** *329*
11:24 believe that *you have* **r** it, *3284*
Lk 6:24 for *you have already* **r** your comfort. *600*
16:25 in your lifetime *you* **r** your good things, *655*
16:25 while Lazarus **r** bad things, *NIG*
18:43 Immediately *he* **r** *his* **sight** *329*
Jn 1:12 Yet to all who **r** him, *3284*
1:16 of his grace we *have* all **r** one blessing *3284*
9:15 also asked him how *he had* **r** *his* **sight.** *329*
9:18 that he had been blind and *had* **r** *his* **sight** *329*
10:18 This command *I* **r** from my Father." *3284*
19:30 When *he had* **r** the drink, Jesus said, *3284*
Ac 2:33 *he has* **r** from the Father the promised *3284*
5:3 for yourself some of the money you **r** for *NIG*
7:38 and he **r** living words to pass on to us. *1312*
7:45 *Having* **r** the tabernacle, *1342*
7:53 *you* who *have* **r** the law that was put *3284*
8:17 and *they* **r** the Holy Spirit. *3284*
10:47 They *have* **r** the Holy Spirit just *3284*
11:1 the Gentiles also *had* **r** the word of God. *1312*
17:11 for they **r** the message with great eagerness *1312*
21:17 at Jerusalem, the brothers **r** us warmly. *622*
21:40 **r** the commander's **permission,** *2205*
28:21 "We *have* not **r** any letters from Judea *1312*
Ro 1:5 *we* **r** grace and apostleship to call people *3284*
1:27 and **r** in themselves the due penalty *655*
4:11 And *he* **r** the sign of circumcision, *3284*
4:13 Abraham and his offspring **r** the promise *NIG*
5:11 whom *we have* now **r** reconciliation. *3284*
8:15 but *you* **r** the Spirit of sonship. *3284*
11:30 to God *have* now **r** **mercy** as a result *1796*
15:28 that they have **r** this fruit, *NIG*
1Co 2:12 We *have* not **r** the spirit of the world but *3284*
6:19 whom you have **r** from God? *NIG*
11:23 For I **r** from the Lord what I also passed on *4161*
15:1 which *you* **r** and on which you have taken *4161*
15:3 For what *I* **r** I passed on to you as of first *4161*
2Co 1:4 the comfort *we* ourselves *have* **r** from God. *4151*
11:4 a different spirit from the one *you* **r**, *3284*
11:24 Five times *I* **r** from the Jews *3284*
Gal 1:12 I **r** it by revelation from Jesus Christ. *NIG*
Eph 4:1 a life worthy *of* the **calling** *you have* **r**. *2813+3104*
Php 4:9 Whatever you have learned or **r** or heard *4161*
4:18 *I have* **r** full **payment** and even more; *600*

Php 4:18 I am amply supplied, now that *I have* r 1312
Col 2: 6 So then, just as *you* r Christ Jesus as Lord, 4161
4:10 *(You have* r instructions about him; 3284
4:17 to it that you complete the work *you have* r 4161
1Th 2:13 *when you* r the word of God, 4161
2Th 3: 6 according to the teaching *you* r **from** us. 4161
1Ti 4: 3 God created to **be r with** thanksgiving 3562
4: 4 to be rejected *if it is* r with thanksgiving, 3284
Heb 2: 2 and disobedience r its just punishment, 3284
6:15 Abraham r what was promised. 2209
8: 6 But the ministry Jesus *has* r is as superior 5593
10:26 on sinning after *we have* r the knowledge of 3284
10:32 *after you had* r the **light,** 5894
11:17 He who *had* r the promises was about 346
11:35 Women r back their dead, 3284
11:39 none of them r what had been promised. 3152
1Pe 2:10 once you *had* not **r mercy,** 1796
2:10 but now *you have* **r mercy.** 1796
4:10 Each one should use whatever gift *he has* r 3284
2Pe 1: 1 of our God and Savior Jesus Christ *have* r 3275
1:17 For *he* r honor and glory from God 3284
1Jn 2:27 anointing *you* r from him remains in you, 3284
Rev 2:27 just as I *have* r authority from my Father. 3284
3: 3 therefore, what *you have* r and heard; 3284
17:12 not yet r a kingdom, 3284
19:20 With these signs he had deluded those who *had* r the mark 3284
20: 4 and *had* not r his mark on their foreheads 3284

RECEIVES (21) [RECEIVE]

Job 27:13 heritage a ruthless man r from the Almighty 4374
Pr 8:35 For whoever finds me finds life and r favor 7049
18:22 a wife finds what is good and r favor from 7049
27:21 but man is tested by the **praise** he *r.* AIT
28:27 to them r many curses. NIH
Eze 16:33 Every prostitute r a fee, 4200+5989
Mt 7: 8 For everyone who asks **r;** 3284
10:40 "He who r you receives me, 1312
10:40 "He who receives you r me, 1312
10:40 he who r me receives the one who sent me. 1312
10:40 he who receives me r the one who sent me. 1312
10:41 Anyone who r a prophet because he is 1312
10:41 and anyone who r a righteous man 1312
13:20 the word and at once r it with joy. 3284
Lk 11:10 For everyone who asks **r;** 3284
Ac 10:43 in him r forgiveness of sins 3284
Gal 6: 6 Anyone who r **instruction in** the word 2994
Heb 6: 7 for whom it is farmed r the blessing 3561
Rev 2:17 known only to him who r it. 3284
14: 9 the beast and his image and r his mark on 3284
14:11 or for anyone who r the mark of his name." 3284

RECEIVES (Anglicized) See also GETS

RECEIVING (9) [RECEIVE]

2Sa 16:12 with good for the cursing I am r today." NIH
Ac 16:24 *Upon* r such orders, 3284
Ro 9: 4 the covenants, the **r of the law,** 3792
2Co 7:15 r him with fear and trembling. 1312
11: 8 *by* r support from them so as to serve you. 3284
Php 4:15 the matter of giving and r, except you only; 3331
Heb 12:28 *we are* r a kingdom that cannot be shaken, 4161
1Pe 1: 9 for *you are* r the goal of your faith, 3152
3Jn 1: 7 r no help from the pagans. 3284

RECENT (1) [RECENTLY]

1Ti 3: 6 He must not be a r **convert,** 3745

RECENTLY (4) [RECENT]

Dt 24: 5 If a man has r married, 2543
32:17 not known, gods that r appeared 2543+4946+7940
Jer 34:15 **R** you repented and did what is right 2021+3427
Ac 18: 2 who had r come from Italy 4711

RECEPTION (1) [RECEIVE]

1Th 1: 9 report what kind of r you gave us. 1658

RECESSES (2)

Job 28: 3 he searches the **farthest** r for ore in 3972+9417
38:16 the sea or walked in the r *of* the deep? 2984

RECHAB, RECHABITES (KJV) See RECAB, RECABITE

RECHAH (KJV) See RECAH

RECITE (4) [RECITED, RECITING]

Dt 27:14 Levites *shall* r to all the people 606+2256+6699
Jdg 5:11 *They* r the righteous acts of the LORD, 5989
Ps 45: 1 a noble theme *as* I r my verses for the king; 606
50:16 "What right have you to r my laws 6218

RECITED (1) [RECITE]

Dt 31:30 And Moses r the words of this song 1819

RECITING (1) [RECITE]

Dt 32:45 When Moses finished r all these words 1819

RECKLESS (5)

Nu 22:32 to oppose you because your path *is a* r *one* 3740
Jdg 9: 4 Abimelech used it to hire r adventurers, 8199
Pr 12:18 **R words** pierce like a sword, 1051
14:16 but a fool is hotheaded and **r.** 1053
Jer 23:32 and lead my people astray with their r lies, 7071

RECKONED (7) [RECKONING]

Ge 21:12 through Isaac that your offspring *will* **be r.** 7924
48: 5 in Egypt before I came to you here will be r NIH
48: 6 in the territory they inherit *they will* **be r** 7924
Nu 18:27 Your offering *will* **be r** to you as grain 3108
18:30 *it will* **be r** to you as the product of 3108
Ro 9: 7 through Isaac that your offspring *will be* **r."** 2813
Heb 11:18 through Isaac that your offspring *will be* **r."** 2813

RECKONING (3) [RECKONED]

Isa 10: 3 What will you do on the day of **r,** 7213
Hos 5: 9 Ephraim will be laid waste on the day of **r.** 9349
9: 7 the days of r are at hand. 8936

RECLAIM (1) [CLAIM]

Isa 11:11 a second time to r the remnant that is left 7864

RECLAIMED (1) [CLAIM]

Est 8: 2 which *he had* r from Haman, 6296

RECLINE (1) [RECLINED, RECLINING]

Lk 12:37 **have** them **r at the table** 369

RECLINED (3) [RECLINE]

Lk 7:36 to the Pharisee's house and **r at the table.** 2884
11:37 so *he* went in and **r at the table.** 404
22:14 Jesus and his apostles **r at the table.** 404

RECLINING (7) [RECLINE]

Est 7: 8 on the couch where Esther was **r.** 6584
Mt 26: 7 on his head *as he was* **r at the table.** 367
26:20 Jesus *was* **r at the table** with the Twelve. 367
Mk 14: 3 **r at the table** in the home of a man known 2879
14:18 *While* they *were* **r at the table** eating, 367
Jn 12: 2 among those **r at the table** with him. 367
13:23 whom Jesus loved, was r next to him. 367

RECOGNITION (3) [RECOGNIZE]

Est 6: 3 "What honor and r has Mordecai received 1525
1Co 16:18 Such men *deserve* **r.** 2105
1Ti 5: 3 **Give** proper **r to** those widows who 5506

RECOGNIZE (16) [RECOGNITION, RECOGNIZED, RECOGNIZES, RECOGNIZING]

Ge 27:23 *He did* not r him, 5795
38:25 *"See if you* r whose seal and cord 5795
42: 8 they *did* not r him. 5795
Dt 33: 9 *He did* not r his brothers 5795
1Sa 24:11 Now understand and r that I am not guilty 8011
Job 2:12 *they could* hardly r him; 5795
Mt 7:16 By their fruit *you will* r them. 2105
7:20 Thus, by their fruit *you will* r them. 2105
17:12 and *they did* not r him, 2105
Lk 19:44 not r the time of God's coming to you." 1182
Jn 1:10 the world *did* not r him. 1182
10: 5 because *they do* not r a stranger's voice." 3857
Ac 13:27 and their rulers *did* not r Jesus, 51
27:39 *they did* not r the land, 2105
1Jn 4: 2 This is how *you can* r the Spirit of God: 1182
4: 6 how *we* r the Spirit of truth and the spirit 1182

RECOGNIZED (24) [RECOGNIZE]

Ge 37:33 *He* r it and said, "It is my son's robe! 5795
38:26 Judah r them and said, 5795
42: 7 soon as Joseph saw his brothers, *he* r them, 5795
42: 8 Although Joseph r his brothers, 5795
Jdg 18: 3 they r the voice of the young Levite; 5795
Ru 3:14 but got up before anyone *could be* **r;** 5795
1Sa 3:20 r that Samuel was attested as a prophet 3359
26:17 Saul r David's voice and said, 5795
1Ki 14: 2 so you won't *be* r as the wife of Jeroboam. 3359
18: 7 Obadiah r him, bowed down to the ground, 5795
20:41 king of Israel r him as one of the prophets. 5795
Jer 28: 9 the prophet who prophesies peace *will* **be r** 3359
La 4: 8 *they* **are** not r in the streets. 5795
Mt 12:33 for a tree *is* r by its fruit. 1182
14:35 And *when* the men of that place r Jesus, 2105
Mk 6:33 But many who saw them leaving r them 2105
6:54 as they got out of the boat, *people* r Jesus. 2105
Lk 6:44 Each tree *is* r by its own fruit. 1182
24:31 their eyes were opened and *they* r him, 2105
24:35 how Jesus *was* r by them when he broke 1182
Ac 3:10 *they* r him as the same man who used 2105
12:14 *When she* r Peter's voice, 2105
Ro 7:13 But in order that sin *might be* r as sin, 5743
Gal 2: 9 of fellowship *when they* r the grace given 1182

RECOGNIZES (1) [RECOGNIZE]

Job 11:11 Surely he r deceitful men; 3359

RECOGNIZING (2) [RECOGNIZE]

Lk 24:16 but they were kept from r him. 2105
1Co 11:29 For anyone who eats and drinks without r 1359

RECOIL (1) [RECOILS]

Ps 54: 5 *Let* evil r on those who slander me; 8740

RECOILS (1) [RECOIL]

Ps 7:16 The trouble he causes r on himself; 8740

RECOMMENDATION (1) [RECOMMENDED]

2Co 3: 1 letters *of* r to you or from you? 5364

RECOMMENDED (1) [RECOMMENDATION]

Est 6:10 Do not neglect anything *you have* **r."** 1819

RECOMPENSE (2)

Isa 40:10 and his r accompanies him. 7190
62:11 and his r accompanies him.' " 7190

RECONCILE (3) [RECONCILED, RECONCILIATION, RECONCILING]

Ac 7:26 *He tried to* r them by saying, 1645+1650+5261
Eph 2:16 *to* r both of them to God through the cross, 639
Col 1:20 and through him *to* r to himself all things, 639

RECONCILED (8) [RECONCILE]

Mt 5:24 First go and *be* r to your brother; 1367
Lk 12:58 try hard *to be* **r to** him on the way, 557
Ro 5:10 *we were* r to him through the death 2904
5:10 how much more, *having been* **r,** 2904
1Co 7:11 she must remain unmarried or else *be* r 2904
2Co 5:18 who r us to himself through Christ 2904
5:20 on Christ's behalf: *Be* r to God. 2904
Col 1:22 now *he has* r you by Christ's physical body 639

RECONCILIATION (4) [RECONCILE]

Ro 5:11 through whom we have now received **r.** 2903
11:15 For if their rejection is the r of the world, 2903
2Co 5:18 and gave us the ministry *of* **r:** 2903
5:19 he has committed to us the message *of* **r.** 2903

RECONCILING (1) [RECONCILE]

2Co 5:19 God was r the world to himself in Christ, 2904

RECONSECRATED (1) [CONSECRATE]

Da 8:14 then the sanctuary *will* **be r."** 7405

RECONSIDER (2) [CONSIDER]

Job 6:29 **r,** for my integrity is at stake. 6388+8740
Jer 18:10 then *I will* r the good I had intended 5714

RECORD (16) [RECORDED, RECORDER, RECORDS]

1Ch 4:33 And *they* **kept a genealogical r.** 3509
5: 1 *could* not **be listed in the genealogical r** 3509
7: 7 **genealogical r listed** 22,034 fighting men. 3509
7: 9 Their **genealogical r** listed the heads 9352
2Ch 24:27 and the r of the restoration of the temple NIH
Ne 7: 5 the genealogical r *of* those who had been 6219
Est 6: 1 the r *of* his reign, 1821
Ps 56: 8 **R** my lament; list my tears on your 6218
56: 8 are they not in your **r?** 6225
87: 4 *"I will* r Rahab and Babylon 2349
130: 3 If *you,* O LORD, **kept a r** *of* sins, O Lord, 9068
Jer 22:30 **"R** this man as if childless, 4180
Eze 24: 2 r this date, this very date, 4180+9005
Hos 13:12 his sins *are* **kept on r.** 7621
Mt 1: 1 A r of the genealogy of Jesus Christ the son 1047
1Co 13: 5 *it keeps* no **r** of wrongs. 3357

RECORDED (22) [RECORD]

Ex 38:21 which **were r** at Moses' command by 7212
Nu 33: 2 the LORD's command Moses r the stages 4180
Dt 28:61 and disaster not r in this Book of the Law, 4180
Jos 24:26 And Joshua r these things in the Book of 4180
1Ki 8: 5 that *they could* not **be r** or counted. 6218
1Ch 9: 1 All Israel was listed in the genealogies r in 4180
24: 6 r their names in the presence of the king 4180
2Ch 5: 6 that *they could* not **be r** or counted. 6218
20:34 which **are r** in the book of the kings 6590
26:22 *are* r *by* the prophet Isaiah son of Amoz. 4180
31:19 all *who* **were r in the genealogies** 3509
Ezr 8:34 and the entire weight **was r** at that time. 4180
Ne 12:22 **were r** in the reign of Darius the Persian. 4180
12:23 of Eliashib **were r** in the book of the annals. 4180
Est 2:23 *All this* **was r** in the book of the annals in 4180
6: 2 It was found r there that Mordecai 4180
9:20 Mordecai r these events, 4180
Job 19:23 "Oh, that my words **were r,** 4180
Isa 4: 3 all who *are* r among the living 4180
Jer 51:60 all that *had* **been r** concerning Babylon. 4180
Jn 20:30 which are not r in this book. 1211
Rev 20:12 to what they had done as r in the books. 1211

RECORDER (9) [RECORD]

2Sa 8:16 Jehoshaphat son of Ahilud *was* **r**; 4654
20:24 Jehoshaphat son of Ahilud was **r**; 4654
1Ki 4:3 Jehoshaphat son of Ahilud—**r**; 4654
2Ki 18:18 Joah son of Asaph the **r** went out to them. 4654
18:37 and Joah son of Asaph the **r** went 4654
1Ch 18:15 Jehoshaphat son of Ahilud was **r**; 4654
2Ch 34:8 with Joah son of Joahaz, the **r**, 4654
Isa 36:3 Joah son of Asaph the **r** went out to him. 4654
36:22 Joah son of Asaph the **r** went to Hezekiah, 4654

RECORDS (35) [RECORD]

Ge 41:49 it was so much that he stopped **keeping r** 6218
Ex 6:16 of the sons of Levi according to their **r**: 9352
6:19 the clans of Levi according to their **r**. 9352
Nu 1:20 by one, according to the **r** *of* their clans 9352
1:22 by one, according to the **r** *of* their clans 9352
1:24 by name, according to the **r** *of* their clans 9352
1:26 by name, according to the **r** *of* their clans 9352
1:28 by name, according to the **r** *of* their clans 9352
1:30 by name, according to the **r** *of* their clans 9352
1:32 by name, according to the **r** *of* their clans 9352
1:34 by name, according to the **r** *of* their clans 9352
1:36 by name, according to the **r** *of* their clans 9352
1:38 by name, according to the **r** *of* their clans 9352
1:40 by name, according to the **r** *of* their clans 9352
1:42 by name, according to the **r** *of* their clans 9352
Ru 4:10 among his family or from the **town r**. 5226+9133
1Ch 4:22 (These **r** are from ancient times.) 1821
5:7 listed according to their **genealogical r**: 9352
5:17 **were entered in the genealogical r** 3509
26:31 to the **genealogical r** of their families. 9352
26:31 a search was made in the **r**, NIH
29:29 they are written in the **r** *of* Samuel the seer, 1821
29:29 the **r** *of* Nathan the prophet and the records 1821
29:29 and the **r** *of* Gad the seer, 1821
2Ch 9:29 not written in the **r** *of* Nathan the prophet, 1821
12:15 the **r** *of* Shemaiah the prophet and of Iddo 1821
31:16 **names** *were* **in the genealogical r**— 3509
31:17 **enrolled** by their families **in the genealogical r** 3509
31:18 **listed in** *these* **genealogical r.** 3509
33:19 all are written in the **r** *of* the seers. 1821
Ezr 2:62 These searched for their family **r**, 4181
4:15 In these **r** you will find that this city 10177+10515
Ne 7:64 These searched for their family **r**, 4181
Est 9:32 and it was written down in the **r**. 6219
Eze 13:9 or be listed in the **r** *of* the house of Israel, 4181

RECOUNT (3) [RECOUNTED]

Ps 40:5 The things you planned for us no *one can* **r** 6885
79:13 to generation *we will* **r** your praise. 6218
119:13 With my lips *I* **r** all the laws that come 6218

RECOUNTED (1) [RECOUNT]

Ps 119:26 *I* **r** my ways and you answered me; 6218

RECOVER (13) [RECOVERED, RECOVERY]

2Ki 1:2 to see if *I will* **r** from this injury." 2649
8:8 ask him, '*Will I* **r** from this illness?' " 2649
8:9 '*Will I* **r** from this illness?' " 2649
8:10 '*You will* **certainly r**'; 2649+2649
8:14 told me that *you would* **certainly r**." 2649+2649
8:29 so King Joram returned to Jezreel to **r** from 8324
9:15 but King Joram had returned to Jezreel to **r** 8324
20:1 you are going to die; *you will* not **r**." 2649
2Ch 14:13 of Cushites fell that they could not **r**; 4695
22:6 to **r** *from* the wounds they had inflicted 8324
Isa 38:1 you are going to die; *you will* not **r**." 2649
38:21 apply it to the boil, and *he will* **r**." 2649
Eze 7:13 The seller *will* not **r** the land he has sold 8740

RECOVERED (12) [RECOVER]

Ge 14:16 *He* **r** all the goods and brought back 8740
38:12 When Judah *had* **r from** his **grief**, 5714
1Sa 30:18 David **r** everything the Amalekites had taken, 5911
30:22 not share with them the plunder *we* **r**. 5911
2Sa 14:14 which cannot **be r**, so we must die. 665
2Ki 13:25 and so *he* **r** the Israelite towns. 8740
14:28 how *he* **r** for Israel both Damascus 8740
16:6 of Aram **r** Elath for Aram by driving out 8740
20:7 so and applied it to the boil, and *he* **r**. 2649
Jer 41:16 the survivors from Mizpah whom *he had* **r** 8740
Eze 38:8 a land *that has* **r** from war, 8740
Rev 18:14 and splendor have vanished, never *to be* **r**.' 2351

RECOVERY (4) [RECOVER]

Isa 38:9 of Judah after his illness and **r**: 2649+2716+4946
39:1 because he had heard of his illness and **r**. 2616
Lk 4:18 the prisoners and **r of sight** for the blind, 330
Ro 11:11 Did they stumble so as to fall beyond **r**? NIG

RECTANGULAR (2)

1Ki 7:5 All the doorways had **r** frames; 8062
Eze 41:21 The outer sanctuary had a **r** doorframe, 8062

RED (54) [REDDISH]

Ge 25:25 The first to come out was **r**, 145
25:30 "Quick, let me have some of that **r** *stew!* 137
Ex 10:19 the locusts and carried them into the **R** Sea. 6068
13:18 around by the desert road toward the **R** Sea. 6068
15:4 are drowned in the **R** Sea. 6068
15:22 the **R** Sea and they went into the Desert 6068
23:31 from the **R** Sea to the Sea of the Philistines, 6068
25:5 ram skins **dyed r** and hides of sea cows; 131
26:14 for the tent a covering of ram skins **dyed r**, 131
35:7 ram skins **dyed r** and hides of sea cows; 131
35:23 ram skins **dyed r** or hides of sea cows 131
36:19 for the tent a covering of ram skins **dyed r**, 131
39:34 of ram skins **dyed r**, the covering of hides 131
Lev 11:14 the **r kite**, any kind of black kite, 1798
Nu 14:25 the desert along the route to the **R** Sea." 6068
19:2 Tell the Israelites to bring you a **r** heifer 137
21:4 along the route to the **R** Sea, 6068
33:10 They left Elim and camped by the **R** Sea. 6068
33:11 the **R** Sea and camped in the Desert of Sin. 6068
Dt 1:40 the desert along the route to the **R** Sea." 6068
2:1 the desert along the route to the **R** Sea, 6068
11:4 of the **R** Sea as they were pursuing you, 6068
14:13 the **r kite**, the black kite, any kind of falcon, 8012
Jos 2:10 the LORD dried up the water of the **R** Sea 6068
4:23 to the **R** Sea when he dried it up before us 6068
24:6 and horsemen as far as the **R** Sea. 6068
Jdg 11:16 Israel went through the desert to the **R** Sea 6068
1Ki 9:26 on the shore of the **R** Sea. 6068
2Ki 3:22 the water looked **r**—like blood. 137
Ne 9:9 you heard their cry at the **R** Sea. 6068
Job 16:16 My face *is* **r** with weeping, 2813
Ps 106:7 and they rebelled by the sea, the **R** Sea. 6068
106:9 He rebuked the **R** Sea, and it dried up; 6068
106:22 of Ham and awesome deeds by the **R** Sea. 6068
136:13 to him who divided the **R** Sea asunder 6068
136:15 swept Pharaoh and his army into the **R** Sea; 6068
Pr 23:31 Do not gaze at wine when *it is* **r**, 131
Isa 1:18 though *they are* **r** as crimson, 131
63:2 Why are your garments **r**, 137
Jer 22:14 panels it with cedar and decorates it in **r**. 9266
49:21 their cry will resound to the **R** Sea. 6068
Eze 23:14 figures of Chaldeans portrayed in **r**, 9266
Na 2:3 The shields of his soldiers *are* **r**; 131
Zec 1:8 there before me was a man riding a **r** horse! 137
1:8 Behind him were **r**, brown and white horses. 137
6:2 The first chariot had **r** horses, 137
Mt 16:2 'It will be fair weather, for the sky *is* **r**,' *4793*
16:3 for the sky *is* **r** and overcast.' *4793*
Ac 7:36 the **R** Sea and for forty years in the desert. *2261*
Heb 11:29 the people passed through the **R** Sea as *2261*
Rev 6:4 another horse came out, a **fiery r** *one.* *4794*
6:12 the whole moon turned **blood r**, *135+6055*
9:17 Their breastplates were **fiery r**, dark blue, *4791*
12:3 an enormous **r** dragon with seven heads *4794*

REDDISH (2) [RED]

Lev 13:49 or any leather article, is greenish or **r**, 140
14:37 and if it has greenish or **r** depressions 140

REDDISH-WHITE (4) [WHITE]

Lev 13:19 a white swelling or **r** spot appears, 140+4237
13:24 **r** or white spot appears in the raw flesh 140+4237
13:42 But if he has a **r** sore on his bald head 140+4237
13:43 on his head or forehead is **r** like 140+4237

REDEEM (53) [KINSMAN-REDEEMER, KINSMAN-REDEEMERS, REDEEMABLE, REDEEMED, REDEEMER, REDEEMS, REDEMPTION]

Ex 6:6 and *I will* **r** you with an outstretched arm 1457
13:13 **R** with a lamb every firstborn donkey, 7009
13:13 but if *you do* not **r** it, break its neck. 7009
13:13 **R** every firstborn among your sons. 7009
13:15 and **r** each of my firstborn sons.' 7009
21:30 he may **r** his life by paying whatever 7018
34:20 **R** the firstborn donkey with a lamb, 7009
34:20 but if *you do* not **r** it, break its neck. 7009
34:20 **R** all your firstborn sons. 7009
Lev 25:25 and **r** what his countryman has sold. 1457
25:26 *to* **r** it *for* him but he himself prospers 1457
25:26 and acquires sufficient means to **r** it, 1460
25:29 During that time he may **r** it. 1460
25:32 the **right to r** their houses in 1460
25:48 One of his relatives *may* **r** him: 1457
25:49 or any blood relative in his clan *may* **r** him. 1457
25:49 Or if he prospers, *he may* **r himself.** 1457
27:13 If the owner *wishes to* **r** the animal, 1457+1457
27:19 who dedicates the field *wishes to* **r** it, 1457+1457
27:20 If, however, *he does* not **r** the field, 1457
27:27 If he *does* not **r** *it*, 1457
Nu 3:46 *To* **r** the 273 firstborn Israelites who exceed 7012
18:15 But *you* **must r** every firstborn son 7009+7009
18:16 *you must* **r** them at the redemption price 7009
18:17 "But *you must* not **r** the firstborn of an ox, 7009
Ru 3:13 and in the morning if *he wants to* **r**, good; 1457
3:13 to redeem, good; *let him* **r**. 1457
4:4 If *you will* **r** it, do so. 1457
4:4 "*I will* **r** it," he said. 1457
4:6 "Then I cannot **r** it because I might 1457
4:6 You **r** it yourself. 1457
2Sa 7:23 on earth that God went out to **r** as a people 7009
1Ch 17:21 on earth whose God went out to **r** a people 7009
Ps 25:22 **R** Israel, O God, from all their troubles! 7009
26:11 **r** me and be merciful to me. 7009
31:5 **r** me, O LORD, the God of truth. 7009
44:26 **r** us because of your unfailing love. 7009
Ps 49:7 No man *can* **r** the life of another or 7009+7009
49:15 But God *will* **r** my life from the grave; 7009
69:18 **r** me because of my foes. 7009
119:134 **R** me from the oppression of men, 7009
119:154 Defend my cause and **r** me; 1457
130:8 *He* himself *will* **r** Israel from all their sins. 7009
Jer 15:21 of the wicked and **r** you from the grasp of 7009
31:11 the LORD will ransom Jacob and **r** them 1457
32:8 Since it is your right to **r** it and possess it, 1460
Hos 7:13 *to* **r** them but they speak lies against me. 7009
13:14 *I will* **r** them from death. 1457
Mic 4:10 the LORD *will* **r** you out of the hand 1457
Zec 10:8 Surely *I will* **r** them; 7009
Lk 24:21 the one who was going to **r** Israel. *3390*
Gal 4:5 to **r** those under law, *1973*
Tit 2:14 to **r** us from all wickedness and to purify *3390*

REDEEMABLE (1) [REDEEM]

Lev 25:33 So the property of the Levites *is* **r**— 1457

REDEEMED (45) [REDEEM]

Ex 15:13 the people *you have* **r**. 1457
21:8 *he must* **let** her **be r**. 7009
Lev 25:30 If *it is* not **r** before a full year has passed, 1457
25:31 They can be **r**, and they are to be returned 1460
25:54 " 'Even if *he* **is** not **r** in any of these ways, 1457
27:20 *it can* never **be r**. 1457
27:28 or family land—may be sold or **r**; 1457
27:33 become holy and cannot **be r**.' " 1457
Nu 3:49 from those who exceeded the number **r** *by* 7009
Dt 7:8 with a mighty hand and **r** you from the land 7009
9:26 your own inheritance that *you* **r** 7009
13:5 who brought you out of Egypt and **r** you 7009
15:15 in Egypt and the LORD your God **r** you. 7009
21:8 whom *you have* **r**, O LORD, 7009
24:18 and the LORD your God **r** you from there. 7009
2Sa 7:23 whom *you* **r** from Egypt? 7009
1Ch 17:21 whom *you* **r** from Egypt? 7009
Ne 1:10 whom *you* **r** by your great strength 7009
Job 33:28 *He* **r** my soul from going down to the pit, 7009
Ps 71:23 I, whom *you have* **r**. 7009
74:2 the tribe of your inheritance, whom *you* **r**— 1457
77:15 With your mighty arm *you* **r** your people, 1457
78:42 the day *he* **r** them from the oppressor, 7009
106:10 from the hand of the enemy *he* **r** them. 1457
107:2 Let the **r** *of* the LORD say this— 1457
107:2 those *he* **r** from the hand of the foe, 1457
Isa 1:27 Zion *will* **be r** with justice, 7009
29:22 who **r** Abraham, says to the house of Jacob: 7009
35:9 But only the **r** will walk there, 1457
43:1 "Fear not, for *I have* **r** you; 1457
44:22 Return to me, for *I have* **r** you." 1457
44:23 for the LORD *has* **r** Jacob, 1457
48:20 say, "The LORD *has* **r** his servant Jacob." 1457
51:10 of the sea so that the **r** might cross over? 1457
52:3 and without money *you will* **be r**." 1457
52:9 *he has* **r** Jerusalem. 1457
62:12 called the Holy People, the **R** *of* the LORD; 1457
63:9 In his love and mercy he **r** them; 1457
La 3:58 you took up my case; *you* **r** my life. 1457
Mic 6:4 I brought you up out of Egypt and **r** you 7009
Lk 1:68 he has come and *has* **r** his people. *3391+4472*
Gal 3:13 Christ **r** us **from** the curse of the law *1973*
3:14 He **r** us in order that the blessing given *NIG*
1Pe 1:18 as silver or gold that *you were* **r** from *3390*
Rev 14:3 who *had been* **r** from the earth. *60*

REDEEMER (17) [REDEEM]

Job 19:25 I know that my **R** lives, 1457
Ps 19:14 O LORD, my Rock and my **R**. 1457
78:35 that God Most High was their **R**. 1457
Isa 41:14 your **R**, the Holy One of Israel. 1457
43:14 your **R**, the Holy One of Israel: 1457
44:6 Israel's King and **R**, the LORD Almighty: 1457
44:24 your **R**, who formed you in the womb: 1457
47:4 Our **R**—the LORD Almighty is his name— 1457
48:17 your **R**, the Holy One of Israel: 1457
49:7 the **R** and Holy One of Israel— 1457
49:26 I, the LORD, am your Savior, your **R**, 1457
54:5 the Holy One of Israel *is* your **R**; 1457
54:8 says the LORD your **R**. 1457
59:20 "The **R** will come to Zion, 1457
60:16 I, the LORD, am your Savior, your **R**, 1457
63:16 our **R** from of old is your name. 1457
Jer 50:34 Yet their **R** is strong; 1457

REDEEMS (4) [REDEEM]

Lev 27:15 If the man who dedicates his house **r** it, 1457
27:31 If a man **r** any of his tithe, 1457+1457
Ps 34:22 The LORD **r** his servants; 7009
103:4 who **r** your life from the pit 1457

REDEMPTION (23) [REDEEM]

Lev 25:24 you must provide for the **r** of the land. 1460
25:29 the **right of r** a full year after its sale. 1460
25:48 the **right of r** after he has sold himself. 1460
25:51 for his **r** a larger share of the price paid 1460
25:52 that and pay for his **r** accordingly. 1460
Nu 3:48 the **r** *of* the additional Israelites to Aaron 7012
3:49 the **r** money from those who exceeded 7017
3:51 the **r** money to Aaron and his sons, 7012
18:16 at the **r** price set at five shekels of silver, 7009
Ru 4:7 **r** and transfer of property to become final, 1460
Ps 111:9 He provided **r** for his people; 7014

Ps 130: 7 and with him is full **r.** 7014
Isa 63: 4 and the year of my **r** has come. 1453
Lk 2:38 to all who were looking forward to the **r** *3391*
21:28 because your **r** is drawing near." *667*
Ro 3:24 through the **r** that came by Christ Jesus. *667*
8:23 our adoption as sons, the **r** of our bodies. *667*
1Co 1:30 that is, our righteousness, holiness and **r.** *667*
Eph 1: 7 In him we have **r** through his blood, *667*
1:14 the **r** of those who are God's possession— *667*
4:30 you were sealed for the day *of* **r.** *667*
Col 1:14 in whom we have **r,** the forgiveness of sins. *667*
Heb 9:12 having obtained eternal **r.** *3391*

REDOUND (KJV) See OVERFLOW

REDUCE (7) [REDUCED, REDUCES]
Ex 5: 8 don't **r** the quota. 1757
5:19 *to* **r the number** *of* bricks required of you 1757
2Ki 10:32 In those days the LORD began to **r** *the* **size** 7894
Job 11: 3 *Will* your idle talk **r** men **to silence?** 3087
24:25 who can prove me false and **r** my words 8492
Isa 41:15 and **r** the hills to chaff. 8492
Jer 10:24 in your anger, lest *you* **r** me **to nothing.** 5070

REDUCED (11) [REDUCE]
Ge 47:21 **r** the people **to servitude,** 4200+6268+6269
Ex 5:11 but your work *will* not **be r** at all.'" 1757
Lev 27:18 and its set value *will* **be r.** 1757
Job 30:19 and *I am* **r to** dust and ashes. 5439
Ps 79: 1 *they have* **r** Jerusalem to rubble. 8492
89:40 through all his walls and **r** his strongholds 8492
102: 5 Because of my loud groaning I *am* **r to** skin 1815
Isa 25: 5 as heat is **r** by the shadow of a cloud, NIH
Eze 16:27 against you and **r** your territory; 1757
28:18 and *I* **r** you to ashes on the ground in 5989
Am 5: 5 and Bethel will be **r** to nothing." NIH

REDUCES (2) [REDUCE]
Pr 6:26 for the prostitute **r** you **to** a loaf of bread, 6330
Isa 40:23 He brings princes to naught and **r** the rulers 6913

REED (12) [REEDS]
1Ki 14:15 that it will be like a **r** swaying in the water. 7866
2Ki 18:21 that splintered **r** of a staff, 7866
Isa 9:14 both palm branch and **r** in a single day; 109
19:15 head or tail, palm branch or **r.** 109
36: 6 that splintered **r** of a staff, 7866
42: 3 A bruised **r** he will not break, 7866
58: 5 for bowing one's head like a **r** and for lying 109
Eze 29: 6 "'You have been a staff of **r** for the house 7866
Mt 11: 7 A **r** swayed by the wind? *2812*
12:20 A bruised **r** he will not break, *2812*
Lk 7:24 A **r** swayed by the wind? *2812*
Rev 11: 1 a **r** like a measuring rod and was told, *2812*

REEDS (10) [REED]
Ge 41: 2 sleek and fat, and they grazed among the **r.** 286
41:18 fat and sleek, and they grazed among the **r.** 286
Ex 2: 3 the child in it and put it among the **r** along 6068
2: 5 among the **r** and sent her slave girl to get it. 6068
Job 8:11 Can **r** thrive without water? 286
40:21 hidden among the **r** in the marsh. 7866
41:20 as from a boiling pot over a fire of **r.** 109
Ps 68:30 Rebuke the beast among the **r,** 7866
Isa 19: 6 The **r** and rushes will wither, 7866
35: 7 grass and **r** and papyrus will grow. 7866

REEKED (1)
Ex 8:14 and the land **r** *of* them. 944

REEL (2) [REELED, REELING, REELS]
Isa 28: 7 also stagger from wine and **r** from beer: 9494
28: 7 befuddled with wine; *they* **r** from beer, 9494

REELAIAH (1)
Ezr 2: 2 Nehemiah, Seraiah, **R,** Mordecai, Bilshan, 8305

REELED (1) [REEL]
Ps 107:27 *They* **r** and staggered like drunken men, 2510

REELING (1) [REEL]
Zec 12: 2 that sends all the surrounding peoples **r.** 8303

REELS (1) [REEL]
Isa 24:20 The earth **r** like a drunkard, 5675+5675

REENTERED (1) [ENTER]
Ne 2:15 and **r** through the Valley Gate. 995+2256+8740

REESTABLISHED (1) [ESTABLISH]
2Ch 29:35 service of the temple of the LORD **was r.** 3922

REFER (1) [REFERRED, REFERRING]
1Jn 5:16 I **r** to those whose sin does not lead *NIG*

REFERRED (1) [REFER]
Gal 3:19 the Seed *to* **whom** the promise *r* had come. *AIT*

REFERRING (2) [REFER]
Ex 4:26 "bridegroom of blood," **r to** circumcision.) 4200
Jn 13:18 "*I am* not **r** to all of you; *3306*

REFINE (3) [REFINED, REFINER, REFINER'S, REFINING]
Jer 9: 7 "See, I *will* **r** and test them, 7671
Zec 13: 9 *I will* **r** them like silver and test them 7671
Mal 3: 3 the Levites and **r** them like gold and silver. 2423

REFINED (10) [REFINE]
1Ch 28:18 and the weight of the **r** gold for the altar 2423
29: 4 and seven thousand talents of **r** silver, 2423
Job 28: 1 for silver and a place where gold *is* **r.** 2423
Ps 12: 6 like silver **r** in a furnace of clay, 7671
66:10 you, O God, tested us; *you* **r** us like silver. 7671
Isa 48:10 See, *I have* **r** you, though not as silver; 7671
Da 11:35 so that they *may be* **r,** 7671
12:10 Many will be purified, made spotless and **r,** 7671
1Pe 1: 7 which perishes even *though* **r** by fire— *1507*
Rev 3:18 I counsel you to buy from me gold **r** in *4792*

REFINER (1) [REFINE]
Mal 3: 3 He will sit as a **r** and purifier of silver; 7671

REFINER'S (1) [REFINE]
Mal 3: 2 he will be like a **r** fire or a launderer's soap. 7671

REFINING (1) [REFINE]
Jer 6:29 but *the* **r goes on** in vain; 7671+7671

REFLECT (3) [REFLECTED, REFLECTION, REFLECTS]
Isa 47: 7 not consider these things or **r on** 2349
2Co 3:18 with unveiled faces all **r** the Lord's glory, *3002*
2Ti 2: 7 **R on** what I am saying, *3783*

REFLECTED (1) [REFLECT]
Ecc 9: 1 So *I* **r on** all this and concluded 448+4213+5989

REFLECTION (1) [REFLECT]
1Co 13:12 Now we see but a poor **r** as in a **mirror;** *2269*

REFLECTS (3) [REFLECT]
Pr 27:19 As water **r a face,** 2021+2021+4200+7156+7156
27:19 so a man's heart **r the man.** 132+2021+4200
Ecc 5:20 *He* seldom **r on** the days of his life, 2349

REFORM (4) [REFORMS]
Jer 7: 3 **R** your ways and your actions, 3512
18:11 and **r** your ways and your actions.' 3512
26:13 Now **r** your ways and your actions 3512
35:15 from your wicked ways and **r** your actions; 3512

REFORMS (1) [REFORM]
Ac 24: 2 and your foresight has brought about **r** *1480*

REFRAIN (10) [REFRAINED]
Dt 23:22 But if *you* **r from** making a vow, 2532
1Sa 18: 8 Saul was very angry; this **r** galled him. 1821
1Ki 22: 6 against Ramoth Gilead, or *shall I* **r?"** 2532
22:15 against Ramoth Gilead, or *shall I* **r?"** 2532
2Ch 18: 5 against Ramoth Gilead, or *shall I* **r?"** 2532
18:14 against Ramoth Gilead, or *shall I* **r?"** 2532
Job 16: 6 and if *I* **r,** it does not go away. 2532
Ps 37: 8 **R** from anger and turn from wrath; 8332
Ecc 3: 5 a time to embrace and a time to **r,** 8178
2Co 12: 6 But *I* **r,** so no one will think more *5767*

REFRAINED (2) [REFRAIN]
2Sa 12: 4 but the rich man **r** *from* taking one 2798
Job 29: 9 the chief men **r** from speaking 6806

REFRAINETH (KJV) See HOLDS

REFRESH (7) [REFRESHED, REFRESHES, REFRESHING]
Jdg 19: 5 **"R** yourself *with* something to eat; 6184
19: 8 the girl's father said, **"R** yourself. 6184
2Sa 16: 2 to **r** those who become exhausted in 9272
SS 2: 5 **r** me with apples, for I am faint with love. 8331
Jer 31:25 *I will* **r** the weary and satisfy the faint." 8115
Phm 1:20 **r** my heart in Christ. *399*
2Pe 1:13 I think it is right *to* **r** your memory as long *1444*

REFRESHED (10) [REFRESH]
Ge 18: 5 you *can be* **r** and then go on your way 4213+6184
Ex 23:12 and the alien as well, *may* **be r.** 5882
2Sa 16:14 And there *he* **r himself.** 5882
Ps 68: 9 you **r** your weary inheritance. 3922
Pr 11:25 he who refreshes others *will* himself **be r.** 3722
Ro 15:32 **together** with you *be* **r.** *5265*
1Co 16:18 For *they* **r** my spirit and yours also. *399*
2Co 7:13 because his spirit *has been* **r** by all of you. *399*
2Ti 1:16 because *he* often **r** me and was not ashamed *434*
Phm 1: 7 brother, *have* **r** the hearts of the saints. *399*

REFRESHES (2) [REFRESH]
Pr 11:25 *he who* **r** others will himself be refreshed. 8115
25:13 *he* **r** the spirit of his masters. 8740

REFRESHING (1) [REFRESH]
Ac 3:19 that times *of* **r** may come from the Lord, *433*

REFUGE (93) [REFUGEES]
Nu 35: 6 the Levites will be cities of **r,** 5236
35:11 select some towns to be your cities of **r,** 5236
35:12 They will be places of **r** from the avenger, 5236
35:13 be your cities of **r.** 5236
35:14 and three in Canaan as cities of **r.** 5236
35:15 These six towns will be a **place of r** 5236
35:25 of blood and send him back to the city of **r** 5236
35:26 of the city of **r** to which he has fled 5236
35:28 The accused must stay in his city of **r** until 5236
35:32 for anyone who has fled to a city of **r** and 5236
Dt 23:15 If a slave *has* **taken r** with you, 5911
32:37 are their gods, the rock *they* **took r** in, 2879
33:27 The eternal God is your **r,** 5104
Jos 20: 2 the Israelites to designate the cities of **r,** 5236
21:13 (a city of **r** *for* one accused of murder), 5236
21:21 of **r** *for* one accused of murder) and Gezer, 5236
21:27 (a city of **r** *for* one accused of murder) and 5236
21:32 (a city of **r** *for* one accused of murder), 5236
21:38 (a city of **r** *for* one accused of murder), 5236
Jdg 9:15 come and **take r** in my shade; 2879
Ru 2:12 whose wings you have come to **take r."** 2879
2Sa 22: 3 my God is my rock, in whom *I* **take r,** 2879
22: 3 He is my stronghold, my **r** and my savior— 4960
22:31 He is a shield for all who **take r** in him. 2879
1Ch 6:57 of Aaron were given Hebron (a city of **r),** 5236
6:67 they were given Shechem (a city of **r),** 5236
Ps 2:12 Blessed are all *who* **take r** in him. 2879
5:11 But let all *who* **take r** in you be glad; 2879
7: 1 O LORD my God, *I* **take r** in you; 2879
9: 9 The LORD is a **r** for the oppressed, 5369
11: 1 In the LORD *I* **take r.** 2879
14: 6 but the LORD is their **r.** 4726
16: 1 Keep me safe, O God, for in you *I* **take r.** 2879
17: 7 by your right hand *those who* **take r** in you 2879
18: 2 my God is my rock, in whom *I* **take r.** 2879
18:30 He is a shield for all who **take r** in him. 2879
25:20 for *I* **take r** in you. 2879
31: 1 In you, O LORD, *I have* **taken r;** 2879
31: 2 be my rock of **r,** a strong fortress 5057
31: 4 for you are my **r.** 5057
31:19 the sight of men on those *who* **take r** in you. 2879
34: 8 blessed is the man *who* **takes r** in him. 2879
34:22 no one will be condemned who **takes r** 2879
36: 7 and low among men **find r** in the shadow 2879
37:40 because *they* **take r** in him. 2879
46: 1 God is our **r** and strength, 4726
57: 1 for in you my soul **takes r.** 2879
57: 1 *I will* **take r** in the shadow of your wings 2879
59:16 my **r** in times of trouble. 4960
61: 3 For you have been my **r,** 4726
61: 4 in your tent forever and **take r** in the shelter 2879
62: 7 he is my mighty rock, my **r.** 4726
62: 8 for God is our **r.** 4726
64:10 in the LORD and **take r** in him; 2879
71: 1 In you, O LORD, *I have* **taken r;** 2879
71: 3 Be my rock of **r,** to which I can always go; 5061
71: 7 but you are my strong **r.** 4726
73:28 I have made the Sovereign LORD my **r;** 4726
91: 2 "He is my **r** and my fortress, my God, 4726
91: 4 and under his wings *you will* **find r;** 2879
91: 9 even the LORD, who is my **r**— 4726
94:22 and my God the rock in whom I take **r.** 4726
104:18 the crags are a **r** for the coneys. 4726
118: 8 to **take r** in the LORD than to trust in man. 2879
118: 9 It is better to **take r** in the LORD than 2879
119:114 You are my **r** and my shield; 6260
141: 8 O Sovereign LORD; in you *I* **take r**— 2879
142: 4 I have no **r;** no one cares for my life. 4960
142: 5 I say, "You are my **r,** 4726
144: 2 my shield, in whom *I* **take r,** 2879
Pr 10:29 way of the LORD is a **r** for the righteous, 5057
14:26 and for his children it will be a **r.** 4726
14:32 but even in death the righteous **have a r.** 2879
22: 3 A prudent man sees danger and **takes r,** 6259
27:12 The prudent see danger and **take r,** 6259
30: 5 he is a shield to those *who* **take r** in him. 2879
Isa 4: 6 **r** and hiding place from the storm and rain. 4726
14:32 and in her his afflicted people *will* **find r."** 2879
25: 4 You have been a **r** for the poor, 5057
25: 4 a **r** for the needy in his distress, 5057
27: 5 Or else let them come to me for **r;** 5057
28:15 a lie our **r** and falsehood our hiding place." 4726
28:17 hail will sweep away your **r,** the lie, 4726
30: 2 to Egypt's shade *for* **r.** 2879
32: 2 be like a shelter from the wind and a **r** *from* 6260
33:16 whose **r** will be the mountain fortress. 5369
57:13 But the *man who* **makes** me *his* **r** will inherit the land 2879
Jer 16:19 my **r** in time of distress, 4960
17:17 you are my **r** in the day of disaster. 4726
21:13 Who can enter our **r?"** 5104
Joel 3:16 But the LORD will be a **r** for his people, 4726
Na 1: 7 The LORD is good, a **r** in times of trouble. 5057
3:11 you will go into hiding and seek **r** from 5057

REFUGEES (2) [REFUGE]

Isa 16: 3 Hide the fugitives, do not betray the **r**. 5610
Jer 50:28 the fugitives and **r** from Babylon declaring 7128

REFUND (1)

Lev 25:27 the value for the years since he sold it and **r** 8740

REFUSAL (1) [REFUSE]

Mk 16:14 for their lack of faith and their **stubborn r** *5016*

REFUSE (50) [REFUSAL, REFUSED, REFUSES, REFUSING]

Ge 23: 6 None of us *will* **r** you his tomb 3973
24:41 be released from my oath even if they **r** 4202
Ex 8: 2 If you **r** to let them go, 4412
9: 2 If you **r** to let them go and continue 4412
10: 3 'How long *will you* **r** to humble yourself 4412
10: 4 If you **r** to let them go, 4412
11: 9 "Pharaoh will **r** to listen to you— 4202
16:28 "How long *will you* **r** 4412
Lev 26:21 " 'If you remain hostile toward me and **r** 14+4202
Nu 14:11 How long will they **r** to believe in me, 4202
Dt 20:12 If they **r** to make peace 4202
1Ki 2:16 *Do* not **r** me." 8740
2:17 ask King Solomon—*he will* not **r** you— 8740
2:20 *"Do* not **r** me." 8740
2:20 *I will* not **r** you." 8740
20: 7 my silver and my gold, *I did* not **r** him." 4979
2Ki 2:17 until he was too ashamed to **r**. NIH
9:37 Jezebel's body will be like **r** on the ground 1961
Job 6: 7 I **r** to touch it; such food makes me ill. 4412
34:33 when *you* **r** to repent? 4415
Ps 26: 5 the assembly of evildoers and **r** to sit with 4202
83:10 at Endor and became like **r** on the ground. 1961
141: 5 My head *will* not **r** it. 5648
Pr 6:35 *he will* **r** the bribe, however great it is. 14+4202
21: 7 for *they* **r** to do what is right. 4412
21:25 because his hands **r** to work. 4412
30: 7 *do* not **r** me before I die: 4979
Isa 5:25 and the dead bodies are like **r** in the streets. 6054
Jer 3: 3 *you* **r** to blush with shame. 4412
8: 2 but will be like **r** lying on the ground. 1961
8: 5 They cling to deceit; *they* **r** to return. 4412
9: 6 in their deceit *they* **r** to acknowledge me," 4412
9:22 " 'The dead bodies of men will lie like **r** on 1961
13:10 who **r** to listen to my words, 4412
16: 4 but will be like **r** lying on the ground. 1961
25:28 But if *they* **r** to take the cup from your hand 4412
25:33 but will be like **r** lying on the ground. 1961
38:21 But if you **r** to surrender, 4412
La 3:45 You have made us scum and **r** among 4400
Eze 3:27 and whoever will **r** let him refuse; 2534
3:27 and whoever will refuse *let him* **r**; 2532
Hos 11: 5 not Assyria rule over them because *they* **r** 4412
Mk 6:26 he did not want *to* **r** her. *119*
Jn 5:40 yet *you* **r** to come to me to have life. *2527+4024*
19:10 "Do you **r** to speak to me?" *4024*
Ac 25:11 *I do* not **r** to die. *4148*
1Co 4:13 the **r** of the world. *4370*
16:11 No one, then, *should* **r to accept** him. *2024*
Heb 12:25 See to it that *you do* not **r** him who speaks. *4148*
Rev 11: 9 on their bodies and **r** them burial. *918+4024*

REFUSED (58) [REFUSE]

Ge 37:35 but *he* **r** to be comforted. 4412
39: 8 But *he* **r**. 4412
39:10 *he* **r** to go to bed with her or even be 4202+9048
48:19 But his father **r** and said, "I know, my son, 4412
Ex 4:23 But *you* **r** to let him go; 4412
13:15 When Pharaoh **stubbornly r** to let us go, 7996
Nu 20:21 Since Edom **r** to let them go 4412
22:13 the LORD *has* **r** to let me go with you." 4412
22:14 "Balaam **r** to come with us." 4412
Dt 2:30 king of Heshbon **r** to let us pass through. 14+4202
Jdg 2:19 They **r** to give up their evil practices 4202
11:17 also to the king of Moab, and *he* **r**. 14+4202
1Sa 8:19 But the people **r** to listen to Samuel. 4412
28:23 *He* **r** and said, "I will not eat." 4412
2Sa 2:23 But Asahel **r** to give up the pursuit; 4412
12:17 but *he* **r**, and he would not eat any food 14+4202
13: 9 but *he* **r** to eat. 4412
13:14 But *he* **r** to listen to her, 14+4202
13:16 But *he* **r** to listen to her. 14+4202
13:25 Absalom urged him, *he still* **r** to go, 14+4202
14:29 but Joab **r** to come to him. 14+4202
14:29 he sent a second time, but *he* **r** to come. 14+4202
23:16 But *he* **r** to drink it; 14+4202
1Ki 12:16 When all Israel saw that the king **r** to listen 4202
20:35 Strike me with your weapon," but the man **r** 4412
21: 4 He lay on his bed sulking and **r** to eat. 4202
21:15 the Jezreelite that *he* **r** to sell you. 4412
22:49 with your men," but Jehoshaphat **r**. 14+4202
2Ki 5:16 And even though Naaman urged him, *he* **r**. 4412
15:16 because they **r** to open their gates. 4202
1Ch 11:18 But he **r** to drink it; 14+4202
2Ch 10:16 When all Israel saw that the king **r** to listen 4202
Ne 9:17 *They* **r** to listen and failed to remember 4412
9:29 became stiff-necked and **r** to listen. 4202
Est 1:12 Queen Vashti **r** to come. 4412
3: 4 Day after day they spoke to him but he **r** 4202
Ps 77: 2 and my soul **r** to be comforted. 4412
78:10 they did not keep God's covenant and **r** 4412
Ecc 2:10 *I* **r** my heart no pleasure. 4979
Jer 5: 3 you crushed them, but *they* **r** correction. 4412
5: 3 harder than stone and **r** to repent. 4412
11:10 who **r** to listen to my words. 4412
Zec 7:11 "But *they* **r** to pay attention; 4412
Mt 18:30 "But he **r**. *2527+4024*
22: 3 but *they* **r** to come. *2527+4024*
27:34 but after tasting it, *he* **r** to drink it. *2527+4024*
Lk 15:28 The older brother became angry and **r** *2527+4024*
18: 4 "For some time *he* **r**. *2527+4024*
Ac 7:39 "But our fathers **r** to obey him. *2527+4024*
14: 2 But the Jews who **r to believe** stirred up *578*
19: 9 *they* **r to believe** and publicly maligned *578*
2Th 2:10 They perish because *they* **r** to love the truth *1312+4024*
Heb 11:24 **r** to be known as the son of Pharaoh's *766*
11:35 Others were tortured and **r** to be released, *4024+4657*
12:25 *when they* **r** him who warned them on earth, *4148*
Rev 13:15 and cause all who **r to worship** the image to be killed. *3590+4686*
16: 9 but *they* **r to repent** and glorify him. *3566+4024*
16:11 but *they* **r to repent** of what they had done. *3566+4024*

REFUSES (7) [REFUSE]

Ex 7:14 *he* **r** to let the people go. 4412
22:17 father **absolutely r** to give her to him, 4412+4412
Dt 25: 7 "My husband's brother **r** to carry 4412
Pr 11:15 but *whoever* **r** to strike hands 8533
Mt 18:17 If *he* **r to listen** *to* them, *4159*
18:17 and if *he* **r to listen** even *to* the church, *4159*
3Jn 1:10 he **r to** welcome the brothers. *4046*

REFUSING (4) [REFUSE]

Jer 31:15 Rachel weeping for her children and **r** to 4412
50:33 captors hold them fast, **r** to let them go. 4412
Da 9:11 and turned away, **r** to obey you. 1194
Mt 2:18 Rachel weeping for her children and **r** *2527+4024*

REFUTE (4) [REFUTED]

Job 32: 3 because they had found no **way to r** Job, 5101
32:13 *let* God **r** him, not man.' 5622
Isa 54:17 *you will* **r** every tongue that accuses you. 8399
Tit 1: 9 and **r** those who oppose it. *1794*

REFUTED (1) [REFUTE]

Ac 18:28 *he* vigorously **r** the Jews in public debate, *1352*

REGAIN (5) [GAIN]

1Sa 29: 4 How better *could* he **r** his master's **favor** than 8354
1Ki 12:21 and to **r** the kingdom for Rehoboam son 8740
2Ch 11: 1 and to **r** the kingdom for Rehoboam. 8740
13:20 Jeroboam *did* not **r** power during 6388+6806
Job 9:18 He would not let me **r** my breath 8740

REGAINED (1) [GAIN]

Ac 9:19 *he* **r** his **strength.** *1932*

REGARD (50) [REGARDED, REGARDING, REGARDLESS, REGARDS]

Ge 31:15 *Does* he not **r** *us as* foreigners? 3108
Lev 5:15 a violation and sins unintentionally **in r to** 4946
5:16 for what he has failed to do **in r to** 4946
11:35 and you *are to* **r** them **as** unclean. 2118+4200
19:23 **r** its fruit **as forbidden.** 6887+6889
21: 8 **R** them **as holy,** 7727
Nu 18:10 You *must* **r** it **as** holy. 2118+4200
Dt 33: 9 *'I* **have** no **r for** them.' 8011
Jos 7: 1 But the Israelites acted unfaithfully **in r to** 928
1Sa 2:12 *they* **had** no **r for** the LORD. 3359
Ezr 7:14 about Judah and Jerusalem **with r to** 10089
Est 9:31 for themselves and their descendants in **r** NIH
Job 21:29 *Have you* **paid** no **r** *to* their accounts— 5795
34:27 from following him and **had** no **r for** any 8505
37:24 for *does he* not **have r for** all the wise 8011
Ps 28: 5 Since *they* **show** no **r** for the works of 1067
41: 1 Blessed is *he who* **has r for** the weak; 8505
54: 3 men without **r** *for* God. 4200+5584+8492
74:20 **Have r for** your covenant, 4200+5564
86:14 men without **r** *for* you. 4200+5584+8492
119:117 *I will* always **have r** for your decrees. 9120
Isa 5:12 *they* **have** no **r for** the deeds of the LORD, 5564
8:13 the one *you are to* **r as holy,** 7727
17: 8 and *they will* **have** no **r for** 8011
22:11 or **have r for** the One who made it, 8011
26:10 of uprightness they go on doing evil and **r** 8011
Jer 24: 5 *I* **r** as good the exiles from Judah, 5795
33:24 no longer **r** them *as* a nation. 2118+4200+7156
Eze 44: 8 Instead of carrying out your **duty** *in r* AIT
Da 11:37 *He will* **show** no **r** for the gods of his fathers 1067
11:37 nor *will he* **r** any god, 1067
Am 5:22 *I will* **have** no **r for** them. 5564
Jn 16: 8 he will convict the world of guilt **in r to** sin *4309*
16: 9 **in r to** sin, because men do not believe *4309*
16:10 **in r to** righteousness, because I am going *4309*
16:11 and **in r to** judgment, *4309*
1Co 4: 1 men *ought to* **r** us as servants of Christ and *3357*
14:20 *In r to* **evil** be infants, *AIT*
2Co 5:16 now on we **r** no one from a worldly point *3857*
Eph 4:22 **with r to** your former way of life, *2848*
Php 3: 5 **in r to** the law, a Pharisee; *2848*
Col 1:24 still lacking in **r** to Christ's afflictions *NIG*
2:16 or **with r to** a religious festival, *1877+3538*
1Th 5:13 Hold them *in* the **highest r** in love because *5655*
2Th 3:15 Yet *do* not **r** him as an enemy, *2451*
Heb 7:14 and **in r to** that tribe Moses said nothing *1650*
11:20 and Esau **in r to** their future. *4309*
1Pe 4: 6 according to men *in r to* the **body,** *AIT*
4: 6 but live according to God *in r to* the **spirit.** *AIT*
5:12 whom *I* **r** as a faithful brother, *3357*

REGARDED (19) [REGARD]

Ex 11: 3 Moses himself was **highly r** in Egypt 1524+4394
Dt 24:13 **r** as a righteous act **in the sight of** 4200+7156
2Sa 16:23 and Absalom **r** all of Ahithophel's advice. 4200
2Ki 5: 1 in the sight of his master and **highly r,** 5951+7156
2Ch 32:23 then on *he* **was highly r** by all the nations. 5951
Job 18: 3 Why **are** *we* **r** as cattle 3108
31:26 if *I have* **r** the sun in its radiance or 8011
Isa 40:15 *they* **are r** as dust on the scales; 3108
40:17 *they* **are r** by him as worthless 3108
Da 4:35 the peoples of the earth **are r** as nothing. 10285
Hos 8:12 but *they* **r** *them* as something alien. 3108
Mk 10:42 "You know that those who are **r** as rulers of *1506*
Ac 5:13 though they *were* **highly r** by the people. *3486*
Ro 2:26 not *be* **r** as though they were circumcised? *3357*
9: 8 the children of the promise who *are* **r** *3357*
2Co 5:16 Though *we once* **r** Christ in this way, *1182*
6: 8 genuine, yet **r as** impostors; *6055*
6: 9 yet **r as** unknown; *6055*
Heb 11:26 *He* **r** disgrace for the sake of Christ as *2451*

REGARDING (6) [REGARD]

Lev 5: 1 to testify **r** something he has seen NIH
Jos 22:20 acted unfaithfully **r** the devoted things 928
Eze 14:22 be consoled **r** the disaster I have brought 6584
44: 5 concerning all the **regulations** *r* the temple AIT
Ro 1: 3 **r** his Son, who as to his human nature was *4309*
4:20 not waver through unbelief **r** the promise *1650*

REGARDLESS (1) [REGARD]

2Ch 5:11 **r** of their divisions. 401+4200+9068

REGARDS (4) [REGARD]

Est 5: 8 If the king **r** *me with* favor and 928+5162+6524
8: 5 "and if he **r** *me with* favor and 4200+5162+7156
Ro 14: 6 He who **r** one day as special, *5858*
14:14 But if anyone **r** something as unclean, *3357*

REGEM (1)

1Ch 2:47 The sons of Jahdai: **R,** Jotham, Geshan, 8084

REGEM-MELECH (1)

Zec 7: 2 people of Bethel had sent Sharezer and **R,** 8085

REGENERATION (KJV) See REBIRTH

REGIMENT (2)

Ac 10: 1 in what was known as the Italian **R.** *5061*
27: 1 *who belonged to* the Imperial **R.** *5061*

REGION (61) [REGIONS]

Ge 10:30 The **r where** they **lived** stretched 4632
20: 1 on from there into the **r** *of* the Negev 824
22: 2 whom you love, and go to the **r** *of* Moriah. 824
35:22 While Israel was living in that **r,** 824
36:20 who were living in the **r:** 824
45:10 You shall live in the **r** *of* Goshen and be 824
46:28 When they arrived in the **r** *of* Goshen, 824
46:34 Then you will be allowed to settle in the **r** 824
47:13 the whole **r** because the famine was severe; 824
47:27 Now the Israelites settled in Egypt in the **r** 824
Dt 2:18 "Today you are to pass by the **r** *of* Moab 1473
3: 4 the whole **r** *of* Argob, 2475
3:13 (The whole **r** *of* Argob in Bashan used to 2475
3:14 the whole **r** *of* Argob as far as the border of 2475
34: 3 and the **whole r** *from* the Valley of Jericho, 3971
Jos 7: 2 and told them, "Go up and spy out the **r."** 824
10:40 So Joshua subdued the whole **r,** 824
10:41 and from the whole **r** *of* Goshen to Gibeon. 824
11: 3 and to the Hivites below Hermon in the **r** 824
11:16 all the Negev, the whole **r** *of* Goshen, 824
13: 4 the **r** *of* the Amorites, 1473
16: 3 the territory of the Japhletites as far as the **r** 1473
17:12 to live in that **r.** 824
17:29 and came out at the sea in the **r** *of* Aczib, 2475
Jdg 20: 6 into pieces and sent one piece to each **r** 8441
2Sa 20:14 and through the **entire** *r of* the Berites, AIT
24: 6 to Gilead and the **r** *of* Tahtim Hodshi, 824
2Ki 4:38 to Gilgal and there was a famine in that **r.** 824
10:33 of the Jordan in all the land of Gilead (the **r** NIH
1Ch 5:10 of the Hagrites throughout the entire **r** east 7156
Ne 3:22 by the priests from the **surrounding r.** 3971
12:28 also were brought together from the **r** 3971
Ps 78:12 in the **r** *of* Zoan. 8441
78:43 his wonders in the **r** *of* Zoan. 8441
Isa 49:12 some from the **r** *of* Aswan." 824
Eze 47: 8 toward the eastern **r** and goes down into 1666
Mt 3: 5 and all Judea and the whole **r** of the Jordan. *4369*
4:25 and the **r** across the Jordan followed him. *NIG*
8:28 When he arrived at the other side in the **r** of *6001*
8:34 they pleaded with him to leave their **r.** *3990*

Mt 9:26 News of this spread through all that **r**. *1178*
9:31 the news about him all over that **r**. *1178*
15:21 Jesus withdrew to the **r** of Tyre and Sidon. *3538*
16:13 to the **r** of Caesarea Philippi, *3538*
19:1 he left Galilee and went into the **r** of Judea *3990*
Mk 1:4 in the **desert r** and preaching a baptism *2245*
1:28 about him spread quickly over the whole **r** *4369*
5:1 across the lake to the **r** of the Gerasenes. *6001*
5:17 to plead with Jesus to leave their **r**. *3990*
6:55 throughout that whole **r** and carried the sick *6001*
7:31 down to the Sea of Galilee and into the **r** of *3990*
8:10 the boat with his disciples and went to the **r** *3538*
10:1 that place and went into the **r** of Judea and *3990*
Lk 4:26 to a widow in Zarephath in the **r** of Sidon. *NIG*
8:26 They sailed to the **r** of the Gerasenes, *6001*
8:37 *of* the **r** of the Gerasenes asked Jesus *4369*
Jn 11:54 Instead he withdrew to a **r** near the desert, *6001*
Ac 13:49 of the Lord spread through the whole **r**. *6001*
13:50 and expelled them from their **r**. *3990*
16:6 throughout the **r** of Phrygia and Galatia, *6001*
18:23 throughout the **r** of Galatia and Phrygia, *6001*

REGIONS (10) [REGION]

Ge 36:40 by name, according to their clans and **r**: 5226
Jos 13:2 all the **r** *of* the Philistines and Geshurites: 1666
13:6 for all the inhabitants of the **mountain r** 2215
Eze 19:8 those from **r** round about. 4519
Joel 3:4 and Sidon and all you **r** *of* Philistia? 1666
Mk 3:8 and the **r across** the Jordan and around Tyre *4305*
Ro 15:23 for me to work in these **r**, *3107*
2Co 10:16 so that we can preach the gospel in the **r** *NIG*
11:10 in the **r** of Achaia will stop this boasting *3107*
Eph 4:9 also descended to the lower, earthly **r**? *3538*

REGISTER (3) [REGISTERED, REGISTRATION]

Ps 87:6 LORD will write in the **r** *of* the peoples: 4180
Lk 2:3 And everyone went to his own town *to* **r**. *616*
2:5 He went there *to* **r** with Mary, *616*

REGISTERED (5) [REGISTER]

1Ch 9:22 They **were r by genealogy** in their villages. 3509
23:24 of families as they **were r** under their names 7212
Ezr 8:1 These are the family heads and *those* **r** 3509
8:3 Zechariah, and with him **were r** 150 men; 3509
8:20 All **were r** by name. 5918

REGISTRATION (1) [REGISTER]

Ne 7:5 and the common people for **r by families.** 3509

REGRET (4)

2Ch 21:20 He passed away, to no one's **r**, 2775
2Co 7:8 caused you sorrow by my letter, *I do* not **r** it *3564*
7:8 Though *I did* **r** it—I see that my letter hurt *3564*
7:10 that leads to salvation and leaves **no r**, *294*

REGROUPED (1) [GROUP]

2Sa 10:15 they had been routed by Israel, *they* **r**. 665+3480

REGULAR (55) [REGULARLY]

Ge 47:22 because they received a **r allotment** 2976
Ex 29:28 be the **r share** from the Israelites for Aaron 2976
Lev 6:18 It is his **r** share of the offerings made to 6409
6:20 an ephah of fine flour as a **r** grain offering, 9458
6:22 It is the LORD's **r** share and is to 6409
7:34 the priest and his sons as their **r** share from 6409
7:36 as their **r** share for the generations to come. 6409
10:15 be the **r** share for you and your children, 6409
14:32 and who cannot afford the **r** offerings NIH
15:19 a woman has her **r flow** *of* blood, 928+1414+2307
16:24 in a holy place and put on his **r** garments. NIH
23:7 a sacred assembly and do no **r work.** 4856+6275
23:8 a sacred assembly and do no **r work.'** 4856+6275
23:21 a sacred assembly and do no **r work.** 4856+6275
23:25 Do no **r work,** 4856+6275
23:35 do no **r work.** 4856+6275
23:36 the closing assembly; do no **r work.** 4856+6275
24:9 of their **r** share of the offerings made to 6409
Nu 4:16 the **r** grain offering and the anointing oil. 9458
8:25 their **r service** and work no longer. 6275+7372
18:8 and your sons as your portion and **r** share. 6409
18:11 and daughters as your **r** share. 6409
18:19 and daughters as your **r** share. 6409
28:3 as a **r** burnt offering each day. 9458
28:6 This is the **r** burnt offering instituted 9458
28:10 the **r** burnt offering and its drink offering. 9458
28:15 the **r** burnt offering with its drink offering, 9458
28:18 a sacred assembly and do no **r work.** 4856+6275
28:23 in addition to the **r** morning burnt offering. 9458
28:24 the **r** burnt offering and its drink offering. 9458
28:25 a sacred assembly and do no **r work.** 4856+6275
28:26 a sacred assembly and do no **r work.** 4856+6275
28:31 the **r** burnt offering and its grain offering. 9458
29:1 a sacred assembly and do no **r work.** 4856+6275
29:11 the **r** burnt offering with its grain offering, 9458
29:12 a sacred assembly and do no **r work.** 4856+6275
29:16 the **r** burnt offering with its grain offering 9458
29:19 the **r** burnt offering with its grain offering, 9458
29:22 the **r** burnt offering with its grain offering 9458
29:25 the **r** burnt offering with its grain offering 9458
29:28 the **r** burnt offering with its grain offering 9458
29:31 the **r** burnt offering with its grain offering 9458
Nu 29:34 the **r** burnt offering with its grain offering 9458
29:35 an assembly and do no **r work.** 4856+6275
29:38 the **r** burnt offering with its grain offering 9458
2Ki 25:30 the king gave Jehoiachin a **r** allowance 9458
2Ch 30:3 not been able to celebrate it at the **r** time 2085S
30:16 up their *r* **positions** as prescribed in the Law AIT
Ezr 3:5 they presented the **r** burnt offerings, 9458
Ne 10:33 the **r** grain offerings and burnt offerings; 9458
Job 1:5 This was Job's **r** custom. 2021+3427+3972
Jer 5:24 who assures us of the **r** weeks of harvest.' 2978
52:34 of Babylon gave Jehoiachin a **r** allowance 9458
Eze 41:17 and on the walls **at r intervals** all around 4500
46:15 by morning for a **r** burnt offering. 9458

REGULARLY (15) [REGULAR]

Ex 29:38 to offer on the altar **r** each day: 9458
29:42 this burnt offering is to be made **r** 9458
30:8 the lamps at twilight so incense will burn **r** 9458
Lev 24:8 to be set out before the LORD **r**, 9458
2Ki 25:29 the rest of his life ate **r** at the king's table. 9458
1Ch 16:6 to blow the trumpets **r** before the ark of 9458
16:37 of the LORD to minister there **r**, 9458
16:40 the LORD on the altar of burnt offering **r**, 9458
23:31 They were to serve before the LORD **r** in 9458
2Ch 2:4 for setting out the consecrated bread **r**, 9458
24:11 did this **r** and collected 928+3427+3427+4200
Jer 52:33 the rest of his life ate **r** at the king's table. 9458
Eze 39:14 " 'Men will be **r** employed to cleanse 9458
Ac 10:2 to those in need and prayed to God **r**. *1328+4246*
Heb 9:6 priests entered **r** into the outer room *1328+4246*

REGULATED (1) [REGULATION]

Ne 11:23 which **r** their daily activity. 591

REGULATION (3) [REGULATED, REGULATIONS]

Ne 8:18 in accordance with the **r**, 5477
Heb 7:16 not on the basis of a **r** as to his ancestry but *3795*
7:18 The former **r** is set aside *1953*

REGULATIONS (45) [REGULATION]

Ex 12:43 "These are the **r** *for* the Passover: 2978
Lev 6:9 'These are the **r** *for* the burnt offering: 9368
6:14 " 'These are the **r** *for* the grain offering: 9368
6:25 'These are the **r** *for* the sin offering: 9368
7:1 " 'These are the **r** *for* the guilt offering, 9368
7:11 the **r** *for* the fellowship offering 9368
7:37 These, then, are the **r** for the burnt offering, 9368
11:46 " 'These are the **r** *concerning* animals, 9368
12:7 the **r** *for* the woman who gives birth to 9368
13:59 the **r** *concerning* contamination by mildew 9368
14:2 "These are the **r** *for* the diseased person at 9368
14:32 These are the **r** *for* anyone who has 9368
14:54 the **r** for any infectious skin disease, 9368
14:57 These are the **r** *for* infectious skin diseases 9368
15:32 These are the **r** *for* a man with a discharge, 9368
26:46 and the **r** that the LORD established 9368
Nu 9:3 in accordance with all its rules and **r**." 5477
9:12 they must follow all the **r**. 2978
9:14 so in accordance with its rules and **r**. 5477
9:14 You must have the same **r** for the alien and 2978
15:16 The same laws and **r** will apply both to you 5477
30:16 These are the **r** the LORD gave Moses 2976
35:24 the avenger of blood according to these **r**. 5477
36:13 and **r** the LORD gave through Moses to 5477
Dt 12:28 to obey all these **r** I am giving you, 1821
1Sa 10:25 Samuel explained to the people the **r** *of* 5477
1Ki 6:12 carry out my **r** and keep all my commands 5477
8:58 decrees and **r** he gave our fathers. 5477
2Ki 23:3 and keep his commands, **r** and decrees 6343
1Ch 6:32 according to the **r** *laid down* for them. 5477
24:19 according to the **r prescribed** *for* them 5477
2Ch 34:31 and keep his commands, **r** and decrees 6343
Ne 9:13 You gave them **r** and laws that are just 5477
10:29 **r** and decrees of the LORD our Lord. 5477
Est 9:32 Esther's decree confirmed these **r** 1821
Eze 43:11 its whole design and all its **r** and laws. 2978
43:11 be faithful to its design and follow all its **r**. 2978
43:18 be the **r** *for* sacrificing burnt offerings 2978
44:5 concerning all the **r** *regarding* the temple of 2978
Lk 1:6 observing all the Lord's commandments and **r** blamelessly. *1468*
Eph 2:15 the law with its commandments and **r**. *1504*
Col 2:14 *with* its **r**, that was against us and *1504*
2:23 **Such r** indeed have an appearance *4015S*
Heb 9:1 Now the first covenant had **r** for worship *1468*
9:10 external **r** applying until the time of *1468*

REHABIAH (4)

1Ch 23:17 The descendants of Eliezer: **R** was the first. 8152
23:17 but the sons of **R** were very numerous. 8152
24:21 for **R**, from his sons: Isshiah was the first. 8153
26:25 **R** his son, Jeshaiah his son, Joram his son, 8153

REHEARSE (KJV) See RECITE

REHOB (10) [BETH REHOB]

Nu 13:21 the land from the Desert of Zin as far as **R**, 8149
Jos 19:28 It went to Abdon, **R**, Hammon and Kanah, 8149
19:30 Ummah, Aphek and **R**. 8149
21:31 and **R**, together with their pasturelands— 8149
Jdg 1:31 or Aczib or Helbah or Aphek or **R**, 8149
2Sa 8:3 David fought Hadadezer son of **R**, 8150
8:12 the plunder taken from Hadadezer son of **R**, 8150
10:8 the Arameans of Zobah and **R** and the men 8149
1Ch 6:75 and **R**, together with their pasturelands; 8149
Ne 10:11 Mica, **R**, Hashabiah, 8150

REHOBOAM (50) [REHOBOAM'S]

1Ki 11:43 And **R** his son succeeded him as king. 8154
12:1 **R** went to Shechem, 8154
12:3 and the whole assembly of Israel went to **R** 8154
12:5 **R** answered, "Go away for three days and NIH
12:6 Then King **R** consulted the elders 8154
12:8 But **R** rejected the advice the elders gave NIH
12:12 and all the people returned to **R**, 8154
12:17 **R** still ruled over them. 8154
12:18 King **R** sent out Adoniram, 8154
12:18 King **R**, however, managed to get into 8154
12:21 When **R** arrived in Jerusalem, 8154
12:21 and to regain the kingdom for **R** son 8154
12:23 "Say to **R** son of Solomon king of Judah, 8154
12:27 **R** king of Judah. 8154
12:27 They will kill me and return to King **R**." 8154
14:21 **R** son of Solomon was king in Judah. 8154
14:25 In the fifth year of King **R**, 8154
14:27 So King **R** made bronze shields 8154
14:30 There was continual warfare between **R** 8154
14:31 And **R** rested with his fathers 8154
15:6 There was war between **R** and Jeroboam 8154
1Ch 3:10 Solomon's son was **R**, Abijah his son, 8154
2Ch 9:31 And **R** his son succeeded him as king. 8154
10:1 **R** went to Shechem, 8154
10:3 he and all Israel went to **R** and said to him: 8154
10:5 **R** answered, "Come back to me NIH
10:6 Then King **R** consulted the elders 8154
10:8 But **R** rejected the advice the elders gave NIH
10:12 and all the people returned to **R**, 8154
10:17 **R** still ruled over them. 8154
10:18 King **R** sent out Adoniram, 8154
10:18 King **R**, however, managed to get into 8154
11:1 When **R** arrived in Jerusalem, 8154
11:1 and to regain the kingdom for **R**. 8154
11:3 "Say to **R** son of Solomon king of Judah 8154
11:5 **R** lived in Jerusalem and built up towns 8154
11:17 the kingdom of Judah and supported **R** son 8154
11:18 **R** married Mahalath, who was the daughter 8154
11:21 **R** loved Maacah daughter of Absalom 8154
11:22 **R** appointed Abijah son of Maacah to be 8154
12:2 in the fifth year of King **R**. 8154
12:5 Then the prophet Shemaiah came to **R** and 8154
12:10 So King **R** made bronze shields 8154
12:12 Because **R** humbled himself, 2257S
12:13 King **R** established himself firmly 8154
12:15 There was continual warfare between **R** 8154
12:16 **R** rested with his fathers and was buried in 8154
13:7 around him and opposed **R** son of Solomon 8154
Mt 1:7 Solomon the father of **R**, *4850*
1:7 **R** the father of Abijah, *4850*

REHOBOAM'S (3) [REHOBOAM]

1Ki 14:29 As for the other events of **R** reign, 8154
2Ch 12:1 After **R** position as king was established 8154
12:15 As for the events of **R** reign, 8154

REHOBOTH (3) [REHOBOTH IR]

Ge 26:22 He named it **R**, saying, 8151
36:37 from **R** *on* the river succeeded him as king. 8151
1Ch 1:48 from **R** *on* the river succeeded him as king. 8151

REHOBOTH IR (1) [REHOBOTH]

Ge 10:11 where he built Nineveh, **R**, Calah 8155

REHUM (8)

Ezr 2:2 Bilshan, Mispar, Bigvai, **R** and Baanah): 8156
4:8 **R** the commanding officer and Shimshai 10662
4:9 **R** the commanding officer and Shimshai 10662
4:17 To **R** the commanding officer, 10662
4:23 the letter of King Artaxerxes was read to **R** 10662
Ne 3:17 by the Levites under **R** son of Bani. 8156
10:25 **R**, Hashabnah, Maaseiah, 8156
12:3 Shecaniah, **R**, Meremoth, 8156

REI (1)

1Ki 1:8 Shimei and **R** and David's special guard did 8298

REIGN (154) [REIGNED, REIGNING, REIGNS]

Ge 37:8 *"Do you* **intend to r** over us? 4887+4887
Ex 15:18 The LORD *will* **r** for ever and ever." 4887
Dt 17:20 he and his descendants **r** a long time **over** 6584
32:25 in their homes terror will **r**. NIH
1Sa 8:9 the king who *will* **r** over them will do." 4887
8:11 the king who *will* **r** over you will do: 4887
11:12 *'Shall* Saul **r** over us?' 4887
2Sa 21:1 During the **r** *of* David, 3427
1Ki 1:35 and sit on my throne and **r** in my place. 4887
6:1 the fourth year of Solomon's **r** over Israel, 4887
11:41 As for the other events of Solomon's **r**— NIH
14:19 The other events of Jeroboam's **r**, NIH
14:29 As for the other events of Rehoboam's **r**, NIH
15:1 of the **r** *of* Jeroboam son of Nebat, 4889
15:7 As for the other events of Abijah's **r**, NIH
15:23 As for all the other events of Asa's **r**, NIH

1Ki 15:29 As soon as he *began to* **r**, 4887
15:31 As for the other events of Nadab's **r**, NIH
16: 5 As for the other events of Baasha's **r**, NIH
16:11 As soon as he *began to* **r** and was seated on 4887
16:14 As for the other events of Elah's **r**, NIH
16:20 As for the other events of Zimri's **r**, NIH
16:27 As for the other events of Omri's **r**, NIH
22:39 As for the other events of Ahab's **r**, NIH
22:45 As for the other events of Jehoshaphat's **r**, NIH
22:46 even after the **r** *of* his father Asa. 3427
2Ki 1:18 As for all the other events of Ahaziah's **r**, NIH
8:16 Jehoram son of Jehoshaphat *began his* **r** 4887
8:23 As for the other events of Jehoram's **r**, NIH
8:25 of Jehoram king of Judah *began to* **r**. 4887
10:34 As for the other events of Jehu's **r**, NIH
11:21 when he *began to* **r**. 4887
12:19 As for the other events of the **r** of Joash, NIH
13: 8 As for the other events of the **r** of Jehoahaz, NIH
13:12 As for the other events of the **r** of Jehoash, NIH
13:22 of Aram oppressed Israel throughout the **r** 3427
14: 1 of Joash king of Judah *began to* **r**. 4887
14:15 As for the other events of the **r** of Jehoash, NIH
14:18 As for the other events of Amaziah's **r**, NIH
14:28 As for the other events of Jeroboam's **r**, NIH
15: 1 of Amaziah king of Judah *began to* **r**. 4887
15: 6 As for the other events of Azariah's **r**, NIH
15:11 of Zechariah's **r** are written in the book of NIH
15:15 The other events of Shallum's **r**, NIH
15:18 *During* his entire **r** he did not turn away 3427
15:21 As for the other events of Menahem's **r**, NIH
15:26 The other events of Pekahiah's **r**, NIH
15:31 As for the other events of Pekah's **r**, NIH
15:32 of Uzziah king of Judah *began to* **r**. 4887
15:36 As for the other events of Jotham's **r**, NIH
16: 1 of Jotham king of Judah *began to* **r**. 4887
16:19 As for the other events of the **r** of Ahaz, NIH
18: 1 of Ahaz king of Judah *began to* **r**. 4887
18:13 the fourteenth year of King Hezekiah's **r**, NIH
20:20 As for the other events of Hezekiah's **r**, NIH
21:17 As for the other events of Manasseh's **r**, NIH
21:25 As for the other events of Amon's **r**, NIH
22: 3 In the eighteenth year of his **r**, 4889
23:28 As for the other events of Josiah's **r**, NIH
23:33 in the land of Hamath so that he *might* not **r** 4887
24: 1 During Jehoiakim's **r**, 3427
24: 5 As for the other events of Jehoiakim's **r**, NIH
24:12 In the eighth year of the **r** of the king 4887
25: 1 So in the ninth year of Zedekiah's **r**, 4887
1Ch 4:31 These were their towns until the **r** 4887
5:10 During Saul's **r** they waged war against 3427
7: 2 During the **r** *of* David, 3427
13: 3 for we did not inquire of it during the **r** 3427
22: 9 and quiet during his **r**. 3427
26:31 fortieth year of David's **r** a search was made 4895
29:29 As for the events of King David's **r**, NIH
29:30 together with the details of his **r** and power, 4895
2Ch 3: 2 in the fourth year of his **r**. 4895
9:29 As for the other events of Solomon's **r**, NIH
12:15 As for the events of Rehoboam's **r**, NIH
13: 1 In the eighteenth year of the **r** *of* Jeroboam, 4889
13:22 The other events of Abijah's **r**, NIH
15:10 of the fifteenth year of Asa's **r**. 4895
15:19 until the thirty-fifth year of Asa's **r**. 4895
16: 1 the thirty-sixth year of Asa's **r** Baasha king 4895
16:11 The events of Asa's **r**, NIH
16:12 of his **r** Asa was afflicted with a disease 4895
16:13 in the forty-first year of his **r** Asa died 4887
17: 7 of his **r** he sent his officials Ben-Hail, 4887
20:34 The other events of Jehoshaphat's **r**, NIH
22: 1 of Jehoram king of Judah *began to* **r**. 4887
23: 3 "The king's son *shall* **r**, 4887
25:26 As for the other events of Amaziah's **r**, NIH
26:22 The other events of Uzziah's **r**, NIH
27: 7 The other events in Jotham's **r**, NIH
28:26 The other events of his **r** and all his ways, NIH
29: 3 In the first month of the first year of his **r**, 4887
32:32 The other events of Hezekiah's **r** NIH
33:18 The other events of Manasseh's **r**, NIH
34: 3 In the eighth year of his **r**, 4887
34: 8 In the eighteenth year of Josiah's **r**, 4887
35:19 in the eighteenth year of Josiah's **r**. 4895
35:26 The other events of Josiah's **r** and his acts NIH
36: 8 The other events of Jehoiakim's **r**, NIH
Ezr 4: 5 and frustrate their plans during the entire **r** 3427
4: 5 and down to the **r** *of* Darius king of Persia. 4895
4: 6 At the beginning of the **r** *of* Xerxes, 4895
4:24 to a standstill until the second year of the **r** 10424
6:15 in the sixth year of the **r** *of* King Darius. 10424
7: 1 during the **r** *of* Artaxerxes king of Persia, 4895
8: 1 up with me from Babylon during the **r** 4895
Ne 12:22 were recorded in the **r** *of* Darius 4895
Est 1: 3 of his **r** he gave a banquet for all his nobles 4887
2:16 in the seventh year of his **r**. 4895
6: 1 the chronicles, the record of his **r**, 3427
Ps 68:16 at the mountain where God chooses to **r**, 3782
Pr 8:15 By me kings **r** and rulers make laws 4887
Isa 9: 7 He will **r** on David's throne and NIH
24:23 the LORD Almighty *will* **r** on Mount Zion 4887
32: 1 a king *will* **r** in righteousness 4887
36: 1 the fourteenth year of King Hezekiah's **r**, NIH
Jer 1: 2 the **r** *of* Josiah son of Amon king of Judah, 4887
1: 3 the **r** *of* Jehoiakim son of Josiah king 3427
3: 6 During the **r** *of* King Josiah, 3427
23: 5 a King *who will* **r** wisely 4887
26: 1 in the **r** *of* Jehoiakim son of Josiah king 4931
27: 1 in the **r** *of* Zedekiah son of Josiah king 4930
28: 1 early in the **r** *of* Zedekiah king of Judah, 4930
Jer 33:21 a descendant *to* **r** on his throne. 4887
35: 1 the LORD during the **r** *of* Jehoiakim son 3427
36: 2 the time I began speaking to you in the **r** 3427
49:34 early in the **r** *of* Zedekiah king of Judah: 4895
51:59 of Judah in the fourth year of his **r**. 4887
52: 4 So in the ninth year of Zedekiah's **r**, 4887
La 5:19 You, O LORD, **r** forever; 3782
Da 1: 1 In the third year of the **r** *of* Jehoiakim king 4895
2: 1 In the second year of his **r**, 4895
5:26 the days of your **r** and brought it to an end. 10424
6:28 So Daniel prospered during the **r** *of* Darius 10424
6:28 of Darius and the **r** *of* Cyrus the Persian. 10424
8: 1 In the third year of King Belshazzar's **r**, I, 4895
8:23 "In the latter part of their **r**, 4895
9: 2 in the first year of his **r**, 4887
Hos 1: 1 the **r** *of* Jeroboam son of Jehoash king 3427
Am 6: 3 You put off the evil day and bring near a **r** 8699
Zep 1: 1 the **r** *of* Josiah son of Amon king of Judah: 3427
Lk 1:33 *he will* **r** over the house of Jacob forever; *996*
3: 1 fifteenth year *of* the **r** of Tiberius Caesar— *2449*
Ac 11:28 (This happened during the **r** of Claudius.) *NIG*
Ro 5:17 of the gift of righteousness **r** in life through *996*
5:21 so also grace *might* **r** through righteousness *996*
6:12 not *let* sin **r** in your mortal body so *996*
1Co 15:25 For he must **r** until he has put all his enemies *996*
2Ti 2:12 if we endure, *we will* also **r with** him. *5203*
Rev 5:10 and *they will* **r** on the earth." *996*
11:15 and *he will* **r** for ever and ever." *996*
11:17 your great power and *have begun to* **r**. *996*
20: 6 be priests of God and of Christ and *will* **r** *996*
22: 5 And *they will* **r** for ever and ever. *996*

REIGNED (94) [REIGN]

Ge 36:31 These were the kings who **r** in Edom 4887
36:31 in Edom before any Israelite king **r**: 4887
Nu 21:34 who **r** in Heshbon." 3782
Dt 1: 4 who **r** in Heshbon, 3782
1: 4 who **r** in Ashtaroth. 3782
3: 2 who **r** in Heshbon." 3782
4:46 who **r** in Heshbon and was defeated 3782
Jos 9:10 of Heshbon, and Og king of Bashan, who **r** NIH
12: 2 who **r** in Heshbon. 3782
12: 4 who **r** in Ashtaroth and Edrei. 3782
13:12 who *had* **r** in Ashtaroth and Edrei 4887
Jdg 4: 2 a king of Canaan, who **r** in Hazor. 4887
1Sa 13: 1 and *he* **r** over Israel [forty-]two years. 4887
2Sa 2:10 and *he* **r** two years. 4887
5: 4 and *he* **r** forty years. 4887
5: 5 In Hebron *he* **r** over Judah seven years 4887
5: 5 and in Jerusalem *he* **r** over all Israel 4887
8:15 David **r** over all Israel, 4887
16: 8 in whose place *you have* **r**. 4887
1Ki 2:11 He *had* **r** forty years over Israel— 4887
11:42 Solomon **r** in Jerusalem 4887
14:20 He **r** for twenty-two years and then rested 4887
14:21 and *he* **r** seventeen years in Jerusalem, 4887
15: 2 and *he* **r** in Jerusalem three years. 4887
15:10 and *he* **r** in Jerusalem forty-one years. 4887
15:25 and *he* **r** over Israel two years. 4887
15:33 and he **r** twenty-four years. NIH
16: 8 and he **r** in Tirzah two years. NIH
16:15 Zimri **r** in Tirzah seven days. 4887
16:23 and *he* **r** twelve years, six of them in Tirzah. 4887
16:29 and he **r** in Samaria 4887
22:42 and *he* **r** in Jerusalem twenty-five years. 4887
22:51 and *he* **r** over Israel two years. 4887
2Ki 3: 1 and *he* **r** twelve years. 4887
8:17 and *he* **r** in Jerusalem eight years. 4887
8:26 and *he* **r** in Jerusalem one year. 4887
10:36 The time that Jehu **r** over Israel 4887
12: 1 and *he* **r** in Jerusalem forty years. 4887
13: 1 and *he* **r** seventeen years. 4887
13:10 and he **r** sixteen years. NIH
14: 2 and *he* **r** in Jerusalem twenty-nine years. 4887
14:23 and he **r** forty-one years. NIH
15: 2 and *he* **r** in Jerusalem fifty-two years. 4887
15: 8 and he **r** six months. NIH
15:13 and *he* **r** in Samaria one month. 4887
15:17 and he **r** in Samaria ten years. NIH
15:23 and he **r** two years. NIH
15:27 and he **r** twenty years. NIH
15:33 and *he* **r** in Jerusalem sixteen years. 4887
16: 2 and *he* **r** in Jerusalem sixteen years. 4887
17: 1 and he **r** nine years. NIH
18: 2 and *he* **r** in Jerusalem twenty-nine years. 4887
21: 1 and *he* **r** in Jerusalem fifty-five years. 4887
21:19 and *he* **r** in Jerusalem two years. 4887
22: 1 and *he* **r** in Jerusalem thirty-one years. 4887
23:31 and *he* **r** in Jerusalem three months. 4887
23:36 and *he* **r** in Jerusalem eleven years. 4887
24: 8 and *he* **r** in Jerusalem three months. 4887
24:18 and *he* **r** in Jerusalem eleven years. 4887
1Ch 1:43 These were the kings who **r** in Edom 4887
1:43 in Edom before any Israelite king **r**: 4887
3: 4 where *he* **r** seven years and six months. 4887
3: 4 David **r** in Jerusalem thirty-three years, 4887
18:14 David **r** over all Israel, 4887
2Ch 1:13 And *he* **r** over Israel. 4887
9:30 Solomon **r** in Jerusalem 4887
12:13 and *he* **r** seventeen years in Jerusalem, 4887
13: 2 and *he* **r** in Jerusalem three years. 4887
20:31 So Jehoshaphat **r** over Judah. 4887
20:31 and *he* **r** in Jerusalem twenty-five years. 4887
21: 5 and *he* **r** in Jerusalem eight years. 4887
21:20 and *he* **r** in Jerusalem eight years. 4887
22: 2 and *he* **r** in Jerusalem one year. 4887
2Ch 24: 1 and *he* **r** in Jerusalem forty years. 4887
25: 1 and *he* **r** in Jerusalem twenty-nine years. 4887
26: 3 and *he* **r** in Jerusalem fifty-two years. 4887
27: 1 and *he* **r** in Jerusalem sixteen years. 4887
27: 8 and *he* **r** in Jerusalem sixteen years. 4887
28: 1 and *he* **r** in Jerusalem sixteen years. 4887
29: 1 and *he* **r** in Jerusalem twenty-nine years. 4887
33: 1 and *he* **r** in Jerusalem fifty-five years. 4887
33:21 and *he* **r** in Jerusalem two years. 4887
34: 1 and *he* **r** in Jerusalem thirty-one years. 4887
36: 2 and *he* **r** in Jerusalem three months. 4887
36: 5 and *he* **r** in Jerusalem eleven years. 4887
36: 9 and *he* **r** in Jerusalem three months 4887
36:11 and *he* **r** in Jerusalem eleven years. 4887
Est 1: 2 At that time King Xerxes **r** from his royal 3782
Jer 37: 1 *he* **r** in place of Jehoiachin son 4887+4889
52: 1 and *he* **r** in Jerusalem eleven years. 4887
Ro 5:14 death **r** from the time of Adam to the time *996*
5:17 death **r** through that one man, *996*
5:21 just as sin **r** in death, *996*
Rev 20: 4 to life and **r** with Christ a thousand years. *996*

REIGNING (1) [REIGN]

Mt 2:22 But when he heard that Archelaus *was* **r** *996*

REIGNS (18) [REIGN]

1Sa 12:14 and the king who **r** over you follow 4887
1Ki 15:16 king of Israel throughout their **r**. 3427
15:32 king of Israel throughout their **r**. 3427
1Ch 5:17 in the genealogical records during the **r** 3427
16:31 among the nations, "The LORD **r!**" 4887
Ps 9: 7 The LORD **r** forever; 3782
47: 8 God **r** over the nations; 4887
93: 1 The LORD **r**, he is robed in majesty; 4887
96:10 Say among the nations, "The LORD **r**." 4887
97: 1 The LORD **r**, let the earth be glad; 4887
99: 1 The LORD **r**, let the nations tremble; 4887
146:10 The LORD **r** forever, your God, O Zion, 4887
Isa 1: 1 that Isaiah son of Amoz saw during the **r** 3427
52: 7 who say to Zion, "Your God **r!**" 4887
Hos 1: 1 during the **r** *of* Uzziah, Jotham, Ahaz 3427
Mic 1: 1 of Moresheth during the **r** *of* Jotham, Ahaz 3427
Lk 22:53 But this is your hour—when darkness **r**." *2026*
Rev 19: 6 For our Lord God Almighty **r**. *996*

REIMBURSE (1)

Lk 10:35 I *will* **r** you for any extra expense *625*

REIN (2)

Job 10: 1 therefore *I will* **give free r** to my complaint 6440
Jas 1:26 **keep a tight r on** his tongue, *5902*

REINFORCE (1) [REINFORCED, REINFORCEMENTS]

Jer 51:12 **R** the guard, station the watchmen, 2616

REINFORCED (2) [REINFORCE]

2Ch 24:13 according to its original design and **r** it. 599
32: 5 He built another wall outside that one and **r** 2616

REINFORCEMENTS (1) [REINFORCE]

Isa 43:17 the army and **r** together, and they lay there, 6450

REJECT (32) [REJECTED, REJECTING, REJECTION, REJECTS]

Lev 26:15 and if you **r** my decrees and abhor my laws 4415
26:44 *I will* not **r** them or abhor them so as 4415
1Sa 12:22 the LORD *will* not **r** his people, 5759
1Ki 9: 7 and *will* **r** this temple I have consecrated 4946+6584+7156+8938
2Ki 23:27 and *I will* **r** Jerusalem, the city I chose, 4415
1Ch 28: 9 if you forsake him, *he will* **r** you forever. 2396
2Ch 6:42 LORD God, *do* not **r** your anointed one. 7156+8740
7:20 and *will* **r** this temple I have consecrated 4946+6584+7156+8959
Job 8:20 "Surely God *does* not **r** a blameless man 4415
Ps 27: 9 *Do* not **r** me or forsake me, 5759
36: 4 and *does* not **r** what is wrong. 4415
44:23 *Do* not **r** us forever. 2396
77: 7 "*Will* the Lord **r** forever? 2396
88:14 *do you* **r** me and hide your face from me? 2396
94:14 For the LORD *will* not **r** his people; 5759
119:118 *You* **r** all who stray from your decrees, 6136
132:10 *do* not **r** your anointed one. 7156+8740
Isa 7:15 and honey when he knows enough *to* **r** 4415
7:16 But before the boy knows enough *to* **r** 4415
31: 7 that day every one of *you will* **r** the idols 4415
Jer 31:37 be searched out *will* **I r** all the descendants 4415
33:26 then *I will* **r** the descendants of Jacob 4415
Hos 4: 6 *I* also **r** you as my priests; 4415
9:17 My God *will* **r** them because they have 4415
Lk 6:22 and insult you and **r** your name as evil, *1675*
Ac 13:46 Since *you* **r** it and do not consider yourselves *723*
Ro 2: 8 who are self-seeking and who **r** the truth *578*
11: 1 I ask then: *Did* God **r** his people? *723*
11: 2 God *did* not **r** his people, *723*
1Th 4: 8 this instruction *does* not **r** man but God, *119*
Tit 1:14 to the commands of those **who r** the truth. *695*
Jude 1: 8 **r** authority and slander celestial beings. *119*

REJECTED (79) [REJECT]

Lev 26:43 for their sins because they r my laws 4415
Nu 11:20 because you have r the LORD, 4415
14:31 in to enjoy the land you have r. 4415
Dt 32:15 the God who made him and r 5571
32:19 and r them because he was angered 5540
1Sa 8: 7 it is not you they have r, 4415
8: 7 but they have r me as their king. 4415
10:19 But you have now r your God, 4415
15:23 you have r the word of the LORD, 4415
15:23 he has r you as king." 4415
15:26 You have r the word of the LORD, 4415
15:26 the LORD has r you as king over Israel!" 4415
16: 1 since I have r him as king over Israel? 4415
16: 7 for I have r him. 4415
1Ki 12: 8 But Rehoboam r the advice 6440
19:10 The Israelites have r your covenant, 6440
19:14 The Israelites have r your covenant, 6440
2Ki 17:15 They r his decrees and the covenant 4415
17:20 the LORD r all the people of Israel; 4415
2Ch 10: 8 But Rehoboam r the advice the elders gave 6440
11:14 because Jeroboam and his sons had r them 2396
Ps 43: 2 Why have you r me? 2396
44: 9 But now you have r and humbled us; 2396
60: 1 You have r us, O God, 2396
60:10 you who have r us and no longer go out 2396
66:20 not r my prayer or withheld his love 6073
74: 1 Why have you r us forever, O God? 2396
78:59 he r Israel completely. 4415
78:67 Then he r the tents of Joseph, 4415
89:38 But you have r, you have spurned, 2396
108:11 you who have r us and no longer go out 2396
118:22 the builders r has become the capstone; 4415
Pr 1:24 But since you r me when I called 4412
Isa 5:24 for they have r the law of the LORD 4415
8: 6 "Because this people has r the gently 4415
14:19 of your tomb like a r branch; 9493
30:12 "Because you have r this message, 4415
41: 9 I have chosen you and have not r you. 4415
49:21 I was exiled and r. 6073
53: 3 He was despised and r by men, 2534
54: 6 a wife who married young, only to be r," 4415
Jer 2:37 for the LORD has r those you trust; 4415
6:19 to my words and have r my law. 4415
6:30 They are called r silver, 4415
6:30 because the LORD has r them." 4415
7:29 on the barren heights, for the LORD has r 4415
8: 9 Since they have r the word of the LORD, 4415
14:19 Have you r Judah completely? 4415+4415
15: 6 You have r me," declares the LORD. 5759
33:24 'The LORD has r the two kingdoms 4415
La 1:15 Lord has r all the warriors in my midst; 6136
2: 7 The Lord has r his altar 2396
5:22 unless you have utterly r us 4415+4415
Eze 5: 6 She has r my laws and has 4415
20:13 not follow my decrees but r my laws— 4415
20:16 because they r my laws and did 4415
20:24 not obeyed my laws but had r my decrees 4415
Hos 4: 6 "Because you have r knowledge, 4415
8: 3 But Israel has r what is good; 2396
Am 2: 4 Because they have r the law of the LORD 4415
Zec 10: 6 They will be as though I had not r them, 2396
Mt 21:42 the builders r has become the capstone; 627
Mk 8:31 of Man must suffer many things and be r 627
9:12 of Man must suffer much and be r? 2022
12:10 the builders r has become the capstone; 627
Lk 7:30 in the law r God's purpose for themselves, 119
9:22 of Man must suffer many things and be r 627
17:25 and be r by this generation. 627
20:17 the builders r has become the capstone'? 627
Ac 4:11 He is " 'the stone you builders r, 2024
7:35 "This is the same Moses whom they had r 766
7:39 they r him and in their hearts turned back 723
1Ti 1:19 Some have r these and 723
4: 4 to be r if it is received with thanksgiving, 612
2Ti 3: 8 who, as far as the faith is concerned, are r. 99
Heb 10:28 Anyone who r the law of Moses died 119
12:17 to inherit this blessing, he was r. 627
1Pe 2: 4 r by men but chosen by God and precious 627
2: 7 the builders r has become the capstone," 627

REJECTING (3) [REJECT]

Dt 31:20 r me and breaking my covenant. 5540
1Ki 12:13 R the advice given him by the elders, 6440
2Ch 10:13 R the advice of the elders, 6440

REJECTION (1) [REJECT]

Ro 11:15 if their r is the reconciliation of the world, 613

REJECTS (8) [REJECT]

Isa 33:15 who r gain from extortion 4415
Lk 10:16 he who r you rejects me; 119
10:16 he who rejects you r me; 119
10:16 but he who r me rejects him who sent me." 119
10:16 but he who rejects me r him who sent me." 119
Jn 3:36 but whoever r the Son will not see life, 578
12:48 a judge for the one who r me and does 119
1Th 4: 8 he who r this instruction does 119

REJOICE (133) [JOY]

Lev 23:40 and r before the LORD your God 8523
Dt 12: 7 you and your families shall eat and shall r 8523
12:12 And there r before the LORD your God, 8523
12:18 to r before the LORD your God 8523
14:26 the presence of the LORD your God and r. 8523
16:11 And r before the LORD your God at 8523
26:11 among you shall r in all the good things 8523
32:43 R, O nations, with his people, 8264
33:18 "R, Zebulun, in your going out, and you, 8523
2Sa 1:20 lest the daughters of the uncircumcised r. 6600
1Ch 16:10 the hearts of those who seek the LORD r. 8523
16:31 Let the heavens r, let the earth be glad; 8523
2Ch 6:41 may your saints r in your goodness. 8523
20:27 given them cause to r over their enemies. 8523
Job 3:22 with gladness and r when they reach 8464
22:19 "The righteous see their ruin and r; 8523
Ps 2:11 the LORD with fear and r with trembling. 1635
5:11 those who love your name may r in you. 6636
9: 2 I will be glad and r in you; 6636
9:14 of Zion and there r in your salvation. 1635
13: 4 and my foes will r when I fall. 1635
14: 7 let Jacob r and Israel be glad! 1635
31: 7 I will be glad and r in your love, 8523
32:11 R in the LORD and be glad, you righteous; 8523
33:21 In him our hearts r, 8523
34: 2 let the afflicted hear and r. 8523
35: 9 Then my soul will r in the LORD 1635
39:13 that I may r again before I depart 1158
40:16 may all who seek you r and be glad in you; 8464
51: 8 let the bones you have crushed r. 1635
53: 6 let Jacob r and Israel be glad! 1635
63:11 But the king will r in God; 8523
64:10 Let the righteous r in the LORD 8523
66: 6 come, let us r in him. 8523
68: 3 the righteous be glad and r before God; 6636
68: 4 and r before him. 6600
70: 4 may all who seek you r and be glad in you; 8464
85: 6 that your people may r in you? 8523
89:16 They r in your name all day long; 1635
89:42 made all his enemies r. 8523
96:11 Let the heavens r, let the earth be glad; 8523
97: 1 let the distant shores r. 1635
97:12 R in the LORD, you who are righteous, 8523
104:31 may the LORD r in his works— 8523
104:34 as I r in the LORD. 8523
105: 3 the hearts of those who seek the LORD r. 8523
107:42 The upright see and r, 8523
109:28 but your servant will r. 8523
118:24 let us r and be glad in it. 1635
119:14 I r in following your statutes 8464
119:74 May those who fear you r 8523
119:162 I r in your promise 8464
149: 2 Let Israel r in their Maker; 8523
149: 5 the saints r in this honor and sing for joy 6600
Pr 2:14 in doing wrong and r in the perverseness 1635
5:18 and may you r in the wife of your youth. 8523
23:16 my inmost being will r 6600
23:25 may she who gave you birth r! 1635
24:17 when he stumbles, do not let your heart r, 1635
29: 2 When the righteous thrive, the people r; 8523
SS 1: 4 We r and delight in you; 1635
Isa 9: 3 they r before you as people rejoice at 8523
9: 3 they rejoice before you as people r at 8525
9: 3 as men r when dividing the plunder. 1635
13: 3 those who r in my triumph. 6611
14:29 Do not r, all you Philistines, that the rod 8523
25: 9 let us r and be glad in his salvation." 1635
29:19 the humble will r in the LORD; 8525
29:19 the needy will r in the Holy One of Israel. 1635
30:29 your hearts will r as when people go up 8525
35: 1 the wilderness will r and blossom. 1635
35: 2 it will r greatly and shout for joy. 677+1635+1638
41:16 But you will r in the LORD and glory in 1635
42:11 let the settlements where Kedar lives r. NIH
49:13 r, O earth; burst into song, O mountains! 1635
61: 7 and instead of disgrace they will r 8264
62: 5 so will your God r over you. 8464
65:13 my servants will r, 8523
65:18 be glad and r forever in what I will create, 1635
65:19 I will r over Jerusalem and take delight 1635
66:10 "R with Jerusalem and be glad for her, 8523
66:10 r greatly with her, 5375+8464
66:14 your heart will r and you will flourish 8464
Jer 11:15 in your wickedness, then you r." 6600
31:12 they will r in the bounty of the LORD— 5642
32:41 I will r in doing them good 8464
50:11 "Because you r and are glad, 8523
La 1:21 they r at what you have done. 8464
4:21 R and be glad, O Daughter of Edom, 8464
Eze 7:12 Let not the buyer r nor the seller grieve, 8523
21:10 " 'Shall we r in the scepter 8464
Hos 9: 1 Do not r, O Israel; 8523
Joel 2:21 Be not afraid, O land; be glad and r. 8523
2:23 r in the LORD your God, 8523
Am 6:13 you who r in the conquest of Lo Debar 8524
Ob 1:12 nor r over the people of Judah in the day 8523
Hab 3:18 yet I will r in the LORD, 6600
Zep 3:11 from this city those who r in their pride. 6611
3:14 Be glad and r with all your heart, 6600
3:17 he will r over you with singing." 1635
Zec 4:10 Men will r when they see the plumb line 8523
9: 9 R greatly, O Daughter of Zion! 1635
10: 7 their hearts will r in the LORD. 1635
Mt 5:12 R and be glad, because great is your reward 5897
Lk 1:14 and many will r because of his birth, 5897
6:23 "R in that day and leap for joy, 5897
10:20 do not r that the spirits submit to you, 5897
10:20 r that your names are written in heaven." 5897
15: 6 'R with me; I have found my lost sheep.' 5176
15: 9 'R with me; I have found my lost coin.' 5176
Jn 16:22 but I will see you again and you will r, 5897
Ro 5: 2 And we r in the hope of the glory of God. 3016
5: 3 Not only so, but we also r in our sufferings, 3016
5:11 but we also r in God through our Lord 3016
12:15 R with those who rejoice; 5897
12:15 Rejoice with those who r; 5897
15:10 Again, it says, "R, O Gentiles, 2370
2Co 2: 3 by those who ought to make me r. 5897
Php 1:18 And because of this I r. 5897
1:18 Yes, and I will continue to r, 5897
2:17 I am glad and r with all of you. 5176
2:18 So you too should be glad and r with me. 5176
3: 1 Finally, my brothers, r in the Lord! 5897
4: 4 R in the Lord always. 5897
4: 4 I will say it again: R! 5897
4:10 I r greatly in the Lord that 5897
Col 1:24 Now I r in what was suffered for you, 5897
1Pe 1: 6 In this you greatly r, 22
4:13 But r that you participate in the sufferings 5897
Rev 12:12 Therefore r, you heavens 2370
18:20 R over her, O heaven! 2370
18:20 R, saints and apostles and prophets! NIG
19: 7 Let us r and be glad and give him glory! 5897

REJOICED (16) [JOY]

1Sa 6:13 they r at the sight. 8523
2Ki 11:20 and all the people of the land r. 8523
1Ch 29: 9 The people r at the willing response 8523
29: 9 David the king also r greatly. 8523+8525
2Ch 15:15 All Judah r about the oath 8523
23:21 and all the people of the land r. 8523
29:36 the people r at what God had brought about 8523
30:25 The entire assembly of Judah r, 8523
Ne 12:43 The women and children also r. 8523
Job 31:25 if I have r over my great wealth, 8523
31:29 "If I have r at my enemy's misfortune 8523
Ps 122: 1 I r with those who said to me, 8523
SS 3:11 the day of his wedding, the day his heart r. 8525
Eze 35:15 Because you r when the inheritance of 8525
Hos 10: 5 those who had r over its splendor, 1635
Jn 8:56 Your father Abraham r at the thought 22

REJOICES (18) [JOY]

1Sa 2: 1 "My heart r in the LORD; 6636
Ps 13: 5 my heart r in your salvation. 1635
16: 9 and my tongue r; 1635
21: 1 O LORD, the king r in your strength. 8523
48:11 Mount Zion r, the villages of Judah 8523
97: 8 Zion hears and r and the villages of Judah 8523
119:14 I rejoice in following your statutes as one r NIH
Pr 11:10 When the righteous prosper, the city r; 6636
Isa 8: 6 and r in Rezin and the son of Remaliah, 5375
61:10 my soul r in my God. 1635
62: 5 as a bridegroom r over his bride, 5375
Eze 35:14 the whole earth r, I will make you desolate. 8523
Hab 1:15 and so he r and is glad. 8523
Lk 1:47 and my spirit r in God my Savior, 22
Jn 16:20 and mourn while the world r. 5897
Ac 2:26 my heart is glad and my tongue r; 22
1Co 12:26 if one part is honored, every part r with it. 5176
13: 6 Love does not delight in evil but r with 5176

REJOICING (24) [JOY]

Nu 10:10 Also at your times of r— 8525
Dt 27: 7 eating them and r in the presence of 8523
2Sa 6:12 of Obed-Edom to the City of David with r. 8525
1Ki 1:40 playing flutes and r greatly, 8524+8525
2Ki 11:14 of the land were r and blowing trumpets. 8524
1Ch 15:25 from the house of Obed-Edom, with r. 8525
2Ch 23:13 of the land were r and blowing trumpets, 8524
23:18 with r and singing, as David had ordered. 8525
30:21 for seven days with great r, 8525
Ne 12:43 r because God had given them great joy. 8523
12:43 of r in Jerusalem could be heard far away. 8525
Job 39:21 He paws fiercely, r in his strength, 8464
Ps 19: 5 like a champion r to run his course. 8464
30: 5 but r comes in the morning. 8262
105:43 He brought out his people with r, 8607
Pr 8:30 r always in his presence, 8471
8:31 r in his whole world and delighting 8471
Jer 30:19 of thanksgiving and the sound of r. 8471
Eze 25: 6 and stamped your feet, r with all the malice 8523
Lk 15: 7 that in the same way there will be more r 5915
15:10 there is r in the presence of the angels 5915
Ac 5:41 r because they had been counted worthy 5897
8:39 but went on his way r. 5897
2Co 6:10 sorrowful, yet always r; 5897

REJOINED (1) [JOIN]

Jdg 14: 9 When he r his parents, he gave them 448+2143

REKEM (5)

Nu 31: 8 Among their victims were Evi, R, Zur, 8390
Jos 13:21 Evi, R, Zur, Hur and Reba— 8390
18:27 R, Irpeel, Taralah, 8389
1Ch 2:43 Korah, Tappuah, R and Shema. 8390
2:44 R was the father of Shammai. 8390

RELATED (11) [RELATING, RELATION, RELATIONS, RELATIONSHIP, RELATIONSHIPS, RELATIVE, RELATIVES]

Lev 21: 4 people r to him by marriage, 1251
Nu 3:26 and everything r to their use. 4200

Nu 3:31 the curtain, and **everything** *r to* their use. AIT
3:36 and **everything** *r to* their use, AIT
4:32 all their equipment and everything **r to** 4200
2Sa 19:42 "We did this because the king is **closely r** 7940
2Ki 8:27 for he was **r by marriage** *to* Ahab's family. 3163
2Ch 4:16 shovels, meat forks and all **r** articles. 2157[S]
Est 8:1 for Esther had told how he was **r to** her. 4200
Ac 19:25 along with the workmen in **r trades,** *5525[S]*
Heb 5:1 to represent them in matters **r** to God, *NIG*

RELATING (1) [RELATED]

Ne 11:24 was the king's agent in all affairs **r to** 4200

RELATION (1) [RELATED]

1Ki 10:1 the fame of Solomon and his **r to** the name 4200

RELATIONS (34) [RELATED]

Ex 19:15 **Abstain from sexual r."** 440+448+851+5602
22:19 "Anyone *who* **has sexual r with** 6640+8886
Lev 18:6 a close relative to **have sexual r.** 1655+6872
18:7 **dishonor** your father **by having sexual r with** 1655+6872
18:7 your mother; *do* **not have r with** her. 1655+6872
18:8 " '*Do* **not have sexual r with** your father's wife; 1655+6872
18:9 " '*Do* **not have sexual r with** your sister, 1655+6872
18:10 " '*Do* **not have sexual r with** your son's daughter 1655+6872
18:11 " '*Do* **not have sexual r with** the daughter 1655+6872
18:12 " '*Do* **not have sexual r with** your father's sister; 1655+6872
18:13 " '*Do* **not have sexual r with** your mother's sister, 1655+6872
18:14 *Do* not **dishonor** your father's brother **by** approaching his wife **to have sexual r;** 1655+6872
18:15 " '*Do* **not have sexual r with** your daughter-in-law. 1655+6872
18:15 *do* **not have r with** her. 1655+6872
18:16 " '*Do* **not have sexual r with** your brother's wife; 1655+6872
18:17 " '*Do* **not have sexual r with** both a woman and her daughter. 1655+6872
18:17 *Do* **not have sexual r with** either 1655+6872
18:18 rival wife and **have sexual r** with her 1655+6872
18:19 **have sexual r** during the uncleanness 1655+6872
18:20 " '*Do* **not have sexual r** 2446+4200+5989+8888
18:23 '*Do* **not have sexual r** with an animal 5989+8888
18:23 to an animal to **have sexual r with** it; 8061
20:15 'If a man **has sexual r** with an animal, 5989+8888
20:16 an animal to **have sexual r with** it, 8061
20:17 and *they* **have sexual r,** it is a disgrace. 906+6872+8011
20:18 and **has sexual r with** her, 906+1655+6872
20:19 " '*Do* **not have sexual r with** the sister of either your mother or 1655+6872
Dt 27:21 "Cursed the man *who* **has sexual r with** any animal." 6640+8886
Jdg 4:17 because there were **friendly r** between 8934
1Ki 1:4 the king **had** no **intimate r with** her. 3359
5:12 There were **peaceful r** between Hiram 8934
Ro 1:26 Even their women exchanged natural **r** *5979*
1:27 also abandoned natural **r** with women *5979*
2Co 1:12 and especially in our **r** with you, *NIG*

RELATIONSHIP (3) [RELATED]

Jdg 18:7 a long way from the Sidonians and had no **r** 1821
18:28 from Sidon and had no **r** with anyone else. 1821
Ro 2:17 on the law and brag about your **r to** God; *1877*

RELATIONSHIPS (1) [RELATED]

Nu 30:16 concerning **r between** a man and his wife, 1068

RELATIVE (22) [RELATED]

Ge 14:14 that his **r** had been taken captive, 278
14:16 the goods and brought back his **r** Lot 278
29:12 a **r** *of* her father and a son of Rebekah. 278
29:15 "Just because you are a **r** *of* mine, 278
Lev 18:6 " 'No one is to approach any **close r** 1414+8638
18:12 she is your father's **close r.** 8638
18:13 because she is your mother's **close r.** 8638
20:19 for that would dishonor a **close r;** 8638
21:2 except for a **close r,** 7940+8638
25:25 his nearest **r** is to come 1457
25:49 An uncle or a cousin or any **blood r** 1414+8638
Nu 5:8 But if that person has no **close r** 1457
27:11 give his inheritance to the nearest **r** 8638
Ru 2:1 Now Naomi had a **r** on her husband's side, 4530
2:20 She added, "That man is our **close r;** 7940
1Ki 16:11 whether **r** or friend. 1457
Jer 23:35 of you keeps on saying to his friend or **r:** 278
32:7 **as nearest r** it is your right and **duty** 1460
Am 6:10 And if a **r** who is to burn the bodies comes 1856
Lk 1:36 Even Elizabeth your **r** is going to have *5151*
Jn 18:26 a **r** of the man whose ear Peter had cut off, *5150*
Ro 16:11 Greet Herodion, my **r.** *5150*

RELATIVES (82) [RELATED]

Ge 24:4 to my country and my own **r** and get a wife 4580
24:27 the journey to the house of my master's **r."** 278
27:37 and have made all his **r** his servants, 278
31:3 to the land of your fathers and to your **r,** 4580
31:23 Taking his **r** with him, 278
31:25 and Laban and his **r** camped there too. 278
31:32 In the presence of our **r,** 278
31:37 Put it here in front of your **r** and mine, 278
31:46 He said to his **r,** "Gather some stones." 278
31:54 the hill country and invited his **r** to a meal. 278
32:9 'Go back to your country and your **r,** 4580
Lev 10:6 But your **r,** all the house of Israel, 278
18:17 they are her **close r.** 8638
25:48 One of his **r** may redeem him: 278
Nu 27:4 Give us property among our father's **r."** 278
27:7 as an inheritance among their father's **r** 278
Jdg 14:3 among your **r** or among all our people? 278
2Ki 10:13 he met *some* **r** *of* Ahaziah king of Judah 278
10:13 They said, "We are **r** *of* Ahaziah, 278
1Ch 5:7 Their **r** by clans, listed according 278
5:13 Their **r,** by families, were: 278
7:5 The **r** who were fighting men belonging 278
7:22 and his **r** came to comfort him. 278
8:32 They too lived near their **r** in Jerusalem. 278
9:38 They too lived near their **r** in Jerusalem. 278
12:32 with all their **r** under their command; 278
15:5 Uriel the leader and 120 **r;** 278
15:6 Asaiah the leader and 220 **r;** 278
15:7 Joel the leader and 130 **r;** 278
15:8 Shemaiah the leader and 200 **r;** 278
15:9 Eliel the leader and 80 **r;** 278
15:10 Amminadab the leader and 112 **r.** 278
25:7 Along with their **r—** 278
25:9 his sons and **r,** 12 the second to Gedaliah, 278
25:9 he and his **r** and sons, 278
25:10 the third to Zaccur, his sons and **r,** 12 278
25:11 the fourth to Izri, his sons and **r,** 12 278
25:12 the fifth to Nethaniah, his sons and **r,** 12 278
25:13 the sixth to Bukkiah, his sons and **r,** 12 278
25:14 the seventh to Jesarelah, his sons and **r,** 12 278
25:15 the eighth to Jeshaiah, his sons and **r,** 12 278
25:16 the ninth to Mattaniah, his sons and **r,** 12 278
25:17 the tenth to Shimei, his sons and **r,** 12 278
25:18 the eleventh to Azarel, his sons and **r,** 12 278
25:19 the twelfth to Hashabiah, his sons and **r,** 12 278
25:20 the thirteenth to Shubael, his sons and **r,** 12 278
25:21 the fourteenth to Mattithiah, his sons and **r,** 278
25:22 the fifteenth to Jerimoth, his sons and **r,** 12 278
25:23 the sixteenth to Hananiah, his sons and **r,** 278
25:24 seventeenth to Joshbekashah, his sons and **r,** 278
25:25 the eighteenth to Hanani, his sons and **r,** 12 278
25:26 the nineteenth to Mallothi, his sons and **r,** 278
25:27 the twentieth to Eliathah, his sons and **r,** 12 278
25:28 the twenty-first to Hothir, his sons and **r,** 278
25:29 twenty-second to Giddalti, his sons and **r,** 278
25:30 twenty-third to Mahazioth, his sons and **r,** 278
25:31 to Romamti-Ezer, his sons and **r,** 278
26:7 his **r** Elihu and Semakiah were 278
26:8 and their sons and their **r** were capable men 278
26:9 Meshelemiah had sons and **r,** 278
26:11 The sons and **r** of Hosah were 13 in all. 278
26:12 just as their **r** had. 278
26:25 His **r** through Eliezer: 278
26:26 and his **r** were in charge of all the treasuries 278
26:28 in the care of Shelomith and his **r.** 278
26:30 From the Hebronites: Hashabiah and his **r—** 278
26:32 Jeriah had twenty-seven hundred **r,** 278
2Ch 5:12 Heman, Jeduthun and their sons and **r—** 278
22:8 of Judah and the sons of Ahaziah's **r,** 278
Pr 19:7 A poor man is shunned by all his **r—** 278
Jer 49:10 His children, **r** and neighbors will perish, 278
Eze 11:15 your brothers who are your **blood r** and 408+1460
Mk 6:4 among his **r** and in his own house is *5150*
Lk 1:58 Her neighbors and **r** heard that *5150*
1:61 "There is no one among your **r** who has *5149*
2:44 for him among their **r** and friends. *5150*
14:12 your brothers or **r,** or your rich neighbors; *5150*
21:16 brothers, **r** and friends, *5150*
Ac 10:24 and had called together his **r** *5150*
Ro 16:7 my **r** who have been in prison with me. *5150*
16:21 as do Lucius, Jason and Sosipater, my **r.** *5150*
1Ti 5:8 If anyone does not provide for **his r,** *2625*

RELEASE (30) [RELEASED, RELEASES]

Lev 14:7 *he is to* **r** the live bird in the open fields. 8938
14:53 *to* **r** the live bird in the open fields outside 8938
16:22 and the man *shall* **r** it in the desert. 8938
25:50 for his **r** is to be based on the rate paid to 4928
Nu 30:5 the LORD *will* **r** her because her father 6142
30:8 and the LORD *will* **r** her. 6142
30:12 and the LORD *will* **r** her. 6142
Dt 15:13 And when *you* **r** him, 8938
Ps 25:15 for only he *will* **r** my feet from the snare. 3655
102:20 of the prisoners and **r** those condemned 7337
Ecc 8:8 not **r** those who practice it. 4880
Isa 42:7 to free captives from prison and to **r** from NIH
61:1 for the captives and **r from darkness** for 7223
Mt 27:15 the governor's custom at the Feast *to* **r** *668*
27:17 "Which one do you want *me to* **r** to you: *668*
27:21 of the two do you want *me to* **r** to you?" *668*
Mk 15:6 *to* **r** a prisoner whom the people requested. *668*
15:9 "Do you want *me to* **r** to you the king of *668*
15:11 the crowd to *have* Pilate **r** Barabbas instead. *668*
Lk 4:18 *to* **r** the oppressed, *690+912+1877*
23:16 *I will* punish him and then **r** him." *668*
23:18 **R** Barabbas to us!" *668*
23:20 Wanting *to* **r** Jesus, *668*
23:22 I will have him punished and then **r** him." *668*
Jn 18:39 for *me to* **r** to you one prisoner at the time *668*
18:39 Do you want *me to* **r** 'the king of the Jews'? *668*
Ac 4:23 *On their* **r,** Peter and John went back *668*
16:35 with the order: **"R** those men." *668*
28:18 They examined me and wanted *to* **r** me, *668*
Rev 9:14 **"R** the four angels who are bound at *3395*

RELEASED (28) [RELEASE]

Ge 24:8 then *you will* **be r** from this oath of mine. 5927
24:41 *you will* **be r** from my oath even 5927
24:41 you will be **r** from my oath.' 5929
Lev 25:41 Then he and his children *are to be* **r,** 3655
25:54 he and his children *are to be* **r** in the Year 3655
27:21 When the field *is* **r** in the Jubilee, 3655
Jos 2:20 be **r** from the oath you made us swear." 5929
2Ki 25:27 *he* **r** Jehoiachin from prison on 5951+8031
2Ch 23:8 the priest *had* not **r** any of the divisions. 7080
Job 12:14 the man he imprisons cannot **be r.** 7337
Ps 105:20 The king sent and **r** him, 6002
Jer 20:3 when Pashhur **r** him from the stocks, 3655
40:1 of the imperial guard *had* **r** him at Ramah. 8938
52:31 *he* **r** Jehoiachin king of Judah and 5951+8031
Mal 4:2 And you will go out and leap like calves **r** NIH
Mt 27:26 Then *he* **r** Barabbas to them. *668*
Mk 15:15 Pilate **r** Barabbas to them. *668*
Lk 23:25 *He* **r** the man who had been thrown *668*
Ac 3:14 and asked that a murderer *be* **r** to you. *5919*
16:36 that *you* and Silas *be* **r.** *668*
22:30 *he* **r** him and ordered the chief priests *3395*
Ro 7:2 *she is* **r** from the law of marriage. *2934*
7:3 she is **r** from that law and is not *1801*
7:6 *we have been* **r** from the law so *2934*
Heb 11:35 Others were tortured and refused to be **r,** *667*
13:23 that our brother Timothy *has been* **r.** *668*
Rev 9:15 and year *were* **r** to kill a third of mankind. *3395*
20:7 Satan *will be* **r** from his prison *3395*

RELEASES (1) [RELEASE]

Lev 16:26 "The *man who* **r** the goat as 8938

RELENT (12) [RELENTED, RELENTS]

Ex 32:12 **r and do not bring** disaster on your 5714
Job 6:29 **R,** do not be unjust; 8740
Ps 7:12 If *he does* not **r,** he will sharpen his sword; 8740
90:13 **R,** O LORD! 8740
Isa 57:6 In the light of these things, *should I* **r?** 5714
Jer 4:28 because I have spoken and *will* not **r,** 5714
18:8 then *I will* **r** and not inflict on it 5714
26:3 Then *I will* **r** and not bring on them 5714
26:13 Then the LORD *will* **r and not bring** 5714
26:19 **r, so that** he *did* **not bring** the disaster 5714
Eze 24:14 I will not have pity, nor *will I* **r.** 5714
Jnh 3:9 God *may* yet **r** and with compassion turn 8740

RELENTED (4) [RELENT]

Ex 32:14 Then the LORD **r and did not** bring 5714
Ps 106:45 and out of his great love *he* **r.** 5714
Am 7:3 So the LORD **r.** 5714
7:6 So the LORD **r.** 5714

RELENTLESS (1)

Isa 14:6 subdued nations with **r** aggression. 1172+3104

RELENTS (2) [RELENT]

Joel 2:13 and *he* **r** from sending calamity. 5714
Jnh 4:2 a God *who* **r** from sending calamity. 5714

RELIABLE (6) [RELY]

1Sa 29:6 as the LORD lives, you have been **r,** 3838
Pr 22:21 teaching you true and **r** words, 622
Isa 8:2 of Jeberekiah as **r** witnesses for me." 586
Jer 2:21 like a choice vine of sound and **r** stock. 622
Jn 8:26 But he who sent me is **r,** *239*
2Ti 2:2 *to* **r** men who will also be qualified *4412*

RELIANCE (1) [RELY]

Pr 25:19 or a lame foot is **r** *on* the unfaithful in times 4440

RELIED (7) [RELY]

Jdg 20:36 because *they* **r** on the ambush they had set 1053
2Ch 13:18 of Judah were victorious because *they* **r** on 9128
16:7 "Because you **r** on the king of Aram and 9128
16:8 Yet when you **r** on the LORD, 9128
Ps 71:6 From birth *I have* **r** on you; 6164
Isa 20:6 'See what has happened to *those* we **r on,** 4438
30:12 **r** on oppression and depended on deceit, 1053

RELIEF (20) [RELIEVE]

Ex 8:15 But when Pharaoh saw that there was **r,** 8121
1Sa 8:18 you will cry out **for r from** 4200+4946+7156
16:23 Then **r** *would* **come** to Saul; 8118
Ezr 9:8 to our eyes and a little **r** in our bondage. 4695
Est 4:14 **r** and deliverance for the Jews will arise 8119
9:16 to protect themselves and **get r** from their 5663
9:22 when the Jews **got r** from their enemies, 5663
Job 16:5 comfort from my lips *would* **bring** you **r.** 3104
32:20 I must speak and **find r;** 8118
35:9 *they* **plead for r** from the arm of 8775
Ps 4:1 **Give** me **r** from my distress; 8143
94:13 you **grant** him **r** from days of trouble, 9200
143:1 and righteousness **come to** my **r.** 6699

Isa 1:24 “Ah, *I will* **get** r from my foes 5714
14:3 the LORD **gives** you r from suffering 5663
La 2:18 give yourself no r, your eyes no rest. 7029
3:49 My eyes will flow unceasingly, without r, 2198
3:56 “Do not close your ears to my cry for r.” 8121
Mic 1:12 waiting for r, because disaster has come 3202
2Th 1:7 and give r to you who are troubled, *457*

RELIES (1) [RELY]

Job 8:14 **what** he r **on** is a spider's web. 4440

RELIEVE (3) [RELIEF, RELIEVED, RELIEVING]

Dt 23:12 the camp where you can go to r yourself. NIH
23:13 and when you r **yourself,** 2575+3782
1Sa 24:3 Saul went in to r **himself.** 906+2257+6114+8079

RELIEVED (2) [RELIEVE]

Job 16:6 “Yet if I speak, my pain is **not** r; 3104
2Co 8:13 Our desire is not that others might be r *457*

RELIEVING (1) [RELIEVE]

Jdg 3:24 “He *must be* r **himself** in the inner room 906+2257+6114+8079

RELIGION (5) [RELIGIOUS]

Ac 25:19 of dispute with him about their own r and *1272*
26:5 that according to the strictest sect *of* our r, *2579*
1Ti 5:4 **put** *their* r **into practice by caring for** *2355*
Jas 1:26 he deceives himself and his r is worthless. *2579*
1:27 R that God our Father accepts as pure *2579*

RELIGIOUS (6) [RELIGION]

Am 5:21 “I hate, I despise your r **feasts;** 2504
8:10 I will turn your r **feasts** into mourning 2504
Ac 17:22 I see that in every way you are **very** r. *1273*
Col 2:16 or with regard to a r **festival,** *2038*
Heb 10:11 and **performs** his r **duties;** *3310*
Jas 1:26 If anyone considers himself r and yet does *2580*

RELISH (1)

Hos 4:8 of my people and r their wickedness. 5883+5951

RELUCTANTLY (1)

2Co 9:7 not r or under compulsion, *1666+3383*

RELY (14) [RELIABLE, RELIANCE, RELIED, RELIES]

2Ch 14:11 O LORD our God, for *we* r on you, 9128
Job 39:11 *Will you* r on him for his great strength? 1053
Isa 10:20 will no longer r on him who struck them 9128
10:20 down but *will* truly r on the LORD, 9128
31:1 *who* r on horses, who trust in the multitude 9128
48:2 the holy city and r on the God of Israel— 6164
50:10 the name of the LORD and r on his God. 9128
59:4 They r on empty arguments and speak lies; 1053
Jer 46:25 and on those *who* r on Pharaoh. 1053
Eze 33:26 *You* r on your sword, 6641
Ro 2:17 if *you* r **on** the law and brag *2058*
2Co 1:9 that *we might* not r on ourselves but on God, *1639+4275*
Gal 3:10 All who r **on** observing the law are *1639+1666*
1Jn 4:16 we know and r **on** the love God has for us. *4409*

REMAIN (116) [REMAINDER, REMAINED, REMAINING, REMAINS]

Ge 15:2 what can you give me since I r childless 2143
24:55 *“Let* the girl r with us ten days or so; 3782
36:7 too great for them *to* r together; 3782
44:33 please *let* your servant r here 3782
Ex 8:9 except for *those that* r in the Nile.” 8636
8:11 *they will* r only in the Nile.” 8636
25:15 The poles *are to* r in the rings of this ark; 2118
34:25 of the sacrifice from the Passover Feast r 4328
Lev 6:9 The burnt offering is to r on the altar hearth NIH
11:37 that are to be planted, they r clean. NIH
22:27 *it is to* r with its mother for seven days. 2118
25:28 what he sold *will* r in the possession of 2118
25:51 If many years r, he must pay for his 6388
25:52 a few years r until the Year of Jubilee, 8636
26:21 “ 'If *you* r hostile toward me and refuse 2143
27:14 value the priest then sets, so *it will* r. 7756
27:18 according to the number of years that r 3855
Nu 4:7 the bread that is continually there *is to* r 2118
9:22 the Israelites *would* r **in camp** and 2837
32:26 our flocks and herds *will* r here in 2118
33:55 those *you* **allow to** r will become barbs 3855
Dt 13:16 *It is to* r a ruin forever, 2118
16:4 the evening of the first day r until morning. 4328
31:26 There *it will* r as a witness against you. 2118
Jos 18:5 Judah *is to* r in its territory on the south 6641
23:4 the land of the nations that r— 8636
23:7 Do not associate with these nations that r 8636
23:12 with the survivors of these nations that r 8636
Jdg 2:23 The LORD *had* **allowed** those nations **to** r; 5663
Ru 1:13 *Would you* r **unmarried** for them? 408+1194+2118+4200+4200+6328
1Sa 16:22 saying, *“Allow* David *to* r in my service, 6641
2Sa 14:14 that a banished person *may* not r **estranged** AIT
2Sa 16:18 his I will be, and *I will* r with him. 3782
1Ki 2:45 and David's throne *will* r secure before 2118
1Ch 21:17 but do not let this plague r on your people.” NIH
2Ch 32:10 that you r in Jerusalem under siege? 3782
33:4 “My Name *will* r in Jerusalem forever.” 2118
Est 4:14 For if *you* r **silent** at this time, 3087+3087
Job 29:20 My glory will r fresh in me, NIH
37:8 *they* r in their dens. 8905
Ps 28:1 For if *you* r **silent,** AIT
30:5 weeping *may* r for a night, 4328
49:11 Their tombs will r their houses forever, NIH
102:26 They will perish, but you r; 6641
102:27 But you r the same, NIH
109:1 O God, whom I praise, *do* not *r* **silent,** AIT
109:15 *May* their sins always r before the LORD, 2118
125:3 the wicked *will* not r over the land allotted 5663
Pr 2:21 and the blameless *will* r in it; 3855
10:30 but the wicked *will* not r *in* the land. 8905
Isa 4:3 who r in Jerusalem, will be called holy, 3855
7:22 All who r in the land will eat curds 3855
10:4 Nothing will r but to cringe among NIH
15:9 the fugitives of Moab and upon *those who* r 8642
17:6 Yet some gleanings *will* r, 8636
18:4 *“I will r* **quiet** and will look on AIT
22:18 and there your splendid chariots will r— NIH
46:3 all you *who* r *of* the house of Israel, 8642
62:1 for Jerusalem's sake *I will* not *r* **quiet,** AIT
Jer 24:8 whether they r in this land or live in Egypt. 8636
27:11 *I will* **let** that nation r in its own land to 5663
27:22 be taken to Babylon and there *they will* r 2118
29:16 on David's throne and all the people who r 3782
32:5 where *he will* r until I deal with him, 2118
51:30 *they* r in their strongholds. 3782
Eze 36:36 the nations around you that r will know 8636
39:14 others will bury those *that* r on the ground. 3855
44:2 “This gate *is to* r shut. 2118
44:2 *It is to* r shut because the LORD, 2118
Da 2:43 be a mixture and *will* not r united, 10201
4:15 r in the ground, in the grass of the field. 10697
4:23 while its roots r in the ground. NIH
11:12 yet *he will* not r **triumphant.** AIT
Hos 9:3 *They will* not r in the LORD's land; 3782
Zec 5:4 *It will* r in his house and destroy it, 4328
12:6 but Jerusalem will r intact in her place. 6388
14:10 But Jerusalem will be raised up and r 3782
Jn 1:32 down from heaven as a dove and r on him. *3531*
1:33 down and r is he who will baptize with *3531*
12:34 the Law that the Christ *will* r forever, *3531*
15:4 R in me, and I will remain in you. *3531*
15:4 Remain in me, and I will r in you. *NIG*
15:4 bear fruit by itself; *it must* r in the vine. *3531*
15:4 Neither can you bear fruit unless *you* r *3531*
15:6 If anyone *does* not r in me, *3531*
15:7 *you* r in me and my words remain in you, *3531*
15:7 If you remain in me and my words r in you, *3531*
15:9 Now r in my love. *3531*
15:10 *you will* r in my love, *3531*
15:10 and r in his love. *3531*
17:11 *I will* r in the world no longer, *1639*
21:22 “If I want him *to* r alive until I return, *3531*
21:23 “If I want him *to* r alive until I return, *3531*
Ac 3:21 He must r in heaven until the time comes *NIG*
11:23 *to* r true to the Lord with all their hearts. *4693*
14:22 and encouraging them *to* r **true to** *1844*
Ro 13:8 *Let* no **debt** r **outstanding,** *4053*
1Co 7:11 *she must* r unmarried or else be reconciled *3531*
7:20 Each one *should* r in the situation *3531*
7:24 *should* r in the situation God called him to. *3531*
7:26 that it is good for you *to* r as you are. *1639*
13:13 now these three r: faith, hope and love. *3531*
14:34 women *should r* **silent** in the churches. *AIT*
Gal 2:5 that the truth of the gospel *might* r with you. *1373*
Php 1:24 but it is more necessary for you that I r in *2152*
1:25 Convinced of this, I know that *I will* r, *3531*
2Ti 2:13 if we are faithless, he *will* r faithful, *3531*
Heb 1:11 They will perish, but you r; *1373*
1:12 But you r the same, and your years will *1639*
8:9 they *did* not r **faithful to** my covenant, *1844*
12:27 so that what cannot be shaken *may* r. *3531*
1Jn 2:24 also *will* r in the Son and in the Father. *3531*
2:27 just as it has taught you, r in him. *3531*
Rev 2:13 Yet *you* r **true to** my name. *3195*
14:12 and r faithful to Jesus. *NIG*
17:10 he does come, he must r for a little while. *3531*

REMAINDER (1) [REMAIN]

Est 9:16 the r *of* the Jews who were in the king's 8637

REMAINED (63) [REMAIN]

Ge 18:22 but Abraham r standing before the LORD. 6388
32:4 with Laban and *have* r there till now. 336
49:24 But his bow r steady, 3782
Ex 8:31 not a fly r. 8636
10:15 Nothing green r on tree or plant in all 3855
17:12 so that his hands r steady till sunset. 2118
20:21 The people r at a distance, 6641
Lev 10:3 Aaron *r* **silent.** AIT
Nu 9:18 *they* r **in camp.** 2837
9:19 the cloud r over the tabernacle a long time, 799
11:26 Eldad and Medad, *had* r in the camp. 8636
36:12 and their inheritance r in their father's clan 2118
Jos 4:10 the priests who carried the ark *r* **standing** in AIT
5:8 *they* r where they were in camp 3782
8:17 Not a man r in Ai or Bethel who did not go 8636
Jdg 1:30 *who* r among them; but they did subject 3782
Jdg 5:17 Asher r on the coast and stayed in his coves 3782
7:3 men left, while ten thousand r. 8636
13:2 a wife who was sterile and r **childless.** 3528+4202
19:4 so *he* r with him three days, 3782
1Sa 5:4 lying on the threshold; only his body r. 8636
7:2 that the ark r at Kiriath Jearim, 3782
13:7 Saul r at Gilgal, and all the troops with him 6388
18:29 and he r his enemy the rest of his days. 2118
23:18 but David r at Horesh. 3782
2Sa 6:11 the LORD r *in* the house of Obed-Edom 3782
11:1 But David r in Jerusalem. 3782
11:12 Uriah r in Jerusalem that day and the next. 3782
1Ki 12:20 Only the tribe of Judah r loyal to the house 2118
22:46 the male shrine prostitutes who r there even 8636
2Ki 2:22 And the water *has r* **wholesome** to this day, AIT
10:11 So Jehu killed everyone in Jezreel who r of 8636
11:3 *He* r hidden with his nurse at the temple of 2118
13:6 the Asherah pole *r* **standing** in Samaria. AIT
18:36 people *r* **silent** and said nothing in reply, AIT
25:11 into exile the people who r in the city, 8636
1Ch 12:29 most of whom *had r* **loyal** *to* Saul's house AIT
13:14 of God r with the family of Obed-Edom 3782
20:1 but David r in Jerusalem. 3782
2Ch 22:12 *He* r hidden with them at the temple of God 2118
Isa 36:21 *people r* **silent** and said nothing in reply, AIT
Jer 35:11 So *we have* r in Jerusalem.” 3782
37:16 where he r a long time. 3782
37:21 So Jeremiah r in the courtyard of the guard. 3782
38:13 Jeremiah r in the courtyard of the guard. 3782
38:28 And Jeremiah r in the courtyard of 3782
39:9 into exile to Babylon the people who r in 8636
39:14 So *he* r among his own people. 3782
52:15 of the poorest people and those *who* r in 8636
Eze 17:6 but its roots r under it. 2118
Da 1:21 And Daniel r there until the first year 2118
2:49 while Daniel himself r at the royal court. NIH
Hos 10:9 O Israel, and there *you have* r. 6641
Mt 11:23 *it* would *have* r to this day. *3531*
26:63 But Jesus *r* **silent.** *AIT*
Mk 3:4 But they *r* **silent.** *AIT*
14:61 But Jesus *r* **silent** and gave no answer. *AIT*
Lk 1:22 to them but r unable to speak. *1373*
1:24 and for five months *r* **in seclusion.** *AIT*
14:4 But they *r* **silent.** *AIT*
Ac 7:45 It r in the land until the time of David, *NIG*
15:35 But Paul and Barnabas r in Antioch, *1417*
1Jn 2:19 *they* would *have* r with us; *3531*

REMAINING (15) [REMAIN]

Ex 28:10 six names on one stone and the r six on 3855
Lev 10:12 Moses said to Aaron and his r sons, 3855
10:16 Aaron's r sons, and asked, 3855
14:17 to put some of the oil r in his palm on 3856
Nu 31:32 The plunder r *from* the spoils that 3856
Jos 7:6 r there till evening. NIH
1Ki 9:21 their descendants r in the land, 3855
1Ch 4:43 the r Amalekites who had escaped, 8642
2Ch 8:8 their descendants r in the land, 3855
Ne 11:1 the r nine were to stay in their own towns. 3338
Isa 10:19 And the r trees of his forests will be so few 8637
Jer 27:18 the LORD Almighty that the furnishings r 3855
Eze 25:16 the Kerethites and destroy those r *along* 8642
48:15 “The r *area,* 5,000 cubits wide and 25,000 3855
Jn 19:23 with the undergarment r. *NIG*

REMAINS (45) [REMAIN]

Ex 22:13 bring in the r as evidence and he will not 3274
Lev 11:36 or a cistern for collecting water r clean, 2118
13:46 as he has the infection he r **unclean.** 3237+3238
27:17 the value that has been set r. 7756
Nu 15:31 his guilt r on him.' ” NIH
16:37 to take the censers out of the **smoldering** r 8599
19:13 his uncleanness r on him. 6388
Dt 24:20 Leave what r for the alien, NIH
24:21 Leave what r for the alien, NIH
Jos 7:26 which r to this day. NIH
8:29 which r to this day. NIH
13:2 “This is the land that r: 8636
2Sa 7:2 while the ark of God r in a tent.” 3782
1Ki 20:10 if **enough** dust r in Samaria to give each AIT
2Ki 6:31 of Shaphat r on his shoulders today!” 6641
Ne 9:10 which r to this day. 3869
Job 19:4 my error r my concern alone. 4328
34:29 But if he r **silent,** who can condemn him? AIT
Ps 146:6 the LORD, who r faithful forever. 9068
Pr 29:1 man *who r* **stiff-necked** after many rebukes AIT
Ecc 1:4 but the earth r forever. 6641
Isa 6:13 And though a tenth r in the land, 6388
29:8 but he awakens, and his hunger r; NIH
Eze 32:5 and fill the valleys with your r. 8239
48:18 What r of the area, 3855
48:21 “What r on both sides of the area formed 3855
Mic 7:2 not one upright man r. NIH
Hag 1:4 while this house r a ruin?” NIH
1:9 “Because of my house, which r a ruin, NIH
2:5 And my Spirit r among you. 6641
Jn 3:36 for God's wrath r on him.” *3531*
6:56 and drinks my blood r in me, *3531*
9:41 that you claim you can see, your guilt r. *3531*
12:24 *it* r only a single seed. *3531*
15:5 *If* a man r in me and I in him, *3531*
1Co 11:21 One *r* **hungry,** another gets drunk. *AIT*
2Co 3:14 for to this day the same veil r when *3531*
Heb 4:6 *It* still r that some will enter that rest, *657*
4:9 *There* r, then, a Sabbath-rest for the people *657*

Heb 7: 3 like the Son of God *he* **r** a priest forever. *3531*
1Jn 2:24 from the beginning **r** in you. *3531*
2:27 anointing you received from him **r** in you, *3531*
3: 9 because God's seed **r** in him; *3531*
3:14 Anyone who does not love **r** in death. *3531*
Rev 3: 2 Strengthen what **r** and is about to die, *3370*

REMALIAH (11) [REMALIAH'S]

2Ki 15:25 One of his chief officers, Pekah son of **R**, 8248
15:27 of **R** became king of Israel in Samaria, 8248
15:30 of Elah conspired against Pekah son of **R**. 8248
15:32 In the second year of Pekah son of **R** king 8248
15:37 of Aram and Pekah son of **R** against Judah.) 8248
16: 1 In the seventeenth year of Pekah son of **R**, 8248
16: 5 and Pekah son of **R** king of Israel marched 8248
2Ch 28: 6 In one day Pekah son of **R** killed a hundred 8248
Isa 7: 1 and Pekah son of **R** king of Israel marched 8248
7: 4 of Rezin and Aram and of the son of **R**. 8248
8: 6 and rejoices over Rezin and the son of **R**, 8248

REMALIAH'S (2) [REMALIAH]

Isa 7: 5 Ephraim and **R** son have plotted your ruin, 8248
7: 9 and the head of Samaria is only **R** son. 8248

REMARKABLE (2)

Lk 5:26 "We have seen **r** *things* today." *4141*
Jn 9:30 The man answered, "Now that is **r**! *2515*

REMARKED (1) [REMARKING]

Ac 17:18 Others **r**, "He seems to be advocating *NIG*

REMARKING (1) [REMARKED]

Lk 21: 5 Some of his disciples *were* **r** about how *3306*

REMEDIES (1) [REMEDY]

Jer 46:11 But you multiply **r** in vain; 8337

REMEDY (6) [REMEDIES]

2Ch 36:16 against his people and there was no **r**. 5340
Pr 6:15 will suddenly be destroyed—without **r**. 5340
29: 1 will suddenly be destroyed—without **r**. 5340
Isa 3: 7 in that day he will cry out, "I have no **r**. 2502
Jer 30:13 no **r** for your sore, no healing for you. 8337
Mic 2:10 it is ruined, **beyond all r**. 5344

REMEMBER (166) [REMEMBERED, REMEMBERING, REMEMBERS, REMEMBRANCE]

Ge 9:15 *I will* **r** my covenant between me and you 2349
9:16 I will see it and **r** the everlasting covenant 2349
31:50 **r** *that* God is a witness between you 8011
40:14 **r** me and show me kindness; 2349
40:23 chief cupbearer, however, *did* not **r** Joseph; 2349
Ex 20: 8 "**R** the Sabbath day by keeping it holy. 2349
32:13 **R** your servants Abraham, Isaac and Israel, 2349
33:13 **R** that this nation is your people." 8011
Lev 26:42 *I will* **r** my covenant with Jacob 2349
26:42 and *I will* **r** the land. 2349
26:45 But for their sake *I will* **r** the covenant 2349
Nu 11: 5 *We* **r** the fish we ate in Egypt at no cost— 2349
15:39 at and so *you will* **r** all the commands of 2349
15:40 Then *you will* **r** to obey all my commands 2349
Dt 4:10 **R** the day you stood before the LORD NIH
5:15 **R** that you were slaves in Egypt and that 2349
7:18 **r well** what the LORD your God did 2349+2349
8: 2 **R** how the LORD your God led you all 2349
8:18 But **r** the LORD your God, 2349
9: 7 **R** this and never forget how you provoked 2349
9:27 **R** your servants Abraham, Isaac and Jacob. 2349
11: 2 **R** today that your children were not 3359
15:15 **R** that you were slaves in Egypt and 2349
16: 3 so that all the days of your life *you may* **r** 2349
16:12 **R** that you were slaves in Egypt, 2349
24: 9 **R** what the LORD your God did to Miriam 2349
24:18 **R** that you were slaves in Egypt and 2349
24:22 **R** that you were slaves in Egypt. 2349
25:17 **R** what the Amalekites did to you along 2349
32: 7 **R** the days of old; 2349
Jos 1:13 "**R** the command that Moses the servant of 2349
23: 4 **R** how I have allotted as an inheritance 8011
Jdg 8:34 and *did* not **r** the LORD their God, 2349
9: 2 **R**, I am your flesh and blood." 2349
16:28 "O Sovereign LORD, **r** me. 2349
1Sa 1:11 look upon your servant's misery and **r** me, 2349
20:23 **r**, the LORD is witness between you 2180
25:31 when the LORD has brought my master success, **r** your servant." 2349
2Sa 19:19 *Do* not **r** how your servant did wrong on 2349
1Ki 2: 8 "And **r**, you have with you Shimei son 2180
2Ki 9:25 **R** how you and I were riding together 2349
20: 3 "**R**, O LORD, how I have walked 2349
1Ch 16:12 **R** the wonders he has done, his miracles, 2349
2Ch 6:42 **R** the great love promised to David 2349
24:22 King Joash *did* not **r** the kindness 2349
Ne 1: 8 "**R** the instruction you gave your servant Moses, 2349
4:14 **R** the Lord, who is great and awesome, 2349
5:19 **R** me with favor, O my God, 2349
6:14 **R** Tobiah and Sanballat, O my God, 2349
6:14 **r** also the prophetess Noadiah and the rest NIH
9:17 and failed *to* **r** the miracles you performed 2349
Ne 13:14 **R** me for this, O my God, 2349
13:22 **R** me for this also, O my God, 2349
13:29 **R** them, O my God, 2349
13:31 **R** me with favor, O my God. 2349
Job 7: 7 **R**, O God, that my life is but a breath; 2349
10: 9 **R** that you molded me like clay. 2349
14:13 you would set a time and then **r** me! 2349
36:24 **R** to extol his work, 2349
41: 8 *you will* **r** the struggle and never do it again! 2349
Ps 20: 3 *May he* **r** all your sacrifices 2349
22:27 All the ends of the earth *will* **r** and turn to 2349
25: 6 **R**, O LORD, your great mercy and love, 2349
25: 7 **R** not the sins of my youth 2349
25: 7 according to your love **r** me, 2349
42: 4 These things *I* **r** as I pour out my soul: 2349
42: 6 therefore *I will* **r** you from the land of 2349
63: 6 On my bed *I* **r** you; 2349
74: 2 **R** the people you purchased of old, 2349
74:18 **R** how the enemy has mocked you, 2349
74:22 **r** how fools mock you all day long. 2349
77:11 *I will* **r** the deeds of the LORD; 2349
77:11 yes, *I will* **r** your miracles of long ago. 2349
78:42 *They did* not **r** his power— 2349
88: 5 whom *you* **r** no more, 2349
89:47 **R** how fleeting is my life. 2349
89:50 **R**, Lord, how your servant has been mocked 2349
103:18 with those who keep his covenant and **r** 2349
105: 5 **R** the wonders he has done, his miracles, 2349
106: 4 **R** me, O LORD, when you show favor 2349
106: 7 *they did* not **r** your many kindnesses, 2349
119:49 **R** your word to your servant, 2349
119:52 *I* **r** your ancient laws, O LORD, 2349
119:55 In the night *I* **r** your name, O LORD, 2349
132: 1 **r** David and all the hardships he endured. 2349
137: 6 to the roof of my mouth if *I do* not **r** you, 2349
137: 7 **R**, O LORD, what the Edomites did on 2349
143: 5 *I* **r** the days of long ago; 2349
Pr 31: 7 and **r** their misery no more. 2349
Ecc 11: 8 But *let him* **r** the days of darkness, 2349
12: 1 **R** your Creator in the days of your youth, 2349
12: 6 **R** him—before the silver cord is severed, NIH
Isa 38: 3 "**R**, O LORD, how I have walked 2349
44:21 "**R** these things, O Jacob, 2349
46: 8 "**R** this, fix it in mind, take it to heart, 2349
46: 9 **R** the former things, those of long ago; 2349
54: 4 of your youth and **r** no more the reproach 2349
64: 5 *who* **r** your ways. 2349
64: 9 *do* not **r** our sins forever. 2349
Jer 2: 2 " '*I* **r** the devotion of your youth, 2349
14:10 now **r** their wickedness and punish them 2349
14:21 **R** your covenant with us and do not break 2349
15:15 O LORD; **r** me and care for me. 2349
17: 2 Even their children **r** their altars 2349
18:20 **R** that I stood before you and spoke 2349
31:20 I often speak against him, *I* still **r** him. 2349+2349
31:34 and *will* **r** their sins no more." 2349
44:21 "*Did* not the LORD **r** and think about 2349
51:50 **R** the LORD in a distant land, 2349
La 3:19 I **r** my affliction and my wandering, 2349
3:20 *I* **well r** them, and my soul is 2349+2349
5: 1 **R**, O LORD, what has happened to us; 2349
Eze 6: 9 those who escape *will* **r** me— 2349
16:22 and your prostitution *you did* not **r** the days 2349
16:43 " 'Because *you did* not **r** the days 2349
16:60 Yet I *will* **r** the covenant I made with you 2349
16:61 Then *you will* **r** your ways and 2349
16:63 *you will* **r** and be ashamed 2349
20:43 There *you will* **r** your conduct and all 2349
23:27 with longing or **r** Egypt anymore. 2349
36:31 Then *you will* **r** your evil ways 2349
Da 6:15 "**R**, O king, that according to the law 10313
Hos 7: 2 not realize that *I* **r** all their evil deeds. 2349
8:13 Now *he will* **r** their wickedness 2349
9: 9 God *will* **r** their wickedness 2349
Mic 6: 5 **r** what Balak king of Moab counseled 2349
6: 5 **R** [your journey] from Shittim to Gilgal, NIH
Hab 3: 2 in wrath **r** mercy. 2349
Zec 10: 9 yet in distant lands *they will* **r** me. 2349
Mal 4: 4 "**R** the law of my servant Moses, 2349
Mt 5:23 and there **r** that your brother has something *3630*
16: 9 Don't *you* **r** the five loaves for *3648*
27:63 "*we* **r** that while he was still alive *3630*
Mk 8:18 And don't *you* **r**? *3648*
Lk 1:72 to our fathers and *to* **r** his holy covenant, *3630*
16:25 "But Abraham replied, 'Son, **r** that *3630*
17:32 **R** Lot's wife! *3648*
23:42 **r** me when you come into your kingdom." *3630*
24: 6 **R** how he told you, *3630*
Jn 15:20 **R** the words I spoke to you: *3648*
16: 4 time comes *you will* **r** that I warned you. *3648*
Ac 20:31 **R** that for three years I never stopped *3648*
Ro 1: 9 is my witness how constantly *I* **r** you *3644+4472*
1Co 1:16 *I* don't **r** if I baptized anyone else.) *3857*
2Co 9: 6 **R this:** Whoever sows sparingly will *1254+4047*
Gal 2:10 that *we should continue to* **r** the poor, *3648*
Eph 2:11 **r** that formerly you who are Gentiles *3648*
2:12 **r** that at that time you were separate *NIG*
Php 1: 3 I thank my God every time I **r** you. *3644*
Col 4:18 **R** my chains. *3648*
1Th 1: 3 *We* continually **r** before our God *3648*
2: 9 *you* **r**, brothers, our toil and hardship; *3648*
2Th 2: 5 Don't *you* **r** that when I was with you *3648*
2Ti 1: 3 *I* constantly **r** you in my prayers. *2400+3644*
2: 8 **R** Jesus Christ, raised from the dead, *3648*
Phm 1: 4 I always thank my God *as* I **r** you *3644+4472*
Heb 8:12 and *will* **r** their sins no more." *3630*
10:17 and lawless acts *I will* **r** no more." *3630*
Heb 10:32 **R** those earlier days after you had received *389*
13: 3 **R** those in prison as if you were their fellow *3630*
13: 7 **R** your leaders, who spoke the word of God *3648*
Jas 5:20 **r** this: Whoever turns a sinner from the *1182*
2Pe 1:15 always be able *to* **r** these things. *3647+4472*
Jude 1:17 **r** what the apostles of our Lord Jesus Christ *3630*
Rev 2: 5 **R** the height from which you have fallen! *3648*
3: 3 **R**, therefore, what you have received *3648*

REMEMBERED (56) [REMEMBER]

Ge 8: 1 But God **r** Noah and all the wild animals 2349
19:29 he **r** Abraham, and he brought Lot out of 2349
30:22 Then God **r** Rachel; he listened to her 2349
41:31 The abundance in the land *will* not **be r**, 3359
42: 9 Then he **r** his dreams about them and said 2349
Ex 2:24 and he **r** his covenant with Abraham, 2349
3:15 the **name by which** I *am to be* **r** from generation to generation. 2352
6: 5 and *I have* **r** my covenant. 2349
17:14 a scroll as **something** to be **r** and make sure 2355
Nu 10: 9 Then *you will* **be r** by the LORD your God 2349
1Sa 1:19 Hannah his wife, and the LORD **r** her. 2349
Est 2: 1 *he* **r** Vashti and what she had done 2349
9:28 These days *should* **be r** and observed 2349
Job 24:20 evil men **are** no longer **r** but are broken like 2349
Ps 77: 3 *I* **r** you, O God, and I groaned; 2349
77: 6 *I* **r** my songs in the night. 2349
78:35 *They* **r** that God was their Rock, 2349
78:39 *He* **r** that they were but flesh, 2349
83: 4 that the name of Israel **be r** no more." 2349
98: 3 *He has* **r** his love and his faithfulness to 2349
105:42 For *he* **r** his holy promise given 2349
106:45 for their sake *he* **r** his covenant and out 2349
109:14 *May* the iniquity of his fathers **be r** before 2349
111: 4 He has caused his wonders to be **r**; 2352
112: 6 a righteous man will be **r** forever. 2352
136:23 to the *One* who **r** us in our low estate 2349
137: 1 and wept when we **r** Zion. 2349
Ecc 1:11 to come will not be **r** by those who follow. 2355
2:16 wise man, like the fool, will not be long **r**; 2355
9:15 But nobody **r** that poor man. 2349
Isa 17:10 *you have* not **r** the Rock, your fortress. 2349
23:16 sing many a song, so that *you will* **be r**." 2349
57:11 and *have* neither **r** me nor pondered this 2349
65:17 The former things *will* not **be r**, 2349
Jer 3:16 It will never enter their minds or *be* **r**; 2349
11:19 that his name **be r** no more." 2349
La 2: 1 not **r** his footstool in the day of his anger. 2349
Eze 3:20 The righteous things he did *will* not **be r**, 2349
18:22 of the offenses he has committed *will* **be r** 2349
18:24 the righteous things he has done *will* **be r**. 2349
21:32 *you will* **be r** no more; 2349
25:10 so that the Ammonites *will* not **be r** among 2349
33:13 the righteous things he has done *will* **be r**; 2349
33:16 of the sins he has committed *will* **be r** 2349
Jnh 2: 7 "When my life was ebbing away, *I* **r** you, 2349
Zec 13: 2 and *they will* **be r** no more," 2349
Mt 26:75 Then Peter **r** the word Jesus had spoken: *3630*
Mk 11:21 Peter **r** and said to Jesus, "Rabbi, look! *389*
14:72 Peter **r** the word Jesus had spoken to him: *389*
Lk 22:61 Then Peter **r** the word the Lord had spoken *5703*
24: 8 Then *they* **r** his words. *3630*
Jn 2:17 His disciples **r** that it is written: *3630*
Ac 10:31 God has heard your prayer and **r** your gifts *3630*
11:16 Then *I* **r** what the Lord had said: *3630*
Rev 16:19 God **r** Babylon the Great and gave her *3630*
18: 5 and God *has* **r** her crimes. *3648*

REMEMBERING (4) [REMEMBER]

Lk 1:54 helped his servant Israel, **r** to be merciful *3630*
Ac 20:35 **r** the words the Lord Jesus himself said: *3648*
1Co 11: 2 I praise you for **r** me in everything and for *3630*
Eph 1:16 **r** you in my prayers. *3644+4472*

REMEMBERS (11) [REMEMBER]

1Ch 16:15 *He* **r** his covenant forever, 2349
Ps 6: 5 No one **r** you when he is dead. 2352
9:12 For he who avenges blood **r**; 2349
103:14 *he* **r** that we are dust. 2349
103:16 and its place **r** it no more. 5795
105: 8 *He* **r** his covenant forever, 2349
111: 5 *he* **r** his covenant forever. 2349
115:12 The LORD **r** us and will bless us: 2349
Isa 43:25 for my own sake, and **r** your sins no more. 2349
La 1: 7 and wandering Jerusalem **r** all the treasures 2349
2Co 7:15 *when he* **r** that you were all obedient, *389*

REMEMBRANCE (5) [REMEMBER]

Ecc 1:11 There is no **r** of men of old, 2355
Mal 3:16 A scroll of **r** was written in his presence 2355
Lk 22:19 my body given for you; do this in **r** of me." *390*
1Co 11:24 body, which is for you; do this in **r** of me." *390*
11:25 do this, whenever you drink it, in **r** of me." *390*

REMETH (1)

Jos 19:21 **R**, En Gannim, En Haddah 8255

REMIND (11) [REMINDED, REMINDER, REMINDERS, REMINDING]

Nu 16:40 to **r** the Israelites that no one except 2355
1Ki 17:18 to **r** me *of* my sin and kill my son?" 2349
Eze 21:23 but he *will* **r** them *of* their guilt 2349
Jn 14:26 will teach you all things and *will* **r** you **of** *5703*

Ro 15:15 as if to **r** you of them **again,** 2057
1Co 4:17 He *will* **r** you **of** my way of life 389
15:1 *I want to* **r** you **of** the gospel I preached 1192
2Ti 1:6 For this reason *I* **r** you to fan into flame 389
Tit 3:1 **R** the people to be subject to rulers 5703
2Pe 1:12 So I will always **r** you of these things, 5703
Jude 1:5 I want *to* **r** you that the Lord delivered 5703

REMINDED (2) [REMIND]

Ge 41:9 "Today I *am* **r** *of* my shortcomings. 2349
2Ti 1:5 *I have been* **r** of your sincere faith, 3284+5704

REMINDER (5) [REMIND]

Ex 13:9 on your hand and a **r** on your forehead that 2355
Nu 5:15 a **r** offering to draw attention to guilt. 2355
5:18 and place in her hands the **r** offering, 2355
Eze 29:16 *be a* **r** *of* their sin in turning to her for help. 2349
Heb 10:3 But those sacrifices are an annual **r** of sins, 390

REMINDERS (1) [REMIND]

2Pe 3:1 both of them as **r** to stimulate you 5704

REMINDING (1) [REMIND]

2Ti 2:14 *Keep* **r** them **of** these things. 5703

REMISSION (KJV) See FORGIVENESS

REMMON (KJV) See RIMMON

REMMON-METHOAR (KJV) See RIMMON, TURNED

REMNANT (65)

Ge 45:7 to preserve for you a **r** on earth 8642
Dt 3:11 (Only Og king of Bashan was left of the **r** 3856
2Ki 19:4 Therefore pray for the **r** that still survives." 8642
19:30 Once more a **r** *of* the house of Judah 7129
19:31 For out of Jerusalem will come a **r,** 8642
21:14 the **r** *of* my inheritance and hand them over 8642
2Ch 34:9 Ephraim and the entire **r** *of* Israel and 8642
34:21 inquire of the LORD for me and for the **r** in 8636
36:20 He carried into exile to Babylon the **r,** 8642
Ezr 9:8 in leaving us a **r** and giving us a firm place 7129
9:13 and have given us a **r** like this. 7129
9:14 leaving us no **r** or survivor? 8642
9:15 We are left this day as a **r.** 7129
Ne 1:2 about the Jewish **r** that survived the exile, 7129
Isa 10:20 In that day the **r** *of* Israel, 8637
10:21 A **r** will return, a remnant of Jacob 8637
10:21 a **r** *of* Jacob will return to the Mighty God. 8637
10:22 only a **r** will return. 8637
11:11 the **r** that is left of his people from Assyria, 8637
11:16 a highway for the **r** *of* his people that is left 8637
17:3 the **r** *of* Aram will be like the glory of 8637
28:5 a beautiful wreath for the **r** *of* his people. 8637
37:4 Therefore pray for the **r** that still survives." 8642
37:31 Once more a **r** *of* the house of Judah 7129
37:32 For out of Jerusalem will come a **r,** 8642
Jer 6:9 the **r** *of* Israel as thoroughly as a vine; 8642
11:23 Not even a **r** will be left to them, 8642
23:3 "I myself will gather the **r** *of* my flock out 8642
31:7 save your people, the **r** *of* Israel.' 8642
40:11 the king of Babylon had left a **r** in Judah 8642
40:15 be scattered and the **r** *of* Judah to perish?" 8642
42:2 to the LORD your God for this entire **r.** 8642
42:15 hear the word of the LORD, O **r** *of* Judah. 8642
42:19 "O **r** *of* Judah, the LORD has told you, 8642
43:5 and all the army officers led away all the **r** 8642
44:7 and so leave yourselves without a **r?** 8642
44:12 the **r** *of* Judah who were determined to go 8642
44:14 of the **r** *of* Judah who have gone to live 8642
44:28 the whole **r** *of* Judah who came to live 8642
47:4 the **r** *from* the coasts of Caphtor. 8642
47:5 O **r** *on* the plain, 8642
50:20 for I will forgive *the* **r** *I* **spare.** 8636
50:26 Completely destroy her and leave her no **r.** 8642
Eze 9:8 the entire **r** *of* Israel in this outpouring 8642
11:13 Will you completely destroy the **r** 8642
Am 5:15 will have mercy on the **r** *of* Joseph. 8642
9:12 so that they may possess the **r** *of* Edom 8642
Mic 2:12 I will surely bring together the **r** *of* Israel. 8642
4:7 I will make the lame a **r,** 8642
5:7 The **r** *of* Jacob will be in the midst 8642
5:8 The **r** *of* Jacob will be among the nations, 8642
7:18 and forgives the transgression of the **r** 8642
Zep 1:4 from this place *every* **r** *of* Baal, the names 8637
2:7 It will belong to the **r** *of* the house 8642
2:9 The **r** *of* my people will plunder them; 8642
3:13 The **r** *of* Israel will do no wrong; 8642
Hag 1:12 the whole **r** *of* the people obeyed the voice 8642
1:14 and the spirit of the whole **r** *of* the people. 8642
2:2 the high priest, and to the **r** *of* the people. 8642
Zec 8:6 to the **r** *of* this people at that time, 8642
8:11 not deal with the **r** *of* this people as I did in 8642
8:12 as an inheritance to the **r** *of* this people. 8642
Ac 15:17 that the **r** of men may seek the Lord, 2905
Ro 9:27 only the **r** will be saved. 5698
11:5 at the present time there is a **r** chosen 3307

REMORSE (1)

Mt 27:3 he *was* **seized with r** and returned 3564

REMOTE (7) [REMOTEST]

Jdg 19:1 a **r area** *in* the hill country of Ephraim took 3752
19:18 to a **r area** *in* the hill country of Ephraim 3752
Mt 14:15 "This is a **r** place, and it's already 2245
15:33 in this **r place** to feed such a crowd?" 2244
Mk 6:35 "This is a **r** place," they said, 2245
8:4 in this **r place** can anyone get enough bread 2244
Lk 9:12 because we are in a **r** place here." 2245

REMOTEST (3) [REMOTE]

2Ki 19:23 I have reached its **r** parts, 7891
Ne 9:22 allotting to them even the **r frontiers.** 6992
Isa 37:24 I have reached its **r** heights, 7891

REMOVAL (2) [REMOVE]

Isa 27:9 will be the full fruitage of the **r** of his sin: 6073
1Pe 3:21 not the **r** of dirt **from** the body but 629

REMOVE (54) [REMOVAL, REMOVED, REMOVES, REMOVING]

Ge 30:32 through all your flocks today and **r** from 6073
Ex 12:15 the first day **r** the yeast from your houses, 8697
27:3 its pots to **r** the **ashes,** and its shovels, 2014
33:23 Then *I will* **r** my hand and you will see 6073
Lev 1:16 *to* **r** the crop with its contents and throw it 6073
3:4 which *he will* **r** with the kidneys. 6073
3:10 which *he will* **r** with the kidneys. 6073
3:15 which *he will* **r** with the kidneys. 6073
4:8 *He shall* **r** all the fat from the bull of 8123
4:9 which *he will* **r** with the kidneys— 6073
4:19 *He shall* **r** all the fat from it and burn it on 8123
4:31 *He shall* **r** all the fat, 6073
4:35 *He shall* **r** all the fat, 6073
6:10 and *shall* **r** the ashes of the burnt offering 8123
26:6 *I will* **r** savage beasts from the land, 8697
Nu 4:13 *They are to* **r** the **ashes** *from* the bronze altar 2014
20:26 **R** Aaron's garments and put them on his 7320
Jos 7:13 against your enemies until you **r** it. 6073
1Ki 15:14 Although *he did* not **r** the high places, 6073
20:24 **R** all the kings from their commands 6073
2Ki 23:4 and the doorkeepers to **r** from the temple of 3655
23:27 *"I will* **r** Judah also from my presence 6073
24:3 to **r** them from his presence because of 6073
2Ch 15:17 Although *he did* not **r** the high places 6073
29:5 **R** all defilement from the sanctuary. 3655
32:12 Hezekiah himself **r** this god's high places 6073
Job 9:34 *someone to* **r** God's rod from me, 6073
22:23 If *you* **r** wickedness **far** from your tent 8178
Ps 39:10 **R** your scourge from me; 6073
119:22 **R** from me scorn and contempt, 1655
Pr 25:4 **R** the dross from the silver, 2048
25:5 **r** the wicked from the king's presence, 2048
27:22 *you will* not **r** his folly from him. 6073
Isa 1:25 and **r** all your impurities. 6073
25:8 *he will* **r** the disgrace of his people 6073
57:14 **R** the obstacles out of the way 8123
62:10 **R** the stones. 6232
Jer 27:10 to you that *will only serve to* **r** you **far** 8178
28:16 *about to* **r** you from the face of the earth. 8938
32:31 and wrath that I *must* **r** it from my sight. 6073
Eze 11:18 return to it and **r** all its vile images 6073
11:19 *I will* **r** from them their heart of stone 6073
21:26 Take off the turban, **r** the crown. 8123
34:10 *I will* **r** them from tending the flock so 8697
36:26 *I will* **r** from you your heart of stone 6073
Hos 2:2 *Let her* **r** the adulterous look from her face 6073
2:17 *I will* **r** the names of the Baals 6073
Zep 3:11 because *I will* **r** from this city those who 6073
3:18 for the appointed feasts *I will* **r** from you; 665
Zec 3:9 'and *I will* **r** the sin of this land in a single 4631
13:2 *"I will* **r** both the prophets and the spirit 6296
Mt 7:5 *to* **r** the speck **from** your brother's eye. 1675
Lk 6:42 *to* **r** the speck **from** your brother's eye. 1675
Rev 2:5 to you and **r** your lampstand from its place. 3075

REMOVED (65) [REMOVE]

Ge 8:13 then **r** the covering from the ark and saw 6073
30:35 That same day *he* **r** all the male goats 6073
48:12 Then Joseph **r** them from Israel's knees 3655
Ex 25:15 *they are* not *to be* **r.** 6073
34:34 *he* **r** the veil until he came out. 6073
Lev 4:10 just as the fat **is r** from the ox sacrificed as 8123
4:31 as the fat **is r** from the fellowship offering, 6073
4:35 just as the fat **is r** from the lamb of 6073
7:4 which *is to be* **r** with the kidneys. 6073
Nu 20:28 Moses **r** Aaron's garments and put them 7320
Dt 26:13 *"I have* **r** from my house the sacred portion 1278
26:14 nor *have I* **r** any of it while I was unclean, 1278
Ru 4:8 And *he* **r** his sandal. 8990
1Sa 21:6 of the Presence that *had* **been r** from before 6073
2Sa 7:15 whom *I* **r** from before you. 6073
20:13 After Amasa *had* **been r** from the road, 3325
1Ki 2:27 So Solomon **r** Abiathar from the priesthood 1763
5:17 *they* **r from** the **quarry** large blocks 5825
20:41 Then the prophet quickly **r** the headband 6073
22:43 The high places, however, *were* not **r,** 6073
2Ki 12:3 The high places, however, *were* not **r;** 6073
14:4 The high places, however, *were* not **r;** 6073
15:4 The high places, however, *were* not **r;** 6073
15:35 The high places, however, *were* not **r;** 6073
16:17 King Ahaz took away the side panels and **r** 6073
16:17 *He* **r** the Sea from the bronze bulls 3718
16:18 and **r** the royal entryway outside the temple NIH
2Ki 17:18 with Israel and **r** them from his presence. 6073
17:23 until the LORD **r** them from his presence, 6073
18:4 He **r** the high places, 6073
18:22 whose high places and altars Hezekiah **r,** 6073
23:11 He **r** from the entrance to the temple of 8697
23:12 He **r** them from there, NIH
23:16 *he* **had** the bones **r** from them and burned on the altar 2256+4374+8938
23:19 Josiah **r** and defiled all the shrines at 6073
23:27 also from my presence as *I* **r** Israel, 6073
24:13 Nebuchadnezzar **r** all the treasures from 3655
2Ch 14:3 *He* **r** the foreign altars and the high places, 6073
14:5 *He* **r** the high places and incense altars 6073
15:8 *He* **r** the detestable idols from the whole 6296
17:6 *he* **r** the high places and the Asherah poles 6073
20:33 The high places, however, *were* not **r,** 6073
29:19 that King Ahaz **r** in his unfaithfulness 2396
30:14 *They* **r** the altars in Jerusalem 6073
33:15 of the foreign gods and **r** the image from NIH
34:33 Josiah **r** all the detestable idols from all 6073
Ezr 5:14 even **r** from the temple of Babylon the gold 10485
Job 19:9 He has stripped me of my honor and **r** 6073
34:20 the mighty *are* **r** without human hand. 6073
Ps 30:11 *you* **r** my sackcloth and clothed me 7337
81:6 *"I* **r** the burden from their shoulders; 6073
103:12 *so* **far** *has he* **r** our transgressions from us. 8178
Pr 27:25 *When* the hay *is* **r** and new growth appears 1655
Isa 10:13 *I* **r** the boundaries of nations, 6073
14:25 and his burden **r** from their shoulders." 6073
36:7 whose high places and altars Hezekiah **r,** 6073
54:10 the mountains be shaken and the hills *be* **r,** 4572
54:10 be shaken nor my covenant of peace *be* **r,"** 4572
54:14 Terror will be far **r;** NIH
Jer 8:1 of Jerusalem *will be* **r** from their graves. 3655
28:3 that Nebuchadnezzar king of Babylon **r** 4374
Eze 24:12 its heavy deposit *has* not *been* **r,** 3655
Jn 20:1 that the stone *had been* **r** from the entrance. 149
2Co 3:14 *It has* not *been* **r,** because only in Christ is it 365
Rev 6:14 and every mountain and island *was* **r** 3075

REMOVES (1) [REMOVE]

1Sa 17:26 and **r** this disgrace from Israel? 6073

REMOVING (2) [REMOVE]

Ac 13:22 *After* **r** Saul, he made David their king. 3496
Heb 12:27 The words "once more" indicate the **r** 3557

REMPHAN (KJV) See REPHAN

REND (2)

Isa 64:1 *you would* **r** the heavens and come down, 7973
Joel 2:13 **R** your heart and not your garments. 7973

RENDER (2) [RENDERING]

Isa 16:3 "Give us counsel, **r** a decision. 6913
Zec 8:16 **r** true and sound **judgment** 5477+9149

RENDERING (1) [RENDER]

Isa 28:7 they stumble when **r decisions.** 7133

RENEGADES (1)

Jdg 12:4 "You Gileadites are **r** from Ephraim 7127

RENEW (8) [RENEWAL, RENEWED, RENEWING]

Ru 4:15 He will **r** your life and sustain you 8740
Ps 51:10 O God, and **r** a steadfast spirit within me. 2542
104:30 and *you* **r** the face of the earth. 2542
Isa 40:31 who hope in the LORD *will* **r** their strength. 2736
41:1 **Let** the nations **r** their strength! 2736
61:4 *they will* **r** the ruined cities 2542
La 5:21 **r** our days as of old 2542
Hab 3:2 **R** them in our day, in our time 2649

RENEWAL (4) [RENEW]

Job 14:14 I will wait for my **r** to come. 2722
Isa 57:10 You found **r** *of* your strength, 2652
Mt 19:28 "I tell you the truth, at the **r** of all things, 4098
Tit 3:5 through the washing of rebirth and **r** by 364

RENEWED (7) [RENEW]

2Ki 23:3 the pillar and **r** the covenant in the presence 4162
2Ch 34:31 and **r** the covenant in the presence of 4162
Job 33:25 then his flesh **is r** like a child's; 8186
Ps 103:5 with good things so that your youth **is r** like 2542
2Co 4:16 yet inwardly we *are being* **r** day by day. 363
Php 4:10 that at last *you have* **r** your concern for me. 352
Col 3:10 which *is being* **r** in knowledge in 363

RENEWING (1) [RENEW]

Ro 12:2 but be transformed *by* the **r** of your mind. 364

RENOUNCE (3) [RENOUNCED, RENOUNCES]

Eze 14:6 and **r** all your detestable practices! 7156+8740
Da 4:27 **R** your sins by doing what is right, 10596
Rev 2:13 *You did* not **r** your faith in me, 766

RENOUNCED (3) [RENOUNCE]

Ps 89:39 *You have* r the covenant with your servant 5545
Mt 19:12 and others *have* r **marriage** because of the kingdom *1571+2335+2336*
2Co 4: 2 *we have* r secret and shameful ways; *584*

RENOUNCES (1) [RENOUNCE]

Pr 28:13 whoever confesses and r them finds mercy. 6440

RENOWN (12) [RENOWNED]

Ge 6: 4 They were the heroes of old, men of r. 9005
Ps 102:12 your r endures through all generations. 2352
135:13 your r, O LORD, through all generations. 2352
Isa 26: 8 and r are the desire of our hearts. 2352
55:13 This will be for the LORD's r, 9005
63:12 to gain for himself everlasting r, 9005
Jer 13:11 'to be my people for my r and praise 9005
32:20 and have gained the r that is still yours. 9005
33: 9 Then this city will bring me r, joy, 9005
49:25 Why has the city of r not been abandoned, 9335
Eze 26:17 " 'How you are destroyed, O city of r, 2146
Hos 12: 5 the LORD is his **name of r!** 2352

RENOWNED (3) [RENOWN]

Isa 23: 8 whose traders *are* r *in* the earth? 3877
23: 9 of all glory and to humble all *who are* r *on* 3877
Eze 34:29 I will provide for them a land r 4200+9005

RENT (1) [RENTED]

Mt 21:41 "and *he will* r the vineyard to other tenants, *1686*

RENTED (4) [RENT]

Mt 21:33 Then *he* r the vineyard to some farmers *1686*
Mk 12: 1 Then *he* r the vineyard to some farmers *1686*
Lk 20: 9 r it to some farmers and went away for *1686*
Ac 28:30 Paul stayed there in his own r **house** *3637*

REOPENED (1)

Ge 26:18 Isaac r the wells that had been 2256+2916+8740

REPAID (9) [PAY]

Ge 44: 4 'Why *have you* r good with evil? 8966
Jdg 9:56 Thus God r the wickedness that Abimelech 8740
2Sa 16: 8 The LORD *has* r you *for* all the blood 8740
Pr 14:14 faithless *will be* **fully** r for their ways, 8425
Jer 18:20 *Should* good **be** r with evil? 8966
Lk 6:34 expecting to be r in full. *655*
14:12 and so you will be r. *501*
14:14 *be* r at the resurrection of the righteous." *500*
Col 3:25 Anyone who does wrong *will be* r *3152*

REPAIR (14) [REPAIRED, REPAIRER, REPAIRING, REPAIRS]

2Ki 12: 5 *be used to* r whatever damage is found in 2616
12: 8 from the people and that they *would* not r 2616
12:12 and dressed stone for the r *of* the temple of 2616
12:14 *who* used it *to* r the temple. 2616
22: 5 have these men pay the workers who r 981+2616
22: 6 and dressed stone to r the temple. 2616
1Ch 26:27 for the r of the temple of the LORD. 2616
2Ch 24: 5 to r the temple of your God. 2616
24:12 workers in iron and bronze to r the temple. 2616
34: 8 to r the temple of the LORD his God. 2616
Ezr 9: 9 the house of our God and r its ruins, 6641
Eze 13: 5 not gone up to the breaks in the wall *to* r it 1553
Am 9:11 *I will* r its broken places, restore its ruins, 1553
Na 3:14 tread the mortar, r the brickwork! 2616

REPAIRED (24) [REPAIR]

1Ki 18:30 and *he* r the altar of the LORD, 8324
2Ki 12: 6 of King Joash the priests *still had* not r 2616
2Ch 15: 8 *He* r the altar of the LORD that was 2542
29: 3 of the temple of the LORD and r them. 2616
34:10 the workers *who* r and restored the temple. 980
Ne 3: 4 the son of Hakkoz, r the next section. 2616
3: 5 The next section *was* r *by* the men 2616
3: 6 The Jeshanah Gate *was* r *by* Joiada son 2616
3: 8 one of the goldsmiths, r the next section; 2616
3: 9 of Jerusalem, r the next section. 2616
3:11 son of Pahath-Moab r another section and 2616
3:12 r the next section with the help 2616
3:13 The Valley Gate *was* r *by* Hanun and 2616
3:13 also r five hundred yards of the wall as far NIH
3:14 The Dung Gate *was* r *by* Malkijah son 2616
3:15 The Fountain Gate *was* r *by* Shallun son 2616
3:15 He also r the wall of the Pool of Siloam, NIH
3:19 ruler of Mizpah, r another section, 2616
3:20 of Zabbai zealously r another section, 2616
3:21 the son of Hakkoz, r another section, 2616
3:24 Binnui son of Henadad r another section, 2616
3:27 the men of Tekoa r another section, 2616
3:30 the sixth son of Zalaph, r another section. 2616
Jer 19:11 potter's jar is smashed and cannot **be** r. 8324

REPAIRER (1) [REPAIR]

Isa 58:12 you will be called R **of** Broken **Walls,** 1553

REPAIRING (4) [REPAIR]

2Ki 12: 7 "Why aren't you r the damage done to 2616
12: 7 but hand it over for r the temple." 981
2Ch 32: 5 Then he worked hard r all the broken 1215
Ezr 4:12 They are restoring the walls and r the 10253

REPAIRS (22) [REPAIR]

2Ch 24:13 and the r progressed under them. 776
Ne 3: 4 the son of Meshezabel, **made** r, 2616
3: 4 to him Zadok son of Baana also **made** r. 2616
3: 7 r *were* **made** *by* men from Gibeon 2616
3: 8 the perfume-makers, **made** r next to that. 2616
3:10 of Harumaph **made** r opposite his house, 2616
3:10 of Hashabneiah **made** r next to him. 2616
3:16 **made** r up to a point opposite the tombs 2616
3:17 *the* r *were* **made** *by* the Levites 2616
3:17 **carried out** r for his district. 2616
3:18 *the* r *were* **made** *by* their countrymen 2616
3:22 r next to him *were* **made** by the priests 2616
3:23 and Hasshub **made** r in front of their house; 2616
3:23 son of Ananish, **made** r beside his house. 2616
3:26 of Ophel made r up to a point opposite NIH
3:28 Above the Horse Gate, the priests **made** r, 2616
3:29 son of Immer **made** r opposite his house. 2616
3:29 the guard at the East Gate, **made** r. 2616
3:30 **made** r opposite his living quarters. 2616
3:31 **made** r as far as the house of 2616
3:32 the goldsmiths and merchants **made** r. 2616
4: 7 the r to Jerusalem's walls had gone ahead 776

REPAY (47) [PAY]

Lev 25:28 if he does not acquire the means *to* r him, 8740
Dt 7:10 But those who hate him *he will* r to their 8966
7:10 *to* r to their face those who hate him. 8966
32: 6 Is this the way *you* r the LORD, 1694
32:35 It is mine to avenge; *I will* r. 8966
32:41 and r those who hate me. 8966
Ru 2:12 the LORD r you *for* what you have done. 8966
2Sa 3:39 *May* the LORD r the evildoer according 8966
16:12 the LORD will see my distress and r me 8740
1Ki 2:32 The LORD *will* r him *for* the blood he shed, 6584+8031+8740
2:44 the LORD *will* r you *for* your wrongdoing. 928+8031+8740
Job 21:19 *Let him* r the man himself, 8966
Ps 28: 4 R them for their deeds and 5989
28: 4 r them for what their hands have done 5989
35:12 *They* r me evil for good 8966
37:21 The wicked borrow and *do* not r, 8966
38:20 *Those who* r my good with evil slander me 8966
41:10 raise me up, that *I may* r them. 8966
94:23 *He will* r them *for* their sins 8740
103:10 not treat us as our sins deserve or r us 1694
109: 5 *They* r me evil for good, 8492
116:12 How *can I* r the LORD for all his goodness 8740
Pr 24:12 *Will he* not r each person according 8740
Isa 59:18 so *will he* r wrath to his enemies 8966
59:18 *he will* r the islands their due. 8966
Jer 16:18 *I will* r them double *for* their wickedness 8966
25:14 *I will* r them according to their deeds and 8966
50:29 R her for her deeds; 8966
51:24 "Before your eyes *I will* r Babylon 8966
51:56 God of retribution; *he will* r **in full.** 8966+8966
Eze 7: 3 and r you *for* all your detestable practices. 5989
7: 4 *I will* surely r you *for* your conduct and 5989
7: 8 and r you *for* all your detestable practices. 5989
7: 9 *I will* r you in accordance with your 5989
Hos 4: 9 for their ways and r them *for* their deeds. 8740
12: 2 according to his ways and r him according 8740
12:14 the guilt of his bloodshed and *will* r him 8740
Joel 2:25 "*I will* r you *for* the years the locusts 8966
Mt 18:25 and all that he had be sold *to* r **the debt.** *625*
Lk 14:14 Although they cannot r you, *500*
Ro 11:35 ever given to God, *that* God *should* r him?" *500*
12:17 *Do* not r anyone evil for evil. *625*
12:19 mine to avenge; I *will* r," says the Lord. *500*
2Ti 4:14 The Lord *will* r him for what he has done. *625*
Heb 10:30 "It is mine to avenge; I *will* r," and again, *500*
1Pe 3: 9 *Do* not r evil with evil or insult with insult, *625*
Rev 2:23 and *I will* r each of you according *1443*

REPAYING (5) [PAY]

2Ch 6:23 r the guilty by bringing down on his own 8740
20:11 *how they are* r us by coming to drive us out 1694
Isa 66: 6 the LORD r his enemies all they deserve. 8966
Joel 3: 4 *Are* you r me *for* something I have done? 8966
1Ti 5: 4 their own family and so r their parents *304+625*

REPAYMENT (1) [PAY]

Lk 6:34 you lend to those from whom you expect r, *3284*

REPAYS (3) [PAY]

Job 21:31 Who r him for what he has done? 8966
34:11 *He* r a man *for* what he has done; 8966
Ps 137: 8 happy is *he* who r you for what you have 8966

REPEALED (3)

Est 1:19 laws of Persia and Media, *which* cannot *be* r 6296
Da 6: 8 the Medes and Persians, which cannot *be* r. 10528
6:12 the Medes and Persians, which cannot *be* r. 10528

REPEAT (2) [REPEATED, REPEATEDLY, REPEATS]

2Co 11:16 *I* r: Let no one take me for a fool. *3306+4099*
13: 2 *I* now r it while absent: *4625*

REPEATED (8) [REPEAT]

Ge 44: 6 *he* r these words to them. 1819
Jdg 9: 3 When the brothers r all this to the citizens 1819
11:11 And he r all his words before the LORD 1819
1Sa 8:21 *he* r it before the LORD. 1819
11: 5 Then *they* r to him what the men 6218
17:27 *They* r to him what they had been saying 606
18:23 They r these words to David. 1819
Heb 10: 1 by the same sacrifices r endlessly year *4712S*

REPEATEDLY (2) [REPEAT]

Jer 46:16 *They will* stumble r; 8049
Lk 8:31 And *they* **begged** him *r* not to order them *AIT*

REPEATS (2) [REPEAT]

Pr 17: 9 *whoever* r the matter separates close friends. 9101
26:11 so a fool r his folly. 9101

REPENT (39) [PENITENT, REPENTANCE, REPENTED, REPENTS]

1Ki 8:47 and r and plead with you in the land 8740
2Ch 6:37 and r and plead with you in the land 8740
Job 34:33 when you refuse to r? NIH
36:10 to correction and commands them *to* r 8740
42: 6 Therefore I despise myself and r in dust 5714
Isa 59:20 to *those* in Jacob *who* r *of* their sins," 8740
Jer 5: 3 harder than stone and refused to r. 8740
15:19 "If *you* r, I will restore you 8740
Eze 14: 6 'This is what the Sovereign LORD says: R! 8740
18:30 declares the Sovereign LORD. **R!** 8740
18:32 declares the Sovereign LORD. **R** and live! 8740
Hos 11: 5 over them because they refuse to r? 8740
Mt 3: 2 **"R,** for the kingdom of heaven is near." *3566*
4:17 **"R,** for the kingdom of heaven is near." *3566*
11:20 because *they did* not r. *3566*
21:32 *you did* not r and believe him. *3564*
Mk 1:15 **R** and believe the good news!" *3566*
6:12 and preached that *people should* r. *3566*
Lk 13: 3 But unless *you* r, you too will all perish. *3566*
13: 5 But unless *you* r, you too will all perish." *3566*
15: 7 righteous persons who do not need *to* r. *3567*
16:30 from the dead goes to them, *they will* r.' *3566*
17: 4 back to you and says, '*I* r,' forgive him." *3566*
Ac 2:38 Peter replied, **"R** and be baptized, *3566*
3:19 **R,** then, and turn to God, *3566*
8:22 **R** of this wickedness and pray to the Lord. *3566*
17:30 he commands all people everywhere *to* r. *3566*
26:20 I preached that they should r and turn *3566*
Rev 2: 5 **R** and do the things you did at first. *3566*
2: 5 If *you do* not r, I will come to you and *3566*
2:16 **R** therefore! Otherwise, I will soon come *3566*
2:21 I have given her time to r of her immorality *3566*
2:22 unless *they* r of her ways. *3566*
3: 3 received and heard; obey it, and r. *3566*
3:19 So be earnest, and r. *3566*
9:20 not killed by these plagues still *did* not r of *3566*
9:21 Nor *did they* r of their murders, *3566*
16: 9 but *they* **refused to** r and glorify him. *3566+4024*
16:11 *they* **refused to** r of what they had done. *3566+4024*

REPENTANCE (21) [REPENT]

Isa 30:15 "In r and rest is your salvation, 8746
Mt 3: 8 Produce fruit in keeping with r. *3567*
3:11 "I baptize you with water for r. *3567*
Mk 1: 4 a baptism *of* r for the forgiveness of sins. *3567*
Lk 3: 3 a baptism *of* r for the forgiveness of sins. *3567*
3: 8 Produce fruit in keeping with r. *3567*
5:32 to call the righteous, but sinners to r." *3567*
24:47 r and forgiveness of sins will be preached *3567*
Ac 5:31 that he might give r and forgiveness of sins *3567*
11:18 even the Gentiles r unto life." *3567*
13:24 John preached r and baptism to all *3567*
19: 4 "John's baptism was a baptism *of* r. *3567*
20:21 **turn** to God **in** r and have faith in our Lord *3567*
26:20 to God and prove their r by their deeds. *3567*
Ro 2: 4 that God's kindness leads you toward r? *3567*
2Co 7: 9 but because your sorrow led you to r. *3567*
7:10 Godly sorrow brings r that leads to *3567*
2Ti 2:25 that God will grant them r leading them to *3567*
Heb 6: 1 the foundation *of* r from acts that lead *3567*
6: 6 if they fall away, to be brought back to r, *3567*
2Pe 3: 9 anyone to perish, but everyone to come to r. *3567*

REPENTED (9) [REPENT]

2Ch 32:26 Then Hezekiah r of the pride of his heart, 4044
Jer 31:19 After I strayed, *I* r; 5714
34:15 Recently you r and did what is right 8740
Zec 1: 6 "Then *they* r and said, 8740
Mt 11:21 *they* would *have* r long ago in sackcloth *3566*
12:41 for *they* r at the preaching of Jonah, *3566*
Lk 10:13 *they* would *have* r long ago, *3566*
11:32 for *they* r at the preaching of Jonah, *3566*
2Co 12:21 and *have* not r of the impurity, *3566*

REPENTS (5) [REPENT]

Jer 8: 6 No one r of his wickedness, saying, 5714
18: 8 and if that nation I warned r of its evil, 8740
Lk 15: 7 rejoicing in heaven over one sinner **who** r *3566*
15:10 the angels of God over one sinner **who** r." *3566*

Lk 17: 3 rebuke him, and if *he* **r**, forgive him. *3566*

REPHAEL (1)

1Ch 26: 7 Othni, **R**, Obed and Elzabad; 8330

REPHAH (1)

1Ch 7:25 **R** was his son, Resheph his son, 8338

REPHAIAH (5)

1Ch 3:21 Pelatiah and Jeshaiah, and the sons of **R**, 8341
4:42 Neariah, **R** and Uzziel, the sons of Ishi, 8341
7: 2 The sons of Tola: Uzzi, **R**, Jeriel, Jahmai, 8341
9:43 **R** was his son, Eleasah his son and 8341
Ne 3: 9 **R** son of Hur, ruler of a half-district of 8341

REPHAIM (8)

Jos 15: 8 at the northern end of the Valley of **R**. 8329
18:16 north of the Valley of **R**. 8329
2Sa 5:18 and spread out in the Valley of **R**; 8329
5:22 up and spread out in the Valley of **R**; 8329
23:13 was encamped in the Valley of **R**. 8329
1Ch 11:15 was encamped in the Valley of **R**. 8329
14: 9 and raided the Valley of **R**; 8329
Isa 17: 5 gleans heads of grain in the Valley of **R**. 8329

REPHAIMS (KJV) See REPHAITES

REPHAITES (10)

Ge 14: 5 and defeated the **R** in Ashteroth Karnaim, 8328
15:20 Hittites, Perizzites, **R**, 8328
Dt 2:11 they too were considered **R**, 8328
2:20 (That too was considered a land of the **R**, 8328
3:11 of Bashan was left of the remnant of the **R**. 8328
3:13 to be known as a land of the **R**. 8328
Jos 12: 4 Og king of Bashan, one of the last of the **R**, 8328
13:12 and had survived as one of the last of the **R**. 8328
17:15 in the land of the Perizzites and **R**." 8328
1Ch 20: 4 Sippai, one of the descendants of the **R**, 8328

REPHAN (1)

Ac 7:43 shrine of Molech and the star of your god **R**, *4818*

REPHIDIM (5)

Ex 17: 1 They camped at **R**, 8340
17: 8 and attacked the Israelites at **R**. 8340
19: 2 After they set out from **R**, 8340
Nu 33:14 They left Alush and camped at **R**, 8340
33:15 They left **R** and camped in the Desert 8340

REPLACE (6) [REPLACED]

Lev 14:42 are to take other stones *to* **r** these 448+995+9393
1Ki 14:27 Rehoboam made bronze shields to **r** them 9393
20:24 and **r** them with other officers. 8492+9393
2Ki 17:24 in the towns of Samaria to **r** the Israelites. 9393
2Ch 12:10 Rehoboam made bronze shields to **r** them 9393
Isa 9:10 but *we will* **r** them *with* cedars." 2736

REPLACED (3) [REPLACE]

1Sa 21: 6 from before the LORD and **r** *by* hot bread 8492
1Ki 2:35 and **r** Abiathar with Zadok the priest. 5989+9393
Da 8:22 The four horns *that* **r** the one 6641+9393

REPLANTED (1) [PLANT]

Eze 36:36 and *have* **r** what was desolate. 5749

REPLENISH (KJV) See FILL

REPLICA (1)

Jos 22:28 Look at the **r** *of* the LORD's altar, 9322

REPLIED (414) [REPLY]

Ge 4: 9 *he* **r**. "Am I my brother's keeper?" 606
19: 9 "Get out of our way," *they* **r**. 606
20:11 Abraham **r**, "I said to myself, 606
21:30 *He* **r**, "Accept these seven lambs 606
22: 1 "Here I am," *he* **r**. 606
22: 7 "Yes, my son?" Abraham **r**. 606
22:11 "Here I am," *he* **r**. 606
23: 5 The Hittites **r** *to* Abraham, 6699
23:10 among his people and he **r** *to* Abraham in 6699
24:40 *"He* **r**, 'The LORD, before whom I have 606
24:55 But her brother and her mother **r**, 606
25:31 Jacob **r**, "First sell me your birthright." 606
27:20 LORD your God gave me success," *he* **r**. 606
27:24 "I am," *he* **r**. 606
29: 4 "We're from Haran," *they* **r**. 606
29: 8 *they* **r**, "until all the flocks are gathered and 606
29:26 Laban **r**, "It is not our custom here to give 606
30:31 "Don't give me anything," Jacob **r**. 606
31:14 Then Rachel and Leah **r**, 6699
32:26 But Jacob **r**, "I will not let you go 606
32:29 But *he* **r**, "Why do you ask my name?" 606
34:13 Jacob's sons **r** deceitfully as they spoke 6699
34:31 But *they* **r**, "Should he have treated our sister like a prostitute?" 606
37:13 "Very well," *he* **r**. 606
37:16 *He* **r**, "I'm looking for my brothers. 606
41:16 "I cannot do it," Joseph **r** *to* Pharaoh, 6699
Ge 42: 7 "From the land of Canaan," *they* **r**, 606
42:13 *they* **r**, "Your servants were twelve brothers, 606
42:22 Reuben **r**, "Didn't I tell you not to sin 6699
43: 7 *They* **r**, "The man questioned us closely 606
43:28 *They* **r**, "Your servant our father is still alive 606
44:16 "What can we say to my lord?" Judah **r**. 606
46: 2 "Here I am," *he* **r**. 606
47: 3 servants are shepherds," *they* **r** to Pharaoh, 606
Ex 4: 2 "A staff," *he* **r**. 606
8:10 Moses **r**, "It will be as you say, 606
9:29 Moses **r**, "When I have gone out of 606
10:29 "Just as you say," Moses **r**, 606
17: 2 Moses **r**, "Why do you quarrel with me? 606
18:17 Moses' father-in-law **r**, "What you are doing 606
19:24 The LORD **r**, "Go down and bring Aaron 606
32:18 Moses **r**: "It is not the sound of victory, 606
32:33 The LORD **r** to Moses, "Whoever has sinned 606
33:14 The LORD **r**, "My Presence will go 606
Lev 10:19 Aaron **r** to Moses, "Today they sacrificed 1819
Nu 11:29 Moses **r**, "Are you jealous for my sake? 606
12:14 The LORD **r** to Moses, "If her father had spit 606
14:20 The LORD **r**, "I have forgiven them, 606
20:19 The Israelites **r**: "We will go along the 606
22:38 "Well, I have come to you now," Balaam **r**. 606
Dt 1:41 Then *you* **r**, "We have sinned against 6699
Jos 2:21 "Agreed," *she* **r**. 606
5:14 *he* **r**, "but as commander of the army of 606
5:15 The commander of the LORD's army **r**, 606
7:20 Achan **r**, "It is true! 6699
15:19 *She* **r**, "Do me a special favor. 606
17:16 The people of Joseph **r**, 606
22:21 the half-tribe of Manasseh **r** *to* the heads of 6699
24:22 "Yes, we are witnesses," *they* **r**. 606
Jdg 1:15 *She* **r**, "Do me a special favor. 606
6:13 Gideon **r**, "if the LORD is with us, 606
6:17 Gideon **r**, "If now I have found favor 606
6:31 Joash **r** to the hostile crowd around him, 606
8: 7 Then Gideon **r**, "Just for that, 606
8:19 Gideon **r**, "Those were my brothers, 606
9:11 "But the fig tree **r**, 'Should I give up my 606
9:36 Zebul **r**, "You mistake the shadows of 606
10:11 The LORD **r**, "When the Egyptians, 606
11:10 elders of Gilead **r**, "The LORD is our witness 606
11:36 *she* **r**, "you have given your word to 606
12: 5 "Are you an Ephraimite?" If *he* **r**, 606
13:16 The angel of the LORD **r**, "Even though 606
13:18 He **r**, "Why do you ask my name? 606
14: 3 His father and mother **r**, 606
14:14 *He* **r**, "Out of the eater, something to eat; 606
14:16 *he* **r**, "so why should I explain it to you?" 606
16:13 *He* **r**, "If you weave the seven braids 606
18:24 *He* **r**, "You took the gods I made, 606
19:12 His master **r**, "No. 606
20:18 The LORD **r**, "Judah shall go first." 606
Ru 1:16 But Ruth **r**, "Don't urge me to leave you or 606
2: 6 The foreman **r**, "She is the Moabitess 6699
2:11 Boaz **r**, "I've been told all about what 6699
3:10 "The LORD bless you, my daughter," *he* **r**. 606
1Sa 1:15 "Not so, my lord," Hannah **r**, 6699
4:17 The man who brought the news **r**, 6699
6: 4 *They* **r**, "Five gold tumors and five gold 606
9: 6 But the servant **r**, "Look, 606
9:19 "I am the seer," Samuel **r**. 6699
10:16 Saul **r**, "He assured us that the donkeys 606
11: 2 But Nahash the Ammonite **r**, 606
12: 4 not cheated or oppressed us," *they* **r**. 606
12:20 "Do not be afraid," Samuel **r**. 606
13:11 Saul **r**, "When I saw that men were 606
14:36 "Do whatever seems best to you," *they* **r**. 606
14:40 "Do what seems best to you," the men **r**. 606
15:16 "Tell me," Saul **r**. 606
15:22 But Samuel **r**: "Does the LORD delight in burnt offerings 606
15:30 Saul **r**, "I have sinned. 606
16: 5 Samuel **r**, "Yes, in peace; 606
17:33 Saul **r**, "You are not able to go out 606
17:55 Abner **r**, "As surely as you live, O king, 606
18:25 Saul **r**, "Say to David, 606
20: 2 "Never!" Jonathan **r**. "You are not 606
21: 5 David **r**, "Indeed women have been kept 6699
21: 9 The priest **r**, "The sword of Goliath 606
23:21 Saul **r**, "The LORD bless you 606
26:14 Abner **r**, "Who are you who calls to 6699
26:17 David **r**, "Yes it is, my lord the king." 606
28: 2 Achish **r**, "Very well, 606
29: 3 Achish **r**, "Is this not David, 606
30:23 David **r**, "No, my brothers, 606
2Sa 7: 3 Nathan **r** to the king, "Whatever you have 606
9: 2 "Your servant," *he* **r**. 606
9: 6 "Your servant," *he* **r**. 606
12:13 Nathan **r**, "The LORD has taken away your 606
12:19 "Yes," *they* **r**, "he is dead." 606
13:25 "No, my son," the king **r**. 606
14:10 The king **r**, "If anyone says anything 606
14:12 "Speak," *he* **r**. 606
15:21 But Ittai **r** *to* the king, "As surely as 6699
17: 7 Hushai **r** to Absalom, "The advice 606
18:12 But the man **r**, "Even if a thousand shekels 606
18:22 But Joab **r**, "My son, 606
18:32 The Cushite **r**, "May the enemies of my lord 606
19:22 David **r**, "What do you and I have 606
20:20 Joab **r**, "Far be it from me to swallow up 6699
24: 3 But Joab **r** to the king, 606
24:24 But the king **r** to Araunah, "No, 606
1Ki 1:52 Solomon **r**, "If he shows himself to be 606
2:14 "You may say it," *she* **r**. 606
2:18 "Very well," Bathsheba **r**, 606
1Ki 2:20 The king **r**, "Make it, my mother; 606
11:22 "Nothing," Hadad **r**, "but do let me go!" 606
12: 7 *They* **r**, "If today you will be a servant 1819
12:10 young men who had grown up with him **r**, 1819
13:14 "I am," *he* **r**. 606
17:12 *she* **r**, "I don't have any bread— 606
17:19 "Give me your son," Elijah **r**. 606
18: 8 "Yes," *he* **r**. 606
18:18 not made trouble for Israel," Elijah **r**. 606
19:10 *He* **r**, "I have been very zealous for the LORD 606
19:14 *He* **r**, "I have been very zealous for the LORD 606
19:20 "Go back," Elijah **r**. 606
20: 9 So *he* **r** to Ben-Hadad's messengers, 606
20:14 The prophet **r**, "This is what 606
21: 3 But Naboth **r**, "The LORD forbid 606
22: 4 Jehoshaphat **r** to the king of Israel, 606
22: 8 not say that," Jehoshaphat **r**. 606
22:25 Micaiah **r**, "You will find out on 606
2Ki 1: 6 "A man came to meet us," *they* **r**. 606
1: 8 *They* **r**, "He was a man with a garment 606
1:12 "If I am a man of God," Elijah **r**, 6699
2: 3 "Yes, I know," Elisha **r**, 606
2: 4 And *he* **r**, "As surely as the LORD lives 606
2: 5 "Yes, I know," *he* **r**, 606
2: 6 And *he* **r**, "As surely as the LORD lives 606
2: 9 a double portion of your spirit," Elisha **r**. 606
2:16 "No," Elisha **r**, "do not send them." 606
3: 7 "I will go with you," *he* **r**. 606
4: 2 Elisha **r** to her, "How can I help you? 606
4: 6 But *he* **r**, "There is not a jar left." 606
4:13 *She* **r**, "I have a home among my own 606
5: 5 "By all means, go," the king of Aram **r**. 606
6: 3 "I will," Elisha **r**. 606
6:27 The king **r**, "If the LORD does not help you, 606
7:19 The man of God *had* **r**, "You will see it 606
8:14 Hazael **r**, "He told me that you would 606
9: 5 "For you, commander," *he* **r**. 606
9:11 and the sort of things he says," Jehu **r**. 606
9:18 What do you have to do with peace?" Jehu **r**. 606
9:19 Jehu **r**, "What do you have to do with peace 606
9:22 "How can there be peace," Jehu **r**, 606
14: 9 of Israel **r** to Amaziah king of Judah: 606+8938
18:27 But the commander **r**, 606
20:14 "From a distant land," Hezekiah **r**. 606
20:19 you have spoken is good," Hezekiah **r**. 606
1Ch 17: 2 Nathan **r** to David, "Whatever you have 606
21: 3 But Joab **r**, "May the LORD multiply 606
21:24 But King David **r** to Araunah, "No, 606
2Ch 2:11 Hiram king of Tyre **r** by letter to Solomon: 606
10: 7 *They* **r**, "If you will be kind to these people 1819
10:10 with him **r**, "Tell the people who have said 1819
18: 3 Jehoshaphat **r**, "I am as you are, 606
18: 7 not say that," Jehoshaphat **r**. 606
18:24 Micaiah **r**, "You will find out on 606
25: 9 The man of God **r**, "The LORD can give 606
25:18 of Israel **r** to Amaziah king of Judah: 606+8938
Ne 2:18 *They* **r**, "Let us start rebuilding." 606
Est 1:16 Then Memucan **r** in the presence of 606
5: 4 "If it pleases the king," **r** Esther, 606
5: 7 Esther **r**, "My petition and my request 6699
8: 7 King Xerxes **r** to Queen Esther and 606
Job 1: 9 "Does Job fear God for nothing?" Satan **r**. 6699
2: 4 "Skin for skin!" Satan **r**. 6699
2:10 *He* **r**, "You are talking like a foolish woman 606
4: 1 Then Eliphaz the Temanite **r**: 6699
6: 1 Then Job **r**: 6699
8: 1 Then Bildad the Shuhite **r**: 6699
9: 1 Then Job **r**: 6699
11: 1 Then Zophar the Naamathite **r**: 6699
12: 1 Then Job **r**: 6699
15: 1 Then Eliphaz the Temanite **r**: 6699
16: 1 Then Job **r**: 6699
18: 1 Then Bildad the Shuhite **r**: 6699
19: 1 Then Job **r**: 6699
20: 1 Then Zophar the Naamathite **r**: 6699
21: 1 Then Job **r**: 6699
22: 1 Then Eliphaz the Temanite **r**: 6699
23: 1 Then Job **r**: 6699
25: 1 Then Bildad the Shuhite **r**: 6699
26: 1 Then Job **r**: 6699
42: 1 Then Job **r** *to* the LORD: 6699
Isa 36:12 But the commander **r**, 606
39: 3 "From a distant land," Hezekiah **r**. 606
39: 8 you have spoken is good," Hezekiah **r** 606
Jer 1:11 I see the branch of an almond tree," *I* **r**. 606
28: 5 Then the prophet Jeremiah **r** to 606
35: 6 But *they* **r**, "We do not drink wine, 606
36:18 Baruch **r**, "he dictated all these words 606
37:17 Jeremiah **r**, "you will be handed over to 606
38:20 "They will not hand you over," Jeremiah **r**. 606
42: 4 "I have heard you," **r** Jeremiah the prophet. 606
Da 2: 5 The king **r** to the astrologers, 10558
2: 7 Once more *they* **r**, "Let the king tell 10558
2:27 Daniel **r**, "No wise man, enchanter, 10558
3:16 Meshach and Abednego **r** to the king, 10558
3:24 *They* **r**, "Certainly, O king." 10558
12: 9 *He* **r**, "Go your way, Daniel, 606
Am 7: 8 "A plumb line," *I* **r**. 606
Jnh 1:12 *he* **r**, "and it will become calm. 606
4: 4 But the LORD **r**, "Have you any right 606
Hab 2: 2 Then the LORD **r**: "Write down the 6699
Hag 2:13 "Yes," the priests **r**, "it becomes defiled." 6699
Zec 4: 5 "No, my lord," *I* **r**. 606
4:13 *He* **r**, "Do you not know what these are?" 606
5: 6 *He* **r**, "It is a measuring basket." 606
5:11 *He* **r**, "To the country of Babylonia to build 606
Mt 2: 5 "In Bethlehem in Judea," they **r**, *3306*

Mt 3:15 Jesus **r**, "Let it be so now; *646*
8: 8 The centurion **r**, "Lord, *646+5774*
8:20 Jesus **r**, "Foxes have holes and birds of *3306*
8:26 *He* **r**, "You of little faith, *3306*
9:28 "Yes, Lord," *they* **r**. *3306*
11: 4 Jesus **r**, "Go back and report *646*
12:48 He **r** to him, "Who is my mother, *646*
13:11 He **r**, "The knowledge of the secrets *646*
13:28 " 'An enemy did this,' he **r**. *5774*
13:51 "Yes," *they* **r**. *3306*
14:16 Jesus **r**, "They do not need to go away. *3306*
14:28 "Lord, if it's you," Peter **r**, *3306*
15: 3 Jesus **r**, "And why do you break *646*
15:13 He **r**, "Every plant that my heavenly *646*
15:26 He **r**, "It is not right to take the children's *646*
15:34 "Seven," they **r**, "and a few small fish." *3306*
16: 2 He **r**, "When evening comes, you say, *646*
16:14 They **r**, "Some say John the Baptist; *3306*
16:17 Jesus **r**, "Blessed are you, *646*
17:11 Jesus **r**, "To be sure, Elijah comes *646*
17:17 Jesus **r**, "how long shall I stay with you? *3306*
17:20 He **r**, "Because you have so little faith. *3306*
17:25 "Yes, he does," *he* **r**. *3306*
19: 4 "Haven't you read," he **r**, *646*
19: 8 Jesus **r**, "Moses permitted you to divorce *3306*
19:11 Jesus **r**, "Not everyone can accept this word, *3306*
19:17 ask me about what is good?" Jesus **r**. *3306*
19:18 Jesus **r**, " 'Do not murder, *3306*
21:16 "Yes," **r** Jesus, "have you never read, *3306*
21:21 Jesus **r**, "I tell you the truth, *646*
21:24 Jesus **r**, "I will also ask you one question. *646*
21:41 a wretched end," *they* **r**, "and he will rent *3306*
22:21 "Caesar's," *they* **r**. *3306*
22:29 Jesus **r**, "You are in error because you do *646*
22:37 Jesus **r**: " 'Love the Lord your God with all *5774*
22:42 "The son of David," *they* **r**. *3306*
25: 9 they **r**, 'there may not be enough for *646*
25:12 "But he **r**, 'I tell you the truth, *646*
25:21 "His master **r**, 'Well done, *5774*
25:23 "His master **r**, 'Well done, *5774*
25:26 "His master **r**, 'You wicked, lazy servant! *646*
26:18 He **r**, "Go into the city to a certain man *3306*
26:23 Jesus **r**, "The one who has dipped his hand *646*
26:33 Peter **r**, "Even if all fall away on account *646*
26:50 Jesus **r**, "Friend, do what you came for." *3306*
26:64 "Yes, it is as you say," Jesus **r**. *3306*
27: 4 "What is that to us?" they **r**. *3306*
27:11 "Yes, it is as you say," Jesus **r**. *5774*
Mk 1:38 Jesus **r**, "Let us go somewhere else— *3306*
5: 9 "My name is Legion," *he* **r**, *3306*
7: 6 He **r**, "Isaiah was right when he prophesied *3306*
7:28 she **r**, "but even the dogs under the table *646*
8: 5 "Seven," they **r**. *3306*
8:19 "Twelve," *they* **r**. *3306*
8:28 They **r**, "Some say John the Baptist; *3306*
9:12 Jesus **r**, "To be sure, Elijah does come first, *5774*
9:19 "O unbelieving generation," Jesus **r**, *646*
9:29 *He* **r**, "This kind can come out only *3306*
10: 3 "What did Moses command you?" he **r**. *646*
10: 5 that Moses wrote you this law," Jesus **r**. *3306*
10:29 "I tell you the truth," Jesus **r**, *5774*
10:37 They **r**, "Let one of us sit at your right and *3306*
11:29 Jesus **r**, "I will ask you one question. *3306*
12:16 "Caesar's," they **r**. *3306*
12:24 Jesus **r**, "Are you not in error *5774*
12:32 "Well said, teacher," the man **r**. *3306*
13: 2 you see all these great buildings?" **r** Jesus. *3306*
14:20 "It is one of the Twelve," he **r**, *3306*
15: 2 "Yes, it is as you say," Jesus **r**. *646*
Lk 3:14 *He* **r**, "Don't extort money *3306*
7:22 So *he* **r** to the messengers, *646*
7:43 Simon **r**, "I suppose the one who had *646*
8:21 He **r**, "My mother and brothers are *646*
8:30 he **r**, because many demons had gone *3306*
9:13 *He* **r**, "You give them something to eat." *3306*
9:19 They **r**, "Some say John the Baptist; *646*
9:41 Jesus **r**, "how long shall I stay with you *646*
9:58 Jesus **r**, "Foxes have holes and birds of *3306*
9:59 But the man **r**, "Lord, *3306*
9:62 Jesus **r**, "No one who puts his hand to *3306*
10:18 *He* **r**, "I saw Satan fall like lightning *3306*
10:26 "What is written in the Law?" he **r**. *3306*
10:28 "You have answered correctly," Jesus **r**. *646*
10:37 The expert in the law **r**, *3306*
11:28 He **r**, "Blessed rather are those who hear *3306*
11:46 Jesus **r**, "And you experts in the law, *3306*
12:14 Jesus **r**, "Man, who appointed me a judge *3306*
13: 8 the man **r**, 'leave it alone *646*
13:32 *He* **r**, "Go tell that fox, *3306*
14:16 Jesus **r**: "A certain man was preparing a *3306*
15:27 'Your brother has come,' he **r**, *3306*
16: 6 " 'Eight hundred gallons of olive oil,' he **r**. *3306*
16: 7 " 'A thousand bushels of wheat,' he **r**. *3306*
16:25 "But Abraham **r**, 'Son, *3306*
16:29 "Abraham **r**, 'They have Moses and *3306*
17: 6 He **r**, "If you have faith as small as *3306*
17:20 the kingdom of God would come, Jesus **r**, *646*
17:37 He **r**, "Where there is a dead body, *3306*
18:27 Jesus **r**, "What is impossible *3306*
18:41 "Lord, I want to see," he **r**. *3306*
19:17 'Well done, my good servant!' his master **r**. *3306*
19:22 "His master **r**, 'I will judge you *3306*
19:26 "He **r**, 'I tell you that to everyone who has, *NIG*
19:34 They **r**, "The Lord needs it." *3306*
19:40 "I tell you," *he* **r**, "if they keep quiet, *646*
20: 3 *He* **r**, "I will also ask you a question. *646*
20:25 "Caesar's," they **r**. *3306*
Lk 20:34 Jesus **r**, "The people of this age marry *3306*
21: 8 He **r**: "Watch out that you are not deceived. *3306*
22:10 He **r**, "As you enter the city, *3306*
22:33 But he **r**, "Lord, I am ready to go with you *3306*
22:38 "That is enough," he **r**. *3306*
22:58 I am not!" Peter **r**. *5774*
22:60 Peter **r**, "Man, I don't know what you're talking about!" *3306*
22:70 He **r**, "You are right in saying I am." *5774*
23: 3 "Yes, it is as you say," Jesus **r**. *646*
24:19 "About Jesus of Nazareth," they **r**. *3306*
Jn 1:23 John **r** in the words of Isaiah the prophet, *5774*
1:26 "I baptize with water," John **r**, *646*
1:39 "Come," *he* **r**, "and you will see." *3306*
2: 4 why do you involve me?" Jesus **r**. *3306*
2:20 The Jews **r**, "It has taken forty-six years *3306*
3:27 To this John **r**, "A man can receive only *646*
4:17 "I have no husband," she **r**. *646*
4:50 Jesus **r**, "You may go. *3306*
5: 7 the invalid **r**, "I have no one to help me *646*
5:11 But he **r**, "The man who made me well said *646*
6:70 Then Jesus **r**, "Have I not chosen you, *646*
7:12 Others **r**, "No, he deceives the people." *3306*
7:52 *They* **r**, "Are you from Galilee, too? *646*
8:19 not know me or my Father," Jesus **r**. *646*
8:25 I have been claiming all along," Jesus **r**. *3306*
8:34 Jesus **r**, "I tell you the truth, *646*
8:54 Jesus **r**, "If I glorify myself, *646*
9:11 He **r**, "The man they call Jesus *646*
9:15 "He put mud on my eyes," the man **r**, *3306*
9:17 The man **r**, "He is a prophet." *3306*
9:25 He **r**, "Whether he is a sinner or not, *646*
9:34 To this *they* **r**, "You were steeped in sin *646*
10:33 **r** the Jews, "but for blasphemy, *646*
11:12 His disciples **r**, "Lord, if he sleeps, *3306*
11:34 "Come and see, Lord," *they* **r**. *3306*
12: 7 "Leave her alone," Jesus **r**. *3306*
12:23 Jesus **r**, "The hour has come for the Son *646*
13: 7 Jesus **r**, "You do not realize *646*
13: 9 Simon Peter **r**, "Not just my feet but *3306*
13:36 Jesus **r**, "Where I am going, *646*
14:23 Jesus **r**, "If anyone loves me, *646*
18: 5 "Jesus of Nazareth," *they* **r**. *646*
18:17 He **r**, "I am not." *3306*
18:20 "I have spoken openly to the world," Jesus **r**. *646*
18:23 "If I said something wrong," Jesus **r**, *646*
18:30 "If he were not a criminal," *they* **r**, *646*
18:35 "Am I a Jew?" Pilate **r**. *646*
Ac 2:38 Peter **r**, "Repent and be baptized, *NIG*
4:19 But Peter and John **r**, "Judge for yourselves *646*
5:29 Peter and the other apostles **r**: *646*
7: 2 To this he **r**: "Brothers and fathers, *5774*
9: 5 Jesus, whom you are persecuting," he **r**. *NIG*
10:14 "Surely not, Lord!" Peter **r**. *3306*
10:22 The men **r**, "We have come from Cornelius *3306*
11: 8 "*I* **r**, 'Surely not, Lord! *3306*
16:31 They **r**, "Believe in the Lord Jesus, *3306*
19: 3 "John's baptism," they **r**. *3306*
21:37 "Do you speak Greek?" he **r**. *5774*
22: 8 whom you are persecuting,' *he* **r**. *3306*
22:19 I **r**, 'these men know that I went *3306*
22:28 "But I was born a citizen," Paul **r**. *5774*
23: 5 Paul **r**, "Brothers, I did not realize *5774*
24:10 for him to speak, Paul **r**: *646*
25:22 *He* **r**, "Tomorrow you will hear him." *5774*
26:15 whom you are persecuting,' the Lord **r**. *3306*
26:25 most excellent Festus," Paul **r**. *5774*
26:29 Paul **r**, "Short time or long— *NIG*
28:21 They **r**, "We have not received any letters *3306*

REPLIES (2) [REPLY]

Ne 6:17 and **r** from Tobiah kept coming to them. 889S
Isa 21:12 The watchman **r**, "Morning is coming, 606

REPLY (27) [REPLIED, REPLIES]

2Ki 18:36 remained silent and **said** nothing **in r**, 6699
Ezr 4:17 The king sent this **r**: To Rehum 10601
5: 5 to Darius and his **written r** be received. 10496
Ne 6: 3 so I sent messengers to them with *this* **r**: 606
6: 8 I sent him *this* **r**: "Nothing like what you 606
Est 4:15 Then Esther sent *this* **r** to Mordecai: 606
Job 13:22 or let me speak, and *you* **r**. 8740
20: 3 and my understanding inspires me *to* **r**. 6699
32:16 now that they stand there with no **r**? 6699
32:20 I must open my lips and **r**. 6699
35: 4 "I would like *to* **r** *to* you and to 4863+8740
40: 4 how *can I* **r** *to* you? 8740
Ps 38:14 whose mouth can offer no **r**. 9350
Pr 15:23 A man finds joy in **giving an apt r**— 5101+7023
16: 1 from the LORD comes the **r** *of* the tongue. 5101
Isa 36:21 remained silent and **said** nothing **in r**, 6699
Jer 18:12 But *they will* **r**, 'It's no use. 606
Joel 2:19 The LORD *will* **r** to them: 6699
Mt 22:46 No one could **say** a word **in r**, *646*
25:40 "The King *will* **r**, 'I tell you the truth, *646*
25:45 "*He will* **r**, 'I tell you the truth, *646*
27:14 But Jesus **made** no **r**, *646*
Mk 7:29 he told her, "For such a **r**, you may go; *3364*
15: 5 But Jesus still **made** no **r**, *646*
Lk 10:30 *In* **r** Jesus said: "A man was going down *5696*
13:27 "But *he will* **r**, 'I don't know you *3306*
Jn 3: 3 **In r** Jesus declared, "I tell you the truth, *646*

REPOINTING (1)

1Sa 13:21 sharpening forks and axes and for **r** goads. 5893

REPORT (48) [REPORTED, REPORTING, REPORTS]

Ge 37: 2 he brought their father a bad **r** *about* them. 1804
Nu 13:32 a **bad r** *about* the land they had explored. 1804
14:15 the nations who have heard this **r** 9051
14:36 against him by spreading a **bad r** about it— 1804
14:37 for spreading the bad **r** *about* the land 1804
Dt 1:22 to spy out the land for us and bring back a **r** 1821
Jos 14: 7 And I brought him back a **r** according 1821
22:33 to hear the **r** and praised God. 1821
1Sa 2:24 not a good **r** that I hear spreading among 9019
2Sa 1: 5 to the young man who **brought** him *the* **r**, 5583
1:13 to the young man who **brought** him *the* **r**, 5583
13:30 the **r** came to David: 9019
13:33 about the **r** that all the king's sons are dead. 1821
1Ki 10: 6 "The **r** I heard in my own country 1821
10: 7 you have far exceeded the **r** I heard. 9019
2Ki 6:13 *The* **r came back**: "He is in Dothan." 5583
7: 9 at once and **r** this *to* the royal palace." 5583
19: 7 in him that when he hears a certain **r**, 9019
19: 9 Sennacherib **received a r** that Tirhakah, 9048
1Ch 21: 2 Then **r back** to me so that I may know 995
2Ch 9: 5 "The **r** I heard in my own country 1821
9: 6 you have far exceeded the **r** I heard. 9019
Ezr 5: 5 a **r** could go to Darius and his written reply 10302
5: 7 The **r** they sent him read as follows: 10601
Ne 6: 7 Now this **r** will get back to the king; 1821
Est 2:23 the **r** was investigated and found to be true, 1821
Job 38:35 *Do they* **r** to you, 'Here we are'? 606
Ecc 10:20 and a bird on the wing *may* **r** what you say. 5583
Isa 21: 6 post a lookout and *have him* **r** what he sees. 5583
23: 5 they will be in anguish at the **r** *from* Tyre. 9051
37: 7 in him so that when he hears a certain **r**, 9019
37: 9 Sennacherib **received a r** that Tirhakah, 9048
Jer 10:22 Listen! The **r** is coming— 9019
20:10 "Terror on every side! **R** him! 5583
20:10 Report him! *Let's* **r** him!" 5583
36:16 *We* **must r** all these words to the king. 5583+5583
37: 5 besieging Jerusalem heard the **r** *about* them, 9051
Mt 2: 8 As soon as you find him, **r** to me, *550*
11: 4 "Go back and **r** to John what you hear *550*
28:14 If this **r** gets to the governor, *NIG*
Lk 7:22 "Go back and **r** to John what you have seen *550*
Jn 11:57 *he should* **r** it so that they might arrest him. *3606*
Ac 5:24 On hearing this **r**, the captain of the temple *3364*
2Co 6: 8 **bad r** and good report; *1556*
6: 8 bad report and **good r**; *2367*
Gal 1:23 They only heard the **r**: *NIG*
1Th 1: 9 for they themselves **r** what kind of reception *550*
2Th 2: 2 **r** or letter supposed to have come from us, *3364*

REPORTED (57) [REPORT]

Ge 14:13 One who had escaped came and **r** this 5583
Ex 6: 9 Moses **r** this to the Israelites, 1819
16:22 the community came and **r** this to Moses. 5583
Nu 13:26 There *they* **r** *to* them and to 1821+8740
14:39 When Moses **r** this to all the Israelites, 1819
Dt 1:25 they brought it down to us and **r**, 1821+8740
Jos 22:32 and Gadites in Gilead and **r** to the 1821+8740
Jdg 9:25 and *this* **was r** to Abimelech. 5583
9:42 and this *was* **r** to Abimelech. 5583
1Sa 11: 4 of Saul and **r** these terms to the people, 1819
11: 9 the messengers went and **r** this to the men 5583
17:31 What David said was overheard and **r** 5583
25:12 When they arrived, *they* **r** every word. 5583
2Sa 7:17 Nathan **r** to David all the words 1819
18:25 to the king and **r** it. 5583
24: 9 Joab **r** the number of the fighting men to 5989
1Ki 2:30 Benaiah **r** *to* the king, 1821+8740
13:25 and they went and **r** it in the city where 1819
18:44 The seventh time the servant **r**, 606
20:17 Ben-Hadad had dispatched scouts, *who* **r**, 5583
2Ki 7:11 and *it was* **r** within the palace. 5583
7:15 the messengers returned and **r** to the king. 5583
9:18 The lookout **r**, "The messenger has 5583
9:20 The lookout **r**, "He has reached them, 5583
17:26 *It was* **r** to the king of Assyria: 606
22: 9 went to the king and **r** *to* him: 1821+8740
1Ch 17:15 Nathan **r** to David all the words 1819
21: 5 Joab **r** the number of the fighting men 5989
2Ch 29:18 Then they went in to King Hezekiah and **r**: 606
34:16 the book to the king and **r** *to* him: 1821+8740
Ne 6: 6 "*It is* **r** among the nations— 9048
Est 2:22 who in turn **r** it to the king, 606
4: 9 and **r** to Esther what Mordecai had said. 5583
4:12 When Esther's words *were* **r** to Mordecai, 5583
9:11 of those slain in the citadel of Susa *was* **r** to 995
Jer 36:20 the king in the courtyard and **r** everything 5583
Zec 1:11 And *they* **r** to the angel of the LORD, 6699
Mt 8:33 went into the town and **r** all this, *550*
28:11 the city and **r** to the chief priests everything *550*
Mk 5:14 Those tending the pigs ran off and **r** this in *550*
6:30 around Jesus and **r** to him all they had done *550*
16:13 These returned and **r** it to the rest; *550*
Lk 8:34 and **r** this in the town and countryside, *550*
9:10 *they* **r** to Jesus what they had done. *1455*
14:21 "The servant came back and **r** this *550*
Ac 4:23 to their own people and **r** all that *550*
5:22 So *they* went back and **r**, *550*
14:27 *they* gathered the church together and **r** all *334*
15: 4 to whom *they* **r** everything God had done *334*
16:38 The officers **r** this to the magistrates, *550*
21:19 and **r** in detail what God had done among *2007*
22:26 he went to the commander and **r** it. *550*
23:22 "Don't tell anyone that *you have* **r** this *1872*

Ac 28:21 from there *has* **r** or said anything bad 550
Ro 1: 8 your faith *is being* **r** all over the world. 2859
3: 8 as *we are being* **slanderously r** as saying 1059
1Co 5: 1 *It is* actually **r** that there is sexual immorality among you, 201

REPORTING (1) [REPORT]
Ne 6:19 they kept **r** to me his good deeds and 606

REPORTS (10) [REPORT]
Ex 23: 1 "Do not spread false **r.** 9051
Dt 2:25 They will hear **r** *of* you and will tremble 9051
Jos 9: 9 For we have heard **r** *of* him: 9053
Ne 6: 6 according to these **r** you are about 1821
Jer 62:24 We have heard **r** *about* them, 9053
50:43 king of Babylon has heard **r** *about* them, 9051
Da 11:44 But **r** from the east and the north 9019
Mt 14: 1 At that time Herod the tetrarch heard the **r** *198*
Ac 9:13 "I have heard many **r** about this man *NIG*
21:24 there is no truth in these **r** about you, *2994*

REPOSE (3) [REPOSES]
Dt 28:65 Among those nations *you will* **find** no **r,** 8089
Isa 28:12 and, "This is the **place of r"**— 5276
34:14 the night creatures *will* also **r** and find 8089

REPOSES (1) [REPOSE]
Pr 14:33 Wisdom **r** in the heart of the discerning and 5663

REPRESENT (6) [REPRESENTATION, REPRESENTATIVE, REPRESENTATIVES, REPRESENTED, REPRESENTING, REPRESENTS]
Lev 24: 7 to **r** the bread and to be an offering made to 4200
Jer 40:10 I myself will stay at Mizpah to **r** you before 6641
Da 8:22 that was broken off **r** four kingdoms NIH
Gal 3:20 does not **r** just one party; but God is one. *NIG*
4:24 for the women **r** two covenants. *1639*
Heb 5: 1 among men and is appointed to **r** them *NIG*

REPRESENTATION (1) [REPRESENT]
Heb 1: 3 of God's glory and the **exact r** of his being, *5917*

REPRESENTATIVE (2) [REPRESENT]
Ex 18:19 You must be the people's **r** before God NIH
2Sa 15: 3 there is no **r** *of* the king to hear you." 907+4946

REPRESENTATIVES (1) [REPRESENT]
2Co 8:23 for our brothers, they are **r** of the churches *693*

REPRESENTED (2) [REPRESENT]
Nu 17: 8 which **r** the house of Levi, 4200
Jdg 18: 2 These men **r** all their clans. 4946

REPRESENTING (2) [REPRESENT]
Ex 24: 4 up twelve stone pillars **r** the twelve tribes 4200
Nu 1:44 each one **r** his family. 4200

REPRESENTS (1) [REPRESENT]
Da 8:20 The two-horned ram that you saw **r** the kings NIH

REPRIMANDED (1)
Jer 29:27 So why *have you* not **r** Jeremiah 1721

REPROACH (21) [REPROACHED]
Jos 5: 9 "Today I have rolled away the **r** *of* Egypt 3075
Ne 5: 9 to avoid the **r** *of* our Gentile enemies? 3075
Job 27: 6 my conscience *will* not **r** me as long 3070
Ps 44:13 You have made us a **r** to our neighbors, 3075
44:16 at the taunts of *those who* **r** and revile me, 3070
79: 4 We are **objects of r** to our neighbors, 3075
79:12 the **r** they have hurled at you, 3075
Isa 51: 7 the **r** *of* men or be terrified by their insults. 3075
54: 4 of your youth and remember no more the **r** 3075
Jer 15:15 think of how I suffer **r** for your sake. 3075
20: 8 insult and **r** all day long. 7841
24: 9 a **r** and a byword, an object of ridicule 3075
29:18 of cursing and horror, of scorn and **r,** 3075
42:18 cursing and horror, of condemnation and **r;** 3075
44: 8 of cursing and **r** among all the nations 3075
44:12 cursing and horror, of condemnation and **r.** 3075
49:13 an object of horror, of **r** and of cursing; 3075
Eze 5:14 and a **r** among the nations around you, 3075
5:15 You will be a **r** and a taunt, 3075
Zep 3:18 they are a burden and a **r** to you. 3075
1Ti 3: 2 Now the overseer must be **above r,** *455*

REPROACHED (1) [REPROACH]
Job 19: 3 Ten times now *you have* **r** me; 4007

REPROBATE, REPROBATES (KJV) See DEPRAVED, FAIL, FAILED, REJECTED, UNFIT

REPROOF, REPROVE (KJV) See ACCUSE, CONVICT, CORRECT, CORRECTION, DECIDE, EXPOSE, PROVE, REBUKE

REPROVES (1)
Am 5:10 you hate the *one who* **r** in court 3519

REPTILES (5)
1Ki 4:33 also taught about animals and birds, **r** 8254
Ac 10:12 as well as **r** of the earth and birds of the air. *2260*
11: 6 wild beasts, **r,** and birds of the air. *2260*
Ro 1:23 and birds and animals and **r.** *2260*
Jas 3: 7 **r** and creatures of the sea are being tamed *2260*

REPULSE (2) [REPULSIVE]
2Ki 18:24 How *can you* **r** one officer of the least 7156+8740
Isa 36: 9 How then *can you* **r** one officer of 7156+8740

REPULSIVE (6) [REPULSE]
1Ki 15:13 because she had made a **r** Asherah pole. 5145
1Ch 21: 6 because the king's command *was* **r** *to* him. 9493
2Ch 15:16 because she had made a **r** Asherah pole. 5145
Job 33:20 so that his very being **finds** food **r** 2299
Ps 88: 8 and have made me **r** to them. 9359
Jer 23:13 the prophets of Samaria I saw this **r thing:** 9524

REPUTATION (4) [REPUTED]
Est 9: 4 his **r** spread throughout the provinces, 9053
Pr 25:10 and you will never lose your **bad r.** 1804
1Ti 3: 7 He must also have a good **r** with outsiders, *3456*
Rev 3: 1 you have a **r** of being alive, *3950*

REPUTED (1) [REPUTATION]
Gal 2: 9 James, Peter and John, those **r** to be pillars, *1506*

REQUEST (31) [REQUESTED, REQUESTING, REQUESTS]
Ge 19:21 "Very well, I will grant this **r** too; 1821
Jdg 6:39 *Let me* **make** just one more **r.** 1819
8: 8 up to Peniel and **made** *the* same **r** of them, 1819
8:24 And he said, *"I do* **have** *one* **r,** 8626+8629
11:37 But grant me this one **r,"** she said. 1821
1Sa 25:35 heard your words and **granted** your **r.** 5951+7156
2Sa 12:20 and *at his* **r** they served him food, 8626
14:22 the king has granted his servant's **r."** 1821
1Ki 2:16 Now *I* **have** one **r to make** 8626+8629
2:20 *"I* **have** one small **r to make** 8626+8629
2:22 "Why *do* you **r** Abishag the Shunammite 8626
2:22 *You might as well* **r** the kingdom for him— 8626
2:23 does not pay with his life for this **r!** 1819+1821
1Ch 4:10 And God granted *his* **r.** 8626
Est 5: 3 What *is* your **r?** Even up to half the 1336
5: 6 And what is your **r?** Even up to half the 1336
5: 7 "My petition and my **r** is this: 1336
5: 8 to grant my petition and fulfill my **r,** 1336
7: 2 What is your **r?** Even up to half the 1336
7: 3 And spare my people—this is my **r.** 1336
9:12 What is your **r?** I will also be granted." 1336
Job 6: 8 "Oh, that I might have my **r,** 8629
Ps 21: 2 and have not withheld the **r** of his lips. 830
Da 2:49 *at* Daniel's **r** the king appointed Shadrach, 10114
9:20 and making my **r** to the LORD my God 9382
Mt 14: 9 he ordered that her **r** be granted *NIG*
15:28 Your **r** is granted." *2527*
Mk 6:25 the girl hurried in to the king with the **r:** *160*
Jn 12:21 from Bethsaida in Galilee, with a **r.** *2263*
Ac 23:21 waiting for your consent to their **r."** *NIG*
24: 4 *I would* **r that** you be kind enough *4151*

REQUESTED (5) [REQUEST]
Ex 12:31 Go, worship the LORD as you *have* **r.** 1819
Ezr 6: 9 as **r** *by* the priests in Jerusalem— 10397
Jer 42: 4 to the LORD your God as you have **r;** 1821
Mk 15: 6 to release a prisoner whom the *people* **r.** *4148*
Ac 25: 3 *They* **urgently r** Festus, as a favor *160+4151*

REQUESTING (1) [REQUEST]
Ac 16:39 from the prison, **r** them to leave the city. *2263*

REQUESTS (7) [REQUEST]
Ne 2: 8 the king **granted** my **r.** 5989
Ps 5: 3 in the morning I lay my **r** before you and NIH
20: 5 May the LORD grant all your **r.** 5399
Da 9:18 We do not make **r** of you 9384
Eph 6:18 with all kinds of prayers and **r.** *1255*
Php 4: 6 with thanksgiving, present your **r** to God. *161*
1Ti 2: 1 I urge, then, first of all, that **r,** prayers, *1255*

REQUIRE (8) [REQUIRED, REQUIREMENT, REQUIREMENTS, REQUIRES, REQUIRING]
Ex 5: 8 But **r** them to make the same number 8492
Dt 15: 2 not **r payment** *from* his fellow Israelite 5601
15: 3 *You may* **r payment** *from* a foreigner, 5601
2Ki 12:15 *They did* not **r an accounting** *from* those 3108
Ps 40: 6 and sin offerings *you did* not **r.** 8626
Eze 18:16 **r a pledge for a loan.** 2471+2478
20:40 There *I will* **r** your offerings 2011
Mic 6: 8 And what *does* the LORD **r** of you? 2011

REQUIRED (25) [REQUIRE]
Ge 50: 3 for that was the **time** *r for* embalming. AIT
Ex 5:13 "Complete the **work** *r of* you for each day, AIT
5:19 the number of **bricks** *r of* you for each day." AIT
22:11 and no **restitution** *is r.* AIT
22:13 as evidence and *he will* not *be r to* **pay** *for* AIT
Lev 23:37 and drink offerings **r** *for* each day. 1821
27:16 to be set according to the amount of **seed** *r* AIT
Nu 7: 7 to the Gershonites, as their work **r,** 7023
7: 8 to the Merarites, as their work **r.** 7023
Jos 16:10 of Ephraim but *are* **r** to do forced labor. 2118
1Ki 8:31 and *is* **r** to take an oath 460+928+5957
2Ch 6:22 and *is* **r** to take an oath 460+928+5957
24: 6 "Why haven't *you* **r** the Levites to 2011+6584
24: 9 that Moses the servant of God had **r of** 6584
24:12 to the men who carried out the work **r** *for* 6275
Ezr 3: 4 the Feast of Tabernacles with the **r** number 1821
Ne 12:44 to bring into the storerooms the **portions** *r* AIT
Jnh 3: 3 very important city—a visit **r** three days. NIH
Lk 2:27 for him what the custom of the Law **r,** *2848*
2:39 and Mary had done everything **r by** the Law *2848*
3:13 "Don't collect any more than you *are* **r** to," *1411*
Ac 15: 5 "The Gentiles must be circumcised and **r** *4133*
Ro 2:14 do by nature things *r by* **the law,** *AIT*
1Co 4: 2 Now *it is* **r** that those who have been given *2426*
Heb 10: 8 (although the law **r** them to be made). *2848*

REQUIRED (Anglicized) See also OBLIGATED

REQUIREMENT (5) [REQUIRE]
Nu 19: 2 "This is a **r** *of* the law that 2978
27:11 This is to be a legal **r** for the Israelites, 2978
31:21 "This is the **r** *of* the law that 2978
2Ch 8:13 to the daily **r** for offerings commanded 1821
8:14 the priests according to each day's **r.** 1821

REQUIREMENTS (19) [REQUIRE]
Ge 26: 5 Abraham obeyed me and kept my **r,** 5466
Lev 18:30 Keep my **r** and do not follow any of 5466
22: 9 " 'The priests are to keep my **r** so 5466
Nu 35:29 " 'These are to be legal **r** for you 2978
Dt 11: 1 Love the LORD your God and keep his **r,** 5466
1Ki 2: 3 and commands, his laws and **r,** 6343
2Ki 23:24 the **r** *of* the law written in the book 1821
1Ch 16:37 according to each day's **r.** 1821
29:19 **r** and decrees and to do everything to build 6343
2Ch 13:11 observing the **r** *of* the LORD our God. 5466
Jer 5: 4 the way of the LORD, the **r** *of* their God. 5477
5: 5 the way of the LORD, the **r** *of* their God." 5477
8: 7 But my people do not know the **r** *of* 5477
Zec 3: 7 you will walk in my ways and keep my **r,** 5466
Mal 3:14 What did we gain by carrying out his **r** 5466
Ac 15:28 with anything beyond the following **r:** *2055*
Ro 2:15 the **r** of the law are written on their hearts, *2240*
2:26 not circumcised keep the law's **r,** *1468*
8: 4 that the **righteous r** of the law might *1468*

REQUIRES (9) [REQUIRE]
Lev 8:35 for seven days and do **what** the LORD **r,** 5466
Nu 7: 5 to the Levites as each man's work **r."** 7023
1Ki 2: 3 **what** the LORD your God **r:** 5466
2Ki 17:26 **what** the god of that country **r.** 5477
17:26 because the people do not know **what** he **r."** 5477
17:27 **what** the god of the land **r."** 5477
Jn 6:28 "What must we do to do the works **God** *r?" AIT*
Heb 7: 5 Now the law **r** the descendants *1953*
9:22 the law **r** that nearly everything be cleansed *2848*

REQUIRING (1) [REQUIRE]
Lev 22:16 and so bring upon them guilt **r payment.** 873

REQUITE, REQUITED, REQUITING (KJV) See PAID BACK, PAY, PAYS BACK, REPAY, REPAYING, SHOW THE SAME FAVOR

REREWARD (KJV) See REAR, REAR GUARD

RESCUE (84) [RESCUED, RESCUES, RESCUING]
Ge 37:21 *he tried to* **r** him from their hands. 5911
37:22 to **r** him from them and take him back 5911
Ex 2:17 and **came to** their **r** and watered their flock. 3828
3: 8 to **r** them from the hand of the Egyptians 5911
Dt 22:27 there was no *one to* **r** her. 4635
25:11 of one of them comes to **r** her husband 5911
28:29 with no *one to* **r** you. 4635
28:31 and no *one will* **r** them. 3828
Jdg 9:17 risked his life *to* **r** you from the hand 5911
10:15 but please **r** us now." 5911
18:28 *to* **r** them because they lived a long way 5911
1Sa 7: 8 that *he may* **r** us from the hand of 3828
11: 3 if no *one* comes *to* **r** us, 4635
12:21 nor *can they* **r** you, because they are useless. 5911
30: 8 overtake them and **succeed in the r."** 5911+5911

2Sa 3:18 'By my servant David I *will* r my people Israel 3828
10:11 then you are to come to my r; 3802
10:11 then I will come to r you. 3828
21:17 Abishai son of Zeruiah **came to** David's r; 6468
1Ch 19:12 then you are to r me; 9591
19:12 then *I will* r you. 3828
2Ch 32:17 of the other lands *did* not r their people 5911
32:17 the god of Hezekiah *will* not r his people 5911
Job 5:19 From six calamities *he will* r you; 5911
10: 7 and that no *one can* r me from your hand? 5911
Ps 7: 2 and rip me to pieces with no *one to* r me. 5911
17:13 r me from the wicked by your sword. 7117
22: 8 *let* the LORD r him. 7117
22:21 R me from the mouth of the lions; 3828
25:20 Guard my life and r me; 5911
31: 2 **come** quickly to my r; 5911
35:10 You r the poor from those too strong 5911
35:17 R my life from their ravages, 8740
43: 1 r me from deceitful and wicked men. 7117
50:22 or I will tear you to pieces, with none *to* r: 5911
69:14 R me from the mire, do not let me sink; 5911
69:18 Come near and r me; 1457
71: 2 R me and deliver me in your righteousness; 5911
71:11 for no *one will* r him." 5911
72:14 *He will* r them from oppression 1457
82: 4 R the weak and needy; 7117
91:14 says the LORD, *"I will* r him; 7117
140: 1 R me, O LORD, from evil men; 2740
142: 6 r me from those who pursue me, 5911
143: 9 R me from my enemies, O LORD, 5911
144: 7 and r me from the mighty waters, 5911
144:11 Deliver me and r me from the hands 5911
Pr 19:19 if *you* r him, you will have to do it again. 5911
24:11 R those being led away to death; 5911
Isa 5:29 and carry it off with no *one to* r. 5911
19:20 and *he will* r them. 5911
31: 5 he will 'pass over' it and *will* r it." 4880
42:22 with no *one to* r them; 5911
46: 2 unable *to* r the burden, 4880
46: 4 I will sustain you and *I will* r you. 4880
50: 2 Do I lack the strength to r you? 5911
Jer 1: 8 for I am with you and *will* r you," 5911
1:19 for I am with you and *will* r you," 5911
15:20 for I am with you to r and save you," 3828
21:12 r from the hand of his oppressor 5911
22: 3 R from the hand of his oppressor 5911
39:17 But *I will* r you on that day, 5911
Eze 34:10 *I will* r my flock from their mouths, 5911
34:12 *I will* r them from all the places 5911
34:27 of their yoke and r them from the hands 5911
Da 3:15 Then what god *will be able to* r you 10706
3:17 and *he will* r us from your hand, O king. 10706
6:14 to r Daniel and made every effort 10706
6:16 whom you serve continually, r you!" 10706
6:20 been able to r you from the lions?" 10706
8: 4 and none *could* r from his power. 5911
8: 7 and none *could* r the ram from his power. 5911
Hos 5:14 with no *one to* r them. 5911
Mic 5: 8 and no *one can* r. 5911
Zep 3:19 *I will* r the lame 3828
Zec 11: 6 and *I will* not r them from their hands." 5911
Mt 27:43 *Let* God r him now if he wants him, *4861*
Lk 1:74 *to* r us from the hand of our enemies, *4861*
Ac 7:25 that God was using him to r them, *1443+5401*
26:17 *I will* r you from your own people and *1975*
Ro 7:24 Who *will* r me from this body of death? *4861*
Gal 1: 4 who gave himself for our sins to r us from *1975*
2Ti 4:18 The Lord *will* r me from every evil attack *4861*
2Pe 2: 9 how *to* r godly men from trials and to hold *4861*

RESCUED (36) [RESCUE]

Ex 2:19 "An Egyptian r us from the shepherds. 5911
5:23 *you have* not r your people **at all."** 5911+5911
18:10 who r you from the hand of the Egyptians 5911
18:10 and who r the people from the hand of 5911
Nu 10: 9 LORD your God and r from your enemies. 3828
Jos 22:31 Now *you have* r the Israelites from 5911
Jdg 8:34 who *had* r them from the hands 5911
1Sa 11:13 for this day the LORD *has* r Israel." 6913+9591
14:23 So the LORD r Israel that day, 3828
14:45 So the men r Jonathan, 7009
17:35 struck it and r the sheep from its mouth. 5911
2Sa 19: 9 he *is* the *one who* r us from the hand of 4880
22:18 *He* r me from my powerful enemy, 5911
22:20 *he* r me because he delighted in me. 2740
22:49 from violent men *you* r me. 5911
2Ki 18:34 *Have they* r Samaria from my hand? 5911
Ne 9:27 *who* r them from the hand of their enemies. 3828
Job 29:12 because *I* r the poor who cried for help, 4880
Ps 18:17 *He* r me from my powerful enemy, 5911
18:19 *he* r me because he delighted in me. 2740
18:48 from violent men *you* r me. 5911
81: 7 In your distress you called and *I* r you, 2740
107:20 *he* r them from the grave. 4880
Pr 11: 8 The righteous man **is** r from trouble, 2740
Isa 36:19 *Have they* r Samaria from my hand? 5911
49:24 or captives r *from* the fierce? 4880
Da 3:28 who has sent his angel and r his servants! 10706
6:27 *He has* r Daniel from the power of 10706
Mic 4:10 there *you will* **be** r. 5911
Ac 7:10 and r him from all his troubles. *1975*
12:11 that the Lord sent his angel and r me *1975*
23:27 but *I* came with my troops and r him, *1975*
Ro 15:31 Pray that *I may be* r from the unbelievers *4861*
Col 1:13 For he *has* r us from the dominion *4861*
2Ti 3:11 Yet the Lord r me from all of them. *4861*
2Pe 2: 7 and if *he* r Lot, a righteous man, *4861*

RESCUES (5) [RESCUE]

1Sa 14:39 As surely as the LORD who r Israel lives, 4635
Pr 12: 6 but the speech of the upright r them. 5911
Jer 20:13 *He* r the life of the needy from the hands of 5911
Da 6:27 *He* r and he saves; he performs signs 10706
1Th 1:10 Jesus, who r us from the coming wrath. *4861*

RESCUING (1) [RESCUE]

Ex 18: 9 in r them from the hand of the Egyptians. 5911

RESEMBLED (3) [RESEMBLING]

Rev 9: 7 and their faces r human faces. *6055*
9:17 The heads of the horses r the heads *6055*
13: 2 The beast I saw r a leopard, *1639+3927*

RESEMBLING (1) [RESEMBLED]

Rev 4: 3 A rainbow, r an emerald, *3927+3970*

RESEN (1)

Ge 10:12 R, which is between Nineveh and Calah; 8271

RESENT (1) [RESENTFUL, RESENTMENT, RESENTS]

Pr 3:11 and *do* not r his rebuke, 7762

RESENTFUL (1) [RESENT]

2Ti 2:24 kind to everyone, able to teach, **not** r. *452*

RESENTMENT (3) [RESENT]

Jdg 8: 3 At this, their r against him subsided. 8120
Job 5: 2 R kills a fool, and envy slays the simple. 4089
36:13 "The godless in heart harbor r; 678

RESENTS (1) [RESENT]

Pr 15:12 A mocker r correction; 170+4202

RESERVE (4) [RESERVED]

Ge 41:36 This food should be **held in** r for 7214
Dt 32:34 not **kept** this **in** r and sealed it in my vaults? 4022
1Ki 19:18 Yet *I* r seven thousand in Israel— 8636
Job 38:23 which *I* r for times of trouble, 3104

RESERVED (6) [RESERVE]

Ge 27:36 "Haven't *you* r any blessing for me?" 724
Isa 26:11 the **fire** *r for* your enemies consume them. AIT
Ro 11: 4 *have* r for myself seven thousand who have not bowed the knee to Baal." *2901*
2Pe 2:17 Blackest darkness *is* r for them. *5498*
3: 7 the present heavens and earth are r for fire, *2564*
Jude 1:13 whom blackest darkness *has been* r forever. *5498*

RESERVOIR (1) [RESERVOIRS]

Isa 22:11 a r between the two walls for the water of 5225

RESERVOIRS (2) [RESERVOIR]

Ex 7:19 over the ponds and all the r'— 4784+5224
Ecc 2: 6 I made r to water groves of 1391+4784

RESETTLE (2) [SETTLE]

1Ch 9: 2 Now the first *to* r on their own property 3782
Eze 36:33 *I will* r your towns, 3782

RESETTLED (2) [SETTLE]

2Ki 17:26 "The people you deported and r in 3782
Eze 38:12 against the r ruins and the people gathered 3782

RESHEPH (1)

1Ch 7:25 Rephah was his son, R his son, 8405

RESIDE (1) [RESIDENCE, RESIDENT, RESIDENTS, RESIDES]

Job 38:19 And where does darkness r? 5226

RESIDENCE (5) [RESIDE]

2Sa 5: 9 then **took up** r in the fortress and called it 3782
1Ch 11: 7 David then **took up** r in the fortress, 3782
Ne 2: 8 the city wall and for the r I will occupy?" 1074
Est 2:16 She was taken to King Xerxes in the royal r 1074
Da 4:30 Babylon I have built as the royal r, 10103

RESIDENT (5) [RESIDE]

Ex 12:45 but a **temporary** r and a hired worker may 9369
Lev 25: 6 the hired worker and **temporary** r who live 9369
25:35 as you would an alien or a **temporary** r, 9369
25:40 as a hired worker or a **temporary** r 9369
25:47 or a **temporary** r among you becomes rich 9369

RESIDENTS (4) [RESIDE]

Lev 25:45 also buy some of the **temporary** r living 9369
Ne 3:13 by Hanun and the r *of* Zanoah. 3782
7: 3 Also appoint r *of* Jerusalem as guards, 3782
Ac 2: 9 r **of** Mesopotamia, Judea and Cappadocia, *2997*

RESIDES (3) [RESIDE]

Job 18:15 Fire r in his tent; 8905
41:22 Strength r in his neck; 4328
Ecc 7: 9 for anger r in the lap of fools. 5663

RESIDUE (KJV) See LEFT, OTHER, REMAINS, REMNANT, REST, SURVIVORS

RESIN (3)

Ge 2:12 **aromatic** r and onyx are also there.) 978
Ex 30:34 **gum** r, onycha and galbanum— 5753
Nu 11: 7 like coriander seed and looked like r. 978

RESIST (13) [RESISTED, RESISTS]

Jdg 2:14 they were no longer able to r. 4200+6641+7156
2Ki 10: 4 "If two kings *could* not r him, 4200+6641+7156
2Ch 13: 7 and not strong enough to r them. 7156
13: 8 you plan to r the kingdom of the LORD, 2616
Pr 28: 4 but those who keep the law r them. 1741
Isa 1:20 but if *you* r and rebel, 4412
Da 11:15 forces of the South will be powerless *to* r; 6641
11:32 the people who know their God *will* firmly r him. 6913
Mt 5:39 But I tell you, *Do* not r an evil person. *468*
Lk 21:15 none of your adversaries will be able *to* r *468*
Ac 7:51 You always r the Holy Spirit! *528*
Jas 4: 7 R the devil, and he will flee from you. *468*
1Pe 5: 9 R him, standing firm in the faith, *468*

RESISTED (3) [RESIST]

Job 9: 4 Who *has* r him and come out unscathed? 7996
Da 10:13 the prince of the Persian kingdom r me 4200+5584+6641
Heb 12: 4 yet r to the point of shedding your blood. *510*

RESISTS (1) [RESIST]

Ro 9:19 For who r his will?" *468*

RESOLUTELY (1)

Lk 9:51 Jesus r set out for Jerusalem. *3836+4725+5114*

RESOLVED (4)

2Ch 20: 3 Jehoshaphat r to inquire of the LORD, 5989+7156
Ps 17: 3 *I have* r that my mouth will not sin. 2372
Da 1: 8 Daniel r not to defile himself 4213+6584+8492
1Co 2: 2 For *I* r to know nothing while I was with *3212*

RESORT (1) [RESORTED]

Nu 24: 1 *he did* not r **to** sorcery as at other times, 2143+4200+7925

RESORTED (1) [RESORT]

Jos 9: 4 they r to a ruse: They went as a delegation 6913

RESOUND (9) [RESOUNDED, RESOUNDING, RESOUNDS]

1Ch 16:32 *Let* the sea r, and all that is in it; 8306
Ps 96:11 *let* the sea r, and all that is in it; 8306
98: 7 *Let* the sea r, and everything in it, 8306
118:15 and victory r in the tents of the righteous: 7754
Jer 6: 7 Violence and destruction r in her; 9048
25:31 The tumult *will* r to the ends of the earth, 995
49:21 their cry *will* r to the Red Sea. 9048
50:46 its cry *will* r among the nations. 9048
51:55 the roar of their voices *will* r. 5989

RESOUNDED (3) [RESOUND]

2Sa 22:14 the voice of the Most High r. 5989
Ps 18:13 the voice of the Most High r. 5989
77:17 the skies r *with* thunder; 5989

RESOUNDING (2) [RESOUND]

Ps 150: 5 praise him with r cymbals. 9558
1Co 13: 1 I am only a r gong or a clanging cymbal. *2490*

RESOUNDS (2) [RESOUND]

1Ki 1:45 gone up cheering, and the city r with it. 2169
Job 37: 4 When his voice r, he holds nothing back. 9048

RESOURCES (1)

1Ch 29: 2 With all my r I have provided for 3946

RESPECT (32) [RESPECTABLE, RESPECTED, RESPECTS]

Ge 41:40 Only with r to the throne will I be greater NIH
Lev 19: 3 of *you must* r his mother and father, 3707
19:32 **show** r for the elderly and revere your God. 2075
22: 2 "Tell Aaron and his sons *to* **treat with** r 5692
Dt 28:50 a fierce-looking nation without r for the old 5951+7156
2Ki 1:13 "please **have** r **for** my life and 928+3700+6524
1:14 But now **have** r **for** my life!" 928+3700+6524
3:14 if I *did* not **have** r **for** the presence of 5951
Est 1:20 all the women *will* r their husbands, 3702+5989

Pr 11:16 A kindhearted woman gains **r**, 3883
Isa 5:12 no **r** *for* the work of his hands. 8011
La 5:12 elders **are shown** no **r**. 2075+7156
Mal 1:6 If I am a master, where is the **r** *due* me?" 4616
Mt 21:37 '*They will* **r** my son,' he said. *1956*
Mk 12:6 saying, '*They will* **r** my son.' *1956*
Lk 20:13 perhaps *they will* **r** him.' *1956*
Ro 13:7 if **r**, then respect; if honor, then honor. *5832*
13:7 if respect, then **r**; if honor, then honor. *5832*
Eph 5:33 and the wife *must* **r** her husband. *5828*
6:5 obey your earthly masters with **r** and fear, *5832*
1Th 4:12 so that your daily life may **win the r** *2361*
5:12 *to* **r** those who work hard among you, *3857*
1Ti 3:4 that his children obey him with proper **r**. *4949*
3:8 likewise, are to be men **worthy of r**, *4948*
3:11 their wives are to be women **worthy of r**, *4948*
6:1 consider their masters worthy *of* full **r**, *5507*
6:2 not *to* **show less r** for them *2969*
Tit 2:2 **worthy of r**, self-controlled, *4948*
1Pe 2:17 **Show proper r to** everyone: *5506*
2:18 submit yourselves to your masters with all **r** *5832*
3:7 and treat them with **r** as the weaker partner *5507*
3:15 But do this with gentleness and **r**, *5832*

RESPECTABLE (1) [RESPECT]

1Ti 3:2 self-controlled, **r**, hospitable, able to teach, *3177*

RESPECTED (10) [RESPECT]

Dt 1:13 wise, understanding and **r** men from each 3359
1:15 wise and **r** men, and appointed them 3359
1Sa 9:6 a man of God; he *is* **highly r**, 3877
22:14 captain of your bodyguard and **highly r** 3877
Pr 31:23 Her husband **is r** at the city gate, 3359
Isa 32:5 nor the scoundrel be **highly r**. 8777
33:8 its witnesses are despised, no one *is* **r**. 3108
Ac 10:22 *who is* **r** by all the Jewish people. *3455*
22:12 a devout observer of the law and highly **r** *3455*
Heb 12:9 and *we* **r** them for it. *1956*

RESPECTER (KJV) See FAVORITISM

RESPECTS (2) [RESPECT]

Pr 13:13 but *he who* **r** a command is rewarded. 3707
Ac 25:13 at Caesarea *to* **pay** *their* **r to** Festus. *832*

RESPITE (1)

Job 20:20 "Surely he will have no **r** from his craving; 8929

RESPLENDENT (2)

Ps 76:4 You *are* **r with light**, 239
132:18 but the crown on his head *will be* **r**." 7437

RESPOND (17) [RESPONDED, RESPONDING, RESPONSE, RESPONSIVE]

1Sa 4:20 But *she did* not **r** or pay any attention. 6699
2Ch 32:25 and he *did* not **r** to the kindness shown him; 8740
Est 1:18 about the queen's conduct *will* **r** to all 606
Ps 102:17 *He will* **r** to the prayer of the destitute; 7155
Pr 29:19 though he understands, he will not **r**. 5101
Isa 14:10 They *will* all **r**, they will say to you, 6699
19:22 and *he will* **r to** their **pleas** and heal them. 6983
Jer 2:30 *they did* not **r to** correction. 4374
17:23 and would not listen or **r to** discipline. 4374
32:33 they would not listen or **r to** discipline. 4374
Hos 2:21 "In that day *I will* **r**," 6699
2:21 "*I will* **r** *to* the skies, 6699
2:21 and they *will* **r** *to* the earth; 6699
2:22 and the earth *will* **r** *to* the grain, 6699
2:22 and they *will* **r** *to* Jezreel. 6699
Ac 16:14 The Lord opened her heart *to* **r to** *4668*
Rev 16:7 And I heard the altar **r**: *3306*

RESPONDED (12) [RESPOND]

Ex 19:8 The people all **r** together, 6699
24:3 they **r** *with* one voice, 6699
24:7 *They* **r**, "We will do everything 606
Jdg 7:14 His friend **r**, "This can be nothing other 6699
20:28 The LORD **r**, "Go, for tomorrow I will 606
2Sa 19:43 of Judah **r** even more harshly than the men 1821
Ezr 10:12 The whole assembly **r** with a loud voice: 6699
Ne 8:6 and all the people lifted their hands and **r**, 6699
Job 9:16 Even if I summoned him and *he* **r**, 6699
Pr 1:23 If *you had* **r** to my rebuke, 8740
Jer 7:28 not obeyed the LORD its God or **r to** 4374
Lk 20:39 Some of the teachers of the law **r**, *646*

RESPONDING (1) [RESPOND]

Ne 12:24 one section **r to** the other, 4200+6645

RESPONSE (8) [RESPOND]

1Ki 18:26 But there was no **r**; no one answered. 7754
18:29 But there was no **r**, no one answered, 7754
2Ki 4:31 but there was no sound or **r**. 7993
1Ch 29:9 The people rejoiced at the **willing r** 5605
Job 19:7 *I* **get** no **r**; though I call for help, 6699
Da 10:12 and I have come **in r to** them. 928
Ro 8:31 What, then, shall we say in **r** to this? *NIG*
Gal 2:2 I went **in r to** a revelation and set before *2848*

RESPONSIBILITIES (4) [RESPONSIBLE]

Nu 8:26 how you are to assign the **r** of the Levites." 5466
1Ch 23:32 the Levites carried out their **r** *for* the Tent 5466
2Ch 31:16 according to their **r** and their divisions. 5466
31:17 according to their **r** and their divisions. 5466

RESPONSIBILITY (13) [RESPONSIBLE]

Nu 4:27 to them as their **r** all they are to carry. 5466
18:1 the **r for offenses** *against* the sanctuary, 6411
18:1 the **r for offenses** *against* the priesthood. 6411
18:23 and bear the **r for offenses** *against* it. 6411
1Ch 9:26 with the **r for** the rooms and treasuries in 6584
9:31 with the **r for** baking the offering bread. 6584
15:22 that was his **r** because he was skillful at it. NIH
Ne 10:32 **assume the r for carrying out** 6584+6641
10:35 also assume **r** for bringing to the house of NIH
Mt 27:4 **"That's your r."** *3972+5148*
27:24 "It is **your r!"** *3972+5148*
Ac 6:3 We will turn this **r** over to them *5970*
18:6 I am clear of my **r**. *NIG*

RESPONSIBLE (45) [RESPONSIBILITIES, RESPONSIBILITY]

Ge 16:5 "You are **r for** the wrong I am suffering. 6584
39:22 and he was *made* **r** *for* all 6913
43:9 *you can* **hold** me personally **r** *for* him. 1335+3338+4946
Ex 21:19 who struck the blow *will* **not be held r** if 5927
21:28 the owner of the bull will **not be held r**. 5929
Lev 5:1 he *will be* **held r**. 5951+6411
5:17 he is guilty and *will be* **held r**. 5951+6411
7:18 of it *will be* **held r**. 5951+6411
17:16 he *will be* **held r.'** " 5951+6411
19:8 Whoever eats it *will be* **held r** 5951+6411
20:17 and *will be* **held r**. 5951+6411
20:19 both of you *would be* **held r**. 5951+6411
20:20 They *will be* **held r**; 2628+5951
24:15 he *will be* **held r**; 2628+5951
Nu 1:53 *to be* **r for** the care of the tabernacle of 9068
3:25 the Gershonites were **r for** the **care** *of* 5466
3:28 The Kohathites were **r** *for* the care of 5466
3:31 They were **r for** the **care** *of* the ark, 5466
3:32 He was appointed over those who were **r** 5466
3:38 They were **r** *for* the care of the sanctuary 5466
7:9 the holy things, *for* which they were **r**. 6275
14:37 these men **r** *for* **spreading** the bad report AIT
18:3 *to be* **r** *to* you and are to perform all 5466+9068
18:4 to join you and *be* **r** *for* the care of the Tent 9068
18:5 *to be* **r** *for* the care of the sanctuary and 9068
30:15 then *he is* **r for** her guilt." 5951
31:30 *who are* **r** *for* the care of the LORD's 9068
31:47 *who were* **r** *for* the care of the LORD's 9068
Jos 2:19 we will **not be r**. 5929
1Sa 22:22 I *am* **r for** the death of your father's 928+6015
23:20 and we will be **r for** handing him over to 4200
1Ch 9:13 **r** *for* ministering in the house of God. 4856
9:19 from his family (the Korahites) were **r** 4856+6275
9:19 the Tent just as their fathers had been **r for** 6584
9:33 from other duties because they were **r for** 6584
16:42 and Jeduthun were **r** for the sounding of NIH
26:30 were **r** in Israel west of the Jordan for all 7213
Ne 11:22 who were the singers **r for** the service 4200+5584
13:10 and singers **r** *for* the service had gone back 6913
13:13 They were made **r** *for* distributing 6584
Jnh 1:7 to find out who is **r for** this calamity." 928+4200+8611
1:8 who is **r for** making all this trouble for us? 889+928+4200
Lk 11:50 *be* **held r for** the blood of all the prophets *1699*
11:51 this generation *will be* **held r** for it all. *1699*
1Co 7:24 Brothers, each man, as **r** to God, *NIG*

RESPONSIVE (2) [RESPOND]

2Ki 22:19 Because your heart was **r** and you humbled 8205
2Ch 34:27 Because your heart was **r** and you humbled 8205

REST (269) [RESTED, RESTING, RESTLESS, RESTS, SABBATH-REST]

Ge 8:4 of the seventh month the ark **came to r** on 5663
14:10 men fell into them and the **r** fled to the hills. 8636
18:4 and then you may all wash your feet and **r** 9128
30:36 while Jacob continued to tend the **r** 3855
30:40 but made the **r** face the streaked 7366[S]
42:16 *the r of* **you** will be kept in prison, AIT
42:19 while *the r of* **you** go and take grain back AIT
44:9 *the r of* **us** will become my lord's slaves." AIT
44:10 *the r of* **you** will be free from blame." AIT
44:17 *The r of* **you**, go back to your father AIT
47:30 but when *I* **r** with my fathers, 8886
49:26 *Let all these* **r** on the head of Joseph, 2118
Ex 4:7 it was restored, like the **r** of his flesh. NIH
16:23 'Tomorrow is to be a **day of r**, 8702
23:12 so that your ox and your donkey *may* **r** and 5663
29:12 pour out the **r** *of* it at the base of the altar. 3972
31:15 but the seventh day is a Sabbath of **r**, 8702
33:14 and *I will* **give** you **r**." 5663
34:21 but on the seventh day *you shall* **r**; 8697
34:21 and harvest *you must* **r**. 8697
35:2 a Sabbath of **r** to the LORD. 8702
Lev 2:3 The **r** of the grain offering belongs 3855
2:10 The **r** of the grain offering belongs 3855
4:7 The **r** *of* the bull's blood he shall pour out 3972
4:12 that is, **all** *the* **r** *of* the bull— AIT
4:18 The **r** *of* the blood he shall pour out at 3972
4:25 and pour out the **r** of the blood at the base NIH
4:30 and pour out the **r** *of* the blood at the base 3972
4:34 and pour out the **r** *of* the blood at the base 3972
5:9 the **r** of the blood must be drained out at 8636
5:13 The **r** of the offering will belong to NIH
6:16 Aaron and his sons shall eat the **r** of it, 3855
8:15 He poured out the **r** of the blood at the base NIH
8:32 burn up the **r** of the meat and the bread. 3855
9:9 the **r** of the blood he poured out at the base NIH
14:9 his eyebrows and the **r** *of* his hair. 3972
14:18 The **r** of the oil in his palm 3855
14:29 The **r** of the oil in his palm 3855
16:31 It is a sabbath of **r**, 8702
23:3 but the seventh day is a Sabbath of **r**, 8702
23:24 to have a **day of r**, 8702
23:32 It is a sabbath of **r** for you, 8702
23:39 the first day is a **day of r**, 8702
23:39 and the eighth day also is a **day of r**. 8702
25:4 the land is to have a sabbath of **r**, 8702
25:5 The land is to have a year of **r**. 8702
26:34 then the land *will* **r** and enjoy its sabbaths. 8697
26:35 the land *will* **have** *the* **r** it did not have 8697
Nu 10:12 the cloud **came to r** in the Desert of Paran. 8905
10:33 to find them a **place to r**. 4957
10:36 Whenever it **came to r**, he said, "Return, 5663
16:9 of Israel has separated you from the **r** of NIH
18:31 You and your households may eat the **r** NIH
23:24 not **r** till he devours his prey and drinks 8886
31:27 in the battle and the **r** *of* the community. 3972
Dt 3:13 The **r** of Gilead and also all of Bashan, 3856
3:20 until the LORD **gives r** to your brothers 5663
5:14 your manservant and maidservant *may* **r**, 5663
12:10 and *he will* **give** you **r** from all your enemies 5663
19:20 The **r** *of the people* will hear of this and 8636
25:19 the LORD your God **gives** you **r** from all 5663
31:16 "You *are going to* **r** with your fathers, 8886
33:12 the beloved of the LORD **r** secure in him, 8905
33:16 *Let all these* **r** on the head of Joseph, 995
Jos 1:13 'The LORD your God is **giving** you **r** 5663
1:15 until the LORD **gives** them **r**, 5663
7:25 and after they had stoned **the r**, 4392[S]
11:23 Then the land **had r** from war. 9200
13:27 with the **r** *of* the realm of Sihon king 3856
14:3 the Levites an inheritance among **the r**, 4392[S]
14:15 Then the land **had r** from war. 9200
17:2 for the **r** of the people of Manasseh— 3855
17:6 to the **r** of the descendants of Manasseh. 3855
21:5 The **r** of Kohath's descendants were allotted 3855
21:20 The **r** of the Kohathite clans of 3855
21:26 and their pasturelands were given to the **r** 3855
21:34 (the **r** of the Levites) were given: 3855
21:40 who *were the* **r** of the Levites, were twelve. 3855
21:44 The LORD **gave** them **r** on every side, 5663
22:4 LORD your God *has* **given** your brothers **r** 5663
23:1 and the LORD *had* **given** Israel **r** from all 5663
Jdg 7:6 All the **r** got down on their knees to drink. 3856
7:8 the **r** *of* the Israelites to their tents but kept 3972[S]
Ru 1:9 that each of you will find **r** in the home 4957
2:7 except for a short **r** in the shelter." 3782
3:18 not **r** until the matter is settled today." 9200
1Sa 13:2 The **r** *of* the men he sent back 3856
15:15 but we totally destroyed the **r**." 3463
18:29 he remained his enemy the **r** *of* his days. 3972
18:30 David met with more success than the **r** 3972
2Sa 4:5 while he *was* **taking** his noonday **r**. 5435+8886
7:1 and the LORD *had* **given** him **r** from all 5663
7:11 also **give** you **r** from all your enemies. 5663
7:12 When your days are over and *you* **r** 8886
10:10 the **r** *of* the men under the command 3856
12:28 Now muster the **r** *of* the troops and besiege 3856
13:27 so he sent with him Amnon and the **r** *of* 3972
14:9 let the blame **r on** me and 6584
14:17 the word of my lord the king bring me **r**, 4957
1Ki 1:21 as soon as my lord the king *is* **laid to r** 8886
2:33 *May* the guilt of their blood **r** on the head 8740
5:4 now the LORD my God *has* **given** me **r** 5663
8:56 who has given **r** to his people Israel just 4957
12:23 and to the **r** *of* the people, 3856
20:15 Then he assembled the **r** *of* the Israelites, 3972
20:30 The **r** of them escaped to the city of Aphek, 3855
22:46 He rid the land of the **r** *of* the male shrine 3856
2Ki 13:7 for the king of Aram had destroyed **the r** 4392[S]
25:11 along with the **r** *of* the populace 3856
25:29 and *for* the **r** *of* his life ate regularly at 3427+3972
1Ch 6:31 of the LORD after the ark **came to r** there. 4955
6:61 The **r** of Kohath's descendants were allotted 3855
6:70 to the **r** of the Kohathite clans. 3855
6:77 (the **r** of the Levites) received the following: 3855
11:8 while Joab restored the **r** *of* the city. 8637
12:38 All the **r** *of* the Israelites were also 8642
13:2 let us send word far and wide to the **r** 8636
16:41 and the **r** *of* those chosen and designated 8637
19:11 the **r** *of* the men under the command 3856
22:9 a son who will be a man of **peace and r**, 4957
22:9 and *I will* **give** him **r** from all his enemies 5663
22:18 *has he* not **granted** you **r** on every side? 5663
23:25 *has* **granted r** to his people and has come 5663
24:20 As for the **r** of the descendants of Levi: 3855
28:2 to build a house as a **place of r** for the ark 4957
2Ch 14:6 for the LORD **gave** him **r**. 5663
14:7 and *he has* **given** us **r** on every side." 5663
15:15 So the LORD **gave** them **r** on every side. 5663
20:30 for his God *had* **given** him **r** on every side. 5663
24:14 they brought the **r** *of* the money to the king 8637
Ezr 2:70 the **r** *of* the Israelites settled in their towns. 3972
3:8 and the **r** *of* their brothers (the priests and 8637

Ezr 4: 3 and the **r** *of* the heads of the families 8637
4: 7 and the **r** *of* his associates wrote a letter 8637
4: 9 together with the **r** *of* their associates— 10692
4: 17 the **r** *of* their associates living in Samaria 10692
6: 16 the Levites and the **r** *of* the exiles— 10692
7: 18 then do whatever seems best with the **r** *of* 10692
Ne 4: 14 the officials and the **r** *of* the people, 3856
4: 19 the officials and the **r** *of* the people, 3856
6: 1 Geshem the Arab and the **r** *of* our enemies 3856
6: 14 the **r** *of* the prophets who have been trying 3856
7: 72 by the **r** *of* the people was 20,000 8642
7: 73 along with certain of the people and the **r** 3972
9: 28 "But as soon as they *were* **at r,** 5663
10: 28 "The **r** *of* the people— 8637
11: 1 and the **r** *of* the people cast lots 8637
11: 20 The **r** *of* the Israelites, 8637
Est 9: 12 in the **r** *of* the king's provinces? 8637
Job 3: 13 I would be asleep and **at r** 5663
3: 17 and there the weary *are* **at r.** 5663
3: 26 *I* **have** no **r,** but only turmoil." 5663
11: 18 you will look about you and **take** *your* **r** 8886
16: 18 may my cry never be laid to **r!** 5226
24: 23 He may let them **r** in a feeling of security, 9128
30: 17 my gnawing pains never **r.** 8886
36: 11 they will spend the **r** of their days NIH
Ps 16: 9 my body also *will* **r** secure, 8905
33: 22 *May* your unfailing love **r** upon us, 2118
55: 6 I would fly away and *be* **at r—** 8905
62: 1 My soul finds **r** in God alone; 1875
62: 5 **Find r,** O my soul, in God alone; 1957
80: 17 *Let* your hand **r** on the man 2118
90: 17 the favor of the Lord our God **r** upon us; 2118
91: 1 *will* **r** in the shadow of the Almighty. 4328
95: 11 "They shall never enter my **r."** 4957
116: 7 Be at **r** once more, O my soul, 4955
Pr 6: 10 a little folding of the hands to **r—** 8886
21: 16 of understanding **comes to r** in the company 5663
24: 33 a little folding of the hands to **r—** 8886
26: 2 an undeserved curse *does* not **come to r.** 995
Ecc 2: 23 even at night his mind *does* not **r.** 8886
6: 5 it has more **r** than does that man— 5739
10: 4 calmness *can* **lay** great errors **to r.** 5663
SS 1: 7 and where *you* **r** your sheep at midday. 8069
Isa 11: 2 The Spirit of the LORD *will* **r** on him— 5663
11: 10 and his **place of r** will be glorious. 4957
13: 20 no shepherd *will* **r** *his* **flocks** there. 8069
14: 7 All the lands *are* **at r** and at peace; 5663
23: 12 even there you *will* **find** no **r."** 5663
25: 10 of the LORD *will* **r** on this mountain; 5663
28: 12 "This is the resting place, *let* the weary **r";** 5663
30: 15 "In repentance and **r** is your salvation, 5739
32: 18 in undisturbed **places of r.** 4957
34: 14 and find for themselves **places of r.** 4955
38: 10 the gates of death and be robbed of the **r** 3856
44: 17 From the **r** he makes a god, his idol; 8642
57: 2 *they* **find r** as they lie in death. 5663
57: 20 which cannot **r,** whose waves cast up mire 9200
62: 6 who call on the LORD, give yourselves no **r,** 1954
62: 7 give him no **r** till he establishes Jerusalem 1954
63: 14 they *were* **given r** *by* the Spirit of 5663
Jer 6: 16 and you will find **r** for your souls. 5273
31: 2 I will come to **give r** *to* Israel." 8089
33: 12 be pastures for shepherds *to* **r** their flocks. 8069
39: 9 and the **r** *of* the people. 3856
41: 10 the **r** *of* the people who were in Mizpah— 8642
45: 3 with groaning and find no **r.'** " 4957
47: 6 'how long till *you* **r?** 9200
47: 7 But how *can it* **r** when the LORD has 9200
48: 11 "Moab *has been* **at r** from youth, 8631
50: 34 so that *he may* **bring r** *to* their land, 8089
52: 15 along with the **r** *of* the craftsmen 3856
52: 16 the **r of** the poorest people of the land 4946
52: 33 and *for* the **r** *of* his life ate regularly at 3427+3972
La 2: 18 give yourself no relief, your eyes no **r.** 1957
5: 5 we are weary and **find** no **r.** 5663
Eze 34: 18 the **r** *of* your pasture with your feet? 3856
34: 18 Must you also muddy the **r** with your feet? 3855
36: 3 that you became the possession of the **r** *of* 8642
36: 4 by the **r** *of* the nations around you— 8642
36: 5 against the **r** *of* the nations, 8642
44: 30 so that a blessing *may* **r** on your household. 5663
48: 23 "As for the **r** *of* the tribes: 3856
Da 2: 18 not be executed with the **r** *of* the wise men 10692
12: 13 *You will* **r,** and then at the end of the days 5663
Mic 5: 3 and the **r** *of* his brothers return to join 3856
Na 3: 18 your nobles **lie down to r.** 8905
Hab 2: 5 he is arrogant and never **at r.** 5657
Zec 1: 11 the earth and found the whole world **at r** 3782
6: 8 the north country *have* **given** my Spirit **r** in 5663
7: 7 and its surrounding towns were **at r** 3782
9: 1 of Hadrach and will **r** *upon* Damascus— 4957
12: 14 and all the **r** *of* the clans and their wives. 8636
14: 2 the **r** *of* the people will not be taken from 3856
Mt 10: 13 *let* your peace **r** on it; *2262*
11: 28 weary and burdened, and I *will* **give** you **r.** *399*
11: 29 and you will find **r** for your souls. *398*
12: 43 through arid places seeking **r** and does *398*
22: 6 The **r** seized his servants, *3370*
27: 49 The **r** said, "Now leave him alone. *3370*
Mk 6: 31 to a quiet place and **get** some **r."** *399*
16: 13 These returned and reported it *to* the **r;** *3370*
Lk 10: 6 your peace *will* **r** on him; *2058*
11: 24 through arid places seeking **r** and does *398*
12: 26 why do you worry about the **r?** *3370*
Jn 11: 16 *to* the **r of the disciples,** *5209*
Ac 2: 3 tongues of fire that separated and **came to r** *2767*
5: 2 brought the **r** and put it at the apostles' feet. *NIG*
Ac 16: 17 This girl followed Paul and the **r** of us, *NIG*
21: 18 The next day Paul and the **r** of us went *NIG*
27: 44 The **r** were to get there on planks or *3370*
28: 9 the **r** of the sick on the island came *3370*
1Co 2: 5 your faith *might* not **r** on men's wisdom, *1639*
7: 12 *To* the **r** I say this (I, not the Lord): *3370*
2Co 7: 5 this body of ours had no **r,** *457*
12: 9 so that Christ's power *may* **r on** me. *2172*
Eph 2: 3 Like the **r,** we were by nature objects *3370*
Php 4: 3 and the **r** of my fellow workers, *3370*
1Th 4: 13 or to grieve like the **r** *of men,* *3370*
Heb 3: 11 'They shall never enter my **r.'** " *2923*
3: 18 that they would never enter his **r** if not *2923*
4: 1 the promise of entering his **r** still stands, *2923*
4: 3 Now we who have believed enter that **r,** *2923*
4: 3 'They shall never enter my **r.'** " *2923*
4: 5 "They shall never enter my **r."** *2923*
4: 6 It still remains that some will enter **that r,** *899S*
4: 8 For if Joshua *had* **given** them **r,** *2924*
4: 10 for anyone who enters God's **r** also rests *2923*
4: 11 therefore, make every effort to enter that **r,** *2923*
1Pe 4: 2 he does not live the **r** of his earthly life *2145*
1Jn 3: 19 **set** our hearts **at r** in his presence *4275*
Rev 2: 24 Now I say *to* the **r** of you in Thyatira, *3370*
9: 20 The **r** of mankind that were not killed *3370*
12: 17 and went off to make war against the **r** *3370*
14: 11 There is no **r** day or night *398*
14: 13 *"they will* **r** from their labor, *399*
19: 21 The **r** of them were killed with the sword *3370*
20: 5 (The **r** of the dead did not come to life until *3370*

RESTED (54) [REST]

Ge 2: 2 on the seventh day *he* **r** from all his work. 8697
2: 3 on it *he* **r** from all the work of creating 8697
Ex 16: 30 So the people **r** on the seventh day. 8697
20: 11 but *he* **r** on the seventh day. 5663
31: 17 seventh day he abstained from work and **r.'** 5882
Nu 11: 25 When the Spirit **r** on them, 5663
11: 26 Yet the Spirit also **r** on them, 5663
1Ki 2: 10 Then David **r** with his fathers 8886
7: 3 above the beams that **r on** the columns— 6584
7: 25 The Sea **r on** top of them, 6584
11: 21 that David **r** with his fathers and that Joab 8886
11: 43 Then he **r** with his fathers and was buried 8886
14: 20 He reigned for twenty-two years and then **r** 8886
14: 31 And Rehoboam **r** with his fathers 8886
15: 8 And Abijah **r** with his fathers 8886
15: 24 Then Asa **r** with his fathers and was buried 8886
16: 6 Baasha **r** with his fathers and was buried 8886
16: 28 Omri **r** with his fathers and was buried 8886
22: 40 Ahab **r** with his fathers. 8886
22: 50 Then Jehoshaphat **r** with his fathers 8886
2Ki 8: 24 Jehoram **r** with his fathers and was buried 8886
10: 35 Jehu **r** with his fathers and was buried 8886
13: 9 Jehoahaz **r** with his fathers and was buried 8886
13: 13 Jehoash **r** with his fathers, 8886
14: 16 Jehoash **r** with his fathers and was buried 8886
14: 22 to Judah after Amaziah **r** with his fathers. 8886
14: 29 Jeroboam **r** with his fathers, 8886
15: 7 Azariah **r** with his fathers and was buried 8886
15: 22 Menahem **r** with his fathers. 8886
15: 38 Jotham **r** with his fathers and was buried 8886
16: 20 Ahaz **r** with his fathers and was buried 8886
20: 21 Hezekiah **r** with his fathers. 8886
21: 18 Manasseh **r** with his fathers and was buried 8886
24: 6 Jehoiakim **r** with his fathers. 8886
2Ch 4: 4 The Sea **r on** top of them, 6584
9: 31 Then he **r** with his fathers and was buried 8886
12: 16 Rehoboam **r** with his fathers 8886
14: 1 And Abijah **r** with his fathers 8886
16: 13 of his reign Asa died and **r** with his fathers. 8886
21: 1 Then Jehoshaphat **r** with his fathers 8886
26: 2 to Judah after Amaziah **r** with his fathers. 8886
26: 23 Uzziah **r** with his fathers and was buried 8886
27: 9 Jotham **r** with his fathers and was buried in 8886
28: 27 Ahaz **r** with his fathers and was buried in 8886
32: 33 Hezekiah **r** with his fathers and was buried 8886
33: 20 Manasseh **r** with his fathers and was buried 8886
36: 21 all the time of its desolation *it* **r,** 8697
Ezr 8: 32 where *we* **r** three days. 3782
Est 9: 17 on the fourteenth they **r** and made it a day 5663
9: 18 and then on the fifteenth they **r** and made it 5663
Eze 32: 27 The punishment for their sins **r** 2118
Am 5: 19 though he entered his house and **r** his hand 6164
Lk 23: 56 But *they* **r** on the Sabbath in obedience to *2483*
Heb 4: 4 the seventh day God **r** from all his work." *2924*

RESTING (23) [REST]

Ge 28: 12 in which he saw a stairway **r** on the earth, 5893
49: 15 When he sees how good is his **r place** and 4957
Dt 12: 9 yet reached the **r place** and the inheritance 4957
28: 65 no **r place** for the sole of your foot. 4955
1Ki 7: 30 each had a basin **r on** four supports, 4946+9393
2Ki 2: 15 said, "The spirit of Elijah *is* **r** on Elisha." 5663
9: 16 because Joram *was* **r** there 8886
2Ch 6: 41 O LORD God, and come to your **r place,** 5665
Ps 132: 8 O LORD, and come to your **r place,** 4957
132: 14 "This is my **r place** for ever and ever; 4957
SS 1: 13 a sachet of myrrh **r** between my breasts. 4328
Isa 22: 16 on the height and chiseling your **r place** in 5438
28: 12 "This is the **r place,** let the weary rest"; 4957
65: 10 the Valley of Achor a **r place** *for* herds, 8070
66: 1 Where will my **r** place be? 4957
Jer 50: 6 and hill and forgot their own **r place.** 8070
La 1: 3 she finds no **r place.** 4955
Eze 25: 5 for camels and Ammon into a **r place** 5271
Mic 2: 10 For this is not your **r place,** 4957
Mt 26: 45 *"Are you* still sleeping and **r?** *399*
Mk 14: 41 "Are you still sleeping and **r?** *399*
Ac 7: 49 Or where will my **r** place be? *2923*
Tit 1: 2 and knowledge **r on** the hope of eternal life, *2093*

RESTITUTION (14)

Ex 22: 3 "A thief **must certainly make r,** 8966+8966
22: 5 *he must* **make r** *from* the best of his own 8966
22: 6 one who started the fire **must make r.** 8966+8966
22: 11 owner is to accept this, and no **r** *is required.* 8966
22: 12 *he must* **make r** to the owner. 8966
22: 14 *he* **must make r.** 8966+8966
Lev 5: 16 *He must* **make r** *for* what he has failed to do 8966
6: 5 *He must* **make r** in full, 8966
22: 14 *he must* **make r** to the priest *for* the offering 5989
24: 18 the life of someone's animal *must* **make r—** 8966
24: 21 Whoever kills an animal *must* **make r,** 8966
Nu 5: 7 *He must* **make full r** *for* his wrong, 928+8031+8740
5: 8 to whom **r** *can be* **made** *for* the wrong, 8740
5: 8 the **r** belongs to the LORD and must 871+8740

RESTLESS (5) [REST]

Ge 4: 12 You will be a **r** wanderer on the earth." 5675
4: 14 I will be a **r** wanderer on the earth, 5675
27: 40 But when *you grow* **r,** 8113
Jer 49: 23 troubled like the **r** sea. 1796
Jas 3: 8 It is a **r** evil, full of deadly poison. *190*

RESTORATION (1) [RESTORE]

2Ch 24: 27 and the record of the **r** *of* the temple of God 3572

RESTORE (61) [RESTORATION, RESTORED, RESTORER, RESTORES, RESTORING]

Ge 40: 13 up your head and **r** you to your position, 8740
Dt 30: 3 the LORD your God *will* **r** your fortunes 8740
2Sa 8: 3 to **r** his control along the Euphrates River. 8740
9: 7 *I will* **r** to you all the land that belonged 8740
2Ch 24: 4 Some time later Joash decided to **r** 2542
24: 12 and carpenters to **r** the LORD's temple, 2542
Ezr 5: 3 to rebuild this temple and **r** this structure?" 10354
5: 9 to rebuild this temple and **r** this structure?" 10354
Ne 4: 2 *Will they* **r** their **wall?** 6441
Job 8: 6 and **r** you *to* your rightful place. 8966
Ps 41: 3 on his sickbed and **r** him from his bed 2200
51: 12 **R** to me the joy of your salvation 8740
60: 1 you have been angry—now **r** us! 8740
69: 4 *I am* **forced to r** what I did not steal. 8740
71: 20 *you will* **r** my **life** again; 2649
80: 3 **R** us, O God; 8740
80: 7 **R** us, O God Almighty; 8740
80: 19 **R** us, O LORD God Almighty; 8740
85: 4 **R** us **again,** O God our Savior, 8740
126: 4 **R** our fortunes, O LORD, 8740
Isa 1: 26 *I will* **r** your judges as in days of old, 8740
44: 26 and of their ruins, *'I will* **r** them,' 7756
49: 6 to **r** the tribes of Jacob and bring back those 7756
49: 8 a covenant for the people, to **r** the land and 7756
57: 18 I will guide him and **r** comfort to him, 8966
61: 4 They will rebuild the ancient ruins and **r** 7756
Jer 15: 19 *I will* **r** you that you may serve me; 8740
16: 15 For *I will* **r** them to the land 8740
27: 22 'Then I will bring them back and **r** them 8740
30: 3 and Judah back from captivity and **r** them 8740
30: 17 But *I will* **r** you to health 6590
30: 18 " '*I will* **r** the fortunes of Jacob's tents 8740
31: 18 **R** me, and I will return, 8740
32: 44 because *I will* **r** their fortunes, 8740
33: 11 For *I will* **r** the fortunes of the land 8740
33: 26 For *I will* **r** their fortunes 8740
42: 12 on you and **r** you to your land.' 8740
48: 47 "Yet *I will* **r** the fortunes of Moab in days 8740
49: 6 *I will* **r** the fortunes of the Ammonites," 8740
49: 39 "Yet *I will* **r** the fortunes of Elam in days 8740
La 1: 16 no *one to* **r** my spirit. 8740
5: 21 **R** us to yourself, O LORD, 8740
Eze 16: 53 *I will* **r** the fortunes of Sodom 8740
Da 9: 25 the decree to **r** and rebuild Jerusalem until 8740
Hos 6: 2 on the third day *he will* **r** us, 7756
6: 11 "Whenever I *would* **r** the fortunes 8740
Joel 3: 1 *I* **r** the fortunes of Judah and Jerusalem, 8740
Am 9: 11 "In that day *I will* **r** David's fallen tent. 7756
9: 11 I will repair its broken places, **r** its ruins, 7756
Na 2: 2 The LORD *will* **r** the splendor of Jacob 8740
Zep 2: 7 *he will* **r** their fortunes. 8740
3: 20 of the earth when I **r** your fortunes 8740
Zec 9: 12 even now I announce that *I will* **r** twice 8740
10: 6 *I will* **r** them because I have compassion 3782
Mt 17: 11 Elijah comes and *will* **r** all things. *635*
Ac 1: 6 *are you* at this time *going to* **r** the kingdom *635*
3: 21 the time comes for God to **r** everything, *640*
9: 12 and place his hands on him to **r** *his* **sight."** *329*
15: 16 Its ruins I will rebuild, and *I will* **r** it, *494*
Gal 6: 1 you who are spiritual *should* **r** him gently. *2936*
1Pe 5: 10 *will* himself **r** you and make you strong, *2936*

RESTORED (39) [RESTORE]

Ge 40: 21 *He* **r** the chief cupbearer to his position, 8740
41: 13 I *was* **r** to my position, 8740
Ex 4: 7 and when he took it out, *it was* **r,** 8740

Nu 21:27 let it be rebuilt; *let* Sihon's city **be r.** 3922
1Sa 7:14 from Israel *were* **r** to her, 8740
1Ki 13: 6 and pray for me that my hand *may be* **r."** 8740
13: 6 and the king's hand *was* **r** and became 8740
2Ki 5:10 and your flesh *will be* **r** and you will 8740
5:14 and his flesh *was* **r** and became clean like 8740
8: 1 to the woman whose son *he had* **r to life,** 2649
8: 5 **r** the dead **to life,** 2649
8: 5 and this is her son whom Elisha **r to life."** 2649
14:22 the one who rebuilt Elath and **r** it to Judah 8740
14:25 the *one who* **r** the boundaries of Israel 8740
1Ch 11: 8 while Joab **r** the rest of the city. 2649
2Ch 26: 2 the one who rebuilt Elath and **r** it to Judah 8740
33:16 Then *he* **r** the altar of the LORD 1215
34:10 the workers who repaired and **r** the temple. 2616
Ezr 4:13 that if this city is built and its walls **are r,** 10354
4:16 that if this city is built and its walls **are r,** 10354
Ne 3: 8 *They* **r** Jerusalem as far as the Broad Wall. 6441
Job 22:23 you return to the Almighty, *you will* **be r:** 1215
33:25 *it is* **r** as in the days of his youth. 8740
33:26 he *is* **r** by God *to* his righteous state. 8740
Ps 85: 1 *you* **r** the fortunes of Jacob. 8740
Isa 38:16 *You* **r** me **to health** and let me live. 2730
Eze 21:27 It *will* not **be r** until he comes 2118
Da 4:26 be **r** to you when you acknowledge 10629
4:34 and my sanity *was* **r.** 10754
4:36 At the same time that my sanity *was* **r,** 10754
4:36 and *I* **was r** to my throne and became 10771
Mic 4: 8 the former dominion *will* **be r** to you; 910
Mt 9:30 and their sight *was* **r.** *487*
12:13 he stretched it out and it *was* **completely r,** *635*
Mk 3: 5 and his hand *was* **completely r.** *635*
8:25 Then his eyes were opened, his sight *was* **r,** *635*
Lk 6:10 He did so, and his hand *was* **completely r.** *635*
Phm 1:22 a guest room for me, because I hope to *be* **r** *5919*
Heb 13:19 to pray so that *I may be* **r** to you soon. *635*

RESTORER (1) [RESTORE]

Isa 58:12 **R** *of* Streets with Dwellings. 8740

RESTORES (4) [RESTORE]

Ps 14: 7 the LORD **r** the fortunes of his people, 8740
23: 3 *he* **r** my soul. He guides me in paths of 8740
53: 6 When God **r** the fortunes of his people, 8740
Mk 9:12 Elijah does come first, and **r** all things. *635*

RESTORING (2) [RESTORE]

2Ki 12:12 met all the other expenses of **r** the temple. 2616
Ezr 4:12 *They are* **r** the walls and repairing 10354

RESTRAIN (5) [RESTRAINED, RESTRAINING, RESTRAINT]

1Sa 3:13 and *he* failed *to* **r** them. 3909
Job 9:13 God *does* not **r** his anger; 8740
Jer 2:24 in her heat who *can* **r** her? 8740
14:10 *they do* not **r** their feet. 3104
31:16 **"R** your voice from weeping and your eyes 4979

RESTRAINED (6) [RESTRAIN]

Ex 36: 6 so the people **were r** from bringing more, 3973
Est 5:10 Haman **r himself** and went home. 706
Ps 76:10 and the survivors of your wrath *are* **r.** 2520
78:38 Time after time he **r** his anger and did not 8740
Eze 31:15 and its abundant waters **were r.** 3973
2Pe 2:16 a man's voice and **r** the prophet's madness. *3266*

RESTRAINING (3) [RESTRAIN]

Pr 27:16 **r** her is like restraining the wind 7621
27:16 like **r** the wind or grasping oil with 7621
Col 2:23 they lack any value **in r** sensual indulgence. *4639*

RESTRAINT (6) [RESTRAIN]

Job 30:11 they throw off **r** in my presence. 8270
Ps 119:51 The arrogant mock me **without r,** 4394+6330
Pr 17:27 A man of knowledge **uses** words **with r,** 3104
23: 4 have the wisdom *to* **show r.** 2532
29:18 the people **cast off r;** 7277
Eze 35:13 against me and spoke against me **without r,** 6984

RESTRICT (1) [RESTRICTED, RESTRICTION]

1Co 7:35 not to **r** you, *1105+2095*

RESTRICTED (1) [RESTRICT]

Jer 36: 5 Then Jeremiah told Baruch, "I *am* **r;** 6806

RESTRICTION (1) [RESTRICT]

Job 36:16 of distress to a spacious place free from **r,** 4608

RESTS (9) [REST]

Dt 33:12 one the LORD loves **r** between his shoulders. 8905
2Ch 28:11 for the LORD's fierce anger **r on** you." 6584
28:13 and his fierce anger **r on** Israel." 6584
36:21 The land enjoyed its **sabbath r;** 8701
Pr 19:23 Then *one* **r** content, untouched by trouble. 4328
21:31 but victory **r with** the LORD. 4200
Lk 2:14 peace to men **on whom** his **favor r."** *2306*
Heb 4:10 for anyone who enters God's rest also **r** *2924*
1Pe 4:14 for the Spirit of glory and of God **r** on you. *399*

RESULT (28)

Ge 38:24 and **as a r** she is now pregnant." 4200
Ex 21:20 a rod and the slave dies **as a direct r,** 3338+9393
Lev 7:16 the **r** of a vow or is a freewill offering, NIH
Nu 25:18 when the plague came **as a r of** Peor." 1821+6584
Ezr 9:13 a **r of** our evil deeds and our great guilt, 928
Mic 7:13 as the **r** *of* their deeds. 7262
Mk 1:45 **As a r,** Jesus could no longer enter *6063*
Lk 21:13 *This will* **r** in your being witnesses *609*
Ac 5:15 **As a r,** people brought the sick into *6063*
25:26 so that *as* **a r** of this investigation *1181*
Ro 3: 8 "Let us do evil that good *may* **r"?** *2262*
5:16 not like **the r of** the one man's sin: *1328*
5:18 as **the r of** one trespass was condemnation *1328*
5:18 so also **the r of** one act of righteousness *1328*
6:21 Those things **r** in death! *5465*
6:22 and the **r** is eternal life. *5465*
11:30 mercy *as a r of* their **disobedience,** *AIT*
11:31 now receive mercy *as a r of* God's **mercy** *AIT*
1Co 9: 1 Are you not the **r** of my work in the Lord? *NIG*
11:34 you meet together it may not **r in** judgment. *1650*
2Co 3: 3 a letter from Christ, the **r of** our ministry, *5679*
9:11 and through us your generosity *will* **r in** *2981*
Gal 4:23 by the free woman was born **as the r of** *1328*
Php 1:13 **As a r,** it has become clear throughout *6063*
2Th 1: 5 as a **r** you will be counted worthy of *1650+3836*
1Ti 6: 4 quarrels about words that **r** in envy, *1181+1666*
1Pe 1: 7 *may be* proved genuine and *may* **r** in praise, *2351*
4: 2 **As a r,** he does not live the rest *1650+3836*

RESURRECTION (40)

Mt 22:23 the Sadducees, who say there is no **r,** *414*
22:28 Now then, at the **r,** whose wife will she be *414*
22:30 the **r** people will neither marry nor be given *414*
22:31 But about the **r** of the dead— *414*
27:53 after Jesus' **r** they went into the holy city *1587*
Mk 12:18 Then the Sadducees, who say there is no **r,** *414*
12:23 At the **r** whose wife will she be, *414*
Lk 14:14 be repaid at the **r** of the righteous." *414*
20:27 the Sadducees, who say there is no **r,** *414*
20:33 Now then, at the **r** whose wife will she be, *414*
20:35 of taking part in that age and *in* the **r** from *414*
20:36 since they are children *of* the **r.** *414*
Jn 11:24 "I know he will rise again in the **r** at *414*
11:25 Jesus said to her, "I am the **r** and the life. *414*
Ac 1:22 a witness with us *of* his **r."** *414*
2:31 he spoke of the **r** of the Christ, *414*
4: 2 the people and proclaiming in Jesus the **r** of *414*
4:33 the apostles continued to testify to the **r** of *414*
17:18 the good news about Jesus and the **r.** *414*
17:32 When they heard about the **r** of the dead, *414*
23: 6 I stand on trial because of my hope *in* the **r** *414*
23: 8 (The Sadducees say that there is no **r,** *414*
24:15 be a **r** of both the righteous and the wicked. *414*
24:21 'It is concerning the **r** of the dead that I am *414*
Ro 1: 4 be the Son of God by his **r** from the dead: *414*
6: 5 also be united with him *in* his **r.** *414*
1Co 15:12 how can some of you say that there is no **r** *414*
15:13 If there is no **r** of the dead, *414*
15:21 the **r** of the dead comes also through a man. *414*
15:29 Now if there is no **r,** *NIG*
15:42 So will it be with the **r** of the dead. *414*
Php 3:10 to know Christ and the power *of* his **r** and *414*
3:11 somehow, to attain to the **r** from the dead. *1983*
2Ti 2:18 They say that the **r** has already taken place, *414*
Heb 6: 2 the laying on of hands, the **r** of the dead, *414*
11:35 so that they might gain a better **r.** *414*
1Pe 1: 3 through the **r** of Jesus Christ from the dead, *414*
3:21 It saves you by the **r** of Jesus Christ, *414*
Rev 20: 5 This is the first **r.** *414*
20: 6 holy are those who have part in the first **r.** *414*

RETAIN (5) [RETAINS]

2Ch 22: 9 the house of Ahaziah powerful enough to **r** 6806
Da 11: 6 but *she will* not **r** her power, 6806
Lk 8:15 **r** it, and by persevering produce a crop. *2988*
Ro 1:28 not think it worthwhile *to* **r** the knowledge *2400*
1Co 7:17 **r the place in life** that the Lord assigned *4344*

RETAINS (2) [RETAIN]

Lev 25:29 he **r** the right of redemption a full year 2118
25:48 he **r** the right of redemption 2118+4200

RETAKE (2) [TAKE]

Jdg 11:26 Why didn't *you* **r** them during that time? 5911
1Ki 22: 3 and yet we are doing nothing *to* **r** it from 4374

RETALIATE (1)

1Pe 2:23 they hurled their insults at him, *he did* not **r;** *518*

RETINUE (2)

1Ki 10:13 and returned with her **r** to her own country. 6269
2Ch 9:12 and returned with her **r** to her own country. 6269

RETIRE (1)

Nu 8:25 *they must* **r** from their regular service 8740

RETORTED (1)

Jn 7:47 he has deceived you also?" the Pharisees **r.** *646*

RETREAT (5) [RETREATED, RETREATING, RETREATS]

Jdg 20:32 *"Let's* **r** and draw them away from the city 5674
Job 41:25 *they* **r** before his thrashing. 2627
Ps 44:10 *You* **made** us **r** before the enemy, 294+8740
74:21 *Do* not *let* the oppressed **r** in disgrace; 8740
Da 11: 9 of the South but *will* **r** to his own country. 8740

RETREATED (1) [RETREAT]

2Sa 23: 9 Then the men of Israel **r,** 6590

RETREATING (1) [RETREAT]

Jer 46: 5 They are terrified, *they are* **r,** 294+6047

RETREATS (1) [RETREAT]

Pr 30:30 mighty among beasts, *who* **r** before nothing; 8740

RETRIBUTION (6)

Ps 69:22 may it become **r** and a trap. 8936
Isa 34: 8 a year of **r,** to uphold Zion's cause. 8936
35: 4 with divine **r** he will come to save you." 1691
59:18 so will he repay wrath to his enemies and **r** 1691
Jer 51:56 LORD is a God of **r;** he will repay in full. 1692
Ro 11: 9 a stumbling block and a **r** for them. *501*

RETRIEVED (1)

Isa 49:25 and plunder **r** *from* the fierce; 4880

RETURN (216) [RETURNED, RETURNING, RETURNS]

Ge 3:19 until you **r** to the ground, since from it you 8740
3:19 for dust you are and to dust *you will* **r."** 8740
8:12 but this time *it did* not **r** to him. 8740
18:10 *"I will* **surely r** to you about this time 8740+8740
18:14 *I will* **r** to you at the appointed time 8740
20: 7 Now **r** the man's wife, for he is a prophet, 8740
20: 7 But if you *do* not **r** her, 8740
28:21 so that *I* **r** safely to my father's house, 8740
29: 3 Then *they would* **r** the stone to its place 8740
29:18 "I'll work for you seven years **in r for** 928
29:27 **in r for** another seven years of work." 928
30:15 "he can sleep with you tonight **in r for** 9393
31:30 because *you* **longed** *to* **r** to your father's AIT
43:12 for *you must* **r** the silver that was put back 8740
44:33 and *let* the boy **r** with his brothers. 6590
45:17 Load your animals and **r** to the land 995+2143
49: 9 *you* **r** from the prey, my son. 6590
50: 5 and bury my father; then *I will* **r.'"** 8740
Ex 4:21 "When you **r** to Egypt, 2143+8740
13:17 they might change their minds and **r** 8740
22:26 **r** it to him by sunset, 8740
33:11 Then Moses *would* **r** to the camp, 8740
Lev 6: 4 *he must* **r** what he has stolen or taken 8740
14:39 the seventh day the priest *shall* **r** to inspect 8740
25:10 of you *is to* **r** to his family property 8740
25:13 " 'In this Year of Jubilee everyone *is to* **r** 8740
Nu 10:36 Whenever it came to rest, he said, **"R,** 8740
18:21 in Israel as their inheritance **in r for** 2739
32:18 *We will* not **r** to our homes 8740
32:22 *you may* **r** and be free from your obligation 8740
35:28 the high priest *may* he **r** to his own property. 8740
Dt 4:30 then in later days *you will* **r** to 8740
5:30 "Go, tell them *to* **r** to their tents. 8740
16: 7 in the morning **r** to your tents. 2143+2256+7155
17:16 or **make** the people **r** to Egypt to get more 8740
23:11 and at sunset *he may* **r** to the camp. 995
24:13 **R** his cloak to him by sunset so 8740+8740
30: 2 when you and your children **r** to the LORD 8740
Jos 2:16 until they **r,** and then go on your way." 8740
18: 4 Then *they will* **r** to me. 995
18: 8 Then **r** to me, and I will cast lots for you 8740
22: 4 **r** to your homes in the land that Moses 7155
22: 8 **"R** to your homes with your great wealth— 8740
22: 9 the Israelites at Shiloh in Canaan to **r** 8740
Jdg 6:18 the LORD said, "I will wait until you **r."** 8740
8: 9 "When I **r** in triumph, 8740
11:31 the door of my house to meet me when I **r** 8740
19: 3 to her to persuade her to **r.** 8740
20: 8 No, not one of *us will* **r** to his house. 6073
Ru 1: 6 *to* **r** home from there. 8740
1:11 But Naomi said, **"R** home, my daughters. 8740
1:12 **R** home, my daughters; 8740
1Sa 6: 3 "If *you* **r** the ark of the god of Israel, 8938
18: 2 and did not let him **r** *to* his father's house. 8740
29: 4 that *he may* **r** to the place you assigned him. 8740
2Sa 1:22 the sword of Saul *did* not **r** unsatisfied. 8740
12:23 I will go to him, but he *will* not **r** to me." 8740
15:34 if *you* **r** *to* the city and say to Absalom, 8740
17: 3 of the man you seek will mean the **r** *of* all; 8740
19:14 They sent word to the king, **"R,** 8740
19:37 *Let* your servant **r,** 8740
1Ki 11:21 that *I may* **r** to my own country." 2143
12:27 and **r** to King Rehoboam." 8740
13: 9 or drink water or **r** by the way you came.' " 8740
13:10 So he took another road and *did* not **r** by 8740
13:17 not eat bread or drink water there or **r** by 8740
17:21 *let* this boy's life **r** to him!" 8740
20:34 *"I will* **r** the cities my father took 8740
22:27 but bread and water until I **r** safely.' " 995
22:28 Micaiah declared, "If *you* **ever r** safely, 8740+8740
2Ki 4:22 go to the man of God quickly and **r."** 8740
19: 7 *he will* **r** to his own country, 8740

2Ki 19:28 *I will* **make** you r by the way you came.' 8740
19:33 By the way that he came *he will* **r;** 8740
2Ch 18:26 but bread and water until I r safely.' " 8740
18:27 Micaiah declared, "If *you* **ever** r safely, 8740+8740
30: 6 "People of Israel, r to the LORD, 8740
30: 6 that *he may* r to you who are left, 8740
30: 9 If you r to the LORD, then your brothers 8740
30: 9 not turn his face from you if *you* r to him." 8740
Ne 1: 9 but if *you* r to me and obey my commands, 8740
7: 5 of those *who had been* the first *to* **r.** 6590
9:17 a leader in order to r to their slavery. 8740
9:29 "You warned them to r to your law, 8740
Est 2:14 the morning r to another part of the harem 8740
2:14 not r to the king unless he was pleased 995+6388
Job 7: 9 he who goes down to the grave *does* not **r.** 6590
10:21 before I go to the place of no **r,** 8740
15:31 for he will get nothing *in* **r.** 9455
16:22 before I go on the journey of no **r.** 8740
22:23 If *you* r to the Almighty, 8740
34:15 and man *would* r to the dust. 8740
39: 4 they leave and *do* not **r.** 8740
Ps 9:17 The wicked r to the grave, 8740
59: 6 *They* r at evening, snarling like dogs, 8740
59:14 *They* r at evening, snarling like dogs, 8740
78:39 a passing breeze *that does* not **r.** 8740
80:14 **R** to us, O God Almighty! 8740
85: 8 but *let them* not r to folly. 8740
90: 3 saying, **"R** to dust, O sons of men." 8740
104:22 they r and lie down in their dens. NIH
104:29 they die and r to the dust. 8740
109: 4 **In r for** my friendship they accuse me, 9393
126: 6 *will* r with songs of joy, 995+995
146: 4 their spirit departs, *they* r to the ground; 8740
Pr 2:19 None who go to her r or attain the paths 8740
Ecc 1: 7 the streams come from, there they **r** again. 2143
3:20 all come from dust, and to dust all **r.** 8740
4: 9 because they have a good **r** for their work: 8510
12: 2 and the clouds **r** after the rain; 8740
Isa 10:21 A remnant *will* **r,** a remnant of Jacob 8740
10:21 remnant of Jacob will r to the Mighty God. NIH
10:22 only a remnant *will* **r.** 8740
13:14 each *will* r to his own people, 7155
23:17 *She will* r to her hire as a prostitute 8740
31: 6 **R** to him you have so greatly revolted 8740
35:10 and the ransomed of the LORD *will* **r.** 8740
37: 7 *he will* r to his own country, 8740
37:29 *I will* **make** you r by the way you came. 8740
37:34 By the way that he came *he will* **r;** 8740
44:22 **R** to me, for I have redeemed you." 8740
51:11 The ransomed of the LORD *will* **r.** 8740
55:10 and *do* not r to it without watering the earth 8740
55:11 *It will* not r to me empty, 8740
63:17 **R** for the sake of your servants, 8740
Jer 3: 1 *should he* r to her again? 8740
3: 1 *would* you now r to me?" 8740
3: 7 that after she had done all this *she would* **r** 8740
3:10 her unfaithful sister Judah *did* not r to me 8740
3:12 " **'R,** faithless Israel,' declares the LORD, 8740
3:14 **"R,** faithless people," declares the LORD, 8740
3:22 **"R,** faithless people; I will cure you of backsliding." 8740
4: 1 "If *you will* **r,** O Israel, return to me," 8740
4: 1 "If you will return, O Israel, r to me," 8740
8: 4 When a man turns away, *does he* not **r?** 8740
8: 5 They cling to deceit; they refuse to **r.** 8740
14: 3 *They* r with their jars unfilled; 8740
22:10 *he will* never r nor see his native land 8740
22:11 *"He will* never **r.** 8740
22:27 to the land you long to r to." 8740
24: 7 for *they will* r to me with all their heart. 8740
31: 8 a great throng *will* **r.** 8740
31:16 *"They will* r from the land of the enemy. 8740
31:17 "Your children *will* r to their own land. 8740
31:18 Restore me, and *I will* **r,** 8740
31:21 **R,** O Virgin Israel, return to your towns. 8740
31:21 Return, O Virgin Israel, r to your towns. 8740
37: 8 the Babylonians *will* r and attack this city; 8740
44:14 to live in Egypt will escape or survive to **r** 8740
44:14 to which they long to r and live; 8740
44:14 none *will* r except a few fugitives." 8740
44:28 and r *to* the land of Judah from Egypt will 8740
47: 6 **R** to your scabbard; cease and be still.' 665
50: 9 skilled warriors *who do* not r empty-handed. 8740
50:16 the sword of the oppressor *let* everyone **r** 7155
La 3:40 and *let us* r to the LORD. 8740
5:21 O LORD, that *we may* **r;** 8740
Eze 11:18 *"They will* r to it and remove all its vile 995
16:55 *will* r to what they were before; 8740
16:55 and you and your daughters *will* **r** 8740
18:12 *He does* not r what he took in pledge. 8740
21: 5 sword from its scabbard; *it will* not r again.' 8740
21:30 **R** the sword to its scabbard. 8740
26:20 and *you will* not r or take your place in 8740
29:14 from captivity and r them to Upper Egypt, 8740
46: 9 *to* r through the gate by which he entered, 8740
Da 10:20 Soon *I will* r to fight against the prince 8740
11:28 of the North *will* r *to* his own country 8740
11:28 against it and then r to his own country. 8740
11:30 *He will* r and show favor 8740
Hos 3: 5 Afterward the Israelites *will* r and seek 8740
5: 4 "Their deeds do not permit them to **r** 8740
6: 1 "Come, *let us* r to the LORD. 8740
7:10 not r to the LORD his God or search for him. 8740
8:13 They *will* r *to* Egypt. 8740
9: 3 Ephraim *will* r *to* Egypt 8740
11: 5 not r to Egypt and will not Assyria rule 8740
Hos 12: 6 But you *must* r to your God; 8740
14: 1 **R,** O Israel, to the LORD your God. 8740
14: 2 Take words with you and r to the LORD. 8740
Joel 2:12 **"r** to me with all your heart, 8740
2:13 **R** to the LORD your God, 8740
3: 4 *I will* swiftly and speedily **r** 8740
3: 7 and *I will* r on your own heads what you 8740
Ob 1:15 your deeds *will* r upon your own head. 8740
Mic 5: 3 of his brothers r to join the Israelites. 8740
Zep 2:10 This is what they will get **in r for** 9393
Zec 1: 3 **'R** to me,' declares the LORD Almighty, 8740
1: 3 'and *I will* r to you,' 8740
1:16 *'I will* r to Jerusalem with mercy, 8740
8: 3 *"I will* r to Zion and dwell in Jerusalem. 8740
9:12 **R** to your fortress, O prisoners of hope; 8740
10: 9 their children will survive, and *they will* **r.** 8740
Mal 3: 7 **R** to me, and I will return to you," 8740
3: 7 Return to me, and *I will* r to you," 8740
3: 7 "But you ask, 'How *are we to* **r?'** 8740
Mt 10:13 if it is not, *let* your peace r to you. *2188*
12:44 Then it says, *'I will* r to the house I left.' *2188*
Lk 8:39 **"R** home and tell how much God has done for you." *1650+5715*
10: 6 if not, *it will* r to you. *366*
10:35 'Look after him,' he said, 'and when I **r,** *2059*
11:24 Then it says, *'I will* r to the house I left.' *5715*
12:36 like men waiting for their master **to r** *386+4536*
17:18 Was no one found to r and give praise *5715*
19:12 have himself appointed king and then *to* **r.** *5715*
Jn 21:22 "If I want him to remain alive until *I* **r,** *2262*
21:23 "If I want him to remain alive until *I* **r,** *2262*
Ac 13:13 where John left them to r to Jerusalem. *5715*
15:16 " 'After this *I will* r and rebuild David's *418*
15:33 the brothers with the blessing of peace to **r** *NIG*
Ro 9: 9 "At the appointed time *I will* **r,** *2262*
1Co 16:11 on his way in peace so that *he may* r to me. *2262*
2Co 1:23 to spare you that *I did* not r to Corinth. *2262*
13: 2 On *my* r I will not spare *1650+2262+3836+4099*
1Th 3: 9 How can we thank God enough for you **in r** *500*
Heb 11:15 they would have had opportunity *to* **r.** *366*

RETURNED (185) [RETURN]

Ge 8: 9 so *it* r to Noah in the ark. 8740
8:11 When the dove r to him in the evening, 995
14:17 After Abram r from defeating Kedorlaomer 8740
18:33 he left, and Abraham r home. 8740
19:27 the next morning Abraham got up and r to NIH
20:14 and *he* r Sarah his wife to him. 8740
21:32 of his forces r to the land of the Philistines. 8740
22:19 Then Abraham r to his servants, 8740
31:55 Then he left and r home. 8740
32: 6 When the messengers r to Jacob, they said, 8740
35: 9 After Jacob r from Paddan Aram, 995
37:29 When Reuben r to the cistern and saw 8740
42:28 "My silver *has* **been r,"** 8740
43:10 *we could have* gone and r twice." 8740
44:13 Then they all loaded their donkeys and r to 8740
50:14 After burying his father, Joseph r to Egypt, 8740
Ex 2:18 When *the girls* r to Reuel their father, 995
2:18 "Why *have you* r so early today?" 995
5:22 Moses r to the LORD and said, "O Lord, 8740
18:27 and Jethro r to his own country. 2143
Lev 25:28 *It will be* r in the Jubilee. 3655
25:30 *It is* not *to be* r in the Jubilee. 3655
25:31 and *they are to be* r in the Jubilee. 3655
25:33 and *is to be* r in the Jubilee, 3655
Nu 11:30 Then Moses and the elders of Israel r to 665
13:25 the end of forty days *they* r from exploring 8740
14:36 *who* r and made the whole community 8740
16:50 Then Aaron r to Moses at the entrance to 8740
22:14 So the Moabite princes r to Balak and said, 995
24:25 and r home and Balak went his own way. 8740
31:14 who r from the battle. 995
Dt 28:31 taken from you and *will* not *be* **r.** 8740
Jos 2:22 along the road and r without finding them. 8740
4:18 the waters of the Jordan r to their place 8740
6:11 Then the people r *to* camp and spent 995
6:14 around the city once and r *to* the camp. 8740
7: 3 When *they* r to Joshua, they said, 8740
8:24 all the Israelites r *to* Ai 8740
10:15 Then Joshua r with all Israel to the camp 8740
10:21 The whole army then r safely to Joshua in 8740
10:43 Then Joshua r with all Israel to the camp 8740
18: 9 and r to Joshua in the camp at Shiloh. 995
22:32 the leaders r to Canaan from their meeting 8740
Jdg 2:19 *the people* r *to* ways even more corrupt 8740
7:15 *He* r to the camp of Israel and called out, 8740
8:13 then r from the battle by the Pass of Heres. 8740
11:34 When Jephthah r to his home in Mizpah, 995
11:39 *she* r to her father and he did to her 8740
14: 2 When *he* **r,** he said to his father and mother, 6590
15:19 his strength r and he revived. 8740
16:18 the rulers of the Philistines r with the silver 6590
17: 3 When *he* r the eleven hundred shekels 8740
17: 4 So *he* r the silver to his mother, 8740
18: 8 When *they* r to Zorah and Eshtaol, 995
21:14 So the Benjamites r at that time 8740
21:23 Then *they* r to their inheritance and rebuilt 8740
Ru 1:22 So Naomi r from Moab accompanied 8740
1Sa 4: 3 When the soldiers r to camp, 995
6:16 of the Philistines saw all this and then **r** 8740
6:21 Philistines *have* r the ark of the LORD. 8740
17:53 the Israelites r from chasing the Philistines, 8740
17:57 as David r from killing the Philistine, 8740
20:38 The boy picked up the arrow and **r** 995
24: 1 After Saul r from pursuing the Philistines, 8740
1Sa 24:22 Then Saul r home, but David 2143
26:25 David went on his way, and Saul r home. 8740
27: 9 Then *he* r to Achish. 8740
2Sa 1: 1 David r from defeating the Amalekites 8740
2:30 Then Joab r from pursuing Abner 8740
3:22 then David's men and Joab r from a raid 995
3:27 Now when Abner r *to* Hebron, 8740
6:20 When David r home to bless his household, 8740
8:13 And David became famous after he **r** 8740
10:14 So Joab r from fighting the Ammonites 8740
12:31 David and his entire army r *to* Jerusalem. 8740
17:20 so *they* r *to* Jerusalem. 8740
19:15 the king r and went as far as the Jordan. 8740
19:24 the king left until the day *he* r safely. 995
19:39 and Barzillai r to his home. 8740
20: 3 When David r to his palace in Jerusalem, 995
23:10 The troops r to Eleazar, 8740
1Ki 2:41 from Jerusalem to Gath and *had* **r,** 8740
3:15 *He* r *to* Jerusalem, 995
10:13 and r with her retinue to her own country. 2143
10:22 Once every three years it **r,** carrying gold, 995
12: 2 he r from Egypt. 8740
12:12 and all the people r to Rehoboam, 995
12:20 the Israelites heard that Jeroboam *had* **r,** 8740
13:19 So the man of God r with him and ate 8740
14:28 afterward *they* r them to the guardroom. 8740
17:22 and the boy's life r to him, and he lived. 8740
2Ki 1: 5 When the messengers r to the king, 8740
2:18 When *they* r to Elisha, 8740
2:25 on to Mount Carmel and from there **r** 8740
3:27 they withdrew and r to their own land. 8740
4:38 Elisha r to Gilgal and there was a famine in 8740
4:39 When *he* **r,** he cut them up into the pot 995
6:23 and *they* r to their master. 2143
7: 8 *They* r and entered another tent 8740
7:15 the messengers r and reported to the king. 8740
8:14 Then Hazael left Elisha and r to his master. 995
8:29 so King Joram r to Jezreel to recover from 8740
9:15 but King Joram *had* r to Jezreel to recover 8740
14:14 He also took hostages and r to Samaria. 8740
16:11 and finished it before King Ahaz **r.** 995
19:36 *He* r to Nineveh and stayed there. 8740
1Ch 16:43 and David r **home** to bless his family. 6015
20: 3 David and his entire army r *to* Jerusalem. 8740
2Ch 9:12 and r with her retinue to her own country. 2143
9:21 Once every three years it **r,** carrying gold, 995
10: 2 he r from Egypt. 8740
10:12 and all the people r to Rehoboam, 995
12:11 afterward *they* r them to the guardroom. 8740
14:15 Then *they* r to Jerusalem. 8740
19: 1 of Judah r safely to his palace in Jerusalem, 8740
20:27 the men of Judah and Jerusalem r joyfully 8740
22: 6 so *he* r to Jezreel to recover from 8740
25:14 When Amaziah r from slaughtering 995
25:24 and r *to* Samaria. 8740
28: 9 and he went out to meet the army when it **r** 995
28:15 the City of Palms, and r *to* Samaria. 8740
31: 1 the Israelites r to their own towns and 8740
Ezr 2: 1 to Babylon *(they* r to Jerusalem and Judah, 8740
3: 8 and the Levites and all who *had* r from 995
6: 5 *are to be* r to their places in the temple 10754
6:21 the Israelites who *had* r from the exile ate it, 8740
8:35 Then the exiles who *had* **r** 995
Ne 4:15 we all r to the wall, each to his own work. 8740
7: 6 of Babylon had taken captive *(they* **r** 8740
8:17 that *had* r from exile built booths and lived 8740
12: 1 These were the priests and Levites who **r** 6590
13: 6 *I had* r to the king. 995
Est 6:12 Afterward Mordecai r to the king's gate. 8740
7: 8 Just as the king r from the palace garden to 8740
Ps 35:13 my prayers r to me **unanswered,** 2668+8740
60: T and *when* Joab r and struck down 8740
Isa 9:13 people *have* not r to him who struck them, 8740
37:37 *He* r to Nineveh and stayed there. 8740
Jer 11:10 *They have* r to the sins of their forefathers, 8740
19:14 Jeremiah then r from Topheth, 995
Da 2:17 Then Daniel r to his house and explained 10016
4:36 my honor and splendor *were* r to me for 10754
6:18 the king r to his palace and spent the night 10016
Am 4: 6 yet *you have* not r to me," 8740
4: 8 yet *you have* not r to me," 8740
4: 9 yet *you have* not r to me," 8740
4:10 yet *you have* not r to me," 8740
4:11 yet *you have* not r to me," 8740
Zec 4: 1 Then the angel who talked with me **r** 8740
Mt 2:12 *they* r to their country by another route. *432*
4:12 John had been put in prison, *he* r to Galilee. *432*
25:19 a long time the master of those servants **r** *2262*
25:27 that *when I* r I would have received it back *2262*
26:40 Then *he* r to his disciples and found them *2262*
26:45 Then *he* r to the disciples and said to them, *2262*
27: 3 with remorse and r the thirty silver coins to *5138*
Mk 14:37 Then *he* r to his disciples and found them *2262*
16:13 These r and reported it to the rest; *599*
Lk 1:23 of service was completed, *he* r home. *599*
1:56 for about three months and then r home. *5715*
2:20 The shepherds **r,** glorifying and praising *5715*
2:39 *they* r to Galilee to their own town *2188*
4: 1 r from the Jordan and was led by the Spirit *5715*
4:14 Jesus r to Galilee in the power of the Spirit, *5715*
7:10 the men who had been sent r to the house *5715*
8:40 Now when Jesus **r,** a crowd welcomed him, *5715*
8:55 Her spirit **r,** and at once she stood up. *2188*
9:10 *When* the apostles **r,** they reported to Jesus *5715*
10:17 The seventy-two r with joy and said, *5715*
19:15 "He was made king, however, and r home. *1877+2059+3836*

Lk 24:33 *They* got up and **r** at once to Jerusalem. *5715*
24:52 and **r** to Jerusalem with great joy. *5715*
Jn 4:27 Just then his disciples **r** and were surprised *2262*
13:12 he put on his clothes and **r to** *his* **place.** *404+4099*
20:17 for *I have* not yet **r** to the Father. *326*
Ac 1:12 Then *they* **r** to Jerusalem from *5715*
8:25 Peter and John **r** to Jerusalem, *5715*
12:25 *they* **r** from Jerusalem, *5715*
14:21 Then *they* **r** to Lystra, *5715*
21:6 we went aboard the ship, and they **r** home. *5715*
22:17 *"When* I **r** to Jerusalem and was praying at *5715*
23:32 while *they* **r** to the barracks. *5715*
Ro 14:9 and **r to life** so that he might be the Lord *2409*
Gal 1:17 into Arabia and later **r** to Damascus. *5715*
1Pe 2:25 but now *you have* **r to** the Shepherd *2188*

RETURNING (12) [RETURN]

Ge 48:7 As I *was* **r** from Paddan, 995
1Sa 7:3 "If you *are* **r** to the LORD 8740
11:5 Just then Saul *was* **r** from the fields, 995
18:6 the men *were* **r** home after David had killed 995
2Sa 20:22 each **r** to his home. NIH
Ecc 1:6 *ever* **r** on its course. 8740
Mic 2:8 like *men* **r** *from* battle. 8740
Mk 14:41 **R** the third time, he said to them, *2262*
Lk 2:43 while his parents *were* **r** home, *5715*
Jn 13:3 and that he had come from God and *was* **r** *5632*
20:17 *'I am* **r** to my Father and your Father, *326*
Heb 7:1 He met Abraham **r** from the defeat of *5715*

RETURNS (11) [RETURN]

Lev 22:13 and *she* **r** to live in her father's house as 8740
Pr 3:14 and **yields** better **r** than gold. 9311
26:11 As a dog **r** to its vomit, 8740
Ecc 12:7 and the dust **r** to the ground it came from, 8740
12:7 and the spirit **r** to God who gave it. 8740
Isa 52:8 When the LORD **r** *to* Zion, 8740
Eze 18:7 but **r** what he took in pledge for a loan. 8740
33:15 **r** what he has stolen, 8966
Mt 24:46 whose master finds him doing so *when he* **r**. *2262*
Lk 12:43 the master finds doing so *when he* **r**. *2262*
2Pe 2:22 "A dog **r to** its vomit," and, *2188*

REU (6)

Ge 11:18 he became the father of **R.** 8293
11:19 And after he became the father of **R,** 8293
11:20 When **R** had lived 32 years, 8293
11:21 **R** lived 207 years and had other sons 8293
1Ch 1:25 Eber, Peleg, **R,** 8293
Lk 3:35 the son *of* **R,** the son of Peleg, *4814*

REUBEN (56) [REUBENITE, REUBENITES]

Ge 29:32 She named him **R,** for she said, 8017
30:14 **R** went out into the fields 8017
35:22 **R** went in and slept with his father's 8017
35:23 **R** the firstborn of Jacob, Simeon, Levi, 8017
37:21 When **R** heard this, he tried to rescue him 8017
37:22 **R** said this to rescue him from them 8017
37:29 When **R** returned to the cistern and saw 8017
42:22 **R** replied, "Didn't I tell you not to sin 8017
42:37 Then **R** said to his father, 8017
46:8 **R** the firstborn of Jacob. 8017
46:9 The sons of **R:** Hanoch, Pallu, Hezron 8017
48:5 just as **R** and Simeon are mine. 8017
49:3 "**R,** you are my firstborn, my might, 8017
Ex 1:2 **R,** Simeon, Levi and Judah; 8017
6:14 of **R** the firstborn son of Israel were Hanoch 8017
6:14 These were the clans of **R.** 8017
Nu 1:5 from **R,** Elizur son of Shedeur; 8017
1:20 From the descendants of **R** the firstborn son 8017
1:21 number from the tribe of **R** was 46,500. 8017
2:10 of the camp of **R** under their standard. 8017
2:10 of the people of **R** is Elizur son of Shedeur. 8017
2:16 All the men assigned to the camp of **R,** 8017
7:30 the leader of the people of **R,** 8017
10:18 The divisions of the camp of **R** went next, 8017
13:4 These are their names: from the tribe of **R,** 8017
26:5 The descendants of **R,** the firstborn son 8017
26:7 These were the clans of **R;** 8018
34:14 because the families of the tribe of **R,** 1201+8018
Dt 27:13 **R,** Gad, Asher, Zebulun, Dan and Naphtali. 8017
33:6 "Let **R** live and not die, 8017
Jos 4:12 The men of **R,** Gad and the half-tribe of 8017
13:15 to the tribe of **R,** clan by clan: 1201+8017
15:6 to the Stone of Bohan son of **R.** 8017
18:7 **R** and the half-tribe of Manasseh 8017
18:17 ran down to the Stone of Bohan son of **R.** 8017
20:8 the desert on the plateau in the tribe of **R,** 8017
21:7 received twelve towns from the tribes of **R,** 8017
21:36 from the tribe of **R,** Bezer, Jahaz, 8017
22:13 **R,** Gad and the half-tribe of Manasseh 1201+8017
22:15 **R,** Gad and the half-tribe of Manasseh 1201+8017
22:21 **R,** Gad and the half-tribe of Manasseh 1201+8017
22:30 heard what **R,** Gad and Manasseh had 1201+8017
22:31 said to **R,** Gad and Manasseh, 1201+8017
Jdg 5:15 the districts of **R** there was much searching 8017
5:16 the districts of **R** there was much searching 8017
2Ki 10:33 of Gad, **R** and Manasseh), from Aroer by 8018
1Ch 2:1 **R,** Simeon, Levi, Judah, Issachar, Zebulun, 8017
5:1 The sons of **R** the firstborn of Israel (he was 8017
5:3 the sons of **R** the firstborn of Israel: 8017
6:63 from the tribes of **R,** 8017
6:78 from the tribe of **R** across the Jordan east 8017
12:37 **men of R,** Gad and the half-tribe of 8018

Eze 48:6 "**R** will have one portion; 8017
48:7 it will border the territory of **R** from east 8017
48:31 on the north side will be the gate of **R,** 8017
Rev 7:5 were sealed, from the tribe *of* **R** 12,000, *4857*

REUBENITE (2) [REUBEN]

Dt 11:6 sons of Eliab the **R,** 1201+8017
1Ch 11:42 Adina son of Shiza the **R,** 8018

REUBENITES (30) [REUBEN]

Nu 16:1 the son of Levi, and certain **R**— 1201+8017
32:1 The **R** and Gadites, 1201+8017
32:6 Moses said to the Gadites and **R,** 1201+8017
32:25 The Gadites and **R** said to Moses, 1201+8017
32:29 He said to them, "If the Gadites and **R,** 1201+8017
32:31 The Gadites and **R** answered, 1201+8017
32:33 the **R** and the half-tribe of Manasseh 1201+8017
32:37 And the **R** rebuilt Heshbon, 1201+8017
Dt 3:12 the **R** and the Gadites the territory north 8018
3:16 But to the **R** and the Gadites I gave 8018
4:43 Bezer in the desert plateau, for the **R;** 8018
29:8 and gave it as an inheritance to the **R,** 8018
Jos 1:12 But to the **R,** the Gadites and the half-tribe 8018
12:6 of the LORD gave their land to the **R,** 8018
13:8 the **R** and the Gadites had received 8018
13:23 The boundary of the **R** was the bank 1201+8017
13:23 the inheritance of the **R,** 1201+8017
22:1 Then Joshua summoned the **R,** 8018
22:9 the **R,** the Gadites and the half-tribe 1201+8017
22:10 the **R,** the Gadites and the half-tribe 1201+8017
22:25 you **R** and Gadites! 1201+8017
22:32 the **R** and Gadites in Gilead and 1201+8017
22:33 to devastate the country where the **R** 1201+8017
22:34 **R** and the Gadites gave the altar this 1201+8017
1Ch 5:6 Beerah was a leader of the **R.** 8018
5:18 The **R,** the Gadites and the half-tribe 1201+8017
5:26 who took the **R,** the Gadites and 8018
11:42 who was chief of the **R,** 8018
26:32 King David put them in charge of the **R,** 8018
27:16 over the **R:** Eliezer son of Zicri; 8018

REUEL (10)

Ge 36:4 to Esau, Basemath bore **R,** 8294
36:10 and **R,** the son of Esau's wife Basemath. 8294
36:13 The sons of **R:** 8294
36:17 The sons of Esau's son **R:** 8294
36:17 These were the chiefs descended from **R** 8294
Ex 2:18 When the girls returned to **R** their father, 8294
Nu 10:29 Now Moses said to Hobab son of **R** 8294
1Ch 1:35 Eliphaz, **R,** Jeush, Jalam and Korah. 8294
1:37 The sons of **R:** 8294
9:8 Meshullam son of Shephatiah, the son of **R,** 8294

REUMAH (1)

Ge 22:24 His concubine, whose name was **R,** 8020

REUNITED (1) [UNITE]

Hos 1:11 and the people of Israel *will* **be r,** 3481+7695

REVEAL (7) [REVEALED, REVEALER, REVEALING, REVEALS, REVELATION, REVELATIONS]

Nu 12:6 *I* **r myself** to him in visions, 3359
1Sa 2:27 *'Did I* not **clearly r myself** 1655+1655
Da 2:11 No one *can* **r** it to the king except the gods, 10252
2:47 for you were able to **r** this mystery." 10144
Mt 11:27 to whom the Son chooses *to* **r** him. *636*
Lk 10:22 to whom the Son chooses *to* **r** him." *636*
Gal 1:16 *to* **r** his Son in me so that I might preach him *636*

REVEALED (62) [REVEAL]

Ge 35:7 because it was there that God **r himself** 1655
41:25 God *has* **r** to Pharaoh what he is about 5583
Dt 29:29 but the *things* **r** belong to us and 1655
1Sa 3:7 The word of the LORD *had* not yet **been r** 1655
3:21 and there he **r himself** to Samuel 1655
9:15 the LORD *had* **r** this *to* Samuel: 265+906+1655
2Sa 7:27 you *have* **r** this *to* your servant, saying, 265+1655
2Ki 8:10 but the LORD *has* **r** *to* me that he will 8011
1Ch 17:25 *have* **r** *to* your servant that you will 265+1655
Est 2:10 Esther *had* not **r** her nationality 5583
Ps 98:2 and **r** his righteousness to the nations. 1655
147:19 *He has* **r** his word to Jacob, 5583
Isa 22:14 The LORD Almighty *has* **r** this 1655
40:5 And the glory of the LORD *will* **be r,** 1655
43:12 I *have* **r** and saved and proclaimed— 5583
53:1 to whom *has* the arm of the LORD **been r**? 1655
56:1 and my righteousness *will* soon **be r.** 1655
65:1 *"I* **r myself** to those who did not ask 2011
Jer 11:18 Because the LORD **r** their plot *to* me, 3359
38:21 this is what the LORD *has* **r** *to* me: 8011
Eze 20:5 of the house of Jacob and **r myself** to them 3359
20:9 among and in whose sight *I had* **r myself** to 3359
Da 2:19 the night the mystery **was r** to Daniel in 10144
2:30 As for me, this mystery *has* **been r** to me, 10144
Hos 7:1 and the crimes of Samaria **r.** NIH
Mt 11:25 and **r** them to little children. *636*
16:17 for this *was* not **r** to you by man, *636*
Lk 2:26 It had been **r** to him by the Holy Spirit *5976*
2:35 that the thoughts of many hearts *will be* **r.** *636*
10:21 and **r** them to little children. *636*
17:30 like this on the day the Son of Man *is* **r.** *636*

Jn 1:31 with water was that *he might be* **r** to Israel." *5746*
2:11 *He* thus **r** his glory, *5746*
12:38 to whom *has* the arm of the Lord *been* **r?"** *636*
17:6 *"I have* **r** you to those whom you gave me *5746*
Ro 1:17 the gospel a righteousness from God *is* **r,** *636*
1:18 wrath of God *is being* **r** from heaven against *636*
2:5 when his righteous judgment will be **r.** *637*
8:18 with the glory that will *be* **r** in us. *636*
8:19 for the sons of God to be **r.** *637*
10:20 *I* **r** *myself* to those who did not ask *1181+1871*
16:26 but now **r** and made known through *5746*
1Co 1:7 for our Lord Jesus Christ to be **r.** *637*
2:10 but God *has* **r** it to us by his Spirit. *636*
3:13 *It will be* **r** with fire, *636*
2Co 4:10 the life of Jesus *may* also *be* **r** in our body. *5746*
4:11 so that his life *may be* **r** in our mortal body. *5746*
Gal 3:23 locked up until faith should *be* **r.** *636*
Eph 3:5 in other generations as *it has* now *been* **r** *636*
2Th 1:7 This will happen when the Lord Jesus is **r** *637*
2:3 and the man of lawlessness *is* **r,** *636*
2:6 so that he *may be* **r** at the proper time. *636*
2:8 And then the lawless one *will be* **r,** *636*
2Ti 1:10 now *been* **r** through the appearing *5746*
1Pe 1:5 of the salvation that is ready *to be* **r** in *636*
1:7 glory and honor when Jesus Christ is **r.** *637*
1:12 *It was* **r** to them that they were *636*
1:13 to be given you when Jesus Christ is **r.** *637*
1:20 but *was* **r** in these last times for your sake. *5746*
4:13 you may be overjoyed when his glory is **r.** *637*
5:1 also will share in the glory to be **r:** *636*
Rev 15:4 for your righteous acts *have been* **r."** *5746*

REVEALER (2) [REVEAL]

Da 2:29 the **r** *of* mysteries showed you what is 10144
2:47 and the Lord of kings and a **r** *of* mysteries, 10144

REVEALING (2) [REVEAL]

Eze 21:24 **r** your sins in all that you do— 8011
Am 3:7 without **r** his plan to his servants 1655

REVEALS (5) [REVEAL]

Nu 23:3 Whatever *he* **r** *to* me I will tell you." 8011
Job 12:22 *He* **r** the deep things of darkness 1655
Da 2:22 He **r** deep and hidden things; 10144
2:28 there is a God in heaven *who* **r** mysteries. 10144
Am 4:13 creates the wind, and **r** his thoughts to man, 5583

REVELATION (16) [REVEAL]

2Sa 7:17 to David all the words of this entire **r.** 2612
1Ch 17:15 to David all the words of this entire **r.** 2606
Pr 29:18 there is no **r,** the people cast off restraint; 2606
Da 10:1 a **r** was given to Daniel 1821
Hab 2:2 "Write down the **r** and make it plain 2606
2:3 For the **r** awaits an appointed time; 2606
Lk 2:32 a light for **r** to the Gentiles and for glory *637*
Ro 16:25 to the **r** of the mystery hidden for long ages *637*
1Co 14:6 unless I bring you some **r** or knowledge *637*
14:26 a **r,** a tongue or an interpretation. *637*
14:30 a **r comes** to someone who is sitting down, *636*
Gal 1:12 rather, I received it by **r** from Jesus Christ. *637*
2:2 in response to a **r** and set before them *637*
Eph 1:17 may give you the Spirit *of* wisdom and **r,** *637*
3:3 the mystery made known to me by **r,** *637*
Rev 1:1 The **r** of Jesus Christ, *637*

REVELATIONS (2) [REVEAL]

2Co 12:1 I will go on to visions and **r** from the Lord. *637*
12:7 because of these surpassingly great **r,** *637*

REVELED (1) [REVELRY]

Ne 9:25 *they* **r** in your great goodness. 6357

REVELERS (3) [REVELRY]

Isa 5:14 and masses with all their brawlers and **r.** 6601
24:8 the noise of the **r** has stopped, 6611
Jer 15:17 I never sat in the company of **r,** 8471

REVELING (3) [REVELRY]

1Sa 30:16 drinking and **r** because of the great amount 2510
Isa 23:12 He said, "No more of your **r,** 6600
2Pe 2:13 **r** in their pleasures while they feast *1960*

REVELRY (6) [REVELED, REVELERS, REVELING]

Ex 32:6 to eat and drink and got up to **indulge in r.** 7464
Isa 22:2 O city of tumult and **r?** 6611
22:13 But see, there is joy and **r,** 8525
23:7 Is this your city of **r,** the old, old city, 6611
32:13 of merriment and for this city of **r.** 6611
1Co 10:7 and got up *to* **indulge in pagan r."** *4089*

REVENGE (11) [VENGEANCE]

Lev 19:18 " *'Do* not **seek r** or bear a grudge against 5933
Jdg 15:7 I won't stop until *I* **get** *my* **r** on you." 5933
16:28 *with* one blow **get r** on the Philistines 5933+5934
1Sa 18:25 to **take r** on his enemies.' " 5933
Ps 44:16 because of the enemy, *who is* **bent on r.** 5933
Pr 6:34 he will show no mercy when he takes **r.** 5934
Jer 20:10 over him and take our **r** on him." 5935
Eze 24:8 **take r** I put her blood on the bare rock, 5933+5934

Eze 25:12 'Because Edom **took** r on the house 5933+5934
25:15 and **took** r with malice in their hearts, 5933+5934
Ro 12:19 *Do* not **take** r, my friends, *1688+4932*

REVENUE (4) [REVENUES]

Isa 23: 3 the harvest of the Nile was the r *of* Tyre, 9311
33:18 Where is the *one who* **took** *the* r? 9202
Ro 13: 7 if r, then revenue; if honor, then honor. *5465*
13: 7 if revenue, then r; if honor, then honor. *5465*

REVENUES (4) [REVENUE]

1Ki 10:15 the r *from* merchants and traders and 5006
2Ch 9:14 not including the r brought in by merchants NIH
Ezr 4:13 and the royal r will suffer. 10063
6: 8 from the r *of* Trans-Euphrates, 10402

REVERE (17) [REVERED, REVERENCE, REVERENT, REVERING]

Lev 19:32 for the elderly and r your God. 3707
Dt 4:10 to r me as long as they live in the land 3707
13: 4 and him *you must* r. 3707
14:23 to r the LORD your God always. 3707
17:19 the days of his life so that he may learn to r 3707
28:58 *do* not r this glorious and awesome name— 3707
Job 37:24 Therefore, men r him, 3707
Ps 22:23 **R** him, all *you* descendants of Israel! 1593
33: 8 *let* all the people of the world r him. 1593
102:15 all the kings of the earth will r your glory. NIH
Ecc 3:14 God does it so that *men will* r him. 3707
Isa 25: 3 cities of ruthless nations *will* r you. 3707
59:19 they will r his glory. NIH
63:17 and harden our hearts so we do not r you? 3711
Jer 10: 7 Who *should* not r you, 3707
Hos 10: 3 "We have no king because *we did* not r 3707
Mal 4: 2 But for you *who* r my name, 3710

REVERED (4) [REVERE]

Jos 4:14 and *they* r him all the days of his life, 3707
4:14 just as *they had* r Moses. 3707
2Ki 4: 1 and you know that he r the LORD. 3707
Mal 2: 5 for reverence and *he* r me and stood in awe 3707

REVERENCE (15) [REVERE]

Lev 19:30 " 'Observe my Sabbaths and **have** r *for* 3707
26: 2 " 'Observe my Sabbaths and **have** r *for* 3707
Jos 5:14 Joshua fell facedown to the ground *in* r, 2556
Ne 5:15 But out of r *for* God I did not act like that. 3711
Ps 5: 7 in r will I bow down 3711
Jer 44:10 not humbled themselves or **shown** r, 3707
Da 6:26 of my kingdom people must fear and r 10167
Mal 2: 5 for r and he revered me and stood in awe 4616
Ac 10:25 Cornelius met him and fell at his feet in r. *4686*
2Co 7: 1 perfecting holiness out of r for God. *5832*
Eph 5:21 Submit to one another out of r for Christ. *5832*
Col 3:22 with sincerity of heart and r **for** the Lord. *5828*
Heb 12:28 so worship God acceptably with r and awe, *2325*
1Pe 3: 2 they see the purity and r of your lives. *5832*
Rev 11:18 and your saints and those who r your name, *5828*

REVERENT (4) [REVERE]

Ecc 8:12 who *are* r before God. 3707
Tit 2: 3 teach the older women to be r in *2640*
Heb 5: 7 he was heard because of his r submission. *2325*
1Pe 1:17 live your lives as strangers here in r **fear.** *5832*

REVERING (2) [REVERE]

Dt 8: 6 walking in his ways and r him. 3707
Ne 1:11 your servants who delight in r your name. 3707

REVERSE (1) [REVERSED]

Isa 43:13 When I act, who *can* r it?" 8740

REVERSED (1) [REVERSE]

Eze 7:13 concerning the whole crowd *will* not *be* r. 8740

REVERT (3)

Lev 27:24 In the Year of Jubilee the field *will* r to 8740
1Ki 12:26 "The kingdom *will* now *likely* r to 8740
Eze 46:17 then *it will* r to the prince. 8697

REVIEW (1)

Isa 43:26 **R the past** *for* me, 2349

REVILE (5) [REVILED, REVILES]

Ps 10:13 Why *does* the wicked man r God? 5540
44:16 the taunts of those who reproach and r me, 1552
55: 3 down suffering upon me and r me 8475
74:10 *Will* the foe r your name forever? 5540
Ecc 10:20 *Do* not r the king even in your thoughts, 7837

REVILED (1) [REVILE]

Ps 74:18 how foolish people *have* r your name. 5540

REVILES (1) [REVILE]

Ps 10: 3 he blesses the greedy and r the LORD. 5540

REVIVE (5) [REVIVED, REVIVING]

Ps 80:18 r us, and we will call on your name. 2649
85: 6 *Will* you not r us again, 2649
Isa 57:15 to r the spirit of the lowly and to revive 2649
57:15 the lowly and to r the heart of the contrite. 2649
Hos 6: 2 After two days *he will* r us; 2649

REVIVED (3) [REVIVE]

Ge 45:27 the spirit of their father Jacob r. 2649
Jdg 15:19 his strength returned and *he* r. 2649
1Sa 30:12 He ate and *was* r, 8120+8740

REVIVING (1) [REVIVE]

Ps 19: 7 law of the LORD is perfect, r the soul. 8740

REVOKE (1) [REVOKED, REVOKING]

Ps 132:11 a sure oath that *he will* not r: 8740

REVOKED (3) [REVOKE]

Est 8: 8 and sealed with his ring *can be* r." 8740
Isa 45:23 in all integrity a word *that will* not *be* r: 8740
Zec 11:11 *It* **was** r on that day, 7296

REVOKING (1) [REVOKE]

Zec 11:10 r the covenant I had made with all the nations. 7296

REVOLT (7) [REVOLTED, REVOLUTIONS]

Ezr 4:19 a long history of r against kings 10492
Ne 6: 6 that you and the Jews are plotting to r, 5277
Isa 59:13 fomenting oppression and r, 6240
Eze 2: 3 and their fathers *have been* **in** r against me 7321
20:38 I will purge you of those *who* r and rebel 5277
Ac 5:37 **led** a band of people **in** r. *923*
21:38 a r and led four thousand terrorists out into *415*

REVOLTED (4) [REVOLT]

Jdg 9:18 (but today you *have* r against my father's 7756
2Ki 8:22 Libnah r at the same time. 7321
2Ch 21:10 Libnah r at the same time, 7321
Isa 31: 6 to him you have so greatly r **against,** 6240

REVOLUTIONS (1) [REVOLT]

Lk 21: 9 When you hear *of* wars and r, *189*

REWARD (55) [REWARDED, REWARDING, REWARDS]

Ge 15: 1 I am your shield, your very great r." 8510
Nu 22:17 *I will* r you **handsomely** 3877+3877+4394
22:37 Am I really not able *to* r you?" 3877
24:11 I said *I would* r you **handsomely,** 3877+3877
1Sa 24:19 *May* the LORD r you well for 8966
2Sa 4:10 r I gave him **for** his **news!** 1415
18:22 *that will* **bring** you **a** r." 5162
19:36 but why *should* the king r me *in* this way? 1694
Job 17: 5 If a man denounces his friends for r, 2750
34:33 *Should* God then r you on your terms, 8966
Ps 17:14 of this world whose r is in this life. 2750
19:11 in keeping them there is great r. 6813
62:12 Surely you *will* r each person according 8966
127: 3 children a r from him. 8510
Pr 9:12 If you are wise, your wisdom will r you; 4200
11:18 he who sows righteousness reaps a sure r. 8512
13:21 but prosperity *is the* r *of* the righteous. 8966
19:17 and *he will* r him *for* what he has done. 8966
25:22 and the LORD *will* r you. 8966
31:31 Give her the r she has **earned,** 3338+7262
Ecc 2:10 and this was the r for all my labor. 2750
9: 5 they have no further r, 8510
Isa 40:10 See, his r is with him, 8510
45:13 but not for a price or r, 8816
49: 4 and my r is with my God." 7190
61: 8 In my faithfulness *I will* r them and 5989+7190
62:11 See, his r is with him, 8510
Jer 17:10 to r a man according to his conduct, 5989
32:19 you r everyone according to his conduct 5989
Eze 29:18 Yet he and his army got no r from 8510
29:20 I have given him Egypt as a r for his efforts 7190
Mt 5:12 because great is your r in heaven, *3635*
5:46 what r will you get? *3635*
6: 1 you will have no r from your Father *3635*
6: 2 they have received their r in full. *3635*
6: 4 who sees what is done in secret, *will* r you. *625*
6: 5 they have received their r in full. *3635*
6: 6 who sees what is done in secret, *will* r you. *625*
6:16 they have received their r in full. *3635*
6:18 who sees what is done in secret, *will* r you. *625*
10:41 a prophet will receive a prophet's r, *3635*
10:41 will receive a righteous man's r. *3635*
10:42 he will certainly not lose his r." *3635*
16:27 and then *he will* r each person according *625*
Mk 9:41 to Christ will certainly not lose his r. *3635*
Lk 6:23 because great is your r in heaven. *3635*
6:35 Then your r will be great, *3635*
Ac 1:18 (With the r he got for his wickedness, *3635*
1Co 3:14 he will receive his r. *3635*
9:17 If I preach voluntarily, I have a r; *3635*
9:18 What then is my r? *3635*
Eph 6: 8 that the Lord *will* r everyone *3152*
Col 3:24 an inheritance from the Lord as a r. *502*
Heb 11:26 because he was looking ahead to his r. *3632*
Rev 22:12 I am coming soon! My r is with me, *3635*

REWARDED (15) [REWARD]

Ge 30:18 "God *has* r me for giving my maidservant 5989+8510
Nu 24:11 but the LORD has kept you from being r." 3883
Ru 2:12 May you be richly r by the LORD, 5382
2Sa 22:21 to the cleanness of my hands *he has* r me. 8740
22:25 The LORD *has* r me according 8740
2Ch 15: 7 for your work will be r." 8510
Ps 18:20 to the cleanness of my hands *he has* r me. 8740
18:24 The LORD *has* r me according 8740
58:11 "Surely the righteous still are r; 7262
Pr 13:13 but he who respects a command **is** r. 8966
14:14 and the good man r for his. NIH
Jer 31:16 for your work will be r," 8510
1Co 3: 8 each *will* **be** r according to his own labor. *3284+3635*
Heb 10:35 your confidence; it will be richly r. *3632*
2Jn 1: 8 but that *you may be* r fully. *655+3635*

REWARDING (1) [REWARD]

Rev 11:18 *for* r your servants the prophets *1443+3635+3836*

REWARDS (5) [REWARD]

1Sa 26:23 The LORD r every man for his righteous 8740
Pr 12:14 as surely as the work of his hands r him. 8740
Da 2: 6 from me gifts and r and great honor. 10454
5:17 and give your r to someone else. 10454
Heb 11: 6 *he* r those who earnestly seek him. *1181+3633*

REZEPH (2)

2Ki 19:12 the gods of Gozan, Haran, **R** and the people 8364
Isa 37:12 the gods of Gozan, Haran, **R** and the people 8364

REZIA (KJV) See RIZIA

REZIN (10) [REZIN'S]

2Ki 15:37 the LORD began to send **R** king of Aram 8360
16: 5 Then **R** king of Aram and Pekah son 8360
16: 6 **R** king of Aram recovered Elath for Aram 8360
16: 9 He deported its inhabitants to Kir and put **R** 8360
Ezr 2:48 **R,** Nekoda, Gazzam, 8360
Ne 7:50 Reaiah, **R,** Nekoda, 8360
Isa 7: 1 King **R** of Aram and Pekah son 8360
7: 4 of **R** and Aram and of the son of Remaliah. 8360
7: 8 and the head of Damascus is only **R.** 8360
8: 6 of Shiloah and rejoices over **R** and the son 8360

REZIN'S (1) [REZIN]

Isa 9:11 But the LORD has strengthened **R** foes 8360

REZON (3)

1Ki 11:23 **R** son of Eliada, 8139
11:25 **R** was Israel's adversary as long NIH
11:25 So **R** ruled in Aram and was hostile NIH

RHEGIUM (1)

Ac 28:13 From there we set sail and arrived at **R.** *4836*

RHESA (1)

Lk 3:27 the son *of* **R,** the son of Zerubbabel, *4840*

RHODA (1)

Ac 12:13 and a servant girl named **R** came to answer *4851*

RHODES (2)

Eze 27:15 " 'The men of **R** traded with you, 8102
Ac 21: 1 The next day we went to **R** and from there *4852*

RIB (1) [RIBS]

Ge 2:22 made a woman from the r he had taken out 7521

RIBAI (2)

2Sa 23:29 Ithai son of **R** from Gibeah in Benjamin, 8192
1Ch 11:31 Ithai son of **R** from Gibeah in Benjamin, 8192

RIBBAND (KJV) See CORD

RIBBON (1)

SS 4: 3 Your lips are like a scarlet r; 2562

RIBLAH (11)

Nu 34:11 from Shepham to **R** on the east side of Ain 8058
2Ki 23:33 at **R** in the land of Hamath so that he might 8058
25: 6 He was taken to the king of Babylon at **R,** 8058
25:20 to the king of Babylon at **R.** 8058
25:21 There at **R,** in the land of Hamath, 8058
Jer 39: 5 to Nebuchadnezzar king of Babylon at **R** in 8058
39: 6 There at **R** the king of Babylon slaughtered 8058
52: 9 He was taken to the king of Babylon at **R** in 8058
52:10 There at **R** the king of Babylon slaughtered 8058
52:26 to the king of Babylon at **R.** 8058
52:27 There at **R,** in the land of Hamath, 8058

RIBS (2) [RIB]

Ge 2:21 he took one of the man's r and closed up 7521
Da 7: 5 it had three r in its mouth between its teeth. 10552

RICH (98) [ENRICH, ENRICHED, RICHER, RICHES, RICHEST, RICHLY, RICHNESS]

Ge 14:23 'I made Abram r.' 6947
26:13 The man *became* r, 1540
49:20 "Asher's food will be r; 9045
Ex 30:15 The r are not to give more than 6938
Lev 25:47 resident among you *becomes* r 3338+5952
Ru 3:10 after the younger men, whether r or poor. 6938
2Sa 12: 1 one r and the other poor. 6938
12: 2 The r *man* had a very large number of sheep 6938
12: 4 "Now a traveler came to the r man, 6938
12: 4 but the r man refrained from taking one NIH
1Ch 4:40 They found r, good pasture, 9045
Job 15:29 *He will* no longer *be* r and his wealth will 6947
21:24 his bones r *with* marrow. 9197
34:19 to princes and does not favor the r over 8777
Ps 21: 3 You welcomed him with r blessings 3202
22:29 the r *of* the earth will feast and worship; 2016
49: 2 both low and high, r and poor alike: 6938
49:16 not be overawed when a man *grows* r, when 6947
76: 4 more majestic than mountains *r with* game. AIT
145: 8 slow to anger and r *in* love. 1524
Pr 10:15 The wealth of the r is their fortified city, 6938
13: 7 *One man* pretends to be r, yet has nothing; 6947
14:20 but the r have many friends. 6938
18:11 The wealth of the r is their fortified city; 6938
18:23 but a r *man* answers harshly. 6938
21:17 and oil *will* never *be* r. 6947
22: 2 R and poor have this in common: 6938
22: 7 The r rule over the poor, 6938
22:16 and he who gives gifts to the r— 6938
23: 4 Do not wear yourself out to *get* r; 6947
24:25 and r blessing will come upon them. 3202
28: 6 a r *man* whose ways are perverse. 6938
28:11 A r man may be wise in his own eyes, 6938
28:20 one eager to get r will not go unpunished. 6947
28:22 A stingy man is eager to get r 2104
Ecc 5:12 abundance of a r *man* permits him no sleep. 6938
10: 6 while the r occupy the low ones. 6938
10:20 or curse the r in your bedroom, 6938
Isa 5:17 lambs will feed among the ruins of the r. 4671
25: 6 a feast of r food for all peoples, a banquet 9043
30:23 the food that comes from the land will be r 2015
33: 6 a r store *of* salvation and wisdom 2890
53: 9 and with the r in his death, 6938
Jer 2: 7 a fertile land to eat its fruit and r produce. 3206
5:27 *they have become* r and powerful 6947
9:23 of his strength or the r *man* boast 6938
49:19 from Jordan's thickets to a r pastureland, 419
50:44 from Jordan's thickets to a r pastureland, 419
51:13 You who live by many waters and are r 8041
Eze 34:14 in a r pasture on the mountains of Israel. 9045
38:12 r *in* livestock and goods, 6913
Hos 12: 8 Ephraim boasts, *"I am* very r; 6947
Mic 2: 8 the r robe from those who pass by without 159
6:12 Her r *men* are violent; 6938
Zec 3: 4 and I will put r garments on you." 4711
11: 3 their r pastures are destroyed! 168
11: 5 'Praise the LORD, *I am* r!' 6947
Mt 19:23 for a r *man* to enter the kingdom of heaven. 4454
19:24 through the eye of a needle than for a r *man* 4454
27:57 there came a r man from Arimathea, 4454
Mk 10:23 for the r to enter the kingdom of God!" 2400+3836+5975
10:25 through the eye of a needle than for a r *man* 4454
12:41 Many r *people* threw in large amounts. 4454
Lk 1:53 but has sent the r away empty. 4456
6:24 "But woe to you who are r, 4454
12:16 "The ground *of* a certain r man produced 4454
12:21 for himself but *is* not r toward God." 4456
14:12 or your r neighbors; 4454
16: 1 a r man whose manager was accused 4454
16:19 "There was a r man who was dressed 4454
16:21 to eat what fell from the r *man's* table. 4454
16:22 The r *man* also died and was buried. 4454
18:24 for the r to enter the kingdom of God! 2400+3836+5975
18:25 through the eye of a needle than for a r *man* 4454
21: 1 Jesus saw the r putting their gifts into 4454
1Co 4: 8 Already *you have become* r! 4456
2Co 6:10 poor, yet making many r; 4457
8: 2 extreme poverty welled up in r generosity. 4458
8: 9 that though he was r, yet for your sake 4454
8: 9 you through his poverty *might become* r. 4456
9:11 *You will be* made r in every way so 4457
Eph 2: 4 God, who is r in mercy, 4454
1Ti 6: 9 *to* get r fall into temptation and a trap and 4456
6:17 Command those who *are* r in this present 4454
6:18 *to be* r in good deeds, 4456
Jas 1:10 But the one who is r should take pride 4454
1:11 the r *man* will fade away even 4454
2: 5 in the eyes of the world to be r in faith and 4454
2: 6 Is it not the r who are exploiting you? 4454
5: 1 Now listen, *you* r *people*, 4454
2Pe 1:11 and you will receive a r welcome into 4455
Rev 2: 9 and your poverty—yet you are r! 4454
3:17 You say, 'I am r; 4454
3:18 so *you can become* r; 4456
6:15 the princes, the generals, the r, the mighty, 4454
13:16 small and great, r and poor, free and slave, 4454
18: 3 and the merchants of the earth grew r 4456
Rev 18:19 all who had ships on the sea *became* r 4456

RICHER (1) [RICH]

Da 11: 2 *who will be* far r than all the others. 6947+6948

RICHES (51) [RICH]

1Ki 3:13 you have not asked for—both r and honor— 6948
10:23 Solomon was greater in r and wisdom than 6948
2Ch 1:11 not asked for wealth, r or honor, nor for 5794
1:12 I will also give you wealth, r and honor, 5794
9:22 in r and wisdom than all the other kings of 6948
32:27 Hezekiah had very great r and honor, 6948
32:29 for God had given him very great r. 8214
Job 20:15 He will spit out the r he swallowed; 2657
36:18 Be careful that no one entices you by r; 6217
Ps 49: 6 in their wealth and boast of their great r? 6948
49:12 But man, despite his r, does not endure; 3702
49:20 A man who has r without understanding is 3702
62:10 though your r increase, 2657
112: 3 Wealth and r are in his house, 6948
119:14 as one rejoices in great r. 2104
Pr 3:16 in her left hand are r and honor. 6948
8:18 With me are r and honor, 6948
11:28 Whoever trusts in his r will fall, 6948
13: 8 A man's r may ransom his life, 6948
22: 1 good name is more desirable than great r; 6948
23: 5 Cast but a glance at r, and they are gone, 2257S
27:24 for r do not endure forever, 2890
30: 8 give me neither poverty nor r, 6948
Isa 10: 3 Where will you leave your r? 3883
30: 6 the envoys carry their r on donkeys' backs, 2657
45: 3 r *stored in* secret places, 4759
60: 5 to you the r *of* the nations will come. 2657
61: 6 and in their r you will boast. 3883
Jer 9:23 or the rich man boast of his r, 6948
17:11 the man who gains r by unjust means. 6948
48: 7 Since you trust in your deeds and r, 238
49: 4 you trust in your r and say, 238
Da 11:43 the treasures of gold and silver and all the r 2776
Joel 2:22 the fig tree and the vine yield their r. 2657
Lk 8:14 r and pleasures, and they do not mature. 4458
16:11 who will trust you with true r? NIG
Ro 2: 4 Or do you show contempt for the r 4458
9:23 the r of his glory known to the objects 4458
11:12 if their transgression means r for the world, 4458
11:12 and their loss means r for the Gentiles, 4458
11:12 much greater r will their fullness bring! NIG
11:33 *of* the r of the wisdom and knowledge 4458
Eph 1: 7 in accordance with the r of God's grace 4458
1:18 the r of his glorious inheritance in 4458
2: 7 the incomparable r of his grace, 4458
3: 8 to the Gentiles the unsearchable r of Christ, 4458
3:16 of his glorious r he may strengthen you 4458
Php 4:19 according to his glorious r in Christ Jesus. 4458
Col 1:27 the Gentiles the glorious r of this mystery, 4458
2: 2 the full r of complete understanding, 4458
Rev 18:14 All your r and splendor have vanished, 3353

RICHEST (3) [RICH]

Ps 63: 5 satisfied as with the r of foods; 2016+2256+2693
Isa 55: 2 and your soul will delight in the r of fare. 2016
Da 11:24 When the r provinces feel secure, 5458

RICHLY (10) [RICH]

Ge 37: 3 and he made a r ornamented robe for him. 7168
37:23 the r ornamented robe he was wearing— 7168
Dt 15: 4 he *will* r bless you, 1385+1385
Ru 2:12 May you be r rewarded by the LORD, 8969
2Sa 13:18 She was wearing a r ornamented robe, 7168
Pr 28:20 A faithful man will be r blessed, 8041
Ro 10:12 of all and r blesses all who call on him, 4456
Col 3:16 Let the word of Christ dwell in you r 4455
1Ti 6:17 who r provides us with everything 4455
Heb 10:35 it will be r rewarded. 3489

RICHNESS (2) [RICH]

Ge 27:28 of heaven's dew and of earth's r— 9044
27:39 dwelling will be away from the earth's r, 9044

RID (32)

Ge 21:10 "Get r of that slave woman and her son, 1763
35: 2 "Get r of the foreign gods you have 6073
Ex 8: 9 and your houses *may* be r of the frogs, 4162
Lev 13:58 that has been washed and *is* r of the mildew 6073
Nu 17: 5 *I will* r myself of this constant grumbling 8896
Jdg 9:29 Then *I would* get r of him. 6073
10:16 Then *they* got r of the foreign gods 6073
1Sa 1:14 Get r of your wine." 6073
7: 3 then r yourselves *of* the foreign gods and 6073
2Sa 4:11 from your hand and r the earth *of* you!" 1278
13:13 Where *could I* get r of my disgrace? 2143
14: 7 then *we will* get r of the heir as well.' 9012
1Ki 15:12 from the land and got r of all 6073
22:46 *He* r the land *of* the rest of the male shrine 1278
2Ki 3: 2 *He* got r of the sacred stone of Baal 6073
23:24 Josiah got r of the mediums and spiritists, 1278
2Ch 19: 3 for *you have* r the land *of* the Asherah poles 1278
33:15 *He* got r of the foreign gods and removed 6073
Eze 18:31 R yourselves *of* all the offenses 4946+6584+8959
20: 7 And I said to them, "Each of you, get r of 8959
20: 8 they *did* not get r of the vile images 8959
34:25 with them and r the land of wild beasts so 8697
Zec 11: 8 In one month *I* got r of the three shepherds 3948
Lk 22: 2 looking for some way *to* get r of Jesus, 359
Ac 16:37 now *do they want to* get r of us quietly? 1675
22:22 "R the earth of him! 149
1Co 5: 7 Get r of the old yeast that you may be 1705
Gal 4:30 "Get r of the slave woman and her son, 1675
Eph 4:31 Get r of all bitterness, rage and anger, 149
Col 3: 8 But now you *must* r *yourselves* of 700
Jas 1:21 get r of all moral filth and the evil that is 700
1Pe 2: 1 r *yourselves* of all malice and all deceit, 700

RIDDEN (4) [RIDE]

Nu 22:30 which *you have* always r, to this day? 8206
Est 6: 8 and a horse the king *has* r, 8206
Mk 11: 2 which no one *has* ever r. 2767
Lk 19:30 which no one *has* ever r. 2767

RIDDLE (8) [RIDDLES]

Jdg 14:12 "Let me tell you a r," Samson said to them. 2648
14:13 "Tell us your r," they said. 2648
14:15 "Coax your husband into explaining the r 2648
14:16 You've given my people a r, 2648
14:17 She in turn explained the r to her people. 2648
14:18 you would not have solved my r." 2648
14:19 to those who had explained the r. 2648
Ps 49: 4 with the harp I will expound my r: 2648

RIDDLES (3) [RIDDLE]

Nu 12: 8 clearly and not in r; 2648
Pr 1: 6 the sayings and r of the wise. 2648
Da 5:12 explain r and solve difficult problems. 10019

RIDE (13) [RIDDEN, RIDER, RIDERS, RIDES, RIDING, RODE]

Ge 41:43 *He* had him r in a chariot 8206
Dt 32:13 *He* made him r on the heights of the land 8206
Jdg 5:10 *"You who* r on white donkeys, 8206
2Sa 16: 2 for the king's household to r on, 8206
19:26 'I will have my donkey saddled and *will* r 8206
2Ki 10:16 Then *he* had him r along in his chariot. 8206
Ps 45: 4 In your majesty r forth victoriously 8206
66:12 *You* let men r over our heads; 8206
Isa 30:16 You said, *'We will* r off on swift horses.' 8206
33:21 No galley with oars *will* r them, 928+2143
58:14 and *I will* cause you to r on the heights 8206
Jer 6:23 They sound like the roaring sea as *they* r 8206
50:42 They sound like the roaring sea as *they* r 8206

RIDER (13) [RIDE]

Ge 49:17 so that its r tumbles backward. 8206
Ex 15: 1 horse and its r he has hurled into the sea. 8206
15:21 horse and its r he has hurled into the sea." 8206
Job 39:18 she laughs at horse and r. 8206
Jer 51:21 with you I shatter horse and r, 8206
Zec 12: 4 with panic and its r with madness," 8206
Rev 6: 2 Its r held a bow, and he was given a crown, 2764+3836
6: 4 Its r was given power to take peace from the earth 2764+3836
6: 5 Its r was holding a pair of scales 2764+3836
6: 8 Its r was named Death, 2764+3836
19:11 r is called Faithful and True. 899+2093+2764
19:19 against the r on the horse and his army. 2764
19:21 that came out of the mouth *of* the r on 2764

RIDERS (9) [RIDE]

2Sa 1: 6 the chariots and r almost upon him. 1251+7304
2Ki 18:23 if you can put r on them! 8206
Isa 21: 7 r *on* donkeys or riders on camels, 8207
21: 7 riders on donkeys or r *on* camels, 8207
36: 8 if you can put r on them! 8206
Eze 39:20 eat your fill of horses and r, 8207
Hag 2:22 horses and their r will fall, 8206
Rev 9:17 The horses and r I saw in my vision looked like this: 2093+2764+3836
19:18 men, of horses and their r, 899+2093+2764

RIDES (6) [RIDE]

Dt 33:26 *who* r on the heavens to help you and on 8206
Ps 68: 4 extol him *who* r on the clouds— 8206
68:33 to him *who* r the ancient skies above, 8206
104: 3 the clouds his chariot and r on the wings of 2143
Isa 19: 1 See, the LORD r on a swift cloud 8206
Rev 17: 7 of the woman and *of* the beast she r, 1002

RIDGE (1) [RIDGES]

Ge 48:22 the r of land I took from the Amorites 8900

RIDGES (1) [RIDGE]

Ps 65:10 You drench its furrows and level its r; 1521

RIDICULE (14) [RIDICULED]

Dt 28:37 of horror and an object of scorn and r to all 9110
1Ki 9: 7 then become a byword and an object of r 9110
2Ki 19: 4 has sent to r the living God, 3070
2Ch 7:20 I will make it a byword and an object of r 9110
Job 19:18 when I appear, *they* r me. 1819
Ps 123: 4 We have endured much r from the proud, 4353
Isa 37: 4 has sent to r the living God, 3070
Jer 24: 9 an object of r and cursing, 9110
48:26 let her be an object of r. 8468

Jer 48:27 Was not Israel the **object of** your r? 8468
48:39 Moab has become an **object of r,** 8468
Mic 2: 4 In that day *men will* r you; 5442+5951
Hab 2: 6 not all of them taunt him with r and scorn, 4886
Lk 14:29 everyone who sees it *will* r him, *1850*

RIDICULED (8) [RIDICULE]

Jdg 9:38 Aren't these the men *you* r? 4415
2Ch 30:10 but the people scorned and r them. 4352
Ne 2:19 they mocked and r us. 1022
4: 1 *He* r the Jews, 4352
Jer 20: 7 I am r all day long; everyone mocks me. 8468
Eze 36: 4 that have been plundered and r by the rest 4353
Hos 7:16 this they *will be* r in the land of Egypt. 4352
Lk 23:11 Herod and his soldiers r and mocked him. *2024*

RIDING (15) [RIDE]

Lev 15: 9 " 'Everything the man sits on when r will 8206
Nu 22:22 Balaam *was* r on his donkey, 8206
1Sa 25:20 As she **came** r her donkey into 8206
2Sa 18: 9 He *was* r his mule, 8206
18: 9 while the mule he was r kept on going. 9393
2Ki 9:25 how you and I *were* r together **in chariots** 8206
Ne 2:12 with me except the one I *was* r on. 8206
Est 8:14 The couriers, r the royal horses, raced out, 8206
Jer 17:25 and their officials *will* come r in chariots 8206
22: 4 r in chariots and on horses, 8206
Eze 38:15 all of them r *on* horses, a great horde, 8206
Zec 1: 8 there before me was a man r a red horse! 8206
9: 9 gentle and r on a donkey, on a colt, 8206
Mt 21: 5 gentle and r on a donkey, on a colt, *2094*
Rev 19:14 r on white horses and dressed in fine linen, *NIG*

RIE (KJV) See SPELT

RIFLED (KJV) See RANSACKED

RIFTS (1)

Jer 2: 6 through a land of deserts and **r,** 8757

RIGGING (2)

Pr 23:34 on the high seas, lying on top of the **r.** 2479
Isa 33:23 Your r hangs loose: 2475

RIGHT (460) [ARIGHT, RIGHTFUL, RIGHTFULLY, RIGHTLY, RIGHTS]

Ge 4: 7 If *you* **do what is r,** 3512
4: 7 But if *you do* not **do what is r,** 3512
13: 9 If you go to the left, *I'll* **go to the r;** 3554
13: 9 if you go to the **r,** I'll go to the left." 3545
18:19 of the LORD by doing *what* is r and just, 7407
18:25 Will not the Judge of all the earth do r?" 5477
24:48 on the r road to get the granddaughter 622
43:23 "It's **all r,**" he said. 8934
48:13 Ephraim on his r toward Israel's left hand 3545
48:13 on his left toward Israel's r hand, 3545
48:14 But Israel reached out his r hand and put it 3545
48:17 Joseph saw his father placing his r hand 3545
48:18 put your r hand on his head." 3545
Ex 8:26 But Moses said, "That *would* not *be* **r.** 3922
9:27 "The LORD is **in the r,** 7404
14:22 a wall of water on their r and on their left. 3545
14:29 a wall of water on their r and on their left. 3545
15: 6 "Your r hand, O LORD, was majestic 3545
15: 6 Your r hand, O LORD, was majestic 3545
15:12 You stretched out your r hand and 3545
15:26 of the LORD your God and do what is r 3838
21: 8 *He* **has** no r to sell her to foreigners, 5440
29:20 of the r ears of Aaron and his sons, 3556
29:20 on the thumbs of their r hands, 3556
29:20 and on the big toes of their r feet. 3556
29:22 with the fat on them, and the r thigh. 3545
Lev 7:32 the r thigh of your fellowship offerings to 3545
7:33 the r thigh as his share. 3545
8:23 and put it on the lobe of Aaron's r ear, 3556
8:23 the thumb of his r hand and on the big toe 3556
8:23 and on the big toe of his r foot. 3556
8:24 of the blood on the lobes of their r ears, 3556
8:24 on the thumbs of their r hands and on 3556
8:24 and on the big toes of their r feet. 3556
8:25 both kidneys and their fat and the r thigh. 3545
8:26 on the fat portions and on the r thigh. 3545
9:21 Aaron waved the breasts and the r thigh 3545
14:14 and put it on the lobe of the r ear of the one 3556
14:14 the thumb of his r hand and on the big toe 3556
14:14 and on the big toe of his r foot. 3556
14:16 dip his r forefinger into the oil in his palm, 3556
14:17 in his palm on the lobe of the r ear of 3556
14:17 the thumb of his r hand and on the big toe 3556
14:17 and on the big toe of his r foot, 3556
14:25 and put it on the lobe of the r ear of the one 3556
14:25 the thumb of his r hand and on the big toe 3556
14:25 and on the big toe of his r foot. 3556
14:27 and with his r forefinger sprinkle some of 3556
14:28 of the r ear of the one to be cleansed, 3556
14:28 be cleansed, on the thumb of his r hand and 3556
14:28 and on the big toe of his r foot. 3556
25:29 the **r of redemption** a full year after its sale. 1460
25:32 the **r to redeem** their houses in 1460
25:48 he retains the **r of redemption** 1460
Nu 11:15 put me to death **r now—** 5528
18:18 the wave offering and the r thigh are yours. 3545
Nu 20:17 the king's highway and not turn to the r or 3545
22:26 either to the r or to the left. 3545
22:29 I would kill you **r now."** 6964
25: 6 to his family a Midianite woman **r before** 4200
27: 7 "What Zelophehad's daughters are saying is **r.** 4026
36: 5 of the descendants of Joseph is saying is **r.** 4026
Dt 2:27 we will not turn aside to the r or to the left. 3545
5:32 do not turn aside to the r or to the left. 3545
6:18 Do what is r and good in the LORD's 3838
11: 6 the earth opened its mouth r in the middle NIH
12:25 because you will be doing what is r in 3838
12:28 and r in the eyes of the LORD your God. 3838
13:18 and doing what is r in his eyes. 3838
17:11 to the r or to the left. 3545
17:20 and turn from the law to the r or to the left. 3545
21: 9 since you have done what is r in the eyes of 3838
21:17 The r *of* the firstborn belongs to him. 5477
28:14 to the r or to the left, 3545
Jos 1: 7 do not turn from it to the r or to the left, 3545
4: 3 the Jordan from **r where** the priests stood 2296
9:25 to us whatever seems good and r to you." 3838
23: 6 without turning aside to the r or to the left. 3545
Jdg 3:16 strapped to his r thigh under his clothing. 3545
3:21 the sword from his r thigh and plunged it 3545
4:18 "Come, my lord, come **r in.** 448
5:26 her r hand for the workman's hammer. 3545
7:20 in their r hands the trumpets they were 3545
11:23 what r have you to take it over? NIH
12: 6 **"All r,** say 'Shibboleth.' " 5528
14: 3 She's the r *one* for me." 3837
15: 3 "This time **/ have a r to get even** 5927
16:29 his r hand on the one and his left hand on 3545
Ru 4: 4 For no one **has the r to do it** except you, 1457[S]
1Sa 6:12 they did not turn to the r or to the left. 3545
11: 2 on the condition that I gouge out the r eye 3545
12: 3 *I will* **make** it **r."** 8740
12:23 I will teach you the way that is good and **r.** 3838
14:13 with his armor-bearer **r behind** him. 339
14:41 the God of Israel, "Give me the **r answer."** 9459
2Sa 2:14 **"All r,** *let them* **do it,"** 7756[S]
2:19 to the r nor to the left as he pursued him. 3545
2:21 "Turn aside to the r or to the left; 3545
8:15 doing what was just and r 7407
14:19 no one can **turn to the r** or to the left 3554
16: 6 and the special guard were on David's r 3545
18:11 to the ground **r there?** 9004
19:28 So what r do I have to make any more 7407
20: 9 by the beard with his r hand to kiss him. 3545
21: 4 "We **have** no r to demand silver or gold 4200
21: 4 nor do we **have the** r to put anyone in Israel 4200
23: 5 "Is not my house r with God? 4026
1Ki 1:25 **R now** they are eating and drinking 2180
2:19 and she sat down at his r hand. 3545
3: 9 and to distinguish between r and wrong. 3202
7:49 the lampstands of pure gold (five on the r 3545
8:36 Teach them the r way to live, 3202
11:33 nor done what is r in my eyes, 3838
11:38 in my ways and do what is r in my eyes 3838
14: 8 doing only what was r in my eyes. 3838
15: 5 For David had done what was r in the eyes 3838
15:11 Asa did what was r in the eyes of 3838
22:19 of heaven standing around him on his r and 3545
22:43 he did what was r in the eyes of the LORD. 3838
2Ki 2: 8 The water divided *to the* r and to the left, 2178[S]
2:14 it divided *to the* r and to the left, 2178[S]
4:23 "It's **all r,"** she said. 8934
4:26 'Are you **all r?** 8934
4:26 Is your husband **all r?** 8934
4:26 Is your child **all r?' "** 8934
4:26 "Everything is **all r,"** she said. 8934
5:21 "Is everything **all r?"** 8934
5:22 "Everything is **all r,"** Gehazi answered. 8934
7: 9 they said to each other, "We're not doing **r.** 4026
9:11 "Is everything **all r?** 8934
10:30 in accomplishing what is r in my eyes 3838
12: 2 Joash did what was r in the eyes of the LORD 3838
12: 9 on the r side as one enters the temple of 3545
14: 3 He did what was r in the eyes of the LORD, 3838
15: 3 He did what was r in the eyes of the LORD, 3838
15:34 He did what was r in the eyes of the LORD, 3838
16: 2 he did not do what was r in the eyes of 3838
17: 9 the LORD their God that were not **r.** 4026
18: 3 He did what was r in the eyes of the LORD, 3838
22: 2 He did what was r in the eyes of the LORD 3838
22: 2 not turning aside to the r or to the left. 3545
1Ch 6:39 who served at his r hand: 3545
13: 4 because it seemed r to all the people. 3837
18:14 doing what was just and r 7407
2Ch 6:27 Teach them the r way to live, 3202
14: 2 Asa did what was good and r in the eyes of 3838
18:18 with all the host of heaven standing on his r 3545
20:32 he did what was r in the eyes of the LORD. 3838
24: 2 Joash did what was r in the eyes of 3838
25: 2 He did what was r in the eyes of the LORD, 3838
26: 4 He did what was r in the eyes of the LORD, 3838
26:18 "It is not **r for** you, Uzziah, 4200
27: 2 He did what was r in the eyes of the LORD, 3838
28: 1 he did not do what was r in the eyes of 3838
29: 2 He did what was r in the eyes of the LORD, 3838
30: 4 The plan seemed r both to the king and to 3837
31:20 doing what was good and r and faithful 3838
34: 2 He did what was r in the eyes of the LORD, 3838
34: 2 not turning aside to the r or to the left. 3545
Ezr 10:12 with a loud voice: "You are **r!** 4026
Ne 2:20 in Jerusalem or any claim or **historic** r 2355
Ne 4:11 *we will* **be r there** among them 995
5: 9 I continued, "What you are doing is not **r.** 3202
8: 4 Beside him on his r stood Mattithiah, 3545
9:13 and laws that are just and **r,** 622
12:31 to proceed on top of the wall to the **r,** 3545
Est 8: 5 with favor and **thinks** *it* the r thing to do, 4178
8:11 the r to assemble and protect themselves; NIH
Job 8: 3 Does the Almighty pervert *what* is **r?** 7406
27: 5 **admit** you are **in the r;** 7405
30:12 On my r the tribe attacks; 3545
32: 9 not only the aged who understand *what* is **r.** 5477
33:12 "But I tell you, in this *you are* not **r,** 7405
33:23 to tell a man *what* is r *for* him, 3841
33:27 'I sinned, and perverted *what* was **r,** 3838
34: 4 Let us discern for ourselves *what* is **r;** 5477
34: 6 Although I am **r,** I am considered a liar; 5477
40:14 to you that your own r hand can save you. 3545
42: 7 you have not spoken of me *what is* **r,** 3922
42: 8 You have not spoken of me *what is* **r.** 3922
Ps 4: 5 Offer r sacrifices and trust in the LORD. 7406
9: 4 For you have upheld my r and my cause; 5477
16: 8 he is at my r hand, I will not be shaken. 3545
16:11 with eternal pleasures at your r hand. 3545
17: 2 may your eyes see *what* is **r.** 4797
17: 7 by your r hand those who take refuge 3545
18:35 and your r hand sustains me; 3545
19: 8 The precepts of the LORD are **r,** 3838
20: 6 with the saving power of his r hand. 3545
21: 8 your r hand will seize your foes. 3545
25: 9 in what is r and teaches them his way. 5477
26:10 whose r hands are full of bribes. 3545
33: 4 For the word of the LORD is **r and true;** 3838
44: 3 it was your r hand, your arm, 3545
45: 4 let your r hand display awesome deeds. 3545
45: 9 at your r hand is the royal bride in gold 3545
48:10 your r hand is filled with righteousness. 3545
50:16 **"What r have you** to recite my 3870+4200+4537
51: 4 so that *you are* **proved** r when you speak 7405
60: 5 Save us and help us with your r hand, 3545
63: 8 your r hand upholds me. 3545
73:23 you hold me by my r hand. 3545
74:11 Why do you hold back your hand, your r hand? 3545
77:10 the years of the r hand *of* the Most High." 3545
78:54 to the hill country his r hand had taken. 3545
80:15 the root your r hand has planted, 3545
80:17 on the man at your r hand, 3545
89:13 your hand is strong, your r hand exalted. 3545
89:25 his r hand over the rivers. 3545
89:42 You have exalted the r hand *of* his foes; 3545
91: 7 ten thousand at your r hand, 3545
98: 1 r hand and his holy arm have worked 3545
99: 4 in Jacob you have done what is just and **r.** 7407
106: 3 who constantly do *what* is **r.** 7407
108: 6 Save us and help us with your r hand, 3545
109: 6 let an accuser stand at his r hand. 3545
109:31 he stands at the r hand *of* the needy one, 3545
110: 1 at my r hand until I make your enemies 3545
110: 5 The Lord is at your r hand; 3545
118:15 LORD's r hand has done mighty things! 3545
118:16 The LORD's r hand is lifted high; 3545
118:16 the LORD's r hand has done mighty things!" 3545
119:128 **consider** all your precepts **r,** 3837
119:137 O LORD, and your laws are **r.** 3838
119:144 Your statutes are forever **r;** 7406
121: 5 the LORD is your shade at your r hand; 3545
137: 5 may my r hand forget [its skill]. 3545
138: 7 with your r hand you save me. 3545
139:10 your r hand will hold me fast. 3545
142: 4 Look to my r and see; 3545
144: 8 whose r hands are deceitful. 3545
144:11 whose r hands are deceitful. 3545
Pr 1: 3 *doing what* is r and just and fair; 7406
2: 9 Then you will understand *what* is r and just 7406
3:16 Long life is in her r hand; 3545
4:27 Do not swerve to the r or the left; 3545
8: 6 I open my lips to speak *what* is **r.** 4797
8: 9 To the discerning all of them are **r;** 5791
12:15 The way of a fool seems **r** to him, 3838
14:12 There is a way that seems **r** to a man, 3838
16:25 There is a way that seems **r** to a man, 3838
18:17 The first to present his case seems **r,** 7404
20:11 by whether his conduct is pure and **r.** 3838
21: 2 All a man's ways seem **r** to him, 3838
21: 3 To do *what* is **r** and just is more acceptable 7407
21: 7 for they refuse to do *what* is **r.** 5477
23:16 when your lips speak *what* is **r.** 4797
23:19 **keep** your heart on the **r** 886
Ecc 7:20 a righteous man on earth who does *what* is **r** 3202
10: 2 The heart of the wise inclines to the **r,** 3545
12:10 Teacher searched to find **just** the **r** words, 2914
SS 1: 4 *How* r they are to adore you! 4797
2: 6 and his r arm embraces me. 3545
8: 3 under my head and his r arm embraces me. 3545
Isa 1: 7 by foreigners **r before** you, 4200+5584
1:17 learn *to* **do r!** 3512
7:15 to reject the wrong and choose the **r.** 3202
7:16 to reject the wrong and choose the **r,** 3202
9:20 On the r they will devour, 3545
28:26 and teaches him the **r way.** 5477
30:10 "Give us no more visions of *what* is **r!** 5791
30:21 Whether *you* **turn to the r** or to the left, 3554
33:15 and speaks *what* is **r,** who rejects gain 4797
40:14 and who taught him the r way? 5477
41:10 I will uphold you with my righteous r hand. 3545
41:13 of your r hand and says to you, Do not fear; 3545
41:26 so we could say, 'He was **r**'? 7404

Isa 43: 9 in their witnesses *to* **prove** *they were* **r**, 7405
44:20 "Is not this thing in my **r** hand a lie?" 3545
45: 1 whose **r** hand I take hold of to subdue 3545
45:19 I declare *what* is **r**. 4797
48:13 and my **r** hand spread out the heavens; 3545
51: 7 "Hear me, you who know *what* is **r**, 7406
54: 3 you will spread out to the **r** and to the left; 3545
56: 1 "Maintain justice and do *what* is **r**, 7407
58: 2 as if they were a nation that does *what* is **r** 7407
62: 8 The LORD has sworn by his **r** hand and 3545
63:12 of power to be at Moses' **r** hand, 3545
64: 5 to the help of those who gladly do **r**, 7406
Jer 8: 6 but they do not say *what* is **r**. 4026
22: 3 Do what is just and **r**. 7407
22:15 He did *what* was **r** and just, 5477
22:24 were a signet ring on my **r** hand, 3545
23: 5 and do what is just and **r** in the land. 7407
26:14 with me whatever you think is good and **r**. 3838
32: 7 as nearest relative it is your **r** and duty 5477
32: 8 it is your **r** to redeem it and possess it, 5477
33:15 he will do what is just and **r** in the land. 7407
34:15 Recently you repented and did *what* is **r** 3838
La 2: 3 He has withdrawn his **r** hand at 3545
2: 4 his **r** hand is ready. 3545
Eze 1:10 on the **r** side each had the face of a lion, 3545
4: 6 lie down again, this time on your **r** side, 3556
18: 5 righteous man who does what is just and **r**. 7407
18:19 Since the son has done what is just and **r** 7407
18:21 and does what is just and **r**, he will surely 7407
18:27 and does what is just and **r**, he will save 7407
21:16 O sword, slash **to the r**, then to the left, 3554
21:22 Into his **r** hand will come the lot 3545
33:14 from his sin and does what is just and **r**— 7407
33:16 He has done what is just and **r**; 7407
33:19 and does what is just and **r**, 7407
39: 3 make your arrows drop from your **r** hand. 3545
45: 9 and oppression and do what is just and **r**. 7407
Da 4:27 Renounce your sins by doing *what* is **r**, 10610
4:37 because everything he does is **r** 10643
12: 7 lifted his **r** hand and his left hand 3545
Hos 14: 9 The ways of the LORD are **r**; 3838
Am 3:10 "They do not know how to do **r**," 5791
Jnh 4: 4 **"Have** you **any r** to be angry?" 3512
4: 9 *"Do* you **have a r** to be angry about 3512
4:11 a hundred twenty thousand people who
cannot tell their **r** hand from their left, 3545
Mic 3: 9 who despise justice and distort all that is **r**; 3838
7: 9 and establishes my **r**. 5477
Hab 2:16 the LORD's **r** hand is coming around 3545
Zec 3: 1 Satan standing at his **r** side to accuse him. 3545
4: 3 the **r** *of* the bowl and the other on its left." 3545
4:11 "What are these two olive trees on the **r** 3545
11:17 May the sword strike his arm and his **r** eye! 3545
11:17 his **r** eye totally blinded!" 3545
12: 6 They will consume **r** and left all 3545
Mt 5:29 If your **r** eye causes you to sin, *1288*
5:30 And if your **r** hand causes you to sin, *1288*
5:39 If someone strikes you on the **r** cheek, *1288*
6: 3 do not let your left hand know what your **r**
hand is doing, *1288*
11:19 But wisdom *is* **proved r** by her actions." *1467*
15: 7 Isaiah was **r** when he prophesied *2822*
15:26 not **r** to take the children's bread and toss it *2819*
20: 4 and I will pay you whatever is **r**.' *1465*
20:15 Don't I **have the r** to do what I want *2003*
20:21 of these two sons of mine may sit at your **r** *1288*
20:23 to sit at my **r** or left is not for me to grant. *1288*
21: 3 and he will send them **r away**." *2317*
22:17 *Is it* **r** to pay taxes to Caesar or not?" *2003*
22:26 **r on down to** the seventh. *2401*
22:44 "Sit at my **r hand** until I put your enemies *1288*
24:33 you know that it is near, **r at** the door. *2093*
25:33 He will put the sheep on his **r** and the goats *1288*
25:34 "Then the King will say to those on his **r**, *1288*
26:58 **r up to** the courtyard of the high priest. *2401*
26:64 sitting at the **r hand** of the Mighty One *1288*
27:29 They put a staff in his **r hand** and knelt *1288*
27:38 one on his **r** and one on his left. *1288*
Mk 5:15 sitting there, dressed and **in** *his* **r mind;** *5404*
6:25 "I want you to give me **r now** the head *1994*
7: 6 "Isaiah was **r** when he prophesied *2822*
7:27 not **r** to take the children's bread and toss it *2819*
10:37 of us sit at your **r** and the other at your left *1288*
10:40 to sit at my **r** or left is not for me to grant. *1288*
12:14 *Is it* **r** to pay taxes to Caesar or not? *2003*
12:32 "You are **r** in saying that God is one *237+2093*
12:36 "Sit at my **r hand** until I put your enemies *1288*
13:29 you know that it is near, **r at** the door. *2093*
14:54 **r into** the courtyard of the high priest.
1650+2276+2401
14:62 sitting at the **r hand** of the Mighty One *1288*
15:27 one on his **r** and one on his left. *1288*
16: 5 in a white robe sitting on the **r side,** *1288*
16:19 into heaven and he sat at the **r hand** of God. *1288*
Lk 1:11 standing at the **r side** of the altar of incense. *1288*
4:30 But he **walked r through** the crowd *1451*
5:19 **r** in front of Jesus. *NIG*
6: 6 man was there whose **r** hand was shriveled. *1288*
7:29 **acknowledged that** God's way *was* **r**, *1467*
7:35 wisdom *is* **proved r** by all her children." *1467*
8:35 dressed and **in** *his* **r mind;** *5404*
12:57 for yourselves what is **r**? *1465*
20:21 know that you speak and teach **what is r**, *3987*
20:22 *Is it* **r** for us to pay taxes to Caesar *2003*
20:42 Lord said to my Lord: "Sit at my **r hand** *1288*
21: 9 but the end will not come **r away**." *2311*
22:50 cutting off his **r** ear. *1288*
Lk 22:69 be seated at the **r hand** of the mighty God." *1288*
22:70 He replied, "You are **r** in saying I am." *NIG*
23:33 one on his **r**, the other on his left. *1288*
Jn 1:12 he gave the **r** to become children of God— *2026*
4:17 to her, "You are **r** when you say *2822*
7: 6 "The **r time** for me has not yet come; *2789*
7: 6 for you any time is **r**. *2289*
7: 8 for me the **r time** has not yet come." *2789*
7:24 and make a **r** judgment." *1465*
8:16 But if I do judge, my decisions are **r**, *240*
8:48 "Aren't we **r** in saying that you are *2822*
18:10 cutting off his **r** ear. *1288*
18:31 "But we **have** no **r** to execute anyone," *2003*
18:37 "You are **r** in saying I am a king. *NIG*
21: 6 "Throw your net on the **r** side of the boat *1288*
Ac 2:25 he is at my **r hand**, I will not be shaken. *1288*
2:33 Exalted *to* the **r hand** of God, *1288*
2:34 Lord said to my Lord: "Sit at my **r hand** *1288*
3: 7 Taking him *by* the **r** hand, *1288*
4:19 for yourselves whether it is **r** in God's sight *1465*
5:31 *to* his own **r hand** as Prince and Savior *1288*
6: 2 not be **r** for us to neglect the ministry of *744*
7:55 and Jesus standing at the **r hand** of God. *1288*
7:56 and the Son of Man standing at the **r hand** *1288*
8:21 because your heart is not **r** before God. *2318*
10:35 who fear him and do **what is r**. *1466*
11:11 **"R then** three men who had been sent to me *1994*
13:10 and an enemy of everything that is **r**! *1466*
13:10 Will you never stop perverting the **r** ways *2318*
25:11 no one *has the* **r** to hand me over to them. *1538*
Ro 3: 4 that *you may be* **proved r** when you speak *1467*
5: 6 **at just the r time,** when we were *2789+2848*
7:21 I want to do good, evil *is* **r there** with me. *4154*
8:22 of childbirth **r up to** the present time. *948*
8:34 at the **r hand** of God and is also interceding *1288*
9:21 Does not the potter have the **r** to make out *2026*
12:17 to do what is **r** in the eyes of everybody. *2819*
13: 3 rulers hold no terror *for* those who do **r**, *19*
13: 3 do what is **r** and he will commend you. *19*
1Co 7:35 a **r** *way* in undivided devotion to the Lord. *2363*
7:37 this man also does **the r thing.** *2822*
7:38 So then, he who marries the virgin does **r**, *2822*
9: 4 Don't we have the **r** to food and drink? *2026*
9: 5 the **r** to take a believing wife along with us, *2026*
9:12 If others have this **r** of support from you, *2026*
9:12 But we did not use this **r**. *2026*
2Co 5:13 if *we are* **in** *our* **r mind,** it is for you. *5404*
6: 7 of righteousness *in* the **r hand** and in *1288*
8:21 For we are taking pains to do what is **r**, *2819*
13: 7 the test but that you will do what is **r** even *2819*
Gal 2: 9 and Barnabas the **r hand** of fellowship *1288*
Eph 1:20 from the dead and seated him at his **r hand** *1288*
6: 1 obey your parents in the Lord, for this is **r**. *1465*
Php 1: 7 It is **r** for me to feel this way about all *1465*
4: 8 whatever is noble, whatever is **r**, *1465*
Col 3: 1 where Christ is seated at the **r hand** of God. *1288*
4: 1 provide your slaves with what is **r** and fair, *1465*
2Th 1: 5 that God's judgment is **r**, *1465*
3: 9 because we do not have the **r** to such help, *2026*
3:13 you, brothers, never tire of **doing what is r**. *2818*
Heb 1: 3 he sat down at the **r hand** of the Majesty *1288*
1:13 "Sit at my **r hand** until I make your enemies *1288*
8: 1 a high priest, who sat down at the **r hand** of *1288*
10:12 he sat down at the **r hand** of God. *1288*
12: 2 sat down at the **r hand** of the throne of God. *1288*
13:10 at the tabernacle have no **r** to eat. *2026*
Jas 2: 8 your neighbor as yourself," you are doing **r**. *2822*
1Pe 2:14 and to commend *those* **who do r**. *18*
3: 6 You are her daughters *if you* **do what is r** *16*
3:14 But even if you should suffer for **what is r**, *1466*
3:22 into heaven and is at God's **r hand**— *1288*
2Pe 1:13 I think it is **r** to refresh your memory *1465*
1Jn 2:29 everyone who does **what is r** has been born *1466*
3: 7 He who does **what is r** is righteous, *1466*
3:10 Anyone who does not do **what is r** is not *1466*
Rev 1:16 In his **r** hand he held seven stars, *1288*
1:17 Then he placed his **r hand** on me and said: *1288*
1:20 the seven stars that you saw in my **r hand** *1288*
2: 1 the seven stars in his **r hand** and walks *1288*
2: 7 I will give the **r** to eat from the tree of life, *NIG*
3:21 the **r** to sit with me on my throne, *NIG*
5: 1 Then I saw in the **r hand** of him who sat on *1288*
5: 7 came and took the scroll from the **r hand** *1288*
10: 2 He planted his **r** foot on the sea *1288*
10: 5 and on the land raised his **r** hand to heaven. *1288*
13:16 a mark on his **r** hand or on his forehead, *1288*
22:11 let him who *does* **r** continue to do right; *1465*
22:11 let him who does right continue to do **r**; *1466*
22:14 the **r** to the tree of life and may go through *2026*

RIGHT-HANDED (1) [HAND]

1Ch 12: 2 to shoot arrows or to sling stones **r** or 3554

RIGHTEOUS (303) [OVERRIGHTEOUS, RIGHTEOUSLY, RIGHTEOUSNESS, RIGHTEOUSNESS']

Ge 6: 9 Noah was a **r** man, 7404
7: 1 I have found you **r** in this generation. 7404
18:23 "Will you sweep away the **r** with 7404
18:24 What if there are fifty **r** *people* in the city? 7404
18:24 the place for the sake of the fifty **r** *people* 7404
18:25 to kill the **r** with the wicked, 7404
18:25 treating the **r** and the wicked alike. 7404
18:26 I find fifty **r** *people* in the city of Sodom, 7404
18:28 if the number of the **r** is five less than fifty? 7404
Ge 38:26 *"She is* more **r** than I, 7405
Ex 23: 8 and twists the words of the **r**. 7404
Nu 23:10 Let me die the death of the **r**, 3838
Dt 4: 8 so great as to have such **r** decrees and laws 7404
16:19 of the wise and twists the words of the **r**. 7404
24:13 be regarded as a **r act** in the sight of 7407
33:21 he carried out the LORD's **r will,** 7407
Jdg 5:11 They recite the **r acts** *of* the LORD, 7407
5:11 the **r acts** *of* his warriors in Israel. 7407
1Sa 12: 7 the **r acts** performed by the LORD for you 7407
24:17 "You are more **r** than I," he said. 7404
1Ki 3: 6 because he was faithful to you and **r** 7407
Ezr 9:15 O LORD, God of Israel, you are **r**! 7404
Ne 9: 8 because you are **r**. 7404
Job 4:17 *'Can* a mortal *be* more **r** than God? 7405
9: 2 But how *can* a mortal *be* **r** before God? 7405
12: 4 though **r** and blameless! 7404
15:14 or one born of woman, that *he could be* **r**? 7405
17: 9 Nevertheless, the **r** will hold to their ways, 7404
22: 3 the Almighty if *you were* **r**? 7405
22:19 "The **r** see their ruin and rejoice; 7404
25: 4 How then *can* a man *be* **r** before God? 7405
27:17 what he lays up the **r** will wear, 7404
32: 1 because he was **r** in his own eyes. 7404
33:26 he is restored by God to his **r state.** 7407
35: 7 If *you are* **r**, what do you give to him, 7405
36: 7 He does not take his eyes off the **r**; 7404
Ps 1: 5 nor sinners in the assembly of the **r**. 7404
1: 6 the LORD watches over the way of the **r**, 7404
4: 1 Answer me when I call you, O my **r** God. 7406
5:12 For surely, O LORD, you bless the **r**; 7404
7: 9 O **r** God, who searches minds and hearts, 7404
7: 9 of the wicked and make the **r** secure. 7404
7:11 God is a **r** judge, 7404
11: 3 what can the **r** do?" 7404
11: 5 The LORD examines the **r**, 7404
11: 7 For the LORD is **r**, he loves justice; 7404
14: 5 for God is present in the company of the **r**. 7404
15: 2 and who does *what* is **r**, 7406
17: 1 Hear, O LORD, my **r** plea; 7406
19: 9 of the LORD are sure and altogether **r**. 7405
31:18 they speak arrogantly against the **r**. 7404
32:11 Rejoice in the LORD and be glad, you **r**; 7404
33: 1 Sing joyfully to the LORD, you **r**; 7404
34:15 the **r** and his ears are attentive to their cry; 7404
34:17 The **r** cry out, and the LORD hears them; NIH
34:19 A **r** *man* may have many troubles, 7404
34:21 the foes of the **r** will be condemned. 7404
37:12 against the **r** and gnash their teeth at them; 7404
37:16 the **r** have than the wealth of many wicked; 7404
37:17 but the LORD upholds the **r**. 7404
37:21 but the **r** give generously; 7404
37:25 yet I have never seen the **r** forsaken 7404
37:29 the **r** will inherit the land and dwell 7404
37:30 The mouth of the **r** *man* utters wisdom, 7404
37:32 The wicked lie in wait for the **r**, 7404
37:39 The salvation of the **r** comes from 7404
51:19 Then there will be **r** sacrifices, 7406
52: 6 The **r** will see and fear; 7404
55:22 he will never let the **r** fall. 7404
58:10 The **r** will be glad when they are avenged, 7404
58:11 "Surely the **r** still are rewarded; 7404
64:10 the **r** rejoice in the LORD and take refuge 7404
68: 3 may the **r** be glad and rejoice before God; 7404
69:28 the book of life and not be listed with the **r**. 7404
71:24 will tell of your **r acts** all day long, 7407
72: 7 In his days the **r** will flourish; 7404
75:10 but the horns of the **r** will be lifted up. 7404
88:12 or your **r deeds** in the land of oblivion? 7407
92:12 The **r** will flourish like a palm tree, 7404
94:21 the **r** and condemn the innocent to death. 7404
97:11 upon the **r** and joy on the upright in heart. 7404
97:12 Rejoice in the LORD, you *who* are **r**, 7404
112: 4 the gracious and compassionate and **r** *man*. 7404
112: 6 a **r** *man* will be remembered forever. 7404
116: 5 The LORD is gracious and **r**; 7404
118:15 and victory resound in the tents of the **r**: 7404
118:20 the LORD through which the **r** may enter. 7404
119: 7 with an upright heart as I learn your **r** laws. 7406
119:62 to give you thanks for your **r** laws. 7406
119:75 I know, O LORD, that your laws are **r**, 7406
119:106 that I will follow your **r** laws. 7406
119:121 I have done *what* is **r** and just; 7406
119:123 looking for your **r** promise. 7406
119:137 **R** are you, O LORD, 7404
119:138 The statutes you have laid down are **r**; 7406
119:160 all your **r** laws are eternal. 7406
119:164 a day I praise you for your **r** laws. 7406
119:172 for all your commands are **r**. 7406
125: 3 not remain over the land allotted to the **r**, 7404
125: 3 then the **r** might use their hands to do evil. 7404
129: 4 But the LORD is **r**; 7404
140:13 Surely the **r** will praise your name and 7404
141: 5 Let a **r** *man* strike me—it is a kindness; 7404
142: 7 Then the **r** will gather about me because 7404
143: 2 for no one living *is* **r** before you. 7405
145:17 The LORD is **r** in all his ways and loving 7404
146: 8 the LORD loves the **r**. 7404
Pr 2:20 of good men and keep to the paths of the **r**. 7404
3:33 but he blesses the home of the **r**. 7404
4:18 The path of the **r** is like the first gleam 7404
9: 9 a **r** *man* and he will add to his learning. 7404
10: 3 the **r** go hungry but he thwarts the craving 7404
10: 6 Blessings crown the head of the **r**, 7404
10: 7 The memory of the **r** will be a blessing, 7404
10:11 The mouth of the **r** is a fountain of life, 7404
10:16 The wages of the **r** bring them life, 7404

Pr 10:20 The tongue of the r is choice silver, 7404
10:21 The lips of the r nourish many, 7404
10:24 what the r desire will be granted. 7404
10:25 but the r stand firm forever. 7404
10:28 The prospect of the r is joy, 7404
10:29 way of the LORD is a refuge for the r, 9448
10:30 The r will never be uprooted, 7404
10:31 The mouth of the r brings forth wisdom, 7404
10:32 The lips of the r know what is fitting, 7404
11: 8 The r *man* is rescued from trouble, 7404
11: 9 but through knowledge the r escape. 7404
11:10 When the r prosper, the city rejoices; 7404
11:19 The truly r *man* attains life, 7407
11:21 but *those who* are r will go free. 2446+7404
11:23 The desire of the r ends only in good, 7404
11:28 but the r will thrive like a green leaf. 7404
11:30 The fruit of the r is a tree of life, 7404
11:31 If the r receive their due on earth, 7404
12: 3 but the r cannot be uprooted. 7404
12: 5 The plans of the r are just, 7404
12: 7 but the house of the r stands firm. 7404
12:10 A r *man* cares for the needs of his animal, 7404
12:12 but the root of the r flourishes. 7404
12:13 but a r *man* escapes trouble. 7404
12:21 No harm befalls the r, 7404
12:26 A r *man* is cautious in friendship, 7404
13: 5 The r hate what is false, 7404
13: 9 The light of the r shines brightly, 7404
13:21 but prosperity is the reward of the r. 7404
13:22 but a sinner's wealth is stored up for the r. 7404
13:25 The r eat to their hearts' content, 7404
14:19 and the wicked at the gates of the r. 7404
14:32 but even in death the r have a refuge. 7404
15: 6 The house of the r contains great treasure, 7404
15:28 The heart of the r weighs its answers, 7404
15:29 the wicked but he hears the prayer of the r. 7404
16:31 it is attained by a r life. 7407
18:10 the r run to it and are safe. 7404
20: 7 The r *man* leads a blameless life; 7404
21:12 The **R One** takes note of the house of 7404
21:15 it brings joy to the r but terror to evildoers. 7404
21:18 The wicked become a ransom for the r, 7404
21:26 but the r give without sparing. 7404
23:24 The father of a r *man* has great joy; 7404
24:15 like an outlaw against a r *man's* house, do 7404
24:16 for though a r *man* falls seven times, 7404
25:26 or a polluted well is a r *man* who gives way 7404
28: 1 but the r are as bold as a lion. 7404
28:12 When the r triumph, there is great elation; 7404
28:28 but when the wicked perish, the r thrive. 7404
29: 2 When the r thrive, the people rejoice; 7404
29: 6 but a r *one* can sing and be glad. 7404
29: 7 The r care about justice for the poor, 7404
29:16 but the r will see their downfall. 7404
29:27 The r detest the dishonest; 7404
Ecc 3:17 "God will bring to judgment both the r and 7404
7:15 a r *man* perishing in his righteousness, 7404
7:20 not a r man on earth who does what is right 7404
8:14 r *men* who get what the wicked deserve, 7404
8:14 wicked men who get what the r deserve. 7404
9: 1 that the r and the wise and what they do are 7404
9: 2 the r and the wicked, the good and the bad, 7404
Isa 3:10 Tell the r it will be well with them, 7404
10:22 Destruction has been decreed, overwhelming and r. 7407
24:16 "Glory to the **R One.**" 7404
26: 2 Open the gates that the r nation may enter, 7404
26: 7 The path of the r is level; 7404
26: 7 you make the way of the r smooth. 7404
41:10 I will uphold you with my r right hand. 7406
45:21 a r God and a Savior; there is none but me. 7404
45:25 the descendants of Israel *will be found* r 7405
53:11 by his knowledge my r servant will justify many, 7404
57: 1 r perish, and no one ponders it in his heart; 7404
57: 1 the r are taken away to be spared from evil. 7404
60:21 be r and they will possess the land forever. 7404
64: 6 and all our r **acts** are like filthy rags; 7407
Jer 3:11 "Faithless Israel *is* more r than unfaithful Judah. 7405
4: 2 a truthful, just and r *way* you swear, 7407
12: 1 You are always r, O LORD, 7404
20:12 you who examine the r and probe the heart 7404
23: 5 "when I will raise up to David a r Branch, 7404
31:23 'The LORD bless you, O r dwelling, 7406
33:15 at that time I will make a r Branch sprout 7407
La 1:18 "The LORD is r, yet I rebelled against his 7404
4:13 who shed within her the blood of the r. 7404
Eze 3:20 when a r *man* turns from his righteousness 7404
3:20 The r **things** he did will not be remembered, 7407
3:21 the r *man* not to sin and he does not sin, 7404
13:22 you disheartened the r with your lies, 7404
16:51 and *have* **made** your sisters **seem** r 7405
16:52 *they* **appear** more r than you. 7405
16:52 for *you have* **made** your sisters **appear** r. 7405
18: 5 a r man who does what is just and right. 7404
18: 9 That man is r; he will surely live, 7404
18:20 of the r *man* will be credited to him, 7404
18:22 of the r **things** he has done, he will live. 7407
18:24 "But if a r *man* turns from his righteousness 7404
18:24 None of the r **things** he has done will 7407
18:26 If a r *man* turns from his righteousness 7404
21: 3 from you both the r and the wicked. 7404
21: 4 I am going to cut off the r and the wicked, 7404
23:45 But r men will sentence them to 7404
33:12 'The righteousness of the r *man* will 7404
33:12 The r *man*, if he sins, 7404
Eze 33:13 If I tell the r *man* that he will surely live, 7404
33:13 none of the r **things** he has done will 7407
33:18 If a r *man* turns from his righteousness 7404
Da 9: 7 you are r, but this day we are covered 7407
9:14 LORD our God is r in everything he does; 7404
9:16 O Lord, in keeping with all your r **acts,** 7407
9:18 not make requests of you because we are r, 7407
Hos 14: 9 the r walk in them, 7404
Am 2: 6 They sell the r for silver, 7404
5:12 the r and take bribes and you deprive 7404
Mic 6: 5 you may know the r **acts** *of* the LORD." 7407
Hab 1: 4 The wicked hem in the r, 7404
1:13 up *those* more r than themselves? 7404
2: 4 but the r will live by his faith— 7404
Zep 3: 5 LORD within her is r; he does no wrong. 7404
Zec 8: 8 be my people, and I will be faithful and r 7407
9: 9 king comes to you, r and having salvation, 7404
Mal 3:18 the distinction between the r and 7404
Mt 1:19 Because Joseph her husband was a r *man* *1465*
5:45 and sends rain on the r and the unrighteous. *1465*
9:13 I have not come to call the r, but sinners." *1465*
10:41 and anyone who receives a r *man* *1465*
10:41 because he is a r *man* will receive *1465*
10:41 will receive a r *man's* reward. *1465*
13:17 and r *men* longed to see what you see *1465*
13:43 the r will shine like the sun in the kingdom *1465*
13:49 and separate the wicked from the r *1465*
23:28 on the outside you appear to people as r but *1465*
23:29 and decorate the graves *of* the r. *1465*
23:35 And so upon you will come all the r blood *1465*
23:35 *of* r Abel to the blood of Zechariah son *1465*
25:37 "Then the r will answer him, 'Lord, *1465*
25:46 but the r to eternal life." *1465*
Mk 2:17 I have not come to call the r, but sinners." *1465*
6:20 knowing him to be a r and holy man. *1465*
Lk 1:17 the disobedient to the wisdom *of* the r— *1465*
2:25 who was r and devout. *1465*
5:32 I have not come to call the r, *1465*
14:14 be repaid at the resurrection *of* the r." *1465*
15: 7 over ninety-nine r *persons* who do not need *1465*
23:47 "Surely this was a r man." *1465*
Jn 17:25 "**R** Father, though the world does *1465*
Ac 3:14 and **R** *One* and asked that a murderer *1465*
7:52 the coming *of* the **R** *One.* *1465*
10:22 He is a r and God-fearing man, *1465*
22:14 to know his will and to see the **R** *One* and *1465*
24:15 a resurrection *of* both the r and the wicked. *1465*
Ro 1:17 "The r will live by faith." *1465*
1:32 Although they know God's r **decree** *1468*
2: 5 when his r **judgment** will be revealed. *1464*
2:13 not those who hear the law who are r *1465*
2:13 the law who *will be* **declared** r. *1467*
3:10 "There is no *one* r, not even one; *1465*
3:20 *be* **declared** r in his sight by observing *1467*
5: 7 Very rarely will anyone die for a r *man,* *1465*
5:19 of the one man the many will be made r. *1465*
7:12 and the commandment is holy, r and good. *1465*
8: 4 that the r **requirements** of the law might *1468*
Gal 3:11 because, "The r will live by faith." *1465*
1Th 2:10 r and blameless we were among you *1469*
1Ti 1: 9 not *for* the r but for lawbreakers and rebels, *1465*
2Ti 4: 8 the r Judge, will award to me on that day— *1465*
Tit 3: 5 not because of r things we had done, *1466+1877*
Heb 10:38 But my r *one* will live by faith. *1465*
11: 4 By faith he was commended as a r *man,* *1465*
12:23 to the spirits *of* r *men* made perfect, *1465*
Jas 1:20 not bring about the r **life** that God desires. *1466*
2:21 *Was* not our ancestor Abraham **considered** r for what he did *1467*
2:25 the prostitute **considered** r for what she did *1467*
5:16 prayer *of* a r *man* is powerful and effective. *1465*
1Pe 3:12 For the eyes of the Lord are on the r *1465*
3:18 the r for the unrighteous, to bring you *1465*
4:18 And, "If it is hard for the r to be saved, *1465*
2Pe 2: 7 Lot, a r *man,* who was distressed by *1465*
2: 8 (for that r *man,* living among them day *1465*
2: 8 in his r soul by the lawless deeds he saw *1465*
1Jn 2: 1 Jesus Christ, the **R** *One.* *1465*
2:29 If you know that he is r, *1465*
3: 7 He who does what is right is r, *1465*
3: 7 what is right is righteous, just as he is r. *1465*
3:12 and his brother's were r. *1465*
Rev 15: 4 for your r **acts** have been revealed." *1468*
19: 8 Fine linen stands for the r **acts** of the saints. *1468*

RIGHTEOUSLY (3) [RIGHTEOUS]

Ps 9: 4 you have sat on your throne, judging r. 7406
Isa 33:15 He who walks r and speaks what is right, 7407
Jer 11:20 you who judge r and test the heart 7406

RIGHTEOUSNESS (239) [RIGHTEOUS]

Ge 15: 6 Abram believed the LORD, and he credited it to him as r. 7407
Dt 6:25 he has commanded us, that will be our r." 7407
9: 4 of this land because of my r." 7407
9: 5 It is not because of your r or your integrity 7407
9: 6 that it is not because of your r that 7407
33:19 and there offer sacrifices of r; 7406
1Sa 26:23 The LORD rewards every man for his r 7407
2Sa 22:21 LORD has dealt with me according to my r; 7407
22:25 LORD has rewarded me according to my r, 7407
23: 3 'When one rules over men in r, 7404
1Ki 10: 9 to maintain justice and r." 7407
2Ch 9: 8 to maintain justice and r." 7407
Job 27: 6 I will maintain my r and never let go of it; 7407
Job 29:14 I put on r as my clothing; 7406
35: 8 and your r only the sons of men. 7407
37:23 in his justice and great r, 7407
Ps 5: 8 in your r because of my enemies— 7407
7: 8 Judge me, O LORD, according to my r, 7406
7:17 of his r and will sing praise to the name of 7406
9: 8 He will judge the world in r; 7406
17:15 And I—in r I will see your face; 7406
18:20 LORD has dealt with me according to my r; 7406
18:24 LORD has rewarded me according to my r, 7406
22:31 They will proclaim his r to a people 7407
23: 3 in paths of r for his name's sake. 7406
31: 1 deliver me in your r. 7407
33: 5 The LORD loves r and justice; 7407
35:24 Vindicate me in your r, O LORD my God; 7406
35:28 of your r and of your praises all day long. 7406
36: 6 Your r is like the mighty mountains, 7407
36:10 your r to the upright in heart. 7407
37: 6 He will make your r shine like the dawn, 7406
40: 9 I proclaim r in the great assembly; 7406
40:10 I do not hide your r in my heart; 7407
45: 4 in behalf of truth, humility and r; 7406
45: 7 You love r and hate wickedness; 7406
48:10 your right hand is filled with r. 7406
50: 6 And the heavens proclaim his r, 7406
51:14 and my tongue will sing of your r. 7407
65: 5 You answer us with awesome deeds of r, 7406
71: 2 Rescue me and deliver me in your r; 7407
71:15 My mouth will tell of your r, 7407
71:16 I will proclaim your r, yours alone. 7407
71:19 Your r reaches to the skies, O God, 7407
72: 1 O God, the royal son with your r. 7407
72: 2 He will judge your people in r, 7406
72: 3 the hills the fruit of r. 7407
85:10 r and peace kiss each other. 7406
85:11 and r looks down from heaven. 7406
85:13 **R** goes before him and prepares the way 7406
89:14 **R** and justice are the foundation 7406
89:16 they exult in your r. 7407
94:15 Judgment will again be founded on r, 7406
96:13 the world in r and the peoples in his truth. 7406
97: 2 r and justice are the foundation 7406
97: 6 The heavens proclaim his r, 7406
98: 2 and revealed his r to the nations. 7407
98: 9 the world in r and the peoples with equity. 7406
103: 6 The LORD works r and justice for all 7407
103:17 and his r with their children's children— 7407
106:31 to him as r for endless generations to come. 7407
111: 3 and his r endures forever. 7407
112: 3 and his r endures forever. 7407
112: 9 his r endures forever; 7407
118:19 Open for me the gates of r; 7406
119:40 Preserve my life in your r. 7407
119:142 Your r is everlasting and your law is true. 7407
132: 9 May your priests be clothed with r; 7406
143: 1 in your faithfulness and r come 7407
143:11 in your r, bring me out of trouble. 7407
145: 7 and joyfully sing of your r. 7407
Pr 8:20 I walk in the way of r, 7407
10: 2 but r delivers from death. 7407
11: 4 but r delivers from death. 7407
11: 5 The r *of* the blameless makes a straight way 7407
11: 6 The r *of* the upright delivers them, 7407
11:18 but he who sows r reaps a sure reward. 7407
12:28 In the way of r there is life; 7407
13: 6 **R** guards the man of integrity, 7407
14:34 **R** exalts a nation, but sin is a disgrace 7407
15: 9 but he loves those who pursue r. 7407
16: 8 a little with r than much gain with injustice. 7407
16:12 for a throne is established through r. 7407
21:21 He who pursues r and love finds life, 7407
25: 5 his throne will be established through r. 7406
Ecc 7:15 a righteous man perishing in his r, 7406
Isa 1:21 r used to dwell in her—but now murderers! 7406
1:26 Afterward you will be called the City of **R,** 7406
1:27 her penitent ones with r. 7407
5: 7 for r, but heard cries of distress. 7407
5:16 holy God will show himself holy by his r. 7407
9: 7 and upholding it with justice and r from 7407
11: 4 but with r he will judge the needy, 7406
11: 5 **R** will be his belt and faithfulness the sash 7406
16: 5 and speeds the cause of r. 7406
26: 9 the people of the world learn r. 7406
26:10 they do not learn r; 7406
28:17 I will make justice the measuring line and r 7407
32: 1 a king will reign in r and rulers will rule 7406
32:16 Justice will dwell in the desert and r live in 7407
32:17 The fruit of r will be peace; 7407
32:17 the effect of r will be quietness 7407
33: 5 he will fill Zion with justice and r. 7407
41: 2 calling him *in* r to his service? 7406
42: 6 the LORD, have called you in r; 7406
42:21 of his r to make his law great and glorious. 7406
45: 8 "You heavens above, rain down r; 7406
45: 8 let salvation spring up, let r grow with it; 7407
45:13 I will raise up Cyrus in my r: 7406
45:24 'In the LORD alone are r and strength.'" 7407
46:12 you who are far from r. 7407
46:13 I am bringing my r near, it is not far away; 7407
48: 1 but not in truth or r— 7407
48:18 your r like the waves of the sea. 7407
51: 1 you who pursue r and who seek 7406
51: 5 My r draws near speedily, 7406
51: 6 my r will never fail. 7407
51: 8 But my r will last forever, 7407
54:14 In r you will be established: 7407
56: 1 at hand and my r will soon be revealed. 7407

Isa 57:12 I will expose your **r** and your works, 7407
58: 8 then your **r** will go before you, 7406
59: 9 and **r** does not reach us. 7407
59:14 and **r** stands at a distance; 7407
59:16 and his own **r** sustained him. 7407
59:17 He put on **r** as his breastplate, 7407
60:17 peace your governor and **r** your ruler. 7407
61: 3 They will be called oaks of **r**, 7406
61:10 of salvation and arrayed me in a robe of **r**, 7407
61:11 so the Sovereign LORD will make **r** 7407
62: 1 till her **r** shines out like the dawn, 7406
62: 2 The nations will see your **r**, 7406
63: 1 "It is I, speaking in **r**, mighty to save." 7407
Jer 9:24 justice and **r** on earth, 7407
23: 6 will be called: The LORD Our **R**. 7406
33:16 will be called: The LORD Our **R**.' 7406
Eze 3:20 when a righteous man turns from his **r** 7406
14:14 they could save only themselves by their **r**, 7407
14:20 They would save only themselves by their **r**. 7407
18:20 The **r** *of* the righteous man will be credited 7407
18:24 "But if a righteous man turns from his **r** 7407
18:26 from his **r** and commits sin, he will die 7407
33:12 'The **r** *of* the righteous man will 7407
33:12 be allowed to live because of **his former r**.' 2023S
33:13 but then he trusts in his **r** and does evil, 7407
33:18 If a righteous man turns from his **r** 7407
Da 9:24 to bring in everlasting **r**, 7406
12: 3 and *those who* **lead** many **to r**, 7405
Hos 2:19 I will betroth you in **r** and justice, 7406
10:12 Sow for yourselves **r**, reap the fruit 7407
10:12 until he comes and showers **r** on you. 7406
Joel 2:23 for he has given you the autumn rains in **r**. 7407
Am 5: 7 into bitterness and cast **r** to the ground 7407
5:24 **r** like a never-failing stream! 7407
6:12 and the fruit of **r** into bitterness— 7407
Mic 7: 9 I will see his **r**. 7407
Zep 2: 3 Seek **r**, seek humility; 7406
Mal 3: 3 Then the LORD will have men who will bring offerings in **r**, 7407
4: 2 sun of **r** will rise with healing in its wings. 7407
Mt 3:15 it is proper for us to do this to fulfill all **r**." *1466*
5: 6 Blessed are those who hunger and thirst for **r**, *1466*
5:10 Blessed are those who are persecuted because *of* **r**, *1466*
5:20 For I tell you that unless your **r** surpasses *1466*
6: 1 not to do your **'acts of r'** before men, *1466*
6:33 But seek first his kingdom and his **r**, *1466*
21:32 to you to show you the way *of* **r**, *1466*
Lk 1:75 in holiness and **r** before him all our days. *1466*
18: 9 To some who were confident of their own **r** *1465*
Jn 16: 8 of guilt in regard to sin and **r** and judgment: *1466*
16:10 to **r**, because I am going to the Father, *1466*
Ac 24:25 As Paul discoursed on **r**, self-control *1466*
Ro 1:17 For in the gospel a **r** from God is revealed, *1466*
1:17 a **r** that is by faith from first to last, *NIG*
3: 5 But if our unrighteousness brings out God's **r** more clearly, *1466*
3:21 But now a **r** from God, apart from law, *1466*
3:22 This **r** from God comes through faith *1466*
4: 3 and it was credited to him as **r**." *1466*
4: 5 his faith is credited as **r**. *1466*
4: 6 to whom God credits **r** apart from works: *1466*
4: 9 Abraham's faith was credited to him as **r**. *1466*
4:11 a seal *of* the **r** that he had by faith *1466*
4:11 in order that **r** might be credited to them. *1466*
4:13 but through the **r** that comes by faith. *1466*
4:22 This is why "it was credited to him as **r**." *1466*
4:24 to whom God will credit **r**— *NIG*
5:17 of grace and of the gift *of* **r** reign in life *1466*
5:18 the result of one **act of r** was justification *1468*
5:21 so also grace might reign through **r** *1466*
6:13 of your body to him as instruments *of* **r**. *1466*
6:16 or to obedience, which leads to **r**? *1466*
6:18 from sin and have become slaves *to* **r**. *1466*
6:19 so now offer them in slavery *to* **r** leading *1466*
6:20 you were free *from* the control of **r**. *1466*
8:10 yet your spirit is alive because of **r**. *1466*
9:30 That the Gentiles, who did not pursue **r**, *1466*
9:30 have obtained it, a **r** that is by faith; *1466*
9:31 who pursued a law *of* **r**, has not attained it. *1466*
10: 3 Since they did not know the **r** that comes *1466*
10: 3 they did not submit *to* God's **r**. *1466*
10: 4 the end of the law so that there may be **r** *1466*
10: 5 Moses describes in this way the **r** that is by *1466*
10: 6 But the **r** that is by faith says: *1466*
14:17 but *of* **r**, peace and joy in the Holy Spirit, *1466*
1Co 1:30 that is, our **r**, holiness and redemption. *1466*
2Co 3: 9 more glorious is the ministry that brings **r**! *1466*
5:21 that in him we might become the **r** of God. *1466*
6: 7 with weapons *of* **r** in the right hand and in *1466*
6:14 what do **r** and wickedness have in common? *1466*
9: 9 his **r** endures forever." *1466*
9:10 and will enlarge the harvest *of* your **r**. *1466*
11:15 if his servants masquerade as servants *of* **r**. *1466*
Gal 2:21 for if **r** could be gained through the law, *1466*
3: 6 and it was credited to him as **r**." *1466*
3:21 **r** would certainly have come by the law. *1466*
5: 5 through the Spirit the **r** for which we hope. *1466*
Eph 4:24 to be like God in true **r** and holiness. *1466*
5: 9 of the light consists in all goodness, **r** *1466*
6:14 with the breastplate *of* **r** in place, *1466*
Php 1:11 *of* **r** that comes through Jesus Christ— *1466*
3: 6 as for legalistic **r**, faultless. *1466*
3: 9 a **r** of my own that comes from the law, but *1466*
3: 9 the **r** that comes from God and is by faith. *1466*
1Ti 6:11 flee from all this, and pursue **r**, godliness, *1466*
2Ti 2:22 Flee the evil desires of youth, and pursue **r**, *1466*
3:16 rebuking, correcting and training in **r**, *1466*
4: 8 there is in store for me the crown *of* **r**, *1466*
Heb 1: 8 and **r** will be the scepter of your kingdom. *2319*
1: 9 You have loved **r** and hated wickedness; *1466*
5:13 not acquainted with the teaching *about* **r**. *1466*
7: 2 First, his name means "king *of* **r**"; *1466*
11: 7 and became heir *of* the **r** that comes *1466*
12:11 it produces a harvest *of* **r** and peace *1466*
Jas 2:23 and it was credited to him as **r**," *1466*
3:18 who sow in peace raise a harvest *of* **r**. *1466*
1Pe 2:24 so that we might die to sins and live *for* **r**; *1466*
2Pe 1: 1 To those who through the **r** of our God *1466*
2: 5 but protected Noah, a preacher *of* **r**, *1466*
2:21 for them not to have known the way *of* **r**, *1466*
3:13 new heaven and a new earth, the home of **r**. *1466*

RIGHTFUL (1) [RIGHT]

Job 8: 6 and restore you to your **r** place. 7406

RIGHTFULLY (1) [RIGHT]

Eze 21:27 until he comes to whom it **r** belongs; 5477

RIGHTLY (3) [RIGHT]

Ge 27:36 Esau said, "Isn't he **r** named Jacob? 3954
Jn 13:13 and **r** so, for that is what I am. *2822*
2Th 1: 3 to thank God for you, brothers, and **r so**, *545+1639*

RIGHTS (18) [RIGHT]

Ex 21: 9 he must grant her the **r** *of* a daughter. 5477
21:10 food, clothing and **marital r**. 6703
Dt 21:16 *he must* **not give the r of the firstborn** 1144
1Ch 5: 1 his **r as firstborn** were given to the sons 1148
5: 2 the **r of the firstborn** belonged 1148
Job 36: 6 but gives the afflicted their **r**. 5477
Ps 82: 3 **maintain** *the* **r** *of* the poor and oppressed. 7405
Pr 31: 5 and deprive all the oppressed of their **r**. 1907
31: 8 for the **r** *of* all who are destitute. 1907
31: 9 **defend** the **r** *of* the poor and needy." 1906
Ecc 5: 8 and justice and **r** denied, 7406
Isa 10: 2 the poor of their **r** and withhold justice 1907
Jer 5:28 they do not defend the **r** *of* the poor. 5477
La 3:35 to deny a man his **r** before the Most High, 5477
1Co 9:15 But I have not used any of these **r**. *NIG*
9:18 so not make use of my **r** in preaching it. *2026*
Gal 4: 5 that we might receive the **full r of sons**. *5625*
Heb 12:16 sold his **inheritance r as the oldest son**. *4757*

RIGID (1)

Mk 9:18 gnashes his teeth and **becomes r**. *3830*

RIGOUR (KJV) See RUTHLESSLY

RIM (24) [RIMS]

Ex 25:25 around it a **r** a handbreadth wide and put 4995
25:25 and put a gold molding on the **r**. 4995
25:27 to the **r** to hold the poles used in carrying 4995
37:12 also made around it a **r** a handbreadth wide 4995
37:12 and put a gold molding on the **r**. 4995
37:14 to the **r** to hold the poles used in carrying 4995
Dt 2:36 From Aroer on the **r** *of* the Arnon Gorge, 8557
4:48 This land extended from Aroer on the **r** *of* 8557
Jos 12: 2 from Aroer on the **r** *of* the Arnon Gorge— 8557
13: 9 from Aroer on the **r** *of* the Arnon Gorge, 8557
13:16 from Aroer on the **r** *of* the Arnon Gorge, 8557
1Ki 7:23 measuring ten cubits from **r** to rim 8557
7:23 measuring ten cubits from rim to **r** 8557
7:24 Below the **r**, gourds encircled it— 8557
7:26 and its **r** was like the rim of a cup, 8557
7:26 and its rim was like the **r** *of* a cup, 8557
2Ch 4: 2 measuring ten cubits from **r** to rim 8557
4: 2 measuring ten cubits from rim to **r** 8557
4: 3 Below **the r**, figures of bulls encircled it— 2257S
4: 5 and its **r** was like the rim of a cup, 8557
4: 5 and its rim was like the **r** *of* a cup, 8557
Eze 43:13 with a **r** of one span around the edge. 1473
43:17 with a **r** of half a cubit and a gutter of 1473
43:20 of the upper ledge and all around the **r**, 1473

RIMMON (13) [EN RIMMON, GATH RIMMON, HADAD RIMMON, RIMMON PEREZ]

Jos 15:32 Lebaoth, Shilhim, Ain and **R**— 8234
19: 7 **R**, Ether and Ashan— 8234
19:13 it came out at **R** and turned toward Neah. 8234
Jdg 20:45 and fled toward the desert to the rock of **R**, 8234
20:47 and fled into the desert to the rock of **R**, 8234
21:13 of peace to the Benjamites at the rock of **R**. 8234
2Sa 4: 2 they were sons of **R** the Beerothite from 8233
4: 5 the sons of **R** the Beerothite, 8233
4: 9 the sons of **R** the Beerothite, 8233
2Ki 5:18 When my master enters the temple of **R** 8235
5:18 when I bow down in the temple of **R**, 8235
1Ch 4:32 Ain, **R**, Token and Ashan— 8234
Zec 14:10 The whole land, from Geba to **R**, 8234

RIMMON PEREZ (2) [PEREZ, RIMMON]

Nu 33:19 They left Rithmah and camped at **R**. 8236
33:20 They left **R** and camped at Libnah. 8236

RIMMONO (1)

1Ch 6:77 **R** and Tabor, together with their 8237

RIMS (3) [RIM]

1Ki 7:33 **r**, spokes and hubs were all of cast metal. 1461
Eze 1:18 Their **r** were high and awesome, 1461
1:18 and all four **r** were full of eyes all around. 1461

RING (23) [RANG, RINGED, RINGS]

Ge 24:22 the man took out a gold **nose r** weighing 5690
24:30 As soon as he had seen the **nose r**, 5690
24:47 the **r** in her nose and the bracelets 5690
41:42 Then Pharaoh took his **signet r** 3192
Ex 26:24 and fitted into a single **r**; 3192
27: 4 a bronze **r** at each of the four corners of 3192
36:29 to the top and fitted into a single **r**; 3192
Jdg 8:25 each man threw a **r** *from* his plunder onto it. 5690
Est 3:10 So the king took his **signet r** from his finger 3192
3:12 and sealed with his own **r**. 3192
8: 2 The king took off his **signet r**, 3192
8: 8 and seal it with the king's **signet r**— 3192
8: 8 the king's name and sealed with his **r** can 3192
8:10 the dispatches with the king's **signet r**, 3192
Job 16:16 deep shadows **r** my eyes; 6584
42:11 a piece of silver and a gold **r**. 5690
Pr 11:22 Like a gold **r** in a pig's snout is 5690
Jer 22:24 were a **signet r** on my right hand, 2597
Eze 16:12 and I put a **r** on your nose, 5690
Da 6:17 and the king sealed it with his own **signet r** 10536
Hag 2:23 'and I will make you like my **signet r**, 2597
Lk 15:22 Put a **r** on his finger and sandals on his feet. *1234*
Jas 2: 2 into your meeting **wearing a gold r** *5993*

RINGED (1) [RING]

Job 41:14 **r about** *with* his fearsome teeth? 6017

RINGLEADER (1) [LEAD]

Ac 24: 5 He is a **r** of the Nazarene sect *4756*

RINGS (42) [RING]

Ge 35: 4 the foreign gods they had and the **r** in their 5690
Ex 25:12 Cast four gold **r** for it and fasten them 3192
25:12 with two **r** on one side and two rings on 3192
25:12 with two rings on one side and two **r** on 3192
25:14 the poles into the **r** on the sides of the chest 3192
25:15 The poles are to remain in the **r** *of* this ark; 3192
25:26 Make four gold **r** for the table 3192
25:27 The **r** are to be close to the rim to hold 3192
26:29 and make gold **r** to hold the crossbars. 3192
27: 7 into the **r** so they will be on two sides of 3192
28:23 Make two gold **r** for it and fasten them 3192
28:24 the two gold chains to the **r** at the corners 3192
28:26 Make two gold **r** and attach them to 3192
28:27 Make two more gold **r** and attach them to 3192
28:28 The **r** *of* the breastpiece are to be tied to 3192
28:28 be tied to the **r** *of* the ephod with blue cord, 3192
30: 4 Make two gold **r** for the altar below 3192
35:22 brooches, earrings, **r** and ornaments. 3192
36:34 and made gold **r** to hold the crossbars. 3192
37: 3 He cast four gold **r** for it and fastened them 3192
37: 3 with two **r** on one side and two rings on 3192
37: 3 with two rings on one side and two **r** on 3192
37: 5 into the **r** on the sides of the ark to carry it. 3192
37:13 They cast four gold **r** for the table 3192
37:14 The **r** were put close to the rim to hold 3192
37:27 They made two gold **r** below 3192
38: 5 They cast bronze **r** to hold the poles for 3192
38: 7 into the **r** so they would be on the sides of 3192
39:16 gold filigree settings and two gold **r**, 3192
39:16 and fastened the **r** to two of the corners of 3192
39:17 They fastened the two gold chains to the **r** 3192
39:19 They made two gold **r** and attached them to 3192
39:20 Then they made two more gold **r** 3192
39:21 the **r** *of* the breastpiece to the rings of 3192
39:21 of the breastpiece to the **r** *of* the ephod 3192
Nu 31:50 armlets, bracelets, **signet r**, 3192
Jdg 8:26 The weight of the gold **r** he asked for came 5690
Est 1: 6 and purple material to silver **r** 1664
Isa 3:21 the **signet r** and nose rings, 3192
3:21 the signet rings and nose **r**, 5690
Da 6:17 with his own signet ring and with the **r** 10536
Hos 2:13 she decked herself with **r** and jewelry, 5690

RINGSTRAKED (KJV) See STREAKED

RINNAH (1)

1Ch 4:20 Amnon, **R**, Ben-Hanan and Tilon. 8263

RINSED (3) [RINSING]

Lev 6:28 the pot is to be scoured and **r** with water. 8851
15:12 any wooden article *is to* **be r** with water. 8851
2Ch 4: 6 to be used for the burnt offerings *were* **r**, 1866

RINSING (1) [RINSED]

Lev 15:11 a discharge touches without **r** his hands 8851

RIOT (3) [RIOTERS, RIOTING, RIOTS]

Mt 26: 5 "or there may be a **r** among the people." *2573*
Mk 14: 2 they said, "or the people *may* **r**." *1639+2573*
Ac 17: 5 formed a mob and *started* a **r** in the city. *2572*

RIOTERS (1) [RIOT]
Ac 21:32 When **the r** saw the commander and *1254+3836*[S]

RIOTING (1) [RIOT]
Ac 19:40 in danger of being charged with **r** because *5087*

RIOTS (2) [RIOT]
Ac 24: 5 stirring up **r** among the Jews all over the world. *5087*
2Co 6: 5 in beatings, imprisonments and **r;** *189*

RIP (3) [RIPPED]
2Ki 8:12 and **r open** their pregnant women." 1324
Ps 7: 2 like a lion and **r** me **to pieces** with no one 7293
Hos 13: 8 attack them and **r** them **open.** 4213+6033+7973

RIPE (13) [RIPEN, RIPENED, RIPENING, RIPENS]
Nu 13:20 (It was the season for the **first r** grapes.) 1137
2Ki 4:42 from the **first r grain,** 1137
Isa 28: 4 will be like a **fig r** before harvest— 1136
Joel 3:13 Swing the sickle, for the harvest *is* **r.** 1418
Am 8: 1 a basket of **r fruit.** 7811
8: 2 "A basket of **r fruit,"** I answered. 7811
8: 2 "The **time is r** for my people Israel; 995+7891
Na 3:12 like fig trees with their **first r fruit;** 1137
Zec 8: 4 and women **of r old age** will sit in 2418
Mk 4:29 As soon as the grain *is* **r,** *4140*
Jn 4:35 They are **r** for harvest. *3328*
Rev 14:15 for the harvest of the earth *is* **r."** *3830*
14:18 because its grapes *are* **r."** *196*

RIPEN (2) [RIPE]
Ex 9:32 were not destroyed, because they **r later.)** 689
Jer 24: 2 like those that **r early;** 1136

RIPENED (3) [RIPE]
Ge 40:10 it blossomed, and its clusters **r** *into* grapes. 1418
Isa 16: 9 The shouts of joy over your **r fruit** and 7811
Jer 48:32 The destroyer has fallen on your **r fruit** 7811

RIPENING (1) [RIPE]
Isa 18: 5 and the flower becomes a **r** grape, 1694

RIPENS (1) [RIPE]
Hos 2: 9 I will take away my grain when it **r,** 6961

RIPHATH (2)
Ge 10: 3 Ashkenaz, **R** and Togarmah. 8196
1Ch 1: 6 Ashkenaz, **R** and Togarmah. 8196

RIPPED (3) [RIP]
2Ki 15:16 and **r open** all the pregnant women. 1324
Hos 13:16 their pregnant women **r open."** 1324
Am 1:13 Because he **r open** the pregnant women 1324

RISE (119) [ARISE, ARISEN, ARISES, AROSE, RAISE, RAISED, RAISES, RAISING, RISEN, RISES, RISING, ROSE, UPRAISED, UPRISING]
Lev 19:32 " **'R** in the presence of the aged, 7756
Nu 10:35 Moses said, **"R up,** O LORD! 7756
23:24 The people **r** like a lioness; 7756
24:17 a scepter *will* **r** out of Israel. 7756
Dt 28: 7 that the enemies who **r up** against you will 7756
28:43 The alien who lives among you *will* **r** 6590
32:38 *Let them* **r up** to help you! 7756
33:11 the loins of *those who* **r up** *against* him; 7756
33:11 strike his foes till *they* **r** no more." 7756
Jos 8: 7 *to* **r up** from ambush and take the city. 7756
Jdg 20:40 column of smoke began to **r** from the city, 6590
1Sa 16:12 Then the LORD said, **"R** and anoint him; 7756
2Sa 18:32 the king and all who **r up** to harm you be 7756
22:39 and *they could* not **r;** 7756
Ezr 10: 4 **R up;** this matter is in your hands. 7756
Job 14:12 so man lies down and *does* not **r;** 7756
20:27 the earth *will* **r up** against him. 7756
24:12 The **groans** of the dying *r* from the city, AIT
25: 3 Upon whom *does* his light not **r?** 7756
Ps 3: 1 How many **r up** against me! 7756
7: 6 **r up** against the rage of my enemies. 5951
17: 1 it does not **r** from deceitful lips. NIH
17:13 **R up,** O LORD, confront them, 7756
18:38 I crushed them so that they could not **r;** 7756
20: 8 but we **r up** and stand firm. 7756
27:12 for false witnesses **r up** against me, 7756
32: 6 mighty waters **r,** they will not reach him. 8852
35:23 Awake, and **r** to my defense! 7810
36:12 thrown down, not able *to* **r!** 7756
44:26 **R up** and help us; 7756
59: 1 protect me from *those who* **r up** *against* me. 7756
66: 7 *let* not the rebellious **r up** against him. 8123
74:22 **R up,** O God, and defend your cause; 7756
82: 8 **R up,** O God, judge the earth, 7756
88:10 *Do* those who are dead **r up** and praise you? 7756
94: 2 **R up,** O Judge of the earth; 5951
94:16 Who *will* **r up** for me against the wicked? 7756
119:62 At midnight *I* **r** to give you thanks 7756
Ps 119:147 *I* **r** before dawn and cry for help; 7709
127: 2 In vain you **r** early and stay up late, 7756
135: 7 *He* **makes** clouds **r** from the ends of the earth; 6590
139: 2 You know when I sit and *when* I **r;** 7756
139: 9 If *I* **r** *on* the wings of the dawn, 5951
139:21 and abhor *those who* **r up** *against* you? 7756
140:10 into miry pits, never *to* **r.** 7756
Pr 28:12 the wicked **r to power,** men go into hiding. 7756
28:28 wicked **r to power,** people go into hiding; 7756
Ecc 12: 4 when *men* **r up** at the sound of birds, 7756
Isa 3: 5 The young *will* **r up** against the old, 8104
5:11 to *those who* **r early** in the morning to run 8899
14: 9 *it* **makes** them **r** from their thrones— 7756
14:21 *to* **r** to inherit the land and cover the earth 7756
14:22 *"I will* **r up** against them," 7756
24:20 that it falls—never *to* **r** again. 7756
26:14 those departed spirits *do* **not r.** 7756
26:19 your dead will live; their bodies *will* **r.** 7756
28:21 The LORD *will* **r up** as he did 7756
31: 2 *He will* **r up** against the house of 7756
32: 9 **r up** and listen to me; 7756
33: 3 when you **r up,** the nations scatter. 8129
34:10 its smoke *will* **r** forever. 6590
43:17 and they lay there, never *to* **r** *again,* 7756
49: 7 "Kings will see you and **r up,** 7756
51:17 **R up,** O Jerusalem, you who have drunk 7756
52: 2 **r up,** sit enthroned, O Jerusalem. 7756
58:10 then your light *will* **r** in the darkness, 2436
Jer 10:13 *he* **makes** clouds **r** from the ends of the earth. 6590
25:27 and vomit, and fall *to* **r** no more because of 7756
46: 8 She says, *'I will* **r** and cover the earth; 6590
49:14 **R up** for battle!" 7756
51:16 *he* **makes** clouds **r** from the ends of the earth. 6590
51:42 The sea *will* **r** over Babylon; 6590
51:64 'So will Babylon sink *to* **r** no more 7756
Eze 1:20 and the wheels *would* **r** along with them, 5951
10:16 when the cherubim spread their wings to **r** 8123
17:14 brought low, unable *to* **r again,** 5951
Da 2:39 "After you, another kingdom *will* **r,** 10624
7:17 *that* will **r** from the earth. 10624
11:14 "In those times many *will* **r** against 6641
11:23 with only a few people *he will* **r** to power. 6590
11:31 "His armed forces *will* **r up** to desecrate 6641
12:13 and then at the end of the days *you will* **r** 6641
Hos 10:14 of battle *will* **r** against your people, so 7756
Joel 2:20 And its stench will go up; its smell *will* **r."** 6590
Am 5: 2 never *to* **r** again, deserted in her own land, 7756
7: 9 with my sword *I will* **r** against the house 7756
8: 8 The whole land *will* **r** like the Nile; 6590
8:14 they will fall, never *to* **r** again." 7756
Ob 1: 1 **"R,** and let us go against her for battle"— 7756
Mic 4:13 **"R** and thresh, O Daughter of Zion, 7756
7: 8 Though I have fallen, *I will* **r.** 7756
Mal 4: 2 the sun of righteousness *will* **r** with healing 2436
Mt 5:45 **causes** his sun **to r** on the evil and the good *422*
12:42 Queen of the South *will* **r** at the judgment *1586*
24: 7 Nation *will* **r** against nation, *1586*
26:46 **R,** let us go! Here comes my betrayer!" *1586*
27:63 'After three days *I will* **r again.'** *1586*
Mk 8:31 be killed and after three days **r again.** *482*
9:31 and after three days *he will* **r."** *482*
10:34 Three days later *he will* **r."** *482*
12:25 When the dead **r,** they will neither marry *482*
13: 8 Nation *will* **r** against nation, *1586*
14:42 **R!** Let us go! Here comes my betrayer!" *1586*
Lk 11:31 of the South *will* **r** at the judgment with *1586*
17:19 Then he said to him, **"R** and go; *482*
18:33 On the third day *he will* **r again."** *482*
20:37 even Moses showed that the dead **r,** *1586*
21:10 "Nation *will* **r** against nation, *1586*
24:38 and why *do* doubts **r** in your minds? *326*
24:46 The Christ will suffer and **r** from the dead *482*
Jn 5:29 those who have done good will **r** to live, *414*
5:29 to live, and those who have done evil will **r** *414*
11:23 "Your brother *will* **r again."** *482*
11:24 "I know *he will* **r again** in the resurrection *482*
20: 9 from Scripture that Jesus had *to* **r** from *482*
Ac 17: 3 that the Christ had to suffer and **r** from *482*
26:23 as the first to **r** from the dead, *414*
Eph 5:14 "Wake up, O sleeper, **r** from the dead, *482*
1Th 4:16 and the dead in Christ *will* **r** first. *482*

RISEN (16) [RISE]
Ge 19:23 the sun *had* **r** over the land. 3655
Dt 34:10 no prophet *has* **r** in Israel like Moses, 7756
2Sa 14: 7 Now the whole clan *has* **r up** 7756
Eze 47: 5 the water *had* **r** and was deep enough 1448
Mic 2: 8 Lately my people *have* **r up** like an enemy. 7756
Mt 11:11 not **r** anyone greater than John the Baptist; *1586*
14: 2 He is not here; he *has* **r** from the dead! *1586*
26:32 But after I *have* **r,** I will go ahead of you *1586*
28: 6 He is not here; *he has* **r,** just as he said. *1586*
28: 7 *'He has* **r** from the dead and is going ahead *1586*
Mk 9: 9 until the Son of Man *had* **r** from the dead. *482*
14:28 But after I *have* **r,** I will go ahead of you *1586*
16: 6 *He has* **r!** He is not here. *1586*
16:14 those who had seen him *after he had* **r.** *1586*
Lk 24: 6 He is not here; *he has* **r!** *1586*
24:34 Lord *has* **r** and has appeared to Simon." *1586*

RISES (33) [RISE]
Jos 11:17 from Mount Halak, which **r** *toward* Seir, 6590
Jos 12: 7 to Mount Halak, which **r** toward Seir 6590
Jdg 5:31 be like the sun *when it* **r** in its strength." 3655
Job 16: 8 my gauntness **r up** and testifies against me. 7756
24:14 murderer **r up** and kills the poor and needy; 7756
41:25 When he **r up,** the mighty are terrified; 8420
Ps 19: 6 It **r** at one end of the heavens 4604
74:23 of your enemies, *which* **r** continually. 6590
104:22 The sun **r,** and they steal away; 2436
Pr 24:16 *he* **r** again, but the wicked are brought down 7756
Ecc 1: 5 The sun **r** and the sun sets, 2436
1: 5 and hurries back to where it **r.** 2436
3:21 the spirit of man **r** upward and if the spirit 6590
10: 4 If a ruler's anger **r** against you, 6590
Isa 2:19 when he **r** to shake the earth. 7756
2:21 when he **r** to shake the earth. 7756
3:13 *he* **r** to judge the people. 6641
30:18 *he* **r** to show you compassion. 8123
60: 1 and the glory of the LORD **r** upon you. 2436
60: 2 but the LORD **r** upon you 2436
Jer 46: 7 "Who is this *that* **r** like the Nile, 6590
46: 8 Egypt **r** like the Nile, 6590
48:34 "The sound of their cry **r** from Heshbon 5989
51: 9 *it* **r** as **high** as the clouds.' 5951
Hos 6: 3 As surely as the **sun r,** he will appear; 8840
7: 4 from the kneading of the dough till it **r.** 2806
Am 9: 5 the whole land **r** like the Nile, 6590
Mic 7: 6 a daughter **r up** against her mother, 7756
Lk 16:31 not be convinced even if someone **r** from *482*
Eph 2:21 and **r** to become a holy temple in the Lord. *889*
Jas 1:11 the sun **r** with scorching heat and withers *422*
2Pe 1:19 until the day dawns and the morning star **r** *422*
Rev 14:11 smoke of their torment **r** for ever and ever. *326*

RISING (20) [RISE]
Ge 19:28 and he saw dense smoke **r** from the land, 6590
Jos 8:20 and saw the smoke of the city **r** against 6590
1Ki 18:44 "A cloud as small as a man's hand *is* **r** 6590
Ps 50: 1 the earth from the **r** *of* the sun to the place 4667
113: 3 the **r** *of* the sun to the place where it sets, 4667
Isa 13:10 The **r** sun will be darkened and 3655
30:28 like a rushing torrent, **r up** to the neck. 2936
41:25 one from the **r** sun who calls on my name. 4667
45: 6 so that from the **r** *of* the sun to the place 4667
59:19 and from the **r** *of* the sun, 4667
Jer 25:32 a mighty storm *is* **r** from the ends of 6424
47: 2 "See how the waters *are* **r** in the north; 6590
Eze 8:11 and a fragrant cloud of incense *was* **r.** 6590
Mal 1:11 from the **r** to the setting of the sun. 4667
Mk 9:10 discussing what **"r** from the dead" meant. *482*
12:26 Now about the dead **r**—have you not read *1586*
Lk 1:78 the **r sun** will come to us from heaven *424*
2:34 to cause the falling and **r** of many in Israel, *414*
12:54 "When you see a cloud **r** in the west, *422*
Rev 14:20 **r** as high as the horses' bridles for *NIG*

RISK (4) [RISKED, RISKING]
2Sa 17:17 for *they* **could** not **r** being seen entering 3523
23:17 not the blood of men who went **at the r of** 928
1Ch 11:19 of these men who went **at the r of** 928
La 5: 9 We get our bread **at the r of** our lives 928

RISKED (5) [RISK]
Jdg 5:18 The people of Zebulun **r** their very lives; 3070+4200+4637
9:17 **r** his life to rescue you from the hand of Midian 4946+5584+8959
1Ch 11:19 Because they **r** their lives to bring it back, 928
Ac 15:26 men *who have* **r** their lives for the name *4140*
Ro 16: 4 They **r** their **lives** for me. *5549+5719*

RISKING (1) [RISK]
Php 2:30 **r** his life to make up for the help you could *4129*

RISSAH (2)
Nu 33:21 They left Libnah and camped at **R.** 8267
33:22 They left **R** and camped at Kehelathah. 8267

RITES (1)
Ac 21:24 Take these men, join in their **purification r** *49*

RITHMAH (2)
Nu 33:18 They left Hazeroth and camped at **R.** 8414
33:19 They left **R** and camped at Rimmon Perez. 8414

RIVAL (4) [RIVALRY]
Lev 18:18 " 'Do not take your wife's sister as a **r wife** 7675
1Sa 1: 6 her **r** kept provoking her in order 7651
1: 7 her **r** provoked her till she wept and would NIH
Eze 31: 8 cedars in the garden of God *could* not **r** it, 6669

RIVALRY (1) [RIVAL]
Php 1:15 that some preach Christ out of envy and **r,** *2251*

RIVER (109) [RIVERBANK, RIVERBED, RIVERS]
Ge 2:10 A **r** watering the garden flowed from Eden; 5643
2:13 The name of the second **r** is the Gihon; 5643
2:14 The name of the third **r** is the Tigris; 5643
2:14 And the fourth **r** is the Euphrates. 5643
15:18 from the **r** *of* Egypt to the great river, 5643

Ge 15:18 from the river of Egypt to the great **r**, 5643
31:21 he fled with all he had, and crossing the **R**, 5643
36:37 from Rehoboth on the **r** succeeded him 5643
41:2 out of the **r** there came up seven cows, 3284
41:18 out of the **r** there came up seven cows, 3284
Ex 2:5 were walking along the **r** bank. 3284
4:9 the **r** will become blood on the ground." 3284
7:18 in the Nile will die, and the **r** will stink; 3284
7:21 and the **r** smelled so bad that 3284
7:24 they could not drink the water of the **r**. 3284
23:31 and from the desert to the **R**. 5643
Nu 22:5 who was at Pethor, near the **R**, 5643
24:6 like gardens beside a **r**, 5643
Dt 1:7 as far as the great **r**, the Euphrates. 5643
3:16 the border) and out to the Jabbok **R**, 5707
11:24 from the Euphrates **R** to the western sea. 5643
Jos 1:2 to cross the Jordan **R** into the land I am NIH
1:4 and from the great **r**, the Euphrates— 5643
2:23 forded the **r** and came to Joshua son of Nun NIH
3:8 go and stand in the **r**.' " 3720
4:18 the priests came up out of the **r** carrying the ark of the covenant 3720
12:2 to the Jabbok **R**, which is the border 5707
13:3 from the Shihor **R** on the east of Egypt to NIH
24:2 of Abraham and Nahor, lived beyond the **R** 5643
24:3 from the land beyond the **R** and led him 5643
24:14 beyond the **R** and in Egypt, 5643
24:15 beyond the **R**, or the gods of the Amorites, 5643
Jdg 4:7 and his troops to the Kishon **R** and give him 5707
4:13 from Harosheth Haggoyim to the Kishon **R**. 5707
5:21 The **r** Kishon swept them away, 5707
5:21 the age-old **r**, the river Kishon. 5707
5:21 the age-old river, the **r** Kishon. 5707
2Sa 8:3 to restore his control along the Euphrates **R**. 5643
10:16 Arameans brought from beyond the **R**; 5643
17:21 "Set out and cross the **r** at once; 4784
1Ki 4:21 from the **R** to the land of the Philistines, 5643
4:24 over all the kingdoms west of the **R**, 5643
14:15 and scatter them beyond the **R**, 5643
2Ki 17:6 the Habor **R** and in the towns of the Medes. 5643
18:11 on the Habor **R** and in towns of the Medes. 5643
23:29 of Egypt went up to the Euphrates **R** to help 5643
24:7 from the Wadi of Egypt to the Euphrates **R**. 5643
1Ch 1:48 from Rehoboth on the **r** succeeded him 5643
5:9 the desert that extends to the Euphrates **R**, 5643
5:26 Habor, Hara and the **r** *of* Gozan, 5643
13:5 the Shihor **R** in Egypt to Lebo Hamath, NIH
18:3 establish his control along the Euphrates **R**. 5643
19:16 Arameans brought from beyond the **R**, 5643
2Ch 9:26 over all the kings from the **R** to the land of 5643
Job 40:23 When the **r** rages, he is not alarmed; 5643
Ps 36:8 you give them drink from your **r** of delights. 5707
46:4 There is a **r** whose streams make glad the city of God, 5643
72:8 He will rule from sea to sea and from the **R** 5643
80:11 its shoots as far as the **R**. 5643
83:9 you did to Sisera and Jabin at the **r** Kishon, 5707
105:41 like a **r** it flowed in the desert. 5643
Isa 7:20 a razor hired from beyond the **R**— 5643
8:7 the mighty floodwaters of the **R**— 5643
11:15 sweep his hand over the Euphrates **R**. 5643
19:5 The waters of the **r** will dry up, 3542
19:7 at the mouth of the **r**. 3284
48:18 your peace would have been like a **r**, 5643
66:12 "I will extend peace to her like a **r**, 5643
Jer 2:18 to Assyria to drink water from the **R**? 5643
46:2 the Euphrates **R** by Nebuchadnezzar king 5643
46:6 the north by the **R** Euphrates they stumble 5643
46:10 in the land of the north by the **R** Euphrates. 5643
51:32 the **r crossings** seized, 5045
La 2:18 let your tears flow like a **r** day and night; 5707
Eze 1:1 I was among the exiles by the Kebar **R**, 5643
1:3 the Kebar **R** in the land of the Babylonians. 5643
3:15 at Tel Abib near the Kebar **R**. 5643
3:23 like the glory I had seen by the Kebar **R**, 5643
10:15 creatures I had seen by the Kebar **R**. 5643
10:20 the God of Israel by the Kebar **R**, 5643
10:22 as those I had seen by the Kebar **R**. 5643
43:3 like the visions I had seen by the Kebar **R**, 5643
47:5 but now it was a **r** that I could not cross, 5707
47:5 a **r** that no one could cross. 5707
47:6 Then he led me back to the bank of the **r**. 5707
47:7 of trees on each side of the **r**. 5707
47:9 creatures will live wherever the **r** flows. 5707
47:9 so where the **r** flows everything will live, 5707
47:12 on both banks of the **r**. 5707
Da 7:10 A **r** of fire was flowing, 10468
10:4 I was standing on the bank of the great **r**, 5643
12:5 of the **r** and one on the opposite bank. 3284
12:6 who was above the waters of the **r**, 3284
12:7 who was above the waters of the **r**, 3284
Am 5:24 But let justice roll on like a **r**, 4784
8:8 it will be stirred up and then sink like the **r** 3284
9:5 then sinks like the **r** *of* Egypt— 3284
Na 2:6 The **r** gates are thrown open and 5643
3:8 The **r** was her defense, the waters her wall. 3542
Zec 9:10 from sea to sea and from the **R** to the ends 5643
Mt 3:6 they were baptized by him in the Jordan **R**. *4532*
Mk 1:5 they were baptized by him in the Jordan **R**. *4532*
Ac 16:13 the city gate to the **r**, *4532*
Rev 9:14 at the great **r** Euphrates." *4532*
12:15 the serpent spewed water like a **r**, *4532*
12:16 by opening its mouth and swallowing the **r** *4532*
16:12 angel poured out his bowl on the great **r** Euphrates, *4532*
22:1 angel showed me the **r** of the water of life, *4532*
22:2 On each side *of* the **r** stood the tree of life, *4532*

RIVERBANK (1) [RIVER]

Ge 41:3 and stood beside those on the **r**. 3284+8557

RIVERBED (2) [RIVER]

Job 14:11 the sea or a **r** becomes parched and dry, 5643
Isa 19:5 and the **r** will be parched and dry. 5643

RIVERS (29) [RIVER]

2Ki 5:12 Abana and Pharpar, the **r** *of* Damascus, 5643
Job 20:17 the **r** *flowing with* honey and cream. 5643+5707
28:11 of the **r** and brings hidden things to light. 5643
Ps 74:15 you dried up the ever flowing **r**. 5643
78:16 and made water flow down like **r**. 5643
78:44 He turned their **r** to blood; 3284
89:25 his right hand over the **r**. 5643
98:8 Let the **r** clap their hands, 5643
107:33 He turned **r** into a desert, 5643
137:1 By the **r** *of* Babylon we sat and wept 5643
SS 8:7 **r** cannot wash it away. 5643
Isa 18:1 to the land of whirring wings along the **r** 5643
18:2 whose land is divided by **r**, 5643
18:7 whose land is divided by **r**— 5643
33:21 be like a place of broad **r** and streams. 5643
41:18 I will make **r** flow on barren heights, 5643
42:15 I will turn **r** into islands and dry up 5643
43:2 and when you pass through the **r**, 5643
50:2 I turn **r** into a desert; 5643
Jer 46:7 like **r** *of* surging waters? 5643
46:8 like **r** *of* surging waters. 5643
Mic 6:7 with ten thousand **r** *of* oil? 5707
Na 1:4 he makes all the **r** run dry. 5643
Hab 3:8 Were you angry with the **r**, O LORD? 5643
3:9 You split the earth with **r**; 5643
Zep 3:10 From beyond the **r** *of* Cush my worshipers, 5643
2Co 11:26 I have been in danger *from* **r**, *4532*
Rev 8:10 fell from the sky on a third *of* the **r** and on *4532*
16:4 on the **r** and springs of water, *4532*

RIZIA (1)

1Ch 7:39 The sons of Ulla: Arah, Hanniel and **R**. 8359

RIZPAH (4)

2Sa 3:7 a concubine named **R** daughter of Aiah. 8366
21:8 the two sons of Aiah's daughter **R**, 8366
21:10 **R** daughter of Aiah took sackcloth 8366
21:11 David was told what Aiah's daughter **R**, 8366

ROAD (98) [CROSSROADS, ROADS, ROADSIDE]

Ge 16:7 the spring that is beside the **r** *to* Shur. 2006
24:48 on the right **r** to get the granddaughter 2006
38:14 which is on the **r** to Timnah. 2006
38:21 the shrine prostitute who was beside the **r** 2006
48:7 So I buried her there beside the **r** 2006
Ex 13:17 God did not lead them on the **r** *through* 2006
13:18 around by the desert **r** toward the Red Sea. 2006
Nu 20:19 "We will go along the **main r**, 5019
21:1 heard that Israel was coming along the **r** 2006
21:33 Then they turned and went up along the **r** 2006
22:22 of the LORD stood in the **r** to oppose him. 2006
22:23 the angel of the LORD standing in the **r** 2006
22:23 she turned off the **r** into a field. 2006
22:23 Balaam beat her to get her back on the **r**. 2006
22:31 the angel of the LORD standing in the **r** 2006
22:34 I did not realize you were standing in the **r** 2006
Dt 1:2 to Kadesh Barnea by the Mount Seir **r**.) 2006
2:8 We turned from the Arabah **r**, 2006
2:8 and traveled along the desert **r** *of* Moab. 2006
2:27 We will stay on the **main r**; 2006+2006
3:1 Next we turned and went up along the **r** 2006
6:7 at home and when you walk along the **r**, 2006
11:19 at home and when you walk along the **r**, 2006
11:30 west of the **r**, toward the setting sun, 2006
22:4 or his ox fallen on the **r**, 2006
22:6 you come across a bird's nest beside the **r**, 2006
27:18 man who leads the blind astray on the **r**." 2006
Jos 2:7 in pursuit of the spies on the **r** that leads to 2006
2:22 the pursuers had searched all along the **r** 2006
10:10 the **r** going up to Beth Horon and cut them 2006
10:11 on the **r down** *from* Beth Horon 4618
Jdg 5:10 and you who walk along the **r**, 2006
21:19 of the **r** that goes from Bethel to Shechem, 5019
Ru 1:7 the **r** that would take them back to the land 2006
1Sa 4:13 on his chair by the side of the **r**, 2006
6:12 keeping on the **r** and lowing all the way; 5019
17:52 along the Shaaraim **r** to Gath and Ekron. 2006
26:3 Saul made his camp beside the **r** on the hill 2006
2Sa 13:34 and saw many people on the **r** west of him, 2006
15:2 by the side of the **r** *leading to* the city gate. 2006
16:13 along the **r** while Shimei was going along 2006
20:12 in his blood in the middle of the **r**, 5019
20:12 from the **r** into a field and threw a garment 5019
20:13 After Amasa had been removed from the **r**, 5019
1Ki 13:10 So he took another **r** and did not return by 2006
13:12 And his sons showed him which **r** the man 2006
13:24 a lion met him on the **r** and killed him, 2006
13:24 and his body was thrown down on the **r**, 2006
13:28 and found the body thrown down on the **r**, 2006
20:38 the prophet went and stood by the **r** waiting 2006
2Ki 2:23 As he was walking along the **r**, 2006
6:19 "This is not the **r** and this is not the city. 2006
7:15 and they found the whole **r** strewn with 2006
9:27 he fled up the **r** *to* Beth Haggan. 2006
2Ki 12:20 on the **r down** *to* Silla. 3718
18:17 on the **r** *to* the Washerman's Field. 5019
1Ch 26:16 and the Shalleketh Gate on the upper **r** fell 5019
26:18 there were four at the **r** and two at 5019
Ezr 8:22 to protect us from enemies on the **r**, 2006
Job 30:13 They break up my **r**; 5986
Pr 26:13 The sluggard says, "There is a lion in the **r**, 2006
Ecc 10:3 Even as he walks along the **r**, 2006
Isa 7:3 on the **r** *to* the Washerman's Field. 5019
15:5 on the **r** *to* Horonaim they lament their destruction. 2006
36:2 on the **r** *to* the Washerman's Field, 5019
51:10 who made a **r** in the depths of the sea 2006
57:14 "Build up, build up, prepare the **r**! 2006
Jer 31:21 "Set up **r signs**; put up guideposts. 7483
31:21 the highway, the **r** *that* you take. 2006
48:5 on the **r down** *to* Horonaim anguished cries 4618
48:19 Stand by the **r** and watch, 2006
Eze 21:19 Make a signpost where the **r** branches off 2006
21:20 Mark out *one* **r** for the sword to come 2006
21:21 of Babylon will stop at the fork in the **r**, 2006
47:15 the Hethlon **r** past Lebo Hamath to Zedad, 2006
48:1 the Hethlon **r** to Lebo Hamath; 2006
Hos 6:9 they murder on the **r** to Shechem, 2006
Na 2:1 Guard the fortress, watch the **r**, 2006
Mt 7:13 and broad is the **r** that leads to destruction, *3847*
7:14 the gate and narrow the **r** that leads to life, *3847*
21:8 on the **r**, while others cut branches from *3847*
21:8 from the trees and spread them on the **r**. *3847*
21:19 Seeing a fig tree by the **r**, *3847*
Mk 9:33 "What were you arguing about on the **r**?" *3847*
10:52 and followed Jesus along the **r**. *3847*
11:8 Many people spread their cloaks on the **r**, *3847*
Lk 9:57 As they were walking along the **r**, *3847*
10:4 and do not greet anyone on the **r**. *3847*
10:31 to be going down the same **r**, *3847*
19:36 people spread their cloaks on the **r**. *3847*
19:37 near the **place where the r goes down** *2853*
24:32 while he talked with us on the **r** and opened *3847*
Ac 8:26 "Go south to the **r**—the desert road— *3847*
8:26 to the road—the desert **r**— *NIG*
8:36 As they traveled along the **r**, *3847*
9:17 to you on the **r** as you were coming here— *3847*
19:1 Paul **took the r through** the interior *1451*
26:13 About noon, O king, as I was on the **r**, *3847*

ROADS (17) [ROAD]

Lev 26:22 few in number that your **r** will be deserted. 2006
Dt 19:3 Build **r** to them and divide into three parts 2006
Jdg 5:6 in the days of Jael, the **r** were abandoned; 784
20:31 in the open field and on the **r**— 5019
20:32 and draw them away from the city to the **r**." 5019
20:45 down five thousand men along the **r**. 5019
Isa 33:8 no travelers are on the **r**. 784
49:9 the **r** and find pasture on every barren hill. 2006
49:11 I will turn all my mountains into **r**, 2006
59:8 They have turned them into crooked **r**; 5986
Jer 6:25 Do not go out to the fields or walk on the **r**, 2006
18:15 They made them walk in bypaths and on **r** 2006
La 1:4 The **r** *to* Zion mourn, 2006
Eze 21:19 mark out two **r** for the sword of the king 2006
21:21 at the junction of the two **r**, 2006
Lk 3:5 The crooked **r** shall become straight, *NIG*
14:23 'Go out to the **r** and country lanes *3847*

ROADSIDE (6) [ROAD]

Ge 38:16 he went over to her by the **r** and said, 2006
49:17 Dan will be a serpent by the **r**, 2006
Jer 3:2 By the **r** you sat waiting for lovers, 2006
Mt 20:30 Two blind men were sitting by the **r**, *3847*
Mk 10:46 was sitting by the **r** begging. *3847*
Lk 18:35 a blind man was sitting by the **r** begging. *3847*

ROAM (4) [ROAMED, ROAMING]

Jdg 11:37 *to* **r** the hills and weep with my friends, 2143+2256+3718
Isa 8:21 *they will* **r** through the land; 6296
Jer 2:31 Why do my people say, '*We are free to* **r**; 8113
50:6 and **caused** them **to r** on the mountains. 8740

ROAMED (2) [ROAM]

1Sa 30:31 where David and his men *had* **r**. 2143
Job 30:3 *they* **r** the parched land in desolate 6908

ROAMING (3) [ROAM]

Job 1:7 "From **r** through the earth and going back 8763
2:2 "From **r** through the earth and going back 8763
Pr 26:13 a fierce lion **r** the streets!" NIH

ROAR (38) [ROARED, ROARING, ROARS]

Job 4:10 The lions may **r** and growl, 8614
37:2 Listen to the **r** *of* his voice, 8075
37:4 After that **comes** the sound of *his* **r**; 8613
Ps 42:7 to deep in the **r** *of* your waterfalls; 7754
46:3 though its waters **r** and foam and 2159
104:21 The lions **r** for their prey 8613
Pr 19:12 A king's rage is like the **r** *of* a lion, 5638
20:2 A king's wrath is like the **r** *of* a lion; 5638
Isa 5:29 Their **r** is like that of the lion, 8614
5:29 *they* **r** like young lions; 8613
5:30 that day *they will* **r** over it like the roaring 5637
17:12 *they* **r** like the roaring of great waters! 8616
17:13 peoples **r** like the roar of surging waters, 8616

Isa 17:13 peoples roar like the r of surging waters, 8623
51:15 who churns up the sea so that its waves r— 2159
Jer 5:22 they may r, but they cannot cross it. 2159
10:13 he thunders, the waters in the heavens r; 2162
11:16 with the r of a mighty storm he will set it 7754
25:30 " 'The LORD will r from on high; 8613
25:30 from his holy dwelling and r mightily 8613+8613
31:35 who stirs up the sea so that its waves r— 2159
51:16 he thunders, the waters in the heavens r; 2162
51:38 Her people all r like young lions, 8613
51:55 the r of their voices will resound. 8623
Eze 1:24 like the r of rushing waters, 7754
19: 9 so his r was heard no longer on 7754
43: 2 His voice was like the r of rushing waters, 7754
Hos 10:14 the r of battle will rise against your people, 8623
11:10 he will r like a lion. 8613
Joel 3:16 The LORD will r from Zion and thunder 8613
Am 3: 4 a lion r in the thicket when he has no prey? 8613
Zec 9:15 They will drink and r as with wine; 2159
11: 3 Listen to the r of the lions; 8614
2Pe 3:10 The heavens will disappear with a r; 4853
Rev 10: 3 he gave a loud shout like the r of a lion. 3681
14: 2 And I heard a sound from heaven like the r 5889
19: 1 I heard what sounded like the r of a 3489+5889
19: 6 the r of rushing waters and like loud peals 5889

ROARED (4) [ROAR]

Ps 74: 4 Your foes r in the place where you met 8613
Jer 2:15 Lions have r; they have growled at him. 8613
Am 3: 8 The lion has r—who will not fear? 8613
Hab 3:10 the deep r and lifted its waves on high. 5989+7754

ROARING (15) [ROAR]

Jdg 14: 5 suddenly a young lion came r toward him. 8613
Ps 22:13 R lions tearing their prey open their mouths 8613
65: 7 who stilled the r of the seas, 8623
65: 7 the r of their waves, 8623
Pr 28:15 Like a r lion or a charging bear is 5637
Isa 5:30 that day they will roar over it like the r of 5639
17:12 they roar like the r of great waters! 8623
Jer 6:23 like the r sea as they ride on their horses; 2159
50:42 like the r sea as they ride on their horses; 2159
51:42 its r waves will cover her. 2162
Eze 19: 7 in it were terrified by his r. 7754+8614
22:25 within her like a r lion tearing its prey; 8613
Zep 3: 3 Her officials are r lions, 8613
Lk 21:25 and perplexity at the r and tossing of 2492
1Pe 5: 8 like a r lion looking for someone to devour. 6054

ROARS (3) [ROAR]

Jer 12: 8 She r at me; therefore I hate her. 928+5989+7754
Hos 11:10 When he r, his children will come trembling 8613
Am 1: 2 "The LORD r from Zion and thunders 8613

ROAST (4) [ROASTED, ROASTS]

Ex 12: 9 but r it over the fire— 7507
Dt 16: 7 R it and eat it at the place 1418
1Sa 2:15 "Give the priest some meat to r; 7499
Pr 12:27 The lazy man does not r his game, 3047

ROASTED (10) [ROAST]

Ex 12: 8 That same night they are to eat the meat r 7507
Lev 2:14 offer crushed heads of new grain r in 7828
23:14 not eat any bread, or r or new grain, 7833
Jos 5:11 unleavened bread and r grain. 7828
Ru 2:14 he offered her some r grain. 7833
1Sa 17:17 of r grain and these ten loaves of bread 7833
25:18 five dressed sheep, five seahs of r grain, 7833
2Sa 17:28 flour and r grain, beans and lentils, 7833
2Ch 35:13 They r the Passover animals over the fire 1418
Isa 44:19 I r meat and I ate. 7499

ROASTS (1) [ROAST]

Isa 44:16 he r his meat and eats his fill. 7499

ROB (12) [ROBBED, ROBBER, ROBBERS, ROBBERY, ROBBING, ROBS]

Lev 19:13 " 'Do not defraud your neighbor or r him. 1608
26:22 r you of your children, 8897
Jdg 9:25 to ambush and r everyone who passed by, 1608
14:15 Did you invite us here to r us?" 3769
Ps 35:10 the poor and needy from those who r them." 1608
Hos 7: 1 bandits r in the streets; 7320
Mal 3: 8 "Will a man r God? Yet you rob me. 7693
3: 8 "Will a man rob God? Yet you r me. 7693
3: 8 "But you ask, 'How do we r you?' 7693
Mt 12:29 Then he can r his house. 1395
Mk 3:27 Then he can r his house. 1395
Ro 2:22 You who abhor idols, do you r temples? 2644

ROBBED (15) [ROB]

Dt 28:29 day after day you will be oppressed and r, 1608
2Sa 17: 8 and as fierce as a wild bear r of her cubs. 8891
Ps 7: 4 with me or without cause have r my foe— 2740
Pr 4:16 they are r of slumber till they make someone fall. 1608
17:12 a bear r of her cubs than a fool in his folly. 8891
Isa 38:10 of death and be r of the rest of my years?" 7212
Jer 21:12 of his oppressor the one who has been r, 1608
22: 3 of his oppressor the one who has been r. 1608
Eze 18:18 r his brother and did what was wrong 1608+1609
Hos 13: 8 Like a bear r of her cubs, 8891
Mk 9:17 by a spirit that has r him of speech. 228
Ac 19:27 will be r of her divine majesty." 2747
19:37 though they have neither r temples 2645
2Co 11: 8 I r other churches by receiving support 5195
1Ti 6: 5 who have been r of the truth and who think 691

ROBBER (1) [ROB]

Jn 10: 1 in by some other way, is a thief and a r. 3334

ROBBERS (13) [ROB]

Jer 7:11 become a den of r to you? 7265
Eze 7:22 r will enter it and desecrate it. 7265
Ob 1: 5 "If thieves came to you, if r in the night— 8720
Mt 21:13 but you are making it a 'den of r.' " 3334
27:38 Two r were crucified with him, 3334
27:44 In the same way the r who were crucified 3334
Mk 11:17 But you have made it 'a den of r.' " 3334
15:27 They crucified two r with him, 3334
Lk 10:30 when he fell into the hands of r. 3334
10:36 to the man who fell into the hands of r?" 3334
18:11 r, evildoers, adulterers— 774
19:46 but you have made it 'a den of r.' " 3334
Jn 10: 8 before me were thieves and r, 3334

ROBBERY (5) [ROB]

Isa 61: 8 I hate r and iniquity. 1610
Eze 18: 7 He does not commit r but gives 1608+1611
18:12 He commits r. 1608+1611
18:16 He does not commit r but gives 1608+1611
22:29 practice extortion and commit r; 1608+1610

ROBBING (2) [ROB]

Isa 10: 2 widows their prey and r the fatherless. 1024
Mal 3: 9 because you are r me. 7693

ROBE (61) [ROBED, ROBES]

Ge 37: 3 and he made a richly ornamented r for him. 4189
37:23 they stripped him of his r— 4189
37:23 the richly ornamented r he was wearing— 4189
37:31 Then they got Joseph's r, 4189
37:31 slaughtered a goat and dipped the r in 4189
37:32 the ornamented r back to their father 4189
37:32 Examine it to see whether it is your son's r. 4189
37:33 "It is my son's r! 4189
Ex 28: 4 a breastpiece, an ephod, a r, a woven tunic, 5077
28:31 the r of the ephod entirely of blue cloth, 5077
28:33 and scarlet yarn around the hem of the r, 2257S
28:34 to alternate around the hem of the r. 5077
29: 5 the tunic, the r of the ephod, 5077
39:22 the r of the ephod entirely of blue cloth— 5077
39:23 with an opening in the center of the r like 5077
39:24 around the hem of the r. 5077
39:26 the hem of the r to be worn for ministering, 5077
Lev 8: 7 clothed him with the r and put the ephod 5077
Jos 7:21 in the plunder a beautiful r from Babylonia, 168
7:24 took Achan son of Zerah, the silver, the r, 168
1Sa 2:19 a little r and took it to him when she went 5077
15:27 Saul caught hold of the hem of his r, 5077
18: 4 the r he was wearing and gave it to David, 5077
24: 4 and cut off a corner of Saul's r. 5077
24: 5 for having cut off a corner of his r. 889S
24:11 look at this piece of your r in my hand! 5077
24:11 the corner of your r but did not kill you. 5077
28:14 "An old man wearing a r is coming up," 5077
2Sa 13:18 She was wearing a richly ornamented r, 4189
13:19 and tore the ornamented r she was wearing. 4189
15:32 his r torn and dust on his head. 4189
1Ch 15:27 David was clothed in a r of fine linen, 5077
Ne 5:13 also shook out the folds of my r and said, 2950
Est 6: 8 have them bring a royal r the king has worn 4230
6: 9 Then let the r and horse be entrusted to one 4230
6: 9 Let them r the man the king delights 4252
6:10 "Get the r and the horse and do just 4230
6:11 So Haman got the r and the horse. 4230
8:15 a large crown of gold and a purple r 9423
Job 1:20 got up and tore his r and shaved his head. 5077
29:14 justice was my r and my turban. 5077
SS 5: 3 I have taken off my r— 4189
Isa 6: 1 and the train of his r filled the temple. 8767
22:21 with your r and fasten your sash 4189
61:10 and arrayed me in a r of righteousness, 5077
Mic 2: 8 the rich r from those who pass by without 8515
Zec 8:23 of one Jew by the hem of his r and say, 4053
Mt 27:28 They stripped him and put a scarlet r 5948
27:31 they took off the r and put his own clothes 5948
Mk 15:17 They put a purple r on him, 4525
15:20 the purple r and put his own clothes 4525
16: 5 a young man dressed in a white r sitting on 5124
Lk 15:22 Bring the best r and put it on him. 5124
23:11 Dressing him in an elegant r, 2264
Jn 19: 2 They clothed him in a purple r 2668
19: 5 the crown of thorns and the purple r, 2668
Heb 1:12 You will roll them up like a r; 4316
Rev 1:13 a r reaching down to his feet 4468
6:11 Then each of them was given a white r, 5124
19:13 He is dressed in a r dipped in blood, 2668
19:16 On his r and on his thigh he has this name 2668

ROBED (5) [ROBE]

Est 6:11 He r Mordecai, and led him on horseback 4252
Ps 93: 1 The LORD reigns, he is r in majesty; 4252
93: 1 the LORD is r in majesty and is armed 4252
Isa 63: 1 Who is this, r in splendor, 4230
Rev 10: 1 He was r in a cloud, 4314

ROBES (41) [ROBE]

Ge 41:42 He dressed him in r of fine linen and put 955
49:11 his r in the blood of grapes. 6078
1Sa 19:24 He stripped off his r and also prophesied 955
1Ki 10: 5 the attending servants in their r, 4860
10:25 articles of silver and gold, r, 8515
22:10 Dressed in their royal r, the king of Israel 955
22:30 but you wear your royal r." 955
2Ki 5: 7 he tore his r and said, "Am I God? 955
5: 8 that the king of Israel had torn his r, 955
5: 8 "Why have you torn your r? 955
6:30 king heard the woman's words, he tore his r. 955
10:22 "Bring r for all the ministers of Baal." 4230
10:22 So he brought out r for them. 4860
11:14 Then Athaliah tore her r and called out, 955
22:11 the Book of the Law, he tore his r. 955
22:19 you tore your r and wept in my presence, 955
2Ch 9: 4 the attending servants in their r, 4860
9: 4 in their r and the burnt offerings he made at 4860
9:24 articles of silver and gold, and r, 8515
18: 9 Dressed in their royal r, 955
18:29 but you wear your royal r." 955
23:13 Athaliah tore her r and shouted, "Treason! 955
34:19 heard the words of the Law, he tore his r. 955
34:27 and tore your r and wept in my presence, 955
Est 5: 1 Esther put on her royal r and stood 4252
Job 2:12 and they tore their r and sprinkled dust 5077
Ps 45: 8 All your r are fragrant with myrrh 955
133: 2 down upon the collar of his r. 4496
Isa 3:22 the fine r and the capes and cloaks, 4711
Eze 26:16 from their thrones and lay aside their r 5077
Da 3:21 So these men, wearing their r, trousers, 10517
3:27 their r were not scorched, 10517
Jnh 3: 6 rose from his throne, took off his royal r, 168
Mk 12:38 They like to walk around in flowing r and 5124
Lk 20:46 around in flowing r and love to be greeted 5124
Ac 9:39 and showing him the r and other clothing 5945
12:21 Herod, wearing his royal r, 2264
Rev 7: 9 They were wearing white r and 5124
7:13 "These in white r—who are they, 5124
7:14 they have washed their r and made them 5124
22:14 "Blessed are those who wash their r, 5124

ROBOAM (KJV) See REHOBOAM

ROBS (2) [ROB]

Pr 19:26 He who r his father and drives out his 8720
28:24 He who r his father or mother and says, 1608

ROCK (117) [ROCKS, ROCKY]

Ge 49:24 because of the Shepherd, the R of Israel, 74
Ex 17: 6 I will stand there before you by the r 7446
17: 6 Strike the r, and water will come out of it 7446
33:21 near me where you may stand on a r. 7446
33:22 a cleft in the r and cover you with my hand 7446
Nu 20: 8 Speak to that r before their eyes 6152
20: 8 You will bring water out of the r for 6152
20:10 in front of the r and Moses said to them, 6152
20:10 must we bring you water out of this r?" 6152
20:11 and struck the r twice with his staff. 6152
24:21 your nest is set in a r; 6152
Dt 8:15 He brought you water out of hard r. 7446
32: 4 He is the R, his works are perfect, 7446
32:13 He nourished him with honey from the r, 6152
32:15 and rejected the R his Savior. 7446
32:18 You deserted the R, who fathered you; 7446
32:30 unless their R had sold them, 7446
32:31 For their r is not like our Rock, 7446
32:31 For their rock is not like our R, 7446
32:37 are their gods, the r they took refuge in, 7446
Jdg 6:20 place them on this r, 6152
6:21 Fire flared from the r, 7446
7:25 They killed Oreb at the r of Oreb, 7446
13:19 and sacrificed it on a r to the LORD. 7446
15: 8 down and stayed in a cave in the r of Etam. 6152
15:11 down to the cave in the r of Etam and said 6152
15:13 and led him up from the r. 6152
20:45 toward the desert to the r of Rimmon, 6152
20:47 into the desert to the r of Rimmon, 6152
21:13 an offer of peace to the Benjamites at the r 6152
1Sa 2: 2 there is no R like our God. 7446
6:14 and there it stopped beside a large r. 74
6:15 and placed them on the large r. 74
6:18 The large r, on which they set the ark of 74
23:25 to the r and stayed in the Desert of Maon. 6152
2Sa 20: 8 While they were at the great r in Gibeon, 74
21:10 and spread it out for herself on a r. 7446
22: 2 He said: "The LORD is my r, 6152
22: 3 my God is my r, in whom I take refuge, 7446
22:32 And who is the R except our God? 7446
22:47 Praise be to my R! 7446
22:47 Exalted be God, the R, my Savior! 7446
23: 3 the R of Israel said to me: 7446
1Ch 11:15 to David to the r at the cave of Adullam, 7446
Ne 9:15 in their thirst you brought them water from the r; 6152
Job 14:18 and as a r is moved from its place, 7446
19:24 or engraved in r forever! 7446
28: 9 the flinty r and lays bare the roots of 2734
28:10 He tunnels through the r; 7446
29: 6 the r poured out for me streams of olive oil. 7446

Jer 41:24 His chest is hard as **r**, 74
Ps 18: 2 The LORD is my **r**, my fortress and 6152
18: 2 my God is my **r**, in whom I take refuge. 7446
18:31 And who is the **R** except our God? 7446
18:46 Praise be to my **R**! 7446
19:14 O LORD, my **R** and my Redeemer. 7446
27: 5 of his tabernacle and set me high upon a **r**. 7446
28: 1 To you I call, O LORD my **R**; 7446
31: 2 be my **r** *of* refuge, a strong fortress 7446
31: 3 Since you are my **r** and my fortress, 6152
40: 2 on a **r** and gave me a firm place to stand. 6152
42: 9 I say to God my **R**, 6152
61: 2 lead me to the **r** that is higher than I. 7446
62: 2 He alone is my **r** and my salvation; 7446
62: 6 He alone is my **r** and my salvation; 7446
62: 7 he is my mighty **r**, my refuge. 7446
71: 3 Be my **r** *of* refuge, to which I can always go 7446
71: 3 for you are my **r** and my fortress. 6152
78:20 When he struck the **r**, water gushed out, 7446
78:35 They remembered that God was their **R**, 7446
81:16 with honey from the **r** I would satisfy you." 7446
89:26 my God, the **R** my Savior.' 7446
92:15 The LORD is upright; he is my **R**, 7446
94:22 and my God the **r** *in whom* I take refuge. 7446
95: 1 let us shout aloud to the **R** *of* our salvation. 7446
105:41 He opened the **r**, and water gushed out; 7446
114: 8 who turned the **r** into a pool, 7446
114: 8 the **hard r** into springs of water. 2734
144: 1 Praise be to the LORD my **R**, 7446
Pr 30:19 the way of a snake on a **r**, 7446
SS 2:14 My dove in the clefts of the **r**, 6152
Isa 8:14 a stone that causes men to stumble and a **r** 7446
10:26 he struck down Midian at the **r** *of* Oreb; 7446
17:10 you have not remembered the **R**, 7446
22:16 and chiseling your resting place in the **r**? 6152
26: 4 the LORD, is the **R** eternal. 7446
30:29 of the LORD, to the **R** *of* Israel. 7446
32: 2 in the desert and the shadow of a great **r** in 6152
44: 8 No, there is no other **R**; I know not one." 7446
48:21 he made water flow for them from the **r**; 7446
48:21 he split the **r** and water gushed out. 7446
51: 1 Look to the **r** *from which* you were cut and 7446
Jer 23:29 like a hammer that breaks a **r** in pieces? 6152
51:26 No **r** will be taken from you for 74
Eze 24: 7 She poured it on the bare **r**; 6152
24: 8 I put her blood on the bare **r**, 6152
26: 4 and make her a bare **r**. 6152
26:14 I will make you a bare **r**, 6152
Da 2:34 While you were watching, a **r** was cut out, 10006
2:35 But the **r** that struck the statue became 10006
2:45 the meaning of the vision of the **r** cut out of 10006
2:45 a **r** that broke the iron, the bronze, the clay, NIH
Hab 1:12 O **R**, you have ordained them to punish. 7446
Zec 12: 3 I will make Jerusalem an immovable **r** 74
Mt 7:24 a wise man who built his house on the **r**. *4376*
7:25 because it had its foundation on the **r**. *4376*
16:18 and on this **r** I will build my church, *4376*
27:60 that he had cut out of the **r**. *4376*
Mk 15:46 and placed it in a tomb cut out *of* **r**. *4376*
Lk 6:48 down deep and laid the foundation on **r**. *4376*
8: 6 Some fell on **r**, and when it came up, *4376*
8:13 on the **r** are the ones who receive the word *4376*
23:53 and placed it in a tomb **cut in the r**, *3292*
Ro 9:33 a stone that causes men to stumble and a **r** *4376*
1Co 10: 4 from the spiritual **r** that accompanied them, *4376*
10: 4 and that **r** was Christ. *4376*
1Pe 2: 8 to stumble and a **r** that makes them fall." *4376*

ROCKS (31) [ROCK]

Dt 8: 9 the **r** are iron and you can dig copper out of 74
Jos 7:26 they heaped up a large pile of **r**, 74
8:29 And they raised a large pile of **r** over it, 74
10:18 "Roll large **r** up to the mouth of the cave, 74
10:27 the mouth of the cave they placed large **r**, 74
1Sa 13: 6 they hid in caves and thickets, among the **r**, 6152
2Sa 18:17 in the forest and piled up a large heap of **r** 74
1Ki 19:11 the mountains apart and shattered the **r** 6152
Job 8:17 around a **pile of r** and looks for a place 1643
18: 4 Or must the **r** be moved from their place? 7446
22:24 your gold of Ophir to the **r** *in* the ravines, 7446
24: 8 by mountain rains and hug the **r** for lack 7446
28: 6 sapphires come from its **r**, 74
30: 6 among the **r** and in holes in the ground. 4091
Ps 78:15 the **r** in the desert and gave them water 7446
137: 9 and dashes them against the **r**. 6152
Isa 2:10 Go into the **r**, hide in the ground 7446
2:19 the **r** and to holes in the ground from dread 7446
2:21 They will flee to caverns in the **r** and to 7446
7:19 and in the crevices in the **r**, 6152
Jer 4:29 some climb up among the **r**. 4091
13: 4 and hide it there in a crevice in the **r**." 6152
16:16 and hill and from the crevices of the **r**. 6152
48:28 and dwell among the **r**, 6152
49:16 you who live in the clefts of the **r**, 6152
Ob 1: 3 the clefts of the **r** and make your home on 6152
Na 1: 6 the **r** are shattered before him. 7446
Mt 27:51 The earth shook and the **r** split. *4376*
Ac 27:29 that we would be dashed against the **r**, *5536+5550*
Rev 6:15 in caves and among the **r** of the mountains. *4376*
6:16 They called *to* the mountains and the **r**, *4376*

ROCKY (10) [ROCK]

Nu 23: 9 From the **r** peaks I see them, 7446
Job 39:28 a **r** crag is his stronghold. 6152
Ps 78:16 of a **r crag** and made water flow down 6152

Jer 18:14 of Lebanon ever vanish from its **r** slopes? 7446
21:13 above this valley on the **r** plateau, declares 7446
Am 6:12 Do horses run on the **r crags?** 6152
Mt 13: 5 Some fell on **r places**, *4378*
13:20 on **r places** is the man who hears the word *4378*
Mk 4: 5 Some fell on **r places**, *4378*
4:16 Others, like seed sown on **r places**, *4378*

ROD (51) [RODS]

Ex 21:20 with a **r** and the slave dies as a direct result, 8657
Lev 27:32 that passes under the **shepherd's r—** 8657
1Sa 17: 7 His spear shaft was like a weaver's **r**, 4962
2Sa 7:14 I will punish him with the **r** *of* men, 8657
21:19 a spear with a shaft like a weaver's **r**. 4962
1Ch 11:23 the Egyptian had a spear like a weaver's **r** 4962
20: 5 a spear with a shaft like a weaver's **r**. 4962
Job 9:34 someone to remove God's **r** from me, 8657
21: 9 the **r** *of* God is not upon them. 8657
Ps 23: 4 your **r** and your staff, they comfort me. 8657
89:32 with the **r**, their iniquity with flogging; 8657
Pr 10:13 but a **r** is for the back of him who lacks judgment. 8657
13:24 He who spares the **r** hates his son, 8657
14: 3 A fool's talk brings a **r** *to* his back, 2643
22: 8 and the **r** *of* his fury will be destroyed. 8657
22:15 **r** *of* discipline will drive it far from him. 8657
23:13 you punish him with the **r**, he will not die. 8657
23:14 with the **r** and save his soul from death. 8657
26: 3 and a **r** for the backs of fools! 8657
29:15 The **r** of correction imparts wisdom, 8657
Isa 9: 4 the **r** *of* their oppressor. 8657
10: 5 "Woe to the Assyrian, the **r** *of* my anger, 8657
10:15 As if a **r** were to wield him who lifts it up, 8657
10:24 who beat you with a **r** and lift up a club 8657
11: 4 the earth with the **r** *of* his mouth; 8657
14: 5 LORD has broken the **r** *of* the wicked, 4751
14:29 that the **r** that struck you is broken; 8657
28:27 caraway is beaten out with a **r**, 4751
30:32 with his punishing **r** will be to the music 4751
La 3: 1 the man who has seen affliction by the **r** 8657
Eze 7:10 Doom has burst forth, the **r** has budded, 4751
7:11 into a **r** *to punish* wickedness; 4751
20:37 of you as you pass under my **r**, 8657
40: 3 a linen cord and a measuring **r** in his hand. 7866
40: 5 The length of the measuring **r** in 7866
40: 5 it was one **measuring r** thick 7866
40: 5 and one **r** high. 7866
40: 6 it was one **r** deep. 7866
40: 7 The alcoves for the guards were one **r** long 7866
40: 7 and one **r** wide, 7866
40: 7 the temple was one **r** deep. 7866
41: 8 It was the length of the **r**, six long cubits. 7866
42:16 the east side with the measuring **r**; 7866
42:17 five hundred cubits by the measuring **r**. 7866
42:18 five hundred cubits by the measuring **r**. 7866
42:19 five hundred cubits by the measuring **r**. 7866
Mic 5: 1 strike Israel's ruler on the cheek with a **r**. 8657
6: 9 "Heed the **r** and the One who appointed it. 4751
Rev 11: 1 a reed like a **measuring r** and was told, *4811*
21:15 a measuring **r** of gold to measure the city, *2812*
21:16 the city *with* the **r** and found it to be 12,000 *2812*

RODANIM (2)

Ge 10: 4 Elishah, Tarshish, the Kittim and the **R**. 8102
1Ch 1: 7 Elishah, Tarshish, the Kittim and the **R**. 8102

RODE (11) [RIDE]

Jdg 10: 4 He had thirty sons, *who* **r** thirty donkeys. 8206
12:14 *who* **r** on seventy donkeys. 8206
1Sa 30:17 except four hundred young men who **r off** 8206
1Ki 13:14 and **r** after the man of God. 2143
18:45 a heavy rain came on and Ahab **r off** 8206
2Ki 9:16 he got into his chariot and **r** to Jezreel, 2143
9:18 The horseman **r off** to meet Jehu and said, 2143
9:21 of Israel and Ahaziah king of Judah **r out**, 3655
Est 8:10 *who* **r** fast horses especially bred for 8206
Hab 3: 8 Did you rage against the sea when *you* **r** 8206
Rev 6: 2 *he* **r out** as a conqueror bent on conquest. *2002*

RODENTS (1)

Isa 2:20 the **r** and bats their idols of silver and idols 2923

RODS (3) [ROD]

Job 40:18 his limbs like **r** *of* iron. 4758
SS 5:14 His arms are **r** *of* gold set with chrysolite. 1664
2Co 11:25 Three times *I was* **beaten with r**, *4810*

ROE (1) [ROEBUCKS]

Dt 14: 5 the gazelle, the **r deer**, the wild goat, 3502

ROEBUCK (KJV) See GAZELLE

ROEBUCKS (1) [ROE]

1Ki 4:23 as well as deer, gazelles, **r** and choice fowl. 3502

ROES (KJV) See GAZELLE

ROGEL See EN ROGEL

ROGELIM (2)

2Sa 17:27 and Barzillai the Gileadite from **R** 8082
19:31 also came down from **R** to cross the Jordan 8082

ROHGAH (1)

1Ch 7:34 Ahi, **R**, Hubbah and Aram. 8108

ROI See BEER LAHAI ROI

ROLL (14) [ROLLED, ROLLING, ROLLS]

Ge 29: 3 the shepherds *would* **r** the stone away from 1670
Jos 10:18 "**R** large rocks up to the mouth of the cave, 1670
1Sa 14:33 "**R** a large stone over here at once." 1670
Pr 26:27 if a man rolls a stone, *it will* **r back** on him. 8740
Isa 22:18 *He will* **r** you **up tightly** like a ball and throw you 7571+7571+7572
Jer 5:22 The waves *may* **r**, but they cannot prevail; 1723
6:26 put on sackcloth and **r** in ashes; 7147
25:34 **r** in the dust, *you* leaders of the flock. 7147
51:25 **r** you off the cliffs, 1670
Eze 27:30 they will sprinkle dust on their heads and **r** 7147
Am 5:24 But *let* justice **r on** like a river, 1670
Mic 1:10 In Beth Ophrah **r** in the dust. 7147
Mk 16: 3 "Who *will* **r** the stone **away** from *653*
Heb 1:12 *You will* **r** them **up** like a robe; *1813*

ROLLED (15) [ROLL]

Ge 29: 8 the stone *has been* **r** away from the mouth 1670
29:10 over and **r** the stone away from the mouth 1670
Jos 5: 9 "Today *I have* **r away** the reproach 1670
2Ki 2: 8 **r** it **up** and struck the water with it. 1676
Isa 9: 5 in battle and every garment **r** in blood will 1670
28:27 nor **is** a cartwheel **r** over cummin; 6015
34: 4 be dissolved and the sky **r up** like a scroll; 1670
38:12 Like a weaver *I have* **r up** my life, 7886
Mt 27:60 **r** a big stone **in front of** the entrance *4685*
28: 2 **r back** the stone and sat on it. *653*
Mk 9:20 *He* fell to the ground and **r around**, *3244*
15:46 Then *he* **r** a stone against the entrance of *4685*
16: 4 which was very large, *had been* **r away**. *653*
Lk 4:20 Then he **r up** the scroll, *4771*
24: 2 They found the stone **r away** from the tomb, *653*

ROLLER (KJV) See SPLINT

ROLLING (2) [ROLL]

Job 30:14 amid the ruins *they* **come r in**. 1670
Rev 6:14 The sky receded like a scroll, **r up**, *1813*

ROLLS (2) [ROLL]

Pr 26:27 if a *man* **r** a stone, it will roll back on him. 1670
Isa 9:18 so that *it* **r upward** *in* a column of smoke. 60

ROMAMTI-EZER (2)

1Ch 25: 4 Hanani, Eliathah, Giddalti and **R**; 8251
25:31 the twenty-fourth to **R**, 8251

ROMAN (13) [ROME]

Lk 2: 1 a census should be taken of the entire **R world**. *3876*
Jn 18:28 to the palace of the **R** governor. *NIG*
Ac 11:28 famine would spread over the entire **R world**. *3876*
16:12 a **R colony** and the leading city of *3149*
16:37 even though we are **R citizens**, *476+4871*
16:38 that Paul and Silas were **R citizens**, *4871*
21:31 the commander *of* the **R troops** that *5061*
22:25 for you to flog a **R citizen** who hasn't *476+4871*
22:26 "This man is a **R citizen.**" *4871*
22:27 "Tell me, are you a **R citizen?**" *4871*
22:29 a **R citizen**, in chains. *4871*
23:27 for I had learned that he is a **R citizen**. *4871*
25:16 not the **R** custom to hand over any man *4871*

ROMANS (3) [ROME]

Jn 11:48 and then the **R** will come and take away *4871*
Ac 16:21 advocating customs unlawful for us **R** *1639+4871*
28:17 in Jerusalem and handed over to the **R**. *4871*

ROME (10) [ROMAN, ROMANS]

Ac 2:10 near Cyrene; visitors from **R** *4871*
18: 2 had ordered all the Jews to leave **R**. *4873*
19:21 he said, "I must visit **R** also." *4873*
23:11 so you must also testify in **R**." *4873*
25:25 to the Emperor I decided to send him to **R**. *NIG*
28:14 And so we came to **R**. *4873*
28:16 When we got to **R**, *4873*
Ro 1: 7 To all in **R** who are loved by God and called *4873*
1:15 the gospel also to you who are at **R**. *4873*
2Ti 1:17 On the contrary, when he was in **R**, *4873*

ROOF (38) [ROOFED, ROOFING, ROOFS]

Ge 6:16 Make a **r** for it and finish the ark to 7415
19: 8 under the protection of my **r**." 7771
Dt 22: 8 around your **r** so that you may not bring 1511
22: 8 on your house if someone falls from the **r**. 5647S
Jos 2: 6 to the **r** and hidden them under the stalks 1511
2: 6 the stalks of flax she had laid out on the **r**.) 1511
2: 8 she went up on the **r** 1511

Jdg 9:51 in and climbed up on the tower r. 1511
16:27 on the r were about three thousand men 1511
1Sa 9:25 with Saul on the r of his house. 1511
9:26 and Samuel called to Saul on the r, 1511
2Sa 11: 2 and walked around on the r of the palace. 1511
11: 2 From the r he saw a woman bathing. 1511
16:22 they pitched a tent for Absalom on the r, 1511
18:24 up to the r of the gateway by the wall. 1511
1Ki 7: 6 of that were pillars and an overhanging r. 6264
2Ki 4:10 Let's make a small room on the r and put 7815
19:26 like grass sprouting on the r, 1511
23:12 the kings of Judah had erected on the r near 1511
Job 29:10 their tongues stuck to the r of their mouths. 2674
Ps 22:15 and my tongue sticks to the r of my mouth; 4918
102: 7 I have become like a bird alone on a r. 1511
129: 6 May they be like grass on the r, 1511
137: 6 May my tongue cling to the r of my mouth 2674
Pr 21: 9 Better to live on a corner of the r than share 1511
25:24 Better to live on a corner of the r than share 1511
Isa 37:27 like grass sprouting on the r, 1511
La 4: 4 to the r of its mouth; 2674
Eze 3:26 to the r of your mouth so that you will 2674
Da 4:29 on the r of the royal palace of Babylon, NIH
Mt 8: 8 not deserve to have you come under my r. 5094
24:17 Let no one on the r of his house go down 1560
Mk 2: 4 they made an opening in the r above Jesus 5094
13:15 Let no one on the r of his house go down 1560
Lk 5:19 the r and lowered him on his mat through 1560
7: 6 not deserve to have you come under my r. 5094
17:31 On that day no one who is on the r 1560
Ac 10: 9 Peter went up on the r to pray. 1560

ROOFED (1) [ROOF]

1Ki 7: 3 It was r with cedar above the beams 6211

ROOFING (2) [ROOF]

1Ki 6: 9 r it with beams and cedar planks. 6211
Ne 3:15 r it over and putting its doors and bolts 3233

ROOFS (9) [ROOF]

Ne 8:16 and built themselves booths on their own r, 1511
Isa 15: 3 the r and in the public squares they all wail, 1511
22: 1 that you have all gone up on the r, 1511
Jer 19:13 where they burned incense on the r to all 1511
32:29 by burning incense on the r to Baal and 1511
48:38 On all the r in Moab and in the public 1511
Zep 1: 5 those who bow down on the r to worship 1511
Mt 10:27 in your ear, proclaim from the r. 1560
Lk 12: 3 be proclaimed from the r. 1560

ROOM (83) [ROOMS, STOREROOM, STOREROOMS]

Ge 24:23 is there r in your father's house for us 5226
24:25 as well as r for you to spend the night." 5226
26:22 "Now the LORD has given us r 8143
34:21 the land has plenty of r for them. 3338+8146
43:30 He went into his private r and wept there. 2540
Lev 26:10 to move it out to make r for the new. 4946+7156
Nu 22:26 in a narrow place where there was no r 2006
Jdg 3:20 the upper r of his summer palace and said, 6608
3:23 of the upper r behind him and locked them. 6608
3:24 and found the doors of the upper r locked. 6608
3:24 "He must be relieving himself in the inner r 2540
3:25 when he did not open the doors of the r, 6608
15: 1 He said, "I'm going to my wife's r." 2540
16: 9 With men hidden in the r, 2540
16:12 Then, with men hidden in the r, 2540
2Sa 18:33 up to the r over the gateway and wept. 6608
1Ki 1:15 to see the aged king in his r, 2540
6:17 in front of this r was forty cubits long. 1074
6:27 the cherubim inside the innermost r of AIT
6:27 touched each other in the middle of the r. 1074
7:50 for the doors of the innermost r, 1074
17:19 to the upper r where he was staying, 6608
17:23 the child and carried him down from the r 6608
20:30 to the city and hid in an inner r. 928+2540+2540
22:25 day you go to hide in an inner r. 928+2540+2540
2Ki 1: 2 through the lattice of his upper r in Samaria 6608
4:10 a small r on the roof and put in it a bed and 6608
4:11 he went up to his r and lay down there. 6608
4:35 and forth in the r and then got on the bed 1074
9: 2 and take him into an inner r. 928+2540+2540
23:11 the r of an official named Nathan-Melech. 4384
23:12 on the roof near the upper r of Ahaz, 6608
2Ch 18:24 day you go to hide in an inner r. 928+2540+2540
Ezr 10: 6 of God and went to the r of Jehohanan son 4384
Ne 2:14 not enough r for my mount to get through; 5226
3:31 and as far as the r above the corner; 6608
3:32 the r above the corner and the Sheep Gate 6608
13: 5 with a large r formerly used to store 4384
13: 7 in providing Tobiah a r in the courts of 5969
13: 8 all Tobiah's household goods out of the r. 4384
Ps 10: 4 in all his thoughts there is no r for God. NIH
SS 3: 4 to the r of the one who conceived me. 2540
Jer 7:32 in Topheth until there is no more r. 5226
19:11 in Topheth until there is no more r. 5226
35: 4 the r of the sons of Hanan son of Igdaliah 4384
35: 4 It was next to the r of the officials, 4384
36:10 From the r of Gemariah son of Shaphan 4384
36:12 to the secretary's r in the royal palace, 4384
36:20 in the r of Elishama the secretary, 4384
36:21 the r of Elishama the secretary and read it 4384
38:11 with him and went to a r under the treasury NIH
Eze 40:38 A r with a doorway was by the portico 4384
40:45 "The r facing south is for 4384
40:46 and the r facing north is for 4384
41: 5 it was six cubits thick, and each side r 7521
Da 6:10 his upstairs r where the windows opened 10547
Joel 2:16 Let the bridegroom leave his r and 2540
Zec 10:10 and there will not be r enough for them. 5162
Mal 3:10 that you will not have r enough for it. 1896
Mt 6: 6 But when you pray, go into your r, 5421
Mk 2: 2 So many gathered that there was no r left, 6003
14:14 Where is my guest r, 2906
14:15 He will show you a large upper r, 333
Lk 2: 7 because there was no r for them in the inn. 5536
14:22 but there is still r.' 5536
22:11 Where is the guest r, 2906
22:12 He will show you a large upper r, 333
Jn 8:37 because you have no r for my word. 6003
21:25 even the whole world would not have r for 6003
Ac 1:13 they went upstairs to the r where 5673
9:37 and placed in an upstairs r. 5673
9:39 he arrived he was taken upstairs to the r. 5673
9:40 Peter sent them all out of the r; NIG
20: 8 in the upstairs r where we were meeting. 5673
25:23 with great pomp and entered the audience r 211
26:31 They left the r, and while talking NIG
Ro 12:19 my friends, but leave r for God's wrath, 5536
2Co 7: 2 Make r for us in your hearts. 6003
Phm 1:22 Prepare a guest r for me, 3825
Heb 9: 2 In its first r were the lampstand, NIG
9: 3 Behind the second curtain was a r called 5008
9: 6 the priests entered regularly into the outer r 5008
9: 7 But only the high priest entered the inner r, NIG

ROOMS (49) [ROOM]

Ge 6:14 make r in it and coat it with pitch inside 7860
1Ki 6: 5 in which there were side r. 7521
6:10 And he built the side r all along the temple. 3666
6:29 in both the inner and outer r, AIT
6:30 both the inner and outer r AIT
1Ch 9:26 for the r and treasuries in the house of God. 4384
9:33 in the r of the temple and were exempt 4384
23:28 to be in charge of the courtyards, the side r, 4384
28:11 its inner r and the place of atonement. 2540
28:12 of the LORD and all the surrounding r, 4384
Ne 13: 9 I gave orders to purify the r, 4384
Pr 24: 4 through knowledge its r are filled with rare 2540
Isa 26:20 enter your r and shut the doors behind you; 2540
Jer 22:13 his upper r by injustice, 6608
22:14 a great palace with spacious upper r.' 6608
35: 2 and invite them to come to one of the side r 4384
Eze 40:17 There I saw some r and a pavement 4384
40:17 there were thirty r along the pavement. 4384
40:44 within the inner court, were two r, 4384
41: 6 The side r were on three levels, 7521
41: 6 to serve as supports for the side r, 7521
41: 7 The side r all around the temple were wider 7521
41: 7 so that the r widened as one went upward. NIH
41: 8 forming the foundation of the side r. 7521
41: 9 of the side r was five cubits thick. 7521
41: 9 The open area between the side r of 7521
41:10 the [priests'] r was twenty cubits wide all 4384
41:11 There were entrances to the side r from 7521
41:26 The side r of the temple 7521
42: 1 to the r opposite the temple courtyard 4384
42: 4 In front of the r was an inner passageway 4384
42: 5 Now the upper r were narrower, 4384
42: 5 from the r on the lower and middle floors NIH
42: 6 The r on the third floor had no pillars, 2177S
42: 7 There was an outer wall parallel to the r 4384
42: 7 it extended in front of the r for fifty cubits. 4384
42: 8 While the row of r on the side next to 4384
42: 9 The lower r had an entrance on 4384
42:10 and opposite the outer wall, were r 4384
42:11 These were like the r on the north; 4384
42:12 were the doorways of the r on the south. 4384
42:12 by which one enters the r. 5527S
42:13 and south r facing the temple courtyard are 4384
42:13 the temple courtyard are the priests' r, 4384+7731
44:19 in and are to leave them in the sacred r, 4384
46:19 of the gate to the sacred r facing north, 4384
Mt 24:26 or, 'Here he is, in the inner r,' 5421
Lk 12: 3 in the ear in the inner r will be proclaimed 5421
Jn 14: 2 In my Father's house are many r; 3665

ROOST (1)

Zep 2:14 and the screech owl will r on her columns. 4328

ROOSTER (13)

Pr 30:31 a strutting r, a he-goat, and a king 2435+5516
Mt 26:34 "this very night, before the r crows, 232
26:74 Immediately a r crowed. 232
26:75 "Before the r crows, you will disown me 232
Mk 13:35 or at midnight, or when the r crows, 231
14:30 before the r crows twice you yourself will disown me three times." 232
14:72 Immediately the r crowed the second time. 232
14:72 "Before the r crows twice you will disown me three times." 232
Lk 22:34 "I tell you, Peter, before the r crows today, 232
22:60 Just as he was speaking, the r crowed. 232
22:61 "Before the r crows today, 232
Jn 13:38 I tell you the truth, before the r crows, 232
18:27 and at that moment a r began to crow. 232

ROOT (35) [ROOTED, ROOTS]

Dt 29:18 make sure there is no r among you 9247
2Ki 19:30 of the house of Judah will take r below 9247
Job 5: 3 I myself have seen a fool taking r, 9245
19:28 since the r of the trouble lies in him,' 9247
30: 4 and their food was the r of the broom tree. 9247
Ps 80: 9 and it took r and filled the land. 9245+9247
80:15 the r your right hand has planted, 4035
Pr 12:12 but the r of the righteous flourishes. 9247
Isa 11:10 the R of Jesse will stand as a banner for 9247
14:29 the r of that snake will spring up a viper, 9247
14:30 But your r I will destroy by famine; 9247
27: 6 In days to come Jacob will take r, 9245
37:31 of the house of Judah will take r below 9247
40:24 no sooner do they take r in the ground 1614+9245
53: 2 and like a r out of dry ground. 9247
Jer 12: 2 and they have taken r; 9245
Hos 9:16 Ephraim is blighted, their r is withered, 9247
Mal 4: 1 "Not a r or a branch will be left to them. 9247
Mt 3:10 The ax is already at the r of the trees, 4844
13: 6 and they withered because they had no r. 4844
13:21 since he has no r, he lasts only a short time. 4844
13:29 you may r up the wheat with them. 1748
Mk 4: 6 and they withered because they had no r. 4844
4:17 they have no r, they last only a short time. 4844
Lk 3: 9 The ax is already at the r of the trees, 4844
8:13 they hear it, but they have no r. 4844
Ro 11:16 if the r is holy, so are the branches. 4844
11:17 in the nourishing sap from the olive r, 4844
11:18 You do not support the r, 4844
11:18 but the r supports you. 4844
15:12 Isaiah says, "The R of Jesse will spring up, 4844
1Ti 6:10 the love of money is a r of all kinds of evil. 4844
Heb 12:15 the grace of God and that no bitter r grows 4844
Rev 5: 5 the R of David, has triumphed. 4844
22:16 I am the R and the Offspring of David, 4844

ROOTED (2) [ROOT]

Eph 3:17 that you, being r and established in love, 4845
Col 2: 7 r and built up in him, strengthened in 4845

ROOTS (21) [ROOT]

Jdg 5:14 whose r were in Amalek; 9247
Job 8:17 it entwines its r around a pile of rocks 9247
14: 8 Its r may grow old in the ground 9247
18:16 His r dry up below 9247
28: 9 and lays bare the r of the mountains. 9247
29:19 My r will reach to the water, 9247
Isa 5:24 so their r will decay and their flowers 9247
11: 1 from his r a Branch will bear fruit. 9247
Jer 17: 8 the water that sends out its r by the stream. 9247
Eze 17: 6 but its r remained under it. 9247
17: 7 now sent out its r toward him from the plot 9247
17: 9 or many people to pull it up by the r. 9247
31: 7 for its r went down to abundant waters. 9247
Da 4:15 But let the stump and its r, 10743
4:23 while its r remain in the ground. 10743
4:26 with its r means that your kingdom will 10743
Hos 14: 5 cedar of Lebanon he will send down his r; 9247
Am 2: 9 I destroyed his fruit above and his r below. 9247
Jnh 2: 6 To the r of the mountains I sank down; 7893
Mt 15:13 not planted will be pulled up by the r. 1748
Mk 11:20 they saw the fig tree withered from the r. 4844

ROPE (6) [ROPES]

Ex 28:14 braided chains of pure gold, like a r, 6310
28:22 braided chains of pure gold, like a r. 6310
39:15 braided chains of pure gold, like a r. 6310
Jos 2:15 So she let them down by a r through 2475
Job 41: 1 or tie down his tongue with a r? 2475
Isa 3:24 instead of a sash, a r; 5940

ROPES (28) [ROPE]

Ex 35:18 and for the courtyard, and their r; 4798
39:40 the r and tent pegs for the courtyard; 4798
Nu 3:26 the tabernacle and altar, and the r— 4798
3:37 with their bases, tent pegs and r. 4798
4:26 the r and all the equipment used 4798
4:32 with their bases, tent pegs, r, 4798
Jdg 15:13 with two new r and led him up from 6310
15:14 The r on his arms became like charred flax, 6310
16:11 "If anyone ties me securely with new r 6310
16:12 Delilah took new r and tied him with them. 6310
16:12 But he snapped the r off his arms as 4392S
2Sa 17:13 then all Israel will bring r to that city, 2475
1Ki 20:31 around our waists and r around our heads. 2475
20:32 and r around their heads, they went to 2475
Job 39: 5 Who untied his r? 4593
Ps 119:61 Though the wicked bind me with r, 2475
Isa 5:18 and wickedness as with cart r, 6310
33:20 nor any of its r broken. 2475
Jer 10:20 My tent is destroyed; all its r are snapped. 4798
38: 6 They lowered Jeremiah by r into 2475
38:11 and let them down with r to Jeremiah in 2475
38:12 under your arms to pad the r." 2475
38:13 with the r and lifted him out of the cistern. 2475
Eze 3:25 And you, son of man, they will tie with r; 6310
4: 8 up with r so that you cannot turn 6310
Ac 27:17 they passed r under the ship itself 1069
27:32 the soldiers cut the r that held the lifeboat 5389
27:40 in the sea and at the same time untied the r 2415

ROSE (62) [RISE]
Ge 7:18 The waters **r** and increased greatly on 1504
7:19 They **r** greatly on the earth, 1504
7:20 The waters **r** and covered the mountains to 1504
23: 3 Then Abraham **r** from beside his dead wife 7756
23: 7 Then Abraham **r** and bowed down before 7756
32:31 The sun **r** above him as he passed Peniel, 2436
37: 7 in the field when suddenly my sheaf **r** 7756
Ex 32: 6 So the next day the people **r early** 8899
33: 8 all the people **r** and stood at the entrances 7756
Nu 16: 2 and **r up** against Moses. 7756
Jos 8:19 in the ambush **r** quickly from their position 7756
Jdg 3:20 As the king **r** from his seat, 7756
6:38 Gideon **r early** the next day; 8899
9:43 *he* **r** to attack them. 7756
10: 1 the son of Dodo, **r** to save Israel. 7756
19: 8 when *he* **r** to go, the girl's father said, 8899
20: 8 All the people **r** as one man, saying, 7756
1Sa 5: 3 the people of Ashdod **r early** the next day, 8899
5: 4 But the following morning *when they* **r**, 8899
9:26 *They* **r** about daybreak and Samuel called 8899
2Sa 18:31 from all who **r up** against you." 7756
22: 9 Smoke **r** from his nostrils; 6590
1Ki 1:49 all Adonijah's guests **r** in alarm 7756
8:54 *he* **r** from before the altar of the LORD, 7756
18:45 the sky grew black with clouds, the wind **r**, NIH
2Ki 3:24 the Israelites **r up** and fought them 7756
8:21 but he **r up** and broke through by night; 7756
1Ch 21: 1 Satan **r up** against Israel and incited David 6641
28: 2 King David **r** to his feet and said: 7756
2Ch 20:23 The men of Ammon and Moab **r up** against 6641
21: 9 but *he* **r up** and broke through by night. 7756
Ezr 9: 5 *I* **r** from my self-abasement, 7756
10: 5 So Ezra **r up** and put the leading priests 7756
Est 5: 9 that *he* neither **r** nor showed fear 7756
Job 29: 8 and stepped aside and the old men **r** 7756
Ps 18: 8 Smoke **r** from his nostrils; 6590
76: 9 O God, **r up** to judge, 7756
78:21 and his wrath **r** against Israel, 6590
78:31 God's anger **r** against them; 6590
SS 2: 1 I am a **r** *of* Sharon, a lily of the valleys. 2483
Eze 1:19 the living creatures **r** from the ground, 5951
1:19 from the ground, the wheels also **r**. 5951
1:21 and when the creatures **r** from the ground, 5951
1:21 the wheels **r** along with them, 5951
10: 4 Then the glory of the LORD **r** from above 8123
10:15 Then the cherubim **r upward.** 8250
10:17 and when the cherubim **r**, 8123
10:17 when the cherubim rose, *they* **r** with them, 8250
10:19 the cherubim spread their wings and **r** from 8250
16:13 You became very beautiful and **r** to be 7503
Jnh 2: 7 LORD, and my prayer **r** to you, 995
3: 6 *he* **r** from his throne, 7756
4: 8 When the sun **r**, God provided a scorching 2436
Mt 7:25 The rain came down, the streams **r**, *2262*
7:27 The rain came down, the streams **r**, *2262*
Mk 16: 9 *When* Jesus **r** early on the first day of *482*
Lk 22:45 *When he* **r** from prayer and went back to *482*
23: 1 whole assembly **r** and led him off to Pilate. *482*
Ac 10:41 by us who ate and drank with him after he **r** *482*
26:30 The king **r**, and with him the governor *482*
1Th 4:14 We believe that Jesus died and **r again** and *482*
Rev 9: 2 smoke **r** from it like the smoke from *326*

ROSH (1)
Ge 46:21 Ashbel, Gera, Naaman, Ehi, **R**, Muppim, 8033

ROT (7) [ROTS, ROTTED, ROTTEN]
Pr 10: 7 but the name of the wicked *will* **r**. 8372
Isa 40:20 an offering selects wood *that will* not **r**. 8372
50: 2 their fish **r** for lack of water and die 944
Hos 5:12 like **r** to the people of Judah. 8373
Zec 14:12 Their flesh *will* **r** while they are still 5245
14:12 their eyes *will* **r** in their sockets, 5245
14:12 and their tongues *will* **r** in their mouths. 5245

ROTS (1) [ROT]
Pr 14:30 gives life to the body, but envy **r** the bones. 8373

ROTTED (1) [ROT]
Jas 5: 2 Your wealth *has* **r**, and moths have eaten *4960*

ROTTEN (2) [ROT]
Job 13:28 "So man wastes away like **something r**, 8373
41:27 like straw and bronze like **r** wood. 8375

ROUGH (4) [ROUGHER, ROUGHS]
Isa 40: 4 the **r ground** shall become level, 6815
42:16 and make the **r places** smooth. 5112
Lk 3: 5 the **r** ways smooth. *5550*
Jn 6:18 and the waters **grew r.** *1444*

ROUGHER (2) [ROUGH]
Jnh 1:11 The sea *was getting* **r and rougher.** 2143+2256+6192
1:11 The sea *was getting* **rougher and r.** 2143+2256+6192

ROUGHS (1) [ROUGH]
Isa 44:13 *he* **r** it **out** with chisels and marks it 6913

ROUND (6) [ROUNDED, ROUNDS]
Jdg 7:13 "A **r loaf** *of* barley bread came tumbling 7501
1Ki 7:31 This opening was **r**, 6318
7:31 The panels of the stands were square, not **r.** 6318
Ecc 1: 6 **r** and round it goes, 6015
1: 6 round and **r** it goes, 6015
Eze 19: 8 those from regions **r about.** 6017

ROUND (Anglicized) See also AROUND

ROUNDABOUT (1) [AROUND]
2Ki 3: 9 After a **r** march of seven days, 6015

ROUNDED (3) [ROUND]
1Ki 10:19 and its back had a **r** top. 6318
SS 7: 2 a **r** goblet that never lacks blended wine. 6044
Ac 17: 5 so *they* **r up** some bad characters from *4689*

ROUNDS (2) [ROUND]
SS 3: 3 *as* they **made** *their* **r** in the city. 6015
5: 7 *as* they **made** *their* **r** in the city. 6015

ROUSE (12) [AROUSE, AROUSED, AROUSES, ROUSED, ROUSES]
Ge 49: 9 like a lioness—who *dares to* **r** him? 7756
Nu 23:24 *they* **r themselves** like a lion that does 5951
24: 9 like a lioness—who *dares to* **r** them? 7756
Job 3: 8 those who are ready *to* **r** Leviathan. 6424
8: 6 even now *he will* **r** *himself* on your behalf 6424
41:10 No one is fierce enough *to* **r** him. 6424
Ps 44:23 Why do you sleep? **R** *yourself!* 7810
59: 5 **r** yourself to punish all the nations; 7810
Isa 28:21 *he will* **r** *himself* as in the Valley 8074
Joel 3: 7 I *am going to* **r** them out of the places 6424
3: 9 **R** the warriors! 6424
Zec 9:13 *I will* **r** your sons, O Zion, 6424

ROUSED (5) [ROUSE]
Job 14:12 men will not awake or **be r** from their sleep. 6424
SS 8: 5 Under the apple tree *I* **r** you; 6424
Eze 7: 6 *It has* **r** *itself* against you. 7810
Joel 3:12 *"Let* the nations **be r;** 6424
Zec 2:13 *he has* **r himself** from his holy dwelling." 6424

ROUSES (1) [ROUSE]
Isa 14: 9 *it* **r** the spirits of the departed 6424

ROUT (3) [ROUTED, ROUTING, ROUTS]
Jdg 1: 5 **putting to r** the Canaanites and Perizzites. 5782
Ps 92:11 my ears have heard the **r** NIH
144: 6 shoot your arrows and **r** them. 2169

ROUTE (8) [ROUTES]
Nu 14:25 and set out toward the desert *along* the **r** *to* 2006
21: 4 They traveled from Mount Hor along the **r** 2006
Dt 1:22 and bring back a report about the **r** we are 2006
1:40 and set out toward the desert along the **r** *to* 2006
2: 1 and set out toward the desert along the **r** *to* 2006
Jdg 8:11 up by the **r** *of* the nomads east of Nobah 2006
2Ki 3: 8 "By what **r** shall we attack?" 2006
Mt 2:12 they returned to their country by another **r.** *3847*

ROUTED (13) [ROUT]
Ge 14:15 to attack them and *he* **r** them, 5782
Jos 7: 4 but *they were* **r** by the men of Ai, 5674
7: 8 that Israel *has been* **r** by its enemies? 2200+6902
Jdg 4:15 the LORD **r** Sisera and all his chariots 2169
1Sa 7:10 panic that *they* **were r** before the Israelites. 5597
2Sa 10:15 Arameans saw that *they had* **been r** by Israel, 5597
22:15 bolts of lightning and **r** them. 2169
2Ki 14:12 Judah **was r** by Israel, 5597
1Ch 19:16 Arameans saw that *they had* **been r** by Israel, 5597
2Ch 13:15 God **r** Jeroboam and all Israel 5597
25:22 Judah **was r** by Israel, 5597
Ps 18:14 great bolts of lightning and **r** them. 2169
Heb 11:34 in battle and **r** foreign armies. *3111*

ROUTES (1) [ROUTE]
Job 6:18 Caravans turn aside from their **r;** 2006

ROUTING (1) [ROUT]
Jdg 8:12 and captured them, **r** their entire army. 3006

ROUTS (1) [ROUT]
Jos 23:10 One of you **r** a thousand, 8103

ROVERS (KJV) See RAIDING

ROVING (1)
Ecc 6: 9 the eye sees than the **r** *of* the appetite. 2143

ROW (15) [ROWED, ROWS]
Ex 28:17 In the first **r** there shall be a ruby, 3215
28:18 in the second **r** a turquoise, a sapphire and 3215
28:19 in the third **r** a jacinth, an agate and 3215
28:20 in the fourth **r** a chrysolite, 3215
39:10 In the first **r** there was a ruby, 3215
39:11 in the second **r** a turquoise, a sapphire and 3215
39:12 in the third **r** a jacinth, an agate and 3215
39:13 in the fourth **r** a chrysolite, 3215
39:37 the pure gold lampstand with its **r** of lamps 5120
Lev 24: 6 Set them in two rows, six in each **r**, 5121
24: 7 Along each **r** put some pure incense as 5121
1Ki 7: 3 forty-five beams, fifteen to a **r.** 3215
Eze 42: 8 While the **r** of rooms on the side next to NIH
42: 8 the **r** on the side nearest the sanctuary was NIH
Jnh 1:13 the men *did their best to* **r** back to land. 3168

ROWED (1) [ROW]
Jn 6:19 When *they had* **r** three or three and *1785*

ROWERS (KJV) See OARSMEN

ROWING (KJV) See AT THE OARS

ROWS (11) [ROW]
Ex 28:17 Then mount four **r** of precious stones on it. 3215
39:10 Then they mounted four **r** 3215
Lev 24: 6 Set them in two **r**, six in each row, 5121
1Ki 7: 2 and thirty high, with four **r** 3215
7:18 in two **r** encircling each network 3215
7:20 pomegranates in **r** all around. 3215
7:24 The gourds were cast in two **r** in one piece 3215
7:42 of network (two **r** of pomegranates 3215
2Ch 4: 3 The bulls were cast in two **r** in one piece 3215
4:13 of network (two **r** of pomegranates 3215
Job 41:15 His back has **r** of shields tightly sealed 692

ROYAL (136) [ROYALTY]
Jos 10: 2 like one of the **r** cities; 4930
11:12 Joshua took all these **r** cities and their kings 4889
13:31 and Ashtaroth and Edrei (the **r** cities of Og 4931
1Sa 27: 5 Why should your servant live in the **r** city 4930
2Sa 8:18 and David's sons were **r advisers.** 3913
12:26 the Ammonites and captured the **r** citadel. 4867
14:26 two hundred shekels by the **r** standard. 4889
1Ki 1: 9 all the men of Judah who were **r** officials, 4889
1:46 Solomon has taken his seat on the **r** throne. 4867
1:47 the **r** officials have come 4889
4: 7 for the king and the **r** household. 2257S
5: 9 by providing food for my **r** household." NIH
9: 1 the temple of the LORD and the **r** palace, 4889
9: 5 I will establish your **r** throne 4930
9:10 of the LORD and the **r** palace— 4889
10:12 of the LORD and for the **r** palace, 4889
10:13 what he had given her out of his **r** bounty. 4889
10:28 the **r** merchants purchased them from Kue. 4889
11: 3 He had seven hundred wives **of r birth** 8576
11:14 from the **r** line of Edom. 4889
11:20 whom Tahpenes brought up in the **r** palace. 7281
14:26 and the treasures of the **r** palace. 4889
14:27 on duty at the entrance to the **r** palace. 4889
16:18 the citadel of the **r** palace and set the palace 4889
22:10 Dressed in their **r** robes, NIH
22:30 but you wear your **r** robes." NIH
2Ki 7: 9 at once and report this to the **r** palace." 4889
10: 6 Now the **r** princes, seventy of them, 4889
11: 1 to destroy the whole **r** family. 4930
11: 2 from among the **r** princes, 4889
11: 5 a third of you guarding the **r** palace, 4889
11:19 king then took his place on the **r** throne, 4889
12:10 the **r** secretary and the high priest came, 4889
12:18 temple of the LORD and of the **r** palace, 4889
14:14 and in the treasuries of the **r** palace. 4889
15:25 in the citadel of the **r** palace at Samaria. 4889
16: 8 the **r** palace and sent it as a gift to the king 4889
16:18 the **r** entryway outside the temple of 4889
18:15 and in the treasuries of the **r** palace. 4889
24:13 of the LORD and from the **r** palace, 4889
25: 9 the **r** palace and all the houses 4889
25:19 of the fighting men and five **r** advisers. 4889
25:25 the son of Elishama, who was of **r** blood, 4867
1Ch 27:25 of Adiel was in charge of the **r** storehouses. 4889
27:34 Joab was the commander of the **r** army. 4889
29:25 and bestowed on him **r** splendor such 4895
2Ch 1:16 the **r** merchants purchased them from Kue. 4889
2: 1 for the Name of the LORD and a **r** palace 4895
7:11 the temple of the LORD and the **r** palace, 4889
7:18 I will establish your **r** throne, 4895
9:11 temple of the LORD and for the **r** palace, 4889
12: 9 and the treasures of the **r** palace. 4889
12:10 on duty at the entrance to the **r** palace. 4889
18: 9 Dressed in their **r** robes, NIH
18:29 but you wear your **r** robes." NIH
22:10 to destroy the whole **r** family of the house 4930
22:11 from among the **r** princes who were about 4889
23: 5 a third of you at the **r** palace and a third at 4889
23:20 and seated the king on the **r** throne, 4930
24:11 the **r** secretary and the officer of 4889
26:11 Hananiah, one of the **r** officials. 4889
28:21 the LORD and from the **r** palace and from 4889
Ezr 4:13 and the **r** revenues will suffer. 10421
4:22 to the detriment of the **r interests?** 10421
5:17 be made in the **r** archives of Babylon to see 10421
6: 4 The costs are to be paid by the **r** treasury. 10421
6: 8 to be fully paid out of the **r** treasury, 10421
7:20 you may provide from the **r** treasury. 10421
8:36 the king's orders to the **r** satraps and to 4889

Est 1: 2 from his r throne in the citadel of Susa, 4895
1: 7 and the r wine was abundant, 4895
1: 9 the women in the r palace of King Xerxes. 4895
1:11 Queen Vashti, wearing her r crown, 4895
1:19 let him issue a r decree and let it be written 4895
1:19 Also let the king give her r **position** 4895
2:16 in the r residence in the tenth month, 4895
2:17 So he set a r crown on her head 4895
2:18 and distributed gifts with r liberality. 4889
3: 2 the r officials at the king's gate knelt down 4889
3: 3 Then the r officials at the king's gate 4889
3: 9 of silver into the r treasury for the men 4889
3:12 the r secretaries were summoned. 4889
4: 7 to pay into the r treasury for the destruction 4889
4:11 and the people of the r provinces know that 4889
4:14 that you have come to r **position** for such 4895
5: 1 on her r robes and stood in the inner court 4895
5: 1 The king was sitting on his r throne in 4895
6: 8 have them bring a r robe the king has worn 4895
6: 8 one with a r crest placed on its head. 4895
8: 9 At once the r secretaries were summoned— 4889
8:14 The couriers, riding the r horses, raced out, 350
8:15 the king's presence wearing r garments 4895
Ps 45: 9 at your right hand is the r **bride** in gold 8712
72: 1 O God, the r son with your righteousness. 4889
SS 6:12 my desire set me among the r chariots 5618
7: 5 Your hair is like r tapestry; NIH
Isa 17: 3 and r **power** from Damascus; 4930
60:16 of nations and be nursed at r breasts. 4889
62: 3 a r diadem in the hand of your God. 4867
Jer 21:11 "Moreover, say to the r house of Judah, 4889
26:10 they went up from the r palace to the house 4889
32: 2 in the courtyard of the guard in the r palace 4889
33: 4 the r palaces of Judah that have been torn 4889
36:12 to the secretary's room in the r palace, 4889
38: 7 a Cushite, an official in the r palace, 4889
39: 8 The Babylonians set fire to the r palace and 4889
41: 1 who was of r blood and had been one of 4867
43:10 he will spread his r **canopy** above them. 9188
52:13 the r palace and all the houses 4889
52:25 the fighting men, and seven r advisers. 4889
Eze 17:13 a member of the r family and made a treaty 4867
Da 1: 3 in some of the Israelites from the r family 4867
1: 8 to defile himself with the r food and wine, 4889
1:13 that of the young men who eat the r food, 4889
1:15 of the young men who ate the r food. 4889
2:49 Daniel himself remained at the r court. 10421
3:27 and r advisers crowded around them. 10421
4:29 on the roof of the r palace of Babylon, 10424
4:30 Babylon I have built as the r residence, 10424
4:31 Your r **authority** has been taken from you. 10424
5: 5 near the lampstand in the r palace. 10421
5:20 from his r throne and stripped of his glory. 10424
6: 7 The r administrators, prefects, satraps, 10424
6:12 and spoke to him about his r decree: 10421
11: 6 together with her r escort and her father NIH
11:20 a tax collector to maintain the r splendor. 4895
11:45 He will pitch his r tents between the seas at 683
Hos 5: 1 Listen, O r house! 4889
Jnh 3: 6 he rose from his throne, took off his r **robes,** 168
Hag 2:22 I will overturn r thrones and shatter 4930
Zec 14:10 the Tower of Hananel to the r winepresses. 4889
Jn 4:46 a certain r **official** whose son lay sick *997*
4:49 The r **official** said, "Sir, come down before *997*
Ac 12:21 Herod, wearing his r robes, *997*
Jas 2: 8 If you really keep the r law found *997*
1Pe 2: 9 you are a chosen people, a r priesthood, *994*

ROYALTY (1) [ROYAL]

Da 11:21 who has not been given the honor of r. 4895

RUB (1) [RUBBED]

Lk 6: 1 r them in their hands and eat the kernels. *6041*

RUBBED (3) [RUB]

2Sa 1:21 the shield of Saul—no longer r with oil. 5417
Eze 16: 4 nor **were** *you* **r with salt** or 4873+4873
29:18 every head **was r bare** and every shoulder 7942

RUBBISH (1)

Php 3: 8 I consider them r, that I may gain Christ *5032*

RUBBLE (16)

2Ki 23:12 smashed them to pieces and threw the r 6760
Ezr 6:11 his house is to be made a **pile of r.** 10470
Ne 4: 2 stones back to life from those heaps of r— 6760
4:10 so much r that we cannot rebuild the wall." 6760
Job 15:28 houses crumbling to r. 1643
Ps 79: 1 they have reduced Jerusalem to r. 6505
Isa 25: 2 You have made the city a **heap of r,** 1643
Jer 26:18 Jerusalem will become a **heap of r,** 6505
Eze 26: 4 I will scrape away her r and make her 6760
26:12 timber and r into the sea. 6760
Da 2: 5 and your houses turned into **piles of r.** 10470
3:29 and their houses be turned into **piles of r,** 10470
Mic 1: 6 "Therefore I will make Samaria a **heap of r,** 6505
3:12 Jerusalem will become a **heap of r,** 6505
Zep 1: 3 The wicked will have only **heaps of r** 4843
2:14 r will be in the doorways, 2997

RUBIES (8) [RUBY]

Job 28:18 the price of wisdom is beyond r. 7165
Pr 3:15 She is more precious than r; 7165
8:11 for wisdom is more precious than r, 7165
20:15 Gold there is, and r in abundance, 7165
31:10 She is worth far more than r. 7165
Isa 54:12 I will make your battlements of r, 3905
La 4: 7 their bodies more ruddy than r, 7165
Eze 27:16 coral and r for your merchandise. 3905

RUBY (3) [RUBIES]

Ex 28:17 In the first row there shall be a r, 138
39:10 In the first row there was a r, 138
Eze 28:13 r, topaz and emerald, chrysolite, 138

RUDDER (1) [RUDDERS]

Jas 3: 4 they are steered by a very small r wherever *4382*

RUDDERS (1) [RUDDER]

Ac 27:40 the ropes that held the r. *4382*

RUDDY (4)

1Sa 16:12 He was r, with a fine appearance 145
17:42 r and handsome, and he despised him. 145
SS 5:10 My lover is radiant and r, 137
La 4: 7 their bodies more r than rubies, 131

RUDE (1)

1Co 13: 5 *It is* not r, it is not self-seeking, *858*

RUDIMENTS (KJV) See BASIC PRINCIPLES

RUE (1)

Lk 11:42 r and all other kinds of garden herbs, *4379*

RUFUS (2)

Mk 15:21 Simon, the father *of* Alexander and R, *4859*
Ro 16:13 Greet R, chosen in the Lord, *4859*

RUGGED (4)

Ps 68:15 r are the mountains of Bashan. 1493
68:16 Why gaze in envy, O r mountains, 1493
SS 2:17 a gazelle or like a young stag on the r hills. 1441
Isa 40: 4 the r **places** a plain. 8221

RUGS (2)

Isa 21: 5 They set the tables, they spread the r, 7620
Eze 27:24 embroidered work and multicolored r 1710

RUHAMAH (KJV) See LOVED ONE

RUIN (82) [RUINED, RUINING, RUINS]

Nu 11:15 and do not let me face my own r." 8288
24:20 but he will come to r at last." 7
24:24 but they too will come to r." 7
Dt 11: 4 how the LORD **brought** lasting r *on* them. 6
13:16 It is to remain a r forever, 9424
28:20 and **come to** sudden r because of 6
28:63 so it will please him to r and destroy you. 6
2Sa 15:14 to overtake us and bring r upon us and put 8288
16: 8 You have come to r because you are a man 8288
2Ki 3:19 and r every good field with stones." 3872
2Ch 34:11 kings of Judah *had* **allowed to fall into r.** 8845
Est 6:13 *you will* **surely come to r!"** 5877+5877
9:24 (that is, the lot) for their r and destruction. 2169
Job 2: 3 though you incited me against him to r him 1180
22:19 "The righteous see their r and rejoice; NIH
31: 3 Is it not r for the wicked, 369
Ps 9: 6 Endless r has overtaken the enemy, 2999
35: 4 may those who plot my r be turned back 8288
35: 8 may r overtake them by surprise— 8739
35: 8 may they fall into the pit, to their r. 8739
38:12 those who would harm me talk of my r; 2095
40:14 may all who desire my r be turned back 8288
52: 5 **bring** you **down to** everlasting r: 5997
64: 8 against them and **bring** them **to** r; 4173
70: 2 may all who desire my r be turned back 8288
73:18 you cast them down to r. 5397
Pr 3:25 of sudden disaster or of the r that overtakes 8739
5:14 I have come to the brink of utter r in 8273
10: 8 but a chattering fool **comes to** r. 4231
10:10 and a chattering fool **comes to** r. 4231
10:14 but the mouth of a fool invites r. 4745
10:15 but poverty is the r *of* the poor. 4745
10:29 but it is the r of those who do evil. 4745
13: 3 but he who speaks rashly will come to r. 4745
18:24 A man of many companions *may* **come to** r, 8318
19:13 A foolish son is his father's r, 2095
21:12 **brings** the wicked **to** r. 2021+4200+6156+8273
26:28 and a flattering mouth works r. 4510
31: 3 your vigor on *those who* r kings. 4681
SS 2:15 the little foxes *that* r the vineyards, 2472
Isa 7: 5 and Remaliah's son have plotted your r, 8288
23:13 its fortresses bare and turned it into a r. 5143
24: 1 *he will* r its face and scatter its inhabitants 6390
25: 2 the fortified town a r, 5143
26:14 and **brought** them **to** r; 9012
51:19 r and destruction, famine and sword— 8719
59: 7 r and destruction mark their ways. 8719
60:18 nor r or destruction within your borders, 8719
Jer 12:10 Many shepherds *will* r my vineyard 8845
13: 9 the same way *I will* r the pride of Judah 8845
19: 7 " 'In this place *I will* r the plans of Judah 1327
22: 5 that this palace will become a r.' " 2999
25: 9 horror and scorn, and an everlasting r. 2999
25:18 to make them a r and an object of horror 2999
27:17 Why should this city become a r? 2999
38: 4 the good of these people but their r." 8288
48:18 up against you and r your fortified cities. 8845
49:13 a r and an object of horror, of reproach and 9014
La 3:47 and pitfalls, r and destruction." 8643
Eze 5:14 "I will make you a r and a reproach among 2999
21:27 A r! A ruin! I will make it a ruin! 6392
21:27 A ruin! A r! I will make it a ruin! 6392
21:27 A ruin! A ruin! I will make it a r! 6392
23:33 the cup of r and desolation, 9014
29:10 the land of Egypt a r and a desolate waste 2999
Hos 2:12 *I will* r her vines and her fig trees, 9037
4:14 without understanding *will* **come to** r! 4231
Am 5: 9 and brings the fortified city to r), 8719
6: 6 but you do not grieve over the r *of* Joseph. 8691
Mic 6:13 *to* r you because of your sins. 9037
6:16 over to r and your people to derision; 9014
Hab 2: 9 to escape the clutches of r! 8273
2:10 You have plotted the r *of* many peoples, 7896
Zep 1:15 a day of trouble and r, 5409
2:15 What a r she has become, 9014
Hag 1: 4 while this house remains a r?" 2992
1: 9 "Because of my house, which remains a r, 2992
Ro 3:16 r and misery mark their ways, *5342*
1Ti 6: 9 and harmful desires that plunge men into r *3897*
Rev 17:16 bring her *to* r and leave her naked; *2246*
18:17 In one hour such great wealth *has been* **brought to r!'** *2246*
18:19 In one hour *she has been* **brought to r!** *2246*

RUINED (44) [RUIN]

Ge 41:36 the country *may* not **be r** by the famine." 4162
Ex 8:24 and throughout Egypt the land **was r** by 8845
10: 7 Do you not yet realize that Egypt *is* r?" 6
Dt 28:51 or lambs of your flocks until you *are* r. 6
Jdg 6: 4 the land and r the crops all the way to Gaza 8845
Job 15:28 he will inhabit r towns and houses 3948
Ps 109:10 may they be driven from their r **homes.** 2999
Pr 14:28 but without subjects a prince is r. 4745
Isa 3:14 "It is you *who have* r my vineyard; 1278
6: 5 *"I am* r! For I am a man of unclean lips, 1950
6:11 the cities **lie** r and without inhabitant, 8615
6:11 the houses are left deserted and the fields r 8615
15: 1 Ar in Moab *is* r, destroyed in a night! 1950
15: 1 Kir in Moab *is* r, destroyed in a night! 1950
24:10 The r city lies desolate; 9332
49:19 "Though you *were* r and made desolate 2999
60:12 it *will be* **utterly** r. 2990+2990
61: 4 the r cities that have been devastated 2997
Jer 4:13 Woe to us! *We* **are** r! 8720
4:27 "The whole land will be r, 9039
9:12 Why *has* the land *been* r and laid waste like 6
9:19 'How r *we are!* 8720
13: 7 but now it *was* r and completely useless. 8845
48: 1 "Woe to Nebo, for *it will* **be** r. 8720
48: 8 *be* r and the plateau destroyed, 6
Eze 6: 6 your idols smashed and r, 8697
29:12 will lie desolate forty years among r cities. 2990
30: 7 and their cities will lie among r cities. 2990
36:38 the r cities be filled with flocks of people. 2992
Joel 1: 7 my vines and r my fig trees. 4200+7914
1:10 The fields *are* r, the ground is dried up; 8720
Am 7: 9 and the sanctuaries of Israel *will be* r; 2990
9:14 they will rebuild the r cities and live 9037
Mic 2: 4 *'We are* **utterly** r; 8720+8720
2:10 because it is defiled, *it is* r, 2256+2472+2476
Na 2: 2 and *have* r their vines. 8845
Zep 1:11 all who trade with silver *will* **be** r. 4162
Zec 11: 2 the stately trees *are* r! 8720
11: 3 the lush thicket of the Jordan *is* r! 8720
Mt 9:17 wine will run out and the wineskins *will be* r. *660*
12:25 kingdom divided against itself *will be* r, *2246*
Mk 2:22 both the wine and the wineskins *will be* r. *660*
Lk 5:37 wine will run out and the wineskins *will be* r. *660*
11:17 kingdom divided against itself *will be* r, *2246*

RUINING (1) [RUIN]

Tit 1:11 *because* they *are* r whole households *426*

RUINS (57) [RUIN]

Lev 26:31 cities into r and lay waste your sanctuaries, 2999
26:33 and your cities will lie **in** r. 2999
Jos 8:28 and made it a permanent **heap of** r, 9424
1Ki 18:30 the altar of the LORD, which *was* **in** r. 2238
1Ch 20: 1 Joab attacked Rabbah and **left** it **in** r. 2238
2Ch 34: 6 and in the r around them, 2999
Ezr 9: 9 the house of our God and repair its r, 2999
Ne 2: 3 where my fathers are buried lies **in** r, 2992
2:17 Jerusalem lies **in** r, 2992
Job 3:14 **places** now **lying in** r, 2999
30:14 amid the r they come rolling in. 8739
Ps 74: 3 Turn your steps toward these everlasting r, 5397
89:40 and reduced his strongholds to r. 4745
102: 6 like an owl among the r. 2999
Pr 19: 3 A man's own folly r his life, 6156
24:31 and the stone wall *was* **in** r. 2238
Ecc 4: 5 The fool folds his hands and r himself. 430
Isa 3: 6 take charge of this **heap of** r!" 4843
5:17 lambs will feed among the r *of* the rich. 2999
17: 1 be a city but will become a heap of r. 5142

Isa 24:12 city is left **in r**, its gate is battered to pieces. 9014
44:26 'They shall be built,' and of their **r**, 2999
51: 3 and will look with compassion on all her **r**; 2999
52: 9 songs of joy together, you **r** *of* Jerusalem, 2999
58:12 Your people will rebuild the ancient **r** 2999
61: 4 They will rebuild the ancient **r** and restore 2999
64:11 and all that we treasured lies in **r**. 2999
Jer 4: 7 Your towns *will* **lie in r** 5898
4:20 the whole land **lies in r**. 8720
4:26 all its towns **lay in r** before the LORD, 5997
9:11 "I will make Jerusalem a **heap of r**, 1643
9:19 because our houses *are* **in r**.' " 8959
30:18 the city will be rebuilt on her **r**, 9424
44: 2 Today they lie deserted and **in r** 2999
44: 6 the desolate **r** they are today. 9039
46:19 for Memphis will be laid waste and **lie in r** 5898
49: 2 it will become a mound of **r**, 9039
49:13 and all its towns will be **in r** forever." 2999
51:37 Babylon will be a **heap of r**, 1643
Eze 13: 4 O Israel, are like jackals among **r**. 2999
26: 2 now that *she* **lies in r** I will prosper,' 2990
26:20 dwell in the earth below, as in ancient **r**, 2999
33:24 in those **r** in the land of Israel are saying, 2999
33:27 as I live, those who are left in the **r** will fall 2999
35: 4 I will turn your towns into **r** and you will 2999
36: 4 to the ravines and valleys, to the desolate **r** 2999
36:10 towns will be inhabited and the **r** rebuilt. 2999
36:33 and the **r** will be rebuilt. 2999
36:35 the cities that were lying **in r**, 2992
38:12 the resettled **r** and the people gathered from 2999
Joel 1:17 The storehouses *are* **in r**, 9037
Am 9:11 I will repair its broken places, restore its **r**, 2232
Na 3: 7 'Nineveh *is* **in r**—who will mourn for her?' 8720
Zep 2: 4 be abandoned and Ashkelon left in **r**. 9039
Mal 1: 4 we will rebuild the **r**." 2999
Ac 15:16 Its **r** I will rebuild, and I will restore it, *2940*
2Ti 2:14 and only **r** those who listen. *2953*

RULE (87) [RULED, RULER, RULER'S, RULERS, RULES, RULING]

Ge 1:26 and *let them* **r** over the fish of the sea and 8097
1:28 **R** over the fish of the sea and the birds of 8097
3:16 and he *will* **r** over you." 5440
37: 8 *Will you* **actually r** us?" 5440+5440
Lev 25:43 *Do* not **r** over them ruthlessly, 8097
25:46 not **r** over your fellow Israelites ruthlessly. 8097
25:53 to it that his owner *does* not **r over** 8097
26:17 those who hate you *will* **r** over you, 8097
Dt 15: 6 *You will* **r** over many nations 5440
15: 6 many nations but none *will* **r** over you. 5440
19: 4 the **r** *concerning* the man who kills another 1821
Jdg 8:22 The Israelites said to Gideon, "**R** over us— 5440
8:23 Gideon told them, "I *will* not **r** over you, 5440
8:23 nor *will* my son **r** over you. 5440
8:23 The LORD *will* **r** over you." 5440
9: 2 *to have* all seventy of Jerub-Baal's sons **r** 5440
13:12 to be the **r** *for* the boy's life and work?" 5477
1Sa 12:12 'No, we want a king *to* **r** over us'— 4887
14:47 After Saul had assumed **r** over Israel, 4867
2Sa 3:21 *you may* **r** over all that your heart desires." 4887
19:10 whom we anointed to **r over** us, 6584
1Ki 2:12 and his **r** was firmly established. 4895
5: 7 for he has given David a wise son to **r over** 6584
8:16 I have chosen David to **r** my people Israel.' 2118+6584
11:37 *you will* **r** over all that your heart desires; 4887
2Ch 6: 6 I have chosen David to **r** my people Israel.' 2118+6584
7:18 'You shall never fail to have a man *to* **r** 5440
9: 8 and placed you on his throne as king to **r** NIH
20: 6 You **r** over all the kingdoms of the nations. 5440
Ne 9:37 *They* **r** over our bodies and our cattle 5440
Ps 2: 9 *You will* **r** them with an iron scepter; 8286
7: 7 **R** over them from on high; 3782
19:13 *may they* not **r** over me. 5440
49:14 The upright *will* **r** over them in 8097
67: 4 for *you* **r** the peoples justly and guide 9149
72: 8 *He will* **r** from sea to sea and from 8097
89: 9 You **r** over the surging sea; 5440
110: 2 *you will* **r** in the midst of your enemies. 8097
119:133 **let** no sin **r** over me. 8948
Pr 8:16 and all nobles *who* **r** *on* earth. 9149
12:24 Diligent hands *will* **r**, 5440
17: 2 wise servant *will* **r** over a disgraceful son, 5440
19:10 much worse for a slave *to* **r** over princes! 5440
22: 7 The rich **r** over the poor, 5440
29: 2 when the wicked **r**, the people groan. 5440
Isa 3:12 oppress my people, women **r** over them. 5440
14: 2 of their captors and **r** over their oppressors. 8097
19: 4 and a fierce king *will* **r** over them," 5440
28:10 For it is: Do and do, do and do, **r** on rule, 7742
28:10 For it is: Do and do, do and do, rule on **r**, 7742
28:10 **r** on rule; a little here, a little there." 7742
28:10 rule on **r**; a little here, a little there." 7742
28:13 Do and do, do and do, **r** on rule, 7742
28:13 Do and do, do and do, rule on **r**, 7742
28:13 do and do, rule on rule, **r** on rule; 7742
28:13 do and do, rule on rule, rule on **r**; 7742
28:14 you scoffers *who* **r** this people in Jerusalem. 5440
32: 1 in righteousness and rulers *will* **r** 8606
52: 5 and *those who* **r** them mock," 5440
Jer 5:31 the priests **r** by their own authority, 8097
22:30 on the throne of David or **r** anymore 5440
33:26 and will not choose one of his sons *to* **r** 5440
51:28 and all the countries they **r**. 4939
La 5: 8 Slaves **r** over us, and there is none to free us 5440
Eze 20:33 *I will* **r** over you with a mighty hand and 4887
29:15 that it *will* never again **r** over the nations. 8097
Da 2:39 one of bronze, *will* **r** over the whole earth. 10715
6: 1 It pleased Darius to appoint 120 satraps to **r** 10542
7: 6 and it was given **authority to r**. 10717
11: 3 *who will* **r** *with* great power and do as 5440
11: 5 *will* **r** his own kingdom with great power. 5440
Hos 11: 5 to Egypt and will not Assyria **r over** them 4889
Mic 4: 7 The LORD *will* **r** over them in Mount Zion 4887
5: 6 *They will* **r** the land of Assyria with 8286
Zec 6:13 be clothed with majesty and will sit and **r** 5440
9:10 His **r** will extend from sea to sea and from 5445
Ro 13: 9 are summed up in this one **r**: *3364*
15:12 one who will arise *to* **r over** the nations; *806*
1Co 7:17 **the r** *I* **lay down** in all the churches. *1411*
Gal 6:16 Peace and mercy to all who follow this **r**, *2834*
Eph 1:21 far above all **r** and authority, *794*
Col 3:15 *Let* the peace of Christ **r** in your hearts, *1093*
2Th 3:10 we were with you, *we* **gave** you this **r**: *4133*
Rev 2:27 '*He will* **r** them with an iron scepter; *4477*
12: 5 who will **r** all the nations with an iron *4477*
17:17 to give the beast their power to **r**, *993*
19:15 "He *will* **r** them with an iron scepter." *4477*

RULED (31) [RULE]

Jos 12: 2 *He* **r** from Aroer on the rim of 5440
12: 3 also **r** over the eastern Arabah from the Sea NIH
12: 5 *He* **r** over Mount Hermon, Salecah, 5440
13:10 king of the Amorites, who **r** in Heshbon, 4887
13:21 king of the Amorites, who **r** at Heshbon. 4887
Jdg 11:19 *who* **r** *in* Heshbon, and said to him, 4889
Ru 1: 1 In the days when the judges **r**, 9149
1Ki 4: 1 So King Solomon **r** over all Israel. 2118+4889
4:21 And Solomon **r** over all the kingdoms from 5440
4:24 For he **r** over all the kingdoms west of 8097
9:19 and throughout all the territory he **r**. 4939
11:25 So Rezon **r** in Aram and was hostile 4887
12:17 Rehoboam *still* **r** over them. 4887
14:19 Jeroboam's reign, his wars and how *he* **r**, 4887
22:47 was then no king in Edom; a deputy **r**. 4889
2Ki 11: 3 the LORD for six years while Athaliah **r** 4887
1Ch 4:22 who **r** in Moab and Jashubi Lehem. 1249
29:27 *He* **r** over Israel forty years— 4887
2Ch 8: 6 and throughout all the territory he **r**. 4939
9:26 He **r** over all the kings from the River to 5440
10:17 Rehoboam *still* **r** over them. 4887
22:12 for six years while Athaliah **r** the land. 4887
Ne 9:28 to the hand of their enemies so that *they* **r** 8097
Est 1: 1 the Xerxes who **r over** 127 provinces 4887
Ps 106:41 and their foes **r** over them. 5440
Ecc 1:16 wisdom more than anyone who has **r over** 6584
Isa 26:13 other lords besides you *have* **r over** us, 1249
63:19 but *you have* not **r** over them, 5440
Jer 34: 1 in the empire he **r** were fighting 3338+4939
Eze 34: 4 *You have* **r** them harshly and brutally. 8097
Ac 13:21 of the tribe of Benjamin, who **r** forty years. *NIG*

RULER (85) [RULE]

Ge 34: 2 son of Hamor the Hivite, the **r** *of* that area, 5954
45: 8 of his entire household and **r** of all Egypt. 5440
45:26 In fact, he *is* **r** of all Egypt." 5440
Ex 2:14 "Who made you **r** and judge over us? 8569
22:28 "Do not blaspheme God or curse the **r** 5954
Nu 24:19 A **r** will come out of Jacob and destroy 8097
2Sa 5: 2 and you will become their **r**.' " 5592
6:21 from his house when he appointed me **r** 5592
7: 8 the flock to be **r** over my people Israel. 5592
1Ki 1:35 I have appointed him **r** over Israel 5592
11:34 I have made him **r** all the days of his life 5954
22:26 the **r** *of* the city and to Joash the king's son 8569
1Ch 5: 2 the strongest of his brothers and a **r** came 5592
11: 2 and you will become their **r**.' " 5592
17: 7 to be **r** over my people Israel. 5592
29:12 you *are* the **r** of all things. 5440
29:22 the LORD to be **r** and Zadok to be priest. 5592
2Ch 18:25 to Amon the **r** *of* the city and to Joash 8569
34: 8 of Azaliah and Maaseiah the **r** *of* the city, 8569
Ne 3: 9 **r** *of* a half-district of Jerusalem, 8569
3:12 **r** *of* a half-district of Jerusalem, 8569
3:14 **r** *of* the district of Beth Hakkerem. 8569
3:15 **r** *of* the district of Mizpah. 8569
3:16 **r** *of* a half-district of Beth Zur, 8569
3:17 Hashabiah, **r** *of* half the district of Keilah, 8569
3:18 **r** *of* the other half-district of Keilah. 8569
3:19 **r** *of* Mizpah, repaired another section, 8569
Est 1:22 be **r** over his own household. 8606
Ps 8: 6 *You* **made** him **r** over the works 5440
82: 7 you will fall like every other **r**." 8569
105:20 the **r** *of* peoples set him free. 5440
105:21 **r** over all he possessed, 5440
Pr 6: 7 It has no commander, no overseer or **r**, 5440
17: 7 how much worse lying lips to a **r**! 5618
19: 6 Many curry favor with a **r**, 5618
23: 1 When you sit to dine with a **r**, 5440
25:15 Through patience a **r** can be persuaded, 7903
28: 3 A **r** who oppresses the poor is like 1505+8031
28:16 A tyrannical **r** lacks judgment, 5592
29:12 If a **r** listens to lies, all his officials 5440
29:26 Many seek an audience with a **r**, 5440
Ecc 9:17 to be heeded than the shouts of a **r** of fools. 5440
10: 5 the sort of error that arises from a **r**: 8954
Isa 16: 1 Send lambs as tribute to the **r** *of* the land, 5440
60:17 and righteousness your **r**. 5601
Jer 30:21 their **r** will arise from among them. 5440
51:46 violence in the land and of **r** against ruler. 5440
51:46 violence in the land and of ruler against **r**. 5440
Eze 28: 2 say to the **r** *of* Tyre, 5592
31:11 I handed it over to the **r** *of* the nations, 380
Da 2:38 *he has* **made** you **r** over them all. 10715
2:48 *He* **made** him **r** over the entire province 10715
5: 7 *be made* the third highest **r** in the kingdom. 10715
5:16 *be made* the third highest **r** in the kingdom. 10715
5:29 and he was proclaimed the third highest **r** 10718
9: 1 who **was made r** over the Babylonian 4887
9:25 the **r**, comes, there will be seven 'sevens,' 5592
9:26 of the **r** who will come will destroy the city 5592
Am 2: 3 I will destroy her **r** and kill all her officials 9149
Mic 5: 1 They will strike Israel's **r** on the cheek with 9149
5: 2 of you will come for me one who will be **r** 5440
7: 3 the **r** demands gifts, the judge accepts 8569
Hab 1:14 like sea creatures that have no **r**. 5440
Zec 10: 4 from him the battle bow, from him every **r**. 5601
Mt 2: 6 for out of you will come a **r** who will be *2451*
9:18 a **r** came and knelt before him and said, *807*
Mk 5:35 from the house of Jairus, the **synagogue r**. *801*
5:36 Jesus told the **synagogue r**, *801*
5:38 to the home *of* the **synagogue r**, *801*
Lk 8:41 a man named Jairus, a **r** of the synagogue, *807*
8:49 from the house of Jairus, the **synagogue r**. *801*
13:14 the **synagogue r** said to the people, *801*
18:18 A certain **r** asked him, "Good teacher, *807*
Ac 7:10 so he made him **r** over Egypt *2451*
7:18 nothing about Joseph, **became r** of Egypt. *482*
7:27 'Who made you **r** and judge over us? *807*
7:35 'Who made you **r** and judge?' *807*
7:35 *to be* their **r** and deliverer by God himself, *807*
18: 8 Crispus, the **synagogue r**, *801*
18:17 on Sosthenes the **synagogue r** and beat him *801*
23: 5 not speak evil about the **r** of your people.' " *807*
Eph 2: 2 of this world and *of* the **r** of the kingdom *807*
1Ti 6:15 God, the blessed and only **R**, *1541*
Rev 1: 5 and the **r** of the kings of the earth. *807*
3:14 the **r** of God's creation. *794*

RULER'S (5) [RULE]

Ge 49:10 nor the **r staff** from between his feet, 2980
Ecc 10: 4 If a **r** anger rises against you, 5440
Eze 19:11 Its branches were strong, fit for a **r** scepter. 5440
19:14 on it fit for a **r** scepter.' 5440
Mt 9:23 the **r** house and saw the flute players and *807*

RULERS (83) [RULE]

Ge 17:20 He will be the father of twelve **r**, 5954
25:16 the names of the twelve tribal **r** according 5954
Jos 13: 3 (the territory of the five Philistine **r** 6249
Jdg 3: 3 the five **r** *of* the Philistines, 6249
5: 3 Listen, you **r**! 8142
15:11 "Don't you realize that the Philistines *are* **r** 5440
16: 5 The **r** *of* the Philistines went to her 6249
16: 8 Then the **r** *of* the Philistines brought her 6249
16:18 she sent word to the **r** *of* the Philistines, 6249
16:18 So the **r** *of* the Philistines returned with 6249
16:23 the **r** *of* the Philistines assembled to offer 6249
16:27 all the **r** *of* the Philistines were there, 6249
16:30 and down came the temple on the **r** and all 6249
1Sa 5: 8 the **r** *of* the Philistines and asked them, 6249
5:11 the **r** *of* the Philistines and said, "Send 6249
6: 4 according to the number of the Philistine **r**, 6249
6: 4 both you and your **r**. 6249
6:12 The **r** *of* the Philistines followed them 6249
6:16 The five **r** *of* the Philistines saw all this 6249
6:18 of Philistine towns belonging to the five **r**— 6249
7: 7 the **r** *of* the Philistines came up 6249
29: 2 As the Philistine **r** marched with their units 6249
29: 6 but the **r** don't approve of you. 6249
29: 7 do nothing to displease the Philistine **r**." 6249
2Sa 7: 7 to any of their **r** whom I commanded 8657
1Ch 12:19 after consultation, their **r** sent him away. 6249
2Ch 23:20 the **r** of the people and all the people of 5440
32:31 by the **r** *of* Babylon to ask him about 8569
Job 3:15 with **r** who had gold, 8569
Ps 2: 2 the **r** gather together against the LORD 8142
2:10 be warned, you **r** *of* the earth. 9149
58: 1 Do you **r** indeed speak justly? 380
76:12 He breaks the spirit of **r**; 5592
105:30 which went up into the bedrooms of their **r**. 4889
110: 6 heaping up the dead and crushing the **r** of 8031
119:23 Though **r** sit together and slander me, 8569
119:161 **R** persecute me without cause, 8569
141: 6 their **r** will be thrown down from the cliffs, 9149
148:11 you princes and all **r** *on* earth, 9149
Pr 8:15 By me kings reign and **r** make laws 8142
28: 2 a country is rebellious, it has many **r**, 8569
31: 4 kings to drink wine, not for **r** to crave beer, 8142
Ecc 7:19 Wisdom makes one wise man more powerful than ten **r** in a city. 8954
Isa 1:10 you **r** *of* Sodom; listen to the law 7903
1:23 Your **r** are rebels, companions of thieves; 8569
14: 5 the rod of the wicked, the scepter of the **r**, 5440
16: 8 The **r** *of* the nations have trampled down 1251
32: 1 in righteousness and **r** will rule 8569
40:23 and reduces the **r** *of* this world to nothing. 9149
41:25 He treads on **r** as if they were mortar, 6036
49: 7 to the servant of **r**: 5440
Da 7:27 and all **r** will worship and obey him.' 10717
9:12 against us and against our **r** by bringing 9149
11:39 *He will* **make** them **r** over many people 5440
Hos 4:18 their **r** dearly love shameful ways. 4482
7: 7 hot as an oven; they devour their **r**. 9149
13:10 Where are your **r** in all your towns, 9149

Mic 3: 1 you r *of* the house of Israel. 7903
3: 9 you r *of* the house of Israel, 7903
Hab 1:10 They deride kings and scoff at **r.** 8142
Zep 3: 3 her **r** are evening wolves, 9149
Mt 2: 6 by no means least among the **r** of Judah; *2450*
20:25 "You know that the **r** of the Gentiles lord it *807*
Mk 5:22 Then one *of* the **synagogue r,** named Jairus, *801*
10:42 as **r** of the Gentiles lord it over them, *806*
Lk 1:52 down **r** from their thrones but has lifted up *1541*
12:11 before synagogues, **r** and authorities, do *794*
23:13 the chief priests, the **r** and the people, *807*
23:35 and the **r** even sneered at him. *807*
24:20 and our **r** handed him over to be sentenced *807*
Jn 7:48 of the **r** or of the Pharisees believed in him? *807*
Ac 4: 5 The next day the **r,** elders and teachers *807*
4: 8 **"R** and elders of the people! *807*
4:26 the **r** gather together against the Lord and *807*
13:15 the **synagogue r** sent word to them, saying, *801*
13:27 The people of Jerusalem and their **r** did *807*
Ro 13: 3 For **r** hold no terror for those who do right, *807*
1Co 2: 6 wisdom of this age or *of* the **r** of this age, *807*
2: 8 None *of* the **r** of this age understood it, *807*
Eph 3:10 be made known *to* the **r** and authorities in *794*
6:12 but against the **r,** against the authorities, *794*
Col 1:16 whether thrones or powers or **r** *794*
Tit 3: 1 Remind the people to be subject *to* **r** *794*

RULES (20) [RULE]

Nu 9: 3 with all its **r** and regulations." 2978
9:14 so in accordance with its **r** and regulations. 2978
15:15 the same **r** for you and for the alien living 2978
2Sa 23: 3 *'When one* **r** over men *in* righteousness, 5440
23: 3 *when he* **r** *in* the fear of God, 5440
1Ki 21:18 Ahab king of Israel, who **r** in Samaria. NIH
2Ch 30:19 even if he is not clean **according to the r** 3869
Ps 22:28 to the LORD and *he* **r** over the nations. 5440
59:13 the ends of the earth that God **r** over Jacob. 5440
66: 7 *He* **r** forever by his power, 5440
103:19 and his kingdom **r** over all. 5440
Isa 29:13 of me is made up only of **r** taught by men. 5184
40:10 and his arm **r** for him. 5440
Da 4:26 when you acknowledge that Heaven **r.** 10718
Mt 15: 9 their teachings are but **r** taught by men.' " *1945*
Mk 7: 7 their teachings are but **r** taught by men.' *1945*
Lk 22:26 and the one who **r** like the one who serves. *2451*
Col 2:20 *do you* **submit** to its **r:** *1505*
2Ti 2: 5 unless he competes **according to the r.** *3789*
Rev 17:18 The woman you saw is the great city that **r** over the kings *993+2400*

RULING (8) [RULE]

Jdg 14: 4 for at that time they *were* **r** over Israel.) 5440
1Ki 3:27 Then the king **gave** *his* **r:** 6699
15:18 the king of Aram, who *was* **r** in Damascus. 3782
2Ch 16: 2 king of Aram, who *was* **r** in Damascus. 3782
Ezr 4:20 Jerusalem has had powerful kings **r** over 10718
Job 34:30 to keep a godless man from **r,** 4887
Pr 28:15 or a charging bear is a wicked man **r** over 5440
Jn 3: 1 a member of the Jewish **r** council. *807*

RUMAH (1)

2Ki 23:36 daughter of Pedaiah; she was from **R.** 8126

RUMBLE (1) [RUMBLING, RUMBLINGS]

Jer 47: 3 at the noise of enemy chariots and the **r** 2162

RUMBLING (3) [RUMBLE]

Job 37: 2 to the **r** that comes from his mouth. 2049
Eze 3:12 and I heard behind me a loud **r** sound— 8323
3:13 the wheels beside them, a loud **r** sound. 8323

RUMBLINGS (4) [RUMBLE]

Rev 4: 5 **r** and peals of thunder. *5889*
8: 5 and there came peals of thunder, **r,** *5889*
11:19 And there came flashes of lightning, **r,** *5889*
16:18 Then there came flashes of lightning, **r,** *5889*

RUMOR (5) [RUMORS]

Job 28:22 'Only a **r** *of* it has reached our ears.' 9051
Jer 51:46 *one* **r** comes this year, another the next, 9019
Eze 7:26 and **r** upon rumor. 9019
7:26 and rumor upon **r.** 9019
Jn 21:23 the **r** spread among the brothers *3364*

RUMORS (4) [RUMOR]

Jer 51:46 not lose heart or be afraid when **r** are heard 9019
51:46 the next, **r** of violence in the land and NIH
Mt 24: 6 You will hear of wars and **r** of wars, *198*
Mk 13: 7 When you hear of wars and **r** of wars, *198*

RUMP (KJV) See FAT TAIL

RUN (73) [OUTRAN, OVERRAN, OVERRUN, RAN, RUNNER, RUNNERS, RUNNING, RUNS]

Ge 19:20 Look, here is a town near enough to **r** to, 5674
31:27 Why *did you* **r off** secretly 1368
39:13 in her hand and *had* **r** out of the house, 5674
Ex 23:27 I will make all your enemies turn their backs and **r.** NIH
Lev 26:36 *They will* **r** as though fleeing from 5674
Nu 34: 7 **r a line** from the Great Sea to Mount Hor 9292
34:10 **r a line** from Hazar Enan to Shepham. 204
Jos 7:12 and **r** because they have been made liable NIH
Ru 3:10 You *have* not **r** after the younger men, 2143
1Sa 8:11 and *they will* **r** in front of his chariots. 8132
14:22 that the Philistines *were* **on the r,** 5674
19:11 "If you don't **r** *for* your life tonight, 4880
20:36 **"R** and find the arrows I shoot." 8132
21:13 and **letting** saliva **r down** his beard. 3718
31: 4 "Draw your sword and **r** me **through,** 1991
31: 4 and **r** me **through** and abuse me." 1991
2Sa 15: 1 a chariot and horses and with fifty men *to* **r** 8132
18:19 *"Let me* **r** and take the news to the king that 8132
18:22 please *let* me **r** behind the Cushite." 8132
18:23 He said, "Come what may, *I want to* **r."** 8132
18:23 So Joab said, **"R!"** 8132
1Ki 1: 5 with fifty men *to* **r** ahead of him. 8132
17:14 be used up and the jug of oil *will* not **r dry** 2893
17:16 not used up and the jug of oil *did* not **r dry,** 2893
2Ki 4:26 **R** to meet her and ask her, 8132
4:29 take my staff in your hand and **r.** 2143
5:20 *I will* **r** after him and get something 8132
9: 3 Then open the door and **r;** don't delay!" 5674
1Ch 10: 4 "Draw your sword and **r** me **through,** 1991
Ne 6:11 But I said, *"Should* a man like me **r away?** 1368
Job 1: 5 When a period of feasting *had* **r** *its* **course,** 5938
39:18 **spreads** *her* **feathers to r,** 928+2021+5257+5294
Ps 16: 4 sorrows of those will increase *who* **r after** 4554
19: 5 like a champion rejoicing to **r** his course. 8132
119:32 *I* **r** *in* the path of your commands, 8132
Pr 4:12 when *you* **r,** you will not stumble. 8132
18:10 the righteous **r** to it and are safe. 8132
Isa 5:11 in the morning *to* **r after** their drinks, 8103
7:25 and **where** sheep **r.** 5330
8: 7 overflow all its channels, **r** over all its banks 2143
10: 3 To whom *will you* **r** for help? 5674
40:31 *they will* **r** and not grow weary, 8132
Jer 2:23 *I have* not **r** after the Baals'? 2143
2:25 **Do not r** until your feet are bare 4979
17:16 not **r** away from being your shepherd; 237
23:21 yet they *have* **r** with their message; 8132
48: 6 **R** *for* your lives; 4880
51: 6 **R** *for* your lives! 4880
51:45 **R** *for* your lives! 4880
51:45 **R** from the fierce anger of the LORD. NIH
Eze 47:15 the north side it will **r** from the Great Sea NIH
47:18 "On the east side the boundary will **r** NIH
47:19 the south side it will **r** from Tamar as far as NIH
48:28 of Gad *will* **r** south from Tamar to 2118
Joel 2: 9 *they* **r** along the wall. 8132
3:18 all the ravines of Judah *will* **r** *with* water. 2143
Am 6:12 *Do* horses **r** on the rocky crags? 8132
Na 1: 4 *he* **makes** all the rivers **r dry.** 2990
Hab 2: 2 on tablets so that a herald *may* **r** with it. 8132
Zec 2: 4 **"R,** tell that young man, 8132
Mt 6:32 For the pagans **r after** all these things, *2118*
9:17 the wine *will* **r out** and the wineskins will *1772*
Lk 5:37 the wine *will* **r out** and the wineskins will *1772*
Jn 10: 5 *they will* **r away** from him because they do *5771*
Ac 27:17 that *they would* **r aground** on the sandbars *1738*
27:26 we must **r aground** on some island." *1738*
27:39 where they decided *to* **r** the ship **aground** *2034*
1Co 9:24 not know that in a race all the runners **r,** *5556*
9:24 **R** in such a way as to get the prize. *5556*
9:26 I *do* not **r** like a man running aimlessly; *5556*
Gal 2: 2 that I was running or *had* **r** *my* **race** in vain. *5556*
Php 2:16 the day of Christ that *I did* not **r** or labor *5556*
Heb 12: 1 and *let us* **r** with perseverance *5556*

RUNNER (1) [RUN]

Job 9:25 "My days are swifter than a **r;** 8132

RUNNERS (1) [RUN]

1Co 9:24 Do you not know that in a race all the **r** run, *5556*

RUNNING (30) [RUN]

Ge 16: 8 "I'm **r away** from my mistress Sarai," 1368
31:20 by not telling him he *was* **r away.** 1368
Ex 32:25 Moses saw that the people *were* **r wild** and 7277
Lev 21:20 or **r sores** or damaged testicles. 3539
22:22 anything with warts or festering or **r sores.** 3539
Jos 8: 6 *'They are* **r away** from us as they did 5674
2Sa 3:29 without *someone who has a* **r sore** or 2307
18:24 As he looked out, he saw a man **r** alone. 8132
18:26 Then the watchman saw another man **r,** 8132
18:26 "Look, another man **r** alone!" 8132
2Ki 5:21 When Naaman saw him **r** toward him, 8132
2Ch 23:12 the noise of the people **r** and cheering 8132
Ps 133: 2 **r down** on the beard, 3718
133: 2 **r** down on Aaron's beard, NIH
Pr 5:15 **r water** from your own well. 5689
Jer 2:23 You are a swift she-camel **r here and there,** 2006+8592
Eze 45: 7 **r** lengthwise from the western to NIH
48:18 on the sacred portion and **r** the length of it, NIH
48:21 Both these areas **r** the length of NIH
Jnh 1:10 (They knew he *was* **r away** from 1368
Mk 9:25 When Jesus saw that a crowd *was* **r** to *2192*
Lk 6:38 pressed down, shaken together and **r over,** *5658*
17:23 *Do* not **go r off** after them. *599+1503+3593*
Jn 20: 2 So *she* came **r** to Simon Peter and *5556*
20: 4 Both *were* **r,** but the other disciple outran Peter *5556*
Ac 3:11 all the people were astonished and **came r** *5340*
21:30 and the people came **r** from all directions. *5282*
1Co 9:26 I do not run like a man **r** aimlessly; *NIG*
Gal 2: 2 that *I was* **r** or had run my race in vain. *5556*
5: 7 *You were* **r** a **good race.** *5556*

RUNS (8) [RUN]

Ge 2:14 it **r along** the east side of Asshur. 2143
2Sa 18:27 the first one **r** like Ahimaaz son of Zadok." 5297
Ps 147:15 his word **r** swiftly. 8132
Eze 16:34 **r after** you **for** your **favors.** 339+2388
Lk 12:30 For the pagan world **r after** all such things, *2118*
Jn 10:12 he abandons the sheep and **r away.** *5771*
10:13 The man **r** away because he is a hired hand *NIG*
2Jn 1: 9 Anyone who **r ahead** and does not continue *4575*

RURAL (1)

Est 9:19 That is why **r** Jews—those living in villages 7253

RUSE (1)

Jos 9: 4 resorted to a **r:** They went as a delegation 6893

RUSH (6) [RUSHED, RUSHES, RUSHING]

Jdg 21:21 then **r** from the vineyards and each 3655
Pr 1:16 for their feet **r** into sin, 8132
6:18 feet that are quick to **r** into evil, 8132
Isa 59: 7 Their feet **r** into sin; 8132
Jer 49: 3 **r here and there** inside the walls, 8763
Joel 2: 9 *They* **r** upon the city; 9212

RUSHED (15) [RUSH]

Jos 8:19 from their position and **r forward.** 8132
Jdg 9:44 and the companies with him **r forward** to 7320
9:44 Then two companies **r** upon those in 7320
1Sa 7:11 of Israel **r out** of Mizpah and pursued 3655
2Sa 19:17 *They* **r** *to* the Jordan, where the king was. 7502
Est 6:12 But Haman **r** home, with his head covered 1894
Mt 8:32 the whole herd **r** down the steep bank into *3994*
Mk 5:13 **r** down the steep bank into the lake *3994*
Lk 8:33 the herd **r** down the steep bank into the lake *3994*
Ac 7:57 at the top of their voices, *they* all **r** at him, *3994*
14:14 *they* tore their clothes and **r out** into *1737*
16:29 **r in** and fell trembling before Paul *1659*
17: 5 *They* **r to** Jason's house in search of Paul *2392*
19:29 and **r** as one man into the theater. *3994*
Jude 1:11 *they have* **r** for profit into Balaam's error; *1772*

RUSHES (3) [RUSH]

Dt 32:35 disaster is near and their doom **r** upon them. 2590
Job 16:14 *he* **r** at me like a warrior. 8132
Isa 19: 6 The reeds and **r** will wither, 6068

RUSHING (11) [RUSH]

Jdg 5:15 **r** after him into the valley. 8938
Job 20:28 **r** waters on the day of God's wrath. 5599
Isa 30:28 His breath *is* like a **r** torrent, 8851
Eze 1:24 like the roar of **r** waters, 8041
43: 2 His voice was like the roar of **r** waters, 8041
Mic 1: 4 like water **r** down a slope. 5599
Na 2: 4 **r back and forth** through the squares. 9212
Rev 1:15 his voice was like the sound *of* **r** waters. *4498*
9: 9 of many horses and chariots **r** into battle. *5556*
14: 2 *of* **r** waters and like a loud peal of thunder. *4498*
19: 6 like the roar *of* **r** waters and like loud peals *4498*

RUST (2)

Mt 6:19 where moth and **r** destroy, *1111*
6:20 where moth and **r** do not destroy, *1111*

RUTH (21)

Ru 1: 4 one named Orpah and the other **R.** 8134
1:14 but **R** clung to her. 8134
1:16 But **R** replied, "Don't urge me to leave you 8134
1:18 that **R** was determined to go with her, 2085S
1:22 from Moab accompanied by **R** 8134
2: 2 And **R** the Moabitess said to Naomi, 8134
2: 8 Boaz said to **R,** "My daughter, listen to me. 8134
2:17 So **R** gleaned in the field until evening. NIH
2:18 **R** also brought out and gave her NIH
2:19 Then **R** told her mother-in-law about NIH
2:21 Then **R** the Moabitess said, 8134
2:22 Naomi said to **R** her daughter-in-law, 8134
2:23 So **R** stayed close to the servant girls NIH
3: 5 "I will do whatever you say," **R** answered. NIH
3: 7 **R** approached quietly, uncovered his feet NIH
3: 9 "I am your servant **R,"** she said. 8134
3:16 When **R** came to her mother-in-law, NIH
4: 5 from Naomi and from **R** the Moabitess, 8134
4:10 I have also acquired **R** the Moabitess, 8134
4:13 So Boaz took **R** and she became his wife. 8134
Mt 1: 5 Obed, whose mother was **R,** *4858*

RUTHLESS (20) [RUTHLESSLY]

Job 6:23 ransom me from the clutches of the **r'?** 6883
15:20 the **r** through all the years stored up 6883
27:13 a **r** *man* receives from the Almighty: 6883
Ps 35:11 **R** witnesses come forward; 2805
37:35 I have seen a wicked and **r** *man* flourishing 6883
54: 3 **r** *men* seek my life— 6883
86:14 a band of **r** *men* seeks my life— 6883
Pr 11:16 but **r** *men* gain only wealth. 6883

Isa 13:11 and will humble the pride of the **r.** 6883
25: 3 cities of **r** nations will revere you. 6883
25: 4 the **r** is like a storm driving against a wall 6883
25: 5 so the song of the **r** is stilled. 6883
29: 5 the **r** hordes like blown chaff. 6883
29:20 The **r** will vanish, 6883
Eze 28: 7 the *most* **r** *of* nations; 6883
30:11 He and his army—the *most* **r** *of* nations— 6883
31:12 the *most* **r** *of* foreign nations cut it down 6883
32:12 the *most* **r** *of* all nations. 6883
Hab 1: 6 that **r** and impetuous people, 5253
Ro 1:31 they are senseless, faithless, heartless, **r.** *446*

RUTHLESSLY (6) [RUTHLESS]

Ex 1:13 and worked them **r.** 928+7266
1:14 the Egyptians used them **r.** 928+7266
Lev 25:43 Do not rule over them **r**, but fear your God. 928+7266
25:46 not rule over your fellow Israelites **r.** 928+7266
25:53 that his owner does not rule over him **r.** 928+7266
Job 30:21 You turn on me **r;** 425+4200

S

SABACHTHANI (2)

Mt 27:46 in a loud voice, "Eloi, Eloi, lama **s**?"— *4876*
Mk 15:34 in a loud voice, "Eloi, Eloi, lama **s**?"— *4876*

SABAOTH (KJV) See ALMIGHTY

SABBATH (133) [SABBATHS]

Ex 16:23 a holy **S** to the LORD. 8701
16:25 "because today is a **S** to the LORD. 8701
16:26 but on the seventh day, the **S,** 8701
16:29 that the LORD has given you the **S;** 8701
20: 8 "Remember the **S** day by keeping it holy. 8701
20:10 seventh day is a **S** to the LORD your God. 8701
20:11 Therefore the LORD blessed the **S** day 8701
31:14 " 'Observe the **S**, because it is holy to you. 8701
31:15 but the seventh day is a **S** *of* rest, 8701
31:15 Whoever does any work on the **S** day must 8701
31:16 The Israelites are to observe the **S,** 8701
35: 2 a **S** *of* rest to the LORD. 8701
35: 3 in any of your dwellings on the **S** day." 8701
Lev 16:31 It is a **s** *of* rest, 8701
23: 3 but the seventh day is a **S** *of* rest, 8701
23: 3 wherever you live, it is a **S** to the LORD. 8701
23:11 priest is to wave it on the day after the **S.** 8701
23:15 " 'From the day after the **S,** 8701
23:16 up to the day after the seventh **S,** 8701
23:32 It is a **s** *of* rest for you, 8701
23:32 *you are to* **observe** your **s.**" 8697+8701
24: 8 before the LORD regularly, **S after Sabbath,** 928+928+2021+2021+3427+3427+8701+8701
24: 8 before the LORD regularly, **Sabbath after S,** 928+928+2021+2021+3427+3427+8701+8701
25: 2 the land itself **must observe a s** 8697+8701
25: 4 in the seventh year the land is to have a **s** 8701
25: 4 a sabbath of rest, a **s** to the LORD. 8701
25: 6 during the **s** year will be food for you— 8701
26:34 the land will enjoy its **s** years all the time 8701
Nu 15:32 gathering wood on the **S** day. 8701
28: 9 " 'On the **S** day, make an offering of two 8701
28:10 the burnt offering for **every S,** 928+8701+8701
Dt 5:12 "Observe the **S** day by keeping it holy, 8701
5:14 seventh day is a **S** to the LORD your God. 8701
5:15 commanded you to observe the **S** day. 8701
2Ki 4:23 "It's not the New Moon or the **S.**" 8701
11: 5 that are going on duty on the **S**— 8701
11: 7 that normally go off **S** duty are all to guard 8701
11: 9 the **S** and those who were going off duty— 8701
16:18 the **S** canopy that had been built at 8701
1Ch 9:32 *for* **every S** the bread set out on the table. 8701+8701
2Ch 23: 4 on the **S** are to keep watch at the doors, 8701
23: 8 the **S** and those who were going off duty— 8701
36:21 The land enjoyed its **s rests;** 8701
Ne 9:14 You made known to them your holy **S** 8701
10:31 or grain to sell on the **S,** 8701
10:31 from them on the **S** or on any holy day. 8701
13:15 treading winepresses on the **S** 8701
13:15 bringing all this into Jerusalem on the **S.** 8701
13:16 and selling them in Jerusalem on the **S** to 8701
13:17 you are doing—desecrating the **S** day? 8701
13:18 wrath against Israel by desecrating the **S.**" 8701
13:19 on the gates of Jerusalem before the **S,** 8701
13:19 and not opened until the **S** was over. 8701
13:19 be brought in on the **S** day. 8701
13:21 that time on they no longer came on the **S.** 8701
13:22 the gates in order to keep the **S** day holy. 8701
Ps 92: T A psalm. A song. For the **S** day. 8701
Isa 56: 2 who keeps the **S** without desecrating it, 8701
56: 6 all who keep the **S** without desecrating it 8701
58:13 "If you keep your feet from breaking the **S** 8701
58:13 if you call the **S** a delight and 8701
Isa 66:23 to another and from *one* **S** to another, 8701
Jer 17:21 Be careful not to carry a load on the **S** day 8701
17:22 of your houses or do any work on the **S,** 8701
17:22 but keep the **S** day holy, 8701
17:24 through the gates of this city on the **S,** 8701
17:24 the **S** day holy by not doing any work on it, 8701
17:27 the **S** day holy by not carrying any load 8701
17:27 the gates of Jerusalem on the **S** day, 8701
Eze 46: 1 the six working days, but on the **S** day and 8701
46: 4 on the **S** day is to be six male lambs and 8701
46:12 as he does on the **S** day. 8701
Hos 2:11 her **S days**—all her appointed feasts. 8701
Am 8: 5 **S** be ended that we may market wheat?"— 8701
Mt 12: 1 through the grainfields *on* the **S.** *4879*
12: 2 Your disciples are doing what is unlawful on the **S.**" *4879*
12: 5 *on* the **S** the priests in the temple desecrate *4879*
12: 8 For the Son of Man is Lord *of* the **S.**" *4879*
12:10 "Is it lawful to heal *on* the **S?**" *4879*
12:11 a sheep and it falls into a pit *on* the **S,** *4879*
12:12 Therefore it is lawful to do good *on* the **S.**" *4879*
24:20 not take place in winter or *on* the **S.** *4879*
28: 1 **After the S,** at dawn on the first day *4067+4879*
Mk 1:21 and when the **S** came, *4879*
2:23 **One S** Jesus was going through *1877+3836+4879*
2:24 are they doing what is unlawful *on* the **S?**" *4879*
2:27 he said to them, "The **S** was made for man, *4879*
2:27 not man for the **S.** *4879*
2:28 So the Son of Man is Lord even *of* the **S.**" *4879*
3: 2 to see if he would heal him *on* the **S.** *4879*
3: 4 "Which is lawful *on* the **S:** to do good or *4879*
6: 2 When the **S** came, he began to teach *4879*
15:42 (that is, the **day before the S**). *4640*
16: 1 When the **S** was over, Mary Magdalene, *4879*
Lk 4:16 on the **S** day he went into the synagogue, *4879*
4:31 and on the **S** began to teach the people. *4879*
6: 1 **One S** Jesus was going through *1877+4879*
6: 2 "Why are you doing what is unlawful *on* the **S?**" *4879*
6: 5 "The Son of Man is Lord *of* the **S.**" *4879*
6: 6 On another **S** he went into the synagogue *4879*
6: 7 to see if he would heal on the **S.** *4879*
6: 9 "I ask you, which is lawful *on* the **S:** *4879*
13:10 On a **S** Jesus was teaching in one of *4879*
13:14 because Jesus had healed *on* the **S,** *4879*
13:14 be healed on those days, not *on* the **S.**" *4879*
13:15 the **S** untie his ox or donkey from the stall *4879*
13:16 *on* the **S** day from what bound her?" *4879*
14: 1 One **S,** when Jesus went to eat in the house *4879*
14: 3 "Is it lawful to heal *on* the **S** or not?" *4879*
14: 5 or an ox that falls into a well on the **S** day, *4879*
23:54 and the **S** was about to begin. *4879*
23:56 the **S** in obedience to the commandment. *4879*
Jn 5: 9 The day on which this took place was a **S,** *4879*
5:10 "It is the **S;** the law forbids you to carry *4879*
5:16 Jesus was doing these things on the **S,** *4879*
5:18 not only was he breaking the **S,** *4879*
7:22 you circumcise a child on the **S.** *4879*
7:23 Now if a child can be circumcised on the **S** *4879*
7:23 for healing the whole man on the **S?** *4879*
9:14 and opened the man's eyes was a **S.** *4879*
9:16 for he does not keep the **S.**" *4879*
19:31 and the next day was to be a special **S.** *4879*
19:31 the bodies left on the crosses during the **S,** *4879*
Ac 1:12 a **S day's walk from** the city. *1584+2400+3847+4879*
13:14 *On* the **S** they entered the synagogue *4879*
13:27 of the prophets that are read every **S.** *4879*
13:42 about these things on the next **S.** *4879*
13:44 the next **S** almost the whole city gathered *4879*
15:21 and is read in the synagogues on every **S.**" *4879*
16:13 *On* the **S** we went outside the city gate *2465+3836+4879*
17: 2 on three **S days** he reasoned with them from *4879*
18: 4 Every **S** he reasoned in the synagogue, *4879*
Col 2:16 a New Moon celebration or a **S day.** *4879*

SABBATH-REST (1) [REST]

Heb 4: 9 then, a **S** for the people of God; *4878*

SABBATHS (30) [SABBATH]

Ex 31:13 'You must observe my **S.** 8701
Lev 19: 3 and you must observe my **S.** 8701
19:30 " 'Observe my **S** and have reverence 8701
23:38 to those for the LORD's **S** and in addition 8701
25: 8 " 'Count off seven **s** *of* years— 8701
25: 8 that the seven **s** *of* years amount to a period 8701
26: 2 " 'Observe my **S** and have reverence 8701
26:34 then the land will rest and enjoy its **s.** 8701
26:35 not have during the **s** you lived in it. 8701
26:43 and will enjoy its **s** while it lies desolate 8701
1Ch 23:31 on **S** and at New Moon festivals and 8701
2Ch 2: 4 and evening and on **S** and New Moons and 8701
8:13 for offerings commanded by Moses for **S,** 8701
31: 3 and for the burnt offerings on the **S,** 8701
Ne 10:33 for the offerings on the **S,** 8701
Isa 1:13 New Moons, **S** and convocations— 8701
56: 4 "To the eunuchs who keep my **S,** 8701
La 2: 6 The LORD has made Zion forget her appointed feasts and her **S;** 8701
Eze 20:12 Also I gave them my **S** as a sign between us, 8701
20:13 and they utterly desecrated my **S.** 8701
20:16 and desecrated my **S.** 8701
20:20 Keep my **S** holy, that they may be a sign 8701
20:21 and they desecrated my **S.** 8701
Eze 20:24 and desecrated my **S,** 8701
22: 8 and desecrated my **S.** 8701
22:26 they shut their eyes to the keeping of my **S,** 8701
23:38 and desecrated my **S.** 8701
44:24 and they are to keep my **S** holy. 8701
45:17 the New Moons and the **S**— 8701
46: 3 On the **S** and New Moons the people of 8701

SABEANS (4)

Job 1:15 and the **S** attacked and carried them off. 8644
Isa 45:14 the merchandise of Cush, and those tall **S**— 6014
Eze 23:42 **S** were brought from the desert along 6014
Joel 3: 8 and they will sell them to the **S,** 8645

SABTA (1)

1Ch 1: 9 Seba, Havilah, **S,** Raamah and Sabteca. 6029

SABTAH (1)

Ge 10: 7 Seba, Havilah, **S,** Raamah and Sabteca. 6030

SABTECA (2)

Ge 10: 7 Seba, Havilah, Sabtah, Raamah and **S.** 6031
1Ch 1: 9 Seba, Havilah, Sabta, Raamah and **S.** 6031

SACAR (2)

1Ch 11:35 Ahiam son of **S** the Hararite, 8511
26: 4 **S** the fourth, Nethanel the fifth, 8511

SACHET (1)

SS 1:13 a **s** *of* myrrh resting between my breasts. 7655

SACK (10) [SACKS]

Ge 42:25 to put each man's silver back in his **s,** 8566
42:27 for the night one of them opened his **s** 8566
42:27 and he saw his silver in the mouth of his **s.** 623
42:28 "Here it is in my **s.**" 623
42:35 in each man's **s** was his pouch of silver! 8566
43:21 in the mouth of his **s.** 623
44: 1 put each man's silver in the mouth of his **s.** 623
44: 2 in the mouth of the youngest one's **s,** 623
44:11 of them quickly lowered his **s** to the ground 623
44:12 And the cup was found in Benjamin's **s.** 623

SACKBUT (KJV) See LYRE

SACKCLOTH (49)

Ge 37:34 on **s** and mourned for his son many days. 8566
Lev 11:32 whether it is made of wood, cloth, hide or **s.** 8566
2Sa 3:31 and put on **s** and walk in mourning in front 8566
21:10 of Aiah took **s** and spread it out for herself 8566
1Ki 20:31 of Israel with **s** around our waists and ropes 8566
20:32 Wearing **s** around their waists and ropes 8566
21:27 he tore his clothes, put on **s** and fasted. 8566
21:27 He lay in **s** and went around meekly. 8566
2Ki 6:30 and there, underneath, he had **s** on his body. 8566
19: 1 he tore his clothes and put on **s** and went 8566
19: 2 and the leading priests, all wearing **s,** to 8566
1Ch 21:16 Then David and the elders, clothed in **s,** 8566
Ne 9: 1 fasting and wearing **s** and having dust 8566
Est 4: 1 he tore his clothes, put on **s** and ashes, 8566
4: 2 no one clothed in **s** was allowed to enter it. 8566
4: 3 Many lay in **s** and ashes. 8566
4: 4 for him to put on instead of his **s,** 8566
Job 16:15 "I have sewed **s** over my skin 8566
Ps 30:11 you removed my **s** and clothed me with joy, 8566
35:13 I put on **s** and humbled myself with fasting. 8566
69:11 when I put on **s,** people make sport of me. 8566
Isa 3:24 instead of fine clothing, **s;** 4680+8566
15: 3 In the streets they wear **s;** 8566
20: 2 the **s** from your body and the sandals 8566
22:12 to tear out your hair and put on **s.** 8566
32:11 **put s around** your waists. 2520
37: 1 he tore his clothes and put on **s** and went 8566
37: 2 and the leading priests, all wearing **s,** 8566
50: 3 with darkness and make **s** its covering." 8566
58: 5 like a reed and for lying on **s** and ashes? 8566
Jer 4: 8 So put on **s,** lament and wail, 8566
6:26 O my people, put on **s** and roll in ashes; 8566
48:37 and every waist is covered with **s.** 8566
49: 3 Put on **s** and mourn; 8566
La 2:10 on their heads and put on **s.** 8566
Eze 7:18 They will put on **s** and be clothed 8566
27:31 because of you and will put on **s.** 8566
Da 9: 3 in fasting, and in **s** and ashes. 8566
Joel 1: 8 in **s** grieving for the husband of her youth. 8566
1:13 Put on **s,** O priests, and mourn; NIH
1:13 Come, spend the night in **s,** 8566
Am 8:10 of you wear **s** and shave your heads. 8566
Jnh 3: 5 from the greatest to the least, put on **s.** 8566
3: 6 covered himself with **s** and sat down in 8566
3: 8 But let man and beast be covered with **s.** 8566
Mt 11:21 they would have repented long ago in **s** *4884*
Lk 10:13 sitting in **s** and ashes. *4884*
Rev 6:12 The sun turned black like **s** made *4884*
11: 3 for 1,260 days, clothed in **s.**" *4884*

SACKED (1)

2Ki 15:16 *He* **s** Tiphsah and ripped open all the 5782

SACKS (10) [SACK]

Ge 42:35 As they were emptying their **s,** 8566
43:12 that was put back into the mouths of your **s.** 623
43:18 that was put back into our s the first time. 623
43:21 for the night we opened our s and each 623
43:22 We don't know who put our silver in our **s."** 623
43:23 has given you treasure in your **s;** 623
44: 1 "Fill the men's s with as much food 623
44: 8 inside the mouths of our **s.** 623
Jos 9: 4 with worn-out s and old wineskins, 8566
1Sa 9: 7 The food in our s is gone. 3998

SACRED (131)

Ex 12:16 On the first day hold a s assembly, 7731
23:24 and break their s **stones** to pieces. 5167
28: 2 Make s garments for your brother Aaron, 7731
28: 4 They are to make these s garments 7731
28:38 in the s **gifts** the Israelites consecrate, 7731
29: 6 on his head and attach the s diadem to 7731
29:29 "Aaron's s garments will belong 7731
29:31 and cook the meat in a s place. 7705
29:33 because they are **s.** 7731
29:34 It must not be eaten, because it is **s.** 7731
30:25 Make these into a s anointing oil, 7731
30:25 It will be the s anointing oil. 7731
30:31 to be my s anointing oil for the generations 7731
30:32 It is **s,** and you are to consider it sacred. 7731
30:32 It is sacred, and you are to consider it **s.** 7731
30:35 It is to be salted and pure and **s.** 7731
31:10 both the s garments for Aaron the priest and 7731
34:13 smash their s **stones** and cut down 5167
35:19 both the s garments for Aaron the priest and 7731
35:21 for all its service, and for the s garments. 7731
37:29 also made the s anointing oil and the pure, 7731
39: 1 They also made s garments for Aaron, 7731
39:30 They made the plate, the s diadem, 7731
39:41 both the s garments for Aaron the priest and 7731
40:13 Then dress Aaron in the s garments, 7731
Lev 8: 9 the s diadem, on the front of it, 7731
12: 4 not touch anything s or go to the sanctuary 7731
16: 4 He is to put on the s linen tunic, 7731
16: 4 These are s garments; 7731
16:32 He is to put on the s linen garments 7731
22: 2 the s **offerings** the Israelites consecrate 7731
22: 3 the s **offerings** that the Israelites consecrate 7731
22: 4 not eat the s **offerings** until he is cleansed. 7731
22: 6 the s **offerings** unless he has bathed himself 7731
22: 7 and after that he may eat the s **offerings,** 7731
22:10 a priest's family may eat the s **offering,** 7731
22:12 she may not eat any of the s contributions. 7731
22:14 " 'If anyone eats a s **offering** by mistake, 7731
22:15 the s **offerings** the Israelites present to 7731
22:16 by allowing them to eat the s **offerings** and 7731
23: 2 which you are to proclaim as s assemblies. 7731
23: 3 a day of s assembly. 7731
23: 4 the s assemblies you are to proclaim 7731
23: 7 a s assembly and do no regular work. 7731
23: 8 And on the seventh day hold a s assembly 7731
23:20 a s **offering** to the LORD for the priest. 7731
23:21 a s assembly and do no regular work. 7731
23:24 a day of rest, a s assembly commemorated 7731
23:27 Hold a s assembly and deny yourselves, 7731
23:35 The first day is a s assembly; 7731
23:36 a s assembly and present an offering made 7731
23:37 as s assemblies for bringing offerings made 7731
26: 1 up an image or a s **stone** for yourselves, 5167
Nu 5: 9 All the s contributions the Israelites bring to 7731
5:10 Each man's s **gifts** are his own, 7731
28:18 a s assembly and do no regular work. 7731
28:25 On the seventh day hold a s assembly 7731
28:26 hold a s assembly and do no regular work. 7731
29: 1 of the seventh month hold a s assembly 7731
29: 7 of this seventh month hold a s assembly. 7731
29:12 hold a s assembly and do no regular work. 7731
Dt 7: 5 down their altars, smash their s **stones,** 5167
12: 3 down their altars, smash their s **stones** 5167
16:22 and do not erect a s **stone,** 5167
26:13 the s **portion** and have given it to 7731
26:14 not eaten any of **the s portion** while I was 5647[S]
Jos 6:19 and the articles of bronze and iron are s to 7731
1Ki 1:39 from the s tent and anointed Solomon. NIH
8: 4 of Meeting and all the s furnishings in it. 7731
14:23 high places, s **stones** and Asherah poles 5167
2Ki 3: 2 He got rid of the s **stone** *of* Baal 5167
10:26 They brought the s **stone** out of the temple 5167
10:27 They demolished the s **stone** *of* Baal 5167
12: 4 the money that is brought as s **offerings** to 7731
12:18 of Judah took all the s **objects** dedicated 7731
17:10 They set up s **stones** and Asherah poles 5167
18: 4 smashed the s **stones** and cut down 5167
23:14 the s **stones** and cut down the Asherah poles 5167
1Ch 16:42 of the other instruments for s song. 466
22:19 of the LORD and the s articles belonging 7731
23:28 of all s **things** and the performance 7731
2Ch 5: 5 of Meeting and all the s furnishings in it. 7731
14: 3 smashed the s **stones** and cut down 5167
24: 7 of God and had used even its s **objects** for 7731
31: 1 smashed the s **stones** and cut down 5167
35: 3 the s ark in the temple that Solomon son 7731
Ezr 2:63 not to eat any of the **most** s *food* until 7731+7731
3: 5 for all the appointed s feasts of the LORD, 7727
8:30 and s articles that had been weighed out to NIH
8:33 and gold and the s articles into the hands NIH
Ne 7:65 not to eat any of the **most** s **food** until 7731+7731
8: 9 "This day is s to the LORD your God. 7705
Ne 8:10 This day is s to our Lord. 7705
8:11 saying, "Be still, for this is a s day. 7705
Ps 89:20 with my s oil I have anointed him. 7731
Isa 1:29 "You will be ashamed because of the **s oaks** 381
14:13 on the utmost heights of the s **mountain.** 7600
64:10 Your s cities have become a desert; 7731
65: 5 for *I am too s for* you!' 7727
Jer 31:23 O righteous dwelling, O s mountain.' 7731
43:13 in Egypt he will demolish the s **pillars** 5167
La 4: 1 The s gems are scattered at the head 7731
Eze 44:19 in and are to leave them in the s rooms, 7731
45: 1 the land as a s *district,* 25,000 cubits long 7731
45: 3 In the s district, measure off a section NIH
45: 4 be the s portion of the land for the priests, 7731
45: 6 cubits long, adjoining the s portion; 7731
45: 7 by the s district and the property of the city. 7731
46:19 of the gate to the s rooms facing north, 7731
48:10 This will be the s portion for the priests. 7731
48:12 be a special gift to them from the s portion NIH
48:18 the s portion and running the length of it, 7731
48:20 the s portion, along with the property of 7731
48:21 of the area formed by the s portion and 7731
48:21 cubits of the s portion to the eastern border, NIH
48:21 the s portion with the temple sanctuary will 7731
Hos 3: 1 to other gods and love the s raisin **cakes."** 862
3: 4 without sacrifice or s **stones,** 5167
10: 1 his land prospered, he adorned his s **stones.** 5167
10: 2 and destroy their s **stones.** 5167
Joel 1:14 Declare a holy fast; call a s **assembly.** 6809
2:15 declare a holy fast, call a s **assembly.** 6809
Mic 5:13 and your s **stones** from among you; 5167
Zec 14:20 the LORD's house will be like the s **bowls** 4670
Mt 7: 6 "Do not give dogs what is **s;** *41*
23:17 gold, or the temple that **makes** the gold **s?** *39*
23:19 the gift, or the altar that **makes** the gift **s?** *39*
Ro 14: 5 One man considers one day more s than another; *NIG*
1Co 3:17 God's temple is **s,** and you are that temple. *41*
2Pe 1:18 when we were with him on the s mountain. *41*
2:21 the s command that was passed on to them. *41*

SACRIFICE (166) [SACRIFICED, SACRIFICES, SACRIFICING]

Ge 22: 2 S him there as a burnt offering on one of 6590
31:54 He offered a s there in the hill country 2285
Ex 5: 8 'Let us go and s to our God.' 2284
5:17 'Let us go and s to the LORD.' 2284
8:25 "Go, s to your God here in the land." 2284
12:27 'It is the Passover s to the LORD, 2285
13:15 This is why I s to the LORD 2284
20:24 and s on it your burnt offerings 2284
23:18 "Do not offer the blood of a s to me along 2285
29:36 S a bull each day as a sin offering 6913
29:41 S the other lamb at twilight with 6913
34:15 to their gods and s to them, 2284
34:25 "Do not offer the blood of a s *to* me along 2285
34:25 of the s *from* the Passover Feast remain 2285
Lev 3: 3 **s made** to the LORD **by fire:** 852
3: 9 **s made** to the LORD **by fire:** 852
7:16 the s shall be eaten on the day he offers it, 2285
7:17 of the s left over till the third day must 2285
7:29 the LORD is to bring part of it as his s to 7933
9: 4 a ram for a fellowship offering to s before 2284
9: 7 "Come to the altar and s your sin offering 6913
9: 7 s the offering that is for the people 6913
14:19 *to* s the sin offering and make atonement 6913
14:30 *he shall* s the doves or the young pigeons, 6913
15:15 The priest *is to* s them, 6913
15:30 The priest *is to* s one for a sin offering and 6913
16: 9 to the LORD and s it for a sin offering. 6913
16:24 and s the burnt offering for himself and 6913
17: 5 and s them as fellowship offerings. 2284
17: 8 who offers a burnt offering or s 2285
17: 9 the entrance to the Tent of Meeting to s it to 6913
19: 5 " 'When *you* s a fellowship offering to 2284
19: 5 s it in such a way that it will be accepted 2284
19: 6 It shall be eaten on the day you s it or on 2285
22:29 "When *you* s a thank offering to 2284
22:29 s it in such a way that it will be accepted 2284
23:12 *you must* s as a burnt offering to 6913
23:19 Then s one male goat for a sin offering 6913
Nu 6:17 and *is to* s the ram as a fellowship offering 6913
6:18 and put it in the fire that is under the s *of* 2285
7:88 for the s *of* the fellowship offering came 2285
15: 5 for the burnt offering or the **s,** 2285
15: 8 a young bull as a burnt offering or **s,** 2285
Dt 12:13 not *to* s your burnt offerings anywhere you please. 6590
15:21 *you must* not s it to the LORD your God. 2284
16: 2 S as the Passover to the LORD your God 2284
16: 4 of the meat *you* s on the evening of 2284
16: 5 You must not s the Passover in any town 2284
16: 6 There *you must* s the Passover in 2284
17: 1 *Do* not s to the LORD your God an ox or 2284
18: 3 from the people *who* s a bull or 2284+2285
27: 7 S fellowship offerings there, 2284
Jos 22:23 or to s fellowship offerings on it, 6913
Jdg 11:31 and *I will* s it as a burnt offering." 6590
16:23 the Philistines assembled to offer a great s 2285
1Sa 1: 3 to worship and s to the LORD Almighty 2284
1: 4 Whenever the day came for Elkanah *to* s, 2284
1:21 up with all his family to offer the annual s 2285
2:13 the people that whenever anyone offered a s 2285
2:19 up with her husband to offer the annual **s.** 2285
2:29 Why do you scorn my s and offering 2285
3:14 of Eli's house will never be atoned for by s 2285
1Sa 9:12 for the people have a s at the high place. 2285
9:13 because he must bless the **s;** 2285
10: 8 down to you to s burnt offerings 6590
15:15 and cattle to s to the LORD your God, 2284
15:21 in order to s them to the LORD your God 2284
15:22 To obey is better than **s,** 2285
16: 2 'I have come to s to the LORD.' 2284
16: 3 Invite Jesse to the **s,** 2285
16: 5 I have come to s to the LORD. 2284
16: 5 Consecrate yourselves and come to the s 2285
16: 5 and his sons and invited them to the s. 2285
20: 6 because an annual s is being made there 2285
20:29 because our family is observing a s in 2285
2Sa 24:24 not s to the LORD my God burnt offerings 6590
1Ki 8:63 Solomon **offered a** s of fellowship offerings 2284
13: 2 On you *he will* s the priests of the high 2284
18:29 until the time for the **evening s.** 4966+6590
18:36 At the time of **s,** the prophet Elijah 4966+6590
18:38 fire of the LORD fell and burned up the **s,** 6592
2Ki 3:20 about the time for offering the **s,** 4966
3:27 and offered him as a s on the city wall. 6592
10:19 I am going to hold a great s for Baal. 2285
17:35 serve them or s to them. 2284
23:10 so no one *could use* it *to* s his son 6296
1Ch 21:24 or s a burnt offering that costs me nothing." 6590
2Ch 7: 5 a s *of* twenty-two thousand head of cattle 2285
28:23 *I will* s to them so they will help me." 2284
29:27 the order to s the burnt offering on the altar. 6590
29:28 the s of the burnt offering was completed. NIH
33:17 however, continued *to* s at the high places, 2284
Ezr 3: 2 the God of Israel to s burnt offerings on it, 6590
7:17 and s them on the altar of the temple 10638
9: 4 And I sat there appalled until the evening **s.** 4966
9: 5 Then, at the evening **s,** 4966
Job 1: 5 in the morning *he would* s a burnt offering 6590
42: 8 to my servant Job and s a burnt offering 6590
Ps 27: 6 at his tabernacle *will I* s *with* shouts 2284+2285
40: 6 S and offering you did not desire, 2285
50: 5 who made a covenant with me by **s."** 2285
50:14 S thank offerings to God, 2284
51:16 You do not delight in **s,** or I would bring it; 2285
54: 6 *I will* s a freewill offering to you; 2284
66:15 *I will* s fat animals to you and 6590+6592
107:22 *Let them* s thank offerings and tell 2284
116:17 *I will* s a thank offering to you and call 2284
141: 2 up of my hands be like the evening **s.** 4966
Pr 15: 8 The LORD detests the s *of* the wicked, 2285
21: 3 more acceptable to the LORD than **s.** 2285
21:27 The s *of* the wicked is detestable— 2285
Ecc 5: 1 to listen rather than to offer the s of fools, 2285
Isa 34: 6 For the LORD has a s in Bozrah and 2285
57: 5 you s your children in the ravines and under 8821
Jer 32:35 in the Valley of Ben Hinnom to s their sons 6296
46:10 will offer a s in the land of the north by 2285
Eze 20:26 the s *of* every firstborn— 6296
20:31 the s *of* your sons in the fire— 6296
39:17 from all around to the s I am preparing 2285
39:17 the great s on the mountains of Israel. 2285
39:19 At the s I am preparing for you, 2285
43:24 on them and s them as a burnt offering to 6590
46: 2 The priests *are to* s his burnt offering 6913
Da 8:11 it took away the **daily** s from him, 9458
8:12 and the **daily** s were given over 9458
8:13 the vision concerning the **daily s,** 9458
9:21 about the time of the evening s. 4966
9:27 In the middle of the 'seven' he will put an end to s 2285
11:31 and will abolish the **daily s.** 9458
12:11 the time that the **daily** s is abolished and 9458
Hos 3: 4 without s or sacred stones, 2285
4:13 *They* s on the mountaintops 2284
4:14 with harlots and s with shrine prostitutes— 2284
6: 6 For I desire mercy, not **s,** 2285
12:11 *Do they* s bulls in Gilgal? 2284
13: 2 *"They* **offer** human s and kiss 2284
Jnh 1:16 a s to the LORD and made vows to him. 2285
2: 9 with a song of thanksgiving, *will* s to you. 2284
Zep 1: 7 The LORD has prepared a **s;** 2285
1: 8 On the day of the LORD's s I will punish 2285
Zec 14:21 and all who come to s will take some of 2284
Mal 1: 8 When you bring blind animals for **s,** 2284
1: 8 When *you* s crippled or diseased animals, 5602
Mt 9:13 'I desire mercy, not **s.'** *2602*
12: 7 'I desire mercy, not **s,'** *2602*
Mk 14:12 it was customary *to* s the Passover lamb, *2604*
Lk 2:24 and to offer a s in keeping with what is said *2602*
Ro 3:25 God presented him as a **s of atonement,** *2663*
1Co 10:19 **s offered to an idol** is anything, *1628*
10:28 "This has been **offered in s,"** *2638*
Eph 5: 2 for us as a fragrant offering and s to God. *2602*
Php 2:17 the s and service coming from your faith, *2602*
4:18 an acceptable **s,** pleasing to God. *NIG*
Heb 9:26 to do away with sin by the s of himself. *2602*
10: 5 **"S** and offering you did not desire, *2602*
10:10 we have been made holy through the s of the body of Jesus Christ *4714*
10:12 for all time one s for sins, *2602*
10:14 *by* one s he has made perfect forever those who are being made holy. *4714*
10:18 there is no longer any s for sin. *4714*
10:26 no s for sins is left, *2602*
11: 4 By faith Abel offered God a better s than *2602*
11:17 when God tested him, **offered** Isaac **as a s.** *4712*
11:17 *was about to* s his one and only son, *4712*
13:15 let us continually offer to God a s of praise *2602*
1Jn 2: 2 He is the **atoning** s for our sins, *2662*
4:10 and sent his Son as an **atoning** s *2662*

SACRIFICED (68) [SACRIFICE]

Ge 8:20 *he* s burnt offerings on it. 6590
22:13 the ram and s it as a burnt offering instead 6590
Ex 24: 5 and s young bulls as fellowship offerings to 2284
32: 6 the people rose early and s burnt offerings 6590
32: 8 They have bowed down to it and s to it 2284
Lev 4:10 just as the fat is removed from the ox s *as* 2285
9:22 And *having* s the sin offering, 6913
10:19 "Today *they* s their sin offering 7928
18:21 " 'Do not give any of your children to *be* s 6296
Nu 7:17 to be s as a fellowship offering. 2285
7:23 to be s as a fellowship offering. 2285
7:29 to be s as a fellowship offering. 2285
7:35 to be s as a fellowship offering. 2285
7:41 to be s as a fellowship offering. 2285
7:47 to be s as a fellowship offering. 2285
7:53 to be s as a fellowship offering. 2285
7:59 to be s as a fellowship offering. 2285
7:65 to be s as a fellowship offering. 2285
7:71 to be s as a fellowship offering. 2285
7:77 to be s as a fellowship offering. 2285
7:83 to be s as a fellowship offering. 2285
22:40 Balak s cattle and sheep, 2284
Dt 32:17 *They* s to demons, which are not God— 2284
Jos 8:31 and s fellowship offerings. 2284
Jdg 6:28 beside it cut down and the second bull s on 6590
13:19 and s it on a rock to the LORD. 6590
1Sa 6:14 the cart and s the cows as a burnt offering 6590
11:15 There *they* s fellowship offerings before 2284
2Sa 6:13 *he* s a bull and a fattened calf. 2284
6:17 and David s burnt offerings 6590
24:25 to the LORD there and s burnt offerings 6590
1Ki 1: 9 Adonijah then s sheep, 2284
1:19 *He has* s great numbers of cattle, 2284
1:25 down and s great numbers of cattle, 2284
3:15 of the Lord's covenant and s burnt offerings 6590
9:25 a year Solomon s burnt offerings 6590
2Ki 16: 3 of the kings of Israel and even s his son in 6296
17:17 *They* s their sons and daughters in the fire. 6296
21: 6 *He* s his own son in the fire, 6296
1Ch 15:26 seven bulls and seven rams *were* s. 2284
21:26 to the LORD there and s burnt offerings 6590
2Ch 8:12 Solomon s burnt offerings to the LORD, 6590
15:11 At that time *they* s to the LORD 2284
28: 3 the Valley of Ben Hinnom and s his sons in 1277
33: 6 He s his sons in the fire in the Valley 6296
33:16 of the LORD and s fellowship offerings 2284
34: 4 over the graves of those *who had* s to them. 2284
Ezr 3: 3 on its foundation and s burnt offerings on it 6590
8:35 from captivity s burnt offerings to the God 7928
Ps 106:37 *They* s their sons and their daughters 2284
106:38 whom *they* s to the idols of Canaan, 2284
Eze 16:20 to me and s them as food to the idols. 2284
16:21 You slaughtered my children and s them to the idols. 928+5989+6296
23:37 *they* even s their children, 6296
23:39 On the very day they s their children 8821
Hos 11: 2 *They* s to the Baals and they burned incense 2284
Lk 22: 7 on which the Passover lamb had *to be* s. *2604*
Ac 15:29 You are to abstain from **food s to idols,** *1628*
21:25 they should abstain from **food s to idols,** *1628*
1Co 5: 7 For Christ, our Passover lamb, *has been* s. *2604*
8: 1 Now about **food s to idols:** *1628*
8: 4 So then, about eating food **s to idols:** *1628*
8: 7 of it as having been s to an idol, *NIG*
8:10 to eat what *has been* **s to idols?** *1628*
Heb 7:27 **He** s for their sins once for all *4472*[S]
9:28 so Christ *was* s once to take away the sins *4712*
Rev 2:14 to sin by eating **food s to idols** and *1628*
2:20 and the eating of **food s to idols.** *1628*

SACRIFICES (142) [SACRIFICE]

Ge 46: 1 he offered s to the God of his father Isaac. 2285
Ex 3:18 *to* **offer** s to the LORD our God.' 2284
5: 3 *to* **offer** s to the LORD our God, 2284
8: 8 and I will let your people go *to* **offer** s to 2284
8:26 *The* s *we* **offer** the LORD our God would 2284
8:26 *we* **offer** s that are detestable in their eyes, 2284
8:27 *to* **offer** s to the LORD our God, 2284
8:28 *to* **offer** s to the LORD your God in 2284
8:29 by not letting the people go to **offer** s to 2284
10:25 to have s and burnt offerings to present to 2285
18:12 brought a burnt offering and other s to God, 2285
22:20 "*Whoever* s to any god other than 2284
34:15 they will invite you and you will eat their s. 2285
Lev 17: 3 Any Israelite who s an ox, 8821
17: 5 to the LORD the s they are now making in 2285
17: 7 They must no longer offer any of their s to 2285
23:37 s and drink offerings required for each day. 2285
Nu 15: 3 whether burnt offerings or s, 2285
25: 2 who invited them to the s *to* their gods. 2285
Dt 12: 6 there bring your burnt offerings and s, 2285
12:11 your burnt offerings and **s,** 2285
12:27 of your s must be poured beside the altar of 2285
12:31 **burn** their sons and daughters in the fire **as** s to their gods. 8596
18:10 among you *who* s his son or daughter in 6296
32:38 the gods who ate the fat of their s and drank 2285
33:19 and there offer s *of* righteousness; 2285
Jos 22:26 but not for burnt offerings or **s.'** 2285
22:27 s and fellowship offerings. 2285
22:28 not for burnt offerings and s, 2285
22:29 grain offerings and **s,** 2285
Jdg 2: 5 There *they* **offered** s to the LORD. 2284
1Sa 6:15 and **made** s to the LORD. 2284+2285
1Sa 15:22 the LORD delight in burnt offerings and s 2285
2Sa 15:12 While Absalom was offering **s,** 2285
15:24 and Abiathar **offered** s until all 6590
1Ki 3: 3 except that he **offered** s and burned incense 2284
3: 4 The king went to Gibeon to **offer s,** 2284
8:62 the king and all Israel with him offered s 2285
11: 8 who burned incense and **offered s** 2284
12:27 If these people go up to offer s at the temple 2285
12:32 and **offered** s on the altar. 6590
12:33 *he* **offered** s on the altar he had built 6590
22:43 and the people continued *to* **offer s** 2284
2Ki 5:17 and s to any other god but the LORD. 2285
10:24 they went in to make s and burnt offerings. 2285
12: 3 *to* **offer** s and burn incense there. 2284
14: 4 *to* **offer** s and burn incense there. 2284
15: 4 *to* **offer** s and burn incense there. 2284
15:35 *to* **offer** s and burn incense there. 2284
16: 4 *He* **offered** s and burned incense at 2284
16:15 the blood of the burnt offerings and **s.** 2285
17:31 **burned** their children in the fire **as s** 8596
17:36 down and to him **offer s.** 2284
1Ch 21:28 *he* **offered** s there. 2284
23:13 to **offer** s before the LORD, 7787
29:21 The next day *they* **made** s to the LORD 2284+2285
29:21 and other s in abundance for all Israel. 2285
2Ch 2: 6 except as a place to **burn** s before him? 7787
7: 1 and consumed the burnt offering and the **s,** 2285
7: 4 the king and all the people offered s before 2285
7:12 this place for myself as a temple for **s.** 2285
11:16 followed the Levites to Jerusalem to **offer** s 2284
25:14 bowed down to them and **burned** s to them. 7787
28: 3 He **burned** s in the Valley of Ben Hinnom 7787
28: 4 *He* **offered** s and burned incense at 2284
28:23 *He* **offered** s to the gods of Damascus, 2284
28:25 in Judah he built high places to **burn** s 7787
29:31 Come and bring s and thank offerings to 2285
29:31 the assembly brought s and thank offerings, 2285
29:33 The animals consecrated as s amounted NIH
32:12 before one altar and **burn** s on it'? 7787
33:22 Amon worshiped and **offered** s to all 2284
Ezr 3: 3 both the morning and evening **s.** 6592
3: 5 the New Moon s and the sacrifices for all NIH
3: 5 and the s for all the appointed sacred feasts NIH
6: 3 the temple be rebuilt as a place to present s, 10157
6:10 so that *they may* **offer** s pleasing to the God 10638
Ne 4: 2 *Will they* **offer s?** 2284
12:43 And on that day they offered great **s,** 2285
Ps 4: 5 Offer right s and trust in the LORD. 2285
20: 3 May he remember all your s 4966
50: 8 for your s or your burnt offerings, 2285
50:23 *He who* s thank offerings honors me, 2284
51:17 The s *of* God are a broken spirit; 2285
51:19 Then there will be righteous s, 2285
106:28 of Peor and ate s *offered to* lifeless gods; 2285
Ecc 9: 2 those *who* **offer** s and those who do not. 2284
Isa 1:11 multitude of your **s**—what are they to me?" 2285
19:21 with s and grain offerings; 2285
43:23 nor honored me with your **s.** 2285
43:24 or lavished on me the fat of your **s.** 2285
56: 7 Their burnt offerings and s will be accepted 2285
57: 7 there you went up to offer your **s.** 2285
65: 3 **offering** s in gardens and burning incense 2284
65: 7 "Because *they* **burned** s on the mountains 7787
66: 3 *whoever* s a bull is like one who kills a man, 8821
Jer 6:20 your s do not please me." 2285
7:21 to your other s and eat the meat yourselves! 2285
7:22 about burnt offerings and **s,** 2285
17:26 bringing burnt offerings and **s,** 2285
19: 4 *they have* **burned** s in it to gods 7787
33:18 to burn grain offerings and to present **s.' "** 2285
Eze 20:28 there they offered their **s,** 2285
20:40 along with all your holy **s.** NIH
40:41 on which *the* s *were* **slaughtered.** 8821
40:42 the burnt offerings and the other **s.** 2285
44:11 they may slaughter the burnt offerings and s 2285
44:15 they are to stand before me to **offer** s *of* fat 7928
46:24 at the temple will cook the s *of* the people." 2285
Hos 4:19 and their s will bring them shame. 2285
8:13 They offer s given to me and they eat 2285
9: 4 nor will their s please him. 2285
9: 4 Such s will be to them like the bread NIH
Am 4: 4 Bring your s every morning, 2285
5:25 "Did you bring me s and offerings 2285
Hab 1:16 Therefore *he* s to his net and burns incense 2284
Mal 1:13 or diseased animals and offer them as s, 4966
1:14 but then s a blemished animal to the Lord. 2284
2: 3 the offal from your **festival s,** 2504
Mk 1:44 show yourself to the priest and **offer** the s *4712*
12:33 love your neighbor as yourself is more important than all burnt offerings and **s."** *2602*
Lk 5:14 show yourself to the priest and **offer** the s *4712*
13: 1 whose blood Pilate had mixed with their **s.** *2602*
Ac 7:41 They brought s to it and held a celebration *2602*
7:42 " 'Did you bring me s and offerings *2602*
14:13 and the crowd wanted *to* **offer** s to them. *2604*
Ro 12: 1 to offer your bodies as living s, *2602*
1Co 10:18 Do not those who eat the s participate in *2602*
10:20 s of pagans *are* **offered** *2604*
Heb 5: 1 to offer gifts and s for sins. *2602*
5: 3 This is why he has to **offer** s *4712*
7:27 he does not need to offer s day after day, *2602*
8: 3 to offer both gifts and s, *2602*
9: 9 the gifts and s being offered were not able *2602*
9:23 to be purified with these s, *NIG*
9:23 *with* better s than these. *2602*
10: 1 *by* the same s repeated endlessly year *2602*
10: 3 But those s are an annual reminder of sins, *NIG*
Heb 10: 8 First he said, "**S** and offerings, *2602*
10:11 again and again he offers the same s, *2602*
13:16 for *with* such s God is pleased. *2602*
1Pe 2: 5 offering spiritual s acceptable to God *2602*

SACRIFICING (12) [SACRIFICE]

1Sa 2:15 and say to the man who *was* s, "Give 2284
7:10 While Samuel was s the burnt offering, 6590
2Sa 6:18 After he had finished s the burnt offerings 6590
1Ki 3: 2 however, *were still* s at the high places, 2284
8: 5 s so many sheep and cattle that they could 2284
12:32 s to the calves he had made. 2284
1Ch 16: 2 After David had finished s 6590
2Ch 5: 6 s so many sheep and cattle that they could 2284
35:14 *were* s the burnt offerings and 6590
Ezr 4: 2 we seek your God and *have been* s to him 2284
Eze 43:18 for s burnt offerings and sprinkling blood 6590
Ac 14:18 the crowd from s to them. *2604*

SACRILEGE (KJV) See ROB TEMPLES

SAD (9) [SADDENED, SADNESS]

Ge 40: 7 "Why are your faces *so* s today?" 8273
Ne 2: 1 I had not been s in his presence before; 8273
2: 2 "Why does your face **look** *so* s 8273
2: 3 Why *should* my face not **look** s when 8317
Ecc 7: 3 because a s face is good for the heart. 8278
Mt 19:22 the young man heard this, he went away **s,** *3382*
26:22 They *were* very s and began to say *3382*
Mk 10:22 went away **s,** because he had great wealth. *3382*
Lk 18:23 When he heard this, he became **very s,** *4337*

SADDENED (1) [SAD]

Mk 14:19 *They were* **s,** and one by one they said *3382*

SADDLE (5) [SADDLEBAGS, SADDLED]

Ge 31:34 inside her camel's s and was sitting on them 4121
Jdg 5:10 sitting on your **s blankets,** 4496
1Ki 13:13 he said to his sons, "**S** the donkey for me." 2502
13:27 "**S** the donkey for me," and they did so. 2502
Eze 27:20 " 'Dedan traded in s blankets with you. 8210

SADDLEBAGS (1) [SADDLE]

Ge 49:14 donkey lying down between **two s.** 5478

SADDLED (10) [SADDLE]

Ge 22: 3 Abraham got up and s his donkey. 2502
Nu 22:21 s his donkey and went with the princes 2502
Jdg 19:10 with his two s donkeys and his concubine. 2502
2Sa 16: 1 He had a string of donkeys s and loaded 2502
17:23 *he* s his donkey and set out for his house 2502
19:26 *'I will* **have** my donkey s and will ride 2502
1Ki 2:40 he s his donkey and went to Achish at Gath 2502
13:13 And when *they had* s the donkey for him, 2502
13:23 the prophet who had brought him back s his donkey 2502
2Ki 4:24 *She* s the donkey and said to her servant, 2502

SADDUCEES (14)

Mt 3: 7 and S coming to where he was baptizing, *4881*
16: 1 and S came to Jesus and tested him *4881*
16: 6 against the yeast of the Pharisees and **S."** *4881*
16:11 against the yeast *of* the Pharisees and **S."** *4881*
16:12 against the teaching *of* the Pharisees and **S.** *4881*
22:23 the **S,** who say there is no resurrection, *4881*
22:34 Hearing that Jesus had silenced the **S,** *4881*
Mk 12:18 Then the S, who say there is no resurrection, *4881*
Lk 20:27 *of* the **S,** who say there is no resurrection, *4881*
Ac 4: 1 of the temple guard and the S came up *4881*
5:17 who were members of the party *of* the **S,** *4881*
23: 6 of them were S and the others Pharisees, *4881*
23: 7 *between* the Pharisees and the S, *4881*
23: 8 (The S say that there is no resurrection, *4881*

SADNESS (1) [SAD]

Ne 2: 2 This can be nothing but s *of* heart." 8278

SADOC (KJV) See ZADOK

SAFE (28) [SAVE]

Dt 29:19 "I will be s, even though I persist in going 8934
1Sa 20: 7 he says, 'Very well,' then your servant is **s.** 8934
20:21 as surely as the LORD lives, you are **s;** 8934
22:23 You will be s with me." 5466
2Sa 18:29 "Is the young man Absalom **s?"** 8934
18:32 "Is the young man Absalom **s?"** 8934
2Ch 15: 5 In those days it was not s to travel about, 8934
Ezr 8:21 before our God and ask him for a s journey 3838
Job 21: 9 Their homes are s and free from fear; 8934
Ps 12: 7 you *will* **keep** us s and protect us 9068
16: 1 **Keep** me s, O God, for in you I take refuge. 9068
27: 5 of trouble *he will* **keep** me s in his dwelling; 7621
31:20 in your dwelling *you* **keep** them s 7621
37: 3 dwell in the land and enjoy s pasture. 575
Pr 11:15 to strike hands in pledge *is* **s.** 1053
18:10 the righteous run to it and *are* **s.** 8435
20:28 Love and faithfulness **keep** a king **s;** 5915
28:18 He whose walk is blameless *is* **kept s,** 3828
28:26 but he who walks in wisdom **is kept s.** 4880
29:25 but whoever trusts in the LORD **is kept s.** 8435

Jer	7:10	and say, *"We are* **s**"—safe to do all these	5911
	7:10	s to do all these detestable things?	NIH
	12: 5	If you stumble in s country,	8934
	12:12	no one will be s.	8934
Lk	11:21	his own house, his possessions are s.	*1645+1877*
	15:27	because he has him back **s and sound.'**	*5617*
Jn	17:12	and **kept** them s by that name you gave me.	*5875*
1Jn	5:18	the one who was born of God **keeps** him s,	*5498*

SAFE-CONDUCT (1) [CONDUCT]

Ne	2: 7	that *they will* **provide** me s until I arrive	6296

SAFEGUARD (1) [GUARD]

Php	3: 1	and it is a s for you.	*855*

SAFEKEEPING (2) [KEEP]

Ex	22: 7	or goods for s and they are stolen from	9068
	22:10	to his neighbor for s and it dies or is injured	9068

SAFELY (18) [SAVE]

Ge	19:16	and of his two daughters and led them s out	5663
	28:21	so that I return s to my father's house,	928+8934
	33:18	he arrived s at the city of Shechem	8969
Lev	25:18	and you will live s in the land.	1055+4200
Jos	10:21	whole army then returned s to Joshua	928+8934
1Sa	20:13	not let you know and send you away s.	4200+8934
2Sa	19:24	the king left until the day he returned s.	928+8934
	19:30	my lord the king has arrived home s."	928+8934
1Ki	22:27	but bread and water until I return s.' "	928+8934
	22:28	Micaiah declared, "If you ever return s,	928+8934
2Ch	18:26	but bread and water until I return s.' "	928+8934
	18:27	Micaiah declared, "If you ever return s,	928+8934
	19: 1	Jehoshaphat king of Judah returned s	928+8934
Ps	78:53	guided them s, so they were unafraid;	1055+4200
Zec	8:10	No one could go about his business s	
		because of his enemy,	2021+4200+8934
Ac	23:24	that *he may be* taken s to Governor Felix."	*1407*
	28: 1	Once s on shore, we found out that	*1407*
2Ti	4:18	from every evil attack and *will* **bring** me s	*5392*

SAFETY (34) [SAVE]

Ge	43: 9	*I* myself *will* **guarantee** his s;	6842
	44:32	Your servant **guaranteed** the boy's s	6842
Lev	25:19	and you will eat your fill and live there in s.	1055
	26: 5	the food you want and live in s	1055
Dt	12:10	around you so that you will live *in* s.	1055
	33:28	So Israel will live *in* s alone;	1055
Jdg	18: 7	that the people were living in s,	1055
1Ki	4:25	from Dan to Beersheba, lived in s,	1055
Job	5: 4	His children are far from s,	3829
	5:11	and those who mourn are lifted to s.	3829
	11:18	about you and take your rest in s.	1055
	30:15	my s vanishes like a cloud.	3802
Ps	4: 8	O LORD, make me dwell in s.	1055
	141:10	while I pass by in s.	NIH
Pr	1:33	but whoever listens to me will live *in* s and	1055
	3:23	Then you will go on your way in s,	1055
Isa	14:30	and the needy will lie down in s.	1055
Jer	4: 6	**Flee for** s without delay!	6395
	6: 1	"**Flee for** s, people of Benjamin!	6395
	23: 6	be saved and Israel will live in s.	1055
	32:37	to this place and let them live in s.	1055
	33:16	be saved and Jerusalem will live in s.	1055
Eze	28:26	They will live there in s	1055
	28:26	they will live in s when I inflict punishment	1055
	34:25	in the desert and sleep in the forests in s.	1055
	34:28	They will live in s,	1055
	38: 8	and now all of them live in s.	1055
	38:14	when my people Israel are living in s,	1055
	39: 6	and on those who live in s in the coastlands,	1055
	39:26	toward me when they lived in s in their land	1055
Hos	2:18	so that all may lie down in s.	1055
Zep	2:15	This is the carefree city that lived in s.	1055
Ac	27:44	In this way everyone reached land **in s.**	*1407*
1Th	5: 3	While people are saying, "Peace and s,"	*854*

SAFFRON (1)

SS	4:14	nard and s, calamus and cinnamon,	4137

SAG (1)

Ecc	10:18	If a man is lazy, the rafters s;	4812

SAHADUTHA See JEGAR SAHADUTHA

SAID (3187) [SAY]

Ge	1: 3	And God s, "Let there be light,"	606
	1: 6	And God s, "Let there be an expanse	606
	1: 9	And God s, "Let the water under the sky	606
	1:11	God s, "Let the land produce vegetation:	606
	1:14	And God s, "Let there be lights in	606
	1:20	And God s, "Let the water teem	606
	1:22	God blessed them and s,	606
	1:24	And God s, "Let the land produce	606
	1:26	Then God s, "Let us make man	606
	1:28	God blessed them and s to them,	606
	1:29	Then God s, "I give you every seed-bearing	606
	2:18	The LORD God s, "It is not good for the man	606
	2:23	The man s, "This is now bone of my bones	606
	3: 1	*He* s to the woman, "Did God really say,	606
	3: 2	The woman s to the serpent, "We may eat	606
	3: 4	not surely die," the serpent s to the woman.	606
Ge	3:11	*he* s, "Who told you that you were naked?	606
	3:12	The man s, "The woman you put here	606
	3:13	Then the LORD God s to the woman,	606
	3:13	The woman s, "The serpent deceived me,	606
	3:14	So the LORD God s to the serpent,	606
	3:16	To the woman *he* s, "I will greatly increase	606
	3:17	To Adam *he* s, "Because you listened	606
	3:22	And the LORD God s, "The man has now	606
	4: 1	*She* s, "With the help of the LORD	606
	4: 6	the LORD s to Cain, "Why are you angry?	606
	4: 8	Now Cain s to his brother Abel,	606
	4: 9	Then the LORD s to Cain, "Where is your	606
	4:10	The LORD s, "What have you done?	606
	4:13	Cain s to the LORD, My punishment	606
	4:15	But the LORD s to him, "Not so;	606
	4:23	Lamech s to his wives, "Adah and Zillah,	606
	5:29	He named him Noah and s,	606
	6: 3	the LORD s, "My Spirit will not contend	606
	6: 7	So the LORD s, "I will wipe mankind,	606
	6:13	So God s to Noah, "I am going to put an end	606
	7: 1	The LORD then s to Noah,	606
	8:15	Then God s to Noah,	1819
	8:21	the pleasing aroma and s in his heart:	606
	9: 8	God s to Noah and to his sons with him:	606
	9:12	God s, "This is the sign of the covenant	606
	9:17	So God s to Noah, "This is the sign	606
	9:25	*he* s, "Cursed be Canaan!	606
	9:26	*He* also s, "Blessed be the LORD,	606
	10: 9	that is why *it* **is** s, "Like Nimrod,	606
	11: 3	*They* s to each other, "Come,	606
	11: 4	Then *they* s, "Come, let us build ourselves	606
	11: 6	The LORD s, "If as one people speaking	606
	12: 1	The LORD *had* s to Abram,	606
	12: 7	The LORD appeared to Abram and s,	606
	12:11	*he* s to his wife Sarai,	606
	12:18	"What have you done to me?" *he* s.	606
	13: 8	So Abram s to Lot,	606
	13:14	The LORD s to Abram after Lot had parted	606
	14:21	The king of Sodom s to Abram,	606
	14:22	But Abram s to the king of Sodom,	606
	15: 2	But Abram s, "O Sovereign LORD,	606
	15: 3	Abram s, "You have given me no children;	606
	15: 5	He took him outside and s,	606
	15: 5	*he* s to him, "So shall your offspring be."	606
	15: 7	*He* also s to him, "I am the LORD,	606
	15: 8	But Abram s, "O Sovereign LORD,	606
	15: 9	So the LORD s to him, "Bring me a heifer,	606
	15:13	Then the LORD s to him, "Know for certain	606
	15:18	LORD made a covenant with Abram and s,	606
	16: 2	so she s to Abram,	606
	16: 2	Abram agreed to **what** Sarai s.	7754
	16: 5	Then Sarai s to Abram,	606
	16: 6	"Your servant is in your hands," Abram s.	606
	16: 8	And *he* s, "Hagar, servant of Sarai,	606
	16:11	The angel of the LORD also s to her:	606
	16:13	"You are the God who sees me," for *she* s,	606
	17: 1	the LORD appeared to him and s,	606
	17: 3	Abram fell facedown, and God s to him,	1819
	17: 9	Then God s to Abraham, "As for you,	606
	17:15	God also s to Abraham, "As for Sarai	606
	17:17	he laughed and s to himself, "Will a son	606
	17:18	And Abraham s to God, "If only Ishmael	606
	17:19	Then God s, "Yes,	606
	18: 3	*He* s, "If I have found favor in your eyes,	606
	18: 6	*he* s, "get three seahs of fine flour	606
	18: 9	"There, in the tent," *he* s.	606
	18:10	Then the LORD s, "I will surely return	606
	18:13	Then the LORD s to Abraham,	606
	18:15	Sarah was afraid, so she lied and s,	606
	18:15	But *he* s, "Yes, you did laugh."	606
	18:17	the LORD s, "Shall I hide from Abraham	606
	18:20	the LORD s, "The outcry against Sodom	606
	18:23	Then Abraham approached him and s:	606
	18:26	The LORD s, "If I find fifty righteous people	606
	18:28	"If I find forty-five there," *he* s,	606
	18:29	*He* s, "For the sake of forty, I will not do it."	606
	18:30	Then *he* s, "May the Lord not be angry,	606
	18:31	Abraham s, "Now that I have been so bold	606
	18:31	*He* s, "For the sake of twenty,	606
	18:32	Then *he* s, "May the Lord not be angry,	606
	19: 2	*he* s, "please turn aside	606
	19: 7	and s, "No, my friends.	606
	19: 9	And *they* s, "This fellow came here as	606
	19:12	The two men s to Lot,	606
	19:14	*He* s, "Hurry and get out of this place,	606
	19:17	*one of them* s, "Flee for your lives!	606
	19:18	But Lot s to them, "No, my lords, please!	606
	19:21	*He* s to him, "Very well,	606
	19:31	the older daughter s to the younger,	606
	19:34	The next day the older daughter s to	606
	20: 2	and there Abraham s of his wife Sarah,	606
	20: 3	in a dream one night and s to him, "You are	606
	20: 4	Abimelech had not gone near her, so *he* s,	606
	20: 6	Then God s to him in the dream, "Yes,	606
	20: 9	Then Abimelech called Abraham in and s,	606
	20:11	Abraham replied, *"I s to myself,*	606
	20:13	*I* s to her, 'This is how you can show your	606
	20:15	And Abimelech s, "My land is before you;	606
	20:16	To Sarah *he* s, "I am giving your brother	606
	21: 1	LORD was gracious to Sarah as *he had* s,	606
	21: 6	Sarah s, "God has brought me laughter,	606
	21: 7	"Who *would have* s to Abraham	4910
	21:10	*she* s to Abraham, "Get rid of that slave	606
	21:12	But God s to him, "Do not be so distressed	606
	21:17	of God called to Hagar from heaven and s	606
	21:22	the commander of his forces s to Abraham,	606
	21:24	Abraham s, "I swear it."	606
Ge	21:26	But Abimelech s, "I don't know who	606
	22: 1	*He* s to him, "Abraham!"	606
	22: 2	Then God s, "Take your son,	606
	22: 5	He s to his servants, "Stay here	606
	22: 7	Isaac spoke up and s to his father Abraham,	606
	22: 7	"The fire and wood are here," Isaac s,	606
	22:12	"Do not lay a hand on the boy," *he* s.	606
	22:14	And to this day *it* **is** s,	606
	22:16	and s, "I swear by myself, declares	606
	23: 3	and spoke to the Hittites. *He* s,	606
	23: 8	*He* s to them, "If you are willing	1819
	23:11	"No, my lord," he s.	606
	23:13	and *he* s to Ephron in their hearing,	1819
	24: 2	He s to the chief servant in his household,	606
	24: 6	not take my son back there," Abraham s.	606
	24:17	The servant hurried to meet her and s,	606
	24:18	"Drink, my lord," *she* s,	606
	24:19	After she had given him a drink, *she* s,	606
	24:30	and had heard Rebekah tell what the man s	1819
	24:31	you who are blessed by the LORD," *he* s.	606
	24:33	Then food was set before him, but *he* s,	606
	24:33	"Then tell us," [Laban] s.	606
	24:34	So *he* s, "I am Abraham's servant.	606
	24:37	my master made me swear an oath, and s,	606
	24:42	"When I came to the spring today, *I* s,	606
	24:45	and *I* s to her, 'Please give me a drink.'	606
	24:46	lowered her jar from her shoulder and s,	606
	24:47	*"She* s, 'The daughter of Bethuel son	606
	24:52	Abraham's servant heard **what** they s,	1821
	24:54	When they got up the next morning, *he* s,	606
	24:56	But *he* s to them, "Do not detain me,	606
	24:57	Then *they* s, "Let's call the girl and ask her	606
	24:58	"I will go," *she* s.	606
	24:60	And they blessed Rebekah and s to her,	606
	25:22	and *she* s, "Why is this happening to me?"	606
	25:23	The LORD s to her, "Two nations are in	606
	25:30	He s to Jacob, "Quick, let me have some	606
	25:32	"Look, I am about to die," Esau s.	606
	25:33	But Jacob s, "Swear to me first."	606
	26: 2	The LORD appeared to Isaac and s,	606
	26: 7	*he* s, "She is my sister,"	606
	26: 9	So Abimelech summoned Isaac and s,	606
	26:10	Abimelech s, "What is this you have done	606
	26:16	Abimelech s to Isaac, "Move away from us;	606
	26:20	with Isaac's herdsmen and s,	606
	26:24	the LORD appeared to him and s,	606
	26:28	so *we* s, 'There ought to be	606
	26:32	*They* s, "We've found water!"	606
	27: 1	he called for Esau his older son and s	606
	27: 2	Isaac s, "I am now an old man	606
	27: 6	Rebekah s to her son Jacob,	606
	27:11	Jacob s to Rebekah his mother,	606
	27:13	His mother s to him, "My son,	606
	27:18	He went to his father and s, "My father."	606
	27:19	Jacob s to his father, "I am Esau	606
	27:21	Then Isaac s to Jacob, "Come near	606
	27:22	who touched him and s,	606
	27:25	Then *he* s, "My son,	606
	27:26	Then his father Isaac s to him, "Come here,	606
	27:27	he blessed him and s, "Ah,	606
	27:31	Then *he* s to him, "My father,	606
	27:33	Isaac trembled violently and s,	606
	27:34	he burst out with a loud and bitter cry and s	606
	27:35	But *he* s, "Your brother came deceitfully	606
	27:36	Esau s, "Isn't he rightly named Jacob?	606
	27:38	Esau s to his father, "Do you have only one	606
	27:41	He s to himself, "The days of mourning	606
	27:42	**what** her older son Esau had s,	1821
	27:42	she sent for her younger son Jacob and s	606
	27:46	Then Rebekah s to Isaac,	606
	28:13	There above it stood the LORD, and *he* s:	606
	28:17	He was afraid and s, "How awesome	606
	29: 5	*He* s to them, "Do you know Laban,	606
	29: 6	"Yes, he is," *they* s,	606
	29: 7	"Look," *he* s, "the sun is still high;	606
	29:14	Then Laban s to him, "You are my own	606
	29:15	Laban s to him, "Just because you are a	606
	29:18	Jacob was in love with Rachel and s,	606
	29:19	Laban s, "It's better that I give her	606
	29:21	Then Jacob s to Laban, "Give me my wife.	606
	29:25	So Jacob s to Laban,	606
	29:32	She named him Reuben, for *she* s,	606
	29:33	and when she gave birth to a son *she* s,	606
	29:34	and when she gave birth to a son *she* s,	606
	29:35	and when she gave birth to a son *she* s,	606
	30: 1	So *she* s to Jacob, "Give me children,	606
	30: 2	Jacob became angry with her and s,	606
	30: 3	*she* s, "Here is Bilhah, my maidservant.	606
	30: 6	Then Rachel s, "God has vindicated me;	606
	30: 8	Then Rachel s, "I have had a great struggle	606
	30:11	Then Leah s, "What good fortune!"	606
	30:13	Then Leah s, "How happy I am!	606
	30:14	Rachel s to Leah, "Please give me some	606
	30:15	But *she* s to her, Wasn't it enough	606
	30:15	"Very well," Rachel s,	606
	30:16	"You must sleep with me," *she* s.	606
	30:18	Then Leah s, "God has rewarded me	606
	30:20	Then Leah s, "God has presented me with	606
	30:23	and gave birth to a son and s,	606
	30:24	She named him Joseph, and s,	606
	30:25	Jacob s to Laban, "Send me on my way	606
	30:27	But Laban s to him, "If I have found favor	606
	30:29	Jacob s to him, "You know how I have	606
	30:34	"Agreed," s Laban.	606
	30:34	"Let it be as you have s."	1821
	31: 3	Then the LORD s to Jacob,	606
	31: 5	*He* s to them, "I see that your father's	606

Ge	31: 8	If *he* s, 'The speckled ones will	606
	31: 8	and if *he* s, 'The streaked ones	606
	31:11	The angel of God s to me in the dream,	606
	31:12	And *he* s, 'Look up and see that all	606
	31:24	the Aramean in a dream at night and s	606
	31:26	Laban s to Jacob, "What have you done?	606
	31:29	last night the God of your father s to me,	606
	31:35	Rachel s to her father, "Don't be angry,	606
	31:46	He s to his relatives, "Gather some stones."	606
	31:48	Laban s, "This heap is a witness	606
	31:49	It was also called Mizpah, because *he* s,	606
	31:51	Laban also s to Jacob, "Here is this heap,	606
	32: 2	When Jacob saw them, *he* s,	606
	32: 6	the messengers returned to Jacob, *they* s,	606
	32: 9	O LORD, who s to me, 'Go back	606
	32:12	But you *have* s, 'I will surely make you	606
	32:16	each herd by itself, and s to his servants,	606
	32:26	the man s, "Let me go, for it is daybreak."	606
	32:28	Then the man s, 'Your name will no longer	606
	32:29	Jacob s, "Please tell me your name."	8626
	33: 8	"To find favor in your eyes, my lord," *he* s.	606
	33: 9	Esau s, "I already have plenty, my brother.	606
	33:10	"No, please!" s Jacob.	606
	33:12	Then Esau s, "Let us be on our way;	606
	33:13	But Jacob s to him, "My lord knows	606
	33:15	Esau s, "Then let me leave some	606
	34: 4	And Shechem s to his father Hamor,	606
	34: 8	But Hamor s to them,	1819
	34:11	Shechem s to Dinah's father and brothers,	606
	34:14	*They* s to them, "We can't do such a thing;	606
	34:19	lost no time in doing what they s,	1821
	34:21	"These men are friendly toward us," they s.	606
	34:30	Then Jacob s to Simeon and Levi,	606
	35: 1	Then God s to Jacob, "Go up to Bethel	606
	35: 2	So Jacob s to his household and	606
	35:10	God s to him, "Your name is Jacob,	606
	35:11	And God s to him, "I am God Almighty;	606
	35:17	the midwife s to her, "Don't be afraid,	606
	37: 6	*He* s to them, "Listen to this dream I had:	606
	37: 8	His brothers s to him,	606
	37: 8	because of his dream and **what** he had s.	1821
	37: 9	"Listen," *he* s, "I had another dream,	606
	37:10	his father rebuked him and s,	606
	37:13	and Israel s to Joseph, "As you know,	606
	37:14	So *he* s to him, "Go and see if all is well	606
	37:19	*they* s to each other.	606
	37:21	"Let's not take his life," *he* s.	606
	37:22	Reuben s this to rescue him from them	606
	37:26	Judah s to his brothers,	606
	37:30	He went back to his brothers and s,	606
	37:32	to their father and s, "We found this.	606
	37:33	He recognized it and s, "It is my son's	606
	37:35	*he* s, "in mourning will I go down to	606
	38: 8	Then Judah s to Onan,	606
	38:11	Judah then s to his daughter-in-law Tamar,	606
	38:16	he went over to her by the roadside and s,	606
	38:17	a young goat from my flock," *he* s.	606
	38:18	*He* s, "What pledge should I give you?"	606
	38:21	been any shrine prostitute here," *they* s.	606
	38:22	So he went back to Judah and s,	606
	38:22	Besides, the men who lived there s,	606
	38:23	Then Judah s, "Let her keep what she has,	606
	38:24	Judah s, "Bring her out	606
	38:25	by the man who owns these," *she* s.	606
	38:26	Judah recognized them and s,	606
	38:28	and tied it on his wrist and s,	606
	38:29	his brother came out, and *she* s,	606
	39: 7	master's wife took notice of Joseph and s,	606
	39:12	She caught him by his cloak and s,	606
	39:14	"Look," *she* s to them,	606
	40: 8	Then Joseph s to them,	606
	40: 9	*He* s to him, "In my dream I saw	606
	40:12	"This is what it means," Joseph s to him.	606
	40:16	*he* s to Joseph, "I too had a dream:	606
	40:18	"This is what it means," Joseph s.	6699
	40:22	*had* s to them **in *his* interpretation.**	7354
	41: 9	Then the chief cupbearer s to Pharaoh,	1819
	41:15	Pharaoh s to Joseph, "I had a dream,	606
	41:15	But I have heard *it* s of you that	606
	41:17	Then Pharaoh s to Joseph, "In my dream	1819
	41:25	Then Joseph s to Pharaoh,	606
	41:28	"It is just as *I* s to Pharaoh:	1819
	41:39	Then Pharaoh s to Joseph, "Since God	606
	41:41	So Pharaoh s to Joseph, "I hereby put you	606
	41:44	Then Pharaoh s to Joseph, "I am Pharaoh,	606
	41:51	Joseph named his firstborn Manasseh and s,	NIH
	41:52	The second son he named Ephraim and s,	NIH
	41:54	famine began, just as Joseph *had* s.	606
	42: 1	grain in Egypt, he s to his sons,	606
	42: 9	his dreams about them and s to them,	606
	42:12	*he* s to them. "You have come to see	606
	42:14	Joseph s to them, "It is just as I told you:	606
	42:18	On the third day, Joseph s to them,	606
	42:21	*They* s to one another,	606
	42:28	*he* s to his brothers.	606
	42:28	to each other trembling and s,	606
	42:29	that had happened to them. *They* s,	606
	42:31	But *we* s to him, 'We are honest men;	606
	42:33	the man who is lord over the land s to us,	606
	42:36	Their father Jacob s to them,	606
	42:37	Then Reuben s to his father,	606
	42:38	But Jacob s, "My son will not go	606
	43: 2	their father s to them, "Go back	606
	43: 3	But Judah s to him, "The man warned us	606
	43: 5	because the man s to us,	606
	43: 8	Then Judah s to Israel his father,	606
	43:11	Then their father Israel s to them,	606
Ge	43:16	*he* s to the steward of his house,	606
	43:20	*they* s, "we came down here the first time	606
	43:23	"It's all right," *he* s.	606
	43:27	and then *he* s, "How is your aged father	606
	43:29	*he* s, "God be gracious to you, my son."	606
	43:31	controlling himself, s, "Serve the food."	606
	44: 2	And he did as Joseph s.	1819
	44: 4	from the city when Joseph s to his steward,	606
	44: 7	But *they* s to him, "Why does my lord say	606
	44:10	"Very well, then," *he* s,	606
	44:15	Joseph s to them, "What is this	606
	44:17	But Joseph s, "Far be it from me to do such	606
	44:18	Then Judah went up to him and s:	606
	44:21	"Then *you* s to your servants,	606
	44:22	And *we* s to my lord,	606
	44:24	**what** my lord had s.	1821
	44:25	"Then our father s, 'Go back	606
	44:26	But *we* s, 'We cannot go down.	606
	44:27	"Your servant my father s to us,	606
	44:28	One of them went away from me, and *I* s,	606
	44:32	I s, 'If I do not bring him back to you,	606
	45: 3	Joseph s to his brothers, "I am Joseph!	606
	45: 4	Then Joseph s to his brothers,	606
	45: 4	When they had done so, *he* s,	606
	45:17	Pharaoh s to Joseph, "Tell your brothers,	606
	45:24	and as they were leaving *he* s to them,	606
	45:27	when they told him everything Joseph *had* s	1819
	45:28	And Israel s, "I'm convinced!	606
	46: 2	to Israel in a vision at night and s,	606
	46: 3	"I am God, the God of your father," *he* s.	606
	46:30	Israel s to Joseph, "Now I am ready to die,	606
	46:31	Then Joseph s to his brothers and to his	606
	47: 4	*They* also s to him, "We have come	606
	47: 5	Pharaoh s to Joseph, "Your father and	606
	47: 9	And Jacob s to Pharaoh, "The years of my	606
	47:15	all Egypt came to Joseph and s,	606
	47:16	"Then bring your livestock," s Joseph.	606
	47:18	they came to him the following year and s,	606
	47:23	Joseph s to the people,	606
	47:25	"You have saved our lives," *they* s.	606
	47:29	he called for his son Joseph and s to him,	606
	47:30	"I will do as you say," *he* s.	606
	47:31	"Swear to me," *he* s.	606
	48: 3	Jacob s to Joseph, "God Almighty appeared	606
	48: 4	and s to me, 'I am going to make you	606
	48: 9	Joseph s to his father.	606
	48: 9	Then Israel s, "Bring them to me	606
	48:11	Israel s to Joseph, "I never expected	606
	48:15	Then he blessed Joseph and s,	606
	48:18	Joseph s to him, "No, my father,	606
	48:19	But his father refused and s, "I know,	606
	48:20	He blessed them that day and s,	606
	48:21	Then Israel s to Joseph, "I am about to die,	606
	49: 1	Then Jacob called for his sons and s:	606
	49:28	and this is what their father s to them	1819
	50: 4	Joseph s to Pharaoh's court,	1819
	50: 5	'My father made me swear an oath and s,	606
	50: 6	Pharaoh s, "Go up and bury your father,	606
	50:11	of Atad, *they* s, "The Egyptians are holding	606
	50:15	that their father was dead, *they* s, "What	606
	50:18	"We are your slaves," *they* s.	606
	50:19	But Joseph s to them, "Don't be afraid.	606
	50:24	Joseph s to his brothers, "I am about to die.	606
	50:25	the sons of Israel swear an oath and s,	606
Ex	1: 9	"Look," *he* s to his people,	606
	1:15	of Egypt s to the Hebrew midwives,	606
	2: 6	"This is one of the Hebrew babies," *she* s.	606
	2: 9	Pharaoh's daughter s to her,	606
	2:14	*The man* s, "Who made you ruler and judge	606
	3: 4	And Moses s, "Here I am."	606
	3: 5	"Do not come any closer," God s.	606
	3: 6	Then *he* s, "I am the God of your father,	606
	3: 7	The LORD s, "I have indeed seen	606
	3:11	But Moses s to God, "Who am I,	606
	3:12	And God s, "I will be with you.	606
	3:13	Moses s to God, "Suppose I go	606
	3:14	God s to Moses, "I AM WHO I AM.	606
	3:15	God also s to Moses, "Say to the Israelites,	606
	3:16	appeared to me and s:	606
	4: 2	Then the LORD s to him, "What is that	606
	4: 3	The LORD s, "Throw it on the ground."	606
	4: 4	Then the LORD s to him, "Reach out your	606
	4: 5	s the LORD, "is so that they may believe	NIH
	4: 6	Then the LORD s, "Put your hand inside	606
	4: 7	"Now put it back into your cloak," *he* s	606
	4: 8	Then the LORD s, "If they do not believe	NIH
	4:10	Moses s to the LORD, "O Lord,	606
	4:11	The LORD s to him, "Who gave man his	606
	4:13	But Moses s, "O Lord,	606
	4:14	anger burned against Moses and *he* s,	606
	4:18	to Jethro his father-in-law and s to him,	606
	4:18	Jethro s, "Go, and I wish you well."	606
	4:19	Now the LORD *had* s to Moses in Midian,	606
	4:21	The LORD s to Moses, "When you return	606
	4:25	a bridegroom of blood to me," *she* s.	606
	4:26	(At that time *she* s "bridegroom of blood,"	606
	4:27	The LORD s to Aaron, "Go into the desert	606
	4:30	the LORD *had* s to Moses.	1819
	5: 1	to Pharaoh and s, "This is what the LORD,	606
	5: 2	Pharaoh s, "Who is the LORD,	606
	5: 3	Then *they* s, "The God of the Hebrews	606
	5: 4	But the king of Egypt s, "Moses and Aaron,	606
	5: 5	Then Pharaoh s, "Look,	606
	5:10	the foremen went out and s to the people,	606
	5:17	Pharaoh s, "Lazy, that's what you are—	606
	5:21	and *they* s, "May the LORD look upon you	606
	5:22	Moses returned to the LORD and s,	606
Ex	6: 1	Then the LORD s to Moses, "Now you will	606
	6: 2	God also s to Moses, "I am the LORD.	1819
	6:10	Then the LORD s to Moses,	1819
	6:12	But Moses s to the LORD,	1819
	6:26	and Moses to whom the LORD s,	606
	6:29	he s to him, "I am the LORD.	1819
	6:30	But Moses s to the LORD, "Since I speak	606
	7: 1	Then the LORD s to Moses, "See,	606
	7: 8	The LORD s to Moses and Aaron,	606
	7:13	just as the LORD *had* s.	1819
	7:14	Then the LORD s to Moses,	606
	7:19	The LORD s to Moses, "Tell Aaron,	606
	7:22	just as the LORD *had* s.	1819
	8: 1	Then the LORD s to Moses, "Go to Pharaoh	606
	8: 5	Then the LORD s to Moses, "Tell Aaron,	606
	8: 8	summoned Moses and Aaron and s,	606
	8: 9	Moses s to Pharaoh, "I leave to you the	606
	8:10	"Tomorrow," Pharaoh s.	606
	8:15	just as the LORD *had* s.	1819
	8:16	Then the LORD s to Moses, "Tell Aaron,	606
	8:19	The magicians s to Pharaoh,	606
	8:19	just as the LORD *had* s.	1819
	8:20	Then the LORD s to Moses, "Get up early	606
	8:25	summoned Moses and Aaron and s,	606
	8:26	But Moses s, "That would not be right.	606
	8:28	Pharaoh s, "I will let you go	606
	9: 1	Then the LORD s to Moses, "Go to Pharaoh	606
	9: 5	The LORD set a time and s,	606
	9: 8	Then the LORD s to Moses and Aaron,	606
	9:12	just as the LORD *had* s to Moses.	1819
	9:13	Then the LORD s to Moses, "Get up early	606
	9:22	Then the LORD s to Moses, "Stretch out	606
	9:27	"This time I have sinned," *he* s to them.	606
	9:35	just as the LORD *had* s through Moses.	1819
	10: 1	Then the LORD s to Moses, "Go to Pharaoh	606
	10: 3	So Moses and Aaron went to Pharaoh and s	606
	10: 7	Pharaoh's officials s to him,	606
	10: 8	"Go, worship the LORD your God," *he* s.	606
	10:10	Pharaoh s, "The LORD be with you—	606
	10:12	And the LORD s to Moses,	606
	10:16	summoned Moses and Aaron and s,	606
	10:21	Then the LORD s to Moses, "Stretch out	606
	10:24	Then Pharaoh summoned Moses and s,	606
	10:25	But Moses s, "You must allow us	606
	10:28	Pharaoh s to Moses, "Get out of my sight!	606
	11: 1	Now the LORD *had* s to Moses,	606
	11: 4	So Moses s, "This is what the LORD says:	606
	11: 9	The LORD *had* s to Moses, "Pharaoh will	606
	12: 1	The LORD s to Moses and Aaron in Egypt,	606
	12:21	the elders of Israel and s to them,	606
	12:31	summoned Moses and Aaron and s,	606
	12:32	Take your flocks and herds, as *you have* s,	1819
	12:33	"For otherwise," *they* s, "we will all die!"	606
	12:43	The LORD s to Moses and Aaron,	606
	13: 1	The LORD s to Moses,	1819
	13: 3	Then Moses s to the people,	606
	13:17	For God s, "If they face war,	606
	13:19	*He had* s, "God will surely come to your aid	606
	14: 1	Then the LORD s to Moses,	1819
	14: 5	changed their minds about them and s,	606
	14:11	*They* s to Moses, "Was it because	606
	14:15	Then the LORD s to Moses, "Why are you	606
	14:25	And the Egyptians s, "Let's get away	606
	14:26	Then the LORD s to Moses,	606
	15:26	*He* s, "If you listen carefully to the voice of	606
	16: 3	The Israelites s to them,	606
	16: 4	Then the LORD s to Moses, "I will rain down	606
	16: 6	So Moses and Aaron s to all the Israelites,	606
	16: 8	Moses also s, "You will know that it was	606
	16:11	The LORD s to Moses,	1819
	16:15	the Israelites saw it, *they* s to each other,	606
	16:15	Moses s to them, "What is it?"	606
	16:19	Then Moses s to them,	606
	16:23	*He* s to them, "This is what the LORD	606
	16:25	"Eat it today," Moses s,	606
	16:28	Then the LORD s to Moses, "How long	606
	16:32	Moses s, "This is what the LORD has	606
	16:33	So Moses s to Aaron, "Take a jar	606
	17: 2	So they quarreled with Moses and s,	606
	17: 3	*They* s, "Why did you bring us up out	606
	17: 9	Moses s to Joshua, "Choose some of	606
	17:14	Then the LORD s to Moses, "Write this	606
	17:16	*He* s, "For hands were lifted up to the throne	606
	18: 3	One son was named Gershom, for Moses s,	606
	18: 4	for he s, "My father's God was my helper;	NIH
	18:10	He s, "Praise be to the LORD,	606
	18:14	the people, *he* s, "What is this you are doing	606
	18:24	to his father-in-law and did everything *he* s.	606
	19: 3	the mountain and s, "This is what you are	606
	19: 8	"We will do everything the LORD *has* s."	1819
	19: 9	The LORD s to Moses, "I am going to come	606
	19: 9	told the LORD **what** the people had s.	1821
	19:10	the LORD s to Moses, "Go to the people	606
	19:15	Then *he* s to the people, "Prepare yourselves	606
	19:21	and the LORD s to him, "Go down and warn	606
	19:23	Moses s to the LORD, "The people cannot	606
	20:19	and s to Moses, "Speak to us yourself	606
	20:20	Moses s to the people, "Do not be afraid.	606
	20:22	LORD s to Moses, "Tell the Israelites this:	606
	23:13	"Be careful to do everything *I have* s	606
	24: 1	Then *he* s to Moses, "Come up	606
	24: 3	"Everything the LORD *has* s we will do."	1819
	24: 4	down everything the LORD had s.	1821
	24: 7	"We will do everything the LORD *has* s;	1819
	24: 8	sprinkled it on the people and s,	606
	24:12	The LORD s to Moses, "Come up to me	606
	24:14	*He* s to the elders, "Wait here for us	606

Ex 25: 1 The LORD s to Moses, 1819
30:11 Then the LORD s to Moses, 1819
30:17 Then the LORD s to Moses, 1819
30:22 Then the LORD s to Moses, 1819
30:34 Then the LORD s to Moses, 606
31: 1 Then the LORD s to Moses, 1819
31:12 Then the LORD s to Moses, 606
32: 1 they gathered around Aaron and s, "Come, 606
32: 4 Then *they* s, "These are your gods, 606
32: 7 Then the LORD s to Moses, "Go down, 1819
32: 8 down to it and sacrificed to it and *have* s, 606
32: 9 "I have seen these people," the LORD s 606
32:11 *he* s, "why should your anger burn 606
32:17 *he* s to Moses, "There is the sound of war 606
32:21 He s to Aaron, "What did these people do 606
32:23 *They* s to me, 'Make us gods 606
32:26 he stood at the entrance to the camp and s, 606
32:27 Then *he* s to them, "This is what the LORD 606
32:29 Then Moses s, "You have been set apart to 606
32:30 The next day Moses s to the people, 606
32:31 So Moses went back to the LORD and s, 606
33: 1 Then the LORD s to Moses, "Leave this 1819
33: 5 For the LORD *had* s to Moses, 606
33:12 Moses s to the LORD, "You have been telling 606
33:12 You *have* s, 'I know you by name 606
33:15 Then Moses s to him, "If your Presence 606
33:17 And the LORD s to Moses, "I will do 606
33:18 Then Moses s, "Now show me your glory." 606
33:19 And the LORD s, "I will cause all 606
33:20 But," *he* s, "you cannot see my face, 606
33:21 Then the LORD s, "There is a place 606
34: 1 The LORD s to Moses, "Chisel out two 606
34: 9 if I have found favor in your eyes," *he* s, 606
34:10 Then the LORD s: "I am making a covenant 606
34:27 Then the LORD s to Moses, "Write down 606
35: 1 the whole Israelite community and s to them, 606
35: 4 Moses s to the whole Israelite community, 606
35:30 Then Moses s to the Israelites, "See, 606
36: 5 and s to Moses, "The people are bringing 606
40: 1 Then the LORD s to Moses: 1819
Lev 1: 1 from the Tent of Meeting. *He* s, 606
4: 1 The LORD s to Moses, 1819
5:14 The LORD s to Moses: 1819
6: 1 The LORD s to Moses: 1819
6: 8 The LORD s to Moses: 1819
6:19 The LORD also s to Moses, 1819
6:24 The LORD s to Moses, 1819
7:22 The LORD s to Moses, 1819
7:28 The LORD s to Moses, 1819
8: 1 The LORD s to Moses, 1819
8: 5 Moses s to the assembly, "This is what 606
8:31 Moses then s to Aaron and his sons, 606
9: 2 *He* s to Aaron, "Take a bull calf 606
9: 6 Then Moses s, "This is what 606
9: 7 Moses s to Aaron, "Come to the altar 606
10: 3 Moses then s to Aaron, "This is what 606
10: 3 what the LORD spoke of when *he* s: 606
10: 4 and s to them, "Come here; 606
10: 6 Then Moses s to Aaron and his sons 606
10: 7 So they did as Moses s. 1821
10: 8 Then the LORD s to Aaron, 1819
10:12 Moses s to Aaron and his remaining sons, 1819
11: 1 The LORD s to Moses and Aaron, 1819
12: 1 The LORD s to Moses, 1819
13: 1 The LORD s to Moses and Aaron, 1819
14: 1 The LORD s to Moses, 1819
14:33 The LORD s to Moses and Aaron, 1819
15: 1 The LORD s to Moses and Aaron, 1819
16: 2 The LORD s to Moses: "Tell your brother 606
17: 1 The LORD s to Moses, 1819
17:14 That is why *I have* s to the Israelites, 606
18: 1 The LORD s to Moses, 1819
19: 1 The LORD s to Moses, 1819
20: 1 The LORD s to Moses, 1819
20:24 *I* s to you, "You will possess their land; 606
21: 1 The LORD s to Moses, 606
21:16 The LORD s to Moses, 1819
22: 1 The LORD s to Moses, 1819
22:17 The LORD s to Moses, 1819
22:26 The LORD s to Moses, 1819
23: 1 The LORD s to Moses, 1819
23: 9 The LORD s to Moses, 1819
23:23 The LORD s to Moses, 1819
23:26 The LORD s to Moses, 1819
23:33 The LORD s to Moses, 1819
24: 1 The LORD s to Moses, 1819
24:13 Then the LORD s to Moses: 1819
25: 1 The LORD s to Moses on Mount Sinai, 1819
27: 1 The LORD s to Moses, 1819
Nu 1: 1 after the Israelites came out of Egypt. *He* s: 606
1:48 The LORD *had* s to Moses: 1819
2: 1 The LORD s to Moses and Aaron: 1819
3: 5 The LORD s to Moses, 1819
3:11 The LORD also s to Moses, 1819
3:14 The LORD s to Moses in the Desert 1819
3:40 The LORD s to Moses, "Count all the 606
3:44 The LORD also s to Moses, 1819
4: 1 The LORD s to Moses and Aaron: 1819
4:17 The LORD s to Moses and Aaron, 1819
4:21 The LORD s to Moses, 1819
5: 1 The LORD s to Moses, 1819
5: 5 The LORD s to Moses, 1819
5:11 Then the LORD s to Moses, 1819
6: 1 The LORD s to Moses, 1819
6:22 The LORD s to Moses, 1819
7: 4 The LORD s to Moses, 606
7:11 For the LORD *had* s to Moses, 606

Nu 8: 1 The LORD s to Moses, 1819
8: 5 The LORD s to Moses: 1819
8:23 The LORD s to Moses, 1819
9: 1 after they came out of Egypt. *He* s, 606
9: 7 and s to Moses, 606
9: 9 Then the LORD s to Moses, 1819
10: 1 The LORD s to Moses: 1819
10:29 Now Moses s to Hobab son of Reuel 606
10:29 for the place about which the LORD s, 606
10:31 But Moses s, "Please do not leave us. 606
10:35 Whenever the ark set out, Moses s, 606
10:36 Whenever it came to rest, *he* s, "Return, 606
11: 4 again the Israelites started wailing and s, 606
11:16 The LORD s to Moses: "Bring me seventy 606
11:21 But Moses s, "Here I am 606
11:24 told the people **what** the LORD had s. 1821
11:28 spoke up and s, "Moses, my lord, 606
12: 4 At once the LORD s to Moses, 606
12: 6 *he* s, "Listen to my words: 606
12:11 and he s to Moses, "Please, my lord, 606
13: 1 The LORD s to Moses, 1819
13:17 Moses sent them to explore Canaan, *he* s, 606
13:30 the people before Moses and s, 606
13:31 But the men who had gone up with him s, 606
13:32 about the land they had explored. They s, 606
14: 2 and the whole assembly s to them, 606
14: 4 And *they* s to each other, 606
14: 7 and s to the entire Israelite assembly, 606
14:11 The LORD s to Moses, "How long 606
14:13 Moses s to the LORD, "Then the Egyptians 606
14:26 The LORD s to Moses and Aaron: 1819
14:31 for your children that *you* s would be taken 606
14:40 "We have sinned," they s. 606
14:41 But Moses s, "Why are you disobeying 606
15: 1 The LORD s to Moses, 1819
15:17 The LORD s to Moses, 1819
15:35 the LORD s to Moses, "The man must die. 606
15:37 The LORD s to Moses, 606
16: 3 to oppose Moses and Aaron and s to them, 606
16: 5 Then *he* s to Korah and all his followers: 1819
16: 8 Moses also s to Korah, "Now listen, 606
16:12 But *they* s, "We will not come! 606
16:15 Then Moses became very angry and s to 606
16:16 Moses s to Korah, "You and all your 606
16:20 The LORD s to Moses and Aaron, 1819
16:23 Then the LORD s to Moses, 1819
16:28 Then Moses s, "This is how you will know 606
16:36 The LORD s to Moses, 1819
16:41 You have killed the LORD's people," *they* s. 606
16:44 and the LORD s to Moses, 1819
16:46 Then Moses s to Aaron, "Take your censer 606
16:47 So Aaron did as Moses s, 1819
17: 1 The LORD s to Moses, 1819
17:10 The LORD s to Moses, "Put back Aaron's 606
17:12 The Israelites s to Moses, "We will die! 606
18: 1 The LORD s to Aaron, "You, your sons 606
18: 8 Then the LORD s to Aaron, 1819
18:20 The LORD s to Aaron, "You will have no 606
18:24 That is why *I* s concerning them: 606
18:25 The LORD s to Moses, 1819
19: 1 The LORD s to Moses and Aaron: 1819
20: 3 They quarreled with Moses and s, 606
20: 7 The LORD s to Moses, 1819
20:10 in front of the rock and Moses s to them, 606
20:12 But the LORD s to Moses and Aaron, 606
20:23 the LORD s to Moses and Aaron, 606
21: 5 and s, "Why have you brought us up out NIH
21: 7 The people came to Moses and s, 606
21: 8 The LORD s to Moses, "Make a snake 606
21:16 the well where the LORD s to Moses, 606
21:34 The LORD s to Moses, "Do not be afraid 606
22: 4 The Moabites s to the elders of Midian, 606
22: 5 Balak s: "A people has come out of Egypt; 606
22: 7 they told him **what** Balak had s. 1821
22: 8 "Spend the night here," Balaam s to them. 606
22:10 Balaam s to God, "Balak son of Zippor, 606
22:12 God s to Balaam, "Do not go with them. 606
22:13 The next morning Balaam got up and s 606
22:14 Moabite princes returned to Balak and s, 606
22:16 They came to Balaam and s: 606
22:20 That night God came to Balaam and s, 606
22:28 donkey's mouth, and *she* s to Balaam, 606
22:30 The donkey s to Balaam, "Am I not 606
22:30 "No," *he* s. 606
22:34 Balaam s to the angel of the LORD, 606
22:35 The angel of the LORD s to Balaam, 606
22:37 Balak s to Balaam, "Did I not send you 606
23: 1 Balaam s, "Build me seven altars here, 606
23: 2 Balak did as Balaam s, 1819
23: 3 Then Balaam s to Balak, "Stay here 606
23: 4 God met with him, and Balaam s, 606
23: 5 put a message in Balaam's mouth and s, 606
23: 7 'Come,' he s, 'curse Jacob for me; NIH
23:11 Balak s to Balaam, "What have you done 606
23:13 Then Balak s to him, "Come with me 606
23:15 Balaam s to Balak, "Stay here 606
23:16 and put a message in his mouth and s, 606
23:23 *It will* now **be** s of Jacob and of Israel, 606
23:25 Then Balak s to Balaam, "Neither curse them 606
23:27 Then Balak s to Balaam, "Come, 606
23:29 Balaam s, "Build me seven altars here, 606
23:30 Balak did as Balaam *had* s, 606
24:10 He struck his hands together and s to him, 606
24:11 *I* s I would reward you handsomely, 606
25: 4 The LORD s to Moses, "Take all the leaders 606
25: 5 So Moses s to Israel's judges, 606
25:10 The LORD s to Moses, 1819

Nu 25:16 The LORD s to Moses, 1819
26: 1 After the plague the LORD s to Moses 606
26: 3 Eleazar the priest spoke with them and s, 606
26:52 The LORD s to Moses, 1819
27: 2 the leaders and the whole assembly, and s, 606
27: 6 and the LORD s to him, 606
27:12 Then the LORD s to Moses, "Go up 606
27:15 Moses s to the LORD, 1819
27:18 So the LORD s to Moses, "Take Joshua 606
28: 1 The LORD s to Moses, 1819
30: 1 Moses s to the heads of the tribes of Israel: 1819
30: 2 but must do everything he s. 3655+4946+7023
31: 1 The LORD s to Moses, 1819
31: 3 So Moses s to the people, "Arm some of 1819
31:21 Then Eleazar the priest s to the soldiers 606
31:25 The LORD s to Moses, 606
31:49 and s to him, "Your servants have counted 606
32: 2 and to the leaders of the community, and s, 606
32: 5 in your eyes," *they* s, "let this land be given 606
32: 6 Moses s to the Gadites and Reubenites, 606
32:16 Then they came up to him and s, 606
32:20 Moses s to them, "If you will do this— 606
32:25 The Gadites and Reubenites s to Moses, 606
32:29 He s to them, "If the Gadites and 606
32:31 servants will do what the LORD *has* s. 1819
33:50 across from Jericho the LORD s to Moses, 1819
34: 1 The LORD s to Moses, 1819
34:16 The LORD s to Moses, 1819
35: 1 across from Jericho, the LORD s to Moses, 1819
35: 9 Then the LORD s to Moses: 1819
36: 2 *They* s, "When the LORD commanded my 606
Dt 1: 6 The LORD our God s to us at Horeb, 1819
1: 9 At that time *I* s to you, "You are too heavy 606
1:20 Then *I* s to you, "You have reached 606
1:22 Then all of you came to me and s, 606
1:27 You grumbled in your tents and s, 606
1:29 Then *I* s to you, "Do not be terrified; 606
1:34 When the LORD heard **what** you s, 1821+7754
1:37 LORD became angry with me also and s, 606
1:39 And the little ones that *you* s would 606
1:42 But the LORD s to me, "Tell them, 606
2: 2 Then the LORD s to me, 606
2: 9 Then the LORD s to me, "Do not harass 606
2:13 And the LORD s, "Now get up and cross NIH
2:17 the LORD s to me, 1819
2:31 The LORD s to me, "See, I have begun 606
3: 2 The LORD s to me, "Do not be afraid of him, 606
3:26 "That is enough," the LORD s. 606
4:10 when he s to me, "Assemble the people 606
5: 1 Moses summoned all Israel and s: 606
5: 5 did not go up the mountain.) And *he* s: 606
5:24 *you* s, "The LORD our God has shown us 606
5:28 when you spoke to me and the LORD s 606
5:28 "I have heard what this people s to you. 1819
5:28 Everything *they* s was good. 1819
6:19 your enemies before you, as the LORD s. 1819
9: 2 You know about them and have heard it s: NIH
9:13 And the LORD s to me, "I have seen this 606
9:23 *he* s, "Go up and take possession of the land 606
9:25 the LORD *had* s he would destroy you. 606
9:26 I prayed to the LORD and s, 606
10: 1 At that time the LORD s to me, 606
10:11 "Go," the LORD s to me, 606
13:12 If you hear *it* s about one of the towns 606
18:16 on the day of the assembly when you s, 606
18:17 The LORD s to me: "What they say is good. 606
22:17 Now he has slandered her and s, 606
27: 9 who are Levites, s to all Israel, "Be silent, 1819
28:68 a journey *I* s you should never make again. 606
29: 2 Moses summoned all the Israelites and s 606
31: 2 The LORD *has* s to me, "You shall not cross 606
31: 3 cross over ahead of you, as the LORD s. 1819
31: 7 and s to him in the presence of all Israel, 606
31:14 The LORD s to Moses, "Now the day 606
31:16 And the LORD s to Moses: 606
32:20 "I will hide my face from them," *he* s, 606
32:26 *I* s I would scatter them and blot out 606
32:46 *he* s to them, "Take to heart all the words 606
33: 2 *He* s: "The LORD came from Sinai 606
33: 7 And this *he* s about Judah: 606
33: 8 About Levi *he* s: 606
33: 9 He s of his father and mother, 606
33:12 About Benjamin *he* s: 606
33:13 About Joseph *he* s: 606
33:18 About Zebulun *he* s: 606
33:20 About Gad *he* s: 606
33:22 About Dan *he* s: 606
33:23 About Naphtali *he* s: 606
33:24 About Asher *he* s: 606
34: 4 Then the LORD s to him, "This is the land 606
34: 4 Abraham, Isaac and Jacob *when* I s, 606
34: 5 as the LORD had s. 7023
Jos 1: 1 the LORD s to Joshua son of Nun, 606
1:12 and the half-tribe of Manasseh, Joshua s, 606
2: 1 "Go, look over the land," he s, 606
2: 4 *She* s, "Yes, the men came to me, 606
2: 9 and s to them, "I know that the LORD has 606
2:16 Now *she had* s to them, 606
2:17 The men s to her, "This oath you made us 606
2:24 *They* s to Joshua, "The LORD has 606
3: 6 Joshua s to the priests, "Take up the ark 606
3: 7 And the LORD s to Joshua, "Today I will 606
3: 9 Joshua s to the Israelites, "Come here 606
4: 1 crossing the Jordan, the LORD s to Joshua, 606
4: 5 and s to them, "Go over before the ark 606
4:15 Then the LORD s to Joshua, 606
4:21 *He* s to the Israelites, "In the future 606

Jos 5: 2 At that time the LORD s to Joshua, 606
5: 9 Then the LORD s to Joshua, "See, 606
6: 2 Then the LORD s to Joshua, "See, 606
6: 6 of Nun called the priests and s to them, 606
6:22 Joshua s to the two men who had spied out 606
7: 3 When they returned to Joshua, *they* s, 606
7: 7 And Joshua s, "Ah, Sovereign LORD, 606
7:10 The LORD s to Joshua, "Stand up! 606
7:19 Then Joshua s to Achan, "My son, 606
7:25 Joshua s, "Why have you brought this 606
8: 1 the LORD s to Joshua, "Do not be afraid; 606
8:18 Then the LORD s to Joshua, "Hold out 606
9: 6 at Gilgal and s to him and the men of Israel, 606
9: 7 The men of Israel s to the Hivites, 606
9: 8 "We are your servants," *they* s to Joshua. 606
9:11 and all those living in our country s to us, 606
9:22 Joshua summoned the Gibeonites and s, 1819
10: 4 up and help me attack Gibeon," he s, 606
10: 8 The LORD s to Joshua, "Do not be afraid 606
10:12 Joshua s to the LORD in the presence 1819
10:18 he s, "Roll large rocks up to the mouth of 606
10:22 Joshua s, "Open the mouth of the cave 606
10:24 he summoned all the men of Israel and s to 606
10:25 Joshua s to them, "Do not be afraid; 606
11: 6 The LORD s to Joshua, "Do not be afraid 606
13: 1 the LORD s to him, "You are very old, 606
14: 6 and Caleb son of Jephunneh the Kenizzite s 606
14: 6 "You know what the LORD s to Moses 1819
14:10 for forty-five years since the time he s this 1819
14:12 I will drive them out just as he s." 1819
15:16 Caleb s, "I will give my daughter Acsah 606
17: 4 Joshua son of Nun, and the leaders and s, 606
17:14 The people of Joseph s to Joshua, 1819
17:17 But Joshua s to the house of Joseph— 606
18: 3 So Joshua s to the Israelites: 606
20: 1 Then the LORD s to Joshua: 1819
21: 2 at Shiloh in Canaan and s to them, 1819
22: 2 and s to them, "You have done all that 606
22:15 the half-tribe of Manasseh—*they* s to them: 1819
22:26 "That is why *we* s, 'Let us get ready 606
22:28 "And *we* s, 'If they ever say this to us, 606
22:31 the priest, s to Reuben, Gad and Manasseh, 606
23: 2 and s to them: "I am old and well advanced 606
24: 2 Joshua s to all the people, "This is what 606
24:19 Joshua s to the people, "You are not able 606
24:21 But the people s to Joshua, "No! 606
24:22 Then Joshua s, "You are witnesses 606
24:23 s Joshua, "throw away the foreign gods NIH
24:24 And the people s to Joshua, 606
24:27 he s to all the people. 606
24:27 It has heard all the words the LORD *has* s 1819
Jdg 1: 3 of Judah s to the Simeonites their brothers, 606
1: 7 Then Adoni-Bezek s, "Seventy kings 606
1:12 Caleb s, "I will give my daughter Acsah 606
1:24 a man coming out of the city and *they* s 606
2: 1 up from Gilgal to Bokim and s, 606
2: 1 *I* s, 'I will never break my covenant 606
2:20 LORD was very angry with Israel and s, 606
3:19 near Gilgal he himself turned back and s, 606
3:19 The king s, "Quiet!" 606
3:20 the upper room of his summer palace and s, 606
3:24 *They* s, "He must be relieving himself in 606
4: 6 of Abinoam from Kedesh in Naphtali and s 606
4: 8 Barak s to her, "If you go with me, 606
4: 9 "Very well," Deborah s, 606
4:14 Then Deborah s to Barak, "Go! 606
4:18 Jael went out to meet Sisera and s to him, 606
4:19 "I'm thirsty," *he* s. 606
4:22 *she* s, "I will show you the man 606
5:23 'Curse Meroz,' s the angel of the LORD. 606
6: 8 *who* s, "This is what the LORD, 606
6:10 *I* s to you, 'I am the LORD your God; 606
6:12 *he* s, "The LORD is with you, 606
6:13 that our fathers told us about when they s, 606
6:14 The LORD turned to him and s, 606
6:18 the LORD s, "I will wait until you return." 606
6:20 The angel of God s to him, "Take the meat 606
6:23 But the LORD s to him, "Peace! 606
6:25 That same night the LORD s to him, 606
6:36 Gideon s to God, "If you will save Israel 606
6:37 will save Israel by my hand, as *you* s." 1819
6:39 Then Gideon s to God, "Do not be angry 606
7: 2 The LORD s to Gideon, "You have too many 606
7: 4 But the LORD s to Gideon, "There are still 606
7: 7 LORD s to Gideon, "With the three hundred 606
7: 9 During that night the LORD s to Gideon, 606
8: 5 *He* s to the men of Succoth, "Give my troops 606
8: 6 But the officials of Succoth s, 606
8: 9 So *he* s to the men of Peniel, 606
8:15 Gideon came and s to the men of Succoth, 606
8:20 Turning to Jether, his oldest son, *he* s, 606
8:21 Zebah and Zalmunna s, "Come, 606
8:22 The Israelites s to Gideon, "Rule over us— 606
8:24 And he s, "I do have one request, 606
9: 1 to his mother's brothers in Shechem and s 1819
9: 3 for *they* s, "He is our brother." 606
9: 8 *They* s to the olive tree, 'Be our king.' 606
9:10 "Next, the trees s to the fig tree, 606
9:12 trees s to the vine, 'Come and be our king.' 606
9:14 "Finally all the trees s to the thornbush, 606
9:15 "The thornbush s to the trees, 606
9:28 Then Gaal son of Ebed s, 606
9:30 of the city heard **what** Gaal son of Ebed s, 1821
9:36 When Gaal saw them, *he* s to Zebul, "Look, 606
9:38 Then Zebul s to him, 606
9:38 "Where is your big talk now, *you* who s, 606
10:15 But the Israelites s to the LORD, 606

Jdg 10:18 of the people of Gilead s to each other, 606
11: 2 in our family," *they* s, "because you are 606
11: 6 "Come," *they* s, "be our commander, 606
11: 7 Jephthah s to them, "Didn't you hate me 606
11: 8 The elders of Gilead s to him, 606
11:19 who ruled in Heshbon, and s to him, 606
11:37 But grant me this one request," *she* s. 606
11:38 "You may go," *he* s. 606
12: 1 crossed over to Zaphon and s to Jephthah, 606
12: 4 down because the Ephraimites *had* s, 606
12: 5 and whenever a survivor of Ephraim s, 606
12: 6 *they* s, "All right, say 'Shibboleth.' " 606
12: 6 If *he* s, "Sibboleth," because he could 606
13: 3 of the LORD appeared to her and s, 606
13: 7 But *he* s to me, 'You will conceive 606
13:11 When he came to the man, *he* s, 606
13:11 "I am," *he* s. 606
13:15 Manoah s to the angel of the LORD, 606
13:22 "We are doomed to die!" he s to his wife. 606
14: 2 he returned, *he* s to his father and mother, 5583
14: 3 But Samson s to his father, "Get her for me. 606
14:12 tell you a riddle," Samson s to them. 606
14:13 "Tell us your riddle," *they* s. 606
14:15 On the fourth day, *they* s to Samson's wife, 606
14:18 on the seventh day the men of the town s 606
14:18 Samson s to them, "If you had not plowed 606
15: 1 *He* s, "I'm going to my wife's room." 606
15: 2 he s, "that I gave her to your friend. 606
15: 3 Samson s to them, "This time I have a right 606
15: 7 Samson s to them, "Since you've acted like 606
15:11 down to the cave in the rock of Etam and s 606
15:12 *They* s to him, "We've come to tie you up 606
15:12 Samson s, "Swear to me 606
15:16 Then Samson s, "With a donkey's jawbone 606
16: 5 rulers of the Philistines went to her and s, 606
16: 6 So Delilah s to Samson, "Tell me the secret 606
16:10 Delilah s to Samson, "You have made a fool 606
16:11 *He* s, "If anyone ties me securely 606
16:13 Delilah then s to Samson, "Until now, 606
16:15 Then *she* s to him, "How can you say, 606
16:17 on my head," *he* s, "because I have been 606
16:26 Samson s to the servant who held his hand, 606
16:30 Samson s, "Let me die with the Philistines!" 606
17: 2 s to his mother, "The eleven hundred 606
17: 2 Then his mother s, "The LORD bless you, 606
17: 3 *she* s, "I solemnly consecrate my silver to 606
17: 9 *he* s, "and I'm looking for a place to stay." 606
17:10 Then Micah s to him, "Live with me and 606
17:13 And Micah s, "Now I know that 606
18: 4 for him, and s, "He has hired me NIH
18: 5 Then *they* s to him, "Please inquire of God 606
18:14 the land of Laish s to their brothers, 606
18:18 the priest s to them, "What are you doing?" 606
18:23 the Danites turned and s to Micah, 606
19: 5 but the girl's father s to his son-in-law, 606
19: 6 Afterward the girl's father s, 606
19: 8 when he rose to go, the girl's father s, 606
19: 9 his father-in-law, the girl's father, s, 606
19:11 the servant s to his master, "Come, 606
19:20 welcome at my house," the old man s. 606
19:23 The owner of the house went outside and s 606
19:28 *He* s to her, "Get up; let's go." 606
19:30 Everyone who saw it s, "Such a thing 606
20: 3 Then the Israelites s, "Tell us how this 606
20: 4 the husband of the murdered woman, s, 6699
20:18 *They* s, "Who of us shall go first to fight 606
20:23 They s, "Shall we go up again to battle 606
20:39 the men of Israel (about thirty), and *they* s, 606
21: 6 one tribe is cut off from Israel," *they* s. 606
21:11 "This is what you are to do," they s. 606
21:16 And the elders of the assembly s, 606
21:17 *they* s, "so that a tribe of Israel will not 606
Ru 1: 8 Then Naomi s to her two daughters-in-law, 606
1:10 and s to her, "We will go back with you 606
1:11 But Naomi s, "Return home, my daughters. 606
1:15 s Naomi, "your sister-in-law is going back 606
2: 2 And Ruth the Moabitess s to Naomi, 606
2: 2 Naomi s to her, "Go ahead, my daughter." 606
2: 7 *She* s, 'Please let me glean and gather 606
2: 8 Boaz s to Ruth, "My daughter, listen to me. 606
2:13 to find favor in your eyes, my lord," *she* s. 606
2:14 At mealtime Boaz s to her, "Come over 606
2:19 the man I worked with today is Boaz," *she* s. 606
2:20 Naomi s to her daughter-in-law. 606
2:21 Then Ruth the Moabitess s, 606
2:21 Ruth the Moabitess said, "*He* even s to me, 606
2:22 Naomi s to Ruth her daughter-in-law, 606
3: 1 One day Naomi her mother-in-law s to her, 606
3: 9 "I am your servant Ruth," *she* s. 606
3:14 and *he* s, "Don't let it be known that 606
3:15 *He* also s, "Bring me the shawl 606
3:18 Then Naomi s, "Wait, my daughter, 606
4: 1 Boaz s, "Come over here, my friend, 606
4: 2 took ten of the elders of the town and s, 606
4: 3 Then *he* s to the kinsman-redeemer, 606
4: 4 "I will redeem it," *he* s. 606
4: 5 Then Boaz s, "On the day you buy the land 606
4: 6 At this, the kinsman-redeemer s, 606
4: 8 So the kinsman-redeemer s to Boaz, 606
4:11 Then the elders and all those at the gate s, 606
4:14 The women s to Naomi: "Praise be 606
4:17 women living there s, "Naomi has a son." 606
1Sa 1:14 and s to her, "How long will you keep on 606
1:18 *She* s, "May your servant find favor 606
1:22 *She* s to her husband, "After the boy is 606
1:26 and *she* s to him, "As surely as you live, 606
2: 1 Then Hannah prayed and s: "My heart 606

1Sa 2:16 If the man s to him, 606
2:23 *he* s to them, "Why do you do such things? 606
2:27 a man of God came to Eli and s to him, 606
3: 5 And he ran to Eli and s, "Here I am; 606
3: 5 But Eli s, "I did not call; 606
3: 6 And Samuel got up and went to Eli and s, 606
3: 6 "My son," Eli s, "I did not call; 606
3: 8 and Samuel got up and went to Eli and s, 606
3:10 Then Samuel s, "Speak, 606
3:11 And the LORD s to Samuel: 606
3:16 but Eli called him and s, 606
3:17 "What was it *he* s to you?" 1819
3:18 Then Eli s, "He is the LORD; 606
4: 7 "A god has come into the camp," *they* s. 606
4:20 the women attending her s, "Don't despair; 1819
4:22 *She* s, "The glory has departed from Israel, 606
5: 7 of Ashdod saw what was happening, *they* s, 606
5:11 of the Philistines and s, "Send the ark of 606
6: 2 for the priests and the diviners and s, 606
7: 3 And Samuel s to the whole house of Israel, 606
7: 5 Then Samuel s, "Assemble all Israel 606
7: 8 They s to Samuel, "Do not stop crying out 606
8: 5 *They* s to him, "You are old, 606
8: 6 But when *they* s, "Give us a king 606
8:11 *He* s, "This is what the king who will reign 606
8:19 "No!" *they* s. "We want a king over us. 606
8:21 When Samuel heard all **that** the people s, 1821
8:22 Then Samuel s to the men of Israel, 606
9: 3 and Kish s to his son Saul, 606
9: 5 Saul s to the servant who was with him, 606
9: 7 Saul s to his servant, "If we go, 606
9: 8 *he* s, "I have a quarter of a shekel of silver. 606
9:10 "Good," Saul s to his servant. 606
9:17 the LORD s *to* him, "This is the man 6699
9:23 Samuel s to the cook, "Bring the piece 606
9:24 Samuel s, "Here is what has been kept 606
9:24 from the time I s, 'I have invited guests.' " 606
9:27 Samuel s to Saul, "Tell the servant to go on 606
10:14 "Looking for the donkeys," *he* s. 606
10:15 Saul's uncle s, "Tell me what Samuel said 606
10:15 "Tell me what Samuel s to you." 606
10:16 not tell his uncle what Samuel *had* s *about* 606
10:18 and s to them, "This is what the LORD, 606
10:19 And *you have* s, 'No, set a king over us.' 606
10:22 And the LORD s, "Yes, he has hidden 606
10:24 Samuel s to all the people, "Do you see 606
10:27 But some troublemakers s, 606
11: 1 And all the men of Jabesh s to him, 606
11: 3 The elders of Jabesh s to him, 606
11: 5 to him **what** the men of Jabesh had s. 1821
11:10 They s to the Ammonites, 606
11:12 The people then s to Samuel, 606
11:13 But Saul s, "No one shall be put 606
11:14 Then Samuel s to the people, "Come, 606
12: 1 Samuel s to all Israel, "I have listened 606
12: 1 "I have listened to everything *you* s to me 606
12: 5 Samuel s to them, "The LORD is witness 606
12: 5 "He is witness," *they* s. 606
12: 6 Then Samuel s to the people, 606
12:10 They cried out to the LORD and s, 606
12:12 *you* s to me, 'No, we want a king to rule 606
12:19 The people all s to Samuel, 606
13: 3 trumpet blown throughout the land and s, 606
13: 9 So he s, "Bring me the burnt offering and 606
13:13 "You acted foolishly," Samuel s. 606
13:19 because the Philistines *had* s, 606
14: 1 One day Jonathan son of Saul s to 606
14: 6 Jonathan s to his young armor-bearer, 606
14: 7 that you have in mind," his armor-bearer s. 606
14: 8 Jonathan s, "Come, then; 606
14:11 s the Philistines. "The Hebrews are crawling 606
14:12 So Jonathan s to his armor-bearer, 606
14:17 Then Saul s to the men who were with him, 606
14:18 Saul s to Ahijah, "Bring the ark of God." 606
14:19 Saul s to the priest, "Withdraw your hand." 606
14:29 Jonathan s, "My father has made trouble 606
14:33 Then *someone* s to Saul, "Look, 5583
14:33 "You have broken faith," *he* s. 606
14:34 Then he s, "Go out among the men 606
14:36 Saul s, "Let us go down after the Philistines 606
14:36 the priest s, "Let us inquire of God here." 606
14:38 Saul therefore s, "Come here, 606
14:39 But not one of the men s **a word.** 6699
14:40 Saul then s to all the Israelites, 606
14:42 Saul s, "Cast the lot between me 606
14:43 Then Saul s to Jonathan, 606
14:44 Saul s, "May God deal with me, 606
14:45 the men s to Saul, "Should Jonathan die— 606
15: 1 Samuel s to Saul, "I am the one 606
15: 6 Then he s to the Kenites, "Go away, 606
15:13 When Samuel reached him, Saul s, 606
15:14 But Samuel s, "What then is this bleating 606
15:16 "Stop!" Samuel s to Saul. 606
15:16 "Let me tell you what the LORD s 1819
15:17 Samuel s, "Although you were once small 606
15:20 "But I did obey the LORD," Saul s. 606
15:24 Then Saul s to Samuel, "I have sinned. 606
15:26 But Samuel s to him, "I will not go back 606
15:28 Samuel s to him, "The LORD has torn 606
15:32 Then Samuel s, "Bring me Agag king of 606
15:33 But Samuel s, "As your sword has made 606
16: 1 The LORD s to Samuel, "How long 606
16: 2 But Samuel s, "How can I go? 606
16: 2 The LORD s, "Take a heifer with you 606
16: 4 Samuel did what the LORD s. 1819
16: 7 But the LORD s to Samuel, "Do not consider 606
16: 8 But Samuel s, "The LORD has not chosen 606

1Sa 16: 9 then had Shammah pass by, but Samuel s, 606
16:10 but Samuel s to him, "The LORD has not 606
16:11 Samuel s, "Send for him; 606
16:12 Then the LORD s, "Rise and anoint him; 606
16:15 Saul's attendants s to him, "See, 606
16:17 So Saul s to his attendants, 606
16:19 Then Saul sent messengers to Jesse and s, 606
17:10 Then the Philistine s, "This day I defy 606
17:17 Now Jesse s to his son David, 606
17:29 "Now what have I done?" s David. 606
17:31 What David s was overheard and reported 1819
17:32 David s to Saul, "Let no one lose heart 606
17:34 But David s to Saul, "Your servant 606
17:37 Saul s to David, "Go, 606
17:39 "I cannot go in these," he s to Saul, 606
17:43 He s to David, "Am I a dog, 606
17:44 he s, "and I'll give your flesh to the birds of 606
17:45 David s to the Philistine, "You come against 606
17:55 he s to Abner, commander of the army, 606
17:56 The king s, "Find out whose son this young 606
17:58 David s, "I am the son of your servant Jesse 606
18:17 Saul s to David, "Here is my older daughter 606
18:17 For Saul s to himself, "I will not raise a hand 606
18:18 But David s to Saul, "Who am I, 606
18:21 So Saul s to David, "Now you have 606
18:23 But David s, "Do you think it is 606
18:24 Saul's servants told him what David had s, 1819
19: 4 and s to him, "Let not the king do wrong 606
19:14 Michal s, "He is ill." 606
19:17 Saul s to Michal, "Why did you deceive me 606
19:17 Michal told him, "He s to me, 606
19:22 "Over in Naioth at Ramah," they s. 606
20: 3 But David took an oath and s, 606
20: 3 and he has s to himself, 606
20: 4 Jonathan s to David, "Whatever you want 606
20: 5 So David s, "Look, tomorrow is 606
20: 9 "Never!" Jonathan s. 606
20:11 Jonathan s, "let's go out into the field." 606
20:12 Then Jonathan s to David: 606
20:18 Then Jonathan s to David: 606
20:26 Saul s nothing that day, for he thought, 1819
20:27 Then Saul s to his son Jonathan, 606
20:29 He s, 'Let me go, 606
20:30 Saul's anger flared up at Jonathan and he s 606
20:36 and he s to the boy, "Run and find the arrows 606
20:40 to the boy and s, "Go, carry them back 606
20:42 Jonathan s to David, "Go in peace, 606
21: 2 with a certain matter and s to me, 606
21: 9 David s, "There is none like it; 606
21:11 But the servants of Achish s to him, 606
21:14 Achish s to his servants, "Look at the man! 606
22: 3 to Mizpah in Moab and s to the king 606
22: 5 But the prophet Gad s to David, 606
22: 7 Saul s to them, "Listen, men of Benjamin! 606
22: 9 who was standing with Saul's officials, s, 6699
22:12 Saul s, "Listen now, son of Ahitub." 606
22:13 Saul s to him, "Why have you conspired 606
22:16 But the king s, "You will surely die, 606
22:22 Then David s to Abiathar: 606
23: 3 But David's men s to him, 606
23: 7 and he s, "God has handed him over to me, 606
23: 9 he s to Abiathar the priest, 606
23:10 David s, "O LORD, God of Israel, 606
23:11 And the LORD s, "He will." 606
23:12 And the LORD s, "They will." 606
23:17 "Don't be afraid," he s. 606
23:19 up to Saul at Gibeah and s, 606
24: 4 The men s, "This is the day 606
24: 4 the day the LORD spoke of when he s 606
24: 6 He s to his men, "The LORD forbid 606
24: 9 He s to Saul, "Why do you listen 606
24:10 I s, 'I will not lift my hand 606
24:17 "You are more righteous than I," he s. 606
25: 5 So he sent ten young men and s to them, 606
25:13 David s to his men, "Put on your swords!" 606
25:21 David had just s, "It's been useless— 606
25:24 She fell at his feet and s: 606
25:32 David s to Abigail, "Praise be to the LORD, 606
25:35 what she had brought him and s, "Go home 606
25:39 David heard that Nabal was dead, he s, 606
25:40 His servants went to Carmel and s 1819
25:41 down with her face to the ground and s, 606
26: 1 The Ziphites went to Saul at Gibeah and s, 606
26: 6 "I'll go with you," s Abishai. 606
26: 8 Abishai s to David, 606
26: 9 David s to Abishai, "Don't destroy him! 606
26:10 As surely as the LORD lives," he s, 606
26:15 David s, "You're a man, aren't you? 606
26:17 Saul recognized David's voice and s, 606
26:19 in the LORD's inheritance and have s, 606
26:21 Then Saul s, "I have sinned. 606
26:25 Then Saul s to David, "May you be blessed, 606
27: 5 Then David s to Achish, 606
27:12 Achish trusted David and s to himself, 606
28: 1 Achish s to David, 606
28: 2 David s, "Then you will see 606
28: 7 Saul then s to his attendants, 606
28: 7 "There is one in Endor," they s. 606
28: 8 "Consult a spirit for me," he s, 606
28: 9 But the woman s to him, 606
28:11 "Bring up Samuel," he s. 606
28:12 she cried out at the top of her voice and s 606
28:13 The king s to her, "Don't be afraid. 606
28:13 The woman s, "I see a spirit coming up out 606
28:14 a robe is coming up," she s. 606
28:15 Samuel s to Saul, "Why have you disturbed 606
28:15 "I am in great distress," Saul s. 606

1Sa 28:16 Samuel s, "Why do you consult me, 606
28:21 and saw that he was greatly shaken, she s, 606
28:23 He refused and s, "I will not eat." 606
29: 4 commanders were angry with him and s, 606
29: 6 So Achish called David and s to him, 606
29: 9 the Philistine commanders have s, 606
30: 7 Then David s to Abiathar the priest, 606
30:13 He s, "I am an Egyptian, 606
30:22 among David's followers s, 6699
31: 4 Saul s to his armor-bearer, 606
2Sa 1: 4 He s, "The men fled from the battle. 606
1: 5 Then David s to the young man 606
1: 6 the young man s, "and there was Saul, 606
1: 7 he called out to me, and I s, 606
1: 9 he s to me, 'Stand over me and kill me! 606
1:13 David s to the young man who brought him 606
1:15 Then David called one of his men and s, 606
1:16 For David had s to him, 606
1:16 mouth testified against you when you s, 606
2: 1 The LORD s, "Go up." 606
2:14 Then Abner s to Joab, 606
2:14 "All right, let them do it," Joab s. 606
2:21 Then Abner s to him, 606
3: 7 And Ish-Bosheth s to Abner, 606
3: 8 of what Ish-Bosheth s and he answered, 1821
3:13 "Good," s David. 606
3:16 Then Abner s to him, "Go back home!" 606
3:17 with the elders of Israel and s, 606
3:21 Then Abner s to David, 606
3:24 So Joab went to the king and s, 606
3:28 Later, when David heard about this, he s, 606
3:31 David s to Joab and all the people with him, 606
3:38 Then the king s to his men, 606
4: 8 of Ish-Bosheth to David at Hebron and s to 606
5: 1 of Israel came to David at Hebron and s, 606
5: 2 And the LORD s to you, 606
5: 6 The Jebusites s to David, 606
5: 8 On that day, David s, 606
5:20 He s, "As waters break out, 606
6: 9 of the LORD that day and s, 606
6:20 of Saul came out to meet him and s, 606
6:21 David s to Michal, "It was before 606
7: 2 he s to Nathan the prophet, 606
7:18 in and sat before the LORD, and he s: 606
9: 2 and the king s to him, "Are you Ziba?" 606
9: 6 David s, "Mephibosheth!" 606
9: 7 "Don't be afraid," David s to him, 606
9: 8 Mephibosheth bowed down and s, 606
9: 9 Saul's servant, and s to him, 606
9:11 Then Ziba s to the king, 606
10: 3 the Ammonite nobles s to Hanun their lord, 606
10: 5 The king s, "Stay at Jericho 606
10:11 Joab s, "If the Arameans are too strong 606
11: 3 The man s, "Isn't this Bathsheba, 606
11: 8 Then David s to Uriah, "Go down to your 606
11:11 Uriah s to David, "The ark and Israel 606
11:12 Then David s to him, "Stay here 606
11:23 The messenger s to David, 606
12: 1 When he came to him, he s, 606
12: 5 with anger against the man and s to Nathan, 606
12: 7 Then Nathan s to David, "You are the man! 606
12:13 Then David s to Nathan, "I have sinned 606
13: 4 Amnon s to him, "I'm in love with Tamar, 606
13: 5 to bed and pretend to be ill," Jonadab s. 606
13: 6 the king came to see him, Amnon s to him, 606
13: 9 "Send everyone out of here," Amnon s. 606
13:10 Then Amnon s to Tamar, "Bring the food 606
13:11 he grabbed her and s, "Come to bed 606
13:12 she s to him. 606
13:15 Amnon s to her, "Get up and get out!" 606
13:16 she s to him. "Don't force me. 606
13:17 He called his personal servant and s, 606
13:20 Her brother Absalom s to her, 606
13:22 Absalom never s a word to Amnon, 1819
13:24 Absalom went to the king and s, 606
13:26 Then Absalom s, "If not, 606
13:32 s, "My lord should not think 6699
13:35 Jonadab s to the king, "See, 606
13:35 it has happened just as your servant s." 1821
14: 2 He s to her, "Pretend you are in mourning. 606
14: 4 and she s, "Help me, O king!" 606
14: 5 She s, "I am indeed a widow; 606
14: 8 The king s to the woman, "Go home, 606
14: 9 But the woman from Tekoa s to him, 606
14:11 She s, "Then let the king invoke 606
14:11 "As surely as the LORD lives," he s, 606
14:12 Then the woman s, "Let your servant speak 606
14:13 The woman s, "Why then have you devised 606
14:18 Then the king s to the woman, 6699
14:18 "Let my lord the king speak," the woman s. 606
14:21 The king s to Joab, "Very well, I will do it. 606
14:22 Joab s, "Today your servant knows 606
14:24 the king s, "He must go to his own house; 606
14:30 Then he s to his servants, "Look, 606
14:31 to Absalom's house and he s to him, 606
14:32 Absalom s to Joab, "Look, 606
14:32 "Look, I sent word to you and s, 606
15: 7 Absalom s to the king, "Let me go to Hebron 606
15: 9 The king s to him, "Go in peace." 606
15:14 Then David s to all his officials who were 606
15:19 The king s to Ittai the Gittite, 606
15:22 David s to Ittai, "Go ahead, march on." 606
15:25 Then the king s to Zadok, 606
15:27 The king also s to Zadok the priest, 606
15:33 David s to him, "If you go with me, 606
16: 3 Ziba s to him, "He is staying in Jerusalem, 606
16: 4 Then the king s to Ziba, 606

2Sa 16: 4 "I humbly bow," Ziba s. 606
16: 7 As he cursed, Shimei s, "Get out, get out, 606
16: 9 Then Abishai son of Zeruiah s to the king, 606
16:10 But the king s, "What do you and I have 606
16:10 he is cursing because the LORD s to him, 606
16:11 David then s to Abishai and all his officials, 606
16:16 went to Absalom and s to him, 606
16:18 Hushai s to Absalom, "No, 606
16:20 Absalom s to Ahithophel, 606
17: 1 Ahithophel s to Absalom, 606
17: 5 But Absalom s, "Summon also Hushai 606
17: 6 When Hushai came to him, Absalom s, 606
17:14 Absalom and all the men of Israel s, 606
17:21 They s to him, "Set out and cross the river 606
17:29 For they s, "The people have become hungry 606
18: 3 But the men s, "You must not go out; 606
18:11 Joab s to the man who had told him this, 606
18:14 Joab s, "I'm not going to wait like this 606
18:19 Now Ahimaaz son of Zadok s, 606
18:21 Then Joab s to a Cushite, "Go, 606
18:22 Ahimaaz son of Zadok again s to Joab, 606
18:23 He s, "Come what may, I want to run." NIH
18:23 So Joab s, "Run!" 606
18:25 The king s, "If he is alone, 606
18:26 The king s, "He must be bringing good news 606
18:27 The watchman s, "It seems to me that 606
18:27 "He's a good man," the king s. 606
18:28 the king with his face to the ground and s, 606
18:30 The king s, "Stand aside and wait here." 606
18:31 Then the Cushite arrived and s, 606
18:33 As he went, he s: "O my son Absalom! 606
19: 2 because on that day the troops heard it s, 606
19: 5 Joab went into the house to the king and s, 606
19:11 since what is being s throughout Israel 1821
19:19 and s to him, "May my lord not hold me 606
19:21 Then Abishai son of Zeruiah s, 6699
19:23 the king s to Shimei, "You shall not die." 606
19:26 He s, "My lord the king, 606
19:26 since I your servant am lame, I s, 606
19:29 The king s to him, "Why say more? 606
19:30 Mephibosheth s to the king, 606
19:33 The king s to Barzillai, 606
19:38 The king s, "Kimham shall cross over 606
20: 4 Then the king s to Amasa, 606
20: 6 David s to Abishai, 606
20: 9 Joab s to Amasa, "How are you, 606
20:11 of Joab's men stood beside Amasa and s, 606
20:17 She s, "Listen to what your servant has 606
20:17 "I'm listening," he s. 606
20:21 The woman s to Joab, 606
21: 1 The LORD s, "It is on account of Saul 606
21: 6 So the king s, "I will give them to you." 606
21:16 s he would kill David. 606
22: 2 He s: "The LORD is my rock, 606
23: 3 the Rock of Israel s to me: 1819
23:15 David longed for water and s, "Oh, 606
23:17 O LORD, to do this!" he s. 606
24: 2 So the king s to Joab and the army 606
24:10 and he s to the LORD, "I have sinned 606
24:13 So Gad went to David and s to him, 5583
24:14 David s to Gad, "I am in deep distress. 606
24:16 and s to the angel who was afflicting 606
24:17 he s to the LORD, "I am the one 606
24:18 that day Gad went to David and s to him, 606
24:21 Araunah s, "Why has my lord 606
24:22 Araunah s to David, "Let my lord the king 606
24:23 Araunah also s to him, 606
1Ki 1: 2 So his servants s to him, 606
1: 5 put himself forward and s, "I will be king." 606
1:14 will come in and confirm what you have s." 1821
1:17 She s to him, "My lord, 606
1:24 Nathan s, "Have you, my lord the king, 606
1:28 Then King David s, "Call in Bathsheba." 6699
1:31 s, "May my lord King David live forever!" 606
1:32 King David s, "Call in Zadok the priest, 606
1:33 he s to them: "Take your lord's servants 606
1:42 Adonijah s, "Come in. 606
1:48 and s, 'Praise be to the LORD, the God 606
1:53 and Solomon s, "Go to your home." 606
2: 2 about to go the way of all the earth," he s. 606
2:15 "As you know," he s, 606
2:16 "You may make it," she s. 606
2:20 to make of you," she s. 606
2:21 So she s, "Let Abishag the Shunammite 606
2:26 To Abiathar the priest the king s, 606
2:30 the tent of the LORD and s to Joab, 606
2:36 Then the king sent for Shimei and s to him, 606
2:38 as my lord the king has s." 1819
2:42 the king summoned Shimei and s to him, 606
2:42 At that time you s to me, 606
2:44 The king also s to Shimei, 606
3: 5 and God s, "Ask for whatever you want me 606
3:11 So God s to him, "Since you have asked 606
3:17 One of them s, "My lord, 606
3:22 The other woman s, "No! 606
3:23 The king s, "This one says, 606
3:24 Then the king s, "Bring me a sword." 606
3:26 with compassion for her son and s to 606
3:26 other s, "Neither I nor you shall have him. 606
5: 5 when he s, 'Your son whom I will put on 606
5: 7 he was greatly pleased and s, 606
8:12 Then Solomon s, "The LORD has said 606
8:12 "The LORD has s that he would dwell in 606
8:15 Then he s: "Praise be to the LORD 606
8:15 to my father David. For he s, 606
8:18 But the LORD s to my father David, 606
8:23 and s: "O LORD, God of Israel, 606

1Ki 8:25 the promises you made to him when you **s,** 606
8:29 this place of which *you* **s,** 606
9: 3 The LORD **s** to him: "I have heard 606
9: 5 as I promised David your father when I **s,** 606
10: 6 *She* **s** to the king, "The report I heard 606
11:11 So the LORD **s** to Solomon, 606
11:21 Then Hadad **s** to Pharaoh, "Let me go, 606
11:31 Then *he* **s** to Jeroboam, "Take ten pieces 606
12: 3 of Israel went to Rehoboam and **s** to him: 1819
12:10 "Tell these people who *have* **s** to you, 1819
12:12 as the king *had* **s,** "Come back to me 1819
12:14 and **s,** "My father made your yoke heavy; 1819
12:28 *He* **s** to the people, "It is too much for you 606
13: 4 from the altar and **s,** "Seize him!" 606
13: 6 Then the king **s** to the man of God, 6699
13: 7 The king **s** to the man of God, 1819
13:11 They also told their father what *he had* **s** to 1819
13:13 So *he* **s** to his sons, "Saddle the donkey 606
13:15 So the prophet **s** to him, 606
13:16 The man of God **s,** "I cannot turn back 606
13:18 angel **s** to me by the word of the LORD: 1819
13:26 of it, *he* **s,** "It is the man of God who defied 606
13:27 The prophet **s** to his sons, 1819
13:30 and they mourned over him and **s,** "Oh, NIH
13:31 After burying him, *he* **s** to his sons, 606
14: 2 and Jeroboam **s** to his wife, 606
14: 4 So Jeroboam's wife did what he **s** and went NIH
14: 6 *he* **s,** "Come in, wife of Jeroboam. 606
14:18 as the LORD *had* **s** through his servant 1819+1821
15:19 between me and you," he **s,** "as there was 606
17: 1 from Tishbe in Gilead, **s** to Ahab, 606
17:13 Elijah **s** to her, "Don't be afraid. 606
17:13 Go home and do as you have **s.** 1821
17:18 *She* **s** to Elijah, "What do you have against 606
17:23 He gave him to his mother and **s,** "Look, 606
17:24 Then the woman **s** to Elijah, 606
18: 5 Ahab *had* **s** to Obadiah, 606
18: 7 and **s,** "Is it really you, my lord Elijah?" 606
18:15 Elijah **s,** "As the LORD Almighty lives, 606
18:17 When he saw Elijah, he **s** to him, 606
18:21 Elijah went before the people and **s,** 606
18:21 But the people **s** nothing. 6699
18:22 Then Elijah **s** to them, 606
18:24 all the people **s,** "What you say is good." 6699
18:25 Elijah **s** to the prophets of Baal, 606
18:27 to taunt them. "Shout louder!" *he* **s.** 606
18:30 Then Elijah **s** to all the people, 606
18:33 Then *he* **s** to them, Fill four large jars 606
18:34 "Do it again," *he* **s,** and they did it again. 606
18:41 And Elijah **s** to Ahab, "Go, eat and drink, 606
18:43 "There is nothing there," *he* **s.** 606
18:43 Seven times Elijah **s,** "Go back." 606
18:44 So Elijah **s,** "Go and tell Ahab, 606
19: 4 "I have had enough, LORD," *he* **s.** 606
19: 5 All at once an angel touched him and **s,** 606
19: 7 a second time and touched him and **s,** 606
19:11 The LORD **s,** "Go out and stand on 606
19:13 Then a voice **s** to him, "What are you doing 606
19:15 The LORD **s** to him, "Go back 606
19:20 *he* **s,** "and then I will come with you." 606
20: 5 The messengers came again and **s,** 606
20: 7 the elders of the land and **s** to them, 606
20:18 *He* **s,** "If they have come out for peace, 606
20:22 the prophet came to the king of Israel and **s,** 606
20:31 His officials **s** to him, "Look, 606
20:32 they went to the king of Israel and **s,** 606
20:33 your brother Ben-Hadad!" *they* **s.** 606
20:33 "Go and get him," the king **s.** 606
20:34 [Ahab **s,**] "On the basis of a treaty NIH
20:35 the sons of the prophets **s** to his companion, 606
20:36 So the prophet **s,** "Because you have not 606
20:37 The prophet found another man and **s,** 606
20:39 someone came to me with a captive and **s,** 606
20:40 "That is your sentence," the king of Israel **s.** 606
20:42 *He* **s** to the king, "This is what the LORD 606
21: 2 Ahab **s** to Naboth, "Let me have your 1819
21: 4 Naboth the Jezreelite *had* **s,** 1819+1821+2021
21: 6 "Because *I* **s** to Naboth the Jezreelite, 1819
21: 6 *he* **s,** 'I will not give you my vineyard.' " 606
21: 7 Jezebel his wife **s,** "Is this how you act 606
21:15 she **s** to Ahab, "Get up and take 606
21:20 Ahab **s** to Elijah, "So you have found me, 606
22: 3 The king of Israel *had* **s** to his officials, 606
22: 5 But Jehoshaphat also **s** to the king of Israel, 606
22: 9 of Israel called one of his officials and **s,** 606
22:12 they **s,** "for the LORD will give it into 606
22:13 to summon Micaiah **s** to him, 1819
22:14 But Micaiah **s,** "As surely as the LORD lives, 606
22:16 The king **s** to him, "How many times 606
22:17 the LORD **s,** 'These people have no master. 606
22:18 The king of Israel **s** to Jehoshaphat, 606
22:20 And the LORD **s,** 'Who will entice Ahab 606
22:21 stood before the LORD and **s,** 606
22:22 spirit in the mouths of all his prophets,' *he* **s.** 606
22:22 succeed in enticing him,' **s** the LORD. 606
22:30 The king of Israel **s** to Jehoshaphat, 606
22:49 At that time Ahaziah son of Ahab **s** 606
2Ki 1: 3 angel of the LORD **s** to Elijah the Tishbite, 1819
1: 6 "And *he* **s** to us, 'Go back 606
1: 8 The king **s,** "That was Elijah the Tishbite." 606
1: 9 and **s** to him, "Man of God, the king says, 1819
1:11 The captain **s** to him, "Man of God, 6699
1:15 The angel of the LORD **s** to Elijah, 1819
2: 2 Elijah **s** to Elisha, "Stay here; 606
2: 2 But Elisha **s,** "As surely as the LORD lives 606
2: 4 Then Elijah **s** to him, "Stay here, Elisha; 606
2: 6 Then Elijah **s** to him, "Stay here; 606

2Ki 2: 9 When they had crossed, Elijah **s** to Elisha, 606
2:10 "You have asked a difficult thing," Elijah **s,** 606
2:15 **s,** "The spirit of Elijah is resting on Elisha." 606
2:16 *they* **s,** "we your servants have fifty able men 606
2:17 So *he* **s,** "Send them." 606
2:18 *he* **s** to them, "Didn't I tell you not to go?" 606
2:19 The men of the city **s** to Elisha, "Look, 606
2:20 "Bring me a new bowl," *he* **s,** 606
2:23 "Go on up, you baldhead!" *they* **s.** 606
3:12 Jehoshaphat **s,** "The word of the LORD is 606
3:13 Elisha **s** to the king of Israel, 606
3:14 Elisha **s,** "As surely as the LORD Almighty 606
3:16 and *he* **s,** "This is what the LORD says: 606
3:23 "That's blood!" *they* **s.** 606
4: 2 *she* **s,** "except a little oil." 606
4: 3 Elisha **s,** "Go around and ask all your 606
4: 6 When all the jars were full, *she* **s** to her son, 606
4: 7 She went and told the man of God, and *he* **s,** 606
4: 9 *She* **s** to her husband, "I know that this man 606
4:12 *He* **s** to his servant Gehazi, 606
4:13 Elisha **s** to him, "Tell her, 606
4:14 Gehazi **s,** "Well, she has no son 606
4:15 Then Elisha **s,** "Call her." 606
4:16 "About this time next year," Elisha **s,** 606
4:19 My head!" *he* **s** to his father. 606
4:22 She called her husband and **s,** 606
4:23 "It's all right," *she* **s.** 606
4:24 the donkey and **s** to her servant, "Lead on; 606
4:25 the man of God **s** to his servant Gehazi, 606
4:26 "Everything is all right," *she* **s.** 606
4:27 but the man of God **s,** "Leave her alone! 606
4:28 for a son, my lord?" *she* **s.** 606
4:29 Elisha **s** to Gehazi, 606
4:30 But the child's mother **s,** 606
4:36 Elisha summoned Gehazi and **s,** 606
4:36 When she came, *he* **s,** "Take your son." 606
4:38 *he* **s** to his servant, 606
4:41 Elisha **s,** "Get some flour." 606
4:41 He put it into the pot and **s,** 606
4:42 "Give it to the people to eat," Elisha **s.** 606
5: 3 *She* **s** to her mistress, 606
5: 4 and told him what the girl from Israel *had* **s.** 1819
5: 7 he tore his robes and **s,** "Am I God? 606
5:11 But Naaman went away angry and **s,** 606
5:13 Naaman's servants went to him and **s,** 1819
5:15 He stood before him and **s,** 606
5:17 "If you will not," **s** Naaman, "please let me, 606
5:19 "Go in peace," Elisha **s.** 606
5:20 the servant of Elisha the man of God, **s** 606
5:23 "By all means, take two talents," **s** Naaman. 606
5:26 But Elisha **s** to him, "Was not my spirit with 606
6: 1 The company of the prophets **s** to Elisha, 606
6: 2 And *he* **s,** "Go." 606
6: 3 Then one of them **s,** "Won't you please come 606
6: 7 "Lift it out," *he* **s.** 606
6: 8 After conferring with his officers, he **s,** 606
6:12 my lord the king," **s** one of his officers, 606
6:20 After they entered the city, Elisha **s,** 606
6:28 She answered, "This woman **s** to me, 606
6:29 The next day *I* **s** to her, 606
6:31 *He* **s,** "May God deal with me, 606
6:32 but before he arrived, Elisha **s** to the elders, 606
6:33 king] **s,** "This disaster is from the LORD. 606
7: 1 Elisha **s,** "Hear the word of the LORD. 606
7: 2 the king was leaning **s** *to* the man of God, 6699
7: 3 *They* **s** to each other, "Why stay here 606
7: 6 so that *they* **s** to one another, "Look, 606
7: 9 Then *they* **s** to each other, 606
7:12 up in the night and **s** to his officers, 606
7:16 as the LORD had **s.** 1821
7:18 It happened as the man of God *had* **s** to 1819
7:19 The officer *had* **s** *to* the man of God, "Look, 6699
8: 1 Now Elisha *had* **s** to the woman whose son 1819
8: 2 to do as the man of God **s.** 1821
8: 4 the servant of the man of God, and *had* **s,** 606
8: 5 Gehazi **s,** "This is the woman, 606
8: 6 assigned an official to her case and **s** to him, 606
8: 8 he **s** to Hazael, "Take a gift with you 606
8: 9 He went in and stood before him, and **s,** 606
8:13 Hazael **s,** "How could your servant, 606
9: 1 the company of the prophets and **s** to him, 606
9: 5 a message for you, commander," *he* **s.** 606
9:12 "That's not true!" *they* **s.** 606
9:12 Jehu **s,** "Here is what he told me: 606
9:15 Jehu **s,** "If this is the way you feel, 606
9:18 The horseman rode off to meet Jehu and **s,** 606
9:19 When he came to them *he* **s,** 606
9:25 Jehu **s** to Bidkar, his chariot officer, 606
9:33 "Throw her down!" Jehu **s.** 606
9:34 "Take care of that cursed woman," *he* **s,** 606
9:36 They went back and told Jehu, *who* **s,** 606
10: 1 the guardians of Ahab's children. He **s,** 606
10: 4 But they were terrified and **s,** 606
10: 9 He stood before all the people and **s,** 606
10:13 *They* **s,** "We are relatives of Ahaziah, 606
10:15 Jehu greeted him and **s,** 606
10:15 "If so," **s** Jehu, "give me your hand." NIH
10:16 Jehu **s,** "Come with me and see my zeal for 606
10:18 and **s** to them, "Ahab served Baal a little; 606
10:20 Jehu **s,** "Call an assembly in honor of Baal." 606
10:22 And Jehu **s** to the keeper of the wardrobe, 606
10:23 Jehu **s** to the ministers of Baal, 606
10:30 The LORD **s** to Jehu, "Because you have done 606
11:15 For the priest *had* **s,** "She must not be put 606
12: 4 Joash **s** to the priests, "Collect all the money 606
13:15 Elisha **s,** "Get a bow and some arrows," 606
13:16 *he* **s** to the king of Israel. 606

2Ki 13:17 "Open the east window," *he* **s,** 606
13:17 "Shoot!" Elisha **s,** and he shot. 606
13:18 Then *he* **s,** "Take the arrows," 606
13:19 The man of God was angry with him and **s,** 606
14:27 since the LORD *had* not **s** he would blot out 1819
17:12 worshiped idols, though the LORD *had* **s,** 606
18:19 The field commander **s** to them, 606
18:26 Shebna and Joah **s** to the field commander, 606
18:36 remained silent and **s** nothing **in reply,** 6699
18:37 told him **what** the field commander had **s.** 1821
19: 6 Isaiah **s** to them, "Tell your master, 606
19:23 And *you have* **s,** "With my many chariots 606
20: 1 of Amoz went to him and **s,** "This is what 606
20: 7 Then Isaiah **s,** "Prepare a poultice of figs." 606
20:10 shadow to go forward ten steps," **s** Hezekiah. 606
20:15 everything in my palace," Hezekiah **s.** 606
20:16 Then Isaiah **s** to Hezekiah, 606
21: 4 of which the LORD *had* **s,** 606
21: 7 of which the LORD *had* **s** to David and 606
21:10 The LORD **s** through his servants 1819
22: 3 to the temple of the LORD. He **s:** 606
22: 8 the high priest **s** to Shaphan the secretary, 606
22:15 *She* **s** to them, "This is what the LORD, 606
23:17 The men of the city **s,** 606
23:18 "Leave it alone," *he* **s.** 606
23:27 So the LORD **s,** "I will remove Judah also 606
23:27 and this temple, about which *I* **s,** 606
25:24 be afraid of the Babylonian officials," *he* **s.** 606
1Ch 10: 4 Saul **s** to his armor-bearer, 606
11: 1 came together to David at Hebron and **s,** 606
11: 2 And the LORD your God **s** to you, 606
11: 5 **s** to David, "You will not get 606
11: 6 David *had* **s,** "Whoever leads the attack on 606
11:17 David longed for water and **s,** "Oh, 606
11:19 that I should do this!" *he* **s.** 606
12:17 David went out to meet them and **s** to them, 6699
12:18 and he **s:** "We are yours, O David! NIH
12:19 They **s,** "It will cost us our heads 606
12:23 as the LORD had **s:** 7023
13: 2 He then **s** to the whole assembly of Israel, 606
14:11 He **s,** "As waters break out, 606
15: 2 Then David **s,** "No one but the Levites 606
15:12 *He* **s** to them, "You are the heads of 606
16:36 Then all the people **s** "Amen" and "Praise 606
17: 1 he **s** to Nathan the prophet, "Here I am, 606
17:16 in and sat before the LORD, and *he* **s:** 606
19: 3 the Ammonite nobles **s** to Hanun, 606
19: 5 The king **s,** "Stay at Jericho 606
19:12 Joab **s,** "If the Arameans are too strong 606
21: 2 So David **s** to Joab and the commanders of 606
21: 8 Then David **s** to God, "I have sinned 606
21: 9 The LORD **s** to Gad, David's seer, 1819
21:11 So Gad went to David and **s** to him, 606
21:13 David **s** to Gad, "I am in deep distress. 606
21:15 and **s** to the angel who was destroying 606
21:17 David **s** to God, "Was it not I 606
21:22 David **s** to him, "Let me have the site 606
21:23 Araunah **s** to David, "Take it! 606
22: 1 Then David **s,** "The house of 606
22: 5 David **s,** "My son Solomon is young 606
22: 7 David **s** to Solomon: "My son, 606
22:11 as *he* **s** you would. 1819
22:18 He **s** to them, "Is not the LORD your God NIH
23: 4 David **s,** "Of these, twenty-four thousand NIH
23:25 For David *had* **s,** "Since the LORD, 606
28: 2 King David rose to his feet and **s:** 606
28: 3 But God **s** to me, 'You are not to build 606
28: 6 *He* **s** to me: 'Solomon your son is the one 606
28:19 David **s,** "I have in writing from the hand NIH
28:20 David also **s** to Solomon his son, 606
29: 1 Then King David **s** to the whole assembly: 606
29:20 Then David **s** to the whole assembly, 606
2Ch 1: 7 That night God appeared to Solomon and **s** 606
1:11 God **s** to Solomon, "Since this is your heart's 606
6: 1 Then Solomon **s,** "The LORD has said 606
6: 1 "The LORD *has* **s** that he would dwell in 606
6: 4 Then *he* **s:** "Praise be to the LORD, 606
6: 4 to my father David. For he **s,** 606
6: 8 But the LORD **s** to my father David, 606
6:14 *He* **s:** "O LORD, God of Israel, 606
6:16 the promises you made to him when you **s,** 606
6:20 which *you* **s** you would put your Name there 606
7:12 the LORD appeared to him at night and **s:** 606
7:18 with David your father when I **s,** 606
8:11 for her, for *he* **s,** "My wife must not live in 606
9: 5 *She* **s** to the king, "The report I heard 606
9: 6 not believe **what** they **s** until I came and 1821
10: 3 and all Israel went to Rehoboam and **s** 1819
10:10 "Tell the people who *have* **s** to you, 1819
10:12 as the king *had* **s,** "Come back to me 1819
10:14 and **s,** "My father made your yoke heavy; 1819
12: 5 and *he* **s** to them, "This is what the LORD 606
12: 6 and the king humbled themselves and **s,** 606
13: 4 in the hill country of Ephraim, and **s,** 606
13:22 what he did and **what** he **s,** 1821
14: 7 "Let us build up these towns," *he* **s** to Judah, 606
14:11 Asa called to the LORD his God and **s,** 606
15: 2 He went out to meet Asa and **s** to him, 606
16: 3 between me and you," he **s,** "as there was 606
16: 7 the seer came to Asa king of Judah and **s** 606
18: 4 But Jehoshaphat also **s** to the king of Israel, 606
18: 8 of Israel called one of his officials and **s,** 606
18:11 they **s,** "for the LORD will give it into 606
18:12 to summon Micaiah **s** to him, 1819
18:13 But Micaiah **s,** "As surely as the LORD lives, 606
18:15 The king **s** to him, "How many times 606
18:16 the LORD **s,** 'These people have no master 606

2Ch 18:17 The king of Israel s to Jehoshaphat, 606
18:19 And the LORD s, 'Who will entice Ahab 606
18:20 stood before the LORD and s, 606
18:21 spirit in the mouths of all his prophets,' *he* s. 606
18:21 succeed in enticing him,' s the LORD. 606
18:29 The king of Israel s to Jehoshaphat, 606
19: 2 went out to meet him and s to the king, 606
20: 6 and s: "O LORD, God of our fathers, 606
20:15 *He* s: "Listen, King Jehoshaphat 606
20:20 As they set out, Jehoshaphat stood and s, 606
21:12 a letter from Elijah the prophet, which s: 606
22: 9 They buried him, for *they* s, 606
23: 3 Jehoiada s to them, "The king's son 606
23:14 and s to them: "Bring her out 606
23:14 For the priest *had* s, "Do not put her 606
24: 5 the priests and Levites and s to them, 606
24: 6 the chief priest and s to him, 606
24:20 He stood before the people and s, 606
24:22 but killed his son, *who* s as he lay dying, 606
25: 7 But a man of God came to him and s, 606
25:15 and he sent a prophet to him, *who* s, 606
25:16 the king s to him, "Have we appointed you 606
25:16 So the prophet stopped but s, 606
26:18 They confronted him and s, 606
26:23 for *people* s, "He had leprosy." 606
28: 9 *He* s to them, "Because the LORD, 606
28:13 not bring those prisoners here," *they* s, 606
29: 5 and s: "Listen to me, 606
29:31 Then Hezekiah s, "You have now dedicated 6699
32: 4 and find plenty of water?" *they* s. 606
32: 8 **what** Hezekiah the king of Judah s. 1821
33: 4 of which the LORD *had* s, 606
33: 7 of which God *had* s to David and 606
34:15 Hilkiah s to Shaphan the secretary, 6699
34:23 *She* s to them, "This is what the LORD, 606
35: 3 *He* s to the Levites, who instructed all Israel 606
35:22 He would not listen to **what** Neco had s 1821
Ezr 4: 2 and to the heads of the families and s, 606
8:28 *I* s to them, "You as well as these articles 606
9: 1 the leaders came to me and s, 606
9:11 your servants the prophets when you s: 606
10: 2 one of the descendants of Elam, s to Ezra, 6699
10:10 Then Ezra the priest stood up and s to them, 606
Ne 1: 3 *They* s to me, "Those who survived the exile 606
1: 5 Then *I* s: "O LORD, God of heaven, 606
2: 3 but *I* s to the king, "May the king live forever 606
2: 4 The king s to me, "What is it you want?" 606
2: 7 *I* also s to him, "If it pleases the king, 606
2:16 yet *I had* s nothing to the Jews or the priests 5583
2:17 *I* s to them, "You see the trouble we are in: 606
2:18 upon me and what the king *had* s to me. 606
4: 2 *he* s, "What are those feeble Jews doing? 606
4: 3 s, "What they are building— 606
4:10 Meanwhile, the people in Judah s, 606
4:11 Also our enemies s, "Before they know it 606
4:14 I stood up and s to the nobles, the officials 606
4:19 Then *I* s to the nobles, the officials 606
4:22 At that time *I* also s to the people, 606
5: 8 and s: "As far as possible, 606
5:12 "We will give it back," *they* s. 606
5:13 I also shook out the folds of my robe and s, 606
5:13 At this the whole assembly s, "Amen," 606
6:10 *He* s, "Let us meet in the house of God, 606
6:11 But *I* s, "Should a man like me run away? 606
6:19 and then telling him **what** I s. 1821
7: 3 *I* s to them, "The gates of Jerusalem 606
8: 9 the people s to them all, 606
8:10 Nehemiah s, "Go and enjoy choice food 606
9: 5 Shebaniah and Pethahiah—s: 606
9:18 for themselves an image of a calf and s, 606
13:17 I rebuked the nobles of Judah and s 606
13:21 But I warned them and s, 606
13:25 an oath in God's name and s: NIH
Est 3: 8 Then Haman s to King Xerxes, 606
3:11 "Keep the money," the king s to Haman, 606
4: 9 reported to Esther **what** Mordecai had s. 1821
5: 5 "Bring Haman at once," the king s, 606
5:14 His wife Zeresh and all his friends s to him, 606
6: 4 The king s, "Who is in the court?" 606
6:13 His advisers and his wife Zeresh s to him, 606
7: 6 Esther s, "The adversary and enemy is 606
7: 9 one of the eunuchs attending the king, s, 606
7: 9 The king s, "Hang him on it!" 606
8: 5 "If it pleases the king," *she* s, 606
9:12 The king s to Queen Esther, 606
Job 1: 7 The LORD s to Satan, "Where have you come 606
1: 8 the LORD s to Satan, "Have you considered 606
1:12 The LORD s to Satan, "Very well, then, 606
1:14 a messenger came to Job and s, 606
1:16 another messenger came and s, 606
1:17 another messenger came and s, 606
1:18 yet another messenger came and s, 606
1:21 and s: "Naked I came from my mother's 606
2: 2 the LORD s to Satan, "Where have you come 606
2: 3 the LORD s to Satan, "Have you considered 606
2: 6 The LORD s to Satan, "Very well, then, 606
2: 9 His wife s to him, "Are you still holding on 606
2:10 In all this, Job did not sin in **what** he s. 8557
2:13 No *one* s a word to him, 1819
3: 2 He s: 6699
3: 3 and the night *it was* s, 'A boy is born!' 606
6:22 *Have I* ever s, 'Give something 606
21:19 [It is s,] 'God stores up a man's punishment NIH
22:17 They s to God, 'Leave us alone! 606
28:28 And *he* s to man, 'The fear of the Lord— 606
31:24 "If I have put my trust in gold or s to pure 606
31:31 if the men of my household *have* never s, 606
Job 32: 6 So Elihu son of Barakel the Buzite s: 6699
33: 8 "But *you have* s in my hearing— 606
34: 1 Then Elihu s: 6699
35: 1 Then Elihu s: 6699
36: 2 that there is more to be s in God's behalf. 4863
36:23 or s to him, 'You have done wrong'? 606
38: 1 LORD answered Job out of the storm. *He* s: 606
38:11 when *I* s, 'This far you may come 606
40: 1 The LORD s *to* Job: 6699
42: 4 ["You s,] 'Listen now, and I will speak; NIH
42: 7 After the LORD *had* s these things to Job, 1819
42: 7 he s to Eliphaz the Temanite, 606
Ps 2: 7 *He* s to me, "You are my Son; 606
16: 2 *I* s to the LORD, "You are my Lord; 606
18: T from the hand of Saul. *He* s: 606
30: 6 I felt secure, I s, "I will never be shaken." 606
31:22 In my alarm I s, "I am cut off 606
32: 5 *I* s, "I will confess my transgressions to 606
38:16 For *I* s, "Do not let them gloat 606
39: 1 *I* s, "I will watch my ways 606
40: 7 Then *I* s, "Here I am, I have come— 606
41: 4 I s, "O LORD, have mercy on me; 606
54: T When the Ziphites had gone to Saul and s, 606
55: 6 *I* s, "Oh, that I had the wings of a dove! 606
73:15 If *I had* s, "I will speak thus," 606
74: 8 *They* s in their hearts, "We will crush them 606
82: 6 "I s, 'You are "gods"; 606
83:12 who s, "Let us take possession of 606
87: 3 Glorious things **are** s of you, O city of God: 1819
87: 5 Indeed, of Zion *it will* **be** s, 606
89: 3 You s, "I have made a covenant NIH
89:19 to your faithful people *you* s: 606
94:18 When *I* s, "My foot is slipping," 606
95:10 *I* s, "They are a people whose hearts go astray, 606
102:24 So *I* s: "Do not take me away, O my God, 606
106:23 So *he* s he would destroy them— 606
116:10 therefore *I* s, "I am greatly afflicted." 1819
116:11 And in my dismay I s, "All men are liars." 606
122: 1 I rejoiced with *those who* s to me, 606
126: 2 Then *it was* s among the nations, 606
137: 3 they s, "Sing us one of the songs of Zion!" NIH
Pr 4: 4 he taught me and s, "Lay hold of my words 606
6: 2 you have been trapped by **what** you s, 609+7023
7:13 and with a brazen face *she* s: 606
Ecc 2: 2 "Laughter," *I* s, "is foolish. 606
2:15 *I* s in my heart, "This too is meaningless." 1819
7:23 All this I tested by wisdom and *I* s, 606
9:16 So I s, "Wisdom is better than strength." 606
SS 2:10 My lover spoke and s to me, "Arise, 606
7: 8 *I* s, "I will climb the palm tree; 606
Isa 6: 7 With it he touched my mouth and s, "See, 606
6: 8 And *I* s, "Here am I. 606
6: 9 *He* s, "Go and tell this people: 606
6:11 Then *I* s, "For how long, O Lord?" 606
7: 3 Then the LORD s to Isaiah, "Go out, 606
7:12 But Ahaz s, "I will not ask; 606
7:13 Isaiah s, "Hear now, you house of David! 606
8: 1 The LORD s to me, "Take a large scroll 606
8: 3 And the LORD s to me, "Name him 606
8:11 not to follow the way of this people. *He* s: 606
14:13 You s in your heart, "I will ascend 606
20: 2 *He* s to him, "Take off the sackcloth 606
20: 3 Then the LORD s, "Just as my servant Isaiah 606
22: 4 Therefore *I* s, "Turn away from me; 606
23:12 *He* s, "No more of your reveling, 606
24:16 But *I* s, "I waste away, I waste away! 606
28:12 to whom *he* s, "This is the resting place, let 606
30:16 *You* s, 'No, we will flee on horses.' 606
30:16 You s, 'We will ride off on swift horses.' NIH
36: 4 The field commander s to them, 606
36:11 Shebna and Joah s to the field commander, 606
36:21 remained silent and s nothing **in reply**, 6699
36:22 told him **what** the field commander had s. 1821
37: 6 Isaiah s to them, "Tell your master 606
37:24 And *you have* s, 'With my many chariots 606
38: 1 Isaiah son of Amoz went to him and s, 606
38:10 I s, "In the prime of my life must I go 606
38:11 *I* s, "I will not again see the LORD, 606
38:21 Isaiah *had* s, "Prepare a poultice of figs 606
39: 4 everything in my palace," Hezekiah s. 606
39: 5 Then Isaiah s to Hezekiah, 606
40: 6 And *I* s, "What shall I cry?" 606
41: 9 *I* s, 'You are my servant'; 606
45:19 *I have* not s to Jacob's descendants, 606
46:11 What *I have* s, that will I bring about; 1819
47: 7 *You* s, 'I will continue forever— 606
47:10 in your wickedness and *have* s, 606
49: 3 *He* s to me, "You are my servant, Israel, 606
49: 4 But I s, "I have labored to no purpose; 606
49:14 But Zion s, "The LORD has forsaken me, 606
51:23 your tormentors, who s to you, 'Fall prostrate 606
57:14 And *it will be* s: "Build up, build up, 606
63: 8 *He* s, "Surely they are my people, 606
65: 1 *I* s, 'Here am I, here am I.' 606
66: 5 *have* s, 'Let the LORD be glorified, 606
Jer 1: 6 "Ah, Sovereign LORD," *I* s, 606
1: 7 But the LORD s to me, "Do not say, 606
1: 9 and touched my mouth and s to me, 606
1:12 The LORD s to me, "You have seen correctly 606
1:14 The LORD s to me, "From the north disaster 606
2:20 *you* s, 'I will not serve you!' 606
2:25 But *you* s, 'It's no use! 606
3: 6 the LORD s to me, "Have you seen what 606
3:11 The LORD s to me, "Faithless Israel is more 606
3:19 "*I* myself s, " 'How gladly would I treat 606
4:10 Then *I* s, "Ah, Sovereign LORD, 606
Jer 5:12 *they* s, "He will do nothing! 606
6:16 But *you* s, 'We will not walk in it.' 606
6:17 I appointed watchmen over you and s, NIH
6:17 But *you* s, 'We will not listen.' 606
9:13 The LORD s, "It is because they have 606
10:19 Yet I s to myself, "This is my sickness, 606
11: 4 *I* s, 'Obey me and do everything I command 606
11: 6 The LORD s to me, "Proclaim all these words 606
11: 9 the LORD s to me, "There is a conspiracy 606
13: 1 This is what the LORD s to me: 606
13: 6 Many days later the LORD s to me, 606
14:11 Then the LORD s to me, "Do not pray for 606
14:13 But *I* s, "Ah, Sovereign LORD, 606
14:14 Then the LORD s to me, "The prophets 606
15: 1 Then the LORD s to me: "Even if Moses 606
15:11 The LORD s, "Surely I will deliver you 606
17:19 This is what the LORD s to me: 606
18:18 *They* s, "Come, let's make plans 606
19:14 the LORD's temple and s to all the people, 606
20: 3 from the stocks, Jeremiah s to him, 606
21: 1 priest Zephaniah son of Maaseiah. They s: 606
22:21 but *you* s, 'I will not listen!' 606
25: 2 the prophet s to all the people of Judah and 1819
25: 5 They s, "Turn now, each of you, 606
25:15 the LORD, the God of Israel, s to me: 606
26: 8 and all the people seized him and s, 606
26:11 the priests and the prophets s to the officials 606
26:12 Then Jeremiah s to all the officials and all 606
26:16 the people s to the priests and the prophets, 606
26:17 the elders of the land stepped forward and s 606
27: 2 This is what the LORD s to me: 606
27:12 I s, "Bow your neck under the yoke of 606
27:16 Then *I* s to the priests and all these people, 1819
28: 1 s to me in the house of the LORD in 606
28: 6 He s, "Amen! 606
28:11 and he s before all the people, "This is what 606
28:15 Then the prophet Jeremiah s to Hananiah 606
29: 3 to King Nebuchadnezzar in Babylon. *It* s: 606
29:25 You s to Zephaniah, 606
32: 6 Jeremiah s, "The word of the LORD came 606
32: 8 "Then, just as the LORD had s, 1821
32: 8 to me in the courtyard of the guard and s, 606
32:24 What *you* s has happened, as you now see. 1819
34:13 out of the land of slavery. I s, 606
35: 5 before the men of the Recabite family and s 606
35:11 *we* s, 'Come, we must go to Jerusalem 606
35:15 They s, "Each of you must turn 606
35:18 Jeremiah s to the family of the Recabites, 606
36:15 *They* s to him, "Sit down, please, 606
36:16 they looked at each other in fear and s to 606
36:19 Then the officials s to Baruch, 606
36:29 You burned that scroll and s, 606
37:13 the son of Hananiah, arrested him and s, 606
37:14 "That's not true!" Jeremiah s. 606
37:18 Then Jeremiah s to King Zedekiah, 606
38: 1 telling all the people *when* he s, 606
38: 4 Then the officials s to the king, 606
38: 8 Ebed-Melech went out of the palace and s 1819
38:12 Ebed-Melech the Cushite s to Jeremiah, 606
38:14 the king s to Jeremiah. "Do not hide 606
38:15 Jeremiah s to Zedekiah, 606
38:17 Then Jeremiah s to Zedekiah, 606
38:19 King Zedekiah s to Jeremiah, 606
38:24 Then Zedekiah s to Jeremiah, 606
38:25 'Tell us what *you* s to the king and what 1819
38:25 to the king and what the king s to you; 1819
38:27 So *they* s **no more** to him, 3087
40: 2 the guard found Jeremiah, *he* s to him, 606
40: 3 he has done just as *he* s he would. 1819
40: 9 be afraid to serve the Babylonians," he s. 606
40:14 and s to him, "Don't you know that 606
40:15 Then Johanan son of Kareah s privately 606
40:16 of Ahikam s to Johanan son of Kareah, 606
41: 6 When he met them, *he* s, 606
41: 8 ten of them s to Ishmael, "Don't kill us! 606
42: 2 Jeremiah the prophet and s to him, 606
42: 5 Then they s to Jeremiah, 606
42: 9 *He* s to them, "This is what the LORD, 606
42:20 and s, 'Pray to the LORD our God for us; 606
43: 2 and all the arrogant men s to Jeremiah, 606
44: 4 *who* s, 'Do not do this detestable thing 606
44:15 in Lower and Upper Egypt, s *to* Jeremiah, 6699
44:17 We will certainly do everything we s we would: 3655+4946+7023
44:20 Then Jeremiah s to all the people, 606
44:24 Then Jeremiah s to all the people, 606
when you s, 'We will certainly carry out 606
45: 3 *You* s, 'Woe to me! 606
45: 4 [The LORD s,] "Say this to him: NIH
50: 7 their enemies s, 'We are not guilty, 606
51:61 He s to Seraiah, "When you get to Babylon, 606
51:62 you *have* s you will destroy this place, 1819
La 3:57 and *you* s, "Do not fear." 606
Eze 2: 1 *He* s to me, "Son of man, 606
2: 3 *He* s: "Son of man, 606
3: 1 And *he* s to me, "Son of man, 606
3: 3 Then *he* s to me, "Son of man, 606
3: 4 *He* then s to me: "Son of man, 606
3:10 And *he* s to me, "Son of man, 606
3:22 and *he* s to me, "Get up and go out 606
3:24 He spoke to me and s: "Go, shut yourself 606
4:13 The LORD s, "In this way the people 606
4:14 Then *I* s, "Not so, Sovereign LORD! 606
4:15 *he* s, "I will let you bake your bread 606
4:16 *He* then s to me: "Son of man, 606
8: 5 Then *he* s to me, "Son of man, 606
8: 6 And *he* s to me, "Son of man, 606

Eze 8: 8 *He* s to me, "Son of man, 606
8: 9 And *he* s to me, "Go in and see 606
8:12 *He* s to me, "Son of man, 606
8:13 *he* s, "You will see them doing things 606
8:15 *He* s to me, "Do you see this, son of man? 606
8:17 *He* s to me, "Have you seen this, 606
9: 4 and s to him, "Go throughout the city 606
9: 5 As I listened, *he* s to the others, 606
9: 7 Then *he* s to them, "Defile the temple 606
10: 2 The LORD s to the man clothed in linen, 606
11: 2 The LORD s to me, "Son of man, 606
11:15 of whom the people of Jerusalem *have* s, 606
16: 6 as you lay there in your blood *I* s to you, 606
20: 5 With uplifted hand I s to them, 606
20: 7 And *I* s to them, "Each of you, 606
20: 8 So *I* s I would pour out my wrath on them 606
20:13 So *I* s I would pour out my wrath on them 606
20:18 *I* s to their children in the desert, 606
20:21 So *I* s I would pour out my wrath on them 606
20:29 Then *I* s to them: What is this high place 606
20:49 Then *I* s, "Ah, Sovereign LORD! 606
23:36 The LORD s to me: "Son of man, 606
23:43 *I* s about the one worn out by adultery, 606
24:20 So *I* s to them, "The word of the LORD came 606
25: 3 Because you s "Aha!" 606
25: 8 'Because Moab and Seir s, "Look, 606
26: 2 because Tyre *has* s of Jerusalem, 'Aha! 606
29: 9 " 'Because *you* s, "The Nile is mine; 606
33:21 from Jerusalem came to me and s, 606
35:10 " 'Because you *have* s, "These two nations 606
35:12 the contemptible things *you have* s against 606
35:12 You s, "They have been laid waste 606
36: 2 The enemy s of you, "Aha! 606
36:20 for *it was* s of them, 'These are the LORD's 606
37: 3 *I* s, "O Sovereign LORD, 606
37: 4 Then *he* s to me, "Prophesy to these bones 606
37: 9 Then *he* s to me, "Prophesy to the breath; 606
37:11 Then *he* s to me: "Son of man, 606
40: 4 The man s to me, "Son of man, 1819
40:45 *He* s to me, "The room facing south 1819
41: 4 *He* s to me, "This is the Most Holy Place." 606
41:22 The man s to me, "This is the table 1819
42:13 Then *he* s to me, "The north and south 606
43: 7 *He* s: "Son of man, 606
43:18 Then *he* s to me, "Son of man, 606
44: 2 LORD s to me, "This gate is to remain shut. 606
44: 5 The LORD s to me, "Son of man, 606
46:20 *He* s to me, "This is the place 606
46:24 *He* s to me, "These are the kitchens 606
47: 8 *He* s to me, "This water flows 606
Da 1:11 Daniel then s to the guard whom 606
2: 3 he s to them, "I have had a dream 606
2:20 and s: "Praise be to the name of God 10042
2:24 and s to him, "Do not execute 10042
2:25 took Daniel to the king at once and s, 10042
2:47 The king s to Daniel, "Surely your God is 10558
3: 9 *They* s to King Nebuchadnezzar, "O king, 10558
3:14 and Nebuchadnezzar s to them, 10558
3:25 *He* s, "Look! I see four men 10558
3:28 Nebuchadnezzar s, "Praise be to the God 10558
4: 9 I s, "Belteshazzar, chief of the magicians, NIH
4:19 So the king s, "Belteshazzar, 10558
4:30 he s, "Is not this the great Babylon 10558
4:33 Immediately **what** had been s 10418
5: 7 astrologers and diviners to be brought and s 10558
5:10 "O king, live forever!" she s. 10558
5:13 and the king s to him, "Are you Daniel, 10558
6: 5 Finally these men s, 10042
6: 6 as a group to the king and s: 10042
6:13 Then *they* s to the king, "Daniel, 10558
6:15 the men went as a group to the king and s 10042
6:16 The king s to Daniel, "May your God, 10558
7: 2 Daniel s: "In my vision at night 10558
8:13 and another holy one s to him, 606
8:14 *He* s to me, "It will take 2,300 evenings 606
8:17 "Son of man," *he* s to me, 606
8:19 *He* s: "I am going to tell you what will 606
9:22 He instructed me and s to me, "Daniel, 1819
10:11 *He* s, "Daniel, you who are highly esteemed, 606
10:11 when he s this to me, I stood up trembling. 1819
10:16 *I* s to the one standing before me, 606
10:19 O man highly esteemed," *he* s. 606
10:19 I was strengthened and s, "Speak, my lord, 606
10:20 So *he* s, "Do you know why I have come 606
12: 6 *One of them* s to the man clothed in linen, 606
Hos 1: 2 the LORD s to him, "Go, take to yourself 606
1: 4 Then the LORD s to Hosea, 606
1: 6 Then the LORD s to Hosea, 606
1: 9 Then the LORD s, "Call him Lo-Ammi, 606
1:10 In the place where *it* **was** s to them, 606
2: 5 *She* s, 'I will go after my lovers, 606
2:12 which *she* s were her pay from her lovers; 606
3: 1 The LORD s to me, "Go, show your love 606
13: 2 *It is* s of these people, 606
13:10 of whom *you* s, 'Give me a king 606
Joel 2:32 will be deliverance, as the LORD *has* s, 606
Am 1: 2 *He* s: "The LORD roars from Zion 606
7: 3 "This will not happen," the LORD s. 606
7: 6 the Sovereign LORD s. 606
7: 8 Then the Lord s, "Look, 606
7:12 Amaziah s to Amos, "Get out, you seer! 606
7:15 from tending the flock and s to me, 606
8: 2 Then the LORD s to me, "The time is ripe 606
9: 1 the Lord standing by the altar, and *he* s: 606
Jnh 1: 6 The captain went to him and s, 606
1: 7 Then the sailors s to each other, "Come, 606
2: 2 *He* s: "In my distress I called to the 606

Jnh 2: 4 I s, 'I have been banished from your sight; 606
4: 2 this not **what** I s when I was still at home? 1821
4: 8 He wanted to die, and s, 606
4: 9 But God s to Jonah, "Do you have any right 606
4: 9 "I do," *he* s. 606
4:10 But the LORD s, "You have been concerned 606
Mic 2: 7 *Should it* **be** s, O house of Jacob: 606
3: 1 Then *I* s, "Listen, you leaders of Jacob, 606
7:10 *she who* s to me, "Where is the LORD 606
Zep 2:15 She s to herself, "I am, 606
3: 7 *I* s to the city, 'Surely you will fear me 606
Hag 2:13 Then Haggai s, "If a person defiled 606
2:14 Then Haggai s, " 'So it is with this people 6699
Zec 1: 6 "Then they repented and s, 606
1:12 Then the angel of the LORD s, 6699
1:14 Then the angel who was speaking to me s, 606
2: 4 and s to him: "Run, tell that young man, 606
3: 2 The LORD s to Satan, "The LORD rebuke you 606
3: 4 The angel s to those who were standing 6699
3: 4 Then *he* s to Joshua, "See, 606
3: 5 Then *I* s, "Put a clean turban on his head." 606
4: 6 So *he* s to me, "This is the word of the LORD 6699
4:13 "No, my lord," *I* s. 606
4:14 So *he* s, "These are the two who are anointed 606
5: 3 And *he* s to me, "This is the curse 606
5: 5 to me came forward and s to me, 606
5: 8 *He* s, "This is wickedness," 606
6: 7 And *he* s, "Go throughout the earth!" 606
11: 9 and s, "I will not be your shepherd. 606
11:13 LORD s to me, "Throw it to the potter"— 606
11:15 Then the LORD s to me, 606
Mal 3:13 "You *have* s harsh *things* against me," 1821
3:13 you ask, 'What *have we* s against you?' 1819
3:14 "*You have* s, 'It is futile to serve God. 606
Mt 1:20 the Lord appeared to him in a dream and s, *3306*
1:22 to fulfill what the Lord *had* s through *3306*
2: 8 *He* sent them to Bethlehem and s, *3306*
2:13 up," *he* s, "take the child and his mother *3306*
2:15 so was fulfilled what the Lord *had* s through *3306*
2:17 Then what *was* s through the prophet *3306*
2:20 and s, "Get up, take the child and his *3306*
2:23 So was fulfilled what *was* s through *3306*
3: 7 *he* s to them: "You brood of vipers! *3306*
3:17 And a voice from heaven s, "This is my Son *3306*
4: 3 The tempter came to him and s, *3306*
4: 6 "If you are the Son of God," *he* s, *3306*
4: 9 "All this I will give you," *he* s, *3306*
4:10 Jesus s to him, "Away from me, Satan! *3306*
4:14 to fulfill what *was* s through the prophet *3306*
4:19 "Come, follow me," Jesus s, *3306*
5:21 that *it was* s to the people long ago, *3306*
5:27 "You have heard that *it was* s, *3306*
5:31 "*It has been* s, 'Anyone who divorces *3306*
5:33 that *it was* s to the people long ago, *3306*
5:38 "You have heard that *it was* s, *3306*
5:43 "You have heard that *it was* s, *3306*
8: 2 came and knelt before him and s, *3306*
8: 3 "I am willing," *he* s. *3306*
8: 4 Then Jesus s to him, "See that you don't tell *3306*
8: 6 *he* s, "my servant lies at home paralyzed *3306*
8: 7 Jesus s to him, "I will go and heal him." *3306*
8:10 and s to those following him, *3306*
8:13 Then Jesus s to the centurion, "Go! *3306*
8:19 a teacher of the law came to him and s, *3306*
8:21 Another disciple s to him, "Lord, *3306*
8:32 *He* s to them, "Go!" *3306*
9: 2 *he* s to the paralytic, "Take heart, son; *3306*
9: 3 of the teachers of the law s to themselves, *3306*
9: 4 Knowing their thoughts, Jesus s, *3306*
9: 6 Then *he* s to the paralytic, "Get up, *3306*
9:12 On hearing this, Jesus s, *3306*
9:18 a ruler came and knelt before him and s, *3306*
9:21 *She* s to herself, "If I only touch his cloak, *3306*
9:22 "Take heart, daughter," *he* s, *3306*
9:24 *he* s, "Go away. The girl is not dead *3306*
9:29 Then he touched their eyes and s, *3306*
9:33 The crowd was amazed and s, *3306*
9:34 Pharisees s, "It is by the prince of demons *3306*
9:37 Then *he* s to his disciples, *3306*
11:25 At that time Jesus s, "I praise you, Father, *3306*
12: 2 When the Pharisees saw this, *they* s to him, *3306*
12:11 He s to them, "If any of you has a sheep *3306*
12:13 *he* s to the man, "Stretch out your hand." *3306*
12:23 All the people were astonished and s, *3306*
12:24 But when the Pharisees heard this, *they* s, *3306*
12:25 Jesus knew their thoughts and s to them, *3306*
12:38 of the Pharisees and teachers of the law s *3306*
12:49 Pointing to his disciples, *he* s, *3306*
13:27 "The owner's servants came to him and s, *3306*
13:36 His disciples came to him and s, *3306*
13:52 He s to them, "Therefore every teacher *3306*
13:57 But Jesus s to them, *3306*
14: 2 and *he* s to his attendants, "This is John *3306*
14: 8 Prompted by her mother, she s, *5774*
14:15 the disciples came to him and s, *3306*
14:18 "Bring them here to me," he s. *3306*
14:26 "It's a ghost," *they* s, and cried out in fear. *3306*
14:27 But Jesus immediately s to them: *3281+3306*
14:29 "Come," he s. *3306*
14:31 "You of little faith," *he* s, *3306*
15: 4 For God s, 'Honor your father and mother' *3306*
15:10 Jesus called the crowd to him and s, *3306*
15:15 Peter s, "Explain the parable to us." *3306*
15:25 "Lord, help me!" she s. *3306*
15:27 she s, "but even the dogs eat the crumbs *3306*
15:32 Jesus called his disciples to him and s, *3306*
16: 6 "Be careful," Jesus s to them. *3306*

Mt 16: 7 discussed this among themselves and s, *3306*
16:22 to rebuke him. "Never, Lord!" he s. *NIG*
16:23 Jesus turned and s to Peter, "Get behind me, *3306*
16:24 Then Jesus s to his disciples, *3306*
17: 4 Peter s to Jesus, "Lord, it is good for us *3306*
17: 5 a voice from the cloud s, "This is my Son, *3306*
17: 7 "Get up," *he* s. *3306*
17:15 "Lord, have mercy on my son," *he* s. *3306*
17:22 he s to them, "The Son of Man is going to *3306*
17:26 "Then the sons are exempt," Jesus s to him. *5774*
18: 3 And *he* s: "I tell you the truth, *3306*
18:32 'You wicked servant,' *he* s, *3306*
19: 5 and s, 'For this reason a man will leave *3306*
19:10 The disciples s to him, *3306*
19:14 Jesus s, "Let the little children come to me, *3306*
19:20 "All these I have kept," the young man s. *3306*
19:23 Then Jesus s to his disciples, *3306*
19:26 Jesus looked at them and s, *3306*
19:28 Jesus s to them, "I tell you the truth, *3306*
20: 7 "*He* s to them, 'You also go and work *3306*
20: 8 the owner of the vineyard s to his foreman, *3306*
20:12 *they* s, 'and you have made them equal *3306*
20:17 the twelve disciples aside and s to them, *3306*
20:21 *She* s, "Grant that one of these two sons *3306*
20:22 Jesus s to them. "Can you drink from the cup *3306*
20:23 Jesus s to them, "You will indeed drink *3306*
20:25 Jesus called them together and s, *3306*
21:13 "It is written," *he* s to them, *3306*
21:19 Then *he* s to it, "May you never bear fruit *3306*
21:25 They discussed it among themselves and s, *3306*
21:27 Then he s, "Neither will I tell you *5774*
21:28 He went to the first and s, 'Son, *3306*
21:30 "Then the father went to the other son and s *3306*
21:31 Jesus s to them, "I tell you the truth, *3306*
21:37 'They will respect my son,' *he* s. *3306*
21:38 tenants saw the son, *they* s to each other, *3306*
21:42 Jesus s to them, "Have you never read in *3306*
22: 4 "Then he sent some more servants and s, *3306*
22: 8 "Then he s to his servants, *3306*
22:16 *they* s, "we know you are a man *3306*
22:18 But Jesus, knowing their evil intent, s, *3306*
22:21 Then *he* s to them, "Give to Caesar what is *3306*
22:24 *they* s, "Moses told us that if a man dies *3306*
22:31 have you not read what God s to you, *3306*
22:43 *He* s to them, "How is it then that David, *3306*
22:44 " 'The Lord s to my Lord: *3306*
23: 1 Jesus s to the crowds and to his disciples: *3281*
24: 3 "Tell us," *they* s, "when will this happen, *3306*
25: 8 The foolish ones s to the wise, *3306*
25:11 others also came. 'Sir! Sir!' *they* s. *3306*
25:20 *he* s, 'you entrusted me with five talents. *3306*
25:22 *he* s, 'you entrusted me with two talents; *3306*
25:24 *he* s, 'I knew that you are a hard man, *3306*
26: 1 *he* s to his disciples, "Sit here while I go *3306*
26: 5 "But not during the Feast," *they* s, *3306*
26:10 Aware of this, Jesus s to them, *3306*
26:21 And while they were eating, *he* s, *3306*
26:25 Judas, the one who would betray him, s, *3306*
26:35 And all the other disciples s the same. *3306*
26:36 and *he* s to them, "Sit here while I go over *3306*
26:38 *he* s to them, "My soul is overwhelmed *3306*
26:45 he returned to the disciples and s to them, *3306*
26:49 Going at once to Jesus, Judas s, "Greetings, *3306*
26:52 Jesus s to him, "for all who draw the sword *3306*
26:55 At that time Jesus s to the crowd, *3306*
26:61 and declared, "This fellow s, 'I am able *5774*
26:62 the high priest stood up and s to Jesus, *3306*
26:63 The high priest s to him, *3306*
26:65 Then the high priest tore his clothes and s, *3306*
26:68 and s, "Prophesy to us, *3306*
26:69 also were with Jesus of Galilee," *she* s. *3306*
26:70 "I don't know what you're talking about," he s. *3306*
26:71 another girl saw him and s to the people *3306*
26:73 those standing there went up to Peter and s, *3306*
27: 4 "I have sinned," *he* s, *3306*
27: 6 The chief priests picked up the coins and s, *3306*
27:24 "I am innocent of this man's blood," *he* s. *3306*
27:29 "Hail, king of the Jews!" *they* s. *3306*
27:42 "He saved others," *they* s, *3306*
27:43 for *he* s, 'I am the Son of God.' " *3306*
27:47 *they* s, "He's calling Elijah." *3306*
27:49 The rest s, "Now leave him alone. *3306*
27:63 *they* s, "we remember that while he was *3306*
27:63 that while he was still alive that deceiver s, *3306*
28: 5 The angel s to the women, "Do not be afraid *3306*
28: 6 He is not here; he has risen, just as *he* s. *3306*
28: 9 "Greetings," *he* s. *3306*
28:10 Then Jesus s to them, "Do not be afraid. *3306*
28:18 Then Jesus came to them and s, *3281*
Mk 1:15 "The time has come," *he* s. *3306*
1:17 "Come, follow me," Jesus s, *3306*
1:25 s Jesus **sternly**. "Come out of him!" *2203*
1:41 "I am willing," *he* s. *3306*
2: 5 *he* s to the paralytic, "Son, your sins are *3306*
2: 8 and *he* s to them, "Why are you thinking *3306*
2:10 *He* s to the paralytic, *3306*
2:17 On hearing this, Jesus s to them, *3306*
2:24 The Pharisees s to him, "Look, *3306*
2:27 Then *he* s to them, "The Sabbath was made *3306*
3: 3 Jesus s to the man with the shriveled hand, *3306*
3: 5 s to the man, "Stretch out your hand." *3306*
3:21 they went to take charge of him, for *they* s, *3306*
3:22 the law who came down from Jerusalem s, *3306*
3:30 He s this because they were saying, *NIG*
3:34 at those seated in a circle around him and s, *3306*
4: 2 by parables, and in his teaching s: *3306*

Mk 4: 9 Then Jesus s, "He who has ears to hear, 3306
4: 11 But to those on the outside everything is s NIG
4: 13 Jesus s to them, "Don't you understand 3306
4: 21 He s to them, "Do you bring in a lamp 3306
4: 26 He also s, "This is what the kingdom 3306
4: 30 Again he s, "What shall we say 3306
4: 35 he s to his disciples, "Let us go over 3306
4: 38 The disciples woke him and s to him, 3306
4: 39 rebuked the wind and s to the waves, 3306
4: 40 He s to his disciples, "Why are you so afraid 3306
5: 8 For Jesus had s to him, "Come out 3306
5: 19 Jesus did not let him, but s, 3306
5: 34 He s to her, "Daughter, your faith 3306
5: 35 "Your daughter is dead," they s. 3306
5: 36 Ignoring what they s, Jesus told 3281
5: 39 He went in and s to them, 3306
5: 41 He took her by the hand and s to her, 3306
6: 4 Jesus s to them, "Only in his hometown, 3306
6: 15 Others s, "He is Elijah." 3306
6: 16 But when Herod heard this, he s, "John, 3306
6: 22 The king s to the girl, "Ask me for anything 3306
6: 24 She went out and s to her mother, 3306
6: 31 he s to them, "Come with me 3306
6: 35 "This is a remote place," they s, 3306
6: 37 They s to him, "You give them something 3306
6: 38 When they found out, they s, "Five— 3306
6: 50 Immediately he spoke to them and s, 3306
7: 9 And he s to them: "You have a fine way 3306
7: 10 For Moses s, 'Honor your father 3306
7: 14 Again Jesus called the crowd to him and s, 3306
7: 34 up to heaven and with a deep sigh s to him, 3306
7: 37 "He has done everything well," they s. 3306
8: 1 Jesus called his disciples to him and s, 3306
8: 12 He sighed deeply and s, 3306
8: 16 They discussed this with one another and s, 3306
8: 21 He s to them, "Do you still not understand?" 3306
8: 24 He looked up and s, "I see people; 3306
8: 33 "Get behind me, Satan!" he s. 3306
8: 34 to him along with his disciples and s: 3306
9: 1 And he s to them, "I tell you the truth, 3306
9: 5 Peter s to Jesus, "Rabbi, it is good for us 3306
9: 23 " 'If you can'?" s Jesus. 3306
9: 25 "You deaf and mute spirit," he s, 3306
9: 26 so much like a corpse that many s, 3306
9: 31 He s to them, "The Son of Man is going to 3306
9: 35 Jesus called the Twelve and s, 3306
9: 36 Taking him in his arms, he s to them, 3306
9: 38 s John, "we saw a man driving out demons 5774
9: 39 "Do not stop him," Jesus s. 3306
10: 4 They s, "Moses permitted a man to write 3306
10: 14 He s to them, "Let the little children come 3306
10: 21 "One thing you lack," he s. 3306
10: 23 Jesus looked around and s to his disciples, 3306
10: 24 But Jesus s again, "Children, how hard it is 3306
10: 26 even more amazed, and s to each other, 3306
10: 27 Jesus looked at them and s, 3306
10: 28 Peter s to him, "We have left everything 3306
10: 33 "We are going up to Jerusalem," he s, NIG
10: 35 they s, "we want you to do for us 3306
10: 38 "You don't know what you are asking,"
Jesus s. 3306
10: 39 Jesus s to them, "You will drink the cup 3306
10: 42 Jesus called them together and s, 3306
10: 49 Jesus stopped and s, "Call him." 3306
10: 51 The blind man s, "Rabbi, I want to see." 3306
10: 52 "Go," s Jesus, "your faith has healed you." 3306
11: 14 Then he s to the tree, 3306
11: 17 as he taught them, he s, "Is it not written: 3306
11: 21 Peter remembered and s to Jesus, "Rabbi, 3306
11: 31 They discussed it among themselves and s, 3306
11: 33 Jesus s, "Neither will I tell you 3306
12: 7 "But the tenants s to one another, 3306
12: 14 They came to him and s, "Teacher, 3306
12: 17 Then Jesus s to them, "Give to Caesar what 3306
12: 19 they s, "Moses wrote for us that if 3306
12: 26 how God s to him, 'I am the God of 3306
12: 32 "Well s, teacher," the man replied. 2822
12: 34 he s to him, "You are not far from the 3306
12: 36 " 'The Lord s to my Lord: 3306
12: 38 As he taught, Jesus s, "Watch out for 3306
12: 43 Calling his disciples to him, Jesus s, 3306
13: 1 one of his disciples s to him, "Look, 3306
13: 5 Jesus s to them: "Watch out that no one 3306
14: 2 "But not during the Feast," they s, 3306
14: 6 "Leave her alone," s Jesus. 3306
14: 18 he s, "I tell you the truth, 3306
14: 19 and one by one they s to him, 3306
14: 24 which is poured out for many," he s to them. 3306
14: 31 And all the others s the same. 3306
14: 32 and Jesus s to his disciples, 3306
14: 34 sorrow to the point of death," he s to them. 3306
14: 36 he s, "everything is possible for you. 3306
14: 37 "Simon," he s to Peter, "are you asleep? 3306
14: 41 Returning the third time, he s to them, 3306
14: 45 Going at once to Jesus, Judas s, "Rabbi!" 3306
14: 48 "Am I leading a rebellion," s Jesus, 3306
14: 62 "I am," s Jesus. 3306
14: 65 struck him with their fists, and s, 3306
14: 67 also were with that Nazarene, Jesus," she s. 3306
14: 68 he s, and went out into the entryway. NIG
14: 69 she s again to those standing around, 3306
14: 70 those standing near s to Peter, 3306
15: 31 "He saved others," they s, 3306
15: 35 they s, "Listen, he's calling Elijah." 3306
15: 36 if Elijah comes to take him down," he s. 3306
15: 39 he s, "Surely this man was the Son of God!" 3306
16: 6 "Don't be alarmed," he s. 3306

Mk 16: 8 They s nothing to anyone, 3306
16: 15 He s to them, "Go into all the world 3306
Lk 1: 13 But the angel s to him: "Do not be afraid, 3306
1: 25 "The Lord has done this for me," she s. 3306
1: 28 The angel went to her and s, "Greetings, 3306
1: 30 But the angel s to her, "Do not be afraid, 3306
1: 36 and she who was s to be barren is 2813
1: 38 "May it be to me as you have s." 4839
1: 45 the Lord has s to her will be accomplished!" 3281
1: 46 And Mary s: "My soul glorifies the Lord 3306
1: 55 even as he s to our fathers." 3281
1: 60 but his mother spoke up and s, 3306
1: 61 They s to her, "There is no one among your 3306
1: 70 he s through his holy prophets of long ago), 3281
2: 10 But the angel s to them, "Do not be afraid. 3306
2: 15 the shepherds s to one another, 3281
2: 18 at what the shepherds s to them. 3281
2: 24 in keeping with what is s in the Law of 3306
2: 33 and mother marveled at what was s 3281
2: 34 Then Simeon blessed them and s to Mary, 3306
2: 48 His mother s to him, "Son, 3306
3: 7 John s to the crowds coming out to 3306
4: 3 The devil s to him, "If you are the Son of 3306
4: 6 And he s to him, "I will give you all their 3306
4: 9 "If you are the Son of God," he s, 3306
4: 23 Jesus s to them, "Surely you will quote 3306
4: 35 Jesus s sternly, "Come out of him!" 2203
4: 36 the people were amazed and s to each other, 5196
4: 43 But he s, "I must preach the good news of 3306
5: 4 he s to Simon, "Put out into deep water, 3306
5: 8 he fell at Jesus' knees and s, 3306
5: 10 Then Jesus s to Simon, "Don't be afraid; 3306
5: 13 "I am willing," he s. 3306
5: 20 When Jesus saw their faith, he s, "Friend, 3306
5: 24 He s to the paralyzed man, "I tell you, 3306
5: 26 They were filled with awe and s, 3306
5: 27 "Follow me," Jesus s to him, 3306
5: 33 They s to him, "John's disciples often fast 3306
6: 5 Then Jesus s to them, "The Son of Man 3306
6: 8 and s to the man with the shriveled hand, 3306
6: 9 Then Jesus s to them, "I ask you, 3306
6: 10 then s to the man, "Stretch out your hand." 3306
6: 20 Looking at his disciples, he s: 3306
7: 9 he s, "I tell you, I have not found such 3306
7: 13 his heart went out to her and he s, 3306
7: 14 He s, "Young man, I say to you, get up!" 3306
7: 16 prophet has appeared among us," they s. 3306
7: 20 When the men came to Jesus, they s, 3306
7: 39 he s to himself, "If this man were a prophet, 3306
7: 40 "Tell me, teacher," he s. 5774
7: 43 "You have judged correctly," Jesus s. 3306
7: 44 Then he turned toward the woman and s 5774
7: 48 Jesus s to her, "Your sins are forgiven." 3306
7: 50 Jesus s to the woman, 3306
8: 8 When he s this, he called out, 3306
8: 10 He s, "The knowledge of the secrets of 3306
8: 22 One day Jesus s to his disciples, 3306
8: 45 When they all denied it, Peter s, "Master, 3306
8: 46 But Jesus s, "Someone touched me; 3306
8: 48 Then he s to her, "Daughter, 3306
8: 49 "Your daughter is dead," he s. 3306
8: 50 Hearing this, Jesus s to Jairus, 646
8: 52 "Stop wailing," Jesus s. 3306
8: 54 But he took her by the hand and s, 5888
9: 9 But Herod s, "I beheaded John. 3306
9: 12 the Twelve came to him and s, 3306
9: 14 But he s to his disciples, "Have them sit 3306
9: 22 And he s, "The Son of Man must suffer 3306
9: 23 Then he s to them all: 3306
9: 28 About eight days after Jesus s this, NIG
9: 33 Peter s to him, "Master, it is good for us 3306
9: 43 he s to his disciples, 3306
9: 48 Then he s to them, "Whoever welcomes 3306
9: 49 s John, "we saw a man driving out demons 3306
9: 50 "Do not stop him," Jesus s, 3306
9: 57 a man s to him, "I will follow you 3306
9: 59 He s to another man, "Follow me." 3306
9: 60 Jesus s to him, "Let the dead bury their own 3306
9: 61 Still another s, "I will follow you, Lord; 3306
10: 17 The seventy-two returned with joy and s, 3306
10: 21 full of joy through the Holy Spirit, s, 3306
10: 23 he turned to his disciples and s privately, 3306
10: 30 In reply Jesus s: "A man was going down 3306
10: 35 'Look after him,' he s, 'and when I return, 3306
10: 39 at the Lord's feet listening to what he s. 3364
11: 1 he finished, one of his disciples s to him, 3306
11: 2 He s to them, "When you pray, say: 3306
11: 5 Then he s to them, "Suppose one of you 3306
11: 15 But some of them s, "By Beelzebub, 3306
11: 17 Jesus knew their thoughts and s to them: 3306
11: 29 As the crowds increased, Jesus s, 3306
11: 39 Then the Lord s to him, "Now then, 3306
11: 49 Because of this, God in his wisdom s, 3306
12: 3 What you have s in the dark will be heard 3306
12: 13 Someone in the crowd s to him, "Teacher, 3306
12: 15 Then he s to them, "Watch out! 3306
12: 18 "Then he s, 'This is what I'll do. 3306
12: 20 "But God s to him, 'You fool! 3306
12: 22 Then Jesus s to his disciples: 3306
12: 54 He s to the crowd: "When you see a cloud 3306
13: 7 So he s to the man who took care of 3306
13: 12 he called her forward and s to her, 3306
13: 14 the synagogue ruler s to the people, 3306
13: 17 When he s this, all his opponents were 3306
13: 23 He s to them, 3306
13: 31 Pharisees came to Jesus and s to him, 3306
14: 12 Then Jesus s to his host, 3306

Lk 14: 15 he s to Jesus, "Blessed is the man who 3306
14: 18 The first s, 'I have just bought a field, 3306
14: 19 "Another s, 'I have just bought five yoke 3306
14: 20 "Still another s, 'I just got married, 3306
14: 22 " 'Sir,' the servant s, 'what you ordered 3306
14: 25 and turning to them he s: 3306
15: 12 The younger one s to his father, 'Father, 3306
15: 17 "When he came to his senses, he s, 5774
15: 21 "The son s to him, 'Father, I have sinned 3306
15: 22 "But the father s to his servants, 'Quick! 3306
15: 31 " 'My son,' the father s, 3306
16: 3 "The manager s to himself, 3306
16: 15 He s to them, "You are the ones who justify 3306
16: 30 " 'No, father Abraham,' he s, 3306
16: 31 "He s to him, 'If they do not listen to Moses 3306
17: 1 Jesus s to his disciples: 3306
17: 5 apostles s to the Lord, "Increase our faith!" 3306
17: 14 When he saw them, he s, "Go, 3306
17: 19 Then he s to him, "Rise and go; 3306
17: 22 Then he s to his disciples, 3306
18: 2 He s: "In a certain town there was a judge 3306
18: 4 But finally he s to himself, 3306
18: 6 And the Lord s, "Listen to what the unjust 3306
18: 13 but beat his breast and s, 'God, 3306
18: 16 But Jesus called the children to him and s, 3306
18: 21 I have kept since I was a boy," he s. 3306
18: 22 When Jesus heard this, he s to him, 3306
18: 24 Jesus looked at him and s, 3306
18: 28 Peter s to him, "We have left all we had 3306
18: 29 "I tell you the truth," Jesus s to them, 3306
18: 42 Jesus s to him, "Receive your sight; 3306
19: 5 he looked up and s to him, "Zacchaeus, 3306
19: 8 But Zacchaeus stood up and s to the Lord, 3306
19: 9 Jesus s to him, "Today salvation has come 3306
19: 12 He s: "A man of noble birth went 3306
19: 13 'Put this money to work,' he s. 3306
19: 16 "The first one came and s, 'Sir, 3306
19: 18 "The second came and s, 'Sir, 3306
19: 20 "Then another servant came and s, 'Sir, 3306
19: 24 "Then he s to those standing by, 3306
19: 25 " 'Sir,' they s, 'he already has ten!' 3306
19: 28 After Jesus had s this, he went on ahead, 3306
19: 39 of the Pharisees in the crowd s to Jesus, 3306
19: 42 and s, "If you, even you, had only known 3306
19: 46 "It is written," he s to them, 3306
20: 2 authority you are doing these things," they s. 3306
20: 5 They discussed it among themselves and s, 3306
20: 8 Jesus s, "Neither will I tell you 3306
20: 13 owner of the vineyard s, 'What shall I do? 3306
20: 14 'This is the heir,' they s. 3306
20: 16 When the people heard this, they s, 3306
20: 20 hoped to catch Jesus in something he s 3364
20: 23 through their duplicity and s to them, 3306
20: 25 He s to them, "Then give to Caesar what is 3306
20: 26 to trap him in what he had s there in public. 4839
20: 28 they s, "Moses wrote for us that if 3306
20: 39 the teachers of the law responded, "Well s, 3306
20: 41 Then Jesus s to them, "How is it that 3306
20: 42 " 'The Lord s to my Lord: 3306
20: 45 Jesus s to his disciples, 3306
21: 3 "I tell you the truth," he s, 3306
21: 5 and with gifts dedicated to God. But Jesus s, 3306
21: 10 Then he s to them: "Nation will rise against 3306
22: 15 And he s to them, "I have eagerly desired to 3306
22: 17 After taking the cup, he gave thanks and s, 3306
22: 25 Jesus s to them, "The kings of the Gentiles 3306
22: 36 He s to them, "But now if you have a purse, 3306
22: 38 The disciples s, "See, Lord, 3306
22: 40 On reaching the place, he s to them, 3306
22: 49 to happen, they s, "Lord, should we strike 3306
22: 52 Then Jesus s to the chief priests, 3306
22: 56 She looked closely at him and s, 3306
22: 57 "Woman, I don't know him," he s. 3306
22: 58 A little later someone else saw him and s, 5774
22: 65 they s many other insulting things to him. 3306
22: 67 "If you are the Christ," they s, "tell us." 3306
22: 71 Then they s, "Why do we need any more
testimony? 3306
23: 14 and s to them, "You brought me this man 3306
23: 28 Jesus turned and s to them, 3306
23: 34 Jesus s, "Father, forgive them, 3306
23: 35 They s, "He saved others; 3306
23: 37 and s, "If you are the king of the Jews, 3306
23: 40 "Don't you fear God," he s, 5774
23: 42 Then he s, "Jesus, remember me 3306
23: 46 When he had s this, he breathed his last. 3306
23: 47 and s, "Surely this was a righteous man." 3306
24: 5 but the men s to them, "Why do you look 3306
24: 23 a vision of angels, who s he was alive. 3306
24: 24 and found it just as the women had s, 3306
24: 25 He s to them, "How foolish you are, 3306
24: 27 he explained to them what was s 1450
24: 36 Jesus himself stood among them and s 3306
24: 38 He s to them, "Why are you troubled, 3306
24: 40 When he had s this, he showed them 3306
24: 44 He s to them, "This is what I told you 3306
Jn 1: 15 saying, "This was he of whom I s, 3306
1: 21 He s, "I am not." 3306
1: 22 Finally they s, "Who are you? 3306
1: 29 toward him and s, "Look, the Lamb of God, 3306
1: 30 This is the one I meant when I s, 3306
1: 36 When he saw Jesus passing by, he s, "Look, 3306
1: 38 They s, "Rabbi" (which means Teacher), 3306
1: 40 of the two who heard what John had s NIG
1: 42 Jesus looked at him and s, "You are Simon 3306
1: 43 Finding Philip, he s to him, "Follow me." 3306
1: 46 "Come and see," s Philip. 3306

Jn	1:47	*he* s of him, "Here is a true Israelite,	*3306*
	1:50	Jesus s, "You believe because I told you	*3306*
	2: 3	Jesus' mother s to him,	*3306*
	2: 5	His mother s to the servants,	*3306*
	2: 7	Jesus s to the servants,	*3306*
	2:10	and s, "Everyone brings out the choice wine	*3306*
	2:16	To those who sold doves *he* s,	*3306*
	2:22	his disciples recalled what *he had* s.	*3306*
	3: 2	He came to Jesus at night and s, "Rabbi,	*3306*
	3:10	"You are Israel's teacher," s Jesus,	*646*
	3:26	They came to John and s to him, "Rabbi,	*3306*
	3:28	You yourselves can testify that *I* s,	*3306*
	4: 7	Jesus s to her, "Will you give me a drink?"	*3306*
	4: 9	The Samaritan woman s to him,	*3306*
	4:11	the woman s, "you have nothing to draw	*3306*
	4:15	The woman s to him, "Sir,	*3306*
	4:17	Jesus s to her, "You are right	*3306*
	4:18	What *you have* just s is quite true."	*3306*
	4:19	the woman s, "I can see that you are	*3306*
	4:25	The woman s, "I know that Messiah"	*3306*
	4:28	the woman went back to the town and s to	*3306*
	4:32	But he s to them, "I have food to eat	*3306*
	4:33	Then his disciples s to each other,	*3306*
	4:34	s Jesus, "is to do the will of him who sent	*3306*
	4:42	*They* s to the woman, "We no longer	*3306*
	4:42	just because of what you s;	*3282*
	4:49	The royal official s, "Sir, come down	*3306*
	4:52	*they* s to him, "The fever left him	*3306*
	4:53	the exact time at which Jesus *had* s to him,	*3306*
	5: 8	Then Jesus s to him, "Get up!	*3306*
	5:10	the Jews s to the man who had been healed,	*3306*
	5:11	"The man who made me well s to me,	*3306*
	5:14	Later Jesus found him at the temple and s	*3306*
	5:17	Jesus s to them, "My Father is always	*646*
	6: 5	*he* s to Philip, "Where shall we buy bread	*3306*
	6:10	Jesus s, "Have the people sit down."	*3306*
	6:12	*he* s to his disciples, "Gather the pieces	*3306*
	6:20	But he s to them, "It is I; don't be afraid."	*3306*
	6:32	Jesus s to them, "I tell you the truth,	*3306*
	6:34	*they* s, "from now on give us this bread."	*3306*
	6:41	to grumble about him because *he* s,	*3306*
	6:42	*They* s, "Is this not Jesus, the son of Joseph,	*3306*
	6:53	Jesus s to them, "I tell you the truth,	*3306*
	6:59	*He* s this while teaching in the synagogue	*3306*
	6:60	On hearing it, many of his disciples s,	*3306*
	6:61	Jesus s to them, "Does this offend you?	*3306*
	7: 3	Jesus' brothers s to him,	*3306*
	7: 9	*Having* s this, he stayed in Galilee.	*3306*
	7:12	Some s, "He is a good man."	*3306*
	7:21	Jesus s to them, "I did one miracle,	*3306*
	7:31	*They* s, "When the Christ comes,	*3306*
	7:33	Jesus s, "I am with you for only a short time	*3306*
	7:35	The Jews s to one another,	*3306*
	7:36	What did he mean when *he* s,	*3306*
	7:37	Jesus stood and s in a loud voice,	*3306*
	7:38	as the Scripture *has* s,	*3306*
	7:40	On hearing his words, *some* of the people s,	*3306*
	7:41	Others s, "He is the Christ."	*3306*
	8: 4	and s to Jesus, "Teacher, this woman	*3306*
	8: 7	he straightened up and s to them,	*3306*
	8:11	"No one, sir," she s.	*3306*
	8:12	When Jesus spoke again to the people, *he* s,	*3306*
	8:21	Once more Jesus s to them,	*3306*
	8:28	So Jesus s, "When you have lifted up	*3306*
	8:31	To the Jews who had believed him, Jesus s,	*3306*
	8:39	"If you were Abraham's children," s Jesus,	*3306*
	8:42	Jesus s to them, "If God were your Father,	*3306*
	8:49	"I am not possessed by a demon," s Jesus,	*646*
	8:55	If *I* s I did not, I would be a liar like you,	*3306*
	8:57	not yet fifty years old," the Jews s to him,	*3306*
	9: 3	s Jesus, "but this happened so that the work	*646*
	9: 6	*Having* s this, he spit on the ground,	*3306*
	9: 9	Others s, "No, he only looks like him."	*3306*
	9:12	"I don't know," *he* s.	*3306*
	9:16	Some of the Pharisees s, "This man is not	*3306*
	9:22	His parents s this because they were afraid	*3306*
	9:23	That was why his parents s, "He is of age;	*3306*
	9:24	"Give glory to God," *they* s.	*3306*
	9:28	Then they hurled insults at him and s,	*3306*
	9:35	*he* s, "Do you believe in the Son of Man?"	*3306*
	9:37	Jesus s, "You have now seen him;	*3306*
	9:38	Then the man s, "Lord, I believe,"	*5774*
	9:39	Jesus s, "For judgment I have come	*3306*
	9:41	Jesus s, "If you were blind,	*3306*
	10: 7	Therefore Jesus s again, "I tell you the truth,	*3306*
	10:20	Many of them s, "He is demon-possessed	*3306*
	10:21	But others s, "These are not the sayings of	*3306*
	10:32	but Jesus s to them, "I have shown you	*646*
	10:34	'I *have* s you are gods'?	*3306*
	10:36	you accuse me of blasphemy because *I* s,	*3306*
	10:41	*They* s, "Though John never performed	*3306*
	10:41	all that John s about this man was true."	*3306*
	11: 4	When he heard this, Jesus s,	*3306*
	11: 7	Then *he* s to his disciples,	*3306*
	11: 8	they s, "a short while ago the Jews tried	*3306*
	11:11	After *he had* s this, he went on to tell them,	*3306*
	11:16	Then Thomas (called Didymus) s to the rest	*3306*
	11:21	"Lord," Martha s to Jesus,	*3306*
	11:23	Jesus s to her, "Your brother will rise again.	*3306*
	11:25	Jesus s to her, "I am the resurrection	*3306*
	11:28	And *after she had* s this,	*3306*
	11:28	"The Teacher is here," *she* s,	*3306*
	11:32	she fell at his feet and s, "Lord,	*3306*
	11:36	Then the Jews s, "See how he loved him!"	*3306*
	11:37	But some of them s, "Could not he who	*3306*
	11:39	"Take away the stone," he s.	*3306*
	11:39	"But, Lord," s Martha, the sister of the dead	*3306*
Jn	11:40	Then Jesus s, "Did I not tell you that	*3306*
	11:41	Then Jesus looked up and s, "Father,	*3306*
	11:42	but *I* s this for the benefit of the people	*3306*
	11:43	*When he had* s this, Jesus called in a loud	*3306*
	11:44	Jesus s to them, "Take off the grave clothes	*3306*
	12:19	So the Pharisees s to one another, "See,	*3306*
	12:21	"Sir," *they* s, "we would like to see Jesus."	*3306*
	12:29	and heard it s it had thundered;	*3306*
	12:29	others s an angel had spoken to him.	*3306*
	12:30	Jesus s, "This voice was for your benefit,	*3306*
	12:33	*He* s this to show the kind of death	*3306*
	12:41	Isaiah s this because he saw Jesus' glory	*3306*
	13: 6	He came to Simon Peter, *who* s to him,	*3306*
	13: 8	s Peter, "you shall never wash my feet."	*3306*
	13:11	that was why *he* s not every one was clean.	*3306*
	13:21	*After he had* s this, Jesus was troubled	*3306*
	13:24	Simon Peter motioned to this disciple and s,	*NIG*
	13:28	at the meal understood why Jesus s this	*3306*
	13:31	When he was gone, Jesus s,	*3306*
	14: 5	Thomas s to him, "Lord, we don't know	*3306*
	14: 8	Philip s, "Lord, show us the Father and	*3306*
	14:22	Then Judas (not Judas Iscariot) s, "But,	*3306*
	14:26	and will remind you of everything I *have* s	*3306*
	16: 6	Because *I have* s these things,	*3281*
	16:15	That is why *I* s the Spirit will take	*3306*
	16:17	*Some* of his disciples s to one another,	*3306*
	16:19	so *he* s to them, "Are you asking	*3306*
	16:19	when *I* s, 'In a little while you will see me	*3306*
	16:29	Jesus' disciples s, "Now you are speaking	*3306*
	17: 1	After Jesus s this, he looked toward heaven	*3281*
	18: 5	"I am he," Jesus s.	*3306*
	18: 6	When Jesus s, "I am he,"	*3306*
	18: 7	And they s, "Jesus of Nazareth."	*3306*
	18:20	*I* s nothing in secret.	*3281*
	18:21	Surely they know what I s."	*3306*
	18:22	*When* Jesus s this, one of the officials	*3306*
	18:23	"If *I* s something wrong," Jesus replied,	*3281*
	18:31	Pilate s, "Take him yourselves	*3306*
	18:36	Jesus s, "My kingdom is not of this world.	*646*
	18:37	"You are a king, then!" s Pilate.	*3306*
	18:38	and s, "I find no basis for a charge	*3306*
	19: 4	Once more Pilate came out and s to	*3306*
	19: 5	Pilate s to them, "Here is the man!"	*3306*
	19:10	"Do you refuse to speak to me?" Pilate s.	*3306*
	19:14	"Here is your king," Pilate s to the Jews.	*3306*
	19:24	"Let's not tear it," *they* s to one another.	*3306*
	19:24	that the scripture might be fulfilled which s,	*3306*
	19:26	*he* s to his mother, "Dear woman,	*3306*
	19:28	Jesus s, "I am thirsty."	*3306*
	19:30	When he had received the drink, Jesus s,	*3306*
	20: 2	the one Jesus loved, and s,	*3306*
	20:13	"They have taken my Lord away," *she* s,	*3306*
	20:15	"Woman," he s, "why are you crying?	*3306*
	20:15	Thinking he was the gardener, she s, "Sir,	*3306*
	20:16	Jesus s to her, "Mary."	*3306*
	20:17	Jesus s, "Do not hold on to me,	*3306*
	20:18	And she told them that *he had* s these things	*3306*
	20:19	Jesus came and stood among them and s,	*3306*
	20:20	*After he* s this, he showed them his hands	*3306*
	20:21	Again Jesus s, "Peace be with you!	*3306*
	20:22	And with that he breathed on them and s,	*3306*
	20:25	But he s to them, "Unless I see the nail	*3306*
	20:26	Jesus came and stood among them and s,	*3306*
	20:27	Then *he* s to Thomas, "Put your finger here;	*3306*
	20:28	Thomas s to him, "My Lord and my God!"	*3306*
	21: 3	Simon Peter told them, and *they* s,	*3306*
	21: 6	He s, "Throw your net on the right side of	*3306*
	21: 7	the disciple whom Jesus loved s to Peter,	*3306*
	21:10	Jesus s to them, "Bring some of the fish	*3306*
	21:12	Jesus s to them, "Come and have breakfast."	*3306*
	21:15	Jesus s to Simon Peter, "Simon son of John,	*3306*
	21:15	Lord," *he* s, "you know that I love you."	*3306*
	21:15	Jesus s, "Feed my lambs."	*3306*
	21:16	Again Jesus s, "Simon son of John,	*3306*
	21:16	Jesus s, "Take care of my sheep."	*3306*
	21:17	The third time *he* s to him,	*3306*
	21:17	*He* s, "Lord, you know all things;	*3306*
	21:17	Jesus s, "Feed my sheep.	*3306*
	21:19	Jesus s this to indicate the kind of death	*3306*
	21:19	Then *he* s to him, "Follow me!"	*3306*
	21:20	against Jesus at the supper and *had* s,	*3306*
	21:23	he only s, "If I want him to remain alive	*NIG*
Ac	1: 7	*He* s to them: "It is not for you to know	*3306*
	1: 9	*After he* s this, he was taken up	*3306*
	1:11	"Men of Galilee," they s,	*3306*
	1:16	and s, "Brothers, the Scripture had to	*3306*
	1:20	s Peter, "it is written in the book of Psalms,	*NIG*
	2:13	Some, however, made fun of them and s,	*3306*
	2:25	David s about him: " 'I saw the Lord	*3306*
	2:34	and yet he s, " 'The Lord said to my Lord:	*3306*
	2:34	and yet he said, " 'The Lord s to my Lord:	*3306*
	2:37	they were cut to the heart and s to Peter and	*3306*
	3: 4	Then Peter s, "Look at us!"	*3306*
	3: 6	Then Peter s, "Silver or gold I do not have,	*3306*
	3:12	When Peter saw this, *he* s to them:	*646*
	3:22	For Moses s, 'The Lord your God will raise	*3306*
	3:25	*He* s to Abraham, 'Through your offspring	*3306*
	4: 8	Peter, filled with the Holy Spirit, s to them:	*3306*
	4:23	the chief priests and elders *had* s to them.	*3306*
	4:24	"Sovereign Lord," *they* s,	*3306*
	5: 3	Then Peter s, "Ananias, how is it that Satan	*3306*
	5: 8	"Yes," she s, "that is the price."	*3306*
	5: 9	Peter s to her, "How could you agree to test	*NIG*
	5:20	"Go, stand in the temple courts," *he* s,	*3306*
	5:25	Then someone came and s, "Look!	*550*
	5:28	not to teach in this name," *he* s.	*3306*
	6: 2	gathered all the disciples together and s,	*3306*
Ac	7: 3	God s, 'and go to the land I will show you.'	*3306*
	7: 7	God s, 'and afterward they will come out of	*3306*
	7:27	the other pushed Moses aside and s,	*3306*
	7:33	the Lord s to him, 'Take off your sandals;	*3306*
	7:56	*he* s, "I see heaven open and the Son	*3306*
	7:60	*When he had* s this, he fell asleep.	*3306*
	8: 6	they all paid close attention *to what* he s.	*3306*
	8:19	and s, "Give me also this ability so	*3306*
	8:24	so that nothing *you have* s may happen	*3306*
	8:26	Now an angel of the Lord s to Philip,	*3281*
	8:31	"How can I," he s,	*3306*
	8:36	they came to some water and the eunuch s,	*5774*
	9:15	But the Lord s to Ananias, "Go!	*3306*
	9:17	Placing his hands on Saul, *he* s,	*3306*
	9:34	"Aeneas," Peter s to him,	*3306*
	9:40	Turning toward the dead woman, *he* s,	*3306*
	10: 3	who came to him and s, "Cornelius!"	*3306*
	10:19	the Spirit s to him, "Simon,	*3306*
	10:21	Peter went down and s to the men,	*3306*
	10:26	"Stand up," *he* s, "I am only a man myself."	*3306*
	10:28	*He* s to them: "You are well aware	*5774*
	10:31	s, 'Cornelius, God has heard your prayer	*5774*
	10:46	and praising God. Then Peter s,	*646*
	11: 3	and s, "You went into the house	*3306*
	11:16	Then I remembered what the Lord *had* s:	*3306*
	12: 7	*he* s, and the chains fell off Peter's wrists.	*3306*
	12: 8	Then the angel s to him,	*3306*
	12:11	Then Peter came to himself and s,	*3306*
	12:15	she kept insisting that it was so, they s,	*3306*
	12:17	*he* s, and then he left for another place.	*3306*
	13: 2	the Holy Spirit s, "Set apart for me	*3306*
	13: 9	looked straight at Elymas and s,	*3306*
	13:16	Paul motioned with his hand and s:	*3306*
	13:25	As John was completing his work, *he* s:	*3306*
	13:40	the prophets *have* s does not happen to you:	*3306*
	14:22	to enter the kingdom of God," they s.	*NIG*
	15: 5	to the party of the Pharisees stood up and s,	*3306*
	15:24	troubling your minds *by* **what** *they* s.	*3364*
	15:32	s much to encourage and strengthen	*3364*
	15:36	Some time later Paul s to Barnabas,	*3306*
	16:15	*she* s, "come and stay at my house."	*3306*
	16:18	so troubled that *he* turned around and s to	*3306*
	16:20	brought them before the magistrates and s,	*3306*
	16:37	But Paul s to the officers:	*5774*
	17: 3	proclaiming to you is the Christ," he s.	*NIG*
	17:11	to see if **what Paul** s was true.	*4047S*
	17:18	They s this because Paul was preaching	*NIG*
	17:19	where *they* s to him,	*3306*
	17:22	up in the meeting of the Areopagus and s:	*5774*
	17:28	As some of your own poets *have* s,	*3306*
	17:32	some of them sneered, but others s,	*3306*
	18: 6	he shook out his clothes in protest and s	*3306*
	18:14	Gallio s to the Jews, "If you Jews were	*3306*
	19: 4	Paul s, "John's baptism was a baptism	*3306*
	19:21	"After I have been there," *he* s,	*3306*
	19:25	with the workmen in related trades, and s:	*3306*
	19:35	The city clerk quieted the crowd and s:	*5774*
	19:41	*After he had* s this, he dismissed the	*3306*
	20: 1	s **good-by** and set out for Macedonia.	*832*
	20:10	"Don't be alarmed," *he* s.	*3306*
	20:18	When they arrived, *he* s to them:	*3306*
	20:35	the words the Lord Jesus himself s:	*3306*
	20:36	*When he had* s this, he knelt down	*3306*
	21:11	tied his own hands and feet with it and s,	*3306*
	21:14	we gave up and s, "The Lord's will be done.	*3306*
	21:20	Then *they* s to Paul:	*3306*
	21:40	*he* s to them in Aramaic:	*4715*
	22: 2	they became very quiet. Then Paul s:	*5774*
	22:10	" 'Get up,' the Lord s,	*3306*
	22:13	*He* stood beside me and s, 'Brother Saul,	*3306*
	22:14	"Then he s: 'The God of our fathers	*3306*
	22:18	he s to me. 'Leave Jerusalem	*NIG*
	22:21	"Then the Lord s to me, 'Go;	*3306*
	22:22	The crowd listened to Paul until he s this.	*NIG*
	22:25	Paul s to the centurion standing there,	*3306*
	22:28	Then the commander s,	*646*
	23: 1	Paul looked straight at the Sanhedrin and s,	*3306*
	23: 3	Then Paul s to him, "God will strike you,	*3306*
	23: 4	Those who were standing near Paul s,	*3306*
	23: 7	*When* he s this, a dispute broke out	*3306*
	23: 9	nothing wrong with this man," *they* s.	*3306*
	23:11	the Lord stood near Paul and s,	*3306*
	23:14	to the chief priests and elders and s,	*3306*
	23:17	Paul called one of the centurions and s,	*5774*
	23:18	The centurion s, "Paul, the prisoner,	*5774*
	23:20	*He* s: "The Jews have agreed to ask	*3306*
	23:35	*he* s, "I will hear your case	*5774*
	24:22	"When Lysias the commander comes," *he* s,	*3306*
	24:25	Felix was afraid and s, "That's enough	*646*
	25: 9	wishing to do the Jews a favor, s to Paul,	*3306*
	25:14	*He* s: "There is a man here	*3306*
	25:22	Then Agrippa s to Festus, "I would like	*NIG*
	25:24	Festus s: "King Agrippa,	*5774*
	26: 1	Agrippa s to Paul, "You have permission	*5774*
	26:22	the prophets and Moses s would happen—	*3281*
	26:28	Then Agrippa s to Paul,	*NIG*
	26:31	and while talking with one another, *they* s,	*3281*
	26:32	Agrippa s to Festus, "This man could have	*5774*
	27:11	instead of listening to what Paul s,	*3306*
	27:21	Paul stood up before them and s:	*3306*
	27:24	and s, 'Do not be afraid, Paul.	*3306*
	27:31	Paul s to the centurion and the soldiers,	*3306*
	27:33	"For the last fourteen days," *he* s,	*3306*
	27:35	*After he* s this, he took some bread	*3306*
	28: 4	*they* s to each other,	*3306*
	28: 6	*they* changed their minds and s he was	*3306*
	28:17	When they had assembled, Paul s to them:	*3306*

Ac 28:21 from there has reported or s anything bad *3281*
28:24 Some were convinced by what he **s,** *3306*
28:25 to your forefathers *when he* s through Isaiah *3306*
Ro 4:18 just as it *had been* s to him, *3306*
7: 7 if the law *had* not s, "Do not covet." *3306*
9:26 in the very place where *it was* s to them, *3306*
9:29 It is just as Isaiah **s previously:** *4625*
15:18 the Gentiles to obey God *by* what I have s *3364*
1Co 6:16 *it is* **s,** "The two will become one flesh." *5774*
11:24 he broke it and **s,** "This is my body, *3306*
14:29 the others should weigh carefully what is **s.** *NIG*
2Co 2:13 So I s **good-by** to them and went on *698*
4: 6 who **s,** "Let light shine out of darkness," *3306*
6:16 As God *has* **s:** "I will live with them *3306*
7: 3 *I have* s **before** that you have such a place *4625*
7:14 But just as everything *we* s to you was true, *3281*
9: 3 as *I* s you would be. *3306*
12: 9 But *he* s to me, "My grace is sufficient *3306*
Gal 1: 9 As *we have* **already s,** so now I say again: *4625*
2:14 *I* s to Peter in front of them all, *3306*
Eph 5:14 This is why *it is* **s:** "Wake up, O sleeper, *3306*
Tit 1:12 Even one of their own prophets *has* **s,** *3306*
Heb 3: 5 *to* what *would be* s *in the future.* *3281*
3:10 with that generation, and *I* **s,** *3306*
3:15 **As has just been s:** "Today, *1877+3306+3836*
4: 3 just as God *has* **s,** "So I declared on oath *3306*
4: 7 as *was* **s before:** "Today, if you hear his *4625*
5: 5 But God s to him, "You are my Son; *3281*
6:16 the oath confirms what is s and puts an end *NIG*
7:13 He of whom these things *are* s belonged to *3306*
7:14 to that tribe Moses s nothing about priests. *3281*
7:15 And what we have s is even more clear *NIG*
7:21 a priest with an oath when God s to him: *3306*
8: 8 But God found fault with the people and **s:** *3306*
9:20 *He* **s,** "This is the blood of the covenant, *3306*
10: 5 when Christ came into the world, *he* **s:** *3306*
10: 7 Then *I* **s,** 'Here I am—it is written about me *3306*
10: 8 First *he* **s,** "Sacrifices and offerings, *3306*
10: 9 Then *he* **s,** "Here I am, I have come to do *3306*
10:30 we know him who **s,** "It is mine to avenge; *3306*
11:18 even though God *had* s to him, *3281*
12:21 The sight was so terrifying that Moses **s,** *3306*
13: 5 because God *has* **s,** "Never will I leave you; *3306*
Jas 2:11 For he who **s,** "Do not commit adultery," *3306*
2:11 also **s,** "Do not murder." *3306*
Jude 1: 9 but **s,** "The Lord rebuke you!" *3306*
1:18 *They* s to you, "In the last times *3306*
Rev 1:11 which **s:** "Write on a scroll what you see *3306*
1:17 Then he placed his right hand on me and **s:** *3306*
4: 1 speaking to me like a trumpet **s,** *3306*
5: 5 one of the elders s to me, "Do not weep! *3306*
5:14 The four living creatures **s,** "Amen," *3306*
7:14 And *he* **s,** "These are they who have come *3306*
9:14 It s to the sixth angel who had the trumpet, *3306*
10: 4 up what the seven thunders *have* s and do *3281*
10: 6 and the sea and all that is in it, and **s,** *NIG*
10: 9 *He* s to me, "Take it and eat it. *3306*
11:15 loud voices in heaven, *which* **s:** *3306*
14: 7 *He* s in a loud voice, "Fear God and give *3306*
14: 8 A second angel followed and **s,** "Fallen! *3306*
14: 9 A third angel followed them and s in *3306*
17: 1 the seven bowls came and s to me, *3281*
17: 7 angel s to me: "Why are you astonished? *3306*
17:15 Then the angel s to me, "The waters *3306*
18:21 and threw it into the sea, and **s:** *3306*
19: 9 Then the angel s to me, "Write: *3306*
19:10 But *he* s to me, "Do not do it! *3306*
21: 5 He who was seated on the throne **s,** *3306*
21: 5 Then *he* **s,** "Write this down, *3306*
21: 6 *He* s to me: "It is done. *3306*
21: 9 of the seven last plagues came and s to me, *3281*
22: 6 The angel s to me, "These words *3306*
22: 9 But *he* s to me, "Do not do it! *3306*

SAIL (18) [FORESAIL, SAILED, SAILING, SAILORS]

1Ki 22:48 but *they* never **set s**—they were wrecked 2143
22:49 said to Jehoshaphat, *"Let* my men s with your men," 641+928+2021+2143
2Ch 20:37 and were not able to **set** s to trade. 2143
Isa 33:21 no mighty ship *will* s them. 6296
33:23 mast is not held secure, the s is not spread. 5812
Eze 27: 7 from Egypt was your s and served 5155
Ac 18:21 Then he **set** s from Ephesus. *343*
20: 3 a plot against him just as he was about to s *343*
20:15 The next day we **set** s from there *676*
20:16 *to* **s past** Ephesus to avoid spending time *4179*
21: 2 went on board and **set s.** *343*
27: 1 When it was decided that we *would* s *676*
27: 2 to s for ports along the coast of the province *4434*
27:12 the majority decided that we *should* s on, *343*
27:21 you should have taken my advice not *to* s *343*
27:24 the lives of all who s with you.' *4434*
28:10 in many ways and *when we were ready to* **s,** *343*
28:13 From there we **set** s and arrived *4311*

SAILED (19) [SAIL]

1Ki 9:28 *They* s to Ophir and brought back 995
2Ch 8:18 s to Ophir and brought back four hundred 995
Jnh 1: 3 and s for Tarshish to flee from the LORD. 995
Lk 8:23 *As* they s, he fell asleep. *4434*
8:26 *They* s to the region of the Gerasenes, *2929*
Ac 13: 4 went down to Seleucia and s from there *676*
13:13 Paul and his companions s to Perga *343*
14:26 From Attalia *they* s back to Antioch, *676*
15:39 Barnabas took Mark and s for Cyprus, *1739*
16:11 From Troas *we* put out to sea and s **straight** *2312*
18:18 Then *he* left the brothers and s for Syria, *1739*
18:18 Before he **s,** he had his hair cut off *NIG*
20: 6 But we s from Philippi after the Feast *1739*
20:13 on ahead to the ship and s for Assos, *343*
21: 1 we put out to sea and s **straight** to Cos. *2312*
21: 3 *we* s on to Syria. *4434*
27: 5 *When we had* s **across** the open sea off *1386*
27: 7 **s to the lee of** Crete, opposite Salome. *5709*
27:13 so *they* weighed anchor and s along *4162*

SAILING (2) [SAIL]

Ac 27: 6 the centurion found an Alexandrian ship s *4434*
27: 9 and s had already become dangerous *4452*

SAILORS (7) [SAIL]

1Ki 9:27 s who knew the sea— 408+641
Eze 27: 9 the sea and their s came alongside to trade 4876
Jnh 1: 5 All the s were afraid and each cried out 4876
1: 7 Then the s said to each other, "Come, NIH
Ac 27:27 the s sensed they were approaching land. *3731*
27:30 the s let the lifeboat down into the sea, *3731*
Rev 18:17 and all who travel by ship, the **s,** *3731*

SAINTS (69)

1Sa 2: 9 He will guard the feet of his **s,** 2883
2Ch 6:41 may your s rejoice in your goodness. 2883
Ps 16: 3 As for the s who are in the land, 7705
30: 4 Sing to the LORD, you s *of* his; 2883
31:23 Love the LORD, all his **s!** 2883
34: 9 Fear the LORD, you his **s,** 7705
52: 9 I will praise you in the presence of your **s.** 2883
79: 2 the flesh of your s to the beasts of the earth. 2883
85: 8 he promises peace to his people, his **s**— 2883
116:15 in the sight of the LORD is the death of his **s.** 2883
132: 9 may your s sing for joy." 2883
132:16 and her s will ever sing for joy. 2883
145:10 your s will extol you. 2883
148:14 the praise of all his **s,** of Israel, 2883
149: 1 his praise in the assembly of the **s.** 2883
149: 5 the s rejoice in this honor and sing for joy 2883
149: 9 This is the glory of all his **s.** 2883
Da 7:18 But the s *of* the Most High will receive 10620
7:21 this horn was waging war against the s 10620
7:22 and pronounced judgment in favor of the s 10620
7:25 against the Most High and oppress his s 10620
7:25 The s will be handed over to him for a time, NIH
7:27 will be handed over to the **s,** 10620
8:12 Because of rebellion, the host [of the s] NIH
Ac 9:13 and all the harm he has done *to* your s *41*
9:32 he went to visit the s in Lydda. *41*
26:10 of the chief priests I put many *of the* s *41*
Ro 1: 7 who are loved by God and called to be **s:** *41*
8:27 the Spirit intercedes for the s in accordance *41*
15:25 to Jerusalem in the service of the s there. *41*
15:26 a contribution for the poor *among* the s *41*
15:31 be acceptable *to* the s there, *41*
16: 2 the s and to give her any help she may need *41*
16:15 and Olympas and all the s with them. *41*
1Co 6: 1 for judgment instead of before the **s?** *41*
6: 2 not know that the s will judge the world? *41*
14:33 As in all the congregations *of* the **s,** *41*
16:15 to the service *of* the **s.** *41*
2Co 1: 1 together with all the s throughout Achaia: *41*
8: 4 of sharing in this service to the **s.** *41*
9: 1 to write to you about this service to the **s.** *41*
13:13 All the s send their greetings. *41*
Eph 1: 1 *To* the s in Ephesus, *41*
1:15 the Lord Jesus and your love for all the **s,** *41*
1:18 of his glorious inheritance in the **s,** *41*
3:18 together with all the **s,** *41*
6:18 and always keep on praying for all the **s.** *41*
Php 1: 1 *To* all the s in Christ Jesus at Philippi, *41*
4:21 Greet all the s in Christ Jesus. *41*
4:22 All the s send you greetings, *41*
Col 1: 4 and of the love you have for all the **s**— *41*
1:12 in the inheritance *of* the s in the kingdom *41*
1:26 but is now disclosed *to* the **s.** *41*
1Ti 5:10 washing the feet *of* the **s,** *41*
Phm 1: 5 in the Lord Jesus and your love for all the **s.** *41*
1: 7 brother, have refreshed the hearts *of* the **s.** *41*
Jude 1: 3 faith that was once for all entrusted *to* the **s.** *41*
Rev 5: 8 which are the prayers *of* the **s.** *41*
8: 3 with the prayers *of* all the **s,** *41*
8: 4 together with the prayers *of* the **s,** *41*
11:18 your servants the prophets and your s *41*
13: 7 against the s and to conquer them. *41*
13:10 and faithfulness *on the part of* the **s.** *41*
14:12 *of* the s who obey God's commandments *41*
16: 6 for they have shed the blood *of* your s *41*
17: 6 woman was drunk with the blood *of* the **s,** *41*
18:20 Rejoice, s and apostles and prophets! *41*
18:24 the blood of prophets and *of* the **s,** *41*
19: 8 for the righteous acts *of* the **s.)** *41*

SAKE (105) [SAKES]

Ge 12:13 be treated well **for** your s and my life will 6288
12:16 He treated Abram well **for** her **s,** 6288
18:24 and not spare the place **for the s of** 5100
18:26 I will spare the whole place **for** their **s."** 6288
18:29 He said, **"For the s of** forty, 6288
18:31 He said, **"For the s of** twenty, 6288
18:32 He answered, **"For the s of** ten, 6288
26:24 of your descendants **for the s of** 6288
Ex 18: 8 and the Egyptians **for** Israel's s 128+6584
Lev 26:45 But **for** their s I will remember 4200
Nu 11:29 Moses replied, "Are you jealous **for** my **s?** 4200
Jos 23: 3 to all these nations **for** your **s;** 4946+7156
1Sa 12:22 **For the s of** his great name the LORD will 6288
2Sa 5:12 exalted his kingdom **for the s of** his people 6288
7:21 **For the s of** your word and according 6288
9: 1 I can show kindness **for** Jonathan's **s?"** 6288
9: 7 surely show you kindness **for the s of** 6288
18: 5 with the young man Absalom **for** my **s."** 4200
18:12 'Protect the young man Absalom **for** my **s.'** 4200
1Ki 11:12 **for the s of** David your father, 5100
11:13 will give him one tribe **for the s of** David 5100
11:13 and **for the s of** Jerusalem, 5100
11:32 But **for the s of** my servant David and 5100
11:34 of his life **for the s of** David my servant, 5100
15: 4 **for** David's s the LORD his God gave him 5100
2Ki 8:19 **for the s of** his servant David, 5100
19:34 **for** my s and for the sake of David 5100
19:34 and **for the s of** David my servant." 5100
20: 6 I will defend this city **for** my s and for 5100
20: 6 and **for the s of** my servant David.' " 5100
1Ch 14: 2 highly exalted **for the s of** his people Israel. 6288
16:21 **for** their s he rebuked kings: 6584
17:19 **For the s of** your servant and according 6288
Ne 10:28 from the neighboring peoples **for the s of** 448
Job 18: 4 is the earth to be abandoned **for** your **s?** 5100
Ps 23: 3 in paths of righteousness **for** his name's **s.** 5100
25:11 **For the s of** your name, O LORD, 5100
31: 3 **for the s of** your name lead and guide me. 5100
44:22 Yet **for** your s we face death all day long; 6584
69: 7 For I endure scorn **for** your **s,** 6584
79: 9 and forgive our sins **for** your name's **s.** 5100
105:14 **for** their s he rebuked kings: 6584
106: 8 Yet he saved them **for** his name's **s,** 5100
106:45 **for** their s he remembered his covenant 4200
109:21 deal well with me **for** your name's **s;** 5100
122: 8 **For the s of** my brothers and friends, 5100
122: 9 **For the s of** the house of the LORD our God 5100
132:10 **For the s of** David your servant, 6288
143:11 **For** your name's **s,** O LORD, 5100
Isa 37:35 **for** my s and for the sake of David 5100
37:35 and **for the s of** David my servant!" 5100
42:21 the LORD **for the s of** his righteousness 5100
43:14 **"For** your s I will send to Babylon 5100
43:25 blots out your transgressions, **for** my own **s,** 5100
45: 4 **For the s of** Jacob my servant, 5100
48: 9 **For** my own name's s I delay my wrath; 5100
48: 9 the s of my praise I hold it back from you, NIH
48:11 **For** my own **s,** for my own sake, I do this. 5100
48:11 For my own sake, **for** my own **s,** I do this. 5100
62: 1 **For** Zion's s I will not keep silent, 5100
62: 1 **for** Jerusalem's s I will not remain quiet, 5100
63:17 Return **for the s of** your servants, 5100
Jer 14: 7 do something **for the s of** your name. 5100
14:21 **For the s of** your name do not despise us; 5100
15:15 think of how I suffer reproach **for** your **s.** 6584
Eze 20: 9 But **for the s of** my name I did what would 5100
20:14 But **for the s of** my name I did what would 5100
20:22 and **for the s of** my name I did what would 5100
20:44 when I deal with you **for** my name's s and 5100
36:22 It is not **for** your **s,** O house of Israel, 5100
36:22 but **for the s of** my holy name, 4200
36:32 to know that I am not doing this **for** your **s,** 5100
Da 9:17 **For** your **s,** O Lord, look with favor 5100
9:19 **For** your **s,** O my God, do not delay, 5100
Mt 10:39 whoever loses his life **for** my s will find it. *1915*
15: 3 of God **for the s of** your tradition? *1328*
15: 6 the word of God **for the s of** your tradition. *1328*
19:29 or children or fields *for* my s will receive *1915*
24:22 but **for the s of** the elect those days will *1328*
Mk 13:20 But **for the s of** the elect, *1328*
Lk 18:29 or children **for the s of** the kingdom of God *1915*
Jn 11:15 and **for** your s I am glad I was not there, *1328*
Ro 1: 5 Through him and **for** his name's **s,** *5642*
8:36 "For your s we face death all day long; *1915*
9: 3 from Christ **for the s of** my brothers, *5642*
14:20 not destroy the work of God **for the s of** *1915*
1Co 9:23 I do all this **for the s of** the gospel, *1328*
10:28 both **for the s of** the man who told you and *1328*
10:28 man who told you and **for** conscience' **s**— *NIG*
2Co 2:10 in the sight of Christ **for** your **s,** *1328*
4: 5 and ourselves as your servants **for** Jesus' **s.** *1328*
4:11 being given over to death **for** Jesus' **s,** *1328*
5:13 it is *for the s of* **God;** *AIT*
12:10 That is why, **for** Christ's **s,** I delight in *5642*
Eph 3: 1 of Christ Jesus **for the s of** you Gentiles— *5642*
Php 3: 7 now consider loss **for the s of** Christ. *1328*
3: 8 **for** whose s I have lost all things. *1328*
Col 1:24 **for the s of** his body, which is the church. *5642*
1Th 1: 5 how we lived among you **for** your **s.** *1328*
2Ti 2:10 Therefore I endure everything **for the s of** *1328*
Tit 1:11 and that **for the s of** dishonest gain. *5920*
Heb 11:26 He regarded disgrace *for the s of* **Christ** as *AIT*
1Pe 1:20 was revealed in these last times **for** your **s.** *1328*
2:13 Submit yourselves **for** the Lord's s *1328*
3Jn 1: 7 It was **for the s of** the Name *5642*

SAKES (1) [SAKE]

2Co 8: 9 yet **for** your s he became poor, *1328*

SAKIA (1)

1Ch 8:10 Jeuz, S and Mirmah. These were his sons, 8499

SALAH (KJV) See SHELAH

SALAMIS (1)
Ac 13: 5 When they arrived at S, 4887

SALATHIEL (KJV) See SHEALTIEL

SALCAH, SALCHAH (KJV) See SALECAH

SALE (4) [SELL]
Lev 25:29 of redemption a full year after its **s.** 4928
Dt 18: 8 though he has received **money from** the **s** 4928
28:68 **offer yourselves for s** to your enemies 4835
Ps 44:12 gaining nothing from their **s.** 4697

SALECAH (4)
Dt 3:10 and all Bashan as far as **S** and Edrei, 6146
Jos 12: 5 He ruled over Mount Hermon, **S,** 6146
13:11 and all Bashan as far as **S**— 6146
1Ch 5:11 next to them in Bashan, as far as **S:** 6146

SALEM (4)
Ge 14:18 king of **S** brought out bread and wine. 8970
Ps 76: 2 His tent is in **S,** his dwelling place in Zion. 8970
Heb 7: 1 This Melchizedek was king *of* **S** and priest 4889
7: 2 "king *of* **S**" means "king of peace." 4889

SALES (1) [SELL]
Ac 4:34 brought the money *from* the **s** 4405

SALIM (1)
Jn 3:23 John also was baptizing at Aenon near **S,** 4890

SALIVA (2)
1Sa 21:13 of the gate and letting **s** run down his beard. 8202
Jn 9: 6 made some mud with the **s,** 4770

SALLAI (1)
Ne 11: 8 and his followers, Gabbai and **S**—928 men. 6144

SALLU (3) [SALLU'S]
1Ch 9: 7 **S** son of Meshullam, the son of Hodaviah, 6132
Ne 11: 7 **S** son of Meshullam, the son of Joed, 6132
12: 7 **S,** Amok, Hilkiah 6139

SALLU'S (1) [SALLU]
Ne 12:20 of **S,** Kallai; of Amok's, Eber; 6139

SALMA (2)
1Ch 2:51 **S** the father of Bethlehem, 8514
2:54 The descendants of **S:** 8514

SALMON (7)
Ru 4:20 Nahshon the father of **S,** 8517
4:21 **S** the father of Boaz, 8517
1Ch 2:11 Nahshon was the father of **S,** 8517
2:11 **S** the father of Boaz, 8517
Mt 1: 4 Nahshon the father of **S,** 4891
1: 5 **S** the father of Boaz, 4891
Lk 3:32 the son *of* **S,** the son of Nahshon, 4885

SALMONE (1)
Ac 27: 7 we sailed to the lee of Crete, opposite **S.** 4892

SALOME (2)
Mk 15:40 of James the younger and of Joses, and **S.** 4897
16: 1 and **S** bought spices so that they might go 4897

SALT (46) [SALTED, SALTINESS, SALTY]
Ge 14: 3 in the Valley of Siddim (the **S** Sea). 4875
19:26 and she became a pillar of **s.** 4875
Lev 2:13 Season all your grain offerings with **s.** 4875
2:13 the **s** *of* the covenant of your God out 4875
2:13 add **s** to all your offerings 4075
Nu 18:19 It is an everlasting covenant of **s** before 4875
34: 3 from the end of the **S** Sea, 4875
34:12 along the Jordan and end at the **S** Sea. 4875
Dt 3:17 to the Sea of the Arabah (the **S** Sea), 4875
29:23 The whole land will be a burning waste of **s** 4875
Jos 3:16 (the **S** Sea) was completely cut off. 4875
12: 3 to the Sea of the Arabah (the **S** Sea), 4875
15: 2 the bay at the southern end of the **S** Sea, 4875
15: 5 the **S** Sea as far as the mouth of the Jordan. 4875
15:62 the City of **S** and En Gedi— 4875
18:19 at the northern bay of the **S** Sea, 4875
Jdg 9:45 he destroyed the city and scattered **s** over it. 4875
2Sa 8:13 in the Valley of **S.** 4875
2Ki 2:20 he said, "and put **s** in it." 4875
2:21 and threw the **s** into it, saying, "This is what 4875
14: 7 the Valley of **S** and captured Sela in battle, 4875
1Ch 18:12 in the Valley of **S.** 4875
2Ch 13: 5 his descendants forever by a covenant of **s?** 4875
25:11 and led his army to the Valley of **S,** 4875
Ezr 6: 9 and wheat, **s,** wine and oil, 10420
7:22 and **s** without limit. 10420
Job 6: 6 Is tasteless food eaten without **s,** 4875
30: 4 In the brush they gathered **s herbs,** 4865
39: 6 the **s flats** as his habitat. 4877
Ps 60: T in the Valley of **S.** 4875
107:34 and fruitful land into a **s waste,** 4877
Jer 17: 6 in a **s** land where no one lives. 4877
48: 9 Put **s** on Moab, for she will be laid waste; 7490
Eze 16: 4 nor **were** *you* **rubbed with s** or 4873+4873
43:24 to sprinkle **s** on them and sacrifice them as 4875
47: 9 and makes the **s** water fresh; NIH
47:11 they will be left for **s.** 4875
Zep 2: 9 a place of weeds and **s** pits, 4875
Mt 5:13 "You are the **s** of the earth. 229
5:13 But if the **s** loses its saltiness, 229
Mk 9:50 "**S** is good, but if it loses its saltiness, 229
9:50 Have **s** in yourselves, 229
Lk 14:34 "**S** is good, but if it loses its saltiness, 229
Col 4: 6 be always full of grace, seasoned *with* **s,** 229
Jas 3:11 Can both fresh water and **s water** flow from 4395
3:12 Neither can a **s spring** produce fresh water. 266

SALTED (2) [SALT]
Ex 30:35 *It is to* **be s** and pure and sacred. 4873
Mk 9:49 Everyone *will be* **s** with fire. 245

SALTINESS (3) [SALT]
Mt 5:13 But if the salt **loses its s,** 3701
Mk 9:50 "Salt is good, but if it loses its **s,** 383
Lk 14:34 "Salt is good, but if it **loses its s,** 3701

SALTY (3) [SALT]
Mt 5:13 how *can it be* **made s** again? 245
Mk 9:50 how *can you* **make** it **s** again? 789
Lk 14:34 how *can it be* **made s** again? 789

SALU (1)
Nu 25:14 the Midianite woman was Zimri son of **S,** 6140

SALUTATION, SALUTATIONS (KJV) See GREETED, GREETING

SALUTE, SALUTED, SALUTETH (KJV) See CALL, GREET, GREETED, GREETINGS, GREETS, PAY RESPECTS

SALVATION (122) [SAVE]
Ex 15: 2 he has become my **s.** 3802
2Sa 22: 3 my shield and the horn of my **s.** 3829
23: 5 Will he not bring to fruition my **s** 3829
1Ch 16:23 proclaim his **s** day after day. 3802
2Ch 6:41 O LORD God, be clothed with **s,** 9591
Ps 9:14 of Zion and there rejoice in your **s.** 3802
13: 5 my heart rejoices in your **s.** 3802
14: 7 that **s** *for* Israel would come out of Zion! 3802
18: 2 He is my shield and the horn of my **s.** 3829
27: 1 The LORD is my light and my **s**— 3829
28: 8 a fortress of **s** *for* his anointed one. 3802
35: 3 Say to my soul, "I am your **s.**" 3802
35: 9 in the LORD and delight in his **s.** 3802
37:39 The **s** *of* the righteous comes from 9591
40:10 I speak of your faithfulness and **s.** 9591
40:16 may those who love your **s** always say, 9591
50:23 so that I may show him the **s** *of* God." 3829
51:12 of your **s** and grant me a willing spirit, 3829
53: 6 that **s** *for* Israel would come out of Zion! 3802
62: 1 my **s** comes from him. 3802
62: 2 He alone is my rock and my **s;** 3802
62: 6 He alone is my rock and my **s;** 3802
62: 7 My **s** and my honor depend on God; 3829
67: 2 your **s** among all nations. 3802
69:13 O God, answer me with your sure **s.** 3829
69:27 do not let them share in your **s.** 7407
69:29 may your **s,** O God, protect me. 3802
70: 4 may those who love your **s** always say, 3802
71:15 of your **s** all day long, 9591
74:12 you bring **s** upon the earth. 3802
85: 7 O LORD, and grant us your **s.** 3829
85: 9 Surely his **s** is near those who fear him, 3829
91:16 and show him my **s.**" 3802
95: 1 let us shout aloud to the Rock of our **s.** 3829
96: 2 proclaim his **s** day after day. 3802
98: 1 and his holy arm *have* **worked s** for him. 3828
98: 2 The LORD has made his **s** known 3802
98: 3 of the earth have seen the **s** *of* our God. 3802
116:13 of **s** and call on the name of the LORD. 3802
118:14 he has become my **s.** 3802
118:21 you have become my **s.** 3802
119:41 your **s** according to your promise; 9591
119:81 My soul faints with longing for your **s,** 9591
119:123 My eyes fail, looking for your **s,** 3802
119:155 **S** is far from the wicked, 3802
119:166 I wait for your **s,** O LORD, 3802
119:174 I long for your **s,** O LORD, 3802
132:16 I will clothe her priests with **s,** 3829
149: 4 he crowns the humble with **s.** 3802
Isa 12: 2 God is my **s;** I will trust and not be afraid. 3802
12: 2 and my song; he has become my **s.**" 3802
12: 3 you will draw water from the wells of **s.** 3802
25: 9 let us rejoice and be glad in his **s.**" 3802
26: 1 God makes **s** its walls and ramparts. 3802
26:18 We have not brought **s** to the earth; 3802
30:15 "In repentance and rest *is your* **s,** 3828
33: 2 our **s** in time of distress. 3802
33: 6 rich store of **s** and wisdom and knowledge; 3802
45: 8 Let the earth open wide, let **s** spring up, 3829
45:17 by the LORD with an everlasting **s;** 9591
46:13 and my **s** will not be delayed. 9591
46:13 I will grant **s** to Zion, my splendor to Israel. 9591
49: 6 that you may bring my **s** to the ends of 3802
49: 8 and in the day of **s** I will help you; 3802
51: 5 my **s** is on the way, 3829
51: 6 But my **s** will last forever, 3802
51: 8 my **s** through all generations." 3802
52: 7 who bring good tidings, who proclaim **s,** 3802
52:10 and all the ends of the earth will see the **s** 3802
56: 1 and do what is right, for my **s** is close 3802
59:16 so his own arm **worked s** for him, 3828
59:17 and the helmet of **s** on his head; 3802
60:18 but you will call your walls **S** 3802
61:10 with garments of **s** and arrayed me in a robe 3829
62: 1 her **s** like a blazing torch. 3802
63: 5 so my own arm **worked s** for me, 3828
Jer 3:23 in the LORD our God is the **s** *of* Israel. 9591
La 3:26 to wait quietly for the **s** *of* the LORD. 9591
Jnh 2: 9 **S** comes from the LORD." 3802
Zec 9: 9 king comes to you, righteous and **having s,** 3828
Lk 1:69 *of* **s** for us in the house of his servant David 5401
1:71 **s** from our enemies and from the hand 5401
1:77 the knowledge *of* **s** through the forgiveness 5401
2:30 For my eyes have seen your **s,** 5403
3: 6 And all mankind will see God's **s.'** " 5403
19: 9 "Today **s** has come to this house, 5401
Jn 4:22 for **s** is from the Jews. 5401
Ac 4:12 **S** is found in no one else, 5401
13:26 to us that this message *of* **s** has been sent. 5401
13:47 you may bring **s** to the ends of the earth.' " 5401
28:28 that God's **s** has been sent to the Gentiles, 5403
Ro 1:16 of God for the **s** of everyone who believes: 5401
11:11 **s** has come to the Gentiles 5401
13:11 because our **s** is nearer now than 5401
2Co 1: 6 it is for your comfort and **s;** 5401
6: 2 and in the day *of* **s** I helped you." 5401
6: 2 now is the day *of* **s.** 5401
7:10 that leads to **s** and leaves no regret, 5401
Eph 1:13 the word of truth, the gospel *of* your **s.** 5401
6:17 the helmet *of* **s** and the sword of the Spirit, 5403
Php 2:12 to work out your **s** with fear and trembling, 5401
1Th 5: 8 and the hope *of* **s** as a helmet. 5401
5: 9 to receive **s** through our Lord Jesus Christ. 5401
2Ti 2:10 that they too may obtain the **s** that is 5401
3:15 which are able to make you wise for **s** 5401
Tit 2:11 the grace of God that brings **s** has appeared 5403
Heb 1:14 to serve those who will inherit **s?** 5401
2: 3 if we ignore such a great **s?** 5401
2: 3 This **s,** which was first announced by NIG
2:10 should make the author *of* their **s** perfect 5401
5: 9 the source *of* eternal **s** for all who obey him 5401
6: 9 things that accompany **s.** 5401
9:28 to bring **s** to those who are waiting for him. 5401
1Pe 1: 5 by God's power until the coming of the **s** 5401
1: 9 the goal of your faith, the **s** of your souls. 5401
1:10 Concerning this **s,** the prophets, 5401
2: 2 so that by it you may grow up in your **s,** 5401
2Pe 3:15 in mind that our Lord's patience means **s,** 5401
Jude 1: 3 to write to you about the **s** we share, 5401
Rev 7:10 "**S** belongs to our God, 5401
12:10 "Now have come the **s** and the power and 5401
19: 1 **S** and glory and power belong to our God, 5401

SALVE (1)
Rev 3:18 and **s** to put on your eyes, so you can see. 3141

SAMARIA (119) [SAMARITAN, SAMARITANS]
1Ki 13:32 in the towns of **S** will certainly come true," 9076
16:24 of **S** from Shemer for two talents of silver 9076
16:24 calling it **S,** after Shemer, 9076
16:28 with his fathers and was buried in **S.** 9076
16:29 in **S** over Israel twenty-two years. 9076
16:32 in the temple of Baal that he built in **S.** 9076
18: 2 Now the famine was severe in **S,** 9076
20: 1 he went up and besieged **S** and attacked it. 9076
20:10 if enough dust remains in **S** to give each 9076
20:17 who reported, "Men are advancing from **S.**" 9076
20:34 as my father did in **S.**" 9076
20:43 the king of Israel went to his palace in **S.** 9076
21: 1 close to the palace of Ahab king of **S.** 9076
21:18 Ahab king of Israel, who rules in **S.** 9076
22:10 by the entrance of the gate of **S,** 9076
22:37 So the king died and was brought to **S,** 9076
22:38 a pool in **S** (where the prostitutes bathed), 9076
22:51 of Ahab became king of Israel in **S** in 9076
2Ki 1: 2 of his upper room in **S** and injured himself. 9076
1: 3 and meet the messengers of the king of **S** 9076
2:25 and from there returned to **S.** 9076
3: 1 of Ahab became king of Israel in **S** in 9076
3: 6 So at that time King Joram set out from **S** 9076
5: 3 would see the prophet who is in **S!** 9076
6:19 And he led them to **S.** 9076
6:20 and there they were, inside **S.** 9076
6:24 and marched up and laid siege to **S.** 9076
7: 1 of barley for a shekel at the gate of **S.**" 9076
7:18 of barley for a shekel at the gate of **S.**" 9076
10: 1 in **S** seventy sons of the house of Ahab. 9076
10: 1 So Jehu wrote letters and sent them to **S:** 9076

2Ki 10:12 Jehu then set out and went toward S. 9076
10:17 When Jehu came to S, he killed all who 9076
10:35 with his fathers and was buried in S. 9076
10:36 over Israel in S was twenty-eight years. 9076
13: 1 of Jehu became king of Israel in S, 9076
13: 6 the Asherah pole remained standing in S. 9076
13: 9 with his fathers and was buried in S. 9076
13:10 of Jehoahaz became king of Israel in S, 9076
13:13 Jehoash was buried in S with the kings 9076
14:14 He also took hostages and returned to S. 9076
14:16 with his fathers and was buried in S with 9076
14:23 of Jehoash king of Israel became king in S, 9076
15: 8 of Jeroboam became king of Israel in S, 9076
15:13 and he reigned in S one month. 9076
15:14 of Gadi went from Tirzah up to S. 9076
15:14 He attacked Shallum son of Jabesh in S, 9076
15:17 and he reigned in S ten years. 9076
15:23 of Menahem became king of Israel in S, 9076
15:25 in the citadel of the royal palace at S. 9076
15:27 of Remaliah became king of Israel in S, 9076
17: 1 of Elah became king of Israel in S, 9076
17: 5 against S and laid siege to it for three years. 9076
17: 6 of Assyria captured S and deported 9076
17:24 in the towns of S to replace the Israelites. 9076
17:24 They took over S and lived in its towns. 9076
17:26 in the towns of S do not know what the god 9076
17:27 the priests you took captive from S go back 9004S
17:28 exiled from S came to live in Bethel 9076
17:29 up in the shrines the **people of** S had made 9085
18: 9 of Assyria marched against S and laid siege 9076
18:10 S was captured in Hezekiah's sixth year, 9076
18:34 Have they rescued S from my hand? 9076
21:13 against S and the plumb line used against 9076
23:18 of the prophet who had come from S. 9076
23:19 in the towns of S that had provoked 9076
2Ch 18: 2 he went down to visit Ahab in S. 9076
18: 9 by the entrance to the gate of S, 9076
22: 9 while he was hiding in S. 9076
25:13 in the war raided Judean towns from S 9076
25:24 and returned to S. 9076
28: 8 which they carried back to S. 9076
28: 9 to meet the army when it returned to S. 9076
28:15 the City of Palms, and returned to S. 9076
Ezr 4:10 and settled in the city of S and elsewhere 10726
4:17 and the rest of their associates living in S 10726
Ne 4: 2 of his associates and the army of S, 9076
Isa 7: 9 The head of Ephraim is S, 9076
7: 9 and the head of S is only Remaliah's son. 9076
8: 4 and the plunder of S will be carried off by 9076
9: 9 Ephraim and the inhabitants of S— 9076
10: 9 and S like Damascus? 9076
10:10 images excelled those of Jerusalem and S— 9076
10:11 as I dealt with S and her idols?' " 9076
36:19 Have they rescued S from my hand? 9076
Jer 23:13 the prophets of S I saw this repulsive thing: 9076
31: 5 you will plant vineyards on the hills of S; 9076
41: 5 and S, bringing grain offerings and incense 9076
Eze 16:46 Your older sister was S, 9076
16:51 S did not commit half the sins you did. 9076
16:53 of Sodom and her daughters and of S 9076
16:55 and S with her daughters, will return 9076
23: 4 Oholah is S, and Oholibah is Jerusalem. 9076
23:33 the cup of your sister S. 9076
Hos 7: 1 and the crimes of S revealed. 9076
8: 5 Throw out your calf-idol, O S! 9076
8: 6 It will be broken in pieces, that calf of S. 9076
10: 5 in S fear for the calf-idol of Beth Aven. 9076
10: 7 S and its king will float away like a twig on 9076
13:16 The people of S must bear their guilt, 9076
Am 3: 9 yourselves on the mountains of S; 9076
3:12 those who sit in S on the edge of their beds 9076
4: 1 you cows of Bashan on Mount S, 9076
6: 1 and to you who feel secure on Mount S, 9076
8:14 They who swear by the shame of S, or say, 9076
Ob 1:19 the fields of Ephraim and S, 9076
Mic 1: 1 the vision he saw concerning S 9076
1: 5 What is Jacob's transgression? Is it not S? 9076
1: 6 "Therefore I will make S a heap of rubble, 9076
Lk 17:11 Jesus traveled along the border between S *4899*
Jn 4: 4 Now he had to go through S. *4899*
4: 5 So he came to a town *in* S called Sychar, *4899*
Ac 1: 8 in Jerusalem, and in all Judea and S, *4899*
8: 1 throughout Judea and S. *4899*
8: 5 a city *in* S and proclaimed the Christ there. *4899*
8: 9 in the city and amazed all the people *of* S. *4899*
8:14 in Jerusalem heard that S had accepted *4899*
9:31 Galilee and S enjoyed a time of peace. *4899*
15: 3 as they traveled through Phoenicia and S, *4899*

SAMARITAN (8) [SAMARIA]

Lk 9:52 into a S village to get things ready for him; *4901*
10:33 S, as he traveled, came where the man was; *4901*
17:16 and thanked him—and he was a S. *4901*
Jn 4: 7 When a S woman came to draw water, *4899*
4: 9 The S woman said to him, *4902*
4: 9 "You are a Jew and I am a S woman. *4902*
8:48 "Aren't we right in saying that you are a S *4901*
Ac 8:25 preaching the gospel in many S villages. *4901*

SAMARITANS (5) [SAMARIA]

Mt 10: 5 the Gentiles or enter any town *of* the S. *4901*
Jn 4: 9 (For Jews do not associate with S.) *4901*
4:22 You S worship what you do not know; *NIG*
4:39 *of* the S from that town believed in him *4901*
4:40 So when the S came to him, *4901*

SAME (267)

Ge 11: 6 the s language they have begun to do this, 285
17:26 both circumcised on that s day. 6795
21:23 as an alien the s kindness I have shown 3869
26:12 and the s year reaped a hundredfold, 2085
26:18 the s names his father had given them. 3869
30:35 **That** s day he removed all the male goats 2085
32:19 the s thing to Esau when you meet him. 3869
40: 3 in the s prison where Joseph was confined. NIH
40: 5 had a dream the s night, 285
41:11 Each of us had a dream the s night, 285
41:25 "The dreams of Pharaoh are **one and the s.** 285
41:26 it is **one and the** s dream. 285
Ex 5: 6 **That** s day Pharaoh gave this order to 2085
5: 8 make the s number of bricks **as** before; 889
6:26 It was **this** s Aaron and Moses to whom 2085
6:27 It was the s Moses and Aaron. 2085
7:11 also did the s *things* by their secret arts: 4027
7:22 But the Egyptian magicians did the s *things* 4027
8: 7 But the magicians did the s *things* 4027
12: 8 **That** s night they are to eat the meat roasted 2296
12:12 "On **that** s night I will pass through Egypt 2296
12:49 The s law applies to the native-born and to 285
22:30 Do the s with your cattle and your sheep. 4027
23:11 Do the s with your vineyard 4027
25:33 the s for all six branches extending from 4027
26: 2 All the curtains are to be the s size— 285
26: 3 and **do the s** *with* the other five. 2489S
26: 4 the s with the end curtain in the other set. 4027
26: 8 All eleven curtains are to be the s size— 285
29:41 the s grain offering and its drink offering as 3869
30:32 and do not make any oil with the s formula. 4017
34:16 **lead** your sons **to do the s.** 339+466+2177+2388S
36: 9 All the curtains were the s size— 285
36:10 and **did the s** *with* the other 285+285+448+2489S
36:11 and the s was done with the end curtain in 4027
36:15 All eleven curtains were the s size— 285
37:19 the s for all six branches extending from 4027
Lev 7: 7 " 'The s law applies to both the sin offering 285
14:28 to put on the s places he put the blood of NIH
16:16 He is to do the s for the Tent of Meeting, 4027
18: 9 **born in the s home** or elsewhere. 1074+4580
22:28 a cow or a sheep and its young on the s day. 285
22:30 It must be eaten **that** s day; 2085
23:21 On that s day you are to proclaim 6795
24:22 You are to have the s law for the alien and 285
Nu 2:17 They will set out **in the s order** 4027
6:11 That s day he is to consecrate his head. 2085
9: 6 they came to Moses and Aaron **that** s day 2085
9:14 You must have the s regulations for 285
10: 7 but not *with the s* **signal.** AIT
13:33 and we looked the s to them." 4027
15:15 the s rules for you and for the alien living 285
15:15 the alien shall be the s before the LORD: 3869
15:16 The s laws and regulations will apply both 285
15:29 **One and the** s law applies to everyone 285
26: 9 The s Dathan and Abiram were 2085
28: 8 along with the s *kind of* grain offering 3869
Dt 2:22 the s for the descendants of Esau, 889+3869
3:21 the s to all the kingdoms over there 4027
7:19 The LORD your God will do the s to all 4027
12:30 We will do the s." 4027
15:17 Do the s for your maidservant. 4027
21:23 Be sure to bury him **that** s day, 2085
22: 3 Do the s if you find your brother's donkey 4027
27:11 the s day Moses commanded the people: 2085
32:48 On that s day the LORD told Moses, 6795
Jos 6:15 around the city seven times in the s manner, 2296
7: 6 The elders of Israel did the **s,** NIH
10:35 They captured it **that** s day and put it to 2085
Jdg 6:25 **That** s night the LORD said to him, 2085
8: 8 to Peniel and made the s request of them, 3869
1Sa 2:34 they will both die on the s day. 285
4:12 **That** s day a Benjamite ran from 2085
6: 4 because the s plague has struck both you 285
6:16 and then returned **that** s day to Ekron. 2085
12:18 and **that** s day the LORD sent thunder 2085
17:30 and brought up the s matter, 3869
28:25 **That** s night they got up and left. 2085
30:24 to be the s **as** that of him who went down to 3869
31: 6 and all his men died together **that** s day. 2085
2Sa 2: 6 the s favor because you have done this. 2296
5: 6 from the *s* **clan** *as* Saul's family came out AIT
1Ki 3:17 this woman and I live in the s house. 285
6:33 **In the s way** he made four-sided jambs 4027
7:18 He did the s for each capital. 4027
7:37 in the s molds and were identical in size 285
8:64 On **that** s day the king consecrated 2085
11: 8 He did the s for all his foreign wives, 4027
13: 3 **That** s day the man of God gave a sign: 2085
22:12 other prophets were prophesying the s *thing.* 4027
2Ki 4:17 about **that** s time she gave birth to a son, 2296
8:22 Libnah revolted at the s time. 2085
1Ch 23:30 They were to do the s in the evening 4027
24:31 were **treated the s as** those of the 4200+6645
2Ch 16:10 At the s time Asa brutally oppressed some 2085
18:11 other prophets were prophesying the s *thing.* 4027
21:10 Libnah revolted at the s time, 2085
27: 5 The Ammonites brought him the s **amount** 2296S
35:12 They did the s with the cattle. 4027
Ne 5: 5 Although we are of the s flesh and blood **as** 3869
6: 4 Four times they sent me the s message, 3869
6: 4 and each time I gave them the s answer. 3869
6: 5 sent his aide to me with the s message, 3869
9: 1 On the twenty-fourth day of the s month, 2296
13:18 Didn't your forefathers do *the s things,* 3907
Est 1:18 to all the king's nobles in the s way. NIH
8: 1 **That** s day King Xerxes gave Queen Esther 2085
9:11 of Susa was reported to the king **that** s day. 2085
Job 9:22 It is **all the s;** that is why I say, 285
31:15 the s **one** form us both within our mothers? 285
Ps 102:27 But you remain the **s,** 2085
Ecc 2:14 that the s fate overtakes them both. 285
3:19 the s fate awaits them both: 285
3:19 All have the s breath; 285
3:20 All go to the s place; 285
6: 6 Do not all go to the s place? 285
9: 3 The s destiny overtakes all. 285
Isa 24: 2 it will be the s *for* priest as for people, 3869
Jer 13: 9 **'In the s way** I will ruin the pride of Judah 3970
14:15 **Those** s prophets will perish by sword 2156
26:20 s things against this city and this land **as** 3869
27:12 the s message to Zedekiah king of Judah. 3869
28: 1 In the fifth month of **that** s year, 2085
28:11 **'In the s way** will I break the yoke 3970
28:17 In the seventh month of **that** s year, 2085
Eze 4: 5 s number of days **as** the years of their sin. 4200
10:22 the s appearance as those I had seen by NIH
18:24 and does the s detestable things 3869
21:19 both starting from the s country. 285
23: 2 daughters of the s mother. 285
23:13 both of them went the s way. 285
23:38 At **that** s time they defiled my sanctuary 2085
40:10 the three had the s measurements, 285
40:10 on each side had the s measurements. 285
40:21 and its portico had the s measurements **as** 3869
40:22 the s measurements **as** those of 3869
40:24 and they had the s measurements **as** 3869
40:28 it had the s measurements **as** the others. 3869
40:29 and its portico had the s measurements **as** 3869
40:32 it had the s measurements **as** the others. 3869
40:33 and its portico had the s measurements **as** 3869
40:35 It had the s measurements **as** the others, 3869
42:11 they had the s length and width, 3869
44: 3 of the gateway and go out the s way." 2257S
45:11 The ephah and the bath are to be the s size, 285
45:20 to do the s on the seventh day of the month 4027
45:25 to make the s provision for sin offerings, 3869
46: 8 and he is to come out the s way. 2257S
46:22 the courts in the four corners was the s size. 285
Da 2:35 the gold were broken to pieces at the s *time* 10248
4:36 At the s time that my sanity was restored, 10192S
8:22 but will not have the s power. 2257S
11:27 will sit at the s table and lie to each other, 285
Am 2: 7 Father and son use **the** *s* girl and AIT
9: 7 Israelites **the** s to me **as** the Cushites? 3869
Zec 6:10 Go the s day to the house of Josiah son 2085
Mt 5:12 for **in the s way** they persecuted *4048*
5:16 **In the s way,** let your light shine *4048*
5:19 and teaches others to do **the s** will *4048*
7: 2 For in **the s way** you judge others, *3210S*
13: 1 **That** s day Jesus went out of the house *1697*
17:12 **In the s way** the Son of Man is going *2779+4048*
18:14 **In the s way** your Father in heaven is *4048*
20: 5 and the ninth hour and did **the s thing.** *6058*
20:14 the man who was hired last **the s as** *2779+6055*
21:30 to the other son and said **the s thing.** *6058*
21:36 and the tenants treated them **the s way.** *6058*
22:23 **That** s day the Sadducees, *1697*
22:26 **The s thing** happened to the second *3931*
23:28 **In the s way,** on the outside you appear *4048*
26:35 And all the other disciples said **the s.** *3931*
26:44 saying the s thing. *899*
27:41 **In the s way** the chief priests, *3931*
27:44 **In** the **s way** the robbers who were crucified *899*
Mk 12:21 It was **the s** with the third. *6058*
14:31 And all the others said **the s.** *6058*
14:39 and prayed the s thing. *899*
15:31 **In the s way** the chief priests and *3931*
Lk 3:11 and the one who has food should do *the* **s."** *3931*
10:31 to be going down the s road, *1697*
14:33 **In the s way,** any of you who does not *4048*
15: 7 **in the s way** there will be more rejoicing *4048*
15:10 **In the s way,** I tell you, there is rejoicing *4048*
17:28 "It was **the s** in the days of Lot. *2777+3931*
20:31 and **in the s way** the seven died, *6058*
22:20 **In the s way,** after supper he took the cup, *6058*
23:40 "since you are under the s sentence? *899*
24:13 Now **that** s day two of them were going to *899*
Jn 6:11 He did **the s** with the fish. *3931*
9: 8 the s man who used to sit and beg?" *NIG*
11: 2 the s one who poured perfume on the Lord *NIG*
12:42 Yet **at the s time** many even among *3940*
21:13 and did **the s** with the fish. *3931*
Ac 1:11 **This** s Jesus, who has been taken from you *4047*
1:11 will come back **in the s way** you have seen him go *4005+5573*
3:10 they recognized him as the s *man* who used *899*
7:35 the s Moses whom they had rejected with *NIG*
11:17 if God gave them the s gift as he gave us, *2698*
24:15 I have the s hope in God **as** these men *2779+4005*
24:26 **At the s time** he was hoping that Paul *275*
27:40 in the sea and **at the s time** untied the ropes *275*
Ro 1:27 **In the s way** the men also abandoned *3931*
2: 1 you who pass judgment do the s *things.* *899*
2: 3 judgment on them and yet do **the** s *things,* *899*
3:30 and the uncircumcised through **that** s faith. *3836*
4: 6 David says **the s thing** when he *2749+2779*
6:11 **In the s way,** count yourselves dead to sin *4048*
8:26 **In the s way,** the Spirit helps us *6058*
9:10 Rebekah's children had one and the s father, *NIG*
9:21 have the right to make out of the s lump *899*
10:12 the s Lord is Lord of all and richly blesses *899*

Ro 12: 4 members do not all have the s function, *899*
1Co 2:11 **In the** s **way** no one knows the thoughts of God except the Spirit *2779+4048*
7: 4 **In the** s **way,** the husband's body does not *3931*
9: 8 Doesn't the Law say **the** s thing? *4047*
9:14 **In the** s **way,** the Lord has commanded *4048*
10: 3 They all ate the s spiritual food *899*
10: 4 and drank the s spiritual drink; *899*
11:25 **In the** s **way,** after supper he took the cup, *6058*
12: 4 different kinds of gifts, but the s Spirit. *899*
12: 5 different kinds of service, but the s Lord. *899*
12: 6 but the s God works all of them in all men. *899*
12: 8 of knowledge by means of the s Spirit, *899*
12: 9 to another faith by the s Spirit, *899*
12:11 the work of one and the s Spirit, *899*
15: 6 five hundred of the brothers **at the** s **time,** *2384*
15:39 All flesh is not the s: *899*
2Co 1: 6 endurance *of* the s sufferings we suffer. *899*
1:17 so that in the s breath I say, *NIG*
3:14 for to this day the s veil remains when *899*
4:13 With that s spirit of faith we also believe *899*
8:16 into the heart of Titus the s concern I have *899*
12:18 act *in* the s spirit and follow the same *899*
12:18 in the same spirit and **follow the** s **course?** *2717*
Gal 4:29 **It is the** s now. *2779+4048*
Eph 5:28 **In this** s **way,** husbands ought to love *2779+4048*
6: 9 And masters, treat your slaves in the s **way.** *899*
Php 1:30 through the s struggle you saw I had, *899*
2: 2 being like-minded, having the s love, *899*
2: 5 Your attitude should be the s as that *NIG*
3: 1 It is no trouble for me to write the **s things** *899*
1Th 2:14 the s *things* those churches suffered from *899*
1Ti 3: 6 and fall under the s judgment as the devil. *NIG*
3:11 **In the** s **way,** their wives are to be worthy *6058*
5:25 **In the** s **way,** good deeds are obvious, *6058*
Heb 1:12 But you remain the **s,** *899*
2:11 who are made holy are of **the** s family. *1651*
6:11 to show this s diligence to the very end, *899*
9:21 **In the** s **way,** he sprinkled with the blood *3931*
10: 1 *by* the s sacrifices repeated endlessly year *899*
10:11 again and again he offers the s sacrifices, *899*
11: 9 who were heirs with him *of* the s promise. *899*
13: 8 Jesus Christ is the s yesterday and today *899*
Jas 1:11 **In the** s **way,** the rich man will fade away *4048*
2:17 **In the** s **way,** faith by itself, *4048*
2:25 **In the** s **way,** was not even Rahab *3931*
3:10 of the s mouth come praise and cursing. *899*
3:11 and salt water flow from the s spring? *899*
1Pe 3: 1 **in the** s **way** be submissive to your husbands *3931*
3: 7 **in the** s **way** be considerate as you live *3931*
4: 1 arm yourselves also with the s attitude, *899*
4: 4 with them into the s flood of dissipation, *899*
5: 5 **in the** s **way** be submissive to those *3931*
5: 9 the world are undergoing the s *kind* *899*
2Pe 3: 7 *By* the s word the present heavens *899*
3:16 He writes **the** s **way** in all his letters, *2779+6055*
Jude 1: 8 **In the** very s **way,** these dreamers pollute *3931*

SAMGAR (1)

Jer 39: 3 Nergal-Sharezer of S, Nebo-Sarsekim a 6161

SAMGAR-NEBO (KJV) See SAMGAR, NEBO-SARSEKIM

SAMLAH (4)

Ge 36:36 S from Masrekah succeeded him as king. 8528
36:37 When S died, Shaul from Rehoboth on 8528
1Ch 1:47 S from Masrekah succeeded him as king. 8528
1:48 When S died, Shaul from Rehoboth on 8528

SAMOS (1)

Ac 20:15 The day after that we crossed over to S, *4904*

SAMOTHRACE (1)

Ac 16:11 we put out to sea and sailed straight for S, *4903*

SAMPLE (1) [SAMPLED]

Pr 23:30 who go to s bowls of mixed wine. 2983

SAMPLED (1) [SAMPLE]

Jos 9:14 The men of Israel s their provisions but did 4374

SAMSON (37) [SAMSON'S]

Jdg 13:24 gave birth to a boy and named him **S.** 9088
14: 1 S went down to Timnah and saw there 9088
14: 3 But S said to his father, "Get her for me. 9088
14: 5 S went down to Timnah together 9088
14:10 And S made a feast there, 9088
14:12 "Let me tell you a riddle," S said to them. 9088
14:18 S said to them, "If you had not plowed NIH
15: 1 S took a young goat and went 9088
15: 3 S said to them, "This time I have a right 9088
15: 6 **"S,** the Timnite's son-in-law, 9088
15: 7 S said to them, "Since you've acted like 9088
15:10 "We have come to take S prisoner," 9088
15:11 the cave in the rock of Etam and said to S, 9088
15:12 S said, "Swear to me that you won't kill me 9088
15:16 Then S said, "With a donkey's jawbone I have made donkeys of them. 9088
15:19 When S drank, his strength returned NIH
15:20 S led Israel for twenty years in the days of NIH
16: 1 One day S went to Gaza, 9088
16: 2 The people of Gaza were told, **"S is here!"** 9088
16: 3 But S lay there only until the middle of 9088
16: 6 So Delilah said to S, "Tell me the secret 9088
16: 7 S answered her, "If anyone ties me 9088
16: 9 **"S,** the Philistines are upon you!" 9088
16:10 Delilah said to S, "You have made a fool 9088
16:12 **"S,** the Philistines are upon you!" 9088
16:13 Delilah then said to **S,** "Until now, 9088
16:14 Again she called to him, **"S,** 9088
16:20 **"S,** the Philistines are upon you!" 9088
16:23 "Our god has delivered **S,** our enemy, 9088
16:25 they shouted, "Bring out S to entertain us." 9088
16:25 So they called S out of the prison, 9088
16:26 S said to the servant who held his hand, 9088
16:27 men and women watching S perform. 9088
16:28 Then S prayed to the LORD, 9088
16:29 S reached toward the two central pillars 9088
16:30 S said, "Let me die with the Philistines!" 9088
Heb 11:32 Barak, S, Jephthah, David, Samuel and *4907*

SAMSON'S (3) [SAMSON]

Jdg 14:15 On the fourth day, they said to S wife, 9088
14:16 Then S wife threw herself on him, sobbing, 9088
14:20 And S wife was given to the friend 9088

SAMUEL (140) [SAMUEL'S]

1Sa 1:20 She named him S, saying, 9017
2:18 But S was ministering before the LORD— 9017
2:21 the boy S grew up in the presence of 9017
2:26 And the boy S continued to grow in stature 9017
3: 1 The boy S ministered before the LORD 9017
3: 3 and S was lying down in the temple of 9017
3: 4 Then the LORD called **S.** 9017
3: 4 S answered, "Here I am." NIH
3: 6 Again the LORD called, **"S!"** 9017
3: 6 And S got up and went to Eli and said, 9017
3: 7 Now S did not yet know the LORD: 9017
3: 8 The LORD called S a third time, 9017
3: 8 and S got up and went to Eli and said, NIH
3: 9 So Eli told **S,** "Go and lie down, 9017
3: 9 So S went and lay down in his place. 9017
3:10 calling as at the other times, **"S!** 9017
3:10 at the other times, **"Samuel! S!"** 9017
3:10 Then S said, "Speak, for your servant is 9017
3:11 And the LORD said to **S:** 9017
3:15 S lay down until morning and then opened 9017
3:16 but Eli called him and said, **"S,** 9017
3:16 S answered, "Here I am." NIH
3:18 So S told him everything, 9017
3:19 The LORD was with S as he grew up, 9017
3:20 to Beersheba recognized that S was attested 9017
3:21 and there he revealed himself to S 9017
7: 3 And S said to the whole house of Israel, 9017
7: 5 Then S said, "Assemble all Israel 9017
7: 6 And S was leader of Israel at Mizpah. 9017
7: 8 They said to **S,** "Do not stop crying out 9017
7: 9 Then S took a suckling lamb and offered it 9017
7:10 While S was sacrificing the burnt offering, 9017
7:12 Then S took a stone and set it up 9017
7:15 S continued as judge over Israel all 9017
8: 1 When S grew old, he appointed his sons 9017
8: 4 of Israel gathered together and came to S 9017
8: 6 a king to lead us," this displeased **S;** 9017
8:10 S told all the words of the LORD to 9017
8:19 But the people refused to listen to **S.** 9017
8:21 When S heard all that the people said, 9017
8:22 Then S said to the men of Israel, 9017
9:14 and as they were entering it, there was **S,** 9017
9:15 the LORD had revealed this to **S:** 9017
9:17 When S caught sight of Saul, 9017
9:18 Saul approached S in the gateway 9017
9:19 "I am the seer," S replied. 9017
9:22 Then S brought Saul and his servant into 9017
9:23 S said to the cook, "Bring the piece of meat 9017
9:24 S said, "Here is what has been kept NIH
9:24 And Saul dined with S that day. 9017
9:25 S talked with Saul on the roof of his house. NIH
9:26 about daybreak and S called to Saul on 9017
9:26 he and S went outside together. 9017
9:27 S said to Saul, "Tell the servant to go on 9017
10: 1 Then S took a flask of oil and poured it 9017
10: 9 As Saul turned to leave **S,** 9017
10:14 not to be found, we went to **S."** 9017
10:15 "Tell me what S said to you." 9017
10:16 not tell his uncle what S had said about 9017
10:17 S summoned the people of Israel to 9017
10:20 S brought all the tribes of Israel near, 9017
10:24 S said to all the people, 9017
10:25 S explained to the people the regulations of 9017
10:25 Then S dismissed the people, 9017
11: 7 of anyone who does not follow Saul and **S."** 9017
11:12 The people then said to **S,** 9017
11:14 Then S said to the people, "Come, 9017
12: 1 S said to all Israel, "I have listened 9017
12: 5 S said to them, "The LORD is witness NIH
12: 6 Then S said to the people, 9017
12:11 sent Jerub-Baal, Barak, Jephthah and **S,** 9017
12:18 Then S called upon the LORD, 9017
12:18 people stood in awe of the LORD and of **S.** 9017
12:19 The people all said to **S,** 9017
12:20 "Do not be afraid," S replied. 9017
13: 8 He waited seven days, the time set by **S;** 9017
13: 8 but S did not come to Gilgal, 9017
13:10 S arrived, and Saul went out to greet him. 9017
13:11 "What have you done?" asked **S.** 9017
13:13 "You acted foolishly," S said. 9017
13:15 Then S left Gilgal and went up to Gibeah 9017
15: 1 S said to Saul, "I am the one the LORD sent 9017
15:10 Then the word of the LORD came to **S:** 9017
15:11 S was troubled, and he cried out to 9017
15:12 Early in the morning S got up and went 9017
15:13 When S reached him, Saul said, 9017
15:14 But S said, "What then is this bleating 9017
15:16 "Stop!" S said to Saul. 9017
15:17 S said, "Although you were once small 9017
15:22 But S replied: "Does the LORD delight in burnt offerings and 9017
15:24 Then Saul said to S, "I have sinned. 9017
15:26 S said to him, "I will not go back with you. 9017
15:27 As S turned to leave, 9017
15:28 S said to him, "The LORD has torn 9017
15:31 So S went back with Saul, 9017
15:32 Then S said, "Bring me Agag king of 9017
15:33 But S said, "As your sword has made women childless, 9017
15:33 And S put Agag to death before the LORD 9017
15:34 Then S left for Ramah, 9017
15:35 Until the day S died, he did not go to see 9017
15:35 though S mourned for him. 9017
16: 1 The LORD said to **S,** "How long will you 9017
16: 2 But S said, "How can I go? 9017
16: 4 S did what the LORD said. 9017
16: 5 S replied, "Yes, in peace; NIH
16: 6 S saw Eliab and thought, NIH
16: 7 But the LORD said to **S,** "Do not consider 9017
16: 8 and had him pass in front of **S.** 9017
16: 8 But S said, "The LORD has not chosen NIH
16: 9 then had Shammah pass by, but S said, NIH
16:10 Jesse had seven of his sons pass before **S,** 9017
16:10 but S said to him, "The LORD has not 9017
16:11 S said, "Send for him; 9017
16:13 So S took the horn of oil and anointed him 9017
16:13 S then went to Ramah. 9017
19:18 he went to S at Ramah and told him all 9017
19:18 he and S went to Naioth and stayed there. 9017
19:20 with S standing there as their leader, 9017
19:22 And he asked, "Where are S and David?" 9017
25: 1 Now S died, and all Israel assembled 9017
28: 3 Now S was dead, and all Israel mourned 9017
28:11 "Bring up **S,"** he said. 9017
28:12 When the woman saw **S,** she cried out 9017
28:14 Then Saul knew it was **S,** 9017
28:15 S said to Saul, "Why have you disturbed me 9017
28:16 S said, "Why do you consult me, 9017
1Ch 6:27 Elkanah his son and S his son. 9017
6:28 The sons of **S:** Joel the firstborn 9017
6:33 the musician, the son of Joel, the son of **S,** 9017
7: 2 Rephaiah, Jeriel, Jahmai, Ibsam and **S—** 9017
9:22 to their positions of trust by David and S 9017
11: 3 as the LORD had promised through **S.** 9017
26:28 And everything dedicated by S the seer and 9017
29:29 they are written in the records of S the seer, 9017
2Ch 35:18 in Israel since the days of the prophet **S;** 9017
Ps 99: 6 S was among those who called 9017
Jer 15: 1 if Moses and S were to stand before me, 9017
Ac 3:24 "Indeed, all the prophets from S on, *4905*
13:20 God gave them judges until the time of S *4905*
Heb 11:32 Jephthah, David, S and the prophets, *4905*

SAMUEL'S (4) [SAMUEL]

1Sa 4: 1 And S word came to all Israel. 9017
7:13 Throughout S lifetime, the hand of the LORD 9017
19:24 and also prophesied in S presence. 9017
28:20 filled with fear because of S words. 9017

SANBALLAT (10)

Ne 2:10 When S the Horonite and Tobiah 6172
2:19 But when S the Horonite, 6172
4: 1 When S heard that we were rebuilding 6172
4: 7 But when **S,** Tobiah, the Arabs, 6172
6: 1 When word came to **S,** Tobiah, 6172
6: 2 S and Geshem sent me this message: 6172
6: 5 S sent his aide to me with the same message 6172
6:12 because Tobiah and S had hired him. 6172
6:14 Remember Tobiah and **S,** O my God, 6172
13:28 the high priest was son-in-law to S 6172

SANCTIFIED (10) [SANCTIFY]

Jn 17:19 that they too *may be* truly s. *39+1639*
Ac 20:32 an inheritance among all those who *are* **s.** *39*
26:18 and a place among those who *are* s by faith *39*
Ro 15:16 s by the Holy Spirit. *39*
1Co 1: 2 to those s in Christ Jesus and called to *39+1639*
6:11 But you were washed, *you were* **s,** *39*
7:14 For the unbelieving husband *has been* s *39*
7:14 and the unbelieving wife *has been* s *39*
1Th 4: 3 It is God's will that you should **be s:** *40*
Heb 10:29 the blood of the covenant that s *him,* *39*

SANCTIFY (4) [SANCTIFIED, SANCTIFYING]

Jn 17:17 S them by the truth; your word is truth. *39*
17:19 For them I s myself, that they too may be *39*
1Th 5:23 God of peace, s you through and through. *39*
Heb 9:13 s them so that they are outwardly clean. *39*

SANCTIFYING (2) [SANCTIFY]

2Th 2:13 to be saved through the s work of the Spirit *40*
1Pe 1: 2 through the s work of the Spirit, *40*

SANCTUARIES (4) [SANCTUARY]

Lev 26:31 into ruins and lay waste your s, 5219
Eze 7:24 and their s will be desecrated. 5219
28:18 dishonest trade you have desecrated your s. 5219
Am 7: 9 be destroyed and the s *of* Israel will 5219

SANCTUARY (177) [SANCTUARIES]

Ex 15:17 you made for your dwelling, the s, O Lord, 5219
25: 8 "Then have them make a s for me, 5219
30:13 according to the s shekel, 7731
30:24 all according to the s shekel— 7731
35:19 garments worn for ministering in the s— 7731
36: 1 of constructing the s are to do the work just 7731
36: 3 to carry out the work of constructing the s. 7731
36: 4 the work on the s left their work 7731
36: 6 as an offering for the s." 7731
38:24 on the s was 29 talents and 730 shekels, 7731
38:24 according to the s shekel. 7731
38:25 shekels, according to the s shekel— 7731
38:26 half a shekel, according to the s shekel, 7731
38:27 the bases for the s and for the curtain— 7731
39: 1 garments for ministering in the s. 7731
39:41 garments worn for ministering in the s, 7731
Lev 4: 6 in front of the curtain of the s. 7731
5:15 according to the s shekel. 7731
10: 4 away from the front of the s." 7731
10:17 the sin offering in the s area? 7731
10:18 you should have eaten the goat in the s area, 7731
12: 4 not touch anything sacred or go to the s 5219
16: 3 "This is how Aaron is to enter the **s area:** 7731
19:30 and have reverence for my s. 5219
20: 3 to Molech, he has defiled my s 5219
21:12 nor leave the s *of* his God or desecrate it, 5219
21:23 and so desecrate my s. 5219
26: 2 and have reverence for my s. 5219
27: 3 according to the s shekel; 7731
27:25 to be set according to the s shekel, 7731
Nu 3:10 anyone else who approaches the s must NIH
3:28 responsible for the care of the s. 7731
3:31 the articles of the s used in ministering, 7731
3:32 responsible for the care of the s. 7731
3:38 They were responsible for the care of the s 5219
3:38 Anyone else who approached the s was to NIH
3:47 according to the s shekel, 7731
3:50 shekels, according to the s shekel. 7731
4:12 the articles used for ministering in the s, 7731
4:19 and his sons are to go into the s and assign NIH
7:13 both according to the s shekel, 7731
7:19 both according to the s shekel, 7731
7:25 both according to the s shekel, 7731
7:31 both according to the s shekel, 7731
7:37 both according to the s shekel, 7731
7:43 both according to the s shekel, 7731
7:49 both according to the s shekel, 7731
7:55 both according to the s shekel, 7731
7:61 both according to the s shekel, 7731
7:67 both according to the s shekel, 7731
7:73 both according to the s shekel, 7731
7:79 both according to the s shekel, 7731
7:85 according to the s shekel. 7731
7:86 according to the s shekel. 7731
8:19 the Israelites when they go near the s." 7731
18: 1 the responsibility for offenses against the s, 5219
18: 3 near the furnishings of the s or the altar, 7731
18: 5 to be responsible for the care of the s and 7731
18: 7 Anyone else who comes near the s must NIH
18:16 according to the s shekel, 7731
19:20 because he has defiled the s *of* the LORD. 5219
28: 7 the drink offering to the LORD at the s. 7731
31: 6 who took with him articles from the s and 7731
Jos 22:27 we will worship the LORD **at** his s 4200+7156[S]
1Ki 6: 5 the main hall and **inner** s he built a structure 1808
6:16 to form within the temple an **inner** s, 1808
6:19 the **inner** s within the temple to set the ark 1808
6:20 The **inner** s was twenty cubits long, 1808
6:21 across the front of the **inner** s, 1808
6:22 the altar that belonged to the **inner** s. 1808
6:23 In the **inner** s he made a pair of cherubim 1808
6:31 of the **inner** s he made doors of olive wood 1808
7:49 in front of the **inner** s); 1808
8: 6 to its place in the **inner** s *of* the temple, 1808
8: 8 in front of the **inner** s, but not from outside 1808
1Ch 9:29 and all the other articles of the s, 7731
22:19 Begin to build the s *of* the LORD God, 5219
24: 5 for there were officials of the s and officials 7731
28:10 to build a temple as a s. 5219
2Ch 4:20 to burn in front of the **inner** s as prescribed; 1808
5: 7 to its place in the **inner** s *of* the temple, 1808
5: 9 could be seen from in front of the **inner** s, 1808
20: 8 They have lived in it and have built in it a s 5219
26:18 Leave the s, for you have been unfaithful; 5219
29: 5 Remove all defilement from the s. 7731
29: 7 or present any burnt offerings at the s to 7731
29:16 The priests went into the s *of* the LORD 1074
29:21 for the s and for Judah. 5219
30: 8 Come to the s, which he has consecrated 5219
30:19 not clean according to the rules of the s." 7731
36:17 with the sword in the s, 1074+5219
Ezr 9: 8 and giving us a firm place in his s, 5226+7731
Ne 10:39 where the articles for the s are kept and 5219
Ps 15: 1 LORD, who may dwell in your s? 185
20: 2 from the s and grant you support from Zion. 7731
60: 6 God has spoken from his s: 7731
63: 2 in the s and beheld your power 7731
68:17 the Lord [has come] from Sinai into his s. 7731
68:24 procession of my God and King into the s. 7731
68:35 You are awesome, O God, in your s; 5219
73:17 till I entered the s *of* God; 5219
74: 3 the enemy has brought on the s. 7731
74: 7 They burned your s to the ground; 5219
78:69 He built his s like the heights, 5219
96: 6 strength and glory are in his s. 5219
102:19 "The LORD looked down from his s 7731
108: 7 God has spoken from his s: 7731
114: 2 Judah became God's s, Israel his dominion. 7731
134: 2 Lift up your hands in the s and praise 7731
150: 1 Praise God in his s; 7731
Isa 8:14 and he will be a s; 5219
60:13 to adorn the place of my s; 5219
62: 9 in the courts of my s." 7731
63:18 our enemies have trampled down your s. 5219
Jer 17:12 is the place of our s. 5219
La 1:10 she saw pagan nations enter her s— 5219
2: 7 rejected his altar and abandoned his s. 5219
2:20 Should priest and prophet be killed in the s 5219
Eze 5:11 because you have defiled my s with all 5219
8: 6 things that will drive me far from my s? 5219
9: 6 Begin at my s." 5219
11:16 for a little while I have been a s for them in 5219
21: 2 against Jerusalem and preach against the s. 5219
23:38 At that same time they defiled my s 5219
23:39 they entered my s and desecrated it. 5219
24:21 I am about to desecrate my s— 5219
25: 3 over my s when it was desecrated and over 5219
37:26 and I will put my s among them forever. 5219
37:28 when my s is among them forever.' " 5219
41: 1 Then the man brought me to the **outer** s 2121
41: 2 He also measured the outer s; NIH
41: 3 Then he went into the **inner** s and measured 7163
41: 4 And he measured the length of the **inner** s; 2257[S]
41: 4 across the end of the **outer** s. 2121
41:15 The **outer** s, the inner sanctuary and 2121
41:15 the **inner** s and the portico facing the court, 7164
41:17 the entrance to the inner s and on the walls 1074
41:17 around the **inner** and outer s 7164
41:20 on the wall of the **outer** s. 2121
41:21 The **outer** s had a rectangular doorframe, 2121
41:23 Both the **outer** s and the Most Holy Place 2121
41:25 of the **outer** s were carved cherubim 2121
42: 8 the row on the side nearest the s was 2121
43:21 of the temple area outside the s. 5219
44: 1 to the outer gate of the s, 5219
44: 5 of the temple and all the exits of the s. 5219
44: 7 in heart and flesh into my s, 5219
44: 8 you put others in charge of my s. 5219
44: 9 in heart and flesh is to enter my s, 5219
44:11 They may serve in my s, 5219
44:15 of my s when the Israelites went astray 5219
44:16 They alone are to enter my s; 5219
44:27 the day he goes into the inner court of the s 7731
44:27 of the sanctuary to minister in the s, 7731
45: 2 section 500 cubits square is to be for the s, 7731
45: 3 In it will be the s, the Most Holy Place. 5219
45: 4 the s and who draw near to minister before 5219
45: 4 as well as a holy place for the s. 5219
45:18 without defect and purify the s. 5219
47:12 because the water from the s flows to them. 5219
48: 8 the s will be in the center of it. 5219
48:10 the center of it will be the s *of* the LORD. 5219
48:21 the sacred portion with the temple s will be 5219
Da 8:11 and the place of his s was brought low. 5219
8:13 and the surrender of the s and of the host 7731
8:14 then the s will be reconsecrated." 7731
9:17 O Lord, look with favor on your desolate s. 5219
9:26 will destroy the city and the s. 7731
Am 7:13 because this is the king's s and the temple 5219
Zep 3: 4 Her priests profane the s and do violence to 7731
Mal 2:11 Judah has desecrated the s the LORD loves, 7731
Lk 11:51 who was killed between the altar and the s. *3875*
Heb 6:19 It enters the inner s behind the curtain, *NIG*
8: 2 and who serves *in* the s, *41*
8: 5 They **serve at a** s that is a copy and shadow *3302*
9: 1 for worship and also an earthly s. *41*
9:24 For Christ did not enter a man-made s *41*

SAND (29) [SANDY]

Ge 22:17 in the sky and as the s on the seashore. 2567
32:12 and will make your descendants like the s 2567
41:49 like the s *of* the sea; 2567
Ex 2:12 he killed the Egyptian and hid him in the s. 2567
Dt 33:19 on the treasures hidden in the s." 2567
Jos 11: 4 as numerous as the s on the seashore. 2567
Jdg 7:12 be counted than the s on the seashore. 2567
1Sa 13: 5 as numerous as the s on the seashore. 2567
2Sa 17:11 as numerous as the s on the seashore— 2567
1Ki 4:20 and Israel were as numerous as the s on 2567
4:29 of understanding as measureless as the s on 2567
Job 6: 3 surely outweigh the s *of* the seas— 2567
29:18 my days as numerous as the **grains of** s. 2567
39:14 on the ground and lets them warm in the s, 6760
Ps 78:27 flying birds like s *on* the seashore. 2567
139:18 they would outnumber the **grains of** s. 2567
Pr 27: 3 Stone is heavy and s a burden, 2567
Isa 10:22 O Israel, be like the s *by* the sea, 2567
35: 7 The **burning** s will become a pool, 9220
48:19 descendants would have been like the s, 2567
Jer 5:22 I made the s a boundary for the sea, 2567
Isa 15: 8 more numerous than the s *of* the sea. 2567
33:22 as measureless as the s *on* the seashore.' " 2567
Hos 1:10 "Yet the Israelites will be like the s *on* 2567
Hab 1: 9 a desert wind and gather prisoners like s. 2567
Mt 7:26 like a foolish man who built his house on s. *302*
Ro 9:27 the number of the Israelites be like the s by *302*
Heb 11:12 the stars in the sky and as countless as the s *302*
Rev 20: 8 In number they are like the s on *302*

SANDAL (6) [SANDALED, SANDALS]

Ge 14:23 not even a thread or the thong of a s, 5837
Ru 4: 7 one party took off his s and gave it to 5837
4: 8 And he removed his s. 5837
Ps 60: 8 upon Edom I toss my s; 5837
108: 9 upon Edom I toss my s; 5837
Isa 5:27 not a s thong is broken. 5837

SANDALED (1) [SANDAL]

SS 7: 1 How beautiful your s feet, 928+2021+5837

SANDALS (28) [SANDAL]

Ex 3: 5 "Take off your s, for the place 5837
12:11 into your belt, your s on your feet 5837
Dt 25: 9 take off one of his s, spit in his face and say, 5837
29: 5 nor did the s on your feet. 5837
Jos 5:15 "Take off your s, for the place 5837
9: 5 The men put worn and patched s 5837
9:13 And our clothes and s are worn out by 5837
1Ki 2: 5 around his waist and the s on his feet. 5837
2Ch 28:15 They provided them with clothes and s, 5836
Isa 11:15 so that men can cross over in s. 5837
20: 2 from your body and the s from your feet." 5837
Eze 16:10 an embroidered dress and **put** leather s **on** 5836
24:17 Keep your turban fastened and your s 5837
24:23 on your heads and your s on your feet. 5837
Am 2: 6 and the needy for a *pair of* s. 5837
8: 6 with silver and the needy for a *pair of* s, 5837
Mt 3:11 whose s I am not fit to carry. *5687*
10:10 or extra tunic, or s or a staff; *5687*
Mk 1: 7 of whose s I am not worthy to stoop down *5687*
6: 9 Wear s but not an extra tunic. *4908*
Lk 3:16 thongs of whose s I am not worthy to untie. *5687*
10: 4 Do not take a purse or bag or s; *5687*
15:22 Put a ring on his finger and s on his feet. *5687*
22:35 "When I sent you without purse, bag or s, *5687*
Jn 1:27 the thongs of whose s I am not worthy *5687*
Ac 7:33 the Lord said to him, 'Take off your s; *5687*
12: 8 "Put on your clothes and s." *4908+5686*
13:25 whose s I am not worthy to untie.' *5687*

SANDBAR (1) [SANDBARS]

Ac 27:41 the ship struck a s and ran aground. *1458+5536*

SANDBARS (1) [SANDBAR]

Ac 27:17 they would run aground on the s **of Syrtis,** *5358*

SANDY (1) [SAND]

Ac 27:39 but they saw a bay with a s **beach,** *129*

SANG (24) [SING]

Ex 15: 1 Then Moses and the Israelites s this song to 8876
15:21 Miriam s to them: "Sing to the LORD, 6702
Nu 21:17 Then Israel s this song: "Spring up, O well! 8876
Jdg 5: 1 and Barak son of Abinoam s *this* **song:** 8876
1Sa 18: 7 As they danced, *they* s: 6702
29: 5 the David *they* s about in their dances: 6702
2Sa 3:33 The king s *this* **lament** for Abner: 7801
22: 1 David s to the LORD the words of this song 1819
2Ch 5:13 in praise to the LORD and s: 9048
29:28 the singers s and the trumpeters played. 8876
29:30 So *they* s **praises** with gladness 2146
30:21 and priests s to the LORD every day, 2146
Ezr 3:11 and thanksgiving *they* s to the LORD: 6702
Ne 12:42 The choirs s under the direction 9048
Job 38: 7 while the morning stars s together and all 8264
Ps 7: T which *he* s to the LORD concerning Cush, 8876
18: T *He* s to the LORD the words of this song 1819
106:12 they believed his promises and s his praise. 8876
Mt 11:17 *we* s **a dirge,** and you did not mourn.' *2577*
Lk 7:32 *we* s **a dirge,** and you did not cry.' *2577*
Rev 5: 9 And *they* s a new song: "You are worthy *106*
5:12 In a loud voice *they* s: "Worthy is the Lamb *3306*
14: 3 And *they* s a new song before the throne *106*
15: 3 and s the song of Moses the servant of God *106*

SANHEDRIN (19)

Mt 5:22 'Raca,' is answerable *to* the S. *5284*
26:59 and the whole S were looking for false *5284*
Mk 14:55 and the whole S were looking for evidence *5284*
15: 1 the teachers of the law and the whole S, *5284*
Jn 11:47 and the Pharisees called a meeting of the S. *5284*
Ac 4:15 from the S and then conferred together. *5284*
5:21 they called together the S— *5284*
5:27 the S to be questioned by the high priest. *5284*
5:34 stood up in the S and ordered that the men *5284*
5:41 The apostles left the S, *5284*
6:12 and brought him before the S. *5284*
6:15 in the S looked intently at Stephen, *5284*
22:30 the chief priests and all the S to assemble. *5284*
23: 1 Paul looked straight at the S and said, *5284*
23: 6 called out in the S, "My brothers, *5284*
23:15 the S petition the commander to bring him *5284*

Ac 23:20 to bring Paul before the S tomorrow on *5284*
23:28 so I brought him to their S. *5284*
24:20 in me when I stood before the S— *5284*

SANITY (2)

Da 4:34 and my s was restored. 10430
4:36 At the same time that my s was restored, 10430

SANK (12) [SINK]

Ge 42:28 Their hearts s and they turned to each other 3655
Ex 15:5 *they* s to the depths like a stone. 3718
15:10 *They* s like lead in the mighty waters. 7510
Nu 21:18 that the nobles of the people s— 4125
Jdg 3:22 Even the handle s **in** after the blade, 995
5:27 At her feet *he* s, he fell; there he lay. 4156
5:27 At her feet *he* s, he fell; 4156
5:27 where *he* s, there he fell—dead. 4156
1Sa 17:49 The stone s into his forehead, 3190
SS 5:6 My heart s at his departure. 3655
Jer 38:6 and Jeremiah s **down** into the mud. 3190
Jnh 2:6 To the roots of the mountains *I* s **down**; 3718

SANK (Anglicized) See also MELTED

SANNAH See KIRIATH SANNAH

SANSANNAH (1)

Jos 15:31 Ziklag, Madmannah, S, 6179

SAP (2) [SAPPED]

Hos 7:9 Foreigners s his strength, 430
Ro 11:17 now share in the nourishing s from the olive *NIG*

SAPH (1)

2Sa 21:18 that time Sibbecai the Hushathite killed S, 6198

SAPHIR (KJV) See SHAPHIR

SAPPED (2) [SAP]

Ps 32:4 my strength **was** s as in the heat of summer. 2200
La 1:14 and the Lord *has* s my strength. 4173

SAPPHIRA (1)

Ac 5:1 together with his wife S, *4912*

SAPPHIRE (7) [SAPPHIRES]

Ex 24:10 like a pavement made of s, 6209
28:18 a s and an emerald; 6209
39:11 a s and an emerald; 6209
Eze 1:26 what looked like a throne of s, 74+6209
10:1 the likeness of a throne of s above 74+6209
28:13 onyx and jasper, s, turquoise and beryl. 6209
Rev 21:19 first foundation was jasper, the second s, *4913*

SAPPHIRES (5) [SAPPHIRE]

Job 28:6 s come from its rocks, 6209
28:16 with precious onyx or s. 6209
SS 5:14 like polished ivory decorated with s. 6209
Isa 54:11 your foundations with s. 6209
La 4:7 their appearance like s. 6209

SARAH (38) [SARAH'S, SARAI]

Ge 17:15 her name will be S. 8577
17:17 Will S bear a child at the age of ninety?" 8577
17:19 "Yes, but your wife S will bear you a son, 8577
17:21 Isaac, whom S will bear to you 8577
18:6 So Abraham hurried into the tent to S. 8577
18:9 "Where is your wife S?" 8577
18:10 and S your wife will have a son." 8577
18:10 S was listening at the entrance to the tent, 8577
18:11 and S were already old and well advanced 8577
18:11 and S was past the age of childbearing. 8577
18:12 So S laughed to herself as she thought, 8577
18:13 "Why did S laugh and say, 8577
18:14 next year and S will have a son." 8577
18:15 S was afraid, so she lied and said, 8577
20:2 and there Abraham said of his wife S, 8577
20:2 Then Abimelech king of Gerar sent for S 8577
20:14 and he **returned** S his wife to him. 8577
20:16 To S he said, "I am giving your brother 8577
20:18 because of Abraham's wife S. 8577
21:1 LORD was gracious to S as he had said, 8577
21:1 LORD did for S what he had promised. 8577
21:2 S became pregnant and bore a son 8577
21:3 the name Isaac to the son S bore him. 8577
21:6 S said, "God has brought me laughter, 8577
21:7 to Abraham that S would nurse children? 8577
21:9 But S saw that the son whom Hagar 8577
21:12 Listen to whatever S tells you, 8577
23:1 S lived to be a hundred and twenty-seven 8577
23:2 and Abraham went to mourn for S and 8577
23:19 Afterward Abraham buried his wife S in 8577
24:36 My master's wife S has borne him a son 8577
24:67 into the tent of his mother S, 8577
25:10 There Abraham was buried with his wife S. 8577
49:31 There Abraham and his wife S were buried, 8577
Isa 51:2 your father, and to S, who gave you birth. 8577
Ro 9:9 and S will have a son." *4925*
Heb 11:11 he was past age—and S herself was barren *4925*
1Pe 3:6 like S, who obeyed Abraham *4925*

SARAH'S (2) [SARAH]

Ge 25:12 whom S maidservant, Hagar the Egyptian, 8577
Ro 4:19 and that S womb was also dead. *4925*

SARAI (15) [SARAH]

Ge 11:29 The name of Abram's wife was S, 8584
11:30 Now S was barren; she had no children. 8584
11:31 and his daughter-in-law S, 8584
12:5 He took his wife S, his nephew Lot, 8584
12:11 he said to his wife S, 8584
12:17 because of Abram's wife S. 8584
16:1 Now S, Abram's wife, had borne him no 8584
16:2 Abram agreed to what S said. 8584
16:3 S his wife took her Egyptian maidservant 8584
16:5 Then S said to Abram, 8584
16:6 S mistreated Hagar; so she fled from her. 8584
16:8 And he said, "Hagar, servant of S, 8584
16:8 "I'm running away from my mistress S," 8584
17:15 *"As for* S your wife, 8584
17:15 you are no longer to call her S; 8584

SARAPH (1)

1Ch 4:22 the men of Cozeba, and Joash and S, 8598

SARDINE (KJV) See CARNELIAN

SARDIS (3)

Rev 1:11 Thyatira, S, Philadelphia and Laodicea." *4915*
3:1 "To the angel of the church in S write: *4915*
3:4 Yet you have a few people in S who have *4915*

SARDITES (KJV) See SEREDITE

SARDIUS (KJV) See RUBY

SARDONYX (1)

Rev 21:20 the fifth s, the sixth carnelian, *4918*

SAREPTA (KJV) See ZAREPHATH

SARGON (1)

Isa 20:1 commander, sent by S king of Assyria, 6236

SARID (2)

Jos 19:10 of their inheritance went as far as S. 8587
19:12 It turned east from S toward the sunrise to 8587

SARON (KJV) See SHARON

SARSECHIM (KJV) See NEBO-SARSEKIM

SARUCH (KJV) See SERUG

SASH (9) [SASHES]

Ex 28:4 a robe, a woven tunic, a turban and a s. 77
28:39 The s is to be the work of an embroiderer. 77
39:29 The s was of finely twisted linen and blue, 77
Lev 8:7 tied the s around him, 77
16:4 he is to tie the linen s around him and put 77
Isa 3:24 instead of a s, a rope; 2514
11:5 and faithfulness the s *around* his waist. 258
22:21 and fasten your s around him 77
Rev 1:13 and with a golden s around his chest. *2438*

SASHES (6) [SASH]

Ex 28:40 s and headbands for Aaron's sons, 77
29:9 Then tie s on Aaron and his sons. 77
Lev 8:13 tied s around them and put headbands 77
Pr 31:24 and supplies the merchants with s. 2512
Isa 3:20 the headdresses and ankle chains and s, 8005
Rev 15:6 and wore golden s around their chests. *2438*

SAT (99) [SIT]

Ge 21:16 Then she went off and s **down** nearby, 3782
21:16 *as she* s there nearby, she began to sob. 3782
37:25 As *they* s **down** to eat their meal, 3782
38:14 and then s **down** at the entrance to Enaim, 3782
48:2 Israel rallied his strength and s **up** on 3782
Ex 2:15 where *he* s **down** by a well. 3782
12:29 Pharaoh, who s on the throne, 3782
16:3 There we s around pots of meat and ate all 3782
17:12 a stone and put it under him and *he* s on it. 3782
32:6 Afterward *they* s **down** to eat and drink 3782
Lev 15:6 with a discharge s on must wash his clothes 3782
Jdg 6:11 The angel of the LORD came and s **down** 3782
19:6 of them s **down** to eat and drink together. 3782
19:15 They went and s in the city square, 3782
20:26 and there *they* s weeping before 3782
21:2 where *they* s before God until evening, 3782
Ru 2:14 When *she* s **down** with the harvesters, 3782
4:1 up to the town gate and s there. 3782
4:1 So he went over and s **down**. 3782
1Sa 20:24 the king s **down** to eat. 3782
20:25 He s in his customary place by the wall, 3782
20:25 and Abner s next to Saul, 3782
28:23 up from the ground and s on the couch. 3782
2Sa 2:13 One group s **down** on one side of the pool 3782
7:18 in and s before the LORD, and he said: 3782
19:28 a place among *those who* s *at* your table. 430
1Ki 2:12 So Solomon s on the throne 3782
2:19 down to her and s **down** on his throne. 3782
2:19 and *she* s **down** at his right hand. 3782
19:4 He came to a broom tree, s **down** under it 3782
21:13 and s opposite him and brought charges 3782
2Ki 4:20 the boy s on her lap until noon, 3782
1Ch 17:16 in and s before the LORD, and he said: 3782
29:23 So Solomon s on the throne of the LORD 3782
Ezr 9:3 from my head and beard and s **down** 3782
9:4 And I s there appalled until 3782
10:16 the first day of the tenth month *they* s **down** 3782
Ne 1:4 *I* s **down** and wept. 3782
Est 3:15 The king and Haman s **down** to drink, 3782
Job 2:8 and scraped himself with it as he s among 3782
2:13 Then *they* s on the ground with him 3782
29:25 the way for them and s as their chief; 3782
Ps 9:4 *you have* s on your throne, 3782
107:10 *Some* s *in* darkness and the deepest gloom, 3782
137:1 By the rivers of Babylon *we* s and wept 3782
Jer 3:2 By the roadside *you* s **waiting** for lovers, 3782
3:2 s like a nomad in the desert. NIH
15:17 *I* never s in the company of revelers, 3782
15:17 *I* s alone because your hand was on me 3782
Eze 3:15 *I* s among them for seven days— 3782
14:1 the elders of Israel came to me and s **down** 3782
20:1 and *they* s **down** in front of me. 3782
23:41 *You* s on an elegant couch, 3782
Jnh 3:6 covered himself with sackcloth and s **down** 3782
4:5 Jonah went out and s **down** at a place east 3782
4:5 s in its shade and waited to see 3782
Zec 5:7 and there in the basket s a woman! 3782
Mt 5:1 he went up on a mountainside and s **down.** *2767*
13:1 went out of the house and s by the lake. *2764*
13:2 around him that he got into a boat and s *2764*
13:48 Then they s **down** and collected *2767*
15:29 *he* went up on a mountainside and s **down.** *2764*
21:7 and Jesus s on them. *2125*
26:55 Every day *I* s in the temple courts *2757*
26:58 *He* entered and s **down** with the guards *2764*
28:2 rolled back the stone and s on it. *2764*
Mk 4:1 that he got into a boat and s in it out on *2764*
6:40 So *they* s **down** in groups of hundreds *404*
11:7 threw their cloaks over it, *he* s on it. *2767*
12:41 Jesus s **down** opposite the place where *2767*
14:54 There *he* s with the guards *1639+5153*
16:19 up into heaven and *he* s at the right hand *2767*
Lk 4:20 gave it back to the attendant and s **down.** *2767*
5:3 Then he s **down** and taught the people from *2767*
7:15 The dead man s **up** and began to talk, *361*
9:15 The disciples did so, and everybody s **down.** *2884*
10:39 who s at the Lord's feet listening *4149*
22:55 of the courtyard and *had* s **down together,** *5154*
22:55 Peter s **down** with them. *2764*
Jn 4:6 s **down** by the well. *2757*
6:3 went up on a mountainside and s **down** *2764*
6:10 and the men s **down,** about five thousand *404*
8:2 and *he* s **down** to teach them. *2767*
12:14 Jesus found a young donkey and s upon it, *2767*
19:13 he brought Jesus out and s **down** on *2767*
Ac 9:40 and seeing Peter *she* s **up.** *361*
12:21 wearing his royal robes, s on his throne *2767*
13:14 they entered the synagogue and s **down.** *2767*
14:8 In Lystra *there* s a man crippled in his feet, *2764*
16:13 We s **down** and began to speak to *2767*
1Co 10:7 "The people s **down** to eat and drink and got *2767*
Heb 1:3 *he* s **down** at the right hand of the Majesty *2767*
8:1 We do have such a high priest, who s **down** *2767*
10:12 *he* s **down** at the right hand of God. *2767*
12:2 and s **down** at the right hand of the throne *2767*
Rev 3:21 as I overcame and s **down** with my Father *2767*
4:3 And the one who s there had the appearance *2764*
5:1 Then I saw in the right hand *of* him who s *2764*
5:7 the scroll from the right hand *of* him who s *2764*

SATAN (53) [SATAN'S]

1Ch 21:1 S rose up against Israel and incited David 8477
Job 1:6 and S also came with them. 8477
1:7 The LORD said to S, "Where have you come 8477
1:7 S answered the LORD, "From roaming 8477
1:8 the LORD said to S, "Have you considered 8477
1:9 Job fear God for nothing?" S replied. 8477
1:12 The LORD said to S, "Very well, then, 8477
1:12 Then S went out from the presence of 8477
2:1 and S also came with them 8477
2:2 the LORD said to S, "Where have you come 8477
2:2 S answered the LORD, "From roaming 8477
2:3 the LORD said to S, "Have you considered 8477
2:4 "Skin for skin!" S replied. 8477
2:6 The LORD said to S, "Very well, then, 8477
2:7 So S went out from the presence of 8477
Zec 3:1 S standing at his right side to accuse him. 8477
3:2 The LORD said to S, "The LORD rebuke you, 8477
3:2 "The LORD rebuke you, S! 8477
Mt 4:10 Jesus said to him, "Away from me, S! *4928*
12:26 If S drives out Satan, *4928*
12:26 If Satan drives out S, *4928*
16:23 and said to Peter, "Get behind me, S! *4928*
Mk 1:13 forty days, being tempted by S. *4928*
3:23 "How can S drive out Satan? *4928*
3:23 "How can Satan drive out S? *4928*
3:26 And if S opposes himself and is divided, *4928*

Mk 4:15 S comes and takes away the word 4928
8:33 "Get behind me, S!" he said. 4928
Lk 10:18 "I saw S fall like lightning from heaven. 4928
11:18 If S is divided against himself, 4928
13:16 this woman, whom S has kept bound 4928
22:3 Then S entered Judas, called Iscariot, 4928
22:31 Simon, S has asked to sift you as wheat. 4928
Jn 13:27 S entered into him. 4928
Ac 5:3 how is it that S has so filled your heart 4928
26:18 and from the power *of* S to God, 4928
Ro 16:20 of peace will soon crush S under your feet. 4928
1Co 5:5 hand this man over *to* S, 4928
7:5 Then come together again so that S will 4928
2Co 2:11 in order that S might not outwit us. 4928
11:14 S himself masquerades as an angel of light. 4928
12:7 a messenger *of* S, to torment me. 4928
1Th 2:18 but S stopped us. 4928
2Th 2:9 in accordance with the work *of* S displayed 4928
1Ti 1:20 whom I have handed over *to* S to be taught 4928
5:15 in fact already turned away to follow S. 4928
Rev 2:9 but are a synagogue *of* S. 4928
2:13 where you live—where S has his throne. 4928
2:13 in your city—where S lives. 4928
3:9 *of* S, who claim to be Jews though they are 4928
12:9 that ancient serpent called the devil, or S, 4928
20:2 that ancient serpent, who is the devil, or S, 4928
20:7 S will be released from his prison 4928

SATAN'S (1) [SATAN]

Rev 2:24 have not learned S so-called deep secrets 4928

SATED (1) [SATISFY]

La 3:15 with bitter herbs and s me with gall. 8115

SATIATE, SATIATED (KJV) See SATISFY, SATISFIED

SATISFACTION (4) [SATISFY]

Est 5:13 But all this **gives** me no s as long as I see 8750
Ecc 2:24 to eat and drink and find s in his work. 3202
3:13 and find s in all his toil— 3202
5:18 to find s in his toilsome labor under the sun 3208

SATISFIED (42) [SATISFY]

Ex 18:23 and all these people will go home s." 928+8934
Lev 10:20 Moses heard this, he *was* s. 928+3512+6524
26:26 You will eat, but *you will* not *be* s. 8425
Dt 6:11 then when you eat and *are* s, 8425
8:10 When you have eaten and *are* s, 8425
8:12 Otherwise, when you eat and *are* s, 8425
11:15 and you will eat and *be* s. 8425
14:29 in your towns may come and eat and *be* s, 8425
26:12 so that they may eat in your towns and *be* s. 8425
Ps 17:15 *I will be* s *with* seeing your likeness. 8425
22:26 The poor will eat and *be* s; 8425
59:15 wander about for food and howl if not s. 8425
63:5 My soul *will be* s as *with* the richest 8425
104:13 the earth *is* s by the fruit of his work. 8425
104:28 *they are* s *with* good things. 8425
105:40 and he brought them quail and s them *with* 8425
Pr 13:4 but the desires of the diligent **are fully** s. 2014
18:20 *with* the harvest from his lips *he is* s. 8425
27:20 Death and Destruction *are* never s, 8425
30:15 "There are three things *that are* never s, 8425
30:16 land, *which is* never s *with* water, and fire, 8425
Ecc 5:10 whoever loves wealth is never s NIH
6:7 yet his appetite **is** never s. 4848
Isa 9:20 on the left they will eat, but not *be* s. 8425
53:11 he will see the light [of life] and *be* s; 8425
66:11 and *be* s at her comforting breasts; 8425
Jer 46:10 The sword will devour till *it is* s, 8425
50:19 *be* s on the hills of Ephraim and Gilead. 8425
Eze 16:28 and even after that, *you* still *were* not s. 8425
16:29 but even with this *you were* not s. 8425
27:33 *you* s many nations; 8425
Hos 13:6 When I fed them, *they were* s; 8425
13:6 *when they were* s, they became proud; 8425
Mic 6:14 You will eat but not *be* s; 8425
Hab 2:5 as the grave and like death is never s, 8425
Mt 14:20 *They* all ate and *were* s, 5963
15:37 *They* all ate and *were* s. 5963
Mk 6:42 They all ate and *were* s, 5963
8:8 The people ate and *were* s. 5963
Lk 6:21 who hunger now, for *you will be* s. 5963
9:17 They all ate and *were* s, 5963
3Jn 1:10 Not s with that, he refuses to welcome 758

SATISFIES (3) [SATISFY]

Ps 103:5 who s your desires with good things so 8425
107:9 for *he* s the thirsty and fills the hungry 8425
147:14 He grants peace to your borders and s you 8425

SATISFY (18) [SATED, SATISFACTION, SATISFIED, SATISFIES]

Job 38:27 to s a desolate wasteland and make it sprout 8425
38:39 for the lioness and s the hunger of the lions 4848
Ps 81:16 with honey from the rock *I would* s you." 8425
90:14 S us in the morning with your unfailing love 8425
91:16 *With* long life *will I* s him 8425
132:15 her poor *will I* s *with* food. 8425
145:16 and s the desires of every living thing. 8425
Pr 5:19 *may* her breasts s you always, 8115
6:30 to s his hunger when he is starving. 4848
Isa 55:2 and your labor on *what* does not s? 8429
58:10 in behalf of the hungry and s the needs of 8425
58:11 *he will* s your needs in a sun-scorched land 8425
Jer 31:14 *I will* s the priests *with* abundance, 8115
31:25 I will refresh the weary and s the faint." 4848
Eze 7:19 not s their hunger or fill their stomachs 8425
Joel 2:19 new wine and oil, *enough to* s you **fully**; 8425
Mt 28:14 we *will* s him and keep you out of trouble." 4275
Mk 15:15 Wanting *to* s the crowd, 2653+4472

SATRAPS (13)

Ezr 8:36 delivered the king's orders to the royal s 346
Est 3:12 Haman's orders to the king's s, 346
8:9 Mordecai's orders to the Jews, and to the s, 346
9:3 And all the nobles of the provinces, the s, 346
Da 3:2 He then summoned the s, prefects, 10026
3:3 So the s, prefects, governors, advisers, 10026
3:27 and the s, prefects, governors 10026
6:1 It pleased Darius to appoint 120 s to rule 10026
6:2 The s were made accountable to them so 10026
6:3 and the s by his exceptional qualities that 10026
6:4 and the s tried to find grounds for charges 10026
6:6 the administrators and the s went as a group 10026
6:7 The royal administrators, prefects, s, 10026

SATYRS (KJV) See WILD GOATS

SAUL (373) [SAUL'S]

1Sa 9:2 He had a son named S, 8620
9:3 and Kish said to his son S, 8620
9:5 S said to the servant who was with him, 8620
9:7 S said to his servant, "If we go, 8620
9:10 "Good," S said to his servant. 8620
9:15 Now the day before S came, 8620
9:17 When Samuel caught sight of S, 8620
9:18 S approached Samuel in the gateway 8620
9:21 S answered, "But am I not a Benjamite, 8620
9:22 Then Samuel brought S and his servant 8620
9:24 with what was on it and set it in front of S. 8620
9:24 And S dined with Samuel that day. 8620
9:25 Samuel talked with S on the roof 8620
9:26 about daybreak and Samuel called to S on 8620
9:26 When S got ready, he and Samuel went 8620
9:27 Samuel said to S, "Tell the servant to go on 8620
10:9 As S turned to leave Samuel, 2257S
10:11 Is S also among the prophets?" 8620
10:12 "Is S also among the prophets?" 8620
10:13 After S stopped prophesying, NIH
10:16 S replied, "He assured us that 8620
10:21 Finally S son of Kish was chosen. 8620
10:26 S also went to his home in Gibeah, 8620
10:27 But S kept silent. NIH
11:4 of S and reported these terms to the people, 8620
11:5 Just then S was returning from the fields, 8620
11:6 When S heard their words, 8620
11:7 the oxen of anyone who does not follow S 8620
11:8 When S mustered them at Bezek, NIH
11:11 The next day S separated his men 8620
11:12 'Shall S reign over us?' 8620
11:13 But S said, "No one shall be put 8620
11:15 and confirmed S as king in the presence of 8620
11:15 and S and all the Israelites held 8620
13:1 S was [thirty] years old when he became 8620
13:2 S chose three thousand men from Israel; 8620
13:3 Then S had the trumpet blown throughout 8620
13:4 "S has attacked the Philistine outpost, 8620
13:4 people were summoned to join S at Gilgal. 8620
13:7 S remained at Gilgal, 8620
13:9 And S offered up the burnt offering. NIH
13:10 and S went out to greet him. 8620
13:11 S replied, "When I saw that the men were 8620
13:15 and S counted the men who were with him. 8620
13:16 S and his son Jonathan and the men 8620
13:22 on the day of the battle not a soldier with S 8620
13:22 only S and his son Jonathan had them. 8620
14:1 One day Jonathan son of S said to 8620
14:2 S was staying on the outskirts of Gibeah 8620
14:17 Then S said to the men who were with him, 8620
14:18 S said to Ahijah, "Bring the ark of God." 8620
14:19 While S was talking to the priest, 8620
14:19 S said to the priest, "Withdraw your hand." 8620
14:20 Then S and all his men assembled 8620
14:21 over to the Israelites who were with S 8620
14:24 S had bound the people under an oath, 8620
14:33 Then someone said to S, "Look, 8620
14:35 Then S built an altar to the LORD; 8620
14:36 S said, "Let us go down after 8620
14:37 So S asked God, "Shall I go down after 8620
14:38 S therefore said, "Come here, 8620
14:40 S then said to all the Israelites, NIH
14:41 Then S prayed to the LORD, 8620
14:41 And Jonathan and S were taken by lot, 8620
14:42 S said, "Cast the lot between me 8620
14:43 Then S said to Jonathan, 8620
14:44 S said, "May God deal with me, 8620
14:45 the men said to S, "Should Jonathan die— 8620
14:46 Then S stopped pursuing the Philistines, 8620
14:47 After S had assumed rule over Israel, 8620
14:52 All the days of S there was bitter war with 8620
14:52 whenever S saw a mighty or brave man, 8620
15:1 said to S, "I am the one the LORD sent 8620
15:4 So S summoned the men 8620
15:5 S went to the city of Amalek and set 8620
15:7 Then S attacked the Amalekites all the way 8620
1Sa 15:9 But S and the army spared Agag and 8620
15:11 "I am grieved that I have made S king, 8620
15:12 Samuel got up and went to meet S, 8620
15:12 but he was told, "S has gone to Carmel. 8620
15:13 When Samuel reached him, S said, 8620
15:15 S answered, "The soldiers brought them 8620
15:16 "Stop!" Samuel said to S. 8620
15:16 "Tell me," S replied. NIH
15:20 "But I did obey the LORD," S said. 8620
15:24 Then S said to Samuel, "I have sinned. 8620
15:27 S caught hold of the hem of his robe, NIH
15:30 S replied, "I have sinned. NIH
15:31 So Samuel went back with S, 8620
15:31 and S worshiped the LORD. 8620
15:34 S went up to his home in Gibeah of Saul. 8620
15:34 Saul went up to his home in Gibeah of S. 8620
15:35 he did not go to see S again, 8620
15:35 that he had made S king over Israel. 8620
16:1 "How long will you mourn for S, 8620
16:2 S will hear about it and kill me." 8620
16:14 Spirit of the LORD had departed from S, 8620
16:17 So S said to his attendants, 8620
16:19 Then S sent messengers to Jesse and said, 8620
16:20 and sent them with his son David to S. 8620
16:21 David came to S and entered his service. 8620
16:21 S liked him very much, NIH
16:22 Then S sent word to Jesse, saying, 8620
16:23 the spirit from God came upon S, 8620
16:23 Then relief would come to S; 8620
17:2 S and the Israelites assembled and camped 8620
17:8 and are you not the servants of S? 8620
17:11 S and all the Israelites were dismayed 8620
17:13 Jesse's three oldest sons had followed S to 8620
17:14 The three oldest followed S, 8620
17:15 and forth from S to tend his father's sheep 8620
17:19 They are with S and all the men of Israel in 8620
17:31 was overheard and reported to S, 8620
17:31 and S sent for him. NIH
17:32 to S, "Let no one lose heart on account 8620
17:33 S replied, "You are not able to go out 8620
17:34 But David said to S, "Your servant 8620
17:37 S said to David, "Go, and the LORD be 8620
17:38 Then S dressed David in his own tunic. 8620
17:39 "I cannot go in these," he said to S, 8620
17:55 As S watched David going out to meet 8620
17:57 Abner took him and brought him before S, 8620
17:58 "Whose son are you, young man?" S asked 8620
18:1 After David had finished talking with S, 8620
18:2 that day S kept David with him and did 8620
18:5 Whatever S sent him to do, 8620
18:5 so successfully that S gave him a high rank 8620
18:6 from all the towns of Israel to meet King S 8620
18:7 "S has slain his thousands, 8620
18:8 S was very angry; this refrain galled him. 8620
18:9 that time on S kept a jealous eye on David. 8620
18:10 from God came forcefully upon S. 8620
18:10 S had a spear in his hand 8620
18:12 S was afraid of David, because the LORD 8620
18:12 the LORD was with David but had left S. 8620
18:15 When S saw how successful he was, 8620
18:17 S said to David, "Here is my older daughter 8620
18:17 S said to himself, "I will not raise a hand 8620
18:18 But David said to S, "Who am I, 8620
18:20 and when they told S about it, 8620
18:21 So S said to David, "Now you have 8620
18:22 Then S ordered his attendants: 8620
18:25 S replied, "Say to David, 8620
18:27 Then S gave him his daughter Michal 8620
18:28 When S realized that the LORD was with 8620
18:29 S became still more afraid of him, 8620
19:1 S told his son Jonathan and all 8620
19:2 "My father S is looking for a chance 8620
19:4 of David to S his father and said to him, 8620
19:6 S listened to Jonathan and took this oath: 8620
19:7 He brought him to S, and David was with 8620
19:7 and David was with S as before. 2257S
19:9 an evil spirit from the LORD came upon S 8620
19:10 S tried to pin him to the wall 8620
19:10 but David eluded him as S drove the spear 8620
19:11 S sent men to David's house to watch it 8620
19:14 When S sent the men to capture David, 8620
19:15 Then S sent the men back to see David 8620
19:17 S said to Michal, "Why did you deceive me 8620
19:18 at Ramah and told him all that S had done 8620
19:19 Word came to S: "David is in Naioth 8620
19:21 S was told about it, and he sent more men, 8620
19:21 S sent men a third time, 8620
19:23 So S went to Naioth at Ramah. NIH
19:24 "Is S also among the prophets?" 8620
20:25 opposite Jonathan, and Abner sat next to S, 8620
20:26 S said nothing that day, for he thought, 8620
20:27 Then S said to his son Jonathan, 8620
20:33 But S hurled his spear at him to kill him. 8620
21:10 from S and went to Achish king of Gath. 8620
21:11 " 'S has slain his thousands, 8620
22:6 Now S heard that David and his men 8620
22:6 And S, spear in hand, was seated 8620
22:7 S said to them, "Listen, men of Benjamin! 8620
22:12 S said, "Listen now, son of Ahitub." 8620
22:13 S said to him, "Why have you conspired 8620
22:21 that S had killed the priests of the LORD. 8620
22:22 I knew he would be sure to tell S. 8620
23:7 S was told that David had gone to Keilah, 8620
23:8 And S called up all his forces for battle, 8620
23:9 When David learned that S was plotting 8620
23:10 that S plans to come to Keilah and destroy 8620
23:11 Will S come down, as your servant has 8620

1Sa 23:12 of Keilah surrender me and my men to S?" 8620
23:13 When S was told that David had escaped 8620
23:14 Day after day S searched for him, 8620
23:15 that S had come out to take his life. 8620
23:17 "My father S will not lay a hand on you. 8620
23:17 Even my father S knows this." 8620
23:19 The Ziphites went up to S at Gibeah 8620
23:21 S replied, "The LORD bless you 8620
23:24 they set out and went to Ziph ahead of S. 8620
23:25 S and his men began the search, 8620
23:25 When S heard this, he went into the Desert 8620
23:26 S was going along one side of 8620
23:26 hurrying to get away from S. 8620
23:26 As S and his forces were closing in 8620
23:27 a messenger came to S, 8620
23:28 Then S broke off his pursuit of David 8620
24: 1 After S returned from pursuing 8620
24: 2 So S took three thousand chosen men 8620
24: 3 and S went in to relieve himself. 8620
24: 7 and did not allow them to attack S. 8620
24: 7 And S left the cave and went his way. 8620
24: 8 went out of the cave and called out to S, 8620
24: 8 When S looked behind him, 8620
24: 9 He said to S, "Why do you listen 8620
24:16 When David finished saying this, S asked, 8620
24:22 So David gave his oath to S. 8620
24:22 Then S returned home, but David 8620
25:44 But S had given his daughter Michal, 8620
26: 1 The Ziphites went to S at Gibeah and said, 8620
26: 2 So S went down to the Desert of Ziph, 8620
26: 3 S made his camp beside the road on the hill 8620
26: 3 he saw that S had followed him there, 8620
26: 4 and learned that S had definitely arrived. 8620
26: 5 and went to the place where S had camped. 8620
26: 5 He saw where S and Abner son of Ner, 8620
26: 5 S was lying inside the camp, 8620
26: 6 will go down into the camp with me to S?" 8620
26: 7 and there was S, lying asleep 8620
26:17 S recognized David's voice and said, 8620
26:21 Then S said, "I have sinned. 8620
26:25 Then S said to David, "May you be blessed 8620
26:25 and S returned home. 8620
27: 1 be destroyed by the hand of S. 8620
27: 1 Then S will give up searching 8620
27: 4 S was told that David had fled to Gath, 8620
28: 3 S had expelled the mediums and spiritists 8620
28: 4 while S gathered all the Israelites and set 8620
28: 5 S saw the Philistine army, he was afraid; 8620
28: 7 S then said to his attendants, 8620
28: 8 So S disguised himself, 8620
28: 9 "Surely you know what S has done. 8620
28:10 S swore to her by the LORD, 8620
28:12 at the top of her voice and said to S, 8620
28:12 you deceived me? You are S!" 8620
28:14 Then S knew it was Samuel, 8620
28:15 Samuel said to S, "Why have you disturbed 8620
28:15 "I am in great distress," S said. 8620
28:20 Immediately S fell full length on 8620
28:21 to S and saw that he was greatly shaken, 8620
28:25 Then she set it before S and his men, 8620
29: 3 who was an officer of S king of Israel? 8620
29: 3 and from the day he left S until now, NIH
29: 5 " 'S has slain his thousands, 8620
31: 2 The Philistines pressed hard after S 8620
31: 3 The fighting grew fierce around S, 8620
31: 4 S said to his armor-bearer, 8620
31: 4 so S took his own sword and fell on it. 8620
31: 5 the armor-bearer saw that S was dead, 8620
31: 6 S and his three sons and his armor-bearer 8620
31: 7 that the Israelite army had fled and that S 8620
31: 8 they found S and his three sons fallen 8620
31:11 of what the Philistines had done to S, 8620
31:12 the bodies of S and his sons from the wall 8620
2Sa 1: 1 After the death of S, David returned 8620
1: 4 And S and his son Jonathan are dead." 8620
1: 5 that S and his son Jonathan are dead?" 8620
1: 6 "and there was S, leaning on his spear, 8620
1:12 till evening for S and his son Jonathan, 8620
1:17 David took up this lament concerning S 8620
1:21 the shield of S—no longer rubbed with oil. 8620
1:22 the sword of S did not return unsatisfied. 8620
1:23 "S and Jonathan—in life they were loved 8620
1:24 "O daughters of Israel, weep for S, 8620
2: 4 of Jabesh Gilead who had buried S, 8620
2: 5 for showing this kindness to S your master 8620
2: 7 for S your master is dead, 8620
2: 8 of S and brought him over to Mahanaim. 8620
2:10 Ish-Bosheth son of S was forty years old 8620
2:12 with the men of Ish-Bosheth son of S, 8620
2:15 for Benjamin and Ish-Bosheth son of S, 8620
3: 1 between the house of S and the house 8620
3: 1 the house of S grew weaker and weaker. 8620
3: 6 During the war between the house of S and 8620
3: 6 his own position in the house of S. 8620
3: 7 Now S had had a concubine named Rizpah 8620
3: 8 the house of your father S and to his family 8620
3:10 the house of S and establish David's throne 8620
3:13 unless you bring Michal daughter of S 8620
3:14 sent messengers to Ish-Bosheth son of S, 8620
4: 1 of S heard that Abner had died in Hebron, 8620
4: 4 (Jonathan son of S had a son who was lame 8620
4: 4 when the news about S and Jonathan came 8620
4: 8 "Here is the head of Ish-Bosheth son of S, 8620
4: 8 the king against S and his offspring." 8620
4:10 when a man told me, 'S is dead,' 8620
5: 2 In the past, while S was king over us, 8620
6:16 Michal daughter of S watched from 8620
2Sa 6:20 Michal daughter of S came out to meet him 8620
6:23 And Michal daughter of S had no children 8620
7:15 as I took it away from S, 8620
9: 1 "Is there anyone still left of the house of S 8620
9: 3 of S to whom I can show God's kindness?" 8620
9: 6 the son of S, came to David, 8620
9: 7 that belonged to your grandfather S, 8620
9: 9 that belonged to S and his family. 8620
12: 7 and I delivered you from the hand of S. 8620
16: 8 the blood you shed in the household of S, 8620
21: 1 of S and his blood-stained house; 8620
21: 2 but S in his zeal for Israel and Judah 8620
21: 4 to demand silver or gold from S 8620
21: 6 before the LORD at Gibeah of S— 8620
21: 7 Mephibosheth son of Jonathan, the son of S, 8620
21: 7 between David and Jonathan son of S. 8620
21: 8 whom she had borne to S, 8620
21:12 of S and his son Jonathan from the citizens 8620
21:12 after they struck S down on Gilboa.) 8620
21:13 of S and his son Jonathan from there, 8620
21:14 the bones of S and his son Jonathan in 8620
22: 1 of all his enemies and from the hand of S. 8620
1Ch 8:33 Kish the father of S, 8620
8:33 and S the father of Jonathan, Malki-Shua, 8620
9:39 Kish the father of S, 8620
9:39 and S the father of Jonathan, Malki-Shua, 8620
10: 2 The Philistines pressed hard after S 8620
10: 3 The fighting grew fierce around S, 8620
10: 4 S said to his armor-bearer, 8620
10: 4 so S took his own sword and fell on it. 8620
10: 5 the armor-bearer saw that S was dead, 8620
10: 6 So S and his three sons died, 8620
10: 7 and that S and his sons had died, 8620
10: 8 they found S and his sons fallen 8620
10:11 of everything the Philistines had done to S, 8620
10:12 and took the bodies of S and his sons 8620
10:13 S died because he was unfaithful to 8620
11: 2 In the past, even while S was king, 8620
12: 1 banished from the presence of S son of Kish 8620
12: 2 they were kinsmen of S from the tribe 8620
12:19 with the Philistines to fight against S. 8620
12:19 if he deserts to his master S.") 8620
13: 3 not inquire of it during the reign of S." 8620
15:29 Michal daughter of S watched from 8620
26:28 by Samuel the seer and by S son of Kish, 8620
Ps 18: T of all his enemies and from the hand of S. 8620
52: T the Edomite had gone to S and told him: 8620
54: T When the Ziphites had gone to S and said, 8620
57: T When he had fled from S into the cave. 8620
59: T When S had sent men to watch David's 8620
Isa 10:29 Ramah trembles; Gibeah of S flees. 8620
Ac 7:58 at the feet *of* a young man named S. *4930*
8: 1 S was there, giving approval to his death. *4930*
8: 3 But S began to destroy the church. *4930*
9: 1 S was still breathing out murderous threats *4930*
9: 4 "S, Saul, why do you persecute me?" *4910*
9: 4 "Saul, S, why do you persecute me?" *4910*
9: 5 "Who are you, Lord?" S asked. *NIG*
9: 7 with S stood there speechless; *899S*
9: 8 S got up from the ground, *4930*
9:11 and ask for a man from Tarsus named S, *4930*
9:17 Placing his hands on S, he said, *899S*
9:17 he said, "Brother S, the Lord— *4930*
9:19 S spent several days with the disciples *NIG*
9:22 Yet S grew more and more powerful *4930*
9:24 but S learned of their plan. *4930*
9:27 how S on his journey had seen the Lord *NIG*
9:28 So S stayed with them and moved *NIG*
11:25 Barnabas went to Tarsus to look for S, *4930*
11:26 for a whole year **Barnabas and** S met with *899S*
11:30 their gift to the elders by Barnabas and S. *4930*
12:25 Barnabas and S had finished their mission, *4930*
13: 1 up with Herod the tetrarch) and S. *4930*
13: 2 "Set apart for me Barnabas and S for *4930*
13: 7 sent for Barnabas and S because he wanted *4930*
13: 9 Then S, who was also called Paul, *4930*
13:21 and he gave them S son of Kish, *4930*
13:22 After removing S, he made David their king *899S*
22: 7 and heard a voice say to me, 'S! *4910*
22: 7 and heard a voice say to me, 'Saul! S! *4910*
22:13 He stood beside me and said, 'Brother S, *4910*
26:14 'S, Saul, why do you persecute me? *4910*
26:14 'Saul, S, why do you persecute me? *4910*

SAUL'S (43) [SAUL]

1Sa 9: 3 belonging to S father Kish were lost, 8620
10: 1 and poured it on S head and kissed him, 2257S
10: 9 God changed S heart, 2257S
10:14 Now S uncle asked him and his servant, 8620
10:15 S uncle said, "Tell me what Samuel said 8620
13: 8 and S men began to scatter. 2021S
14:16 S lookouts at Gibeah in Benjamin saw 4200+8620
14:49 S sons were Jonathan, Ishvi and 8620
14:50 the commander of S army was Abner son 8620
14:50 and Ner was S uncle. 8620
14:51 S father Kish and Abner's father Ner were 8620
16:15 S attendants said to him, "See, 8620
17:12 in S time he was old and well advanced 8620
18: 5 and S officers as well. 8620
18:19 when the time came for Merab, S daughter, 8620
18:20 S daughter Michal was in love with David, 8620
18:24 S servants told him what David had said, 8620
18:25 S plan was to have David fall by the hands 8620
18:30 more success than the rest of S officers, 8620
19:20 upon S men and they also prophesied. 8620
20:30 S anger flared up at Jonathan and he said 8620
1Sa 21: 7 Now one of S servants was there that day, 8620
21: 7 Doeg the Edomite, S head shepherd. 4200+8620
22: 9 who was standing with S officials, said, 8620
23:16 And S son Jonathan went to David 8620
24: 4 and cut off a corner of S robe. 4200+8620
26:12 the spear and water jug near S head, 8620
2Sa 1: 2 the third day a man arrived from S camp, 8620
2: 8 the commander of S army, 4200+8620
4: 2 Now S son had two men who were leaders 8620
9: 2 a servant of S household named Ziba. 8620
9: 9 Then the king summoned Ziba, S servant, 8620
16: 5 from the same clan as S family came out 8620
19:17 the steward of S household, 8620
19:24 Mephibosheth, S grandson, 8620
21: 8 with the five sons of S daughter Merab, 8620
21:11 Rizpah, S concubine, had done, 8620
21:14 in the tomb of S father Kish, 2257S
1Ch 5:10 During S reign they waged war against 8620
12:23 to David at Hebron to turn S kingdom over 8620
12:29 men of Benjamin, S kinsmen—3,000 8620
12:29 of whom had remained loyal to S house 8620
Ac 9:18 something like scales fell from S eyes, *899S*

SAVAGE (2)

Lev 26: 6 I will remove s beasts from the land, 8273
Ac 20:29 s wolves will come in among you and will *987*

SAVE (190) [SAFE, SAFELY, SAFETY, SALVATION, SAVED, SAVES, SAVING, SAVIOR]

Ge 32:11 S me, I pray, from the hand of my brother 5911
45: 5 because it was to s **lives** that God sent me 4695
45: 7 and to s your **lives** by a great deliverance. 2649
Ex 16:23 S whatever is left and keep it 5663
Nu 31:18 but s for yourselves every girl who has never slept with a man. 2649
Dt 4:42 into one of these cities and s *his* **life.** 2649
19: 4 and flees there *to* s *his* **life—** 2649
19: 5 to one of these cities and s *his* **life.** 2649
Jos 2:13 and that *you will* s us from death." 5911
10: 6 Come up to us quickly and s us! 3828
Jdg 6:14 in the strength you have and s Israel out 3828
6:15 Gideon asked, "how *can I* s Israel? 3828
6:31 *Are* you *trying to* s him? 3828
6:36 "If you will s Israel by my hand 3828
6:37 then I will know that *you will* s Israel 3828
7: 7 *I will* s you and give the Midianites 3828
10: 1 the son of Dodo, rose to s Israel. 3828
10:12 *did I* not s you from their hands? 3828
10:13 so I will no longer s you. 3828
10:14 *Let* them s you when you are in trouble!" 3828
12: 2 *you* didn't s me out of their hands. 3828
1Sa 4: 3 and s us from the hand of our enemies." 3828
10:27 "How *can* this fellow s us?" 3828
23: 2 "Go, attack the Philistines and s Keilah." 3828
2Sa 22: 3 from violent men *you* s me. 3828
22:28 *You* s the humble, 3828
22:42 but there was no *one to* s them— 4635
1Ki 1:12 how *you can* s your own life and the life 4880
2Ki 16: 7 up and s me out of the hand of the king 3828
18:35 has been able *to* s his land from me? 5911
19:34 I will defend this city and s it, 3828
1Ch 16:35 Cry out, "S us, O God our Savior; 3828
2Ch 20: 9 and you will hear us and s us.' 3828
25:15 not s their own people from your hand?" 5911
32:11 'The LORD our God *will* s us from 5911
32:14 has been able to s his people from me? 5911
Ne 6:11 like me go into the temple *to* s *his* **life?** 2649
Job 20:20 *he* cannot s *himself* by his treasure. 4880
22:29 then *he will* s the downcast. 3828
40:14 to you that your own right hand *can* s you. 3828
Ps 6: 4 s me because of your unfailing love. 3828
7: 1 s and deliver me from all who pursue me, 3828
17: 7 the wonder of your great love, you *who* s 3828
17:14 by your hand s me from such men, NIH
18:27 You s the humble 3828
18:41 but there was no *one to* s them— 3828
20: 9 O LORD, s the king! 3828
22:21 s me from the horns of the wild oxen. 6699
28: 9 S your people and bless your inheritance; 3828
31: 2 a strong fortress to s me. 3828
31:16 s me in your unfailing love. 3828
33:17 despite all its great strength *it* cannot s. 4880
39: 8 S me from all my transgressions; 5911
40:13 Be pleased, O LORD, to s me; 5911
51:14 S me from bloodguilt, O God, 5911
54: 1 S me, O God, by your name; 3828
59: 2 Deliver me from evildoers and s me 3828
60: 5 S us and help us with your right hand, 3828
69: 1 S me, O God, for the waters have come up 3828
69:35 for God *will* s Zion and rebuild the cities 3828
70: 1 Hasten, O God, to s me; 5911
71: 2 turn your ear to me and s me. 3828
71: 3 give the command to s me, 3828
72: 4 the people and s the children of the needy; 3828
72:13 on the weak and the needy and s the needy 3828
76: 9 to s all the afflicted of the land. 3828
80: 2 Awaken your might; come and s us. 3802
86: 2 s your servant who trusts in you. 3828
86:16 grant your strength to your servant and s 3828
89:48 or s himself from the power of the grave? 4880
91: 3 Surely he *will* s you from the fowler's 5911
106: 4 come to my aid when you s them, 3802
106:47 S us, O LORD our God, 3828
108: 6 S us and help us *with* your right hand, 3828

Ps 109:26 s me in accordance with your love. 3828
109:31 to s his life from those who condemn him. 3828
116: 4 "O LORD, s me!" 4880
118:25 s us; O LORD, grant us success. 3828
119:94 S me, for I am yours; 3828
119:146 s me and I will keep your statutes. 3828
120: 2 S me, O LORD, from lying lips and 5911
138: 7 *with* your right hand *you* s me. 3828
146: 3 in mortal men, who cannot **s.** 9591
Pr 2:12 Wisdom *will* s you from the ways 5911
2:16 It *will* s you also from the adulteress, 5911
23:14 with the rod and s his soul from death. 5911
Isa 33:22 it is he *who will* s us. 3828
35: 4 divine retribution he will come *to* s you." 3828
36:20 has been able *to* s his land from me? 5911
37:35 "I will defend this city and s it, 3828
38:20 The LORD *will* s me, 3828
44:17 He prays to it and says, **"S** me; 5911
44:20 *he* cannot s himself, or say, 5911
45:20 who pray to gods *that* cannot **s.** 3828
46: 7 *it* cannot s him from his troubles. 3828
47:13 *let them* s you from what is coming 3828
47:14 They cannot even s themselves from 5911
47:15 there is not *one that can* s you. 3828
49:25 and your children I *will* **s.** 3828
57:13 *let* your collection [of idols] s you! 5911
59: 1 the arm of the LORD is not too short *to* **s,** 3828
63: 1 speaking in righteousness, mighty to **s."** 3828
Jer 2:27 they say, 'Come and s us!' 3828
2:28 if *they can* s you when you are in trouble! 3828
14: 9 like a warrior powerless to **s?** 3828
15:20 for I am with you to rescue and s you," 5911
15:21 *"I will* s you from the hands of the wicked 5911
17:14 s me and I will be saved, 3828
30:10 'I *will* surely s you out of a distant place, 3828
30:11 I am with you and *will* s you,' 3828
31: 7 s your people, the remnant of Israel.' 3828
39:18 *I will* s you; you will not fall 4880+4880
42:11 with you and *will* s you and deliver you 3828
46:27 I *will* surely s you out of a distant place, 3828
La 4:17 for a nation *that could* not s us. 3828
Eze 3:18 from his evil ways in order to s his **life,** 2649
7:19 to s them in the day of the LORD's wrath. 5911
13:21 I will tear off your veils and s my people 5911
13:22 from their evil ways and so s their **lives,** 2649
13:23 *I will* s my people from your hands. 5911
14:14 were in it, they *could* s only themselves 5911
14:16 not s their own sons or daughters. 5911
14:18 not s their own sons or daughters. 5911
14:20 *they could* s neither son nor daughter. 5911
14:20 They *would* s only themselves 5911
18:27 does what is just and right, he *will* s his life. 2649
33:12 of the righteous man *will* not s him 5911
34:22 *I will* s my flock, 3828
36:29 *I will* s you from all your uncleanness. 3828
37:23 for *I will* s them from all their sinful 3828
Da 3:17 the God we serve is able to s us from it, 10706
3:29 for no other god can s in this way." 10489
6:14 made every effort until sundown to s him. 10489
Hos 1: 7 and *I will* s them—not by bow, 3828
13:10 Where is your king, that *he may* s you? 3828
14: 3 Assyria cannot s us; 3828
Am 2:14 and the warrior *will* not s his life. 4880
2:15 and the horseman *will* not s his life. 4880
Mic 2: 3 from which *you* cannot s yourselves. 4631
6:14 You will store up but s nothing, 7117
6:14 what *you* s I will give to the sword. 7117
Hab 1: 2 but *you do* not **s?** 3828
3:13 to s your anointed one. 3829
Zep 1:18 to s them on the day of the LORD's wrath. 5911
3:17 *he is* mighty *to* **s.** 3828
Zec 8: 7 "I *will* s my people from the countries of 3828
8:13 O Judah and Israel, so *will I* s you, 3828
9:16 The LORD their God *will* s them on 3828
10: 6 "I will strengthen the house of Judah and s 3828
12: 7 "The LORD *will* s the dwellings 3828
Mt 1:21 he *will* s his people from their sins." *5392*
8:25 and woke him, saying, "Lord, s us! *5392*
14:30 beginning to sink, cried out, "Lord, s me!" *5392*
16:25 For whoever wants *to* s his life will lose it, *5392*
27:40 and build it in three days, s yourself! *5392*
27:42 they said, "but he can't s himself! *5392*
27:49 Let's see if Elijah comes *to* s him." *5392*
Mk 3: 4 *to* s life or to kill?" *5392*
8:35 For whoever wants *to* s his life will lose it, *5392*
8:35 for me and for the gospel *will* s it. *5392*
15:30 come down from the cross and s yourself!" *5392*
15:31 they said, "but he can't s himself! *5392*
Lk 6: 9 *to* s life or to destroy it?" *5392*
9:24 For whoever wants *to* s his life will lose it, *5392*
9:24 but whoever loses his life for me *will* s it. *5392*
19:10 to seek and *to* s what was lost." *5392*
23:35 *let him* s himself if he is the Christ of God, *5392*
23:37 "If you are the king of the Jews, s yourself." *5392*
23:39 S yourself and us!" *5392*
Jn 3:17 but to s the world through him. *5392*
12: 7 that *she should* s this perfume for the day *5498*
12:27 'Father, s me from this hour'? *5392*
12:47 not come to judge the world, but to s it. *5392*
Ac 2:40 and he pleaded with them, **"S** *yourselves* *5392*
Ro 11:14 my own people to envy and s some of them. *5392*
1Co 1:21 *to* s those who believe. *5392*
7:16 wife, whether *you will* s your husband? *5392*
7:16 husband, whether *you will* s your wife? *5392*
9:22 that by all possible means *I might* s some. *5392*
2Co 12:14 not have *to* s **up** for their parents, *2564*
1Ti 1:15 Jesus came into the world *to* s sinners— *5392*
1Ti 4:16 *you will* s both yourself and your hearers. *5392*
Heb 5: 7 to the one who could s him from death, *5392*
7:25 *to* s completely those who come to God *5392*
11: 7 in holy fear built an ark to s his family. *5401*
Jas 1:21 the word planted in you, which can s you. *5392*
2:14 Can such faith s him? *5392*
4:12 the one who is able *to* s and destroy. *5392*
5:20 of his way *will* s him from death and cover *5392*
Jude 1:23 snatch others from the fire and s them; *5392*

SAVED (109) [SAVE]

Ge 47:25 *"You have* s our **lives,"** they said. 2649
Ex 14:30 the LORD s Israel from the hands of 3828
16:24 So *they* s it until morning, 5663
18: 4 *he* s me from the sword of Pharaoh." 5911
18: 8 the way and how the LORD *had* s them. 5911
Dt 33:29 Who is like you, a people s by the LORD? 3828
Jos 9:26 So Joshua s them from the Israelites, 5911
Jdg 2:16 *who* s them out of the hands of these raiders. 3828
2:18 with the judge and s them out of the hands 3828
3: 9 Caleb's younger brother, *who* s them. 3828
3:31 He too s Israel. 3828
7: 2 against me that her own strength *has* s her, 3828
8:22 *you have* s us out of the hand of Midian." 3828
1Sa 23: 5 the Philistines and s the people of Keilah. 3828
2Sa 19: 5 who *have* just s your life and the lives 4880
22: 4 and **I am** s from my enemies. 3828
2Ki 14:27 *he* s them by the hand of Jeroboam son 3828
2Ch 32:22 So the LORD s Hezekiah and the people 3828
Job 26: 2 How *you have* s the arm that is feeble! 3828
Ps 18: 3 and *I* **am** s from my enemies. 3828
22: 5 They cried to you and **were s;** 4880
33:16 No king **is** s by the size of his army; 3828
34: 6 *he* s him out of all his troubles. 3828
80: 3 your face shine upon us, that *we may* **be s.** 3828
80: 7 your face shine upon us, that *we may* **be s.** 3828
80:19 your face shine upon us, that *we may* **be s.** 3828
106: 8 Yet *he* s them for his name's sake, 3828
106:10 *He* s them from the hand of the foe; 3828
106:21 They forgot the God *who* s them, 3828
107:13 and *he* s them from their distress. 3828
107:19 and *he* s them from their distress. 3828
116: 6 when I was in great need, *he* s me. 3828
Ecc 9:15 and he s the city by his wisdom. 4880
Isa 25: 9 we trusted in him, and *he* s us. 3828
43:12 I have revealed and s and proclaimed— 3828
45:17 But Israel *will* **be** s by the LORD with 3828
45:22 "Turn to me and **be s,** 3828
63: 9 and the angel of his presence s them. 3828
64: 5 How then *can we* **be s?** 3828
Jer 4:14 wash the evil from your heart and **be s.** 3828
8:20 the summer has ended, and we **are** not **s."** 3828
17:14 save me and *I will* **be s,** 3828
23: 6 In his days Judah *will* **be** s 3828
30: 7 but *he will* **be** s out of it. 3828
33:16 In those days Judah *will* **be** s 3828
Eze 3:19 but you *will have* s yourself. 5911
3:21 and you *will have* s yourself." 5911
14:16 They alone *would* **be s,** 5911
14:18 They alone *would* **be s.** 5911
33: 5 *he would have* s himself. 4880
33: 9 but you *will have* s yourself. 5911
Joel 2:32 calls on the name of the LORD *will* **be s;** 4880
Am 3:12 so *will* the Israelites **be s,** 5911
Mt 10:22 he who stands firm to the end *will be* **s.** *5392*
19:25 "Who then can *be* **s?"** *5392*
24:13 he who stands firm to the end *will be* **s.** *5392*
27:42 *"He* s others," they said, *5392*
Mk 10:26 "Who then can *be* **s?"** *5392*
13:13 he who stands firm to the end *will be* **s.** *5392*
15:31 *"He* s others," they said, *5392*
16:16 Whoever believes and is baptized *will be* **s,** *5392*
Lk 7:50 "Your faith *has* s you; go in peace." *5392*
8:12 so that *they may* not believe and *be* **s.** *5392*
13:23 *are* only a few people *going to be* **s?"** *5392*
18:26 "Who then can *be* **s?"** *5392*
23:35 They said, *"He* s others; *5392*
Jn 2:10 but you *have* s the best till now." *5498*
5:34 but I mention it that you *may be* **s.** *5392*
10: 9 whoever enters through me *will be* **s.** *5392*
Ac 2:21 on the name of the Lord *will be* **s.'** *5392*
2:47 the Lord added to their number daily those
who *were being* **s.** *5392*
4:12 given to men by which we must *be* **s."** *5392*
11:14 and all your household *will be* **s.'** *5392*
15: 1 taught by Moses, you cannot *be* **s."** *5392*
15:11 the grace of our Lord Jesus that *we are* **s,** *5392*
16:17 who are telling you the way to **be s."** *5401*
16:30 "Sirs, what must I do to *be* **s?"** *5392*
16:31 believe in the Lord Jesus, and *you will be* s *5392*
27:20 we finally gave up all hope *of being* **s.** *5392*
27:31 you cannot *be* **s."** *5392*
Ro 5: 9 *be* s from God's wrath through him! *5392*
5:10 *shall we be* s through his life! *5392*
8:24 For in this hope *we were* **s.** *5392*
9:27 only the remnant *will be* **s.** *5392*
10: 1 for the Israelites is that they may **be s.** *1650+5401*
10: 9 raised him from the dead, *you will be* **s.** *5392*
10:10 your mouth that you confess and **are s.** *1650+5401*
10:13 calls on the name of the Lord *will be* **s."** *5392*
11:26 And so all Israel *will be* **s,** as it is written: *5392*
1Co 1:18 but *to us* who *are being* s it is the power *5392*
3:15 *he* himself *will be* **s,** *5392*
5: 5 and his spirit s on the day of the Lord. *5392*
10:33 so that *they may be* **s.** *5392*
15: 2 By this gospel *you are* **s,** *5392*
2Co 2:15 of Christ among those who *are being* s *5392*
Eph 2: 5 it is by grace *you have been* **s.** *1639+5392*
2: 8 For it is by grace *you have been* **s,** *1639+5392*
Php 1:28 but that you will be **s**—and that by God. *5401*
1Th 2:16 to the Gentiles so that *they may be* **s.** *5392*
2Th 2:10 to love the truth and so *be* **s.** *5392*
2:13 from the beginning God chose you to **be s** *5401*
1Ti 2: 4 who wants all men *to be* s and to come to *5392*
2:15 women *will be* s through childbearing— *5392*
2Ti 1: 9 who *has* s us and called us to a holy life— *5392*
Tit 3: 5 *he* s us, not because of righteous things *5392*
3: 5 He s us through the washing of rebirth *NIG*
Heb 10:39 of those who believe and are s. *1650+4348+6034*
1Pe 3:20 eight in all, *were* **s through** water, *1407*
4:18 And, "If it is hard for the righteous *to be* **s,** *5392*

SAVES (20) [SAVE]

1Sa 10:19 who s you out of all your calamities 3828
17:47 not by sword or spear that the LORD **s;** 3828
Job 5:15 *He* s the needy from the sword 3828
5:15 he s them from the clutches of NIH
Ps 7:10 *who* s the upright in heart. 3828
18:48 *who* s me from my enemies. 7117
20: 6 Now I know that the LORD s his anointed; 3828
34:18 and s those who are crushed in spirit. 3828
37:40 from the wicked and s them, 3828
51:14 O God, the God who s me, 9591
55:16 But I call to God, and the LORD s me. 3828
57: 3 He sends from heaven and s me, 3828
68:20 Our God is a God who s; 4636
88: 1 O LORD, the God who s me, 3802
145:19 he hears their cry and s them. 3828
Pr 14:25 A truthful witness s lives, 5911
Da 6:27 He rescues and *he* **s;** 10489
Am 3:12 "As a shepherd s from the lion's mouth 5911
1Pe 3:21 symbolizes baptism that now s you also— *5392*
3:21 It s you by the resurrection of Jesus Christ, *NIG*

SAVING (5) [SAVE]

Ge 50:20 is now being done, the s *of* many lives. 2649
1Sa 14: 6 Nothing can hinder the LORD from **s,** 3828
Ps 20: 6 from his holy heaven with the s power 3829
22: 1 Why are you so far from s me, 3802
1Co 16: 2 in keeping with his income, s it up, so that *NIG*

SAVIOR (55) [SAVE]

Dt 32:15 and rejected the Rock his **S.** 3802
2Sa 22: 3 He is my stronghold, my refuge and my **s**— 4635
22:47 Exalted be God, the Rock, my **S!** 3829
1Ch 16:35 Cry out, "Save us, O God our **S;** 3829
Ps 18:46 Exalted be God my **S!** 3829
24: 5 and vindication from God his **S.** 3829
25: 5 for you are God my **S,** 3829
27: 9 O God my **S.** 3829
38:22 Come quickly to help me, O Lord my **S.** 9591
42: 5 in God, for I will yet praise him, my **S** and 3802
42:11 my **S** and my God. 3802
43: 5 my **S** and my God. 3802
65: 5 O God our **S,** the hope of all the ends of the 3829
68:19 Praise be to the Lord, to God our **S,** 3802
79: 9 Help us, O God our **S,** 3829
85: 4 Restore us again, O God our **S,** 3829
89:26 my God, the Rock my **S.'** 3802
Isa 17:10 You have forgotten God your **S;** 3829
19:20 he will send them a s and defender, 4635
43: 3 your God, the Holy One of Israel, your **S;** 4635
43:11 and apart from me there is no **s.** 4635
45:15 O God and **S** of Israel. 4635
45:21 a righteous God and a **S;** 4635
49:26 the LORD, am your **S,** your Redeemer, 4635
60:16 the LORD, am your **S,** your Redeemer, 4635
62:11 the Daughter of Zion, 'See, your **S** comes! 3829
63: 8 and so he became their **S.** 4635
Jer 14: 8 O Hope of Israel, its **S** in times of distress, 4635
Hos 13: 4 no **S** except me. 4635
Mic 7: 7 I wait for God my **S;** 3829
Hab 3:18 I will be joyful in God my **S.** 3829
Lk 1:47 and my spirit rejoices in God my **S,** *5400*
2:11 in the town of David a **S** has been born *5400*
Jn 4:42 that this man really is the **S** of the world." *5400*
Ac 5:31 to his own right hand as Prince and **S** *5400*
13:23 God has brought to Israel the **S** Jesus, *5400*
Eph 5:23 his body, of which he is the **S.** *5400*
Php 3:20 And we eagerly await a **S** from there, *5400*
1Ti 1: 1 *of* God our **S** and *of* Christ Jesus our hope, *5400*
2: 3 This is good, and pleases God our **S,** *5400*
4:10 who is the **S** of all men, *5400*
2Ti 1:10 through the appearing *of* our **S,** *5400*
Tit 1: 3 to me by the command of God our **S,** *5400*
1: 4 the Father and Christ Jesus our **S.** *5400*
2:10 the teaching *about* God our **S** attractive. *5400*
2:13 appearing *of* our great God and **S,** *5400*
3: 4 kindness and love of God our **S** appeared, *5400*
3: 6 through Jesus Christ our **S,** *5400*
2Pe 1: 1 and **S** Jesus Christ have received a faith *5400*
1:11 of our Lord and **S** Jesus Christ. *5400*
2:20 and **S** Jesus Christ and are again entangled *5400*
3: 2 and the command given *by* our Lord and **S** *5400*
3:18 *of* our Lord and **S** Jesus Christ. *5400*
1Jn 4:14 that the Father has sent his Son to be the **S** *5400*
Jude 1:25 *to* the only God our **S** be glory, *5400*

SAVOUR (KJV) See AROMA

SAVOURY (KJV) See TASTY

SAW (604) [SEE]

Ge 1: 4 God s that the light was good, 8011
1:10 And God s that it was good. 8011
1:12 And God s that it was good. 8011
1:18 And God s that it was good. 8011
1:21 And God s that it was good. 8011
1:25 And God s that it was good. 8011
1:31 God s all that he had made, 8011
3: 6 When the woman s that the fruit of 8011
6: 2 the sons of God s that the daughters 8011
6: 5 The LORD s how great man's wickedness 8011
6:12 God s how corrupt the earth had become, 8011
8:13 from the ark and s that the surface of 8011
9:22 s his father's nakedness and told his two 8011
12:14 the Egyptians s that she was a very beautiful 8011
12:15 And when Pharaoh's officials s her, 8011
13:10 Lot looked up and s that the whole plain of 8011
18: 2 up and s three men standing nearby. 8011
18: 2 When *he* s them, he hurried from the 8011
19: 1 When he s them, he got up to meet them 8011
19:28 and *he* s dense smoke rising from the land, 8011
21: 9 But Sarah s that the son whom Hagar 8011
21:19 Then God opened her eyes and *she* s a well 8011
22: 4 On the third day Abraham looked up and s 8011
22:13 up and there in a thicket *he* s a ram caught 8011
24:63 *he* s camels approaching. 8011
24:64 Rebekah also looked up and s Isaac. 8011
26: 8 and s Isaac caressing his wife Rebekah. 8011
26:28 *"We* s **clearly** that the LORD was 8011+8011
28:12 a dream in which *he* s a stairway resting on 2180
29: 2 There *he* s a well in the field, 8011
29:10 When Jacob s Rachel daughter of Laban, 8011
29:31 the LORD s that Leah was not loved, 8011
30: 1 When Rachel s that she was not bearing 8011
30: 9 Leah s that she had stopped having children, 8011
31:10 up and s *that* the male goats mating with 2180
32: 2 When Jacob s them, he said, 8011
32:25 the man s that he could not overpower him, 8011
32:30 saying, "It is because *I* s God face to face, 8011
33: 5 Then Esau looked up and s the women 8011
34: 2 s her, he took her and violated her. 8011
37: 4 When his brothers s that their father loved 8011
37:18 But *they* s him in the distance, 8011
37:25 up and s a caravan of Ishmaelites coming 8011
37:29 the cistern and s *that* Joseph was not there, 2180
38:14 For *she* s that, though Shelah had now 8011
38:15 When Judah s her, he thought she was 8011
39: 3 When his master s that the LORD was 8011
39:13 When she s that he had left his cloak 8011
40: 6 *he* s that they were dejected. 8011
40: 9 "In my dream I s a vine in front of me, 2180
40:16 the chief baker s that Joseph had given 8011
41:22 "In my dreams *I* also s seven heads 8011
42: 7 As soon as Joseph s his brothers, 8011
42:21 *We* s how distressed he was 8011
42:27 and *he* s his silver in the mouth of his sack. 8011
42:35 they and their father s the money pouches, 8011
43:16 When Joseph s Benjamin with them, 8011
43:29 looked about and s his brother Benjamin, 8011
45:27 and when *he* s the carts Joseph had sent 8011
48: 8 When Israel s the sons of Joseph, he asked, 8011
48:17 Joseph s his father placing his right hand 8011
50:11 When the Canaanites who lived there s 8011
50:15 When Joseph's brothers s that their father 8011
50:23 and s the third generation of Ephraim's 8011
Ex 2: 2 When *she* s that he was a fine child, 8011
2: 5 *She* s the basket among the reeds 8011
2: 6 She opened it and s the baby. 8011
2:11 *He* s an Egyptian beating a Hebrew, 8011
2:13 and s two Hebrews fighting. 2180
3: 2 Moses s that though the bush was 8011
3: 4 the LORD s that he had gone over to look, 8011
8:15 But when Pharaoh s that there was relief, 8011
9:34 When Pharaoh s that the rain and hail 8011
14:30 and Israel s the Egyptians lying dead on 8011
14:31 And when the Israelites s the great power 8011
16:15 When the Israelites s it, 8011
18:14 When his father-in-law s all that Moses 8011
20:18 the people s the thunder and lightning 8011
20:18 and lightning and heard the trumpet and s NIH
24:10 and s the God of Israel. 8011
24:11 *they* s God, and they ate and drank. 2600
32: 1 When the people s that Moses was so long 8011
32: 5 When Aaron s this, he built an altar 8011
32:19 When Moses approached the camp and s 8011
32:25 Moses s that the people were running wild 8011
33:10 the people s the pillar of cloud standing at 8011
34:30 When Aaron and all the Israelites s Moses, 8011
34:35 they s that his face was radiant. 8011
39:43 the work and s that they had done it just as 2180
Lev 9:24 And when all the people s it, 8011
Nu 12:10 toward her and s that she had leprosy; 2180
13:28 *We* even s descendants of Anak there. 8011
13:32 All the people *we* s there are of great size. 8011
13:33 *We* s the Nephilim there (the descendants 8011
14:22 not one of the men who s my glory and 8011
17: 8 of the Testimony and s that Aaron's staff, 2180
22: 2 of Zippor s all that Israel had done to 8011
22:23 When the donkey s the angel of the LORD 8011
22:25 the donkey s the angel of the LORD, 8011
22:27 the donkey s the angel of the LORD, 8011
Nu 22:31 and *he* s the angel of the LORD standing in 8011
22:33 The donkey s me and turned away 8011
22:41 and from there *he* s part of the people. 8011
24: 1 when Balaam s that it pleased the LORD 8011
24: 2 and s Israel encamped tribe by tribe, 8011
24:20 Balaam s Amalek and uttered his oracle: 8011
24:21 Then *he* s the Kenites and uttered his oracle: 8011
25: 7 the priest, s this, he left the assembly, 8011
32: 1 s that the lands of Jazer and Gilead 8011
Dt 1:28 *We* even s the Anakites there.'" 8011
1:31 There *you* s how the LORD your God 8011
4: 3 You s with your own eyes what 8011
4:12 the sound of words but s no form; 8011
4:15 *You* s no form of any kind the day 8011
7:19 *You* s with your own eyes the great trials, 8011
9:16 I s that you had sinned against 2180
10:21 and awesome wonders you s 8011
11: 2 that your children *were* not *the ones* who s 8011
11: 5 not your children who s what he did for you NIH
11: 7 that s all these great things 8011
26: 7 LORD heard our voice and s our misery, 8011
29: 3 With your own eyes *you* s those great trials, 8011
29:17 *You* s among them their detestable images 8011
32:19 The LORD s this and rejected them 8011
Jos 5:13 he looked up and s a man standing in front 8011
7:21 When *I* s in the plunder a beautiful robe 8011
8:14 When the king of Ai s this, 8011
8:20 The men of Ai looked back and s the smoke 2180
8:21 and all Israel s that the ambush had taken 8011
24: 7 *You* s with your own eyes what I did to 8011
Jdg 1:24 the spies s a man coming out of the city 8011
3:25 There they s their lord fallen to the floor, 2180
9:36 When Gaal s them, he said to Zebul, "Look, 8011
9:43 *he* s the people coming out of the city, 8011
9:55 the Israelites s that Abimelech was dead, 8011
11:35 When he s her, he tore his clothes 8011
12: 3 When *I* s that you wouldn't help, 8011
14: 1 Samson went down to Timnah and s there 8011
16: 1 where *he* s a prostitute. 8011
16:18 Delilah s that he had told her everything, 8011
16:24 When the people s him, 8011
17: 6 everyone did as he s fit. 928+6524
18: 7 where *they* s that the people were living 8011
19: 3 and when her father s him, 8011
19:17 When he looked and s the traveler in 8011
19:30 Everyone who s it said, 8011
20:36 the Benjamites s that they were beaten. 8011
20:40 and s the smoke of the whole city going up 2180
21:25 everyone did as he s fit. 928+6524
Ru 2:18 and her mother-in-law s how much she 8011
1Sa 5: 7 the men of Ashdod s what was happening, 8011
6:13 and when they looked up and s the ark, 8011
6:16 of the Philistines s all this and then returned 8011
10:11 had formerly known him s him prophesying 8011
10:14 "But when *we* s they were not to be found, 8011
12:12 "But when you s that Nahash king of 8011
13: 6 of Israel s that their situation was critical 8011
13:11 "When *I* s that the men were scattering, 8011
14:16 Saul's lookouts at Gibeah in Benjamin s 8011
14:26 they s the honey oozing out, 2180
14:52 whenever Saul s a mighty or brave man, 8011
16: 6 Samuel s Eliab and thought, 8011
17:24 When the Israelites s the man, 8011
17:42 over and s that he was only a boy, 8011
17:51 the Philistines s that their hero was dead, 8011
18:15 When Saul s how successful he was, 8011
19: 5 and *you* s it and were glad. 8011
19:20 *they* s a group of prophets prophesying, 8011
22: 9 "*I* s the son of Jesse come to Ahimelech son 8011
25:23 When Abigail s David, 8011
26: 3 When *he* s that Saul had followed him there, 8011
26: 5 He s where Saul and Abner son of Ner, 8011
26:12 No *one* s or knew about it, 8011
28: 5 Saul s the Philistine army, he was afraid; 8011
28:12 When the woman s Samuel, 8011
28:21 to Saul and s that he was greatly shaken, 8011
31: 5 the armor-bearer s that Saul was dead, 8011
31: 7 the valley and those across the Jordan s that 8011
2Sa 1: 7 When he turned around and s me, 8011
6:16 when *she* s King David leaping and dancing 8011
10: 9 Joab s that there were battle lines in front 8011
10:14 When the Ammonites s that the Arameans 8011
10:15 the Arameans s that they had been routed 8011
10:19 of Hadadezer s that they had been defeated 8011
11: 2 From the roof *he* s a woman bathing. 8011
13:34 and s many people on the road west of him, 8011
17:18 But a young man s them and told Absalom. 8011
17:23 When Ahithophel s that his advice had 8011
18:10 When one of the men s this, he told Joab, 8011
18:10 "*I* just s Absalom hanging in an oak tree." 8011
18:11 "What? *You* s him? Why didn't you strike 8011
18:24 As he looked out, *he* s a man running alone. 8011
18:26 Then the watchman s another man running, 8011
18:29 "*I* s great confusion just as Joab was about 8011
20:12 and the man s that all the troops came to 8011
24:17 When David s the angel who was striking 8011
24:20 When Araunah looked and s the king 8011
1Ki 3:21 I s that it wasn't the son I had borne." 2180
3:28 because *they* s that he had wisdom 8011
4:27 **s to it that** nothing **was lacking.** 6372
7: 9 to size and trimmed with a s on their inner 4490
10: 4 When the queen of Sheba s all the wisdom 8011
10: 7 not believe these things until I came and s 8011
11:28 and when Solomon s how well 8011
12:16 When all Israel s that the king refused 8011
13:25 by s the body thrown down there, 8011
16:18 When Zimri s that the city was taken, 8011
1Ki 18:17 When he s Elijah, he said to him, 8011
18:39 When all the people s this, 8011
22:17 "*I* s all Israel scattered on the hills 8011
22:19 *I* s the LORD sitting on his throne 8011
22:32 the chariot commanders s Jehoshaphat, 8011
22:33 the chariot commanders s that he was not 8011
2Ki 2:12 Elisha s this and cried out, "My father! 8011
2:12 And Elisha s him no more. 8011
3:26 the king of Moab s that the battle had gone 8011
4:25 When he s her in the distance, 8011
5:21 When Naaman s him running toward him, 8011
6:17 and he looked and s the hills full of horses 2180
6:21 When the king of Israel s them, 8011
9:17 in Jezreel s Jehu's troops approaching, 8011
9:22 When Joram s Jehu he asked, 8011
9:26 'Yesterday *I* s the blood of Naboth and 8011
9:27 king of Judah s what had happened, 8011
11: 1 When Athaliah the mother of Ahaziah s 8011
12:10 Whenever they s that there was 8011
13: 4 for *he* s how severely the king of Aram 8011
13:21 suddenly *they* s a band of raiders; 8011
16:10 *He* s an altar in Damascus and sent to Uriah 8011
16:12 the king came back from Damascus and s 8011
20:15 "*They* s everything in my palace," 8011
23:16 and when *he* s the tombs that were there on 8011
1Ch 10: 5 the armor-bearer s that Saul was dead, 8011
10: 7 When all the Israelites in the valley s that 8011
15:29 *she* s King David dancing and celebrating, 8011
19:10 Joab s that there were battle lines in front 8011
19:15 When the Ammonites s that the Arameans 8011
19:16 the Arameans s that they had been routed 8011
19:19 of Hadadezer s that they had been defeated 8011
21:15 the LORD s it and was grieved because of 8011
21:16 up and s the angel of the LORD standing 8011
21:20 he turned and s the angel; 8011
21:21 and when Araunah looked and s him, 8011
21:28 when David s that the LORD had answered 8011
2Ch 7: 3 the Israelites s the fire coming down and 8011
9: 3 queen of Sheba s the wisdom of Solomon, 8011
9: 6 until I came and s *with* my own eyes. 8011
10:16 When all Israel s that the king refused NIH
12: 7 the LORD s that they humbled themselves, 8011
13:14 and s that they were being attacked at 2180
15: 9 when they s that the LORD his God was 8011
18:16 "*I* s all Israel scattered on the hills 8011
18:18 *I* s the LORD sitting on his throne 8011
18:31 the chariot commanders s Jehoshaphat, 8011
18:32 when the chariot commanders s that he was 8011
20:24 they s only dead bodies lying on 2180
22:10 When Athaliah the mother of Ahaziah s 8011
24:11 the king's officials and they s that there was 8011
26:20 they s that he had leprosy on his forehead, 2180
31: 8 and his officials came and s the heaps, 8011
32: 2 Hezekiah s that Sennacherib had come 8011
Ezr 3:12 wept aloud when they s the foundation 928+6524
Ne 9: 9 "*You* s the suffering of our forefathers 8011
13:15 In those days *I* s men in Judah treading 8011
13:23 in those days *I* s men of Judah who had 8011
Est 2:15 Esther won the favor of everyone *who* s her. 8011
3: 5 When Haman s that Mordecai would 8011
5: 2 When he s Queen Esther standing in 8011
5: 9 But when he s Mordecai at the king's gate 8011
Job 2:12 When *they* s him from a distance, 906+5951+6524
2:13 because *they* s how great his suffering was. 8011
3:16 like an infant who never s the light of day? 8011
8:18 '*I* never s you.' 8011
10:18 I wish I had died before any eye s me. 8011
20: 9 The eye *that* s him will not see him again; 8812
29: 8 the young men s me and stepped aside and 8011
29:11 and those *who* s me commended me, 8011
32: 5 But when he s that the three men had 8011
42:16 *he* s his children and their children to 8011
Ps 31: 7 for *you* s my affliction and knew 8011
48: 5 they s [her] and were astounded; 8011
73: 3 the arrogant *when I* s the prosperity of 8011
77:16 The waters s you, O God, 8011
77:16 O God, the waters s you and writhed; 8011
107:24 They s the works of the LORD, 8011
139:16 your eyes s my unformed body. 8011
Pr 7: 7 *I* s among the simple, 8011
24:32 and learned a lesson from what *I* s: 8011
Ecc 2:13 I s that wisdom is better than folly, 8011
3:16 And *I* s something else under the sun: 8011
3:22 So *I* s that there is nothing better for 8011
4: 1 Again I looked and s all the oppression 8011
4: 1 I s the tears of the oppressed— 2180
4: 4 And I s that all labor and all achievement 8011
4: 7 Again I s something meaningless under 8011
4:15 *I* s that all who lived and walked under 8011
6: 5 *it* never s the sun or knew anything, 8011
8: 9 All this *I* s, as I applied my mind 8011
8:10 Then too, *I* s the wicked buried— 8011
8:17 then *I* s all that God has done. 8011
9:13 *I* also s under the sun this example 8011
SS 6: 9 The maidens s her and called her blessed; 8011
Isa 1: 1 that Isaiah son of Amoz s during the reigns 2600
2: 1 This is what Isaiah son of Amoz s 2600
5: 7 And he looked for justice, but s bloodshed; 2180
6: 1 *I* s the Lord seated on a throne, 8011
10:15 or the s boast against him who uses it? 5373
13: 1 that Isaiah son of Amoz s: 2600
22: 9 *you* s that the City of David had many 8011
39: 4 "*They* s everything in my palace," 8011
59:16 *He* s that there was no one, 8011
Jer 3: 7 and her unfaithful sister Judah s it. 8011
3: 8 Yet *I* s that her unfaithful sister Judah had 8011
18: 3 and I s him working at the wheel. 2180

Jer 23:13 prophets of Samaria I s this repulsive thing: 8011
39: 4 and all the soldiers s them, they fled; 8011
41:13 with him s Johanan son of Kareah and 8011
44: 2 You s the great disaster I brought 8011
La 1:10 she s pagan nations enter her sanctuary— 8011
Eze 1: 1 the heavens were opened and I s visions 8011
1: 4 I s a windstorm coming out of the north— 2180
1:15 I s a wheel on the ground 2180
1:27 I s that from what appeared to be his waist 8011
1:28 When I s it, I fell facedown, 8011
2: 9 I looked, and I s a hand stretched out to me. 2180
8: 2 I looked, and I s a figure like that of a man. 2180
8: 5 the gate of the altar I s this idol of jealousy. 2180
8: 7 I looked, and I s a hole in the wall. 2180
8: 8 I dug into the wall and s a doorway there. NIH
8:10 and I s portrayed all over the walls all kinds 2180
8:14 and I s women sitting there, 2180
9: 2 And I s six men coming from the direction 2180
10: 1 and I s the likeness of a throne of sapphire 2180
10: 9 and I s beside the cherubim four wheels, 2180
11: 1 and I s among them Jaazaniah son 8011
13:16 and s **visions** of peace for her 2600+2606
16: 6 " 'Then I passed by and s you kicking about 8011
16: 8 and s that you were old enough for love, 2180
19: 5 " 'When she s her hope unfulfilled, 8011
20:28 and they s any high hill or any leafy tree, 8011
23:11 "Her sister Oholibah s this, 8011
23:13 I s that she too defiled herself; 8011
23:14 She s men portrayed on a wall, 8011
23:16 As soon as she s them, 5260+6524
37: 2 and I s a great many bones on the floor of 2180
40: 3 and I s a man whose appearance was 2180
40: 5 I s a wall completely surrounding 2180
40:17 There I s some rooms and a pavement 2180
40:24 to the south side and I s a gate facing south. 2180
41: 8 I s that the temple had a raised base all 8011
43: 2 and I s the glory of the God 2180
43: 3 The vision I s was like the vision 8011
44: 4 and s the glory of the LORD filling 2180
46:21 and I s in each corner another court. 2180
47: 1 and I s water coming out from under 2180
47: 7 I s a great number of trees on each side of 2180
Da 2:26 "Are you able to tell me what I s 10255
2:41 as you s that the feet and toes were partly 10255
2:41 even as you s iron mixed with clay. 10255
2:43 as you s the iron mixed with baked clay, 10255
3:27 They s that the fire had not harmed 10255
4:10 the visions I s while lying in my bed: 10646
4:13 "In the visions I s while lying in my bed, 10646
4:20 The tree you s, which grew large and 10255
4:23 "You, O king, s a messenger, a holy one, 10255
8: 2 In my vision I s myself in the citadel 8011
8: 7 I s him attack the ram furiously, 8011
8:20 The two-horned ram that you s represents 8011
10: 7 I, Daniel, was the only one who s the vision; 8011
Hos 5:13 "When Ephraim s his sickness, 8011
9:10 when I s your fathers, 8011
Am 1: 1 what he s concerning Israel two years 2600
9: 1 I s the Lord standing by the altar, 8011
Jnh 3:10 When God s what they did and 8011
Mic 1: 1 the **vision** he s concerning Samaria 2600
Hab 3: 7 I s the tents of Cushan in distress, 8011
3:10 the mountains s you and writhed. 8011
Hag 2: 3 'Who of you is left who s this house 8011
Mt 2: 2 We s his star in the east and have come 3972
2:10 When they s the star, they were overjoyed. 3972
2:11 they s the child with his mother Mary, 3972
3: 7 But when he s many of the Pharisees 3972
3:16 and he s the Spirit of God descending like 3972
4:18 the Sea of Galilee, he s two brothers, 3972
4:21 he s two other brothers, 3972
5: 1 Now when he s the crowds, 3972
8:14 he s Peter's mother-in-law lying in bed with 3972
8:18 When Jesus s the crowd around him, 3972
8:34 And when they s him, they pleaded 3972
9: 2 When Jesus s their faith, 3972
9: 8 When the crowd s this, 3972
9: 9 he s a man named Matthew sitting at 3972
9:11 When the Pharisees s this, 3972
9:22 Jesus turned and s her. 3972
9:23 the ruler's house and s the flute players and 3972
9:36 When he s the crowds, he had compassion 3972
12: 2 When the Pharisees s this, they said to him, 3972
14:14 When Jesus landed and s a large crowd, 3972
14:26 the disciples s him walking on the lake, 3972
14:30 But when he s the wind, he was afraid and, 1063
15:31 The people were amazed when they s 1063
17: 8 they s no one except Jesus. 3972
18:31 the other servants s what had happened, 3972
20: 3 and s others standing in the marketplace 3972
21:15 of the law s the wonderful things he did and 3972
21:20 When the disciples s this, they were amazed. 3972
21:32 And even after you s this, 3972
21:38 "But when the tenants s the son, 3972
26: 8 When the disciples s this, 3972
26:71 where another girl s him and said to 3972
27: 3 s that Jesus was condemned, 3972
27:24 When Pilate s that he was getting nowhere, 3972
27:54 with him who were guarding Jesus s 3972
28:17 When they s him, they worshiped him; 3972
Mk 1:10 he s heaven being torn open and 3972
1:16 he s Simon and his brother Andrew casting 3972
1:19 he s James son of Zebedee 3972
2: 5 When Jesus s their faith, 3972
2:14 he s Levi son of Alphaeus sitting at 3972
2:16 who were Pharisees s him eating with the 3972
3:11 Whenever the evil spirits s him, 2555
Mk 5: 6 When he s Jesus from a distance, 3972
5:15 they s the man who had been possessed by 2555
5:38 Jesus s a commotion, 2555
6:33 many who s them leaving recognized them 3972
6:34 When Jesus landed and s a large crowd, 3972
6:48 He s the disciples straining at the oars, 3972
6:49 but when they s him walking on the lake, 3972
6:50 because they all s him and were terrified. 3972
7: 2 s some of his disciples eating food 3972
8:25 and he s everything clearly. 1838
9: 8 they no longer s anyone with them 3972
9:14 they s a large crowd around them and 3972
9:15 As soon as all the people s Jesus, 3972
9:20 When the spirit s Jesus, 3972
9:25 When Jesus s that a crowd was running to 3972
9:38 "we s a man driving out demons 3972
10:14 When Jesus s this, he was indignant. 3972
11:20 they s the fig tree withered from the roots. 3972
12:34 When Jesus s that he had answered wisely, 3972
14:67 When she s Peter warming himself, 3972
14:69 When the servant girl s him there, 3972
15:39 heard his cry and s how he died, he said, 3972
15:47 the mother of Joses s where he was laid. 2555
16: 4 when they looked up, they s that the stone, 2555
16: 5 they s a young man dressed in 3972
Lk 1:12 When Zechariah s him, he was startled 3972
2:48 When his parents s him, they were astonished. 3972
5: 2 he s at the water's edge two boats, 3972
5: 8 When Simon Peter s this, 3972
5:12 When he s Jesus, he fell with his face to 3972
5:20 When Jesus s their faith, he said, "Friend, 3972
5:27 Jesus went out and s a tax collector by 2517
7:13 When the Lord s her, his heart went out 3972
7:39 the Pharisee who had invited him s this, 3972
8:28 When he s Jesus, he cried out 3972
8:34 the pigs s what had happened, 3972
9:32 they s his glory and the two men standing 3972
9:49 "we s a man driving out demons 3972
9:54 When the disciples James and John s this, 3972
10:18 "I s Satan fall like lightning from heaven. 2555
10:31 and when he s the man, 3972
10:32 when he came to the place and s him, 3972
10:33 and when he s him, he took pity on him. 3972
13:12 When Jesus s her, he called her forward 3972
15:20 his father s him and was filled 3972
16:23 he looked up and s Abraham far away, 3972
17:14 When he s them, he said, "Go, 3972
17:15 One of them, when he s he was healed, 3972
18:15 When the disciples s this, 3972
18:43 all the people s it, they also praised God. 3972
19: 7 All the people s this and began to mutter, 3972
19:41 As he approached Jerusalem and s the city, 3972
20:14 tenants s him, they talked the matter over. 3972
20:23 He s **through** their duplicity and said 2917
21: 1 Jesus s the rich putting their gifts into 3972
21: 2 He also s a poor widow put 3972
22:49 When Jesus' followers s what was going 3972
22:56 A servant girl s him seated there in 3972
22:58 A little later someone else s him and said, 3972
23: 8 When Herod s Jesus, he was greatly pleased, 3972
23:48 to witness this sight s what took place, 2555
23:55 and s the tomb and how his body was laid 2517
24:12 he s the strips of linen lying by themselves, 1063
24:37 thinking they s a ghost. 2555
Jn 1:29 The next day John s Jesus coming 1063
1:32 "I s the Spirit come down from heaven as 2517
1:36 When he s Jesus passing by, he said, "Look, 1838
1:38 Jesus s them following and asked, 2517
1:39 So they went and s where he was staying, 3972
1:47 When Jesus s Nathanael approaching, 3972
1:48 "I s you while you were still under 3972
1:50 "You believe because I told you I s you 3972
2:23 at the Passover Feast, many people s 2555
5: 6 When Jesus s him lying there and learned 3972
6: 2 of people followed him because they s 2555
6: 5 up and s a great crowd coming toward him, 2517
6:14 After the people s the miraculous sign 3972
6:19 they s Jesus approaching the boat, 2555
6:26 not because you s miraculous signs but 3972
8:56 he s it and was glad." 3972
9: 1 he s a man blind from birth. 3972
11:32 the place where Jesus was and s him, 3972
11:33 When Jesus s her weeping, 3972
12:41 Isaiah said this because he s Jesus' glory 3972
16:19 Jesus s that they wanted to ask him 1182
19: 6 as the chief priests and their officials s him, 3972
19:26 When Jesus s his mother there, 3972
19:35 The man who s it has given testimony, 3972
20: 1 and s that the stone had been removed from 1063
20: 6 He s the strips of linen lying there, 2555
20: 8 He s and believed. 3972
20:12 and s two angels in white, seated where 2555
20:14 turned around and s Jesus standing there, 2555
20:20 The disciples were overjoyed when they s 3972
21: 9 they s a fire of burning coals there with fish 1063
21:20 Peter turned and s **that** the disciple 1063
21:21 When Peter s him, he asked, "Lord, 3972
Ac 2: 3 They s what seemed to be tongues of fire 3972
2:25 " 'I s the Lord always before me. 4632
3: 3 When he s Peter and John about to enter, 3972
3: 9 the people s him walking and praising God, 3972
3:12 When Peter s this, he said to them: 3972
4:13 When they s the courage of Peter and John 2555
6:15 and they s that his face was like the face of 3972
7:24 He s one of them being mistreated by 3972
7:31 When he s this, he was amazed at the sight. 3972
Ac 7:55 looked up to heaven and s the glory of God, 3972
8: 6 When the crowds heard Philip and s 1063
8:13 by the great signs and miracles he s. 2555
8:18 When Simon s that the Spirit was given at 3972
9:35 and Sharon s him and turned to the Lord. 3972
10: 3 He distinctly s an angel of God, 3972
10:11 He s heaven opened and something like 2555
11: 5 and in a trance I s a vision. 3972
11: 5 I s something like a large sheet being let NIG
11: 6 I looked into it and s four-footed animals of 3972
11:23 and s the evidence of the grace of God, 3972
12: 3 When he s that this pleased the Jews, 3972
12:16 and when they opened the door and s him, 3972
13:12 When the proconsul s what had happened, 3972
13:45 When the Jews s the crowds, 3972
14: 9 s that he had faith to be healed 3972
14:11 When the crowd s what Paul had done, 3972
16:27 and when he s the prison doors open, 3972
21:27 some Jews from the province of Asia s Paul 2517
21:32 When the rioters s the commander 3972
22: 9 My companions s the light, 2517
22:18 and s the Lord speaking. 3972
26:13 I s a light from heaven, 3972
27:39 but they s a bay with a sandy beach, 2917
28: 4 When the islanders s the snake hanging 3972
Gal 1:19 I s none of the other apostles— 3972
2: 7 they s that I had been entrusted with 3972
2:14 When I s that they were not acting in line 3972
Php 1:30 through the same struggle you s I had, 3972
Heb 3: 9 and for forty years s what I did. 3972
11:13 they only s them and welcomed them from 3972
11:23 because they s he was no ordinary child, 3972
11:27 because he s him who is invisible. 3972
2Pe 2: 8 by the lawless deeds he s and heard)— 1062
Rev 1: 2 who testifies to everything he s— 3972
1:12 I turned I s seven golden lampstands, 3972
1:17 When I s him, I fell at his feet 3972
1:20 the seven stars that you s in my right hand 3972
5: 1 Then I s in the right hand of him who sat 3972
5: 2 And I s a mighty angel proclaiming in 3972
5: 6 Then I s a Lamb, looking as if 3972
6: 9 I s under the altar the souls of those 3972
7: 1 After this I s four angels standing at 3972
7: 2 I s another angel coming up from the east, 3972
8: 2 I s the seven angels who stand before God, 3972
9: 1 and I s a star that had fallen from the sky 3972
9:17 and riders I s in my vision looked like this: 3972
10: 1 Then I s another mighty angel coming 3972
11:11 and terror struck those who s them. 2555
12:13 When the dragon s that he had been hurled 3972
13: 1 And I s a beast coming out of the sea. 3972
13: 2 The beast I s resembled a leopard, 3972
13:11 I s another beast, coming out of the earth. 3972
14: 6 Then I s another angel flying in midair, 3972
15: 1 I s in heaven another great and marvelous 3972
15: 2 And I s what looked like a sea of glass 3972
16:13 I s three evil spirits that looked like frogs; 3972
17: 3 There I s a woman sitting on 3972
17: 6 I s **that** the woman was drunk with 3972
17: 6 When I s her, I was greatly astonished. 3972
17: 8 The beast, which you s, once was, 3972
17:12 "The ten horns you s are ten kings who have 3972
17:15 the angel said to me, "The waters you s, 3972
17:16 The beast and the ten horns you s will hate 3972
17:18 The woman you s is the great city 3972
18: 1 After this I s another angel coming down 3972
19:11 I s heaven standing open and there 3972
19:17 And I s an angel standing in the sun, 3972
19:19 Then I s the beast and the kings of 3972
20: 1 I s an angel coming down out of heaven, 3972
20: 4 I s thrones on which were seated 3972
20: 4 And I s the souls of those who had been NIG
20:11 Then I s a great white throne 3972
20:12 And I s the dead, great and small, 3972
21: 1 Then I s a new heaven and a new earth, 3972
21: 2 I s the Holy City, the new Jerusalem, 3972
22: 8 am the one who heard and s these things. 1063

SAWDUST (2)

Mt 7: 3 at the **speck of** s in your brother's eye 2847
Lk 6:41 at the **speck of** s in your brother's eye 2847

SAWED (1) [SAWS]

Heb 11:37 They were stoned; they were s **in two;** 4569

SAWN (Anglicized) See SAWED

SAWS (2) [SAWED]

2Sa 12:31 consigning them to labor with s and 4490
1Ch 20: 3 consigning them to labor with s and 4490

SAY (921) [SAID, SAYING, SAYINGS, SAYS]

Ge 3: 1 He said to the woman, "Did God really s, 606
3: 3 but God did s, 'You must not eat fruit 606
12:12 When the Egyptians see you, they will s, 606
12:13 S you are my sister, 606
12:19 Why did you s, 'She is my sister,' 606
14:23 so that you will never be able to s, 606
18: 5 "Very well," they answered, "do as you s." 1819
18:13 "Why did Sarah laugh and s, 606
20: 5 Did he not s to me, 'She is my sister,' 606
20: 5 and didn't she also s, 'He is my brother'? 606
20:13 Everywhere we go, s of me, 606
24:14 May it be that when I s to a girl, 606

Ge 24:33 until I have told you **what I have to s.**" 1821
24:43 a maiden comes out to draw water and *I* s 606
24:50 we can s nothing to you one way or 1819
26: 7 because he was afraid to s, 606
26: 9 Why *did you* s, 'She is my sister'?" 606
27: 6 I overheard your father s 1819
27:13 Just do what I s; go and get them for me." 7754
27:43 Now then, my son, do **what** I s: 7754
31:24 "Be careful not *to* s *anything* to Jacob, 1819
31:29 'Be careful not *to* s anything to Jacob, 1819
32: 4 "This is what *you are to* s 606
32:18 then *you are to* s, 606
32:19 *"You are to* s the same thing to Esau 1819
32:20 And be sure *to* s, 606
37:17 "I heard *them* s, 'Let's go to Dothan.' " 606
37:20 into one of these cisterns and s *that* 606
43: 7 How were we to know *he would* s, 606
44: 4 when you catch up with them, s to them, 606
44: 7 "Why *does* my lord s such things? 1819
44:10 then," he said, "let it be as you **s.** 1821
44:16 "What *can we* s to my lord?" 606
44:16 "What *can we* **s?** 1819
45: 9 Now hurry back to my father and s to him, 606
46:31 up and speak to Pharaoh and *will* s to him, 606
47:30 "I will do as you **s,"** he said. 1821
50:17 'This is what *you are to* s to Joseph: 606
Ex 3:13 "Suppose I go to the Israelites and s 606
3:14 This is what *you are to* s to the Israelites: 606
3:15 God also said to Moses, **"S** to the Israelites, 606
3:16 assemble the elders of Israel and s to them, 606
3:18 to go to the king of Egypt and s to him, 606
4: 1 not believe me or listen to me and **s,** 606
4:12 and will teach you what *to* **s."** 1819
4:22 Then s to Pharaoh, 'This is what 606
4:28 the LORD had sent him to **s,** 1821
6: 6 "Therefore, s to the Israelites: 606
7: 2 You *are to* s everything I command you, 1819
7: 9 'Perform a miracle,' then s to Aaron, 606
7:16 Then s to him, 'The LORD, 606
7:16 has sent me to s to you: 606
8: 1 "Go to Pharaoh and s to him, 606
8:10 Moses replied, "It will be as you **s,** 1821
8:20 to the water and s to him, 'This is what 606
9: 1 "Go to Pharaoh and s to him, 1819
9:13 confront Pharaoh and s to him, 606
10:29 "Just as *you* **s,"** Moses replied, 1819
13:14 s to him, 'With a mighty hand 606
14:12 Didn't *we* s to you in Egypt, 1819+1821
16: 9 **"S** to the entire Israelite community, 606
19: 3 *to* s to the house of Jacob and what you are 606
23:22 to what he says and do all that *I* s, 1819
30:31 **S** to the Israelites, 'This is to be 1819
31:13 **"S** to the Israelites, 'You must observe 1819
32:12 Why *should* the Egyptians **s,** 606
Lev 1: 2 "Speak to the Israelites and s to them: 606
4: 2 **"S** to the Israelites: 'When anyone sins 1819
6:25 **"S** to Aaron and his sons: 1819
7:23 **"S** to the Israelites: 'Do not eat any 1819
7:29 **"S** to the Israelites: 'Anyone who brings 1819
9: 3 Then s to the Israelites: 'Take a male goat 1819
11: 2 **"S** to the Israelites: 'Of all the animals 1819
12: 2 **"S** to the Israelites: 'A woman who 1819
15: 2 "Speak to the Israelites and s to them: 606
17: 2 and his sons and to all the Israelites and s 606
17: 8 **"S** to them: 'Any Israelite 606
17:12 Therefore *I* s to the Israelites, 606
18: 2 "Speak to the Israelites and s to them: 606
19: 2 the entire assembly of Israel and s to them: 606
20: 2 **"S** to the Israelites: 'Any Israelite 606
21: 1 the sons of Aaron, and s to them: 606
21:17 **"S** to Aaron: 'For the generations to come 1819
22: 3 **"S** to them: 'For the generations to come, 606
22:18 and his sons and to all the Israelites and s 606
23: 2 "Speak to the Israelites and s to them: 606
23:10 "Speak to the Israelites and s to them: 606
23:24 **"S** to the Israelites: 'On the first day 1819
23:34 **"S** to the Israelites: 'On the fifteenth day 1819
24:15 **S** to the Israelites: 'If anyone curses 1819
25: 2 "Speak to the Israelites and s to them. 606
27: 2 "Speak to the Israelites and s to them: 606
Nu 5: 6 **"S** to the Israelites: 'When a man or woman 1819
5:12 "Speak to the Israelites and s to them: 606
5:19 the woman under oath and s to her, 606
5:22 " 'Then the woman *is to* s, "Amen. 606
6: 2 "Speak to the Israelites and s to them: 606
6:23 to bless the Israelites. **S** to them: 606
8: 2 "Speak to Aaron and s to him, 606
11:21 and you **s,** 'I will give them meat to eat for 606
11:23 or not *what* I s will come true for you." 1821
14:15 who have heard this report about you *will* **s,** 606
14:28 to you the very things I heard *you* **s:** 1819
15: 2 "Speak to the Israelites and s to them: 606
15:18 "Speak to the Israelites and s to them: 606
15:38 "Speak to the Israelites and s to them: 606
16:24 **"S** to the assembly, 'Move away from 1819
18:26 "Speak to the Levites and s to them: 606
18:30 **"S** to the Levites: 'When you present 606
21:21 Israel sent messengers to s to Sihon king of 606
21:27 That is why the poets **s:** 606
22:17 and do whatever *you* **s.** 606
22:38 "But can I s just anything? 1819
23:17 Balak asked him, "What *did* the LORD **s?"** 1819
24:13 and *I must* s only what the LORD says'? 1819
27: 8 **"S** to the Israelites, 'If a man dies 1819
28: 2 "Give this command to the Israelites and s 606
28: 3 **S** to them: 'This is the offering made by fire 606
33:51 "Speak to the Israelites and s to them: 606
Nu 34: 2 "Command the Israelites and s to them: 606
35:10 "Speak to the Israelites and s to them: 606
Dt 1:28 *They* s, 'The people are stronger 606
4: 6 who will hear about all these decrees and **s,** 606
7:17 *You may* s to yourselves, 606
8:17 *You may* s to yourself, "My power and my 606
9: 4 *do* not s to yourself, "The LORD has 606
9:28 country from which you brought us *will* **s,** 606
12:20 and you crave meat and s, 606
17:14 settled in it, and *you* s, "Let us set a king 606
18:17 "What *they* s is good. 1819
18:20 not commanded him to **s,** 1819
18:21 *You may* s to yourselves, 606
20: 3 *He shall* **s:** "Hear, O Israel, 606
20: 5 The officers *shall* s to the army: 1819
21:20 *They shall* s to the elders, 606
22:16 The girl's father *will* s to the elders, 606
25: 7 to the elders at the town gate and s, 606
25: 9 spit in his face and s, 606
26: 3 and s to the priest in office at the time, 606
26:13 Then s to the LORD your God: 606
27:15 all the people *shall* **s,** "Amen!" 606+2256+6699
27:16 Then all the people *shall* **s,** "Amen!" 606
27:17 Then all the people *shall* **s,** "Amen!" 606
27:18 Then all the people *shall* **s,** "Amen!" 606
27:19 Then all the people *shall* **s,** "Amen!" 606
27:20 Then all the people *shall* **s,** "Amen!" 606
27:21 Then all the people *shall* **s,** "Amen!" 606
27:22 Then all the people *shall* **s,** "Amen!" 606
27:23 Then all the people *shall* **s,** "Amen!" 606
27:24 Then all the people *shall* **s,** "Amen!" 606
27:25 Then all the people *shall* **s,** "Amen!" 606
27:26 Then all the people *shall* **s,** "Amen!" 606
28:67 In the morning *you will* **s,** 606
32:27 lest the adversary misunderstand and **s,** 606
32:37 *He will* **s:** "Now where are their gods, 606
Jos 2:21 "Let it be as you **s."** 1821
6:10 *do* not s a word until the day I tell you to
shout!" 3655+4946+7023
7: 8 O Lord, what *can I* s, 606
8: 6 for *they will* **s,** 'They are running away 606
9:11 go and meet them and s to them, 606
22:24 that some day your descendants *might* s 606
22:27 not *be able to* s to ours, 606
22:28 "And we said, 'If *they* ever s this to us, 606
22:30 Gad and Manasseh *had to* **s,** 1819
Jdg 4:20 'Is anyone here?' s 'No.' " 606
7: 4 If *I* **s,** 'This one shall go with you,' 606
7: 4 but if *I* **s,** 'This one shall not go with you,' 606
9:29 *I would* s to Abimelech, 606
9:54 your sword and kill me, so that *they* can't **s,** 606
11:10 we will certainly do as you **s."** 1821
12: 6 "All right, s 'Shibboleth.' " 606
16:15 Then she said to him, "How *can you* **s,** 606
18:19 **Don't s a word.** 3338+6584+7023+8492
21:22 *we will* s to them, 606
Ru 3: 5 "I will do whatever *you* **s,"** Ruth answered. 606
1Sa 1: 8 Elkanah her husband *would* s to her, 606
2:15 the servant of the priest would come and s 606
3: 9 "Go and lie down, and if he calls you, s, 606
9: 9 *he would* **s,** "Come, let us go to the seer," 606
9:21 Why *do you* s such a thing to me?" 1819
10: 2 *They will* s to you, 'The donkeys you set out 606
11: 9 **"S** to the men of Jabesh Gilead, 606
14: 9 If *they* s to us, 'Wait there until we come 606
14:10 But if *they* **s,** 'Come up to us,' 606
16: 2 "Take a heifer with you and s, 606
18:22 "Speak to David privately and s, 'Look, 606
18:25 Saul replied, **"S** to David, 606
19:24 This is why *people* **s,** "Is Saul also among 606
20:21 Then I will send a boy and **s,** 'Go, NIH
20:21 If *I* s to him, 'Look, 606+606
20:22 But if *I* s to the boy, 'Look, 606
24: 9 "Why do you listen *when* men **s,** 606
25: 6 **S** to him: 'Long life to you! 606
25:24 **what** your servant has to **s.** 1821
27:10 David *would* **s,** "Against the Negev 606
27:11 "They might inform on us and **s,** 606
30:24 Who will listen to **what** you **s?** 1821
2Sa 2: 5 to the men of Jabesh Gilead *to* s to them, 606
3:11 Ish-Bosheth did not dare to s another word 8740
3:12 on his behalf to s to David, 606
5: 8 That is why *they* **s,** "The 'blind and lame' 606
7: 7 *did I* **ever** s *to* any of their rulers 1819+1821
7:20 "What more *can* David s to you? 1819
7:26 Then men *will* **s,** 'The LORD Almighty 606
11:21 If he asks you this, then s to him, 'Also, 606
11:22 David everything Joab had sent him to **s.** NIH
11:25 David told the messenger, **"S** this to Joab: 606
11:25 **S** this to encourage Joab." NIH
13: 5 s to him, 'I would like my sister Tamar 606
13:28 in high spirits from drinking wine and *I* s 606
14: 7 *they* **s,** 'Hand over the one who struck 606
14:15 "And now I have come to s this to my lord 1819
15: 3 Then Absalom *would* s to him, "Look, 606
15:10 throughout the tribes of Israel to **s,** 606
15:10 then **s,** 'Absalom is king in Hebron.' " 606
15:34 if you return to the city and s to Absalom, 606
17: 5 so we can hear what he has to **s."** 7023
17: 9 whoever hears about it *will* **s,** 606
19:10 So why *do* you s **nothing** *about* bringing 3087
19:13 And s to Amasa, 'Are you not my own 606
19:29 The king said to him, "Why s more? 1819+1821
20:17 **what** your servant *has* to **s."** 1821
20:18 continued, "Long ago *they* **used to s,** 1819+1819
1Ki 1:13 Go in to King David and s to him, 606
2:14 he added, "I have **something to** s to you." 1821
2Sa 2:14 *"You may* s it," she replied. 1819
2:38 **"What** you s is good. 1821
2:42 **'What** you s is good. 1821
8:47 in the land of their conquerors and **s,** 606
9: 8 by will be appalled and will scoff and **s,** 606
12: 9 How should we answer these people who s 1819
12:23 "S to Rehoboam son of Solomon king 606
18:11 now you tell me to go to my master and **s,** 606
18:14 now you tell me to go to my master and **s,** 606
18:24 all the people said, "What you s is good." 1821
19: 2 So Jezebel sent a messenger to Elijah to **s,** 606
20: 4 The king of Israel answered, "Just as you **s,** 1821
21:19 **S** to him, 'This is what the LORD says: 1819
21:19 s to him, 'This is what the LORD says: 1819
22: 8 "The king *should* not s that," 606
22:27 and s, 'This is what the king says: 606
2Ki 5:10 Elisha sent a messenger to s to him, "Go, 606
5:22 "My master sent me to **s,** 606
7: 4 If *we* **s,** 'We'll go into the city'— 606
8:10 Elisha answered, "Go and s to him, 606
8:14 "What *did* Elisha s to you?" 606
9:37 so that no *one will be able to* **s,** 606
10: 5 and we will do anything *you* **s.** 606
16: 7 to s to Tiglath-Pileser king of Assyria, 606
18:20 You s you have strategy and military NIH
18:22 And if *you* s to me, 606
18:27 to s these things, and not to the men sitting 1819
19:10 "S to Hezekiah king of Judah: 606
20:14 "What *did* those men **s,** 606
1Ch 16:31 *let them* s among the nations, 606
17: 6 *did I ever* s *to* any of their leaders 1819+1821
17:18 "What more can David s to you NIH
17:24 Then men *will* **s,** 'The LORD Almighty, 606
2Ch 6:37 with you in the land of their captivity and **s,** 606
7:21 all who pass by will be appalled and **s,** 606
10: 9 How should we answer these people who s 1819
11: 3 **"S** to Rehoboam son of Solomon king 606
18: 7 "The king *should* not s that," 606
18:26 and s, 'This is what the king says: 606
25:19 *You* s *to yourself* that you have defeated 606
Ezr 8:17 to s to Iddo and his kinsmen, 1819
9:10 now, O our God, what *can we* s after this? 606
10:12 We must do as you **s.** 1821
Ne 5: 8 because they could find nothing to **s.** 1821
5:12 We will do as you **s."** 606
Est 1:17 so they will despise their husbands and **s,** 606
4:10 Then she instructed him *to* s to Mordecai, 7422
Job 6:26 Do you mean to correct **what** I **s,** 4863
8: 2 "How long *will you* s such things? 4910
9:12 Who *can* s to him, 'What are you doing?' 606
9:22 It is all the same; that is why *I* **s,** 606
9:27 If I **s,** 'I will forget my complaint, 606
10: 2 *I will* s to God: Do not condemn me, 606
11: 4 *You* s to God, 'My beliefs are flawless 606
13:17 let your ears take in **what** I **s.** 289
17:12 in the face of darkness they **s,** NIH
17:14 if *I* s to corruption, 'You are my father,' 7924
19:28 "If *you* **s,** 'How we will hound him, 606
20: 7 those who have seen him *will* **s,** 606
21:14 Yet *they* s to God, 'Leave us alone! 606
21:28 *You* **s,** 'Where now is the great man's house, 606
22:13 Yet *you* **s,** 'What does God know? 606
22:29 When men are brought low and *you* **s,** 606
23: 5 and consider what *he would* **s.** 606
28:22 Destruction and Death **s,** 606
32: 5 that the three men had nothing more to **s,** 5101
32:10 "Therefore *I* **s:** Listen to me; 606
32:13 *Do* not **s,** 'We have found wisdom; 606
32:15 and *have* no more *to* **s;** 6699
32:17 I too *will* **have** my **s;** 2750+6699
33: 1 pay attention to everything I **s.** 1821
33:24 to him and s, 'Spare him from going down 606
33:32 If you have **anything to s,** answer me; 4863
34:16 listen to what I **s.** 4863
34:34 wise men who hear me s to me, 606
35: 2 *You* **s,** 'I will be cleared by God.' 606
35:14 will he listen *when you* s that you do 606
37:19 "Tell us what *we should* s to him; 606
40: 5 twice, but I will s no more." NIH
Ps 2: 3 "Let us break their chains," they **s,** NIH
10:13 Why *does he* s to himself, 606
11: 1 How then *can you* s to me: "Flee like a bird 606
13: 4 my enemy *will* **s,** "I have overcome him," 606
31:14 *I* **s,** "You are my God." 606
35: 3 **S** to my soul, "I am your salvation." 606
35:21 They gape at me and **s,** "Aha! 606
35:25 or **s,** "We have swallowed him up." 606
35:27 *may they* always **s,** "The LORD be exalted, 606
40:15 May those *who* s to me, "Aha! 606
40:16 *may* those who love your salvation always **s,** 606
41: 5 My enemies s of me in malice, 606
42: 3 while men s to me all day long, 606
42: 9 *I* s to God my Rock, "Why have you
forgotten me? 606
58:11 Then men *will* **s,** "Surely the righteous 606
59: 7 and they **s,** "Who can hear us?" NIH
64: 5 *they* **s,** "Who will see them?" 606
64: 6 They plot injustice and **s,** NIH
66: 3 **S** to God, "How awesome are your deeds! 606
70: 3 May those *who* s to me, "Aha! 606
70: 4 *may* those who love your salvation always **s,** 606
71:11 They **s,** "God has forsaken him; 606
73:11 *They* **s,** "How can God know? 606
75: 2 You **s,** "I choose the appointed time; NIH
75: 4 To the arrogant *I* **s,** 'Boast no more,' 606
79:10 Why *should* the nations **s,** 606
83: 4 *they* **s,** "let us destroy them as a nation, 606

Ps 85: 8 I will listen to what God the LORD *will* s; 1819
87: 4 and will s, 'This one was born in Zion.' " NIH
91: 2 *I will* s of the LORD, 606
94: 7 *They* s, "The LORD does not see; 606
96:10 S among the nations, "The LORD reigns." 606
106:48 *Let* all the people s, "Amen!" 606
107: 2 *Let* the redeemed of the LORD s this— 606
115: 2 Why *do* the nations s, 606
118: 2 *Let* Israel s: "His love endures forever." 606
118: 3 *Let* the house of Aaron s: 606
118: 4 *Let* those who fear the LORD s: 606
119:82 I s, "When will you comfort me?" 606
122: 8 sake of my brothers and friends, *I will* s, 1819
124: 1 had not been on our side—*let* Israel s— 606
129: 1 oppressed me from my youth—*let* Israel s— 606
129: 8 *May* those who pass by not s, 606
139:11 If *I* s, "Surely the darkness will hide me 606
140: 6 *I* s to you, "You are my God." 606
141: 7 [They will s,] "As one plows and breaks up NIH
142: 5 I cry to you, O LORD; *I* s, 606
Pr 1:11 If *they* s, "Come along with us; 606
3:28 *Do* not s to your neighbor, 606
4:10 Listen, my son, accept **what** I s, 609
4:20 My son, pay attention to **what** I s; 1821
5: 7 do not turn aside from **what** I s. 609+7023
5:12 *You will* s, "How I hated discipline! 606
7: 4 S to wisdom, "You are my sister," 606
7:24 pay attention to **what** I s. 609+7023
8: 6 Listen, for *I have* worthy things *to* s; 1819
20: 9 Who *can* s, "I have kept my heart pure; 606
20:22 *Do* not s, "I'll pay you back 606
23:35 "They hit me," you will s, NIH
24: 7 at the gate he *has* nothing *to* s. 7023+7337
24:12 If *you* s, "But we knew nothing 606
24:29 not s, "I'll do to him as he has done to me; 606
25: 7 it is better for him *to* s to you, 606
30: 9 and disown you and s, 606
30:15 four *that* never s, 'Enough!': 606
Ecc 1: 8 things are wearisome, more than one can s. 1819
1:10 Is there anything of which *one can* s, 606
5: 6 be angry at **what** you s and destroy the work 7754
6: 3 and does not receive proper burial, *I* s that 606
7:10 *Do* not s, "Why were the old days better 606
7:21 not pay attention to every word *people* s, 1819
8: 2 Obey the king's command, I s, NIH
8: 4 a king's word is supreme, who *can* s to him, 606
8:14 This too, *I* s, is meaningless. 606
10:20 a bird on the wing may report **what** you s. 1821
12: 1 and the years approach when *you will* s, 606
Isa 2: 3 Many peoples will come and s, "Come, 606
3: 6 and s, "You have a cloak, NIH
4: 1 and s, "We will eat our own food 606
5:19 to those *who* s, "Let God hurry, 606
7: 4 S to him, 'Be careful, 606
8: 4 Before the boy knows how *to* s 'My father' 7924
9: 9 *who* s with pride and arrogance of heart, 606
10:12 he will s, "I will punish the king of Assyria NIH
10:29 They go over the pass, and s, NIH
12: 1 In that day *you will* s: "I will praise you, 606
12: 4 In that day *you will* s: "Give thanks to 606
14: 8 the cedars of Lebanon exult over you and s, NIH
14:10 They will all respond, *they will* s to you, 606
19:11 How *can you* s to Pharaoh, 606
20: 6 the people who live on this coast *will* s, 606
22:13 "Let us eat and drink," you s, NIH
22:15 "Go, s to this steward, to Shebna, NIH
25: 9 In that day *they will* s, 606
28:23 pay attention and hear **what** I s. 614
29:11 and s to him, "Read this, please," 606
29:12 and s, "Read this, please," he will answer, 606
29:16 *Shall* what is formed s to him who formed 606
29:16 *Can* the pot s of the potter, 606
30:10 *They* s to the seers, "See no more visions!" 606
30:22 like a menstrual cloth and s to them, 606
32: 9 hear **what I have to s!** 614
33:24 No one living in Zion *will* s, "I am ill"; 606
35: 4 s to those with fearful hearts, 606
36: 5 You s you have strategy NIH
36: 7 And if *you* s to me, 606
36:12 to s these things, and not to the men sitting 1819
37:10 "S to Hezekiah king of Judah: 606
38:15 But what *can I* s? 1819
39: 3 "What *did* those men s, 606
40: 9 s to the towns of Judah, 606
40:27 Why *do you* s, O Jacob, and complain, 606
41:26 so *we could* s, 'He was right'? 606
42:17 those who trust in idols, who s to images, 606
42:22 with no *one to* s, "Send them back." 606
43: 6 *I will* s to the north, 'Give them up!' 606
43: 9 so that others may hear and s, "It is true." 606
44: 5 One *will* s, 'I belong to the LORD'; 606
44:19 the knowledge or understanding to s, "Half 606
44:20 he cannot save himself, or s, 606
44:28 he *will* s of Jerusalem, "Let it be rebuilt," 606
45: 9 *Does* the clay s to the potter, 606
45: 9 Does your work s, 'He has no hands'? NIH
45:24 *They will* s of me, 606
46:10 what is still to come. I s: 606
47:10 and knowledge mislead you when *you* s 606
48: 5 that *you could* not s, 'My idols did them; 606
48: 7 So *you* cannot s, 'Yes, I knew of them.' 606
48:20 Send it out to the ends of the earth; s, 606
49: 9 to s to the captives, 606
49:20 during your bereavement *will* yet s 606
49:21 Then *you will* s in your heart, 606
51:16 and *who* s to Zion, 'You are my people.' " 606
52: 7 who proclaim salvation, *who* s to Zion, 606

Isa 56: 3 who has bound himself to the LORD s, 606
57:10 but *you would* not s, 'It is hopeless.' 606
58: 3 'Why have we fasted,' they s, NIH
58: 9 you will cry for help, and *he will* s: 606
62:11 "S to the Daughter of Zion, 'See, 606
65: 5 who s, 'Keep away; 606
65: 8 and *men* s, 'Don't destroy it, there is 606
Jer 1: 7 But the LORD said to me, *"Do* not s, 606
1: 7 to and s whatever I command you. 1819
1:17 up and s to them whatever I command you. 1819
2:23 "How *can you* s, 'I am not defiled; 606
2:27 *They* s to wood, 'You are my father,' 606
2:27 yet when they are in trouble, *they* s, 606
2:31 Why *do* my people s, 'We are free to roam; 606
2:35 *you* s, 'I am innocent; 606
2:35 I will pass judgment on you because you s, 606
3:16 declares the LORD, *"men will* no longer s, 606
4: 5 in Judah and proclaim in Jerusalem and s: 606
4: 5 Cry aloud and s: 'Gather together! 606
5: 2 Although *they* s, 'As surely as the LORD 606
5:13 so let what they s be done to them." NIH
5:24 *They do* not s to themselves, 606
6:14 'Peace, peace,' they s, 606
7: 4 Do not trust in deceptive words and s, 606
7:10 which bears my Name, and s, 606
7:28 Therefore s to them, 'This is the nation 606
8: 4 "S to them, 'This is what the LORD says: 606
8: 6 but *they do* not s what is right. 1819
8: 8 " 'How *can you* s, "We are wise, 606
8:11 "Peace, peace," they s, 606
9:22 S, "This is what the LORD declares: 1819
13:12 "S to them: 'This is what the LORD, 606
13:12 And if *they* s to you, 606
13:18 S to the king and to the queen mother, 606
13:21 What *will you* s when [the LORD] sets 606
16:11 then s to them, 'It is because your fathers 606
16:14 "when *men will* no longer s, 606
16:15 but they will s, 'As surely as the LORD NIH
16:19 from the ends of the earth and s, 606
17:20 S to them, 'Hear the word of the LORD, 606
18:11 "Now therefore s to the people of Judah 606
19: 3 and s, 'Hear the word of the LORD 606
19:11 and s to them, 'This is what the LORD 606
20: 9 But if *I* s, "I will not mention him or speak 606
21:11 "Moreover, s to the royal house of Judah, NIH
21:13 you who s, "Who can come against us? 606
23: 7 "when *people will* no longer s, 606
23: 8 but they will s, 'As surely as the LORD NIH
23:17 the stubbornness of their hearts *they* s, 606
23:25 the prophets s who prophesy lies 606
23:25 They s, 'I had a dream! 606
23:33 s to them, 'What oracle? 606
25:30 against them and s to them: 606
26: 4 S to them, 'This is what the LORD says: 606
26: 8 the LORD had commanded him to s, 1819
27: 4 and s, 'This is what the LORD Almighty, 606
27:14 to the words of the prophets who s to you, 606
27:16 Do not listen to the prophets *who* s, 606
28: 7 to what I *have to* s in your hearing and in 1819
29:15 *You may* s, "The LORD has raised 606
31: 7 Make your praises heard, and s, 606
31:29 "In those days *people will* no longer s, 606
32: 3 You s, 'This is what the LORD says: 606
32: 7 is going to come to you and s, 606
32:25 you, O Sovereign LORD, s to me, 606
32:43 be bought in this land of which you s, 606
33:10 'You s about this place, 606
36:14 the son of Cushi, to s to Baruch, 606
38:22 Those *women will* s to you: 606
38:25 and they come to you and s, 606
38:27 the king had ordered him to s. 1821
42:13 if you s, 'We will not stay in this land,' 606
42:14 and if you s, 'No, we will go and live in 606
43: 2 The LORD our God has not sent you to s, 606
43:10 Then s to them, 'This is what 606
45: 4 [The LORD said,] "S this to him: 606
46:16 *They will* s, 'Get up, let us go back 606
48:14 "How *can you* s, 'We are warriors, 606
48:17 s, 'How broken is the mighty scepter, 606
49: 4 you trust in your riches and s, NIH
49:14 An envoy was sent to the nations to s, NIH
50: 2 keep nothing back, but s, 606
51:35 s the inhabitants of Zion. 606
51:62 Then s, 'O LORD, you have said you will 606
51:64 Then s, 'So will Babylon sink to rise no more 606
La 2:12 *They* s to their mothers, "Where is bread 606
2:13 What *can I* s *for* you? 6386
2:16 they scoff and gnash their teeth and s, 606
3:18 So *I* s, "My splendor is gone and all 606
3:24 I s *to* myself, "The LORD is my portion; 606
3:41 and our hands to God in heaven, and s: NIH
4:15 *people* among the nations s, 606
Eze 2: 4 S to them, 'This is what 606
2: 6 Do not be afraid of **what** they s 1821
2: 8 you, son of man, listen to what I s to you. 1819
3:11 S to them, 'This is what the Sovereign LORD 606
3:18 When I s to a wicked man, 606
3:27 I will open your mouth and *you shall* s 606
6: 3 and s: 'O mountains of Israel, 606
8:12 *They* s, 'The LORD does not see us; 606
9: 9 *They* s, 'The LORD has forsaken the land; 606
11: 3 They s, 'Will it not soon be time 606
11: 5 and he told me *to* s: 606
11:16 "Therefore s: 'This is what the Sovereign LORD says: 606
11:17 "Therefore s: 'This is what the Sovereign LORD says: 606

Eze 12:10 "S to them, 'This is what the Sovereign LORD says: 606
12:11 S to them, 'I am a sign to you.' 606
12:19 S to the people of the land: 606
12:23 S to them, 'This is what the Sovereign LORD says: 606
12:23 S to them, 'The days are near 1819
12:25 I will fulfill *whatever I* s, 1819+1821
12:28 "Therefore s to them, 'This is what 606
12:28 whatever *I* s will be fulfilled, 1819+1821
13: 2 S to those who prophesy out 606
13: 6 They s, "The LORD declares," 606
13: 7 and uttered lying divinations when you s, 606
13:15 *I will* s to you, "The wall is gone 606
13:18 s, 'This is what the Sovereign LORD says: 606
14: 6 "Therefore s to the house of Israel, 606
14:17 I bring a sword against that country and s, 606
16: 3 s, 'This is what the Sovereign LORD says 606
17: 3 S to them, 'This is what the Sovereign LORD says: 606
17: 9 "S to them, 'This is what the Sovereign LORD says: 606
17:12 "S to this rebellious house, 606
17:12 S to them: 'The king of Babylon went to 606
18:25 *you* s, 'The way of the Lord is not just.' 606
19: 2 and s: " 'What a lioness was your mother 606
20: 3 speak to the elders of Israel and s to them, 606
20: 5 and s to them: 'This is what the Sovereign LORD says: 606
20:27 speak to the people of Israel and s to them, 606
20:30 "Therefore s to the house of Israel: 606
20:32 " 'You s, "We want to be like the nations, 606
20:47 S to the southern forest: 606
21: 3 and s to her: 'This is what the LORD says: 606
21: 7 *you shall* s, 'Because of the news 606
21: 9 and s, 'This is what the Lord says: 606
21:28 "And you, son of man, prophesy and s, 606
22: 3 and s: 'This is what the Sovereign LORD says: 606
22:24 s to the land, 'You are a land that has had no 606
22:28 *They* s, 'This is what 606
24: 3 Tell this rebellious house a parable and s 606
24:21 S to the house of Israel, 'This is what 606
25: 3 S to them, 'Hear the word of the Sovereign 606
26:17 up a lament concerning you and s to you: 606
27: 3 S to Tyre, situated at the gateway to 606
27: 3 " 'You s, O Tyre, "I am perfect in beauty." 606
28: 2 "Son of man, s to the ruler of Tyre, 606
28: 2 " 'In the pride of your heart *you* s, 606
28: 9 *Will you then* s, "I am a god," 606+606
28:12 a lament concerning the king of Tyre and s 606
28:22 and s: 'This is what the Sovereign LORD says: 606
29: 3 Speak to him and s: 'This is what 606
29: 3 *You* s, "The Nile is mine; 606
30: 2 "Son of man, prophesy and s: 606
30: 2 " 'Wail and s, "Alas for that day!" NIH
31: 2 s to Pharaoh king of Egypt and 606
32: 2 concerning Pharaoh king of Egypt and s 606
32:19 S to them, 'Are you more favored than others? NIH
32:21 within the grave the mighty leaders *will* s 1819
33: 2 speak to your countrymen and s to them: 606
33: 8 When I s to the wicked, 'O wicked man, 606
33:10 "Son of man, s to the house of Israel, 606
33:11 S to them, 'As surely as I live, 606
33:12 son of man, s to your countrymen, 606
33:14 And if I s to the wicked man, 606
33:17 "Yet your countrymen s, 606
33:20 Yet, O house of Israel, *you* s, 606
33:25 Therefore s to them, 'This is what 606
33:27 "S this to them: 'This is what the Sovereign 606
34: 2 prophesy and s to them: 'This is what 606
35: 3 s: 'This is what the Sovereign LORD says: 606
36: 1 prophesy to the mountains of Israel and s, 606
36: 3 Therefore prophesy and s, 'This is what 606
36: 6 of Israel and s to the mountains and hills, to 606
36:13 Because *people* s to you, 606
36:22 "Therefore s to the house of Israel, 606
36:35 *They will* s, "This land that was laid waste 606
37: 4 "Prophesy to these bones and s to them, 606
37: 9 prophesy, son of man, and s to it, 606
37:11 *They* s, 'Our bones are dried up 606
37:12 Therefore prophesy and s to them: 606
37:19 s to them, 'This is what the Sovereign 1819
37:21 and s to them, 'This is what the Sovereign 1819
38: 3 s: 'This is what the Sovereign LORD says: 606
38:11 *You will* s, "I will invade a land 606
38:13 of Tarshish and all her villages *will* s 606
38:14 son of man, prophesy and s to Gog: 606
39: 1 "Son of man, prophesy against Gog and s: 606
44: 6 S to the rebellious house of Israel, 606
Da 3:29 or language who s anything against the God 10042
4:35 No one can hold back his hand or s to him: 10042
5:11 your father the king, I s— NIH
11:36 and *will* s unheard-of things against 1819
Hos 2: 1 "S of your brothers, 'My people,' 606
2: 7 Then *she will* s, 'I will go back to my 606
2:23 *I will* s to those called 'Not my people,' 606
2:23 and they *will* s, 'You are my God.' " 606
10: 3 Then *they will* s, "We have no king 606
10: 8 *they will* s to the mountains, "Cover us!" 606
14: 2 S to him: "Forgive all our sins 606
14: 3 *We will* never again s 'Our gods' 606
Joel 2:17 *Let them* s, "Spare your people, O LORD. 606
2:17 Why *should they* s among the peoples, 606
3:10 *Let* the weakling s, "I am strong!" 606

Am 4: 1 and crush the needy and s to your husbands, 606
5:14 will be with you, just as *you* s he is. 606
6:10 and he says, "No," then *he will* s, "Hush! 606
6:13 in the conquest of Lo Debar and s, 606
7:16 You s, " 'Do not prophesy against Israel, 606
8:14 or s, 'As surely as your god lives, O Dan,' 606
9:10 all those *who* s, 'Disaster will not overtake 606
Ob 1: 1 An envoy was sent to the nations to s, NIH
1: 3 you *who* s to yourself, 'Who can bring me 606
Mic 2: 6 "Do not prophesy," their **prophets s.** 5752
3:11 Yet they lean upon the LORD and s, 606
4: 2 Many nations will come and s, "Come, 606
4:11 They s, "Let her be defiled, 606
6: 1 let the hills hear **what** you **have to s.** 7754
Na 3: 7 All who see you will flee from you and s, 606
Hab 2: 1 I will look to see what *he will* s to me, 1819
Zep 3:16 On that day *they will* s to Jerusalem, 606
Hag 1: 2 "These people s, 'The time has not 606
Zec 8:21 of one city will go to another and s, 606
8:23 of one Jew by the hem of his robe and s, 606
11: 5 Those who sell them s, 'Praise the LORD, 606
12: 5 the leaders of Judah *will* s in their hearts, 606
13: 3 to whom he was born, *will* s to him, 606
13: 5 *He will* s, 'I am not a prophet. 606
13: 9 *I will* s, 'They are my people,' 606
13: 9 'They are my people,' and they *will* s, 606
Mal 1: 4 Edom *may* s, "Though we have been crushed 606
1: 5 You will see it with your own eyes and s, 606
1:13 And *you* s, 'What a burden!' 606
Mt 3: 9 And do not think you can s to yourselves, *3306*
5:11 persecute you and falsely s all kinds of evil *3306*
7: 4 How can *you* s to your brother, *3306*
7:22 Many *will* s to me on that day, 'Lord, *3306*
8: 8 But just s the word, and my servant *3306*
8: 9 I s to my servant, 'Do this,' and he does it." *NIG*
8:11 *I* s to you that many will come from *3306*
9: 5 *to* s, 'Your sins are forgiven,' or to say, *3306*
9: 5 or *to* s, 'Get up and walk'? *3306*
10:19 not worry about what *to* s or how to say it. *3281*
10:19 not worry about what to say or how to s it. *NIG*
10:19 At that time you will be given what *to* s, *3281*
11:18 and *they* s, 'He has a demon.' *3306*
11:19 and drinking, and *they* s, 'Here is a glutton *3306*
12:34 how can you who are evil s anything good? *3281*
13:34 *he did* not s anything to them without using *3281*
15: 5 But you s that if a man says to his father *3306*
16: 2 He replied, "When evening comes, *you* s, *3306*
16:13 "Who *do* people s the Son of Man is?" *3306*
16:14 They replied, "Some s John the Baptist; *NIG*
16:14 "Some say John the Baptist; others s Elijah; *NIG*
16:15 "Who *do you* s I am?" *3306*
17:10 of the law s that Elijah must come first?" *3306*
17:20 *you* can s to this mountain, *3306*
21: 5 "S to the Daughter of Zion, *3306*
21:21 but also *you can* s to this mountain, 'Go, *3306*
21:25 "If *we* s, 'From heaven,' he will ask, *3306*
21:26 But if *we* s, 'From men'— *3306*
22:23 *who* s there is no resurrection, *3306*
22:46 No one could s a word **in reply,** *646*
23:16 You s, 'If anyone swears by the temple, *3306*
23:18 You also s, 'If anyone swears by the altar, *NIG*
23:30 And *you* s, 'If we had lived in the days *3306*
23:39 you will not see me again until *you* s, *3306*
25:34 "Then the King *will* s to those on his right, *3306*
25:41 "Then *he will* s to those on his left, *3306*
26:22 and began *to* s to him one after the other, *3306*
26:54 that s it must happen in this way?" *NIG*
26:64 "Yes, it is as you s," Jesus replied. *3306*
26:64 "But *I* s to all of you: *3306*
27:11 "Yes, it is as you s," Jesus replied. *3306*
28:13 "*You are to* s, 'His disciples came *3306*
Mk 2: 9 Which is easier: *to* s to the paralytic, *3306*
2: 9 or *to* s, 'Get up, take your mat and walk'? *3306*
4:30 s the kingdom of God **is like,** *3929*
4:34 *He did* not s anything to them without using *3281*
5:41 (which means, "Little girl, *I* s to you, *3306*
7:11 But you s that if a man says to his father *3306*
8:27 "Who *do* people s I am?" *3306*
8:28 They replied, "Some s John the Baptist; *NIG*
8:28 "Some say John the Baptist; others s Elijah; *NIG*
8:29 "Who *do* you s I am?" *3306*
9: 6 (He did not know what *to* s, *646*
9:11 of the law s that Elijah must come first?" *3306*
9:39 the next moment s anything **bad about** me, *2800*
11:14 And his disciples heard him s it. *NIG*
11:31 "If *we* s, 'From heaven,' he will ask, *3306*
11:32 But if *we* s, 'From men'…." *3306*
12:18 Sadducees, who s there is no resurrection, *3306*
12:35 "How is it that the teachers of the law s that *3306*
13:11 do not worry beforehand about what *to* s. *3281*
13:11 Just s whatever is given you at the time, *3281*
13:37 What *I* s to you, I say to everyone: *3306*
13:37 What I say to you, *I* s to everyone: *3306*
14:14 S to the owner of the house he enters, *3306*
14:40 They did not know what *to* s to him. *646*
14:58 "We heard him s, 'I will destroy this *3306*
15: 2 "Yes, it is as you s," Jesus replied. *3306*
Lk 3: 8 And do not begin *to* s to yourselves, *3306*
5: 5 because you s so, I will let down the nets." *4839*
5:23 *to* s, 'Your sins are forgiven,' or to say, *3306*
5:23 to say, 'Your sins are forgiven,' or *to* s, *3306*
6:42 How can *you* s to your brother, 'Brother, *3306*
6:46 'Lord, Lord,' and do not do what *I* s? *3306*
7: 6 when the centurion sent friends *to* s to him: *3306*
7: 7 s the word, and my servant will be healed. *3306*
7: 8 I s to my servant, 'Do this,' and he does it." *NIG*
7:14 He said, "Young man, *I* s to you, get up!" *3306*
Lk 7:33 and *you* s, 'He has a demon.' *3306*
7:34 and drinking, and *you* s, 'Here is a glutton *3306*
7:49 The other guests began *to* s among *3306*
9:18 "Who *do* the crowds s I am?" *3306*
9:19 They replied, "Some s John the Baptist; *NIG*
9:19 "Some say John the Baptist; others s Elijah; *NIG*
9:20 "Who *do you* s I am?" *3306*
9:61 but first let me go back and **s good-by** *698*
10: 5 "When you enter a house, first s, *3306*
10:10 go into its streets and s, *3306*
11: 2 He said to them, "When you pray, s: *3306*
11: 9 "So I s to you: Ask and it will be given *3306*
11:18 I s this because you claim *NIG*
11:45 *when you* s these things, you insult us also." *3306*
11:54 waiting to catch him in something he
might s. *1666+3836+5125*
12:11 defend yourselves or what *you will* s, *3306*
12:12 at that time what *you* should s." *3306*
12:19 And *I'll* s to myself, *3306*
12:54 immediately *you* s, 'It's going to rain,' *3306*
12:55 And when the south wind blows, *you* s, *3306*
13:26 "Then *you will* s, 'We ate and drank *3306*
13:35 you will not see me again until *you* s, *3306*
14: 6 And they had nothing *to* s. *503*
14: 9 both of you *will* come and s to you, *3306*
14:10 *he will* s to you, 'Friend, *3306*
15:18 and go back to my father and s to him: *3306*
17: 6 *you can* s to this mulberry tree, *3306*
17: 7 *Would he* s to the servant when he comes in *3306*
17: 8 *Would he* not rather s, 'Prepare my supper, *3306*
17:10 *should* s, 'We are unworthy servants; *3306*
17:21 nor *will people* s, 'Here it is,' *3306*
19:14 and sent a delegation after him *to* s, *3306*
20: 5 "If *we* s, 'From heaven,' he will ask, *3306*
20: 6 But if *we* s, 'From men,' *3306*
20:27 who s there is no resurrection, *515*
20:41 "How is it that *they* s the Christ is the Son *3306*
22:11 and s to the owner of the house, *3306*
23: 3 "Yes, it is as you s," Jesus replied. *3306*
23:29 For the time will come when *you will* s, *3306*
23:30 Then " '*they will* s to the mountains, *3306*
Jn 1:22 What *do you* s about yourself?" *3306*
1:37 When the two disciples heard him s this, *3281*
4:17 when you s you have no husband. *3306*
4:35 *Do* you not s, 'Four months more and then *3306*
5:47 how are you going to believe what I **s?"** *4839*
6:14 *they began to* s, "Surely this is the Prophet *3306*
6:42 can *he* now s, 'I came down from heaven'?" *3306*
6:65 *He went on to* s, "This is why I told you *3306*
7:13 But no one *would* s anything publicly *3281*
7:42 not the Scripture s that the Christ will come *3306*
8: 5 Now what *do* you **s?"** *3306*
8:26 "I have much *to* s in judgment of you. *3281*
8:33 How *can* you s that we shall be set free?" *3306*
8:43 Because you are unable to hear what I **s.** *3364*
8:52 yet you s that if anyone keeps your word, *3306*
9:17 "What *have* you *to* s about him? *3306*
9:19 "Is this the one you s was born blind? *3306*
9:40 with him heard him s this and asked, *NIG*
11:51 *He did* not s this on his own, *3306*
12: 6 not s this because he cared about the poor *3306*
12:27 my heart is troubled, and what *shall I* s? *3306*
12:34 so how *can* you s, 'The Son of Man must *3306*
12:49 commanded me what *to* s and how to say it. *3306*
12:49 commanded me what to say and how *to* s it. *3281*
12:50 So whatever I s is just what *3281*
12:50 the Father has told me *to* **s."** *3281*
14: 9 How *can* you s, 'Show us the Father'? *3306*
14:10 The words I s to you are not just my own. *3306*
14:11 Believe me when I s that I am in the Father *NIG*
14:28 "You heard me s, 'I am going away *3306*
16:12 "I have much more *to* s to you, *3306*
17:13 but *I* s these things while I am still in *3281*
21: 7 As soon as Simon Peter heard him s, *NIG*
21:23 But Jesus *did* not s that he would not die; *3306*
Ac 2:14 listen carefully to what I **s.** *4839*
4:14 there was nothing they could **s.** *515*
6:11 they secretly persuaded some men *to* s, *3306*
6:14 For we have heard him s that this Jesus *3306*
9: 4 to the ground and heard a voice s to him, *3306*
10:22 so that he could hear what you have to **s."** *4839*
11:13 an angel appear in his house and s, *3306*
17:18 "What is this babbler trying *to* **s?"** *3306*
19:13 *They would* s, "In the name of Jesus, *3306*
21:37 "May I s something to you?" *3306*
22: 7 to the ground and heard a voice s to me, *3306*
23: 8 Sadducees s that there is no resurrection, *3306*
28:26 " 'Go to this people and s, "You will *3306*
Ro 2:22 You who s that people should *3306*
3: 5 what *shall we* **s?** That God is unjust *3306*
3: 8 Why not **s—**as we are being slanderously
reported *NIG*
3: 8 as saying and as some claim that we **s—** *3306*
4: 1 What then *shall we* s that Abraham, *3306*
4: 3 What *does* the Scripture **s?** *3306*
6: 1 What *shall we* s, then? Shall we go on *3306*
7: 7 What *shall we* s, then? Is the law sin? *3306*
8:31 What, then, *shall we* s in response to this? *3306*
9:14 What then *shall we* **s?** Is God unjust? *3306*
9:19 One of *you will* s to me: *3306*
9:20 "*Shall* what is formed s to him who formed *3306*
9:30 What then *shall we* **s?** That the Gentiles, *3306*
10: 6 "*Do* not s in your heart, 'Who will ascend *3306*
10: 8 But what *does it* **s?** "The word is near you; *3306*
11:19 *You will* s then, "Branches were broken off *3306*
12: 3 the grace given me *I* s to every one of you: *3306*
1Co 1:15 so no one *can* s that you were baptized *3306*
1Co 6: 5 *I* s this to shame you. *3306*
7: 6 *I* s this as a concession, not as a command. *3306*
7: 8 Now to the unmarried and the widows ***I* s:** *3306*
7:12 To the rest *I* s this (I, not the Lord): *3306*
9: 8 *Do I* s this merely from a human point *3281*
9: 8 Doesn't the Law s the same thing? *3306*
10:15 judge for yourselves what ***I* s.** *5774*
11:22 What *shall I* s to you? *3306*
12: 3 "Jesus be cursed," and no one can s, *3306*
12:15 If the foot *should* s, "Because I am not *3306*
12:16 And if the ear *should* s, "Because I am not *3306*
12:21 The eye cannot s to the hand, *3306*
12:21 And the head cannot s to the feet, *NIG*
14:16 who do not understand s "Amen" *3306*
14:23 not s that you are out of your mind? *3306*
14:26 What then *shall we* s, brothers? *1639*
15:12 some of you s that there is no resurrection of *3306*
15:34 *I* s this to your shame. *3281*
2Co 1:17 so that in the same breath I s, "Yes, yes" *NIG*
5: 8 We are confident, I s, and would prefer *NIG*
7: 3 *I do* not s this to condemn you; *3306*
9: 4 not *to* s anything **about** you— *3306*
10:10 For *some* s, "His letters are weighty *5774*
12: 6 is warranted by what I do or **s.** *201+1609+1666*
Gal 1: 9 As we have already said, so now *I* s again: *3306*
3:16 The Scripture *does* not s "and to seeds," *3306*
4:30 But what *does* the Scripture **s?** *3306*
5:16 So *I* s, live by the Spirit, *3306*
Php 3:18 before and now s again even with tears, *3306*
4: 4 *I will* s it again: Rejoice! *3306*
1Th 1: 8 we do not need *to* s anything **about** it, *3281*
2Ti 2: 2 And the things you have heard **me** s in *1609+4123*
2:18 s that the resurrection has already taken
place, *3306*
4: 3 to s what their itching ears want to hear. *NIG*
Tit 2: 8 because they have nothing bad *to* s *3306*
2:12 It teaches us to **s "No" to** ungodliness *766*
Heb 1: 5 For to which of the angels *did* God ever s, *3306*
1:13 To which of the angels *did* God ever s, *3306*
5:11 We have much *to* s about this, *3306*
7: 9 **One might even s** that Levi, *2229+3306+6055*
9:11 that is to s, not a part of this creation. *NIG*
11:14 People who s such things show *3306*
11:32 And what more *shall I* s? *3306*
13: 6 So we s with confidence, *3306*
Jas 1:13 When tempted, no one *should* s, *3306*
2: 3 to the man wearing fine clothes and s, *3306*
2: 3 but s to the poor man, "You stand there" *3306*
2:18 But someone *will* s, "You have faith; *3306*
4:13 Now listen, *you* who s, "Today or tomorrow *3306*
4:15 Instead, you *ought to* s, "If it is the Lord's *3306*
2Pe 3: 4 *They will* s, "Where is this 'coming' he
promised? *3306*
Rev 2: 9 of those who s they are Jews and are not, *3306*
2:24 Now *I* s to the rest of you in Thyatira, *3306*
3:17 *You* s, 'I am rich; I have acquired wealth *3306*
4:10 lay their crowns before the throne and **s:** *3306*
6: 1 of the four living creatures s in a voice *3306*
6: 3 I heard the second living creature s, *3306*
6: 5 I heard the third living creature s, "Come!" *3306*
6: 7 the voice of the fourth living creature s, *3306*
10: 4 but I heard a voice from heaven s, *3306*
12:10 Then I heard a loud voice in heaven **s:** *3306*
14:13 I heard a voice from heaven s, "Write: *3306*
16: 5 I heard the angel in charge of the waters **s:** *3306*
18: 4 Then I heard another voice from heaven **s:** *3306*
18:14 "They will s, 'The fruit you longed *NIG*
22:17 The Spirit and the bride s, "Come!" *3306*
22:17 And *let* him who hears s, "Come!" *3306*

SAYING (285) [SAY]

Ge 4:25 s, "God has granted me another child NIH
9: 1 God blessed Noah and his sons, s to them, 606
14:19 s, "Blessed be Abram by God Most High, 606
19:15 the angels urged Lot, s, "Hurry! 606
24: 7 to me and promised me on oath, s, 606
24:21 **Without s a word,** the man watched her 3087
24:27 s, "Praise be to the LORD, the God 606
26:22 He named it Rehoboth, s, 606
28:20 Then Jacob made a vow, s, 606
31: 1 Jacob heard that Laban's sons *were* s, 1821
32:30 So Jacob called the place Peniel, s, NIH
39:19 s, "This is how your slave treated me," 606
50:16 So they sent word to Joseph, s, 606
Ex 2:10 She named him Moses, s, 606
2:22 and Moses named him Gershom, s, 606
5:13 The slave drivers kept pressing them, s, 606
5:17 That is why you *keep* s, 606
11: 8 bowing down before me and s, 'Go, 606
15:24 So the people grumbled against Moses, s, 606
17: 7 and because they tested the LORD s, 606
33: 1 s, 'I will give it to your descendants.' 606
Lev 8:31 s, 'Aaron and his sons are to eat it.' 606
Nu 11:20 s, "Why did we ever leave Egypt?" " 606
16:31 As soon as he finished s all this, 1819
20:14 from Kadesh to the king of Edom, s: NIH
27: 7 *What* Zelophehad's daughters *are* s is right. 1819
30:14 He confirms them by s **nothing** to her 3087
36: 5 of the descendants of Joseph *is* s is right. 1819
Dt 1: 5 Moses began to expound this law, s: 606
2:26 king of Heshbon offering peace and s, 606
12:30 s, "How do these nations serve their gods? 606
13: 6 entices you, s, "Let us go and worship 606
13:13 their town astray, s, "Let us go and worship 606
22:14 a bad name, s, "I married this woman, 606
25: 8 If he persists *in* s, "I do not want to marry 606

Dt 33:27 He will drive out your enemy before you, s, 606
Jos 9:22 "Why did you deceive us by s, 606
22: 8 s, "Return to your homes 606
Jdg 5:29 indeed, she keeps s to herself, 609+8740
6:32 s, "Let Baal contend with him," 606
7:11 and listen to what they are s. 1819
7:13 "I had a dream," he was s. 606
7:24 throughout the hill country of Ephraim, s, 606
8:15 about whom you taunted me by s, 606
9:31 to Abimelech, s, "Gaal son of Ebed 606
11:15 s: "This is what Jephthah says: 606
11:17 to the king of Edom, s, 'Give us permission 606
16: 2 They made no move during the night, s, 606
16:23 s, "Our god has delivered Samson, 606
16:24 people saw him, they praised their god, s, 606
20: 8 All the people rose as one man, s, 606
20:12 throughout the tribe of Benjamin, s, "What 606
20:32 While the Benjamites were s, 606
20:32 the Israelites were s, "Let's retreat 606
21:20 So they instructed the Benjamites, s, 606
Ru 3:17 s, 'Don't go back to your mother-in-law 606
1Sa 1:11 And she made a vow, s, 606
1:20 She named him Samuel, s, NIH
2:20 Eli would bless Elkanah and his wife, s, 606
4:21 She named the boy Ichabod, s, 606
6:21 s, "The Philistines have returned the ark of 606
7:12 He named it Ebenezer, s, 606
8: 7 "Listen to all that the people are s to you; 606
10: 1 s, "Has not the LORD anointed you leader 606
10:12 So it became a s: "Is Saul also among the 5442
14:24 s, "Cursed be any man who eats food 606
14:28 the army under a strict oath, s, 'Cursed 606
15:18 And he sent you on a mission, s, 606
16:22 Then Saul sent word to Jesse, s, 606
17:25 Now the Israelites had been s, 606
17:27 They repeated to him what they had been s 1821
18:11 s to himself, "I'll pin David to the wall." 606
20:16 s, "May the LORD call David's enemies NIH
20:42 of the LORD, s, 'The LORD is witness 606
23: 2 s, "Shall I go and attack these Philistines?" 606
23:27 a messenger came to Saul, s, 606
24:13 As the old s goes, 'From evildoers come 5442
24:16 When David finished s this, Saul asked, 1819
30:20 s, "This is David's plunder." 606
30:26 who were his friends, s, 606+4200
2Sa 3:35 but David took an oath, s, 606
7: 4 the word of the LORD came to Nathan, s: 606
7:27 you have revealed this to your servant, s, 606
11: 5 and sent word to David, s, 606
12:27 Joab then sent messengers to David, s, 606
19: 9 s, "The king delivered us from the hand 606
19:41 of Israel were coming to the king and s 606
21:17 Then David's men swore to him, s, 606
24: 1 and he incited David against them, s, 606
1Ki 1:25 and drinking with him and s, 606
1:47 to congratulate our lord King David, s, 606
8:55 of Israel in a loud voice, s: 606
18:31 s, "Your name shall be Israel." 606
20: 2 s, "This is what Ben-Hadad says: 606
21:13 the people, s, "Naboth has cursed both God 606
2Ki 1: 2 So he sent messengers, s to them, 606
2:21 s, "This is what the LORD says: 606
10: 6 Then Jehu wrote them a second letter, s, 606
11: 5 He commanded them, s, 606
18:22 s to Judah and Jerusalem, 606
1Ch 4: 9 His mother had named him Jabez, s, 606
17: 3 the word of God came to Nathan, s: 606
29:10 s, "Praise be to you, O LORD, 606
2Ch 7: 3 s, "He is good; his love endures forever." NIH
7: 6 s, "His love endures forever." NIH
20: 8 in it a sanctuary for your Name, s, 606
20:21 as they went out at the head of the army, s: 606
20:37 s, "Because you have made an alliance 606
30:18 But Hezekiah prayed for them, s, 606
32:12 s to Judah and Jerusalem, 606
32:17 the God of Israel, and s this against him: 606
35:21 But Neco sent messengers to him, s, 606
Ne 1: 8 s, 'If you are unfaithful, I will scatter you 606
2:20 I answered them by s, "The God of heaven 606
5: 2 Some were s, "We and our sons 606
5: 3 Others were s, "We are mortgaging our
fields, 606
5: 4 Still others were s, "We have had to borrow 606
6: 8 "Nothing like what you are s is happening; 606
8:11 The Levites calmed all the people, s, 606
Job 22:19 the innocent mock them, s, NIH
Ps 2: 5 and terrifies them in his wrath, s, NIH
3: 2 Many are s of me, "God will not deliver 606
39: 2 not even s anything good, 3120
41: 7 they imagine the worst for me, s, NIH
42:10 s to me all day long, "Where is your God?" 606
52: 6 they will laugh at him, s, NIH
78:19 They spoke against God, s, 606
90: 3 You turn men back to dust, s, 606
Isa 6: 8 Then I heard the voice of the Lord s, 606
7: 5 Remaliah's son have plotted your ruin, s, 606
19:25 The LORD Almighty will bless them, s, 606
30:21 your ears will hear a voice behind you, s, 606
36: 7 s to Judah and Jerusalem, 606
45:14 s, 'Surely God is with you, NIH
47: 8 lounging in your security and s to yourself, 606
Jer 1: 4 The word of the LORD came to me, s, 606
4:10 and Jerusalem by s, 'You will have peace,' 606
4:31 stretching out her hands and s, "Alas! NIH
8: 6 No one repents of his wickedness, s, 606
11: 7 I warned them again and again, s, 606
11:19 s, "Let us destroy the tree and its fruit; NIH
Jer 11:21 and s, 'Do not prophesy in the name of 606
12: 4 Moreover, the people are s, 606
12:16 s, 'As surely as the LORD lives'— NIH
14:15 I did not send them, yet they are s, 606
17:15 They keep s to me, "Where is the word 606
18:19 hear what my accusers are s! 7754
20:10 All my friends are waiting for me to slip, s, NIH
20:15 s, "A child is born to you—a son!" 606
23:17 They keep s to those who despise me, 606+606
23:35 of you keeps on s to his friend or relative: 606
23:37 This is what you keep s to a prophet: 606
31: 3 The LORD appeared to us in the past, s: NIH
31:34 or a man his brother, s, 'Know the LORD,' 606
32: 3 s, "Why do you prophesy as you do? 606
32:36 "You are s about this city, 'By the sword, 606
33:11 s, "Give thanks to the LORD Almighty, 606
33:24 not noticed that these people are s, 1819
35:12 word of the LORD came to Jeremiah, s: 606
38: 4 by the things he is s to them. 1819
40:16 What you are s about Ishmael is not true." 1819
Eze 9:11 s, "I have done as you commanded." 606
11: 5 That is what you are s, O house of Israel, 606
12:27 the house of Israel is s, 'The vision he sees 606
13:10 " 'Because they lead my people astray, s, 606
20:49 They are s of me, 'Isn't he just telling 606
33:10 'This is what you are s: 606
33:24 in those ruins in the land of Israel are s, 606
33:30 s to each other, 'Come and hear 1819
Da 4:23 coming down from heaven and s, 10042
10:15 While he was s this to me, 1819
12: 7 s, "It will be for a time, NIH
Am 7:11 For this is what Amos is s: 606
8: 5 s, "When will the New Moon be over 606
Hab 2: 6 s, " 'Woe to him who piles up stolen goods 606
Mal 1: 7 s that the LORD's table is contemptible. 606
1:12 you profane it by s of the Lord's table, 606
2:17 By s, "All who do evil are good in the eyes 606
Mt 3: 2 and s, "Repent, for the kingdom 3306
3:14 But John tried to deter him, s, 3306
5: 2 and he began to teach them, s: 3306
6:31 So do not worry, s, 'What shall we eat?' 3306
7:28 When Jesus had finished s these things, 3364
8:25 The disciples went and woke him, s, "Lord, 3306
9:18 While he was s this, a ruler came 3281
13: 3 he told them many things in parables, s: 3306
14: 4 for John had been s to him: 3306
14:33 s, "Truly you are the Son of God." 3306
19: 1 When Jesus had finished s these things, 3364
21: 2 s to them, "Go to the village ahead of you, 3306
21:16 "Do you hear what these children are s?" 3306
22: 1 Jesus spoke to them again in parables, s: 3306
26: 1 When Jesus had finished s all these things, 3364
26:26 s, "Take and eat; this is my body." 3306
26:27 gave thanks and offered it to them, s, 3306
26:44 prayed the third time, s the same thing. 3306
27:40 and s, "You who are going to destroy 3306
Mk 2:12 s, "We have never seen anything like this!" 3306
3:30 He said this because they were s, 3306
6:14 Some were s, "John the Baptist has been
raised from the dead, 3306
6:18 For John had been s to Herod, 3306
7:19 (In s this, Jesus declared all foods "clean.") NIG
8:26 Jesus sent him home, s, 3306
11: 2 s to them, "Go to the village ahead of you, 3306
12: 6 He sent him last of all, s, 3306
12:32 in s that God is one and there is no other 3306
14: 4 Some of those present were s indignantly 24
14:22 and gave it to his disciples, s, "Take it; 3306
15:29 shaking their heads and s, "So! 3306
Lk 2:13 appeared with the angel, praising God and s, 3306
2:28 took him in his arms and praised God, s: 3306
2:50 But they did not understand what he was s 3281
4:21 and he began by s to them, 3306
7: 1 When Jesus had finished s all this in 4839
8:24 The disciples went and woke him, s, 3306
8:38 but Jesus sent him away, s, 3306
9: 7 because some were s that John 3306
9:33 (He did not know what he was s.) 3306
9:35 A voice came from the cloud, s, 3306
11:27 As Jesus was s these things, 3306
12: 1 Jesus began to speak first to his disciples, s: NIG
14:30 s, 'This fellow began to build and was 3306
19:29 he sent two of his disciples, s to them, 3306
22: 8 Jesus sent Peter and John, s, 3306
22:19 s, "This is my body given for you; 3306
22:20 after the supper he took the cup, s, 3306
22:70 He replied, "You are right in s I am." 3306
23: 2 And they began to accuse him, s, 3306
24:34 and s, "It is true! The Lord has risen 3306
Jn 1:15 s, "This was he of whom I said, 3306
3: 7 You should not be surprised at my s, 3306
4:37 the s 'One sows and another reaps' is true. 3364
7:26 and they are not s a word to him. 3306+4029
8:48 "Aren't we right in s that you are 3306
10:24 The Jews gathered around him, s, 3306
16:17 "What does he mean by s, 3306+4005
16:18 We don't understand what he is s." 3281
16:26 I am not s that I will ask the Father 3306
18:25 He denied it, s, "I am not." 3306
18:37 "You are right in s I am a king. 3306
19: 3 s, "Hail, king of the Jews!" 3306
Ac 3:18 s that his Christ would suffer. NIG
7:26 He tried to reconcile them by s, 'Men, 3306
11:18 s, "So then, God has granted even 3306
13:15 the synagogue rulers sent word to them, s, 3306
13:45 talked abusively against what Paul was s. 3281
17: 7 s that there is another king, 3306
Ac 21: 6 After s good-by to each other, 571
26:14 and I heard a voice s to me in Aramaic, 3306
26:22 I am s nothing beyond what the prophets 3306
26:25 "What I am s is true and reasonable. 710
Ro 3: 8 as we are being slanderously reported as s NIG
4: 9 We have been s that Abraham's faith 3306
1Co 4: 6 learn from us the meaning of the s, NIG
7:35 I am s this for your own good, 3306
11:25 after supper he took the cup, s, 3306
14: 9 how will anyone know what you are s? 3281
14:11 not grasp the meaning of what someone is s, 5889
14:16 since he does not know what you are s? 3306
15:54 then the s that is written will come true: 3364
Gal 4: 1 What I am s is that as long as the heir is 3306
Php 4:11 I am not s this because I am in need, 3306
1Th 5: 3 While people are s, "Peace and safety," 3306
2Th 2: 2 s that the day of the Lord has already come. NIG
1Ti 1:15 a trustworthy s that deserves full acceptance 3364
3: 1 Here is a trustworthy s: 3364
4: 9 a trustworthy s that deserves full acceptance 3364
5:13 s things they ought not to. 3281
2Ti 2: 7 Reflect on what I am s, 3306
2:11 Here is a trustworthy s: 3364
Tit 3: 8 This is a trustworthy s. 3364
Heb 6:14 s, "I will surely bless you 3306
8: 1 The point of what we are s is this: 3306
8:11 or a man his brother, s, 'Know the Lord,' 3306
2Pe 1:17 s, "This is my Son, whom I love; NIG
1Jn 5:16 I am not s that he should pray about that. 3306
Rev 4: 8 Day and night they never stop s: 3306
6: 6 s, "A quart of wheat for a day's wages, 3306
7:12 s: "Amen! Praise and glory 3306
11:12 Then they heard a loud voice from heaven s 3306
11:17 s: "We give thanks to you, 3306
16: 1 Then I heard a loud voice from the temple s 3306
16:17 a loud voice from the throne, s, 3306
19: 5 Then a voice came from the throne, s: 3306
21: 3 And I heard a loud voice from the throne s, 3306

SAYINGS (10) [SAY]

Ps 49:13 and of their followers, who approve their s. 7023
Pr 1: 6 the s and riddles of the wise. 1821
22:17 Pay attention and listen to the s of the wise; 1821
22:20 Have I not written thirty s for you, NIH
22:20 s of counsel and knowledge, NIH
24:23 These also are s of the wise: NIH
30: 1 The s of Agur son of Jakeh— 1821
31: 1 The s of King Lemuel— 1821
Ecc 12:11 their collected s like firmly embedded 670+1251
Jn 10:21 "These are not the s of a man possessed by 4839

SAYS (742) [SAY]

Ge 24:14 and she s, 'Drink, and I'll water your camels 606
24:44 and if she s to me,'Drink, and I'll water 606
32: 4 'Your servant Jacob s, 606
45: 9 'This is what your son Joseph s: 606
Ex 4:22 say to Pharaoh, 'This is what the LORD s: 606
5: 1 This is what the LORD, the God of Israel, s: 606
5:10 "This is what Pharaoh s: 606
7: 9 "When Pharaoh s to you, 1819
7:17 This is what the LORD s: 606
8: 1 'This is what the LORD s: 606
8:20 'This is what the LORD s: 606
9: 1 the LORD, the God of the Hebrews, s: 606
9:13 the LORD, the God of the Hebrews, s: 606
10: 3 the LORD, the God of the Hebrews, s: 606
11: 4 So Moses said, "This is what the LORD s: 606
22: 9 lost property about which somebody s, 606
23:21 Pay attention to him and listen to what he s. 7754
23:22 If you listen carefully to what he s 7754
32:27 s: 'Each man strap a sword to his side. 606
Nu 20:14 "This is what your brother Israel s: 606
21:14 the Book of the Wars of the LORD s: 606
22:16 "This is what Balak son of Zippor s: 606
23:26 I must do whatever the LORD s?" 1819
24:13 and I must say only what the LORD s'? 1819
30: 4 about her vow or pledge but s nothing 3087
30: 7 about it but s nothing to her, 3087
30:11 but s nothing to her and does not forbid her, 3087
30:14 But if her husband s nothing to her about it
3087+3087
32:27 fight before the LORD, just as our lord s." 1819
Dt 5:27 and listen to all that the LORD our God s. 606
13: 2 which he has spoken takes place, and he s, 606
15:16 But if your servant s to you, 606
Jos 7:13 the God of Israel, s: 606
22:16 "The whole assembly of the LORD s: 606
24: 2 the LORD, the God of Israel, s: 606
Jdg 6: 8 the LORD, the God of Israel, s: 606
11:15 "This is what Jephthah s: 606
1Sa 2:27 "This is what the LORD s: 606
9: 6 and everything he s comes true. 1819
10:18 the LORD, the God of Israel, s: 606
15: 2 This is what the LORD Almighty s: 606
20: 7 he s, 'Very well,' then your servant is safe. 606
2Sa 7: 5 'This is what the LORD s: 606
7: 8 'This is what the LORD Almighty s: 606
12: 7 the LORD, the God of Israel, s: 606
12:11 "This is what the LORD s: 606
14:10 "If anyone s anything to you, 1819
14:13 When the king s this, 1819
14:17 "And now your servant s, 606
14:19 to the left from anything my lord the king s. 1819
15:26 But if he s, 'I am not pleased with you,' 606
17: 6 Should we do what he s? 1821

2Sa 24:12 'This is what the LORD s: 606
1Ki 1:51 *He* s, 'Let King Solomon swear to me today 606
2:30 "The king s, 'Come out!' " 606
2:31 the king commanded Benaiah, "Do as *he* s. 1819
3:23 The king said, "This one s, 606
3:23 while that one s, 'No! 606
11:31 this is what the LORD, the God of Israel, s: 606
12:24 'This is what the LORD s: 606
13:2 This is what the LORD s: 606
13:21 "This is what the LORD s: 606
14:7 this is what the LORD, the God of Israel, s: 606
17:14 this is what the LORD, the God of Israel, s: 606
20:2 saying, "This is what Ben-Hadad s: 606
20:5 "This is what Ben-Hadad s: 606
20:13 "This is what the LORD s: 606
20:14 "This is what the LORD s: 606
20:28 "This is what the LORD s: 606
20:32 "Your servant Ben-Hadad s: 606
20:42 "This is what the LORD s: 606
21:19 Say to him, 'This is what the LORD s: 606
21:19 say to him, 'This is what the LORD s: 606
21:23 "And also concerning Jezebel the LORD s: 1819
22:11 "This is what the LORD s: 606
22:27 'This is what the king s: 606
2Ki 1:4 Therefore this is what the LORD s: 606
1:6 "This is what the LORD s: 606
1:9 "Man of God, the king s, 'Come down!' " 1819
1:11 "Man of God, this is what the king s, 606
1:16 "This is what the LORD s: 606
2:21 saying, "This is what the LORD s: 606
3:16 "This is what the LORD s: 606
3:17 For this is what the LORD s: 606
4:43 For this is what the LORD s: 606
7:1 This is what the LORD s: 606
9:3 'This is what the LORD s: 606
9:6 This is what the LORD, the God of Israel, s: 606
9:11 know the man and the **sort of things he s**," 8490
9:12 'This is what the LORD s: 606
9:18 "This is what the king s: 606
9:19 "This is what the king s: 606
18:19 what the great king, the king of Assyria, s: 606
18:29 This is what the king s: 606
18:30 in the LORD when he s, 'The LORD will 606
18:31 This is what the king of Assyria s: 606
18:32 for he is misleading you when he s, 606
19:3 They told him, "This is what Hezekiah s: 606
19:6 'This is what the LORD s: 606
19:10 god you depend on deceive you when he s, 606
19:20 "This is what the LORD, the God of Israel, s: 606
19:32 "Therefore this is what the LORD s 606
20:1 "This is what the LORD s: 606
20:5 the LORD, the God of your father David, s: 606
20:17 Nothing will be left, s the LORD. 606
21:12 this is what the LORD, the God of Israel, s: 606
22:15 "This is what the LORD, the God of Israel, s: 606
22:16 'This is what the LORD s: 606
22:18 s concerning the words you heard: 606
1Ch 17:4 'This is what the LORD s: 606
17:7 'This is what the LORD Almighty s: 606
21:10 'This is what the LORD s: 606
21:11 "This is what the LORD s: 606
2Ch 11:4 'This is what the LORD s: 606
12:5 "This is what the LORD s, 606
18:10 "This is what the LORD s: 606
18:13 I can tell him only what my God s." 606
18:26 'This is what the king s: 606
20:15 This is what the LORD s to you: 606
21:12 the God of your father David, s: 606
24:20 "This is what God s: 606
32:10 "This is what Sennacherib king of Assyria s: 606
32:11 When Hezekiah s, 'The LORD our God will save us 606
34:23 "This is what the LORD, the God of Israel, s: 606
34:24 'This is what the LORD s: 606
34:26 s concerning the words you heard: 606
36:23 "This is what Cyrus king of Persia s: 606
Ezr 1:2 "This is what Cyrus king of Persia s: 606
Ne 6:6 and Geshem s it is true— 606
Job 8:18 that place disowns it and s, NIH
28:14 The deep s, 'It is not in me'; 606
28:14 the sea s, 'It is not with me.' 606
33:27 Then he comes to men and s, 'I sinned, 606
34:5 "Job s, 'I am innocent, 606
34:9 For *he* s, 'It profits a man nothing 606
34:18 Is he not the *One who* s to kings, 606
34:31 "Suppose *a man* s to God, 606
35:10 But *no one* s, 'Where is God my Maker, 606
37:6 *He* s to the snow, 'Fall on the earth,' 606
Ps 10:6 *He* s to himself, "Nothing will shake me; 606
10:11 *He* s to himself, "God has forgotten; 606
12:4 that s, "We will triumph with our tongues; 606
12:5 I will now arise," s the LORD. 606
14:1 The fool s in his heart, "There is no God." 606
27:8 My heart s of you, "Seek his face!" 606
50:16 But to the wicked, God s: 606
53:1 The fool s in his heart, "There is no God." 606
68:22 Lord s, "I will bring them from Bashan; 606
81:6 He s, "I removed the burden NIH
91:14 "Because he loves me," s the LORD, NIH
110:1 The LORD s to my Lord: 5536
Pr 9:4 *she* s to those who lack judgment. 606
9:16 *she* s to those who lack judgment. 606
20:14 it's no good!" s the buyer; 606
22:13 The sluggard s, "There is a lion outside!" 606
23:7 "Eat and drink," *he* s to you, 606
24:24 *Whoever* s to the guilty, 606
26:13 The sluggard s, "There is a lion in the road, 606

Pr 26:19 is a man who deceives his neighbor and s, 606
28:24 He who robs his father or mother and s, 606
30:16 and fire, *which* never s, 'Enough!' 606
30:20 She eats and wipes her mouth and s, 606
Ecc 1:2 Meaningless!" s the Teacher. 606
7:27 "Look," s the Teacher, 606
12:8 Meaningless!" s the Teacher. 606
Isa 1:11 what are they to me?" s the LORD. 606
1:18 let us reason together," s the LORD. 606
3:16 The LORD s, "The women of Zion are 606
7:7 Yet this is what the Sovereign LORD s: 606
10:8 'Are not my commanders all kings?' *he* s. 606
10:13 For *he* s: " 'By the strength of my hand 606
10:24 the Lord, the LORD Almighty, s: 606
16:14 But now the LORD s: 1819
18:4 This is what the LORD s to me: 606
21:6 This is what the Lord s to me: 606
21:16 This is what the Lord s to me: 606
22:14 s the Lord, the LORD Almighty. 606
22:15 the Lord, the LORD Almighty, s: 606
28:16 So this is what the Sovereign LORD s: 606
29:13 The Lord s: "These people come near to 606
29:22 s to the house of Jacob: 606
30:12 this is what the Holy One of Israel s: 606
30:15 Sovereign LORD, the Holy One of Israel, s: 606
31:4 This is what the LORD s to me: 606
33:10 "Now will I arise," s the LORD. 606
36:4 what the great king, the king of Assyria, s: 606
36:14 This is what the king s: 606
36:15 in the LORD *when* he s, 'The LORD will 606
36:16 This is what the king of Assyria s: 606
36:18 not let Hezekiah mislead you *when* he s, 606
37:3 They told him, "This is what Hezekiah s: 606
37:6 'This is what the LORD s: 606
37:10 god you depend on deceive you *when* he s, 606
37:21 This is what the LORD, the God of Israel, s: 606
37:33 "Therefore this is what the LORD s 606
38:1 "This is what the LORD s: 606
38:5 the God of your father David, s: 606
39:6 Nothing will be left, s the LORD. 606
40:1 Comfort, comfort my people, s your God. 606
40:6 A voice s, "Cry out." 606
40:25 Or who is my equal?" s the Holy One. 606
41:6 each helps the other and s to his brother, 606
41:7 *He* s of the welding, "It is good." 606
41:13 who takes hold of your right hand and s 606
41:21 "Present your case," s the LORD. 606
41:21 "Set forth your arguments," s Jacob's King. 606
42:5 This is what God the LORD s— 606
43:1 But now, this is what the LORD s— 606
43:14 This is what the LORD s— 606
43:16 This is what the LORD s— 606
44:2 This is what the LORD s— 606
44:6 "This is what the LORD s— 606
44:16 He also warms himself and s, "Ah! 606
44:17 He prays to it and s, "Save me; 606
44:24 "This is what the LORD s— 606
44:26 who s of Jerusalem, 'It shall be inhabited,' 606
44:27 who s to the watery deep, 606
44:28 who s of Cyrus, 'He is my shepherd 606
45:1 "This is what the LORD s to his anointed, 606
45:10 Woe to *him who* s to his father, 606
45:11 "This is what the LORD s— 606
45:13 s the LORD Almighty." 606
45:14 This is what the LORD s: 606
45:18 For this is what the LORD s— 606
45:18 but formed it to be inhabited—he s: NIH
48:17 This is what the LORD s— 606
48:22 "There is no peace," s the LORD, 606
49:5 And now the LORD s— 606
49:6 *he* s: "It is too small a thing for you 606
49:7 This is what the LORD s— 606
49:8 This is what the LORD s: 606
49:22 This is what the Sovereign LORD s: 606
49:25 But this is what the LORD s: 606
50:1 This is what the LORD s: 606
51:22 This is what your Sovereign LORD s, 606
52:3 For this is what the LORD s: 606
52:4 For this is what the Sovereign LORD s: 606
54:1 of her who has a husband," s the LORD. 606
54:6 only to be rejected," s your God. 606
54:8 s the LORD your Redeemer. 606
54:10 s the LORD, who has compassion on you. 606
56:1 This is what the LORD s: 606
56:4 For this is what the LORD s: 606
57:15 For this is what the high and lofty *One* s 606
57:19 peace, to those far and near," s the LORD. 606
57:21 "There is no peace," s my God, 606
59:21 this is my covenant with them," s the LORD. 606
59:21 from this time on and forever," s the LORD. 606
65:7 and the sins of your fathers," s the LORD. 606
65:8 This is what the LORD s: 606
65:13 the Sovereign LORD s: 606
65:25 on all my holy mountain," s the LORD. 606
66:1 This is what the LORD s: 606
66:9 and not give delivery?" s the LORD. 606
66:9 when I bring to delivery?" s your God. 606
66:12 For this is what the LORD s: 606
66:20 and on mules and camels," s the LORD. 606
66:21 of them also to be priests and Levites," s 606
66:23 and bow down before me," s the LORD. 606
Jer 2:5 This is what the LORD s: 606
4:3 the LORD s to the men of Judah and 606
4:27 This is what the LORD s: 606
5:14 the LORD God Almighty s: 606
6:6 This is what the LORD Almighty s: 606
6:9 This is what the LORD Almighty s: 606

Jer 6:15 down when I punish them," s the LORD. 606
6:16 This is what the LORD s: 606
6:21 Therefore this is what the LORD s: 606
6:22 This is what the LORD s: 606
7:3 the God of Israel, s: 606
7:20 the Sovereign LORD s: 606
7:21 the God of Israel, s: 606
8:4 "Say to them, 'This is what the LORD s: 606
8:12 be brought down when they are punished, s 606
9:7 the LORD Almighty s: 606
9:15 the God of Israel, s: 606
9:17 This is what the LORD Almighty s: 606
9:23 This is what the LORD s: 606
10:1 Hear what the LORD s to you, 1819
10:2 This is what the LORD s: 606
10:18 For this is what the LORD s: 606
11:3 the God of Israel, s: 606
11:11 Therefore this is what the LORD s: 606
11:21 "Therefore this is what the LORD s about 606
11:22 the LORD Almighty s: 606
12:14 This is what the LORD s: 606
13:9 "This is what the LORD s: 606
13:12 the God of Israel, s: 606
13:13 then tell them, 'This is what the LORD s: 606
14:10 the LORD s about this people: 606
14:15 this is what the LORD s about 606
15:2 tell them, 'This is what the LORD s: 606
15:19 Therefore this is what the LORD s: 606
16:3 For this is what the LORD s about the sons 606
16:5 For this is what the LORD s: 606
16:9 the God of Israel, s: 606
17:5 This is what the LORD s: 606
17:21 This is what the LORD s: 606
18:11 'This is what the LORD s: Look! 606
18:13 Therefore this is what the LORD s: 606
18:18 and pay no attention to anything he s." 1821
19:1 This is what the LORD s: 606
19:3 the God of Israel, s: Listen! 606
19:11 'This is what the LORD Almighty s: 606
19:15 the God of Israel, s: 'Listen! 606
20:4 For this is what the LORD s: 606
21:4 the God of Israel, s: 606
21:8 tell the people, 'This is what the LORD s: 606
21:12 this is what the LORD s: 606
22:1 This is what the LORD s: 606
22:3 This is what the LORD s: 606
22:6 the LORD s about the palace of the king 606
22:11 the LORD s about Shallum son of Josiah, 606
22:14 He s, 'I will build myself a great palace 606
22:18 Therefore this is what the LORD s 606
22:30 This is what the LORD s: 606
23:2 s to the shepherds who tend my people: 606
23:15 this is what the LORD Almighty s 606
23:16 This is what the LORD Almighty s: 606
23:17 'The LORD s: You will have peace.' 1819
23:38 this is what the LORD s: 606
24:5 the God of Israel, s: 606
24:8 so bad they cannot be eaten,' s the LORD, 606
25:8 Therefore the LORD Almighty s this: 606
25:27 the God of Israel, s: 606
25:28 'This is what the LORD Almighty s: 606
25:32 This is what the LORD Almighty s: 606
26:2 "This is what the LORD s: 606
26:4 Say to them, 'This is what the LORD s: 606
26:18 'This is what the LORD Almighty s: 606
27:4 the God of Israel, s: 606
27:16 "This is what the LORD s: 606
27:19 the LORD Almighty s about the pillars, 606
27:21 s about the things that are left in the house 606
28:2 the God of Israel, s: 606
28:11 "This is what the LORD s: 606
28:13 'This is what the LORD s: 606
28:14 the God of Israel, s: 606
28:16 Therefore, this is what the LORD s: 606
29:4 s to all those I carried into exile 606
29:8 the God of Israel, s: 606
29:10 This is what the LORD s: 606
29:16 the LORD s about the king who sits 606
29:17 this is what the LORD Almighty s: 606
29:21 s about Ahab son of Kolaiah 606
29:25 the God of Israel, s: 606
29:31 'This is what the LORD s about Shemaiah 606
29:32 this is what the LORD s: 606
30:2 the God of Israel, s: 606
30:3 to possess,' s the LORD." 606
30:5 "This is what the LORD s: 606
30:12 "This is what the LORD s: 606
30:18 "This is what the LORD s: 606
31:2 This is what the LORD s: 606
31:7 This is what the LORD s: 606
31:15 This is what the LORD s: 606
31:16 This is what the LORD s: 606
31:23 the God of Israel, s: 606
31:35 This is what the LORD s, 606
31:37 This is what the LORD s: 606
32:3 You say, 'This is what the LORD s: 606
32:14 the God of Israel, s: 606
32:15 the God of Israel, s: 606
32:28 Therefore, this is what the LORD s: 606
32:36 the God of Israel, s: 606
32:42 "This is what the LORD s: 606
33:2 "This is what the LORD s, he who made 606
33:4 s about the houses in this city and 606
33:10 "This is what the LORD s: 606
33:11 the land as they were before,' s the LORD. 606
33:12 "This is what the LORD Almighty s: 606
33:13 of the one who counts them,' s the LORD. 606

Jer	33:17	For this is what the LORD s:	606
	33:20	"This is what the LORD s:	606
	33:25	This is what the LORD s:	606
	34: 2	the God of Israel, s:	606
	34: 2	'This is what the LORD s:	606
	34: 4	This is what the LORD s concerning you:	606
	34:13	the God of Israel, s:	606
	34:17	"Therefore, this is what the LORD s:	606
	35:13	the God of Israel, s:	606
	35:17	the God of Israel, s: 'Listen!	606
	35:18	the God of Israel, s:	606
	35:19	the God of Israel, s:	606
	36:29	'This is what the LORD s:	606
	36:30	the LORD s about Jehoiakim king	606
	37: 7	the God of Israel, s:	606
	37: 9	"This is what the LORD s:	606
	38: 2	"This is what the LORD s:	606
	38: 3	And this is what the LORD s:	606
	38:17	the God of Israel, s:	606
	39:16	the God of Israel, s:	606
	42: 4	the LORD s and will keep nothing back	6699
	42: 9	to present your petition, s:	606
	42:15	the God of Israel, s:	606
	42:18	the God of Israel, s:	606
	42:20	tell us everything he s and we will do it.'	606
	43:10	the God of Israel, s:	606
	44: 2	the God of Israel, s:	606
	44: 7	the God of Israel, s:	606
	44:11	the God of Israel, s:	606
	44:25	the God of Israel, s:	606
	44:26	'I swear by my great name,' s the LORD,	606
	44:30	This is what the LORD s:	606
	45: 2	the God of Israel, s to you, Baruch:	606
	45: 4	'This is what the LORD s:	606
	46: 8	*She* s, 'I will rise and cover the earth;	606
	46:25	The LORD Almighty, the God of Israel, s:	606
	47: 2	This is what the LORD s:	606
	48: 1	s: "Woe to Nebo, for it will be ruined.	606
	48:40	This is what the LORD s: "Look!	606
	49: 1	This is what the LORD s:	606
	49: 2	out those who drove her out," s the LORD.	606
	49: 7	This is what the LORD Almighty s:	606
	49:12	This is what the LORD s:	606
	49:18	s the LORD, "so no one will live there;	606
	49:28	This is what the LORD s:	606
	49:35	This is what the LORD Almighty s:	606
	50:18	the God of Israel, s:	606
	50:33	This is what the LORD Almighty s:	606
	51: 1	This is what the LORD s:	606
	51:33	the God of Israel, s:	606
	51:35	those who live in Babylonia," s Jerusalem.	606
	51:36	Therefore, this is what the LORD s:	606
	51:58	This is what the LORD Almighty s:	606
Eze	2: 4	'This is what the Sovereign LORD s.'	606
	3:11	'This is what the Sovereign LORD s,'	606
	3:27	'This is what the Sovereign LORD s.'	606
	5: 5	"This is what the Sovereign LORD s:	606
	5: 7	this is what the Sovereign LORD s:	606
	5: 8	this is what the Sovereign LORD s:	606
	6: 3	the Sovereign LORD s to the mountains	606
	6:11	" 'This is what the Sovereign LORD s:	606
	7: 2	this is what the Sovereign LORD s to	606
	7: 5	"This is what the Sovereign LORD s:	606
	11: 5	"This is what the LORD s:	606
	11: 7	the Sovereign LORD s:	606
	11:16	'This is what the Sovereign LORD s:	606
	11:17	'This is what the Sovereign LORD s:	606
	12:10	'This is what the Sovereign LORD s:	606
	12:19	the Sovereign LORD s about those living	606
	12:23	'This is what the Sovereign LORD s:	606
	12:28	'This is what the Sovereign LORD s:	606
	13: 3	This is what the Sovereign LORD s:	606
	13: 8	this is what the Sovereign LORD s:	606
	13:13	this is what the Sovereign LORD s:	606
	13:18	'This is what the Sovereign LORD s:	606
	13:20	this is what the Sovereign LORD s:	606
	14: 4	'This is what the Sovereign LORD s:	606
	14: 6	'This is what the Sovereign LORD s:	606
	14:21	"For this is what the Sovereign LORD s:	606
	15: 6	this is what the Sovereign LORD s:	606
	16: 3	the Sovereign LORD s to Jerusalem:	606
	16:36	This is what the Sovereign LORD s:	606
	16:59	" 'This is what the Sovereign LORD s:	606
	17: 3	'This is what the Sovereign LORD s:	606
	17: 9	'This is what the Sovereign LORD s:	606
	17:19	this is what the Sovereign LORD s:	606
	17:22	" 'This is what the Sovereign LORD s:	606
	18:29	Yet the house of Israel s,	606
	20: 3	'This is what the Sovereign LORD s:	606
	20: 5	'This is what the Sovereign LORD s:	606
	20:27	'This is what the Sovereign LORD s:	606
	20:30	'This is what the Sovereign LORD s:	606
	20:39	this is what the Sovereign LORD s:	606
	20:47	This is what the Sovereign LORD s:	606
	21: 3	'This is what the LORD s:	606
	21: 9	prophesy and say, 'This is what the Lord s:	606
	21:24	this is what the Sovereign LORD s:	606
	21:26	this is what the Sovereign LORD s:	606
	21:28	'This is what the Sovereign LORD s about	606
	22: 3	'This is what the Sovereign LORD s:	606
	22:19	this is what the Sovereign LORD s:	606
	22:28	'This is what the Sovereign LORD s'—	606
	23:22	this is what the Sovereign LORD s:	606
	23:28	"For this is what the Sovereign LORD s:	606
	23:32	"This is what the Sovereign LORD s:	606
	23:35	this is what the Sovereign LORD s:	606
	23:46	"This is what the Sovereign LORD s:	606
Eze	24: 3	'This is what the Sovereign LORD s:	606
	24: 6	" 'For this is what the Sovereign LORD s:	606
	24: 9	this is what the Sovereign LORD s:	606
	24:21	'This is what the Sovereign LORD s:	606
	25: 3	This is what the Sovereign LORD s:	606
	25: 6	For this is what the Sovereign LORD s:	606
	25: 8	"This is what the Sovereign LORD s:	606
	25:12	"This is what the Sovereign LORD s:	606
	25:13	this is what the Sovereign LORD s:	606
	25:15	"This is what the Sovereign LORD s:	606
	25:16	this is what the Sovereign LORD s:	606
	26: 3	this is what the Sovereign LORD s:	606
	26: 7	"For this is what the Sovereign LORD s:	606
	26:15	"This is what the Sovereign LORD s	606
	26:19	"This is what the Sovereign LORD s:	606
	27: 3	'This is what the Sovereign LORD s:	606
	28: 2	'This is what the Sovereign LORD s:	606
	28: 6	this is what the Sovereign LORD s:	606
	28:12	'This is what the Sovereign LORD s:	606
	28:22	'This is what the Sovereign LORD s:	606
	28:25	" 'This is what the Sovereign LORD s:	606
	29: 3	'This is what the Sovereign LORD s:	606
	29: 8	this is what the Sovereign LORD s:	606
	29:13	" 'Yet this is what the Sovereign LORD s:	606
	29:19	this is what the Sovereign LORD s:	606
	30: 2	'This is what the Sovereign LORD s:	606
	30: 6	" 'This is what the LORD s:	606
	30:10	" 'This is what the Sovereign LORD s:	606
	30:13	" 'This is what the Sovereign LORD s:	606
	30:22	this is what the Sovereign LORD s:	606
	31:10	this is what the Sovereign LORD s:	606
	31:15	" 'This is what the Sovereign LORD s:	606
	32: 3	" 'This is what the Sovereign LORD s:	606
	32:11	" 'For this is what the Sovereign LORD s:	606
	33:25	'This is what the Sovereign LORD s:	606
	33:27	'This is what the Sovereign LORD s:	606
	34: 2	'This is what the Sovereign LORD s:	606
	34:10	This is what the Sovereign LORD s:	606
	34:11	" 'For this is what the Sovereign LORD s:	606
	34:17	this is what the Sovereign LORD s:	606
	34:20	the Sovereign LORD s to them:	606
	35: 3	'This is what the Sovereign LORD s:	606
	35:14	This is what the Sovereign LORD s:	606
	36: 2	This is what the Sovereign LORD s:	606
	36: 3	'This is what the Sovereign LORD s:	606
	36: 4	the Sovereign LORD s to the mountains	606
	36: 5	this is what the Sovereign LORD s:	606
	36: 6	'This is what the Sovereign LORD s:	606
	36: 7	this is what the Sovereign LORD s:	606
	36:13	" 'This is what the Sovereign LORD s:	606
	36:22	'This is what the Sovereign LORD s:	606
	36:33	" 'This is what the Sovereign LORD s:	606
	36:37	"This is what the Sovereign LORD s:	606
	37: 5	the Sovereign LORD s to these bones:	606
	37: 9	'This is what the Sovereign LORD s:	606
	37:12	'This is what the Sovereign LORD s:	606
	37:19	'This is what the Sovereign LORD s:	606
	37:21	'This is what the Sovereign LORD s:	606
	38: 3	'This is what the Sovereign LORD s:	606
	38:10	" 'This is what the Sovereign LORD s:	606
	38:14	'This is what the Sovereign LORD s:	606
	38:17	" 'This is what the Sovereign LORD s:	606
	39: 1	'This is what the Sovereign LORD s:	606
	39:17	this is what the Sovereign LORD s:	606
	39:25	the Sovereign LORD s:	606
	43:18	this is what the Sovereign LORD s:	606
	44: 6	'This is what the Sovereign LORD s:	606
	44: 9	This is what the Sovereign LORD s:	606
	45: 9	" 'This is what the Sovereign LORD s:	606
	45:18	" 'This is what the Sovereign LORD s:	606
	46: 1	" 'This is what the Sovereign LORD s:	606
	46:16	" 'This is what the Sovereign LORD s:	606
	47:13	This is what the Sovereign LORD s:	606
Am	1: 3	This is what the LORD s:	606
	1: 5	of Aram will go into exile to Kir," s	606
	1: 6	This is what the LORD s:	606
	1: 8	s the Sovereign LORD.	606
	1: 9	This is what the LORD s:	606
	1:11	This is what the LORD s:	606
	1:13	This is what the LORD s:	606
	1:15	he and his officials together," s the LORD.	606
	2: 1	This is what the LORD s:	606
	2: 3	and kill all her officials with him," s	606
	2: 4	This is what the LORD s:	606
	2: 6	This is what the LORD s:	606
	3:11	this is what the Sovereign LORD s:	606
	3:12	This is what the LORD s:	606
	5: 3	This is what the Sovereign LORD s:	606
	5: 4	This is what the LORD s to the house	606
	5:16	the LORD God Almighty, s:	606
	5:17	for I will pass through your midst," s	606
	5:27	beyond Damascus," s the LORD,	606
	6:10	and *he* s, "No," then he will say, "Hush!	606
	7:17	"Therefore this is what the LORD s:	606
	9:15	s the LORD your God.	606
Ob	1: 1	the Sovereign LORD s about Edom—	606
Mic	2: 3	Therefore, the LORD s:	606
	2:11	If a liar and deceiver comes and s,	NIH
	3: 5	This is what the LORD s:	606
	6: 1	Listen to what the LORD s:	606
Na	1:12	This is what the LORD s:	606
Hab	2:19	Woe to *him who* s to wood, 'Come to life!'	606
Zep	3:20	before your very eyes," s the LORD.	606
Hag	1: 2	This is what the LORD Almighty s:	606
	1: 5	Now this is what the LORD Almighty s:	606
	1: 7	This is what the LORD Almighty s:	606
	1: 8	in it and be honored," s the LORD.	606
Hag	2: 6	"This is what the LORD Almighty s:	606
	2: 7	s the LORD Almighty.	606
	2: 9	s the LORD Almighty.	606
	2:11	"This is what the LORD Almighty s:	606
	2:11	'Ask the priests what the law s:	606
Zec	1: 3	This is what the LORD Almighty s:	606
	1: 3	s the LORD Almighty.	606
	1: 4	This is what the LORD Almighty s:	606
	1:14	This is what the LORD Almighty s:	606
	1:16	"Therefore, this is what the LORD s:	606
	1:17	This is what the LORD Almighty s:	606
	2: 8	For this is what the LORD Almighty s:	606
	3: 7	"This is what the LORD Almighty s:	606
	3: 9	s the LORD Almighty,	5536
	4: 6	but by my Spirit,' s the LORD Almighty.	606
	5: 3	for according to what it s on one side,	NIH
	5: 3	and according to what it s on the other,	NIH
	6:12	this is what the LORD Almighty s:	606
	7: 9	"This is what the LORD Almighty s:	606
	7:13	I would not listen,' s the LORD Almighty.	606
	8: 2	This is what the LORD Almighty s:	606
	8: 3	This is what the LORD s:	606
	8: 4	This is what the LORD Almighty s:	606
	8: 6	This is what the LORD Almighty s:	606
	8: 7	This is what the LORD Almighty s:	606
	8: 9	This is what the LORD Almighty s:	606
	8:14	This is what the LORD Almighty s:	606
	8:14	s the LORD Almighty,	606
	8:19	This is what the LORD Almighty s:	606
	8:20	This is what the LORD Almighty s:	606
	8:23	This is what the LORD Almighty s:	606
	11: 4	This is what the LORD my God s:	606
Mal	1: 2	"I have loved you," s the LORD.	606
	1: 2	the LORD s. "Yet I have loved Jacob,	5536
	1: 4	But this is what the LORD Almighty s:	606
	1: 6	s the LORD Almighty.	606
	1: 8	s the LORD Almighty.	606
	1: 9	s the LORD Almighty.	606
	1:10	s the LORD Almighty,	606
	1:11	s the LORD Almighty.	606
	1:13	s the LORD Almighty.	606
	1:13	accept them from your hands?" s the LORD.	606
	1:14	I am a great king," s the LORD Almighty,	606
	2: 2	s the LORD Almighty,	606
	2: 4	s the LORD Almighty.	606
	2: 8	s the LORD Almighty.	606
	2:16	s the LORD God of Israel,	606
	2:16	s the LORD Almighty.	606
	3: 1	will come," s the LORD Almighty.	606
	3: 5	s the LORD Almighty.	606
	3: 7	s the LORD Almighty.	606
	3:10	Test me in this," s the LORD Almighty,	606
	3:11	s the LORD Almighty.	606
	3:12	s the LORD Almighty.	606
	3:13	said harsh things against me," s the LORD.	606
	3:17	s the LORD Almighty,	606
	4: 1	s the LORD Almighty.	606
	4: 3	s the LORD Almighty.	606
Mt	5:22	Again, anyone who s to his brother, 'Raca,'	*3306*
	5:22	But anyone who s, 'You fool!'	*3306*
	7:21	"Not everyone who s to me, 'Lord, Lord,'	*3306*
	12:44	Then *it* s, 'I will return to the house I left.'	*3306*
	15: 5	But you say that if a man s to his father	*3306*
	21: 3	If anyone s anything to you,	*3306*
	22:43	calls him 'Lord'? For he s,	*NIG*
	24:23	At that time if anyone s to you, 'Look,	*3306*
	24:48	But suppose that servant is wicked and s	*3306*
	26:18	'The Teacher s: My appointed time is near.	*3306*
Mk	7:11	But you say that if a man s to his father	*3306*
	11:23	if anyone s to this mountain, 'Go,	*3306*
	11:23	but believes that what *he* s will happen,	*3281*
	13:21	At that time if anyone s to you, 'Look,	*3306*
Lk	4:12	Jesus answered, "*It* s: 'Do	*3306*
	5:39	for *he* s, 'The old is better.' "	*3306*
	11: 5	and he goes to him at midnight and s,	*3306*
	11:24	Then *it* s, 'I will return to the house I left.'	*3306*
	12:45	But suppose the servant s to himself,	*3306*
	15: 6	and neighbors together and s, 'Rejoice	*3306*
	15: 9	and neighbors together and s, 'Rejoice	*3306*
	17: 4	and seven times comes back to you and s,	*3306*
	18: 6	"Listen to what the unjust judge s.	*3306*
Jn	8:22	Is that why *he* s, 'Where I go,	*3306*
	8:47	He who belongs to God hears what God s.	*4839*
	12:39	because, as Isaiah s elsewhere:	*3306*
	19:37	as another scripture s, "They will look on	*3306*
Ac	2:17	God s, I will pour out my Spirit	*3306*
	7:48	As the prophet s:	*3306*
	7:49	house will you build for me? s the Lord.	*3306*
	15:17	the Gentiles who bear my name, s the Lord,	*3306*
	19:26	*He* s that man-made gods are no gods at all.	*3306*
	21:11	"The Holy Spirit s, 'In this way	*3306*
Ro	3:19	Now we know that whatever the law s,	*3306*
	3:19	*it* s to those who are under the law,	*3281*
	4: 6	David s the same thing when he speaks of	*NIG*
	9:15	For *he* s to Moses, "I will have mercy	*3306*
	9:17	For the Scripture s to Pharaoh:	*3306*
	9:25	As *he* s in Hosea: "I will call them	*3306*
	10: 6	But the righteousness that is by faith s:	*3306*
	10:11	As the Scripture s, "Anyone who trusts	*3306*
	10:16	For Isaiah s, "Lord, who has believed	*3306*
	10:19	Moses s, "I will make you envious	*3306*
	10:20	And Isaiah boldly s, "I was found	*3306*
	10:21	But concerning Israel *he* s,	*3306*
	11: 2	Scripture s in the poassage **about** Elijah—	*3306*
	11: 9	David s: "May their table become a snare	*3306*
	12:19	I will repay," s the Lord.	*3306*
	14:11	" 'As surely as I live,' s the Lord,	*3306*

Ro 15:10 Again, *it* s, "Rejoice, O Gentiles, *3306*
15:12 Isaiah **s**, "The Root of Jesse will spring up, *3306*
1Co 1:12 One of you **s**, "I follow Paul"; *3306*
3: 4 For when one **s**, "I follow Paul," *3306*
9:10 Surely *he* s this for us, doesn't he? *3306*
10:28 But if anyone s to you, *3306*
12: 3 who is speaking by the Spirit of God **s**, *3306*
14:13 that he may interpret what he s. *NIG*
14:21 then they will not listen to me," s the Lord. *3306*
14:34 but must be in submission, as the Law **s**. *3306*
15:27 when *it* s that "everything" has been put *3306*
2Co 6: 2 For *he* s, "In the time of my favor *3306*
6:17 from them and be separate, s the Lord. *3306*
6:18 s the Lord Almighty." *3306*
Gal 4:21 are you not aware of what the law **s?** *NIG*
Eph 4: 8 This is why *it* **s**: "When he ascended *3306*
1Ti 4: 1 The Spirit clearly s that in later times *3306*
5:18 For the Scripture **s**, "Do not muzzle *3306*
Heb 1: 6 *he* **s**, "Let all God's angels worship him." *3306*
1: 7 In speaking of the angels *he* **s**, *3306*
1: 8 But about the Son he **s**, "Your throne, *NIG*
1:10 He also **s**, "In the beginning, O Lord, *NIG*
2:12 *He* **s**, "I will declare your name *3306*
2:13 And again he **s**, "Here am I, *NIG*
3: 7 So, as the Holy Spirit **s**: "Today, if you *3306*
4: 5 And again in the passage above he **s**, *NIG*
5: 6 And *he* s in another place, *3306*
10:15 Spirit also testifies about this. First *he* **s**: *3306*
10:16 with them after that time, s the Lord. *3306*
Jas 1:22 and so deceive yourselves. Do what it **s**. *NIG*
1:23 to the word but does not do what it s is like *NIG*
2:16 *If* one of you s to him, "Go, *3306*
2:23 And the scripture was fulfilled that **s**, *3306*
3: 2 If anyone is never at fault in **what** he **s**, *3364*
4: 5 Or do you think Scripture s without reason *3306*
4: 6 That is why Scripture **s**: "God opposes *3306*
1Pe 2: 6 For in Scripture *it* **s**: "See, I lay a stone *4321*
1Jn 2: 4 The man who **s**, "I know him," *3306*
4:20 If anyone **s**, "I love God," *3306*
Rev 1: 8 s the Lord God, "who is, and who was, *3306*
2: 7 let him hear what the Spirit s to the churches *3306*
2:11 let him hear what the Spirit s to the churches *3306*
2:17 let him hear what the Spirit s to the churches *3306*
2:29 let him hear what the Spirit s to the churches *3306*
3: 6 let him hear what the Spirit s to the churches *3306*
3:13 let him hear what the Spirit s to the churches *3306*
3:22 let him hear what the Spirit s to the churches *3306*
14:13 s the Spirit, "they will rest from their labor, *3306*
22:20 He who testifies to these things **s**, "Yes, *3306*

SCAB, SCABBED (KJV) See FESTERING SORES, RASH, RUNNING SORES, SORES

SCABBARD (5)

1Sa 17:51 and drew it from the **s**. 9509
Jer 47: 6 Return to your **s**; cease and be still.' 9509
Eze 21: 3 I will draw my sword from its **s** and cut off 9509
21: 5 I the LORD have drawn my sword from its **s**; 9509
21:30 Return the sword to its **s**. 9509

SCABS (1)

Job 7: 5 My body is clothed with worms and **s**, 1599+6760

SCAFFOLD (KJV) See PLATFORM

SCALE (4) [SCALES]

1Sa 17: 5 his head and wore a **coat of s armor** 7989+9234
2Sa 22:30 with my God *I can* s a wall. 1925
Ps 18:29 with my God *I can* s a wall. 1925
Joel 2: 7 *they* s walls like soldiers. 6590

SCALES (25) [SCALE]

Lev 11: 9 you may eat any that have fins and **s**. 7989
11:10 that do not have fins and **s**— 7989
11:12 the water that does not have fins and s is to 7989
19:36 Use honest s and honest weights, 4404
Dt 14: 9 you may eat any that has fins and **s**. 7989
14:10 that does not have fins and s you may 7989
Job 6: 2 and all my misery be placed on the **s!** 4404
31: 6 let God weigh me in honest s 4404
Pr 11: 1 The LORD abhors dishonest **s**, 4404
16:11 Honest s and balances are from the LORD; 4404
20:23 and dishonest s do not please him. 4404
Isa 40:12 or weighed the mountains on the s and 7144
40:15 they are regarded as dust on the **s**; 4404
46: 6 and weigh out silver on the **s**; 7866
Jer 32:10 and weighed out the silver on the **s**. 4404
Eze 5: 1 take a **set of s** and divide up the hair. 4404+5486
29: 4 the fish of your streams stick to your **s**. 7989
29: 4 with all the fish sticking to your **s**. 7989
45:10 You are to use accurate **s**, 4404
Da 5:27 You have been weighed on the s 10396
Hos 12: 7 The merchant uses dishonest **s**; 4404
Am 8: 5 the price and cheating with dishonest **s**, 4404
Mic 6:11 Shall I acquit a man with dishonest **s**, 4404
Ac 9:18 something like s fell from Saul's eyes, *3318*
Rev 6: 5 Its rider was holding a **pair of s** in his hand. *2433*

SCALL (KJV) See SORE

SCALP (1) [SCALPS]

Lev 13:41 If he has lost his hair from the front of his s 7156

SCALPS (1) [SCALP]

Isa 3:17 the LORD will make their s bald." 7327

SCANT (KJV) See SHORT

SCAPEGOAT (4) [GOAT]

Lev 16: 8 for the LORD and the other for the **s**. 6439
16:10 But the goat chosen by lot as the s shall 6439
16:10 by sending it into the desert as a **s**. 6439
16:26 a **s** must wash his clothes and bathe himself 6439

SCAR (2)

Lev 13:23 it is only a *s from* the boil, 7648
13:28 it is only a *s from* the burn. 7648

SCARCE (2) [SCARCELY, SCARCER, SCARCITY]

Dt 8: 9 not *be* **s** and you will lack nothing; 430+928+5017
Eze 4:17 for food and water *will be* **s**. 2893

SCARCELY (4) [SCARCE]

Ge 27:30 and Jacob had **s** left his father's presence, 421
Job 29:24 When I smiled at them, they **s** believed it; 4202
SS 3: 4 **S** had I passed them when I found 3869+5071
Lk 9:39 It **s ever** leaves him and is destroying him. *3653*

SCARCER (1) [SCARCE]

Isa 13:12 *I will* **make** man **s** than pure gold, 3700

SCARCITY (2) [SCARCE]

Pr 6:11 like a bandit and s like an armed man. 4728
24:34 like a bandit and s like an armed man. 4728

SCARECROW (1)

Jer 10: 5 Like a **s** *in* a melon patch, 9473

SCARLET (49)

Ge 38:28 a **s thread** and tied it on his wrist and said, 9106
38:30 who had the **s thread** on his wrist, 9106
Ex 25: 4 purple and **s yarn** and fine linen; 9106+9357
26: 1 purple and **s yarn**, 9106+9357
26:31 and **s yarn** and finely twisted linen, 9106+9357
26:36 and **s yarn** and finely twisted linen— 9106+9357
27:16 and **s yarn** and finely twisted linen— 9106+9357
28: 5 purple and **s yarn**, and fine linen. 9106+9357
28: 6 and of blue, purple and **s yarn**, 9106+9357
28: 8 and with blue, purple and **s yarn**, 9106+9357
28:15 gold, and of blue, purple and **s yarn**, 9106+9357
28:33 and **s yarn** around the hem of the robe, 9106+9357
35: 6 purple and **s yarn** and fine linen; 9106+9357
35:23 or **s yarn** or fine linen, or goat hair, 9106+9357
35:25 blue, purple or **s yarn** or fine linen. 9106+9357
35:35 purple and **s yarn** and fine linen, 9106+9357
36: 8 purple and **s yarn**, 9106+9357
36:35 and **s yarn** and finely twisted linen, 9106+9357
36:37 and **s yarn** and finely twisted linen— 9106+9357
38:18 and **s yarn** and finely twisted linen— 9106+9357
38:23 purple and **s yarn** and fine linen.) 9106+9357
39: 1 and **s yarn** they made woven garments 9106+9357
39: 2 and of blue, purple and **s yarn**, 9106+9357
39: 3 purple and **s yarn** and fine linen— 9106+9357
39: 5 and with blue, purple and **s yarn**, 9106+9357
39: 8 of gold, and of blue, purple and **s yarn**, 9106+9357
39:24 and **s yarn** and finely twisted linen 9106+9357
39:29 purple and **s yarn—** 9106+9357
Lev 14: 4 **s yarn** and hyssop be brought for the 9106+9357
14: 6 the **s yarn** and the hyssop, 9106+9357
14:49 **s yarn** and hyssop. 9106+9357
14:51 hyssop, the **s yarn** and the live bird, 9106+9357
14:52 cedar wood, the hyssop and the **s yarn**. 9106+9357
Nu 4: 8 Over these they are to spread a **s** cloth, 9106+9357
19: 6 hyssop and **s wool** and throw them 9106+9357
Jos 2:18 you have tied this **s** cord in the window 9106
2:21 And she tied the **s** cord in the window. 9106
2Sa 1:24 who clothed you in **s** and finery, 9106
Pr 31:21 for all of them are clothed in **s**. 9106
SS 4: 3 Your lips are like a **s** ribbon; 9106
Isa 1:18 "Though your sins are like **s**, 9106
Jer 4:30 Why dress yourself in **s** and put on jewels 9106
Na 2: 3 the warriors *are* **clad in s**. 9443
Mt 27:28 They stripped him and put a **s** robe on him, *3132*
Heb 9:19 **s** wool and branches of hyssop, *3132*
Rev 17: 3 There I saw a woman sitting on a **s** beast *3132*
17: 4 The woman was dressed in purple and **s**, *3132*
18:12 fine linen, purple, silk and **s** cloth; *3132*
18:16 purple and **s**, and glittering with gold, *3132*

SCATTER (39) [SCATTERED, SCATTERING, SCATTERS]

Ge 49: 7 *I will* s them in Jacob and disperse them 2745
Lev 26:33 *I will* s you among the nations 2430
Nu 16:37 and s the coals some distance away, for 2430
Dt 4:27 The LORD *will* s you among the peoples, 7046
28:64 the LORD *will* s you among all nations, 7046
32:26 I said *I would* s them and blot out 6990
1Sa 13: 8 and Saul's men *began to* **s**. 7046
1Ki 14:15 that he gave to their forefathers and s them 2430
Ne 1: 8 I *will* s you among the nations, 7046
Ps 68:30 S the nations who delight in war. 1029
106:27 among the nations and s them throughout 2430
144: 6 Send forth lightning and s [the enemies]; 7046
Ecc 3: 5 a time to s stones and a time to gather them, 8959
Isa 24: 1 he will ruin its face and s its inhabitants— 7046
28:25 does he not sow caraway and s cummin? 2450
33: 3 when you rise up, the nations **s**. 5880
Jer 9:16 *I will* s them among nations 7046
13:24 *"I will* s you like chaff driven by 7046
18:17 *I will* s them before their enemies; 7046
30:11 the nations among which *I* s you, 7046
46:28 the nations among which *I* s you, 5615
49:32 *I will* s to the winds those who are 2430
49:36 *I will* s them to the four winds, 2430
Eze 5: 2 And s a third to the wind. 2430
5:10 and *will* s all your survivors to the winds. 2430
5:12 a third *I will* s to the winds and pursue 2430
6: 5 *I will* s your bones around your altars. 2430
10: 2 from among the cherubim and s them over 2450
12:14 *I will* s to the winds all those 2430
12:15 among the nations and s them through 2430
20:23 among the nations and s them through 2430
22:15 the nations and s you through the countries; 2430
29:12 the Egyptians among the nations and s them 2430
30:23 the Egyptians among the nations and s them 2430
30:26 the Egyptians among the nations and s them 2430
Da 4:14 strip off its leaves and s its fruit. 10095
Hab 3:14 when his warriors stormed out to s us, 7046
Zec 1:21 against the land of Judah to s its people." 2430
10: 9 Though *I* s them among the peoples, 2445

SCATTERED (85) [SCATTER]

Ge 9:19 from them came *the people who were* **s** *over* 5880
10:18 Later the Canaanite clans **s** 7046
11: 4 for ourselves and not *be* s over the face of 7046
11: 8 So the LORD s them from there over all 7046
11: 9 From there the LORD s them over the face 7046
Ex 5:12 the people s all over Egypt to gather stubble 7046
32:20 to powder, s it on the water and made 2430
Nu 10:35 *May* your enemies *be* **s**; 7046
Dt 30: 3 from all the nations where he s you. 7046
Jdg 9:45 he destroyed the city and s salt *over* it. 2445
1Sa 11:11 Those who survived *were* **s**, 7046
30:16 and there they were, **s** over the countryside, 5759
2Sa 17:19 the opening of the well and s grain over it. 8848
22:15 He shot arrows and s [the enemies], 7046
1Ki 22:17 "I saw all Israel s on the hills like sheep 7046
2Ki 23: 6 to powder and s the dust over the graves of 8959
25: 5 **were** separated from him and **s**, 7046
2Ch 18:16 "I saw all Israel s on the hills like sheep 7046
34: 4 These he broke to pieces and s over 2450
Est 3: 8 "There is a certain people dispersed and **s** 7233
Job 4:11 and the cubs of the lioness **are s**. 7233
18:15 burning sulfur is s over his dwelling. 2430
38:24 or the place where the east winds *are* s over 7046
Ps 18:14 He shot his arrows and s [the enemies], 7046
44:11 be devoured like sheep and *have* s us among 2430
53: 5 God s the bones of those who attacked you; 7061
68: 1 May God arise, *may* his enemies *be* **s**; 7046
68:14 When the Almighty s the kings in the land, 7298
89:10 with your strong arm *you* s your enemies. 7061
92: 9 all evildoers *will* **be s**. 7233
112: 9 *He has* **s abroad** his gifts to the poor, 7061
141: 7 so our bones *have* **been** s at the mouth of 7061
Isa 11:12 he will assemble the s *people of* Judah 7046
Jer 3:13 *you have* s your favors to foreign gods 7061
10:21 not prosper and all their flock **is s**. 7046
23: 2 "Because you *have* s my flock 7046
31:10 *'He who* s Israel will gather them 2430
40:12 all the countries where *they had* **been s**. 5615
40:15 *to* **be s** and the remnant of Judah to perish?" 7046
43: 5 from all the nations where *they had* **been s**. 5615
50:17 a s flock that lions have chased away. 7061
52: 8 **were** separated from him and **s**, 7046
La 4: 1 The sacred gems *are* s at the head 9161
4:16 The LORD himself *has* s them; 2745
Eze 6: 8 the sword when you **are s** among the lands 2430
11:16 the nations and s them among the countries, 7046
11:17 from the countries where *you have* **been s**, 7046
17:21 and the survivors *will* **be** s to the winds. 7298
20:34 from the countries where *you have* **been s**— 7046
20:41 from the countries where *you have* **been s**, 7046
28:25 from the nations where *they have* **been s**, 7046
29:13 from the nations where *they* **were s**. 7046
34: 5 *they were* s because there was no shepherd, 7046
34: 5 when *they were* s they became food for all 7046
34: 6 They **were** s over the whole earth, 7046
34:12 after his s flock when he is with them, 7298
34:12 from all the places where *they* **were** s on 7046
36:19 and *they* **were** s through the countries; 2430
Da 9: 7 the countries where *you have* s us because 5615
Joel 3: 2 for *they* s my people among the nations 7061
Na 3:18 Your people *are* s on the mountains 7056
Zep 3:10 my s people, will bring me offerings. 7046
3:19 the lame and gather those *who have* **been s**. 5615
Zec 1:19 "These are the horns that s Judah, 2430
1:21 "These are the horns that s Judah so 2430
2: 6 *I have* s you to the four winds of heaven," 7298
7:14 *'I have* s them **with a whirlwind** 6192
13: 7 and the sheep *will* **be s**, 7046
Mt 25:24 and gathering where *you have* not **s seed**. *1399*
25:26 and gather where *I have* not **s seed?** *1399*
26:31 and the sheep of the flock *will be* **s**.' *1399*
Mk 14:27 and the sheep *will be* **s**.' *1399*

Lk 1:51 *he has* s those who are proud *1399*
Jn 2:15 *he* s the coins of the money changers *1772*
7:35 go where our **people live** s **among** *1402+3836*
11:52 for that nation but also for the s children *1399*
16:32 and has come, when *you will be* s, *5025*
Ac 5:37 and all his followers *were* s. *1399*
8:1 the apostles *were* s throughout Judea *1401*
8:4 Those who *had been* s preached *1401*
11:19 Now those who *had been* s by *1401*
1Co 10:5 their bodies *were* s over the desert. *2954*
2Co 9:9 *"He has* s **abroad** his gifts to the poor; *5025*
Jas 1:1 To the twelve tribes s among the nations: *1402*
1Pe 1:1 in the world, s **throughout** Pontus, *1402*

SCATTERING (5) [SCATTER]

1Sa 13:11 "When I saw that the men *were* s, 5880
Jer 23:1 to the shepherds who are destroying and s 7046
Mt 13:4 As he *was* s **the seed,** *5062*
Mk 4:4 As he *was* s **the seed,** *5062*
Lk 8:5 As he *was* s **the seed,** *5062*

SCATTERS (7) [SCATTER]

Job 36:30 See how *he* s his lightning about him, 7298
37:11 *he* s his lightning *through* them. 7046
Ps 147:16 He spreads the snow like wool and s 7061
Mt 12:30 and he who does not gather with me s. *5025*
Mk 4:26 A man's seed on the ground. *965*
Lk 11:23 and he who does not gather with me, s. *5025*
Jn 10:12 Then the wolf attacks the flock and s it. *5025*

SCENE (1)

Mk 9:25 that a crowd was running to the s, *NIG*

SCENT (2)

Job 14:9 yet at the s *of* water it will bud 8194
39:25 *He* **catches the** s *of* battle from afar, 8193

SCEPTER (27) [SCEPTERS]

Ge 49:10 The s will not depart from Judah, 8657
Nu 24:17 a s will rise out of Israel. 8657
Est 4:11 to this is for the king to extend the gold s 9222
5:2 and held out to her the gold s that was 9222
5:2 and touched the tip of the s. 9222
8:4 the gold s to Esther and she arose and stood 9222
Ps 2:9 You will rule them with an iron **s;** 8657
45:6 a s *of* justice will be the scepter 8657
45:6 of justice will be the s *of* your kingdom. 8657
60:7 Ephraim is my helmet, Judah my s. 2980
108:8 Ephraim is my helmet, Judah my s. 2980
110:2 The LORD will extend your mighty s 4751
125:3 The s *of* the wicked will not remain over 8657
Isa 14:5 the s *of* the rulers, 8657
30:31 with his s he will strike them down. 8657
Jer 48:17 say, 'How broken is the mighty s, 4751
Eze 19:11 Its branches were strong, fit for a ruler's s. 8657
19:14 on it fit for a ruler's **s.'** 8657
21:10 in the s *of* my son [Judah]? 8657
21:13 And what if the s [of Judah], 8657
Am 1:5 and the one who holds the s in Beth Eden. 8657
1:8 and the one who holds the s in Ashkelon. 8657
Zec 10:11 down and Egypt's s will pass away. 8657
Heb 1:8 and righteousness will be the s *4811*
Rev 2:27 'He will rule them with an iron **s;** *4811*
12:5 who will rule all the nations with an iron s. *4811*
19:15 "He will rule them with an iron **s."** *4811*

SCEPTERS (1) [SCEPTER]

Nu 21:18 the nobles with s and staffs." 2980

SCEVA (1)

Ac 19:14 Seven sons *of* **S**, a Jewish chief priest, *5005*

SCHEME (4) [SCHEMER, SCHEMES, SCHEMING]

Est 9:25 that the evil s Haman had devised against 4742
Ecc 7:25 to search out wisdom and the s **of things** 3113
7:27 to another to discover the s **of things—** 3113
Eze 38:10 and you will devise an evil **s.** 4742

SCHEMER (1) [SCHEME]

Pr 24:8 who plots evil will be known as a s. 1251+4659

SCHEMES (20) [SCHEME]

Ex 21:14 a man s and kills another man deliberately, 2326
Job 5:13 and the s *of* the wily are swept away. 6783
10:3 while you smile on the s *of* the wicked? 6783
18:7 his own s throw him down. 6783
21:27 the s by which you would wrong me. 4659
Ps 10:2 who are caught in the s he devises. 4659
21:11 and devise **wicked s,** they cannot succeed; 4659
26:10 in whose hands are **wicked s,** 2365
37:7 when they carry out their **wicked s.** 4659
119:150 Those who devise **wicked** s are near, 2365
Pr 1:31 and be filled with the fruit of their **s.** 4600
6:18 a heart that devises wicked **s,** 4742
24:9 s *of* folly are sin, and men detest a mocker. 2365
Ecc 7:29 but men have gone in search of many **s."** 3115
8:11 of the people are filled with s to do wrong. NIH
Isa 32:7 he makes up **evil** s to destroy the poor 2365
Jer 6:19 disaster on this people, the fruit of their s, 4742
Jer 11:15 in my temple as she works out her **evil s** 4659
2Co 2:11 For we are not unaware of his **s.** *3784*
Eph 6:11 take your stand against the devil's **s.** *3497*

SCHEMING (2) [SCHEME]

Ne 6:2 But they *were* s to harm me; 3108
Eph 4:14 and craftiness of men in their deceitful **s.** *3497*

SCHISM (KJV) See DIVISION

SCHOLAR (1)

1Co 1:20 Where is the wise man? Where is the **s?** *1208*

SCHOOL (KJV) See LECTURE HALL

SCHOOLMASTER (KJV) See SUPERVISION, PUT IN CHARGE

SCIENCE (KJV) See KNOWLEDGE

SCOFF (10) [SCOFFED, SCOFFERS, SCOFFING, SCOFFS]

1Ki 9:8 all who pass by will be appalled and *will* s 9239
Ps 59:8 *you* s at all those nations. 4352
73:8 *They* s, and speak with malice; 4610
Jer 19:8 all who pass by will be appalled and *will* s 9239
49:17 all who pass by will be appalled and *will* s 9239
50:13 and s because of all her wounds. 9239
La 2:15 *they* s and shake their heads at the Daughter 9239
2:16 *they* s and gnash their teeth and say, 9239
Hab 1:10 They deride kings and s at rulers. 5377
Zep 2:15 All who pass by her s and shake their fists. 9239

SCOFFED (1) [SCOFF]

2Ch 36:16 despised his words and s at his prophets 9506

SCOFFERS (4) [SCOFF]

Isa 28:14 you s who rule this people in Jerusalem. 408+4371
Ac 13:41 *you* **s,** wonder and perish, *2970*
2Pe 3:3 that in the last days s will come, *1851*
Jude 1:18 there will be s who will follow their own ungodly desires." *1851*

SCOFFING (1) [SCOFF]

2Pe 3:3 s and following their own evil desires. *1848*

SCOFFS (2) [SCOFF]

Ps 2:4 in heaven laughs; the Lord s at them. 4352
Pr 29:9 the fool rages and **s,** and there is no peace. 8471

SCOOP (1) [SCOOPED, SCOOPING, SCOOPS]

Pr 6:27 *Can* a man s fire into his lap 3149

SCOOPED (1) [SCOOP]

Jdg 14:9 which *he* s **out** with his hands and ate 8098

SCOOPING (1) [SCOOP]

Isa 30:14 for taking coals from a hearth or s water out 3106

SCOOPS (1) [SCOOP]

Ps 7:15 and s **it out** falls into the pit he has made. 2916

SCORCH (1) [SCORCHED, SCORCHING, SUN-SCORCHED]

Rev 16:8 sun was given power *to* s people with fire. *3009*

SCORCHED (11) [SCORCH]

Ge 41:6 thin and s *by* the east wind. 8728
41:23 withered and thin and s *by* the east wind. 8728
41:27 so are the seven worthless heads of grain s 8728
2Ki 19:26 s before it grows up. 8729
Pr 6:28 on hot coals without his feet **being s?** 3917
Isa 9:19 of the LORD Almighty the land *will* **be s** 6977
37:27 s before it grows up. 8729
Eze 20:47 from south to north *will* **be** s by it. 7646
Da 3:27 their robes *were* not s, 10731
Mt 13:6 when the sun came up, the plants *were* **s,** *3009*
Mk 4:6 when the sun came up, the plants *were* **s,** *3009*

SCORCHING (8) [SCORCH]

Dt 28:22 with s **heat** and drought, 3031
Ps 11:6 a s wind will be their lot. 2363
Pr 16:27 and his speech is like a s fire. 7647
Isa 11:15 with a s wind he will sweep his hand over 6522
Jer 4:11 "A s wind from the barren heights in 7456
Jnh 4:8 God provided a s east wind, 3046
Jas 1:11 sun rises with s **heat** and withers the plant; *3014*
Rev 7:16 sun will not beat upon them, nor any s **heat.** *3008*

SCORN (38) [SCORNED, SCORNFULLY, SCORNING, SCORNS]

Dt 28:37 of horror and an **object of** s and ridicule 5442
1Sa 2:29 Why *do you* s my sacrifice and offering 1246
2Ch 29:8 an object of dread and horror and **s,** 9240
Job 16:10 they strike my cheek in s and unite together 3075
19:18 Even the little boys s me; 4415
34:7 who drinks s like water? 4353
Ps 39:8 do not make me the s *of* fools. 3075
44:13 the s and derision of those around us. 4353
64:8 who see them *will* **shake** *their* **heads in s.** 5653
69:7 For I endure s for your sake, 3075
69:10 When I weep and fast, I must endure **s;** 3075
69:20 **S** has broken my heart 3075
71:13 to harm me be covered with s and disgrace. 3075
79:4 of s and derision to those around us. 4353
89:41 he has become the s of his neighbors. 3075
109:25 I am an **object of** s to my accusers; 3075
119:22 Remove from me s and contempt, 3075
Pr 23:9 for *he will* s the wisdom of your words. 996
Isa 43:28 to destruction and Israel to s. 1526
Jer 18:16 an **object of** lasting **s;** 9241
19:8 and make it an **object of s;** 9240
25:9 and make them an object of horror and **s,** 9240
25:18 and an object of horror and s and cursing, 9240
29:18 cursing and horror, of s and reproach, 9240
48:27 that *you* **shake** *your* **head in s** 5653
51:37 a haunt of jackals, an object of horror and **s,** 9240
Eze 22:4 Therefore I will make you an **object of** s to 3075
23:32 it will bring s and derision, 7465
34:29 in the land or bear the s *of* the nations. 4009
36:6 because you have suffered the s *of* 4009
36:7 the nations around you will also suffer **s.** 4009
36:15 the s *of* the peoples or cause your nation 3075
Da 9:16 and your people an **object of** s to all those 3075
Joel 2:17 not make your inheritance an **object of s,** 3075
2:19 never again will I make you an **object of** s 3075
Mic 6:16 you will bear the s *of* the nations." 3075
Hab 2:6 of them taunt him with ridicule and **s,** 2648
Gal 4:14 *you did* not treat me with contempt or **s.** *1746*

SCORNED (7) [SCORN]

2Ch 30:10 but the people s and ridiculed them. 8471
Est 3:6 he s **the idea** of killing only Mordecai. 928+1022+6524
Ps 22:6 s *by* men and despised by the people. 3075
69:19 You know how I am **s,** 3075
SS 8:7 it *would be* **utterly s.** 996+996
Eze 16:31 because you s payment. 7840
16:57 *you are* now s *by* the daughters of Edom 3075

SCORNFULLY (1) [SCORN]

Job 34:37 s *he* **claps** *his* **hands** among us 6215

SCORNING (1) [SCORN]

Heb 12:2 s its shame, and sat down at the right hand *2969*

SCORNS (2) [SCORN]

Pr 13:13 *He who* s instruction will pay for it, 996
30:17 *that* s obedience to a mother, 996

SCORPION (5) [SCORPIONS]

Nu 34:4 cross south of **S** Pass, 6832
Jos 15:3 crossed south of **S** Pass, 6832
Jdg 1:36 of the Amorites was from **S** Pass to Sela 6832
Lk 11:12 Or if he asks for an egg, will give him a **s?** *5026*
Rev 9:5 like that of the sting *of* a s when it strikes *5026*

SCORPIONS (9) [SCORPION]

Dt 8:15 with its venomous snakes and **s.** 6832
1Ki 12:11 I will scourge you with **s.' "** 6832
12:14 I will scourge you with **s."** 6832
2Ch 10:11 I will scourge you with **s.' "** 6832
10:14 I will scourge you with **s."** 6832
Eze 2:6 around you and you live among **s.** 6832
Lk 10:19 and s and to overcome all the power of *5026*
Rev 9:3 and were given power like that of s of *5026*
9:10 They had tails and stings like **s,** *5026*

SCOUNDREL (4) [SCOUNDREL'S, SCOUNDRELS]

2Sa 16:7 get out, you man of blood, you **s!** 408+1175+2021
Pr 6:12 A s and villain, who goes about with 132+1175
16:27 A s plots evil, and his speech is like 408+1175
Isa 32:5 nor the s highly respected. 3964

SCOUNDREL'S (1) [SCOUNDREL]

Isa 32:7 The s methods are wicked, 3964

SCOUNDRELS (3) [SCOUNDREL]

1Ki 21:10 But seat two s opposite him 1175+1201
21:13 Then two s came and sat opposite him 1175+1201
2Ch 13:7 Some worthless s gathered around him 1175+1201

SCOURED (1)

Lev 6:28 the pot *is to* **be** s and rinsed with water. 5347

SCOURGE (8) [SCOURGED]

1Ki 12:11 I *will* s you with scorpions.' " 3579
12:14 I *will* s you with scorpions." 3579
2Ch 10:11 I will s you with scorpions.' " NIH
10:14 I will s you with scorpions." NIH

Job 9:23 When a s brings sudden death, 8765
Ps 39:10 Remove your s from me; 5596
Isa 28:15 When an overwhelming s sweeps by, 8765
28:18 When the overwhelming s sweeps by, 8765

SCOURGED (4) [SCOURGE]

1Ki 12:11 My father s you with whips; 3579
12:14 My father s you with whips; 3579
2Ch 10:11 My father s you with whips; 3579
10:14 My father s you with whips; 3579

SCOURGES, SCOURGETH, SCOURGING, SCOURGINGS (KJV) See FLOG, FLOGGED, FLOGGING, LASH, PUNISHES, PUNISHMENT, SCOURGE, WHIP, WHIPS

SCOUTS (2)

1Sa 26:4 he sent out s and learned that Saul 8078
1Ki 20:17 Now Ben-Hadad had dispatched s, NIH

SCRAPE (1) [SCRAPED]

Eze 26:4 *I will* s **away** her rubble and make her 6081

SCRAPED (4) [SCRAPE]

Lev 14:41 **have** all the inside walls of the house s 7909
14:41 and the material that *is* s **off** dumped into 7894
14:43 and the house s and plastered, 7894
Job 2:8 a piece of broken pottery and s **himself** 1740

SCRAPS (2)

Jdg 1:7 and big toes cut off *have* **picked up** s 4377
Eze 13:19 for a few handfuls of barley and s *of* bread. 7336

SCRAWNY (1)

Ge 41:19 s and very ugly and lean. 1924

SCRAWNY (Anglicized) See also RAWBONED

SCREAM (2) [SCREAMED, SCREAMS]

Ge 39:15 he heard me s **for help,** 2256+7754+7924+8123
Dt 22:24 in a town and *did* not s **for help,** 7590

SCREAMED (3) [SCREAM]

Ge 39:14 He came in here to sleep with me, but *I* s. 928+1524+7754+7924
39:18 as soon as I s **for help,** 2256+7754+7924+8123
Dt 22:27 and though the betrothed girl s, 7590

SCREAMS (1) [SCREAM]

Lk 9:39 A spirit seizes him and *he* suddenly s; *3189*

SCREECH (4)

Lev 11:16 the s **owl,** the gull, any kind of hawk, 9379
Dt 14:15 the s **owl,** the gull, any kind of hawk, 9379
Isa 34:11 The desert owl and s **owl** will possess it; 7887
Zep 2:14 and the s **owl** will roost on her columns. 7887

SCRIBE (11) [SCRIBE'S, SCRIBES]

1Ch 24:6 The s Shemaiah son of Nethanel, a Levite, 6221
27:32 was a counselor, a man of insight and a s. 6221
Ne 8:1 They told Ezra the s to bring out the Book 6221
8:4 the s stood on a high wooden platform built 6221
8:9 Ezra the priest and s, 6221
8:13 gathered around Ezra the s to give attention 6221
12:26 the governor and of Ezra the priest and s. 6221
12:36 Ezra the s led the procession. 6221
13:13 I put Shelemiah the priest, Zadok the s, 6221
Jer 36:26 to arrest Baruch the s and Jeremiah 6221
36:32 and gave it to the s Baruch son of Neriah, 6221

SCRIBE'S (1) [SCRIBE]

Jer 36:23 a s knife and threw them into the firepot, 6221

SCRIBES (3) [SCRIBE]

1Ch 2:55 and the clans of s who lived at Jabez: 6221
2Ch 34:13 of the Levites were secretaries, s 8853
Jer 8:8 the lying pen of the s has handled it falsely? 6221

SCRIP (KJV) See BAG

SCRIPT (5)

Ezr 4:7 in Aramaic s and in the Aramaic language. 4181
Est 1:22 to each province in its own s and 4181
3:12 the s *of* each province and in the language 4181
8:9 in the s *of* each province and the language 4181
8:9 to the Jews in their own s and language. 4181

SCRIPTURE (33) [SCRIPTURES]

Mk 12:10 Haven't you read this s: *1210*
Lk 4:21 "Today this s is fulfilled in your hearing." *1210*
Jn 2:22 the S and the words that Jesus had spoken. *1210*
7:38 Whoever believes in me, as the S has said, *1210*
Jn 7:42 not the S say that the Christ will come *1210*
10:35 and the S cannot be broken— *1210*
13:18 But this is to fulfill the s: *1210*
17:12 to destruction so that S would be fulfilled. *1210*
19:24 that the s might be fulfilled which said, *1210*
19:28 and so that the S would be fulfilled, *1210*
19:36 These things happened so that the s would *1210*
19:37 as another s says, "They will look on the *1210*
20:9 not understand from S that Jesus had to rise *1210*
Ac 1:16 the S had to be fulfilled which *1210*
8:32 The eunuch was reading this passage *of* S: *1210*
8:35 with that very passage *of* S and told him *1210*
Ro 4:3 What does the S say? *1210*
9:17 For the S says to Pharaoh: "I raised you up *1210*
10:11 As the S says, "Anyone who trusts in him *1210*
11:2 the S says in the passage about Elijah— *1210*
Gal 3:8 The S foresaw that God would justify *1210*
3:16 The S does not say "and to seeds," *NIG*
3:22 But the S declares that the whole world is *1210*
4:30 But what does the S say? *1210*
1Ti 4:13 devote yourself to the public reading of S, *NIG*
5:18 For the S says, "Do not muzzle the ox *1210*
2Ti 3:16 All S is God-breathed and is useful *1210*
Jas 2:8 If you really keep the royal law found in S, *1210*
2:23 And the s was fulfilled that says, *1210*
4:5 Or do you think S says without reason that *1210*
4:6 That is why S says: "God opposes the proud *NIG*
1Pe 2:6 For in S it says: "See, I lay a stone in Zion, *1210*
2Pe 1:20 that no prophecy *of* S came about by *1210*

SCRIPTURES (21) [SCRIPTURE]

Da 9:2 I, Daniel, understood from the S, 6219
Mt 21:42 "Have you never read in the S: *1210*
22:29 in error because you do not know the S or *1210*
26:54 the S be fulfilled that say it must happen *1210*
Mk 12:24 not in error because you do not know the S *1210*
14:49 But the S must be fulfilled." *1210*
Lk 24:27 to them what was said in all the S *1210*
24:32 with us on the road and opened the S *1210*
24:45 so they could understand the S. *1210*
Jn 5:39 the S because you think that *1210*
5:39 These are the S that testify about me, *NIG*
Ac 17:2 he reasoned with them from the S, *1210*
17:11 and examined the S every day to see *1210*
18:24 with a thorough knowledge of the S. *1210*
18:28 from the S that Jesus was the Christ. *1210*
Ro 1:2 through his prophets in the Holy S *1210*
15:4 *of* the S we might have hope. *1210*
1Co 15:3 Christ died for our sins according to the S, *1210*
15:4 on the third day according to the S, *1210*
2Ti 3:15 from infancy you have known the holy S, *1207*
2Pe 3:16 as they do the other S, *1210*

SCROLL (66) [SCROLLS]

Ex 17:14 on a s as something to be remembered 6219
Nu 5:23 " 'The priest is to write these curses on a s 6219
Dt 17:18 he is to write for himself on a s a copy 6219
Jos 18:9 They wrote its description on a s, 6219
1Sa 10:25 He wrote them down on a s and deposited it 6219
Ezr 6:2 A s was found in the citadel of Ecbatana in 10399
Job 19:23 that they were written on a s, 6219
Ps 40:7 it is written about me in the s. 4479+6219
56:8 Record my lament; list my tears on your s— 5532
Isa 8:1 "Take a large s and write on it with 1663
29:11 but words sealed in a s. 6219
29:11 if you give **the** s to someone who can read, 2257[S]
29:12 you give the s to someone who cannot read, 6219
29:18 the deaf will hear the words of the s, 6219
30:8 inscribe it on a s, 6219
34:4 be dissolved and the sky rolled up like a s; 6219
34:16 Look in the s *of* the LORD and read: 6219
Jer 36:2 "Take a s and write on it all 4479+6219
36:4 Baruch wrote them on the s. 4479+6219
36:6 and read to the people from the s the words 4479
36:8 the words of the LORD from the s. 6219
36:10 the words of Jeremiah from the s. 6219
36:11 the words of the LORD from the s, 6219
36:13 Baruch read to the people from the s, 6219
36:14 "Bring the s from which you have read to 4479
36:14 son of Neriah went to them with the s 4479
36:18 and I wrote them in ink on the s." 6219
36:20 After they put the s in the room of Elishama 4479
36:21 The king sent Jehudi to get the s, 4479
36:23 three or four columns of the s, NIH
36:23 until the entire s was burned in the fire. 4479
36:25 urged the king not to burn the s, 4479
36:27 the king burned the s containing the words 4479
36:28 "Take another s and write on it all 4479
36:28 on it all the words that were on the first s, 4479
36:29 You burned that s and said, 4479
36:32 So Jeremiah took another s and gave it to 4479
36:32 Baruch wrote on it all the words of the s 6219
45:1 a s the words Jeremiah was then dictating: 6219
51:60 a s about all the disasters that would come 6219
51:63 When you finish reading this s, 6219
Eze 2:9 In it was a s, 4479+6219
3:1 eat what is before you, eat this s; 4479
3:2 and he gave me the s to eat. 4479
3:3 eat this s I am giving you 4479
Da 12:4 up and seal the words of the s until the time 6219
Zec 5:1 and there before me was a flying s! 4479
5:2 I answered, "I see a flying s, 4479
Mal 3:16 A s *of* remembrance was written 6219
Lk 4:17 The s of the prophet Isaiah was handed *1046*
4:20 Then he rolled up the s, *1046*
Heb 9:19 and sprinkled the s and all the people. *1046*
10:7 it is written about me in the s— *1046*
Rev 1:11 "Write on a s what you see and send it to *1046*
5:1 on the throne a s with writing on both sides *1046*
5:2 to break the seals and open the s?" *1046*
5:3 on earth or under the earth could open the s *1046*
5:4 to open the s or look inside. *1046*
5:5 He is able to open the s and its seven seals." *1046*
5:7 He came and took the s from the right hand *NIG*
5:9 "You are worthy to take the s and *1046*
6:14 The sky receded like a s, rolling up, *1046*
10:2 He was holding a **little** s, *1044*
10:8 "Go, take the s that lies open in the hand of *1046*
10:9 and asked him to give me the **little** s. *1044*
10:10 I took the **little** s from the angel's hand *1044*

SCROLLS (3) [SCROLL]

Ac 19:19 A number who had practiced sorcery brought their s together *1047*
19:19 When they calculated the value **of the** s, *899*[S]
2Ti 4:13 and my s, especially the parchments. *1046*

SCULPTURED (1)

2Ch 3:10 he made a pair of s cherubim and 5126+7589

SCUM (2)

La 3:45 You have made us s and refuse among 6082
1Co 4:13 Up to this moment we have become the s of *4326*

SCURVY (KJV) See FESTERING SORE

SCYTHIAN (1)

Col 3:11 barbarian, S, slave or free, but Christ is all, *5033*

SEA (353) [SEAFARERS, SEAMEN, SEAS, SEASHORE]

Ge 1:21 the great **creatures of the** s and every living 9490
1:26 and let them rule over the fish of the s and 3542
1:28 over the fish of the s and the birds of the air 3542
9:2 and upon all the fish of the s; 3542
14:3 in the Valley of Siddim (the Salt S). 3542
32:12 like the sand of the s, 3542
41:49 like the sand of the s; 3542
Ex 10:19 the locusts and carried them into the Red S. 3542
13:18 by the desert road toward the Red S. 3542
14:2 between Migdol and the s. 3542
14:2 They are to encamp by the s, 3542
14:9 and overtook them as they camped by the s 3542
14:16 over the s to divide the water so that 3542
14:16 so that the Israelites can go through the s 3542
14:21 Moses stretched out his hand over the s, 3542
14:21 that night the LORD drove the s back with 3542
14:22 Israelites went through the s on dry ground, 3542
14:23 and horsemen followed them into the s. 3542
14:26 the s so that the waters may flow back over 3542
14:27 Moses stretched out his hand over the s, 3542
14:27 and at daybreak the s went back to its place. 3542
14:27 and the LORD swept them into the s. 3542
14:28 that had followed the Israelites into the s. 3542
14:29 Israelites went through the s on dry ground, 3542
15:1 and its rider he has hurled into the s. 3542
15:4 and his army he has hurled into the s. 3542
15:4 officers are drowned in the Red S. 3542
15:8 deep waters congealed in the heart of the s. 3542
15:10 and the s covered them. 3542
15:19 chariots and horsemen went into the s, 3542
15:19 the LORD brought the waters of the s back 3542
15:19 but the Israelites walked through the s 3542
15:21 and its rider he has hurled into the s." 3542
15:22 the Red S and they went into the Desert 3542
20:11 the s, and all that is in them, 3542
23:31 the Red S to the Sea of the Philistines, 3542
23:31 the Red Sea to the S *of* the Philistines, 3542
25:5 ram skins dyed red and hides of **s cows;** 9391
26:14 and over that a covering of hides of **s cows.** 9391
35:7 ram skins dyed red and hides of **s cows;** 9391
35:23 or hides of **s cows** brought them. 9391
36:19 and over that a covering of hides of **s cows.** 9391
39:34 of hides of **s cows** and the shielding curtain; 9391
Nu 4:6 they are to cover this with hides of **s cows,** 9391
4:8 that with hides of **s cows** and put its poles 9391
4:10 a covering of hides of **s cows** and put it on 9391
4:11 that with hides of **s cows** and put its poles 9391
4:12 cover that with hides of **s cows** and put them 9391
4:14 of hides of **s cows** and put its poles in place. 9391
4:25 and the outer covering of **hides of s cows,** 9391
11:22 the fish in the s were caught for them?" 3542
11:31 the LORD and drove quail in from the s. 3542
13:29 and the Canaanites live near the s and along 3542
14:25 the desert along the route to the Red S." 3542
21:4 along the route to the Red S, 3542
33:8 and passed through the s into the desert, 3542
33:10 They left Elim and camped by the Red S. 3542
33:11 the Red S and camped in the Desert of Sin. 3542
34:3 from the end of the Salt S, 3542
34:5 join the Wadi of Egypt and end at the S. 3542
34:6 be the coast of the Great S. 3542
34:7 run a line from the Great S to Mount Hor 3542
34:11 along the slopes east of the S *of* Kinnereth. 3542
34:12 along the Jordan and end at the Salt S. 3542
Dt 1:40 the desert along the route to the Red S." 3542
2:1 the desert along the route to the Red S, 3542
3:17 from Kinnereth to the S *of* the Arabah 3542

Dt 3:17 to the Sea of the Arabah (the Salt **S**), 3542
4:49 as far as the **S** *of* the Arabah, 3542
11: 4 of the Red **S** as they were pursuing you, 3542
11:24 from the Euphrates River to the western **s**. 3542
30:13 Nor is it beyond the **s**, 3542
30:13 the **s** to get it and proclaim it to us 3542
34: 2 all the land of Judah as far as the western **s**, 3542
Jos 1: 4 to the Great **S** on the west. 3542
2:10 the LORD dried up the water of the Red **S** 3542
3:16 while the water flowing down to the **S** *of* 3542
3:16 (the Salt **S**) was completely cut off. 3542
4:23 to the Red **S** when he dried it up before us 3542
9: 1 the Great **S** as far as Lebanon (the kings of 3542
12: 3 the **S** *of* Kinnereth to the Sea of the Arabah 3542
12: 3 the Sea of Kinnereth to the **S** *of* the Arabah 3542
12: 3 to the Sea of the Arabah (the Salt **S**), 3542
13:27 up to the end of the **S** *of* Kinnereth). 3542
15: 2 the bay at the southern end of the Salt **S**, 3542
15: 4 the Wadi of Egypt, ending at the **s**. 3542
15: 5 the Salt **S** as far as the mouth of the Jordan. 3542
15: 5 the bay of the **s** at the mouth of the Jordan, 3542
15:11 The boundary ended at the **s**. 3542
15:12 the coastline of the Great **S**. 3542
15:47 of Egypt and the coastline of the Great **S**. 3542
16: 3 and on to Gezer, ending at the **s**. 3542
16: 6 and continued to the **s**. 3542
16: 8 to the Kanah Ravine and ended at the **s**. 3542
17: 9 of the ravine and ended at the **s**. 3542
17:10 The territory of Manasseh reached the **s** 3542
18:19 at the northern bay of the Salt **S**, 3542
19:29 turned toward Hosah and came out at the **s** 3542
23: 4 the Jordan and the Great **S** in the west. 3542
24: 6 out of Egypt, you came to the **s**, 3542
24: 6 and horsemen as far as the Red **S**. 3542
24: 7 the **s** over them and covered them. 3542
Jdg 11:16 Israel went through the desert to the Red **S** 3542
2Sa 22:16 the **s** were exposed and the foundations of 3542
1Ki 5: 9 down from Lebanon to the **s**, 3542
5: 9 in rafts by **s** to the place you specify. 3542
7:23 He made the **S** of cast metal, 3542
7:24 in two rows in one piece with the **S**. 3542
7:25 The **S** stood on twelve bulls, NIH
7:25 The **S** rested on top of them, 3542
7:39 He placed the **S** on the south side, 3542
7:44 the **S** and the twelve bulls under it; 3542
9:26 on the shore of the Red **S**. 3542
9:27 sailors who knew the **s**— 3542
10:22 of trading ships at **s** along with the ships 3542
18:43 "Go and look toward the **s**," 3542
18:44 as a man's hand is rising from the **s**." 3542
2Ki 14:25 from Lebo Hamath to the **S** *of* the Arabah, 3542
16:17 He removed the **S** from the bronze bulls 3542
25:13 and the bronze **S** that were at the temple of 3542
25:16 the **S** and the movable stands, 3542
1Ch 16:32 Let the **s** resound, and all that is in it; 3542
18: 8 which Solomon used to make the bronze **S**, 3542
2Ch 2:16 and will float them in rafts by **s** down 3542
4: 2 He made the **S** of cast metal, 3542
4: 3 in two rows in one piece with the **S**. 3542
4: 4 The **S** stood on twelve bulls, NIH
4: 4 The **S** rested on top of them, 3542
4: 6 but the **S** was to be used by the priests 3542
4:10 He placed the **S** on the south side, 3542
4:15 the **S** and the twelve bulls under it; 3542
8:18 men who knew the **s**. 3542
20: 2 from the other side of the **S**. 3542
Ezr 3: 7 so that they would bring cedar logs by **s** 3542
Ne 9: 9 you heard their cry at the Red **S**. 3542
9:11 You divided the **s** before them, 3542
Job 7:12 Am I the **s**, or the monster of the deep, 3542
9: 8 and treads on the waves of the **s**. 3542
11: 9 the earth and wider than the **s**. 3542
12: 8 or let the fish of the **s** inform you. 3542
14:11 from the **s** or a riverbed becomes parched 3542
26:12 By his power he churned up the **s**; 3542
28:14 the **s** says, 'It is not with me.' 3542
36:30 bathing the depths of the **s**. 3542
38: 8 the **s** behind doors when it burst forth from 3542
38:16 "Have you journeyed to the springs of the **s** 3542
41:31 like a boiling caldron and stirs up the **s** like 3542
Ps 8: 8 the birds of the air, and the fish of the **s**, 3542
18:15 the **s** were exposed and the foundations of 4784
33: 7 He gathers the waters of the **s** into jars; 3542
46: 2 the mountains fall into the heart of the **s**, 3542
66: 6 He turned the **s** into dry land, 3542
68:22 I will bring them from the depths of the **s**, 3542
72: 8 from **s** to sea and from the River to the ends 3542
72: 8 from sea to **s** and from the River to the ends 3542
74:13 It was you who split open the **s** 3542
77:19 Your path led through the **s**, 3542
78:13 He divided the **s** and led them through; 3542
78:53 but the **s** engulfed their enemies. 3542
80:11 It sent out its boughs to the **S**, 3542
89: 9 You rule over the surging **s**; 3542
89:25 I will set his hand over the **s**, 3542
93: 4 mightier than the breakers of the **s**— 3542
95: 5 The **s** is his, for he made it, 3542
96:11 let the **s** resound, and all that is in it; 3542
98: 7 Let the **s** resound, and everything in it, 3542
104:25 There is the **s**, vast and spacious, 3542
106: 7 and they rebelled by the **s**, the Red Sea. 3542
106: 7 and they rebelled by the sea, the Red **S**. 3542
106: 9 He rebuked the Red **S**, and it dried up; 3542
106:22 of Ham and awesome deeds by the Red **S**. 3542
107:23 Others went out on the **s** in ships; 3542
107:29 the waves of **the s** were hushed. 2157S
114: 3 **s** looked and fled, the Jordan turned back; 3542
Ps 114: 5 Why was it, O **s**, that you fled, O Jordan, 3542
136:13 to him who divided the Red **S** asunder 3542
136:15 and his army into the Red **S**; 3542
139: 9 if I settle on the far side of the **s**, 3542
146: 6 the **s**, and everything in them— 3542
148: 7 you **great s creatures** and all ocean depths, 9490
Pr 8:29 the **s** its boundary so the waters would 3542
Ecc 1: 7 All streams flow into the **s**, 3542
1: 7 yet the **s** is never full. 3542
Isa 5:30 over it like the roaring of the **s**. 3542
9: 1 by the way of the **s**, along the Jordan— 3542
10:22 O Israel, be like the sand by the **s**, 3542
11: 9 of the LORD as the waters cover the **s**. 3542
11:11 from Hamath and from the islands of the **s**. 3542
11:15 up the gulf of the Egyptian **s**; 3542
16: 8 and went as far as the **s**. 3542
17:12 they rage like the raging **s**! 3542
18: 2 which sends envoys by **s** in papyrus boats 3542
21: 1 An oracle concerning the Desert by the **S**: 3542
23: 4 O fortress of the **s**, for the sea has spoken: 3542
23: 4 O fortress of the sea, for the **s** has spoken: 3542
23:11 over the **s** and made its kingdoms tremble. 3542
24:15 the God of Israel, in the islands of the **s**. 3542
27: 1 he will slay the monster of the **s**. 3542
42:10 you who go down to the **s**, 3542
43:16 he who made a way through the **s**, 3542
48:18 your righteousness like the waves of the **s**. 3542
50: 2 By a mere rebuke I dry up the **s**, 3542
51:10 Was it not you who dried up the **s**, 3542
51:10 who made a road in the depths of the **s** so 3542
51:15 up the **s** so that its waves roar— 3542
57:20 But the wicked are like the tossing **s**, 3542
63:11 is he who brought them through the **s**, 3542
Jer 5:22 I made the sand a boundary for the **s**, 3542
6:23 They sound like the roaring **s** as they ride 3542
15: 8 more numerous than the sand of the **s**. 3542
25:22 the kings of the coastlands across the **s**; 3542
27:19 about the pillars, the **S**, the movable stands 3542
31:35 who stirs up the **s** so that its waves roar— 3542
46:18 like Carmel by the **s**. 3542
48:32 Your branches spread as far as the **s**; 3542
48:32 they reached as far as the **s** *of* Jazer. 3542
49:21 their cry will resound to the Red **S**. 3542
49:23 troubled like the restless **s**. 3542
50:42 They sound like the roaring **s** as they ride 3542
51:36 up her **s** and make her springs dry. 3542
51:42 The **s** will rise over Babylon; 3542
52:17 and the bronze **S** that were at the temple of 3542
52:20 the **S** and the twelve bronze bulls under it, 3542
La 2:13 Your wound is as deep as the **s**. 3542
Eze 26: 3 like the **s** casting up its waves. 3542
26: 5 Out in the **s** she will become a place 3542
26:12 timber and rubble into the **s**. 4784
26:17 O city of renown, peopled by men of the **s**! 3542
26:18 in the **s** are terrified at your collapse.' 3542
27: 3 situated at the gateway to the **s**, 3542
27: 9 of the **s** and their sailors came alongside 3542
27:25 with heavy cargo in the heart of the **s**. 3542
27:26 to pieces in the heart of the **s**. 3542
27:27 on board will sink into the heart of the **s** on 3542
27:32 like Tyre, surrounded by the **s**?" 3542
27:34 by the **s** in the depths of the waters; 3542
38:20 The fish of the **s**, the birds of the air, 3542
39:11 of those who travel east toward the **S**. 3542
47: 8 where it enters the **S**. 3542
47: 8 When it empties into the **S**, 3542
47:10 like the fish of the Great **S**. 3542
47:15 the north side it will run from the Great **S** 3542
47:17 The boundary will extend from the **s** 3542
47:18 to the eastern **s** and as far as Tamar. 3542
47:19 along the Wadi [of Egypt] to the Great **S**. 3542
47:20 the Great **S** will be the boundary to 3542
48:28 along the Wadi [of Egypt] to the Great **S**. 3542
Da 7: 2 of heaven churning up the great **s**. 10322
7: 3 from the others, came up out of the **s**. 10322
Hos 4: 3 of the air and the fish of the **s** are dying. 3542
Joel 2:20 into the eastern **s** and those in the rear into 3542
2:20 and those in the rear into the western **s**. 3542
Am 5: 8 of the **s** and pours them out over the face of 3542
8:12 from **s** to sea and wander from north to east, 3542
8:12 from sea to **s** and wander from north to east, 3542
9: 3 from me at the bottom of the **s**, 3542
9: 6 of the **s** and pours them out over the face of 3542
Jnh 1: 4 Then the LORD sent a great wind on the **s**, 3542
1: 5 the cargo into the **s** to lighten the ship. 3542
1: 9 who made the **s** and the land." 3542
1:11 The **s** was getting rougher and rougher. 3542
1:11 to you to make the **s** calm down for us?" 3542
1:12 "Pick me up and throw me into the **s**," 3542
1:13 for the **s** grew even wilder than before. 3542
1:15 and the raging **s** grew calm. 3542
Mic 7:12 from Egypt to the Euphrates and from **s** 3542
7:12 to the Euphrates and from sea to **s** and 3542
7:19 into the depths of the **s**. 3542
Na 1: 4 He rebukes the **s** and dries it up; 3542
Hab 1:14 You have made men like fish in the **s**, 3542
1:14 like **s creatures** that have no ruler. 8254
2:14 as the waters cover the **s**. 3542
3: 8 Did you rage against the **s** when you rode 3542
3:15 You trampled the **s** with your horses, 3542
Zep 1: 3 the birds of the air and the fish of the **s**. 3542
2: 5 Woe to you who live by the **s**, 3542
2: 6 The land by the **s**, 3542
Hag 2: 6 the **s** and the dry land. 3542
Zec 9: 4 and destroy her power on the **s**, 3542
9:10 from **s** to sea and from the River to the ends 3542
9:10 from sea to **s** and from the River to the ends 3542
Zec 10:11 They will pass through the **s** *of* trouble; 3542
10:11 the surging **s** will be subdued and all 3542
14: 8 to the eastern **s** and half to the western sea, 3542
14: 8 to the eastern sea and half to the western **s**, 3542
Mt 4:15 the way *to* the **s**, along the Jordan, *2498*
4:18 As Jesus was walking beside the **S** *2498*
15:29 Jesus left there and went along the **S** *2498*
18: 6 and to be drowned in the depths *of* the **s**. *2498*
21:21 'Go, throw yourself into the **s**,' *2498*
23:15 over land and **s** to win a single convert, *2498*
Mk 1:16 As Jesus walked beside the **S** of Galilee, *2498*
7:31 to the **S** of Galilee and into the region of *2498*
9:42 be better for him to be thrown into the **s** *2498*
11:23 'Go, throw yourself into the **s**,' *2498*
Lk 17: 2 to be thrown into the **s** with a millstone tied *2498*
17: 6 'Be uprooted and planted in the **s**,' *2498*
21:25 at the roaring and tossing *of* the **s**. *2498*
Jn 6: 1 to the far shore *of* the **S** of Galilee (that is, *2498*
6: 1 (that is, the **S** of Tiberias), *NIG*
21: 1 by the **S** of Tiberias. *2498*
Ac 4:24 the heaven and the earth and the **s**, *2498*
7:36 the Red **S** and for forty years in the desert. *2498*
10: 6 whose house is by the **s**." *2498*
10:32 Simon the tanner, who lives by the **s**.' *2498*
14:15 and earth and **s** and everything in them. *2498*
16:11 From Troas we **put out to s** *343*
21: 1 we **put out to s** and sailed straight to Cos. *343*
27: 2 and *we* **put out to s**. *343*
27: 4 From there we **put out to s** again *343*
27: 5 When we had sailed across the **open s** off *4283*
27:17 they lowered the **s anchor** and let the ship *5007*
27:27 across the **Adriatic S**, *102*
27:30 the sailors let the lifeboat down into the **s**, *2498*
27:38 the ship by throwing the grain into the **s**. *2498*
27:40 the **s** and at the same time untied the ropes *2498*
28: 4 for though he escaped from the **s**, *2498*
28:11 After three months *we* **put out to s** in *343*
Ro 9:27 of the Israelites be like the sand *by* the **s**, *2498*
1Co 10: 1 and that they all passed through the **s**. *2498*
10: 2 into Moses in the cloud and in the **s**. *2498*
2Co 11:25 I spent a night and a day in the **open s**, *1113*
11:26 in danger in the country, in danger at **s**; *2498*
Heb 11:29 the people passed through the Red **S** as *2498*
Jas 1: 6 he who doubts is like a wave *of* the **s**, *2498*
3: 7 and **creatures of** the **s** are being tamed *1879*
Jude 1:13 They are wild waves *of* the **s**, *2498*
Rev 4: 6 the throne there was what looked like a **s** *2498*
5:13 under the earth and on the **s**, and all that is *2498*
7: 1 from blowing on the land or on the **s** or *2498*
7: 2 to harm the land and the **s**: *2498*
7: 3 "Do not harm the land or the **s** or the trees *2498*
8: 8 all ablaze, was thrown into the **s**. *2498*
8: 8 A third *of* the **s** turned into blood, *2498*
8: 9 a third of the living creatures in the **s** died, *2498*
10: 2 on the **s** and his left foot on the land, *2498*
10: 5 Then the angel I had seen standing on the **s** *2498*
10: 6 and the **s** and all that is in it, and said, *2498*
10: 8 of the angel who is standing on the **s** and on *2498*
12:12 But woe to the earth and the **s**, *2498*
13: 1 And the dragon stood on the shore *of* the **s**. *2498*
13: 1 And I saw a beast coming out of the **s**. *2498*
14: 7 the earth, the **s** and the springs of water." *2498*
15: 2 like a **s** of glass mixed with fire and, *2498*
15: 2 standing beside the **s**, those who had been *2498*
16: 3 on the **s**, and it turned into blood like that *2498*
16: 3 and every living thing in the **s** died. *2498*
18:17 "Every **s captain**, and all who travel *3237*
18:17 and all who earn their living from the **s**, *2498*
18:19 on the **s** became rich through her wealth! *2498*
18:21 of a large millstone and threw it into the **s**, *2498*
20:13 The **s** gave up the dead that were in it, *2498*
21: 1 and there was no longer any **s**. *2498*

SEAFARERS (1) [SEA]

Isa 23: 2 of Sidon, whom the **s** have enriched. 3542+6296

SEAH (3) [SEAHS]

2Ki 7: 1 a **s** *of* flour will sell for a shekel 6006
7:16 So a **s** *of* flour sold for a shekel, 6006
7:18 a **s** *of* flour will sell for a shekel 6006

SEAHS (6) [SEAH]

Ge 18: 6 "get three **s** *of* fine flour and knead it 6006
1Sa 25:18 five dressed sheep, five **s** of roasted grain, 6006
1Ki 18:32 around it large enough to hold *two* **s** 6006
2Ki 7: 1 for a shekel and *two* **s** of barley for a shekel 6006
7:16 and *two* **s** *of* barley sold for a shekel, 6006
7:18 for a shekel and *two* **s** of barley for a shekel 6006

SEAL (35) [SEALED, SEALING, SEALS]

Ge 38:18 "Your **s** and its cord, 2597
38:25 "See if you recognize whose **s** and cord 3160
Ex 28:11 the way a gem cutter engraves a **s**. 2597
28:21 each engraved like a **s** with the name of one 2597
28:36 of pure gold and engrave on it as on a **s**: 2597
39: 6 like a **s** with the names of the sons of Israel. 2597
39:14 each engraved like a **s** with the name of one 2597
39:30 like an inscription on a **s**: 2597
1Ki 21: 8 **placed** his **s** *on* them, 928+2597+3159
Est 8: 8 and **s** it with the king's signet ring— 3159
Job 38:14 The earth takes shape like clay under a **s**; 2597
Ps 40: 9 *I do* not **s** my lips, as you know, O LORD. 3973
SS 8: 6 Place me like a **s** over your heart, 2597
8: 6 like a **s** on your arm; 2597

Isa 8:16 Bind up the testimony and s **up** the law 3159
Da 8:26 but s **up** the vision, 6258
9:24 to s **up** vision and prophecy and to anoint 3159
12:4 close up and s the words of the scroll until 3159
Mt 27:66 the tomb secure *by* **putting a s on** the stone *5381*
Jn 6:27 **On** him God the Father *has* **placed** *his* s *5381*
Ro 4:11 a s of the righteousness that he had by faith *5382*
1Co 9:2 you are the s of my apostleship in the Lord. *5382*
2Co 1:22 **set** his **s of ownership on** us, *5381*
Eph 1:13 *you were* **marked** in him **with a s,** *5381*
Rev 6:3 When the Lamb opened the second **s,** *5382*
6:5 When the Lamb opened the third **s,** *5382*
6:7 When the Lamb opened the fourth **s,** *5382*
6:9 When he opened the fifth **s,** *5382*
6:12 I watched as he opened the sixth **s.** *5382*
7:2 having the s of the living God. *5382*
7:3 the trees until *we* **put a s** on the foreheads *5381*
8:1 When he opened the seventh **s,** *5382*
9:4 not have the s of God on their foreheads. *5382*
10:4 but I heard a voice from heaven say, **"S up** *5381*
22:10 *"Do* not **s up** the words of the prophecy *5381*

SEALED (23) [SEAL]

Dt 32:34 "Have I not kept this in reserve and s it 3159
Ne 10:1 Those *who* s it were: 3159
Est 3:12 in the name of King Xerxes himself and s 3159
8:8 in the king's name and s with his ring 3159
8:10 the dispatches with the king's signet ring, 3159
Job 14:17 My offenses *will* **be s up** in a bag; 3159
41:15 of shields tightly **s together;** 2597+6037
SS 4:12 you are a spring enclosed, a s fountain. 5835
Isa 29:10 *He has* s your eyes (the prophets); 6794
29:11 is nothing but words s in a scroll. 3159
29:11 he will answer, "I can't; it *is* **s."** 3159
Jer 32:10 I signed and s the deed, had it witnessed, 3159
32:11 the s *copy* containing the terms 3159
32:14 both the s and unsealed copies of the deed 3159
32:44 s and witnessed in the territory 3159
Da 6:17 and the king s it with his own signet ring 10291
12:9 the words are closed up and s until the time 3159
Eph 4:30 with whom *you were* s for the day *5381*
2Ti 2:19 **s with** this inscription: "The Lord *2400+5382*
Rev 5:1 a scroll with writing on both sides and s *2958*
7:4 I heard the number *of* those who *were* **s:** *5381*
7:5 From the tribe of Judah 12,000 *were* **s,** *5381*
20:3 and locked and s it over him, *5381*

SEALING (1) [SEAL]

Dt 29:12 with you this day and s with an oath, NIH

SEALS (7) [SEAL]

Ne 9:38 and our priests *are* **affixing** their s to it." 3159
Job 9:7 *he* **s off** the light of the stars. 1237+3159
Rev 5:1 on both sides and sealed *with* seven **s.** *5382*
5:2 "Who is worthy to break the s and open *5382*
5:5 He is able to open the scroll and its seven **s.** *5382*
5:9 to take the scroll and to open its **s,** *5382*
6:1 as the Lamb opened the first of the seven **s.** *5382*

SEAM (2) [SEAMS]

Ex 28:27 the s just above the waistband of the ephod. 4678
39:20 the s just above the waistband of the ephod. 4678

SEAMEN (4) [SEA]

Eze 27:8 O Tyre, were aboard as your **s.** 2480
27:27 your mariners, s and shipwrights, 2480
27:28 shorelands will quake when your s cry out. 2480
27:29 the mariners and all the s will stand on 2480+3542

SEAMLESS (1)

Jn 19:23 This garment was s, woven in one piece *731*

SEAMS (1) [SEAM]

Eze 27:9 on board as shipwrights to caulk your **s.** 981

SEARCH (48) [SEARCHED, SEARCHES, SEARCHING]

Ge 44:12 Then the steward *proceeded to* **s,** 2924
Dt 1:33 to **s out** places for you to camp and 9365
Jdg 17:8 that town *in* **s** *of* some other place to stay. 5162
1Sa 16:16 *to* **s for** someone who can play the harp. 1335
23:25 Saul and his men began the **s,** 1335
26:2 to s there **for** David. 1335
2Sa 5:17 they went up in full force to **s for** him, 1335
1Ki 2:40 to Achish at Gath **in s of** his slaves. 1335
20:6 to send my officials *to* s your palace and 2924
1Ch 4:39 of the valley **in s of** pasture for their flocks. 1335
14:8 they went up in full force to **s for** him, 1335
26:31 David's reign *a* **s was made** in the records, 2011
2Ch 22:9 *He* then **went in s** of Ahaziah, 1335
Ezr 4:15 so that a **s** *may be* **made** 10118
4:19 I issued an order and **a s** *was* **made,** 10118
5:17 *let* **a s be made** in the royal archives 10118
Est 2:2 *Let* **a s** *be* **made for** beautiful young virgins 1335
Job 3:21 *who* **s for** it more than for hidden treasure, 2916
7:21 *you will* **s for** me, but I will be no more." 8838
10:6 that *you must* **s out** my faults and probe 1335
Ps 4:4 s your hearts and be silent. 606+928
139:23 S me, O God, and know my heart; 2983
Pr 2:4 for silver and **s for** it as for hidden treasure, 2924
25:2 *to* **s out** a matter is the glory of kings. 2983
Ecc 3:6 a time to s and a time to give up, 1335
7:25 *to* **s out** wisdom and the scheme of things 1335
7:29 but men *have* **gone in s of** many schemes." 1335
8:17 Despite all his efforts to **s** *it* **out,** 1335
SS 3:2 *I will* **s for** the one my heart loves. 1335
Isa 41:12 Though *you* **s for** your enemies, 1335
41:17 "The poor and needy **s for** water, 1335
Jer 5:1 and consider, s through her squares. 1335
17:10 "I the LORD s the heart and examine 2983
50:20 **"s** *will* **be made for** Israel's guilt, 1335
La 1:11 All her people groan *as they* **s for** bread; 1335
Eze 34:8 and because my shepherds *did* not **s for** 2011
34:11 I myself *will* **s for** my sheep and look 2011
34:16 *I will* **s for** the lost and bring back 1335
39:14 the seven months *they will begin their* **s.** 2983
Hos 7:10 not return to the LORD his God or **s for** 1335
Zep 1:12 At that time *I will* s Jerusalem with lamps 2924
Mt 2:8 "Go and **make a** careful **s** for the child. *2004*
2:13 for Herod is going to **s for** the child *2426*
10:11 **s for** some worthy person there and stay *2004*
Lk 15:8 the house and s carefully until she finds it? *2426*
Jn 6:24 the boats and went to Capernaum **in s of** *2426*
Ac 12:19 Herod had **a thorough s made for** him *2118*
17:5 They rushed to Jason's house **in s of** Paul *2426*

SEARCHED (22) [SEARCH]

Ge 31:34 Laban **s through** everything in the tent 5491
31:35 So *he* s but could not find 2924
31:37 Now that *you have* **s through** all my goods, 5491
Jos 2:22 until the pursuers *had* s all along the road 1335
1Sa 23:14 Day after day Saul **s for** him, 1335
27:4 he no longer **s for** him. 1335
2Sa 17:20 The men s but found no one, 1335
1Ki 1:3 s throughout Israel **for** a beautiful girl 1335
2Ki 2:17 *who* s for three days but did not find him. 1335
Ezr 2:62 These **s for** their family records, 1335
6:1 and *they* s in the archives stored in 10118
Ne 7:64 These **s for** their family records, 1335
Ps 139:1 *you have* s me and you know me. 2983
Ecc 12:9 and **s out** and set in order many proverbs. 2983
12:10 The Teacher s to find just the right words, 1335
Jer 31:37 of the earth below **be s out** will I reject all 2983
La 1:19 in the city while *they* **s for** food 1335
Eze 20:6 of Egypt into a land *I had* **s out** for them, 9365
34:4 not brought back the strays or **s for** the lost. 1335
34:6 and no *one* s or looked for them. 2011
2Ti 1:17 *he* s hard **for** me until he found me. *2426*
1Pe 1:10 **s intently and with the greatest care,** *1699+2001+2779*

SEARCHES (11) [SEARCH]

1Ch 28:9 for the LORD s every heart 2011
Job 28:3 *he* s the farthest recesses **for** ore 2983
28:11 *He* s the sources of the rivers 2924
39:8 for his pasture and s for any green thing. 2011
Ps 7:9 O righteous God, *who* s minds and hearts, 1043
Pr 11:27 but evil comes to him *who* **s for** it. 2011
20:27 lamp of the LORD s the spirit of a man; 2924
20:27 it s out his inmost being. NIH
Ro 8:27 And he who s our hearts knows the mind of *2236*
1Co 2:10 The Spirit s all things, *2236*
Rev 2:23 that I am he who s hearts and minds, *2236*

SEARCHING (8) [SEARCH]

Jdg 5:15 In the districts of Reuben there was much s 2984
5:16 In the districts of Reuben there was much s 2984
1Sa 27:1 Then Saul will give up **s for** me anywhere 1335
Job 32:11 while *you were* **s for** words, 2983
Ecc 7:28 while I *was* still s but not finding— 1335
Am 8:12 **s for** the word of the LORD, 1335
Lk 2:48 Your father and I *have been* anxiously **s for** *2426*
2:49 "Why *were you* **s for** me?" *2426*

SEARED (2) [SEARING]

1Ti 4:2 consciences *have been* **s as with a hot iron.** *3013*
Rev 16:9 They *were* **s** by the intense heat *3009*

SEARING (1) [SEARED]

Ps 38:7 My back is filled with **s pain;** 7828

SEAS (29) [SEA]

Ge 1:10 and the gathered waters he called "**s.**" 3542
1:22 in number and fill the water in the **s,** 3542
Lev 11:9 the creatures living in the water of the s and 3542
11:10 But all creatures in the s or streams that do 3542
Dt 33:19 they will feast on the abundance of the **s,** 3542
Ne 9:6 the s and all that is in them. 3542
Job 6:3 It would surely outweigh the sand of the **s**— 3542
Ps 8:8 all that swim the paths of the **s.** 3542
24:2 the s and established it upon the waters. 3542
65:5 the ends of the earth and of the farthest **s,** 3542
65:7 who stilled the roaring of the **s,** 3542
69:34 the s and all that move in them, 3542
78:15 and gave them water as abundant as the **s;** 9333
93:3 The s have lifted up, O LORD, 5643
93:3 O LORD, the s have lifted up their voice; 5643
93:3 the s have lifted up their pounding waves. 5643
135:6 in the s and all their depths. 3542
Pr 23:34 be like one sleeping on the **high s,** 3542+4213
30:19 the way of a ship on the **high s,** 3542+4213
Isa 60:5 the wealth on the s will be brought to you, 3542
Eze 26:17 You were a power on the **s,** 3542
27:4 Your domain was on the **high s;** 3542+4213
27:26 Your oarsmen take you out to the high **s.** 4784
27:33 When your merchandise went out on the **s,** 3542
28:2 on the throne of a god in the heart of the **s."** 3542
28:8 a violent death in the heart of the **s.** 3542
32:2 in the s thrashing about in your streams, 3542
Da 11:45 He will pitch his royal tents between the s 3542
Jnh 2:3 into the very heart of the **s,** 3542

SEASHORE (13) [SEA]

Ge 22:17 in the sky and as the sand on the **s.** 3542+8557
49:13 "Zebulun will live by the s and 2572+3542
Jos 11:4 as numerous as the sand on the **s.** 3542+8557
Jdg 7:12 be counted than the sand on the **s.** 3542+8557
1Sa 13:5 as numerous as the sand on the **s.** 3542+8557
2Sa 17:11 as numerous as the sand on the **s**— 3542
1Ki 4:20 as numerous as the sand on the **s;** 3542
4:29 as measureless as the sand on the **s.** 3542+8557
Ps 78:27 flying birds like sand on the **s.** 3542
Jer 33:22 and as measureless as the sand on the **s.'** " 3542
Hos 1:10 the Israelites will be like the sand on the **s,** 3542
Heb 11:12 as countless as the sand on the **s.** *2498+3836+5927*
Rev 20:8 In number they are like the sand *on* the **s.** *2498*

SEASON (20) [SEASONED, SEASONS]

Ge 31:10 "In breeding s I once had a dream 6961
Ex 34:21 the **plowing s** and harvest you must rest. 3045
Lev 2:13 S all your grain offerings with salt. 4873
26:4 I will send you rain in its **s,** 6961
Nu 13:20 (It was the s *for* the first ripe grapes.) 3427
Dt 11:14 then I will send rain on your land in its **s,** 6961
28:12 in s and to bless all the work of your hands. 6961
Ezr 10:13 and it is the rainy **s;** 6961
Job 5:26 like sheaves gathered in **s.** 6961
6:17 but that cease to flow in the dry **s,** 6961
Ps 1:3 in s and whose leaf does not wither. 6961
Pr 20:4 A sluggard does not plow in **s;** 3074
Ecc 3:1 and a s for every activity under heaven: 6961
SS 2:12 the s of singing has come, 6961
Jer 5:24 who gives autumn and spring rains in **s,** 6961
Eze 34:26 I will send down showers in **s;** 6961
Mk 11:13 because it was not the s for figs. *2789*
2Ti 4:2 be prepared **in** s and out of season; *2323*
4:2 be prepared in season and **out of s;** *178*
Tit 1:3 and at his **appointed** s he brought his word *2789*

SEASONED (1) [SEASON]

Col 4:6 be always full of grace, s with salt, *789*

SEASONS (7) [SEASON]

Ge 1:14 as signs to mark s and days and years, 4595
Job 38:32 in their s or lead out the Bear with its cubs? 6961
Ps 104:19 The moon marks off the **s,** 4595
Jer 8:7 the stork in the sky knows her **appointed s,** 4595
Da 2:21 He changes times and **s;** 10232
Ac 14:17 from heaven and crops **in** *their* **s;** *2789*
Gal 4:10 and months and s and years! *2789*

SEAT (26) [SEATED, SEATING, SEATS]

Ex 18:13 The next day Moses **took** *his* s to serve 3782
Jdg 3:20 As the king rose from his **s,** 4058
1Sa 20:18 because your s will be empty. 4632
2Sa 19:8 king got up and **took** *his* s in the gateway. 3782
1Ki 1:46 Solomon *has* **taken** *his* s on the royal 3782
10:19 On both sides of the s were armrests, 5226+8699
21:9 "Proclaim a day of fasting and s Naboth in 3782
21:10 But s two scoundrels opposite him 3782
2Ki 25:28 and gave him a **s of honor** higher than those 4058
2Ch 9:18 On both sides of the s were armrests, 5226+8699
Est 3:1 and giving him a **s of honor** higher than that 4058
Job 29:7 the city and took my s in the public square, 4632
Ps 1:1 or stand in the way of sinners or sit in the s 4632
Pr 9:14 on a s *at* the highest point of the city, 4058
31:23 he **takes** his s among the elders of the land. 3782
SS 3:10 Its s was upholstered with purple, 5323
Isa 22:23 be a s *of* honor for the house of his father. 4058
Jer 52:32 and gave him a **s of honor** higher than those 4058
Da 7:9 and the Ancient of Days **took** *his* **s.** 10338
Mt 23:2 of the law and the Pharisees sit in Moses' **s.** *2756*
27:19 While Pilate was sitting on the **judge's s,** *1037*
Lk 14:9 'Give this man your **s.'** *5536*
Jn 19:13 down on the **judge's s** at a place known as *1037*
Ro 14:10 we will all stand before God's **judgment s.** *1037*
2Co 5:10 before the **judgment** s of Christ, *1037*
Jas 2:3 "Here's a good s for you," *2764*

SEATED (29) [SEAT]

Ge 43:33 The men *had been* s before him in the order 3782
Ru 4:4 of these s here and in the presence of 3782
1Sa 9:22 his servant into the hall and s them 5226+5989
22:6 *was* s under the tamarisk tree on the hill 3782
1Ki 16:11 As soon as he began to reign and *was* s on 3782
21:12 and s Naboth in a prominent place among 3782
2Ch 23:20 through the Upper Gate and s the king on 3782
Ps 47:8 God *is* s on his holy throne. 3782
Isa 6:1 I saw the Lord s on a throne, 3782
Da 7:10 court *was* s, and the books were opened. 10338
Zec 3:8 O high priest Joshua and your associates s 3782
Mk 3:34 at those s in a circle around him and said, *2764*
Lk 22:56 A servant girl saw him s there in *2764*
22:69 be s at the right hand of the mighty God." *2764*
Jn 6:11 and distributed *to* those who *were* s *367*
12:15 your king is coming, s on a donkey's colt." *2764*
20:12 s where Jesus' body had been, *2757*

Ac 20: 9 S in a window *was* a young man named *2757*
Eph 1:20 from the dead and s him at his right hand in *2767*
2: 6 and s us **with** him in the heavenly realms *5154*
Col 3: 1 where Christ is s at the right hand of God. *2764*
Rev 4: 4 and s on them *were* twenty-four elders. *2764*
11:16 who *were* s on their thrones before God, *2764*
14:14 s on the cloud *was one* "like a son of man" *2764*
14:16 So he who *was* s on the cloud swung his *2764*
19: 4 who *was* s on the throne. *2764*
20: 4 *were* s those who had been given authority *2767*
20:11 a great white throne and him who *was* s *2764*
21: 5 He who *was* s on the throne said, *2764*

SEATING (2) [SEAT]
1Ki 10: 5 the s *of* his officials, the attending servants 4632
2Ch 9: 4 the s *of* his officials, the attending servants 4632

SEATS (7) [SEAT]
1Sa 2: 8 *he* s them with princes and has them inherit 3782
Ps 113: 8 he s them with princes, with the princes of 3782
Jer 39: 3 of the king of Babylon came and **took** s in 3782
Mt 23: 6 the **most important** s in the synagogues; *4751*
Mk 12:39 the **most important** s in the synagogues and *4751*
Lk 11:43 because you love the **most important** s in *4751*
20:46 the **most important** s in the synagogues and *4751*

SEAWEED (1) [WEED]
Jnh 2: 5 s was wrapped around my head. 6068

SEBA (4)
Ge 10: 7 S, Havilah, Sabtah, Raamah and Sabteca. 6013
1Ch 1: 9 S, Havilah, Sabta, Raamah and Sabteca. 6013
Ps 72:10 kings of Sheba and S will present him gifts. 6013
Isa 43: 3 Cush and S in your stead. 6013

SEBAM (1)
Nu 32: 3 Heshbon, Elealeh, S, Nebo and Beon— 8423

SEBAT (KJV) See SHEBAT

SECACAH (1)
Jos 15:61 In the desert: Beth Arabah, Middin, S, 6117

SECHU (KJV) See SECU

SECLUSION (1)
Lk 1:24 and for five months *remained* **in s.** *4332*

SECOND (163) [TWO]
Ge 1: 8 and there was morning—the s day. 9108
2:13 The name of the s river is the Gihon; 9108
7:11 on the seventeenth day of the s month— 9108
8:14 the s month the earth was completely dry. 9108
22:15 to Abraham from heaven a s **time** 9108
30: 7 and bore Jacob a s son. 9108
30:12 Leah's servant Zilpah bore Jacob a s son. 9108
32:19 He also instructed the s, 9108
41: 5 He fell asleep again and had a s dream: 9108
41:52 The s son he named Ephraim and said, 9108
Ex 4: 8 they may believe the s. 340
16: 1 of the s month after they had come out 9108
25:19 on one end and the s cherub on the other; 285
25:35 a s bud under the second pair, NIH
25:35 a second bud under the s pair, NIH
28:18 in the s row a turquoise, a sapphire and 9108
37: 8 on one end and the s cherub on the other; 285
37:21 a s bud under the second pair, NIH
37:21 a second bud under the s pair, NIH
39:11 in the s row a turquoise, a sapphire and 9108
40:17 the first day of the first month in the s year. 9108
Lev 19:10 **go over** your vineyard **a s time** 6618
Nu 1: 1 of Sinai on the first day of the s month of 9108
1: 1 of the s year after the Israelites came out 9108
1:18 on the first day of the s month. 9108
2:16 They will set out s. 9108
7:18 On the s day Nethanel son of Zuar, 9108
8: 8 to take a s young bull for a sin offering. 9108
9: 1 of the s year after they came out of Egypt. 9108
9:11 on the fourteenth day of the s month 9108
10: 6 At the sounding of a s blast, 9108
10:11 On the twentieth day of the s month of 9108
10:11 of the second month of the s year, 9108
28: 8 Prepare the s lamb at twilight, 9108
29:17 " 'On the s day prepare twelve young bulls, 9108
Dt 24: 3 and her s husband dislikes her 340
24:20 *do* not **go over the branches a s time.** 339+6994
Jos 6:14 the s day they marched around the city once 9108
10:32 and Joshua took it on the s day. 9108
19: 1 The s lot came out for the tribe of Simeon, 9108
Jdg 6:25 "Take the s bull from your father's herd, 9108
6:26 offer the s bull as a burnt offering." 9108
6:28 beside it cut down and the s bull sacrificed 9108
20:24 Israelites drew near to Benjamin the s day. 9108
1Sa 8: 2 and the name of his s was Abijah, 5467
17:13 the s, Abinadab; and the third, Shammah. 5467
18:21 a s *opportunity* to become my son-in-law." 9109
20:27 But the next day, the s day *of* the month, 9108
20:34 on that s day of the month he did not eat, 9108
23:17 and I will be s to you. 5467
2Sa 3: 3 his s, Kileab the son of Abigail the widow 5467
2Sa 14:29 So he sent a s time, but he refused to come. 9108
1Ki 6: 1 in the month of Ziv, the s month, 9108
6:25 The s cherub also measured ten cubits, 9108
9: 2 the LORD appeared to him a **s time,** 9108
15:25 of Israel in the s year of Asa king of Judah, 9109
19: 7 The angel of the LORD came back a **s time** 9108
2Ki 1:17 Joram succeeded him as king in the s year 9109
9:19 So the king sent out a s horseman. 9108
10: 6 Then Jehu wrote them a s letter, saying, 9108
14: 1 the s year of Jehoash son of Jehoahaz king 9109
15:32 In the s year of Pekah son of Remaliah king 9109
19:29 and the s year what springs from that. 9108
22:14 She lived in Jerusalem, in the **S District.** 5467
1Ch 2:13 the s son was Abinadab, the third Shimea, 9108
3: 1 the **s,** Daniel the son of Abigail of Carmel; 9108
3:15 Johanan the firstborn, Jehoiakim the s son, 9108
5:12 Shapham the s, then Janai and Shaphat, 5467
6:28 Joel the firstborn and Abijah the s son. 9108
8: 1 Ashbel the s son, Aharah the third, 9108
8:39 Jeush the s son and Eliphelet the third. 9108
12: 9 Obadiah the **s in command,** Eliab the third, 9108
16: 5 Zechariah s, then Jeiel, Shemiramoth, 5467
23:11 Jahath was the first and Ziza the **s,** 9108
23:19 Jeriah the first, Amariah the s, 9108
23:20 Micah the first and Isshiah the **s.** 9108
24: 7 the s to Jedaiah, 9108
24:23 Jeriah the first, Amariah the s, 9108
25: 9 the s to Gedaliah, he and his relatives and 9108
26: 2 Zechariah the firstborn, Jediael the s, 9108
26: 4 Shemaiah the firstborn, Jehozabad the s, 9108
26:11 the s, Tabaliah the third and Zechariah 9108
27: 4 of the division for the s month was Dodai 9108
29:22 Solomon son of David as king a **s time,** 9108
2Ch 3: 2 on the s day of the second month in 9108
3: 2 the s month in the fourth year of his reign. 9108
3:12 of the s cherub was five cubits long 337
21:19 at the end of the s year, his bowels came out 9109
27: 5 the same amount also in the s and third 9108
28: 7 and Elkanah, s *to* the king. 5467
30: 2 to celebrate the Passover in the s month. 9108
30:13 of Unleavened Bread in the s month. 9108
30:15 on the fourteenth day of the s month. 9108
34:22 She lived in Jerusalem, in the **S District.** 5467
Ezr 3: 8 In the s month of the second year 9108
3: 8 of the s year after their arrival at the house 9108
4:24 until the s year of the reign of Darius king 10775
Ne 8:13 On the s day of the month, 9108
11: 9 of Hassenuah was over the **S District** of 5467
11:17 Bakbukiah, s among his associates; 5467
12:38 The s choir proceeded in 9108
Est 2:19 When the virgins were assembled a **s time,** 9108
7: 2 as they were drinking wine on that s day, 9108
9:29 to confirm this s letter concerning Purim. 9108
10: 3 the Jew was **s in rank** to King Xerxes, 5467
Job 42:14 the s Keziah and the third Keren-Happuch. 9108
Isa 11:11 a s **time** to reclaim the remnant that is left 9108
37:30 and the s year what springs from that. 9108
Jer 13: 3 word of the LORD came to me a **s time:** 9108
33: 1 word of the LORD came to him a **s time:** 9108
Eze 10:14 the s the face of a man, 9108
43:22 "On the s day you are to offer a male goat 9108
Da 2: 1 In the s year of his reign, 9109
7: 5 "And there before me was a s beast, 10765
Am 7: 1 and just as the s **crop** was coming up. 4381
Jnh 3: 1 word of the LORD came to Jonah a **s time:** 9108
Na 1: 9 trouble will not come a *s* **time.** AIT
Hag 1: 1 In the s year of King Darius, 9109
1:15 of the sixth month in the s year 9109
2:10 in the s year of Darius, 9109
2:20 to Haggai a **s time** on the twenty-fourth day 9108
Zec 1: 1 In the eighth month of the s year of Darius, 9109
1: 7 in the s year of Darius, 9109
6: 2 The first chariot had red horses, the s black, 9108
11:14 Then I broke my s staff called Union, 9108
Mt 22:26 The same thing happened to the s *1311*
22:39 And the s is like it: *1311*
26:42 went away a **s time** and prayed, *1311+1666+4099*
Mk 12:21 The s one married the widow, *1311*
12:31 s is this: 'Love your neighbor as yourself.' *1311*
14:72 the rooster crowed the **s time.** *1311+1666*
Lk 12:38 even if he comes in the s or third watch of *1311*
16: 7 "Then he asked the s, *NIG*
19:18 "The s came and said, 'Sir, *1311*
20:30 The s *1311*
Jn 3: 4 a **s time** into his mother's womb to *1309*
4:54 This was the s miraculous sign that Jesus performed, *1311+4099*
9:24 A **s time** they summoned the man *1311+1666*
Ac 7:13 On their s *visit,* Joseph told his brothers *1311*
10:15 The voice spoke to him a **s time** *1311+1666+4099*
11: 9 The voice spoke from heaven a **s time** *1311+1666*
12:10 They passed the first and s guards and came *1311*
13:33 As it is written in the s Psalm: *1311*
1Co 12:28 first of all apostles, s prophets, third *1309*
15:47 the s man from heaven. *1311*
2Co 13: 2 a warning when I was with you the **s time.** *1309*
Tit 3:10 and then warn him a s *time.* *1311*
Heb 9: 3 Behind the s curtain was a room called *1311*
9:28 will appear a **s time,** not to bear sin, *1311+1666*
10: 9 He sets aside the first to establish the **s.** *1311*
2Pe 3: 1 Dear friends, this is now my s letter to you. *1311*
Rev 2:11 not be hurt at all by the s death. *1311*
4: 7 the s was like an ox, *1311*
6: 3 When the Lamb opened the s seal, *1311*
6: 3 I heard the s living creature say, "Come!" *1311*
8: 8 The s angel sounded his trumpet, *1311*
11:14 The s woe has passed; *1311*
Rev 14: 8 A s angel followed and said, "Fallen! *1311*
16: 3 The s angel poured out his bowl on the sea, *1311*
20: 6 The s death has no power over them, *1311*
20:14 The lake of fire is the s death. *1311*
21: 8 This is the s death." *1311*
21:19 first foundation was jasper, the s sapphire, *1311*

SECOND-IN-COMMAND (1) [COMMAND]
Ge 41:43 He had him ride in a chariot as his s, 5467

SECRET (44) [SECRETLY, SECRETS]
Ex 7:11 also did the same things by their s **arts:** 4268
7:22 the same things by their **s arts,** 4319
8: 7 the same things by their s **arts;** 4319
8:18 to produce gnats by their s **arts,** 4319
Dt 27:15 and sets it up in **s."** 6260
29:29 The s *things* belong to the LORD our God, 6259
Jdg 3:19 "I have a s message for you, O king." 6260
16: 5 showing you the s of his great strength 928+4537
16: 6 "Tell me the s of your great strength 928+4537
16: 9 So the s of his strength was not discovered. NIH
16:15 a fool of me and haven't told me the s 928+4537
2Sa 12:12 You did it in s, but I will do this thing 6260
15:10 Absalom sent s **messengers** throughout 8078
Est 2:20 But Esther *had* **kept** s her family background 401+5583
Ps 10: 8 watching *in* s for his victims. 7621
90: 8 our s sins in the light of your presence. 6623
101: 5 Whoever slanders his neighbor in s, 6260
139:15 from you when I was made in the s **place.** 6260
Pr 9:17 food eaten in s is delicious!" 6260
11:13 but a trustworthy man keeps a s. 1821
17:23 a bribe in s to pervert the course of justice. 2668
21:14 A gift given in s soothes anger, 6260
Isa 45: 3 riches stored in **s places,** 5041
45:19 I have not spoken in s, 6260
48:16 I have not spoken in **s;** 6260
65: 4 and spend their nights **keeping s vigil;** 5915
Jer 13:17 I will weep in s because of your pride; 5041
23:24 in **s places** so that I cannot see him?" 5041
Eze 28: 3 Is no s hidden from you? 6259
Mt 6: 4 so that your giving may be in **s.** *3220*
6: 4 your Father, who sees what is done in **s,** *3220*
6: 6 your Father, who sees what is done in **s,** *3220*
6:18 your Father, who sees what is done in **s,** *3224*
Mk 4:11 "The s of the kingdom of God *3696*
7:24 yet he could not **keep** his presence **s.** *3291*
Jn 7: 4 to become a public figure acts in **s.** *3220*
7:10 he went also, not publicly, but in **s.** *3220*
18:20 I said nothing in **s.** *3220*
1Co 2: 7 No, we speak of God's s wisdom, *1877+3696*
4: 1 as those entrusted with the s *things* of God. *3696*
2Co 4: 2 we have renounced s and shameful ways; *3220*
Eph 5:12 to mention what the disobedient do *in* **s.** *3225*
Php 4:12 *I have* **learned the** s of being content *3679*
2Th 2: 7 s power of lawlessness is already at work; *3696*

SECRETARIES (4) [SECRETARY]
1Ki 4: 3 and Ahijah, sons of Shisha—**s;** 6221
2Ch 34:13 Some of the Levites were s, 6221
Est 3:12 the first month the royal s were summoned. 6221
8: 9 At once the royal s were summoned— 6221

SECRETARY (32) [SECRETARIES, SECRETARY'S]
2Sa 8:17 of Abiathar were priests; Seraiah was **s;** 6221
20:25 Sheva was **s;** Zadok and Abiathar were 6221
2Ki 12:10 the royal s and the high priest came, 6221
18:18 the palace administrator, Shebna the s, 6221
18:37 Shebna the s and Joah son of Asaph 6221
19: 2 Shebna the s and the leading priests, 6221
22: 3 King Josiah sent the **s,** 6221
22: 8 the high priest said to Shaphan the **s,** 6221
22: 9 the s went to the king and reported to him: 6221
22:10 Then Shaphan the s informed the king, 6221
22:12 the s and Asaiah the king's attendant: 6221
25:19 He also took the s who was chief officer 6221
1Ch 18:16 of Abiathar were priests; Shavsha was **s;** 6221
2Ch 24:11 the royal s and the officer of the chief priest 6221
26:11 to their numbers as mustered by Jeiel the s 6221
34:15 Hilkiah said to Shaphan the **s,** 6221
34:18 Then Shaphan the s informed the king, 6221
34:20 the s and Asaiah the king's attendant: 6221
Ezr 4: 8 the s wrote a letter against Jerusalem 10516
4: 9 and Shimshai the s, together with the rest 10516
4:17 the commanding officer, Shimshai the s and 10516
4:23 and Shimshai the s and their associates, 10516
Isa 36: 3 the palace administrator, Shebna the s, 6221
36:22 the palace administrator, Shebna the s, 6221
37: 2 Shebna the **s,** and the leading priests, 6221
Jer 36:10 of Gemariah son of Shaphan the **s,** 6221
36:12 Elishama the **s,** Delaiah son of Shemaiah, 6221
36:20 the scroll in the room of Elishama the **s,** 6221
36:21 from the room of Elishama the s and read it 6221
37:15 in the house of Jonathan the **s,** 6221
37:20 to the house of Jonathan the **s,** 6221
52:25 He also took the s who was chief officer 6221

SECRETARY'S (1) [SECRETARY]
Jer 36:12 to the s room in the royal palace, where all 6221

SECRETLY (16) [SECRET]
Ge 31:27 Why did you run off s and deceive me? 2461

Dt 13: 6 your closest friend s entices you, 928+2021+6260
27:24 man who kills his neighbor **s.**" 928+2021+6260
28:57 to eat them s during the siege 928+2021+6260
Jos 2: 1 Then Joshua son of Nun s sent two spies 3089
2Sa 21:12 *(They had* **taken** them s from the public 1704
2Ki 17: 9 The Israelites s **did** things against 2901
Job 4:12 "A word **was** s **brought** to me, 1704
13:10 if you s showed partiality. 928+2021+6260
31:27 so that my heart was s enticed 928+2021+6260
Jer 38:16 King Zedekiah swore this oath s 928+2021+6260
Mt 2: 7 the Magi s and found out from them *3277*
Jn 19:38 but s because he feared the Jews. *3221*
Ac 6:11 Then *they* s **persuaded** some men to say, *5680*
2Pe 2: 1 They *will* s **introduce** destructive heresies, *4206*
Jude 1: 4 *have* s **slipped in** among you. *4208*

SECRETS (7) [SECRET]

Job 11: 6 and disclose to you the s *of* wisdom, 9502
Ps 44:21 since he knows the s *of* the heart? 9502
Mt 13:11 "The knowledge of the s of the kingdom *3696*
Lk 8:10 the s of the kingdom of God has been given *3696*
Ro 2:16 on the day when God will judge men's s *3220*
1Co 14:25 and the s of his heart will be laid bare. *3220*
Rev 2:24 have not learned Satan's so-called deep s *NIG*

SECT (5)

Lk 5:30 **who belonged to their** s complained *899*
Ac 24: 5 He is a ringleader *of* the Nazarene s *146*
24:14 the Way, which they call a **s.** *146*
26: 5 according to the strictest s of our religion, *146*
28:22 people everywhere are talking against this **s.** *146*

SECTION (20) [SECTIONS]

2Ki 14:13 a s about six hundred feet long. NIH
2Ch 25:23 a s about six hundred feet long. NIH
Ne 3: 2 men of Jericho built the **adjoining s,** 3338+6584
3: 4 the son of Hakkoz, repaired the **next s.** 3338+6584
3: 5 The **next** s was repaired by the men 3338+6584
3: 8 of the goldsmiths, repaired the **next s;** 3338+6584
3: 9 repaired the **next s.** 3338+6584
3:11 of Pahath-Moab repaired another s and 4500
3:12 **next** s with the help of his daughters. 3338+6584
3:19 ruler of Mizpah, repaired another **s,** 4500
3:20 of Zabbai zealously repaired another **s,** 4500
3:21 the son of Hakkoz, repaired another **s,** 4500
3:24 Binnui son of Henadad repaired another **s,** 4500
3:27 the men of Tekoa repaired another **s,** 4500
3:30 the sixth son of Zalaph, repaired another **s.** 4500
12:24 *one* s responding to the other, 5464
Eze 42: 3 the s twenty cubits from the inner court and NIH
42: 3 from the inner court and in the s opposite NIH
45: 2 a s 500 cubits square is to be for NIH
45: 3 measure off a s 25,000 cubits long NIH

SECTIONS (3) [SECTION]

1Ki 22:34 and hit the king of Israel between the s 1817
2Ch 18:33 and hit the king of Israel between the s 1817
32: 5 repairing all the **broken** *s* of the wall AIT

SECU (1)

1Sa 19:22 and went to the great cistern at **S.** 8497

SECUNDUS (1)

Ac 20: 4 Aristarchus and **S** from Thessalonica, *4941*

SECURE (40) [SECURED, SECURELY, SECURES, SECURITY]

Nu 24:21 "Your dwelling place is **s,** 419
Dt 33:12 the beloved of the LORD rest s in him, 1055
33:28 Jacob's spring is s in a land of grain NIH
Jdg 18: 7 like the Sidonians, unsuspecting and **s.** 1053
1Ki 2:45 and David's throne will remain s before 3922
Job 5:24 You will know that your tent is **s;** 8934
11:18 *You will be* **s,** because there is hope; 1053
12: 6 and those who provoke God are **s**— 1058
21:23 completely s and at ease, 8916
40:23 *he is* **s,** though the Jordan should surge 1053
Ps 7: 9 of the wicked and **make** the righteous **s.** 3922
16: 5 you *have* **made** my lot **s.** 9461
16: 9 my body also will rest **s,** 1055
30: 6 I **felt s,** I said, "I will never be shaken." 8930
48: 8 God **makes** her s forever 3922
112: 8 His heart *is* **s,** he will have no fear; 6164
122: 6 *"May* those who love you *be* **s.** 8922
Pr 14:26 He who fears the LORD has a s fortress, 4440
20:28 through love his throne *is* **made s.** 6184
27:24 and a crown is not s for all generations. NIH
29:14 his throne *will* always **be s.** 3922
Isa 32: 9 you daughters *who* **feel s,** 1053
32:10 a year you *who* **feel** s will tremble; 1053
32:11 shudder, you daughters *who* **feel s!** 1053
32:18 in s homes, in undisturbed places of rest. 4440
33:23 mast *is* not **held s,** the sail is not spread. 2616
Jer 22:21 I warned you when you **felt s,** 8932
Eze 34:27 the people will be s in their land. 1055
Da 8:25 When they **feel s,** he will destroy many 8932
11:21 the kingdom when its people **feel s,** 8932
11:24 When the richest provinces **feel s,** 8932
Am 6: 1 and to *you who* **feel** s on Mount Samaria, 1053
Zec 1:15 with the nations that **feel s.** 8633
14:11 Jerusalem will be **s.** 1055
Mt 27:64 So give the order for the tomb *to be* **made** s *856*
27:65 **make** the tomb as s as you know how." *856*
27:66 and **made** the tomb s by putting a seal on *856*
Ac 27:16 we were hardly able to make the lifeboat **s.** *4331*
Heb 6:19 as an anchor for the soul, firm and **s.** *1010*
2Pe 3:17 and fall from your s **position.** *5113*

SECURED (2) [SECURE]

2Sa 23: 5 arranged and s in every part? 9068
Ac 12:20 *Having* **s the support** of Blastus, *4275*

SECURELY (8) [SECURE]

Jdg 16:11 "If *anyone* **ties** me s with new ropes 673+673
1Sa 12:11 so that you lived **s.** 1055
25:29 of my master will be **bound** s in the bundle 7674
1Ki 2:24 he who has established me s on the throne 3782
Pr 8:28 above and **fixed** s the fountains of the deep, 6451
10: 9 The man of integrity walks **s,** 1055
Mic 5: 4 And *they will* **live s,** 3782
Ac 5:23 the jail s locked, with the guards *854+1877+4246*

SECURES (1) [SECURE]

Ps 140:12 that the LORD s justice for the poor 6913

SECURITY (20) [SECURE]

Dt 24: 6 *Do* not **take** a pair of millstones—not even the upper one—**as s for a debt,** 2471
24: 6 **taking** a man's livelihood **as s.** 2471
2Ki 20:19 not be peace and s in my lifetime?" 622
Job 17: 3 Who else *will* **put up** s *for* me? 3338+4200+9546
18:14 the s *of* his tent and marched off to the king 4440
22: 6 *You* **demanded** s *from* your brothers 2471
24:23 He may let them rest in a **feeling of s,** 1055
31:24 or said to pure gold, 'You are my **s,'** 4440
Ps 122: 7 May there be peace within your walls and **s** 8932
Pr 6: 1 if *you have* **put up** s for your neighbor, 6842
11:15 *He who* **puts up** s *for* another will 6842
17:18 and **puts up** s for his neighbor. 6842+6859
20:16 Take the garment of *one who* **puts up** s *for* 6842
22:26 in pledge or **puts up** s *for* debts; 6842
27:13 Take the garment of one *who* **puts up** s *for* 6842
Isa 39: 8 "There will be peace and s in my lifetime." 622
47: 8 lounging in your s and saying to yourself, 1055
Jer 30:10 Jacob will again have peace and **s,** 8631
33: 6 will let them enjoy abundant peace and **s.** 622
46:27 Jacob will again have peace and **s,** 8631

SEDITION (1)

Ezr 4:19 and has been a place of rebellion and **s.** 10083

SEDITIONS (KJV) See DISSENSIONS

SEDUCE (1) [SEDUCED, SEDUCES, SEDUCTIVE]

2Pe 2:14 *they* s the unstable; *1284*

SEDUCED (1) [SEDUCE]

Pr 7:21 *she* s him with her smooth talk. 5615

SEDUCES (1) [SEDUCE]

Ex 22:16 "If a man s a virgin who is not pledged to 7331

SEDUCTIVE (2) [SEDUCE]

Pr 2:16 from the wayward wife with her s words, 2744
7: 5 from the wayward wife with her s words. 2744

SEE (796) [NEARSIGHTED, SAW, SEEING, SEEN, SEES, SIGHT, SIGHTING, SIGHTLESS, SIGHTS]

Ge 2:19 to the man to s what he would name them; 8011
8: 8 a dove to s if the water had receded from 8011
9:16 *I will* s it and remember 8011
9:23 *they would* not s their father's nakedness. 8011
11: 5 But the LORD came down to s the city 8011
12:12 When the Egyptians s you, they will say, 8011
13:15 All the land that you s I will give to you 8011
18:16 s them **on their way.** 8938
18:21 down and s if what they have done is as bad 8011
24:13 **S,** I am standing beside this spring, 2180
24:43 **S,** I am standing beside this spring; 2180
27: 1 so weak that *he could* no longer **s,** 8011
31: 5 "I s that your father's attitude toward me is 8011
31:12 and s that all the male goats mating with 8011
31:32 s for yourself whether there is anything 5795
31:43 All you s is mine. 8011
32:20 later, when *I* s him, 7156+8011
33:10 For *to* s your face is like seeing the face 8011
37:14 "Go and s if all is well with your brothers 8011
37:20 Then *we'll* s what comes of his dreams." 8011
37:32 **Examine** it **to** s whether it is your son's robe." 5795
38:25 *"S if you* **recognize** whose seal and cord AIT
42: 9 to s where our land is unprotected." 8011
42:12 to s where our land is unprotected." 8011
42:16 be tested to s if you are telling the truth. NIH
43: 3 not s my face again unless your brother is 8011
43: 5 not s my face again unless your brother is 8011
44:21 down to me so *I can* s him for myself.' 6524+8492
44:23 *you will* not s my face again.' 8011
44:26 We cannot s the man's face 8011
44:34 *Do* not *let me* s the misery that would come 8011
45:12 *"You can* s **for yourselves,** 4013+6524+8011
45:28 I will go and s him before I die." 8011
48:10 and he could hardly **s.** 8011
48:11 "I never expected *to* s your face again, 8011
48:11 God *has* **allowed** me **to** s your children too. 8011
Ex 2: 4 a distance to s what would happen to him. 3359
3: 3 "I will go over and s this strange sight— 8011
4:18 in Egypt *to* s if any of them are still alive." 8011
4:21 s that you perform before Pharaoh all 8011
6: 1 *you will* s what I will do to Pharaoh: 8011
7: 1 Then the LORD said to Moses, **"S,** 8011
10:23 No one *could* s anyone else 8011
10:28 The day you s my face you will die." 8011
12:13 and when *I* s the blood, I will pass over 8011
12:23 *he will* s the blood on the top and sides of 8011
14:13 Stand firm and *you will* s the deliverance 8011
14:13 The Egyptians *you* s today you will never 8011
14:13 you see today *you will* never s again. 8011
16: 4 s whether they will follow my instructions. NIH
16: 7 and in the morning *you will* s the glory of 8011
16:32 to come, so *they can* s the bread I gave you 8011
19:21 not force their way through to s the LORD 8011
21:19 **s that** *he* **is completely healed.** 8324+8324
23: 5 If *you* s the donkey of someone who hates 8011
23: 8 for a bribe blinds *those who* s and twists 7221
23:20 **"S,** I am sending an angel ahead of you 2180
25:40 **S** that you make them according to 8011
31: 2 **"S,** I have chosen Bezalel son of Uri, 8011
33:20 But," he said, "you cannot s my face, 8011
33:20 for no one *may* s me and live." 8011
33:23 and *you will* s my back; 8011
34:10 among *will* s how awesome is the work 8011
35:30 Then Moses said to the Israelites, **"S,** 8011
Lev 13:12 so far as the priest can **s,** 5260+6524
25:53 you must **s to it** that his owner does 4200+6524
Nu 4:18 *"S that* the Kohathite tribal clans *are* not **cut off** AIT
11: 6 we never s anything but this manna!" 448+6524
11:23 *You will* now s whether or 8011
13:18 **S** what the land is like and whether 8011
14:23 not one of them *will ever* s the land 8011
14:23 treated me with contempt *will ever* s it. 8011
23: 9 From the rocky peaks *I* s them, 8011
23: 9 I s a people who live apart and do 2176
23:13 to another place where *you can* s them; 8011
23:13 *you will* s only a part but not all of them. 8011
23:23 **'S** what God has done!' NIH
24:17 *"I* s him, but not now; 8011
27:12 up this mountain in the Abarim range and s 8011
28: 2 **'S** that you present to me at the appointed 9068
32:11 of Egypt *will* s the land I promised on oath 8011
Dt 1: 8 **S,** I have given you this land. 8011
1:21 **S,** the LORD your God has given you 8011
1:35 "Not a man of this evil generation *shall* s 8011
1:36 He *will* s it, and I will give him 8011
2:24 **S,** I have given into your hand Sihon 8011
2:31 The LORD said to me, **"S,** 8011
3:25 Let me go over and s the good land beyond 8011
3:28 to inherit the land that *you will* **s."** 8011
4: 5 **S,** I have taught you decrees and laws as 8011
4:19 when you look up to the sky and s the sun, 8011
4:28 which cannot s or hear or eat or smell. 8011
11:26 **S,** I am setting before you today a blessing 8011
12:32 **S** that you do all I command you; 9068
18:16 nor s this great fire anymore, 8011
20: 1 to war against your enemies and s horses 8011
21: 7 nor *did* our eyes s it done. 8011
22: 1 *you* s your brother's ox or sheep straying, 8011
22: 4 If *you* s your brother's donkey 8011
23:14 not s among you anything indecent 8011
28:10 on earth *will* s that you are called by 8011
28:34 The sights *you* s will drive you mad. 8011
28:67 and the sights that your eyes *will* **s.** 8011
29: 4 a mind that understands or eyes that s 8011
29:22 from distant lands *will* s the calamities 8011
30:15 **S,** I set before you today life 8011
32:20 he said, "and s what their end will be; 8011
32:39 **"S** now that I myself am He! 8011
32:52 *you will* s the land only from a distance; 8011
34: 4 *I have* **let** you s it with your eyes, 8011
Jos 3: 3 "When you s the ark of the covenant of 8011
3:11 **S,** the ark of the covenant of the Lord of all 2180
5: 6 to them that they *would* not s the land 8011
6: 2 Then the LORD said to Joshua, **"S,** 8011
8: 8 **S** *to* it; you have my orders." 8011
9:12 But now s how dry and moldy it is. 2180
9:13 but s how cracked they are. 2180
24:27 **"S!"** he said to all the people. 2180
Jdg 1:24 *we will s that* you *are* **treated** well." AIT
2:22 to test Israel and s whether they will keep NIH
3: 4 the Israelites to s whether they would obey 3359
13: 4 Now **s to it** that you drink no wine 9068
14:10 Now his father went down to s the woman. NIH
16: 5 *"S if you can* **lure** him into showing you AIT
1Sa 2:32 and *you will* s distress in my dwelling. 5564
3: 2 so weak that he could barely **s,** 8011
3:11 And the LORD said to Samuel: **"S,** 2180
4:15 so that he could not **s.** 8011
10:24 *"Do you* s the man the LORD has chosen? 8011
12:13 **s,** the LORD has set a king over you. 2180
12:16 and s this great thing the LORD is about 8011
14: 8 over toward the men and **let** them s *us.* 1655
14:17 "Muster the forces and s who has left us." 8011
14:29 **S** how my eyes brightened when I tasted 8011
15:35 *he did* not go to s Saul again, 8011
16:15 Saul's attendants said to him, **"S,** 2180

1Sa 17:18 **S** how your brothers are 7212
17:25 *"Do you* **s** how this man keeps coming out? 8011
19:15 Then Saul sent the men back to **s** David 8011
20:29 let me get away *to* **s** my brothers.' 8011
24:11 **S,** my father, look at this piece of your robe 8011
25:17 Now think it over and **s** what you can do, 8011
25:25 *I did* not **s** the men my master sent. 8011
28: 2 "Then *you will* **s** for yourself 3359
28:13 What *do you* **s?"** 8011
28:13 *"I* **s** a spirit coming up out of the ground." 8011
2Sa 3:13 of Saul when you come to **s** me." 8011
13: 5 "When your father comes to **s** you, 8011
13: 6 When the king came to **s** him, 8011
13:34 *"I* **s** men in the direction of Horonaim, 8011
13:35 Jonadab said to the king, **"S,** 2180
14:24 *he must* not **s** my face." 8011
14:24 to his own house and *did* not **s** the face of 8011
14:32 Now then, *I want to* **s** the king's face, 8011
15: 4 *I would* **s that** he **gets justice."** 7405
15:25 he will bring me back and **let** me **s** it 8011
16:12 be that the LORD *will* **s** my distress 8011
19: 6 *I* **s** that you would be pleased 3359
24: 3 and *may* the eyes of my lord the king **s** it. 8011
1Ki 1:15 So Bathsheba went to **s** the aged king NIH
1:48 who has allowed my eyes *to* **s** a successor 8011
9:12 to **s** the towns that Solomon had given him, 8011
11:31 **'S,** I am going to tear the kingdom out 2180
14: 4 Now Ahijah could not **s;** 8011
15:19 **S,** I am sending you a gift of silver 2180
20: 7 **"S** how this man is looking for trouble! 2256+3359+8011
20:13 *'Do you* **s** this vast army? 8011
20:22 and **s** what must be done, 2256+3359+8011
22: 2 of Judah went down to **s** the king of Israel. NIH
2Ki 1: 2 to **s** if I will recover from this injury." NIH
1:14 **S,** fire has fallen from heaven 2180
2:10 if *you* **s** me when I am taken from you, 8011
2:19 this town is well situated, as you *can* **s,** 8011
3:17 *You will* **s** neither wind nor rain, 8011
5: 3 "If only my master would **s** 4200+7156
5: 7 **S** how he is trying to pick a quarrel with me!" 2256+3359+8011
6:17 "O LORD, open his eyes so *he may* **s."** 8011
6:20 open the eyes of these men so *they can* **s."** 8011
6:32 to the elders, "Don't *you* **s** 8011
7: 2 "You *will* **s** it with your own eyes," 8011
7:19 "You *will* **s** it with your own eyes, 8011
8:29 down to Jezreel to **s** Joram son of Ahab, 8011
9:16 of Judah had gone down to **s** him. 8011
9:17 he called out, "I **s** some troops coming." 8011
10:16 with me and **s** my zeal for the LORD." 8011
10:19 **S** that no one is missing, NIH
10:23 "Look around and **s** that no servants of 8011
13:14 Jehoash king of Israel went down to **s** him NIH
19:16 open your eyes, O LORD, and **s;** 8011
20:15 "What *did they* **s** in your palace?" 8011
22:20 not **s** all the disaster I am going to bring 8011
23:17 "What is that tombstone I **s?"** 8011
1Ch 12:17 the God of our fathers **s** it and judge you." 8011
2Ch 16: 3 **S,** I am sending you silver and gold. 2180
20:11 **S** how they are repaying us by coming 2180
20:17 stand firm and **s** the deliverance 8011
22: 6 down to Jezreel to **s** Joram son of Ahab 8011
24:22 the LORD **s** this and call you to account." 8011
29: 8 as you *can* **s** with your own eyes. 8011
30: 7 an object of horror, as you **s.** 8011
34:28 not **s** all the disaster I am going to bring 8011
Ezr 4:14 to the palace and it is not proper for us to **s** 10255
5:17 to **s** if King Cyrus did in fact issue a decree NIH
Ne 2:17 I said to them, "You **s** the trouble we are in: 8011
4:11 "Before they know it or **s** us, 8011
8: 5 All the people could **s** him 4200+6524
9:36 "But **s,** we are slaves today, 2180
Est 3: 4 to **s** whether Mordecai's behavior would 8011
5:13 as long as I **s** that Jew Mordecai sitting at 8011
8: 6 can I bear *to* **s** disaster fall on my people? 8011
8: 6 How can I bear *to* **s** the destruction 8011
Job 3: 9 for daylight in vain and not **s** the first rays 8011
6:21 *you* **s** something dreadful and are afraid. 8011
7: 7 my eyes *will* never **s** happiness again. 8011
7: 8 eye that now sees me *will* **s** me no longer; 8800
9:11 When he passes me, *I* cannot **s** him; 8011
10: 4 *Do you* **s** as a mortal sees? 8011
14:21 if they are brought low, *he does* not **s** it. 1067
15:17 Who *can* **s** any hope for me? 8800
19:26 yet in my flesh *I will* **s** God; 2600
19:27 I myself *will* **s** him with my own eyes— 2600
20: 9 The eye that saw him will not **s** him again; NIH
21: 8 They **s** their children established 4200+7156
21:20 *Let* his own eyes **s** his destruction; 8011
22:11 why it is so dark *you* cannot **s,** 8011
22:12 And **s** how lofty *are* the highest stars! 8011
22:14 so *he does* not **s** us as he goes about in 8011
22:19 "The righteous **s** their ruin and rejoice; 8011
23: 9 he is at work in the north, *I do* not **s** him; 296
24:15 he thinks, 'No eye *will* **s** me,' 8800
28:10 his eyes **s** all its treasures. 8011
31: 4 not **s** my ways and count my every step? 8011
34:26 where *everyone can* **s** them, 8011
34:29 If he hides his face, who *can* **s** him? 8800
34:32 Teach me what *I* cannot **s;** 2600
35: 5 Look up at the heavens and **s;** 8011
35:14 when you say that *you do* not **s** him, 8800
36:30 **S** how he scatters his lightning about him, 2176
Ps 9:13 **s** how my enemies persecute me! 8011
10:14 But you, O God, *do* **s** trouble and grief; 8011
11: 7 upright men *will* **s** his face. 2600
Ps 14: 2 of men to **s** if there are any who understand, 8011
16:10 nor will you let your Holy One **s** decay. 8011
17: 2 *may* your eyes **s** what is right. 2600
17:15 in righteousness *I will* **s** your face; 2600
22: 7 All *who* **s** me mock me; 8011
25:19 **S** how my enemies have increased and 8011
27:13 I *will* **s** the goodness of the LORD in 8011
31:11 *those who* **s** me on the street flee from me. 8011
34: 8 Taste and **s** that the LORD is good; 8011
34:12 and desires to **s** many good days, 8011
36: 9 in your light *we* **s** light. 8011
36:12 **S** how the evildoers lie fallen— 9004
37:34 when the wicked are cut off, *you will* **s** it. 8011
40: 3 Many *will* **s** and fear and put their trust in 8011
40:12 my sins have overtaken me, and I cannot **s.** 8011
41: 6 Whenever one comes to **s** me, 8011
46: 8 Come and **s** the works of the LORD, 2600
49: 9 he should live on forever and not **s** decay. 8011
49:10 For *all can* **s** that wise men die; 8011
49:19 *who will* never **s** the light [of life]. 8011
50:18 When *you* **s** a thief, you join with him; 8011
52: 6 The righteous *will* **s** and fear; 8011
53: 2 of men to **s** if there are any who understand, 8011
55: 9 for *I* **s** violence and strife in the city. 8011
58: 8 like a stillborn child, *may they* not **s** the sun. 2600
59: 3 **S** how they lie in wait for me! 2180
59: 7 **S** what they spew from their mouths— 2180
64: 5 they say, "Who *will* **s** them?" 8011
64: 8 all *who* **s** them will shake their heads 8011
66: 5 Come and **s** what God has done, 8011
69:23 be darkened so they cannot **s,** 8011
69:32 The poor *will* **s** and be glad— 8011
71:20 Though *you have* **made** me **s** troubles, 8011
80:14 Look down from heaven and **s!** 8011
83: 2 **S** how your enemies are astir, 2180
86:17 my enemies *may* **s** it and be put to shame, 8011
89:48 What man can live and not **s** death, 8011
91: 8 You will only observe with your eyes and **s** 8011
94: 7 They say, "The LORD *does* not **s;** 8011
94: 9 *Does he* who formed the eye not **s?** 5564
97: 6 and all the peoples **s** his glory. 8011
107:42 The upright **s** and rejoice, 8011
109:25 *when they* **s** me, they shake their heads. 8011
112:10 The wicked man *will* **s** and be vexed, 8011
115: 5 but cannot speak, eyes, but *they* cannot **s;** 8011
119:18 that *I may* **s** wonderful things in your law. 5564
119:74 who fear you rejoice *when they* **s** me, 8011
119:96 To all perfection *I* **s** a limit; 8011
119:159 **S** how I love your precepts; 8011
128: 5 *may you* **s** the prosperity of Jerusalem, 8011
128: 6 *may you* live to **s** your children's children. 8011
135:16 but cannot speak, eyes, but *they* cannot **s;** 8011
139:24 **S** if there is any offensive way in me, 8011
142: 4 Look to my right and **s;** 8011
Pr 20:12 Ears that hear and eyes *that* **s—** 8011
22:29 *Do you* **s** a man skilled in his work? 2600
23:33 Your eyes *will* **s** strange *sights* 8011
24:18 or the LORD *will* **s** and disapprove 8011
26:12 *Do you* **s** a man wise in his own eyes? 8011
27:12 The prudent **s** danger and take refuge, 8011
29:16 but the righteous *will* **s** their downfall. 8011
29:20 *Do you* **s** a man who speaks in haste? 2600
Ecc 2: 3 *to* **s** what was worthwhile for men to do 8011
2:24 This too, I **s,** is from the hand of God, 8011
3:18 so that they *may* **s** that they are like 8011
3:22 to **s** what will happen after him? 8011
5: 8 If *you* **s** the poor oppressed in a district, 8011
7:11 is a good thing and benefits *those who* **s** 8011
11: 7 and it pleases the eyes to **s** the sun. 8011
11: 9 of your heart and *whatever* your eyes **s,** 5260
SS 2:11 **S!** The winter is past; 2180
6:11 to **s** if the vines had budded or 8011
7:12 the vineyards *to* **s** if the vines have budded, 8011
Isa 1:21 **S how** the faithful city has become a harlot! 377
3: 1 **S** now, the Lord, the LORD Almighty, 2180
5:19 let him hasten his work so *we may* **s** it. 8011
5:30 he will **s** darkness and distress; 2180
6: 7 With it he touched my mouth and said, **"S,** 2180
6:10 Otherwise *they might* **s** with their eyes, 8011
8:22 the earth and **s** only distress and darkness 2180
10:33 **S,** the Lord, the LORD Almighty, 2180
13: 9 **S,** the day of the LORD is coming— 2180
13:17 **S,** I will stir up against them the Medes, 2180
14:16 *Those who* **s** you stare at you, 8011
17: 1 An oracle concerning Damascus: **"S,** 2180
18: 3 *you will* **s** it, and when a trumpet sounds, 8011
19: 1 An oracle concerning Egypt: **S,** 2180
20: 6 **'S** what has happened to those we relied 2180
21: 3 I am bewildered by *what* I **s.** 8011
22:13 But **s,** there is joy and revelry, 2180
24: 1 **S,** the LORD is going to lay waste 2180
26:11 your hand is lifted high, but *they do* not **s** it. 2600
26:11 *Let them* **s** your zeal for your people and 2600
26:21 **S,** the LORD is coming out 2180
28: 2 **S,** the Lord has one who is powerful 2180
28:16 **"S,** I lay a stone in Zion, a tested stone, 2180
29:18 and darkness the eyes of the blind *will* **s.** 8011
29:23 When they **s** among them their children, 8011
30:10 They say to the seers, **"S** no *more* **visions!"** 8011
30:20 *with* your own eyes you *will* **s** them. 8011
30:27 **S,** the Name of the LORD comes 2180
30:30 and *will* **make** them **s** his arm coming down 8011
32: 1 **S,** a king will reign in righteousness 2176
32: 3 Then the eyes of *those who* **s** will no longer 8011
33:17 Your eyes *will* **s** the king in his beauty 2600
33:19 *You will* **s** those arrogant people no more, 8011
33:20 your eyes *will* **s** Jerusalem, 8011
Isa 34: 5 **s,** it descends in judgment on Edom, 2180
35: 2 they *will* **s** the glory of the LORD, 8011
37:17 open your eyes, O LORD, and **s;** 8011
38:11 I said, *"I will* not again **s** the LORD, 8011
39: 4 "What *did they* **s** in your palace?" 8011
40: 5 and all mankind together *will* **s** it. 8011
40:10 **S,** the Sovereign LORD comes 2180
40:10 **S,** his reward is with him, 2180
41:15 **"S,** I will make you into a threshing sledge, 2180
41:20 so that people *may* **s** and know, 8011
41:29 **S,** they are all false! 2176
42: 9 **S,** the former things have taken place, 2180
42:18 "Hear, you deaf; look, you blind, and **s!** 8011
43:19 **S,** I am doing a new thing! 2180
44:16 I am warm; *I* **s** the fire." 8011
44:18 over so they cannot **s,** 8011
48:10 **S,** I have refined you, though not as silver; 2180
49: 7 "Kings *will* **s** you and rise up, 8011
49: 7 princes will **s** and bow down, NIH
49:12 **S,** they will come from afar— 2180
49:16 **S,** I have engraved you on the palms 2176
49:22 **"S,** I will beckon to the Gentiles, 2180
51:22 **"S,** I have taken out of your hand the cup 2180
52: 8 *they will* **s** it with their own eyes. 8011
52:10 the earth *will* **s** the salvation of our God. 8011
52:13 **S,** my servant will act wisely; 2180
52:15 For what they were not told, *they will* **s,** 8011
53:10 *he will* **s** his offspring 8011
53:11 *he will* **s** the light [of life] and be satisfied; 8011
54:16 **"S,** it is I who created the blacksmith 2180
55: 4 **S,** I have made him a witness to 2176
58: 7 when *you* **s** the naked, to clothe him, 8011
60: 2 **S,** darkness covers the earth 2180
61: 9 All *who* **s** them will acknowledge 8011
62: 2 The nations *will* **s** your righteousness, 8011
62:11 "Say to the Daughter of Zion, **'S,** 2180
62:11 **S,** his reward is with him, 2180
63:15 from heaven and **s** from your lofty throne, 8011
65: 6 **"S,** it stands written before me: 2180
66: 5 that *we may* **s** your joy!' 8011
66:14 When *you* **s** this, your heart will rejoice 8011
66:15 **S,** the LORD is coming with fire, 2180
66:18 and they will come and **s** my glory. 8011
Jer 1:10 **S,** today I appoint you over nations 8011
1:11 "What *do you* **s,** Jeremiah?" 8011
1:11 "I **s** the branch of an almond tree," 8011
1:12 *s that* my word *is* **fulfilled."** AIT
1:13 "What *do you* **s?"** 8011
1:13 "I **s** a boiling pot, 8011
2:10 **s** if there has ever been anything like this: 8011
2:23 **S** how you behaved in the valley; 8011
3: 2 "Look up to the barren heights and **s.** 8011
4:21 How long *must I* **s** the battle standard 8011
5:12 *we will* never **s** sword or famine. 8011
5:21 who have eyes but *do* not **s,** 8011
7:12 and **s** what I did to it because of 8011
7:17 not **s** what they are doing in the towns 8011
8:17 **"S,** I will send venomous snakes 2180
9: 7 **"S,** I will refine and test them, 2180
9:15 **"S,** I will make this people eat bitter food 2180
11:20 *let me* **s** your vengeance upon them, 8011
12: 3 *you* **s** me and test my thoughts about you. 8011
12: 4 *"He will* not **s** what happens to us." 8011
13:20 and **s** those who are coming from the north. 8011
14:13 *'You will* not **s** the sword or suffer famine. 8011
14:18 I **s** those slain by the sword; 2180
14:18 I **s** the ravages of famine. 2180
16:12 **S** how each of you is following 2180
17: 6 *he will* not **s** prosperity when it comes. 8011
20: 4 with your own eyes you *will* **s** them fall by 8011
20:12 *let me* **s** your vengeance upon them, 8011
20:18 to **s** trouble and sorrow and to end my days 8011
21: 8 **S,** I am setting before you the way of life 2180
22:10 nor **s** his native land again. 8011
22:12 *he will* not **s** this land again." 8011
23:18 of the LORD *to* **s** or to hear his word? 8011
23:19 **S,** the storm of the LORD will burst out 2180
23:24 in secret places so that I cannot **s** him?" 8011
24: 3 the LORD asked me, "What *do you* **s,** 8011
25:29 **S,** I am beginning to bring disaster on 2180
29:32 nor *will he* **s** the good things I will do 8011
30: 6 Ask and **s:** Can a man bear children? 8011
30: 6 Then why *do I* **s** every strong man 8011
30:23 **S,** the storm of the LORD will burst out 2180
31: 8 **S,** I will bring them from the land of 2180
32: 4 to face and **s** him with his own eyes. 8011
32:24 **"S** how the siege ramps are built up to take 2180
32:24 What you said has happened, as you now **s.** 8011
34: 3 You *will* **s** the king of Babylon 8011
42: 2 For as you now **s,** though we were once many, 6524+8011
42:14 not **s** war or hear the trumpet or be hungry 8011
42:18 *you will* never **s** this place again.' 8011
44:23 disaster has come upon you, as you now **s."** NIH
46: 5 What *do I* **s?** 8011
47: 2 **"S** how the waters are rising in the north; 2180
49:35 **"S,** I will break the bow of Elam, 2180
50:31 **"S,** I am against you, O arrogant one," 2180
51: 1 This is what the LORD says: **"S,** 2180
51:36 **"S,** I will defend your cause 2180
51:61 **s** that you read all these words aloud. 8011
La 1:12 Look around and **s.** 8011
1:20 **"S,** O LORD, how distressed I am! 8011
2:16 we have lived *to* **s** it." 8011
3:36 *would* not the Lord **s** such things? 8011
3:51 **What** I **s** brings grief to my soul because 6524
5: 1 look, and **s** our disgrace. 8011

Eze 8: 6 do you s what they are doing— 8011
8: 6 But you will s things that are 8011
8: 9 "Go in and s the wicked 8011
8:12 They say, 'The LORD does not s us; 8011
8:13 "You will s them doing things that are 8011
8:15 He said to me, "Do you s this, son of man? 8011
8:15 You will s things that are even more 8011
9: 9 the LORD does not s.' 8011
12: 2 They have eyes to s but do not see and ears 8011
12: 2 but do not s and ears to hear but do not hear, 8011
12: 6 Cover your face so that you cannot s 8011
12:12 He will cover his face so that he cannot s 2021+4200+6524+8011
12:13 but he will not s it, and there he will die. 8011
13: 9 be against the prophets who s false **visions** 2600
13:23 therefore you will no longer s false **visions** 2600
14:22 when you s their conduct and their actions, 8011
14:23 when you s their conduct and their actions, 8011
16:37 and they will s all your nakedness. 8011
20:48 Everyone will s that I the LORD have kindled 8011
22: 6 " 'S how each of the princes 2180
32:31 will s them and he will be consoled 8011
34:20 S, I myself will judge between 2180
39:21 the nations will s the punishment I inflict 8011
40: 4 Tell the house of Israel everything you s." 8011
47: 6 He asked me, "Son of man, do you s this?" 8011
Da 1:10 Why should he s you looking worse than 8011
1:13 in accordance with what you s." 8011
3:25 I s four men walking around in the fire, 10255
5:23 which cannot s or hear or understand. 10255
9:18 open your eyes and s the desolation of 8011
10: 7 the men with me did not s it, 8011
Joel 2:28 your young men will s visions. 8011
3: 7 "S, I am going to rouse them out of 2180
Am 3: 9 s the great unrest within her and 8011
7: 8 LORD asked me, "What do you s, Amos?" 8011
8: 2 "What do you s, Amos?" 8011
Ob 1: 2 "S, I will make you small among 2180
Jnh 4: 5 and waited to s what would happen to 8011
Mic 7: 9 I will s his righteousness. 8011
7:10 Then my enemy will s it and will 8011
7:10 My eyes will s her downfall; 8011
7:16 Nations will s and be ashamed, 8011
Na 3: 7 All who s you will flee from you and say, 8011
Hab 2: 1 I will look to s what he will say to me, 8011
2: 4 "S, he is puffed up; 2180
Hag 1: 9 "You expected much, but s, 2180
Zec 3: 4 Then he said to Joshua, "S, 8011
3: 9 S, the stone I have set in front of Joshua! 2180
4: 2 He asked me, "What do you s?" 8011
4: 2 "I s a solid gold lampstand with a bowl at 8011
4:10 when they s the plumb line in the hand 8011
5: 2 He asked me, "What do you s?" 8011
5: 2 I answered, "I s a flying scroll, 8011
5: 5 up and s what this is that is appearing." 8011
9: 5 Ashkelon will s it and fear; 8011
9: 9 S, your king comes to you, 2180
10: 2 diviners s **visions** that lie; 2600
10: 7 Their children will s it and be joyful; 8011
Mal 1: 5 You will s it with your own eyes and say, 8011
3: 1 "S, I will send my messenger, 2180
3:10 "and s if I will not throw open NIH
3:18 And you will again s the distinction 8011
4: 5 "S, I will send you the prophet Elijah 2180
Mt 5: 8 Blessed are the pure in heart, for they will s God. 3972
5:16 that they may s your good deeds 3972
6:28 S how the lilies of the field grow. 2908
7: 5 and then you will s **clearly** to remove 1332
8: 4 "**S that** you don't tell anyone. 3972
9:30 "**S that** no one knows about this." 3972
11: 4 and report to John what you hear and s: 1063
11: 7 "What did you go out into the desert to s? 2517
11: 8 If not, what did you go out to s? 3972
11: 9 Then what did you go out to s? 3972
12:22 so that he could both talk and s. 1063
12:38 we want to s a miraculous sign from you." 3972
13:13 "Though seeing, they do not s; 1063
13:15 Otherwise they might s with their eyes, 3972
13:16 But blessed are your eyes because they s, 1063
13:17 to s what you see but did not see it, 3972
13:17 to see what you s but did not see it, 1063
13:17 to see what you see but did not s it, 3972
15:17 "Don't you s that whatever enters 3783
16:28 before they s the Son of Man coming 3972
18:10 "S that you do not look down on one 3972
18:10 that their angels in heaven always s the face 1063
21: 5 'S, your king comes to you, 2627
22:11 "But when the king came in to s the guests, 2517
23: 5 "Everything they do is done for men to s: 2517
23:39 you will not s me again until you say, 3972
24: 2 "Do you s all these things?" 1063
24: 6 but s **to it** that you are not alarmed. 3972
24:15 "So when you s standing in the holy place 3972
24:25 S, I have told you ahead of time. 2627
24:30 They will s the Son of Man coming on 3972
24:33 Even so, when you s all these things, 3972
25:20 S, I have gained five more.' 3972
25:22 s, I have gained two more.' 3972
25:25 S, here is what belongs to you.' 3972
25:37 when did we s you hungry and feed you, 3972
25:38 When did we s you a stranger and invite you 3972
25:39 When did we s you sick or in prison and go 3972
25:44 when did we s you hungry or thirsty or 3972
26:58 down with the guards to s the outcome. 3972
26:64 In the future you will s the Son 3972
27:49 Let's s if Elijah comes to save him." 3972
Mt 28: 6 Come and s the place where he lay. 3972
28: 7 There you will s him.' 3972
28:10 there they will s me." 3972
Mk 1:44 "**S that** you don't tell this to anyone. 3972
3: 2 to s if he would heal him on the Sabbath. NIG
5:14 people went out to s what had happened. 3972
5:31 "You s the people crowding against you," 1063
5:32 around to s who had done it. 3972
6:38 he asked. "Go and s." 3972
7:18 "Don't you s that nothing that enters a man 3783
8:17 Do you still not s or understand? 3783
8:18 Do you have eyes but fail to s, 1063
8:23 Jesus asked, "Do you s anything?" 1063
8:24 He looked up and said, "I s people; 1063
9: 1 not taste death before they s the kingdom 3972
10:51 The blind man said, "Rabbi, I want to s." 329
13: 2 "Do you s all these great buildings?" 1063
13:14 "When you s 'the abomination 3972
13:26 "At that time men will s the Son 3972
13:29 so, when you s these things happening, 3972
14:62 "And you will s the Son of Man sitting at 3972
15: 4 S how many things they are accusing you 3972
15:24 they cast lots to s what each would get. NIG
15:32 that we may s and believe." 3972
15:36 Let's s if Elijah comes to take him down," 3972
16: 6 S the place where they laid him. 3972
16: 7 There you will s him, 3972
Lk 2:15 "Let's go to Bethlehem and s this thing 3972
3: 6 And all mankind will s God's salvation.' " 3972
6: 7 to s if he would heal on the Sabbath. NIG
6:42 when you yourself fail to s the plank 1063
6:42 and then you will s **clearly** to remove 1332
7:24 "What did you go out into the desert to s? 2517
7:25 If not, what did you go out to s? 3972
7:26 But what did you go out to s? 3972
7:44 "Do you s this woman? 1063
8:10 so that, " 'though seeing, they may not s; 1063
8:16 so that those who come in can s the light. 1063
8:19 Jesus' mother and brothers came to s him, NIG
8:20 standing outside, wanting to s you." 3972
8:35 people went out to s what had happened. 3972
9: 9 And he tried to s him. 3972
9:27 not taste death before they s the kingdom 3972
10:23 "Blessed are the eyes that s what you see. 1063
10:23 "Blessed are the eyes that see what you s. 1063
10:24 and kings wanted to s what you see but did 3972
10:24 and kings wanted to see what you s but did 1063
10:24 to see what you see but did not s it, 3972
11:33 so that those who come in may s the light. 1063
11:35 **S to it,** then, that the light within you is 5023
12:54 "When you s a cloud rising in the west, 3972
13:28 when you s Abraham, Isaac and Jacob 3972
13:35 you will not s me again until you say, 3972
14:18 and I must go and s it. 3972
14:28 the cost **to s if** he has enough money 1623
17:22 when you will long to s one of the days of 3972
17:22 but you will not s it. 3972
18: 5 **s that** she **gets justice,** 1688
18: 8 I tell you, he will s that they get justice, NIG
18:41 "Lord, I want to s," he replied. 329
19: 3 He wanted to s who Jesus was, 3972
19: 4 and climbed a sycamore-fig tree to s him, 3972
21: 6 "As for what you s **here,** the time will 2555+4047
21:20 "When you s Jerusalem being surrounded 3972
21:27 At that time they will s the Son of Man 3972
21:30 you can s for yourselves and know 1063
21:31 so, when you s these things happening, 3972
22:38 The disciples said, "S, Lord, 2627
23: 8 a long time he had been wanting to s him. 3972
23: 8 he hoped to s him perform some miracle. 3972
23:15 **as** you **can** s, he has done nothing to deserve 2627
24:24 but him they did not s." 3972
24:39 Touch me and s; a ghost does not have flesh 3972
24:39 as you s I have." 2555
Jn 1:33 'The man on whom you s the Spirit come 3972
1:39 "Come," he replied, "and you will s." 3972
1:46 "Come and s," said Philip. 3972
1:50 You shall s greater things than that." 3972
1:51 you shall s heaven open, 3972
3: 3 no one can s the kingdom of God 3972
3:36 but whoever rejects the Son will not s life, 3972
4:19 "I **can** s that you are a prophet. 2555
4:29 s a man who told me everything I ever did. 3972
4:48 "Unless you people s miraculous signs 3972
5:14 "S, you are well again. 3972
6:30 then will you give that we may s it 3972
6:62 What if you s the Son of Man ascend to 2555
7: 3 so that your disciples may s 2555
8:51 he will never s death." 2555
9:11 So I went and washed, and then I could s." 329
9:15 "and I washed, and now I s." 1063
9:19 How is it that now he can s?" 1063
9:21 But how he can s now, 1063
9:25 I was blind but now I s!" 1063
9:39 so that the blind will s 1063
9:39 and those who s will become blind." 1063
9:41 you claim you can s, your guilt remains. 1063
11:34 "Come and s, Lord," they replied. 3972
11:36 Then the Jews said, "S how he loved him!" 3972
11:40 you would s the glory of God?" 3972
12: 9 only because of him but also to s Lazarus, 3972
12:15 s, your king is coming, 2627
12:19 So the Pharisees said to one another, "S, 2555
12:21 they said, "we would like to s Jesus." 3972
12:40 so they can neither s with their eyes, 3972
14:19 long, the world will not s me anymore, 2555
14:19 but you will s me. 2555
Jn 16:10 where you can s me no longer; 2555
16:16 "In a little while you will s me no more, 2555
16:16 then after a little while you will s me." 3972
16:17 'In a little while you will s me no more, 2555
16:17 and then after a little while you will s me,' 3972
16:19 'In a little while you will s me no more, 2555
16:19 then after a little while you will s me'? 3972
16:22 I will s you again and you will rejoice, 3972
16:30 Now we **can** s that you know all things and 3857
17:24 and to s my glory, the glory you have given 2555
18:26 "Didn't I s you with him in 3972
20:25 "Unless I s the nail marks in his hands 3972
20:27 "Put your finger here; s my hands. 3972
Ac 2:17 your young men will s visions, 3972
2:27 nor will you let your Holy One s decay. 3972
2:31 nor did his body s decay. 3972
2:33 and has poured out what you now s 1063
3:16 this man whom you s 2555
3:16 as **you can** all s. 595+5148
4:14 But since they could s 1063
7:56 "I s heaven open and the Son 2555
8:23 For I s that you are full of bitterness 3972
8:39 and the eunuch did not s him again, 3972
9: 7 they heard the sound but did not s anyone. 2555
9: 8 he opened his eyes he could s nothing. 1063
9:17 so that you may s **again** and be filled with 329
9:18 and he could s **again.** 329
13:11 you will **be unable to** s the light 1063+3590
13:35 " 'You will not let your Holy One s decay.' 3972
13:37 from the dead did not s decay. 3972
15: 2 s the apostles and elders **about** 4309
15:36 of the Lord and s how they are doing." NIG
17:11 and examined the Scriptures every day to s NIG
17:16 he was greatly distressed to s that 2555
17:22 s that in every way you are very religious. 2555
18: 2 Paul went to s them, NIG
19:26 And you s and hear 2555
20:25 the kingdom will ever s me again. 3972
20:38 that they would never s his face again. 2555
21:18 and the rest of us went to s James, NIG
21:20 Then they said to Paul: "You s, brother, 2555
22:12 "A man named Ananias came to s me. NIG
22:13 at that very moment I was **able to** s him. 329
22:14 to s the Righteous One and to hear words 3972
25:24 all who are present with us, you s this man! 2555
26: 7 This is the promise our twelve tribes are hoping to s **fulfilled** 2918
27:10 I can s that our voyage is going to be 2555
28: 8 Paul went in to s him and, after prayer, NIG
28:20 For this reason I have asked to s you 3972
28:27 Otherwise they might s with their eyes, 3972
28:30 and welcomed all who came to s him. NIG
Ro 1:11 I long to s you so that I may impart 3972
5: 6 **You** s, at just the right time, 1142
7:23 but I s another law at work in the members 1063
9:33 As it is written: "S, I lay in Zion a stone 2627
11: 8 not s and ears so that they could not hear, 1063
11:10 be darkened so they cannot s, 1063
15:21 not told about him will s, 3972
15:23 for many years to s you, 2262+4639
1Co 13:12 Now we s but a poor reflection as in 1063
13:12 then we shall s face to face. NIG
16: 7 I do not want to s you now and make only 3972
16:10 s **to it** that he has nothing to fear 1063
2Co 2: 9 to s **if** you would stand the test and 1182
4: 4 so that they cannot s the light of the gospel 878
7: 8 I s that my letter hurt you, 1063
7:11 S what this godly sorrow has produced 2627
7:11 **readiness to** s **justice done.** 1689
7:12 that before God you could s for yourselves 5746
7:13 we were especially delighted to s NIG
8: 7 s that you also **excel** in everything— AIT
8:24 so that the churches **can** s **it.** 4725[S]
13: 5 Examine yourselves to s whether you are in NIG
13: 7 Not that people will s that we have stood 5743
Gal 1:17 to Jerusalem **to** s those who were apostles 4639
6:11 S what large letters I use as I write to you 3972
Php 1:27 whether I come and s you or only hear 3972
2:23 to send him as soon as I s how things go 927
2:28 that when you s him again you may be glad 3972
Col 2: 5 and delight to s how orderly you are and 1063
2: 8 S **to it** that no one takes you captive 1063
4:16 s that it is also read in the church of 4472
4:17 "S **to it** that you complete the work 1063
1Th 2:17 we made every effort to s you. 3972
3: 6 of us and that you long to s us, 3972
3: 6 just as we also long to s you. NIG
3:10 that we may s you again 3972
1Ti 3: 4 **manage** his own family well **and** s **that** 4613
4:15 so that everyone may s your progress. 5745
6:16 whom no one has seen or can s. 3972
2Ti 1: 4 Recalling your tears, I long to s you, 3972
Tit 3:13 the lawyer and Apollos on their way and s NIG
Heb 2: 8 at present we do not s everything subject 3972
2: 9 But we s Jesus, who was made a little lower 1063
3:12 S **to it,** brothers, that none of you has 1063
3:19 So we s that they were not able to enter, 1063
8: 5 "S **to it** that you make everything 3972
10:25 all the more as you s the Day approaching. 1063
11: 1 for and certain of what we do not s. 1063
12:14 without holiness no one will s the Lord. 3972
12:15 S **to it** that no one misses the grace of God 2174
12:16 S that no one is sexually immoral, NIG
12:25 S **to it** that you do not refuse him 1063
13:23 I will come with him to s you. 3972
Jas 2:22 You s that his faith and his actions 1063
2:24 You s that a person is justified by what he 3972

Jas 5: 7 **S how** the farmer waits for the land *2627*
1Pe 1: 8 and *even though you do* not s him now, *3972*
2: 6 For in Scripture it says: **"S,** I lay a stone in *2627*
2:12 they may s your good deeds *2227*
3: 2 *when they* s the purity and reverence *2227*
3:10 and s good days must keep his tongue *3972*
2Pe 1:15 to s that after my departure you will always *NIG*
1Jn 2:24 *S that* what you have heard from the beginning **remains** in you. *AIT*
3: 2 for *we shall* s him as he is. *3972*
4: 1 the spirits to s whether they are from God, *NIG*
3Jn 1:14 I hope *to* s you soon, *3972*
Jude 1:14 **"S,** the Lord is coming with thousands *2627*
Rev 1: 7 and every eye *will* s him, *3972*
1:11 "Write on a scroll what *you* s and send it to *1063*
1:12 around *to* s the voice that was speaking *1063*
3: 8 **S,** I have placed before you an open door *2627*
3:18 and salve to put on your eyes, so *you can* **s.** *1063*
5: 5 **S,** the Lion of the tribe of Judah, *2627*
9:20 idols that cannot s or hear or walk. *1063*
17: 8 of the world will be astonished *when they* s *1063*
18: 9 with her and shared her luxury s the smoke *1063*
18:18 *When they* s the smoke of her burning, *1063*
21:22 *I did* not s a temple in the city, *3972*
22: 4 *They will* s his face, and his name will be *3972*

SEED (81) [SEED-BEARING, SEEDS, SEEDTIME]

Ge 1:11 and trees on the land that bear fruit with s 2446
1:12 plants bearing s according to their kinds 2446
1:12 and trees bearing fruit with s in it according 2446
1:29 every tree that has fruit with s in it. 2445+2446
47:19 Give us s so that we may live and not die, 2446
47:23 here is s for you so you can plant 2446
47:24 The other four-fifths you may keep as s *for* 2446
Ex 16:31 like coriander s and tasted like wafers made 2446
Lev 11:38 But if water has been put on the s and 2446
19:19 not **plant** your field **with** two kinds of **s.** 2445
26:16 You will plant s in vain, 2446
27:16 according to the amount of s *required* 2446
27:16 of silver to a homer of barley **s.** 2446
Nu 11: 7 The manna was like coriander s and looked 2446
24: 7 their s will have abundant water. 2446
Dt 11:10 where you planted your s and irrigated it 2446
22: 9 *Do* not **plant** two kinds of s in your 2445
28:38 You will sow much s in the field 2446
1Ki 18:32 large enough to hold two seahs of **s.** 2446
2Ki 6:25 a quarter of a cab of s **pods** for five shekels. 1807
Ps 126: 6 goes out weeping, carrying **s to sow,** 2446+5433
Ecc 11: 6 Sow your s in the morning, 2446
Isa 5:10 a homer of s only an ephah of grain." 2446
6:13 so the holy s will be the stump in the land." 2446
30:23 He will also send you rain for the s you sow 2446
32:20 **sowing** *your* s by every stream, 2445
55:10 that it yields s for the sower and bread for 2446
Jer 35: 7 sow s or plant vineyards; 2446
Eze 17: 5 the s *of* your land and put it in fertile soil. 2446
Hag 2:19 Is there yet any s left in the barn? 2446
Zec 8:12 "The s will grow well, 2446
Mt 13: 3 "A farmer went out *to* **sow** his **s.** *5062*
13: 4 As he *was* **scattering** the **s,** *5062*
13: 7 Other s fell among thorns, *NIG*
13: 8 Still other s fell on good soil, *NIG*
13:19 This is the s **sown** along the path. *5062*
13:20 **received** the **s that fell** on rocky places *5062*
13:22 **received** the **s that fell** among the thorns *5062*
13:23 **received** the **s that fell** on good soil *5062*
13:24 of heaven is like a man who sowed good s *5065*
13:27 'Sir, didn't you sow good s in your field? *5065*
13:31 kingdom of heaven is like a mustard **s,** *3133*
13:37 "The one who sowed the good s is the Son *5065*
13:38 good s stands for the sons of the kingdom. *5065*
17:20 if you have faith as small as a mustard **s,** *3133*
25:24 where *you have* not **scattered s.** *1399*
25:26 and gather where *I have* not **scattered s?** *1399*
Mk 4: 3 "Listen! A farmer went out *to* **sow** his **s.** *5062*
4: 4 As he *was* **scattering the s,** *5062*
4: 7 Other s fell among thorns, *NIG*
4: 8 Still other s fell on good soil. *NIG*
4:15 Some people are like s along the path, *NIG*
4:16 Others, like **s sown** on rocky places, *5062*
4:18 Still others, like **s sown** among thorns, *5062*
4:20 Others, like **s sown** on good soil, *5062*
4:26 A man scatters s on the ground. *5078*
4:27 the s sprouts and grows, *5078*
4:31 It is like a mustard **s,** *3133*
4:31 the smallest s you plant in the ground. *5065*
Lk 8: 5 "A farmer went out to sow his **s.** *5078*
8: 5 As he *was* **scattering the s,** *5062*
8: 7 Other s fell among thorns, *NIG*
8: 8 Still other s fell on good soil. *NIG*
8:11 The s is the word of God. *5078*
8:14 The s that fell among thorns stands *NIG*
8:15 But the s on good soil stands for those with *NIG*
13:19 It is like a mustard **s,** *3133*
17: 6 "If you have faith as small as a mustard **s,** *3133*
Jn 12:24 it remains only a single **s.** *NIG*
1Co 3: 6 I planted the **s,** Apollos watered it, *NIG*
9:11 If we *have* **sown** spiritual s among you, *5062*
15:37 but just a **s,** perhaps of wheat or of *3133*
15:38 to each kind *of* s he gives its own body. *5065*
2Co 9:10 Now he who supplies s to the sower *5078*
9:10 and increase your store of s and will *3836+5078*
Gal 3:16 spoken to Abraham and *to* his **s.** *5065*
3:16 meaning many people, but "and *to* your **s,"** *5065*
3:19 of transgressions until the S to whom *5065*
3:29 then you are Abraham's **s,** *5065*
1Pe 1:23 not of perishable **s,** but of imperishable, *5076*
1Jn 3: 9 because God's s remains in him; *5065*

SEED-BEARING (2) [SEED]

Ge 1:11 s plants and trees on the land that bear 2445+2446
1:29 "I give you every s plant on the face 2445+2446

SEEDS (7) [SEED]

Lev 11:37 If a carcass falls on any s that are to 2433+2446
Nu 6: 4 not even the s or skins. 3079
Isa 61:11 the sprout come up and a garden causes s 2433
Joel 1:17 The s are shriveled beneath the clods. 7237
Mt 13:32 Though it is the smallest of all your **s,** *5065*
Jn 12:24 But if it dies, it produces many **s.** *2843*
Gal 3:16 The Scripture does not say "and *to* **s,"** *5065*

SEEDTIME (1) [SEED]

Ge 8:22 long as the earth endures, s and harvest, 2446

SEEING (29) [SEE]

Ge 33:10 to see your face is like s the face of God, 8011
Ex 2:12 Glancing this way and that and s no one, 8011
Nu 35:23 or, without s him, drops a stone on him 8011
Jdg 13:20 S this, Manoah and his wife fell 8011
18:26 s that they were too strong for him, 8011
2Sa 14:28 in Jerusalem without s the king's face. 8011
Ps 17:15 I will be satisfied with s your likeness. NIH
Ecc 1: 8 The eye never has enough of **s,** 8011
8:16 his eyes not s sleep day or night— 8011
Isa 6: 9 *be* **ever s,** but never perceiving.' 8011+8011
28: 7 they stagger when s **visions,** 8015
Hos 9:10 it was like s the early fruit on the fig tree. NIH
Mt 13:13 *"Though* **s,** they do not see; *1063*
13:14 *you will be* **ever** s but never perceiving. *1063+1063*
15:31 the lame walking and the blind **s.** *1063*
21:19 S a fig tree by the road, *3972*
Mk 4:12 " *'they may be* **ever** s but never perceiving, *1063+1063*
5:22 S Jesus, he fell at his feet *3972*
11:13 S in the distance a fig tree in leaf, *3972*
Lk 8:10 so that, " *'though* **s,** they may not see; *1063*
8:47 woman, s that she could not go unnoticed, *3972*
23:47 The centurion, s what had happened, *3972*
Jn 8:56 at the thought of s my day; *3972*
9: 7 man went and washed, and came home **s.** *1063*
Ac 2:31 **S what was ahead,** he spoke of the *4632*
9:40 She opened her eyes, and s Peter she sat up. *3972*
12: 9 he thought *he was* s a vision. *1063*
28: 6 a long time and s nothing unusual happen *2555*
28:26 *you will be* **ever** s but never perceiving." *1063+1063*

SEEK (128) [SEEKING, SEEKS, SELF-SEEKING, SOUGHT]

Ex 18:15 the people come to me to s God's **will.** 2011
Lev 19:18 not s **revenge** or bear a grudge against one 5933
19:31 not turn to mediums or s **out** spiritists, 1335
Dt 4:29 if from there *you* s the LORD your God, 1335
12: 5 But *you are to* s the place 2011
23: 6 *Do* not s a treaty of friendship with them 2011
2Sa 17: 3 of the man you s will mean the return of all; 1335
1Ki 22: 5 "First s the counsel of the LORD." 2011
1Ch 16:10 of *those who* s the LORD rejoice. 1335
16:11 s his face always. 1335
28: 9 If *you* s him, he will be found by you; 2011
2Ch 7:14 and pray and s my face and turn 1335
14: 4 He commanded Judah to s the LORD, 2011
15: 2 If *you* s him, he will be found by you, 2011
15:12 They entered into a covenant to s 2011
15:13 All who *would* not s the LORD, 2011
16:12 even in his illness *he did* not s **help** *from* 2011
18: 4 "First s the counsel of the LORD." 2011
20: 4 of Judah came together to **s help** from 1335
20: 4 from every town in Judah to s him. 1335
34: 3 he began to s the God of his father David. 2011
Ezr 4: 2 *we* s your God and have been sacrificing 2011
6:21 of their Gentile neighbors in order to s 2011
9:12 *Do* not s a treaty of friendship with them 2011
Ps 4: 2 you love delusions and s false gods? 1335
9:10 have never forsaken *those who* s you. 2011
10: 4 In his pride the wicked *does* not s him; 2011
14: 2 any who understand, *any who* s God. 2011
22:26 *they who* s the LORD will praise him— 2011
24: 6 Such is the generation of *those who* s him, 2011
24: 6 *who* s your face, O God of Jacob. 1335
27: 4 this is what *I* **s:** that I may dwell in 1335
27: 4 upon the beauty of the LORD and to s him 1329
27: 8 My heart says of you, **"S** his face!" 1335
27: 8 Your face, LORD, *I will* **s.** 1335
34:10 *those who* s the LORD lack no good thing. 2011
34:14 s peace and pursue it. 1335
35: 4 May *those who* s my life be disgraced 1335
38:12 *Those who* s my life set their traps, 1335
40:14 *May* all *who* s to take my life be put 1335
40:16 But may all *who* s you rejoice and be glad 1335
45:12 men of wealth *will* s your **favor.** 2704+7156
53: 2 any who understand, *any who* s God. 2011
54: 3 ruthless men s my life— 1335
63: 1 you are my God, **earnestly** *I* s you; 8838
63: 9 They *who* s my life will be destroyed; 1335
69: 4 *those who* **s to destroy** me. 7551
Ps 69: 6 may *those who* s you not be put to shame 1335
69:32 you *who* s God, may your hearts live! 2011
70: 2 May *those who* s my life be put to shame 1335
70: 4 But may all *who* s you rejoice and be glad 1335
78:34 Whenever God slew them; *they would* s him 2011
83:16 with shame so that *men will* s your name, 1335
104:21 The lions roar for their prey and s their food 1335
105: 3 of *those who* s the LORD rejoice. 1335
105: 4 s his face always. 1335
119: 2 and s him with all their heart. 2011
119:10 *I* s you with all my heart; 2011
119:155 for *they do* not **s out** your decrees. 2011
119:176 S your servant, for I have not forgotten 1335
122: 9 *I will* s your prosperity. 1335
Pr 8:17 and *those who* s me find me. 8838
18:15 the ears of the wise **s** it **out.** 1335
25:27 nor is it honorable to s one's own honor. 2984
28: 5 *those who* s the LORD understand it fully. 1335
29:10 a man of integrity and **s to** kill the upright. 1335
29:26 Many **s an audience with** a ruler, 1335+7156
Isa 1:17 S justice, encourage the oppressed. 2011
31: 1 or s **help** *from* the LORD. 2011
45:19 to Jacob's descendants, **'S** me in vain.' 1335
51: 1 you who pursue righteousness and *who* s 1335
55: 6 S the LORD while he may be found; 2011
58: 2 For day after day *they* s me **out;** 2011
65: 1 I was found by *those who did* not s me. 1335
65:10 for my people who s me. 2011
Jer 4:30 Your lovers despise you; *they* s your life. 1335
19: 7 at the hands of *those who* s their lives, 1335
19: 9 on them by the enemies *who* s their lives.' 1335
21: 7 and to their enemies *who* s their lives. 1335
22:25 to *those who* s your life, those you fear— 1335
26:19 the LORD and s his **favor?** 906+2704+7156
29: 7 s the peace and prosperity of the city 2011
29:13 *You will* s me and find me 1335
29:13 when *you* s me with all your heart. 2011
34:20 over to their enemies *who* s their lives. 1335
34:21 over to their enemies *who* s their lives, 1335
44:30 of Egypt over to his enemies *who* s his life, 1335
45: 5 then s great things for yourself? 1335
45: 5 S them not. 1335
46:26 over to *those who* s their lives, 1335
49:37 before *those who* s their lives; 1335
50: 4 of Judah together will go in tears *to* s 1335
Eze 7:25 When terror comes, *they will* s peace, 1335
21:21 to **s an omen:** He will cast lots 7876+7877
Hos 3: 5 Afterward the Israelites will return and s 1335
5: 6 with their flocks and herds to s the LORD, 1335
5:15 And *they will* s my face; 1335
5:15 in their misery *they will* **earnestly** s me." 8838
10:12 for it is time to s the LORD, 2011
Am 5: 4 **"S** me and live; 2011
5: 5 *do* not s Bethel, do not go to Gilgal, 2011
5: 6 S the LORD and live, 2011
5:14 S good, not evil, that you may live. 2011
Na 3:11 you will go into hiding and s refuge from 1335
Zep 1: 6 from following the LORD and neither s 1335
2: 3 S the LORD, all you humble of the land, 1335
2: 3 S righteousness, seek humility; 1335
2: 3 Seek righteousness, s humility; 1335
Zec 8:21 the LORD and s the LORD Almighty. 1335
8:22 to Jerusalem to s the LORD Almighty and 1335
11:16 or s the young, or heal the injured, 1335
Mal 2: 7 from his mouth *men should* s instruction— 1335
Mt 6:33 s first his kingdom and his righteousness, *2426*
7: 7 s and you will find; *2426*
Lk 11: 9 s and you will find; *2426*
12:31 But s his kingdom, and these things will be *2426*
19:10 For the Son of Man came *to* s and to save *2426*
Jn 5:30 and my judgment is just, for *I* s not to please *2426*
Ac 15:17 that the remnant of men *may* s the Lord, *1699*
17:27 God did this so that men would s him *2426*
Ro 2: 7 by persistence in doing good s glory, *2426*
10:20 "I was found by those who *did* not s me; *2426*
1Co 7:27 Are you married? *Do* not s a divorce. *2426*
10:24 Nobody *should* s his own good, *2426*
Gal 2:17 "If, *while* we s to be justified in Christ, *2426*
Heb 11: 6 that he rewards those who **earnestly** s him. *1699*
1Pe 3:11 *he must* s peace and pursue it. *2426*
Rev 9: 6 During those days men *will* s death, *2426*

SEEKING (25) [SEEK]

Jdg 14: 4 who *was* s an occasion to confront 1335
18: 1 in those days the tribe of the Danites *was* s 1335
1Sa 22:23 *man* who *is* s your life is seeking mine also. 1335
22:23 man who is seeking your life *is* s mine also. 1335
1Ki 12:28 **s advice,** the king made two golden calves. 3619
2Ki 16:15 I will use the bronze altar for **s guidance."** 1329
1Ch 22:19 Now devote your heart and soul to s 2011
2Ch 11:16 tribe of Israel who set their hearts on s 1335
12:14 because he had not set his heart on s 2011
19: 3 and have set your heart on s God." 2011
30:19 who sets his heart *on* s God— 2011
Est 9: 2 to attack *those* s their destruction. 1335
Ps 37:32 in wait for the righteous, s their very lives; 1335
Pr 20:18 Make plans by s advice; NIH
Jer 11:21 of Anathoth who *are* s your life and saying, 1335
38: 4 This man *is* not s the good of these people 2011
38:16 over to those who *are* s your life." 1335
44:30 the enemy *who was* s his life.' " 1335
Mal 2:15 Because *he was* s godly offspring. 1335
3: 1 the Lord you *are* s will come to his temple; 1335
Mt 12:43 it goes through arid places s rest and does *2426*
Lk 11:24 it goes through arid places s rest and does *2426*
Jn 8:50 I *am* not s glory for myself; *2426*

Ac 13:11 s someone to lead him by the hand. 2426
1Co 10:33 not s my own good but the good of many, 2426

SEEKS (14) [SEEK]

Job 39:29 From there *he* s **out** his food; 2916
Ps 86:14 a band of ruthless men s my life— 1335
Pr 11:27 *He who* s good finds goodwill, 8838
14:6 The mocker s wisdom and finds none, 1335
15:14 The discerning heart s knowledge, 1335
Isa 16:5 in judging s justice and speeds the cause 2011
56:11 each s his own gain. 4200
Jer 5:1 but one person who deals honestly and s 1335
La 3:25 to the one *who* s him; 2011
Mt 7:8 who asks receives; he who s finds; 2426
Lk 11:10 who asks receives; he who s finds; 2426
Jn 4:23 the kind of worshipers the Father s. 2426
8:50 there is one who s it, and he is the judge. 2426
Ro 3:11 no one who understands, no one who s God. 1699

SEEM (18) [SEEMED, SEEMS]

Lev 13:31 it does not s to be more than skin deep 5260
Ne 9:32 *do* not *let* all this hardship *s* **trifling** AIT
Job 8:7 Your beginnings *will* s humble, 2118
36:21 which *you s to* **prefer** to affliction. AIT
Pr 16:2 All a man's ways s innocent *to* him, 928+6524
21:2 All a man's ways s right *to* him, 928+6524
Isa 5:28 their horses' hoofs s like flint, 3108
29:17 and the fertile field s like a forest? 3108
58:2 *they s* **eager** to know my ways, AIT
58:2 They ask me for just decisions and *s* **eager** AIT
Eze 16:51 **made** your sisters s **righteous** by all these 7405
21:23 *It will* s like a false omen 928+2118+6524
Hag 2:3 Does it not s *to* you like nothing? 928+4017+6524
Zec 8:6 "It may s marvelous *to* the remnant 928+6524
8:6 but will it s marvelous *to* me?" 928+6524
1Co 12:22 that s to be weaker are indispensable, 1506
2Co 10:9 not want *to* s to be trying to frighten you 1506
13:7 even though we may s to have failed. 6055

SEEMED (17) [SEEM]

Ge 29:20 but *they* s like only a few days *to* him 928+2118+6524
34:18 Their proposal s good to Hamor 928+6524
41:37 The plan s good *to* Pharaoh and 928+6524
Nu 13:33 *We* s like grasshoppers in our own eyes, 2118
Dt 1:23 The idea s good *to* me; 928+6524
2Sa 13:2 it s impossible for him to do anything 928+6524
17:4 This plan s good *to* Absalom and to all 928+6524
1Ch 13:4 because it s right *to* all the people. 928+6524
2Ch 30:4 The plan s right both *to* the king and to 928+6524
Jer 18:4 shaping it as s best *to* him. 928+6524
Lk 1:3 *it* **s good** also to me to write 1506
24:11 their words s to them like nonsense. 5743
Ac 2:3 They saw **what s to be** tongues of fire 6059
15:28 *It* **s good** to the Holy Spirit and to us not 1506
Gal 2:2 *to* those who **s to be leaders,** 1506
2:6 As for those who s to be important— 1506
Rev 13:3 One of the heads of the beast s to have had 6055

SEEMLY (KJV) See FITTING

SEEMS (23) [SEEM]

Jos 9:25 to us whatever s good and right *to* you. 928+6524
24:15 if serving the LORD s undesirable *to* you, 928+6524
1Sa 1:23 "Do what s best *to* you," 928+6524
11:10 can do to us whatever s good *to* you." 928+6524
14:36 "Do whatever s best *to* you," 928+6524
14:40 "Do what s best *to* you," the men 928+6524
2Sa 15:26 him do to me whatever s good *to* him." 928+6524
18:4 "I will do whatever s best to you." 928+6524
18:27 *"It* s *to* me that the first one runs 8011
1Ch 13:2 "If it s good to you and if it is the will of NIH
Ezr 7:18 then do whatever s **best** with the rest of 10320
Est 8:8 in behalf of the Jews as s best *to* you, 928+6524
Job 15:21 when all s well, marauders attack him. NIH
41:29 A club s to him but a piece of straw; 3108
Pr 12:15 The way of a fool s right *to* him, 928+6524
14:12 There is a way that s right **to** a man, 4200+7156
16:25 There is a way that s right **to** a man, 4200+7156
18:17 The first to present his case s right, NIH
Isa 32:15 and the fertile field s like a forest. 3108
Ac 17:18 *"He* s to be advocating foreign gods." 1506
1Co 4:9 For it s to *me* that God has put us apostles 1506
16:4 If *it s* **advisable** for me to go also, AIT
Heb 12:11 No discipline s pleasant at the time, 1506

SEEN (218) [SEE]

Ge 16:13 *"I have* now s the One who sees me." 8011
24:30 As soon as *he had* s the nose ring, 8011
29:32 "It is because the LORD *has* s my misery. 8011
31:12 for *I have* s all that Laban has been doing 8011
31:42 But God *has* s my hardship and the toil 8011
41:19 *I had* never s such ugly cows in all the land 8011
44:28 And *I have* not s him since. 8011
45:13 in Egypt and about everything *you have* s. 8011
46:30 since *I have* s **for myself** that you 7156+8011
Ex 3:7 *"I have* **indeed** s the misery of my people in Egypt. 8011+8011
3:9 and *I have* s the way the Egyptians are 8011
3:16 *I have* **watched over** you **and** *have* s 7212+7212
4:31 about them and *had* s their misery, 8011
10:5 the face of the ground so that it cannot *be* s. 8011
Ex 10:6 nor your forefathers *have ever* s from 8011
13:7 with yeast in it *is to* **be** s among you, 8011
13:7 nor *shall* any yeast **be** s anywhere 8011
19:4 *'You* yourselves *have* s what I did to Egypt, 8011
20:22 *'You have* s for yourselves that I have 8011
32:9 *"I have* s these people," 8011
33:23 but my face *must* not **be s."** 8011
34:3 with you or **be** s anywhere on the mountain; 8011
Lev 5:1 to testify regarding something *he has* s 8011
14:35 'I *have* s something that looks like mildew 8011
Nu 14:14 O LORD, *have* **been** s face to face, 8011
23:21 "No misfortune *is* s in Jacob, 5564
27:13 After *you have* s it, 8011
Dt 1:19 and dreadful desert that *you have* **s,** 8011
3:21 "You *have* s *with* your own eyes all that 8011
4:9 the things your eyes *have* s or let them slip 8011
5:24 Today *we have* s that a man can live even 8011
9:13 the LORD said to me, *"I have* s this people, 8011
29:2 Your eyes *have* s all that the LORD did 8011
Jos 23:3 *You* yourselves *have* s everything 8011
Jdg 2:7 and who *had* s all the great things 8011
5:8 or spear **was** s among forty thousand 8011
6:22 *I have* s the angel of the LORD face 8011
9:48 Do what *you have* s me do!" 8011
13:22 *"We have* s God!" 8011
14:2 *"I have* s a Philistine woman in Timnah; 8011
18:9 *We have* s that the land is very good. 8011
19:30 "Such a thing *has* never **been** s or done, 8011
1Sa 16:18 *"I have* s a son of Jesse of Bethlehem 8011
23:22 and who *has* s him there. 8011
24:10 This day *you have* s with your own eyes 8011
2Sa 17:17 they could not risk **being** s entering the city. 8011
18:21 "Go, tell the king what *you have* **s."** 8011
1Ki 6:18 Everything was cedar; no stone *was to* **be s.** 8011
8:8 so long that their ends *could* **be** s from 8011
10:12 or s since that day.) 8011
2Ki 14:26 The LORD *had* s how bitterly everyone 8011
20:5 I have heard your prayer and s your tears; 8011
23:24 the other detestable things s in Judah 8011
1Ch 29:17 And now *I have* s with joy how willingly 8011
2Ch 5:9 *could* **be** s *from* in front of the inner 8011
9:11 Nothing like them *had* ever **been** s in Judah. 8011
Ezr 3:12 who *had* s the former temple, 8011
Est 9:26 in this letter and because of what *they had* s 8011
Job 5:3 *I* myself *have* s a fool taking root, 8011
13:1 "My eyes *have* s all this, 8011
15:17 let me tell you what *I have* **s,** 2600
20:7 *those who have* s him will say, 8011
27:12 You *have* all s this yourselves. 2600
28:7 no falcon's eye *has* s it. 8812
31:19 if *I have* s anyone perishing for lack of 8011
36:25 All mankind *has* s it; 2600
38:17 *Have you* s the gates of the shadow 8011
38:22 of the snow or s the storehouses of the hail, 8011
42:5 heard of you but now my eyes *have* s you. 8011
Ps 35:21 *With* our own eyes *we have* s it." 8011
35:22 O LORD, *you have* s this; be not silent. 8011
37:25 yet *I have* never s the righteous forsaken 8011
37:35 *I have* s a wicked and ruthless man 8011
48:8 so *have we* s in the city of the LORD 8011
63:2 *I have* s you in the sanctuary 2600
77:19 though your footprints **were** not s. 3359
90:15 for as many years as *we have* s trouble. 8011
92:11 My eyes *have* s the defeat of my 5564
95:9 though *they had* s what I did. 8011
98:3 of the earth *have* s the salvation of our God. 8011
Pr 25:7 What *you have* s *with* your eyes 8011
Ecc 1:14 *I have* s all the things that are done under 8011
3:10 *I have* s the burden God has laid on men. 8011
4:3 who *has* not s the evil that is done under 8011
5:13 *I have* s a grievous evil under the sun: 8011
6:1 *I have* s another evil under the sun, 8011
7:15 In this meaningless life of mine *I have* s 8011
9:11 *I have* s something else under the sun: 8011
10:5 There is an evil *I have* s under the sun, 8011
10:7 *I have* s slaves on horseback, 8011
SS 3:3 *"Have you* s the one my heart loves?" 8011
Isa 6:5 and my eyes *have* s the King, 8011
9:2 The people walking in darkness *have* s 8011
38:5 I have heard your prayer and s your tears; 8011
41:5 The islands *have* s it and fear; 8011
42:20 *You have* s many things, 8011
57:18 *I have* s his ways, but I will heal him; 8011
58:3 they say, 'and *you have* not s it? 8011
64:4 no eye *has* s any God besides you, 8011
66:8 Who *has ever* s such things? 8011
66:19 not heard of my fame or s my glory. 8011
Jer 1:12 "You have s correctly, 8011
3:6 *"Have you* s what faithless Israel has done? 8011
13:26 over your face that your shame *may* **be s—** 8011
13:27 *I have* s your detestable acts on the hills 8011
23:14 of Jerusalem *I have* s something horrible: 8011
La 1:8 for *they have* s her nakedness; 8011
3:1 I am the man *who has* s affliction by the rod 8011
3:59 *You have* **s,** O LORD, the wrong done to me. 8011
3:60 *You have* s the depth of their vengeance, 8011
Eze 3:23 like the glory *I had* s by the Kebar River, 8011
8:4 as in the vision *I had* s in the plain. 8011
8:12 *have you* s what the elders of the house 8011
8:17 said to me, *"Have you* s this, son of man? 8011
10:8 of the cherubim *could* **be** s what looked like 8011
10:15 These were the living creatures *I had* s by 8011
10:20 the living creatures *I had* s beneath the God 8011
10:22 the same appearance as those *I had* s by 8011
11:24 Then the vision *I had* s went up from me, 8011
13:3 follow their own spirit and *have* s nothing! 8011
13:7 *Have you* not s false visions 2600
Eze 16:50 I did away with them as *you have* **s.** 8011
43:3 The vision I saw was like the vision *I had* s 8011
43:3 like the visions *I had* s by the Kebar River, 8011
Da 8:6 toward the two-horned ram *I had* s standing 8011
9:21 the man *I had* s in the earlier vision, 8011
11:19 he will stumble and fall, *to* **be** s no more. 5162
Hos 6:10 *I have* s a horrible thing in the house 8011
9:13 *I have* s Ephraim, like Tyre, 8011
Mt 2:9 the star *they had* s in the east went ahead 3972
4:16 the people living in darkness *have* s 3972
6:1 before men, to *be* s by them. 2517
6:5 and on the street corners to **be** s by men. 5743
9:33 like this *has* ever *been* s in Israel." 5743
17:9 "Don't tell anyone what you have **s,** 3969
Mk 2:12 *"We have* never s anything like this!" 3972
5:16 Those who *had* s it told the people 3972
9:9 to tell anyone what *they had* s until the Son 3972
16:11 that Jesus was alive and that she *had* s *him,* 2517
16:14 to believe those who *had* s him 2517
Lk 1:22 They realized *he had* s a vision in the temple, 3972
2:17 *When they had* s him, they spread the word 3972
2:20 for all the things they had heard and **s,** 3972
2:26 not die before *he had* s the Lord's Christ. 3972
2:30 For my eyes *have* s your salvation, 3972
5:26 *"We have* **s** remarkable things today." 3972
7:22 to John what *you have* s and heard: 3972
8:36 Those who *had* s it told the people how 3972
9:36 and told no one at that time what *they had* **s.** 3972
19:37 loud voices for all the miracles *they had* **s:** 3972
24:23 told us that *they had* s a vision of angels, 3972
Jn 1:14 *We have* s his glory, the glory of the One 2517
1:18 No one *has* ever s God, 3972
1:34 *I have* s and I testify that this is the Son 3972
3:11 and we testify to what *we have* **s,** 3972
3:21 so that *it may be* s **plainly** that what he has 5746
3:32 He testifies to what *he has* s and heard, 3972
4:45 *They had* s all that he had done in Jerusalem 3972
5:37 have never heard his voice nor s his form, 3972
6:36 *you have* s me and still you do not believe. 3972
6:46 No one *has* s the Father except the one 3972
6:46 only he *has* s the Father. 3972
8:38 I am telling you what I *have* s in 3972
8:57 "and *you have* s Abraham!" 3972
9:8 who *had* formerly s him begging asked, 2555
9:37 Jesus said, *"You have* now s him; 3972
11:45 and *had* s what Jesus did, 2517
14:7 you do know him and *have* s him." 3972
14:9 Anyone who *has* s me has seen the Father. 3972
14:9 Anyone who has seen me *has* s the Father. 3972
15:24 But now *they have* s these miracles, 3972
20:18 with the news: *"I have* s the Lord!" 3972
20:25 disciples told him, *"We have* s the Lord!" 3972
20:29 Jesus told him, "Because *you have* s me, 3972
20:29 blessed are those who *have* not s and 3972
Ac 1:11 in the same way *you have* s him go 2517
4:20 about what *we have* s and heard." 3972
7:34 *I have* **indeed** s the oppression of my people in Egypt. 3972+3972
7:44 according to the pattern *he had* **s.** 3972
9:12 In a vision *he has* s a man named Ananias 3972
9:27 He told them how Saul on his journey *had* s 3972
10:40 on the third day and caused him to be s. 1871
10:41 He was not s by all the people, NIG
11:13 how *he had* s an angel appear in his house 3972
13:31 and for many days he *was* s 3972
16:10 After Paul *had* s the vision, 3972
21:29 *(They had* **previously** s Trophimus 1639+4632
22:15 to all men of what *you have* s and heard. 3972
26:16 and as a witness of what *you have* **s of** me 3972
Ro 1:20 and divine nature—*have been* **clearly s,** 2775
8:24 But hope *that is* s is no hope at all. 1063
1Co 2:9 However, as it is written: "No eye *has* **s,** 3972
9:1 *Have I* not s Jesus our Lord? 3972
2Co 4:18 So we fix our eyes not on what *is* **s,** 1063
4:18 For what *is* s is temporary, 1063
5:12 in what is s rather than in what is in 4725
Php 4:9 or s in me—put it into practice. 3972
Col 2:18 into great detail about what *he has* **s,** 3972
1Ti 3:16 a body, was vindicated by the Spirit, was s 3972
6:16 whom no one *has* s or can see. 3972
Heb 11:3 so that what *is* s was not made out 1063
11:7 when warned about things not yet **s,** 1063
Jas 5:11 of Job's perseverance and *have* s what 3972
1Pe 1:8 *Though you have* not s him, you love him; 3972
1Jn 1:1 which *we have* s with our eyes, 3972
1:2 *we have* s it and testify to it, 3972
1:3 We proclaim to you what *we have* s 3972
2:8 its truth is s in him and you, NIG
3:6 to sin *has* either s him or known him. 3972
4:12 No one *has* ever s God; 2517
4:14 And we *have* s and testify that 2517
4:20 whom *he has* s, cannot love God, 3972
4:20 cannot love God, whom *he has* not **s.** 3972
3Jn 1:11 who does what is evil *has* not s God. 3972
Rev 1:19 "Write, therefore, what *you have* **s,** 3972
10:5 the angel *I had* s standing on the sea and on 3972
11:19 and within his temple *was* s the ark 3972
22:8 And when I had heard and s them, 1063

SEER (21) [SEER'S, SEERS]

1Sa 9:9 he would say, "Come, let us go to the **s,"** 8014
9:9 the prophet of today used to be called a **s.)** 8014
9:11 and they asked them, "Is the s here?" 8014
9:19 "I am the **s,"** Samuel replied. 8014
2Sa 15:27 said to Zadok the priest, "Aren't you a **s?** 8014

2Sa 24:11 to Gad the prophet, David's s: 2602
1Ch 9:22 of trust by David and Samuel the s. 8014
21: 9 The LORD said to Gad, David's s, 2602
25: 5 All these were sons of Heman the king's s. 2602
26:28 And everything dedicated by Samuel the s 8014
29:29 in the records of Samuel the s, 8014
29:29 the prophet and the records of Gad the s, 2602
2Ch 9:29 the Shilonite and in the visions of Iddo the s 2602
12:15 of Shemaiah the prophet and of Iddo the s 2602
16: 7 At that time Hanani the s came to Asa king 8014
16:10 Asa was angry with the s because of this; 8014
19: 2 Jehu the s, the son of Hanani, went out 2602
29:25 by David and Gad the king's s and Nathan 2602
29:30 the words of David and of Asaph the s. 2602
35:15 Asaph, Heman and Jeduthun the king's s. 2602
Am 7:12 Amaziah said to Amos, "Get out, you s! 2602

SEER'S (1) [SEER]

1Sa 9:18 please tell me where the s house is?" 8014

SEERS (6) [SEER]

2Ki 17:13 and Judah through all his prophets and s: 2602
2Ch 33:18 to his God and the words the s spoke to him 2602
33:19 all are written in the records of the s. 2602
Isa 29:10 he has covered your heads (the s). 2602
30:10 They say to the s, "See no more visions!" 8014
Mic 3: 7 The s will be ashamed and the diviners 2602

SEES (52) [SEE]

Ge 16:13 "You are the God *who* s me," for she said, 8024
16:13 "I have now seen the *One who* s me." 8011
44:31 s that the boy isn't there, he will die. 8011
49:15 When *he* s how good is his resting place and 8011
Ex 4:14 and his heart will be glad when *he* s you. 8011
Lev 13: 5 if he s that the sore is unchanged and 928+6524
13:15 When the priest s the raw flesh, 8011
Nu 12: 8 *he* s the form of the LORD. 5564
24: 3 the oracle of one whose eye s **clearly,** 9280
24: 4 who s a vision from the Almighty, 2600
24:15 the oracle of one whose eye s **clearly,** 9280
24:16 *who* s a vision from the Almighty, 2600
Dt 12: 8 everyone as he s fit, 928+6524
32:36 when *he* s their strength is gone 8011
Job 7: 8 eye *that now* s me will see me no longer; 8011
10: 4 Do you see as a mortal s? 8011
11:11 and when *he* s evil, does he not take note? 8011
28:24 the ends of the earth and s everything under 8011
33:26 *he* s God's face and shouts for joy; 8011
34:21 *he* s their every step. 8011
Ps 10:11 he covers his face and never s." 8011
33:13 the LORD looks down and s all mankind; 8011
97: 4 the earth s and trembles. 8011
Pr 22: 3 A prudent man s danger and takes refuge, 8011
28:11 a poor man who has discernment s **through** 2983
31:18 *She* s that her trading is profitable, 3247
Ecc 6: 9 Better **what** the eye s than the roving of 5260
Isa 11: 3 not judge by **what** he s *with* his eyes, 5260
21: 6 a lookout and have him report what *he* s. 8011
21: 7 When *he* s chariots with teams of horses, 8011
28: 4 as someone s it and takes it in his hand, 8011
29:15 in darkness and think, "Who s us? 8011
47:10 and have said, 'No *one* s me.' 8011
La 3:50 the LORD looks down from heaven and s. 8011
Eze 12:27 vision he s is for many years from now, 2600
18:14 a son *who* s all the sins his father commits, 8011
18:14 and though *he* s them, he does not do such 8011
33: 3 and *he* s the sword coming against the land 8011
33: 6 the watchman s the sword coming and does 8011
39:15 the land and *one of them* s a human bone, 8011
Mt 6: 4 your Father, who s what is done in secret, *1063*
6: 6 your Father, who s what is done in secret, *1063*
6:18 your Father, who s what is done in secret, *1063*
Lk 14:29 everyone who s it will ridicule him, *2555*
Jn 5:19 he can do only what *he* s his Father doing, *1063*
10:12 So when *he* s the wolf coming, *2555*
11: 9 for *he* s by this world's light. *1063*
12:45 he looks at me, *he* s the one who sent me. *2555*
14:17 because *it* neither s him nor knows him. *2555*
1Co 8:10 with a weak conscience s you who have this knowledge eating *3972*
1Jn 3:17 and s his brother in need but has no pity *2555*
5:16 If anyone s his brother commit a sin *3972*

SEGUB (3)

1Ki 16:34 at the cost of his youngest son S, 8437
1Ch 2:21 and she bore him S. 8437
2:22 S was the father of Jair, 8437

SEIR (39)

Ge 14: 6 and the Horites in the hill country of S, 8541
32: 3 of him to his brother Esau in the land of S, 8541
33:14 until I come to my lord in S." 8541
33:16 that day Esau started on his way back to S. 8541
36: 8 Edom) settled in the hill country of S. 8541
36: 9 of the Edomites in the hill country of S. 8541
36:20 These were the sons of S the Horite, 8543
36:21 of S in Edom were Horite chiefs. 8543
36:30 according to their divisions, in the land of S. 8541
Nu 24:18 Edom will be conquered; S, his enemy, 8541
Dt 1: 2 to Kadesh Barnea by the Mount S road.) 8541
1:44 and beat you down from S all the way 8541
2: 1 around the hill country of S. 8541
2: 4 the descendants of Esau, who live in S. 8541
2: 5 I have given Esau the hill country of S 8541
Dt 2: 8 the descendants of Esau, who live in S. 8541
2:12 Horites used to live in S, 8541
2:22 the descendants of Esau, who lived in S, 8541
2:29 the descendants of Esau, who live in S, 8541
33: 2 from Sinai and dawned over them from S; 8541
Jos 11:17 which rises toward S, 8541
12: 7 toward S (their lands Joshua gave as 8541
15:10 from Baalah to Mount S, 8542
24: 4 I assigned the hill country of S to Esau, 8541
Jdg 5: 4 "O LORD, when you went out from S, 8541
1Ch 1:38 The sons of S: Lotan, Shobal, Zibeon, 8543
4:42 invaded the hill country of S. 8541
2Ch 20:10 and Mount S, whose territory you would 8541
20:22 and Mount S who were invading Judah, 8541
20:23 against the men from Mount S to destroy 8541
20:23 finished slaughtering the men from S, 8541
25:11 where he killed ten thousand men of S. 8541
25:14 the gods of the people of S. 8541
Isa 21:11 Someone calls to me from S, "Watchman, 8541
Eze 25: 8 'Because Moab and S said, "Look, 8541
35: 2 set your face against Mount S; 8541
35: 3 I am against you, Mount S, 8541
35: 7 I will make Mount S a desolate waste 8541
35:15 You will be desolate, O Mount S, 8541

SEIRAH (1)

Jdg 3:26 He passed by the idols and escaped to S. 8545

SEIZE (29) [SEIZED, SEIZES, SEIZING, SEIZURES]

Ge 43:18 and s us as slaves and take our donkeys." 4374
Jdg 7:24 "Come down against the Midianites and s 4334
21:21 the vineyards and each of you s a wife from 2642
1Ki 13: 4 from the altar and said, "S him!" 9530
18:40 "S the prophets of Baal. 9530
20: 6 *They will* s everything you value 928+3338+8492
1Ch 7:21 when they went down to s their livestock. 4374
Job 3: 6 That night—*may* thick darkness s it; 4374
Ps 21: 8 your right hand *will* s your foes. 5162
71:11 pursue him and s him, 9530
109:11 *May* a creditor s all he has; 5943
Isa 3: 6 A man *will* s one of his brothers 9530
5:29 as *they* s their prey and carry it off 296
10: 6 to s loot and snatch plunder, 8964
13: 8 **Terror** *will* s *them,* pain 987
21: 3 pangs s me, like those of a woman in labor; 296
Jer 12:14 "As for all my wicked neighbors who s 5595
Eze 38:13 and goods and to s much plunder?" ' 8964
Da 11: 8 He will also s their gods, NIH
11:21 and *he will* s it through intrigue. 2616
Am 9: 3 there I will hunt them down and s them. 4374
Ob 1:13 nor s their wealth in the day 8938
Mic 2: 2 They covet fields and s them, and houses, 1608
Hab 1: 6 across the whole earth to s dwelling places 3769
Zec 14:13 Each man *will* s the hand of another, 2616
Jn 7:30 At this they tried *to* s him, *4389*
7:44 Some wanted *to* s him, *4389*
10:39 Again they tried *to* s him, *4389*
Ac 12: 3 he proceeded *to* s Peter also. *5197*

SEIZED (53) [SEIZE]

Ge 14:11 The four kings s all the goods of Sodom 4374
21:25 of water that Abimelech's servants *had* s. 1608
34:28 *They* s their flocks and herds and donkeys 4374
Ex 15:15 leaders of Moab *will be* s *with* trembling, 296
Jdg 12: 6 *they* s him and killed him at the fords of 296
16:21 Then the Philistines s him, 296
1Sa 17:35 When it turned on me, *I* s it by its hair, 2616
2Sa 4:10 *I* s him and put him to death in Ziklag. 296
10: 4 So Hanun s David's men, 4374
1Ki 18:40 *They* s them, and Elijah had them brought 9530
21:19 not murdered a man and s his **property?'** 3769
2Ki 11:16 So *they* s her as she reached the place 3338+8492
17: 4 Shalmaneser s him and put him in prison. 6806
1Ch 5:21 *They* s the livestock of the Hagrites— 8647
19: 4 So Hanun s David's men, shaved them, 4374
2Ch 23:15 *they* s her as she reached the entrance 3338+8492
Est 8:17 because fear of the Jews *had* s them. 5877+6584
9: 3 because fear of Mordecai *had* s them. 5877+6584
Job 4:14 fear and trembling s me 7925
16:12 *he* s me by the neck and crushed me. 296
18:20 men of the east *are* s with horror. 296
20:19 *he has* s houses he did not build. 1608
24: 9 the infant of the poor *is* s **for a debt.** 2471
Ps 48: 6 Trembling s them there, 296
56: T When the Philistines *had* s him in Gath. 296
Isa 10:10 As my hand s the kingdoms of the idols, 5162
Jer 26: 8 the prophets and all the people s him 9530
49:24 anguish and pain *have* s her, 296
51:32 the river crossings s, the marshes set on fire, 9530
51:41 the boast of the whole earth s! 9530
Mt 21:35 "The tenants s his servants; *3284*
22: 6 The rest s his servants, *3195*
26:50 s Jesus and arrested him. *2093+2095+3836+5931*
27: 3 he *was* s **with remorse** and returned *3564*
Mk 12: 3 But they s him, beat him and sent him away *3284*
14:46 men s Jesus and arrested him. *2095+3836+5931*
14:51 When *they* s him, *3195*
Lk 8:29 Many times *it had* s him, *5275*
23:26 led him away, *they* s Simon from Cyrene, *2138*
Jn 8:20 Yet no one s him, because his time had not *4389*
Ac 4: 3 *They* s Peter and John, *2095+3836+5931*
5: 5 great fear s all who heard what had happened. *1181+2093*
Ac 5:11 Great fear s the whole church *1181+2093*
6:12 *They* s Stephen and brought him before *5275*
16:19 they s Paul and Silas and dragged them into *2138*
19:17 they *were* all s **with fear,** *2158+5832*
19:29 The people s Gaius and Aristarchus, *5275*
21:27 They stirred up the whole crowd and s him, *2093+2095+3836+5931*
23:27 This man *was* s by the Jews and they were *5197*
24: 6 tried to desecrate the temple, so *we* s him. *3195*
26:21 the Jews s me in the temple courts and tried *5197*
1Co 10:13 No temptation *has* s you except what is common to man. *3284*
Rev 20: 2 *He* s the dragon, that ancient serpent, *3195*

SEIZES (8) [SEIZE]

Dt 25:11 and s him by his private parts, 2616
Job 18: 9 A trap s him by the heel; 296
21: 6 I am terrified; trembling s my body. 296
Ps 137: 9 *he* who s your infants and dashes them 296
Pr 26:17 Like *one who* s a dog by the ears is 2616
Mic 4: 9 pain s you like that of a woman in labor? 2616
Mk 9:18 Whenever *it* s him, it throws him to the *2898*
Lk 9:39 A spirit s him and he suddenly screams; *3284*

SEIZING (4) [SEIZE]

Lk 22:54 Then s him, they led him away *5197*
Ac 21:30 S Paul, they dragged him from the temple, *2138*
Ro 7: 8 But sin, s the opportunity afforded by *3284*
7:11 For sin, s the opportunity afforded by *3284*

SEIZURES (2) [SEIZE]

Mt 4:24 the demon-possessed, those *having* s, *4944*
17:15 *"He has* s and is suffering greatly. *4944*

SELA (4) [SELA HAMMAHLEKOTH]

Jdg 1:36 the Amorites was from Scorpion Pass to S 6153
2Ki 14: 7 the Valley of Salt and captured S in battle, 6153
Isa 16: 1 from S, across the desert, 6153
42:11 Let the people of S sing for joy; 6153

SELA HAMMAHLEKOTH (1) [SELA]

1Sa 23:28 That is why they call this place S. 6154

SELAH (74)

Ps 3: 2 "God will not deliver him." S 6138
3: 4 he answers me from his holy hill. S 6138
3: 8 blessing be on your people. S 6138
4: 2 love delusions and seek false gods? S 6138
4: 4 search your hearts and be silent. S 6138
7: 5 make me sleep in the dust. S 6138
9:16 by the work of their hands. Higgaion. S 6138
9:20 nations know they are but men. S 6138
20: 3 and accept your burnt offerings. S 6138
21: 2 not withheld the request of his lips. S 6138
24: 6 who seek your face, O God of Jacob. S 6138
24:10 he is the King of glory. S 6138
32: 4 in the heat of summer. S 6138
32: 5 you forgave the guilt of my sin. S 6138
32: 7 surround me with songs of deliverance. S 6138
39: 5 each man's life is but a breath. S 6138
39:11 each man is but a breath. S 6138
44: 8 we will praise your name forever. S 6138
46: 3 mountains quake with their surging. S 6138
46: 7 the God of Jacob is our fortress. S 6138
46:11 the God of Jacob is our fortress. S 6138
47: 4 the pride of Jacob, whom he loved. S 6138
48: 8 God makes her secure forever. S 6138
49:13 who approve their sayings. S 6138
49:15 he will surely take me to himself. S 6138
50: 6 for God himself is judge. S 6138
52: 3 rather than speaking the truth. S 6138
52: 5 uproot you from the land of the living. S 6138
54: 3 men without regard for God. S 6138
55: 7 and stay in the desert; S 6138
55:19 will hear and afflict them—S 6138
57: 3 rebuking those who hotly pursue me; S 6138
57: 6 fallen into it themselves. S 6138
59: 5 mercy to wicked traitors. S 6138
59:13 that God rules over Jacob. S 6138
60: 4 against the bow. S 6138
61: 4 the shelter of your wings. S 6138
62: 4 in their hearts they curse. S 6138
62: 8 God is our refuge. S 6138
66: 4 sing praise to your name." S 6138
66: 7 rise up against him. S 6138
66:15 will offer bulls and goats. S 6138
67: 1 and make his face shine upon us, S 6138
67: 4 the nations of the earth. S 6138
68: 7 through the wasteland, S 6138
68:19 bears our burdens. S 6138
68:32 sing praise to the Lord, S 6138
75: 3 who hold its pillars firm. S 6138
76: 3 the weapons of war. S 6138
76: 9 the afflicted of the land. S 6138
77: 3 and my spirit grew faint. S 6138
77: 9 in anger withheld his compassion?" S 6138
77:15 descendants of Jacob and Joseph. S 6138
81: 7 at the waters of Meribah. S 6138
82: 2 show partiality to the wicked? S 6138
83: 8 to the descendants of Lot. S 6138
84: 4 they are ever praising you. S 6138
84: 8 listen to me, O God of Jacob. S 6138
85: 2 and covered all their sins. S 6138

Ps 87: 3 O city of God: S 6138
87: 6 "This one was born in Zion." S 6138
88: 7 overwhelmed me with all your waves. S 6138
88:10 rise up and praise you? S 6138
89: 4 throne firm through all generations.' " S 6138
89:37 faithful witness in the sky." S 6138
89:45 with a mantle of shame. S 6138
89:48 the power of the grave? S 6138
140: 3 poison of vipers is on their lips. S 6138
140: 5 set traps for me along my path. S 6138
140: 8 or they will become proud. S 6138
143: 6 soul thirsts for you like a parched land. S 6138
Hab 3: 3 the Holy One from Mount Paran. S 6138
3: 9 you called for many arrows. S 6138
3:13 you stripped him from head to foot. S 6138

SELDOM (2)
Pr 25:17 S *set* foot in your neighbor's house— 3700
Ecc 5:20 He s reflects on the days of his life, 2221+4202

SELECT (6) [SELECTED, SELECTS]
Ex 12:21 at once and s the animals for your families 4374
18:21 But s capable men from all the people— 2600
Nu 31:30 s one out of every fifty, whether persons, 4374
35:11 s some towns to be your cities of refuge, 7936
Est 3: 7 in the presence of Haman to **s a day** and a month. 3427+3427+4200+4946
Isa 66:21 And *I will* s some of them also to 4374

SELECTED (12) [SELECT]
Ge 18: 7 Then he ran to the herd and s a choice, 4374
32:13 and from what he had with him *he* s a gift 4374
Ex 21: 8 the master who *has* s her for himself, 3585
Nu 18: 6 *I* myself *have* s your fellow Levites from 4374
31:47 Moses s one out of every fifty persons 4374
Dt 1:23 *I* s twelve of you, one man from each tribe. 4374
2Sa 10: 9 so *he* s some of the best troops in Israel 1047
2Ki 7:14 So *they* s two chariots with their horses, 4374
1Ch 19:10 so *he* s some of the best troops in Israel 1047
Ezr 10:16 the priest s men who were family heads, 976
Est 2: 9 to her seven maids s from the king's palace 8011
Heb 5: 1 Every high priest *is* s from among men *3284*

SELECTS (3) [SELECT]
Ex 21: 9 If *he* s her for his son, 3585
Pr 31:13 *She* s wool and flax and works 2011
Isa 40:20 to present such an offering s wood that will 1047

SELED (2)
1Ch 2:30 The sons of Nadab: S and Appaim. 6135
2:30 S died without children. 6135

SELEUCIA (1)
Ac 13: 4 down to S and sailed from there to Cyprus. *4942*

SELF (9) [HERSELF, HIMSELF, ITSELF, MYSELF, ONESELF, OURSELVES, SELFISH, SELVES, THEMSELVES, YOURSELF, YOURSELVES]
Ex 32:13 to whom you swore by **your own s:** 3870
Lk 9:25 and yet lose or forfeit **his** very **s?** *1571*
Ro 6: 6 that our old s was crucified with him so that *476*
Eph 4:22 to put off your old s, *476*
4:24 and to put on the new s, *476*
Col 3: 9 since you have taken off your old s *476*
3:10 and have put on the new s, *NIG*
Phm 1:19 to mention that you owe me **your very s.** *4932*
1Pe 3: 4 it should be that of your inner s, *476+2840+3836*

SELF-ABASEMENT (1)
Ezr 9: 5 at the evening sacrifice, I rose from my s, 9504

SELF-CONDEMNED (1) [CONDEMN]
Tit 3:11 such a man is warped and sinful; he is s. *896*

SELF-CONFIDENCE (1) [CONFIDENCE]
Ne 6:16 were afraid and **lost** their s, 928+4394+5877+6524

SELF-CONFIDENT (1) [CONFIDENCE]
2Co 11:17 In this s boasting I am not talking as *5712*

SELF-CONTROL (7) [CONTROL]
Pr 25:28 down is a man who lacks s. 4200+5110+8120
Ac 24:25 righteousness, s and the judgment to come, *1602*
1Co 7: 5 not tempt you because of your **lack of s.** *202*
Gal 5:23 gentleness and s. Against such things *1602*
2Ti 3: 3 unforgiving, slanderous, **without s,** brutal, *203*
2Pe 1: 6 and to knowledge, s; *1602*
1: 6 and to s, perseverance; *1602*

SELF-CONTROLLED (11) [CONTROL]
1Th 5: 6 who are asleep, but *let us be* alert and s. *3768*
5: 8 since we belong to the day, *let us be* s, *3768*
1Ti 3: 2 the husband of but one wife, temperate, s, *5409*
Tit 1: 8 **who is s,** upright, holy and disciplined. *5409*
2: 2 worthy of respect, s, and sound in faith, *5409*
2: 5 to be s and pure, to be busy at home, *5409*
2: 6 encourage the young men *to be* s. *5404*
Tit 2:12 and to live s, upright and godly lives *5407*
1Pe 1:13 prepare your minds for action; *be* s; *3768*
4: 7 *be* clear minded and s so that you can pray. *3768*
5: 8 *Be* s and alert. *3768*

SELF-DISCIPLINE (1) [DISCIPLINE]
2Ti 1: 7 but a spirit of power, of love and *of* s. *5406*

SELF-IMPOSED (1) [IMPOSE]
Col 2:23 with their s **worship,** *1615*

SELF-INDULGENCE (2) [INDULGE]
Mt 23:25 but inside they are full of greed and s. *202*
Jas 5: 5 You have lived on earth in luxury and s. *5059*

SELF-SEEKING (2) [SEEK]
Ro 2: 8 for those who are s and who reject the truth *2249*
1Co 13: 5 It is not rude, *it is* not s, *1571+2426+3836*

SELFISH (7) [SELF]
Ps 119:36 toward your statutes and not toward s **gain.** 1299
Pr 18: 1 An unfriendly man pursues s **ends;** 9294
Gal 5:20 discord, jealousy, fits of rage, s **ambition,** *2249*
Php 1:17 The former preach Christ out of s **ambition,** *2249*
2: 3 of s **ambition** or vain conceit, *2249*
Jas 3:14 if you harbor bitter envy and s **ambition** *2249*
3:16 For where you have envy and s **ambition,** *2249*

SELFSAME (KJV) See SAME, VERY

SELL (39) [SALE, SALES, SELLER, SELLERS, SELLING, SELLS, SOLD]
Ge 23: 4 S me some property for a burial site here 5989
23: 9 so *he will* s me the cave of Machpelah, 5989
23: 9 Ask him *to* s it to me for the full price as 5989
25:31 Jacob replied, "First s me your birthright." 4835
37:27 *let's* s him to the Ishmaelites and 4835
47:16 *"I will* s you food in exchange 5989
47:22 That is why *they did* not s their land. 4835
Ex 21: 8 He has no right to s her to foreigners, 4835
21:35 *to* s the live one and divide both the money 4835
Lev 25:14 " 'If *you* s **land** to one of your 4835+4928
25:15 *to* s to you on the basis of the number 4835
25:37 at interest or s him food at a profit. 5989
Dt 2:28 S us food to eat and water to drink 8690
14:21 or you *may* s it to a foreigner. 4835
21:14 *You* **must** not s her or treat her as a slave, 928+2021+4084+4835+4835
1Ki 21: 6 'S me your vineyard; 928+4084+5989
21:15 that he refused to s you. 928+4084+5989
2Ki 4: 7 "Go, s the oil and pay your debts. 4835
7: 1 a seah of flour will s for a shekel NIH
7:18 a seah of flour *will* s **for** a shekel 928+2118
1Ch 21:22 S it to me at the full price." 5989
Ne 10:31 or grain to s on the Sabbath, 4835
Pr 11:26 but blessing crowns *him who is willing to* s. 8690
23:23 Buy the truth and *do* not s it; 4835
Isa 50: 1 Or to which of my creditors *did I* s you? 4835
Eze 30:12 I will dry up the streams of the Nile and s 4835
48:14 *They must* not s or exchange any of it. 4835
Joel 3: 8 *I will* s your sons and daughters to 4835
3: 8 and *they will* s them to the Sabeans, 4835
Am 2: 6 They s the righteous for silver, 4835
8: 5 be over that *we may* s grain, and the Sabbath 8690
Zec 11: 5 *Those who* s them say, 'Praise the LORD, 4835
Mt 19:21 go, s your possessions and give to the poor, *4797*
25: 9 go to those who s oil and buy some *4797*
Mk 10:21 s everything you have and give to the poor. *4797*
Lk 12:33 S your possessions and give to the poor. *4797*
18:22 S everything you have and give to the poor, *4797*
22:36 s your cloak and buy one. *4797*
Rev 13:17 so that no one could buy or s unless he had *4797*

SELLER (3) [SELL]
Isa 24: 2 for mistress as for maid, for s as for buyer, 4835
Eze 7:12 Let not the buyer rejoice nor the s grieve, 4835
7:13 The s will not recover the land he has sold 4835

SELLERS (1) [SELL]
Ne 13:20 or twice the merchants and s *of* all kinds 4835

SELLING (16) [SELL]
Ge 25:33 an oath to him, s his birthright to Jacob. 4835
45: 5 not be angry with yourselves for s me here, 4835
Lev 25:16 he *is* really s you is the number of crops. 4835
Ru 4: 3 *is* s the piece of land that belonged 4835
Ne 5: 8 Now you *are* s your brothers, 4835
13:15 I warned them against s food on that day. 4835
13:16 of merchandise and s them in Jerusalem on 4835
Am 8: 6 s even the sweepings with the wheat. 8690
Mt 21:12 drove out all who *were* buying and s there. *60*
21:12 and the benches *of* those s doves. *4797*
Mk 11:15 driving out those who were buying and s *60*
11:15 and the benches *of* those s doves, *4797*
Lk 17:28 buying and s, planting and building. *4797*
19:45 and began driving out those who *were* s. *4797*
Jn 2:14 In the temple courts he found men s cattle, *4797*
Ac 2:45 S their possessions and goods, *4405*

SELLS (10) [SELL]
Ex 21: 7 "If a man s his daughter as a servant, 4835
21:16 and either s him or still has him 4835
22: 1 an ox or a sheep and slaughters it or s it, 4835
Lev 25:25 and s some of his property, 4835
25:29 " 'If a man s a house in a walled city, 4835
25:39 among you and s **himself** to you, 4835
25:47 and s **himself** to the alien living among you 4835
Dt 15:12 s **himself** to you and serves you six years, 4835
24: 7 and treats him as a slave or s him, 4835
Pr 31:24 She makes linen garments and s them, 4835

SELVEDGE (KJV) See END

SELVES (1) [SELF]
Ro 6:19 because you are weak *in* your **natural s.** *4922*

SEM (KJV) See SHEM

SEMAKIAH (1)
1Ch 26: 7 his relatives Elihu and S were 6165

SEMEIN (1)
Lk 3:26 the son of Mattathias, the son *of* S, *4946*

SEMEN (6)
Ge 38: 9 with his brother's wife, he spilled his s on NIH
Lev 15:16 " 'When a man has an emission of s, 2446
15:17 Any clothing or leather that has s on it must 2446
15:18 with a woman and there is an emission of s, 2446
15:32 unclean by an emission of s, 2446
22: 4 or by anyone who has an emission of s, 2446

SENAAH (2)
Ezr 2:35 of S 3,630 6171
Ne 7:38 of S 3,930 6171

SENATE (KJV) See FULL ASSEMBLY

SEND (264) [SENDING, SENDS, SENT]
Ge 7: 4 Seven days from now I *will* s **rain** on 4763
24: 7 he *will* s his angel before you so 8938
24:40 *will* s his angel with you and 8938
24:54 **"S** me **on** my **way** to my master." 8938
24:56 **S** me **on** my **way** so I may go to my master. 8938
27:45 *I'll* s **word** *for* you to come back 8938
30:25 **"S** me **on** my **way** so I can go back 8938
31:27 so *I could* s you **away** with joy and singing 8938
37:13 Come, *I am going to* s you to them." 8938
38:17 "I'll s you a young goat from my flock," 8938
38:17 something as a pledge until you s it?" 8938
38:23 After all, *I did* s her this young goat, 8938
42: 4 But Jacob *did* not s Benjamin, 8938
42:16 **S** one of your number to get your brother; 8938
43: 4 If you will s our brother along with us, 8938
43: 5 But if you will not s him, 8938
43: 8 **"S** the boy along with me and we will go 8938
Ex 4:13 "O Lord, please s someone else to do it." 8938
8:21 I *will* s swarms of flies on you 8938
9:14 or this time I *will* s the full force of my 8938
9:18 at this time tomorrow I *will* s the worst 4763
23:27 *"I will* s my terror ahead of you and throw 8938
23:28 *I will* s the hornet ahead of you to drive 8938
33: 2 *I will* s an angel before you and drive out 8938
33:12 not let me know whom *you will* s 8938
33:15 *do* not s us **up** from here. 6590
Lev 16:21 *He shall* s the goat **away** into the desert in 8938
25:21 *I will* s you such a blessing in the sixth year 7422
26: 4 *I will* s you rain in its season, 5989
26:22 *I will* s wild animals against you, 8938
26:25 *I will* s a plague among you, 8938
Nu 5: 2 *to* s **away** from the camp anyone who has 8938
5: 3 **S away** male and female alike; 8938
5: 3 s them outside the camp so they will 8938
13: 2 **"S** some men to explore the land 8938
13: 2 From each ancestral tribe s one 8938
22:37 *"Did I* not s you an **urgent** summons? 8938+8938
31: 4 **S** into battle a thousand men from each of 8938
35:25 and s him **back** to the city of refuge 8740
Dt 1:22 *"Let us* s men ahead to spy out the land 8938
7:20 the LORD your God *will* s the hornet 8938
11:14 *I will* s rain on your land in its season, 5989
15:13 *do* not s him away empty-handed. 8938
19:12 the elders of his town *shall* s **for** him, 8938
28: 8 The LORD *will* s a blessing 7422
28:12 to s rain on your land in season and 5989
28:20 The LORD *will* s on you curses, 8938
28:59 the LORD *will* s **fearful** plagues on you 7098
28:68 The LORD *will* s you **back** in ships 8740
32:24 *I will* s wasting famine against them, 8938
32:24 I will s against them the fangs of wild NIH
Jos 1:16 and wherever *you* s us we will go. 8938
7: 3 S two or three thousand men to take it 6590
18: 4 *I will* s them **out** to make a survey of 8938
Jdg 20:38 with the ambush that they *should* s **up** 6590
1Sa 5:11 **"S** the ark of the god of Israel **away;** 8938
6: 2 how *we should* s it **back** to its place." 8938
6: 3 *do* not s it **away** empty, 8938
6: 3 **by all means** s a guilt offering to him. 8740+8740
6: 4 "What guilt offering *should we* s to him?" 8740
6: 6 not s the Israelites **out** so they could go 8938

1Sa 6: 8 S it on its way, 8938
9:16 "About this time tomorrow I will s you 8938
9:26 s you on your way." 8938
11: 3 so we can s messengers throughout Israel; 8938
12:17 I will call upon the LORD to s thunder 5989
16:11 Samuel said, "S for him; 2256+4374+8938
16:19 "S me your son David, 8938
19:17 and s my enemy away so that he escaped?" 8938
20:12 will I not s you word and let you know? 8938
20:13 not let you know and s you away safely. 8938
20:21 Then I will s a boy and say, 'Go, 8938
20:31 Now s and bring him to me, 8938
29: 4 "S the man back, that he may return 8740
2Sa 11: 6 "S me Uriah the Hittite." 8938
11:12 and tomorrow I will s you back." 8938
13: 9 "S everyone out of here," Amnon said. 3655
14:29 for Joab in order to s him to the king, 8938
14:32 'Come here so I can s you to the king 8938
15:36 S them to me with anything you hear." 8938
17:16 Now s a message immediately 8938
18:29 as Joab was about to s the king's servant 8938
19:31 and to s him on his way from there. 8938
1Ki 8:36 and s rain on the land you gave your people 5989
8:44 wherever you s them, and when they pray 8938
18: 1 and I will s rain on the land." 5989
20: 6 to s my officials to search your palace and 8938
22:26 s him back to Amon the ruler of the city 8740
2Ki 2:16 "No," Elisha replied, "do not s them." 8938
2:17 So he said, "S them." 8938
4:22 "Please s me one of the servants and 8938
5: 5 "I will s a letter to the king of Israel." 8938
5: 7 Why does this fellow s someone to me to 8938
6:13 "so I can s men and capture him." 8938
7:13 let us s them to find out what happened." 8938
9:17 "S him to meet them and ask, 8938
15:37 the LORD began to s Rezin king of Aram 8938
1Ch 13: 2 let us s word far and wide to the rest 8938
2Ch 2: 3 "S me cedar logs as you did NIH
2: 7 "S me, therefore, a man skilled to work 8938
2: 8 "S me also cedar, pine and algum logs 8938
2:15 "Now let my lord s his servants the wheat 8938
6:27 and s rain on the land you gave your people 5989
6:34 wherever you s them, and when they pray 8938
7:13 or s a plague among my people, 8938
18:25 s him back to Amon the ruler of the city 8740
28:11 S back your fellow countrymen you have 8740
30: 5 to s a proclamation throughout Israel, 6296
Ezr 5:17 let the king s us his decision in this matter. 10714
10: 3 before our God to s away all these women 3655
Ne 2: 5 let him s me to the city in Judah 8938
2: 6 It pleased the king to s me; so I set a time. 8938
8:10 s some to those who have nothing prepared. 8938
8:12 to s portions of food and to celebrate 8938
Job 1: 5 Job would s and have them purified. 8938
14:20 change his countenance and s him away. 8938
21:11 They s forth their children as a flock; 8938
38:35 Do you s the lightning bolts on their way? 8938
Ps 20: 2 May he s you help from the sanctuary 8938
43: 3 S forth your light and your truth, 8938
104:30 When you s your Spirit, they are created, 8938
144: 6 S forth lightning and scatter 1397+1398
Pr 10:26 so is a sluggard to those who s him. 8938
24:22 for those two will s sudden destruction 7756
25:13 a trustworthy messenger to those who s him; 8938
SS 7:13 The mandrakes s out their fragrance, 5989
Isa 6: 8 "Whom shall I s? 8938
6: 8 "Here am I. S me!" 8938
10: 6 I s him against a godless nation, 8938
10:16 will s a wasting disease upon his sturdy 8938
16: 1 S lambs as tribute to the ruler of the land, 8938
19:20 he will s them a savior and defender, 8938
30:23 also s you rain for the seed you sow in 5989
34: 3 their dead bodies will s up a stench; 6590
42:19 and deaf like the messenger I s? 8938
42:22 with no one to say, "S them back." 8740
43:14 "For your sake I will s to Babylon 8938
48:20 S it out to the ends of the earth; 3655
66:19 and I will s some of those who survive to 8938
Jer 1: 7 You must go to everyone I s you to 8938
2:10 s to Kedar and observe closely; 8938
8:17 I will s venomous snakes among you, 8938
9:17 s for the most skillful of them. 8938
14: 3 The nobles s their servants for water; 8938
14:15 I did not s them, yet they are saying, 8938
14:22 Do the skies themselves s down showers? 5989
15: 1 S them away from my presence! 8938
15: 3 "I will s four kinds of destroyers 7212
16:16 "But now I will s for many fishermen," 8938
16:16 After that I will s for many hunters, 8938
22: 7 I will s destroyers against you, 7727
23:21 I did not s these prophets, 8938
23:32 yet I did not s or appoint them. 8938
24:10 I will s the sword, 8938
25:15 the nations to whom I s you drink it. 8938
25:16 and go mad because of the sword I will s 8938
25:27 because of the sword I will s among you.' 8938
27: 3 Then s word to the kings of Edom, Moab, 8938
29:17 "I will s the sword, 8938
29:31 "S this message to all the exiles: 8938
29:31 even though I did not s him, 8938
37:20 Do not s me back to the house of Jonathan 8740
38:26 not to s me back to Jonathan's house 8740
43:10 I will s for my servant 2256+4374+8938
48:12 "when I will s men who pour from jars, 8938
51: 2 I will s foreigners to Babylon 8938
51:27 s up horses like a swarm of locusts. 6590
51:53 I will s destroyers against her," 907+995+4946
Eze 5:17 I will s famine and wild beasts 8938
13:11 and I will s hailstones hurtling down, 5989
14:13 to cut off its food supply and s famine 8938
14:15 "Or if I s wild beasts through that country 6296
14:19 "Or if I s a plague into that land 8938
14:21 How much worse will it be when I s 8938
28:23 I will s a plague upon her 8938
34:26 I will s down showers in season; 3718
39: 2 and s you against the mountains of Israel. 995
39: 6 I will s fire on Magog and 8938
Da 11:20 "His successor will s out a tax collector 6296
Hos 8:14 But I will s fire upon their cities 8938
14: 5 Like a cedar of Lebanon he will s down 5782
Joel 3: 6 you might s them far from their homeland. 8178
Am 1: 4 I will s fire upon the house of Hazael 8938
1: 7 I will s fire upon the walls of Gaza 8938
1:10 I will s fire upon the walls of Tyre 8938
1:12 I will s fire upon Teman 8938
2: 2 I will s fire upon Moab that will consume 8938
2: 5 I will s fire upon Judah that will consume 8938
5:27 Therefore I will s you into exile 1655
8:11 I will s a famine through the land— 8938
Zec 5: 4 'I will s it out, and it will enter the house 3655
Mal 2: 2 "I will s a curse upon you, 8938
3: 1 "See, I will s my messenger, 8938
4: 5 I will s you the prophet Elijah before 8938
Mt 8:31 s us into the herd of pigs." 690
9:38 to s out workers into his harvest field." 1675
11:10 " 'I will s my messenger ahead of you, 690
13:41 The Son of Man will s out his angels, 690
14:15 S the crowds away, 668
15:23 "S her away, for she keeps crying out 668
15:32 I do not want to s them away hungry, 668
19: 7 a certificate of divorce and s her away?" 668
21: 3 and he will s them right away." 690
24:31 And he will s his angels with 690
Mk 1: 2 "I will s my messenger ahead of you, 690
3:14 be with him and that he might s them out 690
5:10 and again not to s them out of the area. 690
5:12 "S us among the pigs; 4287
6:36 S the people away so they can go to 668
8: 3 If I s them home hungry, 668
10: 4 a certificate of divorce and s her away." 668
11: 3 and will s it back here shortly.' " 690
12: 6 "He had one left to s, a son, NIG
13:27 And he will s his angels and gather 690
Lk 7:27 " 'I will s my messenger ahead of you, 690
9:12 "S the crowd away so they can go to 668
10: 2 to s out workers into his harvest field. 1675
11:49 'I will s them prophets and apostles, 690
14:32 he will s a delegation while the other is still 690
16:24 have pity on me and s Lazarus to dip the tip 4287
16:27 father, s Lazarus to my father's house, 4287
20:13 I will s my son, whom I love; 4287
24:49 to s you what my Father has promised; 690
Jn 3:17 For God did not s his Son into the world 690
13:20 whoever accepts anyone I s accepts me; 4287
14:26 whom the Father will s in my name, 4287
15:26 whom I will s to you from the Father, 4287
16: 7 but if I go, I will s him to you. 4287
Ac 3:20 and that he may s the Christ, 690
7:34 Now come, I will s you back to Egypt.' 690
7:37 'God will s you a prophet like me 482
7:43 Therefore I will s you into exile' 3579
10: 5 Now s men to Joppa to bring back 4287
10:32 S to Joppa for Simon who is called Peter. 4287
11:13 'S to Joppa for Simon who is called Peter. 690
15:22 of their own men and s them to Antioch 4287
15:25 to choose some men and s them to you 4287
22:21 I will s you far away to the Gentiles.' ' 1990
24:25 When I find it convenient, I will s for you." 3559
25:21 I ordered him held until I could s him 402
25:25 to the Emperor I decided to s him to Rome. 4287
25:27 to s on a prisoner without specifying 4287
Ro 16:16 All the churches of Christ s greetings. 832
16:23 our brother Quartus s you their greetings. 832
1Co 1:17 For Christ did not s me to baptize, 690
16: 3 and s them with your gift to Jerusalem. 4287
16:11 S him on his way in peace 4636
16:19 in the province of Asia s you greetings. 832
16:20 All the brothers here s you greetings. 832
2Co 1:16 have you s me on my way to Judea. 4636
13:13 All the saints s their greetings. 832
Php 2:19 in the Lord Jesus to s Timothy to you soon, 4287
2:23 to s him as soon as I see how things go 4287
2:25 But I think it is necessary to s back 4287
2:28 Therefore I am all the more eager to s him, 4287
4:21 The brothers who are with me s greetings. 832
4:22 All the saints s you greetings, 832
Col 4:14 Luke, the doctor, and Demas s greetings. 832
Tit 3:12 As soon as I s Artemas or Tychicus to you, 4287
Heb 13:24 Those from Italy s you their greetings. 832
2Jn 1:13 of your chosen sister s their greetings. 832
3Jn 1: 6 s them on their way in a manner worthy 4636
1:14 The friends here s their greetings. 832
Rev 1:11 "Write on a scroll what you see and s it to 4287

SENDING (44) [SEND]

Ge 32: 5 Now I am s this message to my lord, 8938
32:20 "I will pacify him with these gifts I am s on 2143
Ex 3:10 I am s you to Pharaoh to bring my people 8938
23:20 I am s an angel ahead of you to guard you 8938
Lev 16:10 to be used for making atonement by s it into 8938
Jdg 6:14 Am I not s you?" 8938
1Sa 6: 8 beside it put the gold objects you are s back 8740
16: 1 I am s you to Jesse of Bethlehem. 8938
2Sa 10: 3 by s men to you to express sympathy? 8938
13:16 "S me away would be 8938
1Ki 15:19 See, I am s you a gift of silver and gold. 8938
2Ki 1: 6 that you are s men to consult Baal-Zebub, 8938
5: 6 "With this letter I am s my servant Naaman 8938
6:32 you see how this murderer is s someone 8938
1Ch 19: 3 by s men to you to express sympathy? 8938
2Ch 2:13 "I am s you Huram-Abi, a man of great skill 8938
16: 3 See, I am s you silver and gold. 8938
Ezr 4:14 we are s this message to inform the king, 10714
Ne 6:17 of Judah were s many letters to Tobiah, 2143
Pr 26: 6 or drinking violence is the s of a message 8938
Jer 42: 6 whom we are s you, so that it will go well 8938
Eze 2: 3 "Son of man, I am s you to the Israelites, 8938
2: 4 to whom I am s you are obstinate 8938
17:15 by s his envoys to Egypt to get horses and 8938
Joel 2:13 and he relents from s calamity. NIH
2:19 "I am s you grain, new wine and oil, 8938
Jnh 4: 2 a God who relents from s calamity. NIH
Mt 10:16 I am s you out like sheep among wolves. 690
23:34 Therefore I am s you prophets and wise men 690
Lk 10: 3 I am s you out like lambs among wolves. 690
Jn 20:21 As the Father has sent me, I am s you." 4287
Ac 11:30 s their gift to the elders by Barnabas 690
15:27 Therefore we are s Judas and Silas 690
26:17 I am s you to them 690
Ro 8: 3 God did by s his own Son in the likeness 4287
1Co 4:17 For this reason I am s to you Timothy, 4287
2Co 8:18 And we are s along with him the brother 5225
8:22 In addition, we are s with them our brother 5225
9: 3 But I am s the brothers in order that 4287
Eph 6:22 I am s him to you for this very purpose, 4287
Col 4: 8 I am s him to you for the express purpose 4287
Phm 1:12 I am s him—who is my very heart—back 402
Rev 1: 1 by s his angel to his servant John, 690
11:10 and will celebrate by s each other gifts, 4287

SENDS (30) [SEND]

Dt 24: 1 gives it to her and s her from his house, 8938
24: 3 gives it to her and s her from his house, 8938
28:48 you will serve the enemies the LORD s 8938
1Sa 2: 7 The LORD s poverty and wealth; 3769
Job 5:10 he s water upon the countryside. 8938
12:24 he s them wandering through a trackless 9494
37: 3 and s it to the ends of the earth. NIH
Ps 57: 3 He s from heaven and saves me, 8938
57: 3 God s his love and his faithfulness. 8938
135: 7 he s lightning with the rain and brings out 6913
147:15 He s his command to the earth; 8938
147:18 He s his word and melts them; 8938
Isa 18: 2 which s envoys by sea in papyrus boats 8938
Jer 10:13 He s lightning with the rain and brings out 6913
17: 8 the water that s out its roots by the stream. 8938
42: 5 with everything the LORD your God s you 8938
51:16 He s lightning with the rain and brings out 6913
Hos 12: 1 with Assyria and s olive oil to Egypt. 3297
Joel 2:23 He s you abundant showers, 3718
Zec 12: 2 to make Jerusalem a cup that s all AIT
Mt 5:45 s rain on the righteous and the unrighteous. 1101
Ro 16:21 my fellow worker, s his greetings to you, 832
16:23 s you his greetings. 832
Col 4:10 Aristarchus s you his greetings, 832
4:11 Jesus, who is called Justus, also s greetings. NIG
4:12 and a servant of Christ Jesus, s greetings. 832
2Th 2:11 For this reason God s them a powerful 4287
Tit 3:15 Everyone with me s you greetings. 832
Phm 1:23 prisoner in Christ Jesus, s you greetings. 832
1Pe 5:13 together with you, s you her greetings, 832

SENEH (1)

1Sa 14: 4 one was called Bozez, and the other S. 6175

SENIR (4) [HERMON]

Dt 3: 9 the Amorites call it S.) 8536
1Ch 5:23 that is, to S (Mount Hermon). 8536
SS 4: 8 from the top of S, the summit of Hermon, 8536
Eze 27: 5 of pine trees from S; 8536

SENNACHERIB (15) [SENNACHERIB'S]

2Ki 18:13 S king of Assyria attacked all 6178
19: 9 Now S received a report that Tirhakah, NIH
19:16 listen to the words S has sent to insult 6178
19:20 I have heard your prayer concerning S king 6178
19:36 So S king of Assyria broke camp 6178
2Ch 32: 1 S king of Assyria came and invaded Judah. 6178
32: 2 When Hezekiah saw that S had come and 6178
32: 9 when S king of Assyria and all his forces 6178
32:10 "This is what S king of Assyria says: 6178
32:22 from the hand of S king of Assyria 6178
Isa 36: 1 S king of Assyria attacked all 6178
37: 9 Now S received a report that Tirhakah, NIH
37:17 listen to all the words S has sent to insult 6178
37:21 to me concerning S king of Assyria, 6178
37:37 So S king of Assyria broke camp 6178

SENNACHERIB'S (1) [SENNACHERIB]

2Ch 32:16 S officers spoke further against the LORD 2257^{S}

SENSE (5) [SENSED, SENSELESS, SENSES, SENSIBLE, SENSITIVE, SENSITIVITY]

Dt 32:28 They are a nation without s, 6783

Job 39:17 with wisdom or give her a share of good s. 1069
Ecc 10: 3 the fool lacks s and shows everyone 4213
1Co 12:17 where would the s of hearing be? 198
12:17 where would the s of smell be? 4018

SENSED (1) [SENSE]
Ac 27:27 the sailors s they were approaching land. 5706

SENSELESS (13) [SENSE]
Ps 49:10 and the s alike perish and leave their wealth 1280
73:22 I was s and ignorant; I was a brute beast 1280
92: 6 The s man does not know, 1280
94: 8 Take heed, you s ones among the people; 1279
Isa 19:11 wise counselors of Pharaoh give s advice. 1279
Jer 4:22 They are s children; 6119
5:21 you foolish and s people, 401+4213
10: 8 They are all s and foolish; 1279
10:14 Everyone is s and without knowledge; 1279
10:21 The shepherds are s and do not inquire of 1279
51:17 "Every man is s and without knowledge; 1279
Hos 7:11 easily deceived and s— 401+4213
Ro 1:31 they are s, faithless, heartless, ruthless. 852

SENSES (3) [SENSE]
Lk 15:17 "When he came to his s, he said, 1571
1Co 15:34 Come back to your s as you ought, 1729
2Ti 2:26 that they will come to their s and escape 392

SENSIBLE (2) [SENSE]
Job 18: 2 Be s, and then we can talk. 1067
1Co 10:15 I speak to s people; 5861

SENSITIVE (3) [SENSE]
Dt 28:54 Even the most gentle and s man 6697
28:56 The most gentle and s woman among you— 6697
28:56 so s and gentle that she would not venture 6695

SENSITIVITY (1) [SENSE]
Eph 4:19 Having lost all s, they have given themselves 556

SENSUAL (2) [SENSUALITY]
Col 2:23 lack any value in restraining s indulgence. 4922
1Ti 5:11 s desires overcome their dedication to 2952

SENSUALITY (1) [SENSUAL]
Eph 4:19 they have given themselves over to s so as 816

SENT (654) [SEND]
Ge 2: 5 the LORD God had not s rain on the earth 4763
8: 1 and he s a wind over the earth, 6296
8: 7 and s out a raven, and it kept flying 8938
8: 8 Then he s out a dove to see if 8938
8:10 He waited seven more days and again s out 8938
8:12 and s the dove out again, 8938
12:20 and they s him on his way, 906+8938
19:13 against its people is so great that he has s us 8938
20: 2 Then Abimelech king of Gerar s for Sarah 8938
21:14 on her shoulders and then s her off with 8938
24:59 s their sister Rebekah on her way, 8938
25: 6 the sons of his concubines and s them away 8938
26:27 you were hostile to me and s me away?" 8938
26:29 but always treated you well and s you away 8938
26:31 Then Isaac s them on their way, 8938
27:42 she s for her younger son Jacob 2256+7924+8938
28: 5 Then Isaac s Jacob on his way, 8938
28: 6 had s him to Paddan Aram to take a wife 8938
31: 4 So Jacob s word to Rachel and Leah to
come out 2256+7924+8938
31:42 surely have s me away empty-handed. 8938
32: 3 Jacob s messengers ahead of him 8938
32:18 They are a gift s to my lord Esau, 8938
32:23 After he had s them across the stream, 6296
32:23 he s over all his possessions. 6296
37:14 he s him off from the Valley of Hebron. 8938
38:20 Meanwhile Judah s the young goat 8938
38:25 she s a message to her father-in-law. 8938
41: 8 so he s for all the magicians and wise men
2256+7924+8938
41:14 So Pharaoh s for Joseph, 2256+7924+8938
44: 3 the men were s on their way with their 8938
45: 5 because it was to save lives that God s me 8938
45: 7 But God s me ahead of you to preserve 8938
45: 8 then, it was not you who s me here, but God. 8938
45:23 And this is what he s to his father: 8938
45:24 Then he s his brothers away, 8938
45:27 the carts Joseph had s to carry him back, 8938
46: 5 carts that Pharaoh had s to transport him. 8938
46:28 Now Jacob s Judah ahead of him to Joseph 8938
50:16 So they s word to Joseph, saying, 7422
Ex 2: 5 the reeds and s her slave girl to get it. 8938
3:12 the sign to you that it is I who have s you: 8938
3:13 'The God of your fathers has s me to you,' 8938
3:14 'I AM has s me to you.' " 8938
3:15 the God of Jacob—has s me to you.' 8938
4:28 the LORD had s him to say, 8938
5:22 Is this why you s me? 8938
7:16 God of the Hebrews, has s me to say to you: 8938
9: 7 Pharaoh s men to investigate and found that 8938
9:23 the LORD s thunder and hail, 5989
18: 2 After Moses had s away his wife Zipporah, 8933
18: 6 Jethro had s word to him, 606
Ex 18:27 Moses s his father-in-law on his way, 8938
24: 5 Then he s young Israelite men, 8938
36: 6 s this word throughout the camp: 6296
Lev 26:41 toward them so that I s them into the land 995
Nu 5: 4 they s them outside the camp. 8938
13: 3 the LORD's command Moses s them out 8938
13:16 the names of the men Moses s to explore 8938
13:17 When Moses s them to explore Canaan, 8938
13:27 "We went into the land to which you s us, 8938
14:36 So the men Moses had s to explore the land, 8938
16:28 the LORD has s me to do all these things 8938
16:29 then the LORD has not s me. 8938
20:14 Moses s messengers from Kadesh to 8938
20:16 and s an angel and brought us out of Egypt. 8938
21: 6 LORD s venomous snakes among them; 8938
21:21 Israel s messengers to say to Sihon king of 8938
21:32 After Moses had s spies to Jazer, 8938
22: 5 s messengers to summon Balaam son 8938
22:10 king of Moab, s me this message: 8938
22:15 Then Balak s other princes, 8938
24:12 "Did I not tell the messengers you s me, 8938
31: 6 Moses s them into battle, 8938
32: 8 This is what your fathers did when I s them 8938
Dt 2:26 of Kedemoth I s messengers to Sihon king 8938
6:22 the LORD s miraculous signs 5989
9:23 the LORD s you out from Kadesh Barnea, 8938
24: 5 not be s to war or have any other duty laid 3655
34:11 and wonders the LORD s him to do 8938
Jos 2: 1 of Nun secretly s two spies from Shittim. 8938
2: 3 the king of Jericho s this message to Rahab: 8938
2:21 So she s them away and they departed. 8938
6:17 because she hid the spies we s. 8938
6:25 the men Joshua had s as spies to Jericho— 8938
7: 2 Now Joshua s men from Jericho to Ai, 8938
7:22 So Joshua s messengers, 8938
8: 3 of his best fighting men and s them out 8938
8: 9 Then Joshua s them off, 8938
10: 6 then s word to Joshua in the camp at Gilgal: 8938
11: 1 he s word to Jobab king of Madon, 8938
14: 7 when Moses the servant of the LORD s me 8938
14:11 as strong today as the day Moses s me out; 8938
22: 6 Then Joshua blessed them and s them away, 8938
22: 7 When Joshua s them home, 8938
22:13 So the Israelites s Phinehas son of Eleazar, 8938
22:14 With him they s ten of the chief men, NIH
24: 5 " 'Then I s Moses and Aaron, 8938
24: 9 he s for Balaam son of Beor to put a curse
on you. 2256+4200+7924+8938
24:12 I s the hornet ahead of you, 8938
24:28 Then Joshua s the people away, 8938
Jdg 1:23 When they s men to spy out Bethel 9365
3:15 The Israelites s him with tribute 8938
3:18 he s on their way the men who had 8938
4: 6 She s for Barak son of Abinoam from
Kedesh 2256+4200+7924+8938
6: 8 he s them a prophet, who said, 8938
6:35 He s messengers throughout Manasseh, 8938
7: 8 So Gideon s the rest of the Israelites 8938
7:24 Gideon s messengers throughout 8938
9:23 God s an evil spirit between Abimelech and 8938
9:31 Under cover he s messengers to Abimelech, 8938
11:12 Then Jephthah s messengers to 8938
11:14 Jephthah s back messengers to 8938
11:17 Israel s messengers to the king of Edom, 8938
11:17 They s also to the king of Moab, 8938
11:19 "Then Israel s messengers to Sihon king of 8938
11:28 to the message Jephthah s him. 8938
13: 8 let the man of God you s to us come again 8938
16:18 she s word to the rulers of the Philistines, 8938
18: 2 So the Danites s five warriors from Zorah 8938
19:25 and s her outside to them, 3655
19:29 and s them into all the areas of Israel. 8938
20: 6 into pieces and s one piece to each region 8938
20:12 The tribes of Israel s men throughout 8938
21:10 assembly s twelve thousand fighting men 8938
21:13 the whole assembly s an offer of peace to 8938
1Sa 4: 4 So the people s men to Shiloh, 8938
4:13 the whole town s up a cry. 2410
5:10 So they s the ark of God to Ekron. 8938
6:17 These are the gold tumors the Philistines s 8740
6:21 Then they s messengers to the people 8938
11: 7 and s the pieces by messengers 8938
12: 8 and the LORD s Moses and Aaron, 8938
12:11 Then the LORD s Jerub-Baal, Barak, 8938
12:18 and that same day the LORD s thunder 5989
13: 2 rest of the men he s back to their homes. 8938
14:15 It was a panic s by God. AIT
15: 1 the one the LORD s to anoint you king 8938
15:18 And he s you on a mission, saying, 8938
16:12 So he s and had him brought in. 8938
16:19 Then Saul s messengers to Jesse and said, 8938
16:20 a young goat and s them with his son David 8938
16:22 Then Saul s word to Jesse, saying, 8938
17:31 and Saul s for him. 4374
18: 5 Whatever Saul s him to do, 8938
18:13 So he s David away from him 6073
19:11 Saul s men to David's house to watch it and 8938
19:14 When Saul s the men to capture David, 8938
19:15 Then Saul s the men back to see David 8938
19:20 so he s men to capture him. 8938
19:21 Saul was told about it, and he s more men, 8938
19:21 Saul s men a third time, 8938
20:22 because the LORD has s you away. 8938
22:11 king s for the priest Ahimelech 4200+7924+8938
25: 5 So he s ten young men and said to them, 8938
25:14 "David s messengers from the desert 8938
25:25 I did not see the men my master s. 8938
1Sa 25:32 who has s you today to meet me. 8938
25:39 Then David s word to Abigail, 8938
25:40 "David has s us to you to take you 8938
26: 4 he s out scouts and learned that Saul 8938
30:26 he s some of the plunder to the elders 8938
30:27 He s it to those who were in Bethel, NIH
31: 9 and they s messengers throughout the land 8938
2Sa 2: 5 he s messengers to the men 8938
3:12 Then Abner s messengers on his behalf 8938
3:14 Then David s messengers to Ish-Bosheth 8938
3:21 David s Abner away, and he went in peace. 8938
3:22 because David had s him away, 8938
3:23 and that the king had s him away 8938
3:26 Joab then left David and s messengers 8938
5:11 Hiram king of Tyre s messengers to David, 8938
8:10 he s his son Joram to King David 8938
10: 2 So David s a delegation to express his 8938
10: 3 Hasn't David s them to you to explore 8938
10: 4 and s them away. 8938
10: 5 he s messengers to meet the men, 8938
10: 7 David s Joab out with the entire army 8938
11: 1 David s Joab out with the king's men and 8938
11: 3 and David s someone to find out about her. 8938
11: 4 Then David s messengers to get her. 8938
11: 5 The woman conceived and s word to David,
2256+5583+8938
11: 6 So David s this word to Joab: 8938
11: 6 And Joab s him to David. 8938
11: 8 and a gift from the king was s after him. 3655
11:14 a letter to Joab and s it with Uriah. 8938
11:18 Joab s David a full account of the battle. 8938
11:22 he told David everything Joab had s him 8938
12: 1 The LORD s Nathan to David. 8938
12:25 he s word through Nathan the prophet 8938
12:27 Joab then s messengers to David, saying, 8938
13: 7 David s word to Tamar at the palace: 8938
13:27 so he s with him Amnon and the rest of 8938
14: 2 So Joab s someone to Tekoa and had 8938
14:29 Then Absalom s for Joab in order 8938
14:29 he s a second time, but he refused to come. 8938
14:32 "Look, I s word to you and said, 8938
15:10 Then Absalom s secret messengers 8938
15:12 he also s for Ahithophel the Gilonite, 8938
18: 2 David s the troops out— 8938
19:11 King David s this message to Zadok 8938
19:14 They s word to the king, "Return, 8938
24:13 how I should answer the one who s me." 8938
24:15 So the LORD s a plague on Israel from 5989
1Ki 1:44 The king has s with him Zadok the priest, 8938
1:53 Then King Solomon s men, 8938
2:36 Then the king s for Shimei and said to him,
2256+4200+7924+8938
4:34 s by all the kings of the world, 907+4946
5: 1 he s his envoys to Solomon, 8938
5: 2 Solomon s back this message to Hiram: 8938
5: 8 So Hiram s word to Solomon: 8938
5: 8 "I have received the message you s me 8938
5:14 He s them off to Lebanon in shifts 8938
7:13 King Solomon s to Tyre and brought Huram 8938
8:66 On the following day he s the people away. 8938
9:14 Hiram had s to the king 120 talents of gold. 8938
9:27 And Hiram s his men—sailors who knew 8938
12: 3 So they s for Jeroboam, 2256+4200+7924+8938
12:18 King Rehoboam s out Adoniram, 8938
12:20 they s and called him to the assembly 8938
14: 6 I have been s to you with bad news. 8938
15:18 He entrusted it to his officials and s them 8938
15:20 and s the commanders of his forces against 8938
18:10 where my master has not s someone to look 8938
18:20 So Ahab s word throughout all Israel 8938
19: 2 So Jezebel s a messenger to Elijah to say, 8938
20: 2 He s messengers into the city to Ahab king 8938
20: 5 'I s to demand your silver and gold, 8938
20: 7 When he s for my wives and my children, 8938
20:10 Ben-Hadad s another message to Ahab: 8938
21: 8 and s them to the elders and nobles 8938
21:14 Then they s word to Jezebel: 8938
2Ki 1: 2 So he s messengers, saying to them, 8938
1: 6 to the king who s you and tell him, 8938
1: 9 Then he s to Elijah a captain 8938
1:11 At this the king s to Elijah another captain 8938
1:13 the king s a third captain with his fifty men. 8938
1:16 to consult that you have s messengers 8938
2: 2 the LORD has s me to Bethel." 8938
2: 4 the LORD has s me to Jericho," 8938
2: 6 the LORD has s me to the Jordan." 8938
2:17 And they s fifty men, 8938
3: 7 He also s this message to Jehoshaphat king 8938
5: 8 he s him this message: 8938
5:10 Elisha s a messenger to say to him, "Go, 8938
5:22 "My master s me to say, 8938
5:24 He s the men away and they left. 8938
6: 9 of God s word to the king of Israel: 8938
6:14 Then he s horses and chariots and 8938
6:23 he s them away, 8938
6:32 The king s a messenger ahead, 8938
7:14 the king s them after the Aramean army. 8938
8: 9 of Aram has s me to ask, 8938
9:19 So the king s out a second horseman. 8938
10: 1 Jehu wrote letters and s them to Samaria: 8938
10: 5 the elders and the guardians s this message 8938
10: 7 They put their heads in baskets and s them 8938
10:21 Then he s word throughout Israel, 8938
11: 4 In the seventh year Jehoiada s for the
commanders 2256+4374+8938
12:18 and he s them to Hazael king of Aram, 8938
14: 8 Then Amaziah s messengers to Jehoash son 8938

2Ki 14: 9 "A thistle in Lebanon s a message to 8938
14:19 but *they* s men after him to Lachish 8938
16: 7 Ahaz s messengers to say 8938
16: 8 the royal palace and s it as a gift to the king 8938
16:10 He saw an altar in Damascus and s to Uriah 8938
16:11 with all the plans that King Ahaz *had* s 8938
17: 4 for *he had* s envoys to So king of Egypt, 8938
17:25 so he s lions among them 8938
17:26 *He has* s lions among them, 8938
18:14 So Hezekiah king of Judah s this message 8938
18:17 of Assyria s his supreme commander, 8938
18:27 that my master s me to say these things, and 8938
19: 2 *He* s Eliakim the palace administrator, 8938
19: 4 *has* s to ridicule the living God, 8938
19: 9 So he again s messengers to Hezekiah 8938
19:16 to the words Sennacherib *has* s to insult 8938
19:20 Then Isaiah son of Amoz s a message 8938
20:12 of Babylon s Hezekiah letters and a gift, 8938
22: 3 King Josiah s the secretary, 8938
22:15 Tell the man who s you to me, 8938
22:18 who s you to inquire of the LORD, 8938
24: 2 The LORD s Babylonian, Aramean, 8938
24: 2 *He* s them to destroy Judah, 8938
1Ch 6:15 s Judah and Jerusalem **into exile** 1655
10: 9 and s **messengers** throughout the land of 8938
12:19 after consultation, their rulers s him **away.** 8938
14: 1 Hiram king of Tyre s messengers to David, 8938
18:10 *he* s his son Hadoram to King David 8938
19: 2 So David s a delegation to express his 8938
19: 4 and s them **away.** 8938
19: 5 *he* s messengers to meet them, 8938
19: 6 and the Ammonites s a thousand talents 8938
19: 8 David s Joab **out** with the entire army 8938
19:16 routed by Israel, *they* s messengers 8938
21:12 how I should answer the *one who* s me." 8938
21:14 So the LORD s a plague on Israel, 5989
21:15 And God s an angel to destroy Jerusalem. 8938
2Ch 2: 3 Solomon s this message to Hiram king 8938
2: 3 for my father David when *you* s him cedar 8938
7:10 of the seventh month *he* s the people 8938
8:18 And Hiram s him ships commanded 8938
10: 3 So *they* s **for** Jeroboam, 2256+4200+7924+8938
10:18 King Rehoboam s **out** Adoniram, 8938
13:13 Jeroboam *had* s troops **around** to the rear, 6015
16: 2 and s it to Ben-Hadad king of Aram, 8938
16: 4 and s the commanders of his forces against 8938
17: 7 of his reign *he* s his officials Ben-Hail, 8938
23:14 the priest s **out** the commanders of units of 3655
24:19 the LORD s prophets to the people 8938
24:23 *They* s all the plunder to their king 8938
25:10 to him from Ephraim and s them home. 2143
25:13 the troops that Amaziah *had* **s back** 8740
25:15 and *he* s a prophet to him, who said, 8938
25:17 *he* s this challenge to Jehoash son 8938
25:18 "A thistle in Lebanon s a message to 8938
25:27 but *they* s men after him to Lachish 8938
28:16 At that time King Ahaz s to the king 8938
30: 1 Hezekiah s **word** to all Israel and Judah and 8938
32: 9 he s his officers to Jerusalem 8938
32:21 And the LORD s an angel, 8938
32:31 But when envoys *were* s by the rulers 8938
34: 8 *he* s Shaphan son of Azaliah and Maaseiah 8938
34:22 the king had s with him went to speak to NIH
34:23 Tell the man who s you to me, 8938
34:26 who s you to inquire of the LORD, 8938
35:21 But Neco s messengers to him, saying, 8938
36:10 King Nebuchadnezzar s *for* him 8938
36:15 **s word** to them through his messengers 8938
Ezr 4:11 (This is a copy of the letter *they* s him.) 10714
4:17 The king s this reply: 10714
4:18 The letter *you* s us has been read 10714
5: 6 s to King Darius. 10714
5: 7 The report *they* s him read as follows: 10714
6:13 because of the decree King Darius *had* **s,** 10714
7:14 You **are** s by the king and his seven 10714
8:17 and *I* s them to Iddo, the leader in 7422
Ne 2: 9 also s army officers and cavalry with me. 8938
6: 2 Sanballat and Geshem s me this message: 8938
6: 3 so *I* s messengers to them with this reply: 8938
6: 4 Four times *they* s me the same message, 8938
6: 5 Sanballat s his aide to me with the same 8938
6: 8 *I* s him this reply: 8938
6:12 I realized that God *had* not s him, 8938
6:19 And Tobiah s letters to intimidate me. 8938
9:10 *You* s miraculous signs and wonders 5989
Est 1:22 *He* s dispatches to all parts of the kingdom, 8938
3:13 Dispatches **were** s by couriers to all 8938
4: 4 *She* s clothes *for* him to put on instead 8938
4:13 he **s back** this answer: 8740
4:15 Then Esther s this reply to Mordecai: 8740
8:10 and s them by mounted couriers, 8938
9:20 and *he* s letters to all the Jews throughout 8938
9:30 And Mordecai s letters to all the Jews in 8938
Job 22: 9 And *you* s widows **away** empty-handed 8938
Ps 59: T When Saul *had* s men to watch David's 8938
78:25 *he* s them all the food they could eat. 8938
78:45 *He* s swarms of flies that devoured them, 8938
78:61 *He* s [the ark of] his might into captivity, 5989
80:11 *It* **s out** its boughs to the Sea, 8938
105:17 and *he* s a man before them— 8938
105:20 The king s and released him, 8938
105:26 *He* s Moses his servant, and Aaron, 8938
105:28 *He* s darkness and made the land dark— 8938
106:15 but s a wasting disease upon them. 8938
107:20 *He* s **forth** his word and healed them; 8938
135: 9 *He* s his signs and wonders into your midst, 8938
Pr 9: 3 *She has* s **out** her maids, 8938

Pr 17:11 a merciless official *will* **be** s against him. 8938
22:21 can give sound answers to *him who* s you? 8938
Isa 6:12 until the LORD *has* s everyone **far away** 8178
9: 8 The Lord *has* s a message against Jacob; 8938
20: 1 s *by* Sargon king of Assyria, 8938
36: 2 the king of Assyria s his field commander 8938
36:12 that my master s me to say these things, and 8938
37: 2 *He* s Eliakim the palace administrator, 8938
37: 4 *has* s to ridicule the living God, 8938
37: 9 *he* s messengers to Hezekiah with this word: 8938
37:17 to all the words Sennacherib *has* s to insult 8938
37:21 Then Isaiah son of Amoz s a message 8938
39: 1 of Babylon s Hezekiah letters and a gift, 8938
48:16 Sovereign LORD *has* s me, with his Spirit. 8938
50: 1 of divorce with which *I* s her **away?** 8938
50: 1 because of your transgressions your mother **was s away.** 8938
55:11 and achieve the purpose for which *I* s it. 8938
57: 9 *You* s your ambassadors far away; 8938
61: 1 *He has* s me to bind up the brokenhearted, 8938
63:12 *who* s his glorious arm of power to be 2143
Jer 3: 8 and s her **away** because of all her adulteries. 8938
7:25 again and again *I* s you my servants 8938
14:14 not s them or appointed them or spoken 8938
19:14 where the LORD *had* s him to prophesy, 8938
21: 1 when King Zedekiah s to him Pashhur son 8938
24: 5 from Judah, whom *I* s **away** from this place 8938
25: 4 though the LORD *has* s all his servants 8938
25:17 the nations to whom he s me drink it: 8938
26: 5 whom I *have* s to you again and again 8938
26:12 "The LORD s me to prophesy 8938
26:15 for in truth the LORD *has* s me to you 8938
26:22 however, s Elnathan son of Acbor to Egypt, 8938
27:15 *'I have* not s them,' declares the LORD. 8938
28: 9 as one truly s *by* the LORD only 8938
28:15 The LORD *has* not s you, 8938
29: 1 that the prophet Jeremiah s from Jerusalem 8938
29: 3 of Judah s to King Nebuchadnezzar 8938
29: 9 *I have* not s them," declares the LORD. 8938
29:19 "words that *I* s to them again and again 8938
29:20 all you exiles whom *I have* s **away** 8938
29:25 You s letters in your own name to all 8938
29:28 *He has* s this message to us in Babylon: 8938
35:15 and again *I* s all my servants the prophets 8938
36:14 all the officials s Jehudi son of Nethaniah, 8938
36:21 The king s Jehudi to get the scroll, 8938
37: 3 s Jehucal son of Shelemiah with 8938
37: 7 who s you to inquire of me, 8938
37:17 Then King Zedekiah s **for** him 8938
38:14 Then King Zedekiah s **for** Jeremiah 8938
39:14 s and had Jeremiah taken out of 8938
40:14 of the Ammonites *has* s Ishmael son 8938
42: 9 to whom *you* s me to present your petition, 8938
42:20 when you s me to the LORD your God 8938
42:21 the LORD your God in all *he* s me 8938
43: 1 the LORD *had* s him to tell them— 8938
43: 2 The LORD our God *has* not s you to say, 8938
44: 4 and again *I* s my servants the prophets, 8938
49:14 An envoy **was** s to the nations to say, 8938
La 1:13 "From on high *he* s fire, 8938
1:13 s it **down** into my bones. 3718
Eze 3: 5 not **being** s to a people of obscure speech 8938
3: 6 Surely if *I had* s you to them, 8938
11:16 Although *I* s them **far away** among 8178
13: 6 when the LORD *has* not s them; 8938
17: 7 The vine now **s out** its roots toward him 4102
23:16 she lusted after them and s messengers 8938
23:40 *"They* even s messengers for men who came 8938
31: 4 around its base and s their channels to all 8938
39:28 I s them **into exile** among the nations, 1655
Da 2:13 and *men were* s *to* **look for** Daniel AIT
3:28 who *has* s his angel and rescued his 10714
5:24 Therefore he s the hand that wrote 10714
6:22 My God s his angel, and shut the mouths 10714
10:11 and stand up, for *I have* now **been** s to you." 8938
Hos 5:13 s to the great king **for help.** 8938
Joel 2:25 my great army that *I* s among you. 8938
Am 4: 7 *I* **s rain** on one town, 4763
4:10 *"I* s plagues among you as I did to Egypt. 8938
7:10 of Bethel s a message to Jeroboam king 8938
Ob 1: 1 An envoy **was** s to the nations to say, "Rise, 8938
Jnh 1: 4 Then the LORD s a great wind on the sea, 3214
Mic 6: 4 *I* s Moses to lead you, 8938
Hag 1:12 because the LORD their God *had* s him. 8938
Zec 1:10 the ones the LORD *has* s to go throughout 8938
2: 8 "After he has honored me and *has* s me 8938
2: 9 that the LORD Almighty *has* s me. 8938
2:11 that the LORD Almighty *has* s me to you. 8938
4: 9 that the LORD Almighty *has* s me to you. 8938
6:15 that the LORD Almighty *has* s me to you. 8938
7: 2 The people of Bethel *had* s Sharezer 8938
7:12 to the words that the LORD Almighty *had* s 8938
Mal 2: 4 that *I have* s you this admonition so 8938
Mt 2: 8 He s them to Bethlehem and said, *4287*
10: 5 These twelve Jesus **s out** with the following *690*
10:40 receives me receives the one who s me. *690*
11: 2 what Christ was doing, *he* s his disciples *4287*
14:35 *they* **s word** to all the surrounding country. *690*
15:24 *"I* **was** s only to the lost sheep of Israel." *690*
15:39 *After* Jesus *had* s the crowd **away,** *668*
20: 2 for the day and s them into his vineyard. *690*
21: 1 Jesus s two disciples, *690*
21:34 *he* s his servants to the tenants *690*
21:36 Then *he* s other servants to them, *690*
21:37 Last of all, *he* s his son to them. *690*
22: 3 *He* s his servants to those who had been *690*
22: 4 "Then *he* s some more servants and said, *690*

Mt 22: 7 He s his army and destroyed those *4287*
22:16 *They* s their disciples to him along with *690*
23:37 you who kill the prophets and stone those s *690*
26:47 s from the chief priests and the elders of *NIG*
27:19 his wife s him this **message:** *690*
Mk 1:12 At once the Spirit s him **out** into the desert, *1675*
1:43 Jesus s him **away** at once with a strong *1675*
3:31 *they* s someone in to call him. *690*
6: 7 *he* s them **out** two by two *690*
6:27 So he immediately s an executioner *690*
8: 9 And *having* s them **away,** *668*
8:26 Jesus s him home, saying, *690*
9:37 not welcome me but the one who s me." *690*
11: 1 Jesus s two of his disciples, *690*
12: 2 At harvest time *he* s a servant to the tenants *690*
12: 3 beat him and s him **away** empty-handed. *690*
12: 4 Then *he* s another servant to them; *690*
12: 5 *He* s still another, and that one they killed. *690*
12: 5 He s many others; some of them they beat, *NIG*
12: 6 *He* s him last of all, saying, *690*
12:13 Later *they* s some of the Pharisees *690*
14:13 So *he* s two of his disciples, telling them, *690*
14:43 s from the chief priests, *NIG*
Lk 1:19 and *I have been* s to speak to you and *690*
1:26 God s the angel Gabriel to Nazareth, *690*
1:53 but *has* s the rich **away** empty. *1990*
4:18 *He has* s me to proclaim freedom for *690*
4:26 Yet Elijah *was* not s to any of them, *4287*
4:43 because that is why *I was* **s."** *690*
7: 3 of Jesus and s some elders of the Jews *690*
7: 6 from the house when the centurion s friends *4287*
7:10 Then the men who *had been* s returned to *4287*
7:19 *he* s them to the Lord to ask, *4287*
7:20 "John the Baptist s us to you to ask, *690*
8:38 but Jesus s him **away,** saying, *668*
9: 2 and *he* s them **out** to preach the kingdom *690*
9:48 welcomes me welcomes the one who s me. *690*
9:52 And *he* s messengers on ahead, *690*
10: 1 and s them two by two ahead of him *690*
10:16 he who rejects me rejects him who s me." *690*
13:34 you who kill the prophets and stone those s *690*
14: 4 he healed him and s him **away.** *668*
14:17 At the time of the banquet *he* s his servant *690*
15:15 *who* s him to his fields to feed pigs. *4287*
19:14 and s a delegation after him to say, *690*
19:15 Then *he* s **for** the servants *3306+5888*
19:29 *he* s two of his disciples, saying to them, *690*
19:32 Those who *were* s ahead went *690*
20:10 At harvest time *he* s a servant to the tenants *690*
20:10 and s him **away** empty-handed. *1990*
20:11 *He* s another servant, *4287+4707*
20:11 and s **away** empty-handed. *1990*
20:12 *He* s still a third, *4287+4707*
20:20 Keeping a close watch on him, *they* s spies, *690*
22: 8 Jesus s Peter and John, saying, *690*
22:35 "When *I* s you without purse, *690*
23: 7 Herod's jurisdiction, *he* s him to Herod, *402*
23:11 *they* s him **back** to Pilate. *402*
23:15 Neither has Herod, for *he* s him **back** to us; *402*
Jn 1: 6 There came a man *who was* s from God; *690*
1:19 the Jews of Jerusalem s priests and Levites *690*
1:22 an answer to take back *to* those who s us. *4287*
1:24 Now some Pharisees who had been s *690*
1:33 except that the one who s me to baptize *4287*
3:28 'I am not the Christ but am s ahead of him.' *690*
3:34 the one whom God *has* s speaks the words *690*
4:34 *of* him who s me and to finish his work. *4287*
4:38 I s you to reap what you have *690*
5:23 not honor the Father, who s him. *4287*
5:24 and believes him who s me has eternal life *4287*
5:30 not to please myself but him who s me. *4287*
5:33 "You *have* s to John and he has testified to *690*
5:36 testifies that the Father *has* s me. *690*
5:37 the Father *who* s me has himself testified *4287*
5:38 for you do not believe the one he **s.** *690*
6:29 to believe in the one he *has* **s."** *690*
6:38 but to do the will *of* him who s me. *4287*
6:39 And this is the will *of* him who s me, *4287*
6:44 unless the Father who s me draws him, *4287*
6:57 the living Father s me and I live because of *690*
7:16 It comes *from* him who s me. *4287*
7:18 for the honor *of* the one who s him is a man *4287*
7:28 but he who s me is true. *4287*
7:29 because I am from him and he s me." *690*
7:32 the Pharisees s temple guards to arrest him. *690*
7:33 and then I go to the one who s me. *4287*
8:16 I stand with the Father, who s me. *4287*
8:18 my other witness is the Father, who s me." *4287*
8:26 But he who s me is reliable, *4287*
8:29 The one who s me is with me; *4287*
8:42 I have not come on my own; but he s me. *690*
9: 4 we must do the work *of* him who s me. *4287*
9: 7 the Pool of Siloam" (this word means **S).** *690*
9:18 and had received his sight until *they* **s for** *5888*
10:36 the Father set apart as his very own and s *690*
11: 3 So the sisters s word to Jesus, "Lord, *690*
11:42 that they may believe that you s me." *690*
12:44 but in the one who s me. *4287*
12:45 he looks at me, he sees the one who s me. *4287*
12:49 the Father who s me commanded me what *4287*
13:16 messenger greater than the one who s him. *4287*
13:20 accepts me accepts the one who s me." *4287*
14:24 they belong to the Father who s me. *4287*
15:21 for they do not know the One who s me. *4287*
16: 5 "Now I am going to him who s me, *4287*
17: 3 and Jesus Christ, whom *you have* **s.** *690*
17: 8 and they believed that you s me. *690*

Jn 17:18 As *you* s me into the world, *690*
17:18 I *have* s them into the world. *690*
17:21 the world may believe that you *have* s me. *690*
17:23 that you s me and have loved them even *690*
17:25 and they know that you *have* s me. *690*
18:24 Then Annas s him, still bound, *690*
20:21 As the Father *has* s me, I am sending you." *690*
Ac 3:26 *he* s him first to you to bless you *690*
5:21 and s to the jail for the apostles. *690*
7: 4 God s him to this land where you are *3579*
7:12 *he* s our fathers on their first visit. *1990*
7:14 Joseph s **for** his father Jacob *690+3559*
7:35 He *was* s to be their ruler and deliverer *690*
8:14 *they* s Peter and John to them. *690*
9:17 *has* s me so that you may see again and *690*
9:30 down to Caesarea and s him **off** to Tarsus. *1990*
9:38 *they* s two men to him and urged him, *690*
9:40 Peter s them all out of the room; *1675*
10: 8 that had happened and s them to Joppa. *690*
10:17 the men s by Cornelius found out *690*
10:20 go with them, for I *have* s them." *690*
10:29 So *when I was* s **for,** I came *3569*
10:29 May I ask why *you* s **for** me?" *3569*
10:33 So *I* s for you immediately, *4287*
10:36 You know the message God s to the people *690*
11:11 "Right then three men *who had been* s to me *690*
11:22 and *they* s Barnabas to Antioch. *1990*
12:11 without a doubt that the Lord s his angel *1990*
13: 3 placed their hands on them and s them **off.** *668*
13: 4 s **on** *their* **way** by the Holy Spirit, *1734*
13: 7 s **for** Barnabas and Saul because he wanted *4673*
13:15 the synagogue rulers s word to them, *690*
13:26 that this message of salvation *has been* s. *1990*
15: 3 The church s *them* **on** *their* **way,** *4636*
15:23 With them *they* s **the** following **letter:** *1211*
15:30 The men *were* s **off** and went down *668*
15:33 *they were* s **off** by the brothers with *668*
15:33 of peace to return to those who *had* s them. *690*
16:35 the magistrates s their officers to the jailer *690*
17:10 brothers s Paul and Silas **away** to Berea. *1734*
17:14 The brothers immediately s Paul to *1990*
19:22 *He* s two of his helpers, *690*
19:31 s him a message begging him not to venture *4287*
20: 1 Paul s **for** the disciples and, *3569*
20:17 Paul s to Ephesus for the elders of the church. *4287*
23:18 s **for** me and asked me to bring this young *4673*
23:30 *I* s him to you at once. *4287*
24:24 *He* s **for** Paul and listened to him *3569*
24:26 so he s **for** him frequently and talked *3569*
28:28 to know that God's salvation *has been* s to *690*
Ro 10:15 how can they preach unless *they are* s? *690*
2Co 2:17 with sincerity, like men s from God. *NIG*
12:17 through any of the men *I* s you? *690*
12:18 to go to you and *I* s our brother **with** him. *5273*
Gal 1: 1 s not from men nor by man, *NIG*
4: 4 the time had fully come, God s his Son, *1990*
4: 6 God s the Spirit of his Son into our hearts, *1990*
Php 2:25 whom you s to take care of my needs. *NIG*
4:16 *you* s me aid again and again when I was *4287*
4:18 from Epaphroditus the gifts you s. *NIG*
1Th 3: 2 *We* s Timothy, who is our brother *4287*
3: 5 *I* s to find out about your faith. *4287*
2Ti 4:12 *I* s Tychicus to Ephesus. *690*
Heb 1:14 Are not all angels ministering spirits s *690*
Jas 2:25 and s them **off** in a different direction? *1675*
1Pe 1:12 to you by the Holy Spirit s from heaven. *690*
2:14 *who are* s by him to punish those who do *4287*
2Pe 2: 4 when they sinned, but s them **to hell,** *5434*
1Jn 4: 9 He s his one and only Son into the world *690*
4:10 but that he loved us and s his Son as *690*
4:14 the Father *has* s his Son to be the Savior of *690*
Rev 5: 6 which are the seven spirits of God s **out** *690*
22: 6 s his angel to show his servants the things *690*
22:16 *have* s my angel to give you this testimony *4287*

SENTENCE (12) [SENTENCED]

1Ki 20:40 "That is your **s,**" the king of Israel said. 5477
2Ki 25: 6 where s was pronounced on him. 5477
Ps 149: 9 to carry out the s written against them. 5477
Ecc 8:11 the s for a crime is not quickly carried out, 7330
Jer 39: 5 where he pronounced s on him. 5477
52: 9 where he pronounced s on him. 5477
Eze 16:38 *I will* s you *to* the punishment 9149
23:45 But righteous men *will* s them *to* 9149
Lk 23:40 he said, "since you are under the same s? *3210*
Ac 13:28 found no proper ground *for* a **death s,** *2505*
Ro 9:28 For the Lord will carry out his s on earth *3364*
2Co 1: 9 Indeed, in our hearts we felt the s of death. *645*

SENTENCED (3) [SENTENCE]

Jer 26:11 be s *to* death because he has prophesied 5477
26:16 "This man should not be s *to* death! 5477
Lk 24:20 to be s to death, and they crucified him; *3210*

SENTENCES (KJV) See INTRIGUE, RIDDLES

SENTRIES (1)

Ac 12: 6 and s stood guard at the entrance. *5874*

SENUAH (KJV) See HASSENUAH

SEORIM (1)

1Ch 24: 8 the third to Harim, the fourth to **S,** 8556

SEPARATE (26) [SEPARATED, SEPARATES, SEPARATION]

Ge 1: 6 between the waters *to* s water from water." 976
1:14 in the expanse of the sky to s the day from 976
1:18 and to s light from darkness. 976
30:40 Thus he made s flocks for himself and 963+4200
Ex 26:33 The curtain *will* s the Holy Place from 976
Lev 15:31 *'You must* **keep** the Israelites s from things 5692
Nu 16:21 **"S yourselves** from this assembly 976
Jdg 7: 5 **"S** those who lap the water 963+3657+4200
2Sa 14: 6 and no *one was there to* s them. 1068+5911
1Ki 5: 9 There *I will* s them and you can take them 5879
2Ki 15: 5 and he lived in a s house. 2931
2Ch 26:21 He lived in a s house— 2931
Ezr 9: 1 *have* not **kept themselves** s from 976
10:11 **S yourselves** from the peoples around you 976
Eze 42:20 to s the holy from the common. 976
Mt 13:49 The angels will come and s the wicked *928*
19: 6 what God has joined together, *let* man not **s.** *6004*
25:32 and *he will* s the people one from another *928*
Mk 10: 9 what God has joined together, *let* man not **s.** *6004*
Jn 20: 7 by itself, s **from** the linen. *3552+4024*
Ro 8:35 Who *shall* s us from the love of Christ? *6004*
8:39 be able *to* s us from the love of God that is *6004*
1Co 7:10 A wife *must* not s from her husband. *6004*
2Co 6:17 "Therefore come out from them and *be* **s,** *928*
Gal 2:12 *he began to* draw back and s himself from *928*
Eph 2:12 remember that at that time you were **s from** *6006*

SEPARATED (19) [SEPARATE]

Ge 1: 4 and he s the light from the darkness. 976
1: 7 So God made the expanse and s the water 976
2:10 from there *it* **was** s into four headwaters. 7233
25:23 two peoples from within you *will* **be s;** 7233
Nu 16: 9 the God of Israel *has* s you from the rest of 976
1Sa 11:11 The next day Saul s his men 8492
2Ki 2:11 horses of fire appeared and s the two 1068+7233
25: 5 All his soldiers were **s from** him 4946+6584
1Ch 24: 3 David s them **into divisions** 2745
Ezr 6:21 all who *had* s **themselves** from the unclean 976
Ne 4:19 and we *are* widely s from each other along 7233
9: 2 *Those of* Israelite descent *had* **s themselves** 976
10:28 temple servants and all who s **themselves** 976
Isa 59: 2 your iniquities *have* s you from your God; 976
Jer 52: 8 All his soldiers were **s from** him 4946+6584
Eze 46:18 so that none of my people *will be* **s** 7046
Ac 2: 3 to be tongues of fire *that* s and came to rest *1374*
Eph 4:18 in their understanding and s from the life *558*
Phm 1:15 Perhaps the reason *he was* **s from** you for *6004*

SEPARATES (5) [SEPARATE]

Ru 1:17 if anything but death s you and me." 7233
Pr 16:28 and a gossip s close friends. 7233
17: 9 whoever repeats the matter s close friends. 7233
Eze 14: 7 in Israel s **himself** from me and sets up idols 5692
Mt 25:32 from another as a shepherd s the sheep from *928*

SEPARATION (10) [SEPARATE]

Nu 6: 2 a vow of s to the LORD as a Nazirite, 5687
6: 5 vow of s no razor may be used on his head. 5694
6: 5 He must be holy until the period of *his* s to 5693
6: 6 of his s to the LORD he must not go near 5693
6: 7 the **symbol of** his s *to* God is on his head. 5694
6: 8 of his s he is consecrated to the LORD. 5694
6:12 for the period of his s and must bring 5694
6:12 because he became defiled during his **s.** 5694
6:13 when the period of his s is over. 5694
6:21 to the LORD in accordance with his **s,** 5694

SEPHAR (1)

Ge 10:30 stretched from Mesha toward **S,** 6223

SEPHARAD (1)

Ob 1:20 from Jerusalem who are in S will possess 6224

SEPHARVAIM (6) [SEPHARVITES]

2Ki 17:24 and **S** and settled them in the towns 6226
17:31 and Anammelech, the gods of **S.** 6226
18:34 Where are the gods of **S,** Hena and Ivvah? 6226
19:13 the king of Arpad, the king of the city of **S,** 6226
Isa 36:19 Where are the gods of **S?** 6226
37:13 the king of Arpad, the king of the city of **S,** 6226

SEPHARVITES (1) [SEPHARVAIM]

2Ki 17:31 and the S burned their children in the fire 6227

SEPHER See KIRIATH SEPHER

SEPULCHRE, SEPULCHRES (KJV) See GRAVE, GRAVES, TOMB, TOMBS

SERAH (3) [TIMNATH SERAH]

Ge 46:17 Their sister was **S.** 8580
Nu 26:46 (Asher had a daughter named **S.**) 8580
1Ch 7:30 Their sister was **S.** 8580

SERAIAH (18) [SERAIAH'S]

2Sa 8:17 of Abiathar were priests; **S** was secretary; 8588
2Ki 25:18 of the guard took as prisoners **S** 8588
25:23 **S** son of Tanhumeth the Netophathite, 8588
1Ch 4:13 The sons of Kenaz: Othniel and **S.** 8588
4:14 **S** was the father of Joab, 8588
4:35 Jehu son of Joshibiah, the son of **S,** 8588
6:14 Azariah the father of **S,** 8588
6:14 and **S** the father of Jehozadak. 8588
Ezr 2: 2 Nehemiah, **S,** Reelaiah, Mordecai, Bilshan, 8588
7: 1 Ezra son of **S,** the son of Azariah, 8588
Ne 10: 2 **S,** Azariah, Jeremiah, 8588
11:11 **S** son of Hilkiah, 8588
12: 1 of Shealtiel and with Jeshua: **S,** 8588
Jer 36:26 **S** son of Azriel and Shelemiah son 8589
40: 8 the sons of Kareah, **S** son of Tanhumeth, 8588
51:59 to the staff officer **S** son of Neriah, 8588
51:61 He said to **S,** "When you get to Babylon, 8588
52:24 of the guard took as prisoners **S** 8588

SERAIAH'S (1) [SERAIAH]

Ne 12:12 of **S** family, Meraiah; of Jeremiah's, 8588

SERAPHS (2)

Isa 6: 2 Above him were **s,** each with six wings: 8597
6: 6 of the s flew to me with a live coal 8597

SERAPHIMS (KJV) See SERAPHS

SERED (2) [SEREDITE]

Ge 46:14 The sons of Zebulun: **S,** Elon and Jahleel. 6237
Nu 26:26 through **S,** the Seredite clan; 6237

SEREDITE (1) [SERED]

Nu 26:26 through Sered, the **S** clan; 6238

SERGIUS (1) [PAULUS]

Ac 13: 7 an attendant of the proconsul, **S** Paulus. *4950*

SERIOUS (8) [SERIOUSNESS]

Ge 12:17 the LORD inflicted s diseases on Pharaoh 1524
Ex 21:22 but there is no **s injury,** 656
21:23 But if there is **s injury,** 656
Dt 15:21 is lame or blind, or has any s flaw, 8273
Jer 6:14 wound of my people as though *it were* **not s** 7837
8:11 wound of my people as though *it were* **not s** 7837
Ac 18:14 about some misdemeanor or s crime, *4505*
25: 7 bringing many s charges against him, *987*

SERIOUSNESS (1) [SERIOUS]

Tit 2: 7 In your teaching show integrity, s *4949*

SERPENT (17) [SERPENT'S, SERPENTS]

Ge 3: 1 Now the s was more crafty than any of 5729
3: 2 The woman said to the **s,** 5729
3: 4 the s said to the woman. 5729
3:13 The woman said, "The s deceived me, 5729
3:14 So the LORD God said to the **s,** 5729
49:17 Dan will be a s by the roadside, 5729
Job 26:13 his hand pierced the gliding **s.** 5729
Ps 91:13 you will trample the great lion and the **s.** 9490
Isa 14:29 its fruit will be a darting, **venomous s.** 8597
27: 1 Leviathan the gliding **s,** 5729
27: 1 Leviathan the coiling **s;** 5729
Jer 46:22 a fleeing s as the enemy advances in force; 5729
51:34 Like a s he has swallowed us 9490
Am 9: 3 there I will command the s to bite them. 5729
Rev 12: 9 that ancient s called the devil, or Satan, *4058*
12:15 Then from his mouth the s spewed water *4058*
20: 2 He seized the dragon, that ancient **s,** *4058*

SERPENT'S (4) [SERPENT]

Ps 140: 3 They make their tongues as sharp as a **s;** 5729
Isa 65:25 but dust will be the s food. 5729
2Co 11: 3 as Eve was deceived by the s cunning, *899+4058*
Rev 12:14 times and half a time, out of the s reach. *4058*

SERPENTS (3) [SERPENT]

Dt 32:33 Their wine is the venom of **s,** 9490
Job 20:14 it will become the venom of s within him. 7352
20:16 He will suck the poison of **s;** 7352

SERUG (6)

Ge 11:20 he became the father of **S.** 8578
11:21 And after he became the father of **S,** 8578
11:22 When **S** had lived 30 years, 8578
11:23 **S** lived 200 years and had other sons 8578
1Ch 1:26 **S,** Nahor, Terah 8578
Lk 3:35 the son *of* **S,** the son of Reu, *4952*

SERVANT (516) [MAIDSERVANT, MAIDSERVANTS, MANSERVANT, MENSERVANTS, SERVANT'S, SERVANTS, SERVANTS']

Ge 15: 3 so a **s** *in* my household will be my heir." 1201
16: 5 I put my s in your arms, 9148
16: 6 "Your s is in your hands," Abram said. 9148

Ge 16: 8 And he said, "Hagar, s *of* Sarai, 9148
18: 3 my lord, do not pass your s by. 6269
18: 5 now that you have come to your **s."** 6269
18: 7 tender calf and gave it to a s, 5853
19:19 Your s has found favor in your eyes, 6269
24: 2 He said to the chief s in his household, 6269
24: 5 The s asked him, "What if the woman 6269
24: 9 So the s put his hand under the thigh 6269
24:10 s took ten of his master's camels and left, 6269
24:14 the one you have chosen for your s Isaac. 6269
24:17 The s hurried to meet her and said, 6269
24:34 So he said, "I am Abraham's **s.** 6269
24:52 When Abraham's s heard what they said, 6269
24:53 the s brought out gold and silver jewelry 6269
24:59 along with her nurse and Abraham's s 6269
24:61 So the s took Rebekah and left. 6269
24:65 and asked the **s,** "Who is that man 6269
24:65 "He is my master," the s answered. 6269
24:66 Then the s told Isaac all he had done. 6269
26:24 for the sake of my s Abraham." 6269
29:24 And Laban gave his **s girl** Zilpah 9148
29:29 Laban gave his **s girl** Bilhah 9148
30: 4 So she gave him her s Bilhah as a wife. 9148
30: 7 Rachel's s Bilhah conceived again 9148
30:10 Leah's s Zilpah bore Jacob a son. 9148
30:12 Leah's s Zilpah bore Jacob a second son. 9148
32: 4 'Your s Jacob says, I have been staying 6269
32:10 and faithfulness you have shown your **s.** 6269
32:18 'They belong to your s Jacob. 6269
32:20 'Your s Jacob is coming behind us.' " 6269
33: 5 children God has graciously given your **s."** 6269
33:14 So let my lord go on ahead of his **s,** 6269
41:12 a s of the captain of the guard. 6269
43:28 "Your s our father is still alive and well." 6269
44:18 my lord, let your s speak a word to my lord. 6269
44:18 Do not be angry with your **s,** 6269
44:24 When we went back to your s my father, 6269
44:27 "Your s my father said to us, 6269
44:30 with us when I go back to your s my father 6269
44:32 Your s guaranteed the boy's safety 6269
44:33 please let your s remain here 6269
Ex 4:10 past nor since you have spoken to your **s.** 6269
14:31 put their trust in him and in Moses his **s.** 6269
21: 2 "If you buy a Hebrew **s,** 6269
21: 5 "But if the s declares, 6269
21: 6 Then *he will be* his s for life. 6268
21: 7 "If a man sells his daughter as a **s,** 563
21:26 he must let **the** s go free to compensate for 5647S
21:27 he must let **the** s go free to compensate for 5647S
Nu 11:11 "Why have you brought this trouble on your **s?** 6269
12: 7 But this is not true of my s Moses; 6269
12: 8 not afraid to speak against my s Moses?" 6269
14:24 because my s Caleb has a different spirit 6269
Dt 3:24 to show to your s your greatness 6269
15:16 But if your s says to you, NIH
15:17 and he will become your s for life. 6269
15:18 not consider it a hardship to set your s free, 2257S
34: 5 And Moses the s *of* the LORD died there 6269
Jos 1: 1 the death of Moses the s *of* the LORD, 6269
1: 2 "Moses my s is dead. 6269
1: 7 to obey all the law my s Moses gave you; 6269
1:13 "Remember the command that Moses the s 6269
1:15 the s *of* the LORD gave you east of 6269
5:14 What message does my Lord have for his s? 6269
8:31 Moses the s *of* the LORD had commanded 6269
8:33 as Moses the s *of* the LORD had formerly 6269
9:24 LORD your God had commanded his s Moses 6269
11:12 Moses the s *of* the LORD had commanded. 6269
11:15 As the LORD commanded his s Moses, 6269
12: 6 Moses, the s *of* the LORD, 6269
12: 6 Moses the s *of* the LORD gave their land to 6269
13: 8 as he, the s *of* the LORD, had assigned 6269
14: 7 I was forty years old when Moses the s *of* 6269
18: 7 Moses the s *of* the LORD gave it to them." 6269
22: 2 "You have done all that Moses the s *of* 6269
22: 4 to your homes in the land that Moses the s 6269
22: 5 that Moses the s *of* the LORD gave you: 6269
24:29 Joshua son of Nun, the s *of* the LORD, 6269
Jdg 2: 8 Joshua son of Nun, the s *of* the LORD, 6269
7:10 go down to the camp with your s Purah 5853
7:11 and Purah his s went down to the outposts 5853
9:54 So his s ran him through, and he died. 5853
15:18 "You have given your s this great victory. 6269
16:26 Samson said to the s who held his hand, 5853
19: 3 He had with him his s and two donkeys. 5853
19: 9 the man, with his concubine and his **s,** 5853
19:11 the s said to his master, "Come, 5853
Ru 2: 8 Stay here with my **s girls.** 5855
2:13 and have spoken kindly to your **s—** 9148
2:13 the standing of one of your **s girls."** 9148
2:23 the **s girls** *of* Boaz to glean until the barley 5855
3: 2 with whose **s girls** you have been, 5855
3: 9 "I am your s Ruth," she said. 563
1Sa 1:11 and not forget your s but give her a son, 563
1:16 Do not take your s for a wicked woman; 563
1:18 "May your s find favor in your eyes." 9148
2:13 the s *of* the priest would come with 5853
2:15 the s *of* the priest would come and say to 5853
2:16 the s would then answer, "No, NIH
3: 9 'Speak, LORD, for your s is listening.' " 6269
3:10 "Speak, for your s is listening." 6269
9: 5 Saul said to the s who was with him, 5853
9: 6 But the s replied, "Look, in this town NIH
9: 7 Saul said to his s, "If we go, 5853
9: 8 The s answered him again. 5853
1Sa 9:10 "Good," Saul said to his **s.** 5853
9:22 Then Samuel brought Saul and his s into 5853
9:27 "Tell the s to go on ahead of us"— 5853
9:27 and the s did so— NIH
10:14 Now Saul's uncle asked him and his **s,** 5853
17:32 your s will go and fight him." 6269
17:34 "Your s has been keeping his father's sheep. 6269
17:36 Your s has killed both the lion and the bear; 6269
17:58 the son of your s Jesse of Bethlehem." 6269
19: 4 "Let not the king do wrong to his s David; 6269
20: 7 If he says, 'Very well,' then your s is safe. 6269
20: 8 As for you, show kindness to your **s,** 6269
22: 8 that my son has incited my s to lie in wait 6269
22:15 Let not the king accuse your s or any 6269
22:15 for your s knows nothing at all 6269
23:10 your s has heard definitely that Saul plans 6269
23:11 Will Saul come down, as your s has heard? 6269
23:11 O LORD, God of Israel, tell your **s."** 6269
25:24 Please let your s speak to you; 563
25:24 hear what your s has to say. 563
25:25 But as for me, your s, I did not see the men 563
25:27 which your s has brought to my master, 9148
25:31 when the LORD has brought my master success, remember your **s."** 563
25:39 He has kept his s from doing wrong 6269
26:18 he added, "Why is my lord pursuing his **s?** 6269
27: 5 Why should your s live in the royal city 6269
27:12 the Israelites, that he will be my s forever." 6269
28: 2 for yourself what your s can do." 6269
28:22 to your s and let me give you some food 9148
29: 8 "What have you found against your s from 6269
2Sa 3:18 'By my s David I will rescue my people 6269
7: 5 "Go and tell my s David, 'This is what 6269
7: 8 "Now then, tell my s David, 6269
7:19 about the future of the house of your **s.** 6269
7:20 For you know your **s,** O Sovereign LORD. 6269
7:21 and made it known to your **s.** 6269
7:25 concerning your s and his house. 6269
7:26 And the house of your s David will 6269
7:27 you have revealed this to your **s,** saying, 6269
7:27 So your s has found courage 6269
7:28 have promised these good things to your **s.** 6269
7:29 be pleased to bless the house of your **s,** 6269
7:29 the house of your s will be blessed forever." 6269
9: 2 a s of Saul's household named Ziba. 6269
9: 2 "Your **s,"** he replied. 6269
9: 6 "Your **s,"** he replied. 6269
9: 8 "What is your s, that you should notice 6269
9: 9 Then the king summoned Ziba, Saul's **s,** 5853
9:11 "Your s will do whatever my lord 6269
9:11 the king commands his s to do." 6269
11:21 'Also, your s Uriah the Hittite is dead.' " 6269
11:24 Moreover, your s Uriah the Hittite is dead." 6269
13:17 He called his **personal** s and said, 5853+9250
13:18 So his s put her out and bolted the door 9250
13:24 "Your s has had shearers come. 6269
13:35 it has happened just as your s said." 6269
14: 6 I your s had two sons. 9148
14: 7 the whole clan has risen up against your **s;** 9148
14:12 "Let your s speak a word to my lord 9148
14:15 Your s thought, 'I will speak to the king; 9148
14:15 perhaps he will do what his s asks. 563
14:16 Perhaps the king will agree to deliver his s 563
14:17 "And now your s says, 9148
14:19 it was your s Joab who instructed me 6269
14:19 all these words into the mouth of your **s.** 9148
14:20 Your s Joab did this to change 6269
14:22 "Today your s knows that he has found 6269
15: 2 "Your s is from one of the tribes of Israel." 6269
15: 8 While your s was living at Geshur in Aram, 6269
15:21 there will your s be." 6269
15:34 'I will be your **s,** O king; 6269
15:34 I was your father's s in the past, 6269
15:34 but now I will be your **s,'** 6269
17:17 A **s girl** was to go and inform them, 9148
18:29 as Joab was about to send the king's s 6269
18:29 your **s,** but I don't know what it was." 6269
19:19 Do not remember how your s did wrong on 6269
19:20 For I your s know that I have sinned, 6269
19:26 "My lord the king, since I your s am lame, 6269
19:26 But Ziba my s betrayed me. 6269
19:27 he has slandered your s to my lord the king. 6269
19:28 but you gave your s a place 6269
19:35 Can your s taste what he eats and drinks? 6269
19:35 Why should your s be an added burden 6269
19:36 Your s will cross over the Jordan with 6269
19:37 Let your s return, that I may die in my own 6269
19:37 But here is your s Kimham. 6269
20:17 She said, "Listen to what your s has to say." 563
24:10 I beg you, take away the guilt of your **s.** 6269
24:21 "Why has my lord the king come to his **s?"** 6269
1Ki 1:13 did you not swear to me your **s:** 563
1:17 swore to me your s by the LORD your God: 563
1:19 but he has not invited Solomon your **s.** 6269
1:26 But me your **s,** and Zadok the priest, 6269
1:26 and your s Solomon he did not invite. 6269
1:51 not put his s to death with the sword.' " 6269
2:38 Your s will do as my lord the king 6269
3: 6 "You have shown great kindness to your **s,** 6269
3: 7 you have made your s king in place 6269
3: 8 Your s is here among the people 6269
3: 9 So give your s a discerning heart 6269
3:20 from my side while I your s was asleep. 563
8:24 to your s David my father; 6269
8:25 keep for your s David my father the 6269
8:26 promised your s David my father come true. 6269
8:28 the cry and the prayer that your s is praying 6269
1Ki 8:29 so that you will hear the prayer your s prays 6269
8:30 Hear the supplication of your s and 6269
8:53 just as you declared through your s Moses 6269
8:56 good promises he gave through his s Moses. 6269
8:59 that he may uphold the cause of his s and 6269
8:66 for his s David and his people Israel. 6269
11:13 for the sake of David my s and for the sake 6269
11:32 But for the sake of my s David and the city 6269
11:34 of his life for the sake of David my **s,** 6269
11:36 so that David my s may always have a lamp 6269
11:38 as David my s did, I will be with you. 6269
12: 7 "If today you will be a s to these people 6269
14: 8 but you have not been like my s David, 6269
14:18 as the LORD had said through his s 6269
15:29 of the LORD given through his s Ahijah 6269
18: 9 "that you are handing your s over to Ahab 6269
18:12 Yet I your s have worshiped the LORD 6269
18:36 God in Israel and that I am your s 6269
18:43 "Go and look toward the sea," he told his **s.** 5853
18:44 The seventh time the s reported, NIH
19: 3 he left his s there, 5853
20: 9 'Your s will do all you demanded 6269
20:32 "Your s Ben-Hadad says: 6269
20:39 "Your s went into the thick of the battle, 6269
20:40 While your s was busy here and there, 6269
2Ki 4: 1 "Your s my husband is dead, 6269
4: 2 "Your s has nothing there at all," she said, 9148
4:12 He said to his s Gehazi, 5853
4:16 "Don't mislead your **s,** O man of God!" 9148
4:19 His father told a **s,** "Carry him to his mother 5853
4:20 the s had lifted him up and carried him NIH
4:24 She saddled the donkey and said to her **s,** 5853
4:25 the man of God said to his s Gehazi, 5853
4:38 he said to his **s,** "Put on the large pot 5853
4:43 this before a hundred men?" his s asked. 9250
5: 6 "With this letter I am sending my s Naaman 6269
5:15 Please accept now a gift from your **s."** 6269
5:17 said Naaman, "please let me, your **s,** 6269
5:17 your s will never again make burnt offerings 6269
5:18 But may the LORD forgive your s 6269
5:18 may the LORD forgive your s for this." 6269
5:20 the s *of* Elisha the man of God, 5853
5:25 "Your s didn't go anywhere," 6269
6:15 When the s *of* the man of God got up 9250
6:15 what shall we do?" the s asked. 5853
8: 4 the s *of* the man of God, and had said, 5853
8:13 Hazael said, "How could your **s,** 6269
8:19 Nevertheless, for the sake of his s David, 6269
9:36 that he spoke through his s Elijah 6269
10:10 what he promised through his s Elijah." 6269
14:25 spoken through his s Jonah son of Amittai, 6269
16: 7 "I am your s and vassal. 6269
18:12 that Moses the s *of* the LORD commanded. 6269
19:34 for my sake and for the sake of David my **s.** 6269
20: 6 for my sake and for the sake of my s David. 6269
21: 8 that my s Moses gave them." 6269
1Ch 2:34 He had an Egyptian s named Jarha. 6269
2:35 his daughter in marriage to his s Jarha, 6269
6:49 that Moses the s *of* God had commanded. 6269
16:13 O descendants of Israel his **s,** 6269
17: 4 "Go and tell my s David, 'This is what 6269
17: 7 "Now then, tell my s David, 6269
17:17 about the future of the house of your **s.** 6269
17:18 say to you for honoring your **s?** 6269
17:18 For you know your **s,** 6269
17:19 sake of your s and according to your will, 6269
17:23 concerning your s and his house 6269
17:24 And the house of your s David will 6269
17:25 have revealed to your s that you will build 6269
17:25 So your s has found courage to pray to you. 6269
17:26 have promised these good things to your **s.** 6269
17:27 of your **s,** that it may continue forever 6269
21: 8 I beg you, take away the guilt of your **s.** 6269
2Ch 1: 3 which Moses the LORD's s had made in 6269
6:15 to your s David my father; 6269
6:16 keep for your s David my father 6269
6:17 that you promised your s David come true. 6269
6:19 the cry and the prayer that your s is praying 6269
6:20 the prayer your s prays toward this place. 6269
6:21 Hear the supplications of your s and 6269
6:42 the great love promised to David your **s."** 6269
24: 6 the s *of* the LORD and by the assembly 6269
24: 9 to the LORD the tax that Moses the s 6269
32:16 the LORD God and against his s Hezekiah. 6269
Ne 1: 6 the prayer your s is praying before you day 6269
1: 7 decrees and laws you gave your s Moses. 6269
1: 8 the instruction you gave your s Moses, 6269
1:11 to the prayer of this your s and to the prayer 6269
1:11 Give your s success today 6269
2: 5 and if your s has found favor in his sight, 6269
9:14 decrees and laws through your s Moses. 6269
10:29 the Law of God given through Moses the s 6269
Job 1: 8 "Have you considered my s Job? 6269
2: 3 "Have you considered my s Job? 6269
19:16 I summon my **s,** but he does not answer, 6269
42: 7 spoken of me what is right, as my s Job has. 6269
42: 8 to my s Job and sacrifice a burnt offering 6269
42: 8 My s Job will pray for you, 6269
42: 8 spoken of me what is right, as my s Job has. 6269
Ps 18: T Of David the s *of* the LORD. 6269
19:11 By them is your s warned; 6269
19:13 Keep your s also from willful sins; 6269
27: 9 do not turn your s away in anger; 6269
31:16 Let your face shine on your **s;** 6269
35:27 who delights in the well-being of his **s."** 6269
36: T Of David the s *of* the LORD. 6269
69:17 Do not hide your face from your **s;** 6269

Ps 78:70 He chose David his s and took him from 6269
86: 2 save your s who trusts in you. 6269
86: 4 Bring joy to your s, for to you, O Lord, 6269
86:16 grant your strength to your s and save 6269
89: 3 I have sworn to David my s, 6269
89:20 I have found David my s; 6269
89:39 with your s and have defiled his crown in 6269
89:50 Lord, how your s has been mocked, 6269
105: 6 O descendants of Abraham his s, 6269
105:26 He sent Moses his s, and Aaron, 6269
105:42 his holy promise given to his s Abraham. 6269
109:28 but your s will rejoice. 6269
116:16 O LORD, truly I am your s; 6269
116:16 I am your s, the son of your maidservant; 6269
119:17 Do good to your s, and I will live; 6269
119:23 your s will meditate on your decrees. 6269
119:38 Fulfill your promise to your s, 6269
119:49 Remember your word to your s, 6269
119:65 Do good to your s according to your word, 6269
119:76 according to your promise to your s. 6269
119:84 How long must your s wait? 6269
119:124 Deal with your s according to your love 6269
119:125 I am your s; give me discernment 6269
119:135 upon your s and teach me your decrees. 6269
119:140 and your s loves them. 6269
119:176 Seek your s, for I have not forgotten 6269
132:10 For the sake of David your s, 6269
136:22 an inheritance to his s Israel; 6269
143: 2 Do not bring your s into judgment, 6269
143:12 destroy all my foes, for I am your s. 6269
144:10 who delivers his s David from the deadly 6269
Pr 11:29 and the fool will be s to the wise. 6269
12: 9 be a nobody and yet have a s than pretend 6269
14:35 A king delights in a wise s, 6269
14:35 but a shameful s incurs his wrath. NIH
17: 2 A wise s will rule over a disgraceful son, 6269
22: 7 and the borrower is s to the lender. 6269
27:27 and to nourish your **s girls.** 5855
29:19 A s cannot be corrected by mere words; 6269
29:21 If a man pampers his s from youth, 6269
30:10 "Do not slander a s to his master, 6269
30:22 a s who becomes king, 6269
31:15 for her family and portions for her **s girls.** 5855
Ecc 7:21 or you may hear your s cursing you— 6269
10:16 a s and whose princes feast in the morning. 5853
Isa 16:14 a **s bound by contract** would count them, 8502
20: 3 "Just as my s Isaiah has gone stripped 6269
21:16 as a **s bound by contract** would count it, 8502
22:20 "In that day I will summon my s, 6269
24: 2 for master as for s, for mistress as for maid, 6269
37:35 my sake and for the sake of David my s!" 6269
41: 8 "But you, O Israel, my s, Jacob, 6269
41: 9 I said, 'You are my s'; 6269
42: 1 "Here is my s, whom I uphold, 6269
42:19 Who is blind but my s, 6269
42:19 blind like the s *of* the LORD? 6269
43:10 "and my s whom I have chosen, 6269
44: 1 "But now listen, O Jacob, my s, Israel, 6269
44: 2 Do not be afraid, O Jacob, my s, Jeshurun, 6269
44:21 O Jacob, for you are my s, O Israel. 6269
44:21 I have made you, you are my s; 6269
45: 4 For the sake of Jacob my s, 6269
48:20 "The LORD has redeemed his s Jacob." 6269
49: 3 He said to me, "You are my s, Israel, 6269
49: 5 in the womb to be his s to bring Jacob back 6269
49: 6 "It is too small a thing for you to be my s 6269
49: 7 to the s *of* rulers: "Kings will see you 6269
50:10 the LORD and obeys the word of his s? 6269
52:13 See, my s will act wisely; 6269
53:11 by his knowledge my righteous s will justify many, 6269
Jer 2:14 Is Israel a s, a slave by birth? 6269
25: 9 of the north and my s Nebuchadnezzar king 6269
27: 6 to my s Nebuchadnezzar king of Babylon; 6269
30:10 " 'So do not fear, O Jacob my s; 6269
33:21 then my covenant with David my s— 6269
33:22 of David my s and the Levites who minister 6269
33:26 the descendants of Jacob and David my s 6269
43:10 for my s Nebuchadnezzar king of Babylon, 6269
46:27 "Do not fear, O Jacob my s; 6269
46:28 Do not fear, O Jacob my s, 6269
Eze 28:25 which I gave to my s Jacob. 6269
34:23 my s David, and he will tend them; 6269
34:24 and my s David will be prince among them. 6269
37:24 " 'My s David will be king over them, 6269
37:25 in the land I gave to my s Jacob, 6269
37:25 and David my s will be their prince forever. 6269
46:17 **the** s may keep it until the year of freedom; 2257S
Da 6:20 "Daniel, s *of* the living God, has your God, 10523
9:11 the s *of* God, have been poured out on us, 6269
9:17 hear the prayers and petitions of your s. 6269
10:17 How can I, your s, talk with you, my lord? 6269
Hag 2:23 my s Zerubbabel son of Shealtiel,' 6269
Zec 3: 8 I am going to bring my s, the Branch. 6269
Mal 1: 6 "A son honors his father, and a s his master. 6269
4: 4 "Remember the law of my s Moses, 6269
Mt 8: 6 "my s lies at home paralyzed and *4090*
8: 8 just say the word, and my s will be healed. *4090*
8: 9 I say *to* my s, 'Do this,' and he does it." *1528*
8:13 And his s was healed at that very hour. *4090*
10:24 nor a s above his master. *1528*
10:25 and the s like his master. *1528*
12:18 "Here is my s whom I have chosen, *4090*
18:26 "The s fell on his knees before him. *1528*
18:28 "But when that s went out, *1528*
18:29 "His **fellow** s fell to his knees *5281*
18:32 "Then the master called **the** s in. *899S*
Mt 18:32 'You wicked s,' he said, *1528*
18:33 on your **fellow** s just as I had on you?' *5281*
20:26 to become great among you must be your s, *1356*
23:11 The greatest among you will be your s. *1356*
24:45 "Who then is the faithful and wise s, *1528*
24:46 for that s whose master finds him doing so *1528*
24:48 But suppose that s is wicked and says *1528*
24:50 *of* that s will come on a day when he does *1528*
25:21 'Well done, good and faithful s! *1528*
25:23 'Well done, good and faithful s! *1528*
25:26 "His master replied, '*You* wicked, lazy s! *1528*
25:30 And throw that worthless s outside, *1528*
26:51 and struck the s of the high priest, *1528*
26:69 and a **s girl** came to him. *4087*
Mk 9:35 he must be the very last, and the s of all." *1356*
10:43 to become great among you must be your s, *1356*
12: 2 a s to the tenants to collect from them some *1528*
12: 4 Then he sent another s to them; *1528*
14:47 near drew his sword and struck the s of *1528*
14:66 *of* the **s girls** of the high priest came by. *4087*
14:69 When the **s girl** saw him there, *4087*
Lk 1:38 "I am the Lord's s," Mary answered. *1527*
1:48 been mindful of the humble state *of* his s. *1527*
1:54 He has helped his s Israel, *4090*
1:69 for us in the house *of* his s David *4090*
2:29 you now dismiss your s in peace. *1528*
7: 2 There a centurion's s, whom his master *1528*
7: 3 asking him to come and heal his s. *1528*
7: 7 But say the word, and my s will be healed. *4090*
7: 8 I say *to* my s, 'Do this,' and he does it." *1528*
7:10 to the house and found the s well. *1528*
12:43 for that s whom the master finds doing so *1528*
12:45 But suppose the s says to himself, *1528*
12:46 *of* that s will come on a day when he does *1528*
12:47 "That s who knows his master's will *1528*
14:17 At the time of the banquet he sent his s *1528*
14:21 "The s came back and reported this *1528*
14:21 became angry and ordered his s, *1528*
14:22 the s said, 'what you ordered has been done, *1528*
14:23 "Then the master told his s, *1528*
16:13 "No s can serve two masters. *3860*
17: 7 of you had a s plowing or looking after *1528*
17: 7 *to* **the** s when he comes in from the field, *899S*
17: 9 the s because he did what he was told *1528*
19:17 " 'Well done, my good s!' *1528*
19:20 "Then another s came and said, 'Sir, *NIG*
19:22 by your own words, *you* wicked s! *1528*
20:10 At harvest time he sent a s to the tenants *1528*
20:11 He sent another s, *1528*
22:50 one of them struck the s of the high priest, *1528*
22:56 A **s girl** saw him seated there in *4087*
Jn 12:26 and where I am, my s also will be. *1356*
13:16 no s is greater than his master, *1528*
15:15 a s does not know his master's business. *1528*
15:20 'No s is greater than his master.' *1528*
18:10 drew it and struck the high priest's s, *1528*
Ac 3:13 has glorified his s Jesus. *4090*
3:26 When God raised up his s, *4090*
4:25 the mouth *of* your s, our father David: *4090*
4:27 to conspire against your holy s Jesus, *4090*
4:30 through the name *of* your holy s Jesus." *4090*
12:13 and a **s girl** named Rhoda came to answer *4087*
12:20 Blastus, a **trusted personal** s of the king, *2093+3131+3836*
26:16 I have appeared to you to appoint you as a s *5677*
Ro 1: 1 Paul, a s of Christ Jesus, *1528*
13: 4 For he is God's s to do you good. *1356*
13: 4 He is God's s, an agent of wrath *1356*
14: 4 Who are you to judge someone else's s? *3860*
15: 8 For I tell you that Christ has become a s of *1356*
16: 1 a s of the church in Cenchrea. *1356*
Gal 1:10 I would not be a s of Christ. *1528*
Eph 3: 7 I became a s of this gospel by the gift *1356*
6:21 the dear brother and faithful s in the Lord, *1356*
Php 2: 7 taking the very nature *of* a s, *1528*
Col 1: 7 from Epaphras, our dear **fellow** s, *5281*
1:23 and of which I, Paul, have become a s. *1356*
1:25 I have become its s by the commission *1356*
4: 7 a faithful minister and **fellow** s in the Lord. *5281*
4:12 who is one of you and a s of Christ Jesus, *1528*
2Ti 2:24 And the Lord's s must not quarrel; *1528*
Tit 1: 1 Paul, a s of God and an apostle of Jesus Christ for the faith *1528*
Heb 3: 5 Moses was faithful as a s in all God's *2544*
Jas 1: 1 James, a s of God and of the Lord Jesus *1528*
2Pe 1: 1 Simon Peter, a s and apostle of Jesus Christ, *1528*
Jude 1: 1 Jude, a s of Jesus Christ and a brother of James, *1528*
Rev 1: 1 by sending his angel *to* his s John, *1528*
15: 3 and sang the song of Moses the s of God *1528*
19:10 **fellow s with** you and with your brothers *5281*
22: 9 **fellow s with** you and with your brothers *5281*

SERVANT'S (12) [SERVANT]

Ge 19: 2 he said, "please turn aside to your s house. 6269
1Sa 1:11 if you will only look upon your s misery 563
25:28 Please forgive your s offense, 563
26:19 the king listen to his s words. 6269
2Sa 14:22 because the king has granted his s request." 6269
1Ki 8:28 to your s prayer and his plea for mercy, 6269
8:52 "May your eyes be open to your s plea and 6269
2Ki 6:17 Then the LORD opened the s eyes, 5853
2Ch 6:19 to your s prayer and his plea for mercy, 6269
Ps 119:122 Ensure your s well-being; 6269
Mt 18:27 The s master took pity on him, *1528*
Jn 18:10 (The s name was Malchus.) *1528*

SERVANTS (264) [SERVANT]

Ge 21:25 of water that Abimelech's s had seized. 6269
22: 3 with him two of his s and his son Isaac. 5853
22: 5 He said to his s, "Stay here with the donkey 5853
22:19 Then Abraham returned to his s, 5853
26:14 He had so many flocks and herds and s that 6276
26:15 So all the wells that his father's s had dug 6269
26:19 Isaac's s dug in the valley and discovered 6269
26:25 and there his s dug a well. 6269
26:32 That day Isaac's s came and told him about 6269
27:37 and have made all his relatives his s, 6269
32:16 He put them in the care of his s, 6269
32:16 each herd by itself, and said to his s, 6269
39:11 and none of the household s was inside. 408
39:14 she called her household s. 408
41:10 Pharaoh was once angry with his s, 6269
42:10 "Your s have come to buy food. 6269
42:11 Your s are honest men, not spies." 6269
42:13 they replied, "Your s were twelve brothers, 6269
44: 7 be it from your s to do anything like that! 6269
44: 9 If any of your s is found to have it, 6269
44:19 My lord asked his s, 'Do you have a father 6269
44:21 "Then you said to your s, 'Bring him down 6269
44:23 But you told your s, 'Unless your youngest 6269
44:31 Your s will bring the gray head 6269
46:34 'Your s have tended livestock 6269
47: 3 "Your s are shepherds," 6269
47: 4 So now, please let your s settle in Goshen." 6269
50:17 the sins of the s *of* the God of your father." 6269
Ex 5:15 "Why have you treated your s this way? 6269
5:16 Your s are given no straw, yet we are told, 6269
5:16 Your s are being beaten, 6269
32:13 Remember your s Abraham, Isaac and 6269
Lev 25:42 Because the Israelites are my s, 6269
25:55 for the Israelites belong to me as s. 6269
25:55 They are my s, whom I brought out of 6269
Nu 22:22 and his two s were with him. 5853
31:49 "Your s have counted the soldiers 6269
32: 4 and your s have livestock. 6269
32: 5 be given to your s as our possession. 6269
32:25 "We your s will do as our lord commands. 6269
32:27 But your s, every man armed for battle, 6269
32:31 "Your s will do what the LORD has said. 6269
Dt 9:27 Remember your s Abraham, Isaac and 6269
32:36 on his s when he sees their strength is gone 6269
32:43 for he will avenge the blood of his s; 6269
Jos 9: 8 "We are your s," they said to Joshua. 6269
9: 9 "Your s have come from a very distant 6269
9:11 "We are your s; make a treaty with us." ' 6269
9:24 "Your s were clearly told how 6269
10: 6 "Do not abandon your s. 6269
Jdg 3:24 the s came and found the doors of 6269
6:27 of his s and did as the LORD told him. 6269
19:19 and bread and wine for ourselves your s— 6269
1Sa 9: 3 of the s with you and go and look for 5853
12:19 "Pray to the LORD your God for your s so 6269
16:16 Let our lord command his s here to search 6269
16:18 One of the s answered, 5853
17: 8 and are you not the s of Saul? 6269
18:24 Saul's s told him what David had said, 6269
21: 7 Now one of Saul's s was there that day, 6269
21:11 But the s *of* Achish said to him, 6269
21:14 Achish said to his s, "Look at the man! 6269
22:14 "Who of all your s is as loyal as David, 6269
25: 8 Ask your own s and they will tell you. 5853
25: 8 Please give your s and your son David 6269
25:10 Nabal answered David's s, 6269
25:10 Many s are breaking away from their 6269
25:14 One of the s told Nabal's wife Abigail: 5853
25:19 Then she told her s, "Go on ahead; 5853
25:40 His s went to Carmel and said to Abigail, 6269
25:41 and wash the feet of my master's s." 6269
29:10 along with your master's s who have come 6269
2Sa 6:20 of his s as any vulgar fellow would!" 6269
9:10 You and your sons and your s are to farm 6269
9:10 (Now Ziba had fifteen sons and twenty s.) 6269
9:12 the members of Ziba's household were s 6269
11: 9 to the palace with all his master's s and did 6269
11:13 to sleep on his mat among his master's s; 6269
11:24 Then the archers shot arrows at your s from 6269
12:18 David's s were afraid to tell him that 6269
12:19 David noticed that his s were whispering 6269
12:21 His s asked him, "Why are you acting this 6269
13:31 all his s stood by with their clothes torn. 6269
13:36 too, and all his s wept very bitterly. 6269
14:30 Then he said to his s, "Look, 6269
14:30 So Absalom's s set the field on fire. 6269
14:31 "Why have your s set my field on fire?" 6269
15:15 "Your s are ready to do whatever our lord 6269
19:17 and his fifteen sons and twenty s. 6269
1Ki 1: 2 So his s said to him, 6269
1:27 without letting his s know who should sit 6269
1:33 "Take your lord's s with you 6269
8:23 with your s who continue wholeheartedly 6269
8:32 Judge between your s, 6269
8:36 from heaven and forgive the sin of your s, 6269
10: 5 the attending s in their robes, 9250
12: 7 they will always be your s." 6269
2Ki 1:13 and the lives of these fifty men, your s! 6269
2:16 they said, "we your s have fifty able men. 6269
4:22 of the s and a donkey so I can go to the man 5853
5:13 Naaman's s went to him and said, 6269
5:23 He gave them to two of his s, 5853
5:24 from **the** s and put them away in the house. 4392S
6: 3 "Won't you please come with your s?" 6269
9: 7 of my s the prophets and the blood of all 6269

2Ki 9: 7 and the blood of all the LORD's s shed 6269
9:28 His s took him by chariot to Jerusalem 6269
10: 5 "We are your s and we will do anything 6269
10:23 and see that no s *of* the LORD are here 6269
17:13 and that I delivered to you through my s 6269
17:23 as he had warned through all his s 6269
18:26 "Please speak to your s in Aramaic, 6269
21:10 The LORD said through his s the prophets: 6269
23:30 Josiah's s brought his body in a chariot 6269
24: 2 the word of the LORD proclaimed by his s 6269
1Ch 9: 2 priests, Levites and **temple s.** 5987
2Ch 2:10 I will give your s, the woodsmen who cut 6269
2:15 "Now let my lord send his s the wheat 6269
6:14 with your s who continue wholeheartedly 6269
6:23 Judge between your s, 6269
6:27 from heaven and forgive the sin of your s, 6269
9: 4 the attending s in their robes, 9250
10: 7 they will always be your s." 6269
36:20 and they became s to him and his sons until 6269
Ezr 2:43 The **temple s:** the descendants of Ziha, 5987
2:55 The descendants of the s *of* Solomon: 6269
2:58 The **temple** s and the descendants of 5987
2:58 the descendants of the s *of* Solomon 392 6269
2:70 and the **temple** s settled in their own towns, 5987
4:11 To King Artaxerxes, From your s, 10523
5:11 the s of the God of heaven and earth, 10523
7: 7 Levites, singers, gatekeepers and **temple s,** 5987
7:24 **temple** s or other workers at this house 10497
8:17 the **temple** s in Casiphia, 5987
8:20 They also brought 220 of the **temple s—** 5987
9:11 through your s the prophets when you said: 6269
Ne 1: 6 before you day and night for your s, 6269
1:10 "They are your s and your people, 6269
1:11 and to the prayer of your s who delight 6269
2:20 We his s will start rebuilding, 6269
3:26 and the **temple** s living on the hill 5987
3:31 of the **temple** s and the merchants, opposite 5987
7:46 The **temple s:** the descendants of Ziha, 5987
7:57 The descendants of the s *of* Solomon: 6269
7:60 The **temple** s and the descendants of 5987
7:60 the descendants of the s *of* Solomon 392 6269
7:73 the singers and the **temple s,** 5987
10:28 **temple** s and all who separated themselves 5987
11: 3 **temple s** and descendants 5987
11: 3 of Solomon's s lived in the towns of Judah, 6269
11:21 The **temple** s lived on the hill of Ophel, 5987
Job 1: 3 and had a large number of s. 6276
1:15 They put the s to the sword, 5853
1:16 the sky and burned up the sheep and the s, 5853
1:17 They put the s to the sword, 5853
4:18 If God places no trust in his s, 6269
Ps 34:22 The LORD redeems his s; 6269
69:36 the children of his s will inherit it, 6269
79: 2 They have given the dead bodies of your s 6269
79:10 the outpoured blood of your s. 6269
90:13 Have compassion on your s. 6269
90:16 May your deeds be shown to your s, 6269
102:14 For her stones are dear to your s; 6269
102:28 of your s will live in your presence; 6269
103:21 you his s who do his will. 9250
104: 4 flames of fire his s. 9250
105:25 to conspire against his s. 6269
113: 1 Praise, O s *of* the LORD, 6269
134: 1 all you s *of* the LORD who minister 6269
135: 1 praise him, you s *of* the LORD, 6269
135: 9 O Egypt, against Pharaoh and all his s. 6269
135:14 and have compassion on his s. 6269
Isa 36:11 "Please speak to your s in Aramaic, 6269
44:26 of his s and fulfills the predictions 6269
54:17 This is the heritage of the s *of* **the LORD,** 6269
63:17 Return for the sake of your s, 6269
65: 8 so will I do in behalf of my s; 6269
65: 9 and there will my s live. 6269
65:13 "My s will eat, but you will go hungry; 6269
65:13 my s will drink, but you will go thirsty; 6269
65:13 my s will rejoice, but you will be put 6269
65:14 My s will sing out of the joy of their hearts, 6269
65:15 but to his s he will give another name. 6269
66:14 of the LORD will be made known to his s, 6269
Jer 7:25 and again I sent you my s the prophets. 6269
14: 3 The nobles send their s for water; 7582
25: 4 the LORD has sent all his s the prophets 6269
26: 5 not listen to the words of my s the prophets, 6269
29:19 that I sent to them again and again by my s 6269
35:15 Again and again I sent all my s the prophets 6269
44: 4 Again and again I sent my s the prophets, 6269
Eze 38:17 the one I spoke of in former days by my s 6269
46:17 to one of his s, the servant may keep it until 6269
Da 1:12 "Please test your s for ten days: 6269
1:13 and treat your s in accordance with what 6269
2: 4 Tell your s the dream, 10523
2: 7 "Let the king tell his s the dream, 10523
3:26 s *of* the Most High God, come out! 10523
3:28 who has sent his angel and rescued his s! 10523
9: 6 We have not listened to your s the prophets, 6269
9:10 or kept the laws he gave us through his s 6269
Joel 2:29 Even on my s, both **men** and women, 6269
Am 3: 7 without revealing his plan to his s 6269
Zec 1: 6 which I commanded my s the prophets, 6269
Mt 13:27 "The owner's s came to him and said, 'Sir, *1528*
13:28 "The s asked him, 'Do you want us to go *1528*
18:23 to settle accounts with his s. *1528*
18:28 one *of* his **fellow** s who owed him *5281*
18:31 When the other s saw what had happened, *5281*
21:34 he sent his s to the tenants *1528*
21:35 "The tenants seized his s; *1528*
21:36 Then he sent other s to them, *1528*
Mt 22: 3 He sent his s to those who had been invited *1528*
22: 4 "Then he sent some more s and said, *1528*
22: 6 The rest seized his s, mistreated them and *1528*
22: 8 "Then he said *to* his s, *1528*
22:10 So the s went out into the streets *1528*
24:45 in charge of the s **in** his **household** *3859*
24:49 then begins to beat his **fellow** s and to eat *5281*
25:14 who called his s and entrusted his property *1528*
25:19 a long time the master *of* those s returned *1528*
Mk 13:34 He leaves his house and puts his s *1528*
Lk 1: 2 from the first were eyewitnesses and s of *5677*
12:37 those s whose master finds them watching *1528*
12:38 for those s whose master finds them ready, *NIG*
12:42 of his s to give them their food allowance at *2542*
15:22 "But the father said to his s, 'Quick! *1528*
15:26 *of* the s and asked him what was going on. *4090*
17:10 should say, 'We are unworthy s; *1528*
19:13 of his s and gave them ten minas. *1528*
19:15 for the s to whom he had given the money, *1528*
Jn 2: 5 His mother said *to* the s, *1356*
2: 7 Jesus said *to* **the s,** "Fill the jars with water" *899S*
2: 9 the s who had drawn the water knew. *1356*
4:51 his s met him with the news *1528*
15:15 I no longer call you s, *1528*
18:18 and the s and officials stood around *1528*
18:26 One of the high priest's s, *1528*
18:36 my s would fight to prevent my arrest by *5677*
Ac 2:18 Even on my s, both men and women, *1528*
4:29 consider their threats and enable your s *1528*
10: 7 *of* his s and a devout soldier who was one *3860*
16:17 "These men are s of the Most High God, *1528*
Ro 13: 6 for the authorities are God's s, *3313*
1Co 3: 5 Only s, through whom you came *1356*
4: 1 men ought to regard us as s of Christ and *5677*
2Co 4: 5 and ourselves as your s for Jesus' sake. *1528*
6: 4 as s of God we commend ourselves *1356*
11:15 if his s masquerade as servants of *1356*
11:15 servants masquerade as s of righteousness. *1356*
11:23 Are they s of Christ? *1356*
Php 1: 1 Paul and Timothy, s of Christ Jesus, *1528*
Heb 1: 7 his s flames of fire." *3313*
1Pe 2:16 live as s of God. *1528*
Rev 1: 1 to show his s what must soon take place. *1528*
2:20 By her teaching she misleads my s *1528*
6:11 of their **fellow** s and brothers who were to *5281*
7: 3 until we put a seal on the foreheads *of* the s *1528*
10: 7 just as he announced *to* his s the prophets." *1528*
11:18 and for rewarding your s the prophets *1528*
19: 2 He has avenged on her the blood *of* his **s."** *1528*
19: 5 "Praise our God, all you his s, *1528*
22: 3 and his s will serve him. *1528*
22: 6 sent his angel to show his s the things *1528*

SERVANTS' (2) [SERVANT]

Ge 44:16 God has uncovered your s' guilt. 6269
47: 4 and your s' flocks have no pasture. 4200+6269

SERVE (219) [SERVED, SERVES, SERVICE, SERVICES, SERVING, SERVITUDE]

Ge 1:14 and *let them* s as signs to mark seasons 2118
15:14 the nation *they* s **as slaves,** 6268
25:23 and the older *will* s the younger." 6268
27:29 *May* nations s you and peoples bow down 6268
27:40 by the sword and *you will* s your brother. 6268
31:44 and *let it* s as a witness between us." 2118
43:31 controlling himself, said, **"S** the food." 8492
Ex 14:12 *let us* s the Egyptians'? 6268
14:12 for us *to* s the Egyptians than to die in 6268
18:13 to s **as judge** *for* the people, 9149
18:22 *Have them* s **as judges** *for* the people 9149
21: 2 *he is to* s you for six years. 6268
28: 1 so they *may* s me **as priests.** 3912
28: 3 so he *may* s me **as priest.** 3912
28: 4 so they *may* s me **as priests.** 3912
28:41 so *they may* s me **as priests.** 3912
29: 1 so *they may* s me **as priests:** 3912
29:44 and his sons to s me **as priests.** 3912
30:30 so they *may* s me **as priests.** 3912
31:10 for his sons when *they* s **as priests,** 3912
35:19 for his sons when *they* s **as priests."** 3912
40:13 consecrate him so *he may* s me **as priest.** 3912
40:15 so *they may* s me **as priests.** 3912
Lev 7:35 s the LORD **as priests.** 3912
Nu 1: 3 or more *who are able to* s *in* the army. 3655
1:20 *to* s *in* the army were listed by name, 3655
1:22 *to* s *in* the army were counted and listed 3655
1:24 *to* s *in* the army were listed by name, 3655
1:26 *to* s *in* the army were listed by name, 3655
1:28 *to* s *in* the army were listed by name, 3655
1:30 *to* s *in* the army were listed by name, 3655
1:32 *to* s *in* the army were listed by name, 3655
1:34 *to* s *in* the army were listed by name, 3655
1:36 *to* s *in* the army were listed by name, 3655
1:38 *to* s *in* the army were listed by name, 3655
1:40 *to* s *in* the army were listed by name, 3655
1:42 *to* s *in* the army were listed by name, 3655
1:45 *to* s *in* Israel's army were counted 3655
3: 3 who were ordained to s **as priests.** 3912
3:10 Appoint Aaron and his sons *to* s as priests; 9068
4: 3 s *in* the work in the Tent of Meeting. 6913+7372
4:23 s in the work at the Tent of Meeting. 7371+7372
4:30 to s in the work at the Tent of Meeting. 7372
4:35 to s in the work in the Tent of Meeting, 7372
4:39 to s in the work at the Tent of Meeting, 7372
Nu 4:43 to s in the work at the Tent of Meeting, 7372
18: 7 and your sons *may* s as priests in connection 9068
26: 2 or more *who are able to* s **in** the army 3655
Dt 6:13 s him only and take your oaths in his name. 6268
7: 4 from following me *to* s other gods, 6268
7:16 on them with pity and *do* not s their gods, 6268
10:12 to love him, to s the LORD your God 6268
10:20 Fear the LORD your God and s him. 6268
11:13 to love the LORD your God and to s him 6268
12:30 saying, "How *do* these nations s their gods? 6268
13: 4 s him and hold fast to him. 6268
18: 7 like all his fellow Levites who s there in 6641
28:47 not s the LORD your God joyfully 6268
28:48 *you will* s the enemies the LORD sends 6268
Jos 4: 6 to s **as** a sign among you. 2118
9:23 to s as woodcutters and water carriers for 6269
22: 5 to him and to s him with all your heart 6268
23: 7 *You must* not s them or bow down to them. 6268
23:16 go and s other gods and bow down to them, 6268
24:14 the LORD and s him with all faithfulness. 6268
24:14 and s the LORD. 6268
24:15 for yourselves this day whom *you will* s, 6268
24:15 me and my household, *we will* s the LORD." 6268
24:16 to forsake the LORD to s other gods! 6268
24:18 We too *will* s the LORD, 6268
24:19 "You are not able to s the LORD. 6268
24:20 you forsake the LORD and s foreign gods, 6268
24:21 *We will* s the LORD." 6268
24:22 that you have chosen to s the LORD." 6268
24:24 *"We will* s the LORD our God 6268
Jdg 9:28 S the men of Hamor, Shechem's father! 6268
9:28 Why *should* we s Abimelech? 6268
18:19 Isn't it better that you s a tribe and 2118+4200
1Sa 7: 3 to the LORD and s him only, 6268
8:11 will take your sons and **make** them s 4200+8492
12:10 and *we will* s you.' 6268
12:14 If you fear the LORD and s and obey him 6268
12:20 but s the LORD with all your heart. 6268
12:24 and s him faithfully with all your heart; 6268
17: 9 you will become our subjects and s us." 6268
18:17 only s me bravely and fight the battles of 2118
25:41 ready to s you and wash the feet 9148
26:19 and have said, 'Go, s other gods.' 6268
29: 6 I would be pleased *to have* you s 995+2256+3655
2Sa 16:19 Furthermore, whom *should* I **s?** 6268
16:19 Should I not s the son? 4200+7156
16:19 your father, so *I will* s you." 2118+4200+7156
1Ki 9: 6 *to* s other gods and worship them, 6268
9:27 to s in the fleet with Solomon's men. NIH
12: 4 and *we will* s you." 6268
12: 7 to these people and s them and give them 6268
16:31 and began *to* s Baal and worship him. 6268
17: 1 God of Israel, lives, whom *I* s, 4200+6641+7156
18:15 "As the LORD Almighty lives, whom *I* s, 4200+6641+7156
2Ki 3:14 as the LORD Almighty lives, whom *I* s, 4200+6641+7156
4:41 **"S** it to the people to eat." 3668
5:16 "As surely as the LORD lives, whom *I* s, 4200+6641+7156
10:18 Jehu *will* s him much. 6268
17:35 s them or sacrifice to them. 6268
18: 7 the king of Assyria and *did* not s him. 6268
23: 9 of the high places *did* not s at the altar of 6590
25:24 down in the land and s the king of Babylon, 6268
1Ch 12:38 were fighting men *who* **volunteered to s** 6370
23:31 They were to s before the LORD regularly NIH
28: 9 and s him with wholehearted devotion and 6268
2Ch 7:19 *to* s other gods and worship them, 6268
10: 4 and *we will* s you." 6268
13:10 The priests *who* s the LORD are sons 9250
19: 9 *"You must* s faithfully and wholeheartedly 6913
19:11 the Levites *will* **s as officials** before you. 8853
29:11 to stand before him and s him, 9250
30: 8 S the LORD your God, 6268
33:16 and told Judah to s the LORD, 6268
34:33 **had** all who were present in Israel s 6641
35: 3 Now s the LORD your God 6268
Ne 4:22 so *they can* s us as guards by night 2118
9:35 not s you or turn from their evil ways. 6268
Est 1: 8 to s each man what he wished. 6913
Job 21:15 Who is the Almighty, that *we should* s him? 6268
36:11 If they obey and s him, 6268
39: 9 "Will the wild ox consent *to* s you? 6268
Ps 2:11 S the LORD with fear and rejoice 6268
22:30 Posterity *will* s him; 6268
72:11 down to him and all nations *will* s him. 6268
119:91 for all things s you. 6269
Pr 22:29 *He will* s before kings; 3656
22:29 *he will* not s before obscure men. 3656
Isa 56: 6 to the LORD to s him, to love the name of 9250
60: 7 the rams of Nebaioth *will* s you; 9250
60:10 and their kings *will* s you. 9250
60:12 or kingdom that *will* not s you will perish; 6268
Jer 2:20 you said, *'I will* not s you!' 6268
5:19 so now *you will* s foreigners in a land 6268
11:10 They have followed other gods to s them. 6268
13:10 after other gods to s and worship them, will 6268
15:19 I will restore you *that you may* s me; 4200+6641+7156
16:13 there *you will* s other gods day and night, 6268
25: 6 Do not follow other gods to s 6268
25:11 and these nations *will* s the king 6268
27: 7 All nations *will* s him and his son 6268
27: 8 not s Nebuchadnezzar king of Babylon 6268
27: 9 *'You will* not s the king of Babylon.' 6268
27:10 *that will only* s *to* **remove** you **far** AIT

Jer 27:11 the yoke of the king of Babylon and s him, 6268
27:12 s him and his people, and you will live. 6268
27:13 that will not s the king of Babylon? 6268
27:14 'You will not s the king of Babylon,' 6268
27:17 S the king of Babylon, and you will live. 6268
28:14 to make them s Nebuchadnezzar king 6268
28:14 and they will s him. 6268
30: 9 they will s the LORD their God 6268
35:15 do not follow other gods to s them. 6268
35:19 fail to have a man to s me.' " 4200+6641+7156
40: 9 "Do not be afraid to s the Babylonians," 6268
40: 9 down in the land and s the king of Babylon, 6268
Eze 20:32 who s wood and stone." 9250
20:39 Go and s your idols, every one of you! 6268
20:40 the entire house of Israel will s me, 6268
27:25 of Tarshish s as carriers for your wares. AIT
41: 6 the wall of the temple to s as supports for 2118
44:11 They may s in my sanctuary, 2118
44:11 and stand before the people and s them. 9250
44:13 They are not to come near to s me as priests 3912
44:24 the priests are to s as judges and decide it 6641
45: 5 Levites, who s in the temple, 9250
47:12 Their fruit will s for food and their leaves 2118
Da 1: 4 and qualified to s in the king's palace. 6641
3:12 They neither s your gods nor worship 10586
3:14 that you do not s my gods or worship 10586
3:17 the God we s is able to save us from it, 10586
3:18 that we will not s your gods or worship 10586
3:28 to give up their lives rather than s 10586
6:16 "May your God, whom you s continually, 10586
6:20 has your God, whom you s continually, 10586
Zep 3: 9 the LORD and s him shoulder to shoulder. 6268
Zec 4:14 "These are the two who are anointed to s the Lord 6584+6641
Mal 3:14 "You have said, 'It is futile to s God. 6268
3:18 between those who s God 6268
Mt 4:10 the Lord your God, and s him only.' " 3302
6:24 "No one can s two masters. 1526
6:24 You cannot s both God and Money. 1526
20:28 to be served, but to s, and to give his life 1354
Mk 10:45 to be served, but to s, and to give his life 1354
Lk 1:74 and to enable us to s him without fear 3302
4: 8 the Lord your God and s him only.' " 3302
12:37 he will dress himself to s, 4322
16:13 "No servant can s two masters. 1526
16:13 You cannot s both God and Money." 1526
Ac 7: 7 I will punish the nation they s as slaves,' 1526
26: 7 to see fulfilled as they earnestly s God day 3302
27:23 of the God whose I am and whom I s stood 3302
Ro 1: 9 God, whom I s with my whole heart 3302
7: 6 from the law so that we s in the new way of 1526
9:12 "The older will s the younger." 1526
12: 7 If it is serving, let him s; 1355
1Co 9:13 and those who s at the altar share 4204
2Co 11: 8 receiving support from them so as to s you. 1355
13: 4 we will live with him to s you. 1650
Gal 5:13 rather, s one another in love. 1526
Eph 6: 7 S wholeheartedly, as if you were serving 1526
1Th 1: 9 from idols to s the living and true God, 1526
1Ti 3:10 let them s as deacons. 1354
6: 2 Instead, they are to s them even better, 1526
2Ti 1: 3 I thank God, whom I s, 3302
Heb 1:14 to s those who will inherit salvation? 1355
8: 5 They s at a sanctuary that is a copy 3302
9:14 so that we may s the living God! 3302
1Pe 4:10 Each one should use whatever gift he has received to s others, 1354
5: 2 not greedy for money, but eager to s; NIG
Jude 1: 7 They s as an example of those who suffer 4618
Rev 1: 6 to be a kingdom and priests to s his God NIG
5:10 to be a kingdom and priests to s our God, NIG
7:15 the throne of God and s him day and night 3302
22: 3 and his servants will s him. 3302

SERVED (70) [SERVE]

Ge 29:20 So Jacob s seven years to get Rachel, 6268
29:25 I s you for Rachel, didn't I? 6268
30:26 wives and children, for whom I have s you, 6268
43:32 They s him by himself, 8492
43:34 portions were s to them from Joseph's table, 5951
Ex 18:26 They s as judges for the people at all times. 9149
38: 8 the women who s at the entrance to the Tent of Meeting. 7371+7371
Nu 3: 4 and Ithamar s as priests during the lifetime 3912
4:37 of all those in the Kohathite clans who s in 6268
4:41 in the Gershonite clans who s at the Tent 6268
26:10 And they s as a warning sign. 2118
Jos 24:15 whether the gods your forefathers s beyond 6268
24:31 Israel s the LORD throughout the lifetime 6268
Jdg 2: 7 The people s the LORD throughout 6268
2:11 in the eyes of the LORD and s the Baals. 6268
2:13 because they forsook him and s Baal and 6268
3: 6 daughters to their sons, and s their gods. 6268
3: 7 the LORD their God and s the Baals and 6268
10: 6 They s the Baals and the Ashtoreths, 6268
10: 6 forsook the LORD and no longer s him, 6268
10:13 But you have forsaken me and s other gods, 6268
10:16 of the foreign gods among them and s 6268
1Sa 2:22 and how they slept with the women who s 7371
7: 4 Baals and Ashtoreths, and s the LORD only. 6268
8: 2 and they s at Beersheba. 9149
12:10 we have forsaken the LORD and s the Baals 6268
2Sa 12:20 and at his request they s him food, 8492
13: 9 Then she took the pan and s him the bread, 3668
16:19 Just as I s your father, so I will serve you." 6268
1Ki 11:17 some Edomite officials who had s his father. 6269
1Ki 12: 6 the elders who had s his father Solomon 907+6641+7156
22:53 He s and worshiped Baal and provoked 6268
2Ki 5: 2 and she s Naaman's wife. 2118+4200+7156
10:18 "Ahab s Baal a little; 6268
17:33 also s their own gods in accordance with 6268
1Ch 6:10 of Azariah (it was he who s as priest in 3912
6:33 Here are the men who s, 6641
6:39 who s at his right hand: 6641
23:24 or more who s in the temple of the LORD. 6275
24: 2 so Eleazar and Ithamar s as the priests. 3912
27: 1 and their officers, who s the king in all 9250
2Ch 10: 6 the elders who had s his father Solomon 4200+6641+7156
17:19 These were the men who s the king, 9250
35:13 caldrons and pans and s them quickly to all 8132
Ne 12:26 They s in the days of Joiakim son NIH
Est 1: 7 Wine was s in goblets of gold, 9197
1:10 the seven eunuchs who s him— 9250
Jer 5:19 and s foreign gods in your own land, 6268
8: 2 and s and which they have followed 6268
16:11 'and followed other gods and s 6268
22: 9 and have worshiped and s other gods.' " 6268
34:14 After he has s you six years, 6268
52:12 who s the king of Babylon, 4200+6641+7156
Eze 27: 7 was your sail and s as your banner; 2118
27:10 Lydia and Put s as soldiers in your army. 2118
44:12 But because they s them in the presence 9250
Hos 12:12 Israel s to get a wife, 6268
Mt 20:28 as the Son of Man did not come to be s, 1354
Mk 10:45 even the Son of Man did not come to be s, 1354
Jn 12: 2 Martha s, while Lazarus was among those 1354
13: 2 The evening meal was being s, NIG
Ac 1:16 Judas, who s as guide for those who 1181
13:36 "For when David had s God's purpose 5676
17:25 And he is not s by human hands, 2543
20:19 I s the Lord with great humility and 1526
Ro 1:25 and s created things rather than the Creator 3302
Php 1:12 that what has happened to me has really s 2262
2:22 with his father he has s with me in the work 1526
1Ti 3:13 Those who have s well gain an excellent 1354
Heb 7:13 and no one from that tribe has ever s at 4668

SERVES (11) [SERVE]

Dt 15:12 sells himself to you and s you six years, 6268
Mal 3:17 a man spares his son who s him. 6268
Lk 22:26 and the one who rules like the one who s. 1354
22:27 one who is at the table or the one who s? 1354
22:27 But I am among you as one who s. 1354
Jn 12:26 Whoever s me must follow me; 1354
12:26 My Father will honor the one who s me. 1354
Ro 14:18 because anyone who s Christ in this way 1526
1Co 9: 7 Who s as a soldier at his own expense? 5129
Heb 8: 2 and who s in the sanctuary, 3313
1Pe 4:11 If anyone s, he should do it with the strength 1354

SERVICE (76) [SERVE]

Ge 41:46 when he entered the s of Pharaoh king of Egypt. 4200+6641+7156
50: 2 Then Joseph directed the physicians in his s 6269
Ex 27:19 All the other articles used in the s of 6275
30:16 the Israelites and use it for the s of the Tent 6275
35:21 for all its s, and for the sacred garments. 6275
Nu 4:24 the s of the Gershonite clans as they work 6275
4:26 and all the equipment used in its s. 6275
4:27 All their s, whether carrying or doing 6275
4:28 the s of the Gershonite clans at the Tent 6275
4:31 as they perform s at the Tent of Meeting: 6275
4:33 the s of the Merarite clans as they work at 6275
8:25 retire from their regular s and work 6275+7372
18: 7 I am giving you the s of the priesthood as 6275
Dt 15:18 to set your servant free, because his s 6269
Jos 18: 7 because the priestly s of the LORD is their 3914
1Sa 14:52 or brave man, he took him into his s. 665
16:21 David came to Saul and entered his s. 4200+6641+7156
16:22 "Allow David to remain in my s, 4200+7156
1Ki 8:11 And the priests could not perform their s 9250
2Ki 25:14 the bronze articles used in the temple s. 9250
1Ch 5:18 men ready for military s— 3655+7372
9:28 of the articles used in the temple s; 6275
23:26 or any of the articles used in its s." 6275
23:28 to help Aaron's descendants in the s of 6275
23:32 for the s of the temple of the LORD. 6275
25: 1 the list of the men who performed this s: 6275
26:30 of the LORD and for the king's s. 6275
28: 1 the commanders of the divisions in the s of 9250
28:13 well as for all the articles to be used in its s. 6275
28:14 used in various kinds of s, 2256+6275+6275
28:14 used in various kinds of s: 2256+6275+6275
28:20 until all the work for the s of the temple of 6275
2Ch 5:14 not perform their s because of the cloud, 9250
17:16 volunteered himself for the s of the LORD, 5605
24:14 articles for the s and for the burnt offerings, 9250
25: 5 there were three hundred thousand men ready for military s, 3655+7372
29:35 So the s of the temple of the LORD 6275
30:22 who showed good understanding of the s of 4200
31:21 that he undertook in the s of God's temple 6275
35: 2 to their duties and encouraged them in the s 6275
35:10 The s was arranged and the priests stood 6275
35:16 the entire s of the LORD was carried out 6275
Ezr 6:18 the Levites in their groups for the s of God 10525
Ne 10:32 of a shekel each year for the s of the house 6275
11:22 who were the singers responsible for the s 4856
Ne 12:45 They performed the s of their God and 5466
12:45 of their God and the s of purification, 5466
13:10 for the s had gone back to their own fields. 4856
Job 7: 1 "Does not man have hard s on earth? 7372
14:14 of my hard s I will wait for my renewal 7372
Isa 40: 2 to her that her hard s has been completed, 7372
41: 2 calling him in righteousness to his s? 8079
Jer 52:18 the bronze articles used in the temple s. 9250
Eze 44:16 to minister before me and perform my s. 5466
Da 1: 5 they were to enter the king's s. 4200+6641+7156
1:19 so they entered the king's s. 4200+6641+7156
Lk 1:23 When his time of s was completed, 3311
9:62 and looks back is fit for s in the kingdom 2310
12:35 "Be dressed ready for s and 3836+4019+4322
Jn 16: 2 kills you will think he is offering a s to God. 3301
Ro 15:17 I glory in Christ Jesus in my s to God. NIG
15:25 I am on my way to Jerusalem in the s of 1354
15:31 that my s in Jerusalem may be acceptable to 1355
1Co 12: 5 There are different kinds of s, 1355
16:15 and they have devoted themselves to the s 1355
2Co 8: 4 with us for the privilege of sharing in this s 1355
8:18 by all the churches for his s to the gospel. NIG
9: 1 to write to you about this s to the saints. 1355
9:12 This s that you perform 1355+3311+3836+4047
9:13 the s by which you have proved yourselves, 1355
Eph 4:12 to prepare God's people for works of s, 1355
Php 2:17 the sacrifice and s coming from your faith, 3311
1Ti 1:12 me faithful, appointing me to his s. 1355
6: 2 those who benefit from their s are believers, 2307
Heb 2:17 a merciful and faithful high priest in s NIG
Rev 2:19 your s and perseverance, 1355

SERVICES (3) [SERVE]

Ex 14: 5 let the Israelites go and have lost their s!" 6268
Ne 12: 9 stood opposite them in the s. 5466
13:14 done for the house of my God and its s. 5464

SERVILE (KJV) See REGULAR

SERVING (28) [SERVE]

Ex 39:41 the garments for his sons when s as priests. 3912
Nu 4:47 to do the work of s and carrying the Tent 6275
18:21 in return for the work they do while s at 6275
Dt 28:14 following other gods and s them. 6268
Jos 20: 6 until the death of the high priest who is s at 2118
24:15 if s the LORD seems undesirable to you, 6268
Jdg 2:19 and s and worshiping them. 6268
10:10 forsaking our God and s the Baals." 6268
1Sa 8: 8 forsaking me and s other gods, 6268
1Ki 9: 9 other gods, worshiping and s them— 6268
12: 8 who had grown up with him and were s him. 4200+6641+7156
2Ki 17:41 they were s their idols. 6268
1Ch 28:13 the work of s in the temple of the LORD, 6275
2Ch 7:22 other gods, worshiping and s them— 6268
10: 8 who had grown up with him and were s him. 4200+6641+7156
12: 8 the difference between s me and serving 6275
12: 8 the difference between serving me and s 6275
Eze 44:11 of the gates of the temple and s in it; 9250
48:11 who were faithful in s me and did 5466
Lk 1: 8 on duty and he was s as priest before God, 2634
Ro 12: 7 If it is s, let him serve; 1355
12:11 but keep your spiritual fervor, s the Lord. 1526
16:18 For such people are not s our Lord Christ, 1526
Eph 6: 7 as if you were s the Lord, not men, NIG
Col 3:24 It is the Lord Christ you are s. 1526
2Ti 2: 4 No one s as a soldier gets involved 5129
1Pe 1:12 that they were not s themselves but you, 1354
5: 2 that is under your care, s as overseers— 2174

SERVITOR (KJV) See SERVANT

SERVITUDE (1) [SERVE]

Ge 47:21 Joseph reduced the people to s, 4200+6268+6269

SET (610) [SETS, SETTING, SETTINGS]

Ge 1:17 God s them in the expanse of the sky 5989
8: 9 the dove could find no place to s its feet 4955
9:13 I have s my rainbow in the clouds, 5989
11:31 and together they s out from Ur of 3655
12: 4 when he s out from Haran. 3655
12: 5 and they s out for the land of Canaan, 3655
12: 9 Then Abram s out and continued toward 5825
13:11 of the Jordan and s out toward the east. 5825
15:17 When the sun had s and darkness had fallen, 995
18: 8 and s these before them. 5989
21:14 He s them on her shoulders and 8492
21:28 Abraham s apart seven ewe lambs from 5893
21:29 of these seven ewe lambs you have s apart 5893
22: 3 he s out for the place God had told him 2143
22:19 and they s off together for Beersheba. 2143
24:10 He s out for Aram Naharaim 7756
24:33 Then food was s before him, but he said, 8492
28:10 Jacob left Beersheba and s out for Haran. 2143
28:11 for the night because the sun had s. 995
28:18 and s it up as a pillar and poured oil on top 8492
28:22 and this stone that I have s up as a pillar 8492
30:40 s apart the young of the flock by themselves, 7233
31:45 So Jacob took a stone and s it up as a pillar. 8123
31:51 and here is this pillar I have s up 3721
33:20 There he s up an altar and called it 5893

Ge 34: 8 "My son Shechem *has* his heart **s** on your 3137
35: 5 Then *they* **s out,** and the terror of God 5825
35:14 Jacob **s up** a stone pillar at the place 5893
35:20 Over her tomb Jacob **s up** a pillar, 5893
43: 9 not bring him back to you and **s** him here 3657
46: 1 So Israel **s out** with all that was his, 5825
49:21 a doe **s free** that bears beautiful fawns. 8938
Ex 9: 5 The LORD **s** a time and said, 8492
9:17 You still **s yourself** against my people 6147
16: 1 The whole Israelite community **s out** from 5825
17: 1 The whole Israelite community **s out** from 5825
19: 2 After *they* **s out** from Rephidim, 5825
19: 7 the people and **s** before them all the words 8492
19:23 the mountain and **s** it **apart as holy.'** " 7727
21: 1 the laws *you are to* **s** before them: 8492
24: 4 and **s** up twelve stone pillars representing NIH
24:13 Then Moses **s out** with Joshua his aide, 7756
25:37 "Then make its seven lamps and **s** them **up** 6590
26: 4 along the edge of the end curtain in one **s,** 2501
26: 4 the same with the end curtain in the other **s.** 4678
26: 5 on the end curtain of the other **s,** 4678
26: 9 five of the curtains together **into one s** 963+4200
26: 9 and the other six **into another s.** 963+4200
26:10 the edge of the end curtain in one **s** and also 2501
26:10 the edge of the end curtain in the other **s.** 2501
26:17 two projections **s parallel** to each other. 8917
26:30 **"S up** the tabernacle according to the plan 7756
31: 5 to cut and **s** stones, to work in wood, 4848
32:29 "You *have been* **s apart** to the LORD 3338+4848
35:33 to cut and **s** stones, to work in wood, 4848
36:11 along the edge of the end curtain in one **s,** 4678
36:11 with the end curtain in the other **s.** 4678
36:12 on the end curtain of the other **s,** 4678
36:16 into *one* **s** and the other six into another set. 963
36:16 into one set and the other six into *another* **s.** 963
36:17 the edge of the end curtain in one **s** and also 4678
36:17 the edge of the end curtain in the other **s.** 2501
36:22 with two projections **s parallel** 8917
40: 2 **"S up** the tabernacle, the Tent of Meeting, 7756
40: 4 Bring in the table and **s out** what belongs 6885
40: 4 bring in the lampstand and **s up** its lamps. 6590
40: 8 **S up** the courtyard around it and put 8492
40:17 So the tabernacle **was s up** on the first day 7756
40:18 When Moses **s up** the tabernacle, 7756
40:18 inserted the crossbars and **s up** the posts. 7756
40:23 **s out** the bread on it before the LORD, 6885+6886
40:25 and **s up** the lamps before the LORD, 6590
40:29 *He* **s** the altar of burnt offering near 8492
40:33 Then Moses **s up** the courtyard around 7756
40:36 above the tabernacle, *they would* **s out;** 5825
40:37 *they did* not **s out—**until the day it lifted. 5825
Lev 8: 9 on Aaron's head and **s** the gold plate, 8492
17:10 *I will* **s** my face against that person who 5989
20: 3 I *will* **s** my face against that man 5989
20: 5 I *will* **s** my face against that man 8492
20: 6 " *'I will* **s** my face against the person 5989
20:24 who *has* **s** you **apart** from the nations. 976
20:25 those which *I have* **s apart** as unclean 976
20:26 and *I have* **s** you **apart** from the nations to 976
24: 6 **S** them in two rows, six in each row, 8492
24: 8 *to be* **s out** before the LORD regularly, 6885
26: 1 " 'Do not make idols or **s up** an image or 7756
26:17 *I will* **s** my face against you so 5989
27: 3 **s** the value of a male between the ages 2118
27: 4 **s** her value at thirty shekels. 2118
27: 5 **s** the value of a male at twenty shekels and 2118
27: 6 **s** the value of a male at five shekels 2118
27: 7 **s** the value of a male at fifteen shekels and 2118
27: 8 who *will* **s** *the* **value** *for* him according 6885
27:16 its value *is to be* **s** according to 2118
27:17 the value that has been **s** remains. NIH
27:18 and its **s value** will be reduced. 6886
27:25 *to be* **s** according to the sanctuary shekel, 2118
27:27 he may buy it back at its **s value,** 6886
27:27 it is to be sold at its **s value.** 6886
Nu 1:51 and whenever the tabernacle *is to be* **s up,** 2837
1:52 The Israelites *are to* **s** up their **tents** 2837
1:53 *to* **s up** their **tents** around the tabernacle of 2837
2: 9 *They will* **s out** first. 5825
2:16 *They will* **s out** second. 5825
2:17 of the Levites *will* **s out** in the middle of 5825
2:17 *They will* **s out** in the same order 5825
2:24 *They will* **s out** third. 5825
2:31 *They will* **s out** last, under their standards. 5825
2:34 and that is the way *they* **s out,** 5825
3:13 *I* **s apart** for myself every firstborn 7727
8: 2 'When you **s up** the seven lamps, 6590
8: 3 *he* **s up** the lamps so that they faced forward 6590
8:14 In this way *you are to* **s** the Levites **apart** 976
8:17 *I* **s** them **apart** for myself. 7727
9:15 the Tent of the Testimony, *was* **s up,** 7756
9:17 from above the Tent, the Israelites **s out;** 5825
9:18 the LORD's command the Israelites **s out,** 5825
9:19 the LORD's order and *did* not **s out.** 5825
9:20 and then at his command *they would* **s out.** 5825
9:21 when it lifted in the morning, *they* **s out.** 5825
9:21 whenever the cloud lifted, *they* **s out.** 5825
9:22 would remain in camp and not **s out;** 5825
9:22 but when it lifted, *they would* **s out.** 5825
9:23 and at the LORD's command *they* **s out.** 5825
10: 2 and for **having** the camps **s** out. 5023
10: 5 the tribes camping on the east *are to* **s out.** 5825
10: 6 the camps on the south *are to* **s out.** 5825
10:12 the Israelites **s out** from the Desert of Sinai 5825
10:13 *They* **s out,** this first time, 5825
10:17 and Merarites, who carried it, **s out.** 5825
10:21 Kohathites **s out,** carrying the holy things. 5825
Nu 10:21 *to be* **s up** before they arrived. 7756
10:25 the divisions of the camp of Dan **s out,** 5825
10:28 for the Israelite divisions as *they* **s out.** 5825
10:33 So *they* **s out** from the mountain of 5825
10:34 over them by day when they **s out** from 5825
10:35 Whenever the ark **s out,** Moses said, 5825
14:25 and **s out** *toward* the desert along the route 5825
16: 3 Why then *do you* **s yourselves** above 5951
18:11 *whatever* is **s aside** *from* the gifts of all 9556
18:16 at the redemption **price s** *at* five shekels 6886
18:19 Whatever is **s aside** *from* the holy offerings 9556
20:22 The whole Israelite community **s out** 5825
21:11 Then *they* **s out** from Oboth and camped 5825
21:13 *They* **s out** from there and camped 5825
24:21 your nest *is* **s** in a rock; 8492
31:28 **s apart** as tribute for the LORD one out 8123
31:42 which Moses **s apart** from that of 2936
33: 3 The Israelites **s out** from Rameses on 5825
Dt 1:13 and *I will* **s** them over you." 8492
1:19 *we* **s out** from Horeb and went toward 5825
1:36 and his descendants the land *he* **s** *his* **feet** 2005
1:40 and **s out** toward the desert *along* the route 5825
2: 1 and **s out** toward the desert *along* the route 5825
2:24 *"S* **out** now and cross the Arnon Gorge. AIT
4:41 Moses **s aside** three cities east of the Jordan, 976
4:44 the law Moses **s** before the Israelites. 8492
5:21 not **s** *your* **desire on** your neighbor's house 203
7: 7 The LORD *did* not **s** *his* **affection** on you 3137
7:26 will be **s apart for destruction.** 3051
7:26 for it is **s apart for destruction.** 3051
10: 8 At that time the LORD **s apart** the tribe 976
10:15 Yet the LORD **s** *his* **affection** on your 3137
11:24 Every place where *you* **s** your foot will 2005
14:22 **Be sure to s aside a tenth** of all 6923+6923
15:18 a hardship *to* **s** your servant **free,** 2930+8938
15:19 **S apart** for the LORD your God every firstborn male 7727
16:21 not **s up** any wooden Asherah pole beside 5749
17:14 *"Let us* **s** a king over us like all the nations 8492
19: 2 then **s aside** for yourselves three cities 976
19: 7 This is why I command you *to* **s aside** 976
19: 9 then you are to **s** aside three more cities. NIH
19:14 move your neighbor's boundary stone **s up** 1487
26: 4 from your hands and **s** it **down** in front of 5663
26:19 He has declared that he *will* **s** you 5989
27: 2 **s up** some large stones and coat them 7756
27: 4 **s up** these stones on Mount Ebal, 7756
27: 8 of this law on these stones you have **s** up." NIH
28: 1 the LORD your God *will* **s** you high 5989
28:36 and the king *you* **s** over you to 7756
30: 1 and curses *I have* **s** before you come 5989
30:15 *I* **s** before you today life and prosperity, 5989
30:19 that *I have* **s** before you life and death, 5989
32: 8 *he* **s up** boundaries for the peoples 5893
32:22 and its harvests and **s afire** the foundations 4265
Jos 1: 3 every place where *you* **s** your foot, 2005
2: 7 So the men **s out in pursuit** of the spies *on* 8103
3: 1 the Israelites **s out** from Shittim and went 5825
3:13 **s** foot in the Jordan, its waters flowing 5663
4: 9 Joshua **s up** the twelve stones that had been 7756
4:18 No sooner *had* they **s** their feet on 5998
4:20 And Joshua **s up** at Gilgal 7756
6:26 at the cost of his youngest *will he* **s up** 5893
8: 2 **S** an ambush behind the city." 8492
8: 4 You *are to* **s an ambush** behind the city. 741
8: 8 When you have taken the city, **s** it **on fire.** 836+928+2021+3675
8:11 *They* **s up camp** north of Ai, 2837
8:12 and **s** them in ambush between Bethel 8492
8:14 that an **ambush** *had been* **s** against him 741
8:19 and captured it and quickly **s** it **on fire.** 836+928+2021+3675
9:17 So the Israelites **s out** and on 5825
16: 9 that were **s aside** for the Ephraimites within 4426
18: 1 of the Israelites gathered at Shiloh and **s up** 8905
20: 7 So *they* **s apart** Kedesh in Galilee in 7727
24:26 a large stone and **s** it **up** there under the oak 7756
Jdg 1: 8 They put the city to the sword and **s** it 8938
6:18 and bring my offering and **s** it before you." 5663
8:33 *They* **s up** Baal-Berith as their god 8492
9:25 to him these citizens of Shechem **s** men on 8492
9:34 and all his troops **s out** by night and took 7756
9:43 into three companies and **s an ambush** in 741
9:49 against the stronghold and **s** it **on fire** over 836+928+2021+3675
9:52 the entrance to the tower to **s** it **on fire,** 836+928+2021+8596
13: 5 to be a **Nazirite,** *s apart to* God from birth, AIT
16:17 "because I have been a **Nazirite** *s apart* AIT
16:21 they **s** *him to* grinding in the prison. 2118
18:11 **s out** from Zorah and Eshtaol. 5825
18:12 On their way *they* **s up camp** 2837
18:30 the Danites **s up** for themselves the idols, 7756
19:14 sun **s** as they neared Gibeah in Benjamin. 995
19:28 the man put her on his donkey and **s out** 2143
20:29 Then Israel **s** an ambush around Gibeah. 8492
20:36 on the ambush *they had* **s** near Gibeah. 8492
20:48 the towns they came across *they* **s** on fire. 8938
Ru 1: 7 where she had been living and **s out** on 2143
1Sa 2: 8 upon them he *has* **s** the world. 8883
4:15 and whose eyes *were* **s** so that he could 7756
5: 2 into Dagon's temple and **s** it beside Dagon. 3657
6:18 on which *they* **s** the ark of the LORD, 5663
7:12 and **s** it up between Mizpah and Shen. 8492
9:10 So *they* **s out** for the town where the man 2143
9:24 with what was on it and **s** it in front of Saul. 8492
9:24 *it* **was s aside** for you for this occasion, 9068
1Sa 10: 2 'The donkeys *you* **s out** to look for 2143
10:19 And you have said, 'No, **s** a king over us.' 8492
12: 1 to me and *have* **s a king** over you. 4887+4889
12:13 see, the LORD *has* **s** a king over you. 5989
13: 8 the **time s** by Samuel; 4595
13:11 that you did not come at the **s time,** 3427+4595
15: 5 of Amalek and **s an ambush** in the ravine. 741
15:12 There *he has* **s up** a monument 5893
17:20 loaded up and **s out,** as Jesse had directed. 2143
21: 5 as usual whenever I **s out.** 3655
23:24 *they* **s out** and went to Ziph ahead of Saul. 7756
24: 2 from all Israel and **s out** to look for David 2143
26: 5 Then David **s out** and went to the place 7756
28: 4 and came and **s up camp** at Shunem, 2837
28: 4 the Israelites and **s up camp** at Gilboa. 2837
28: 9 Why *have* you **s a trap** for my life to bring 5943
28:25 Then *she* **s** it before Saul and his men, 5602
2Sa 4: 5 **s out** for the house of Ish-Bosheth, 2143
6: 2 and all his men **s out** from Baalah of Judah 2143
6: 3 *They* **s** the ark of God on a new cart 8206
6:17 They brought the ark of the LORD and **s** it 3657
11:22 The messenger **s out,** and when he arrived 2143
12:30 and it was **s** with precious stones— NIH
14:30 Go and **s** it **on fire."** 836+928+2021+3675
14:30 **s** the field **on fire.** 836+928+2021+3675
14:31 **s** my field **on fire?"** 836+928+2021+3675
15:16 The king **s out,** with his entire household 3655
15:17 So the king **s out,** with all the people 3655
15:24 *They* **s down** the ark of God, 3668
17: 1 and **s out** tonight in pursuit of David. 7756
17:21 **"S out** and cross the river at once; 7756
17:22 So David and all the people with him **s out** 7756
17:23 and **s out** for his house in his hometown. 2143
20: 5 he took longer than the time the king *had* **s** 3585
1Ki 1:33 and **s** Solomon my son on my own mule 8206
5: 6 for your men whatever wages *you* **s.** 606
6:19 the inner sanctuary within the temple to **s** 5989
7: 8 the palace in which he was to live, **s farther back,** 337+2021+2958
7:16 of cast bronze to **s** on the tops of the pillars; 5989
9:16 *He had* **s** it **on fire.** 836+928+2021+8596
11:18 *They* **s out** from Midian and went to Paran. 7756
12:29 One *he* **s up** in Bethel, and the other in Dan. 8492
14:12 When you **s** foot in your city, 995
14:23 They also **s up** for themselves high places, 1215
16:18 and **s** the palace **on fire** around him. 836+928+2021+8596
16:32 *He* **s up** an altar for Baal in the temple 7756
16:34 and *he* **s up** its gates at the cost of his 5893
18:23 and put it on the wood but not **s** fire *to* it. 8492
18:23 and put it on the wood but not **s** fire *to* it. 8492
19:21 Then *he* **s out** to follow Elijah 7756
20:16 *They* **s out** at noon while Ben-Hadad and 3655
20:34 *"You may* **s up** your own market areas 8492
20:34 "On the basis of a treaty I *will* **s** you **free."** 8938
20:42 *'You have* **s free** a man 3338+4946+8938
22:48 but *they* never **s sail—** 2143
2Ki 2:16 and **s** him **down** on some mountain or 8959
3: 6 at that time King Joram **s out** from Samaria 3655
3: 9 of Israel **s out** with the king of Judah and 2143
4:25 So *she* **s out** and came to the man of God 2143
4:43 "How *can I* **s** this before a hundred men?" 5989
4:44 Then *he* **s** it before them, 5989
6: 8 "I will **s up** my **camp** in such and such 9381
6:22 **S** food and water before them so 8492
8:12 *"You will* **s fire to** their fortified places, 836+928+2021+8938
8:20 and **s up** its own **king.** 4887+4889
10: 3 and **s** him on his father's throne. 8492
10:12 Jehu then **s out** and went toward Samaria. 995
16:17 the bronze bulls that supported it and **s** it on 5989
17:10 *They* **s up** sacred stones and Asherah poles 5893
17:29 and **s** them **up** in the shrines the people 5663
25: 9 *He* **s fire to** the temple of the LORD, 8596
1Ch 9:32 the bread **s out on the table.** 5121
16: 1 They brought the ark of God and **s** it inside 3657
17:14 *I will* **s** him over my house 6641
20: 2 and it was **s with** precious stones— 928
23:13 Aaron **was s apart,** he and his descendants 976
23:29 the bread **s out on the table,** 5121
25: 1 **s apart** some of the sons of Asaph, 976
2Ch 11:16 from every tribe of Israel who **s** their hearts 5989
12:14 He did evil because *he had* not **s** his heart 3922
13:11 They **s out** the bread on the ceremonially 5121
19: 3 the Asherah poles and *have* **s** your heart **on** 3922
20:20 As they **s out,** Jehoshaphat stood and said, 3655
20:22 the LORD **s** ambushes against the men 5989
20:33 and the people still *had* not **s** their hearts on 3922
20:37 and were not able to **s sail** to trade. 2143
21: 8 and **s up** its own **king.** 4887+4889
25:14 *He* **s** them **up** as his own gods, 6641
28:24 the doors of the LORD's temple and **s up** 6913
29:12 Then these Levites **s to work:** 7756
33:19 the sites where he built high places and **s up** 6641
35:12 *They* **s aside** the burnt offerings to give 6073
35:20 when Josiah *had* **s** the temple **in order,** 3922
36:19 *They* **s fire to** God's temple and broke 8596
Ezr 4: 4 around them *s out to* **discourage** AIT
5: 2 **s to work** to rebuild the house of God in Jerusalem. 10221+10624+10742
8:24 *I* **s apart** twelve of the leading priests, 976
8:31 the twelfth day of the first month *we* **s out** 5825
10:14 married a foreign woman come at a **s** time, 2374
Ne 2: 6 pleased the king to send me; so *I* **s** a time. 5989
2:12 I **s out** during the night with a few men. 7756
3: 1 They dedicated it and **s** its doors **in place,** 6641
6: 1 though up to that time *I had* not **s** the doors 6641

Ne 7: 1 and *I* s the doors **in place,** 6641
10:33 the bread s **out on the table;** 5121
10:34 to the house of our God at s times each year 2374
12:47 **s aside** the portion for the other Levites, 7727
12:47 and the Levites s **aside** the portion for 7727
Est 2:17 So *he* s a royal crown on her head 8492
Job 2:11 they s **out** from their homes 995
14: 5 and *have* s limits he cannot exceed. 6913
14:13 If only *you would* s me a time and 8883
24: 1 the Almighty not s times for judgment? 7621
28: 8 Proud beasts *do* not s **foot on** it, 2005
38: 6 On what **were** its footings **s,** 3190
38:10 and s its doors and bars **in place,** 8492
38:33 *Can you* s **up** [God's] dominion over 8492
Ps 4: 3 that the LORD *has* s **apart** the godly 7111
8: 1 *You have* s your glory above the heavens. 5989
8: 3 which *you have* s **in place,** 3922
11: 2 *they* s their arrows against the strings 3922
16: 8 *I have* s the LORD always before me. 8751
27: 5 his tabernacle and s me **high** upon a rock. 8123
31: 4 Free me from the trap that *is* s for me, 3243
31: 8 over to the enemy but *have* s my feet in 6641
38:12 Those who seek my life s *their* **traps,** 5943
40: 2 *he* s my feet on a rock and gave me 7756
41:12 In my integrity you uphold me and s me 5893
45: 7 therefore God, your God, has s you NIH
62:10 *do* not s your heart on them. 8883
69:22 the table s before them become a snare; NIH
74: 4 *they* s **up** their standards as signs. 8492
74:17 It was you *who* s all the boundaries of 5893
78:60 the tent *he had* s **up** among men. 8905
81: 6 their hands *were* s **free** from the basket. 6296
84: 5 who have s their hearts **on** pilgrimage. 928
85: 3 *You* s **aside** all your wrath and turned 665
87: 1 He has s his foundation on the holy NIH
88: 5 I am s **apart** with the dead, 2930
89:25 *I will* s his hand over the sea, 8492
90: 8 *You have* s our iniquities before you, 8883
101: 3 *I will* s before my eyes no vile thing. 8883
104: 5 *He* s the earth on its foundations; 3569
104: 9 *You* s a boundary they cannot cross; 8492
105:20 the ruler of peoples s him **free.** 7337
119:30 *I have* s *my* **heart** *on* your laws. 8751
119:32 for *you have* s my heart **free.** 8143
119:110 The wicked *have* s a snare for me, 5989
119:112 My heart *is* s *on* keeping your decrees to 5742
132:17 a horn grow for David and s **up** a lamp 6885
140: 5 the cords of their net and *have* s traps for me 8883
141: 2 *May* my prayer **be** s before you like incense; 3922
141: 3 S a guard over my mouth, O LORD; 8883
141: 9 from the **traps** *s by* evildoers. AIT
142: 7 S me **free** from my prison, 3655
148: 6 *He* s them **in place** for ever and ever; 6641
Pr 1:15 *do* **not** s foot on their paths; 4979
3:19 by understanding *he* s the heavens **in place;** 3922
4: 9 *She will* s a garland of grace on your head 5989
4:14 *Do* not s **foot** on the path of the wicked 995
7: 9 as the dark of night s in. NIH
8:27 I was there when *he* s the heavens **in place,** 3922
9: 2 *she has* also s her table. 6885
22:28 not move an ancient boundary stone s **up** 6913
25:17 **Seldom** *s* foot in your neighbor's house— AIT
30:14 and whose jaws are s with knives to devour NIH
Ecc 3:11 *He has* also s eternity in the hearts of men; 5989
12: 9 and s **in order** many proverbs. 9545
SS 5:14 His arms are rods of gold s with chrysolite. 4848
5:15 His legs are pillars of marble s on bases 3569
6:12 my desire s me *among* the royal chariots 8492
Isa 17:10 *though you* s **out** the finest plants 5749
17:11 though on the day you s them **out,** 5750
21: 5 They s the tables, they spread the rugs, 6885
23:18 and her earnings will be s **apart** for 7731
27: 4 *I would* s them all **on fire.** 7455
28: 1 s on the head of a fertile valley— NIH
28: 4 **s on** the head of a fertile valley, 6584
29: 3 and s **up** my siege works against you. 7756
33:12 like cut thornbushes *they will be* s **ablaze."** 836+928+2021+3675
40:20 a skilled craftsman to s **up** an idol that will 3922
41:19 *I will* s pines in the wasteland, 8492
41:21 **"S forth** your arguments," 5602
43: 2 the flames *will* not s you **ablaze.** 1277
45:13 and s my exiles **free,** 8938
46: 7 *they* s **it up** in its place, and there it stands. 5663
50: 7 Therefore *have I* s my face like flint, 8492
50:11 and of the torches *you have* s **ablaze.** 1277
51:14 cowering prisoners *will* soon **be s free;** 7337
51:16 I who s the heavens **in place,** 5749
58: 6 cords of the yoke, *to* s the oppressed free 8938
60:20 Your sun *will* never s again, 995
63:11 is he *who* s his Holy Spirit among them, 8492
66:19 *"I will* s a sign among them, 8492
Jer 1: 5 before you were born *I* s you **apart;** 7727
1:15 and s **up** their thrones in the entrance of 5989
4: 7 a destroyer of nations *has* s **out.** 5825
5:26 and like *those who* s traps to catch men. 5893
7:30 *They have* s **up** their detestable idols in 8492
9:13 which *I* s before them; 5989
10:20 now to pitch my tent or *to* s **up** my shelter. 7756
11:13 and the altars *you have* s **up** to burn incense 8492
11:16 of a mighty storm *he will* s it **on fire,** 836+3675
12: 3 S them **apart** for the day of slaughter! 7727
15: 9 Her sun *will* s while it is still day; 995
22:17 and your heart are s only **on** dishonest gain, 6584
26: 4 follow my law, which *I have* s before you, 5989
31:21 **"S up** road signs; put up guideposts. 5893
31:29 and the children's teeth *are* s **on edge.'** 7733

Jer 31:30 his own teeth *will be* s **on edge.** 7733
32:29 come in and s it **on fire;** 836+928+2021+3675
32:34 *They* s **up** their abominable idols in 8492
34:10 They agreed, and s them **free.** 8938
34:16 the male and female slaves *you had* s free 8938
35: 5 Then *I* s bowls full of wine and some cups 5989
39: 8 The Babylonians s **fire to** the royal palace 836+928+2021+8596
41:10 and s **out** to cross over to the Ammonites. 2143
43:10 of Babylon, and *I will* s his throne 8492
43:12 *He will* s **fire** to the temples of the gods 836+3675
44:10 the decrees *I* s before you and your fathers. 5989
49: 2 its surrounding villages *will be* s **on fire.** 836+928+2021+3675
49:27 *"I will* s **fire** to the walls of Damascus; 836+3675
49:38 *I will* s my throne in Elam 8492
50:24 *I* s **a trap** for you, O Babylon, 3704
51:30 Her dwellings *are* s **on fire;** 3675
51:32 the marshes s **on fire,** 836+928+2021+8596
51:39 *I will* s **out** a feast for them 8883
51:58 and her high gates s **on fire;** 836+928+2021+3675
52:13 *He* s **fire to** the temple of the LORD, 8596
Eze 4: 2 **s up** camps against it and put battering rams 5989
4:10 and eat it **at s times.** 4946+6330+6961+6961
4:11 and drink it **at s times.** 4946+6330+6961+6961
5: 1 a **s of scales** and divide up the hair. 4404+5486
5: 5 which *I have* s in the center of the nations, 8492
6: 2 s your face against the mountains of Israel; 8492
12: 3 **s out** and go from where you are 1655
13:17 s your face against the daughters of your 8492
13:20 *I will* s **free** the people that you ensnare 8938
14: 3 these men *have* s **up** idols in their hearts 6590
14: 8 *I will* s my face against that man 5989
15: 7 *I will* s my face against them. 5989
15: 7 And when I s my face against them, 8492
17: 2 **s forth** an allegory and tell the house 2554
18: 2 and the children's teeth *are* s **on edge'?** 7733
20: 7 of the vile images you have s your eyes on, NIH
20: 8 of the vile images they had s their eyes on, NIH
20:46 s your face toward the south; 8492
20:47 I *am about to* s **fire** to you, 836+3675
21: 2 s your face against Jerusalem and preach 8492
21:22 where he is to s **up** battering rams, 8492
21:22 to s battering rams against the gates, 8492
24:11 Then s the empty pot on the coals 6641
25: 2 s your face against the Ammonites 8492
25: 4 *They will* s **up** their camps 3782
26: 8 *he will* s **up** siege works against you, 5989
28:21 s your face against Sidon; 8492
29: 2 s your face against Pharaoh king of Egypt 8492
30: 8 when I s fire to Egypt and all her helpers 5989
30:14 s fire to Zoan and inflict punishment 5989
30:16 *I will* s fire to Egypt; 5989
35: 2 s your face against Mount Seir; 8492
37: 1 of the LORD and s me in the middle of 5663
38: 2 s your face against Gog, 8492
39:15 *he will* s **up** a marker beside it until 1215
40: 2 of Israel and s me on a very high mountain, 5663
48:20 **As a special gift** *you will* **s aside** 8123
Da 1:18 of the time s *by* the king to bring them in, 606
2:44 the God of heaven *will* s **up** a kingdom 10624
3: 1 and s it **up** on the plain of Dura in 10624
3: 2 to the dedication of the image he *had* s **up.** 10624
3: 3 image that King Nebuchadnezzar *had* s **up,** 10624
3: 5 gold that King Nebuchadnezzar *has* s **up.** 10624
3: 7 gold that King Nebuchadnezzar *had* s **up.** 10624
3:12 But there are some Jews whom *you have* s 10431
3:12 the image of gold *you have* s **up."** 10624
3:14 or worship the image of gold *I have* s **up?** 10624
3:18 the image of gold *you have* s **up."** 10624
5:23 *you have* s *yourself* **up** against the Lord 10659
6: 3 that the king planned to s him over 10624
7: 9 "As I looked, "thrones **were** s **in place,** 10667
7:25 and try to change the s **times** and the laws. 10232
8:11 *It* s *itself* **up to be** as **great** as the Prince 1540
9:27 he will s up an abomination that causes NIH
10:10 A hand touched me and s me **trembling** 5675
10:12 that *you* s your mind to gain understanding 5989
11:28 be s **against** the holy covenant. 6584
11:31 Then *they will* s **up** the abomination 5989
11:44 and *he will* s **out** in a great rage to destroy 3655
12:11 that causes desolation *is* s **up,** 5989
Hos 8: 4 They s **up kings** without my consent; 4887
Am 1:14 *I will* s **fire** to the walls of Rabbah 836+3675
3: 5 on the ground where no snare has been s? NIH
Ob 1: 7 those who eat your bread *will* s a trap 8492
1:18 and *they will* s it **on fire** and consume it. 1944
Mic 3: 6 The sun *will* s for the prophets, 995
Hab 2: 9 by unjust gain to s his nest on high, 8492
Zec 3: 9 See, the stone *I have* s in front of Joshua! 5989
5:11 the basket *will* **be** s there in its place." 5663
6:11 and s it on the head of the high priest, 8492
12: 9 On that day *I will* s **out** to destroy all 1335
Mal 2: 2 *you do* not s your heart to honor my name," 8492
2: 2 you *have* not s your heart to honor me. 8492
4: 1 that day that is coming *will* s them **on fire,"** 4265
Mt 27: 9 **price s on** him by the people of Israel, *5506+5507*
27:29 a crown of thorns and s it **on** his head. *2202*
Mk 6:41 to his disciples to s **before** the people. *4192*
8: 6 and gave them to his disciples to s **before** *4192*
15:17 a crown of thorns and s it **on** him. *4363*
Lk 8:22 So they got into a boat and s **out.** *343*
9: 6 they s **out** and went from village to village, *2002*
9:16 to the disciples *to* s **before** the people. *4192*
9:51 Jesus resolutely s **out** for Jerusalem. *4513*
10: 8 eat what *is* s **before** you. *4192*
11: 6 and I have nothing *to* s **before** him.' *4192*

Lk 12:29 not s *your* **heart on** what you will eat *2426*
13:12 *you are* s **free** from your infirmity." *668*
13:16 *be* s **free** on the Sabbath day *3395*
15:13 **s off** for a distant country *623*
15:18 I will s **out** and go back to my father *482*
Jn 5:45 on whom your **hopes are s.** *1827*
6:17 where they got into a boat and **s off** across *2262*
8:32 and the truth *will* s you **free."** *1802*
8:33 How can you say that we shall be **s free?"** *1801*
10:36 the Father **s apart** as his very own and sent *39*
13:15 *I have* s you an example that you should do *1443*
19:12 From then on, Pilate tried *to* s Jesus **free,** *668*
Ac 1: 7 to know the times or dates the Father *has* s *5502*
2:23 *by* God's s purpose and foreknowledge; *3988*
7:34 and have come down *to* s them **free.** *1975*
13: 2 **"S apart** for me Barnabas and Saul for *928*
16:34 his house and **s a meal before** them; *4192+5544*
17:26 and he determined the times s for them and *4705*
17:31 For *he has* s a day when he will judge *2705*
18:21 Then *he* s **sail** from Ephesus. *343*
18:23 Paul s **out** from there and traveled *2002*
20: 1 said good-by and s **out** for Macedonia. *2002*
20:15 The next day we s **sail** from there *676*
21: 2 went on board and s **sail.** *343*
26:32 "This man could *have been* s **free** if he had *668*
28:13 From there we s **sail** and arrived *4311*
Ro 1: 1 to be an apostle and s **apart** for the gospel *928*
6:18 *You have been* s **free** from sin *1802*
6:22 But now *that you have been* s **free** from sin *1802*
8: 2 of the Spirit of life s me **free** from the law *1802*
8: 5 the sinful nature *have their* **minds** s **on** what *5858*
8: 5 with the Spirit have their minds s on what *NIG*
1Co 16: 2 one of you *should* s **aside** a sum of money *5502*
2Co 1:10 On him *we have* s *our* **hope** *1827*
1:22 s his **seal of ownership on** us, *5381*
Gal 1:15 who s me **apart** from birth and called me *928*
2: 2 to a revelation and s **before** them the gospel *423*
2:21 *I do* not s **aside** the grace of God, *119*
3:15 Just as no one *can* s **aside** or add to *119*
3:17 *does* not s **aside** the covenant previously *218*
4: 2 and trustees until the **time** s by his father. *4607*
5: 1 It is for freedom that Christ *has* s us **free.** *1802*
Php 4:15 when *I* s **out** from Macedonia, *2002*
Col 3: 1 s *your* **hearts on** things above, *2426*
3: 2 S *your* **minds on** things above, not on *5858*
1Ti 4:12 s an example for the believers in speech, *1181*
Tit 2: 7 In everything s them an example *4218*
Heb 1: 9 therefore God, your God, has s you *NIG*
4: 7 Therefore God again s a certain day, *3988*
7:18 The former regulation is **s aside** *120*
7:26 blameless, pure, s **apart** from sinners, *6004*
8: 2 the true tabernacle s **up** by the Lord, *4381*
9: 2 A tabernacle *was* s **up.** *2941*
9:15 that he has died as a ransom to s them free *NIG*
12: 2 for the joy s **before** him endured the cross, *4618*
Jas 3: 5 Consider what a great forest *is* s **on fire** by *409*
3: 6 and *is* itself s **on fire** by hell. *5824*
1Pe 1:13 s *your* **hope** fully on the grace to *1827*
3:15 But in your hearts s **apart** Christ as Lord. *39*
1Jn 3:19 and how *we* s our hearts **at rest** *4275*
Rev 13:14 He ordered them *to* s **up** an image in honor *4472*
20: 3 he must *be* s **free** for a short time. *3395*

SETH (9)

Ge 4:25 she gave birth to a son and named him **S,** 9269
4:26 **S** also had a son, and he named him Enosh. 9269
5: 3 in his own image; and he named him **S.** 9269
5: 4 After **S** was born, Adam lived 800 years 9269
5: 6 When **S** had lived 105 years, 9269
5: 7 **S** lived 807 years and had other sons 9269
5: 8 Altogether, **S** lived 912 years, 9269
1Ch 1: 1 Adam, **S,** Enosh, 9269
Lk 3:38 the son *of* **S,** the son of Adam, *4953*

SETHUR (1)

Nu 13:13 from the tribe of Asher, S son of Michael; 6256

SETS (46) [SET]

Ge 45:22 shekels of silver and five s *of* clothes. 2722
Ex 36:13 to fasten the *two* s *of* **curtains** together so AIT
Lev 27:12 Whatever value the priest then s, NIH
27:14 Whatever value the priest then s, 6885
Dt 27:15 craftsman's hands—and s it **up** in secret." 8492
Jdg 14:12 linen garments and thirty s *of* clothes. 2722
14:13 linen garments and thirty s *of* clothes." 2722
2Sa 3:35 or anything else before the sun s!" 995
22:49 *who* s me **free** from my enemies. 3655
1Ki 7: 4 Its windows were placed high in s *of* three, 3215
7: 5 they were in the front part in s of three, 7193
7:41 the **two** s of network decorating AIT
7:42 for the **two** s of network (two rows AIT
2Ki 5: 5 six thousand shekels of gold and ten s 2722
5:22 Please give them a talent of silver and two s 2722
5:23 silver in two bags, with two s *of* clothing. 2722
2Ch 4:12 the **two** s of network decorating AIT
4:13 for the **two** s *of* network (two rows AIT
30:19 *who* s his heart on seeking God— 3922
Job 5:11 The lowly he s on high, 8492
34:24 the mighty and s **up** others in their place. 6641
41:21 His breath s coals **ablaze.** 4265
Ps 50: 1 the rising of the sun to the **place where** it **s.** 4427
68: 6 God s the lonely in families, 3782
83:14 s the mountains **ablaze,** 4265
113: 3 the rising of the sun to the **place where** it s, 4427
146: 7 The LORD s prisoners **free,** 6002

Pr 31:17 *She* s **about** her **work** vigorously; 2520+5516
Ecc 1: 5 The sun rises and the sun s, 995
Isa 9:18 s the forest thickets **ablaze,** 3675
30:33 like a stream of burning sulfur, s it **ablaze.** 1277
64: 2 *when* fire s twigs **ablaze** and causes water 7706
Jer 9: 8 but in his heart *he* s a trap for him. 8492
13:21 What will you say when [the LORD] s over 7212
Eze 14: 4 When any Israelite s **up** idols in his heart 6590
14: 7 in Israel separates himself from me and s **up** 6590
Da 2:21 *he* s **up** kings and deposes them. 10624
4:17 and gives them to anyone he wishes and s 10624
5:21 of men and s over them anyone he wishes. 10624
Am 9: 6 and s its foundation on the earth, who calls 3569
Jn 8:36 the Son s you **free,** you will be free indeed. *1802*
2Co 10: 5 *that* s *itself* **up** against the knowledge *2048*
2Th 2: 4 so that he s *himself* **up** in God's temple, *2767*
1Ti 3: 1 If anyone s his **heart on being** an overseer, *3977*
Heb 10: 9 *He* s **aside** the first to establish the second. *359*
Jas 3: 6 s the whole course of his life **on fire,** *5824*

SETTER (KJV) See ADVOCATING

SETTING (23) [SET]

Ge 15:12 As the sun *was* s, Abram fell into a deep sleep, 995
Ex 8: 9 leave to you the honor of s **the time** for me to pray 4200+5503
Nu 7: 1 When Moses finished s **up** the tabernacle, 7756
10: 6 The blast will be the signal for s **out.** 5023
10:29 "We *are* s **out** for the place about which 5825
Dt 4: 8 and laws as this body of laws I *am* s 5989
11:26 I *am* s before you today a blessing and 5989
11:30 west of the road, toward the s sun, 4427
11:32 you obey all the decrees and laws I *am* s 5989
26:12 you have finished s **aside a tenth** 5130+6923
2Sa 2:24 and *as* the sun *was* s, they came 995
1Ki 22:36 As the sun *was* s, a cry spread 995
2Ch 2: 4 for s out the consecrated bread regularly, NIH
29:18 table for s **out the consecrated bread,** 5121
Ps 118: 5 and he answered by s me **free.** 5303
Isa 45: 6 to the **place of** its s men may know there is none besides me. 5115
Jer 21: 8 See, I *am* s before you the way of life and 5989
Am 7: 8 I *am* s a plumb line among my people Israel; 8492
Mal 1:11 from the rising to the s *of* the sun. 4427
Mk 7: 9 a fine way of s **aside** the commands of God *119*
Lk 4:40 *When* the sun *was* s, the people brought *1544*
1Co 10: 6 as examples to keep us from s our **hearts on** *2122*
2Co 4: 2 by s **forth** the truth **plainly** we commend *5748*

SETTINGS (12) [SET]

Ex 28:11 Then mount the stones in gold filigree s 6015
28:13 Make gold **filigree** s 5401
28:14 like a rope, and attach the chains to the s. 5401
28:20 Mount them in gold **filigree s.** 8687
28:25 the other ends of the chains to the two s, 5401
39: 6 in gold filigree s and engraved them like 6015
39:13 They were mounted in gold filigree **s.** 4853
39:16 They made two gold **filigree** s 5401
39:18 the other ends of the chains to the two s, 5401
1Ch 29: 2 as well as onyx for the s, turquoise, 4854
Pr 25:11 like apples of gold in s *of* silver. 5381
Eze 28:13 Your s and mountings were made of gold; 4856+9513

SETTLE (43) [RESETTLE, RESETTLED, SETTLED, SETTLEMENT, SETTLEMENTS, SETTLES]

Ge 34:10 *You can* s among us; 3782
34:16 *We'll* s among you and become one people 3782
34:23 and *they will* s among us." 3782
35: 1 "Go up to Bethel and s there, 3782
46:34 *be allowed to* s in the region of Goshen, 3782
47: 4 please *let* your servants s in Goshen." 3782
47: 6 s your father and your brothers in the best 3782
Nu 33:53 Take possession of the land and s in it, 3782
Dt 8:12 when you build fine houses and **s down,** 3782
12:10 But you will cross the Jordan and s in 3782
Jdg 18: 1 a place of their own where they *might* s, 3782
2Ki 25:24 **"S down** in the land and serve the king 3782
2Ch 19: 8 the law of the LORD and to s disputes. NIH
Job 3: 5 *may* a cloud s over it; 8905
Ps 69:35 Then *people will* s there and possess it; 3782
107: 4 finding no way to a city **where** they could s. 4632
107: 7 a straight way to a city **where** they could **s.** 4632
107:36 and they founded a city **where** they could **s.** 4632
139: 9 if *I* s on the far side of the sea, 8905
Isa 2: 4 and *will* **s disputes** for many peoples. 3519
7:19 and s in the steep ravines and in 5663
14: 1 and *will* s them in their own land. 5663
23: 7 whose feet have taken her to s in far-off 1591
54: 3 and s **in** their desolate cities. 3782
Jer 29: 5 "Build houses and **s down;** 3782
29:28 Therefore build houses and s **down;** 3782
40: 9 **"S down** in the land and serve the king 3782
42:15 to go to Egypt and you do go to s there, 1591
42:17 to Egypt to s there will die by the sword, 1591
42:22 in the place where you want to go to **s."** 1591
43: 2 'You must not go to Egypt to s there.' 1591
44:12 determined to go to Egypt to s there. 1591
Eze 32: 4 **let** all the birds of the air s on you 8905
32:14 Then *I will* **let** her waters s 9205
36:11 *I will* s *people* **on** you as in the past 3782
Eze 37:14 and *I will* s you in your own land. 5663
Hos 11:11 *I will* s them in their homes," 3782
Mic 4: 3 between many peoples and *will* **s disputes** 3519
Na 3:17 like swarms of locusts that s in the walls on 2837
Mt 5:25 **"S matters** quickly with your *1639+2333*
18:23 like a king who wanted *to* s accounts *5256*
Ac 18:15 **s the matter** yourselves. *3972*
2Th 3:12 to s **down** and earn the bread they eat. *2484+3552*

SETTLED (72) [SETTLE]

Ge 11: 2 they found a plain in Shinar and s there. 3782
11:31 But when they came to Haran, *they* s there. 3782
19:30 Lot and his two daughters left Zoar and s in 3782
25:18 His descendants **s in** the area from Havilah 8905
26:17 in the Valley of Gerar and s there. 3782
36: 8 Edom) s in the hill country of Seir. 3782
47:11 So Joseph s his father and his brothers 3782
47:27 Now the Israelites s in Egypt in the region 3782
Ex 10: 6 from the day they s in this land till now.'" 2118
10:14 and **s down** in every area of the country 5663
16:35 until they came to a land *that was* **s;** 3782
22:11 between them *will be* s *by* the taking of 2118
24:16 the glory of the LORD s on Mount Sinai. 8905
40:35 the Tent of Meeting because the cloud *had* s 8905
Nu 9:17 wherever the cloud s, 8905
11: 9 When the dew s on the camp at night, 3718
21:31 So Israel s in the land of the Amorites. 3782
22: 5 the face of the land and *have* s next to me. 3782
31:10 the towns where the Midianites had **s,** 4632
32:40 and *they* s there. 3782
Dt 2:12 from before them and s in their place, 3782
2:21 who drove them out and s in their place. 3782
2:23 from Caphtor destroyed them and s 3782
12:29 But when you have driven them out and s 3782
17:14 and have taken possession of it and s in it, 3782
19: 1 and when you have driven them out and s 3782
26: 1 and have taken possession of it and s in it, 3782
Jos 19:47 *They* s in Leshem and named it Dan 3782
19:50 And he built up the town and s there. 3782
21:43 and they took possession of it and s there. 3782
Jdg 7:12 the other eastern peoples *had* s in the valley, 5877
11: 3 So Jephthah fled from his brothers and s in 3782
18:28 The Danites rebuilt the city and s there. 3782
21:23 and rebuilt the towns and s in them. 3782
Ru 3:18 not rest until the matter *is* s today." 3983
1Sa 12: 8 of Egypt and s them in this place. 3782
27: 3 David and his men s in Gath with Achish. 3782
2Sa 2: 3 and *they* s in Hebron and its towns. 3782
7: 1 After the king *was* s in his palace and 3782
20:18 'Get your answer at Abel,' and that s *it.* 9462
1Ki 11:24 where *they* s and took control. 3782
2Ki 17: 6 *He* s them in Halah, in Gozan 3782
17:24 and Sepharvaim and s them in the towns 3782
17:29 in the several towns where they **s,** 3782
18:11 to Assyria and s them in Halah, 5663
1Ch 4:41 Then *they* s in their place, 3782
5: 8 They s in the area from Aroer to Nebo 3782
5:23 *they* s in the land from Bashan 3782
17: 1 After David *was* s in his palace, 3782
2Ch 8: 2 and s Israelites in them. 3782
15: 9 and Simeon *who had* s among them, 1591
Ezr 2:70 the gatekeepers and the temple servants s 3782
2:70 the rest of the Israelites s in their towns. NIH
3: 1 and the Israelites had s in their towns, NIH
4:10 and honorable Ashurbanipal deported and s 10338
Ne 7:73 the Israelites, s in their own towns. 3782
7:73 and the Israelites had s in their towns, NIH
11: 1 the leaders of the people s in Jerusalem, 3782
11: 3 the provincial leaders who s in Jerusalem 3782
11:36 of the divisions of the Levites of Judah s NIH
Ps 68:10 Your people s in it, and from your bounty, 3782
78:55 *he* s the tribes of Israel in their homes. 8905
Pr 8:25 before the mountains **were s in place,** 3190
Isa 29: 1 Ariel, Ariel, the city where David s! 2837
Eze 31:13 All the birds of the air s on the fallen tree, 8905
47:22 for yourselves and for the aliens who *have* s 1591
Zec 7: 7 Negev and the western foothills *were* **s?'"** 3782
Mt 25:19 returned and s **accounts** with them. *3364+5256*
Ac 7: 4 "So *he* left the land of the Chaldeans and s *2997*
7:29 where he s **as a foreigner** and had two sons. *4230*
19:39 *it* **must be** s in a legal assembly. *2147*
1Co 7:37 who *has* s **the matter** in his own mind, *1612+2705*

SETTLEMENT (2) [SETTLE]

Isa 27:10 an abandoned **s,** forsaken like the desert; 5659
Mt 18:24 As he began the **s,** a man who owed him 5256

SETTLEMENTS (29) [SETTLE]

Ge 25:16 the twelve tribal rulers according to their s 2958
36:43 to their s in the land they occupied. 4632
Nu 21:25 and all its **surrounding s.** 1426
21:32 the Israelites captured its **surrounding** s 1426
32:41 a descendant of Manasseh, captured their s 2557
32:42 and its **surrounding** s and called it Nobah 1426
Jos 13:30 all the s *of* Jair in Bashan, sixty towns, 2557
15:45 Ekron, with its **surrounding** s and villages; 1426
15:47 Ashdod, its **surrounding** s and villages; 1426
15:47 and Gaza, its s and villages, 1426
17:11 together with their **surrounding** s (the third 1426
17:16 and its s and those in the Valley of Jezreel." 1426
Jdg 1:27 or Megiddo and their **surrounding** s, 1426
11:26 the **surrounding** s and all the towns along 1426
1Ki 4:13 in Ramoth Gilead (the s *of* Jair son 2557
1Ch 2:23 as well as Kenath with its **surrounding** s— 1426
4:33 These were their s. 4632
1Ch 6:54 These were the locations of their s allotted 4632
7:28 Their lands and s included Bethel 4632
Ne 11:25 in Kiriath Arba and its **surrounding s,** 1426
11:25 in Dibon and its s, 1426
11:27 in Hazar Shual, in Beersheba and its s, 1426
11:28 in Ziklag, in Meconah and its s, 1426
11:30 and in Azekah and its s. 1426
11:31 Aija, Bethel and its s, 1426
Isa 42:11 let the s where Kedar lives rejoice. 2958
Eze 26: 6 and her s on the mainland will be ravaged 1426
26: 8 He will ravage your s on the mainland with 1426
34:13 in the ravines and in all the s *in* the land. 4632

SETTLES (4) [SETTLE]

2Sa 17:12 we will fall on him as dew s on the ground. 5877
Ps 113: 9 *He* s the barren woman in her home as 3782
Pr 18:18 Casting the lot s disputes 8697
Eze 47:23 In whatever tribe the alien s, 1591

SEVEN (391) [SEVENFOLD, SEVENS, SEVENTH]

Ge 4:15 he will suffer vengeance s *times over."* 8679
4:24 If Cain is avenged s *times,* 8679
7: 2 s of every kind of clean animal, 8679+8679
7: 3 and also s of every kind of bird, 8679+8679
7: 4 S days from now I will send rain on 8679
7:10 And after the s days the floodwaters came 8679
8:10 He waited s more days and again sent out 8679
8:12 He waited s more days and sent 8679
21:28 Abraham set apart s ewe lambs from 8679
21:29 of these s ewe lambs you have set apart 8679
21:30 "Accept these s lambs from my hand as 8679
29:18 "I'll work for you s years in return 8679
29:20 So Jacob served s years to get Rachel, 8679
29:27 in return for another s years of work." 8679
29:30 And he worked for Laban another s years. 8679
31:23 he pursued Jacob for s days and caught up 8679
33: 3 and bowed down to the ground s times 8679
41: 2 when out of the river there came up s cows, 8679
41: 3 After them, s other cows, ugly and gaunt, 8679
41: 4 that were ugly and gaunt ate up the s sleek, 8679
41: 5 S heads of grain, healthy and good, 8679
41: 6 s other heads of grain sprouted— 8679
41: 7 of grain swallowed up the s healthy, 8679
41:18 when out of the river there came up s cows, 8679
41:19 After them, s other cows came up— 8679
41:20 ugly cows ate up the s fat cows that came 8679
41:22 "In my dreams I also saw s heads of grain, 8679
41:23 After them, s other heads sprouted— 8679
41:24 of grain swallowed up the s good heads. 8679
41:26 The s good cows are seven years, 8679
41:26 The seven good cows are s years, 8679
41:26 the s good heads of grain are seven years; 8679
41:26 the seven good heads of grain are s years; 8679
41:27 The s lean, ugly cows that came 8679
41:27 that came up afterward are s years, and 8679
41:27 the s worthless heads of grain scorched by 8679
41:27 They are s years of famine. 8679
41:29 S years of great abundance are coming 8679
41:30 but s years of famine will follow them. 8679
41:34 of Egypt during the s years of abundance. 8679
41:36 during the s years of famine that will come 8679
41:47 During the s years of abundance 8679
41:48 in those s years of abundance in Egypt 8679
41:53 The s years of abundance in Egypt came to 8679
41:54 and the s years of famine began, 8679
46:25 to his daughter Rachel—s in all. 8679
Ex 2:16 Now a priest of Midian had s daughters, 8679
7:25 S days passed after the LORD struck 8679
12:15 For s days you are to eat bread made 8679
12:19 For s days no yeast is to be found 8679
13: 6 For s days eat bread made without yeast 8679
13: 7 Eat unleavened bread during those s days; 8679
22:30 Let them stay with their mothers for s days, 8679
23:15 for s days eat bread made without yeast, 8679
25:37 "Then make its s lamps and set them up 8679
29:30 in the Holy Place is to wear them s days. 8679
29:35 taking s days to ordain them. 8679
29:37 For s days make atonement for the altar 8679
34:18 For s days eat bread made without yeast, 8679
37:23 They made its s lamps, 8679
Lev 4: 6 the blood and sprinkle some of it s times 8679
4:17 the LORD s times in front of the curtain. 8679
8:11 of the oil on the altar s times, 8679
8:33 to the Tent of Meeting for s days, 8679
8:33 for your ordination will last s days. 8679
8:35 for s days and do what the LORD requires, 8679
12: 2 be ceremonially unclean for s days, 8679
13: 4 the infected person in isolation for s days. 8679
13: 5 to keep him in isolation another s days. 8679
13:21 priest is to put him in isolation for s days. 8679
13:26 priest is to put him in isolation for s days. 8679
13:31 the infected person in isolation for s days. 8679
13:33 to keep him in isolation another s days. 8679
13:50 and isolate the affected article for s days. 8679
13:54 Then he is to isolate it for another s days. 8679
14: 7 S times he shall sprinkle the one to 8679
14: 8 but he must stay outside his tent for s days. 8679
14:16 sprinkle some of it before the LORD s times. 8679
14:27 from his palm s times before the LORD. 8679
14:38 of the house and close it up for s days. 8679
14:51 and sprinkle the house s times. 8679
15:13 he is to count off s days 8679
15:19 of her monthly period will last s days, 8679
15:24 he will be unclean for s days; 8679

Lev 15:28 she must count off s days, 8679
16:14 of it with his finger s times before 8679
16:19 of the blood on it with his finger s times 8679
22:27 it is to remain with its mother for s days. 8679
23: 6 for s days you must eat bread made 8679
23: 8 For s days present an offering made to 8679
23:15 count off s full weeks. 8679
23:18 Present with this bread s male lambs, 8679
23:34 Tabernacles begins, and it lasts for s days. 8679
23:36 For s days present offerings made to 8679
23:39 the festival to the LORD for s days; 8679
23:40 before the LORD your God for s days. 8679
23:41 to the LORD for s days each year. 8679
23:42 Live in booths for s days: 8679
25: 8 " 'Count off s sabbaths of years— 8679
25: 8 sabbaths of years—s times seven years— 8679
25: 8 sabbaths of years—seven times s years— 8679
25: 8 the s sabbaths of years amount to a period 8679
26:18 punish you for your sins s *times* over. 8679
26:21 I will multiply your afflictions s *times* 8679
26:24 afflict you for your sins s *times over.* 8679
26:28 punish you for your sins s *times over.* 8679
Nu 8: 2 'When you set up the s lamps, 8679
12:14 not have been in disgrace for s days? 8679
12:14 Confine her outside the camp for s days; 8679
12:15 confined outside the camp for s days, 8679
13:22 (Hebron had been built s years before Zoan 8679
19: 4 on his finger and sprinkle it s times toward 8679
19:11 of anyone will be unclean for s days. 8679
19:14 in it will be unclean for s days, 8679
19:16 will be unclean for s days. 8679
23: 1 Balaam said, "Build me s altars here, 8679
23: 1 and prepare s bulls and seven rams for me." 8679
23: 1 and prepare seven bulls and s rams for me." 8679
23: 4 and Balaam said, "I have prepared s altars, 8679
23:14 and there he built s altars and offered a bull 8679
23:29 Balaam said, "Build me s altars here, 8679
23:29 and prepare s bulls and seven rams for me." 8679
23:29 and prepare seven bulls and s rams for me." 8679
28:11 one ram and s male lambs a year old, 8679
28:17 for s days eat bread made without yeast. 8679
28:19 one ram and s male lambs a year old, 8679
28:21 and with each of the s lambs, one-tenth. 8679
28:24 for s days as an aroma pleasing to 8679
28:27 one ram and s male lambs a year old as 8679
28:29 and with each of the s lambs, one-tenth. 8679
29: 2 one ram and s male lambs a year old, 8679
29: 4 and with each of the s lambs, one-tenth. 8679
29: 8 one ram and s male lambs a year old, 8679
29:10 and with each of the s lambs, one-tenth. 8679
29:12 a festival to the LORD for s days. 8679
29:32 " 'On the seventh day prepare s bulls, 8679
29:36 one ram and s male lambs a year old, 8679
31:19 stay outside the camp s days. 8679
Dt 7: 1 s nations larger and stronger than you— 8679
15: 1 of every s years you must cancel debts. 8679
16: 3 but for s days eat unleavened bread, 8679
16: 4 in all your land for s days. 8679
16: 9 Count off s weeks from the time you begin 8679
16:13 the Feast of Tabernacles for s days 8679
16:15 For s days celebrate the Feast to the LORD 8679
28: 7 from one direction but flee from you in **s.** 8679
28:25 from one direction but flee from them in **s,** 8679
31:10 "At the end of every s years, 8679
Jos 6: 4 Have s priests carry trumpets 8679
6: 4 march around the city s times, 8679
6: 6 and have s priests carry trumpets in front 8679
6: 8 the s priests carrying the seven trumpets 8679
6: 8 the seven priests carrying the s trumpets 8679
6:13 The s priests carrying the seven trumpets 8679
6:13 the s trumpets went forward, 8679
6:15 around the city s times in the same manner, 8679
6:15 on that day they circled the city s times. 8679
18: 2 there were still s Israelite tribes who had 8679
18: 5 You are to divide the land into s parts. 8679
18: 6 descriptions of the s parts of the land, 8679
18: 9 town by town, in s parts, 8679
Jdg 6: 1 and for s years he gave them into the hands 8679
6:25 the one s years old. 8679
12: 9 Ibzan led Israel s years. 8679
14:12 the answer within the s days of the feast, 8679
14:17 She cried the whole s days of the feast. 8679
16: 7 "If anyone ties me with s fresh thongs 8679
16: 8 of the Philistines brought her s fresh thongs 8679
16:13 "If you weave the s braids of my head into 8679
16:13 Delilah took the s braids of his head, 8679
16:19 a man to shave off the s braids of his hair, 8679
20:15 to s hundred chosen men from those living 8679
20:16 Among all these soldiers there were s
hundred chosen men who were left-handed, 8679
Ru 4:15 and who is better to you than s sons, 8679
1Sa 2: 5 She who was barren has borne s children, 8679
6: 1 in Philistine territory s months, 8679
10: 8 but you must wait s days until I come 8679
11: 3 "Give us s days so we can send messengers 8679
13: 8 He waited s days, the time set by Samuel; 8679
16:10 Jesse had s *of* his sons pass before Samuel, 8679
31:13 and they fasted s days. 8679
2Sa 2:11 of Judah was s years and six months. 8679
5: 5 In Hebron he reigned over Judah s years 8679
8: 4 s thousand charioteers and twenty thousand 8679
10:18 and David killed s hundred of their 8679
21: 6 let s of his male descendants be given to us 8679
21: 9 *All* s *of* them fell together; 8679
1Ki 2:11 s years in Hebron and thirty-three in 8679
6: 6 and the third floor **s.** 8679
6:38 He had spent s years building it. 8679
1Ki 7:17 s for each capital. 8679
8:65 before the LORD our God for s days 8679
8:65 for seven days and s days more, 8679
11: 3 He had s hundred wives of royal birth 8679
16:15 Zimri reigned in Tirzah s days. 8679
18:43 S times Elijah said, "Go back." 8679
19:18 Yet I reserve s thousand in Israel— 8679
20:29 For s days they camped opposite each other, 8679
2Ki 3: 9 After a roundabout march of s days, 8679
3:26 with him s hundred swordsmen to break 8679
4:35 The boy sneezed s times 8679
5:10 "Go, wash yourself s times in the Jordan, 8679
5:14 and dipped himself in the Jordan s times, 8679
8: 1 a famine in the land that will last s years." 8679
8: 2 in the land of the Philistines s years. 8679
8: 3 the s years she came back from the land of 8679
11:21 Joash was s years old when he began 8679
24:16 the entire force of s thousand fighting men, 8679
1Ch 3: 4 where he reigned s years and six months. 8679
3:24 Delaiah and Anani—s in all. 8679
5:13 Zia and Eber—s in all. 8679
10:12 and they fasted s days. 8679
11:23 was s **and a half feet** tall. 564+928+2021+2822
15:26 s bulls and seven rams were sacrificed. 8679
15:26 seven bulls and s rams were sacrificed. 8679
18: 4 s thousand charioteers and twenty thousand 8679
19:18 and David killed s thousand of their 8679
29: 4 and s thousand talents of refined silver, 8679
29:27 s in Hebron and thirty-three in Jerusalem. 8679
2Ch 7: 8 for s days, and all Israel with him— 8679
7: 9 the dedication of the altar for s days and 8679
7: 9 and the festival for s days more. 8679
13: 9 and s rams may become a priest of what are 8679
15:11 to the LORD s hundred head of cattle 8679
15:11 of cattle and s thousand sheep and goats 8679
17:11 s thousand seven hundred rams 8679
17:11 seven thousand s hundred rams 8679
17:11 and s thousand seven hundred goats. 8679
17:11 and seven thousand s hundred goats. 8679
24: 1 Joash was s years old 8679
29:21 They brought s bulls, seven rams, 8679
29:21 They brought seven bulls, s rams, 8679
29:21 s male lambs and seven male goats as 8679
29:21 seven male lambs and s male goats as 8679
30:21 the Feast of Unleavened Bread for s days 8679
30:22 the s days they ate their assigned portion 8679
30:23 to celebrate the festival s more days; 8679
30:23 for another s days they celebrated joyfully. 8679
30:24 a thousand bulls and s thousand sheep 8679
35:17 the Feast of Unleavened Bread for s days. 8679
Ezr 6:22 For s days they celebrated with joy 8679
7:14 You are sent by the king and his s advisers 10696
Ne 8:18 They celebrated the feast for s days, 8679
Est 1: 5 the king gave a banquet, lasting s days, 8679
1:10 the s eunuchs who served him— 8679
1:14 and Memucan, the s nobles of Persia 8679
2: 9 He assigned to her s maids selected from 8679
Job 1: 2 He had s sons and three daughters, 8679
1: 3 and he owned s thousand sheep, 8679
2:13 with him for s days and seven nights. 8679
2:13 with him for seven days and s nights. 8679
5:19 in s no harm will befall you. 8679
42: 8 So now take s bulls and seven rams and go 8679
42: 8 So now take seven bulls and s rams and go 8679
42:13 And he also had s sons and three daughters. 8685
Ps 12: 6 in a furnace of clay, purified s *times.* 8679
79:12 into the laps of our neighbors s *times* 8679
119:164 S *times* a day I praise you 8679
Pr 6:16 s that are detestable to him: 8679
9: 1 she has hewn out its s pillars. 8679
24:16 for though a righteous man falls s *times,* 8679
26:16 than s men who answer discreetly. 8679
26:25 for s abominations fill his heart. 8679
Ecc 11: 2 Give portions to **s,** yes to eight, 8679
Isa 4: 1 that day s women will take hold of one man 8679
11:15 up into s streams so that men can cross over 8679
30:26 and the sunlight will be s *times brighter,* 8679
30:26 like the light of s full days, 8679
Jer 15: 9 of s will grow faint and breathe her last. 8679
52:25 and s royal advisers. 8679
Eze 3:15 I sat among them for s days— 8679
3:16 of s days the word of the LORD came 8679
39: 9 For s years they will use them for fuel. 8679
39:12 " 'For s months the house of Israel will 8679
39:14 of the s months they will begin their search, 8679
40:22 S steps led up to it, 8679
40:26 S steps led up to it, 8679
41: 3 on each side of it were s cubits wide. 8679
43:25 "For s days you are to provide 8679
43:26 For s days they are to make atonement for 8679
44:26 After he is cleansed, he must wait s days. 8679
45:21 Passover, a feast lasting s days, 8651
45:23 during the s days of the Feast he is 8679
45:23 of the Feast he is to provide s bulls 8679
45:23 to provide seven bulls and s rams 8679
45:25 " 'During the s days of the Feast, 8679
Da 3:19 the furnace heated s times hotter than usual 10696
4:16 till s times pass by for him. 10696
4:23 until s times pass by for him.' 10696
4:25 S times will pass by for you 10696
4:32 S times will pass by for you 10696
9:25 the ruler, comes, there will be s 'sevens,' 8679
9:27 a covenant with many *for* one **'s.'** 8651
9:27 In the middle of the **'s'** he will put an end 8651
Mic 5: 5 we will raise against him s shepherds, 8679
Zec 3: 9 There are s eyes on that one stone, 8679
4: 2 with a bowl at the top and s lights on it, 8679
Zec 4: 2 with s channels to the lights. 8679
4:10 "(These s are the eyes of the LORD, 8679
Mt 12:45 s other spirits more wicked than itself, *2231*
15:34 **"S,"** they replied, "and a few small fish." *2231*
15:36 Then he took the s loaves and the fish, *2231*
15:37 the disciples picked up s basketfuls *2231*
16:10 Or the s loaves for the four thousand, *2231*
18:21 when he sins against me? Up to s **times?"** *2232*
18:22 Jesus answered, "I tell you, not s **times,** *2232*
22:25 Now there were s brothers among us. *2231*
22:28 whose wife will she be *of* the s, *2231*
Mk 8: 5 **"S,"** they replied. *2231*
8: 6 When he had taken the s loaves *2231*
8: 8 the disciples picked up s basketfuls *2231*
8:20 I broke the s loaves for the four thousand, *2231*
8:20 They answered, **"S."** *2231*
12:20 Now there were s brothers. *2231*
12:22 In fact, none of the s left any children. *2231*
12:23 since the s were married to her?" *2231*
16: 9 out of whom he had driven s demons. *2231*
Lk 2:36 with her husband s years after her marriage, *2231*
8: 2 from whom s demons had come out; *2231*
11:26 takes s other spirits more wicked than itself, *2231*
17: 4 If he sins against you s **times** in a day, *2232*
17: 4 and s **times** comes back to you and says, *2232*
20:29 Now there were s brothers. *2231*
20:31 and in the same way the s died, *2231*
20:33 since the s were married to her?" *2231*
24:13 about s **miles** from Jerusalem. *2008+5084*
Ac 6: 3 choose s men from among you *2231*
13:19 he overthrew s nations in Canaan *2231*
19:14 S sons of Sceva, a Jewish chief priest, *2231*
20: 6 Troas, where we stayed s days. *2231*
21: 4 we stayed with them s days. *2231*
21: 8 Philip the evangelist, one of the **S.** *2231*
21:27 When the s days were nearly over, *2231*
Ro 11: 4 for myself s **thousand** who have not bowed *2233*
Heb 11:30 had marched around them for s days. *2231*
2Pe 2: 5 a preacher of righteousness, and s others; *NIG*
Rev 1: 4 *To* the s churches in the province of Asia: *2231*
1: 4 and from the s spirits before his throne, *2231*
1:11 and send it *to* the s churches: *2231*
1:12 when I turned I saw s golden lampstands, *2231*
1:16 In his right hand he held s stars, *2231*
1:20 *of* the s stars that you saw in my right hand *2231*
1:20 and of the s golden lampstands is this: *2231*
1:20 s stars are the angels of the seven churches, *2231*
1:20 seven stars are the angels *of* the s churches, *2231*
1:20 the s lampstands are the seven churches. *2231*
1:20 the seven lampstands are the s churches. *2231*
2: 1 the words of him who holds the s stars *2231*
2: 1 and walks among the s golden lampstands: *2231*
3: 1 of him who holds the s spirits of God and *2231*
3: 1 the seven spirits of God and the s stars. *2231*
4: 5 Before the throne, s lamps were blazing. *2231*
4: 5 These are the s spirits of God. *2231*
5: 1 on both sides and sealed *with* s seals. *2231*
5: 5 He is able to open the scroll and its s seals." *2231*
5: 6 He had s horns and seven eyes, *2231*
5: 6 He had seven horns and s eyes, *2231*
5: 6 which are the s spirits of God sent out *2231*
6: 1 as the Lamb opened the first of the s seals. *2231*
8: 2 I saw the s angels who stand before God, *2231*
8: 2 and to them were given s trumpets. *2231*
8: 6 Then the s angels who had *2231*
8: 6 the s trumpets prepared to sound them. *2231*
10: 3 the voices of the s thunders spoke. *2231*
10: 4 the s thunders spoke, I was about to write; *2231*
10: 4 up what the s thunders have said and do *2231*
11:13 S thousand people were killed in *2231*
12: 3 an enormous red dragon with s heads *2231*
12: 3 and ten horns and s crowns on his heads. *2231*
13: 1 He had ten horns and s heads, *2231*
15: 1 s angels with the seven last plagues— *2231*
15: 1 seven angels with the s last plagues— *2231*
15: 6 Out of the temple came the s angels with *2231*
15: 6 the seven angels with the s plagues. *2231*
15: 7 the s angels seven golden bowls filled with *2231*
15: 7 the seven angels s golden bowls filled with *2231*
15: 8 the temple until the s plagues of *2231*
15: 8 *of* the s angels were completed. *2231*
16: 1 from the temple saying *to* the s angels, *2231*
16: 1 the s bowls of God's wrath on the earth." *2231*
17: 1 the s angels who had the seven bowls came *2231*
17: 1 the seven angels who had the s bowls came *2231*
17: 3 with blasphemous names and had s heads *2231*
17: 7 which has the s heads and ten horns. *2231*
17: 9 The s heads are seven hills on which *2231*
17: 9 The seven heads are s hills on which *2231*
17:10 They are also s kings. *2231*
17:11 to the s and is going to his destruction. *2231*
21: 9 the s angels who had the seven bowls full *2231*
21: 9 the seven angels who had the s bowls full *2231*
21: 9 *of* the s last plagues came and said to me, *2231*

SEVEN-DAY (2) [DAY]

Ge 50:10 a s period of mourning for his father. 3427+8679
1Ch 9:25 share their duties for s **periods.** 2021+3427+8679

SEVENFOLD (1) [SEVEN]

Pr 6:31 Yet if he is caught, he must pay **s,** 8679

SEVENS (4) [SEVEN]

Da 9:24 "Seventy **'s'** are decreed for your people 8651
9:25 the ruler, comes, there will be seven **'s,'** 8651

Da 9:25 will be seven 'sevens,' and sixty-two **'s.'** 8651
9:26 After the sixty-two **'s,'** the Anointed One 8651

SEVENTEEN (8) [SEVENTEENTH]

Ge 37:2 Joseph, a young man *of* s, 6926+8679
47:28 Jacob lived in Egypt s years, 6926+8679
Jdg 8:26 gold rings he asked for came to s **hundred** shekels, 547+2256+4395+8679
1Ki 14:21 and he reigned s years in Jerusalem, 6926+8679
2Ki 13:1 and he reigned s years. 6926+8679
1Ch 26:30 s **hundred** able men— 547+2256+4395+8679
2Ch 12:13 and he reigned s years in Jerusalem, 6926+8679
Jer 32:9 and weighed out for him s shekels of silver. 2256+6927+8679

SEVENTEENTH (6) [SEVENTEEN]

Ge 7:11 on the s day of the second month— 6925+8679
8:4 on the s day of the seventh month the ark came to rest 6925+8679
1Ki 22:51 s year of Jehoshaphat king of Judah, 6926+8679
2Ki 16:1 the s year of Pekah son of Remaliah, 6926+8679
1Ch 24:15 the s to Hezir, the eighteenth to 6925+8679
25:24 the s to Joshbekashah, 6925+8679

SEVENTH (116) [SEVEN]

Ge 2:2 By the s day God had finished the work 8668
2:2 so on the s day he rested from all his work. 8668
2:3 God blessed the s day and made it holy, 8668
8:4 and on the seventeenth day of the s month 8668
Ex 12:15 the first day through the s must be cut off 8668
12:16 and another one on the s day. 8668
13:6 on the s day hold a festival to the LORD. 8668
16:26 but on the s day, the Sabbath, 8668
16:27 some of the people went out on the s day 8668
16:29 to stay where he is on the s day; 8668
16:30 So the people rested on the s day. 8668
20:10 s day is a Sabbath to the LORD your God. 8668
20:11 but he rested on the s day. 8668
21:2 But in the s year, he shall go free, 8668
23:11 during the s year let the land lie unplowed 8668
23:12 but on the s day do not work, 8668
24:16 the s day the LORD called to Moses from 8668
31:15 but the s day is a Sabbath of rest, 8668
31:17 and on the s day he abstained from work 8668
34:21 but on the s day you shall rest; 8668
35:2 but the s day shall be your holy day, 8668
Lev 13:5 On the s day the priest is to examine him, 8668
13:6 the s day the priest is to examine him again, 8668
13:27 On the s day the priest is to examine him, 8668
13:32 On the s day the priest is to examine the sore, 8668
13:34 the s day the priest is to examine the itch, 8668
13:51 On the s day he is to examine it, 8668
14:9 On the s day he must shave off all his hair; 8668
14:39 the s day the priest shall return to inspect 8668
16:29 the s month you must deny yourselves and 8668
23:3 but the s day is a Sabbath of rest, 8668
23:8 And on the s day hold a sacred assembly 8668
23:16 up to the day after the s Sabbath, 8668
23:24 of the s month you are to have a day of rest, 8668
23:27 "The tenth day of this s month is the Day 8668
23:34 'On the fifteenth day of the s month 8668
23:39 of the s month, after you have gathered 8668
23:41 celebrate it in the s month. 8668
25:4 in the s year the land is to have a sabbath 8668
25:9 on the tenth day of the s month; 8668
25:20 "What will we eat in the s year if we do 8668
Nu 6:9 the day of his cleansing—the s day. 8668
7:48 On the s day Elishama son of Ammihud, 8668
19:12 the water on the third day and on the s day; 8668
19:12 not purify himself on the third and s days, 8668
19:19 the unclean person on the third and s days, 8668
19:19 and on the s day he is to purify him. 8668
28:25 On the s day hold a sacred assembly 8668
29:1 " 'On the first day of the s month hold 8668
29:7 " 'On the tenth day of this s month hold 8668
29:12 " 'On the fifteenth day of the s month, 8668
29:32 " 'On the s day prepare seven bulls, 8668
31:19 and s days you must purify yourselves 8668
31:24 the s day wash your clothes and you will 8668
Dt 5:14 s day is a Sabbath to the LORD your God. 8668
15:9 "The s year, the year for canceling debts, 8679
15:12 in the s year you must let him go free. 8668
16:8 and on the s day hold an assembly to 8668
Jos 6:4 On the s day, march around the city seven 8668
6:15 On the s day, they got up at daybreak 8668
6:16 The s time around, when the priests 8668
19:40 The s lot came out for the tribe of Dan, 8668
Jdg 14:17 So on the s day he finally told her, 8668
14:18 the s day the men of the town said to him, 8668
2Sa 12:18 On the s day the child died. 8668
1Ki 8:2 in the month of Ethanim, the s month. 8668
18:44 The s time the servant reported, 8668
20:29 and on the s day the battle was joined. 8668
2Ki 11:4 In the s year Jehoiada sent for 8668
12:1 In the s year of Jehu, Joash became king, 8679
18:9 the s year of Hoshea son of Elah king 8668
25:8 On the s day of the fifth month, 8679
25:25 In the s month, however, 8668
1Ch 2:15 the sixth Ozem and the s David. 8668
12:11 Attai the sixth, Eliel the s, 8668
24:10 the s to Hakkoz, the eighth to Abijah, 8668
25:14 the s to Jesarelah, his sons and relatives, 12 8668
26:3 Jehohanan the sixth and Eliehoenai the **s.** 8668
26:5 Issachar the s and Peullethai the eighth. 8668
27:10 The s, for the seventh month, 8668
1Ch 27:10 The seventh, for the s month, 8668
2Ch 5:3 at the time of the festival in the s month. 8668
7:10 the twenty-third day of the s month he sent 8668
23:1 In the s year Jehoiada showed his strength. 8668
31:7 the third month and finished in the s month. 8668
Ezr 3:1 When the s month came and 8668
3:6 On the first day of the s month they began 8668
7:7 also came up to Jerusalem in the s year 8679
7:8 in Jerusalem in the fifth month of the s year 8668
Ne 7:73 When the s month came and 8668
8:2 the s month Ezra the priest brought the Law 8668
8:14 in booths during the feast of the s month 8668
10:31 Every s year we will forgo working the land 8668
Est 1:10 On the s day, when King Xerxes was 8668
2:16 in the s year of his reign. 8679
Jer 28:17 In the s month of that same year, 8668
34:14 'Every s year each of you must free any 8679
41:1 In the s month Ishmael son of Nethaniah, 8668
52:28 in the s year, 3,023 Jews; 8679
Eze 20:1 In the s year, in the fifth month 8668
30:20 in the first month on the s day, 8679
45:20 to do the same on the s day of the month 8679
45:25 in the s month on the fifteenth day, 8668
Hag 2:1 On the twenty-first day of the s month, 8668
Zec 7:5 and mourned in the fifth and s months for 8668
8:19 s and tenth months will become joyful 8668
Mt 22:26 right on down to the **s.** *2231*
Jn 4:52 "The fever left him yesterday at the s hour." *1575*
Heb 4:4 about the s day in these words: *1575*
4:4 on the s day God rested from all his work." *1575*
Jude 1:14 Enoch, the s from Adam, *1575*
Rev 8:1 When he opened the s seal, *1575*
10:7 the s angel is about to sound his trumpet, *1575*
11:15 The s angel sounded his trumpet, *1575*
16:17 The s angel poured out his bowl into *1575*
21:20 the sixth carnelian, the s chrysolite, *1575*

SEVENTY (58) [70]

Ge 46:27 which went to Egypt, were s in all. 8679
50:3 And the Egyptians mourned for him s days. 8679
Ex 1:5 The descendants of Jacob numbered s 8679
15:27 twelve springs and s palm trees, 8679
24:1 and s of the elders of Israel. 8679
24:9 and the s elders of Israel went up 8679
Nu 7:13 silver sprinkling bowl weighing s shekels, 8679
7:19 silver sprinkling bowl weighing s shekels, 8679
7:25 silver sprinkling bowl weighing s shekels, 8679
7:31 silver sprinkling bowl weighing s shekels, 8679
7:37 silver sprinkling bowl weighing s shekels, 8679
7:43 silver sprinkling bowl weighing s shekels, 8679
7:49 silver sprinkling bowl weighing s shekels, 8679
7:55 silver sprinkling bowl weighing s shekels, 8679
7:61 silver sprinkling bowl weighing s shekels, 8679
7:67 silver sprinkling bowl weighing s shekels, 8679
7:73 silver sprinkling bowl weighing s shekels, 8679
7:79 silver sprinkling bowl weighing s shekels, 8679
7:85 and each sprinkling bowl s shekels. 8679
11:16 "Bring me s of Israel's elders who are 8679
11:24 He brought together s of their elders 8679
11:25 on him and put the Spirit on the s elders. 8679
33:9 twelve springs and s palm trees, 8679
Dt 10:22 who went down into Egypt were s in all, 8679
Jdg 1:7 "S kings with their thumbs 8679
8:30 He had s sons of his own, 8679
9:2 to have all s of Jerub-Baal's sons rule 8679
9:4 They gave him s shekels of silver from 8679
9:5 and on one stone murdered his s brothers, 8679
9:18 murdered his s sons on a single stone, 8679
9:24 that the crime against Jerub-Baal's s sons, 8679
9:56 to his father by murdering his s brothers. 8679
12:14 who rode on s donkeys. 8679
1Sa 6:19 putting s of them to death 8679
2Sa 24:15 and s thousand of the people from Dan 8679
1Ki 5:15 Solomon had s thousand carriers 8679
2Ki 10:1 in Samaria s sons of the house of Ahab. 8679
10:6 Now the royal princes, s of them, 8679
10:7 the princes and slaughtered all s of them. 8679
1Ch 21:5 including four hundred and s thousand 8679
21:14 and s thousand men of Israel fell dead. 8679
2Ch 2:2 He conscripted s thousand men as carriers 8679
29:32 the assembly brought was s bulls, 8679
36:21 the s years were completed in fulfillment of 8679
Ps 90:10 The length of our days is s years— 8679
Isa 23:15 that time Tyre will be forgotten for s years, 8679
23:15 But at the end of these s years, 8679
23:17 At the end of s years, the LORD will deal 8679
Jer 25:11 will serve the king of Babylon s years. 8679
25:12 "But when the s years are fulfilled, 8679
29:10 "When s years are completed for Babylon, 8679
Eze 8:11 In front of them stood s elders of the house 8679
41:12 on the west side was s cubits wide. 8679
Da 9:2 desolation of Jerusalem would last s years. 8679
9:24 **"S** 'sevens' are decreed for your people 8679
Zec 1:12 you have been angry with these s years?" 8679
7:5 and seventh months for the past s years, 8679
Ac 23:23 s horsemen and two hundred spearmen *1573*

SEVENTY-FIVE (7) [75]

Ge 12:4 Abram was s years old when he set out from Haran. 2256+2822+8679
25:7 Abraham lived a hundred and s years. 2256+2822+8679
Est 5:14 "Have a gallows built, s **feet** high, 564+2822
7:9 gallows s **feet** high stands by Haman's 564+2822
9:16 They killed s thousand of them 2256+2822+8679
Jn 19:39 of myrrh and aloes, about s **pounds.** *1669+3354*
Ac 7:14 Jacob and his whole family, s in all. *1573+4297*

SEVENTY-SEVEN (4)

Ge 4:24 then Lamech s *times*." 2256+8679+8679
Jdg 8:14 the names of the s officials 2256+8679+8679
Ezr 8:35 ninety-six rams, s male lambs 2256+8679+8679
Mt 18:22 I tell you, not seven times, but s **times.** *1574+2231*

SEVENTY-TWO (2) [72]

Lk 10:1 After this the Lord appointed s others *1545+1573*
10:17 The s returned with joy and said, *1545+1573*

SEVERAL (7)

2Ki 17:29 own gods in the *s* **towns** where they settled, AIT
Da 8:27 was exhausted and lay ill *for s* **days.** AIT
11:13 and after s **years,** he will advance with a AIT
Ac 9:19 Saul spent s days with the disciples *5516*
16:12 And we stayed there s days. *5516*
24:17 "After an absence *of* s years, *4498*
24:24 S days later Felix came with his wife *5516*

SEVERE (22) [SEVERELY]

Ge 12:10 there for a while because the famine was **s.** 3878
41:31 the famine that follows it will be so **s.** 3878
41:56 for the famine *was* s throughout Egypt. 2616
41:57 because the famine *was* s in all the world. 2616
43:1 Now the famine was still s in the land. 3878
47:4 because the famine is s in Canaan 3878
47:13 region because the famine was s; 3878+4394
47:20 because the famine *was too* s for them. 2616
Nu 11:33 and he struck them with a s plague. 4394+8041
Dt 28:59 and s and lingering illnesses. 8273
1Ki 18:2 Now the famine was s in Samaria, 2617
2Ki 25:3 *so* s that there was no food for the people 2616
2Ch 16:12 Though his disease was s, 2025+4200+5087
Jer 52:6 *so* s that there was no food for the people 2616
Mt 4:24 those suffering s **pain,** *992*
Lk 4:25 and a half years and there was a s famine *3489*
15:14 there was a s famine in that whole country, *2708*
Ac 11:28 that a s famine would spread over *3489*
2Co 8:2 Out of the most s **trial,** *1509+2568*
1Th 1:6 in spite of s suffering, *4498*
Rev 11:13 that very hour there was a s earthquake and *3489*
16:18 peals of thunder and a s earthquake. *3489*

SEVERED (1) [SEVERING]

Ecc 12:6 before the silver cord **is s,** 8178

SEVERELY (22) [SEVERE]

Ru 1:17 May the LORD deal with me, *be it* ever so **s,** 3578
1Sa 3:17 May God deal with you, *be it* ever so **s,** 3578
14:44 "May God deal with me, *be it* ever so **s,** 3578
20:13 may the LORD deal with me, *be it* ever so **s,** 3578
25:22 May God deal with David, *be it* ever so **s,** 3578
2Sa 3:9 May God deal with Abner, *be it* ever so **s,** 3578
3:35 "May God deal with me, *be it* ever so **s,** 3578
19:13 May God deal with me, *be it* ever so **s,** 3578
1Ki 2:23 "May God deal with me, *be it* ever so **s,** 3578
19:2 May the gods deal with me, *be it* ever so **s,** 3578
20:10 May the gods deal with me, *be it* ever so **s,** 3578
2Ki 6:31 "May God deal with me, *be it* ever so **s,** 3578
13:4 s the king of Aram *was* **oppressing** 4315+4316
2Ch 24:25 they left Joash s wounded. 8041
Ps 118:18 The LORD *has* **chastened** me s, 3579+3579
Mk 12:40 Such men will be punished **most s."** *4358*
Lk 20:47 Such men will be punished **most s."** *4358*
Ac 16:23 After they had been s flogged, *4498*
20:19 *although* I was s **tested** by the plots of *AIT*
2Co 2:5 to some extent—not to **put it too s.** *2096*
11:23 been flogged **more s,** *5649*
Heb 10:29 How much **more** s do you think a man *5937*

SEVERING (2) [SEVERED]

Lev 1:17 by the wings, not s it **completely,** 976
5:8 from its neck, not s it **completely,** 976

SEW (1) [SEWED, SEWS]

Eze 13:18 Woe to *the women who* s magic charms 9529

SEWED (2) [SEW]

Ge 3:7 so *they* s fig leaves **together** 9529
Job 16:15 *"I have* s sackcloth over my skin 9529

SEWS (3) [SEW]

Mt 9:16 "No one s a patch of unshrunk cloth **on** *2095*
Mk 2:21 "No one s a patch of unshrunk cloth on *2165*
Lk 5:36 from a new garment and s it **on** an old one. *2095*

SEX (2) [SEXUAL, SEXUALLY]

Ge 19:5 to us so that *we can* **have** s **with** them." 3359
Jdg 19:22 to your house so *we can* **have** s **with** him." 3359

SEXUAL (47) [SEX]

Ex 19:15 **Abstain from** s **relations."** 440+448+851+5602
22:19 "Anyone *who* **has** s **relations with** 6640+8886
Lev 18:6 any close relative to **have** s **relations.** 1655+6872
18:7 *Do* not **dishonor** your father **by having** s **relations with** your mother. 1655+6872

Lev 18: 8 " '*Do* not **have s relations with** your father's wife; 1655+6872
18: 9 " '*Do* not **have s relations with** your sister, 1655+6872
18:10 " '*Do* not **have s relations with** your son's daughter 1655+6872
18:11 " '*Do* not **have s relations with** the daughter of your father's wife 1655+6872
18:12 " '*Do* not **have s relations with** your father's sister; 1655+6872
18:13 " '*Do* not **have s relations with** your mother's sister, 1655+6872
18:14 " '*Do* not **dishonor** your father's brother **by** approaching his wife **to have s relations;** 1655+6872
18:15 " '*Do* not **have s relations with** your daughter-in-law. 1655+6872
18:16 " '*Do* not **have s relations with** your brother's wife; 1655+6872
18:17 " '*Do* not **have s relations with** both a woman and her daughter. 1655+6872
18:17 *Do* not **have s relations with** either 1655+6872
18:18 a rival wife and **have s relations** with 1655+6872
18:19 to **have s relations** during the uncleanness of her monthly period. 1655+6872
18:20 " '*Do* not **have s relations** with your neighbor's wife 2446+4200+5989+8888
18:23 not **have s relations** with an animal 5989+8888
18:23 to an animal to **have s relations with** it; 8061
20:15 a man **has s relations** with an animal, 5989+8888
20:16 an animal to **have s relations with** it, 8061
20:17 and *they* **have s relations,** 906+6872+8011
20:18 and **has s relations with** her, 906+1655+6872
20:19 " '*Do* not **have s relations with** the sister of either your mother 1655+6872
Nu 25: 1 the men began to **indulge in s immorality** 2388
Dt 27:21 "Cursed is the man *who* **has s relations with** any animal." 6640+8886
Mt 15:19 murder, adultery, **s immorality,** theft, *4518*
Mk 7:21 come evil thoughts, **s immorality,** theft, *4518*
Ac 15:20 by idols, from **s immorality,** from the meat *4518*
15:29 strangled animals and *from* **s immorality.** *4518*
21:25 strangled animals and from **s immorality."** *4518*
Ro 1:24 of their hearts to **s impurity** for *174*
13:13 not *in* **s immorality** and debauchery, *3130*
1Co 5: 1 that there is **s immorality** among you, and *4518*
6:13 The body is not *meant for* **s immorality,** *4518*
6:18 Flee from **s immorality.** *4518*
10: 8 *We should* not **commit s immorality,** *4519*
2Co 12:21 have not repented of the impurity, **s sin** *4518*
Gal 5:19 **s immorality,** impurity and debauchery; *4518*
Eph 5: 3 not be even a hint of **s immorality,** *4518*
Col 3: 5 **s immorality,** impurity, lust, *4518*
1Th 4: 3 that you should avoid **s immorality;** *4518*
Jude 1: 7 **gave** themselves **up to s immorality** *1745*
Rev 2:14 and by **committing s immorality.** *4519*
2:20 misleads my servants into **s immorality** and *4519*
9:21 their **s immorality** or their thefts. *4518*

SEXUALLY (8) [SEX]

1Co 5: 9 not to associate with **s immoral** *people*— *4521*
5:11 a brother but is **s immoral** or greedy, *4521*
6: 9 the **s immoral** nor idolaters nor adulterers *4521*
6:18 but he who **sins s** sins against his own body. *4519*
Heb 12:16 See that no one *is* **s immoral,** *4521*
13: 4 the adulterer and all the **s immoral.** *4521*
Rev 21: 8 the vile, the murderers, the **s immoral,** *4521*
22:15 the **s immoral,** the murderers, *4521*

SHAALABBIN (1)

Jos 19:42 **S,** Aijalon, Ithlah, 9125

SHAALBIM (2)

Jdg 1:35 to hold out in Mount Heres, Aijalon and **S,** 9124
1Ki 4: 9 **S,** Beth Shemesh and Elon Bethhanan; 9124

SHAALBONITE (2)

2Sa 23:32 Eliahba the **S,** the sons of Jashen, Jonathan 9126
1Ch 11:33 Azmaveth the Baharumite, Eliahba the **S,** 9126

SHAALIM (1)

1Sa 9: 4 They went on into the district of **S,** 9127

SHAAPH (2)

1Ch 2:47 Jotham, Geshan, Pelet, Ephah and **S.** 9131
2:49 to **S** the father of Madmannah and to Sheva 9131

SHAARAIM (3)

Jos 15:36 **S,** Adithaim and Gederah 9139
1Sa 17:52 Their dead were strewn along the **S** road 9139
1Ch 4:31 Hazar Susim, Beth Biri and **S.** 9139

SHAASHGAZ (1)

Est 2:14 of the harem to the care of **S,** 9140

SHABBETHAI (3)

Ezr 10:15 supported by Meshullam and **S** the Levite, 8703
Ne 8: 7 Jeshua, Bani, Sherebiah, Jamin, Akkub, **S,** 8703
11:16 **S** and Jozabad, two of the heads of 8703

SHABBY (1)

Jas 2: 2 and a poor man in **s** clothes also comes in. *4865*

SHACHIA (KJV) See SAKIA

SHACKLES (12)

Jdg 16:21 Binding him with **bronze** *s,* AIT
2Ki 25: 7 with **bronze s** and took him to Babylon. 5733
2Ch 33:11 with **bronze s** and took him to Babylon. 5733
36: 6 and bound him with **bronze s** to take him 5733
Job 12:18 He takes off the **s** *put on by* kings and ties 4591
13:27 You fasten my feet in **s;** 6040
33:11 He fastens my feet in **s;** 6040
Ps 105:18 They bruised his feet with **s,** 3890
149: 8 their nobles with **s** *of* iron, 3890
Jer 39: 7 and bound him with **bronze s** to take him 5733
52:11 with **bronze s** and took him to Babylon, 5733
Na 1:13 from your neck and tear your **s** away." 4593

SHADE (19)

Jdg 9:15 come and take refuge in my **s;** 7498
Ne 8:15 palms and **s** trees, to make booths"— 6290
Ps 80:10 The mountains were covered with its **s,** 7498
121: 5 the LORD is your **s** at your right hand; 7498
SS 2: 3 I delight to sit in his **s,** 7498
Isa 4: 6 be a shelter and **s** from the heat of the day, 7498
25: 4 from the storm and a **s** from the heat. 7498
30: 2 to Egypt's **s** for refuge. 7498
30: 3 Egypt's **s** will bring you disgrace. 7498
Jer 4:30 Why **s** your eyes with paint? 7973
Eze 17:23 they will find shelter in the **s** 7498
31: 6 all the great nations lived in its **s.** 7498
31:12 of the earth came out from under its **s** 7498
31:17 Those who lived in its **s,** 7498
Hos 4:13 where the **s** is pleasant. 7498
14: 7 Men will dwell again in his **s.** 7498
Jnh 4: 5 sat in its **s** and waited to see what would 7498
4: 6 to give **s** for his head to ease his discomfort, 7498
Mk 4:32 that the birds of the air can perch in its **s."** *5014*

SHADOW (40) [SHADOWS]

2Ki 20: 9 Shall the **s** go forward ten steps, 7498
20:10 for the **s** to go forward ten steps," 7498
20:11 the **s** go back the ten steps it had gone down 7498
1Ch 29:15 Our days on earth are like a **s,** 7498
Job 3: 5 and **deep s** claim it once more; 7516
8: 9 and our days on earth are but a **s.** 7498
10:21 to the land of gloom and **deep s,** 7516
10:22 of deepest night, of **deep s** and disorder, 7516
14: 2 like a fleeting **s,** he does not endure. 7498
17: 7 my whole frame is but a **s.** 7498
34:22 There is no dark place, no **deep s,** 7516
38:17 Have you seen the gates of the **s of death?** 7516
40:22 The lotuses conceal him in their **s;** 7498
Ps 17: 8 hide me in the **s** *of* your wings 7498
23: 4 I walk through the valley of the **s of death,** 7516
36: 7 and low among men find refuge in the **s** 7498
57: 1 I will take refuge in the **s** *of* your wings 7498
63: 7 I sing in the **s** *of* your wings. 7498
91: 1 Most High will rest in the **s** *of* the Almighty. 7498
102:11 My days are like the evening **s;** 7498
109:23 I fade away like an evening **s;** 7498
144: 4 his days are like a fleeting **s.** 7498
Ecc 6:12 days he passes through like a **s?** 7498
8:13 and their days will not lengthen like a **s.** 7498
Isa 9: 2 on those living in the land of the **s of death** 7516
16: 3 Make your **s** like night—at high noon. 7498
25: 5 as heat is reduced by the **s** *of* a cloud, 7498
32: 2 like streams of water in the desert and the **s** 7498
34:15 for her young under the **s** *of* her wings; 7498
38: 8 I will make the **s** cast by the sun go back 7498
49: 2 in the **s** *of* his hand he hid me; 7498
51:16 and covered you with the **s** *of* my hand— 7498
Jer 48:45 "In the **s** *of* Heshbon the fugitives stand 7498
La 4:20 We thought that under his **s** we would live 7498
Mt 4:16 on those living in the land of the **s** of death *5014*
Lk 1:79 on those living in darkness and in the **s** *5014*
Ac 5:15 at least Peter's **s** might fall on some of them *5014*
Col 2:17 These are a **s** of the things that were *5014*
Heb 8: 5 at a sanctuary that is a copy and **s** of what is *5014*
10: 1 a **s** of the good things that are coming— *5014*

SHADOWS (11) [SHADOW]

Jdg 9:36 "You mistake the **s** *of* the mountains 7498
Ne 13:19 When **evening s fell** *on* the gates 7511
Job 7: 2 Like a slave longing for the **evening s,** 7498
12:22 of darkness and brings **deep s** into the light. 7516
16:16 **deep s** ring my eyes; 7516
Ps 11: 2 the strings to shoot from the **s** at the upright 694
SS 2:17 Until the day breaks and the **s** flee, turn, 7498
4: 6 Until the day breaks and the **s** flee, 7498
Isa 59: 9 for brightness, but we walk in **deep s.** 696
Jer 6: 4 and the **s** *of* evening grow long. 7498
Jas 1:17 who does not change like shifting **s.** *5572*

SHADRACH (14)

Da 1: 7 the name Belteshazzar; to Hananiah, **S;** 8731
2:49 at Daniel's request the king appointed **S,** 10701
3:12 **S,** Meshach and Abednego— 10701
3:13 Nebuchadnezzar summoned **S,** 10701
3:14 "Is it true, **S,** Meshach and Abednego, 10701
3:16 **S,** Meshach and Abednego replied to 10701
3:19 Then Nebuchadnezzar was furious with **S,** 10701
3:20 in his army to tie up **S,** Meshach and 10701
3:22 the fire killed the soldiers who took up **S,** 10701
3:26 **"S,** Meshach and Abednego, servants of 10701
3:26 So **S,** Meshach and Abednego came out of 10701
3:28 "Praise be to the God of **S,** Meshach and 10701
3:29 against the God of **S,** Meshach and 10701
3:30 Then the king promoted **S,** Meshach and 10701

SHAFT (9)

Ex 25:31 of pure gold and hammer it out, base and **s;** 7866
37:17 and hammered it out, base and **s;** 7866
1Sa 17: 7 His spear's **s** was like a weaver's rod, 6770
2Sa 5: 8 the Jebusites will have to use the **water s** 7562
21:19 a spear with a **s** like a weaver's rod. 6770
23: 7 a tool of iron or the **s** *of* a spear; 6770
1Ch 20: 5 a spear with a **s** like a weaver's rod. 6770
Job 28: 4 Far from where people dwell he cuts a **s,** 5707
Rev 9: 1 The star was given the key *to* the **s** of *5853*

SHAGEE (1)

1Ch 11:34 Jonathan son of **S** the Hararite, 8707

SHAGGY (1)

Da 8:21 The **s** goat is the king of Greece, 8537

SHAHAR See ZERETH SHAHAR

SHAHARAIM (1)

1Ch 8: 8 Sons were born to **S** in Moab 8844

SHAHAZUMAH (1)

Jos 19:22 The boundary touched Tabor, **S** and 8833

SHAKE (31) [SHAKEN, SHAKES, SHAKING, SHOOK]

Jdg 16:20 "I'll go out as before and **s myself free."** 5850
Ne 5:13 "In this way *may* God **s out** of his house 5850
Job 4:14 and **made** all my bones **s.** 7064
16: 4 against you and **s** my head at you. 5675
38:13 the earth by the edges and **s** the wicked out 5850
Ps 10: 6 He says to himself, "Nothing *will* **s** *me;* 4572
44:14 the peoples **s** their heads at us. 4954
64: 8 who see them *will* **s** *their* **heads in scorn.** 5653
99: 1 between the cherubim, *let* the earth **s.** 5667
109:25 when they see me, *they* **s** their heads. 5675
Isa 2:19 when he rises to **s** the earth. 6907
2:21 when he rises to **s** the earth. 6907
5:25 The mountains **s,** and the dead bodies are 8074
10:32 *they will* **s** their fist at the mount of 5677
13:13 the earth *will* **s** from its place at the wrath 8321
24:18 the foundations of the earth **s.** 8321
52: 2 **S off** your dust; rise up, sit enthroned, 5850
Jer 18:16 by will be appalled and *will* **s** their heads. 5653
48:27 that *you* **s** *your* **head in scorn** 5653
La 2:15 they scoff and **s** their heads at the Daughter 5675
Am 9: 1 of the pillars so that the thresholds **s.** 8321
9: 9 and *I will* **s** the house of Israel among all 5675
Zep 2:15 All who pass by her scoff and **s** their fists. 5675
Hag 2: 6 while I *will* once more **s** the heavens and 8321
2: 7 *I will* **s** all nations, 8321
2:21 that I *will* **s** the heavens and the earth. 8321
Mt 10:14 **s** the dust **off** your feet when you leave *1759*
Mk 6:11 **s** the dust **off** your feet when you leave, *1759*
Lk 6:48 torrent struck that house but could not **s** it, *4888*
9: 5 **s** the dust **off** your feet when you leave *701*
Heb 12:26 "Once more I *will* **s** not only the earth but *4940*

SHAKEN (33) [SHAKE]

1Sa 28:21 to Saul and saw that *he* **was** greatly **s,** 987
2Sa 18:33 The king *was* **s.** 8074
Ne 5:13 So may such a man be **s out** and emptied!" 5850
Job 34:20 the people **are s** and they pass away; 1723
Ps 15: 5 He who does these things *will* never **be s.** 4572
16: 8 he is at my right hand, *I will* not **be s.** 4572
21: 7 of the Most High *he will* not **be s.** 4572
30: 6 I felt secure, I said, *"I will never* **be s."** 4572
60: 2 *You have* **s** the land and torn it open; 8321
62: 2 he is my fortress, *I will* never **be s.** 4572
62: 6 he is my fortress, *I will* not **be s.** 4572
82: 5 all the foundations of the earth **are s.** 4572
109:23 *I* **am s off** like a locust. 5850
112: 6 Surely *he will* never **be s;** 4572
125: 1 *which* cannot **be s** but endures forever. 4572
Isa 7: 2 so the hearts of Ahaz and his people *were* **s,** 5675
7: 2 as the trees of the forest *are* **s** by the wind. 5675
24:19 the earth **is thoroughly s.** 4572+4572
54:10 mountains *be* **s** and the hills be removed, 4631
54:10 yet my unfailing love for you *will* not *be* **s** 4631
Am 9: 9 of Israel among all the nations as grain is **s** 5675
Na 3:12 when *they are* **s,** the figs fall into the mouth 5675
Mt 24:29 and the heavenly bodies *will be* **s.'** *4888*
Mk 13:25 and the heavenly bodies *will be* **s.'** *4888*
Lk 6:38 pressed down, **s together** and running over, *4888*
21:26 for the heavenly bodies *will be* **s.** *4888*
Ac 2:25 he is at my right hand, *I will* not *be* **s.** *4888*
4:31 the place where they were meeting *was* **s.** *4888*
16:26 that the foundations of the prison *were* **s.** *4888*
Heb 12:27 the removing of what *can be* **s**— *4888*
12:27 so that what cannot *be* **s** may remain. *4888*
12:28 a kingdom that **cannot be s,** *810*

Rev 6:13 as late figs drop from a fig tree *when* s by *4940*

SHAKES (6) [SHAKE]
Job 9: 6 He s the earth from its place 8074
15:25 because *he* s his fist at God 5742
Ps 29: 8 The voice of the LORD s the desert; 2655
29: 8 the LORD s the Desert of Kadesh. 2655
Isa 30:28 He s the nations in the sieve of destruction; 5677
Joel 2:10 Before them the earth s, the sky trembles, 8074

SHAKING (3) [SHAKE]
Ps 22: 7 they hurl insults, s their heads: 5675
Mt 27:39 by hurled insults at him, s their heads *3075*
Mk 15:29 s their heads and saying, "So! *3075*

SHALIM (KJV) See SHAALIM

SHALISHA (1)
1Sa 9: 4 of Ephraim and through the area around S, 8995

SHALISHAH See BAAL SHALISHAH

SHALL (467) See Index of Articles Etc.

SHALLEKETH (1)
1Ch 26:16 The lots for the West Gate and the S Gate 8962

SHALLOW (2)
Mt 13: 5 It sprang up quickly, because the soil *was* s. *958+2400+3590*
Mk 4: 5 It sprang up quickly, because the soil was s. *958+3590*

SHALLUM (25) [SHALLUM'S]
2Ki 15:10 S son of Jabesh conspired against 8935
15:13 S son of Jabesh became king in the 8935
15:14 He attacked S son of Jabesh in Samaria, 8935
22:14 who was the wife of S son of Tikvah, 8935
1Ch 2:40 Sismai the father of S, 8935
2:41 S the father of Jekamiah, 8935
3:15 Zedekiah the third, S the fourth. 8935
4:25 S was Shaul's son, 8935
6:12 Zadok the father of S, 8935
6:13 S the father of Hilkiah, 8935
9:17 The gatekeepers: S, Akkub, Talmon, 8935
9:17 and their brothers, S their chief 8935
9:19 S son of Kore, the son of Ebiasaph, 8935
9:31 the firstborn son of S the Korahite, 8935
2Ch 28:12 of Meshillemoth, Jehizkiah son of S, 8935
34:22 who was the wife of S son of Tokhath, 8935
Ezr 2:42 the descendants of S, Ater, Talmon, 8935
7: 2 the son of S, the son of Zadok, 8935
10:24 From the gatekeepers: S, Telem and Uri. 8935
10:42 S, Amariah and Joseph. 8935
Ne 3:12 S son of Hallohesh, 8935
7:45 the descendants of S, Ater, Talmon, 8935
Jer 22:11 the LORD says about S son of Josiah, 8935
32: 7 of S your uncle is going to come to you 8935
35: 4 which was over that of Maaseiah son of S 8935

SHALLUM'S (1) [SHALLUM]
2Ki 15:15 The other events of S reign, 8935

SHALLUN (1)
Ne 3:15 The Fountain Gate was repaired by S son 8937

SHALMAI (2)
Ezr 2:46 Hagab, S, Hanan, 8978
Ne 7:48 Lebana, Hagaba, S, 8978

SHALMAN (1)
Hos 10:14 as S devastated Beth Arbel on the day 8986

SHALMANESER (3) [SHALMANESER'S]
2Ki 17: 3 S king of Assyria came up 8987
17: 4 S seized him and put him in prison. 855+4889S
18: 9 S king of Assyria marched against Samaria 8987

SHALMANESER'S (1) [SHALMANESER]
2Ki 17: 3 Hoshea, who had been S vassal 2257+4200S

SHAMA (1)
1Ch 11:44 S and Jeiel the sons of Hotham 9052

SHAMARIAH (KJV) See SHEMARIAH

SHAMBLES (KJV) See MEAT MARKET

SHAME (128) [ASHAMED, SHAMED, SHAMEFUL, SHAMEFULLY, SHAMELESS, SHAMELESSLY, SHAMING]
Ge 2:25 were both naked, and *they* **felt** no s. 1017
Dt 32: 5 to their s they are no longer his children, 4583
1Sa 20:30 sided with the son of Jesse to your own s 1425
20:30 to the s *of* the mother who bore you? 1425+6872
2Ki 19:26 are dismayed and **put to s.** 1017
Job 8:22 Your enemies will be clothed in s, 1425
10:15 I am full of s and drowned in my affliction. 7830
11:15 then you will lift up your face without s; 4583
Ps 4: 2 O men, will you turn my glory into s? 4009
25: 2 *Do* not *let me be* **put to s,** 1017
25: 3 whose hope is in you *will* ever *be* **put to s,** 1017
25: 3 *be* **put to s** who are treacherous 1017
25:20 *let me* not *be* **put to s,** 1017
31: 1 *let me* never *be* **put to s;** 1017
31:17 *Let me* not *be* **put to s,** O LORD, 1017
31:17 the wicked *be* **put to s** and lie silent in 1017
34: 5 their faces *are* never **covered with s.** 2917
35: 4 be disgraced and **put to s;** 4007
35:26 over my distress *be* **put to s** and confusion; 1017
35:26 over me be clothed with s and disgrace. 1425
40:14 to take my life *be* **put to s** and confusion; 1017
40:15 be appalled at their own s. 1425
44: 7 **put** our adversaries **to s.** 1017
44:15 and my face is covered with s 1425
53: 5 *you* **put** them **to s,** for God despised them. 1017
69: 6 *may* those who seek you not *be* **put to s** 4007
69: 7 and s covers my face. 4009
70: 2 *May* those who seek my life *be* **put to s** 1017
70: 3 turn back because of their s. 1425
71: 1 *let me* never *be* **put to s.** 1017
71:13 May my accusers perish *in* s; 1017
71:24 to harm me *have been* **put to s** 1017
78:66 he put them to everlasting s. 3075
83:16 with s so that men will seek your name, 7830
86:17 my enemies may see it and *be* **put to s,** 1017
89:45 you have covered him with a mantle of s. 1019
97: 7 All who worship images *are* **put to s,** 1017
109:28 when they attack *they will be* **put to s,** 1017
109:29 be clothed with disgrace and wrapped in s 1425
119: 6 Then *I would* not *be* **put to s** 1017
119:31 *do* not **let me be put to s.** 1017
119:46 before kings and *will* not *be* **put to s,** 1017
119:78 the arrogant *be* **put to s** for wronging me 1017
119:80 that *I may* not *be* **put to s.** 1017
127: 5 not *be* **put to s** when they contend 1017
129: 5 May all who hate Zion be turned back *in* s. 1017
132:18 I will clothe his enemies with s, 1425
Pr 3:35 but fools he holds up to s. 7830
6:33 and his s will never be wiped away; 3075
13: 5 but the wicked **bring** s and disgrace. 944
13:18 ignores discipline comes to poverty and s, 7830
18: 3 and with s comes disgrace. 7830
18:13 that is his folly and his s. 4009
19:26 a son *who* **brings** s and disgrace. 1017
25: 8 in the end if your neighbor **puts** you **to s?** 4007
25:10 or he who hears it *may* s you 2873
Isa 20: 4 with buttocks bared—*to* Egypt's s. 6872
20: 5 in Egypt will be afraid and **put to s.** 1017
26:11 for your people and *be* **put to s;** 1017
30: 3 But Pharaoh's protection will be to your s, 1425
30: 5 **be put to s** because of a people useless 1017
30: 5 but only s and disgrace." 1425
37:27 are dismayed and **put to s.** 1017
42:17 will be turned back *in* **utter s.** 1017+1425
44: 9 they are ignorant, to *their own* s. 1017
44:11 *He* and his kind *will be* **put to s;** 1017
45:16 All the makers of idols *will be* **put to s** 1017
45:17 *you will* never *be* **put to s** or disgraced, 1017
45:24 will come to him and *be* **put to s.** 1017
47: 3 be exposed and your s uncovered. 3075
50: 7 and I know *I will* not *be* **put to s.** 1017
54: 4 "Do not be afraid; *you will* not **suffer s.** 1017
54: 4 the s *of* your youth and remember no more 1425
61: 7 Instead of their s my people will receive 1425
65:13 but you *will be* **put to s.** 1017
66: 5 Yet they *will be* **put to s.** 1017
Jer 3: 3 you refuse *to* **blush with s.** 4007
3:25 Let us lie down in our s, 1425
6:15 No, *they* **have** no **s at all;** 1017+1017
7:19 harming themselves, to their own s? 1425
8: 9 The wise *will be* **put to s;** 1017
8:12 No, *they* **have** no **s at all;** 1017+1017
9:19 How great *is our* **s!** 1017
12:13 So **bear** *the* s of your harvest because of 1017
13:26 over your face that your s may be seen— 7830
17:13 all who forsake you *will be* **put to s.** 1017
17:18 *Let* my persecutors *be* **put to s,** 1017
17:18 but *keep* me from **s;** 1017
20:18 and sorrow and to end my days in s? 1425
23:40 everlasting s that will not be forgotten." 4010
46:12 The nations will hear of your s; 7830
46:24 The Daughter of Egypt *will be* **put to s,** 1017
48:39 How Moab turns her back *in* **s!** 1017
50: 2 Bel *will be* **put to s,** 1017
50: 2 **be put to s** and her idols filled with terror.' 1017
51:51 and s covers our faces, 4009
Eze 7:18 be covered with s and their heads will 1019
23:29 the s *of* your prostitution will be exposed. 6872
32:24 They bear their s with those who go down 4009
32:25 they bear their s with those who go down to 4009
32:30 and bear their s with those who go down to 4009
39:26 They will forget their s and all 4009
44:13 the s *of* their detestable practices. 4009
Da 9: 7 but this day we are covered with s— 1425
9: 8 with s because we have sinned against you. 1425
12: 2 others to s and everlasting contempt. 3075
Hos 4:19 and their sacrifices *will* **bring** *them* s. 1017
Am 8:14 They who swear by the s *of* Samaria, 873
Ob 1:10 you will be covered with s; 1019
Mic 1:11 Pass on in nakedness and s, 1425
7:10 and will be covered with s, 1019
Na 3: 5 and the kingdoms your s. 7830
Hab 2:16 You will be filled with s instead of glory. 7830
Zep 3: 5 yet the unrighteous know no s. 1425
3:11 that day *you will* not *be* **put to s** for all 1017
3:19 in every land where they were put to s. 1425
Ro 9:33 who trusts in him *will* never *be* **put to s."** *2875*
10:11 who trusts in him *will* never *be* **put to s."** *2875*
1Co 1:27 the foolish things of the world to s the wise; *2875*
1:27 God chose the weak things of the world to s *2875*
4:14 I am not writing this *to* s you, *1956*
6: 5 I say this to s you. *1959*
15:34 I say this to your s. *1959*
2Co 11:21 **To my s** I admit that we were too weak *871+2848*
Php 3:19 and their glory is in their s. *158*
Heb 12: 2 endured the cross, scorning its s, *158*
1Pe 2: 6 who trusts in him *will* never *be* **put to s."** *2875*
Jude 1:13 wild waves of the sea, foaming up their s; *158*

SHAMED (5) [SHAME]
Ps 69:19 how I am scorned, disgraced and s; 4009
Jer 10:14 every goldsmith *is* s by his idols. 1017
51:17 every goldsmith *is* s by his idols. 1017
Joel 2:26 never again *will* my people *be* s. 1017
2:27 never again *will* my people *be* s. 1017

SHAMEFACEDNESS (KJV) See DECENCY

SHAMEFUL (15) [SHAME]
1Sa 20:34 at his father's s **treatment** *of* David. 4007
Job 31:11 that would have been s, a sin to be judged. 2365
Pr 14:35 but a s servant incurs his wrath. 1017
Jer 3:24 From our youth s **gods** have consumed 1425
11:13 to that s **god** Baal are as many as the streets 1425
Hos 4:18 their rulers dearly love s **ways.** 7830
6: 9 the road to Shechem, committing s **crimes.** 2365
9:10 they consecrated themselves to that s **idol** 1425
Zep 2: 1 gather together, O s nation, 4083+4202
Ro 1:26 of this, God gave them over to s lusts. *871*
2Co 4: 2 we have renounced secret and s ways; *158*
Eph 5:12 For it is s even to mention what *156*
2Pe 2: 2 Many will follow their s *ways* *816*
Rev 3:18 so you can cover your s nakedness; *158*
21:27 will anyone who does **what is** s or deceitful, *1007*

SHAMEFULLY (4) [SHAME]
Eze 22:11 another s defiles his daughter-in-law, 928+2365
Mk 12: 4 on the head and **treated** him s. *870*
Lk 20:11 and **treated** s and sent away empty-handed. *869*
Rev 16:15 he may not go naked and be s exposed." *859*

SHAMELESS (1) [SHAME]
Jer 13:27 and lustful neighings, your s prostitution! 2365

SHAMELESSLY (1) [SHAME]
Job 19: 3 reproached me; s you attack me. 1017+4202

SHAMER (KJV) See SHEMER, SHOMER

SHAMGAR (2)
Jdg 3:31 After Ehud came S son of Anath, 9011
5: 6 "In the days of S son of Anath, 9011

SHAMHUTH (1)
1Ch 27: 8 was the commander S the Izrahite. 9016

SHAMING (1) [SHAME]
Hab 2:10 s your own house and forfeiting your life. 1425

SHAMIR (4)
Jos 15:48 In the hill country: S, Jattir, Socoh, 9034
Jdg 10: 1 He lived in S, in the hill country of Ephraim 9034
10: 2 then he died, and was buried in S. 9034
1Ch 24:24 from the sons of Micah: S. 9033

SHAMMA (1)
1Ch 7:37 Bezer, Hod, S, Shilshah, Ithran and Beera. 9007

SHAMMAH (9)
Ge 36:13 Nahath, Zerah, S and Mizzah. 9015
36:17 Chiefs Nahath, Zerah, S and Mizzah. 9015
1Sa 16: 9 Jesse then had S pass by, but Samuel said, 9015
17:13 and the third, S. 9015
2Sa 23:11 to him was S son of Agee the Hararite. 9007
23:12 S took his stand in the middle of the field. NIH
23:25 S the Harodite, Elika the Harodite, 9015
23:33 son of S the Hararite, 9015
1Ch 1:37 Nahath, Zerah, S and Mizzah. 9015

SHAMMAI (5) [SHAMMAI'S]
1Ch 2:28 The sons of Onam: S and Jada. 9025
2:28 The sons of S: Nadab and Abishur. 9025
2:44 Rekem was the father of S. 9025
2:45 The son of S was Maon, 9025
4:17 S and Ishbah the father of Eshtemoa. 9025

SHAMMAI'S (1) [SHAMMAI]
1Ch 2:32 The sons of Jada, S brother: 9025

SHAMMOTH (1)
1Ch 11:27 S the Harorite, Helez the Pelonite, 9021

SHAMMUA (6)
Nu 13: 4 from the tribe of Reuben, S son of Zaccur; 9018
2Sa 5:14 S, Shobab, Nathan, Solomon, 9018
1Ch 3: 5 S, Shobab, Nathan and Solomon. 9055
14: 4 S, Shobab, Nathan, Solomon, 9018
Ne 11:17 and Abda son of S, the son of Galal, 9018
12:18 of Bilgah's, S; of Shemaiah's, Jehonathan; 9018

SHAMSHERAI (1)
1Ch 8:26 S, Sheharíah, Athaliah, 9091

SHAN See BETH SHAN

SHAPE (12) [SHAPED, SHAPES, SHAPING]
Ex 32: 4 made it into an idol cast in the **s of a calf,** 6319
32: 8 an idol cast in the **s of a calf.** 6319
Dt 4:16 an idol, an image of any **s,** 6166
9:16 an idol cast in the **s of a calf.** 6319
1Ki 6:25 two cherubim were identical in size and **s.** 7893
7:19 of the pillars in the portico were in the s 5126
7:22 The capitals on top were in the s *of* lilies. 5126
7:23 the Sea of cast metal, **circular in s,** 6017+6318
7:37 and were identical in size and **s.** 7893
2Ki 17:16 two idols cast in the **s of calves,** 6319
2Ch 4: 2 the Sea of cast metal, **circular in s,** 6017+6318
Job 38:14 The earth **takes** s like clay under a seal; 2200

SHAPED (5) [SHAPE]
Ex 25:33 Three cups **s like almond flowers** 5481
25:34 four cups **s like almond flowers** 5481
37:19 Three cups **s like almond flowers** 5481
37:20 four cups **s like almond flowers** 5481
Job 10: 8 "Your hands s me and made me. 6771

SHAPES (4) [SHAPE]
Isa 44:10 Who s a god and casts an idol, 3670
44:12 *he* s an idol with hammers, 3670
44:13 *He* s it in the form of man, 6913
Jer 10: 3 and a craftsman s it with his chisel. 3338+5126

SHAPHAM (1)
1Ch 5:12 S the second, then Janai and Shaphat, 9171

SHAPHAN (30)
2Ki 22: 3 S son of Azaliah, the son of Meshullam, 9177
22: 8 the high priest said to S the secretary, 9177
22: 8 He gave it to S, who read it. 9177
22: 9 Then S the secretary went to the king 9177
22:10 Then S the secretary informed the king, 9177
22:10 S read from it in the presence of the king. 9177
22:12 Ahikam son of S, Acbor son of Micaiah, 9177
22:12 S the secretary and Asaiah 9177
22:14 S and Asaiah went to speak to 9177
25:22 Gedaliah son of Ahikam, the son of S, 9177
2Ch 34: 8 he sent S son of Azaliah and Maaseiah 9177
34:15 Hilkiah said to S the secretary, 9177
34:15 He gave it to S. 9177
34:16 Then S took the book to the king 9177
34:18 Then S the secretary informed the king, 9177
34:18 S read from it in the presence of the king. 9177
34:20 Ahikam son of S, Abdon son of Micah, 9177
34:20 S the secretary and Asaiah 9177
Jer 26:24 Ahikam son of S supported Jeremiah, 9177
29: 3 He entrusted the letter to Elasah son of S 9177
36:10 From the room of Gemariah son of S 9177
36:11 Micaiah son of Gemariah, the son of S, 9177
36:12 Elnathan son of Acbor, Gemariah son of S, 9177
39:14 the son of S, to take him back to his home. 9177
40: 5 Gedaliah son of Ahikam, the son of S, 9177
40: 9 Gedaliah son of Ahikam, the son of S, 9177
40:11 the son of S, as governor over them, 9177
41: 2 the son of S, with the sword, 9177
43: 6 Gedaliah son of Ahikam, the son of S, 9177
Eze 8:11 and Jaazaniah son of S was standing 9177

SHAPHAT (8)
Nu 13: 5 from the tribe of Simeon, S son of Hori; 9151
1Ki 19:16 of S from Abel Meholah to succeed you 9151
19:19 from there and found Elisha son of S. 9151
2Ki 3:11 "Elisha son of S is here. 9151
6:31 of S remains on his shoulders today!" 9151
1Ch 3:22 Hattush, Igal, Bariah, Neariah and S— 9151
5:12 Shapham the second, then Janai and S, 9151
27:29 S son of Adlai was in charge of the herds in 9151

SHAPHER (KJV) See SHEPHER

SHAPHIR (1)
Mic 1:11 in nakedness and shame, you who live in S. 9160

SHAPING (2) [SHAPE]
Jer 18: 4 the pot he *was* s from the clay was marred 6913
Jer 18: 4 into another pot, s it as seemed best to him. 6913

SHARAI (1)
Ezr 10:40 Macnadebai, Shashai, S, 9232

SHARAIM (KJV) See SHAARAIM

SHARAR (1)
2Sa 23:33 Ahiam son of S the Hararite, 9243

SHARE (102) [SHARED, SHARERS, SHARES, SHARING]
Ge 14:24 the s *that belongs to* the men who went 2750
14:24 Let them have their **s."** 2750
21:10 slave woman's son *will* never **s in the inheritance** with my son Isaac." 3769
31:14 "Do we still have any s in the inheritance 2750
Ex 12: 4 they *must* s one with their nearest neighbor, 4374
18:22 because *they will* s it with you. 5951
29:26 and it will be your **s.** 4950
29:28 the **regular** s from the Israelites for Aaron 2976
Lev 6:17 as their s of the offerings made to me 2750
6:18 It is his regular s of the offerings made to 2976
6:22 It is the LORD's regular s and is to 2976
7:33 the right thigh as his **s.** 4950
7:34 the priest and his sons as their regular s 2976
7:36 to them as their regular s for the generations 2978
8:29 Moses' s of the ordination ram— 4950
10:13 because it is your s and your sons' share of 2976
10:13 because it is your share and your sons' s of 2976
10:14 to you and your children as your s of 2976
10:15 be the regular s for you and your children, 2976
19:17 so *you will* not **s in** his guilt. 5951+6584
24: 9 of their regular s *of* the offerings made to 2976
25:51 a **larger s of** the price paid for him. 4946
Nu 10:32 *we will* s with you whatever good things 3512
18: 8 and your sons as your portion and regular **s.** 2976
18:11 and daughters as your regular **s.** 2976
18:19 and daughters as your regular **s.** 2976
18:20 nor will you have any s among them; 2750
18:20 I am your s and your inheritance among 2750
31:29 from their **half** s and give it to Eleazar 4734
31:36 The half s *of* those who fought in 2750
Dt 10: 9 the Levites have no s or inheritance 2750
18: 3 This is the s *due* the priests from 5477
18: 8 *He is to* s equally **in** their benefits, 430
21:17 as the firstborn by giving him a double s 7023
Jos 14: 4 The Levites received no s of the land 2750
17: 5 Manasseh's s consisted of ten tracts 2475
19: 9 of the Simeonites was taken from the s 2475
22:19 and s the land with us. 296
22:25 You have no s in the LORD.' 2750
22:27 'You have no s in the LORD.' 2750
Jdg 8:24 an earring from your **s of the plunder."** 8965
1Sa 26:19 They have now driven me from my s in 6202
30:22 not s with them the plunder we recovered. 5989
30:24 The s *of* the man who stayed with 2750
30:24 *All will* s alike." 2745
2Sa 20: 1 "We have no s in David, 2750
1Ki 12:16 "What s do we have in David, 2750
1Ch 9:25 **s their duties** for seven-day periods. 465+6640
2Ch 10:16 "What s do we have in David, 2750
Ne 2:20 you have no s in Jerusalem or any claim 2750
Job 39:17 with wisdom or **give** her **a** s of good sense. 2745
Ps 68:23 the tongues of your dogs have their **s."** 4945
69:27 *do* not *let them* s in your salvation. 995
106: 5 that I *may* s in the **joy** *of* your nation 8523+8525
Pr 1:14 and we *will* s a common purse"— 2118+4200
14:10 and no one else *can* s its joy. 6843
16:19 among the oppressed than *to* s plunder with 2745
17: 2 and *will* s the inheritance as one of 2745
21: 9 on a corner of the roof than s a house **with** 2490
25:24 to live on a corner of the roof than s a house 2490
Ecc 9: 2 All s a common destiny— 889+3869+4200
Isa 58: 7 Is it not *to* s your food with the hungry and 7271
Jer 37:12 **get** his **s of the property** among the people 2745
Eze 18:19 the son not s the guilt of his father?' 928+5951
18:20 The son *will* not s the guilt of the father, 928+5951
18:20 nor *will* the father s the guilt of the son. 928+5951
Am 7: 1 after the **king's** *s* had been harvested and AIT
Mt 21:41 **give him** *his* **s of the** crop at harvest time." 625
25:21 Come and s your master's happiness!' NIG
25:23 Come and s your master's happiness!' NIG
Lk 3:11 "The man with two tunics *should* **s with** 3556
15:12 'Father, give me my s of the estate.' 2095+3538
Ac 8:21 You have no part or s in this ministry, 3102
Ro 8:17 with Christ, if indeed *we* **s in** his **sufferings** 5224
8:17 in order that *we may* also **s in** his **glory.** 5280
11:17 and now s in the nourishing sap 1181+5171
12:13 **S with** God's people who are in need. 3125
15:27 *to* s with them their material blessings. 3310
1Co 9:13 at the altar s in what is offered on the altar? 5211
9:23 that *I may* s in its blessings. 1181+5171
2Co 1: 7 because we know that just as *you* s 1639+3128
1: 7 so also you s in our comfort. NIG
2: 3 that you would all s my joy. NIG
Gal 4:30 slave woman's son *will* never **s in the inheritance** with the free woman's 3099
6: 6 in the word *must* s all good things 3125
Eph 4:28 that he may have something *to* s with those 3556
Php 1: 7 all of you s in God's grace **with** me. 1639+5171
4:14 Yet it was good of you *to* s in my troubles. 5170
Col 1:12 to s in the inheritance of the saints in 3535
1Th 2: 8 so much that we were delighted *to* **s with** 3556
2Th 2:14 that you might s in the glory 4348
1Ti 5:22 and *do* not **s in** the sins of others. 3125
6:18 and to be generous and willing to **s.** 3127
2Ti 2: 6 be the first *to* **receive a** s of the crops. 3561
Heb 3: 1 holy brothers, **who s in** the heavenly calling, 3581
3:14 to **s in** Christ if we hold firmly till the end 3581
12:10 that we *may* **s in** his holiness. 3561
13:16 not forget to do good and to s with others, 3126
1Pe 5: 1 and one who also will s in the glory to 3128
Jude 1: 3 to write to you about the salvation we **s,** 3123
Rev 18: 4 so that *you will* not s in her sins, 5170
22:19 from him his s in the tree of life and in 3538

SHARED (12) [SHARE]
2Sa 12: 3 *It* s his food, drank from his cup 430
1Ki 2:26 s all my father's **hardships.** 889+928+6700+6700
Ps 41: 9 whom I trusted, *he who* s my bread, 430
Pr 5:17 never to be s **with** strangers. 907
Lk 1:58 and *they* s her **joy.** 5176
Ac 1:17 and s in this ministry." 3102+3275+3836
4:32 but they s everything they had. 3123
Ro 15:27 For if the Gentiles *have* **s in** the Jews' 3125
Php 4:15 not one church s with me in the matter 3125
Heb 2:14 he too **s in** their humanity so that 3576
6: 4 who *have* **s in** the Holy Spirit, 1181+3581
Rev 18: 9 with her and s her **luxury** see the smoke 5139

SHARERS (1) [SHARE]
Eph 3: 6 **s together in** the promise in Christ Jesus. 5212

SHARES (5) [SHARE]
2Sa 19:43 "We have ten s in the king; 3338
Pr 22: 9 for *he* s his food with the poor. 5989
Jn 13:18 'He who s my bread has lifted up his heel 5592
19:23 **dividing** them **into** four **s,** 3538+4472
2Jn 1:11 Anyone who welcomes him **s in** his wicked 3125

SHAREZER (3)
2Ki 19:37 his sons Adrammelech and S cut him down 8570
Isa 37:38 his sons Adrammelech and S cut him down 8570
Zec 7: 2 of Bethel had sent S and Regem-Melech, 8570

SHARING (6) [SHARE]
Job 31:17 not s it *with* the fatherless— 430+4946
1Co 9:10 to do so in the hope *of* **s in** the harvest. 3576
2Co 8: 4 with us for the privilege of s in this service 3126
9:13 and for your generosity *in* s with them and 3126
Php 3:10 and the **fellowship of** s in his sufferings, 3126
Phm 1: 6 that you may be active in s your faith, 3126

SHARON (7) [SHARONITE]
1Ch 5:16 and on all the pasturelands of S as far 9227
27:29 in charge of the herds grazing in S. 9227
SS 2: 1 I am a rose of S, a lily of the valleys. 9227
Isa 33: 9 S is like the Arabah, 9227
35: 2 the splendor of Carmel and S; 9227
65:10 S will become a pasture for flocks, 9227
Ac 9:35 and S saw him and turned to the Lord. 4926

SHARONITE (1) [SHARON]
1Ch 27:29 the S was in charge of the herds grazing 9228

SHARP (19) [SHARPEN, SHARPENED, SHARPENING, SHARPENS, SHARPER, SHARPLY]
Ps 45: 5 Let your s arrows pierce the hearts of 9111
57: 4 whose tongues are s swords. 2521
120: 4 punish you with a warrior's s arrows, 9111
140: 3 *They* **make** their tongues as s as a serpent's; 9111
Pr 5: 4 s as a double-edged sword. 2521
25:18 Like a club or a sword or a s arrow is 9111
Isa 5:28 Their arrows *are* **s,** all their bows are strung; 9111
41:15 new and s, with many teeth. 3023
Eze 5: 1 take a s sword and use it as a barber's razor 2521
28:24 who are painful briers and s thorns 3872
Ac 15: 2 and Barnabas into s dispute and debate 3900+4024
15:39 a s **disagreement** that they parted company. 4237
Rev 1:16 of his mouth came a s double-edged sword. 3955
2:12 These are the words of him who has the **s,** 3955
14:14 a crown of gold on his head and a s sickle 3955
14:17 and he too had a s sickle. 3955
14:18 in a loud voice to him who had the s sickle, 3955
14:18 "Take your s sickle and gather the clusters 3955
19:15 Out of his mouth comes a s sword with 3955

SHARPEN (4) [SHARP]
Dt 32:41 when *I* s my flashing sword 9111
Ps 7:12 If he does not relent, *he will* s his sword; 4323
64: 3 *They* s their tongues like swords 9111
Jer 51:11 "S the arrows, take up the shields! 1406

SHARPENED (6) [SHARP]
1Sa 13:20 mattocks, axes and sickles **s.** 4323
Ps 52: 2 it is like a s razor, you who practice deceit. 4323
Isa 49: 2 He made my mouth like a s sword, 2521
Eze 21: 9 " 'A sword, a sword, s and polished— 2523
21:10 s for the slaughter, polished to flash 2523
21:11 it **is s** and polished, made ready for the hand 2523

SHARPENING (2) [SHARP]

1Sa 13:21 of a shekel for s plowshares and mattocks, 7201
13:21 and a third of a shekel for s forks and axes NIH

SHARPENS (2) [SHARP]

Pr 27:17 As iron s iron, so one man sharpens another. 2527
27:17 As iron sharpens iron, so one man s another. 2527

SHARPER (1) [SHARP]

Heb 4:12 S than any double-edged sword, *5533*

SHARPLY (3) [SHARP]

Jdg 8: 1 And they criticized him s. 928+2622
Jn 6:52 Jews *began to* **argue** s among themselves, *3481*
Tit 1:13 Therefore, rebuke them s, *705*

SHARPNESS (KJV) See HARSH

SHARUHEN (1)

Jos 19: 6 Beth Lebaoth and S— 9226

SHASHAI (1)

Ezr 10:40 Macnadebai, S, Sharai, 9258

SHASHAK (2)

1Ch 8:14 Ahio, S, Jeremoth, 9265
8:25 Iphdeiah and Penuel were the sons of S. 9265

SHATTER (13) [SHATTERED, SHATTERING, SHATTERS]

Isa 30:31 The voice of the LORD *will* s Assyria; 3169
Jer 49:37 *I will* s Elam before their foes, 3169
51:20 with you *I* s nations, 5879
51:21 with you *I* s horse and rider, 5879
51:21 with you *I* s chariot and driver, 5879
51:22 with you *I* s man and woman, 5879
51:22 with you *I* s old man and youth, 5879
51:22 with you *I* s young man and maiden, 5879
51:23 with you *I* s shepherd and flock, 5879
51:23 with you *I* s farmer and oxen, 5879
51:23 with you *I* s governors and officials. 5879
Eze 32:12 *They will* s the pride of Egypt, 8720
Hag 2:22 and s the power of the foreign kingdoms. 9012

SHATTERED (24) [SHATTER]

Ex 15: 6 Your right hand, O LORD, s the enemy. 8320
Jdg 5:26 *she* s and pierced his temple. 4730
10: 8 *who* that year s and crushed them. 8320
1Sa 2:10 those who oppose the LORD *will* **be** s. 3169
1Ki 19:11 the mountains apart and s the rocks before 8689
Job 16:12 All was well with me, but *he* s me; 7297
17:11 My days have passed, my plans **are** s, 5998
Ps 48: 7 You destroyed them like ships of Tarshish s NIH
105:33 and fig trees and s the trees of their country. 8689
Ecc 12: 6 before the pitcher **is** s at the spring, 8689
Isa 7: 8 Ephraim *will* **be** too s to be a people. 3169
8: 9 Raise the war cry, you nations, and *be* s! 3169
8: 9 Prepare for battle, and *be* s! 3169
8: 9 Prepare for battle, and *be* s! 3169
9: 4 *you have* s the yoke that burdens them, 3169
21: 9 All the images of its gods *lie* s on 8689
30:14 s so mercilessly that among its pieces not 4198
Jer 25:34 you will fall and *be* s like fine pottery. 9518
48: 1 the stronghold will be disgraced and s. 3169
48:20 Moab is disgraced, for *she is* s. 3169
48:39 "How s *she is!* How they wail! 3169
50:23 and s *is* the hammer of the whole earth! 8689
Eze 27:34 Now *you are* s by the sea in the depths of 8689
Na 1: 6 the rocks *are* s before him. 5997

SHATTERING (1) [SHATTER]

Da 8: 7 striking the ram and s his two horns. 8689

SHATTERS (2) [SHATTER]

Job 34:24 Without inquiry *he* s the mighty and sets 8318
Ps 46: 9 he breaks the bow and s the spear, 7915

SHAUL (9) [SHAUL'S, SHAULITE]

Ge 36:37 S from Rehoboth on the river 8620
36:38 When S died, Baal-Hanan son 8620
46:10 Zohar and S the son of a Canaanite woman. 8620
Ex 6:15 Zohar and S the son of a Canaanite woman. 8620
Nu 26:13 through S, the Shaulite clan. 8620
1Ch 1:48 S from Rehoboth on the river 8620
1:49 When S died, Baal-Hanan son 8620
4:24 Nemuel, Jamin, Jarib, Zerah and S; 8620
6:24 Uriel his son, Uzziah his son and S his son. 8620

SHAUL'S (1) [SHAUL]

1Ch 4:25 Shallum was S son, 2257S

SHAULITE (1) [SHAUL]

Nu 26:13 through Shaul, the S clan. 8621

SHAVE (19) [SHAVED]

Lev 14: 8 **s off** all his hair and bathe with water; 1662
14: 9 the seventh day *he must* s **off** all his hair; 1662
14: 9 *he must* s his head, his beard, 1662
21: 5 " 'Priests **must** not s their heads or 7942+7947
21: 5 their heads or s **off** the edges of their beards 1662
Nu 6: 9 *he must* s his head on the day 1662
6:18 the Nazirite *must* s **off** the hair 1662
8: 7 then **have** *them* s their whole bodies 6296+9509
Dt 14: 1 s the front of your heads for the dead, 7947+8492
21:12 into your home and *have her* s her head, 1662
Jdg 16:19 a man *to* **s off** the seven braids of his hair, 1662
Isa 7:20 *to* s your head and the hair of your legs, 1662
Jer 16: 6 and no one will cut himself or s *his* **head** 7942
47: 5 Gaza *will* s *her* **head in mourning;** 995+7947
Eze 5: 1 and use it as a barber's razor *to* s your head 6296
27:31 *They will* s *their* **heads** because of you 7942+7947
44:20 not s their heads or let their hair grow long, 1662
Am 8:10 you wear sackcloth and s your heads. 6584+7947
Mic 1:16 S *your* **heads** in mourning for the 1605+7942

SHAVED (16) [SHAVE]

Ge 41:14 When *he had* s and changed his clothes, 1662
Lev 13:33 *he must* **be** s except for the diseased area, 1662
Nu 6:19 Nazirite *has* **s off** the hair of his dedication, 1662
Jdg 16:17 If my head **were** s, my strength would leave 1662
16:22 to grow again after *it had* **been** s. 1662
2Sa 10: 4 **s off** half of each man's beard, 1662
1Ch 19: 4 So Hanun seized David's men, s them, 1662
Job 1:20 Job got up and tore his robe and s his head. 1605
Isa 15: 2 Every head is s and every beard cut off. 7947
Jer 2:16 the men of Memphis and Tahpanhes *have* s 8286
41: 5 eighty men *who had* **s off** their beards, 1662
48:37 Every head is s and every beard cut off; 7947
Eze 7:18 with shame and their heads will be s. 7947
Ac 21:24 so that *they can have* their heads s. *3834*
1Co 11: 5 it is just as though her head *were* s. *3834*
11: 6 for a woman *to have her* hair cut or **s off,** *3834*

SHAVEH (1) [SHAVEH KIRIATHAIM]

Ge 14:17 to meet him in the Valley of S (that is, 8753

SHAVEH KIRIATHAIM (1) [KIRIATHAIM, SHAVEH]

Ge 14: 5 the Zuzites in Ham, the Emites in S 8754

SHAVSHA (1)

1Ch 18:16 of Abiathar were priests; S was secretary; 8807

SHAWL (1) [SHAWLS]

Ru 3:15 the s you are wearing and hold it out." 4762

SHAWLS (1) [SHAWL]

Isa 3:23 and the linen garments and tiaras and s. 8100

SHE (1011) [HER, HERS, HERSELF, SHE'S] See Index of Articles Etc.

SHE'S (1) [SHE]

Jdg 14: 3 S the right one for me." 2085

SHE-CAMEL (1) [CAMEL]

Jer 2:23 You are a swift s running here and there, 1149

SHEAF (6) [SHEAVES]

Ge 37: 7 when suddenly my s rose and stood upright, 524
Lev 23:10 a **s of** the first **grain** you harvest. 6684
23:11 to wave the s before the LORD so it will 6684
23:12 On the day you wave the s, 6684
23:15 day you brought the s *of* the wave offering, 6684
Dt 24:19 in your field and you overlook a s, 6684

SHEAL (1)

Ezr 10:29 Malluch, Adaiah, Jashub, S and Jeremoth. 8627

SHEALTIEL (13)

1Ch 3:17 of Jehoiachin the captive: S his son, 8630
Ezr 3: 2 son of S and his associates began to build 8630
3: 8 Zerubbabel son of S, 8630
5: 2 of S and Jeshua son of Jozadak set to work 10691
Ne 12: 1 with Zerubbabel son of S and with Jeshua: 8630
Hag 1: 1 the prophet Haggai to Zerubbabel son of S, 8630
1:12 Then Zerubbabel son of S, 9003
1:14 up the spirit of Zerubbabel son of S, 9003
2: 2 "Speak to Zerubbabel son of S, 9003
2:23 my servant Zerubbabel son of S,' 8630
Mt 1:12 Jeconiah was the father of S, *4886*
1:12 S the father of Zerubbabel, *4886*
Lk 3:27 the son of Zerubbabel, the son *of* S, *4886*

SHEAR (3) [SHEARED, SHEARER, SHEARERS, SHEARING, SHEEP-SHEARING, SHEEPSHEARERS, SHORN]

Ge 31:19 When Laban had gone to s his sheep, 1605
38:13 on his way to Timnah to s his sheep," 1605
Dt 15:19 and *do* not s the firstborn of your sheep. 1605

SHEAR-JASHUB (1)

Isa 7: 3 "Go out, you and your son S, 8639

SHEARED (1) [SHEAR]

Isa 22:25 *it will* **be s off** and will fall, 1548

SHEARER (1) [SHEAR]

Ac 8:32 and as a lamb before the s is silent, *3025*

SHEARERS (3) [SHEAR]

1Sa 25:11 and the meat I have slaughtered for my s, 1605
2Sa 13:24 "Your servant has had s come. 1605
Isa 53: 7 and as a sheep before her s is silent, 1605

SHEARIAH (2)

1Ch 8:38 Azrikam, Bokeru, Ishmael, S, 9138
9:44 Azrikam, Bokeru, Ishmael, S, 9138

SHEARING (4) [SHEAR]

Ge 38:12 to the *men who were* s his sheep, 1605
Dt 18: 4 the first **wool from** *the* s *of* your sheep, 1600
1Sa 25: 2 which he was s in Carmel. 1605
25: 4 he heard that Nabal *was* s sheep. 1605

SHEATH (3) [SHEATHED]

2Sa 20: 8 at his waist was a belt with a dagger in its s. 9509
20: 8 he stepped forward, it dropped out of its s. NIH
1Ch 21:27 and he put his sword back into its s. 5620

SHEATHED (1) [SHEATH]

Ps 68:13 the wings of [my] dove **are** s with silver, 2902

SHEAVES (9) [SHEAF]

Ge 37: 7 We were binding **s of grain** out in the field 524
37: 7 while your s gathered around mine 524
Ru 2: 7 'Please let me glean and gather among the s 6684
2:15 "Even if she gathers among the s, 6684
Job 5:26 like s gathered in season. 1538
24:10 they carry the s, but still go hungry. 6684
Ps 126: 6 return with songs of joy, carrying s *with* him. 524
Mic 4:12 he who gathers them like s to the threshing 6658
Zec 12: 6 like a flaming torch among s. 6658

SHEBA (34)

Ge 10: 7 The sons of Raamah: S and Dedan. 8644
10:28 Obal, Abimael, S, 8644
25: 3 Jokshan was the father of S and Dedan; 8644
Jos 19: 2 It included: Beersheba (or S), Moladah, 8681
2Sa 20: 1 Now a troublemaker named S son of Bicri, 8680
20: 2 of Israel deserted David to follow S son 8680
20: 6 to Abishai, "Now S son of Bicri 8680
20: 7 from Jerusalem to pursue S son of Bicri. 8680
20:10 and his brother Abishai pursued S son 8680
20:13 the men went on with Joab to pursue S son 8680
20:14 S passed through all the tribes of Israel NIH
20:15 the troops with Joab came and besieged S 2257S
20:21 A man named S son of Bicri, 8680
20:22 and they cut off the head of S son of Bicri 8680
1Ki 10: 1 When the queen of S heard about the fame 8644
10: 4 When the queen of S saw all the wisdom 8644
10:10 the queen of S gave to King Solomon. 8644
10:13 the queen of S all she desired and asked 8644
1Ch 1: 9 The sons of Raamah: S and Dedan. 8644
1:22 Obal, Abimael, S, 8644
1:32 The sons of Jokshan: S and Dedan. 8644
5:13 Michael, Meshullam, S, Jorai, Jacan, 8680
2Ch 9: 1 the queen of S heard of Solomon's fame, 8644
9: 3 queen of S saw the wisdom of Solomon, 8644
9: 9 the queen of S gave to King Solomon. 8644
9:12 queen of S all she desired and asked for; 8644
Job 6:19 the traveling merchants of S look in hope. 8644
Ps 72:10 kings of S and Seba will present him gifts. 8644
72:15 May gold from S be given him. 8644
Isa 60: 6 And all from S will come, 8644
Jer 6:20 about incense from S or sweet calamus 8644
Eze 27:22 " 'The merchants of S and Raamah traded 8644
27:23 Canneh and Eden and merchants of S, 8644
38:13 S and Dedan and the merchants of Tarshish 8644

SHEBAH (KJV) See SHIBAH

SHEBAM (KJV) See SEBAM

SHEBANIAH (6)

1Ch 15:24 S, Joshaphat, Nethanel, Amasai, Zechariah, 8677
Ne 9: 4 Jeshua, Bani, Kadmiel, S, Bunni, 8676
9: 5 Sherebiah, Hodiah, S and Pethahiah— 8676
10: 4 Hattush, S, Malluch, 8676
10:10 S, Hodiah, Kelita, Pelaiah, Hanan, 8676
10:12 Zaccur, Sherebiah, S, 8676

SHEBAT (1)

Zec 1: 7 the eleventh month, the month of S, 8658

SHEBER (1)

1Ch 2:48 the mother of S and Tirhanah. 8693

SHEBNA (9)

2Ki 18:18 the palace administrator, S the secretary, 8675
18:26 S and Joah said to the field commander, 8675
18:37 S the secretary and Joah son of Asaph 8674
19: 2 S the secretary and the leading priests, 8674
Isa 22:15 "Go, say to this steward, to **S**, 8674
36: 3 the palace administrator, S the secretary, 8674
36:11 S and Joah said to the field commander, 8674
36:22 the palace administrator, S the secretary, 8674
37: 2 S the secretary, and the leading priests, 8674

SHEBUEL (KJV) See SHUBAEL

SHECANIAH (10) [SHECANIAH'S]

1Ch 3:21 of Arnan, of Obadiah and of **S**. 8908
3:22 The descendants of **S:** 8908
24:11 the ninth to Jeshua, the tenth to **S**, 8909
2Ch 31:15 and S assisted him faithfully in the towns 8909
Ezr 8: 3 of the descendants of **S;** 8908
8: 5 S son of Jahaziel, and with him 300 men; 8908
10: 2 Then S son of Jehiel, 8908
Ne 3:29 Next to him, Shemaiah son of **S**, 8908
6:18 since he was son-in-law to S son of Arah, 8908
12: 3 **S**, Rehum, Meremoth, 8908

SHECANIAH'S (1) [SHECANIAH]

Ne 12:14 of Malluch's, Jonathan; of **S**, Joseph; 8908

SHECHEM (62) [SHECHEM'S, SHECHEMITE]

Ge 12: 6 as the site of the great tree of Moreh at **S**. 8901
33:18 of S in Canaan and camped within sight of 8901
33:19 the sons of Hamor, the father of **S**, 8902
34: 2 When S son of Hamor the Hivite, 8902
34: 4 And S said to his father Hamor, 8902
34: 7 because S had done a disgraceful thing NIH
34: 8 "My son S has his heart set on your 8902
34:11 Then S said to Dinah's father and brothers, 8902
34:13 as they spoke to S and his father Hamor. 8902
34:18 seemed good to Hamor and his son **S**. 8902
34:20 and his son S went to the gate of their city 8902
34:24 with Hamor and his son **S**, 8902
34:26 They put Hamor and his son S to the sword 8902
35: 4 and Jacob buried them under the oak at **S**. 8901
37:12 to graze their father's flocks near **S**, 8901
37:13 your brothers are grazing the flocks near **S**. 8901
37:14 When Joseph arrived at **S**, 8901
Nu 26:31 through S, the Shechemite clan; 8903
Jos 17: 2 the clans of Abiezer, Helek, Asriel, **S**, 8903
17: 7 from Asher to Micmethath east of **S**. 8901
20: 7 S in the hill country of Ephraim, 8901
21:21 hill country of Ephraim they were given S 8901
24: 1 assembled all the tribes of Israel at **S**. 8901
24:25 at S he drew up for them decrees and laws. 8901
24:32 at S in the tract of land that Jacob bought 8901
24:32 sons of Hamor, the father of **S**. 8902
Jdg 8:31 His concubine, who lived in **S**, 8901
9: 1 to his mother's brothers in S and said 8901
9: 2 "Ask all the citizens of S, 'Which is better 8901
9: 3 repeated all this to the citizens of S, 8901
9: 6 the citizens of S and Beth Millo gathered 8901
9: 6 at the pillar in S to crown Abimelech king. 8901
9: 7 "Listen to me, citizens of **S**, 8901
9:18 of S because he is your brother)— 8901
9:20 citizens of S and Beth Millo, 8901
9:20 citizens of S and Beth Millo, 8901
9:23 between Abimelech and the citizens of **S**, 8901
9:24 and on the citizens of **S**, 8901
9:25 of S set men on the hilltops to ambush 8901
9:26 of Ebed moved with his brothers into **S**, 8901
9:28 "Who is Abimelech, and who is **S**, 8902
9:31 to S and are stirring up the city against you. 8901
9:34 and took up concealed positions near S 8901
9:39 the citizens of S and fought Abimelech. 8901
9:41 Zebul drove Gaal and his brothers out of **S**. 8901
9:42 The next day the people of S went out to NIH
9:46 of S went into the stronghold of the temple 8901
9:49 So all the people in the tower of **S**, 8901
9:57 the men of S pay for all their wickedness. 8901
21:19 of the road that goes from Bethel to **S**, 8901
1Ki 12: 1 Rehoboam went to **S**, 8901
12:25 Then Jeroboam fortified S in the hill 8901
1Ch 6:67 hill country of Ephraim they were given S 8901
7:19 Ahian, **S**, Likhi and Aniam. 8903
7:28 and S and its villages all the way to Ayyah 8901
2Ch 10: 1 Rehoboam went to **S**, 8901
Ps 60: 6 "In triumph I will parcel out S 8901
108: 7 "In triumph I will parcel out S 8901
Jer 41: 5 and cut themselves came from **S**, 8901
Hos 6: 9 they murder on the road to **S**, 8901
Ac 7:16 Their bodies were brought back to S *5374*
7:16 of Hamor at S for a certain sum of money. *5374*

SHECHEM'S (3) [SHECHEM]

Ge 34: 6 S father Hamor went out to talk with Jacob. 8902
34:26 to the sword and took Dinah from S house 8902
Jdg 9:28 Serve the men of Hamor, S father! 8902

SHECHEMITE (1) [SHECHEM]

Nu 26:31 through Shechem, the S clan; 8904

SHED (46) [SHEDDING, SHEDS]

Ge 9: 6 by man *shall* his blood **be s;** 9161
37:22 "Don't s any blood. 9161
Lev 17: 4 *he has* s blood and must be cut off 9161
Nu 35:33 for the land on which blood *has* **been s**, 9161
35:33 except by the blood of the *one who* s it. 9161
Dt 19:10 Do this so that innocent blood *will* not **be s** 9161
21: 7 "Our hands *did* not s this blood, 9161
2Sa 16: 8 the **blood** you s *in* the household of Saul, 1947
1Ki 2:31 the guilt of the innocent blood that Joab **s**. 9161
2:32 LORD will repay him for the blood he s, NIH
2Ki 9: 7 blood of all the LORD's servants **s by** 3338+4946
21:16 Manasseh also s so much innocent blood 9161
1Ch 22: 8 *'You have* s much blood 9161
22: 8 because *you have* s much blood on 9161
28: 3 you are a warrior and *have* s blood.' 9161
Ps 97:11 Light **is** s upon the righteous and joy on 2445
106:38 *They* s innocent blood, 9161
Pr 1:16 they are swift to s blood. 9161
6:17 a lying tongue, hands *that* s innocent blood, 9161
Isa 26:21 The earth will disclose the **blood** *s* AIT
59: 7 they are swift to s innocent blood. 9161
Jer 7: 6 or the widow and *do* not s innocent blood 9161
22: 3 and *do* not s innocent blood in this place. 9161
La 4:13 who s within her the blood of the righteous. 9161
Eze 16:38 who commit adultery and *who* s blood; 9161
21:32 your blood will be s in your land, NIH
22: 4 because of the blood *you have* s 9161
22: 6 in you uses his power to s blood. 9161
22:12 In you men accept bribes to s blood; 9161
22:13 and at the blood *you have* s in your midst. 2118
22:27 they s blood and kill people 9161
23:45 and s blood, because they are adulterous 9161
24: 7 " 'For the blood she s is in her midst: NIH
24:16 Yet do not lament or weep or s any tears. 995
33:25 in it and look to your idols and s blood, 9161
36:18 because *they had* s blood in the land 9161
Joel 3:19 in whose land *they* s innocent blood. 9161
Mic 7: 2 All men lie in wait to s blood; NIH
Hab 2: 8 For you have s man's blood; NIH
2:17 For you have s man's blood; NIH
Mt 23:35 the righteous blood *that has been* s *1772*
Lk 11:50 the blood of all the prophets that *has been* s *1772*
Ac 22:20 the blood of your martyr Stephen *was* s, *1772*
Ro 3:15 "Their feet are swift to s blood; *1772*
Col 1:20 peace through his blood, s on the cross. *NIG*
Rev 16: 6 for *they have* s the blood of your saints *1772*

SHEDDING (12) [SHED]

Dt 19:13 from Israel the **guilt of** s innocent **blood**, 1947
21: 9 yourselves the **guilt of** s innocent **blood**, 1947
Jdg 9:24 the s **of** their **blood**, might be avenged 1947
1Ki 2: 5 s their blood in peacetime as if in battle, 8492
2Ki 24: 4 including the s *of* innocent blood. 9161
Job 15:33 like an olive tree s its blossoms. 8959
Jer 22:17 on s innocent blood and on oppression 9161
Eze 22: 3 by s blood in her midst and defiles herself 9161
22: 9 In you are slanderous men bent on s blood; 9161
Mt 23:30 not have taken part with them in s the blood *NIG*
Heb 9:22 and without the **s of blood** there is no forgiveness. *136*
12: 4 yet resisted to the point of s your **blood**. *135*

SHEDEUR (5)

Nu 1: 5 from Reuben, Elizur son of **S;** 8725
2:10 of the people of Reuben is Elizur son of **S**. 8725
7:30 On the fourth day Elizur son of **S**, 8725
7:35 This was the offering of Elizur son of **S**. 8725
10:18 Elizur son of S was in command. 8725

SHEDS (2) [SHED]

Ge 9: 6 *"Whoever* s the blood of man, by man 9161
Eze 18:10 *who* s blood or does any of these other 9161

SHEEP (204) [SHEEP'S, SHEEPSKINS]

Ge 12:16 and Abram acquired s and cattle, 7366
20:14 Then Abimelech brought s and cattle 7366
21:27 So Abraham brought s and cattle 7366
24:35 He has given him s and cattle, 7366
29: 2 with three flocks of s lying near it because 7366
29: 3 from the well's mouth and water the s. 7366
29: 6 here comes his daughter Rachel with the **s**." 7366
29: 7 Water the s and take them back to pasture." 7366
29: 8 Then we will water the **s**." 7366
29: 9 Rachel came with her father's **s**, 7366
29:10 his mother's brother, and Laban's **s**, 7366
29:10 of the well and watered his uncle's **s**. 7366
30:32 from them every speckled or spotted **s**, 8445
31:19 When Laban had gone to shear his **s**, 7366
31:38 Your s and goats have not miscarried, 8161
32: 5 I have cattle and donkeys, **s and goats**, 7366
38:12 to the men who were shearing his **s**, 7366
38:13 on his way to Timnah to shear his **s**," 7366
47:17 their **s and goats**, their cattle and 5238+7366
Ex 9: 3 and on your cattle and **s and goats**. 7366
12: 5 you may take them from the s or the goats. 3897
20:24 your **s and goats** and your cattle. 7366
22: 1 a man steals an ox or a s and slaughters it 8445
22: 1 of cattle for the ox and four s for the sheep. 7366
22: 1 of cattle for the ox and four sheep for the **s**. 8445
22: 4 whether ox or donkey or **s—** 8445
22: 9 a donkey, a **s**, a garment, 8445
22:10 a s or any other animal to his neighbor 8445
22:30 Do the same with your cattle and your **s**. 7366
Lev 1:10 from either the s or the goats, 4166
7:23 not eat any of the fat of cattle, s or goats. 4166
22:19 s or goats in order that it may be accepted 4166
22:23 present as a freewill offering an ox or a s 8445
22:28 a cow or a s and its young on the same day. 8445
27:26 whether an ox or a s, it is the LORD's. 8445
Nu 18:17 a s or a goat; they are holy. 4166
22:40 Balak sacrificed cattle and **s**, 7366
27:17 so the LORD's people will not be like s 7366
31:28 cattle, donkeys, **s or goats.** 7366
31:30 cattle, donkeys, **s, goats or** other animals. 7366
31:32 that the soldiers took was 675,000 **s**, 7366
31:36 in the battle was: 337,500 **s**, 7366
31:43 the community's half—was 337,500 **s**, 7366
Dt 14: 4 the ox, the **s**, the goat, 4166+8445
14: 5 the ibex, the antelope and the **mountain s.** 2378
14:26 cattle, **s**, wine or other fermented drink, 7366
15:19 and do not shear the firstborn of your **s**. 7366
17: 1 an ox or a s that has any defect or flaw in it, 8445
18: 3 from the people who sacrifice a bull or a **s:** 8445
18: 4 the first wool from the shearing of your **s**, 7366
22: 1 If you see your brother's ox or s straying, 8445
28:31 Your s will be given to your enemies, 7366
Jos 6:21 young and old, cattle, **s** and donkeys. 8445
7:24 donkeys and **s**, his tent and all that he had, 7366
Jdg 6: 4 neither s nor cattle nor donkeys. 8445
1Sa 14:32 They pounced on the plunder and, taking **s**, 7366
14:34 'Each of you bring me your cattle and **s**, 8445
15: 3 cattle and **s**, camels and donkeys.' " 8445
15: 9 the s and cattle, the fat calves and lambs— 7366
15:14 "What then is this bleating of s in my ears? 7366
15:15 the best of the s and cattle to sacrifice to 7366
15:21 The soldiers took s and cattle from 7366
16:11 Jesse answered, "but he is tending the **s**." 7366
16:19 who is with the **s**." 7366
17:15 and forth from Saul to tend his father's **s** 7366
17:28 And with whom did you leave those few s 7366
17:34 servant has been keeping his father's **s**. 7366
17:34 a lion or a bear came and carried off a s 8445
17:35 struck it and rescued the s from its mouth. NIH
22:19 and its cattle, donkeys and **s**. 8445
24: 3 He came to the s pens along the way; 7366
25: 2 a thousand goats and three thousand **s**, 7366
25: 4 he heard that Nabal was shearing **s**. 7366
25:16 the time we were herding our s near them. 7366
25:18 five dressed **s**, five seahs of roasted grain, 7366
27: 9 but took s and cattle, donkeys and camels, 7366
2Sa 12: 2 The rich man had a very large number of s 7366
12: 4 of his own s or cattle to prepare a meal for 7366
17:29 and curds, **s**, and cheese from cows' milk 7366
24:17 These are but **s**. What have they done? 7366
1Ki 1: 9 Adonijah then sacrificed **s**, 7366
1:19 and **s**, and has invited all the king's sons, 7366
1:25 of cattle, fattened calves, and **s**. 7366
4:23 and a hundred **s and goats**, 7366
8: 5 so many s and cattle that they could not 7366
8:63 a hundred and twenty thousand **s and goats**. 7366
22:17 "I saw all Israel scattered on the hills like s 7366
2Ki 3: 4 Now Mesha king of Moab **raised s**, 5924
1Ch 5:21 two hundred fifty thousand s 7366
12:40 oil, cattle and **s**, for there was joy in Israel. 7366
21:17 These are but **s**. What have they done? 7366
2Ch 5: 6 so many s and cattle that they could not 7366
7: 5 a hundred and twenty thousand **s and goats**. 7366
14:15 and carried off droves of **s and goats** 7366
15:11 of cattle and seven thousand **s and goats** 7366
18: 2 Ahab slaughtered many s and cattle for him 7366
18:16 "I saw all Israel scattered on the hills like s 7366
29:33 and three thousand **s and goats**. 7366
30:24 and seven thousand **s and goats** for 7366
30:24 and ten thousand **s and goats**. 7366
35: 7 a total of thirty thousand s and goats 3897+7366
Ne 3: 1 to work and rebuilt the S Gate. 7366
3:32 the room above the corner and the S Gate 7366
5:18 Each day one ox, six choice s 7366
12:39 as far as the S Gate. 7366
Job 1: 3 and he owned seven thousand **s**, 7366
1:16 fell from the sky and burned up the s 7366
30: 1 disdained to put with my s dogs. 7366
31:20 for warming him with the fleece from my **s**, 3897
42:12 He had fourteen thousand **s**, 7366
Ps 44:11 to be devoured like s and have scattered us 7366
44:22 we are considered as s to be slaughtered. 7366
49:14 Like s they are destined for the grave, 7366
74: 1 Why does your anger smolder against the s 7366
78:52 he led them like s through the desert. 6373
78:70 and took him from the s pens; 7366
78:71 from tending the s he brought him to be 6402
79:13 Then we your people, the s *of* your pasture, 7366
100: 3 we are his people, the s *of* his pasture. 7366
119:176 I have strayed like a lost **s**. 8445
144:13 Our s will increase by thousands, 7366
SS 1: 7 and where you rest your s at midday. NIH
1: 8 of the s and graze your young goats by 7366
4: 2 Your teeth are like a flock of **s just shorn**, 7892
6: 6 Your teeth are like a flock of s coming up 8161
Isa 5:17 Then s will graze as in their own pasture; 3897
7:25 cattle are turned loose and where s run. 8445
13:14 like s without a shepherd, 7366
22:13 slaughtering of cattle and killing of **s**, 7366
43:23 not brought me s for burnt offerings, 8445
53: 6 We all, like **s**, have gone astray, 7366
53: 7 and as a s before her shearers is silent, 8161
Jer 12: 3 Drag them off like s to be butchered! 7366
13:20 the s *of* which you boasted? 7366
23: 1 and scattering the s *of* my pasture!" 7366
50: 6 "My people have been lost **s;** 7366

Eze 25: 5 and Ammon into a resting place for s. 7366
34: 6 My s wandered over all the mountains and 7366
34:11 I myself will search for my s and look 7366
34:12 so will I look after my s. 7366
34:15 I myself will tend my s and have them lie 7366
34:17 I will judge between *one* s and another, 8445
34:20 See, I myself will judge between the fat s 8445
34:20 between the fat sheep and the lean s. 8445
34:21 butting all the weak s with your horns NIH
34:22 I will judge between *one* s and another. 8445
34:31 You my s, the sheep of my pasture, 7366
34:31 You my sheep, the s *of* my pasture, 7366
36:37 I will make their people as numerous as s, 7366
45:15 Also one s is to be taken from every flock 8445
Hos 12:12 and to pay for her *he* **tended s.** 9068
Joel 1:18 even the flocks of s are suffering. 7366
Mic 2:12 I will bring them together like s *in* a pen, 7366
5: 8 like a young lion among flocks of s, 7366
Hab 3:17 though there are no s in the pen 7366
Zep 2: 6 will be a place for shepherds and s pens. 7366
Zec 10: 2 the people wander like s oppressed for lack 7366
11:16 but will eat the meat of the **choice** s, 1374
13: 7 and the s will be scattered, 7366
Mt 9:36 like s without a shepherd. *4585*
10: 6 Go rather to the lost s of Israel. *4585*
10:16 I am sending you out like s among wolves. *4585*
12:11 "If any of you has a s and it falls into a pit *4585*
12:12 How much more valuable is a man *than* a s! *4585*
15:24 "I was sent only to the lost s of Israel." *4585*
18:12 If a man owns a hundred s, *4585*
18:13 about **that one** s than about the ninety-nine *899S*
25:32 from another as a shepherd separates the s *4585*
25:33 He will put the s on his right and the goats *4585*
26:31 and the s of the flock will be scattered.' *4585*
Mk 6:34 they were like s without a shepherd. *4585*
14:27 and the s will be scattered.' *4585*
Lk 15: 4 "Suppose one of you has a hundred s *4585*
15: 4 in the open country and go after the lost s *NIG*
15: 6 I have found my lost s.' *4585*
17: 7 a servant plowing or **looking after** the s. *4477*
Jn 2:14 found men selling cattle, s and doves, *4585*
2:15 from the temple area, both s and cattle; *4585*
5: 2 Now there is in Jerusalem near the S **Gate** *4583*
10: 1 the man who does not enter the s pen by *4585*
10: 2 by the gate is the shepherd *of* his **s.** *4585*
10: 3 and the s listen to his voice. *4585*
10: 3 He calls his own s by name *4585*
10: 4 and his s follow him *4585*
10: 7 "I tell you the truth, I am the gate *for* the s. *4585*
10: 8 but the s did not listen to them. *4585*
10:11 good shepherd lays down his life for the **s.** *4585*
10:12 not the shepherd who owns the s. *4585*
10:12 he abandons the s and runs away. *4585*
10:13 a hired hand and cares nothing for the s. *4585*
10:14 I know my s and my sheep know me— *NIG*
10:14 I know my sheep and my s know me— *NIG*
10:15 and I lay down my life for the s. *4585*
10:16 I have other s that are not of this sheep pen. *4585*
10:16 I have other sheep that are not of this **s pen.** *885*
10:26 do not believe because you are not my s. *4585*
10:27 My s listen to my voice; *4585*
21:16 Jesus said, "Take care of my **s."** *4585*
21:17 Jesus said, "Feed my s. *4585*
Ac 8:32 "He was led like a s to the slaughter, *4585*
Ro 8:36 we are considered as s to be slaughtered." *4585*
Heb 13:20 Lord Jesus, that great Shepherd *of* the s, *4585*
1Pe 2:25 For you were like s going astray, *4585*
Rev 18:13 fine flour and wheat; cattle and **s;** *4585*

SHEEP'S (1) [SHEEP]

Mt 7:15 They come to you in s clothing, *4585*

SHEEP-SHEARING (1) [SHEAR]

1Sa 25: 7 " 'Now I hear that *it is* **s time.** 1605

SHEEPCOTE (KJV) See PASTURE, SHEEP PENS

SHEEPFOLD (KJV) See CAMPFIRES, SHEEP PEN, SHEEP PENS

SHEEPMASTER (KJV) See RAISED SHEEP

SHEEPSHEARERS (1) [SHEAR]

2Sa 13:23 when Absalom's s were at Baal Hazor near 1605

SHEEPSKINS (1) [SHEEP]

Heb 11:37 They went about in s and goatskins, *3603*

SHEER (1)

Isa 28:19 of this message will bring s terror. 8370

SHEERAH (1) [UZZEN SHEERAH]

1Ch 7:24 His daughter was S, 8641

SHEET (4) [SHEETS]

Isa 25: 7 the s that covers all nations; 5012
Ac 10:11 and something like a large s being let down *3855*
10:16 and immediately the s was taken back *5007*
11: 5 like a large s being let down from heaven *3855*

SHEETS (2) [SHEET]

Ex 39: 3 They hammered out **thin** s *of* gold 7063
Nu 16:38 Hammer the censers into s to overlay 7063

SHEHARIAH (1)

1Ch 8:26 Shamsherai, S, Athaliah, 8843

SHEKEL (41) [SHEKELS]

Ex 30:13 to those already counted is to give a half s, 9203
30:13 according to the sanctuary s, 9203
30:13 This half s is an offering to the LORD. 9203
30:15 to give more than a half s and the poor are 9203
30:24 all according to the sanctuary s— 9203
38:24 according to the sanctuary s. 9203
38:25 shekels, according to the sanctuary s— 9203
38:26 half a s, according to the sanctuary shekel, 9203
38:26 half a shekel, according to the sanctuary s, 9203
Lev 5:15 according to the sanctuary s. 9203
27: 3 according to the sanctuary s; 9203
27:25 to be set according to the sanctuary s, 9203
27:25 twenty gerahs to the s. 9203
Nu 3:47 according to the sanctuary s, 9203
3:50 shekels, according to the sanctuary s. 9203
7:13 both according to the sanctuary s, 9203
7:19 both according to the sanctuary s, 9203
7:25 both according to the sanctuary s, 9203
7:31 both according to the sanctuary s, 9203
7:37 both according to the sanctuary s, 9203
7:43 both according to the sanctuary s, 9203
7:49 both according to the sanctuary s, 9203
7:55 both according to the sanctuary s, 9203
7:61 both according to the sanctuary s, 9203
7:67 both according to the sanctuary s, 9203
7:73 both according to the sanctuary s, 9203
7:79 both according to the sanctuary s, 9203
7:85 according to the sanctuary s. 9203
7:86 according to the sanctuary s. 9203
18:16 according to the sanctuary s, 9203
1Sa 9: 8 he said, "I have a quarter of a s *of* silver. 9203
13:21 **two thirds of a s** for sharpening plowshares 7088
13:21 a third of a s for sharpening forks and axes NIH
2Ki 7: 1 for a s and two seahs of barley for a shekel 9203
7: 1 for a shekel and two seahs of barley for a s 9203
7:16 So a seah of flour sold for a s, 9203
7:16 and two seahs of barley sold for a **s,** 9203
7:18 for a s and two seahs of barley for a shekel 9203
7:18 for a shekel and two seahs of barley for a s 9203
Ne 10:32 of a s each year for the service of the house 9203
Eze 45:12 The s is to consist of twenty gerahs. 9203

SHEKELS (105) [SHEKEL]

Ge 20:16 "I am giving your brother a thousand s NIH
23:15 the land is worth four hundred s *of* silver, 9203
23:16 four hundred s *of* silver, 9203
24:22 and two gold bracelets weighing ten s. NIH
37:28 for twenty s of silver to the Ishmaelites, NIH
45:22 but to Benjamin he gave three hundred s NIH
Ex 21:32 the owner must pay thirty s of silver to 9203
30:23 500 s of liquid myrrh, half as much (that is, NIH
30:23 (that is, 250 s) of fragrant cinnamon, NIH
30:23 250 s of fragrant cane, NIH
30:24 500 s of cassia— NIH
38:24 on the sanctuary was 29 talents and 730 s, 9203
38:25 1,775 s, according to the sanctuary shekel— 9203
38:28 1,775 s to make the hooks for the posts, NIH
38:29 wave offering was 70 talents and 2,400 s. 9203
Lev 27: 3 and sixty at fifty s *of* silver, according to 9203
27: 4 and if it is a female, set her value at thirty s. 9203
27: 5 at twenty s and of a female at ten shekels. 9203
27: 5 at twenty shekels and of a female at ten s. 9203
27: 6 the value of a male at five s *of* silver and 9203
27: 6 and that of a female at three s *of* silver. 9203
27: 7 at fifteen s and of a female at ten shekels. 9203
27: 7 at fifteen shekels and of a female at ten s. 9203
27:16 fifty s *of* silver to a homer of barley seed. 9203
Nu 3:47 collect five s for each one, 9203
3:50 **s,** according to the sanctuary shekel. NIH
7:13 plate weighing a hundred and thirty s, NIH
7:13 silver sprinkling bowl weighing seventy s, 9203
7:14 one gold dish weighing ten **s,** filled NIH
7:19 plate weighing a hundred and thirty s, NIH
7:19 silver sprinkling bowl weighing seventy s, 9203
7:20 one gold dish weighing ten **s,** filled NIH
7:25 plate weighing a hundred and thirty s, NIH
7:25 silver sprinkling bowl weighing seventy s, 9203
7:26 one gold dish weighing ten **s,** filled NIH
7:31 plate weighing a hundred and thirty s, NIH
7:31 silver sprinkling bowl weighing seventy s, 9203
7:32 one gold dish weighing ten **s,** filled NIH
7:37 plate weighing a hundred and thirty s, NIH
7:37 silver sprinkling bowl weighing seventy s, 9203
7:38 one gold dish weighing ten **s,** filled NIH
7:43 plate weighing a hundred and thirty s, NIH
7:43 silver sprinkling bowl weighing seventy s, 9203
7:44 one gold dish weighing ten **s,** filled NIH
7:49 plate weighing a hundred and thirty s, NIH
7:49 silver sprinkling bowl weighing seventy s, 9203
7:50 one gold dish weighing ten **s,** filled NIH
7:55 plate weighing a hundred and thirty s, NIH
7:55 silver sprinkling bowl weighing seventy s, 9203
7:56 one gold dish weighing ten **s,** filled NIH
Nu 7:61 plate weighing a hundred and thirty s, NIH
7:61 silver sprinkling bowl weighing seventy s, 9203
7:62 one gold dish weighing ten **s,** filled NIH
7:67 plate weighing a hundred and thirty s, NIH
7:67 silver sprinkling bowl weighing seventy s, 9203
7:68 one gold dish weighing ten **s,** filled NIH
7:73 plate weighing a hundred and thirty s, NIH
7:73 silver sprinkling bowl weighing seventy s, 9203
7:74 one gold dish weighing ten **s,** filled NIH
7:79 plate weighing a hundred and thirty s, NIH
7:79 silver sprinkling bowl weighing seventy s, 9203
7:80 one gold dish weighing ten **s,** filled NIH
7:85 plate weighing a hundred and thirty s, NIH
7:85 and each sprinkling bowl seventy s. NIH
7:85 silver dishes weighed two thousand four hundred s, NIH
7:86 with incense weighed ten s each, NIH
7:86 dishes weighed a hundred and twenty s. NIH
18:16 the redemption price set at five s of silver, 9203
31:52 as a gift to the LORD weighed 16,750 s. 9203
Dt 22:19 They shall fine him a hundred s of silver NIH
22:29 he shall pay the girl's father fifty s of silver. NIH
Jos 7:21 two hundred s *of* silver and a wedge 9203
7:21 and a wedge of gold weighing fifty s, 9203
Jdg 8:26 for came to seventeen hundred s, NIH
9: 4 They gave him seventy s of silver from NIH
16: 5 of us will give you eleven hundred s NIH
17: 2 "The eleven hundred s of silver NIH
17: 3 the eleven hundred s of silver to his mother, NIH
17: 4 and she took two hundred s of silver NIH
17:10 and I'll give you ten s of silver a year, NIH
1Sa 17: 5 of bronze weighing five thousand s; 9203
17: 7 and its iron point weighed six hundred **s.** 9203
2Sa 14:26 and its weight was two hundred s by 9203
18:11 Then I would have had to give you ten s NIH
18:12 "Even if a thousand s were weighed out 4084
21:16 bronze spearhead weighed three hundred s NIH
24:24 the oxen and paid fifty s of silver for them. 9203
1Ki 10:29 from Egypt for six hundred s of silver, NIH
2Ki 5: 5 six thousand s of gold and ten sets NIH
6:25 a donkey's head sold for eighty s of silver, NIH
6:25 a quarter of a cab of seed pods for five **s.** 4084
15:20 Every wealthy man had to contribute fifty s 9203
1Ch 21:25 So David paid Araunah six hundred s 9203
2Ch 1:17 from Egypt for six hundred s of silver, NIH
3: 9 The gold nails weighed fifty s. 9203
Ne 5:15 on the people and took forty s of silver 9203
SS 8:11 Each was to bring for its fruit a thousand s NIH
8:12 the thousand s are for you, O Solomon, NIH
Isa 7:23 a thousand vines worth a thousand silver **s,** NIH
Jer 32: 9 and weighed out for him seventeen s 9203
Eze 4:10 Weigh out twenty s of food to eat each day 9203
45:12 Twenty s plus twenty-five shekels plus fifteen shekels equal one mina. 9203
45:12 Twenty shekels plus twenty-five s plus fifteen shekels equal one mina. 9203
45:12 Twenty shekels plus twenty-five shekels plus fifteen s equal one mina. 9203
Hos 3: 2 for fifteen s of silver and about a homer and NIH

SHELAH (19) [SHELANITE]

Ge 10:24 Arphaxad was the father of **S,** 8941
10:24 and **S** the father of Eber. 8941
11:12 he became the father of **S.** 8941
11:13 And after he became the father of **S,** 8941
11:14 When **S** had lived 30 years, 8941
11:15 **S** lived 403 years and had other sons 8941
38: 5 to still another son and named him **S.** 8925
38:11 until my son **S** grows up." 8925
38:14 she saw that, though **S** had now grown up, 8925
38:26 since I wouldn't give her to my son **S."** 8925
46:12 The sons of Judah: Er, Onan, **S,** 8925
Nu 26:20 through **S,** the Shelanite clan; 8925
1Ch 1:18 Arphaxad was the father of **S,** 8941
1:18 and **S** the father of Eber. 8941
1:24 Shem, Arphaxad, **S,** 8941
2: 3 The sons of Judah: Er, Onan and **S.** 8925
4:21 The sons of **S** son of Judah: 8925
Ne 11: 5 the son of Zechariah, a descendant **of S.** 8989
Lk 3:35 the son of Eber, the son *of* **S,** *4885*

SHELANITE (1) [SHELAH]

Nu 26:20 through Shelah, the **S** clan; 8989

SHELEMIAH (10)

1Ch 26:14 The lot for the East Gate fell to **S.** 8983
Ezr 10:39 **S,** Nathan, Adaiah, 8982
10:41 Azarel, **S,** Shemariah, 8983
Ne 3:30 Next to him, Hananiah son of **S,** 8982
13:13 I put **S** the priest, Zadok the scribe, 8982
Jer 36:14 the son of **S,** the son of Cushi, 8983
36:26 Seraiah son of Azriel and **S** son of Abdeel 8983
37: 3 of **S** with the priest Zephaniah son 8982
37:13 whose name was Irijah son of **S,** 8982
38: 1 Gedaliah son of Pashhur, Jehucal son of **S,** 8983

SHELEPH (2)

Ge 10:26 Joktan was the father of Almodad, **S,** 8991
1Ch 1:20 Joktan was the father of Almodad, **S,** 8991

SHELESH (1)

1Ch 7:35 Zophah, Imna, **S** and Amal. 8994

SHELISHIYAH See EGLATH SHELISHIYAH

SHELOMI (1)
Nu 34:27 Ahihud son of S, the leader from the tribe 8979

SHELOMITH (8)
Lev 24:11 (His mother's name was S, 8985
1Ch 3:19 S was their sister. 8985
23:18 The sons of Izhar: S was the first. 8984
26:25 Joram his son, Zicri his son and S his son. 8984
26:26 S and his relatives were in charge of all 8984
26:28 in the care of S and his relatives. 8984
2Ch 11:20 who bore him Abijah, Attai, Ziza and S. 8984
Ezr 8:10 S son of Josiphiah, and with him 160 men; 8984

SHELOMOTH (3)
1Ch 23: 9 The sons of Shimei: S, Haziel and Haran— 8977
24:22 S; from the sons of Shelomoth: Jahath. 8977
24:22 from the sons of S: Jahath. 8977

SHELTER (24) [SHELTERED, SHELTERS]
Ex 9:19 **bring** your livestock and everything you have in the field **to a place of s**, 6395
Dt 32:38 *Let them* **give** you s! 2118+6261
Ru 2: 7 except for a short rest in the s." 1074
1Ch 28:18 and s the ark of the covenant of the LORD. 6114
Job 24: 8 and hug the rocks for lack of s. 4726
Ps 27: 5 in the s *of* his tabernacle and set me high 6260
31:20 the s *of* your presence you hide them from 6260
55: 8 I would hurry to my **place of s**, 5144
61: 4 in your tent forever and take refuge in the s 6260
91: 1 He who dwells in the s *of* the Most High 6260
Ecc 7:12 Wisdom is a s as money is a shelter, 7498
7:12 Wisdom is a shelter as money is a s, 7498
Isa 1: 8 The Daughter of Zion is left like a s in 6109
4: 6 be a s and shade from the heat of the day, 6109
16: 4 be their s from the destroyer." 6260
25: 4 s from the storm and a shade from the heat. 4726
32: 2 Each man will be like a s *from* the wind and 4675
58: 7 and to provide the poor wanderer with s— 1074
Jer 4:20 my tents are destroyed, my s in a moment. 3749
10:20 now to pitch my tent or to set up my s. 3749
Eze 17:23 *they will* **find** s in the shade 8905
Da 4:12 Under it the beasts of the field **found** s, 10300
4:21 *giving* s to the beasts of the field, 10163
Jnh 4: 5 There he made himself a s, 6109

SHELTERED (1) [SHELTER]
Zep 2: 3 perhaps *you will* **be** s on the day of the 6259

SHELTERS (6) [SHELTER]
Ge 33:17 for himself and made s for his livestock. 6109
Jdg 6: 2 the Israelites prepared s for themselves 4953
Jer 49:29 their s will be carried off 3749
Mt 17: 4 If you wish, I will put up three s— *5008*
Mk 9: 5 Let us put up three s— *5008*
Lk 9:33 Let us put up three s— *5008*

SHELUMIEL (5)
Nu 1: 6 from Simeon, S son of Zurishaddai; 8981
2:12 The leader of the people of Simeon is S son 8981
7:36 On the fifth day S son of Zurishaddai, 8981
7:41 the offering of S son of Zurishaddai. 8981
10:19 S son of Zurishaddai was over the division 8981

SHEM (20)
Ge 5:32 he became the father of S, 9006
6:10 Noah had three sons: S, Ham and Japheth. 9006
7:13 On that very day Noah and his sons, S, 9006
9:18 of Noah who came out of the ark were S, 9006
9:23 But S and Japheth took a garment 9006
9:26 "Blessed be the LORD, the God of S! 9006
9:26 May Canaan be the slave of S. 4564S
9:27 may Japheth live in the tents of S, 9006
10: 1 This is the account of S, Ham and Japheth, 9006
10:21 Sons were also born to S, 9006
10:21 S was the ancestor of all the sons of Eber. 2085S
10:22 The sons of S: Elam, Asshur, 9006
10:31 the sons of S by their clans and languages, 9006
11:10 This is the account of S. 9006
11:10 when S was 100 years old, 9006
11:11 S lived 500 years and had other sons 9006
1Ch 1: 4 The sons of Noah: S, Ham and Japheth. 9006
1:17 The sons of S: Elam, Asshur, 9006
1:24 S, Arphaxad, Shelah, 9006
Lk 3:36 the son of Arphaxad, the son *of* S, *4954*

SHEMA (6)
Jos 15:26 Amam, S, Moladah, 9054
1Ch 2:43 Korah, Tappuah, Rekem and S. 9050
2:44 S was the father of Raham, 9050
5: 8 the son of S, the son of Joel. 9050
8:13 and Beriah and S, 9050
Ne 8: 4 S, Anaiah, Uriah, Hilkiah and Maaseiah; 9050

SHEMAAH (1)
1Ch 12: 3 and Joash the sons of S the Gibeathite; 9057

SHEMAIAH (39) [SHEMAIAH'S]
1Ki 12:22 word of God came to S the man of God: 9061
1Ch 3:22 S and his sons: Hattush, Igal, 9061
4:37 the son of Shimri, the son of S. 9061
5: 4 S his son, Gog his son, Shimei his son, 9061
9:14 S son of Hasshub, the son of Azrikam, 9061
9:16 Obadiah son of S, the son of Galal, the son 9061
15: 8 S the leader and 200 relatives; 9061
15:11 Joel, S, Eliel and Amminadab the Levites. 9061
24: 6 The scribe S son of Nethanel, a Levite, 9061
26: 4 Obed-Edom also had sons: S the firstborn, 9061
26: 6 His son S also had sons, 9061
26: 7 The sons of S: Othni, Rephael, 9061
2Ch 11: 2 of the LORD came to S the man of God: 9062
12: 5 Then the prophet S came to Rehoboam and 9061
12: 7 this word of the LORD came to S: 9061
12:15 in the records of S the prophet and of Iddo 9061
17: 8 With them were certain Levites—S, 9062
29:14 the descendants of Jeduthun, S and Uzziel. 9061
31:15 Eden, Miniamin, Jeshua, S, 9062
35: 9 Also Conaniah along with S and Nethanel, 9062
Ezr 8:13 whose names were Eliphelet, Jeuel and S, 9061
8:16 So I summoned Eliezer, Ariel, S, Elnathan, 9061
10:21 Maaseiah, Elijah, S, Jehiel and Uzziah. 9061
10:31 Eliezer, Ishijah, Malkijah, S, Shimeon, 9061
Ne 3:29 Next to him, S son of Shecaniah, 9061
6:10 One day I went to the house of S son 9061
10: 8 Bilgai and S. These were the priests. 9061
11:15 S son of Hasshub, the son of Azrikam, 9061
12: 6 S, Joiarib, Jedaiah, 9061
12:34 Judah, Benjamin, S, Jeremiah, 9061
12:35 the son of S, the son of Mattaniah, 9061
12:36 S, Azarel, Milalai, Gilalai, Maai, Nethanel, 9061
12:42 S, Eleazar, Uzzi, Jehohanan, Malkijah, 9061
Jer 26:20 (Now Uriah son of S from Kiriath Jearim 9062
29:24 Tell S the Nehelamite, 9062
29:31 the LORD says about S the Nehelamite: 9061
29:31 Because S has prophesied to you, 9061
29:32 I will surely punish S the Nehelamite 9061
36:12 Elishama the secretary, Delaiah son of S, 9062

SHEMAIAH'S (1) [SHEMAIAH]
Ne 12:18 of Bilgah's, Shammua; of S, Jehonathan; 9061

SHEMARIAH (4)
1Ch 12: 5 Bealiah, S and Shephatiah the Haruphite; 9080
2Ch 11:19 She bore him sons: Jeush, S and Zaham. 9079
Ezr 10:32 Benjamin, Malluch and S. 9079
10:41 Azarel, Shelemiah, S, 9079

SHEMEBER (1)
Ge 14: 2 Shinab king of Admah, S king of Zeboiim, 9008

SHEMED (1)
1Ch 8:12 Eber, Misham, S (who built Ono and Lod 9013

SHEMER (3)
1Ki 16:24 of Samaria from S for two talents of silver 9070
16:24 calling it Samaria, after S, 9070
1Ch 6:46 the son of Bani, the son of S, 9070

SHEMESH (1) See BETH SHEMESH, EN SHEMESH, IR SHEMESH
Jos 15: 7 along to the waters of **En S** and came 6539+9087

SHEMIDA (3) [SHEMIDAITE]
Nu 26:32 through S, the Shemidaite clan; 9026
Jos 17: 2 Helek, Asriel, Shechem, Hepher and S. 9026
1Ch 7:19 The sons of S were: 9026

SHEMIDAITE (1) [SHEMIDA]
Nu 26:32 through Shemida, the S clan; 9027

SHEMINITH (3)
1Ch 15:21 play the harps, directing according to s. 9030
Ps 6: T According to s. A Psalm of David. 9030
12: T According to s. A Psalm of David. 9030

SHEMIRAMOTH (4)
1Ch 15:18 Zechariah, Jaaziel, S, Jehiel, Unni, Eliab, 9035
15:20 Aziel, S, Jehiel, Unni, Eliab, 9035
16: 5 Zechariah second, then Jeiel, S, Jehiel, 9035
2Ch 17: 8 Shemaiah, Nethaniah, Zebadiah, Asahel, S, 9035

SHEMUEL (1)
Nu 34:20 S son of Ammihud, from the tribe 9017

SHEN (1)
1Sa 7:12 and set it up between Mizpah and S. 9095

SHENAZZAR (1)
1Ch 3:18 S, Jekamiah, Hoshama and Nedabiah. 9100

SHENIR (KJV) See SENIR

SHEPHAM (2)
Nu 34:10 run a line from Hazar Enan to S. 9172
34:11 from S to Riblah on the east side of Ain 9172

SHEPHATIAH (13)
2Sa 3: 4 the fifth, S the son of Abital; 9152
1Ch 3: 3 S the son of Abital; 9152
9: 8 and Meshullam son of S, the son of Reuel, 9152
12: 5 Bealiah, Shemariah and S the Haruphite; 9153
27:16 S son of Maacah; 9153
2Ch 21: 2 Zechariah, Azariahu, Michael and S. 9153
Ezr 2: 4 of S 372 9152
2:57 S, Hattil, Pokereth-Hazzebaim and Ami 9152
8: 8 of the descendants of S, Zebadiah son 9152
Ne 7: 9 of S 372 9152
7:59 S, Hattil, Pokereth-Hazzebaim and Amon 9152
11: 4 the son of S, the son of Mahalalel, 9152
Jer 38: 1 S son of Mattan, Gedaliah son of Pashhur, 9152

SHEPHER (2)
Nu 33:23 left Kehelathah and camped at Mount S. 9184
33:24 They left Mount S and camped at Haradah. 9184

SHEPHERD (62) [SHEPHERD'S, SHEPHERDED, SHEPHERDESS, SHEPHERDS]
Ge 48:15 the God who *has been* my s all my life 8286
49:24 because of the S, the Rock of Israel, 8286
Nu 27:17 not be like sheep without a s." 8286
1Sa 17:20 in the morning David left the flock with a s, 9068
21: 7 he was Doeg the Edomite, Saul's head s. 8286
2Sa 5: 2 'You *will* s my people Israel, 8286
7: 7 whom I commanded to s my people Israel, 8286
1Ki 22:17 on the hills like sheep without a s, 8286
1Ch 11: 2 'You *will* s my people Israel, 8286
17: 6 whom I commanded to s my people, 8286
2Ch 18:16 on the hills like sheep without a s, 8286
Ps 23: 1 The LORD *is* my s, I shall not be in want. 8286
28: 9 *be* their s and carry them forever. 8286
78:71 he brought him to *be* the s of his people 8286
80: 1 Hear us, O S *of* Israel, 8286
Ecc 12:11 firmly embedded nails—given by one S. 8286
Isa 13:14 like sheep without a s, 7695
13:20 no s will rest his flocks there. 8286
40:11 He tends his flock like a s: 8286
44:28 'He is my s and will accomplish all 8286
61: 5 Aliens *will* s your flocks; 8286
63:11 with the s *of* his flock? 8286
Jer 17:16 I have not run away from *being* your s; 8286
31:10 and will watch over his flock like a s.' 8286
43:12 As a s wraps his garment around him, 8286
49:19 And what s can stand against me?" 8286
50:44 And what s can stand against me?" 8286
51:23 with you I shatter s and flock, 8286
Eze 34: 5 they were scattered because *there was* no s, 8286
34: 8 because my flock lacks a s and 8286
34:12 a s looks after his scattered flock when he is 8286
34:16 *I will* s the flock with justice. 8286
34:23 I will place over them one s, 8286
34:23 he will tend them and be their s. 8286
37:24 and they will all have one s. 8286
Am 3:12 "As a s saves from the lion's mouth only 8286
7:14 but I was a s, and I also took care of 1012
Mic 5: 4 and s *his* **flock** in the strength of the LORD 8286
7:14 S your people with your staff, 8286
Zec 10: 2 like sheep oppressed for lack of a s. 8286
11: 9 *"I will* not *be* your s. 8286
11:15 "Take again the equipment of a foolish s. 8286
11:16 up a s over the land who will not care for 8286
11:17 "Woe to the worthless s, 8286
13: 7 "Awake, O sword, against my s, 8286
13: 7 the s, and the sheep will be scattered, 8286
Mt 2: 6 a ruler who *will* **be the s of** *4477*
9:36 like sheep without a s. *4478*
25:32 the people one from another as a s separates *4478*
26:31 " 'I will strike the s, and the sheep will be *4478*
Mk 6:34 because they were like sheep without a s. *4478*
14:27 " 'I will strike the s, and the sheep will be *4478*
Jn 10: 2 The man who enters by the gate is the s *4478*
10:11 "I am the good s. *4478*
10:11 The good s lays down his life for the sheep. *4478*
10:12 hired hand is not the s who owns the sheep. *4478*
10:14 "I am the good s; I know my sheep *4478*
10:16 and there shall be one flock and one s. *4478*
Heb 13:20 our Lord Jesus, that great S of the sheep, *4478*
1Pe 2:25 to the S and Overseer of your souls. *4478*
5: 4 And when the **Chief S** appears, *799*
Rev 7:17 at the center of the throne *will* **be** their s; *4477*

SHEPHERD'S (3) [SHEPHERD]
Lev 27:32 that passes under the s **rod**— 8657
1Sa 17:40 put them in the pouch of his s bag and, 8286
Isa 38:12 a s tent my house has been pulled down 8286

SHEPHERDED (1) [SHEPHERD]
Ps 78:72 And David s them with integrity of heart; 8286

SHEPHERDESS (1) [SHEPHERD]
Ge 29: 9 with her father's sheep, for she *was a* s. 8286

SHEPHERDS (50) [SHEPHERD]
Ge 29: 3 the s would roll the stone away from NIH
29: 4 Jacob asked **the s**, "My brothers, 2157S
46:32 The men *are* s; they tend livestock, 7366+8286

Ge 46:34 all s are detestable to the Egyptians." 7366+8286
47: 3 "Your servants are s," 7366+8286
Ex 2:17 Some s came along and drove them away, 8286
2:19 "An Egyptian rescued us from the s. 8286
Nu 14:33 Your children will be s here for forty years, 8286
1Sa 25: 7 When your s were with us, 8286
2Ki 10:12 At Beth Eked of the S, 8286
SS 1: 8 by the tents of the s. 8286
Isa 31: 4 though a whole band of s is called together 8286
56:11 They *are* s who lack understanding; 8286
Jer 3:15 Then I will give you s after my own heart, 8286
6: 3 S with their flocks will come against her; 8286
10:21 The s are senseless and do not inquire of 8286
12:10 Many s will ruin my vineyard and trample 8286
22:22 The wind will drive all your s away, 8286
23: 1 to the s who are destroying and scattering 8286
23: 2 says to the s who tend my people: 8286
23: 4 I will place s over them who will tend them 8286
25:34 Weep and wail, you s; 8286
25:35 The s will have nowhere to flee, 8286
25:36 Hear the cry of the s, 8286
33:12 be pastures for s to rest their flocks. 8286
50: 6 their s have led them astray 8286
Eze 34: 2 prophesy against the s *of* Israel; 8286
34: 2 Woe to the s *of* Israel who only take care 8286
34: 2 Should not s take care of the flock? 8286
34: 7 you s, hear the word of the LORD: 8286
34: 8 because my s did not search for my flock 8286
34: 9 O s, hear the word of the LORD: 8286
34:10 the s and will hold them accountable 8286
34:10 so that the s can no longer feed themselves. 8286
Am 1: 1 words of Amos, one of the s of Tekoa— 5924
1: 2 the pastures of the s dry up, 8286
Mic 5: 5 we will raise against him seven s, 8286
Na 3:18 O king of Assyria, your s slumber; 8286
Zep 2: 6 will be a place for s and sheep pens. 8286
Zec 10: 3 "My anger burns against the s, 8286
11: 3 Listen to the wail of the s; 8286
11: 5 Their own s do not spare them. 8286
11: 8 In one month I got rid of the three s. 8286
Lk 2: 8 there were s living out in the fields nearby, *4478*
2:15 the s said to one another, *4478*
2:18 at what the s said to them. *4478*
2:20 The s returned, glorifying and praising God *4478*
Ac 20:28 **Be s of** the church of God, *4477*
1Pe 5: 2 **Be s of** God's flock that is under your care, *4477*
Jude 1:12 s who feed only themselves. *4477*

SHEPHO (2)
Ge 36:23 Alvan, Manahath, Ebal, S and Onam. 9143
1Ch 1:40 Alvan, Manahath, Ebal, S and Onam. 9143

SHEPHUPHAN (1)
1Ch 8: 5 Gera, S and Huram. 9146

SHERAH (KJV) See SHEERAH

SHERD, SHERDS (KJV) See FRAGMENT, PIECES

SHEREBIAH (8) [SHEREBIAH'S]
Ezr 8:18 they brought us S, a capable man, 9221
8:24 of the leading priests, together with S, 9221
Ne 8: 7 The Levites—Jeshua, Bani, S, Jamin, 9221
9: 4 Shebaniah, Bunni, S, Bani and Kenani— 9221
9: 5 Jeshua, Kadmiel, Bani, Hashabneiah, S, 9221
10:12 Zaccur, S, Shebaniah, 9221
12: 8 Kadmiel, S, Judah, and also Mattaniah, 9221
12:24 leaders of the Levites were Hashabiah, S, 9221

SHEREBIAH'S (1) [SHEREBIAH]
Ezr 8:18 the son of Israel, and S sons and brothers, 2257S

SHERESH (1)
1Ch 7:16 His brother was named S, 9246

SHEREZER (KJV) See SHAREZER

SHERIFFS (KJV) See MAGISTRATES

SHESHACH (2)
Jer 25:26 all of them, the king of S will drink it too. 9263
51:41 "How S will be captured, 9263

SHESHAI (3)
Nu 13:22 S and Talmai, the descendants of Anak, 9259
Jos 15:14 S, Ahiman and Talmai— 9259
Jdg 1:10 and defeated S, Ahiman 9259

SHESHAN (4)
1Ch 2:31 Ishi, who was the father of S. 9264
2:31 S was the father of Ahlai. 9264
2:34 S had no sons—only daughters. 9264
2:35 S gave his daughter in marriage 9264

SHESHBAZZAR (4)
Ezr 1: 8 who counted them out to S the prince 9256
1:11 S brought all these along when the exiles 9256
5:14 King Cyrus gave them to a man named S, 10746
5:16 So this S came and laid the foundations of 10746

SHETH (1)
Nu 24:17 the skulls of all the sons of S. 9269

SHETHAR (1)
Est 1:14 Carshena, S, Admatha, Tarshish, Meres, 9285

SHETHAR-BOZENAI (4)
Ezr 5: 3 and S and their associates went to them 10750
5: 6 and S and their associates, 10750
6: 6 and S and you, their fellow officials 10750
6:13 and S and their associates carried it out 10750

SHEVA (2)
2Sa 20:25 S was secretary; Zadok and Abiathar 8737
1Ch 2:49 and to S the father of Macbenah and Gibea. 8737

SHEWBREAD (KJV) See BREAD OF THE PRESENCE

SHIBAH (1)
Ge 26:33 He called it S, and to this day the name 8683

SHIBBOLETH (1)
Jdg 12: 6 they said, "All right, say 'S.' " 8672

SHIBMAH (KJV) See SIBMAH

SHICRON (KJV) See SHIKKERON

SHIELD (51) [SHIELDED, SHIELDING, SHIELDS]
Ge 15: 1 I am your s, your very great reward." 4482
Ex 40: 3 the ark of the Testimony in it and s the ark 6114
Dt 13: 8 Do not spare him or s him. 4059
33:29 He is your s and helper 4482
Jdg 5: 8 a s or spear was seen among forty thousand 4482
1Sa 17: 7 His s bearer went ahead of him. 7558
17:41 with his s bearer in front of him, 7558
2Sa 1:21 For there the s *of* the mighty was defiled, 4482
1:21 the s *of* Saul—no longer rubbed with oil. 4482
22: 3 my s and the horn of my salvation. 4482
22:31 He is a s for all who take refuge in him. 4482
22:36 You give me your s *of* victory; 4482
1Ki 10:16 six hundred bekas of gold went into each s. 7558
10:17 with three minas of gold in each s. 4482
2Ki 19:32 He will not come before it *with* s or build 4482
1Ch 5:18 able-bodied men who could handle s 4482
12: 8 for battle and able to handle the s and spear. 7558
12:24 carrying s and spear—6,800 armed for 7558
2Ch 9:15 of hammered gold went into each s. 7558
9:16 with three hundred bekas of gold in each s. 4482
25: 5 able to handle the spear and s. 7558
Job 15:26 against him with a thick, strong s. 4482
Ps 3: 3 But you are a s around me, O LORD; 4482
5:12 with your favor as with a s. 7558
7:10 My s is God Most High, 4482
18: 2 He is my s and the horn of my salvation, 4482
18:30 He is a s for all who take refuge in him. 4482
18:35 You give me your s *of* victory, 4482
28: 7 The LORD is my strength and my s; 4482
33:20 he is our help and our s. 4482
35: 2 Take up s and buckler; 4482
59:11 But do not kill them, O Lord our s, 4482
84: 9 Look upon our s, O God; 4482
84:11 For the LORD God is a sun and s; 4482
89:18 Indeed, our s belongs to the LORD, 4482
91: 4 his faithfulness will be your s and rampart. 7558
115: 9 trust in the LORD—he is their help and s. 4482
115:10 trust in the LORD—he is their help and s. 4482
115:11 trust in the LORD—he is their help and s. 4482
119:114 You are my refuge and my s; 4482
144: 2 my stronghold and my deliverer, my s, 4482
Pr 2: 7 he is a s to those whose walk is blameless, 4482
30: 5 he is a s to those who take refuge in him. 4482
Isa 22: 6 Kir uncovers the s. 4482
31: 5 the LORD Almighty *will* s Jerusalem; 1713
31: 5 he *will* s it and deliver it, 1713
37:33 He will not come before it *with* s or build 4482
Na 2: 5 the **protective** s is put in place. 6116
Zec 9:15 and the LORD Almighty *will* s them. 1713
12: 8 that day the LORD *will* s those who live 1713
Eph 6:16 In addition to all this, take up the s of faith, *2599*

SHIELDED (3) [SHIELD]
Ex 40:21 and hung the shielding curtain and s the ark 6114
Dt 32:10 *He* s him and cared for him; 6015
1Pe 1: 5 through faith *are* s by God's power until *5864*

SHIELDING (3) [SHIELD]
Ex 39:34 of hides of sea cows and the s curtain; 5009
40:21 and hung the s curtain and shielded the ark 5009
Nu 4: 5 in and take down the s curtain and cover 5009

SHIELDS (43) [SHIELD]
Ex 35:12 and the curtain that s it; 5009
Dt 33:12 for *he* s him all day long, 2910
2Sa 8: 7 the gold s that belonged to the officers 8949
1Ki 10:16 King Solomon made two hundred **large** s 7558
10:17 He also made three hundred **small** s 4482
14:26 including all the gold s Solomon had made. 4482
14:27 So King Rehoboam made bronze s 4482
14:28 the guards bore **the** s, 4392S
2Ki 11:10 and s that had belonged to King David and 8949
1Ch 12:34 37,000 men carrying s and spears; 7558
18: 7 David took the gold s carried by the officers 8949
2Ch 9:15 King Solomon made two hundred **large** s 7558
9:16 He also made three hundred **small** s 4482
11:12 He put s and spears in all the cities, 7558
12: 9 including the gold s Solomon had made. 4482
12:10 So King Rehoboam made bronze s 4482
12:11 the guards went with him, bearing **the** s, 4392S
14: 8 equipped with **large** s and with spears, 7558
14: 8 armed with **small** s and with bows. 4482
17:17 with 200,000 men armed with bows and s; 4482
23: 9 the large and **small** s that had belonged 8949
26:14 Uzziah provided s, spears, helmets, 4482
32: 5 also made large numbers of weapons and s. 4482
32:27 spices, s and all kinds of valuables. 4482
Ne 4:16 the other half were equipped with spears, s, 4482
Job 41:15 of s tightly sealed together; 4482
Ps 46: 9 he burns the s with fire. 6317
76: 3 the s and the swords, the weapons of war. 4482
140: 7 *who* s my head in the day of battle— 6114
SS 4: 4 on it hang a thousand s, 4482
4: 4 all of them s *of* warriors. 8949
Isa 21: 5 Get up, you officers, oil the s! 4482
Jer 46: 3 s, both large and **small**, 4482
46: 9 men of Cush and Put who carry s, 4482
51:11 "Sharpen the arrows, take up the s! 8949
Eze 23:24 with large and **small** s and with helmets. 4482
26: 8 up to your walls and raise his s against you. 7558
27:10 They hung their s and helmets 4482
27:11 They hung their s around your walls; 8949
38: 4 and a great horde with large and **small** s, 4482
38: 5 all with s and helmets, 4482
39: 9 the **small** and large s, 4482
Na 2: 3 The s *of* his soldiers are red; 4482

SHIFTING (1) [SHIFTS, SHIFTLESS]
Jas 1:17 who does not change like s shadows. *684*

SHIFTLESS (1) [SHIFTING]
Pr 19:15 and the s man goes hungry. 8244

SHIFTS (1) [SHIFTING]
1Ki 5:14 to Lebanon in s of ten thousand a month, 2722

SHIGGAION (1)
Ps 7: T A s of David, which he sang to the LORD 8710

SHIGIONOTH (1)
Hab 3: 1 A prayer of Habakkuk the prophet. On s. 8710

SHIHON (KJV) See SHION

SHIHOR (4) [SHIHOR LIBNATH]
Jos 13: 3 from the S River on the east of Egypt to 8865
1Ch 13: 5 the S River *in* Egypt to Lebo Hamath, 8865
Isa 23: 3 the great waters came the grain of the S; 8865
Jer 2:18 to Egypt to drink water from the S? 8865

SHIHOR LIBNATH (1) [SHIHOR]
Jos 19:26 the boundary touched Carmel and S. 8866

SHIKKERON (1)
Jos 15:11 toward S, passed along to Mount Baalah 8914

SHILHI (2)
1Ki 22:42 mother's name was Azubah daughter of S. 8944
2Ch 20:31 mother's name was Azubah daughter of S. 8944

SHILHIM (1)
Jos 15:32 S, Ain and Rimmon— 8946

SHILLEM (3) [SHILLEMITE]
Ge 46:24 Jahziel, Guni, Jezer and S. 8973
Nu 26:49 through S, the Shillemite clan. 8973
1Ch 7:13 Jahziel, Guni, Jezer and S— 8973

SHILLEMITE (1) [SHILLEM]
Nu 26:49 through Shillem, the S clan. 8980

SHILOAH (1)
Isa 8: 6 the gently flowing waters of S and rejoices 8942

SHILOH (32) [TAANATH SHILOH]
Jos 18: 1 at S and set up the Tent of Meeting there. 8926
18: 8 and I will cast lots for you here at S in 8926
18: 9 and returned to Joshua in the camp at S. 8926
18:10 then cast lots for them in S in the presence 8926
19:51 the tribal clans of Israel assigned by lot at S 8926
21: 2 at S in Canaan and said to them, 8926

Jos 22: 9 the Israelites at S in Canaan to return 8926
22:12 the whole assembly of Israel gathered at S 8926
Jdg 18:31 all the time the house of God was in S. 8926
21:12 they took them to the camp at S in Canaan. 8926
21:19 the annual festival of the LORD in S, 8931
21:21 When the girls of S come out to join in 8870
21:21 a wife from the girls of S and go to the land 8870
1Sa 1: 3 and sacrifice to the LORD Almighty at S, 8926
1: 9 finished eating and drinking in S, 8926
1:24 to the house of the LORD at S. 8931
2:14 the Israelites who came to S. 8926
3:21 The LORD continued to appear at S, 8926
4: 3 the ark of the LORD's covenant from S, 8926
4: 4 So the people sent men to S, 8926
4:12 from the battle line and went to S, 8926
14: 3 the son of Eli, the LORD's priest in S. 8931
1Ki 2:27 the word the LORD had spoken at S about 8926
11:29 and Ahijah the prophet **of S** met him on 8872
14: 2 Then go to S. Ahijah the prophet is there— 8926
14: 4 and went to Ahijah's house in S. 8926
Ps 78:60 He abandoned the tabernacle of S, 8931
Jer 7:12 the place in S where I first made a dwelling 8870
7:14 what I did to S I will now do to the house 8931
26: 6 like S and this city an object of cursing 8926
26: 9 be like S and this city will be desolate 8931
41: 5 and cut themselves came from Shechem, S 8926

SHILONI (KJV) See SHELAH

SHILONITE (4) [SHILONITES]
1Ki 12:15 of Nebat through Ahijah the S. 8872
15:29 through his servant Ahijah the S— 8872
2Ch 9:29 of Ahijah the S and in the visions of Iddo 8872
10:15 of Nebat through Ahijah the S. 8872

SHILONITES (1) [SHILONITE]
1Ch 9: 5 Of the S: Asaiah the firstborn and his sons. 8872

SHILSHAH (1)
1Ch 7:37 Bezer, Hod, Shamma, S, Ithran and Beera. 8996

SHIMEA (4)
1Ch 2:13 the second son was Abinadab, the third S, 9055
6:30 S his son, Haggiah his son 9055
6:39 Asaph son of Berekiah, the son of S, 9055
20: 7 When he taunted Israel, Jonathan son of S, 9055

SHIMEAH (4)
2Sa 13: 3 a friend named Jonadab son of S, 9056
13:32 But Jonadab son of S, David's brother, 9056
21:21 When he taunted Israel, Jonathan son of S, 9056
1Ch 8:32 who was the father of S. 9009

SHIMEAM (1)
1Ch 9:38 Mikloth was the father of S. 9010

SHIMEATH (2) [SHIMEATHITES]
2Ki 12:21 of S and Jehozabad son of Shomer. 9064
2Ch 24:26 son of S an Ammonite woman, 9064

SHIMEATHITES (1) [SHIMEATH]
1Ch 2:55 the Tirathites, S and Sucathites. 9065

SHIMEI (44) [SHIMEI'S, SHIMEITES]
Ex 6:17 by clans, were Libni and S. 9059
Nu 3:18 of the Gershonite clans: Libni and S. 9059
2Sa 16: 5 His name was S son of Gera, 9059
16: 7 As he cursed, S said, "Get out, get out, 9059
16:13 along the road while S was going along 9059
19:16 S son of Gera, the Benjamite 9059
19:18 When S son of Gera crossed the Jordan, 9059
19:21 "Shouldn't S be put to death for this? 9059
19:23 So the king said to S, "You shall not die." 9059
1Ki 1: 8 S and Rei and David's special guard did 9059
2: 8 you have with you S son of Gera, 9059
2:36 Then the king sent for S and said to him, 9059
2:38 S answered the king, "What you say is good 9059
2:38 And S stayed in Jerusalem for a long time. 9059
2:39 and S was told, "Your slaves are in Gath." 9059
2:40 So S went away and brought 9059
2:41 When Solomon was told that S had gone 9059
2:42 the king summoned S and said to him, 9059
2:44 The king also said to S, 9059
2:46 and he went out and struck S down 2257S
4:18 S son of Ela—in Benjamin; 9059
1Ch 3:19 The sons of Pedaiah: Zerubbabel and S. 9059
4:26 Zaccur his son and S his son. 9059
4:27 S had sixteen sons and six daughters, 9059
5: 4 Shemaiah his son, Gog his son, S his son, 9059
6:17 of Gershon: Libni and S. 9059
6:29 Mahli, Libni his son, S his son, 9059
6:42 the son of Zimmah, the son of S, 9059
8:21 Beraiah and Shimrath were the sons of S. 9059
23: 7 to the Gershonites: Ladan and S. 9059
23: 9 The sons of S: Shelomoth, Haziel and 9059
23:10 sons of S: Jahath, Ziza, Jeush and Beriah. 9059
23:10 These were the sons of S—four in all. 9059
25: 3 Gedaliah, Zeri, Jeshaiah, S, 9059
25:17 the tenth to S, his sons and relatives, 12 9059
27:27 S the Ramathite was in charge of 9059
2Ch 29:14 the descendants of Heman, Jehiel and S; 9059
31:12 and his brother S was next in rank. 9059
31:13 under Conaniah and S his brother, 9059
Ezr 10:23 Jozabad, S, Kelaiah (that is, Kelita), 9059
10:33 Zabad, Eliphelet, Jeremai, Manasseh and S. 9059
10:38 From the descendants of Binnui: S, 9059
Est 2: 5 named Mordecai son of Jair, the son of S, 9059
Zec 12:13 the clan of S and their wives, 9060

SHIMEI'S (1) [SHIMEI]
1Ki 2:39 two of S slaves ran off to Achish son 4200+9059

SHIMEITES (1) [SHIMEI]
Nu 3:21 the clans of the Libnites and S; 9060

SHIMEON (1)
Ezr 10:31 Eliezer, Ishijah, Malkijah, Shemaiah, S, 9058

SHIMHI, SHIMI (KJV) See SHIMEI

SHIMITES (KJV) See SHIMEITES

SHIMMA (KJV) See SHIMEA

SHIMMERING (1)
Isa 18: 4 like s heat in the sunshine, 7456

SHIMON (1)
1Ch 4:20 The sons of S: Amnon, Rinnah, Ben-Hanan 8873

SHIMRATH (1)
1Ch 8:21 Beraiah and S were the sons of Shimei. 9086

SHIMRI (4)
1Ch 4:37 the son of S, the son of Shemaiah. 9078
11:45 Jediael son of S, his brother Joha 9078
26:10 S the first (although he was not the 9078
2Ch 29:13 the descendants of Elizaphan, S and Jeiel; 9078

SHIMRITH (1)
2Ch 24:26 and Jehozabad, son of S a Moabite woman. 9083

SHIMRON (5) [SHIMRONITE, SHIMRON MERON]
Ge 46:13 Tola, Puah, Jashub and S. 9075
Nu 26:24 through S, the Shimronite clan. 9075
Jos 11: 1 to the kings of S and Acshaph, 9074
19:15 Included were Kattath, Nahalal, S, 9074
1Ch 7: 1 Tola, Puah, Jashub and S—four in all. 9075

SHIMRON MERON (1) [SHIMRON]
Jos 12:20 the king of S one the king of Acshaph one 9077

SHIMRONITE (1) [SHIMRON]
Nu 26:24 through Shimron, the S clan. 9084

SHIMSHAI (4)
Ezr 4: 8 Rehum the commanding officer and S 10729
4: 9 and S the secretary, together with the rest 10729
4:17 the commanding officer, S the secretary 10729
4:23 and S the secretary and their associates, 10729

SHINAB (1)
Ge 14: 2 S king of Admah, Shemeber king of 9098

SHINAR (4)
Ge 10:10 Erech, Akkad and Calneh, in S. 824+9114
11: 2 they found a plain in S and settled 824+9114
14: 1 At this time Amraphel king of S, 9114
14: 9 Amraphel king of S and Arioch king 9114

SHINE (36) [SHINES, SHINING, SHONE]
Nu 6:25 the LORD **make** his face s upon you and 239
Ne 9:19 by night to s on the way they were to take. 239
Job 3: 4 *may* no light s upon it. 3649
9: 7 He speaks to the sun and *it does* not s; 2436
22:28 and light *will* s on your ways. 5585
33:30 that the light of life *may* s *on* him. 239
Ps 4: 6 **Let** the light of your face s upon us, 5951
31:16 *Let* your face s on your servant; 239
37: 6 **make** your righteousness s like the dawn, 3655
67: 1 and bless us and **make** his face s upon us, 239
80: 1 between the cherubim, **s forth** 3649
80: 3 **make** your face s upon us, 239
80: 7 **make** your face s upon us, 239
80:19 **make** your face s upon us, 239
94: 1 O God who avenges, **s forth.** 3649
104:15 oil to **make** his face s, 7413
118:27 and *he has* **made** *his* **light** s upon us. 239
119:135 **Make** your face s upon your servant 239
139:12 the night *will* s like the day, 239
Isa 30:26 The moon *will* s like the sun, 240+2118
60: 1 "Arise, s, for your light has come, 239
60:19 nor *will* the brightness of the moon s 239
Jer 31:35 he who appoints the sun to s by day, 239
31:35 and stars to s by night, who stirs up the sea 239
Da 12: 3 Those who are wise *will* s like 2301
Joel 2:10 and the stars **no longer s.** 665+5586
3:15 and the stars **no longer s.** 665+5586
Mt 5:16 *let* your light s before men, *3290*
13:43 Then the righteous *will* s like the sun in *1719*
Lk 1:79 *to* **s on** those living in darkness and in *2210*
2Co 4: 6 who said, *"Let* light s out of darkness," *3290*
4: 6 **made** his light s in our hearts to give us *3290*
Eph 5:14 and Christ *will* **s on** you." *2213*
Php 2:15 in which *you* s like stars in the universe *5743*
Rev 18:23 of a lamp *will* never s in you again. *5743*
21:23 not need the sun or the moon to s on it, *5743*

SHINES (5) [SHINE]
Ps 50: 2 From Zion, perfect in beauty, God s **forth.** 3649
Pr 13: 9 The light of the righteous s **brightly,** 8523
Isa 62: 1 till her righteousness s **out** like the dawn, 3655
Lk 11:36 as when the light of a lamp s **on** you." *5894*
Jn 1: 5 The light s in the darkness, *5743*

SHINING (12) [SHINE]
2Ki 3:22 the sun *was* s on the water. 2436
Ps 68:13 its feathers with s gold." 3768
148: 3 sun and moon, praise him, all you s stars. 240
Pr 4:18 **s ever brighter** till the full light of day. 239+2143+2256
Eze 28: 7 and wisdom and pierce your s **splendor.** 3650
32: 8 All the s lights in the heavens I will darken 240
Lk 23:45 for the sun **stopped s.** *1722*
Ac 10:30 a man in s clothes stood before me *3287*
2Pe 1:19 as to a light s in a dark place, *5743*
1Jn 2: 8 and the true light *is* already s. *5743*
Rev 1:16 like the sun s in all its brilliance. *5743*
15: 6 They were dressed in clean, s linen *3287*

SHION (1)
Jos 19:19 Hapharaim, S, Anaharath, 8858

SHIP (28) [SHIP'S, SHIPS, SHIPWRIGHTS]
Pr 30:19 the way of a s on the high seas, 641
Isa 2:16 every **trading** s and every stately vessel 641+9576
33:21 no mighty s will sail them. 7469
Jnh 1: 3 where he found a s bound for that port. 641
1: 4 a violent storm arose that the s threatened 641
1: 5 the cargo into the sea to lighten the s. NIH
Ac 20:13 on ahead to the s and sailed for Assos, *4450*
20:38 Then they accompanied him to the **s.** *4450*
21: 2 We found a s crossing over to Phoenicia, *4450*
21: 3 where our s was to unload its cargo. *4450*
21: 6 we went aboard the s, *4450*
27: 2 We boarded a s from Adramyttium about *4450*
27: 6 an Alexandrian s sailing for Italy and put us *4450*
27:10 to be disastrous and bring great loss to s *4450*
27:11 of the pilot and of the **owner of the s.** *3729*
27:15 The s was caught by the storm and could *4450*
27:17 under the s itself to hold it together. *4450*
27:17 the sea anchor and let the s be driven along. *NIG*
27:22 only the s will be destroyed. *4450*
27:30 In an attempt to escape from the s, *4450*
27:31 "Unless these men stay with the s, *4450*
27:38 they lightened the s by throwing the grain *4450*
27:39 where they decided to run the s aground *4450*
27:41 But the s struck a sandbar and ran aground. *3730*
27:44 to get there on planks or on pieces of the s. *4450*
28:11 to sea in a s that had wintered in the island. *4450*
28:11 It was an Alexandrian s with the figurehead *NIG*
Rev 18:17 and all who **travel by s,** the sailors, *4434*

SHIP'S (1) [SHIP]
Ac 27:19 they threw the s tackle overboard *4450*

SHIPHI (1)
1Ch 4:37 and Ziza son of S, the son of Allon, 9181

SHIPHMITE (1)
1Ch 27:27 Zabdi the S was in charge of the produce of 9175

SHIPHRAH (1)
Ex 1:15 whose names were S and Puah, 9186

SHIPHTAN (1)
Nu 34:24 Kemuel son of S, the leader from the tribe 9154

SHIPMASTER (KJV) See CAPTAIN

SHIPMEN (KJV) See SAILORS

SHIPPING (KJV) See BOATS

SHIPS (30) [SHIP]
Ge 49:13 by the seashore and become a haven for **s;** 641
Nu 24:24 S will come from the shores of Kittim; 7469
Dt 28:68 The LORD will send you back in s 641
Jdg 5:17 And Dan, why did he linger by the s? 641
1Ki 9:26 King Solomon also built s at Ezion Geber, 639
10:11 (Hiram's s brought gold from Ophir; 639
10:22 The king had a **fleet of trading** s at sea 639+9576
10:22 at sea along with the s *of* Hiram. 639

1Ki 22:48 a **fleet of trading** s to go to Ophir 641+9576
2Ch 8:18 And Hiram sent him s commanded 641
9:21 The king had a **fleet of trading** s manned by Hiram's men. 641+2143+9576
20:36 He agreed with him to construct a **fleet of trading s.** 641+2143+4200+9576
20:37 The s were wrecked and were not able 641
Ps 48: 7 like s *of* Tarshish shattered by an east wind. 641
104:26 There the s go to and fro, and the leviathan, 641
107:23 Others went out on the sea in s; 641
Pr 31:14 She is like the merchant s, 641
Isa 23: 1 Wail, O s *of* Tarshish! 641
23:14 Wail, you s *of* Tarshish; 641
43:14 in the s *in which* they took pride. 641
60: 9 in the lead are the s *of* Tarshish, 641
Eze 27: 9 All the s *of* the sea and their sailors 641
27:25 " 'The s *of* Tarshish serve as carriers 641
27:29 the oars will abandon their s; 641
30: 9 from me in s to frighten Cush out 7469
Da 11:30 S *of* the western coastlands will oppose him, 7469
11:40 and cavalry and a great **fleet of s.** 641
Jas 3: 4 Or take s as an example. *4450*
Rev 8: 9 and a third *of* the s were destroyed. *4450*
18:19 where all who had s on the sea became rich *4450*

SHIPWRECK (1) [WRECKED]
Eze 27:27 the heart of the sea on the day of your s. 5147

SHIPWRECKED (2) [WRECKED]
2Co 11:25 once I was stoned, three times *I was* s, *3728*
1Ti 1:19 and so *have* s their faith. *3728*

SHIPWRIGHTS (2) [SHIP]
Eze 27: 9 on board as s to caulk your seams. NIH
27:27 your mariners, seamen and s, 981+2616

SHISHA (1)
1Ki 4: 3 and Ahijah, sons of S— 8881

SHISHAK (7)
1Ki 11:40 but Jeroboam fled to Egypt, to S the king, 8882
14:25 S king of Egypt attacked Jerusalem. 8882
2Ch 12: 2 S king of Egypt attacked Jerusalem in 8882
12: 5 of S, and he said to them, "This is what 8882
12: 5 therefore, I now abandon you to S.' " 8882
12: 7 not be poured out on Jerusalem through S. 8882
12: 9 When S king of Egypt attacked Jerusalem, 8882

SHITRAI (1)
1Ch 27:29 S the Sharonite was in charge of the herds 8855

SHITTAH See BETH SHITTAH

SHITTIM (4) [ABEL SHITTIM]
Nu 25: 1 While Israel was staying in S, 8850
Jos 2: 1 of Nun secretly sent two spies from S. 8850
3: 1 the Israelites set out from S and went to 8850
Mic 6: 5 Remember [your journey] from S to Gilgal, 8850

SHIVERS (KJV) See PIECES

SHIZA (1)
1Ch 11:42 Adina son of S the Reubenite, 8862

SHOA (1)
Eze 23:23 the men of Pekod and S and Koa, 8778

SHOBAB (4)
2Sa 5:14 Shammua, S, Nathan, Solomon, 8744
1Ch 2:18 These were her sons: Jesher, S and Ardon. 8744
3: 5 Shammua, S, Nathan and Solomon. 8744
14: 4 Shammua, S, Nathan, Solomon, 8744

SHOBACH (2)
2Sa 10:16 they went to Helam, with S the commander 8747
10:18 He also struck down S the commander 8747

SHOBAI (2)
Ezr 2:42 Hatita and S 139 8662
Ne 7:45 Hatita and S 138 8662

SHOBAL (9)
Ge 36:20 Lotan, S, Zibeon, Anah, 8748
36:23 The sons of S: Alvan, Manahath, 8748
36:29 These were the Horite chiefs: Lotan, S, 8748
1Ch 1:38 The sons of Seir: Lotan, S, Zibeon, Anah, 8748
1:40 The sons of S: Alvan, Manahath, 8748
2:50 S the father of Kiriath Jearim, 8748
2:52 of S the father of Kiriath Jearim were: 8748
4: 1 Perez, Hezron, Carmi, Hur and S. 8748
4: 2 Reaiah son of S was the father of Jahath, 8748

SHOBEK (1)
Ne 10:24 Hallohesh, Pilha, S, 8749

SHOBI (1)
2Sa 17:27 S son of Nahash from Rabbah of 8661

SHOCHO, SHOCO (KJV) See SOCO

SHOCHOH (KJV) See SOCOH

SHOCKED (1) [SHOCKING, SHOCKS]
Eze 16:27 who **were** s by your lewd conduct. 4007

SHOCKING (1) [SHOCKED]
Jer 5:30 "A horrible and s **thing** has happened in 9136

SHOCKS (2) [SHOCKED]
Ex 22: 6 so that it burns s **of grain** or standing grain 1538
Jdg 15: 5 He burned up the s and standing grain, 1538

SHOD (KJV) See FITTED, SANDALS, WEAR

SHOE, SHOE'S, SHOES (KJV) See SANDAL, SANDALED, SANDALS, UNSANDALED

SHOELATCHET (KJV) See THONG

SHOHAM (1)
1Ch 24:27 Beno, S, Zaccur and Ibri. 8733

SHOMER (3)
2Ki 12:21 of Shimeath and Jehozabad son of S. 9071
1Ch 7:32 S and Hotham and of their sister Shua. 9071
7:34 The sons of S: Ahi, Rohgah, Hubbah 9071

SHONE (6) [SHINE]
Dt 33: 2 *he* s **forth** from Mount Paran. 3649
Job 29: 3 when his lamp s upon my head and 2145
Mt 17: 2 His face s like the sun, *3290*
Lk 2: 9 and the glory of the Lord s **around** them, *4334*
Ac 12: 7 an angel of the Lord appeared and a light s *3290*
Rev 21:11 *It* s **with** the **glory** of God, *1518+2400*

SHOOK (18) [SHAKE]
Jdg 5: 4 the earth s, the heavens poured, 8321
1Sa 4: 5 a great shout that the ground s. 2101
14:15 and raiding parties—and the ground s. 8074
2Sa 22: 8 the foundations of the heavens s; 8074
1Ki 1:40 so that the ground s with the sound. 1324
Ne 5:13 *I* also s **out** the folds of my robe and said, 5850
Ps 18: 7 and the foundations of the mountains s; 8074
68: 8 the earth s, the heavens poured down rain, 8321
Isa 6: 4 and thresholds s and the temple was filled 5675
14:16 "Is this the man *who* s the earth 8074
Hab 3: 6 He stood, and s the earth; 4571
Mt 27:51 The earth s and the rocks split. *4940*
28: 4 so afraid of him that *they* s and became *4940*
Mk 1:26 The evil spirit s the man **violently** *5057*
Ac 13:51 So they s the dust **from** their feet in protest *1759*
18: 6 *he* s **out** his clothes in protest and said *1759*
28: 5 But Paul s the snake **off** into the fire *701*
Heb 12:26 At that time his voice s the earth, *4888*

SHOOT (24) [SHOOTING, SHOOTS, SHOT]
1Sa 20:20 I *will* s three arrows *to* the side of it, 3721
20:36 "Run and find the arrows I s." 3721
2Sa 11:20 Didn't you know *they would* s **arrows** from 3721
2Ki 13:17 "S!" Elisha said, and he shot. 3721
19:32 not enter this city or s an arrow here. 3721
1Ch 12: 2 to s arrows or to sling stones 928+2021+8008
2Ch 26:15 and on the corner defenses to s arrows 3721
Job 41:19 from his mouth; sparks of fire s **out.** 4880
Ps 11: 2 they set their arrows against the strings to s 3721
64: 4 They s from ambush *at* the innocent man; 3721
64: 4 *they* s *at* him suddenly, without fear. 3721
64: 7 But God *will* s them with arrows; 3721
144: 6 s your arrows and rout them. 8938
Isa 11: 1 A s will come up from the stump of Jesse; 2643
37:33 not enter this city or s an arrow here. 3721
53: 2 He grew up before him like a **tender** s, 3437
60:21 They are the s I have planted, 5916
Jer 9: 3 **make ready** their tongue like a bow, **to** s 2005
50:14 S at her! Spare no arrows, 3343
Eze 5:16 When I s at you with my deadly and 8938
5:16 *I will* s to destroy you. 8938
17: 4 he broke off its topmost s and carried it 3566
17:22 I myself will take a s from the very top *of* 7550
Ro 11:17 and you, *though* a **wild olive** s, *66*

SHOOTING (2) [SHOOT]
1Sa 20:20 as though I *were* s at a target. 8938
Pr 26:18 a madman s firebrands or deadly arrows 3721

SHOOTS (12) [SHOOT]
2Ki 19:26 like **tender** green s, 3764
Job 8:16 spreading its s over the garden; 3438
14: 7 and its **new** s will not fail. 3438
14: 9 the scent of water it will bud and put forth s 7908
15:30 a flame will wither his s, 3438
Ps 80:11 its s as far as the River. 3438
128: 3 be like olive s around your table. 9277
Isa 16: 8 Their s spread out and went as far as 8943
18: 5 he will cut off the s with pruning knives, 2360
37:27 like **tender** green **s,** like grass sprouting 3764
Eze 17:22 from its topmost s and plant it on a high 3438
Hos 14: 6 his **young** s will grow. 3438

SHOPHACH (2)
1Ch 19:16 with S the commander of Hadadezer's army 8791
19:18 also killed S the commander of their army. 8791

SHOPHAN See ATROTH SHOPHAN

SHORE (18) [ASHORE, SHORES]
Ex 14:30 the Egyptians lying dead on the s. 3542+8557
1Ki 9:26 on the s *of* the Red Sea. 8557
Eze 27:29 and all the seamen will stand on the s. 824
47:10 Fishermen will stand along **the s;** 2257[S]
Zep 2:11 The nations on every s will worship him, 362
Mt 13: 2 while all the people stood on the s. *129*
13:48 the fishermen pulled it up on the s. *129*
Mk 4: 1 while all the people were along the s at *1178*
Lk 5: 3 and asked him to put out a little from **s.** *1178*
5:11 So they pulled their boats up on s, *1178*
Jn 6: 1 **to the far** s of the Sea of Galilee (that is, *4305*
6:21 and immediately the boat reached the s *1178*
6:22 the crowd that had stayed **on the opposite** s *4305*
21: 4 Early in the morning, Jesus stood on the s, *129*
21: 8 for they were not far from s, *1178*
Ac 27:13 and sailed **along the** s of Crete. *839*
28: 1 Once safely on **s,** we found out that *NIG*
Rev 13: 1 And the dragon stood on the s of the sea. *302*

SHORELANDS (1) [LAND]
Eze 27:28 The s will quake when your seamen cry out. 4494

SHORES (4) [SHORE]
Nu 24:24 Ships will come from the s *of* Kittim; 3338
Est 10: 1 throughout the empire, to its **distant s.** 362+3542
Ps 72:10 and of **distant** s will bring tribute to him; 362
97: 1 let the distant s rejoice. 362

SHORN (1) [SHEAR]
SS 4: 2 Your teeth are like a flock of **sheep just s,** 7892

SHORT (33) [SHORTENED, SHORTER, SHORTLY]
Nu 11:23 *"Is* the LORD's arm **too s?** 7918
Ru 2: 7 except for a s rest in the shelter." 5071
1Sa 2:31 when *I will* **cut** s your strength and 1548
21:15 Am I *so* s *of* madmen that you have 2894
2Sa 16: 1 When David had gone a **s distance** beyond 5071
19:36 the Jordan with the king for a s **distance,** 5071
Job 17: 1 My spirit is broken, my days **are cut s,** 2403
Ps 89:45 *You have* **cut** s the days of his youth; 7918
102:23 *he* **cut** s my days. 7918
Pr 10:27 but the years of the wicked *are* **cut s.** 7918
Isa 28:20 The bed *is* too s to stretch out on, 7918
29:17 **In a very s time,** will not 4663+5071+6388
50: 2 *Was* my arm too s to ransom you? 7918+7918
59: 1 the arm of the LORD *is* not too s to save, 7918
Mic 6:10 your ill-gotten treasures and the s ephah, 8137
Mt 13:21 since he has no root, he lasts **only a s time.** *4672*
24:22 If those days *had* not *been* **cut s,** *3143*
Mk 4:17 they have no root, they last **only a s time.** *4672*
13:20 If the Lord *had* not **cut** s those days, *3143*
Lk 19: 3 but being a s *man* he could not, *2461+3625+3836*
Jn 7:33 Jesus said, "I am with you for only a s time, *3625*
11: 8 **"a s while ago** the Jews tried to stone you, *3814*
Ac 26:28 that in such **a s time** you can persuade me to *3900*
26:29 Paul replied, **"S time** or long— *1877+3900*
27:28 A s time later they took soundings again *1099*
Ro 3:23 for all have sinned and **fall** s of the glory *5728*
1Co 7:29 What I mean, brothers, is that the time is s. *5319*
1Th 2:17 we were torn away from you for a s time *6052*
Heb 4: 1 of you be found *to have* **fallen** s of it. *5728*
11:25 to enjoy the pleasures of sin *for* **a s time.** *4672*
13:22 for I have written you only a s letter. *1099+1328*
Rev 12:12 because he knows that his time *is* **s."** *2400+3900*
20: 3 After that, he must be set free *for* a s time. *3625*

SHORT-SIGHTED (Anglicized) See NEARSIGHTED

SHORTCOMINGS (1)
Ge 41: 9 "Today I am reminded of my s. 2628

SHORTENED (2) [SHORT]
Mt 24:22 the sake of the elect those days *will be* **s.** *3143*
Mk 13:20 whom he has chosen, *he has* s them. *3143*

SHORTER (1) [SHORT]
Ex 13:17 the Philistine country, though that was s. 7940

SHORTLY (2) [SHORT]
Jer 28:12 **S after** the prophet Hananiah had broken 339

Mk 11: 3 Lord needs it and will send it back here s.' " 2317

SHOT (9) [SHOOT]

Ge 49:23 *they* s *at* him with hostility. 8046
Ex 19:13 He shall surely be stoned or s **with arrows;** 3721+3721
1Sa 20:36 As the boy ran, he s an arrow beyond him. 3721
2Sa 11:24 Then the archers s **arrows** at your servants 3721
22:15 *He* s arrows and scattered [the enemies], 8938
2Ki 9:24 Then Jehu drew his bow and s Joram 5782
13:17 "Shoot!" Elisha said, and *he* s. 3721
2Ch 35:23 Archers s King Josiah, 3721
Ps 18:14 *He* s his arrows and scattered [the enemies], 8938

SHOULD (371) [SHOULDN'T]

Ge 20: 9 have done things to me that s not **be done."** AIT
27:45 Why *s I* **lose** both of you in one day?" AIT
29:15 *s you* **work for** me for nothing? AIT
29:15 Tell me what your wages s be." NIH
34: 7 a *thing that s* not **be done.** AIT
34:31 *"S he have* **treated** our sister like AIT
38:18 He said, "What pledge *s I* **give** you?" AIT
41:35 *They s* **collect** all the food AIT
41:36 This food *s* **be** held in reserve for AIT
46:34 *you s* **answer,** 'Your servants have tended AIT
47:15 Why *s we* **die** before your eyes? AIT
47:19 Why *s we* **perish** before your eyes— AIT
Ex 3:11 that *I s* **go** to Pharaoh and bring AIT
5: 2 that *I s* **obey** him and let Israel go? AIT
16: 7 that *you s* **grumble** against us?" AIT
32:11 "why *s* your anger **burn** AIT
32:12 Why *s* the Egyptians **say,** AIT
Lev 10:18 *you s have* **eaten** the goat in AIT
13:16 *S* the raw flesh change and **turn** AIT
24:12 of the LORD *s be* **made clear** to them. AIT
27:10 if *he s* **substitute** one animal for another, AIT
Nu 9: 7 *s we* **be kept from** presenting the LORD's AIT
10:31 You know where *we s* **camp** in the desert, AIT
13:30 *"We* s **go up** and take possession of 6590+6590
14: 4 *We s* **choose** a leader and go back to Egypt." AIT
15:34 it was not clear what *s* **be done** to him. AIT
16:11 Who is Aaron that *you s* **grumble** AIT
16:40 of Aaron *s* **come** to burn incense before AIT
20: 4 that we and our livestock *s* **die** here? AIT
23:19 God is not a man, that *he s* **lie,** AIT
23:19 nor a son of man, that *he s* **change** *his* **mind.** AIT
27: 4 *s* our father's name **disappear** from his clan AIT
Dt 1:33 and to show you the way *you s* **go.** AIT
5:25 But now, why *s we* **die?** AIT
15: 4 However, *there s* **be** no poor among you, AIT
16:16 No man *s* **appear** before the LORD AIT
20:19 that you *s* **besiege** them? AIT
28:68 on a journey I said you *s* never **make again.** AIT
Jdg 8: 6 Why *s we* **give** bread to your troops?" AIT
8:15 Why *s we* **give** bread to your exhausted men? AIT
9: 9 olive tree answered, *'S I* **give up** my oil, AIT
9:11 the fig tree replied, *'S I* **give up** my fruit, AIT
9:13 the vine answered, *'S I* **give up** my wine, AIT
9:28 that *we s be* **subject to** him? AIT
9:28 Why *s* we **serve** Abimelech? AIT
9:32 the night you and your men *s* **come** and lie AIT
9:38 'Who is Abimelech that *we s be* **subject to** AIT
11:34 *who s* **come out** to meet him AIT
14:16 he replied, "so *why s I* **explain** it to you?" AIT
20:38 that they *s* **send up** a great cloud of smoke AIT
21: 3 *s* one tribe *be* **missing** from Israel AIT
21: 5 *s* **certainly be put to death.** AIT
Ru 3: 1 *s I* not **try to find** a home for you, AIT
4: 4 *s* **bring** the matter to your **attention** AIT
1Sa 6: 2 Tell us how *we s* **send** it **back** to its place." AIT
6: 4 "What guilt offering *s we* **send** to him?" AIT
9:13 *you s* **find** him about this time." AIT
12:23 that I *s* **sin** against the LORD by failing AIT
14:45 But the men said to Saul, *"S* Jonathan **die—** AIT
15:29 he is not a man, that *he s* **change** *his* **mind."** AIT
17:26 that *he s* **defy** the armies of the living God? AIT
18:18 that *I s* **become** the king's son-in-law?" AIT
19:17 Why *s I* **kill** you?' " AIT
20:32 *s he* **be put to death?** AIT
24: 6 that *I s* **do** such a thing to my master, AIT
25:11 Why *s I* **take** my bread and water, AIT
26:11 But the LORD forbid that I *s* **lay** a hand AIT
27: 5 Why *s* your servant **live** in the royal city AIT
2Sa 2:22 Why *s I* **strike** you down? AIT
3:33 *"S* Abner *have* **died** as the lawless die? AIT
4:11 *s I* not now **demand** his blood from your AIT
9: 8 that *you s* **notice** a dead dog like me?" AIT
12:23 But now that he is dead, why *s* I **fast?** AIT
13:12 Such a thing *s* not **be done** in Israel! AIT
13:25 "All of us *s* not **go;** AIT
13:26 "Why *s he* **go** with you?" AIT
13:32 "My lord *s* not **think** that they killed all AIT
13:33 the king *s* not *be* **concerned about** AIT
15:19 "Why *s* you **come** along with us? AIT
16: 9 *s* this dead dog **curse** my lord AIT
16:19 Furthermore, whom *s I* **serve?** AIT
16:19 **S** I not serve the son? NIH
16:20 What *s we* **do?"** AIT
17: 6 *S we* **do** what he says? AIT
17: 9 If *he s* **attack** your troops first, AIT
19:11 the elders of Judah, 'Why *s you* **be** the last AIT
19:12 So why *s you* **be** the last to bring back AIT
19:22 *S* anyone **be put to death** in Israel today? AIT
19:34 that *I s* **go up** to Jerusalem with the king? AIT
19:35 Why *s* your servant **be** an added burden AIT
2Sa 19:36 but why *s* the king **reward** me *in* this way? AIT
24:13 think it over and decide how *I s* **answer** AIT
1Ki 1:27 without letting his servants know who *s* **sit** AIT
12: 9 How *s we* **answer** these people who say AIT
20:11 'One who puts on his armor *s* not **boast** AIT
20:42 a man I had **determined s die.** 3051
21: 3 "The LORD forbid that I *s* **give** you AIT
22: 8 "The king *s* not **say** that," AIT
2Ki 6:33 Why *s I* **wait** for the LORD any longer?" AIT
7: 2 *even if* the LORD *s* **open** the floodgates AIT
7:19 *even if* the LORD *s* **open** the floodgates AIT
13:19 "You *s have* **struck** the ground five AIT
1Ch 11:19 "God forbid that I *s* **do** this!" AIT
11:19 *"S I* **drink** the blood of these men who went AIT
12:32 the times and knew what Israel *s* **do—** AIT
21: 3 Why *s he* **bring** guilt on Israel?" AIT
21:12 how *I s* **answer** the one who sent me." AIT
22: 5 for the LORD *s be* of **great** magnificence AIT
29:14 *we s be* **able** to give as generously as this? AIT
2Ch 10: 9 How *s we* **answer** these people who say AIT
18: 7 "The king *s* not **say** that," AIT
19: 2 *"S you* **help** the wicked and love those who AIT
24: 9 in Judah and Jerusalem that they *s* **bring** to AIT
32: 4 "Why *s* the kings of Assyria **come** AIT
Ezr 4:12 The king *s* **know** that the Jews who came up AIT
4:13 the king *s* **know** that if this city is built AIT
5: 8 The king *s* **know** that we went to the district AIT
7:23 Why *s there* **be** wrath against the realm of AIT
Ne 2: 3 Why *s* my face not **look sad** AIT
6: 3 Why *s* the work **stop** while I leave it AIT
6:11 *"S* a man like me **run away?** AIT
6:11 Or *s* one like me **go** into the temple AIT
7:65 until there **s** be a priest ministering with NIH
8:15 and that *they s* **proclaim** this word AIT
13: 1 or Moabite *s* ever *be* **admitted** into AIT
Est 1:22 in each people's tongue that every man *s* **be** AIT
6: 6 "What *s be* **done** for the man whom the king AIT
9:25 *s* **come back** onto his own head, AIT
9:25 he and his sons *s be* **hanged** on the gallows. AIT
9:27 *s* without **fail** observe these two days every AIT
9:28 These days *s* **be remembered** and observed AIT
9:28 of Purim *s* never **cease** to be celebrated by AIT
9:28 *s* the memory of them **die out** AIT
Job 4: 6 **S** not your piety be your confidence NIH
6:11 that *I s still* **hope?** AIT
6:11 What prospects, that I *s be* **patient?** AIT
6:14 "A despairing man **s** have the devotion NIH
9:29 why *s I* **struggle** in vain? AIT
19:29 *you s* **fear** the sword yourselves; AIT
21: 4 Why *s* I not *be* **impatient?** AIT
21:15 Who is the Almighty, that *we s* **serve** him? AIT
32: 7 I thought, 'Age *s* **speak;** AIT
32: 7 advanced years *s* **teach** wisdom.' AIT
33: 7 No fear of me *s* **alarm** you, AIT
33: 7 nor *s* my hand *be* **heavy** upon you. AIT
34:23 that they *s* **come** before him for judgment. AIT
34:33 *S* God then **reward** you on your terms, AIT
37:19 "Tell us what *we s* **say** to him; AIT
37:20 *S* he **be told** that I want to speak? AIT
40:23 the Jordan *s* **surge** against his mouth. AIT
Ps 32: 8 and teach you in the way *you s* **go;** AIT
49: 5 Why *s I* **fear** when evil days come, AIT
49: 9 *he s* **live** on forever and not see decay. AIT
79:10 Why *s* the nations **say,** AIT
143: 8 Show me the way *I s* **go,** AIT
Pr 5:16 *S* your springs **overflow** AIT
16:10 and his mouth *s* not **betray** justice. AIT
22: 6 a child **in the way** he **s go,** 2006+6584+7023
Ecc 5: 6 Why *s* God *be* **angry** at what you say AIT
7: 2 the living *s* **take** this to heart. AIT
SS 1: 7 Why *s I* be like a veiled woman beside AIT
Isa 1: 5 Why *s you* **be beaten** anymore? AIT
8:19 *s* not a people **inquire of** their God? AIT
48:17 who directs you in the way *you s* **go.** AIT
53: 2 in his appearance that *we s* **desire** him. AIT
57: 6 In the light of these things, *s I* **relent?** AIT
Jer 3: 1 *s he* **return** to her again? AIT
5: 7 "Why *s I* **forgive** you? AIT
5: 9 *S I* not **punish** them for this?" AIT
5: 9 *"S I* not **avenge** myself on such a nation AIT
5:22 *S you* not **fear** me?" AIT
5:22 *"S you* not **tremble** in my presence? AIT
5:29 *S I* not **punish** them for this?" AIT
5:29 *"S I* not **avenge** myself on such a nation AIT
9: 9 *S I* not **punish** them for this?" AIT
9: 9 *"S I* not **avenge** myself on such a nation AIT
10: 7 Who *s* not **revere** you, AIT
13:12 Every wineskin *s* **be filled** *with* wine.' AIT
13:12 that every wineskin *s* **be filled** *with* wine?' AIT
18:20 *S* good **be repaid** with evil? AIT
26:11 "This man **s** be sentenced to death NIH
26:16 "This man **s** not be sentenced to death! NIH
27:17 Why *s* this city **become** a ruin? AIT
29:26 *you s* **put** any madman who acts like AIT
32:35 that they *s* **do** such a detestable thing and AIT
38: 4 *s* **be put to death.** AIT
40:15 Why *s he* **take** your life and cause all AIT
42: 3 where *we s* **go** and what we should do." AIT
42: 3 where we should go and what *we s* **do."** AIT
45: 5 *S* you then **seek** great things for yourself? AIT
49:12 *s* you **go unpunished?** AIT
La 2:20 *S* women **eat** their offspring, AIT
2:20 *S* priest and prophet **be killed** AIT
3:39 Why *s* any living man **complain** AIT
Eze 13:19 you have killed those who *s* not *have* **died** AIT
13:19 and have spared those who *s* not **live.** AIT
14: 3 *S I* **let** them **inquire of** *me* **at all?** AIT
Eze 16:16 *Such things s* not **happen,** AIT
16:16 nor *s they ever* **occur.** AIT
33:25 *s you* then **possess** the land? AIT
33:26 *S you* then **possess** the land?' AIT
34: 2 *S* not shepherds **take care of** the flock? AIT
Da 1:10 Why *s he* **see** you looking worse than AIT
6: 7 that the king *s* **issue** an edict and enforce AIT
Hos 1: 6 that *I s* **at all forgive** them. AIT
Joel 2:17 Why *s they* **say** among the peoples, AIT
Ob 1:12 *You s* not **look down on** your brother AIT
1:13 *You s* not **march** through the gates AIT
1:14 *You s* not **wait** at the crossroads to cut AIT
Jnh 1:11 "What *s we* **do** to you to make the sea calm AIT
4:11 *S* I not *be* **concerned** about that great city? AIT
Mic 2: 7 *S it* **be said,** O house of Jacob: AIT
3: 1 *S* you not **know** justice, AIT
Zec 7: 3 *"S I* **mourn** and fast in the fifth month, AIT
Mal 1:13 *s I* **accept** them from your hands?" AIT
2: 7 and from his mouth *men s* **seek** instruction AIT
Mt 6: 9 "This, then, is how you *s* **pray:** *AIT*
11: 3 or *s we* **expect** someone else?" *AIT*
18:14 that any of these little ones *s be* **lost.** *AIT*
18:34 until *he s* **pay back** all he owed. *AIT*
19:12 The one who can accept this *s* **accept** it." *AIT*
23:23 You s *have* practiced the latter, *1256*
25:27 you s *have* put my money on deposit with *1256*
Mk 6:12 and preached that *people s* **repent.** *AIT*
12:15 *S we* **pay** or shouldn't we?" *AIT*
Lk 1:43 that the mother of my Lord *s* **come** to me? *AIT*
2: 1 that a **census** *s* **be taken of** the entire *AIT*
3:10 "What *s we* **do** then?" the crowd asked. *AIT*
3:11 "The man with two tunics *s* **share with** *AIT*
3:11 and the one who has food *s* **do the same."** *AIT*
3:12 "Teacher," they asked, "what *s we* **do?"** *AIT*
3:14 "And what *s* we **do?"** *AIT*
7:19 or *s we* **expect** someone else?" *AIT*
7:20 or *s we* **expect** someone else?' " *AIT*
11:42 You **s** have practiced the latter *1256*
12: 5 But I will show you whom *you s* **fear:** *AIT*
12:12 at that time what you **s** say." *1256*
13: 7 Why *s it* **use up** the soil?' *AIT*
13:16 Then **s** not this woman, *1256*
17:10 *s* **say,** 'We are unworthy servants; *AIT*
17:31 *s* **go down** to get them. *AIT*
17:31 no one in the field *s* **go** back for anything. *AIT*
18: 1 to show them that they **s** always pray and *1256*
22:26 greatest among you *s* **be** like the youngest, *AIT*
22:49 "Lord, *s we* **strike** with our swords?" *AIT*
Jn 3: 7 *You s* not *be* **surprised** at my saying, *AIT*
11:57 *he s* **report** it so that they might arrest him. *AIT*
12: 7 that *she s* **save** this perfume for the day *AIT*
12:46 so that no one who believes in me *s* **stay** *AIT*
13:14 you also **s** wash one another's feet. *4053*
13:15 an example that you *s* **do** as I have done. *AIT*
Ac 4:28 and will had decided beforehand *s* **happen.** *AIT*
10:28 that I *s* not **call** any man impure *AIT*
15:19 that *we s* not **make it difficult for** *AIT*
15:20 Instead *we s* **write** to them, *AIT*
17:26 that *they s* **inhabit** the whole earth; *AIT*
17:26 and the exact places where they **s** live. *NIG*
17:29 *we* **s** not think that the divine being is *4053*
21:25 that they *s* **abstain from** food sacrificed *AIT*
24:20 who are here *s* **state** what crime they found *AIT*
26: 8 Why *s* any of you **consider** it incredible *AIT*
26:20 I preached that they **s** repent and turn *NIG*
27:12 the majority decided that we *s* **sail** on, *AIT*
27:21 "Men, you **s** have taken my advice not *1256*
Ro 2:22 that people *s* not **commit adultery,** *AIT*
6: 6 that *we s* no longer *be* **slaves** to sin— *AIT*
11:35 *that* God *s* **repay** him?" *AIT*
14: 5 Each one *s be* **fully convinced** in his own *AIT*
15: 2 of us *s* **please** his neighbor for his good, *AIT*
1Co 3:10 But each one *s be* **careful** how he builds. *AIT*
3:18 *he s* **become** a "fool" so that he may become wise. *AIT*
7: 2 each man *s* **have** his own wife, *AIT*
7: 3 The husband *s* **fulfill** his marital duty *AIT*
7: 9 *they s* **marry,** for it is better to marry than *AIT*
7:17 *s* **retain the place in life** that the Lord *AIT*
7:18 *He s* not **become uncircumcised.** *AIT*
7:18 *He s* not **be circumcised.** *AIT*
7:20 Each one *s* **remain** in the situation which *AIT*
7:24 *s* **remain** in the situation God called him to. *AIT*
7:29 now on those who have wives *s* **live** as if *AIT*
7:36 *he s* **do** as he wants. *AIT*
7:36 *They s* **get married.** *AIT*
9:14 *s* **receive** *their* **living** from the gospel. *AIT*
10: 8 *s* not **commit sexual immorality,** *AIT*
10: 9 *We s* not **test** the Lord, *AIT*
10:24 Nobody *s* **seek** his own good, *AIT*
10:29 For why *s* my freedom *be* **judged** *AIT*
11: 6 *she s have* her hair **cut off;** *AIT*
11: 6 *she s* **cover** her head. *AIT*
11:34 If anyone is hungry, *he s* **eat** at home, *AIT*
12:15 If the foot *s* **say,** "Because I am not a hand, *AIT*
12:16 And if the ear *s* **say,** "Because I am not *AIT*
12:25 so that *there s* **be** no division in the body, *AIT*
12:25 but that its parts *s* **have** equal **concern** *AIT*
14:13 in a tongue *s* **pray** that he may interpret *AIT*
14:27 **s** speak, one at a time, *NIG*
14:28 *s keep* **quiet** in the church and **speak** *AIT*
14:29 Two or three prophets *s* **speak,** *AIT*
14:29 the others *s* **weigh carefully** what is said. *AIT*
14:30 the first speaker *s* **stop.** *AIT*
14:34 women *s remain* **silent** in the churches. *AIT*
14:35 *they s* **ask** their own husbands at home; *AIT*
14:40 But everything *s be* **done** in a fitting *AIT*

1Co 16: 2 each one of you s set aside a sum of money AIT
16:11 No one, then, s refuse to accept him. AIT
2Co 2: 3 so that when I came I s not be distressed AIT
5:15 that those who live s no longer live AIT
9: 3 in this matter s not prove hollow, AIT
9: 7 Each man s give what he has decided NIG
10: 7 he s consider again that we belong AIT
10:11 Such people s realize that what we are AIT
12: 6 Even if I s choose to boast, AIT
12:14 children s not have to save up 4053
Gal 1: 8 from heaven s preach a gospel other than AIT
2: 9 They agreed that we s go to the Gentiles, NIG
2:10 that we s continue to remember the poor, AIT
3:23 locked up until faith s be revealed. 3516
6: 1 you who are spiritual s restore him gently. AIT
6: 4 Each one s test his own actions. AIT
6: 5 for each one s carry his own load. AIT
Eph 3:10 of God s be made known to the rulers AIT
5: 4 Nor s there be obscenity, NIG
5:24 so also wives s submit to their husbands NIG
6:20 Pray that I may declare it fearlessly, as I s. 1256
Php 2: 4 you s look not only to your own interests, AIT
2: 5 Your attitude s be the same as that AIT
2:10 that at the name of Jesus every knee s bow, 2828
2:18 So you too s be glad and rejoice with me. AIT
3:15 are mature s take such a view of things. AIT
4: 1 that is how you s stand firm in the Lord, AIT
Col 4: 4 Pray that I may proclaim it clearly, as I s. 1256
1Th 4: 3 It is God's will that you s be sanctified: NIG
4: 3 that you s avoid sexual immorality; NIG
4: 4 of you s learn to control his own body in NIG
4: 6 in this matter no one s wrong his brother NIG
5: 4 in darkness so that this day s surprise you AIT
1Ti 2:11 A woman s learn in quietness AIT
5: 4 these s learn first of all to put their religion AIT
5:16 she s help them and not let the church AIT
6: 1 of slavery s consider their masters worthy AIT
2Ti 2: 6 The hardworking farmer s be the first 1256
4:15 You too s be on your guard against AIT
Tit 2:15 These, then, are the things you s teach. AIT
Heb 2:10 s make the author of their salvation perfect AIT
12: 9 How much more s we submit to the Father AIT
13: 4 Marriage s be honored by all, NIG
Jas 1: 5 If any of you lacks wisdom, he s ask God, AIT
1: 7 That man s not think he will receive anything from the Lord; AIT
1:10 But the one who is rich s take pride NIG
1:13 When tempted, no one s say, AIT
1:19 Everyone s be quick to listen, AIT
3: 1 Not many of you s presume to be teachers, NIG
3:10 My brothers, this s not be. 5973
5:13 Is any one of you in trouble? He s pray. AIT
5:14 He s call the elders of the church to pray AIT
5:19 if one of you s wander from the truth AIT
5:19 the truth and someone s bring him back, AIT
1Pe 2:15 doing good you s silence the ignorant talk AIT
2:21 that you s follow in his steps. AIT
3: 3 Your beauty s not come from outward AIT
3: 4 Instead, it s be that of your inner self, NIG
3:14 But even if you s suffer for what is right, AIT
4:10 Each one s use whatever gift he has received NIG
4:11 he s do it as one speaking the very words NIG
4:11 he s do it with the strength God provides, NIG
4:15 it s not be as a murderer or thief NIG
4:19 to God's will s commit themselves AIT
1Jn 3: 1 that we s be called children of God! AIT
3:11 We s love one another. AIT
5:16 he s pray and God will give him life. AIT
5:16 I am not saying that he s pray about that. AIT

SHOULDER (25) [SHOULDERS]

Ge 24:15 Rebekah came out with her jar on her s. 8900
24:45 Rebekah came out, with her jar on her s. 8900
24:46 "She quickly lowered her jar from her s NIH
49:15 he will bend his s to the burden and submit 8900
Ex 28: 7 It is to have two s pieces attached to two 4190
28:12 and fasten them on the s pieces of the ephod 4190
28:25 attaching them to the s pieces of the ephod 4190
28:27 attach them to the bottom of the s pieces 4190
39: 4 They made s pieces for the ephod, 4190
39: 7 Then they fastened them on the s pieces of 4190
39:18 attaching them to the s pieces of the ephod 4190
39:20 to the bottom of the s pieces on the front of 4190
Nu 6:19 the priest is to place in his hands a boiled s 2432
Dt 18: 3 the s, the jowls and the inner parts. 2432
Jos 4: 5 Each of you is to take up a stone on his s, 8900
Job 31:22 then let my arm fall from the s, 8900
31:36 Surely I would wear it on my s, 8900
Isa 22:22 I will place on his s the key to the house 8900
Eze 12: 6 Put them on your s as they are watching 4190
12:12 among them will put his things on his s 4190
24: 4 the choice pieces—the leg and the s. 4190
29:18 and every s made raw. 4190
34:21 Because you shove with flank and s, 4190
Zep 3: 9 the LORD and serve him s to shoulder. 285+8900
3: 9 the LORD and serve him shoulder to s. 285+8900

SHOULDERS (24) [SHOULDER]

Ge 9:23 took a garment and laid it across their s; 8900
21:14 on her s and then sent her off with the boy. 8900
Ex 12:34 on their s in kneading troughs wrapped 8900
28:12 on his s as a memorial before the LORD. 4190
Nu 7: 9 because they were to carry on their s 4190
Dt 33:12 one the LORD loves rests between his s." 4190
Jdg 9:48 some branches, which he lifted to his s. 8900
Jdg 16: 3 He lifted them to his s and carried them to 4190
2Ki 6:31 of Shaphat remains on his s today!" NIH
9:24 and shot Joram between the s. 2432
1Ch 15:15 the ark of God with the poles on their s, 4190
2Ch 35: 3 It is not to be carried about on your s. 4190
Ne 3: 5 but their nobles would not put their s to 7418
Ps 81: 6 "I removed the burden from their s; 8900
Isa 9: 4 the bar across their s, the rod of their 8900
9: 6 and the government will be on his s. 8900
10:27 from your s, their yoke from your neck; 8900
14:25 and his burden removed from their s." 8900
46: 7 They lift it to their s and carry it; 4190
49:22 and carry your daughters on their s. 4190
Eze 12: 7 carrying them on my s while they watched. 4190
29: 7 you splintered and you tore open their s; 4190
Mt 23: 4 up heavy loads and put them on men's s, 6049
Lk 15: 5 when he finds it, he joyfully puts it on his s 6049

SHOULDN'T (7) [NOT, SHOULD]

2Sa 19:21 "S Shimei be put to death for this? 4202
Ne 5: 9 S you walk in the fear of our God to avoid 4202
Mt 18:33 S you have had mercy on your fellow 1256+4024
Mk 12:15 Should we pay or s we?" 3590
Ac 8:36 Why s I be baptized?" 3266
1Co 5: 2 S you rather have been filled with grief 4049
9:12 s we have it all the more? 4024

SHOUT (61) [SHOUTED, SHOUTING, SHOUTS]

Nu 23:21 the s of the King is among them. 9558
Jos 6: 5 have all the people give a loud s; 8131+9558
6:10 not say a word until the day I tell you to s. 8131
6:10 until the day I tell you to shout. Then s!" 8131
6:16 Joshua commanded the people, "S! 8131
6:20 when the people gave a loud s, 8131+9558
Jdg 7:18 from all around the camp blow yours and s, 606
1Sa 4: 5 raised such a great s that the ground 8131+9558
17:52 of Israel and Judah surged forward with a s 8131
1Ki 1:34 Blow the trumpet and s, 606
18:27 began to taunt them. "S louder!" 928+7754+7924
Ezr 3:11 all the people gave a great s of praise 8131+9558
Job 3: 7 may no s of joy be heard in it. 8265
3:18 they no longer hear the slave driver's s. 7754
39: 7 he does not hear a driver's s. 9583
39:25 the s of commanders and the battle cry. 8308
Ps 20: 5 We will s for joy when you are victorious 8264
33: 3 play skillfully, and s for joy. 9558
35:27 in my vindication s for joy and gladness; 8264
47: 1 s to God with cries of joy. 8131
60: 8 over Philistia I s in triumph." 8131
65:13 they s for joy and sing. 8131
66: 1 S with joy to God, all the earth! 8131
71:23 My lips will s for joy when I sing praise 8264
81: 1 s aloud to the God of Jacob! 8131
95: 1 let us s aloud to the Rock 8131
98: 4 S for joy to the LORD, all the earth, 8131
98: 6 s for joy before the LORD, the King. 8131
100: 1 S for joy to the LORD, all the earth. 8131
108: 9 over Philistia I s in triumph." 8131
Isa 12: 6 S aloud and sing for joy, people of Zion, 7412
13: 2 a banner on a bare hilltop, s to them; 7754+8123
24:14 They raise their voices, they s for joy; 8264
26:19 wake up and s for joy. 8264
35: 2 it will rejoice greatly and s for joy. 8264
35: 6 and the mute tongue s for joy. 8264
40: 9 lift up your voice with a s, lift it up, 3946
42: 2 He will not s or cry out, 7590
42:11 let them s from the mountaintops. 7423
42:13 with a s he will raise the battle cry 8131
44:23 s aloud, O earth beneath. 8131
49:13 S for joy, O heavens; 8264
52: 8 together they s for joy. 8264
54: 1 burst into song, s for joy, 7412
58: 1 "S it aloud, do not hold back. 928+1744+7924
Jer 25:30 He will s like those who tread the grapes, 2116
25:30 s against all who live on the earth. 6699
31: 7 s for the foremost of the nations. 7412
31:12 and s for joy on the heights of Zion; 8264
49:29 Men will s to them, 'Terror on every side!' 7924
50:15 S against her on every side! 8131
51:14 and they will s in triumph over you. 2116+6702
51:39 so that they s with laughter— 6600
51:48 in them will s for joy over Babylon, 8264
La 2: 7 a s in the house of the LORD as on the day 7754
Eze 8:18 Although they s in my ears, I will not listen to them." 1524+7754+7924
Zep 3:14 Sing, O Daughter of Zion; s aloud, 8131
Zec 2:10 "S and be glad, O Daughter of Zion. 8264
9: 9 S, Daughter of Jerusalem! 8131
Mk 10:47 he began to s, "Jesus, Son of David, 3189
Rev 10: 3 he gave a loud s like the roar of a lion. 3189+5889

SHOUTED (53) [SHOUT]

Ge 41:43 and men s before him, "Make way!" 7924
Lev 9:24 they s for joy and fell facedown. 8264
Jos 6:20 When the trumpets sounded, the people s, 8131
Jdg 7:20 they s, "A sword for the LORD and for 7924
9: 7 on the top of Mount Gerizim and s to them, 2256+5951+7754+7924
16:25 While they were in high spirits, they s, 606
18:23 As they s after them, the Danites turned 7924
19:22 they s to the old man who owned the house, 606
1Sa 10:24 Then the people s, "Long live the king!" 8131
14:12 The men of the outpost s to Jonathan 6699
1Sa 17: 8 Goliath stood and s to the ranks of Israel, 7924
17:23 from his lines and s his usual defiance, 1819
20:38 Then he s, "Hurry! 7924
2Sa 20: 1 He sounded the trumpet and s, 606
1Ki 1:39 the trumpet and all the people s, 606
18:26 "O Baal, answer us!" they s. 606
18:28 So they s louder and slashed 928+7754+7924
2Ki 7:11 The gatekeepers s the news, 7924
9:13 Then they blew the trumpet and s, 606
11:12 and the people clapped their hands and s, 606
2Ch 23:11 They anointed him and s, 606
23:13 Athaliah tore her robes and s, "Treason! 606
Ezr 3:12 many others s for joy. 928+7754+8123+9558
Job 30: 5 s at as if they were thieves. 8131
38: 7 and all the angels s for joy? 8131
Isa 21: 8 And the lookout s, "Day after day, my lord, 7924
Da 3:26 the opening of the blazing furnace and s, 10558
Mt 8:29 do you want with us, Son of God?" they s. 3189
20:30 they s, "Lord, Son of David, 3189
20:31 but they s all the louder, "Lord, 3189
21: 9 ahead of him and those that followed s, 3189
27:23 But they s all the louder, "Crucify him!" 3189
Mk 5: 7 He s at the top of his voice, 3189
10:48 but he s all the more, "Son of David, have mercy on me!" 3189+3437+4498
11: 9 ahead and those who followed s, 3189
15:13 "Crucify him!" they s. 3189
15:14 But they s all the louder, "Crucify him!" 3189
Lk 18:39 but he s all the more, "Son of David, 3189
Jn 18:40 They s back, "No, not him! 3198
19: 6 and their officials saw him, they s, 3198
19:15 But they s, "Take him away! 3198
Ac 12:22 They s, "This is the voice of a god, 2215
14:11 s in the Lycaonian language, 2048+3836+5889
16:28 Paul s, "Don't harm yourself! 3489+5888+5889
19:33 some of the crowd s instructions to him. NIG
19:34 all s in unison for about two hours: 1181+3189
21:34 in the crowd s one thing and some another, 2215
22:22 Then they raised their voices and s, 3306
24:21 unless it was this one thing I s as I stood 3189
26:24 "You are out of your mind, Paul!" he s. 3489+3836+5774+5889
Rev 10: 3 When he s, the voices of the seven thunders 3189
18: 2 With a mighty voice he s: "Fallen! 3189
19: 3 And again they s: "Hallelujah! 3306

SHOUTING (27) [SHOUT]

Ex 32:17 Joshua heard the noise of the people s, 8275
Nu 16:34 s, "The earth is going to swallow us too!" 606
Jdg 15:14 the Philistines came toward him s. 8131
1Sa 4: 6 What's all this s in the Hebrew camp? 7754+9558
17:20 to its battle positions, s the war cry. 8131
2Ki 9:27 Jehu chased him, s, "Kill him too!" 606
2Ch 15:14 with s and with trumpets and horns. 9558
Isa 16:10 for I have put an end to the s. 2116
Zep 1:14 the s of the warrior there. 7658
Mt 21:15 and the children s in the temple area, 3189
Lk 4:41 demons came out of many people, s, 3198
8:28 s at the top of his voice, 3306+3489+5889
23:21 But they kept s, "Crucify him! 2215
Jn 12:13 and went out to meet him, s, "Hosanna!" 3198
19:12 but the Jews kept s, "If you let his man go, 3198
Ac 14:14 and rushed out into the crowd, s: 3189
16:17 This girl followed Paul and the rest of us, s, 3189
17: 6 before the city officials, s: "These men 1066
19:28 they were furious and began s: 3189
19:32 Some were s one thing, some another. 3189
21:28 s, "Men of Israel, help us! 3189
21:36 The crowd that followed kept s, 3189
22:23 As they were s and throwing off their cloaks 3198
22:24 to find out why the people were s at him 2215
25:24 s that he ought not to live any longer. 1066
Rev 19: 1 the roar of a great multitude in heaven s: 3306
19: 6 and like loud peals of thunder, s: 3306

SHOUTS (22) [SHOUT]

2Sa 6:15 brought up the ark of the LORD with s 9558
1Ch 15:28 the ark of the covenant of the LORD with s, 9558
Ezr 3:13 No one could distinguish the sound of the s 9558
Job 8:21 with laughter and your lips with s of joy. 9558
33:26 he sees God's face and s for joy; 9558
Ps 27: 6 will I sacrifice with s of joy; 9558
42: 4 with s of joy and thanksgiving 7754+8262
47: 5 God has ascended amid s of joy, 9558
105:43 his chosen ones with s of joy; 8262
118:15 S of joy and victory resound in the tents of 8262
Pr 11:10 when the wicked perish, there are s of joy. 8262
Ecc 9:17 be heeded than the s of a ruler of fools. 2411
Isa 16: 9 The s of joy over your ripened fruit and 2116
16:10 no one sings or s in the vineyards; 8131
31: 4 against him, he is not frightened by their s 7754
48:20 with s of joy and proclaim it. 7754+8262
Jer 48:33 no one treads them with s of joy. 2116
48:33 there are s, they are not shouts of joy. 2116
48:33 there are shouts, they are not s of joy. 2116
Zec 4: 7 Then he will bring out the capstone to s 9583
Lk 23:23 But with loud s they insistently demanded 5889
23:23 that he be crucified, and their s prevailed. 5889

SHOVE (1) [SHOVES]

Eze 34:21 Because you s with flank and shoulder, 2074

SHOVEL (1) [SHOVELS]

Isa 30:24 spread out with fork and s. 4665

SHOVELS (9) [SHOVEL]

Ex 27: 3 its pots to remove the ashes, and its s, 3582
38: 3 its pots, s, sprinkling bowls, 3582
Nu 4:14 meat forks, s and sprinkling bowls. 3582
1Ki 7:40 the basins and s and sprinkling bowls. 3582
7:45 s and sprinkling bowls. 3582
2Ki 25:14 They also took away the pots, s, 3582
2Ch 4:11 the pots and s and sprinkling bowls. 3582
4:16 s, meat forks and all related articles. 3582
Jer 52:18 They also took away the pots, s, 3582

SHOVES (2) [SHOVE]

Nu 35:20 anyone with malice aforethought s another 2074
35:22 if without hostility someone suddenly s another 2074

SHOW (200) [SHOWED, SHOWING, SHOWN, SHOWS]

Ge 12: 1 and go to the land I will s you. 8011
20:13 'This is how you can s your love to me: 6913
21:23 S to me and the country where you are 6913
24:12 and s kindness to my master Abraham. 6913
24:49 Now if you will s kindness and faithfulness 6913
40:14 remember me and s me kindness; 6913
47:29 and promise that you will s me kindness 6913
Ex 9:16 that I might s you my power and 8011
18:20 and s them the way to live and 3359
23: 3 and do not s favoritism to a poor man 2075
25: 9 like the pattern I will s you. 8011
33:18 Then Moses said, "Now s me your glory." 8011
Lev 10: 3 " 'Among those who approach me I will s myself holy; 7727
19:15 do not s partiality to the poor or 5951+7156
19:32 s respect for the elderly 2075
Nu 16: 5 the LORD will s who belongs to him 3359
Dt 1:17 Do not s partiality in judging; 5795+7156
1:33 and to s you the way you should go. 8011
3:24 to s to your servant your greatness 8011
4: 6 this will s your wisdom and understanding 6524
7: 2 and s them no mercy. 2858
13: 8 S him no pity. 2571+6524
13:17 he will s you mercy, have compassion 5989
15: 9 you do not s ill will toward your needy brother 6524+8317
16:19 Do not pervert justice or s partiality. 5795+7156
19:13 S him no pity. 2571+6524
19:21 S no pity: life for life, eye for eye, 2571+6524
25:12 shall cut off her hand. S her no pity. 2571+6524
Jos 2:12 by the LORD that you will s kindness 6913
Jdg 1:24 "S us how to get into the city 8011
4:22 "I will s you the man you're looking for." 8011
8:35 They also failed to s kindness to the family 6913
13:21 not s himself again to Manoah and his wife, 8011
Ru 1: 8 May the LORD s kindness to you, 6913
1Sa 16: 3 and I will s you what to do. 3359
20: 8 As for you, s kindness to your servant, 6913
20:14 But s me unfailing kindness like that of 6913
2Sa 2: 6 now s you kindness and faithfulness, 6913
2: 6 and I too will s you the same favor 6913
9: 1 of Saul to whom I can s kindness 6913
9: 3 of Saul to whom I can s God's kindness?" 6913
9: 7 "for I will surely s you kindness for 6913+6913
10: 2 "I will s kindness to Hanun son of Nahash, 6913
12:14 you have made the enemies of the LORD s utter contempt, 5540+5540
16:17 "Is this the love you s your friend? 907
22:26 "To the faithful you s yourself faithful, 2874
22:26 to the blameless you s yourself blameless, 9462
22:27 to the pure you s yourself pure, 1405
22:27 but to the crooked you s yourself shrewd. 7349
1Ki 2: 2 "So be strong, s yourself a man, 2118+4200
2: 7 "But s kindness to the sons of Barzillai 6913
8:50 cause their conquerors to s them mercy; 8163
2Ki 20:13 that Hezekiah did not s them. 8011
20:15 among my treasures that I did not s them." 8011
1Ch 19: 2 "I will s kindness to Hanun son of Nahash, 6913
Ezr 2:59 not s that their families were descended 5583
Ne 7:61 not s that their families were descended 5583
13:22 s mercy to me according to your great love. 2571
Est 4: 8 to s to Esther and explain it to her, 8011
Job 6:24 s me where I have been wrong 1067
13: 8 Will you s him partiality? 5951+7156
13:23 S me my offense and my sin. 3359
24:21 and to the widow s no kindness. 3512
32:21 I will s partiality to no one, 5951+7156
36: 2 with me a little longer and I will s you 2555
37:13 or to water his earth and s his love. NIH
Ps 4: 6 "Who can s us any good?" 8011
17: 7 S the wonder of your great love, 7098
18:25 To the faithful you s yourself faithful, 2874
18:25 to the blameless you s yourself blameless, 9462
18:26 to the pure you s yourself pure, 1405
18:26 but to the crooked you s yourself shrewd. 7349
25: 4 S me your ways, O LORD, 3359
28: 5 Since they s no regard for the works of 1067
39: 4 "S me, O LORD, my life's end and 3359
50:23 and he prepares the way so that I may s him 8011
59: 5 s no mercy to wicked traitors. 2858
68:28 s us your strength, O God, 6451
77: 7 Will he never s his favor again? 8354
82: 2 unjust and s partiality to the wicked? 5951+7156
85: 7 S us your unfailing love, O LORD, 8011
88:10 Do you s your wonders to the dead? 6913
91:16 and s him my salvation." 8011
Ps 102:13 for it is time to s favor to her; 2858
106: 4 when you s favor to your people, NIH
143: 8 S me the way I should go, 3359
Pr 6:34 he will s no mercy when he takes revenge. 2798
23: 4 have the wisdom to s restraint. 2532
24:23 To s partiality in judging is not good: 5795+7156
28:21 To s partiality is not good— 5795+7156
SS 2:14 s me your face, let me hear your voice; 8011
Isa 5:16 and the holy God will s himself holy 7727
13:10 their constellations will not s their light. 2145
19:12 Let them s you and make known what 5583
30:18 he rises to s you compassion. 8163
39: 2 that Hezekiah did not s them. 8011
39: 4 among my treasures that I did not s them." 8011
60:10 in favor I will s you compassion. 8163
Jer 6:23 they are cruel and s no mercy. 8163
15: 6 I can no longer s compassion. 5714
16: 5 do not go to mourn or s sympathy, 5653
16:13 for I will s you no favor.' 5989
18:17 I will s them my back and not my face in 8011
21: 7 he will s them no mercy or pity 2571
32:18 You s love to thousands but bring 6913
42:12 I will s you compassion so 5989
La 3:32 he brings grief, he will s compassion, 8163
Eze 20:41 and I will s myself holy among you in 7727
28:22 on her and s myself holy within her. 7727
28:25 I will s myself holy among them in 7727
36:23 I will s the holiness of my great name, 7727
36:23 when I s myself holy through you 7727
38:16 when I s myself holy through you 7727
38:23 so I will s my greatness and my holiness, 1540
39:27 I will s myself holy through them in 7727
40: 4 to everything I am going to s you, 8011
44:23 s them how to distinguish between the 3359
Da 1: 9 God had caused the official to s favor 4200+7156
11:30 and s favor to those who forsake 1067
11:37 He will s no regard for the gods 1067
Hos 1: 6 for I will no longer s love to the house 8163
1: 7 Yet I will s love to the house of Judah; 8163
2: 4 I will not s my love to her children, 8163
2:23 I will s my love to the one I called 8163
3: 1 "Go, s your love to your wife again, 170
Joel 2:30 I will s wonders in the heavens and on 5989
Mic 7:15 I will s them my wonders." 8011
7:18 but delight to s mercy. NIH
7:20 and s mercy to Abraham, 5989
Na 3: 5 I will s the nations your nakedness and 8011
Zec 1: 9 "I will s you what they are." 8011
7: 9 s mercy and compassion to one another. 6913
Mal 1: 6 O priests, who s contempt for my name. 1022
Mt 6:16 to s men they are fasting. 5743
8: 4 But go, s yourself to the priest and 1259
16: 1 and tested him by asking him to s them 2109
18:15 sins against you, go and s him his fault, 1794
21:32 to you to s you the way of righteousness, NIG
22:19 S me the coin used for paying the tax." 2109
Mk 1:44 But go, s yourself to the priest and 1259
12:40 and for a s make lengthy prayers. 4733
14:15 He will s you a large upper room, 1259
Lk 1:72 to s mercy to our fathers and 4472
5:14 s yourself to the priest and offer 1259
6:47 I will s you what he is like who comes 5683
12: 5 But I will s you whom you should fear: 5683
17:14 he said, "Go, s yourselves to the priests." 2109
18: 1 a parable to s them that they should 3836+4639
20:21 and that you do not s partiality but 3284+4725
20:24 "S me a denarius. 1259
20:47 and for a s make lengthy prayers. 4733
22:12 He will s you a large upper room, 1259
Jn 2:18 "What miraculous sign can you s us to prove your authority 1259
5:20 to your amazement he will s him 1259
7: 4 s yourself to the world." 5746
12:33 to s the kind of death he was going to die. 4955
14: 8 s us the Father and that will be enough 1259
14: 9 How can you say, 'S us the Father'? 1259
14:21 and I too will love him and s myself 1872
14:22 why do you intend to s yourself to us and 1872
Ac 1:24 S us which of these two you have chosen 344
2:19 I will s wonders in the heaven above 1443
7: 3 'and go to the land I will s you.' 1259
9:16 I will s him how much he must suffer 5683
10:34 that God does not s favoritism 1639+4720
26:16 of me and what I will s you. 3972
Ro 2: 4 Or do you s contempt for the riches 2969
2:11 For God does not s favoritism. 1639+4721
2:15 since they s that the requirements of 1892
9:22 to s his wrath and make his power known, 1892
1Co 11:19 s which of you have God's approval. 1181+5745
12:31 now I will s you the most excellent way. 1259
2Co 3: 3 You s that you are a letter from Christ, 5746
4: 7 But we have this treasure in jars of clay to s NIG
8:19 the Lord himself and to s our eagerness NIG
8:24 Therefore s these men the proof 1892
11:30 of the things that s my weakness. NIG
Eph 2: 7 in order that in the coming ages he might s 1892
Php 4:10 but you had no opportunity to s it. NIG
1Ti 6: 2 not to s less respect for them 2969
2Ti 1:16 May the Lord s mercy to the household 1443
Tit 2: 7 In your teaching s integrity, NIG
2:10 but to s that they can be fully trusted, 1892
3: 2 and to s true humility toward all men. 1892
Heb 6:11 to s this same diligence to the very end, 1892
11:14 People who say such things s that 1872
Jas 2: 1 as believers in our glorious Lord Jesus Christ, don't s favoritism. 1877+4721
2: 3 If you s special attention to the man 2098
Jas 2: 9 But if you s favoritism, you sin 4719
2:18 S me your faith without deeds, 1259
2:18 and I will s you my faith by what I do. 1259
3:13 Let him s it by his good life, 1259
1Pe 2:17 S proper respect to everyone: 5506
3Jn 1: 8 therefore to s hospitality to such men so 5696
Jude 1:23 to others s mercy, mixed with fear— 1796
Rev 1: 1 to s his servants what must soon take place. 1259
4: 1 and I will s you what must take place 1259
17: 1 I will s you the punishment of the great 1259
21: 9 "Come, I will s you the bride, 1259
22: 6 sent his angel to s his servants the things 1259

SHOWED (59) [SHOW]

Ge 39:21 he s him kindness and granted him favor in 5742
Ex 15:25 and the LORD s him a piece of wood. 3723
Nu 13:26 the whole assembly and s them the fruit of 8011
20:13 and where he s himself holy among them. 7727
Dt 4:36 On earth he s you his great fire, 8011
34: 1 There the LORD s him the whole land— 8011
Jdg 1:25 So he s them, and they put the city to the 8011
Ru 3:10 greater than that which you s earlier: NIH
1Sa 14:11 So both of them s themselves to 1655
15: 6 for you s kindness to all the Israelites 6913
2Sa 10: 2 just as his father s kindness to me." 6913
1Ki 3: 3 Solomon s his love for the LORD 170
13:12 And his sons s him which road the man 8011
2Ki 6: 6 When he s him the place, 8011
11: 4 Then he s them the king's son. 8011
13:23 and had compassion and s concern for 448+7155
20:13 and s them all that was in his storehouses— 8011
1Ch 19: 2 because his father s kindness to me." 6913
2Ch 23: 1 In the seventh year Jehoiada s his strength. 2616
30:22 who s good understanding of the 8505+8507
Est 5: 9 and observed that he neither rose nor s fear 2316
Job 10:12 You gave me life and s me kindness, 6913
13:10 if you secretly s partiality. 5951+7156
Ps 31:21 for he s his wonderful love to me 7098
85: 1 You s favor to your land, O LORD; 8354
Isa 39: 2 and s them what was in his storehouses— 8011
40:14 that taught him knowledge or s him 3359
47: 6 and you s them no mercy. 8492
Jer 11:18 at that time he s me what they were doing. 8011
24: 1 the LORD s me two baskets of figs placed 8011
36:24 who heard all these words s no fear, 7064
Eze 35:11 the anger and jealousy you s in your hatred 6913
39:26 the unfaithfulness they s toward me 5085+5086
46:19 and s me a place at the western end. 2180
Da 2:29 of mysteries s you what is going to happen. 10313
Am 7: 1 This is what the Sovereign LORD s me: 8011
7: 4 This is what the Sovereign LORD s me: 8011
7: 7 This is what he s me: 8011
8: 1 This is what the Sovereign LORD s me: 8011
Mic 6: 8 He has s you, O man, what is good. 5583
Zec 1:20 Then the LORD s me four craftsmen. 8011
3: 1 Then he s me Joshua the high priest 8011
8:14 to bring disaster upon you and s no pity 5714
Mt 4: 8 and s him all the kingdoms of the world 1259
Lk 4: 5 up to a high place and s him in an instant all 1259
20:37 even Moses s that the dead rise, 3606
24:40 he s them his hands and feet. 1259
Jn 13: 1 he now s them the full extent of his love. 26
20:20 he s them his hands and side. 1259
Ac 1: 3 he s himself to these men 4225
15: 8 s that he accepted them by giving 3455
15:14 how God at first s his concern by taking 2170
18:17 But Gallio s no concern whatever. 3508
20:35 I s you that by this kind 5683
28: 2 The islanders s us unusual kindness. 4218
1Jn 2:19 but their going s that none of them belonged 5746
4: 9 This is how God s his love among us: 5746
Rev 21:10 and s me the Holy City, Jerusalem, 1259
22: 1 the angel s me the river of the water of life, 1259

SHOWER (2) [SHOWERING, SHOWERS]

Job 37: 6 and to the rain s, 'Be a mighty downpour.' 1773
Isa 45: 8 let the clouds s it down. 5688

SHOWERING (1) [SHOWER]

2Sa 16:13 and throwing stones at him and s him 6759

SHOWERS (15) [SHOWER]

Dt 32: 2 like s on new grass, 8540
Job 29:23 for me as for s and drank in my words as 4764
36:28 down their moisture and abundant s fall 8319
Ps 65:10 you soften it with s and bless its crops. 8053
68: 9 You gave abundant s, O God; 1773
72: 6 like s watering the earth. 8053
Jer 3: 3 Therefore the s have been withheld, 8053
14:22 Do the skies themselves send down s? 8053
Eze 22:24 'You are a land that has had no rain or s in 1775
34:26 I will send down s in season; 1773
34:26 there will be s of blessing. 1773
Hos 10:12 until he comes and s righteousness on you. 3722
Joel 2:23 He sends you abundant s, 1773
Mic 5: 7 like s on the grass, 8053
Zec 10: 1 He gives s of rain to men, 4764

SHOWING (13) [SHOW]

Ex 20: 6 but s love to a thousand [generations] 6913
Dt 5:10 but s love to a thousand [generations] 6913
Jdg 16: 5 into s you the secret of his great strength 8011
Ru 2:20 not stopped s his kindness to the living and 6440
2Sa 2: 5 "The LORD bless you for s this kindness 6913

Eze 9: 5 without s **pity** or compassion. 2571+6524
Da 1: 4 s **aptitude** for every kind of learning, 8505
Jn 15: 8 s yourselves to be my disciples. *NIG*
Ac 9:39 and s him the robes and other clothing *2109*
Ro 12: 8 if it is s **mercy,** let him do it cheerfully. *1796*
1Ti 5:10 such as bringing up children, s **hospitality,** *3827*
Heb 9: 8 The Holy Spirit *was* s by this that the way *1317*
Rev 22: 8 at the feet of the angel who *had been* s them *1259*

SHOWN (56) [SHOW]

Ge 19:19 and you have s great kindness to me 6913
21:23 as an alien the same kindness *I have* s 6913
24:14 that *you have* s kindness to my master." 6913
32:10 and faithfulness *you have* s your servant. 6913
41:28 God *has* s Pharaoh what he is about to do. 8011
Ex 25:40 to the pattern s you on the mountain. 8011
26:30 the tabernacle according to the plan s *you* 8011
27: 8 be made just as you *were* s on the mountain. 8011
Lev 13: 7 after *he has* s himself to the priest 8011
13:49 it is a spreading mildew and *must* **be** s *to* 8011
Nu 8: 4 like the pattern the LORD *had* s Moses. 8011
Dt 4:35 You **were** s these things so 8011
5:24 "The LORD our God *has* s us his glory 8011
34:12 For no one has ever s the mighty power NIH
Jos 2:12 because *I have* s kindness to you. 6913
Jdg 13:23 nor s us all these things or 8011
Ru 1: 8 as *you have* s to your dead and to me. 6913
1Ki 3: 6 "You *have* s great kindness to your servant, 6913
2Ki 8:13 "The LORD *has* s me that you will become 8011
2Ch 1: 8 "You *have* s great kindness to David 6913
24:22 the kindness Zechariah's father Jehoiada *had* s him 6913
30: 9 and your children will be s compassion NIH
32:25 not respond to the **kindness** *s* him; AIT
Ezr 9: 9 *He has* s us kindness in the sight of the kings 5742
Job 38:12 or s the dawn its place, 3359
38:17 *Have* the gates of death **been** s to you? 1655
Ps 48: 3 *he has* s **himself** to be her fortress. 3359
60: 3 *You have* s your people desperate times; 8011
78:11 the wonders *he had* s them. 8011
90:16 *May* your deeds **be** s to your servants, 8011
111: 6 *He has* s his people the power of his works, 5583
Isa 21: 2 A dire vision *has* **been** s to me: 5583
26:10 Though **grace is** s *to* the wicked, 2858
66:14 but *his* **fury** *will* **be** s to his foes. 2404
Jer 44:10 not humbled themselves or s **reverence,** 3707
44:25 You and your wives *have* s 4848
La 4:16 priests *are* s no **honor,** the elders no 5951+7156
5:12 elders **are** s no **respect.** 2075+7156
Eze 11:25 the exiles everything the LORD *had* s me. 8011
Da 2:28 *He has* s King Nebuchadnezzar what will 10313
2:45 "The great God *has* s the king what will 10313
Mal 1: 6 'How *have we* s **contempt** *for* your name?' 1022
2: 9 but *have* s **partiality** in matters of 5951+7156
Mt 5: 7 Blessed are the merciful, for they *will be* s **mercy.** *1796*
Lk 1:25 "In these days *he has* s *his* **favor** *2078*
1:58 that the Lord *had* s her **great** mercy, *3486*
Jn 10:32 *"I have* s you many great miracles from *1259*
Ac 4: 9 an **act of kindness** s **to** a cripple *2307*
10:28 But God *has* s me that I should not call *1259*
14:17 *He has* s **kindness** by giving you rain *14*
1Co 3:13 his work will be s for what it is, *5745*
1Ti 1:13 *I was* s **mercy** because I acted in ignorance *1796*
1:16 for that very reason *I was* s **mercy** so that *1796*
Heb 6:10 the love *you have* s him as you have helped *1892*
8: 5 to the pattern s you on the mountain." *1259*
Jas 2:13 without mercy will be s to anyone who has *NIG*

SHOWS (16) [SHOW]

Dt 10:17 s no **partiality** and accepts no bribes. 5951+7156
17:12 The man who s contempt for the judge or 6913
2Sa 22:51 *he* s unfailing kindness to his anointed, 6913
1Ki 1:52 "If *he* s *himself* **to be** a worthy man, 2118+4200
Job 34:19 who s no **partiality** *to* princes and 5951+7156
Ps 18:50 *he* s unfailing kindness to his anointed, 6913
123: 2 till *he* s us *his* **mercy.** 2858
Pr 10:17 He who heeds discipline s the way to life, NIH
11:22 a beautiful woman *who* s **no** discretion. 6073
12:16 A fool s his annoyance at once, 3359
14:31 He who oppresses the poor s **contempt** 3070
15: 5 but whoever heeds correction s **prudence.** 6891
17: 5 the poor s **contempt** *for* their Maker; 3070
Ecc 10: 3 fool lacks sense and s everyone how stupid 606
Isa 27:11 and their Creator s them no **favor.** 2858
Jn 5:20 Father loves the Son and s him all he does. *1259*

SHRED (KJV) See CUT UP

SHREWD (5) [SHREWDLY]

2Sa 13: 3 Jonadab was a very s man. 2682
22:27 but to the crooked *you* **show yourself** s. 7349
Ps 18:26 but to the crooked *you* **show yourself** s. 7349
Mt 10:16 be as s as snakes and as innocent as doves. *5861*
Lk 16: 8 the people of this world are *more* s *5642+5861*

SHREWDLY (2) [SHREWD]

Ex 1:10 *we must* **deal** s with them or they will 2681
Lk 16: 8 dishonest manager because he had acted s. *5862*

SHRIEK (1) [SHRIEKED, SHRIEKS]

Mk 1:26 and came out of him *with* a s. *3489+5888+5889*

SHRIEKED (1) [SHRIEK]

Mk 9:26 The spirit s, convulsed him violently *3189*

SHRIEKS (1) [SHRIEK]

Ac 8: 7 *With* s, evil spirits came out of many, *1066+3489+5889*

SHRINE (17) [SHRINES]

Ge 38:21 "Where is the s **prostitute** who was beside 7728
38:21 "There hasn't been any s **prostitute** here," 7728
38:22 'There hasn't been any s **prostitute** here.' " 7728
Dt 23:17 or woman is to become a s **prostitute.** 7728
Jdg 17: 5 Now this man Micah had a s, 466+1074
1Ki 14:24 There were even *male* s **prostitutes** in 7728
15:12 He expelled the *male* s **prostitutes** from 7728
22:46 the *male* s **prostitutes** who remained there 7728
2Ki 10:25 the bodies out and then entered the **inner** s 6551
23: 7 the quarters of the *male* s **prostitutes,** 7728
Isa 16:12 she goes to her s to pray, it is to no avail. 5219
44:13 that it may dwell in a s. 1074
Eze 8:12 each at the s *of* his own idol? 2540
16:24 and made a **lofty** s in every public square. 8229
Hos 4:14 with harlots and sacrifice with s **prostitutes** 7728
Am 5:26 You have lifted up the s *of* your king, 6109
Ac 7:43 You have lifted up the s of Molech and *5008*

SHRINES (15) [SHRINE]

1Ki 12:31 Jeroboam built s *on* high places 1074
13:32 the altar in Bethel and against all the s *on* 1074
2Ki 17:29 up in the s the people of Samaria had made 1074
17:32 to officiate for them as priests in the s *at* 1074
23: 8 He broke down the s *at* the gates— 1195
23:19 and defiled all the s *at* the high places that 1074
Job 36:14 among *male* **prostitutes of the s.** 7728
Eze 16:25 of every street you built your **lofty** s 8229
16:31 of every street and made your **lofty** s 8229
16:39 and destroy your **lofty s.** 8229
18: 6 He does not eat at the **mountain** s or 2215
18:11 "He eats at the **mountain s.** 2215
18:15 "He does not eat at the **mountain** s or 2215
22: 9 in you are those who eat at the **mountain** s 2215
Ac 19:24 who made silver s of Artemis, *3724*

SHRINK (2) [SHRINKS]

Heb 10:39 not *of* those who s **back** and are destroyed, *5714*
Rev 12:11 they did not love their lives so much as to s *NIG*

SHRINKS (1) [SHRINK]

Heb 10:38 if *he* s **back,** I will not be pleased with him. *5713*

SHRIVEL (2) [SHRIVELED]

Isa 64: 6 we all s **up** like a leaf, 5570
Eze 19:12 The east wind **made** *it* s, 3312

SHRIVELED (9) [SHRIVEL]

1Ki 13: 4 hand he stretched out toward the man s **up,** 3312
Isa 34: 4 like s figs from the fig tree. 5570
La 4: 8 Their skin *has* s on their bones; 7594
Joel 1:17 The seeds *are* s beneath the clods. 6308
Mt 12:10 and a man with a s hand was there. *3831*
Mk 3: 1 and a man with a s hand was there. *3830*
3: 3 Jesus said to the man with the s hand, *3831*
Lk 6: 6 a man was there whose right hand was s. *3831*
6: 8 and said to the man with the s hand, *3831*

SHROUD (2) [SHROUDED]

Job 40:13 s their faces in the grave. 2502
Isa 25: 7 the s that enfolds all peoples, the sheet 4287

SHROUDED (2) [SHROUD]

Job 19: 8 *he has* s my paths *in* darkness. 8492
Ecc 6: 4 and in darkness its name **is s.** 4059

SHRUB (1)

Ge 2: 5 and no s *of* the field had yet appeared 3972+8489

SHUA (4)

Ge 38: 2 the daughter of a Canaanite man named S. 8781
38:12 long time Judah's wife, the daughter of S, 8781
1Ch 2: 3 a Canaanite woman, the daughter of S. 8781
7:32 Shomer and Hotham and of their sister S. 8783

SHUAH (2)

Ge 25: 2 Jokshan, Medan, Midian, Ishbak and S. 8756
1Ch 1:32 Jokshan, Medan, Midian, Ishbak and S. 8756

SHUAL (2) [HAZAR SHUAL]

1Sa 13:17 toward Ophrah in the vicinity of S, 8787
1Ch 7:36 The sons of Zophah: Suah, Harnepher, S, 8786

SHUBAEL (6)

1Ch 23:16 descendants of Gershom: S was the first. 8649
24:20 S; from the sons of Shubael: Jehdeiah. 8742
24:20 from the sons of S: Jehdeiah. 8742
25: 4 Mattaniah, Uzziel, S and Jerimoth; 8649
25:20 the thirteenth to S, 8742
26:24 S, a descendant of Gershom son of Moses, 8649

SHUDDER (7)

Isa 19:16 *They will* s with fear at the uplifted hand 3006
32:11 s, *you* daughters who feel secure! 8074
Jer 2:12 O heavens, and s *with* great horror," 8547
Eze 12:18 and s in fear as you drink your water. 8077
27:35 their kings s *with* horror 8547
32:10 and their kings *will* s *with* horror because 8547
Jas 2:19 Even the demons believe that—and s. *5857*

SHUHAH'S (1)

1Ch 4:11 Kelub, S brother, was the father of Mehir, 8758

SHUHAM (1) [SHUHAMITE]

Nu 26:42 through S, the Shuhamite clan. 8761

SHUHAMITE (2) [SHUHAM]

Nu 26:42 through Shuham, the S clan. 8762
26:43 All of them were S clans; 8762

SHUHITE (5)

Job 2:11 Bildad the S and Zophar the Naamathite, 8760
8: 1 Then Bildad the S replied: 8760
18: 1 Then Bildad the S replied: 8760
25: 1 Then Bildad the S replied: 8760
42: 9 the S and Zophar the Naamathite did what 8760

SHULAMMITE (2)

SS 6:13 Come back, come back, O S; 8769
6:13 on the S as on the dance of Mahanaim? 8769

SHUMATHITES (1)

1Ch 2:53 the Ithrites, Puthites, S and Mishraites. 9092

SHUN (2) [SHUNNED, SHUNS]

Job 28:28 and *to* s evil is understanding.' " 6073
Pr 3: 7 fear the LORD and s evil. 6073

SHUNAMMITE (8)

1Ki 1: 3 Abishag, a S, and brought her to the king. 8774
1:15 where Abishag the S was attending him. 8774
2:17 to give me Abishag the S as my wife." 8774
2:21 "Let Abishag the S be given in marriage 8774
2:22 "Why do you request Abishag the S 8774
2Ki 4:12 He said to his servant Gehazi, "Call the S." 8774
4:25 "Look! There's the S! 8774
4:36 and said, "Call the S." 8774

SHUNEM (3)

Jos 19:18 territory included: Jezreel, Kesulloth, S, 8773
1Sa 28: 4 and came and set up camp at S, 8773
2Ki 4: 8 One day Elisha went to S. 8773

SHUNI (2) [SHUNITE]

Ge 46:16 The sons of Gad: Zephon, Haggi, S, 8771
Nu 26:15 through S, the Shunite clan; 8771

SHUNITE (1) [SHUNI]

Nu 26:15 through Shuni, the S clan; 8772

SHUNNED (3) [SHUN]

Job 1: 1 he feared God and s evil. 6073
Pr 14:20 The poor **are** s even by their neighbors, 8533
19: 7 A poor man *is* s *by* all his relatives— 8533

SHUNS (4) [SHUN]

Job 1: 8 a man who fears God and s evil." 6073
2: 3 a man who fears God and s evil. 6073
Pr 14:16 A wise man fears the LORD and s evil, 6073
Isa 59:15 and *whoever* s evil becomes a prey. 6073

SHUPHAM (1) [SHUPHAMITE]

Nu 26:39 through S, the Shuphamite clan; 8792

SHUPHAMITE (1) [SHUPHAM]

Nu 26:39 through Shupham, the S clan; 8793

SHUPPIM (1)

1Ch 26:16 on the upper road fell to S and Hosah. 9157

SHUPPITES (2)

1Ch 7:12 The S and Huppites were the descendants 9158
7:15 a wife from among the Huppites and S. 9158

SHUR (6)

Ge 16: 7 the spring that is beside the road to S. 8804
20: 1 and lived between Kadesh and S. 8804
25:18 in the area from Havilah to S, 8804
Ex 15:22 and they went into the Desert of S. 8804
1Sa 15: 7 the way from Havilah to S, 8804
27: 8 in the land extending to S and Egypt.) 8804

SHUSHAN (KJV) See SUSA

SHUT (54) [SHUTS]

Ge 7:16 Then the LORD s him in. 6037
19: 6 to meet them and s the door behind him 6037
19:10 and pulled Lot back into the house and s 6037
Dt 11:17 and *he will* s the heavens so that it will 6806
Jos 2: 7 pursuers had gone out, the gate *was* **s.** 6037
6: 1 Now Jericho *was* **tightly s up** 2256+6037+6037
Jdg 3:23 *he* s the doors of the upper room behind him 6037
1Sa 12: 3 a bribe *to* **make** *me* s my eyes? 6623
1Ki 8:35 the heavens *are* **s up** and there is no rain 6806
2Ki 4: 4 Then go inside and s the door behind you 6037
4: 5 She left him and afterward s the door 6037
4:21 then s the door and went out. 6037
4:33 s the door on the two of them and prayed to 6037
6:32 s the door and hold it shut against him. 6037
6:32 shut the door and **hold** it s *against* him. 4315
2Ch 6:26 the heavens *are* **s up** and there is no rain 6806
7:13 *I* **s up** the heavens so that there is no rain, 6806
28:24 *He* s the doors of the LORD's temple 6037
29: 7 also s the doors of the portico and put out 6037
Ne 6:10 who **was s in** at his home. 6806
7: 3 *have them* s the doors and bar them. 1589
13:19 I ordered the doors *to* **be** s and not opened 6037
Job 3:10 for *it did* not s the doors of the womb 6037
24:16 but by day *they* s themselves **in;** 3159
38: 8 "Who s **up** the sea behind doors 6114
Ps 107:42 but all the wicked s their mouths. 7890
Isa 22:22 what he opens no *one can* s, 6037
24:22 *they will* **be s up** in prison and be punished 6037
26:20 enter your rooms and s the doors 6037
45: 1 before him so that gates *will* not **be s:** 6037
52:15 kings *will* s their mouths because of him. 7890
60:11 *they will* never **be s,** day or night, 6037
Jer 13:19 The cities in the Negev *will* **be s up,** 6037
20: 9 a fire **s up** in my bones. 6806
Eze 3:24 "Go, s **yourself** inside your house. 6037
22:26 and *they* s their eyes to the keeping 6623
44: 1 the one facing east, and it *was* **s.** 6037
44: 2 "This gate is to remain **s.** 6037
44: 2 It is to remain s because the LORD, 6037
46: 1 of the inner court facing east is to be s on 6037
46: 2 but the gate *will* not **be s** until evening. 6037
46:12 after he has gone out, the gate *will be* **s.** 6037
Da 6:22 and *he* s the mouths of the lions. 10506
Mal 1:10 that one of you *would* s the temple doors, 6037
Mt 23:13 *You* s the kingdom of heaven in men's faces *3091*
25:10 And the door *was* **s.** *3091*
Lk 4:25 the sky *was* s for three and a half years *3091*
Ac 21:30 and immediately the gates *were* **s.** *3091*
2Th 1: 9 and s out from the presence of the Lord and *NIG*
Heb 11:33 who s the mouths of lions, *5852*
Rev 3: 7 What he opens no one can s, *3091*
3: 8 before you an open door that no one can **s.** *3091*
11: 6 These men have power *to* s up the sky so *3091*
21:25 On no day *will* its gates ever *be* **s,** *3091*

SHUTHELAH (4) [SHUTHELAHITE]

Nu 26:35 through **S,** the Shuthelahite clan; 8811
26:36 These were the descendants of **S:** 8811
1Ch 7:20 **S,** Bered his son, Tahath his son, 8811
7:21 Zabad his son and **S** his son. 8811

SHUTHELAHITE (1) [SHUTHELAH]

Nu 26:35 through Shuthelah, the **S** clan; 9279

SHUTS (6) [SHUT]

Job 5:16 poor have hope, and injustice s its mouth. 7890
Pr 21:13 If a *man* s his ears to the cry of the poor, 357
Isa 22:22 and what *he* s no one can open. 6037
33:15 and s his eyes against contemplating evil— 6794
La 3: 8 *he* **s out** my prayer. 8608
Rev 3: 7 and what he s no one can open. *3091*

SHUTTLE (1)

Job 7: 6 "My days are swifter than a **weaver's s,** 756

SHY (1)

Job 39:22 *he does* not **s away** from the sword. 8740

SIA (1)

Ne 7:47 Keros, **S,** Padon, 6103

SIAHA (1)

Ezr 2:44 Keros, **S,** Padon, 6104

SIBBECAI (4)

2Sa 21:18 At that time **S** the Hushathite killed Saph, 6021
1Ch 11:29 **S** the Hushathite, Ilai the Ahohite, 6021
20: 4 At that time **S** the Hushathite killed Sippai, 6021
27:11 for the eighth month, was **S** the Hushathite, 6021

SIBBOLETH (1)

Jdg 12: 6 **"S,"** because he could not pronounce 6027

SIBMAH (5)

Nu 32:38 (these names were changed) and **S.** 8424
Jos 13:19 **S,** Zereth Shahar on the hill in the valley, 8424
Isa 16: 8 The fields of Heshbon wither, the vines of **S** 8424
16: 9 as Jazer weeps, for the vines of **S.** 8424
Jer 48:32 as Jazer weeps, O vines of **S.** 8424

SIBRAIM (1)

Eze 47:16 Berothah and **S** (which lies on the border 6028

SICK (43) [SICKNESS, SICKNESSES]

Pr 13:12 Hope deferred **makes** the heart **s,** 2703
Isa 10:18 as when a s *man* wastes away. 5823
19:10 and all the wage earners will be s *at* heart. 108
Eze 34: 4 not strengthened the weak or healed the s 2703
Mt 8:16 with a word and healed all the **s.** *2400+2809*
9:12 healthy who need a doctor, but the **s.** *2400+2809*
10: 8 Heal the s, raise the dead, *820*
12:15 and he healed all their s, *NIG*
14:14 had compassion on them and healed their **s.** *779*
14:35 People brought all their s to him *2400+2809*
14:36 to let the s just touch the edge of his cloak, *NIG*
25:36 *I was* s and you looked after me, *820*
25:39 When did we see you s or in prison and go *820*
25:43 I was s and in prison and you did not look *822*
25:44 or a stranger or needing clothes or s or *822*
Mk 1:32 Jesus all the s and demon-possessed. *2400+2809*
2:17 healthy who need a doctor, but the **s.** *2400+2809*
6: 5 except lay his hands on a few s *people* *779*
6:13 and anointed many s *people* with oil *779*
6:55 whole region and carried the s on mats *2400+2809*
6:56 they placed the s in the marketplaces. *820*
16:18 they will place their hands on s *people,* *779*
Lk 5:17 the Lord was present for him to heal the **s.** *NIG*
5:31 healthy who need a doctor, but the **s.** *2400+2809*
7: 2 **was** s and about to die. *2400+2809*
9: 2 the kingdom of God and to heal the **s.** *822*
10: 9 Heal the s who are there and tell them, *822*
Jn 4:46 a certain royal official whose son **lay** s *820*
6: 2 miraculous signs he had performed on the **s.** *820*
11: 1 Now a man named Lazarus was **s.** *820*
11: 2 whose brother Lazarus now **lay s,** *820*
11: 3 "Lord, the one you love *is* **s."** *820*
11: 6 Yet when he heard that Lazarus *was* **s,** *820*
Ac 5:15 the s into the streets and laid them on beds *822*
5:16 bringing their s and those tormented *822*
9:37 About that time *she became* s and died, *820*
19:12 that had touched him were taken to the s, *820*
28: 8 His father was **s in bed,** *2879*
28: 9 the s on the island came and were cured. *819+2400*
1Co 11:30 many among you are weak and s, *779*
2Ti 4:20 and I left Trophimus s in Miletus. *820*
Jas 5:14 *Is* any one of you **s?** *820*
5:15 offered in faith will make the s *person* well; *2827*

SICHEM (KJV) See SHECHEM

SICKBED (1) [BED]

Ps 41: 3 The LORD will sustain him on his s 1867+6911

SICKLE (12) [SICKLES]

Dt 16: 9 from the time you begin to put the s to 3058
23:25 you must not put a s to his standing grain. 3058
Jer 50:16 and the reaper with his s at harvest. 4478
Joel 3:13 Swing the s, for the harvest is ripe. 4478
Mk 4:29 as the grain is ripe, he puts the s to it, *1535*
Rev 14:14 a crown of gold on his head and a sharp s *1535*
14:15 "Take your s and reap, *1535*
14:16 on the cloud swung his s over the earth, *1535*
14:17 and he too had a sharp s. *1535*
14:18 in a loud voice to him who had the sharp **s,** *1535*
14:18 "Take your sharp s and gather the clusters *1535*
14:19 The angel swung his s on the earth, *1535*

SICKLES (1) [SICKLE]

1Sa 13:20 mattocks, axes and s sharpened. 3058

SICKNESS (11) [SICK]

Ex 23:25 I will take away s from among you, 4701
Dt 28:61 of s and disaster not recorded in this Book 2716
Pr 18:14 A man's spirit sustains him in s, 4700
Jer 6: 7 her s and wounds are ever before me. 2716
10:19 Yet I said to myself, "This is my s, 2716
Hos 5:13 "When Ephraim saw his s, 2716
Mt 4:23 and healing every disease and s among *3433*
9:35 and healing every disease and s. *3433*
10: 1 and to heal every disease and s. *3433*
Lk 4:40 to Jesus all who had various kinds *of* **s,** *820+3798*
Jn 11: 4 Jesus said, "This s will not end in death. *819*

SICKNESSES (2) [SICK]

Lk 5:15 to hear him and to be healed of their s. *819*
7:21 many who had diseases, s and evil spirits, *3465*

SIDDIM (3)

Ge 14: 3 in the Valley of **S** (the Salt Sea). 8443
14: 8 up their battle lines in the Valley of **S** 8443
14:10 Now the Valley of **S** was full of tar pits, 8443

SIDE (293) [ASIDE, BESIDE, FIVE-SIDED, FOUR-SIDED, SIDED, SIDES, SIDEWALLS, SIDING]

Ge 2:14 it runs along the **east** *s of* Asshur. AIT
3:24 the **east** *s* of the Garden of Eden cherubim AIT
6:16 a door in the s *of* the ark and make lower, 7396
31:52 not go past this heap to **your** *s* to harm you AIT
31:52 past this heap and pillar to **my** *s* to harm me. AIT
Ex 3: 1 the **far** s *of* the desert and came to Horeb, 339
14:20 the cloud brought darkness to the one s NIH
14:20 to the one side and light to the other **s;** NIH
17:12 one on *one* s, one on the other— 2296[S]
25:12 with two rings on one s and two rings on 7521
25:32 three on one s and three on the other. 7396
26:18 Make twenty frames for the south s of 6991
26:20 For the other **s,** the north side 7521
26:20 the north s *of* the tabernacle, 6991
26:26 for the frames on one s *of* the tabernacle, 7521
26:27 five for those on the other **s,** 7521
26:35 the curtain on the north s *of* the tabernacle 7521
26:35 the lampstand opposite it on the south **s.** 7521
27: 9 The south s shall be a hundred cubits long 6991
27:11 The north s shall also be a hundred cubits 6991
27:14 to be on one s of the entrance, 4190
27:15 to be on the other **s,** 4190
32:27 'Each man strap a sword to his s. 3751
36:23 They made twenty frames for the south s of 6991
36:25 For the other s, the north side 7521
36:25 the north s *of* the tabernacle, 6991
36:31 for the frames on one s *of* the tabernacle, 7521
36:32 five for those on the other s, 7521
37: 3 with two rings on one s and two rings on 7521
37:18 three on one s and three on the other. 7396
38: 9 The south s was a hundred cubits long 6991
38:11 The north s was also a hundred cubits long 6991
38:14 Curtains fifteen cubits long were on one s 4190
38:15 the other s of the entrance to the courtyard, 4190
40:22 in the Tent of Meeting on the north s *of* 3751
40:24 of Meeting opposite the table on the south s 3751
Lev 1:11 the north s *of* the altar before the LORD, 3751
1:15 its blood shall be drained out on the s *of* 7815
1:16 with its contents and throw it to the east s 725
5: 9 the blood of the sin offering against the s *of* 7815
13:55 the mildew has affected one s or the other. 7949[S]
Nu 3:29 to camp on the south s *of* the tabernacle. 3751
3:35 to camp on the north s *of* the tabernacle. 3751
32:19 **on the other s of** the Jordan, 2134+2256+4946+6298
32:19 to us on the east s *of* the Jordan." 4946+6298
32:32 property we inherit will be **on this s of** 4946+6298
34: 3 " 'Your southern s will include some of 6991
34:11 to Riblah on the **east** *s* of Ain and continue AIT
34:12 with its boundaries **on every s.' "** 6017
34:15 on the east s of the Jordan of Jericho, 6298
35: 5 measure three thousand feet on the east s, 6991
35: 5 three thousand on the south s, 6991
35:14 Give three on **this** s of the Jordan and three 6298
36:11 their **cousins on their father's s.** 1201+1856
Jos 4:11 and the priests **came to the other** s 6296
7: 7 to stay on the **other** s *of* the Jordan! 6298
12: 1 including all the **eastern** *s of* the Arabah: AIT
12: 7 on the west s *of* the Jordan, from Baal Gad 6298
13:27 of Sihon king of Heshbon (the east s *of* 6298
17: 9 the **northern** *s* of the ravine and ended at AIT
18: 7 on the east s of the Jordan. 6298
18:12 On the north s their boundary began at 6991
18:14 the western s and came out at Kiriath Baal 6991
18:14 This was the western **s.** 6991
18:15 The southern s began at the outskirts 6991
18:20 the boundary on the eastern s. 6991
20: 8 On the east s of the Jordan 6298
21:44 The LORD gave them rest on **every s,** 6017
22: 4 of the LORD gave you on the **other** s *of* 6298
22: 7 the tribe Joshua gave land on the west s *of* 6298
22:11 near the Jordan on the Israelite s, 6298
Jdg 8:34 hands of all their enemies **on every s.** 4946+6017
10: 8 the Israelites on the **east** s *of* the Jordan 6298
11:18 along the eastern s of the country of Moab, NIH
11:18 and camped on the **other** s *of* the Arnon. 6298
Ru 2: 1 Naomi had a relative **on** her husband's s, 4200
1Sa 4:13 there was Eli sitting on his chair by the s *of* 3338
4:18 Eli fell backward off his chair by the s *of* 3338
12:11 from the hands of your enemies **on every s,** 6017
14: 1 over to the Philistine outpost on the **other s.** 6298
14: 4 **On each** s *of* the pass 2021+2021+2296+2296+4946+4946+4946+4946+6298+6298
14:47 he fought against their enemies **on every s:** 6017
20:20 I will shoot three arrows to the s *of* it, 7396
20:21 'Look, the arrows are **on this** s of you; 2178
20:41 David got up from the south s 725
22:17 Then the king ordered the guards **at** his s: 6584
23:26 Saul was going along one s *of* 7396
23:26 and David and his men were on the other s, 7396
26:13 Then David crossed over to the **other** s 6298
2Sa 2:13 down on *one* s of the pool and one group 2296[S]
2:13 of the pool and one group on the *other* s. 2296[S]
2:16 and thrust his dagger into his opponent's s, 7396
3: 8 "Am I a dog's head—**on** Judah's **s?** 4200
13:34 coming down the s *of* the hill. 7396
13:34 direction of Horonaim, on the s *of* the hill." 7396
15: 2 He would get up early and stand by the s *of* 3338
1Ki 3:20 from my s while I your servant was asleep. 725
5: 4 on **every s,** and there is no adversary 6017
6: 5 in which there were s **rooms.** 7521
6: 8 to the lowest floor was on the south s *of* 4190
6:10 he built the s **rooms** all along the temple. 3666
7:28 They had s **panels** attached to uprights. 4995
7:30 cast with wreaths on each **s.** 6298
7:39 He placed five of the stands on the south s 4190
7:39 He placed the Sea on the south s, 4190
2Ki 4: 4 as each is filled, **put it to one s."** 5825
6:11 of us is **on the s of** the king of Israel?" 448
9:32 "Who is **on** my **s?** 907
10: 6 "If you are **on** my s and will obey me, 4200
11:11 the altar and the temple, from the south s to 4190

2Ki 11:11 the south side to the north s *of* the temple. 4190
12: 9 on the right s as one enters the temple of NIH
16:14 and put it on the north s *of* the new altar. 3751
16:17 the s **panels** and removed the basins from 4995
1Ch 18:17 chief officials at the king's **s.** 3338
22: 9 from all his enemies **on every s.** 4946+6017
22:18 he not granted you rest **on every s?** 4946+6017
23:28 be in charge of the courtyards, the **s rooms,** 4384
2Ch 4: 6 for washing and placed five on the **south** *s* AIT
4: 7 five on the **south** *s* and five on the north. AIT
4: 8 five on the **south** *s* and five on the north. AIT
4:10 He placed the Sea on the south **s,** 4190
5:12 stood on the **east** *s* of the altar, AIT
14: 7 and he has given us rest **on every s."** 4946+6017
15:15 the LORD gave them rest **on every s.** 4946+6017
20: 2 from the **other** s of the Sea. 6298
20:30 his God had given him rest **on every s.** 4946+6017
23:10 the altar and the temple, from the south s to 4190
23:10 the south side to the north s *of* the temple. 4190
29: 4 assembled them in the square on the **east** *s* AIT
32:22 He took care of them **on every s.** 4946+6017
32:30 and channeled the water down to the **west** *s* AIT
Ne 4: 3 Tobiah the Ammonite, who was **at** his **s,** 725
4:18 of the builders wore his sword at his s 5516
Job 15:10 The gray-haired and the aged are **on** our **s,** 928
18:11 Terrors startle him **on every** s 6017
19:10 He tears me down **on every** s till I am gone; 6017
21:26 **S by side** they lie in the dust, 3480
21:26 **Side by** s they lie in the dust, 3480
33:23 if there is an angel **on** his s as a mediator, 6584
39:23 The quiver rattles **against** his **s,** 6584
Ps 3: 6 drawn up against me **on every s.** 6017
31:13 there is terror **on every s;** 4946+6017
45: 3 Gird your sword upon your **s,** 3751
91: 7 A thousand may fall at your **s,** 7396
97: 3 and consumes his foes **on every s.** 6017
118:11 They surrounded me **on every s,** 6015
124: 1 If the LORD had not been **on** our **s—** 4200
124: 2 not been **on** our s when men attacked us, 4200
139: 9 if I settle on the **far** s *of* the sea, 344
Pr 8:30 Then I was the craftsman **at** his **s.** 725
Ecc 4: 1 power was on the s *of* their oppressors— 3338
SS 3: 8 each with his sword at his **s,** 3751
Jer 6:25 and there is terror **on every s.** 4946+6017
20:10 "Terror **on every s!** 4946+6017
35: 2 to come to one of the **s rooms** of the house 4384
46: 5 and there is terror **on every s,"** 4946+6017
49:29 'Terror **on every s!'** 4946+6017
49:32 on them from every **s,"** 6298
50:15 Shout against her **on every s!** 6017
51: 2 they will oppose her **on every** s in 4946+6017
La 2:22 against me terrors **on every s.** 4946+6017
Eze 1:10 on the right s each had the face of a lion, NIH
1:11 the wing of another creature on either **s,** NIH
4: 4 on your left **s** and put the sin of the house 7396
4: 4 for the number of days you lie on **your s.** 2257[S]
4: 6 lie down again, this time on your right **s,** 7396
4: 8 that you cannot turn from one s to the other 7396
4: 9 during the 390 days you lie on your **s.** 7396
9: 2 in linen who had a writing kit at his **s.** 5516
9: 3 in linen who had the writing kit at his s 5516
9:11 the writing kit at his s brought back word, 5516
10: 3 the cherubim were standing on the **south** *s* AIT
10:16 the wheels did not leave their **s.** 725
21:14 **closing in** on them **from every s.** 2539
23:22 against you from **every s—** 6017
23:24 up positions against you **on every s** 6017
27:11 and Helech manned your walls **on every s;** 6017
28:23 with the sword against her **on every s.** 4946+6017
36: 3 and hounded you **from every s** so 4946+6017
40: 2 on whose **south** *s* were some buildings AIT
40:10 Inside the east gate were three alcoves **on each s;** 2256+4946+4946+7024+7024
40:10 projecting walls **on each** s had the same 2256+4946+4946+7024+7024
40:19 a hundred cubits on the **east** *s* as well as on AIT
40:21 Its alcoves—three **on each s—** 2256+4946+4946+7024+7024
40:24 to the south **s** and I saw a gate facing south. 2006
40:26 the faces of the projecting walls **on each s.** 2256+4946+4946+7024+7024
40:27 to the outer gate on the south **s;** 2006
40:32 on the east **s,** and he measured the gateway; 2006
40:34 palm trees decorated the jambs **on either s,** 2256+4946+4946+7024+7024
40:37 palm trees decorated the jambs **on either s,** 2256+4946+4946+7024+7024
40:39 portico of the gateway were two tables **on each s,** 2256+4946+4946+7024+7024
40:40 on the other s of the steps were two tables. 4190
40:41 So there were four tables on *one* s of 7024
40:44 at the s *of* the north gate and facing south, 4190
40:44 at the s *of* the south gate and facing north. 4190
40:48 they were five cubits wide **on either s.** 2256+4946+4946+7024+7024
40:48 its projecting walls were three cubits wide **on either s.** 2256+4946+4946+7024+7024
40:49 there were pillars **on each** s of the jambs. 2256+4946+4946+7024+7024
41: 1 width of the jambs was six cubits **on each s.** 2256+4946+4946+7024+7024
41: 2 and the projecting walls **on each** s 2256+4946+4946+7024+7024
41: 3 on each s of it were seven cubits wide. NIH
41: 5 it was six cubits thick, and each **s room** 7521
41: 6 The **s rooms** were on three levels, 7521
41: 6 to serve as supports for the **s rooms,** 7521
Eze 41: 7 The **s rooms** all around the temple 7521
41: 8 forming the foundation of the **s rooms.** 7521
41: 9 of the **s rooms** was five cubits thick. 7521
41: 9 The open area between the **s rooms** of 7521
41:11 There were entrances to the **s rooms** from 7521
41:12 *on* the west **s** was seventy cubits wide. 6991
41:15 including its galleries **on each s;** 2256+4946+4946+7024+7024
41:19 the palm tree on one s and the face of a lion 7024
41:26 with palm trees carved **on each s.** 2256+4946+4946+7024+7024
41:26 The **s rooms** *of* the temple also had 7521
42: 1 and opposite the outer wall on the **north** *s.* AIT
42: 8 While the row of rooms on the s next to NIH
42: 8 the row on the s nearest the sanctuary was NIH
42: 9 on the **east** *s* as one enters them from AIT
42:10 On the south s along the length of the wall 2006
42:16 the east s with the measuring rod; 8120
42:17 He measured the north **s;** 8120
42:18 He measured the south **s;** 8120
42:19 Then he turned to the west s and measured; 8120
45: 7 the land **bordering each** s of the area formed by 2256+2296+2296+4946+4946[S]
45: 7 the west s and eastward from the east side, 6991
45: 7 the west side and eastward from the east **s,** 6991
46:19 through the entrance at the s *of* the gate to 4190
47: 1 down from under the south s *of* the temple, 4190
47: 2 and the water was flowing from the south **s.** 4190
47: 7 I saw a great number of trees **on each** s *of* the river. 2256+2296+2296+4946+4946[S]
47:15 the north s it will run from the Great Sea by 6991
47:18 "On the east s the boundary will run 6991
47:19 the south s it will run from Tamar as far as 6991
47:20 "On the west **s,** the Great Sea 6991
48: 1 be part of its border from the **east** *s* to AIT
48: 1 from the east side to the **west** *s.* AIT
48:10 It will be 25,000 cubits long on the **north** *s,* AIT
48:10 10,000 cubits wide on the **west** *s,* AIT
48:10 10,000 cubits wide on the **east** *s* AIT
48:10 and 25,000 cubits long on the **south** *s.* AIT
48:16 the north s 4,500 cubits, 6991
48:16 the south s 4,500 cubits, the east side 4,500 6991
48:16 the east s 4,500 cubits, 6991
48:16 and the west s 4,500 cubits. 6991
48:18 will be 10,000 cubits on the **east** *s* and AIT
48:18 10,000 cubits on the **west** *s.* AIT
48:20 25,000 cubits **on each s.** 928
48:23 from the east **s** to the west side. 6991
48:23 from the east side to the west **s.** 6991
48:30 Beginning on the north **s,** which is 4,500 6991
48:31 on the **north** *s* will be the gate of Reuben, AIT
48:32 "On the east **s,** which is 4,500 cubits long, 6991
48:33 "On the south **s,** which measures 4,500 6991
48:34 "On the west **s,** which is 4,500 cubits long, 6991
Joel 3:11 all you nations **from every s,** 4946+6017
3:12 to judge all the nations **on every s.** 4946+6017
Zec 3: 1 Satan standing at his right s to accuse him. NIH
5: 3 for according to what it says on *one* **s,** 2296[S]
Mt 8:18 he gave orders to cross to the **other** s of *4305*
8:28 the **other** s in the region of the Gadarenes, *4305*
14:22 and go on ahead of him to the **other s,** *4305*
19: 1 into the region of Judea to the **other** s of *4305*
Mk 4:35 "Let us go over to the **other s."** *4305*
5:21 over by boat to the **other** s of the lake, *4305*
8:13 into the boat and crossed to the **other s.** *4305*
16: 5 in a white robe sitting on the **right s,** *1288*
Lk 1:11 at the **right** s of the altar of incense. *1288*
8:22 "Let's go over to the **other** s **of** the lake." *4305*
10:31 *he* **passed by on the other s.** *524*
10:32 **passed by on the other s.** *524*
16:22 and the angels carried him to Abraham's **s.** *3146*
16:23 Abraham far away, with Lazarus by his **s.** *3146*
19:43 and hem you in **on every s.** *4119*
Jn 1:18 who is at the Father's **s,** *3146*
1:28 This all happened at Bethany **on the other s** *4305*
3:26 was with you **on the other** s of the Jordan *4305*
6:25 When they found him **on the other** s of *4305*
18: 1 **On the other** s there was an olive grove, *3963[S]*
18:37 Everyone on the **s** of truth listens to me." *NIG*
19:18 **one on each** s and Jesus in the middle. *1949+1949+2779*
19:34 of the soldiers pierced Jesus' s with a spear, *4433*
20:20 he showed them his hands and **s.** *4433*
20:25 and put my hand into his **s,** *4433*
20:27 Reach out your hand and put it into my **s.** *4433*
21: 6 "Throw your net on the right s of the boat *3538*
Ac 12: 7 He struck Peter on the s and woke him up. *4433*
2Co 4: 8 We are hard pressed on **every** *s,* *AIT*
Php 4: 3 help these women who *have* **contended at** my s in the cause of the gospel, *5254*
2Ti 4:17 Lord **stood at** my s and gave me strength, *4225*
Heb 10:33 at other times you stood **s by side** *3128*
10:33 at other times you stood **side by s** *3128*
Rev 22: 2 **On each** s of the river stood the tree of life, *1696+1949+2779*

SIDED (4) [SIDE]

1Sa 20:30 you *have* s **with** the son of Jesse 1047+4200
22:17 because they too have s **with** David. 3338+6640
2Ch 11:13 from all their districts throughout Israel s 3656
Ac 14: 4 some **s with** the Jews, others with *1639+5250*

SIDES (50) [SIDE]

Ex 12: 7 to take some of the blood and put it on the s 9109
12:22 on the top and on **both** s *of* the doorframe. 9109
Ex 12:23 the blood on the top and s *of* the doorframe 9109
25:14 the poles into the rings on the s *of* the chest 7521
25:32 Six branches are to extend from the s *of* 7396
26:13 a cubit longer **on both s;** 2256+2296+2296+4946[S]
26:13 the s *of* the tabernacle so as to cover it. 7396
27: 7 be on two s *of* the altar when it is carried. 7521
29:16 and sprinkle it against the altar **on all s.** 6017
29:20 sprinkle blood against the altar **on all s.** 6017
30: 3 Overlay the top and all the s and the horns 7815
30: 4 two on **opposite s—**to hold the poles 7396+7521
32:15 They were inscribed on both **s,** 6298
37: 5 into the rings on the s *of* the ark to carry it. 7521
37:18 Six branches extended from the s *of* 7396
37:26 and all the s and the horns with pure gold, 7815
37:27 two on **opposite s—**to hold the poles 7396+7521
38: 7 into the rings so they would be on the s *of* 7521
Lev 1: 5 against the altar **on all** s at the entrance to 6017
1:11 against the altar **on all s.** 6017
3: 2 the blood against the altar **on all s.** 6017
3: 8 against the altar **on all s.** 6017
3:13 against the altar **on all s.** 6017
7: 2 to be sprinkled against the altar **on all s.** 6017
8:19 the blood against the altar **on all s.** 6017
8:24 against the altar **on all s.** 6017
9:12 he sprinkled it against the altar **on all s.** 6017
9:18 he sprinkled it against the altar **on all s.** 6017
19:27 " 'Do not cut the hair at the s *of* your head 6991
Nu 22:24 between two vineyards, with walls **on both s.** 2256+2296+2296+4946+4946[S]
33:55 in your eyes and thorns in your **s.** 7396
Jos 8:22 caught in the middle, with Israelites **on both s.** 2256+2296+2296+4946+4946[S]
8:33 were standing **on both** s of the ark of the covenant 2256+2296+2296+4946+4946[S]
18:20 of the clans of Benjamin **on all s.** 6017
Jdg 2: 3 be [thorns] in your s and their gods will be 7396
1Ki 4:24 and had peace on all **s.** 4946+6017+6298
5: 3 **waged against** my father David **from all s,** 6015
10:19 **On both** s of the seat were armrests, 2256+2296+2296+4946+4946[S]
1Ch 9:24 The gatekeepers were on the four **s:** 8120
2Ch 9:18 **On both** s of the seat were armrests, 2256+2296+2296+4946+4946[S]
Job 11: 6 for true wisdom has **two s.** 4101
Jer 52:23 were ninety-six pomegranates on the **s;** 8120
Eze 1: 8 on their four s they had the hands of a man. 8063
2:10 **On both** s of it were written words of lament and mourning 294+2256+7156
40:18 It abutted the s *of* the gateways and was 4190
41:22 its corners, its base and its s were of wood. 7815
42:20 So he measured the area on all four **s.** 8120
48:21 "What remains **on both** s of the area formed by 2256+2296+2296+4946+4946[S]
Da 7: 5 It was raised up on one of its **s,** 10680
Rev 5: 1 a scroll with writing **on both s** *2277+2779+3957*

SIDEWALLS (1) [SIDE]

Eze 41:26 the s *of* the portico were narrow windows 4190

SIDING (1) [SIDE]

Ex 23: 2 do not pervert justice by s with the crowd, 5742

SIDON (32) [GREATER SIDON, SIDONIANS]

Ge 10:15 Canaan was the father of **S** his firstborn, 7477
10:19 and the borders of Canaan reached from S 7477
49:13 his border will extend toward **S.** 7477
Jdg 1:31 or S or Ahlab or Aczib or Helbah or Aphek 7477
10: 6 and the gods of Aram, the gods of **S,** 7477
18:28 a long way from S and had no relationship 7477
2Sa 24: 6 and on to Dan Jaan and around toward **S.** 7477
1Ki 17: 9 at once to Zarephath of S and stay there. 7477
1Ch 1:13 Canaan was the father of S his firstborn, 7477
Ezr 3: 7 and oil to the **people of S** and Tyre, 7479
Isa 23: 2 of the island and you merchants of **S,** 7477
23: 4 Be ashamed, O **S,** and you, 7477
23:12 O Virgin Daughter of **S,** now crushed! 7477
Jer 25:22 all the kings of Tyre and **S;** 7477
27: 3 and S through the envoys who have come 7477
47: 4 to cut off all survivors who could help Tyre and **S.** 7477
Eze 27: 8 Men of S and Arvad were your oarsmen; 7477
28:21 "Son of man, set your face against **S;** 7477
28:22 " 'I am against you, O **S,** 7477
Joel 3: 4 and S and all you regions of Philistia? 7477
Zec 9: 2 which borders on it, and upon Tyre and **S,** 7477
Mt 11:21 in you had been performed in Tyre and **S,** *4972*
11:22 be more bearable *for* Tyre and S on the day *4972*
15:21 to the region *of* Tyre and **S.** *4972*
Mk 3: 8 across the Jordan and around Tyre and **S.** *4972*
7:31 the vicinity of Tyre and went through **S,** *4972*
Lk 4:26 to a widow in Zarephath *in* the region of **S.** *4972*
6:17 and from the coast of Tyre and **S,** *4972*
10:13 in you had been performed in Tyre and **S,** *4972*
10:14 But it will be more bearable *for* Tyre and S *4972*
Ac 12:20 *with* the people of Tyre and **S;** *4973*
27: 3 The next day we landed at **S;** *4972*

SIDONIANS (15) [SIDON]

Dt 3: 9 (Hermon is called Sirion by the **S;** 7479
Jos 13: 4 from Arah of the S as far as Aphek, 7479
13: 6 Misrephoth Maim, that is, all the **S,** 7479
Jdg 3: 3 all the Canaanites, the **S,** 7479
10:12 the **S,** the Amalekites and the Maonites 7479

Jdg 18: 7 like the S, unsuspecting and secure. 7479
18: 7 from the S and had no relationship 7479
1Ki 5: 6 so skilled in felling timber as the S." 7479
11: 1 Ammonites, Edomites, S and Hittites. 7479
11: 5 followed Ashteroth the goddess of the S, 7479
11:33 worshiped Ashteroth the goddess of the S, 7479
16:31 of Ethbaal king of the S, 7479
2Ki 23:13 for Ashtoreth the vile goddess of the S, 7479
1Ch 22: 4 for the S and Tyrians had brought large 7479
Eze 32:30 of the north and all the S are there; 7479

SIEGE (49) [BESIEGE, BESIEGED, BESIEGES, BESIEGING, SIEGEWORKS]

Dt 20:12 engage you in battle, **lay** s to that city. 7443
20:19 When *you* **lay** s to a city for a long time, 7443
20:20 not fruit trees and use them to build s **works** 5189
28:52 *They will* **lay** s to all the cities 7674
28:53 enemy will inflict on you during the s, 5189
28:55 on you during the s of all your cities. 5189
28:57 to eat them secretly during the s and in 5189
2Sa 11:16 So while Joab *had* the city **under** s, 9068
20:15 They built a s **ramp** up to the city, 6149
1Ki 16:17 from Gibbethon and **laid** s to Tirzah. 7443
2Ki 6:24 and marched up and **laid** s to Samaria. 7443
6:25 *the* s lasted so long that a donkey's head 7443
17: 5 marched against Samaria and **laid** s to it 7443
18: 9 against Samaria and **laid** s to it. 7443
19:32 with shield or build a s **ramp** against it. 6149
24:10 Jerusalem and **laid** s *to* it, 928+995+2021+5189
25: 1 the city and built s **works** all around it. 1911
25: 2 The city was kept under s until 5189
2Ch 32: 1 *He* **laid** s **to** the fortified cities, 2837+6584
32: 9 and all his forces were laying s to Lachish, NIH
32:10 that you remain in Jerusalem under s? 5189
Job 19:12 they build a s **ramp** against me and encamp 2006
30:12 they build their s **ramps** against me. 369+784
Isa 1: 8 in a field of melons, like a city **under** s. 7443
21: 2 Elam, attack! Media, **lay** s! 7443
23:13 they raised up their s **towers**, 1032
29: 3 and set up my s **works** against you. 5193
37:33 with shield or build a s **ramp** against it. 6149
Jer 6: 6 "Cut down the trees and build s **ramps** 6149
10:17 to leave the land, you who live under s. 5189
19: 9 during the stress of the s imposed on them 5189
32:24 the s **ramps** are built up to take the city. 6149
33: 4 torn down to be used against the s **ramps** 6149
39: 1 with his whole army and **laid** s to it. 7443
52: 4 the city and built s **works** all around it. 1911
52: 5 The city was kept under s until the 5189
Eze 4: 2 Then lay s to it: Erect siege works 5189
4: 2 lay siege to it: Erect s **works** against it, 1911
4: 3 It will be under s, and you shall besiege it. 5189
4: 7 Turn your face toward the s *of* Jerusalem 5189
4: 8 until you have finished the days of your s. 5189
5: 2 When the days of your s come to an end, 5189
17:17 and s **works** erected to destroy many lives. 1911
21:22 to build a ramp and to erect s **works**. 1911
24: 2 because the king of Babylon *has* **laid** s 6164
26: 8 he will set up s **works** against you, 1911
Da 11:15 the North will come and build up s **ramps** 6149
Mic 5: 1 O city of troops, for a s is laid against us. 5189
Na 3:14 Draw water for the s, strengthen your 5189

SIEGEWORKS (1) [SIEGE]

Ecc 9:14 surrounded it and built huge s against it. 5189

SIEVE (2)

Isa 30:28 the nations in the s *of* destruction; 5864
Am 9: 9 the nations as grain is shaken in a s, 3895

SIFT (2)

Jdg 7: 4 and *I will* s them for you there. 7671
Lk 22:31 Simon, Satan has asked *to* s you as wheat. *4985*

SIGH (1) [SIGHED, SIGHING]

Mk 7:34 up to heaven and **with a deep** s said to him, *5100*

SIGHED (1) [SIGH]

Mk 8:12 *He* s **deeply** and said, *417+3836+4460*

SIGHING (5) [SIGH]

Job 3:24 For s comes to me instead of food; 635
Ps 5: 1 O LORD, consider my s. 2052
38: 9 my s is not hidden from you. 635
Isa 35:10 and sorrow and s will flee away. 635
51:11 and sorrow and s will flee away. 635

SIGHT (143) [SEE]

Ge 6:11 Now the earth was corrupt in God's s 7156
33:18 and camped **within** s of the city. 907+7156
38: 7 was wicked in the LORD's s; 6524
38:10 What he did was wicked in the LORD's s; 6524
43:30 Deeply moved **at the** s **of** his brother, 448
Ex 3: 3 "I will go over and see this strange s— 5260
4:11 Who gives him s or makes him blind? 7221
10:28 Pharaoh said to Moses, "Get out of **my** *s!* AIT
17: 6 So Moses did this in the s *of* the elders 6524
19:11 on Mount Sinai in the s *of* all the people. 6524
40:38 in the s *of* all the house of Israel 6524
Lev 10: 3 the s *of* all the people I will be honored.' " 7156
26:16 and fever that will destroy your s 6524
Lev 26:45 in the s *of* the nations to be their God. 6524
Nu 20:12 in me enough to honor me as holy in the s 6524
20:27 They went up Mount Hor in the s *of* 6524
32:13 who had done evil in his s was gone. 6524
Dt 6:18 right and good in the LORD's s, 6524
9:18 doing what was evil in the LORD's s and 6524
24:13 **regarded** as a righteous act **in the** s **of** 4200+7156
31:29 upon you because you will do evil in the s 6524
34:12 the awesome deeds that Moses did in the s 6524
Jos 4:14 That day the LORD exalted Joshua in the s 6524
1Sa 2:17 was very great **in the** LORD's s, 907+7156
6:13 saw the ark, they rejoiced at the s. 8011
9:17 When Samuel **caught** s of Saul, 8011
2Sa 6:20 in the s *of* the slave girls of his servants 6524
7:19 And as if this were not enough in your s, 6524
7:29 that it may continue forever in your s; 7156
10:12 The LORD will do what is good in his s." 6524
13: 5 in my s so I may watch her and then eat it 6524
13: 6 and make some special bread in my s, 6524
13: 8 made the bread in his s and baked it. 6524
16:22 with his father's concubines in the s 6524
22:25 according to my cleanness in his s. 6524
1Ki 14: 4 his s was gone because of his age. 6524
2Ki 5: 1 in the s *of* his master and highly regarded, 7156
1Ch 2: 3 was wicked in the LORD's s; 6524
17:17 And as if this were not enough in your s, 6524
17:27 that it may continue forever in your s; 7156
19:13 The LORD will do what is good in his s." 6524
21: 7 This command was also evil in the s 6524
22: 5 and splendor **in the** s **of** all the nations. 4200
22: 8 shed much blood on the earth in my s. 7156
28: 8 in the s *of* all Israel and of the assembly of 6524
29:15 We are aliens and strangers in your s, 7156
29:25 in the s *of* all Israel and bestowed 6524
Ezr 9: 9 He has shown us kindness in the s *of* 7156
Ne 2: 5 and if your servant has found favor in his s, 7156
4: 5 or blot out their sins from your s, 4200+7156
9:28 they again did what was evil in your s. 7156
Job 11: 4 and I am pure in your s.' 6524
18: 3 as cattle and considered stupid in your s? 6524
41: 9 the mere s *of* him is overpowering. 5260
Ps 18:24 to the cleanness of my hands in his s. 6524
19:14 of my heart be pleasing in your s, 7156
31:19 which you bestow **in the** s **of** men 5584
31:22 "I am cut off from your s!" 6524
51: 4 and done what is evil in your s, 6524
72:14 for precious is their blood in his s. 6524
78:12 He did miracles **in the** s **of** their fathers in 5584
90: 4 in your s are like a day that has just gone 6524
116:15 Precious in the s *of* the LORD is the death 6524
146: 8 the LORD **gives** s *to* the blind, 7219
Pr 3: 4 and a good name in the s *of* God and man. 6524
3:21 do not let them out of your s; 6524
4:21 Do not let them out of your s, 6524
29:13 The LORD **gives** s *to* the eyes of both. 239
Isa 1:16 Take your evil deeds out of my s! 6524
5:21 in their own eyes and clever in their own s. 7156
31: 9 at s of the battle standard their commanders will panic," NIH
43: 4 you are precious and honored in my s, 6524
52:10 his holy arm in the s *of* all the nations, 6524
59:12 For our offenses are many **in** your s, 5584
65:12 evil in my s and chose what displeases me." 6524
66: 4 evil in my s and chose what displeases me." 6524
Jer 4: 1 out of my s and no longer go astray, 7156
18:10 it does evil in my s and does not obey me, 6524
18:23 or blot out their sins from your s. 4200+7156
31:36 if these decrees vanish from my s," 4200+7156
32:30 but evil in my s from their youth; 6524
32:31 and wrath that I must remove it from my s. 7156
34:15 and did what is right in my s: 6524
Eze 4:12 bake it in the s *of* the people, 6524
4:17 They will be appalled at the s of each other NIH
5: 8 and I will inflict punishment on you in the s 6524
5:14 in the s *of* all who pass by. 6524
16:41 and inflict punishment on you in the s 6524
20: 9 and in whose s I had revealed myself to 6524
20:14 in whose s I had brought them out. 6524
20:22 in whose s I had brought them out. 6524
20:41 among you in the s *of* the nations. 6524
28:18 in the s *of* all who were watching. 6524
28:25 among them in the s *of* the nations. 6524
36:17 a woman's monthly uncleanness in my s. 7156
36:34 of lying desolate in the s *of* all who pass 6524
38:23 and I will make myself known in the s 6524
39:27 through them in the s *of* many nations. 6524
Da 6:22 because I was found innocent **in** his s. 10621
Joel 2: 6 At the s *of* them, nations are in anguish; 7156
Jnh 2: 4 I said, 'I have been banished from your s; 6524
Hag 2:14 with this people and this nation in my s,' 7156
Mt 9:30 and their s was restored. *4057*
11: 5 The blind **receive** s, the lame walk, *329*
20:33 "Lord," they answered, "we want our s." *4057*
20:34 Immediately *they* **received** *their* s *329*
Mk 8:25 his eyes were opened, his s was restored, *NIG*
10:52 Immediately *he* **received** *his* s *329*
Lk 1: 6 Both of them were upright **in the** s of God, *1883*
1:15 for he will be great **in the** s of the Lord. *1967*
2:31 which you have prepared in the s of all *4725*
4:18 for the prisoners and **recovery of** s for *330*
7:21 and gave s to many who were blind. *1063*
7:22 The blind **receive** s, the lame walk, *329*
16:15 among men is detestable **in** God's s. *1967*
18:42 Jesus said to him, "**Receive** *your* s; *329*
18:43 Immediately *he* **received** *his* s *329*
23:48 to witness this s saw what took place, *2556*
24:31 and he disappeared from their s. *NIG*
Jn 9:15 also asked him how *he had* **received** *his* s. *329*
9:18 he had been blind and *had* **received** *his* s *329*
Ac 1: 9 and a cloud hid him from their s. *4057*
4:19 for yourselves whether it is right *in* God's s *1967*
7:31 When he saw this, he was amazed at the s. *3969*
9:12 place his hands on him to **restore** *his* s." *329*
22:13 'Brother Saul, **receive** *your* s!' *329*
28:15 *At* **the** s **of** these men Paul thanked God *3972*
Ro 2:13 not those who hear the law who are righteous **in God's** s, *2536+3836+4123*
3:20 declared righteous **in his** s by observing *899+1967*
4:17 He is our father **in the** s of God, *2978*
1Co 3:19 this world is foolishness **in God's** s. *2536+4123*
2Co 2:10 I have forgiven in the s of Christ *4725*
4: 2 to every man's conscience **in the** s of God. *1967*
5: 7 We live by faith, not by s. *1626*
12:19 We have been speaking **in the** s of God *2978*
Eph 1: 4 the world to be holy and blameless **in** his s. *2979*
Col 1:22 through death to present you holy in his s, *2979*
1Ti 5:21 **in the** s of God and Christ Jesus and *1967*
6:13 **In the** s of God, who gives life to everything *1967*
Heb 4:13 in all creation is hidden from God's s *1967*
12:21 The s was so terrifying that Moses said, *5751*
1Pe 3: 4 which is of great worth in God's s. *1967*
Rev 3: 2 not found your deeds complete **in the** s of *1967*

SIGHTING (1) [SEE]

Ac 21: 3 *After* s Cyprus and passing to the south *428*

SIGHTLESS (1) [SEE]

Isa 29: 9 blind yourselves and *be* s; 9129

SIGHTS (3) [SEE]

Dt 28:34 The s you see will drive you mad. 5260+6524
28:67 the terror that will fill your hearts and the s 5260
Pr 23:33 Your eyes *will* **see** strange *s* AIT

SIGN (87) [SIGNED, SIGNS]

Ge 9:12 "This is the s *of* the covenant I am making 253
9:13 be the s *of* the covenant between me and 253
9:17 the s *of* the covenant I have established 253
17:11 the s *of* the covenant between me and you. 253
49: 3 my might, the **first** *s of* my strength, AIT
Ex 3:12 the s to you that it is I who have sent you: 253
4: 8 or pay attention to the first **miraculous** s, 253
8:23 This **miraculous** s will occur tomorrow.' " 253
12:13 be a s for you on the houses where you are; 253
13: 9 This observance will be for you like a s 253
13:16 And it will be like a s on your hand and 253
31:13 a s between me and you for the generations 253
31:17 a s between me and the Israelites forever, 253
Nu 16:38 Let them be a s to the Israelites." 253
17:10 to be kept as a s to the rebellious. 253
26:10 And they served as a **warning** s. 5812
Dt 13: 1 and announces to you a **miraculous** s 253
13: 2 if the s or wonder of which he has spoken 253
21:17 the first s **of** his father's **strength.** 226
28:46 They will be a s and a wonder to you 253
Jos 2:12 Give me a sure s 253
4: 6 to serve as a s among you. 253
Jdg 6:17 give me a s that it is really you talking 253
1Sa 2:34 Hophni and Phinehas, will be a s to you— 253
14:10 be our s that the LORD has given them 253
1Ki 13: 3 That same day the man of God gave a s: 4603
13: 3 "This is the s the LORD has declared: 4603
13: 5 according to the s given by the man of God 4603
20:33 The men **took** *this* **as a good** s 5727
2Ki 19:29 "This will be the s for you, O Hezekiah: 253
20: 8 be the s that the LORD will heal me and 253
20: 9 "This is the LORD's s to you that 253
2Ch 32:24 and gave him a **miraculous** s. 4603
32:31 about the **miraculous** s that had occurred in 4603
Job 31:35 I s now my defense— 9338
Ps 86:17 Give me a s of your goodness, 253
Isa 7:11 "Ask the LORD your God for a s, 253
7:14 the Lord himself will give you a s: 253
19:20 be a s and witness to the LORD Almighty 253
20: 3 as a s and portent against Egypt and Cush, 253
37:30 "This will be the s for you, O Hezekiah: 253
38: 7 " 'This is the LORD's s to you that 253
38:22 be the s that I will go up to the temple of 253
55:13 for an everlasting s, which will not be 253
66:19 "I will set a s among them, 253
Jer 44:29 be the s to you that I will punish you 253
Eze 4: 3 This will be a s to the house of Israel. 253
12: 6 I have made you a s to the house of Israel." 4603
12:11 Say to them, 'I am a s *to* you.' 4603
20:12 Also I gave them my Sabbaths as a s 253
20:20 that they may be a s between us. 253
24:24 Ezekiel will be a s to you; 4603
24:27 So you will be a s to them, 4603
Mt 12:38 we want to see a **miraculous** s from you." *4956*
12:39 generation asks for a **miraculous** s! *4956*
12:39 But none will be given it except the s of *4956*
16: 1 asking him to show them a s from heaven. *4956*
16: 4 generation looks for a **miraculous** s, *4956*
16: 4 none will be given it except the s of Jonah." *4956*
24: 3 and what will be the s of your coming and *4956*
24:30 the s of the Son of Man will appear in *4956*
Mk 8:11 they asked him for a s from heaven. *4956*
8:12 does this generation ask for a **miraculous** s? *4956*
8:12 I tell you the truth, no s will be given to it." *4956*
13: 4 the s that they are all about to be fulfilled?" *4956*

Lk 2:12 This will be a s to you: *4956*
Lk 2:34 and to be a s that will be spoken against, *4956*
11:16 Others tested him by asking for a s *4956*
11:29 It asks for a **miraculous s,** *4956*
11:29 none will be given it except the s of Jonah. *4956*
11:30 For as Jonah was a s to the Ninevites, *4956*
21:7 be the s that they are about to take place?" *4956*
Jn 2:18 "What **miraculous** s can you show us *4956*
4:54 This was the second **miraculous s** *4956*
6:14 After the people saw the **miraculous** s *4956*
6:30 "What **miraculous** s then will you give *4956*
10:41 John never performed a **miraculous s,** *4956*
12:18 that he had given this **miraculous s,** *4956*
19:20 Many of the Jews read this **s,** *5518*
19:20 and the s was written in Aramaic, *NIG*
Ro 4:11 And he received the s of circumcision, *4956*
1Co 11:10 the woman ought to have a s of authority *NIG*
14:22 Tongues, then, are a s, not for believers *4956*
Php 1:28 a s to them that they will be destroyed, but *1893*
Rev 12:1 A great and **wondrous** s appeared in heaven *4956*
12:3 Then another s appeared in heaven: *4956*
15:1 in heaven another great and marvelous s: *4956*

SIGNAL (7) [SIGNALED, SIGNALING, SIGNALS]

Nu 10:6 The blast *will be the* s for setting out. 9546
10:7 blow the trumpets, but not *with the same* **s.** 8131
Jer 4:6 Raise the s to go to Zion! 5812
6:1 Raise the s over Beth Hakkerem! 5368
Zec 10:8 *I will* s for them and gather them in. 9239
Mt 26:48 the betrayer had arranged a s with them: *4956*
Mk 14:44 the betrayer had arranged a s with them: *5361*

SIGNALED (1) [SIGNAL]

Lk 5:7 So *they* s their partners in the other boat *2916*

SIGNALING (1) [SIGNAL]

Nu 31:6 from the sanctuary and the trumpets for **s.** 9558

SIGNALS (1) [SIGNAL]

Pr 6:13 s with his feet and motions with his fingers, 4911

SIGNED (3) [SIGN]

Jer 32:10 *I* s and sealed the deed, had it witnessed, 4180
32:12 and of the witnesses who *had* s the deed and 4180
32:44 and deeds *will be* s, sealed and witnessed 4180

SIGNET (10)

Ge 41:42 Then Pharaoh took his s **ring** 3192
Nu 31:50 armlets, bracelets, s **rings,** 3192
Est 3:10 So the king took his s **ring** from his finger 3192
8:2 The king took off his **s ring,** 3192
8:8 and seal it with the king's **s ring—** 3192
8:10 sealed the dispatches with the king's **s ring,** 3192
Isa 3:21 the s **rings** and nose rings, 3192
Jer 22:24 were a **s ring** on my right hand, 2597
Da 6:17 and the king sealed it with his own **s ring** 10536
Hag 2:23 'and I will make you like my **s ring,** 2597

SIGNIFICATION (KJV) See MEANING

SIGNIFY (KJV) See GIVE NOTICE, PETITION, POINTING, SPECIFYING

SIGNPOST (1)

Eze 21:19 a s where the road branches off to the city. 3338

SIGNS (76) [SIGN]

Ge 1:14 as s to mark seasons and days and years, 253
Ex 4:9 if they do not believe these two s or listen 253
4:17 so you can perform **miraculous s** with it." 253
4:28 the **miraculous** s he had commanded him 253
4:30 He also performed the s before the people, 253
7:3 and though I multiply my **miraculous s** 253
10:1 so that I may perform these **miraculous s** 253
10:2 the Egyptians and how I performed my s 253
Nu 14:11 of all the **miraculous s** I have performed 253
14:22 the **miraculous s** I performed in Egypt and 253
Dt 4:34 by testings, by **miraculous s** and wonders, 253
6:22 the LORD sent **miraculous** s and wonders, 253
7:19 the **miraculous** s and wonders, 253
11:3 the s he performed and the things he did in 253
26:8 with great terror and with **miraculous s** 253
29:3 those **miraculous s** and great wonders. 253
34:11 who did all those **miraculous** s and wonders 253
Jos 24:17 performed those great s before our eyes. 253
1Sa 10:7 Once these s are fulfilled, 253
10:9 and all these s were fulfilled that day. 253
Ne 9:10 You sent **miraculous** s and wonders 253
Ps 74:4 they set up their standards as s. 253
74:9 We are given no **miraculous s;** 253
78:43 the day he displayed his **miraculous s** 253
105:27 They performed his **miraculous s** 253
135:9 He sent his s and wonders into your midst, 253
Isa 8:18 We are s and symbols in Israel from 253
44:25 the s *of* false prophets and makes fools 253
Jer 10:2 or be terrified by s in the sky, 253
31:21 "Set up **road s;** put up guideposts. 7483
32:20 You performed **miraculous** s and wonders 253
32:21 Israel out of Egypt with s and wonders, 253

Da 4:2 about the **miraculous** s and wonders that 10084
Da 4:3 How great are his **s,** 10084
6:27 he performs s and wonders in the heavens 10084
Mt 16:3 but you cannot interpret the s of the times. *4956*
24:24 and perform great s and miracles to deceive *4956*
Mk 13:22 and perform s and miracles to deceive *4956*
16:17 these s will accompany those who believe: *4956*
16:20 with them and confirmed his word by the s *4956*
Lk 1:22 for he *kept* **making** s to them *1377+1639*
1:62 Then *they* **made** s to his father, *1935*
21:11 and fearful events and great s from heaven. *4956*
21:25 "There will be s in the sun, moon and stars. *4956*
Jn 2:11 This, the first *of* his **miraculous s,** *4956*
2:23 people saw the **miraculous** s he was doing *4956*
3:2 the **miraculous** s you are doing if God were *4956*
4:48 "Unless you people see **miraculous s** *4956*
6:2 the **miraculous** s he had performed on *4956*
6:26 not because you saw **miraculous** s but *4956*
7:31 Christ comes, will he do more **miraculous** s than this man?" *4956*
9:16 "How can a sinner do such **miraculous s?"** *4956*
11:47 this man performing many **miraculous s.** *4956*
12:37 after Jesus had done all these **miraculous s** *4956*
20:30 Jesus did many other **miraculous** s in *4956*
Ac 2:19 the heaven above and s on the earth below, *4956*
2:22 by God to you *by* miracles, wonders and **s,** *4956*
2:43 and **miraculous** s were done by *4956*
4:30 and perform **miraculous** s and wonders *4956*
5:12 The apostles performed many **miraculous s** *4956*
6:8 did great wonders and **miraculous** s among *4956*
7:36 of Egypt and did wonders and **miraculous s** *4956*
8:6 and saw the **miraculous** s he did, *4956*
8:13 by the great s and miracles he saw. *4956*
14:3 by enabling them to do **miraculous s** *4956*
15:12 and Paul telling about the **miraculous s** *4956*
Ro 15:19 by the power *of* s and miracles, *4956*
1Co 1:22 Jews demand **miraculous** s and Greeks *4956*
2Co 12:12 s, wonders and miracles— *4956*
2Th 2:9 of counterfeit miracles, s and wonders, *4956*
Heb 2:4 God also testified to it *by* **s,** *4956*
Rev 13:13 And he performed great and **miraculous s,** *4956*
13:14 the s he was given power to do on behalf of *4956*
16:14 of demons performing **miraculous s,** *4956*
19:20 the **miraculous** s on his behalf. *4956*
19:20 With these s he had deluded those who had received the mark of the beast *NIG*

SIHON (34) [SIHON'S]

Nu 21:21 Israel sent messengers to say to S king of 6095
21:23 But S would not let Israel pass 6095
21:26 the city of S king of the Amorites, 6095
21:28 a blaze from the city of **S.** 6095
21:29 his daughters as captives to S king of 6095
21:34 Do to him what you did to S king of 6095
32:33 of S king of the Amorites and the kingdom 6095
Dt 1:4 This was after he had defeated S king of 6095
2:24 I have given into your hand S the Amorite, 6095
2:26 of Kedemoth I sent messengers to S king 6095
2:30 But S king of Heshbon refused 6095
2:31 I have begun to deliver S and his country 6095
2:32 When S and all his army came out 6095
3:2 Do to him what you did to S king of 6095
3:6 as we had done with S king of Heshbon, 6095
4:46 in the land of S king of the Amorites, 6095
29:7 S king of Heshbon and Og king of 6095
31:4 to them what he did to S and Og, 6095
Jos 2:10 and what you did to S and Og, 6095
9:10 S king of Heshbon, and Og king of Bashan, 6095
12:2 S king of the Amorites, 6095
12:5 and half of Gilead to the border of S king 6095
13:10 all the towns of S king of the Amorites, 6095
13:21 the entire realm of S king of the Amorites, 6095
13:21 princes allied with **S—** 6095
13:27 the rest of the realm of S king of Heshbon 6095
Jdg 11:19 "Then Israel sent messengers to S king of 6095
11:20 **S,** however, did not trust Israel to pass 6095
11:21 gave S and all his men into Israel's hands, 6095
1Ki 4:19 (the country of S king of the Amorites and 6095
Ne 9:22 over the country of S king of Heshbon and 6095
Ps 135:11 S king of the Amorites, Og king of Bashan 6095
136:19 S king of the Amorites 6095
Jer 48:45 a blaze from the midst of **S;** 6095

SIHON'S (1) [SIHON]

Nu 21:27 let it be rebuilt; let S city be restored. 6095

SIHOR (KJV) See SHIHOR

SILAS (21)

Ac 15:22 and **S,** two men who were leaders among *4976*
15:27 Therefore we are sending Judas and S *4976*
15:32 Judas and **S,** who themselves were prophets, *4976*
15:40 but Paul chose S and left, *4976*
16:19 they seized Paul and S and dragged them *4976*
16:22 in the attack against **Paul and S,** *899S*
16:25 About midnight Paul and S were praying *4976*
16:29 in and fell trembling before Paul and **S.** *4976*
16:36 that you and S be released. *NIG*
16:38 that Paul and S were Roman citizens, *NIG*
16:40 After Paul and S came out of the prison, *NIG*
17:4 were persuaded and joined Paul and **S,** *4976*
17:5 to Jason's house in search of **Paul and S** *899S*
17:10 the brothers sent Paul and S away to Berea. *4976*
17:14 but S and Timothy stayed at Berea. *4976*
17:15 for S and Timothy to join him as soon *4976*
Ac 18:5 When S and Timothy came from *4976*
2Co 1:19 who was preached among you by me and S *4977*
1Th 1:1 Paul, S and Timothy, To the church of *4977*
2Th 1:1 Paul, S and Timothy, To the church of *4977*
1Pe 5:12 With the help of **S,** whom I regard *4977*

SILENCE (17) [SILENCED, SILENCES, SILENT]

Job 11:3 *Will* your idle talk **reduce** men to **s?** 3087
29:21 **waiting in** s for my counsel. 1957
Ps 8:2 to s the foe and the avenger. 8697
94:17 I would soon have dwelt in the s **of death.** 1872
101:5 him *will I* **put to s;** 7551
101:8 Every morning *I will* **put to** s all the wicked 7551
115:17 those who go down to **s;** 1872
143:12 In your unfailing love, s my enemies; 7551
Isa 25:5 *You* s the uproar of foreigners; 4044
47:5 "Sit *in* **s,** go into darkness, 1876
Jer 51:55 *he will* s her noisy din. 6
La 2:10 of Zion sit on the ground *in* **s;** 1949
3:28 Let him sit alone *in* **s,** 1957
Am 8:3 many bodies—flung everywhere! **S!"** 2187
Ac 19:33 for s in order to make a defense before *NIG*
1Pe 2:15 by doing good *you should* s the ignorant **talk** of foolish men. *5821*
Rev 8:1 there was s in heaven for about half an hour. *4968*

SILENCED (13) [SILENCE]

Nu 13:30 Caleb s the people before Moses and said, 2188
1Sa 2:9 but the wicked *will* **be s** in darkness. 1957
Job 23:17 Yet *I am* not s by the darkness, 7551
Ps 31:18 *Let* their lying lips **be s,** 519
63:11 while the mouths of liars *will* **be s.** 6126
Jer 47:5 Ashkelon *will* **be s.** 1949
48:2 *You* too, O Madmen, *will be* **s;** 1957
49:26 all her soldiers *will* **be s** in that day," 1959
50:30 all her soldiers *will* **be s** in that day," 1957
Eze 27:32 "Who was ever s like Tyre, 1951
Mt 22:34 Hearing that Jesus *had* s the Sadducees, *5821*
Ro 3:19 *be* s and the whole world held accountable *5852*
Tit 1:11 They must *be* **s,** because they are ruining *2187*

SILENCES (1) [SILENCE]

Job 12:20 *He* s the lips of trusted advisers 6073

SILENT (59) [SILENCE]

Lev 10:3 Aaron *remained* **s.** 1957
Dt 27:9 said to all Israel, *"Be* **s,** O Israel, and listen! 6129
1Sa 10:27 But Saul kept s. 3087
2Ki 18:36 people *remained* s and said nothing in reply, 3087
Est 4:14 For if *you* **remain** s at this time, 3087+3087
Job 7:11 "Therefore I *will* not **keep s;** 3104+7023
13:5 If only *you would be* **altogether s!** 3087+3087
13:13 *"Keep* s and let me speak; 3087
13:19 If so, *I will be* s and die. 3087
31:34 that *I kept* s and would not go outside 1957
32:16 Must I wait, now that *they are* **s,** 1819+4202
33:31 *be* **s,** and I will speak. 3087
33:33 *be* **s,** and I will teach you wisdom." 3087
34:29 if he *remains* **s,** who can condemn him? 9200
Ps 4:4 search your hearts and *be* **s.** 1957
22:2 by night, and am not s. 1875
28:1 For if *you remain* **s,** 3120
30:12 that my heart may sing to you and not *be* **s.** 1957
31:17 the wicked be put to shame and *lie* s in 1957
32:3 When *I kept* **s,** my bones wasted away 3087
35:22 O LORD, you have seen this; *be* not s. 3087
39:2 But *when I was* s and still, 519
39:9 *I was* **s;** I would not open my mouth, 519
50:3 Our God comes and *will* not *be* **s;** 3087
50:21 These things you have done and *I kept* **s;** 3087
83:1 O God, do not keep **s;** 1954
109:1 O God, whom I praise, *do* not *remain* **s,** 3087
Pr 17:28 Even a fool is thought wise if *he* **keeps s,** 3087
Ecc 3:7 a time to *be* s and a time to speak, 3120
Isa 23:2 *Be* **s,** *you* people of the island 1957
24:8 the joyful harp *is* **s.** 2532
36:21 *people remained* s and said nothing in reply, 3087
41:1 *"Be* s before me, you islands! 3087
42:14 "For a long time *I have kept* **s,** 3120
53:7 and as a sheep before her shearers *is* **s,** 519
57:11 not because I *have* long *been* s that you do 3120
62:1 For Zion's sake *I will* not *keep* **s,** 3120
62:6 *they will* never *be* s day or night. 3120
64:12 *Will you keep* s and punish us 3120
65:6 *I will* not *keep* s but will pay back in full; 3120
Jer 4:19 My heart pounds within me, *I* cannot *keep* **s.** 3087
Eze 3:26 of your mouth so that *you will be* s 519
24:27 with him and *will* no longer *be* **s.** 519
33:22 mouth was opened and *I was* no longer **s.** 519
Hab 1:13 Why *are you* s while the wicked swallow 3087
2:20 *let* all the earth **be** s before him." 2187
Zep 1:7 **Be** s before the Sovereign LORD, 2187
Mt 26:63 But Jesus *remained* **s.** *4995*
Mk 3:4 But they *remained* **s.** *4995*
14:61 But Jesus *remained* s and gave no answer. *4995*
Lk 1:20 now you will be s and not able to speak *4995*
14:4 But they *remained* **s.** *2483*
20:26 astonished by his answer, *they became* **s.** *4967*
Ac 8:32 and as a lamb before the shearer is **s,** *936*
15:12 The whole assembly *became* **s** *4967*
18:9 keep on speaking, *do* not *be* **s.** *4995*
21:40 When they were **all s,** *4498+4968*

1Co 14:34 women *should remain* s in the churches. 4967
1Ti 2:12 or have authority over a man; she must be s. 2484

SILK (1)

Rev 18:12 fine linen, purple, s and scarlet cloth; 4986

SILLA (1)

2Ki 12:20 at Beth Millo, on the road down to S. 6133

SILLY (KJV) See SENSELESS, SIMPLE, WEAK-WILLED

SILOAH (KJV) See SILOAM

SILOAM (4)

Ne 3:15 He also repaired the wall of the Pool of S, 8940
Lk 13: 4 when the tower in S fell on them— 4978
Jn 9: 7 in the Pool *of* S" (this word means Sent). 4978
9:11 He told me to go to S and wash. 4978

SILVER (343)

Ge 13: 2 wealthy in livestock and in s and gold. 4084
20:16 a thousand shekels of s. 4084
23:15 the land is worth four hundred shekels of s, 4084
23:16 four hundred shekels of s, 4084
24:35 s and gold, menservants and maidservants, 4084
24:53 the servant brought out gold and s jewelry 4084
33:19 For a hundred **pieces of s**, 7988
37:28 for twenty shekels of s to the Ishmaelites, 4084
42:25 to put each man's s back in his sack, 4084
42:27 and he saw his s in the mouth of his sack. 4084
42:28 "My s has been returned," 4084
42:35 in each man's sack was his pouch of s! 4084
43:12 Take double the amount of s with you, 4084
43:12 for you must return the s that was put back 4084
43:15 the gifts and double the amount of s, 4084
43:18 of the s that was put back into our sacks 4084
43:21 and each of us found his s— 4084
43:22 We have also brought additional s with us 4084
43:22 We don't know who put our s 4084
43:23 I received your s." 4084
44: 1 put each man's s in the mouth of his sack. 4084
44: 2 Then put my cup, the s one, 4084
44: 2 along with the s *for* his grain." 4084
44: 8 of Canaan the s we found inside the mouths 4084
44: 8 So why would we steal s or gold 4084
45:22 of s and five sets of clothes. 4084
Ex 3:22 for articles of s and gold and for clothing, 4084
11: 2 to ask their neighbors for articles of s 4084
12:35 the Egyptians for articles of s and gold and 4084
20:23 not make for yourselves gods of s or gods 4084
21:32 the owner must pay thirty shekels of s to 4084
22: 7 "If a man gives his neighbor s or goods 4084
25: 3 gold, s and bronze; 4084
26:19 and make forty s bases to go under them— 4084
26:21 and forty s bases—two under each frame. 4084
26:25 be eight frames and sixteen s bases— 4084
26:32 with gold and standing on four s bases. 4084
27:10 and twenty bronze bases and with s hooks 4084
27:11 and twenty bronze bases and with s hooks 4084
27:17 around the courtyard are to have s bands 4084
31: 4 to make artistic designs for work in gold, s 4084
35: 5 to bring to the LORD an offering of gold, s 4084
35:24 of s or bronze brought it as an offering to 4084
35:32 to make artistic designs for work in gold, s 4084
36:24 and made forty s bases to go under them— 4084
36:26 and forty s bases—two under each frame. 4084
36:30 sixteen s bases—two under each frame. 4084
36:36 for them and cast their four s bases. 4084
38:10 and with s hooks and bands on the posts. 4084
38:11 with s hooks and bands on the posts. 4084
38:12 with s hooks and bands on the posts. 4084
38:17 The hooks and bands on the posts were s, 4084
38:17 and their tops were overlaid with s; 4084
38:17 all the posts of the courtyard had s bands. 4084
38:19 Their hooks and bands were s, 4084
38:19 and their tops were overlaid with s. 4084
38:25 The s *obtained from* those of 4084
38:27 The 100 talents of s were used to cast 4084
Lev 5:15 without defect and of the proper value in s, 4084
27: 3 and sixty at fifty shekels of s, according to 4084
27: 6 the value of a male at five shekels of s and 4084
27: 6 and that of a female at three shekels of s. 4084
27:16 fifty shekels of s to a homer of barley seed. 4084
Nu 3:50 the Israelites he collected s weighing 1,365 4084
7:13 His offering was one s plate weighing 4084
7:13 one s sprinkling bowl weighing seventy 4084
7:19 offering he brought was one s plate 4084
7:19 one s sprinkling bowl weighing seventy 4084
7:25 His offering was one s plate weighing 4084
7:25 one s sprinkling bowl weighing seventy 4084
7:31 His offering was one s plate weighing 4084
7:31 one s sprinkling bowl weighing seventy 4084
7:37 His offering was one s plate weighing 4084
7:37 one s sprinkling bowl weighing seventy 4084
7:43 His offering was one s plate weighing 4084
7:43 one s sprinkling bowl weighing seventy 4084
7:49 His offering was one s plate weighing 4084
7:49 one s sprinkling bowl weighing seventy 4084
7:55 His offering was one s plate weighing 4084
7:55 one s sprinkling bowl weighing seventy 4084
7:61 His offering was one s plate weighing 4084
7:61 one s sprinkling bowl weighing seventy 4084
7:67 His offering was one s plate weighing 4084
Nu 7:67 one s sprinkling bowl weighing seventy 4084
7:73 His offering was one s plate weighing 4084
7:73 one s sprinkling bowl weighing seventy 4084
7:79 His offering was one s plate weighing 4084
7:79 one s sprinkling bowl weighing seventy 4084
7:84 when it was anointed: twelve s plates, 4084
7:84 twelve s sprinkling bowls 4084
7:85 Each s plate weighed a hundred and thirty 4084
7:85 the s dishes weighed two thousand four hundred shekels, 4084
10: 2 "Make two trumpets of hammered s, 4084
18:16 the redemption price set at five shekels of s, 4084
22:18 if Balak gave me his palace filled with s 4084
24:13 if Balak gave me his palace filled with s 4084
31:22 Gold, s, bronze, iron, tin, lead 4084
Dt 2: 6 to pay them in s for the food you eat and 4084
2:28 to eat and water to drink for their price in s. 4084
7:25 Do not covet the s and gold on them, 4084
8:13 and flocks grow large and your s 4084
14:25 then exchange your tithe for s, 4084
14:25 and take the s with you and go to the place 4084
14:26 Use the s to buy whatever you like: 4084
17:17 He must not accumulate large amounts of s 4084
22:19 They shall fine him a hundred shekels of s 4084
22:29 the girl's father fifty shekels of s. 4084
29:17 idols of wood and stone, of s and gold. 4084
Jos 6:19 All the s and gold and the articles of bronze 4084
6:24 but they put the s and gold and the articles 4084
7:21 two hundred shekels of s and a wedge 4084
7:21 with the s underneath." 4084
7:22 hidden in his tent, with the s underneath. 4084
7:24 took Achan son of Zerah, the s, the robe, 4084
22: 8 with large herds of livestock, with s, gold, 4084
24:32 that Jacob bought for a hundred **pieces of s** 7988
Jdg 5:19 but they carried off no s, no plunder. 4084
9: 4 They gave him seventy shekels of s from 4084
16: 5 will give you eleven hundred shekels of s." 4084
16:18 of the Philistines returned with the s 4084
17: 2 of s that were taken from you and 4084
17: 2 I have that s with me; I took it." 4084
17: 3 the eleven hundred shekels of s 4084
17: 3 "I solemnly consecrate my s to the LORD 4084
17: 4 So he returned the s to his mother, 4084
17: 4 and she took two hundred shekels of s 4084
17:10 and I'll give you ten shekels of s a year, 4084
1Sa 2:36 down before him for a piece of s and a crust 4084
9: 8 he said, "I have a quarter of a shekel of s. 4084
2Sa 8:10 with him articles of s and gold and bronze. 4084
8:11 as he had done with the s and gold from all 4084
18:11 to give you ten shekels of s and 4084
21: 4 "We have no right to demand s or gold 4084
24:24 and the oxen and paid fifty shekels of s 4084
1Ki 7:51 the s and gold and the furnishings— 4084
10:21 Nothing was made of s, 4084
10:21 because s was considered of little value NIH
10:22 s and ivory, and apes and baboons. 4084
10:25 articles of s and gold, robes, 4084
10:27 The king made s as common in Jerusalem 4084
10:29 from Egypt for six hundred shekels of s, 4084
15:15 the temple of the LORD the s and gold and 4084
15:18 the s and gold that was left in the treasuries 4084
15:19 See, I am sending you a gift of s and gold. 4084
16:24 of Samaria from Shemer for two talents of s 4084
20: 3 'Your s and gold are mine, 4084
20: 5 'I sent to demand your s and gold, 4084
20: 7 my s and my gold, I did not refuse him." 4084
20:39 or you must pay a talent of s.' 4084
2Ki 5: 5 taking with him ten talents of s, 4084
5:22 Please give them a talent of s and two sets 4084
5:23 then tied up the two talents of s in two bags, 4084
6:25 for eighty shekels of s, 4084
7: 8 They ate and drank, and carried away s, 4084
12:13 not spent for making s basins, 4084
12:13 of gold or s for the temple of the LORD; 4084
14:14 the gold and s and all the articles found in 4084
15:19 a thousand talents of s to gain his support 4084
15:20 to contribute fifty shekels of s to be given 4084
16: 8 And Ahaz took the s and gold found in 4084
18:14 of Judah three hundred talents of s 4084
18:15 the s that was found in the temple of 4084
20:13 the s, the gold, the spices and the fine oil— 4084
23:33 a levy of a hundred talents of s and a talent 4084
23:35 Jehoiakim paid Pharaoh Neco the s 4084
23:35 he taxed the land and exacted the s and gold 4084
25:15 all that were made of pure gold or s. 4084+4084
1Ch 18:10 of articles of gold and s and bronze. 4084
18:11 with the s and gold he had taken 4084
19: 6 the Ammonites sent a thousand talents of s 4084
22:14 a million talents of s, 4084
22:16 in gold and s, bronze and iron— 4084
28:14 and the weight of s for all the silver articles NIH
28:14 and the weight of silver for all the s articles 4084
28:15 of s for each silver lampstand and its lamps, 4084
28:15 of silver for each s lampstand and its lamps, NIH
28:16 the weight of s for the silver tables; 4084
28:16 the weight of silver for the s tables; 4084
28:17 the weight of s for each silver dish; 4084
28:17 the weight of silver for each s dish; NIH
29: 2 gold for the gold work, s for the silver, 4084
29: 2 gold for the gold work, silver for the s, 4084
29: 3 and s for the temple of my God, over and 4084
29: 4 and seven thousand talents of refined s, 4084
29: 5 for the gold work and the s *work*, 4084
29: 7 ten thousand talents of s, 4084
2Ch 1:15 The king made s and gold as common 4084
1:17 from Egypt for six hundred shekels of s, 4084
2: 7 a man skilled to work in gold and s, 4084
2Ch 2:14 He is trained to work in gold and s, 4084
5: 1 the s and gold and all the furnishings— 4084
9:14 of the land brought gold and s to Solomon. 4084
9:20 Nothing was made of s, 4084
9:20 because s was considered of little value NIH
9:21 s and ivory, and apes and baboons. 4084
9:24 articles of s and gold, and robes, 4084
9:27 The king made s as common in Jerusalem 4084
15:18 into the temple of God the s and gold and 4084
16: 2 the s and gold out of the treasuries of 4084
16: 3 See, I am sending you s and gold. 4084
17:11 gifts and s as tribute, and 4084
21: 3 Their father had given them many gifts of s 4084
24:14 also dishes and other objects of gold and s. 4084
25: 6 from Israel for a hundred talents of s. 4084
25:24 the gold and s and all the articles found in 4084
27: 5 a hundred talents of s, 4084
32:27 and he made treasuries for his s and gold 4084
36: 3 a levy of a hundred talents of s and a talent 4084
Ezr 1: 4 now be living are to provide him with s 4084
1: 6 with articles of s and gold, 4084
1: 9 gold dishes 30 s dishes 1,000 4084
1: 9 gold dishes 30 silver dishes 1,000 s pans 29 NIH
1:10 gold bowls 30 matching s bowls 410 4084
1:11 there were 5,400 articles of gold and of s. 4084
2:69 5,000 minas of s and 100 priestly garments. 4084
5:14 the gold and s articles of the house of God, 10362
6: 5 the gold and s articles of the house of God, 10362
7:15 to take with you the s and gold that the king 10362
7:16 with all the s and gold you may obtain from 10362
7:18 with the rest of the s and gold, 10362
7:22 up to a hundred talents of s, 10362
8:25 and I weighed out to them the offering of s 4084
8:26 I weighed out to them 650 talents of s, 4084
8:26 s articles weighing 100 talents, 4084
8:28 The s and gold are a freewill offering to 4084
8:30 Then the priests and Levites received the s 4084
8:33 the s and gold and the sacred articles into 4084
Ne 5:15 on the people and took forty shekels of s 4084
7:71 drachmas of gold and 2,200 minas of s. 4084
7:72 minas of s and 67 garments for priests. 4084
Est 1: 6 of white linen and purple material to s rings 4084
1: 6 and s on a mosaic pavement of porphyry, 4084
3: 9 and I will put ten thousand talents of s into 4084
Job 3:15 who filled their houses with s. 4084
22:25 the choicest s for you. 4084
27:16 up s like dust and clothes like piles of clay, 4084
27:17 and the innocent will divide his s. 4084
28: 1 for s and a place where gold is refined. 4084
28:15 nor can its price be weighed in s. 4084
42:11 and each one gave him a **piece of s** and 7988
Ps 12: 6 like s refined in a furnace of clay, 4084
66:10 you, O God, tested us; you refined us like s. 4084
68:13 the wings of [my] dove are sheathed with s, 4084
68:30 Humbled, may it bring bars of s. 4084
105:37 laden with s and gold, 4084
115: 4 But their idols are s and gold, 4084
119:72 to me than thousands of pieces of s 4084
135:15 The idols of the nations are s and gold, 4084
Pr 2: 4 and if you look for it as for s 4084
3:14 for she is more profitable than s 4084
8:10 Choose my instruction instead of s, 4084
8:19 what I yield surpasses choice s. 4084
10:20 The tongue of the righteous is choice s, 4084
16:16 to choose understanding rather than s! 4084
17: 3 The crucible for s and the furnace for gold, 4084
22: 1 to be esteemed is better than s or gold. 4084
25: 4 Remove the dross from the s, 4084
25:11 like apples of gold in settings of s. 4084
27:21 The crucible for s and the furnace for gold, 4084
Ecc 2: 8 I amassed s and gold for myself, 4084
12: 6 before the s cord is severed, 4084
SS 1:11 of gold, studded with s. 4084
3:10 Its posts he made of s, its base of gold. 4084
8: 9 we will build towers of s on her. 4084
8:11 to bring for its fruit a thousand shekels of s. 4084
Isa 1:22 Your s has become dross, 4084
2: 7 Their land is full of s and gold; 4084
2:20 and bats their idols of s and idols of gold, 4084
7:23 a thousand s shekels, 4084
13:17 not care for s and have no delight in gold. 4084
30:22 with s and your images covered with gold; 4084
31: 7 of s and gold your sinful hands have made. 4084
39: 2 the s, the gold, the spices, the fine oil, 4084
40:19 with gold and fashions s chains for it. 4084
46: 6 from their bags and weigh out s on 4084
48:10 See, I have refined you, though not as s; 4084
60: 9 with their s and gold, 4084
60:17 and s in place of iron. 4084
Jer 6:30 They are called rejected s, 4084
10: 4 They adorn it with s and gold; 4084
10: 9 Hammered s is brought from Tarshish 4084
32: 9 for him seventeen shekels of s. 4084
32:10 and weighed out the s on the scales. 4084
32:25 'Buy the field with s and have 4084
32:44 Fields will be bought for s, 4084
52:19 all that were made of pure gold or s. 4084+4084
Eze 7:19 They will throw their s into the streets, 4084
7:19 Their s and gold will not be able 4084
16:13 So you were adorned with gold and s; 4084
16:17 the jewelry made of my gold and s, 4084
22:18 They are but the dross of s. 4084
22:20 As men gather s, copper, iron, 4084
22:22 As s is melted in a furnace, 4084
27:12 they exchanged s, iron, tin and lead 4084
28: 4 and amassed gold and s in your treasuries. 4084

38:13 to carry off s and gold, 4084
Da 2:32 its chest and arms of s, 10362
2:35 the s and the gold were broken to pieces at 10362
2:45 the clay, the s and the gold to pieces. 10362
5:2 to bring in the gold and s goblets 10362
5:4 they praised the gods of gold and s, 10362
5:23 You praised the gods of s and gold, 10362
11:8 of s and gold and carry them off to Egypt. 4084
11:38 to his fathers he will honor with gold and s, 4084
11:43 the treasures of gold and s and all the riches 4084
Hos 2:8 who lavished on her the s and gold— 4084
3:2 So I bought her for fifteen shekels of s and 4084
8:4 With their s and gold they make idols 4084
9:6 Their treasures of s will be taken over 4084
13:2 for themselves from their s, 4084
Joel 3:5 For you took my s and my gold 4084
Am 2:6 They sell the righteous for s, 4084
8:6 with s and the needy for a pair of sandals, 4084
Na 2:9 Plunder the s! 4084
Hab 2:19 It is covered with gold and s; 4084
Zep 1:11 all who trade with s will be ruined. 4084
1:18 Neither their s nor their gold will be able 4084
Hag 2:8 'The s is mine and the gold is mine,' 4084
Zec 6:10 "Take [s and gold] from the exiles Heldai, NIH
6:11 Take the s and gold and make a crown, 4084
9:3 she has heaped up s like dust, 4084
11:12 So they paid me thirty pieces of s. 4084
11:13 the thirty pieces of s and threw them into 4084
13:9 I will refine them like s and test them 4084
14:14 great quantities of gold and s and clothing. 4084
Mal 3:3 He will sit as a refiner and purifier of s; 4084
3:3 the Levites and refine them like gold and s. 4084
Mt 10:9 along any gold or s or copper in your belts; 738
26:15 So they counted out for him thirty **s coins.** 736
27:3 with remorse and returned the thirty **s coins** 736
27:9 "They took the thirty **s coins,** 736
Lk 10:35 The next day he took out two **s coins** 1324
15:8 a woman has ten **s coins** and loses one. 1534
Ac 3:6 Then Peter said, "S or gold I do not have, 736
17:29 the divine being is like gold or s or stone— 738
19:24 who made s shrines of Artemis, 735
20:33 not coveted anyone's s or gold or clothing. 736
1Co 3:12 s, costly stones, wood, hay or straw, 738
2Ti 2:20 of gold and s, but also of wood and clay; 735
Jas 5:3 Your gold and s are corroded. 738
1Pe 1:18 not with perishable things such as s or gold 736
Rev 9:20 s, bronze, stone and wood— 735
18:12 s, precious stones and pearls; 738

SILVERSMITH (3)

Jdg 17:4 shekels of silver and gave them to a s, 7671
Pr 25:4 and out comes material for the s; 7671
Ac 19:24 A s named Demetrius, 737

SIMEON (43) [SIMEONITE, SIMEONITES]

Ge 29:33 So she named him S. 9058
34:25 two of Jacob's sons, S and Levi, 9058
34:30 Then Jacob said to S and Levi, 9058
35:23 Reuben the firstborn of Jacob, S, Levi, 9058
42:24 He had S taken from them and bound 9058
42:36 Joseph is no more and S is no more, 9058
43:23 Then he brought S out to them. 9058
46:10 The sons of S: Jemuel, Jamin, Ohad, 9058
48:5 just as Reuben and S are mine. 9058
49:5 "S and Levi are brothers— 9058
Ex 1:2 Reuben, S, Levi and Judah; 9058
6:15 The sons of S were Jemuel, Jamin, Ohad, 9058
6:15 These were the clans of S. 9058
Nu 1:6 from S, Shelumiel son of Zurishaddai; 9058
1:22 From the descendants of S: 9058
1:23 number from the tribe of S was 59,300. 9058
2:12 The tribe of S will camp next to them. 9058
2:12 of S is Shelumiel son of Zurishaddai. 9058
7:36 the leader of the people of S, 9058
10:19 over the division of the tribe of S, 1201+9058
13:5 from the tribe of S, Shaphat son of Hori; 9058
26:12 The descendants of S by their clans were: 9058
26:14 These were the clans of S; 9063
34:20 from the tribe of S; 1201+9058
Dt 27:12 S, Levi, Judah, Issachar, 9058
Jos 19:1 second lot came out for the tribe of S, 1201+9058
21:4 from the tribes of Judah, S and Benjamin. 9063
21:9 S they allotted the following towns 1201+9058
1Ch 2:1 Reuben, S, Levi, Judah, Issachar, Zebulun, 9058
4:24 The descendants of S: 9058
6:65 S and Benjamin they allotted 1201+9058
12:25 men of S, warriors ready for battle— 9058
2Ch 15:9 and S who had settled among them, 9058
34:6 In the towns of Manasseh, Ephraim and S, 9058
Eze 48:24 "S will have one portion; 9058
48:25 it will border the territory of S from east 9058
48:33 the gate of S, the gate of Issachar and 9058
Lk 2:25 there was a man in Jerusalem called S, 5208
2:28 S took him in his arms and praised God, 899S
2:34 Then S blessed them and said to Mary, 5208
3:30 the son of S, the son of Judah, 5208
Ac 13:1 Barnabas, S called Niger, 5208
Rev 7:7 from the tribe of S 12,000, 5208

SIMEONITE (1) [SIMEON]

Nu 25:14 the leader of a S family. 9063

SIMEONITES (8) [SIMEON]

Jos 19:8 the inheritance of the tribe of the S, 1201+9058
19:9 S was taken from the share of Judah, 1201+9058
Jos 19:9 So the S received their inheritance 1201+9058
Jdg 1:3 men of Judah said to the S their brothers, 9058
1:3 So the S went with them. 9058
1:17 of Judah went with the S their brothers 9058
1Ch 4:42 And five hundred of these S, 1201+9058
27:16 over the S: Shephatiah son of Maacah; 9063

SIMILAR (10) [SIMILARLY]

1Ki 7:8 set farther back, was s *in* design. 3869
2Ki 25:17 The other pillar, with its network, was s. 3869
Jer 36:32 And many s words were added to them. 3869
52:22 with its pomegranates, was s. 3869
Eze 41:21 one at the front of the Most Holy Place was s. 2021+3869+5260
42:11 with s exits and dimensions. 3869
42:11 S *to* the doorways on the north 3869
Zec 14:15 A s plague will strike the horses and mules, 4027
Mk 4:33 *With* many s parables Jesus spoke the word 5525
Jude 1:7 In a s way, Sodom and Gomorrah 3927

SIMILARLY (4) [SIMILAR]

2Ch 3:12 S one wing of the second cherub 2256
1Co 7:22 s, he who was a free man 3931
2Ti 2:5 S, if anyone competes as an athlete, 1254
Tit 2:6 S, encourage the young men to be 6058

SIMON (74) [PETER, SIMON'S]

Mt 4:18 S called Peter and his brother Andrew. 4981
10:2 first, S (who is called Peter) 4981
10:4 S the Zealot and Judas Iscariot, 4981
13:55 and aren't his brothers James, Joseph, S 4981
16:16 S Peter answered, "You are the Christ, 4981
16:17 "Blessed are you, S son of Jonah, 4981
17:25 "What do you think, S?" 4981
26:6 the home *of* a man known as S the Leper, 4981
27:32 they met a man from Cyrene, named S, 4981
Mk 1:16 he saw S and his brother Andrew casting 4981
1:29 and John to the home *of* S and Andrew. 4981
1:36 S and his companions went to look for him, 4981
3:16 S (to whom he gave the name Peter); 4981
3:18 of Alphaeus, Thaddaeus, S the Zealot 4981
6:3 Joseph, Judas and S? 4981
14:3 the table in the home *of* a man known as S 4981
14:37 "S," he said to Peter, "are you asleep? 4981
15:21 A certain man from Cyrene, S, 4981
Lk 4:38 the synagogue and went to the home *of* S. 4981
5:3 the boats, the one **belonging to S,** 1639+4981
5:4 he said to S, "Put out into deep water, 4981
5:5 S answered, "Master, we've worked hard 4981
5:8 When S Peter saw this, 4981
5:10 Then Jesus said to S, "Don't be afraid; 4981
6:14 S (whom he named Peter), 4981
6:15 S who was called the Zealot, 4981
7:40 Jesus answered him, "S, 4981
7:43 S replied, "I suppose the one who had 4981
7:44 he turned toward the woman and said *to* S, 4981
22:31 "S, Simon, Satan has asked to sift you 4981
22:31 S, Satan has asked to sift you as wheat. 4981
22:32 But I have prayed for you, S, NIG
23:26 they seized S from Cyrene, 4981
24:34 The Lord has risen and has appeared *to* S." 4981
Jn 1:40 Andrew, S Peter's brother, 4981
1:41 to find his brother S and tell him, 4981
1:42 "You are S son of John. 4981
6:8 Andrew, S Peter's brother, spoke up, 4981
6:68 S Peter answered him, "Lord, 4981
6:71 (He meant Judas, *the son of* S Iscariot, 4981
13:2 Judas Iscariot, *son of* S, to betray Jesus. 4981
13:6 He came to S Peter, who said to him, 4981
13:9 "Then, Lord," S Peter replied, 4981
13:24 S Peter motioned to this disciple and said, 4981
13:26 he gave it to Judas Iscariot, *son of* S. 4981
13:36 S Peter asked him, "Lord, 4981
18:10 Then S Peter, who had a sword, 4981
18:15 S Peter and another disciple were following Jesus. 4981
18:25 As S Peter stood warming himself, 4981
20:2 So she came running to S Peter and 4981
20:6 Then S Peter, who was behind him, 4981
21:2 S Peter, Thomas (called Didymus), 4981
21:3 "I'm going out to fish," S Peter told them, 4981
21:7 As soon as S Peter heard him say, 4981
21:11 S Peter climbed aboard and dragged 4981
21:15 Jesus said *to* S Peter, "Simon son of John, 4981
21:15 Jesus said to Simon Peter, "S son of John, 4981
21:16 Again Jesus said, "S son of John, 4981
21:17 third time he said to him, "S son of John, 4981
Ac 1:13 James son of Alphaeus and S the Zealot, 4981
8:9 a man named S had practiced sorcery in 4981
8:13 S himself believed and was baptized. 4981
8:18 When S saw that the Spirit was given at 4981
8:24 Then S answered, "Pray to the Lord for me 4981
9:43 for some time with a tanner named S. 4981
10:5 a man named S who is called Peter. 4981
10:6 He is staying with S the tanner, 4981
10:18 asking if S who was known 4981
10:19 "S, three men are looking for you. NIG
10:32 Send to Joppa for S who is called Peter. 4981
10:32 He is a guest in the home *of* S the tanner, 4981
11:13 'Send to Joppa for S who is called Peter. 4981
15:14 S has described to us how God 5208
2Pe 1:1 S Peter, a servant and apostle 5208

SIMON'S (4) [SIMON]

Mk 1:30 S mother-in-law was in bed with a fever, 4981
Lk 4:38 Now S mother-in-law was suffering from 4981
5:10 the sons of Zebedee, S partners. 4981
Ac 10:17 where S house was and stopped at the gate. 4981

SIMPLE (21) [SIMPLEHEARTED, SIMPLY]

Ex 18:22 the s cases they can decide themselves. 7785
18:26 but the s ones they decided themselves. 7785
2Ki 20:10 *"It is a* s *matter* for the shadow to go 7837
Job 5:2 and envy slays the s. 7331
Ps 19:7 are trustworthy, making wise the s. 7343
119:130 it gives understanding to the s. 7343
Pr 1:4 for giving prudence to the s, knowledge 7343
1:22 "How long will you s *ones* love your simple ways? 7343
1:22 "How long will you simple ones love your **s ways?** 7344
1:32 For the waywardness of the s will kill them, 7343
7:7 I saw among the s, I noticed among the 7343
8:5 You who are s, gain prudence; 7343
9:4 "Let all who are s come in here!" 7343
9:6 Leave your s **ways** and you will live; 7344
9:16 "Let all who are s come in here!" 7343
14:15 A s *man* believes anything, 7343
14:18 The s inherit folly, 7343
19:25 and the s will learn prudence; 7343
21:11 a mocker is punished, the s gain wisdom; 7343
22:3 but the s keep going and suffer for it. 7343
27:12 but the s keep going and suffer for it. 7343

SIMPLEHEARTED (1) [SIMPLE, HEART]

Ps 116:6 The LORD protects the s; 7343

SIMPLY (5) [SIMPLE]

Ge 43:7 We s answered his questions. 6584+7023
Mt 5:37 S let your 'Yes' be 'Yes,' and your 'No,' 1254
Ac 8:16 they had s been baptized into the name of 3668
1Co 9:17 I am s discharging the trust committed NIG
1Th 1:5 our gospel came to you not s with words, 3668

SIMRI (KJV) See SHIMRI

SIN (473) [SIN'S, SINFUL, SINFULNESS, SINNED, SINNER, SINNER'S, SINNERS, SINNING, SINS]

Ge 4:7 s is crouching at your door; 2633
15:16 for the s *of* the Amorites has not yet reached 6411
18:20 and Gomorrah is so great and their s so 2633
31:36 "What s *have* I *committed* 2633
39:9 then could I do such a wicked thing and s 2627
42:22 "Didn't I tell you not *to* s against the boy? 2627
Ex 10:17 Now forgive my s once more and pray to 2633
16:1 from Elim and came to the Desert of S, 6097
17:1 set out from the Desert of S, 6097
20:5 the children for the s *of* the fathers to 6411
23:33 or *they will* **cause** you **to** s against me, 2627
29:14 It is a **s offering.** 2633
29:36 Sacrifice a bull each day as a **s offering** 2633
30:10 with the blood of the atoning **s offering** for 2633
32:21 that you led them into such great **s?"** 2631
32:30 "You *have* **committed a** great s. 2627+2631
32:30 perhaps I can make atonement for your **s."** 2633
32:31 what **a** great s these people *have* **committed!** 2627+2631
32:32 But now, please forgive their **s—** 2633
32:34 I will punish them for their **s."** 2633
34:7 and forgiving wickedness, rebellion and s. 10258
34:7 and their children for the s *of* the fathers to 6411
34:9 forgive our wickedness and our s, 2633
Lev 4:3 a young bull without defect as a **s offering** 2633
4:3 as a sin offering for the s he has committed. 2633
4:8 the fat from the bull of the **s offering—** 2633
4:14 they become aware of the s they committed, 2633
4:14 a **s offering** and present it before the Tent 2633
4:20 as he did with the bull for the **s offering.** 2633
4:21 This is the **s offering** *for* the community. 2633
4:23 he is made aware of the s he committed, 2633
4:24 It is a **s offering.** 2633
4:25 the s **offering** with his finger and put it on 2633
4:26 make atonement for the man's **s,** 2633
4:28 he is made aware of the s he committed, 2633
4:28 as his offering for the s he committed 2633
4:29 the **s offering** and slaughter it at the place 2633
4:32 " 'If he brings a lamb as his s offering, 2633
4:33 and slaughter it for a **s offering** at the place 2633
4:34 the **s offering** with his finger and put it on 2633
4:35 for him for the s he has committed, 2633
5:6 as a penalty for the s he has committed, 2633
5:6 or goat from the flock as a **s offering;** 2633
5:6 make atonement for him for his **s.** 2633
5:7 to the LORD as a penalty for his **s—** 2627
5:7 one for a **s offering** and the other for 2633
5:8 the one for the **s offering.** 2633
5:9 the blood of the **s offering** against the side 2633
5:9 It is a **s offering.** 2633
5:10 for him for the s he has committed, 2633
5:11 for his s a tenth of an ephah of fine flour for 2627
5:11 of an ephah of fine flour for a **s offering.** 2633
5:11 because it is a **s offering.** 2633
5:12 It is a **s offering.** 2633
6:3 he **commits** any such s that people may do 2627

Lev 6:17 Like the s **offering** and the guilt offering, 2633
6:25 the regulations for the s **offering:** 2633
6:25 The s **offering** is to be slaughtered before 2633
6:30 But any s **offering** whose blood is brought 2633
7: 7 both the s **offering** and the guilt offering: 2633
7:37 the grain offering, the s **offering,** 2633
8: 2 the bull for the s **offering,** 2633
8:14 then presented the bull for the s **offering,** 2633
9: 2 "Take a bull calf for your s **offering** and 2633
9: 3 'Take a male goat for a s **offering,** 2633
9: 7 to the altar and sacrifice your s **offering** 2633
9: 8 and slaughtered the calf as a s **offering** 2633
9:10 of the liver from the s **offering,** as 2633
9:15 He took the goat for the people's s **offering** 2633
9:15 and **offered** it **for** a **s offering** 2627
9:22 And having sacrificed the s **offering,** 2633
10:16 about the goat of the s **offering** and found 2633
10:17 "Why didn't you eat the s **offering** in 2633
10:19 "Today they sacrificed their s **offering** 2633
10:19 if I had eaten the s **offering** today?" 2633
12: 6 a young pigeon or a dove for a s **offering.** 2633
12: 8 and the other for a s **offering.** 2633
14:13 in the holy place where the s **offering** and 2633
14:13 the s **offering,** the guilt offering belongs to 2633
14:19 the s **offering** and make atonement for 2633
14:22 one for a s **offering** and the other for 2633
14:31 one as a s **offering** and the other as 2633
15:15 the one for a s **offering** and the other for 2633
15:30 to sacrifice one for a s **offering** and 2633
16: 3 a s **offering** and a ram for a burnt offering. 2633
16: 5 a s **offering** and a ram for a burnt offering. 2633
16: 6 for his own s **offering** to make atonement 2633
16: 9 the LORD and sacrifice it for a s **offering.** 2633
16:11 for his own s **offering** to make atonement 2633
16:11 to slaughter the bull for his own s **offering.** 2633
16:15 then slaughter the goat for the s **offering** 2633
16:25 He shall also burn the fat of the s **offering** 2633
16:27 The bull and the goat for the s **offerings,** 2633
18:25 so I punished it for its s, 6411
19:22 the LORD for the s he has committed, 2633
19:22 and his s will be forgiven. 2633
23:19 for a s **offering** and two lambs, 2633
26:41 and they pay for their s, 6411
Nu 5: 7 and must confess the s he has committed. 2633
5:31 bear the **consequences of** her s.' " 6411
6:11 to offer one as a s **offering** and the other as 2633
6:14 without defect for a s **offering,** 2633
6:16 before the LORD and make the s **offering** 2633
7:16 one male goat for a s **offering;** 2633
7:22 one male goat for a s **offering;** 2633
7:28 one male goat for a s **offering;** 2633
7:34 one male goat for a s **offering;** 2633
7:40 one male goat for a s **offering;** 2633
7:46 one male goat for a s **offering;** 2633
7:52 one male goat for a s **offering;** 2633
7:58 one male goat for a s **offering;** 2633
7:64 one male goat for a s **offering;** 2633
7:70 one male goat for a s **offering;** 2633
7:76 one male goat for a s **offering;** 2633
7:82 one male goat for a s **offering;** 2633
7:87 goats were used for the s **offering.** 2633
8: 8 a second young bull for a s **offering.** 2633
8:12 a s **offering** to the LORD and the other for 2633
9:13 bear the **consequences of** his s. 2628
12:11 the s we have so foolishly committed. 2633
14:18 in love and forgiving s and rebellion. 6411
14:18 the children for the s *of* the fathers to 6411
14:19 forgive the s *of* these people, 6411
15:24 and a male goat for a s **offering.** 2633
15:25 an offering made by fire and a s **offering.** 2633
15:27 a year-old female goat for a s **offering.** 2633
18: 9 whether grain or s or guilt offerings, 2633
18:22 or they will bear the **consequences of** their s 2628
19: 9 it is for **purification from s.** 2633
27: 3 but he died for his own s and left no sons. 2628
28:15 be presented to the LORD as a s **offering.** 2633
28:22 as a s **offering** to make atonement for you. 2633
29: 5 as a s **offering** to make atonement for you. 2633
29:11 Include one male goat as a s **offering,** 2633
29:11 in addition to the s **offering** *for* atonement 2633
29:16 Include one male goat as a s **offering,** 2633
29:19 Include one male goat as a s **offering,** 2633
29:22 Include one male goat as a s **offering,** 2633
29:25 Include one male goat as a s **offering,** 2633
29:28 Include one male goat as a s **offering,** 2633
29:31 Include one male goat as a s **offering,** 2633
29:34 Include one male goat as a s **offering,** 2633
29:38 Include one male goat as a s **offering,** 2633
32:23 be sure that your s will find you out. 2633
33:11 the Red Sea and camped in the Desert of S. 6097
33:12 the Desert of S and camped at Dophkah. 6097
Dt 5: 9 the children for the s *of* the fathers to 6411
9:18 because of all the s you had committed, 2633
9:27 their wickedness and their s. 2633
15: 9 and you will be found **guilty of s.** 2628
20:18 *you will* s against the LORD your God. 2627
22:26 she has committed no s *deserving* death. 2628
23:21 of you and you will be **guilty of s.** 2628
24: 4 *Do* not **bring** s *upon* the land 2627
24:15 and you will be **guilty of s.** 2628
24:16 each is to die for his own **s.** 2628
Jos 22:17 Was not the s *of* Peor enough for us? 6411
22:17 not cleansed ourselves from that s, NIH
22:20 not the only one who died for his s.' " 6411
1Sa 2:17 This s *of* the young men was very great in 2633
3:13 because of the s he knew about; 6411
12:23 from me that I *should* s against the LORD 2627
1Sa 14:34 *Do* not s against the LORD by eating meat 2627
14:38 let us find out what s has been committed today. 2633
15:23 For rebellion is like the s *of* divination, 2633
15:25 forgive my s and come back with me, 2633
2Sa 12:13 "The LORD has taken away your s. 2633
22:24 before him and have kept myself from **s.** 6411
1Ki 8:34 then hear from heaven and forgive the s 2633
8:35 confess your name and turn from their s 2633
8:36 then hear from heaven and forgive the s 2633
8:46 "When *they* s against you— 2627
8:46 for there is no one who *does* not s— 2627
12:30 And this thing became a s; 2633
13:34 This was the s *of* the house of Jeroboam 2633
15:26 in the ways of his father and in his s, 2633
15:34 in the ways of Jeroboam and in his s, 2633
16: 2 **caused** my people Israel **to** s 2627
16:19 of Jeroboam and in the s he had committed 2633
16:26 of Jeroboam son of Nebat and in his s, 2633
17:18 to remind me of my s and kill my son?" 6411
21:22 to anger and *have* **caused** Israel **to** s.' 2627
22:52 who **caused** Israel **to s.** 2627
2Ki 12:16 from the guilt offerings and s **offerings** was 2633
17:21 and caused them to commit a great **s.** 2631
21:11 and *has* **led** Judah **into** s with his idols. 2627
21:16 the s that he had caused Judah to commit, 2633
23:17 including the s he committed, 2633
23:15 who *had* **caused** Israel **to s—** 2627
2Ch 6:25 then hear from heaven and forgive the s 2633
6:26 confess your name and turn from their s 2633
6:27 then hear from heaven and forgive the s 2633
6:36 "When *they* s against you— 2627
6:36 for there is no one who *does* not **s—** 2627
7:14 from heaven and will forgive their s 2633
19:10 to warn them not *to* s against the LORD; 870
19:10 Do this, and *you will* not **s.** 870
28:13 Do you intend to add to our s and guilt? 2633
29:21 and seven male goats as a s **offering** for 2633
29:23 the s **offering** were brought before the king 2633
29:24 **presented** their blood on the altar **for a s offering** 2627
29:24 the burnt offering and the s **offering** 2633
Ezr 6:17 as a s **offering** for all Israel, 10260
8:35 as a s **offering,** twelve male goats. 2633
Ne 6:13 to intimidate me so that *I would* **commit a s** 2627
10:33 for s **offerings** to make atonement 2633
13:26 even he *was* **led into** s *by* foreign women. 2627
Job 1:22 not s by charging God with wrongdoing. 2627
2:10 In all this, Job *did* not s in what he said. 2627
8: 4 gave them over to the **penalty of** their s. 7322
10: 6 and probe after my s— 2633
11: 6 God has even forgotten some of your s. 6411
11:14 the s that is in your hand and allow no evil 224
13:23 Show me my offense and my s. 2633
14:16 but not keep track of my s. 2633
14:17 you will cover over my s. 6411
15: 5 Your s prompts your mouth; 6411
31:11 a s to be judged. 6411
31:30 to s by invoking a curse against his life— 2627
31:33 if I have concealed my s as men do, 7322
33: 9 'I am pure and without s; 7322
34:37 To his s he adds rebellion; 2633
35: 6 If *you* s, how does that affect him? 2627
Ps 4: 4 In your anger *do* not s; 2627
17: 3 I have resolved that my mouth *will* not s. 6296
18:23 before him and have kept myself from s. 6411
32: 2 the man whose s the LORD does not count 6411
32: 5 Then I acknowledged my s to you and did 2633
32: 5 and you forgave the guilt of my s. 2633
36: 2 to detect or hate his s. 6411
38: 3 bones have no soundness because of my **s.** 2633
38:18 I am troubled by my s. 2633
39: 1 and keep my tongue from s; 2627
39:11 You rebuke and discipline men for their **s;** 6411
40: 6 burnt offerings and s **offerings** you did 2631
51: 2 and cleanse me from my s. 2633
51: 3 and my s is always before me. 2633
59: 3 against me for no offense or s *of* mine, 2633
66:18 If I had cherished s in my heart, 224
78:17 But they continued to s against him, 2627
89:32 I will punish their s with the rod, 7322
106:43 and they wasted away in their s. 6411
109:14 the s *of* his mother never be blotted out. 2633
119:11 in my heart that *I might* not s against you. 2627
119:133 let no s rule over me. 224
Pr 1:16 for their feet rush into s, 8273
5:22 the cords of his s hold him fast. 2633
10:19 When words are many, s is not absent, 7322
14: 9 Fools mock at **making amends for s,** 871
14:34 but s is a disgrace to any people. 2633
16: 6 love and faithfulness s is atoned for; 6411
17:19 He who loves a quarrel loves s; 7322
20: 9 I am clean and without s"? 2633
21: 4 the lamp of the wicked, are s! 2633
24: 9 The schemes of folly are s, 2633
29: 6 An evil man is snared by his own s, 7322
29:16 When the wicked thrive, so does s, 7322
Ecc 5: 6 Do not let your mouth **lead** you **into s.** 2627
Isa 3: 9 they parade their s like Sodom; 2633
5:18 Woe to those who draw s along with cords 6411
6: 7 and your s atoned for." 2633
22:14 "Till your dying day this s will not 6411
27: 9 be the full fruitage of the removal of his s: 2633
30: 1 but not by my Spirit, heaping s upon sin; 2633
30: 1 but not by my Spirit, heaping sin upon s; 2633
30:13 this s will become for you like a high wall, 6411
40: 2 that her s has been paid for, 6411
Isa 53:12 For he bore the s *of* many, 2628
59: 7 Their feet rush into s; 8273
64: 5 But when *we* continued *to* s against them, 2627
Jer 9: 3 They go from *one* s to another; 8288
9: 7 for what else can I do because of the s NIH
16:10 What s have we committed against 2633
16:17 nor is their s concealed from my eyes. 6411
16:18 for their wickedness and their s, 2633
17: 1 "Judah's s is engraved with an iron tool, 2633
17: 3 because of s throughout your country. 2633
31:30 Instead, everyone will die for his own s; 6411
32:35 a detestable thing and so **make** Judah **s.** 2627
33: 8 the s they have committed against me 6411
36: 3 I will forgive their wickedness and their **s."** 2633
La 2:14 they did not expose your s 6411
4:22 he will punish your s 6411
Eze 3:18 that wicked man will die for his s, 6411
3:19 he will die for his s; 6411
3:20 you did not warn him, he will die for his **s.** 2633
3:21 if you do warn the righteous man not to s 2627
3:21 not to sin and he *does* not s, 2627
4: 4 on your left side and put the s *of* the house 6411
4: 4 You are to bear their s for the number 6411
4: 5 of days as the years of their s. 6411
4: 5 So for 390 days you will bear the s *of* 6411
4: 6 and bear the s *of* the house of Judah. 6411
4:17 and will waste away because of their **s.** 6411
7:19 for it has made them stumble into **s.** 6411
9: 9 "The s *of* the house of Israel 6411
16:49 " 'Now this was the s *of* your sister Sodom: 6411
18:17 He withholds his hand from s 6404
18:17 He will not die for his father's s; 6411
18:18 But his father will die for his own s, 6411
18:24 from his righteousness and commits s 6404
18:26 from his righteousness and commits s, 6404
18:26 of the s he has committed he will die. 6404
18:30 then s will not be your downfall. 6411
29:16 but will be a reminder of their s in turning 6411
33: 6 man will be taken away because of his s, 6411
33: 8 that wicked man will die for his s, 6411
33: 9 he will die for his s, 6411
33:14 from his s and does what is just and right— 2633
39:23 of Israel went into exile for their s, 6411
40:39 on which the burnt offerings, s **offerings** 2633
42:13 the s **offerings** and the guilt offerings— 2633
43:19 You are to give a young bull as a s **offering** 2633
43:21 You are to take the bull for the s **offering** 2633
43:22 a male goat without defect for a s **offering,** 2633
43:25 a male goat daily for a s **offering;** 2633
44:10 must bear the **consequences of** their s. 6411
44:12 and made the house of Israel fall into s, 6411
44:12 must bear the **consequences of** their s, 6411
44:27 he is to offer a s **offering** for himself, 2633
44:29 the s **offerings** and the guilt offerings; 2633
45:17 He will provide the s **offerings,** 2633
45:19 the s **offering** and put it on the doorposts of 2633
45:22 a bull as a s **offering** for himself and for all 2633
45:23 and a male goat for a s **offering.** 2633
45:25 to make the same provision for s **offerings,** 2633
46:20 the s **offering** and bake the grain offering, 2633
Da 9:20 confessing my s and the sin of my people 2633
9:20 and the s *of* my people Israel 2633
9:24 to put an end to s, to atone for wickedness, 2633
Hos 5: 5 even Ephraim, stumble in their s; 6411
8:11 Ephraim built many altars for s **offerings,** 2627
10: 8 it is the s *of* Israel. 2633
10:10 to put them in bonds for their double s. 6411
12: 8 not find in me any iniquity or s." 2628
13: 2 Now *they* s more and more; 2627
Am 4: 4 "Go to Bethel and s; 7321
4: 4 go to Gilgal and s yet more. 7321
Mic 1:13 the beginning of s to the Daughter of Zion, 2633
3: 8 to Jacob his transgression, to Israel his **s.** 2633
6: 7 the fruit of my body for the s *of* my soul? 2633
7:18 Who is a God like you, who pardons s 6411
Zec 3: 4 "See, I have taken away your **s,** 6411
3: 9 'and I will remove the s *of* this land in 6411
13: 1 to cleanse them from s and impurity. 2633
Mal 2: 6 and turned many from s. 6411
Mt 5:29 If your right eye **causes** you *to* s, *4997*
5:30 And if your right hand **causes** you **to s,** *4997*
6:14 you forgive men when they **s against** you, *4183*
12:31 every s and blasphemy will be forgiven *281*
13:41 of his kingdom everything that **causes** s *4998*
18: 6 anyone **causes** one of these little ones who believe in me **to s,** *4997*
18: 7 the **things that cause** people **to s!** *4998*
18: 8 If your hand or your foot **causes** you **to s,** *4997*
18: 9 And if your eye **causes** you **to s,** *4997*
23:32 the measure of the s of your forefathers! *NIG*
Mk 3:29 he is guilty *of* an eternal s." *280*
9:42 anyone **causes** one of these little ones who believe in me **to s,** *4997*
9:43 If your hand **causes** you **to s,** cut it off. *4997*
9:45 And if your foot **causes** you to s, cut it off. *4997*
9:47 if your eye **causes** you **to s,** pluck it out. *4997*
Lk 17: 1 that **cause people to s** are bound to come, *4998*
17: 2 to **cause** one of these little ones **to s.** *4997*
Jn 1:29 who takes away the s of the world! *281*
8: 7 "If any one of you is **without s,** *387*
8:11 and **leave your life of s."** *279+3600*
8:21 and you will die in your s. *281*
8:34 everyone who sins is a slave *to* s. *281*
8:46 Can any of you prove me guilty of s? *281*
9:34 "You were steeped in s at birth; *281*
9:41 *you* would not **be guilty of s;** *281+2400*
15:22 *they would* not **be guilty of s.** *281+2400*

Jn 15:22 however, they have no excuse for their s. *281*
15:24 *they would* not **be guilty of s.** *281+2400*
16: 8 of guilt in regard to s and righteousness *281*
16: 9 in regard to s, because men do not believe *281*
19:11 *is* **guilty of** a greater s." *281+2400*
Ac 7:60 "Lord, do not hold this s against them." *281*
8:23 of bitterness and captive *to* s." *94*
Ro 2:12 All who s apart from the law will *279*
2:12 and all who s under the law will be judged *279*
3: 9 that Jews and Gentiles alike are all under s. *281*
3:20 through the law we become conscious *of* s. *281*
4: 8 the man whose s the Lord will never count *281*
5:12 as s entered the world through one man, *281*
5:12 through s, and in this way death came *281*
5:13 before the law was given, s was in the world. *281*
5:13 But s is not taken into account when there is *281*
5:14 even over those who *did* not s by breaking *279*
5:16 not like the result of the one man's s: *279*
5:16 The judgment followed one s *NIG*
5:20 But where s increased, grace increased *281*
5:21 just as s reigned in death, *281*
6: 2 We died *to* s; how can we live in it *281*
6: 6 so that the body *of* s might be done away *281*
6: 6 that we should no longer be slaves *to* s— *281*
6: 7 anyone who has died has been freed from s. *281*
6:10 The death he died, he died *to* s once for all; *281*
6:11 count yourselves dead *to* s but alive to God *281*
6:12 not let s reign in your mortal body so *281*
6:13 Do not offer the parts of your body *to* s, *281*
6:14 For s shall not be your master, *281*
6:15 *Shall we* s because we are not under law *279*
6:16 whether you are slaves to s, *281*
6:17 though you used to be slaves *to* s, *281*
6:18 from s and have become slaves *281*
6:20 When you were slaves *to* s, *281*
6:22 But now that you have been set free from s *281*
6:23 For the wages *of* s is death, *281*
7: 7 Is the law s? Certainly not! *281*
7: 7 not have known **what** s **was** except through *281*
7: 8 But s, seizing the opportunity afforded by *281*
7: 8 For apart from law, s is dead. *281*
7: 9 s sprang to life and I died. *281*
7:11 For s, seizing the opportunity afforded by *281*
7:13 in order that s might be recognized as sin, *281*
7:13 in order that sin might be recognized as s, *281*
7:13 through the commandment s might become utterly sinful. *281*
7:14 but I am unspiritual, sold as a slave to s. *281*
7:17 but it is s living in me. *281*
7:20 but it is s living in me that does it. *281*
7:23 the law *of* s at work within my members. *281*
7:25 in the sinful nature a slave to the law *of* s. *281*
8: 2 Spirit of life set me free from the law *of* s *281*
8: 3 the likeness of sinful man to be a s **offering.** *281*
8: 3 And so he condemned s in sinful man, *281*
8:10 your body is dead because of s, *281*
14:23 that does not come from faith is s. *281*
1Co 8:12 *When you* s against your brothers *279*
8:12 *you* s against Christ. *279*
8:13 I eat **causes** my brother *to* **fall into** s, *4997*
15:56 The sting of death is s, *281*
15:56 and the power *of* s is the law. *281*
2Co 5:21 God made him who had no s to be sin *281*
5:21 God made him who had no sin to be s *281*
11: 7 Was it a s for me to lower myself *281+4472*
11:29 Who *is* **led into** s, and I do not inwardly *4997*
12:21 the impurity, **sexual** s and debauchery *4518*
Gal 2:17 does that mean that Christ **promotes** s? *281+1356*
3:22 that the whole world is a prisoner of s, *281*
6: 1 Brothers, if someone is caught in a s, *4183*
Eph 4:26 "In your anger *do* not s": *279*
1Ti 5:20 Those who s are to be rebuked publicly, *279*
Heb 4:15 just as we are—yet was without s. *281*
9:26 at the end of the ages to do away *with* s by *281*
9:28 he will appear a second time, not to bear s, *281*
10: 6 and s **offerings** you were not pleased. *281+4309*
10: 8 burnt offerings and s **offerings** you did *281+4309*
10:18 there is no longer any sacrifice for s. *281*
11:25 to enjoy the pleasures *of* s for a short time. *281*
12: 1 and the s that so easily entangles, *281*
12: 4 In your struggle against s, *281*
13:11 into the Most Holy Place as a s **offering,** *281*
Jas 1:15 desire has conceived, it gives birth to s; *281*
1:15 and s, when it is full-grown, *281*
2: 9 *you* s and are convicted by the law *281+2237*
1Pe 2:22 "He committed no s, and no deceit was *281*
4: 1 who has suffered in his body is done with s. *281*
1Jn 1: 7 blood of Jesus, his Son, purifies us from all s. *281*
1: 8 If we claim to be **without** s, *281+4024*
2: 1 I write this to you so that *you will* not s. *279*
2: 1 But if anybody *does* s, *279*
3: 4 in fact, s is lawlessness. *281*
3: 5 And in him is no s. *281*
3: 6 No one who *continues to* s has either seen *279*
3: 9 No one who is born of God *will continue to* s, *281+4472*
5:16 If anyone sees his brother **commit a** s *279+281*
5:16 *to* those whose s does not lead to death. *279*
5:16 There is a s that leads to death. *281*
5:17 All wrongdoing is s, *281*
5:17 and there is s that does not lead to death. *281*
5:18 anyone born of God *does* not *continue to* s; *279*
Rev 2:14 the Israelites to s by eating food sacrificed *NIG*

SIN'S (1) [SIN]

Heb 3:13 of you may be hardened by s deceitfulness. *281*

SINA (KJV) See SINAI

SINAI (39) [HOREB]

Ex 16: 1 which is between Elim and S, 6099
19: 1 they came to the Desert of S. 6099
19: 2 they entered the Desert of S, 6099
19:11 the LORD will come down on Mount S in 6099
19:18 Mount S was covered with smoke, 6099
19:20 of Mount S and called Moses to the top of 6099
19:23 "The people cannot come up Mount S, 6099
24:16 glory of the LORD settled on Mount S. 6099
31:18 speaking to Moses on Mount S, 6099
34: 2 and then come up on Mount S. 6099
34: 4 the first ones and went up Mount S early in 6099
34:29 down from Mount S with the two tablets of 6099
34:32 the LORD had given him on Mount S. 6099
Lev 7:38 which the LORD gave Moses on Mount S 6099
7:38 to the LORD, in the Desert of S. 6099
25: 1 The LORD said to Moses on Mount S, 6099
26:46 that the LORD established on Mount S 6099
27:34 the LORD gave Moses on Mount S for 6099
Nu 1: 1 of S on the first day of the second month of 6099
1:19 And so he counted them in the Desert of S: 6099
3: 1 the LORD talked with Moses on Mount S. 6099
3: 4 before him in the Desert of S. 6099
3:14 to Moses in the Desert of S, 6099
9: 1 of S in the first month of the second year 6099
9: 5 of S at twilight on the fourteenth day of 6099
10:12 of S and traveled from place to place until 6099
26:64 the Israelites in the Desert of S. 6099
28: 6 instituted at Mount S as a pleasing aroma, 6099
33:15 and camped in the Desert of S. 6099
33:16 of S and camped at Kibroth Hattaavah. 6099
Dt 33: 2 from S and dawned over them from Seir; 6099
Jdg 5: 5 the One of S, before the LORD, 6099
Ne 9:13 "You came down on Mount S; 6099
Ps 68: 8 before God, the One of S, before God, 6099
68:17 Lord [has come] from S into his sanctuary. 6099
Ac 7:30 a burning bush in the desert near Mount S. *4982*
7:38 to him on Mount S, and with our fathers; *4982*
Gal 4:24 from Mount S and bears children who are *4982*
4:25 for Mount S in Arabia and corresponds to *4982*

SINCE (266)

Ge 3:19 s from it you were taken; 3954
4:25 s Cain killed him." 3954
14:12 s he was living in Sodom. 2256
15: 2 what can you give me s I remain childless 2256
26:27 s you were hostile to me 2256
38:26 s I wouldn't give her to my son 3954+4027+6584
41:39 "S God has made all this known to you, 339
42:23 s he was using an interpreter. 3954
44:28 And I have not seen him s. 2178+6330
46:30 s I have seen for myself 339
47:16 s your money is gone." 561
47:18 the fact that s our money is gone 561
Ex 4:10 nor s you have spoken to your servant. 255+4946
5:23 **Ever** s I went to Pharaoh to speak 255+4946
6:12 s I speak with faltering lips?" 2256
6:30 "S I speak with faltering lips, 2176
9:24 land of Egypt s it had become a nation. 255+4946
9:31 s the barley had headed and the flax was 3954
10:11 s that's what you have been asking for." 3954
21:21 s the slave is his property. 3954
23:21 s my Name is in him. 3954
Lev 10:18 S its blood was not taken into 2176
11:11 **And** s you are to detest them, 2256
13:13 S it has all turned white, he is clean. NIH
21: 3 on him s she has no husband— 889
25:15 on the basis of the number of years s 339
25:27 **the years** *s* he sold it and refund the balance AIT
27:26 s the firstborn already belongs to 889
Nu 5:13 (s there is no witness against her 2256
11:28 who had been Moses' aide s youth, 4946
14:25 S the Amalekites and Canaanites are living 2256
20:21 S Edom refused to let them go 2256
22:20 "S these men have come to summon you, 561
35:23 then s he was not his enemy and he did 2256
Dt 3:27 s you are not going to cross this Jordan. 3954
9:24 the LORD **ever** s I have known you. 3427+4946
12: 9 s you have not yet reached the resting place 3954
19: 6 s he did it to his neighbor 3954
21: 9 s you have done what is right in the eyes of 3954
21:14 s you have dishonored her. 889+9393
34:10 S **then,** no prophet has risen in Israel 6388
Jos 3: 4 s you have never been this way before. 3954
5: 6 s they had not obeyed the LORD. 889
7:26 called the Valley of Achor **ever** s. 2021+2021+2296+3427+6330
10:14 a day like it before or s, 339
13:14 s the offerings made by fire to the LORD, NIH
14:10 he has kept me alive for forty-five years s 4946
14:14 belonged to Caleb of Jephunneh the Kenizzite **ever** s, 2021+2021+2296+3427+6330
15:19 S you have given me land in the Negev, 3954
Jdg 1:15 S you have given me land in the Negev, 3954
11:23 "Now s the LORD, the God of Israel, 2256
15: 7 "S you've acted like this, 561
16:17 a Nazirite set apart to God s birth. 4946
17:13 s this Levite has become my priest." 3954
18: 7 And s their land lacked nothing, NIH
19:23 S this man is my guest, 339+889
19:30 not s the day the Israelites came up out 4946
21: 7 s we have taken an oath by the LORD not 2256
21:18 s we Israelites have taken this oath: 3954
Jdg 21:22 s you did not give your daughters 3954
Ru 2:11 mother-in-law s the death of your husband 339
3: 9 s you are a kinsman-redeemer." 3954
1Sa 16: 1 s I have rejected him as king over Israel? 2256
21: 6 s there was no bread there except the bread 3954
25: 8 s we come at a festive time. 3954
25:26 "Now s the LORD has kept you, 2256
27: 6 belonged to the kings of Judah **ever** s. 2021+2021+2296+3427+6330
2Sa 7:11 and have done **ever** s the time 4946
13:14 **and** s he was stronger than she, 2256
13:32 Absalom's expressed intention **ever** s 4946
19:11 to bring the king back to his palace, s 2256
19:26 s I your servant am lame, I said, 3954
1Ki 3:11 "S you have asked for this and not 889+3610
8:16 'S the day I brought my people Israel out 4946
8:39 s you know his heart (for you alone know 889
10:12 or seen s that day.) 6330
11:11 "S this is your attitude and you have 889+3610
18:12 worshiped the LORD s my youth. 4946
18:25 s there are so many of you. 3954
21: 2 s it is close to my palace. 3954
2Ki 10: 2 s your master's sons are with you 2256
14:27 **And** s the LORD had not said 2256
18:26 s we understand it. 3954
23:22 Not s the days of the judges who led Israel, 4946
1Ch 17:10 and have done **ever** s the time 4946
23:25 For David had said, "S the LORD, NIH
2Ch 1:11 "S this is your heart's desire and you 889+3610
1:11 and s you have not asked for a long life but 1685
2: 6 s the heavens, even the highest heavens, 3954
6: 5 'S the day I brought my people out 4946
6:30 s you know his heart (for you alone know 889
12: 7 "S they have humbled themselves, NIH
14: 6 s the land was at peace. 3954
14:14 s there was much booty there. 3954
22: 1 king in his place, s the raiders, 3954
28:23 for he thought, "S the gods of the kings 3954
30:17 S many in the crowd had 3954
30:26 for s the days of Solomon son 4946
31:10 "S the people began to bring their 4946
35:18 in Israel s the days of the prophet Samuel; 4946
Ezr 4: 2 and have been sacrificing to him s the time 4946
4:14 Now s we are under obligation to the palace 10168+10353+10619
Ne 6:18 s he was son-in-law to Shecaniah son 3954
Est 1:13 S it was customary for the king 3954
4:11 But thirty days have passed s I was called 4202
6:13 and his wife Zeresh said to him, "S 561
Job 9:29 S I am already found guilty, NIH
19:28 s the root of the trouble lies in him,' 2256
20: 4 **ever** s man was placed on the earth, 4974
21:22 s he judges even the highest? 2256
30: 2 s their vigor had gone from them? NIH
Ps 22: 8 Let him deliver him, s he delights in him." 3954
28: 5 S they show no regard for the works of 3954
31: 3 S you are my rock and my fortress, 3954
35: 7 S they hid their net for me without cause 3954
44:21 s he knows the secrets of the heart? 3954
45: 2 s God has blessed you forever. 4027+6584
71: 5 my confidence s my youth. 4946
71:17 S my youth, O God, you have taught me, 4946
Pr 1:24 **But** s you rejected me when I called 3610
1:25 s you ignored all my advice and would 2256
1:29 S they hated knowledge and did not 3954+9393
1:30 s they would not accept my advice NIH
6: 3 s you have fallen into your neighbor's 3954
17:16 s he has no desire to get wisdom? 2256
Ecc 5:16 s he toils for the wind? 8611
8: 4 S a king's word is supreme, 889+928
8: 7 S no man knows the future, 3954
9: 6 and their jealousy have **long** s vanished; 3893
Isa 7:17 a time unlike any s Ephraim broke away from Judah— 3427+4200+4946
36:11 s we understand it. 3954
40:21 not understood s the earth was founded? NIH
43: 4 S you are precious and honored 889+4946
44: 7 and lay out before me what has happened s 4946
46: 3 whom I have upheld s you were conceived, 4974
46: 3 and have carried s your birth. 4974
47:12 which you have labored at s childhood. 4946
47:15 with and trafficked with s childhood. 4946
64: 4 S ancient times no one has heard, 4946
Jer 8: 9 S they have rejected the word of 2180
8:21 S my people are crushed, I am crushed; 6584
32: 8 S it is your right to redeem it 3954
44:18 But **ever** s we stopped burning incense 255+4946
48: 7 S you trust in your deeds and riches, 3610+3954
50:15 S this is the vengeance of the LORD, 3954
Eze 3:20 S you did not warn him, 3954
18:19 S the son has done what is just and right 2256
23:35 S you have forgotten me and thrust me 3610
33: 5 S he heard the sound of the trumpet but did NIH
33:25 S you eat meat with the blood still in it NIH
35: 6 S you did not hate bloodshed, 561
Da 10:12 S the first day that you set your mind 4946
10:19 my lord, s you have given me strength." 3954
Hos 10: 9 "S the days of Gibeah, you have sinned, 4946
Mic 1: 7 S she gathered her gifts from the wages 3954
Hab 2:18 s a man has carved it? 3954
Zec 13: 5 the land has been my livelihood s 4946
Mal 3: 7 **Ever** s the time of your forefathers 4200+4946
Mt 13:21 s he has no root, he lasts only a short time. *NIG*
13:35 I will utter things hidden s the creation of *608*
18:25 *S he was* not **able** to pay, *AIT*
22:25 and *s he* **had** no children, *AIT*
22:28 s all of them were married to her?" *1142*

Mt 25:34 the kingdom prepared for you s the creation 608
27: 6 s it is blood money." 2075
Mk 2: 4 S they could not get him to Jesus because AIT
4:17 But s they have no root, NIG
8: 1 S they had nothing to eat, NIG
10:20 "all these I have kept s I was a boy." 1666
11:11 but s it was already late, AIT
12:23 s the seven were married to her?" 1142
Lk 1: 3 s I myself have carefully investigated NIG
1:34 Mary asked the angel, "s I am a virgin?" 2075
11:50 of all the prophets that has been shed s 608
12:26 S you cannot do this very little thing, 1623
16:16 S that time, the good news of the kingdom 608
18:21 "All these I have kept s I was a boy," 1666
19: 4 s Jesus was coming that way. 4022
20:33 s the seven were married to her?" 1142
20:36 s they are children of the resurrection. AIT
23:40 "s you are under the same sentence? 4022
24:21 it is the third day s all this took place. 608+4005
Jn 5:47 But s you do not believe what he wrote, 1623
7: 4 S you are doing these things, 1623
7:39 s Jesus had not yet been glorified. 4022
13:29 S Judas had charge of the money, 2075
19:42 of Preparation and s the tomb was nearby, 4022
Ac 4:14 But s they could see the man AIT
13:46 S you reject it and do not consider 2076
17:29 "Therefore s we are God's offspring, AIT
18:15 But s it involves questions about words 1623
19:36 Therefore, s these facts are undeniable, AIT
19:40 s there is no reason for it." AIT
21:34 s the commander could not get at the truth AIT
22:30 s the commander wanted to find out AIT
25:14 S they were spending many days there, 6055
26: 4 the way I have lived ever s I was a child, 1666
27:12 S the harbor was unsuitable to winter in, AIT
Ro 1:19 s what may be known about God is plain 1484
1:20 For s the creation of the world 608
1:28 s they did not think it worthwhile to retain 2777
2:15 s they show that the requirements of NIG
3:30 s there is only one God, 1642
4:19 s he was about a hundred years old— AIT
5: 1 s we have been justified through faith, AIT
5: 9 S we have now been justified by his blood, AIT
6: 9 For we know that s Christ was raised from AIT
10: 3 S they did not know the righteousness AIT
15:23 and s I have been longing for many years AIT
1Co 1:21 For s in the wisdom of God the world 2076
3: 3 For s there is jealousy and quarreling 3963
7: 2 But s there is so much immorality, 1328
8: 7 and s their conscience is weak, it is defiled. NIG
11: 7 s he is the image and glory of God; AIT
14:12 S you are eager to have spiritual gifts, 2075
14:16 s he does not know what you are saying? 2076
15:21 For s death came through a man, 2076
2Co 3:12 s we have such a hope, we are very bold. AIT
4: 1 Therefore, s through God's mercy we have this ministry, 2777
5:11 S, then, we know what it is to fear the Lord, AIT
7: 1 S we have these promises, dear friends, AIT
8: 6 s he had earlier made a beginning, 2777
9: 2 that s last year you in Achaia were ready 608
11:18 S many are boasting in the way 2075
11:19 You gladly put up with fools s you are AIT
13: 3 s you are demanding proof 2075
Gal 4: 7 and s you are a son, 1623
5:25 S we live by the Spirit, 1623
Eph 1:15 ever s I heard about your faith in AIT
6: 9 s you know that he who is both their Master AIT
Php 1: 7 s I have you in my heart; 1328
1:30 s you are going through the same struggle 2400
Col 1: 6 just as it has been doing among you s 608+4005
1: 9 s the day we heard about you, 608
2:20 S you died with Christ to the basic principles of this world, 1623
3: 1 S, then, you have been raised with Christ, 1623
3: 9 s you have taken off your old self AIT
3:15 s as members of one body you were called NIG
3:24 s you know that you will receive AIT
1Th 3: 8 s you are standing firm in the Lord. 1569
5: 8 But s we belong to the day, AIT
Tit 1: 7 S an overseer is entrusted with God's work, 1142
Heb 2:14 S the children have flesh and blood, 2075
4: 1 s the promise of entering his rest still stands, AIT
4: 3 And yet his work has been finished s 608
4:14 s we have a great high priest who has gone AIT
5: 2 s he himself is subject to weakness. 2075
6:13 s there was no one greater for him to swear 2075
7:23 s death prevented them from 1328+3836
9:26 to suffer many times s the creation of 608
10:13 S that time he waits for his enemies to 3370+3836
10:19 s we have confidence to enter the Most Holy AIT
10:21 and s we have a great priest over the house NIG
12: 1 s we are surrounded by such a great cloud AIT
12:28 s we are receiving a kingdom that cannot AIT
1Pe 1:17 S you call on a Father who judges each 1623
4: 1 Therefore, s Christ suffered in his body, AIT
2Pe 3: 4 Ever s our fathers died, 608+4005
3: 4 everything goes on as it has s the beginning 608
3:11 S everything will be destroyed AIT
3:14 s you are looking forward to AIT
3:17 dear friends, s you already know this, AIT
1Jn 2: 7 which you have had s the beginning. 608
4:11 Dear friends, s God so loved us, 1623
Rev 3:10 S you have kept my command 4022
16:18 No earthquake like it has ever occurred s man has been on the earth, 608+4005

SINCERE (11) [SINCERITY, SINCERELY]

Da 11:34 and many who are not s will join them. 2761
Ac 2:46 and ate together with glad and s hearts, 911
Ro 12: 9 Love must be s. 537
2Co 6: 6 in the Holy Spirit and in s love; 537
11: 3 from your s and pure devotion to Christ. 605
1Ti 1: 5 and a good conscience and a s faith. 537
3: 8 are to be men worthy of respect, s, 1474+3590
2Ti 1: 5 I have been reminded of your s faith, 537
Heb 10:22 near to God with a s heart in full assurance 240
Jas 3:17 of mercy and good fruit, impartial and s. 537
1Pe 1:22 by obeying the truth so that you have s love 537

SINCERELY (2) [SINCERE]

Job 33: 3 my lips s speak what I know. 1359
Php 1:17 preach Christ out of selfish ambition, not s, 56

SINCERITY (6) [SINCERE]

1Co 5: 8 the bread of s and truth. 1636
2Co 1:12 in the holiness and s that are from God. 1636
2:17 in Christ we speak before God with s, 1636
8: 8 to test the s of your love by comparing it 1188
Eph 6: 5 with respect and fear, and with s of heart, 605
Col 3:22 with s of heart and reverence for the Lord. 605

SINEWS (4)

Job 10:11 and knit me together with bones and s? 1630
40:17 the s of his thighs are close-knit. 1630
Isa 48: 4 the s of your neck were iron, 1630
Col 2:19 and held together by its ligaments and s, 5278

SINFUL (54) [SIN]

Dt 9:21 Also I took that s thing of yours, 2633
Ps 36: 4 he commits himself to a s course and 3202+4202
38: 5 and are loathsome because of my s folly. 222
51: 5 Surely I was s at birth, 6411
51: 5 s from the time my mother conceived me. 2628
Pr 12:13 An evil man is trapped by his s talk, 7322
Isa 1: 4 Ah, s nation, a people loaded with guilt, 2627
31: 7 of silver and gold your s hands have made. 2628
57:17 I was enraged by his s greed; 6411
Eze 37:23 save them from all their s backsliding, 2627
Hos 9:15 Because of their s deeds, 8278
Am 9: 8 the Sovereign LORD are on the s kingdom. 2629
Mk 8:38 in this adulterous and s generation, 283
Lk 5: 8 I am a s man!" 283
7:37 When a woman who had lived a s life in 283
24: 7 be delivered into the hands of s men, 283
Ro 1:24 over in the s desires of their hearts 2123
7: 5 when we were controlled by the s nature, 4922
7: 5 the s passions aroused by the law were 281
7:13 commandment sin might become utterly s. 283
7:18 lives in me, that is, in my s nature. 4922
7:25 but in the s nature a slave to the law of sin. 4922
8: 3 in that it was weakened by the s nature, 4922
8: 3 in the likeness of s man to be a sin offering. 281
8: 3 And so he condemned sin in s man, 4922
8: 4 to the s nature but according to the Spirit. 4922
8: 5 to the s nature have their minds set on what 4922
8: 6 The mind of s man is death, 4922
8: 7 the s mind is hostile to God. 4922
8: 8 by the s nature cannot please God. 4922
8: 9 are controlled not by the s nature but by 4922
8:12 but it is not to the s nature, 4922
8:13 For if you live according to the s nature, 4922
13:14 how to gratify the desires of the s nature. 4922
1Co 5: 5 so that the s nature may be destroyed 4922
Gal 5:13 use your freedom to indulge the s nature; 4922
5:16 not gratify the desires of the s nature. 4922
5:17 For the s nature desires what is contrary to 4922
5:17 the Spirit what is contrary to the s nature. 4922
5:19 The acts of the s nature are obvious: 4922
5:24 to Christ Jesus have crucified the s nature 4922
6: 8 The one who sows to please his s nature, 4922
Eph 2: 3 of our s nature and following its desires 4922
Col 2:11 in the putting off of the s nature, 4922
2:13 and in the uncircumcision of your s nature, 4922
1Ti 1: 9 ungodly and s, the unholy and irreligious; 283
Tit 3:11 be sure that such a man is warped and s; 279
Heb 3:12 See to it, brothers, that none of you has a s, 4505
12: 3 from s men, so that you will not grow weary 283
1Pe 2:11 to abstain from s desires, 4920
2Pe 2:10 of the s nature and despise authority. 4922
2:18 to the lustful desires of s human nature, 4922
1Jn 2:16 the cravings of s man, 4922
3: 8 He who does what is s is of the devil, 281

SINFULNESS (1) [SIN]

Ps 36: 1 concerning the s of the wicked: 7322

SING (122) [SANG, SINGER, SINGERS, SINGING, SINGS, SONG, SONGS, SUNG]

Ex 15: 1 "I will s to the LORD, 8876
15:21 "S to the LORD, for he is highly exalted. 8876
Nu 21:17 O well! S about it, 6702
Dt 31:19 the Israelites and have them s it, 928+7023+8492
Jdg 5: 3 I will s to the LORD, I will sing; 8876
5: 3 I will sing to the LORD, I will s; NIH
1Sa 21:11 the one they s about in their dances: 6702
2Sa 22:50 I will s praises to your name. 2376
1Ch 15:16 their brothers as singers to s joyful songs, 928+4200+7754+8123+9048
1Ch 16: 9 S to him, sing praise to him; 8876
16: 9 Sing to him, s praise to him; 2376
16:23 S to the LORD, all the earth; 8876
16:33 Then the trees of the forest will s, NIH
16:33 they will s for joy before the LORD, 8264
2Ch 20:21 to s to the LORD and to praise him for 8876
20:22 As they began to s and praise, 8262
31: 2 to give thanks and to s praises 2146
Job 21:12 They s to the music of tambourine and harp; 5951
29:13 I made the widow's heart s. 8264
Ps 5:11 let them ever s for joy. 8264
7:17 and will s praise to the name of the LORD 2376
9: 2 I will s praise to your name, 2376
9:11 S praises to the LORD, enthroned in Zion; 2376
13: 6 I will s to the LORD, 8876
18:49 I will s praises to your name. 2376
21:13 we will s and praise your might. 8876
27: 6 I will s and make music to the LORD. 8876
30: 4 S to the LORD, you saints of his; 2376
30:12 my heart may s to you and not be silent. 2376
32:11 s, all you who are upright in heart! 8264
33: 1 S joyfully to the LORD, 8264
33: 3 S to him a new song; 8876
47: 6 S praises to God, sing praises; 2376
47: 6 Sing praises to God, s praises; 2376
47: 6 s praises to our King, sing praises. 2376
47: 6 sing praises to our King, s praises. 2376
47: 7 s to him a psalm of praise. 2376
51:14 my tongue will s of your righteousness. 8264
57: 7 I will s and make music. 8876
57: 9 I will s of you among the peoples. 2376
59:16 But I will s of your strength, 8876
59:16 in the morning I will s of your love; 8264
59:17 O my Strength, I s praise to you; 2376
61: 8 Then will I ever s praise to your name 2376
63: 7 I s in the shadow of your wings. 8264
65:13 they shout for joy and s. 8876
66: 2 S the glory of his name; 2376
66: 4 they s praise to you, 2376
66: 4 they s praise to your name." 2376
67: 4 May the nations be glad and s for joy, 8264
68: 4 S to God, sing praise to his name, 8876
68: 4 Sing to God, s praise to his name, 2376
68:32 S to God, O kingdoms of the earth, 8876
68:32 s praise to the Lord, 2376
71:22 I will s praise to you with the lyre, 2376
71:23 My lips will shout for joy when I s praise 2376
75: 9 I will s praise to the God of Jacob. 2376
81: 1 S for joy to God our strength; 8264
87: 7 As they make music they will s, 8876
89: 1 I will s of the LORD's great love forever; 8876
89:12 Tabor and Hermon s for joy at your name. 8264
90:14 we may s for joy and be glad all our days. 8264
92: 4 I s for joy at the works of your hands. 8264
95: 1 Come, let us s for joy to the LORD; 8264
96: 1 S to the LORD a new song; 8876
96: 1 s to the LORD, all the earth. 8876
96: 2 S to the LORD, praise his name; 8876
96:12 all the trees of the forest will s for joy; 8264
96:13 they will s before the LORD, NIH
98: 1 S to the LORD a new song, 8876
98: 8 let the mountains s together for joy; 8264
98: 9 let them s before the LORD, NIH
101: 1 I will s of your love and justice; 8876
101: 1 to you, O LORD, I will s praise. 2376
104:12 they s among the branches. 5989+7754
104:33 I will s to the LORD all my life; 8876
104:33 I will s praise to my God as long as I live. 2376
105: 2 S to him, sing praise to him; 8876
105: 2 Sing to him, s praise to him; 2376
108: 1 I will s and make music with all my soul. 8876
108: 3 I will s of you among the peoples. 2376
119:172 May my tongue s of your word, 6702
132: 9 may your saints s for joy." 8264
132:16 and her saints will ever s for joy. 8264+8264
135: 3 s praise to his name, for that is pleasant. 2376
137: 3 they said, "S us one of the songs of Zion!" 8876
137: 4 How can we s the songs of the LORD 8876
138: 1 before the "gods" I will s your praise. 2376
138: 5 May they s of the ways of the LORD, 8876
144: 9 I will s a new song to you, O God; 8876
145: 7 and joyfully s of your righteousness. 8264
146: 2 I will s praise to my God as long as I live. 2376
147: 1 How good it is to s praises to our God, 2376
147: 7 S to the LORD with thanksgiving; 6702
149: 1 S to the LORD a new song, 8876
149: 5 in this honor and s for joy on their beds. 8264
Pr 29: 6 but a righteous one can s and be glad. 8264
Isa 5: 1 I will s for the one I love a song 8876
12: 5 S to the LORD, for he has done glorious 2376
12: 6 Shout aloud and s for joy, people of Zion, 8264
23:16 play the harp well, s many a song, NIH
27: 2 In that day—"S about a fruitful vineyard: 6702
30:29 And you will s as on the night you celebrate 8877
38:18 death cannot s your praise; 2146
38:20 and we will s with stringed instruments all 5594
42:10 S to the LORD a new song, 8876
42:11 Let the people of Sela s for joy; 8264
44:23 S for joy, O heavens, 8264
54: 1 "S, O barren woman, you who never bore 8264
65:14 My servants will s out of the joy 8264
Jer 20:13 S to the LORD! 8876
31: 7 "S with joy for Jacob; 8264
Hos 2:15 There she will s as in the days 6702
Zep 3:14 S, O Daughter of Zion; 8264
Ro 15: 9 I will s hymns to your name." 6010
15:11 and s praises to him, all you peoples." 2046

1Co 14:15 *I will* s with my spirit, *6010*
14:15 but *I will* also s with my mind. *6010*
Eph 5:19 S and make music in your heart to the Lord, *106*
Col 3:16 and *as you* s psalms, hymns and *106*
Heb 2:12 of the congregation *I will* s your **praises.**" *5630*
Jas 5:13 *Let him* s **songs of praise.** *6010*

SINGED (1)
Da 3:27 nor **was** a hair of their heads s; 10283

SINGER (1) [SING]
2Sa 23: 1 by the God of Jacob, Israel's s *of* songs: 5834

SINGERS (31) [SING]
Jdg 5:11 the voice of the s at the watering places. 2952
2Sa 19:35 the voices of *men* and women s? 8876
1Ch 15:16 of the Levites to appoint their brothers as s 8876
15:27 and as were the s, and Kenaniah, 8876
2Ch 5:13 The trumpeters and s joined in unison, 8876
23:13 and blowing trumpets, and s 8876
29:28 while the s sang and the trumpeters played. 8877
35:25 the *men* and women s commemorate Josiah 8876
Ezr 2:41 The s: the descendants of Asaph 128 8876
2:65 and they also had 200 *men* and women s. 8876
2:70 The priests, the Levites, the s, 8876
7: 7 Levites, s, gatekeepers and temple servants, 8876
7:24 Levites, s, gatekeepers, temple servants 10234
10:24 From the s: Eliashib. 8876
Ne 7: 1 and the s and the Levites were appointed. 8876
7:44 The s: the descendants of Asaph 148 8876
7:67 and they also had 245 *men* and women s. 8876
7:73 the s and the temple servants, 8876
10:28 priests, Levites, gatekeepers, s, 8876
10:39 the gatekeepers and the s stay. 8876
11:22 who *were* the s responsible for the service 8876
11:23 The s were under the king's orders, 8876
12:28 The s also were brought together from 1201+8876
12:29 for the s had built villages for themselves 8876
12:45 as did also the s and gatekeepers, 8876
12:46 there had been directors for the s and for 8876
12:47 the daily portions for the s and gatekeepers. 8876
13: 5 for the Levites, s and gatekeepers, as well 8876
13:10 and that all the Levites and s responsible 8876
Ps 68:25 In front are the s, after them the musicians; 8876
Ecc 2: 8 I acquired *men* and women s, 8876

SINGING (20) [SING]
Ge 31:27 with joy and s to the music of tambourines 8877
Ex 32:18 it is the sound of s that I hear." 6702
1Sa 18: 6 the towns of Israel to meet King Saul with s 8876
1Ch 15:22 the head Levite was in charge of the s; 5362
15:27 who was in charge of the s *of* the choirs. 5362
2Ch 23:18 with rejoicing and s, as David had ordered. 8877
29:27 s *to* the LORD began also, 8877
Ps 63: 5 with s lips my mouth will praise you. 8265
68: 6 he leads forth the prisoners with s; 3938
98: 5 with the harp and the sound of s, 2379
SS 2:12 the season of s has come, 2369
Isa 14: 7 they break into s. 8262
24:16 From the ends of the earth we hear s: 2369
35:10 They will enter Zion with s; 8262
51: 3 thanksgiving and the sound of s. 2379
51:11 They will enter Zion with s; 8262
Am 8:10 into mourning and all your s into weeping. 8877
Zep 3:17 he will rejoice over you with s." 8262
Ac 16:25 and Silas *were* praying and s **hymns** to God, *5630*
Rev 5:13 and all that is in them, s: *3306*

SINGLE (24) [SINGLED, SINGLENESS]
Ge 41: 5 were growing on a s stalk. 285
41:22 full and good, growing on a s stalk. 285
Ex 23:29 But I will not drive them out in a s year, 285
26:24 and fitted into a s ring; 285
36:29 the way to the top and fitted into a s ring; 285
Nu 13:23 they cut off a branch bearing a s cluster 285
Dt 29:21 The LORD *will* s him **out** from all the 976
Jdg 9:18 murdered his seventy sons on a s stone, 285
1Ki 16:11 He did not spare a *s* **male,** AIT
Est 3:13 on a s day, the thirteenth day of the month 285
Isa 9:14 both palm branch and reed in a s day; 285
10:17 a s day it will burn and consume his thorns 285
47: 9 on a s day: loss of children and widowhood. 285
Eze 37:19 making them a s stick of wood, 285
Zec 3: 9 I will remove the sin of this land in a s day. 285
Mt 6:27 Who of you by worrying can add **a** s hour *1651*
23:15 over land and sea to win **a** s convert, *1651*
27:14 not even to **a** s charge— *1651*
Lk 12:25 Who of you by worrying can add **a** s hour *1651*
Jn 12:24 it remains **only a** s seed. *3668*
Ac 27:34 of you will lose a s hair from his head." *NIG*
Gal 5:14 law is summed up in **a** s command: *1651*
Heb 12:16 who for **a** s meal sold his inheritance rights *1651*
Rev 21:21 each gate made of **a** s pearl. *1651*

SINGLED (1) [SINGLE]
1Ki 8:53 For you s them **out** from all the nations of 976

SINGLENESS (1) [SINGLE]
Jer 32:39 I will give them s of heart and action, 285

SINGS (3) [SING]
Pr 25:20 is *one who* s songs to a heavy heart. 8876
Isa 16:10 no *one* s or shouts in the vineyards; 8264
Eze 33:32 nothing more than one who s love songs NIH

SINITES (2)
Ge 10:17 Hivites, Arkites, S, 6098
1Ch 1:15 Hivites, Arkites, S, 6098

SINK (8) [SANK, SINKING, SINKS, SUNK]
Dt 28:43 but you *will* s lower and lower. 3718
Ps 69: 2 *I* s in the miry depths, 3190
69:14 Rescue me from the mire, *do not let me* s; 3190
Jer 51:64 'So *will* Babylon s to rise no more because 9205
Eze 27:27 on board *will* s into the heart of the sea on 5877
Am 8: 8 it will be stirred up and then s like the river 9205
Mt 14:30 beginning *to* s, cried out, "Lord, save me!" *2931*
Lk 5: 7 both boats so full that they *began to* s. *1112*

SINK (Anglicized) See also MELT WITH FEAR

SINKING (1) [SINK]
Ac 20: 9 *who was* s into a deep sleep as Paul talked *2965*

SINKS (2) [SINK]
Isa 5:24 and as dry grass s **down** in the flames, 8332
Am 9: 5 then s like the river of Egypt— 9205

SINNED (89) [SIN]
Ex 9:27 "This time *I have* s," he said to them. 2627
9:34 and thunder had stopped, *he* s again: 2627
10:16 *"I have* s against the LORD your God and 2627
32:33 "Whoever *has* s against me I will blot out 2627
Lev 5: 5 he must confess in what way *he has* s 2627
Nu 6:11 to make atonement for him because *he* s 2627
14:40 "We *have* s," they said. 2627
16:38 of the men who s at the cost of their lives. 2629
21: 7 *"We* s when we spoke against the LORD 2627
22:34 to the angel of the LORD, *"I have* s. 2627
Dt 1:41 you replied, *"We have* s against the LORD. 2627
9:16 that *you had* s against the LORD your God; 2627
Jos 7:11 Israel *has* s; they have violated my covenant 2627
7:20 I *have* s against the LORD, 2627
Jdg 10:10 *"We have* s against you, 2627
10:15 the Israelites said to the LORD, *"We have* s. 2627
1Sa 7: 6 *"We have* s against the LORD." 2627
12:10 to the LORD and said, *'We have* s; 2627
15:24 Then Saul said to Samuel, *"I have* s. 2627
15:30 Saul replied, *"I have* s. 2627
26:21 Then Saul said, *"I have* s. 2627
2Sa 12:13 *"I have* s against the LORD." 2627
19:20 For I your servant know that I *have* s, 2627
24:10 *"I have* s greatly in what I have done. 2627
24:17 "I *am the one who has* s and done wrong. 2627
1Ki 8:33 an enemy because *they have* s against you, 2627
8:35 because your people *have* s against you, 2627
8:47 *'We have* s, we have done wrong, 2627
8:50 who *have* s against you; 2627
16:25 of the LORD and s more than all those 8317
2Ki 17: 7 because the Israelites *had* s against 2627
1Ch 21: 8 *"I have* s greatly by doing this. 2627
21:17 I am the one who *has* s and done wrong. 2627
2Ch 6:24 an enemy because *they have* s against you 2627
6:26 because your people *have* s against you, 2627
6:37 *'We have* s, we have done wrong 2627
6:39 who *have* s against you. 2627
Ezr 10:13 because we have s greatly in this thing. 7321
Ne 9:29 *They* s against your ordinances, 2627
13:26 like these that Solomon king of Israel s? 2627
Job 1: 5 "Perhaps my children *have* s 2627
7:20 If *I have* s, what have I done to you, 2627
8: 4 When your children s against him, 2627
10:14 If *I* s, you would be watching me 2627
24:19 the grave snatches away *those who have* s. 2627
33:27 Then he comes to men and says, *'I* s, 2627
36: 9 that they have s arrogantly. 7322
Ps 41: 4 heal me, for *I have* s against you." 2627
51: 4 *have I* s and done what is evil in your sight, 2627
106: 6 *We have* s, even as our fathers did; 2627
Isa 42:24 against whom *we have* s? 2627
43:27 Your first father s; 2627
Jer 2:35 because you say, *'I have* not s.' 2627
3:25 *We have* s against the LORD our God, 2627
8:14 because *we have* s against him. 2627
14: 7 *we have* s against you. 2627
14:20 *we have* indeed s against you. 2627
40: 3 because *you people* s against the LORD 2627
44:23 and *have* s against the LORD and have 2627
50: 7 for *they* s against the LORD, 2627
50:14 for *she has* s against the LORD. 2627
La 1: 8 Jerusalem *has* **s greatly** and 2627+2628
3:42 "*We have* s and rebelled and you have 7321
5: 7 Our fathers s and are no more, 2627
5:16 Woe to us, for *we have* s! 2627
Eze 28:16 with violence, and *you* s. 2627
Da 9: 5 *we have* s and done wrong. 2627
9: 8 with shame because *we have* s against you. 2627
9:11 because *we have* s against you. 2627
9:15 *we have* s, we have done wrong. 2627
Hos 4: 7 the more *they* s against me; 2627
10: 9 "Since the days of Gibeah, *you have* s, 2627
Mic 7: 9 Because *I have* s against him, 2627
Zep 1:17 because *they have* s against the LORD. 2627
Mt 27: 4 *"I have* s," he said, *279*
Lk 15:18 *I have* s against heaven and against you. *279*
15:21 *I have* s against heaven and against you. *279*
Jn 9: 2 His disciples asked him, "Rabbi, who s, *279*
9: 3 "Neither this man nor his parents s," *279*
Ro 3:23 all *have* s and fall short of the glory of God, *279*
5:12 death came to all men, because all s— *279*
1Co 7:28 But if you do marry, *you have* not s; *279*
7:28 and if a virgin marries, *she has* not s. *279*
2Co 12:21 be grieved over many who *have* s **earlier** *4579*
13: 2 not spare those who s **earlier** or any of *4579*
Heb 3:17 Was it not *with* those who s, *279*
Jas 5:15 If *he has* s, he will be forgiven. *281+1639+4472*
2Pe 2: 4 For if God did not spare angels *when they* s, *279*
1Jn 1:10 If we claim *we have* not s, *279*

SINNER (20) [SIN]
Pr 11:31 how much more the ungodly and the s! 2627
13: 6 but wickedness overthrows the s. 2633
13:21 Misfortune pursues the s, 2629
Ecc 2:26 but to the s he gives the task of gathering 2627
7:26 but the s she will ensnare. 2627
9: 2 As it is with the good man, so with the s; 2627
9:18 but one s destroys much good. 2627
Lk 7:39 what kind of woman she is—that she is a s." *283*
15: 7 in heaven over one s who repents than *283*
15:10 the angels of God over one s who repents." *283*
18:13 'God, have mercy on me, a s.' *283*
19: 7 "He has gone to be the guest of a 's.' " *283+467*
Jn 9:16 "How can a s do such miraculous signs?" *283+476*
9:24 "We know this man is a s." *283*
9:25 He replied, "Whether he is a s or not, *283*
Ro 3: 7 why am I still condemned as a s?" *283*
1Co 14:24 **convinced** by all **that** *he* **is a s** *1794*
1Ti 2:14 woman who was deceived and became a s. *4126*
Jas 5:20 turns a s from the error of his way will save *283*
1Pe 4:18 what will become of the ungodly and the s?" *283*

SINNER'S (1) [SIN]
Pr 13:22 but a s wealth is stored up for the righteous. 2627

SINNERS (44) [SIN]
Nu 32:14 "And here you are, a brood of s, 2629
Ps 1: 1 in the way of s or sit in the seat of mockers. 2629
1: 5 nor s in the assembly of the righteous. 2629
25: 8 therefore he instructs s in his ways. 2629
26: 9 Do not take away my soul along with s, 2629
37:38 But all s will be destroyed; 7321
51:13 and s will turn back to you. 2629
104:35 But may s vanish from the earth and 2629
Pr 1:10 My son, if s entice you, 2629
23:17 Do not let your heart envy s, 2629
Isa 1:28 But rebels and s will both be broken, 2629
13: 9 the land desolate and destroy the s within it. 2629
33:14 The s in Zion are terrified; 2629
Am 9:10 All the s *among* my people will die by 2629
Mt 9:10 many tax collectors and "s" came and ate *283*
9:11 with tax collectors and 's'?" *283*
9:13 I have not come to call the righteous, but s." *283*
11:19 a friend *of* tax collectors and "s." ' *283*
26:45 Son of Man is betrayed into the hands *of* s. *283*
Mk 2:15 many tax collectors and "s" were eating *283*
2:16 with the "s" and tax collectors, *283*
2:16 with tax collectors and 's'?" *283*
2:17 I have not come to call the righteous, but s." *283*
14:41 Son of Man is betrayed into the hands *of* s. *283*
Lk 5:30 and drink with tax collectors and 's'?" *283*
5:32 to call the righteous, but s to repentance." *283*
6:32 Even 's' love those who love them. *283*
6:33 Even 's' do that. *283*
6:34 Even 's' lend to 'sinners,' *283*
6:34 Even 'sinners' lend *to* 's,' *283*
7:34 a friend of tax collectors and "s." ' *283*
13: 2 that these Galileans were worse s than all *283*
15: 1 the tax collectors and "s" were all gathering *283*
15: 2 "This man welcomes s and eats with them." *283*
Jn 9:31 We know that God does not listen to s. *283*
Ro 5: 8 While we were still s, Christ died for us. *283*
5:19 of the one man the many were made s, *283*
Gal 2:15 Jews by birth and not 'Gentile s' *283*
2:17 it becomes evident that we ourselves are s, *283*
1Ti 1:15 Christ Jesus came into the world to save s— *283*
1:16 so that in me, the worst of s, *NIG*
Heb 7:26 set apart from s, exalted above the heavens. *283*
Jas 4: 8 Wash your hands, *you* s, *283*
Jude 1:15 the harsh words ungodly s have spoken *283*

SINNING (20) [SIN]
Ge 13:13 of Sodom were wicked and were s greatly 2629
20: 6 and so I have kept you from s against me. 2627
Ex 20:20 be with you to keep *you* from s." 2627
Nu 15:28 for the one who erred by s unintentionally, 2630
32:23 *you will be* s against the LORD; 2627
1Sa 14:33 the men *are* s against the LORD 2627
Job 35: 3 and what do I gain by not s?' 2633
Ps 78:32 In spite of all this, *they* kept on s; 2627
Jer 9: 5 they weary themselves with s. 6390
Hos 8:11 these have become altars for s. 2627
Jn 5:14 Stop s or something worse may happen *279*
Ro 6: 1 on s so that grace may increase? *281*
1Co 7:36 *He is* not s. They should get married. *279*
11:27 be **guilty of** s **against** the body and blood *1944*
15:34 to your senses as you ought, and stop s; *279*
Heb 10:26 *on* s after we have received the knowledge *279*
2Pe 2:14 eyes full of adultery, they never stop s; *281*

1Jn 3: 6 No one who lives in him *keeps on* s. *279*
3: 8 the devil *has been* s from the beginning. *279*
3: 9 he cannot *go on* s, because he has been born *279*

SINS (292) [SIN]

Ge 50:17 I ask you to forgive your brothers the s and 7322
50:17 Now please forgive the s *of* the servants of 7322
Lev 4: 2 'When anyone s unintentionally 2627
4: 3 " 'If the anointed priest s, 2627
4:13 Israelite community s **unintentionally** 8706
4:22 " 'When a leader s unintentionally 2627
4:27 of the community s unintentionally 2627
5: 1 " 'If a person s because he does not speak 2627
5:13 for any of these s he has committed, 2633
5:15 a violation and s unintentionally in regard 2627
5:17 "If a person s and does what is forbidden 2627
6: 2 "If anyone s and is unfaithful to the LORD 2627
6: 4 when *he* thus s and becomes guilty, 2627
16:16 whatever their s have been. 2633
16:21 all their s—and put them on the goat's head. 2633
16:22 The goat will carry on itself all their s to 6411
16:30 you will be clean from all your s. 2633
16:34 to be made once a year for all the s *of* 2633
26:18 punish you for your s seven times over. 2633
26:21 seven times over, as your s deserve. 2633
26:24 afflict you for your s seven times over. 2633
26:28 punish you for your s seven times over. 2633
26:39 of their enemies because of their s; 6411
26:39 of their fathers' s they will waste away. 6411
26:40 if they will confess their s and the sins 6411
26:40 if they will confess their sins and the s 6411
26:43 for their s because they rejected my laws 6411
Nu 14:34 for your s and know what it is like 6411
15:27 " 'But if just one person s unintentionally, 2627
15:29 everyone *who* s **unintentionally,** 928+6913+8705
15:30 anyone who s **defiantly,** 928+3338+6913+8123
16:22 the entire assembly when only one man s?" 2627
16:26 be swept away because of all their s." 2633
Jos 24:19 not forgive your rebellion and your s. 2633
1Sa 2:25 If a man s against another man, 2627
2:25 but if a man s against the LORD, 2627
12:19 for we have added to all our other s the evil 2633
1Ki 14:16 because of the s Jeroboam has committed 2633
14:22 By the s they committed they stirred 2633
15: 3 He committed all the s his father had done 2633
15:30 because of the s Jeroboam had committed 2633
16: 2 and to provoke me to anger by their s. 2633
16:13 because of all the s Baasha and his son 2633
16:19 because of the s he had committed, 2633
16:31 to commit the s *of* Jeroboam son of Nebat, 2633
2Ki 3: 3 he clung to the s *of* Jeroboam son of Nebat, 2633
10:29 not turn away from the s *of* Jeroboam son 2628
10:31 not turn away from the s *of* Jeroboam, 2633
13: 2 by following the s *of* Jeroboam son of 2633
13: 6 But they did not turn away from the s *of* 2633
13:11 and did not turn away from any of the s 2633
14: 6 each is to die for his own s." 2628
14:24 and did not turn away from any of the s 2633
15: 9 not turn away from the s *of* Jeroboam son 2633
15:18 not turn away from the s *of* Jeroboam son 2633
15:24 not turn away from the s *of* Jeroboam son 2633
15:28 not turn away from the s *of* Jeroboam son 2633
17:22 the s *of* Jeroboam and did not turn away 2633
21:11 of Judah has committed these **detestable s.** 9359
24: 3 of the s *of* Manasseh and all he had done, 2633
2Ch 25: 4 each is to die for his own s." 2628
28:10 But aren't you also **guilty of s** against 873
33:19 as well as all his s and unfaithfulness, 2633
Ezr 9: 6 because our s are higher than our heads 6411
9: 7 Because of our s, we and our kings 6411
9:13 you have punished us less than our s have deserved 6411
Ne 1: 6 I confess the s we Israelites, 2633
4: 5 not cover up their guilt or blot out their s 2633
9: 2 and confessed their s and the wickedness 2633
9:37 Because of our s, its abundant harvest goes 2633
Job 7:21 not pardon my offenses and forgive my s? 6411
13:23 How many wrongs and s have I committed? 2633
13:26 and make me inherit the s *of* my youth. 6411
22: 5 Are not your s endless? 6411
31:28 then these also would be s to be judged, 6411
35: 6 your s are many, what does that do to him? 7322
Ps 5:10 Banish them for their many s, 7322
19:13 Keep your servant also from **willful s;** 2294
25: 7 the s *of* my youth and my rebellious ways; 2633
25:18 and my distress and take away all my s. 2633
32: 1 are forgiven, whose s are covered. 2631
40:12 my s have overtaken me, and I cannot see. 6411
51: 9 from my s and blot out all my iniquity. 2628
59:12 For the s *of* their mouths, 2633
65: 3 When we were overwhelmed by s, 1821+6411
68:21 hairy crowns of those who go on in their s. 871
79: 8 Do not hold against us the s *of* the fathers; 6411
79: 9 and forgive our s for your name's sake. 2633
85: 2 of your people and covered all their s. 2633
90: 8 our secret s in the light of your presence. NIH
94:23 He will repay them for their s 224
103: 3 who forgives all your s and heals all your 6411
103:10 not treat us as our s deserve or repay us 2628
109:15 May their s always remain before NIH
130: 3 If you, O LORD, kept a record of s, 6411
130: 8 redeem Israel from all their s. 6411
Pr 14:21 He who despises his neighbor s, 2627
28:13 He who conceals his s does not prosper, 7322
29:22 and a hot-tempered one commits many s. 7322
Ecc 7:20 on earth who does what is right and never s. 2627
Isa 1:18 "Though your s are like scarlet, 2628
13:11 the world for its evil, the wicked for their s. 6411
14:21 a place to slaughter his sons for the s 6411
26:21 to punish the people of the earth for their s. 6411
33:24 s of those who dwell there will be forgiven. 6411
38:17 you have put all my s behind your back. 2628
40: 2 the LORD's hand double for all her s. 2633
43:24 But you have burdened me with your s 2633
43:25 and remembers your s no more. 2633
44:22 your s like the morning mist. 2633
50: 1 Because of your s you were sold; 6411
58: 1 and to the house of Jacob their s. 2633
59: 2 your s have hidden his face from you, 2633
59:12 and our s testify against us. 2633
59:20 to those in Jacob who repent of their s," 7322
64: 6 and like the wind our s sweep us away. 6411
64: 7 and made us waste away because of our s. 6411
64: 9 do not remember our s forever. 6411
65: 7 both your s and the sins of your fathers," 6411
65: 7 both your sins and the s *of* your fathers," 6411
Jer 2:13 "My people have committed two s: 8288
5:25 your s have deprived you of good. 2633
11:10 to the s *of* their forefathers, 6411
13:22 it is because of your many s 6411
14: 7 Although our s testify against us, 6411
14:10 and punish them for their s." 2633
15:13 of all your s throughout your country. 2633
18:23 not forgive their crimes or blot out their s 2633
30:14 your guilt is so great and your s so many. 2633
30:15 and many s I have done these things to you. 2633
31:34 and will remember their s no more." 2633
32:18 the fathers' s into the laps of their children 6411
33: 8 and will forgive all their s of rebellion 6411
50:20 and for the s *of* Judah, 2633
51: 6 Do not be destroyed because of her s. 6411
La 1: 5 because of her many s. 7322
1:14 "My s have been bound into a yoke; 7322
1:22 with me because of all my s. 7322
3:39 when **punished for** his s? 2628
4:13 of the s *of* her prophets and the iniquities 2633
Eze 7:13 Because of their s, not one of them 6411
7:16 each because of his s. 6411
14:11 defile themselves anymore with all their s. 7322
14:13 a country s against me by being unfaithful 2627
16:51 Samaria did not commit half the s you did. 2633
16:52 Because your s were more vile than theirs, 2633
18: 4 The soul who s is the one who will die. 2627
18:14 a son who sees all the s his father commits, 2633
18:20 The soul who s is the one who will die. 2627
18:21 from all the s he has committed 2633
18:24 of and because of the s he has committed, 2633
21:24 revealing your s in all that you do— 2633
23:49 the **consequences of** your s *of* idolatry. 2628
24:23 of your s and groan among yourselves. 6411
28:18 By your many s and dishonest trade 6411
32:27 The **punishment for** their s rested 6411
33:10 "Our offenses and s weigh us down, 2633
33:12 The righteous man, if he s, 2627
33:16 the s he has committed will be remembered 2633
36:31 and you will loathe yourselves for your s 6411
36:33 On the day I cleanse you from all your s, 6411
43:10 that they may be ashamed of their s. 6411
45:20 for anyone *who* s **unintentionally** or 8706
Da 4:27 Renounce your s by doing what is right, 10259
9:13 the LORD our God by turning from our s 6411
9:16 Our s and the iniquities of our fathers 2628
Hos 4: 8 They feed on the s *of* my people 2633
7: 1 the s *of* Ephraim are exposed and 6411
7: 2 Their s engulf them; 5095
8:13 their wickedness and punish their s: 2633
9: 7 Because your s are so many 6411
9: 9 wickedness and punish them for their s. 2633
13:12 his s are kept on record. 2633
14: 1 Your s have been your downfall! 6411
14: 2 "Forgive all our s and receive us graciously, 6411
Am 1: 3 "For three s *of* Damascus, even for four, 7322
1: 6 "For three s *of* Gaza, even for four, 7322
1: 9 "For three s *of* Tyre, even for four, 7322
1:11 "For three s *of* Edom, even for four, 7322
1:13 "For three s *of* Ammon, even for four, 7322
2: 1 "For three s *of* Moab, even for four, 7322
2: 4 "For three s *of* Judah, even for four, 7322
2: 6 "For three s *of* Israel, even for four, 7322
3: 2 therefore I will punish you for all your s." 6411
3:14 "On the day I punish Israel for her s, 7322
5:12 and how great your s. 2633
Mic 1: 5 because of the s *of* the house of Israel. 2633
6:13 to ruin you because of your s. 2633
7:19 you will tread our s underfoot 6411
Mt 1:21 he will save his people from their s." *281*
3: 6 Confessing their s, they were baptized *281*
6:15 But if you do not forgive men their s, *4183*
6:15 your Father will not forgive your s. *4183*
9: 2 your s are forgiven." *281*
9: 5 to say, 'Your s are forgiven,' or to say, *281*
9: 6 of Man has authority on earth to forgive s." *281*
18:15 "If your brother s against you, *279*
18:21 when *he* s against me? *279*
26:28 for many for the forgiveness *of* s. *281*
Mk 1: 4 of repentance for the forgiveness *of* s. *281*
1: 5 Confessing their s, they were baptized *281*
2: 5 "Son, your s are forgiven." *281*
2: 7 Who can forgive s but God alone?" *281*
2: 9 'Your s are forgiven,' or to say, 'Get up, *281*
2:10 of Man has authority on earth to forgive s." *281*
3:28 all the s and blasphemies of men will *280*
11:25 Father in heaven may forgive you your s." *4183*
Lk 1:77 through the forgiveness *of* their s, *281*
3: 3 of repentance for the forgiveness *of* s. *281*
5:20 he said, "Friend, your s are forgiven." *281*
5:21 Who can forgive s but God alone?" *281*
5:23 to say, 'Your s are forgiven,' or to say, *281*
5:24 of Man has authority on earth to forgive s." *281*
7:47 I tell you, her many s have been forgiven— *281*
7:48 Jesus said to her, "Your s are forgiven." *281*
7:49 "Who is this who even forgives s?" *281*
11: 4 Forgive us our s, for we also forgive *281*
11: 4 we also forgive everyone *who* s against us. *4053*
17: 3 "If your brother s, rebuke him, *279*
17: 4 If *he* s against you seven times in a day, *279*
24:47 and repentance and forgiveness *of* s will *281*
Jn 8:24 I told you that you would die in your s; *281*
8:24 you will indeed die in your s." *281*
8:34 everyone who s is a slave to sin. *281+3836+4472*
20:23 you forgive anyone his s, they are forgiven; *281*
Ac 2:38 for the forgiveness *of* your s. *281*
3:19 so that your s may be wiped out, *281*
5:31 and forgiveness *of* s to Israel. *281*
10:43 in him receives forgiveness *of* s *281*
13:38 the forgiveness *of* s is proclaimed to you. *281*
22:16 Get up, be baptized and wash your s away, *281*
26:18 that they may receive forgiveness *of* s and *281*
Ro 3:25 the s committed beforehand unpunished— *280*
4: 7 are forgiven, whose s are covered. *281*
4:25 over to death for our s and was raised to life *4183*
11:27 with them when I take away their s." *281*
1Co 6:18 other s a man commits are outside his body, *280*
6:18 but he who s **sexually** sins against his own *4519*
6:18 who sins sexually s against his own body. *279*
15: 3 that Christ died for our s according to *281*
15:17 you are still in your s. *281*
2Co 5:19 not counting men's s against them. *4183*
Gal 1: 4 who gave himself for our s to rescue us *281*
Eph 1: 7 through his blood, the forgiveness *of* s, *4183*
2: 1 *in* your transgressions and s, *281*
Col 1:14 we have redemption, the forgiveness *of* s. *281*
2:13 When you were dead in your s and in *4183*
2:13 He forgave us all our s, *4183*
1Th 2:16 In this way they always heap up their s to *281*
4: 6 The Lord will punish men for all **such s,** *4047S*
1Ti 5:22 and do not share in the s of others. *281*
5:24 The s of some men are obvious, *281*
5:24 the s of others trail behind them. *NIG*
2Ti 3: 6 who are loaded down *with* s and are swayed *281*
Heb 1: 3 After he had provided purification *for* s, *281*
2:17 and that he might make atonement for the s *281*
5: 1 to offer gifts and sacrifices for s. *281*
5: 3 to offer sacrifices for his own s, *281*
5: 3 as well as for the s of the people. *NIG*
7:27 first for his own s, and then for the sins of *281*
7:27 and then for the s of the people. *NIG*
7:27 He sacrificed for their s once for all *NIG*
8:12 and will remember their s no more." *281*
9: 7 s the people had **committed in ignorance.** *52*
9:15 to set them free *from* the s committed under *4126*
9:28 to take away the s of many people; *281*
10: 2 would no longer have felt guilty *for* their s. *281*
10: 3 an annual reminder *of* s, *281*
10: 4 the blood of bulls and goats to take away s. *281*
10:11 which can never take away s. *281*
10:12 offered for all time one sacrifice for s, *281*
10:17 s and lawless acts I will remember no *281*
10:26 no sacrifice for s is left, *281*
Jas 4:17 he ought to do and doesn't do it, s. *281+1639*
5:16 Therefore confess your s to each other *281*
5:20 from death and cover over a multitude *of* s. *281*
1Pe 2:24 He himself bore our s in his body on *281*
2:24 so that we might die *to* s and live *281*
3:18 For Christ died for s once for all, *281*
4: 8 because love covers over a multitude *of* s. *281*
2Pe 1: 9 that he has been cleansed *from* his past s. *281*
1Jn 1: 9 If we confess our s, he is faithful and just *281*
1: 9 and will forgive us our s and purify us *281*
2: 2 He is the atoning sacrifice for our s, *281*
2: 2 and not only for ours but also for the s of *NIG*
2:12 because your s have been forgiven *281*
3: 4 Everyone who s breaks the law; *281+3836+4472*
3: 5 so that he might take away our s. *281*
4:10 as an atoning sacrifice for our s. *281*
Rev 1: 5 and has freed us from our s by his blood, *281*
18: 4 so that you will not share *in* her s, *281*
18: 5 for her s are piled up to heaven, *281*

SION (KJV) See SIYON, ZION

SIPHMOTH (1)

1Sa 30:28 to those in Aroer, S, Eshtemoa 8560

SIPPAI (1)

1Ch 20: 4 that time Sibbecai the Hushathite killed S, 6205

SIR (26) [SIRS]

Ge 23: 6 "S, listen to us. You are a mighty prince 123
43:20 s," they said, "we came down here 123
Jdg 6:13 "But s," Gideon replied, 123
Mt 13:27 and said, 'S, didn't you sow good seed *3261*
21:30 He answered, 'I will, s,' but he did not go. *3261*
25:11 "Later the others also came. 'S! *3261*
25:11 "Later the others also came. 'Sir! S!' *3261*
27:63 "S," they said, "we remember that *3261*
Lk 13: 8 " 'S,' the man replied, *3261*

Lk 13:25 **'S,** open the door for us.' *3261*
14:22 " **'S,'** the servant said, *3261*
19:16 "The first one came and said, **'S,** *3261*
19:18 "The second came and said, **'S,** *3261*
19:20 "Then another servant came and said, **'S,** *3261*
19:25 " **'S,'** they said, 'he already has ten!' *3261*
Jn 4:11 **"S,"** the woman said, "you have nothing *3261*
4:15 The woman said to him, **"S,** *3261*
4:19 **"S,"** the woman said, "I can see that you are *3261*
4:49 The royal official said, **"S,** *3261*
5:7 **"S,"** the invalid replied, *3261*
6:34 **"S,"** they said, "from now *3261*
8:11 "No one, **s,"** she said. *3261*
9:36 "Who is he, **s?"** *3261*
12:21 **"S,"** they said, "we would like to see Jesus." *3261*
20:15 Thinking he was the gardener, she said, **"S,** *3261*
Rev 7:14 I answered, **"S,** you know." *3261*

SIRAH (1)

2Sa 3:26 they brought him back from the well of **S.** 6241

SIRION (2) [HERMON]

Dt 3:9 (Hermon is called **S** by the Sidonians; 8590
Ps 29:6 **S** like a young wild ox. 8590

SIRS (1) [SIR]

Ac 16:30 He then brought them out and asked, **"S,** *3261*

SISAMAI (KJV) See SISMAI

SISERA (20) [SISERA'S]

Jdg 4:2 The commander of his army was **S,** 6102
4:7 I will lure **S,** the commander of Jabin's 6102
4:9 the LORD will hand **S** over to a woman." 6102
4:12 When they told **S** that Barak son 6102
4:13 **S** gathered together his nine hundred iron chariots 6102
4:14 the LORD has given **S** into your hands. 6102
4:15 the LORD routed **S** and all his chariots 6102
4:15 **S** abandoned his chariot and fled on foot. 6102
4:16 All the troops of **S** fell by the sword; 6102
4:17 **S,** however, fled on foot to the tent of Jael, 6102
4:18 Jael went out to meet **S** and said to him, 6102
4:22 Barak came by in pursuit of **S,** 6102
4:22 and there lay **S** with the tent peg 6102
5:20 from their courses they fought against **S.** 6102
5:26 She struck **S,** she crushed his head, 6102
5:30 colorful garments as plunder for **S,** 6102
1Sa 12:9 so he sold them into the hand of **S,** 6102
Ezr 2:53 Barkos, **S,** Temah, 6102
Ne 7:55 Barkos, **S,** Temah, 6102
Ps 83:9 you did to **S** and Jabin at the river Kishon, 6102

SISERA'S (1) [SISERA]

Jdg 5:28 "Through the window peered **S** mother; 6102

SISMAI (2)

1Ch 2:40 Eleasah the father of **S,** 6183
2:40 **S** the father of Shallum, 6183

SISTER (106) [SISTER-IN-LAW, SISTER'S, SISTERS]

Ge 4:22 Tubal-Cain's **s** was Naamah. 295
12:13 Say you are my **s,** so that I will be treated 295
12:19 Why did you say, 'She is my **s,'** 295
20:2 said of his wife Sarah, "She is my **s."** 295
20:5 Did he not say to me, 'She is my **s,'** 295
20:12 Besides, she really is my **s,** 295
24:59 So they sent their **s** Rebekah on her way, 295
24:60 "Our **s,** may you increase to thousands 295
25:20 the Aramean from Paddan Aram and **s** 295
26:7 "She is my **s,"** because he was afraid to say, 295
26:9 Why did you say, 'She is my **s'?"** 295
28:9 the **s** *of* Nebaioth and daughter 295
30:1 she became jealous of her **s.** 295
30:8 "I have had a great struggle with my **s,** 295
34:13 Because their **s** Dinah had been defiled, 295
34:14 we can't give our **s** to a man who is 295
34:17 we'll take our **s** and go." 1426
34:27 the city where their **s** had been defiled. 295
34:31 "Should he have treated our **s** like 295
36:3 also Basemath daughter of Ishmael and **s** 295
36:22 Timna was Lotan's **s.** 295
46:17 Their **s** was Serah. 295
Ex 2:4 His **s** stood at a distance 295
2:7 Then his **s** asked Pharaoh's daughter, 295
6:20 Amram married his **father's s** Jochebed, 1860
6:23 daughter of Amminadab and **s** *of* Nahshon, 295
15:20 Then Miriam the prophetess, Aaron's **s,** 295
Lev 18:9 " 'Do not have sexual relations with your **s,** 295
18:11 born to our father; she is your **s.** 295
18:12 sexual relations with your father's **s;** 295
18:13 sexual relations with your mother's **s,** 295
18:18 " 'Do not take your wife's **s** as a rival wife 295
20:17 " 'If a man marries his **s,** 295
20:17 He has dishonored his **s** and will 295
20:19 the **s** *of* either your mother or your father, 295
21:3 or an unmarried **s** who is dependent on him 295
Nu 6:7 or mother or brother or **s** dies, 295
25:18 in the affair of Peor and their **s** Cozbi, 295
26:59 Moses and their **s** Miriam. 295
Dt 27:22 "Cursed is the man who sleeps with his **s,** 295
Jdg 15:2 Isn't her younger **s** more attractive? 295
2Sa 13:1 the beautiful **s** of Absalom son of David. 295
13:2 of illness on account of his **s** Tamar, 295
13:4 Tamar, my brother Absalom's **s."** 295
13:5 'I would like my **s** Tamar to come 295
13:6 "I would like my **s** Tamar to come 295
13:11 "Come to bed with me, my **s."** 295
13:20 Be quiet now, my **s;** he is your brother. 295
13:22 because he had disgraced his **s** Tamar. 295
13:32 since the day Amnon raped his **s** Tamar. 295
17:25 the daughter of Nahash and **s** *of* Zeruiah 295
1Ki 11:19 so pleased with Hadad that he gave him a **s** 295
11:20 The **s** *of* Tahpenes bore him 295
2Ki 11:2 the daughter of King Jehoram and **s** 295
1Ch 1:39 Timna was Lotan's **s.** 295
3:9 And Tamar was their **s.** 295
3:19 Shelomith was their **s.** 295
4:3 Their **s** was named Hazzelelponi. 295
4:19 The sons of Hodiah's wife, the **s** *of* Naham: 295
7:18 His **s** Hammoleketh gave birth to Ishhod, 295
7:30 Their **s** was Serah. 295
7:32 Shomer and Hotham and of their **s** Shua. 295
2Ch 22:11 of the priest Jehoiada, was Ahaziah's **s,** 295
Job 17:14 and to the worm, 'My mother' or 'My **s,'** 295
Pr 7:4 Say to wisdom, "You are my **s,"** 295
SS 4:9 You have stolen my heart, my **s,** my bride; 295
4:10 delightful is your love, my **s,** my bride! 295
4:12 You are a garden locked up, my **s,** 295
5:1 I have come into my garden, my **s,** 295
5:2 My lover is knocking: "Open to me, my **s,** 295
8:8 We have a young **s,** 295
8:8 for our **s** for the day she is spoken for? 295
Jer 3:7 and her unfaithful **s** Judah saw it. 295
3:8 that her unfaithful **s** Judah had no fear; 295
3:10 her unfaithful **s** Judah did not return to me 295
22:18 'Alas, my brother! Alas, my **s!'** 295
Eze 16:45 and you are a true **s** *of* your sisters, 295
16:46 Your older **s** was Samaria, 295
16:46 and your younger **s,** who lived to the south 295
16:48 your **s** Sodom and her daughters 295
16:49 " 'Now this was the sin of your **s** Sodom: 295
16:56 You would not even mention your **s** Sodom 295
22:11 and another violates his **s,** 295
23:4 and her **s** was Oholibah. 295
23:11 "Her **s** Oholibah saw this, 295
23:11 lust and prostitution she was more depraved than her **s.** 295
23:18 just as I had turned away from her **s.** 295
23:31 You have gone the way of your **s;** 295
23:33 the cup of your **s** Samaria. 295
23:42 on the arms of **the woman and her s** 2177S
44:25 son or daughter, brother or unmarried **s,** 295
Mt 12:50 in heaven is my brother and **s** and mother." *80*
Mk 3:35 God's will is my brother and **s** and mother." *80*
Lk 10:39 She had a **s** called Mary, *80*
10:40 don't you care that my **s** has left me to do *80*
Jn 11:1 the village of Mary and her **s** Martha. *80*
11:5 Jesus loved Martha and her **s** and Lazarus. *80*
11:28 she went back and called her **s** Mary aside. *80*
11:39 Lord," said Martha, the **s** of the dead man, *80*
19:25 his mother's **s,** Mary the wife of Clopas, *80*
Ac 23:16 when the son of Paul's **s** heard of this plot, *80*
Ro 16:1 I commend to you our **s** Phoebe, *80*
16:15 Greet Philologus, Julia, Nereus and his **s,** *80*
Phm 1:2 *to* Apphia our **s,** *80*
Jas 2:15 Suppose a brother or **s** is without clothes *80*
2Jn 1:13 *of* your chosen **s** send their greetings. *80*

SISTER'S (4) [SISTER]

Ge 24:30 and the bracelets on his **s** arms, 295
29:13 Jacob, his **s** son, he hurried to meet him. 295
1Ch 7:15 His **s** name was Maacah. 295
Eze 23:32 "You will drink your **s** cup, 295

SISTER-IN-LAW (1) [SISTER]

Ru 1:15 "your **s** is going back to her people 3304

SISTERS (19) [SISTER]

Jos 2:13 my father and mother, my brothers and **s,** 295
1Ch 2:16 Their **s** were Zeruiah and Abigail. 295
Job 1:4 and they would invite their three **s** to eat 295
42:11 and **s** and everyone who had known him 295
Eze 16:45 and you are a true sister of your **s,** 295
16:51 and have made your **s** seem righteous 295
16:52 have furnished some justification for your **s.** 295
16:52 for you have made your **s** appear righteous. 295
16:55 And your **s,** Sodom with her daughters 295
16:61 and be ashamed when you receive your **s,** 295
Hos 2:1 and of your **s,** 'My loved one.' 295
Mt 13:56 Aren't all his **s** with us? *80*
19:29 or **s** or father or mother or children or fields *80*
Mk 6:3 Aren't his **s** here with us?" *80*
10:29 or **s** or mother or father or children or fields *80*
10:30 brothers, **s,** mothers, children and fields— *80*
Lk 14:26 his wife and children, his brothers and **s—** *80*
Jn 11:3 So the **s** sent word to Jesus, "Lord, *80*
1Ti 5:2 and younger women as **s,** *80*

SISTRUMS (1)

2Sa 6:5 lyres, tambourines, **s** and cymbals. 4983

SIT (106) [SAT, SITS, SITTING]

Ge 27:19 Please **s** up and eat some of my game so 3782
27:31 "My father, **s up** and eat some of my game, 7756
Ex 18:14 Why *do* you alone **s as judge,** 3782
Nu 32:6 to war while you **s** here? 3782
Dt 6:7 Talk about them when you **s** at home and 3782
11:19 talking about them when you **s** at home and 3782
Ru 4:1 "Come over here, my friend, and **s down."** 3782
4:2 **"S** here," and they did so. 3782
1Sa 16:11 *we will* not **s down** until he arrives." 6015
1Ki 1:13 and he *will* **s** on my throne"? 3782
1:17 and he *will* **s** on my throne.' 3782
1:20 to learn from you who *will* **s** on the throne 3782
1:24 and that he *will* **s** on your throne? 3782
1:27 who *should* **s** on the throne of my lord 3782
1:30 and he *will* **s** on my throne in my place." 3782
1:35 and **s** on my throne and reign in my place. 3782
3:6 I have given him a son *to* **s** on his throne this very day. 3782
8:20 and now *I* **s** on the throne of Israel, 3782
8:25 to have a man *to* **s** before me on the throne 3782
2Ki 10:30 your descendants *will* **s** on the throne 3782
15:12 "Your descendants *will* **s** on the throne 3782
1Ch 28:5 he has chosen my son Solomon to **s** on 3782
2Ch 6:10 and now *I* **s** on the throne of Israel, 3782
6:16 'You shall never fail to have a man *to* **s** before me on the throne of Israel, 3782
Ps 1:1 of sinners or **s** in the seat of mockers. 3782
26:4 *I do* not **s** with deceitful men, 3782
26:5 the assembly of evildoers and refuse *to* **s** 3782
69:12 *Those who* **s** *at* the gate mock me, 3782
80:1 you who **s enthroned** *between* the cherubim 3782
102:12 But you, O LORD, **s enthroned** forever; 3782
110:1 **"S** at my right hand until I make your 3782
119:23 Though rulers **s** *together* and slander me, 3782
132:12 then their sons *will* **s** on your throne 3782
132:14 here *I will* **s enthroned,** 3782
139:2 You know *when* I **s** and when I rise; 3782
Pr 23:1 When *you* **s** to dine with a ruler, 3782
SS 2:3 I delight *to* **s** in his shade, 3782
Isa 3:26 destitute, *she will* **s** on the ground. 3782
14:13 *I will* **s enthroned** on the mount 3782
16:5 in faithfulness *a man will* **s** on it— 3782
42:7 and to release from the dungeon *those who* **s** 3782
47:1 "Go down, **s** in the dust, 3782
47:1 **s** on the ground without a throne, 3782
47:5 **"S** in silence, go into darkness, 3782
47:14 here is no fire to **s** by. 3782
52:2 rise up, **s enthroned,** O Jerusalem. 3782
65:4 who **s** among the graves 3782
Jer 13:13 in this land, including the kings who **s** 3782
16:8 a house where there is feasting and **s down** 3782
17:25 then kings *who* **s** on David's throne 3782
22:2 you who **s** on David's throne— 3782
22:4 then kings *who* **s** on David's throne 3782
22:30 of his offspring will prosper, none *will* **s** 3782
33:17 'David will never fail to have a man *to* **s** on 3782
36:15 They said to him, **"S down,** please, 3782
36:30 He will have no *one to* **s** on the throne 3782
48:18 "Come down from your glory and **s** on 3782
La 2:10 of the Daughter of Zion **s** on the ground 3782
3:28 *Let him* **s** alone in silence, 3782
Eze 26:16 *they will* **s** on the ground, 3782
28:2 *I* **s** *on* the throne of a god in the heart of 3782
33:31 and **s** before you to listen to your words, 3782
44:3 prince himself is the only one *who may* **s** 3782
Da 7:26 " 'But the court *will* **s,** 10338
11:27 will **s** at the same table and lie to each NIH
Joel 3:12 for there *I will* **s** to judge all the nations 3782
Am 3:12 so will the Israelites be saved, those *who* **s** 3782
Mic 4:4 Every man *will* **s** under his own vine and 3782
7:8 Though *I* **s** in darkness, 3782
Zec 3:10 of you will invite his neighbor to **s** NIH
6:13 be clothed with majesty and *will* **s** and rule 3782
8:4 and women of ripe old age *will* **s** in 3782
Mal 3:3 *He will* **s** as a refiner and purifier of silver; 3782
Mt 14:19 And he directed the people *to* **s down** on *369*
15:35 He told the crowd *to* **s down** on the ground. *404*
19:28 you who have followed me *will* also **s** *2764*
20:21 of mine *may* **s** at your right and the other *2767*
20:23 but *to* **s** at my right or left is not for me *2767*
22:44 **"S** at my right hand until I put your *2764*
23:2 "The teachers of the law and the Pharisees **s** *2767*
25:31 *he will* **s** on his throne in heavenly glory. *2767*
26:36 **"S** here while I go over there and pray." *2767*
Mk 6:39 **have** all the people **s down** *369*
8:6 He told the crowd *to* **s down** on the ground. *404*
10:37 "Let one of us **s** at your right and the other *2767*
10:40 but *to* **s** at my right or left is not for me *2767*
12:36 **"S** at my right hand until I put your *2764*
14:32 **"S** here while I pray." *2767*
Lk 9:14 *"Have* them **s down** in groups of about *2884*
14:28 not first **s down** and estimate the cost to see *2767*
14:31 Will he not first **s down** *2767*
16:6 **s down** quickly, and make it four hundred.' *2767*
17:7 'Come along now and **s down to eat'?** *404*
20:42 **"S** at my right hand *2764*
22:30 and drink at my table in my kingdom and **s** *2764*
Jn 6:10 Jesus said, "Have the people **s down."** *404*
9:8 the same man who *used to* **s** and beg?" *2764*
Ac 2:34 **"S** at my right hand *2764*
3:10 as the same man who *used to* **s** begging at *2764*
8:31 So he invited Philip to come up and **s** *2767*
23:3 You **s** there to judge me according to *2764*
1Co 9:3 *to* those who **s in judgment on** me. *373*
Heb 1:13 **"S** at my right hand *2764*
Jas 2:3 "You stand there" or **"S** on the floor *2764*
Rev 3:21 the right *to* **s** with me on my throne, *2767*
18:7 In her heart she boasts, *'I* **s** as queen; *2764*

SITE (13) [SITES]
Ge 12: 6 as far as the s *of* the great tree of Moreh 5226
23: 4 for a **burial** s here so I can bury my dead." 7700
23: 9 to sell it to me for the full price as a burial s 299
23:20 to Abraham by the Hittites as a burial **s.** 299
Nu 21:15 the ravines that lead to the s *of* Ar and lie 8699
1Ki 6: 7 at the temple s while it was being built. NIH
1Ch 17: 5 I have moved from one **tent** s to another, 185
21:22 the s *of* your threshing floor so I can build 5226
21:25 six hundred shekels of gold for the **s.** 5226
Ezr 2:68 the rebuilding of the house of God on its **s.** 4806
5:15 And rebuild the house of God on its **s.'** 10087
6: 7 rebuild this house of God on its **s.** 10087
Zec 14:10 from the Benjamin Gate to the s *of* 5226

SITES (2) [SITE]
2Ki 23:14 down the Asherah poles and covered the s 5226
2Ch 33:19 and the s where he built high places and set 5226

SITH (KJV) See SINCE

SITHRI (1)
Ex 6:22 of Uzziel were Mishael, Elzaphan and **S.** 6262

SITNAH (1)
Ge 26:21 over that one also; so he named it **S.** 8479

SITS (27) [SIT]
Ex 11: 5 of Pharaoh, who s on the throne, 3782
Lev 15: 4 and anything *he* s on will be unclean. 3782
15: 6 Whoever s on anything that the man with 3782
15: 9 the man s on when riding will be unclean, 5323
15:20 and anything *she* s on will be unclean. 3782
15:22 Whoever touches anything *she* s on 3782
15:26 and anything *she* s on will be unclean, 3782
Est 6:10 Mordecai the Jew, who s at the king's gate. 3782
Ps 29:10 The LORD s **enthroned** over the flood; 3782
99: 1 *he* s **enthroned** *between* the cherubim, 3782
113: 5 the One who s **enthroned** on high, 3782
Pr 9:14 *She* s at the door of her house, 3782
20: 8 *When* a king s on his throne to judge, 3782
Isa 28: 6 a spirit of justice to him *who* s in judgment, 3782
40:22 He s **enthroned** above the circle of the earth 3782
Jer 29:16 the king who s on David's throne and all 3782
Mt 19:28 the Son of Man s on his glorious throne, *2767*
23:22 by God's throne and by the one who s on it. *2764*
Rev 4: 9 *to* him who s on the throne and who lives *2764*
4:10 down before him who s on the throne, *2764*
5:13 *"To* him who s on the throne and to *2764*
6:16 and hide us from the face *of* him who s on *2764*
7:10 who s on the throne, and to the Lamb." *2764*
7:15 and he who s on the throne *2764*
17: 1 great prostitute, who s on many waters. *2764*
17: 9 on which the woman **s.** *2764*
17:15 where the prostitute **s,** are peoples, *2764*

SITTING (75) [SIT]
Ge 18: 1 while he *was* s *at* the entrance to his tent in 3782
19: 1 and Lot *was* s in the gateway of the city. 3782
23:10 Ephron the Hittite *was* s among his people 3782
31:34 inside her camel's saddle and *was* s 3782
Lev 15:23 Whether it is the bed or anything she *was* s 3782
Dt 22: 6 and the mother *is* s on the young or on 8069
Jdg 3:20 then approached him while he *was* s alone 3782
5:10 s on your saddle blankets, 3782
1Sa 1: 9 the priest *was* s on a chair by the doorpost 3782
4:13 there was Eli s on his chair by the side of 3782
19: 9 the LORD came upon Saul as he *was* s 3782
2Sa 18:24 While David *was* s between the inner 3782
19: 8 "The king *is* s in the gateway," 3782
1Ki 13:14 He found him s under an oak tree 3782
13:20 While they were s at the table, 3782
22:10 and Jehoshaphat king of Judah *were* s 3782
22:19 the LORD s on his throne with all the host 3782
2Ki 1: 9 *who was* s on the top of a hill, 3782
6:32 Now Elisha *was* s in his house, 3782
6:32 and the elders *were* s with him. 3782
9: 5 he found the army officers s together. 3782
18:27 and not to the men s on the wall— 3782
2Ch 18: 9 and Jehoshaphat king of Judah *were* s 3782
18:18 the LORD s on his throne with all the host 3782
Ezr 10: 9 all the people *were* s in the square before 3782
Ne 2: 6 Then the king, with the queen s beside him, 3782
Est 2:19 Mordecai *was* s at the king's gate. 3782
2:21 the time Mordecai *was* s at the king's gate, 3782
5: 1 The king *was* s on his royal throne in 3782
5:13 that Jew Mordecai s at the king's gate." 3782
Isa 36:12 and not to the men s on the wall— 3782
Jer 8:14 "Why *are* we s here? 3782
32:12 the Jews s in the courtyard of the guard. 3782
36:12 where all the officials *were* **s:** 3782
36:22 It was the ninth month and the king *was* s in 3782
38: 7 While the king *was* s in the Benjamin Gate, 3782
La 3:63 S or standing, they mock me in their songs. 3782
Eze 8: 1 *while* I *was* s in my house and the elders 3782
8: 1 in my house and the elders of Judah *were* s 3782
8:14 and I saw women s there, 3782
Mt 9: 9 he saw a man named Matthew s at *2764*
11:16 They are like children s in the marketplaces *2764*
20:30 Two blind men were s by the roadside, *2764*
24: 3 *As* Jesus *was* s on the Mount of Olives, *2764*
26:64 In the future you will see the Son of Man s *2764*
26:69 Now Peter *was* s out in the courtyard, *2764*
27:19 *While* Pilate *was* s on the judge's seat, *2764*
27:36 **s down,** they kept watch over him there. *2764*
27:61 and the other Mary were s there opposite *2764*
Mk 2: 6 Now some teachers of the law were s there, *2764*
2:14 of Alphaeus s at the tax collector's booth. *2764*
3:32 A crowd *was* s around him, *2764*
5:15 s there, dressed and in his right mind; *2764*
9:35 **S down,** Jesus called the Twelve and said, *2767*
10:46 *was* s by the roadside begging. *2764*
13: 3 *As* Jesus *was* s on the Mount of Olives *2764*
14:62 "And you will see the Son of Man s at *2764*
16: 5 a young man dressed in a white robe s on *2764*
Lk 2:46 in the temple courts, s among the teachers, *2757*
5:17 from Judea and Jerusalem, were s there. *2764*
5:27 by the name of Levi s at his tax booth. *2764*
7:32 They are like children s in the marketplace *2764*
8:35 s at Jesus' feet, dressed and *2764*
10:13 s in sackcloth and ashes. *2764*
18:35 a blind man *was* s by the roadside begging. *2764*
Jn 2:14 and others s at tables exchanging money. *2764*
Ac 2: 2 the whole house where they were **s.** *2764*
6:15 All who *were* s in the Sanhedrin *2757*
8:28 and on his way home *was* s in his chariot *2764*
26:30 the governor and Bernice and those **s with** *5153*
1Co 14:30 revelation comes to someone *who is* **s down** *2764*
Jas 4:11 but **s in judgment** on it. *3216*
Rev 4: 2 a throne in heaven with *someone* s on it. *2764*
14:15 and called in a loud voice *to* him who *was* s *2764*
17: 3 There I saw a woman s on a scarlet beast *2764*

SITUATED (3) [SITUATION]
2Ki 2:19 our lord, this town is well **s,** as you can see, 4632
Eze 27: 3 Say to Tyre, s at the gateway to the sea, 3782
Na 3: 8 Are you better than Thebes, s on the Nile, 3782

SITUATION (9) [SITUATED, SITUATIONS]
Ge 31:40 *This* **was** *my s:* The heat consumed me AIT
1Sa 13: 6 of Israel saw that their s was critical and NIH
2Sa 14:20 Joab did this to change the present **s.** 1821
Da 2: 9 hoping the s will change. 10530
6:17 so that Daniel's s might not be changed. 10606
Mt 19:10 "If this is the s between a husband and wife, *162*
1Co 7:20 in the s which he was in when God called *3104*
7:24 should remain in **the** s God called him to. *4005*
Php 4:12 of being content in any and **every** *s,* *AIT*

SITUATIONS (1) [SITUATION]
2Ti 4: 5 But you, keep your head in **all** *s,* *AIT*

SIVAN (1)
Est 8: 9 of the third month, the month of **S.** 6094

SIX (126) [SIXTH]
Ge 7: 6 Noah was s hundred years old when 9252
7:11 In the s hundredth year of Noah's life, 9252
8:13 of the first month of Noah's s hundred 9252
30:20 because I have borne him s sons." 9252
31:41 for your two daughters and s years 9252
Ex 12:37 There were about s hundred thousand men 9252
14: 7 He took s hundred of the best chariots, 9252
16:26 S days you are to gather it, 9252
20: 9 S days you shall labor 9252
20:11 in s days the LORD made the heavens and 9252
21: 2 he is to serve you for s years. 9252
23:10 "For s years you are to sow your fields 9252
23:12 "S days do your work, 9252
24:16 For s days the cloud covered the mountain, 9252
25:32 S branches are to extend from the sides of 9252
25:33 the same for all s branches extending from 9252
25:35 the third pair—s branches in all. 9252
26: 9 into one set and the other s into another set. 9252
26:22 Make s frames for the far end, that is, 9252
28:10 s names on one stone and the remaining six 9252
28:10 six names on one stone and the remaining s 9252
31:15 For s days, work is to be done, 9252
31:17 in s days the LORD made the heavens and 9252
34:21 "S days you shall labor, 9252
35: 2 For s days, work is to be done, but 9252
36:16 into one set and the other s into another set. 9252
36:27 They made s frames for the far end, that is, 9252
37:18 S branches extended from the sides of 9252
37:19 the same for all s branches extending from 9252
37:21 the third pair—s branches in all. 9252
Lev 23: 3 " 'There are s days when you may work, 9252
24: 6 Set them in two rows, s *in* each row, 9252
25: 3 For s years sow your fields, 9252
25: 3 and for s years prune your vineyards 9252
Nu 7: 3 before the LORD s covered carts 9252
11:21 "Here I am among s hundred thousand men 9252
35: 6 **"S** *of* the towns you give the Levites will 9252
35:13 These s towns you give will be your cities 9252
35:15 These s towns will be a place of refuge 9252
Dt 3:11 thirteen feet long and s **feet** wide. 564+752
5:13 S days you shall labor 9252
15:12 sells himself to you and serves you s years, 9252
15:18 to you these s years has been worth twice 9252
16: 8 For s days eat unleavened bread and on 9252
Jos 6: 3 Do this for s days. 9252
6:14 They did this for s days. 9252
15:59 s towns and their villages. 9252
15:62 s towns and their villages. 9252
Jdg 3:31 who struck down s hundred Philistines with 9252
12: 7 Jephthah led Israel s years. 9252
18:11 s hundred men from the clan of the Danites, 9252
18:16 The s hundred Danites, armed for battle, 9252
18:17 and the s hundred armed men stood at 9252
20:47 But s hundred men turned and fled into 9252
Ru 3:15 he poured into it s measures of barley 9252
3:17 "He gave me these s measures of barley, 9252
1Sa 13: 5 s thousand charioteers, and soldiers as 9252
13:15 They numbered about s hundred. 9252
14: 2 With him were about s hundred men, 9252
17: 7 its iron point weighed s hundred shekels. 9252
23:13 about s hundred in number, 9252
27: 2 the s hundred men with him left and went 9252
30: 9 and the s hundred men with him came to 9252
2Sa 2:11 of Judah was seven years and s months. 9252
5: 5 over Judah seven years and s months, 9252
6:13 the ark of the LORD had taken s steps, 9252
15:18 s hundred Gittites who had accompanied 9252
21:20 with s fingers on each hand and six toes 9252
21:20 with six fingers on each hand and s toes 9252
1Ki 6: 6 the middle floor s cubits and 9252
10:16 s hundred bekas of gold went 9252
10:19 The throne had s steps, 9252
10:20 Twelve lions stood on the s steps, 9252
10:29 from Egypt for s hundred shekels of silver, 9252
11:16 the Israelites stayed there for s months, 9252
16:23 s *of* them in Tirzah. 9252
2Ki 5: 5 s thousand shekels of gold and ten sets 9252
11: 3 the LORD for s years while Athaliah ruled 9252
13:19 the ground five or s times; 9252
14:13 **about s hundred feet** long. 564+752+4395
15: 8 and he reigned s months. 9252
1Ch 3: 4 These s were born to David in Hebron, 9252
3: 4 where he reigned seven years and s months. 9252
3:22 and Shaphat—s in all. 9252
4:27 Shimei had sixteen sons and s daughters, 9252
8:38 Azel had s sons, 9252
9:44 Azel had s sons, 9252
20: 6 with s fingers on each hand and six toes 9252
20: 6 with six fingers on each hand and s toes 9252
21:25 So David paid Araunah s hundred shekels 9252
23: 4 of the LORD and s thousand are to 9252
25: 3 Shimei, Hashabiah and Mattithiah, s in all, 9252
26:17 There were s Levites a day on the east, 9252
2Ch 1:17 from Egypt for s hundred shekels of silver, 9252
3: 8 inside with s hundred talents of fine gold. 9252
9:15 s hundred bekas of hammered gold went 9252
9:18 The throne had s steps, 9252
9:19 Twelve lions stood on the s steps, 9252
22:12 with them at the temple of God for s years 9252
25:23 **about s hundred feet** long. 564+752+4395
29:33 to s hundred bulls and three thousand sheep 9252
Ne 5:18 Each day one ox, s choice sheep 9252
Est 2:12 s months with oil of myrrh and six 9252
2:12 with oil of myrrh and s with perfumes 9252
Job 5:19 From s calamities he will rescue you; 9252
42:12 s thousand camels, a thousand yoke of oxen 9252
Pr 6:16 There are s things the LORD hates, 9252
Isa 6: 2 were seraphs, each with s wings: 9252
Jer 34:14 After he has served you s years, 9252
Eze 9: 2 And I saw s men coming from the direction 9252
40: 5 in the man's hand was s long cubits, 9252
40:12 and the alcoves were s cubits square. 9252
41: 1 of the jambs was s cubits on each side. 9252
41: 3 The entrance was s cubits wide, 9252
41: 5 it was s cubits thick, 9252
41: 8 It was the length of the rod, s long cubits. 9252
46: 1 to be shut on the s working days, 9252
46: 4 the Sabbath day is to be s male lambs and 9252
46: 6 s lambs and a ram, all without defect. 9252
Mt 17: 1 After s days Jesus took with him Peter, *1971*
Mk 9: 2 After s days Jesus took Peter, *1971*
Lk 13:14 "There are s days for work. *1971*
Jn 2: 6 Nearby stood s stone water jars, *1971*
12: 1 S days before the Passover, *1971*
Ac 11:12 These s brothers also went with me, *1971*
Rev 4: 8 of the four living creatures had s wings *1971*

SIXSCORE (KJV) See 120

SIXTEEN (18) [SIXTEENTH]
Ge 46:18 to his daughter Leah—s in all. 6926+9252
Ex 26:25 be eight frames and s silver bases— 6925+9252
36:30 eight frames and s silver bases— 6925+9252
Jos 15:41 s towns and their villages. 6926+9252
19:22 There were s towns and their villages. 6926+9252
2Ki 13:10 and he reigned s years. 6926+9252
14:21 who was s years old, 6926+9252
15: 2 was s years old when he became king, 6926+9252
15:33 and he reigned in Jerusalem s years. 6926+9252
16: 2 and he reigned in Jerusalem s years. 6926+9252
1Ch 4:27 Shimei had s sons and six daughters, 6925+9252
24: 4 s heads of families 6925+9252
2Ch 13:21 had twenty-two sons and s daughters. 6926+9252
26: 1 who was s years old, 6926+9252
26: 3 Uzziah was s years old 6926+9252
27: 1 and he reigned in Jerusalem s years. 6926+9252
27: 8 and he reigned in Jerusalem s years. 6926+9252
28: 1 and he reigned in Jerusalem s years. 6926+9252

SIXTEENTH (3) [SIXTEEN]
1Ch 24:14 the fifteenth to Bilgah, the s to Immer, 6925+9252
25:23 the s to Hananiah, his sons and 6925+9252
2Ch 29:17 on the s day of the first month. 6925+9252

SIXTH (44) [SIX]
Ge 1:31 and there was morning—the s day. 9261
30:19 and bore Jacob a s son. 9261
Ex 16: 5 On the s day they are to prepare 9261
16:22 the s day, they gathered twice as much— 9261
16:29 that is why on the s day he gives you bread 9261
26: 9 the s curtain double at the front of the tent. 9261
Lev 25:21 I will send you such a blessing in the s year 9261
Nu 7:42 On the s day Eliasaph son of Deuel, 9261
29:29 " 'On the s day prepare eight bulls, 9261
Jos 19:32 s lot came out for Naphtali, clan by clan: 9261
2Sa 3: 5 and the s, Ithream the son 9261
2Ki 18:10 Samaria was captured in Hezekiah's s year, 9252
1Ch 2:15 the s Ozem and the seventh David. 9261
3: 3 and the s, Ithream, by his wife Eglah. 9261
12:11 Attai the s, Eliel the seventh, 9261
24: 9 the fifth to Malkijah, the s to Mijamin, 9261
25:13 the s to Bukkiah, his sons and relatives, 9261
26: 3 Jehohanan the s and Eliehoenai the seventh. 9261
26: 5 the s, Issachar the seventh and Peullethai 9261
27: 9 The s, for the sixth month, 9261
27: 9 The sixth, for the s month, 9261
Ezr 6:15 in the s year of the reign of King Darius. 10747
Ne 3:30 and Hanun, the s son of Zalaph, 9261
Eze 4:11 Also measure out a s *of* a hin of water 9261
8: 1 In the s year, in the sixth month 9261
8: 1 in the s month on the fifth day, 9261
45:13 a s *of* an ephah from each homer of wheat 9261
45:13 an ephah from each homer of wheat and a s 9257
46:14 consisting of a s *of* an ephah with a third of 9261
Hag 1: 1 on the first day of the s month, 9261
1:15 on the twenty-fourth day of the s month in 9261
Mt 20: 5 about the s hour and the ninth hour and did *1761*
27:45 From the s hour until the ninth hour *1761*
Mk 15:33 At the s hour darkness came over *1761*
Lk 1:26 In the s month, God sent the angel Gabriel *1761*
1:36 to be barren is in her s month. *1761*
23:44 It was now about the s hour, *1761*
Jn 4: 6 It was about the s hour. *1761*
19:14 about the s hour. *1761*
Rev 6:12 I watched as he opened the s seal. *1761*
9:13 The s angel sounded his trumpet, *1761*
9:14 It said *to* the s angel who had the trumpet, *1761*
16:12 The s angel poured out his bowl on *1761*
21:20 the s carnelian, the seventh chrysolite, *1761*

SIXTY (28) [60]
Ge 25:26 Isaac was s years old when Rebekah 9252
Lev 27: 3 and s at fifty shekels of silver, according to 9252
27: 7 If it is a person s years old or more, 9252
Nu 7:88 to twenty-four oxen, s rams, 9252
7:88 s male goats and sixty male lambs 9252
7:88 sixty male goats and s male lambs 9252
Dt 3: 4 There was not one of the s cities that we did 9252
Jos 13:30 the settlements of Jair in Bashan, s towns, 9252
2Sa 2:31 and s Benjamites who were with Abner. 9252
1Ki 4:13 in Bashan and its s large walled cities 9252
4:22 of fine flour and s cors of meal, 9252
6: 2 for the LORD was s cubits long, 9252
2Ki 25:19 of conscripting the people of the land and s 9252
1Ch 2:21 when he was s years old), 9252
2:23 with its surrounding settlements—s towns.) 9252
2Ch 3: 3 the temple of God was s cubits long 9252
11:21 he had eighteen wives and s concubines, 9252
11:21 twenty-eight sons and s daughters. 9252
12: 3 and s thousand horsemen and 9252
SS 3: 7 escorted by s warriors, the noblest of Israel, 9252
6: 8 S queens there may be, 9252
Jer 52:25 of conscripting the people of the land and s 9252
Eze 40:14 of the gateway—s cubits. 9252
Mt 13: 8 s or thirty *times* what was sown. *2008*
13:23 s or thirty *times* what was sown." *2008*
Mk 4: 8 s, or even a hundred *times*." *2008*
4:20 s or even a hundred *times* what was sown." *2008*
1Ti 5: 9 on the list of widows unless she is over s, *2008*

SIXTY-EIGHT (1)
1Ch 16:38 and his s associates to minister 2256+9046+9252

SIXTY-FIVE (1) [65]
Isa 7: 8 Within s years Ephraim will 2256+2822+9252

SIXTY-SIX (2)
Ge 46:26 numbered s persons. 2256+9252+9252
Lev 12: 5 Then she must wait s days to be purified 2256+9252+9252

SIXTY-TWO (3) [62]
Da 5:31 at the age of s. 10221+10749+10775
9:25 seven 'sevens,' and s 'sevens.' 2256+9109+9252
9:26 After the s 'sevens,' 2256+9109+9252

SIYON (1) [HERMON]
Dt 4:48 on the rim of the Arnon Gorge to Mount S 8481

SIZE (15)
Ex 26: 2 All the curtains are to be the same s— 4500
26: 8 All eleven curtains are to be the same s— 4500
36: 9 All the curtains were the same s— 4500
36:15 All eleven curtains were the same s— 4500
Nu 13:32 All the people we saw there are of **great s.** 4500
1Ki 6:25 for the two cherubim were identical in s 4500
7: 9 blocks of high-grade stone cut to s 4500
7:11 Above were high-grade stones, cut to s, 4500
7:37 in the same molds and were identical in s 4500
2Ki 10:32 the LORD began to **reduce** *the* s of Israel. 7894
1Ch 23:29 and all measurements of quantity and s. 4500
Ps 33:16 No king is saved by the s *of* his army; 8044
Eze 45:11 ephah and the bath are to be the same s, 9420
46:22 in the four corners was the same s. 4500
Rev 18:21 a mighty angel picked up a boulder **the s of** *6055*

SKETCH (1)
2Ki 16:10 and sent to Uriah the priest a s of the altar, 1952

SKIES (21) [SKY]
Dt 28:24 down from the s until you are destroyed. 9028
Job 26: 7 the northern [s] over empty space; NIH
26:13 By his breath the s became fair; 9028
37:18 can you join him in spreading out the s, 8836
37:21 the s after the wind has swept them clean. 8836
Ps 19: 1 the s proclaim the work of his hands. 8385
36: 5 your faithfulness to the s. 8836
57:10 your faithfulness reaches to the s. 8836
68:33 to him who rides the ancient s **above,** 9028+9028
68:34 whose power is in the s. 8836
71:19 Your righteousness reaches to the s, O God, 5294
77:17 the s resounded with thunder; 8836
78:23 Yet he gave a command to the s above 8836
89: 6 the s **above** can compare with the LORD? 8836
108: 4 your faithfulness reaches to the s. 8836
148: 4 and you waters above the s. 9028
Jer 14:22 Do the s themselves send down showers? 9028
51: 9 for her judgment reaches to the s, 9028
Hos 2:21 "I will respond to the s, 9028
Mt 11:23 Capernaum, will you be lifted up to the s? *4041*
Lk 10:15 Capernaum, will you be lifted up to the s? *4041*

SKILL (13) [SKILLED, SKILLFUL, SKILLFULLY, SKILLS]
Ex 31: 3 with s, ability and knowledge in all kinds 2683
31: 6 Also I have given s to all the craftsmen 2683
35:26 and had the s spun the goat hair. 2683
35:31 with s, ability and knowledge in all kinds 2683
35:35 s to do all kinds of work as craftsmen, 2683+4213
36: 1 to whom the LORD has given s and ability 2683
2Ch 2:13 Huram-Abi, a man of **great s,** 1069+2682+3359
Ps 137: 5 may my right hand forget [its s]. NIH
Ecc 2:19 into which I have poured my effort and s 2681
2:21 do his work with wisdom, knowledge and s, 4179
10:10 but s will bring success. 2683
Eze 28: 5 By your great s in trading you have 2683
Ac 17:29 an image made by man's design and s. *5492*

SKILLED (35) [SKILL]
Ex 26: 1 worked into them by a s **craftsman.** 3110
26:31 worked into it by a s **craftsman.** 3110
28: 3 s *men* to whom I have given wisdom 2682+4213
28: 6 the work of a s **craftsman.** 3110
28:15 the work of a s **craftsman.** 3110
35:10 "All *who* are s among you are to come 2682+4213
35:25 Every s woman spun with her hands 2682+4213
36: 1 Oholiab and every s person to whom 2682+4213
36: 2 Oholiab and every s person to whom 2682+4213
36: 4 So all the s **craftsmen** who were doing all 2682
36: 8 All the s *men* among the workmen 2682+4213
36: 8 worked into them by a s **craftsman.** 3110
36:35 worked into it by a s **craftsman.** 3110
39: 3 the work of a s **craftsman.** 3110
39: 8 the work of a s **craftsman.** 3110
1Ki 5: 6 that we have no one *so* s *in* felling timber 3359
7:14 Huram was highly s and experienced 2683
1Ch 22:15 as well as men s in every kind of work 2682
25: 7 all of them trained and s in music for 1067
28:21 and every willing man s 2683
2Ch 2: 7 a man s to work in gold and silver, 2682
2: 7 and Jerusalem with my s **craftsmen,** 2682
2: 8 that your men *are* s *in* cutting timber there. 3359
34:12 *who were* s *in* playing musical instruments 1067
Job 32:22 for if I *were* s *in* flattery, 3359
Pr 22:29 Do you see a man s in his work? 4542
Isa 3: 3 s craftsman and clever enchanter. 2682
40:20 He looks for a s craftsman to set up an idol 2682
Jer 2:33 How s *you are* at pursuing love! 2006+3512
4:22 They are s in doing evil; 2682
10: 9 all made by s *workers.* 2682
50: 9 Their arrows will be like s warriors who do 8505
Eze 21:31 I will hand you over to brutal men, *men* s 3093
27: 8 your s *men,* O Tyre, were aboard as your 2682
Mic 7: 3 Both hands *are* s in doing evil; 3512

SKILLFUL (8) [SKILL]
Ge 25:27 and Esau became a s hunter, 3359
1Ch 15:22 that was his responsibility because he *was* s 1067
2Ch 26:15 by **s men** for use on the towers and on 3110
Ps 45: 1 my tongue is the pen of a s writer. 4542
58: 5 however s the enchanter may be. 2681
78:72 with s hands he led them. 9312
Jer 9:17 send for the *most* s *of them.* 2682
Zec 9: 2 though *they are* very s. 2681

SKILLFULLY (5) [SKILL]
Ex 28: 8 Its s **woven** waistband is to be like it— 682
29: 5 the ephod on him by its s woven waistband. NIH
39: 5 Its s **woven** waistband was like it— 682
Lev 8: 7 the ephod to him by its s **woven waistband;** 3109
Ps 33: 3 play s, and shout for joy. 3512

SKILLS (1) [SKILL]
Dt 33:11 Bless all his s, O LORD, 2657

SKIM (1)
Job 9:26 *They* s **past** like boats of papyrus, 2736

SKIMPING (1)
Am 8: 5 s the measure, boosting the price 7781

SKIN (75) [SKINNED, SKINS, SMOOTH-SKINNED]
Ge 3:21 The LORD God made garments of s 6425
21:14 and a s *of* water and gave them to Hagar. 2827
21:15 When the water in the s was gone, 2827
21:19 and filled the s with water and gave the boy 2827
27:11 and I'm a man *with* **smooth** *s.* AIT
Lev 1: 6 *He is to* s the burnt offering and cut it 7320
13: 2 or a rash or a bright spot on his s 1414+6425
13: 2 that may become an infectious s **disease,** 7669
13: 3 priest is to examine the sore on his s, 1414+6425
13: 3 sore appears to be more than s deep, 1414+6425
13: 3 it is an infectious s **disease.** 7669
13: 4 on his s is white but does not appear 1414+6425
13: 4 to be more than s deep and the hair in it has 6425
13: 5 and has not spread in the s, 6425
13: 6 sore has faded and has not spread in the s, 6425
13: 7 in his s after he has shown himself to 6425
13: 8 and if the rash has spread in the s, 6425
13: 9 "When anyone has an infectious s **disease,** 7669
13:10 in the s that has turned the hair white and 6425
13:11 it is a chronic s **disease** and 7669
13:12 "If the disease breaks out all over his s and, 6425
13:12 it covers all the s *of* the infected person 6425
13:18 "When someone has a boil on his s 1414+6425
13:20 and if it appears to be more than s deep and 6425
13:20 an infectious s **disease** that has broken out 7669
13:21 not more than s deep and has faded, 6425
13:22 If it is spreading in the s, 6425
13:24 "When someone has a burn on his s 1414+6425
13:25 and it appears to be more than s deep, 6425
13:25 it is an infectious s **disease.** 7669
13:26 in the spot and if it is not more than s deep 6425
13:27 and if it is spreading in the s, 6425
13:27 it is an infectious s **disease.** 7669
13:28 in the s but has faded, it is a swelling from 6425
13:30 and if it appears to be more than s deep and 6425
13:31 it does not seem to be more than s deep 6425
13:32 not appear to be more than s deep, 6425
13:34 and if it has not spread in the s and appears 6425
13:34 and appears to be no more than s deep, 6425
13:35 in the s after he is pronounced clean, 6425
13:36 and if the itch has spread in the s, 6425
13:38 or woman has white spots on the s, 1414+6425
13:39 that has broken out on the s; 6425
13:43 like an infectious s disease, 1414+6425
14: 3 of his infectious s **disease,** 7669
14:32 for anyone who has an infectious s **disease** 7669
14:54 the regulations for any infectious s **disease,** 7669
14:57 **infectious s diseases and mildew.** 7669
22: 4 **has an infectious s disease** or 7665
Nu 5: 2 **has an infectious s disease** 7665
Jdg 4:19 She opened a s *of* milk, gave him a drink, 5532
1Sa 1:24 an ephah of flour and a s *of* wine, 5574
10: 3 and another a s *of* wine. 5574
16:20 a s *of* wine and a young goat and sent them 5532
2Sa 16: 1 a hundred cakes of figs and a s *of* wine. 5574
2Ch 29:34 were too few to s all the burnt offerings; 7320
Job 2: 4 **"S for skin!"** Satan replied. 6425
2: 4 "Skin for s**!"** Satan replied. 6425
7: 5 my s is broken and festering. 6425
10:11 with s and flesh and knit me together 6425
16:15 over my s and buried my brow in the dust. 1654
18:13 It eats away parts of his **s;** 6425
19:20 I am **nothing but** s and bones; 1414+2256+6425
19:20 I have escaped with only the s *of* my teeth. 6425
19:26 And after my s has been destroyed, 6425
30:30 My s grows black and peels; 6425
Ps 102: 5 of my loud groaning I am reduced to s 1414
Jer 13:23 Can the Ethiopian change his s or 6425
La 3: 4 He has made my s and my flesh grow old 1414
4: 8 Their s has shriveled on their bones; 6425
5:10 Our s is hot as an oven, 6425
Eze 37: 6 upon you and cover you with **s;** 6425
37: 8 on them and s covered them, 6425
Mic 3: 2 who tear the s from my people and the flesh 6425
3: 3 strip off their s and break their bones 6425

SKINK (1)
Lev 11:30 the wall lizard, the s and the chameleon. 2793

SKINNED (1) [SKIN]
2Ch 35:11 while the Levites s the animals. 7320

SKINS (11) [SKIN]
Ex 25: 5 ram s dyed red and hides of sea cows; 6425
26:14 for the tent a covering of ram s dyed red, 6425
35: 7 ram s dyed red and hides of sea cows; 6425
35:23 ram s dyed red or hides of sea cows 6425
36:19 for the tent a covering of ram s dyed red, 6425

Ex 39:34 of ram s dyed red, the covering of hides 6425
Nu 6: 4 not even the seeds or **s.** 2293
1Sa 25:18 two s *of* wine, five dressed sheep, 5574
Mt 9:17 If they do, the s will burst, *829*
Mk 2:22 If he does, the wine will burst the s, *829*
Lk 5:37 If he does, the new wine will burst the s, *829*

SKIP (1) [SKIPPED]
Ps 29: 6 *He* **makes** Lebanon s like a calf, 8376

SKIPPED (2) [SKIP]
Ps 114: 4 the mountains s like rams, 8376
114: 6 that *you* s like rams, you hills, like lambs? 8376

SKIRTED (1) [SKIRTS]
Jdg 11:18 s the lands of Edom and Moab, 6015

SKIRTS (5) [SKIRTED]
Isa 47: 2 Lift up your **s**, bare your legs, 8670
Jer 13:22 that your s have been torn off 8767
13:26 I will pull up your s over your face 8767
La 1: 9 Her filthiness clung to her **s;** 8767
Na 3: 5 "I will lift your s over your face. 8767

SKULL (6) [SKULLS]
Jdg 9:53 on his head and cracked his **s.** 1653
2Ki 9:35 they found nothing except her s, 1653
Mt 27:33 Golgotha (which means The Place *of* the **S**). *3191*
Mk 15:22 Golgotha (which means The Place *of* the **S**). *3191*
Lk 23:33 When they came to the place called the **S**, *3191*
Jn 19:17 he went out to the place of the S (which *3191*

SKULLS (2) [SKULL]
Nu 24:17 the s *of* all the sons of Sheth. 7721
Jer 48:45 the s *of* the noisy boasters. 7721

SKY (74) [SKIES]
Ge 1: 8 God called the expanse **"s."** 9028
1: 9 "Let the water under the s be gathered 9028
1:14 be lights in the expanse of the s to separate 9028
1:15 in the expanse of the s to give light on 9028
1:17 in the expanse of the s to give light on 9028
1:20 above the earth across the expanse of the **s."** 9028
8: 2 and the rain had stopped falling from the **s.** 9028
22:17 in the s and as the sand on the seashore. 9028
26: 4 in the s and will give them all these lands, 9028
Ex 9:22 the s so that hail will fall all over Egypt— 9028
9:23 Moses stretched out his staff toward the s, 9028
10:21 toward the s so that darkness will spread 9028
10:22 Moses stretched out his hand toward the s, 9028
24:10 made of sapphire, clear as the s itself. 9028
32:13 as numerous as the stars in the s 9028
Lev 26:19 down your stubborn pride and make the s 9028
Dt 1:10 as many as the stars in the s. 9028
1:28 the cities are large, with walls up to the s. 9028
4:19 when you look up to the s and see the sun, 9028
9: 1 with large cities that have walls up to the s. 9028
10:22 as numerous as the stars in the **s.** 9028
17: 3 to the sun or the moon or the stars of the s, 9028
28:23 The s over your head will be bronze, 9028
28:62 as numerous as the stars in the s will be left 9028
Jos 8:20 the smoke of the city rising against the s, 9028
10:11 large hailstones down on them from the s, 9028
10:13 the middle of the s and delayed going down 9028
Jdg 20:40 of the whole city going up into the **s.** 9028
2Sa 22:12 the dark rain **clouds of the s.** 6265+8836
1Ki 18:45 Meanwhile, the s grew black with clouds, 9028
1Ch 27:23 as numerous as the stars in the **s.** 9028
Ne 9:23 as numerous as the stars in the s, 9028
Job 1:16 "The fire of God fell from the s and burned 9028
Ps 18:11 the dark rain **clouds of the s.** 6265+8836
89:37 the faithful witness in the **s."** 8836
147: 8 He covers the s with clouds; 9028
Pr 23: 5 surely sprout wings and fly off to the s like 9028
30:19 the way of an eagle in the s, 9028
Isa 34: 4 be dissolved and the s rolled up like 9028
50: 3 I clothe the s with darkness 9028
Jer 4:25 every bird in the s had flown away. 9028
8: 7 stork in the s knows her appointed seasons, 9028
10: 2 the nations or be terrified by signs in the s, 9028
33:22 before me as countless as the stars of the s 9028
51:53 the s and fortifies her lofty stronghold, 9028
La 4:19 pursuers were swifter than eagles in the **s;** 9028
Da 4:11 and strong and its top touched the **s;** 10723
4:20 with its top touching the s, 10723
4:22 until it reaches the s, 10723
Joel 2:10 the earth shakes, the s trembles, the sun 9028
3:16 the earth and the s will tremble. 9028
Na 3:16 till they are more than the stars of the s, 9028
Mt 16: 2 'It will be fair weather, for the s is red,' *4041*
16: 3 for the s is red and overcast.' *4041*
16: 3 how to interpret the appearance *of* the s, *4041*
24:29 the stars will fall from the s, *4041*
24:30 of the Son of Man will appear in the s, *4041*
24:30 Son of Man coming on the clouds *of* the s, *4041*
Mk 13:25 the stars will fall from the s, *4041*
Lk 4:25 the s was shut for three and a half years *4041*
12:56 the appearance *of* the earth and the **s.** *4041*
17:24 and lights up the s from one end to *4041*
Ac 1:10 They were looking intently up into the s *4041*
1:11 "why do you stand here looking into the s? *4041*
Heb 11:12 *in* the s and as countless as the sand on *4041*
Rev 6:13 and the stars *in* the s fell to earth, *4041*
6:14 The s receded like a scroll, rolling up, *4041*
8:10 fell from the s on a third of the rivers and *4041*
9: 1 and I saw a star that had fallen from the s to *4041*
9: 2 The sun and s were darkened by the smoke *113*
11: 6 These men have power to shut up the s so *4041*
12: 4 of the stars *out of* the s and flung them to *4041*
16:21 From the s huge hailstones of about *4041*
20:11 Earth and s fled from his presence, *4041*

SLACK (1)
Pr 18: 9 *One who is* s in his work is brother 8332

SLAIN (61) [SLAY]
Dt 21: 1 If a man is found **s**, lying in a field 2728
32:42 the blood of the s and the captives, 2728
Jos 11: 6 hand all of them over to Israel, **s.** 2728
13:22 In addition to *those* **s in battle,** 2728
Jdg 16:24 and multiplied our **s."** 2728
1Sa 18: 7 "Saul *has* s his thousands, 5782
21:11 " 'Saul *has* s his thousands, 5782
29: 5 " 'Saul *has* s his thousands, 5782
31: 1 and many fell s on Mount Gilboa. 2728
2Sa 1:19 O Israel, lies s on your heights. 2728
1:22 From the blood of the **s,** 2728
1:25 Jonathan lies s on your heights. 2728
2Ki 11:20 because Athaliah *had been* s with the sword 4637
1Ch 5:22 and many others fell **s,** 2728
10: 1 and many fell s on Mount Gilboa. 2728
2Ch 23:21 because Athaliah *had been* s with the sword. 4637
Est 9:11 The number of those s in the citadel 2222
Job 39:30 and where the s are, there is he." 2728
Ps 88: 5 like the s who lie in the grave, 2728
89:10 You crushed Rahab like *one of* the s; 2728
Pr 7:26 her s are a mighty throng. 2222
Isa 10: 4 among the captives or fall among the **s.** 2222
14:19 you are covered with the s, 2222
22: 2 Your s were not killed by the sword, 2728
26:21 she will conceal her s no longer. 2222
34: 3 Their s will be thrown out, 2728
66:16 and many will be *those* s *by* the LORD. 2728
Jer 9: 1 I would weep day and night for the s 2728
14:18 I see *those* s *by* the sword; 2728
18:21 their young men s *by* the sword in battle. 5782
25:33 At that time *those* s *by* the LORD will 2728
51: 4 They will fall down s in Babylon, 2728
51:47 be disgraced and her s will all lie fallen 2728
51:49 "Babylon must fall because of Israel's s, 2728
51:49 as the s *in* all the earth have fallen because 2728
La 2: 4 Like a foe *he has* s all who were pleasing to 2222
2:21 *You have* s them in the day of your anger; 2222
3:43 *you have* s without pity. 2222
Eze 6: 7 Your people will fall s among you, 2728
6:13 when their *people* lie s among their idols 2728
9: 7 the temple and fill the courts with the **s.** 2728
21:29 on the necks of the wicked who are to be s, 2728
28:23 The s will fall within her, 2728
30: 4 When the s fall in Egypt, 2728
30:11 against Egypt and fill the land with the **s.** 2728
32:22 she is surrounded by the graves of all her **s,** 2728
32:23 in the land of the living are s, 2728
32:24 All of them are s, fallen by the sword. 2728
32:25 A bed is made for her among the s, 2728
32:25 they are laid among the **s.** 2728
32:30 the s in disgrace despite the terror caused 2728
35: 8 I will fill your mountains with the **s;** 2728
37: 9 O breath, and breathe into these s, 2222
Da 5:30 king of the Babylonians, **was s,** 10625
7:11 until the beast was s and its body destroyed 10625
Zep 2:12 O Cushites, will be s *by* my sword." 2728
Rev 5: 6 I saw a Lamb, looking as if *it had been* s, *5377*
5: 9 and to open its seals, because *you were* s, *5377*
5:12 "Worthy is the Lamb, who *was* s, *5377*
6: 9 the altar the souls *of* those who *had been* s *5377*
13: 8 to the Lamb that *was* s from the creation of *5377*

SLANDER (27) [SLANDERED, SLANDERER, SLANDERERS, SLANDERING, SLANDEROUS, SLANDEROUSLY, SLANDERS]
Lev 19:16 about **spreading** s among your people. 8215
Ps 15: 3 and *has* no s on his tongue, 8078
31:13 For I hear the s *of* many; 1804
38:20 with evil s me when I pursue what is good. 8476
41: 6 he speaks falsely, while his heart gathers **s;** 224
50:20 and s your own mother's son. 1984+5989
54: 5 Let evil recoil on *those who* s me; 8806
59:10 and will let me gloat over *those who* s me. 8806
119:23 Though rulers sit together and s me, 1819
Pr 10:18 and whoever spreads s is a fool. 1804
30:10 *"Do* not s a servant to his master, 4387
Jer 6:28 hardened rebels, going about to s. 8215
Eze 36: 3 the object of people's malicious talk and s, 1804
Mt 15:19 sexual immorality, theft, false testimony, s. *1060*
Mk 7:22 lewdness, envy, **s,** arrogance and folly. *1060*
2Co 12:20 factions, s, gossip, arrogance and disorder. *2896*
Eph 4:31 rage and anger, brawling and s, *1060*
Col 3: 8 **s,** and filthy language from your lips. *1060*
1Ti 5:14 and to give the enemy no opportunity for **s.** *3367*
Tit 3: 2 *to* s no one, to be peaceable and considerate *1059*
Jas 4:11 Brothers, *do* not s one another. *2895*
1Pe 2: 1 hypocrisy, envy, and s of every kind. *2896*
3:16 in Christ may be ashamed of their **s.** *2895*
2Pe 2:10 not afraid to s celestial beings; *1059*
Jude 1: 8 reject authority and s celestial beings. *1059*
Rev 2: 9 the s of those who say they are Jews and are *1060*
13: 6 and *to* s his name and his dwelling place *1059*

SLANDERED (5) [SLANDER]
Dt 22:17 Now he *has* s her and said, 1821+6613+8492
2Sa 19:27 *he has* s your servant to my lord the king. 8078
Ps 35:15 *They* s me without ceasing. 7973
1Co 4:13 *when we are* **s,** we answer kindly. *1555*
1Ti 6: 1 God's name and our teaching *may* not *be* **s.** *1059*

SLANDERER (2) [SLANDER]
Jer 9: 4 and every friend a **s.** 2143+8215
1Co 5:11 an idolater or a **s,** a drunkard or a swindler. *3368*

SLANDERERS (5) [SLANDER]
Ps 56: 2 My s pursue me all day long; 8806
140:11 Let s not be established in the land; 408+4383
Ro 1:30 **s,** God-haters, insolent, arrogant *2897*
1Co 6:10 nor s nor swindlers will inherit the kingdom *3368*
Tit 2: 3 not to be s or addicted to much wine, *1333*

SLANDERING (1) [SLANDER]
Jas 2: 7 the ones who *are* s the noble name of him *1059*

SLANDEROUS (4) [SLANDER]
Eze 22: 9 In you are s men bent on shedding blood; 8215
2Ti 3: 3 unforgiving, **s,** without self-control, brutal, *1333*
2Pe 2:11 not bring s accusations against such beings *1061*
Jude 1: 9 not dare to bring a s accusation against him, *1060*

SLANDEROUSLY (1) [SLANDER]
Ro 3: 8 as *we are being* **s reported** as saying and *1059*

SLANDERS (2) [SLANDER]
Dt 22:14 s her and gives her a bad name, 1821+6613+8492
Ps 101: 5 *Whoever* s his neighbor in secret, 4387

SLANG (KJV) See SLUNG

SLAPPED (3) [SLAPS]
1Ki 22:24 went up and s Micaiah in the face. 5782
2Ch 18:23 went up and s Micaiah in the face. 5782
Mt 26:67 struck him with their fists. Others s him *4824*

SLAPS (1) [SLAPPED]
2Co 11:20 pushes himself forward or s you in the face. *1296*

SLASH (1) [SLASHED]
Eze 21:16 O sword, s to the right, then to the left, 2523

SLASHED (2) [SLASH]
1Ki 18:28 and s **themselves** with swords and spears, 1517
Jer 48:37 every hand is s and every waist is covered 1523

SLAUGHTER (63) [SLAUGHTERED, SLAUGHTERING, SLAUGHTERS]
Ge 43:16 s an animal and prepare dinner; 3180
Ex 12: 6 of the community of Israel *must* s them 8821
12:21 for your families and s the Passover lamb. 8821
29:11 **S** it in the LORD's presence at 8821
29:16 **S** it and take the blood and sprinkle it 8821
29:20 **S** it, take some of its blood and put it on 8821
Lev 1: 5 *to* s the young bull before the LORD, 8821
1:11 *to* s it at the north side of the altar before 8821
3: 2 of his offering and s it at the entrance to 8821
3: 8 on the head of his offering and s it in front 8821
3:13 to lay his hand on its head and s it in front 8821
4: 4 to lay his hand on its head and s it before 8821
4:24 to lay his hand on the goat's head and s it at 8821
4:29 and s it at the place of the burnt offering. 8821
4:33 and s it for a sin offering at the place where 8821
14:13 *He is to* s the lamb in the holy place where 8821
14:19 the priest *shall* s the burnt offering 8821
14:25 *He shall* s the lamb for the guilt offering 8821
16:11 *he is to* s the bull for his own sin offering. 8821
16:15 *"He shall* then s the goat for the sin offering 8821
22:28 *Do* not s a cow or a sheep and its young on 8821
Dt 12:15 *you may* s your animals in any of your 2284
12:21 *you may* s animals from the herds 2284
1Sa 4:10 The s was very great; 4804
14:30 Would not the s of the Philistines have been 4804
14:34 and s them here and eat them. 8821
2Sa 17: 9 a s among the troops who follow Absalom.' 4487
2Ch 35: 6 **S** the Passover lambs, 8821
Est 7: 4 for destruction and s and annihilation. 2222
Pr 7:22 like an ox going to the s, 3181
24:11 hold back those staggering toward **s.** 2223
Isa 14:21 Prepare a **place to s** his sons for the sins 4749
30:25 In the day of great **s,** when the towers fall, 2223
34: 2 he will give them over to **s.** 3181
34: 6 a sacrifice in Bozrah and a great s in Edom. 3181
53: 7 he was led like a lamb to the s, 3181
65:12 and you will all bend down for the **s;** 3181
Jer 7:32 but the Valley of **S,** for they will bury 2224
11:19 I had been like a gentle lamb led to the s; 3180
12: 3 Set them apart for the day of **s!** 2224
19: 6 but the Valley of **S.** 2224

Jer 48:15 her finest young men will go down in the s, 3181
50:27 let them go down to the s! 3181
51:40 "I will bring them down like lambs to the s, 3180
Eze 9: 6 S old men, young men and 2222+4200+5422
21:10 sharpened for the s, polished to flash 3180+3181
21:14 It is a sword for s—a sword for great 2728
21:14 a sword for great s, 2728
21:15 the sword *for* s at all their gates. 18
21:15 it is grasped for s. 3181
21:22 to give the command to s, 8358
21:28 " 'A sword, a sword, drawn for the s, 3181
26:15 wounded groan and *the* s **takes place** 2222+2223
34: 3 with the wool and s the choice animals, 2284
44:11 they *may* s the burnt offerings and sacrifices 8821
Da 11:12 with pride and *will* s many thousands, 5877
Hos 5: 2 The rebels are deep in s. 8823
Ob 1: 9 mountains will be cut down in the s. 7780
Zec 11: 4 "Pasture the flock marked for s. 2224
11: 5 Their buyers s them and go unpunished. 2222
11: 7 So I pastured the flock marked for s, 2224
Ac 8:32 "He was led like a sheep to the s, *5375*
Jas 5: 5 fattened yourselves in the day *of* s. *5375*

SLAUGHTERED (52) [SLAUGHTER]

Ge 37:31 s a goat and dipped the robe in the blood. 8821
Lev 4:15 and the bull *shall be* s before the LORD. 8821
4:24 the burnt offering *is* s before the LORD. 8821
4:33 at the place where the burnt offering *is* s. 8821
6:25 *to* **be** s before the LORD in the place 8821
6:25 in the place the burnt offering *is* s; 8821
7: 2 The guilt offering *is to be* s in the place 8821
7: 2 in the place where the burnt offering *is* s, 8821
8:15 Moses s the bull and took some of 8821
8:19 Then Moses s the ram and sprinkled 8821
8:23 Moses s the ram and took some of its blood 8821
9: 8 So Aaron came to the altar and s the calf as 8821
9:12 Then *he* s the burnt offering. 8821
9:15 and s it and offered it for a sin offering 8821
9:18 *He* s the ox and the ram as 8821
14:13 the sin offering and the burnt offering *are* s. 8821
Nu 11:22 if flocks and herds **were** s for them? 8821
14:16 so *he* s them in the desert.' 8821
19: 3 it is to be taken outside the camp and s 8821
Dt 28:31 Your ox *will* **be** s before your eyes, 3180
Jdg 15: 8 He attacked them viciously and s many 4804
1Sa 1:25 When *they had* s the bull, 8821
11:11 into the camp of the Ammonites and s them 5782
14:34 brought his ox that night and s it there. 8821
25:11 and the meat *I have* s for my shearers, 3180
1Ki 18:40 down to the Kishon Valley and s there. 8821
19:21 He took his yoke of oxen and s them. 2284
2Ki 3:23 kings must have fought and s each other. 5782
3:24 And the Israelites invaded the land and s 5782
10: 7 these men took the princes and s all seventy 8821
10:14 and s them by the well of Beth Eked— 8821
23:20 Josiah s all the priests of those high places 2284
2Ch 18: 2 Ahab s many sheep and cattle for him and 2284
28: 9 But *you have* s them in a rage that reaches 2222
29:22 So *they* s the bulls, and the priests took 8821
29:22 next *they* s the rams and sprinkled 8821
29:22 then *they* s the lambs and sprinkled 8821
29:24 then s the goats and presented their blood 8821
30:15 *They* s the Passover lamb on 8821
35: 1 and the Passover lamb *was* s on 8821
35:11 The Passover lambs *were* s, 8821
Ezr 6:20 The Levites s the Passover lamb for all 8821
Ps 44:22 we are considered as sheep to be s. 3186
Jer 25:34 For your time *to be* s has come; 3180
39: 6 the king of Babylon s the sons of Zedekiah 8821
41: 7 and the men who were with him s them 8821
52:10 the king of Babylon s the sons of Zedekiah 8821
La 2:21 *you have* s them without pity. 3180
Eze 16:21 *You* s my children and sacrificed them to 8821
40:39 sin offerings and guilt offerings *were* s. 8821
40:41 on which *the* **sacrifices** *were* s. 8821
Ro 8:36 we are considered as sheep *to be* s." *5375*

SLAUGHTERED (Anglicized) See also BUTCHERED

SLAUGHTERING (5) [SLAUGHTER]

1Sa 7:11 s them along the way to a point below 5782
2Ch 20:23 After they finished s the men from Seir, NIH
25:14 When Amaziah returned from s 5782
Isa 22:13 s *of* cattle and killing of sheep, 2222
Eze 40:42 the utensils *for* s the burnt offerings and 8821

SLAUGHTERS (1) [SLAUGHTER]

Ex 22: 1 "If a man steals an ox or a sheep and s it 3180

SLAVE (89) [ENSLAVE, ENSLAVED, ENSLAVES, ENSLAVING, SLAVERY, SLAVES, SLAVING]

Ge 9:26 May Canaan be the s of Shem. 6269
9:27 and may Canaan be his s." 6269
20:17 healed Abimelech, his wife and his s **girls** 563
21:10 "Get rid of that s **woman** and her son, 563
21:10 for that s **woman's** son will never share in 563
39:17 "That Hebrew s you brought us came to me 6269
39:19 saying, "This is how your s treated me," 6269
44:10 found to have it will become my s; 6269
44:17 found to have the cup will become my s. 6269
Ge 44:33 as my lord's s in place of the boy, 6269
Ex 1:11 So they put s masters over them 4989
2: 5 the reeds and sent her s **girl** to get it. 563
3: 7 because of their s **drivers**, 5601
5: 6 to the s **drivers** and foremen in charge of 5601
5:10 the s **drivers** and the foremen went out 5601
5:13 The s **drivers** kept pressing them, saying, 5601
5:14 by Pharaoh's s **drivers** were beaten 5601
11: 5 to the firstborn son of the s **girl**, 9148
12:44 Any s you have bought may eat of it 6269
21:20 a man beats his **male** or female s with a rod 6269
21:20 or female slave with a rod and the s dies as NIH
21:21 but he is not to be punished if the s gets up NIH
21:21 since **the** s is his property. 2085[S]
21:32 If the bull gores a **male** or female s, 6269
21:32 shekels of silver to the master of **the** s, 2257[S]
23:12 s **born in** your **household**, 563+1201
Lev 19:20 with a woman who is a s **girl** promised 9148
22:11 But if a priest buys a s with money, 5883
22:11 or if a s is born in his household, NIH
22:11 **that** s may eat his food. 2085[S]
25:39 do not make him work **as a** s. 6269+6275
Dt 21:14 You must not sell her or **treat** her **as a** s, 6683
23:15 If a s has taken refuge with you, 6269
24: 7 **treats** him **as a** s or sells him, 6683
32:36 and no one is left, s or free. 6806
Jdg 9:18 and made Abimelech, the son of his s **girl**, 563
1Sa 30:13 "I am an Egyptian, the s of an Amalekite. 6269
2Sa 6:20 in the sight of the s **girls** *of* his servants 563
6:22 But by these s **girls** you spoke of, 563
1Ki 9:21 Solomon conscripted for his s labor force, 6268
14:10 every last male in Israel—s or free. 6806
21:21 every last male in Israel—s or free. 6806
2Ki 9: 8 every last male in Israel—s or free. 6806
14:26 whether s or free, was suffering; 6806
2Ch 8: 8 Solomon conscripted for his s **labor force,** 4989
Job 3:18 they no longer hear the s **driver's** shout. 5601
3:19 and the s is freed from his master. 6269
7: 2 Like a s longing for the evening shadows, 6269
41: 4 with you for you to take him as your s 6269
Ps 105:17 Joseph, sold as a s. 6269
Pr 12:24 but laziness ends in s **labor.** 4989
19:10 much worse for a s to rule over princes! 6269
Jer 2:14 Is Israel a servant, a s **by birth?** 1074+3535
La 1: 1 among the provinces has now become a s. 4989
Na 2: 7 Its s **girls** moan like doves and beat 563
Mt 20:27 whoever wants to be first must be your s— *1528*
Mk 10:44 whoever wants to be first must be s of all. *1528*
Jn 8:34 everyone who sins is a s to sin. *1528*
8:35 a s has no permanent place in the family, *1528*
Ac 7: 9 they sold him as a s into Egypt. *NIG*
16:16 we were met by a s **girl** who had a spirit *4087*
16:19 When the owners *of* **the** s **girl** realized *899*[S]
Ro 7:14 but I am unspiritual, sold as a s to sin. *NIG*
7:25 I myself in my mind *am* a s to God's law, *1526*
7:25 but in the sinful nature a s to the law of sin. *NIG*
8:15 not receive a spirit that **makes** you **a** s again *1525*
1Co 7:21 Were you a s when you were called? *1528*
7:22 For he who was a s when he was called by *1528*
7:22 a free man when he was called is Christ's s. *1528*
9:19 *I* **make** myself **a** s to everyone, *1530*
9:27 I beat my body and **make** it my s so that *1524*
12:13 whether Jews or Greeks, s or free— *1528*
Gal 3:28 There is neither Jew nor Greek, s nor free, *1528*
4: 1 he is no different from a s, *1528*
4: 7 So you are no longer a s, but a son; *1528*
4:22 one by the s **woman** and the other by *4087*
4:23 the s **woman** was born in the ordinary way; *4087*
4:30 "Get rid of the s **woman** and her son, *4087*
4:30 for the s **woman's** son will never share in *4087*
4:31 we are not children *of* the s **woman,** *4087*
Eph 6: 8 whether he is s or free. *1528*
Col 3:11 s or free, but Christ is all, and is in all. *1528*
1Ti 1:10 *for* s **traders** and liars and perjurers— *435*
Phm 1:16 no longer as a s, but better than a slave, *1528*
1:16 but better than a s, as a dear brother. *1528*
2Pe 2:19 a man *is a* s to whatever has mastered him. *1530*
Rev 6:15 and every s and every free man hid in caves *1528*
13:16 small and great, rich and poor, free and s, *1528*
19:18 and the flesh *of* all people, free and s, *1528*

SLAVERY (24) [SLAVE]

Ex 2:23 The Israelites groaned in their s 6275
2:23 for help because of their s went up to God. 6275
13: 3 out of Egypt, out of the land of s. 6269
13:14 out of Egypt, out of the land of s. 6269
20: 2 out of Egypt, out of the land of s. 6269
Dt 5: 6 out of Egypt, out of the land of s. 6269
6:12 out of Egypt, out of the land of s. 6269
7: 8 and redeemed you from the land of s, 6269
8:14 out of Egypt, out of the land of s. 6269
13: 5 and redeemed you from the land of s; 6269
13:10 out of Egypt, out of the land of s. 6269
Jos 24:17 out of Egypt, from that land of s, 6269
Jdg 6: 8 out of Egypt, out of the land of s. 6269
Ne 5: 5 to subject our sons and daughters to s. 6269
9:17 a leader in order to return to their s. 6285
Jer 34:13 out of Egypt, out of the land of s. 6269
Mic 6: 4 and redeemed you from the land of s. 6269
Ro 6:19 the parts of your body **in** s to impurity and *1529*
6:19 so now offer them **in** s to righteousness *1529*
Gal 4: 3 we were **in** s under the basic principles of *1530*
4:25 because *she is* **in** s with her children. *1526*
5: 1 be burdened again by a yoke *of* s. *1525*
1Ti 6: 1 of s should consider their masters worthy *1528*
Heb 2:15 free those who all their lives were held *in* s *1525*

SLAVES (71) [SLAVE]

Ge 9:25 The **lowest of** s will he be to his brothers." 6269+6269
15:14 But I will punish the nation *they* **serve as** s, 6268
20:14 and **male** and female s and gave them 6269
43:18 and seize us as s and take our donkeys." 6269
44: 9 and the rest of us will become my lord's s." 6269
44:16 We are now my lord's s— 6269
50:18 "We are your s," they said. 6269
Ex 6: 6 I will free you from being s to them, 6275
9:20 to bring their s and their livestock inside. 6269
9:21 of the LORD left their s and livestock in 6269
Lev 25:42 they must not be sold as s. 6269
25:44 " 'Your **male** and female s are to come 6269
25:44 from them you may buy s. 563+2256+6269
25:46 as inherited property and *can* **make** them s 6268
26:13 of Egypt so that you would no longer be s 6269
Dt 5:15 Remember that you were s in Egypt and 6269
6:21 tell him: "We were s of Pharaoh in Egypt, 6269
15:15 Remember that you were s in Egypt and 6269
16:12 Remember that you were s in Egypt, 6269
24:18 Remember that you were s in Egypt and 6269
24:22 Remember that you were s in Egypt. 6269
28:68 to your enemies as **male** and female s, 6269
1Sa 8:17 and you yourselves will become his s. 6269
1Ki 2:39 two of Shimei's s ran off to Achish son 6269
2:39 and Shimei was told, "Your s are in Gath." 6269
2:40 to Achish at Gath in search of his s. 6269
2:40 and brought the s back from Gath. 6269
9:22 But Solomon *did* not make s of any of 6269
2Ki 4: 1 to take my two boys as his s." 6269
2Ch 8: 9 not make s of the Israelites for his work; 6269
28:10 **make** the **men** and women of Judah and Jerusalem your s. 3899+6269
Ezr 9: 9 Though we are s, 6269
Ne 9:36 "But see, we are s today, 6269
9:36 s in the land you gave our forefathers 6269
Est 7: 4 sold as **male** and female s, 6269
Ps 123: 2 of s look to the hand of their master, 6269
Ecc 2: 7 I bought **male** and female s 6269
2: 7 and had other s who were born NIH
10: 7 I have seen s on horseback, 6269
10: 7 while princes go on foot like s. 6269
Jer 34: 8 in Jerusalem to proclaim **freedom for** *the* s. 2002
34: 9 to free his Hebrew s, both **male** 6269
34:10 they would free their **male** and female s 6269
34:11 took back the s they had freed 2256+6269+9148
34:16 the **male** and female s you had set free 6269
34:16 to become your s again. 2256+6269+9148
La 5: 8 S rule over us, and there is none to free us 6269
Eze 27:13 they exchanged s and articles of bronze 132+5883
Zec 2: 9 so that their s will plunder them. 6269
Jn 8:33 and *have* never *been* s of anyone. *1526*
Ac 7: 7 But I will punish the nation *they* **serve as** s,' *1526*
Ro 6: 6 that we *should* no longer *be* s to sin— *1526*
6:16 to someone to obey him as s, you are slaves *1528*
6:16 you are s to the one whom you obey— *1528*
6:16 whether you are s to sin, *NIG*
6:17 though you used to be s to sin, *1528*
6:18 and *have* **become** s to righteousness. *1530*
6:20 When you were s to sin, *1528*
6:22 from sin and *have* **become** s to God, *1530*
1Co 7:23 do not become s of men. *1528*
Gal 2: 4 in Christ Jesus and to **make** us s. *2871*
4: 8 *you were* s to those who by nature are *1526*
4:24 and bears children who are to be s: *1525*
Eph 6: 5 S, obey your earthly masters with respect *1528*
6: 6 but like s of Christ, *1528*
6: 9 And masters, treat **your** s in the same way. *899*[S]
Col 3:22 S, obey your earthly masters in everything; *1528*
4: 1 provide your s with what is right and fair, *1528*
Tit 2: 9 Teach s to be subject to their masters *1528*
1Pe 2:18 S, submit yourselves to your masters *3860*
2Pe 2:19 while they themselves are s of depravity— *1528*

SLAVING (1) [SLAVE]

Lk 15:29 All these years *I've been* s for you *1526*

SLAY (16) [SLAIN, SLAYER, SLAYS, SLEW]

Ge 22:10 and took the knife to s his son. 8821
Job 13:15 Though *he* s me, yet will I hope in him; 7779
Ps 34:21 Evil *will* s the wicked; 4637
37:14 to s those whose ways are upright. 3180
94: 6 *They* s the widow and the alien; 2222
139:19 If only *you would* s the wicked, O God! 7779
Isa 11: 4 the breath of his lips *he will* s the wicked. 4637
14:30 *it will* s your survivors. 2222
27: 1 *he will* s the monster of the sea. 2222
Jer 33: 5 of the men *I will* s in my anger and wrath. 5782
Eze 6: 4 *I will* s your people in front of your idols. 5877
28: 9 not a god, in the hands of *those who* s you. 2726
Hos 2: 3 and s her with thirst. 4637
9:16 *I will* s their cherished offspring." 4637
Am 9: 4 there I will command the sword *to* s them. 2222
Rev 6: 4 the earth and to make men s each other. *5377*

SLAYER (2) [SLAY]

Eze 21:11 made ready for the hand of the s. 2222
Hos 9:13 But Ephraim will bring out their children to the s." 2222

SLAYS (1) [SLAY]

Job 5: 2 Resentment kills a fool, and envy s the simple. 4637

SLEDGE (3) [SLEDGES]
Job 41:30 leaving a trail in the mud like a **threshing s.** 3023
Isa 28:27 Caraway is not threshed with a **s,** 3023
41:15 "See, I will make you into a **threshing s,** 4617

SLEDGES (3) [SLEDGE]
2Sa 24:22 and here are **threshing s** and ox yokes for 4617
1Ch 21:23 the **threshing s** for the wood, 4617
Am 1: 3 she threshed Gilead with s *having* iron teeth, 3023

SLEEK (6)
Ge 41: 2 seven cows, s and fat, and they grazed 3637+5260
41: 4 ugly and gaunt ate up the seven **s,** 3637+5260
41:18 seven cows, fat and **s,** and they grazed 3637+9307
Dt 32:15 filled with food, he became heavy and **s.** 4170
Jer 5:28 and have grown fat and **s.** 6950
Eze 34:16 but the s and the strong I will destroy. 9045

SLEEP (73) [ASLEEP, SLEEPER, SLEEPING, SLEEPLESS, SLEEPS, SLEEPY, SLEPT]
Ge 2:21 the man to fall into a **deep s;** 9554
15:12 Abram fell into a **deep s,** 9554
16: 2 **Go, s with** my maidservant; 448+995
28:11 he put it under his head and **lay down to s.** 8886
28:16 When Jacob awoke from his **s,** he thought, 9104
30: 3 **S with** her so that she can bear children 448+995
30:15 *"he can* **s with** you tonight in return 6640+8886
30:16 *"You must* **s with** me," she said. 448+995
31:40 and s fled from my eyes. 9104
38:16 "Come now, *let me* **s with** you." 448+995
38:16 what will you give me *to* **s with** *you?"* 448+995
38:26 And *he did* not **s with** her again. 3359
39:14 He came in here to **s with** me, 6640+8886
Ex 22:27 What else *will he* **s** in? 8886
Dt 24:12 *do* not **go to s** with his pledge 8886
24:13 to him by sunset so that *he may* **s** in it. 8886
Jdg 16:14 He awoke from his s and pulled up the pin 9104
16:19 *Having* **put** him **to s** on her lap, 3822
16:20 He awoke from his s and thought, 9104
1Sa 26:12 the LORD had put them into a **deep s.** 9554
2Sa 3: 7 "Why *did you* **s with** my father's 448+995
11:13 the evening Uriah went out to s on his mat 8886
Est 6: 1 That night the king could not **s;** 9104
Job 4:13 when **deep s** falls on men, 9554
14:12 not awake or be roused from their **s.** 9104
31:10 and *may* other men **s with** her. 4156+6584
33:15 when **deep s** falls on men as they slumber 9554
Ps 3: 5 I lie down and **s;** 3822
4: 8 I will lie down and s in peace, 3822
7: 5 to the ground and **make** me **s** in the dust. 8905
13: 3 or *I will* **s** *in* death; 3822
44:23 Awake, O Lord! Why *do you* **s?** 3822
68:13 Even while *you* **s** among the campfires, 8886
76: 5 *they* **s** their last sleep; 5670
76: 5 they sleep their last **s;** 9104
78:65 Then the Lord awoke as from **s,** 3825
90: 5 You sweep men away in the **s of death;** 9104
121: 4 over Israel will neither slumber nor **s.** 3822
127: 2 for he grants s to those he loves. 9097
132: 4 I will allow no s to my eyes, 9104
Pr 3:24 when you lie down, your s will be sweet. 9104
4:16 For *they* cannot s till they do evil; 3822
6: 4 Allow no s to your eyes, 9104
6: 9 When will you get up from your **s?** 9104
6:10 A little **s,** a little slumber, 9104
6:22 when you **s,** they will watch over you; 8886
19:15 Laziness brings on **deep s,** 9554
20:13 Do not love s or you will grow poor; 9104
24:33 A little **s,** a little slumber, a little folding of 9104
Ecc 5:12 The s *of* a laborer is sweet, 9104
5:12 abundance of a rich man permits him no **s.** 3822
8:16 his eyes not seeing s day or night— 9104
Isa 29:10 LORD has brought over you a **deep s:** 8120+9554
56:10 they lie around and dream, they love to **s.** 5670
Jer 31:26 My s had been pleasant to me. 9104
51:39 then s forever and not awake," 3822+9104
51:57 *they will* s forever and not awake," 3822+9104
Eze 23:44 As *men* **s with** a prostitute, 448+995
34:25 so that they may live in the desert and s in 3822
Da 2: 1 his mind was troubled and he could not **s.** 9104
6:18 And he could not **s.** 10733
8:18 *I was* **in a deep s,** with my face to the 8101
10: 9 **fell into a deep s,** my face to the ground. 8101
12: 2 Multitudes *who* **s** *in* the dust of the earth 3825
Jnh 1: 5 and **fell into a deep s.** 8101
1: 6 "How *can* you **s?** 8101
Zec 4: 1 as a man is wakened from his **s.** 9104
Jn 11:13 his disciples thought he meant **natural s.** 3122+3836+3836+5678
Ac 20: 9 *into* a deep s as Paul talked on and on. 5678
1Co 15:51 I tell you a mystery: *We will* not all **s,** 3121
2Co 11:27 and **have** often **gone without s;** 71+1877
1Th 5: 7 For those who **s,** sleep at night, 2761
5: 7 For those who sleep, **s** at night, 2761

SLEEPER (1) [SLEEP]
Eph 5:14 This is why it is said: "Wake up, O **s,** 2761

SLEEPING (22) [SLEEP]
Ge 2:21 while *he was* **s,** he took one of the man's 3822
Nu 5:13 *by* **s with** another man, 907+2446+8886+8887
Nu 5:20 *by* **s with** a man other than your husband"— 928+5989+8888
Dt 22:22 is found **s with** another man's wife, 6640+8886
Jdg 16:13 So *while he was* **s,** Delilah took 3822
19: 4 eating and drinking, and s there. 4328
1Sa 26:12 They *were* all **s,** because the LORD had put 3825
1Ki 18:27 Maybe he is s and must be awakened." 3825
Pr 23:34 You will be like *one* s on the high seas, 8886
Mt 8:24 But Jesus *was* **s.** 2761
13:25 But *while* everyone *was* **s,** 1877+2761
26:40 to his disciples and found them **s.** 2761
26:43 he again found them **s,** 2761
26:45 *"Are you* still s and resting? 2761
Mk 4:38 Jesus was in the stern, s on a cushion. 2761
13:36 do not let him find you **s.** 2761
14:37 to his disciples and found them **s.** 2761
14:40 he again found them **s,** 2761
14:41 he said to them, *"Are you* still s and resting? 2761
Lk 22:46 "Why *are you* **s?"** 2761
Ac 12: 6 Peter was s between two soldiers, 3121
2Pe 2: 3 and their destruction *has* not *been* **s.** 3818

SLEEPLESS (1) [SLEEP]
2Co 6: 5 in hard work, **s nights** and hunger; 71

SLEEPS (15) [SLEEP]
Ex 22:16 a virgin who is not pledged to be married and **s with** her, 6640+8886
Lev 14:47 Anyone *who* s or eats in the house 8886
19:20 " 'If a man **s with** a woman who is a slave girl 907+2446+8886+8887
20:11 " 'If a man **s with** his father's wife, 907+8886
20:12 " 'If a man **s with** his daughter-in-law, 907+8886
20:20 " 'If a man **s with** his aunt, 907+8886
Dt 22:23 pledged to be married and *he* **s with** 6640+8886
27:20 the man *who* **s with** his father's wife, 6640+8886
27:22 is the man *who* **s with** his sister, 6640+8886
27:23 man *who* **s with** his mother-in-law." 6640+8886
Pr 6:29 So is he *who* **s with** another man's wife; 448+995
10: 5 *he who* s during harvest is a disgraceful son. 8101
Isa 5:27 not one slumbers or **s;** 3822
Mk 4:27 Night and day, whether *he* s or gets up, 2761
Jn 11:12 His disciples replied, "Lord, if *he* **s,** 3121

SLEEPY (1) [SLEEP]
Lk 9:32 Peter and his companions were **very s,** 976+5678

SLEET (1)
Ps 78:47 with hail and their sycamore-figs with s. 2857

SLEIGHT (KJV) See SCHEMING

SLEPT (21) [SLEEP]
Ge 16: 4 *He* **s with** Hagar, and she conceived. 448+995
19: 8 I have two daughters who *have* never **s with** 3359
26:10 men might well have **s with** your wife, 907+8886
30: 4 Jacob **s with** her, 448+995
30:16 So *he* **s with** her that night. 6640+8886
35:22 **s with** his father's concubine Bilhah, 907+8886
38:18 So he gave them to her and **s with** her, 448+995
Nu 5:19 "If no other man *has* **s with** you 907+8886
31:17 And kill every woman *who has* **s with** a man, 408+3359+4200+5435
31:18 every girl who *has* never **s with** 3359+5435
31:35 who *had* never **s with** a man. 2351+3359+5435
Dt 22:22 both the man who **s with** her and 6640+8886
Jdg 21:12 in Jabesh Gilead four hundred young women who *had* never **s with** 2351+3359+4200+5435
1Sa 2:22 how *they* **s with** the women who served 907+8886
2Sa 11: 4 She came to him, and *he* **s with** her. 6640+8886
11: 9 But Uriah **s** *at* the entrance to the palace 8886
12: 3 drank from his cup and even s in his arms. 8886
SS 5: 2 I s but my heart was awake. 3825
Eze 23: 8 when during her youth *men* **s with** her, 907+8886
23:44 And *they* **s with** her. 448+995
23:44 so *they* **s with** those lewd women, 448+995

SLEW (1) [SLAY]
Ps 78:34 Whenever God s them, they would seek him 2222

SLIGHTEST (1)
Jude 1:12 eating with you **without the s qualm—** 925

SLIDE (KJV) See SLIP, WAVERING

SLIME (1) [SLIMY]
Job 9:31 you would plunge me into a **s pit** so that 8846

SLIMEPITS (KJV) See TAR PITS

SLIMY (1) [SLIME]
Ps 40: 2 He lifted me out of the **s pit,** 1014+8622

SLING (6) [SLINGS, SLUNG]
Jdg 20:16 each of whom *could* s a stone at a hair and 7843
1Sa 17:40 with his s in his hand, approached the 7845
17:50 over the Philistine with a s and a stone; 7845
25:29 hurl away as from the pocket of a s. 7845
1Ch 12: 2 to shoot arrows or to **s stones** 74+928+2021
Pr 26: 8 a stone in a s is the giving of honor to 5275

SLINGS (1) [SLING]
2Ki 3:25 but **men armed with s** surrounded it 7847

SLINGSTONES (3) [STONE]
2Ch 26:14 bows and s for the entire army. 74+7845
Job 41:28 s are like chaff to him. 74+7845
Zec 9:15 They will destroy and overcome with **s.** 74+7845

SLIP (7) [SLIPPED, SLIPPERY, SLIPPING, SLIPS]
Dt 4: 9 or *let them* s from your heart as long 6073
32:35 In due time their foot *will* **s;** 4572
1Sa 27: 1 and *I will* **s out** of his hand." 4880
2Ki 9:15 don't *let* anyone **s out** of the city to go 3655
Ps 37:31 his feet *do* not **s.** 5048
121: 3 He will not let your foot s— 4572
Jer 20:10 All my friends are waiting for me to **s,** 7520

SLIPPED (6) [SLIP]
2Sa 4: 6 Then Recab and his brother Baanah **s away.** 4880
Ps 17: 5 my feet *have* not s. 4572
73: 2 But as for me, my feet *had* almost s; 5742
Jn 5:13 for Jesus *had* **s away** into the crowd 1728
2Co 11:33 from a window in the wall and **s through** 1767
Jude 1: 4 *have* **secretly s in** among you. 4208

SLIPPERY (3) [SLIP]
Ps 35: 6 may their path be dark and s, 2761
73:18 Surely you place them on s *ground;* 2747
Jer 23:12 "Therefore their path will become s; 2761

SLIPPING (4) [SLIP]
Job 12: 5 as the fate of *those* whose feet *are* **s.** 5048
Ps 66: 9 and kept our feet from **s.** 4572
94:18 When I said, "My foot *is* **s,"** your love, 4572
Jn 8:59 **s away from** the temple grounds. 2002

SLIPS (1) [SLIP]
Ps 38:16 exalt themselves over me when my foot **s."** 4572

SLOPE (9) [SLOPES]
Jos 15: 8 the southern s *of* the Jebusite city (that is, 4190
15:10 ran along the northern s *of* Mount Jearim 4190
15:11 It went to the northern s *of* Ekron, 4190
18:12 the northern s *of* Jericho and headed west 4190
18:13 From there it crossed to the south s *of* Luz 4190
18:16 the Hinnom Valley along the southern s *of* 4190
18:18 the northern s *of* Beth Arabah and on down 4190
18:19 then went to the northern s *of* Beth Hoglah 4190
Mic 1: 4 like water rushing down a **s.** 4618

SLOPES (12) [SLOPE]
Nu 21:15 and the s *of* the ravines that lead to the site 844
34:11 along the s east *of* the Sea of Kinnereth. 4190
Dt 3:17 below the s *of* Pisgah. 844
4:49 below the s *of* Pisgah. 844
33: 2 from his **mountain s.** 850
Jos 7: 5 and struck them down on the **s.** 4618
10:40 the western foothills and the **mountain s,** 844
12: 3 and then southward below the s *of* Pisgah. 844
12: 8 the **mountain s,** the desert and the Negev— 844
13:20 the s *of* Pisgah, and Beth Jeshimoth 844
Isa 11:14 They will swoop down on the s *of* Philistia 4190
Jer 18:14 of Lebanon ever vanish from its rocky **s?** 8442

SLOTHFUL (KJV) See HESITATE, LACKING, LAZINESS, LAZY, SLACK, SLUGGARD

SLOW (19) [SLOWLY, SLOWNESS]
Ex 4:10 I am s *of* speech and tongue." 3878
34: 6 gracious God, s *to* anger, abounding in love 800
Nu 14:18 'The LORD is s *to* anger, abounding in love 800
Dt 7:10 *he will* not *be* s to repay 336
23:21 do not be s to pay it, 336
2Ki 4:24 don't **s down** for me unless 4200+6806+8206
Ne 9:17 s *to* anger and abounding in love. 800
Ps 86:15 gracious God, s *to* anger, abounding in love 800
103: 8 s *to* anger, abounding in love. 800
145: 8 s *to* anger and rich in love. 800
Joel 2:13 s *to* anger and abounding in love, 800
Jnh 4: 2 s *to* anger and abounding in love, 800
Na 1: 3 LORD is s *to* anger and great in power; 800
Lk 24:25 and **how s** of heart to believe all that 1096
Ac 27: 7 *We* **made s headway** for many days 1095
Heb 5:11 but it is hard to explain because you are s 3821
Jas 1:19 s to speak and slow to become angry, 1096
1:19 slow to speak and s to become angry, 1096
2Pe 3: 9 The Lord *is* not s in keeping his promise, 1094

SLOWLY (1) [SLOW]
Ge 33:14 I move along s at the pace of the droves 351+4200

SLOWNESS (1) [SLOW]
2Pe 3: 9 The Lord is not slow in keeping his promise, as some understand **s.** 1097

SLUG (1)
Ps 58: 8 Like a s melting away as it moves along, 8671

SLUGGARD (13) [SLUGGARD'S]
Pr 6: 6 Go to the ant, you s; 6789
6: 9 How long will you lie there, you s? 6789
10:26 so is a s to those who send him. 6789
13: 4 The s craves and gets nothing, 6789
15:19 The way of the s is blocked with thorns, 6789
19:24 The s buries his hand in the dish; 6789
20: 4 A s does not plow in season; 6789
22:13 The s says, "There is a lion outside!" 6789
24:30 I went past the field of the s, 6789
26:13 The s says, "There is a lion in the road, 6789
26:14 so a s turns on his bed. 6789
26:15 The s buries his hand in the dish; 6789
26:16 The s is wiser in his own eyes than 6789

SLUGGARD'S (1) [SLUGGARD]
Pr 21:25 The s craving will be the death of him, 6789

SLUMBER (10) [SLUMBERS]
Job 33:15 when deep sleep falls on men as they s 9484
Ps 121: 3 he who watches over you *will* not s; 5670
121: 4 he who watches over Israel *will* neither s 5670
132: 4 no s to my eyelids, 9484
Pr 4:16 of s till they make someone fall. 9104
6: 4 no s to your eyelids. 9484
6:10 a little s, a little folding of the hands to rest 9484
24:33 a little s, a little folding of the hands to rest 9484
Na 3:18 O king of Assyria, your shepherds s; 5670
Ro 13:11 for you to wake up from your s, *5678*

SLUMBERS (1) [SLUMBER]
Isa 5:27 not *one* s or sleeps; 5670

SLUMPED (1)
2Ki 9:24 The arrow pierced his heart and *he* s **down** 4156

SLUNG (2) [SLING]
1Sa 17: 6 a bronze javelin was s **on** his **back.** 1068+4190
17:49 *he* s it and struck the Philistine on the 7843

SLUR (1)
Ps 15: 3 and casts no s on his fellowman, 3075

SLY (3)
Pr 25:23 so a s tongue brings angry looks. 6260
Mt 26: 4 to arrest Jesus *in* some s **way** and kill him. *1515*
Mk 14: 1 some s way to arrest Jesus and kill *1515+1877*

SMALL (70) [SMALLER, SMALLEST]
Ge 19:20 town near enough to run to, and it is s. 5203
19:20 Let me flee to it—it is *very* s, isn't it? 5203
Ex 12: 4 If any household *is* too s for a whole lamb, 5070
Nu 22:18 not do anything great or s to go beyond 7783
Dt 1:17 hear both s and great alike. 7785
25:14 measures in your house—one large, one s. 7783
Jos 17:15 "and if the hill country of Ephraim *is too* s 237
1Sa 15:17 you were once s in your own eyes, 7785
18:23 *a* s *matter* to become the king's son-in-law? 7829
20: 2 my father doesn't do anything, great or s, 7785
20:35 He had a s boy with him, 7785
1Ki 2:20 "I have one s request to make of you," 7783
8:64 altar before the LORD was too s to hold 7785
10:17 He also made three hundred s **shields** 4482
17:13 But first make a s cake of bread for me 7783
18:44 as s as a man's hand is rising from the sea." 7783
20:27 like two s **flocks** *of* goats, 3105
22:31 "Do not fight with anyone, s or great, 7785
2Ki 4:10 a s room on the roof and put in it a bed and 7783
6: 1 the place where we meet with you is too s 7639
2Ch 9:16 He also made three hundred s **shields** 4482
14: 8 armed with s **shields** and with bows. 4482
15:13 were to be put to death, whether s or great, 7785
18:30 "Do not fight with anyone, s or great, 7785
23: 9 the large and s **shields** that had belonged 8949
36:18 from the temple of God, both large and s, 7783
Job 3:19 The s and the great are there, 7785
Ps 104:25 living things both large and **s.** 7783
115:13 who fear the LORD—s and great alike. 7783
148:10 s **creatures** and flying birds, 8254
Pr 24:10 how s is your strength! 7639
30:24 "Four things on earth are s, 7783
Ecc 9:14 a s city with only a few people in it. 7783
Isa 49: 6 *"It is* too s *a thing for* you to 7837
49:19 now *you will be* too s for your people, 7674
49:20 'This place is too s for us; 7639
Jer 46: 3 "Prepare your **shields,** both large and s, 4482
49:15 "Now I will make you s among the nations, 7785
Eze 23:24 with large and s **shields** and with helmets. 4482
38: 4 and a great horde with large and s **shields,** 4482
39: 9 the s and large **shields,** the bows and 4482
Da 8: 9 which started s but grew in power to 7582
Am 6:11 the great house into pieces and the s house 7785
7: 2 How can Jacob survive? He is so **s!"** 7785
7: 5 How can Jacob survive? He is so **s!"** 7785
Ob 1: 2 I will make you s among the nations; 7785
Mic 5: 2 though you are s among the clans of Judah, 7582
Zec 4:10 "Who despises the day of s *things?* 7783
Mt 7:14 But s is the gate and narrow the road *5101*
15:34 "Seven," they replied, "and a few s **fish."** *2715*
17:20 if you have faith as s as a mustard seed, *NIG*
Mk 3: 9 to have a s **boat** ready for him, *4449*
8: 7 They had a few s **fish** as well; *2715*
12:42 and put in two very s **copper coins,** *3321*
Lk 17: 6 "If you have faith as s as a mustard seed, *NIG*
19:17 trustworthy in a **very** s *matter,* *1788*
21: 2 in two very s **copper coins.** *3321*
Jn 6: 9 "Here is a boy with five s **barley** loaves *3209*
6: 9 with five small barley loaves and two s **fish,** *4066*
Ac 12:18 there was no s commotion among *3900*
26:22 and so I stand here and testify *to* s *3625*
27:16 to the lee of a s **island** called Cauda, *3761*
Jas 3: 4 by a **very** s rudder wherever the pilot wants *1788*
3: 5 Likewise the tongue is a s part of the body, *3625*
3: 5 a great forest is set on fire by a s spark. *2462*
Rev 11:18 reverence your name—both s and great— *3625*
13:16 He also forced everyone, s and great, *3625*
19: 5 you who fear him, both s and great!" *3625*
19:18 free and slave, s and great." *3625*
20:12 And I saw the dead, great and s, *3625*

SMALLER (7) [SMALL]
Nu 26:54 and to a s *group* a smaller one; 5071
26:54 and to a smaller group a s one; 5070
26:56 by lot among the larger and s groups." 5071
33:54 and to a s *group* a smaller one. 5071
33:54 and to a smaller group a s one. 5070
Eze 42: 6 so *they were* s in floor space than those on 724
43:14 and from the s ledge up to 7783

SMALLEST (5) [SMALL]
1Sa 9:21 a Benjamite, from the s tribe of Israel, 7783
Isa 60:22 become a thousand, the s a mighty nation. 7582
Mt 5:18 not **the s letter,** not the least stroke of a pen, *2740*
13:32 Though it is the s of all your seeds, *3625*
Mk 4:31 which is the s seed you plant in the ground. *3625*

SMART (KJV) See SUFFER

SMASH (7) [SMASHED, SMASHES]
Ex 34:13 s their sacred stones and cut down 8689
Dt 7: 5 down their altars, s their sacred stones, 8689
12: 3 s their sacred stones and burn their 8689
Jer 13:14 *I will* s them one against the other, 5879
19:11 *I will* s this nation and this city just 8689
48:12 they will empty her jars and s her jugs. 5879
Am 6:11 and *he will* s the great house *into* pieces 5782

SMASHED (14) [SMASH]
Jdg 7:20 blew the trumpets and s the jars. 8689
2Ki 11:18 *They* s the altars and idols to pieces 8689
18: 4 s the sacred stones and cut down 8689
23:12 s them **to pieces** and threw the rubble into 8368
23:14 Josiah s the sacred stones and cut down 8689
2Ch 14: 3 s the sacred stones and cut down 8689
23:17 *They* s the altars and idols 8689
31: 1 s the sacred stones and cut down 8689
34: 4 and s the Asherah poles, 8689
Ps 74: 6 *They* s all the carved paneling 2150
Jer 19:11 and this city just as this potter's jar *is* s 8689
Eze 6: 4 and your incense altars *will* **be** s; 8689
6: 6 your idols s and ruined, 8689
Da 2:34 on its feet of iron and clay and s them. 10182

SMASHES (1) [SMASH]
Da 2:40 for iron breaks and s everything— 10290

SMEAR (1) [SMEARED]
Job 13: 4 You, however, s me *with* lies; 3260

SMEARED (1) [SMEAR]
Ps 119:69 Though the arrogant *have* s me *with* lies, 3260

SMELL (11) [SMELLED]
Ge 27:27 Isaac **caught the** s *of* his clothes, 8193+8194
27:27 the s *of* my son is like the smell of a field 8194
27:27 the s *of* a field that the LORD has blessed. 8194
Ex 16:20 but it was full of maggots and *began to* s. 944
Dt 4:28 which cannot see or hear or eat or s. 8193
Ps 115: 6 but cannot hear, noses, but *they* cannot s; 8193
Ecc 10: 1 As dead flies **give** perfume **a bad** s, 944+5580
Da 3:27 and there was no s *of* fire on them. 10666
Joel 2:20 And its stench will go up; its s will rise." 7462
1Co 12:17 where would the **sense of** s be? *4018*
2Co 2:16 To the one we are the s of death; *4011*

SMELLED (2) [SMELL]
Ge 8:21 The LORD s the pleasing aroma and said 8193
Ex 7:21 the river s so **bad** that the Egyptians could 944

SMELTED (1)
Job 28: 2 and copper **is** s *from* ore. 3668

SMILE (2) [SMILED]
Job 9:27 I will change my expression, and s,' 1158
10: 3 while *you* s on the schemes of the wicked? 3649

SMILED (1) [SMILE]
Job 29:24 *When I* s at them, they scarcely believed it; 8471

SMITE (1) [SMITTEN]
Dt 33:11 S the loins of those who rise up 4730

SMITTEN (1) [SMITE]
Isa 53: 4 stricken by God, s *by* him, and afflicted. 5782

SMOKE (47) [SMOKING]
Ge 19:28 and he saw **dense** s rising *from* the land, 7798
19:28 like s *from* a furnace. 7798
Ex 19:18 Mount Sinai *was* **covered with s,** 6939
19:18 The s billowed up from it like smoke from 6940
19:18 The smoke billowed up from it like s *from* 6940
20:18 the trumpet and saw the mountain **in s,** 6942
Lev 16:13 and the s *of* the incense will conceal 6727
Jos 8:20 The men of Ai looked back and saw the s 6940
8:21 and that s was going up from the city, 6940
Jdg 20:38 that they should send up a great cloud of s 6940
20:40 the column of s began to rise from the city, 6940
20:40 and saw the s of the whole city going up 5368
2Sa 22: 9 S rose from his nostrils; 6940
Job 41:20 S pours from his nostrils as from 6940
Ps 18: 8 S rose from his nostrils; 6940
37:20 they will vanish—vanish like s. 6940
68: 2 As s is blown away by the wind, 6940
102: 3 For my days vanish like **s;** 6940
104:32 who touches the mountains, and *they* s. 6939
119:83 Though I am like a wineskin in the **s,** 7798
144: 5 touch the mountains, so that *they* s. 6939
Pr 10:26 As vinegar to the teeth and s to the eyes, 6940
SS 3: 6 up from the desert like a column of s, 6940
Isa 4: 5 over those who assemble there a cloud of s 6940
6: 4 and the temple was filled with s. 6940
9:18 so that it rolls upward in a column of s. 6940
14:31 A **cloud of** s comes from the north, 6940
30:27 with burning anger and dense **clouds of s;** 5366
34:10 its s will rise forever. 6940
51: 6 the heavens will vanish like **s,** 6940
65: 5 Such people are s in my nostrils, 6940
Hos 13: 3 like s escaping through a window. 6940
Joel 2:30 blood and fire and billows of s. 6940
Na 2:13 "I will burn up your chariots in **s,** 6940
Ac 2:19 blood and fire and billows *of* s. *2837*
Rev 8: 4 The s of the incense, *2837*
9: 2 s rose from it like the smoke from *2837*
9: 2 from it like the s from a gigantic furnace. *2837*
9: 2 The sun and sky were darkened by the s *2837*
9: 3 of the s locusts came down upon the earth *2837*
9:17 of their mouths came fire, s and sulfur. *2837*
9:18 s and sulfur that came out of their mouths. *2837*
14:11 s of their torment rises for ever and ever. *2837*
15: 8 the temple was filled *with* s from the glory *2837*
18: 9 with her and shared her luxury see the s *2837*
18:18 When they see the s of her burning, *2837*
19: 3 The s from her goes up for ever and ever." *2837*

SMOKING (1) [SMOKE]
Ge 15:17 a s firepot with a blazing torch appeared 6940

SMOLDER (2) [SMOLDERING, SMOLDERS]
Ps 74: 1 Why *does* your anger s against the sheep 6939
80: 4 how long *will your* **anger** s against 6939

SMOLDERING (4) [SMOLDER]
Nu 16:37 the censers out of the s **remains** and scatter 8599
Isa 7: 4 because of these two s stubs of firewood— 6942
42: 3 and a s wick he will not snuff out. 3910
Mt 12:20 and a s wick he will not snuff out, *5606*

SMOLDERS (1) [SMOLDER]
Hos 7: 6 Their passion s all night; 3822

SMOOTH (11) [SMOOTH-SKINNED, SMOOTHER, SMOOTHLY, SMOOTHS]
Ge 27:11 and I'm a man *with* s *skin.* 2747
27:16 She also covered his hands and the s *part* 2753
1Sa 17:40 chose five s stones from the stream, 2752
Ps 55:21 His speech *is* s as butter, 2744
Pr 6:24 from the s tongue of the wayward wife. 2753
7:21 she seduced him with her s talk. 2749
Isa 26: 7 **make** the way of the righteous **s.** 7142
42:16 before them and make the rough places **s.** 4793
57: 6 the s stones *of* the ravines are your portion; 2747
Lk 3: 5 shall become straight, the rough ways **s.** *3308*
Ro 16:18 By s **talk** and flattery they deceive *5981*

SMOOTH-SKINNED (2) [SKIN, SMOOTH]
Isa 18: 2 swift messengers, to a people tall and s, 5307
18: 7 a people tall and s, from a people feared far 5307

SMOOTHER (1) [SMOOTH]
Pr 5: 3 and her speech is s than oil; 2747

SMOOTHLY (1) [SMOOTH]
Pr 23:31 in the cup, when it goes down s! 928+4797

SMOOTHS (1) [SMOOTH]
Isa 41: 7 and *he who* s *with* the hammer spurs 2744

SMYRNA (2)
Rev 1:11 to Ephesus, **S**, Pergamum, Thyatira, Sardis, *5044*
2: 8 "To the angel of the church in S write: *5044*

SNAIL (KJV) See SKINK, SLUG

SNAKE (24) [SNAKES]
Ex 4: 3 on the ground and it became a **s**, 5729
4: 4 Moses reached out and took hold of **the s** 2257[S]
7: 9 and it will become a **s**." 9490
7:10 and it became a **s**. 9490
7:12 down his staff and it became a **s**. 9490
7:15 the staff that was changed into a **s**. 5729
Nu 21: 8 "Make a s and put it up on a pole; 8597
21: 9 So Moses made a bronze s and put it up on 5729
21: 9 when anyone was bitten by a s and looked 5729
21: 9 by a snake and looked at the bronze **s**, 5729
2Ki 18: 4 into pieces the bronze s Moses had made, 5729
Ps 58: 4 Their venom is like the venom of a **s**, 5729
Pr 23:32 In the end it bites like a s and poisons like 5729
30:19 the way of a s on a rock, 5729
Ecc 10: 8 through a wall may be bitten by a **s**. 5729
10:11 If a s bites before it is charmed, 5729
Isa 14:29 the root of that s will spring up a viper, 5729
Am 5:19 on the wall only to have a s bite him. 5729
Mic 7:17 They will lick dust like a **s**, 5729
Mt 7:10 Or if he asks for a fish, will give him a **s**? *4058*
Lk 11:11 ask for a fish, will give him a s instead? *4058*
Jn 3:14 Just as Moses lifted up the s in the desert, *4058*
Ac 28: 4 the s hanging from his hand, they said *2563*
28: 5 But Paul shook the s off into the fire *2563*

SNAKES (11) [SNAKE]
Nu 21: 6 the LORD sent venomous s among them; 5729
21: 7 the LORD will take the s away from us." 5729
Dt 8:15 with its venomous s and scorpions. 5729
Isa 30: 6 of adders and darting **s**, 8597
Jer 8:17 "See, I will send **venomous** s among you, 5729
Mt 10:16 be as shrewd as s and as innocent as doves. *4058*
23:33 *"You* **s**! You brood of vipers! *4058*
Mk 16:18 they will pick up s with their hands; *4058*
Lk 10:19 I have given you authority to trample on s *4058*
1Co 10: 9 and were killed by **s**. *4058*
Rev 9:19 for their tails were like **s**, *4058*

SNAPPED (3) [SNAPS]
Jdg 16: 9 But *he* s the thongs as easily as a piece 5998
16:12 But *he* s the ropes off his arms as 5998
Jer 10:20 My tent is destroyed; all its ropes **are s**. 5998

SNAPS (1) [SNAPPED]
Jdg 16: 9 as a piece of string s when it comes close to 5998

SNARE (35) [ENSNARE, ENSNARED, SNARED, SNARES]
Ex 10: 7 "How long will this man be a s to us? 4613
23:33 of their gods will certainly be a s to you." 4613
34:12 or they will be a s among you. 4613
Dt 7:16 for that will be a s to you. 4613
Jdg 2: 3 in your sides and their gods will be a s 4613
8:27 and it became a s to Gideon and his family. 4613
1Sa 18:21 "so that she may be a s to him and so that 4613
Job 18: 9 a s holds him fast. 7545
Ps 25:15 for only he will release my feet from the **s**. 8407
69:22 May the table set before them become a **s**; 7062
91: 3 Surely he will save you from the fowler's s 7062
106:36 which became a s to them. 4613
119:110 The wicked have set a s for me, 7062
124: 7 like a bird out of the fowler's **s**; 7062
124: 7 s has been broken, and we have escaped. 7062
140: 5 Proud men have hidden a s for me; 7062
142: 3 the path where I walk men have hidden a s 7062
Pr 6: 5 like a bird from the s *of* the fowler. 3338
7:23 like a bird darting into a **s**, 7062
18: 7 and his lips are a s *to* his soul. 4613
21: 6 a fleeting vapor and a deadly **s**. 1335
29:25 Fear of man will prove to be a **s**, 4613
Ecc 7:26 the woman who is a **s**, 5178
9:12 or birds are taken in a **s**, 7062
Isa 8:14 of Jerusalem he will be a trap and a **s**. 4613
24:17 Terror and pit and s await you, 7062
24:18 of the pit will be caught in a **s**. 7062
Jer 5:26 in wait like **men who s birds** and 3687
48:43 Terror and pit and s await you, 7062
48:44 of the pit will be caught in a **s**; 7062
Eze 12:13 and he will be caught in my **s**; 5180
17:20 and he will be caught in my **s**. 5180
Hos 5: 1 You have been a s at Mizpah, 7062
Am 3: 5 on the ground where no s has been set? 4613
Ro 11: 9 "May their table become a s and a trap, *4075*

SNARED (4) [SNARE]
Pr 3:26 and will keep your foot from being **s**. 4335
29: 6 An evil man is s by his own sin, 4613
Isa 8:15 *they will* **be** s and captured." 3704
28:13 be injured and s and captured. 3704

SNARES (13) [SNARE]
Jos 23:13 they will become s and traps for you, 7062
2Sa 22: 6 the s *of* death confronted me. 4613
Job 22:10 That is why s are all around you, 7062
30:12 *they* **lay** s *for* my feet, 8938
34:30 from laying s *for* the people. 4613
Ps 18: 5 the s *of* death confronted me. 4613
64: 5 they talk about hiding their **s**; 4613
141: 9 Keep me from the s they have laid for me, 7062
Pr 13:14 turning a man from the s *of* death. 4613
14:27 turning a man from the s *of* death. 4613
22: 5 In the paths of the wicked lie thorns and **s**, 7062
Jer 18:22 a pit to capture me and have hidden s 7062
Hos 9: 8 yet s await him on all his paths, 3687+7062

SNARLING (2)
Ps 59: 6 s like dogs, and prowl about the city. 2159
59:14 s like dogs, and prowl about the city. 2159

SNATCH (9) [SNATCHED, SNATCHES]
Job 24:19 heat and drought s **away** the melted snow, 1608
30:22 *You* s me **up** and drive me before the wind; 5951
Ps 52: 5 *He will* s you **up** and tear you 3149
119:43 *Do* not s the word of truth from my mouth, 5911
Isa 3:18 that day the Lord *will* s **away** their finery: 6073
10: 6 to seize loot and s plunder, 1024
Jn 10:28 no one *can* s them out of my hand. *773*
10:29 no one can s them out of my Father's hand. *773*
Jude 1:23 s others from the fire and save them; *773*

SNATCHED (10) [SNATCH]
Jdg 6: 9 *I* s you from the power of Egypt and from 5911
2Sa 23:21 *He* s the spear from the Egyptian's hand 1608
1Ch 11:23 *He* s the spear from the Egyptian's hand 1608
Job 24: 9 The fatherless child *is* s from the breast; 1608
29:17 the fangs of the wicked and s the victims 8959
Pr 22:27 your very bed *will be* s from under you. 4374
Joel 1: 5 for *it has* **been** s from your lips. 4162
Am 4:11 You were like a burning stick s from 5911
Zec 3: 2 Is not this man a burning stick s from 5911
Rev 12: 5 her child *was* s **up** to God and to his throne. *773*

SNATCHES (4) [SNATCH]
Job 9:12 If *he* s **away**, who can stop him? 3166
24:19 so the grave s away those who have sinned. NIH
27:20 a tempest s him **away** in the night. 1704
Mt 13:19 and s **away** what was sown in his heart. *773*

SNEER (1) [SNEERED, SNEERING, SNEERS]
Isa 57: 4 At whom *do you* s and stick out your 7023+8143

SNEERED (2) [SNEER]
Lk 23:35 and the rulers even s **at** him. *1727*
Ac 17:32 some of them **s**, but others said, *5949*

SNEERING (1) [SNEER]
Lk 16:14 heard all this and *were* s **at** Jesus. *1727*

SNEERS (1) [SNEER]
Ps 10: 5 *he* s at all his enemies. 7032

SNEEZED (1)
2Ki 4:35 The boy s seven times and opened his eyes. 2453

SNIFF (1) [SNIFFING]
Mal 1:13 and *you* s *at* it **contemptuously**," 5870

SNIFFING (1) [SNIFF]
Jer 2:24 s the wind in her craving— 8634

SNORTING (3) [SNORTS]
Job 39:20 striking terror with his proud **s**? 5724
41:18 His s throws out flashes of light; 6490
Jer 8:16 s *of* the enemy's horses is heard from Dan; 5725

SNORTS (1) [SNORTING]
Job 39:25 At the blast of the trumpet *he* **s**, 'Aha!' 606

SNOUT (1)
Pr 11:22 Like a gold ring in a pig's s is 678

SNOW (20) [SNOWS, SNOWY]
Ex 4: 6 it was leprous, like **s**. 8920
Nu 12:10 there stood Miriam—leprous, like **s**. 8920
2Ki 5:27 he was leprous, as white as **s**. 8920
Job 6:16 by thawing ice and swollen with melting **s**, 8920
24:19 heat and drought snatch away the melted **s**, 8920
37: 6 He says to the **s**, 'Fall on the earth,' 8920
38:22 "Have you entered the storehouses of the s 8920
Ps 51: 7 wash me, and I will be whiter than **s**. 8920
68:14 *it was like* **s fallen** on Zalmon. 8919
147:16 He spreads the s like wool and scatters 8920
148: 8 and hail, s and clouds, stormy winds 8920
Pr 25:13 Like the coolness of s at harvest time is 8920
26: 1 Like s in summer or rain in harvest, 8920
Isa 1:18 they shall be as white as **s**; 8920
55:10 the rain and the s come down from heaven, 8920
Jer 18:14 Does the s *of* Lebanon ever vanish 8920
La 4: 7 Their princes were brighter than s 8920
Da 7: 9 His clothing was as white as **s**; 10758
Mt 28: 3 and his clothes were white as **s**. *5946*
Rev 1:14 white like wool, as white as **s**, *5946*

SNOWS (1) [SNOW]
Pr 31:21 When it **s**, she has no fear for her household 8920

SNOWY (2) [SNOW]
2Sa 23:20 down into a pit on a s day and killed a lion. 8920
1Ch 11:22 down into a pit on a s day and killed a lion. 8920

SNUFF (3) [SNUFFED]
Isa 42: 3 and a smoldering wick *he will* not **s out**. 3882
Eze 32: 7 When I s you **out**, I will cover the heavens 3882
Mt 12:20 and a smoldering wick *he will* not **s out**, *4931*

SNUFFDISHES (KJV) See TRAYS

SNUFFED (6) [SNUFF]
Job 18: 5 "The lamp of the wicked *is* **s out**; 1980
21:17 the lamp of the wicked **s out**? 1980
Pr 13: 9 but the lamp of the wicked is **s out**. 1980
20:20 his lamp *will be* **s out** in pitch darkness. 1980
24:20 and the lamp of the wicked *will be* **s out**. 1980
Isa 43:17 extinguished, **s out** like a wick: 3882

SNUFFERS (KJV) See WICK TRIMMERS

SO (1 of 3003) For SO as a Conjunction, See Index of Articles Etc. (See Introduction p. xi)
2Ki 17: 4 for he had sent envoys to S king of Egypt, 6046

SO-CALLED (2) [CALL]
1Co 8: 5 For even if there are s gods, *3306*
Rev 2:24 have not learned Satan's s deep secrets *3306+6055*

SOAKED (4) [SOAK]
2Ki 8:15 he took a thick cloth, s it in water 3188
Isa 34: 3 the mountains *will* **be** s with their blood. 5022
34: 7 and the dust *will* **be** s with fat. 2014
Jn 19:29 so they s a sponge in it, put the sponge on *3550*

SOAP (3)
Job 9:30 with s and my hands with washing soda, 8921
Jer 2:22 with soda and use an abundance of **s**, 1383
Mal 3: 2 be like a refiner's fire or a launderer's **s**. 1383

SOAR (4) [SOARED]
Job 39:27 *Does* the eagle s at your command 1467
Isa 40:31 *They will* s *on* wings like eagles; 6590
Jer 49:22 An eagle *will* s and swoop down, 6590
Ob 1: 4 Though *you* s like the eagle 1467

SOARED (2) [SOAR]
2Sa 22:11 *he* s on the wings of the wind. 1797
Ps 18:10 *he* s on the wings of the wind. 1797

SOB (1) [SOBBING]
Ge 21:16 And as she sat there nearby, she began *to* **s**. 1134

SOBBING (1) [SOB]
Jdg 14:16 Samson's wife threw herself on him, **s**, 1134

SOBER (2)
1Sa 25:37 when Nabal *was* **s**, 2021+3516+3655+4946
Ro 12: 3 of yourself with **s judgment**, *5404*

SOBRIETY (KJV) See PROPRIETY

SOCHO (KJV) See SOCO

SOCHOH (KJV) See SOCOH

SOCKET (3) [SOCKETS]
Ge 32:25 he touched the s *of* Jacob's hip so 4090
32:32 the tendon attached to the s *of* the hip, 4090
32:32 because the s *of* Jacob's hip was touched 4090

SOCKETS (3) [SOCKET]
1Ki 6:34 each having two leaves *that* **turned in s**. 1664
7:50 gold s for the doors of the innermost room, 7327
Zec 14:12 their eyes will rot in their **s**, 2986

SOCO (3)
1Ch 4:18 Heber the father of **S**, 8459
2Ch 11: 7 Beth Zur, **S**, Adullam, 8459
28:18 Aijalon and Gederoth, as well as **S**, 8459

SOCOH (5)
Jos 15:35 Jarmuth, Adullam, **S**, Azekah, 8458

Jos 15:48 In the hill country: Shamir, Jattir, S, 8458
1Sa 17: 1 for war and assembled at S in Judah. 8458
17: 1 between S and Azekah. 8458
1Ki 4:10 in Arubboth (S and all the land 8458

SOD, SODDEN (KJV) See BOILED, COOKED, COOKING

SODA (3)

Job 9:30 with soap and my hands with **washing s,** 1342
Pr 25:20 or like vinegar poured on s, 6003
Jer 2:22 Although you wash yourself with s and use 6003

SODERING (KJV) See WELDING

SODI (1)

Nu 13:10 from the tribe of Zebulun, Gaddiel son of S; 6052

SODOM (47)

Ge 10:19 and then toward S, Gomorrah, 6042
13:10 (This was before the LORD destroyed S 6042
13:12 of the plain and pitched his tents near S. 6042
13:13 of S were wicked and were sinning greatly 6042
14: 2 went to war against Bera king of S, 6042
14: 8 Then the king of S, the king of Gomorrah, 6042
14:10 when the kings of S and Gomorrah fled, 6042
14:11 The four kings seized all the goods of S 6042
14:12 since he was living in S. 6042
14:17 of S came out to meet him in the Valley 6042
14:21 The king of S said to Abram, 6042
14:22 But Abram said to the king of S, 6042
18:16 they looked down toward S, 6042
18:20 "The outcry against S and Gomorrah is 6042
18:22 The men turned away and went toward S, 6042
18:26 fifty righteous people in the city of S, 6042
19: 1 The two angels arrived at S in the evening, 6042
19: 4 all the men from every part of the city of S 6042
19:24 down burning sulfur on S and Gomorrah— 6042
19:28 He looked down toward S and Gomorrah, 6042
Dt 29:23 be like the destruction of S and Gomorrah, 6042
32:32 Their vine comes from the vine of S and 6042
Isa 1: 9 we would have become like S, 6042
1:10 the word of the LORD, you rulers of S; 6042
3: 9 they parade their sin like S; 6042
13:19 will be overthrown by God like S 6042
Jer 23:14 They are all like S to me; 6042
49:18 As S and Gomorrah were overthrown, 6042
50:40 As God overthrew S and Gomorrah along 6042
La 4: 6 of my people is greater than that of S, 6042
Eze 16:46 the south of you with her daughters, was S. 6042
16:48 the Sovereign LORD, your sister S 6042
16:49 " 'Now this was the sin of your sister S: 6042
16:53 the fortunes of S and her daughters and 6042
16:55 S with her daughters and Samaria 6042
16:56 You would not even mention your sister S 6042
Am 4:11 "I overthrew some of you as I overthrew S 6042
Zep 2: 9 "surely Moab will become like S, 6042
Mt 10:15 be more bearable *for* S and Gomorrah *1178+5047*
11:23 in you had been performed in S, *5047*
11:24 *for* S on the day of judgment than for *1178+5047*
Lk 10:12 be more bearable on that day *for* S than for *5047*
17:29 But the day Lot left S, *5047*
Ro 9:29 we would have become like S, *5047*
2Pe 2: 6 *of* S and Gomorrah by burning them *5047*
Jude 1: 7 S and Gomorrah and the surrounding towns *5047*
Rev 11: 8 which is figuratively called S and Egypt, *5047*

SODOMA (KJV) See SODOM

SODOMITE, SODOMITES (KJV) See MALE SHRINE PROSTITUTES, SHRINE PROSTITUTE

SOFT (KJV) See FAINT, FINE, GENTLE, SOFTEN

SOFTEN (1)

Ps 65:10 *you* s it with showers and bless its crops. 4570

SOIL (38) [SOILED]

Ge 4: 2 Abel kept flocks, and Cain worked the **s.** 141
4: 3 of the s as an offering to the LORD. 141
9:20 Noah, a man of the **s,** proceeded to plant 141
Ex 23:19 "Bring the best of the firstfruits of your s to 141
34:26 "Bring the best of the firstfruits of your s to 141
Lev 26:20 because your s will not yield its crops, 824
27:30 from the s or fruit from the trees, belongs to 824
Nu 13:20 How is the s? 824
Dt 26: 2 that you produce from the s of the land 141
26:10 now I bring the firstfruits of the s that you, 141
1Ki 18:38 the wood, the stones and the s, 6760
2Ch 26:10 for he loved the s. 141
Job 5: 6 For hardship does not spring from the s, 6760
8:19 and from the s other plants grow. 6760
14: 8 in the ground and its stump die in the s, 6760
14:19 and torrents wash away the s, 824+6760
21:33 The s *in* the valley is sweet to him; 8073
Ps 37:35 like a green tree in its **native s,** 275
105:35 ate up the produce of their s. 141
SS 5: 3 *must I* s them again? 3245
Isa 28:24 on breaking up and harrowing the s? 141
30:24 and donkeys that work the s will eat fodder 141
61:11 For as the s makes the sprout come up and 824
Eze 17: 5 the seed of your land and put it in fertile s. 8441
17: 8 in good s by abundant water so 8441
Mt 13: 5 where it did not have much s. *1178*
13: 5 because the s was shallow. *1178*
13: 8 Still other seed fell on good s, *1178*
13:23 on good s is the man who hears the word *1178*
Mk 4: 5 where it did not have much s. *1178*
4: 5 because the s was shallow. *1178*
4: 8 Still other seed fell on good s. *1178*
4:20 Others, like seed sown on good s, *1178*
4:28 All by itself the s produces grain— *1178*
Lk 8: 8 Still other seed fell on good s. *1178*
8:15 But the seed on good s stands for those with *1178*
13: 7 Why should it use up the **s?'** *1178*
14:35 for the s nor for the manure pile; *1178*

SOILED (1) [SOIL]

Rev 3: 4 in Sardis who *have* not s their clothes. *3662*

SOJOURN, SOJOURNED, SOJOURNER, SOJOURNERS, SOJOURNETH, SOJOURNING (KJV) See ALIEN, ALIENS, DWELL, GUEST, LIVE, LIVED, LIVES, LIVING, SETTLED, STAY, STAYED, STAYING, TEMPORARY RESIDENT

SOLACE (KJV) See ENJOY

SOLD (69) [SELL]

Ge 31:15 Not only *has he* s us, 4835
37:28 of the cistern and s him for twenty shekels 4835
37:36 Midianites s Joseph in Egypt to Potiphar, 4835
41:56 Joseph opened the storehouses and **s grain** 8690
42: 6 the *one who* **s grain** to all its people. 8690
45: 4 the one *you* s into Egypt! 4835
47:20 The Egyptians, one and all, s their fields, 4835
Ex 22: 3 *he must* **be s** to pay for his theft. 4835
Lev 25:23 " 'The land *must* not **be s** permanently, 4835
25:25 **what** his countryman has **s.** 4928
25:27 since he s it and refund the balance to 4928
25:27 the balance to the man to whom *he* s it; 4835
25:28 **what** he s will remain in the possession of 4928
25:33 that is, a house s in any town they hold— 4928
25:34 to their towns *must* not **be s;** 4835
25:42 *they* **must** not **be s** as slaves. 4835+4929
25:48 of redemption after *he has* **s himself.** 4835
25:50 to count the time from the year he s **himself** 4835
27:20 or if *he has* s it to someone else, 4835
27:27 *it is to* **be s** at its set value. 4835
27:28 *may* **be s** or redeemed; 4835
Dt 32:30 unless their Rock *had* s them, 4835
Jdg 2:14 *He* s them to their enemies all around, 4835
3: 8 against Israel so that *he* s them into 4835
4: 2 the LORD s them into the hands of Jabin, 4835
10: 7 *He* s them into the hands of the Philistines 4835
1Sa 12: 9 so *he* s them into the hand of Sisera, 4835
1Ki 21:20 "because you *have* **s yourself** to do evil in 4835
21:25 who s **himself** to do evil in the eyes of 4835
2Ki 6:25 a donkey's head **s for** eighty shekels 928+2118
7:16 So a seah of flour **s for** a shekel, 928+2118
7:16 and two seahs of barley s for a shekel, NIH
17:17 and sorcery and s **themselves** to do evil in 4835
Ne 5: 8 we have bought back our Jewish brothers who **were s** 4835
5: 8 only for *them to* **be s back** to us!" 4835
Est 7: 4 and my people *have* **been s** for destruction 4835
7: 4 If *we had* merely **been s** as male 4835
Ps 44:12 *You* s your people for a pittance, 4835
105:17 Joseph, s as a slave. 4835
Isa 50: 1 Because of your sins *you* **were s;** 4835
52: 3 *"You were* s for nothing, 4835
Jer 34:14 free any fellow Hebrew who *has* **s himself** 4835
Eze 7:13 not recover the **land** he has s as long as 4928
Hos 8: 9 Ephraim *has* s *herself to* lovers. 9479
8:10 Although *they have* s *themselves* among 9479
Joel 3: 3 *they* s girls for wine that they might drink. 4835
3: 6 *You* s the people of Judah and Jerusalem to 4835
3: 7 of the places to which *you* s them, 4835
Am 1: 6 and s them to Edom, 6037
1: 9 Because she s whole communities 6037
Mt 10:29 *Are* not two sparrows s for a penny? *4797*
13:44 in his joy went and **s** all he had and bought *4797*
13:46 and s everything he had and bought it. *4405*
18:25 and all that he had *be* s to repay the debt. *4405*
26: 9 "This perfume could *have been* s at *4405*
Mk 14: 5 It could have *been* s for more than *4405*
Lk 12: 6 *Are* not five sparrows s for two pennies? *4797*
Jn 2:16 *To* those who s doves he said, *4797*
12: 5 "Why wasn't this perfume s and *4405*
Ac 4:34 those who owned lands or houses s them, *4797*
4:37 s a field he owned and brought the money *4797*
5: 1 also s a piece of property. *4797*
5: 4 Didn't it belong to you before it was s? *NIG*
5: 4 And *after it was* s, *4405*
7: 9 *they* s him as a slave into Egypt. *625*
Ro 7:14 but I am unspiritual, s as a slave to sin. *4405*
1Co 10:25 Eat anything s in the meat market *4797*
Heb 12:16 for a single meal s his inheritance rights as *625*
Rev 18:15 The merchants who s these things *NIG*

SOLDIER (13) [SOLDIERS]

Nu 31:53 Each s had taken plunder for himself. 408+7372
1Sa 13:22 So on the day of the battle not a s with Saul 6639
2Sa 17:10 Then even the **bravest s,** 1201+2657
2Ki 5: 1 He was a **valiant s,** but he had leprosy. 1475+2657
2Ch 17:17 From Benjamin: Eliada, a **valiant s,** 1475+2657
Am 2:15 the fleet-footed s will not get away, 2257[S]
Ac 10: 7 of his servants and a devout s who was one *5132*
28:16 to live by himself, with a s to guard him. *5132*
1Co 9: 7 Who **serves as a s** at his own expense? *5129*
Php 2:25 my brother, fellow worker and **fellow s,** *5369*
2Ti 2: 3 Endure hardship with us like a good s *5132*
2: 4 No one **serving as a s** gets involved *5129*
Phm 1: 2 *to* Archippus our **fellow s** and to *5369*

SOLDIERS (79) [SOLDIER]

Nu 31:21 said to the s who had gone into battle, 408+7372
31:27 the s who took part in the battle and 4878+9530
31:28 From the s who fought in the battle, 408+4878
31:32 from the spoils that the s took was 6639+7372
31:49 "Your servants have counted the s 408+4878
Jos 8:13 They had the s take up their positions— 6639
17: 1 because the Makirites were **great s.** 408+4878
Jdg 9:35 and his s came out from their hiding place. 6639
20: 2 four hundred thousand s armed 408+8081
20:16 Among all these s there were seven hundred chosen men who were left-handed, 6639
1Sa 4: 3 When the s returned to camp, 6639
4:10 Israel lost thirty thousand **foot s.** 8081
13: 5 s as numerous as the sand on the seashore. 6639
14:28 Then one of the s told him, 6639
15: 4 two hundred thousand **foot s** 8081
15:15 "The s brought them from the Amalekites; 6639
15:21 The s took sheep and cattle from 6639
26: 7 Abner and the s were lying around him. 6639
2Sa 3:23 When Joab and all the s with him arrived, 7372
8: 4 and twenty thousand **foot s.** 408+8081
10: 6 they hired twenty thousand Aramean **foot s** 8081
10:18 and forty thousand of their **foot s.** 8081
11: 7 how the s were and how the war was going. 6639
1Ki 20:29 on the Aramean **foot s** in one day. 8081
2Ki 13: 7 ten chariots and ten thousand **foot s,** 8081
25: 5 All his s were separated from him 2657
1Ch 12:33 **experienced** s prepared for battle 3655+7372
12:36 **experienced** s prepared for battle— 3655+7372
18: 4 and twenty thousand **foot s.** 408+8081
19:18 and forty thousand of their **foot s.** 408+8081
2Ch 28: 6 and twenty thousand s in Judah— 1201+2657
28:14 So the s gave up the prisoners and plunder 2741
Ezr 8:22 the king for s and horsemen to protect us 2657
Jer 38: 4 He is discouraging the s who are left 408+4878
39: 4 and all the s saw them, they fled; 408+4878
41: 3 as the Babylonian s who were there. 408+4878
41:16 the s, women, children 408+1505+4878
49:26 all her s will be silenced in that day," 408+4878
50:30 all her s will be silenced in that day," 408+4878
51:32 marshes set on fire, and the s terrified." 408+4878
52: 8 All his s were separated from him 2657
Eze 27:10 Lydia and Put served as s in your army. 408+4878
27:27 your merchants and all your s, 408+4878
39:20 mighty men and s of every kind,' 408+4878
Da 3:20 some of the **strongest** s in his army 10132+10264
3:22 the fire killed the s who took up Shadrach, 10131
Joel 2: 7 they scale walls like s. 408+4878
Na 2: 3 The shields of his s are red; 1475
Mt 8: 9 a man under authority, with s under me. *5132*
27:27 Then the governor's s took Jesus into *5132*
27:27 and gathered the whole **company of s** *5061*
28:12 they gave the s a large sum of money, *5132*
28:15 So **the** s took the money and did *3836[S]*
Mk 15:16 The s led Jesus away into the palace *5132*
15:16 called together the whole **company of s.** *5061*
Lk 3:14 Then some s asked him, *5129*
7: 8 a man under authority, with s under me. *5132*
23:11 Herod and his s ridiculed and mocked him. *5128*
23:36 The s also came up and mocked him. *5132*
Jn 18: 3 a **detachment of s** and some officials from *5061*
18:12 the **detachment of s** with its commander *5061*
19: 2 The s twisted together a crown of thorns *5132*
19:16 So the s took charge of Jesus. *NIG*
19:23 When the s crucified Jesus, *5132*
19:24 So this is what the s did. *5132*
19:32 The s therefore came and broke the legs of *5132*
19:34 *of* the s pierced Jesus' side with a spear, *5132*
Ac 12: 4 be guarded by four squads *of* four s each. *5132*
12: 6 Peter was sleeping between two s, *5132*
12:18 there was no small commotion among the s *5132*
21:32 He at once took some officers and s and ran *5132*
21:32 the rioters saw the commander and his s, *5132*
21:35 so great he had to be carried by the s. *5132*
21:37 As the s were about to take Paul into *NIG*
23:23 "Get ready a detachment of two hundred **s,** *5132*
23:31 So the s, carrying out their orders, *5132*
27:31 Then Paul said *to* the centurion and the s, *5132*
27:32 So the s cut the ropes that held the lifeboat *5132*
27:42 The s planned to kill the prisoners *5132*

SOLE (4) [SOLES]

Dt 28:56 to touch the ground with the s *of* her foot— 4090
28:65 no resting place for the s *of* your foot. 4090
2Sa 14:25 to the s *of* his foot there was no blemish 4090
Isa 1: 6 From the s *of* your foot to the top 4090

SOLEMN (5) [SOLEMNLY]

Ge 50:11 "The Egyptians are holding a s ceremony 3878
Jos 6:26 **pronounced** *this* **s oath:** 8678
Jdg 21: 5 a s oath that anyone who failed to assemble 1524
Eze 16: 8 **gave** you *my* **s oath** 8678
Ac 23:14 *"We have* **taken a s oath** not to eat *353+354*

SOLEMNITIES, SOLEMNITY (KJV) See APPOINTED FEASTS, FEAST, FESTIVAL, FESTIVALS

SOLEMNLY (7) [SOLEMN]

Ge 43: 3 said to him, "The man **warned** us **s,** 6386+6386
Dt 1:34 he was angry and **s swore:** 8678
4:21 and *he* **s swore** that I would not cross 8678
32:46 the words I *have* **s declared** to you this day, 6386
Jos 5: 6 he *had* **s promised** their fathers to give us, 8678
Jdg 17: 3 *"I* **s consecrate** my silver to the LORD 7727+7727
1Sa 8: 9 but **warn** them s and let them know 6386+6386

SOLES (7) [SOLE]

Dt 28:35 spreading from the s *of* your feet to the top 4090
2Ki 19:24 With the s *of* my feet I have dried up all 4090
Job 2: 7 from the s *of* his feet to the top of his head. 4090
13:27 on all my paths by putting marks on the s 9247
Isa 37:25 With the s *of* my feet I have dried up all 4090
Eze 43: 7 of my throne and the place for the s 4090
Mal 4: 3 be ashes under the s *of* your feet on the day 4090

SOLID (7)

Nu 4: 6 a cloth of s blue over that and put the poles 4003
2Ch 4:21 and lamps and tongs (they were s gold); 4816
Zec 4: 2 a s gold lampstand with a bowl at the top 3972
1Co 3: 2 I gave you milk, not **s food,** *1109*
2Ti 2:19 God's s foundation stands firm, *5104*
Heb 5:12 You need milk, not s food! *5104*
5:14 But s food is for the mature, *5104*

SOLITARY (6)

Lev 16:22 on itself all their sins to a s place; 10141
Mt 14:13 he withdrew by boat privately to a s place. *2245*
Mk 1:35 left the house and went off to a s place, *2245*
6:32 by themselves in a boat to a s place. *2245*
Lk 4:42 At daybreak Jesus went out to a s place. *2245*
8:29 by the demon into **s places.** *2245*

SOLOMON (248) [SOLOMON'S]

2Sa 5:14 Shammua, Shobab, Nathan, S, 8976
12:24 and they named him S. 8976
1Ki 1:10 or the special guard or his brother S. 8976
1:12 and the life of your son S. 8976
1:13 "Surely S your son shall be king after me, 8976
1:17 'S your son shall be king after me, 8976
1:19 but he has not invited S your servant. 8976
1:21 and my son S will be treated as criminals." 8976
1:26 and your servant S he did not invite. 8976
1:30 S your son shall be king after me, 8976
1:33 and set S my son on my own mule 8976
1:34 'Long live King S!' 8976
1:37 with S to make his throne even greater than 8976
1:38 and the Pelethites went down and put S 8976
1:39 of oil from the sacred tent and anointed S. 8976
1:39 "Long live King S!" 8976
1:43 "Our lord King David has made S king. 8976
1:46 S has taken his seat on the royal throne. 8976
1:50 But Adonijah, in fear of S, 8976
1:51 Then S was told, 'Adonijah is afraid 8976
1:51 of King S and is clinging to the horns of 8976
1:51 'Let King S swear to me today that he will 8976
1:52 S replied, "If he shows himself to be 8976
1:53 Then King S sent men, 8976
1:53 and bowed down to King S, 8976
1:53 and S said, "Go to your home." 8976
2: 1 he gave a charge to S his son. 8976
2:12 So S sat on the throne of his father David, 8976
2:17 So he continued, "Please ask King S— 8976
2:19 When Bathsheba went to King S to speak 8976
2:22 King S answered his mother, 8976
2:23 Then King S swore by the LORD: 8976
2:25 So King S gave orders to Benaiah son 8976
2:27 So S removed Abiathar from 8976
2:29 King S was told that Joab had fled to 8976
2:29 Then S ordered Benaiah son of Jehoiada, 8976
2:41 When S was told that Shimei had gone 8976
2:45 But King S will be blessed, 8976
3: 1 S made an alliance with Pharaoh king 8976
3: 3 S showed his love for the LORD 8976
3: 4 and S offered a thousand burnt offerings on 8976
3: 5 the LORD appeared to S during the night 8976
3: 6 S answered, "You have shown great kindness to your servant, 8976
3:10 The Lord was pleased that S had asked 8976
3:15 Then S awoke—and he realized it had been a dream. 8976
4: 1 So King S ruled over all Israel. 8976
4: 7 S also had twelve district governors 8976
4:11 (he was married to Taphath daughter of S); 8976
4:15 (he had married Basemath daughter of S); 8976
4:21 And S ruled over all the kingdoms from 8976
4:26 S had four thousand stalls for chariot horses 8976
4:27 supplied provisions for King S 8976
4:29 God gave S wisdom and very great insight, 8976
1Ki 5: 1 that S had been anointed king 2257^S
5: 1 he sent his envoys to S, 8976
5: 2 S sent back this message to Hiram: 8976
5: 8 So Hiram sent word to S: 8976
5:10 In this way Hiram kept S supplied with all 8976
5:11 and S gave Hiram twenty thousand cors 8976
5:11 S continued to do this for Hiram year 8976
5:12 The LORD gave S wisdom, 8976
5:12 peaceful relations between Hiram and S, 8976
5:13 King S conscripted laborers 8976
5:15 S had seventy thousand carriers 8976
5:18 The craftsmen of S and Hiram and the men 8976
6: 2 The temple that King S built for 8976
6:11 The word of the LORD came to S: 8976
6:14 So S built the temple and completed it. 8976
6:21 S covered the inside of the temple 8976
7: 1 It took S thirteen years, however, 8976
7: 8 S also made a palace like this hall 8976
7:13 King S sent to Tyre and brought Huram, 8976
7:14 to King S and did all the work assigned 8976
7:40 the work he had undertaken for King S in 8976
7:45 that Huram made for King S for the temple 8976
7:47 S left all these things unweighed, 8976
7:48 S also made all the furnishings that were in 8976
7:51 the work King S had done for the temple of 8976
8: 1 Then King S summoned into his presence 8976
8: 2 the men of Israel came together to King S 8976
8: 5 and King S and the entire assembly 8976
8:12 Then S said, "The LORD has said 8976
8:22 Then S stood before the altar of the LORD 8976
8:54 When S had finished all these prayers 8976
8:63 S offered a sacrifice of fellowship offerings 8976
8:65 So S observed the festival at that time, 8976
9: 1 When S had finished building the temple of 8976
9:10 during which S built these two buildings— 8976
9:11 King S gave twenty towns in Galilee 8976
9:12 to see the towns that S had given him, 8976
9:15 of the forced labor King S conscripted 8976
9:17 And S rebuilt Gezer.) 8976
9:21 these S conscripted for his slave labor 8976
9:22 But S did not make slaves of any of 8976
9:24 the City of David to the palace S had built NIH
9:25 a year S sacrificed burnt offerings 8976
9:26 King S also built ships at Ezion Geber, 8976
9:28 which they delivered to King S. 8976
10: 1 the fame of S and his relation to the name 8976
10: 2 she came to S and talked with him about all 8976
10: 3 S answered all her questions; 8976
10: 4 the queen of Sheba saw all the wisdom of S 8976
10:10 the queen of Sheba gave to King S. 8976
10:13 King S gave the queen of Sheba all she 8976
10:14 that S received yearly was 666 talents, 8976
10:16 King S made two hundred large shields 8976
10:23 King S was greater in riches 8976
10:24 The whole world sought audience with S 8976
10:26 S accumulated chariots and horses; 8976
11: 1 King S, however, loved many foreign women besides Pharaoh's daughter— 8976
11: 2 Nevertheless, S held fast to them in love. 8976
11: 4 As S grew old, his wives turned his heart 8976
11: 6 So S did evil in the eyes of the LORD; 8976
11: 7 S built a high place for Chemosh 8976
11: 9 with S because his heart had turned away 8976
11:10 he had forbidden S to follow other gods, 2257^S
11:10 S did not keep the LORD's command. NIH
11:11 So the LORD said to S, 8976
11:14 LORD raised up against S an adversary, 8976
11:23 God raised up against S another adversary, 2257^S
11:25 Israel's adversary as long as S lived, 8976
11:27 S had built the supporting terraces 8976
11:28 and when S saw how well 8976
11:40 S tried to kill Jeroboam, 8976
11:41 not written in the book of the annals of S? 8976
11:42 S reigned in Jerusalem over all Israel 8976
12: 2 where he had fled from King S), 8976
12: 6 the elders who had served his father S 8976
12:21 the kingdom for Rehoboam son of S. 8976
12:23 "Say to Rehoboam son of S king of Judah, 8976
14:21 Rehoboam son of S was king in Judah. 8976
14:26 including all the gold shields S had made. 8976
2Ki 21: 7 to David and to his son S, 8976
23:13 the ones S king of Israel had built 8976
24:13 that S king of Israel had made for 8976
25:16 which S had made for the temple of 8976
1Ch 3: 5 Shammua, Shobab, Nathan and S. 8976
6:10 in the temple S built in Jerusalem), 8976
6:32 until S built the temple of the LORD 8976
14: 4 Shammua, Shobab, Nathan, S, 8976
18: 8 which S used to make the bronze Sea, 8976
22: 5 "My son S is young and inexperienced, 8976
22: 6 for his son S and charged him to build 8976
22: 7 David said to S: "My son, 8976
22: 9 His name will be S, 8976
22:17 the leaders of Israel to help his son S. 8976
23: 1 he made his son S king over Israel. 8976
28: 5 he has chosen my son S to sit on the throne 8976
28: 6 'S your son is the one who will build 8976
28: 9 "And you, my son S, 8976
28:11 Then David gave his son S the plans for 8976
28:20 David also said to S his son, 8976
29: 1 "My son S, the one whom God has chosen, 8976
29:19 give my son S the wholehearted devotion 8976
29:22 Then they acknowledged S son of David 8976
29:23 So S sat on the throne of the LORD 8976
29:24 pledged their submission to King S. 8976
29:25 The LORD highly exalted S in the sight 8976
29:28 His son S succeeded him as king. 8976
2Ch 1: 1 S son of David established himself firmly 8976
1: 2 Then S spoke to all Israel— 8976
1: 3 and S and the whole assembly went to 8976
1: 5 S and the assembly inquired of him there. 8976
1: 6 S went up to the bronze altar before 8976
1: 7 That night God appeared to S and said 8976
1: 8 S answered God, "You have shown great kindness to David 8976
1:11 God said to S, "Since this is your heart's 8976
1:13 Then S went to Jerusalem from 8976
1:14 S accumulated chariots and horses; 8976
2: 1 S gave orders to build a temple for 8976
2: 3 S sent this message to Hiram king of Tyre: 8976
2:11 Hiram king of Tyre replied by letter to S: 8976
2:17 S took a census of all the aliens who were 8976
3: 1 Then S began to build the temple of 8976
3: 3 The foundation S laid for building 8976
4:11 the work he had undertaken for King S in 8976
4:16 that Huram-Abi made for King S for 8976
4:18 All these things that S made amounted to 8976
4:19 S also made all the furnishings that were 8976
5: 1 the work S had done for the temple of 8976
5: 2 Then S summoned to Jerusalem the elders 8976
5: 6 and King S and the entire assembly 8976
6: 1 Then S said, "The LORD has said 8976
6:12 Then S stood before the altar of the LORD NIH
7: 1 When S finished praying, 8976
7: 5 And King S offered a sacrifice 8976
7: 7 S consecrated the middle part of 8976
7: 8 So S observed the festival at that time 8976
7:10 the LORD had done for David and S and 8976
7:11 When S had finished the temple of 8976
8: 1 during which S built the temple of 8976
8: 2 S rebuilt the villages that Hiram 8976
8: 3 S then went to Hamath Zobah 8976
8: 8 these S conscripted for his slave labor 8976
8: 9 But S did not make slaves of the Israelites 8976
8:11 S brought Pharaoh's daughter up from 8976
8:12 S sacrificed burnt offerings to the LORD, 8976
8:17 Then S went to Ezion Geber and Elath on 8976
8:18 which they delivered to King S. 8976
9: 1 to S and talked with him about all she had 8976
9: 2 S answered all her questions; 8976
9: 3 the queen of Sheba saw the wisdom of S, 8976
9: 9 the queen of Sheba gave to King S. 8976
9:10 and the men of S brought gold from Ophir; 8976
9:12 King S gave the queen of Sheba all she 8976
9:13 that S received yearly was 666 talents, 8976
9:14 of the land brought gold and silver to S. 8976
9:15 King S made two hundred large shields 8976
9:22 King S was greater in riches 8976
9:23 of the earth sought audience with S to hear 8976
9:25 S had four thousand stalls for horses 8976
9:30 S reigned in Jerusalem over all Israel 8976
10: 2 where he had fled from King S), 8976
10: 6 the elders who had served his father S 8976
11: 3 "Say to Rehoboam son of S king of Judah 8976
11:17 supported Rehoboam son of S three years, 8976
11:17 the ways of David and S during this time. 8976
12: 9 including the gold shields S had made. 8976
13: 6 an official of S son of David, 8976
13: 7 of S when he was young and indecisive 8976
30:26 for since the days of S son of David king 8976
33: 7 to David and to his son S, 8976
35: 3 "Put the sacred ark in the temple that S son 8976
35: 4 by David king of Israel and by his son S. 8976
Ezr 2:55 The descendants of the servants of S: 8976
2:58 the descendants of the servants of S 392 8976
Ne 7:57 The descendants of the servants of S: 8976
7:60 the descendants of the servants of S 392 8976
12:45 to the commands of David and his son S. 8976
13:26 because of marriages like these that S king 8976
Ps 72: T Of S. 8976
127: T A song of ascents. Of S. 8976
Pr 1: 1 proverbs of S son of David, king of Israel: 8976
10: 1 The proverbs of S: 8976
25: 1 These are more proverbs of S, 8976
SS 1: 5 like the tent curtains of S. 8976
3: 9 King S made for himself the carriage; 8976
3:11 and look at King S wearing the crown, 8976
8:11 S had a vineyard in Baal Hamon; 8976
8:12 the thousand shekels are for you, O S, 8976
Jer 52:20 which King S had made for the temple of 8976
Mt 1: 6 David was the father of S, *5048*
1: 7 S the father of Rehoboam, *5048*
6:29 not even S in all his splendor was dressed *5048*
12:42 and now one greater than S is here. *5048*
Lk 11:31 and now one greater than S is here. *5048*
12:27 not even S in all his splendor was dressed *5048*
Ac 7:47 But it was S who built the house for him. *5048*

SOLOMON'S (41) [SOLOMON]

1Ki 1:11 Then Nathan asked Bathsheba, S mother, 8976
1:47 'May your God make S name more famous 8976
2:13 went to Bathsheba, S mother. 8976
2:46 now firmly established in S hands. 8976
4:21 and were S subjects all his life. 8976
4:22 S daily provisions were thirty cors 8976
4:25 During S lifetime Judah and Israel, 8976
4:30 S wisdom was greater than the wisdom 8976
4:34 of all nations came to listen to S wisdom, 8976
5: 7 When Hiram heard S message, 8976
6: 1 in the fourth year of S reign over Israel, 8976
9:16 as a wedding gift to his daughter, S wife. 8976
9:23 chief officials in charge of S projects 4200+8976
9:27 to serve in the fleet with S men. 8976

1Ki 10:21 All King S goblets were gold, 8976
10:21 was considered of little value in S days. 8976
10:28 S horses were imported from Egypt 4200+8976
11:26 He was one of S officials, 4200+8976
11:31 out of S hand and give you ten tribes. 8976
11:33 and laws as David, S father, did. 2257[S]
11:34 not take the whole kingdom out of S hand; 2257[S]
11:40 and stayed there until S death. 8976
11:41 As for the other events of S reign— 8976
1Ch 3:10 S son was Rehoboam, Abijah his son, 8976
2Ch 1:16 S horses were imported from Egypt 4200+8976
8:10 They were also King S chief officials 4200+8976
8:16 All S work was carried out, 8976
8:18 with S men, sailed to Ophir 8976
9:1 When the queen of Sheba heard of S fame, 8976
9:20 All King S goblets were gold, 8976
9:20 silver was considered of little value in S day 8976
9:28 S horses were imported from Egypt 4200+8976
9:29 As for the other events of S reign, 8976
Ne 11:3 of S servants lived in the towns of Judah, 8976
SS 1:1 S Song of Songs. 4200+8976
3:7 It is S carriage, escorted by 4200+8611+8976
Mt 12:42 the ends of the earth to listen to S wisdom, *5048*
Lk 11:31 the ends of the earth to listen to S wisdom, *5048*
Jn 10:23 in the temple area walking in S Colonnade. *5048*
Ac 3:11 to them in the place called S Colonnade. *5048*
5:12 to meet together in S Colonnade. *5048*

SOLVE (2) [SOLVED]

Da 5:12 explain riddles and s difficult problems. 10742
5:16 interpretations and to s difficult problems. 10742

SOLVED (1) [SOLVE]

Jdg 14:18 *you would* not *have* s my riddle." 5162

SOMBER (1)

Mt 6:16 *do* not **look** s as the hypocrites do, *1181+5034*

SOME (568) [SOMEBODY, SOMEHOW, SOMEONE, SOMEONE'S, SOMETHING, SOMETIMES, SOMEWHAT, SOMEWHERE]

Ge 3:6 she took s and ate it. 4946
3:6 She also gave s to her husband, NIH
3:12 she gave me s fruit from the tree, 4946
4:3 Cain brought s *of* the fruits of the soil 4946
4:4 But Abel brought fat portions from s *of* 4946
8:20 taking s *of* all the clean animals 4946
9:21 When he drank s *of* its wine, 4946
14:10 *s of the men* **fell** into them AIT
18:6 flour and knead it and bake *s* **bread."** AIT
18:8 then brought *s* **curds** and milk and the calf AIT
21:14 the next morning Abraham took *s* **food** and AIT
22:1 **S time later** God tested Abraham. 339+465+1821+2021+2021
22:20 **S time later** Abraham was told, 339+465+1821+2021+2021
23:4 Sell me *s* **property** *for* a burial site here AIT
25:29 Once when Jacob was cooking *s* **stew,** AIT
25:30 "Quick, let me have s *of* that red stew! 4946
25:34 Then Jacob gave Esau *s* **bread** AIT
25:34 some bread and *s* lentil **stew.** AIT
27:3 to the open country to hunt *s* **wild game** AIT
27:7 'Bring me *s* **game** and prepare me AIT
27:7 and prepare me *s* **tasty food** to eat, AIT
27:9 I can prepare *s* **tasty food** for your father, AIT
27:14 and she prepared *s* **tasty food,** AIT
27:19 Please sit up and eat s *of* my game so 4946
27:25 "My son, bring me s *of* your game to eat, 4946
27:25 and he brought *s* **wine** and he drank. AIT
27:31 He too prepared *s* **tasty food** AIT
27:31 "My father, sit up and eat s *of* my game, 4946
29:19 that I give her to you than to *s* **other** man. AIT
30:14 the fields and found *s* **mandrake plants,** AIT
30:14 "Please give me s *of* your son's mandrakes. 4946
30:21 **S time later** she gave birth to a daughter 339
31:46 He said to his relatives, "Gather *s* **stones."** AIT
32:16 and keep *s* **space** between the herds." AIT
33:15 "Then let me leave s *of* my men with you." 4946
35:16 While they were still **s distance** 824+2021+3896
36:6 **s distance from** his brother Jacob. 4946+7156
37:33 S ferocious animal has devoured him. NIH
40:1 **S time later,** the cupbearer and the baker 339+465+1821+2021+2021
40:4 After they had been in custody *for* **s time,** 3427
42:2 Go down there and buy s for us, NIH
43:11 Put s *of* the best products of the land 4946
43:11 a little balm and a little honey, *s* **spices** AIT
43:11 *s* **pistachio nuts** and almonds. AIT
45:19 Take *s* **carts** from Egypt for your children AIT
48:1 **S time later** Joseph was told, 339+465+1821+2021+2021
Ex 2:17 S shepherds came along 2021[S]
4:9 take s water from the Nile and pour it on 4946
10:26 We have to use s *of* them in worshiping 4946
12:7 to take s *of* the blood and put it on the sides 4946
12:10 if s is left till morning, you must burn it. 4946
12:22 the basin and put s *of* the blood on the top 4946
16:17 *s* **gathered** much, some little. AIT
16:17 some gathered much, s little. NIH
16:20 **s of them** paid no attention to Moses; 408[S]
16:27 s *of* the people went out on the seventh day 4946
17:5 with you s *of* the elders of Israel and take 4946
17:9 "Choose *s of* our **men** and go out to fight AIT
Ex 18:19 now to me and *I will* **give** you *s* **advice,** AIT
29:12 Take s *of* the bull's blood and put it on 4946
29:20 take s *of* its blood and put it on the lobes of 4946
29:21 And take s *of* the blood on the altar 4946
29:21 and s *of* the anointing oil and sprinkle it 4946
30:36 Grind s *of* it to powder and place it in front 4946
33:7 outside the camp s **distance away,** 4946+8178
34:16 And when you choose s *of* their daughters 4946
Lev 4:5 Then the anointed priest shall take s *of* 4946
4:6 the blood and sprinkle s *of* it seven times 4946
4:7 The priest shall then put s *of* the blood on 4946
4:16 to take s *of* the bull's blood into the Tent 4946
4:18 He is to put s *of* the blood on the horns of 4946
4:25 Then the priest shall take s *of* the blood of 4946
4:30 Then the priest is to take s *of* the blood 4946
4:34 Then the priest shall take s *of* the blood of 4946
5:9 to sprinkle s *of* the blood of the sin offering 4946
8:11 He sprinkled s *of* the oil on 4946
8:12 He poured s *of* the anointing oil 4946
8:15 the bull and took *s of* the **blood,** AIT
8:23 the ram and took s *of* its blood and put it on 4946
8:24 and put s *of* the blood on the lobes 4946
8:30 Then Moses took s *of* the anointing oil 4946
8:30 of the anointing oil and s *of* the blood from 4946
11:4 " 'There are s that only chew the cud 4946
11:21 s winged creatures that walk on all 3972+4946
11:40 Anyone who eats s *of* the carcass 4946
14:4 that two live clean birds and *s* cedar **wood,** AIT
14:14 to take s *of* the blood of the guilt offering 4946
14:15 The priest shall then take s *of* the log of oil, 4946
14:16 and with his finger sprinkle s *of* it before 4946
14:17 to put s *of* the oil remaining in his palm on 4946
14:25 for the guilt offering and take s *of* its blood 4946
14:26 The priest is to pour s *of* the oil into 4946
14:27 and with his right forefinger sprinkle s *of* 4946
14:28 S *of* the oil in his palm he is to put on 4946
14:49 to take two birds and *s* cedar **wood,** AIT
16:14 He is to take s *of* the bull's blood and 4946
16:14 then he shall sprinkle s *of* it 4946
16:18 He shall take s *of* the bull's blood 4946
16:18 of the bull's blood and s *of* the goat's blood 4946
16:19 He shall sprinkle s *of* the blood on it 4946
24:7 Along each row put *s* pure **incense** as AIT
25:25 and sells s *of* his property, 4946
25:45 also buy s *of* the temporary residents living 4946
Nu 2:2 the Tent of Meeting s **distance** from it, 5584
5:17 Then he shall take s holy water in a clay jar NIH
5:17 and put s dust from the tabernacle floor into 4946
9:6 But s *of them* could not celebrate 408[S]
11:1 and consumed s *of* the outskirts of 928
13:2 "Send *s* **men** to explore the land of Canaan, AIT
13:20 Do your best to bring back s *of* the fruit of 4946
13:23 along with s pomegranates and figs. 4946
16:37 and scatter the coals s **distance away,** for 2134
19:4 Then Eleazar the priest is to take s 4946
19:6 The priest is to take *s* cedar **wood,** AIT
19:17 put s ashes from the burned purification 4946
19:18 to take *s* **hyssop,** dip it in the water AIT
21:1 he attacked the Israelites and captured s 4946
22:40 and gave s to Balaam and NIH
27:20 Give him s *of* your authority so 4946
30:15 he nullifies them **s time after** he hears 339
31:3 "Arm s *of* your men to go to war 907+4946
34:3 " 'Your southern side will include s *of* 4946
35:11 select *s* **towns** to be your cities of refuge, AIT
Dt 1:13 Choose *s* **wise,** understanding AIT
1:25 Taking with them s *of* the fruit of the land, 4946
12:20 "I would like *s* **meat,"** AIT
26:2 take s *of* the firstfruits of all 4946
27:2 set up *s* large **stones** and coat them AIT
Jos 2:2 S *of* the Israelites have come here tonight 408[S]
5:11 they ate s *of* the produce of the land: 4946
7:1 of the tribe of Judah, took **s of** them. 4946
7:11 They have taken s *of* the devoted things; 4946
10:18 and post *s* **men** there to guard it. AIT
22:24 that **s day** your descendants might say 4737
Jdg 4:19 "Please give me s water." 5071
5:14 S came from Ephraim, NIH
8:5 "Give my troops *s* **bread;** AIT
9:48 He took an ax and cut off *s* **branches,** AIT
11:4 **S time later,** when the Ammonites made war on Israel, 3427+4946
14:8 **S time later,** when he went back 3427+4946
14:8 In it was a swarm of bees and *s* **honey,** AIT
14:9 he gave them **s,** and they too ate it. NIH
16:4 **S time later,** he fell in love 339+4027
17:5 and *s* **idols** and installed one of his sons AIT
17:8 that town in search of **s other place** to stay. 889[S]
18:22 When they *had* **gone s distance** 8178
18:25 or s hot-tempered **men** will attack you, AIT
19:22 s *of* the wicked men of the city surrounded 408[S]
Ru 2:14 Have s bread and dip it in 4946
2:14 he offered her *s* **roasted grain.** AIT
2:14 She ate all she wanted and **had s left over.** 3855
2:16 pull out s stalks for her from the bundles NIH
1Sa 2:15 "Give the priest *s* **meat** to roast; AIT
2:36 to s priestly office so I can have food 285
6:19 down s *of* the men of Beth Shemesh, 928
8:12 S he will assign to be commanders NIH
9:11 they met *s* **girls** coming out to draw water, AIT
10:27 But *s* **troublemakers** said, AIT
13:7 *S* **Hebrews** even crossed the Jordan to AIT
14:14 and his armor-bearer killed s twenty men in 3869
14:30 if the men had eaten today s *of* 4946
17:18 and bring back *s* **assurance** *from* them. AIT
19:13 with a garment and putting s goats' hair at 2021[S]
19:16 and at the head was s goats' hair. 2021[S]
1Sa 21:4 there is *s* consecrated **bread** here— AIT
24:10 **S urged** me to kill you, but I spared you; AIT
26:13 on top of the hill s **distance away;** 4946+8158
28:22 and let me give you s food so you may eat 7326
28:24 She took *s* **flour,** kneaded it and AIT
30:9 where s stayed behind, 3855
30:26 he sent s *of* the plunder to the elders 4946
2Sa 2:14 s of the **young men** get up and AIT
3:17 **"For s time** you have wanted to make David your king. 1685+1685+8997+9453
4:6 of the house as if to get *s* **wheat,** AIT
10:9 selected s *of* the best troops in Israel 3972+4946
11:17 s of the men in David's army fell; 4946
11:24 and s *of* the king's men died. 4946
13:6 and make s special bread in my sight, 9109[S]
13:7 of your brother Amnon and prepare s food 2021[S]
13:8 She took s dough, kneaded it, 2021[S]
15:17 and they halted at a place s **distance away.** 5305
17:9 now, he is hidden in a cave or s **other** place. 285[S]
1Ki 7:10 s measuring ten cubits and some eight. 74[S]
7:10 some measuring ten cubits and s eight. 74[S]
11:17 with s Edomite officials who had served his father. 4946
13:25 *S* **people** who passed by saw the body AIT
14:3 *s* **cakes** and a jar of honey, and go to him. AIT
17:7 **S time** later the brook dried up 3427
17:17 **S time later** the son 339+465+1821+2021+2021
18:5 Maybe we can find *s* **grass** to keep AIT
20:20 on horseback with *s* of his **horsemen.** AIT
21:1 **S time later** there was an incident 339+465+1821+2021+2021
2Ki 2:16 down on s mountain or in some valley." 285
2:16 down on some mountain or in s valley." 285
2:23 *s* **youths** came out of the town and jeered AIT
4:38 "Put on the large pot and cook *s* **stew** AIT
4:39 He gathered s *of* its gourds and filled 4946
4:41 Elisha said, "Get *s* **flour."** AIT
4:42 along with *s* **heads of new grain.** AIT
4:43 'They will eat and **have** *s* **left over.'** " AIT
4:44 and they ate and **had** *s* **left over,** AIT
5:13 prophet had told you to do *s* **great thing,** AIT
5:19 After Naaman had traveled s **distance,** 824+3896
6:24 **S time later,** Ben-Hadad king 339+4027
7:8 and took s things from it and hid them also. NIH
7:13 *"Have s* **men take** five of the horses AIT
9:17 he called out, "I see *s* **troops** coming." AIT
9:33 and s *of* her blood spattered the wall and 4946
10:13 he met *s* **relatives** *of* Ahaziah king AIT
13:15 Elisha said, "Get a bow and *s* **arrows,"** AIT
13:21 while *s* **Israelites** were burying a man, AIT
17:25 among them and they killed s *of* 928
20:18 And s *of* your descendants, 4946
25:12 behind s *of* the poorest people of the land 4946
1Ch 4:40 S Hamites had lived there formerly. 4946
6:66 S *of* the Kohathite clans were given 4946
9:2 in their own towns were *s* **Israelites,** AIT
9:28 S *of* them were in charge of 4946
9:30 But s *of* the priests took care of mixing 4946
9:32 S *of* their Kohathite brothers were 4946
12:8 S Gadites defected to David 4946
12:16 *s* **men** from Judah also **came** AIT
12:19 S *of* the men of Manasseh defected 4946
16:4 He appointed s *of* the Levites to minister 4946
19:10 selected s *of* the best troops in Israel 3972+4946
25:1 set apart s *of* the sons of Asaph, 4200
26:27 S *of* the plunder taken in battle 4946
2Ch 11:23 dispersing s *of* his sons throughout 3972+4946
12:12 Indeed, there was s good in Judah. 1821
13:7 S worthless scoundrels gathered 408[S]
16:10 the same time Asa brutally oppressed s *of* 4946
17:11 S Philistines brought Jehoshaphat gifts 4946
18:2 **S years later** he went down 4200+7891+9102
19:3 There is, however, s good in you, 1821
19:8 Jehoshaphat appointed s *of* the Levites, 4946
20:1 with s *of* the Meunites came to make war 4946
20:2 *S* **men came** and told Jehoshaphat, AIT
20:19 Then s Levites from the Kohathites 2021[S]
21:4 to the sword along with s *of* the princes 4946
24:4 **S time later** Joash decided to restore 339+4027
28:12 Then s of the leaders in Ephraim— 408[S]
28:21 Ahaz **took s of the things** from the temple 2745
30:11 Nevertheless, *s* **men** of Asher, AIT
32:21 s *of* his sons cut him down with the sword. 4946
34:13 S *of* the Levites were secretaries, 4946
Ezr 2:68 s *of* the heads of the families 4946
2:70 along with s *of* the other people, 4946
7:7 S *of* the Israelites, including priests, 4946
9:2 They have taken s *of* their daughters 4946
10:44 and s *of* them had children by these wives. 4946
Ne 1:2 came from Judah with *s other* **men,** AIT
1:4 *For s* **days** I mourned and fasted and prayed AIT
4:13 Therefore I stationed *s of* the **people** AIT
5:2 S were saying, "We and our sons 889[S]
5:5 S *of* our daughters have already been enslaved, 4946
5:18 and *s* **poultry** were prepared for me, AIT
7:3 s at their posts and some near their own 408[S]
7:3 at their posts and s near their own houses." 408[S]
7:70 S *of* the heads of the families 4946+7921
7:71 S *of* the heads of the families gave to 4946
8:10 send s to those who have nothing prepared. 4950[S]
11:3 in Jerusalem (now *s* **Israelites,** AIT
11:25 s *of* the people of Judah lived 4946
11:36 S *of* the divisions of the Levites 4946
12:35 as well as s priests with trumpets, 4946
13:6 **S time** later I asked his permission 3427
13:19 I stationed s *of* my own men at the gates so 4946

Ne 13:25 I beat s *of* the men 4946
Job 11: 6 God has even forgotten s *of* your sin. 4946
39:15 that s wild animal may trample them. NIH
Ps 20: 7 S trust in chariots and some in horses, 465
20: 7 Some trust in chariots and s in horses, 465
107: 4 *S* **wandered** in desert wastelands, AIT
107:10 *S* **sat** *in* darkness and the deepest gloom, AIT
107:17 *S* became **fools** through their rebellious AIT
Pr 1:11 let's waylay s harmless soul; NIH
Ecc 5:14 or wealth lost through *s* **misfortune,** AIT
Isa 1: 9 LORD Almighty had left us s survivors, 3869+5071
17: 6 Yet *s* **gleanings** will remain, AIT
39: 7 And **s of** your descendants, 4946
43:12 I, and not *s* **foreign** god among you. AIT
44:15 s *of* it he takes and warms himself, 4946
46: 6 S pour out gold from their bags 2021S
49:12 s from the north, some from the west, 465
49:12 some from the north, s from the west, NIH
49:12 s from the region of Aswan." 465
65: 8 'Don't destroy it, there is yet *s* **good** in it,' AIT
66:19 and I will send s *of* those who survive to 4946
66:21 And I will select s *of* them also to 4946
Jer 4:29 *S* **go** into the thickets; AIT
4:29 *s* **climb up** among the rocks. AIT
19: 1 Take along s *of* the elders of the people and 4946
26:17 S of the elders of the land stepped forward 408S
26:22 along with *s* other **men.** AIT
35: 5 Then I set bowls full of wine and *s* **cups** AIT
35: 5 and said to them, "Drink *s* **wine."** AIT
38:11 He took *s* old **rags** and worn-out clothes AIT
39:10 the guard left behind in the land of Judah s 4946
43: 9 take *s* large **stones** with you and bury them AIT
52:15 of the guard carried into exile s *of* 4946
Eze 6: 8 " 'But I will spare **s,** NIH
6: 8 for s *of* you will escape the sword 4200
10: 7 He took up s of it and put it into the hands NIH
14: 1 S of the elders of Israel came to me and sat 408S
14:22 Yet *there will be* s survivors— 3855
16:16 You took s *of* your garments 4946
16:52 **furnished** *s* **justification** for your sisters. AIT
17: 5 " 'He took s *of* the seed of your land 4946
20: 1 s of the elders of Israel came to inquire of 408S
39:14 *S will* **go** throughout the land and, AIT
40: 2 on whose south side were *s* **buildings** AIT
40:17 There I saw *s* **rooms** and a pavement AIT
43:20 You are to take s *of* its blood and put it on 4946
45:19 to take s *of* the blood of the sin offering 4946
Da 1: 2 with s *of* the articles from the temple 4946+7921
1: 3 in s *of* the Israelites from the royal family 4946
1: 6 Among these were s from Judah: 1201S
2:41 it will have s *of* the strength of iron in it, 10427
3: 8 At this time s astrologers came forward 10131S
3:12 But there are s Jews whom you have set 10131S
3:20 and commanded s *of* the strongest soldiers 10131S
8:10 and it threw s *of* the starry host down to 4946
11: 6 After *s* **years,** they will become allies. AIT
11: 8 *For s* **years** he will leave the king of AIT
11:35 S *of* the wise will stumble, 4946
12: 2 s to everlasting life, others to shame 465
Am 4: 1 "Bring us *s* **drinks!"** AIT
4:11 "I overthrew **s of** you 928
Hag 2:12 and that fold touches s bread or stew, 2021S
2:12 s wine, oil or other food, 2021S
Zec 14:21 and all who come to sacrifice will take s *of* 4946
Mt 8:30 **S distance** from them a large herd 3426
9: 2 *S men* **brought** to him a paralytic, AIT
9: 3 s of the teachers of the law said 5516
10:11 search for s worthy person there and stay 5516
12: 1 to pick s heads of grain and eat them. NIG
12:38 Then s of the Pharisees and teachers of 5516
13: 4 s fell along the path, 3525+4005
13: 5 S fell on rocky places, 257+1254
14:15 to the villages and buy themselves s food." NIG
15: 1 Then s Pharisees and teachers of the law NIG
16:14 They replied, **"S** say John the Baptist; 3525+3836
16:28 s who are standing here will not taste death 5516
19: 3 S Pharisees came to him to test him. NIG
19:12 For s are eunuchs because they were born 4015
21:33 the vineyard to s farmers and went away on NIG
22: 4 "Then he sent **s more** servants and said, 257
23:34 **S of** them you will kill and crucify; 1666
25: 8 'Give us **s of** your oil; 1666
25: 9 go to those who sell oil and buy s NIG
26: 4 and they plotted to arrest Jesus in s sly way NIG
27:47 When s of those standing there heard this, 5516
28:11 s of the guards went into the city 5516
28:17 they worshiped him; but s doubted. 3836
Mk 2: 3 S men came, **bringing** to him a paralytic, NIG
2: 6 s teachers of the law were sitting there, 5516
2:18 *S people* **came** and asked Jesus, AIT
2:23 they began to pick s heads of grain. 3836
2:26 And he also gave s to his companions." NIG
3: 2 S of them were looking for a reason NIG
4: 4 s fell along the path, 3525+4005
4: 5 S fell on rocky places, 257
4:15 *S people* are like seed along the path, 4047
5:35 *s men* **came** from the house of Jairus, AIT
6:14 *S were* **saying,** "John the Baptist has been AIT
6:31 to a quiet place and get s rest." 3900
7: 1 The Pharisees and s of the teachers of 5516
7: 2 saw s of his disciples eating food 5516
7:32 There *s people* **brought** to him AIT
8: 3 s of them have come a long distance." 5516
8:22 and *s people* **brought** a blind man AIT
8:28 They replied, **"S** say John the Baptist; NIG
9: 1 s who are standing here will not taste death 5516
10: 2 S Pharisees came and tested him by asking, NIG

Mk 11: 5 s *people* standing there asked, 5516
12: 1 the vineyard to s farmers and went away on NIG
12: 2 from them s of the fruit of the vineyard. NIG
12: 5 s of them they beat, others they killed. 3525+4005
12:13 Later they sent s of the Pharisees 5516
14: 1 for s sly **way** to arrest Jesus and kill him. 4802
14: 4 S of those present were saying indignantly 5516
14:57 Then s stood up and gave this false 5516
14:65 Then s began to spit at him; 5516
15:35 When s of those standing near heard this, 5516
15:40 S women were watching from a distance. NIG
15:46 So Joseph bought s linen cloth, NIG
Lk 3:14 Then s soldiers asked him, NIG
5:18 S men came carrying a paralytic on a mat NIG
6: 1 his disciples began to pick s heads of grain, 3836
6: 2 S of the Pharisees asked, 5516
6: 4 And he also gave s to his companions." NIG
7: 3 of Jesus and sent s elders of the Jews NIG
8: 2 and also s women who had been cured 5516
8: 5 s fell along the path; 3525+4005
8: 6 S fell on rock, and when it came up, 2283
9: 7 because s were saying 5516
9:19 They replied, **"S** say John the Baptist; NIG
9:27 s who are standing here will not taste death 5516
11:15 But s of them said, "By Beelzebub, 5516
11:49 s of whom they will kill 2779
13: 1 Now there were s present at 5516
13:31 that time s Pharisees came to Jesus and said 5516
18: 4 "For s **time** he refused. 5989
18: 9 To s who were confident 5516
19:39 S of the Pharisees in the crowd said 5516
20: 9 to s farmers and went away for a long time. NIG
20:10 to the tenants so they would give him **s of** 608
20:27 S of the Sadducees, 5516
20:39 S of the teachers of the law responded, 5516
21: 5 S of his disciples were remarking about 5516
21:16 and they will put **s of** you to death. 1666
22: 2 were looking for s **way** to get rid 3836+4802
23: 8 he hoped to see him perform s miracle. 5516
24:22 In addition, s of our women amazed us. 5516
24:24 Then s of our companions went to the tomb 5516
Jn 1:24 Now s Pharisees who had been sent NIG
2: 8 "Now draw s out and take it to the master NIG
3:22 where *he* **spent** s **time** with them, 1417
3:25 An argument developed between **s of** 1666
5: 1 **S time later,** Jesus went up to Jerusalem 3552+4047
6: 1 **S time after** this, Jesus crossed 3552
6:23 Then s boats from Tiberias landed near 257
6:64 Yet there are s of you who do not believe." 5516
7:12 S said, "He is a good man." 3525+3836
7:25 At that point s of the people 5516
7:40 *s* of the people **said,** AIT
7:44 S wanted to seize him, 5516
9: 6 made s mud with the saliva, NIG
9: 9 S claimed that he was. 257
9:11 "The man they call Jesus made s mud NIG
9:16 S of the Pharisees said, 5516
9:40 S Pharisees **who** were with him heard him 3836
10: 1 but climbs in by s other way, NIG
11:37 But s of them said, 5516
11:46 But s of them went to the Pharisees 5516
12:20 Now there were s Greeks 5516
13:29 s thought Jesus was telling him 5516
16:17 *S* of his disciples **said** to one another, AIT
18: 3 a detachment of soldiers and s officials NIG
21: 6 of the boat and you will find **s."** NIG
21: 9 with fish on it, and s bread. NIG
21:10 "Bring s of the fish you have just caught." 608
Ac 2:13 **S,** however, made fun of them and said, 2283
5: 3 for yourself s of the money you received for 608
5:15 that at least Peter's shadow might fall on s 5516
5:36 **S time ago** Theudas appeared, 2465+3836+4047+4574
6:11 Then they secretly persuaded s men to say, NIG
8: 9 Now **for s time** a man named Simon 4732
8:36 they came to s water and the eunuch said, 5516
9:19 and after taking s food, NIG
9:43 *for* s time with a tanner named Simon. 2653
10:23 s of the brothers from Joppa went along. 5516
11:20 S of them, however, men from Cyprus 5516
11:27 During this time s prophets came down NIG
12: 1 that King Herod arrested s who belonged to 5516
14: 4 s sided with the Jews, 3525+3836
14:19 Then s Jews came from Antioch NIG
15: 1 *S men* came down from Judea to Antioch 5516
15: 2 along with s other believers, 5516
15: 5 Then s of the believers who belonged to 5516
15: 7 you know that **s time ago** God 608+792+2465
15:22 to choose s of their own men and send them NIG
15:24 We have heard that s went out from us 5516
15:25 to choose s men and send them to you NIG
15:33 After spending s time there, NIG
15:36 S time later Paul said to Barnabas, 5516
17: 4 S of the Jews were persuaded 5516
17: 5 up s bad characters from the marketplace, 5516
17: 6 they dragged Jason and s other brothers 5516
17:18 S of them asked, 5516
17:20 You are bringing s strange ideas to our ears, 5516
17:28 As s of your own poets have said, 5516
17:32 s of them sneered, but others said, 3525+3836
18:14 about s misdemeanor or serious crime, 5516
18:18 Paul stayed on in Corinth *for* s time. 2653
18:23 After spending s time in Antioch, 5516
19: 1 There he found s disciples 5516
19: 9 But s *of them* became obstinate; 5516
19:13 S Jews who went around driving out 5516

Ac 19:31 Even s of the officials of the province, 5516
19:32 S were shouting one thing, some another. 3525
19:32 Some were shouting one thing, s another. 257
19:33 *s* of the crowd shouted **instructions to** AIT
21:16 S of the disciples from Caesarea NIG
21:27 s Jews from the province of Asia saw Paul 3836
21:32 at once took s officers and soldiers and ran NIG
21:34 S in the crowd shouted one thing 257
21:34 the crowd shouted one thing and s another, NIG
21:38 the desert **s time ago?"** 2465+3836+4047+4574
23: 6 that s of them were Sadducees 1651+3538+3836
23: 9 and s of the teachers of the law 5516
24: 1 down to Caesarea with s of the elders and 5516
24:19 there are s Jews from the province of Asia, 5516
24:23 under guard but to give him s freedom NIG
25: 5 Let s of your leaders come with me 3836
25:19 they had s points of dispute with him 5516
27: 1 and s other prisoners were handed over to 5516
27:26 we must run aground on s island." 5516
27:30 to lower s anchors from the bow. NIG
27:34 Now I urge you to take s food. NIG
27:35 he took s bread and gave thanks to God NIG
27:36 and ate s food themselves. NIG
28:14 There we found s brothers who invited us NIG
28:24 S were convinced by what he said, 3525+3836
Ro 1:11 to you s spiritual gift to make you strong— 5516
3: 3 What if s did not have faith? 5516
3: 8 as saying and as s claim that we say— 5516
9:21 of clay s pottery for noble purposes 3525+4005
9:21 noble purposes **and** s for common use? 1254+4005
11:14 to envy and save s of them. 5516
11:17 If s of the branches have been broken off, 5516
15:15 written you quite boldly **on s points,** 608+3538
1Co 1:11 My brothers, s from Chloe's NIG
4:18 S of you have become arrogant, 5516
6:11 And that is what s of you were. 5516
8: 7 *S people* are still so accustomed to idols 5516
9:22 so that by all possible means I might save **s.** 5516
10: 7 Do not be idolaters, as s of them were; 5516
10: 8 as s of them did—and in one day 5516
10: 9 as s of them did—and were killed 5516
10:10 And do not grumble, as s of them did— 5516
10:27 If s unbeliever invites you to a meal 5516
11:18 and to s extent I believe it. 5516
14: 6 unless I bring you s revelation 2445
14:23 **s who do not understand** or some 2626
14:23 not understand or s unbelievers come in, NIG
15: 6 though s have fallen asleep. 5516
15:12 how can s of you say 5516
15:34 for there are s who are ignorant of God— 5516
16: 7 I hope to spend s time with you, 5516
2Co 2: 5 **to s extent**—not to put it too 247+608+3538
3: 1 Or do we need, like *s people,* 5516
10: 2 as I expect to be toward *s people* who think 5516
10:10 For *s* **say,** "His letters are weighty AIT
10:12 *with* s who commend themselves. 5516
Gal 1: 7 Evidently *s people* are throwing you 5516
2: 4 s false brothers had infiltrated our ranks 4015
Eph 4:11 It was he who gave s to be apostles, 3525
4:11 s to be prophets, some to be evangelists, 1254
4:11 some to be prophets, s to be evangelists, 1254
4:11 **and** s to be pastors and teachers, 1254
Php 1:15 that s preach Christ out of envy and rivalry, 5516
3:15 And if on **s point** you think differently, 5516
1Th 3: 5 I was afraid that **in s way** the tempter 4803
2Th 2: 2 unsettled or alarmed by s prophecy, NIG
3:11 We hear that s among you are idle. 5516
1Ti 1: 6 S have wandered away from these 5516
1:19 S have rejected these and 5516
4: 1 that in later times s will abandon the faith 5516
4: 8 For physical training is of s value, 3900
5:15 S have in fact already turned away 5516
5:24 The sins *of* s men are obvious, 5516
6:10 S *people,* eager for money, 5516
6:21 which s have professed and in 5516
2Ti 2:18 and they destroy the faith *of* **s.** 5516
2:20 s are for noble purposes and some 3525+4005
2:20 for noble purposes **and** s for ignoble. 1254+4005
Phm 1:20 I may have s benefit from you in the Lord; NIG
Heb 4: 6 It still remains that s will enter that rest, 5516
10:25 as s are in the habit of doing, 5516
11:36 S faced jeers and flogging, 2283
13: 2 so doing *s people* have entertained angels 5516
2Pe 3: 9 as s understand slowness. 5516
3:16 His letters contain s *things* that are hard 5516
2Jn 1: 4 It has given me great joy to find **s of** 1666
3Jn 1: 3 to have s brothers come and tell NIG
Rev 2:10 devil will put **s of** you in prison to test you, 1666
2:17 I will give *s of* **the** hidden manna. AIT

SOMEBODY (5) [BODY, SOME]

Ex 22: 9 any other lost property about which *s* **says,** AIT
Pr 12: 9 and yet have a servant than **pretend to be s** 3877
Ac 5:36 Theudas appeared, claiming to be **s,** 5516
Gal 6: 4 without comparing himself to **s else,** 2283
Heb 9:17 a will is in force only when s has died; NIG

SOMEHOW (5) [HOW, SOME]

Ro 11:14 the hope that I may s arouse my own people 4803
1Co 12: 2 **s or other** you were influenced 323+6055
2Co 11: 3 your minds may s be led astray NIG
Gal 4:11 that s I have wasted my efforts on you. 4803
Php 3:11 and so, **s,** to attain to the resurrection 1623+4803

SOMEONE (120) [ONE, SOME]

Ex 4:13 "O Lord, please send s else to do it." 928+3338[S]
12:30 for there was not a house without *s* **dead.** AIT
23: 5 the donkey of *s who* **hates** you fallen down AIT
Lev 2: 1 " 'When s brings a grain offering to 5883
13:18 "When s has a boil on his skin and it heals, 2257
13:24 "When s has a burn on his skin and NIH
15: 8 with the discharge spits on s *who* is clean, 2021
27:20 or if he has sold it to s else, 408
Nu 6: 9 " 'If s dies suddenly in his presence, 4637[S]
19:16 the open who touches s who has been killed 2021
19:16 *s who has* **died a natural death,** AIT
19:18 or a grave or s who has been killed 2021[S]
19:18 or s who has died a natural death. 2021[S]
35: 6 a person who has killed s may flee. NIH
35:11 who has killed s accidentally may flee. 5883
35:16 " 'If a man strikes s with an iron object so 2084
35:17 and he strikes s so that he dies, 2084
35:18 and he hits s so that he dies, 2084
35:22 without hostility *s* suddenly **shoves** another AIT
36: 8 in any Israelite tribe must marry s 285
Dt 20: 5 in battle and s else may dedicate it. 408
20: 6 or he may die in battle and s else enjoy it. 408
20: 7 in battle and s else marry her." 408
22: 8 on your house if s falls from 2021+5877[S]
22:26 of s who attacks and murders his neighbor, 408
Jos 20: 9 who killed s accidentally could flee 5883
Jdg 4:20 "If s comes by and asks you, 408
6:31 he can defend himself when *s* **breaks down** AIT
Ru 2:22 in **s else's** field you might be harmed." 337
1Sa 14:33 Then *s* **said** to Saul, "Look, AIT
16:16 to search for s who can play the harp. 408
16:17 "Find s who plays well and bring him 408
17:30 He then turned away to **s else** and brought 337
25:29 though **s** is pursuing you to take your life, 132
26:15 S came to destroy your lord 285+2021+6639
2Sa 3:29 *s who has a* **running sore** AIT
11: 3 and David sent s to find out about her. NIH
14: 2 So Joab sent s to Tekoa and had NIH
23:15 that s would get me a drink of water from 4769
1Ki 14: 5 *she will* **pretend to be s else."** 5796
18:10 or kingdom where my master has not sent s NIH
20:39 and s came to me with a captive and said, 408
22:34 But s drew his bow at random and hit 408
2Ki 5: 7 Why does this fellow send s to me to 408
6:32 how this murderer is sending s NIH
1Ch 11:17 that s would get me a drink of water from 4769
19: 5 *s* **came** and told David about the men, AIT
2Ch 18:33 But s drew his bow at random and hit 408
Ne 2:10 that s had come to promote the welfare of 132
Est 1:19 to **s else** who is better than she. 8295
Job 4: 2 "If *s* **ventures** a word with you, AIT
9:33 only there were *s to* **arbitrate** between us, AIT
9:34 *s to* **remove** God's rod from me, AIT
31:35 that I had *s to* **hear** me! AIT
Pr 4:16 robbed of slumber till they make s fall. NIH
27: 2 **s else,** and not your own lips. 5799
Ecc 2:21 then he must leave all he owns to s who has 132
Isa 21:11 *S* **calls** to me from Seir, "Watchman, AIT
28: 4 as s sees it and takes it in his hand, 2021+8011[S]
29:11 if you give the scroll to *s who* **can read,** AIT
29:12 if you give the scroll to s who cannot read, 889
Eze 43: 6 I heard *s* **speaking** to me from inside AIT
Da 5:17 and give your rewards to **s else.** 10025
Zec 13: 6 If *s* **asks** him, 'What are these wounds AIT
Mt 5:39 If s strikes you on the right cheek, *4015*
5:40 if s wants to sue you and take your tunic, *3836*
5:41 If s forces you to go one mile, *4015*
11: 3 or should we expect **s else?"** *2283*
12:47 S told him, "Your mother *5516*
Mk 3:31 Standing outside, they sent s in to call him. *NIG*
Lk 6:29 If s strikes you on one cheek, *3836*
6:29 If s takes your cloak, *3836*
7:19 or should we expect **s else?"** *257*
7:20 or should we expect **s else?' "** *257*
8:20 S told him, "Your mother *NIG*
8:46 But Jesus said, **"S** touched me; *5516*
8:49 s came from the house of Jairus, *5516*
11:22 *s* **stronger** attacks and overpowers him, *AIT*
12:13 S in the crowd said to him, "Teacher, *5516*
13:23 S asked him, "Lord, are only *5516*
14: 8 "When s invites you to a wedding feast, *5516*
16:12 not been trustworthy with **s else's** property, *259*
16:30 'but if s from the dead goes to them, *5516*
16:31 they will not be convinced even if s rises *5516*
22:58 A little later *s* **else** saw him and said, *AIT*
Jn 4:33 "Could s have brought him food?" *5516*
5: 7 **s else** goes down ahead of me. *257*
5:43 but if **s else** comes in his own name, *257*
21:18 and **s else** will dress you and lead you *257*
Ac 5:25 Then s came and said, "Look! *5516*
8: 9 He boasted that he was s great, *5516*
8:31 he said, "unless s explains it to me?" *5516*
8:34 prophet talking about, himself or s else?" *5516*
13:11 **s to lead** him **by the hand.** *5933*
13:41 would never believe, even if s told you.' " *5516*
Ro 2: 1 you who pass judgment on s else, *NIG*
3: 7 S might argue, "If my falsehood enhances God's truthfulness *NIG*
5: 7 for a good man s might possibly dare to die. *5516*
6:16 *to* s to obey him as slaves, you are slaves to *4005*
10:14 can they hear without *s* **preaching** to them? *AIT*
14: 4 Who are you to judge **s else's** servant? *259*
14:20 for a man to eat anything that causes s else *NIG*
15:20 not be building on **s else's** foundation. *259*
1Co 3:10 and **s else** is building on it. *257*
14:11 not grasp the meaning *of* what **s is saying,** *5889*
14:24 **s who does not understand** comes in *2626*
14:27 one at a time, and s must interpret. *1651*
14:30 revelation comes *to* s who is sitting down, *257*
15:35 But s may ask, "How are the dead raised? *5516*
2Co 11: 4 For if s comes to you and preaches *3836*
Gal 6: 1 Brothers, if s is caught in a sin, *476*[S]
Heb 2: 6 But there is a place where s has testified: *5516*
3: 4 For every house is built by **s,** *5516*
5:12 you need s to teach you the elementary *5516*
6:16 Men swear by *s* **greater than** themselves, *AIT*
Jas 2:18 s will say, "You have faith; I have deeds." *5516*
5:19 from the truth and s should bring him back, *5516*
1Pe 5: 8 like a roaring lion looking for s to devour. *5516*
Rev 1:13 and among the lampstands was s "like a son *NIG*
4: 2 a throne in heaven with *s* **sitting** on it. *AIT*

SOMEONE'S (3) [ONE, SOME]

Lev 3: 1 " 'If s offering is a fellowship offering, 2257
24:18 the life of s animal must make restitution— NIH
Pr 1:11 let's lie in wait for s blood, NIH

SOMETHING (110) [SOME, THING]

Ge 18: 5 Let me get you **s to eat,** 4312+7326
30:30 when *may* I **do** *s* for my own household?" AIT
38:17 "Will you give me s as a pledge NIH
Ex 2:20 Invite him to have s to eat." 4312[S]
10: 6 s neither your fathers 889
17:14 a scroll as s to be **remembered** 2355
24:10 *s* like a pavement **made** *of* sapphire, AIT
Lev 5: 1 to testify regarding s he has seen or learned NIH
6: 2 by deceiving his neighbor about **s entrusted** 7214
7:21 If anyone touches s unclean— 3972
11:32 When one of them dies and falls on **s,** 2257[S]
14:35 'I have seen s that looks like mildew NIH
14:57 to determine when s is clean or unclean. 2021[S]
22: 4 also be unclean if he touches s defiled by 3972
27:14 " 'If a man dedicates his house as **s holy** to 7731
27:23 on that day as **s holy** to the LORD. 7731
Nu 11: 8 And it tasted like **s made** *with* olive oil. 4382
16:30 if the LORD brings about **s totally new,** 1375
18:10 Eat it as s most holy; every male shall eat it. 2021[S]
35:20 or throws s at him intentionally so NIH
35:22 or throws s at him unintentionally 3972+3998
Dt 8:16 s your fathers had never known, 889
23:13 of your equipment have **s to dig with,** 3845
24: 1 because he finds s indecent about her, 1821
Jdg 14:14 He replied, "Out of the eater, **s to eat;** 4407
14:14 out of the strong, *s* **sweet."** AIT
18: 9 **Aren't** you *going to* **do s?** 3120
19: 5 "Refresh yourself with **s to eat;** 4312+7326
19:21 *they had s to* **eat** and drink. AIT
Ru 3: 8 the middle of the night *s* **startled** the man, AIT
1Sa 1:18 Then she went her way and ate s, NIH
3:11 I am about to do s in Israel that will make 1821
20:26 **"S** must have **happened** 5247
2Sa 3:35 Then they all came and urged David to eat s 4312[S]
12:18 He may do s **desperate."** 8288
13: 5 like my sister Tamar to come and give me s 4312[S]
1Ki 1:27 Is this s my lord the king has done 1821
2:14 Then he added, "I have **s to say** to you." 1821
13: 7 "Come home with me and **have s to eat,** 6184
17:13 and then make s for yourself and your son. NIH
2Ki 5:20 I will run after him and get s from him." 4399
Job 6:21 you see **s dreadful** and are afraid. 3170
6:22 Have I ever said, 'Give s on my behalf, NIH
13:28 "So man wastes away like **s rotten,** 8373
Pr 20:25 for a man to dedicate s rashly and only later NIH
Ecc 1:10 This is s new"? 2085[S]
3:16 And I saw **s else** under the sun: 6388
4: 7 Again I saw *s* **meaningless** under the sun: AIT
8:14 There is s else meaningless that occurs NIH
9:11 I have seen **s else** under the sun: 8740
Isa 41:23 **Do** *s,* whether **good** or bad, AIT
Jer 7:31 s I did not command, 889
14: 7 O LORD, **do s** for the sake of your name. 6913
19: 5 s I did not command or mention, 889
23:14 of Jerusalem I have seen **s horrible:** 9136
38:14 "I am going to ask you **s,"** 1821
Eze 15: 5 how much less can it be made into **s useful** 4856
Da 6: 5 unless it has **s to do with** the law 10089
Hos 4: 7 exchanged their Glory for *s* **disgraceful.** AIT
8:12 but they regarded them as **s alien.** AIT
Joel 3: 4 Are you repaying me for s I have **done?** 1691
Hab 1: 5 to do s in your days that you would 7189
Mt 5:23 and there remember that your brother has s *5516*
14:16 You give them s to eat." *NIG*
25:35 For I was hungry and you gave me s to eat, *NIG*
25:35 I was thirsty and you gave me s to drink, *NIG*
25:37 or thirsty and give you s to drink? *NIG*
Mk 5:43 and told them to give her s to eat. *NIG*
6:36 and villages and buy themselves s to eat." *5515*
6:37 But he answered, "You give them s to eat." *NIG*
Lk 7:40 "Simon, I have s to tell you." *5516*
8:55 Then Jesus told them to give her s to eat. *NIG*
9:13 He replied, "You give them **s** to eat." *NIG*
11:54 waiting to catch him in s he might say. *5516*
20:20 **s he said** so that they might hand him over *3364*
Jn 4:31 his disciples urged him, "Rabbi, eat **s."** *NIG*
5:14 Stop sinning or s worse may happen *5516*
13:29 or to give s to the poor. *5516*
18:23 "If I said s wrong," Jesus replied, *NIG*
Ac 3: 5 expecting to get s from them. *5516*
9:18 s like scales fell from Saul's eyes, *NIG*
10:10 He became hungry and wanted s to eat, *NIG*
10:11 and s like a large sheet being let down *5516*
11: 5 I saw s like a large sheet being let down *5516*
13:41 for I am going to do s in your days *2240*
17:23 *as s* **unknown** I am going to proclaim *AIT*
21:37 "May I say s to you?" *5516*
23:17 he has s to tell him." *5516*
23:18 to you because he has s to tell you." *5516*
25:26 as a result of this investigation I may have s *5515*
Ro 4: 2 he had **s to boast about—** *3017*
12:20 if he is thirsty, give him s to drink. *NIG*
14:14 But if anyone regards s as unclean, *5516*
1Co 7:30 those who buy **s,** as if it were not theirs *NIG*
8: 2 The man who thinks he knows s does not *5516*
10:30 because of s I thank God for? *4005*
14:35 If they want to inquire about **s,** *5516*
15:37 perhaps of wheat or *of* s else. *5516*
2Co 11: 9 And when I was with you and needed **s,** *NIG*
Gal 1:11 s that **man made up.** *476+2848*
6: 3 If anyone thinks he is s when he is nothing, *5516*
Eph 4:28 doing s useful with his own hands, *3836*
4:28 he may have s to share with those in need. *NIG*
Php 2: 6 equality with God **s to be grasped,** *772*
Heb 8: 3 for this one also to have s to offer. *5516*
11:40 God had planned s better for us so *5516*
Jas 4: 2 You want s but don't get it. *NIG*
1Pe 4:12 as though *s* **strange** were happening to you. *AIT*
Rev 8: 8 and s like a huge mountain, all ablaze, *NIG*
9: 7 On their heads they wore s like crowns *6055*

SOMETIME (KJV) See ONCE

SOMETIMES (3) [SOME]

Nu 9:20 S the cloud was over the tabernacle 889+3780
9:21 S the cloud stayed only from evening 889+3780
Heb 10:33 S you were publicly exposed to insult *3525+4047*

SOMEWHAT (1) [SOME, WHAT]

2Co 10: 8 even if I boast s freely about the authority *5516*

SOMEWHERE (4) [SOME, WHERE]

Isa 45:19 from s *in* a land of darkness; 5226
Mk 1:38 Jesus replied, "Let us go **s else—** *250*
Lk 13:31 "Leave this place and go s else. *NIG*
Heb 4: 4 For s he has spoken about the seventh day *4543*

SON (2331) [GRANDSON, GRANDSONS, SON'S, SON-IN-LAW, SONS, SONS', SONS-IN-LAW, SONSHIP]

Ge 4:17 and he named it after his s Enoch. 1201
4:22 Zillah also **had a s,** Tubal-Cain, 3528
4:25 she gave birth to a s and named him Seth, 1201
4:26 Seth also had a **s,** and he named him Enosh. 1201
5: 3 *he* **had a s** in his own likeness, 3528
5:28 Lamech had lived 182 years, he had a **s.** 1201
9:24 and found out what his youngest s had done 1201
11:31 Terah took his s Abram, 1201
11:31 his grandson Lot s *of* Haran, 1201
11:31 the wife of his s Abram, 1201
15: 4 but a s coming from your own body will 889[S]
16:11 now with child and you will have a **s.** 1201
16:15 So Hagar bore Abram a **s,** 1201
16:15 the name Ishmael to the s she had borne. 1201
17:16 I will bless her and will surely give you a s 1201
17:17 a **s be born** to a man a hundred years old? 3528
17:19 "Yes, but your wife Sarah will bear you a **s,** 1201
17:23 that very day Abraham took his s Ishmael 1201
17:25 and his s Ishmael was thirteen; 1201
17:26 and his s Ishmael were both circumcised on 1201
18:10 and Sarah your wife will have a **s."** 1201
18:14 and Sarah will have a **s."** 1201
19:37 The older daughter had a **s,** 1201
19:38 The younger daughter also had a **s,** 1201
21: 2 and bore a s to Abraham in his old age, 1201
21: 3 the name Isaac to the s Sarah bore him. 1201
21: 4 When his s Isaac was eight days old, 1201
21: 5 when his s Isaac was born to him. 1201
21: 7 Yet I have borne him a s in his old age." 1201
21: 9 the s whom Hagar the Egyptian had borne 1201
21:10 "Get rid of that slave woman and her **s,** 1201
21:10 for that slave woman's s will never share in 1201
21:10 in the inheritance with my s Isaac." 1201
21:11 because it concerned his **s.** 1201
21:13 the s *of* the maidservant into a nation also, 1201
22: 2 Then God said, "Take your s, 1201
22: 2 God said, "Take your son, your **only s,** 3495
22: 3 of his servants and his s Isaac. 1201
22: 6 and placed it on his s Isaac, 1201
22: 7 "Yes, my **s?"** Abraham replied. 1201
22: 8 the lamb for the burnt offering, my **s."** 1201
22: 9 He bound his s Isaac and laid him on 1201
22:10 and took the knife to slay his **s.** 1201
22:12 you have not withheld from me your s, 1201
22:12 from me your son, your **only s."** 3495
22:13 as a burnt offering instead of his **s.** 1201
22:16 and have not withheld your **s,** 1201
22:16 not withheld your son, your **only s,** 3495
23: 8 to me and intercede with Ephron s *of* Zohar 1201
24: 3 not get a wife for my s from the daughters 1201
24: 4 and get a wife for my s Isaac." 1201
24: 5 Shall I then take your s back to 1201
24: 6 that you do not take my s back there," 1201
24: 7 that you can get a wife for my s from there. 1201
24: 8 Only do not take my s back there." 1201

Ge 24:15 the daughter of Bethuel s *of* Milcah, 1201
24:24 the s that Milcah bore to Nahor." 1201
24:36 My master's wife Sarah has borne him a s 1201
24:37 not get a wife for my s from the daughters 1201
24:38 and get a wife for my s.' 1201
24:40 a wife for my s from my own clan and 1201
24:44 the LORD has chosen for my master's s.' 1201
24:47 'The daughter of Bethuel s *of* Nahor, 1201
24:48 of my master's brother for his s. 1201
24:51 let her become the wife of your master's s, 1201
25:6 and sent them away from his s Isaac to 1201
25:9 the field of Ephron s *of* Zohar the Hittite, 1201
25:11 God blessed his s Isaac, 1201
25:12 This is the account of Abraham's s Ishmael, 1201
25:19 This is the account of Abraham's s Isaac. 1201
27:1 he called for Esau his older s and said 1201
27:1 and said to him, "My s." 1201
27:5 as Isaac spoke to his s Esau. 1201
27:6 Rebekah said to her s Jacob, 1201
27:8 my s, listen carefully 1201
27:13 His mother said to him, "My s, 1201
27:15 the best clothes of Esau her older s, 1201
27:15 and put them on her younger s Jacob. 1201
27:17 to her s Jacob the tasty food and 1201
27:18 "Yes, my s," he answered. 1201
27:20 Isaac asked his s, 1201
27:20 "How did you find it so quickly, my s?" 1201
27:21 "Come near so I can touch you, my s, 1201
27:21 to know whether you really are my s Esau 1201
27:24 "Are you really my s Esau?" 1201
27:25 Then he said, "My s, 1201
27:26 "Come here, my s, and kiss me." 1201
27:27 the smell of my s is like the smell of a field 1201
27:32 "I am your s," he answered, "your firstborn, 1201
27:37 So what can I possibly do for you, my s?" 1201
27:42 Rebekah was told what her older s Esau 1201
27:42 she sent for her younger s Jacob and said 1201
27:43 Now then, my s, do what I say: 1201
28:5 to Laban s *of* Bethuel the Aramean, 1201
28:9 and daughter of Ishmael s *of* Abraham, 1201
29:12 a relative of her father and a s *of* Rebekah. 1201
29:13 his sister's s, he hurried to meet him. 1201
29:32 Leah became pregnant and gave birth to a s. 1201
29:33 and when she gave birth to a s she said, 1201
29:34 and when she gave birth to a s she said, 1201
29:35 and when she gave birth to a s she said, 1201
30:5 and she became pregnant and bore him a s. 1201
30:6 he has listened to my plea and given me a s. 1201
30:7 and bore Jacob a second s. 1201
30:10 Leah's servant Zilpah bore Jacob a s. 1201
30:12 servant Zilpah bore Jacob a second s. 1201
30:17 and bore Jacob a fifth s. 1201
30:19 and bore Jacob a sixth s. 1201
30:23 She became pregnant and gave birth to a s 1201
30:24 "May the LORD add to me another s." 1201
34:2 When Shechem s *of* Hamor the Hivite, 1201
34:8 "My s Shechem has his heart set 1201
34:18 to Hamor and his s Shechem. 1201
34:20 So Hamor and his s Shechem went to 1201
34:24 with Hamor and his s Shechem, 1201
34:26 They put Hamor and his s Shechem to 1201
35:17 "Don't be afraid, for you have another s." 1201
35:18 she named **her** s Ben-Oni. 2257S
36:10 Eliphaz, the s *of* Esau's wife Adah, 1201
36:10 and Reuel, the s *of* Esau's wife Basemath. 1201
36:12 Esau's s Eliphaz also had 1201
36:17 The sons of Esau's s Reuel: 1201
36:32 Bela s *of* Beor became king of Edom. 1201
36:33 Jobab s *of* Zerah from Bozrah 1201
36:35 When Husham died, Hadad s *of* Bedad, 1201
36:38 Baal-Hanan s *of* Acbor succeeded him 1201
36:39 When Baal-Hanan s *of* Acbor died, 1201
37:34 and mourned for his s many days. 1201
37:35 down to the grave to my s." 1201
38:3 she became pregnant and gave birth to a s, 1201
38:4 and gave birth to a s and named him Onan. 1201
38:5 to still another s and named him Shelah. 1201
38:11 until my s Shelah grows up." 1201
38:26 since I wouldn't give her to my s Shelah." 1201
41:52 The second s he named Ephraim and said, NIH
42:38 "My s will not go down there with you; 1201
43:29 his own mother's s, he asked, 1201
43:29 he said, "God be gracious to you, my s." 1201
44:20 a young s *born* to him *in* his old age. 3529
45:9 'This is what your s Joseph says: 1201
45:28 My s Joseph is still alive. 1201
46:10 and Shaul the s *of* a Canaanite woman. 1201
46:23 The s *of* Dan: Hushim. 1201
47:29 he called for his s Joseph and said to him, 1201
48:2 "Your s Joseph has come to you," 1201
48:19 his father refused and said, "I know, my s, 1201
49:9 you return from the prey, my s. 1201
50:23 of Makir s *of* Manasseh were placed 1201
Ex 2:2 she became pregnant and gave birth to a s. 1201
2:10 to Pharaoh's daughter and he became her s. 1201
2:22 Zipporah gave birth to a s, 1201
4:22 Israel is my firstborn s, 1201
4:23 "Let my s go, so he may worship me." 1201
4:23 so I will kill your firstborn s.' " 1201
6:14 the **firstborn** *s of* Israel were Hanoch AIT
6:15 and Shaul the s *of* a Canaanite woman. 1201
6:25 Eleazar s *of* Aaron married one of 1201
11:5 Every **firstborn** *s* in Egypt will die, AIT
11:5 from the **firstborn** *s of* Pharaoh, AIT
11:5 to the **firstborn** *s of* the slave girl, AIT
13:8 On that day tell your s, 1201
13:14 "In days to come, when your s asks you, 1201
Ex 18:3 One s was named Gershom, for Moses said, NIH
20:10 neither you, nor your s or daughter, 1201
21:9 If he selects her for his s, 1201
21:31 This law also applies if the bull gores a s 1201
29:30 The s who succeeds him as priest 1201
31:2 I have chosen Bezalel s *of* Uri, 1201
31:2 the s *of* Hur, of the tribe of Judah, 1201
31:6 I have appointed Oholiab s *of* Ahisamach, 1201
33:11 but his young aide Joshua s *of* Nun did 1201
35:30 the LORD has chosen Bezalel s *of* Uri, 1201
35:30 the s *of* Hur, of the tribe of Judah, 1201
35:34 And he has given both him and Oholiab s 1201
38:21 the Levites under the direction of Ithamar s 1201
38:22 (Bezalel s *of* Uri, the son of Hur, 1201
38:22 (Bezalel son of Uri, the s *of* Hur, 1201
38:23 with him was Oholiab s *of* Ahisamach, of 1201
Lev 6:22 The s who is to succeed him 1201
7:33 The s *of* Aaron who offers the blood and 1201
12:2 to a s will be ceremonially unclean 2351
12:6 " 'When the days of her purification for a s 1201
21:2 his s or daughter, his brother, 1201
24:10 Now the s *of* an Israelite mother and 1201
24:11 The s *of* the Israelite woman blasphemed 1201
Nu 1:5 from Reuben, Elizur s *of* Shedeur; 1201
1:6 from Simeon, Shelumiel s *of* Zurishaddai; 1201
1:7 from Judah, Nahshon s *of* Amminadab; 1201
1:8 from Issachar, Nethanel s *of* Zuar; 1201
1:9 from Zebulun, Eliab s *of* Helon; 1201
1:10 from Ephraim, Elishama s *of* Ammihud; 1201
1:10 from Manasseh, Gamaliel s *of* Pedahzur; 1201
1:11 from Benjamin, Abidan s *of* Gideoni; 1201
1:12 from Dan, Ahiezer s *of* Ammishaddai; 1201
1:13 from Asher, Pagiel s *of* Ocran; 1201
1:14 from Gad, Eliasaph s *of* Deuel; 1201
1:15 from Naphtali, Ahira s *of* Enan." 1201
1:20 the descendants of Reuben the **firstborn** *s* AIT
2:3 of Judah is Nahshon s *of* Amminadab. 1201
2:5 of the people of Issachar is Nethanel s 1201
2:7 the people of Zebulun is Eliab s *of* Helon. 1201
2:10 of the people of Reuben is Elizur s 1201
2:12 of Simeon is Shelumiel s *of* Zurishaddai. 1201
2:14 of the people of Gad is Eliasaph s *of* Deuel. 1201
2:18 of Ephraim is Elishama s *of* Ammihud. 1201
2:20 of Manasseh is Gamaliel s *of* Pedahzur. 1201
2:22 of the people of Benjamin is Abidan s 1201
2:25 of Dan is Ahiezer s *of* Ammishaddai. 1201
2:27 of the people of Asher is Pagiel s *of* Ocran. 1201
2:29 the people of Naphtali is Ahira s *of* Enan. 1201
3:24 of the Gershonites was Eliasaph s *of* Lael. 1201
3:30 of the Kohathite clans was Elizaphan s 1201
3:32 of the Levites was Eleazar s *of* Aaron, 1201
3:35 the Merarite clans was Zuriel s *of* Abihail; 1201
4:16 "Eleazar s *of* Aaron, the priest, 1201
4:28 under the direction of Ithamar s *of* Aaron, 1201
4:33 of Meeting under the direction of Ithamar s 1201
7:8 under the direction of Ithamar s *of* Aaron, 1201
7:12 the first day was Nahshon s *of* Amminadab 1201
7:17 the offering of Nahshon s *of* Amminadab. 1201
7:18 On the second day Nethanel s *of* Zuar, 1201
7:23 This was the offering of Nethanel s 1201
7:24 On the third day, Eliab s *of* Helon, 1201
7:29 This was the offering of Eliab s *of* Helon. 1201
7:30 On the fourth day Elizur s *of* Shedeur, 1201
7:35 the offering of Elizur s *of* Shedeur. 1201
7:36 the fifth day Shelumiel s *of* Zurishaddai, 1201
7:41 the offering of Shelumiel s *of* Zurishaddai. 1201
7:42 On the sixth day Eliasaph s *of* Deuel, 1201
7:47 the offering of Eliasaph s *of* Deuel. 1201
7:48 the seventh day Elishama s *of* Ammihud, 1201
7:53 the offering of Elishama s *of* Ammihud. 1201
7:54 On the eighth day Gamaliel s *of* Pedahzur, 1201
7:59 the offering of Gamaliel s *of* Pedahzur. 1201
7:60 On the ninth day Abidan s *of* Gideoni, 1201
7:65 the offering of Abidan s *of* Gideoni. 1201
7:66 the tenth day Ahiezer s *of* Ammishaddai, 1201
7:71 the offering of Ahiezer s *of* Ammishaddai. 1201
7:72 On the eleventh day Pagiel s *of* Ocran, 1201
7:77 This was the offering of Pagiel s *of* Ocran. 1201
7:78 On the twelfth day Ahira s *of* Enan, 1201
7:83 This was the offering of Ahira s *of* Enan. 1201
10:14 Nahshon s *of* Amminadab was 1201
10:15 Nethanel s *of* Zuar was over the division of 1201
10:16 and Eliab s *of* Helon was over the division 1201
10:18 Elizur s *of* Shedeur was in command. 1201
10:19 Shelumiel s *of* Zurishaddai was over 1201
10:20 and Eliasaph s *of* Deuel was over 1201
10:22 Elishama s *of* Ammihud was in command. 1201
10:23 Gamaliel s *of* Pedahzur was over 1201
10:24 and Abidan s *of* Gideoni was over 1201
10:25 Ahiezer s *of* Ammishaddai was 1201
10:26 Pagiel s *of* Ocran was over the division of 1201
10:27 and Ahira s *of* Enan was over the division 1201
10:29 Now Moses said to Hobab s *of* Reuel 1201
11:28 Joshua s *of* Nun, 1201
13:4 Shammua s *of* Zaccur; 1201
13:5 Shaphat s *of* Hori; 1201
13:6 Caleb s *of* Jephunneh; 1201
13:7 from the tribe of Issachar, Igal s *of* Joseph; 1201
13:8 Hoshea s *of* Nun; 1201
13:9 Palti s *of* Raphu; 1201
13:10 Gaddiel s *of* Sodi; 1201
13:11 Gaddi s *of* Susi; 1201
13:12 Ammiel s *of* Gemalli; 1201
13:13 Sethur s *of* Michael; 1201
13:14 Nahbi s *of* Vophsi; 1201
13:15 from the tribe of Gad, Geuel s *of* Maki. 1201
13:16 (Moses gave Hoshea s *of* Nun the name 1201
Nu 14:6 Joshua s *of* Nun and Caleb son 1201
14:6 of Nun and Caleb s *of* Jephunneh, 1201
14:30 except Caleb s *of* Jephunneh 1201
14:30 of Jephunneh and Joshua s *of* Nun. 1201
14:38 only Joshua s *of* Nun and Caleb son 1201
14:38 of Nun and Caleb s *of* Jephunneh survived. 1201
16:1 Korah s *of* Izhar, the son of Kohath, 1201
16:1 Korah son of Izhar, the s *of* Kohath, 1201
16:1 the s *of* Levi, and certain Reubenites— 1201
16:1 sons of Eliab, and On s *of* Peleth— 1201
16:37 "Tell Eleazar s *of* Aaron, the priest, to take 1201
18:15 But you must redeem every firstborn s 132
20:25 Get Aaron and his s Eleazar and take them 1201
20:26 on his s Eleazar, for Aaron will be gathered 1201
20:28 and put them on his s Eleazar. 1201
22:2 Now Balak s *of* Zippor saw all 1201
22:4 So Balak s *of* Zippor, 1201
22:5 messengers to summon Balaam s *of* Beor, 1201
22:10 Balaam said to God, "Balak s *of* Zippor, 1201
22:16 "This is what Balak s *of* Zippor says: 1201
23:18 hear me, s *of* Zippor. 1201
23:19 that he should lie, nor a s *of* man, 1201
24:3 "The oracle of Balaam s *of* Beor, 1201
24:15 "The oracle of Balaam s *of* Beor, 1201
25:7 When Phinehas s *of* Eleazar, 1201
25:7 Phinehas son of Eleazar, the s *of* Aaron, 1201
25:11 "Phinehas s *of* Eleazar, the son of Aaron, 1201
25:11 the s *of* Aaron, the priest, 1201
25:14 the Midianite woman was Zimri s *of* Salu, 1201
26:1 the LORD said to Moses and Eleazar s 1201
26:5 the **firstborn** *s of* Israel, were: AIT
26:8 The s *of* Pallu was Eliab, 1201
26:33 (Zelophehad s *of* Hepher had no sons; 1201
26:65 and not one of them was left except Caleb s 1201
26:65 of Jephunneh and Joshua s *of* Nun. 1201
27:1 The daughters of Zelophehad s *of* Hepher, 1201
27:1 the s *of* Gilead, the son of Makir, 1201
27:1 the s *of* Makir, the son of Manasseh, 1201
27:1 the son of Makir, the s *of* Manasseh, 1201
27:1 to the clans of Manasseh s *of* Joseph. 1201
27:4 from his clan because he had no s? 1201
27:8 'If a man dies and leaves no s, 1201
27:18 "Take Joshua s *of* Nun, 1201
31:6 along with Phinehas s *of* Eleazar, 1201
31:8 They also killed Balaam s *of* Beor with 1201
32:12 not one except Caleb s *of* Jephunneh 1201
32:12 of Jephunneh the Kenizzite and Joshua s 1201
32:28 to Eleazar the priest and Joshua s *of* Nun 1201
32:33 and the half-tribe of Manasseh s *of* Joseph 1201
32:39 of Makir s *of* Manasseh went to Gilead, 1201
34:17 Eleazar the priest and Joshua s *of* Nun. 1201
34:19 Caleb s *of* Jephunneh, 1201
34:20 Shemuel s *of* Ammihud, from the tribe 1201
34:21 Elidad s *of* Kislon, from the tribe 1201
34:22 Bukki s *of* Jogli, the leader from the tribe 1201
34:23 Hanniel s *of* Ephod, the leader from 1201
34:23 from the tribe of Manasseh s *of* Joseph; 1201
34:24 Kemuel s *of* Shiphtan, the leader from 1201
34:24 from the tribe of Ephraim s of Joseph; NIH
34:25 Elizaphan s *of* Parnach, the leader from 1201
34:26 Paltiel s *of* Azzan, the leader from the tribe 1201
34:27 Ahihud s *of* Shelomi, the leader from 1201
34:28 Pedahel s *of* Ammihud, 1201
36:1 The family heads of the clan of Gilead s 1201
36:1 the s *of* Manasseh, 1201
36:12 the clans of the descendants of Manasseh s 1201
Dt 1:31 as a father carries his s, 1201
1:36 except Caleb s *of* Jephunneh. 1201
1:38 But your assistant, Joshua s *of* Nun, 1201
5:14 neither you, nor your s or daughter, 1201
6:20 In the future, when your s asks you, 1201
8:5 in your heart that as a man disciplines his s, 1201
10:6 and Eleazar his s succeeded him as priest. 1201
13:6 or your s or daughter, or the wife you love, 1201
18:10 among you who sacrifices his s or daughter 1201
21:15 but the firstborn is the s of the wife he does 1201
21:16 of the firstborn to the s *of* the wife he loves 1201
21:16 the s *of* the wife he does not love. 1201
21:17 the s *of* his unloved wife as the firstborn 1201
21:17 **That** s is the first sign of his father's 2085S
21:18 a stubborn and rebellious s who does 1201
21:20 "This s *of* ours is stubborn and rebellious. 1201
23:4 and they hired Balaam s *of* Beor 1201
25:5 and one of them dies without a s, 1201
25:6 The **first** *s* she bears shall carry on AIT
28:56 the husband she loves and her own s 1201
31:23 The LORD gave this command to Joshua s 1201
32:44 with Joshua s *of* Nun and spoke all 1201
34:9 Now Joshua s *of* Nun was filled with 1201
Jos 1:1 the LORD said to Joshua s *of* Nun, 1201
2:1 Then Joshua s *of* Nun secretly sent two 1201
2:23 to Joshua s *of* Nun and told him everything 1201
6:6 So Joshua s *of* Nun called the priests 1201
6:26 "At the cost of his **firstborn** *s* will he lay AIT
7:1 Achan s *of* Carmi, the son of Zimri, 1201
7:1 Achan son of Carmi, the s *of* Zimri, 1201
7:1 the s *of* Zerah, of the tribe of Judah, 1201
7:18 and Achan s *of* Carmi, the son of Zimri, 1201
7:18 and Achan son of Carmi, the s *of* Zimri, 1201
7:18 the s *of* Zerah, of the tribe of Judah, 1201
7:19 Then Joshua said to Achan, "My s, 1201
7:24 took Achan s *of* Zerah, the silver, the robe, 1201
13:22 the Israelites had put to the sword Balaam s 1201
13:31 the descendants of Makir s *of* Manasseh— 1201
14:1 Joshua s *of* Nun and the heads of 1201
14:6 and Caleb s *of* Jephunneh 1201
14:13 Then Joshua blessed Caleb s *of* Jephunneh 1201

Jos 14:14 to Caleb s *of* Jephunneh the Kenizzite ever 1201
15: 6 of Beth Arabah to the Stone of Bohan s 1201
15:13 Joshua gave to Caleb s *of* Jephunneh 1201
15:17 Othniel s *of* Kenaz, Caleb's brother, 1201
17: 2 the other male descendants of Manasseh s 1201
17: 3 Now Zelophehad s *of* Hepher, 1201
17: 3 Zelophehad son of Hepher, the s *of* Gilead, 1201
17: 3 the s *of* Makir, the son of Manasseh, 1201
17: 3 the son of Makir, the s *of* Manasseh, 1201
17: 4 Joshua s *of* Nun, and the leaders and said, 1201
18:17 down to the Stone of Bohan s *of* Reuben. 1201
19:49 the Israelites gave Joshua s *of* Nun 1201
19:51 Joshua s *of* Nun and the heads of 1201
21: 1 Joshua s *of* Nun, and the heads of 1201
21:12 to Caleb s *of* Jephunneh as his possession. 1201
22:13 So the Israelites sent Phinehas s *of* Eleazar, 1201
22:20 When Achan s *of* Zerah acted unfaithfully 1201
22:31 And Phinehas s *of* Eleazar, the priest, 1201
22:32 Then Phinehas s *of* Eleazar, the priest, 1201
24: 9 When Balak s *of* Zippor, the king of Moab, 1201
24: 9 for Balaam s *of* Beor to put a curse on you. 1201
24:29 After these things, Joshua s *of* Nun, 1201
24:33 And Eleazar s *of* Aaron died 1201
24:33 which had been allotted to his s Phinehas in 1201
Jdg 1:13 Othniel s *of* Kenaz, Caleb's younger 1201
2: 8 Joshua s *of* Nun, the servant of the LORD, 1201
3: 9 Othniel s *of* Kenaz, Caleb's younger 1201
3:11 until Othniel s *of* Kenaz died. 1201
3:15 the s *of* Gera the Benjamite. 1201
3:31 After Ehud came Shamgar s *of* Anath, 1201
4: 6 for Barak s *of* Abinoam from Kedesh 1201
4:12 that Barak s *of* Abinoam had gone up 1201
5: 1 and Barak s *of* Abinoam sang this song: 1201
5: 6 "In the days of Shamgar s *of* Anath, 1201
5:12 your captives, O s *of* Abinoam.' 1201
6:11 where his s Gideon was threshing wheat in 1201
6:29 they were told, "Gideon s *of* Joash did it." 1201
6:30 "Bring out your s. 1201
7:14 be nothing other than the sword of Gideon s 1201
8:13 Gideon s *of* Joash then returned from 1201
8:20 Turning to Jether, his **oldest** *s*, he said, AIT
8:22 you, your s and your grandson— 1201
8:23 nor will my s rule over you. 1201
8:29 Jerub-Baal s *of* Joash went back home 1201
8:31 who lived in Shechem, also bore him a s, 1201
8:32 Gideon s *of* Joash died at a good old age 1201
9: 1 Abimelech s *of* Jerub-Baal went 1201
9: 5 But Jotham, the youngest s *of* Jerub-Baal, 1201
9:18 Abimelech, the s *of* his slave girl, 1201
9:26 Now Gaal s *of* Ebed moved with his 1201
9:28 Then Gaal s *of* Ebed said, 1201
9:28 Isn't he Jerub-Baal's s, 1201
9:30 of the city heard what Gaal s *of* Ebed said, 1201
9:31 "Gaal s *of* Ebed and his brothers 1201
9:35 Now Gaal s *of* Ebed had gone out 1201
9:57 The curse of Jotham s *of* Jerub-Baal came 1201
10: 1 Tola s *of* Puah, the son of Dodo, 1201
10: 1 the s *of* Dodo, rose to save Israel. 1201
11: 2 "because you are the s *of* another woman." 1201
11:25 Are you better than Balak s *of* Zippor, 1201
11:34 for her he had neither s nor daughter. 1201
12:13 After him, Abdon s *of* Hillel, 1201
12:15 Then Abdon s *of* Hillel died, 1201
13: 3 but you are going to conceive and have a s. 1201
13: 5 you will conceive and give birth to a s. 1201
13: 7 'You will conceive and give birth to a s. 1201
17: 2 "The LORD bless you, my s!" 1201
17: 3 for my s to make a carved image and 1201
18:30 and Jonathan s *of* Gershom, 1201
18:30 Gershom, the s *of* Moses, 1201
20:28 with Phinehas s *of* Eleazar, 1201
20:28 the s *of* Aaron, ministering before it.) 1201
Ru 4:13 and she gave birth to a s. 1201
4:17 women living there said, "Naomi has a s." 1201
1Sa 1: 1 whose name was Elkanah s *of* Jeroham, 1201
1: 1 the s *of* Elihu, the son of Tohu, 1201
1: 1 the son of Elihu, the s *of* Tohu, 1201
1: 1 the son of Tohu, the s *of* Zuph, 1201
1:11 not forget your servant but give her a s, 408+2446
1:20 and gave birth to a s. 1201
1:23 the woman stayed at home and nursed her s 1201
3: 6 "My s," Eli said, "I did not call; 1201
3:16 but Eli called him and said, "Samuel, my s." 1201
4:16 Eli asked, "What happened, my s?" 1201
4:20 you have given birth to a s." 1201
7: 1 on the hill and consecrated Eleazar his s 1201
9: 1 whose name was Kish s *of* Abiel, 1201
9: 1 the s *of* Zeror, the son of Becorath, 1201
9: 1 the son of Zeror, the s *of* Becorath, 1201
9: 1 the s *of* Aphiah of Benjamin. 1201
9: 2 He had a s named Saul, 1201
9: 3 and Kish said to his s Saul, 1201
10: 2 "What shall I do about my s?"' 1201
10:11 "What is this that has happened to the s 1201
10:21 Finally Saul s *of* Kish was chosen. 1201
13:16 Saul and his s Jonathan and the men 1201
13:22 only Saul and his s Jonathan had them. 1201
14: 1 One day Jonathan s *of* Saul said to 1201
14: 3 He was a s *of* Ichabod's brother Ahitub son 1201
14: 3 Ichabod's brother Ahitub s *of* Phinehas, 1201
14: 3 the s *of* Eli, the LORD's priest in Shiloh. 1201
14:39 even if it lies with my s Jonathan, 1201
14:40 I and Jonathan my s will stand over here." 1201
14:42 the lot between me and Jonathan my s." 1201
14:50 the commander of Saul's army was Abner s 1201
16:18 a s of Jesse of Bethlehem who knows how 1201
16:19 "Send me your s David, 1201

1Sa 16:20 and sent them with his s David to Saul. 1201
17:12 the s *of* an Ephrathite named Jesse, 1201
17:17 Now Jesse said to his s David, 1201
17:55 "Abner, whose s is that young man?" 1201
17:56 "Find out whose s this young man is." 1201
17:58 "Whose s are you, young man?" 1201
17:58 the s *of* your servant Jesse of Bethlehem." 1201
19: 1 Saul told his s Jonathan and all 1201
20:27 Then Saul said to his s Jonathan, 1201
20:27 "Why hasn't the s *of* Jesse come to 1201
20:30 "You s *of* a perverse and rebellious woman! 1201
20:30 Don't I know that you have sided with the s 1201
20:31 As long as the s *of* Jesse lives on this earth, 1201
22: 7 Will the s *of* Jesse give all of you fields 1201
22: 8 when my s makes a covenant with the son 1201
22: 8 son makes a covenant with the s *of* Jesse. 1201
22: 8 or tells me that my s has incited my servant 1201
22: 9 the s *of* Jesse come to Ahimelech son 1201
22: 9 of Jesse come to Ahimelech s *of* Ahitub 1201
22:11 the king sent for the priest Ahimelech s 1201
22:12 Saul said, "Listen now, s *of* Ahitub." 1201
22:13 you and the s *of* Jesse, 1201
22:20 Abiathar, a s of Ahimelech son of Ahitub, 1201
22:20 Abiathar, a son of Ahimelech s *of* Ahitub, 1201
23: 6 (Now Abiathar s *of* Ahimelech had brought 1201
23:16 And Saul's s Jonathan went to David 1201
24:16 "Is that your voice, David my s?" 1201
25: 8 and your s David whatever you can find 1201
25:10 Who is this s *of* Jesse? 1201
25:44 to Paltiel s *of* Laish, who was from Gallim. 1201
26: 5 He saw where Saul and Abner s *of* Ner, 1201
26: 6 the Hittite and Abishai s *of* Zeruiah, 1201
26:14 He called out to the army and to Abner s 1201
26:17 "Is that your voice, David my s?" 1201
26:21 Come back, David my s. 1201
26:25 "May you be blessed, my s David; 1201
27: 2 and went over to Achish s *of* Maoch king 1201
30: 7 the s *of* Ahimelech, "Bring me the ephod." 1201
2Sa 1: 4 And Saul and his s Jonathan are dead." 1201
1: 5 that Saul and his s Jonathan are dead?" 1201
1:12 till evening for Saul and his s Jonathan, 1201
1:13 "I am the s *of* an alien, an Amalekite," 1201
1:17 concerning Saul and his s Jonathan, 1201
2: 8 Meanwhile, Abner s *of* Ner, 1201
2: 8 had taken Ish-Bosheth s *of* Saul 1201
2:10 Ish-Bosheth s *of* Saul was forty years old 1201
2:12 Abner s *of* Ner, together with the men of 1201
2:12 with the men of Ish-Bosheth s *of* Saul, 1201
2:13 Joab s *of* Zeruiah and David's men 1201
2:15 twelve men for Benjamin and Ish-Bosheth s 1201
3: 2 His firstborn was Amnon the s of Ahinoam NIH
3: 3 Kileab the s of Abigail the widow of Nabal NIH
3: 3 the s *of* Maacah daughter of Talmai king 1201
3: 4 Adonijah the s *of* Haggith; 1201
3: 4 the fifth, Shephatiah the s *of* Abital; 1201
3: 5 Ithream the s of David's wife Eglah. NIH
3:14 to Ish-Bosheth s *of* Saul, 1201
3:15 from her husband Paltiel s *of* Laish. 1201
3:23 he was told that Abner s *of* Ner had come 1201
3:25 You know Abner s *of* Ner; 1201
3:28 concerning the blood of Abner s *of* Ner. 1201
3:37 in the murder of Abner s *of* Ner. 1201
4: 1 When Ish-Bosheth s *of* Saul heard 1201
4: 2 Saul's s had two men who were leaders 1201
4: 4 (Jonathan s *of* Saul had a son who was lame 1201
4: 4 (Jonathan son of Saul had a s who was lame 1201
4: 8 "Here is the head of Ish-Bosheth s *of* Saul, 1201
7:14 I will be his father, and he will be my s. 1201
8: 3 David fought Hadadezer s *of* Rehob, 1201
8:10 he sent his s Joram to King David 1201
8:12 the plunder taken from Hadadezer s 1201
8:16 Joab s *of* Zeruiah was over the army; 1201
8:16 Jehoshaphat s *of* Ahilud was recorder; 1201
8:17 Zadok s *of* Ahitub and Ahimelech son 1201
8:17 and Ahimelech s *of* Abiathar were priests; 1201
8:18 Benaiah s *of* Jehoiada was over 1201
9: 3 "There is still a s *of* Jonathan; 1201
9: 4 "He is at the house of Makir s *of* Ammiel 1201
9: 5 from the house of Makir s *of* Ammiel. 1201
9: 6 When Mephibosheth s *of* Jonathan, 1201
9: 6 the s *of* Saul, came to David, 1201
9:12 Mephibosheth had a young s named Mica, 1201
10: 1 and his s Hanun succeeded him as king. 1201
10: 2 "I will show kindness to Hanun s 1201
11:21 Who killed Abimelech s *of* Jerub-Besheth? 1201
11:27 and she became his wife and bore him a s. 1201
12:14 the s born to you will die." 1201
12:24 She gave birth to a s, 1201
13: 1 Amnon s *of* David fell in love with Tamar, 1201
13: 1 the beautiful sister of Absalom s *of* David. 1201
13: 3 Now Amnon had a friend named Jonadab s 1201
13: 4 "Why do you, the king's s, 1201
13:25 "No, my s," the king replied. 1201
13:32 But Jonadab s *of* Shimeah, 1201
13:37 and went to Talmai s *of* Ammihud, 1201
13:37 King David mourned for his s every day. 1201
14: 1 Joab s *of* Zeruiah knew that 1201
14:11 so that my s will not be destroyed." 1201
14:13 king has not brought back his banished s? NIH
14:16 to cut off both me and my s from 1201
15:27 with your s Ahimaaz and Jonathan son 1201
15:27 with your son Ahimaaz and Jonathan s 1201
15:36 Ahimaaz s of Zadok and Jonathan son NIH
15:36 Ahimaaz son of Zadok and Jonathan s NIH
16: 5 His name was Shimei s *of* Gera, 1201
16: 8 the kingdom over to your s Absalom. 1201
16: 9 Then Abishai s *of* Zeruiah said to the king, 1201

2Sa 16:11 "My s, who is of my own flesh, 1201
16:19 Should I not serve the s? 1201
17:25 Amasa was the s *of* a man named Jether, 1201
17:27 Shobi s *of* Nahash from Rabbah of 1201
17:27 and Makir s *of* Ammiel from Lo Debar, 1201
18: 2 under Joab's brother Abishai s *of* Zeruiah, 1201
18:12 not lift my hand against the king's s. 1201
18:18 "I have no s to carry on the memory 1201
18:19 Now Ahimaaz s *of* Zadok said, 1201
18:20 because the king's s is dead." 1201
18:22 Ahimaaz s *of* Zadok again said to Joab, 1201
18:22 But Joab replied, "My s, 1201
18:27 to me that the first one runs like Ahimaaz s 1201
18:33 As he went, he said: "O my s Absalom! 1201
18:33 My s, my son Absalom! 1201
18:33 My son, my s Absalom! 1201
18:33 O Absalom, my s, my son!" 1201
18:33 O Absalom, my son, my s!" 1201
19: 2 "The king is grieving for his s." 1201
19: 4 "O my s Absalom! 1201
19: 4 O Absalom, my s, my son!" 1201
19: 4 O Absalom, my son, my s!" 1201
19:16 Shimei s *of* Gera, the Benjamite 1201
19:18 When Shimei s *of* Gera crossed the Jordan, 1201
19:21 Then Abishai s *of* Zeruiah said, 1201
20: 1 a troublemaker named Sheba s *of* Bicri, 1201
20: 1 no part in Jesse's s! 1201
20: 2 of Israel deserted David to follow Sheba s 1201
20: 6 to Abishai, "Now Sheba s *of* Bicri 1201
20: 7 from Jerusalem to pursue Sheba s *of* Bicri. 1201
20:10 and his brother Abishai pursued Sheba s 1201
20:13 on with Joab to pursue Sheba s *of* Bicri. 1201
20:21 A man named Sheba s *of* Bicri, 1201
20:22 the head of Sheba s *of* Bicri and threw it 1201
20:23 Benaiah s *of* Jehoiada was over 1201
20:24 Jehoshaphat s *of* Ahilud was recorder; 1201
21: 7 The king spared Mephibosheth s *of* 1201
21: 7 son of Jonathan, the s *of* Saul, 1201
21: 7 the LORD between David and Jonathan s 1201
21: 8 to Adriel s *of* Barzillai the Meholathite. 1201
21:12 of Saul and his s Jonathan from the citizens 1201
21:13 of Saul and his s Jonathan from there, 1201
21:14 the bones of Saul and his s Jonathan in 1201
21:17 But Abishai s *of* Zeruiah came 1201
21:19 Elhanan s *of* Jaare-Oregim 1201
21:21 he taunted Israel, Jonathan s *of* Shimeah, 1201
23: 1 "The oracle of David s *of* Jesse, 1201
23: 9 to him was Eleazar s *of* Dodai the Ahohite. 1201
23:11 Next to him was Shammah s *of* Agee 1201
23:18 of Joab s *of* Zeruiah was chief of the Three. 1201
23:20 Benaiah s *of* Jehoiada was a valiant fighter 1201
23:22 the exploits of Benaiah s *of* Jehoiada; 1201
23:24 Elhanan s *of* Dodo from Bethlehem, 1201
23:26 Ira s *of* Ikkesh from Tekoa, 1201
23:29 Heled s *of* Baanah the Netophathite, 1201
23:29 Ithai s *of* Ribai from Gibeah in Benjamin, 1201
23:33 s *of* Shammah the Hararite, 1201
23:33 Ahiam s *of* Sharar the Hararite, 1201
23:34 Eliphelet s *of* Ahasbai the Maacathite, 1201
23:34 Eliam s *of* Ahithophel the Gilonite, 1201
23:36 Igal s *of* Nathan from Zobah, 1201
23:36 Nathan from Zobah, the s *of* Hagri, 1201
23:37 the armor-bearer of Joab s *of* Zeruiah, 1201
1Ki 1: 7 Adonijah conferred with Joab s *of* Zeruiah 1201
1: 8 Zadok the priest, Benaiah s *of* Jehoiada, 1201
1:11 Adonijah, the s *of* Haggith, 1201
1:12 and the life of your s Solomon. 1201
1:13 "Surely Solomon your s shall be king 1201
1:17 'Solomon your s shall be king after me, 1201
1:21 I and my s Solomon will be treated 1201
1:26 and Benaiah s *of* Jehoiada, 1201
1:30 Solomon your s shall be king after me, 1201
1:32 the prophet and Benaiah s *of* Jehoiada." 1201
1:33 and set Solomon my s on my own mule 1201
1:36 Benaiah s *of* Jehoiada answered the king, 1201
1:38 Nathan the prophet, Benaiah s *of* Jehoiada, 1201
1:42 Jonathan s *of* Abiathar the priest arrived. 1201
1:44 Nathan the prophet, Benaiah s *of* Jehoiada, 1201
2: 1 he gave a charge to Solomon his s. 1201
2: 5 "Now you yourself know what Joab s 1201
2: 5 Abner s *of* Ner and Amasa son of Jether. 1201
2: 5 Abner son of Ner and Amasa s *of* Jether. 1201
2: 8 you have with you Shimei s *of* Gera, 1201
2:13 Now Adonijah, the s *of* Haggith, 1201
2:22 and for Abiathar the priest and Joab s 1201
2:25 So King Solomon gave orders to Benaiah s 1201
2:29 Solomon ordered Benaiah s *of* Jehoiada, 1201
2:32 Both of them—Abner s *of* Ner, 1201
2:32 and Amasa s *of* Jether, 1201
2:34 So Benaiah s *of* Jehoiada went up 1201
2:35 The king put Benaiah s *of* Jehoiada over 1201
2:39 two of Shimei's slaves ran off to Achish s 1201
2:46 Then the king gave the order to Benaiah s 1201
3: 6 a s to sit on his throne this very day. 1201
3:19 "During the night this woman's s died 1201
3:20 up in the middle of the night and took my s 1201
3:20 and put her dead s by my breast. 1201
3:21 The next morning, I got up to nurse my s— 1201
3:21 I saw that it wasn't the s I had borne." 1201
3:22 The living one is my s; 1201
3:23 'My s is alive and your son is dead,' 1201
3:23 'My son is alive and your s is dead.' 1201
3:23 Your s is dead and mine is alive.'" 1201
3:26 The woman whose s was alive was filled 1201
3:26 with compassion for her s and said to 1201
4: 2 Azariah s *of* Zadok— 1201
4: 3 Jehoshaphat s *of* Ahilud— 1201

1Ki 4: 4 Benaiah s of Jehoiada—commander in chief 1201
4: 5 Azariah s of Nathan—in charge of 1201
4: 5 Zabud s of Nathan—a priest and 1201
4: 6 Adoniram s of Abda—in charge of 1201
4:12 Baana s of Ahilud—in Taanach and 1201
4:13 (the settlements of Jair s of Manasseh 1201
4:14 Ahinadab s of Iddo—in Mahanaim; 1201
4:16 Baana s of Hushai—in Asher and 1201
4:17 Jehoshaphat s of Paruah—in Issachar; 1201
4:18 Shimei s of Ela—in Benjamin; 1201
4:19 Geber s of Uri—in Gilead 1201
5: 5 'Your s whom I will put on the throne 1201
5: 7 a wise s to rule over this great nation." 1201
8:19 your s, who is your own flesh and blood— 1201
11:12 I will tear it out of the hand of your s. 1201
11:20 of Tahpenes bore him a s named Genubath, 1201
11:23 another adversary, Rezon s of Eliada, 1201
11:26 Jeroboam s of Nebat rebelled against 1201
11:36 I will give one tribe to his s so 1201
11:43 Rehoboam his s succeeded him as king. 1201
12: 2 When Jeroboam s of Nebat 1201
12:15 to Jeroboam s of Nebat through Ahijah 1201
12:16 what part in Jesse's s? 1201
12:21 and to regain the kingdom for Rehoboam s 1201
12:23 to Rehoboam s of Solomon king of Judah, 1201
13: 2 'A s named Josiah will be born to the house 1201
14: 1 that time Abijah s of Jeroboam became ill, 1201
14: 5 to ask you about her s, 1201
14:20 And Nadab his s succeeded him as king. 1201
14:21 Rehoboam s of Solomon was king 1201
14:31 And Abijah his s succeeded him as king. 1201
15: 1 of the reign of Jeroboam s of Nebat, 1201
15: 4 a lamp in Jerusalem by raising up a s 1201
15: 8 And Asa his s succeeded him as king. 1201
15:18 to Ben-Hadad s of Tabrimmon, 1201
15:20 the s of Hezion, the king of Aram, 1201
15:24 Jehoshaphat his s succeeded him as king. 1201
15:25 Nadab s of Jeroboam became king of Israel 1201
15:27 Baasha s of Ahijah of the house of 1201
15:33 Baasha s of Ahijah became king 1201
16: 1 of the LORD came to Jehu s of Hanani 1201
16: 3 like that of Jeroboam s of Nebat. 1201
16: 6 And Elah his s succeeded him as king. 1201
16: 7 the prophet Jehu s of Hanani to Baasha 1201
16: 8 Elah s of Baasha became king of Israel, 1201
16:13 and his s Elah had committed 1201
16:21 half supported Tibni s of Ginath for king, 1201
16:22 than those of Tibni s of Ginath. 1201
16:26 in all the ways of Jeroboam s of Nebat and 1201
16:28 And Ahab his s succeeded him as king. 1201
16:29 Ahab s of Omri became king of Israel, 1201
16:30 Ahab s of Omri did more evil in the eyes of 1201
16:31 to commit the sins of Jeroboam s of Nebat, 1201
16:34 at the cost of his **firstborn** s Abiram, AIT
16:34 at the cost of his **youngest** s Segub, AIT
16:34 the word of the LORD spoken by Joshua s 1201
17:12 for myself and my s, that we may eat it— 1201
17:13 make something for yourself and your s. 1201
17:17 the s of the woman who owned 1201
17:18 to remind me of my sin and kill my s?" 1201
17:19 "Give me your s," Elijah replied. 1201
17:20 by causing her s to die?" 1201
17:23 "Look, your s is alive!" 1201
19:16 anoint Jehu s of Nimshi king over Israel, 1201
19:16 and anoint Elisha s of Shaphat 1201
19:19 from there and found Elisha s of Shaphat. 1201
21:22 like that of Jeroboam s of Nebat and that 1201
21:22 of Nebat and that of Baasha s of Ahijah, 1201
21:29 on his house in the days of his s." 1201
22: 8 He is Micaiah s of Imlah." 1201
22: 9 "Bring Micaiah s of Imlah at once." 1201
22:11 Now Zedekiah s of Kenaanah 1201
22:24 Then Zedekiah s of Kenaanah went up 1201
22:26 of the city and to Joash the king's s 1201
22:40 And Ahaziah his s succeeded him as king. 1201
22:41 Jehoshaphat s of Asa became king of Judah 1201
22:49 At that time Ahaziah s of Ahab said 1201
22:50 And Jehoram his s succeeded him. 1201
22:51 Ahaziah s of Ahab became king of Israel 1201
22:52 and mother and in the ways of Jeroboam s 1201
2Ki 1:17 Because Ahaziah had no s, 1201
1:17 of Jehoram s of Jehoshaphat king of Judah. 1201
3: 1 Joram s of Ahab became king of Israel 1201
3: 3 to the sins of Jeroboam s of Nebat, 1201
3:11 "Elisha s of Shaphat is here. 1201
3:27 Then he took his firstborn s, 1201
4: 6 she said to her s, "Bring me another one." 1201
4:14 "Well, she has no s and her husband is old." 1201
4:16 "you will hold a s in your arms." 1201
4:17 about that same time she gave birth to a s, 1201
4:28 "Did I ask you for a s, my lord?" 1201
4:36 When she came, he said, "Take your s." 1201
4:37 Then she took her s and went out. 1201
6:28 'Give up your s so we may eat him today, 1201
6:28 and tomorrow we'll eat my s.' 1201
6:29 So we cooked my s and ate him. 1201
6:29 'Give up your s so we may eat him,' 1201
6:31 if the head of Elisha s of Shaphat remains 1201
8: 1 the woman whose s he had restored to life, 1201
8: 5 the woman whose s Elisha had brought back 1201
8: 5 this is her s whom Elisha restored to life." 1201
8: 9 "Your s Ben-Hadad king of Aram 1201
8:16 In the fifth year of Joram s of Ahab king 1201
8:16 Jehoram s of Jehoshaphat began his reign 1201
8:24 And Ahaziah his s succeeded him as king. 1201
8:25 In the twelfth year of Joram s of Ahab king 1201
8:25 Ahaziah s of Jehoram king of Judah began 1201
2Ki 8:28 Ahaziah went with Joram s of Ahab to war 1201
8:29 Then Ahaziah s of Jehoram king 1201
8:29 down to Jezreel to see Joram s of Ahab, 1201
9: 2 look for Jehu s of Jehoshaphat, 1201
9: 2 Jehoshaphat, the s of Nimshi. 1201
9: 9 of Jeroboam s of Nebat and like the house 1201
9: 9 and like the house of Baasha s of Ahijah. 1201
9:14 So Jehu s of Jehoshaphat, 1201
9:14 Jehu son of Jehoshaphat, the s of Nimshi, 1201
9:20 The driving is like that of Jehu s 1201
9:29 (In the eleventh year of Joram s of Ahab, 1201
10:15 he came upon Jehonadab s of Recab, 1201
10:23 Then Jehu and Jehonadab s of Recab went 1201
10:29 not turn away from the sins of Jeroboam s 1201
10:35 And Jehoahaz his s succeeded him as king. 1201
11: 1 of Ahaziah saw that her s was dead, 1201
11: 2 took Joash s of Ahaziah and stole him away 1201
11: 4 Then he showed them the king's s. 1201
11:12 Jehoiada brought out the king's s and put 1201
12:21 The officials who murdered him were
Jozabad s of Shimeath 1201
12:21 of Shimeath and Jehozabad s of Shomer. 1201
12:21 And Amaziah his s succeeded him as king. 1201
13: 1 of Joash s of Ahaziah king of Judah, 1201
13: 1 Jehoahaz s of Jehu became king of Israel 1201
13: 2 by following the sins of Jeroboam s 1201
13: 3 of Aram and Ben-Hadad his s. 1201
13: 9 And Jehoash his s succeeded him as king. 1201
13:10 Jehoash s of Jehoahaz became king 1201
13:11 of the sins of Jeroboam s of Nebat, 1201
13:24 Ben-Hadad his s succeeded him as king. 1201
13:25 Then Jehoash s of Jehoahaz recaptured 1201
13:25 of Jehoahaz recaptured from Ben-Hadad s 1201
14: 1 of Jehoash s of Jehoahaz king of Israel, 1201
14: 1 Amaziah s of Joash king of Judah began 1201
14: 8 to Jehoash s of Jehoahaz, the son 1201
14: 8 the s of Jehu, king of Israel, 1201
14: 9 'Give your daughter to my s in marriage.' 1201
14:13 the s of Joash, the son of Ahaziah, 1201
14:13 the s of Ahaziah, at Beth Shemesh. 1201
14:16 And Jeroboam his s succeeded him as king. 1201
14:17 Amaziah s of Joash king of Judah lived 1201
14:17 for fifteen years after the death of Jehoash s 1201
14:23 of Amaziah s of Joash king of Judah, 1201
14:23 Jeroboam s of Jehoash king of Israel 1201
14:24 of the sins of Jeroboam s of Nebat, 1201
14:25 through his servant Jonah s of Amittai, 1201
14:27 he saved them by the hand of Jeroboam s 1201
14:29 And Zechariah his s succeeded him as king. 1201
15: 1 Azariah s of Amaziah king of Judah began 1201
15: 5 the king's s had charge of the palace 1201
15: 7 And Jotham his s succeeded him as king. 1201
15: 8 Zechariah s of Jeroboam became king 1201
15: 9 not turn away from the sins of Jeroboam s 1201
15:10 Shallum s of Jabesh conspired against 1201
15:13 Shallum s of Jabesh became king in 1201
15:14 Then Menahem s of Gadi went from Tirzah 1201
15:14 He attacked Shallum s of Jabesh 1201
15:17 Menahem s of Gadi became king of Israel, 1201
15:18 not turn away from the sins of Jeroboam s 1201
15:22 And Pekahiah his s succeeded him as king. 1201
15:23 Pekahiah s of Menahem became king 1201
15:24 not turn away from the sins of Jeroboam s 1201
15:25 Pekah s of Remaliah, conspired against 1201
15:27 Pekah s of Remaliah became king of Israel 1201
15:28 not turn away from the sins of Jeroboam s 1201
15:30 Then Hoshea s of Elah conspired against 1201
15:30 conspired against Pekah s of Remaliah. 1201
15:30 in the twentieth year of Jotham s of Uzziah. 1201
15:32 of Pekah s of Remaliah king of Israel, 1201
15:32 Jotham s of Uzziah king of Judah began 1201
15:37 and Pekah s of Remaliah against Judah.) 1201
15:38 And Ahaz his s succeeded him as king. 1201
16: 1 In the seventeenth year of Pekah s 1201
16: 1 Ahaz s of Jotham king of Judah began 1201
16: 3 the kings of Israel and even sacrificed his s 1201
16: 5 of Aram and Pekah s of Remaliah king 1201
16:20 And Hezekiah his s succeeded him as king. 1201
17: 1 Hoshea s of Elah became king of Israel 1201
17:21 they made Jeroboam s of Nebat their king. 1201
18: 1 In the third year of Hoshea s of Elah king 1201
18: 1 Hezekiah s of Ahaz king of Judah began 1201
18: 9 the seventh year of Hoshea s of Elah king 1201
18:18 and Eliakim s of Hilkiah 1201
18:18 and Joah s of Asaph the recorder went out 1201
18:26 Then Eliakim s of Hilkiah, 1201
18:37 Then Eliakim s of Hilkiah 1201
18:37 Shebna the secretary and Joah s of Asaph 1201
19: 2 to the prophet Isaiah s of Amoz. 1201
19:20 Then Isaiah s of Amoz sent a message 1201
19:37 Esarhaddon his s succeeded him as king. 1201
20: 1 The prophet Isaiah s of Amoz went to him 1201
20:12 At that time Merodach-Baladan s of 1201
20:21 And Manasseh his s succeeded him as king. 1201
21: 6 He sacrificed his own s in the fire, 1201
21: 7 to David and to his s Solomon, 1201
21:18 And Amon his s succeeded him as king. 1201
21:24 they made Josiah his s king in his place. 1201
21:26 And Josiah his s succeeded him as king. 1201
22: 3 Shaphan s of Azaliah, 1201
22: 3 Azaliah, the s of Meshullam, 1201
22:12 Ahikam s of Shaphan, 1201
22:12 Acbor s of Micaiah, Shaphan the secretary 1201
22:14 who was the wife of Shallum s of Tikvah, 1201
22:14 the s of Harhas, keeper of the wardrobe. 1201
23:10 to sacrifice his s or daughter in the fire 1201
23:15 the high place made by Jeroboam s of 1201
2Ki 23:30 And the people of the land took Jehoahaz s 1201
23:34 Pharaoh Neco made Eliakim s of Josiah 1201
24: 6 Jehoiachin his s succeeded him as king. 1201
25:22 king of Babylon appointed Gedaliah s of 1201
25:22 son of Ahikam, the s of Shaphan, 1201
25:23 Ishmael s of Nethaniah, 1201
25:23 Ishmael son of Nethaniah, Johanan s 1201
25:23 Seraiah s of Tanhumeth the Netophathite, 1201
25:23 Jaazaniah the s of the Maacathite, 1201
25:25 however, Ishmael s of Nethaniah, 1201
25:25 the s of Elishama, who was of royal blood, 1201
1Ch 1:41 The s of Anah: Dishon. 1201
1:43 Bela s of Beor, whose city was named 1201
1:44 Jobab s of Zerah from Bozrah 1201
1:46 When Husham died, Hadad s of Bedad, 1201
1:49 Baal-Hanan s of Acbor succeeded him 1201
2: 7 The s of Carmi: Achar, who brought trouble 1201
2: 8 The s of Ethan: Azariah. 1201
2:13 the second s was Abinadab, NIH
2:18 Caleb s of Hezron had children 1201
2:31 The s of Appaim: Ishi, 1201
2:42 the father of Ziph, and his s Mareshah, 1201
2:45 The s of Shammai was Maon, 1201
3: 1 The firstborn was Amnon the s of Ahinoam NIH
3: 1 second, Daniel the s of Abigail of Carmel; NIH
3: 2 the s of Maacah daughter of Talmai king 1201
3: 2 the fourth, Adonijah the s of Haggith; 1201
3: 3 Shephatiah the s of Abital; NIH
3:10 Solomon's s was Rehoboam, 1201
3:10 Abijah his s, Asa his son, 1201
3:10 Asa his s, Jehoshaphat his son, 1201
3:10 Asa his son, Jehoshaphat his s, 1201
3:11 Jehoram his s, Ahaziah his son, 1201
3:11 Ahaziah his s, Joash his son, 1201
3:11 Ahaziah his son, Joash his s, 1201
3:12 Amaziah his s, Azariah his son, 1201
3:12 Azariah his s, Jotham his son, 1201
3:12 Azariah his son, Jotham his s, 1201
3:13 Ahaz his s, Hezekiah his son, 1201
3:13 Hezekiah his s, Manasseh his son, 1201
3:13 Hezekiah his son, Manasseh his s, 1201
3:14 Amon his s, Josiah his son. 1201
3:14 Amon his son, Josiah his s. 1201
3:15 Jehoiakim the second s, Zedekiah the third, NIH
3:16 Jehoiachin his s, and Zedekiah. 1201
3:17 of Jehoiachin the captive: Shealtiel his s, 1201
4: 2 Reaiah s of Shobal was the father 1201
4: 8 and of the clans of Aharhel s of Harum. 1201
4:15 The sons of Caleb s of Jephunneh: 1201
4:15 The s of Elah: Kenaz. 1201
4:21 The sons of Shelah s of Judah: 1201
4:25 Shallum was Shaul's s, 1201
4:25 Mibsam his s and Mishma his son. 1201
4:25 Mibsam his son and Mishma his s. 1201
4:26 Hammuel his s, Zaccur his son 1201
4:26 Zaccur his s and Shimei his son. 1201
4:26 Zaccur his son and Shimei his s. 1201
4:34 Meshobab, Jamlech, Joshah s of Amaziah, 1201
4:35 Jehu s of Joshibiah, the son of Seraiah, 1201
4:35 Jehu son of Joshibiah, the s of Seraiah, 1201
4:35 the son of Seraiah, the s of Asiel, 1201
4:37 and Ziza s of Shiphi, 1201
4:37 the s of Allon, the son of Jedaiah, 1201
4:37 the s of Jedaiah, the son of Shimri, 1201
4:37 the s of Shimri, the son of Shemaiah. 1201
4:37 the son of Shimri, the s of Shemaiah. 1201
5: 1 to the sons of Joseph s of Israel; 1201
5: 4 The descendants of Joel: Shemaiah his s, 1201
5: 4 Shemaiah his son, Gog his s, 1201
5: 4 Gog his son, Shimei his s, 1201
5: 5 Micah his s, Reaiah his son, Baal his son, 1201
5: 5 Micah his son, Reaiah his s, Baal his son, 1201
5: 5 Micah his son, Reaiah his son, Baal his s, 1201
5: 6 and Beerah his s, whom Tiglath-Pileser 1201
5: 8 and Bela s of Azaz, the son of Shema, 1201
5: 8 the s of Shema, the son of Joel. 1201
5: 8 the son of Shema, the s of Joel. 1201
5:14 These were the sons of Abihail s of Huri, 1201
5:14 the s of Jaroah, the son of Gilead, 1201
5:14 the s of Gilead, the son of Michael, 1201
5:14 the s of Michael, the son of Jeshishai, 1201
5:14 the son of Michael, the s of Jeshishai, 1201
5:14 the son of Jeshishai, the s of Jahdo, 1201
5:14 the son of Jahdo, the s of Buz. 1201
5:15 Ahi s of Abdiel, the son of Guni, 1201
5:15 Ahi son of Abdiel, the s of Guni, 1201
6:20 Libni his s, Jehath his son, Zimmah his son, 1201
6:20 Libni his son, Jehath his s, Zimmah his son, 1201
6:20 Libni his son, Jehath his son, Zimmah his s, 1201
6:21 Joah his s, Iddo his son, Zerah his son 1201
6:21 Iddo his s, Zerah his son 1201
6:21 Zerah his s and Jeatherai his son. 1201
6:21 Zerah his son and Jeatherai his s. 1201
6:22 Amminadab his s, Korah his son, 1201
6:22 Amminadab his son, Korah his s, 1201
6:22 Korah his son, Assir his s, 1201
6:23 Elkanah his s, Ebiasaph his son, 1201
6:23 Ebiasaph his s, Assir his son, 1201
6:23 Ebiasaph his son, Assir his s, 1201
6:24 Tahath his s, Uriel his son, Uzziah his son 1201
6:24 Uriel his s, Uzziah his son 1201
6:24 Uzziah his s and Shaul his son. 1201
6:24 Uzziah his son and Shaul his s. 1201
6:26 Elkanah his s, Zophai his son, 1201
6:26 Zophai his s, Nahath his son, 1201
6:26 Zophai his son, Nahath his s, 1201
6:27 Eliab his s, Jeroham his son, 1201

1Ch	6:27	Jeroham his **s**, Elkanah his son	1201
	6:27	Elkanah his **s** and Samuel his son.	1201
	6:27	Elkanah his son and Samuel his **s**.	1201
	6:28	Joel the firstborn and Abijah the second **s**.	NIH
	6:29	Mahli, Libni his **s**, Shimei his son,	1201
	6:29	Mahli, Libni his son, Shimei his **s**,	1201
	6:29	Libni his son, Shimei his son, Uzzah his **s**,	1201
	6:30	Shimea his **s**, Haggiah his son	1201
	6:30	Haggiah his **s** and Asaiah his son.	1201
	6:30	Haggiah his son and Asaiah his **s**.	1201
	6:33	Heman, the musician, the **s** *of* Joel,	1201
	6:33	the son of Joel, the **s** *of* Samuel,	1201
	6:34	the **s** *of* Elkanah, the son of Jeroham,	1201
	6:34	the **s** *of* Jeroham, the son of Eliel,	1201
	6:34	the son of Jeroham, the **s** *of* Eliel,	1201
	6:34	the son of Eliel, the **s** *of* Toah,	1201
	6:35	the **s** *of* Zuph, the son of Elkanah,	1201
	6:35	the **s** *of* Elkanah, the son of Mahath,	1201
	6:35	the son of Elkanah, the **s** *of* Mahath,	1201
	6:35	the son of Mahath, the **s** *of* Amasai,	1201
	6:36	the **s** *of* Elkanah, the son of Joel,	1201
	6:36	the **s** *of* Joel, the son of Azariah,	1201
	6:36	the **s** *of* Azariah, the son of Zephaniah,	1201
	6:36	the son of Azariah, the **s** *of* Zephaniah,	1201
	6:37	the **s** *of* Tahath, the son of Assir,	1201
	6:37	the **s** *of* Assir, the son of Ebiasaph,	1201
	6:37	the **s** *of* Ebiasaph, the son of Korah,	1201
	6:37	the son of Ebiasaph, the **s** *of* Korah,	1201
	6:38	the **s** *of* Izhar, the son of Kohath, the son	1201
	6:38	the **s** *of* Kohath, the son of Levi,	1201
	6:38	the son of Kohath, the **s** *of* Levi,	1201
	6:38	the son of Levi, the **s** *of* Israel;	1201
	6:39	Asaph **s** *of* Berekiah, the son of Shimea,	1201
	6:39	Asaph son of Berekiah, the **s** *of* Shimea,	1201
	6:40	the **s** *of* Michael, the son of Baaseiah,	1201
	6:40	the **s** *of* Baaseiah, the son of Malkijah,	1201
	6:40	the son of Baaseiah, the **s** *of* Malkijah,	1201
	6:41	the **s** *of* Ethni, the son of Zerah,	1201
	6:41	the **s** *of* Zerah, the son of Adaiah,	1201
	6:41	the son of Zerah, the **s** *of* Adaiah,	1201
	6:42	the **s** *of* Ethan, the son of Zimmah,	1201
	6:42	the **s** *of* Zimmah, the son of Shimei,	1201
	6:42	the son of Zimmah, the **s** *of* Shimei,	1201
	6:43	the **s** *of* Jahath, the son of Gershon, the son	1201
	6:43	the **s** *of* Gershon, the son of Levi;	1201
	6:43	the son of Gershon, the **s** *of* Levi;	1201
	6:44	Ethan **s** *of* Kishi, the son of Abdi,	1201
	6:44	Ethan son of Kishi, the **s** *of* Abdi,	1201
	6:44	the son of Abdi, the **s** *of* Malluch,	1201
	6:45	the **s** *of* Hashabiah, the son of Amaziah,	1201
	6:45	the **s** *of* Amaziah, the son of Hilkiah,	1201
	6:45	the son of Amaziah, the **s** *of* Hilkiah,	1201
	6:46	the **s** *of* Amzi, the son of Bani,	1201
	6:46	the **s** *of* Bani, the son of Shemer,	1201
	6:46	the son of Bani, the **s** *of* Shemer,	1201
	6:47	the **s** *of* Mahli, the son of Mushi,	1201
	6:47	the **s** *of* Mushi, the son of Merari,	1201
	6:47	the son of Mushi, the **s** *of* Merari,	1201
	6:47	the son of Merari, the **s** *of* Levi.	1201
	6:50	Eleazar his **s**, Phinehas his son,	1201
	6:50	Eleazar his son, Phinehas his **s**,	1201
	6:50	Phinehas his son, Abishua his **s**,	1201
	6:51	Bukki his **s**, Uzzi his son, Zerahiah his son,	1201
	6:51	Bukki his son, Uzzi his **s**, Zerahiah his son,	1201
	6:51	Bukki his son, Uzzi his son, Zerahiah his **s**,	1201
	6:52	Meraioth his **s**, Amariah his son,	1201
	6:52	Amariah his **s**, Ahitub his son,	1201
	6:52	Amariah his son, Ahitub his **s**,	1201
	6:53	Zadok his **s** and Ahimaaz his son.	1201
	6:53	Zadok his son and Ahimaaz his **s**.	1201
	6:56	around the city were given to Caleb **s**	1201
	7:3	The **s** *of* Uzzi: Izrahiah.	1201
	7:10	The **s** *of* Jediael: Bilhan.	1201
	7:16	Makir's wife Maacah gave birth to a **s**	1201
	7:17	The **s** *of* Ulam: Bedan.	1201
	7:17	These were the sons of Gilead **s** *of* Makir,	1201
	7:17	son of Makir, the **s** *of* Manasseh.	1201
	7:20	Shuthelah, Bered his **s**, Tahath his son,	1201
	7:20	Shuthelah, Bered his son, Tahath his **s**,	1201
	7:20	Eleadah his **s**, Tahath his son,	1201
	7:20	Eleadah his son, Tahath his **s**,	1201
	7:21	Zabad his **s** and Shuthelah his son.	1201
	7:21	Zabad his son and Shuthelah his **s**.	1201
	7:23	she became pregnant and gave birth to a **s**.	1201
	7:25	Rephah was his **s**, Resheph his son,	1201
	7:25	Rephah was his son, Resheph his **s**,	NIH
	7:25	Resheph his son, Telah his **s**,	1201
	7:25	Telah his son, Tahan his **s**,	1201
	7:26	Ladan his **s**, Ammihud his son,	1201
	7:26	Ammihud his **s**, Elishama his son,	1201
	7:26	Ammihud his son, Elishama his **s**,	1201
	7:27	Nun his **s** and Joshua his son.	1201
	7:27	Nun his son and Joshua his **s**.	1201
	7:29	The descendants of Joseph **s** *of* Israel lived	1201
	8:1	Ashbel the second **s**, Aharah the third,	NIH
	8:30	and his firstborn **s** was Abdon,	1201
	8:34	The **s** *of* Jonathan: Merib-Baal,	1201
	8:37	Raphah was his **s**,	1201
	8:37	Eleasah his **s** and Azel his son.	1201
	8:37	Eleasah his son and Azel his **s**.	1201
	8:39	Jeush the second **s** and Eliphelet the third.	NIH
	9:4	Uthai **s** *of* Ammihud, the son of Omri,	1201
	9:4	the **s** *of* Omri, the son of Imri,	1201
	9:4	the son of Omri, the **s** *of* Imri,	1201
	9:4	the son of Imri, the **s** *of* Bani,	1201
	9:4	a descendant of Perez **s** *of* Judah.	1201
	9:7	Sallu **s** *of* Meshullam, the son of Hodaviah,	1201
1Ch	9:7	Sallu son of Meshullam, the **s** *of* Hodaviah,	1201
	9:7	the son of Hodaviah, the **s** *of* Hassenuah;	1201
	9:8	Ibneiah **s** *of* Jeroham;	1201
	9:8	Elah **s** *of* Uzzi, the son of Micri;	1201
	9:8	Elah son of Uzzi, the **s** *of* Micri;	1201
	9:8	and Meshullam **s** *of* Shephatiah,	1201
	9:8	the **s** *of* Reuel, the son of Ibnijah.	1201
	9:8	the son of Reuel, the **s** *of* Ibnijah.	1201
	9:11	Azariah **s** *of* Hilkiah, the son of Meshullam,	1201
	9:11	the **s** *of* Meshullam, the son of Zadok,	1201
	9:11	the son of Meshullam, the **s** *of* Zadok,	1201
	9:11	the **s** *of* Meraioth, the son of Ahitub,	1201
	9:11	the son of Meraioth, the **s** *of* Ahitub,	1201
	9:12	Adaiah **s** *of* Jeroham, the son of Pashhur,	1201
	9:12	the **s** *of* Pashhur, the son of Malkijah;	1201
	9:12	the son of Pashhur, the **s** *of* Malkijah;	1201
	9:12	and Maasai **s** *of* Adiel, the son of Jahzerah,	1201
	9:12	and Maasai son of Adiel, the **s** *of* Jahzerah,	1201
	9:12	the son of Jahzerah, the **s** *of* Meshullam,	1201
	9:12	the **s** *of* Meshillemith, the son of Immer.	1201
	9:12	the son of Meshillemith, the **s** *of* Immer.	1201
	9:14	Of the Levites: Shemaiah **s** *of* Hasshub,	1201
	9:14	the **s** *of* Azrikam, the son of Hashabiah,	1201
	9:14	the son of Azrikam, the **s** *of* Hashabiah,	1201
	9:15	Heresh, Galal and Mattaniah **s** *of* Mica,	1201
	9:15	the **s** *of* Zicri, the son of Asaph;	1201
	9:15	the son of Zicri, the **s** *of* Asaph;	1201
	9:16	Obadiah **s** *of* Shemaiah, the son of Galal,	1201
	9:16	the **s** *of* Galal, the son of Jeduthun;	1201
	9:16	the son of Galal, the **s** *of* Jeduthun;	1201
	9:16	and Berekiah **s** *of* Asa, the son of Elkanah,	1201
	9:16	and Berekiah son of Asa, the **s** *of* Elkanah,	1201
	9:19	Shallum **s** *of* Kore, the son of Ebiasaph,	1201
	9:19	Shallum son of Kore, the **s** *of* Ebiasaph,	1201
	9:19	the son of Ebiasaph, the **s** *of* Korah,	1201
	9:20	In earlier times Phinehas **s** *of* Eleazar was	1201
	9:21	Zechariah **s** *of* Meshelemiah was	1201
	9:31	the firstborn **s** of Shallum the Korahite,	NIH
	9:36	and his firstborn **s** was Abdon,	1201
	9:40	The **s** *of* Jonathan: Merib-Baal,	1201
	9:43	Rephaiah was his **s**,	1201
	9:43	Eleasah his **s** and Azel his son.	1201
	9:43	Eleasah his son and Azel his **s**.	1201
	10:14	and turned the kingdom over to David **s**	1201
	11:6	Joab **s** *of* Zeruiah went up first,	1201
	11:12	to him was Eleazar **s** *of* Dodai the Ahohite,	1201
	11:22	Benaiah **s** *of* Jehoiada was a valiant fighter	1201
	11:24	the exploits of Benaiah **s** *of* Jehoiada;	1201
	11:26	Elhanan **s** *of* Dodo from Bethlehem,	1201
	11:28	Ira **s** *of* Ikkesh from Tekoa,	1201
	11:30	Heled **s** *of* Baanah the Netophathite,	1201
	11:31	Ithai **s** *of* Ribai from Gibeah in Benjamin,	1201
	11:34	Jonathan **s** *of* Shagee the Hararite,	1201
	11:35	Ahiam **s** *of* Sacar the Hararite,	1201
	11:35	Eliphal **s** *of* Ur,	1201
	11:37	Hezro the Carmelite, Naarai **s** *of* Ezbai,	1201
	11:38	Mibhar **s** *of* Hagri,	1201
	11:39	the armor-bearer of Joab **s** *of* Zeruiah,	1201
	11:41	Uriah the Hittite, Zabad **s** *of* Ahlai,	1201
	11:42	Adina **s** *of* Shiza the Reubenite,	1201
	11:43	Hanan **s** *of* Maacah,	1201
	11:45	Jediael **s** *of* Shimri,	1201
	12:1	from the presence of Saul **s** *of* Kish	1201
	12:18	We are with you, O **s** *of* Jesse!	1201
	15:17	So the Levites appointed Heman **s** *of* Joel;	1201
	15:17	from his brothers, Asaph **s** *of* Berekiah;	1201
	15:17	from their brothers the Merarites, Ethan **s**	1201
	16:38	Obed-Edom **s** *of* Jeduthun, and also Hosah,	1201
	17:13	I will be his father, and he will be my **s**.	1201
	18:10	he sent his **s** Hadoram to King David	1201
	18:12	Abishai **s** *of* Zeruiah struck down	1201
	18:15	Joab **s** *of* Zeruiah was over the army;	1201
	18:15	Jehoshaphat **s** *of* Ahilud was recorder;	1201
	18:16	Zadok **s** *of* Ahitub and Ahimelech son	1201
	18:16	and Ahimelech **s** *of* Abiathar were priests;	1201
	18:17	Benaiah **s** *of* Jehoiada was over	1201
	19:1	and his **s** succeeded him as king.	1201
	19:2	"I will show kindness to Hanun **s**	1201
	20:5	Elhanan **s** *of* Jair killed Lahmi the brother	1201
	20:7	he taunted Israel, Jonathan **s** *of* Shimea,	1201
	22:5	"My **s** Solomon is young and inexperienced	1201
	22:6	for his **s** Solomon and charged him to build	1201
	22:7	David said to Solomon: "My **s**,	1201
	22:9	But you will have a **s** who will be a man	1201
	22:10	He will be my **s**, and I will be his father.	1201
	22:11	"Now, my **s**, the LORD be with you,	1201
	22:17	the leaders of Israel to help his **s** Solomon.	1201
	23:1	he made his **s** Solomon king over Israel.	1201
	24:6	The scribe Shemaiah **s** *of* Nethanel,	1201
	24:6	Zadok the priest, Ahimelech **s** *of* Abiathar	1201
	24:24	The **s** *of* Uzziel: Micah;	1201
	24:26	The **s** *of* Jaaziah: Beno.	1201
	24:29	From Kish: the **s** *of* Kish: Jerahmeel.	1201
	26:1	Meshelemiah **s** *of* Kore,	1201
	26:6	His **s** Shemaiah also had sons,	1201
	26:14	Then lots were cast for his **s** Zechariah,	1201
	26:24	a descendant of Gershom **s** *of* Moses,	1201
	26:25	Rehabiah his **s**, Jeshaiah his son,	1201
	26:25	Rehabiah his son, Jeshaiah his **s**,	1201
	26:25	Jeshaiah his son, Joram his **s**,	1201
	26:25	Zicri his **s** and Shelomith his son.	1201
	26:25	Zicri his son and Shelomith his **s**.	1201
	26:28	by Samuel the seer and by Saul **s** *of* Kish,	1201
	26:28	Abner **s** *of* Ner and Joab son of Zeruiah,	1201
	26:28	Abner son of Ner and Joab **s** *of* Zeruiah,	1201
	27:2	was Jashobeam **s** *of* Zabdiel.	1201
	27:5	was Benaiah **s** *of* Jehoiada the priest.	1201
1Ch	27:6	His **s** Ammizabad was in charge	1201
	27:7	his **s** Zebadiah was his successor.	1201
	27:9	was Ira the **s** *of* Ikkesh the Tekoite.	1201
	27:16	over the Reubentes: Eliezer **s** *of* Zicri;	1201
	27:16	over the Simeonites: Shephatiah **s** *of* Maacah;	1201
	27:17	over Levi: Hashabiah **s** *of* Kemuel;	1201
	27:18	over Issachar: Omri **s** *of* Michael;	1201
	27:19	over Zebulun: Ishmaiah **s** *of* Obadiah;	1201
	27:19	over Naphtali: Jerimoth **s** *of* Azriel;	1201
	27:20	over the Ephraimites: Hoshea **s** *of* Azaziah;	1201
	27:20	of Manasseh: Joel **s** *of* Pedaiah;	1201
	27:21	Manasseh in Gilead: Iddo **s** *of* Zechariah;	1201
	27:21	over Benjamin: Jaasiel **s** *of* Abner;	1201
	27:22	over Dan: Azarel **s** *of* Jeroham.	1201
	27:24	Joab **s** *of* Zeruiah began to count the men	1201
	27:25	Azmaveth **s** *of* Adiel was in charge of	1201
	27:25	Jonathan **s** *of* Uzziah was in charge of	1201
	27:26	Ezri **s** *of* Kelub was in charge of	1201
	27:29	Shaphat **s** *of* Adlai was in charge of	1201
	27:32	Jehiel **s** *of* Hacmoni took care of	1201
	27:34	by Jehoiada **s** *of* Benaiah and by Abiathar.	1201
	28:5	he has chosen my **s** Solomon to sit on	1201
	28:6	'Solomon your **s** is the one who will build	1201
	28:6	for I have chosen him to be my **s**,	1201
	28:9	"And you, my **s** Solomon,	1201
	28:11	Then David gave his **s** Solomon the plans	1201
	28:20	David also said to Solomon his **s**,	1201
	29:1	to the whole assembly: "My **s** Solomon,	1201
	29:19	give my **s** Solomon wholehearted devotion	1201
	29:22	Then they acknowledged Solomon **s**	1201
	29:26	David **s** *of* Jesse was king over all Israel.	1201
	29:28	His **s** Solomon succeeded him as king.	1201
2Ch	1:1	Solomon **s** *of* David established himself firmly over his kingdom,	1201
	1:5	But the bronze altar that Bezalel **s** *of* Uri,	1201
	1:5	the **s** *of* Hur, had made was in Gibeon	1201
	2:12	He has given King David a wise **s**,	1201
	6:9	your **s**, who is your own flesh and blood—	1201
	9:29	the seer concerning Jeroboam **s** *of* Nebat?	1201
	9:31	Rehoboam his **s** succeeded him as king.	1201
	10:2	When Jeroboam **s** *of* Nebat heard this	1201
	10:15	to Jeroboam **s** *of* Nebat through Ahijah	1201
	10:16	what part in Jesse's **s**?	1201
	11:3	to Rehoboam **s** *of* Solomon king of Judah	1201
	11:17	of Judah and supported Rehoboam **s**	1201
	11:18	who was the daughter of David's **s** Jerimoth	1201
	11:18	the daughter of Jesse's **s** Eliab.	1201
	11:22	Rehoboam appointed Abijah **s** *of* Maacah	1201
	12:16	And Abijah his **s** succeeded him as king.	1201
	13:6	Yet Jeroboam **s** *of* Nebat,	1201
	13:6	an official of Solomon **s** *of* David,	1201
	13:7	and opposed Rehoboam **s** *of* Solomon	1201
	14:1	Asa his **s** succeeded him as king,	1201
	15:1	The Spirit of God came upon Azariah **s**	1201
	15:8	and the prophecy of Azariah **s** *of* Oded	1201
	17:1	Jehoshaphat his **s** succeeded him as king	1201
	17:16	Amasiah **s** *of* Zicri,	1201
	18:7	He is Micaiah **s** *of* Imlah."	1201
	18:8	"Bring Micaiah **s** *of* Imlah at once."	1201
	18:10	Now Zedekiah **s** *of* Kenaanah	1201
	18:23	Then Zedekiah **s** *of* Kenaanah went up	1201
	18:25	of the city and to Joash the king's **s**,	1201
	19:2	Jehu the seer, the **s** *of* Hanani,	1201
	19:11	and Zebadiah **s** *of* Ishmael,	1201
	20:14	of the LORD came upon Jahaziel **s**	1201
	20:14	the **s** *of* Benaiah, the son of Jeiel,	1201
	20:14	the **s** *of* Jeiel, the son of Mattaniah,	1201
	20:14	the son of Jeiel, the **s** *of* Mattaniah,	1201
	20:34	in the annals of Jehu **s** *of* Hanani,	1201
	20:37	Eliezer **s** *of* Dodavahu	1201
	21:1	And Jehoram his **s** succeeded him as king.	1201
	21:3	to Jehoram because he was his **firstborn** *s*.	AIT
	21:17	Not a **s** was left to him except Ahaziah,	1201
	22:1	Jehoram's youngest **s**, king in his place,	1201
	22:1	So Ahaziah **s** *of* Jehoram king of Judah	1201
	22:5	with Joram **s** *of* Ahab king of Israel to war	1201
	22:6	Then Ahaziah **s** *of* Jehoram king of Judah	1201
	22:6	down to Jezreel to see Joram **s** *of* Ahab	1201
	22:7	he went out with Joram to meet Jehu **s**	1201
	22:9	for they said, "He was a **s** *of* Jehoshaphat,	1201
	22:10	of Ahaziah saw that her **s** was dead,	1201
	22:11	took Joash **s** *of* Ahaziah and stole him away	1201
	23:1	Azariah **s** *of* Jeroham,	1201
	23:1	Ishmael **s** *of* Jehohanan,	1201
	23:1	son of Jehohanan, Azariah **s** *of* Obed,	1201
	23:1	Maaseiah **s** *of* Adaiah,	1201
	23:1	and Elishaphat **s** *of* Zicri.	1201
	23:3	"The king's **s** shall reign,	1201
	23:11	the king's **s** and put the crown on him;	1201
	24:20	of God came upon Zechariah **s** *of* Jehoiada	1201
	24:22	but killed his **s**, who said as he lay dying,	1201
	24:25	against him for murdering the **s** *of* Jehoiada	1201
	24:26	**s** *of* Shimeath an Ammonite woman,	1201
	24:26	**s** *of* Shimrith a Moabite woman.	1201
	24:27	And Amaziah his **s** succeeded him as king.	1201
	25:17	he sent this challenge to Jehoash **s**	1201
	25:17	the **s** *of* Jehu, king of Israel:	1201
	25:18	'Give your daughter to my **s** in marriage.'	1201
	25:23	the **s** *of* Joash, the son of Ahaziah,	1201
	25:23	the **s** *of* Ahaziah, at Beth Shemesh.	1201
	25:25	Amaziah **s** *of* Joash king of Judah lived	1201
	25:25	for fifteen years after the death of Jehoash **s**	1201
	26:21	Jotham his **s** had charge of the palace	1201
	26:22	are recorded by the prophet Isaiah **s**	1201
	26:23	And Jotham his **s** succeeded him as king.	1201
	27:9	And Ahaz his **s** succeeded him as king.	1201
	28:6	In one day Pekah **s** *of* Remaliah killed	1201

2Ch 28: 7 killed Maaseiah the king's s, 1201
28:12 Azariah s *of* Jehohanan, 1201
28:12 Berekiah s *of* Meshillemoth, 1201
28:12 Jehizkiah s *of* Shallum, 1201
28:12 and Amasa s *of* Hadlai— 1201
28:27 And Hezekiah his s succeeded him as king. 1201
29:12 from the Kohathites, Mahath s *of* Amasai 1201
29:12 Mahath son of Amasai and Joel s 1201
29:12 from the Merarites, Kish s *of* Abdi 1201
29:12 of Abdi and Azariah s *of* Jehallelel; 1201
29:12 Joah s *of* Zimmah and Eden son of Joah; 1201
29:12 Joah son of Zimmah and Eden s *of* Joah; 1201
30:26 since the days of Solomon s *of* David king 1201
31:14 Kore s *of* Imnah the Levite, 1201
32:20 and the prophet Isaiah s *of* Amoz cried out 1201
32:32 the prophet Isaiah s *of* Amoz in the book of 1201
32:33 And Manasseh his s succeeded him as king. 1201
33: 7 to David and to his s Solomon, 1201
33:20 And Amon his s succeeded him as king. 1201
33:25 they made Josiah his s king in his place. 1201
34: 8 he sent Shaphan s *of* Azaliah and Maaseiah 1201
34: 8 with Joah s *of* Joahaz, the recorder, 1201
34:20 Ahikam s *of* Shaphan, 1201
34:20 Abdon s *of* Micah, Shaphan the secretary 1201
34:22 who was the wife of Shallum s *of* Tokhath, 1201
34:22 the s *of* Hasrah, keeper of the wardrobe. 1201
35: 3 in the temple that Solomon s *of* David king 1201
35: 4 of Israel and by his s Solomon. 1201
36: 1 And the people of the land took Jehoahaz s 1201
36: 8 Jehoiachin his s succeeded him as king. 1201
Ezr 3: 2 Then Jeshua s *of* Jozadak 1201
3: 2 and his fellow priests and Zerubbabel s 1201
3: 8 Zerubbabel s *of* Shealtiel, 1201
3: 8 Jeshua s *of* Jozadak and the rest of their 1201
5: 2 Then Zerubbabel s *of* Shealtiel and 10120
5: 2 and Jeshua s *of* Jozadak set to work 10120
7: 1 Ezra s *of* Seraiah, the son of Azariah, 1201
7: 1 Ezra son of Seraiah, the s *of* Azariah, 1201
7: 1 the son of Azariah, the s *of* Hilkiah, 1201
7: 2 the s *of* Shallum, the son of Zadok, 1201
7: 2 the s *of* Zadok, the son of Ahitub, 1201
7: 2 the son of Zadok, the s *of* Ahitub, 1201
7: 3 the s *of* Amariah, the son of Azariah, 1201
7: 3 the s *of* Azariah, the son of Meraioth, 1201
7: 3 the son of Azariah, the s *of* Meraioth, 1201
7: 4 the s *of* Zerahiah, the son of Uzzi, 1201
7: 4 the s *of* Uzzi, the son of Bukki, 1201
7: 4 the son of Uzzi, the s *of* Bukki, 1201
7: 5 the s *of* Abishua, the son of Phinehas, 1201
7: 5 the s *of* Phinehas, the son of Eleazar, 1201
7: 5 the son of Phinehas, the s *of* Eleazar, 1201
7: 5 the s *of* Aaron the chief priest— 1201
8: 4 Eliehoenai s *of* Zerahiah, 1201
8: 5 Shecaniah s *of* Jahaziel, 1201
8: 6 Ebed s *of* Jonathan, and with him 50 men; 1201
8: 7 Jeshaiah s *of* Athaliah, 1201
8: 8 Zebadiah s *of* Michael, 1201
8: 9 Obadiah s *of* Jehiel, and with him 218 men; 1201
8:10 Shelomith s *of* Josiphiah, 1201
8:11 Zechariah s *of* Bebai, and 1201
8:12 Johanan s *of* Hakkatan, 1201
8:18 from the descendants of Mahli s *of* Levi, 1201
8:18 the s *of* Israel, and Sherebiah's sons 1201
8:33 into the hands of Meremoth s *of* Uriah, 1201
8:33 Eleazar s *of* Phinehas was with him, 1201
8:33 so were the Levites Jozabad s *of* Jeshua 1201
8:33 of Jeshua and Noadiah s *of* Binnui. 1201
10: 2 Then Shecaniah s *of* Jehiel, 1201
10: 6 to the room of Jehohanan s *of* Eliashib. 1201
10:15 Only Jonathan s *of* Asahel and 1201
10:15 Only Jonathan son of Asahel and Jahzeiah s 1201
10:18 of Jeshua s *of* Jozadak, and his brothers: 1201
Ne 1: 1 The words of Nehemiah s *of* Hacaliah: 1201
3: 2 and Zaccur s *of* Imri built next to them. 1201
3: 4 Meremoth s *of* Uriah, the son of Hakkoz, 1201
3: 4 Meremoth son of Uriah, the s *of* Hakkoz, 1201
3: 4 Next to him Meshullam s *of* Berekiah, 1201
3: 4 the s *of* Meshezabel, made repairs, 1201
3: 4 to him Zadok s *of* Baana also made repairs. 1201
3: 6 The Jeshanah Gate was repaired by Joiada s 1201
3: 6 of Paseah and Meshullam s *of* Besodeiah. 1201
3: 8 Uzziel s *of* Harhaiah, one of the goldsmiths, 1201
3: 9 Rephaiah s *of* Hur, 1201
3:10 Adjoining this, Jedaiah s *of* Harmaph 1201
3:10 and Hattush s *of* Hashabneiah made repairs 1201
3:11 Malkijah s *of* Harim and Hasshub son 1201
3:11 Malkijah son of Harim and Hasshub s 1201
3:12 Shallum s *of* Hallohesh, 1201
3:14 The Dung Gate was repaired by Malkijah s 1201
3:15 by Shallun s *of* Col-Hozeh, 1201
3:16 Beyond him, Nehemiah s *of* Azbuk, 1201
3:17 by the Levites under Rehum s *of* Bani. 1201
3:18 by their countrymen under Binnui s 1201
3:19 Next to him, Ezer s *of* Jeshua, 1201
3:20 Next to him, Baruch s *of* Zabbai 1201
3:21 Next to him, Meremoth s *of* Uriah, 1201
3:21 the s *of* Hakkoz, repaired another section, 1201
3:23 and next to them, Azariah s *of* Maaseiah, 1201
3:23 Azariah son of Maaseiah, the s *of* Ananiah, 1201
3:24 Next to him, Binnui s *of* Henadad 1201
3:25 and Palal s *of* Uzai worked opposite 1201
3:25 Next to him, Pedaiah s *of* Parosh 1201
3:29 Next to them, Zadok s *of* Immer 1201
3:29 Next to him, Shemaiah s *of* Shecaniah, 1201
3:30 Next to him, Hananiah s *of* Shelemiah, 1201
3:30 and Hanun, the sixth s *of* Zalaph, 1201
3:30 Next to them, Meshullam s *of* Berekiah 1201
Ne 6:10 One day I went to the house of Shemaiah s 1201
6:10 the s *of* Mehetabel, 1201
6:18 he was son-in-law to Shecaniah s *of* Arah, 1201
6:18 and his s Jehohanan had married 1201
6:18 the daughter of Meshullam s *of* Berekiah. 1201
8:17 the days of Joshua s *of* Nun until that day, 1201
10: 1 Nehemiah the governor, the s *of* Hacaliah. 1201
10: 9 The Levites: Jeshua s *of* Azaniah, 1201
11: 4 Athaiah s *of* Uzziah, the son of Zechariah, 1201
11: 4 Athaiah son of Uzziah, the s *of* Zechariah, 1201
11: 4 the s *of* Amariah, the son of Shephatiah, 1201
11: 4 the s *of* Shephatiah, the son of Mahalalel, 1201
11: 4 the s *of* Mahalalel, a descendant of Perez; 1201
11: 5 and Maaseiah s *of* Baruch, 1201
11: 5 the s *of* Col-Hozeh, the son of Hazaiah, 1201
11: 5 the son of Col-Hozeh, the s *of* Hazaiah, 1201
11: 5 the son of Hazaiah, the s *of* Adaiah, 1201
11: 5 the s *of* Joiarib, the son of Zechariah, 1201
11: 5 the s *of* Zechariah, a descendant of Shelah. 1201
11: 7 Sallu s *of* Meshullam, the son of Joed, 1201
11: 7 Sallu son of Meshullam, the s *of* Joed, 1201
11: 7 the s *of* Pedaiah, the son of Kolaiah, 1201
11: 7 the s *of* Kolaiah, the son of Maaseiah, 1201
11: 7 the son of Kolaiah, the s *of* Maaseiah, 1201
11: 7 the son of Maaseiah, the s *of* Ithiel, 1201
11: 7 the son of Ithiel, the s *of* Jeshaiah, 1201
11: 9 Joel s *of* Zicri was their chief officer, 1201
11: 9 and Judah s *of* Hassenuah was over 1201
11:10 From the priests: Jedaiah; the s *of* Joiarib; 1201
11:11 Seraiah s *of* Hilkiah, 1201
11:11 the s *of* Meshullam, the son of Zadok, 1201
11:11 the son of Meshullam, the s *of* Zadok, 1201
11:11 the s *of* Meraioth, the son of Ahitub, 1201
11:11 the son of Meraioth, the s *of* Ahitub, 1201
11:12 Adaiah s *of* Jeroham, the son of Pelaliah, 1201
11:12 Adaiah son of Jeroham, the s *of* Pelaliah, 1201
11:12 the s *of* Amzi, the son of Zechariah, 1201
11:12 the s *of* Zechariah, the son of Pashhur, 1201
11:12 the son of Zechariah, the s *of* Pashhur, 1201
11:12 the son of Pashhur, the s *of* Malkijah, 1201
11:13 Amashsai s *of* Azarel, the son of Ahzai, 1201
11:13 Amashsai son of Azarel, the s *of* Ahzai, 1201
11:13 the s *of* Meshillemoth, the son of Immer, 1201
11:13 the son of Meshillemoth, the s *of* Immer, 1201
11:14 Their chief officer was Zabdiel s 1201
11:15 From the Levites: Shemaiah s *of* Hasshub, 1201
11:15 the s *of* Azrikam, the son of Hashabiah, 1201
11:15 the son of Azrikam, the s *of* Hashabiah, 1201
11:15 the son of Hashabiah, the s *of* Bunni; 1201
11:17 Mattaniah s *of* Mica, the son of Zabdi, 1201
11:17 the s *of* Zabdi, the son of Asaph, 1201
11:17 the son of Zabdi, the s *of* Asaph, 1201
11:17 and Abda s *of* Shammua, the son of Galal, 1201
11:17 and Abda son of Shammua, the s *of* Galal, 1201
11:17 the son of Galal, the s *of* Jeduthun. 1201
11:22 of the Levites in Jerusalem was Uzzi s 1201
11:22 the s *of* Hashabiah, the son of Mattaniah, 1201
11:22 the son of Hashabiah, the s *of* Mattaniah, 1201
11:22 the son of Mattaniah, the s *of* Mica. 1201
11:24 Pethahiah s *of* Meshezabel, 1201
11:24 one of the descendants of Zerah s *of* Judah, 1201
12: 1 and Levites who returned with Zerubbabel s 1201
12:23 of Johanan s *of* Eliashib were recorded in 1201
12:24 Jeshua s *of* Kadmiel, and their associates, 1201
12:26 They served in the days of Joiakim s *of* 1201
12:26 son of Jeshua, the s *of* Jozadak, 1201
12:35 and also Zechariah s *of* Jonathan, 1201
12:35 the s *of* Shemaiah, the son of Mattaniah, 1201
12:35 the son of Shemaiah, the s *of* Mattaniah, 1201
12:35 the son of Mattaniah, the s *of* Micaiah, 1201
12:35 the son of Micaiah, the s *of* Zaccur, 1201
12:35 the son of Zaccur, the s *of* Asaph, 1201
12:45 the commands of David and his s Solomon. 1201
13:13 of the storerooms and made Hanan s 1201
13:13 the s *of* Mattaniah, their assistant, 1201
13:28 One of the sons of Joiada s *of* Eliashib 1201
Est 2: 5 of Benjamin, named Mordecai s *of* Jair, 1201
2: 5 the s *of* Shimei, the son of Kish, 1201
2: 5 the son of Shimei, the s *of* Kish, 1201
3: 1 King Xerxes honored Haman s *of* 1201
3:10 and gave it to Haman s *of* Hammedatha, 1201
8: 5 that Haman s *of* Hammedatha, 1201
9:10 the ten sons of Haman s *of* Hammedatha, 1201
9:24 For Haman s *of* Hammedatha, the Agagite, 1201
Job 25: 6 a s *of* man, who is only a worm!" 1201
32: 2 But Elihu s *of* Barakel the Buzite, 1201
32: 6 So Elihu s *of* Barakel the Buzite said: 1201
Ps 2: 7 He said to me, "You are my S; 1201
2:12 Kiss the S, lest he be angry and you 1337
3: T When he fled from his s Absalom. 1201
8: 4 the s *of* man that you care for him? 1201
9: T To [the tune of] "The Death of the S." 1201
50:20 and slander your own mother's s. 1201
72: 1 O God, the royal s with your righteousness. 1201
72:20 This concludes the prayers of David s *of* 1201
80:15 the s you have raised up for yourself. 1201
80:17 the s *of* man you have raised up 1201
86:16 and save the s *of* your maidservant. 1201
116:16 the s *of* your maidservant; 1201
144: 3 the s *of* man that you think of him? 1201
Pr 1: 1 The proverbs of Solomon s *of* David, 1201
1: 8 my s, to your father's instruction and do 1201
1:10 My s, if sinners entice you, 1201
1:15 my s, do not go along with them, do 1201
2: 1 My s, if you accept my words and store 1201
3: 1 My s, do not forget my teaching, 1201
3:11 My s, do not despise the LORD's discipline 1201
Pr 3:12 as a father the s he delights in. 1201
3:21 My s, preserve sound judgment 1201
4:10 Listen, my s, accept what I say, 1201
4:20 My s, pay attention to what I say; 1201
5: 1 My s, pay attention to my wisdom, 1201
5:20 Why be captivated, my s, by an adulteress? 1201
6: 1 My s, if you have put up security 1201
6: 3 my s, to free yourself, 1201
6:20 My s, keep your father's commands and do 1201
7: 1 My s, keep my words and store 1201
10: 1 A wise s brings joy to his father, 1201
10: 1 but a foolish s grief to his mother. 1201
10: 5 who gathers crops in summer is a wise s, 1201
10: 5 sleeps during harvest is a disgraceful s. 1201
13: 1 A wise s heeds his father's instruction, 1201
13:24 He who spares the rod hates his s, 1201
15:20 A wise s brings joy to his father, 1201
17: 2 wise servant will rule over a disgraceful s, 1201
17:21 To **have a** fool *for a* s brings grief; 3528
17:25 A foolish s brings grief to his father 1201
19:13 A foolish s is his father's ruin, 1201
19:18 Discipline your s, for in that there is hope; 1201
19:26 a s who brings shame and disgrace. 1201
19:27 Stop listening to instruction, my s, 1201
23:15 My s, if your heart is wise, 1201
23:19 Listen, my s, and be wise, 1201
23:24 *he who* **has** a wise s delights in him. 3528
23:26 My s, give me your heart 1201
24:13 Eat honey, my s, for it is good; 1201
24:21 Fear the LORD and the king, my s, 1201
27:11 Be wise, my s, and bring joy to my heart; 1201
28: 7 He who keeps the law is a discerning s, 1201
29:17 Discipline your s, and he will give you peace; 1201
30: 1 The sayings of Agur s *of* Jakeh— 1201
30: 4 What is his name, and the name of his s? 1201
31: 2 "O my s, O son of my womb, O son 1337
31: 2 O s *of* my womb, O son of my vows, 1337
31: 2 O son of my womb, O s *of* my vows, 1337
Ecc 1: 1 The words of the Teacher, s *of* David, 1201
4: 8 he had neither s nor brother. 1201
5:14 so that when he has a s there is nothing left 1201
12:12 my s, of anything in addition to them. 1201
Isa 1: 1 that Isaiah s *of* Amoz saw during the reigns 1201
2: 1 This is what Isaiah s *of* Amoz saw 1201
7: 1 When Ahaz s *of* Jotham, the son of Uzziah, 1201
7: 1 When Ahaz son of Jotham, the s *of* Uzziah, 1201
7: 1 of Aram and Pekah s *of* Remaliah king 1201
7: 3 "Go out, you and your s Shear-Jashub, 1201
7: 4 and Aram and of the s *of* Remaliah. 1201
7: 5 and Remaliah's s have plotted your ruin, 1201
7: 6 and make the s *of* Tabeel king over it." 1201
7: 9 the head of Samaria is only Remaliah's s. 1201
7:14 be with child and will give birth to a s, 1201
8: 2 the priest and Zechariah s *of* Jeberekiah 1201
8: 3 and she conceived and gave birth to a s. 1201
8: 6 of Shiloah and rejoices over Rezin and the s 1201
9: 6 For to us a child is born, to us a s is given, 1201
13: 1 An oracle concerning Babylon that Isaiah s 1201
14:12 O morning star, s *of* the dawn! 1201
20: 2 that time the LORD spoke through Isaiah s 1201
22:20 my servant, Eliakim s *of* Hilkiah. 1201
36: 3 Eliakim s *of* Hilkiah the palace 1201
36: 3 and Joah s *of* Asaph the recorder went out 1201
36:22 Then Eliakim s *of* Hilkiah the palace 1201
36:22 and Joah s *of* Asaph the recorder went 1201
37: 2 to the prophet Isaiah s *of* Amoz. 1201
37:21 Then Isaiah s *of* Amoz sent a message 1201
37:38 Esarhaddon his s succeeded him as king. 1201
38: 1 The prophet Isaiah s *of* Amoz went to him 1201
39: 1 At that time Merodach-Baladan s *of* 1201
66: 7 the pains come upon her, she delivers a s. 2351
Jer 1: 1 The words of Jeremiah s *of* Hilkiah, 1201
1: 2 in the thirteenth year of the reign of Josiah s 1201
1: 3 of Jehoiakim s *of* Josiah king of Judah, 1201
1: 3 of Zedekiah s *of* Josiah king of Judah, 1201
6:26 mourn with bitter wailing as for an **only** s, 3495
15: 4 of the earth because of what Manasseh s 1201
20: 1 When the priest Pashhur s *of* Immer, 1201
20:15 "A child is born to you—a s!" 2351
21: 1 when King Zedekiah sent to him Pashhur s 1201
21: 1 and the priest Zephaniah s *of* Maaseiah. 1201
22:11 the LORD says about Shallum s *of* Josiah, 1201
22:18 about Jehoiakim s *of* Josiah king of Judah: 1201
22:24 Jehoiachin s *of* Jehoiakim king of Judah, 1201
24: 1 After Jehoiachin s *of* Jehoiakim king 1201
25: 1 of Judah in the fourth year of Jehoiakim s 1201
25: 3 from the thirteenth year of Josiah s 1201
26: 1 in the reign of Jehoiakim s *of* Josiah king 1201
26:20 (Now Uriah s *of* Shemaiah from 1201
26:22 sent Elnathan s *of* Acbor to Egypt, 1201
26:24 Ahikam s *of* Shaphan supported Jeremiah, 1201
27: 1 in the reign of Zedekiah s *of* Josiah king 1201
27: 7 and his s and his grandson until the time 1201
27:20 not take away when he carried Jehoiachin s 1201
28: 1 the prophet Hananiah s *of* Azzur, 1201
28: 4 to this place Jehoiachin s *of* Jehoiakim king 1201
29: 3 the letter to Elasah s *of* Shaphan and 1201
29: 3 of Shaphan and to Gemariah s *of* Hilkiah, 1201
29:21 about Ahab s *of* Kolaiah and Zedekiah son 1201
29:21 about Ahab son of Kolaiah and Zedekiah s 1201
29:25 to Zephaniah s *of* Maaseiah the priest, 1201
31: 9 and Ephraim is my **firstborn** s. AIT
31:20 Is not Ephraim my dear s, 1201
32: 7 Hanamel s *of* Shallum your uncle is going 1201
32:12 and I gave this deed to Baruch s *of* Neriah, 1201
32:12 Baruch son of Neriah, the s *of* Mahseiah, 1201

Jer 32:16 the deed of purchase to Baruch s *of* Neriah, 1201
35: 1 the LORD during the reign of Jehoiakim s 1201
35: 3 So I went to get Jaazaniah s *of* Jeremiah, 1201
35: 3 the s *of* Habazziniah, and his brothers 1201
35: 4 the room of the sons of Hanan s *of* Igdaliah 1201
35: 4 of Maaseiah s *of* Shallum the doorkeeper. 1201
35: 6 because our forefather Jonadab s 1201
35: 8 We have obeyed everything our forefather
Jonadab s *of* Recab commanded 1201
35:14 'Jonadab s *of* Recab ordered his sons not 1201
35:16 of Jonadab s *of* Recab have carried out 1201
35:19 'Jonadab s *of* Recab will never fail to have 1201
36: 1 of Jehoiakim s *of* Josiah king of Judah, 1201
36: 4 So Jeremiah called Baruch s *of* Neriah, 1201
36: 8 Baruch s *of* Neriah did everything Jeremiah 1201
36: 9 the fifth year of Jehoiakim s *of* Josiah king 1201
36:10 From the room of Gemariah s *of* Shaphan 1201
36:11 When Micaiah s *of* Gemariah, 1201
36:11 the s *of* Shaphan, heard all the words 1201
36:12 Delaiah s *of* Shemaiah, 1201
36:12 of Shemaiah, Elnathan s *of* Acbor, 1201
36:12 Gemariah s *of* Shaphan, 1201
36:12 Zedekiah s *of* Hananiah, 1201
36:14 all the officials sent Jehudi s *of* Nethaniah, 1201
36:14 the s *of* Shelemiah, the son of Cushi, 1201
36:14 the son of Shelemiah, the s *of* Cushi, 1201
36:14 So Baruch s *of* Neriah went to them with 1201
36:26 Jerahmeel, a s *of* the king, 1201
36:26 Seraiah s *of* Azriel and Shelemiah son 1201
36:26 and Shelemiah s *of* Abdeel to arrest Baruch 1201
36:32 and gave it to the scribe Baruch s 1201
37: 1 Zedekiah s *of* Josiah was made king 1201
37: 1 in place of Jehoiachin s *of* Jehoiakim. 1201
37: 3 sent Jehucal s *of* Shelemiah with 1201
37: 3 of Shelemiah with the priest Zephaniah s 1201
37:13 whose name was Irijah s *of* Shelemiah, 1201
37:13 the s *of* Hananiah, arrested him and said, 1201
38: 1 Shephatiah s *of* Mattan, 1201
38: 1 Gedaliah s *of* Pashhur, 1201
38: 1 Jehucal s *of* Shelemiah, 1201
38: 1 of Shelemiah, and Pashhur s *of* Malkijah 1201
38: 6 the king's **s**, which was in the courtyard of 1201
39:14 They turned him over to Gedaliah s *of* 1201
39:14 the s *of* Shaphan, 1201
40: 5 "Go back to Gedaliah s *of* Ahikam, 1201
40: 5 the s *of* Shaphan, to take him back 1201
40: 6 So Jeremiah went to Gedaliah s *of* Ahikam 1201
40: 7 of Babylon had appointed Gedaliah s *of* 1201
40: 8 Ishmael s *of* Nethaniah, 1201
40: 8 Seraiah s *of* Tanhumeth, 1201
40: 8 and Jaazaniah the s *of* the Maacathite, 1201
40: 9 Gedaliah s *of* Ahikam, the son of Shaphan, 1201
40: 9 Gedaliah son of Ahikam, the s *of* Shaphan, 1201
40:11 and had appointed Gedaliah s *of* Ahikam, 1201
40:11 the s *of* Shaphan, as governor over them, 1201
40:13 Johanan s *of* Kareah and all 1201
40:14 of the Ammonites has sent Ishmael s 1201
40:14 But Gedaliah s *of* Ahikam did 1201
40:15 Then Johanan s *of* Kareah said privately 1201
40:15 and kill Ishmael s *of* Nethaniah, 1201
40:16 But Gedaliah s *of* Ahikam said 1201
40:16 of Ahikam said to Johanan s *of* Kareah, 1201
41: 1 the seventh month Ishmael s *of* Nethaniah, 1201
41: 1 the s *of* Elishama, who was of royal blood 1201
41: 1 with ten men to Gedaliah s *of* Ahikam 1201
41: 2 Ishmael s *of* Nethaniah and 1201
41: 2 up and struck down Gedaliah s *of* Ahikam, 1201
41: 2 the s *of* Shaphan, with the sword, 1201
41: 6 Ishmael s *of* Nethaniah went out 1201
41: 6 he said, "Come to Gedaliah s *of* Ahikam." 1201
41: 7 Ishmael s *of* Nethaniah and 1201
41: 9 Ishmael s *of* Nethaniah filled it with 1201
41:10 imperial guard had appointed Gedaliah s 1201
41:10 Ishmael s *of* Nethaniah took them captive 1201
41:11 When Johanan s *of* Kareah and all 1201
41:11 all the crimes Ishmael s *of* Nethaniah 1201
41:12 and went to fight Ishmael s *of* Nethaniah. 1201
41:13 with him saw Johanan s *of* Kareah and 1201
41:14 and went over to Johanan s *of* Kareah. 1201
41:15 But Ishmael s *of* Nethaniah and eight 1201
41:16 Then Johanan s *of* Kareah and all 1201
41:16 recovered from Ishmael s *of* Nethaniah 1201
41:16 after he had assassinated Gedaliah s 1201
41:18 They were afraid of them because Ishmael s 1201
41:18 of Nethaniah had killed Gedaliah s 1201
42: 1 including Johanan s *of* Kareah 1201
42: 1 of Kareah and Jezaniah s *of* Hoshaiah, 1201
42: 8 So he called together Johanan s *of* Kareah 1201
43: 2 Azariah s *of* Hoshaiah and Johanan son 1201
43: 2 Azariah son of Hoshaiah and Johanan s 1201
43: 3 But Baruch s *of* Neriah is inciting you 1201
43: 4 So Johanan s *of* Kareah and all 1201
43: 5 Johanan s *of* Kareah and all 1201
43: 6 the imperial guard had left with Gedaliah s 1201
43: 6 the s *of* Shaphan, and Jeremiah the prophet 1201
43: 6 and Jeremiah the prophet and Baruch s *of* 1201
45: 1 the prophet told Baruch s *of* Neriah in 1201
45: 1 of Neriah in the fourth year of Jehoiakim s 1201
46: 2 of Jehoiakim s *of* Josiah king of Judah: 1201
51:59 to the staff officer Seraiah s *of* Neriah, 1201
51:59 the s *of* Mahseiah, when he went to Babylon 1201
Eze 1: 3 Ezekiel the priest, the s *of* Buzi, 1201
2: 1 He said to me, "S *of* man, stand up 1201
2: 3 He said: "S *of* man, I am sending you 1201
2: 6 And you, s *of* man, do not be afraid of them 1201
2: 8 you, s *of* man, listen to what I say to you. 1201
3: 1 And he said to me, "S *of* man, 1201

Eze 3: 3 Then he said to me, "S *of* man, 1201
3: 4 He then said to me: "S *of* man, 1201
3:10 And he said to me, "S *of* man, 1201
3:17 "S *of* man, I have made you a watchman 1201
3:25 And you, s *of* man, they will tie with ropes; 1201
4: 1 "Now, s *of* man, take a clay tablet, 1201
4:16 He then said to me: "S *of* man, 1201
5: 1 s *of* man, take a sharp sword and use it as 1201
6: 2 "S *of* man, set your face against 1201
7: 2 "S *of* man, this is what the Sovereign 1201
8: 5 Then he said to me, "S *of* man, 1201
8: 6 And he said to me, "S *of* man, 1201
8: 8 He said to me, "S *of* man, 1201
8:11 and Jaazaniah s *of* Shaphan was standing 1201
8:12 He said to me, "S *of* man, 1201
8:15 He said to me, "Do you see this, s *of* man? 1201
8:17 "Have you seen this, s *of* man? 1201
11: 1 and I saw among them Jaazaniah s 1201
11: 1 of Azzur and Pelatiah s *of* Benaiah, 1201
11: 2 The LORD said to me, "S *of* man, 1201
11: 4 prophesy against them; prophesy, s *of* man." 1201
11:13 Pelatiah s *of* Benaiah died. 1201
11:15 "S *of* man, your brothers— 1201
12: 2 "S *of* man, you are living among 1201
12: 3 "Therefore, s *of* man, pack your belongings 1201
12: 9 "S *of* man, did not that rebellious house 1201
12:18 "S *of* man, tremble as you eat your food, 1201
12:22 "S *of* man, what is this proverb you have 1201
12:27 "S *of* man, the house of Israel is saying, 1201
13: 2 "S *of* man, prophesy against the prophets 1201
13:17 "Now, s *of* man, set your face against 1201
14: 3 "S *of* man, these men have set up idols 1201
14:13 "S *of* man, if a country sins against me 1201
14:20 they could save neither s nor daughter. 1201
15: 2 "S *of* man, how is the wood of 1201
16: 2 "S *of* man, confront Jerusalem 1201
17: 2 "S *of* man, set forth an allegory and tell 1201
18: 4 the father as well as the **s**— 1201
18:10 "Suppose he has a violent **s**, 1201
18:14 "But suppose this s has a son who sees all NIH
18:14 a s who sees all the sins his father commits, 1201
18:19 the s not share the guilt of his father?' 1201
18:19 Since the s has done what is just and right 1201
18:20 The s will not share the guilt of the father, 1201
18:20 nor will the father share the guilt of the **s**. 1201
20: 3 "S *of* man, speak to the elders of Israel 1201
20: 4 Will you judge them, s *of* man? 1201
20:27 s *of* man, speak to the people of Israel 1201
20:46 "S *of* man, set your face toward the south; 1201
21: 2 "S *of* man, set your face against Jerusalem 1201
21: 6 "Therefore groan, s *of* man! 1201
21: 9 "S *of* man, prophesy and say, 'This is what 1201
21:10 in the scepter of my s [Judah]? 1201
21:12 Cry out and wail, s *of* man, 1201
21:14 "So then, s *of* man, 1201
21:19 "S *of* man, mark out two roads for 1201
21:28 "And you, s *of* man, prophesy and say, 1201
22: 2 "S *of* man, will you judge her? 1201
22:18 "S *of* man, the house of Israel has become 1201
22:24 "S *of* man, say to the land, 'You are a land 1201
23: 2 "S *of* man, there were two women, 1201
23:36 The LORD said to me: "S *of* man, 1201
24: 2 "S *of* man, record this date, this very date, 1201
24:16 "S *of* man, with one blow I am about 1201
24:25 "And you, s *of* man, 1201
25: 2 "S *of* man, set your face against 1201
26: 2 "S *of* man, because Tyre has said 1201
27: 2 "S *of* man, take up a lament 1201
28: 2 "S *of* man, say to the ruler of Tyre, 1201
28:12 "S *of* man, take up a lament concerning 1201
28:21 "S *of* man, set your face against Sidon; 1201
29: 2 "S *of* man, set your face against Pharaoh 1201
29:18 "S *of* man, Nebuchadnezzar king 1201
30: 2 "S *of* man, prophesy and say: 1201
30:21 "S *of* man, I have broken the arm 1201
31: 2 "S *of* man, say to Pharaoh king of Egypt 1201
32: 2 "S *of* man, take up a lament 1201
32:18 "S *of* man, wail for the hordes of Egypt 1201
33: 2 "S *of* man, speak to your countrymen 1201
33: 7 "S *of* man, I have made you a watchman 1201
33:10 "S *of* man, say to the house of Israel, 1201
33:12 s *of* man, say to your countrymen, 1201
33:24 "S *of* man, the people living in those ruins 1201
33:30 "As for you, s *of* man, 1201
34: 2 "S *of* man, prophesy against the shepherds 1201
35: 2 "S *of* man, set your face against Mount Seir 1201
36: 1 "S *of* man, prophesy to the mountains 1201
36:17 "S *of* man, when the people 1201
37: 3 He asked me, "S *of* man, 1201
37: 9 prophesy, s *of* man, and say to it, 1201
37:11 Then he said to me: "S *of* man, 1201
37:16 "S *of* man, take a stick of wood and write 1201
38: 2 "S *of* man, set your face against Gog, of 1201
38:14 s *of* man, prophesy and say to Gog: 1201
39: 1 "S *of* man, prophesy against Gog and say: 1201
39:17 "S *of* man, this is what the Sovereign 1201
40: 4 The man said to me, "S *of* man, 1201
43: 7 He said: "S *of* man, this is the place 1201
43:10 "S *of* man, describe the temple to 1201
43:18 Then he said to me, "S *of* man, 1201
44: 5 The LORD said to me, "S *of* man, 1201
44:25 s or daughter, brother or unmarried sister, 1201
47: 6 He asked me, "S *of* man, do you see this?" 1201
Da 3:25 and the fourth looks like a s *of* the gods." 10120
5:22 "But you his s, O Belshazzar, 10120
7:13 before me was one like a s *of* man, 10120
8:17 "S *of* man," he said to me, 1201

Da 9: 1 the first year of Darius s *of* Xerxes (a Mede 1201
Hos 1: 1 the LORD that came to Hosea s *of* Beeri 1201
1: 1 of Jeroboam s *of* Jehoash king of Israel: 1201
1: 3 and she conceived and bore him a s. 1201
1: 8 Gomer had another s. 1201
11: 1 I loved him, and out of Egypt I called my **s**. 1201
Joel 1: 1 The word of the LORD that came to Joel s 1201
Am 1: 1 and Jeroboam s *of* Jehoash was king 1201
2: 7 Father and s use the same girl and 408
7:14 "I was neither a prophet nor a prophet's **s**, 1201
8:10 an **only** s and the end of it like a bitter day. 3495
Jnh 1: 1 of the LORD came to Jonah s *of* Amittai: 1201
Mic 6: 5 of Moab counseled and what Balaam s 1201
7: 6 For a s dishonors his father, 1201
Zep 1: 1 that came to Zephaniah s *of* Cushi, the son 1201
1: 1 the s *of* Gedaliah, the son of Amariah, 1201
1: 1 the s *of* Amariah, the son of Hezekiah, 1201
1: 1 the son of Amariah, the s *of* Hezekiah, 1201
1: 1 during the reign of Josiah s *of* Amon king 1201
Hag 1: 1 through the prophet Haggai to Zerubbabel s 1201
1: 1 and to Joshua s *of* Jehozadak, 1201
1:12 Then Zerubbabel s *of* Shealtiel, 1201
1:12 Joshua s *of* Jehozadak, the high priest, 1201
1:14 up the spirit of Zerubbabel s *of* Shealtiel, 1201
1:14 and the spirit of Joshua s *of* Jehozadak, 1201
2: 2 "Speak to Zerubbabel s *of* Shealtiel, 1201
2: 2 to Joshua s *of* Jehozadak, the high priest, 1201
2: 4 'Be strong, O Joshua s *of* Jehozadak, 1201
2:23 my servant Zerubbabel s *of* Shealtiel,' 1201
Zec 1: 1 the LORD came to the prophet Zechariah s 1201
1: 1 Zechariah son of Berekiah, the s *of* Iddo: 1201
1: 7 the LORD came to the prophet Zechariah s 1201
1: 7 Zechariah son of Berekiah, the s *of* Iddo. 1201
6:10 Go the same day to the house of Josiah s 1201
6:11 high priest, Joshua s *of* Jehozadak. 1201
6:14 and Hen s *of* Zephaniah as a memorial in 1201
12:10 for him as one grieves for a **firstborn** *s*. AIT
Mal 1: 6 "A s honors his father, 1201
3:17 a man spares his s who serves him. 1201
Mt 1: 1 *of* Jesus Christ the s of David, the son *5626*
1: 1 the son of David, the s of Abraham: *5626*
1:20 "Joseph s of David, do not be afraid *5626*
1:21 She will give birth to a **s**, *5626*
1:23 to a **s**, and they will call him Immanuel"— *5626*
1:25 with her until she gave birth to a **s**. *5626*
2:15 "Out of Egypt I called my **s**." *5626*
3:17 a voice from heaven said, "This is my **S**, *5626*
4: 3 "If you are the S of God, *5626*
4: 6 "If you are the S of God," he said, *5626*
4:21 James s of Zebedee and his brother John. *3836*
7: 9 "Which of you, if his s asks for bread, *5626*
8:20 the S of Man has no place to lay his head." *5626*
8:29 "What do you want with us, S of God?" *5626*
9: 2 "Take heart, **s**; your sins are forgiven." *5451*
9: 6 that the S of Man has authority on earth *5626*
9:27 "Have mercy on us, S of David!" *5626*
10: 2 James s of Zebedee, and his brother John; *3836*
10: 3 James s of Alphaeus, and Thaddeus; *3836*
10:23 through the cities of Israel before the S *5626*
10:37 anyone who loves his s or daughter more *5626*
11:19 The S of Man came eating and drinking, *5626*
11:27 No one knows the S except the Father, *5626*
11:27 the Father except the S and those to whom *5626*
11:27 the Son and those to whom the S chooses *5626*
12: 8 For the S of Man is Lord of the Sabbath." *5626*
12:23 "Could this be the S of David?" *5626*
12:32 Anyone who speaks a word against the S *5626*
12:40 so the S of Man will be three days *5626*
13:37 "The one who sowed the good seed is the S *5626*
13:41 The S of Man will send out his angels, *5626*
13:55 "Isn't this the carpenter's **s**? *5626*
14:33 saying, "Truly you are the S of God." *5626*
15:22 "Lord, S of David, have mercy on me! *5626*
16:13 "Who do people say the S of Man is?" *5626*
16:16 "You are the Christ, the S of the living
God." *5626*
16:17 "Blessed are you, Simon **s of Jonah**, *980*
16:27 For the S of Man is going to come *5626*
16:28 the S of Man coming in his kingdom." *5626*
17: 5 "This is my **S**, whom I love; *5626*
17: 9 until the S of Man has been raised from *5626*
17:12 In the same way the S of Man is going *5626*
17:15 "Lord, have mercy on my **s**," he said. *5626*
17:22 "The S of Man is going to be betrayed into *5626*
19:28 the S of Man sits on his glorious throne, *5626*
20:18 and the S of Man will be betrayed to *5626*
20:28 as the S of Man did not come to be served, *5626*
20:30 "Lord, S of David, have mercy on us!" *5626*
20:31 "Lord, S of David, have mercy on us!" *5626*
21: 9 "Hosanna *to* the S of David!" *5626*
21:15 "Hosanna *to* the S of David," *5626*
21:28 He went to the first and said, '**S**, *5451*
21:30 to the other s and said the same thing. *NIG*
21:37 Last of all, he sent his s to them. *5626*
21:37 'They will respect my **s**,' he said. *5626*
21:38 "But when the tenants saw the **s**, *5626*
22: 2 a wedding banquet *for* his **s**. *5626*
22:42 Whose s is he?" *5626*
22:42 "The s of David," they replied. *NIG*
22:45 how can he be his **s**?" *5626*
23:15 you make him twice as much a s of hell *5626*
23:35 to the blood of Zechariah s of Berekiah, *5626*
24:27 so will be the coming *of* the S of Man. *5626*
24:30 the sign *of* the S of Man will appear in *5626*
24:30 They will see the S of Man coming on *5626*
24:36 not even the angels in heaven, nor the S, *5626*
24:37 so it will be at the coming *of* the S of Man. *5626*

Mt 24:39 how it will be at the coming *of* the S of Man 5626
24:44 because the S of Man will come at an hour 5626
25:31 "When the S of Man comes in his glory, 5626
26: 2 and the S of Man will be handed over to 5626
26:24 The S of Man will go just as it is written 5626
26:24 woe to that man who betrays the S of Man! 5626
26:45 and the S of Man is betrayed into the hands 5626
26:63 Tell us if you are the Christ, the S of God." 5626
26:64 the future you will see the S of Man sitting 5626
27:40 if you are the S of God!" 5626
27:43 for he said, 'I am the S of God.' " 5626
27:54 "Surely he was the S of God!" 5626
28:19 the name of the Father and *of* the S and of 5626
Mk 1: 1 the gospel about Jesus Christ, the S of God. 5626
1:11 "You are my S, whom I love; 5626
1:19 he saw James s of Zebedee 3836
2: 5 "S, your sins are forgiven." 5451
2:10 that the S of Man has authority on earth 5626
2:14 he saw Levi s of Alphaeus sitting at 3836
2:28 the S of Man is Lord even of the Sabbath." 5626
3:11 "You are the S of God." 5626
3:17 James s of Zebedee and his brother John 3836
3:18 Thomas, James s of Alphaeus, Thaddaeus, 3836
5: 7 Jesus, S of the Most High God? 5626
6: 3 Isn't this Mary's s and the brother of James, 5626
8:31 that the S of Man must suffer many things 5626
8:38 the S of Man will be ashamed of him 5626
9: 7 "This is my S, whom I love. 5626
9: 9 until the S of Man had risen from the dead. 5626
9:12 that the S of Man must suffer much and 5626
9:17 "Teacher, I brought you my s, 5626
9:31 "The S of Man is going to be betrayed into 5626
10:33 "and the S of Man will be betrayed to 5626
10:45 the S of Man did not come to be served, 5626
10:46 Bartimaeus (that is, the S of Timaeus), 5626
10:47 "Jesus, S of David, have mercy on me!" 5626
10:48 but he shouted all the more, "S of David, 5626
12: 6 "He had one left to send, a s, 5626
12: 6 saying, 'They will respect my s.' 5626
12:35 of the law say that the Christ is the s 5626
12:37 How then can he be his s?" 5626
13:26 "At that time men will see the S of Man 5626
13:32 not even the angels in heaven, nor the S, 5626
14:21 The S of Man will go just as it is written 5626
14:21 woe to that man who betrays the S of Man! 5626
14:41 the S of Man is betrayed into the hands 5626
14:61 the S of the Blessed One?" 5626
14:62 "And you will see the S of Man sitting at 5626
15:39 "Surely this man was the S of God!" 5626
Lk 1:13 Your wife Elizabeth will bear you a s, 5626
1:31 You will be with child and give birth to a s, 5626
1:32 He will be great and will be called the S of 5626
1:35 the holy one to be born will be called the S 5626
1:57 she gave birth to a s. 5626
2: 7 and she gave birth to her firstborn, a s. 5626
2:48 His mother said to him, "S, 5451
3: 2 of God came to John s of Zechariah in 5626
3:22 "You are my S, whom I love; 5626
3:23 He was the s, so it was thought, of Joseph, 5626
3:23 so it was thought, of Joseph, **the s** of Heli, 3836
3:24 **the s** of Matthat, the son of Levi, 3836
3:24 **the s** of Levi, the son of Melki, 3836
3:24 **the s** of Melki, the son of Jannai, 3836
3:24 **the s** of Jannai, the son of Joseph, 3836
3:24 the son of Jannai, **the s** of Joseph, 3836
3:25 **the s** of Mattathias, the son of Amos, 3836
3:25 **the s** of Amos, the son of Nahum, 3836
3:25 the son of Amos, **the s** of Nahum, 3836
3:25 the son of Nahum, **the s** of Esli, 3836
3:25 the son of Esli, **the s** of Naggai, 3836
3:26 **the s** of Maath, the son of Mattathias 3836
3:26 **the s** of Mattathias, the son of Semein, 3836
3:26 the son of Mattathias, **the s** of Semein, 3836
3:26 the son of Semein, **the s** of Josech, 3836
3:26 the son of Josech, **the s** of Joda, 3836
3:27 **the s** of Joanan, the son of Rhesa, 3836
3:27 **the s** of Rhesa, the son of Zerubbabel, 3836
3:27 **the s** of Zerubbabel, the son of Shealtiel, 3836
3:27 the son of Zerubbabel, **the s** of Shealtiel, 3836
3:27 the son of Shealtiel, **the s** of Neri, 3836
3:28 **the s** of Melki, the son of Addi, 3836
3:28 **the s** of Addi, the son of Cosam, 3836
3:28 **the s** of Cosam, the son of Elmadam, 3836
3:28 the son of Cosam, **the s** of Elmadam, 3836
3:28 the son of Elmadam, **the s** of Er, 3836
3:29 **the s** of Joshua, the son of Eliezer, 3836
3:29 the s of Eliezer, the son of Jorim, *NIG*
3:29 **the s** of Jorim, the son of Matthat, 3836
3:29 the son of Jorim, **the s** of Matthat, 3836
3:29 the son of Matthat, **the s** of Levi, 3836
3:30 **the s** of Simeon, the son of Judah, 3836
3:30 **the s** of Judah, the son of Joseph, 3836
3:30 **the s** of Joseph, the son of Jonam, 3836
3:30 **the s** of Jonam, the son of Eliakim, 3836
3:30 the son of Jonam, **the s** of Eliakim, 3836
3:31 **the s** of Melea, the son of Menna, 3836
3:31 **the s** of Menna, the son of Mattatha, 3836
3:31 **the s** of Mattatha, the son of Nathan, 3836
3:31 the son of Mattatha, **the s** of Nathan, 3836
3:31 the son of Nathan, **the s** of David, 3836
3:32 **the s** of Jesse, the son of Obed, 3836
3:32 **the s** of Obed, the son of Boaz, 3836
3:32 **the s** of Boaz, the son of Salmon, 3836
3:32 **the s** of Salmon, the son of Nahshon, 3836
3:32 the son of Salmon, **the s** of Nahshon, 3836
3:33 **the s** of Amminadab, the son of Ram, 3836
3:33 **the s** of Ram, the son of Hezron, 3836

Lk 3:33 **the s** of Hezron, the son of Perez, 3836
3:33 the son of Hezron, **the s** of Perez, 3836
3:33 the son of Perez, **the s** of Judah, 3836
3:34 **the s** of Jacob, the son of Isaac, 3836
3:34 **the s** of Isaac, the son of Abraham, 3836
3:34 **the s** of Abraham, the son of Terah, 3836
3:34 the son of Abraham, **the s** of Terah, 3836
3:34 the son of Terah, **the s** of Nahor, 3836
3:35 **the s** of Serug, the son of Reu, 3836
3:35 **the s** of Reu, the son of Peleg, 3836
3:35 **the s** of Peleg, the son of Eber, 3836
3:35 **the s** of Eber, the son of Shelah, 3836
3:35 the son of Eber, **the s** of Shelah, 3836
3:36 **the s** of Cainan, the son of Arphaxad, 3836
3:36 **the s** of Arphaxad, the son of Shem, 3836
3:36 the son of Arphaxad, **the s** of Shem, 3836
3:36 **the s** of Noah, the son of Lamech, 3836
3:36 the son of Noah, **the s** of Lamech, 3836
3:37 **the s** of Methuselah, the son of Enoch, 3836
3:37 **the s** of Enoch, the son of Jared, 3836
3:37 **the s** of Jared, the son of Mahalalel, 3836
3:37 **the s** of Mahalalel, the son of Kenan, 3836
3:37 the son of Mahalalel, **the s** of Kenan, 3836
3:38 **the s** of Enosh, the son of Seth, 3836
3:38 **the s** of Seth, the son of Adam, 3836
3:38 the son of Seth, **the s** of Adam, 3836
3:38 the son of Adam, **the s** of God. 3836
4: 3 "If you are the S of God, 5626
4: 9 "If you are the S of God," he said, 5626
4:22 "Isn't this Joseph's s?" 5626
4:41 shouting, "You are the S of God!" 5626
5:24 that the S of Man has authority on earth 5626
6: 5 "The S of Man is Lord of the Sabbath." 5626
6:15 Thomas, James *s of* **Alphaeus,** 271
6:16 Judas *s of* **James,** *AIT*
6:22 because of the S of Man. 5626
7:12 only s of his mother, and she was a widow. 5626
7:34 The S of Man came eating and drinking, 5626
8:28 Jesus, S of the Most High God? 5626
9:22 "The S of Man must suffer many things 5626
9:26 the S of Man will be ashamed of him 5626
9:35 "This is my S, whom I have chosen; 5626
9:38 "Teacher, I beg you to look at my s, 5626
9:41 Bring your s here." 5626
9:44 The S of Man is going to be betrayed into 5626
9:58 the S of Man has no place to lay his head." 5626
10:22 No one knows who the S is except 5626
10:22 the S and those to whom the Son chooses 5626
10:22 the Son and those to whom the S chooses 5626
11:11 if your s asks for a fish, 5626
11:30 will the S of Man be to this generation. 5626
12: 8 the S of Man will also acknowledge him 5626
12:10 against the S of Man will be forgiven, 5626
12:40 because the S of Man will come at an hour 5626
12:53 father against s and son against father, 5626
12:53 father against son and s against father, 5626
14: 5 "If one of you has a s or an ox that falls into 5626
15:13 the younger s got together all he had, 5626
15:19 I am no longer worthy to be called your s; 5626
15:20 he ran to his s, threw his arms around him *NIG*
15:21 "The s said to him, 'Father, I have sinned 5626
15:21 I am no longer worthy to be called your s.' 5626
15:24 this s of mine was dead and is alive again; 5626
15:25 "Meanwhile, the older s was in the field. 5626
15:30 when this s of yours who has squandered 5626
15:31 " 'My s,' the father said, 5451
16:25 "But Abraham replied, 'S, 5451
17:22 to see one of the days *of* the S of Man, 5626
17:24 For the S of Man in his day will be like 5626
17:26 also will it be in the days *of* the S of Man. 5626
17:30 "It will be just like this on the day the S of 5626
18: 8 However, when the S of Man comes, 5626
18:31 that is written by the prophets *about* the S 5626
18:38 He called out, "Jesus, S of David, 5626
18:39 but he shouted all the more, "S of David, 5626
19: 9 because this man, too, is a s of Abraham. 5626
19:10 For the S of Man came to seek and 5626
20:13 I will send my s, whom I love; 5626
20:41 "How is it that they say the Christ is the S 5626
20:44 How then can he be his s?" 5626
21:27 the S of Man coming in a cloud with power 5626
21:36 that you may be able to stand before the S 5626
22:22 The S of Man will go as it has been decreed 5626
22:48 are you betraying the S of Man with 5626
22:69 the S of Man will be seated at the right hand 5626
22:70 "Are you then the S of God?" 5626
24: 7 'The S of Man must be delivered into 5626
Jn 1:34 seen and I testify that this is the S of God." 5626
1:42 "You are Simon s of John. 5626
1:45 Jesus of Nazareth, the s of Joseph." 5626
1:49 "Rabbi, you are the S of God; 5626
1:51 ascending and descending on the S of Man. 5626
3:13 who came from heaven—the S of Man. 5626
3:14 so the S of Man must be lifted up, 5626
3:16 the world that he gave his one and only S, 5626
3:17 For God did not send his S into the world 5626
3:18 in the name of God's one and only S. 5626
3:35 The Father loves the S and has placed 5626
3:36 Whoever believes in the S has eternal life, 5626
3:36 but whoever rejects the S will not see life, 5626
4: 5 of ground Jacob had given *to* his s Joseph. 5626
4:46 a certain royal official whose s lay sick 5626
4:47 and begged him to come and heal his s, 5626
4:50 Your s will live." 5626
4:52 as to the time when his s got better, *NIG*
4:53 "Your s will live." 5626
5:19 the S can do nothing by himself; 5626

Jn 5:19 whatever the Father does the S also does. 5626
5:20 loves the S and shows him all he does. 5626
5:21 so the S gives life to whom he is pleased 5626
5:22 but has entrusted all judgment *to* the S, 5626
5:23 that all may honor the S just as they honor 5626
5:23 not honor the S does not honor the Father, 5626
5:25 when the dead will hear the voice *of* the S 5626
5:26 he has granted the S to have life in himself. 5626
5:27 to judge because he is the S of Man. 5626
6:27 which the S of Man will give you. 5626
6:40 that everyone who looks to the S 5626
6:42 "Is this not Jesus, the s of Joseph, 5626
6:53 unless you eat the flesh *of* the S of Man 5626
6:62 What if you see the S of Man ascend to 5626
6:71 (He meant Judas, *the s of* **Simon** Iscariot, *AIT*
8:28 "When you have lifted up the S of Man, 5626
8:35 but a s belongs to it forever. 5626
8:36 the S sets you free, you will be free indeed. 5626
9:19 "Is this your s?" 5626
9:20 "We know he is our s," 5626
9:35 he said, "Do you believe in the S of Man?" 5626
10:36 blasphemy because I said, 'I am God's S'? 5626
11: 4 that God's S may be glorified through it." 5626
11:27 believe that you are the Christ, the S of God, 5626
12:23 "The hour has come for the S of Man to 5626
12:34 'The S of Man must be lifted up'? 5626
12:34 Who is this 'S of Man'?" 5626
13: 2 Judas Iscariot, *s of* **Simon,** to betray Jesus. *AIT*
13:26 he gave it to Judas Iscariot, *s of* **Simon.** *AIT*
13:31 the S of Man glorified and God is glorified 5626
13:32 God will glorify **the S** in himself, 899[S]
14:13 so that the S may bring glory to the Father. 5626
17: 1 the time has come. Glorify your S, 5626
17: 1 that your S may glorify you. 5626
19: 7 because he claimed to be the S of God." 5626
19:26 "Dear woman, here is your s," 5626
20:31 believe that Jesus is the Christ, the S of God 5626
21:15 "Simon *s of* **John,** do you truly love me *AIT*
21:16 Again Jesus said, "Simon *s of* **John,** *AIT*
21:17 "Simon *s of* **John,** do you love me?" *AIT*
Ac 1:13 James *s of* **Alphaeus** and Simon the Zealot, *AIT*
1:13 and Judas *s of* **James.** *AIT*
4:36 apostles called Barnabas (which means S of Encouragement), 5626
7:21 and brought him up as her own s. 5626
7:56 and the S of Man standing at the right hand 5626
9:20 the synagogues that Jesus is the S of God. 5626
13:21 and he gave them Saul s of Kish, 5626
13:22 'I have found David s of Jesse a man 3836
13:33 " 'You are my S; today I have become your 5626
20: 4 by Sopater *s of* **Pyrrhus** from Berea, *AIT*
23: 6 I am a Pharisee, the s of a Pharisee. 5626
23:16 the s of Paul's sister heard of this plot, 5626
Ro 1: 3 regarding his S, who as to human nature 5626
1: 4 to be the S of God by his resurrection from 5626
1: 9 in preaching the gospel *of* his S, 5626
5:10 to him through the death *of* his S, 5626
8: 3 by sending his own S in the likeness 5626
8:29 to be conformed to the likeness *of* his S, 5626
8:32 He who did not spare his own S, 5626
9: 9 and Sarah will have a s." 5626
1Co 1: 9 *with* his S Jesus Christ our Lord, 5626
4:17 Timothy, my s whom I love, 5451
15:28 then the S himself will be made subject 5626
2Co 1:19 For the S of God, Jesus Christ, 5626
Gal 1:16 to reveal his S in me so that I might preach 5626
2:20 I live by faith *in* the S of God, 5626
4: 4 the time had fully come, God sent his S, 5626
4: 6 God sent the Spirit *of* his S into our hearts, 5626
4: 7 So you are no longer a slave, but a s; 5626
4: 7 you are a s, God has made you also an heir. 5626
4:23 **His s** by the slave woman was born 3525+3836[S]
4:23 but **his s** by the free woman was born as 3836[S]
4:29 At that time **the s** born in the ordinary way 3836[S]
4:29 **the s** born by the power of the Spirit. 3836[S]
4:30 "Get rid of the slave woman and her s, 5626
4:30 for the slave woman's s will never share in 5626
4:30 in the inheritance with the free woman's s." 5626
Eph 4:13 in the faith and in the knowledge *of* the S 5626
Php 2:22 as a s with his father he has served with me 5451
Col 1:13 into the kingdom *of* the S he loves, 5626
1Th 1:10 for his S from heaven, whom he raised 5626
1Ti 1: 2 To Timothy my true s in the faith: 5451
1:18 my s, I give you this instruction in keeping 5451
2Ti 1: 2 *To* Timothy, my dear s: 5451
2: 1 then, my s, be strong in the grace that is 5451
Tit 1: 4 To Titus, my true s in our common faith: 5451
Phm 1:10 I appeal to you for my s Onesimus, 5451
1:10 who became my s while I was in chains. *NIG*
Heb 1: 2 last days he has spoken to us by his S, 5626
1: 3 **The S** is the radiance of God's glory and 4005[S]
1: 5 "You are my S; today I have become your 5626
1: 5 "I will be his Father, and he will be my S"? 5626
1: 8 But about the S he says, "Your throne, 5626
2: 6 the s of man that you care for him? 5626
3: 6 Christ is faithful as a s over God's house. 5626
4:14 Jesus the S of God, let us hold firmly to 5626
5: 5 But God said to him, "You are my S; 5626
5: 8 Although he was a s, he learned obedience 5626
6: 6 to their loss they are crucifying the S 5626
7: 3 the S of God he remains a priest forever. 5626
7:28 which came after the law, appointed the S, 5626
10:29 to be punished who has trampled the S 5626
11:17 about to sacrifice his **one and only s,** 3666
11:24 to be known as the s of Pharaoh's daughter. 5626
12: 5 "My s, do not make light of the Lord's 5626
12: 6 and he punishes everyone he accepts as a s." 5626

Heb 12: 7 For what s is not disciplined by his father? 5626
12:16 sold his **inheritance rights as the oldest s.** 4757
Jas 2:21 for what he did when he offered his s Isaac 5626
1Pe 5:13 and so does my s Mark. 5626
2Pe 1:17 saying, "This is my S, whom I love; 5626
2:15 to follow the way of Balaam s of Beor, 3836
1Jn 1: 3 with the Father and with his S, 5626
1: 7 and the blood *of* Jesus, his S, purifies us 5626
2:22 he denies the Father and the S. 5626
2:23 No one who denies the S has the Father; 5626
2:23 whoever acknowledges the S has the Father 5626
2:24 also will remain in the S and in the Father. 5626
3: 8 The reason the S of God appeared was 5626
3:23 to believe in the name *of* his S, 5626
4: 9 He sent his one and only S into the world 5626
4:10 but that he loved us and sent his S as 5626
4:14 the Father has sent his S to be the Savior of 5626
4:15 If anyone acknowledges that Jesus is the S 5626
5: 5 Only he who believes that Jesus is the S 5626
5: 9 which he has given about his S. 5626
5:10 in the S of God has this testimony 5626
5:10 the testimony God has given about his S. 5626
5:11 and this life is in his S. 5626
5:12 He who has the S has life; 5626
5:12 not have the S of God does not have life. 5626
5:13 to you who believe in the name *of* the S 5626
5:20 We know also that the S of God has come 5626
5:20 even in his S Jesus Christ. 5626
2Jn 1: 3 and from Jesus Christ, the Father's S, will 5626
1: 9 the teaching has both the Father and the S. 5626
Rev 1:13 was someone "like a s of man," 5626
2:18 These are the words of the S of God, 5626
12: 5 She gave birth to a s, a male child, 5626
14:14 on the cloud was one "like a s of man" with 5626
21: 7 and I will be his God and he will be my s. 5626

SON'S (12) [SON]

Ge 30:14 give me some of your s mandrakes." 1201
30:15 Will you take my s mandrakes too?" 1201
30:15 in return for your s mandrakes." 1201
30:16 "I have hired you with my s mandrakes." 1201
37:32 Examine it to see whether it is your s robe." 1201
37:33 He recognized it and said, "It is my s robe! 1201
Ex 4:25 cut off her s foreskin and touched 1201
Lev 18:10 sexual relations with your s daughter 1201
18:15 She is your s wife; do not have sexual 1201
18:17 with either her s daughter or her daughter's 1201
2Sa 14:11 "not one hair of your s head will fall to 1201
1Ki 11:35 from his s hands and give you ten tribes. 1201

SON-IN-LAW (11) [SON]

Jdg 15: 6 they were told, "Samson, the Timnite's s, 3163
19: 5 but the girl's father said to his s, 3163
1Sa 18:18 that I should become the king's s?" 3163
18:21 a second opportunity *to become* my s." 3161
18:22 now *become* his s.' " 3161
18:23 a small matter *to become* the king's s? 3161
18:26 he was pleased to *become* the king's s. 3161
18:27 so that *he might become* the king's s. 3161
22:14 the king's s, captain of your bodyguard 3163
Ne 6:18 since he was s to Shecaniah son of Arah, 3163
13:28 the high priest was s to Sanballat 3163

SONG (81) [SING]

Ex 15: 1 Then Moses and the Israelites sang this s to 8878
15: 2 The LORD is my strength and my s; 2379
Nu 21:17 Then Israel sang this s: "Spring up, O well! 8878
Dt 31:19 down for yourselves this s and teach it to 8878
31:21 this s will testify against them, 8878
31:22 So Moses wrote down this s that day 8878
31:30 the words of this s from beginning to end in 8878
32:44 of Nun and spoke all the words of this s in 8878
Jdg 5: 1 and Barak son of Abinoam **sang** *this* s: 8876
5:12 Wake up, wake up, break out in s! 8877
2Sa 22: 1 words of this s when the LORD delivered 8878
1Ch 16:42 of the other instruments for sacred s. 8877
Job 30: 9 "And now their sons **mock** me **in** s; 5593
36:24 which men *have* **praised in** s. 8876
Ps 18: T He sang to the LORD the words of this s 8878
28: 7 for joy and I will give thanks to him in s. 8877
30: T A psalm. A s. 8877
33: 3 Sing to him a new s; 8877
40: 3 He put a new s in my mouth, 8877
42: 8 at night his s is with me— 8877
45: T A maskil. A wedding s. 8877
46: T According to alamoth. A s. 8877
48: T A s. A psalm of the Sons of Korah. 8877
65: T A psalm of David. A s. 8877
66: T For the director of music. A s. A psalm. 8877
67: T With stringed instruments. A psalm. A s. 8877
68: T Of David. A psalm. A s. 8877
69:12 and I am the s *of* the drunkards. 5593
69:30 in s and glorify him with thanksgiving. 8877
75: T A psalm of Asaph. A s. 8877
76: T A psalm of Asaph. A s. 8877
83: T A s. A psalm of Asaph. 8877
87: T Of the Sons of Korah. A psalm. A s. 8877
88: T A s. A psalm of the Sons of Korah. 8877
92: T A psalm. A s. For the Sabbath day. 8877
95: 2 and extol him with **music and** s. 2369
96: 1 Sing to the LORD a new s; 8877
98: 1 Sing to the LORD a new s, 8877
98: 4 burst into **jubilant** s with music; 8264
108: T A s. A psalm of David. 8877
118:14 The LORD is my strength and my s; 2379
Ps 119:54 the **theme of** my s wherever I lodge. 2369
120: T A s *of* ascents. 8877
121: T A s of ascents. 8877
122: T A s *of* ascents. Of David. 8877
123: T A s *of* ascents. 8877
124: T A s *of* ascents. Of David. 8877
125: T A s *of* ascents. 8877
126: T A s *of* ascents. 8877
127: T A s *of* ascents. Of Solomon. 8877
128: T A s *of* ascents. 8877
129: T A s *of* ascents. 8877
130: T A s *of* ascents. 8877
131: T A s *of* ascents. Of David. 8877
132: T A s *of* ascents. 8877
133: T A s *of* ascents. Of David. 8877
134: T A s *of* ascents. 8877
144: 9 I will sing a new s to you, O God; 8877
149: 1 Sing to the LORD a new s, 8877
Ecc 7: 5 a wise man's rebuke than to listen to the s 8877
SS 1: 1 Solomon's S *of* Songs. 8877
Isa 5: 1 for the one I love a s about his vineyard: 8878
12: 2 the LORD, is my strength and my s; 2379
23:15 to Tyre as in the s *of* the prostitute: 8878
23:16 play the harp well, sing many a s, 8877
24: 9 No longer do they drink wine with a s; 8877
25: 5 so the s *of* the ruthless is stilled. 2369
26: 1 In that day this s will be sung in the land 8877
42:10 Sing to the LORD a new s, 8877
44:23 Burst into s, you mountains, 8262
49:13 burst into s, O mountains! 8262
54: 1 burst into s, shout for joy, 8262
55:12 the mountains and hills will burst into s 8262
La 3:14 they **mock** me **in** s all day long. 5593
Jnh 2: 9 But I, with a s *of* thanksgiving, 7754
Mic 2: 4 they will taunt you with this **mournful** s: 5631
Rev 5: 9 And they sang a new s: "You are worthy 6046
14: 3 And they sang a new s before the throne 6046
14: 3 No one could learn the s except the 144,000 6046
15: 3 and sang the s of Moses the servant of God 6046
15: 3 the servant of God and the s of the Lamb: 6046

SONGS (36) [SING]

1Sa 18: 6 with **joyful** s and with tambourines 8525
2Sa 6: 5 with s and with harps, lyres, tambourines, 8877
23: 1 by the God of Jacob, Israel's singer of s: 2369
1Ki 4:32 and his s numbered a thousand and five. 8877
1Ch 13: 8 with s and with harps, lyres, tambourines, 8877
15:16 as singers *to* **sing** joyful s,
928+4200+7754+8123+9048
Ne 12: 8 was in charge of the s **of thanksgiving.** 2117
12:27 with s **of thanksgiving** and with the music 9343
12:46 for the s *of* praise and thanksgiving to God. 8877
Job 35:10 who gives s in the night, 2369
Ps 32: 7 and surround me with s *of* deliverance. 8260
65: 8 and evening fades *you* **call forth** s **of joy.** 8264
77: 6 I remembered my s in the night. 5593
78:63 and their maidens **had** no **wedding** s; 2146
100: 2 come before him with **joyful** s. 8265
107:22 and tell of his works with s **of joy.** 8262
126: 2 our tongues with s **of joy.** 8262
126: 5 who sow in tears will reap with s **of joy.** 8262
126: 6 will return with s **of joy,** 8262
137: 3 for there our captors asked us for s, 1821+8877
137: 3 our tormentors demanded s of joy; NIH
137: 3 they said, "Sing us one of the s *of* Zion!" 8877
137: 4 How can we sing the s *of* the LORD while 8877
Pr 25:20 is one who sings s to a heavy heart. 8877
Ecc 12: 4 but all their s grow faint; 1426+8877
SS 1: 1 Solomon's Song of S. 8877
Isa 52: 9 Burst into s **of joy** together, 8264
Jer 30:19 From them will come s **of thanksgiving** and 9343
La 3:63 they **mock** me **in** their s. 4947
Eze 26:13 I will put an end to your noisy s, 8877
33:32 nothing more than one who sings love s 8877
Am 5:23 Away with the noise of your s! 8877
8: 3 "the s *in* the temple will turn to wailing. 8878
Eph 5:19 with psalms, hymns and spiritual s. 6046
Col 3:16 and spiritual s with gratitude in your hearts 6046
Jas 5:13 *Let him* **sing** s **of praise.** 6010

SONS (878) [SON]

Ge 5: 4 Adam lived 800 years and had other s 1201
5: 7 Seth lived 807 years and had other s 1201
5:10 Enosh lived 815 years and had other s 1201
5:13 Kenan lived 840 years and had other s 1201
5:16 Mahalalel lived 830 years and had other s 1201
5:19 Jared lived 800 years and had other s 1201
5:22 with God 300 years and had other s 1201
5:26 Methuselah lived 782 years and had other s 1201
5:30 Lamech lived 595 years and had other s 1201
6: 2 the s *of* God saw that the daughters 1201
6: 4 the s *of* God went to the daughters of men 1201
6:10 Noah had three s: Shem, Ham and Japheth. 1201
6:18 you and your s and your wife 1201
7: 7 And Noah and his s and his wife 1201
7:13 On that very day Noah and his s, Shem, 1201
7:13 with his wife and the wives of his three s, 1201
8:16 and your wife and your s and their wives. 1201
8:18 with his s and his wife and his sons' wives. 1201
9: 1 Then God blessed Noah and his s, 1201
9: 8 God said to Noah and to his s with him: 1201
9:18 The s *of* Noah who came out of the ark 1201
9:19 These were the three s *of* Noah, 1201
10: 1 Shem, Ham and Japheth, Noah's s, 1201
10: 1 who themselves had s after the flood. 1201
Ge 10: 2 The s *of* Japheth: 1201
10: 3 The s *of* Gomer: 1201
10: 4 The s *of* Javan: 1201
10: 6 The s *of* Ham: 1201
10: 7 The s *of* Cush: 1201
10: 7 The s *of* Raamah: Sheba and Dedan. 1201
10:20 the s *of* Ham by their clans and languages, 1201
10:21 *S* **were** also **born** to Shem, AIT
10:21 Shem was the ancestor of all the s *of* Eber. 1201
10:22 The s *of* Shem: 1201
10:23 The s *of* Aram: 1201
10:25 Two s were born to Eber: 1201
10:29 All these were s *of* Joktan. 1201
10:31 the s *of* Shem by their clans and languages, 1201
10:32 These are the clans of Noah's s, 1201
11:11 Shem lived 500 years and had other s 1201
11:13 Arphaxad lived 403 years and had other s 1201
11:15 Shelah lived 403 years and had other s 1201
11:17 Eber lived 430 years and had other s 1201
11:19 Peleg lived 209 years and had other s 1201
11:21 Reu lived 207 years and had other s 1201
11:23 Serug lived 200 years and had other s 1201
11:25 Nahor lived 119 years and had other s 1201
19:12 sons-in-law, s or daughters, 1201
22:20 she has borne s to your brother Nahor: 1201
22:23 Milcah bore **these** eight *s* to AIT
22:24 whose name was Reumah, also **had** s: 3528
25: 4 The s *of* Midian were Ephah, Epher, 1201
25: 6 the s *of* his concubines and sent them away 1201
25: 9 His s Isaac and Ishmael buried him in 1201
25:13 These are the names of the s *of* Ishmael, 1201
25:16 These were the s *of* Ishmael, 1201
27:29 and may the s *of* your mother bow down 1201
29:34 because I have borne him three s." 1201
30:20 because I have borne him six s." 1201
30:35 and he placed them in the care of his s. 1201
31: 1 Jacob heard that Laban's s were saying, 1201
32:22 and his eleven s and crossed the ford of 3529
33:19 he bought from the s *of* Hamor, 1201
34: 5 his s were in the fields with his livestock; 1201
34: 7 Now Jacob's s had come in from the fields 1201
34:13 Jacob's s replied deceitfully as they spoke 1201
34:25 two of Jacob's s, Simeon and Levi, 1201
34:27 The s *of* Jacob came upon the dead bodies 1201
35:22 Jacob had twelve s: 1201
35:23 The s *of* Leah: Reuben the firstborn 1201
35:24 The s *of* Rachel: Joseph and Benjamin. 1201
35:25 The s *of* Rachel's maidservant Bilhah: 1201
35:26 The s *of* Leah's maidservant Zilpah: 1201
35:26 These were the s *of* Jacob, 1201
35:29 And his s Esau and Jacob buried him. 1201
36: 5 These were the s *of* Esau, 1201
36: 6 and s and daughters and all the members 1201
36:10 These are the names of Esau's s: 1201
36:11 The s *of* Eliphaz: 1201
36:13 The s *of* Reuel: 1201
36:14 The s *of* Esau's wife Oholibamah daughter 1201
36:15 The s *of* Eliphaz the firstborn of Esau: 1201
36:17 The s *of* Esau's son Reuel: 1201
36:18 The s *of* Esau's wife Oholibamah: 1201
36:19 These were the s *of* Esau (that is, Edom), 1201
36:20 These were the s *of* Seir the Horite, 1201
36:21 These s *of* Seir in Edom were Horite chiefs. 1201
36:22 The s *of* Lotan: Hori and Homam. 1201
36:23 The s *of* Shobal: 1201
36:24 The s *of* Zibeon: Aiah and Anah. 1201
36:26 The s *of* Dishon: 1201
36:27 The s *of* Ezer: Bilhan, Zaavan and Akan. 1201
36:28 The s *of* Dishan: Uz and Aran. 1201
37: 2 the sons of Bilhah and the sons of Zilpah, 1201
37: 2 the sons of Bilhah and the s *of* Zilpah, 1201
37: 3 of his *other* s, because he had been born 1201
37:35 All his s and daughters came to comfort him 1201
41:50 two s were born to Joseph by Asenath 1201
42: 1 there was grain in Egypt, he said to his s, 1201
42: 5 So Israel's s were among those who went 1201
42:11 We are all the s *of* one man. 1201
42:13 the s *of* one man, 1201
42:32 We were twelve brothers, s *of* one father. 1201
42:37 "You may put both of my s to death if I do 1201
44:20 and he is the only one of his mother's s left, NIH
44:27 'You know that my wife bore me **two** *s.* AIT
45:21 So the s *of* Israel did this. 1201
46: 5 and Israel's s took their father Jacob 1201
46: 7 with him to Egypt his s and grandsons 1201
46: 8 These are the names of the s *of* Israel 1201
46: 9 The s *of* Reuben: Hanoch, Pallu, 1201
46:10 The s *of* Simeon: Jemuel, Jamin, 1201
46:11 The s *of* Levi: Gershon, Kohath and Merari. 1201
46:12 The s *of* Judah: Er, Onan, Shelah, 1201
46:12 The s *of* Perez: Hezron and Hamul. 1201
46:13 The s *of* Issachar: Tola, Puah, 1201
46:14 The s *of* Zebulun: Sered, Elon and Jahleel. 1201
46:15 the s Leah bore to Jacob in Paddan Aram, 1201
46:15 These s and daughters of his were 1201
46:16 The s *of* Gad: Zephon, Haggi, Shuni, 1201
46:17 The s *of* Asher: Imnah, Ishvah, 1201
46:17 The s *of* Beriah: Heber and Malkiel. 1201
46:19 The s *of* Jacob's wife Rachel: 1201
46:21 The s *of* Benjamin: Bela, Beker, 1201
46:22 These were the s *of* Rachel who were born 1201
46:24 The s *of* Naphtali: Jahziel, Guni, 1201
46:25 These were the s born to Jacob *by* Bilhah, 1201
46:27 the two s who had been born to Joseph 1201
48: 1 So he took his two s Manasseh and Ephraim 1201
48: 5 your two s born to you in Egypt 1201
48: 8 When Israel saw the s *of* Joseph, he asked, 1201

Ge 48: 9 “They are the s God has given me here,” 1201
48:10 So Joseph brought his s close to him, 4392S
49: 1 Then Jacob called for his s and said: 1201
49: 2 “Assemble and listen, s *of* Jacob; 1201
49: 8 your father's s will bow down to you. 1201
49:33 to his s, he drew his feet up into 1201
50:12 Jacob's s did as he had commanded them: 1201
50:25 And Joseph made the s *of* Israel swear 1201
Ex 1: 1 the names of the s *of* Israel who went 1201
3:22 which you will put on your s and daughters. 1201
4:20 So Moses took his wife and s, 1201
6:14 The s *of* Reuben the firstborn son 1201
6:15 The s *of* Simeon were Jemuel, Jamin, 1201
6:16 of the s *of* Levi according to their records: 1201
6:17 The s *of* Gershon, by clans, 1201
6:18 The s *of* Kohath were Amram, Izhar, 1201
6:19 The s *of* Merari were Mahli and Mushi. 1201
6:21 The s *of* Izhar were Korah, 1201
6:22 The s *of* Uzziel were Mishael, 1201
6:24 The s *of* Korah were Assir, 1201
10: 9 with our s and daughters, 1201
13:13 Redeem every firstborn among your s. 1201
13:15 and redeem each of my firstborn s.’ 1201
13:19 with him because Joseph had made the s 1201
18: 3 and her two s. 1201
18: 5 together with Moses' s and wife, 1201
18: 6 to you with your wife and her two s.” 1201
21: 4 a wife and she bears him s or daughters, 1201
22:29 “You must give me the firstborn of your s. 1201
27:21 and his s are to keep the lamps burning 1201
28: 1 along with his s Nadab and Abihu, 1201
28: 4 for your brother Aaron and his s, 1201
28: 9 and engrave on them the names of the s 1201
28:11 of the s *of* Israel on the two stones the way 1201
28:12 of the ephod as memorial stones for the s 1201
28:21 one for each of the names of the s *of* Israel, 1201
28:29 the names of the s *of* Israel over his heart 1201
28:40 sashes and headbands for Aaron's s, 1201
28:41 on your brother Aaron and his s, 1201
28:43 his s must wear them whenever they enter 1201
29: 4 Then bring Aaron and his s to the entrance 1201
29: 8 Bring his s and dress them in tunics 1201
29: 9 Then tie sashes on Aaron and his s. 1201
29: 9 this way you shall ordain Aaron and his s. 1201
29:10 and his s shall lay their hands on its head. 1201
29:15 and his s shall lay their hands on its head. 1201
29:19 and his s shall lay their hands on its head. 1201
29:20 of the right ears of Aaron and his s, 1201
29:21 on Aaron and his garments and on his s 1201
29:21 Then he and his s and their garments will 1201
29:24 Put all these in the hands of Aaron and his s 1201
29:27 that belong to Aaron and his s: 1201
29:28 from the Israelites for Aaron and his s. 1201
29:32 and his s are to eat the meat of the ram and 1201
29:35 his s everything I have commanded you, 1201
29:44 and will consecrate Aaron and his s 1201
30:19 and his s are to wash their hands and feet 1201
30:30 and his s and consecrate them 1201
31:10 and the garments for his s when they serve 1201
32: 2 your s and your daughters are wearing, 1201
32:29 you were against your own s and brothers, 1201
34:16 of their daughters as wives for your s 1201
34:16 they will lead your s to do the same. 1201
34:20 Redeem all your firstborn s. 1201
35:19 and the garments for his s when they serve 1201
39: 6 like a seal with the names of the s *of* Israel. 1201
39: 7 of the ephod as memorial stones for the s 1201
39:14 one for each of the names of the s *of* Israel, 1201
39:27 For Aaron and his s, 1201
39:41 and the garments for his s when serving 1201
40:12 “Bring Aaron and his s to the entrance to 1201
40:14 Bring his s and dress them in tunics. 1201
40:31 and Moses and Aaron and his s used it 1201
Lev 1: 5 and then Aaron's s the priests shall bring 1201
1: 7 The s *of* Aaron the priest are to put fire on 1201
1: 8 Then Aaron's s the priests shall arrange 1201
1:11 the altar before the LORD, and Aaron's s 1201
2: 2 and take it to Aaron's s the priests. 1201
2: 3 to Aaron and his s; 1201
2:10 to Aaron and his s; 1201
3: 2 Then Aaron's s the priests shall sprinkle 1201
3: 5 Then Aaron's s are to burn it on the altar 1201
3: 8 Then Aaron's s shall sprinkle its blood 1201
3:13 Then Aaron's s shall sprinkle its blood 1201
6: 9 “Give Aaron and his s this command: 1201
6:14 Aaron's s are to bring it before the LORD, 1201
6:16 Aaron and his s shall eat the rest of it, 1201
6:20 the offering Aaron and his s are to bring to 1201
6:25 “Say to Aaron and his s: 1201
7:10 belongs equally to all the s *of* Aaron. 1201
7:31 but the breast belongs to Aaron and his s. 1201
7:34 the priest and his s as their regular share 1201
7:35 by fire that were allotted to Aaron and his s 1201
8: 2 “Bring Aaron and his s, 1201
8: 6 and his s forward and washed them 1201
8:13 Then he brought Aaron's s forward, 1201
8:14 Aaron and his s laid their hands on its head. 1201
8:18 Aaron and his s laid their hands on its head. 1201
8:22 Aaron and his s laid their hands on its head. 1201
8:24 Moses also brought Aaron's s forward 1201
8:27 of Aaron and his s and waved them before 1201
8:30 on Aaron and his garments and on his s 1201
8:30 and his s and their garments. 1201
8:31 Moses then said to Aaron and his s, 1201
8:31 saying, ‘Aaron and his s are to eat it.’ 1201
8:36 So Aaron and his s did everything 1201
9: 1 and his s and the elders of Israel. 1201
Lev 9: 9 His s brought the blood to him, 1201
9:12 His s handed him the blood, 1201
9:18 His s handed him the blood, 1201
10: 1 Aaron's s Nadab and Abihu took their censers, 1201
10: 4 s *of* Aaron's uncle Uzziel, 1201
10: 6 Then Moses said to Aaron and his s Eleazar 1201
10: 9 “You and your s are not to drink wine 1201
10:12 Moses said to Aaron and his remaining s, 1201
10:14 and your s and your daughters may eat 1201
10:16 Aaron's remaining s, and asked, 1201
13: 2 to Aaron the priest or to one of his s who is 1201
16: 1 the death of the two s *of* Aaron who died 1201
17: 2 to Aaron and his s and to all the Israelites 1201
21: 1 “Speak to the priests, the s *of* Aaron, 1201
21:24 to Aaron and his s and to all the Israelites. 1201
22: 2 “Tell Aaron and his s to treat with respect 1201
22:18 to Aaron and his s and to all the Israelites 1201
24: 9 It belongs to Aaron and his s, 1201
26:29 of your s and the flesh of your daughters. 1201
Nu 1:10 from the s *of* Joseph: from Ephraim 1201
1:32 From the s *of* Joseph: From the 1201
3: 2 of the s *of* Aaron were Nadab the firstborn 1201
3: 3 Those were the names of Aaron's s, 1201
3: 4 They had no s; 1201
3: 9 Give the Levites to Aaron and his s; 1201
3:10 Appoint Aaron and his s to serve as priests; 1201
3:17 These were the names of the s *of* Levi: 1201
3:38 Moses and Aaron and his s were to camp to 1201
3:48 the additional Israelites to Aaron and his s.” 1201
3:51 the redemption money to Aaron and his s, 1201
4: 5 Aaron and his s are to go in and take down 1201
4:15 and his s have finished covering 1201
4:19 Aaron and his s are to go into the sanctuary 1201
4:27 under the direction of Aaron and his s. 1201
6:23 “Tell Aaron and his s, 1201
8:13 the Levites stand in front of Aaron and his s 1201
8:18 the Levites in place of all the **firstborn** *s* AIT
8:19 as gifts to Aaron and his s to do the work at 1201
8:22 under the supervision of Aaron and his s. 1201
10: 8 “The s *of* Aaron, the priests, 1201
16: 1 Dathan and Abiram, s *of* Eliab, 1201
16:12 Dathan and Abiram, the s *of* Eliab. 1201
18: 1 your s and your father's family are to bear 1201
18: 1 and you and your s alone are to bear 1201
18: 2 and your s minister before the Tent of 1201
18: 7 But only you and your s may serve 1201
18: 8 to you and your s as your portion 1201
18: 9 that part belongs to you and your s. 1201
18:11 I give this to you and your s and daughters 1201
18:19 to the LORD I give to you and your s 1201
21:29 given up his s as fugitives and his daughters 1201
21:35 together with his s and his whole army, 1201
24:17 the skulls of all the s *of* Sheth. 1201
26: 9 and the s *of* Eliab were Nemuel, 1201
26:19 Er and Onan were s *of* Judah, 1201
26:33 (Zelophehad son of Hepher had no s; 1201
27: 3 but he died for his own sin and left no s. 1201
Dt 2:33 together with his s and his whole army. 1201
7: 3 Do not give your daughters to their s 1201
7: 3 or take their daughters for your s, 1201
7: 4 for they will turn your s away 1201
11: 6 s *of* Eliab the Reubenite, 1201
12:12 you, your s and daughters, 1201
12:18 you, your s and daughters, 1201
12:31 even burn their s and daughters in the fire 1201
16:11 you, your s and daughters, 1201
16:14 you, your s and daughters, 1201
21: 5 The priests, the s *of* Levi, 1201
21:15 both bear him s but the firstborn is the son 1201
21:16 when he wills his property to his s, 1201
28:32 Your s and daughters will be given 1201
28:41 You will have s and daughters but you will 1201
28:53 the flesh of the s and daughters 1201
31: 9 to the priests, the s *of* Levi, 1201
32: 8 according to the number of the s *of* Israel. 1201
32:19 because he was angered by his s 1201
33:24 “Most blessed of s is Asher; 1201
Jos 5: 7 So he raised up their s in their place, 1201
7:24 the gold wedge, his s and daughters, 1201
13:31 for half of the s *of* Makir, clan by clan. 1201
14: 4 the s *of* Joseph had become two tribes— 1201
17: 3 had no s but only daughters, 1201
17: 6 received an inheritance among the s. 1201
24: 4 but Jacob and his s went down to Egypt. 1201
24:32 for a hundred pieces of silver from the s 1201
Jdg 1:20 who drove from it the three s *of* Anak. 1201
3: 6 and gave their own daughters to their s, 1201
8:19 my brothers, the s *of* my own mother. 1201
8:30 He had seventy s of his own, 1201
9: 2 to have all seventy *of* Jerub-Baal's s rule 1201
9: 5 seventy brothers, the s *of* Jerub-Baal. 1201
9:18 murdered his seventy s on a single stone, 1201
9:24 the crime against Jerub-Baal's seventy s, 1201
10: 4 He had thirty s, who rode thirty donkeys. 1201
11: 2 Gilead's wife also bore him s, 1201
12: 9 He had thirty s and thirty daughters. 1201
12: 9 for his s he brought in thirty young women 1201
12:14 He had forty s and thirty grandsons, 1201
17: 5 and some idols and installed one of his s 1201
17:11 the young man was to him like one of his s. 1201
18:30 and his s were priests for the tribe of Dan 1201
Ru 1: 1 together with his wife and two s, 1201
1: 2 and the names of his two s were Mahlon 1201
1: 3 died, and she was left with her two s. 1201
1: 5 and Naomi was left without her two s 3529
1:11 Am I going to have any more s, 1201
Ru 1:12 a husband tonight and then gave birth to s— 1201
4:15 and who is better to you than seven s, 1201
1Sa 1: 3 Hophni and Phinehas, the two s *of* Eli, 1201
1: 4 to his wife Peninnah and to all her s 1201
1: 8 Don't I mean more to you than ten s?” 1201
2: 5 but she who has had many s pines away. 1201
2:12 Eli's s were wicked men; 1201
2:21 and gave birth to three s and two daughters. 1201
2:22 heard about everything his s were doing 1201
2:24 my s; it is not a good report that I hear 1201
2:25 His s, however, did not listen NIH
2:29 Why do you honor your s more than me 1201
2:34 “ ‘And what happens to your two s, 1201
3:13 his s made themselves contemptible, 1201
4: 4 And Eli's two s, Hophni and Phinehas, 1201
4:11 and Eli's two s, Hophni and Phinehas, died. 1201
4:17 Also your two s, Hophni and Phinehas, 1201
8: 1 he appointed his s as judges for Israel. 1201
8: 3 But his s did not walk in his ways. 1201
8: 5 and your s do not walk in your ways; 1201
8:11 He will take your s and make them serve 1201
12: 2 and my s are here with you. 1201
14:49 Saul's s were Jonathan, Ishvi and 1201
14:51 and Abner's father Ner were s *of* Abiel. 1201
16: 1 I have chosen one of his s to be king.” 1201
16: 5 and his s and invited them to the sacrifice. 1201
16:10 Jesse had seven of his s pass 1201
16:11 “Are these all the s you have?” 5853
17:12 Jesse had eight s, and in Saul's time 1201
17:13 Jesse's three oldest s had followed Saul to 1201
28:19 tomorrow you and your s will be with me. 1201
30: 3 and s and daughters taken captive. 1201
30: 6 each one was bitter in spirit because of his s 1201
31: 2 pressed hard after Saul and his s, 1201
31: 2 and they killed his s Jonathan, 1201
31: 6 So Saul and his three s and his armor-bearer 1201
31: 7 and that Saul and his s had died, 1201
31: 8 and his three s fallen on Mount Gilboa. 1201
31:12 the bodies of Saul and his s from the wall 1201
2Sa 2:18 The three s *of* Zeruiah were there: 1201
3: 2 S were born to David in Hebron: 1201
3:39 these s *of* Zeruiah are too strong for me. 1201
4: 2 they were s *of* Rimmon the Beerothite from 1201
4: 5 the s *of* Rimmon the Beerothite, 1201
4: 9 the s *of* Rimmon the Beerothite, 1201
5:13 and more s and daughters were born to him. 1201
6: 3 Uzzah and Ahio, s *of* Abinadab, 1201
8:18 and David's s were royal advisers. 1201
9:10 and your s and your servants are to farm 1201
9:10 Ziba had fifteen s and twenty servants.) 1201
9:11 at David's table like one of the king's s. 1201
13:23 he invited all the king's s to come there. 1201
13:27 and the rest of the king's s. 1201
13:29 Then all the king's s got up, 1201
13:30 “Absalom has struck down all the king's s; 1201
13:33 the report that all the king's s are dead. 1201
13:35 “See, the king's s are here; 1201
13:36 the king's s came in, wailing loudly. 1201
14: 6 I your servant had two s. 1201
14:27 Three s and a daughter were born 1201
15:27 You and Abiathar take your two s with you. 1201
15:36 Their two s, Ahimaaz son of Zadok 1201
16:10 and I have in common, you s *of* Zeruiah? 1201
19: 5 and the lives of your s and daughters and 1201
19:17 and his fifteen s and twenty servants. 1201
19:22 and I have in common, you s *of* Zeruiah? 1201
21: 8 the two s *of* Aiah's daughter Rizpah, 1201
21: 8 with the five s *of* Saul's daughter Merab, 1201
23:32 the s *of* Jashen, Jonathan 1201
1Ki 1: 9 He invited all his brothers, the king's s, 1201
1:19 and sheep, and has invited all the king's s, 1201
1:25 He has invited all the king's s, 1201
2: 7 the s *of* Barzillai of Gilead and let them be 1201
4: 3 and Ahijah, s *of* Shisha— 1201
4:31 Calcol and Darda, the s *of* Mahol. 1201
8:25 if only your s are careful in all they do 1201
9: 6 if you or your s turn away from me and do 1201
13:11 whose s came and told him all that the man 1201
13:12 And his s showed him which road the man 1201
13:13 So he said to his s, “Saddle the donkey 1201
13:27 The prophet said to his s, “When I die, 1201
13:31 After burying him, he said to his s, 1201
20:35 the s *of* the prophets said to his companion, 1201
2Ki 4: 4 and shut the door behind you and your s. 1201
4: 5 the door behind her and her s. 1201
4: 7 You and your s can live on what is left.” 1201
9:26 the blood of Naboth and the blood of his s, 1201
10: 1 in Samaria seventy s of the house of Ahab. 1201
10: 2 since your master's s are with you 1201
10: 3 the best and most worthy of your master's s 1201
10: 6 take the heads of your master's s and come 1201
14: 6 Yet he did not put the s *of* the assassins 1201
17:17 They sacrificed their s and daughters in 1201
19:37 his s Adrammelech and Sharezer cut him 1201
25: 7 the s *of* Zedekiah before his eyes. 1201
1Ch 1: 4 The s *of* Noah: Shem, Ham and Japheth. 1201
1: 5 The s *of* Japheth: Gomer, Magog, Madai, 1201
1: 6 The s *of* Gomer: Ashkenaz, 1201
1: 7 The s *of* Javan: Elishah, Tarshish, 1201
1: 8 s *of* Ham: Cush, Mizraim, Put and Canaan. 1201
1: 9 The s *of* Cush: Seba, Havilah, 1201
1: 9 The s *of* Raamah: Sheba and Dedan. 1201
1:17 The s *of* Shem: Elam, Asshur, 1201
1:17 The s *of* Aram: Uz, Hul, Gether 1201
1:19 Two s were born to Eber: 1201
1:23 All these were s *of* Joktan. 1201
1:28 The s *of* Abraham: Isaac and Ishmael. 1201

1Ch 1:31 These were the s *of* Ishmael. 1201
1:32 The s born to Keturah, 1201
1:32 The s *of* Jokshan: Sheba and Dedan. 1201
1:33 The s *of* Midian: Ephah, Epher, 1201
1:34 The s *of* Isaac: Esau and Israel. 1201
1:35 The s *of* Esau: Eliphaz, Reuel, 1201
1:36 The s *of* Eliphaz: Teman, Omar, 1201
1:37 The s *of* Reuel: Nahath, Zerah, 1201
1:38 The s *of* Seir: Lotan, Shobal, 1201
1:39 The s *of* Lotan: Hori and Homam. 1201
1:40 The s *of* Shobal: Alvan, Manahath, 1201
1:40 The s *of* Zibeon: Aiah and Anah. 1201
1:41 The s *of* Dishon: Hemdan, Eshban, 1201
1:42 The s *of* Ezer: Bilhan, Zaavan and Akan. 1201
1:42 The s *of* Dishan: Uz and Aran. 1201
2:1 These were the s *of* Israel: 1201
2:3 The s *of* Judah: Er, Onan and Shelah. 1201
2:4 Judah had five s in all. 1201
2:5 The s *of* Perez: Hezron and Hamul. 1201
2:6 The s *of* Zerah: Zimri, Ethan, 1201
2:9 The s born to Hezron were: 1201
2:16 Zeruiah's three s were Abishai, 1201
2:18 These were her s: Jesher, Shobab 1201
2:25 The s *of* Jerahmeel the firstborn of Hezron: 1201
2:27 The s *of* Ram the firstborn of Jerahmeel: 1201
2:28 The s *of* Onam: Shammai and Jada. 1201
2:28 The s *of* Shammai: Nadab and Abishur. 1201
2:30 The s *of* Nadab: Seled and Appaim. 1201
2:32 The s *of* Jada, Shammai's brother: 1201
2:33 The s *of* Jonathan: Peleth and Zaza. 1201
2:34 Sheshan had no s—only daughters. 1201
2:42 The s *of* Caleb the brother of Jerahmeel: 1201
2:43 The s *of* Hebron: Korah, Tappuah, 1201
2:47 The s *of* Jahdai: Regem, Jotham, 1201
2:50 The s *of* Hur the firstborn of Ephrathah: 1201
3:1 These were the s *of* David born to him 1201
3:9 All these were the s *of* David, 1201
3:9 besides his s *by* his concubines. 1201
3:15 The s *of* Josiah: Johanan the firstborn, 1201
3:19 The s *of* Pedaiah: Zerubbabel and Shimei. 1201
3:19 The s *of* Zerubbabel: Meshullam and 1201
3:21 and the s *of* Rephaiah, of Arnan, 1201
3:22 Shemaiah and his s: 1201
3:23 The s *of* Neariah: Elioenai, Hizkiah 1201
3:24 The s *of* Elioenai: Hodaviah, 1201
4:3 These were the s *of* Etam: 1201S
4:7 The s *of* Helah: Zereth, Zohar, Ethnan, 1201
4:13 The s *of* Kenaz: Othniel and Seraiah. 1201
4:13 The s *of* Othniel: Hathath and Meonothai. 1201
4:15 The s *of* Caleb son of Jephunneh: 1201
4:16 The s *of* Jehallelel: Ziph, Ziphah, 1201
4:17 The s *of* Ezrah: Jether, Mered, 1201
4:19 The s *of* Hodiah's wife, 1201
4:20 The s *of* Shimon: Amnon, Rinnah, 1201
4:21 The s *of* Shelah son of Judah: 1201
4:27 Shimei had sixteen s and six daughters, 1201
4:42 Neariah, Rephaiah and Uzziel, the s *of* Ishi, 1201
5:1 The s *of* Reuben the firstborn 1201
5:1 his rights as firstborn were given to the s 1201
5:3 the s *of* Reuben the firstborn of Israel: 1201
5:14 These were the s *of* Abihail son of Huri, 1201
6:1 s *of* Levi: Gershon, Kohath and Merari. 1201
6:2 The s *of* Kohath: Amram, Izhar, 1201
6:3 The s *of* Aaron: Nadab, Abihu, 1201
6:16 s *of* Levi: Gershon, Kohath and Merari. 1201
6:17 These are the names of the s *of* Gershon: 1201
6:18 The s *of* Kohath: Amram, Izhar, 1201
6:19 The s *of* Merari: Mahli and Mushi. 1201
6:28 The s *of* Samuel: Joel the firstborn 1201
6:33 together with their s: 1201
7:1 The s *of* Issachar: Tola, Puah, 1201
7:2 The s *of* Tola: Uzzi, Rephaiah, 1201
7:3 The s *of* Izrahiah: Michael, Obadiah, 1201
7:6 Three s of Benjamin: Bela, Beker NIH
7:7 The s *of* Bela: Ezbon, Uzzi, 1201
7:8 The s *of* Beker: Zemirah, Joash, 1201
7:8 All these were the s *of* Beker. 1201
7:10 The s *of* Bilhan: Jeush, Benjamin, 1201
7:11 All these s *of* Jediael were heads 1201
7:13 The s *of* Naphtali: Jahziel, Guni, 1201
7:16 and his s were Ulam and Rakem. 1201
7:17 These were the s *of* Gilead son of Makir, 1201
7:19 The s *of* Shemida were: 1201
7:30 The s *of* Asher: Imnah, Ishvah, 1201
7:31 The s *of* Beriah: Heber and Malkiel, 1201
7:33 The s *of* Japhlet: Pasach, Bimhal 1201
7:33 These were Japhlet's s. 1201
7:34 The s *of* Shomer: Ahi, Rohgah, 1201
7:35 The s *of* his brother Helem: 1201
7:36 The s *of* Zophah: Suah, Harnepher, 1201
7:38 The s *of* Jether: Jephunneh, 1201
7:39 The s *of* Ulla: Arah, Hanniel and Rizia. 1201
8:3 The s of Bela were: Addar, Gera, Abihud, 1201
8:8 S were born to Shaharaim in Moab NIH
8:10 These were his s, heads of families. 1201
8:12 The s *of* Elpaal: Eber, Misham, 1201
8:16 Ishpah and Joha were the s *of* Beriah. 1201
8:18 Izliah and Jobab were the s *of* Elpaal. 1201
8:21 Beraiah and Shimrath were the s *of* Shimei. 1201
8:25 Iphdeiah and Penuel were the s *of* Shashak. 1201
8:27 Elijah and Zicri were the s *of* Jeroham. 1201
8:35 The s *of* Micah: Pithon, Melech, 1201
8:38 Azel had six s, and these were their names: 1201
8:38 All these were the s *of* Azel. 1201
8:39 The s *of* his brother Eshek: 1201
8:40 The s *of* Ulam were brave warriors who could handle the bow. 1201
1Ch 8:40 They had many s and grandsons— 1201
9:5 Asaiah the firstborn and his s. 1201
9:41 The s *of* Micah: Pithon, Melech, 1201
9:44 Azel had six s, and these were their names: 1201
9:44 These were the s *of* Azel. 1201
10:2 pressed hard after Saul and his s, 1201
10:2 and they killed his s Jonathan, 1201
10:6 So Saul and his three s died, 1201
10:7 and that Saul and his s had died, 1201
10:8 and his s fallen on Mount Gilboa. 1201
10:12 and his s and brought them to Jabesh. 1201
11:34 the s *of* Hashem the Gizonite, 1201
11:44 and Jeiel the s *of* Hotham the Aroerite, 1201
11:46 Jeribai and Joshaviah the s *of* Elnaam, 1201
12:3 and Joash the s *of* Shemaah the Gibeathite; 1201
12:3 Jeziel and Pelet the s *of* Azmaveth; 1201
12:7 and Zebadiah the s *of* Jeroham from Gedor. 1201
14:3 the father of more s and daughters. 1201
16:13 O s *of* Jacob, his chosen ones. 1201
16:42 The s *of* Jeduthun were stationed at 1201
17:11 to succeed you, one of your own s, 1201
18:17 and David's s were chief officials at 1201
21:20 his four s who were with him hid 1201
23:6 into groups corresponding to the s *of* Levi: 1201
23:8 The s *of* Ladan: Jehiel the first, 1201
23:9 The s *of* Shimei: Shelomoth, 1201
23:10 And the s *of* Shimei: Jahath, Ziza, 1201
23:10 These were the s *of* Shimei—four in all. 1201
23:11 but Jeush and Beriah did not have many s; 1201
23:12 The s *of* Kohath: Amram, Izhar, 1201
23:13 The s *of* Amram: Aaron and Moses. 1201
23:14 The s *of* Moses the man of God were 1201
23:15 The s *of* Moses: Gershom and Eliezer. 1201
23:17 Eliezer had no other s, 1201
23:17 but the s *of* Rehabiah were very numerous. 1201
23:18 The s *of* Izhar: Shelomith was the first. 1201
23:19 The s *of* Hebron: Jeriah the first, 1201
23:20 The s *of* Uzziel: Micah the first 1201
23:21 The s *of* Merari: Mahli and Mushi. 1201
23:21 The s *of* Mahli: Eleazar and Kish. 1201
23:22 Eleazar died without having s: 1201
23:22 Their cousins, the s *of* Kish, married them. 1201
23:23 The s *of* Mushi: Mahli, Eder 1201
24:1 These were the divisions of the s *of* Aaron: 1201
24:1 The s *of* Aaron were Nadab, Abihu, 1201
24:2 and they had no s; 1201
24:20 from the s *of* Amram: Shubael; 1201
24:20 from the s *of* Shubael: Jehdeiah. 1201
24:21 Rehabiah, from his s: Isshiah was the first. 1201
24:22 from the s *of* Shelomoth: Jahath. 1201
24:23 The s *of* Hebron: Jeriah the first, 1201
24:24 from the s *of* Micah: Shamir. 1201
24:25 from the s *of* Isshiah: Zechariah. 1201
24:26 The s *of* Merari: Mahli and Mushi. 1201
24:27 The s *of* Merari: from Jaaziah: 1201
24:28 From Mahli: Eleazar, who had no s. 1201
24:30 the s *of* Mushi: Mahli, Eder and Jerimoth. 1201
25:1 set apart some of the s *of* Asaph, 1201
25:2 From the s *of* Asaph: Zaccur, Joseph, 1201
25:2 The s *of* Asaph were under the supervision 1201
25:3 As for Jeduthun, from his s: 1201
25:4 As for Heman, from his s: 1201
25:5 All these were s *of* Heman the king's seer. 1201
25:5 God gave Heman fourteen s 1201
25:9 fell to Joseph, his s and relatives, 1201
25:9 to Gedaliah, he and his relatives and s, 1201
25:10 the third to Zaccur, his s and relatives, 1201
25:11 the fourth to Izri, his s and relatives, 1201
25:12 the fifth to Nethaniah, his s and relatives, 1201
25:13 the sixth to Bukkiah, his s and relatives, 1201
25:14 the seventh to Jesarelah, his s and relatives, 1201
25:15 the eighth to Jeshaiah, his s and relatives, 1201
25:16 the ninth to Mattaniah, his s and relatives, 1201
25:17 the tenth to Shimei, his s and relatives, 1201
25:18 the eleventh to Azarel, his s and relatives, 1201
25:19 the twelfth to Hashabiah, his s and relatives, 1201
25:20 thirteenth to Shubael, his s and relatives, 1201
25:21 fourteenth to Mattithiah, his s and relatives, 1201
25:22 fifteenth to Jerimoth, his s and relatives, 1201
25:23 sixteenth to Hananiah, his s and relatives, 1201
25:24 to Joshbekashah, his s and relatives, 1201
25:25 eighteenth to Hanani, his s and relatives, 1201
25:26 nineteenth to Mallothi, his s and relatives, 1201
25:27 twentieth to Eliathah, his s and relatives, 1201
25:28 to Hothir, his s and relatives, 1201
25:29 to Giddalti, his s and relatives, 1201
25:30 to Mahazioth, his s and relatives, 1201
25:31 to Romamti-Ezer, his s and relatives, 1201
26:1 one of the s *of* Asaph. 1201
26:2 Meshelemiah had s: Zechariah the firstborn, 1201
26:4 Obed-Edom also had s: 1201
26:6 His son Shemaiah also had s, 1201
26:7 The s *of* Shemaiah: Othni, 1201
26:8 they and their s and their relatives 1201
26:9 Meshelemiah had s and relatives, 1201
26:10 Hosah the Merarite had s: 1201
26:11 The s and relatives of Hosah were 13 in all. 1201
26:15 and the lot for the storehouse fell to his s. 1201
26:22 the s *of* Jehieli, 1201
26:29 and his s were assigned duties away from 1201
27:32 of Hacmoni took care of the king's s. 1201
28:1 to the king and his s, 1201
28:4 and from my father's s he was pleased 1201
28:5 Of all my s—and the LORD has given me 1201
29:24 as well as all of King David's s, 1201
2Ch 5:12 Jeduthun and their s and relatives— 1201
6:16 if only your s are careful in all they do 1201
2Ch 11:14 and his s had rejected them as priests of 1201
11:19 She bore him s: 1201
11:21 twenty-eight s and sixty daughters. 1201
11:23 of his s throughout the districts of Judah 1201
13:9 the s *of* Aaron, and the Levites, 1201
13:10 The priests who serve the LORD are s 1201
13:21 and had twenty-two s and sixteen daughters. 1201
21:2 Jehoram's brothers, the s *of* Jehoshaphat, 1201
21:2 All these were s *of* Jehoshaphat king 1201
21:14 to strike your people, your s, your wives 1201
21:17 together with his s and wives. 1201
22:1 had killed all the older s. NIH
22:8 of Judah and the s *of* Ahaziah's relatives, 1201
23:11 and his s brought out the king's son and put 1201
24:3 and he had s and daughters. 1201
24:7 Now the s *of* that wicked woman Athaliah 1201
24:27 The account of his s, 1201
25:4 Yet he did not put their s to death, 1201
28:3 of Ben Hinnom and sacrificed his s in 1201
28:8 two hundred thousand wives, s and 1201
29:9 by the sword and why our s and daughters 1201
29:11 My s, do not be negligent now, 1201
31:18 and the s and daughters of 1201
32:21 of his s cut him down with the sword. 3665+5055
33:6 He sacrificed his s in the fire in the Valley 1201
36:20 and his s until the kingdom of Persia came 1201
Ezr 3:9 Jeshua and his s and brothers and Kadmiel 1201
3:9 and his s (descendants of Hodaviah) and 1201
3:9 and the s *of* Henadad and their sons 1201
3:9 of Henadad and their s and brothers— 1201
3:10 the Levites (the s *of* Asaph) with cymbals, 1201
6:10 for the well-being of the king and his s. 10120
7:23 against the realm of the king and of his s? 10120
8:18 and Sherebiah's s and brothers, 18 men; 1201
9:2 as wives for themselves and their s, 1201
9:12 in marriage to their s or take their daughters 1201
9:12 or take their daughters for your s. 1201
Ne 3:3 The Fish Gate was rebuilt by the s 1201
4:14 your s and your daughters, 1201
5:2 "We and our s and daughters are numerous; 1201
5:5 as our countrymen and though our s are 1201
5:5 yet we have to subject our s and daughters 1201
9:23 You made their s as numerous as the stars 1201
9:24 Their s went in and took possession of 1201
10:9 Binnui of the s *of* Henadad, Kadmiel, 1201
10:28 and all their s and daughters who are able 1201
10:30 around us or take their daughters for our s. 1201
10:36 we will bring the firstborn of our s and 1201
13:25 your daughters in marriage to their s, 1201
13:25 in marriage for your s or for yourselves. 1201
13:28 One of the s *of* Joiada son of Eliashib 1201
Est 5:11 to them about his vast wealth, his many s, 1201
9:10 the ten s *of* Haman son of Hammedatha, 1201
9:12 the ten s *of* Haman in the citadel of Susa. 1201
9:13 let Haman's ten s be hanged on gallows." 1201
9:14 and they hanged the ten s *of* Haman. 1201
9:25 and his s should be hanged on the gallows. 1201
Job 1:2 He had seven s and three daughters, 1201
1:4 His s used to take turns holding feasts 1201
1:13 when Job's s and daughters were feasting 1201
1:18 "Your s and daughters were feasting 1201
14:21 If his s are honored, he does not know it; 1201
21:19 up a man's punishment for his s.' 1201
30:9 "And now **their** s mock me in song; 4392S
35:8 and your righteousness only the s *of* men. 1201
42:13 he also had seven s and three daughters. 1201
Ps 11:4 He observes the s *of* men; 1201
14:2 down from heaven on the s *of* men to see 1201
17:14 their s have plenty, and they store up wealth 1201
42:T A maskil of the S *of* Korah. 1201
44:T Of the S *of* Korah. 1201
45:T Of the S *of* Korah. 1201
45:16 Your s will take the place of your fathers; 1201
46:T Of the S *of* Korah. 1201
47:T Of the S *of* Korah. 1201
48:T A song. A psalm of the S *of* Korah. 1201
49:T Of the S *of* Korah. 1201
53:2 down from heaven on the s *of* men to see 1201
69:8 an alien to my own mother's s; 1201
82:6 you are all s *of* the Most High.' 1201
84:T Of the S *of* Korah. 1201
85:T Of the S *of* Korah. 1201
87:T Of the S *of* Korah. A psalm. A song. 1201
88:T A psalm of the S *of* Korah. 1201
89:30 "If his s forsake my law and do 1201
90:3 saying, "Return to dust, O s *of* men." 1201
105:6 O s *of* Jacob, his chosen ones. 1201
106:37 They sacrificed their s and their daughters 1201
106:38 the blood of their s and daughters, 1201
127:3 S are a heritage from the LORD, 1201
127:4 of a warrior are s *born in* one's youth. 1201
128:3 your s will be like olive shoots 1201
132:12 if your s keep my covenant and 1201
132:12 then their s will sit on your throne for ever 1201
144:12 Then our s in their youth will be 1201
Pr 4:1 Listen, my s, to a father's instruction; 1201
5:7 Now then, my s, listen to me; 1201
7:24 Now then, my s, listen to me; 1201
8:32 "Now then, my s, listen to me; 1201
SS 1:6 My mother's s were angry with me 1201
Isa 14:21 Prepare a place to slaughter his s for 1201
23:4 I have neither reared s nor brought 1033
37:38 his s Adrammelech and Sharezer cut him 1201
43:6 Bring my s from afar and my daughters 1201
49:17 Your s hasten back, 1201
49:18 all **your** s gather and come to you. 4392S
49:22 they will bring your s in their arms 1201

Isa 51:12 the s *of* men, who are but grass, 1201
51:18 the s she bore there was none to guide her; 1201
51:18 the s she reared there was none to take her 1201
51:20 Your s have fainted; 1201
54:13 All your s will be taught by the LORD, 1201
56: 5 and a name better than s and daughters; 1201
57: 3 come here, you s *of* a sorceress, 1201
60: 4 your s come from afar, 1201
60: 9 bringing your s from afar, 1201
60:14 The s *of* your oppressors will come bowing 1201
62: 5 so will your s marry you; 1201
63: 8 s who will not be false to me"; 1201
Jer 3:19 " 'How gladly would I treat you like s 1201
3:24 and herds, their s and daughters. 1201
5:17 devour your s and daughters; 1201
6:21 Fathers and s alike will stumble over them; 1201
7:31 in the Valley of Ben Hinnom to burn their s 1201
10:20 My s are gone from me and are no more; 1201
11:22 their s and daughters by famine. 1201
13:14 fathers and s alike, declares the LORD. 1201
14:16 their s or their daughters. 1201
16: 2 and have s or daughters in this place." 1201
16: 3 For this is what the LORD says about the s 1201
19: 5 the high places of Baal to burn their s in 1201
19: 9 I will make them eat the flesh of their s 1201
29: 6 Marry and have s and daughters; 1201
29: 6 for your s and give your daughters 1201
29: 6 so that they too may have s and daughters. 1201
32:35 to sacrifice their s and daughters to Molech, 1201
33:26 and will not choose one of his s to rule over 2446
35: 3 and his brothers and all his **s—** 1201
35: 4 the room of the s *of* Hanan son of Igdaliah 1201
35: 8 Neither we nor our wives nor our s 1201
35:14 of Recab ordered his s not to drink wine 1201
39: 6 of Babylon slaughtered the s *of* Zedekiah 1201
40: 8 Johanan and Jonathan the s *of* Kareah, 1201
40: 8 the s *of* Ephai the Netophathite, 1201
48:46 your s are taken into exile 1201
49: 1 "Has Israel no s? 1201
52:10 of Babylon slaughtered the s *of* Zedekiah 1201
La 4: 2 How the precious s *of* Zion, 1201
Eze 14:16 not save their own s or daughters. 1201
14:18 not save their own s or daughters. 1201
14:22 s and daughters who will be brought out 1201
16:20 " 'And you took your s and daughters 1201
20:31 the sacrifice of your s in the fire— 1201
23: 4 They were mine and gave birth to s 1201
23:10 took away her s and daughters 1201
23:25 They will take away your s and daughters, 1201
23:47 they will kill their s and daughters and burn 1201
24:21 The s and daughters you left 1201
24:25 and their s and daughters as well— 1201
40:46 These are the s *of* Zadok, 1201
46:16 from his inheritance to one of his s, it will 1201
46:17 His inheritance belongs to his s only; 1201
46:18 He is to give his s their inheritance out 1201
Da 11:10 His s will prepare for war and assemble 1201
Hos 1:10 they will be called 's *of* the living God.' 1201
Joel 2:28 Your s and daughters will prophesy, 1201
3: 8 I will sell your s and daughters to 1201
Am 2:11 also raised up prophets from among your s 1201
7:17 your s and daughters will fall by the sword. 1201
Zep 1: 8 and the king's s and all those clad 1201
Zec 9:13 I will rouse your s, O Zion, 1201
9:13 O Zion, against your s, O Greece, 1201
Mt 5: 9 for they will be called s of God. 5626
5:45 that you may be s of your Father in heaven. 5626
13:38 good seed stands for the s of the kingdom. 5626
13:38 The weeds are the s of the evil one, 5626
17:25 from their own s or from others?" 5626
17:26 "Then the s are exempt," Jesus said to him. 5626
20:20 *of* Zebedee's s came to Jesus with her sons 5626
20:20 of Zebedee's sons came to Jesus with her s 5626
20:21 of these two s of mine may sit at your right 5626
21:28 There was a man who had two s. 5451
26:37 and the two s of Zebedee along with him, 5626
27:56 and the mother of Zebedee's s. 5626
Mk 3:17 which means S of Thunder); 5626
10:35 Then James and John, the s of Zebedee, 5626
Lk 5:10 the s of Zebedee, Simon's partners. 5626
6:35 and you will be s of the Most High, 5626
15:11 "There was a man who had two s. 5626
Jn 4:12 as did also his s and his flocks and herds?" 5626
12:36 so that you may become s of light." 5626
21: 2 **the** *s* of Zebedee, and the two other AIT
Ac 2:17 Your s and daughters will prophesy, 5626
7:16 that Abraham had bought from the s 5626
7:29 he settled as a foreigner and had two s. 5626
19:14 Seven s of Sceva, a Jewish chief priest, 5626
Ro 8:14 by the Spirit of God are s of God. 5626
8:19 in eager expectation for the s of God to 5626
8:23 as we wait eagerly for our **adoption as** s, 5625
9: 4 Theirs is the **adoption as** s; 5625
9:26 they will be called 's of the living God.' " 5626
2Co 6:18 and you will be my s and daughters, 5626
Gal 3:26 You are all s of God through faith 5626
4: 5 that we might receive the **full rights of** s. 5625
4: 6 Because you are s, God sent the Spirit 5626
4:22 For it is written that Abraham had two s, 5626
Eph 1: 5 to be **adopted as** his s through Jesus Christ, 5625
1Th 5: 5 You are all s of the light and sons of 5626
5: 5 You are all sons of the light and s of 5626
Heb 2:10 In bringing many s to glory, 5626
11:21 blessed each of Joseph's s, 5626
12: 5 of encouragement that addresses you as s: 5626
12: 7 God is treating you as s. 5626
12: 8 you are illegitimate children and not true s. 5626

SONS-IN-LAW (3) [SON]

Ge 19:12 s, sons or daughters, or anyone else in 3163
19:14 So Lot went out and spoke to his s, 3163
19:14 But his s thought he was joking. 3163

SONS' (5) [SON]

Ge 6:18 and your wife and your s' wives with you. 1201
7: 7 and his s' wives entered the ark to escape 1201
8:18 with his sons and his wife and his s' wives. 1201
46:26 not counting his s' wives— 1201
Lev 10:13 because it is your share and your s' share of 1201

SONSHIP (1) [SON]

Ro 8:15 but you received the Spirit *of* s. 5625

SOON (105) [SOONER]

Ge 19:17 **As s as** they had brought them out, 3869
24:30 **As s as** he had seen the nose ring, 3869
29:13 **As s as** Laban heard the news about Jacob, 3869
34: 7 in from the fields **as s as** they heard 3869
39:18 But **as s as** I screamed for help, 3869
40:10 **As s as** it budded, it blossomed, 3869
41:32 and God will do it s. 4554
42: 7 **As s as** Joseph saw his brothers, 2256
46:29 **As s as** Joseph appeared before him, 2256
Ex 8:29 Moses answered, **"As s as** I leave you, 2180
Nu 16:31 **As s as** he finished saying all this, 3869
Dt 11:17 and you will s perish from the good land 4559
31:16 these people will s prostitute themselves 7756
Jos 2: 7 and **as s as** the pursuers had gone out, 889+3869
3:13 And **as s as** the priests who carry the ark of 3869
3:15 Yet **as s as** the priests who carried 3869
4:11 and **as s as** all of them had crossed, 889+3869
8:19 **As s as** he did this, 3869
1Sa 9:13 **As s as** you enter the town, 3869+4027
17:57 **As s as** David returned from killing 3869
29:10 and leave in the morning **as s as** it is light." 2256
2Sa 5:24 **As s as** you hear the sound of marching in 3869
15:10 **"As s as** you hear the sound of the trumpets, 3869
19:41 S all the men of Israel were coming to 2180
22:45 **as s as** they hear me, they obey me. 4200
1Ki 1:21 **as s as** my lord the king is laid to rest 3869
14:17 As s as she stepped over the threshold of NIH
15:29 **As s as** he began to reign, 3869
16:11 **As s as** he began to reign and was seated on 928
20:36 **as s as** you leave me a lion will kill you." 2180
21:15 **As s as** Jezebel heard 3869
2Ki 5: 7 **As s as** the king of Israel read the letter, 3869
10: 2 **"As s as** this letter reaches you, 3869
10:25 **As s as** Jehu had finished making 3869
1Ch 14:15 **As s as** you hear the sound of marching in 3869
2Ch 12: 7 but will s give them deliverance. 3869+5071
31: 5 **As s as** the order went out, 3869
Ezr 4:23 **As s as** the copy of the letter 10008+10168+10427
Ne 9:28 "But **as s as** they were at rest, 3869
Est 7: 8 As s as the word left the king's mouth, NIH
Job 7:21 For I will s lie down in the dust; 6964
32:22 my Maker would s take me away. 3869+5071
Ps 18:44 **As s as** they hear me, they obey me; 4200
37: 2 for like the grass they will s wither, 4559
37: 2 like green plants they will s die away. NIH
37:36 but *he s* **passed away** and was no more; AIT
94:17 I would s have dwelt in the silence of death. 3869+5071
106:13 But they s forgot what he had done and did 4554
Isa 10:25 **Very** s my anger against you will end 4663+5071+6388
28: 4 **as s as** someone sees it and takes it 889
30:19 **As s as** he hears, he will answer you. 3869
51:14 The cowering prisoners will s be set free; 4554
56: 1 and my righteousness will s be revealed. NIH
Jer 26: 8 But **as s as** Jeremiah finished telling all 3869
27:16 not listen to the prophets who say, **'Very s** 4559
51:33 the time to harvest her will s come." 5071+6388
Eze 11: 3 'Will it not s be time to build houses?' 928+7940
16:47 in all your ways you s became more depraved than they. 3869+5071+7775
23:16 **As s as** she saw them, 4200
36: 8 for they will s come home. 7928
Da 3: 5 **As s as** you hear the sound of the horn, 10002+10089+10168+10530
3: 7 **as s as** they heard the sound of the horn 10002+10168+10232+10341
9:23 **As s as** you began to pray, 928
10:20 S I will return to fight against the prince 6964
Hos 1: 4 I will s punish the house of Jehu 5071+6388
Mt 2: 8 **As s as** you find him, report to me, *2054*
3:16 **As s as** Jesus was baptized, *2317*
24:32 **As s as** its twigs get tender *4020*
Mk 1:29 **As s as** they left the synagogue, *2317*
4:15 **As s as** they hear it, *2317+4020*
4:29 **As s as** the grain is ripe, *2317+4020*
6:54 **As s as** they got out of the boat, *2317*
7:25 In fact, **as s as** she heard about him, *2317*
9:15 **As s as** all the people saw Jesus, *2317*
13:28 **As s as** its twigs get tender *2453+4020*
Lk 1:44 **As s as** the sound of your greeting *6055*
7:11 **S afterward,** Jesus went to *1877+2009+3836*
Jn 13:27 **As s as** Judas took the bread, *5538*
13:30 **As s as** Judas had taken the bread, *2317*
19: 6 **As s as** the chief priests and their officials *4021*
21: 7 *s as* Simon Peter **heard** him say, *AIT*
Ac 17:10 **As s as** it was night, *2311*
17:15 and Timothy to join him as s *as possible*. *5441*
19:29 S the whole city was in an uproar. *2779*
25: 4 and I myself am going there s. *1877+5443*
Ro 16:20 The God of peace will s crush Satan under your feet. *1877+5443*
1Co 4:19 But I will come to you **very** s, *5441*
Php 2:19 in the Lord Jesus to send Timothy to you s, *5441*
2:23 to send him **as s as** I see how things go *323+6055*
2:24 in the Lord that I myself will come s. *5441*
1Ti 3:14 Although I hope to come to you s, *1877+5443*
Tit 3:12 **As s as** I send Artemas or Tychicus to you, *4020*
Heb 8:13 what is obsolete and aging will s disappear. *1584*
13:19 to pray so that I may be restored to you s. *5441*
13:23 If he arrives s, I will come with him to see *5441*
2Pe 1:14 because I know that I will s put it aside, *5442*
3Jn 1:14 I hope to see you s, *2311*
Rev 1: 1 to show his servants what must s take place. *1877+5443*
2:16 I will s come to you and will fight *5444*
3:11 I am coming s. Hold on to what you have, *5444*
11:14 the third woe is coming s. *5444*
22: 6 the things that must s take place." *1877+5443*
22: 7 "Behold, I am coming s! *5444*
22:12 "Behold, I am coming s! *5444*
22:20 "Yes, I am coming s." *5444*

SOONER (6) [SOON]

Jos 4:18 **No s** had they set their feet on the dry ground **than** the waters 3869
Jdg 8:33 **No s** had Gideon died **than** 889+3869
Isa 40:24 **No s** are they planted, 677+1153
40:24 **no s** are they sown, 677+1153
40:24 **no s** do they take root in the ground, 677+1153
66: 8 **no s** is Zion in labor **than** she gives birth 1685

SOOT (3)

Ex 9: 8 of s *from* a furnace and have Moses toss it 7086
9:10 So they took s *from* a furnace and stood 7086
La 4: 8 But now they are blacker than s; 8818

SOOTHED (1) [SOOTHES, SOOTHING]

Isa 1: 6 not cleansed or bandaged or s with oil. 8216

SOOTHES (1) [SOOTHED]

Pr 21:14 A gift given in secret s anger, 4092

SOOTHING (1) [SOOTHED]

Ps 55:21 his words *are* more s than oil, 8216

SOOTHSAYER (1) [SOOTHSAYERS']

Isa 3: 2 the judge and prophet, the s and elder, 7876

SOOTHSAYERS' (1) [SOOTHSAYER]

Jdg 9:37 from the direction of the s' tree." 6726

SOP (KJV) See PIECE OF BREAD

SOPATER (1)

Ac 20: 4 He was accompanied by S son of Pyrrhus *5396*

SOPE (KJV) See LAUNDERER'S SOAP

SOPHERETH (1)

Ne 7:57 the descendants of Sotai, S, Perida, 6072

SORCERER (2) [SORCERY]

Ac 13: 6 There they met a Jewish s and false prophet *3407*
13: 8 But Elymas the s (for that is what his name *3407*

SORCERERS (4) [SORCERY]

Ex 7:11 Pharaoh then summoned wise men and s, 4175
Jer 27: 9 your mediums or your s who tell you, 4177
Da 2: 2 the magicians, enchanters, s and astrologers 4175
Mal 3: 5 I will be quick to testify against s, 4175

SORCERESS (2) [SORCERY]

Ex 22:18 "Do not allow a s to live. 4175
Isa 57: 3 "But you—come here, you sons of a s, 6726

SORCERIES (3) [SORCERY]

Isa 47: 9 of your many s and all your potent spells. 4176
47:12 your magic spells and with your many s, 4176
Na 3: 4 alluring, the mistress of s, 4176

SORCERY (10) [SORCERER, SORCERERS, SORCERESS, SORCERIES]

Lev 19:26 " 'Do not practice divination or s. 6726
Nu 23:23 There is no s against Jacob, 5728
24: 1 he did not resort to s as at other times, 5728
Dt 18:10 who practices divination or s, 6726
18:14 to *those who* **practice** s or divination. 6726
2Ki 17:17 and s and sold themselves to do evil in 5727
21: 6 **practiced** s and divination, 6726
2Ch 33: 6 **practiced** s, divination and witchcraft, 6726
Ac 8: 9 a man named Simon *had* **practiced** s in *3405*
19:19 who had practiced s brought their scrolls *4319*

SORE (14) [SORES]

Lev 13: 3 The priest is to examine the s on his skin, 5596
13: 3 and if the hair in the s has turned white and 5596
13: 3 the sore has turned white and the s appears 5596
13: 5 that the s is unchanged and has not spread 5596
13: 6 s has faded and has not spread in the skin, 5596
13:29 "If a man or woman has a s on the head or 5596
13:30 to examine the s, and if it appears to 5596
13:31 priest examines **this kind of s,** 2021+5596+5999
13:32 the priest is to examine the s, 5596
13:42 if he has a reddish-white s on his bald head 5596
13:43 and if the swollen s on his head 5596
13:44 because of the s on his head. 5596
2Sa 3:29 be without *someone who has a* **running** s 2307
Jer 30:13 no remedy for your s, no healing for you. 4649

SOREK (1)

Jdg 16: 4 the Valley of S whose name was Delilah. 8604

SORELY (KJV) See ANGUISH, BITTERNESS

SORES (13) [SORE]

Lev 13:17 and if the s have turned white, 5596
21:20 or **running** s or damaged testicles. 3539
22:22 with warts or festering or **running s.** 3539
Dt 28:27 **festering** s and the itch, 1734
Job 2: 7 the LORD and afflicted Job with painful s 8825
Isa 1: 6 only wounds and welts and open s, 4804
3:17 the Lord *will* **bring s on** the heads of 8558
Hos 5:13 Ephraim saw his sickness, and Judah his s, 4649
5:13 not able to heal your s. 4649
Lk 16:20 a beggar named Lazarus, **covered with s** *1815*
16:21 Even the dogs came and licked his s. *1814*
Rev 16: 2 and ugly and painful s broke out on *1814*
16:11 of heaven because of their pains and their s, *1814*

SORROW (36) [SORROWFUL, SORROWS]

Ge 42:38 down to the grave in s." 3326
44:31 of our father down to the grave in s. 3326
48: 7 to my s Rachel died in the land of Canaan NIH
Est 9:22 the month when their s was turned into joy 3326
Ps 6: 7 My eyes grow weak with s; 4088
13: 2 with my thoughts and every day have s 3326
31: 9 my eyes grow weak with s, 4088
90:10 yet their span is but trouble and s, 224
107:39 by oppression, calamity and s; 3326
116: 3 I was overcome by trouble and s. 3326
119:28 My soul is weary with s; 9342
Pr 23:29 Who has woe? Who has s? 16
Ecc 1:18 For with much wisdom comes much s; 4088
7: 3 S is better than laughter, 4088
Isa 35:10 and s and sighing will flee away. 3326
51:11 and s and sighing will flee away. 3326
60:20 and your days of s will end. 65
Jer 8:18 O my Comforter in s, 3326
20:18 to see trouble and s and to end my days 3326
31:12 and they will s no more. 1790
31:13 and joy instead of s. 3326
45: 3 The LORD has added s to my pain; 3326
Eze 23:33 You will be filled with drunkenness and s, 3326
Mt 26:38 "My soul is **overwhelmed with** s to the point of death. *4337*
Mk 14:34 "My soul is **overwhelmed with** s to the point of death," *4337*
Lk 22:45 he found them asleep, exhausted from s. *3383*
Ro 9: 2 I have great s and unceasing anguish *3383*
2Co 2: 7 he will not be overwhelmed *by* excessive s. *3383*
7: 7 your **deep** s, your ardent concern for me, *3851*
7: 8 Even if *I* **caused** you s by my letter, *3382*
7: 9 but because *your* s led you to repentance. *3382*
7:10 Godly s brings repentance that leads *3383*
7:10 but worldly s brings death. *3383*
7:11 See what this godly s has produced in you: *3382*
Php 2:27 to spare me s upon sorrow. *3383*
2:27 to spare me sorrow upon s. *3383*

SORROWFUL (3) [SORROW]

Mt 26:37 and he began *to be* s and troubled. *3382*
2Co 6:10 s, yet always rejoicing; *3382*
7: 9 For *you became* s as God intended and *3382*

SORROWS (4) [SORROW]

Ps 16: 4 The s *of* those will increase who run 6780
Isa 53: 3 a man of s, and familiar with suffering. 4799
53: 4 he took up our infirmities and carried our s, 4799
Zep 3:18 The s for the appointed feasts I will remove 5652

SORRY (2)

Ex 2: 6 He was crying, and *she* **felt** s for him. 2798
2Co 7: 9 not because *you were* **made** s, *3382*

SORT (4) [SORTS]

2Ki 9:11 and the s **of things he says,"** 8490
Ecc 10: 5 the s *of* error that arises from a ruler: 3869
2Th 2:10 and in **every** s of evil that deceives those *AIT*
Rev 18:12 **every** *s* of citron wood, *AIT*

SORTS (5) [SORT]

1Ki 12:31 and appointed priests from **all s** 7896
1Ki 13:33 for the high places from **all s** *of* people. 7896
2Ki 17:32 appointed **all s** *of* their own *people* 4946+7896
Pr 1:13 we will get **all** *s of* valuable things AIT
1Co 14:10 Undoubtedly there are all s of languages in *1169*

SOSIPATER (1)

Ro 16:21 as do Lucius, Jason and S, my relatives. *5399*

SOSTHENES (2)

Ac 18:17 on S the synagogue ruler and beat him *5398*
1Co 1: 1 and our brother S, *5398*

SOTAI (2)

Ezr 2:55 the descendants of S, Hassophereth, 6055
Ne 7:57 the descendants of S, Sophereth, Perida, 6055

SOTTISH (KJV) See SENSELESS

SOUGHT (37) [SEEK]

Ex 32:11 Moses **s the favor of** the LORD his God. 906+2704+7156
1Sa 7: 2 and all the people of Israel mourned and s NIH
13:12 *I have* not s the LORD's **favor.'** 2704+7156
13:14 the LORD *has* s **out** a man 1335
2Sa 21: 1 so David s the face of the LORD. 1335
1Ki 10:24 The whole world s audience with Solomon 1335
2Ki 13: 4 Jehoahaz s the LORD's **favor,** 906+2704+7156
2Ch 9:23 the earth s audience with Solomon to hear 1335
14: 7 because *we have* s the LORD our God; 2011
14: 7 *we* s him and he has given us rest 2011
15: 4 and s him, and he was found by them. 1335
15:15 *They* s God eagerly, 1335
17: 4 but s the God of his father 2011
22: 9 who s the LORD with all his heart." 2011
25:20 because *they* s the gods of Edom. 2011
26: 5 He s God during the days of Zechariah, 2011
26: 5 As long as he s the LORD, 2011
31:21 he s his God and worked wholeheartedly. 2011
33:12 In his distress *he* **s the favor of** 906+2704+7156
Ne 12:27 the Levites *were* **s out** from 1335
Ps 34: 4 *I* s the LORD, and he answered me; 2011
77: 2 When I was in distress, *I* s the Lord; 2011
119:45 for *I have* **s out** your precepts. 2011
119:58 *I have* s your face with all my heart; 2704
119:94 *I have* **s out** your precepts. 2011
Isa 9:13 nor *have they* s the LORD Almighty. 2011
62:12 and you will be called S **After,** 2011
Jer 26:21 the king **s to** put him to death. 1335
Eze 25:15 with ancient hostility s to destroy Judah, NIH
26:21 *You will* **be s,** but you will never again 1335
Da 4:36 My advisers and nobles s me **out,** 10114
9:13 *we have* not s **the favor of** the LORD our God 906+2704+7156
Ac 12:20 they now joined together and **s an audience** *4205*
Ro 10: 3 from God and s to establish their own, *2426*
11: 7 What Israel s **so earnestly** it did not obtain, *2118*
Heb 8: 7 no place would *have been* **s for** another. *2426*
12:17 though *he* s the blessing with tears. *1699*

SOUL (129) [SOULS]

Dt 4:29 with all your heart and with all your s. 5883
6: 5 with all your heart and with all your s and 5883
10:12 with all your heart and with all your s, 5883
11:13 with all your heart and with all your s— 5883
13: 3 with all your heart and with all your s. 5883
26:16 with all your heart and with all your s. 5883
30: 2 with all your heart and with all your s 5883
30: 6 with all your heart and with all your s, 5883
30:10 with all your heart and with all your s. 5883
Jos 22: 5 with all your heart and all your s." 5883
23:14 with all your heart and s that not one of all 5883
Jdg 5:21 March on, my s; be strong! 5883
1Sa 1:10 In bitterness of s Hannah wept much and 5883
1:15 I was pouring out my s to the LORD. 5883
14: 7 I am with you **heart and s."** 3869+4222
1Ki 2: 4 before me with all their heart and s, 5883
8:48 to you with all their heart and s in the land 5883
2Ki 23: 3 and decrees with all his heart and all his s, 5883
23:25 and with all his s and with all his strength, 5883
1Ch 22:19 Now devote your heart and s to seeking 5883
2Ch 6:38 to you with all their heart and s in the land 5883
15:12 with all their heart and s. 5883
34:31 and decrees with all his heart and all his s, 5883
Job 3:20 and life to the bitter of s, 5883
7:11 I will complain in the bitterness of my s. 5883
10: 1 and speak out in the bitterness of my s. 5883
21:25 Another man dies in bitterness of s, 5883
27: 2 who has made me taste bitterness of s, 5883
30:25 Has not my s grieved for the poor? 5883
33:18 to preserve his s from the pit, 5883
33:20 and his s loathes the choicest meal. 5883
33:22 His s draws near to the pit, 5883
33:28 He redeemed my s from going down to 5883
33:30 to turn back his s from the pit, 5883
Ps 6: 3 My s is in anguish. 5883
11: 5 and those who love violence his s hates. 5883
19: 7 law of the LORD is perfect, reviving the s. 5883
23: 3 he restores my s. 5883
24: 4 up his s to an idol or swear by what is false. 5883
25: 1 To you, O LORD, I lift up my s; 5883
26: 9 Do not take away my s along with sinners, 5883
31: 7 and knew the anguish of my s. 5883
31: 9 my s and my body with grief. 5883
Ps 34: 2 My s will boast in the LORD; 5883
35: 3 Say to my s, "I am your salvation." 5883
35: 9 Then my s will rejoice in the LORD 5883
35:12 for good and leave my s forlorn. 5883
42: 1 so my s pants for you, O God. 5883
42: 2 My s thirsts for God, for the living God. 5883
42: 4 as I pour out my s: 5883
42: 5 Why are you downcast, O my s? 5883
42: 6 My s is downcast within me; 5883
42:11 Why are you downcast, O my s? 5883
43: 5 Why are you downcast, O my s? 5883
57: 1 for in you my s takes refuge. 5883
57: 8 Awake, my s! 3883
62: 1 My s finds rest in God alone; 5883
62: 5 O my s, in God alone; 5883
63: 1 my s thirsts for you, my body longs for you, 5883
63: 5 My s will be satisfied as with the richest 5883
63: 8 My s clings to you; 5883
77: 2 and my s refused to be comforted. 5883
84: 2 My s yearns, even faints, 5883
86: 4 for to you, O Lord, I lift up my s. 5883
88: 3 For my s is full of trouble 5883
94:19 your consolation brought joy to my s. 5883
103: 1 Praise the LORD, O my s; 5883
103: 2 Praise the LORD, O my s, 5883
103:22 Praise the LORD, O my s. 5883
104: 1 Praise the LORD, O my s. 5883
104:35 Praise the LORD, O my s. 5883
108: 1 I will sing and make music with all my s. 3883
116: 7 Be at rest once more, O my s, 5883
116: 8 O LORD, have delivered my s from death, 5883
119:20 My s is consumed with longing 5883
119:28 My s is weary with sorrow; 5883
119:81 My s faints with longing for your salvation, 5883
130: 5 I wait for the LORD, my s waits, 5883
130: 6 My s waits for the Lord more than 5883
131: 2 But I have stilled and quieted my s; 5883
131: 2 like a weaned child is my s within me. 5883
143: 6 my s thirsts for you like a parched land. 5883
143: 8 for to you I lift up my s. 5883
146: 1 Praise the LORD, O my s. 5883
Pr 1:11 let's waylay some **harmless s;** 2855+5929
2:10 and knowledge will be pleasant to your s. 5883
13:19 A longing fulfilled is sweet to the s, 5883
16:24 sweet to the s and healing to the bones. 5883
18: 7 and his lips are a snare to his s. 5883
19: 8 He who gets wisdom loves his own s; 5883
22: 5 he who guards his s stays far from them. 5883
23:14 with the rod and save his s from death. 5883
24:14 Know also that wisdom is sweet to your s; 5883
25:25 a weary s is good news from a distant land. 5883
29:17 he will bring delight to your s. 5883
Isa 1:14 and your appointed feasts my s hates. 5883
26: 9 My s yearns for you in the night; 5883
38:15 because of this anguish of my s. 5883
53:11 After the suffering of his s, 5883
55: 2 and your s will delight in the richest of fare. 5883
55: 3 hear me, that your s may live. 5883
61:10 my s rejoices in my God. 5883
Jer 32:41 in this land with all my heart and s. 5883
La 3:20 and my s is downcast within me. 5883
3:51 What I see brings grief to my s because 5883
Eze 18: 4 For every **living** s belongs to me, 5883
18: 4 The s who sins is the one who will die. 5883
18:20 The s who sins is the one who will die. 5883
27:31 with anguish of s and with bitter mourning. 5883
Mic 6: 7 the fruit of my body for the sin of my s? 5883
Mt 10:28 the body but cannot kill the s. *6034*
10:28 of the One who can destroy both s and body *6034*
16:26 gains the whole world, yet forfeits his s? *6034*
16:26 a man give in exchange for his s? *6034*
22:37 and with all your s and with all your mind.' *6034*
26:38 "My s is overwhelmed with sorrow to *6034*
Mk 8:36 to gain the whole world, yet forfeit his s? *6034*
8:37 a man give in exchange for his s? *6034*
12:30 with all your s and with all your mind and *6034*
14:34 "My s is overwhelmed with sorrow to *6034*
Lk 1:46 And Mary said: "My s glorifies the Lord *6034*
2:35 And a sword will pierce your own s too." *6034*
10:27 with all your heart and with all your s and *6034*
1Th 5:23 s and body be kept blameless at the coming *6034*
Heb 4:12 it penetrates even to dividing s and spirit, *6034*
6:19 We have this hope as an anchor *for* the s, *6034*
1Pe 2:11 which war against your s. *6034*
2Pe 2: 8 was tormented in his righteous s by *6034*
3Jn 1: 2 even as your s is getting along well. *6034*

SOULS (10) [SOUL]

Job 24:12 and the s *of* the wounded cry out for help. 5883
Pr 11:30 and he who wins s is wise. 5883
Isa 66: 3 and their s delight in their abominations; 5883
Jer 6:16 and you will find rest for your s. 5883
Mt 11:29 and you will find rest *for* your s. *6034*
1Pe 1: 9 goal of your faith, the salvation *of* your s. *6034*
2:25 to the Shepherd and Overseer *of* your s. *6034*
Rev 6: 9 the altar the s of those who had been slain *6034*
18:13 and bodies and s of men. *6034*
20: 4 the s of those who had been beheaded *6034*

SOUND (124) [FINE-SOUNDING, SOUNDED, SOUNDING, SOUNDINGS, SOUNDNESS, SOUNDS]

Ge 3: 8 and his wife heard the s *of* the LORD God 7754
Ex 19:19 and the s *of* the trumpet grew louder 7754
28:35 The s *of* the bells will be heard 7754

Ex 32:17 "There is the s *of* war in the camp." 7754
32:18 replied: "It is not the s *of* victory, 6702+7754
32:18 it is not the s *of* defeat; 6702+7754
32:18 it is the s *of* singing that I hear." 7754
Lev 25: 9 on the Day of Atonement s the trumpet 6296
26:36 that the s *of* a windblown leaf will put them 7754
Nu 10: 9 **s a blast** on the trumpets. 8131
10:10 *to* s the trumpets over your burnt offerings 9546
29: 1 It is a day for you to **s the trumpets.** 9558
Dt 4:12 You heard the s *of* words but saw no form; 7754
Jos 6: 5 When you hear them s a **long** blast on 5432
6:20 and at the s *of* the trumpet, 7754
Jdg 11:34 dancing to the s of tambourines! NIH
1Sa 20:12 *I will* surely **s out** my father by this time 2983
2Sa 5:24 as you hear the s *of* marching in the tops of 7754
6:15 the ark of the LORD with shouts and the s 7754
15:10 "As soon as you hear the s *of* the trumpets, 7754
1Ki 1:40 so that the ground shook with the **s.** 7754
1:41 On hearing the s *of* the trumpet, 7754
14: 6 when Ahijah heard the s *of* her footsteps at 7754
18:41 for there is the s *of* a heavy rain." 7754
2Ki 4:31 but there was no s or response. 7754
6:32 Is not the s *of* his master's footsteps 7754
7: 6 to hear the s *of* chariots and horses and 7754
7:10 not a s *of* anyone— 7754
1Ch 14:15 as you hear the s *of* marching in the tops of 7754
15:19 and Ethan were to s the bronze cymbals; 9048
16: 5 Asaph *was to* s the cymbals, 9048
2Ch 13:12 with their trumpets *will* s the battle cry 8131
13:15 At the **s of** their **battle cry,** 8131
Ezr 3:13 the s *of* the shouts of joy from the sound 7754
3:13 of the shouts of joy from the s *of* weeping, 7754
3:13 And the s was heard far away. 7754
Ne 4:20 Wherever you hear the s *of* the trumpet, 7754
12:43 s of rejoicing in Jerusalem *could* **be heard** 9048
Job 21:12 they make merry to the s *of* the flute. 7754
30:31 and my flute to the s *of* wailing. 7754
37: 4 After that comes the s of his roar; 7754
Ps 66: 8 O peoples, let the s *of* his praise be heard; 7754
81: 3 **S** the ram's horn at the New Moon, 9546
98: 5 with the harp and the s *of* singing, 7754
104: 7 at the s *of* your thunder they took to flight; 7754
115: 7 nor *can they* **utter a s** with their throats. 2047
Pr 3:21 preserve s **judgment** and discernment, 9370
4: 2 I give you s learning, 3202
8:14 Counsel and s **judgment** are mine; 9370
18: 1 he defies all **s judgment.** 9370
22:21 so that you can give s answers 622
Ecc 12: 4 the doors to the street are closed and the s 7754
12: 4 when men rise up at the s *of* birds, 7754
Isa 6: 4 At the s *of* their voices the doorposts 7754
24:18 Whoever flees at the s *of* terror will fall 7754
27:13 And in that day a great trumpet *will* **s.** 9546
51: 3 thanksgiving and the s *of* singing. 7754
65:19 the s *of* weeping and of crying will 7754
66: 6 It is the s *of* the LORD repaying his enemies 7754
Jer 2:21 like a choice vine of s and reliable stock. 3972
4: 5 '**S** the trumpet throughout the land!' 9546
4:19 For I have heard the s *of* the trumpet; 7754
4:21 the battle standard and hear the s *of* 7754
4:29 At the s *of* horsemen and archers 7754
6: 1 **S** the trumpet in Tekoa! 9546
6:17 'Listen to the s *of* the trumpet!' 7754
6:23 They s like the roaring sea as they ride 7754
9:19 The s *of* wailing is heard from Zion: 7754
25:10 s *of* millstones and the light of the lamp. 7754
30:19 of thanksgiving and the s *of* rejoicing. 7754
47: 3 at the s *of* the hoofs of galloping steeds, 7754
48:34 "The s *of* their cry rises from Heshbon 7754
49: 2 "when *I will* s the battle cry 9048
49:21 At the s *of* their fall the earth will tremble; 7754
50:42 They s like the roaring sea as they ride 7754
50:46 At the s *of* Babylon's capture 7754
51:54 "The s *of* a cry comes from Babylon, 7754
51:54 the s of great destruction from the land of NIH
Eze 1:24 I heard the s *of* their wings, 7754
3:12 and I heard behind me a loud rumbling **s**— 7754
3:13 the s *of* the wings of the living creatures 7754
3:13 against each other and the s *of* the wheels 7754
3:13 the wheels beside them, a loud rumbling **s.** 7754
10: 5 The s *of* the wings of the cherubim could 7754
21:22 to slaughter, to s the battle cry, 7754+8123
26:15 the coastlands tremble at the s *of* your fall, 7754
31:16 at the s *of* its fall when I brought it down to 7754
33: 5 Since he heard the s *of* the trumpet but did 7754
37: 7 a **rattling s,** and the bones came together, 8323
Da 3: 5 As soon as you hear the s *of* the horn, 10631
3: 7 as soon as they heard the s *of* the horn, 10631
3:10 that everyone who hears the s *of* the horn, 10631
3:15 Now when you hear the s *of* the horn, flute, 10631
10: 6 and his voice like the s *of* a multitude. 7754
Hos 5: 8 "**S** the trumpet in Gibeah, 9546
Joel 2: 1 s *the* **alarm** on my holy hill. 8131
Hab 3:16 my lips quivered at the **s;** 7754
Zec 8:16 and render true and s judgment 8934
9:14 The Sovereign LORD *will* s the trumpet; 9546
Mt 12:13 completely restored, just as s as the other. *5618*
Lk 1:44 as the s of your greeting reached my ears, *5889*
15:27 because he has him back **safe and s.'** *5617*
Jn 3: 8 You hear its **s,** but you cannot tell where *5889*
Ac 2: 2 a s like the blowing of a violent wind came *2491*
2: 6 When they **heard** this **s,** *1181+5889*
9: 7 they heard the s but did not see anyone. *5889*
20: 9 *When he was* **s asleep,** *608+2965+3836+5678*
1Co 14: 8 Again, if the trumpet *does* not s a clear call, *1443*
15:52 For the **trumpet** *will* **s,** the dead will be *4895*
1Ti 1:10 whatever else is contrary *to* the s doctrine *5617*
1Ti 6: 3 to the s instruction of our Lord Jesus Christ *5617*
2Ti 1:13 keep as the pattern *of* s teaching, *5617*
4: 3 when men will not put up with s doctrine. *5617*
Tit 1: 9 that he can encourage others by s doctrine *5617*
1:13 so that *they will be* s in the faith *5617*
2: 1 in accord *with* s doctrine. *5617*
2: 2 and s in faith, in love and in endurance. *5617*
Rev 1:15 his voice was like the s of rushing waters. *5889*
8: 6 the seven trumpets prepared to s them. *4895*
9: 9 the s of their wings was like the thundering *5889*
10: 7 the seventh angel is about to s *his* **trumpet,** *4895*
14: 2 And I heard a s from heaven like the roar *5889*
14: 2 The s I heard was like that of harpists *5889*
18:22 The s of a millstone will never be heard *5889*

SOUNDED (23) [SOUND]

Lev 25: 9 Then **have** the trumpet s everywhere on 6296
Nu 10: 3 When both *are* s, the whole community 9546
10: 4 If only one *is* s, the leaders— 9546
10: 5 When a trumpet blast *is* s, 9546
Jos 6:16 when the priests s the trumpet **blast,** 9546
6:20 When the trumpets **s,** the people shouted, 9546
Jdg 7:22 When the three hundred trumpets **s,** 9546
2Sa 18:16 Then Joab **s** the trumpet, 9546
20: 1 *He* s the trumpet and shouted, 9546
20:22 So *he* s the trumpet, 9546
1Ki 1:39 Then *they* s the trumpet and all 9546
Ne 4:18 the *man who* s the trumpet stayed with me. 9546
Rev 6: 6 Then I heard what s like a voice among *NIG*
8: 7 The first angel s *his* **trumpet,** *4895*
8: 8 The second angel s *his* **trumpet,** *4895*
8:10 The third angel s *his* **trumpet,** *4895*
8:12 The fourth angel s *his* **trumpet,** *4895*
8:13 because of the trumpet blasts about to *be* s *4895*
9: 1 The fifth angel s *his* **trumpet,** *4895*
9:13 The sixth angel s *his* **trumpet,** *4895*
11:15 The seventh angel s *his* **trumpet,** *4895*
19: 1 After this I heard **what s like** the roar of *6055*
19: 6 Then I heard what s like a great multitude, *5889*

SOUNDING (8) [SOUND]

Nu 10: 6 At the s *of* a second blast, 9546
Jos 6: 9 All this time the trumpets *were* s. 9546
6:13 while the trumpets kept **s.** 9546
1Ch 15:28 with the s *of* rams' horns and trumpets, 7754
16:42 and Jeduthun were responsible for *the* s *of* 9048
2Ch 5:12 by 120 priests s trumpets. 2955
Ps 47: 5 the LORD amid the s *of* trumpets. 7754
150: 3 Praise him with the s *of* the trumpet, 9547

SOUNDINGS (2) [SOUND]

Ac 27:28 They **took** s and found that the water was *1075*
27:28 A short time later they **took** s again *1075*

SOUNDNESS (3) [SOUND]

Ps 38: 3 my bones have no s because of my sin. 8934
Isa 1: 6 to the top of your head there is no **s**— 5507
Tit 2: 8 and s of speech that cannot be condemned, *5618*

SOUNDS (10) [SOUND]

Ex 19:13 ram's horn s **a long blast** may they go 5432
Job 15:21 Terrifying s fill his ears; 7754
39:24 he cannot stand still when the trumpet **s.** 7754
Isa 18: 3 and when a trumpet **s,** you will hear it. 9546
Jer 7:34 the s *of* joy and gladness and to the voices 7754
16: 9 and in your days I will bring an end to the s 7754
25:10 from them the s *of* joy and gladness, 7754
33:11 the s *of* joy and gladness, the voices 7754
Am 3: 6 When a trumpet s in a city, 9546
1Co 14: 7 in the case of lifeless things that make **s,** *5889*

SOUR (6)

Job 20:14 yet his food will turn s in his stomach; NIH
Jer 31:29 'The fathers have eaten s **grapes,** 1235
31:30 whoever eats s **grapes**— 1235
Eze 18: 2 " 'The fathers eat s **grapes,** 1235
Rev 10: 9 *It will* **turn** your stomach **s,** *4393*
10:10 when I had eaten it, my stomach **turned s.** *4393*

SOURCE (6) [SOURCES]

Ge 26:35 a **s of grief** to Isaac and Rebekah. 5289+8120
Lev 20:18 he has exposed the **s of** her flow, 5227
Ps 80: 6 You have made us a **s of contention** 4506
Isa 28: 6 a **s of strength** to those who turn back 1476
Eze 29:16 be a **s of confidence** for the people of Israel 4440
Heb 5: 9 he became the s of eternal salvation *165*

SOURCES (2) [SOURCE]

Job 28:11 the s *of* the rivers and brings hidden things 4441
Jer 18:14 from **distant** s ever cease to flow? 2424

SOUTH (126) [SOUTHERN, SOUTHERNMOST, SOUTHLAND, SOUTHWARD]

Ge 13:14 where you are and look north and s, 2025+5582
28:14 to the north and to the **s.** 5582
Ex 26:18 Make twenty frames for the s side of 2025+2025+5582+9402
26:35 the lampstand opposite it on the s side. 2025+9402
27: 9 s side shall be a hundred cubits 2025+5582+9402
Ex 36:23 They made twenty frames for the s side of 2025+5582+9402
38: 9 s side was a hundred cubits long 2025+5582+9402
40:24 opposite the table on the s side 2025+5582
Nu 2:10 On the s will be the divisions of the camp 9402
3:29 to camp on the s side of the tabernacle. 2025+9402
10: 6 the camps on the s are to set out. 9402
34: 4 cross s of Scorpion Pass, 5582
34: 4 on to Zin and go s of Kadesh Barnea. 5582
35: 5 three thousand on the s side, 5582
Dt 3:27 Pisgah and look west and north and s 2025+9402
33: 2 with myriads of holy ones from the **s,** 3545
Jos 11: 2 in the Arabah s *of* Kinnereth, 5582
13: 4 from the **s,** all the land of the Canaanites, 9402
15: 1 to the Desert of Zin in the extreme **s.** 5582+9402
15: 3 crossed s of Scorpion Pass, 5582
15: 3 continued on to Zin and went over to the s 5582
15: 7 which faces the Pass of Adummim s 4946+5582
17: 9 continued s to the Kanah Ravine. 2025+5582
17:10 On the s the land belonged to Ephraim, 5582
18: 5 the s and the house of Joseph in its territory 5582
18:13 From there it crossed to the s slope of Luz 5582
18:13 down to Ataroth Addar on the hill s 4946+5582
18:14 on the s the boundary turned south along 5582
18:14 on the south the boundary turned s 2025+5582
18:19 at the mouth of the Jordan in the **s.** 5582
19:34 It touched Zebulun on the **s,** 5582
Jdg 21:19 and to the s of Lebonah." 5582
1Sa 14: 5 the other to the s toward Geba. 5582
20:41 David got up from the s side 5582
23:19 on the hill of Hakilah, s *of* Jeshimon? 3545+4946
23:24 in the Arabah s *of* Jeshimon. 3545
2Sa 24: 5 s *of* the town in the gorge, 3545
1Ki 6: 8 to the lowest floor was on the s side of 3556
7:21 to the s he named Jakin and the one to 3556
7:25 three facing s and three facing east. 2025+5582
7:39 placed five of the stands on the s side 3545+4946
7:39 He placed the Sea on the s side, 3556
2Ki 11:11 the temple, from the s side to the north side 3556
23:13 that were east of Jerusalem on the s of 3545
1Ch 9:24 east, west, north and s. 2025+5582
26:15 The lot for the S Gate fell to Obed-Edom, 5582
26:17 four a day on the s and 2025+5582
2Ch 3:17 one to the s and one to the north. 3545
3:17 *to the* s he named Jakin and the one to 3556
4: 4 three facing s and three facing east. 2025+5582
4: 6 for washing and placed five on the s *side* 3545
4: 7 five on the s *side* and five on the north. 3545
4: 8 five on the s *side* and five on the north. 3545
4:10 He placed the Sea on the s side, 3556
23:10 the temple, from the s side to the north side 3556
Job 9: 9 the Pleiades and the constellations of the s. 9402
23: 9 he turns to the s, I catch no glimpse of him. 3545
37:17 when the land lies hushed under the **s wind,** 1999
39:26 and spread his wings toward the **s?** 9402
Ps 78:26 from the heavens and led forth the **s wind** 9402
89:12 You created the north and the **s;** 3545
107: 3 from east and west, from north and s. 3542
Ecc 1: 6 wind blows to the s and turns to the north; 1999
11: 3 Whether a tree falls to the s or to the north, 1999
SS 4:16 Awake, north wind, and come, **s wind!** 9402
Isa 43: 6 and to the s, 'Do not hold them back.' 9402
Eze 10: 3 the cherubim were standing on the s *side* of 3545
16:46 and your younger sister, who lived to the s 3545
20:46 set your face toward the **s;** 2025+9402
20:46 against the s and prophesy against the forest 1999
20:47 from s to north will be scorched by it. 5582
21: 4 be unsheathed against everyone from s 5582
40: 2 on whose s *side* were some buildings 4946+5582
40:24 to the s side and I saw a gate facing south. 1999
40:24 to the south side and I saw a gate facing **s.** 1999
40:27 The inner court also had a gate facing **s,** 1999
40:27 to the outer gate on the s side; 1999
40:28 the s gate, and he measured the south gate; 1999
40:28 and he measured the s gate; 1999
40:44 at the side of the north gate and facing **s,** 1999
40:44 at the side of the s gate and facing north. 1999
40:45 "The room facing s is for 1999
41:11 one on the north and another on the **s;** 1999
42:10 On the s side along the length of the wall of 1999
42:12 were the doorways of the rooms on the **s.** 1999
42:13 and s rooms facing the temple courtyard are 1999
42:18 He measured the s side; 1999
46: 9 to worship is to go out the s gate; 5582
46: 9 by the s gate is to go out the north gate. 5582
47: 1 down from under the s side of the temple, 3556
47: 1 of the temple, s of the altar. 4946+5582
47: 2 and the water was flowing from the s side. 3556
47:19 "On the s side it will run from Tamar 5582+9402
47:19 will be the s boundary. 2025+2025+5582+9402
48:10 25,000 cubits long on the s *side.* 5582
48:16 the north side 4,500 cubits, the s side 4,500 5582
48:17 250 cubits on the **s,** 250 cubits on the east, 5582
48:28 will run s from Tamar to the waters 2025+9402
48:33 "On the s side, which measures 4,500 5582
Da 8: 4 toward the west and the north and the **s.** 5582
8: 9 in power to the s and to the east and toward 5582
11: 5 "The king of the S will become strong, 5582
11: 6 The daughter of the king of the S will go to 5582
11: 9 of the S but will retreat to his own country. 5582
11:11 of the S will march out in a rage and fight 5582
11:12 **the king of the S** will be filled with pride 2257S
11:14 many will rise against the king of the **S.** 5582
11:15 The forces of the S will be powerless 5582
11:17 an alliance with **the king of the S.** 2257S
11:25 and courage against the king of the **S.** 5582
11:25 The king of the S will wage war with 5582

Da 11:29 the S again, but this time the outcome will 5582
11:40 the king of the S will engage him in battle, 5582
Zec 6: 6 one with the dappled horses toward the s." 9402
9:14 he will march in the storms of the s, 9402
14: 4 and half moving s. 2025+5582
14:10 from Geba to Rimmon, s *of* Jerusalem, 5582
Mt 12:42 *of* the S will rise at the judgment *3803*
Lk 11:31 the S will rise at the judgment with the men *3803*
12:55 And when the s wind blows, you say, *3803*
13:29 from east and west and north and s, *3803*
Ac 8:26 "Go s to the road— *3540*
21: 3 and passing to the s **of** it, *2381*
27:13 When a gentle s **wind** began to blow, *3803*
28:13 The next day the s **wind** came up, *3803*
Rev 21:13 three on the s and three on the west. *3803*

SOUTHEAST (2) [EAST]

1Ki 7:39 at the s corner of the temple. 2025+5582+7711
2Ch 4:10 at the s corner. 2025+2025+5582+7711

SOUTHERN (11) [SOUTH]

Nu 34: 3 " 'Your s side will include some of 5582
34: 3 your s boundary will start from the end of 5582
Jos 15: 2 Their s boundary started from the bay at 5582
15: 2 the bay at the s end of the Salt Sea, 2025+5582
15: 4 This is their s boundary. 5582
15: 8 Valley of Ben Hinnom along the s 4946+5582
18:15 The s side began at the outskirts 2025+5582
18:16 along the s slope of the Jebusite city 2025+5582
18:19 This was the s boundary. 5582
Eze 20:47 Say to the s forest: 5582
48:28 "The s boundary of Gad will run 448+5582+6991

SOUTHERNMOST (1) [SOUTH, MOST]

Jos 15:21 The s towns of the tribe of Judah in 4946+7895

SOUTHLAND (2) [SOUTH]

Isa 21: 1 Like whirlwinds sweeping through the s, 5582
Eze 20:46 prophesy against the forest of the s. 5582+8441

SOUTHWARD (3) [SOUTH]

Dt 33:23 he will inherit s to the lake." 1999
Jos 12: 3 and then s below the slopes of Pisgah. 4946+9402
17: 7 The boundary ran s from there 448+2021+3545

SOUTHWEST (1) [WEST]

Ac 27:12 facing both s and northwest. *3355*

SOVEREIGN (303) [SOVEREIGNTY]

Ge 15: 2 But Abram said, "O S LORD, 151
15: 8 But Abram said, "O S LORD, 151
Ex 23:17 the men are to appear before the S LORD. 123
34:23 to appear before the S LORD, 123
Dt 3:24 "O S LORD, you have begun to show 151
9:26 "O S LORD, do not destroy your people, 151
Jos 7: 7 And Joshua said, "Ah, S LORD, 151
Jdg 6:22 he exclaimed, "Ah, S LORD! 151
16:28 "O S LORD, remember me. 151
2Sa 7:18 "Who am I, O S LORD, 151
7:19 O S LORD, you have also spoken about 151
7:19 of dealing with man, O S LORD? 151
7:20 For you know your servant, O S LORD. 151
7:22 "How great you are, O S LORD! 151
7:28 O S LORD, you are God! 151
7:29 for you, O S LORD, have spoken, 151
1Ki 2:26 of the S LORD before my father David 151
8:53 O S LORD, brought our fathers out 151
Ps 68:20 the S LORD comes escape from death. 151
71: 5 For you have been my hope, O S LORD, 151
71:16 and proclaim your mighty acts, O S LORD; 151
73:28 I have made the S LORD my refuge; 151
109:21 But you, O S LORD, deal well with me 151
140: 7 O S LORD, my strong deliverer, 151
141: 8 But my eyes are fixed on you, O S LORD; 151
Isa 7: 7 Yet this is what the S LORD says: 151
25: 8 The S LORD will wipe away the tears 151
28:16 So this is what the S LORD says: 151
30:15 This is what the S LORD, 151
40:10 See, the S LORD comes with power, 151
48:16 the S LORD has sent me, with his Spirit. 151
49:22 This is what the S LORD says: 151
50: 4 The S LORD has given me 151
50: 5 The S LORD has opened my ears, 151
50: 7 Because the S LORD helps me, 151
50: 9 It is the S LORD who helps me. 151
51:22 This is what your S LORD says, 151
52: 4 For this is what the S LORD says: 151
56: 8 The S LORD declares— 151
61: 1 The Spirit of the S LORD is on me, 151
61:11 so the S LORD will make righteousness 151
65:13 Therefore this is what the S LORD says: 151
65:15 the S LORD will put you to death, 151
Jer 1: 6 "Ah, S LORD," I said, 151
2:22 declares the S LORD. 151
4:10 Then I said, "Ah, S LORD, 151
7:20 the S LORD says: 151
14:13 But I said, "Ah, S LORD, 151
32:17 S LORD, you have made the heavens and 151
32:25 you, O S LORD, say to me, 151
44:26 "As surely as the S LORD lives." 151
50:25 for the S LORD Almighty has work to do 151
Eze 2: 4 'This is what the S LORD says.' 151
3:11 'This is what the S LORD says,' 151
3:27 'This is what the S LORD says.' 151
4:14 Then I said, "Not so, S LORD! 151
5: 5 "This is what the S LORD says: 151
5: 7 "Therefore this is what the S LORD says: 151
5: 8 "Therefore this is what the S LORD says: 151
5:11 declares the S LORD, 151
6: 3 hear the word of the S LORD. 151
6: 3 the S LORD says to the mountains 151
6:11 " 'This is what the S LORD says: 151
7: 2 this is what the S LORD says to the land 151
7: 5 "This is what the S LORD says: Disaster! 151
8: 1 of the S LORD came upon me there. 151
9: 8 crying out, "Ah, S LORD! 151
11: 7 "Therefore this is what the S LORD says: 151
11: 8 declares the S LORD. 151
11:13 in a loud voice, "Ah, S LORD! 151
11:16 'This is what the S LORD says: 151
11:17 'This is what the S LORD says: 151
11:21 declares the S LORD." 151
12:10 'This is what the S LORD says: 151
12:19 the S LORD says about those living 151
12:23 'This is what the S LORD says: 151
12:25 declares the S LORD.' " 151
12:28 'This is what the S LORD says: 151
12:28 declares the S LORD.' " 151
13: 3 This is what the S LORD says: 151
13: 8 the S LORD says: 151
13: 8 I am against you, declares the S LORD. 151
13: 9 you will know that I am the S LORD. 151
13:13 the S LORD says: 151
13:16 declares the S LORD." ' 151
13:18 'This is what the S LORD says: 151
13:20 the S LORD says: 151
14: 4 'This is what the S LORD says: 151
14: 6 'This is what the S LORD says: Repent! 151
14:11 declares the S LORD.' " 151
14:14 declares the S LORD. 151
14:16 declares the S LORD, 151
14:18 declares the S LORD, 151
14:20 declares the S LORD, even if Noah, 151
14:21 "For this is what the S LORD says: 151
14:23 declares the S LORD." 151
15: 6 "Therefore this is what the S LORD says: 151
15: 8 declares the S LORD." 151
16: 3 the S LORD says to Jerusalem: 151
16: 8 declares the S LORD, 151
16:14 declares the S LORD. 151
16:19 declares the S LORD. 151
16:23 Woe to you, declares the S LORD. 151
16:30 declares the S LORD, 151
16:36 This is what the S LORD says: 151
16:43 declares the S LORD. 151
16:48 As surely as I live, declares the S LORD, 151
16:59 " 'This is what the S LORD says: 151
16:63 declares the S LORD.' " 151
17: 3 'This is what the S LORD says: 151
17: 9 'This is what the S LORD says: 151
17:16 surely as I live, declares the S LORD, 151
17:19 the S LORD says: 151
17:22 " 'This is what the S LORD says: 151
18: 3 "As surely as I live, declares the S LORD, 151
18: 9 he will surely live, declares the S LORD. 151
18:23 declares the S LORD. 151
18:30 declares the S LORD. 151
18:32 declares the S LORD. 151
20: 3 'This is what the S LORD says: 151
20: 3 declares the S LORD.' 151
20: 5 'This is what the S LORD says: 151
20:27 'This is what the S LORD says: 151
20:30 'This is what the S LORD says: 151
20:31 As surely as I live, declares the S LORD, 151
20:33 As surely as I live, declares the S LORD, 151
20:36 so I will judge you, declares the S LORD. 151
20:39 this is what the S LORD says: 151
20:40 declares the S LORD, 151
20:44 declares the S LORD.' " 151
20:47 This is what the S LORD says: 151
20:49 Then I said, "Ah, S LORD! 151
21: 7 declares the S LORD." 151
21:13 declares the S LORD.' 151
21:24 "Therefore this is what the S LORD says: 151
21:26 this is what the S LORD says: 151
21:28 the S LORD says about the Ammonites 151
22: 3 'This is what the S LORD says: 151
22:12 declares the S LORD. 151
22:19 Therefore this is what the S LORD says: 151
22:28 'This is what the S LORD says'— 151
22:31 declares the S LORD." 151
23:22 Oholibah, this is what the S LORD says: 151
23:28 "For this is what the S LORD says: 151
23:32 "This is what the S LORD says: 151
23:34 I have spoken, declares the S LORD. 151
23:35 "Therefore this is what the S LORD says: 151
23:46 "This is what the S LORD says: 151
23:49 you will know that I am the S LORD." 151
24: 3 'This is what the S LORD says: 151
24: 6 " 'For this is what the S LORD says: 151
24: 9 "Therefore this is what the S LORD says: 151
24:14 declares the S LORD.' " 151
24:21 'This is what the S LORD says: 151
24:24 you will know that I am the S LORD.' 151
25: 3 'Hear the word of the S LORD. 151
25: 3 This is what the S LORD says: 151
25: 6 For this is what the S LORD says: 151
25: 8 "This is what the S LORD says: 151
25:12 "This is what the S LORD says: 151
Eze 25:13 therefore this is what the S LORD says: 151
25:14 declares the S LORD.' " 151
25:15 "This is what the S LORD says: 151
25:16 therefore this is what the S LORD says: 151
26: 3 therefore this is what the S LORD says: 151
26: 5 for I have spoken, declares the S LORD. 151
26: 7 "For this is what the S LORD says: 151
26:14 declares the S LORD. 151
26:15 "This is what the S LORD says to Tyre: 151
26:19 "This is what the S LORD says: 151
26:21 declares the S LORD." 151
27: 3 'This is what the S LORD says: 151
28: 2 'This is what the S LORD says: 151
28: 6 "Therefore this is what the S LORD says: 151
28:10 I have spoken, declares the S LORD.' " 151
28:12 'This is what the S LORD says: 151
28:22 'This is what the S LORD says: 151
28:24 they will know that I am the S LORD. 151
28:25 " 'This is what the S LORD says: 151
29: 3 'This is what the S LORD says: 151
29: 8 the S LORD says: 151
29:13 " 'Yet this is what the S LORD says: 151
29:16 they will know that I am the S LORD.' " 151
29:19 Therefore this is what the S LORD says: 151
29:20 declares the S LORD. 151
30: 2 'This is what the S LORD says: 151
30: 6 declares the S LORD. 151
30:10 " 'This is what the S LORD says: 151
30:13 " 'This is what the S LORD says: 151
30:22 Therefore this is what the S LORD says: 151
31:10 " 'Therefore this is what the S LORD says: 151
31:15 " 'This is what the S LORD says: 151
31:18 declares the S LORD.' " 151
32: 3 " 'This is what the S LORD says: 151
32: 8 declares the S LORD. 151
32:11 " 'For this is what the S LORD says: 151
32:14 declares the S LORD. 151
32:16 declares the S LORD." 151
32:31 declares the S LORD. 151
32:32 declares the S LORD." 151
33:11 'As surely as I live, declares the S LORD, 151
33:25 'This is what the S LORD says: 151
33:27 'This is what the S LORD says: 151
34: 2 'This is what the S LORD says: 151
34: 8 declares the S LORD, 151
34:10 This is what the S LORD says: 151
34:11 " 'For this is what the S LORD says: 151
34:15 declares the S LORD. 151
34:17 my flock, this is what the S LORD says: 151
34:20 " 'Therefore this is what the S LORD says 151
34:30 are my people, declares the S LORD. 151
34:31 declares the S LORD.' " 151
35: 3 'This is what the S LORD says: 151
35: 6 declares the S LORD, 151
35:11 declares the S LORD, 151
35:14 This is what the S LORD says: 151
36: 2 This is what the S LORD says: 151
36: 3 'This is what the S LORD says: 151
36: 4 hear the word of the S LORD: 151
36: 4 the S LORD says to the mountains 151
36: 5 this is what the S LORD says: 151
36: 6 'This is what the S LORD says: 151
36: 7 Therefore this is what the S LORD says: 151
36:13 " 'This is what the S LORD says: 151
36:14 declares the S LORD. 151
36:15 declares the S LORD.' " 151
36:22 'This is what the S LORD says: 151
36:23 declares the S LORD, 151
36:32 declares the S LORD. 151
36:33 " 'This is what the S LORD says: 151
36:37 "This is what the S LORD says: 151
37: 3 I said, "O S LORD, you alone know." 151
37: 5 the S LORD says to these bones: 151
37: 9 'This is what the S LORD says: 151
37:12 'This is what the S LORD says: 151
37:19 'This is what the S LORD says: 151
37:21 'This is what the S LORD says: 151
38: 3 'This is what the S LORD says: 151
38:10 " 'This is what the S LORD says: 151
38:14 'This is what the S LORD says: 151
38:17 " 'This is what the S LORD says: 151
38:18 declares the S LORD. 151
38:21 declares the S LORD. 151
39: 1 'This is what the S LORD says: 151
39: 5 for I have spoken, declares the S LORD. 151
39: 8 declares the S LORD. 151
39:10 declares the S LORD. 151
39:13 declares the S LORD. 151
39:17 this is what the S LORD says: 151
39:20 declares the S LORD. 151
39:25 "Therefore this is what the S LORD says: 151
39:29 declares the S LORD." 151
43:18 this is what the S LORD says: 151
43:19 declares the S LORD. 151
43:27 I will accept you, declares the S LORD." 151
44: 6 'This is what the S LORD says: 151
44: 9 This is what the S LORD says: 151
44:12 declares the S LORD. 151
44:15 declares the S LORD. 151
44:27 declares the S LORD. 151
45: 9 " 'This is what the S LORD says: 151
45: 9 declares the S LORD. 151
45:15 declares the S LORD. 151
45:18 " 'This is what the S LORD says: 151
46: 1 " 'This is what the S LORD says: 151
46:16 " 'This is what the S LORD says: 151
47:13 This is what the S LORD says: 151

Eze 47:23 declares the S LORD. 151
48:29 declares the S LORD. 151
Da 4:17 living may know that the Most High is s 10718
4:25 that the Most High is s over the kingdoms 10718
4:32 that the Most High is s over the kingdoms 10718
5:21 the Most High God is s over the kingdoms 10718
7:14 He was given authority, glory and s **power;** 10424
Am 1:8 says the S LORD. 151
3:7 Surely the S LORD does nothing without 151
3:8 The S LORD has spoken— 151
3:11 Therefore this is what the S LORD says: 151
4:2 The S LORD has sworn by his holiness: 151
4:5 declares the S LORD. 151
5:3 This is what the S LORD says: 151
6:8 The S LORD has sworn by himself— 151
7:1 This is what the S LORD showed me: 151
7:2 I cried out, "S LORD, forgive! 151
7:4 This is what the S LORD showed me: 151
7:4 The S LORD was calling for judgment 151
7:5 I cried out, "S LORD, I beg you, stop! 151
7:6 will not happen either," the S LORD said. 151
8:1 This is what the S LORD showed me: 151
8:3 "In that day," declares the S LORD, 151
8:9 "In that day," declares the S LORD, 151
8:11 declares the S LORD, 151
9:8 of the S LORD are on the sinful kingdom. 151
Ob 1:1 the S LORD says about Edom— 151
Mic 1:2 that the S LORD may witness against you, 151
Hab 3:19 The S LORD is my strength; 151
Zep 1:7 Be silent before the S LORD, 151
Zec 9:14 The S LORD will sound the trumpet; 151
Lk 2:29 **"S Lord,** as you have promised, you *1305*
Ac 4:24 **"S Lord,"** they said, "you made the heaven *1305*
2Pe 2:1 denying the s **Lord** who bought them— *1305*
Jude 1:4 and deny Jesus Christ our only **S** and Lord. *1305*
Rev 6:10 "How long, **S Lord,** holy and true, *1305*

SOVEREIGNTY (2) [SOVEREIGN]

Da 5:18 Most High God gave your father Nebuchadnezzar s and greatness 10424
7:27 the s, power and greatness of the kingdoms 10424

SOW (31) [SOWED, SOWER, SOWING, SOWN, SOWS]

Ex 23:10 "For six years *you are to* s your fields 2445
23:16 with the firstfruits of the crops you s 2445
Lev 25:3 For six years s your fields, 2445
25:4 not s your fields or prune your vineyards. 2445
25:11 not s and do not reap what grows of itself 2445
Dt 28:38 *You will* s much seed *in* the field 3655
2Ki 19:29 But in the third year s and reap, 2445
Job 4:8 and *those who* s trouble reap it. 2445
Ps 126:5 Those *who* s in tears will reap with songs 2445
126:6 goes out weeping, carrying **seed to s,** 2446+5433
Ecc 11:6 S your seed in the morning, 2445
Isa 28:25 *does he* not s caraway and scatter cummin? 7046
30:23 also send you rain for the seed *you* s *in* 2445
37:30 But in the third year s and reap, 2445
Jer 4:3 up your unplowed ground and *do* not s 2445
12:13 *They will* s wheat but reap thorns; 2445
35:7 s seed or plant vineyards; 2445
Hos 8:7 "*They* s the wind and reap the whirlwind. 2445
10:12 S for yourselves righteousness, 2445
Mt 6:26 they *do* not s or reap or store away in barns, *5062*
13:3 "A farmer went out *to* s his **seed.** *5062*
13:27 'Sir, didn't *you* s good seed in your field? *5062*
Mk 4:3 "Listen! A farmer went out *to* s his **seed.** *5062*
Lk 8:5 "A farmer went out *to* s his seed. *5062*
12:24 Consider the ravens: *They do* not s or reap, *5062*
19:21 not put in and reap what *you did* not **s.'** *5062*
19:22 and reaping what *I did* not **s?** *5062*
1Co 15:36 What you s does not come to life *5062*
15:37 When *you* s, you do not plant the body *5062*
Jas 3:18 Peacemakers who s in peace raise a harvest *5062*
2Pe 2:22 and, "A s that is washed goes back to her *5725*

SOWED (4) [SOW]

Ps 107:37 *They* s fields and planted vineyards 2445
Mt 13:24 of heaven is like a man *who* s good seed *5062*
13:25 his enemy came and s weeds among *2178*
13:37 "The one who s the good seed is the Son *5062*

SOWER (5) [SOW]

Isa 55:10 so that it yields seed for the s and bread for 2445
Jer 50:16 Cut off from Babylon the s, 2445
Mt 13:18 then to what the parable *of* the s means: *5062*
Jn 4:36 the s and the reaper may be glad together. *5062*
2Co 9:10 *to* the s and bread for food will also supply *5062*

SOWING (1) [SOW]

Isa 32:20 s *your* **seed** by every stream, 2445

SOWN (23) [SOW]

Job 31:8 then may others eat what *I have* **s,** 2445
Isa 19:7 Every s **field** *along* the Nile will become 4669
40:24 no sooner *are they* **s,** 2445
Jer 2:2 through the desert, through a land not s. 2445
Eze 36:9 you will be plowed and **s,** 2445
Mt 13:8 a hundred, sixty or thirty times what was **s.** *NIG*
13:19 and snatches away what *was* s in his heart. *5062*
13:19 This is the **seed** s along the path. *5062*
13:23 sixty or thirty times what was **s."** *NIG*
25:24 where *you have* not s and gathering *5062*
Mt 25:26 that I harvest where *I have* not s and gather *5062*
Mk 4:15 along the path, where the word *is* **s.** *5062*
4:15 and takes away the word that *was* s in them. *5062*
4:16 Others, like **seed** s on rocky places, *5062*
4:18 Still others, like **seed** s among thorns, *5062*
4:20 Others, like **seed** s on good soil, *5062*
4:20 sixty or even a hundred times what was **s."** *NIG*
Lk 8:8 a hundred times more than was **s."** *NIG*
1Co 9:11 If we *have* s spiritual **seed** among you, *5062*
15:42 The body that *is* s is perishable, *5062*
15:43 *it is* s in dishonor, it is raised in glory; *5062*
15:43 *it is* s in weakness, it is raised in power; *5062*
15:44 *it is* s a natural body, it is raised a spiritual *5062*

SOWS (10) [SOW]

Pr 11:18 *he who* s righteousness reaps a sure reward. 2445
22:8 *He who* s wickedness reaps trouble, 2445
Mt 13:39 and the enemy who s them is the devil. *5062*
Mk 4:14 The farmer s the word. *5062*
Jn 4:37 the saying 'One s and another reaps' is true. *5062*
2Co 9:6 Whoever s sparingly will also reap *5062*
9:6 and whoever s generously will also reap *5062*
Gal 6:7 A man reaps what *he* **s.** *5062*
6:8 The one who s to please his sinful nature, *5062*
6:8 the one who s to please the Spirit, *5062*

SPACE (10) [SPACIOUS]

Ge 32:16 and keep *some* s between the herds." 8119
Ex 25:37 up on it so that they light the s in front of it. 6298
1Sa 26:13 there was a wide s between them. 5226
1Ki 7:36 on the panels, in every **available s,** 5113
Job 26:7 the northern [skies] over **empty s;** 9332
Isa 5:8 to field till no s is left and you live alone in 5226
49:20 **give us more s** to live in.' 5602
Eze 41:17 In the s above the outside of the entrance to NIH
42:5 the galleries **took** more s from them than 430
42:6 so they were smaller in **floor** s than those 824

SPACIOUS (11) [SPACE]

Ex 3:8 a good and s land, a land flowing with milk 8146
Jdg 18:10 a s land that God has put into your hands, 3338+8146
2Sa 22:20 He brought me out into a s **place;** 5303
1Ch 4:40 and the land was s, peaceful and quiet. 3338+8146
Ne 7:4 Now the city was large and **s,** 3338+8146
9:35 in the s and fertile land you gave them, 8146
Job 36:16 from the jaws of distress to a s **place** free 8144
Ps 18:19 He brought me out into a s **place;** 5303
31:8 but have set my feet in a s **place.** 5303
104:25 There is the sea, vast and **s,** 3338+8146
Jer 22:14 a great palace with s upper rooms.' 8118

SPAIN (2)

Ro 15:24 I plan to do so when I go to **S.** *5056*
15:28 I will go to S and visit you on the way. *5056*

SPAN (9)

Ex 23:26 I will give you a full **life s.** 3427+5031
28:16 square—a s long and a span wide— 2455
28:16 square—a span long and a s wide— 2455
39:9 It was square—a s long and a span wide— 2455
39:9 It was square—a span long and a s wide— 2455
Ps 39:5 the **s of** my **years** is as nothing before you. 2698
90:10 yet their s is but trouble and sorrow, 8145
Isa 23:15 for seventy years, the **s of** a king's **life.** 3427
Eze 43:13 with a rim of one s around the edge. 2455

SPARE (48) [SPARED, SPARES, SPARING, SPARINGLY]

Ge 18:24 Will you really sweep it away and not s 5951
18:26 *I will* s the whole place for their sake." 5951
Dt 13:8 *Do* not s him or shield him. 2798
Jos 2:13 that *you will* s *the* **lives** *of* my father 2649
22:22 *do* not s us this day. 3828
Jdg 6:4 the way to Gaza and *did* not s a living thing 8636
1Sa 15:3 *Do* not s them; put to death men and women 2798
2Sa 21:7 the Israelites had sworn to [s] them, NIH
1Ki 16:11 *He did* not s a single male, 8636
20:31 Perhaps *he will* s your life." 2649
2Ki 7:4 If *they* s us, we live; 2649
2Ch 31:10 we have had enough to eat and plenty *to* s, 3855
Est 4:11 the gold scepter to him and s *his* **life.** 2649
7:3 And s my people—this is my request. NIH
Job 2:6 but *you must* s his life." 9068
33:24 'S him from going down to the pit; 7021
Ps 78:50 *he did* not s them from death but gave them 3104
Pr 20:13 stay awake and *you will* **have** food **to s.** 8425
Isa 9:19 no one *will* s his brother. 2798
47:3 I will take vengeance; *I will* s no one." 7003
Jer 50:14 S no arrows, for she has sinned against 2798
50:20 for I will forgive *the* **remnant** *I* **s.** 8636
51:3 *Do* not s her young men; 2798
Eze 5:11 I will not look on you with pity or s you. 2798
6:8 " 'But *I will* s some, for some of you 3855
7:4 I will not look on you with pity or s you; 2798
7:9 I will not look on you with pity or s you; 2798
8:18 I will not look on them with pity or s them. 2798
9:10 not look on them with pity or s them, 2798
12:16 *I will* s a few of them from the sword, 3855
Da 5:19 those he wanted to s, he spared; NIH
Joel 2:17 Let them say, "S your people, O LORD. 2571
Am 7:8 *I will* s them no longer. 6296
8:2 *I will* s them no longer. 6296
Zec 11:5 Their own shepherds *do* not s them. 2798
Mal 3:17 *I will* s them, just as in compassion a man 2798
Lk 15:17 of my father's hired men **have** food **to s,** *4355*
Ac 20:29 in among you and *will* not s the flock. *5767*
27:43 But the centurion wanted *to* s Paul's life *1407*
Ro 8:32 He who *did* not s his own Son, *5767*
11:21 For if God *did* not s the natural branches, *5767*
11:21 *he will* not s you either. *5767*
1Co 7:28 and I want to s you this. *5767*
2Co 1:23 as my witness that it was *in order to* s you *5767*
13:2 not s those who sinned earlier or any of *5767*
Php 2:27 to s me sorrow upon sorrow. *2400+3590*
2Pe 2:4 if God *did* not s angels when they sinned, *5767*
2:5 not s the ancient world when he brought *5767*

SPARED (26) [SPARE]

Ge 12:13 for your sake and my life *will be* s because 2649
19:20 Then my life *will be* **s."** 2649
32:30 and yet my life **was s."** 5911
Ex 12:27 of the Israelites in Egypt and s our homes 5911
Nu 22:33 but *I would have* s her." 2649
Jos 6:17 with her in her house *shall be* **s,** 2649
6:25 But Joshua s Rahab the prostitute, 2649
Jdg 1:25 they put the city to the sword but s the man 8938
8:19 the LORD lives, if *you had* s their **lives,** 2649
21:14 of Jabesh Gilead who *had been* **s.** 2649
1Sa 2:33 be s only to blind your eyes with tears and NIH
15:9 But Saul and the army s Agag and the best 2798
15:15 *they* s the best of the sheep and cattle 2798
24:10 Some urged me to kill you, but I s you; 2571
2Sa 21:7 The king s Mephibosheth son of Jonathan, 2798
2Ki 23:18 So *they* s his bones and those of 4880
2Ch 36:17 and s neither young man nor young woman, 2798
Job 21:30 the evil man **is** s from the day of calamity, 3104
Ps 30:3 *you* s me from going down into the pit. 2649
Isa 57:1 righteous are taken away to be **s from** 4946+7156
Jer 38:17 of the king of Babylon, your life *will be* s 2649
38:20 and your life *will be* **s.** 2649
Eze 6:12 he that survives and **is** s will die of famine. 5915
13:19 not have died and *have* s those who should 2649
Da 5:19 those he wanted to spare, *he* **s;** 10262
Ac 27:21 you would have s yourselves this damage *3045*

SPARES (2) [SPARE]

Pr 13:24 *He who* s the rod hates his son, 3104
Mal 3:17 just as **in compassion** a man s his son 2798

SPARING (4) [SPARE]

Ge 19:19 great kindness to me in s my life. 2649
Jos 11:11 destroyed them, not s anything that breathed 3855
11:14 destroyed them, not s anyone that breathed. 8636
Pr 21:26 but the righteous give without **s.** 3104

SPARINGLY (2) [SPARE]

2Co 9:6 Whoever sows s will also reap sparingly, *5768*
9:6 Whoever sows sparingly will also reap **s,** *5768*

SPARK (2) [SPARKS]

Isa 1:31 man will become tinder and his work a **s;** 5773
Jas 3:5 a great forest is set on fire by a small **s.** *4786*

SPARKLE (1) [SPARKLED, SPARKLES, SPARKLING]

Zec 9:16 *They will* s in his land like jewels in a crown 5824

SPARKLED (2) [SPARKLE]

Eze 1:16 They s like chrysolite, 6524
10:9 the wheels s like chrysolite. 6524

SPARKLES (1) [SPARKLE]

Pr 23:31 when it is red, when *it* **s** in the cup, 5989+6524

SPARKLING (2) [SPARKLE]

Isa 54:12 of rubies, your gates of s **jewels,** 74+734
Eze 1:22 an expanse, s like ice, and awesome. 6524

SPARKS (2) [SPARK]

Job 5:7 to trouble as surely as s fly upward. 1201+8404
41:19 stream from his mouth; s *of* fire shoot out. 3958

SPARROW (2) [SPARROWS]

Ps 84:3 Even the s has found a home, 7606
Pr 26:2 Like a fluttering s or a darting swallow, 7606

SPARROWS (4) [SPARROW]

Mt 10:29 Are not two s sold for a penny? *5141*
10:31 you are worth more than many **s.** *5141*
Lk 12:6 Are not five s sold for two pennies? *5141*
12:7 you are worth more than many **s.** *5141*

SPAT (Anglicized) See SPIT

SPATTERED (3)

Lev 6:27 and if any of the blood **is** s on a garment, 5684
2Ki 9:33 of her blood s the wall and the horses 5684
Isa 63:3 their blood s my garments, 5684

SPEAK (322) [SPEAKER, SPEAKING, SPEAKS, SPOKE, SPOKEN, SPOKESMAN, SPOKESMEN]

Ge 18:27 that I have been so bold as to s to the Lord, 1819
18:30 "May the Lord not be angry, but *let me* s. 1819
18:31 that I have been so bold as to s to the Lord, 1819
18:32 but *let me* s just once more. 1819
19:21 I will not overthrow the town *you* s *of.* 1819
34:20 of their city *to* s to their fellow townsmen. 1819
37:4 they hated him and could not s a kind *word* 1819
44:18 *let* your servant s a word to my lord. 1819
46:31 "I will go up and s to Pharaoh and will say 5583
50:4 s to Pharaoh for me. 1819
Ex 4:12 I will help you s and will teach you what 7023
4:14 I know he *can* s **well.** 1819+1819
4:15 *You shall* s to him and put words 1819
4:15 both of you s and will teach you what to do. 7023
4:16 He *will* s to the people for you, 1819
5:23 since I went to Pharaoh to s in your name, 1819
6:12 since I s with faltering lips?" NIH
6:30 "Since I s with faltering lips, NIH
19:6 the words *you are to* s to the Israelites." 1819
19:7 the LORD had commanded him to **s.** NIH
20:19 **"S** to us yourself and we will listen. 1819
20:19 But *do* not *have* God s to us or we will die." 1819
29:42 There I will meet you and s to you; 1819
33:11 The LORD *would* s to Moses face to face, 1819
34:34 the LORD's presence to s with him, 1819
34:35 over his face until he went in to s with 1819
Lev 1:2 **"S** to the Israelites and say to them: 1819
5:1 " 'If a person sins because *he does* not s **up** 5583
15:2 **"S** to the Israelites and say to them: 1819
17:2 **"S** to Aaron and his sons and to all 1819
18:2 **"S** to the Israelites and say to them: 1819
19:2 **"S** to the entire assembly of Israel and say 1819
21:1 **"S** to the priests, the sons of Aaron, 606
22:18 **"S** to Aaron and his sons and to all 1819
23:2 **"S** to the Israelites and say to them: 1819
23:10 **"S** to the Israelites and say to them: 1819
25:2 **"S** to the Israelites and say to them: 1819
27:2 **"S** to the Israelites and say to them: 1819
Nu 5:12 **"S** to the Israelites and say to them: 1819
6:2 **"S** to the Israelites and say to them: 1819
7:89 the Tent of Meeting to s with the LORD, 1819
8:2 **"S** to Aaron and say to him, 1819
11:17 I will come down and s with you there, 1819
12:6 *I* s to him in dreams. 1819
12:8 With him *I* s face to face, 1819
12:8 not afraid to s against my servant Moses?" 1819
15:2 **"S** to the Israelites and say to them: 1819
15:18 **"S** to the Israelites and say to them: 1819
15:38 **"S** to the Israelites and say to them: 1819
17:2 **"S** to the Israelites and get twelve staffs 1819
18:26 **"S** to the Levites and say to them: 1819
20:8 S to that rock before their eyes 1819
22:35 but s only what I tell you." 1819
22:38 *I must* s only what God puts 1819
23:12 not s what the LORD puts in my mouth?" 1819
23:19 *Does* he s and then not act? 606
33:51 **"S** to the Israelites and say to them: 1819
35:10 **"S** to the Israelites and say to them: 1819
Dt 3:26 *"Do* not s to me anymore about this matter. 1819
18:20 But a prophet who presumes to s 1819
31:28 so that *I can* s these words in their hearing 1819
32:1 Listen, O heavens, and *I will* **s;** 1819
Jdg 20:7 **s up** and give your verdict." 1821
1Sa 2:3 or *let* your mouth s such arrogance, 3655
3:9 **'S,** LORD, for your servant is listening.' " 1819
3:10 Then Samuel said, **"S,** for your servant 1819
17:29 said David. "Can't I even **s?"** 1821
18:22 **"S** to David privately and say, 'Look, 1819
19:3 I'll s to him about you 1819
25:24 Please *let* your servant s to you; 1819
2Sa 3:27 as though to s with him privately. 1819
13:13 Please s to the king; 1819
14:3 go to the king and s these words to him." 1819
14:12 *"Let* your servant s a word to my lord 1819
14:12 **"S,"** he replied. 1819
14:15 *'I will* s to the king; 1819
14:18 *"Let* my lord the king **s,"** the woman said. 1819
19:43 the first to s *of* bringing back our king?" 1821
20:16 Tell Joab to come here so *I can* s to him." 1819
1Ki 2:18 "I *will* s to the king for you." 1819
2:19 to King Solomon to s to him for Adonijah, 1819
22:13 with theirs, and s favorably." 1819
22:24 go when he went from me to s to you?" 1819
2Ki 2:3 Elisha replied, "but *do* **not** s *of* it." 3120
2:5 I know," he replied, "but *do* **not** s *of* it." 3120
4:13 *Can* we s on your behalf to the king or 1819
6:12 tells the king of Israel the very words *you* s 1819
18:20 but *you* s only empty words. 606
18:26 "Please s to your servants in Aramaic, 1819
18:26 Don't s to us in Hebrew in the hearing of 1819
22:14 Shaphan and Asaiah went *to* s to 1819
2Ch 18:12 with theirs, and s favorably." 1819
18:23 go when he went from me to s to you?" 1819
34:22 the king had sent with him went *to* s to 1819
Ne 13:24 not know how to s the language of Judah. 1819
Est 6:4 the outer court of the palace to s to the king 606
Job 7:11 *I will* s **out** in the anguish of my spirit, 1819
9:35 Then *I would* s **up** without fear of him, 1819
10:1 to my complaint and s **out** in the bitterness 1819
11:5 Oh, how I wish that God *would* **s,** 1819
12:8 or s to the earth, and it will teach you, 8488
13:3 *to* s to the Almighty and to argue my case 1819
Job 13:7 *Will you* s wickedly on God's behalf? 1819
13:7 *Will you* s deceitfully for him? 1819
13:13 "Keep silent and *let* me **s;** 1819
13:22 summon me and I will answer, or *let me* **s,** 1819
16:4 I also *could* s like you, 1819
16:6 "Yet if *I* **s,** my pain is not relieved; 1819
21:3 Bear with me while I **s,** 1819
27:4 my lips *will* not s wickedness, 1819
32:7 I thought, 'Age *should* **s;** 1819
32:20 *I must* s and find relief; 1819
33:3 my lips sincerely s what I know. 4910
33:14 For God *does* **s**—now one way, now 1819
33:16 *he may* s *in* their ears and terrify them 1655
33:31 be silent, and I *will* **s.** 1819
33:32 **s up,** for I want you to be cleared. 1819
37:20 Should he be told that *I want to* **s?** 1819
41:3 s to you **with gentle words?** 1819
41:12 *"I will* not **fail to** s *of* his limbs, 3087
42:4 'Listen now, and I *will* **s;** 1819
Ps 5:9 *with* their tongue *they* s **deceit.** 2744
12:2 their flattering lips s with deception. 1819
17:10 and their mouths s with arrogance. 1819
28:3 *who* s cordially with their neighbors 1819
31:18 with pride and contempt they s arrogantly 1819
35:20 *They do* not s peaceably, 1819
35:28 My tongue *will* s *of* your righteousness 2047
40:5 *were I to* s and tell of them, 5583
40:10 *I* s *of* your faithfulness and salvation. 606
49:3 My mouth *will* s words of wisdom; 1819
50:7 O my people, and *I will* **s,** O Israel, 1819
50:20 *You* s continually against your brother 1819
51:4 when you s and justified when you judge. 1819
58:1 *Do you* rulers indeed s justly? 1819
58:3 the womb they are wayward and s lies. 1819
71:10 For my enemies s against me; 606
73:8 They scoff, and s with malice; 1819
73:15 If I had said, *"I will* s thus," 6218
75:5 *do* not s with outstretched neck.' " 1819
77:4 I was too troubled *to* **s.** 1819
109:20 to those *who* s evil of me. 1819
115:5 They have mouths, but cannot **s,** eyes, 1819
119:46 *I will* s of your statutes before kings 1819
120:7 but when *I* **s,** they are for war. 1819
135:16 They have mouths, but cannot **s,** eyes, 1819
139:20 *They* s *of* you with evil intent; 606
145:5 *They will* s *of* the glorious splendor 1819
145:11 of your kingdom and s *of* your might, 1819
145:21 My mouth *will* s in praise of the LORD. 1819
Pr 6:22 when you awake, they *will* s *to* you. 8488
8:6 I open my lips to s what is right. NIH
16:10 The lips of a king s as an oracle, NIH
20:15 but **lips** *that* s knowledge are a rare jewel. AIT
23:9 *Do* not s to a fool, 1819
23:16 when your lips s what is right. 1819
31:8 **"S up** for those who cannot speak 7023+7337
31:8 up for **those who cannot** s *for themselves,* 522
31:9 **S up** and judge fairly; 7023+7337
Ecc 3:7 a time to be silent and a time to **s,** 1819
Isa 8:20 If *they do* not s according to this word, 606
19:18 in Egypt *will* s the language of Canaan 1819
28:11 and strange tongues God *will* s 1819
29:4 Brought low, *you will* s from the ground; 1819
36:5 but *you* s only empty words. 606
36:11 "Please s to your servants in Aramaic, 1819
36:11 Don't s to us in Hebrew in the hearing of 1819
40:2 S tenderly *to* Jerusalem, 1819
41:1 Let them come forward and **s;** 1819
44:9 **Those who** would **s up for** 6332
45:19 I, the LORD, s the truth; 1819
53:8 And who *can* s *of* his descendants? 8488
59:4 They rely on empty arguments and s lies; 1819
Jer 1:6 I said, "I do not know how *to* **s;** 1819
5:5 So I will go to the leaders and s *to* them; 1819
6:10 To whom *can I* s and give warning? 1819
10:5 their idols cannot **s;** 1819
12:1 Yet *I would* s with you about your justice: 1819
12:6 though *they* s well of you. 1819
14:17 **"S** this word to them: 606
20:8 Whenever *I* **s,** I cry out proclaiming violence 1819
20:9 "I will not mention him or s any more 1819
23:16 *They* s visions from their own minds, 1819
23:21 *I did* not s to them, 1819
23:28 the one who has my word s it faithfully. 1819
26:2 the LORD's house and s to all the people 1819
26:7 the people heard Jeremiah s these words in 1819
26:15 to you to s all these words in your hearing." 1819
31:20 I often s against him, I still remember him. 1819
32:4 and *will* s *with* him face to face 1819
34:3 and he *will* s *with* you face to face. 1819
48:27 in scorn whenever you s of her? 1821
La 3:37 Who *can* s and have it happen if 606
Eze 2:1 stand up on your feet and *I will* s to you." 1819
2:7 *You must* s my words to them, 1819
3:1 then go and s to the house of Israel." 1819
3:4 the house of Israel and s my words to them. 1819
3:10 and take to heart all the words *I* s to you. 1819
3:11 to your countrymen in exile and s to them. 1819
3:17 so hear the word I s and give them warning 4946+7023
3:18 or s **out** to dissuade him from his evil ways 1819
3:22 and there *I will* s to you." 1819
3:27 But when I s to you, 1819
12:25 But I the LORD *will* s what I will, 1819
14:4 Therefore s to them and tell them, 1819
20:3 s to the elders of Israel and say to them, 1819
20:27 s to the people of Israel and say to them, 1819
Eze 24:27 *you will* s with him and will no longer 1819
29:3 S to him and say: 1819
33:2 s to your countrymen and say to them: 1819
33:7 so hear the word I s and give them warning 4946+7023
33:8 not s **out** to dissuade him from his ways, 1819
36:6 I s in my jealous wrath 1819
Da 7:25 *He will* s against the Most High 10418+10425
10:11 the words I *am about to* s to you, 1819
10:16 and I opened my mouth and *began to* **s.** 1819
10:19 I was strengthened and said, **"S,** my lord, 1819
Hos 1:2 the LORD began *to* s through Hosea, 1819
2:14 I will lead her into the desert and s tenderly 1819
7:13 to redeem them but they s lies against me. 1819
Mic 6:12 and their tongues s deceitfully. 928+7023
Hab 2:18 he makes idols **that cannot s.** 522
Zep 3:13 *they will* s no lies, nor will deceit be found 1819
Hag 2:2 **"S** to Zerubbabel son of Shealtiel, 606
Zec 8:16 S the truth to each other, 1819
10:2 The idols s deceit, diviners see visions 1819
Mt 10:27 I tell you in the dark, s in the daylight; *3306*
11:7 Jesus began *to* s to the crowd about John: *3306*
12:46 stood outside, wanting *to* s to him. *3281*
12:47 standing outside, wanting *to* s to you." *3281*
13:10 "Why *do you* s to the people in parables?" *3281*
13:13 This is why *I* s to them in parables: *3281*
17:25 Jesus was the first *to* **s.** *3306*
Mk 1:34 but he would not let the demons s *3281*
7:35 and *he began* **to s** plainly. *3281*
7:37 even makes the deaf hear and the mute **s."** *3281*
12:1 He then began *to* s to them in parables: *3281*
16:17 *they will* s in new tongues; *3281*
Lk 1:19 *to* s to you and to tell you this good news. *3281*
1:20 and not able *to* s until the day this happens, *3281*
1:22 When he came out, he could not s to them. *3281*
1:22 to them but remained **unable to s.** *3273*
1:64 and *he began to* **s,** praising God. *3281*
4:41 and would not allow them *to* **s,** *3281*
6:26 Woe to you when all men s well **of** you, *3306*
7:24 Jesus began *to* s to the crowd about John: *3306*
8:10 but to others I s in parables, so that, *NIG*
12:1 Jesus began *to* s first to his disciples, *3306*
20:21 we know that *you* s and teach what is right, *3306*
Jn 3:11 I tell you the truth, *we* s of what we know, *3281*
3:12 will you believe if *I* s **of** heavenly things? *3306*
4:26 Jesus declared, "I who s to you am he." *3281*
7:17 from God or whether I s on my own. *3281*
8:28 that I do nothing on my own but s just what *3281*
9:21 He is of age; he *will* s for himself." *3281*
10:25 miracles I do in my Father's name s for me, *3455*
12:49 For I *did* not s of my own accord, *3281*
14:30 *I will* not s with you much longer, *3281*
16:13 *He will* not s on his own; *3281*
16:13 *he will* s only what he hears, *3281*
19:10 *"Do you* refuse *to* s to me?" *3281*
Ac 1:4 which you have heard me s about. *NIG*
2:4 with the Holy Spirit and began *to* s *3281*
4:17 we must warn these men *to* s no longer *3281*
4:18 not *to* s or teach at all in the name of Jesus. *5779*
4:29 and enable your servants *to* s your word *3281*
5:40 Then they ordered them not *to* s in *3281*
6:11 "We have heard Stephen s words *3281*
8:33 Who *can* s **of** his descendants? *1455*
10:34 Then Peter **began to s:** *487+3306+3836+5125*
11:15 "As I began *to* **s,** the Holy Spirit came on *3281*
11:20 went to Antioch and *began to* s to Greeks *3281*
13:15 of encouragement for the people, please **s."** *3306*
13:42 the people invited them *to* s further **about** *3281*
13:46 "We had *to* s the word of God to you first. *3281*
16:13 *to* s to the women who had gathered there. *3281*
18:14 Just as Paul was about to **s,** *487+3836+5125*
18:26 He began *to* s **boldly** in the synagogue. *4245*
21:37 *"Do you* s Greek?" *1182*
21:39 Please let me s to the people." *3281*
22:2 When they heard *him* s to them in Aramaic, *4715*
23:5 not s evil **about** the ruler of your people.' " *3306*
24:10 When the governor motioned for him *to* **s,** *3306*
25:18 When his accusers got up to **s,** *NIG*
26:1 "You have permission *to* s for yourself." *3306*
26:26 and *I* can s freely to him. *3281*
Ro 3:4 when you s and prevail when you judge." *3364*
9:1 *I* s the truth in Christ— *3306*
15:18 I will not venture *to* s of anything except *3281*
1Co 2:6 s a message of wisdom among the mature, *3281*
2:7 No, *we* s of God's secret wisdom, *3281*
2:13 This is what *we* **s,** not in words taught us by *3281*
10:15 *I* s to sensible people; judge for yourselves *3306*
12:30 Do all s in tongues? Do all interpret? *3281*
13:1 If *I* s in the tongues of men and of angels, *3281*
14:2 in a tongue *does* not s to men but to God. *3281*
14:5 like every one of you *to* s in tongues, *3281*
14:6 brothers, if I come to you and s in tongues, *3281*
14:9 *you* s intelligible words with your tongue, *1443*
14:18 that *I* s in tongues more than all of you. *3281*
14:19 I would rather s five intelligible words *3281*
14:21 and through the lips of foreigners *I will* s *3281*
14:27 should **s,** one at a time, and someone must *NIG*
14:28 in the church and s to himself and God. *3281*
14:29 Two or three prophets *should* **s,** *3281*
14:34 They are not allowed *to* **s,** *3281*
14:35 for it is disgraceful for a woman *to* s in *3281*
2Co 2:17 in Christ *we* s before God with sincerity, *3281*
4:13 of faith we also believe and therefore **s,** *3281*
6:13 *I* s as to my children— *3306*
Eph 4:25 and s truthfully to his neighbor, *3281*
5:19 S to one another with psalms, hymns and *3281*
Php 1:14 *to* s the word of God more courageously *3281*

1Th 2: 4 *we* s as men approved by God to *3281*
Heb 6: 9 Even though *we* s like this, dear friends, *3281*
Jas 1:19 slow to s and slow to become angry, *3281*
2:12 S and act as those who are going to *3281*
1Pe 3:16 **s maliciously against** your good behavior *2092*
1Jn 4: 5 therefore s from the viewpoint of the world, *3281*
3Jn 1:12 We also **s well of** him, *3455*
Jude 1:10 Yet these men **s abusively against** *1059*
Rev 13:15 so that it *could* s and cause all who refused *3281*

SPEAKER (5) [SPEAK]

Ac 14:12 because he was the chief **s.** *3364*
1Co 14:11 I am a foreigner *to* the s, *3281*
14:28 the s should keep quiet in the church *NIG*
14:30 the first s should stop. *NIG*
2Co 11: 6 I may not be a trained **s,** but I do have *3364*

SPEAKING (102) [SPEAK]

Ge 11: 6 "If as one people s the same language NIH
17:22 When he had finished s with Abraham, 1819
18:33 When the LORD had finished s with Abraham, 1819
45:12 that it is really I who *am* s to you. 1819
Ex 16:10 While Aaron *was* s to the whole Israelite 1819
19: 9 so that the people will hear me **s** with you 1819
31:18 When the LORD finished s to Moses 1819
34:33 When Moses finished s to them, 1819
Nu 7:89 he heard the voice s to him from between 1819
Dt 4:33 the voice of God s out of fire, 1819
5:26 the voice of the living God s out of fire, 1819
20: 9 the officers have finished s to the army, 1819
Jdg 15:17 When he finished **s,** he threw away 1819
1Sa 17:28 heard him s with the men, 1819
2Sa 13:36 As he finished **s,** the king's sons came in, 1819
1Ki 1:22 While she *was* still s with the king, 1819
1:42 Even as he *was* s, Jonathan son of 1819
2Ch 25:16 While he was still **s,** the king said to him, 1819
Job 1:16 While he *was* still **s,** another messenger 1819
1:17 While he *was* still **s,** another messenger 1819
1:18 While he *was* still **s,** yet another messenger 1819
4: 2 But who can keep from **s?** 4863
29: 9 refrained from s and covered their mouths 4863
32: 4 Now Elihu had waited before s to Job 1821
Ps 34:13 from evil and your lips from s lies. 1819
52: 3 falsehood rather than s the truth. 1819
Isa 58:13 and not doing as you please or s idle words, 1819
63: 1 "It is I, s in righteousness, mighty to save." 1819
65:24 while they *are* still s I will hear. 1819
Jer 36: 2 from the time *I began* s to you in the reign 1819
Eze 1:28 and I heard the voice of *one* **s.** 1819
2: 2 and I heard *him* s to me. 1819
43: 6 I heard *someone* s to me from inside 1819
Da 7:11 of the boastful words the horn *was* **s.** 10425
8:13 Then I heard a holy one **s,** 1819
8:18 While he *was* s to me, I was in a deep sleep, 1819
9:20 While I *was* s and praying, 1819
10: 9 Then I heard him **s,** 1821+7754
Zec 1:14 Then the angel who *was* s to me said, 1819
1:19 I asked the angel who *was* s to me, 1819
2: 3 Then the angel who *was* s to me left, 1819
5: 5 the angel who *was* s to me came forward 1819
5:10 I asked the angel who *was* s to me. 1819
6: 4 I asked the angel who *was* s to me, 1819
Mt 10:20 for it will not be you s, but the Spirit *3281*
10:20 but the Spirit of your Father s through you. *3281*
15:31 when they saw the mute **s,** *3281*
17: 5 *While* he *was* still **s,** a bright cloud *3281*
22:43 "How is it then that David, s by the Spirit, *3306*
26:47 *While* he *was* still **s,** Judas, *3281*
Mk 5:35 *While* Jesus *was* still **s,** some men came *3281*
12:36 David himself, s by the Holy Spirit, *NIG*
13:11 for it is not you s, but the Holy Spirit. *3281*
14:43 Just as he *was* **s,** Judas, one of the Twelve, *3281*
Lk 5: 4 When he had finished **s,** he said to Simon, *3281*
8:49 *While* Jesus *was* still **s,** someone came *3281*
9:34 *While* he *was* **s,** a cloud appeared *3306*
11:37 When Jesus had finished **s,** *3281*
22:47 *While* he *was* still s a crowd came up, *3281*
22:60 Just as he *was* **s,** the rooster crowed. *3281*
Jn 7:26 Here he is, s publicly, and they are not *3281*
9:37 in fact, he is the one s with you." *3281*
11:13 Jesus *had been* s of his death, *3306*
12:36 When he *had finished* **s,** *3281*
16:25 "Though *I have been* s figuratively, *3281*
16:29 "Now *you are* s clearly and without figures *3281*
Ac 2: 6 each one heard them s in his own language. *3281*
2: 7 "Are not all these men who *are* s Galileans? *3281*
4: 1 and John *while* they *were* s to the people. *3281*
4:20 For we cannot **help s about** what we *3281+3590*
6:13 "This fellow never stops s against this *3281*
9:28 **s boldly** in the name of the Lord. *4245*
10:44 *While* Peter *was* still s these words, *3281*
10:46 For they heard them s in tongues *3281*
14: 3 **s boldly** for the Lord, *4245*
14: 9 He listened to Paul *as he was* **s.** *3281*
18: 9 *keep on* **s,** do not be silent. *3281*
20: 2 s many words of **encouragement to** *4151*
22: 9 not understand the voice *of* him who *was* s *3281*
22:18 and saw the Lord **s.** *3306*
Ro 7: 1 for *I am* s to men who know the law— *3281*
1Co 1: 5 in all your s and in all your knowledge— *3364*
12: 3 Therefore I tell you that no one *who is* s by *3281*
12:10 **s in** different kinds of **tongues,** *1185*
12:28 *those* **s in** different kinds *of* **tongues.** *1185*
14: 9 You will just be s into the air. *3281*
14:39 and do not forbid s in tongues. *3281*
2Co 10:10 and his s amounts to nothing." *3364*
11:21 *I am* s as a fool—I also dare to boast about. *3306*
12: 6 because *I would be* s the truth. *3306*
12:19 *We have been* s in the sight of God as those *3281*
13: 3 that Christ *is* s through me. *3281*
Eph 4:15 Instead, s *the* **truth** in love, *238*
1Th 2:16 from s to the Gentiles so that they may *3281*
Heb 1: 7 In s of the angels he says, *NIG*
2: 5 about which *we are* **s.** *3281*
11:19 the dead, and **figuratively s,** *1877+4130*
12:19 to a trumpet blast or to such a voice s words *NIG*
1Pe 4:11 he should do it as one s the very words *NIG*
2Pe 3:16 s in them of these matters. *3281*
Rev 1:12 I turned around to see the voice that *was* s *3281*
4: 1 And the voice I had first heard s to me like *3281*

SPEAKS (51) [SPEAK]

Ex 33:11 face to face, as a man s with his friend. 1819
Dt 5:24 that a man can live even if God s with him. 1819
18:19 to my words that the prophet s in my name, 1819
18:20 a prophet who s in the name of other gods, 1819
1Sa 16:18 He s well and is a fine-looking man. 1821
Job 9: 7 He s to the sun and it does not shine; 606
34:35 'Job s without knowledge; 1819
36:15 *he* s *to* them in their affliction. 265+1655
Ps 15: 2 *who* s the truth from his heart 1819
37:30 and his tongue s what is just. 1819
41: 6 *he* s falsely, while his heart gathers slander; 1819
50: 1 s and summons the earth from the rising of 1819
101: 7 no *one who* s falsely will stand 1819
Pr 8: 7 My mouth s what is true, 2047
13: 3 but he *who* **s rashly** will come to ruin. 7316+8557
16:13 they value a *man who* s the truth. 1819
29:20 Do you see a man who s in haste? 1821
31:26 She s with wisdom, 7023+7337
Isa 9:17 every mouth s vileness. 1819
32: 6 the fool s folly, his mind is busy with evil: 1819
33:15 and s what is right, who rejects gain 1819
Jer 9: 5 and no *one* s the truth. 1819
9: 8 tongue is a deadly arrow; *it* s *with* deceit. 1819
9: 8 With his mouth *each* s cordially 1819
Eze 10: 5 like the voice of God Almighty when he s. 1819
Hab 2: 3 *it* s of the end and will not prove false. 7032
Mt 12:32 Anyone who s a word against the Son *3306*
12:32 but anyone who s against the Holy Spirit *3306*
12:34 of the overflow of the heart the mouth **s.** *3281*
Lk 5:21 "Who is this fellow who s blasphemy? *3281*
6:45 out of the overflow of his heart his mouth **s.** *3281*
12:10 And everyone who s a word against the Son *3306*
Jn 3:31 and s as one from the earth. *3281*
3:34 For the one whom God has sent s the words *3281*
7:18 He who s on his own does so to gain honor *3281*
8:44 When he lies, *he* s his native language, *3281*
Ro 4: 6 when he **s of** the blessedness of the man *3306*
1Co 14: 2 For anyone who s in a tongue does *3281*
14: 3 But everyone who prophesies s to men *3281*
14: 4 He who s in a tongue edifies himself, *3281*
14: 5 He who prophesies is greater than one who s in tongues, *3281*
14:13 For this reason anyone who s in a tongue *3281*
14:23 and everyone s in tongues, *3281*
14:27 If anyone s in a tongue, two— *3281*
Heb 11: 4 by faith *he* still s, even though he is dead. *3281*
12:24 the sprinkled blood that s a better word than *3281*
12:25 See to it that you do not refuse him who **s.** *3281*
Jas 4:11 Anyone who s **against** his brother *2895*
4:11 against his brother or judges him s **against** *2895*
1Pe 4:11 If anyone **s,** he should do it as one speaking *3281*
1Jn 2: 1 **one who s** to the Father **in** *our* **defense—** *4156*

SPEAR (47) [SPEARHEAD, SPEARMEN, SPEARS]

Nu 25: 7 he left the assembly, took a s in his hand 8242
25: 8 He drove the s through both of them— NIH
Jdg 5: 8 or s was seen among forty thousand 8242
1Sa 13:22 and Jonathan had a sword or s in his hand; 2851
17: 7 His s shaft was like a weaver's rod, 2851
17:45 against me with sword and s and javelin, 2851
17:47 not by sword or s that the LORD saves; 2851
18:10 Saul had a s in his hand 2851
19: 9 as he was sitting in his house with his s 2851
19:10 Saul tried to pin him to the wall with his **s,** 2851
19:10 but David eluded him as Saul drove the s 2851
20:33 But Saul hurled his s at him to kill him. 2851
21: 8 "Don't you have a s or a sword here? 2851
22: 6 And Saul, s in hand, 2851
26: 7 with his **s** stuck in the ground near his head. 2851
26: 8 to the ground with one thrust of my **s;** 2851
26:11 the s and water jug that are near his head, 2851
26:12 the s and water jug near Saul's head, 2851
26:16 Where are the king's s and water jug 2851
26:22 "Here is the king's **s,"** David answered. 2851
2Sa 1: 6 "and there was Saul, leaning on his **s,** 2851
2:23 the butt of his s into Asahel's stomach, 2851
2:23 and the s came out through his back. 2851
21:19 a s with a shaft like a weaver's rod. 2851
23: 7 a tool of iron or the shaft of a **s;** 2851
23: 8 he raised his s against eight hundred men, 2851
23:18 He raised his s against three hundred men, 2851
23:21 Although the Egyptian had a s in his hand, 2851
23:21 He snatched the s from the Egyptian's hand 2851
23:21 and killed him with his own **s.** 2851
1Ch 11:11 he raised his s against three hundred men, 2851
11:20 He raised his s against three hundred men, 2851
11:23 the Egyptian had a s like a weaver's rod 2851
1Ch 11:23 He snatched the s from the Egyptian's hand 2851
11:23 and killed him with his own **s.** 2851
12: 8 and able to handle the shield and **s.** 8242
12:24 men of Judah, carrying shield and **s—** 8242
20: 5 a s with a shaft like a weaver's rod. 2851
2Ch 25: 5 able to handle the s and shield. 8242
Job 39:23 along with the flashing s and lance. 2851
41:26 nor does the s or the dart or the javelin. 2851
Ps 35: 3 Brandish s and javelin against those who 2851
46: 9 he breaks the bow and shatters the **s,** 2851
Jer 6:23 They are armed with bow and **s;** 3959
Hab 3:11 at the lightning of your flashing **s.** 2851
3:14 With his own s you pierced his head 4751
Jn 19:34 of the soldiers pierced Jesus' side *with* a **s,** *3365*

SPEARHEAD (1) [SPEAR]

2Sa 21:16 bronze s weighed three hundred shekels 7802

SPEARMEN (1) [SPEAR]

Ac 23:23 seventy horsemen and two hundred s to go *1287*

SPEARS (21) [SPEAR]

1Sa 13:19 the Hebrews will make swords or **s!"** 2851
1Ki 18:28 and slashed themselves with swords and **s,** 8242
2Ki 11:10 Then he gave the commanders the s 2851
1Ch 12:34 men carrying shields and **s;** 2851
2Ch 11:12 He put shields and s in all the cities, 8242
14: 8 equipped with large shields and with **s,** 8242
23: 9 the commanders of units of a hundred the s 2851
26:14 Uzziah provided shields, **s,** helmets, 8242
Ne 4:13 with their swords, s and bows. 8242
4:16 while the other half were equipped with **s,** 8242
4:21 the work with half the men holding **s,** 8242
Job 41: 7 with harpoons or his head with fishing **s?** 7528
Ps 57: 4 men whose teeth are s and arrows, 2851
Isa 2: 4 and their s into pruning hooks. 2851
Jer 46: 4 Polish your **s,** put on your armor! 8242
50:42 They are armed with bows and **s;** 3959
Eze 39: 9 the bows and arrows, the war clubs and **s.** 8242
Joel 3:10 into swords and your pruning hooks into **s.** 8242
Mic 4: 3 and their s into pruning hooks. 2851
Na 2: 3 the **s of pine** are brandished. 1360
3: 3 flashing swords and glittering **s!** 2851

SPECIAL (33) [ESPECIALLY]

Ge 47: 6 know of any among them with **s ability,** 2657
Lev 22:21 to the LORD to **fulfill a s** vow or as 5624+7098
27: 2 'If anyone **makes a s vow** to dedicate 5624+7098
Nu 6: 2 or woman *wants* to **make a s vow,** 5623+7098
15: 3 for **s vows** or freewill offerings 5624+7098
15: 8 for **a s vow** or a fellowship offering to 5624+7098
Dt 12: 6 your tithes and **s gifts,** 3338+9556
12:11 your tithes and **s gifts,** 3338+9556
12:17 or your freewill offerings or **s gifts.** 3338+9556
Jos 15:19 She replied, "Do me a **s favor.** 1388
Jdg 1:15 She replied, "Do me a **s favor.** 1388
2Sa 13: 6 and **make** some **s bread** in my sight, 4221+4223
16: 6 the **s guard** were on David's right and left. 1475
1Ki 1: 8 and David's **s guard** did not join Adonijah. 1475
1:10 or the **s guard** or his brother Solomon. 1475
Est 1:14 Persia and Media *who* **had s access to** 7156+8011
2: 9 with her beauty treatments and **s food.** 4950
Jer 13:21 those you cultivated as your s allies? 8031
Eze 44:30 of all your **s gifts** will belong to the priests. 9556
45:13 " 'This is the **s gift** you are to offer: 9556
45:16 of the land will participate in this **s gift** for 9556
48: 8 **portion** you are to present **as a s gift.** 9556
48: 9 "The **s portion** you are to offer to 9556
48:12 be a **s gift** to them from the sacred portion 9557
48:20 **As a s gift** *you will* **set aside** 8123
Jn 19:31 and the next day was to be a s Sabbath. *3489*
Ro 14: 6 He who regards one day as **s,** *NIG*
1Co 12:23 less honorable we treat with s honor. *4358*
12:23 unpresentable are treated with s modesty, *4358*
12:23 our presentable parts need no **s treatment.** *5507*
Gal 4:10 You are observing s days and months *NIG*
2Th 3:14 **take s note** of him. *4957*
Jas 2: 3 *If you* **show s attention to** *2098*

SPECIFIC (1) [SPECIFY]

Nu 4:32 to each man the **s things** he is to carry. 3998+5466

SPECIFICATIONS (2) [SPECIFY]

1Ki 6:38 finished in all its details according to its **s.** 5477
2Ch 4: 7 according to the s *for* them and placed them 5477

SPECIFIED (9) [SPECIFY]

Lev 27: 8 is too poor to pay the s **amount,** 6886
Nu 29: 6 grain offerings and drink offerings as **s.** 5477
29:18 drink offerings according to the number **s.** 5477
29:21 drink offerings according to the number **s.** 5477
29:24 drink offerings according to the number **s.** 5477
29:27 drink offerings according to the number **s.** 5477
29:30 drink offerings according to the number **s.** 5477
29:33 drink offerings according to the number **s.** 5477
29:37 drink offerings according to the number **s.** 5477

SPECIFY (1) [SPECIFIC, SPECIFICATIONS, SPECIFIED, SPECIFYING]

1Ki 5: 9 float them in rafts by sea to the place *you* **s.** 8938

SPECIFYING (1) [SPECIFY]
Ac 25:27 to send on a prisoner without s the charges *4955*

SPECK (6) [SPECKLED]
Mt 7: 3 at the **s of sawdust** in your brother's eye *2847*
7: 4 'Let me take the s out of your eye,' *2847*
7: 5 then you will see clearly to remove the s *2847*
Lk 6:41 at the **s of sawdust** in your brother's eye *2847*
6:42 'Brother, let me take the s out of your eye,' *2847*
6:42 then you will see clearly to remove the s *2847*

SPECKLED (10) [SPECK]
Ge 30:32 from them every s or spotted sheep, 5923
30:32 and every spotted or s goat. 5923
30:33 in my possession that is not s or spotted, 5923
30:35 and all the s or spotted female goats 5923
30:39 that were streaked or s or spotted. 5923
31: 8 If he said, 'The s *ones* will be your wages,' 5923
31: 8 then all the flocks gave birth to s *young;* 5923
31:10 with the flock were streaked, s or spotted. 5923
31:12 with the flock are streaked, s or spotted, 5923
Jer 12: 9 to me like a s bird of prey that other birds 7380

SPECTACLE (4)
Eze 28:17 I made a s of you before kings. 8019
Na 3: 6 treat you with contempt and make you a **s.** 8024
1Co 4: 9 We have been made a s to the whole *2519*
Col 2:15 *he* **made** a public s of them, *1258*

SPED (1) [SPEED]
Eze 1:14 The creatures s back and **forth** like flashes 8351

SPEECH (33) [SPEECHES]
Ge 11: 1 world had one language and a common **s.** 1821
Ex 4:10 I am slow of s and tongue." 7023
Ps 19: 2 Day after day they pour forth **s;** 608
19: 3 There is no s or language where their voice 608
55: 9 O Lord, confound their **s,** 4383
55:21 His s is smooth as butter, 7023
Pr 1:21 gateways of the city *she* **makes** her **s:** 606+609
5: 3 and her s is smoother than oil; 2674
8:13 evil behavior and perverse s. 7023
12: 6 but the s *of* the upright rescues them. 7023
16:27 and his s is like a scorching fire. 8557
22:11 and whose s is gracious will have the king 8557
26:25 Though his s is charming, 7754
Ecc 5: 3 the s *of* a fool when there are many words. 7754
Isa 18: 2 an aggressive nation of **strange s,** 7743+7743
18: 7 an aggressive nation of **strange s,** 7743+7743
29: 4 your s will mumble out of the dust. 614
29: 4 out of the dust your s will whisper. 614
33:19 those people of an obscure s, 8557
Jer 5:15 *whose* s you do not understand. 1819+4537
Eze 3: 5 people of obscure s and difficult language, 8557
3: 6 peoples of obscure s and difficult language, 8557
Mk 9:17 by a spirit that has **robbed him of s.** *228*
Jn 10: 6 Jesus used this **figure of s,** *4231*
16:29 and without **figures of s.** *4231*
Ac 5:40 His s persuaded them. *NIG*
7:22 of the Egyptians and was powerful in s *3364*
2Co 6: 7 in truthful s and in the power of God; *3364*
8: 7 in faith, *in* s, in knowledge, *3364*
1Ti 4:12 but set an example for the believers in **s,** *3364*
Tit 2: 8 soundness of s that cannot be condemned, *3364*
1Pe 3:10 from evil and his lips from deceitful **s.** *3281*
2Pe 2:16 by a donkey—a beast **without s—** *936*

SPEECHES (4) [SPEECH]
Job 15: 3 useless words, with s that have no value? 4863
16: 3 Will your long-winded s never end? 1821
16: 4 *I could* **make fine s** against you 928+2488+4863
18: 2 "When will you end these **s?** 4863

SPEECHLESS (3)
Da 10:15 with my face toward the ground and *was* **s.** 519
Mt 22:12 The man *was* **s.** *5821*
Ac 9: 7 The men traveling with Saul stood there **s;** *1917*

SPEED (2) [SPED, SPEED, SPEEDS]
Ro 9:28 his sentence on earth *with* s and finality." *5335*
2Pe 3:12 forward to the day of God and s its coming. *5067*

SPEEDILY (3) [SPEED]
Isa 5:26 Here they come, swiftly and s! 7824
51: 5 My righteousness draws near s, NIH
Joel 3: 4 I will swiftly and s return on your own 4559

SPEEDS (1) [SPEED]
Isa 16: 5 justice and s the cause of righteousness. 4542

SPELL (1) [SPELLS]
Rev 18:23 By your **magic** s all the nations were led *5758*

SPELLS (4) [SPELL]
Dt 18:11 or **casts s,** or who is a medium or 2489+2490
Isa 47: 9 your many sorceries and all your potent **s.** 2490
47:12 "Keep on, then, with your **magic** s and 2490
Mic 5:12 and you will no longer **cast s.** 6726

SPELT (3)
Ex 9:32 The wheat and **s,** however, 4081
Isa 28:25 barley in its plot, and s in its field? 4081
Eze 4: 9 beans and lentils, millet and **s;** 4081

SPEND (42) [SPENDING, SPENT]
Ge 19: 2 You can wash your feet and s **the night** and 4328
19: 2 *"we will* s **the night** in the square." 4328
24:23 in your father's house for us to s **the night?** 4328
24:25 as well as room for you to s **the night."** 4328
Nu 22: 8 "S the night here," Balaam said to them, 4328
Dt 32:23 upon them and s my arrows against them. 3983
Jdg 16: 1 **went in to** s **the night with** her. 448+995
19: 9 **S the night** here; the day is nearly over. 4328
19:11 at this city of the Jebusites and s **the night."** 4328
19:13 to reach Gibeah or Ramah and s **the night** 4328
19:15 There they stopped to s **the night.** 4328
19:20 Only don't s **the night** in the square." 4328
20: 4 to Gibeah in Benjamin to s **the night.** 4328
2Sa 17: 8 *he will* not s **the night** with the troops. 4328
17:16 not s the night at the fords in the desert; 4328
1Ch 9:27 *They would* s **the night** stationed around 4328
Ne 13:21 "Why *do* you s **the night** by the wall? 4328
Job 21:13 *They* s their years in prosperity and go 3983
24: 7 Lacking clothes, *they* s **the night** naked; 4328
31:32 but no stranger *had to* s **the night** in 4328
36:11 *they will* s the rest of their days 3983
Ps 25:13 He *will* s *his* **days** in prosperity, 4328
Pr 31: 3 *do* not s your strength on women, 5989
SS 7:11 *let us* s **the night** in the villages. 4328
Isa 55: 2 Why s money on what is not bread, 9202
58:10 if *you* s yourselves in behalf of the hungry 7049
65: 4 and s *their* **nights** keeping secret vigil; 4328
Eze 6:12 So *will I* s my wrath upon them. 3983
7: 8 on you and s my anger against you; 3983
13:15 So *I will* s my wrath against the wall and 3983
20: 8 and s my anger against them in Egypt. 3983
20:21 and s my anger against them in the desert. 3983
Joel 1:13 Come, **s the night** in sackcloth, 4328
Mk 6:37 to go and s that much on bread and give it *60*
Lk 21:37 and each evening *he* went out to **s the night** *887*
Ac 18:20 they asked him *to* s more **time** *2093+3531+5989*
28:14 who invited us *to* s a week with them. *2152*
1Co 16: 6 or even **s the winter,** *4199*
16: 7 I hope *to* s some **time** with you, *2152+5989*
2Co 12:15 So I *will* very gladly s for you everything *1251*
Jas 4: 3 *you may* s what you get on your pleasures. *1251*
4:13 s a year there, carry on business *4472*

SPENDING (5) [SPEND]
Ac 15:33 *After* s some time there, *4472*
18:23 *After* s some time in Antioch, *4472*
20:16 to avoid s **time** in the province *1181+5990*
25: 6 *After* s eight or ten days with them, *1417*
25:14 Since *they were* s many days there, *1417*

SPENT (33) [SPEND]
Ge 24:54 and drank and s **the night** there. 4328
31:54 After they had eaten, *they* s **the night** there. 4328
32:13 *He* s the night there, 4328
32:21 but *he* himself s the night in the camp. 4328
Lev 26:20 Your strength *will be* s in vain, 9462
Dt 1:46 all the time *you* s there. 3782
Jos 6:11 to camp and s **the night** there. 4328
8: 9 but Joshua s that night with the people. 4328
Jdg 18: 2 where *they* s **the night.** 4328
2Sa 12:16 and s **the nights** lying on the ground. 4328
14: 2 a woman who *has* s many days **grieving** AIT
1Ki 5:14 so that *they* s one month in Lebanon 2118
6:38 *He had* s seven years **building** it. AIT
19: 9 There he went into a cave and s **the night.** 4328
2Ki 12:13 **was** not **s for making** silver basins. 4946+6913
1Ch 12:39 *The men* s three days there with David, 2118
Ne 9: 3 *s* another quarter *in* **confession** AIT
13:20 of goods s **the night** outside Jerusalem. 4328
Pr 5:11 when your flesh and body *are* s. 3983
Isa 49: 4 *I have* s my strength in vain and 3983
Eze 5:13 And when I *have* s my wrath upon them, 3983
Da 6:18 to his palace and s **the night** without eating 10102
Mt 21:17 to Bethany, where *he* s **the night.** *887*
Mk 5:26 of many doctors and *had* s all she had, *1251*
Lk 6:12 and s **the night** praying to God. *1381+1639*
15:14 *After* he *had* s everything, *1251*
Jn 1:39 and s that day with him. *3531*
3:22 where *he* s **some time** with them, *1417*
Ac 9:19 Saul s several days with the disciples *1181*
14: 3 and Barnabas s considerable time there, *1417*
17:21 foreigners who lived there s *their* **time** doing nothing *2320*
2Co 11:25 *I* s a night and a day in the open sea, *4472*
1Pe 4: 3 For you have s enough time in the *NIG*

SPEW (3) [SPEWED]
Ps 59: 7 See what *they* s from their mouths— 5580
59: 7 they s out swords from their lips, NIH
Jer 51:44 and **make** him **s out** what he has swallowed. 3655+4946+7023

SPEWED (3) [SPEW]
Jer 51:34 and then *has* s us **out.** 5615
Rev 12:15 Then from his mouth the serpent s water *965*
12:16 that the dragon *had* s out of his mouth. *965*

SPICE (4) [SPICED, SPICES]
SS 4:10 the fragrance of your perfume than any **s!** 1411
5: 1 I have gathered my myrrh with my **s.** 1411
5:13 like beds of s yielding perfume. 1411
Rev 18:13 and **s,** of incense, myrrh and frankincense, *319*

SPICE-LADEN (1) [LOAD]
SS 8:14 or like a young stag on the s mountains. 1411

SPICED (1) [SPICE]
SS 8: 2 I would give you s wine to drink, 8380

SPICERY (KJV) See SPICES

SPICES (32) [SPICE]
Ge 37:25 Their camels were loaded with s, 5780
43:11 a little balm and a little honey, *some* s 5780
Ex 25: 6 s for the anointing oil and for 1411
30:23 "Take the following fine **s:** 1411
30:34 LORD said to Moses, "Take **fragrant s—** 6160
35: 8 s for the anointing oil and for 1411
35:28 also brought s and olive oil for the light and 1411
1Ki 10: 2 with camels carrying s, 1411
10:10 large quantities of **s,** and precious stones. 1411
10:10 so many s brought in as those the queen 1411
10:25 weapons and **s,** and horses and mules. 1411
2Ki 20:13 the silver, the gold, the s and the fine oil— 1411
1Ch 9:29 and the oil, incense and **s.** 1411
9:30 of the priests took care of mixing the **s.** 1411
2Ch 9: 1 with camels carrying s, 1411
9: 9 large quantities of **s,** and precious stones. 1411
9: 9 There had never been such s as those 1411
9:24 weapons and **s,** and horses and mules. 1411
16:14 They laid him on a bier covered with s 1411
32:27 **s,** shields and all kinds of valuables. 1411
Ps 75: 8 a cup full of foaming wine **mixed with s;** 5008
SS 3: 6 with myrrh and incense made from all the s 86
4:14 with myrrh and aloes and all the finest **s.** 1411
6: 2 to the beds of **s,** to browse in the gardens 1411
Isa 39: 2 the silver, the gold, the **s,** the fine oil, 1411
Eze 24:10 Cook the meat well, mixing in the **s;** 5350
27:22 of all kinds of s and precious stones, 1411
Mt 23:23 You give a tenth of your **s—mint,** *2455*
Mk 16: 1 and Salome bought s so that they might go *808*
Lk 23:56 Then they went home and prepared s *808*
24: 1 the women took the s they had prepared *808*
Jn 19:40 the two of them wrapped it, with the s, *808*

SPIDER (KJV) See LIZARD

SPIDER'S (2)
Job 8:14 what he relies on is a s web. 6571
Isa 59: 5 the eggs of vipers and spin a s web. 6571

SPIED (4) [SPY]
Jos 6:22 Joshua said to the two men who *had* s **out** 8078
7: 2 So the men went up and s **out** Ai. 8078
Jdg 18:14 Then the five men who *had* s **out** the land 8078
18:17 The five men who *had* s **out** the land went 8078

SPIES (17) [SPY]
Ge 42: 9 about them and said to them, "You *are* **s!** 8078
42:11 Your servants are honest men, not **s."** 8078
42:14 as I told you: You *are* **s!** 8078
42:16 then as surely as Pharaoh lives, you are **s!"** 8078
42:31 'We are honest men; we are not **s.** 8078
42:34 to me so I will know that you *are* not s 8078
Nu 21:32 After Moses had sent s to Jazer, 8078
Jos 2: 1 Joshua son of Nun secretly sent two s 408+8078
2: 7 **the s** on the road that leads to the fords of 2157[S]
2: 8 Before **the s** lay down for the night, 2156[S]
6:17 because she hid the s we sent. 4855
6:25 the men Joshua had sent as s to Jericho— 8078
Jdg 1:24 the s saw a man coming out of the city 9068
Lk 20:20 Keeping a close watch on him, they sent **s,** *1588*
20:21 So the s questioned him: *NIG*
Heb 11:31 Rahab, because she welcomed the s, *2946*
Jas 2:25 when she gave lodging to the s *34*

SPIKENARD (KJV) See NARD

SPILLED (4) [SPILLS]
Ge 38: 9 with his brother's wife, *he* s his semen on 8845
2Sa 14:14 Like water s on the ground, 5599
20:10 and his intestines **s out** on the ground. 9161
Ac 1:18 and all his intestines **s out.** *1772*

SPILLS (1) [SPILLED]
Job 16:13 he pierces my kidneys and s my gall on 9161

SPIN (3) [SPINDLE, SPUN]
Isa 59: 5 the eggs of vipers and s a spider's web. 755
Mt 6:28 They do not labor or s. *3756*
Lk 12:27 They do not labor or s. *3756*

SPINDLE (1) [SPIN]
Pr 31:19 the distaff and grasps the s with her fingers. 7134

SPIRIT (533) [SPIRIT'S, SPIRITIST, SPIRITISTS, SPIRITS, SPIRITUAL, SPIRITUALLY]

Ge 1: 2 the S *of* God was hovering over the waters. 8120
6: 3 "My S will not contend with man forever, 8120
41:38 one in whom is the s *of* God?" 8120
45:27 the s *of* their father Jacob revived. 8120
Ex 31: 3 and I have filled him with the S *of* God, 8120
35:31 and he has filled him with the S *of* God, 8120
Nu 11:17 of the S that is on you and put the Spirit 8120
11:17 of the Spirit that is on you and put the S NIH
11:25 the S that was on him and put the Spirit on 8120
11:25 on him and put the S on the seventy elders. NIH
11:25 When the S rested on them, 8120
11:26 Yet the S also rested on them, 8120
11:29 that the LORD would put his S on them!" 8120
14:24 because my servant Caleb has a different s 8120
24: 2 the S *of* God came upon him 8120
27:18 a man in whom is the s, 8120
Dt 2:30 LORD your God had made his s stubborn 8120
34: 9 of Nun was filled with the s *of* wisdom 8120
Jdg 3:10 The S *of* the LORD came upon him, 8120
6:34 the S *of* the LORD came upon Gideon, 8120
9:23 God sent an evil s between Abimelech and 8120
11:29 the S *of* the LORD came upon Jephthah. 8120
13:25 and the S *of* the LORD began to stir him 8120
14: 6 The S *of* the LORD came upon him 8120
14:19 S *of* the LORD came upon him in power. 8120
15:14 The S *of* the LORD came upon him 8120
1Sa 10: 6 The S *of* the LORD will come upon you 8120
10:10 the S *of* God came upon him in power, 8120
11: 6 the S *of* God came upon him in power, 8120
16:13 from that day on the S *of* the LORD came 8120
16:14 S *of* the LORD had departed from Saul, 8120
16:14 an evil s from the LORD tormented him. 8120
16:15 "See, an evil s *from* God is tormenting you. 8120
16:16 when the evil s *from* God comes upon you, 8120
16:23 Whenever the s *from* God came upon Saul, 8120
16:23 and the evil s would leave him. 8120
18: 1 Jonathan became one in s with David, 5883
18:10 an evil s *from* God came forcefully 8120
19: 9 an evil s *from* the LORD came upon Saul 8120
19:20 the S *of* God came upon Saul's men 8120
19:23 But the S *of* God came even upon him, 8120
28: 8 "Consult a s for me," he said, 200
28:13 "I see a s coming up out of the ground." 466
30: 6 each one was bitter in s because of his sons 5883
2Sa 13:39 the s *of* the king longed to go to Absalom, 8120
23: 2 "The S *of* the LORD spoke through me; 8120
1Ki 18:12 where the S *of* the LORD may carry you 8120
22:21 Finally, a s came forward, 8120
22:22 a lying s in the mouths of all his prophets,' 8120
22:23 a lying s in the mouths of all these prophets 8120
22:24 "Which way did the s *from* the LORD go 8120
2Ki 2: 9 "Let me inherit a double portion of your s," 8120
2:15 said, "The s *of* Elijah is resting on Elisha." 8120
2:16 the S *of* the LORD has picked him up 8120
5:26 not my s with you when the man got down 4213
19: 7 to put such a s in him that when he hears 8120
1Ch 5:26 stirred up the s *of* Pul king of Assyria 8120
12:18 Then the S came upon Amasai, 8120
28:12 that the S had put in his mind for the courts 8120
2Ch 15: 1 The S *of* God came upon Azariah son 8120
18:20 Finally, a s came forward, 8120
18:21 a lying s in the mouths of all his prophets,' 8120
18:22 the LORD has put a lying s in the mouths 8120
18:23 "Which way did the s *from* the LORD go 8120
20:14 Then the S *of* the LORD came upon 8120
24:20 the S *of* God came upon Zechariah son 8120
Ne 9:20 You gave your good S to instruct them. 8120
9:30 By your S you admonished them 8120
Job 4:15 A s glided past my face, 8120
6: 4 my s drinks in their poison; 8120
7:11 I will speak out in the anguish of my s, 8120
10:12 and in your providence watched over my s. 8120
17: 1 My s is broken, my days are cut short, 8120
26: 4 And whose s spoke from your mouth? 5972
31:39 without payment or broken the s 5883
32: 8 But it is the s in a man, 8120
32:18 and the s within me compels me; 8120
33: 4 The S *of* God has made me; 8120
34:14 and he withdrew his s and breath, 8120
Ps 31: 5 Into your hands I commit my s; 8120
32: 2 against him and in whose s is no deceit. 8120
34:18 and saves those who are crushed in s. 8120
51:10 O God, and renew a steadfast s within me. 8120
51:11 from your presence or take your Holy S 8120
51:12 of your salvation and grant me a willing s, 8120
51:17 The sacrifices of God are a broken s; 8120
73:21 my heart was grieved and my s embittered, 4000
76:12 He breaks the s *of* rulers; 8120
77: 3 I mused, and my s grew faint. 8120
77: 6 My heart mused and my s inquired: 8120
104:30 When you send your S, they are created, 8120
106:33 for they rebelled against the S *of* God, 8120
139: 7 Where can I go from your S? 8120
142: 3 When my s grows faint within me, 8120
143: 4 So my s grows faint within me; 8120
143: 7 O LORD; my s fails. 8120
143:10 may your good S lead me on level ground. 8120
146: 4 their s departs, they return to the ground; 8120
Pr 15: 4 but a deceitful tongue crushes the s. 8120
15:13 but heartache crushes the s. 8120
16:18 a haughty s before a fall. 8120
16:19 be lowly in s and among the oppressed than 8120
Pr 17:22 but a crushed s dries up the bones. 8120
18:14 A man's s sustains him in sickness, 8120
18:14 but a crushed s who can bear? 8120
20:27 The lamp of the LORD searches the s *of* 5972
25:13 he refreshes the s *of* his masters. 5883
29:23 but a man of lowly s gains honor. 8120
Ecc 3:21 if the s *of* man rises upward and if the spirit 8120
3:21 and if the s *of* the animal goes down 8120
7: 9 Do not be quickly provoked in your s, 8120
12: 7 and the s returns to God who gave it. 8120
Isa 4: 4 from Jerusalem by a s *of* judgment and 8120
4: 4 by a spirit of judgment and a s *of* fire. 8120
11: 2 The S *of* the LORD will rest on him— 8120
11: 2 the S *of* wisdom and *of* understanding, 8120
11: 2 the S *of* counsel and *of* power, 8120
11: 2 and of power, the S *of* knowledge and *of* 8120
19:14 The LORD has poured into them a s 8120
26: 9 in the morning my s longs for you. 8120
28: 6 a s *of* justice to him who sits in judgment, 8120
29:24 in s will gain understanding; 8120
30: 1 but not by my S, heaping sin upon sin; 8120
31: 3 their horses are flesh and not s. 8120
32:15 till the S is poured upon us from on high, 8120
34:16 and his S will gather them together. 8120
37: 7 to put a s in him so that when he hears 8120
38:16 and my s finds life in them too. 8120
42: 1 I will put my S on him 8120
44: 3 I will pour out my S on your offspring, 8120
48:16 Sovereign LORD has sent me, with his S. 8120
54: 6 a wife deserted and distressed in s— 8120
57:15 with him who is contrite and lowly in s, 8120
57:15 the s *of* the lowly and to revive the heart of 8120
57:16 the s of man would grow faint before me— 8120
59:21 "My S, who is on you, 8120
61: 1 The S *of* the Sovereign LORD is on me, 8120
61: 3 garment of praise instead of a s *of* despair. 8120
63:10 Yet they rebelled and grieved his Holy S. 8120
63:11 is he who set his Holy S among them, 8120
63:14 they were given rest by the S *of* the LORD. 8120
65:14 of heart and wail in brokenness of s. 8120
66: 2 he who is humble and contrite in s, 8120
Jer 51: 1 up the s *of* a destroyer against Babylon and 8120
La 1:16 no one to restore my s. 5883
Eze 1:12 Wherever the s would go, they would go, 8120
1:20 Wherever the s would go, they would go, 8120
1:20 s *of* the living creatures was in the wheels. 8120
1:21 s *of* the living creatures was in the wheels. 8120
2: 2 the S came into me and raised me 8120
3:12 Then the S lifted me up, 8120
3:14 The S then lifted me up and took me away, 8120
3:14 in bitterness and in the anger of my s, 8120
3:24 S came into me and raised me to my feet. 8120
8: 3 The S lifted me up between earth 8120
10:17 the s *of* the living creatures was in them. 8120
11: 1 Then the S lifted me up and brought me to 8120
11: 5 Then the S *of* the LORD came upon me, 8120
11:19 an undivided heart and put a new s in them; 8120
11:24 The S lifted me up and brought me to 8120
11:24 in Babylonia in the vision given by the S 8120
13: 3 the foolish prophets who follow their own s 8120
18:31 and get a new heart and a new s. 8120
21: 7 every s will become faint 8120
36:26 I will give you a new heart and put a new s 8120
36:27 And I will put my S in you and move you 8120
37: 1 by the S *of* the LORD and set me in 8120
37:14 I will put my S in you and you will live, 8120
39:29 I will pour out my S on the house of Israel, 8120
43: 5 Then the S lifted me up and brought me 8120
Da 4: 8 and the s *of* the holy gods is in him.) 10658
4: 9 I know that the s *of* the holy gods is in you, 10658
4:18 because the s *of* the holy gods is in you." 10658
5:11 a man in your kingdom who has the s *of* 10658
5:14 I have heard that the s *of* the gods is in you 10658
7:15 "I, Daniel, was troubled in s, 10658
Hos 4:12 A s *of* prostitution leads them astray; 8120
5: 4 A s *of* prostitution is in their heart; 8120
Joel 2:28 I will pour out my S on all people. 8120
2:29 I will pour out my S in those days. 8120
Mic 2: 7 "Is the S *of* the LORD angry? 8120
3: 8 with the S *of* the LORD, 8120
Hag 1:14 up the s *of* Zerubbabel son of Shealtiel, 8120
1:14 and the s *of* Joshua son of Jehozadak, 8120
1:14 the s *of* the whole remnant of the people. 8120
2: 5 And my S remains among you. 8120
Zec 4: 6 'Not by might nor by power, but by my S,' 8120
6: 8 the north country have given my S rest in 8120
7:12 that the LORD Almighty had sent by his S 8120
12: 1 and who forms the s *of* man within him, 8120
12:10 of Jerusalem a s *of* grace and supplication. 8120
13: 2 "I will remove both the prophets and the s 8120
Mal 2:15 In flesh and s they are his. 8120
2:15 So guard yourself in your s, 8120
2:16 So guard yourself in your s, 8120
Mt 1:18 to be with child through the Holy S. *4460*
1:20 what is conceived in her is from the Holy S. *4460*
3:11 He will baptize you with the Holy S and *4460*
3:16 and he saw the S of God descending like *4460*
4: 1 Then Jesus was led by the S into the desert *4460*
5: 3 "Blessed are the poor *in* s, *4460*
10:20 the S of your Father speaking through you. *4460*
12:18 I will put my S on him, *4460*
12:28 But if I drive out demons by the S of God, *4460*
12:31 but the blasphemy against the S will not *4460*
12:32 against the Holy S will not be forgiven, *4460*
12:43 "When an evil s comes out of a man, *4460*
22:43 speaking by the S, calls him 'Lord'? *4460*
26:41 The s is willing, but the body is weak." *4460*
Mt 27:50 he gave up his s. *4460*
28:19 and of the Son and *of* the Holy S, *4460*
Mk 1: 8 but he will baptize you with the Holy S." *4460*
1:10 and the S descending on him like a dove. *4460*
1:12 At once the S sent him out into the desert, *4460*
1:23 who was possessed by an evil s cried out, *4460*
1:26 The evil s shook the man violently *4460*
2: 8 Immediately Jesus knew *in* his s *4460*
3:29 against the Holy S will never be forgiven; *4460*
3:30 "He has an evil s." *4460*
5: 2 an evil s came from the tombs to meet him. *4460*
5: 8 "Come out of this man, *you* evil s!" *4460*
7:25 by an evil s came and fell at his feet. *4460*
9:17 who is possessed by a s that has robbed him *4460*
9:18 I asked your disciples to drive out **the** s, *899S*
9:20 When the s saw Jesus, *4460*
9:25 he rebuked the evil s. *4460*
9:25 "You deaf and mute s," he said, *4460*
9:26 The s shrieked, convulsed him violently *NIG*
12:36 David himself, speaking by the Holy S, *4460*
13:11 for it is not you speaking, but the Holy S. *4460*
14:38 The s is willing, but the body is weak." *4460*
Lk 1:15 and he will be filled *with* the Holy S even *4460*
1:17 in the s and power of Elijah, *4460*
1:35 "The Holy S will come upon you, *4460*
1:41 and Elizabeth was filled *with* the Holy S. *4460*
1:47 and my s rejoices in God my Savior, *4460*
1:67 *with* the Holy S and prophesied: *4460*
1:80 the child grew and became strong *in* s; *4460*
2:25 and the Holy S was upon him. *4460*
2:26 to him by the Holy S that he would not die *4460*
2:27 Moved by the S, he went into the temple *4460*
3:16 He will baptize you with the Holy S and *4460*
3:22 and the Holy S descended on him *4460*
4: 1 Jesus, full *of* the Holy S, returned from *4460*
4: 1 and was led by the S in the desert, *4460*
4:14 returned to Galilee in the power *of* the S, *4460*
4:18 "The S of the Lord is on me, *4460*
4:33 a man possessed by a demon, an evil s. *4460*
8:29 For Jesus had commanded the evil s *4460*
8:55 Her s returned, and at once she stood up. *4460*
9:39 A s seizes him and he suddenly screams; *4460*
9:42 But Jesus rebuked the evil s, *4460*
10:21 full of joy through the Holy S, said, *4460*
11:13 the Holy S to those who ask him!" *4460*
11:24 "When an evil s comes out of a man, *4460*
12:10 against the Holy S will not be forgiven. *4460*
12:12 for the Holy S will teach you at that time *4460*
13:11 by a s for eighteen years. *4460*
23:46 "Father, into your hands I commit my s." *4460*
Jn 1:32 the S come down from heaven as a dove *4460*
1:33 'The man on whom you see the S come *4460*
1:33 who will baptize with the Holy S.' *4460*
3: 5 unless he is born of water and the S. *4460*
3: 6 but the S gives birth to spirit. *4460*
3: 6 but the Spirit gives birth to s. *4460*
3: 8 So it is with everyone born of the S." *4460*
3:34 for God gives the S without limit. *4460*
4:23 the Father in s and truth, *4460*
4:24 God is s, and his worshipers must worship *4460*
4:24 and his worshipers must worship in s and *4460*
6:63 S gives life; the flesh counts for nothing. *4460*
6:63 The words I have spoken to you are s *4460*
7:39 By this he meant the S, *4460*
7:39 Up to that time the S had not been given, *4460*
11:33 he was deeply moved *in* s and troubled. *4460*
13:21 Jesus was troubled *in* s and testified, *4460*
14:17 the S of truth. The world cannot accept him, *4460*
14:26 But the Counselor, the Holy S, *4460*
15:26 S of truth who goes out from the Father, *4460*
16:13 But when he, the S of truth, comes, *4460*
16:15 the S will take from what is mine *NIG*
19:30 he bowed his head and gave up his s. *4460*
20:22 "Receive the Holy S. *4460*
Ac 1: 2 after giving instructions through the Holy S *4460*
1: 5 be baptized with the Holy S." *4460*
1: 8 when the Holy S comes on you; *4460*
1:16 the Holy S spoke long ago through *4460*
2: 4 All of them were filled *with* the Holy S *4460*
2: 4 in other tongues as the S enabled them. *4460*
2:17 I will pour out my S on all people. *4460*
2:18 I will pour out my S in those days, *4460*
2:33 from the Father the promised Holy S *4460*
2:38 you will receive the gift *of* the Holy S. *4460*
4: 8 Peter, filled *with* the Holy S, said to them: *4460*
4:25 You spoke by the Holy S through *4460*
4:31 And they were all filled *with* the Holy S *4460*
5: 3 the Holy S and have kept for yourself some *4460*
5: 9 could you agree to test the S of the Lord? *4460*
5:32 and so is the Holy S, whom God has given *4460*
6: 3 to be full *of* the S and wisdom. *4460*
6: 5 a man full of faith and *of* the Holy S; *4460*
6:10 not stand up against his wisdom or the S *4460*
7:51 You always resist the Holy S! *4460*
7:55 But Stephen, full *of* the Holy S, *4460*
7:59 Stephen prayed, "Lord Jesus, receive my s." *4460*
8:15 that they might receive the Holy S, *4460*
8:16 Holy S had not yet come upon any of them; *NIG*
8:17 and they received the Holy S. *4460*
8:18 When Simon saw that the S was given at *4460*
8:19 I lay my hands may receive the Holy S." *4460*
8:29 The S told Philip, "Go to that chariot *4460*
8:39 S of the Lord suddenly took Philip away, *4460*
9:17 and be filled *with* the Holy S." *4460*
9:31 and encouraged *by* the Holy S, *4460*
10:19 the S said to him, "Simon, three men are *4460*
10:38 anointed Jesus of Nazareth *with* the Holy S *4460*

Ac 10:44 Holy S came on all who heard the message. *4460*
10:45 *of* the Holy S had been poured out even on *4460*
10:47 They have received the Holy S just *4460*
11:12 The S told me to have no hesitation *4460*
11:15 the Holy S came on them as he had come *4460*
11:16 but you will be baptized with the Holy S.' *4460*
11:24 full *of* the Holy S and faith, *4460*
11:28 stood up and through the S predicted that *4460*
13: 2 the Holy S said, "Set apart for me *4460*
13: 4 sent on their way by the Holy S, *4460*
13: 9 filled *with* the Holy S, *4460*
13:52 with joy and *with* the Holy S. *4460*
15: 8 that he accepted them by giving the Holy S *4460*
15:28 It seemed good *to* the Holy S and to us not *4460*
16: 6 by the Holy S from preaching the word in *4460*
16: 7 but the S of Jesus would not allow them to. *4460*
16:16 s by **which** she **predicted the future.** *4460+4780*
16:18 that he turned around and said *to* the s, *4460*
16:18 At that moment the s left her. *NIG*
19: 2 the Holy S when you believed?" *4460*
19: 2 not even heard that there is a Holy S." *4460*
19: 6 the Holy S came on them, *4460*
19:15 the evil s answered them, "Jesus I know, *4460*
19:16 the man who had the evil s jumped on them *4460*
20:22 "And now, compelled *by* the S, *4460*
20:23 that in every city the Holy S warns me *4460*
20:28 the Holy S has made you overseers. *4460*
21: 4 Through the S they urged Paul not to go on *4460*
21:11 "The Holy S says, 'In this way, *4460*
23: 9 if a s or an angel has spoken to him?" *4460*
28:25 "The Holy S spoke the truth to your *4460*
Ro 1: 4 the S of holiness was declared with power *4460*
2:29 by the S, not by the written code. *4460*
5: 5 his love into our hearts by the Holy S, *4460*
7: 6 so that we serve in the new way *of* the S, *4460*
8: 2 the S of life set me free from the law of sin *4460*
8: 4 to the sinful nature but according to the S. *4460*
8: 5 with the S have their minds set on what *4460*
8: 5 minds set on what the S desires. *4460*
8: 6 mind controlled *by* the S is life and peace; *4460*
8: 9 not by the sinful nature but by the S, *4460*
8: 9 if the S of God lives in you. *4460*
8: 9 if anyone does not have the S of Christ, *4460*
8:10 yet your s is alive because of righteousness. *4460*
8:11 And if the S of him who raised Jesus from *4460*
8:11 to your mortal bodies through his S, *4460*
8:13 if *by* the S you put to death the misdeeds of *4460*
8:14 because those who are led *by* the S *4460*
8:15 not receive a s that makes you a slave again *4460*
8:15 but you received the S of sonship. *4460*
8:16 The S himself testifies with our spirit *4460*
8:16 with our s that we are God's children. *4460*
8:23 who have the firstfruits *of* the S, *4460*
8:26 the S helps us in our weakness. *4460*
8:26 the S himself intercedes for us with groans *4460*
8:27 knows the mind *of* the S, *4460*
8:27 because the S intercedes for the saints *NIG*
9: 1 my conscience confirms it in the Holy S— *4460*
11: 8 "God gave them a s of stupor, *4460*
14:17 peace and joy in the Holy S, *4460*
15: 5 give you a s **of unity** among *899+3836+5858*
15:13 with hope by the power *of* the Holy S. *4460*
15:16 sanctified by the Holy S. *4460*
15:19 and miracles, through the power *of* the S. *4460*
15:30 and by the love *of* the S, *4460*
1Co 2:10 but God has revealed it to us by his S. *4460*
2:10 The S searches all things, *4460*
2:11 the thoughts of a man except the man's s *4460*
2:11 the thoughts of God except the S of God. *4460*
2:12 We have not received the s of the world but *4460*
2:12 of the world but the S who is from God, *4460*
2:13 but in words taught *by* the S, *4460*
2:14 The man **without the** S does not accept *6035*
2:14 not accept the things that *come from* the S *4460*
3:16 and that God's S lives in you? *4460*
4:21 or in love and with a gentle s? *4460*
5: 3 I am with you *in* s. *4460*
5: 4 of our Lord Jesus and I am with you in s, *4460*
5: 5 be destroyed and his s saved on the day of *4460*
6:11 of the Lord Jesus Christ and by the S *4460*
6:17 with the Lord is one with him in s. *4460*
6:19 that your body is a temple *of* the Holy S, *4460*
7:34 be devoted to the Lord *in* both body and s. *4460*
7:40 and I think that I too have the S of God. *4460*
12: 3 that no one who is speaking by the S *4460*
12: 3 "Jesus is Lord," except by the Holy S. *4460*
12: 4 different kinds of gifts, but the same S. *4460*
12: 7 *of* the S is given for the common good. *4460*
12: 8 through the S the message of wisdom, *4460*
12: 8 of knowledge by means of the same S, *4460*
12: 9 to another faith by the same S, *4460*
12: 9 to another gifts of healing by that one S, *4460*
12:11 the work of one and the same S, *4460*
12:13 For we were all baptized by one S *4460*
12:13 and we were all given the one S to drink. *4460*
14: 2 he utters mysteries *with* his s. *4460*
14:14 For if I pray in a tongue, my s prays, *4460*
14:15 I will pray *with* my s, *4460*
14:15 I will sing *with* my s, *4460*
14:16 If you are praising God with your s, *4460*
15:45 the last Adam, a life-giving s. *4460*
16:18 For they refreshed my s and yours also. *4460*
2Co 1:22 and put his S in our hearts as a deposit, *4460*
3: 3 with ink but *with* the S of the living God, *4460*
3: 6 not of the letter but *of* the S; *4460*
3: 6 for the letter kills, but the S gives life. *4460*
3: 8 *of* the S be even more glorious? *4460*
2Co 3:17 Now the Lord is the S, *4460*
3:17 and where the S of the Lord is, *4460*
3:18 which comes from the Lord, who is the S. *4460*
4:13 With that same s of faith we also believe *4460*
5: 5 for this very purpose and has given us the S *4460*
6: 6 in the Holy S and in sincere love; *4460*
7: 1 that contaminates body and s, *4460*
7:13 his s has been refreshed by all of you. *4460*
11: 4 a different s from the one you received, *4460*
12:18 *in* the same s and follow the same course? *4460*
13:14 fellowship *of* the Holy S be with you all. *4460*
Gal 3: 2 Did you receive the S by observing *4460*
3: 3 After beginning *with* the S, *4460*
3: 5 Does God give you his S *4460*
3:14 might receive the promise *of* the S. *4460*
4: 6 God sent the S of his Son into our hearts, *4460*
4: 6 the S who calls out, "Abba, Father." *NIG*
4:29 the son born by the power of the S. *4460*
5: 5 the S the righteousness for which we hope. *4460*
5:16 So I say, live *by* the S, *4460*
5:17 desires what is contrary to the S, *4460*
5:17 the S what is contrary to the sinful nature. *4460*
5:18 But if you are led *by* the S, *4460*
5:22 But the fruit *of* the S is love, joy, peace, *4460*
5:25 Since we live *by* the S, *4460*
5:25 let us keep in step *with* the S. *4460*
6: 8 the one who sows to please the S, *4460*
6: 8 from the S will reap eternal life. *4460*
6:18 of our Lord Jesus Christ be with your s, *4460*
Eph 1:13 with a seal, the promised Holy S, *4460*
1:17 the S of wisdom and revelation, *4460*
2: 2 the s who is now at work *4460*
2:18 both have access to the Father by one S. *4460*
2:22 a dwelling in which God lives by his S. *4460*
3: 5 the S to God's holy apostles and prophets. *4460*
3:16 through his S in your inner being, *4460*
4: 3 to keep the unity *of* the S through the bond *4460*
4: 4 There is one body and one S— *4460*
4:30 And do not grieve the Holy S of God, *4460*
5:18 Instead, be filled with the S. *4460*
6:17 of salvation and the sword *of* the S, *4460*
6:18 in the S on all occasions with all kinds *4460*
Php 1:19 and the help given *by* the S of Jesus Christ, *4460*
1:27 I will know that you stand firm in one s, *4460*
2: 1 if any fellowship *with* the S, *4460*
2: 2 being one in s and purpose. *5249*
3: 3 we who worship *by* the S of God, *4460*
4:23 of the Lord Jesus Christ be with your s. *4460*
Col 1: 8 and who also told us of your love in the S. *4460*
2: 5 *in* s and delight to see how orderly you are *4460*
1Th 1: 5 with the Holy S and with deep conviction. *4460*
1: 6 with the joy *given by* the Holy S. *4460*
4: 8 who gives you his Holy S. *4460*
5:23 May your whole s, soul and body be kept *4460*
2Th 2:13 through the sanctifying work *of* the S and *4460*
1Ti 3:16 was vindicated by the S, *4460*
4: 1 The S clearly says that in later times *4460*
2Ti 1: 7 For God did not give us a s of timidity, *4460*
1: 7 but a s of power, of love and *NIG*
1:14 the help *of* the Holy S who lives in us. *4460*
4:22 The Lord be with your s. *4460*
Tit 3: 5 of rebirth and renewal *by* the Holy S, *4460*
Phm 1:25 of the Lord Jesus Christ be with your s. *4460*
Heb 2: 4 *of* the Holy S distributed according *4460*
3: 7 So, as the Holy S says: "Today, *4460*
4:12 it penetrates even to dividing soul and s, *4460*
6: 4 who have shared in the Holy S, *4460*
9: 8 The Holy S was showing by this that *4460*
9:14 the eternal S offered himself unblemished *4460*
10:15 The Holy S also testifies to us about this. *4460*
10:29 and who has insulted the S of grace? *4460*
Jas 2:26 As the body without the s is dead, *4460*
4: 5 without reason that the s he caused to live *4460*
1Pe 1: 2 through the sanctifying *work of* the S, *4460*
1:11 and circumstances to which the S of Christ *4460*
1:12 to you by the Holy S sent from heaven. *4460*
3: 4 the unfading beauty *of* a gentle and quiet s, *4460*
3:18 in the body but made alive *by* the S, *4460*
4: 6 but live according to God *in regard to* the s. *4460*
4:14 for the S of glory and of God rests on you. *4460*
2Pe 1:21 as they were carried along by the Holy S. *4460*
1Jn 3:24 We know it by the S he gave us. *4460*
4: 1 Dear friends, do not believe every s, *4460*
4: 2 how you can recognize the S of God: *4460*
4: 2 Every s that acknowledges that Jesus Christ *4460*
4: 3 but every s that does not acknowledge Jesus *4460*
4: 3 This is the s of the antichrist, *NIG*
4: 6 This is how we recognize the S of truth and *4460*
4: 6 the Spirit of truth and the s of falsehood. *4460*
4:13 because he has given us of his S. *4460*
5: 6 And it is the S who testifies, *4460*
5: 6 because the S is the truth. *4460*
5: 8 the S, the water and the blood; *4460*
Jude 1:19 and do not have the S. *4460*
1:20 and pray in the Holy S. *4460*
Rev 1:10 On the Lord's Day I was in the S, *4460*
2: 7 let him hear what the S says to the churches. *4460*
2:11 let him hear what the S says to the churches. *4460*
2:17 let him hear what the S says to the churches. *4460*
2:29 let him hear what the S says to the churches. *4460*
3: 6 let him hear what the S says to the churches. *4460*
3:13 let him hear what the S says to the churches. *4460*
3:22 let him hear what the S says to the churches. *4460*
4: 2 At once I was in the S, *4460*
14:13 says the S, "they will rest from their labor, *4460*
17: 3 Then the angel carried me away in the S *4460*
18: 2 for demons and a haunt *for* every evil s, *4460*
Rev 19:10 the testimony of Jesus is the s of prophecy." *4460*
21:10 in the S to a mountain great and high, *4460*
22:17 The S and the bride say, "Come!" *4460*

SPIRIT'S (2) [SPIRIT]

1Co 2: 4 but with a demonstration *of* the S power, *4460*
1Th 5:19 Do not put out the S fire; *4460*

SPIRITIST (2) [SPIRIT]

Lev 20:27 " 'A man or woman who is a medium or s 3362
Dt 18:11 or who is a medium or s or who consults 3362

SPIRITISTS (9) [SPIRIT]

Lev 19:31 " 'Do not turn to mediums or seek out s, 3362
20: 6 the person who turns to mediums and s 3362
1Sa 28: 3 Saul had expelled the mediums and s from 3362
28: 9 He has cut off the mediums and s from 3362
2Ki 21: 6 and consulted mediums and s. 3362
23:24 Josiah got rid of the mediums and s, 3362
2Ch 33: 6 and consulted mediums and s. 3362
Isa 8:19 men tell you to consult mediums and s, 3362
19: 3 spirits of the dead, the mediums and the s. 3362

SPIRITS (47) [SPIRIT]

Nu 16:22 "O God, God of the s of all mankind, 8120
27:16 the God of the s of all mankind, 8120
Jdg 16:25 While they *were* **in high s,** 3201+4213
Ru 3: 7 and drinking and *was* **in good s,** 3512+4213
1Sa 25:36 He *was* **in high s** and very drunk. 3201+4213
2Sa 13:28 When Amnon *is* **in high s** 3201+4213
Est 1:10 King Xerxes *was* **in high s** from wine, 3201+4213
5: 9 that day happy and **in high s.** 3201+4213
Ps 78: 8 whose s were not faithful to him. 8120
Pr 2:18 to death and her paths to the **s of the dead.** 8327
Isa 14: 9 the **s of the departed** to greet you— 8327
19: 3 the idols and the **s of the dead,** 356
26:14 *those* **departed** s do not rise. 8327
Zec 6: 5 "These are the four s *of* heaven, 8120
Mt 8:16 the s with a word and healed all the sick. *4460*
10: 1 to drive out evil s and to heal every disease *4460*
12:45 seven other s more wicked than itself, *4460*
Mk 1:27 He even gives orders *to* evil s *4460*
3:11 Whenever the evil s saw him, *4460*
5:13 the evil s came out and went into the pigs. *4460*
6: 7 by two and gave them authority over evil s. *4460*
Lk 4:36 and power he gives orders *to* evil s *4460*
6:18 Those troubled by evil s were cured, *4460*
7:21 who had diseases, sicknesses and evil s, *4460*
8: 2 who had been cured of evil s and diseases: *4460*
10:20 do not rejoice that the s submit to you, *4460*
11:26 takes seven other s more wicked than itself, *4460*
Ac 5:16 and those tormented by evil s, *4460*
8: 7 With shrieks, evil s came out of many, *4460*
19:12 and the evil s left them. *4460*
19:13 around **driving out evil** s tried to invoke *2020*
23: 8 and that there are neither angels nor s, *4460*
1Co 12:10 to another distinguishing between s, *4460*
14:32 The s of prophets are subject to the control *4460*
1Ti 4: 1 and follow deceiving s and things taught *4460*
Heb 1:14 Are not all angels ministering s sent *4460*
12: 9 to the Father *of* our s and live! *4460*
12:23 *to* the s of righteous men made perfect, *4460*
1Pe 3:19 also he went and preached *to* the s *4460*
1Jn 4: 1 test the s to see whether they are from God, *4460*
Rev 1: 4 and from the seven s before his throne, *4460*
3: 1 of him who holds the seven s of God and *4460*
4: 5 These are the seven s of God. *4460*
5: 6 which are the seven s of God sent out *4460*
16:13 I saw three evil s that looked like frogs; *4460*
16:14 They are s of demons performing *4460*
22: 6 The Lord, the God *of* the s of the prophets, *4460*

SPIRITUAL (30) [SPIRIT]

Ro 1:11 to you some s gift to make you strong— *4461*
7:14 We know that the law is s; *4461*
12: 1 this is your s act of worship. *3358*
12:11 but keep your s fervor, serving the Lord. *4460*
15:27 have shared in the Jews' s blessings, *4461*
1Co 1: 7 not lack any s **gift** as you eagerly wait *5922*
2:13 expressing s truths in spiritual words. *4461*
2:13 expressing spiritual truths *in* s words. *4461*
2:15 The s man makes judgments *4461*
3: 1 not address you as s but as worldly— *4461*
9:11 If we have sown s seed among you, *4461*
10: 3 They all ate the same s food *4461*
10: 4 and drank the same s drink; *4461*
10: 4 from the s rock that accompanied them, *4461*
12: 1 Now about s gifts, brothers, *4461*
14: 1 the way of love and eagerly desire s gifts, *4461*
14:12 Since you are eager to have s gifts, *4460*
15:44 sown a natural body, it is raised a s body. *4461*
15:44 a natural body, there is also a s body. *4461*
15:46 The s did not come first, but the natural, *4461*
15:46 but the natural, and after that the s. *4461*
Gal 6: 1 you who are s should restore him gently. *4461*
Eph 1: 3 the heavenly realms with every s blessing *4461*
5:19 with psalms, hymns and s songs. *4461*
6:12 the s forces of evil in the heavenly realms. *4461*
Col 1: 9 through all s wisdom and understanding. *4461*
3:16 and s songs with gratitude in your hearts *4461*
1Pe 2: 2 Like newborn babies, crave pure s milk, *3358*
2: 5 into a s house to be a holy priesthood, *4461*
2: 5 offering s sacrifices acceptable to God *4461*

SPIRITUALLY (2) [SPIRIT]

1Co 2:14 because they are s discerned. *4462*
14:37 anybody thinks he is a prophet or s gifted, *4461*

SPIT (15) [SPITS, SPITTING]

Nu 12:14 "If her father *had* s in her face, 3762+3762
Dt 25: 9 one of his sandals, s in his face and say, 3762
Job 17: 6 a man in whose face people **s.** 9531
20:15 *He will* **s out** the riches he swallowed; 7794
30:10 they do not hesitate to s in my face. 8371
Mt 26:67 Then *they* s in his face and struck him *1870*
27:30 *They* s on him, and took the staff and *1870*
Mk 7:33 Then he s and touched the man's tongue. *4772*
8:23 *When he had* s on the man's eyes *4772*
10:34 who will mock him and **s on** him, *1870*
14:65 Then some began *to* **s at** him; *1870*
15:19 on the head with a staff and **s on** him. *1870*
Lk 18:32 They will mock him, insult him, **s on** *him,* *1870*
Jn 9: 6 Having said this, *he* s on the ground, *4772*
Rev 3:16 I am about to s you out of my mouth. *1840*

SPITE (15)

Lev 26:23 " 'If **in s of** these things you do 928
26:27 " 'If **in s of** this you still do not listen to me 928
26:44 Yet **in s of** this, when they are in the land 1685
Nu 14:11 **in s of** all the miraculous signs 928
Dt 1:32 **In s of** this, you did not trust in the LORD 928
Ezr 10: 2 But **in s of** this, there is still hope for Israel. 6584
Ne 5:18 **In s of** all this, I never demanded the food 6640
Job 23: 2 his hand is heavy **in s of** my groaning. 6584
Ps 78:32 **In s of** all this, they kept on sinning; 928
78:32 **in s of** his wonders, they did not believe. 928
Isa 47: 9 **in s of** your many sorceries 928
Jer 2:34 Yet **in s of** all this 6584
3:10 **In s of** all this, her unfaithful sister Judah 928
1Th 1: 6 **in s of** severe suffering, you welcomed *1877*
2: 2 tell you his gospel in s of strong opposition. *NIG*

SPITS (1) [SPIT]

Lev 15: 8 the discharge s on someone who is clean, 8394

SPITTING (1) [SPIT]

Isa 50: 6 I did not hide my face from mocking and **s.** 8371

SPLENDID (3) [SPLENDOR]

Isa 22:18 and there your s chariots will remain— 3883
Eze 17: 8 bear fruit and become a s vine.' 168
17:23 and bear fruit and become a s cedar. 129

SPLENDOR (76) [SPLENDID]

1Ch 16:27 S and majesty are before him; 2086
16:29 worship the LORD in the s *of* his holiness. 2079
22: 5 be of great magnificence and fame and s in 9514
29:11 and the glory and the majesty and the **s,** 2086
29:25 and bestowed on him royal s such 2086
2Ch 20:21 for the s *of* his holiness as they went out at 2079
Est 1: 4 the vast wealth of his kingdom and the s 3702
Job 13:11 Would not his s terrify you? 8420
31:23 for fear of his s I could not do such things. 8420
31:26 in its radiance or the moon moving *in* s, 3701
37:22 Out of the north he comes in golden **s;** NIH
40:10 Then adorn yourself with glory and **s,** 1470
Ps 21: 5 you have bestowed on him s and majesty. 2086
29: 2 worship the LORD in the s *of* his holiness. 2079
45: 3 clothe yourself with s and majesty. 2086
49:16 when the s *of* his house increases; 3883
49:17 his s will not descend with him. 3883
71: 8 declaring your s all day long. 9514
78:61 his s into the hands of the enemy. 9514
89:44 to his s and cast his throne to the ground. 3199
90:16 your s to their children. 2077
96: 6 S and majesty are before him; 2086
96: 9 the LORD in the s *of* his holiness; 2079
104: 1 you are clothed with s and majesty. 2086
145: 5 of the glorious s *of* your majesty, 2077
145:12 of your mighty acts and the glorious s 2077
148:13 his s is above the earth and the heavens. 2086
Pr 4: 9 and present you with a crown of **s."** 9514
16:31 Gray hair is a crown of **s;** 9514
20:29 gray hair the s *of* the old. 2077
Isa 2:10 of the LORD and the s *of* his majesty! 2077
2:19 of the LORD and the s *of* his majesty, 2077
2:21 of the LORD and the s *of* his majesty, 2077
10:18 The s *of* his forests and fertile fields 3883
16:14 Moab's s and all her many people 3883
35: 2 the s *of* Carmel and Sharon; 2077
35: 2 the glory of the LORD, the s *of* our God. 2077
46:13 I will grant salvation to Zion, my s to Israel. 9514
49: 3 Israel, in whom *I will* **display** *my* **s."** 6995
52: 1 Put on your garments of **s,** O Jerusalem, 9514
55: 5 for *he has* **endowed** you **with s."** 6995
60: 9 for *he has* **endowed** you **with s.** 6995
60:21 work of my hands, for *the* **display** of my **s.** 6995
61: 3 of the LORD for *the* **display** *of* his **s.** 6995
62: 3 be a crown of s in the LORD's hand, 9514
63: 1 Who is this, robed in **s,** 2075
Jer 22:18 'Alas, my master! Alas, his **s!'** 2086
La 1: 6 All the s has departed from the Daughter 2077
2: 1 down the s *of* Israel from heaven to earth; 9514
3:18 "My s is gone and all that I had hoped from 5905
Eze 16:14 s I had given you made your beauty perfect, 2077
27:10 and helmets on your walls, bringing you **s.** 2077
28: 7 and wisdom and pierce your **shining s.** 3650
28:17 corrupted your wisdom because of your **s.** 3650
31:18 be compared with you in s and majesty? 3883
Da 4:36 my honor and s were returned to me for 10228
5:18 and greatness and glory and **s.** 10199
11:20 a tax collector to maintain the royal **s.** 2078
Hos 10: 5 those who had rejoiced over its **s,** 3883
14: 6 His s will be like an olive tree, 2086
Na 2: 2 The LORD will restore the s *of* Jacob like 1454
2: 2 the splendor of Jacob like the s *of* Israel, 1454
Hab 3: 4 His **s** was like the sunrise; 5586
Mt 4: 8 the kingdoms of the world and their **s.** *1518*
6:29 not even Solomon in all his s was dressed *1518*
Lk 4: 6 "I will give you all their authority and **s,** *1518*
9:31 appeared in **glorious s,** talking with Jesus. *1518*
12:27 not even Solomon in all his s was dressed *1518*
1Co 15:40 but the s of the heavenly bodies is one kind, *1518*
15:40 and the s of the earthly bodies is another. *NIG*
15:41 The sun has one kind of **s,** *1518*
15:41 and star differs from star in **s.** *1518*
2Th 2: 8 the breath of his mouth and destroy *by* the s *2211*
Rev 18: 1 and the earth was illuminated by his s. *1518*
18:14 All your riches and s have vanished, *3287*
21:24 kings of the earth will bring their s into it. *1518*

SPLINT (1)

Eze 30:21 or put in a s so as to become strong enough 3151

SPLINTERED (3)

2Ki 18:21 depending on Egypt, that s reed of a staff, 8368
Isa 36: 6 depending on Egypt, that s reed of a staff, 8368
Eze 29: 7 *you* s and you tore open their shoulders; 8368

SPLIT (24) [SPLITS]

Lev 11: 3 *a* s hoof completely divided and that chews 7271
11: 4 the cud or only *have* a s hoof, 7271
11: 4 *does* not *have* a s hoof; it is ceremonially 7271
11: 5 *does* not *have* a s hoof; it is unclean for you. 7271
11: 6 *does* not *have* a s hoof; it is unclean for you. 7271
11: 7 though it *has* a s hoof completely divided, 7271
11:26 a s hoof not completely divided or that does 7271
Nu 16:31 the ground under them **s apart** 1324
Dt 14: 6 *a* s hoof divided in two and that chews 7271
14: 7 a s hoof completely divided you may 7271
14: 7 *they do* not *have a* s hoof; 7271
14: 8 although it *has a* s hoof, 7271
1Ki 13: 3 The altar *will* **be s apart** and the ashes 7973
13: 5 the altar **was s apart** and its ashes poured 7973
16:21 people of Israel **were** s into two factions; 2745
Ps 74:13 It was you *who* **s open** the sea 7297
78:15 *He* s the rocks in the desert 1324
Isa 24:19 is broken up, the earth **is s asunder,** 7297+7297
48:21 *he* s the rock and water gushed out. 1324
Mic 1: 4 and the valleys **s apart,** 1324
Hab 3: 9 *You* s the earth with rivers; 1324
Zec 14: 4 and the Mount of Olives *will* **be** s in two 1324
Mt 27:51 The earth shook and the rocks **s.** *5387*
Rev 16:19 The great city s into three parts, *1181*

SPLITS (1) [SPLIT]

Ecc 10: 9 *whoever* s logs may be endangered by them. 1324

SPOIL (3) [DESPOIL, SPOILS]

Ps 119:162 in your promise like one who finds great **s.** 8965
Jer 30:16 all *who* **make** s *of* you I will despoil. 1024
1Pe 1: 4 an inheritance that can never perish, s or *299*

SPOILS (10) [SPOIL]

Ex 15: 9 I will divide the **s;** 8965
Nu 31:11 They took all the plunder and **s,** 4917
31:12 s and plunder to Moses and Eleazar 4917
31:27 the s between the soldiers who took part in 4917
31:32 the s that the soldiers took was 675,000 4917
Jdg 5:30 'Are they not finding and dividing the **s:** 8965
Isa 33:23 Then an abundance of s will be divided and 8965
53:12 and he will divide the s with the strong, 8965
Lk 11:22 the man trusted and divides up the **s.** *5036*
Jn 6:27 Do not work for food that s, *660*

SPOKE (184) [SPEAK, SPOKES]

Ge 16:13 She gave this name to the LORD who s 1819
18:27 Then Abraham **s up** again: 6699
18:29 Once again *he* s to him, 1819
19:14 So Lot went out and s to his sons-in-law, 1819
22: 7 Isaac **s up** and said to his father Abraham, 606
23: 3 beside his dead wife and s to the Hittites. 1819
24: 7 and who s to me and promised me on oath, 1819
27: 5 Now Rebekah was listening as Isaac s 1819
34: 3 and he loved the girl and s tenderly to her. 1819
34:13 as *they* s *to* Shechem and his father Hamor. 1819
39:10 And though she s to Joseph day after day, 1819
42: 7 to be a stranger and s harshly to them. 1819
42:24 but then turned back and s to them again. 1819
42:30 over the land s harshly to us and treated us 1819
43:19 So they went up to Joseph's steward and s 1819
46: 2 God s to Israel in a vision at night and said, 606
50:21 he reassured them and s kindly to them. 1819
Ex 6:13 the LORD s to Moses and Aaron about 1819
6:27 They *were* the *ones who* s to Pharaoh king 1819
6:28 Now when the LORD s to Moses in Egypt, 1819
7: 7 and Aaron eighty-three when they s to 1819
19:19 Then Moses s and the voice of God 1819
20: 1 And God s all these words: 1819
32:34 lead the people to the place *I* s *of,* 1819
33: 9 while the LORD s with Moses. 1819
34:31 and he s to them. 1819
Lev 1: 1 The LORD called to Moses and s to him 1819
10: 3 the LORD s *of* when he said: 1819
16: 1 The LORD s to Moses after the death of 1819
24:23 Then Moses s to the Israelites, 1819
Nu 1: 1 The LORD s to Moses in the Tent 1819
7:89 And *he* s with him. 1819
9: 1 The LORD s to Moses in the Desert 1819
11:25 the LORD came down in the cloud and s 1819
11:28 **s up** and said, "Moses, my lord, stop them!" 6699
17: 6 So Moses s to the Israelites, 1819
21: 5 they s against God and against Moses, 1819
21: 7 "We sinned when *we* s against the LORD 1819
26: 3 and Eleazar the priest s with them and said, 1819
36: 1 came and s before Moses and the leaders, 1819
Dt 1: 1 These are the words Moses s to all Israel in 1819
4:12 Then the LORD s to you out of the fire. 1819
4:15 the day the LORD s to you at Horeb out of 1819
5: 4 The LORD s to you face to face out of 1819
5:28 The LORD heard you when you s to me 1819
31: 1 Then Moses went out and s these words 1819
32:44 with Joshua son of Nun and s all the words 1819
Jdg 9:37 But Gaal **s up** again: 1819
1Sa 3:12 carry out against Eli everything *I* s 1819
9:17 "This is the man *I* s to you *about;* 606
19: 4 Jonathan s well of David to Saul his father 1819
24: 4 the day the LORD s *of* when he said NIH
2Sa 3:19 Abner also s *to* the Benjamites in person. 1819
6:22 But by these slave girls *you* s *of,* 606
12:18 *we* s to David but he would not listen to us. 1819
21: 2 The king summoned the Gibeonites and s 606
23: 2 "The Spirit of the LORD s through me; 1819
23: 3 The God of Israel **s,** 606
1Ki 4:32 *He* s three thousand proverbs 1819
2Ki 9:36 "This is the word of the LORD that *he* s 1819
25:28 *He* s kindly to him and gave him a seat 1819
1Ch 21:27 Then the LORD s to the angel, 606
2Ch 1: 2 Then Solomon s to all Israel— 606
30:22 Hezekiah s encouragingly *to* all 1819
32:16 Sennacherib's officers s further against 1819
32:19 *They* s about the God of Jerusalem 1819
33:10 The LORD s to Manasseh and his people, 1819
33:18 to his God and the words the seers s to him 1819
34:27 when you heard **what** he s against this place 1821
36:12 who **s the word** *of* the LORD. 4946+7023
Ne 9:13 *you* s to them from heaven. 1819
13:24 of their children s the language of Ashdod 1819
Est 1:13 he s with the wise men who understood 606
3: 4 Day after day they s to him but he refused 606
7: 9 who **s up** to help the king." 1819
10: 3 of his people and **s up** *for* the welfare of all 1819
Job 26: 4 And whose spirit s from your mouth? 3655
29:11 Whoever heard me **s well of** me, 887
29:22 After I had spoken, they s no more; NIH
32:11 I waited while you **s,** 1821
40: 5 *I* s once, but I have no answer— 1819
40: 6 Then the LORD s *to* Job out of the storm: 6699
42: 3 Surely *I* s *of* things I did not understand, 5583
Ps 33: 9 For he **s,** and it came to be; 606
39: 3 then *I* s with my tongue: 1819
66:14 vows my lips promised and my mouth s 1819
78:19 *They* s against God, saying, 1819
89:19 Once *you* s in a vision, 1819
99: 7 *He* s to them from the pillar of cloud; 1819
105:31 *He* **s,** and there came swarms of flies, 606
105:34 *He* **s,** and the locusts came, 606
107:25 For *he* s and stirred up a tempest 606
SS 2:10 My lover s and said to me, "Arise, 6699
Isa 7:10 Again the LORD s to Ahaz, 1819
8: 5 The LORD s to me again: 1819
8:11 The LORD s to me with his strong hand 606
20: 2 at that time the LORD s through Isaiah son 1819
65:12 *I* s but you did not listen. 1819
66: 4 when I called, no one answered, *when I* **s,** 1819
Jer 7:13 *I* s to you again and again, 1819
7:22 of Egypt and s *to* them, 1819
18:20 that I stood before you and s in their behalf 1819
30: 4 the LORD s concerning Israel and Judah: 1819
35:17 *I* s to them, but they did not listen; 1819
46:13 the message the LORD s to Jeremiah 1819
50: 1 the LORD s through Jeremiah the prophet 1819
52:32 *He* s kindly to him and gave him a seat 1819
Eze 2: 2 As *he* **s,** the Spirit came into me 1819
3:24 *He* s to me and said: 1819
24:18 So *I* s to the people in the morning, 1819
35:13 You boasted against me and s against me 1821
38:17 Are you not the one *I* s *of* in former days 1819
Da 2:14 Daniel s to him *with* wisdom and tact. 10754
6:12 So they went to the king and s to him 10042
7: 8 of a man and a mouth *that* s boastfully. 10425
7:20 that had eyes and a mouth *that* s boastfully. 10425
9: 6 who s in your name to our kings, 1819
10:19 When he s to me, I was strengthened 1819
Hos 12:10 *I* s to the prophets, gave them many visions 1819
13: 1 When Ephraim **s,** men trembled; 1819
Zec 1:13 So the LORD s kind and comforting words 6699
Mt 9:33 the man who had been mute s. *3281*
13:34 Jesus s all these things to the crowd *3281*
22: 1 Jesus s to them again in parables, saying: *3306*
Mk 3:23 Jesus called them and s to them in parables: *3306*
4:33 With many similar parables Jesus s *3281*
6:50 Immediately he s to them and said, *3281*
8:32 *He* s plainly **about** this, *3281*
Lk 1:60 but his mother **s up** and said, *646*

Lk 2:38 she gave thanks to God and s about *3281*
4:22 All **s well of** him and were amazed at *3455*
9:11 and s to them about the kingdom of God, *3281*
9:31 *They* **s about** his departure, *3306*
11:14 the man who had been mute s, *3281*
23:22 For the third time he s to them: "Why? *3306*
Jn 6:8 Andrew, Simon Peter's brother, s up, *3306*
7:46 "No one ever s the way this man does," *3281*
8:12 When Jesus s again to the people, he said, *3281*
8:20 *He* s these words while teaching in *3281*
8:30 *Even as* he s, many put their faith in him. *3281*
9:29 We know that God s to Moses, *3281*
11:49 who was high priest that year, **s up,** *3306*
12:34 The crowd **s up,** "We have heard from the *646*
12:41 because he saw Jesus' glory and s *3281*
12:48 very word which *I* s will condemn him *3281*
15:20 Remember the words I s to you: *3306*
18:16 s to the girl on duty there *3306*
18:23 But if I s the truth, why did you strike me?" *NIG*
Ac 1:3 to them over a period of forty days and s *3306*
1:16 the Holy Spirit **s long ago** through *4625*
2:31 *he* s of the resurrection of the Christ, *3281*
4:25 You s by the Holy Spirit through the mouth *3306*
4:31 with the Holy Spirit and s the word *3281*
6:10 or the Spirit by whom *he* s. *3281*
7:6 God s to him in this way: *3281*
7:38 the angel who s to him on Mount Sinai, and *3281*
10:7 When the angel who s to him had gone, *3281*
10:15 The voice s to him a second time, *NIG*
11:9 "The voice s from heaven a second time, *646*
14:1 There *they* s so effectively that *3281*
15:13 When they finished, James **s up:** *646*
16:2 at Lystra and Iconium **s well of** him. *3455*
16:32 Then *they* s the word of the Lord to him *3281*
18:9 One night the Lord s to Paul in a vision: *3306*
18:25 and *he* s with great fervor and taught *3281*
19:6 and *they* s in tongues and prophesied. *3281*
19:8 and s **boldly** there for three months, *4245*
20:7 Paul **s to** the people and, *1363*
24:24 He sent for Paul and listened to him as he s *NIG*
28:25 "The Holy Spirit s the truth to your *3281*
Heb 1:1 In the past God s to our forefathers through *3281*
4:7 when a long time later *he* s through David, *3306*
11:4 *when* God **s well** of his offerings. *3455*
11:22 s about the exodus of the Israelites *3648*
13:7 who s the word of God to you. *3281*
Jas 5:10 the prophets who s in the name of the Lord. *3281*
1Pe 1:10 who s of the grace that was to come to you, *4736*
1:12 when they s of the things that have *NIG*
2Pe 1:21 but men s from God as they were carried *3281*
2:16 who s with a man's voice and restrained *5779*
Rev 10:3 the voices of the seven thunders **s.** *3281*
10:4 the seven thunders s, I was about to write; *3281*
10:8 the voice that I had heard from heaven s *3281*
13:11 horns like a lamb, but *he* s like a dragon. *3281*

SPOKEN (160) [SPEAK]

Ex 4:10 past nor since you *have* s to your servant. 1819
20:22 'You have seen for yourselves that *I have* s 1819
34:29 that his face was radiant because he *had* s 1819
Nu 12:2 *"Has* the LORD s only through Moses?" 1819
12:2 "Hasn't *he* also s through us?" 1819
12:8 I, the LORD, *have* s, 1819
Dt 13:2 or wonder of which he *has* s takes place, 1819
18:21 a message *has* not *been* s by the LORD?" 1819
18:22 that is a message the LORD *has* not **s.** 1819
18:22 That prophet *has* s presumptuously. 1819
Jos 6:8 When Joshua *had* s to the people, 606
Jdg 2:4 the angel of the LORD *had* s these things 1819
Ru 2:13 and *have* s **kindly** *to* your servant— 1819+4213+6584
2Sa 2:27 "As surely as God lives, if *you had* not s, 1819
7:19 also s about the future of the house 1819
7:29 for you, O Sovereign LORD, *have* s, 1819
1Ki 2:27 the LORD *had* s at Shiloh about the house 1819
12:15 the word the LORD *had* s to Jeroboam son 1819
14:11 The LORD *has* **s!'** 1819
16:12 the word of the LORD s against Baasha 1819
16:34 the word of the LORD s by Joshua son 1819
17:16 in keeping with the word of the LORD s 1819
22:28 the LORD *has* not s through me." 1819
2Ki 1:17 to the word of the LORD that Elijah *had* **s.** 1819
2:22 according to the word Elisha *had* **s.** 1819
10:10 a word the LORD *has* s against the house 1819
10:17 according to the word of the LORD s 1819
14:25 s through his servant Jonah son of Amittai, 1819
15:12 of the LORD s to Jehu was fulfilled: 1819
19:21 the word that the LORD *has* s against him: 1819
20:19 of the LORD *you have* s is good," 1819
22:19 the LORD when you heard what *I have* s 1819
1Ch 17:17 *you have* s about the future of the house 1819
21:19 up in obedience to the word that Gad *had* s 1819
2Ch 10:15 the word the LORD *had* s to Jeroboam son 1819
18:27 the LORD *has* not s through me." 1819
36:21 in fulfillment of the word of the LORD s 7023
36:22 in order to fulfill the word of the LORD s 7023
Ezr 1:1 in order to fulfill the word of the LORD s 7023
Job 15:11 not enough for you, **words** *s* gently to you? AIT
21:3 and after I *have* **s,** mock on. 1819
29:22 After I had s, they spoke no more; 1821
42:7 because *you have* not s of me what is right, 1819
42:8 *You have* not s of me what is right, 1819
Ps 60:6 God *has* s from his sanctuary: 1819
62:11 One thing God *has* s, two things I have 1819
108:7 God *has* s from his sanctuary: 1819
109:2 *they have* s against me *with* lying tongues. 1819
Ps 141:6 that my words were well s. NIH
Pr 25:11 A word aptly s is like apples of gold 1819
SS 8:8 for our sister for the day she **is** s for? 1819
Isa 1:2 For the LORD *has* s: 1819
1:20 For the mouth of the LORD *has* **s.** 1819
16:13 the LORD *has* already s concerning Moab. 1819
21:17 The LORD, the God of Israel, *has* **s.** 1819
22:25 The LORD *has* **s.** 1819
23:4 O fortress of the sea, for the sea *has* **s:** 606
24:3 The LORD *has* s this word. 1819
25:8 The LORD *has* **s.** 1819
37:22 the word the LORD *has* s against him: 1819
38:15 *He has* s to me, and he himself has done this 606
39:8 of the LORD *you have* s is good," 1819
40:5 For the mouth of the LORD *has* **s."** 1819
45:19 *I have* not s in secret, 1819
48:15 I, even I, *have* **s;** yes, I have called him. 1819
48:16 "From the first announcement *I have* not s 1819
58:14 The mouth of the LORD *has* **s.** 1819
59:3 Your lips *have* s lies, 1819
Jer 4:28 because *I have* s and will not relent, 1819
5:14 "Because the people *have* s these words, 1819
13:15 do not be arrogant, for the LORD *has* **s.** 1819
14:14 I have not sent them or appointed them or s 1819
23:35 or 'What *has* the LORD **s?'** 1819
23:37 or 'What *has* the LORD **s?'** 1819
25:3 of the LORD has come to me and *I have* s 1819
25:13 that land all the things *I have* s against it, 1819
26:16 *He has* s to us in the name of the LORD 1819
29:23 and in my name *have* s lies, 1819+1821
30:2 in a book all the words *I have* s to you. 1819
35:14 But I *have* s to you again and again, 1819
36:2 and write on it all the words *I have* s to you 1819
36:4 the words the LORD *had* s to him, 1819
37:2 the LORD *had* s through Jeremiah 1819
44:16 not listen to the message *you have* s to us in 1819
48:8 because the LORD *has* **s.** 606
Eze 5:13 they will know that I the LORD *have* s 1819
5:15 I the LORD *have* **s.** 1819
5:17 I the LORD *have* **s."** 1819
13:7 though I *have* not s? 1819
17:21 you will know that I the LORD *have* **s.** 1819
17:24 " 'I the LORD *have* **s,** and I will do it.' " 1819
21:17 I the LORD *have* **s."** 1819
21:32 for I the LORD *have* **s.' "** 1819
22:14 I the LORD *have* **s,** and I will do it. 1819
22:28 when the LORD *has* not **s.** 1819
23:34 I *have* **s,** declares the Sovereign LORD. 1819
24:14 " 'I the LORD *have* **s.** 1819
26:5 for I *have* **s,** declares the Sovereign LORD. 1819
26:14 for I the LORD *have* **s,** 1819
28:10 I *have* **s,** declares the Sovereign LORD.' " 1819
30:12 I the LORD *have* **s.** 1819
34:24 I the LORD *have* **s.** 1819
36:5 In my burning zeal *I have* s against the rest 1819
36:36 I the LORD *have* **s,** and I will do it.' 1819
37:14 you will know that I the LORD *have* **s,** 1819
39:5 You will fall in the open field, for I *have* **s,** 1819
39:8 This is the day *I have* s *of.* 1819
Da 9:12 You have fulfilled the words s against us 1819
Joel 3:8 The LORD *has* **s.** 1819
Am 3:1 the LORD *has* s against you, O people 1819
3:8 The Sovereign LORD *has* **s—** 1819
Ob 1:18 The LORD *has* **s.** 1819
Mic 4:4 for the LORD Almighty *has* **s.** 1819+7023
Zec 8:9 "You who now hear these words s by 7023
Mt 3:3 This is he who *was* **s of** through *3306*
8:17 This was to fulfill what *was* s through *3306*
12:17 This was to fulfill what *was* s through *3306*
12:36 for every careless word *they have* **s.** *3281*
13:35 So was fulfilled what *was* s through *3306+3306*
21:4 This took place to fulfill what *was* s through *3306*
24:15 **s of** through the prophet Daniel— *3306*
26:65 *"He has* s **blasphemy!** *1059*
26:75 Peter remembered the word Jesus *had* **s:** *3306*
27:9 Then what *was* s by Jeremiah *3306*
Mk 12:12 to arrest him because they knew *he had* s *3306*
14:72 the word Jesus *had* s to him: *3306*
16:19 After the Lord Jesus *had* s to them, *3281*
Lk 2:34 and to be a sign *that will be* **s against,** *515*
9:36 When the voice *had* **s,** *1181*
20:19 knew *he had* s this parable against them. *3306*
22:61 the word the Lord *had* s to him: *3306*
24:25 to believe all that the prophets *have* **s!** *3281*
Jn 2:21 But the temple he *had* s of was his body. *3306*
2:22 the Scripture and the words that Jesus *had* **s.** *3306*
3:12 *I have* s to you of earthly things *3306*
6:63 The words I *have* s to you are spirit *3281*
12:29 others said an angel *had* s to him. *3281*
14:25 "All this *I have* s while still with you. *3281*
15:3 because of the word *I have* s to you. *3281*
15:22 If I had not come and s to them, *3281*
18:9 that the words *he had* s would be fulfilled: *3306*
18:20 "*I have* s openly to the world," *3281*
18:32 the words Jesus *had* s indicating the kind *3306*
Ac 2:16 No, this is what *was* s by the prophet Joel: *3306*
3:24 as many as *have* s, have foretold these days. *3281*
9:27 the Lord and that the Lord *had* s to him, *3281*
23:9 "What if a spirit or an angel *has* s to him?" *3281*
Ro 14:16 what you consider good *to be* **s of as evil.** *1059*
2Co 1:20 And so through him the "Amen" is s by us *NIG*
4:13 It is written: "I believed; therefore *I have* **s."** *3281*
6:11 We *have* s **freely** to you, *487+3836+5125*
Gal 3:16 The promises *were* s to Abraham and *3306*
Heb 1:2 in these last days *he has* s to us by his Son, *3281*
2:2 For if the message s by angels was binding, *3281*
4:4 For somewhere *he has* s about the seventh *3306*
Heb 4:8 not *have* s later about another day. *3281*
12:19 that no **further word** *be* s to them, *3364+4707*
2Pe 3:2 the words **s in the past** by the holy prophets *4625*
3Jn 1:12 Demetrius *is* **well s of** by everyone— *3455*
Jude 1:15 the harsh words ungodly sinners *have* s *3281*

SPOKES (1) [SPOKE]

1Ki 7:33 rims, s and hubs were all of cast metal. 3140

SPOKESMAN (1) [SPEAK, MAN]

Jer 15:19 you will be my **s.** 3869+7023

SPOKESMEN (1) [SPEAK, MAN]

Isa 43:27 your s rebelled against me. 4885

SPONGE (4)

Mt 27:48 Immediately one of them ran and got a **s.** *5074*
Mk 15:36 One man ran, filled a s with wine vinegar, *5074*
Jn 19:29 so they soaked a s in it, *5074*
19:29 put the s on a stalk of the hyssop plant, *NIG*

SPONTANEOUS (1)

Phm 1:14 favor you do will be s and not forced. *1730+2848*

SPOON, SPOONS (KJV) See DISH, DISHES

SPORT (3)

Ge 39:14 has been brought to us to **make** s of us! 7464
39:17 brought us came to me to **make** s of me. 7464
Ps 69:11 people **make** s **of** *me.* 2118+4200+5442

SPORTING (KJV) See CARESSING, REVELING

SPOT (17) [SPOTLESS, SPOTS, SPOTTED]

Lev 13:2 a swelling or a rash or a **bright** s on his skin 994
13:4 If the s on his skin is white but does 994
13:19 a white swelling or reddish-white s appears, 994
13:23 if the s is unchanged and has not spread, 994
13:24 and a reddish-white or white s appears in 994
13:25 the priest is to examine the s, 994
13:26 and there is no white hair in the s and if it is 994
13:28 the s is unchanged and has not spread in 994
14:56 and for a swelling, a rash or a **bright s,** 994
Jos 4:9 in the middle of the Jordan **at the** s where 9393
2Sa 2:23 He fell there and died **on the s.** 9393
2Ki 5:11 over the s and cure me of my leprosy. 5226
Job 8:18 But when it is torn from its s, 5226
Isa 28:8 with vomit and there is not a s without filth. 5226
46:7 From that s it cannot move. 5226
Lk 19:5 When Jesus reached the **s,** *5536*
1Ti 6:14 to keep this command **without** s or blame *834*

SPOTLESS (3) [SPOT]

Da 11:35 and **made** s until the time of the end, 4235
12:10 Many will be purified, **made** s and refined, 4235
2Pe 3:14 make every effort to be found **s,** *834*

SPOTS (3) [SPOT]

Lev 13:38 a man or woman has white s on the skin, 994
13:39 and if the s are dull white, 994
Jer 13:23 change his skin or the leopard its **s?** 2494

SPOTTED (8) [SPOT]

Ge 30:32 from them every speckled or s sheep, 3229
30:32 every dark-colored lamb and every s 3229
30:33 in my possession that is not speckled or s, 3229
30:35 the male goats that were streaked or s, 3229
30:35 and all the speckled or s *female* goats 3229
30:39 that were streaked or speckled or **s.** 3229
31:10 with the flock were streaked, speckled or **s.** 1353
31:12 with the flock are streaked, speckled or **s,** 1353

SPOUSE (KJV) See BRIDE

SPRANG (4) [SPRING]

Jnh 4:10 *It* **s up** overnight and died overnight. 2118
Mt 13:5 *It* **s up** quickly, because the soil was shallow *1984*
Mk 4:5 *It* **s up** quickly, because the soil was shallow *1984*
Ro 7:9 sin **s to life** and I died. *348*

SPREAD (156) [OUTSPREAD, SPREADING, SPREADS, WIDESPREAD]

Ge 10:5 (From these the maritime peoples **s out** 7233
10:32 From these the nations **s out** over the earth 7233
28:14 *you will* **s out** to the west and to the east, 7287
41:56 the famine *had* s over the whole country, 2118
Ex 1:12 the more they multiplied and **s;** 7287
9:29 *I will* **s out** my hands in prayer to 7298
9:33 *He* **s out** his hands toward the LORD; 7298
10:21 toward the sky so that darkness *will* s 2118
23:1 "*Do* not s false reports. 5951
25:20 to have their wings s upward, 7298
29:2 and wafers s with oil. 5417
37:9 The cherubim had their wings s upward, 7298

Ex 40:19 Then *he* s the tent over the tabernacle 7298
Lev 2: 4 wafers made without yeast and s with oil. 5417
7:12 wafers made without yeast and s with oil, 5417
13: 5 that the sore is unchanged and *has* not s in 7313
13: 6 the sore has faded and *has* not s in the skin, 7313
13: 7 But if the rash *does* s in his skin 7313+7313
13: 8 and if the rash *has* s in the skin, 7313
13:23 But if the spot is unchanged and *has* not s, 7313
13:28 and *has* not s in the skin but has faded, it is 7313
13:32 the itch *has* not s and there is no yellow hair 7313
13:34 and if it *has* not s in the skin and appears to 7313
13:35 But if the itch *does* s in the skin 7313+7313
13:36 and if the itch *has* s in the skin, 7313
13:51 and if the mildew *has* s in the clothing, 7313
13:53 the mildew *has* not s in the clothing, 7313
13:55 even though it *has* not s, it is unclean. 7313
14:39 If the mildew *has* s on the walls, 7313
14:44 if the mildew *has* s in the house, 7313
14:48 to examine it and the mildew *has* not s after 7313
Nu 4: 6 s a cloth of solid blue over that and put 7298
4: 7 of the Presence *they are to* s a blue cloth 7298
4: 8 Over these *they are to* s a scarlet cloth, 7298
4:11 *to* s a blue cloth and cover that with hides 7298
4:13 the bronze altar and s a purple cloth over it. 7298
4:14 Over it *they are to* s a covering of hides 7298
6:15 and wafers s with oil. 5417
11:32 *they* s them **out** all around the camp. 8848+8848
13:32 And *they* s among the Israelites 3655
24: 6 "Like valleys *they* s **out,** 5742
Jos 6:27 and his fame s throughout the land. 2118
7:23 and all the Israelites and s them **out** before 3668
Jdg 8:25 So *they* s **out** a garment, 7298
20:37 s **out** and put the whole city to the sword. 5432
Ru 3: 9 "**S** the corner of your garment over me, 7298
1Sa 4: 2 and *as* the battle s, Israel was defeated 5759
2Sa 5:18 Now the Philistines had come and s **out** in 5759
5:22 up and s **out** in the Valley of Rephaim; 5759
17:19 a covering and s it **out** over the opening of 7298
18: 8 The battle s **out** over the whole 7046
21:10 of Aiah took sackcloth and s it **out** 5742
1Ki 4:31 his fame s to all the surrounding nations. 2118
6:27 with their wings s **out.** 7298
8: 7 The cherubim s their wings over the place 7298
8:22 s **out** his hands *toward* heaven 7298
8:54 with his hands s **out** *toward* heaven. 7298
22:36 a cry s through the army: 6296
2Ki 8:15 in water and s it over the king's face, 7298
9:13 and took their cloaks and s them under him 8492
19:14 the LORD and s it **out** before the LORD. 7298
1Ch 14:17 So David's fame s throughout every land, 3655
28:18 *that* s their wings and shelter the ark of 7298
2Ch 5: 8 The cherubim s their wings over the place 7298
6:12 assembly of Israel and s **out** his hands. 7298
6:13 and s **out** his hands toward heaven. 7298
26: 8 and his fame s as far as the border of Egypt, 2143
26:15 His fame s far and wide, 3655
Ezr 9: 5 with my hands s **out** to the LORD my God 7298
Ne 4:19 "The work is extensive and s **out,** 8146
8:15 that they should proclaim this word and s it 6296
Est 9: 4 his reputation s throughout the provinces, 2143
Job 1:10 so that his flocks and herds *are* s throughout 7287
15:29 nor *will* his possessions s over the land. 5742
17:13 if *I* s **out** my bed in darkness, 8331
39:26 by your wisdom and s his wings toward 7298
Ps 5:11 S *your* **protection** over them, 6114
44:20 the name of our God or s **out** our hands to 7298
57: 6 *They* s a net for my feet— 3922
78:19 saying, "Can God s a table in the desert? 6885
88: 9 *I* s **out** my hands to you. 8848
105:39 *He* s **out** a cloud as a covering, 7298
136: 6 *who* s **out** the earth upon the waters, 8392
140: 5 *they have* s **out** the cords of their net 7298
143: 6 *I* s **out** my hands to you; 7298
Pr 1:17 How useless *to* s a net in full view of all 2430
15: 7 The lips of the wise s knowledge; 2430
SS 1:12 my perfume s its fragrance. 5989
2:13 the blossoming vines s their fragrance. 5989
4:16 that its fragrance *may* s **abroad.** 5688
Isa 1:15 When you s **out** your hands in prayer, 7298
14:11 maggots **are** s **out** beneath you 3667
16: 8 which once reached Jazer and s *toward* 9494
16: 8 Their shoots s **out** and went as far as 5759
21: 5 They set the tables, they s the rugs, 7596
25:11 *They will* s **out** their hands in it, 7298
30:24 s **out** with fork and shovel. 2430
33:23 mast is not held secure, the sail *is* not s. 7298
37:14 the LORD and s it **out** before the LORD. 7298
42: 5 and stretched them out, *who* s **out** the earth 8392
44:24 *who* s **out** the earth by myself, 8392
48:13 and my right hand s **out** the heavens; 3253
54: 3 *you will* s **out** *to* the right and *to* the left; 7287
65:11 who s a table for Fortune and fill bowls 6885
Jer 23:15 the prophets of Jerusalem ungodliness *has* s 3655
43:10 *he will* s his royal canopy above them. 5742
48:32 Your branches s as far as the sea; 6296
La 1:13 *He* s a net for my feet and turned me back. 7298
Eze 1:11 Their wings *were* s **out** upward; 7233
1:22 **S out** above the heads of the living creatures 5742
5: 4 A fire *will* s from there to the whole house 3655
10:16 and when the cherubim s their wings to rise 5951
10:19 the cherubim s their wings and rose from 5951
11:22 with the wheels beside them, s their wings, 5951
12:13 *I will* s my net for him, 7298
16: 8 *I* s the corner of my garment over you 7298
16:14 And your fame s among the nations 3655
17:20 *I will* s my net for him, 7298
19: 8 *They* s their net for him, 7298
Eze 19:14 Fire s from one of its main branches 3655
23:41 a table s before it on which you had placed 6885
26: 5 she will become a **place to** s fishnets, 5427
26:14 and you will become a **place to** s fishnets. 5427
30:13 and *I will* s fear throughout the land. 5989
32: 5 *I will* s your flesh on the mountains 5989
32:23 All who *had* s terror in the land of 5989
32:24 All who *had* s terror in the land of 5989
32:25 their terror *had* s in the land of the living, 5989
32:26 by the sword because *they* s their terror in 5989
32:32 *I had* him s terror in the land of the living, 5989
Hos 5: 1 a net s **out** on Tabor. 7298
Mal 2: 3 *I will* s on your faces the offal 2430
Mt 4:24 News about him s all over Syria, *599*
9:26 News of this s through all that region. *2002*
9:31 But they went out and **s the news about** *1424*
21: 8 A very large crowd s their cloaks on the *5143*
21: 8 from the trees and s them on the road. *5143*
Mk 1:28 about him s quickly over the whole region *2002*
11: 8 Many people s their cloaks on the road, *5143*
11: 8 others s branches they had cut in the fields. *NIG*
Lk 2:17 *they* s the word concerning what had been *1192*
4:14 about him s through the whole countryside. *2002*
4:37 And the news about him s throughout *1744*
5:15 Yet the news about him s all the more, *1451*
7:17 This news about Jesus s throughout Judea *2002*
19:36 *people* s their cloaks on the road. *5716*
Jn 12:17 from the dead *continued to* **s the word.** *3455*
21:23 the rumor s among the brothers *2002*
Ac 6: 7 So the word of God **s.** *889*
11:28 that a severe famine would s over *1639*
12:24 word of God continued to increase and **s.** *4437*
13:49 of the Lord s through the whole region. *1422*
19:20 In this way the word of the Lord s **widely** *889*
2Th 3: 1 that the message of the Lord *may* s **rapidly** *5556*
2Ti 2:17 Their teaching *will* s like gangrene. *2400+3786*
Rev 7:15 on the throne *will* s *his* **tent** over them. *5012*

SPREADING (41) [SPREAD]

Lev 13:22 If *it is* s in the skin, 7313+7313
13:27 and if *it is* s in the skin, 7313+7313
13:49 a s **mildew** and must be shown to **the priest.** 7669
13:57 or in the leather article, it *is* s, 7255
14:34 And I put a s **mildew** in a house 5596+7669
19:16 not go about s **slander** among your people. 8215
Nu 14:36 against him by s a bad report about it— 3655
14:37 these men *responsible for* s the bad report 3655
Dt 12: 2 on the hills and under every s tree where 8316
28:35 **s from** the soles of your feet to the top AIT
Jdg 15: 9 and camped in Judah, s **out** near Lehi. 5759
1Sa 2:24 it is not a good report that I hear s **among** 6296
1Ki 8:38 and s **out** his hands toward this temple— 7298
14:23 on every high hill and under every s tree. 8316
2Ki 16: 4 on the hilltops and under every s tree. 8316
17:10 on every high hill and under every s tree. 8316
2Ch 6:29 and s **out** his hands toward this temple— 7298
28: 4 on the hilltops and under every s tree. 8316
Job 8:16 s its shoots over the garden; 3655
26: 9 the full moon, s his clouds over it. 7299
37:18 *can you* join him in s **out** the skies, 8392
Pr 29: 5 Whoever flatters his neighbor *is* s a net 7298
Isa 18: 5 and cut down and take away the s **branches.** 5746
57: 5 among the oaks and under every s tree; 8316
Jer 2:20 and under every s tree you lay down as 8316
3: 6 up on every high hill and under every s tree 8316
3:13 to foreign gods under every s tree, 8316
17: 2 and Asherah poles beside the s trees and on 8316
25:32 Disaster *is* s from nation to nation; 3655
48:40 s its wings over Moab. 7298
49:22 s its wings over Bozrah. 7298
Eze 6:13 under every s tree and every leafy oak— 8316
17: 6 and it sprouted and became a low, s vine. 6243
31: 5 s because of abundant waters. 8938
31: 7 It was majestic in beauty, with its s boughs, 802
47:10 there will be **places for** s nets. 5427
Hos 10: 1 Israel *was* a s vine; he brought forth fruit 1328
Joel 2: 2 Like dawn s across the mountains a large 7298
Mk 1:45 and began to talk freely, s the news. *1424*
Ac 4:17 to stop *this* thing from s any further among *1376*
1Th 3: 2 and God's fellow worker in s the **gospel** *2295*

SPREADS (12) [SPREAD]

Ex 22: 6 "If a fire breaks out and s *into* thornbushes 5162
Dt 32:11 *that* s its wings to catch them 7298
Job 26: 7 *He* s **out** the northern [skies] over empty 5742
36:29 Who can understand how he s **out** 5155
39:18 s *her* **feathers to run,** 928+2021+5257+5294
Ps 41: 6 then he goes out and s it abroad. 1819
147:16 He s the snow like wool and scatters 5989
Pr 10:18 and *whoever* s slander is a fool. 3655
Isa 25:11 as a swimmer s **out** his hands to swim. 7298
32: 6 He practices ungodliness and s error 1819
40:22 and s them **out** like a tent to live in. 5501
2Co 2:14 and through us s everywhere the fragrance *5746*

SPRIG (1)

Eze 17:22 a **tender** *s* from its topmost shoots AIT

SPRING (61) [SPRANG, SPRINGING, SPRINGS, SPRINGTIME, SPRUNG, WELLSPRING]

Ge 16: 7 found Hagar near a s in the 2021+4784+6524
16: 7 it was the s that is beside the road to Shur. 6524
Ge 24:13 See, I am standing beside this **s,** 4784+6524
24:16 She went down to the **s,** 6524
24:29 and he hurried out to the man at the **s.** 6524
24:30 by the camels near the **s.** 6524
24:42 "When I came to the **s** today, I said, 6524
24:43 See, I am standing beside this **s;** 4784+6524
24:45 She went down to the s and drew water, 6524
49:22 a fruitful vine near a **s,** 6524
Lev 11:36 A **s,** however, or a cistern for collecting 5078
Nu 21:17 Then Israel sang this song: "**S up,** O well! 6590
Dt 11:14 both autumn and **s rains,** 4919
33:28 Jacob's s is secure in a land of grain 6524
Jos 15: 9 toward the s *of* the waters of Nephtoah, 5078
18:15 and the boundary came out at the s *of* 5078
Jdg 7: 1 and all his men camped at the s *of* Harod. 6524
15:19 So **the** s was called En Hakkore, 2023S
1Sa 29: 1 and Israel camped by the s in Jezreel. 6524
2Sa 11: 1 In the **s,** at the time when kings go off 9102+9588
1Ki 20:22 because next s the king 2021+9102+9588
20:26 The next s Ben-Hadad mustered 9102+9588
2Ki 2:21 Then he went out to the s and threw 4604+4784
13:20 to enter the country **every s.** 995+9102
1Ch 20: 1 In the **s,** at the time when kings go off to war, 6961+9102+9588
2Ch 32:30 the Gihon s and channeled the water down 4784
33:14 west of the Gihon s in the valley, NIH
36:10 In the s, King Nebuchadnezzar sent 9102+9588
Job 5: 6 For hardship *does* not s from the soil, 3655
29:23 and drank in my words as the **s rain.** 4919
Ps 92: 7 that though the wicked **s up** like grass 7255
Pr 16:15 his favor is like a **rain** cloud **in s.** 4919
25:26 Like a muddied s or a polluted well is 5078
Ecc 4: 4 and all achievement s from man's envy NIH
12: 6 before the pitcher is shattered at the **s,** 4432
SS 4:12 you are a s enclosed, a sealed fountain. 5078
Isa 14:29 the root of that snake *will* **s up** a viper, 3655
42: 9 before *they* **s into being** I announce them 7541
44: 4 *They will* **s up** like grass in a meadow, 7541
45: 8 Let the earth open wide, *let* salvation **s up,** 7238
58:11 like a s whose waters never fail. 4604+4784
61:11 *will* **make** righteousness and praise **s up** 7541
Jer 2:13 have forsaken me, the s *of* living water, 5227
3: 3 and no **s rains** have fallen. 4919
5:24 who gives autumn and s rains in season, 4919
9: 1 a **s of water** and my eyes a fountain 4784
15:18 like a s that fails? 4784
17:13 forsaken the LORD, the s *of* living water. 5227
Hos 6: 3 like the **s rains** that water the earth." 4919
10: 4 therefore lawsuits **s up** like poisonous 7255
13:15 his s will fail and his well dry up. 5227
Joel 2:23 both autumn and **s rains,** as before. 4919
Am 3: 5 *Does* a trap **s up** from the earth 6590
Jn 4:14 the water I give him will become in him a s *4380*
Ro 15:12 Isaiah says, "The Root of Jesse will s up, *NIG*
Col 1: 5 and love that s from the hope that is stored *NIG*
1Th 2: 3 the appeal we make does not s from error *NIG*
Jas 3:11 and salt water flow from the same **s?** *3956*
3:12 Neither can a **salt** s produce fresh water. *266*
5: 7 how patient he is for the autumn and s rains. *4069*
Rev 21: 6 to drink without cost from the s of the water *4380*

SPRINGING (1) [SPRING]

Dt 33:22 "Dan is a lion's cub, s **out** of Bashan." 2397

SPRINGS (43) [SPRING]

Ge 7:11 the s *of* the great deep burst forth, 5078
8: 2 Now the s *of* the deep and the floodgates of 5078
36:24 the **hot** s in the desert while he was grazing 3553
Ex 15:27 Elim, where there were twelve s and 4784+6524
Nu 33: 9 Elim, where there were twelve s and 4784+6524
Dt 8: 7 with s flowing in the valleys and hills; 9333
Jos 15:19 give me also s *of* water." 1657
15:19 So Caleb gave her the upper and lower **s.** 1657
Jdg 1:15 give me also s *of* water." 1657
1:15 Then Caleb gave her the upper and lower **s.** 1657
1Ki 18: 5 "Go through the land to all the s and 4784+5078
2Ki 3:19 stop up all the **s,** and ruin every 4784+5078
3:25 stopped up all the s and cut down 4784+5078
19:29 and the second year **what s from** *that.* 6084
2Ch 32: 3 the water from the s outside the city, 6524
32: 4 and they blocked all the s and the stream 5078
Job 14: 2 *He* **s up** like a flower and withers away; 3655
38:16 the s *of* the sea or walked in the recesses of 5569
Ps 74:15 It was you who opened up s and streams; 5078
84: 6 they make it a place of **s;** 5078
85:11 Faithfulness **s forth** from the earth, 7541
90: 6 though in the morning *it* **s up** new, 7437
104:10 He makes s pour water into the ravines; 5078
107:33 **flowing** s into thirsty ground, 4604+4784
107:35 the parched ground into **flowing s;** 4604+4784
114: 8 the hard rock into s *of* water. 5078
Pr 5:16 Should your s overflow in the streets, 5078
8:24 when there were no s abounding 5078
27: 9 of one's friend s from his earnest counsel. NIH
Isa 35: 7 the thirsty ground **bubbling s.** 4432+4784
37:30 and the second year **what s from** *that.* 8826
41:18 and s within the valleys. 5078
41:18 and the parched ground into **s.** 4604+4784
43:19 Now *it* **s up;** do you not perceive it? 7541
49:10 and lead them beside s *of* water. 4432
Jer 51:36 I will dry up her sea and make her s dry. 5227
Eze 31: 4 **deep** s made it grow tall; 9333
31:15 down to the grave I covered the **deep** s 9333
2Pe 2:17 These men are s without water *4380*
Rev 7:17 he will lead them to s of living water. *4380*

Rev 8:10 a third of the rivers and on the s of water— *4380*
14: 7 the earth, the sea and the s of water." *4380*
16: 4 his bowl on the rivers and s of water, *4380*

SPRINGTIME (1) [SPRING]

Zec 10: 1 Ask the LORD for rain in the s; 4919+6961

SPRINKLE (31) [SPRINKLED, SPRINKLES, SPRINKLING]

Ex 29:16 and take the blood and s it against the altar 2450
29:20 Then s blood against the altar on all sides. 2450
29:21 and s it on Aaron and his garments and 5684
Lev 1: 5 the priests shall bring the blood and s it 2450
1:11 the priests *shall* s its blood against the altar 2450
3: 2 Then Aaron's sons the priests *shall* s 2450
3: 8 Then Aaron's sons *shall* s its blood against 2450
3:13 Then Aaron's sons *shall* s its blood against 2450
4: 6 into the blood and s some of it seven times 5684
4:17 and s it before the LORD seven times 5684
5: 9 *to* s some of the blood of the sin offering 5684
14: 7 Seven times *he shall* s the one to 5684
14:16 and with his finger s some of it before 5684
14:27 with his right forefinger s some of the oil 5684
14:51 and s the house seven times. 5684
16:14 the bull's blood and with his finger s it on 5684
16:14 then *he shall* s some of it 5684
16:15 *He shall* s it on the atonement cover and 5684
16:19 *He shall* s some of the blood on it 5684
17: 6 The priest *is to* s the blood against 2450
Nu 8: 7 S the water of cleansing on them; 5684
18:17 S their blood on the altar and burn their fat 2450
19: 4 on his finger and s it seven times toward 5684
19:18 and s the tent and all the furnishings and 5684
19:18 He must also s anyone who has touched NIH
19:19 *to* s the unclean person on the third 5684
2Ki 16:15 S on the altar all the blood of 2450
Isa 52:15 so *will he* s many nations, 5684
Eze 27:30 *they will* s dust on their heads and roll 6590
36:25 *I will* s clean water on you, 2450
43:24 *to* s salt on them and sacrifice them as 8959

SPRINKLED (26) [SPRINKLE]

Ex 24: 6 and the other half *he* s on the altar. 2450
24: 8 s it on the people and said, 2450
Lev 7: 2 and its blood *is to be* s against the altar 2450
8:11 *He* s some of the oil on the altar 5684
8:19 the ram and s the blood against the altar 2450
8:24 he s blood against the altar on all sides. 2450
8:30 and s them on Aaron and his garments and 5684
9:12 and *he* s it against the altar on all sides. 2450
9:18 and *he* s it against the altar on all sides. 2450
Nu 19:13 water of cleansing *has* not **been** s on him, 2450
19:20 water of cleansing *has* not **been** s on him, 2450
Jos 7: 6 and s dust on their heads. 6590
2Ki 16:13 and s the blood of his fellowship offerings 2450
2Ch 29:22 priests took the blood and s it on the altar; 2450
29:22 the rams and s their blood on the altar; 2450
29:22 the lambs and s their blood on the altar. 2450
30:16 The priests s the blood handed to them by 2450
35:11 and the priests s the blood handed to them, 2450
Job 2:12 and they tore their robes and s dust 2450
La 2:10 *they have* s dust on their heads and put 6590
Hos 7: 9 His hair *is* s *with* gray, 2450
Heb 9:13 and bulls and the ashes of a heifer s **on** *4822*
9:19 and s the scroll and all the people. *4822*
9:21 *he* s with the blood both the tabernacle *4822*
10:22 *having* our hearts s **to cleanse** us from *4822*
12:24 to the s blood that speaks a better word than *4823*

SPRINKLES (2) [SPRINKLE]

Lev 7:14 it belongs to the priest who s the blood of 2450
Nu 19:21 "The *man who* s the water of cleansing must 5684

SPRINKLING (32) [SPRINKLE]

Ex 27: 3 s **bowls,** meat forks and firepans. 4670
38: 3 its pots, shovels, s **bowls,** 4670
Nu 4:14 meat forks, shovels and s **bowls.** 4670
7:13 one silver s **bowl** weighing seventy shekels, 4670
7:19 one silver s **bowl** weighing seventy shekels, 4670
7:25 one silver s **bowl** weighing seventy shekels, 4670
7:31 one silver s **bowl** weighing seventy shekels, 4670
7:37 one silver s **bowl** weighing seventy shekels, 4670
7:43 one silver s **bowl** weighing seventy shekels, 4670
7:49 one silver s **bowl** weighing seventy shekels, 4670
7:55 one silver s **bowl** weighing seventy shekels, 4670
7:61 one silver s **bowl** weighing seventy shekels, 4670
7:67 one silver s **bowl** weighing seventy shekels, 4670
7:73 one silver s **bowl** weighing seventy shekels, 4670
7:79 one silver s **bowl** weighing seventy shekels, 4670
7:84 twelve silver plates, twelve silver s **bowls** 4670
7:85 and each s **bowl** seventy shekels. 4670
1Ki 7:40 the basins and shovels and s **bowls.** 4670
7:45 the pots, shovels and s **bowls.** 4670
7:50 s **bowls,** dishes and censers; 4670
2Ki 12:13 wick trimmers, s **bowls,** 4670
25:15 the censers and s **bowls—** 4670
1Ch 28:17 s **bowls** and pitchers; 4670
2Ch 4: 8 He also made a hundred gold s **bowls.** 4670
4:11 the pots and shovels and s **bowls.** 4670
4:22 s **bowls,** dishes and censers; 4670
Jer 52:18 shovels, wick trimmers, s **bowls,** 4670
52:19 censers, s **bowls,** pots, lampstands, 4670
Eze 43:18 and s blood upon the altar when it is built: 2450

Zec 9:15 be full like a **bowl used for** s the corners of 4670
Heb 11:28 By faith he kept the Passover and the s of *4717*
1Pe 1: 2 for obedience to Jesus Christ and s by his *4823*

SPROUT (8) [SPROUTED, SPROUTING, SPROUTS]

Nu 17: 5 staff belonging to the man I choose *will* s, 7255
Job 5: 6 nor *does* trouble s from the ground. 7541
14: 7 If it is cut down, *it will* s again, 2736
38:27 to satisfy a desolate wasteland and **make** it s 7541
Pr 23: 5 for *they will* **surely** s wings and fly off 6913+6913
Isa 61:11 the s come up and a garden causes seeds 7542
Jer 33:15 *I will* **make** a righteous Branch s 7541
Lk 21:30 When *they* s **leaves,** you can see *4582*

SPROUTED (5) [SPROUT]

Ge 41: 6 After them, seven other heads of grain s— 7541
41:23 After them, seven other heads s— 7541
Nu 17: 8 *had* not only s but had budded, 7255
Eze 17: 6 and *it* s and became a low, 7541
Mt 13:26 When the wheat s and formed heads, *1056*

SPROUTING (3) [SPROUT]

Dt 29:23 nothing planted, nothing s, 7541
2Ki 19:26 like **grass** *s on* the roof, AIT
Isa 37:27 like **grass** *s on* the roof, AIT

SPROUTS (1) [SPROUT]

Mk 4:27 the seed s and grows, *1056*

SPRUNG (1) [SPRING]

Ge 2: 5 and no plant of the field *had* yet s **up,** 7541

SPUE, SPUED (KJV) See SPIT, VOMIT, VOMITED

SPUN (3) [SPIN]

Ex 35:25 Every skilled woman s with her hands 3211
35:25 with her hands and brought **what** she had s 4757
35:26 and had the skill s the goat hair. 3211

SPUNGE (KJV) See SPONGE

SPUR (1) [SPURRED, SPURS]

Heb 10:24 we may s one another **on** toward love *1650+4237*

SPURN (1) [SPURNED, SPURNS]

Job 10: 3 *to* s the work of your hands, 4415

SPURNED (6) [SPURN]

Ps 89:38 *you have* s, you have been very angry 4415
Pr 1:30 not accept my advice and s my rebuke, 5540
5:12 How my heart s correction! 5540
Isa 1: 4 *they have* s the Holy One of Israel 5540
5:24 and s the word of the Holy One of Israel. 5540
La 2: 6 in his fierce anger *he has* s both king 5540

SPURNS (1) [SPURN]

Pr 15: 5 A fool s his father's discipline, 5540

SPURRED (3) [SPUR]

Est 3:15 S **on** by the king's command, 1894
8:14 raced out, s **on** by the king's command. 1894
Isa 9:11 against them and *has* s their enemies **on.** 6056

SPURS (1) [SPUR]

Isa 41: 7 the hammer s on him who strikes the anvil. NIH

SPY (9) [SPIED, SPIES, SPYING]

Dt 1:22 "Let us send men ahead *to* s **out** the land 2916
Jos 2: 2 come here tonight to s **out** the land." 2916
2: 3 they have come to s **out** the whole land." 2916
7: 2 "Go up and s **out** the region." 8078
Jdg 1:23 When they **sent** *men* **to** s **out** Bethel 9365
18: 2 and Eshtaol to s **out** the land and explore it. 8078
2Sa 10: 3 the city and s it **out** and overthrow it?" 8078
1Ch 19: 3 and s **out** the country and overthrow it?" 8078
Gal 2: 4 *to* s **on** the freedom we have in Christ Jesus *2945*

SPYING (2) [SPY]

Ge 42:30 treated us as though we *were* s on the land. 8078
Jos 6:23 So the young men who *had done the* s went 8078

SQUADS (1)

Ac 12: 4 be guarded *by* **four** s of four soldiers each. *5482*

SQUALL (2)

Mk 4:37 A furious s came up, *449+3278*
Lk 8:23 A s came down on the lake, *449+3278*

SQUANDERED (2) [SQUANDERS]

Lk 15:13 for a distant country and there s his wealth *1399*
15:30 this son of yours who *has* s your property *2983*

SQUANDERS (1) [SQUANDERED]

Pr 29: 3 but a companion of prostitutes s his wealth. 6

SQUARE (32) [SQUARES]

Ge 19: 2 "we will spend the night in the s." 8148
Ex 27: 1 it is to be s, five cubits long 8062
28:16 It is to be s—a span long and a span wide 8062
30: 2 It is to be s, a cubit long and a cubit wide, 8062
37:25 *It was* s, a cubit long and a cubit wide, 8062
38: 1 *it was* s, five cubits long 8062
39: 9 It was s—a span long and a span wide 8062
Dt 13:16 of the town into the middle of the **public** s 8148
Jdg 19:15 They went and sat in the city s, 8148
19:17 he looked and saw the traveler in the city s, 8148
19:20 Only don't spend the night in the s." 8148
2Sa 21:12 from the **public** s *at* Beth Shan, 8148
1Ki 7:31 The panels of the stands *were* s, not round. 8062
2Ch 29: 4 assembled them in the s *on* the east side 8148
32: 6 and assembled them before him in the s *at* 8148
Ezr 10: 9 all the people were sitting in the s *before* 8148
Ne 8: 1 as one man in the s before the Water Gate. 8148
8: 3 the s before the Water Gate in the presence 8148
8:16 and in the s *by* the Water Gate and the one 8148
Est 4: 6 to Mordecai in the **open** s *of* the city 8148
Job 29: 7 the city and took my seat in the **public** s, 8148
Eze 16:24 and made a lofty shrine in every **public** s. 8148
16:31 made your lofty shrines in every **public** s, 8148
40:12 and the alcoves were six cubits s. 2256+4946+4946+7024+7024
40:47 Then he measured the court: *It was* s— 8062
41:22 and two cubits s; 802+2256+8145
43:16 The altar hearth *is* s, 448+752+8062+8063
43:17 The upper ledge also is s, 448+752+8063
45: 2 a section 500 cubits s is to be for 8062
48:20 The entire portion will be a s, 25,000 cubits 8055
Am 5:16 and cries of anguish in every **public** s. 8148
Rev 21:16 The city was laid out like a s, *5481*

SQUARES (9) [SQUARE]

Pr 1:20 she raises her voice in the **public** s; 8148
5:16 your streams of water in the **public** s? 8148
7:12 now in the s, at every corner she lurks.) 8148
SS 3: 2 through its streets and s; 8148
Isa 15: 3 the roofs and in the **public** s they all wail, 8148
Jer 5: 1 search through her s. 8148
9:21 and the young men from the **public** s. 8148
48:38 the **public** s there is nothing but mourning, 8148
Na 2: 4 rushing back and forth through the s. 8148

SQUEEZED (2)

Ge 40:11 s them into Pharaoh's cup and put the cup 8469
Jdg 6:38 *he* s the fleece and wrung out the dew— 2318

STAB (1) [STABBED]

Zec 13: 3 his own parents *will* s him. 1991

STABBED (4) [STAB]

2Sa 3:27 Joab s him *in* the stomach, and he died. 5782
4: 6 and *they* s him in the stomach. 5782
4: 7 After *they* s and killed him, 5782
20:10 Without being s again, Amasa died. NIH

STABILITY (1)

Pr 29: 4 By justice a king **gives** a country s, 6641

STABLE (KJV) See FIRMLY ESTABLISHED, PASTURE

STABLISH, STABLISHED, STABLISHETH (KJV) See ESTABLISH, ESTABLISHED, ESTABLISHES, FULFILL, SET IN PLACE, STAND FIRM, STRENGTHEN, STRENGTHENED

STACHYS (1)

Ro 16: 9 and my dear friend S. *5093*

STACKS (KJV) See SHOCKS

STACTE (KJV) See GUM RESIN

STADIA (2)

Rev 14:20 the horses' bridles for a distance of 1,600 s. *5084*
21:16 be 12,000 s in length, and as wide and high *5084*

STAFF (67) [FLAGSTAFF, STAFFS]

Ge 32:10 I had only my s when I crossed this Jordan, 5234
38:18 and the s in your hand," she answered. 4751
38:25 whose seal and cord and s these are." 4751
47:31 as he leaned on the top of his s. 4751
49:10 nor the **ruler's** s from between his feet, 2980
Ex 4: 2 "A s," he replied. 4751
4: 4 of the snake and it turned back into a s 4751
4:17 But take this s in your hand 4751
4:20 And he took the s *of* God in his hand. 4751
7: 9 'Take your s and throw it down 4751

Ex 7:10 Aaron threw his s down in front of Pharaoh 4751
7:12 Each one threw down his s and it became 4751
7:12 But Aaron's s swallowed up their staffs. 4751
7:15 in your hand the s that was changed into 4751
7:17 With the s that is in my hand I will strike 4751
7:19 'Take your s and stretch out your hand over 4751
7:20 He raised his s in the presence of Pharaoh 4751
8:5 'Stretch out your hand with your s over 4751
8:16 'Stretch out your s and strike the dust of 4751
8:17 with the s and struck the dust of the ground, 4751
9:23 Moses stretched out his s toward the sky, 4751
10:13 So Moses stretched out his s over Egypt, 4751
12:11 on your feet and your s in your hand. 5234
14:16 Raise your s and stretch out your hand over 4751
17:5 in your hand the s with which you struck 4751
17:9 of the hill with the s *of* God in my hands." 4751
21:19 up and walks around outside with his s; 5475
Nu 17:2 Write the name of each man on his s. 4751
17:3 On the s *of* Levi write Aaron's name, 4751
17:3 be one s for the head of each ancestral tribe. 4751
17:5 The s *belonging to* the man I choose 4751
17:6 and Aaron's s was among them. 4751
17:8 of the Testimony and saw that Aaron's s, 4751
17:9 and each man took his own s. 4751
17:10 "Put back Aaron's s in front of the Testimony, 4751
20:8 "Take the s, and you and your brother 4751
20:9 the s from the LORD's presence, 4751
20:11 and struck the rock twice with his s. 4751
22:27 and he was angry and beat her with his s. 5234
Jdg 5:14 Zebulun those who bear a commander's s. 8657
6:21 With the tip of the s that was in his hand, 5475
1Sa 14:27 the s that was in his hand and dipped it into 4751
14:43 a little honey with the end of my s. 4751
17:40 Then he took his s in his hand, 5234
2Ki 4:29 take my s in your hand and run. 5475
4:29 Lay my s on the boy's face." 5475
4:31 on ahead and laid the s on the boy's face, 5475
18:21 that splintered reed of a s, 5475
2Ch 32:3 and **military s** about blocking off the water 1475
Ps 23:4 your rod and your s, they comfort me. 5475
Isa 10:26 and he will raise his s over the waters, 4751
36:6 that splintered reed of a s, 5475
Jer 48:17 how broken the glorious s!' 5234
51:59 to the s officer Seraiah son of Neriah, 4957
Eze 12:14 his s and all his troops— 6469
29:6 " 'You have been a s *of* reed for the house 5475
Mic 7:14 Shepherd your people with your s, 8657
Zec 11:10 Then I took my s called Favor and broke it, 5234
11:14 Then I broke my second s called Union, 5234
Mt 10:10 or extra tunic, or sandals or a s; *4811*
27:29 They put a s in his right hand and knelt *2812*
27:30 the s and struck him on the head again *2812*
Mk 6:8 "Take nothing for the journey except a s— *4811*
15:19 on the head *with* a s and spit on him. *2812*
Lk 9:3 no s, no bag, no bread, no money, *4811*
Heb 9:4 Aaron's s that had budded, *4811*
11:21 worshiped as he leaned on the top *of* his s. *4811*

STAFFS (7) [STAFF]

Ex 7:12 But Aaron's staff swallowed up their s. 4751
Nu 17:2 to the Israelites and get twelve s from them, 4751
17:6 and their leaders gave him twelve s, 4751
17:7 Moses placed the s before the LORD in 4751
17:9 the s from the LORD's presence to all 4751
21:18 the nobles with scepters and s." 5475
Zec 11:7 Then I took two s and called one Favor and 5234

STAG (3)

SS 2:9 My lover is like a gazelle or a **young s**. 385+6762
2:17 and be like a gazelle or like a **young s** 385+6762
8:14 and be like a gazelle or like a **young s** 385+6762

STAGE (2) [STAGES]

Jos 3:15 Jordan *is* **at flood s** all during harvest. 1536+3972+4848+6584
4:18 and ran **at flood s** as before. 1536+3972+6584

STAGES (4) [STAGE]

Nu 33:1 the **s in** the **journey** *of* the Israelites 5023
33:2 Moses recorded the s in their journey. 4604
33:2 This is their journey by s: 4604
Eze 41:7 the temple was built **in ascending s**, 2025+2025+4200+4200+5087+5087

STAGGER (12) [STAGGERED, STAGGERING, STAGGERS]

Job 12:25 *he* **makes** them s like drunkards. 9494
Ps 60:3 you have given us wine *that* **makes** us s. 9570
Isa 19:14 *they* **make** Egypt s in all that she does, 9494
28:7 these also s from wine and reel from beer: 8706
28:7 and prophets s from beer and are befuddled 8706
28:7 *they* s when seeing visions, 8706
29:9 but not from wine, s, but not from beer. 5675
51:17 to its dregs the goblet that **makes** men s. 9570
51:22 of your hand the cup that **made** you s; 9570
Jer 25:16 *they will* s and go mad because of 1723
La 5:13 boys s under loads of wood. 4173
Am 8:12 *Men will* s from sea to sea and wander 5675

STAGGERED (3) [STAGGER]

Ps 107:27 They reeled and s like drunken men; 5675
Isa 21:3 *I* **am** s by what I hear, 6390
Am 4:8 People s from town to town for water 5675

STAGGERING (2) [STAGGER]

1Sa 25:31 not have on his conscience the s **burden** of needless bloodshed 2256+4842+7050
Pr 24:11 hold back *those* s toward slaughter. 4572

STAGGERS (2) [STAGGER]

Isa 3:8 Jerusalem s, Judah is falling; 4173
19:14 as a drunkard s **around** in his vomit. 9494

STAIN (2) [STAINED]

Jer 2:22 the s of your guilt *is still* before me," 4187
Eph 5:27 without s or wrinkle or any other blemish, *5070*

STAINED (6) [STAIN]

1Ki 2:5 *with* that blood s the belt around his waist 5989
Isa 59:3 For your hands **are** s with blood, 1458
63:1 from Bozrah, with his garments **s crimson?** 2808
63:3 and *I* s all my clothing. 1458
Hos 6:8 *s with* **footprints** of blood. AIT
Jude 1:23 even the clothing s by corrupted flesh. *5071*

STAIRS (2) [DOWNSTAIRS, STAIRWAY, UPSTAIRS]

Ne 9:4 Standing on the s were the Levites— 5090
Eze 40:49 It was reached by a **flight of s**, 5092

STAIRWAY (5) [STAIRS]

Ge 28:12 He had a dream in which he saw a s resting 6150
1Ki 6:8 a s led up to the middle level and 4294
2Ki 20:11 the ten steps it had gone down on the s 5092
Isa 38:8 the ten steps it has gone down on the s 5092
Eze 41:7 A s went up from the lowest floor to NIH

STAKE (1) [STAKES]

Job 6:29 reconsider, for my integrity is **at s**. 928

STAKES (2) [STAKE]

Isa 33:20 its s will never be pulled up, 3845
54:2 lengthen your cords, strengthen your s. 3845

STALK (6) [STALKED, STALKS]

Ge 41:5 were growing on a single s. 7866
41:22 full and good, growing on a single s. 7866
Job 10:16 *you* s me like a lion and again display your 7421
Hos 8:7 The s has no head; it will produce no flour. 7850
Mk 4:28 first the s, then the head, *5965*
Jn 19:29 put the sponge on a s of the hyssop plant, *NIG*

STALKED (2) [STALK]

La 4:18 *Men* s us *at* every step, 7421
Eze 32:27 of these warriors had s through the land of NIH

STALKS (3) [STALK]

Jos 2:6 up to the roof and hidden them under the s 6770
Ru 2:16 pull out some s for her from the bundles NIH
Ps 91:6 nor the pestilence *that* s in the darkness, 2143

STALL (3) [STALLS]

Ps 50:9 from your s or of goats from your pens, 1074
Mal 4:2 and leap like calves released from the s. 5272
Lk 13:15 from the s and lead it out to give it water? *5764*

STALL-FED (1) [FEED]

1Ki 4:23 ten head of s cattle, twenty of pasture-fed 1374

STALLIONS (3)

Jer 5:8 They are well fed, lusty s, 6061
8:16 of their s the whole land trembles. 52
50:11 a heifer threshing grain and neigh like s, 52

STALLS (4) [STALL]

1Ki 4:26 Solomon had four thousand s for chariot 774
2Ch 9:25 Solomon had four thousand s *for* horses 774
32:28 and he made s for various kinds of cattle, 774
Hab 3:17 no sheep in the pen and no cattle in the s, 8348

STAMMERING (1)

Isa 32:4 and the s tongue will be fluent and clear. 6589

STAMP (1) [STAMPED]

Eze 6:11 Strike your hands together and s your feet 8392

STAMPED (1) [STAMP]

Eze 25:6 you have clapped your hands and s your feet 8392

STANCHED (KJV) See STOPPED

STAND (257) [STANDING, STANDS, STOOD]

Ge 31:35 that I cannot **s up** in your presence; 7756
Ex 9:11 The magicians could not s before Moses 6641
14:13 **S firm** and you will see the deliverance 3656
17:6 I *will* s there before you by the rock 6641
17:9 Tomorrow I *will* s on top of the hill with 5893
18:14 while all these people s around you 5893
18:23 you will be able *to* **s the strain**, 6641
30:18 with its bronze **s**, for washing. 4029
30:28 and the basin with its **s**. 4029
31:9 the basin with its **s**— 4029
33:21 a place near me where *you may* s on a rock. 5893
35:16 the bronze basin with its **s**; 4029
38:8 the bronze basin and its bronze **s** from 4029
39:39 the basin with its **s**; 4029
40:11 the basin and its **s** and consecrate them. 4029
Lev 8:11 and all its utensils and the basin with its **s**, 4029
26:37 not be **able to** s before your enemies. 9538
Nu 5:16 " 'The priest shall bring her and **have** her s 6641
5:18 After the priest *has* **had** the woman's s before 6641
5:30 *to* **have** her s before the LORD and is 6641
8:13 **Have** the Levites s in front of Aaron 6641
11:16 that *they may* s there with you. 3656
11:24 of their elders and **had** them s around 6641
16:9 and to s before the community and minister 6641
27:19 **Have** him s before Eleazar the priest and 6641
27:21 *He is to* s before Eleazar the priest, 6641
27:22 and **had** him s before Eleazar the priest and 6641
30:4 by which she obligated herself *will* **s**. 7756
30:5 by which she obligated herself *will* **s**; 7756
30:7 by which she obligated herself *will* **s**. 7756
30:11 by which she obligated herself *will* **s**. 7756
30:12 or pledges that came from her lips *will* **s**. 7756
Dt 7:24 No one *will be able to* **s up** against you; 3656
9:2 "Who *can* **s up** against the Anakites?" 3656
10:8 to s before the LORD to minister and 6641
11:25 No man *will be able to* s against you. 3656
18:5 of all your tribes to s and minister in 6641
19:16 If a malicious witness **takes the s** to 928+7756
19:17 the two men involved in the dispute *must* s 6641
27:12 these tribes *shall* s on Mount Gerizim 6641
27:13 And these tribes *shall* s on Mount Ebal 6641
Jos 1:5 *to* **s up** against you all the days of your life. 3656
3:8 the Jordan's waters, go and s in the river.' " 6641
3:13 will be cut off and **s up** in a heap." 6641
7:10 The LORD said to Joshua, **"S up!** 7756
7:12 the Israelites cannot s against their enemies; 7756
7:13 You cannot s against your enemies 7756
10:12 "O sun, **s still** over Gibeon, O moon, 1957
20:4 *he is to* **s** *in* the entrance of the city gate 6641
Jdg 4:20 **"S** *in* the doorway of the tent," he told her. 6641
1Sa 6:20 "Who can s in the presence of the LORD, 6641
12:3 Here I **s**. Testify against me in the presence NIH
12:7 s here, because I am going to confront you 3656
12:16 "Now then, **s still** and see this great thing 3656
14:40 "You s over there; I and Jonathan 2118
14:40 I and Jonathan my son *will* s over here." 2118
17:16 and evening and **took** *his* **s**. 3656
19:3 I will go out and s with my father in 6641
2Sa 1:9 he said to me, 'S over me and kill me! 6641
2:25 a group and **took** *their* s on top of a hill. 6641
15:2 He would get up early and s by the side of 6641
18:30 The king said, **"S aside** and wait here." 6015
22:34 *he* **enables** me **to** s on the heights. 6641
23:12 But Shammah **took** *his* s in the middle of 3656
1Ki 7:30 Each s had four bronze wheels 4807
7:31 inside of **the s** there was an opening that 2084[S]
7:32 axles of the wheels were attached to the s. 4807
7:34 Each s had four handles, 4807
7:34 one on each corner, projecting from the s. 4807
7:35 of the s there was a circular band half 4807
7:35 and panels were attached to the top of the s. 4807
10:8 who continually s before you 6641
19:11 and s on the mountain in the presence of 6641
2Ki 5:11 that he would surely come out to me and s 6641
1Ch 11:14 *they* **took** *their* s in the middle of the field. 3656
23:30 They *were* also to s every morning to thank 6641
2Ch 9:7 officials, who continually s before you 6641
20:9 *we will* s in your presence 6641
20:17 **s firm** and see the deliverance 6641
29:11 the LORD has chosen you to s before him 6641
35:5 **"S** in the holy place with a group of Levites 6641
Ezr 9:15 of it not one of us *can* s in your presence." 6641
10:13 so we cannot s outside. 6641
Ne 9:5 **"S up** and praise the LORD your God, 7756
Est 6:13 *you* **cannot s** against him— 3523+4202
9:2 No one *could* s against them, 6641
Job 11:15 *you will* s firm and without fear. 2118
19:25 and that in the end *he will* s upon the earth. 7756
21:16 I **s aloof** from the counsel of the wicked. 8178
22:18 I **s aloof** from the counsel of the wicked. 8178
30:20 *I* **s up**, but you merely look at me. 6641
30:28 *I* **s up** in the assembly and cry for help. 7756
32:16 now that *they* s there with no reply? 6641
38:14 its features **s out** like those of a garment. 3656
39:24 *he* cannot **s still** when the trumpet sounds. 586
40:12 crush the wicked **where** they s. 9393
41:10 Who then *is able to* s against me? 3656
Ps 1:1 in the counsel of the wicked or s in the way 6641
1:5 the wicked *will* not s in the judgment, 7756
2:2 The kings of the earth **take** *their* s and 3656
5:5 The arrogant cannot s in your presence; 3656
10:1 O LORD, *do you* s far off? 6641
18:33 *he* **enables** me **to** s on the heights. 6641
20:8 but we rise up and **s firm**. 6386
24:3 Who *may* s in his holy place? 7756
26:12 My feet s on level ground; 6641
30:7 *you* **made** my mountain s firm; 6641
33:11 But the plans of the LORD **s firm** forever, 6641
40:2 on a rock and gave me a firm **place to s**. 892
76:7 Who *can* s before you when you are angry? 6641

Ps 78:13 he made the water s firm 5893
93: 5 Your statutes s firm; 586+4394
94:16 Who will take a s for me 3656
101: 7 no one who speaks falsely will s 3922
109: 6 let an accuser s at his right hand. 6641
119:120 I s in awe of your laws. 3707
122: 5 There the thrones for judgment s, 3782
127: 1 the watchmen s guard in vain. 9193
130: 3 O Lord, who could s? 6641
Pr 8: 2 where the paths meet, she takes her s; 5893
10:25 but the righteous s firm forever. 3572
27: 4 but who can s before jealousy? 6641
Ecc 5: 7 Therefore s in awe of God. 3707
8: 3 Do not s up for a bad cause, 6641
Isa 7: 9 If you do not s firm in your faith, 586
7: 9 you will not s at all.' " 586
8:10 propose your plan, but it will not s, 7756
11:10 of Jesse will s as a banner for the peoples; 6641
14:24 and as I have purposed, so it will s. 7756
21: 8 my lord, I s on the watchtower; 6641
28:18 your agreement with the grave will not s. 7756
29:23 and will s in awe of the God of Israel. 6907
44:11 all come together and take their s; 6641
46:10 I say: My purpose will s, 7756
48:13 I summon them, they all s up together. 6641
60:11 Your gates will always s open, AIT
Jer 1:17 S up and say to them whatever I command 7756
1:18 a bronze wall to s against the whole land— NIH
6:16 "S at the crossroads and look; 6641
7: 2 "S at the gate of the LORD's house 6641
7:10 then come and s before me in this house, 6641
14: 6 Wild donkeys s on the barren heights 6641
15: 1 if Moses and Samuel were to s before me, 6641
17:19 "Go and s at the gate of the people, 6641
17:19 s also at all the other gates of Jerusalem. NIH
26: 2 S in the courtyard of the LORD's house 6641
30:18 and the palace will s in its proper place. 3782
33:18 to have a man to s before me continually NIH
44:28 in Egypt will know whose word will s— 7756
44:29 of harm against you will surely s.' 7756+7756
46:15 cannot s, for the LORD will push them down. 6641
46:21 they will not s their ground, 6641
48:19 S by the road and watch, 6641
48:45 of Heshbon the fugitives s helpless, 6641
49:19 And what shepherd can s against me?" 6641
50:44 And what shepherd can s against me?" 6641
51:29 the LORD's purposes against Babylon s— 7756
Eze 2: 1 s up on your feet and I will speak to you." 6641
13: 5 the house of Israel so that it will s firm in 6641
22:30 and s before me in the gap on behalf of 6641
27:29 the mariners and all the seamen will s on 6641
44:11 and sacrifices for the people and s before 6641
44:15 they are to s before me to offer sacrifices 6641
46: 2 through the portico of the gateway and s by 6641
47:10 Fishermen will s along the shore; 6641
Da 8: 4 No animal could s against him, 6641
8: 7 The ram was powerless to s against him; 6641
8:25 and take his s against the Prince of princes. 6641
10:11 and s up, for I have now been 6584+6641+6642
11: 1 I took my s to support and protect him.) 6641
11:15 will not have the strength to s. 6641
11:16 no one will be able to s against him. 6641
11:25 be able to s because of the plots devised 6641
Am 2:15 The archer will not s his ground, 6641
5:21 I cannot s your assemblies. 8193
Mic 5: 4 He will s and shepherd his flock in 6641
6: 1 Listen to what the LORD says: "S up, 7756
Hab 2: 1 I will s at my watch and station myself on 6641
3: 2 I s in awe of your deeds, O LORD. 3707
Zep 3: 8 "for the day I will s up to testify. 7756
Zec 14: 4 On that day his feet will s on the Mount 6641
Mal 3: 2 Who can s when he appears? 6641
Mt 4: 5 and had him s on the highest point of 2705
5:15 Instead they put it on its s, 3393
12:25 household divided against itself will not s. 2705
12:26 How then can his kingdom s? 2705
12:41 men of Nineveh will s up at the judgment 482
18: 2 a little child and had him s among them. 2705
Mk 3: 3 "S up in front of everyone." 1586
3:24 divided against itself, that kingdom cannot s 2705
3:25 divided against itself, that house cannot s. 2705
3:26 he cannot s; his end has come. 2705
4:21 Instead, don't you put it on its s? 3393
9:36 a little child and had him s among them. 2705
11:25 And when you s praying, 2705
13: 9 account of me you will s before governors 2705
Lk 1:19 I s in the presence of God, 4225
4: 9 and had him s on the highest point of 2705
6: 8 "Get up and s in front of everyone." 2705
8:16 Instead, he puts it on a s, 3393
9:47 took a little child and had him s beside him. 2705
11:18 against himself, how can his kingdom s? 2705
11:32 men of Nineveh will s up at the judgment 482
11:33 Instead he puts it on its s, 3393
13:25 you will s outside knocking and pleading, 2705
21:28 s up and lift up your heads, 376
21:36 that you may be able to s before the Son 2705
Jn 8: 3 They made her s before the group 2705
8:16 I s with the Father, who sent me. NIG
Ac 1:11 "why do you s here looking into the sky? 2705
4:26 The kings of the earth take their s and 4225
5:20 "Go, s in the temple courts," he said, 2705
6:10 but they could not s up against his wisdom 468
10:26 "S up," he said, "I am only a man myself." 482
14:10 "S up on your feet!" 482+3981
22:30 he brought Paul and had him s before them. 2705
23: 6 I s on trial because of my hope in 3212
Ac 25: 9 to Jerusalem and s trial before me there 3212
25:20 to go to Jerusalem and s trial there 3212
26: 2 to s before you today as I make my defense NIG
26:16 'Now get up and s on your feet. 2705
26:22 and so I s here and testify to small 2705
27:24 You must s trial before Caesar; 4225
Ro 5: 2 by faith into this grace in which we now s. 2705
9:11 that God's purpose in election might s: 3531
11:20 because of unbelief, and you s by faith. 2705
14: 4 And he will s, for the Lord is able to make 2705
14: 4 for the Lord is able to make him s. 2705
14:10 we will all s before God's judgment seat. 4225
1Co 10:13 a way out so that you can s up under it. 5722
15: 1 and on which you have taken your s. 2705
15:58 Therefore, my dear brothers, s firm. 1181+1612
16:13 Be on your guard; s firm in the faith; 2705
2Co 1:21 God who makes both us and you s firm 1011
1:24 because it is by faith you s firm. 2705
2: 9 if you would s the test and be obedient 1509
Gal 5: 1 S firm, then, and do not let yourselves 2705
Eph 6:11 of God so that you can take your s against 2705
6:13 you may be able to s your ground, 468
6:13 and after you have done everything, to s. 2705
6:14 S firm then, with the belt of truth buckled 2705
Php 1:27 I will know that you s firm in one spirit, 2705
4: 1 that is how you should s firm in the Lord, 2705
Col 4:12 that you may s firm in all the will of God, 2705
1Th 3: 1 So when we could s it no longer, 5095
3: 5 For this reason, when I could s it no longer, 5095
2Th 2:15 s firm and hold to the teachings we passed 2705
Jas 2: 3 "You s there" or "Sit on the floor 2705
5: 8 You too, be patient and s firm, 2840+3836+5114
1Pe 5:12 the true grace of God. S fast in it. 2705
Rev 3:20 I s at the door and knock. 2705
6:17 their wrath has come, and who can s?" 2705
8: 2 I saw the seven angels who s before God, 2705
11: 4 the two lampstands that s before the Lord 2705
18:10 they will s far off and cry: " 'Woe! 2705
18:15 gained their wealth from her will s far off, 2705
18:17 their living from the sea, will s far off. 2705

STANDARD (16) [STANDARDS]

Nu 1:52 each man in his own camp under his own s. 1840
2: 2 under his s with the banners of his family." 1840
2: 3 of Judah are to encamp under their s. 1840
2:10 of the camp of Reuben under their s. 1840
2:17 each in his own place under his s. 1840
2:18 of the camp of Ephraim under their s. 1840
2:25 of the camp of Dan, under their s. 1840
10:14 the camp of Judah went first, under their s. 1840
10:18 of Reuben went next, under their s. 1840
10:22 of Ephraim went next, under their s. 1840
10:25 of the camp of Dan set out, under their s. 1840
2Sa 14:26 two hundred shekels by the royal s. 74
2Ch 3: 3 (using the cubit of the old s). 4500
Isa 31: 9 the battle s their commanders will panic," 5812
Jer 4:21 How long must I see the battle s and hear 5812
Eze 45:11 the homer is to be the s measure for both. 5504

STANDARDBEARER (KJV) See SICK MAN (Isa 10:18)

STANDARDS (12) [STANDARD]

Lev 19:35 not use dishonest s when measuring length, 5477
Nu 2:31 They will set out last, under their s. 1840
2:34 that is the way they encamped under their s, 1840
Ps 74: 4 they set up their s as signs. 253
Eze 5: 7 not even conformed to the s of the nations 5477
7:27 and by their own s I will judge them. 5477
11:12 but have conformed to the s of the nations 5477
23:24 they will punish you according to their s. 5477
Jn 8:15 You judge by human s; 3836+4922
1Co 1:26 Not many of you were wise by human s; 2848
3:18 of you thinks he is wise by the s of this age, NIG
2Co 10: 2 that we live by the s of this world. 2848

STANDING (154) [STAND]

Ge 18: 2 looked up and saw three men s nearby. 5893
18:22 Abraham remained s before the LORD. 6641
24:13 See, I am s beside this spring, 5893
24:30 the man and found him s by the camels near 6641
24:31 "Why are you s out here? 6641
24:43 See, I am s beside this spring; 5893
41: 1 He was s by the Nile, 6641
41:17 "In my dream I was s on the bank of 6641
Ex 3: 5 the place where you are s is holy ground." 6641
22: 6 so that it burns shocks of grain or s grain or 7850
26:32 of acacia wood overlaid with gold and s NIH
33:10 the people saw the pillar of cloud s at 6641
Nu 16:27 and Abiram had come out and were s 5893
22:23 the angel of the LORD s in the road with 5893
22:31 and he saw the angel of the LORD s in 5893
22:34 I did not realize you were s in the road 5893
23: 6 to him and found him s beside his offering, 5893
23:17 to him and found him s beside his offering, 5893
32:14 s in the place of your fathers and making 7756
Dt 16: 9 to put the sickle to the s grain. 7850
23:25 but you must not put a sickle to his s grain. 7850
29:10 All of you are s today in the presence of 5893
29:12 You are s here in order to enter into NIH
29:15 who are s here with us today in 6641
Jos 4:10 the priests who carried the ark remained s in 6641
5:13 a man s in front of him with a drawn sword 6641
5:15 for the place where you are s is holy." 6641
Ex 8:33 were s on both sides of the ark of 6641
20: 9 by the avenger of blood prior to s trial 6641
Jdg 9:35 of Ebed had gone out and was s at 6641
15: 5 and let the foxes loose in the s grain of 7850
15: 5 He burned up the shocks and s grain, 7850
Ru 2: 1 from the clan of Elimelech, a man of s, 1475+2657
2:13 not have the s of one of your servant girls." 3869
4:11 May you have s in Ephrathah and 2657
1Sa 9: 1 There was a Benjamite, a man of s, 2657
17:26 David asked the men s near him, 6641
19:20 with Samuel s there as their leader, 6641
22: 6 with all his officials s around him. 5893
22: 9 who was s with Saul's officials, said, 5893
2Sa 13:34 Now the man s watch looked up 7595
1Ki 8:14 the whole assembly of Israel was s there, 6641
10:19 with a lion s beside each of them. 6641
11:28 Now Jeroboam was a man of s, 1475+2657
13: 1 as Jeroboam was s by the altar to make 6641
13:24 both the donkey and the lion s beside it. 6641
13:25 with the lion s beside the body, 6641
13:28 with the donkey and the lion s beside it. 6641
22:19 the host of heaven s around him on his right 6641
2Ki 9:17 When the lookout s on the tower 6641
11:14 s by the pillar, as the custom was. 6641
13: 6 the Asherah pole remained s in Samaria. 6641
1Ch 21:15 the LORD was then s at the threshing floor 6641
21:16 of the LORD s between heaven and earth, 6641
2Ch 6: 3 the whole assembly of Israel was s there, 6641
7: 6 and all the Israelites were s. 6641
9:18 with a lion s beside each of them. 6641
18:18 on his throne with all the host of heaven s 6641
23:13 s by his pillar at the entrance. 6641
Ne 8: 5 the people could see him because he was s 2118
8: 7 in the Law while the people were s there. 6642
9: 4 S on the stairs were the Levites— 7756
Est 5: 2 When he saw Queen Esther s in the court, 6641
6: 5 "Haman is s in the court." 6641
Ps 122: 2 Our feet are s in your gates, O Jerusalem. 6641
Isa 17: 5 a reaper gathers the s grain and harvests 7850
27: 9 or incense altars will be left s. 7756
Jer 28: 5 the priests and all the people who were s in 6641
36:21 and read it to the king and all the officials s 6641
La 3:63 Sitting or s, they mock me in their songs. 7800
Eze 3:23 And the glory of the LORD was s there, 6641
8:11 and Jaazaniah son of Shaphan was s 6641
10: 3 Now the cherubim were s on the south side 6641
40: 3 he was s in the gateway with a linen cord 6641
43: 6 While the man was s beside me, 6641
Da 7:16 I approached one of those s there 10624
8: 3 s beside the canal, and the horns were long. 6641
8: 6 toward the two-horned ram I had seen s 6641
8:17 he came near the place where I was s, 6642
10: 4 as I was s on the bank of the great river, NIH
10:16 I said to the one s before me, 6641
Am 7: 7 The Lord was s by a wall 5893
9: 1 I saw the Lord s by the altar, and he said: 5893
Zec 1: 8 He was s among the myrtle trees in a ravine. 6641
1:10 man s among the myrtle trees explained, 6641
1:11 who was s among the myrtle trees, 6641
3: 1 Then he showed me Joshua the high priest s 6641
3: 1 and Satan s at his right side to accuse him. 6641
3: 4 The angel said to those who were s 6641
3: 7 I will give you a place among these s here. 6641
6: 5 going out from s in the presence of the Lord 3656
14:12 Their flesh will rot while they are still s 6641
Mt 6: 5 for they love to pray s in the synagogues 2705
12:47 "Your mother and brothers are s outside, 2705
16:28 some who are s here will not taste death 2705
20: 3 the third hour he went out and saw others s 2705
20: 6 and found still others s around. 2705
20: 6 'Why have you been s here all day long 2705
24:15 "So when you see s in the holy place 2705
26:73 those s there went up to Peter and said, 2705
27:47 When some of those s there heard this, 2705
Mk 3:31 S outside, they sent someone in to call him. 2705
9: 1 some who are s here will not taste death 2705
11: 5 some people s there asked, 2705
13:14 'the abomination that causes desolation' s 2705
14:47 of those s near drew his sword and struck 4225
14:69 she said again to those s around, 4225
14:70 those s near said to Peter, 4225
15:35 When some of those s near heard this, 4225
Lk 1:11 s at the right side of the altar of incense. 2705
5: 1 as Jesus was s by the Lake of Gennesaret, 2705
8:20 "Your mother and brothers are s outside, 2705
9:27 some who are s here will not taste death 2705
9:32 they saw his glory and the two men s with 5319
19:24 "Then he said to those s by, 4225
21:19 By s firm you will gain life. 5705
23:10 and the teachers of the law were s there, 2705
Jn 8: 9 with the woman still s there. 1639
11:42 for the benefit of the people s here, 4325
18: 5 the traitor was s there with them.) 2705
18:18 Peter also was s with them, 2705
19:26 and the disciple whom he loved s nearby, 4225
20:14 she turned around and saw Jesus s there, 2705
Ac 4:14 the man who had been healed s there 2705
5:23 with the guards s at the doors; 2705
5:25 in jail are s in the temple courts teaching 2705
7:33 the place where you are s is holy ground. 2705
7:55 and Jesus s at the right hand of God. 2705
7:56 the Son of Man s at the right hand of God." 2705
13:16 S up, Paul motioned with his hand 482
13:50 of high s and the leading men of the city. 2363
16: 9 man of Macedonia s and begging him, 1639+2705
22:25 Paul said to the centurion s there, 2705
23: 2 the high priest Ananias ordered those s near 4225

Ac 23: 4 Those who *were* s **near** Paul said, *4225*
25:10 "I am now s before Caesar's court, *2705*
1Co 10:12 So, if you think *you are* s **firm,** *2705*
1Th 3: 8 since you *are* s **firm** in the Lord. *2705*
1Ti 3:13 an excellent s and great assurance *957*
Heb 9: 8 as long as the first tabernacle was still **s.** *5087*
Jas 5: 9 The Judge *is* s at the door! *2705*
1Pe 5: 9 Resist him, **s firm** in the faith, *5104*
Rev 4: 1 before me was a door **s open** in heaven. *487*
5: 6 s in the center of the throne, *2705*
7: 1 After this I saw four angels s at *2705*
7: 9 s before the throne and in front of *2705*
7:11 All the angels *were* s around the throne and *2705*
10: 5 Then the angel I had seen s on the sea and *2705*
10: 8 in the hand of the angel who *is* s on the sea *2705*
14: 1 s on Mount Zion, and with him 144,000 *2705*
15: 2 s beside the sea, those who had been *2705*
19:11 I saw heaven **s open** and there before me *487*
19:17 And I saw an angel s in the sun, *2705*
20:12 s before the throne, and books were opened. *2705*

STANDS (52) [STAND]

Nu 35:12 of murder may not die before he s trial 6641
Dt 17:12 or for the priest who s ministering there to 6641
Jos 22:19 where the LORD's tabernacle **s,** 8905
22:29 the altar of the LORD our God that s NIH
Jdg 6:24 To this day it s in Ophrah of the Abiezrites. 6388
1Sa 16: 6 "Surely the LORD's anointed s here NIH
1Ki 7:27 He also made ten **movable** s of bronze; 4807
7:28 This is how the s were made: 4807
7:31 The panels of **the** s were square, not round. 2157S
7:37 This is the way he made the ten **s.** 4807
7:38 one basin to go on each of the ten **s.** 4807
7:39 He placed five of the s on the south side of 4807
7:43 the ten s with their ten basins; 4807
2Ki 16:17 the basins from the **movable s.** 4807
25:13 the **movable** s and the bronze Sea that were 4807
25:16 the Sea and the **movable s,** 4807
2Ch 4:14 the s with their basins; 4807
Est 7: 9 "A gallows seventy-five feet high s 6641
Job 9:35 but as it now s with me, I cannot. NIH
23:13 "But he s alone, and who can oppose him? NIH
Ps 89: 2 I will declare that your love s **firm** forever, 1215
109:31 For *he* s at the right hand of the needy one, 6641
119:89 is eternal; *it* s **firm** in the heavens. 5893
Pr 12: 7 but the house of the righteous **s firm.** 6641
SS 2: 9 There *he* s behind our wall, 6641
Isa 27:10 The fortified city s desolate, NIH
32: 8 and by noble deeds he s. 7756
40: 8 but the word of our God s forever." 7756
46: 7 they set it up in its place, and there *it* **s.** 6641
59:14 and righteousness s at a distance; 6641
65: 6 "See, *it* s **written** before me: AIT
Jer 27:19 the **movable** s and the other furnishings 4807
52:17 the **movable** s and the bronze Sea that were 4807
52:20 and the **movable s,** which King Solomon 4807
Da 6:12 The king answered, "The decree s— 10327
Mt 10:22 but he who s **firm** to the end will be saved. *5702*
13:38 good seed s **for** the sons of the kingdom. *1639*
24:13 but he who s **firm** to the end will be saved. *5702*
Mk 13:13 but he who s **firm** to the end will be saved. *5702*
Lk 8:14 that fell among thorns s **for** those who hear, *1639*
8:15 But the seed on good soil s **for** those with *1639*
Jn 1:26 "but among you s one you do not know. *2705*
3:18 does not believe *s* **condemned** already *AIT*
16:11 the prince of this world *now s* **condemned.** *AIT*
Ac 4:10 that this man s before you healed. *4225*
Ro 14: 4 To his own master *he* s or falls. *2705*
Gal 4:25 Now Hagar s **for** Mount Sinai in Arabia *1639*
2Ti 2:19 God's solid foundation s **firm,** *2705*
Heb 4: 1 the promise of entering his rest *still* **s,** *2901*
10:11 Day after day every priest s *2705*
1Pe 1:25 but the word of the Lord s forever." *3531*
Rev 19: 8 (Fine linen s **for** the righteous acts of *1639*

STANDSTILL (1)

Ezr 4:24 the house of God in Jerusalem **came to a s** 10098

STAR (17) [STARGAZERS, STARRY, STARS]

Nu 24:17 A s will come out of Jacob; 3919
Isa 14:12 you have fallen from heaven, O **morning s,** 2122
Am 5:26 pedestal of your idols, the s *of* your god— 3919
Mt 2: 2 We saw his s in the east and have come *843*
2: 7 the exact time the s had appeared. *843*
2: 9 the s they had seen in the east went ahead *843*
2:10 When they saw the **s,** they were overjoyed. *843*
Ac 7:43 of Molech and the s of your god Rephan, *849*
1Co 15:41 and s differs from star in splendor. *843*
15:41 and star differs *from* s in splendor. *843*
2Pe 1:19 until the day dawns and the **morning** s rises *5892*
Rev 2:28 I will also give him the morning s. *843*
8:10 and a great **s,** blazing like a torch, *843*
8:11 the name *of* the s is Wormwood. *843*
9: 1 and I saw a s that had fallen from the sky to *843*
9: 1 **The** s was given the key to the shaft of *899S*
22:16 and the bright Morning **S."** *843*

STARE (4) [STARED, STARES]

Ps 22:17 people s and gloat over me. 5564
SS 1: 6 *Do* not s *at* me because I am dark, 8011
Isa 14:16 Those who see you s at you, 8708
Ac 3:12 Why *do you* s **at** us as if by our own power *867*

STARED (3) [STARE]

2Ki 8:11 *He* s *at* him **with a fixed gaze** until Hazael felt ashamed. 906+2256+6641+7156+8492
Jn 13:22 His disciples s at one another, *1063*
Ac 10: 4 Cornelius s **at** him in fear. *867*

STARES (1) [STARE]

Ps 55: 3 voice of the enemy, at the s *of* the wicked; 6821

STARGAZERS (1) [STAR]

Isa 47:13 s who make predictions month 928+2600+3919

STARRY (15) [STAR]

2Ki 17:16 They bowed down to all the s hosts, 9028
21: 3 down to all the s hosts and worshiped them. 9028
21: 5 he built altars to all the s hosts. 9028
23: 4 for Baal and Asherah and all the s hosts. 9028
23: 5 to the constellations and to all the s hosts. 9028
2Ch 33: 3 down to all the s hosts and worshiped them. 9028
33: 5 he built altars to all the s hosts. 9028
Ne 9: 6 and all their s **host,** 7372
Ps 33: 6 their **s host** by the breath of his mouth. 7372
Isa 34: 4 the **s host** will fall like withered leaves from 7372
40:26 He who brings out the **s host** one by one, 7372
45:12 I marshaled their **s hosts.** 7372
Jer 19:13 the s hosts and poured out drink offerings 9028
Da 8:10 of the s host down to the earth and trampled 3919
Zep 1: 5 down on the roofs to worship the s host, 9028

STARS (55) [STAR]

Ge 1:16 He also made the **s.** 3919
15: 5 "Look up at the heavens and count the s— 3919
22:17 as numerous as the s *in* the sky and as 3919
26: 4 as numerous as the s *in* the sky 3919
37: 9 and moon and eleven s were bowing down 3919
Ex 32:13 as numerous as the s *in* the sky 3919
Dt 1:10 so that today you are as many as the s *in* 3919
4:19 the sun, the moon and the s— 3919
10:22 as numerous as the s *in* the sky. 3919
17: 3 to the sun or the moon or the s *of* the sky, 7372
28:62 as numerous as the s *in* the sky will be left 3919
Jdg 5:20 From the heavens the s fought, 3919
1Ch 27:23 to make Israel as numerous as the s *in* 3919
Ne 4:21 the first light of dawn till the s came out. 3919
9:23 You made their sons as numerous as the s 3919
Job 3: 9 May its morning s become dark; 3919
9: 7 he seals off the light of the s. 3919
22:12 And see how lofty are the highest **s!** 3919
25: 5 not bright and the s are not pure in his eyes, 3919
38: 7 while the morning s sang together and all 3919
Ps 8: 3 the moon and the **s,** which you have set in 3919
136: 9 the moon and s to govern the night; 3919
147: 4 the number of the s and calls them each 3919
148: 3 praise him, all you shining s. 3919
Ecc 12: 2 the light and the moon and the s grow dark, 3919
SS 6:10 majestic as the s in procession? NIH
Isa 13:10 The s *of* heaven and their constellations 3919
14:13 I will raise my throne above the s *of* God; 3919
34: 4 the s *of* the heavens will be dissolved and 7372
Jer 8: 2 and the moon and all the s *of* the heavens, 7372
31:35 and s to shine by night, who stirs up the sea 3919
33:22 before me as countless as the s *of* the sky 7372
Eze 32: 7 I will cover the heavens and darken their **s;** 3919
Da 12: 3 like the s for ever and ever. 3919
Joel 2:10 and the s no longer shine. 3919
3:15 and the s no longer shine. 3919
Ob 1: 4 the eagle and make your nest among the **s,** 3919
Na 3:16 till they are more than the s *of* the sky, 3919
Mt 24:29 the s will fall from the sky, *843*
Mk 13:25 the s will fall from the sky, *843*
Lk 21:25 "There will be signs in the sun, moon and **s.** *843*
Ac 27:20 nor s appeared for many days and *843*
1Co 15:41 the moon another and the s another; *843*
Php 2:15 in which you shine like s in the universe *5891*
Heb 11:12 the s in the sky and as countless as the sand *843*
Jude 1:13 wandering **s,** for whom the blackest darkness *843*
Rev 1:16 In his right hand he held seven s, *843*
1:20 the seven s that you saw in my right hand *843*
1:20 The seven s are the angels of the seven *843*
2: 1 the words of him who holds the seven s *843*
3: 1 the seven spirits of God and the seven **s.** *843*
6:13 and the s in the sky fell to earth, *843*
8:12 a third of the moon, and a third *of* the **s,** *843*
12: 1 under her feet and a crown *of* twelve s *843*
12: 4 His tail swept a third *of* the s out of the sky *843*

START (5) [STARTED, STARTING]

Nu 34: 3 your southern boundary *will* s from 2118
1Sa 9: 5 the donkeys and *s* **worrying** about us." AIT
1Ki 20:14 "And who *will* s the battle?" 673
Ne 2:18 They replied, *"Let us* s rebuilding." 7756
2:20 We his servants *will* s rebuilding, 7756

STARTED (23) [START]

Ge 33:16 So that day Esau s on his way **back** to Seir. 8740
Ex 4:20 put them on a donkey and **s back** to Egypt. 8740
22: 6 the *one who* s the fire must make restitution. 1277
Nu 11: 4 and again the Israelites *s* **wailing** and said, AIT
16:46 from the LORD; the plague *has* **s."** 2725
16:47 The plague *had already* s among the people, 2725
Jos 2:23 Then the two men **s back.** 8740
15: 2 Their southern boundary s from the bay at 2118
15: 5 The northern boundary s from the bay 4200+6991
18: 8 the men s on their way to map out the land, 7756
Est 6:13 before whom your downfall *has* **s,** 2725
Jer 37:12 Jeremiah *s to* **leave** the city to go to the AIT
Da 8: 9 which s small but grew in power to 4946
Jnh 3: 4 On the first day, Jonah s into the city. 2725
Mk 10:17 *As* Jesus s on his way, *1744*
Lk 9:46 An argument s among the disciples as *1656*
23: 5 *He* s in Galilee and has come all *806*
Jn 8: 6 But Jesus bent down and *s to* **write** on *AIT*
20: 3 Peter and the other disciple s for the tomb. *2002*
Ac 8:27 So *he* **s out,** and on his way he met an *4513*
10:23 The next day Peter **s out** with them, *482+2002*
17: 5 formed a mob and *s* a **riot** in the city. *AIT*
21:38 "Aren't you the Egyptian who *s* a **revolt** *AIT*

STARTING (4) [START]

2Ki 15:16 At that time Menahem, **s out from** Tirzah, 4946
Pr 17:14 **S** a quarrel is like breaching a dam; 8040
Eze 21:19 both s from the same country. 3655
Mt 27:24 but that instead an uproar *was* **s,** *1181*

STARTLE (1) [STARTLED]

Job 18:11 Terrors s him on every side 1286

STARTLED (3) [STARTLE]

Ru 3: 8 In the middle of the night *something* s 3006
Lk 1:12 *he was* s and was gripped with fear. *5429*
24:37 They were s and frightened, *4765*

STARVATION (2) [STARVE]

Jer 15: 2 those for **s,** to starvation; 8280
15: 2 those for starvation, to s; 8280

STARVE (2) [STARVATION, STARVING]

Ex 16: 3 into this desert to s this entire assembly 8280
Jer 38: 9 where he will s to death 8280

STARVING (5) [STARVE]

Ge 42:19 and take grain back for your s households. 8282
42:33 and take food for your s households and go. 8282
2Ki 7:12 They know we are s; 8281
Pr 6:30 to satisfy his hunger when *he is* **s.** 8279
Lk 15:17 and here I *am* s **to death!** *660+3350*

STATE (7) [STATED, STATEMENT, STATEMENTS]

Jos 20: 4 the city gate and s his case before the elders 1819
Job 23: 4 *I would* s my case before him 6885
33:26 he is restored by God to his **righteous s.** 7407
Isa 14:18 the kings of the nations **lie in s,** 928+3883+8886
43:26 s the case for your innocence. 6218
Lk 1:48 for he has been mindful of the **humble** s *5428*
Ac 24:20 are here *should* s what crime they found *3306*

STATED (3) [STATE]

Ac 13:34 never to decay, *is* s in these words: *3306*
13:35 So *it is* s elsewhere: "You will not let your *3306*
Ro 9: 9 For this was how the promise was **s:** *3364*

STATELY (4)

Pr 30:29 *that are* s *in* their stride, four that move 3512
30:29 four that move *with* **s bearing:** 3512
Isa 2:16 for every trading ship and every s vessel. 2775
Zec 11: 2 the s trees are ruined! 129

STATEMENT (2) [STATE]

Ac 20:38 What grieved them most was his s *3364*
28:25 leave *after* Paul *had* **made** this final **s:** *3306+4839*

STATEMENTS (1) [STATE]

Mk 14:56 against him, but their s did not agree. *3456*

STATION (4) [STATIONED]

2Ki 11: 8 **S yourselves** around the king, 5938
2Ch 23: 7 The Levites *are to* s **themselves** around 5938
Jer 51:12 Reinforce the guard, s the watchmen, 7756
Hab 2: 1 at my watch and s **myself** on the ramparts; 3656

STATIONED (16) [STATION]

Jdg 20:22 where *they had* s *themselves* the first day. 6885
2Ki 3:21 who could bear arms was called up and s on 6641
11:11 s *themselves* around the king— 6641
1Ch 9:18 being s **at** the King's Gate on the east, 928
9:27 They would spend the night s **around** 6017
16:42 The sons of Jeduthun were s **at** the gate. 4200
2Ch 17: 2 *He* s troops in all the fortified cities of Judah 5989
17:19 besides those he s in the fortified cities 5989
23:10 *He* s all the men, each with his weapon 6641
23:19 *He* also s doorkeepers at the gates of 6641
29:25 *He* s the Levites in the temple of the LORD 6641
33:14 *He* s military commanders in all 8492
Ne 4:13 Therefore *I* s some of the people behind 6641
13:11 Then I called them together and s them 6641
13:19 *I* s some of my own men at the gates so 6641
Eze 21:15 *I have* s the sword for slaughter 5989

STATUE (5)

Da 2:31 O king, and there before you stood a large s 10614
2:31 an enormous, dazzling s, 10614
2:32 The head of the s was made of pure gold, 10614
2:34 It struck the s on its feet of iron and clay 10614
2:35 that struck the s became a huge mountain 10614

STATURE (3)

1Sa 2:26 And the boy Samuel continued to grow *in* s 1541
SS 7:7 Your s is like that of the palm, 7757
Lk 2:52 And Jesus grew *in* wisdom and s, *2461*

STATUTE (3) [STATUTES]

1Sa 30:25 David made this a s and ordinance for Israel 2976
Ps 81:5 as a s for Joseph when he went out 6343
122:4 according to the s given to Israel. 6343

STATUTES (39) [STATUTE]

1Ki 3:3 the LORD by walking according to the s 2978
3:14 And if you walk in my ways and obey my s 2976
11:33 nor kept my s and laws as David, 2978
11:34 and who observed my commands and s. 2978
11:38 by keeping my s and commands, 2978
Ps 19:7 The s *of* the LORD are trustworthy, 6343
78:5 He decreed s for Jacob and established 6343
78:56 they did not keep his s. 6343
89:30 and do not follow my s, 5477
93:5 Your s stand firm; 6343
99:7 they kept his s and the decrees he gave them 6343
119:2 Blessed are they who keep his s 6343
119:14 I rejoice in following your s as one rejoices 6343
119:22 for I keep your s. 6343
119:24 Your s are my delight; 6343
119:31 I hold fast to your s, O LORD; 6343
119:36 toward your s and not toward selfish gain. 6343
119:46 I will speak of your s before kings and will 6343
119:59 and have turned my steps to your s. 6343
119:79 those who understand your s. 6343
119:88 and I will obey the s *of* your mouth. 6343
119:95 but I will ponder your s. 6343
119:99 for I meditate on your s. 6343
119:111 Your s are my heritage forever; 6343
119:119 therefore I love your s. 6343
119:125 that I may understand your s. 6343
119:129 Your s are wonderful; 6343
119:138 The s you have laid down are righteous; 6343
119:144 Your s are forever right; 6343
119:146 save me and I will keep your s. 6343
119:152 from your s that you established them 6343
119:157 but I have not turned from your s. 6343
119:167 I obey your s, for I love them greatly. 6343
119:168 I obey your precepts and your s, 6343
132:12 and the s I teach them, 6343
Isa 24:5 they have disobeyed the laws, violated the s 2976
Eze 20:18 the s *of* your fathers or keep their laws 2976
20:25 also gave them over to s that were not good 2976
Mic 6:16 You have observed the s *of* Omri and all 2978

STAVES (KJV) See CLUBS, POLES, SPEAR, STAFF, STAFFS, STICKS

STAY (127) [STAYED, STAYING, STAYS]

Ge 13:6 that they were not able to s together. 3782
19:30 for he was afraid to s in Zoar. 3782
22:5 "S here with the donkey while I and 3782
26:3 S in this land **for a while,** 1591
27:44 S with him for a while 3782
29:19 S *here* with me." 3782
30:27 found favor in your eyes, please s. NIH
38:1 Judah left his brothers and went down *to* s 5742
42:19 *let* one of your brothers s here in prison, 673
Ex 2:21 Moses agreed to s with the man, 3782
9:28 *you* don't *have to* s any longer." 6641
16:29 *to* s where he is on the seventh day; 3782
22:30 *Let them* s with their mothers 2118
24:12 up to me on the mountain and s here, 2118
33:9 the pillar of cloud would come down and s 6641
Lev 8:35 *You must* s at the entrance to the Tent 3782
14:8 *he must* s outside his tent for seven days. 3782
Nu 22:19 Now s here tonight as the others did, 3782
23:3 "S here beside your offering while I go 3656
23:15 "S here beside your offering while I meet 3656
31:19 touched anyone who was killed *must* s outside the camp 2837
35:25 *He must* s there until the death of 3782
35:28 The accused *must* s in his city of refuge 3782
Dt 2:27 *We will* s on the main road; 2143
3:19 your livestock (I know you have much livestock) *may* s 3782
5:31 But you s here with me so 6641
23:10 he is to go outside the camp and s there. 995+4202
24:5 be free to s at home and bring happiness to NIH
24:11 S outside and let the man 6641
Jos 1:14 your children and your livestock *may* s in 3782
4:3 down at the place where *you* s tonight." 4328
7:7 *to* s on the other side of the Jordan! 3782
20:6 *to* s in that city until he has stood trial 3782
Jdg 5:16 Why *did you* s among the campfires to hear 3782
13:15 *"We would like you to* s until we prepare 6806
17:8 that town in search of some other place to s. 1591
17:9 he said, "and I'm looking for a place to s." 1591
19:4 the girl's father, prevailed upon him to s; NIH
19:6 "Please s **tonight** and enjoy yourself." 4328
Jdg 19:9 S and enjoy yourself. 4328
19:10 But, unwilling to s another **night,** 4328
Ru 1:16 and where *you* s I will stay. 4328
1:16 and where you stay *I will* **s.** 4328
2:8 S here with my servant girls. 1815
2:21 'S with my workers 1815
3:13 S here for the night, 4328
1Sa 1:23 "S here until you have weaned him; 3782
5:7 of the god of Israel *must* not s here with us, 3782
9:27 "but you s here awhile, 6641
14:9 *we will* s where we are and not go up 6641
19:2 go into hiding and **s there.** 2461
22:3 and mother come and s with you NIH
22:5 *"Do* not s in the stronghold. 3782
22:23 S with me; don't be afraid; 3782
2Sa 10:5 "S at Jericho till your beards have grown, 3782
11:12 David said to him, "S here one more day, 3782
15:19 Go back and s with King Absalom. 3782
19:32 He had provided for the king during his s 8859
19:33 over with me and s with me in Jerusalem, NIH
1Ki 17:9 at once to Zarephath of Sidon and s there. 3782
2Ki 2:2 Elijah said to Elisha, "S here; 3782
2:4 Then Elijah said to him, "S here, Elisha; 3782
2:6 Then Elijah said to him, "S here; 3782
4:8 who urged him to s **for a meal.** 430+4312
4:10 *he can* s there whenever he comes to us." 6073
7:3 "Why s here until we die? 3782
7:4 And if *we* s here, we will die. 3782
8:1 and s **for a while** wherever you can, 1591
11:8 S close to the king wherever he goes." 2118
14:10 Glory in your victory, but s at home! 3782
19:27 *where* you s and when you come and go and 3782
1Ch 19:5 "S at Jericho till your beards have grown, 3782
2Ch 23:7 S close to the king wherever he goes." 2118
25:19 But s at home! 3782
Ezr 6:6 s away from there. 10201
Ne 4:22 s inside Jerusalem **at night,** 4328
5:2 in order for us to eat and **s alive,** 2649
10:39 the gatekeepers and the singers s. NIH
11:1 while the remaining nine were to s NIH
Job 24:13 who do not know its ways or s in its paths. 3782
39:9 s by your manger **at night?** 4328
Ps 38:11 my neighbors s far away. 6641
55:7 I would flee far away and s in the desert; 4328
92:14 *they will* s fresh and green, 2118
119:148 My eyes s **open** *through* the watches of 7709
127:2 In vain you rise early and s **up** late, 3782
Pr 7:11 her feet never s at home; 8905
14:7 S away from a foolish man, 2143
20:13 s **awake** and you will have food 6524+7219
Isa 5:11 *who* s **up late** at night till they are inflamed 336
16:4 *Let* the Moabite fugitives s with you; 1591
21:8 every night I s at my post. 5893
37:28 *where* you s and when you come and go and 3782
Jer 25:5 and *you can* s in the land the LORD gave 3782
40:10 *I* myself *will* s at Mizpah to represent you 3782
42:10 'If *you* s in this land, I will build you 3782+3782
42:13 if you say, *'We will* not s in this land,' 3782
43:4 the LORD's command to s in the land 3782
49:30 S **in** deep caves, you who live in Hazor," 3782
La 4:15 *"They can* s here no longer." 1591
Mic 7:18 *You do* not s angry forever but delight 2616
Mt 2:13 S there until I tell you, *1639*
10:11 search for some worthy person there and s *3531*
17:17 "how long *shall I* s with you? *1639*
26:38 S here and keep watch with me." *3531*
Mk 6:10 s there until you leave that town. *3531*
9:19 "how long *shall I* s with you? *1639*
14:34 "S here and keep watch." *3531*
Lk 9:4 s there until you leave that town. *3531*
9:41 "how long *shall I* s with you and put up *1639*
10:7 S in that house, eating and drinking *3531*
19:5 I must s at your house today." *3531*
24:29 But they urged him strongly, "S with us, *3531*
24:29 So he went in *to* s with them. *3531*
24:49 but s in the city until you have been clothed *2767*
Jn 4:40 they urged him *to* s with them, *3531*
12:46 so that no one who believes in me *should* s *3531*
Ac 8:29 "Go to that chariot and s **near** it." *3140*
10:48 Then they asked Peter *to* s with them for *2152*
13:17 the people prosper during their s in Egypt, *4229*
16:15 she said, "come and s at my house." *3531*
21:16 home of Mnason, where *we were to* **s.** *3826*
27:31 "Unless these men s with the ship, *3531*
1Co 7:8 It is good for them *to* s unmarried, as I am. *3531*
16:6 Perhaps *I will* s with you **awhile,** *4169*
16:8 But *I will* **s on** at Ephesus until Pentecost, *2152*
1Ti 1:3 s there in Ephesus so that you may *4693*

STAYED (94) [STAY]

Ge 13:6 not support them while they s together, 3782
20:1 **For a while** *he* s in Gerar, 1591
21:34 And Abraham s in the land of the Philistines 1591
22:19 And Abraham s in Beersheba. 3782
26:6 So Isaac s in Gerar. 3782
29:14 After Jacob *had* s with him *for* 3782
35:27 Hebron), where Abraham and Isaac *had* s. 1591
37:1 in the land where his father *had* s, 4472
49:24 his strong arms *s* **limber,** AIT
50:22 Joseph s in Egypt, along with all his 3782
Ex 20:18 *They* s at a distance 6641
24:18 And he s on the mountain forty days 2118
Nu 9:18 As long as the cloud s over the tabernacle, 8905
9:21 the cloud s only from evening till morning, 2118
9:22 cloud s over the tabernacle for two days 799+8905
11:35 the people traveled to Hazeroth and s there. 2118
Nu 20:1 and they s at Kadesh. 3782
22:8 So the Moabite princes s with him. 3782
Dt 1:6 "You *have* s long enough at this mountain. 3782
1:46 And so *you* s in Kadesh many days— 3782
3:29 So *we* s in the valley near Beth Peor. 3782
9:9 *I* s on the mountain forty days 3782
10:10 Now I *had* s on the mountain forty days 6641
Jos 2:1 of a prostitute named Rahab and s there. 8886
2:22 into the hills and s there three days, 3782
Jdg 5:17 Gilead s beyond the Jordan. 8905
5:17 Asher remained on the coast and s 8905
9:41 Abimelech s in Arumah, 3782
11:17 So Israel s at Kadesh. 3782
15:8 down and s in a cave in the rock of Etam. 3782
19:7 so *he* s there *that* **night.** 2256+3782+4328
20:47 where *they* s four months. 3782
Ru 2:23 So Ruth s **close** to the servant girls of Boaz 1815
1Sa 1:23 So the woman **s at home** and nursed her son 3782
19:18 he and Samuel went to Naioth and s there. 3782
22:4 and *they* s with him as long as David was in 3782
23:14 David s in the desert strongholds and in 3782
23:25 to the rock and s in the Desert of Maon. 3782
25:13 while two hundred s with the supplies. 3782
26:3 but David s in the desert. 3782
30:9 Besor Ravine, where some **s behind,** 6641
30:24 of the *man who* s with the supplies is to be 3782
2Sa 1:1 the Amalekites and s in Ziklag two days. 3782
13:38 went to Geshur, *he* s there three years. 2118
15:29 of God back to Jerusalem and s there. 3782
20:2 the men of Judah s by their king all the way 1815
1Ki 2:38 And Shimei s in Jerusalem for a long time. 3782
11:16 and all the Israelites s there for six months, 3782
11:40 and s there until Solomon's death. 2118
17:5 east of the Jordan, and s there. 3782
2Ki 8:2 and her family went away and s in the land 1591
10:21 of Baal came; not one s **away.** 995+4202
15:20 So the king of Assyria withdrew and s in 6641
19:36 He returned to Nineveh and s there. 3782
1Ch 4:23 *they* s there and worked for the king. 3782
9:33 s in the rooms of the temple NIH
Ne 4:18 man who sounded the trumpet s with me. NIH
Est 7:7 **s behind** to beg Queen Esther for his life. 6641
Ecc 2:9 In all this my wisdom s with me. 6641
Isa 37:37 He returned to Nineveh and s there. 3782
Jer 40:6 to Gedaliah son of Ahikam at Mizpah and s 3782
Mt 2:15 where *he* s until the death of Herod. *1639*
Mk 1:45 but s outside in lonely places. *1639*
Lk 1:21 and wondering why he s **so long** in *5988*
1:56 Mary s with Elizabeth for about three *3531*
2:43 the boy Jesus s **behind** in Jerusalem, *5702*
24:53 And *they* s continually at the temple, *1639*
Jn 2:12 There *they* s for a few days. *3531*
4:40 and *he* s two days. *1695+3531*
6:22 the crowd that *had* s on the opposite shore *2705*
7:9 Having said this, he s in Galilee. *3531*
10:40 in the early days. Here *he* s *3531*
11:6 *he* s where he was two more days. *3531*
11:20 but Mary s at home. *2757*
11:54 where *he* s with his disciples. *3531*
Ac 9:28 So Saul s with them and moved *1639*
9:43 Peter s in Joppa for some time with *3531*
12:19 from Judea to Caesarea and s there **a while.** *1417*
14:28 *they* s there a long time with the disciples. *1417*
16:12 And *we* s there several days. *1417*
17:14 but Silas and Timothy s at Berea. *5702*
18:3 *he* s and worked with them. *3531*
18:11 So Paul s for a year and a half, *2767*
18:18 Paul s on in Corinth for some time. *4693*
19:22 he s in the province of Asia **a little longer.** *2091+5989*
20:3 where *he* s three months. *4472*
20:6 Troas, where *we* s seven days. *1417*
21:4 *we* s with them seven days. *2152*
21:7 the brothers and s with them for a day. *3531*
21:8 and s at the house of Philip the evangelist, *3531*
28:12 in at Syracuse and s there three days. *2152*
28:30 For two whole years Paul s there **in** *1844*
Gal 1:18 with Peter and s with him fifteen days. *2152*
2Ti 4:20 Erastus s in Corinth, *3531*

STAYING (24) [STAY]

Ge 25:27 Jacob was a quiet man, s *among* the tents. 3782
32:4 'Your servant Jacob says, *I have been* s 1591
36:7 where they were s could not support them 4472
Nu 25:1 While Israel *was* s in Shittim, 3782
Jdg 19:26 to the house where her master was **s,** NIH
1Sa 13:16 with them *were* s in Gibeah in Benjamin, 3782
14:2 Saul *was* s on the outskirts of Gibeah under 3782
2Sa 11:11 "The ark and Israel and Judah *are* s in tents, 3782
16:3 Ziba said to him, *"He is* s in Jerusalem, 3782
17:17 Jonathan and Ahimaaz *were* s at En Rogel. 6641
1Ki 17:19 to the upper room where he *was* **s,** 3782
17:20 also upon this widow I *am* s with, 1591
2Ki 2:18 who *was* s in Jericho, he said to them, 3782
Ne 2:11 to Jerusalem, and after s there three days 2118
Mt 24:48 'My master *is* **s away a long time,'** *5988*
Jn 1:38 (which means Teacher), "where *are you* **s?"** *3531*
1:39 So they went and saw where *he was* s, *3531*
7:1 purposely **s away from** Judea *1877+4024+4344*
Ac 1:13 to the room where *they* were s. *2910*
2:5 Now there were s in Jerusalem *2997*
10:6 He *is* s with Simon the tanner, *3826*
10:18 Simon who was known as Peter *was* s there. *3826*
11:11 stopped at the house where I was s. *NIG*
28:23 larger numbers to the **place where** *he* was **s.** *3825*

STAYS (8) [STAY]

Nu 14:14 that your cloud s over them, 6641
Job 39:28 He dwells on a cliff and s there **at night;** 4328
Pr 22: 5 he who guards his soul s **far** from them. 8178
Jer 14: 8 like a traveler *who* s **only a night?** 4328+5742
21: 9 Whoever s in this city will die by 3782
38: 2 'Whoever s in this city will die by 3782
1Co 7:40 she is happier if *she* s as she is— *3531*
Rev 16:15 Blessed is he who s **awake** *1213*

STEAD (1) [INSTEAD]

Isa 43: 3 Cush and Seba **in** your s. 9393

STEADFAST (9) [STEADFASTLY]

Ps 51:10 O God, and renew a s spirit within me. 3922
57: 7 My heart *is* s, O God; 3922
57: 7 my heart *is* s; I will sing and make music. 3922
108: 1 My heart *is* s, O God; 3922
111: 8 *They are* s for ever and ever, 6164
112: 7 his heart *is* s, trusting in the LORD. 3922
119: 5 my ways *were* s in obeying your decrees! 3922
Isa 26: 3 in perfect peace him whose mind *is* s, 6164
1Pe 5:10 and make you strong, firm and s. *2530*

STEADFASTLY (1) [STEADFAST]

2Ch 27: 6 Jotham grew powerful because he walked s 3922

STEADILY (3) [STEADY]

Ge 8: 3 The water **receded** s from the earth. 2143+2256+8740+8740
Ru 2: 7 and *has* **worked** *s* from morning till now, AIT
2Co 3: 7 the Israelites could not **look** s at the face *867*

STEADY (4) [STEADILY]

Ge 49:24 But his bow remained s, 419
Ex 17:12 so that his hands remained s till sunset. 575
1Ch 13: 9 Uzzah reached out his hand to s the ark, 296
Isa 35: 3 s the knees that give way; 599

STEAL (25) [STEALING, STEALS, STOLE, STOLEN]

Ge 31:30 But why *did you* s my gods?" 1704
44: 8 So why *would we* s silver or gold 1704
Ex 20:15 *"You shall* not s. 1704
Lev 19:11 " *'Do* not s. 1704
Dt 5:19 *"You shall* not s. 1704
2Sa 19: 3 that day as men s **in** who are ashamed 1704
19:41 s the king **away** and bring him 1704
Ps 69: 4 I am forced to restore what *I did* not s. 1608
104:22 The sun rises, and *they* s **away;** 665
Pr 30: 9 Or I may become poor and s, 1704
Jer 7: 9 " *'Will you* s and murder, 1704
23:30 "I am against the prophets *who* s 1704
49: 9 not s only as much as they wanted? 8845
Ob 1: 5 not s only as much as they wanted? 1704
Mt 6:19 and where thieves break in and s. *3096*
6:20 and where thieves do not break in and s. *3096*
19:18 *do* not s, do not give false testimony, *3096*
27:64 his disciples may come and s the body *3096*
Mk 10:19 *do* not s, do not give false testimony, *3096*
Lk 18:20 *do* not s, do not give false testimony, *3096*
Jn 10:10 thief comes only to s and kill and destroy; *3096*
Ro 2:21 against stealing, *do you* s? *3096*
13: 9 "Do not murder," *"Do* not s," *3096*
Eph 4:28 He who has been stealing *must* s no longer, *3096*
Tit 2:10 and not to s from them, *3802*

STEALING (3) [STEAL]

Hos 4: 2 lying and murder, s and adultery; 1704
Ro 2:21 You who preach against s, do you steal? *3096*
Eph 4:28 He who *has been* s must steal no longer, *3096*

STEALS (3) [STEAL]

Ex 22: 1 a man s an ox or a sheep and slaughters it 1704
Job 24:14 in the night *he* s **forth** like a thief. 2118
Pr 6:30 a thief if *he* s to satisfy his hunger 1704

STEALTH (KJV) See STOLE

STEDFAST (KJV) See ENDURES, FAITHFUL, FIRM, FIRMLY, SECURE

STEEDS (3)

Jdg 5:22 galloping, galloping go his mighty s. NIH
Jer 46: 4 Harness the horses, mount the s! 7304
47: 3 at the sound of the hoofs of galloping s, 52

STEEL (KJV) See BRONZE

STEEP (4) [STEEPED]

Isa 7:19 in the s ravines and in the crevices in 1431
Mt 8:32 the whole herd rushed down the s **bank** into *3204*
Mk 5:13 the s **bank** into the lake and were drowned. *3204*
Lk 8:33 the s **bank** into the lake and was drowned. *3204*

STEEPED (1) [STEEP]

Jn 9:34 "You were s in sin at birth; *3910*

STEERED (1)

Jas 3: 4 *they are* s by a very small rudder wherever *3555*

STEM (KJV) See STUMP

STENCH (10) [STINK]

Ge 34:30 on me by **making** me a s to the Canaanites 944
Ex 5:21 *You have* **made** us a s to Pharaoh 944+8194
1Sa 13: 4 Israel *has become a* s to the Philistines." 944
2Sa 10: 6 that *they had become a* s in David's nostrils, 944
16:21 that *you have* **made yourself a** s 944
1Ch 19: 6 that *they had become a* s in David's nostrils, 944
Isa 3:24 Instead of fragrance there will be a s; 5215
34: 3 their dead bodies will send up a s; 945
Joel 2:20 And its s will go up; its smell will rise." 945
Am 4:10 I filled your nostrils with the s 945

STEP (14) [FOOTSTEPS, OVERSTEP, STEPPED, STEPPING, STEPS]

Dt 21: 5 the sons of Levi, *shall* s **forward,** 5602
1Sa 5: 5 at Ashdod s on the threshold. 2005
20: 3 there is only a s between me and death." 7315
1Ki 10:20 one at either end of each s. NIH
2Ch 9:19 one at either end of each s. NIH
Job 18: 7 The vigor of his s is weakened; 7576
18:11 on every side and dog his *every* s. 8079
31: 4 not see my ways and count my every s? 7576
31:37 an account of my *every* s; 7576
34:21 he sees their every s. 7576
Ps 89:51 with which they have mocked *every* s 6811
La 4:18 Men stalked us at *every* s, 7576
Eze 26:16 of the coast *will* s **down** from their thrones 3718
Gal 5:25 *let us* **keep in** s with the Spirit. *5123*

STEPHANAS (3)

1Co 1:16 (Yes, I also baptized the household *of* S; *5107*
16:15 the household *of* S were the first converts *5107*
16:17 I was glad when S, Fortunatus and *5107*

STEPHEN (11)

Ac 6: 5 They chose S, a man full of faith and of *5108*
6: 8 Now S, a man full of God's grace *5108*
6: 9 These men began to argue with S, *5108*
6:11 "We have heard S speak words *899S*
6:12 They seized S and brought him before *899S*
6:15 in the Sanhedrin looked intently at S, *899S*
7:55 But S, full of the Holy Spirit, *NIG*
7:59 While they were stoning him, S prayed, *NIG*
8: 2 Godly men buried S and mourned deeply *5108*
11:19 in connection with S traveled as far *5108*
22:20 when the blood of your martyr S was shed, *5108*

STEPPED (14) [STEP]

Lev 9:22 and the fellowship offering, *he* s **down.** 3718
Nu 12: 5 When both of them s **forward,** 3655
Jdg 8:21 So Gideon s **forward** and killed them, 7756
19:27 the house and s **out** to continue on his way, 3655
1Sa 17:23 s **out** from his lines 6590
2Sa 18:30 So *he* s **aside** and stood there. 6015
20: 8 he s **forward,** it dropped out of its sheath. 3655
1Ki 14:17 as she s over the threshold of the house, 995
18:36 the prophet Elijah s **forward** and prayed: 5602
Job 29: 8 the young men saw me and s **aside** and 2461
Jer 26:17 of the elders of the land s **forward** and said 7756
Mt 9: 1 Jesus s into a boat, crossed over *1832*
26:50 Then the *men* s **forward,** seized Jesus *4665*
Lk 8:27 *When* Jesus s ashore, he was met by *2002*

STEPPING (2) [STEP]

Pr 7:22 like a deer s into a noose NIH
Zep 1: 9 On that day I will punish all who **avoid** s 1925

STEPS (47) [STEP]

Ex 20:26 And do not go up to my altar on s, 5092
2Sa 6:13 the ark of the LORD *had* **taken** six s, 7575+7576
1Ki 10:19 The throne had six s, 5092
10:20 Twelve lions stood on the six s, 5092
2Ki 9:13 and spread them under him on the bare s. 5092
20: 9 Shall the shadow go forward ten s, 5092
20: 9 or shall it go back ten s?" 5092
20:10 for the shadow to go forward ten s," 5092
20:10 "Rather, have it go back ten s." 5092
20:11 the ten s it had gone down on the stairway 5092
2Ch 9:11 The king used the algumwood to make s for 5019
9:18 The throne had six s, 5092
9:19 Twelve lions stood on the six s, 5092
Ne 3:15 as the s going down from the City of David. 5092
12:37 up the s *of* the City of David on the ascent 5092
Job 14:16 then you will count my s but not keep track 7576
23:11 My feet have closely followed his s; 892
31: 7 if my s have turned from the path, 892
Ps 17: 5 My s have held to your paths; 892
37:23 he makes his s firm; 5202
56: 6 They conspire, they lurk, they watch my s, 6811
74: 3 Turn your s toward these everlasting ruins, 7193
85:13 before him and prepares the way for his s. 7193
119:59 and have turned my s to your statutes. 8079
Pr 4:12 you walk, your s will not be hampered; 7576
5: 5 her s lead straight to the grave. 7576
14:15 but a prudent man gives thought to his s. 892
16: 9 but the LORD determines his s. 7576
20:24 A man's s are directed by the LORD. 5202
Ecc 5: 1 Guard your s when you go to the house 8079
Isa 3:16 **tripping along with mincing** s, 2143+2256+3262
38: 8 shadow cast by the sun go back the ten s 5092
38: 8 went back the ten s it had gone down. 5092
Jer 10:23 it is not for man to direct his s. 7576
Eze 40: 6 He climbed its s and measured 5092
40:22 Seven s led up to it, 5092
40:26 Seven s led up to it, 5092
40:31 and eight s led up to it. 5092
40:34 and eight s led up to it. 5092
40:37 and eight s led up to it. 5092
40:40 near the s at the entrance to 6590
40:40 on the other side of the s were two tables. NIH
43:17 The s *of* the altar face east." 5092
Hab 3: 5 pestilence followed his s. 8079
Ac 21:35 When Paul reached the s, *325*
21:40 stood on the s and motioned to the crowd. *325*
1Pe 2:21 that you should follow *in* his s. *2717*

STERILE (2)

Jdg 13: 2 a wife who was s and remained childless. 6829
13: 3 "You are s and childless, 6829

STERN (4) [STERNLY, STERN-FACED, STERNNESS]

Pr 15:10 S discipline awaits him who leaves 8273
Mk 4:38 Jesus was in the s, sleeping on a cushion. *4744*
Ac 27:29 they dropped four anchors from the s *4744*
27:41 the s was broken to pieces by the pounding *4744*

STERN-FACED (1) [STERN, FACE]

Da 8:23 s king, a master of intrigue, will arise. 6434+7156

STERNLY (3) [STERN]

Mt 9:30 Jesus **warned** them s, "See that no one *1839*
Mk 1:25 **said** Jesus s. "Come out of him!" *2203*
Lk 4:35 Jesus **said** s. "Come out of him!" *2203*

STERNNESS (2) [STERN]

Ro 11:22 Consider therefore the kindness and s *704*
11:22 s to those who fell, but kindness to you, *704*

STEW (7)

Ge 25:29 Once when Jacob was cooking *some* s, 5686
25:30 "Quick, let me have some of that **red** *s!* AIT
25:34 some bread and *some* lentil s. 5686
2Ki 4:38 "Put on the large pot and cook *some* s 5686
4:39 he cut them up into the pot of s, 5686
4:40 The s was poured out for the men, 5686
Hag 2:12 and that fold touches some bread or s, 5686

STEWARD (9) [STEWARDS]

Ge 43:16 he said to **the** s *of* his house, 889+6584S
43:19 So they went up to Joseph's s and spoke 408+889+1074+2021+6584S
43:24 The s took the men into Joseph's house, 408S
44: 1 Joseph gave these instructions to **the** s 889+6584S
44: 4 city when Joseph said to his s, 889+1074+6584S
44:12 Then the s proceeded to search, NIH
2Sa 16: 1 there was Ziba, the s *of* Mephibosheth, 5853
19:17 along with Ziba, the s *of* Saul's household, 5853
Isa 22:15 "Go, say to this s, to Shebna, 6125

STEWARDS (1) [STEWARD]

Est 1: 8 for the king instructed all the **wine** s 1074+8042

STICK (21) [STICKING, STICKS, STUCK]

2Ki 6: 6 Elisha cut a s and threw it there, 6770
Job 33:21 and his bones, once hidden, now s **out.** 9142
38:38 and the clods of earth s **together?** 1815
Isa 28:27 and cummin with a s. 8657
57: 4 and s **out** your tongue? 799
La 4: 8 it has become as dry as a s. 6770
Eze 3:26 *I will* **make** your tongue s to the roof 1815
21:10 The sword despises every such s. 6770
29: 4 **make** the fish of your streams s 1815
37:16 take a s **of wood** and write on it, 6770
37:16 Then take another s **of wood,** 6770
37:16 and write on it, 'Ephraim's s, 6770
37:17 into one s so that they will become one 6770
37:19 I am going to take the s *of* Joseph— 6770
37:19 and join it to Judah's s, 6770
37:19 making them a single s **of wood,** 6770
Hos 4:12 and are answered by a s **of wood.** 5234
Am 4:11 You were like a **burning** s snatched from 202
Zec 3: 2 Is not this man a **burning** s snatched from 202
Mt 27:48 He filled it with wine vinegar, put it on a s, *2812*
Mk 15:36 put it on a s, and offered it to Jesus *2812*

STICKING (1) [STICK]

Eze 29: 4 with all the fish s to your scales. 1815

STICKS (8) [STICK]

1Sa 17:43 "Am I a dog, that you come at me with s?" 5234
1Ki 17:10 a widow was there gathering s. 6770
17:12 a few s to take home and make a meal 6770
Ps 22:15 and my tongue s *to* the roof of my mouth; 1815
Pr 18:24 but there is a friend *who* s **closer** than 1816

La 4: 4 Because of thirst the infant's tongue s to 1815
Eze 37:20 before their eyes the s you have written on 6770
Lk 10:11 of your town that s to our feet we wipe off *3140*

STIFF-NECKED (19) [NECK]

Ex 32: 9 "and they are a s people. 6902+7997
33: 3 a s people and I might destroy you on 6902+7997
33: 5 Tell the Israelites, 'You are a s people. 6902+7997
34: 9 Although this is a s people, 6902+7997
Dt 9: 6 for you are a s people. 6902+7997
9:13 and they are a s people indeed! 6902+7997
10:16 therefore, and *do* not *be* s any longer. 6902+7996
31:27 I know how rebellious and s you are. 6902+7997
2Ki 17:14 they would not listen and *were* as s 6902+7996
2Ch 30: 8 *Do* not *be* s, as your fathers were; 6902+7996
36:13 *He became* s and hardened his heart 6902+7996
Ne 9:16 forefathers, became arrogant and s, 6902+7996
9:17 *They became* s and 6902+7996
9:29 *became* s and refused to listen. 6902+7996
Pr 29: 1 A man *who remains* s 6902+7996
Jer 7:26 *They were* s and did more evil than 6902+7996
17:23 *they were* s and would not listen or 6902+7996
19:15 *they were* s and would not listen 6902+7996
Ac 7:51 "You s *people*, with uncircumcised hearts *5019*

STIFFHEARTED (KJV) See STUBBORN

STIFLING (1)

Am 1:11 his brother with a sword, s all compassion, 8845

STILL (287) [STILLED]

Ge 9: 4 not eat meat that has its lifeblood s in it. NIH
11:28 **While** his father Terah was **s alive,** 6584+7156
16:14 **it is s there,** between Kadesh and Bered. 2180
25: 6 But while he was s living, 6388
29: 7 "Look," he said, "the sun is s high; 6388
29: 9 **While** he was s talking with them, 6388
31:14 "Do we s have any share in the inheritance 6388
34:25 while all of them were *s* **in pain,** AIT
35:16 While they were s some distance 6388
38: 5 **s another** son and named him Shelah. 3578+6388
43: 1 Now the famine was s severe in the land. NIH
43: 7 'Is your father s living?' 6388
43:27 Is he s living?" 6388
43:28 "Your servant our father is s alive 6388
44:14 Joseph was s in the house when Judah 6388
45: 3 Is my father s living?" 6388
45:11 because five years of famine are s *to come.* 6388
45:26 They told him, "Joseph is s alive! 6388
45:28 My son Joseph is s alive. 6388
46:30 I have seen for myself that you are s alive." 6388
47:26 **s in force** today—that a fifth of the 6330
48: 7 in the land of Canaan while we were s on 6388
Ex 4:18 in Egypt to see if any of them are s alive." 6388
9:17 You s set yourself against my people 6388
9:19 that has not been brought in and *is* **s out** in 5162
9:30 that you and your officials s do **not** fear 3270
14:14 you *need only to be* **s."** 3087
15:16 By the power of your arm *they will be* as s 1957
21:16 or s has him when he is caught must be put NIH
22:17 *he must s* **pay** the bride-price for virgins. AIT
Lev 10: 5 s in their tunics, outside the camp, NIH
19:26 " 'Do not eat any meat with the blood s NIH
26:10 *You will s be* **eating** last year's harvest AIT
26:27 in spite of this *you s do* not **listen** to me AIT
Nu 9:10 on a journey, *they may s* **celebrate** AIT
11:33 **while** the meat was s between their teeth 6388
30: 3 "When a young woman is s living in her NIH
30:16 a father and his young daughter s living NIH
Dt 3:11 It is s in Rabbah of the Ammonites.) NIH
4: 4 to the LORD your God are s alive today. NIH
10: 8 as they s do today. 6330
22:21 in Israel by being promiscuous while s NIH
31:27 the LORD while I am s alive and with you, 6388
Jos 5: 7 They were s uncircumcised 3954
10:12 "O sun, **stand s** over Gibeon, O moon, 1957
10:13 So the sun **stood s,** and the moon stopped, 1957
13: 1 and *there are* s very large areas of land to 8636
14:11 I am s as strong today as the day 6388
18: 2 *there were* seven Israelite tribes who had 3855
Jdg 7: 4 "There are s too many men. 6388
8: 5 and I *am s* **pursuing** Zebah and Zalmunna, AIT
15:19 it is s there in Lehi. 2021+2021+2296+3427+6330
Ru 1:12 Even if I thought there was s hope for me— NIH
1Sa 8:12 and s others to make weapons of war NIH
12:16 **stand** s and see this great thing 3656
14:34 the LORD by eating meat with blood s NIH
16:11 *"There is* s the youngest," 6388+8636
17:57 with David s holding the Philistine's head. NIH
18:29 Saul became s more afraid of him, 6388
2Sa 1: 9 in the throes of death, but I'm s alive.' 3972+6388
3:35 to eat something while it was s day; 6388
9: 1 "Is there anyone s left of the house of Saul 6388
9: 3 "Is there no one s left of the house of Saul 6388
9: 3 "There is s a son of Jonathan; 6388
12:18 "While the child **was** s living, AIT
12:22 He answered, "While the child was s alive, 6388
13:25 Absalom urged him, *he s* **refused** to go, AIT
14:32 be better for me if I were s there!" ' 6388
18:14 Absalom's heart **while** Absalom was s alive 6388
19:35 Can I s hear the voices of men 6388
21:20 In **s another** battle, which took place 6388
1Ki 1:14 **While** you are s there talking to the king, 6388
1:22 **While** she was s speaking with the king, 6388
1Ki 3: 2 *were s* **sacrificing** at the high places, AIT
8: 8 and they are s there today. 6330
11:17 But Hadad, s only a boy, NIH
12: 2 son of Nebat heard this (he was s in Egypt, 6388
12:17 Rehoboam *s* **ruled** over them. AIT
20:32 The king answered, "Is he s alive? 6388
22: 8 "There is s one man through whom 6388
2Ki 6:33 **While** he was s talking to them, 6388
12: 6 of King Joash the priests *s had* not **repaired** AIT
17:23 they are s there. 2021+2021+2296+3427+6330
19: 4 pray for the remnant that *s* **survives."** AIT
25:19 Of *those* s in the city, 5162
1Ch 20: 6 In **s another** battle, which took place 6388
2Ch 5: 9 and they are s there today. 6330
10:17 Rehoboam *s* **ruled** over them. AIT
14: 7 The land is s ours, 6388
18: 7 "There is s one man through whom 6388
20:33 and the people s had not set their hearts on 6388
25:16 **While** he was *s* speaking, AIT
34: 3 **while** he was s young, 6388
Ezr 10: 2 in spite of this, **there is** *s* hope for Israel. AIT
Ne 5: 4 S others were saying, 2256
7: 3 While the gatekeepers *are s* **on duty,** AIT
8:11 saying, **"Be s,** for this is a sacred day. 2187
Est 6:14 **While** they were s talking with him, 6388
Job 1:16 **While** he was s speaking, 6388
1:17 **While** he was s speaking, 6388
1:18 **While** he was s speaking, 6330
2: 3 And he s maintains his integrity, 6388
2: 9 "Are you s holding on to your integrity? 6388
6:10 Then I would s have this consolation— 6388
6:11 that *I should s* **hope?** AIT
8:12 **While** s growing and uncut, 6388
9:28 *I s* **dread** all my sufferings, AIT
23:14 and many such plans he s has in store. NIH
24:10 they carry the sheaves, but s go hungry. NIH
29: 5 when the Almighty was s with me 6388
39:24 *he* cannot **stand** s when the trumpet sounds. 586
Ps 17:14 *You* s *the* **hunger** *of* those you cherish; 1061+4848
27:13 I am s confident of this: 4295
37: 7 **Be** s before the LORD and wait patiently 1957
39: 2 But when I was silent and s, 1875
46:10 *"Be* s, and know that I am God; 8332
58:11 "Surely the righteous s are rewarded; NIH
76: 6 both horse and chariot **lie s.** 8101
78:30 even **while** it was s in their mouths, 6388
83: 1 be not quiet, O God, *be* not **s.** 9200
89: 9 when its waves mount up, you s them. 8656
92:14 They will s bear fruit in old age, 6388
139:18 When I awake, I am s with you. 6388
Pr 4: 3 I was a boy in my father's house, s tender, NIH
9: 9 Instruct a wise man and he will be wiser s; 6388
31:15 She gets up while it is s dark; 6388
Ecc 2: 3 my mind *s* **guiding** me with wisdom. AIT
4: 2 are happier than the living, who are s alive. 6364
5: 8 and over them both are others higher s. NIH
7:28 **while** I was s searching but not finding— 6388
8:12 a hundred crimes **and** s lives a long time, 2256
Isa 5:25 not turned away, his hand is **s** upraised. 6388
9:12 not turned away, his hand is **s** upraised. 6388
9:17 not turned away, his hand is **s** upraised. 6388
9:20 but *s be* **hungry;** AIT
9:21 not turned away, his hand is **s** upraised. 6388
10: 4 not turned away, his hand is **s** upraised. 6388
15: 9 but I will bring **s more** upon Dimon— 3578
22: 3 while the enemy was s far away. NIH
37: 4 pray for the remnant that *s* **survives."** AIT
44: 5 s another will write on his hand, 2256
46:10 from ancient times, what *is* **s to come.** 4202+6913
56: 8 "I will gather *s* **others** to them besides AIT
65: 8 when juice is *s* **found** in a cluster of grapes AIT
65:24 **while** they are s speaking I will hear. 6388
Jer 2:22 **stain** of your guilt *is s* before me," AIT
5: 2 s they are swearing falsely." 4027+4200
15: 9 Her sun will set while it is s day; 6388
22:24 I would s pull you off. 3954
31:20 I s remember him. 6388
32:20 and have gained the renown that is s yours. 2021+2021+2296+3427+3869
33: 1 **While** Jeremiah was s confined in 6388
34: 7 of Judah that *were s* **holding out—** AIT
40: 7 the army officers and their men who were s NIH
40:13 of Kareah and all the army officers s in NIH
42:21 but *you s have* not **obeyed** the LORD AIT
47: 6 Return to your scabbard; cease and **be s.'** 1957
52:25 Of those **s** in the city, 5162
Eze 1:21 when the creatures **stood s,** 6641
1:21 the creatures stood still, *they* also **stood s;** 6641
1:24 they **stood s,** they lowered their wings. 6641
10:17 the cherubim **stood s,** they also stood still; 6641
10:17 the cherubim stood still, *they* also **stood s;** 6641
16:28 after that, you s were not satisfied. 1685+2256
23: 5 in prostitution while she was s mine; NIH
23:14 **carried** her prostitution **s further.** 3578
33:25 with the blood s in it and look to your idols NIH
Da 4:31 The words were **s** on his lips when 10531
6:13 *He s* **prays** three times a day." AIT
9:21 **while** I was s in prayer, 6388
11:27 an end will s come at the appointed time. 6388
11:35 for it will s come at the appointed time. 6388
Am 4: 7 when the harvest was s three months away. 6388
6:10 of the house and asks anyone s hiding there, 6388
Jnh 4: 2 not what I said when I was s at home? 6330
Mic 6:10 Am I s to forget, O wicked house, 6388
6:14 your stomach will s be empty. NIH
Hab 3:11 and moon **stood** s in the heavens at the glint 6641
Zep 3: 7 But *they were s* **eager** to act corruptly AIT
Zec 2:13 **Be** s before the LORD, all mankind, 2187
13: 3 And if anyone s prophesies, 6388
14:12 while they *are s* **standing** on their feet, AIT
Mt 5:25 Do it while you are s with him on the way, *NIG*
12:46 While Jesus was s talking to the crowd, *2285*
13: 8 S other seed fell on good soil, *1254*
13:33 He told them s **another** parable: *257*
15:16 "Are you s so dull?" Jesus asked them. *197*
16: 9 Do you s **not** understand? *4037*
16:14 **s others,** Jeremiah or one of the prophets." *2283*
17: 5 While he was s speaking, *2285*
19:20 "What do I s lack?" *2285*
20: 6 and found *s* **others** standing around. *AIT*
24: 6 but the end is **s to come.** *4037*
26:45 "Are you s sleeping and resting? *3370+3836*
26:47 While he was s speaking, Judas, *2285*
27:63 that **while** he was s alive that deceiver said, *2285*
Mk 1:35 **while it was s dark,** Jesus got up, *1939*
1:45 the people s came to him from everywhere. *NIG*
4: 8 S other seed fell on good soil. *2779*
4:18 S others, like seed sown among thorns, *2779*
4:39 and said to the waves, "Quiet! *Be* **s!"** *5821*
4:40 Do you s have **no** faith?" *4037*
5:35 While Jesus was s speaking, *2285*
6:15 And **s others** claimed, "He is a prophet, *257*
8:17 Do you s **not** see or understand? *4037*
8:21 "Do you s **not** understand?" *4037*
8:28 and **s others,** one of the prophets." *257*
12: 5 He sent **s another,** and that one they killed. *257*
13: 7 but the end is **s to come.** *4037*
14:41 "Are you s sleeping and resting? *3370+3836*
15: 5 But Jesus s made **no** reply, *4033*
Lk 7:14 and those carrying it stood **s.** *NIG*
8: 8 S other seed fell on good soil. *2779*
8:49 While Jesus was s speaking, *2285*
9: 8 and *s* **others** that one of the prophets *AIT*
9:19 and *s* **others,** that one of the prophets *AIT*
9:61 S another said, "I will follow you, Lord; *2779*
14:20 **"S** another said, 'I just got married, *2779*
14:22 but there is s room.' *2285*
14:32 the other is s a long way off and will ask *2285*
15:20 "But while he was s a long way off, *2285*
18:22 he said to him, "You s lack one thing. *2285*
20:12 He sent s a third, *2779*
22:47 While he was s speaking a crowd came up, *2285*
24: 6 while he was s with you in Galilee: *2285*
24:17 They stood s, their faces downcast. *NIG*
24:36 *While* they were *s* **talking about** this, *AIT*
24:41 And while they s did not believe it because *2285*
24:44 "This is what I told you while I was s *2285*
Jn 1:48 "I saw you while you were s under *NIG*
3:11 **but** s you people do not accept our *2779*
4:51 While he was s on the way, *2453*
6:36 you have seen me **and** s you do not believe. *2779*
7:28 Then Jesus, *s* **teaching** in the temple courts, *AIT*
7:31 **S,** many in the crowd put their faith in him. *1254*
7:41 **S others** asked, "How can the Christ come from Galilee? *1254+3836*
8: 9 with the woman *s* **standing** there. *AIT*
9:18 The Jews s did not believe *4036*
11:30 but was s at the place where Martha had met *2285*
12:37 they s would not believe in him. *NIG*
14:25 "All this I have spoken *while* s with you. *3531*
17:11 but they are s in the world, *NIG*
17:13 I say these things while I am s in the world, *NIG*
18:24 Then Annas sent him, *s* **bound,** *AIT*
20: 1 while it was s dark, Mary Magdalene went *2285*
20: 9 (They s did not understand from Scripture *4031*
Ac 7: 2 to our father Abraham while he was s *NIG*
9: 1 Saul was s breathing out murderous threats *2285*
9:39 that Dorcas had made while she was s *NIG*
10:19 *While* Peter *was s* **thinking** about the vision, *AIT*
10:44 While Peter was s speaking these words, *2285*
27:27 fourteenth night we were *s being* **driven** *AIT*
Ro 3: 7 why am I s condemned as a sinner?" *2285*
4:11 by faith while he was s uncircumcised. *NIG*
5: 6 when we were s powerless, Christ died for *2285*
5: 8 While we were s sinners, Christ died for us. *2285*
7: 3 *while* her husband *is s* **alive,** *AIT*
9:19 "Then why does God s blame us? *2285*
1Co 1:12 **s another,** "I follow Christ." *1254*
3: 2 Indeed, you are s not ready. *2285+3814*
3: 3 You are s worldly. *2285*
8: 7 people are s so accustomed to idols *785+2401*
12:10 to s another the interpretation of tongues. *NIG*
15: 6 most of whom are s living, *785+2401*
15:17 you are s in your sins. *2285*
2Co 2:13 I s had no peace of mind, *NIG*
Gal 1:10 If I were s trying to please men, *2285*
5:11 Brothers, if I am s preaching circumcision, *2285*
5:11 why am I s being persecuted? *2285*
Eph 4:26 the sun go down while you are s angry, *NIG*
Php 1:30 and now hear that I s have. *NIG*
Col 1:24 up in my flesh what is s lacking in regard *NIG*
2:20 why, as though *you s* **belonged** to it, *AIT*
1Th 4:15 we tell you that we who *are s* **alive,** *AIT*
4:17 we who *are s* **alive** and are left will *AIT*
Heb 4: 1 the promise of entering his rest *s* **stands,** *AIT*
4: 6 It s remains that some will enter that rest, *NIG*
5:13 who lives on milk, being s an infant, *NIG*
7:10 Levi was s in the body of his ancestor. *2285*
7:11 why was there s need for another priest *2285*
9: 8 **as long as** the first tabernacle was s *2285*
11: 4 And by faith he s speaks, *2285*
11:13 All these people were s living by faith *NIG*
11:36 while s others were chained and put *2285*
1Jn 2: 9 but hates his brother is s in the darkness. *785+2401*

Rev 9:20 not killed by these plagues s did not repent NIG
14:18 S another angel, who had charge of the fire, 2779

STILLBORN (4) [BEAR]
Nu 12:12 a s infant coming from its mother's womb 4637
Job 3:16 not hidden in the ground like a s child, 5878
Ps 58:8 like a s child, may they not see the sun. 851+5878
Ecc 6:3 I say that a s child is better off than he. 5878

STILLED (7) [STILL]
Ps 65:7 who s the roaring of the seas, 8656
107:29 He s the storm to a whisper; 7756
131:2 But I have s and quieted my soul; 8750
Isa 16:9 and over your harvests have been s. 5877
24:8 The gaiety of the tambourines is s, 8697
25:5 so the song of the ruthless is s. 6700
1Co 13:8 where there are tongues, they will be s; 4264

STIMULATE (1)
2Pe 3:1 both of them as reminders to s you to 1444

STING (3) [STINGING, STINGS]
1Co 15:55 Where, O death, is your s?" 3034
15:56 The s of death is sin, 3034
Rev 9:5 of the s of a scorpion when it strikes a man. 990

STINGING (1) [STING]
Eze 5:15 in anger and in wrath and with s rebuke. 2779

STINGS (1) [STING]
Rev 9:10 They had tails and s like scorpions, 3034

STINGY (2)
Pr 23:6 Do not eat the food of a s man, 6524+8273
28:22 A s man is eager to get rich and 6524+8273

STINK (3) [STENCH]
Ex 7:18 fish in the Nile will die, and the river will s; 944
16:24 and it did not s or get maggots in it. 944
Isa 19:6 The canals will s; the streams of Egypt will 2395

STIPULATIONS (4)
Dt 4:45 These are the s, decrees and laws 6343
6:17 and the s and decrees he has given you. 6343
6:20 "What is the meaning of the s, 6343
Jer 44:23 or followed his law or his decrees or his s, 6343

STIR (17) [ASTIR, STIRRED, STIRRING, STIRS]
Jdg 13:25 and the Spirit of the LORD began to s him 7192
Ne 4:8 and fight against Jerusalem and s up trouble 6913
Ps 78:38 and did not s up his full wrath. 6424
140:2 in their hearts and s up war every day. 1592
Pr 29:8 Mockers s up a city, 7032
Isa 13:17 See, I will s up against them the Medes, 6424
19:2 "I will s up Egyptian against Egyptian— 6056
42:13 like a warrior he will s up his zeal; 6424
Jer 50:9 For I will s up and bring against Babylon 6424
51:1 "See, I will s up the spirit of a destroyer 6424
Eze 23:22 I will s up your lovers against you, 6424
24:8 To s up wrath and take revenge 6590
Da 11:2 he will s up everyone against the kingdom 6424
11:25 a large army he will s up his strength 6424
Hos 7:4 like an oven whose fire the baker need not s 6424
Am 6:14 "I will s up a nation against you, 7756
Php 1:17 that they can s up trouble for me while I am 1586

STIRRED (22) [STIR]
Ru 1:19 the whole town was s because of them, 2101
1Ki 14:22 s up his jealous anger more than their 7861
1Ch 5:26 the God of Israel s up the spirit of Pul king 6424
Ps 45:1 My heart is s by a noble theme 8180
107:25 and s up a tempest that lifted high 6641
Ecc 12:5 along and desire no longer is s. 7296
Isa 41:2 "Who has s up one from the east, 6424
41:25 "I have s up one from the north, 6424
Jer 6:22 a great nation is being s up from the ends 6424
50:41 and many kings are being s up from 6424
51:11 LORD has s up the kings of the Medes, 6424
Eze 32:13 to be s by the foot of man or muddied by 1931
Am 8:8 it will be s up and then sink like the river 1764
Hag 1:14 So the LORD s up the spirit of Zerubbabel 6424
Mt 21:10 the whole city was s and asked, 4940
Mk 15:11 But the chief priests s up the crowd 411
Jn 5:7 into the pool when the water is s. 5429
Ac 6:12 So they s up the people and the elders and 5167
13:50 s up persecution against Paul and 2074
14:2 But the Jews who refused to believe s up 2074
21:27 They s up the whole crowd and seized him, 5177
2Co 9:2 enthusiasm has s most of them to action. 2241

STIRRING (6) [STIR]
Jdg 9:31 and are s up the city against you. 7443
Ne 13:18 Now you are s up more wrath against Israel 3578
Pr 30:33 so s up anger produces strife." 4790
Ac 17:13 agitating the crowds and s them up. 5429
24:5 s up riots among the Jews all over 3075
24:12 or s up a crowd in the synagogues 2180+4472

STIRS (13) [STIR]
Dt 32:11 that s up its nest and hovers over its young, 6424
Job 41:31 a boiling caldron and s up the sea like a pot 8492
Ps 147:18 he s up his breezes, and the waters flow. 5959
Pr 6:14 he always s up dissension. 8938
6:19 a man who s up dissension among brothers. 8938
10:12 Hatred s up dissension, 6424
15:1 but a harsh word s up anger. 6590
15:18 A hot-tempered man s up dissension, 1741
16:28 A perverse man s up dissension, 8938
28:25 A greedy man s up dissension, 1741
29:22 An angry man s up dissension, 1741
Jer 31:35 who s up the sea so that its waves roar— 8088
Lk 23:5 "He s up the people all over Judea 411

STOCK (2) [STOCKS]
Job 5:24 you will take s of your property 7212
Jer 2:21 like a choice vine of sound and reliable s. 2446

STOCKS (4) [STOCK]
Jer 20:2 in the s at the Upper Gate of Benjamin at 4551
20:3 when Pashhur released him from the s, 4551
29:26 like a prophet into the s and neck-irons. 4551
Ac 16:24 and fastened their feet in the s. 3833

STOIC (1)
Ac 17:18 A group of Epicurean and S philosophers 5121

STOLE (6) [STEAL]
Ge 31:19 Rachel s her father's household gods. 1704
2Sa 15:6 and so he s the hearts of the men of Israel. 1704
19:3 The men s into the city that day 995+1704+4200
2Ki 11:2 took Joash son of Ahaziah and s him away 1704
2Ch 22:11 took Joash son of Ahaziah and s him away 1704
Mt 28:13 and s him away while we were asleep.' 3096

STOLEN (16) [STEAL]
Ge 30:33 will be considered s." 1704
31:32 Now Jacob did not know that Rachel had s 1704
31:39 from me for whatever was s by day or night. 1704
Ex 22:4 s animal is found alive in his possession— 1706
22:7 and they are s from the neighbor's house, 1704
22:12 if the animal was s from the neighbor, 1704+1704
Lev 6:2 to him or left in his care or s, 1610
6:4 he must return what he has s or taken 1608+1611
Jos 7:11 they have s, they have lied, 1704
Job 24:2 they pasture flocks they have s. 1608
Ps 62:10 in extortion or take pride in s goods; 1610
Pr 9:17 "S water is sweet; food eaten in secret 1704
SS 4:9 You have s my heart, my sister, my bride; 4220
4:9 you have s my heart with one glance 4220
Eze 33:15 returns what he has s, follows the decrees 1611
Hab 2:6 to him who piles up s goods 2257+4200+4202

STOMACH (20) [STOMACHS]
2Sa 2:23 thrust the butt of his spear into Asahel's s, 2824
3:27 Joab stabbed him in the s, and he died. 2824
4:6 and they stabbed him in the s. 2824
Job 20:14 yet his food will turn sour in his s; 5055
20:15 God will make his s vomit them up. 1061
Pr 13:25 but the s of the wicked goes hungry. 1061
18:20 the fruit of his mouth a man's s is filled; 1061
Jer 30:6 with his hands on his s like a woman 2743
51:34 and filled his s with our delicacies, 4160
Eze 3:3 and fill your s with it." 5055
Mic 6:14 your s will still be empty. 7931
Mt 15:17 the mouth goes into the s and then out of 3120
Mk 7:19 it doesn't go into his heart but into his s, 3120
Lk 15:16 He longed to fill his s with the pods that 3120
1Co 6:13 for the s and the stomach for food"— 3120
6:13 for the stomach and the s for food"— 3120
Php 3:19 their god is their s, 3120
1Ti 5:23 and use a little wine because of your s 5126
Rev 10:9 It will turn your s sour, 3120
10:10 but when I had eaten it, my s turned sour. 3120

STOMACHS (2) [STOMACH]
Eze 7:19 not satisfy their hunger or fill their s with it, 5055
Am 4:6 "I gave you empty s in every city 5931+9094

STONE (186) [CAPSTONE, CORNERSTONE, CORNERSTONES, FIELDSTONES, MILLSTONE, MILLSTONES, SLINGSTONES, STONE'S, STONECUTTERS, STONED, STONEMASONS, STONES, STONING, TOMBSTONE]
Ge 11:3 They used brick instead of s, 74
28:18 the s he had placed under his head and set it 74
28:22 and this s that I have set up as a pillar will 74
29:2 The s over the mouth of the well was large. 74
29:3 the s away from the well's mouth and water 74
29:3 the s to its place over the mouth of the well. 74
29:8 the s has been rolled away from the mouth 74
29:10 over and rolled the s away from the mouth 74
31:45 So Jacob took a s and set it up as a pillar. 74
35:14 a s pillar at the place where God had talked 74
Ex 7:19 even in the wooden buckets and s jars." 74
8:26 detestable in their eyes, will they not s us? 6232
15:5 they sank to the depths like a s. 74
15:16 of your arm they will be as still as a s— 74
17:4 They are almost ready to s me." 6232
17:12 a s and put it under him and he sat on it. 74
21:18 with a s or with his fist and he does not die 74
24:4 and set up twelve s pillars representing 5167
24:12 and I will give you the tablets of s, 74
28:10 on one s and the remaining six on the other. 74
31:18 tablets of s inscribed by the finger of God. 74
34:1 "Chisel out two s tablets like the first ones, 74
34:4 So Moses chiseled out two s tablets like 74
34:4 he carried the two s tablets in his hands. 74
Lev 20:2 The people of the community are to s him. 74+928+2021+8083
20:27 You are to s them; 74+928+2021+8083
24:14 and the entire assembly is to s him. 8083
24:16 The entire assembly must s him. 8083+8083
26:1 up an image or a sacred s for yourselves, 5167
26:1 not place a carved s in your land to bow 74
Nu 15:35 The whole assembly must s him outside the camp." 74+928+2021+8083
35:17 if anyone has a s in his hand that could kill, 74
35:23 drops a s on him that could kill him, 74
Dt 4:13 and then wrote them on two s tablets. 74
4:28 man-made gods of wood and s, 74
5:22 on two s tablets and gave them to me. 74
9:9 on the mountain to receive the tablets of s, 74
9:10 The LORD gave me two s tablets inscribed 74
9:11 the LORD gave me the two s tablets, 74
10:1 "Chisel out two s tablets like the first ones 74
10:3 and chiseled out two s tablets like 74
13:10 S him to death, because he tried to turn you 6232
16:22 and do not erect a sacred s, 5167
17:5 and s that person to death. 74+928+2021+6232
19:14 Do not move your neighbor's boundary s 1473
21:21 his town shall s him to death. 74+928+2021+8083
22:21 her town shall s her to death. 74+928+2021+6232
22:24 the gate of that town and s them to death— 6232
27:17 man who moves his neighbor's boundary s. 1473
28:36 worship other gods, gods of wood and s. 74
28:64 worship other gods—gods of wood and s, 74
29:17 and idols of wood and s, 74
Jos 4:5 of you is to take up a s on his shoulder, 74
7:5 as the s quarries and struck them down on 8696
15:6 of Beth Arabah to the S of Bohan son 74
18:17 ran down to the S of Bohan son of Reuben. 74
24:26 a large s and set it up there under the oak 74
24:27 "This s will be a witness against us. 74
Jdg 9:5 and on one s murdered his seventy brothers, 74
9:18 murdered his seventy sons on a single s, 74
20:16 each of whom could sling a s at a hair and 74
1Sa 7:12 a s and set it up between Mizpah and Shen. 74
14:33 "Roll a large s over here at once." 74
17:49 Reaching into his bag and taking out a s, 74
17:49 The s sank into his forehead, 74
17:50 over the Philistine with a sling and a s; 74
20:19 and wait by the s Ezel. 74
20:41 David got up from the south side [of the s] NIH
25:37 his heart failed him and he became like a s. 74
1Ki 1:9 and fattened calves at the S of Zoheleth 74
5:17 from the quarry large blocks of quality s 74
5:17 a foundation of dressed s for the temple. 74
5:18 of Gebal cut and prepared the timber and s 74
6:18 Everything was cedar; no s was to be seen. 74
6:36 of three courses of dressed s and one course 1607
7:9 were made of blocks of high-grade s cut 74
7:12 of three courses of dressed s and one course 1607
8:9 the two s tablets that Moses had placed in it 74
21:10 Then take him out and s him to death." 6232
2Ki 3:2 He got rid of the sacred s of Baal 5167
3:25 a s on every good field until it was covered. 74
10:26 They brought the sacred s out of the temple 5167
10:27 They demolished the sacred s of Baal 5167
12:12 and dressed s for the repair of the temple of 74
16:17 that supported it and set it on a s base. 74
19:18 they were not gods but only wood and s, 74
19:25 turned fortified cities into piles of s. 1643+5898
22:6 and dressed s to repair the temple. 74
1Ch 22:2 to prepare dressed s for building the house 74
22:14 too great to be weighed, and wood and s. 74
29:2 and all kinds of fine s and marble— 74
2Ch 2:14 bronze and iron, s and wood, 74
34:11 and builders to purchase dressed s, 74
Ne 9:11 like a s into mighty waters. 74
Job 6:12 Do I have the strength of s? 74
38:30 when the waters become hard as s, 74
Ps 91:12 you will not strike your foot against a s. 74
118:22 The s the builders rejected has become 74
Pr 22:28 Do not move an ancient boundary s set up 1473
23:10 Do not move an ancient boundary s 1473
24:31 and the s wall was in ruins. 74
26:8 a s in a sling is the giving of honor to 74
26:27 if a man rolls a s, it will roll back on him. 74
27:3 S is heavy and sand a burden, 74
Isa 8:14 but for both houses of Israel he will be a s 74
9:10 but we will rebuild with dressed s; 1607
28:16 "See, I lay a s in Zion, a tested stone, 74
28:16 "See, I lay a stone in Zion, a tested s, 74
37:19 they were not gods but only wood and s, 74
37:26 turned fortified cities into piles of s. 1643+5898
Jer 2:27 and to s, 'You gave me birth.' 74
3:9 and committed adultery with s and wood. 74
5:3 They made their faces harder than s 6152
51:26 nor any s for a foundation, 74
51:63 tie a s to it and throw it into the Euphrates. 74
La 3:9 He has barred my way with blocks of s; 1607
Eze 3:9 I will make your forehead like the hardest s 9032

Eze 11:19 remove from them their heart of s and give 74
16:40 *who will* s you and hack you to pieces 74+928+2021+8083
20:32 who serve wood and s." 74
23:47 The mob *will* s them and cut them down 74+8083
28:13 every precious s adorned you: 74
36:26 I will remove from you your heart of s 74
40:42 There were also four tables of dressed s for 74
46:23 of each of the four courts was a **ledge of s,** 3215
Da 5:4 of bronze, iron, wood and **s.** 10006
5:23 of bronze, iron, wood and **s,** 10006
6:17 A s was brought and placed over the mouth 10006
Am 5:11 though you have built s mansions, 1607
Hab 2:19 Or to lifeless s, 'Wake up!' 74
Hag 2:15 how things were before one s was laid 74
Zec 3:9 See, the s I have set in front of Joshua! 74
3:9 There are seven eyes on that one s, 74
Mt 4:6 you will not strike your foot against a **s.'** " *3345*
7:9 if his son asks for bread, will give him a s? *3345*
21:42 " 'The s the builders rejected has become *3345*
21:44 He who falls on this s will be broken *3345*
23:37 you who kill the prophets and s those sent *3344*
24:2 not *one* s here will be left on another; *3345*
27:60 He rolled a big s in front of the entrance to *3345*
27:66 the tomb secure by putting a seal on the s *3345*
28:2 rolled back the s and sat on it. *3345*
Mk 12:10 " 'The s the builders rejected has become *3345*
13:2 "Not one s here will be left on another; *3345*
15:46 Then he rolled a s against the entrance of *3345*
16:3 "Who will roll the s away from the entrance *3345*
16:4 when they looked up, they saw that the s, *3345*
Lk 4:3 tell this s to become bread." *3345*
4:11 you will not strike your foot against a **s.'** " *3345*
13:34 you who kill the prophets and s those sent *3344*
19:44 They will not leave one s on another, *3345*
20:6 'From men,' all the people *will* s us, *2902*
20:17 " 'The s the builders rejected has become *3345*
20:18 Everyone who falls on that s will be broken *3345*
21:6 the time will come when not one s will *3345*
24:2 They found the s rolled away from *3345*
Jn 2:6 Nearby stood six s water jars, *3343*
8:5 Moses commanded us *to* s such women. *3342*
8:7 let him be the first to throw a s at her." *3345*
8:59 At this, they picked up stones to s him, *965+2093*
10:31 Again the Jews picked up stones to s him, *3342*
10:32 For which of these *do you* s me?" *3342*
11:8 "a short while ago the Jews tried *to* s you, *3342*
11:38 a cave with a s laid across the entrance. *3345*
11:39 "Take away the **s,"** he said. *3345*
11:41 So they took away the s. *3345*
19:13 at a place known as the **S Pavement** (which *3346*
20:1 the s had been removed from the entrance. *3345*
Ac 4:11 He is " 'the s you builders rejected, *3345*
5:26 they feared that the people *would* s them. *3342*
7:58 out of the city and *began to* s him. *3344*
14:5 to mistreat them and s them. *3344*
17:29 the divine being is like gold or silver or **s—** *3345*
Ro 9:32 They stumbled over the "stumbling **s."** *3345*
9:33 I lay in Zion a s that causes men to stumble *3345*
2Co 3:3 not on tablets of **s** but on tablets *3343*
3:7 which was engraved in letters *on* **s,** *3345*
Heb 9:4 and the **s tablets** of the covenant. *4419*
1Pe 2:4 As you come to him, the living **S—** *3345*
2:6 "See, I lay a s in Zion, *3345*
2:7 Now to you who believe, this s is precious. *NIG*
2:7 "The s the builders rejected has become *3345*
2:8 "A s that causes men to stumble and a rock *3345*
Rev 2:17 a white s with a new name written on it, *6029*
9:20 silver, bronze, s and wood— *3343*
21:19 *with* every kind of precious **s.** *3345*

STONE'S (1) [STONE]

Lk 22:41 He withdrew about a s throw beyond them, *3345*

STONECUTTERS (6) [STONE]

1Ki 5:15 and eighty thousand s in the hills, 2935
2Ki 12:12 the masons and s. 74+2935
1Ch 22:2 and from among them he appointed s 2935
22:15 You have many workmen: s, 2935
2Ch 2:2 and eighty thousand as s in the hills 2935
2:18 and 80,000 to be s in the hills, 2935

STONED (19) [STONE]

Ex 19:13 *He shall* **surely be** s or shot with 6232+6232
21:28 the bull **must be s to death,** 6232+6232
21:29 the bull *must* **be** s and the owner also must 6232
21:32 and the bull *must* **be s.** 6232
Lev 24:23 blasphemer outside the camp and s him. 74+8083
Nu 15:36 the camp and s him to death, 74+928+2021+8083
Jos 7:25 Then all Israel s him, 74+8083
7:25 and after *they had* s the rest, 74+928+2021+6232
1Ki 12:18 but all Israel s him to death. 74+8083
21:13 the city and s him to death. 74+928+2021+6232
21:14 "Naboth *has* **been** s and is dead." 6232
21:15 as Jezebel heard that Naboth *had* **been s** 6232
2Ch 10:18 but the Israelites s him to death. 74+8083
24:21 by order of the king *they* s him **to death** 74+8083
Mt 21:35 they beat one, killed another, and s a third. *3344*
Ac 14:19 They s Paul and dragged him outside *3342*
2Co 11:25 once *I was* **s,** three times I was shipwrecked, *3342*
Heb 11:37 *They were* **s;** they were sawed in two; *3342*
12:20 touches the mountain, *it must be* **s."** *3344*

STONEMASONS (2) [STONE]

2Sa 5:11 cedar logs and carpenters and s, 74+3093+7815
1Ch 14:1 s and carpenters to build a palace for 3093+7815

STONES (128) [STONE]

Ge 28:11 Taking one of the s there, 74
31:46 He said to his relatives, "Gather *some* **s."** 74
31:46 So they took s and piled them in a heap, 74
Ex 20:25 If you make an altar of s for me, 74
20:25 do not build it with **dressed s,** 1607
23:24 and break their **sacred** s to pieces. 5167
25:7 and onyx s and other gems to be mounted 74
28:9 "Take two onyx s and engrave on them 74
28:11 the names of the sons of Israel on the two s 74
28:11 Then mount **the** s in gold filigree settings 4392[S]
28:12 of the ephod as memorial s for the sons 74
28:17 Then mount four rows of precious s on it. 74
28:21 There are to be twelve s, 74
31:5 to cut and set **s,** to work in wood, 74
34:13 smash their **sacred** s and cut 5167
35:9 and onyx s and other gems to be mounted 74
35:27 The leaders brought onyx s and other gems 74
35:33 to cut and set **s,** to work in wood, 74
39:6 the onyx s in gold filigree settings 74
39:7 of the ephod as memorial s for the sons 74
39:10 they mounted four rows of precious s on it. 74
39:14 There were twelve **s,** one for each of 74
Lev 14:40 to order that the contaminated s be torn out 74
14:42 to take other s to replace these 74
14:43 the house after the s have been torn out and 74
14:45 its **s,** timbers and all the plaster— 74
Dt 7:5 down their altars, smash their **sacred s,** 5167
12:3 smash their **sacred** s and burn their Asherah 5167
27:2 up *some* large s and coat them with plaster. 74
27:4 set up these s on Mount Ebal, 74
27:5 to the LORD your God, an altar of **s.** 74
27:8 of this law on these s you have set up." 74
Jos 4:3 up twelve s from the middle of the Jordan 74
4:6 'What do these s mean?' 74
4:7 These s are to be a memorial to the people 74
4:8 They took twelve s from the middle of 74
4:9 up the twelve s that had been in the middle 74
4:20 up at Gilgal the twelve s they had taken out 74
4:21 'What do these s mean?' 74
8:31 an altar of uncut **s,** on which no iron tool 74
8:32 Joshua copied on s the law of Moses, 74
1Sa 17:40 chose five smooth s from the stream, 74
2Sa 12:30 and it was set with precious **s—** 74
16:6 and all the king's officials with **s,** 74
16:13 and throwing s at him and showering him 74
1Ki 7:10 The foundations were laid with large s 74
7:11 Above were high-grade **s,** cut to size, 74
10:2 large quantities of gold, and precious **s—** 74
10:10 large quantities of spices, and precious **s.** 74
10:11 of almugwood and precious **s.** 74
10:27 as common in Jerusalem as **s,** 74
14:23 high places, **sacred** s and Asherah poles 5167
15:22 and they carried away *from* Ramah the s 74
18:31 Elijah took twelve s, one for each of the 74
18:32 With the s he built an altar in the name of 74
18:38 the wood, the s and the soil, 74
2Ki 3:19 and ruin every good field with **s."** 74
3:25 Only Kir Hareseth was left with its s 74
17:10 They set up **sacred** s and Asherah poles 5167
18:4 smashed the **sacred** s and cut down 5167
23:14 **sacred s** and cut down the Asherah poles 5167
1Ch 12:2 arrows or to **sling** s right-handed or 74+928+2021
20:2 and it was set with precious **s—** 74
29:2 turquoise, s *of* various colors, 74
29:8 Any who had precious s gave them to 74
2Ch 1:15 and gold as common in Jerusalem as **s,** 74
3:6 He adorned the temple with precious **s.** 74
9:1 large quantities of gold, and precious **s—** 74
9:9 large quantities of spices, and precious **s.** 74
9:10 also brought algumwood and precious **s.** 74
9:27 as common in Jerusalem as **s,** 74
14:3 smashed the **sacred** s and cut down 5167
16:6 the s and timber Baasha had been using. 74
26:15 to shoot arrows and hurl large **s.** 74
31:1 smashed the **sacred** s and cut down 5167
32:27 and gold and for his precious **s,** 74
Ezr 5:8 with **large** s and placing the timbers 10006+10146
6:4 with three courses of **large** s and 10006+10146
Ne 4:2 the s back to life from those heaps 74
4:3 he would break down their wall of **s!"** 74
Est 1:6 mother-of-pearl and other **costly s.** 6090
Job 5:23 For you will have a covenant with the s *of* 74
8:17 of rocks and looks for a place among the s. 74
14:19 as water wears away s 74
24:2 Men move **boundary s;** 1474
Ps 102:14 For her s are dear to your servants; 74
Ecc 3:5 time to scatter s and a time to gather them, 74
10:9 Whoever quarries s may be injured 74
Isa 5:2 and **cleared** it **of s** and planted it with 6232
14:19 those who descend to the s *of* the pit. 74
27:9 the altar s to be like chalk stones crushed 74
27:9 the altar stones to be like chalk s crushed 74
54:11 I will build you with s *of* turquoise, 74
54:12 and all your walls of precious **s.** 74
57:6 [The idols] among the smooth s of NIH
60:17 and iron in place of s. 74
62:10 Remove the s. 74
Jer 43:9 take *some* large s with you and bury them 74
43:10 over these s I have buried here; 74
La 3:53 to end my life in a pit and threw s at me; 74
Eze 26:12 and throw your **s,** timber and rubble into 74
27:22 of all kinds of spices and precious **s,** 74
28:14 you walked among the fiery **s.** 74
28:16 O guardian cherub, from among the fiery **s.** 74
Da 11:38 with precious s and costly gifts. 74
Hos 3:4 without sacrifice or **sacred s,** 5167
5:10 like those who move **boundary s.** 1473
10:1 his land prospered, he adorned his **sacred s.** 5167
10:2 and destroy their **sacred s.** 5167
12:11 Their altars will be like **piles of s** on 1643
Mic 1:6 I will pour her s into the valley 74
5:13 and your **sacred** s from among you; 5167
Hab 2:11 The s of the wall will cry out, 74
Zec 5:4 both its timbers and its **s.'** " 74
Mt 3:9 I tell you that out *of* these s God can raise *3345*
4:3 tell these s to become bread." *3345*
Mk 5:5 and cut himself *with* **s.** *3345*
13:1 What massive **s!** What magnificent *3345*
Lk 3:8 that out of these s God can raise up children *3345*
19:40 "if they keep quiet, the s will cry out." *3345*
21:5 the temple was adorned *with* beautiful s and *3345*
Jn 8:59 At this, they picked up s to stone him, *3345*
10:31 Again the Jews picked up s to stone him, *3345*
1Co 3:12 silver, costly **s,** wood, hay or straw, *3345*
1Pe 2:5 also, like living **s,** are being built into *3345*
Rev 17:4 glittering with gold, precious s and pearls. *3345*
18:12 cargoes of gold, silver, precious s and pearls *3345*
18:16 glittering with gold, precious s and pearls! *3345*

STONING (4) [STONE]

Nu 14:10 the whole assembly talked about s them. 74+928+2021+8083
1Sa 30:6 because the men were talking of s him; 6232
Jn 10:33 *"We are* not s you for any of these," *3342*
Ac 7:59 *While they were* s him, Stephen prayed, *3344*

STOOD (216) [STAND]

Ge 18:8 While they ate, he s near them under a tree. 6641
19:27 the place where *he had* s before the LORD. 6641
28:13 There above it s the LORD, and he said: 5893
37:7 and s **upright,** while your sheaves gathered 5893
41:3 came up out of the Nile and s beside those 6641
Ex 2:4 His sister s at a distance to see 3656
9:10 So they took soot from a furnace and s 6641
14:19 of cloud also moved from in front and s 6641
15:8 The surging waters s **firm** like a wall; 5893
18:13 and they s around him from morning 6641
19:17 and *they* s at the foot of the mountain. 3656
32:26 he s at the entrance to the camp and said, 6641
33:8 all the people rose and s at the entrances 5893
33:10 they all s and worshiped, 7756
34:5 down in the cloud and s there with him 3656
Lev 9:5 the entire assembly came near and s before 6641
Nu 12:5 *he* s *at* the entrance to the Tent 6641
12:10 there s Miriam—leprous, like snow. NIH
16:18 and s with Moses and Aaron at the entrance 6641
16:48 *He* s between the living and the dead, 6641
22:22 of the LORD s in the road to oppose him. 3656
22:24 the angel of the LORD s in a narrow path 6641
22:26 of the LORD moved on ahead and s in 6641
27:2 to the Tent of Meeting and s before Moses, 6641
Dt 4:10 the day *you* s before the LORD your God 6641
4:11 near and s at the foot of the mountain 6641
5:5 that time I s between the LORD and you 6641
31:15 the cloud s over the entrance to the Tent. 6641
Jos 3:17 of the LORD s firm on dry ground in 6641
4:3 from right where the priests s 3922+5163+8079
4:9 the ark of the covenant had **s.** 5163+8079
8:33 of the people s in front of Mount Gerizim NIH
10:13 So the sun s **still,** and the moon stopped, 1957
20:6 to stay in that city until he *has* s trial before 6641
Jdg 16:25 When *they* s him among the pillars, 6641
16:29 two central pillars on which the temple **s.** 3922
18:16 s *at* the entrance to the gate. 5893
18:17 the priest and the six hundred armed men s 5893
1Sa 1:9 and drinking in Shiloh, Hannah s **up.** 7756
1:26 the woman who s here beside you praying 5893
3:10 The LORD came and s there, 3656
10:23 and *as he* s among the people he was 3656
12:18 So all the people s **in awe** *of* the LORD 3707+4394
14:5 One cliff s to the north toward Micmash, 5187
17:8 Goliath s and shouted to the ranks of Israel, 6641
17:51 David ran and s over him. 6641
26:13 and s on top of the hill some distance away; 6641
2Sa 1:10 "So *I* s over him and killed him, 6641
2:15 So *they* **s up** and were counted off— 7756
12:17 of his household s beside him to get him up 7756
13:31 The king **s up,** tore his clothes and lay 7756
13:31 all his servants **s by** with their clothes torn. 5893
18:4 So the king s beside the gate while all 6641
18:30 So he stepped aside and s there. 6641
20:11 of Joab's men s beside Amasa and said, 6641
20:15 and *it* s against the outer fortifications. 6641
23:10 but he s *his* **ground** and struck down 7756
1Ki 1:28 So she came into the king's presence and s 6641
2:7 *They* s by me when I fled 7928
2:19 the king **s up** to meet her, 7756
3:15 s before the ark of the Lord's covenant 6641
3:16 Now two prostitutes came to the king and s 6641
7:25 The Sea s on twelve bulls, 6641
8:22 Then Solomon s before the altar of 6641
8:55 *He* s and blessed the whole assembly 6641
10:20 Twelve lions s on the six steps, 6641
19:13 and went out and s at the mouth of the cave. 6641
20:38 and s by the road **waiting** for the king. 6641

1Ki 22:21 came forward, s before the LORD and said, 6641
2Ki 2: 7 of the company of the prophets went and s 6641
2:13 from Elijah and went back and s on 6641
4:12 So he called her, and *she* s before him. 6641
4:15 So he called her, and *she* s in the doorway. 6641
5:15 *He* s before him and said, 6641
5:25 he went in and s before his master Elisha. 6641
8: 9 He went in and s before him, and said, 6641
10: 9 *He* s before all the people and said, 6641
13:21 the man came to life and **s up** on his feet. 7756
16:14 that s before the LORD he brought from NIH
18:28 the commander s and called out in Hebrew: 6641
23: 3 The king s by the pillar and renewed 6641
2Ch 3:13 They s on their feet, facing the main hall. 6641
4: 4 The Sea s on twelve bulls, 6641
5:12 s on the east side of the altar, 6641
6:12 Then Solomon s before the altar of 6641
6:13 *He* s on the platform and then knelt down 6641
9:19 Twelve lions s on the six steps, 6641
13: 4 Abijah s on Mount Zemaraim, 7756
18:20 came forward, s before the LORD and said, 6641
20: 5 Then Jehoshaphat **s up** in the assembly 6641
20:13 s there before the LORD. 6641
20:14 as he s in the assembly. NIH
20:19 and Korahites **s up** and praised the LORD, 7756
20:20 As they set out, Jehoshaphat s and said, 6641
24:20 *He* s before the people and said, 6641
29:26 Levites s *ready* with David's instruments, 6641
30:27 The priests and the Levites s to bless 7756
34:31 The king s by his pillar and renewed 6641
35:10 the priests s in their places with the Levites 6641
Ezr 10:10 Then Ezra the priest **s up** and said to them, 7756
Ne 4:14 *I* **s up** and said to the nobles, 7756
8: 4 Ezra the scribe s on a high wooden platform 6641
8: 4 Beside him on his right s Mattithiah, 6641
8: 5 and as he opened it, the people all **s up.** 6641
9: 2 *They* **s in** *their* **places** and confessed 6641
9: 3 *They* s where they were and read from 7756
12: 9 s opposite them in the services. NIH
12:24 who s opposite them to give praise NIH
Est 5: 1 on her royal robes and s in the inner court 6641
8: 4 to Esther and she arose and s before him. 6641
Job 4:15 and the hair on my body **s on end.** 6169
4:16 A form s before my eyes, NIH
Ps 33: 9 he commanded, and *it* **s firm.** 6641
104: 6 the waters s above the mountains. 6641
106:23 s in the breach before him to keep his wrath 6641
106:30 But Phinehas **s up** and intervened, 6641
Isa 36:13 the commander s and called out in Hebrew, 6641
Jer 18:20 that I s before you and spoke in their behalf 6641
19:14 and s in the court of the LORD's temple 6641
23:18 of *them has* s in the council of the LORD 6641
23:22 But if *they had* s in my council, 6641
Eze 1:21 when the creatures **s still,** 6641
1:21 the creatures stood still, *they* also **s still;** 6641
1:24 they **s still,** they lowered their wings. 6641
1:25 above the expanse over their heads as they s 6641
8: 3 where the idol that provokes to jealousy **s.** 4632
8:11 of them s seventy elders of the house 6641
9: 2 They came in and s beside the bronze altar. 6641
10: 6 the man went in and s beside a wheel. 6641
10:17 the cherubim **s still,** they also stood still; 6641
10:17 the cherubim stood still, *they* also **s still;** 6641
37:10 they came to life and **s up** on their feet— 6641
Da 2: 2 When they came in and s before the king, 6641
2:31 and there before you s a large statue— 10624
3: 3 and *they* s before it. 10624
4:10 and there before me s a tree in the middle of NIH
7: 4 from the ground so that *it* s on two feet 10624
7:10 ten thousand times ten thousand s before 10624
8:15 before me s one who looked like a man. 6641
10:11 when he said this to me, *I* **s up** trembling. 6641
12: 5 looked, and there before me s two others, 6641
Ob 1:11 On the day you s aloof 6641
Hab 3: 6 *He* s, and shook the earth; 6641
3:11 Sun and moon **s still** in the heavens at 6641
Zec 3: 3 in filthy clothes as *he* s before the angel. 6641
3: 5 while the angel of the LORD **s by.** 6641
Mal 2: 5 he revered me and **s in awe** of my name. 3169
Mt 12:46 his mother and brothers s outside, *2705*
13: 2 while all the people s on the shore. *2705*
26:62 Then the high priest **s up** and said to Jesus, *482*
27:11 Meanwhile Jesus s before the governor, *2705*
Mk 5:42 Immediately the girl **s up** and walked *482*
9:27 lifted him to his feet, and *he* **s up.** *482*
14:57 some **s up** and gave this false testimony *482*
14:60 Then the high priest **s up** before them *482*
15:39 the centurion, who s **there** in front of Jesus, *4225*
Lk 4:16 And *he* **s up** to read. *482*
5:25 Immediately he **s up** in front of them, *482*
6: 8 So he got up and s there. *482*
6:17 down with them and s on a level place. *2705*
7:14 and those carrying it s still. *2705*
7:38 and *as she* s behind him at his feet weeping, *2705*
8:55 Her spirit returned, and at once *she* **s up.** *482*
10:25 On one occasion an expert in the law **s up** *482*
17:12 They s at a distance *2705*
18:11 Pharisee **s up** and prayed about himself: *2705*
18:13 "But the tax collector s at a distance. *2705*
19: 8 But Zacchaeus **s up** and said to the Lord, *2705*
22:28 You are those who *have* s by me *1373*
23:35 The people s watching, *2705*
23:49 s at a distance, watching these things. *2705*
24: 4 that gleamed like lightning s **beside** them. *2392*
24:17 *They* s still, their faces downcast. *2705*
24:36 Jesus himself s among them and said *2705*
Jn 2: 6 Nearby s six stone water jars, *1639+3023*
Jn 7:37 Jesus s and said in a loud voice, *2705*
11:56 and *as they* s in the temple area *2705*
18:18 and officials s around a fire they had made *2705*
18:25 As Simon Peter s warming himself, *1639+2705*
19:25 Near the cross of Jesus s his mother, *2705*
20:11 but Mary s outside the tomb crying. *2705*
20:19 Jesus came and s among them and said, *2705*
20:26 Jesus came and s among them and said, *2705*
21: 4 Early in the morning, Jesus s on the shore, *2705*
Ac 1:10 two men dressed in white **s beside** them. *4225*
1:15 In those days Peter **s up** among *482*
2:14 Then Peter **s up** with the Eleven, *2705*
5:34 **s up** in the Sanhedrin and ordered that *482*
9: 7 men traveling with Saul s there speechless; *2705*
9:39 All the widows s **around** him, *4225*
10:30 a man in shining clothes s before me *2705*
11:28 **s up** and through the Spirit predicted that *482*
12: 6 and sentries s guard at the entrance. *5498*
15: 5 to the party of the Pharisees **s up** and said, *1985*
17:22 then **s up** in the meeting of the Areopagus *2705*
21:40 Paul s on the steps and motioned to *2705*
22:13 He **s beside** me and said, 'Brother Saul, *2392*
22:20 I s there giving my approval and *1639+2392*
23: 9 of the law who were Pharisees **s up** *482*
23:11 The following night the Lord **s near** Paul *2392*
24:20 in me *when* I s before the Sanhedrin— *2705*
24:21 unless it was this one thing I shouted *as I* s *2705*
25: 7 down from Jerusalem s **around** him, *4325*
27:21 Paul **s up** before them and said: *2705*
27:23 and whom I serve **s beside** me *4225*
2Co 13: 7 that people will see that we have **s the test** *1511*
Col 2:14 against us and that s **opposed** to us; *1639+5641*
2Ti 4:17 the Lord **s at** my **side** and gave me strength, *4225*
Heb 10:32 when *you* s *your* **ground** in a great contest *5702*
10:33 at other times *you* s side by side *1181*
Jas 1:12 because *when he has* s the test, *1181*
Rev 8: 3 came and s at the altar. *2705*
11:11 and *they* s on their feet, and terror struck *2705*
12: 4 The dragon s in front of the woman *2705*
13: 1 And the dragon s on the shore of the sea. *2705*
22: 2 On each side of the river s the tree of life, *NIG*

STOOL (1) [FOOTSTOOL]

Ex 1:16 and observe them on the **delivery s,** 78

STOOP (5) [STOOPED, STOOPS]

2Sa 22:36 you **s down** to make me great. 6700
Ps 18:35 you **s down** to make me great. 6708
Ecc 12: 3 and the strong men **s,** when the grinders 6430
Isa 46: 2 *They* s and bow down together; 7970
Mk 1: 7 of whose sandals I am not worthy to **s down** *3252*

STOOPED (1) [STOOP]

Jn 8: 8 Again *he* **s down** and wrote on the ground. *2893*

STOOPS (2) [STOOP]

Ps 113: 6 who **s down** to look on the heavens and 9164
Isa 46: 1 Bel bows down, Nebo **s low;** 7970

STOP (67) [STOPPED, STOPPING, STOPS]

Ge 19:17 and don't s anywhere in the plain! 6641
Ex 9:29 The thunder *will* s and there will 2532
Nu 11:28 "Moses, my lord, s them!" 3973
Jos 10:19 But don't s! Pursue your enemies, 6641
22:25 descendants *might* **cause** ours **to s** fearing 8697
Jdg 15: 7 *I* won't s until I get my revenge on you." 2532
19:11 *let's* s at this city of the Jebusites 6073
1Sa 7: 8 "*Do* not s crying out to the LORD our God 3087
9: 5 or my father *will* s thinking about 2532
15:16 **"S!"** Samuel said to Saul. 8332
20:38 "Hurry! Go quickly! Don't **s!"** 6641
2Sa 2:21 But Asahel would not s chasing him. 6073
2:22 Abner warned Asahel, **"S** chasing me! 6073
2:26 your men to s pursuing their brothers?" 8740
2Ki 3:19 **s up** all the springs, and ruin every good 6258
2Ch 25:16 **S!** Why be struck down?" 2532
35:21 so s opposing God, who is with me, 2532
Ezr 4:21 Now issue an order to these men to **s work,** 10098
4:23 and compelled them by force *to* **s.** 10098
6: 8 so that the work *will* not s. 10098
Ne 5:10 But *let* the exacting of usury **s!** 6440
6: 3 the work s while I leave it and go down 8697
Job 9:12 If he snatches away, who *can* **s him?** 8740
13:21 and s frightening me with your terrors. 440
37:14 s and consider God's wonders. 6641
Pr 19:27 S listening to instruction, my son, 2532
Isa 1:13 S bringing meaningless offerings! 3578+4202
1:16 out of my sight! S doing wrong, 2532
2:22 **S trusting in** man, 2532+4946
28:22 Now s your mocking, 440
30:11 and s confronting us with the Holy One 8697
33: 1 When you s destroying, 9462
33: 1 when you s betraying, you will be betrayed. 5801
Jer 15: 5 Who *will* s to ask how you are? 6073
32:40 *I will* never s doing good to them, 8740
44: 5 from their wickedness or s burning incense 1194
Eze 16:41 *I will* **put a s** to your prostitution, 8697
21:21 of Babylon *will* s at the fork in the road, at 6641
23:27 So *I will* **put a s** *to* the lewdness 8697
45: 9 S dispossessing my people, 8123
Hos 2:11 *I will* s all her celebrations: 8697
Am 7: 5 "Sovereign LORD, I beg you, **s!** 2532
7:16 and s preaching against the house of Isaac.' 4202
Na 2: 8 **"S!** Stop!" they cry, but no one turns back. 6641
Na 2: 8 "Stop! **S!"** they cry, but no one turns back. 6641
Mk 9:38 in your name and *we* **told** him **to s,** *3266*
9:39 "*Do* not s him," Jesus said. *3266*
Lk 6:29 *do* not s him **from taking** your tunic. *3266*
8:52 **"S** wailing," Jesus said. *3590*
9:49 in your name and *we tried to* s him, *3266*
9:50 "*Do* not s him," Jesus said, *3266*
Jn 5:14 S sinning or something worse may happen *3600*
6:43 **"S** grumbling among yourselves," *3590*
7:24 **S** judging by mere appearances, *3590*
20:27 **S** doubting and believe." *3590*
Ac 4:17 to s this thing from spreading any further *3590*
5:39 you will not be able *to* s these men; *2907*
8:38 And he gave orders *to* s the chariot. *2705*
13:10 *Will you* never s perverting the right ways *4264*
Ro 14:13 let us s passing judgment on one another. *3600*
1Co 14:20 Brothers, s thinking like children. *3590*
14:30 the first speaker *should* **s.** *4967*
2Co 11:10 the regions of Achaia *will* s this boasting *5852*
1Ti 5:23 S drinking only water, and use a little wine *3600*
2Pe 2:14 eyes full of adultery, they **never** s sinning; *188*
Rev 4: 8 Day and night *they* never s saying: *398+2400*
9:20 they did not s worshiping demons, *NIG*

STOPPED (78) [STOP]

Ge 8: 2 and the rain *had* **s falling** from the sky. 3973
11: 8 and *they* s building the city. 2532
26:15 the Philistines **s up,** filling them with earth. 6258
26:18 the Philistines *had* **s up** after Abraham died, 6258
28:11 *he* **s for the night** because the sun had set. 4328
29:35 Then *she* s having children. 6641
30: 9 Leah saw that *she had* s having children, 6641
41:49 it was so much that *he* s keeping records 2532
42:27 At **place where they s for the night** 4869
43:21 But at **place where we s for the night** 4869
Ex 9:33 the thunder and hail **s,** 2532
9:34 and hail and thunder *had* **s,** he sinned again: 2532
Nu 16:48 and the plague **s.** 6806
16:50 for the plague *had* **s.** 6806
25: 8 Then the plague against the Israelites **was s;** 6806
Jos 3:16 the water from upstream s flowing. 6641
5:12 The manna s the day after they ate this food 8697
10:13 So the sun stood still, and the moon **s,** 6641
10:13 The sun s in the middle of the sky 6641
Jdg 19:15 There *they* s to spend the night. 6073
Ru 1:18 determined to go with her, *she* s urging her. 2532
2:20 not **s showing** his kindness *to* the living and 6440
1Sa 6:14 and there *it* **s** beside a large rock. 6641
10: 2 now your father *has* **s thinking** *about* them 5759
10:13 After Saul s prophesying, 3983
14:46 Then Saul s pursuing the Philistines, 4946+6590
2Sa 2:23 And every man s when he came to the place 6641
18:16 and the troops s pursuing Israel, 8740
20:12 that everyone who came up to Amasa **s,** 6641
24:21 that the plague on the people *may* **be s."** 6806
24:25 and the plague on Israel **was s.** 6806
1Ki 15:21 *he* s building Ramah and withdrew 2532
17:17 and finally s breathing. 3855+4202
22:33 not the king of Israel and s pursuing him. 8740
2Ki 2: 7 where Elijah and Elisha *had* s at the Jordan. 6641
3:25 *They* **s up** all the springs and cut 6258
4: 6 Then the oil s flowing. 6641
4: 8 So whenever he came by, *he* s there to eat. 6073
5: 9 with his horses and chariots and s at 6641
6:23 Aram s raiding Israel's territory. 3578+4202+6388
13:18 He struck it three times and **s.** 6641
18:17 and s at the aqueduct of the Upper Pool, 6641
1Ch 21:22 that the plague on the people *may* **be s.** 6806
2Ch 16: 5 *he* s building Ramah and abandoned his 2532
18:32 *they* s pursuing him. 8740
25:16 So the prophet s but said, 2532
Ezr 5: 5 and they *were* not s until a report could go 10098
Ne 12:39 At the Gate of the Guard *they* **s.** 6641
Job 4:16 *It* **s,** but I could not tell what it was. 6641
32: 1 So these three men s answering Job, 8697
Ps 58: 4 like that of a cobra *that has* s its ears, 357
Isa 24: 8 the noise of the revelers *has* **s,** 8697
36: 2 When the commander s at the aqueduct of 6641
Jer 44:18 since *we* s burning incense to the Queen 2532
48:33 *I have* s the flow of wine from the presses; 8697
51:30 Babylon's warriors *have* s fighting; 2532
La 5:14 the young men have s their music. 4946
Eze 10:18 from over the threshold of the temple and s 6641
10:19 *They* s at the entrance to the east gate of 6641
11:23 the city and s above the mountain east of it. 6641
Zec 7:11 they turned their backs and **s up** 3877+4946+9048
Mt 2: 9 the east went ahead of them until *it* s over *2705*
20:32 Jesus s and called them. *2705*
Mk 5:29 Immediately her bleeding s and she felt *3830*
10:49 Jesus s and said, "Call him." *2705*
Lk 7:45 the time I entered, *has* not s kissing my feet. *1364*
8:44 and immediately her bleeding **s.** *2705*
18:40 Jesus s and ordered the man to be brought *2705*
23:45 for the sun **s shining.** *1722*
Ac 5:42 *they* never s teaching and proclaiming *4264*
10:17 where Simon's house was and s **at** the gate. *2392*
11:11 to me from Caesarea s at the house *2392*
20:31 that for three years *I* never s warning each *4264*
21:32 and his soldiers, *they* s beating Paul. *4264*
Eph 1:16 *I have* not s giving thanks for you, *4264*
Col 1: 9 not s praying for you and asking God *4264*
1Th 2:18 did, again and again—but Satan s us. *1601*
Heb 10: 2 would *they* not *have* s being offered? *4264*

STOPPING (2) [STOP]
Ex 5: 5 and *you are* s them from working." 8697
Jer 41:17 s at Geruth Kimham near Bethlehem 3782

STOPS (8) [STOP]
1Ki 18:44 and go down before the rain s you.' " 6806
Job 18: 5 the flame of his fire s burning. 4202
30:27 The churning inside me never s; 1957
37: 7 *he* s every man from his labor. 3159
Isa 33:15 *who* s his ears against plots of murder 357
44:19 No one s **to think,** 448+4213+8740
Ac 6:13 "This fellow never s speaking *4264*
3Jn 1:10 *He* also s those who want to do so *3266*

STORAGE (2) [STORE]
Jer 40:10 and put them in your s **jars,** 3998
Eze 4: 9 in a s **jar** and use them to make bread 3998

STORE (29) [STORAGE, STORED, STORES, STORING]
Ge 6:21 and s it **away** as food for you and for them." 665
41:35 that are coming and s **up** the grain under 7392
Ex 1:11 and Rameses as s cities for Pharaoh. 5016
Dt 14:28 that year's produce and s it in your towns, 5663
1Ki 9:19 as well as all his s cities and the towns 5016
2Ch 8: 4 in the desert and all the s cities he had built 5016
8: 6 as well as Baalath and all his s cities, 5016
16: 4 Abel Maim and all the s cities of Naphtali. 5016
17:12 he built forts and s cities in Judah 5016
32:28 He also made **buildings to** s the harvest 5016
Ne 13: 5 with a large room formerly used *to* s 5989
Job 23:14 and many such plans he still has **in s.** 6640
Ps 17:14 and *they* s **up** wealth for their children. 5663
Pr 2: 1 and s **up** my commands within you, 7621
2: 7 *He* **holds** victory **in** s for the upright, 7621
7: 1 keep my words and s **up** my commands 7621
10:14 Wise men s **up** knowledge, 7621
30:25 yet *they* s **up** their food in the summer; 3922
Isa 2:12 The LORD Almighty has a day **in** s **for** all 6584
10:28 *they* s supplies at Micmash. 7212
33: 6 a **rich** s *of* salvation and wisdom 2890
Mic 6:14 *You will* s **up** but save nothing, 6047
Mt 6:19 not s **up** for yourselves treasures on earth, *2564*
6:20 But s **up** for yourselves treasures in heaven, *2564*
6:26 they do not sow or reap or s **away** in barns, *5251*
Lk 12:17 I have no place *to* s my crops.' *5251*
12:18 there *I will* s all my grain and my goods. *5251*
2Co 9:10 and increase your s of seed and will enlarge *NIG*
2Ti 4: 8 Now *there is* **in** s for me the crown *641*

STORED (19) [STORE]
Ge 41:48 of abundance in Egypt and s it in the cities. 5989
41:49 Joseph s **up** huge quantities of grain, 7392
2Ki 20:17 all that your fathers *have* s **up** until this day, 732
Ezr 6: 1 in the archives s in the treasury at Babylon. 10474
Job 15:20 the ruthless through all the years s **up** 7621
Ps 31:19 which *you have* s **up** for those who fear you, 7621
Pr 13:22 a sinner's wealth **is** s **up** for the righteous. 7621
SS 7:13 both new and old, that *I have* s **up** for you, 7621
Isa 15: 7 and s **up** they carry away over the Ravine of 7213
22: 9 *you* s **up** water in the Lower Pool. 7695
23:18 *they will* not **be** s **up** or hoarded. 732
39: 6 all that your fathers *have* s **up** until this day, 732
45: 3 **riches** *s in* secret places, AIT
Hos 13:12 The guilt of Ephraim *is* s **up,** 7674
Mt 12:35 good things out of the good s **up** in him, *2565*
12:35 evil things out of the evil s **up** in him. *2565*
Lk 6:45 things out of the good s **up** in his heart, *2565*
6:45 evil things out of the evil s **up** in his heart. *2565*
Col 1: 5 from the hope that is s **up** for you in heaven *641*

STOREHOUSE (5) [HOUSE]
Dt 28:12 the heavens, the s *of* his bounty, 238
1Ch 26:15 and the lot for the s fell to his sons. 667+1074
26:17 on the south and two at a time at the s. 667
Hos 13:15 His s will be plundered of all its treasures. 238
Mal 3:10 Bring the whole tithe into the s, 238+1074

STOREHOUSES (12) [HOUSE]
Ge 41:56 Joseph opened **the** s and 889+928+2157+3972[S]
2Ki 20:13 showed them all that was in his **s—** 1074+5800
1Ch 27:25 of Adiel was in charge of the royal **s.** 238
27:25 in charge of the s in the outlying districts, 238
Job 38:22 the s *of* the snow or seen the storehouses of 238
38:22 the storehouses of the snow or seen the **s** *of* 238
Ps 33: 7 he puts the deep into **s.** 238
135: 7 the rain and brings out the wind from his **s.** 238
Isa 39: 2 and showed them what was in his **s—** 1074+5800
Jer 10:13 the rain and brings out the wind from his **s.** 238
51:16 the rain and brings out the wind from his **s.** 238
Joel 1:17 The s are in ruins, 238

STOREROOM (2) [ROOM]
Mt 13:52 of his s new treasures as well as old." *2565*
Lk 12:24 they have no s or barn; yet God feeds them. *5421*

STOREROOMS (11) [ROOM]
1Ch 28:11 its buildings, its **s,** its upper parts, 1711
2Ch 31:11 to prepare s in the temple of the LORD, 4384
Ne 10:37 we will bring to the s *of* the house 4384
10:38 house of our God, to the s of the treasury. 4384
10:39 new wine and oil to the s where the articles 4384
12:25 who guarded the s *at* the gates. 667
12:44 of the s for the contributions, 238+4200+5969
12:44 into **the** s the portions required by the Law 2157[S]
13: 4 the priest had been put in charge of the s *of* 4384
13:12 new wine and oil into the **s.** 238
13:13 **put** Shelemiah the priest, Zadok the scribe, and a Levite named Pedaiah **in charge of the s** 238+732+6584

STORES (4) [STORE]
Job 21:19 'God s **up** a man's punishment for his sons.' 7621
Pr 6: 8 yet *it* s its provisions in summer 3922
21:20 the house of the wise are s *of* choice food 238
Lk 12:21 be with anyone who s **up** things for himself *2564*

STORIES (2) [STORY]
2Pe 1:16 We did not follow cleverly invented s *3680*
2: 3 exploit you *with* s they have made up. *3364*

STORING (2) [STORE]
Ecc 2:26 of gathering and s **up wealth** to hand it over 4043
Ro 2: 5 *you are* s **up** wrath against yourself for *2564*

STORK (6)
Lev 11:19 the s, any kind of heron, the hoopoe and 2884
Dt 14:18 the s, any kind of heron, the hoopoe and 2884
Job 39:13 with the pinions and feathers of the **s.** 2884
Ps 104:17 the s has its home in the pine trees. 2884
Jer 8: 7 s in the sky knows her appointed seasons, 2884
Zec 5: 9 They had wings like those of a **s,** 2884

STORM (34) [STORMED, STORMS, STORMY, THUNDERSTORM, WINDSTORM]
Ex 9:24 It was the worst s in all the land of Egypt 1352
Job 9:17 a s and multiply my wounds for no reason. 8554
30:22 you toss me about in the **s.** 9583
36:33 His thunder announces **the coming s;** 2257[S]
38: 1 Then the LORD answered Job out of the **s.** 6194
40: 6 Then the LORD spoke to Job out of the **s:** 6194
Ps 55: 8 far from the tempest and **s."** 6193
83:15 and terrify them with your **s.** 6070
107:29 He stilled the s to a whisper; 6194
Pr 1:27 when calamity overtakes you like a **s,** 8739
10:25 When the s has swept by, 6070
Isa 4: 6 refuge and hiding place from the s and rain. 2443
25: 4 from the s and a shade from the heat. 2443
25: 4 the breath of the ruthless is like a s *driving* 2443
32: 2 from the wind and a refuge from the **s,** 2443
Jer 11:16 But with the roar of a mighty s he will set it 2167
23:19 the s *of* the LORD will burst out in wrath, 6194
25:32 a mighty s is rising from the ends of 6193
30:23 the s *of* the LORD will burst out in wrath, 6194
Eze 30:16 Thebes will be **taken by s;** 1324
38: 9 you will go up, advancing like a **s;** 8739
Da 11:40 and the king of the North *will* s **out** 8548
Jnh 1: 4 a violent s arose that the ship threatened 6193
1:12 that it is my fault that this great s has come 6193
Na 1: 3 His way is in the whirlwind and the **s,** 8554
2: 4 The chariots s through the streets, 2147
Zec 10: 1 it is the LORD who makes the s **clouds.** 2613
Mt 8:24 a furious s came up on the lake, *4939*
Lk 8:24 the s subsided, and all was calm. *NIG*
Ac 27:15 by the s and could not **head into the wind;** *NIG*
27:18 **took** such a violent **battering from the s** *5928*
27:20 for many days and the s continued raging, *5930*
Heb 12:18 to darkness, gloom and **s;** *2590*
2Pe 2:17 without water and mists driven by a **s.** *3278*

STORMED (2) [STORM]
Jdg 9:52 Abimelech went to the tower and s it. 4309
Hab 3:14 when his warriors s **out** to scatter us, 6192

STORMS (2) [STORM]
Isa 54:11 **lashed by** s and not comforted, 6192
Zec 9:14 he will march in the s *of* the south, 6194

STORMY (3) [STORM]
Ps 148: 8 s winds that do his bidding, 6194
Am 1:14 amid violent winds on a s day. 6070
Mt 16: 3 'Today it will be s, *5930*

STORY (4) [STORIES]
Ge 39:17 Then she told him this **s:** 1821
39:19 the s his wife told him, 1821
Mt 28:15 And this s has been widely circulated *3364*
Ac 20: 9 he fell to the ground from the **third** s and *5566*

STOUT (KJV) See HARSH, IMPOSING, WILLFUL PRIDE

STOUTHEARTED (1) [HEART]
Ps 138: 3 you made me bold and **s.** 5883+6437

STRAGGLER (1)
Isa 14:31 and there is not a s in its ranks. 969

STRAIGHT (40) [STRAIGHTEN, STRAIGHTENED]
Jos 6: 5 and the people will go up, every man s **in."** 5584
6:20 so every man charged s **in,** 5584
1Sa 6:12 the cows **went** s *up* toward Beth Shemesh, 3837
2Sa 5:23 and he answered, *"Do* not **go** s **up,** 6590
1Ch 14:14 and God answered him, *"Do* not **go** s **up,** 6590
Job 10:19 s from the womb **to** the grave! 4200
Ps 5: 8 **make** s your way before me. 3837
27:11 in a s path because of my oppressors. 4793
107: 7 by a s way to a city where they could settle. 3838
Pr 2:13 who leave the s paths to walk in dark ways, 3841
3: 6 and he *will* **make** your paths **s.** 3837
4:11 of wisdom and lead you along s paths. 3841
4:25 Let your eyes look s **ahead,** 4200+5790
5: 5 her steps **lead** s *to* the grave. 9461
9:15 who **go** s *on* their way. 3837
11: 5 of the blameless **makes** *a* s way for them, 3837
15:21 a man of understanding **keeps** a s course. 3837
SS 7: 9 May the wine go s to my lover, 4797
Isa 40: 3 **make** s in the wilderness a highway for 3837
45:13 *I will* **make** all his ways **s.** 3837
Jer 31:39 The measuring line will stretch from there s 5584
Eze 1: 7 Their legs were **s;** 3838
1: 9 Each one went s **ahead;** 448+6298+7156
1:12 Each one went s **ahead.** 448+6298+7156
10:22 Each one went s **ahead.** 448+6298+7156
Joel 2: 8 each marches **s ahead.** 5019
Am 4: 3 You will each go s out **through** breaks in 5584
Mt 3: 3 way for the Lord, make s paths for him.' " *2318*
Mk 1: 3 way for the Lord, make s paths for him.' " *2318*
Lk 3: 4 way for the Lord, make s paths for him. *2318*
3: 5 The crooked roads shall become **s,** *2318*
22:61 The Lord turned and **looked** s **at** Peter. *1838*
Jn 1:23 **'Make** s the way for the Lord.' " *2316*
Ac 3: 4 Peter **looked** s at him, as did John. *867*
9:11 the house of Judas on S Street and ask for *2318*
13: 9 **looked** s at Elymas and said, *867*
16:11 From Troas *we* put out to sea and **sailed** s *2312*
21: 1 we put out to sea and **sailed** s to Cos. *2312*
23: 1 Paul **looked** s at the Sanhedrin and said, *867*
2Pe 2:15 They have left the s way and wandered off *2318*

STRAIGHTEN (3) [STRAIGHT]
Ecc 7:13 Who can s what he has made crooked? 9545
Lk 13:11 She was bent over and could not s **up** at all. *376*
Tit 1: 5 *you might* s **out** what was left unfinished *2114*

STRAIGHTENED (4) [STRAIGHT]
Ecc 1:15 What is twisted cannot *be* s; 9545
Lk 13:13 and immediately *she* s **up** and praised God. *494*
Jn 8: 7 *he* s **up** and said to them, *376*
8:10 Jesus s **up** and asked her, "Woman, *376*

STRAIGHTWAY (KJV) See AS SOON AS, AT ONCE, AT THAT MOMENT, HURRIED, IMMEDIATELY, RIGHT AWAY, WITHOUT DELAY

STRAIN (2) [STRAINING]
Ex 18:23 you will be able *to* **stand the s,** 6641
Mt 23:24 You s **out** a gnat but swallow a camel. *1494*

STRAINING (3) [STRAIN]
Zec 6: 7 *they were* s to go throughout the earth. 1335
Mk 6:48 He saw the disciples s at the oars, *989*
Php 3:13 Forgetting what is behind and s **toward** *2085*

STRANDS (3)
Ex 39: 3 of gold and cut s to be worked into the blue, 7348
Ecc 4:12 A cord of **three** *s* is not quickly broken. AIT
Eze 5: 3 But take a few s of hair and tuck them away NIH

STRANGE (12) [ESTRANGED, STRANGER, STRANGER'S, STRANGERS]
Ex 3: 3 "I will go over and see this s sight— 1524
Pr 23:33 Your eyes will see s sights 2424
Isa 18: 2 an aggressive nation of **s speech,** 7743+7743
18: 7 an aggressive nation of **s speech,** 7743+7743
28:11 and s tongues God will speak to this people, 337
28:21 to do his work, his s work, 2424
33:19 with their **s,** incomprehensible tongue. 4352
Ac 17:20 You are bringing some s *ideas* to our ears, *3826*
1Co 14:21 "Through *men of* **s tongues** and through *2280*
Heb 13: 9 be carried away by all kinds of s teachings. *3828*
1Pe 4: 4 *They* **think it** s that you do not plunge *3826*
4:12 though *something* s were happening to you. *3828*

STRANGER (18) [STRANGE]
Ge 23: 4 "I am an alien and a s among you. 9369
42: 7 **pretended to be a** s and spoke harshly 5796
Job 19:15 and my maidservants count me a **s;** 2424
29:16 I took up the case of the **s.** 3359+4202
31:32 but no s had to spend the night in the street, 1731
Ps 39:12 For I dwell with you as an alien, a **s,** 9369
69: 8 I am a s to my brothers, 2319
119:19 I am a s on earth; 1731
Pr 20:16 garment of one who puts up security for a **s;** 2424
27:13 garment of one who puts up security for a **s;** 2424

Ecc 6: 2 and a s enjoys them instead. 5799
Jer 14: 8 why are you like a s in the land, 1731
Mt 25:35 I was a s and you invited me in, *3828*
25:38 When did we see you a s and invite you in, *3828*
25:43 I was a s and you did not invite me in, *3828*
25:44 a s or needing clothes or sick or in prison, *3828*
Jn 10: 5 But they will never follow a **s;** *259*
Heb 11: 9 in the promised land like a s in *259*

STRANGER'S (1) [STRANGE]

Jn 10: 5 because they do not recognize a s voice." *259*

STRANGERS (19) [STRANGE]

Ge 15:13 that your descendants will be s in a country 1731
1Ch 16:19 few in number, few indeed, and s in it, 1591
29:15 We are aliens and s in your sight, 9369
Ps 54: 3 S are attacking me; 2424
105:12 few in number, few indeed, and s in it, 1591
109:11 may s plunder the fruits of his labor. 2424
Pr 5:10 lest s feast on your wealth 2424
5:17 never to be shared with **s.** 2424
Isa 1: 7 laid waste as when overthrown by **s.** 2424
Eze 16:32 You prefer s to your own husband! 2424
Ob 1:11 while s carried off his wealth 2424
Zec 7:14 all the nations, where they *were* **s.** 3359+4202
Ac 7: 6 'Your descendants will be s in a country *4230*
Heb 11:13 that they were aliens and s on earth. *4215*
13: 2 Do not forget to **entertain s,** *5810*
1Pe 1: 1 s in the world, scattered throughout Pontus, *4215*
1:17 live your lives as s here in reverent fear. *4229*
2:11 I urge you, as aliens and s in the world, *4215*
3Jn 1: 5 even though they are s to you. *3828*

STRANGLED (4) [STRANGLING]

Na 2:12 The lion killed enough for his cubs and s 2871
Ac 15:20 from the **meat of s animals** and from blood. *4465*
15:29 from blood, *from* the **meat of s animals** *4465*
21:25 from blood, *from* the **meat of s animals** *4465*

STRANGLING (1) [STRANGLED]

Job 7:15 so that I prefer s and death, 4725

STRAP (1) [STRAPPED, STRAPS]

Ex 32:27 'Each man s a sword to his side. 8492

STRAPPED (2) [STRAP]

Jdg 3:16 which *he* s to his right thigh under his 2520
2Sa 20: 8 and s over it at his waist was a belt with 7537

STRAPS (1) [STRAP]

Jer 27: 2 a **yoke** *out* **of** s and crossbars and put it 4593

STRATEGY (3)

2Ki 18:20 You say you have s and military strength— 6783
Isa 8:10 Devise your s, but it will be thwarted; 6783
36: 5 You say you have s and military strength— 6783

STRAW (22)

Ge 24:25 "We have plenty of s and fodder, 9320
24:32 S and fodder were brought for the camels, 9320
Ex 5: 7 the people with s for making bricks; 9320
5: 7 let them go and gather their own **s.** 9320
5:10 'I will not give you any more **s.** 9320
5:11 get your own s wherever you can find it, 9320
5:12 over Egypt to gather stubble to use for **s.** 9320
5:13 just as when you had **s."** 9320
5:16 Your servants are given no **s,** 9320
5:18 You will not be given any **s,** 9320
Jdg 19:19 We have both s and fodder for our donkeys 9320
1Ki 4:28 the proper place their quotas of barley and s 9320
Job 21:18 How often are they like s before the wind, 9320
41:27 like s and bronze like rotten wood. 9320
41:29 A club seems to him but a **piece of s;** 7990
Isa 5:24 of fire lick up s and as dry grass sinks down 7990
11: 7 and the lion will eat s like the ox. 9320
25:10 be trampled under him as s is trampled 5495
33:11 You conceive chaff, you give birth to **s;** 7990
65:25 and the lion will eat s like the ox, 9320
Jer 23:28 For what has s to do with grain?" 9320
1Co 3:12 silver, costly stones, wood, hay or **s,** *2811*

STRAWED (KJV) See SCATTERED

STRAY (9) [ASTRAY, STRAYED, STRAYING, STRAYS]

Ex 22: 5 or vineyard and **lets** them s and they graze 8938
1Ki 22:43 in the ways of his father Asa and *did* not s 6073
2Ch 20:32 in the ways of his father Asa and *did* not s 6073
Ps 119:10 *do* not **let** me s from your commands. 8706
119:21 and who s from your commands. 8706
119:118 You reject all *who* s from your decrees, 8706
Pr 7:25 Do not let your heart turn to her ways or s 9494
19:27 you *will* s from the words of knowledge. 8706
Eze 14:11 people of Israel *will* no longer s from me, 9494

STRAYED (6) [STRAY]

Ps 44:18 our feet *had* not s from your path. 5742
119:110 but *I have* not s from your precepts. 9494
119:176 *I have* s like a lost sheep. 9494
Jer 2: 5 that *they* s *so* **far** from me? 8178
31:19 After I **s,** I repented; 8740
Hos 7:13 Woe to them, because *they have* s from me! 5610

STRAYING (1) [STRAY]

Dt 22: 1 If you see your brother's ox or sheep **s,** 5615

STRAYS (5) [STRAY]

Pr 21:16 A man *who* s from the path 9494
27: 8 Like a bird *that* s from its nest is a man 5610
27: 8 from its nest is a man *who* s from his home. 5610
Eze 34: 4 not brought back the s or searched for 5615
34:16 for the lost and bring back the **s.** 5615

STREAKED (7)

Ge 30:35 the male goats that were s or spotted, 6819
30:39 that were s or speckled or spotted. 6819
30:40 the rest face the s and dark-colored animals 6819
31: 8 if he said, 'The s *ones* will be your wages,' 6819
31: 8 then all the flocks bore s *young.* 6819
31:10 male goats mating with the flock were **s,** 6819
31:12 the male goats mating with the flock are **s,** 6819

STREAM (16) [DOWNSTREAM, STREAMING, STREAMS, UPSTREAM]

Ge 32:23 After he had sent them across the **s,** 5707
Dt 9:21 as fine as dust and threw the dust into a s 5707
21: 4 or planted and where there is a **flowing s.** 419
1Sa 17:40 chose five smooth stones from the **s,** 5707
2Ch 32: 4 and they blocked all the springs and the s 5707
Job 30: 6 They were forced to live in the dry **s beds,** 5707
40:22 the poplars by the s surround him. 5707
41:19 Firebrands s from his mouth; 2143
Isa 2: 2 and all nations *will* s to it. 5641
30:33 like a s *of* burning sulfur, sets it ablaze. 5707
32:20 sowing your seed by every **s,** 4784
66:12 and the wealth of nations like a flooding **s;** 5707
Jer 17: 8 the water that sends out its roots by the **s.** 3414
51:44 The nations *will* no longer s to him. 5641
Am 5:24 righteousness like a never-failing **s!** 5707
Mic 4: 1 and peoples *will* s to it. 5641

STREAMING (1) [STREAM]

SS 4:15 of flowing water **s down** from Lebanon. 5688

STREAMS (61) [STREAM]

Ge 2: 6 but s came up from the earth and watered 116
Ex 7:19 over the s and canals, 5643
8: 5 with your staff over the s and canals 5643
Lev 11: 9 in the water of the seas and the **s,** 5707
11:10 But all creatures in the seas or s that do 5707
Dt 8: 7 a land with s and pools *of* water, 5707
10: 7 a land with s *of* water. 5707
2Ki 19:24 the soles of my feet I have dried up all the s 3284
Job 6:15 as undependable as **intermittent s,** 5707
6:15 as the s that overflow 692+5707
20:17 He will not enjoy the **s,** 7106
29: 6 the rock poured out for me s *of* olive oil. 7104
36:27 which distill as rain to the **s;** 116
Ps 1: 3 He is like a tree planted by s *of* water, 7104
42: 1 As the deer pants for s *of* water, 692
46: 4 There is a river whose s make glad the city 7104
65: 9 The s *of* God are filled with water 7104
74:15 It was you who opened up springs and **s;** 5707
78:16 he brought s out of a rocky crag 5689
78:20 water gushed out, and s flowed abundantly. 5707
78:44 they could not drink from their **s.** 5689
119:136 S *of* tears flow from my eyes, 7104
126: 4 O LORD, like s in the Negev. 692
Pr 5:16 your s *of* water in the public squares? 7104
Ecc 1: 7 All s flow into the sea, 5707
1: 7 To the place the s come from, 5707
SS 5:12 His eyes are like doves by the water **s,** 692
Isa 7:18 the distant s *of* Egypt and for bees from 3284
11:15 up into seven s so that men can cross over 5707
19: 6 the s *of* Egypt will dwindle and dry up. 3284
30:25 s *of* water will flow on every high 7104
32: 2 like s *of* water in the desert and the shadow 7104
33:21 It will be like a place of broad rivers and **s.** 3284
34: 9 Edom's s will be turned into pitch, 5707
35: 6 in the wilderness and s in the desert. 5707
37:25 the soles of my feet I have dried up all the s 3284
43:19 a way in the desert and s in the wasteland. 5643
43:20 because I provide water in the desert and s 5643
44: 3 and s on the dry ground; 5689
44: 4 like poplar trees by **flowing s.** 3298+4784
44:27 'Be dry, and I will dry up your **s,'** 5643
47: 2 bare your legs, and wade through the **s.** 5643
Jer 9:18 till our eyes overflow with tears and water s 5688
31: 9 I will lead them beside s *of* water on 5707
La 3:48 S *of* tears flow from my eyes 7104
Eze 29: 3 you great monster lying among your **s.** 3284
29: 4 the fish of your s stick to your scales. 3284
29: 4 I will pull you out from among your **s,** 3284
29: 5 you and all the fish of your **s.** 3284
29:10 against you and against your **s,** 3284
30:12 I will dry up the **s of the Nile** and sell 3284
31: 4 their s flowed all around its base 5643
31:15 I held back its **s,** and its abundant waters 5643
32: 2 in the seas thrashing about in your **s,** 5643
32: 2 with your feet and muddying the **s.** 5643
32:14 and make her s flow like oil, 5643
Joel 1:20 the s *of* water have dried up 692
Hab 3: 8 Was your wrath against the **s?** 5643
Mt 7:25 The rain came down, the s rose, *4532*
7:27 The rain came down, the s rose, *4532*
Jn 7:38 s of living water will flow from *4532*

STREET (26) [STREETS]

Dt 32:25 In the s the sword will make them childless; 2575
Jos 2:19 the **s,** his blood will be on his own head; 2575
2Ch 28:24 up altars at every **s corner** in Jerusalem. 7157
Job 31:32 in the **s,** for my door was always open to 2575
Ps 31:11 those who see me on the s flee from me. 2575
Pr 1:20 Wisdom calls aloud in the **s,** 2575
7: 8 He was going down the s near her corner, 8798
7:12 now in the **s,** now in the squares, 2575
Ecc 12: 4 the doors to the s are closed and the sound 8798
Isa 51:20 they lie at the head of every **s,** 2575
51:23 like a s to be walked over." 2575
Jer 6:11 "Pour it out on the children in the s and on 2575
37:21 of the guard and given bread from the s *of* 2575
La 2:19 from hunger at the head of every **s.** 2575
4: 1 scattered at the head of every **s.** 2575
Eze 16:25 of every s you built your lofty shrines 2006
16:31 of every s and made your lofty shrines 2006
Na 3:10 to pieces at the head of every **s.** 2575
Mt 6: 5 in the synagogues and on the s corners to *4423*
22: 9 Go to the s corners and invite to *3847*
Mk 11: 4 They went and found a colt outside in the **s,** *316*
Ac 9:11 to the house of Judas on Straight S and ask *4860*
12:10 When they had walked *the length of* one **s,** *4860*
Rev 11: 8 Their bodies will lie in the s of the great *4423*
21:21 The **great s** of the city was of pure gold, *4423*
22: 2 down the middle *of* the **great s** of the city. *4423*

STREETS (65) [STREET]

2Sa 1:20 proclaim it not in the s *of* Ashkelon, 2575
22:43 and trampled them like mud in the **s.** 2575
Est 6: 9 on the horse through the city **s,** 8148
6:11 led him on horseback through the city **s,** 8148
Ps 18:42 I poured them out like mud in the **s.** 2575
55:11 threats and lies never leave its **s.** 8148
144:14 no cry of distress in our **s.** 8148
Pr 1:21 the noisy s she cries out, in the gateways of NIH
5:16 Should your springs overflow in the **s,** 2575
22:13 or, "I will be murdered in the **s!"** 8148
26:13 a fierce lion roaming the **s!"** 8148
Ecc 12: 5 of heights and of dangers in the **s;** 2006
12: 5 and mourners go about the **s.** 8798
SS 3: 2 through its s and squares; 8798
Isa 5:25 and the dead bodies are like refuse in the **s.** 2575
10: 6 to trample them down like mud in the **s.** 2575
15: 3 In the s they wear sackcloth; 2575
24:11 In the s they cry out for wine; 2575
33: 7 Look, their brave men cry aloud in the **s;** 2575
42: 2 or raise his voice in the **s.** 2575
58:12 Restorer of S with Dwellings. 5986
59:14 truth has stumbled in the **s,** 8148
Jer 5: 1 "Go up and down the s *of* Jerusalem, 2575
7:17 towns of Judah and in the s *of* Jerusalem? 2575
7:34 the towns of Judah and the s *of* Jerusalem, 2575
9:21 the children from the s and the young men 2575
11: 6 of Judah and in the s *of* Jerusalem: 2575
11:13 that shameful god Baal are as many as the s 2575
14:16 the s *of* Jerusalem because of the famine 2575
33:10 the towns of Judah and the s *of* Jerusalem 2575
44: 6 the towns of Judah and the s *of* Jerusalem 2575
44: 9 in the land of Judah and the s *of* Jerusalem? 2575
44:17 of Judah and in the s *of* Jerusalem. 2575
44:21 the s *of* Jerusalem by you and your fathers, 2575
49:26 Surely, her young men will fall in the **s;** 8148
50:30 Therefore, her young men will fall in the **s;** 8148
51: 4 fatally wounded in her **s.** 2575
La 2:11 because children and infants faint in the s 8148
2:12 as they faint like wounded men in the s *of* 8148
2:21 and old lie together in the dust of the **s;** 2575
4: 5 once ate delicacies are destitute in the **s.** 2575
4: 8 they are not recognized in the **s.** 2575
4:14 through the s like men who are blind. 2575
4:18 so we could not walk in our **s.** 8148
Eze 7:19 They will throw their silver into the **s,** 2575
11: 6 in this city and filled its s with the dead. 2575
26:11 hoofs of his horses will trample all your **s;** 2575
28:23 upon her and make blood flow in her **s.** 2575
Da 9:25 It will be rebuilt with s and a trench, 8148
Hos 7: 1 bandits rob in the **s;** 2575
Am 5:16 "There will be wailing in all the s and cries 2575
Mic 7:10 be trampled underfoot like mire in the **s.** 2575
Na 2: 4 The chariots storm through the **s,** 2575
Zep 3: 6 I have left their s deserted, 2575
Zec 8: 4 and women of ripe old age will sit in the s 8148
8: 5 The city s will be filled with boys 8148
9: 3 and gold like the dirt of the **s.** 2575
10: 5 be like mighty men trampling the muddy s 2575
Mt 6: 2 in the synagogues and on the **s,** *4860*
12:19 no one will hear his voice in the **s.** *4423*
22:10 So the servants went out into the s *3847*
Lk 10:10 go into its s and say, *4423*
13:26 and you taught in our **s.'** *4423*
14:21 into the s and alleys of the town and bring *4423*
Ac 5:15 the s and laid them on beds and mats so that *4423*

STRENGTH (183) [STRONG]

Ge 31: 6 I've worked for your father with all my **s,** 3946
48: 2 Israel **rallied** *his* s and sat up on the bed. 2616
49: 3 the first sign of my **s,** excelling in honor, 226
Ex 15: 2 The LORD is my s and my song; 6437

Ex 15:13 In your s you will guide them 6437
Lev 26:20 Your s will be spent in vain, 3946
Nu 14:17 "Now may the Lord's s be displayed, 3946
23:22 they have the s *of* a wild ox. 9361
24: 8 they have the s *of* a wild ox. 9361
Dt 4:37 of Egypt by his Presence and his great **s,** 3946
6: 5 and with all your soul and with all your **s.** 4394
8:17 "My power and the s *of* my hands have 6797
11: 8 so that *you may* **have** *the* **s** *to* go in and take 2616
21:17 That son is the first **sign of** his father's **s.** 226
32:36 on his servants when he sees their s is gone 3338
33:25 and your s will equal your days. 1801
34: 7 yet his eyes were not weak nor his s gone. 4301
Jdg 5:31 be like the sun when it rises in its **s."** 1476
6:14 "Go in the s you have and save Israel out 3946
7: 2 against me that her own s has saved her, 3338
8:21 'As is the man, so is his **s.'** " 1476
15:19 his s returned and he revived. 8120
16: 5 into showing you the secret of his great s 3946
16: 6 of your great s and how you can be tied up 3946
16: 9 So the secret of his s was not discovered. 3946
16:15 haven't told me the secret of your great **s."** 3946
16:17 head were shaved, my s would leave me, 3946
16:19 And his s left him. 3946
1Sa 2: 4 but those who stumbled are armed with **s.** 2657
2: 9 "It is not by s that one prevails; 3946
2:10 "He will give s to his king and exalt 6437
2:31 when I will cut short your s and the strength 2432
2:31 when I will cut short your strength and the s 2432
23:16 and **helped** him **find** s in God. 906+2616+3338
28:20 His s was gone, for he had eaten nothing 3946
28:22 so you may eat and have the s to go 3946
30: 4 until they had no s left to weep. 3946
30: 6 But David **found** s in the LORD his God. 2616
2Sa 15:12 And so the conspiracy gained **s,** 579
22:33 with s and makes my way perfect. 2657
22:40 You armed me with s for battle; 2657
2Ki 18:20 You say you have strategy and military **s—** 1476
19: 3 of birth and there is no s to deliver them. 3946
23:25 and with all his soul and with all his **s,** 4394
1Ch 16:11 Look to the LORD and his **s;** 6437
16:27 s and joy in his dwelling place. 6437
16:28 ascribe to the LORD glory and **s,** 6437
26: 8 with the s to do the work— 3946
29:12 In your hands are s and power to exalt 3946
29:12 and power to exalt and **give** s to all. 2616
2Ch 13:21 But Abijah **grew in s.** 2616
23: 1 In the seventh year Jehoiada **showed** *his* **s.** 2616
25:11 then **marshaled** *his* s and led his army to 2616
Ne 1:10 by your great s and your mighty hand. 3946
4:10 "The s *of* the laborers is giving out, 3946
8:10 for the joy of the LORD is your **s."** 5057
Job 6:11 "What s do I have, that I should still hope? 3946
6:12 Do I have the s *of* stone? 3946
9:19 If it is a matter of **s,** he is mighty! 3946
12:16 To him belong s and victory; 6437
22: 9 and broke the s *of* the fatherless. 2432
30: 2 Of what use was the s *of* their hands to me, 3946
39:11 Will you rely on him for his great **s?** 3946
39:19 Do you give the horse his s or 1476
39:21 He paws fiercely, rejoicing in his **s,** 3946
40:16 What s he has in his loins, 3946
41:12 his s and his graceful form. 1476
41:22 S resides in his neck; 6437
Ps 10:10 they collapse; they fall under his **s.** 6786
18: 1 I love you, O LORD, my **s.** 2619
18:32 with s and makes my way perfect. 2657
18:39 You armed me with s for battle; 2657
21: 1 O LORD, the king rejoices in your **s.** 6437
21:13 Be exalted, O LORD, in your **s;** 6437
22:15 My s is dried up like a potsherd, 3946
22:19 O my **S,** come quickly to help me. 394
28: 7 The LORD is my s and my shield; 6437
28: 8 The LORD is the s of his people, 6437
29: 1 ascribe to the LORD glory and **s.** 6437
29:11 The LORD gives s to his people; 6437
31:10 my s fails because of my affliction, 3946
32: 4 my s was sapped as in the heat of summer. 4382
33:16 no warrior escapes by his great **s.** 3946
33:17 despite all its great s it cannot save. 2657
38:10 My heart pounds, my s fails me; 3946
46: 1 God is our refuge and **s,** 6437
59: 9 O my **S,** I watch for you; 6437
59:16 But I will sing of your **s,** 6437
59:17 O my **S,** I sing praise to you; 6437
65: 6 having armed yourself with **s,** 1476
68:28 **show** us *your* **s,** O God, 6451
68:35 of Israel gives power and s to his people. 9508
71: 9 do not forsake me when my s is gone. 3946
73:26 the s *of* my heart and my portion forever. 7446
79:11 by the s *of* your arm preserve those
condemned to die. 1542
81: 1 Sing for joy to God our **s;** 6437
83: 8 Even Assyria has joined them to lend s to 2432
84: 5 Blessed are those whose s is in you, 6437
84: 7 They go from s to strength, 2657
84: 7 They go from strength to **s,** 2657
86:16 grant your s to your servant and save 6437
88: 4 I am like a man without **s.** 384
89:17 For you are their glory and **s,** 6437
89:19 "I have bestowed s on a warrior; 6469
90:10 or eighty, if we have the **s;** 1476
93: 1 in majesty and is armed with **s.** 6437
96: 6 s and glory are in his sanctuary. 6437
96: 7 ascribe to the LORD glory and **s.** 6437
102:23 In the course of my life he broke my **s;** 3946
105: 4 Look to the LORD and his **s;** 6437
Ps 118:14 The LORD is my s and my song; 6437
147:10 His pleasure is not in the s *of* the horse, 1476
Pr 5: 9 lest you give your **best** s to others 2086
14: 4 the s *of* an ox comes an abundant harvest. 3946
20:29 The glory of young men is their **s,** 3946
24: 5 and a man of knowledge increases **s;** 3946
24:10 how small is your **s!** 3946
30:25 Ants are creatures of little **s,** yet they store 6434
31: 3 do not spend your s on women, 2657
31:25 She is clothed with s and dignity; 6437
Ecc 9:16 So I said, "Wisdom is better than **s."** 1476
10:10 *more* s is needed but skill will bring success. 2657
10:17 for s and not for drunkenness. 1476
Isa 10:13 " 'By the s *of* my hand I have done this, 3946
12: 2 the LORD, is my s and my song; 6437
28: 6 a **source of** s to those who turn back 1476
30:15 in quietness and trust is your **s,** 1476
31: 1 and in the great s of their horsemen, 6793
33: 2 Be our s every morning, 2432
36: 5 You say you have strategy and military **s—** 1476
37: 3 of birth and there is no s to deliver them. 3946
40:26 Because of his great power and mighty **s,** 3946
40:29 He gives s to the weary and increases 3946
40:31 in the LORD will renew their **s.** 3946
41: 1 Let the nations renew their **s!** 3946
44:12 He gets hungry and loses his **s;** 3946
45:24 the LORD alone are righteousness and **s.'** " 6437
49: 4 I have spent my s in vain and for nothing. 3946
49: 5 of the LORD and my God has been my **s—** 6437
50: 2 Do I lack the s to rescue you? 3946
51: 9 Clothe yourself with **s,** 6437
52: 1 awake, O Zion, clothe yourself with **s.** 6437
57:10 You found renewal of your **s,** 3338
63: 1 striding forward in the greatness of his **s?** 3946
Jer 9:23 of his s or the rich man boast of his riches, 1476
16:19 O LORD, my s and my fortress, 6437
17: 5 for his s and whose heart turns away from 2432
51:30 Their s is exhausted; 1476
La 1:14 and the Lord has sapped my **s.** 3946
Eze 30: 6 of Egypt will fall and her proud s will fail. 6437
30:18 there her proud s will come to an end. 6437
33:28 and her proud s will come to an end, 6437
Da 2:41 yet it will have some of the s of iron in it, 10487
10: 8 I had no s left, my face turned deadly pale 3946
10:17 My s is gone and I can hardly breathe." 3946
10:18 like a man touched me and **gave** me **s.** 2616
10:19 my lord, since *you have* **given** me **s."** 2616
11:15 even their best troops will not have the s 3946
11:25 up his s and courage against the king of 3946
Hos 7: 9 Foreigners sap his **s,** 3946
10:13 Because you have depended on your own s 2006
Am 2:14 the strong will not muster their **s,** 3946
6:13 "Did we not take Karnaim by our own **s?"** 2620
Mic 5: 4 and shepherd his flock in the s *of* 6437
Na 2: 1 brace yourselves, marshal all your **s!** 3946
3: 9 Cush and Egypt were her boundless **s;** 6797
Hab 1:11 guilty men, whose own s is their god." 3946
3:19 The Sovereign LORD is my **s;** 2657
Mk 12:30 and with all your mind and with all your **s.'** *2709*
12:33 all your understanding and with all your **s,** *2709*
Lk 10:27 and with all your s and with all your mind'; *2709*
Ac 9:19 after taking some food, *he* **regained** his **s.** *1932*
1Co 1:25 weakness of God is stronger than man's **s.** *NIG*
Eph 1:19 power is like the working *of* his mighty **s,** *3197*
Php 4:13 through him who **gives** me **s.** *1904*
1Ti 1:12 Christ Jesus our Lord, who *has* **given** me **s,** *1904*
2Ti 4:17 the Lord stood at my side and **gave** me **s,** *1904*
Heb 11:34 whose weakness *was* **turned to s;** *1540*
1Pe 4:11 he should do it with the s God provides, *2709*
Rev 3: 8 I know that you have little **s,** *1539*
5:12 and wealth and wisdom and s and honor *2709*
7:12 and honor and power and s be to our God *2709*
14:10 which has been poured **full** s into the cup *204*

STRENGTHEN (32) [STRONG]

Dt 3:28 and encourage and s him, 599
Jdg 16:28 O God, please s me just once more, 2616
1Ki 20:22 **"S** *your* **position** and see what must 2616
2Ki 15:19 to gain his support and s his own hold on 2616
2Ch 16: 9 to s those whose hearts are fully committed 2616
Ne 6: 9 [But I prayed,] "Now s my hands." 2616
Job 8:20 a blameless man or s the hands of evildoers. 2616
Ps 89:21 surely my arm *will* s him. 599
119:28 s me according to your word. 7756
SS 2: 5 S me with raisins, refresh me with apples, 6164
Isa 22:10 in Jerusalem and tore down houses to s 1307
35: 3 S the feeble hands, steady the knees 2616
41:10 *I will* s you and help you; 599
45: 5 *I will* s you, though you have not 273
54: 2 lengthen your cords, s your stakes. 2616
58:11 a sun-scorched land and *will* s your frame. 2741
Jer 23:14 *They* s the hands of evildoers, 2616
Eze 30:24 *I will* s the arms of the king of Babylon 2616
30:25 *I will* s the arms of the king of Babylon, 2616
34:16 I will bind up the injured and **s** the weak, 2616
Na 3:14 Draw water for the siege, s your defenses! 2616
Zec 10: 6 *"I will* s the house of Judah and save 1504
10:12 *I will* s them in the LORD and 1504
Lk 22:32 you have turned back, s your brothers." *5114*
Ac 15:32 said much to encourage and s the brothers. *2185*
Eph 3:16 out of his glorious riches *he may* s you *1443+3194*
1Th 3: 2 to s and encourage you in your faith, *5114*
3:13 *May he* s your hearts so that you will *5114*
2Th 2:17 and s you in every good deed and word. *5114*
3: 3 and he *will* s and protect you from *5114*
Heb 12:12 s your feeble arms and weak knees. *494*
Rev 3: 2 S what remains and is about to die, *5114*

STRENGTHENED (18) [STRONG]

2Sa 16:21 the hands of everyone with you *will be* **s."** 2616
1Ki 19: 8 S by that food, he traveled forty days and 3946
2Ch 11:11 *He* s their defenses and put commanders 2616
11:17 *They* s the kingdom of Judah 2616
17: 1 as king and **s himself** against Israel. 2616
Job 4: 3 how *you have* s feeble hands. 2616
4: 4 *you have* s faltering knees. 599
Isa 9:11 the LORD *has* s Rezin's foes against them 8435
Eze 34: 4 not s the weak or healed the sick or bound 2616
Da 10:19 When he spoke to me, *I* **was** s and said, 2616
Hos 7:15 I trained them and s them, 2432+2616
Lk 22:43 from heaven appeared to him and s him. *1932*
Ac 9:31 *It was* **s;** and encouraged by the Holy Spirit, *3868*
16: 5 So the churches *were* s in the faith *5105*
Ro 4:20 but *was* s in his faith and gave glory to God, *1904*
Col 1:11 *being* s with all power according *1540*
2: 7 s in the faith as you were taught, *1011*
Heb 13: 9 It is good for our hearts *to be* s by grace, *1011*

STRENGTHENING (7) [STRONG]

2Sa 3: 6 Abner had been s **his own position** in 2616
Ac 14:22 s the disciples and encouraging them *2185*
15:41 through Syria and Cilicia, s the churches. *2185*
18:23 s all the disciples. *2185*
1Co 14: 3 who prophesies speaks to men for their **s,** *3869*
14:26 All of these must be done for the s of *3869*
2Co 12:19 dear friends, is for your **s.** *3869*

STRENGTHENS (1) [STRONG]

Ps 147:13 for *he* s the bars of your gates 2616

STRESS (2)

Jer 19: 9 during the s of the siege imposed on them 5186
Tit 3: 8 And I want you *to* s these things, *1331*

STRETCH (35) [OUTSTRETCHED, STRETCHED, STRETCHES, STRETCHING]

Ex 3:20 So *I will* **s out** my hand and strike 8938
7: 5 that I am the LORD when I **s out** my hand 5742
7:19 'Take your staff and **s out** your hand over 5742
8: 5 **'S out** your hand with your staff over 5742
8:16 **'S out** your staff and strike the dust of 5742
9:22 **"S out** your hand toward the sky so 5742
10:12 **"S out** your hand over Egypt so 5742
10:21 **"S out** your hand toward the sky so 5742
14:16 and **s out** your hand over the sea to divide 5742
14:26 **"S out** your hand over the sea so that 5742
2Ki 21:13 *I will* **s out** over Jerusalem the measuring 5742
Job 1:11 But **s out** your hand and strike everything 8938
2: 5 But **s out** your hand and strike his flesh 8938
11:13 to him and **s out** your hands to him, 7298
Ps 138: 7 *you* **s out** your hand against the anger 8938
Isa 28:20 The bed is too short *to* **s out** *on,* 8594
34:11 God *will* **s out** over Edom the measuring 5742
54: 2 s your tent curtains **wide,** 5742
Jer 6:12 when *I* **s out** my hand against those who 5742
31:39 The measuring line *will* s from there 3655
51:25 *"I will* **s out** my hand against you, 5742
Eze 6:14 And *I will* **s out** my hand against them 5742
14: 9 and *I will* **s out** my hand against him 5742
14:13 by being unfaithful and *I* **s out** my hand 5742
25: 7 therefore I *will* **s out** my hand against you 5742
25:13 *I will* **s out** my hand against Edom 5742
25:16 *to* **s out** my hand against the Philistines, 5742
35: 3 and *I will* **s out** my hand against you 5742
Zep 1: 4 *"I will* **s out** my hand against Judah and 5742
2:13 *He will* **s out** his hand against the north 5742
Mt 12:13 he said to the man, **"S out** your hand." *1753*
Mk 3: 5 said to the man, **"S out** your hand." *1753*
Lk 6:10 said to the man, **"S out** your hand." *1753*
Jn 21:18 you are old *you will* **s out** your hands, *1753*
Ac 4:30 **S out** your hand to heal and perform *1753*

STRETCHED (38) [STRETCH]

Ge 10:30 The region where they lived s from Mesha 2118
Ex 8: 6 So Aaron **s out** his hand over the waters 5742
8:17 when Aaron **s out** his hand with the staff 5742
9:15 For by now *I could have* **s out** my hand 8938
9:23 When Moses **s out** his staff toward the sky, 5742
10:13 So Moses **s out** his staff over Egypt, 5742
10:22 So Moses **s out** his hand toward the sky, 5742
14:21 Then Moses **s out** his hand over the sea, 5742
14:27 Moses **s out** his hand over the sea, 5742
15:12 *You* **s out** your right hand and 5742
2Sa 24:16 angel **s out** his hand to destroy Jerusalem, 8938
1Ki 13: 4 *he* **s out** his hand from the altar and said, 8938
13: 4 hand *he* **s out** toward the man shriveled up, 8938
17:21 Then *he* **s himself out** on the boy 4499
2Ki 4:34 As *he* **s** *himself* **out** upon him, 1566
4:35 the room and then got on the bed and **s out** 1566
Job 38: 5 Who s a measuring line across it? 5742
Ps 77: 2 at night I **s out** untiring hands 5599
Pr 1:24 *when I* **s out** my hand, 5742
Isa 14:26 this is the hand **s out** over all nations. 5742
14:27 His hand *is* **s out,** and who can turn it back? 5742
23:11 The LORD *has* **s out** his hand over the sea 5742
42: 5 he who created the heavens and s them **out,** 5742
44:24 *who* alone **s out** the heavens, 5742

Isa 45:12 My own hands **s out** the heavens; 5742
51:13 *who* **s out** the heavens and laid 5742
Jer 10:12 and **s out** the heavens by his understanding. 5742
51:15 and **s out** the heavens by his understanding. 5742
La 2: 8 *He* **s out** a measuring line and did 5742
Eze 1:23 the expanse their wings were **s out** one 3838
2: 9 I looked, and I saw a hand **s out** to me. 8938
8: 3 *He* **s out** what looked like a hand 8938
16:27 So *I* **s out** my hand against you 5742
17: 7 where it was planted and **s out** its branches 8938
Zec 1:16 And the measuring line *will* **be s out** 5742
Mt 12:13 *he* **s it out** and it was completely restored, *1753*
Mk 3: 5 *He* **s it out,** and his hand was completely *1753*
Ac 22:25 As *they* **s** him **out** to flog him, *4727*

STRETCHES (7) [STRETCH]

Job 9: 8 He alone **s out** the heavens and treads on 5742
Ps 104: 2 *he* **s out** the heavens like a tent 5742
Isa 31: 3 When the LORD **s out** his hand, 5742
33:17 in his beauty and view a land that **s afar.** 5305
40:22 He **s out** the heavens like a canopy, 5742
La 1:17 Zion **s out** her hands, 7298
Zec 12: 1 The LORD, *who* **s out** the heavens, 5742

STRETCHING (3) [STRETCH]

Est 1: 1 over 127 provinces *s* **from** India to Cush: AIT
8: 9 of the 127 provinces *s* **from** India to Cush. AIT
Jer 4:31 **s out** her hands and saying, "Alas! 7298

STREWN (2)

1Sa 17:52 Their dead *were* s along the Shaaraim road 5877
2Ki 7:15 and they found the whole road **s with** 4849

STRICKEN (3) [STRIKE]

Isa 53: 4 yet we considered him s *by* God, 5595
53: 8 for the transgression of my people he was **s.** 5596
Zec 14:13 men *will be* s by the LORD *with* **great** panic. AIT

STRICT (5) [STRICTEST, STRICTLY]

1Sa 14:28 **bound** the army **under a s oath,** 8678+8678
Mk 3:12 But he gave them s orders not to tell *4498*
5:43 He gave s orders not to let anyone know *4498*
Ac 5:28 *"We* **gave** you **s orders** not to teach *4132+4133*
1Co 9:25 in the games goes into s training. *4246*

STRICTEST (1) [STRICT]

Ac 26: 5 that according to the s sect of our religion, *207*

STRICTLY (2) [STRICT]

Lk 9:21 Jesus **s warned** them not to tell this *2203+4133*
Jas 3: 1 that we who teach will be judged more **s.** *NIG*

STRIDE (1) [STRIDING, STRODE]

Pr 30:29 three things that are stately in their **s,** 7576

STRIDING (1) [STRIDE]

Isa 63: 1 **s forward** in the greatness of his strength? 7579

STRIFE (12) [STRIVE]

Ps 55: 9 for I see violence and s in the city. 8190
Pr 17: 1 a house full of feasting, with **s.** 8190
18: 6 A fool's lips bring him **s,** 8190
20: 3 It is to a man's honor to avoid **s,** 8190
22:10 Drive out the mocker, and out goes **s;** 4506
23:29 Who has **s?** 4506
26:21 so is a quarrelsome man for kindling **s.** 8190
30:33 so stirring up anger produces **s."** 8190
Isa 58: 4 Your fasting ends in quarreling and **s,** 5175
Hab 1: 3 there is **s,** and conflict abounds. 8190
Ro 1:29 They are full of envy, murder, **s,** *2251*
1Ti 6: 4 about words that result in envy, **s,** *2251*

STRIKE (81) [STRICKEN, STRIKES, STRIKING, STROKE, STRUCK]

Ge 3:15 crush your head, and you *will* s his heel." 8790
Ex 3:20 and s the Egyptians with all the wonders 5782
5: 3 *he may* s us with plagues or with the sword. 7003
7:17 in my hand I *will* s the water of the Nile, 5782
8:16 'Stretch out your staff and s the dust of 5782
12:12 through Egypt and **s down** every firstborn— 5782
12:13 will touch you when I s Egypt. 5782
12:23 the LORD goes through the land to **s down** 5597
12:23 to enter your houses and s you **down.** 5597
17: 6 S the rock, and water will come out of it 5782
Nu 8:19 so that no plague *will* s the Israelites 928+2118
14:12 *I will* s them **down** with a plague 5782
Dt 28:22 LORD *will* s you with wasting disease, 5782
33:11 s his foes till they rise no more." NIH
Jdg 6:16 and *you will* **s down** all the Midianites 5782
1Sa 17:46 and *I'll* s you **down** and cut off your head. 5782
22:17 not willing to raise a hand to s the priests of 7003
22:18 "You turn and **s down** the priests." 7003
26: 8 *I* won't s him **twice."** 9101
26:10 he said, "the LORD *himself will* s him; 5597
2Sa 1:15 of his men and said, "Go, s him **down!"** 7003
2:22 Why *should I* s you down? 5782
5:24 the LORD has gone out in front of you to s 5782
13:28 **'S Amnon down,'** then kill him. 5782
17: 2 *I would* s him **with terror,** 3006
2Sa 17: 2 *I would* **s down** only the king 5782
18:11 Why didn't *you* s him to the ground 5782
1Ki 2:29 son of Jehoiada, "Go, s him **down!"** 7003
2:31 S him **down** and bury him, 7003
14:15 And the LORD *will* s Israel, 5782
20:35 **"S** me with your weapon," 5782
20:37 prophet found another man and said, **"S** me, 5782
2Ki 6:18 **"S** these people with blindness." 5782
13:18 Elisha told him, **"S** the ground." 5782
1Ch 14:15 in front of you to s the Philistine army." 5782
2Ch 21:14 the LORD *is about to* s your people, 5597
Job 1:11 your hand and s everything he has, 5595
2: 5 But stretch out your hand and s his flesh 5595
16:10 *they* s my cheek in scorn and unite together 5782
36:32 and commands it *to* s its **mark.** 7003
Ps 3: 7 S all my enemies *on* the jaw; 5782
9:20 S them *with* terror, O LORD; 8883
81: 2 Begin the music, s the tambourine, 5989
89:23 I will crush his foes before him and **s down** 5597
91:12 *you will* not s your foot against a stone. 5597
141: 5 *Let* a righteous man s me— 2150
Pr 11:15 to **s hands in pledge** is safe. 9364
Isa 11: 4 *He will* s the earth with the rod 5782
13:18 Their bows *will* **s down** the young men; 8187
19:22 The LORD *will* s Egypt **with a plague;** 5597
19:22 *he will* s them and heal them. 5597
30:31 with his scepter *he will* s them **down.** 5782
Jer 21: 6 *I will* **s down** those who live in this city— 5782
La 3:30 offer his cheek to *one who would* s him, 5782
Eze 5: 2 and s it with the sword all around the city. 5782
6:11 S your hands **together** and stamp your feet 5782
21:14 prophesy and s your hands together. 5782
21:14 *Let* the sword **s twice,** even three times. 4100
21:17 I too *will* s my hands together, 5782
22:13 " *'I will* surely s my hands **together** at 5782
32:15 when I **s down** all who live there, 5782
39: 3 Then *I will* s your bow from your left hand 5782
Am 9: 1 **"S** the tops of the pillars so that 5782
Mic 5: 1 *They will* s Israel's ruler on the cheek with 5782
Zec 11:17 May the sword s his arm and his right eye! 6584
12: 4 that day *I will* s every horse with panic 5782
13: 7 **"S** the shepherd, and the sheep will 5782
14:12 the plague with which the LORD *will* s all 5597
14:15 A similar plague *will* s the horses 2118
Mal 4: 6 or else I will come and s the land *with* 5782
Mt 4: 6 *you will* not s your foot against a stone.' " *4684*
26:31 " *'I will* s the shepherd, and the sheep *4250*
Mk 14:27 " *'I will* s the shepherd, and the sheep *4250*
Lk 4:11 *you will* not s your foot against a stone.' " *4684*
22:49 "Lord, *should we* s with our swords?" *4250*
Jn 18:23 if I spoke the truth, why *did you* s me?" *1296*
Ac 23: 2 near Paul *to* s him on the mouth. *5597*
23: 3 Then Paul said to him, "God will s you, *5597*
Rev 2:23 *I will* s her children **dead.** *650*
11: 6 and *to* s the earth with every kind of plague *4250*
19:15 a sharp sword with which to **s down** *4250*

STRIKER (KJV) See VIOLENT

STRIKES (16) [STRIKE]

Ex 21:12 *"Anyone who* s a man and kills him shall 5782
Nu 35:16 " 'If *a man* s someone with an iron object so 5782
35:17 and *he* s someone so that he dies, 5782
Job 4: 5 *it* s you, and you are dismayed. 5595
Ps 29: 7 of the LORD s with flashes of lightning. 2934
Pr 17:18 in judgment **s hands in pledge** and puts 9546
22:26 not be a *man who* s hands **in pledge** or puts 9546
27:10 when disaster s you— NIH
Isa 5:25 his hand is raised and *he* s them **down.** 5782
41: 7 the hammer spurs on *him who* s the anvil. 2150
Jer 11:12 not help them at all when disaster **s.** NIH
Eze 7: 9 that it is I the LORD *who* **s the blow.** 5782
17:10 when the east wind s it— 5595
Mt 5:39 If someone s you on the right cheek, *4824*
Lk 6:29 *If* someone s you on one cheek, *5597*
Rev 9: 5 of the sting of a scorpion when *it* s a man. *4091*

STRIKING (6) [STRIKE]

1Sa 14:20 s each other with their swords. 928+2118
2Sa 8:13 from **s down** eighteen thousand Edomites in 5782
24:17 When David saw the angel who *was* **s down** 5782
Job 39:20 s terror with his proud snorting? NIH
Isa 58: 4 and in s each other with wicked fists. 5782
Da 8: 7 s the ram and shattering his two horns. 5782

STRING (4) [STRINGED, STRINGS, STRUNG, TEN-STRINGED]

Jdg 16: 9 as a **piece of s** snaps when it comes 5861+7348
2Sa 16: 1 He had a s *of* donkeys saddled and loaded 7538
Ps 7:12 he will bend and s his bow. 3922
Jer 51: 3 *Let* not the archer s his bow, 2005

STRINGED (9) [STRING]

Ps 4: T With **s instruments.** 5593
6: T With **s instruments.** 5593
54: T With **s instruments.** 5593
55: T With **s instruments.** 5593
61: T With **s instruments.** 5593
67: T With **s instruments.** 5593
76: T With **s instruments.** 5593
Isa 38:20 with **s instruments** all the days of our lives 5593
Hab 3:19 On my **s instruments.** 5593

STRINGS (4) [STRING]

Ps 11: 2 they set their arrows against the s to shoot 3857
45: 8 the **music of** the **s** makes you glad. 4944
150: 4 praise him with the s and flute, 4944
SS 1:10 your neck with **s of jewels.** 3016

STRIP (19) [STRIPPED, STRIPS]

1Sa 31: 8 when the Philistines came to s the dead, 7320
2Sa 2:21 take on one of the young men and s him **of** 4374
23:10 but only to s **the dead.** 7320
1Ch 10: 8 when the Philistines came to s the dead, 7320
Job 41:13 Who *can* **s off** his outer coat? 1655
Isa 27:10 *they* s its branches **bare.** 3983
32:11 **S off** *your* **clothes,** 2256+6910+7320
45: 1 to subdue nations before him and *to* s kings 7337
Jer 5:10 **S off** her branches, 6073
49:10 But I *will* s Esau **bare;** 3106
Eze 16:37 and *will* s you in front of them, 1655+6872
16:39 *They will* s you *of* your clothes 7320
23:26 *They will* also s you *of* your clothes 7320
32:15 When I make Egypt desolate and s the land 9037
Da 4:14 **s off** its leaves and scatter its fruit. 10499
Hos 2: 3 Otherwise *I will* s her naked and make her 7320
Mic 2: 8 *You* s off the rich robe from those who pass 7320
3: 3 **s off** their skin and break their bones 7320
Na 3:16 but like locusts *they* s the land and 7320

STRIPE, STRIPES (KJV) See BEATINGS, BLOWS, BRUISE, FLOGGED, FLOGGING, FLOGGINGS, LASHES, WOUNDS

STRIPES (1)

Ge 30:37 and plane trees and made white s on them 7203

STRIPLING (KJV) See YOUNG MAN

STRIPPED (33) [STRIP]

Ge 37:23 *they* s him *of* his robe— 7320
Ex 9:25 in the fields and s every tree. 8689
33: 6 So the Israelites **s off** their ornaments 5911
Jdg 14:19 s them *of* their belongings 4374
1Sa 19:24 He **s off** his robes and also prophesied 7320
31: 9 They cut off his head and **s off** his armor, 7320
2Ki 18:16 At this time Hezekiah king of Judah **s off** 7915
1Ch 10: 9 *They* s him and took his head 7320
Job 12:17 He leads counselors away s 8768
12:19 He leads priests away s 8768
15:33 He will be like a vine s *of* its unripe grapes, 2803
19: 9 *He has* s me *of* my honor and removed 7320
22: 6 *you* s men *of* their clothing, 7320
Isa 1: 7 your fields *are being* s *by* foreigners right 430
20: 2 And he did so, going around s and barefoot. 6873
20: 3 "Just as my servant Isaiah has gone s 6873
20: 4 of Assyria will lead away s and barefoot 6873
22: 8 the defenses of Judah *are* **s away.** 1655
23:13 *they* s its fortresses **bare** and turned it into 6910
La 4:21 you will be drunk and s **naked.** 6867
Eze 12:19 for their land *will be* s of everything in it 9037
17: 9 Will it not be uprooted and s *of* its fruit so 7878
19:12 *it* **was** s *of* its fruit; 7293
23:10 They s her naked, took away her sons and 1655
Da 5:20 he was deposed from his royal throne and s 10528
7:12 (The other beasts *had been* s of their 10528
Joel 1: 7 *It has* **s off** their **bark** and thrown it 3106+3106
Am 7: 2 When *they had* s the land **clean,** I cried out, 430
Na 2:10 She is pillaged, plundered, **s!** 1191
Hab 3:13 *you* s him from head to foot. 6867
Mt 27:28 They s him and put a scarlet robe on him, *1694*
Lk 10:30 They s him **of** his **clothes,** beat him and *1694*
Ac 16:22 the magistrates ordered them *to be* s and beaten. *2668+3836+4351*

STRIPS (6) [STRIP]

Ps 29: 9 the oaks and s the forests **bare.** 3106
Lk 24:12 he saw the **s of linen** lying by themselves, *3856*
Jn 11:44 and feet wrapped *with* **s of linen,** *3024*
19:40 with the spices, *in* **s of linen.** *3856*
20: 5 the **s of linen** lying there but did not go in *3856*
20: 6 He saw the **s of linen** lying there, *3856*

STRIVE (2) [STRIFE, STRIVES, STRIVING]

Ac 24:16 So I s always to keep my conscience clear *828*
1Ti 4:10 (and for this we labor and **s),** *76*

STRIVES (2) [STRIVE]

Isa 64: 7 No one calls on your name or s to lay hold 6424
Jer 15:10 with whom the whole land s and contends! 8190

STRIVING (1) [STRIVE]

Ecc 2:22 and **anxious s** with which he labors 4213+8301

STRODE (1) [STRIDE]

Hab 3:12 In wrath *you* **s through** the earth and 7575

STROKE (4) [STRIKE]

Job 5:20 and in battle from the s *of* the sword. 3338
Isa 30:32 Every s the LORD lays on them 5044
Mt 5:18 not **least s of a pen,** will by any means *3037*
Lk 16:17 for **least s of a pen** to drop out of the Law. *3037*

STROKES (KJV) See BEATING

STRONG (157) [STRENGTH, STRENGTHEN, STRENGTHENED, STRENGTHENING, STRENGTHENS, STRONGER, STRONGEST, STRONGLY]

Ge 30:42 to Laban and the s *ones* to Jacob. 8003
49:24 his s **arms** stayed limber, 2432+3338
Ex 10:19 the wind to a very s west wind, 2617
14:21 the sea back with a s east wind and turned it 6434
Nu 13:18 and whether the people who live there are s 2617
24:18 will be conquered, but Israel will grow s. 2657
Dt 2:10 a people s and numerous, 1524
2:21 They were a people s and numerous, 1524
2:36 not one town was too s for us. 8435
3:24 your greatness and your s hand. 2617
9: 2 The people are s and tall—Anakites! 1524
31: 6 *Be* s and courageous. 2616
31: 7 "*Be* s and courageous, 2616
31:23 "*Be* s and courageous, 2616
Jos 1: 6 "*Be* s and courageous, 2616
1: 7 *Be* s and very courageous. 2616
1: 9 *Be* s and courageous. 2616
1:18 Only *be* s and courageous!" 2616
10:25 *Be* s and courageous. 2616
14:11 as s today as the day Moses sent me out; 2617
17:18 though they are s, you can drive them out." 2617
23: 6 "*Be* very s; be careful to obey all that 2616
Jdg 1:28 When Israel *became* s, 2616
3:29 all vigorous and s; not a man escaped. 2657
5:21 March on, my soul; be s! 6437
9:51 Inside the city, however, was a s tower, 6437
14:14 out of the s, something sweet." 6434
18:26 seeing that they were too s for him, 2617
1Sa 4: 9 *Be* s, Philistines! Be men, 2616
2Sa 2: 7 Now then, *be* s and brave, 2616+3338
3:39 and these sons of Zeruiah are too s for me. 7997
10:11 "If the Arameans *are* too s for me, 2616
10:11 but if the Ammonites *are* too s for you, 2616
10:12 *Be* s and let us fight bravely for our people 2616
13:28 *Be* s and brave." 2616
22:18 from my foes, *who were* too s for me. 599
1Ki 2: 2 "So *be* s, show yourself a man, 2616
15: 4 to succeed him and by **making** Jerusalem s. 6641
20:23 That is why *they were* too s for us. 2616
2Ki 6:14 and chariots and a s force there. 3878
24:16 seven thousand fighting men, s and fit for 1475
1Ch 11:10 **gave** his kingship **s support** 2616+6640
19:12 "If the Arameans *are* too s for me, 2616
19:12 but if the Ammonites *are* too s for you, 2616
19:13 *Be* s and let us fight bravely for our people 2616
22:13 *Be* s and courageous. 2616
28:10 *Be* s and do the work." 2616
28:20 "*Be* s and courageous, and do the work. 2616
2Ch 11:12 and **made** them very s. 2616
12: 1 and he had **become** s, he and all Israel 2621
13: 7 and indecisive and not s *enough* 2616
15: 7 But as for you, *be* s and do not give up, 2616
32: 7 "*Be* s and courageous. 2616
Ezr 9:12 that *you may be* s and eat the good things of 2616
Job 15:26 against him with a thick, s shield. 1461
39: 4 Their young thrive and **grow** s in the wilds; 2730
Ps 18:17 from my foes, *who were* too s for me. 599
22:12 s bulls *of* Bashan encircle me. 52
24: 8 The LORD s and mighty, 6450
27:14 *be* s and take heart and wait for the LORD. 2616
31: 2 a **s fortress** to save me. 1074+5181
31:24 *Be* s and take heart, 2616
35:10 You rescue the poor from *those* too s 2617
52: 7 but trusted in his great wealth and *grew* s 6395
61: 3 a s tower against the foe. 6437
62:11 that you, O God, are s, 6437
71: 7 but you are my s refuge. 6437
73: 4 their bodies are healthy and s. 9447
89:10 with your s arm you scattered your enemies. 6437
89:13 your hand *is* s, your right hand exalted. 6451
140: 7 O Sovereign LORD, my s deliverer, 6437
142: 6 for *they are* too s for me. 599
Pr 18:10 The name of the LORD is a s tower; 6437
18:18 and keeps s *opponents* apart. 6786
23:11 for their Defender is s; 2617
31:17 her arms *are* s for her tasks. 599
Ecc 9:11 or the battle to the s, nor does food come to 1475
12: 3 and the s men stoop, 2657
SS 8: 6 for love is as s as death, 6434
Isa 8:11 The LORD spoke to me with his s hand 2621
17: 9 In that day their s cities, 5057
25: 3 Therefore s peoples will honor you; 6434
26: 1 We have a s city; 6434
28: 2 the Lord has one who is powerful and s. 579
35: 4 "*Be* s, do not fear; 2616
41: 6 the other and says to his brother, "*Be* s!" 2616
53:12 and he will divide the spoils with the s, 6786
59:10 among the s, we are like the dead. 875
Jer 4:12 a wind too s for that comes from me. 4849
9:23 or the s **man** boast of his strength or 1475
30: 6 Then why do I see every s **man** 1505
46: 6 "The swift cannot flee nor the s escape. 1475
50:34 Yet their Redeemer is s; 2617
Eze 3:14 with the s hand of the LORD upon me. 2617
17: 9 not take a s arm or many people to pull it 1524
19: 3 and he became a s **lion.** 4097
19: 5 of her cubs and made him a s **lion.** 4097
19: 6 for he was now a s **lion.** 4097
19:11 Its branches were s, fit for a ruler's scepter. 6437
19:12 its s branches withered 6437
19:14 No s branch is left on it fit for 6437
22:14 or your hands *be* s in the day I deal 2616
26:11 and your s pillars will fall to the ground. 6437
30:21 in a splint so as to *become* s *enough* to hold 2616
34:16 but the sleek and the s I will destroy. 2617
Da 2:40 there will be a fourth kingdom, s as iron— 10768
2:42 so this kingdom will be partly s 10768
4:11 and s and its top touched the sky; 10772
4:20 The tree you saw, which grew large and s, 10772
4:22 You have become great and s; 10772
8:24 *He will become* **very** s, 3946+6793
10:19 *Be* s now; be strong." 2616
10:19 Be strong now; *be* s." 2616
11: 5 "The king of the South *will become* s, 2616
Joel 3:10 Let the weakling say, "I am s!" 1475
Am 2: 9 he was tall as the cedars and s as the oaks. 2891
2:14 the s will not muster their strength, 2617
5: 3 "The city that marches out a thousand s NIH
5: 3 a hundred s will have only ten left." NIH
8:13 **s young men** will faint because of thirst. 1033
Mic 4: 3 and will settle disputes for s nations far 6786
4: 7 those driven away a s nation. 6786
Hag 2: 4 *be* s, O Zerubbabel,' declares the LORD. 2616
2: 4 '*Be* s, O Joshua son of Jehozadak, 2616
2: 4 *Be* s, all you people of the land,' 2616
Zec 8: 9 *let* your hands *be* s so that the temple may 2616
8:13 Do not be afraid, but *let* your hands *be* s." 2616
12: 5 'The people of Jerusalem are s, 602
Mt 12:29 how can anyone enter a s *man's* house *2708*
12:29 unless he first ties up the s *man?* *2708*
Mk 1:43 sent him away at once *with* a s **warning:** *1839*
3:27 no one can enter a s *man's* house *2708*
3:27 unless he first ties up the s *man.* *2708*
5: 4 No one *was* s enough to subdue him. *2710*
Lk 1:80 And the child grew and *became* s in spirit; *3194*
2:40 And the child grew and **became** s; *3194*
11:21 "When a s *man,* fully armed, *2708*
16: 3 *I'm* not s enough to dig, *2710*
Jn 6:18 A s wind was blowing and *3489*
Ac 3: 7 the man's feet and ankles *became* s. *5105*
3:16 whom you see and know *was made* s. *5105*
Ro 1:11 to you some spiritual gift to **make** you s— *5114*
15: 1 We who are s ought to bear with *1543*
1Co 1: 8 He *will* **keep** you s to the end, *1011*
1:27 the weak things of the world to shame the s. *2708*
4:10 We are weak, but you are s! *2708*
16:13 be men of courage; *be* s. *3194*
2Co 12:10 For when I am weak, then I am s. *1543*
13: 9 whenever we are weak but you are s; *1543*
Eph 6:10 *be* s in the Lord and in his mighty power. *1904*
1Th 2: 2 tell you his gospel in spite of s opposition. *4498*
2Ti 2: 1 *be* s in the grace that is in Christ Jesus. *1904*
Jas 3: 4 they are so large and are driven by s winds, *5017*
1Pe 5:10 *will* himself restore you and **make** you s, *5114*
1Jn 2:14 young men, because you are s, *2708*
Rev 6:13 from a fig tree when shaken by a s wind. *3489*
12: 8 But *he was* not s enough, *2710*

STRONGER (30) [STRONG]

Ge 25:23 one people *will be* s than the other, 599
30:41 Whenever the s *females* were in heat, 8003
Nu 13:31 they are s than we are." 2617
14:12 into a nation greater and s than they." 6786
Dt 1:28 'The people are s and taller than we are; 1524
4:38 before you nations greater and s than you 6786
7: 1 seven nations larger and s than you— 6786
7:17 "These nations are s than we are. 8041
9: 1 dispossess nations greater and s than you, 6786
9:14 a nation s and more numerous than they." 6786
11:23 dispossess nations larger and s than you. 6786
Jos 17:13 However, when the Israelites *grew* s, 2616
Jdg 4:24 Israelites **grew s and stronger** 2143+2256+7997
4:24 Israelites **grew stronger and** s 2143+2256+7997
14:18 What is s than a lion?" 6434
2Sa 1:23 *they were* s than lions. 1504
3: 1 David **grew** s **and stronger,** 2143+2256+2618
3: 1 David **grew stronger and** s, 2143+2256+2618
13:14 and since *he was* s than she, he raped her. 2616
1Ki 16:22 But Omri's followers **proved** s *than* those 2616
20:23 surely *we will be* s than they. 2616
20:25 Then surely *we will be* s than they." 2616
Job 17: 9 and *those with* clean hands *will* **grow** s. 601+3578
Ecc 6:10 with one who is s than he. 9544
Jer 31:11 from the hand of *those* s than they. 2617
Da 11: 5 *even* s than he and will rule his own 2616
Lk 11:22 *someone* s attacks and overpowers him, *2708*
1Co 1:25 weakness of God is s *than* man's strength. *2708*
10:22 Are we s **than** he? *2708*
2Pe 2:11 although they are s and more powerful, *2709*

STRONGEST (3) [STRONG]

2Sa 11:16 where he knew the s **defenders** were. 408+2657
1Ch 5: 2 and though Judah *was the* s of his brothers 1504
Da 3:20 commanded some of the s **soldiers** 10132+10264

STRONGHOLD (31) [STRONGHOLDS]

Jdg 9:46 in the tower of Shechem went into the s *of* 7663
9:49 They piled them against the s and set it 7663
1Sa 22: 4 with him as long as David was in the s. 5181
22: 5 "Do not stay in the s. 5181
24:22 but David and his men went up to the s. 5181
2Sa 5:17 about it and went down to the s. 5181
22: 3 He is my s, my refuge and my savior— 5369
23:14 At that time David was in the s, 5181
1Ch 11:16 At that time David was in the s, 5181
12: 8 Some Gadites defected to David at his s in 5171
12:16 from Judah also came to David in his s. 5171
Job 39:28 a rocky crag is his s. 5181
Ps 9: 9 for the oppressed, a s in times of trouble. 5369
18: 2 and the horn of my salvation, my s. 5369
27: 1 The LORD is the s *of* my life— 5057
37:39 he is their s in time of trouble. 5057
43: 2 You are God my s. 5057
52: 7 is the man who did not make God his s 5057
144: 2 my s and my deliverer, my shield, 5369
Pr 21:22 the city of the mighty and pulls down the s 6437
Isa 25: 2 the foreigners' s a city no more; 810
31: 9 Their s will fall because of terror; 6152
Jer 48: 1 the s will be disgraced and shattered. 5369
51:53 reaches the sky and fortifies her lofty s, 6437
Eze 24:21 the s *in which* you take pride, 6437
24:25 son of man, on the day I take away their s, 5057
30:15 my wrath on Pelusium, the s *of* Egypt, 5057
Joel 3:16 a s for the people of Israel. 5057
Am 5: 9 he flashes destruction on the s and 6434
Mic 4: 8 O s *of* the Daughter of Zion, 6755
Zec 9: 3 Tyre has built herself a s; 5190

STRONGHOLDS (19) [STRONGHOLD]

Jdg 6: 2 in mountain clefts, caves and s. 5171
1Sa 23:14 David stayed in the desert s and in the hills 5171
23:19 "Is not David hiding among us in the s 5171
23:29 up from there and lived in the s *of* En Gedi. 5171
2Sa 22:46 they come trembling from their s. 4995
Ps 18:45 they come trembling from their s. 4995
89:40 through all his walls and reduced his s 4448
Isa 13:22 Hyenas will howl in her s, 528
34:13 nettles and brambles her s. 4448
Jer 48:41 Kerioth will be captured and the s taken. 5171
51:30 they remain in their s. 5171
La 2: 2 in his wrath he has torn down the s *of* 4448
2: 5 up all her palaces and destroyed her s. 4448
Eze 19: 7 down their s and devastated their towns. 810
33:27 and those in s and caves will die of 5171
Am 3:11 down your s and plunder your fortresses." 6437
Mic 5:11 of your land and tear down all your s. 4448
Zep 3: 6 their s are demolished. 7157
2Co 10: 4 they have divine power to demolish s. *4065*

STRONGLY (4) [STRONG]

Ge 19: 3 But he insisted *so* s that they did go 4394
Lk 24:29 But *they* **urged** him s, "Stay with us, *4128*
1Co 16:12 I s urged him to go to you with the brothers. *4498*
2Ti 4:15 because he s opposed our message. *3336*

STRUCK (146) [STRIKE]

Ge 19:11 Then *they* s the men who were at the door 5782
Ex 7:20 and his officials and s the water of the Nile, 5782
7:25 Seven days passed after the LORD s 5782
8:17 with the staff and s the dust of the ground, 5782
9:15 and s you and your people with a plague 5782
9:25 Throughout Egypt hail s everything in 5782
12:27 and spared our homes when he s **down** 5597
12:29 the LORD **s down** all the firstborn 5782
17: 5 in your hand the staff with which *you* s 5782
21:19 the *one who* **s the blow** will not 5782
22: 2 "If a thief is caught breaking in and **is s** so 5782
32:35 the LORD **s** the people **with a plague** 5597
Nu 3:13 When I **s down** all the firstborn in Egypt, 5782
8:17 When I **s down** all the firstborn in Egypt, 5782
11:33 and he s them *with* a severe plague. 5782
14:37 the land *were* **s down and died** of a plague 4637
20:11 and s the rock twice with his staff. 5782
21:35 So *they* s him **down,** 5782
24:10 *He* s his hands **together** and said to him, 6215
31:16 so that a plague s the LORD's people. 928+2118
33: 4 whom the LORD *had* **s down** among them; 5782
Dt 2:33 over to us and *we* s him **down,** 5782
3: 3 *We* s them **down,** leaving no survivors. 5782
Jos 7: 5 as far as the stone quarries and s them **down** 5782
10:26 Then Joshua s and killed the kings 5782
11:17 and s them **down,** 5782
Jdg 1: 4 and *they* **s down** ten thousand men at Bezek. 5782
3:29 At that time *they* **s down** 5782
3:31 *who* **s down** six hundred Philistines with 5782
5:26 *She* s Sisera, she crushed his head, 2150
7:13 *It* s the tent with such force that 5782
9:44 upon those in the fields and s them **down.** 5782
12: 4 The Gileadites s them **down** because 5782
14:19 **s down** thirty of their men, 5782
15:15 he grabbed it and **s down** a thousand men. 5782
20:35 and on that day the Israelites **s down** 25,100 8845
20:45 the Benjamites as far as Gidom and **s down** 5782
1Sa 4: 8 the gods who s the Egyptians with all kinds 5782
6: 4 same plague has s both you and your rulers. 4200
6: 9 not his hand that s us and that it happened 5595
6:19 But God **s down** some of the men 5782
14:15 Then panic s the whole army— 928+2118
14:31 the Israelites *had* **s down** the Philistines 5782
17:35 s it and rescued the sheep from its mouth. 5782
17:35 I seized it by its hair, s it and killed it. 5782
17:49 and s the Philistine on the forehead. 5782
17:50 a sword in his hand *he* **s down** the Philistine 5782
19: 8 *He* s them *with* such force that they fled 5782
22:18 Doeg the Edomite turned and s them **down.** 7003
25:38 the LORD s Nabal and he died. 5597
2Sa 1:15 So *he* s him **down,** and he died. 5782
5:25 and *he* **s down** the Philistines all the way 5782

2Sa 6: 7 therefore God s him **down** and he died there 5782
8: 5 David s **down** twenty-two thousand of them 5782
10:18 *He* also s **down** Shobach the commander 5782
11:15 from him so *he will* **be s down** and die." 5782
12: 9 *You* s **down** Uriah the Hittite with the sword 5782
12:15 the LORD s the child that Uriah's wife had 5597
13:30 "Absalom *has* s **down** all the king's sons; 5782
14: 6 One s the other and killed him. 5782
14: 7 'Hand over the *one who* s his brother **down,** 5782
18:15 surrounded Absalom, s him and killed him. 5782
21:12 after they s Saul **down** on Gilboa.) 5782
21:17 *he* s the Philistine **down** and killed him. 5782
23:10 but he stood his ground and s **down** 5782
23:12 He defended it and s the Philistines **down,** 5782
23:20 He s **down** two of Moab's best men. 5782
23:21 And he s **down** a huge Egyptian. 5782
1Ki 2:25 and *he* s **down** Adonijah and he died. 7003
2:34 of Jehoiada went up and s **down** Joab 7003
2:46 and he went out and s Shimei **down** 7003
11:15 *had* s **down** all the men in Edom. 5782
15:27 and he s him **down** at Gibbethon, 5782
16:10 Zimri came in, s him **down** and killed him 5782
20:20 and each one s **down** his opponent. 5782
20:37 So the man s him and wounded him. 5782+5782
2Ki 2: 8 rolled it up and s the water with it. 5782
2:14 that had fallen from him and s the water 5782
2:14 When *he* s the water, it divided 5782
6:18 So *he* s them with blindness, 5782
13:18 *He* s it three times and stopped. 5782
13:19 "You *should have* s the ground five 5782
1Ch 11:14 They defended it and s the Philistines **down,** 5782
11:22 He s **down** two of Moab's best men. 5782
11:23 And he s **down** an Egyptian who was 5782
13:10 burned against Uzzah, and *he* s him **down** 5782
14:16 and *they* s **down** the Philistine army, 5782
18: 5 David s **down** twenty-two thousand of them 5782
18:12 Abishai son of Zeruiah s **down** 5782
2Ch 13:20 And the LORD s him **down** and he died. 5597
14:12 The LORD s **down** the Cushites before Asa 5597
25:16 Stop! Why *be* s **down?"** 5782
Est 9: 5 The Jews s **down** all their enemies 4804+5782
Job 1:19 in from the desert and s the four corners of 5595
19:21 have pity, for the hand of God *has* s me. 5595
Ps 60: T and s **down** twelve thousand Edomites in 5782
64: 7 suddenly they will be s **down.** 4804
78:20 When *he* s the rock, water gushed out, 5782
78:51 *He* s **down** all the firstborn of Egypt, 5782
105:33 *he* s **down** their vines and fig trees 5782
105:36 *he* s **down** all the firstborn in their land, 5782
135: 8 He s **down** the firstborn of Egypt, 5782
135:10 He s **down** many nations 5782
136:10 to *him who* s **down** the firstborn 5782
136:17 *who* s **down** great kings, 5782
Pr 6: 1 if *you have* s hands **in pledge** for another, 9546
Isa 9:13 people have not returned to him *who* s them, 5782
10:20 will no longer rely on *him who* s them **down** 5782
10:26 when he s **down** Midian at the rock of Oreb; 4804
14: 6 *which* in anger s **down** peoples 5782
14:29 that the rod *that* s you is broken; 5782
27: 7 *Has* [the LORD] s her as he struck 5782
27: 7 Has [the LORD] struck her as he s **down** 4804
27: 7 as he struck down *those who* s her? 5782
60:10 Though in anger *I* s you, 5782
Jer 5: 3 *You* s them, but they felt no pain; 5782
26:23 *who* **had** him s **down** with a sword 5782
30:14 *I have* s you as an enemy would 5782
41: 2 with him got up and s **down** Gedaliah son 5782
Da 2:34 *It* s the statue on its feet of iron and clay 10411
2:35 that s the statue became a huge mountain 10411
Am 4: 9 "Many times *I* s your gardens 5782
4: 9 I s them with blight and mildew. NIH
Hag 2:17 *I* s all the work of your hands with blight, 5782
Zec 13: 8 "two-thirds *will* **be s down** and perish; 4162
Mt 26:51 and s the servant of the high priest, *4250*
26:67 s him **with** *their* **fists.** *3139*
27:30 and s him on the head again and again. *5597*
Mk 12: 4 s this man **on the head** *3052*
14:47 of those standing near drew his sword and s *4091*
14:65 s him **with their fists,** *3139*
15:19 *Again and again they* s him on the head *5597*
Lk 6:48 torrent s that house but could not shake it, *4703*
6:49 The moment the torrent s that house, *4703*
22:50 one of them s the servant of the high priest, *4250*
Jn 18:10 drew it and s the high priest's servant, *4091*
18:22 one of the officials nearby s him **in the face.** *1443+4825*
19: 3 And *they* s him **in the face.** *1443+4825*
Ac 7:11 Then a famine s all Egypt and Canaan, *2093+2262*
12: 7 He s Peter on the side and woke him up. *4250*
12:23 an angel of the Lord s him **down,** *4250*
23: 3 violate the law by commanding that I *be* s!" *5597*
27:41 But the ship s a sandbar and ran aground. *4346*
2Co 4: 9 s **down,** but not destroyed. *2850*
Rev 8:12 and a third of the sun *was* s, *4448*
11:11 and terror s those who saw them. *2158*

STRUCTURE (7) [STRUCTURES]
1Ki 6: 5 he built a s around the building, 3666
1Ch 29: 1 this **palatial** s is not for man but for the LORD God. 1072
29:19 to do everything to build the **palatial** s 1072
Ezr 5: 3 to rebuild this temple and restore this **s?"** 10082
5: 9 to rebuild this temple and restore this **s?"** 10082
Eze 1:16 the appearance and s *of* the wheels: 5126
41: 7 The *s* **surrounding** the temple was built AIT

STRUCTURES (1) [STRUCTURE]
1Ki 7: 9 All **these** *s,* from the outside to the great AIT

STRUGGLE (8) [STRUGGLED, STRUGGLES, STRUGGLING]
Ge 30: 8 *"I have* **had a** great s with my sister, 5887+7349
Jdg 12: 2 "I and my people were engaged in a great s 8190
Job 9:29 why *should I* s in vain? 3333
41: 8 will remember the s and never do it again! 4878
Ro 15:30 **join** me **in** my s by praying to God for me. *5253*
Eph 6:12 For our s is not against flesh and blood, *4097*
Php 1:30 through the same s you saw I had, *74*
Heb 12: 4 *In your* s against sin, you have not yet *497*

STRUGGLED (3) [STRUGGLE]
Ge 32:28 because *you have* s with God and with men 8575
Hos 12: 3 as a man *he* s with God. 8575
12: 4 *He* s with the angel and overcame him; 8575

STRUGGLES (1) [STRUGGLE]
Ps 73: 4 They have no s; their bodies are healthy and 3078

STRUGGLING (2) [STRUGGLE]
Col 1:29 To this end I labor, s with all his energy, *76*
2: 1 how much I am s for you and for those *74*

STRUM (1)
Am 6: 5 *You* s **away** on your harps like David 7260

STRUNG (2) [STRING]
Isa 5:28 Their arrows are sharp, all their bows *are* s; 2005
La 2: 4 Like an enemy *he has* s his bow; 2005

STRUT (1) [STRUTTING]
Ps 12: 8 The wicked **freely** s about when what is vile 2143

STRUTTING (1) [STRUT]
Pr 30:31 a s **rooster,** a he-goat, and a king 2435+5516

STUBBLE (7)
Ex 5:12 over Egypt to gather s to use for straw. 7990
15: 7 it consumed them like **s.** 7990
Isa 47:14 they are like s; the fire will burn them up. 7990
Joel 2: 5 like a crackling fire consuming **s,** 7990
Ob 1:18 the house of Esau will be s, 7990
Na 1:10 they will be consumed like dry s. 7990
Mal 4: 1 the arrogant and every evildoer will be s, 7990

STUBBORN (15) [STUBBORN-HEARTED, STUBBORNLY, STUBBORNNESS]
Lev 26:19 I will break down your s pride and make 6437
Dt 2:30 the LORD your God *had* **made** his spirit s 7996
21:18 a man has a s and rebellious son who does 6253
21:20 "This son of ours *is* s and rebellious. 6253
Jdg 2:19 to give up their evil practices and s ways. 7997
Ps 78: 8 a s and rebellious generation, 6253
81:12 to their s hearts to follow their own devices. 9244
Isa 48: 4 For I knew how s you were; 7997
Jer 5:23 these people have s and rebellious hearts; 6253
7:24 instead, they followed the s inclinations 9244
Eze 2: 4 The people to whom I am sending you are obstinate and s. 2617+4213
Hos 4:16 The Israelites *are* s, like a stubborn heifer. 6253
4:16 The Israelites are stubborn, like a s heifer. 6253
Mk 3: 5 deeply distressed at their s hearts, *4801*
16:14 for their lack of faith and their s **refusal** *5016*

STUBBORN-HEARTED (1) [HEART, STUBBORN]
Isa 46:12 Listen to me, you s, you who are far 52+4213

STUBBORNLY (3) [STUBBORN]
Ex 13:15 When Pharaoh s **refused** to let us go, 7996
Ne 9:29 S they turned their backs on you, 6253
Zec 7:11 s they turned **their backs** and stopped 6253

STUBBORNNESS (9) [STUBBORN]
Dt 9:27 Overlook the s *of* this people, 8001
Jer 3:17 No longer will they follow the s *of* their 9244
9:14 they have followed the s *of* their hearts; 9244
11: 8 they followed the s *of* their evil hearts. 9244
13:10 the s *of* their hearts and go after other gods 9244
16:12 See how each of you is following the s *of* 9244
18:12 of us will follow the s *of* his evil heart.' " 9244
23:17 who follow the s *of* their hearts they say, 9244
Ro 2: 5 of your s and your unrepentant heart, *5018*

STUBS (1)
Isa 7: 4 of these two smoldering s *of* firewood— 2387

STUCK (3) [STICK]
1Sa 26: 7 with his spear s in the ground near his head. 5080
Job 29:10 their tongues s to the roof of their mouths. 1815
Ac 27:41 The bow s **fast** and would not move, *2242*

STUDDED (1)
SS 1:11 earrings of gold, s with silver. 5925

STUDENT (4) [STUDY]
1Ch 25: 8 Young and old alike, teacher as well as s, 9441
Mt 10:24 "A s is not above his teacher, *3412*
10:25 It is enough *for* the s to be like his teacher, *3412*
Lk 6:40 A s is not above his teacher, *3412*

STUDIED (1) [STUDY]
Jn 7:15 "How did this man get such learning without *having* **s?"** *3443*

STUDY (4) [STUDENT, STUDIED]
Ezr 7:10 s and observance of the Law of the LORD, 2011
Ecc 1:13 I devoted myself to s and to explore 2011
12:12 and much s wearies the body. 4261
Jn 5:39 *You* **diligently** s the Scriptures because *2236*

STUDY (KJV) See also DO BEST

STUFF (KJV) See BAGGAGE, BELONGINGS, GOODS, POSSESSIONS, SUPPLIES, THINGS

STUMBLE (43) [STUMBLED, STUMBLES, STUMBLING]
Lev 26:37 *They will* s over one another as though 4173
Ps 9: 3 *they* s and perish before you. 4173
27: 2 they *will* s and fall. 4173
37:24 though *he* s, he will not fall, for the LORD 5877
119:165 and nothing can **make** them **s.** 4842
Pr 3:23 and your foot *will* not s; 5597
4:12 when you run, *you will* not **s.** 4173
4:19 they do not know what *makes them* **s.** 4173
Isa 8:14 be a stone that **causes** men **to** s and a rock 5598
8:15 Many of them *will* s; they will fall 4173
28: 7 *they* s when rendering decisions. 7048
31: 3 he who helps *will* s, 4173
40:30 and young men s **and fall;** 4173+4173
59:10 At midday *we* s as if it were twilight; 4173
63:13 Like a horse in open country, *they did* not s; 4173
Jer 6:21 Fathers and sons alike *will* s over them; 4173
12: 5 If you s in safe country, 1054
13:16 before your feet s on the darkening hills. 5597
18:15 *which* **made** them s in their ways and in 4173
20:11 so my persecutors *will* s and not prevail. 4173
31: 9 on a level path where *they will* not s, 4173
46: 6 In the north by the River Euphrates *they* s 4173
46:12 One warrior *will* s over another; 4173
46:16 They will s repeatedly; 4173
50:32 The arrogant one *will* s and fall 4173
Eze 7:19 for it has made them s *into* sin. 4842
Da 11:19 the fortresses of his own country but *will* s 4173
11:35 Some of the wise *will* s, 4173
Hos 4: 5 *You* s day and night, 4173
4: 5 and the prophets s with you. 4173
5: 5 the Israelites, even Ephraim, s in their sin; 4173
14: 9 but the rebellious s in them. 4173
Na 2: 5 yet *they* s on their way. 4173
Mal 2: 8 by your teaching *have* **caused** many **to s;** 4173
Jn 11: 9 A man who walks by day *will* not s, *4684*
Ro 9:33 I lay in Zion a stone that **causes men to** s *4682*
11:11 *Did they* s so as to fall beyond recovery? *4760*
14:20 that causes someone else to s. *4682*
1Co 10:32 *Do* **not cause** anyone **to** s, whether Jews, *718*
Jas 3: 2 *We* all s **in** many ways. *4760*
1Pe 2: 8 "A stone that **causes men to** s and a rock *4682*
2: 8 They s because they disobey the message— *4684*
1Jn 2:10 and there is nothing in him to make him **s.** *4998*

STUMBLED (8) [STUMBLE]
1Sa 2: 4 but *those who* s are armed with strength. 4173
2Sa 6: 6 because the oxen **s.** 9023
1Ch 13: 9 because the oxen **s.** 9023
Job 4: 4 Your words have supported *those who* **s;** 4173
Ps 35:15 But when I s, they gathered in glee; 7520
107:12 *they* **s,** and there was no one to help. 4173
Isa 59:14 truth *has* s in the streets, 4173
Ro 9:32 *They* **s over** the "stumbling stone." *4684*

STUMBLES (5) [STUMBLE]
Pr 24:17 when he **s,** do not let your heart rejoice, 4173
Isa 5:27 Not one of them grows tired or **s,** 4173
Hos 5: 5 Judah also s with them. 4173
Jn 11:10 It is when he walks by night that *he* **s,** *4684*
Jas 2:10 For whoever keeps the whole law and yet s *4760*

STUMBLING (15) [STUMBLE]
Lev 19:14 not curse the deaf or put a s **block** in front 4842
Ps 56:13 from death and my feet from **s,** 1892
116: 8 my eyes from tears, my feet from **s,** 1892
Eze 3:20 and I put a s **block** before him, he will die. 4842
14: 3 and put wicked **s blocks** before their faces. 4842
14: 4 and puts a wicked **s block** before his face 4842
14: 7 and puts a wicked **s block** before his face 4842
Na 3: 3 *people* s over the corpses— 4173
Mt 16:23 You are a **s block** to me; *4998*
Ro 9:32 They stumbled over the **"s** stone." *4682*

Ro 11: 9 a s **block** and a retribution for them. *4998*
14:13 make up your mind not to put any s **block** *4682*
1Co 1:23 a s **block** to Jews and foolishness to *4998*
8: 9 of your freedom does not become a s **block** *4682*
2Co 6: 3 We put no s **block** in anyone's path, *4683*

STUMP (6) [STUMPS]
Job 14: 8 in the ground and its s die in the soil, 1614
Isa 6:13 so the holy seed will be the s *in* the land." 5169
11: 1 A shoot will come up from the s *of* Jesse; 1614
Da 4:15 But let the s and its roots, 10567
4:23 but leave the s, bound with iron and bronze, 10567
4:26 The command to leave the s of the tree 10567

STUMPS (1) [STUMP]
Isa 6:13 and oak leave s when they are cut down, 5169

STUNNED (2)
Ge 45:26 Jacob *was* s; he did not believe them. 4213+7028
Isa 29: 9 *Be* s and amazed, blind yourselves and 9449

STUNTED (1)
Lev 22:23 an ox or a sheep that is deformed or s, 7832

STUPID (4) [STUPIDITY]
Job 18: 3 as cattle and **considered** s in your sight? 3241
Pr 12: 1 but he who hates correction is s. 1280
Ecc 10: 3 and shows everyone *how* s he is. 6119
2Ti 2:23 to do with foolish and s arguments, *553*

STUPIDITY (1) [STUPID]
Ecc 7:25 and to understand the s of wickedness and 4073

STUPOR (2)
Ps 78:65 as a man **wakes from** *the* s of wine. 8130
Ro 11: 8 "God gave them a spirit *of* s, *2919*

STURDIEST (1) [STURDY]
Ps 78:31 he put to death the s among them, 5458

STURDY (1) [STURDIEST]
Isa 10:16 a wasting disease upon his s *warriors;* 5458

SUAH (1)
1Ch 7:36 The sons of Zophah: **S**, Harnepher, Shual, 6053

SUBDIVISION (1) [DIVIDE]
2Ch 35: 5 a group of Levites for *each* s *of* the families 7107

SUBDIVISIONS (1) [DIVIDE]
2Ch 35:12 the s of the families of the people to offer to 5141

SUBDUE (10) [SUBDUED, SUBDUES, SUBDUING]
Ge 1:28 increase in number; fill the earth and s it. 3899
Nu 24:24 *they will* s Asshur and Eber, 6700
Dt 9: 3 he *will* s them before you. 4044
Jdg 16: 5 so we may tie him up and s him. 6700
16:19 and so began to s him. 6700
1Ch 17:10 *I will* also s all your enemies. 4044
Ps 81:14 how quickly *would I* s their enemies 4044
Isa 45: 1 to s nations before him and to strip kings 3718
Da 7:24 *he will* s three kings. 10737
Mk 5: 4 No one was strong enough *to* s him. *1238*

SUBDUED (19) [SUBDUE]
Nu 32: 4 the LORD s before the people of Israel— 5782
32:22 then when the land **is** s before the LORD, 3899
32:29 then when the land **is** s before you, 3899
Jos 10:40 So Joshua s the whole region, 5782
10:41 Joshua s them from Kadesh Barnea to Gaza 5782
Jdg 4:23 On that day God s Jabin, 4044
8:28 Thus Midian **was** s before the Israelites 4044
11:33 Thus Israel s Ammon. 4044
16: 6 and how you can be tied up and **s."** 6700
1Sa 7:13 So the Philistines **were** s and did 4044
2Sa 8: 1 David defeated the Philistines and s them, 4044
8:11 and gold from all the nations *he had* **s:** 3899
1Ch 18: 1 David defeated the Philistines and s them, 4044
2Ch 13:18 The men of Israel **were** s on that occasion, 4044
Ne 9:24 *You* s before them the Canaanites, 4044
Ps 47: 3 *He* s nations under us, 1818
Isa 10:13 like a mighty one *I* s their kings. 3718
14: 6 in fury s nations with relentless aggression. 8097
Zec 10:11 the surging sea *will be* s and all the depths 5782

SUBDUES (3) [SUBDUE]
Ps 18:47 *who* s nations under me, 1818
144: 2 who s peoples under me. 8096
Isa 41: 2 He hands nations over to him and s kings 8097

SUBDUING (1) [SUBDUE]
Job 41: 9 Any hope of s him is false; NIH

SUBJECT (42) [SUBJECTED, SUBJECTING, SUBJECTS]
Ge 14: 4 *For* twelve years *they had been* **s to** 6268
Dt 20:11 all the people in it shall be **s to** forced labor 4200
Jdg 1:30 but they did s them to forced labor. NIH
3: 8 **to** whom the Israelites *were* s for eight years 6268
3:14 The Israelites *were* s to Eglon king of Moab 6268
3:30 Moab *was* **made** s to Israel, 3338+4044+9393
9:28 Shechem, that *we should be* **s to** him? 6268
9:38 'Who is Abimelech that *we should be* **s to** 6268
1Sa 4: 9 Be men, or *you will be* s to the Hebrews, 6268
11: 1 and *we will be* **s to** you." 6268
2Sa 8: 2 So the Moabites became s to David 6269
8: 6 and the Arameans became s to him 6269
8:14 and all the Edomites became s to David. 6269
10:19 with the Israelites and *became* s *to* them. 6268
22:44 People I did not know *are* **s** to me, 6268
1Ch 18: 2 they became s to him and brought tribute. 6269
18: 6 and the Arameans became s to him 6269
18:13 and all the Edomites became s to David. 6269
19:19 they made peace with David and *became* s 6268
22:18 land **is** s to the LORD and to his people. 3899
2Ch 12: 8 They will, however, become s to him, 6269
Ne 5: 5 yet we *have to* s our sons and daughters 3899
Ps 18:43 people I did not know *are* **s** to me. 6268
89:22 No enemy *will* s him **to tribute;** 5957
Isa 11:14 and the Ammonites will be **s to** them. 5463
Jer 27: 6 I will make even the wild animals **s to** him. 6268
Mt 5:21 and anyone who murders will be s *1944*
5:22 with his brother will be s to judgment. *1944*
9:20 then a woman *who had been* **s to bleeding** *137*
Mk 5:25 woman was there who had been **s to**
bleeding for twelve years. *135+1877+4868*
Lk 8:43 woman was there who had been **s to**
bleeding for twelve years. *135+1877+4868*
Ac 17:32 "We want to hear you again on **this** *s*." *AIT*
1Co 2:15 he himself is not **s to** any man's judgment: *5679*
14:32 The spirits of prophets *are* **s to the control** *5718*
15:28 *be made* s to him who put everything *5718*
Gal 4: 2 He is **s to** guardians and trustees until *5679*
Tit 2: 5 to be kind, and to be s to their husbands, *5718*
2: 9 *to be* s to their masters in everything, *5718*
3: 1 the people *to be* s to rulers and authorities, *5718*
Heb 2: 8 God left nothing that is **not** s to him. *538*
2: 8 Yet at present we do not see everything s *5718*
5: 2 since *he* himself *is* **s to** weakness. *4329*

SUBJECTED (7) [SUBJECT]
Jos 17:13 *they* s the Canaanites to forced labor 5989
Ezr 9: 7 and our kings and our priests *have* **been** s 5989
Ps 106:42 Their enemies oppressed them and s *them* 4044
107:12 So *he* s them to bitter labor; 4044
Ro 8:20 For the creation *was* s to frustration, *5718*
8:20 but by the will of the one who s it, *5718*
Heb 2: 5 to angels that *he has* s the world to come, *5718*

SUBJECTING (1) [SUBJECT]
Heb 6: 6 and s him **to public disgrace.** *4136*

SUBJECTION (KJV) See SUBMISSIVE

SUBJECTS (7) [SUBJECT]
1Sa 17: 9 we will become your **s;** 6269
17: 9 you will become our s and serve us." 6269
1Ki 4:21 and *were* Solomon's s all his life. 6268
1Ch 21: 3 are they not all my lord's **s?** 6269
Pr 14:28 but without s a prince is ruined. 4211
Mt 8:12 s of the kingdom will be thrown outside, *5626*
Lk 19:14 "But his s hated him and sent a delegation *4489*

SUBJUGATE (1) [SUBJUGATED]
Jer 27: 7 and great kings *will* s him. 6268

SUBJUGATED (1) [SUBJUGATE]
1Ch 20: 4 and the Philistines **were s.** 4044

SUBMISSION (6) [SUBMIT]
1Ch 29:24 pledged their s *to* King Solomon. 9393
Da 11:43 with the Libyans and Nubians in **s.** 5202
1Co 14:34 but *must be* **in s,** as the Law says. *5718*
1Ti 2:11 woman should learn in quietness and full **s.** *5717*
Heb 5: 7 and he was heard because of his reverent **s.** *NIG*
1Pe 3:22 authorities and powers in **s** to him. *5718*

SUBMISSIVE (4) [SUBMIT]
Jas 3:17 then peace-loving, considerate, s, *2340*
1Pe 3: 1 the same way *be* s to your husbands so that, *5718*
3: 5 *They were* s to their own husbands, *5718*
5: 5 the same way *be* s to those who are older. *5718*

SUBMIT (24) [SUBMISSION, SUBMISSIVE, SUBMITS, SUBMITTED]
Ge 16: 9 "Go back to your mistress and s to her." 6700
41:40 and all my people are *to* s to your orders. 5976
49:15 to the burden and s to forced labor. 6268
2Ch 30: 8 as your fathers were; s to the LORD. 3338+5989
Job 22:21 "S to God and be at peace with him; 6122
Ps 68:31 Cush *will* s herself to God. 3338+8132
81:11 Israel *would* not s to me. 14
Lk 10:17 even the demons s to us in your name." *5718*
10:20 do not rejoice that the spirits s to you, *5718*
Ro 8: 7 *It does* not s to God's law, *5718*
10: 3 *they did* not s to God's righteousness. *5718*
13: 1 Everyone *must* s *himself* to *5718*
13: 5 it is necessary *to* s to the authorities, *5718*
1Co 16:16 to s to such as these and to everyone who *5718*
Eph 5:21 S to one another out of reverence *5718*
5:22 Wives, s to your husbands as to the Lord. *NIG*
5:24 so also wives should s to their husbands *NIG*
Col 2:20 *do you* **s to** its **rules:** *1505*
3:18 Wives, s to your husbands, as is fitting *5718*
Heb 12: 9 How much more *should we* s to the Father *5718*
13:17 Obey your leaders and s to their authority. *5640*
Jas 4: 7 S *yourselves*, then, to God. *5718*
1Pe 2:13 S *yourselves* for the Lord's sake to every *5718*
2:18 Slaves, s *yourselves* to your masters *5718*

SUBMITS (1) [SUBMIT]
Eph 5:24 Now as the church s to Christ, *5718*

SUBMITTED (1) [SUBMIT]
La 5: 6 *We* s *to* Egypt and Assyria 3338+5989

SUBORDINATES (1)
1Ki 11:11 from you and give it to one of your s. 6269

SUBORNED (KJV) See SECRETLY PERSUADED

SUBSCRIBE (KJV) See SIGNED, WRITE

SUBSIDE (3) [SUBSIDED, SUBSIDES]
Eze 5:13 and my wrath against them *will* s, 5663
16:42 Then my wrath against you *will* s 5663
21:17 and my wrath *will* s. 5663

SUBSIDED (5) [SUBSIDE]
Jdg 8: 3 At this, their resentment against him **s.** 8332
Est 2: 1 Later when the anger of King Xerxes *had* s, 8896
7:10 Then the king's fury s. 8896
Eze 24:13 until my wrath against you *has* **s.** 5663
Lk 8:24 the storm **s,** and all was calm. *4264*

SUBSIDES (1) [SUBSIDE]
Ge 27:44 for a while until your brother's fury **s.** 8740

SUBSTANCE (1)
Da 7: 1 He wrote down the s of his dream. 10418+10646

SUBSTITUTE (4) [SUBSTITUTION]
Lev 27:10 He must not exchange it or s a good one for 4614
27:10 if *he should* s one animal for another, 4614+4614
27:10 both it and the s become holy. 9455
27:33 both the animal and its s become holy 9455

SUBSTITUTION (2) [SUBSTITUTE]
Lev 27:33 the good from the bad or **make** any s. 4614
27:33 If *he does* **make a s,** 4614+4614

SUBTIL (KJV) See CRAFTY

SUBTRACT (1)
Dt 4: 2 not add to what I command you and *do* not s 1757

SUBURBS (KJV) See FARM LANDS, OPEN LAND, PASTURELAND, SHORELANDS

SUBVERT (KJV) See DEPRIVE, RUINING

SUBVERTING (1)
Lk 23: 2 "We have found this man s our nation. *1406*

SUCATHITES (1)
1Ch 2:55 the Tirathites, Shimeathites and **S.** 8460

SUCCEED (28) [SUCCEEDED, SUCCEEDS, SUCCESS, SUCCESSFUL, SUCCESSFULLY, SUCCESSIVE, SUCCESSOR, SUCCESSORS]
Lev 6:22 to s him as anointed priest shall prepare it. 9393
16:32 and ordained to s his father as high priest is 9393
Nu 14:41 This *will* not **s!** 7503
1Sa 30: 8 overtake them and s **in the rescue."** 5911+5911
2Sa 7:12 I will raise up your offspring to s you, 339
1Ki 5: 1 anointed king to s his father David, 9393
15: 4 to s him and by making Jerusalem strong. 339
19:16 from Abel Meholah to s you as prophet. 9393
22:22 " *'You will* s in enticing him,' 3523
2Ki 3:27 firstborn son, who was to s him as king, 9393
1Ch 17:11 I will raise up your offspring to s you, 339
2Ch 13:12 the God of your fathers, for *you will* not **s."** 7503
18:21 " *'You will* s in enticing him,' 3523
Job 30:13 *they* s in destroying me— 3603

Ps 20: 4 and **make** all your plans **s.** 4848
21:11 and devise wicked schemes, *they* cannot **s;** 3523
37: 7 do not fret when men s *in* their ways, 7503
140: 8 *do* not **let** their plans **s,** 7049
Pr 15:22 but with many advisers *they* **s.** 7756
16: 3 and your plans *will* **s.** 3922
21:30 no plan that can s **against** the LORD. 4200+5584
Ecc 11: 6 for you do not know which *will* **s,** 4178
Isa 47:12 Perhaps you will **s,** perhaps you will cause 3603
48:15 and *he will* s *in* his mission. 7503
Jer 32: 5 against the Babylonians, *you will* not **s.'** " 7503
Eze 17:15 *Will he* **s?** Will he who does such things 7503
Da 8:24 and *will* s in whatever he does. 7503
11:17 but his plans *will* not s or help him. 6641

SUCCEEDED (73) [SUCCEED]

Ge 36:33 Jobab son of Zerah from Bozrah s him 9393
36:34 the land of the Temanites s him as king. 9393
36:35 in the country of Moab, s him as king. 9393
36:36 Samlah from Masrekah s him as king. 9393
36:37 from Rehoboth on the river s him as king. 9393
36:38 Baal-Hanan son of Acbor s him as king. 9393
36:39 Hadad s him as king. 9393
Dt 10: 6 and Eleazar his son s him as priest. 9393
2Sa 10: 1 and his son Hanun s him as king. 9393
1Ki 8:20 *I have* s David my father and now I sit 7756+9393
11:43 And Rehoboam his son s him as king. 9393
14:20 And Nadab his son s him as king. 9393
14:31 And Abijah his son s him as king. 9393
15: 8 And Asa his son s him as king. 9393
15:24 And Jehoshaphat his son s him as king. 9393
15:28 of Asa king of Judah and s him as king. 9393
16: 6 And Elah his son s him as king. 9393
16:10 Then he s him as king. 9393
16:28 And Ahab his son s him as king. 9393
22:40 And Ahaziah his son s him as king. 9393
22:50 And Jehoram his son s him. 9393
2Ki 1:17 Joram s him as king in the second year 9393
8:15 Then Hazael s him as king. 9393
8:24 And Ahaziah his son s him as king. 9393
10:35 And Jehoahaz his son s him as king. 9393
12:21 And Amaziah his son s him as king. 9393
13: 9 And Jehoash his son s him as king. 9393
13:13 and Jeroboam s him on the throne. 3782
13:24 and Ben-Hadad his son s him as king. 9393
14:16 And Jeroboam his son s him as king. 9393
14:29 And Zechariah his son s him as king. 9393
15: 7 And Jotham his son s him as king. 9393
15:10 assassinated him and s him as king. 9393
15:14 assassinated him and s him as king. 9393
15:22 And Pekahiah his son s him as king. 9393
15:25 Pekah killed Pekahiah and s him as king. 9393
15:30 and then s him as king in the twentieth year 9393
15:38 And Ahaz his son s him as king. 9393
16:20 And Hezekiah his son s him as king. 9393
19:37 And Esarhaddon his son s him as king. 9393
20:21 And Manasseh his son s him as king. 9393
21:18 And Amon his son s him as king. 9393
21:26 And Josiah his son s him as king. 9393
24: 6 And Jehoiachin his son s him as king. 9393
1Ch 1:44 Jobab son of Zerah from Bozrah s him 9393
1:45 the land of the Temanites s him as king. 9393
1:46 in the coutnry of Moab, s him as king. 9393
1:47 Samlah from Masrekah s him as king. 9393
1:48 from Rehoboth on the river s him as king. 9393
1:49 Baal-Hanan son of Acbor s him as king. 9393
1:50 Baal-Hanan died, Hadad s him as king. 9393
19: 1 and his son s him as king. 9393
27:34 Ahithophel was s *by* Jehoiada son 339
29:28 His son Solomon s him as king. 9393
2Ch 6:10 *I have* s David my father and now I sit 7756+9393
7:11 *had* **s in carrying out** all he had in mind 7503
9:31 And Rehoboam his son s him as king. 9393
12:16 And Abijah his son s him as king. 9393
14: 1 Asa his son s him as king, 9393
17: 1 Jehoshaphat his son s him as king 9393
21: 1 And Jehoram his son s him as king. 9393
24:27 And Amaziah his son s him as king. 9393
26:23 And Jotham his son s him as king. 9393
27: 9 And Ahaz his son s him as king. 9393
28:27 And Hezekiah his son s him as king. 9393
32:30 He s in everything he undertook. 7503
32:33 And Manasseh his son s him as king. 9393
33:20 And Amon his son s him as king. 9393
36: 8 And Jehoiachin his son s him as king. 9393
Isa 37:38 And Esarhaddon his son s him as king 9393
Jer 22:11 who s his father as king of Judah 9393
Da 11:21 *be* s *by* a contemptible person 4030+6584+6641
Ac 24:27 Felix *was* s by Porcius Festus, *1345+3284*

SUCCEEDS (2) [SUCCEED]

Ex 29:30 The son who s him as priest and comes to 9393
Pr 17: 8 wherever he turns, *he* **s.** 8505

SUCCESS (25) [SUCCEED]

Ge 24:12 of my master Abraham, **give** me s today, 7936
24:40 with you and **make** your journey a **s,** 7503
24:42 please **grant** s *to* the journey 7503
24:56 the LORD *has* **granted** s *to* my journey. 7503
27:20 "The LORD your God **gave** me **s,"** 7936
39: 3 with him and that the LORD **gave** him s 7503
39:23 and **gave** him s *in* whatever he did. 7503
1Sa 18:14 In everything he did he **had great s,** 8505
18:30 David **met with** more s than the rest 8505
25:31 when the LORD *has* **brought** my master **s,** 3512
1Ki 22:13 the other prophets are predicting s for 3202
1Ch 12:18 **S,** success to you, and success to those 8934
12:18 s to you, and success to those who help you, 8934
12:18 and s to those who help you, 8934
22:11 and *may you* **have** s and build the house of 7503
22:13 Then *you will* **have** s if you are careful 7503
2Ch 18:12 the other prophets are predicting s for 3202
26: 5 God **gave** him **s.** 7503
Ne 1:11 **Give** your servant s today 7503
2:20 "The God of heaven *will* **give** us **s.** 7503
Job 5:12 so that their hands achieve no s. 9370
6:13 now that s has been driven from me? 9370
Ps 118:25 O LORD, save us; O LORD, **grant** us **s.** 7503
Ecc 10:10 strength is needed but skill will bring **s.** 3862
Da 11:14 in fulfillment of the vision, but **without s.** 4173

SUCCESSFUL (8) [SUCCEED]

Ge 24:21 or not the LORD *had* **made** his journey **s.** 7503
Jos 1: 7 that *you may be* s wherever you go. 8505
1: 8 Then you will be prosperous and **s.** 8505
Jdg 18: 5 to learn whether our journey *will be* **s."** 7503
1Sa 18:15 When Saul saw how s he *was,* 8505
2Ki 18: 7 *he was* s in whatever he undertook. 8505
2Ch 20:20 in his prophets and *you will be* **s."** 7503
Da 11:36 *be* s until the time of wrath is completed, 7503

SUCCESSFULLY (1) [SUCCEED]

1Sa 18: 5 *so* s that Saul gave him a high rank in 8505

SUCCESSIVE (2) [SUCCEED]

2Sa 21: 1 was a famine *for* three s **years;** 339+9102+9102
Eze 41: 7 all around the temple were wider **at each s level.** 2025+2025+4200+4200+5087+5087

SUCCESSOR (6) [SUCCEED]

1Ki 1:48 who has allowed my eyes to see a s 3782
1Ch 27: 7 his son Zebadiah was his **s.** 339
Ecc 2:12 What more can the king's s do than what has already been done? 132+339+995+8611
4:15 followed the youth, the king's **s.** 6641+9393
4:16 came later were not pleased with **the s.** 2257[S]
Da 11:20 "His s will send out a tax collector to maintain 4030+6584+6641

SUCCESSORS (1) [SUCCEED]

1Ch 3:16 The s *of* Jehoiakim: Jehoiachin his son, 1201

SUCCOUR, SUCCOURED, SUCCOURER (KJV) See HELP, HELPED, RESCUE, SUPPORT

SUCCOTH (18) [SUCCOTH BENOTH]

Ge 33:17 Jacob, however, went to S, 6111
33:17 That is why the place is called S. 6111
Ex 12:37 Israelites journeyed from Rameses to **S.** 6111
13:20 After leaving S they camped at Etham on 6111
Nu 33: 5 Israelites left Rameses and camped at **S.** 6111
33: 6 They left S and camped at Etham, 6111
Jos 13:27 S and Zaphon with the rest of the realm 6111
Jdg 8: 5 He said to the men of S, 6111
8: 6 But the officials of S said, 6111
8: 8 but they answered as the men of S had. 6111
8:14 a young man of S and questioned him, 6111
8:14 of the seventy-seven officials of S, 6111
8:15 Gideon came and said to the men of **S,** 6111
8:16 the town and taught the men of S a lesson 6111
1Ki 7:46 of the Jordan between S and Zarethan. 6111
2Ch 4:17 of the Jordan between S and Zarethan. 6111
Ps 60: 6 and measure off the Valley of **S.** 6111
108: 7 and measure off the Valley of **S.** 6111

SUCCOTH BENOTH (1) [SUCCOTH]

2Ki 17:30 The men from Babylon made S, 6112

SUCH (227)

Ge 18:25 Far be it from you to do s a thing— 3869
20: 9 that you have brought *s* **great** guilt AIT
34:14 They said to them, "We can't do s a thing; 2296
39: 9 could I do s a wicked thing and sin 1524+2296
41:19 I had never seen s ugly cows in all the land 3869
44: 7 "Why does my lord say s things? 3869
44:17 "Far be it from me to do s *a thing!* 2296
Ex 10:14 had there been s a plague of locusts, 4017+4027
28: 3 in s matters that they are to make garments NIH
32:21 that you led them into *s* **great** sin?" AIT
Lev 6: 3 he commits any s sin that people may do— 2179
10:19 but s things **as** this have happened to me. 3869
11:34 but has water on it from s a pot is unclean, 3972
13:45 "The person with s an infectious disease 889
18:29 s persons must be cut off from their people. 2021+6913[S]
19: 5 sacrifice it **in s a way that** it will be 4200
21: 2 **s as** his mother or father, 4200
22: 6 The one who touches **any s thing** will 2257[S]
22:25 you must not accept s animals from 3972+4946
22:29 sacrifice it **in s a way that** it will be 4200
25:21 I will send you s a blessing in the sixth year NIH
27: 9 s an animal given to the LORD becomes holy. 889
Dt 4: 8 s righteous decrees and laws **as** this 3869
13:11 among you will do s an evil thing again. 3869
19:20 and never again will s an evil thing be done 3869
29:18 among you that produces s bitter poison. NIH
29:19 When s a person hears the words NIH
33:17 S are the ten thousands of Ephraim; 2156[S]
33:17 s are the thousands of Manasseh." 2156[S]
Jdg 7:13 with **s force** that the tent overturned 5877[S]
16:16 With s nagging she prodded him day 1821[S]
19:24 don't do s a disgraceful thing." 2296
19:30 **"S** a thing has never been seen or done, 3869
Ru 2:10 "Why have I found s favor in your eyes NIH
1Sa 2: 3 or let your mouth speak s arrogance, NIH
2:23 he said to them, "Why do you do s things? 3869
4: 5 all Israel raised s a great shout that NIH
6:10 They took two s cows and hitched them to 6402[S]
7:10 and **threw** them **into** *s* **a panic** that AIT
8: 5 **s as** all the other nations have." 3869
9:21 Why do you say s a thing to me?" 3869
19: 8 He struck them with s force that they fled 1524
24: 6 that I should do s a thing to my master, 2296
25:17 He is s a wicked man that no one can talk NIH
27:11 And s was his practice as long as he lived 3907
2Sa 11:11 surely as you live, I will not do s a thing!" 2296
12: 6 because he did s a thing and had no pity." 2296
13:12 S *a thing* should not be done in Israel! 4027
17:15 the elders of Israel to do s and such, 2296+3869
17:15 the elders of Israel to do such and **s,** 2296+3869
17:21 Ahithophel has advised s **and such** 3970
17:21 Ahithophel has advised **such and** s 3970
23:17 S were the exploits of the three mighty men. 465
23:22 S were the exploits of Benaiah son 465
24: 3 But why does my lord the king want to do s 2296
1Ki 9: 8 the LORD done s *a thing* to this land and 3970
14: 5 are to give her s and such an answer. 2297+3869
14: 5 are to give her such and s an answer. 2296+3869
2Ki 6: 8 "I will set up my camp in s **and such** 532+7141
6: 8 "I will set up my camp in **such and** s 532+7141
6:10 so that he was on his guard **in s places.** 9004[S]
8:13 a mere dog, accomplish s a feat?" 2296
18:21 S is Pharaoh king of Egypt 4027
19: 7 to put s a spirit in him that when he hears NIH
21:12 I am going to bring s disaster on Jerusalem NIH
23:22 had any s Passover been observed. 3869
1Ch 11:19 S were the exploits of the three mighty men. 465
11:24 S were the exploits of Benaiah son 465
29:25 and bestowed on him royal splendor *s* **as** AIT
2Ch 1:12 s as no king who was before you ever had 4027
7:21 the LORD done **s a thing** to this land and 3970
9: 9 There had never been s spices as those 3869
14:13 S a great number of Cushites fell NIH
35:18 of the kings of Israel had ever celebrated s 3869
Ezr 9:14 peoples who commit s detestable practices? 465
Ne 5:13 So *may s a man* **be** shaken out and emptied! AIT
Est 4:14 to royal position for s a time as this?" 3869
7: 4 no s distress would justify disturbing 2021
7: 5 Where is the man who has dared to do s 4027
Job 6: 7 I refuse to touch it; s food makes me ill. 3869
8: 2 "How long will you say s *things?* 465
8:13 S is the destiny of all who forget God; 4027
14: 3 Do you fix your eye on s *a one?* 2296
15:13 and pour out *s* **words** from your mouth? AIT
18:21 Surely s is the dwelling of an evil man; 465
18:21 s is the place of one who knows not God." 2296
20:29 S is the fate God allots the wicked, 2296
22:13 Does he judge through s darkness? NIH
23:14 and many s plans he still has in store. 3869
24: 1 who know him look in vain for s days? 2257[S]
31:23 fear of his splendor I could not do s things. NIH
Ps 12: 7 and protect us from s people forever. 2306
17:14 by your hand save me from s men, NIH
24: 6 S is the generation of those who seek him, 2296
139: 6 *S* **knowledge** is too wonderful for me, AIT
Pr 1:19 S is the end of all who go after ill-gotten 4027
29: 7 but the wicked **have** no *s* **concern.** AIT
Ecc 5: 8 do not be surprised at **s things;** 2914[S]
7:10 For it is not wise to ask **s questions.** 2296[S]
Isa 36: 6 S is Pharaoh king of Egypt 4027
38:16 Lord, by **s things** men live; 2157[S]
38:17 for my benefit that I suffered *s* **anguish.** AIT
40:20 to **present** *s* **an offering** selects wood AIT
65: 5 S *people* are smoke in my nostrils, 465
66: 8 Who has ever heard of s a thing? 3869
66: 8 Who has ever seen s things? 3869
Jer 5: 9 not avenge myself on s a nation **as** this? 3869
5:29 not avenge myself on s a nation as this? 3869
9: 9 not avenge myself on s a nation as this?" 3869
16:10 the LORD decreed s a great disaster 2296
22: 8 'Why has the LORD done **s a thing** 3970
32:35 that they should do s a detestable thing and 2296
40:16 "Don't do s a thing! 2296
44: 7 Why bring *s* **great** disaster on yourselves AIT
La 3:36 would not the Lord see s things? NIH
Eze 1:11 S were their faces. NIH
16:16 *S things should* **not happen,** AIT
17:15 Will he who does s *things* escape? 465
18:13 *Will s a man* **live?** AIT
18:14 he does not do s things: 3869
21:10 The sword despises every s stick. NIH
31:14 are ever to reach *s* **a height;** AIT
43:12 S is the law of the temple. 2296
Da 2:10 ever asked s a thing of any magician 10180+10341
2:15 "Why did the king issue *s* a **harsh** decree?" AIT
10: 7 but s terror overwhelmed them that they fled 1524
12: 1 be a time of distress **s as** has not happened 889
Hos 9: 4 S sacrifices will be to them like the bread NIH
Joel 2: 2 **s as** never was of old nor ever will be 4017
Am 5:13 the prudent man keeps quiet in s times, 2085
Jnh 1: 4 and s a violent storm arose that NIH

Mic 2: 7 Does he do s *things?"* 465
Mal 1: 9 With s **offerings** from your hands, 2296[S]
Mt 8:10 anyone in Israel with s **great** faith. *5537*
9: 8 who had given s authority to men. *5525*
13: 2 S large crowds gathered around him *NIG*
15:33 in this remote place to feed s a crowd?" *5537*
18: 7 **S things** must come, but woe to *3836+4998*[S]
19:14 kingdom of heaven belongs to **s as these."** *5525*
24: 6 S things must happen, but the end is still *NIG*
Mk 4:32 with s big branches that the birds of *NIG*
7: 4 s as the washing of cups, *NIG*
7:29 he told her, "For s a reply, you may go; *4047*
10:14 the kingdom of God belongs *to* **s as these.** *5525*
12:40 S *men* will be punished most severely." *4047*
13: 7 S things must happen, but the end is still *NIG*
Lk 5: 6 they caught s a large number of fish *NIG*
7: 9 not found s **great** faith even in Israel." *5537*
9: 9 Who, then, is this I hear s *things* about?" *5525*
12:30 For the pagan world runs after all s *things*, *4047*
18:16 the kingdom of God belongs to **s as these.** *5525*
20:47 S *men* will be punished most severely." *4047*
Jn 7:15 "How did this man get s learning *NIG*
7:32 the crowd whispering s *things* about him. *4047*
8: 5 Moses commanded us to stone s *women*. *5525*
8:40 Abraham did not do s *things*. *4047*
9:16 "How can a sinner do s miraculous signs?" *5525*
14: 9 after I have been among you s a long time? *5537*
15: 6 s branches are picked up, thrown into the *899*
16: 3 They will do s *things* because they have *4047*
Ac 5: 4 What made you think of doing s a thing? *4047*
8:22 Perhaps he will forgive you for having **s a** *3836*
15:39 They had s a sharp disagreement that *NIG*
16:24 Upon receiving s orders, *5525*
16:26 there was s a violent earthquake **that** *6063*
17:30 In the past God overlooked s ignorance, *3836*
18:15 I will not be a judge *of* s *things."* *4047*
19:16 He gave them s a beating that they ran out *NIG*
25:20 at a loss how to investigate s *matters;* *4047*
26:28 in s a short time you can persuade me to be *NIG*
27:18 We took s a **violent** battering from *5380*
Ro 1:32 that those who do s *things* deserve death, *5525*
2: 2 against those who do s *things* is based *5525*
2:29 **S a man's** praise is not from men, *4005*[S]
16:18 s *people* are not serving our Lord Christ, *5525*
1Co 5:11 With **s a man** do not even eat. *5525*
6: 4 if you have disputes about s **matters,** *1053*[S]
7:15 not bound in s *circumstances;* *5525*
8: 7 to idols that when they eat s **food** they think *1628*
9:15 in the hope that you will do **s things** for me. *4048*
9:24 **Run in s a way** as to get the prize. *4048*
14: 7 **s as** the flute or harp, *1664*
16:16 *to* **s as these** and to everyone who joins in *5525*
16:18 S *men* deserve recognition. *5525*
2Co 1:10 He has delivered us from s a deadly peril, *5496*
2:16 And who is equal to s a *task?* *4047*
3: 4 S confidence as this is ours through Christ *5525*
3:12 since we have s a hope, we are very bold. *5525*
7: 3 I have said before that *you* **have s a place** *1639*
10:11 S *people* should realize that what we are *5525*
11:13 For s *men* are false apostles, *5525*
Gal 5:23 Against s *things* there is no law. *5525*
Eph 5: 5 **s a man** is an idolater— *4005*
5: 6 for because of s *things* God's wrath comes *4047*
Php 3: 4 I myself have reasons for s confidence. *NIG*
3:15 mature *should* **take s a view of things.** *5858*
4: 8 or praiseworthy—think about s *things*. *4047*
Col 2:18 S a person goes into great detail *NIG*
2:23 **S regulations** indeed have an appearance *4015*[S]
3: 8 now you must rid yourselves of all s things *NIG*
1Th 4: 6 The Lord will punish men for all **s sins,** *4047*[S]
2Th 3: 9 because we do not have the right to s help, *NIG*
3:12 S *people* we command and urge in *5525*
1Ti 4: 2 S teachings come through hypocritical liars, *NIG*
5:10 s as bringing up children, *NIG*
5:11 *do* **not put** them **on s a list.** *4148*
Tit 3:11 be sure that **s a man** is warped and sinful; *5525*
Heb 2: 3 if we ignore s a **great** salvation? *5496*
7:26 **S a** high priest meets our need— *5525*
8: 1 We do have s a high priest, *5525*
11:14 People who say s *things* show *5525*
12: 1 since we are surrounded by s a **great** cloud *5537*
12: 3 Consider him who endured s opposition *5525*
12:19 or to s a voice speaking words *NIG*
13:16 for *with* s sacrifices God is pleased. *5525*
Jas 2:14 Can s faith save him? *3836*
3:15 S "wisdom" does not come down *4047*
4:16 All s boasting is evil. *5525*
1Pe 1:18 with perishable things s as silver or gold *NIG*
2:12 Live s good lives among the pagans that, *NIG*
3: 3 s as braided hair and the wearing *NIG*
2Pe 2:11 against s **beings** in the presence of the Lord. *899*
1Jn 2:22 S a *man* is the antichrist— *4047*
2Jn 1: 7 **Any s person** is the deceiver and *4047*
3Jn 1: 8 to s *men* so that we may work together for *5525*
Rev 18:17 In one hour s **great** wealth has been brought *5537*
18:21 **"With** s violence the great city *4048*

SUCHATHITES (KJV) See SUCATHITES

SUCK (1) [SUCKLING]

Job 20:16 *He will* s the poison of serpents; 3567

SUCK, SUCKED, SUCKING (KJV) See also FEAST, NOURISHED, NURSE, NURSED, NURSING

SUCKLING (1) [SUCK]

1Sa 7: 9 Then Samuel took a s lamb and offered it 2692

SUCKLING, SUCKLINGS (KJV) See also INFANT, INFANTS

SUDDEN (11) [SUDDENLY]

Lev 26:16 I will bring upon you s **terror,** 988
Dt 28:20 to s ruin because of the evil you have done 4554
Jdg 20:37 in ambush made a s dash into Gibeah, 2590
Job 9:23 When a scourge brings s death, 7328
22:10 why s peril terrifies you, 7328
Ps 6:10 they will turn back in s disgrace. 8092
Pr 3:25 of s disaster or of the ruin that overtakes 7328
24:22 for those two will send s destruction 7328
Isa 17:14 In the evening, **s terror!** 1166
Zep 1:18 for he will make a s end of all who live in 987
Jn 19:34 bringing a s flow of blood and water. *2317*

SUDDENLY (45) [SUDDEN]

Ge 37: 7 when s my sheaf rose and stood upright, 2180
Nu 6: 9 If someone dies s in his presence, 928+7328+7353
16:42 s the cloud covered it and the glory of 2180
35:22 if without hostility someone s shoves 928+7353
Jos 11: 7 and his whole army came against them s at 7328
Jdg 14: 5 s a young lion came roaring toward him. 2180
2Ki 2:11 s a chariot of fire and horses of fire **appeared** 2180
13:21 s they saw a band of raiders; 2180
Job 1:19 when s a mighty wind swept in from 2180
5: 3 but s his house was cursed. 7328
Ps 64: 4 they shoot at him **s**, without fear. 7328
64: 7 s they will be struck down. 7328
73:19 How s are they destroyed, 3869+8092
Pr 6:15 he will s be destroyed—without remedy. 7353
28:18 *he* whose ways are perverse will s fall. 285+928
29: 1 after many rebukes will s be destroyed— 7353
Isa 29: 5 like blown chaff. **S,** in an instant, 7328
30:13 cracked and bulging, that collapses **s,** 7328
47:11 catastrophe you cannot foresee will s come 7328
48: 3 then s I acted, and they came to pass. 7328
Jer 6:26 for s the destroyer will come upon us. 7328
15: 8 s I will bring down on them anguish 7328
18:22 when you s bring invaders against them, 7328
51: 8 Babylon will s fall and be broken. 7328
Da 5: 5 S the fingers of a human hand appeared 10191+10734
8: 5 s a goat with a prominent horn 2180
Hab 2: 7 Will not your debtors s arise? 7353
Mal 3: 1 Then s the Lord you are seeking will come 7328
Mt 28: 9 S Jesus met them. 2627+2779
Mk 9: 8 **S,** when they looked around, *1988*
13:36 If he comes **s,** do not let him find you *1978*
Lk 2:13 S a great company of the heavenly host *1978*
9:39 A spirit seizes him and he s screams; *1978*
24: 4 s two men in clothes that gleamed *2627*
Ac 1:10 when s two men dressed in white stood *2627*
2: 2 S a sound like the blowing of a violent wind *924*
8:39 the Spirit of the Lord s **took** Philip **away,** *773*
9: 3 s a light from heaven flashed around him. *1978*
10:30 S a man in shining clothes stood before me *2627*
12: 7 S an angel of the Lord appeared and *2627*
12:10 s the angel left him. *2311*
16:26 S there was such a violent earthquake that *924*
22: 6 s a bright light from heaven flashed *1978*
28: 6 expected him to swell up or s fall dead, *924*
1Th 5: 3 destruction will come on them **s,** *167*

SUE (1)

Mt 5:40 And if someone wants *to* s you *3212*

SUFFER (50) [LONG-SUFFERING, SUFFERED, SUFFERING, SUFFERINGS, SUFFERS]

Ge 4:15 *he will* s **vengeance** seven times over." 5933
Nu 14:34 *you will* s **for** your sins 5951
Dt 26: 6 the Egyptians mistreated us and **made** us **s,** 6700
Ezr 4:13 and the royal revenues *will* **s.** 10472
Job 24:11 they tread the winepresses, yet s **thirst.** 7532
36:15 *those who* s he delivers in their suffering; 6714
Ps 42:10 My bones s mortal agony 928
Pr 9:12 if you are a mocker, you alone *will* **s."** 5951
11:15 up security for another *will* **surely s,** 8273+8317
22: 3 but the simple keep going and s for it. 6740
27:12 but the simple keep going and s for it. 6740
Isa 47: 8 be a widow or s the loss of children.' 3359
53:10 to crush him and **cause** him **to s,** 2703
54: 4 "Do not be afraid; *you will* not s **shame.** 1017
Jer 14:13 'You will not see the sword or s famine. 2118
15:15 think of *how* I s reproach for your sake. 5951
Eze 23:49 *will* s the penalty for your lewdness 5989+6584
36: 7 the nations around you *will* also s scorn. 5951
36:15 and no longer *will you* s the scorn of 5951
36:30 that *you will* no longer s disgrace among 4374
Da 6: 2 to them so that the king *might* not s **loss.** 10472
Mt 16:21 to Jerusalem and s many things at the hands *4248*
17:12 the Son of Man is going to s at their hands." *4248*
Mk 8:31 that the Son of Man must s many things and *4248*
9:12 Son of Man must s much and be rejected? *4248*
Lk 9:22 "The Son of Man must s many things and *4248*
17:25 But first he must s many things and *4248*
22:15 to eat this Passover with you before I s. *4248*
24:26 *to* s these things and then enter his glory?" *4248*
24:46 The Christ *will* s and rise from the dead on *4248*
Ac 3:18 saying that his Christ *would* **s.** *4248*
9:16 I will show him how much he must s *4248*
17: 3 the Christ had *to* s and rise from the dead. *4248*
26:23 that the Christ would s and, *4078*
1Co 3:15 If it is burned up, *he will* **s loss;** *2423*
2Co 1: 6 of the same sufferings we **s.** *4248*
Php 1:29 but also *to* s for him, *4248*
1Th 5: 9 For God did not appoint us to s wrath but *NIG*
Heb 9:26 *to* s many times since the creation of *4248*
1Pe 1: 6 a little while you may have had *to* s **grief** *3382*
2:20 if *you* s for doing good and you endure it, *4248*
3:14 But even if *you should* s for what is right, *4248*
3:17 *to* s for doing good than for doing evil. *4248*
4:15 If you **s,** it should not be as a murderer *4248*
4:16 However, if you s as a Christian, *NIG*
4:19 those who s according to God's will *4248*
Jude 1: 7 an example of those who s the punishment *5674*
Rev 2:10 not be afraid of what you are about *to* **s.** *4248*
2:10 *you will* s **persecution** for ten days. *2400+2568*
2:22 who commit adultery with her s intensely, *2568*

SUFFERED (29) [SUFFER]

1Sa 4:17 and the army *has* s heavy losses. 928+2118
Ps 88:15 *I have* s your terrors and am in despair. 5951
107:17 and s **affliction** because of their iniquities. 6700
119:107 *I have* s much; preserve my life, O LORD, 6700
Isa 38:17 it was for my benefit that I s such anguish. 5352
Jer 14:17 *has* s a grievous wound, a crushing blow. 8689
44:17 of food and were well off and s no harm. 8011
La 3:47 We *have* s terror and pitfalls, 2118+4200
Eze 36: 6 because *you have* s the scorn of the nations. 5951
Mt 27:19 for *I have* s a great deal today in a dream *4248*
Mk 5:26 *She had* s a great deal under the care *4248*
Lk 13: 2 because *they* s this way? *4248*
Ac 28: 5 into the fire and s no ill effects. *4248*
2Co 1: 8 the hardships we s in the province of Asia. *1181*
Gal 3: 4 *Have you* s so much for nothing— *4248*
Col 1:24 Now I rejoice in what was s for you, *4077*
1Th 2: 2 *We had* **previously** s and been insulted *4634*
2:14 You s from your own countrymen *4248*
2:14 the same things those churches s from *NIG*
Heb 2: 9 with glory and honor because he s death, *4077*
2:18 Because *he* himself s when he was tempted, *4248*
5: 8 he learned obedience from what he s *4248*
13:12 so Jesus also s outside the city gate to make *4248*
1Pe 2:21 because Christ s for you, *4248*
2:23 *when he* **s,** he made no threats. *4248*
4: 1 Therefore, *since* Christ s in his body, *4248*
4: 1 he who *has* s in his body is done with sin. *4248*
5:10 *after you have* s a little while, *4248*
Rev 9: 5 the agony they s was like that of the sting *NIG*

SUFFERING (53) [SUFFER]

Ge 16: 5 "You are responsible for the **wrong** I am *s.* AIT
41:52 has made me fruitful in the land of my **s."** 6715
Ex 3: 7 and I am concerned about their s. 4799
Nu 5:24 this water will enter her and cause **bitter s.** 5253
5:27 it will go into her and cause **bitter s;** 5253
14:33 **s for** your unfaithfulness, 5951
Dt 28:53 of the s that your enemy will inflict on you 5186
28:55 the s your enemy will inflict on you during 5186
2Ki 13:14 Now Elisha *was* s *from* the illness 2703
14:26 was **s;** there was no one to help them. 6715
Ne 9: 9 "You saw the s *of* our forefathers in Egypt; 6715
Job 2:13 because they saw how great his s was. 3873
30:16 now my life ebbs away; days of s grip me. 6715
30:27 days of s confront me. 6715
36:15 But those who suffer he delivers in their **s;** 6715
Ps 22:24 For he has not despised or disdained the s 6713
55: 3 for they bring down s upon me 224
107:10 prisoners s in iron chains, 6715
119:50 My comfort in my s is this: 6715
119:153 Look upon my s and deliver me, 6715
Isa 14: 3 the day the LORD gives you relief from s 6778
53: 3 a man of sorrows, and familiar with s. 2716
53:11 After the s *of* his soul, he will see the light 6662
La 1:12 Is any s like my suffering that was inflicted 4799
1:12 Is any suffering like my s that was inflicted 4799
1:18 Listen, all you peoples; look upon my s. 4799
Joel 1:18 even the flocks of sheep *are* **s.** 870
Mt 4:24 those s severe pain, the demon-possessed, *5309*
8: 6 at home paralyzed and in terrible **s."** *989*
15:22 s terribly **from demon-possession."** *1227*
17:15 "He has seizures and *is* s greatly. *4248*
Mk 5:29 in her body that she was freed from her **s.** *3465*
5:34 Go in peace and be freed from your **s."** *3465*
Lk 4:38 Now Simon's mother-in-law was s from *5309*
14: 2 in front of him was a man **s from dropsy.** *5622*
Ac 1: 3 After his **s,** he showed himself to these men *4248*
5:41 counted worthy *of* **s disgrace** for the Name. *869*
7:11 all Egypt and Canaan, bringing great **s,** *2568*
28: 8 **s from** fever and dysentery. *5309*
Ro 5: 3 we know that s produces perseverance; *2568*
1Th 1: 6 in spite of severe **s,** you welcomed the *2568*
2Th 1: 5 the kingdom of God, for which *you are* **s.** *4248*
2Ti 1: 8 But **join** with me **in** s for the gospel, *5155*
1:12 That is why *I am* s as I am. *4248*
2: 9 for which *I am* s even to the point of being *2802*
Heb 2:10 author of their salvation perfect through s. *4077*
10:32 in a great contest in the face *of* **s.** *4077*

Heb 13: 3 as if you yourselves were s. *NIG*
Jas 5:10 as an example of patience in the face *of* s, *2801*
1Pe 2:19 the pain *of* unjust s because he is conscious *4248*
4:12 be surprised at the painful trial you *are* s, *1181*
Rev 1: 9 in the s and kingdom and patient endurance *2568*
2:22 So I will cast her on a **bed of s,** *3109*

SUFFERINGS (14) [SUFFER]

Job 9:28 I still dread all my s, 6780
Ro 5: 3 Not only so, but we also rejoice in our s, *2568*
8:17 with Christ, if indeed *we* **share in** his s *5224*
8:18 that our present s are not worth comparing *4077*
2Co 1: 5 as the s of Christ flow over into our lives, *4077*
1: 6 patient endurance *of* the same s we suffer. *4077*
1: 7 we know that just as you share *in* our s, *4077*
Eph 3:13 to be discouraged because of my s for you, *2568*
Php 3:10 and the fellowship of sharing *in* his s, *4077*
2Ti 3:11 persecutions, s—what kinds of things *4077*
1Pe 1:11 when he predicted the s of Christ and *4077*
4:13 But rejoice that you participate *in* the s *4077*
5: 1 *of* Christ's s and one who also will share in *4077*
5: 9 undergoing the same kind *of* s. *4077*

SUFFERS (4) [SUFFER]

Job 15:20 All his days the wicked man s **torment,** 2655
Pr 13:20 but a companion of fools s **harm.** 8317
1Co 12:26 If one part s, every part suffers with it; *4248*
12:26 If one part suffers, every part s **with** it; *5224*

SUFFICE, SUFFICED, SUFFICETH (KJV) See ALL WANTED, ENOUGH

SUFFICIENT (5)

Lev 25:26 and acquires s **means** to redeem it, 1896+3869
Isa 40:16 Lebanon is not s *for* altar fires, 1896
2Co 2: 6 on him by the majority is s for him. *2653*
12: 9 But he said to me, "My grace *is* s for you, *758*
Php 1:20 but will have s courage so that now *4246*

SUGGEST (1) [SUGGESTED, SUGGESTION]

Ru 4: 4 to your attention and s that you buy it in 606

SUGGESTED (5) [SUGGEST]

1Ki 22:20 "One s this, and another that. 606
2Ch 18:19 "One s this, and another that. 606
Ezr 10: 5 all Israel under oath to do what had been s. 1821+2021+2021+2296
Est 2:15 who was in charge of the harem, s. 606
6:10 and the horse and do just as *you have* s 1819

SUGGESTION (1) [SUGGEST]

Est 5:14 This s delighted Haman, 1821

SUIT (1) [SUITABLE]

2Ti 4: 3 Instead, **to** s their own desires, *2848*

SUITABLE (4) [SUIT]

Ge 2:18 I will make a helper s **for** him." 3869+5584
2:20 But for Adam no s helper was found, 3869+5584
Nu 32: 1 of Jazer and Gilead were s *for* livestock. 5226
32: 4 are s *for* livestock, and your servants have 824

SUKKIIMS (KJV) See SUKKITES

SUKKITES (1)

2Ch 12: 3 S and Cushites that came with him 6113

SULFUR (15)

Ge 19:24 down burning s on Sodom and Gomorrah— 1730
Dt 29:23 be a burning waste of salt and s— 1730
Job 18:15 **burning** s is scattered over his dwelling. 1730
Ps 11: 6 On the wicked he will rain fiery coals and **burning s;** 1730
Isa 30:33 like a stream of **burning s,** sets it ablaze. 1730
34: 9 her dust into **burning s;** 1730
Eze 38:22 of rain, hailstones and burning s on him and 1730
Lk 17:29 fire and s rained down from heaven *2520*
Rev 9:17 dark blue, and **yellow as s.** *2523*
9:17 of their mouths came fire, smoke and s, *2520*
9:18 smoke and s that came out of their mouths. *2520*
14:10 be tormented with burning s in the presence *2520*
19:20 into the fiery lake of burning s. *2520*
20:10 was thrown into the lake of burning s, *2520*
21: 8 be in the fiery lake of burning s. *2520*

SULKING (1)

1Ki 21: 4 He lay on his bed s and refused 906+6015+7156

SULLEN (3)

1Ki 20:43 S and angry, the king of Israel went 6234
21: 4 went home, s and angry because Naboth 6234
21: 5 "Why are you so s? 6234

SUM (4) [SUMMED, SUMS]

Ps 139:17 How vast is the s *of* them! 8031
Mt 28:12 they gave the soldiers a **large** s of money, *2653*
Ac 7:16 at Shechem *for* a certain s of money. *5507*
1Co 16: 2 a **s of money** in keeping with his income, *2564*

SUMMED (2) [SUM]

Ro 13: 9 *are* s **up** in this one rule: "Love your neighbor as yourself." *368*
Gal 5:14 The entire law *is* s **up** in a single command: *4444*

SUMMER (19)

Ge 8:22 cold and heat, s and winter, 7811
Jdg 3:20 in the upper room of his s **palace** and said, 5249
Ps 32: 4 my strength was sapped as in the heat of s. 7811
74:17 you made both s and winter. 7811
Pr 6: 8 in s and gathers its food at harvest. 7811
10: 5 He who gathers crops in s is a wise son, 7811
26: 1 Like snow in s or rain in harvest, 7811
30:25 yet they store up their food in the s; 7811
Isa 18: 6 the birds *will* feed on them **all s,** 7810
Jer 8:20 "The harvest is past, the s has ended, 7811
40:10 harvest the wine, s **fruit** and oil, 7811
40:12 an abundance of wine and s **fruit.** 7811
Da 2:35 like chaff on a threshing floor in the s. 10627
Am 3:15 the winter house along with the s house; 7811
Mic 7: 1 like one who gathers s **fruit** at the gleaning 7811
Zec 14: 8 to the western sea, in s and in winter. 7811
Mt 24:32 you know that s is near. *2550*
Mk 13:28 you know that s is near. *2550*
Lk 21:30 for yourselves and know that s is near. *2550*

SUMMIT (4)

2Sa 15:32 When David arrived at the s, 8031
16: 1 a short distance beyond the s, 8031
SS 4: 8 from the top of Senir, the s of Hermon, NIH
Jer 22: 6 like the s *of* Lebanon, 8031

SUMMON (27) [SUMMONED, SUMMONING, SUMMONS]

Nu 22: 5 sent messengers to s Balaam son of Beor, 7924
22:20 "Since these men have come to s you, 7924
Dt 25: 8 the elders of his town *shall* s him and talk 7924
33:19 *They will* s peoples *to* the mountain 7924
2Sa 17: 5 Absalom said, "S also Hushai the Arkite, 7924
20: 4 "S the men of Judah to come to me 2410
20: 5 But when Amasa went to s Judah, 2410
1Ki 18:19 Now s the people from all over Israel 8938
22:13 who had gone to s Micaiah said to him, 7924
2Ki 10:19 Now s all the prophets of Baal, 7924
2Ch 18:12 who had gone to s Micaiah said to him, 7924
Job 9:19 a matter of justice, who *will* s him? 3585
13:22 Then s me and I will answer, 7924
19:16 *I* s my servant, but he does not answer, 7924
Ps 68:28 S your power, O God; 7422
Isa 22:20 "In that day *I will* s my servant, 7924
45: 4 *I* s you by name and bestow on you a title 7924
46:11 From the east I s a bird of prey; 7924
48:13 *when* I s them, they all stand up together. 7924
55: 5 Surely *you will* s nations you know not, 7924
Jer 1:15 I *am about to* s all the peoples of the 7924
25: 9 I *will* s all the peoples of the 2256+4374+8938
50:29 "S archers against Babylon, 9048
51:27 s against her these kingdoms: 9048
La 2:22 "As *you* s *to* a feast day, 7924
Eze 38:21 *I will* s a sword against Gog 7924
Joel 1:14 S the elders and all who live in the land to 665

SUMMONED (65) [SUMMON]

Ge 12:18 So Pharaoh s Abram. 7924
20: 8 next morning Abimelech s all his officials, 7924
26: 9 So Abimelech s Isaac and said, 7924
Ex 1:18 of Egypt s the midwives and asked them, 7924
7:11 Pharaoh then s wise men and sorcerers, 7924
8: 8 Pharaoh s Moses and Aaron and said, 7924
8:25 Then Pharaoh s Moses and Aaron and said, 7924
9:27 Pharaoh s Moses and Aaron. 2256+7924+8938
10:16 Pharaoh quickly s Moses and Aaron 7924
10:24 Then Pharaoh s Moses and said, "Go, 7924
12:21 Then Moses s all the elders of Israel 7924
12:31 the night Pharaoh s Moses and Aaron 7924
19: 7 So Moses went back and s the elders of 7924
36: 2 Then Moses s Bezalel and Oholiab 7924
Lev 9: 1 the eighth day Moses s Aaron and his sons 7924
10: 4 Moses s Mishael and Elzaphan, 7924
Nu 12: 5 at the entrance to the Tent and s Aaron 7924
16:12 Moses s Dathan and Abiram, 4200+7924+8938
24:10 *"I* s you to curse my enemies, 7924
Dt 5: 1 Moses s all Israel and said: 7924
29: 2 Moses s all the Israelites and said to them: 7924
31: 7 Then Moses s Joshua and said to him in 7924
Jos 9:22 Then Joshua s the Gibeonites and said, 7924
10:24 he s all the men of Israel and said to 7924
22: 1 Then Joshua s the Reubenites, 7924
23: 2 s all Israel—their elders, leaders, 7924
24: 1 *He* s the elders, leaders, 7924
Jdg 4:10 where he s Zebulun and Naphtali. 2410
1Sa 10:17 Samuel s the people of Israel to the LORD 7590
13: 4 the people **were** s to join Saul at Gilgal. 7590
15: 4 So Saul s the men and mustered them 9048
2Sa 9: 9 Then the king s Ziba, Saul's servant, 7924
14:33 Then the king s Absalom, 7924
21: 2 The king s the Gibeonites and spoke 7924
1Ki 2:42 king s Shimei and said to him, 2256+7924+8938
8: 1 Then King Solomon s into his presence 7735
18: 3 and Ahab *had* s Obadiah, 7924
1Ki 20: 7 The king of Israel s all the elders of the land 7924
20:15 So Ahab s the young officers of 7212
2Ki 4:36 Elisha s Gehazi and said, 7924
6:11 *He* s his officers and demanded of them, 7924
9: 1 The prophet Elisha s a man from 7924
12: 7 Therefore King Joash s Jehoiada the priest 7924
1Ch 15:11 David s Zadok and Abiathar the priests, 7924
28: 1 s all the officials of Israel **to assemble** 7735
2Ch 5: 2 Solomon s to Jerusalem the elders of Israel, 7735
24: 6 the king s Jehoiada the chief priest and said 7924
Ezr 8:16 So *I* s Eliezer, Ariel, Shemaiah, Elnathan, 8938
Ne 5:12 Then *I* s the priests and made the nobles 7924
Est 2:14 unless he was pleased with her and s *her* 7924
3:12 the first month the royal secretaries **were** s. 7924
4: 5 Then Esther s Hathach, 7924
4:11 the inner court without **being** s the king has 7924
8: 9 At once the royal secretaries **were** s— 7924
Job 9:16 Even if *I* s him and he responded, 7924
Isa 13: 3 *I have* s my warriors 7924
43: 1 *I have* s you by name; you are mine. 7924
La 1:15 *he has* s an army against me 7924
2:22 so you s against me terrors on every side. NIH
Da 2: 2 So the king s the magicians, enchanters, 7924
3: 2 He then s the satraps, 10359+10378+10714
3:13 Nebuchadnezzar s Shadrach, 10042+10085+10378
Am 5:16 *be* s to weep and the mourners to wail. 7924
Jn 9:24 A second time *they* s the man who *5888*
18:33 s Jesus and asked him, "Are you the king *5888*

SUMMONING (2) [SUMMON]

Jdg 6:34 s the Abiezrites to follow him. 2410
Mk 15:44 S the centurion, he asked him *4673*

SUMMONS (5) [SUMMON]

Nu 22:37 "Did I not send you an urgent s? 7924
Ps 50: 1 and s the earth from the rising of the sun to 7924
50: 4 *He* s the heavens above, and the earth, 7924
Isa 45: 3 the God of Israel, who s you by name. 7924
Na 2: 5 *He* s his picked troops, 2349

SUMPTUOUSLY (KJV) See LUXURY

SUMS (1) [SUM]

Mt 7:12 for this s **up** the Law and the Prophets. *1639*

SUN (142) [SUNDOWN, SUNRISE, SUNSET, SUNSHINE]

Ge 15:12 As the s was setting, Abram fell into a deep 9087
15:17 When the s had set and darkness had fallen, 9087
19:23 the s had risen over the land. 9087
28:11 for the night because the s had set. 9087
29: 7 "Look," he said, "the s is still high; 3427
32:31 The s rose above him as he passed Peniel, 9087
37: 9 and this time the s and moon 9087
Ex 16:21 and when the s grew hot, it melted away. 9087
Lev 22: 7 When the s goes down, he will be clean, 9087
Dt 4:19 when you look up to the sky and see the s, 9087
11:30 west of the road, toward the setting s, 9087
16: 6 when the s goes down, 9087
17: 3 to the s or the moon or the stars of the sky, 9087
33:14 the best the s brings forth and the finest 9087
Jos 10:12 "O s, stand still over Gibeon, O moon, 9087
10:13 So the s stood still, and the moon stopped, 9087
10:13 The s stopped in the middle of the sky 9087
Jdg 5:31 be like the s when it rises in its strength." 9087
19:14 s set as they neared Gibeah in Benjamin. 9087
1Sa 11: 9 'By the time the s is hot tomorrow, 9087
2Sa 2:24 and as the s was setting, 9087
3:35 or anything else before the s sets!" 9087
1Ki 22:36 As the s was setting, 9087
2Ki 3:22 the s was shining on the water. 9087
23: 5 to the s and moon, 9087
23:11 the kings of Judah had dedicated to the s. 9087
23:11 then burned the chariots dedicated to the s. 9087
Ne 7: 3 not to be opened until the s is hot. 9087
Job 9: 7 He speaks to the s and it does not shine; 3064
30:28 I go about blackened, but not by the s; 2780
31:26 if I have regarded the s in its radiance or 240
37:21 Now no one can look at the s, 240
Ps 19: 4 the heavens he has pitched a tent for the s, 9087
37: 6 the justice of your cause like the **noonday** s. 7416
50: 1 the rising of the s to the place where it sets. 9087
58: 8 may they not see the s. 9087
72: 5 He will endure as long as the s, 9087
72:17 may it continue as long as the s. 9087
74:16 you established the s and moon. 9087
84:11 For the LORD God is a s and shield; 9087
89:36 and his throne endure before me like the s; 9087
104:19 and the s knows when to go down. 9087
104:22 The s rises, and they steal away; 9087
113: 3 the rising of the s to the place where it sets. 9087
121: 6 the s will not harm you by day, 9087
136: 8 the s to govern the day, 9087
148: 3 Praise him, s and moon, praise him, 9087
Ecc 1: 3 at which he toils under the s? 9087
1: 5 The s rises and the sun sets, 9087
1: 5 The sun rises and the s sets, 9087
1: 9 there is nothing new under the s. 9087
1:14 the things that are done under the s; 9087
2:11 nothing was gained under the s. 9087
2:17 that is done under the s was grievous to me. 9087
2:18 the things I had toiled for under the s, 9087
2:19 poured my effort and skill under the s. 9087

Ecc 2:20 over all my toilsome labor under the s. 9087
2:22 with which he labors under the s? 9087
3:16 And I saw something else under the s: 9087
4: 1 that was taking place under the s: 9087
4: 3 not seen the evil that is done under the s. 9087
4: 7 I saw something meaningless under the s: 9087
4:15 and walked under the s followed the youth, 9087
5:13 I have seen a grievous evil under the s: 9087
5:18 in his toilsome labor under the s during 9087
6: 1 I have seen another evil under the s, 9087
6: 5 it never saw the s or knew anything, 9087
6:12 will happen under the s after he is gone? 9087
7:11 and benefits those who see the s. 9087
8: 9 to everything done under the s. 9087
8:15 a man under the s than to eat and drink and 9087
8:15 of the life God has given him under the s. 9087
8:17 comprehend what goes on under the s. 9087
9: 3 in everything that happens under the s: 9087
9: 6 a part in anything that happens under the s. 9087
9: 9 that God has given you under the s— 9087
9: 9 and in your toilsome labor under the s. 9087
9:11 I have seen something else under the s: 9087
9:13 under the s this example of wisdom 9087
10: 5 There is an evil I have seen under the s, 9087
11: 7 and it pleases the eyes to see the s. 9087
12: 2 before the s and the light and the moon and 9087
SS 1: 6 because I am darkened by the s. 9087
6:10 fair as the moon, bright as the s, 2780
Isa 13:10 The rising s will be darkened and 9087
24:23 The moon will be abashed, the s ashamed; 2780
30:26 The moon will shine like the s, 2780
38: 8 the s go back the ten steps it has gone down 9087
41:25 from the rising s who calls on my name. 9087
45: 6 so that from the rising of the s to the place 9087
49:10 the desert heat or the s beat upon them. 9087
59:19 and from the rising of the s, 9087
60:19 The s will no more be your light by day, 9087
60:20 Your s will never set again, 9087
Jer 8: 2 They will be exposed to the s and the moon 9087
15: 9 Her s will set while it is still day; 9087
31:35 he who appoints the s to shine by day, 9087
43:13 of the s in Egypt he will demolish 9087
Eze 8:16 they were bowing down to the s in the east. 9087
32: 7 I will cover the s with a cloud, 9087
Hos 6: 3 As surely as the s **rises**, he will appear; 8840
Joel 2:10 the s and moon are darkened, 9087
2:31 The s will be turned to darkness and 9087
3:15 The s and moon will be darkened, 9087
Am 8: 9 the s go down at noon and darken the earth 9087
Jnh 4: 8 When the s rose, God provided a scorching 9087
4: 8 and the s blazed on Jonah's head so 9087
Mic 3: 6 The s will set for the prophets, 9087
Na 3:17 but when the s appears they fly away, 9087
Hab 3:11 S and moon stood still in the heavens at 9087
Mal 1:11 from the rising to the setting of the s. 9087
4: 2 the s *of* righteousness will rise with healing 9087
Mt 5:45 He causes his s to rise on the evil and *2463*
13: 6 But when the s came up, *2463*
13:43 Then the righteous will shine like the s in *2463*
17: 2 His face shone like the s, *2463*
24:29 " 'the s will be darkened, and the moon will *2463*
Mk 4: 6 But when the s came up, *2463*
13:24 " 'the s will be darkened, and the moon will *2463*
Lk 1:78 the **rising** s will come to us from heaven *424*
4:40 When the s was setting, *2463*
21:25 "There will be signs in the s, *2463*
23:45 for the s stopped shining. *2463*
Ac 2:20 The s will be turned to darkness and *2463*
13:11 be unable to see the light of the s." *2463*
26:13 a light from heaven, brighter than the s, *2463*
27:20 When neither s nor stars appeared *2463*
1Co 15:41 The s has one kind of splendor, *2463*
Eph 4:26 the s go down while you are still angry, *2463*
Jas 1:11 the s rises with scorching heat and withers *2463*
Rev 1:16 like the s shining in all its brilliance. *2463*
6:12 The s turned black like sackcloth made *2463*
7:16 The s will not beat upon them, *2463*
8:12 and a third *of* the s was struck, *2463*
9: 2 The s and sky were darkened by the smoke *2463*
10: 1 his face was like the s, *2463*
12: 1 a woman clothed with the s, *2463*
16: 8 on the s, and the sun was given power *2463*
16: 8 and **the** s was given power to scorch people *899S*
19:17 And I saw an angel standing in the s, *2463*
21:23 not need the s or the moon to shine on it, *2463*
22: 5 the light of a lamp or the light *of* the s, *2463*

SUN-SCORCHED (2) [SCORCH]

Ps 68: 6 but the rebellious live in a s **land.** 7461
Isa 58:11 in a s **land** and will strengthen your frame. 7463

SUNDER (KJV) See AWAY, PIECES, SHATTERS, THROUGH

SUNDOWN (1) [SUN]

Da 6:14 and made every effort until s to save him. 10002+10436+10728

SUNDRY (KJV) See MANY

SUNG (3) [SING]

Isa 26: 1 In that day this song *will* **be** s in the land 8876
Mt 26:30 *When they had* s **a hymn,** *5630*
Mk 14:26 *When they had* s **a hymn,** *5630*

SUNK (3) [SINK]

Jer 38:22 Your feet *are* s in the mud; 3190
La 2: 9 Her gates *have* s into the ground; 3190
Hos 9: 9 *They have* s **deep** *into* corruption, 6676

SUNLIGHT (2) [LIGHT]

Isa 30:26 and the s will be seven times brighter, 240+2780
38: 8 s went back the ten steps it had gone down. 9087

SUNRISE (13) [SUN]

Ex 22: 3 but if it happens *after* s, 2021+2436+9087
27:13 On the east end, toward the s, 4667
38:13 The east end, toward the s, 4667
Nu 2: 3 On the east, toward the s, 4667
3:38 of the tabernacle, toward the s, in front of 4667
21:11 desert that faces Moab toward the s. 4667+9087
34:15 of the Jordan of Jericho, toward the s." 4667
Jos 1:15 of the Jordan toward the s." 4667+9087
19:12 turned east from Sarid, *toward* the s 4667+9087
Jdg 9:33 In the morning at s, advance 2021+2436+9087
2Sa 23: 4 at s *on* a cloudless morning, 2436+9087
Hab 3: 4 His splendor was like the s; 240
Mk 16: 2 first day of the week, **just after** s *422+2463+3836*

SUNSET (10) [SUN]

Ex 17:12 his hands remained steady till s. 995+2021+9087
22:26 return it to him by s, 995+2021+9087
Dt 23:11 at s he may return to the camp. 995+2021+9087
24:13 by s so that he may sleep in it. 995+2021+9087
24:15 Pay him his wages each day before s, 995+2021+9087
Jos 8:29 At s, Joshua ordered them to take 995+2021+9087
10:27 At s Joshua gave the order 995+2021+6961+9087
Jdg 14:18 Before s on the seventh day 995+2021+3064
2Ch 18:34 Then at s he died. 995+2021+6961+9087
Mk 1:32 That evening after s the people *1544+2463*

SUNSHINE (2) [SUN]

Job 8:16 He is like a well-watered plant in the s, 9087
Isa 18: 4 like shimmering heat in the s, 240

SUP (KJV) See ADVANCE, EAT

SUPER-APOSTLES (2) [APOSTLE]

2Co 11: 5 I am in the least inferior to those **"s."** *693+5663*
12:11 I am not in the least inferior to the **"s,"** *693+5663*

SUPERFLUITY, SUPERFLUOUS (KJV) See DEFORMED, NO NEED, PREVALENT

SUPERIOR (7)

Da 8:25 and *he will* consider himself s. 1540
Ro 2:18 of what *is* s because you are instructed by *1422*
1Co 2: 1 not come with eloquence or s **wisdom** *5053+5667*
Heb 1: 4 So he became as much s **to** the angels as *3202*
1: 4 the angels as the name he has inherited is s *1427*
8: 6 But the ministry Jesus has received is *as* s *1427*
8: 6 covenant of which he is mediator is s **to** *3202*

SUPERSCRIPTION (KJV) See INSCRIPTION, WRITTEN NOTICE

SUPERSTITIONS (1)

Isa 2: 6 They are full of s from the East; NIH

SUPERVISE (5) [SUPERVISED, SUPERVISING, SUPERVISION, SUPERVISOR, SUPERVISORS]

2Ki 12:11 to the men appointed *to* s the work on 6913
22: 5 to the men appointed *to* s the work on 6913
1Ch 23: 4 to s the work of the temple of the LORD 5904
2Ch 34:10 *to* s the work on the LORD's temple. 6913
Ezr 3: 8 and older to s the building of the house of 5904

SUPERVISED (2) [SUPERVISE]

1Ki 5:16 as thirty-three hundred foremen who s 6584
2Ch 34:13 the laborers and s all the workers from job 5904

SUPERVISING (3) [SUPERVISE]

1Ki 9:23 550 officials s the men who did the work. 928
2Ch 8:10 two hundred and fifty officials s the men. 928
Ezr 3: 9 in s those working on the house of God. 5904

SUPERVISION (7) [SUPERVISE]

Nu 8:22 Tent of Meeting **under** the s *of* Aaron 4200+7156
1Ch 25: 2 sons of Asaph were under the s *of* Asaph, 3338
25: 2 who prophesied under the king's s. 3338
25: 3 under the s *of* their father Jeduthun, 3338
25: 6 under the s *of* their fathers for the music of 3338
25: 6 Jeduthun and Heman were under the s *of* 3338
Gal 3:25 we are no longer under the s of the law. *4080*

SUPERVISOR (1) [SUPERVISE]

Ne 11:11 the son of Ahitub, s *in* the house of God, 5592

SUPERVISORS (4) [SUPERVISE]

2Ki 22: 9 and have entrusted it to the workers and s at 7212
2Ch 31:13 and Benaiah were s under Conaniah 7224
34:17 and have entrusted it to the s and workers." 7212
Ne 3: 5 their shoulders to the work under their s. 123

SUPH (1)

Dt 1: 1 opposite S, between Paran and Tophel, 6069

SUPHAH (1)

Nu 21:14 "...Waheb in S and the ravines, 6071

SUPPER (7)

Lk 17: 8 he not rather say, 'Prepare **my** s, *1268+5515*
22:20 In the same way, after the s he took the cup, *1268*
Jn 21:20 who leaned back against Jesus at the s *1270*
1Co 11:20 it is not the Lord's S you eat, *1270*
11:25 In the same way, after s he took the cup, *1268*
Rev 19: 9 to the wedding s of the Lamb!' " *1270*
19:17 gather together for the great s of God, *1270*

SUPPLANT (KJV) See DECEIVER

SUPPLE (Anglicized) See LIMBER

SUPPLE (KJV) See MAKE CLEAN

SUPPLICATION (5) [SUPPLICATIONS]

1Ki 8:30 Hear the s *of* your servant and 9382
8:33 praying and **making** s to you in this temple, 2858
2Ch 6:24 and **making** s before you in this temple, 2858
Ps 119:170 May my s come before you; 9382
Zec 12:10 of Jerusalem a spirit of grace and s. 9384

SUPPLICATIONS (2) [SUPPLICATION]

1Ki 8:54 all these prayers and s to the LORD, 9382
2Ch 6:21 Hear the s *of* your servant and of your 9384

SUPPLIED (14) [SUPPLY]

Nu 31: 5 *were* s from the clans of Israel. 5034
1Ki 4: 7 *who* s **provisions** *for* the king and 3920
4:27 s **provisions** *for* King Solomon 3920
5:10 In this way Hiram *kept* Solomon s *with* all 5989
9:11 because Hiram *had* s him with all the cedar 5951
18: 4 and *had* s them *with* food and water.) 3920
18:13 and s them *with* food and water. 3920
1Ch 12:39 for their families *had* s **provisions** for them. 3922
Isa 33:16 His bread *will* **be** s, and water will not fail 5989
Jer 5: 7 *I* s **all** their **needs,** yet they committed 8425
Ac 20:34 these hands of mine *have* s my own needs *5676*
1Co 16:17 they *have* s what was lacking from you. *405*
2Co 11: 9 who came from Macedonia s what I needed. *4650*
Php 4:18 *I am* **amply** s, now that I have received *4444*

SUPPLIES (18) [SUPPLY]

Jos 1:11 'Get your s ready. 7476
1Sa 17:22 David left his things with the keeper of s, 3998
25:13 while two hundred stayed with the s. 3998
30:24 of the man who stayed with the s is to be 3998
1Ki 4: 7 Each one had to **provide** s *for* one month in 3920
1Ch 12:40 There were plentiful s of flour, fig cakes, 4407
27:28 Joash was in charge of the s *of* olive oil. 238
2Ch 11:11 with s *of* food, olive oil and wine. 238
17:13 and had large s in the towns of Judah. 4856
Ne 13:13 for **distributing** *the* s to their brothers. 2745
Ps 105:16 the land and destroyed all their s *of* food; 4751
147: 8 he s the earth *with* rain and makes grass 3922
Pr 31:24 and s the merchants *with* sashes. 5989
Isa 3: 1 all s *of* food and all supplies of water, 5472
3: 1 all supplies of food and all s *of* water, 5472
10:28 they store s at Micmash. 3998
Ac 28:10 they furnished us with the s we needed. *NIG*
2Co 9:10 Now he who s seed to the sower and bread *2220*

SUPPLY (23) [SUPPLIED, SUPPLIES, SUPPLYING]

Ex 5: 7 "You are no longer to s the people 5989
Lev 26:26 When I cut off your s *of* bread, 4751
Nu 4: 9 and all its jars for the oil used *to* s it. 9250
Dt 15:14 S him **liberally** from your flock, 6735+6735
Jos 9: 5 All the bread of their **food** s was dry 7474
Jdg 19:20 "Let me s whatever you need. NIH
2Sa 12:27 against Rabbah and taken its **water** s. 4784
1Ki 17: 9 a widow in that place to s you **with food."** 3920
2Ki 3: 4 and *he had to* s the king of Israel *with* 8740
Ezr 7:20 that you may have occasion to s, 10498
Ne 5:18 and every ten days an **abundant** s of wine 2221
Ps 78:20 *Can he* s meat for his people?" 3922
Isa 3: 1 to take from Jerusalem and Judah both s 5473
Eze 4:16 I will cut off the s *of* food in Jerusalem. 4751
5:16 upon you and cut off your s *of* food. 4751
14:13 to cut off its food s and send famine upon it 4751
48:18 Its produce *will* s food for the workers 2118+4200
Na 2: 9 The s is endless, the wealth from all its 9414
Ac 12:20 on the king's country for their **food** s. *5555*

2Co 8:14 your plenty *will* s what they need, *1181*
8:14 in turn their plenty *will* s what you need. *NIG*
9:10 for food *will* also s and increase your store *5961*
1Th 3:10 and s what is lacking in your faith. *2936*

SUPPLYING (1) [SUPPLY]

2Co 9:12 not only s the needs of God's people but is *4650*

SUPPORT (24) [SUPPORTED, SUPPORTING, SUPPORTS]

Ge 13:6 not s them while they stayed together, 5951
36:7 not s them both because of their livestock. 5951
Lev 25:35 and *is* **unable to** s himself among you, 3338+4572
Jdg 16:26 "Put me where I can feel the pillars that s 3922
2Sa 18:3 It would be better now for you to **give** us s 6468
22:19 but the LORD was my **s.** 5472
1Ki 1:7 and *they* **gave** him *their* **s.** 339+6468
2Ki 15:19 a thousand talents of silver to **gain** his s 907+2118+3338
1Ch 11:10 **gave** his kingship **strong** s 2616+6640
2Ch 28:13 to s the king against his enemies. 6468
Ezr 10:4 We will s you, so take courage and do it." 6640
Ps 18:18 but the LORD was my **s.** 5472
20:2 the sanctuary and **grant** you s from Zion. 6184
Pr 28:17 a fugitive till death; *let* no *one* s him. 9461
Isa 3:1 and Judah both supply and **s:** 5474
63:5 I was appalled that no *one* **gave s;** 6164
Jer 37:7 which has marched out to s you, 6476
Da 11:1 I took my stand to s and protect him.) 2616
Lk 8:3 These women *were* **helping to** s them out *1354*
Ac 12:20 *Having* **secured the** s of Blastus, *4275*
Ro 11:18 You *do* not s the root, *1002*
1Co 9:12 If others have this right of s from you, *NIG*
2Co 11:8 I robbed other churches by receiving s *4072*
2Ti 4:16 At my first defense, no one **came to** my **s,** *4134*

SUPPORTED (11) [SUPPORT]

1Ki 16:21 half s Tibni son of Ginath for king, 339+2118
16:21 and the other half s Omri. 339
2Ki 16:17 from the bronze bulls that s it and set it on 9393
2Ch 11:17 the kingdom of Judah and s Rehoboam son 599
Ezr 10:15 s *by* Meshullam and Shabbethai the Levite, 6468
Job 4:4 Your words *have* s those who stumbled; 7756
Ps 89:43 of his sword and *have* not s him in battle. 7756
94:18 your love, O LORD, s me. 6184
Jer 26:24 son of Shaphan s Jeremiah, 907+2118+3338
Da 11:6 and her father and the *one who* s her. 2616
Col 2:19 s and held together by its ligaments *2220*

SUPPORTING (8) [SUPPORT]

2Sa 5:9 from the s **terraces** inward. 4864
1Ki 7:2 of cedar columns s trimmed cedar beams. 6584
9:15 the s **terraces,** the wall of Jerusalem, 4864
9:24 he constructed the s **terraces.** 4864
11:27 the s **terraces** and had filled in the gap in 4864
1Ch 11:8 from the s **terraces** to the surrounding wall, 4864
2Ch 32:5 and reinforced the **s terraces** *of* the City 4864
Eph 4:16 and held together by every s ligament, *2221*

SUPPORTS (8) [SUPPORT]

1Ki 7:30 and each had a basin resting on four **s,** 4190+7193
7:35 The s and panels were attached to the top of 3338
7:36 lions and palm trees on the surfaces of the s 3338
10:12 The king used the almugwood to make s for 5026
Eze 41:6 the temple to serve as s for the side rooms, 296
41:6 so that the s were not inserted into the wall 296
Da 10:21 (No one s me against them except Michael, your prince. 2616+6640
Ro 11:18 do not support the root, but the root s you. *NIG*

SUPPOSE (21) [SUPPOSED, SUPPOSEDLY, SUPPOSING]

Ex 3:13 **"S** I go to the Israelites and say to them, 2180
Nu 36:3 Now s they marry men NIH
Jdg 11:9 **"S** you take me back to fight 561
Job 34:31 **"S** a man says to God, 3954
Eze 18:5 **"S** there is a righteous man who does what 3954
18:10 **"S** he has a violent son, 2256
18:14 "But s this son has a son who sees all 2180
Mt 10:34 *"Do* not s that I have come to bring peace to *3787*
24:48 s that servant is wicked and says to himself, *1569*
Lk 7:43 *"I* s the one who had the bigger debt *5696*
11:5 he said to them, **"S one** of you has a friend, *5515*
12:45 But s the servant says to himself, *1569*
14:28 **"S one** of you wants to build a tower. *5515*
14:31 "Or s a king is about to go to war *5515*
15:4 **"S one** of you has a hundred sheep *476+5515*
15:8 "Or s a woman has ten silver coins *1569+5515*
17:7 **"S one** of you had a servant plowing *5515*
Jn 21:25 *I* s that even the whole world would *3887*
Ac 2:15 These men are not drunk, as you **s.** *5696*
Jas 2:2 S a man comes into your meeting *1142+1569*
2:15 S a brother or sister is without clothes *1569*

SUPPOSED (2) [SUPPOSE]

1Sa 20:5 and I *am* **s to dine** with the king; 430+3782+3782
2Th 2:2 report or letter s to have come from us, *6055*

SUPPOSEDLY (1) [SUPPOSE]

Jer 23:30 prophets who steal from one another words s from me. NIH

SUPPOSING (2) [SUPPOSE]

Jn 11:31 s she was going to the tomb to mourn there. *1506*
Php 1:17 s that they can stir up trouble for me *3887*

SUPPRESS (1)

Ro 1:18 of men who s the truth by their wickedness, *2988*

SUPREMACY (1) [SUPREME]

Col 1:18 so that in everything he might have the **s.** *4750*

SUPREME (5) [SUPREMACY]

2Ki 18:17 The king of Assyria sent his **s commander,** 9580
Pr 4:7 Wisdom is **s;** therefore get wisdom. 8040
Ecc 8:4 Since a king's word is **s,** 8950
Isa 20:1 In the year that the **s commander,** 9580
1Pe 2:13 whether to the king, as the **s authority,** *5660*

SUR (1)

2Ki 11:6 at the S Gate, and a third at the gate behind 6075

SURE (62) [SURELY]

Ge 20:7 *you may* **be s** that you and all yours will die. 3359
24:6 **"Make s** *that* you do take my son back 9068
32:20 And **be s** to say, 2180
Ex 8:29 *s that* Pharaoh *does* not **act deceitfully** AIT
10:28 **Make s** you do not appear before me again! 9068
17:14 **make s** *that* Joshua **hears** 265+928+8492
23:4 **be s to take** it **back** to him. 8740+8740
23:5 **be s** *you* **help** him with it. 6441+6441
Nu 26:55 **Be s** that the land is distributed by lot. 421
28:31 Be s the animals are without defect. NIH
32:23 *you may* **be s** that your sin will find you out. 3359
Dt 5:1 Learn them and **be s** to follow them. 9068
6:17 **Be s to keep** the commands of 9068+9068
11:32 **be s** that you obey all the decrees 9068
12:23 But **be s** you do not eat the blood, 2616
14:22 **Be s to set aside a tenth** 6923+6923
17:15 **be s to appoint** over you the king 8492+8492
21:23 **Be s to bury** him that same day, 7699+7699
22:1 **be s to take** it **back** to him. 8740+8740
22:7 **be s to let** the mother **go,** 8938+8938
23:23 Whatever your lips utter *you must* **be s** 9068
28:66 never s of your life. 586
29:18 Make s there is no man or woman, NIH
29:18 make s there is no root among you NIH
31:29 *you are* **s to become utterly corrupt** 8845+8845
Jos 2:12 Give me a s sign 622
13:6 **Be s** to allocate this land to Israel for 8370
23:13 then *you may* **be s** that the LORD 3359+3359
Jdg 15:2 *"I was* **so s** you thoroughly hated her," 606+606
1Sa 12:24 But *be s to* **fear** the LORD and serve AIT
20:7 *you can* **be s** that he is determined 3359
22:22 I knew *he would* **be s to tell** Saul. 5583+5583
1Ki 2:37 *you can* **be s** you will die; 3359+3359
2:42 *you can* **be s** you will die'? 3359+3359
Ezr 7:17 With this money **be s** to buy bulls, 10056
Ps 19:9 the LORD are s and altogether righteous. 622
69:13 O God, answer me with your s salvation. 622
132:11 a s oath that he will not revoke: 622
Pr 11:14 but many advisers make victory **s.** NIH
11:18 he who sows righteousness reaps a s reward. 622
11:21 **Be s of this:** The wicked will not go unpunished, 3338+3338+4200
16:5 **Be s of this:** They will not go unpunished. 3338+3338+4200
27:23 **Be s** *you* **know** the condition of your flocks, 3359+3359
Isa 28:16 a precious cornerstone for a s foundation; 3569
33:6 He will be the **s foundation** *for* your times, 575
Jer 42:19 **Be s** *of* this: I warn you today 3359+3359
42:22 **be s** *of* this: you will die by the sword, 3359+3359
Eze 30:9 Egypt's doom, for it is s to come. 2180
Mt 17:11 Jesus replied, **"To be s,** Elijah comes and *3525*
Mk 9:12 Jesus replied, "To be **s,** Elijah does come *NIG*
Lk 1:18 "How *can I* **be s of** this? *1182*
10:11 *be* **s of** this: The kingdom of God is near.' *1182*
Ac 13:34 and s blessings promised to David.' *4412*
Ro 15:28 and *have* **made s that** they have received *5381*
2Co 13:4 **For to be s,** he was crucified in weakness, *1142*
Eph 5:5 For of this *you can be* **s:** *1182+3857*
1Th 5:15 **Make s that** nobody pays back wrong *3972*
Tit 3:11 *be* s that such a man is warped and sinful; *3857*
Heb 6:11 in order to make your hope **s.** *4443*
11:1 Now faith is *being* s of what we hope for *5712*
13:18 *We are* s that we have a clear conscience *4275*
2Pe 1:10 to make your calling and election **s.** *1010*

SURELY (304) [SURE]

Ge 2:17 for when you eat of it *you will* **s die."** 4637+4637
3:4 *"You will* not **s die,"** 4637+4637
6:13 I am s going to destroy both them and 2180
9:5 And for your lifeblood I will s demand 421
17:16 I will bless her and will s give you a son 1685
17:20 I will s bless him; 2180
18:10 *"I will* **s return** to you 8740+8740
18:18 Abraham *will* **s become** a great 2118+2118
20:11 'There is s no fear of God in this place, 8370
22:17 *I will* **s bless** you 1385+1385
26:11 *shall* **s be put to death."** 4637+4637
28:16 he thought, **"S the** LORD is in this place, 434
29:32 S my husband will love me now." 3954
31:16 **S** all the wealth that God took away 3954
31:42 you would s have sent me away 3954+6964
32:12 *'I will* **s make** you **prosper** 3512+3512
37:33 Joseph *has* **s been torn to pieces."** 3271+3271
42:15 **As s as** Pharaoh **lives,** 2644
42:16 **as s as** Pharaoh **lives,** 2644
42:21 **"S** we are being punished because 66
44:28 and I said, "He has s been torn to pieces." 421
46:4 and I *will* **s bring** you **back** again. 6590+6590
50:24 God *will* **s come to** your **aid** 7212+7212
50:25 God *will* **s come to** your **aid,** 7212+7212
Ex 4:25 **"S** you are a bridegroom of blood to me," 3954
13:19 "God *will* **s come to** your **aid,** 7212+7212
19:12 *He shall* **s be put to death.** 4637+4637
19:13 *He shall* **s be stoned** or shot with 6232+6232
21:12 *shall* **s be put to death.** 4637+4637
Nu 14:21 **as s as I live** and as surely as the glory of 2644
14:21 as surely as I live and as s as the glory of NIH
14:28 **'As s as I live,** declares the LORD, 2644
14:35 and I will s do these things 561+4202
15:31 that person **must s be cut off;** 4162+4162
26:65 the LORD had told those Israelites *they would* **s die** 4637+4637
35:31 He must s be put to death. 3954
Dt 4:6 **"S** this great nation is a wise 8370
8:19 that *you will* **s be destroyed.** 6+6
32:40 **As s as I live** forever, 2645
33:3 S it is you who love the people; 677
Jos 2:24 "The LORD has s given the whole land 3954
10:14 S the LORD was fighting for Israel! 3954
Jdg 8:19 **As s as** the LORD **lives,** 2644
Ru 3:13 **as s as** the LORD **lives** 2644
1Sa 1:26 **"As s as** you **live,** 2644+5883
10:8 I will s come down to you 2180
14:39 **As s as** the LORD who rescues Israel **lives,** 2644
14:45 **As s as** the LORD **lives,** 2644
15:32 thinking, **"S** the bitterness of death is past." 434
16:6 "S the LORD's anointed stands here 421
17:55 **"As s as** you **live,** 2644
19:6 **"As s as** the LORD **lives,** 2644
20:3 **as s as** the LORD **lives** 2644
20:12 "By the LORD, the God of Israel, I will s 3954
20:21 **as s as** the LORD **lives,** 2644
20:26 s he is unclean." 3954
22:16 But the king said, *"You will* **s die,** 4637+4637
24:20 I know that *you will* **s be king** and that 4887+4887
25:26 **as s as** the LORD **lives** 2644
25:34 **as s as** the LORD, the God of Israel, **lives,** 2644
26:10 **As s as** the LORD **lives,"** 2644
26:16 **As s as** the LORD **lives,** 2644
26:21 S I have acted like a fool 2180
26:24 As s as I valued your life today, 2180
26:25 will do great things and **s triumph."** 3523+3523
28:9 "S you know what Saul has done. 2180
28:10 **"As s as** the LORD **lives,** 2644
29:6 **"As s as** the LORD **lives,** 2644
2Sa 2:27 **"As s as** God **lives,** 2644
4:9 **"As s as** the LORD **lives,** 2644
5:19 **s hand** the Philistines **over** 928+3338+5989+5989
9:7 "for *I will* **s show** you kindness for 6913+6913
11:11 **As s as** you **live,** 2256+2644+2644+5883
12:5 **"As s as** the LORD **lives,** 2644
14:11 **"As s as** the LORD **lives,"** 2644
14:19 **"As s as** you **live,** 2644+5883
15:21 **"As s as** the LORD **lives,** 2644
18:2 *"I myself will* **s march out** with you." 3655+3655
1Ki 1:13 **"S** Solomon your son shall be king 3954
1:29 **"As s as** the LORD **lives,** 2644
1:30 I will s carry out today what I swore to you 3954
2:24 **as s as** the LORD **lives—** 2644
11:2 **because** they will s turn your hearts 434
17:12 **"As s as** the LORD your God **lives,"** 2644
18:10 **As s as** the LORD your God **lives,** 2644
18:15 I will s present myself to Ahab today." 3954
18:27 "S he is a god! 3954
20:23 s we will be stronger than they. 561+4202
20:25 Then s we will be stronger than they." 561+4202
22:14 **"As s as** the LORD **lives,** 2644
22:32 they thought, **"S** this is the king of Israel." 421
2Ki 2:2 **"As s as** the LORD **lives** 2644
2:4 **"As s as** the LORD **lives** 2644
2:6 **"As s as** the LORD **lives** 2644
3:14 **"As s as** the LORD Almighty **lives,** 2644
4:30 **"As s as** the LORD **lives** 2644
5:11 "I thought that *he would* **s come out** to 3655+3655
5:16 **"As s as** the LORD **lives,** 2644
5:20 **As s as** the LORD **lives,** 2644
7:12 thinking, 'They will s come out, 3954
9:26 I will s make you pay for it on this plot 561+4202
18:30 'The LORD *will* **s deliver** us; 5911+5911
19:11 **S** you have heard what the kings 2180
20:17 The time will s come when everything 2180
24:3 **S** these things happened to Judah according 421
2Ch 18:13 **"As s as** the LORD **lives,** 2644
Ezr 7:26 law of the king must s be punished 10056
Est 6:13 *you will* **s come to ruin!"** 5877+5877
Job 1:11 and he will s curse you to your face." 561+4202
2:5 and he will s curse you to your face." 561+4202
5:7 to trouble **as s as** sparks fly upward. 2256
6:3 It would s outweigh the sand of the seas— 3954
8:19 **S** its life withers away, 2176
8:20 **"S** God does not reject a blameless man 2176
11:11 **S** he recognizes deceitful men; 3954
11:16 You will s forget your trouble, 3954
13:10 *He would* **s rebuke** you 3519+3519
13:15 I will s defend my ways to his face. 421
14:16 **S** then you will count my steps but 3954
16:7 **S,** O God, you have worn me out; 421+6964

Job 17: 2 S mockers surround me; 561+4202
18:21 S such is the dwelling of an evil man; 421
20: 4 "S you know how it has been from of old, 2022
20:20 "S he will have no respite from his craving; 3954
22:20 'S our foes are destroyed, 561+4202
22:26 S then you will find delight in 3954
27: 2 "**As s as** God **lives,** 2644
30:24 "S no one lays a hand on a broken man 421
31:36 S I would wear it on my shoulder, 561+4202
38: 5 S you know! 3954
38:21 S you know, for you were already born! 3954
42: 3 S I spoke of things I did not understand, 4027+4200
Ps 5:12 **For s,** O LORD, you bless the righteous; 3954
16: 6 s I have a delightful inheritance. 677
21: 6 S you have granted him eternal blessings 3954
23: 6 S goodness and love will follow me all 421
32: 6 s when the mighty waters rise, 8370
49:15 he will s take me to himself. 3954
51: 5 S I was sinful at birth, 2176
51: 6 S you desire truth in the inner parts; 2176
52: 5 S God will bring you down 1685
54: 4 S God is my help; 2180
58:11 "S the righteous still are rewarded; 421
58:11 s there is a God who judges the earth." 421
62:12 S you will reward each person according 3954
64: 6 S the mind and heart of man are cunning. 2256
66:19 but God has s listened and heard my voice 434
68:21 S God will crush the heads of his enemies, 421
73: 1 S God is good to Israel, 421
73:13 S in vain have I kept my heart pure; 421
73:18 S you place them on slippery ground; 421
76:10 S your wrath against men brings you praise, 3954
85: 9 S his salvation is near those who fear him, 421
89:21 s my arm will strengthen him. 677
91: 3 S he will save you from the fowler's snare 3954
92: 9 For s your enemies, O LORD, 2180
92: 9 O LORD, s your enemies will perish; 2180
112: 6 S he will never be shaken; 3954
139:11 "S the darkness will hide me and 421
140:13 S the righteous will praise your name and 421
Pr 11:15 up security for another *will* **s suffer,** 8273+8317
12:14 a man is filled with good things **as s as** 2256
21: 5 the diligent lead to profit **as s as** haste leads 421
23: 5 *they will* **s sprout** wings and fly off 6913+6913
23:18 There is s a future hope for you, 561+3954
Isa 5: 9 "S the great houses will become desolate, 561+4202
9:18 S wickedness burns like a fire; 3954
12: 2 S God is my salvation; 2180
14:24 The LORD Almighty has sworn, "S, 561+4202
25: 9 "S this is our God; 2180
36:15 'The LORD *will* **s deliver** us; 5911+5911
37:11 S you have heard what the kings 2180
38:17 S it was for my benefit that I suffered 2180
39: 6 The time will s come when everything 2180
40: 7 S the people are grass. 434
40:15 S the nations are like a drop in a bucket; 2176
41:11 "All who rage against you will s be ashamed NIH
45:14 'S God is with you, and there is no other; 421
47:14 S they are like stubble; 2180
49:18 **As s as I live,"** 2644
51: 3 The LORD will s comfort Zion 3954
53: 4 S he took up our infirmities 434
55: 5 S you will summon nations you know not, 2176
56: 3 "The LORD *will* **s exclude** me 976+976
59: 1 S the arm of the LORD is not too short 2176
60: 9 S the islands look to me; 3954
63: 8 He said, "S they are my people, 421
Jer 3:23 S the [idolatrous] commotion on the hills 434
3:23 s in the LORD our God is the salvation 434
4: 2 '**As s as** the LORD **lives,'** 2644
5: 2 '**As s as** the LORD **lives,'** 2644
5: 5 s they know the way of the LORD, 3954
12:16 '**As s as** the LORD **lives'—** 2644
15:11 S I will deliver you for a good purpose; 561+4202
15:11 s I will make your enemies plead with you 561+4202
16:14 '**As s as** the LORD **lives,** 2644
16:15 '**As s as** the LORD **lives,** 2644
22: 6 I will s make you like a desert, 561+4202
22:24 "**As s as I live,"** 2644
23: 7 '**As s as** the LORD **lives,** 2644
23: 8 '**As s as** the LORD **lives,** 2644
23:39 I *will* **s forget** you and cast you out 5960+5960
29:32 I will s punish Shemaiah the Nehelamite 2180
30:10 'I will s save you out of a distant place, 3954
31:18 *"I have* **s heard** Ephraim's moaning: 9048+9048
32:37 I will s gather them from all the lands 2180
34: 3 *will* **s be captured** and handed over 9530+9530
37: 9 'The Babylonians *will* **s leave** us.' 2143+2143+4946+6584
38:16 "**As s as** the LORD **lives,** 2644
44:26 "**As s as** the Sovereign LORD **lives."** 2644
44:29 of harm against you *will* **s stand.'** 7756+7756
46:18 "**As s as I live,"** 2644
46:27 I will s save you out of a distant place, 3954
49:26 S, her young men will fall in the streets; 4027+4200
51:14 I will s fill you with men, 561+3954
51:47 For the time will s come when I will punish 2180
Eze 3: 6 S if I had sent you to them, 4202
3:18 I say to a wicked man, *'You will* **s die,'** 4637+4637
3:21 *he will* **s live** because he took warning, 2649+2649
5:11 **as s as I live,** declares the Sovereign LORD, 2644
7: 4 I will s repay you for your conduct and 3954
14:16 **as s as I live,** declares the Sovereign LORD, 2644
Eze 14:18 **as s as I live,** declares the Sovereign LORD, 2644
14:20 **as s as I live,** declares the Sovereign LORD, 2644
16:43 I will s bring down on your head 2026
16:48 **As s as I live,** declares the Sovereign LORD, 2644
17:16 '**As s as I live,** declares the Sovereign LORD, 2644
17:19 **As s as I live,** I will bring down on his head 2644
18: 3 **As s as I live,** declares the Sovereign LORD, 2644
18: 9 That man is righteous; *he will* **s live,** 2649+2649
18:13 **s be put to death** 4637+4637
18:17 for his father's sin; *he will* **s live.** 2649+2649
18:19 keep all my decrees, *he will* **s live.** 2649+2649
18:21 *he will* **s live;** he will not die. 2649+2649
18:28 *he will* **s live;** he will not die. 2649+2649
20: 3 **As s as I live,** I will not let you 2644
20:31 **As s as I live,** declares the Sovereign LORD, 2644
20:33 **As s as I live,** declares the Sovereign LORD, 2644
20:39 But afterward you will s listen to me 401+561
21: 7 *It will* **s take place,** 2118
21:13 " 'Testing will s come. 3954
22:13 " 'I will s strike my hands together at 2180
33: 8 'O wicked man, *you will* **s die,'** 4637+4637
33:11 '**As s as I live,** declares the Sovereign LORD, 2644
33:13 the righteous man that *he will* **s live,** 2649+2649
33:14 to the wicked man, *'You will* **s die,'** 4637+4637
33:15 and does no evil, *he will* **s live;** 2649+2649
33:16 what is just and right; *he will* **s live.** 2649+2649
33:24 s the land has been given to us NIH
33:27 **As s as I live,** those who are left 2644
33:33 "When all this comes true—and it s will— 2180
34: 8 **As s as I live,** declares the Sovereign LORD, 2644
35: 6 **as s as I live,** declares the Sovereign LORD, 2644
35:11 **as s as I live,** declares the Sovereign LORD, 2644
39: 8 It will s take place, 2180
Da 2:47 "S your God is the God of gods and the Lord of kings 10168+10427+10643
Hos 4:15 '**As s as** the LORD **lives!'** 2644
6: 3 **As s as** the sun rises, he will appear; 3869
Joel 1:12 S the joy of mankind is withered away. 3954
2:20 S he has done great things. 3954
2:21 S the LORD has done great things. 3954
Am 3: 7 S the Sovereign LORD does nothing 3954
4: 2 "The time will s come when you will 3954
5: 5 For Gilgal *will* **s go into exile,** 1655+1655
7:11 and Israel *will* **s go into exile,** 1655+1655
8:14 '**As s as** your god **lives,** 2644
8:14 '**As s as** the god of Beersheba **lives'—** 2644
9: 8 "S the eyes of the Sovereign LORD are on 2180
Mic 2:12 *"I will* **s gather** all of you, O Jacob; 665+665
2:12 *I will* **s bring together** the remnant 7695+7695
Zep 2: 9 **as s as I live,"** declares the LORD Almighty, 2644
2: 9 "s Moab will become like Sodom, 3954
3: 7 'S you will fear me and accept correction!' 421
Zec 2: 9 I will s raise my hand against them so 3954
10: 8 S I will redeem them; 3954
Mal 4: 1 "S the day is coming; 2180+3954
Mt 26:22 to say to him one after the other, "S not I, *NIG*
26:25 said, "**S not** I, Rabbi?" *3614*
26:73 "S you are one of them, *242*
27:54 and exclaimed, "S he was the Son of God!" *242*
28:20 And s I am with you always, *2627*
Mk 14:19 and one by one they said to him, "**S not** I?" *3614*
14:70 "S you are one of them, *242*
15:39 he said, "S this man was the Son of God!" *242*
Lk 4:23 "S you will quote this proverb to me: *4122*
13:33 for s no prophet can die outside Jerusalem! *NIG*
23:47 "S this was a righteous man." *3953*
Jn 3: 4 "S he cannot enter a second time *NIG*
6:14 "S this is the Prophet who is to come into *242*
7:40 "S this man is the Prophet." *242*
18:21 S they know what I said." *3972*
Ac 10:14 "**S not,** Lord!" Peter replied. *3592*
11: 8 "I replied, '**S not,** Lord! *3592*
Ro 14:11 " '**As s as I live,'** says the Lord, *1609+2409*
1Co 9: 2 an apostle to others, s I am to you! *247+1145*
9:10 S he says this for us, doesn't he? *4122*
15:31 **I mean that,** brothers—**just as s** as I glory *3755*
2Co 1:18 But as s as God is faithful, *NIG*
11:10 As s as the truth of Christ is in me, *NIG*
Eph 3: 2 S you have heard about the administration of God's grace *1145+1623*
4:21 S you heard of him and were taught *1145+1623*
1Th 2: 9 S you remember, brothers, *1142*
Heb 2:16 For s it is not angels he helps, *1327*
6:14 "I will s bless you and give you many *1623+3605*

SURETY (KJV) See CERTAIN, ENSURE, GUARANTEE, GUARANTEED, PLEDGE, REALLY, SECURITY, WITHOUT DOUBT

SURF (1)

Ac 27:41 broken to pieces by the pounding *of* the s. *3246*

SURFACE (12) [SURFACES]

Ge 1: 2 darkness was over the s *of* the deep, 7156
2: 6 and watered the whole s *of* the ground— 7156
7:18 and the ark floated on the s *of* the water. 7156
8: 8 to see if the water had receded from the s 7156
8: 9 because there was water over all the s *of* 7156
8:13 the covering from the ark and saw that the s 7156
Lev 14:37 that appear to be deeper than the s of NIH
Job 24:18 "Yet they are foam on the s *of* the water; 7156
38:30 when the s *of* the deep is frozen? 7156
Isa 28:25 When he has leveled the s, 7156
Hos 10: 7 like a twig on the s *of* the waters. 7156

2Co 10: 7 are looking only on the s of things. *2848+4725*

SURFACES (1) [SURFACE]

1Ki 7:36 lions and palm trees on the s of the supports 4283

SURFEITING (KJV) See DISSIPATION

SURGE (2) [SURGED, SURGING]

Job 40:23 the Jordan *should* s against his mouth. 1631
Isa 54: 8 In a s *of* anger I hid my face from you for 9192

SURGED (1) [SURGE]

1Sa 17:52 Then the men of Israel and Judah **s forward** 7756

SURGING (7) [SURGE]

Ex 15: 8 The s waters stood firm like a wall; 5689
Ps 46: 3 and the mountains quake with their s. 1452
89: 9 You rule over the s sea; 1455
Isa 17:13 the peoples roar like the roar of s waters, 8041
Jer 46: 7 like rivers of s waters? 1723
46: 8 like rivers of s waters. 1723
Zec 10:11 the s sea will be subdued and all the depths 1644

SURLY (1)

1Sa 25: 3 a Calebite, was s and mean in his dealings. 7997

SURMISINGS (KJV) See SUSPICIONS

SURMOUNTED (1)

Eze 40:16 inside the gateway were **s by** 448

SURNAME (KJV) See CALLED, NAME

SURPASS (1) [ALL-SURPASSING, SURPASSED, SURPASSES, SURPASSING, SURPASSINGLY]

Pr 31:29 women do noble things, but you s them all." 6590

SURPASSED (2) [SURPASS]

Jn 1:15 'He who comes after me *has* s me *1181+1869*
1:30 'A man who comes after me *has* s me *1181+1869*

SURPASSES (3) [SURPASS]

Pr 8:19 what I yield s choice silver. 4946
Mt 5:20 that unless your righteousness s that of *4355+4498*
Eph 3:19 and to know this love *that* s knowledge— *5650*

SURPASSING (4) [SURPASS]

Ps 150: 2 praise him for his s greatness. 8044
2Co 3:10 now in comparison with the s glory. *5650*
9:14 because of the s grace God has given you. *5650*
Php 3: 8 a loss compared to the **s greatness** *5660*

SURPASSINGLY (1) [SURPASS]

2Co 12: 7 *because of* these **s great** revelations, *5651*

SURPRISE (6) [SURPRISED, SURPRISING]

Jos 10: 9 Joshua took them **by s.** 7328
Ps 35: 8 may ruin overtake them **by s—** 3359+4202
55:15 *Let* death **take** my enemies **by s;** 5958
Jer 14: 9 Why are you like a man **taken by s,** 1850
Ac 3:12 "Men of Israel, why *does* this s *you?* *2513*
1Th 5: 4 not in darkness so that this day *should* s you *2898*

SURPRISED (7) [SURPRISE]

Ecc 5: 8 *do* not *be* s at such things; 9449
Mk 15:44 Pilate *was* s to hear that he was already dead *2513*
Lk 11:38 not first wash before the meal, *was* **s.** *2513*
Jn 3: 7 *You should* not *be* s at my saying, *2513*
4:27 Just then his disciples returned and *were* s *2513*
1Pe 4:12 *be* s at the painful trial you are suffering, *3826*
1Jn 3:13 *Do* not *be* s, my brothers, *2513*

SURPRISING (1) [SURPRISE]

2Co 11:15 *It is* not s, then, if his servants masquerade *3489*

SURRENDER (14) [SURRENDERED, SURRENDERS]

Jos 20: 5 *they must* not s the one accused, 928+3338+6037
Jdg 20:13 Now s those wicked men of Gibeah so 5989
1Sa 11: 3 no one comes to rescue us, *we will* s to you. 3655
11:10 "Tomorrow *we will* s to you, 3655
23:11 *Will* the citizens of Keilah s me to him? 6037
23:12 the citizens of Keilah s me and my men 6037
2Ki 7: 4 over to the camp of the Arameans and s. 5877
Ps 41: 2 he will bless him in the land and not s him 5989
Isa 54:15 whoever attacks you *will* s to you. 5877
Jer 38:17 'If *you* s to the officers of the king 3655+3655
38:18 if *you will* not s to the officers of the king 3655
38:21 But if you refuse to s, this is what 3655
Da 8:13 and the s *of* the sanctuary and of the host 5989
1Co 13: 3 to the poor and s my body to the flames, *4140*

SURRENDERED (2) [SURRENDER]
2Ki 24:12 his nobles and his officials *all* s to him. 3655
Lk 23:25 and s Jesus to their will. *4140*

SURRENDERS (2) [SURRENDER]
Jer 21: 9 whoever goes out and s to the Babylonians 5877
50:15 *She* s, her towers fall, 3338+5989

SURROUND (21) [SURROUNDED, SURROUNDING, SURROUNDS]
Jos 7: 9 and *they will* s us and wipe out our name 6015
Job 16:13 his archers s me. 6015
17: 2 Surely mockers s me; 6643
40:22 the poplars by the stream s him. 6015
Ps 5:12 *you* s them *with* your favor as with 6496
17: 9 from my mortal enemies *who* s me. 5938
17:11 *they* now s me, with eyes alert, 6015
22:12 Many bulls s me; 6015
27: 6 be exalted above the enemies *who* s me; 6017
32: 7 you will protect me from trouble and s me 6015
40:12 For troubles without number s me; 705
49: 5 *when* wicked deceivers s me— 6015
88:17 All day long *they* s me like a flood; 6015
89: 7 he is more awesome than all *who* s him. 6017
97: 2 Clouds and thick darkness s him; 6017
109: 3 *With* words of hatred *they* s me; 6015
125: 2 As the mountains s Jerusalem, 6017
140: 9 the heads of *those who* s me be covered with 4990
Jer 4:17 *They* s her like men guarding a field, 2118+4946+6017
12: 9 that other birds of prey s and attack? 6017
31:22 a woman *will* s a man." 6015

SURROUNDED (28) [SURROUND]
Ge 19: 4 both young and old—s the house. 6015
Jdg 16: 2 So *they* s the place and lay in wait 6015
19:22 of the wicked men of the city s the house. 6015
20: 5 of Gibeah came after me and s the house, 6015
20:43 *They* s the Benjamites, 4193
2Sa 18:15 ten of Joab's armor-bearers s Absalom, 6015
1Ki 7:12 The great courtyard was s *by* a wall 6017
2Ki 3:25 with slings s it and attacked it as well. 6015
6:14 They went by night and s the city. 5938
6:15 an army with horses and chariots *had* s 6015
8:21 The Edomites s him and his chariot 6015
1Ch 29:30 and the circumstances that s him and Israel 6296
2Ch 21: 9 The Edomites s him and his chariot 6015
Ps 22:16 Dogs *have* s me; a band of evil men 6015
118:10 All the nations s me, 6015
118:11 *They* s me on every side, 6015
Ecc 9:14 s it and built huge siegeworks against it. 6015
La 3: 5 and s me *with* bitterness and hardship. 5938
Eze 1: 4 flashing lightning and s by brilliant light. 6017
1:27 and brilliant light s him. 6017
27:32 "Who was ever silenced like Tyre, **s by** 928+9348
32:22 she is s *by* the graves of all her slain, 6017
Hos 11:12 Ephraim *has* s me with lies, 6015
Jnh 2: 5 waters threatened me, the deep s me; 6015
Lk 21:20 "When you see Jerusalem *being* s *3240*
Jn 5: 2 and which *is* s **by** five covered colonnades. *2400*
Heb 12: 1 since we are s by such a great cloud *4329*
Rev 20: 9 the earth and s the camp of God's people, *3238*

SURROUNDING (57) [SURROUND]
Ge 41:48 the food grown in the fields s it. 6017
Ex 38:20 and of the s courtyard were bronze. 6017
38:31 for the s courtyard and those for its entrance 6017
38:31 the tabernacle and those for the s courtyard. 6017
Nu 3:26 the curtain at the entrance to the courtyard s 6017
3:37 the posts of the s courtyard with their bases, 6017
4:26 of the courtyard s the tabernacle and altar, 6017
4:32 the posts of the s courtyard with their bases, 6017
21:25 Heshbon and all its s **settlements.** 1426
21:32 the Israelites captured its s **settlements** 1426
32:42 and its s **settlements** and called it Nobah 1426
Jos 15:45 Ekron, with its s **settlements** and villages; 1426
15:47 its s **settlements** and villages; 1426
17:11 together with their s **settlements** (the third 1426
21:11 Hebron), with its s pastureland, 6017
21:42 Each of these towns had pasturelands s it; 6017
Jdg 1:27 or Megiddo and their s **settlements,** 1426
11:26 the s **settlements** and all the towns along 1426
1Ki 4:31 And his fame spread to all the s nations. 6017
2Ki 25: 4 though the Babylonians were s the city. 6017
1Ch 2:23 as well as Kenath with its s **settlements** — 1426
4:32 Their s **villages** were Etam, Ain, 2958
6:55 in Judah with its s pasturelands. 6017
7:28 Bethel and its s **villages,** 1426
8:12 and Lod with its s **villages),** 1426
11: 8 from the supporting terraces to the s *wall,* 6017
18: 1 and he took Gath and its s **villages** from 1426
28:12 of the LORD and all the s rooms, 6017
2Ch 13:19 and Ephron, with their s **villages.** 1426
17:10 on all the kingdoms of the lands s Judah, 6017
28:18 Timnah and Gimzo, with their s **villages.** 1426
Ne 3:22 by the priests from the s **region.** 3971
5:17 as those who came to us from the s nations. 6017
6:16 all the s nations were afraid 6017
11:25 in Kiriath Arba and its s **settlements,** 1426
Jer 1:15 they will come against all her s walls and 6017
25: 9 and against all the s nations. 6017
34: 1 against Jerusalem and all its s towns, NIH
49: 2 and its s **villages** will be set on fire. 1426
Jer 52: 7 though the Babylonians were s the city. 6017
52:23 of pomegranates above the s network was 6017
Eze 34:26 I will bless them and the *places* s my hill. 6017
40: 5 I saw a wall **completely** s the temple 6017+6017
41: 7 The *structure* s the temple was built 6015
43:12 All the s area on top of the mountain 6017+6017
Zec 7: 7 when Jerusalem and its s towns were at rest 6017
12: 2 a cup that sends all the s peoples reeling. 6017
12: 6 and left all the s peoples, 6017
14:14 of all the s nations will be collected— 6017
Mt 14:35 they sent word to all the s **country.** *4369*
Mk 6:36 so they can go to the s countryside *3241*
Lk 4:37 about him spread throughout the s area. *4369*
7:17 throughout Judea and the s **country.** *4369*
9:12 the s villages and countryside and find food *3241*
Ac 14: 6 of Lystra and Derbe and to the s **country,** *4369*
Jude 1: 7 and the s towns gave themselves up *899+4309*
Rev 4: 4 S the throne were twenty-four other thrones, *3239*

SURROUNDS (3) [SURROUND]
Ps 32:10 but the LORD's unfailing love s the man who 6015
89: 8 O LORD, and your faithfulness s you. 6017
125: 2 so the LORD s his people both now 6017

SURVEY (2) [SURVEYED]
Jos 18: 4 send them out *to* **make a** s **of** the land 928+2143
18: 8 "Go and **make a** s **of** the land and write 928+2143

SURVEYED (1) [SURVEY]
Ecc 2:11 Yet *when* I s all that my hands had done 7155

SURVIVE (16) [SURVIVED, SURVIVES, SURVIVING, SURVIVOR, SURVIVORS]
Dt 4:27 of *you will* s among the nations to which 8636
Jos 11:22 only in Gaza, Gath and Ashdod *did any* s. 8636
2Sa 1:10 that after he had fallen *he could* not s. 2649
Job 27:15 The plague will bury *those who* s him, 8586
Isa 66:19 and I will send some of those *who* s to 7128
Jer 21: 7 and the people in this city who s the plague, 8636
31: 2 "The people *who* s the sword will find favor 8586
42:17 not one of them will s or escape 8586
44:14 to live in Egypt will escape or s to return to 8586
Eze 7:16 All *who* s and escape will be in 7117
Am 7: 2 How *can* Jacob s? He is so small!" 7756
7: 5 How *can* Jacob s? He is so small!" 7756
Zec 10: 9 *They* and their children *will* s, 2649
Mt 24:22 had not been cut short, no one *would* s, *323+5392*
Mk 13:20 not cut short those days, no one would s. *5392*
Ac 27:34 take some food. You need it to s. *5401*

SURVIVED (9) [SURVIVE]
Ex 14:28 Not one of them s. 8636
Nu 14:38 son of Nun and Caleb son of Jephunneh s. 2649
Dt 5:26 speaking out of fire, as we have, and s? 2649
Jos 13:12 and *had* s as one of the last of the Rephaites. 8636
1Sa 11:11 Those *who* s were scattered, 8636
Ne 1: 2 about the Jewish remnant that s the exile, 8636
1: 3 "Those who s the exile and are back in 8636
Ps 106:11 not one of them s. 3855
La 2:22 of the LORD's anger no one escaped or s; 8586

SURVIVES (4) [SURVIVE]
2Ki 19: 4 pray for the remnant that *still* s." 5162
Isa 37: 4 pray for the remnant that *still* s." 5162
Eze 6:12 he *that* s and is spared will die of famine. 8636
1Co 3:14 If what he has built s, he will receive *3531*

SURVIVING (3) [SURVIVE]
Dt 28:54 wife he loves or his s children, 889+3855+3856
Jer 29: 1 to the s elders among the exiles and to 3856
Eze 17:14 s only by keeping his treaty. 6641

SURVIVOR (5) [SURVIVE]
Jdg 12: 5 and whenever a s *of* Ephraim said, 7127
2Ki 10:11 leaving him no s. 8586
10:14 *He* **left** no s. 8636
Ezr 9:14 leaving us no remnant or s? 7129
Job 18:19 no s where once he lived. 8586

SURVIVORS (41) [SURVIVE]
Nu 21:35 his whole army leaving them no s. 8586
24:19 of Jacob and destroy the s of the city." 8586
Dt 2:34 We left no s. 8586
3: 3 We struck them down, leaving no s. 8586
7:20 the s who hide from you have perished. 8636
Jos 8:22 leaving them neither s nor fugitives. 8586
10:28 destroyed everyone in it. He left no s. 8586
10:30 Joshua put to the sword. He left no s there. 8586
10:33 until no s were left. 8586
10:37 and everyone in it. They left no s. 8586
10:39 they totally destroyed. They left no s. 8586
10:40 together with all their kings. He left no s. 8586
11: 8 until no s were left. 8586
23:12 with the s *of* these nations that remain 3856
Jdg 21:17 The Benjamite s must have heirs," 7129
2Sa 21: 2 a part of Israel but were s of the Amorites; 3856
2Ki 19:31 and out of Mount Zion a **band of s.** 7129
Ezr 1: 4 of any place where s may now be living are 8636
Ps 76:10 and the s *of* your wrath are restrained. 8642
Isa 1: 9 the LORD Almighty had left us some s, 8586
4: 2 the land will be the pride and glory of the s 7129
Isa 10:20 the s *of* the house of Jacob, 7129
14:22 from Babylon her name and s, 8637
14:30 it will slay your s. 8642
16:14 and her s will be very few and feeble." 8637
21:17 The s *of* the bowmen, 8637
37:32 and out of Mount Zion a **band of s.** 7129
Jer 8: 3 all the s of this evil nation will prefer death 8642
15: 9 the s to the sword before their enemies," 8642
24: 8 his officials and the s *from* Jerusalem, 8642
41:16 the s from Mizpah whom he had recovered 8642
47: 4 and to cut off all s who could help Tyre 8586
Eze 5:10 and will scatter all your s to the winds. 8642
14:22 Yet there will be some s— 7129
17:21 and the s will be scattered to the winds. 8636
Joel 2:32 among the s whom the LORD calls. 8586
Ob 1:14 over their s in the day of their trouble. 8586
1:18 There will be no s from the house of Esau." 8586
Zep 2: 9 the s *of* my nation will inherit their land." 3856
Zec 14:16 Then the s from all the nations 3855
Rev 11:13 and the s were terrified and gave glory to *3370*

SUSA (22)
Ezr 4: 9 Erech and Babylon, the Elamites **of** S, 10704
Ne 1: 1 while I was in the citadel of S, 8809
Est 1: 2 from his royal throne in the citadel of S, 8809
1: 5 who were in the citadel of S. 8809
2: 3 into the harem at the citadel of S. 8809
2: 5 Now there was in the citadel of S a Jew of 8809
2: 8 many girls were brought to the citadel of S 8809
3:15 and the edict was issued in the citadel of S. 8809
3:15 but the city of S was bewildered. 8809
4: 8 which had been published in S, 8809
4:16 gather together all the Jews who are in S, 8809
8:14 the edict was also issued in the citadel of S. 8809
8:15 And the city of S held a joyous celebration. 8809
9: 6 In the citadel of S, the Jews killed and 8809
9:11 in the citadel of S was reported to the king 8809
9:12 the ten sons of Haman in the citadel of S. 8809
9:13 "give the Jews in S permission 8809
9:14 An edict was issued in S, 8809
9:15 in S came together on the fourteenth day of 8809
9:15 they put to death in S three hundred men, 8809
9:18 The Jews in S, however, had assembled 8809
Da 8: 2 in the citadel of S in the province of Elam; 8809

SUSAH SEE HAZAR SUSAH

SUSANCHITES (KJV) See SUSA

SUSANNA (1)
Lk 8: 3 of Herod's household; S; and many others. *5052*

SUSI (1)
Nu 13:11 (a tribe of Joseph), Gaddi son of S; 6064

SUSIM See HAZAR SUSIM

SUSPECTS (3) [SUSPICIONS]
Nu 5:14 and *he* s his wife and she is impure— 7861
5:14 if he is jealous and s her even though she is 7861
5:30 over a man because *he* s his wife. 7861

SUSPENDS (1)
Job 26: 7 *he* s the earth over nothing. 9434

SUSPENSE (3)
Dt 28:66 You will live *in* constant s, 9428
Jn 10:24 "How long *will you* **keep** us **in** s? *149+3836+6034*
Ac 27:33 "you have been in constant s and have gone *4659*

SUSPICIONS (1) [SUSPECTS]
1Ti 6: 4 in envy, strife, malicious talk, evil s *5707*

SUSTAIN (10) [SUSTAINED, SUSTAINING, SUSTAINS]
Ru 4:15 He will renew your life and s you 3920
Job 36:19 or even all your mighty efforts s you 6885
Ps 41: 3 The LORD *will* s him on his sickbed 6184
51:12 and grant me a willing spirit, *to* s me. 6164
55:22 your cares on the LORD and he *will* s you; 3920
89:21 My hand *will* s him; 3922
119:116 S me according to your promise, 6164
119:175 and *may* your laws s me. 6468
Isa 46: 4 I am he *who will* s you. 6022
46: 4 I *will* s you and I will rescue you. 6022

SUSTAINED (4) [SUSTAIN]
Ge 27:37 and *I have* s him *with* grain and new wine. 6164
Ne 9:21 For forty years *you* s them in the desert; 3920
Isa 59:16 and his own righteousness s him. 6164
63: 5 and my own wrath s me. 6164

SUSTAINING (1) [SUSTAIN]
Heb 1: 3 s all things by his powerful word. *5770*

SUSTAINS (8) [SUSTAIN]
Ps 3: 5 I wake again, because the LORD s me. 6164
18:35 and your right hand s me; 6184

Ps 54: 4 the Lord is the *one who* s me. 6164
104:15 and bread *that* s his heart. 6184
146: 9 The LORD watches over the alien and s 6386
147: 6 The LORD s the humble but casts 6386
Pr 18:14 A man's spirit s him in sickness, 3920
Isa 50: 4 to know the word *that* s the weary. 6431

SUSTENANCE (KJV) See FOOD, LIVING THING

SWADDLED, SWADDLING, SWADDLINGBAND (KJV) See CARED FOR, WRAPPED IN CLOTHS

SWALLOW (14) [SWALLOWED, SWALLOWING, SWALLOWS]
Nu 14: 9 because we will s them **up.** 4312
16:34 shouting, "The earth *is going to* s us too!" 1180
2Sa 20:19 you want *to* s **up** the LORD's inheritance?" 1180
20:20 "Far be it from me *to* s **up** or destroy! 1180
Ps 21: 9 In his wrath the LORD *will* s them **up,** 1180
69:15 the depths s me **up** or the pit close its mouth 1180
84: 3 and the s a nest for herself, 2000
Pr 1:12 *let's* s them alive, like the grave, 1180
26: 2 Like a fluttering sparrow or a darting **s,** 2000
Isa 25: 8 *he will* s **up** death forever. 1180
Hos 8: 7 foreigners *would* s it **up.** 1180
Jnh 1:17 the LORD provided a great fish to s Jonah, 1180
Hab 1:13 Why are you silent while the wicked s **up** 1180
Mt 23:24 You strain out a gnat but s a camel. *2927*

SWALLOWED (22) [SWALLOW]
Ge 41: 7 heads of grain s **up** the seven healthy, 1180
41:24 heads of grain s **up** the seven good heads. 1180
Ex 7:12 But Aaron's staff s **up** their staffs. 1180
15:12 and the earth s them. 1180
Nu 16:32 and the earth opened its mouth and s them, 1180
26:10 The earth opened its mouth and s them 1180
Dt 11: 6 in the middle of all Israel and s them **up** 1180
2Sa 17:16 and all the people with him *will* **be** s **up.'** " 1180
Job 20:15 He will spit out the riches *he* s; 1180
37:20 Would any man ask *to* **be** s **up?** 1180
Ps 35:25 or say, *"We have* s him **up."** 1180
106:17 The earth opened up and s Dathan; 1180
124: 3 *they would have* s us alive; 1180
Jer 51:34 a serpent *he has* s us and filled his stomach 1180
51:44 and make him spew out **what** he has s. 1183
La 2: 2 the Lord *has* s **up** all the dwellings of Jacob; 1180
2: 5 Lord is like an enemy; *he has* s **up** Israel. 1180
2: 5 *He has* s **up** all her palaces 1180
2:16 *"We have* s her **up.** 1180
Hos 8: 8 Israel **is** s **up;** now she is among the nations 1180
1Co 15:54 "Death *has been* s **up** in victory." *2927*
2Co 5: 4 so that what is mortal *may be* s **up** by life. *2927*

SWALLOWING (1) [SWALLOW]
Rev 12:16 by opening its mouth and s the river that *2927*

SWALLOWS (2) [SWALLOW]
Nu 16:30 and the earth opens its mouth and s them, 1180
Isa 28: 4 and takes it in his hand, *he* s it. 1180

SWAMPED (2) [SWAMPLAND, SWAMPS]
Mk 4:37 so that it *was* nearly **s.** *1153*
Lk 8:23 so that the boat *was being* **s,** *5230*

SWAMPLAND (1) [SWAMPED]
Isa 14:23 into a place for owls and into **s;** 106+4784

SWAMPS (1) [SWAMPED]
Eze 47:11 the s and marshes will not become fresh; 1289

SWARM (11) [SWARMED, SWARMING, SWARMS]
Ge 7:21 all the creatures that s over the earth, 9237
Ex 10:12 over Egypt so that locusts *will* s over 6590
Dt 1:44 a s **of bees** and beat you down from Seir all 1805
14:19 All flying **insects that** s are unclean to you; 9238
Jdg 14: 8 In it was a s *of* bees and some honey, 6337
Isa 33: 4 like a s *of* locusts men pounce on it. 5480
Jer 12:12 the desert destroyers *will* **s,** for the sword 995
51:14 fill you with men, as with a **s of locusts,** 3540
51:27 send up horses like a s of locusts. 6170
Joel 1: 4 What the **locust** s has left the great locusts 1612
2:25 the other locusts and the **locust** s— 1612

SWARMED (1) [SWARM]
Ps 118:12 *They* s **around** me like bees, 6015

SWARMING (1) [SWARM]
Lev 11:10 whether among all the s **things** or among all 9238

SWARMS (10) [SWARM]
Ex 8:21 I will send **s of flies** on you 6856
8:22 no **s of flies** will be there, 6856
8:24 Dense **s of flies** poured into Pharaoh's 6856
Dt 28:42 **S of locusts** will take over all your trees 7526
Jdg 6: 5 and their tents like s *of* locusts. 1896
Ps 78:45 He sent **s of flies** that devoured them, 6856
105:31 He spoke, and there came **s of flies,** 6856
Eze 47: 9 S of living creatures will live wherever 9237
Am 7: 1 He was preparing **s of locusts** after 1479
Na 3:17 your officials like s *of* locusts that settle in 1571

SWAN (KJV) See WHITE OWL

SWARE (KJV) See SWORE

SWAY (4) [SWAYED, SWAYING, SWAYS]
Jdg 9: 9 to **hold** s over the trees?' 5675
9:11 to **hold** s over the trees?' 5675
9:13 to **hold** s over the trees?' 5675
Ps 72:16 on the tops of the hills *may it* **s.** 8321

SWAYED (5) [SWAY]
Mt 11: 7 A reed s by the wind? *4888*
22:16 You aren't s by men, because you pay no *3508*
Mk 12:14 You aren't s by men, because you pay no *3508*
Lk 7:24 A reed s by the wind? *4888*
2Ti 3: 6 who are loaded down with sins and *are* s *72*

SWAYING (2) [SWAY]
1Ki 14:15 so that it will be like a reed s in the water. 5653
Jer 4:24 they were quaking; all the hills *were* **s.** 7837

SWAYS (3) [SWAY]
Job 28: 4 far from men he dangles and **s.** 5675
40:17 His tail s like a cedar; 2912
Isa 24:20 *it* s like a hut in the wind; 5653

SWEAR (53) [SWEARING, SWEARS, SWORE, SWORN]
Ge 21:23 Now s to me here before God *that* you will 8678
21:24 Abraham said, "I s it." 8678
22:16 *"I* s by myself, declares the LORD, 8678
24: 3 *I* **want** you **to** s by the LORD, 8678
24:37 And my master **made** me **s an oath,** 8678
25:33 But Jacob said, **"S** to me first." 8678
47:31 **"S** to me," he said. 8678
50: 5 'My father **made** me **s an oath** 8678
50: 6 as *he* **made** you **s** *to do."* 8678
50:25 Joseph **made** the sons of Israel **s an oath** 8678
Ex 13:19 *had* **made** the sons of Israel **s an oath.** 8678+8678
Lev 5: 4 in any matter one might carelessly s about— 8652
19:12 not s falsely by my name and so profane 8678
Jos 2:12 please s to me by the LORD 8678
2:17 "This oath *you* **made** us s will not 8678
2:20 be released from the oath *you* **made** us **s."** 8678
23: 7 do not invoke the names of their gods or s 8678
Jdg 15:12 Samson said, **"S** to me that you won't kill 8678
1Sa 24:21 Now s to me by the LORD that you will 8678
30:15 **"S** to me before God that you will 8678
2Sa 19: 7 *I* s by the LORD that if you don't go out, 8678
1Ki 1:13 *did* you not s to me your servant: 8678
1:51 *'Let* King Solomon s to me today 8678
2:42 not **make** you s by the LORD and warn you, 8678
18:10 *he* **made** them s they could not find you. 8678
22:16 "How many times *must* **I make** you s 8678
2Ch 18:15 "How many times *must* **I make** you s 8678
Ps 24: 4 who does not lift up his soul to an idol or s 8678
63:11 all who s by God's name will praise him, 8678
Isa 19:18 and s **allegiance** to the LORD Almighty. 8678
45:23 by me every tongue *will* **s.** 8678
65:16 he who takes an oath in the land *will* s by 8678
Jer 4: 2 just and righteous way *you* **s,** 8678
12:16 the ways of my people and s by my name, 8678
12:16 they once taught my people to s by Baal— 8678
22: 5 *I* s by myself that this palace will become 8678
44:26 'I s by my great name,' says the LORD, 8678
44:26 or **s,** "As surely as the Sovereign LORD 606
49:13 *I* s by myself," declares the LORD, 8678
Eze 36: 7 I **s with uplifted** hand that the nations 5951
Da 12: 7 and I heard him s by him who lives forever, 8678
Hos 4:15 And *do* not **s,** 'As surely as the LORD 8678
Am 8:14 They *who* s by the shame of Samaria, 8678
Zep 1: 5 those who bow down and s by the LORD 8678
1: 5 by the LORD and who also s by Molech, 8678
Zec 8:17 and do not love to s falsely. 8652
Mt 5:34 But I tell you, *Do* not s at all: *3923*
5:36 And *do* not s by your head, *3923*
Mk 5: 7 **S** to God that you won't torture me!" *3991*
Heb 3:18 And to whom *did* God s that they would *3923*
6:13 there was no one greater for him *to* **s by,** *3923*
6:16 Men s by someone greater than themselves, *3923*
Jas 5:12 *do* not **s—**not **by** heaven or by earth or *3923*

SWEARING (1) [SWEAR]
Jer 5: 2 as the LORD lives,' still *they are* s falsely." 8678

SWEARS (15) [SWEAR]
Lev 6: 3 and lies about it, or if *he* s falsely, 8678
1Ki 8:31 to take an oath and he comes and **s the oath** 457
2Ch 6:22 to take an oath and he comes and **s the oath** 457
Zec 5: 3 everyone who **s falsely** will be banished. 8678
5: 4 the house of him *who* s falsely by my name. 8678
Mt 23:16 You say, 'If anyone s by the temple, *3923*
23:16 but if anyone s by the gold of the temple, *3923*
23:18 You also say, 'If anyone s by the altar, *3923*
Mt 23:18 but if anyone s by the gift on it, *3923*
23:20 he who s by the altar swears by it and *3923*
23:20 by the altar s by it and by everything on it. *3923*
23:21 And he who s by the temple swears by it *3923*
23:21 And he who swears by the temple s by it *3923*
23:22 And he who s by heaven swears by God's *3923*
23:22 by heaven s by God's throne and by *3923*

SWEAT (2)
Ge 3:19 the s *of* your brow you will eat your food 2399
Lk 22:44 and his s was like drops of blood falling to *2629*

SWEEP (22) [SWEEPING, SWEEPINGS, SWEEPS, SWEPT]
Ge 18:23 *"Will you* s **away** the righteous with 6200
18:24 *Will you* really s it **away** and not spare 6200
Ps 90: 5 *You* s men **away** in the sleep of death; 2441
Isa 8: 8 and s **on** into Judah, swirling over it, 2736
11:15 with a scorching wind *he will* s his hand 5677
14:23 *I will* s her with the broom of destruction," 3173
28:17 hail *will* s **away** your refuge, the lie, 3589
28:19 by day and by night, *it will* s **through."** 6296
43: 2 *they will* not s **over** you. 8851
64: 6 and like the wind our sins s us **away.** 5951
Eze 5:17 Plague and bloodshed *will* s through you, 6296
Da 11:10 *which will* s **on** like an irresistible flood 995+995
11:40 and s **through** them like a flood. 6296
Hos 4:19 A whirlwind *will* s them **away,** 928+4053+7674
Am 5: 6 or *he will* s **through** the house of Joseph 7502
Hab 1: 6 who s across the whole earth 2143
1:11 Then *they* s **past** like the wind and go on— 2736
Zep 1: 2 *"I will* s **away** everything from the face 665+6066
1: 3 *"I will* s **away** both men and animals; 6066
1: 3 *I will* s **away** the birds of the air and 6066
Lk 15: 8 s the house and search carefully *4924*
Rev 12:15 s her **away with the torrent.** *4472+4533*

SWEEPING (1) [SWEEP]
Isa 21: 1 Like whirlwinds s through the southland, 2736

SWEEPINGS (1) [SWEEP]
Am 8: 6 selling even the s *with* the wheat. 5139

SWEEPS (7) [SWEEP]
Job 27:21 *it* s him **out** of his place. 8548
Pr 1:27 when disaster s **over** you like a whirlwind, 910
13:23 but injustice s it **away.** 6200
Isa 28:15 When an overwhelming scourge **s by,** 6296
28:18 When the overwhelming scourge **s by,** 6296
40:24 and a whirlwind s them **away** like chaff. 5951
Zep 2: 2 the appointed time arrives and that day s **on** 6296

SWEET (26) [SWEETER, SWEETNESS]
Ex 15:25 and the water *became* **s.** 5517
Jdg 9:11 so good and **s,** to hold sway over the trees?' 5519
14:14 out of the strong, *something* **s."** 5498
Ne 8:10 "Go and enjoy choice food and s drinks, 4941
Job 20:12 "Though evil *is* s in his mouth 5517
21:33 The soil in the valley *is* s to him; 5517
Ps 55:14 with whom *I once* **enjoyed** s fellowship 5517
119:103 How s *are* your words to my taste, 4914
Pr 3:24 when you lie down, your sleep *will be* **s.** 6844
9:17 "Stolen water *is* s; food eaten in secret 5517
13:19 A longing fulfilled *is* s to the soul, 6844
16:24 s to the soul and healing to the bones. 5498
20:17 Food gained by fraud **tastes** s to a man, 6853
24:13 honey from the comb is s to your taste. 5498
24:14 Know **also** that wisdom is s to your soul; 4027[S]
27: 7 to the hungry even what is bitter tastes **s.** 5498
Ecc 5:12 The sleep of a laborer is **s,** 5498
11: 7 Light is **s,** and it pleases the eyes to see 5498
SS 2: 3 and his fruit is s to my taste. 5498
2:14 for your voice is **s,** and your face is lovely. 6853
Isa 5:20 who put bitter for s and sweet for bitter. 5498
5:20 who put bitter for sweet and s for bitter. 5498
Jer 6:20 about incense from Sheba or s calamus 3203
Eze 3: 3 and it tasted as s as honey in my mouth. 5498
Rev 10: 9 but in your mouth it will be as s as honey." *1184*
10:10 *It* **tasted** as s as honey in my mouth, *1184+1639*

SWEETER (3) [SWEET]
Jdg 14:18 "What is s than honey? 5498
Ps 19:10 they are s than honey, than honey from the 5498
119:103 s than honey to my mouth! NIH

SWEETNESS (2) [SWEET]
SS 4:11 Your lips drop **s as the honeycomb,** 5885
5:16 His mouth is s *itself;* 4941

SWEETSMELLING (KJV) See FRAGRANT

SWELL (5) [SWELLING, SWELLS, SWOLLEN]
Nu 5:21 to waste away and your abdomen to **s.** 7379
5:27 her abdomen *will* s and her thigh waste 7377
Dt 8: 4 not wear out and your feet *did* not s 1301
Isa 60: 5 your heart will throb and **s with joy;** 8143
Ac 28: 6 The people expected him to **s up** *4399*

SWELLING (6) [SWELL]
Lev 13: 2 a s or a rash or a bright spot on his skin 8421
13:10 a white s in the skin that has turned 8421
13:10 and if there is raw flesh in the **s,** 8421
13:19 a white s or reddish-white spot appears, 8421
13:28 it is a s *from* the burn, 8421
14:56 and for a **s,** a rash or a bright spot, 8421

SWELLS (1) [SWELL]
Nu 5:22 so that your abdomen s and your thigh 7377

SWELTER (1)
Job 37:17 You who s in your clothes when 2768

SWEPT (32) [SWEEP]
Ge 19:15 or *you will* **be s away** when the city 6200
19:17 to the mountains or *you will* **be s away!"** 6200
Ex 14:27 and the LORD s them into the sea. 5850
Nu 16:26 or *you will* **be s away** because 6200
Jdg 5:21 The river Kishon s them **away,** 1759
1Sa 12:25 both you and your king *will* **be s away."** 6200
1Ch 21:12 of **being s away** before your enemies, 6200
Job 1:17 and **s down** on your camels 7320
1:19 when suddenly a mighty wind **s in** from 995
5:13 and the schemes of the wily **are s away.** 4554
21:18 like chaff **s away** *by* a gale? 1704
37:21 in the skies after the wind *has* s them clean. 6296
Ps 42: 7 all your waves and breakers *have* s over me. 6296
58: 9 the wicked *will be* **s away.** 8548
73:19 completely **s away** by terrors! 6200
88:16 Your wrath *has* s over me; 6296
124: 4 the torrent *would have* s over us, 6296
124: 5 the raging waters *would have* s us **away.** 6296
136:15 s Pharaoh and his army into the Red Sea; 5850
Pr 10:25 When the storm *has* **s by,** 6296
Isa 44:22 *I have* **s away** your offenses like a cloud, 4681
Da 2:35 The wind s them **away** without leaving 10492
11:22 an overwhelming army *will* **be s away** 8851
11:26 his army *will be* **s away,** 8851
Jnh 2: 3 all your waves and breakers s over me. 6296
Mic 7: 2 The godly *have been* s from the land; 6
Hab 3:10 Torrents of water **s by;** 6296
Mt 8:24 so that the waves **s over** the boat. *2821*
12:44 **s clean** and put in order. *4924*
Lk 11:25 it finds the house **s clean** and put in order. *4924*
Ac 27:14 the "northeaster," s down from the island. *965*
Rev 12: 4 His tail s a third of the stars out of the sky *5359*

SWERVE (2) [SWERVING]
Pr 4: 5 do not forget my words or s from them. 5742
4:27 *Do* not s *to* the right or the left; 5742

SWERVING (1) [SWERVE]
Joel 2: 7 march in line, not s *from* their course. 6293

SWIFT (16) [SWIFTER, SWIFTLY]
1Ch 12: 8 they were as s as gazelles in the mountains. 4554
Pr 1:16 *they are* s to shed blood. 4554
Ecc 9:11 The race is not to the s or the battle to 7824
Isa 18: 2 Go, s messengers, to a people tall 7824
19: 1 on a s cloud and is coming to Egypt. 7824
30:16 You said, 'We will ride off on s horses.' 7824
30:16 Therefore your pursuers *will be* **s!** 7837
38:14 I cried like a s or thrush, 6101
59: 7 *they are* s to shed innocent blood. 4554
Jer 2:23 a s she-camel running here and there, 7824
8: 7 the s and the thrush observe the time 6101
46: 6 "The s cannot flee nor the strong escape. 7824
Da 9:21 came to me in **s flight** about the time 3616+3618
Am 2:14 The s will not escape, 7824
Ro 3:15 "Their feet are s to shed blood; *3955*
2Pe 2: 1 bringing s destruction on themselves. *5442*

SWIFTER (6) [SWIFT]
2Sa 1:23 *They were* s than eagles, 7837
Job 7: 6 "My days *are* s than a weaver's shuttle, 7837
9:25 "My days *are* s than a runner; 7837
Jer 4:13 his horses *are* s than eagles. 7837
La 4:19 Our pursuers were s than eagles in the sky; 7824
Hab 1: 8 Their horses *are* s than leopards, 7837

SWIFTLY (4) [SWIFT]
Ps 147:15 his word runs **s.** 4559+6330
Isa 5:26 Here they come, s and speedily! 4559
60:22 in its time *I will* **do** this **s."** 2590
Joel 3: 4 I will s and speedily return on your own 7824

SWIM (4) [SWIMMER, SWIMMING]
Ps 8: 8 all *that* s the paths of the seas. 6296
Isa 25:11 as a swimmer spreads out his hands to **s.** 8466
Eze 47: 5 and was **deep enough to s in—** 8467
Ac 27:43 He ordered those who could s *3147*

SWIMMER (1) [SWIM]
Isa 25:11 as a s spreads out his hands to swim. 8466

SWIMMING (1) [SWIM]
Ac 27:42 to prevent any of them *from* **s away** *1713*

SWINDLER (1) [SWINDLERS]
1Co 5:11 an idolater or a slanderer, a drunkard or a **s.** *774*

SWINDLERS (2) [SWINDLER]
1Co 5:10 or the greedy and **s,** or idolaters. *774*
6:10 nor s will inherit the kingdom of God. *774*

SWINE (KJV) See PIG

SWING (3) [SWINGS, SWUNG]
Ex 28:28 so that the breastpiece *will* not **s out** from 2322
39:21 that the breastpiece *would* not **s out** from 2322
Joel 3:13 S the sickle, for the harvest is ripe. 8938

SWINGS (2) [SWING]
Dt 19: 5 and as he s his ax to fell a tree, 5616
Isa 10:15 Does the ax raise itself above him *who* s it, 2933

SWIRL (1) [SWIRLED, SWIRLING]
Job 37:12 At his direction they s around over the face 2200

SWIRLED (2) [SWIRL]
2Sa 22: 5 "The waves of death **s about** me; 705
Jnh 2: 3 and the currents **s about** me; 6015

SWIRLING (4) [SWIRL]
Isa 8: 8 and sweep on into Judah, **s over** it, passing 8851
Jer 23:19 a whirlwind **s down** on the heads of 2565
30:23 a driving wind **s down** on the heads of 2565
Hos 13: 3 like chaff s from a threshing floor, 6192

SWOLLEN (3) [SWELL]
Lev 13:43 and if the s sore on his head 8421
Ne 9:21 not wear out nor *did* their feet *become* **s.** 1301
Job 6:16 by thawing ice and s with melting snow, 6623

SWOON, SWOONED (KJV) See FAINT

SWOOP (2) [SWOOPING]
Isa 11:14 *They will* **s down** on the slopes of Philistia 6414
Jer 49:22 An eagle will soar and **s down,** 1797

SWOOPING (4) [SWOOP]
Dt 28:49 like an eagle **s down,** 1797
Job 9:26 like eagles **s down** on their prey. 3216
Jer 48:40 An eagle *is* **s down,** spreading its wings 1797
Hab 1: 8 They fly like a vulture s to devour; 2590

SWORD (402) [SWORDS, SWORDSMEN]
Ge 3:24 a flaming s flashing back and forth to guard 2995
27:40 by the s and you will serve your brother. 2995
34:26 put Hamor and his son Shechem to the s 2995
48:22 from the Amorites with my s and my bow." 2995
Ex 5: 3 he may strike us with plagues or with the **s."** 2995
5:21 to Pharaoh and his officials and have put a s 2995
15: 9 I will draw my s and my hand will destroy 2995
17:13 the Amalekite army with the **s.** 2995
18: 4 he saved me from the s *of* Pharaoh." 2995
22:24 and I will kill you with the **s;** 2995
32:27 'Each man strap a s to his side. 2995
Lev 26: 6 the s will not pass through your country. 2995
26: 7 and they will fall by the s before you. 2995
26: 8 your enemies will fall by the s before you. 2995
26:25 And I will bring the s upon you to avenge 2995
26:33 among the nations and will draw out my s 2995
26:36 They will run as though fleeing from the **s,** 2995
26:37 as though fleeing from the **s,** 2995
Nu 14: 3 to this land only to let us fall by the **s?** 2995
14:43 not be with you and you will fall by the **s."** 2995
19:16 with a s or someone who has died 2995
20:18 and attack you with the **s."** 2995
21:24 put him to the s and took over his land from 2995
22:23 in the road with a drawn s in his hand, 2995
22:29 If I had a s in my hand, 2995
22:31 in the road with his s drawn. 2995
31: 8 also killed Balaam son of Beor with the **s.** 2995
Dt 13:15 you must certainly put to the s all who live 2995
20:13 put to the s all the men in it. 2995
32:25 In the street the s will make them childless; 2995
32:41 when I sharpen my flashing s 2995
32:42 while my s devours flesh: 2995
33:29 and helper and your glorious **s.** 2995
Jos 5:13 in front of him with a drawn s in his hand. 2995
6:21 and destroyed with the s every living thing 2995
8:24 every one of them had been put to the **s,** 2995
10:28 to the s and totally destroyed everyone in it. 2995
10:30 and everyone in it Joshua put to the **s.** 2995
10:32 The city and everyone in it he put to the **s,** 2995
10:35 to the s and totally destroyed everyone in it, 2995
10:37 They took the city and put it to the **s,** 2995
10:39 and put them to the **s.** 2995
11:10 and put its king to the **s.** 2995
11:11 Everyone in it they put to the **s.** 2995
11:12 and their kings and put them to the **s.** 2995
11:14 the s until they completely destroyed them, 2995
13:22 the Israelites had put to the s Balaam son 2995
19:47 took it, put it to the s and occupied it. 2995
24:12 You did not do it with your own s and bow. 2995
Jdg 1: 8 They put the city to the s and set it on fire. 2995
1:25 and they put the city to the s but spared 2995
3:16 Now Ehud had made a double-edged s 2995
3:21 the s from his right thigh and plunged it 2995
3:22 Ehud did not pull the s out, 2995
4:15 and all his chariots and army by the **s,** 2995
4:16 All the troops of Sisera fell by the **s;** 2995
7:14 be nothing other than the s *of* Gideon son 2995
7:20 "A s for the LORD and for Gideon!" 2995
8:20 But Jether did not draw his **s,** 2995
9:54 "Draw your s and kill me, 2995
18:27 They attacked them with the s and burned 2995
20:37 spread out and put the whole city to the **s.** 2995
20:48 to Benjamin and put all the towns to the **s,** 2995
21:10 and put to the s those living there, 2995
1Sa 13:22 not a soldier with Saul and Jonathan had a s 2995
15: 8 all his people he totally destroyed with the **s.** 2995
15:33 "As your s has made women childless, 2995
17:39 on his s over the tunic and tried walking 2995
17:45 against me with s and spear and javelin, 2995
17:47 not by s or spear that the LORD saves; 2995
17:50 a s in his hand he struck down the Philistine 2995
17:51 of the Philistine's s and drew it from 2995
17:51 he killed him, he cut off his head with **the s.** 2023S
18: 4 and even his **s,** his bow and his belt. 2995
21: 8 "Don't you have a spear or a s here? 2995
21: 8 I haven't brought my s or any other weapon, 2995
21: 9 "The s *of* Goliath the Philistine, 2995
21: 9 there is no s here but that one." 337S
22:10 he also gave him provisions and the s 2995
22:13 giving him bread and a s and inquiring 2995
22:19 He also put to the s Nob, 2995
31: 4 "Draw your s and run me through, 2995
31: 4 so Saul took his own s and fell on it. 2995
31: 5 he too fell on his s and died with him. 2995
2Sa 1:12 because they had fallen by the **s.** 2995
1:22 the s *of* Saul did not return unsatisfied. 2995
2:26 "Must the s devour forever? 2995
3:29 or who falls by the s or who lacks food." 2995
11:25 the s devours one as well as another. 2995
12: 9 with the s and took his wife to be your own. 2995
12: 9 with the s *of* the Ammonites. 2995
12:10 the s will never depart from your house, 2995
15:14 upon us and put the city to the **s."** 2995
18: 8 claimed more lives that day than the **s.** 2995
21:16 and who was armed with a new **[s],** NIH
23:10 till his hand grew tired and froze to the **s.** 2995
24: 9 able-bodied men who could handle a **s,** 2995
1Ki 1:51 not put his servant to death with the **s.' "** 2995
2: 8 'I will not put you to death by the **s.'** 2995
2:32 and killed them with the **s.** 2995
3:24 Then the king said, "Bring me a **s."** 2995
3:24 So they brought a s for the king. 2995
19: 1 he had killed all the prophets with the **s.** 2995
19:10 and put your prophets to death with the **s.** 2995
19:14 and put your prophets to death with the **s.** 2995
19:17 Jehu will put to death any who escape the s 2995
19:17 to death any who escape the s *of* Jehu. 2995
2Ki 6:22 with your own s or bow? 2995
8:12 kill their young men with the **s,** 2995
10:25 So they cut them down with the **s.** 2995
11:15 and put to the s anyone who follows her." 2995
11:20 because Athaliah had been slain with the s 2995
19: 7 there I will have him cut down with the **s.' "** 2995
19:37 and Sharezer cut him down with the **s,** 2995
1Ch 5:18 handle shield and **s,** who could use a bow, 2995
10: 4 "Draw your s and run me through, 2995
10: 4 so Saul took his own s and fell on it. 2995
10: 5 he too fell on his s and died. 2995
21: 5 men who could handle a **s,** 2995
21:12 or three days of the s *of* the LORD— 2995
21:16 with a drawn s in his hand extended 2995
21:27 and he put his s back into its sheath. 2995
21:30 because he was afraid of the s *of* the angel 2995
2Ch 20: 9 whether the s *of* judgment, 2995
21: 4 to the s along with some of the princes 2995
23:14 and put to the s anyone who follows her." 2995
23:21 because Athaliah had been slain with the **s.** 2995
29: 9 This is why our fathers have fallen by the s 2995
32:21 some of his sons cut him down with the **s.** 2995
36:17 who killed their young men with the s in 2995
36:20 who escaped from the **s,** 2995
Ezr 9: 7 and our priests have been subjected to the s 2995
Ne 4:18 of the builders wore his s at his side 2995
Est 9: 5 down all their enemies with the **s,** 2995
Job 1:15 They put the servants to the **s,** 2995
1:17 They put the servants to the **s,** 2995
5:15 the needy from the s in their mouth; 2995
5:20 and in battle from the stroke of the **s.** 2995
15:22 he is marked for the **s.** 2995
19:29 you should fear the s yourselves; 2995
19:29 for wrath will bring punishment by the **s,** 2995
27:14 their fate is the **s;** 2995
33:18 his life from perishing by the **s.** 8939
36:12 by the s and die without knowledge. 8939
39:22 he does not shy away from the **s.** 2995
40:19 yet his Maker can approach him with his **s.** 2995
41:26 The s that reaches him has no effect, 2995
Ps 7:12 If he does not relent, he will sharpen his **s;** 2995
17:13 rescue me from the wicked by your **s.** 2995
22:20 Deliver my life from the **s,** 2995
37:14 The wicked draw the s and bend the bow 2995
44: 3 It was not by their s that they won the land, 2995
44: 6 my s does not bring me victory; 2995
45: 3 Gird your s upon your side, O mighty one; 2995
63:10 over to the s and become food for jackals. 2995
78:62 He gave his people over to the **s;** 2995
78:64 their priests were put to the **s,** 2995

Ps 89:43 You have turned back the edge of his s 2995
144:10 his servant David from the deadly s. 2995
149: 6 be in their mouths and a double-edged s 2995
Pr 5: 4 sharp as a double-edged s. 2995
12:18 Reckless words pierce like a s, 2995
25:18 Like a club or a s or a sharp arrow is 2995
SS 3: 8 all of them wearing the s, 2995
3: 8 each with his s at his side, 2995
Isa 1:20 you will be devoured by the s." 2995
2: 4 Nation will not take up s against nation, 2995
3:25 Your men will fall by the s, 2995
13:15 all who are caught will fall by the s. 2995
14:19 with those pierced by the s, 2995
21:15 They flee from the s, 2995
21:15 flee from the sword, from the drawn s, 2995
22: 2 Your slain were not killed by the s, 2995
27: 1 the LORD will punish with his s, 2995
27: 1 his fierce, great and powerful s, NIH
31: 8 "Assyria will fall by a s that is not of man; 2995
31: 8 a s, not of mortals, will devour them. 2995
31: 8 before the s and their young men will 2995
34: 5 My s has drunk its fill in the heavens; 2995
34: 6 The s of the LORD is bathed in blood, 2995
37: 7 there I will have him cut down with the s.' " 2995
37:38 and Sharezer cut him down with the s, 2995
41: 2 He turns them to dust with his s, 2995
49: 2 He made my mouth like a sharpened s, 2995
51:19 ruin and destruction, famine and s— 2995
65:12 for the s, and you will all bend down for 2995
66:16 For with fire and with his s 2995
Jer 2:30 Your s has devoured your prophets like 2995
4:10 when the s is at our throats." 2995
5:12 we will never see s or famine. 2995
5:17 the s they will destroy the fortified cities 2995
6:25 for the enemy has a s, 2995
9:16 with the s until I have destroyed them." 2995
11:22 Their young men will die by the s, 2995
12:12 for the s of the LORD will devour 2995
14:12 Instead, I will destroy them with the s, 2995
14:13 'You will not see the s or suffer famine. 2995
14:15 'No s or famine will touch this land.' 2995
14:15 Those same prophets will perish by s 2995
14:16 of Jerusalem because of the famine and s. 2995
14:18 I see those slain by the s; 2995
15: 2 those for the s, to the sword; 2995
15: 2 those for the sword, to the s; 2995
15: 3 "the s to kill and the dogs to drag away and 2995
15: 9 the survivors to the s before their enemies," 2995
16: 4 They will perish by s and famine, 2995
18:21 hand them over to the power of the s. 2995
18:21 their young men slain by the s in battle. 2995
19: 7 fall by the s before their enemies, 2995
20: 4 fall by the s *of* their enemies. 2995
20: 4 away to Babylon or put them to the s. 2995
21: 7 s and famine, to Nebuchadnezzar king 2995
21: 7 He will put them to the s; 2995
21: 9 Whoever stays in this city will die by the s, 2995
24:10 I will send the s, famine and plague 2995
25:16 because of the s I will send among them." 2995
25:27 to rise no more because of the s I will send 2995
25:29 for I am calling down a s upon all who live 2995
25:31 and put the wicked to the s,' " 2995
25:38 of the s *of* the oppressor and because of 2995
26:23 down with a s and his body thrown into 2995
27: 8 I will punish that nation with the s, 2995
27:13 Why will you and your people die by the s, 2995
29:17 "I will send the s, famine and plague 2995
29:18 I will pursue them with the s, famine 2995
31: 2 the s will find favor in the desert; 2995
32:24 Because of the s, famine and plague, 2995
32:36 "You are saying about this city, 'By the s, 2995
33: 4 to be used against the siege ramps and the s 2995
34: 4 You will not die by the s; 2995
34:17 'freedom' to fall by the s, plague and 2995
38: 2 in this city will die by the s, famine or 2995
39:18 you will not fall by the s but will escape 2995
41: 2 the son of Shaphan, with the s, 2995
42:16 then the s you fear will overtake you there, 2995
42:17 to Egypt to settle there will die by the s, 2995
42:22 You will die by the s, famine and plague 2995
43:11 and the s to those destined for the sword. 2995
43:11 and the sword to those destined for the s. 2995
44:12 they will fall by the s or die from famine. 2995
44:12 they will die by s or famine. 2995
44:13 in Egypt with the s, famine and plague. 2995
44:18 and have been perishing by s and famine." 2995
44:27 by s and famine until they are all destroyed. 2995
44:28 Those who escape the s and return to 2995
46:10 The s will devour till it is satisfied, 2995
46:14 for the s devours those around you.' 2995
46:16 away from the s *of* the oppressor.' 2995
47: 6 " 'Ah, s of the LORD,' 2995
48: 2 the s will pursue you. 2995
48:10 on him who keeps his s from bloodshed! 2995
49:37 with the s until I have made an end of them. 2995
50:16 of the s *of* the oppressor let everyone return 2995
50:35 "A s against the Babylonians!" 2995
50:36 A s against her false prophets! 2995
50:36 A s against her warriors! 2995
50:37 A s against her horses and chariots and all 2995
50:37 A s against her treasures! 2995
51:50 You who have escaped the s, 2995
La 1:20 Outside, the s bereaves; 2995
2:21 and maidens have fallen by the s. 2995
4: 9 by the s are better off than those who die 2995
5: 9 of our lives because of the s *in* the desert. 2995
Eze 5: 1 take a sharp s and use it as a barber's razor 2995

Eze 5: 2 and strike it with the s all around the city. 2995
5: 2 For I will pursue them with drawn s. 2995
5:12 a third will fall by the s outside your walls; 2995
5:12 to the winds and pursue with drawn s. 2995
5:17 and I will bring the s against you. 2995
6: 3 I am about to bring a s against you, 2995
6: 8 the s when you are scattered among 2995
6:11 for they will fall by the s, 2995
6:12 and he that is near will fall by the s, 2995
7:15 the s, inside are plague and famine; 2995
7:15 those in the country will die by the s, 2995
11: 8 You fear the s, and the sword is what 2995
11: 8 and the s is what I will bring against you, 2995
11:10 You will fall by the s, 2995
12:14 and I will pursue them with drawn s. 2995
12:16 But I will spare a few of them from the s, 2995
14:17 if I bring a s against that country and say, 2995
14:17 'Let the s pass throughout the land,' 2995
14:21 s and famine and wild beasts and plague— 2995
17:21 All his fleeing troops will fall by the s, 2995
21: 3 I will draw my s from its scabbard 2995
21: 4 my s will be unsheathed against everyone 2995
21: 5 that I the LORD have drawn my s 2995
21: 9 " 'A s, a sword, sharpened and polished— 2995
21: 9 " 'A sword, a s, sharpened and polished— 2995
21:10 The s despises every such stick. NIH
21:11 " 'The s is appointed to be polished, 2995
21:12 They are thrown to the s along 2995
21:13 which the s despises, does not continue? NIH
21:14 Let the s strike twice, even three times. 2995
21:14 It is a s *for* slaughter— 2995
21:14 a s *for* great slaughter, 2995
21:15 the s for slaughter at all their gates. 2995
21:16 O s, slash to the right, then to the left, NIH
21:19 mark out two roads for the s *of* the king 2995
21:20 Mark out one road for the s to come 2995
21:28 " 'A s, a sword, drawn for the slaughter, 2995
21:28 " 'A sword, a s, drawn for the slaughter, 2995
21:30 Return the s to its scabbard. NIH
23:10 and daughters and killed her with the s. 2995
23:25 those of you who are left will fall by the s. 2995
24:21 behind will fall by the s. 2995
25:13 to Dedan they will fall by the s. 2995
26: 6 on the mainland will be ravaged by the s. 2995
26: 8 on the mainland with the s; 2995
26:11 he will kill your people with the s, 2995
28:23 with the s against her on every side. 2995
29: 8 a s against you and kill your men 2995
30: 4 A s will come against Egypt, 2995
30: 5 of the covenant land will fall by the s along 2995
30: 6 to Aswan they will fall by the s within her, 2995
30:17 and Bubastis will fall by the s, 2995
30:21 so as to become strong enough to hold a s. 2995
30:22 and make the s fall from his hand. 2995
30:24 of Babylon and put my s in his hand, 2995
30:25 when I put my s into the hand of the king 2995
31:17 joining those killed by the s. 2995
31:18 with those killed by the s. 2995
32:10 of you when I brandish my s before them. 2995
32:11 " 'The s *of* the king of Babylon will come 2995
32:20 They will fall among those killed by the s. 2995
32:20 The s is drawn; 2995
32:21 with those killed by the s.' 2995
32:22 all who have fallen by the s. 2995
32:23 are slain, fallen by the s. 2995
32:24 All of them are slain, fallen by the s. 2995
32:25 uncircumcised, killed by the s. 2995
32:26 by the s because they spread their terror in 2995
32:28 with those killed by the s. 2995
32:29 they are laid with those killed by the s. 2995
32:30 by the s and bear their shame 2995
32:31 for all his hordes that were killed by the s, 2995
32:32 with those killed by the s, 2995
33: 2 'When I bring the s against a land, 2995
33: 3 and he sees the s coming against the land 2995
33: 4 but does not take warning and the s comes 2995
33: 6 the s coming and does not blow the trumpet 2995
33: 6 and the s comes and takes the life of one 2995
33:26 You rely on your s, 2995
33:27 in the ruins will fall by the s, 2995
35: 5 and delivered the Israelites over to the s at 2995
35: 8 those killed by the s will fall on your hills 2995
38:21 a s against Gog on all my mountains, 2995
38:21 Every man's s will be against his brother. 2995
39:23 and they all fell by the s. 2995
Da 11:33 the s or be burned or captured or plundered. 2995
Hos 1: 7 not by bow, s or battle, 2995
2:18 Bow and s and battle I will abolish from 2995
7:16 by the s because of their insolent words. 2995
13:16 They will fall by the s; 2995
Am 1:11 Because he pursued his brother with a s, 2995
4:10 I killed your young men with the s, 2995
7: 9 with my s I will rise against the house 2995
7:11 " 'Jeroboam will die by the s, 2995
7:17 your sons and daughters will fall by the s. 2995
9: 1 those who are left I will kill with the s. 2995
9: 4 there I will command the s to slay them. 2995
9:10 among my people will die by the s, 2995
Mic 4: 3 Nation will not take up s against nation, 2995
5: 6 the land of Assyria with the s, 2995
5: 6 the land of Nimrod with **drawn s.** 7347
6:14 because what you save I will give to the s. 2995
Na 2:13 and the s will devour your young lions. 2995
3:15 the s will cut you down and, 2995
Zep 2:12 O Cushites, will be slain by my s." 2995
Hag 2:22 each by the s *of* his brother. 2995
Zec 9:13 O Greece, and make you like a warrior's s. 2995

Zec 11:17 May the s strike his arm and his right eye! 2995
13: 7 "Awake, O s, against my shepherd, 2995
Mt 10:34 I did not come to bring peace, but a s. *3479*
26:51 one of Jesus' companions reached for his s, *3479*
26:52 "Put your s back in its place," *3479*
26:52 all who draw the s will die by the sword. *3479*
26:52 all who draw the sword will die by the s. *3479*
Mk 14:47 of those standing near drew his s and struck *3479*
Lk 2:35 And a s will pierce your own soul too." *4855*
21:24 They will fall *by* the s and *3479+5125*
22:36 and if you don't have a s, *3479*
Jn 18:10 Then Simon Peter, who had a s, *3479*
18:11 Jesus commanded Peter, "Put your s away! *3479*
Ac 12: 2 the brother of John, put to death *with* the s. *3479*
16:27 he drew his s and was about to kill himself *3479*
Ro 8:35 or famine or nakedness or danger or s? *3479*
13: 4 for he does not bear the s for nothing. *3479*
Eph 6:17 Take the helmet of salvation and the s of *3479*
Heb 4:12 Sharper than any double-edged s, *3479*
11:34 and escaped the **edge** *of* the s; *3479+5125*
11:37 they were put to death *by* the s. *3479*
Rev 1:16 of his mouth came a sharp double-edged s. *4855*
2:12 of him who has the sharp, double-edged s. *4855*
2:16 to you and will fight against them with the s *4855*
6: 4 To him was given a large s. *3479*
6: 8 over a fourth of the earth to kill by s, *4855*
13:10 If anyone is to be killed with the s, *3479*
13:10 with the s he will be killed. *3479*
13:14 of the beast who was wounded *by* the s and *3479*
19:15 of his mouth comes a sharp s with which *4855*
19:21 of them were killed with the s that came out *4855*

SWORDS (40) [SWORD]

Ge 34:25 took their s and attacked 2995
49: 5 their s are weapons of violence. 4839
Jos 10:11 the hailstones than were killed by the s of 2995
Jdg 7:22 the camp to turn on each other with their s. 2995
20: 2 four hundred thousand soldiers armed with s 2995
20:25 all of them armed with s. 2995
20:35 Benjamites, all armed with s. 2995
1Sa 13:19 "Otherwise the Hebrews will make s 2995
14:20 striking each other with their s. 2995
25:13 David said to his men, "Put on your s!" 2995
25:13 So they put on their s, 2995
1Ki 18:28 and slashed themselves with s and spears, 2995
1Ch 21:12 with their s overtaking you, 2995
Ne 4:13 posting them by families, with their s, 2995
Ps 37:15 But their s will pierce their own hearts, 2995
55:21 yet they are **drawn s.** 7347
57: 4 whose tongues are sharp s. 2995
59: 7 they spew out s from their lips, 2995
64: 3 They sharpen their tongues like s 2995
76: 3 the shields and the s, the weapons of war. 2995
Pr 30:14 those whose teeth are s and whose jaws 2995
Isa 2: 4 They will beat their s into plowshares 2995
Eze 16:40 and hack you to pieces with their s. 2995
23:47 and cut them down with their s; 2995
28: 7 they will draw their s against your beauty 2995
30:11 They will draw their s against Egypt 2995
32:12 I will cause your hordes to fall by the s 2995
32:27 whose s were placed under their heads? 2995
38: 4 all of them brandishing their s. 2995
Hos 11: 6 S will flash in their cities, 2995
Joel 3:10 into s and your pruning hooks into spears. 2995
Mic 4: 3 They will beat their s into plowshares 2995
Na 3: 3 flashing s and glittering spears! 2995
Mt 26:47 With him was a large crowd armed with s *3479*
26:55 that you have come out with s and clubs *3479*
Mk 14:43 With him was a crowd armed with s *3479*
14:48 "that you have come out with s and clubs *3479*
Lk 22:38 "See, Lord, here are two s." *3479*
22:49 "Lord, should we strike with our s?" *3479*
22:52 that you have come with s and clubs? *3479*

SWORDSMEN (5) [SWORD]

Jdg 8:10 a hundred and twenty thousand s had fallen. 408+2995+8990
20:15 Benjamites mobilized twenty-six thousand s 408+2995+8990
20:17 mustered four hundred thousand s, 408+2995+8990
20:46 that day twenty-five thousand Benjamite s fell, 408+2995+8990
2Ki 3:26 with him seven hundred s to 408+2995+8990

SWORE (60) [SWEAR]

Ge 21:31 because the two men **s an oath** there. 8678
24: 9 and **s an oath** to him concerning this matter. 8678
25:33 So *he* **s an oath** to him, 8678
26: 3 the oath *I* s to your father Abraham. 8678
26:31 Early the next morning *the men* **s an oath** 8678
47:31 Then Joseph s to him, 8678
Ex 6: 8 to the land I **s with uplifted** hand to give 5951
13: 5 the land *he* s to your forefathers to give you, 8678
32:13 to whom *you* s by your own self: 8678
Lev 6: 5 or whatever it was *he* s falsely about. 8678
Nu 14:30 the land I **s with uplifted** hand to make 5951
32:10 that day and *he* s *this* **oath:** 8678
Dt 1: 8 of the land that the LORD s he would give 8678
1:34 he was angry and **solemnly s:** 8678
1:35 the good land *I* s to give your forefathers, 8678
4:21 and *he* **solemnly s** that I would not cross 8678
6:10 into the land *he* s to your fathers, 8678
7: 8 the LORD loved you and kept the oath *he* s 8678
7:12 as *he* s to your forefathers. 8678

Dt 7:13 in the land that *he* s to your forefathers 8678
8:18 which *he* s to your forefathers, as it is today. 8678
9:5 to accomplish what he s to your fathers, 8678
10:11 and possess the land that *I* s to their fathers 8678
11:9 that the LORD s to your forefathers to give 8678
11:21 that the LORD s to give your forefathers, 8678
26:3 the LORD s to our forefathers to give us." 8678
28:11 in the land he s to your forefathers 8678
29:13 be your God as he promised you and as *he* s 8678
30:20 in the land he s to give to your fathers, 8678
31:7 that the LORD s to their forefathers 8678
Jos 1:6 to inherit the land *I* s to their forefathers 8678
9:20 on us for breaking the oath *we* s to them." 8678
14:9 So on that day Moses s to me, 8678
Jdg 2:1 the land that *I* s to give to your forefathers. 8678
1Sa 3:14 Therefore, *I* s to the house of Eli, 8678
28:10 Saul s to her by the LORD, 8678
2Sa 21:17 Then David's men s to him, saying, 8678
1Ki 1:17 *you* yourself s to me your servant by 8678
1:30 surely carry out today what *I* s to you by 8678
2:8 *I* s to him by the LORD: 8678
2:23 Then King Solomon s by the LORD: 8678
1Ch 16:16 the **oath** he s to Isaac. 8652
Ps 89:49 *which* in your faithfulness *you* s to David? 8678
105:9 the oath he s to Isaac. NIH
106:26 So *he* s to them **with uplifted** hand 5951
132:2 He s **an oath** to the LORD and made 8678
132:11 The LORD s **an oath** to David, 8678
Isa 54:9 when *I* s that the waters 8678
Jer 11:5 I will fulfill the oath *I* s to your forefathers, 8678
38:16 But King Zedekiah s *this* **oath** secretly 8678
Eze 20:5 I s **with uplifted** hand to the descendants 5951
20:6 On that day *I* s to them 3338+5951
20:15 **with uplifted** hand I s to them in the desert 5951
20:23 **with uplifted** hand I s to them in the desert 5951
47:14 Because I s **with uplifted** hand to give it 5951
Mt 26:74 down curses on himself and he s to them, *3923*
Mk 14:71 and *he* s to them, "I don't know this man *3923*
Lk 1:73 the oath *he* s to our father Abraham: *3923*
Heb 6:13 for him to swear by, *he* s by himself, *3923*
Rev 10:6 *he* s by him who lives for ever and ever, *3923*

SWORN (31) [SWEAR]

Ge 26:28 we said, 'There ought to be a s **agreement** 460
Nu 30:13 or any s pledge to deny herself. 8652
Dt 2:14 as the LORD *had* s to them. 8678
Jos 5:6 the LORD *had* s to them that they would 8678
9:18 the leaders of the assembly *had* s **an oath** 8678
21:43 the LORD gave Israel all the land *he had* s 8678
21:44 just as *he had* s to their forefathers. 8678
Jdg 2:15 just as *he had* s to them. 8678
1Sa 20:42 for we *have* s friendship with each other in 8678
2Sa 21:2 the Israelites *had* s to [spare] them, 8678
2Ch 15:15 because *they had* s it wholeheartedly. 8678
Ne 9:15 of the land *you had* s **with uplifted** hand 5951
Ps 89:3 *I have* s to David my servant, 8678
89:35 Once for all, *I have* s by my holiness— 8678
110:4 LORD *has* s and will not change his mind: 8678
Isa 14:24 The LORD Almighty *has* **s,** "Surely, 8678
45:23 By myself *I have* s, 8678
54:9 So now *I have* s not to be angry with you, 8678
62:8 The LORD *has* s by his right hand and 8678
Jer 5:7 Your children have forsaken me and s 8678
32:22 You gave them this land *you had* s 8678
51:14 The LORD Almighty *has* s by himself: 8678
Eze 20:28 into the land I *had* s to give them 906+3338+5951
20:42 the land I *had* s **with uplifted** hand to give 5951
21:23 to those *who have* s **allegiance** to him, 8652+8678
44:12 therefore I *have* s **with uplifted** hand 5951
Da 9:11 the curses and s **judgments** written in 8652
Am 4:2 Sovereign LORD *has* s by his holiness: 8678
6:8 The Sovereign LORD *has* s by himself— 8678
8:7 The LORD *has* s by the Pride of Jacob: 8678
Heb 7:21 Lord *has* s and will not change his mind: *3923*

SWUNG (3) [SWING]

Eze 26:2 and its doors *have* **s open** to me; 6015
Rev 14:16 on the cloud s his sickle over the earth, *965*
14:19 The angel s his sickle on the earth, *965*

SYCAMINE (KJV) See MULBERRY

SYCAMORE-FIG (6) [FIG]

1Ki 10:27 cedar as plentiful as s **trees** in the foothills. 9204
1Ch 27:28 the olive and s **trees** in the western foothills. 9204
2Ch 1:15 cedar as plentiful as s **trees** in the foothills. 9204
9:27 cedar as plentiful as s **trees** in the foothills. 9204
Am 7:14 and I also took care of s **trees.** 9204
Lk 19:4 ahead and climbed a s **tree** to see him, *5191*

SYCAMORE-FIGS (1) [FIG]

Ps 78:47 with hail and their s with sleet. 9204

SYCHAR (1)

Jn 4:5 So he came to a town in Samaria called S, *5373*

SYCHEM (KJV) See SHECHEM

SYCOMORE (KJV) See SYCAMORE-FIG

SYENE (KJV) See ASWAN

SYMBOL (2) [SYMBOLIC, SYMBOLIZES, SYMBOLS]

Ex 13:16 on your hand and a s on your forehead that 3213
Nu 6:7 **s of** his **separation** *to* God is on his head. 5694

SYMBOLIC (1) [SYMBOL]

Zec 3:8 who are men s **of things to come:** 4603

SYMBOLIZES (1) [SYMBOL]

1Pe 3:21 and this water s baptism that now saves you *531*

SYMBOLS (4) [SYMBOL]

Dt 6:8 Tie them as s on your hands and bind them 253
11:18 tie them as s on your hands and bind them 253
Isa 8:18 and s in Israel from the LORD Almighty, 4603
57:8 your doorposts you have put your **pagan s.** 2355

SYMPATHETIC (1) [SYMPATHY]

1Pe 3:8 *be* s, love as brothers, be compassionate *5218*

SYMPATHIZE (2) [SYMPATHY]

Job 2:11 and met together by agreement to go and s 5653
Heb 4:15 a high priest who is unable *to* s **with** *5217*

SYMPATHIZED (1) [SYMPATHY]

Heb 10:34 *You* s **with** those in prison *5217*

SYMPATHY (8) [SYMPATHETIC, SYMPATHIZE, SYMPATHIZED]

2Sa 10:2 So David sent a delegation to **express** his s 5714
10:3 by sending men to you *to* **express** s? 5714
1Ch 19:2 So David sent a delegation to **express** his s 5714
19:2 in the land of the Ammonites to **express** s 5714
19:3 by sending men to you *to* **express** s? 5714
Ps 69:20 I looked for s, but there was none, 5653
Jer 16:5 do not go to mourn or **show** s, 5653
Da 1:9 the official to show favor and s to Daniel, 8171

SYNAGOGUE (45) [SYNAGOGUES]

Mt 12:9 he went into their s, *5252*
13:54 he began teaching the people in their s, *5252*
Mk 1:21 Jesus went into the s and began to teach. *5252*
1:23 then a man in their s who was possessed by *5252*
1:29 As soon as they left the s, *5252*
3:1 Another time he went into the s, *5252*
5:22 Then one *of* the **s rulers,** named Jairus, *801*
5:35 from the house of Jairus, the **s ruler.** *801*
5:36 Jesus told the **s ruler,** "Don't be afraid; *801*
5:38 to the home *of* the **s ruler,** *801*
6:2 he began to teach in the s, *5252*
Lk 4:16 and on the Sabbath day he went into the s, *5252*
4:20 The eyes of everyone in the s were fastened *5252*
4:28 in the s were furious when they heard this. *5252*
4:33 In the s there was a man possessed by *5252*
4:38 the s and went to the home of Simon. *5252*
6:6 On another Sabbath he went into the s *5252*
7:5 he loves our nation and has built our **s."** *5252*
8:41 Then a man named Jairus, a ruler *of* the s, *5252*
8:49 from the house of Jairus, the **s ruler.** *801*
13:14 the **s ruler** said to the people, *801*
Jn 6:59 while teaching in the s in Capernaum. *5252*
9:22 was the Christ would be **put out of the s.** *697*
12:42 for fear they would be **put out of the s;** *697*
16:2 *They will* **put** you **out of the s;** *697+4472*
Ac 6:9 the S of the Freedmen (as it was called)— *5252*
13:14 On the Sabbath they entered the s *5252*
13:15 the **s rulers** sent word to them, saying, *801*
13:42 As Paul and Barnabas were leaving the s, *5252*
14:1 went as usual into the Jewish s. *5252*
17:1 where there was a Jewish **s.** *5252*
17:2 As his custom was, Paul went into the s, *NIG*
17:10 they went to the Jewish **s.** *5252*
17:17 So he reasoned in the s with the Jews and *5252*
18:4 Every Sabbath he reasoned in the s, *5252*
18:7 Then Paul left **the** s and went next door to *1696S*
18:8 Crispus, the **s ruler,** and his entire *801*
18:17 on Sosthenes the **s ruler** and beat him *801*
18:19 He himself went into the s and reasoned *5252*
18:26 He began to speak boldly in the s. *5252*
19:8 Paul entered the s and spoke boldly there *5252*
22:19 'these men know that I went from one s *5252*
26:11 I went **from one s to another** *2848+4246+5252*
Rev 2:9 Jews and are not, but are a s of Satan. *5252*
3:9 I will make those who are of the s of Satan, *5252*

SYNAGOGUES (23) [SYNAGOGUE]

Mt 4:23 teaching in their s, preaching the good news *5252*
6:2 the hypocrites do in the s and on the streets, *5252*
6:5 in the s and on the street corners to be seen *5252*
9:35 teaching in their s, preaching the good news *5252*
10:17 to the local councils and flog you in their **s.** *5252*
23:6 and the most important seats in the s; *5252*
23:34 others you will flog in your s and pursue *5252*
Mk 1:39 in their s and driving out demons. *5252*
12:39 in the s and the places of honor at banquets. *5252*
13:9 to the local councils and flogged in the **s.** *5252*
Lk 4:15 He taught in their s, and everyone praised *5252*
4:44 And he kept on preaching in the s of Judea. *5252*
11:43 in the s and greetings in the marketplaces. *5252*
12:11 "When you are brought before s, *5252*
13:10 Jesus was teaching in one *of* the **s,** *5252*
20:46 in the s and the places of honor at banquets. *5252*
21:12 They will deliver you to s and prisons, *5252*
Jn 18:20 "I always taught in s or at the temple, *5252*
Ac 9:2 asked him for letters to the s in Damascus, *5252*
9:20 to preach in the s that Jesus is the Son *5252*
13:5 the word of God in the Jewish **s.** *5252*
15:21 from the earliest times and is read in the s *5252*
24:12 stirring up a crowd in the s or anywhere else *5252*

SYNTYCHE (1)

Php 4:2 with S to agree with each other in the Lord. *5345*

SYRACUSE (1)

Ac 28:12 We put in at S and stayed there three days. *5352*

SYRIA (8) [SYRIAN]

Mt 4:24 News about him spread all over **S,** *5353*
Lk 2:2 while Quirinius was governor *of* **S.)** *5353*
Ac 15:23 S and Cilicia: Greetings. *5353*
15:41 He went through S and Cilicia, *5353*
18:18 Then he left the brothers and sailed for **S,** *5353*
20:3 as he was about to sail for **S,** *5353*
21:3 we sailed on to **S.** *5353*
Gal 1:21 Later I went to S and Cilicia. *5353*

SYRIA-DAMASCUS (KJV) See ARAMEAN KINGDOM OF DAMASCUS

SYRIA-MAACHAH (KJV) See ARAM MAACAH

SYRIACK (KJV) See ARAMAIC

SYRIAN (1) [SYRIA]

Lk 4:27 of them was cleansed—only Naaman the S. *5354*

SYRIAN PHOENICIA (1) [PHOENICIA, SYRIA]

Mk 7:26 The woman was a Greek, born in S. *5355*

SYRIANS (KJV) See ARAMEANS

SYROPHENICIAN (KJV) See SYRIAN PHOENICIA

SYRTIS (1)

Ac 27:17 would run aground on the **sandbars of S,** *5358*

T

TAANACH (7)

Jos 12:21 the king of T one the king of Megiddo one 9505
17:11 Endor, **T** and Megiddo, 9505
21:25 the tribe of Manasseh they received **T** 9505
Jdg 1:27 not drive out the people of Beth Shan or **T** 9505
5:19 of Canaan fought at **T** by the waters 9505
1Ki 4:12 in **T** and Megiddo, and in all 9505
1Ch 7:29 of Manasseh were Beth Shan, **T,** Megiddo 9505

TAANATH SHILOH (1)

Jos 16:6 the north it curved eastward to **T,** 9304

TABALIAH (1)

1Ch 26:11 **T** the third and Zechariah the fourth. 3189

TABBAOTH (2)

Ezr 2:43 the descendants of Ziha, Hasupha, **T,** 3191
Ne 7:46 the descendants of Ziha, Hasupha, **T,** 3191

TABBATH (1)

Jdg 7:22 as the border of Abel Meholah near T. 3195

TABEEL (2)

Ezr 4:7 **T** and the rest of his associates wrote 3175
Isa 7:6 and make the son of **T** king over it." 3174

TABERAH (2)

Nu 11:3 So that place was called **T,** 9323
Dt 9:22 You also made the LORD angry at **T,** 9323

TABERING (KJV) See BEAT

TABERNACLE (114) [TABERNACLES]

Ex 25: 9 Make this **t** and all its furnishings exactly 5438
26: 1 "Make the **t** with ten curtains 5438
26: 6 the curtains together so that the **t** is a unit. 5438
26: 7 of goat hair for the tent over the **t**— 5438
26:12 over is to hang down at the rear of the **t.** 5438
26:13 what is left will hang over the sides of the **t** 5438
26:15 of acacia wood for the **t.** 5438
26:17 Make all the frames of the **t** in this way. 5438
26:18 for the south side of the **t** 5438
26:20 For the other side, the north side of the **t,** 5438
26:22 that is, the west end of the **t,** 5438
26:26 five for the frames on one side of the **t,** 5438
26:27 at the far end of the **t.** 5438
26:30 the **t** according to the plan shown you on 5438
26:35 the **t** and put the lampstand opposite it on 5438
27: 9 "Make a courtyard for the **t.** 5438
27:19 articles used in the service of the **t,** 5438
35:11 the **t** with its tent and its covering, 5438
35:15 for the doorway at the entrance to the **t;** 5438
35:18 the **t** and for the courtyard, and their ropes; 5438
36: 8 the workmen made the **t** with ten curtains 5438
36:13 of curtains together so that the **t** was a unit. 5438
36:14 of goat hair for the tent over the **t**— 5438
36:20 frames of acacia wood for the **t.** 5438
36:22 They made all the frames of the **t** 5438
36:23 for the south side of the **t** 5438
36:25 For the other side, the north side of the **t,** 5438
36:27 that is, the west end of the **t,** 5438
36:28 for the corners of the **t** at the far end. 5438
36:31 five for the frames on one side of the **t,** 5438
36:32 at the far end of the **t.** 5438
38:20 All the tent pegs of the **t** and of 5438
38:21 the amounts of the materials used for the **t,** 5438
38:21 the **t** *of* the Testimony, 5438
38:31 and all the tent pegs for the **t** and those for 5438
39:32 So all the work on the **t,** 5438
39:33 Then they brought the **t** to Moses: 5438
39:40 all the furnishings for the **t,** 5438
40: 2 "Set up the **t,** the Tent of Meeting, 5438
40: 5 and put the curtain at the entrance to the **t.** 5438
40: 6 the entrance to the **t,** the Tent of Meeting; 5438
40: 9 "Take the anointing oil and anoint the **t** 5438
40:17 So the **t** was set up on the first day of 5438
40:18 When Moses set up the **t,** 5438
40:19 Then he spread the tent over the **t** and put 5438
40:21 into the **t** and hung the shielding curtain 5438
40:22 the north side of the **t** outside the curtain 5438
40:24 the table on the south side of the **t** 5438
40:28 up the curtain at the entrance to the **t.** 5438
40:29 of burnt offering near the entrance to the **t,** 5438
40:33 the courtyard around the **t** and altar and put 5438
40:34 and the glory of the LORD filled the **t.** 5438
40:35 and the glory of the LORD filled the **t.** 5438
40:36 from above the **t,** they would set out; 5438
40:38 cloud of the LORD was over the **t** by day, 5438
Lev 8:10 and anointed the **t** and everything in it, 5438
17: 4 an offering to the LORD in front of the **t** 5438
Nu 1:50 to be in charge of the **t** *of* the Testimony— 5438
1:50 to carry the **t** and all its furnishings; 5438
1:51 Whenever the **t** is to move, 5438
1:51 and whenever the **t** is to be set up, 5438
1:53 the **t** *of* the Testimony so that wrath will 5438
1:53 to be responsible for the care of the **t** *of* 5438
3: 7 of Meeting by doing the work of the **t.** 5438
3: 8 of the Israelites by doing the work of the **t.** 5438
3:23 to camp on the west, behind the **t.** 5438
3:25 for the care of the **t** and tent, 5438
3:26 the courtyard surrounding the **t** and altar, 5438
3:29 to camp on the south side of the **t.** 5438
3:35 to camp on the north side of the **t.** 5438
3:36 to take care of the frames of the **t,** 5438
3:38 to camp to the east of the **t,** 5438
4:16 be in charge of the entire **t** and everything 5438
4:25 They are to carry the curtains of the **t,** 5438
4:26 the courtyard surrounding the **t** and altar, 5438
4:31 to carry the frames of the **t,** its crossbars, 5438
5:17 and put some dust from the **t** floor into 5438
7: 1 When Moses finished setting up the **t,** 5438
7: 3 These they presented before the **t.** 5438
9:15 On the day the **t,** the Tent of the Testimony, 5438
9:15 till morning the cloud above the **t** looked 5438
9:18 As long as the cloud stayed over the **t,** 5438
9:19 the cloud remained over the **t** a long time, 5438
9:20 the cloud was over the **t** only a few days; 5438
9:22 the cloud stayed over the **t** for two days or 5438
10:11 the cloud lifted from above the **t** *of* 5438
10:17 Then the **t** was taken down, 5438
10:21 The **t** was to be set up before they arrived. 5438
16: 9 the work at the LORD's **t** and to stand 5438
17:13 Anyone who even comes near the **t** *of* 5438
19:13 to purify himself defiles the LORD's **t.** 5438
31:30 for the care of the LORD's **t.**" 5438
31:47 for the care of the LORD's **t.** 5438
Jos 22:19 where the LORD's **t** stands, 5438
22:29 the LORD our God that stands before his **t.**" 5438
1Ch 6:32 They ministered with music before the **t,** 5438
6:48 to all the other duties of the **t,** 5438
16:39 the priest and his fellow priests before the **t** 5438
21:29 The **t** *of* the LORD, which Moses had made 5438
23:26 the Levites no longer need to carry the **t** 5438
2Ch 1: 5 in Gibeon in front of the **t** *of* the LORD; 5438
Ps 27: 5 in the shelter of his **t** and set me high upon 185
27: 6 at his **t** will I sacrifice with shouts of joy; 185
78:60 He abandoned the **t** *of* Shiloh, 5438
Ac 7:44 the **t** of the Testimony with them in *5008*
Ac 7:45 Having received **the t,** *4005^S*
Heb 8: 2 the true **t** set up by the Lord, not by man. *5008*
8: 5 when he was about to build the **t:** *5008*
9: 2 A **t** was set up. *5008*
9: 8 as long as the first **t** was still standing. *5008*
9:11 and more perfect **t** that is not man-made, *5008*
9:21 the blood both the **t** and everything used *5008*
13:10 who minister *at* the **t** have no right to eat. *5008*
Rev 15: 5 that is, the **t** of the Testimony, was opened. *5008*

TABERNACLES (10) [TABERNACLE]

Lev 23:34 the LORD's Feast of **T** begins, 6109
Dt 16:13 of **T** for seven days after you have gathered 6109
16:16 the Feast of Weeks and the Feast of **T.** 6109
31:10 for canceling debts, during the Feast of **T,** 6109
2Ch 8:13 the Feast of Weeks and the Feast of **T.** 6109
Ezr 3: 4 the Feast of **T** with the required number 6109
Zec 14:16 and to celebrate the Feast of **T.** 6109
14:18 not go up to celebrate the Feast of **T.** 6109
14:19 not go up to celebrate the Feast of **T.** 6109
Jn 7: 2 But when the Jewish Feast of **T** was near, *5009*

TABITHA (2)

Ac 9:36 In Joppa there was a disciple named **T** *5412*
9:40 the dead woman, he said, "**T,** get up." *5412*

TABLE (86) [TABLES]

Ge 43:34 were served to them from Joseph's **t,** 7156^S
Ex 25:23 "Make a **t** *of* acacia wood— 8947
25:26 Make four gold rings for **the t** 2257^S
25:27 to hold the poles used in carrying the **t.** 8947
25:28 overlay them with gold and carry the **t** 8947
25:30 Put the bread of the Presence on this **t** to 8947
26:35 the **t** outside the curtain on the north side 8947
30:27 the **t** and all its articles, 8947
31: 8 the **t** and its articles, 8947
35:13 the **t** with its poles and all its articles and 8947
37:10 They made the **t** of acacia wood— 8947
37:13 They cast four gold rings for **the t** 2257^S
37:14 to hold the poles used in carrying the **t.** 8947
37:15 The poles for carrying the **t** were made 8947
37:16 from pure gold the articles for the **t**— 8947
39:36 the **t** with all its articles and the bread of 8947
40: 4 Bring in the **t** and set out what belongs 8947
40:22 Moses placed the **t** in the Tent of Meeting 8947
40:24 of Meeting opposite the **t** on the south side 8947
Lev 24: 6 on the **t** of pure gold before the LORD. 8947
Nu 3:31 the **t,** the lampstand, the altars, 8947
4: 7 the **t** *of* the Presence they are to spread 8947
Jdg 1: 7 have picked up scraps under my **t.** 8947
1Sa 20:29 why he has not come to the king's **t.**" 8947
20:34 Jonathan got up from the **t** in fierce anger; 8947
2Sa 9: 7 and you will always eat at my **t.**" 8947
9:10 will always eat at my **t.**" 8947
9:11 So Mephibosheth ate at David's **t** like one 8947
9:13 because he always ate at the king's **t,** 8947
19:28 a place among those who sat at your **t.** 8947
1Ki 2: 7 be among those who eat at your **t.** 8947
4:27 and all who came to the king's **t.** 8947
7:48 the golden **t** on which was the bread of 8947
10: 5 the food on his **t,** the seating of his officials, 8947
13:20 While they were sitting at the **t,** 8947
18:19 of Asherah, who eat at Jezebel's **t.**" 8947
2Ki 4:10 on the roof and put in it a bed and a **t,** 8947
25:29 of his life ate regularly **at** the king's **t.** 4200+7156^S
1Ch 9:32 the bread **set out on the t.** 5121
23:29 the bread **set out on the t,** 5121
28:16 **each t** for consecrated bread; 2256+8947+8947
2Ch 9: 4 the food on his **t,** the seating of his officials, 8947
13:11 the bread on the ceremonially clean **t** 8947
29:18 the **t** *for* setting out the consecrated bread, 8947
Ne 5:17 and fifty Jews and officials ate at my **t,** 8947
10:33 for the bread **set out on the t;** 5121
Job 36:16 of your **t** laden with choice food. 8947
Ps 23: 5 You prepare a **t** before me in the presence 8947
69:22 May the **t** set before them become a snare; 8947
78:19 saying, "Can God spread a **t** in the desert? 8947
128: 3 be like olive shoots around your **t.** 8947
Pr 9: 2 she has also set her **t.** 8947
SS 1:12 While the king was at his **t,** 4990
Isa 65:11 who spread a **t** for Fortune and fill bowls 8947
Jer 52:33 of his life ate regularly at the king's **t.** 4200+7156^S
Eze 23:41 an elegant couch, with a **t** spread before it 8947
39:20 At my **t** you will eat your fill of horses 8947
41:22 "This is the **t** that is before the LORD." 8947
44:16 to come near my **t** to minister before me 8947
Da 1: 5 of food and wine from the king's **t.** 5492
11:27 will sit at the same **t** and lie to each other, 8947
Mal 1: 7 that the LORD's **t** is contemptible. 8947
1:12 you profane it by saying of the Lord's **t,** 8947
Mt 15:27 the crumbs that fall from their masters' **t.**" *5544*
26: 7 on his head *as he was* **reclining at the t.** *367*
26:20 Jesus *was* **reclining at the t** with *367*
Mk 7:28 under the **t** eat the children's crumbs." *5544*
14: 3 **reclining at the t** in the home of a man *2879*
14:18 *While* they *were* **reclining at the t** eating, *367*
Lk 7:36 the Pharisee's house and **reclined at the t.** *2884*
11:37 so *he* went in and **reclined at the t.** *404*
12:37 **have them recline at the t** and will come *369*
14: 7 guests picked the **places of honor at the t,** *4752*
14:15 *of* those **at the t with** him heard this, *5263*
16:21 to eat what fell from the rich man's **t.** *5544*
22:14 Jesus and his apostles **reclined at the t.** *404*
22:21 to betray me is with mine on the **t.** *5544*
22:27 one who *is* **at the t** or the one who serves? *367*
Lk 22:27 Is it not the one who *is* **at the t?** *367*
22:30 at my **t** in my kingdom and sit on thrones, *5544*
24:30 When he *was* **at the t** with them, *2884*
Jn 12: 2 among those **reclining at the t** with him. *367*
Ro 11: 9 "May their **t** become a snare and a trap, *5544*
1Co 10:21 you cannot have a part *in* both the Lord's **t** *5544*
10:21 both the Lord's table and the **t** of demons. *5544*
Heb 9: 2 the **t** and the consecrated bread; *5544*

TABLES (18) [TABLE]

1Ch 28:16 the weight of silver for the silver **t;** 8947
2Ch 4: 8 He made ten **t** and placed them in 8947
4:19 the **t** on which was the bread of the Presence 8947
Est 9: 1 but now **the t were turned** and the Jews got 2200
Isa 21: 5 They set the **t,** they spread the rugs, 8947
28: 8 the **t** are covered with vomit and there is 8947
Eze 40:39 In the portico of the gateway were two **t** 8947
40:40 to the north gateway were two **t,** 8947
40:40 on the other side of the steps were two **t.** 8947
40:41 So there were four **t** on one side of 8947
40:41 eight **t** in all—on which the sacrifices 8947
40:42 There were also four **t** of dressed stone for 8947
40:43 The **t** were for the flesh of the offerings. 8947
Mt 21:12 He overturned the **t** of the money changers *5544*
Mk 11:15 He overturned the **t** of the money changers *5544*
Jn 2:14 and others sitting at **t** exchanging money. *NIG*
2:15 the money changers and overturned their **t.** *5544*
Ac 6: 2 of the word of God in order to wait on **t.** *5544*

TABLET (5) [TABLETS]

Pr 3: 3 write them on the **t** *of* your heart. 4283
7: 3 write them on the **t** *of* your heart. 4283
Isa 30: 8 Go now, write it on a **t** for them, 4283
Eze 4: 1 "Now, son of man, take a **clay t,** 4246
Lk 1:63 He asked for a **writing t,** *4400*

TABLETS (36) [TABLET]

Ex 24:12 and I will give you the **t** *of* stone, 4283
31:18 he gave him the two **t** *of* the Testimony, 4283
31:18 **t** *of* stone inscribed by the finger of God. 4283
32:15 the two **t** *of* the Testimony in his hands. 4283
32:16 The **t** were the work of God; 4283
32:16 the writing of God, engraved on the **t.** 4283
32:19 his anger burned and he threw the **t** out 4283
34: 1 "Chisel out two stone **t** like the first ones, 4283
34: 1 on them the words that were on the first **t,** 4283
34: 4 So Moses chiseled out two stone **t** like 4283
34: 4 and he carried the two stone **t** in his hands. 4283
34:28 on the **t** the words of the covenant— 4283
34:29 down from Mount Sinai with the two **t** *of* 4283
Dt 4:13 and then wrote them on two stone **t.** 4283
5:22 on two stone **t** and gave them to me. 4283
9: 9 on the mountain to receive the **t** *of* stone, 4283
9: 9 the **t** *of* the covenant that the LORD made 4283
9:10 The LORD gave me two stone **t** inscribed 4283
9:11 the LORD gave me the two stone **t,** 4283
9:11 two stone tablets, the **t** *of* the covenant. 4283
9:15 two **t** *of* the covenant were in my hands. 4283
9:17 the two **t** and threw them out of my hands, 4283
10: 1 "Chisel out two stone **t** like the first ones 4283
10: 2 I will write on the **t** the words that were on 4283
10: 2 the words that were on the first **t,** 4283
10: 3 and chiseled out two stone **t** like the first 4283
10: 3 the mountain with the two **t** in my hands. 4283
10: 4 on these **t** what he had written before, 4283
10: 5 down the mountain and put the **t** in the ark 4283
1Ki 8: 9 the two stone **t** that Moses had placed in it 4283
2Ch 5:10 the two **t** that Moses had placed in it 4283
Jer 17: 1 on the **t** *of* their hearts and on the horns 4283
Hab 2: 2 the revelation and make it plain on **t** so that 4283
2Co 3: 3 not on **t** of stone but on tablets of human *4419*
3: 3 of stone but on **t** of human hearts. *4419*
Heb 9: 4 and the **stone t** of the covenant. *4419*

TABOR (10) [AZNOTH TABOR, KISLOTH TABOR]

Jos 19:22 The boundary touched **T,** 9314
Jdg 4: 6 and Zebulun and lead the way to Mount **T.** 9314
4:12 of Abinoam had gone up to Mount **T,** 9314
4:14 So Barak went down Mount **T,** 9314
8:18 "What kind of men did you kill at **T?**" 9314
1Sa 10: 3 until you reach the great tree of **T.** 9314
1Ch 6:77 Kartah, Rimmono and **T,** 9314
Ps 89:12 **T** and Hermon sing for joy at your name. 9314
Jer 46:18 "one will come who is like **T** among 9314
Hos 5: 1 a net spread out on **T.** 9314

TABRET, TABRETS (KJV) See TAMBOURINES

TABRIMMON (1)

1Ki 15:18 and sent them to Ben-Hadad son of **T,** 3193

TACHES (KJV) See CLASP

TACHMONITE (KJV) See TAHKEMONITE

TACKLE (1)

Ac 27:19 they threw the ship's **t** overboard *5006*

TACT (1)
Da 2:14 Daniel spoke to him with wisdom and **t.** 10302

TADMOR (2)
1Ki 9:18 and **T** in the desert, within his land, 9330
2Ch 8: 4 He also built up **T** in the desert and all 9330

TAHAN (2) [TAHANITE]
Nu 26:35 through **T**, the Tahanite clan. 9380
1Ch 7:25 Resheph his son, Telah his son, **T** his son, 9380

TAHANITE (1) [TAHAN]
Nu 26:35 through Tahan, the **T** clan. 9385

TAHAPANES (KJV) See TAHPANHES

TAHASH (1)
Ge 22:24 Tebah, Gaham, **T** and Maacah. 9392

TAHATH (6)
Nu 33:26 They left Makheloth and camped at **T.** 9395
33:27 They left **T** and camped at Terah. 9395
1Ch 6:24 **T** his son, Uriel his son, Uzziah his son 9394
6:37 the son of **T**, the son of Assir, 9394
7:20 Shuthelah, Bered his son, **T** his son, 9394
7:20 Tahath his son, Eleadah his son, **T** his son, 9394

TAHKEMONITE (1)
2Sa 23: 8 Josheb-Basshebeth, a **T,** 9376

TAHPANHES (7)
Jer 2:16 and **T** have shaved the crown of your head. 9387
43: 7 to the LORD and went as far as **T.** 9387
43: 8 In **T** the word of the LORD came 9387
43: 9 at the entrance to Pharaoh's palace in **T.** 9387
44: 1 in Migdol, **T** and Memphis— 9387
46:14 proclaim it also in Memphis and **T:** 9387
Eze 30:18 Dark will be the day at **T** when I break 9387

TAHPENES (3)
1Ki 11:19 sister of his own wife, Queen **T,** in marriage 9388
11:20 sister of **T** bore him a son named Genubath, 9388
11:20 whom **T** brought up in the royal palace. 9388

TAHREA (1)
1Ch 9:41 Pithon, Melech, **T** and Ahaz. 9390

TAHTIM HODSHI (1)
2Sa 24: 6 to Gilead and the region of **T,** 9398

TAIL (15) [TAILS]
Ex 4: 4 "Reach out your hand and take it by the **t.**" 2387
29:22 "Take from this ram the fat, the **fat t,** 487
Lev 3: 9 entire **fat t** cut off close to the backbone, 487
7: 3 the **fat t** and the fat that covers 487
8:25 He took the fat, the **fat t,** 487
9:19 the **fat t,** the layer of fat, 487
Dt 28:13 will make you the head, not the **t.** 2387
28:44 He will be the head, but you will be the **t.** 2387
Jdg 15: 4 and tied them **t** to tail in pairs. 2387
15: 4 and tied them tail to **t** in pairs. 2387
Job 40:17 His **t** sways like a cedar; 2387
Isa 9:14 and **t,** both palm branch and reed in 2387
9:15 the prophets who teach lies are the **t.** 2387
19:15 head or **t,** palm branch or reed. 2387
Rev 12: 4 His **t** swept a third of the stars out of *4038*

TAILS (5) [TAIL]
Jdg 15: 4 He then fastened a torch to every pair of **t,** 2387
Rev 9:10 They had **t** and stings like scorpions, *4038*
9:10 in their **t** they had power to torment people *4038*
9:19 in their mouths and in their **t;** *4038*
9:19 for their **t** were like snakes, *4038*

TAKE (861) [RETAKE, TAKEN, TAKES, TAKING, TOOK]
Ge 2:15 Garden of Eden to work it and **t care of** it 9068
3:22 he allowed to reach out his hand and **t** also 4374
6:21 *to* **t** every kind of food that is to be eaten 4374
7: 2 **T** with you seven of every kind of clean 4374
12:19 **T** her and go!" 4374
15: 7 to give you this land to **t possession** *of* it." 3769
19:15 **T** your wife and your two daughters who 4374
21:18 Lift the boy up and **t** him by the hand, 2616
22: 2 Then God said, "**T** your son, your only son, 4374
22:17 Your descendants *will* **t possession** *of* 3769
24: 5 *Shall I then* **t** your son **back** to 8740+8740
24: 6 that *you do* not **t** my son **back** there," 8740
24: 8 Only *do* not **t** my son **back** there." 8740
24:51 Here is Rebekah; **t** her and go, 4374
27:10 Then **t** it to your father to eat, 995
28: 2 **T** a wife for yourself there, 4374
28: 4 so that you *may* **t possession** *of* the land 3769
28: 6 to Paddan Aram to **t** a wife from there, 4374
29: 7 the sheep and **t** them **back** *to* pasture." 2143
30:15 *Will you* **t** my son's mandrakes too?" 4374
31:31 **t** your daughters away from me **by force.** 1608
31:32 of yours here with me; and if so, **t** it." 4374
31:50 if *you* **t** any wives besides my daughters, 4374
34: 9 give us your daughters and **t** our daughters 4374
34:16 and **t** your daughters for ourselves. 4374
34:17 *we'll* **t** our sister and go." 4374
37:21 "*Let's* not **t** his life," he said. 5782
37:22 to rescue him from them and **t** him **back** 8740
37:25 and they were on their way to **t** them **down** 3718
41:34 *to* **t a fifth** *of* the harvest of Egypt during 2821
42:19 while the rest of you go and **t** grain **back** 995
42:33 of your brothers here with me, and **t** food 4374
42:36 and now *you want to* **t** Benjamin. 4374
43:11 in your bags and **t** them **down** to the man *as* 3718
43:12 **T** double the amount of silver with you, 4374
43:13 **T** your brother also and go back to the man 4374
43:16 "**T** these men to my house, 995
43:18 and seize us as slaves and **t** our donkeys." NIH
44:29 If *you* **t** this one from me too 4374
45:19 **T** some carts from Egypt for your children 4374
48:21 but God will be with you and **t** you **back** to 8740
50:24 to your aid and **t** you **up** out of this land to 6590
Ex 2: 9 "**T** this baby and nurse him for me, 2143
3: 5 "**T off** your sandals, 5970
3:18 *Let us* **t** a three-day journey into 2143
4: 4 "Reach out your hand and **t** it by the tail." 296
4: 9 **t** some water from the Nile and pour it on 4374
4: 9 The water *you* **t** from the river will become 4374
4:17 But **t** this staff in your hand 4374
5: 3 Now *let us* **t** a three-day journey into 2143
6: 7 *I will* **t** you as my own people, 4374
7: 9 '**T** your staff and throw it down 4374
7:15 and **t** in your hand the staff 4374
7:19 '**T** your staff and stretch out your hand 4374
7:23 and *did* not **t** even this *to* heart. 8883
8: 8 to the LORD *to* **t** the frogs **away** from me 6073
8:27 *We must* **t** a three-day journey into 2143
9: 8 "**T** handfuls of soot from a furnace 4374
10:17 **t** this deadly plague **away** from me." 6073
12: 3 of this month each man *is to* **t** a lamb 4374
12: 5 and *you may* **t** them from the sheep or 4374
12: 6 **T care of** them until the fourteenth day 2118+4200+5466
12: 7 Then *they are to* **t** some of the blood 4374
12:22 **T** a bunch of hyssop, 4374
12:32 **T** your flocks and herds, as you have said, 4374
12:46 **t** none of the meat outside the house. 3655
12:48 then *he may* **t part** like one born in 6913+7928
16:16 **T** an omer for each person you have 4374
16:32 '**T** an omer of manna and keep it for 4850
16:33 "**T** a jar and put an omer of manna in it. 4374
17: 5 **T** with you some of the elders of Israel 4374
17: 5 with you some of the elders of Israel and **t** 4374
21: 6 his master *must* **t** him before the judges. 5602
21: 6 *He shall* **t** him to the door or the doorpost 5602
21:14 **t** him away from my altar and put him 4374
21:23 *you are to* **t** life for life, 5989
22:22 not **t advantage of** a widow or an orphan. 6700
22:26 **t** your neighbor's cloak **as a pledge,** 2471+2471
23: 4 **be sure to t** it **back** to him. 8740+8740
23:25 *I will* **t away** sickness from among you, 6073
23:30 *to* **t possession** *of* the land. 5706
28: 9 "**T** two onyx stones and engrave on them 4374
29: 1 **T** a young bull and two rams 4374
29: 5 **T** the garments and dress Aaron with 4374
29: 7 **T** the anointing oil and anoint him 4374
29:12 **T** some of the bull's blood and put it on 4374
29:13 Then **t** all the fat around the inner parts, 4374
29:15 "**T** one of the rams, 4374
29:16 Slaughter it and **t** the blood and sprinkle it 4374
29:19 "**T** the other ram, 4374
29:20 **t** some of its blood and put it on the lobes 4374
29:21 And **t** some of the blood on the altar 4374
29:22 "**T** from this ram the fat, the fat tail, 4374
29:23 which is before the LORD, **t** a loaf, NIH
29:25 Then **t** them from their hands 4374
29:26 After *you* **t** the breast of the ram 4374
29:31 "**T** the ram for the ordination and cook 4374
30:12 "When *you* **t a census** *of* the Israelites 906+5951+8031
30:23 "**T** the following fine spices: 4374
30:34 said to Moses, "**T** fragrant spices— 4374
32: 2 "**T off** the gold earrings that your wives, 7293
32:24 'Whoever has any gold jewelry, **t** it **off.**' 7293
33: 5 Now **t off** your ornaments 3718+4946+6584
33: 7 Moses *used to* **t** a tent and pitch it outside 4374
34: 9 **t** us **as** *your* **inheritance.**" 5706
35: 5 **t** an offering for the LORD. 4374
40: 9 "**T** the anointing oil and anoint 4374
Lev 2: 2 and **t** it to Aaron's sons the priests. 995
2: 2 The priest *shall* **t a handful** of 4850+7858+7859
2: 8 *who shall* **t** it to the altar. 5602
2: 9 He *shall* **t out** the memorial portion from 8123
4: 5 Then the anointed priest *shall* **t** some of 4374
4:12 *he must* **t** outside the camp to 3655
4:16 *to* **t** some of the bull's blood into the Tent 995
4:21 Then *he shall* **t** the bull outside the camp 3655
4:25 Then the priest *shall* **t** some of the blood 4374
4:30 Then the priest *is to* **t** some of the blood 4374
4:34 Then the priest *shall* **t** some of the blood 4374
5:12 who *shall* **t a handful** of it as 4850+7858+7859
6:11 Then *he is to* **t off** these clothes and put 7320
6:15 The priest *is to* **t** a handful of fine flour 8123
9: 2 "**T** a bull calf for your sin offering and 4374
9: 3 '**T** a male goat for a sin offering, 4374
10:12 "**T** the grain offering left over from 4374
10:17 to you to **t away** the guilt of the community 5951
14: 6 *He is* then *to* **t** the live bird and dip it, 4374
14:12 *to* **t** one of the male lambs and offer it as 4374
14:14 *to* **t** some of the blood of the guilt offering 4374
14:15 priest *shall* then **t** some of the log of oil, 4374
14:21 *he must* **t** one male lamb as a guilt offering 4374
14:24 *to* **t** the lamb for the guilt offering, 4374
14:25 the lamb for the guilt offering and **t** some 4374
14:42 *to* **t** other stones to replace these 4374
14:42 to replace these and **t** new clay and plaster 4374
14:49 To purify the house *he is to* **t** two birds 4374
14:51 Then *he is to* **t** the cedar wood, 4374
15:14 On the eighth day *he must* **t** two doves 4374
15:29 On the eighth day *she must* **t** two doves 4374
16: 5 *to* **t** two male goats for a sin offering and 4374
16: 7 *to* **t** the two goats and present them before 4374
16:12 *He is to* **t** a censer full of burning coals 4374
16:12 and **t** them behind the curtain. 995
16:14 *He is to* **t** some of the bull's blood and 4374
16:15 and **t** its blood behind the curtain and do 995
16:18 *He shall* **t** some of the bull's blood 4374
16:23 to go into the Tent of Meeting and **t off** 7320
18:18 " '*Do* not **t** your wife's sister as a rival wife 4374
23:40 the first day *you are to* **t** choice fruit from 4374
24: 5 "**T** fine flour and bake twelve loaves 4374
24:14 "**T** the blasphemer outside the camp. 3655
25:14 *do* not **t advantage of** each other. 3561
25:17 *Do* not **t advantage of** each other, 3561
25:36 *Do* not **t** interest of any kind from him, 4374
26:31 and *I will* **t** no **delight** in the pleasing aroma 8193
Nu 1: 2 "**T a census** *of* the whole Israelite 5951+8031
1:50 *to* **t care of** it and encamp around it. 9250
1:51 the Levites *are to* **t** it **down,** 3718
3: 8 *They are to* **t care of** all the furnishings of 9068
3:36 The Merarites were appointed to **t care of** 5466
3:41 **T** the Levites for me in place of all 4374
3:45 "**T** the Levites in place of all the firstborn 4374
4: 2 "**T a census** *of* the Kohathite 906+5951+8031
4: 5 Aaron and his sons are to go in and **t down** 3718
4: 9 *to* **t** a blue cloth and cover the lampstand 4374
4:12 *to* **t** all the articles used for ministering in 4374
4:22 "**T a census** also *of* the Gershonites 5951+8031
5:15 then he *is to* **t** his wife to the priest. 995
5:15 also **t** an offering of a tenth of an ephah 995
5:17 Then he *shall* **t** some holy water in 4374
5:25 *to* **t** from her hands the grain offering 4374
5:26 then *to* **t a handful** of the grain offering 7858
6:18 *to* **t** the hair and put it in the fire that is 4374
8: 6 "**T** the Levites from among the other 4374
8: 8 *Have them* **t** a young bull 4374
8: 8 *to* **t** a second young bull for a sin offering. 4374
8:24 shall come to **t part** in the work at 7371+7372
11:17 and *I will* **t** of the Spirit that is on you 724
13:30 "We should go up and **t possession** *of* 3769
16: 6 followers are to do this: **T** censers 4374
16:17 *to* **t** his censer and put incense in it— 4374
16:37 *to* **t** the censers out of the smoldering 8123
16:46 "**T** your censer and put incense in it, 4374
19: 4 Then Eleazar the priest *is to* **t** some 4374
19: 6 The priest *is to* **t** some cedar wood, 4374
19:18 ceremonially clean *is to* **t** some hyssop, 4374
20: 8 "**T** the staff, and you and your brother 4374
20:25 and his son Eleazar and **t** them **up** 6590
21: 7 that the LORD *will* **t** the snakes **away** 6073
23:27 "Come, *let me* **t** you to another place. 4374
25: 4 "**T** all the leaders of these people, 4374
26: 2 "**T a census** *of* the whole 906+5951+8031
26: 4 "**T** a census of the men twenty years old NIH
27:18 "**T** Joshua son of Nun, 4374
31: 2 "**T vengeance** on the Midianites *for* 5933+5935
31:29 **T** this tribute from their half share 4374
33:53 **T possession** *of* the land and settle in it, 3769
35: 8 **T many** towns from a tribe that has many, 8049
Dt 1: 8 Go in and **t possession** *of* the land that 3769
1:21 Go up and **t possession** *of* it as the LORD, 3769
1:22 a report about the route *we are to* **t** and 6590
1:39 to them and they *will* **t possession** *of* it. 3769
2:24 Begin *to* **t possession** *of* it and engage him 3769
3: 4 not one of the sixty cities that *we did* not **t** 4374
3:18 given you this land to **t possession** *of* it. 3769
4: 1 and may go in and **t possession** *of* the land 3769
4: 5 in the land you are entering to **t possession** 3769
4:22 over and **t possession** *of* that good land. 3769
4:34 to **t** for himself one nation out of another 4374
4:39 Acknowledge and **t** to heart this day that 8740
6:13 serve him only and **t** *your* **oaths** 8678
6:18 with you and you may go in and **t over** 3769
7: 3 or **t** their daughters for your sons, 4374
7:11 Therefore, **t care** to follow the commands, 9068
7:25 and *do* not **t** it for yourselves, 4374
9: 4 to **t possession** *of* this land because 3769
9: 5 that you are going in to **t possession** 3769
9:23 "Go up and **t possession** *of* the land 3769
9:28 the LORD was not able to **t** them into 995
10:20 to him and **t** *your* **oaths** in his name. 8678
11: 8 in and **t over** the land that you are crossing 3769
11:10 The land you are entering to **t over** is not 3769
11:11 to **t possession** *of* is a land of mountains 3769
11:31 to cross the Jordan to enter and **t possession** 3769
12:26 But **t** your consecrated things 5951
12:32 do not add to it or **t away** from it. 1757
14:25 and **t** the silver with you and go to 7443
15:17 then **t** an awl and push it through his ear 4374
17: 5 **t** the man or woman who has done this evil 3655
17: 8 **t** them to the place the LORD your God will 6590
17:17 *He must* not **t many** wives, 8049
18:22 the LORD *does* not **t place** or come true, 2118
20:14 *you may* **t** these as plunder for yourselves. 1024
21: 3 the town nearest the body *shall* **t** a heifer 4374

Dt 21:10 into your hands and *you* **t captives,** 8647+8660
21:11 *you may* **t** her as your wife. 4374
21:19 his father and mother *shall* **t hold** of him 9530
22: 1 **be sure to t** it **back** to him. 8740+8740
22: 2 **t** it home with you and keep it 665
22: 6 *do* not **t** the mother with the young. 4374
22: 7 *You may* **t** the young, 4374
22:18 the elders *shall* **t** the man and punish him. 4374
22:24 *you shall* **t** both of them to the gate of 3655
24: 6 not **t** a pair of millstones—not even the upper one—**as security for a debt,** 2471
24:14 *Do* not **t advantage** *of* a hired man 6943
24:17 or **t** the cloak of the widow **as a pledge.** 2471
25: 1 *to* **t** it to court and the judges will decide 5602
25: 5 Her husband's brother *shall* **t** her 995+6584
25: 9 **t off** one of his sandals, 2740
26: 2 **t** some of the firstfruits of all 4374
26: 4 The priest *shall* **t** the basket 4374
28:30 but another will **t** her and ravish her. NIH
28:42 of locusts *will* **t over** all your trees and 3769
30: 1 before you come upon you and *you* **t** them 8740
30: 5 and *you will* **t possession** *of* it. 3769
31: 3 and *you will* **t possession** *of* their land. 3769
31:26 **"T** this Book of the Law and place it beside 4374
32:41 *I will* **t vengeance** on my adversaries 5934+8740
32:43 *he will* **t vengeance** on his enemies 5934+8740
32:46 **"T** to heart all the words I have solemnly 8492
Jos 1:11 the Jordan here to go in and **t possession** *of* 3769
3: 6 **"T up** the ark of the covenant and pass on 5951
4: 3 *to* **t up** twelve stones from the middle of 5951
4: 5 of you *is to* **t up** a stone on his shoulder, 8123
5:15 **"T off** your sandals, for the place 5970
6: 6 **"T up** the ark of the covenant of the LORD 5951
7: 3 Send two or three thousand men *to* **t** it 5782
8: 1 **T** the whole army with you, 4374
8: 7 to rise up from ambush and **t** the city. 3769
8:13 **had** the soldiers **t up** *their* **positions—** 8492
8:29 Joshua ordered them *to* **t** his body from 3718
9:11 **'T** provisions for your journey; 4374
18: 3 before you begin to **t possession** *of* the land 3769
23: 5 and *you will* **t possession** *of* their land, 3769
Jdg 2: 6 they went to **t possession** *of* the land, 3769
4: 6 **t** with you ten thousand men of Naphtali 4374
5: 2 "When the princes in Israel **t the lead,** 7276
5:12 **T captive** your captives, 8647
6:20 **"T** the meat and the unleavened bread, 4374
6:25 **"T** the second bull from your father's herd, 4374
7: 4 **T** them **down** to the water, 3718
9:15 come and **t refuge** in my shade; 2879
11: 9 "Suppose you **t** me **back** to fight 8740
11:15 Israel *did* not **t** the land of Moab or 4374
11:23 what right have you *to* **t** it **over?** 3769
11:24 not **t** what your god Chemosh gives you? 3769
15: 2 **T** *her* instead." 2118+4200
15:10 "We have come to **t** Samson **prisoner,"** 673
18: 9 Don't hesitate to go there and **t** it **over.** 3769
20:10 *We'll* **t** ten men out of every hundred 4374
Ru 1: 7 the road that *would* **t** them **back** to the land 8740
2:12 whose wings you have come to **t refuge."** 2879
1Sa 1:16 *Do* not **t** your servant **for** a wicked woman; 4200+5989+7156
1:22 *I will* **t** him and present him before the LORD 995
2:14 and the priest *would* **t** for himself whatever 4374
2:16 and then **t** whatever you want," 4374
2:16 if you don't, *I'll* **t** it by force." 4374
2:20 to **t the place of** the one she prayed for 9393
6: 7 but **t** their calves **away** and pen them up. 8740
6: 8 **T** the ark of the LORD and put it on 4374
6:21 Come down and **t** it **up** to your place." 6590
8:11 *He will* **t** your sons and make them serve 4374
8:13 *He will* **t** your daughters to be perfumers 4374
8:14 *He will* **t** the best of your fields 4374
8:15 *He will* **t a tenth** *of* your grain and 6923
8:16 and donkeys *he will* **t** for his own use. 4374
8:17 *He will* **t a tenth** *of* your flocks, 6923
9: 3 **"T** one of the servants with you and go 4374
9: 6 Perhaps he will tell us what way *to* **t."** 2143
9: 7 We have no gift to **t** to the man of God. 995
9: 8 of God so that he will tell us what way to **t."** NIH
16: 2 **"T** a heifer with you and say, 4374
16:23 David *would* **t** his harp and play. 4374
17:17 **"T** this ephah of roasted grain 4374
17:18 **T along** these ten cheeses to the 995
18:25 to **t revenge** on his enemies.' " 5933
20: 1 that *he is* **trying to t** my life?" 1335
21: 9 If you want it, **t** it; 4374
23:15 that Saul had come out to **t** his life. 1335
24:11 but you are hunting me down to **t** my life. 4374
25:11 Why *should I* **t** my bread and water, 4374
25:29 someone is pursuing you to **t** your life, 1335
25:40 to you to **t** you to become his wife." 4374
30:15 and *I will* **t** you **down** to them." 3718
30:22 each man *may* **t** his wife and children 5627
2Sa 2:21 **t on** one of the young men and strip him 296
4: 8 your enemy, who **tried to t** your life. 1335
6:10 to **t** the ark of the LORD to be with him in 6073
12:11 Before your very eyes *I will* **t** your wives 4374
12:28 Otherwise I *will* **t** the city, 4334
13:20 Don't **t** this thing *to* heart." 8883
14:14 But God *does* not **t away** life; 5951
15: 5 **t hold** of him and kiss him. 2616
15:16 but he left ten concubines to **t care of** 9068
15:20 Go back, and **t** your countrymen. 8740
15:25 **"T** the ark of God **back** into the city. 8740
15:27 and Abiathar **t** your two sons with you. NIH
16:11 *is* **trying to t** my life. 1335
16:21 whom he left to **t care of** the palace. 9068
2Sa 18:19 "Let me run and **t the news** *to* the king that 1413
18:20 "You are not the one to **t** the news today," NIH
18:20 *"You may* **t the news** another time, 1413
19:18 at the ford to **t** the king's household **over** 6296
19:30 *"Let him* **t** everything, 4374
20: 3 the ten concubines he had left to **t care of** 9068
20: 6 **T** your master's men and pursue him, 4374
22: 3 my God is my rock, in whom *I* **t refuge,** 2879
22:31 He is a shield for all who **t refuge** in him. 2879
24: 1 "Go and **t a census** *of* Israel and Judah." 4948
24:10 I beg you, **t away** the guilt of your servant. 6296
24:22 my lord the king **t** whatever pleases him 4374
1Ki 1: 2 to attend the king and **t care of** him. 2118+6125
1:33 **"T** your lord's servants with you 4374
1:33 on my own mule and **t** him **down** to Gihon. 3718
5: 9 and you *can* **t** them **away.** 5951
8:31 and is required to **t an oath** and he comes 457
11:31 **"T** ten pieces for yourself, 4374
11:34 " 'But *I will* not **t** the whole kingdom out 4374
11:35 *I will* **t** the kingdom from his son's hands 4374
11:37 However, as for you, *I will* **t** you, 4374
14: 3 **T** ten loaves of bread with you, 4374
17:12 a few sticks *to* **t home** and make a meal 995
19: 4 he said. **"T** my life; 4374
20:18 they have come out for peace, **t** them alive; 9530
20:18 they have come out for war, **t** them alive." 9530
21:10 Then **t** him **out** and stone him to death." 3655
21:15 and **t possession** *of* the vineyard of Naboth 3769
21:16 down to **t possession** *of* Naboth's vineyard. 3769
21:18 where he has gone to **t possession** *of* it. 3769
22:26 **"T** Micaiah and send him back to Amon 4374
2Ki 2: 1 *to* **t** Elijah **up** to heaven in a whirlwind, 6590
2: 3 that the LORD *is going to* **t** your master 4374
2: 5 that the LORD *is going to* **t** your master 4374
4: 1 to **t** my two boys as his slaves." 4374
4:29 **t** my staff in your hand and run. 4374
4:36 When she came, he said, **"T** your son." 5951
5:23 "By all means, **t** two talents," 4374
5:26 Is this the time to **t** money, 4374
7:12 and then *we will* **t** them alive and get into 9530
7:13 *"Have some men* **t** five of the horses 4374
8: 8 **"T** a gift with you and go to meet the man 4374
9: 1 **t** this flask of oil with you and go 4374
9: 2 and **t** him **into** an inner room. 995
9: 3 Then **t** the flask and pour the oil 4374
9:34 **"T care of** that cursed woman," he said, 7212
10: 6 **t** the heads of your master's sons and come 4374
10:14 **"T** them alive!" he ordered. 9530
11: 6 who **t turns** guarding the temple— 5005
12: 7 **T** no more money from your treasurers, 4374
13:16 **"T** the bow in your hands," 8206
13:18 Then he said, **"T** the arrows," 4374
18:32 and **t** you to a land like your own, 4374
19:30 of the house of Judah will **t** root below NIH
1Ch 9:29 to **t care of** the furnishings and all 6584
13:13 not **t** the ark to be with him in the City 6073
17:13 *I will* never **t** my love **away** from him, 6073
21: 1 and incited David to **t a census** *of* Israel. 4948
21: 8 I beg you, **t away** the guilt of your servant. 6296
21:11 This is what the LORD says: **'T** your **choice:** 7691
21:23 Araunah said to David, **"T** it! 4374
21:24 *I will* not **t** for the LORD what is yours, 5951
27:23 David *did* not **t** the number of the men who 5951
2Ch 2:16 You *can* then **t** them **up** *to* Jerusalem." 6590
6:22 and is required to **t an oath** and he comes 457
18:25 **"T** Micaiah and send him back to Amon 4374
20:17 **T up** *your* **positions;** 3656
20:25 more than *they could* **t away.** 5362+5911
25:13 *to* **t part** in the war raided Judean 2143+6640
35:23 and he told his officers, **"T** me **away;** 6296
36: 6 with bronze shackles to **t** him to Babylon. 2143
36:13 *had* **made** him **t an oath** in God's name. 8678
Ezr 5:15 **'T** these articles and go and deposit them 10492
7:15 you are to **t** with you the silver and gold 10308
9:12 or **t** their daughters for your sons. 5951
10: 4 so **t courage** and do it." 2616
Ne 2: 6 asked me, "How long *will* your journey **t,** 2118
5:12 **made** the nobles and officials **t an oath** 8678
9:12 on the way *they were to* **t.** 2143
9:15 and **t possession** *of* the land you had sworn 3769
9:19 to shine on the way *they were to* **t.** 2143
10:30 around us or **t** their daughters for our sons. 4374
13:25 *I* **made** them **t an oath** in God's name 8678
13:25 nor *are you* **t** their daughters **in marriage** 5951
Est 2:13 Anything she wanted was given her to **t** 995
Job 1: 4 **t turns** holding feasts in their homes, 2143+3427
5:24 *you will* **t stock** *of* your property 7212
11:11 and when he sees evil, *does he* not **t note?** 1067
11:18 you will look about you and **t** *your* **rest** 8886
13:14 in jeopardy and **t** my life in my hands? 8492
13:17 let your ears **t in** what I say. 928
23:10 But he knows the way that I **t;** NIH
24: 3 **t** the widow's ox **in pledge.** 2471
32:22 my Maker *would* soon **t** me **away.** 5951
35:15 not **t** the least **notice** of wickedness. 3359
36: 7 *He does* not **t** his eyes off the righteous; 1757
37: 8 The animals **t** cover; 995+1198
38:13 that *it might* **t** the earth by the edges 296
38:20 *Can you* **t** them to their places? 4374
39:26 *"Does* the hawk **t flight** by your wisdom 87
41: 4 an agreement with you for *you to* **t** him 4374
42: 8 now **t** seven bulls and seven rams and go 4374
Ps 2: 2 The kings of the earth **t** *their* **stand** and 3656
2:12 Blessed are all *who* **t refuge** in him. 2879
5:11 But let all *who* **t refuge** in you be glad; 2879
7: 1 O LORD my God, *I* **t refuge** in you; 2879
10:14 you consider it to **t** it in hand. 5989
Ps 11: 1 In the LORD *I* **t refuge.** 2879
16: 1 O God, for in you *I* **t refuge.** 2879
16: 4 not pour out their libations of blood or **t up** 5951
17: 7 by your right hand *those who* **t refuge** 2879
18: 2 my God is my rock, in whom *I* **t refuge.** 2879
18:30 He is a shield for all who **t refuge** in him. 2879
25:18 and my distress and **t away** all my sins. 5951
25:20 for *I* **t refuge** in you. 2879
26: 9 *Do* not **t away** my soul along with sinners, 665
27:14 and **t heart** and wait for the LORD. 599+4213
31:13 against me and plot to **t** my life. 4374
31:19 in the sight of men on those *who* **t refuge** 2879
31:24 Be strong and **t heart,** 599+4222
35: 2 **T up** shield and buckler; 2616
37:40 because *they* **t refuge** in him. 2879
40:14 to **t** my life be put to shame and confusion; 6200
45:16 Your sons *will* **t the place of** 2118+9393
49:15 *he will* surely **t** me to himself. 4374
49:17 *he will* **t** nothing with him when he dies, 4374
50:16 to recite my laws or **t** my covenant 5951
51:11 from your presence or **t** your Holy Spirit 4374
51:16 *you do* not **t pleasure in** burnt offerings. 8354
55:15 *Let* death **t** my enemies **by surprise;** 5958
56: 6 they watch my steps, eager to **t** my life. NIH
57: 1 *I will* **t refuge** in the shadow 2879
61: 4 to dwell in your tent forever and **t refuge** in 2879
62: 4 *they* **t delight in** lies. 8354
62:10 in extortion or **t pride** in stolen goods; 2038
64:10 in the LORD and **t refuge** in him; 2879
72:13 *He will* **t pity** on the weak and the needy 2571
73: 9 and their tongues **t possession** of the earth. 2143
73:24 and afterward *you will* **t** me *into* glory. 4374
74:11 **T** it from the folds of your garment NIH
83:12 *"Let us* **t possession** *of* the pasturelands 3769
89:33 but *I will* not **t** my love from him, 7296
94: 8 **T heed,** *you* senseless ones among 1067
94:16 Who *will* **t a stand** for me 3656
94:22 and my God the rock in whom I **t** refuge. NIH
102:24 So I said: *"Do* not **t** me **away,** O my God, 6590
104:29 *when you* **t away** their breath, 665
109: 8 *may* another **t** his place of leadership. 4374
109:12 to him or **t pity** on his fatherless children. 2858
118: 8 It is better to **t refuge** in the LORD than 2879
118: 9 It is better to **t refuge** in the LORD than 2879
119:39 **T away** the disgrace I dread, 6296
119:109 Though I constantly **t** my life in my hands, NIH
141: 4 to **t part in** wicked deeds 6618
141: 8 in you *I* **t refuge—** 2879
144: 2 my shield, in whom *I* **t refuge,** 2879
Pr 4:26 for your feet and **t** only ways that are firm. NIH
13:10 but wisdom is found in *those who* **t advice.** 3619
16:13 Kings **t** pleasure in honest lips; NIH
20:16 **T** the garment of one who puts up security 4374
22:23 for the LORD *will* **t up** their case 8189
23:11 he *will* **t up** their case against you. 8189
27:12 The prudent see danger and **t refuge,** 6259
27:13 **T** the garment of one who puts up security 4374
30: 5 he is a shield to those *who* **t refuge** in him. 2879
Ecc 4:13 who no longer knows how to **t warning.** 2302
7: 2 the living *should* **t** this to heart. 5989
9: 2 as it is with those *who* **t oaths,** 8678
9: 2 so with those who are afraid to **t** them. NIH
SS 1: 4 **T** me **away** with you—let us hurry! 5432
1: 6 and made me **t care of** the vineyards; 5757
7: 8 *I will* **t hold** of its fruit." 296
Isa 1:16 **T** your evil deeds out of my sight! 6073
2: 4 Nation *will* not **t up** sword against nation, 5951
3: 1 *to* **t** from Jerusalem and Judah both supply 6073
3: 6 **t charge of** this heap of ruins!" 3338+9393
4: 1 In that day seven women *will* **t hold** 2616
4: 1 **T away** our disgrace!" 665
5: 5 I *will* **t away** its hedge, 6073
7: 7 " *'It will* not **t place,** it will not happen, 7756
7:20 and *to* **t off** your beards also. 6200
8: 1 **"T** a large scroll and write on it with 4374
9:17 Therefore the Lord *will* **t** no **pleasure** in 8523
10:31 the people of Gebim **t cover.** 6395
14: 2 Nations *will* **t** them and bring them 4374
14: 4 *you will* **t up** this taunt against the king 5951
18: 5 down and **t away** the spreading branches. 6073
20: 2 **"T off** the sackcloth from your body and 7337
22:17 to **t firm hold** *of* you and hurl you 6487+6487
23:16 **"T up** a harp, walk through 4374
27: 6 In days to come Jacob *will* **t root,** 9245
31: 2 *he does* not **t back** his words. 6073
36:17 and **t** you to a land like your own— 4374
37:31 of the house of Judah will **t** root below NIH
40:24 no sooner *do they* **t root** in the ground, 1614+9245
42: 6 *I will* **t hold** of your hand. 2616
42:25 but *they did* not **t** it to heart. 8492
44: 5 and *will* **t** the name Israel. 4033
44:11 all come together and **t** *their* **stand;** 6641
45: 1 whose right hand *I* **t hold** *of* 2616
45:21 *let them* **t counsel** together. 3619
46: 8 fix it in mind, **t** it to heart, *you* rebels. 8740
47: 2 **T** millstones and grind flour; 4374
47: 2 **t off** your veil. 1655
47: 3 *I will* **t** vengeance; I will spare no one." 4374
48: 1 you who **t oaths** in the name of the LORD 8678
51:18 the sons she reared there was none *to* **t** her 2616
62: 4 for the LORD *will* **t delight** in you, 2911
65:19 I will rejoice over Jerusalem and **t delight** 8464
Jer 6: 8 **T warning,** O Jerusalem, 3579
7:29 **t up** a lament on the barren heights, 5951
8:13 " *'I will* **t away** their harvest, 665
9:10 for the mountains and **t** up a lament NIH
13: 4 **"T** the belt you bought and are wearing 4374

Jer 15:15 You are long-suffering—*do* not **t** me **away;** 4374
19: 1 **T** along some of the elders of the people NIH
20: 5 *They will* **t** it **away** as plunder 4374
20:10 over him and **t** our revenge on him." 4374
25:15 "**T** from my hand this cup filled with 4374
25:28 if they refuse to **t** the cup from your hand 4374
27:20 not **t away** when he carried Jehoiachin son 4374
31: 4 Again *you will* **t up** your tambourines 6335
31:21 **T note** of the highway, 4213+8883
31:21 the highway, the road that *you* **t.** 2143
32: 5 *He will* **t** Zedekiah *to* Babylon, 2143
32:14 **T** these documents, both the sealed 4374
32:24 "See how the siege ramps are built up to **t** 4334
34:22 **t** it and burn it down. 4334
36: 2 "**T** a scroll and write on it all 4374
36:28 "**T** another scroll and write on it all 4374
38:10 "**T** thirty men from here with you 4374
39: 7 with bronze shackles to **t** him to Babylon. 995
39:12 "**T** him and look after him; 4374
39:14 to **t** him **back** to his home. 3655
40:14 of Nethaniah to **t** your life?" 5782
40:15 Why *should he* **t** your life and cause all 5782
43: 9 **t** some large stones with you 4374
43:12 and **t** their gods **captive.** 8647
44:12 *I will* **t away** the remnant 4374
46: 4 **T** *your* **positions** with helmets on! 3656
46:14 '**T** *your* **positions** and get ready, 3656
50: 9 *They will* **t up** *their* **positions** against her, 6885
50:14 "**T up** *your* **positions** around Babylon, 6885
50:15 **t vengeance** on her; do to her as she has 5933
51:11 "Sharpen the arrows, **t up** the shields! 4848
51:11 The LORD will **t** vengeance, NIH
Eze 3:10 and **t** to heart all the words I speak to you. 4374
4: 1 "Now, son of man, **t** a clay tablet, 4374
4: 3 Then **t** an iron pan, 4374
4: 9 "**T** wheat and barley, beans and lentils, 4374
5: 1 **t** a sharp sword and use it as 4374
5: 1 **t** a set of scales and divide up the hair. 4374
5: 2 **T** a third and strike it with the sword all 4374
5: 3 But **t** a few strands of hair 4374
5: 4 **t** a few of these and throw them into 4374
7:24 the nations *to* **t possession** *of* their houses; 3769
10: 6 "**T** fire from among the wheels, 4374
12: 5 **t** your belongings **out** through it. 3655
16:39 of your clothes and **t** your fine jewelry 4374
17: 9 not **t** a strong arm or many people to pull it NIH
17:22 *I* myself *will* **t** a shoot from the very top 4374
18: 8 not lend at usury or **t** excessive interest. 4374
18:23 *Do I* **t any pleasure in** the death of 2911+2911
18:32 *I* **t** no **pleasure** in the death of anyone, 2911
19: 1 "**T up** a lament concerning the princes 5951
20:37 *I will* **t note** *of* you **as you pass** 6296
21: 7 *It will* **surely t place,** 2118
21:19 for the sword of the king of Babylon to **t,** 995
21:23 of their guilt and **t** them **captive.** 9530
21:26 **T off** the turban, remove the crown. 6073
22:12 *you* **t** usury and excessive interest 4374
22:25 they devour people, **t** treasures 4374
23:24 *they will* **t up positions** against you 8492
23:25 They *will* **t away** your sons and daughters, 4374
23:26 of your clothes and **t** your fine jewelry. 4374
23:29 **t away** everything you have worked for. 4374
23:48 that all women *may* **t warning** and 3579
24: 5 **t** the pick of the flock. 4374
24: 8 To stir up wrath and **t revenge** 5933+5934
24:16 *about to* **t away** from you the delight 4374
24:21 the stronghold in which you **t** pride, NIH
24:25 on the day I **t away** their stronghold, 4374
25:14 *I will* **t** vengeance on Edom by the hand 5989
25:17 when I **t** vengeance on them.' " 5989
26:16 and **t off** their embroidered garments. 7320
26:17 Then *they will* **t up** a lament 5951
26:20 and you will not return or **t** *your* **place** in 3656
27: 2 **t up** a lament concerning Tyre. 5951
27:26 Your oarsmen **t** you **out** to the high seas. 995
27:32 *they will* **t up a lament** concerning you: 7801
28:12 **t up** a lament concerning the king of Tyre 5951
30: 9 Anguish *will* **t hold of** them on the day 928+2118
32: 2 **t up** a lament concerning Pharaoh king 5951
33: 4 the trumpet but *does* not **t warning** and 2302
33: 5 of the trumpet but *did* not **t warning,** 2302
33:11 *I* **t** no **pleasure** in the death of the wicked, 2911
34: 2 the shepherds of Israel who *only* **t care of** 8286
34: 2 *Should* not shepherds **t care of** the flock? 8286
34: 3 but *you do* not **t care of** the flock. 8286
35:10 be ours and *we will* **t possession** *of* them," 3769
36:24 " 'For *I will* **t** you out of the nations; 4374
37:16 **t** a stick of wood and write on it, 4374
37:16 Then **t** another stick of wood, 4374
37:19 I *am going to* **t** the stick of Joseph— 4374
37:21 I *will* **t** the Israelites out of the nations 4374
38: 7 and **t command** of them. 2118+4200+5464
38:13 to **t away** livestock and goods and 4374
38:14 *will you* not **t notice** *of* it? 3359
39: 8 *It will* surely **t place,** 2118
43:20 *You are to* **t** some of its blood and put it on 4374
43:21 *to* **t** the bull for the sin offering and burn it 4374
44:19 *they are to* **t off** the clothes they have been 7320
45:18 *to* **t** a young bull without defect and purify 4374
45:19 *to* **t** some of the blood of the sin offering 4374
46:18 not **t** any of the inheritance of the people, 4374
Da 2:24 **T** me to the king, 10549
2:45 the king what *will* **t place** in the future. 10201
8:13 "How long will it **t** for the vision to NIH
8:14 He said to me, "It will **t** 2,300 NIH
8:25 he will destroy many and **t** *his* **stand** 6641
11: 7 her family line will arise to **t** her place. NIH

Da 11:18 to the coastlands and *will* **t** many of them, 4334
11:28 *He will* **t action** against it and then return 6913
11:36 what has been determined *must* **t place.** 6913
Hos 1: 2 **t** to yourself an adulterous wife 4374
2: 9 "Therefore *I will* **t away** my grain 4374
2: 9 *I will* **t back** my wool and my linen, 5911
2:10 no one *will* **t** her out of my hands. 5911
4:11 *which* **t away** the understanding 4374
10: 4 **t** false **oaths** and make agreements; 457
14: 2 **T** words with you and return to the LORD. 4374
Joel 2:18 for his land and **t pity** on his people. 2798
Am 5: 1 this lament I **t up** concerning you: 5951
5:12 the righteous and **t** bribes and you deprive 4374
6:13 not **t** Karnaim by our own strength?" 4374
9: 2 from there my hand *will* **t** them. 4374
Jnh 1: 6 Maybe he *will* **t notice** of us, 6951
4: 3 Now, O LORD, **t** away my life, 4374
Mic 2: 2 and houses, and **t** them. 5951
2: 9 *You* **t away** my blessing from their children 4374
4: 3 Nation *will* not **t up** sword against nation, 5951
5:15 *I will* **t** vengeance in anger and wrath 6913
Zep 3:17 *He will* **t great delight** in you, 928+8464+8525
Hag 1: 8 *I may* **t pleasure** in it and be honored," 8354
2:23 *'I will* **t** you, my servant Zerubbabel 4374
Zec 3: 4 "**T off** his filthy clothes." 6073
6:10 "**T** [silver and gold] from the exiles Heldai, 4374
6:11 **T** the silver and gold and make a crown, 4374
8:23 and nations *will* **t firm hold** *of* one Jew 2616
9: 4 But the Lord *will* **t away** her **possessions** 3769
9: 7 *I will* **t** the blood from their mouths, 6073
9:10 *I will* **t away** the chariots from Ephraim 4162
11:15 "**T** again the equipment of a foolish 4374
14:18 Egyptian people do not go up and **t part,** 995
14:21 and all who come to sacrifice *will* **t** some 4374
Mt 1:20 not be afraid *to* **t** Mary home as your wife, *4161*
2:13 "**t** the child and his mother and escape *4161*
2:20 **t** the child and his mother and go to *4161*
2:20 for those who *were* **trying to t** *2426*
5:40 someone wants to sue you and **t** your tunic, *3284*
7: 4 'Let *me* **t** the speck **out** of your eye,' *1675*
7: 5 first **t** the plank **out** of your own eye, *1675*
8:11 **t** *their* **places at the feast** with Abraham, *369*
9: 2 "**T heart,** son; your sins are forgiven." *2510*
9: 6 "Get up, **t** your mat and go home." *149*
9:22 "**T heart,** daughter," he said, *2510*
10: 9 not **t along** any gold or silver or copper *3227*
10:10 **t** no bag for the journey, or extra tunic, *NIG*
10:38 not **t** his cross and follow me is not worthy *3284*
11:29 **T** my yoke upon you and learn from me, *149*
12:11 *will you* not **t hold of** it and lift it out? *3195*
14:27 immediately said to them: "**T courage!** *2510*
15:26 "It is not right *to* **t** the children's bread *3284*
16: 5 the disciples forgot *to* **t** bread. *3284*
16:24 he must deny himself and **t up** his cross *149*
17:27 **T** the first fish you catch; *149*
17:27 **T** it and give it to them for my tax *3284*
18:16 **t** one or two others along, *4161*
20:14 **T** your pay and go. *149*
21:38 Come, let's kill him and **t** his inheritance.' *2400*
24:17 of his house go down *to* **t** anything out of *149*
24:20 that your flight *will* not **t place** in winter *1181*
25: 3 but *did* not **t** any oil with them. *3284*
25:28 " '**T** the talent from him and give it to *149*
25:34 **t** *your* **inheritance,** the kingdom prepared *3099*
26:26 saying, "**T** and eat; this is my body." *3284*
27:65 "**T** a guard," Pilate answered. *2400*
Mk 2: 9 or to say, 'Get up, **t** your mat and walk'? *149*
2:11 get up, **t** your mat and go home." *149*
3:21 they went *to* **t charge of** him, for they said, *3195*
6: 8 "**T** nothing for the journey except a staff— *149*
6:37 would **t** eight months of a man's wages! *NIG*
6:50 he spoke to them and said, "**T courage!** *2510*
7:27 "for it is not right *to* **t** the children's bread *3284*
8:34 after me, he must deny himself and **t up** *149*
9:22 **t pity** on us and help us." *5072*
13:15 down or enter the house *to* **t** anything out. *149*
13:18 Pray that *this will* not **t place** in winter, *1181*
14:22 and gave it to his disciples, saying, "**T** it; *3284*
14:36 **T** this cup from me. *4195*
15:23 but he *did* not **t** it. *3284*
15:36 Let's see if Elijah comes *to* **t** him **down,"** *2747*
Lk 1:15 *He is* never *to* **t** wine or other fermented *4403*
5:18 a paralytic on a mat and tried *to* **t** him **into** *1662*
5:24 get up, **t** your mat and go home." *149*
6:42 *let me* **t** the speck **out** of your eye,' *1675*
6:42 first **t** the plank **out** of your eye, *1675*
9: 3 He told them: "**T** nothing for the journey— *149*
9:23 after me, he must deny himself and **t up** *149*
10: 4 *Do* not **t** a purse or bag or sandals; *1002*
12:19 **T life easy;** eat, drink and be merry." ' *399*
13:29 **t** *their* **places at the feast** in the kingdom *369*
14: 8 *do* not **t** the place of honor, *1650+2884*
14: 9 *to* **t** the least important place. *2988*
14:10 when you are invited, **t** the lowest place *404+1650*
16: 6 "The manager told him, '**T** your bill, *1312*
16: 7 '**T** your bill and make it eight hundred.' *1312*
19:17 **t** charge of ten cities.' *1639+2400*
19:19 'You **t charge of** five cities.' *1181+2062*
19:21 *You* **t out** what you did not put in *149*
19:24 '**T** his mina **away** from him and give it to *149*
21: 7 the sign that they are about to **t place?"** *1181*
21:28 When these things begin *to* **t place,** *1181*
22:17 "**T** this and divide it among you. *3284*
22:36 "But now if you have a purse, **t** it, *149*
22:42 if you are willing, **t** this cup from me; *4195*
Jn 1:22 an answer to **t back** to those who sent us. *1443*
2: 8 "Now draw some out and **t** it to the master *5770*

Jn 6:21 they were willing *to* **t** him into the boat, *3284*
7: 1 the Jews there were waiting *to* **t** his **life.** *650*
10:17 I lay down my life—only *to* **t** it **up** again. *3284*
10:18 to lay it down and authority *to* **t** it **up** *3284*
11:39 "**T away** the stone," he said. *149*
11:44 "**T off** the grave clothes and let him go." *3395*
11:48 and then the Romans will come and **t away** *149*
11:53 from that day on they plotted *to* **t** *his* **life.** *650*
14: 3 and **t** you to be with me that you also may *4161*
16:15 the Spirit *will* **t** from what is mine *3284*
16:22 and no one *will* **t away** your joy. *149*
16:33 But **t heart!** I have overcome the world." *2510*
17:15 not that *you* **t** them out of the world but *149*
18:31 "**T** him yourselves and judge him *3284*
19: 6 "You **t** him and crucify him. *3284*
19:15 But they shouted, "**T** him **away!** *149*
19:15 **T** him **away!** Crucify him!" *149*
21:16 Jesus said, "**T care of** my sheep." *4477*
Ac 1:20 " *'May* another **t** his place of leadership.' *3284*
1:25 *to* **t over** this apostolic ministry, *3284*
4:26 The kings of the earth **t** *their* **stand** and *4225*
7:33 the Lord said to him, '**T off** your sandals; *3395*
9: 2 *he might* **t** them as prisoners to Jerusalem. *72*
9:21 to **t** them as prisoners to the chief priests?" *72*
9:34 Get up and **t care of** *your* **mat."** *4932+5143*
13:40 **T care** that what the prophets have said *1063*
15:37 wanted *to* **t** John, also called Mark, **with** *5221*
15:38 but Paul did not think it wise *to* **t** him, *5221*
16: 3 Paul wanted *to* **t** him along on the journey, *2002*
20:13 where we were going to **t** Paul **aboard.** *377*
21:24 **T** these men, join in their purification rites *4161*
21:37 As the soldiers were about to **t** Paul **into** *1652*
23:10 **t** him away from them **by force** *773*
23:11 near Paul and said, "**T courage!** *2510*
23:17 "**T** this young man to the commander; *552*
24:23 permit his friends *to* **t care of** his **needs.** *5676*
27:34 Now I urge you *to* **t** some food. *3561*
Ro 2:16 This will **t** place on the day when God *NIG*
11:27 with them when *I* **t away** their sins." *904*
12:19 *Do* not **t revenge,** my friends, *1688+4932*
1Co 4: 6 not **t pride** in one man over against another. *5881*
6: 1 **t** it before the ungodly *for* **judgment** *3212*
6:15 Shall I then **t** the members of Christ *149*
9: 5 the right to **t** a believing wife **along** *4310*
10:30 If I **t part** in the meal with thankfulness, *3576*
2Co 5:12 but are giving you an opportunity to **t** pride *NIG*
5:12 so that you can answer those who **t pride** *3016*
7: 4 I **t** great pride in you. *NIG*
10: 5 and *we* **t captive** every thought *170*
11:16 I repeat: *Let* no one **t** me **for** a fool. *1506+1639*
12: 8 with the Lord to **t** it **away from** me. *923*
Gal 3:15 *let me* **t an example** from everyday life. *3306*
5:10 in the Lord that *you will* **t** no other **view.** *5858*
6: 4 Then he can **t** pride in himself, *2400*
Eph 6:11 of God so that you can **t** your **stand** against *2705*
6:16 **t up** the shield of faith, with which you can *377*
6:17 **T** the helmet of salvation and the sword of *1312*
Php 2:25 whom you sent to **t care** of my needs. *3313*
3:12 but I press on to **t hold** of that *2898*
3:15 mature *should* **t such a view of things.** *5858*
3:17 and **t note** of those who live according to *5023*
1Th 4: 6 wrong his brother or **t advantage of** him. *4430*
2Th 3:14 **t special note** of him. *4957*
1Ti 3: 5 how *can he* **t care of** God's church?) *2150*
5:20 so that the others *may* **t** warning. *2400*
6: 7 and we can **t** nothing **out of** it. *1766*
6:12 **T hold** of the eternal life *2138*
6:19 *they may* **t hold** of the life that is truly life. *2138*
Phm 1:13 that he could **t** your **place** in helping me *5642*
Heb 5: 5 *did* not **t** upon himself the **glory** *1519*
6:18 *to* **t hold** of the hope offered to us may *3195*
9:28 so Christ was sacrificed once *to* **t away** *429*
10: 4 the blood of bulls and goats *to* **t away** sins. *904*
10:11 which can never **t away** sins. *4311*
Jas 1: 9 in humble circumstances *ought to* **t pride** *3016*
1:10 But the one who is rich should **t** pride *NIG*
1:19 My dear brothers, **t note of** this: *3857*
3: 4 Or **t** ships as an example. *NIG*
5:10 **t** the prophets who spoke in the name of *3284*
1Jn 3: 5 so that *he might* **t away** our sins. *149*
2Jn 1:10 not **t** him into your house or welcome him. *3284*
Rev 1: 1 show his servants what must soon **t place.** *1181*
1: 3 and **t to heart** what is written in it, *5498*
1:19 what is now and what will **t place** later *1181*
3:11 so that no one *will* **t** your crown. *3284*
4: 1 and I will show you what must **t place** *1181*
5: 9 "You are worthy *to* **t** the scroll and *3284*
6: 4 Its rider was given power *to* **t** peace from *3284*
10: 8 "Go, **t** the scroll that lies open in the hand *3284*
10: 9 He said to me, "**T** it and eat it. *3284*
14:15 "**T** your sickle and reap, *4287*
14:18 "**T** your sharp sickle and gather the clusters *4287*
22: 6 the things that must soon **t place."** *1181*
22:17 *let him* **t** the free gift of the water of life. *3284*
22:19 God *will* **t away from** him his share in *904*

TAKEN (268) [TAKE]

Ge 2:22 woman from the rib *he had* **t** out of the man, 4374
2:23 'woman,' for she **was t** out of man." 4374
3:19 since from it *you* **were t;** 4374
3:23 the ground from which *he had* **been t.** 4374
12:15 and she **was t** *into* his palace. 4374
14:14 that his relative *had* **been t captive,** 8647
14:22 *"I have* **raised** my hand to the LORD, God
Most High, Creator of heaven and earth,
and *have* **t an oath** 8123

Ge 20: 3 as dead because of the woman *you have* **t;** 4374
27:36 and now *he's* **t** my blessing!" 4374
30:23 "God *has* **t away** my disgrace." 665
31: 1 "Jacob *has* **t** everything our father owned 4374
31: 9 So God *has* **t away** your father's livestock 5911
31:34 Now Rachel *had* **t** the household gods 4374
39: 1 Now Joseph *had* **been t down** to Egypt. 3718
39: 1 from the Ishmaelites who *had* **t** him there. 3718
42:24 *He had* Simeon **t** from them and bound 4374
43:18 the men were frightened when *they* **were t** 995
Ex 12: 4 having **t into account** the number 928
22:10 or **is t away** while no one is looking, 8647
Lev 6: 4 what he has stolen or **t by extortion,** 6943+6945
7:34 *I have* **t** the breast that is waved and 4374
10:18 its blood **was** not **t** into the Holy Place, 995
14:45 and **t out** of the town to an unclean place. 3655
16:27 *must be* **t** outside the camp; 3655
25:12 eat only **what is t** directly from the fields. 9311
Nu 3:12 "I *have* **t** the Levites from among 4374
8:16 *I have* **t** them as my own in place of 4374
8:18 And *I have* **t** the Levites in place of all 4374
10:17 Then the tabernacle **was t down,** 3718
14: 3 and children *will be* **t** as plunder. 2118
14:31 for your children that you said *would be* **t** 2118
16:15 not **t** so much as a donkey from them, 5951
19: 3 *to be* **t** outside the camp and slaughtered 3655
21:26 against the former king of Moab and *had* **t** 4374
30: 9 "Any vow or **obligation t** by a widow 673
31:53 Each soldier *had* **t plunder** for himself. 1024
36: 3 then their inheritance *will* **be t** 1757
36: 3 inheritance allotted to us *will* **be t away.** 1757
36: 4 and their property *will* **be t** from 1757
Dt 1:39 **be t captive,** your children who do not 1020
3:20 and they too *have* **t over** the land that 3769
11:31 *you have* **t** it **over** and are living there, 3769
17:14 and *have* **t possession** *of* it and settled in it, 3769
17:18 **t from** that of the priests, 4200+4946+7156
23:15 If a slave *has* **t refuge** with you, 5911
26: 1 as an inheritance and *have* **t possession** *of* it 3769
28:31 Your donkey *will* **be forcibly t** from you 1608
Jos 1:15 until they too *have* **t possession** *of* the land 3769
2: 4 woman *had* **t** the two men and hidden them. 4374
2: 6 (But she *had* **t** them **up** to the roof 6590
4:20 up at Gilgal the twelve stones *they had* **t** out 4374
7:11 *They have* **t** some of the devoted things; 4374
7:16 came forward by tribes, and Judah **was t.** 4334
7:17 came forward by families, and Zimri **was t.** 4334
7:18 of the tribe of Judah, **was t.** 4334
8: 8 When you *have* **t** the city, set it on fire. 9530
8:12 Joshua *had* **t** about five thousand men 4374
8:21 and all Israel saw that the ambush *had* **t** 4334
10: 1 that Joshua *had* **t** Ai and totally destroyed it, 4334
13: 1 very large areas of land to *be* **t over.** 3769
13:12 Moses had defeated them and **t over** 3769
19: 9 The inheritance of the Simeonites was **t** NIH
Jdg 14: 9 not tell them that *he had* **t** the honey from 8098
17: 2 of silver that **were t** from you and 4374
19:18 No one *has* **t** me into his house. 665
21: 1 The men of Israel *had* **t an oath** at Mizpah: 8678
21: 5 For they *had* **t** a solemn oath 2118
21: 7 since we *have* **t an oath** by the LORD not 8678
21:18 since *we* Israelites *have* **t** *this* **oath:** 8678
1Sa 12: 3 Whose ox *have I* **t?** 4374
12: 3 Whose donkey *have I* **t?** 4374
12: 4 not **t** anything from anyone's hand." 4374
14:41 And Jonathan and Saul **were t** by lot, 4334
14:42 And Jonathan **was t.** 4334
21: 6 by hot bread on the day it **was t away.** 4374
30: 2 and *had* **t captive** the women 8647
30: 3 and sons and daughters **t captive.** 8647
30:16 the great amount of plunder *they had* **t** from 4374
30:18 the Amalekites *had* **t,** 4374
30:19 plunder or anything else *they had* **t.** 4374
2Sa 2: 8 *had* **t** Ish-Bosheth son of Saul 4374
3:15 and *had* her **t away** from her husband 4374
6:13 the ark of the LORD *had* **t six steps,** 7575+7576
7:15 my love *will* never *be* **t away** from him, 6073
8:12 the plunder **t** from Hadadezer son of Rehob, NIH
12:13 "The LORD *has* **t away** your sin. 6296
12:27 against Rabbah and **t** its water supply. 4334
18:18 During his lifetime Absalom *had* **t** a pillar 4374
19:24 *He had* not **t care of** his feet 6913
19:40 the troops of Israel *had* **t** the king **over.** 6296
19:42 *Have we* **t anything** for ourselves?" 5951+5951
21:12 *(They had* **t** them **secretly** from 1704
1Ki 1:46 Solomon *has* **t** *his* **seat** on the royal throne. 3782
13:12 the man of God from Judah *had* **t.** 2143
16:18 When Zimri saw that the city **was t,** 4334
18: 4 Obadiah *had* **t** a hundred prophets 4374
2Ki 2: 9 what can I do for you before *I* **am t** 4374
2:10 "yet if you see me when I **am t** from you, 4374
5: 2 from Aram had gone out and *had* **t captive** 8647
13:16 When *he had* **t** it, Elishah put his hands 8206
13:25 of Hazael the towns *he had* **t** in battle 4374
17:23 **t** from their homeland **into exile** 1655
20:18 that will be born to you, *will be* **t away,** 4374
24: 7 the king of Babylon *had* **t** all his territory, 4374
25: 6 He *was* **t** to the king of Babylon at Riblah, 6590
1Ch 9: 1 The people of Judah **were t captive** 1655
9:28 in and *when they were* **t out.** 3655
18:11 and gold *he had* **t** from all these nations: 5951
22:14 "I have **t great pains** to provide for 928+6715
24: 6 one family **being t** from Eleazar and 296
26:27 the plunder **t** *in* battle they dedicated for 4946
2Ch 2:17 **census** his father David *had* **t;** 6218+6222
6:38 of their captivity where they *were* **t,** 8647
28:11 countrymen *you have* **t as prisoners,** 8647+8664
2Ch 34:14 the money that *had* **been t into** the temple 995
Ezr 2: 1 king of Babylon *had* **t captive** to Babylon 1655
5:14 which Nebuchadnezzar *had* **t** from 10485
8:30 *be* **t** to the house of our God in Jerusalem. 995
9: 2 **t** some of their daughters **as wives** 5951
10:13 this matter cannot be **t** care of in a day NIH
Ne 7: 6 of Babylon *had* **t captive** (they returned 1655
Est 1:15 of King Xerxes that the eunuchs have **t** 928+3338
2: 6 among those **t captive** with Jehoiachin 1655
2: 7 and Mordecai *had* **t** her as his own daughter 4374
2: 8 Esther also **was t** to the king's palace 4374
2:16 She **was t** to King Xerxes in the royal 4374
Job 1:21 and the LORD *has* **t away;** 4374
28: 2 Iron **is t** from the earth, 4374
33: 6 I too *have* **been t** from clay. 7975
36:17 judgment and justice *have* **t hold** of you. 9461
Ps 31: 1 In you, O LORD, *I have* **t refuge;** 2879
71: 1 In you, O LORD, *I have* **t refuge;** 2879
78:54 to the hill country his right hand *had* **t.** 7864
88: 8 *You have* **t** from me my closest friends 8178
88:18 *You have* **t** my companions and loved ones 8178
102:10 for *you have* **t** me **up** and thrown me aside. 5951
119:106 *I have* **t an oath** and confirmed it, 8678
Pr 27:14 *it will* **be t** as a curse. 3108
Ecc 3:14 nothing can be added to it and nothing **t** 1757
5: 9 The increase from the land is **t** by all; NIH
9:12 or birds **are t** in a snare, 296
SS 2: 4 *He has* **t** me to the banquet hall, 995
5: 3 *I have* **t off** my robe— 7320
Isa 6: 6 which *he had* **t** with tongs from the altar. 4374
6: 7 your guilt *is* **t away** and your sin atoned for. 6073
14:25 His yoke *will be* **t** from my people, 6073
16:10 and gladness **are t away** from the orchards; 665
22: 3 All you who were caught **were t prisoner** together, 673
23: 7 whose feet *have* **t** her to settle in far-off 3297
28: 9 to *those just* **t** from the breast? 6972
38:12 has been pulled down and **t** from me. 1655
39: 7 who will be born to you, *will be* **t away,** 4374
42: 9 See, the former things *have* **t place,** 995
49:24 *Can* plunder **be t** from warriors, 4374
49:25 "Yes, captives *will* **be t** *from* warriors, 4374
51:22 "See, *I have* **t** out of your hand the cup 4374
52: 5 my people *have* **been t away** for nothing, 4374
53: 8 By oppression and judgment *he* **was t away.** 4374
57: 1 devout men **are t away,** 665
57: 1 that the righteous **are t away** to be spared 665
Jer 8:13 What I have given them *will* **be t from** 6296
12: 2 and *they have* **t root;** 9245
13:17 the LORD's flock *will* **be t captive.** 8647
14: 9 Why are you like a man **t by surprise,** 1850
27:18 the king of Judah and in Jerusalem not *be* **t** 995
27:22 *'They will* **be t** to Babylon 995
34:16 each of *you has* **t back** the male 8740
38:28 This is how Jerusalem **was t:** 4334
39:14 sent and *had* Jeremiah **t** out of the courtyard 4374
40:10 and live in the towns *you have* **t over."** 9530
41:14 All the people Ishmael *had* **t captive** 8647
48: 7 you too *will* **be t captive,** 4334
48:41 be captured and the strongholds **t.** 9530
48:46 your sons **are t** into exile 4374
49: 1 Why then *has* Molech **t possession** *of* Gad? 3769
49:29 Their tents and their flocks *will be* **t;** 4374
50:28 how the LORD our God has **t** vengeance, NIH
51:26 No rock *will* **be t** from you for 4374
52: 9 He *was* **t** to the king of Babylon at Riblah 6590
52:30 745 Jews **t into exile** *by* Nebuzaradan 1655
Eze 15: 3 **Is** wood *ever* **t** from it to make anything 4374
21:24 *you will* **be t captive.** 928+2021+4090+9530
30:16 Thebes will be **t by storm;** 1324
33: 5 If he *had* **t warning,** 2302
33: 6 that man *will* **be t away** because of his sin, 4374
45:15 be **t** from every flock of two hundred from NIH
Da 4:31 Your royal authority *has been* **t** from you. 10528
5: 2 that Nebuchadnezzar his father *had* **t** from 10485
5: 3 in the gold goblets that *had been* **t** from 10485
7:26 and his power *will be* **t away** 10528
Hos 9: 6 Their treasures of silver *will be* **t over** 3769
10: 5 because *it is* **t** from them **into exile.** 1655
Am 2: 8 beside every altar on garments **t in pledge.** 2471
2: 8 In the house of their god they drink **wine** *t* AIT
4: 2 surely come when you *will* **be t away** 5951
Mic 1:11 its protection *is* **t** from you. 4374
Na 3:10 Yet she was **t** captive and went into exile. 4200
Zep 3:15 The LORD *has* **t away** your punishment, 6073
Zec 3: 4 "See, *I have* **t away** your sin, 6296
14: 2 of the people *will* not **be t** from the city. 4162
Mt 9:15 when the bridegroom *will be* **t from** them; *554*
13:12 even what he has *will be* **t** from him. *149*
21:43 of God *will be* **t away** from you and given *149*
23:30 not *have* **t part** with them in shedding *1639+3128*
24:40 one *will be* **t** and the other left. *4161*
24:41 one *will be* **t** and the other left. *4161*
25:29 even what he has *will be* **t** from him. *149*
26:39 if it is possible, *may* this cup **be t** from me. *4216*
26:42 if it is not possible for this cup *to* **be t away** *4216*
26:56 But this *has* all **t place** that the writings of *1181*
Mk 2:20 when the bridegroom *will be* **t from** them, *554*
4:25 even what he has *will be* **t** from him." *149*
8: 6 *When he had* **t** the seven loaves *3284*
16:19 *he was* **t up** into heaven and he sat at *377*
Lk 1:25 and **t away** my disgrace among *904*
2: 1 **census** *should* **be t of** the entire Roman *616*
5: 9 at the catch of fish *they had* **t,** *5197*
5:35 when the bridegroom *will be* **t from** them; *554*
8:18 even what he thinks he has *will be* **t** *149*
9:51 As the time approached for him to be **t up** *378*
Lk 10:42 and it *will* not *be* **t away from** her." *904*
11:52 *you have* **t away** the key to knowledge. *149*
17:34 one *will be* **t** and the other left. *4161*
17:35 one *will be* **t** and the other left." *4161*
19:26 even what he has *will be* **t away.** *149*
21:24 the sword and *will be* **t as prisoners** to all *170*
24:51 he left them and *was* **t up** into heaven. *429*
Jn 2:20 "It has **t** forty-six years to build this *NIG*
13:30 As soon as Judas *had* **t** the bread, *3284*
18:40 **had t part in a rebellion.** *1639+3334*
19:31 the legs broken and the bodies **t down.** *149*
20: 2 *"They have* **t** the Lord out of the tomb, *149*
20:13 *"They have* **t** my Lord **away,"** she said, *149*
21: 7 (for he had **t it off)** and jumped into *1218*
Ac 1: 2 until the day *he was* **t up** to heaven, *377*
1: 9 *he was* **t up** before their very eyes, *2048*
1:11 who *has been* **t** from you into heaven, *377*
1:22 to the time when Jesus *was* **t up** from us. *377*
8:33 For his life *was* **t** from the earth." *149*
9:39 he arrived *he was* **t upstairs** to the room. *343*
10:16 and immediately the sheet *was* **t back** *377*
18:18 at Cenchrea because of a vow *he had* **t.** *2400*
19:12 and aprons that had touched him *were* **t** to *708*
21:34 he ordered that Paul *be* **t** into the barracks. *72*
22:24 the commander ordered Paul *to be* **t into** *1652*
23:14 *"We have* **t a solemn oath** not *353+354*
23:21 They *have* **t an oath** not to eat or drink *354*
23:24 that he may be **t** safely to Governor Felix." *2097*
27:21 "Men, you should *have* **t** my **advice** not *4272*
Ro 5:13 not **t into account** when there is no law. *1824*
1Co 15: 1 and on which *you have* **t** *your* **stand.** *2705*
2Co 3:14 because only in Christ *is it* **t away.** *2934*
3:16 turns to the Lord, the veil *is* **t away.** *4311*
Gal 4:24 These things may be **t figuratively,** *251*
Php 3:13 not consider myself yet *to have* **t hold of** *2898*
Col 3: 9 *since you have* **t off** your old self *588*
2Th 2: 7 to do so till *he is* **t** out of the way. *1181*
1Ti 3:16 believed on in the world, *was* **t up** in glory. *377*
2Ti 2:18 that the resurrection *has* already **t place,** *1181*
2:26 who *has* them **t captive** to do his will. *2436*
Heb 11: 5 By faith Enoch *was* **t from** this life, *3572*
11: 5 because God *had* **t** him **away.** *3572*
11: 5 For before he *was* **t,** he was commended *3557*
Jude 1:11 *They have* **t** the way of Cain; *4513*
Rev 5: 8 And when *he had* **t** it, *3284*
11:17 because *you have* **t** your great power *3284*
12: 6 where she *might be* **t care of** for 1,260 *5555*
12:14 where she *would be* **t care of** for a time, *5555*

TAKES (72) [TAKE]

Ge 27:46 If Jacob **t** a wife from among the women 4374
Lev 5: 4 " 'Or if a person thoughtlessly **t an oath** 8678
24:17 'If anyone **t** the **life** *of* a human being, 5782+5883
24:18 *Anyone who* **t** the **life** *of* someone's 5782+5883
Nu 24:22 be destroyed when Asshur **t** you **captive."** 8647
30: 2 or **t an oath** to obligate himself 8652+8678
Dt 1: 2 (It **t** eleven days to go from Horeb NIH
13: 2 of which he has spoken **t place,** 995
17:18 When he **t** the throne of his kingdom, 3782+6584
19:16 If a malicious witness **t the stand** to 928+7756
22:13 If a man **t** a wife and, after lying with her, 4374
Jos 7:14 that the LORD **t** shall come forward clan 4334
7:14 the LORD **t** shall come forward family 4334
7:14 that the LORD **t** shall come forward man 4334
2Sa 15: 8 'If the LORD **t** me **back** *to* Jerusalem, 8740+8740
1Ki 8:46 *who* **t** them **captive** to his own land, 8647+8647
20:11 not boast like *one who* **t** it **off.'** " 7337
2Ch 6:36 to the enemy, *who* **t** them **captive** to 8647+8647
Job 12:18 *He* **t off** the shackles put on by kings 7337
12:20 the lips of trusted advisers and **t away** 4374
27: 8 when God **t away** his life? 8923
34:25 Because *he* **t note** of their deeds, 5795
38:14 The earth **t shape** like clay under a seal; 2200
Ps 5: 4 You are not a God *who* **t pleasure in** evil; 2913
34: 8 blessed is the man *who* **t refuge** in him. 2879
34:22 no one will be condemned who **t refuge** 2879
57: 1 for in you my soul **t refuge.** 2879
149: 4 For the LORD **t delight** in his people; 8354
Pr 1:19 *it* **t away** the lives of those who get it. 4374
3:32 for the LORD detests a perverse man but **t** NIH
6:34 he will show no mercy when he **t** revenge. NIH
8: 2 where the paths meet, *she* **t** *her* **stand;** 5893
10: 9 *he who* **t crooked** paths will be found out. 6835
16:32 a man who controls his temper than *one who* **t** a city. 4334
21:12 The Righteous One **t note** of the house of 8505
22: 3 A prudent man sees danger and **t refuge,** 6259
25:20 Like *one who* **t away** a garment on 6334
31:23 he **t** his **seat** among the elders of the land. 3782
Ecc 5:15 *He* **t** nothing from his labor 5951
Isa 3:13 The LORD **t** *his* **place** in court; 5893
21: 2 The traitor betrays, the looter **t loot.** 8720
22: 6 Elam **t up** the quiver, 5951
28: 4 as someone sees it and **t** it in his hand, NIH
41:13 *who* **t hold** *of* your right hand and says 2616
44:12 The blacksmith **t** a tool and works with it NIH
44:15 some of it *he* **t** and warms himself, 4374
65:16 he *who* **t an oath** in the land will swear by 8678
Jer 4:29 and archers every town **t to flight.** 1368
Eze 18:13 He lends at usury and **t** excessive interest. 4374
18:17 and **t** no usury or excessive interest. 4374
26:15 and *the* **slaughter t place** in you? 2222+2223
33: 4 and the sword comes and **t** his **life,** 4374
33: 6 and the sword comes and **t** the life of one 4374
Mic 2: 4 *He* **t** it from me! He assigns our fields 4631
Na 1: 2 the LORD **t vengeance** and is filled 5933

Na 1: 2 The LORD t **vengeance** on his foes 5933
Hab 2: 5 to himself all the nations and t **captive** all 7695
Mt 12:45 Then it goes and t with it *4161*
Mk 4:15 and t **away** the word that was sown *149*
Lk 6:29 *If* someone t your cloak, *149*
6:30 and *if* anyone t what belongs to you, *149*
8:12 then the devil comes and t **away** the word *149*
11:22 *he* t **away** the armor in which *149*
11:26 t seven other spirits more wicked than itself, *4161*
Jn 1:29 who t **away** the sin of the world! *149*
10:18 No one t it from me, but I lay it down *149*
2Co 11:20 or exploits you or t **advantage of** you *3284*
Php 2:20 who t a genuine **interest** in your welfare. *3534*
Col 2: 8 no one t you **captive** through hollow *1639+5194*
Heb 5: 4 No one t this honor upon himself; *3284*
9:17 it never t **effect** while the one who made it *2710*
Rev 22:19 And if anyone t words **away from** this book *904*

TAKING (59) [TAKE]

Ge 8:20 t some of all the clean animals 4374
24:10 t **with** him all kinds of good things 928+3338
28:11 T one of the stones there, 4374
28:20 over me on this journey I *am* t 2143
31:23 T his relatives with him, 4374
34:29 t **as plunder** everything in the houses. 1024
42:38 to him on the journey *you are* t, 2143
50: 3 t a **full** forty days, 4848
Ex 5: 4 why *are you* t the people **away** 7277
22:11 by the t of an oath before the LORD that NIH
29:35 t seven days to ordain them. NIH
Nu 15:18 you enter the land to which I *am* t you 995
22: 7 t **with** them the fee for divination. 928+3338
Dt 1:25 T with them some of the fruit of the land, 4374
24: 6 t a man's livelihood **as security.** 2471
Jos 6:18 about your own destruction *by* t any 4374
19:47 **had difficulty** t **possession of** their 3655+4946
Jdg 3:28 t **possession** *of* the fords of the Jordan 4334
1Sa 14:32 They pounced on the plunder and, t sheep, 4374
17:49 Reaching into his bag and t out a stone, 4374
29: 4 by t the heads of our own men? NIH
2Sa 4: 5 while he *was* t his noonday **rest.** 5435+8886
4: 7 T it with them, 4374
12: 4 but the rich man refrained from t one 4374
1Ki 11:18 Then t men from Paran with them, 4374
2Ki 5: 5 t with him ten talents of silver, 4374
8: 9 t with him as a gift forty camel-loads of all 4374
15:25 T fifty men of Gilead with him, NIH
1Ch 2: 7 by violating the ban on t devoted things. NIH
2Ch 17: 9 t with them the Book of the Law of NIH
Job 5: 3 I myself have seen a fool t **root,** 9245
5: 5 t it even from among thorns, 4374
Ecc 4: 1 the oppression that *was* t **place** under 6913
Isa 30:14 a fragment will be found for t coals from 3149
Eze 17: 3 T **hold** *of* the top of a cedar, 4374
Hos 11: 3 t them by the arms; 4374
Jnh 1:14 please do not let us die for t this man's life. NIH
Zec 5:10 "Where *are* they t the basket?" 2143
Mt 5:25 **adversary who is** t you **to court.** *508*
14:19 T the five loaves and the two fish *3284*
Mk 6:41 T the five loaves and the two fish *3284*
9:36 T him **in his arms,** *1878*
Lk 6: 4 and t the consecrated bread, *3284*
6:29 *do* not **stop** him **from** t your tunic. *3266*
9:16 T the five loaves and the two fish *3284*
12:45 'My master *is* t **a long time** in coming,' *5988*
14: 4 So t **hold of** the man, *2138*
16: 3 My master *is* t **away** my job. *904*
19:22 t **out** what I did not put in, *149*
20:35 of t **part** in that age and in the resurrection *5593*
22:17 *After* t the cup, he gave thanks and said, *1312*
Jn 16:14 He will bring glory to me by t from what is *3284*
19:40 T Jesus' body, the two of them wrapped it, *3284*
Ac 3: 7 T him by the right hand, he helped him up, *4389*
9:19 and *after* t some food, he regained *3284*
12:25 t **with** *them* John, also called Mark. *5221*
15:14 *by* t from the Gentiles a people for himself. *3284*
2Co 8:21 For *we are* t **pains** to do what is right, *4629*
Php 2: 7 t the very nature of a servant, *3284*

TALENT (14) [TALENTS]

Ex 25:39 A t *of* pure gold is to be used for 3971
37:24 and all its accessories from *one* t 3971
38:27 one t for each base. 3971
2Sa 12:30 its weight was a t *of* gold, 3971
1Ki 20:39 or you must pay a t *of* silver.' 3971
2Ki 5:22 Please give them a t *of* silver and two sets 3971
23:33 a levy of a hundred talents of silver and a t 3971
1Ch 20: 2 its weight was found to be a t *of* gold, 3971
2Ch 36: 3 a levy of a hundred talents of silver and a t 3971
Mt 25:15 and to another one t, *NIG*
25:18 man who had received the one t went off, *NIG*
25:24 the man who had received the one t came. *5419*
25:25 So I was afraid and went out and hid your t *5419*
25:28 " 'Take the t from him and give it to *5419*

TALENTS (49) [TALENT]

Ex 38:24 on the sanctuary was 29 t and 730 shekels, 3971
38:25 in the census was 100 t and 1,775 shekels, 3971
38:27 The 100 t *of* silver were used to cast 3971
38:27 100 bases from the 100 t, 3971
38:29 from the wave offering was 70 t and 2,400 3971
1Ki 9:14 Hiram had sent to the king 120 t *of* gold. 3971
9:28 to Ophir and brought back 420 t of gold, 3971
10:10 And she gave the king 120 t *of* gold, 3971
10:14 that Solomon received yearly was 666 t, 3971
16:24 of Samaria from Shemer for *two* t *of* silver 3971
2Ki 5: 5 taking with him ten t *of* silver, 3971
5:23 "By all means, take *two* t," said Naaman. 3971
5:23 then tied up the *two* t of silver in two bags, 3971
15:19 a thousand t *of* silver to gain his support 3971
18:14 of Judah three hundred t *of* silver 3971
18:14 of silver and thirty t *of* gold. 3971
23:33 a levy of a hundred t *of* silver and a talent 3971
1Ch 19: 6 the Ammonites sent a thousand t *of* silver 3971
22:14 the LORD a hundred thousand t *of* gold, 3971
22:14 a million t of silver, 3971
29: 4 three thousand t *of* gold (gold of Ophir) 3971
29: 4 and seven thousand t *of* refined silver, 3971
29: 7 on the temple of God five thousand t 3971
29: 7 ten thousand t of silver, 3971
29: 7 eighteen thousand t of bronze and 3971
29: 7 of bronze and a hundred thousand t of iron. 3971
2Ch 3: 8 the inside with six hundred t of fine gold. 3971
8:18 and brought back four hundred and fifty t 3971
9: 9 Then she gave the king 120 t *of* gold, 3971
9:13 that Solomon received yearly was 666 t, 3971
25: 6 from Israel for a hundred t *of* silver. 3971
25: 9 "But what about the hundred t I paid 3971
27: 5 the Ammonites paid him a hundred t 3971
36: 3 a levy of a hundred t *of* silver and a talent 3971
Ezr 7:22 up to a hundred t of silver, 10352
8:26 I weighed out to them 650 t of silver, 3971
8:26 silver articles weighing 100 t, 3971
8:26 100 t of gold, 3971
Est 3: 9 and I will put ten thousand t *of* silver into 3971
Mt 18:24 who owed him ten thousand t was brought *5419*
25:15 To one he gave five t **of money,** *5419*
25:15 to another two t, and to another one talent, *NIG*
25:16 The man who had received the five t went *5419*
25:17 the one with the two t gained two more. *NIG*
25:20 the five t brought the other five. *5419*
25:20 he said, 'you entrusted me with five t. *5419*
25:22 "The man with the two t also came. *5419*
25:22 he said, 'you entrusted me with two t; *5419*
25:28 and give it to the one who has the ten t. *5419*

TALE (KJV) See COUNTED, FULL QUOTA, SAME NUMBER

TALEBEARER (KJV) See GOSSIP, SPREADING SLANDER

TALES (1)

1Ti 4: 7 with godless myths and **old wives'** t; *1212*

TALITHA (1)

Mk 5:41 **"T** koum!" (which means, "Little girl, *5420*

TALK (43) [TALKED, TALKER, TALKERS, TALKING, TALKS]

Ge 34: 6 Hamor went out to t with Jacob. 1819
Nu 12: 1 and Aaron *began to* t against Moses 1819
Dt 6: 7 T about them when you sit at home and 1819
25: 8 elders of his town shall summon him and t 1819
Jdg 9:38 "Where is your **big** t now, you who said, 7023
1Sa 25:17 He is such a wicked man that no *one can* t 1819
Job 11: 3 Will your **idle** t reduce men to silence? 966
18: 2 Be sensible, and then *we can* t. 1819
27:12 Why then this **meaningless** t? 2038+2039
35:16 So Job opens his mouth with **empty** t; 2039
Ps 38:12 those who would harm me t *of* my ruin; 1819
64: 5 *they* t *about* hiding their snares; 6218
69:26 For they persecute those you wound and t 6218
Pr 4:24 keep **corrupt** t far from your lips. 4299
7:21 she seduced him with her smooth t. 8557
12:13 An evil man is trapped by his sinful t, 8557
14: 3 A fool's t brings a rod to his back, 7023
14:23 but **mere** t leads only to poverty. 1821+8557
24: 2 and their lips t *about* making trouble. 1819
Isa 58: 9 with the pointing finger and malicious t, 1819
Jer 3: 5 This is how *you* t, 1819
Eze 36: 3 and the **object of** people's **malicious** t 4383+6584+6590+8557
Da 10:17 How can I, your servant, t with you, 1819
Mt 9:32 and **could not** t was brought to Jesus. *3273*
12:22 so that he *could* both t and see. *3281*
Mk 1:45 Instead he went out and began *to* t freely, *3062*
2: 7 "Why *does* this fellow t like that? *3281*
7:32 a man who was deaf and **could hardly** t, *3652*
Lk 7:15 The dead man sat up and began *to* t, *3281*
Jn 18:34 "or *did* others t to you about me?" *3306*
Ac 28:20 I asked to see you and t **with** you. *4688*
Ro 9:20 But who are you, O man, to t **back** to God? *503*
16:18 By **smooth** t and flattery they deceive *5981*
1Co 4:20 For the kingdom of God is not a matter of t *3364*
2Co 11:23 (*I* am out of my mind *to* t like this.) *3281*
Eph 4:29 Do not let any unwholesome t come out *3364*
5: 4 **foolish** t or coarse joking, *3703*
1Ti 1: 6 from these and turned to **meaningless** t. *3467*
6: 4 that result in envy, strife, **malicious** t, *1060*
Tit 2: 9 to try to please them, not to t **back** to them, *515*
1Pe 2:15 **silence** the ignorant t of foolish men. *5821*
2Jn 1:12 to visit you and t with you face to face, *3281*
3Jn 1:14 and *we will* t face to face. *3281*

TALKED (29) [TALK]

Ge 35:13 at the place where *he had* t with him. 1819
35:14 a stone pillar at the place where God *had* t 1819
35:15 the place where God *had* t with him Bethel. 1819
45:15 Afterward his brothers t with him. 1819
Nu 3: 1 the LORD t with Moses on Mount Sinai. 1819
14:10 the whole assembly t *about* stoning them. 606
Jos 22:33 And *they* t no more *about* going to war 606
Jdg 13:11 "Are you the one who t to my wife?" 1819
14: 7 Then he went down and t with the woman, 1819
1Sa 9:25 Samuel t with Saul on the roof 1819
1Ki 10: 2 and t with him *about* all that she had 1819
2Ch 9: 1 she came to Solomon and t with him 1819
Jer 38:25 If the officials hear that *I* t with you, 1819
Da 1:19 The king t with them, 1819
Hos 12: 4 at Bethel and t with him there— 1819
Zec 1:13 and comforting words to the angel who t 1819
4: 1 Then the angel who t with me returned 1819
4: 4 I asked the angel who t with me, 1819
Mal 3:16 Then those who feared the LORD t with each 1819
Lk 20:14 saw him, *they* t **the matter over.** *253+1368+4639*
24:15 As they t and discussed these things *3917*
24:32 not our hearts burning within us while *he* t *3281*
Ac 9:29 *He* t and debated with the Grecian Jews, *3281*
13:43 who t **with** them and urged them *4688*
13:45 with jealousy and t abusively **against** *515*
20: 9 into a deep sleep *as* Paul t on and on. *1363*
24:26 *he* sent for him frequently and t with him. *3917*
1Co 13:11 When I was a child, *I* t like a child, *3281*
Rev 21:15 The angel who t with me had a measuring *3281*

TALKER (1) [TALK]

Job 11: 2 Is this t to be vindicated? 408+8557

TALKERS (2) [TALK]

1Ti 3:11 not **malicious** t but temperate and *1333*
Tit 1:10 rebellious people, **mere** t and deceivers, *3468*

TALKING (48) [TALK]

Ge 29: 9 While he *was* still t with them, 1819
Dt 11:19 t about them when you sit at home and 1819
Jdg 6:17 give me a sign that it is really you t to me. 1819
1Sa 2: 3 "Do not keep t so proudly 1819
14:19 While Saul *was* t to the priest, 1819
17:23 As he *was* t with them, Goliath, 1819
18: 1 After David had finished t with Saul, 1819
30: 6 because the men *were* t *of* stoning him; 606
1Ki 1:14 While you *are* still there t to the king, 1819
2Ki 2:11 As they were walking along and t together, 1819
6:33 While he *was* still t to them, 1819
8: 4 The king *was* t to Gehazi, 1819
Est 6:14 While they *were* still t with him, 1819
Job 2:10 He replied, *"You are* t like a foolish woman 1819
Eze 33:30 your countrymen *are* t **together** about you 1819
Zec 1: 9 The angel who *was* t with me answered, 1819
Mt 12:46 *While* Jesus *was* still t to the crowd, *3281*
16: 8 why *are you* t among yourselves *1368*
16:11 that *I was* not t to you about bread? *3306*
17: 3 before them Moses and Elijah, t **with** Jesus. *5196*
17:13 Then the disciples understood that *he was* t *3306*
21:45 they knew *he was* t about them. *3306*
26:70 "I don't know what *you're* t **about,"** *3306*
Mk 7:36 the more they *kept* t **about** it. *3062*
8:17 "Why *are you* t **about** having no bread? *1368*
9: 4 Elijah and Moses, who were t **with** Jesus. *5196*
14:68 or understand what you're t **about,"** *3306*
14:71 "I don't know this man *you're* t **about."** *3306*
Lk 1:65 of Judea *people were* t **about** *1362*
9:31 in glorious splendor, t **with** Jesus. *5196*
18:34 they did not know what *he was* t **about.** *3306*
22:60 "Man, I don't know what *you're* t **about!"** *3306*
24:14 They *were* t with each other *3917*
24:36 *While* they *were still* t **about** this, *3281*
Jn 4:27 and were surprised to find *him* t with *3281*
4:27 or "Why *are you* t with her?" *3281*
Ac 8:34 please, who *is* the prophet t about, *3306*
10:27 T **with** him, Peter went inside and found *5326*
17:21 but t **about** and listening to the latest ideas.) *3306*
20: 7 kept on t until midnight. *3364*
20:11 *After* t until daylight, he left. *3917*
26:31 and *while* t with one another, they said, *3306*
28:22 that people everywhere *are* t **against** *515*
Ro 11:13 *I am* t to you Gentiles. *3306*
1Co 4:19 not only how these arrogant people *are* t, *3364*
2Co 11:17 In this self-confident boasting *I am* not t as *3281*
Eph 5:32 but I *am* t about Christ and the church. *3306*
1Ti 1: 7 not know what *they are* t **about** *3306*

TALKS (1) [TALK]

Pr 20:19 so avoid a *man who* t **too much.** 7331+8557

TALL (15) [TALLER, TALLEST]

Dt 2:10 and as t as the Anakites. 8123
2:21 and as t as the Anakites. 8123
9: 2 The people *are* strong and t**—Anakites!** 8123
1Sa 17: 4 He was over nine feet t. 1470
1Ch 11:23 Egyptian who was seven and a half feet t. 4500
Job 8:11 *Can* papyrus **grow** t where there is no 1448
Isa 2:13 t and lofty, and all the oaks of Bashan, 8123
10:33 the t *ones* will be brought low. 1469
18: 2 to a people t and smooth-skinned, 5432
18: 7 from a people t and smooth-skinned, from 5432
45:14 and those t Sabeans—they will come 408+4500
Eze 17:24 the LORD bring down the t tree and make 1469
17:24 **make** the low tree **grow** t. 1467
31: 4 deep springs **made** it **grow** t; 8123

Am 2: 9 though he was **t** as the cedars and strong as 1470

TALLER (3) [TALL]

Dt 1:28 'The people are stronger and **t** than we are; 8123
1Sa 9: 2 a head **t** than any of the others. 1469
10:23 among the people *he was* a head **t** than any 1467

TALLEST (2) [TALL]

2Ki 19:23 I have cut down its **t** cedars, 7757
Isa 37:24 I have cut down its **t** cedars, 7757

TALMAI (6)

Nu 13:22 Sheshai and **T**, the descendants of Anak, 9440
Jos 15:14 Sheshai, Ahiman and **T**— 9440
Jdg 1:10 and defeated Sheshai, Ahiman and **T**. 9440
2Sa 3: 3 of Maacah daughter of **T** king of Geshur; 9440
13:37 Absalom fled and went to **T** son of 9440
1Ch 3: 2 of Maacah daughter of **T** king of Geshur; 9440

TALMON (5)

1Ch 9:17 The gatekeepers: Shallum, Akkub, **T**, 3236
Ezr 2:42 the descendants of Shallum, Ater, **T**, 3236
Ne 7:45 the descendants of Shallum, Ater, **T**, 3236
11:19 Akkub, **T** and their associates, 3236
12:25 Obadiah, Meshullam, **T** 3236

TAMAH (KJV) See TEMAH

TAMAR (26) [BAAL TAMAR, HAZAZON TAMAR]

Ge 38: 6 his firstborn, and her name was **T**. 9470
38:11 Judah then said to his daughter-in-law **T**, 9470
38:11 So **T** went to live in her father's house. 9470
38:13 When **T** was told, 9470
38:24 "Your daughter-in-law **T** is guilty 9470
Ru 4:12 whom **T** bore to Judah." 9470
2Sa 13: 1 Amnon son of David fell in love with **T**, 9470
13: 2 of illness on account of his sister **T**, 9470
13: 4 Amnon said to him, "I'm in love with **T**, 9470
13: 5 'I would like my sister **T** to come 9470
13: 6 'I would like my sister **T** to come 9470
13: 7 David sent word to **T** at the palace: 9470
13: 8 **T** went to the house of her brother Amnon, 9470
13:10 Then Amnon said to **T**, 9470
13:10 And **T** took the bread she had prepared 9470
13:19 **T** put ashes on her head and tore 9470
13:20 **T** lived in her brother Absalom's house, 9470
13:22 because he had disgraced his sister **T**. 9470
13:32 since the day Amnon raped his sister **T**. 9470
14:27 The daughter's name was **T**, 9470
1Ch 2: 4 **T**, Judah's daughter-in-law, 9470
3: 9 And **T** was their sister. 9470
Eze 47:18 to the eastern sea and as far as **T**. 9471
47:19 "On the south side it will run from **T** as far 9471
48:28 of Gad will run south from **T** to the waters 9471
Mt 1: 3 whose mother was **T**, *2500*

TAMARISK (3)

Ge 21:33 Abraham planted a **t tree** in Beersheba, 869
1Sa 22: 6 was seated under the **t tree** on the hill 869
31:13 and buried them under a **t tree** at Jabesh, 869

TAMBOURINE (5) [TAMBOURINES]

Ex 15:20 Aaron's sister, took a **t** in her hand, 9512
Job 21:12 They sing to the **music of t** and harp; 9512
Ps 81: 2 Begin the music, strike the **t**, 9512
149: 3 and make music to him with **t** and harp. 9512
150: 4 praise him with **t** and dancing, 9512

TAMBOURINES (12) [TAMBOURINE]

Ge 31:27 and singing to the **music of t** and harps? 9512
Ex 15:20 women followed her, with **t** and dancing. 9512
Jdg 11:34 his daughter, dancing to the sound of **t**! 9512
1Sa 10: 5 with lyres, **t**, flutes and harps being played 9512
18: 6 with joyful songs and with **t** and lutes. 9512
2Sa 6: 5 with songs and with harps, lyres, **t**, 9512
1Ch 13: 8 with songs and with harps, lyres, **t**, 9512
Ps 68:25 with them are the maidens **playing t**. 9528
Isa 5:12 **t** and flutes and wine, 9512
24: 8 The gaiety of the **t** is stilled, 9512
30:32 be to the **music of t** and harps, 9512
Jer 31: 4 Again you will take up your **t** and go out 9512

TAME (1) [TAMED]

Jas 3: 8 but no man can **t** the tongue. *1238*

TAMED (2) [TAME]

Jas 3: 7 reptiles and creatures of the sea *are being* **t** *1238*
3: 7 of the sea are being tamed and *have been* **t** *1238*

TAMMUZ (1)

Eze 8:14 I saw women sitting there, mourning for **T**. 9452

TANACH (KJV) See TAANACH

TANHUMETH (2)

2Ki 25:23 Seraiah son of **T** the Netophathite, 9489
Jer 40: 8 the sons of Kareah, Seraiah son of **T**, 9489

TANNER (3)

Ac 9:43 for some time with a **t** named Simon. *1114*
10: 6 He is staying with Simon the **t**, *1114*
10:32 He is a guest in the home *of* Simon the **t**, *1114*

TAPESTRY (1)

SS 7: 5 Your hair is like royal **t**; 763

TAPHATH (1)

1Ki 4:11 (he was married to **T** daughter of Solomon); 3264

TAPPUAH (6) [BETH TAPPUAH, EN TAPPUAH]

Jos 12:17 the king of **T** one the king of Hepher one 9517
15:34 Zanoah, En Gannim, **T**, Enam, 9517
16: 8 From **T** the border went west to 9517
17: 8 (Manasseh had the land of **T**, 9517
17: 8 but **T** itself, on the boundary of Manasseh, 9517
1Ch 2:43 Korah, **T**, Rekem and Shema. 9516

TAR (3)

Ge 11: 3 brick instead of stone and **t** for mortar. 2819
14:10 the Valley of Siddim was full of **t** pits, 2819
Ex 2: 3 for him and coated it with **t** and pitch. 2819

TARAH (KJV) See TERAH

TARALAH (1)

Jos 18:27 Rekem, Irpeel, **T**, 9550

TARE (KJV) See CONVULSION, MAULED, TORE

TAREA (1)

1Ch 8:35 Pithon, Melech, **T** and Ahaz. 9308

TARES (KJV) See WEEDS

TARGET (4)

1Sa 20:20 as though I were shooting at a **t**. 4766
Job 7:20 Why have you made me your **t**? 5133
16:12 He has made me his **t**; 4766
La 3:12 He drew his bow and made me the **t** 4766

TARPELITES (KJV) See TRIPOLIS

TARRIED, TARRIEST, TARRIETH, TARRY, TARRYING (KJV) See HALTED, LONG TIME, REST, SPEND TIME, SPENT TIME, STAYED, SUSPENSE, WAIT, WAITED

TARSHISH (19)

Ge 10: 4 Elishah, **T**, the Kittim and the Rodanim. 9576
1Ch 1: 7 Elishah, **T**, the Kittim and the Rodanim. 9576
7:10 Ehud, Kenaanah, Zethan, **T** and Ahishahar. 9578
Est 1:14 Carshena, Shethar, Admatha, **T**, Meres, 9578
Ps 48: 7 like ships of **T** shattered by an east wind. 9578
72:10 of **T** and of distant shores will bring tribute 9576
Isa 23: 1 Wail, O ships of **T**! 9576
23: 6 Cross over to **T**; wail, you people 9576
23:10 O Daughter of **T**, for you no longer have 9576
23:14 Wail, you ships of **T**; 9576
60: 9 in the lead are the ships of **T**, 9576
66:19 to **T**, to the Libyans and Lydians 9576
Jer 10: 9 Hammered silver is brought from **T** 9576
Eze 27:12 " '**T** did business with you because 9576
27:25 ships of **T** serve as carriers for your wares. 9576
38:13 Sheba and Dedan and the merchants of **T** 9576
Jnh 1: 3 from the LORD and headed for **T**. 9576
1: 3 and sailed for **T** to flee from the LORD. 9576
4: 2 That is why I was so quick to flee to **T**. 9576

TARSUS (5)

Ac 9:11 and ask for a **man from T** named Saul, *5432*
9:30 down to Caesarea and sent him off to **T**. *5433*
11:25 Then Barnabas went to **T** to look for Saul, *5433*
21:39 "I am a Jew, **from T** in Cilicia, *5432*
22: 3 "I am a Jew, born in **T** of Cilicia, *5433*

TARTAK (1)

2Ki 17:31 the Avvites made Nibhaz and **T**, 9581

TARTAN (KJV) See SUPREME COMMANDER

TASK (16) [TASKS]

Ge 31:36 Jacob was angry and **took** Laban **to t**. 8189
Lev 16:21 in the care of a man **appointed for the t**. 6967
1Ch 29: 1 The **t** is great, because this palatial structure 4856
2Ch 29:34 until the **t** was finished and 4856
Ne 13:30 each to his own **t**. 4856
Ecc 2:26 but to the sinner he gives the **t** of gathering 6721
Isa 28:21 his strange work, and perform his **t**, 6275
28:21 and perform his task, his alien **t**. 6275
Mk 13:34 each with his assigned **t**, *2240*
Ac 20:24 the **t** the Lord Jesus has given me— *1355*
20:24 **t** of testifying to the gospel of God's grace. *NIG*
Ro 15:28 So after I have completed **this** *t* *AIT*
1Co 3: 5 as the Lord has assigned to each his **t**. *NIG*
2Co 2:16 And who is equal to **such** a *t?* *AIT*
Gal 2: 7 with the **t** of preaching the gospel to *NIG*
1Ti 3: 1 on being an overseer, he desires a noble **t**. *2240*

TASKMASTERS (KJV) See SLAVE MASTERS, SLAVE DRIVERS

TASKS (2) [TASK]

2Ch 31:16 the daily duties of their *various* **t**, 6275
Pr 31:17 her arms are strong for her **t**. NIH

TASSEL (1) [TASSELS]

Nu 15:38 with a blue cord on each **t**. 7492

TASSELS (4) [TASSEL]

Nu 15:38 to make **t** on the corners of your garments, 7492
15:39 You will have these **t** to look at and 7492
Dt 22:12 Make **t** on the four corners of 1544
Mt 23: 5 and the **t** on their garments long; *3192*

TASTE (17) [TASTED, TASTELESS, TASTES, TASTING, TASTY]

Ge 25:28 Isaac, who had a **t** *for* wild game, 7023
2Sa 3:35 with me, be it ever so severely, if *I* **t** bread 3247
19:35 *Can* your servant **t** what he eats 3247
Job 27: 2 *who has* **made** me **t bitterness** of soul, 5352
Ps 34: 8 **T** and see that the LORD is good; 3247
119:103 How sweet are your words to my **t**, 2674
Pr 24:13 honey from the comb is sweet to your **t**. 2674
SS 2: 3 and his fruit is sweet to my **t**. 2674
4:16 into his garden and **t** its choice fruits. 430
Jnh 3: 7 **t** anything; do not let them eat or drink. 3247
Mt 16:28 not **t** death before they see the Son *1174*
Mk 9: 1 not **t** death before they see the kingdom *1174*
Lk 9:27 not **t** death before they see the kingdom *1174*
14:24 of those men who were invited *will* **get a t** *1174*
Jn 8:52 *he will* never **t** death. *1174*
Col 2:21 "Do not handle! *Do* not **t**! Do not touch!"? *1174*
Heb 2: 9 so that by the grace of God *he might* **t** death *1174*

TASTED (11) [TASTE]

Ex 16:31 like coriander seed and **t** like wafers made 3248
Nu 11: 8 it **t** like something made with olive oil. 3248
1Sa 14:24 So none of the troops **t** food. 3247
14:29 how my eyes brightened when *I* **t** a little 3247
14:43 "*I* **merely t** a little honey with the end 3247+3247
Eze 3: 3 and *it* **t** as sweet as honey in my mouth. 2118
Jn 2: 9 and the master of the banquet **t** the water *1174*
Heb 6: 4 who *have* **t** the heavenly gift, *1174*
6: 5 who *have* **t** the goodness of the word *1174*
1Pe 2: 3 now that *you have* **t** that the Lord is good. *1174*
Rev 10:10 *It* **t** as **sweet** as honey in my mouth, *1184+1639*

TASTELESS (1) [TASTE]

Job 6: 6 Is **t** *food* eaten without salt, 9522

TASTES (5) [TASTE]

Job 12:11 not the ear test words as the tongue **t** food? 3247
34: 3 the ear tests words as the tongue **t** food. 3247
Pr 20:17 Food gained by fraud **t sweet** to a man, 6853
27: 7 to the hungry even what is bitter **t** sweet. NIH
Jer 48:11 So she **t** as she did, 3248

TASTING (1) [TASTE]

Mt 27:34 but *after* **t** it, he refused to drink it. *1174*

TASTY (6) [TASTE]

Ge 27: 4 the kind of **t food** I like and bring it to me 4761
27: 7 and prepare me *some* **t food** to eat, 4761
27: 9 I can prepare *some* **t food** for your father, 4761
27:14 and she prepared *some* **t food**, 4761
27:17 the **t food** and the bread she had made. 4761
27:31 He too prepared *some* **t food** and brought it 4761

TATTENAI (4)

Ezr 5: 3 At that time **T**, governor of 10779
5: 6 This is a copy of the letter that **T**, 10779
6: 6 Now then, **T**, governor of Trans-Euphrates, 10779
6:13 **T**, governor of Trans-Euphrates, 10779

TATTLERS (KJV) See GOSSIPS

TATTOO (1)

Lev 19:28 for the dead or put **t** marks on yourselves. 7882

TAUGHT (59) [TEACH]

Dt 4: 5 *I have* **t** you decrees and laws as 4340
31:22 wrote down this song that day and **t** it *to* 4340
Jdg 8:16 and **t** the men of Succoth **a lesson** 3359
2Sa 1:18 men of Judah *be* **t** this lament of the bow 4340

1Ki 4:33 He also t about animals and birds, 1819
2Ki 17:28 and t them how to worship the LORD. 2118+3723
2Ch 17: 9 They t throughout Judah, 4340
17: 9 to all the towns of Judah and t the people. 4340
Ps 71:17 Since my youth, O God, you have t me, 4340
119:102 for you yourself have t me. 3723
Pr 4: 4 he t me and said, "Lay hold of my words 3723
31: 1 an oracle his mother t him: 3579
SS 8: 2 to my mother's house—she who has t me. 4340
Isa 29:13 of me is made up only of rules t by men. 4340
40:14 and who t him the right way? 4340
40:14 that t him knowledge or showed him 4340
50: 4 wakens my ear to listen like one being t. 4341
54:13 All your sons will be t by the LORD, 4341
Jer 9: 5 They have t their tongues to lie; 4340
9:14 as their fathers t them." 4340
10: 8 they are t by worthless wooden idols. 4592
12:16 they once t my people to swear by Baal— 4340
32:33 though I t them again and again, 4340
Hos 11: 3 It was I who t Ephraim to walk, 8078
Mt 7:29 because he t as one who had authority, 1438+1639
15: 9 their teachings are but rules t by men.' " NIG
Mk 1:22 he t them as one who had authority, 1438+1639
4: 2 He t them many things by parables, 1438
6:30 to him all they had done and t. 1438
7: 7 their teachings are but rules t by men.' NIG
10: 1 and as was his custom, he t them. 1438
11:17 And as he t them, he said, "Is it not written: 1438
12:38 As he t, Jesus said, "Watch out for 1439
Lk 1: 4 the certainty of the things you have been t. 2994
4:15 He t in their synagogues, 1438
5: 3 he sat down and t the people from the boat. 1438
11: 1 just as John t his disciples." 1438
13:26 and you t in our streets.' 1438
Jn 6:45 'They will all be t by God.' 1435
8:28 but speak just what the Father has t me. 1438
18:20 "I always t in synagogues or at the temple, 1438
Ac 11:26 the church and t great numbers of people. 1438
15: 1 according to the custom t by Moses, NIG
15:35 and many others t and preached the word 1438
18:25 and he spoke with great fervor and t 1438
20:20 be helpful to you but have t you publicly 1438
28:31 of God and t about the Lord Jesus Christ. 1438
1Co 2:13 not in words t us by human wisdom but 1435
2:13 by human wisdom but in words t by 1435
Gal 1:12 not receive it from any man, nor was I t it; 1438
Eph 4:21 Surely you heard of him and were t in him 1438
4:22 You were t, with regard to your former way NIG
Col 2: 7 strengthened in the faith as you were t, 1438
1Th 4: 9 for you yourselves have been t by God 2531
1Ti 1:20 whom I have handed over to Satan to be t 4084
4: 1 and follow deceiving spirits and things t 1436
Tit 1: 9 to the trustworthy message as it has been t, 1439
1Jn 2:27 just as it has t you, remain in him. 1438
Rev 2:14 who t Balak to entice the Israelites to sin 1438

TAUNT (8) [TAUNTED, TAUNTS]
Dt 32:27 but I dreaded the t of the enemy, lest 4088
1Ki 18:27 At noon Elijah began to t them. 2252
Ps 42:10 suffer mortal agony as my foes t me, 3070
102: 8 All day long my enemies t me; 3070
Isa 14: 4 you will take up this t against the king 5442
Eze 5:15 You will be a reproach and a t, 1527
Mic 2: 4 they will t you with this mournful song: 5629
Hab 2: 6 Will not all of them t him with ridicule 5442+5951

TAUNTED (4) [TAUNT]
Jdg 8:15 about whom you t me by saying, 3070
2Sa 21:21 When he t Israel, Jonathan son of Shimeah, 3070
23: 9 when they t the Philistines gathered 3070
1Ch 20: 7 When he t Israel, Jonathan son of Shimea, 3070

TAUNTS (6) [TAUNT]
Ps 44:16 the t of those who reproach and revile me, 7754
89:50 I bear in my heart the t of all the nations, 8190
89:51 t with which your enemies have mocked, NIH
119:42 then I will answer the one who t me, 3070
Eze 36:15 No longer will I make you hear the t of 4009
Zep 2: 8 "I have heard the insults of Moab and the t 1526

TAVERNS See THREE TAVERNS

TAX (33) [TAXED, TAXES]
2Ch 24: 6 in from Judah and Jerusalem the t imposed 5368
24: 9 to the LORD the t that Moses the servant 5368
Ne 5: 4 the king's t on our fields and vineyards. 4501
Da 11:20 a t collector to maintain the royal splendor. 5601
Mt 5:46 Are not even the t collectors doing that? 5467
9: 9 Matthew sitting at the t collector's booth. 5468
9:10 many t collectors and "sinners" came 5467
9:11 with t collectors and 'sinners'?" 5467
10: 3 Thomas and Matthew the t collector; 5467
11:19 a friend of t collectors and "sinners." ' 5467
17:24 collectors of the two-drachma t 3284
17:24 "Doesn't your teacher pay the temple t?" NIG
17:27 and give it to them for my t and yours." NIG
18:17 as you would a pagan or a t collector. 5467
21:31 the t collectors and the prostitutes 5467
21:32 the t collectors and the prostitutes did. 5467
22:19 Show me the coin used for paying the t." 3056
Mk 2:14 sitting at the t collector's booth. 5468
2:15 at Levi's house, many t collectors 5467
2:16 with the "sinners" and t collectors, 5467
2:16 "Why does he eat with t collectors 5467
Lk 3:12 T collectors also came to be baptized. 5467
5:27 a t collector by the name of Levi sitting 5467
5:27 by the name of Levi sitting at his t booth. 5468
5:29 of t collectors and others were eating 5467
5:30 with t collectors and 'sinners'?" 5467
7:29 (All the people, even the t collectors, 5467
7:34 a friend of t collectors and "sinners." ' 5467
15: 1 Now the t collectors and "sinners." 5467
18:10 a Pharisee and the other a t collector. 5467
18:11 or even like this t collector. 5467
18:13 "But the t collector stood at a distance. 5467
19: 2 a chief t collector and was wealthy. 803

TAXED (1) [TAX]
2Ki 23:35 he t the land and exacted the silver 6885

TAXES (12) [TAX]
1Sa 17:25 exempt his father's family from t 2930+6913
Ezr 4:13 no more t, tribute or duty will be paid, 10402
4:20 and t, tribute and duty were paid to them. 10402
7:24 that you have no authority to impose t, 10402
Mt 17:25 the kings of the earth collect duty and t— 3056
22:17 Is it right to pay t to Caesar or not?" 3056
Mk 12:14 Is it right to pay t to Caesar or not? 3056
Lk 20:22 Is it right for us to pay t to Caesar or not?" 5843
23: 2 of t to Caesar and claims to be Christ, 5843
Ro 13: 6 This is also why you pay t, 5843
13: 7 If you owe t, pay taxes; 5843
13: 7 If you owe taxes, pay t; 5843

TAXING (KJV) See CENSUS

TEACH (123) [TAUGHT, TEACHER, TEACHERS, TEACHES, TEACHING, TEACHINGS]
Ex 4:12 I will help you speak and will t you what 3723
4:15 of you speak and will t you what to do. 3723
18:20 T them the decrees and laws, 2302
33:13 t me your ways so I may know you 3359
35:34 of the tribe of Dan, the ability to t others. 3723
Lev 10:11 and you must t the Israelites all the decrees 3723
Dt 4: 1 the decrees and laws I am about to t you. 4340
4: 9 T them to your children and 3359
4:10 the land and may t them to their children." 4340
4:14 to t you the decrees and laws you are 4340
5:31 and laws you are to t them to follow in 4340
6: 1 the LORD your God directed me to t you 4340
8: 3 to t you that man does not live on bread 3359
11:19 T them to your children, 4340
17:11 Act according to the law they t you and 3723
20:18 they will t you to follow all 4340
31:19 down for yourselves this song and t it to 4340
Jdg 3: 2 to t warfare to the descendants of 4340
13: 8 to t us how to bring up the boy who is to 3723
1Sa 12:23 And I will t you the way that is good 3723
14:12 "Come up to us and we'll t you a lesson." 3359
1Ki 8:36 T them the right way to live, 3723
2Ki 17:27 to live there and t the people what the god 3723
2Ch 6:27 T them the right way to live, 3723
15: 3 without a priest to t and without the law. 3723
17: 7 and Micaiah to t in the towns of Judah. 4340
Ezr 7:25 you are to t any who do not know them. 10313
Job 6:24 "T me, and I will be quiet; 3723
12: 7 "But ask the animals, and they will t you, 3723
12: 8 or speak to the earth, and it will t you, 3723
21:22 "Can anyone t knowledge to God, 4340
27:11 "I will t you about the power of God; 3723
32: 7 advanced years should t wisdom.' 3359
33:33 be silent, and I will t you wisdom." 544
34:32 T me what I cannot see; 3723
Ps 25: 4 O LORD, t me your paths; 4340
25: 5 guide me in your truth and t me, 4340
27:11 T me your way, O LORD; 3723
32: 8 and t you in the way you should go; 3723
34:11 I will t you the fear of the LORD. 4340
51: 6 you t me wisdom in the inmost place. 3359
51:13 Then I will t transgressors your ways, 4340
78: 5 our forefathers to t their children, 3359
86:11 T me your way, O LORD, 3723
90:12 T us to number our days aright, 3359
94:12 O LORD, the man you t from your law; 4340
105:22 as he pleased and t his elders wisdom 2681
119:12 t me your decrees. 4340
119:26 t me your decrees. 4340
119:33 T me, O LORD, to follow your decrees; 3723
119:64 t me your decrees. 4340
119:66 T me knowledge and good judgment, 4340
119:68 t me your decrees. 4340
119:108 and t me your laws. 4340
119:124 to your love and t me your decrees. 4340
119:135 upon your servant and t me your decrees. 4340
119:171 for you t me your decrees. 4340
132:12 and the statutes I t them, 4340
143:10 T me to do your will, for you are my God; 4340
Pr 9: 9 t a righteous man and he will add to his 3359
22:17 apply your heart to what I t, 1981
22:19 I t you today, even you. 3359
Isa 2: 3 He will t us his ways, 3723
9:15 the prophets who t lies are the tail. 3723
28: 9 "Who is it he is trying to t? 1978+3723
Jer 9:20 T your daughters how to wail; 4340
9:20 t one another a lament. NIH
16:21 "Therefore I will t them— 3359
16:21 this time I will t them my power 3359
31:34 No longer will a man t his neighbor, 4340
Eze 22:26 they t that there is no difference between 3359
44:23 They are to t my people the difference 3723
Da 1: 4 to t them the language and literature of 4340
Mic 3:11 her priests t for a price, 3723
4: 2 He will t us his ways, 3723
Mt 5: 2 and he began to t them, saying: 1438
11: 1 on from there to t and preach in the towns 1438
22:16 of integrity and that you t the way of God 1438
Mk 1:21 into the synagogue and began to t. 1438
2:13 and he began to t them. 1438
4: 1 Again Jesus began to t by the lake. 1438
6: 2 he began to t in the synagogue, 1438
8:31 He then began to t them that the Son 1438
12:14 but you t the way of God in accordance 1438
Lk 4:31 and on the Sabbath began to t the people. 1438
11: 1 "Lord, t us to pray, 1438
12:12 for the Holy Spirit will t you at 1438
20:21 that you speak and t what is right, 1438
20:21 but t the way of God in accordance with 1438
Jn 7:14 up to the temple courts and begin to t. 1438
7:35 among the Greeks, and t the Greeks? 1438
8: 2 and he sat down to t them. 1438
14:26 will t you all things and will remind you 1438
Ac 1: 1 about all that Jesus began to do and to t 1438
4:18 to speak or t at all in the name of Jesus. 1438
5:21 and began to t the people. 1438
5:28 "We gave you strict orders not to t 1438
21:21 They have been informed that you t all 1438
Ro 2:21 who t others, do you not teach yourself? 1438
2:21 who teach others, do you not t yourself? 1438
12: 7 if it is teaching, let him t; 1436
15: 4 in the past was written to t us, 1436
1Co 4:17 with what I t everywhere in every church. 1438
11:14 of things t you that if a man has long hair, 1438
Col 3:16 of Christ dwell in you richly as you t 1438
1Ti 1: 3 not to t false doctrines any longer 2281
2:12 a woman to t or to have authority over 1438
3: 2 respectable, hospitable, able to t, 1434
4:11 Command and t these things. 1438
6: 2 These are the things you are to t and urge 1438
2Ti 2: 2 also be qualified to t others. 1438
2:24 he must be kind to everyone, able to t, 1434
Tit 1:11 by teaching things they ought not to t— NIG
2: 1 You must t what is in accord 3281
2: 2 T the older men to be temperate, NIG
2: 3 t the older women to be reverent in NIG
2: 3 but to t what is good. 2815
2: 9 T slaves to be subject to their masters NIG
2:15 These, then, are the things you should t. 3281
Heb 5:12 to t you the elementary truths 1438
8:11 No longer will a man t his neighbor, 1438
Jas 3: 1 that we who t will be judged more strictly. NIG
1Jn 2:27 and you do not need anyone to t you. 1438

TEACHER (68) [TEACH]
1Ch 25: 8 Young and old alike, t as well as student, 1067
Ezr 7: 6 a t well versed in the Law of Moses, 6221
7:11 and t, a man learned in matters concerning 6221
7:12 a t of the Law of the God of heaven: 10516
7:21 a t of the Law of the God of heaven, 10516
Job 36:22 Who is a t like him? 4621
Ecc 1: 1 The words of the T, son of David, 7738
1: 2 "Meaningless! Meaningless!" says the T. 7738
1:12 I, the T, was king over Israel in Jerusalem. 7738
7:27 says the T, "this is what I have discovered: 7738
12: 8 "Meaningless! Meaningless!" says the T. 7738
12: 9 Not only was the T wise, 7738
12:10 The T searched to find just the right words, 7738
Mt 8:19 Then a t of the law came to him and said, 1208
8:19 "T, I will follow you wherever you go." 1437
9:11 "Why does your t eat with tax collectors 1437
10:24 "A student is not above his t, 1437
10:25 It is enough for the student to be like his t, 1437
12:38 of the law said to him, "T, we want to see 1437
13:52 every t of the law who has been instructed 1208
17:24 "Doesn't your t pay the temple tax?" 1437
19:16 a man came up to Jesus and asked, "T, 1437
22:16 "T," they said, "we know you are a man 1437
22:24 "T," they said, "Moses told us that if 1437
22:36 "T, which is the greatest commandment in 1437
23:10 Nor are you to be called 't,' 2762
23:10 for you have one T, the Christ. 2762
26:18 'The T says: My appointed time is near. 1437
Mk 4:38 "T, don't you care if we drown?" 1437
5:35 "Why bother the t any more?" 1437
9:17 A man in the crowd answered, "T, 1437
9:38 "T," said John, "we saw a man driving out 1437
10:17 "Good t," he asked, "what must I do 1437
10:20 "T," he declared, "all these I have kept 1437
10:35 "T," they said, "we want you to do 1437
12:14 They came to him and said, "T, 1437
12:19 "T," they said, "Moses wrote for us that if 1437
12:32 "Well said, t," the man replied. 1437
13: 1 one of his disciples said to him, "Look, T! 1437
14:14 of the house he enters, 'The T asks: 1437
Lk 3:12 "T," they asked, "what should we do?" 1437
6:40 A student is not above his t, 1437
6:40 who is fully trained will be like his t. 1437
7:40 "Tell me, t," he said. 1437
8:49 "Don't bother the t any more." 1437
9:38 A man in the crowd called out, "T, 1437
10:25 "T," he asked, "what must I do 1437
11:45 "T, when you say these things, 1437
12:13 Someone in the crowd said to him, "T, 1437

Lk 18:18 A certain ruler asked him, "Good t, 1437
19:39 "T, rebuke your disciples!" 1437
20:21 So the spies questioned him: "T, 1437
20:28 "T," they said, "Moses wrote for us that if 1437
20:39 of the law responded, "Well said, t!" 1437
21: 7 "T," they asked, "When will these things 1437
22:11 to the owner of the house, 'The T asks: 1437
Jn 1:38 They said, "Rabbi" (which means T), 1437
3: 2 we know you are a t who has come 1437
3:10 "You are Israel's t," said Jesus, 1437
8: 4 to Jesus, "T, this woman was caught in 1437
11:28 "The T is here," she said, 1437
13:13 "You call me 'T' and 'Lord,' 1437
13:14 Now that I, your Lord and T, 1437
20:16 "Rabboni!" (which means T). 1437
Ac 5:34 Pharisee named Gamaliel, a t of the law, 3791
Ro 2:20 a t of infants, because you have in the law 1437
1Ti 2: 7 and a t of the true faith to the Gentiles. 1437
2Ti 1:11 a herald and an apostle and a t. 1437

TEACHERS (73) [TEACH]

Ps 119:99 I have more insight than all my t, 4340
Pr 5:13 not obey my t or listen to my instructors. 4621
Isa 30:20 your t will be hidden no more; 4621
Mt 2: 4 the people's chief priests and t of the law, 1208
5:20 that of the Pharisees and the t of the law, 1208
7:29 and not as their t of the law. 1208
9: 3 some of the t of the law said to themselves, 1208
12:38 the Pharisees and t of the law said to him, 1208
15: 1 and t of the law came to Jesus 1208
16:21 chief priests and t of the law, 1208
17:10 "Why then do the t of the law say 1208
20:18 to the chief priests and the t of the law. 1208
21:15 the chief priests and the t of the law saw 1208
23: 2 "The t of the law and the Pharisees sit 1208
23:13 "Woe to you, t of the law and Pharisees, 1208
23:15 "Woe to you, t of the law and Pharisees, 1208
23:23 "Woe to you, t of the law and Pharisees, 1208
23:25 "Woe to you, t of the law and Pharisees, 1208
23:27 "Woe to you, t of the law and Pharisees, 1208
23:29 "Woe to you, t of the law and Pharisees, 1208
23:34 sending you prophets and wise men and t. 1208
26:57 t of the law and the elders had assembled. 1208
27:41 the chief priests, the t of the law and 1208
Mk 1:22 who had authority, not as the t of the law. 1208
2: 6 Now some t of the law were sitting there, 1208
2:16 t of the law who were Pharisees saw him eating 1208
3:22 And the t of the law who came down 1208
7: 1 some of the t of the law who had come 1208
7: 5 the Pharisees and t of the law asked Jesus, 1208
8:31 chief priests and t of the law, 1208
9:11 "Why do the t of the law say 1208
9:14 around them and the t of the law arguing 1208
10:33 to the chief priests and t of the law. 1208
11:18 and the t of the law heard this 1208
11:27 the t of the law and the elders came 1208
12:28 One of the t of the law came 1208
12:35 that the t of the law say that the Christ is 1208
12:38 "Watch out for the t of the law. 1208
14: 1 and the t of the law were looking 1208
14:43 the t of the law, and the elders. 1208
14:53 elders and t of the law came together. 1208
15: 1 the t of the law and the whole Sanhedrin, 1208
15:31 and the t of the law mocked him 1208
Lk 2:46 sitting among the t, listening to them 1437
5:17 Pharisees and t of the law, 3791
5:21 and the t of the law began thinking 1208
5:30 and the t of the law who belonged 1208
6: 7 the t of the law were looking for a reason 1208
9:22 chief priests and t of the law, 1208
11:53 the Pharisees and the t of the law began 1208
15: 2 and the t of the law muttered, 1208
19:47 the t of the law and the leaders among 1208
20: 1 the chief priests and the t of the law, 1208
20:19 The t of the law and the chief priests 1208
20:39 Some of the t of the law responded, 1208
20:46 "Beware of the t of the law. 1208
22: 2 and the t of the law were looking 1208
22:66 both the chief priests and t of the law, 1208
23:10 and the t of the law were standing there, 1208
Jn 8: 3 The t of the law and the Pharisees brought 1208
Ac 4: 5 elders and t of the law met in Jerusalem. 1208
6:12 and the elders and the t of the law. 1208
13: 1 at Antioch there were prophets and t: 1437
23: 9 the t of the law who were Pharisees stood 1208
1Co 12:28 third t, then workers of miracles, 1437
12:29 Are all prophets? Are all t? 1437
Eph 4:11 and some to be pastors and t, 1437
1Ti 1: 7 They want to be t of the law, 3791
2Ti 4: 3 of t to say what their itching ears want 1437
Heb 5:12 though by this time you ought to be t, 1437
Jas 3: 1 Not many of you should presume to be t, 1437
2Pe 2: 1 just as there will be false t among you. 6015
2: 3 In their greed these t will exploit you NIG

TEACHES (14) [TEACH]

Dt 33:10 He t your precepts to Jacob and your law 3723
Job 35:11 who t more to us than to the beasts of 544
Ps 25: 9 in what is right and t them his way. 4340
94:10 Does he who t man lack knowledge? 4340
Pr 15:33 The fear of the LORD t a man wisdom, 4592
Isa 28:26 His God instructs him and t him 3723
48:17 who t you what is best for you, 4340
Hab 2:18 Or an image that t lies? 3723
Mt 5:19 of these commandments and t others to do 1438
5:19 and t these commands will be called great 1438
Ac 21:28 This is the man who t all men everywhere 1438
1Ti 6: 3 If anyone t false doctrines and does 2281
Tit 2:12 It t us to say "No" to ungodliness 4084
1Jn 2:27 But as his anointing t you about all things 1438

TEACHING (89) [TEACH]

Dt 32: 2 Let my t fall like rain and my words 4375
Ezr 7:10 and to t its decrees and laws in Israel. 4340
Ps 60: T A miktam of David. For t. 4340
78: 1 O my people, hear my t; 9368
119:27 Let me understand the t of your precepts; 2006
Pr 1: 8 and do not forsake your mother's t. 9368
3: 1 My son, do not forget my t, 9368
4: 2 so do not forsake my t. 9368
6:20 and do not forsake your mother's t. 9368
6:23 commands are a lamp, this t is a light, 9368
13:14 The t of the wise is a fountain of life, 9368
22:21 t you true and reliable words, 3359
Jer 18:18 t of the law by the priest will not be lost, 9368
Eze 7:26 the t of the law by the priest will be lost, 9368
Mal 2: 8 the way and by your t have caused many 9368
Mt 4:23 t in their synagogues, 1438
7:28 the crowds were amazed at his t, 1439
9:35 t in their synagogues, 1438
13:54 he began t the people in their synagogue, 1438
16:12 the t of the Pharisees and Sadducees. 1439
21:23 and, while he was t, 1438
22:33 they were astonished at his t. 1439
26:55 Every day I sat in the temple courts t, 1438
28:20 and t them to obey everything I have 1438
Mk 1:22 The people were amazed at his t, 1439
1:27 A new t—and with authority! 1439
4: 2 by parables, and in his t said: 1439
6: 6 Jesus went around t from village to village. 1438
6:34 So he began t them many things. 1438
9:31 because he was t his disciples. 1438
11:18 the whole crowd was amazed at his t. 1439
12:35 While Jesus was t in the temple courts, 1438
14:49 t in the temple courts, 1438
Lk 4:32 They were amazed at his t, 1439
4:36 "What is this t? With authority and power 3364
5:17 One day as he was t, 1438
6: 6 into the synagogue and was t, 1438
13:10 On a Sabbath Jesus was t in one of 1438
13:22 t as he made his way to Jerusalem. 1438
19:47 Every day he was t at the temple. 1438
20: 1 as he was t the people in the temple courts 1438
21:37 Each day Jesus was t at the temple, 1438
23: 5 up the people all over Judea by his t. 1438
Jn 6:59 while t in the synagogue in Capernaum. 1438
6:60 "This is a hard t. Who can accept it?" 3364
7:16 Jesus answered, "My t is not my own. 1439
7:17 he will find out whether my t comes 1439
7:28 Then Jesus, still t in the temple courts, 1438
8:20 while t in the temple area near the place 1438
8:31 Jesus said, "If you hold to my t, 3364
14:23 "If anyone loves me, he will obey my t. 3364
14:24 not love me will not obey my t. 3364
15:20 If they obeyed my t, they will obey yours 3364
18:19 about his disciples and his t. 1439
Ac 2:42 They devoted themselves to the apostles' t 1439
4: 2 because the apostles were t the people 1438
5:25 in jail are standing in the temple courts t 1438
5:28 "Yet you have filled Jerusalem with your t 1439
5:42 they never stopped t and proclaiming 1438
13:12 for he was amazed at the t about the Lord. 1439
15: 1 down from Judea to Antioch and were t 1438
17:19 "May we know what this new t is 1439
18:11 t them the word of God. 1438
Ro 6:17 the form of t to which you were entrusted. 1439
12: 7 if it is t, let him teach; 1438
16:17 that are contrary to the t you have learned. 1439
Eph 4:14 by every wind of t and by the cunning 1436
Col 1:28 and t everyone with all wisdom, 1438
2Th 3: 6 according to the t you received from us. 4142
1Ti 4: 6 and of the good t that you have followed. 1436
4:13 to preaching and to t. 1436
5:17 especially those whose work is preaching and t. 1436
6: 1 so that God's name and our t may not be 1436
6: 3 of our Lord Jesus Christ and to godly t, 1436
2Ti 1:13 keep as the pattern of sound t, 3364
2:17 Their t will spread like gangrene. 3364
3:10 You, however, know all about my t, 1436
3:16 God-breathed and is useful for t, 1436
Tit 1:11 by t things they ought not to teach— 1438
2: 7 In your t show integrity, 1436
2:10 so that in every way they will make the t 1436
Heb 5:13 with the t about righteousness. 3364
2Jn 1: 9 in the t of Christ does not have God; 1439
1: 9 in the t has both the Father and the Son. 1439
1:10 comes to you and does not bring this t, 1439
Rev 2:14 You have people there who hold to the t 1439
2:15 also have those who hold to the t of 1439
2:20 By her t she misleads my servants 1438
2:24 to you who do not hold to her t and have 1439

TEACHINGS (9) [TEACH]

Pr 7: 2 guard my t as the apple of your eye. 9368
Mt 15: 9 their t are but rules taught by men.'" 1436+1438
Mk 7: 7 their t are but rules taught by men.' 1436+1438
1Co 11: 2 in everything and for holding to the t, 4142
Col 2:22 they are based on human commands and t. 1436
2Th 2:15 stand firm and hold to the t we passed on 1438
1Ti 4: 2 Such t come through hypocritical liars, NIG
Heb 6: 1 the elementary t about Christ and go on 3364
13: 9 be carried away by all kinds of strange t. 1439

TEAM (2) [TEAMS]

Isa 21: 9 here comes a man in a chariot with a t 7538
Mic 1:13 harness the t to the chariot. 8224

TEAMS (1) [TEAM]

Isa 21: 7 When he sees chariots with t of horses, 7538

TEAR (54) [TEARING, TEARS, TORE, TORN]

Ex 28:32 so that it will not t. 7973
39:23 so that it would not t. 7973
Lev 1:17 He shall t it open by the wings, 9117
10: 6 and do not t your clothes, 7268
13:56 he is to t the contaminated part out of 7973
21:10 his hair become unkempt or t his clothes. 7268
Jdg 6:25 T down your father's altar to Baal and cut 2238
8: 7 I will t your flesh with desert thorns 1889
8: 9 I will t down this tower." 5997
2Sa 3:31 "T your clothes and put on sackcloth 7973
1Ki 11:11 most certainly t the kingdom away 7973+7973
11:12 I will t it out of the hand of your son. 7973
11:13 I will not t the whole kingdom from him, 7973
11:31 to t the kingdom out of Solomon's hand 7973
Job 18: 4 You who t yourself to pieces in your anger, 3271
Ps 7: 2 or they will t me like a lion and rip me 3271
28: 5 he will t them down and never build them 2238
50:22 or I will t you to pieces, 3271
52: 5 He will snatch you up and t you 5815
58: 6 t out, O LORD, the fangs of the lions! 5997
137: 7 "T it down," they cried, 6867
137: 7 they cried, "t it down to its foundations!" 6867
Ecc 3: 3 a time to t down and a time to build, 7287
3: 7 a time to t and a time to mend, 7973
Isa 7: 6 let us t it apart and divide it among 7763
22:12 to t out your hair and put on sackcloth. 7947
Jer 1:10 and kingdoms to uproot and t down, 5997
5: 6 to t to pieces any who venture out, 3271
24: 6 I will build them up and not t them down; 2238
30: 8 and will t off their bonds; 5998
31:28 over them to uproot and t down, 5997
36:24 nor did they t their clothes. 7973
42:10 I will build you up and not t you down; 2238
La 2: 8 The LORD determined to t down the wall 8845
Eze 13:14 I will t down the wall you have covered 2238
13:20 and I will t them from your arms; 7973
13:21 I will t off your veils and save my people 7973
16:39 and they will t down your mounds 2238
19: 3 to t the prey and he devoured men. 3271
19: 6 to t the prey and he devoured men. 3271
23:34 you will dash it to pieces and t your breasts. 5998
Hos 5:14 I will t them to pieces and go away; 3271
13: 8 a wild animal will t them apart. 1324
Am 3:15 I will t down the winter house along with 5782
Mic 3: 2 who t the skin from my people and the flesh 1608
5:11 the cities of your land and t down 2238
Na 1:13 from your neck and t your shackles away." 5998
Mt 7: 6 and then turn and t you to pieces. 4838
9:16 away from the garment, making the t worse. 5388
Mk 2:21 pull away from the old, making the t worse. 5388
Lk 12:18 I will t down my barns and build 2747
Jn 19:24 "Let's not t it," they said to one another. 5387
Rev 7:17 And God will wipe away every t 1232
21: 4 He will wipe every t from their eyes. 1232

TEARING (6) [TEAR]

Dt 33:20 like a lion, t at arm or head. 3271
Ps 22:13 Roaring lions t their prey open their mouths 3271
Eze 22:25 within her like a roaring lion t its prey; 3271
22:27 within her are like wolves t their prey; 3271
Zec 11:16 of the choice sheep, t off their hoofs. 7293
2Co 13:10 for building you up, not for t you down. 2746

TEARS (45) [TEAR]

1Sa 2:33 be spared only to blind your eyes with t NIH
2Ki 20: 5 I have heard your prayer and seen your t; 1965
Job 12:14 What he t down cannot be rebuilt; 2238
16: 9 and t me in his anger and gnashes his teeth 3271
16:20 as my eyes pour out t to God; 1940
19:10 He t me down on every side till I am gone; 5997
31:38 and all its furrows are wet with t, 1134
Ps 6: 6 with weeping and drench my couch with t. 1965
42: 3 My t have been my food day and night, 1965
56: 8 list my t on your scroll— 1965
80: 5 You have fed them with the bread of t; 1965
80: 5 you have made them drink t by 1965
102: 9 as my food and mingle my drink with t 1140
116: 8 my eyes from t, my feet from stumbling, 1965
119:136 Streams of t flow from my eyes, 4784
126: 5 Those who sow in t will reap with songs 1965
Pr 14: 1 the foolish one t hers down. 2238
15:25 The LORD t down the proud man's house 5815
29: 4 but one who is greedy for bribes t it down. 2238
Ecc 4: 1 I saw the t of the oppressed— 1965
Isa 16: 9 O Elealeh, I drench you with t! 1965
25: 8 LORD will wipe away the t from all faces; 1965
38: 5 I have heard your prayer and seen your t; 1965
Jer 9: 1 of water and my eyes a fountain of t! 1965
9:18 with t and water streams from our eyelids. 1965

Jer 13:17 with **t**, because the LORD's flock will 1965
14:17 with **t** night and day without ceasing; 1965
31:16 from weeping and your eyes from **t**, 1965
50: 4 the people of Judah together will go *in* **t** 1134
La 1: 2 **t** are upon her cheeks. 1965
1:16 and my eyes overflow with **t**. 4784
2:18 let your **t** flow like a river day and night; 1965
3:48 Streams of **t** flow from my eyes 4784
Eze 24:16 Yet do not lament or weep or shed any **t**. 1965
Mal 2:13 You flood the LORD's altar with **t**. 1965
Lk 5:36 "No one **t** a patch from a new garment *5387*
7:38 she began to wet his feet *with* her **t**. *1232*
7:44 *with* her **t** and wiped them with her hair. *1232*
Ac 20:19 the Lord with great humility and with **t**, *1232*
20:31 of you night and day with **t**. *1232*
2Co 2: 4 and anguish of heart and with many **t**, *1232*
Php 3:18 before and now say again even **with t**, *3081*
2Ti 1: 4 Recalling your **t**, I long to see you, *1232*
Heb 5: 7 and petitions with loud cries and **t** to *1232*
12:17 though he sought the blessing with **t**. *1232*

TEATS (KJV) See BREASTS

TEBAH (3)

Ge 22:24 **T**, Gaham, Tahash and Maacah. 3182
2Sa 8: 8 From **T** and Berothai, 3183
1Ch 18: 8 From **T** and Cun, 3187

TEBALIAH (KJV) See TABALIAH

TEBETH (1)

Est 2:16 in the tenth month, the month of **T**, 3194

TEDIOUS (KJV) See WEARY

TEEM (2) [TEEMED, TEEMING, TEEMS]

Ge 1:20 *"Let* the water **t** *with* living creatures, 9237+9238
Ex 8: 3 The Nile *will* **t** *with* frogs. 9237

TEEMED (1) [TEEM]

Ps 105:30 Their land **t** *with* frogs, which went up into 9237

TEEMING (1) [TEEM]

Ps 104:25 **t** with **creatures** beyond number— 8254

TEEMS (1) [TEEM]

Ge 1:21 and moving thing with which the water **t**, 9237

TEETH (42) [TOOTH]

Ge 49:12 his **t** whiter than milk. 9094
Nu 11:33 while the meat was still between their **t** 9094
Job 4:10 yet the **t** *of* the great lions are broken. 9094
16: 9 and tears me in his anger and gnashes his **t** 9094
19:20 I have escaped with only the skin of my **t**. 9094
29:17 and snatched the victims from their **t**. 9094
41:14 ringed about with his fearsome **t**? 9094
Ps 3: 7 break the **t** *of* the wicked. 9094
35:16 they gnashed their **t** at me. 9094
37:12 the righteous and gnash their **t** at them; 9094
57: 4 men whose **t** are spears and arrows, 9094
58: 6 Break the **t** in their mouths, O God; 9094
112:10 he will gnash his **t** and waste away; 9094
124: 6 who has not let us be torn by their **t**. 9094
Pr 10:26 As vinegar to the **t** and smoke to the eyes, 9094
30:14 those whose **t** are swords 9094
SS 4: 2 Your **t** are like a flock of sheep just shorn, 9094
6: 6 Your **t** are like a flock of sheep coming up 9094
7: 9 flowing gently over lips and **t**. 9094
Isa 41:15 new and sharp, with **many t**. 7092
Jer 31:29 and the children's **t** are set on edge.' 9094
31:30 his own **t** will be set on edge. 9094
La 2:16 they scoff and gnash their **t** and say, 9094
3:16 He has broken my **t** with gravel; 9094
Eze 18: 2 and the children's **t** are set on edge'? 9094
Da 7: 5 it had three ribs in its mouth between its **t**. 10730
7: 7 It had large iron **t**; 10730
7:19 with its iron **t** and bronze claws— 10730
Joel 1: 6 it has the **t** *of* a lion, the fangs of a lioness. 9094
Am 1: 3 with sledges having iron **t**, NIH
Zec 9: 7 the forbidden food from between their **t**. 9094
Mt 8:12 there will be weeping and gnashing *of* **t**." *3848*
13:42 there will be weeping and gnashing *of* **t** *3848*
13:50 there will be weeping and gnashing *of* **t**. *3848*
22:13 be weeping and gnashing *of* **t**.' *3848*
24:51 there will be weeping and gnashing *of* **t**. *3848*
25:30 there will be weeping and gnashing *of* **t**.' *3848*
Mk 9:18 gnashes his **t** and becomes rigid. *3848*
Lk 13:28 be weeping there, and gnashing *of* **t**, *3848*
Ac 7:54 they were furious and gnashed their **t** *3848*
Rev 9: 8 and their **t** were like lions' teeth. *3848*
9: 8 and their teeth were like lions' **t**. *NIG*

TEHAPHNEHES (KJV) See TAHPANHES

TEHINNAH (1)

1Ch 4:12 Paseah and **T** the father of Ir Nahash. 9383

TEIL (KJV) See TEREBINTH

TEKEL (2)

Da 5:25 that was written: MENE, MENE, **T**, PARSIN 10770
5:27 **T**: You have been weighed on the scales 10770

TEKOA (13) [TEKOITE]

2Sa 14: 2 to **T** and had a wise woman brought 9541
14: 4 When the woman **from T** went to the king, 9542
14: 9 But the woman **from T** said to him, 9542
23:26 Helez the Paltite, Ira son of Ikkesh **from T**, 9542
1Ch 2:24 of Hezron bore him Ashhur the father of **T**. 9541
4: 5 Ashhur the father of **T** had two wives, 9541
11:28 Ira son of Ikkesh **from T**, 9542
2Ch 11: 6 Bethlehem, Etam, **T**, 9541
20:20 in the morning they left for the Desert of **T**. 9541
Ne 3: 5 section was repaired by the **men of T**, 9542
3:27 the **men of T** repaired another section, 9542
Jer 6: 1 Sound the trumpet in **T**! 9541
Am 1: 1 words of Amos, one of the shepherds of **T** 9541

TEKOITE (1) [TEKOA]

1Ch 27: 9 was Ira the son of Ikkesh the **T**. 9542

TEL ABIB (1)

Eze 3:15 I came to the exiles who lived at **T** 9425

TEL ASSAR (2)

2Ki 19:12 the people of Eden who were in **T**? 9431
Isa 37:12 the people of Eden who were in **T**? 9431

TEL HARSHA (2) [HARSHA]

Ezr 2:59 **T**, Kerub, Addon and Immer, 9426
Ne 7:61 **T**, Kerub, Addon and Immer, 9426

TEL MELAH (2)

Ezr 2:59 of **T**, Tel Harsha, Kerub, Addon 9427
Ne 7:61 of **T**, Tel Harsha, Kerub, Addon 9427

TELAH (1)

1Ch 7:25 Resheph his son, **T** his son, Tahan his son, 9436

TELAIM (1)

1Sa 15: 4 the men and mustered them at **T**— 3230

TELEM (2)

Jos 15:24 Ziph, **T**, Bealoth, 3234
Ezr 10:24 From the gatekeepers: Shallum, **T** and Uri. 3235

TELL (576) [TELLING, TELLS, TOLD]

Ge 12:18 "Why didn't *you* **t** me she was your wife? 5583
21:26 You *did* not **t** me, and I heard about it 5583
22: 2 of the mountains *I will* **t** you *about.*" 606
24:23 Please **t** me, is there room 5583
24:30 and had heard Rebekah **t** what 606+1821
24:33 "Then **t** us," [Laban] said. 1819
24:49 and faithfulness to my master, **t** me; 5583
24:49 **t** me, so I may know which way to turn." 5583
26: 2 live in the land where *I* **t** you to live. 606
27: 8 listen carefully and do what I **t** you: 7422
29:15 **T** me what your wages should be." 5583
31:27 Why didn't *you* **t** me, so I could send you 5583
32:29 Jacob said, "Please **t** me your name." 5583
37:16 *Can you* **t** me where they are 5583
40: 8 **T** me your dreams." 6218
41:21 no *one could* **t** that they had done so; 3359
42:22 "Didn't *I* **t** you not to sin against the boy? 606
45:13 **T** my father *about* all the honor 5583
45:17 Pharaoh said to Joseph, "**T** your brothers, 606
45:19 "You are also directed to **t** them, 'Do this: NIH
49: 1 around so *I can* **t** you what will happen 5583
50: 4 speak to Pharaoh for me. **T** him, 606
Ex 3:13 Then what *shall I* **t** them?" 606
6:11 **t** Pharaoh king of Egypt to let 1819
6:29 **T** Pharaoh king of Egypt everything I tell 1819
6:29 king of Egypt everything I **t** you." 1819
7: 2 and your brother Aaron *is to* **t** Pharaoh 1819
7:19 The LORD said to Moses, "**T** Aaron, 606
8: 5 Then the LORD said to Moses, "**T** Aaron, 606
8:16 Then the LORD said to Moses, "**T** Aaron, 606
10: 2 that *you may* **t** your children 6218
11: 2 **T** the people that men and women 265+928+1819
12: 3 **T** the whole community of Israel that on 1819
12:27 then **t** them, 'It is the Passover sacrifice to 606
13: 8 On that day **t** your son, 5583
14: 2 "**T** the Israelites to turn back and encamp 1819
14:15 **T** the Israelites to move on. 1819
16:12 **T** them, 'At twilight you will eat meat, 1819
19: 3 and what *you are to* **t** the people of Israel: 5583
19:12 around the mountain and **t** them, 606
20:22 "**T** the Israelites this: 606
25: 2 "**T** the Israelites to bring me an offering. 1819
28: 3 **T** all the skilled men to whom I have given 1819
33: 5 For the LORD had said to Moses, "**T** 606
Lev 14:35 the owner of the house must go and **t** 5583
16: 2 "**T** your brother Aaron not to come 1819
22: 2 "**T** Aaron and his sons to treat with respect 1819
Nu 6:23 "**T** Aaron and his sons, 1819
9:10 "**T** the Israelites: 'When any of you 1819
11:12 Why *do you* **t** me to carry them 606
11:18 "**T** the people: 'Consecrate yourselves 606
14:14 And *they will* **t** the inhabitants of this land 606
14:28 So **t** them, 'As surely as I live, 606
16:37 "**T** Eleazar son of Aaron, the priest, to take 606
19: 2 **T** the Israelites to bring you a red heifer 1819
22:19 find out what else the LORD *will* **t** me." 1819
22:20 go with them, but do only what *I* **t** you." 1819
22:35 but speak only what *I* **t** you." 1819
23: 3 Whatever he reveals to me *I will* **t** you." 5583
23:26 *"Did I* not **t** you I must do whatever 1819
24:12 *"Did I* not **t** the messengers you sent me, 1819
25:12 Therefore **t** him I am making my covenant 606
Dt 1:42 But the LORD said to me, "**T** them, 606
5:27 Then **t** us whatever the LORD tells you. 1819
5:30 "Go, **t** them to return to their tents. 606
6:21 **t** him: "We were slaves of Pharaoh 606
17:11 Do not turn aside from what *they* **t** you, 5583
18:18 *he will* **t** them everything I command him. 1819
32: 7 Ask your father and *he will* **t** you, 5583
Jos 1:11 "Go through the camp and **t** the people, 7422
2:14 "If *you* don't **t** what we are doing, 5583
2:20 But if *you* **t** what we are doing, 5583
3: 8 **T** the priests who carry the ark of 7422
4: 3 and **t** them to take up twelve stones from 7422
4: 7 **t** them that the flow of the Jordan 606
4:22 **t** them, 'Israel crossed the Jordan on dry 3359
6:10 do not say a word until the day I **t** you 606
7:13 **T** them, 'Consecrate yourselves 606
7:19 **T** me what you have done; 5583
20: 2 "**T** the Israelites to designate the cities 1819
Jdg 2: 3 Now therefore *I* **t** you that I will 606
13: 6 and *he* didn't **t** me his name. 5583
13:10 The woman hurried *to* **t** her husband, 5583
14: 9 not **t** them that he had taken the honey 5583
14:12 *"Let me* **t** you a riddle," 2554
14:13 If you can't **t** me *the* **answer,** 5583
14:13 "**T** us your riddle," they said. 2554
16: 6 "**T** me the secret of your great strength and 5583
16:10 Come now, **t** me how you can be tied." 5583
16:13 **T** me how you can be tied." 5583
19:30 **T** us what to do!" 1819
20: 3 "**T** us how this awful thing happened." 1819
Ru 3: 4 He *will* **t** you what to do." 5583
4: 4 But if you will not, **t** me, so I will know. 5583
1Sa 3:15 He was afraid *to* **t** Eli the vision, 5583
6: 2 **T** us how we should send it back 3359
9: 6 Perhaps *he will* **t** us what way to take." 5583
9: 8 so that *he will* **t** us what way to take." 5583
9:18 *"Would you* please **t** me where 5583
9:19 and *will* **t** you all that is in your heart. 5583
9:27 "**T** the servant to go on ahead of us"— 606
10: 8 until I come to you and **t** you what you are 3359
10:15 "**T** me what Samuel said to you." 5583
10:16 not **t** his uncle what Samuel had said about 5583
14: 1 But *he did* not **t** his father. 5583
14:34 "Go out among the men and **t** them, 606
14:43 "**T** me what you have done." 5583
15:16 *"Let me* **t** you what the LORD said 5583
15:16 "**T** me," Saul replied. 1819
19: 3 about you and *will* **t** you what I find out." 5583
20: 6 If your father misses me at all, **t** him, 606
20: 9 to harm you, wouldn't *I* **t** you?" 5583
20:10 "Who *will* **t** me if your father answers you 5583
22:17 yet *they did* not **t** me." 265+906+1655
22:22 I knew *he would* **be sure to t** Saul. 5583+5583
23:11 O LORD, God of Israel, **t** your servant." 5583
23:22 *They* **t** me he is very crafty. 606
25: 8 and *they will* **t** you. 5583
25:19 But *she did* not **t** her husband Nabal. 5583
28:15 I have called on you to **t** me what to do." 3359
2Sa 1: 4 David asked. "**T** me." 5583
1:20 "**T** it not in Gath, 5583
3:19 to Hebron to **t** David everything that Israel 1819
7: 5 "Go and **t** my servant David, 'This is what 606
7: 8 "Now then, **t** my servant David, 606
12:18 David's servants were afraid to **t** him that 5583
12:18 How *can we* **t** him the child is dead? 606
13: 4 Won't *you* **t** me?" 5583
15:35 **T** them anything you hear in 5583
17:16 a message immediately and **t** David, 'Do 5583
17:17 and they were to go and **t** King David, 5583
18:21 "Go, **t** the king what you have seen." 5583
19:35 *Can I* **t the difference** between what is good 3359
20:16 **T** Joab to come here so I can speak 606
24:12 "Go and **t** David, 'This is what 1819
1Ki 12:10 "**T** these people who have said to you, 606
12:10 but make our yoke lighter'—**t** them, 1819
14: 3 He *will* **t** you what will happen to 5583
14: 7 **t** Jeroboam that this is what the LORD, 606
18: 8 "Go **t** your master, 'Elijah is here.' " 606
18:11 now you **t** me to go to my master and say, 606
18:12 If I go and **t** Ahab and he doesn't find you, 5583
18:14 now you **t** me to go to my master and say, 606
18:44 So Elijah said, "Go and **t** Ahab, 606
20: 9 "**T** my lord the king, 606
20:11 The king of Israel answered, "**T** him: 1819
22:14 *I can* **t** him only what the LORD tells me." 1819
22:16 *to* **t** me nothing but the truth in the name 1819
22:18 "Didn't *I* **t** you that he never prophesies 606
2Ki 1: 6 and **t** him, "This is what the LORD says: 1819
2: 9 Elijah said to Elisha, "**T** me, 8626
2:18 "Didn't *I* **t** you not to go?" 606
4: 2 **T** me, what do you have in your house?" 5583
4:13 Elisha said to him, "**T** her, 606
4:24 don't slow down for me unless *I* **t** you." 606
4:28 "Didn't *I* **t** you, 'Don't raise my hopes'?" 606
6:11 *"Will you* not **t** me which of us is on 5583
7:12 *"I will* **t** you what the Arameans have done 5583
8: 4 "**T** me *about* all the great things Elisha 6218

2Ki 9:12 “That's not true!” they said. “T us.” 5583
9:15 of the city to go and t the news in Jezreel.” 5583
18:19 “T Hezekiah: “ ‘This is what 606
19: 6 “T your master, ‘This is what 606
20: 5 “Go back and t Hezekiah, the leader 606
22:15 T the man who sent you to me, 606
22:18 T the king of Judah, who sent you 606
1Ch 16: 9 t of all his wonderful acts. 8488
17: 4 “Go and t my servant David, ‘This is what 606
17: 7 “Now then, t my servant David, 606
21:10 “Go and t David, ‘This is what 1819
21:18 the LORD ordered Gad to t David to go 606
2Ch 10:10 “T the people who have said to you, 606
10:10 but make our yoke lighter’—t them, 606
18:13 *I can* t him only what my God says.” 1819
18:15 *to* t me nothing but the truth in the name 1819
18:17 “Didn't *I* t you that he never prophesies 606
34:23 T the man who sent you to me, 606
34:26 T the king of Judah, who sent you 606
Job 1:15 the only one who has escaped to t you!” 5583
1:16 the only one who has escaped to t you!” 5583
1:17 the only one who has escaped to t you!” 5583
1:19 the only one who has escaped to t you!” 5583
4:16 It stopped, but *I could* not t what it was. 5795
8:10 Will they not instruct you and t you? 606
10: 2 t me what charges you have against me. 3359
12: 7 or the birds of the air, and *they will* t you; 5583
15:17 *let me* t you what I have seen, 6218
32: 6 not daring *to* t you what I know. 2555
32:10 I too *will* t you what I know. 2555
32:17 I too *will* t what I know. 2555
33:12 “But *I* t you, in this you are not right, 6699
33:23 to t a man what is right for him, 5583
34:33 so t me what you know. 1819
37:19 “T us what we should say to him; 3359
38: 4 T me, if you understand. 5583
38:18 T me, if you know all this. 5583
Ps 5: 6 You destroy *those who* t lies; 1819
9: 1 *I will* t *of* all your wonders. 6218
40: 5 were I to speak and t of them, 1819
48:13 *you may* t of them to the next generation. 6218
50:12 If I were hungry *I would* not t you, 606
66:16 *let me* t you what he has done for me. 6218
71:15 My mouth *will* t *of* your righteousness, 6218
71:24 My tongue *will* t *of* your righteous acts 2047
73:28 I *will* t *of* all your deeds. 6218
75: 1 *men* t *of* your wonderful deeds. 6218
78: 4 we *will* t the next generation 6218
78: 6 and *they* in turn *would* t their children. 6218
105: 2 t of all his wonderful acts. 8488
107:22 Let them sacrifice thank offerings and t 6218
142: 2 before him *I* t my trouble. 5583
145: 4 *they will* t *of* your mighty acts. 5583
145: 6 *They will* t *of* the power of your awesome 606
145:11 *They will* t *of* the glory of your kingdom 606
Pr 30: 4 T me if you know! NIH
Ecc 6:12 Who *can* t him what will happen under 5583
8: 7 who *can* t him what is to come? 5583
10:14 who *can* t him what will happen after him? 5583
SS 1: 7 T me, you whom I love, 5583
5: 8 you find my lover, what *will you* t him? 5583
5: 8 T him I am faint with love. NIH
Isa 3:10 T the righteous it will be well with them, 606
5: 5 Now *I will* t you what I am going to do 3359
6: 9 He said, “Go and t this people: 606
8:19 When *men* t you to consult mediums 606
21:10 *I* t you what I have heard from 5583
30:10 T us pleasant things, prophesy illusions. 1819
36: 4 “T Hezekiah, “ ‘This is what the great king 606
37: 6 “T your master, ‘This is what the LORD 606
38: 5 and t Hezekiah, ‘This is what the LORD, 606
38:19 fathers t their children about your 3359
41:22 “Bring in [your idols] *to* t us what is going 5583
41:22 T us what the former things were, 5583
41:23 t us what the future holds, 5583
41:27 I was the first to t Zion, ‘Look, NIH
48: 6 now on *I will* t you *of* new things, 9048
63: 7 *I will* t *of* the kindnesses of the LORD, 2349
Jer 4:16 “T this to the nations, 2349
5:19 *you will* t them, ‘As you have forsaken me 606
7:27 “When *you* t them all this, 1819
10:11 “T them this: ‘These gods, who did not 10042
11: 2 to the terms of this covenant and t them to 1819
11: 3 T them that this is what the LORD, 606
13:13 then t them, ‘This is what the LORD says: 606
15: 2 t them, ‘This is what the LORD says: 606
16:10 “When *you* t these people all this 5583
19: 2 There proclaim the words *I* t you, 1819
21: 3 But Jeremiah answered them, “T Zedekiah, 606
21: 8 “Furthermore, t the people, ‘This is what 606
23:27 dreams *they* t one another will make my people forget my name, 6218
23:28 the prophet who has a dream t his dream, 6218
23:32 “*They* t them and lead my people astray 6218
25:27 “Then t them, ‘This is what the LORD 606
25:28 t them, ‘This is what the LORD Almighty 606
26: 2 T them everything I command you; 1819
27: 4 “T this to your masters: 606
27: 9 your mediums or your sorcerers who t you, 606
28:13 “Go and t Hananiah, ‘This is what the LORD 606
29:23 which *I did* not t them to do. 7422
29:24 T Shemaiah the Nehelamite, 606
33: 3 and I will answer you and t you great 5583
34: 2 Go to Zedekiah king of Judah and t him, 606
35:13 Go and t the men of Judah and the people 606
36:17 Then they asked Baruch, “T us, 5583
36:29 Also t Jehoiakim king of Judah, 606
Jer 37: 7 T the king of Judah, ‘This is what the LORD 606
38:20 “Obey the LORD by doing what I t you. 1819
38:25 ‘T us what you said to the king and what 5583
38:26 then t them, ‘I was pleading with the king 606
39:16 “Go and t Ebed-Melech the Cushite, 606
42: 3 Pray that the LORD your God *will* t us 5583
42: 4 *I will* t you everything the LORD says 5583
42: 5 the LORD your God sends you to t us. NIH
42:20 t us everything he says and we will do it.’ 5583
42:21 in all he sent me to t you. NIH
43: 1 the LORD had sent him to t them— NIH
51:10 come, *let us* t in Zion what the LORD 6218
Eze 13:11 t those who cover it with whitewash 606
14: 4 Therefore speak to them and t them, 606
17: 2 set forth an allegory and t the house 5439
24: 3 T this rebellious house a parable and say 5439
24:19 “Won't *you* t us what these things have 5583
24:26 on that day a fugitive will come to t you NIH
33:13 If I t the righteous man that he will 606
37:18 ‘Won't *you* t us what you mean by this?’ 5583
40: 4 T the house of Israel everything you see.” 5583
44: 5 and give attention to everything I t you 1819
Da 2: 2 to t him what he had dreamed. 5583
2: 4 T your servants the dream, 10042
2: 5 If *you do* not t me what my dream was 10313
2: 6 But if *you* t me the dream and explain it, 10252
2: 6 So t me the dream and interpret it for me.” 10252
2: 7 “*Let* the king t his servants the dream, 10042
2: 9 If *you do* not t me the dream, 10313
2: 9 You have conspired to t me misleading 10042
2: 9 So then, t me the dream, 10042
2:25 among the exiles from Judah who *can* t 10313
2:26 “Are you able to t me what I saw 10313
4: 2 to t you *about* the miraculous signs 10252
4:18 Now, Belteshazzar, t me what it means, 10042
5: 8 but they could not read the writing or t 10313
5:12 and *he will* t you what the writing means.” 10252
5:15 and t me what it means, 10313
5:16 and t me what it means, 10313
5:17 for the king and t him what it means. 10313
8:16 t this man **the meaning** of the vision.” 1067
8:19 *to* t you what will happen later in the time 3359
9:23 which I have come to t you, 5583
10:21 but first *I will* t you what is written in 5583
11: 2 “Now then, *I* t you the truth: 5583
Joel 1: 3 T it to your children, 6218
1: 3 and let your children t it to their children, NIH
Jnh 1: 8 So they asked him, “T us, 5583
4:11 a hundred and twenty thousand people who cannot t their right hand 3359
Mic 1:10 T it not in Gath; weep not at all. 5583
3:11 and her prophets t **fortunes** for money. 7876
Hag 2:21 “T Zerubbabel governor of Judah 606
Zec 1: 3 Therefore t the people: 606
2: 4 “Run, t that young man, 1819
6:12 T him this is what the LORD Almighty 606
10: 2 *they* t dreams that are false, 1819
Mt 2:13 Stay there until *I* t you, *3306*
3: 9 *I* t you that out of these stones *3306*
4: 3 t these stones to become bread.” *3306*
5:18 *I* t you the truth, until heaven and earth *3306*
5:20 For *I* t you that unless your righteousness *3306*
5:22 But I t you that anyone who is angry *3306*
5:26 *I* t you the truth, you will not get out *3306*
5:28 But I t you that anyone who looks at *3306*
5:32 I t you that anyone who divorces his wife, *3306*
5:34 But I t you, Do not swear at all: *3306*
5:39 But I t you, Do not resist an evil person. *3306*
5:44 But I t you: Love your enemies *3306*
6: 2 *I* t you the truth, they have received *3306*
6: 5 *I* t you the truth, they have received *3306*
6:16 *I* t you the truth, they have received *3306*
6:25 “Therefore *I* t you, do not worry *3306*
6:29 Yet *I* t you that not even Solomon *3306*
7:23 Then *I will* t them **plainly,** *3933*
8: 4 “See that *you* don't t anyone. *3306*
8: 9 *I* t this one, ‘Go,’ and he goes; *3306*
8:10 “*I* t you the truth, I have not found anyone *3306*
10:15 *I* t you the truth, it will be more bearable *3306*
10:23 *I* t you the truth, you will not finish going *3306*
10:27 What *I* t you in the dark, *3306*
10:42 *I* t you the truth, he will certainly not lose *3306*
11: 9 Yes, *I* t you, and more than a prophet. *3306*
11:11 *I* t you the truth: Among those born of *3306*
11:22 But *I* t you, it will be more bearable *3306*
11:24 But *I* t you that it will be more bearable *3306*
12: 6 *I* t you that one greater than the temple *3306*
12:16 warning them not to t who he was. *4472+5745*
12:31 And so *I* t you, every sin and blasphemy *3306*
12:36 But *I* t you that men will have *3306*
13:17 For *I* t you the truth, many prophets and *3306*
13:30 At that time *I will* t the harvesters: *3306*
14:28 “t me to come to you on the water.” *3027*
16:18 And I t you that you are Peter, *3306*
16:20 not *to* t anyone that he was the Christ. *3306*
16:28 *I* t you the truth, some who are standing *3306*
17: 9 “Don't t anyone what you have seen, *3306*
17:12 But *I* t you, Elijah has already come, *3306*
17:20 *I* t you the truth, if you have faith as small *3306*
18: 3 And he said: “*I* t you the truth, *3306*
18:10 For *I* t you that their angels *3306*
18:13 And if he finds it, *I* t you the truth, *3306*
18:17 t it to the church; and if he refuses *3306*
18:18 “*I* t you the truth, whatever you bind on *3306*
18:19 *I* t you that if two of you on earth agree *3306*
18:22 Jesus answered, “*I* t you, not seven times, *3306*
19: 9 *I* t you that anyone who divorces his wife, *3306*
Mt 19:23 “*I* t you the truth, it is hard for a rich man *3306*
19:24 Again *I* t you, it is easier for a camel *3306*
19:28 Jesus said to them, “*I* t you the truth, *3306*
21: 3 t him that the Lord needs them, *3306*
21:21 Jesus replied, “*I* t you the truth, *3306*
21:24 I *will* t you by what authority I am doing *3306*
21:27 “Neither *will* I t you by what authority *3306*
21:31 Jesus said to them, “*I* t you the truth, *3306*
21:43 “Therefore *I* t you that the kingdom *3306*
22: 3 to the banquet *to* t them to come, *2813*
22: 4 ‘T those who have been invited *3306*
22:17 T us then, what is your opinion? *3306*
23: 3 and do everything *they* t you. *3306*
23:36 *I* t you the truth, all this will come upon this *3306*
23:39 For *I* t you, you will not see me again until *3306*
24: 2 “*I* t you the truth, not one stone here will be *3306*
24: 3 “T us,” they said, “when will this happen, *3306*
24:34 *I* t you the truth, this generation *3306*
24:47 *I* t you the truth, he will put him in charge *3306*
25:12 “But he replied, ‘*I* t you the truth, *3306*
25:40 “The King will reply, ‘*I* t you the truth, *3306*
25:45 “He will reply, ‘*I* t you the truth, *3306*
26:13 *I* t you the truth, wherever this gospel is *3306*
26:18 into the city to a certain man and t him, *3306*
26:21 they were eating, he said, “*I* t you the truth, *3306*
26:29 *I* t you, I will not drink of this fruit of *3306*
26:34 “*I* t you the truth,” Jesus answered, *3306*
26:63 T us if you are the Christ, the Son of God.” *3306*
27:64 and t the people that he has been raised *3306*
28: 7 Then go quickly and t his disciples: *3306*
28: 8 and ran *to* t his disciples. *550*
28:10 Go and t my brothers to go to Galilee; *550*
Mk 1:44 “See that *you* don't t this to anyone. *3306*
2:11 “*I* t you, get up, take your mat *3306*
3:12 not to t who he was. *4472+5745*
3:28 *I* t you the truth, *3306*
5:19 and t them how much the Lord has done *550*
5:20 So the man went away and began *to* t in *3062*
7:36 Jesus commanded them not to t anyone. *3306*
8:12 *I* t you the truth, all sins and blasphemies *3306*
8:30 Jesus warned them not *to* t anyone *3306*
9: 1 And he said to them, “*I* t you the truth, *3306*
9: 9 not *to* t anyone what they had seen until *1455*
9:13 But *I* t you, Elijah has come, *3306*
9:41 *I* t you the truth, anyone who gives you *3306*
10:15 *I* t you the truth, anyone who will not *3306*
10:29 “*I* t you the truth,” Jesus replied, *3306*
11: 3 t him, ‘The Lord needs it *3306*
11:23 “*I* t you the truth, if anyone says to this *3306*
11:24 Therefore *I* t you, whatever you ask for *3306*
11:29 *I will* t you by what authority I am doing *3306*
11:30 from heaven, or from men? T me!” *646*
11:33 “Neither *will* I t you by what authority *3306*
12:43 Jesus said, “*I* t you the truth, *3306*
13: 4 “T us, when will these things happen? *3306*
13:30 *I* t you the truth, this generation *3306*
14: 9 *I* t you the truth, wherever this gospel is *3306*
14:18 he said, “*I* t you the truth, *3306*
14:25 “*I* t you the truth, I will not drink again *3306*
14:30 “*I* t you the truth,” Jesus answered, *3306*
16: 7 But go, t his disciples and Peter, *3306*
Lk 1:19 and to t you this **good news.** *2294*
3: 8 For *I* t you that out of these stones God can *3306*
4: 3 t this stone to become bread.” *3306*
4:24 “*I* t you the truth,” he continued, *3306*
5:14 Then Jesus ordered him, “Don't t anyone, *3306*
5:24 He said to the paralyzed man, “*I* t you, *3306*
6:27 “But *I* t you who hear me: *3306*
7: 8 *I* t this one, ‘Go,’ and he goes; *3306*
7: 9 he said, “*I* t you, I have not found such *3306*
7:26 Yes, *I* t you, and more than a prophet. *3306*
7:28 *I* t you, among those born of women *3306*
7:40 “Simon, I have something *to* t you.” *3306*
7:40 “T me, teacher,” he said. *3306*
7:47 *I* t you, her many sins have been forgiven— *3306*
8:39 and t how much God has done for you.” *1455*
8:56 not *to* t anyone what had happened. *3306*
9:21 Jesus strictly warned them not *to* t this *3306*
9:27 *I* t you the truth, some who are standing *3306*
9:44 to what I **am about to** t *you:* *3364+3836+4047*
10: 9 Heal the sick who are there and t them, *3306*
10:12 *I* t you, it will be more bearable on *3306*
10:24 For *I* t you that many prophets *3306*
10:40 T her to help me!” *3306*
11: 8 *I* t you, though he will not get up *3306*
11:51 *I* t you, this generation will be held *3306*
12: 4 “*I* t you, my friends, do not be afraid of *3306*
12: 5 Yes, *I* t you, fear him. *3306*
12: 8 “*I* t you, whoever acknowledges me *3306*
12:13 t my brother to divide the inheritance *3306*
12:22 “Therefore *I* t you, do not worry *3306*
12:27 Yet *I* t you, not even Solomon in all his *3306*
12:37 *I* t you the truth, he will dress himself to *3306*
12:44 *I* t you the truth, he will put him in charge *3306*
12:51 No, *I* t you, but division. *3306*
12:59 *I* t you, you will not get out until you have *3306*
13: 3 *I* t you, no! *3306*
13: 5 *I* t you, no! *3306*
13:24 because many, *I* t you, will try to enter *3306*
13:32 He replied, “Go t that fox, *3306*
13:35 *I* t you, you will not see me again *3306*
14:17 *to* t those who had been invited, *3306*
14:24 *I* t you, not one of those men *3306*
15: 7 *I* t you that in the same way there will *3306*
15:10 In the same way, *I* t you, there is rejoicing *3306*
16: 9 I t you, use worldly wealth to gain friends *3306*
17:23 *Men will* t you, ‘There he is!’ *3306*

Lk 17:34 *I* t you, on that night two people will be *3306*
18: 8 *I* t you, he will see that they get justice, *3306*
18:14 "*I* t you that this man, rather than the other, *3306*
18:17 *I* t you the truth, anyone who will not *3306*
18:29 "*I* t you the truth," Jesus said to them, *3306*
19:11 *he* went on *to* t them a parable, *3306*
19:26 '*I* t you that to everyone who has, *3306*
19:31 t him, 'The Lord needs it.' " *3306*
19:40 "*I* t you," he replied, "if they keep quiet, *3306*
20: 2 "T us by what authority you are doing these things," *3306*
20: 3 "I will also ask you a question. T me, *3306*
20: 8 "Neither *will* I t you by what authority *3306*
20: 9 He went on *to* t the people this parable: *3306*
21: 3 "*I* t you the truth," he said, *3306*
21:32 "*I* t you the truth, *3306*
22:16 For *I* t you, this generation *3306*
22:18 For *I* t you I will not drink again of *3306*
22:34 Jesus answered, "*I* t you, Peter, *3306*
22:37 *I* t you that this must be fulfilled in me. *3306*
22:67 "If you are the Christ," they said, "t us." *3306*
22:67 Jesus answered, "If *I* t you, *3306*
23:43 Jesus answered him, "*I* t you the truth, *3306*
Jn 1:41 to find his brother Simon and t him, *3306*
1:51 He then added, "*I* t you the truth, *3306*
3: 3 In reply Jesus declared, "*I* t you the truth, *3306*
3: 5 Jesus answered, "*I* t you the truth, *3306*
3: 8 but *you* cannot t where it comes from or *3857*
3:11 *I* t you the truth, we speak of what we know *3306*
4:35 *I* t you, open your eyes and look at *3306*
5:19 "*I* t you the truth, the Son can do nothing by *3306*
5:24 "*I* t you the truth, whoever hears my word *3306*
5:25 *I* t you the truth, a time is coming *3306*
6:26 Jesus answered, "*I* t you the truth, *3306*
6:32 Jesus said to them, "*I* t you the truth, *3306*
6:47 *I* t you the truth, he who believes has *3306*
6:53 Jesus said to them, "*I* t you the truth, *3306*
8:26 and what I have heard from him *I* t *3281*
8:34 Jesus replied, "*I* t you the truth, *3306*
8:45 I t the truth, you do not believe me! *3306*
8:51 *I* t you the truth, if anyone keeps my word, *3306*
8:58 "*I* t you the truth," Jesus answered, *3306*
9:36 "T me so that I may believe in him." *NIG*
10: 1 "*I* t you the truth, the man who does not *3306*
10: 7 Jesus said again, "*I* t you the truth, *3306*
10:24 If you are the Christ, t us plainly." *3306*
10:25 Jesus answered, "*I did* t you, *3306*
11:11 *he* went on *to* t them, "Our friend Lazarus *3306*
11:40 "*Did I* not t you that if you believed, *3306*
12:22 Philip went *to* t Andrew; *3306*
12:24 *I* t you the truth, unless a kernel of wheat *3306*
13:16 *I* t you the truth, no servant is greater than *3306*
13:20 *I* t you the truth, whoever accepts anyone *3306*
13:21 "*I* t you the truth, one of you is going to *3306*
13:33 and just as I told the Jews, so *I* t you now: *3306*
13:38 *I* t you the truth, before the rooster crows, *3306*
14:12 *I* t you the truth, anyone who has faith in me *3306*
16: 4 *I did* not t you this at first because I was *3306*
16: 7 But I t you the truth: It is for your good *3306*
16:13 and *he will* t you what is yet to come. *334*
16:20 *I* t you the truth, you will weep *3306*
16:23 *I* t you the truth, my Father will give you *3306*
16:25 but *will* t you plainly about my Father. *550*
20:15 t me where you have put him, *3306*
20:17 Go instead to my brothers and t them, *3306*
21:18 *I* t you the truth, when you were younger *3306*
Ac 2:29 *I* can t you confidently that the patriarch *3306*
5: 8 Peter asked her, "T me, is this the price *3306*
5:20 "and t the people the full message *3281*
8:34 The eunuch asked Philip, "T me, please, *NIG*
10:33 the Lord has commanded you to t us." *NIG*
12:17 "T James and the brothers about this," *550*
13:32 "*We* t you the good news: *2294*
21:23 so do what *we* t you. *3306*
22:27 "T me, are you a Roman citizen?" *3306*
23:17 he has something *to* t him." *550*
23:18 because he has something *to* t you." *3281*
23:19 "What is it you want *to* t me?" *550*
23:22 and cautioned him, "Don't t anyone *1718*
Ro 15: 8 For *I* t you that Christ has become *3306*
1Co 12: 3 Therefore *I* t you that no one who is *1192*
15:51 Listen, *I* t you a mystery: *3306*
2Co 6: 2 I t you, now is the time of God's favor, *2627*
12: 4 things that man is not permitted *to* t. *3281*
Gal 4:21 T me, you who want to be under the law, *3306*
5: 2 Paul, t you that if you let yourselves be *3306*
Eph 4:17 So *I* t you this, and insist on it in the Lord, *3306*
6:21 *will* t you everything, so that you also may *1192*
Col 2: 4 *I* t you this so that no one may deceive you *3306*
4: 7 Tychicus *will* t you all the news *1192*
4: 9 *They will* t you everything *1192*
4:17 T Archippus: "See to it that you complete *3306*
1Th 1: 9 They t how you turned to God from idols *NIG*
2: 2 of our God we dared *to* t you his gospel *3281*
4:15 *we* t you that we who are still alive, *3306*
2Th 2: 5 with you *I used to* t you these things? *3306*
Heb 11:32 I do not have time *to* t about Gideon, *1455*
3Jn 1: 3 and t about your faithfulness to the truth *3455*
Rev 2:10 I t you, the devil will put some of you *2627*

TELLING (36) [TELL]

Ge 31:20 by not t him he was running away. 5583
42:16 be tested to see if you are t the truth. NIH
43: 6 "Why did you bring this trouble on me by t 5583
Ex 33:12 "You *have been* t me, 'Lead these people,' 606
Jdg 7:13 Gideon arrived just as a man *was* t a friend 6218
2Ki 8: 5 Just as Gehazi was t the king 6218
Ne 6:19 and then t him what I said. 3655
Ps 26: 7 proclaiming aloud your praise and t 6218
Jer 14:13 the prophets *keep* t them, 606
26: 8 But as soon as Jeremiah finished t all 1819
38: 1 of Malkijah heard what Jeremiah *was* t all 1819
43: 1 When Jeremiah finished t the people all 1819
Eze 20:49 'Isn't he *just* t parables?' " 5439
Mt 16:12 not t them to guard against the yeast used *3306*
28:13 t them, "You are to say, 'His disciples came *3306*
Mk 14:13 So he sent two of his disciples, t them, *3306*
Lk 12:41 "Lord, *are you* t this parable to us, *3306*
Jn 8:27 not understand that *he was* t them about *3306*
8:38 *I am* t you what I have seen in *3281*
8:46 If *I am* t the truth, why don't you believe *3306*
10: 6 not understand what he was t them. *3281*
13:19 "*I am* t you now before it happens, *3306*
13:29 some thought Jesus *was* t him *3306*
Ac 10:36 t the good news of peace through Jesus *2294*
11: 7 Then I heard a voice t me, 'Get up, Peter. *3306*
11:19 t the message only to Jews. *3281*
11:20 t them the good news about the Lord Jesus. *2294*
14:15 t you to turn from these worthless things to *NIG*
15:12 and Paul t about the miraculous signs *2007*
15:20 t them to abstain from food polluted *NIG*
16:17 who *are* t you the way to be saved." *2859*
21:21 t them not to circumcise their children *3306*
2Co 9: 2 t them that since last year you in Achaia *NIG*
Gal 4:16 become your enemy *by* t you the truth? *238*
1Th 3: 4 *we kept* t you that we would be persecuted. *4625*
1Ti 2: 7 *I am* t the truth, I am not lying— *3306*

TELLS (17) [TELL]

Ge 21:12 Listen to whatever Sarah t you, 606
41:55 "Go to Joseph and do what *he* t you." 606
Dt 5:27 tell us whatever the LORD our God t you. 1819
1Sa 22: 8 No *one* t me when my son makes 265+906+1655
22: 8 None of you is concerned about me or t me 265+906+1655
1Ki 22:16 I can tell him only what the LORD t me." 606
2Ki 5:13 How much more, then, when *he* t you, 606
6:12 t the king of Israel the very words 5583
Job 36: 9 *he* t them what they have done— 5583
Pr 12:17 but a false witness t lies. NIH
Da 5: 7 and t me what it means will be clothed 10252
Am 5:10 in court and despise *him who* t the truth. 1819
Mt 24:26 "So if anyone t you, 'There he is, *3306*
Mk 13:34 and t the one at the door to keep watch. *1948*
Jn 2: 5 "Do whatever *he* t you." *3306*
19:35 He knows that *he* t the truth, *3306*
Ac 3:22 you must listen to everything *he* t you. *3281*

TEMA (5)

Ge 25:15 Hadad, T, Jetur, Naphish and Kedemah. 9401
1Ch 1:30 Mishma, Dumah, Massa, Hadad, T, 9401
Job 6:19 The caravans of T look for water, 9401
Isa 21:14 you who live in T, bring food 824+9401
Jer 25:23 T, Buz and all who are in distant places; 9401

TEMAH (2)

Ezr 2:53 Barkos, Sisera, T, 9457
Ne 7:55 Barkos, Sisera, T, 9457

TEMAN (11) [TEMANITE, TEMANITES]

Ge 36:11 T, Omar, Zepho, Gatam and Kenaz. 9403
36:15 Chiefs T, Omar, Zepho, Kenaz, 9403
36:42 Kenaz, T, Mibzar, 9403
1Ch 1:36 T, Omar, Zepho, Gatam and Kenaz; 9403
1:53 Kenaz, T, Mibzar, 9403
Jer 49: 7 "Is there no longer wisdom in T? 9403
49:20 against those who live in T: 9403
Eze 25:13 and from T to Dedan they will fall by 9403
Am 1:12 I will send fire upon T that will consume 9403
Ob 1: 9 Your warriors, O T, will be terrified, 9403
Hab 3: 3 God came from T, the Holy One from 9403

TEMANITE (6) [TEMAN]

Job 2:11 When Job's three friends, Eliphaz the T, 9404
4: 1 Then Eliphaz the T replied: 9404
15: 1 Then Eliphaz the T replied: 9404
22: 1 Then Eliphaz the T replied: 9404
42: 7 he said to Eliphaz the T, 9404
42: 9 the T, Bildad the Shuhite and Zophar 9404

TEMANITES (2) [TEMAN]

Ge 36:34 the land of the T succeeded him as king. 9404
1Ch 1:45 the land of the T succeeded him as king. 9404

TEMENI (1)

1Ch 4: 6 Hepher, T and Haahashtari. 9405

TEMPER (2) [EVEN-TEMPERED, HOT-TEMPERED, ILL-TEMPERED, QUICK-TEMPERED]

1Sa 20: 7 But if *he* loses his t, you can be sure 3013+3013
Pr 16:32 a man who controls his t than one who takes 8120

TEMPERANCE (KJV) See SELF-CONTROL

TEMPERATE (3)

1Ti 3: 2 t, self-controlled, respectable, hospitable, *3767*
3:11 not malicious talkers but t and trustworthy *3767*
Tit 2: 2 Teach the older men to be t, *3767*

TEMPERED (KJV) See COMBINED, MIXED

TEMPEST (7)

Job 27:20 a t snatches him away in the night. 6070
37: 9 The t comes out from its chamber, 6070
Ps 50: 3 and around him a t rages. 4394+8548
55: 8 far from the t and storm." 6185+8120
83:15 with your t and terrify them 6193
107:25 and stirred up a t that lifted high 6194+8120
Isa 29: 6 and t and flames of a devouring fire. 6194

TEMPLE (683) [TEMPLES]

Jdg 4:21 the peg through his t into the ground, 8377
4:22 with the tent peg through his t— 8377
5:26 she shattered and pierced his t. 8377
9: 4 of silver from the t *of* Baal-Berith, 1074
9:27 they held a festival in the t *of* their god. 1074
9:46 into the stronghold of the t *of* El-Berith. 1074
16:26 the pillars that support the t, 1074
16:27 the t was crowded with men and women; 1074
16:29 the two central pillars on which the t stood. 1074
16:30 and down came the t on the rulers and all 1074
1Sa 1: 9 a chair by the doorpost of the LORD's t. 2121
3: 3 Samuel was lying down in the t *of* the LORD 2121
5: 2 Then they carried the ark into Dagon's t 1074
5: 5 nor any others who enter Dagon's t 1074
31: 9 the Philistines to proclaim the news in the t 1074
31:10 They put his armor in the t *of* the Ashtoreths 1074
2Sa 22: 7 From his t he heard my voice; 2121
1Ki 1: 9 building his palace and the t *of* the LORD, 1074
3: 2 a t had not yet been built for the Name of 1074
5: 3 a t for the Name of the LORD his God 1074
5: 5 a t for the Name of the LORD my God, 1074
5: 5 on the throne in your place will build the t 1074
5:17 a foundation of dressed stone for the t. 1074
5:18 and stone for the building of the t. 1074
6: 1 he began to build the t of the LORD. 1074
6: 2 The t that King Solomon built for the Name 1074
6: 3 the main hall of the t extended the width of 1074
6: 3 of the temple extended the width of the t, 1074
6: 3 from the front of the t. 1074
6: 4 made narrow clerestory windows in the t. 1074
6: 6 the t so that nothing would be inserted into 1074
6: 6 be inserted into the t walls. 1074
6: 7 In building the t, only blocks dressed at 1074
6: 7 at the t site while it was being built. 1074
6: 8 on the south side of the t; 1074
6: 9 So he built the t and completed it, 1074
6:10 And he built the side rooms all along the t. 1074
6:10 and they were attached to the t by beams 1074
6:12 "As for this t you are building, 1074
6:14 So Solomon built the t and completed it. 1074
6:15 paneling them from the floor of the t to 1074
6:15 and covered the floor of the t with planks 1074
6:16 of the t with cedar boards from floor 1074
6:16 from floor to ceiling to form within the t 1074
6:18 The inside of the t was cedar, 1074
6:19 within the t to set the ark of the covenant 1074
6:21 Solomon covered the inside of the t 1074
6:27 inside the innermost room of the t, 1074
6:29 On the walls all around the t, 1074
6:30 of both the inner and outer rooms of the t 1074
6:37 of the t *of* the LORD was laid in 1074
6:38 the t was finished in all its details 1074
7:12 the inner courtyard of the t *of* the LORD 1074
7:21 the pillars at the portico of the t. 2121
7:39 of the stands on the south side of the t 1074
7:39 at the southeast corner of the t. 1074
7:40 for King Solomon in the t *of* the LORD: 1074
7:45 for King Solomon for the t *of* the LORD 1074
7:48 that were in the LORD's t: 1074
7:50 also for the doors of the main hall of the t. 1074
7:51 the work King Solomon had done for the t 1074
7:51 in the treasuries of the LORD's t. 1074
8: 6 to its place in the inner sanctuary of the t, 1074
8:10 the cloud filled the t *of* the LORD 1074
8:11 for the glory of the LORD filled his t. 1074
8:13 I have indeed built a magnificent t for you, 1074
8:16 a city in any tribe of Israel to have a t built 1074
8:17 to build a t for the Name of the LORD, 1074
8:18 'Because it was in your heart to build a t 1074
8:19 you are not the one to build the t, 1074
8:19 the one who will build the t for my Name.' 1074
8:20 the LORD promised, and I have built the t 1074
8:27 How much less this t I have built! 1074
8:29 May your eyes be open toward this t night 1074
8:31 the oath before your altar in this t, 1074
8:33 and making supplication to you in this t, 1074
8:38 and spreading out his hands toward this t— 1074
8:42 when he comes and prays toward this t, 1074
8:44 and the t I have built for your Name, 1074
8:48 and the t I have built for your Name; 1074
8:63 and all the Israelites dedicated the t *of* 1074
8:64 of the courtyard in front of the t *of* 1074
9: 1 When Solomon had finished building the t 1074
9: 3 I have consecrated this t, 1074
9: 7 and will reject this t I have consecrated 1074
9: 8 And though this t is now imposing, 1074
9: 8 a thing to this land and to this t?' 1074

1Ki 9:10 the t of the LORD and the royal palace— 1074
9:15 to build the LORD's t, his own palace, 1074
9:25 and so fulfilled the t obligations. 1074
10: 5 and the burnt offerings he made at the t of 1074
10:12 the almugwood to make supports for the t 1074
12:27 up to offer sacrifices at the t of the LORD 1074
14:26 of the t of the LORD and the treasures of 1074
14:28 the king went to the LORD's t, 1074
15:15 into the t of the LORD the silver and gold 1074
15:18 of the LORD's t and of his own palace. 1074
16:32 He set up an altar for Baal in the t of Baal 1074
2Ki 5:18 When my master enters the t of Rimmon 1074
5:18 when I bow down in the t of Rimmon, 1074
10:21 the t of Baal until it was full from one end 1074
10:23 son of Recab went into the t of Baal. 1074
10:25 and then entered the inner shrine of the t 1074
10:26 They brought the sacred stone out of the t 1074
10:27 of Baal and tore down the t of Baal, 1074
11: 3 He remained hidden with his nurse at the t 1074
11: 4 and had them brought to him at the t of 1074
11: 4 with them and put them under oath at the t 1074
11: 6 who take turns guarding the t— 1074
11: 7 to guard the t for the king. 1074
11:10 to King David and that were in the t of 1074
11:11 near the altar and the t, 1074
11:11 the south side to the north side of the t. 1074
11:13 to the people at the t of the LORD. 1074
11:15 not be put to death in the t of the LORD." 1074
11:18 the people of the land went to the t of Baal 1074
11:18 the priest posted guards at the t of 1074
11:19 down from the t of the LORD and went 1074
12: 4 that is brought as sacred offerings to the t 1074
12: 4 and the money brought voluntarily to the t. 1074
12: 5 repair whatever damage is found in the t." 1074
12: 6 the priests still had not repaired the t. 1074
12: 7 the damage done to the t? 1074
12: 7 but hand it over for repairing the t." 1074
12: 8 that they would not repair the t themselves. 1074
12: 9 on the right side as one enters the t of 1074
12: 9 that was brought to the t of the LORD. 1074
12:10 the money that had been brought into the t 1074
12:11 to supervise the work on the t. 1074
12:11 those who worked on the t of the LORD— 1074
12:12 and dressed stone for the repair of the t of 1074
12:12 the other expenses of restoring the t. 1074
12:13 The money brought into the t was 1074
12:13 of gold or silver for the t of the LORD; 1074
12:14 who used it to repair the t. 1074
12:16 and sin offerings was not brought into the t 1074
12:18 the treasuries of the t of the LORD and of 1074
14:14 the t of the LORD and in the treasuries of 1074
15:35 Jotham rebuilt the Upper Gate of the t of 1074
16: 8 the t of the LORD and in the treasuries of 1074
16:14 from the front of the t— 1074
16:14 the new altar and the t of the LORD— 1074
16:18 that had been built at the t and removed 1074
16:18 the royal entryway outside the t of 1074
18:15 the t of the LORD and in the treasuries of 1074
18:16 and doorposts of the t of the LORD, 2121
19: 1 and put on sackcloth and went into the t of 1074
19:14 up to the t of the LORD and spread it out 1074
19:37 while he was worshiping in the t 1074
20: 5 now you will go up to the t of the LORD. 1074
20: 8 and that I will go up to the t of the LORD 1074
21: 4 He built altars in the t of the LORD, 1074
21: 5 In both courts of the t of the LORD, 1074
21: 7 and put it in the t, 1074
21: 7 "In this t and in Jerusalem, 1074
22: 3 to the t of the LORD. 1074
22: 4 the money that has been brought into the t 1074
22: 5 to supervise the work on the t. 1074
22: 5 the workers who repair the t of the LORD— 1074
22: 6 and dressed stone to repair the t. 1074
22: 8 "I have found the Book of the Law in the t 1074
22: 9 the money that was in the t of the LORD 1074
22: 9 to the workers and supervisors at the t." 1074
23: 2 the t of the LORD with the men of Judah, 1074
23: 2 which had been found in the t of 1074
23: 4 and the doorkeepers to remove from the t 2121
23: 6 the Asherah pole from the t of the LORD 1074
23: 7 which were in the t of the LORD and 1074
23:11 He removed from the entrance to the t of 1074
23:12 in the two courts of the t of the LORD. 1074
23:24 the priest had discovered in the t of 1074
23:27 and this t, about which I said, 1074
24:13 the treasures from the t of the LORD and 1074
24:13 of Israel had made for the t of the LORD. 2121
25: 9 He set fire to the t of the LORD, 1074
25:13 and the bronze Sea that were at the t of 1074
25:14 the bronze articles used in the t service. NIH
25:16 which Solomon had made for the t of 1074
1Ch 6:10 in the t Solomon built in Jerusalem), 1074
6:32 until Solomon built the t of the LORD 1074
9: 2 priests, Levites and t servants. 5987
9:28 of the articles used in the t service; NIH
9:33 of the t and were exempt from other duties NIH
10:10 the t of their gods and hung up his head in 1074
10:10 of their gods and hung up his head in the t 1074
22:14 to provide for the t of the LORD 1074
22:19 into the t that will be built for the Name of 1074
23: 4 the t of the LORD and six thousand are to 1074
23:24 or more who served in the t of the LORD. 1074
23:28 in the service of the t of the LORD: 1074
23:32 for the service of the t of the LORD. 1074
24:19 of ministering when they entered the t of 1074
25: 6 of their fathers for the music of the t of 1074
26:12 for ministering in the t of the LORD, 1074

1Ch 26:22 of the treasuries of the t of the LORD. 1074
26:27 for the repair of the t of the LORD. 1074
26:29 from the t, as officials and judges NIH
28:10 for the LORD has chosen you to build a t 1074
28:11 the plans for the portico of the t, NIH
28:12 the courts of the t of the LORD and all 1074
28:12 for the treasuries of the t of God and for 1074
28:13 the work of serving in the t of the LORD, 1074
28:20 until all the work for the service of the t of 1074
28:21 for all the work on the t of God, 1074
29: 2 I have provided for the t of my God— 1074
29: 3 in my devotion to the t of my God I 1074
29: 3 and silver for the t of my God, over and 1074
29: 3 I have provided for this holy t: 1074
29: 7 on the t of God five thousand talents 1074
29: 8 to the treasury of the t of the LORD in 1074
29:16 that we have provided for building you a t 1074
2Ch 2: 1 to build a t for the Name of the LORD 1074
2: 4 Now I am about to build a t for the Name 1074
2: 5 "The t I am going to build will be great, 1074
2: 6 But who is able to build a t for him, 1074
2: 6 Who then am I to build a t for him, 1074
2: 9 the t I build must be large and magnificent. 1074
2:12 a t for the LORD and a palace for himself. 1074
3: 1 to build the t of the LORD in Jerusalem 1074
3: 3 the t of God was sixty cubits long 1074
3: 4 at the front of the t was twenty cubits long NIH
3: 6 He adorned the t with precious stones. 1074
3: 7 walls and doors of the t with gold, 1074
3: 8 to the width of the t— 1074
3:11 and touched the t wall, 1074
3:12 and touched the other t wall, 1074
3:15 In the front of the t he made two pillars, 1074
3:17 He erected the pillars in the front of the t, 2121
4: 7 for them and placed them in the t, 2121
4: 8 and placed them in the t, 2121
4:11 for King Solomon in the t of God: 1074
4:16 for King Solomon for the t of 1074
4:19 the furnishings that were in God's t: 1074
4:22 and the gold doors of the t: 1074
5: 1 the work Solomon had done for the t of 1074
5: 1 he placed them in the treasuries of God's t. 1074
5: 7 to its place in the inner sanctuary of the t, 1074
5:13 t of the LORD was filled with a cloud, 1074
5:14 the glory of the LORD filled the t of God. 1074
6: 2 I have built a magnificent t for you, 1074
6: 5 a city in any tribe of Israel to have a t built 1074
6: 7 to build a t for the Name of the LORD, 1074
6: 8 'Because it was in your heart to build a t 1074
6: 9 you are not the one to build the t, 1074
6: 9 the one who will build the t for my Name.' 1074
6:10 and I have built the t for the Name of 1074
6:18 How much less this t I have built! 1074
6:20 May your eyes be open toward this t day 1074
6:22 the oath before your altar in this t, 1074
6:24 making supplication before you in this t, 1074
6:29 and spreading out his hands toward this t— 1074
6:32 when he comes and prays toward this t, 1074
6:34 and the t I have built for your Name, 1074
6:38 toward the t I have built for your Name; 1074
7: 1 and the glory of the LORD filled the t. 1074
7: 2 the t of the LORD because the glory of 1074
7: 3 and the glory of the LORD above the t, 1074
7: 5 the king and all the people dedicated the t 1074
7: 7 of the courtyard in front of the t of 1074
7:11 the t of the LORD and the royal palace, 1074
7:11 the t of the LORD and in his own palace, 1074
7:12 for myself as a t for sacrifices. 1074
7:16 I have chosen and consecrated this t so 1074
7:20 and will reject this t I have consecrated 1074
7:21 And though this t is now so imposing, 1074
7:21 a thing to this land and to this t?' 1074
8: 1 the t of the LORD and his own palace, 1074
8:16 from the day the foundation of the t of 1074
8:16 So the t of the LORD was finished. 1074
9: 4 and the burnt offerings he made at the t of 1074
9:11 to make steps for the t of the LORD and 1074
12: 9 of the t of the LORD and the treasures of 1074
12:11 the king went to the LORD's t, 1074
15: 8 in front of the portico of the LORD's t. NIH
15:18 into the t of God the silver and gold and 1074
16: 2 of the LORD's t and of his own palace 1074
20: 5 and Jerusalem at the t of the LORD in 1074
20: 9 we will stand in your presence before this t 1074
20:28 and went to the t of the LORD with harps 1074
22:12 with them at the t of God for six years 1074
23: 3 a covenant with the king at the t of God. 1074
23: 5 be in the courtyards of the t of the LORD. 1074
23: 6 the t of the LORD except the priests 1074
23: 7 Anyone who enters the t must be put 1074
23: 9 to King David and that were in the t 1074
23:10 near the altar and the t, 1074
23:10 the south side to the north side of the t. 1074
23:12 she went to them at the t of the LORD. 1074
23:14 "Do not put her to death at the t of 1074
23:17 All the people went to the t of Baal 1074
23:18 Then Jehoiada placed the oversight of the t 1074
23:18 in the t, to present the burnt offerings of 1074
23:19 of the LORD's t so that no one who was 1074
23:20 the king down from the t of the LORD. 1074
24: 4 to restore the t of the LORD. 1074
24: 5 to repair the t of your God. 1074
24: 7 into the t of God and had used 1074
24: 8 at the gate of the t of the LORD. 1074
24:12 the work required for the t of the LORD. 1074
24:12 and carpenters to restore the LORD's t, 1074
24:12 workers in iron and bronze to repair the t. 1074

2Ch 24:13 They rebuilt the t of God according to 1074
24:14 made articles for the LORD's t: 1074
24:14 presented continually in the t of the LORD. 1074
24:16 had done in Israel for God and his t. 1074
24:18 They abandoned the t of the LORD, 1074
24:21 in the courtyard of the LORD's t. 1074
24:27 the t of God are written in the annotations 1074
25:24 and silver and all the articles found in the t 1074
26:16 the t of the LORD to burn incense on 2121
26:19 before the incense altar in the LORD's t, 1074
26:21 and excluded from the t of the LORD. 1074
27: 2 but unlike him he did not enter the t of 2121
27: 3 Jotham rebuilt the Upper Gate of the t of 1074
28:21 Ahaz took some of the things from the t of 1074
28:24 from the t of God and took them away. 1074
28:24 He shut the doors of the LORD's t 1074
29: 3 he opened the doors of the t of the LORD 1074
29: 5 now and consecrate the t of the LORD, 1074
29:15 they went in to purify the t of the LORD, 1074
29:16 of the LORD's t everything unclean 1074
29:16 that they found in the t of the LORD. 2121
29:17 For eight more days they consecrated the t 1074
29:18 "We have purified the entire t of the LORD 1074
29:20 and went up to the t of the LORD. 1074
29:25 in the t of the LORD with cymbals, harps 1074
29:31 and thank offerings to the t of the LORD. 1074
29:35 of the t of the LORD was reestablished. 1074
30: 1 to the t of the LORD in Jerusalem 1074
30:15 and brought burnt offerings to the t of 1074
31:10 to bring their contributions to the t of 1074
31:11 to prepare storerooms in the t of the LORD, 1074
31:13 and Azariah the official in charge of the t 1074
31:16 all who would enter the t of the LORD 1074
31:21 of God's t and in obedience to the law and 1074
32:21 And when he went into the t of his god, 1074
33: 4 He built altars in the t of the LORD, 1074
33: 5 In both courts of the t of the LORD, 1074
33: 7 and put it in God's t, 1074
33: 7 "In this t and in Jerusalem, 1074
33:15 from the t of the LORD, as well as all 1074
33:15 as all the altars he had built on the t hill 1074
34: 8 to purify the land and the t, 1074
34: 8 to repair the t of the LORD his God. 1074
34: 9 the money that had been brought into the t 1074
34:10 to supervise the work on the LORD's t. 1074
34:10 who repaired and restored the t. 1074
34:14 the money that had been taken into the t of 1074
34:15 "I have found the Book of the Law in the t 1074
34:17 the money that was in the t of the LORD 1074
34:30 the t of the LORD with the men of Judah, 1074
34:30 which had been found in the t of the LORD. 1074
35: 2 in the service of the LORD's t. 1074
35: 3 in the t that Solomon son of David king 1074
35: 8 the administrators of God's t, 1074
35:20 all this, when Josiah had set the t in order, 1074
36: 7 also took to Babylon articles from the t of 1074
36: 7 of the LORD and put them in his t there. 2121
36:10 together with articles of value from the t 1074
36:14 of the nations and defiling the t of the LORD, 1074
36:18 to Babylon all the articles from the t 1074
36:18 and the treasures of the LORD's t and 1074
36:19 They set fire to God's t and broke down 1074
36:23 to build a t for him at Jerusalem in Judah. 1074
Ezr 1: 2 to build a t for him at Jerusalem in Judah. 1074
1: 3 up to Jerusalem in Judah and build the t of 1074
1: 4 and with freewill offerings for the t of God 1074
1: 7 the articles belonging to the t of the LORD, 1074
1: 7 from Jerusalem and had placed in the t 1074
2:42 The gatekeepers of the t: NIH
2:43 The t servants: the descendants of Ziha, 5987
2:58 The t servants and the descendants of 5987
2:70 the gatekeepers and the t servants settled 5987
3: 6 the foundation of the LORD's t had not 2121
3:10 the builders laid the foundation of the t of 2121
3:12 who had seen the former t, 1074
3:12 the foundation of this t being laid, 1074
4: 1 the exiles were building a t for the LORD, 2121
4: 3 "You have no part with us in building a t 1074
5: 3 to rebuild this t and restore this structure?" 10103
5: 8 to the t of the great God. 10103
5: 9 to rebuild this t and restore this structure?" 10103
5:11 and earth, and we are rebuilding the t 10103
5:12 who destroyed this t and deported 10103
5:14 the t of Babylon the gold and silver articles 10206
5:14 from the t in Jerusalem and brought to 10206
5:14 in Jerusalem and brought to the t 10206
5:15 and deposit them in the t in Jerusalem. 10206
6: 3 the king issued a decree concerning the t 10103
6: 3 Let the t be rebuilt as a place to present 10103
6: 5 the t in Jerusalem and brought to Babylon, 10206
6: 5 are to be returned to their places in the t 10206
6: 7 Do not interfere with the work on this t 10103
6:12 to change this decree or to destroy this t 10103
6:14 the t according to the command of the God NIH
6:15 The t was completed on the third day of 10103
7: 7 singers, gatekeepers and t servants, 5987
7:16 for the t of their God in Jerusalem. 10103
7:17 the altar of the t of your God in Jerusalem. 10103
7:19 to you for worship in the t of your God. 10103
7:20 And anything else needed for the t 10103
7:23 be done with diligence for the t of the God 10103
7:24 t servants or other workers at this house 10497
8:17 the t servants in Casiphia, 5987
8:20 They also brought 220 of the t servants— 5987
Ne 2: 8 of the citadel by the t and for the city wall 1074
3:26 and the t servants living on the hill 5987
3:31 the t servants and the merchants, opposite 5987

Ne 6:10 the **t**, and let us close the temple doors, 2121
6:10 and let us close the **t** doors, 2121
6:11 like me go into the **t** to save his life? 2121
7:46 The **t servants:** the descendants of Ziha, 5987
7:60 The **t servants** and the descendants of 5987
7:73 the singers and the **t servants,** 5987
10:28 gatekeepers, singers, **t servants** 5987
11:3 **t servants** and descendants of Solomon's 5987
11:12 who carried on work for the **t**— 1074
11:21 The **t servants** lived on the hill of Ophel, 5987
13:5 and incense and **t** articles, NIH
Ps 5:7 will I bow down toward your holy **t.** 2121
11:4 The LORD is in his holy **t;** 2121
18:6 From his **t** he heard my voice; 2121
27:4 of the LORD and to seek him in his **t.** 2121
29:9 And in his **t** all cry, "Glory!" 2121
30:T For the dedication of the **t.** 1074
48:9 Within your **t,** O God, we meditate 2121
65:4 of your house, of your holy **t.** 2121
66:13 I will come to your **t** with burnt offerings 1074
68:29 Because of your **t** at Jerusalem 2121
79:1 they have defiled your holy **t,** 2121
138:2 I will bow down toward your holy **t** 2121
Ecc 5:6 And do not protest to the **[t]** messenger, NIH
Isa 2:2 the LORD's **t** will be established as chief 1074
6:1 and the train of his robe filled the **t.** 2121
6:4 and thresholds shook and the **t** was filled 1074
15:2 Dibon goes up to its **t,** 1074
37:1 and put on sackcloth and went into the **t** *of* 1074
37:14 up to the **t** *of* the LORD and spread it out 1074
37:38 while he was worshiping in the **t** 1074
38:20 of our lives in the **t** *of* the LORD. 1074
38:22 that I will go up to the **t** *of* the LORD?" 1074
43:28 So I will disgrace the dignitaries of your **t,** 7731
44:28 and of the **t,** "Let its foundations be laid." ' 2121
56:5 within my **t** and its walls a memorial and 1074
60:7 and I will adorn my glorious **t.** 1074
64:11 Our holy and glorious **t,** 1074
66:6 hear that noise from the **t!** 2121
66:20 grain offerings, to the **t** *of* the LORD 1074
Jer 7:4 "This is the **t** *of* the LORD, 2121
7:4 the **t** *of* the LORD, 2121
7:4 the **t** *of* the LORD!" 2121
7:14 **the t** you trust in, the place I gave to you 889[S]
11:15 in my **t** as she works out her evil schemes 1074
19:14 the court of the LORD's **t** and said to all 1074
20:1 the chief officer in the **t** *of* the LORD, 1074
20:2 Upper Gate of Benjamin at the LORD's **t.** 1074
23:11 even in my **t** I find their wickedness," 1074
24:1 of figs placed in front of the **t** *of* the LORD. 2121
26:18 of rubble, the **t** hill a mound overgrown 1074
36:5 I cannot go to the LORD's **t.** 1074
36:8 at the LORD's **t** he read the words of 1074
36:10 at the entrance of the New Gate of the **t,** 1074
36:10 the LORD's **t** the words of Jeremiah from 1074
38:14 the third entrance to the **t** *of* the LORD. 1074
43:13 the **t** *of* the sun in Egypt he will demolish 1074
50:28 has taken vengeance, vengeance for his **t.** 2121
51:11 will take vengeance, vengeance for his **t.** 2121
52:13 He set fire to the **t** *of* the LORD, 1074
52:17 at the **t** *of* the LORD and they carried all 1074
52:18 the bronze articles used in the **t** service. NIH
52:20 which King Solomon had made for the **t** 1074
Eze 8:16 and there at the entrance to the **t,** 2121
8:16 the **t** *of* the LORD and their faces toward 2121
9:3 and moved to the threshold of the **t.** 1074
9:6 with the elders who were in front of the **t.** 1074
9:7 the **t** and fill the courts with the slain. 1074
10:3 the south side of the **t** when the man went 1074
10:4 and moved to the threshold of the **t.** 1074
10:4 The cloud filled the **t,** 1074
10:18 of the **t** and stopped above the cherubim. 1074
40:5 a wall completely surrounding the **t** area. 1074
40:7 the portico facing the **t** was one rod deep. 1074
40:9 The portico of the gateway faced the **t.** 1074
40:45 for the priests who have charge of the **t,** 1074
40:47 And the altar was in front of the **t.** 1074
40:48 the portico of the **t** and measured the jambs 1074
41:5 Then he measured the wall of the **t;** 1074
41:5 around the **t** was four cubits wide. 1074
41:6 the wall of the **t** to serve as supports for 1074
41:6 not inserted into the wall of the **t.** 1074
41:7 The side rooms all around the **t** were wider NIH
41:7 The structure surrounding the **t** was built 1074
41:8 that the **t** had a raised base all around it, 1074
41:9 between the side rooms of the **t** 1074
41:10 twenty cubits wide all around the **t.** 1074
41:12 The building facing the **t** courtyard on NIH
41:13 Then he measured the **t;** 1074
41:13 a hundred cubits long, and the **t** courtyard NIH
41:14 The width of the **t** courtyard on the east, NIH
41:14 including the front of the **t,** 1074
41:15 at the rear of **the t,** including its galleries 2023[S]
41:19 They were carved all around the whole **t.** 1074
41:26 of the **t** also had overhangs. 1074
42:1 the **t** courtyard and opposite the outer wall NIH
42:10 the **t** courtyard and opposite the outer wall, NIH
42:13 and south rooms facing the **t** courtyard are NIH
42:15 the **t area,** he led me out by the east gate 1074
43:4 The glory of the LORD entered the **t** 1074
43:5 and the glory of the LORD filled the **t.** 1074
43:6 speaking to me from inside the **t.** 1074
43:10 describe the **t** to the people of Israel, 1074
43:11 make known to them the design of the **t**— 1074
43:12 "This is the law of the **t:** 1074
43:12 Such is the law of the **t.** 1074
43:21 in the designated part of the **t area** outside 1074
Eze 44:4 of the north gate to the front of the **t.** 1074
44:4 of the LORD filling the **t** *of* the LORD, 1074
44:5 the regulations regarding the **t** *of* the LORD. 1074
44:5 to the entrance of the **t** and all the exits of 1074
44:7 into my sanctuary, desecrating my **t** 1074
44:11 of the gates of the **t** and serving in it; 1074
44:14 of the **t** and all the work that is to be done 1074
44:17 the gates of the inner court or inside the **t.** 1074
45:5 the Levites, who serve in the **t,** 1074
45:19 and put it on the doorposts of the **t,** 1074
45:20 so you are to make atonement for the **t.** 1074
46:24 where those who minister at the **t** will cook 1074
47:1 to the entrance of the **t,** 1074
47:1 under the threshold of the **t** toward the east 1074
47:1 toward the east (for the **t** faced east). 1074
47:1 down from under the south side of the **t,** 1074
48:21 the sacred portion with the **t** sanctuary will 1074
Da 1:2 along with some of the articles from the **t** 1074
1:2 to the **t** *of* his god in Babylonia and put in 1074
5:2 father had taken from the **t** in Jerusalem, 10206
5:3 that had been taken from the **t** of God 10206
5:23 You had the goblets from his **t** brought 10103
9:27 [of the **t**] he will set up an abomination NIH
11:31 to desecrate the **t** fortress and will abolish 5219
Hos 9:4 it will not come into the **t** *of* the LORD. 1074
Joel 2:17 weep between the **t porch** and the altar. 395
Am 7:13 the king's sanctuary and the **t** *of* 1074
8:3 "the songs in the **t** will turn to wailing. 2121
Jnh 2:4 yet I will look again toward your holy **t.**' 2121
2:7 and my prayer rose to you, to your holy **t.** 2121
Mic 1:2 the Lord from his holy **t.** 2121
1:7 all her **t gifts** will be burned with fire; 924
3:12 the **t** hill a mound overgrown with thickets. 1074
4:1 the LORD's **t** will be established as chief 1074
Na 1:14 that are in the **t** *of* your gods. 1074
Hab 2:20 But the LORD is in his holy **t;** 2121
Zep 1:9 who fill the **t** *of* their gods with violence 1074
Hag 2:15 stone was laid on another in the LORD's **t.** 2121
2:18 the foundation of the LORD's **t** was laid. 2121
Zec 4:9 have laid the foundation of this **t;** 1074
6:12 from his place and build the **t** *of* the LORD. 2121
6:13 It is he who will build the **t** *of* the LORD, 2121
6:14 of Zephaniah as a memorial in the **t** *of* 2121
6:15 and help to build the **t** *of* the LORD, 2121
8:9 let your hands be strong so that the **t** may 2121
Mal 1:10 that one of you would shut the **t** doors, NIH
3:1 Then suddenly the Lord you are seeking
will come to his **t;** 2121
Mt 4:5 on the highest point *of* the **t.** *2639*
12:5 on the Sabbath the priests in the **t** desecrate *2639*
12:6 I tell you that one greater than the **t** is here. *2639*
17:24 "Doesn't your teacher pay the **t** tax?" *NIG*
21:12 Jesus entered the **t area** and drove out *2639*
21:14 and the lame came to him at the **t,** *2639*
21:15 and the children shouting in the **t area,** *2639*
21:23 Jesus entered the **t courts,** and, *2639*
23:16 You say, 'If anyone swears by the **t,** *3724*
23:16 but if anyone swears by the gold *of* the **t,** *3724*
23:17 gold, or the **t** that makes the gold sacred? *3724*
23:21 And he who swears by the **t** swears by it *3724*
23:35 whom you murdered between the **t** and *3724*
24:1 Jesus left the **t** and was walking away *2639*
26:55 Every day I sat in the **t courts** teaching, *2639*
26:61 the **t** of God and rebuild it in three days.' " *3724*
27:5 Judas threw the money into the **t** and left. *3724*
27:40 to destroy the **t** and build it in three days, *3724*
27:51 that moment the curtain *of* the **t** was torn *3724*
Mk 11:11 Jesus entered Jerusalem and went to the **t.** *2639*
11:15 Jesus entered the **t area** and began *2639*
11:16 to carry merchandise through the **t courts.** *2639*
11:27 while Jesus was walking in the **t courts,** *2639*
12:35 While Jesus was teaching in the **t courts,** *2639*
12:41 putting their money into the **t treasury.** *1126*
13:1 As he was leaving the **t,** *2639*
13:3 on the Mount of Olives opposite the **t,** *2639*
14:49 I was with you, teaching in the **t courts,** *2639*
14:58 'I will destroy this man-made **t** and *3724*
15:29 to destroy the **t** and build it in three days, *3724*
15:38 the **t** was torn in two from top to bottom. *3724*
Lk 1:9 into the **t** of the Lord and burn incense. *3724*
1:21 why he stayed so long in the **t.** *3724*
1:22 They realized he had seen a vision in the **t,** *3724*
2:27 he went into the **t courts.** *2639*
2:37 She never left the **t** but worshiped night *2639*
2:46 they found him in the **t courts,** *2639*
4:9 had him stand on the highest point *of* the **t.** *2639*
18:10 "Two men went up to the **t** to pray, *2639*
19:45 Then he entered the **t area** and began *2639*
19:47 Every day he was teaching at the **t.** *2639*
20:1 in the **t courts** and preaching the gospel, *2639*
21:1 putting their gifts into the **t treasury.** *1126*
21:5 the **t** was adorned with beautiful stones and *2639*
21:37 Each day Jesus was teaching at the **t,** *2639*
21:38 in the morning to hear him at the **t.** *2639*
22:4 and the **officers of the t guard** *5130*
22:52 the officers of the **t** guard, and the elders, *2639*
22:53 Every day I was with you in the **t courts,** *2639*
23:45 And the curtain *of* the **t** was torn in two. *3724*
24:53 And they stayed continually at the **t,** *2639*
Jn 2:14 In the **t courts** he found men selling cattle, *2639*
2:15 and drove all from the **t area,** *2639*
2:19 Jesus answered them, "Destroy this **t,** *3724*
2:20 "It has taken forty-six years to build this **t,** *3724*
2:21 But the **t** he had spoken of was his body. *3724*
5:14 Later Jesus found him at the **t** and said *2639*
7:14 the Feast did Jesus go up to the **t courts** *2639*
7:28 Then Jesus, still teaching in the **t courts,** *2639*
Jn 7:32 the Pharisees sent **t guards** to arrest him. *5677*
7:45 the **t guards** went back to the chief priests *5677*
8:2 At dawn he appeared again in the **t courts,** *2639*
8:20 while teaching in the **t area** near the place *2639*
8:59 slipping away from the **t grounds.** *2639*
10:23 and Jesus was in the **t area** walking *2639*
11:56 in the **t area** they asked one another, *2639*
18:20 "I always taught in synagogues or at the **t,** *2639*
Ac 2:46 to meet together in the **t courts.** *2639*
3:1 and John were going up to the **t** at the time *2639*
3:2 to the **t** gate called Beautiful, *2639*
3:2 to beg from those going into the **t courts.** *2639*
3:8 Then he went with them into the **t courts,** *2639*
3:10 to sit begging at the **t** gate called Beautiful, *2639*
4:1 *of* the **t** guard and the Sadducees came up *2639*
5:20 "Go, stand in the **t courts,"** he said, *2639*
5:21 At daybreak they entered the **t courts,** *2639*
5:24 the captain *of* the **t guard** and *2639*
5:25 in jail are standing in the **t courts** teaching *2639*
5:42 in the **t courts** and from house to house, *2639*
14:13 Zeus, whose **t** was just outside the city, *NIG*
19:27 that the **t** of the great goddess Artemis will *2639*
19:35 the city of Ephesus is the **guardian of the t** *3753*
21:26 to the **t** to give notice of the date when *2639*
21:27 the province of Asia saw Paul at the **t.** *2639*
21:28 into the **t area** and defiled this holy place." *2639*
21:29 that Paul had brought him into the **t area.)** *2639*
21:30 Seizing Paul, they dragged him from the **t,** *2639*
22:17 to Jerusalem and was praying at the **t,** *2639*
24:6 and even tried to desecrate the **t;** *2639*
24:12 not find me arguing with anyone at the **t,** *2639*
24:18 they found me in the **t courts** doing this. *2639*
25:8 against the law of the Jews or against the **t** *2639*
26:21 in the **t courts** and tried to kill me. *2639*
Ro 9:4 the **t worship** and the promises. *3301*
1Co 3:16 that you yourselves are God's **t** and *3724*
3:17 If anyone destroys God's **t,** God will *3724*
3:17 God's **t** is sacred, and you are that temple. *3724*
3:17 God's temple is sacred, and you are **that t.** *4015[S]*
6:19 know that your body is a **t** of the Holy Spirit *3724*
8:10 have this knowledge eating in an **idol's t,** *1627*
9:13 that those who work in the **t** get their food *2641*
9:13 in the temple get their food from the **t,** *2639*
2Co 6:16 What agreement is there between the **t** *3724*
6:16 For we are the **t** of the living God. *3724*
Eph 2:21 and rises to become a holy **t** in the Lord. *3724*
2Th 2:4 so that he sets himself up in God's **t,** *3724*
Rev 3:12 I will make a pillar in the **t** of my God. *3724*
7:15 and serve him day and night in his **t;** *3724*
11:1 and measure the **t** of God and the altar, *3724*
11:19 Then God's **t** in heaven was opened, *3724*
11:19 and within his **t** was seen the ark *3724*
14:15 Then another angel came out of the **t** *3724*
14:17 Another angel came out of the **t** in heaven, *3724*
15:5 After this I looked and in heaven the **t,** *3724*
15:6 Out of the **t** came the seven angels with *3724*
15:8 the **t** was filled with smoke from the glory *3724*
15:8 and no one could enter the **t** until *3724*
16:1 Then I heard a loud voice from the **t** saying *3724*
16:17 of the **t** came a loud voice from the throne, *3724*
21:22 I did not see a **t** in the city, *3724*
21:22 Lord God Almighty and the Lamb are its **t.** *3724*

TEMPLES (9) [TEMPLE]

SS 4:3 Your **t** behind your veil are like the halves 8377
6:7 Your **t** behind your veil are like the halves 8377
Jer 43:12 He will set fire to the **t** *of* the gods 1074
43:12 he will burn **their t** and take their gods 4392[S]
43:13 the sacred pillars and will burn down the **t** 1074
Joel 3:5 and carried off my finest treasures to your **t.** 2121
Ac 17:24 and does not live in **t** built by hands. *3724*
19:37 *though they have* neither **robbed t** *2645*
Ro 2:22 You who abhor idols, *do you* **rob t?** *2644*

TEMPORAL (KJV) See TEMPORARY

TEMPORARY (7)

Ex 12:45 a **t resident** and a hired worker may not eat 9369
Lev 25:6 the hired worker and **t resident** who live 9369
25:35 as you would an alien or a **t resident,** 9369
25:40 be treated as a hired worker or a **t resident** 9369
25:45 also buy some of the **t residents** living 9369
25:47 or a **t resident** among you becomes rich 9369
2Co 4:18 For what is seen is **t,** but what is unseen *4672*

TEMPT (2) [TEMPTATION, TEMPTED, TEMPTER, TEMPTING]

1Co 7:5 so that Satan *will* not **t** you because of your *4279*
Jas 1:13 be tempted by evil, nor *does* he **t** anyone; *4279*

TEMPTATION (8) [TEMPT]

Mt 6:13 And lead us not into **t,** but deliver us from *4280*
26:41 and pray so that you will not fall into **t.** *4280*
Mk 14:38 and pray so that you will not fall into **t.** *4280*
Lk 11:4 And lead us not into **t.**' " *4280*
22:40 "Pray that you will not fall into **t."** *4280*
22:46 up and pray so that you will not fall into **t."** *4280*
1Co 10:13 No **t** has seized you except what is common *4280*
1Ti 6:9 People who want to get rich fall into **t** and *4280*

TEMPTED (13) [TEMPT]

Mt 4:1 the Spirit into the desert *to be* **t** by the devil. *4279*
Mk 1:13 in the desert forty days, *being* **t** by Satan. *4279*

Lk 4: 2 where for forty days *he was* **t** by the devil. *4279*
1Co 10:13 not let you *be* **t** beyond what you can bear. *4279*
10:13 But **when** you **are t,** he will also provide a way out *3836+4280+5250*
Gal 6: 1 But watch yourself, or you also *may be* **t.** *4279*
1Th 3: 5 in some way the tempter might *have* **t** you *4279*
Heb 2:18 Because he himself suffered *when he was* **t,** *4279*
2:18 he is able to help those who *are being* **t.** *4279*
4:15 we have *one who has been* **t** in every way, *4279*
Jas 1:13 *When* **t,** no one should say, "God is *4279*
1:13 For God **cannot** be **t** by evil, nor does he *585*
1:14 but each one *is* **t** when, by his own evil *4279*

TEMPTER (2) [TEMPT]

Mt 4: 3 The **t** came to him and said, *4279*
1Th 3: 5 in some way the **t** might have tempted you *4279*

TEMPTING (2) [TEMPT]

Lk 4:13 When the devil had finished all this **t,** *4280*
Jas 1:13 tempted, no one should say, "God *is* **t** *me.*" *4279*

TEN (199) [ONE-TENTH, TENS, TENTH, TITHE, TITHES, TWO-TENTHS]

Ge 16: 3 Abram had been living in Canaan **t** years, 6924
18:32 What if only **t** can be found there?" 6927
18:32 He answered, "For the sake of **t,** 6927
24:10 the servant took **t** of his master's camels 6927
24:22 and two gold bracelets weighing **t** shekels. 6927
24:55 "Let the girl remain with us **t** days or so; 6917
31: 7 by changing my wages **t** times. 6930
31:41 and you changed my wages **t** times. 6930
32:15 forty cows and **t** bulls, 6927
32:15 and **t** male donkeys. 6927
42: 3 Then **t** of Joseph's brothers went down 6927
45:23 **t** donkeys loaded with the best things 6927
45:23 and **t** female donkeys loaded with grain 6924
50:22 He lived a hundred and **t** years 6924
50:26 Joseph died at the age of a hundred and **t.** 6924
Ex 26: 1 with **t** curtains of finely twisted linen 6924
26:16 Each frame is to be **t** cubits long and 6924
27:12 with **t** posts and ten bases. 6927
27:12 with ten posts and **t** bases. 6924
34:28 the **T** Commandments. 6930
36: 8 with **t** curtains of finely twisted linen 6924
36:21 Each frame was **t** cubits long and a cubit 6924
38:12 with **t** posts and ten bases, 6927
38:12 with ten posts and **t** bases, 6927
Lev 26: 8 a hundred of you will chase **t thousand,** 8047
26:26 **t** women will be able to bake your bread 6924
27: 5 and of a female at **t** shekels. 6930
27: 7 and of a female at **t** shekels. 6927
Nu 7:14 one gold dish weighing **t** shekels, filled 6927
7:20 one gold dish weighing **t** shekels, filled 6927
7:26 one gold dish weighing **t** shekels, filled 6927
7:32 one gold dish weighing **t** shekels, filled 6927
7:38 one gold dish weighing **t** shekels, filled 6927
7:44 one gold dish weighing **t** shekels, filled 6927
7:50 one gold dish weighing **t** shekels, filled 6927
7:56 one gold dish weighing **t** shekels, filled 6927
7:62 one gold dish weighing **t** shekels, filled 6927
7:68 one gold dish weighing **t** shekels, filled 6927
7:74 one gold dish weighing **t** shekels, filled 6927
7:80 one gold dish weighing **t** shekels, filled 6927
7:86 with incense weighed **t** shekels each, 6927
11:19 or two days, or five, **t** or twenty days, 6927
11:32 No one gathered less than **t** homers. 6927
14:22 and tested me **t** times— 6924
29:23 " 'On the fourth day prepare **t** bulls, 6927
Dt 4:13 his covenant, the **T** Commandments, 6930
10: 4 the **T** Commandments he had proclaimed 6930
32:30 or two put **t thousand** to flight, 8047
33:17 Such are the **t thousands** *of* Ephraim; 8047
Jos 15:57 **t** towns and their villages. 6924
17: 5 Manasseh's share consisted of **t** tracts 6927
21: 5 Kohath's descendants were allotted **t** towns 6924
21:26 All these **t** towns and their pasturelands 6924
22:14 With him they sent **t** *of* the chief men, 6927
24:29 died at the age of a hundred and **t.** 6924
Jdg 1: 4 and they struck down **t** thousand men 6930
2: 8 died at the age of a hundred and **t.** 6924
3:29 about **t** thousand Moabites, all vigorous 6930
4: 6 take with you **t** thousand men of Naphtali 6930
4:10 **T** thousand men followed him, 6930
4:14 followed by **t** thousand men. 6930
6:27 So Gideon took **t** of his servants and did as 6927
7: 3 while **t** thousand remained. 6930
12:11 Elon the Zebulunite led Israel **t** years. 6924
17:10 and I'll give you **t** shekels of silver a year, 6930
20:10 We'll take **t** men out of every hundred 6924
20:10 and a thousand from **t thousand,** 8047
20:34 Then **t** thousand of Israel's finest men 6930
Ru 1: 4 After they had lived there about **t** years, 6924
4: 2 Boaz took **t** of the elders of the town 6927
1Sa 1: 8 Don't I mean more to you than **t** sons?" 6924
15: 4 and **t** thousand men from Judah. 6930
17:17 of roasted grain and these **t** loaves of bread 6927
17:18 along these **t** cheeses to the commander 6930
25: 5 So he sent **t** young men and said to them, 6927
25:38 About **t** days later, the LORD struck Nabal 6930
2Sa 15:16 but he left **t** concubines to take care of 6924
18: 3 but you are worth **t** thousand of us. 6927
18:11 to give you **t** shekels of silver and 6927
18:15 And **t** of Joab's armor-bearers surrounded Absalom, 6927
2Sa 19:43 "We have **t** shares in the king; 6924
20: 3 the **t** concubines he had left to take care of 6924
1Ki 4:23 **t** head of stall-fed cattle, 6927
5:14 to Lebanon in shifts of **t** thousand a month, 6930
6: 3 and projected **t** cubits from the front of 6924
6:23 cherubim of olive wood, each **t** cubits high. 6924
6:24 **t** cubits from wing tip to wing tip. 6924
6:25 The second cherub also measured **t** cubits, 6924
6:26 The height of each cherub was **t** cubits. 6924
7:10 some measuring **t** cubits and some eight. 6924
7:23 measuring **t** cubits from rim to rim 6924
7:24 gourds encircled it—**t** to a cubit. 6924
7:27 He also made **t** movable stands of bronze; 6924
7:37 This is the way he made the **t** stands. 6924
7:38 He then made **t** bronze basins, 6927
7:38 one basin to go on each of the **t** stands. 6924
7:43 the **t** stands with their ten basins; 6924
7:43 the ten stands with their **t** basins; 6927
11:31 "Take **t** pieces for yourself, 6927
11:31 of Solomon's hand and give you **t** tribes. 6927
11:35 from his son's hands and give you **t** tribes. 6930
14: 3 Take **t** loaves of bread with you, 6927
2Ki 5: 5 taking with him **t** talents of silver, 6924
5: 5 six thousand shekels of gold and **t** sets 6924
13: 7 **t** chariots and ten thousand foot soldiers, 6927
13: 7 ten chariots and **t** thousand foot soldiers, 6930
14: 7 the one who defeated **t** thousand Edomites 6930
15:17 and he reigned in Samaria **t** years. 6924
20: 9 Shall the shadow go forward **t** steps, 6924
20: 9 or shall it go back **t** steps?" 6924
20:10 for the shadow to go forward **t** steps," 6924
20:10 "Rather, have it go back **t** steps." 6924
20:11 the shadow go back the **t** steps it had gone 6924
24:14 and artisans—a total of **t** thousand. 6930
25:25 came with **t** men and assassinated Gedaliah 6927
1Ch 6:61 Kohath's descendants were allotted **t** towns 6924
29: 7 and **t thousand** darics of gold, 8052
29: 7 **t** thousand talents of silver, 6930
2Ch 4: 1 twenty cubits wide and **t** cubits high. 6924
4: 2 measuring **t** cubits from rim to rim 6924
4: 3 figures of bulls encircled it—**t** to a cubit. 6924
4: 6 He then made **t** basins for washing 6927
4: 7 He made **t** gold lampstands according to 6924
4: 8 He made **t** tables and placed them in 6927
14: 1 the country was at peace for **t** years. 6924
25:11 where he killed **t** thousand men of Seir. 6930
25:12 also captured **t** thousand men alive, 6930
27: 5 **t** thousand cors of wheat 6930
27: 5 of wheat and **t** thousand cors of barley. 6930
30:24 with a thousand bulls and **t** thousand sheep 6930
36: 9 in Jerusalem three months and **t** days. 6930
Ezr 8:24 Hashabiah and **t** of their brothers, 6927
Ne 4:12 near them came and told us **t** times over, 6924
5:18 and every **t** days an abundant supply 6930
11: 1 to bring one out of every **t** to live 6927
Est 3: 9 and I will put **t** thousand talents of silver 6930
9:10 the **t** sons of Haman son of Hammedatha, 6930
9:12 the **t** sons of Haman in the citadel of Susa. 6930
9:13 let Haman's **t** sons be hanged on gallows." 6930
9:14 and they hanged the **t** sons of Haman. 6930
Job 19: 3 **T** times now you have reproached me; 6924
Ps 91: 7 **t thousand** at your right hand, 8047
Ecc 7:19 Wisdom makes one wise man more powerful than **t** rulers 6927
SS 5:10 outstanding among **t thousand.** 8047
Isa 38: 8 by the sun go back the **t** steps it has gone 6924
38: 8 the **t** steps it had gone down. 6924
Jer 41: 1 with **t** men to Gedaliah son of Ahikam 6927
41: 2 and the **t** men who were with him got up 6930
41: 8 **t** of them said to Ishmael, "Don't kill us! 6927
42: 7 **T** days later the word of the LORD came 6930
Eze 40:11 it was **t** cubits and its length was thirteen 6924
41: 2 The entrance was **t** cubits wide, 6924
42: 4 an inner passageway **t** cubits wide and 6924
45:14 from each cor (which consists of **t** baths 6930
45:14 for **t** baths are equivalent to a homer). 6930
Da 1:12 "Please test your servants for **t** days: 6927
1:14 to this and tested them for **t** days. 6927
1:15 the end of the **t** days they looked healthier 6927
1:20 he found them **t** times better than all 6924
7: 7 the former beasts, and it had **t** horns. 10573
7:10 **t thousand** *times* ten thousand stood 10649
7:10 ten thousand times **t thousand** stood 10649
7:20 to know about the **t** horns on its head and 10573
7:24 The **t** horns are ten kings who will come 10573
7:24 The ten horns are **t** kings who will come 10573
Am 5: 3 a hundred strong will have only **t** left." 6927
6: 9 If **t** men are left in one house, 6927
Mic 6: 7 with **t thousand** rivers of oil? 8047
Hag 2:16 of twenty measures, there were only **t.** 6927
Zec 8:23 "In those days **t** men from all languages 6927
Mt 18:24 owed him **t thousand** talents was brought *3691*
20:24 When the **t** heard about this, *1274*
25: 1 be like **t** virgins who took their lamps *1274*
25:28 and give it to the one who has the **t** talents. *1274*
Mk 10:41 When the **t** heard about this, *1274*
Lk 14:31 with **t** thousand men to oppose the one *1274*
15: 8 a woman has **t** silver coins and loses one. *1274*
17:12 **t** men who had leprosy met him. *1274*
17:17 Jesus asked, "Were not all **t** cleansed? *1274*
19:13 So he called **t** of his servants *1274*
19:13 of his servants and gave them **t** minas. *1274*
19:16 'Sir, your mina has earned **t** more.' *1274*
19:17 take charge of **t** cities.' *1274*
19:24 and give it to the one who has **t** minas.' *1274*
19:25 " 'Sir,' they said, 'he already has **t!**' *1274*
Ac 25: 6 After spending eight or **t** days with them, *1274*
1Co 4:15 though you have **t thousand** guardians *3692*
14:19 to instruct others than **t thousand** words in *3692*
Rev 2:10 and you will suffer persecution *for* **t** days. *1274*
5:11 and **t thousand** times ten thousand. *3689*
5:11 and ten thousand times **t thousand.** *3689*
12: 3 and **t** horns and seven crowns on his heads. *1274*
13: 1 He had **t** horns and seven heads, *1274*
13: 1 with **t** crowns on his horns, *1274*
17: 3 and had seven heads and **t** horns. *1274*
17: 7 which has the seven heads and **t** horns. *1274*
17:12 The **t** horns you saw are ten kings who have *1274*
17:12 The ten horns you saw are **t** kings who have *1274*
17:16 The beast and the **t** horns you saw will hate *1274*

TEN-ACRE (1) [ACRE]

Isa 5:10 A **t** vineyard will produce only a bath 6930+7538

TEN-STRINGED (3) [STRING]

Ps 33: 2 make music to him on the **t** lyre. 6917
92: 3 to the music of the **t** lyre and the melody of 6917
144: 9 on the **t** lyre I will make music to you, 6917

TENANTS (16)

Lev 25:23 and you are but aliens and my **t.** 9369
Job 31:39 or broken the spirit of its **t,** 1251
SS 8:11 he let out his vineyard to **t.** 5757
Mt 21:34 he sent his servants to the **t** *1177*
21:35 "The **t** seized his servants; *1177*
21:36 and the **t** treated them the same way. *NIG*
21:38 "But when the **t** saw the son, *1177*
21:40 what will he do *to* those **t?**" *1177*
21:41 "and he will rent the vineyard to other **t,** *1177*
Mk 12: 2 the **t** to collect from them some of the fruit *1177*
12: 7 the **t** said to one another, 'This is the heir. *1177*
12: 9 He will come and kill those **t** and give *1177*
Lk 20:10 At harvest time he sent a servant to the **t** *1177*
20:10 But the **t** beat him and sent him away *1177*
20:14 the **t** saw him, they talked the matter over. *1177*
20:16 He will come and kill those **t** and give *1177*

TEND (12) [TENDED, TENDING, TENDS]

Ge 30:36 Jacob *continued to* **t** the rest of Laban's 8286
46:32 are shepherds; *they* **t livestock,** 408+2118+5238
Lev 24: 3 Aaron *is to* **t** the lamps before the LORD 6885
1Sa 17:15 and forth from Saul to **t** his father's sheep 8286
SS 8:12 two hundred are for *those who* **t** its fruit. 5757
Jer 23: 2 says to the shepherds who **t** my people: 8286
23: 4 place shepherds over them *who will* **t** them, 8286
Eze 34:14 *I will* **t** them in a good pasture, 8286
34:15 *I* myself *will* **t** my sheep 8286
34:23 my servant David, and *he will* **t** them; 8286
34:23 he *will* **t** them and be their shepherd. 8286
Jnh 4:10 though *you did* not **t** it or make it grow. 6661

TENDED (3) [TEND]

Ge 46:34 'Your servants *have* **t livestock** 408+2118+5238
Lev 24: 4 before the LORD *must be* **t** continually. 6885
Hos 12:12 and to pay for her *he* **t sheep.** 9068

TENDER (12) [TENDERLY, TENDERNESS]

Ge 18: 7 **t** calf and gave it to a servant, 8205
33:13 "My lord knows that the children are **t** and 8205
Dt 32: 2 like abundant rain on **t plants.** 6912
2Ki 19:26 like **t** green **shoots,** 3764
Pr 4: 3 I was a boy in my father's house, still **t,** 8205
Isa 37:27 like **t** green **shoots,** 3764
47: 1 No more will you be called **t** or delicate. 8205
53: 2 He grew up before him like a **t shoot,** 3437
Eze 17:22 a **t** *sprig* from its topmost shoots 8205
Mt 24:32 as its twigs get **t** and its leaves come out, *559*
Mk 13:28 as its twigs get **t** and its leaves come out, *559*
Lk 1:78 because of the **t mercy** of our God, *1799+5073*

TENDERHEARTED (KJV) See COMPASSIONATE, INDECISIVE

TENDERLY (3) [TENDER]

Ge 34: 3 he loved the girl and spoke **t** *to* her. 4213+6584
Isa 40: 2 Speak **t** to Jerusalem, 4213+6584
Hos 2:14 lead her into the desert and speak **t** 4213+6584

TENDERNESS (2) [TENDER]

Isa 63:15 Your **t** and compassion are withheld 2162+5055
Php 2: 1 if any **t** and compassion, *5073*

TENDING (11) [TEND]

Ge 30:31 go on **t** your flocks and watching over them: 8286
37: 2 was **t** the flocks with his brothers, 8286
Ex 3: 1 Now Moses was **t** the flock of Jethro 8286
1Sa 16:11 Jesse answered, "but *he is* **t** the sheep." 8286
Ps 78:71 from **t** the sheep he brought him to be 339
Jer 6: 3 each **t** his own portion." 8286
Eze 34:10 I will remove them from **t** the flock so that 8286
Am 7:15 But the LORD took me from **t** the flock 339
Mt 8:33 Those **t** the pigs ran off, went into the town *1081*
Mk 5:14 Those **t** the pigs ran off and reported this in *1081*
Lk 8:34 those **t** the pigs saw what had happened, *1081*

TENDON (2) [TENDONS]

Ge 32:32 Israelites do not eat the **t** attached to 1630+5962
32:32 of Jacob's hip was touched near the **t.** 1630+5962

TENDONS (2) [TENDON]

Eze 37: 6 I will attach **t** to you and make flesh come 1630
37: 8 and **t** and flesh appeared on them 1630

TENDS (4) [TEND]

Ex 30: 7 every morning when he **t** the lamps. 3512
Pr 27:18 *He who* **t** a fig tree will eat its fruit, 5915
Isa 40:11 *He* **t** his flock like a shepherd: 8286
1Co 9: 7 Who **t** a flock and does not drink of *4477*

TENONS (KJV) See PROJECTIONS

TENS (10) [TEN]

Ex 18:21 thousands, hundreds, fifties and **t.** 6930
18:25 thousands, hundreds, fifties and **t.** 6930
Dt 1:15 of fifties and of **t** and as tribal officials. 6930
1Sa 18: 7 and David his **t of thousands."** 8047
18: 8 credited David with **t of thousands,"** 8047
21:11 and David his **t of thousands'?"** 8047
29: 5 and David his **t of thousands'?"** 8047
Ps 3: 6 I will not fear the **t of thousands** drawn up 8047
68:17 of God are **t of thousands** and thousands 8052
144:13 *by* **t of thousands** in our fields; 8045

TENT (286) [TENTMAKER, TENTS]

Ge 9:21 and lay uncovered inside his **t.** 185
12: 8 the hills east of Bethel and pitched his **t,** 185
13: 3 and Ai where his **t** had been earlier 185
18: 1 while he was sitting at the entrance to his **t** 185
18: 2 of his **t** to meet them and bowed low to 185
18: 6 So Abraham hurried into the **t** to Sarah. 185
18: 9 "There, in the **t,"** he said. 185
18:10 Sarah was listening at the entrance to the **t,** 185
24:67 brought her into the **t** *of* his mother Sarah, 185
26:25 There he pitched his **t,** 185
31:25 Jacob had pitched his **t** in the hill country 185
31:33 into Jacob's **t** and into Leah's tent and into 185
31:33 into Jacob's tent and into Leah's **t** and into 185
31:33 and into the **t** *of* the two maidservants, 185
31:33 After he came out of Leah's **t,** 185
31:33 he entered Rachel's **t.** 185
31:34 Laban searched through everything in the **t** 185
33:19 the plot of ground where he pitched his **t.** 185
35:21 Israel moved on again and pitched his **t** 185
Ex 16:16 for each person you have in your **t.'"** 185
18: 7 and then went into the **t.** 185
26: 7 of goat hair for the **t** over the tabernacle— 185
26: 9 curtain double at the front of the **t.** 185
26:11 the loops to fasten the **t** together as a unit. 185
26:12 for the additional length of the **t** curtains, 185
26:13 The **t** curtains will be a cubit longer on 185
26:14 for the **t** a covering of ram skins dyed red, 185
26:36 the entrance to the **t** make a curtain of blue, 185
27:19 the **t pegs** *for* it and those for the courtyard, 3845
27:21 In the **T** *of* Meeting, outside the curtain 185
28:43 the **T** *of* Meeting or approach the altar 185
29: 4 and his sons to the entrance to the **T** 185
29:10 the bull to the front of the **T** *of* Meeting, 185
29:11 at the entrance to the **T** *of* Meeting. 185
29:30 and comes to the **T** *of* Meeting to minister 185
29:32 At the entrance to the **T** *of* Meeting, 185
29:42 at the entrance to the **T** *of* Meeting before 185
29:44 "So I will consecrate the **T** *of* Meeting and 185
30:16 for the service of the **T** *of* Meeting. 185
30:18 between the **T** *of* Meeting and the altar, 185
30:20 Whenever they enter the **T** *of* Meeting, 185
30:26 Then use it to anoint the **T** *of* Meeting, 185
30:36 of the Testimony in the **T** *of* Meeting, 185
31: 7 the **T** *of* Meeting, the ark of the Testimony 185
31: 7 and all the other furnishings of the **t—** 185
33: 7 to take a **t** and pitch it outside 185
33: 7 calling it the **"t** *of* meeting." 185
33: 7 to the **t** *of* meeting outside the camp. 185
33: 8 And whenever Moses went out to the **t,** 185
33: 8 watching Moses until he entered the **t.** 185
33: 9 As Moses went into the **t,** 185
33:10 of cloud standing at the entrance to the **t,** 185
33:10 each at the entrance to his **t.** 185
33:11 Joshua son of Nun did not leave the **t** 185
35:11 the tabernacle with its **t** and its covering, 185
35:18 the **t pegs** *for* the tabernacle and for 3845
35:21 the LORD for the work on the **T** *of* Meeting, 185
36:14 of goat hair for the **t** over the tabernacle— 185
36:18 to fasten the **t** together as a unit. 185
36:19 for the **t** a covering of ram skins dyed red, 185
36:37 to the **t** they made a curtain of blue, purple 185
38: 8 at the entrance to the **T** *of* Meeting. 185
38:20 All the **t pegs** of the tabernacle and of 3845
38:30 to make the bases for the entrance to the **T** 185
38:31 and those for its entrance and all the **t pegs** 3845
39:32 the **T** *of* Meeting, was completed. 185
39:33 the **t** and all its furnishings, its clasps, 185
39:38 and the curtain for the entrance to the **t;** 185
39:40 the ropes and **t pegs** *for* the courtyard; 3845
39:40 all the furnishings for the tabernacle, the **T** 185
40: 2 the tabernacle, the **T** *of* Meeting, 185
40: 6 the tabernacle, the **T** *of* Meeting; 185
40: 7 place the basin between the **T** *of* Meeting 185
40:12 and his sons to the entrance to the **T** 185
Ex 40:19 Then he spread the **t** over the tabernacle 185
40:19 and put the covering over the **t,** 185
40:22 Moses placed the table in the **T** *of* Meeting 185
40:24 the lampstand in the **T** *of* Meeting opposite 185
40:26 in the **T** *of* Meeting in front of the curtain 185
40:29 the tabernacle, the **T** *of* Meeting, 185
40:30 the basin between the **T** *of* Meeting and 185
40:32 They washed whenever they entered the **T** 185
40:34 Then the cloud covered the **T** *of* Meeting, 185
40:35 Moses could not enter the **T** *of* Meeting 185
Lev 1: 1 and spoke to him from the **T** *of* Meeting. 185
1: 3 He must present it at the entrance to the **T** 185
1: 5 the altar on all sides at the entrance to the **T** 185
3: 2 and slaughter it at the entrance to the **T** 185
3: 8 and slaughter it in front of the **T** 185
3:13 on its head and slaughter it in front of the **T** 185
4: 4 the bull at the entrance to the **T** *of* Meeting 185
4: 5 of the bull's blood and carry it into the **T** 185
4: 7 before the LORD in the **T** *of* Meeting. 185
4: 7 of burnt offering at the entrance to the **T** 185
4:14 as a sin offering and present it before the **T** 185
4:16 to take some of the bull's blood into the **T** 185
4:18 the altar that is before the LORD in the **T** 185
4:18 of burnt offering at the entrance to the **T** 185
6:16 they are to eat it in the courtyard of the **T** 185
6:26 in the courtyard of the **T** *of* Meeting. 185
6:30 into the **T** *of* Meeting to make atonement 185
8: 3 the entire assembly at the entrance to the **T** 185
8: 4 at the entrance to the **T** *of* Meeting. 185
8:31 to the **T** *of* Meeting and eat it there with 185
8:33 not leave the entrance to the **T** *of* Meeting 185
8:35 at the entrance to the **T** *of* Meeting day 185
9: 5 to the front of the **T** *of* Meeting, 185
9:23 Moses and Aaron then went into the **T** 185
10: 7 not leave the entrance to the **T** *of* Meeting 185
10: 9 into the **T** *of* Meeting, 185
12: 6 to the **T** *of* Meeting a year-old lamb for 185
14: 8 he must stay outside his **t** for seven days. 185
14:11 before the LORD at the entrance to the **T** 185
14:23 at the entrance to the **T** *of* Meeting, 185
15:14 before the LORD to the entrance to the **T** 185
15:29 at the entrance to the **T** *of* Meeting. 185
16: 7 before the LORD at the entrance to the **T** 185
16:16 He is to do the same for the **T** *of* Meeting, 185
16:17 No one is to be in the **T** *of* Meeting from 185
16:20 the **T** *of* Meeting and the altar, 185
16:23 "Then Aaron is to go into the **T** *of* Meeting 185
16:33 for the **T** *of* Meeting and the altar, 185
17: 4 of bringing it to the entrance to the **T** 185
17: 5 to the **T** *of* Meeting and sacrifice them 185
17: 6 the entrance to the **T** *of* Meeting and burn 185
17: 9 to the **T** *of* Meeting to sacrifice it to 185
19:21 to the **T** *of* Meeting for a guilt offering to 185
24: 3 of the Testimony in the **T** *of* Meeting, 185
Nu 1: 1 to Moses in the **T** *of* Meeting in the Desert 185
2: 2 "The Israelites are to camp around the **T** 185
2:17 Then the **T** *of* Meeting and the camp of 185
3: 7 the whole community at the **T** *of* Meeting 185
3: 8 of all the furnishings of the **T** *of* Meeting, 185
3:25 At the **T** *of* Meeting the Gershonites were 185
3:25 for the care of the tabernacle and **t,** 185
3:25 at the entrance to the **T** *of* Meeting, 185
3:37 their bases, **t pegs** and ropes. 3845
3:38 in front of the **T** *of* Meeting. 185
4: 3 to serve in the work in the **T** *of* Meeting. 185
4: 4 "This is the work of the Kohathites in the **T** 185
4:15 to carry those things that are in the **T** 185
4:23 to serve in the work at the **T** *of* Meeting. 185
4:25 the tabernacle, the **T** *of* Meeting, 185
4:25 for the entrance to the **T** *of* Meeting, 185
4:28 the service of the Gershonite clans at the **T** 185
4:30 to serve in the work at the **T** *of* Meeting. 185
4:31 as they perform service at the **T** 185
4:32 **t pegs,** ropes, all their equipment 3845
4:33 of the Merarite clans as they work at the **T** 185
4:35 to serve in the work in the **T** *of* Meeting, 185
4:37 in the Kohathite clans who served in the **T** 185
4:39 to serve in the work at the **T** *of* Meeting, 185
4:41 in the Gershonite clans who served at the **T** 185
4:43 to serve in the work at the **T** *of* Meeting, 185
4:47 of serving and carrying the **T** *of* Meeting 185
6:10 at the entrance to the **T** *of* Meeting. 185
6:13 He is to be brought to the entrance to the **T** 185
6:18 at the entrance to the **T** *of* Meeting, 185
7: 5 that they may be used in the work at the **T** 185
7:89 When Moses entered the **T** *of* Meeting 185
8: 9 the Levites to the front of the **T** *of* Meeting 185
8:15 they are to come to do their work at the **T** 185
8:19 the **T** *of* Meeting on behalf of the Israelites 185
8:22 to do their work at the **T** *of* Meeting under 185
8:24 in the work at the **T** *of* Meeting, 185
8:26 in performing their duties at the **T** 185
9:15 the **T** *of* the Testimony, was set up, 185
9:17 from above the **T,** the Israelites set out; 185
10: 3 at the entrance to the **T** *of* Meeting. 185
11:10 each at the entrance to his **t.** 185
11:16 Have them come to the **T** *of* Meeting, 185
11:24 and had them stand around the **T.** 185
11:26 but did not go out to the **T.** 185
12: 4 "Come out to the **T** *of* Meeting, 185
12: 5 to the **T** and summoned Aaron and Miriam. 185
12:10 When the cloud lifted from above the **T,** 185
14:10 the glory of the LORD appeared at the **T** 185
16:18 at the entrance to the **T** *of* Meeting. 185
16:19 at the entrance to the **T** *of* Meeting, 185
16:42 and turned toward the **T** *of* Meeting, 185
16:43 and Aaron went to the front of the **T** 185
Lev 16:50 at the entrance to the **T** *of* Meeting, 185
17: 4 Place them in the **T** *of* Meeting in front of 185
17: 7 the staffs before the LORD in the **T** *of* 185
17: 8 The next day Moses entered the **T** *of* 185
18: 2 and your sons minister before the **T** *of* 185
18: 3 and are to perform all the duties of the **T,** 185
18: 4 and be responsible for the care of the **T** 185
18: 4 all the work at the **T—** 185
18: 6 to the LORD to do the work at the **T** 185
18:21 for the work they do while serving at the **T** 185
18:22 on the Israelites must not go near the **T** 185
18:23 the Levites who are to do the work at the **T** 185
18:31 for it is your wages for your work at the **T** 185
19: 4 toward the front of the **T** *of* Meeting. 185
19:14 that applies when a person dies in a **t:** 185
19:14 the **t** and anyone who is in it will 185
19:18 dip it in the water and sprinkle the **t** and all 185
20: 6 from the assembly to the entrance to the **T** 185
25: 6 at the entrance to the **T** *of* Meeting. 185
25: 8 and followed the Israelite into the **t.** 7688
27: 2 the entrance to the **T** *of* Meeting and stood 185
31:54 into the **T** *of* Meeting as a memorial for 185
Dt 31:14 Call Joshua and present yourselves at the **T** 185
31:14 and presented themselves at the **T** 185
31:15 the LORD appeared at the **T** in a pillar 185
31:15 the cloud stood over the entrance to the **T.** 185
Jos 7:21 They are hidden in the ground inside my **t,** 185
7:22 and they ran to the **t,** and there it was, 185
7:22 hidden in his **t,** with the silver underneath. 185
7:23 They took the things from the **t,** 185
7:24 his **t** and all that he had, 185
18: 1 and set up the **T** *of* Meeting there. 185
19:51 of the LORD at the entrance to the **T** 185
Jdg 4:11 and pitched his **t** by the great tree 185
4:17 however, fled on foot to the **t** *of* Jael, 185
4:18 So he entered her **t,** and she put a covering 185
4:20 "Stand in the doorway of the **t,"** he told her. 185
4:21 up a **t** peg and a hammer and went quietly 185
4:22 with the **t peg** through his temple— 3845
5:26 Her hand reached for the **t peg,** 3845
7:13 It struck the **t** with such force that 185
7:13 that the **t** overturned and collapsed." 185
1Sa 2:22 at the entrance to the **T** *of* Meeting. 185
4:10 and every man fled to his **t.** 185
17:54 the Philistine's weapons in his own **t.** 185
2Sa 6:17 inside the **t** that David had pitched for it, 185
7: 2 while the ark of God remains in a **t."** 3749
7: 6 to place with a **t** as my dwelling. 185
16:22 they pitched a **t** for Absalom on the roof, 185
20: 1 Every man to his **t,** O Israel!" 185
1Ki 1:39 from the sacred **t** and anointed Solomon. 185
2:28 to the **t** *of* the LORD and took hold of 185
2:29 that Joab had fled to the **t** *of* the LORD 185
2:30 So Benaiah entered the **t** *of* the LORD 185
8: 4 the LORD and the **T** *of* Meeting and all 185
2Ki 7: 8 and entered another **t** and took some things 185
1Ch 6:32 the tabernacle, the **T** *of* Meeting, 185
9:19 for guarding the thresholds of the **T** just 185
9:21 the gatekeeper at the entrance to the **T** 185
9:23 the house called the **T.** 185
15: 1 a place for the ark of God and pitched a **t** 185
16: 1 inside the **t** that David had pitched for it, 185
17: 1 of the covenant of the LORD is under a **t."** 3749
17: 5 I have moved from one **t site** to another, 185
23:32 responsibilities for the **T** *of* Meeting, 185
2Ch 1: 3 for God's **T** *of* Meeting was there, 185
1: 4 he had pitched a **t** for it in Jerusalem. 185
1: 6 the bronze altar before the LORD in the **T** 185
1:13 from before the **T** *of* Meeting. 185
5: 5 up the ark and the **T** *of* Meeting and all 185
24: 6 and by the assembly of Israel for the **T** *of* 185
Job 4:21 Are not the **cords of** their **t** pulled up, 3857
5:24 You will know that your **t** is secure; 185
11:14 and allow no evil to dwell in your **t,** 185
18: 6 The light in his **t** becomes dark; 185
18:14 from the security of his **t** and marched off 185
18:15 Fire resides in his **t;** 185
19:12 against me and encamp around my **t.** 185
20:26 and devour what is left in his **t.** 185
22:23 If you remove wickedness far from your **t** 185
Ps 19: 4 the heavens he has pitched a **t** for the sun, 185
52: 5 snatch you up and tear you from your **t;** 185
61: 4 to dwell in your **t** forever and take refuge 185
76: 2 His **t** is in Salem, his dwelling place in Zion. 6108
78:60 the **t** he had set up among men. 185
91:10 no disaster will come near your **t.** 185
104: 2 he stretches out the heavens like a **t** 3749
Pr 14:11 but the **t** *of* the upright will flourish. 185
SS 1: 5 like the **t curtains** *of* Solomon. 3749
Isa 13:20 no Arab *will* **pitch** *his* **t** there, 182
33:20 a **t** that will not be moved; 185
38:12 a shepherd's **t** my house has been pulled 185
40:22 and spreads them out like a **t** to live in. 185
54: 2 "Enlarge the place of your **t,** 185
54: 2 stretch your **t** curtains wide, 5438
Jer 10:20 My **t** is destroyed; 185
10:20 now to pitch my **t** or to set up my shelter. 185
La 2: 4 like fire on the **t** *of* the Daughter of Zion. 185
Am 9:11 "In that day I will restore David's fallen **t.** 6109
Zec 10: 4 From Judah will come the cornerstone,
from him the **t peg,** 3845
Ac 15:16 and rebuild David's fallen **t.** *5008*
2Co 5: 1 that if the earthly **t** we live in is destroyed, *5011*
5: 4 For while we are in this **t,** *5008*
2Pe 1:13 as long as I live in the **t** of this body, *5013*
Rev 7:15 and he who sits on the throne *will* **spread**
his **t** over them. *5012*

TENT-DWELLING (1) [DWELL]
Jdg 5:24 most blessed of t women. 185+928+2021

TENTH (68) [TEN]
Ge 8: 5 continued to recede until the t month, 6920
8: 5 and on the first day of the t month the tops 6920
14:20 Then Abram gave him a t of everything. 5130
28:22 that you give me *I will* **give** you **a t."** 6923+6923
Ex 12: 3 that on the t day of this month each man is 6917
16:36 (An omer is *one* t *of* an ephah.) 6920
29:40 With the first lamb offer a t *of* an ephah 6928
Lev 5:11 for his sin a t *of* an ephah of fine flour for 6920
6:20 a t *of* an ephah of fine flour as 6920
14:21 a t of an ephah of fine flour mixed with oil 6928
16:29 On the t day of the seventh month 6917
23:27 "The t day of this seventh month is 6917
25: 9 on the t day of the seventh month; 6917
27:32 every t animal that passes under 6920
Nu 5:15 also take an offering of a t *of* an ephah 6920
7:66 On the t day Ahiezer son of Ammishaddai, 6920
15: 4 of a t *of* an ephah of fine flour mixed with 6928
18:26 as your inheritance, you must present a t of 5130
28: 5 of a t *of* an ephah of fine flour mixed with 6920
28:13 a t of an ephah of fine flour mixed with oil. 6928
29: 7 " 'On the t day of this seventh month hold 6917
Dt 14:22 **Be sure to set aside a** t of all that 6923+6923
23: 2 even down to the t generation. 6920
23: 3 even down to the t generation. 6920
26:12 you have finished **setting aside a t** 5130+6923
Jos 4:19 the t day of the first month the people went 6917
1Sa 8:15 *He will* **take a** t *of* your grain and 6923
8:17 *He will* **take a** t *of* your flocks, 6923
2Ki 25: 1 on the t day of the tenth month, 6917
25: 1 on the tenth day of the t month, 6920
1Ch 12:13 Jeremiah the t and Macbannai 6920
24:11 the ninth to Jeshua, the t to Shecaniah, 6920
25:17 the t to Shimei, his sons and relatives, 12 6920
27:13 The t, for the tenth month, 6920
27:13 The tenth, for the t month, 6920
Ezr 10:16 of the t month they sat down to investigate 6920
Ne 10:38 the Levites are to bring a t *of* the tithes up 5130
Est 2:16 in the royal residence in the t month, 6920
Isa 6:13 And though a t remains in the land, 6920
Jer 32: 1 the LORD in the t year of Zedekiah king 6920
39: 1 in the t month, Nebuchadnezzar king of 6920
52: 4 on the t day of the tenth month, 6917
52: 4 on the tenth day of the t month, 6920
52:12 On the t day of the fifth month, 6917
Eze 20: 1 in the fifth month on the t day, 6917
24: 1 in the t month on the tenth day, 6920
24: 1 in the tenth month on the t day, 6917
29: 1 In the t year, in the tenth month on 6920
29: 1 in the t month on the twelfth day, 6920
33:21 in the t month on the fifth day, 6920
40: 1 on the t of the month, in the fourteenth 6917
45:11 a t *of* a homer and the ephah a tenth of 5130
45:11 of a homer and the ephah a t *of* a homer; 6920
45:14 a t *of* a bath from each cor (which consists 5130
Zec 8:19 seventh and t months will become joyful 6920
Mt 23:23 *You* **give a t of** your spices— *620*
Lk 11:42 because *you* **give God a t of** your mint, *620*
18:12 I fast twice a week and **give a t of** *620*
Jn 1:39 It was about the t hour. *1281*
Heb 7: 2 and Abraham gave him a t of everything. *1281*
7: 4 Even the patriarch Abraham gave him a t *1281*
7: 5 *to* **collect a t from** the people— *620+2400*
7: 6 yet *he* **collected a t** from Abraham *1282*
7: 8 the t is collected by men who die; *1281*
7: 9 that Levi, who collects the t, *1281*
7: 9 **paid the** t through Abraham, *1282*
Rev 11:13 a severe earthquake and a t of the city *1281*
21:20 the t chrysoprase, the eleventh jacinth, *1281*

TENTMAKER (1) [TENT]
Ac 18: 3 and because he was a t as they were, *5010*

TENTS (58) [TENT]
Ge 4:20 of those who live in t and raise livestock. 185
9:27 may Japheth live in the t *of* Shem, 185
13: 5 also had flocks and herds and t. 185
13:12 of the plain and **pitched** *his* t near Sodom. 182
13:18 So Abram **moved** *his* t and went to live 182
25:27 a quiet man, staying among the t. 185
Ex 33: 8 and stood at the entrances to their t, 185
Nu 1:52 The Israelites *are to* **set up** their t 2837
1:53 *are to* **set up** their t around the tabernacle 2837
16:24 'Move away from the t *of* Korah, 5438
16:26 from the t *of* these wicked men! 185
16:27 So they moved away from the t *of* Korah, 5438
16:27 and little ones at the entrances to their t. 185
24: 5 "How beautiful are your t, 185
Dt 1:27 You grumbled in your t and said, 185
5:30 "Go, tell them to return to their t. 185
11: 6 their t and every living thing that belonged 185
16: 7 Then in the morning return to your t. 185
33:18 and you, Issachar, in your t. 185
Jdg 6: 5 with their livestock and their t like swarms 185
7: 8 the rest of the Israelites to their t but kept 185
2Sa 11:11 ark and Israel and Judah are staying in t, 6109
1Ki 12:16 To your t, O Israel! 185
20:12 and the kings were drinking in their t, 6109
20:16 with him were in their t getting drunk. 6109
2Ki 7: 7 and fled in the dusk and abandoned their t 185
7: 8 of the camp and entered one of the t. 185
2Ki 7:10 and the t left just as they were." 185
2Ch 10:16 To your t, O Israel! 185
Job 8:22 and the t *of* the wicked will be no more." 185
12: 6 The t of marauders are undisturbed, 185
15:34 the t *of* those who love bribes. 185
21:28 the t where wicked men lived?' 185
Ps 69:25 let there be no one to dwell in their t. 185
78:28 inside their camp, all around their t. 5438
78:51 the firstfruits of manhood in the t *of* Ham. 185
78:67 Then he rejected the t *of* Joseph, 185
83: 6 the t *of* Edom and the Ishmaelites, 185
84:10 the house of my God than dwell in the t *of* 185
106:25 They grumbled in their t and did not obey 185
118:15 Shouts of joy and victory resound in the t 185
120: 5 that I live among the t *of* Kedar! 185
SS 1: 5 dark like the t *of* Kedar, 185
1: 8 and graze your young goats by the t *of* 5438
Jer 4:20 In an instant my t are destroyed, 185
6: 3 they will pitch their t around her, 185
30:18 " 'I will restore the fortunes of Jacob's t 185
35: 7 but must always live in t. 185
35:10 We have lived in t and have fully obeyed 185
37:10 and only wounded men were left in their t, 185
49:29 Their t and their flocks will be taken; 185
Eze 25: 4 set up their camps and pitch their t among 5438
Da 11:45 He will pitch his royal t between the seas 185
Hos 9: 6 and thorns will overrun their t. 185
12: 9 I will make you live in t again, 185
Hab 3: 7 I saw the t *of* Cushan in distress, 185
Mal 2:12 may the LORD cut him off from the t *of* Jacob 185
Heb 11: 9 he lived in t, as did Isaac and Jacob, *5008*

TERAH (13)
Ge 11:24 he became the father of T. 9561
11:25 And after he became the father of T, 9561
11:26 After T had lived 70 years, 9561
11:27 This is the account of T. 9561
11:27 T became the father of Abram, 9561
11:28 While his father T was still alive, 9561
11:31 T took his son Abram, 9561
11:32 T lived 205 years, and he died in Haran. 9561
Nu 33:27 They left Tahath and camped at T. 9562
33:28 They left T and camped at Mithcah. 9562
Jos 24: 2 'Long ago your forefathers, including T 9561
1Ch 1:26 Serug, Nahor, T 9561
Lk 3:34 the son of Abraham, the son *of* T, *2508*

TEREBINTH (2)
Isa 6:13 But as the t and oak leave stumps 461
Hos 4:13 poplar and t, where the shade is pleasant. 461

TERESH (2)
Est 2:21 at the king's gate, Bigthana and T, two of 9575
6: 2 that Mordecai had exposed Bigthana and T, 9575

TERMS (14)
Ge 23:16 Abraham **agreed** to Ephron's *t* AIT
Dt 29: 1 These are the t *of* the covenant 1821
29: 9 Carefully follow the t *of* this covenant, 1821
1Sa 11: 4 of Saul and reported these t to the people, 1821
1Ki 5: 1 because he had always been **on friendly** t 170
Job 34:33 Should God then reward you **on** your t 4946+6640
Jer 11: 2 "Listen to the t *of* this covenant and 1821
11: 3 'Cursed is the man who does not obey the t 1821
11: 4 **the** t I commanded your forefathers 889[S]
11: 6 to the t *of* this covenant and follow them. 1821
32:11 the sealed copy containing the t and 5184
34:18 the t *of* the covenant they made before me, 1821
Lk 14:32 a long way off and will ask for t of peace. *3836*
Ro 6:19 **I put this in human** t because you are *474+3306*

TERRACES (8)
2Sa 5: 9 from the **supporting** t inward. 4864
1Ki 9:15 the **supporting** t, the wall of Jerusalem, 4864
9:24 he constructed the **supporting** t. 4864
11:27 the **supporting** t and had filled in the gap 4864
1Ch 11: 8 the **supporting** t to the surrounding wall, 4864
2Ch 32: 5 and reinforced the **supporting** t *of* the City 4864
Job 24:11 They crush olives among the t; 8805
Jer 31:40 the t out to the Kidron Valley on the east 8727

TERRESTRIAL (KJV) See EARTHLY

TERRIBLE (11) [TERROR]
Ex 9: 3 will bring a t plague on your livestock 3878+4394
Nu 20: 5 bring us up out of Egypt to this t place? 8273
Dt 6:22 signs and wonders—great and t— 8273
Ne 13:27 that you too are doing all this t wickedness 1524
Jer 4: 6 from the north, even t destruction." 1524
6: 1 looms out of the north, even t destruction. 1524
21: 6 and they will die of a t plague. 1524
26:19 about to bring a t disaster on ourselves!" 1524
Mt 8: 6 at home paralyzed and in t suffering." *1267*
2Ti 3: 1 There will be t times in the last days. *5901*
Rev 16:21 because the plague was so t. *3489*

TERRIBLY (1) [TERROR]
Mt 15:22 My daughter is suffering t from *2809*

TERRIFIED (51) [TERROR]
Ge 45: 3 because *they were* t at his presence. 987
Ex 14:10 *They were* t and cried out to the LORD. 3707+4394
15:15 The chiefs of Edom *will be* t, 987
Nu 22: 3 and Moab *was* t because there were 1593
Dt 1:29 Then I said to you, *"Do* not *be* t; 6907
7:21 *Do* not *be* t by them, 6907
20: 3 not *be* t or give way to panic before them. 2905
31: 6 Do not be afraid or t because of them, 6907
Jos 1: 9 *Do* not *be* t; do not be discouraged, 6907
Jdg 20:41 and the men of Benjamin *were* t, 987
1Sa 17:11 all the Israelites were dismayed and t. 3707+4394
31: 4 his armor-bearer *was* t and would not 3707+4394
2Ki 10: 4 But *they were* t and said, 3707+4394+4394
1Ch 10: 4 his armor-bearer *was* t and would not 3707+4394
Est 7: 6 Haman *was* t before the king and queen. 1286
Job 21: 6 When I think about this, *I am* t; 987
23:15 That is why *I am* t before him; 987
23:16 the Almighty *has* t me. 987
41:25 When he rises up, the mighty *are* t; 1593
Ps 90: 7 by your anger and t by your indignation. 987
104:29 When you hide your face, *they are* t; 987
Isa 19:17 to whom Judah is mentioned *will be* t, 7064
33:14 The sinners in Zion *are* t; 7064
51: 7 Do not fear the reproach of men or *be* t 3169
Jer 1:17 *Do* not *be* t by them, 3169
10: 2 the ways of the nations or *be* t by signs in 3169
10: 2 though the nations *are* t by them. 3169
17:18 *let* them *be* t, but keep me from terror. 3169
23: 4 and they will no longer be afraid or t, 3169
46: 5 They are t, they are retreating, 3146
51:32 the marshes set on fire, and the soldiers t." 987
Eze 2: 6 not be afraid of what they say or t by them, 3169
3: 9 Do not be afraid of them or t by them, 3169
19: 7 and all who were in it **were** t by his roaring. 9037
26:18 in the sea *are* t at your collapse.' 987
Da 4: 5 that passed through my mind t me. 10097
4:19 and his thoughts t him. 10097
5: 9 even more t and his face grew more pale. 10097
8:17 *I was* t and fell prostrate. 1286
Ob 1: 9 Your warriors, O Teman, *will be* t, 3169
Jnh 1:10 This t them and they asked, 1524+3707+3711
Mt 14:26 saw him walking on the lake, *they were* t. *5429*
17: 6 they fell facedown to the ground, t. *5379+5828*
27:54 *they were* t, and exclaimed, *5379+5828*
Mk 4:41 *They were* t and asked each other, *3489+5828+5832*
6:50 because *they* all saw him and *were* t. *5429*
Lk 2: 9 glory of the Lord shone around them and *they were* t. *3489+5828+5832*
Jn 6:19 walking on the water, and *they were* t. *5828*
Rev 11:13 and the survivors were t and gave glory to *1873*
18:10 T at her torment, they will stand far off *5832*
18:15 will stand far off, t at her torment. *1328+5832*

TERRIFIES (2) [TERROR]
Job 22:10 why sudden peril t you, 987
Ps 2: 5 in his anger and t them in his wrath, 987

TERRIFY (9) [TERROR]
2Ch 32:18 to t them and make them afraid in order 3707
Job 7:14 then you frighten me with dreams and t me 1286
13:11 *Would* not his splendor t you? 1286
33:16 in their ears and t them with warnings, 3169
Ps 10:18 who is of the earth, *may* t no more. 6907
83:15 your tempest and t them with your storm. 987
Jer 1:17 or *I will* t you before them. 3169
Hab 2:17 your destruction of animals *will* t you. 3169
Zec 1:21 to t them and throw down these horns of 3006

TERRIFYING (4) [TERROR]
Job 15:21 T sounds fill his ears; 7065
Da 7: 7 t and frightening and very powerful. 10167
7:19 the others and most t, with its iron teeth 10167
Heb 12:21 The sight was so t that Moses said, *5829*

TERRITORIES (5) [TERRITORY]
Ge 10: 5 the maritime peoples spread out into their t 824
10:20 in their t and nations. 824
10:31 in their t and nations. 824
Jos 19:51 These are the t that Eleazar the priest, 5709
1Ch 13: 2 to the rest of our brothers throughout the t 824

TERRITORY (97) [TERRITORIES]
Ge 9:27 *May* God **extend the** t of Japheth; 7332
14: 7 and they conquered the whole t *of* the 8441
48: 6 in the t they **inherit** they will be reckoned 5709
Ex 34:24 before you and enlarge your t, 1473
Nu 20:16 a town on the edge of your t. 1473
20:17 until we have passed through your t." 1473
20:21 to let them go through their t, 1473
21:13 in the desert extending into Amorite t. 1473
21:22 until we have passed through your t." 1473
21:23 not let Israel pass through his t. 1473
22:36 the Arnon border, at the edge of his t. 1473
32:33 the whole land with its cities and the t 1473
Dt 1: 5 East of the Jordan in the t *of* Moab, 824
2: 4 the t *of* your brothers the descendants 1473
3: 8 of the Amorites the t east of the Jordan, 824
3:12 the Reubenites and the Gadites the t north 889[S]
3:16 and the Gadites I gave the t extending NIH
11:24 Your t will extend from the desert 1473
11:30 in the t *of* those Canaanites living in 824
12:20 the LORD your God has enlarged your t 1473
19: 8 If the LORD your God enlarges your t, 1473
34: 2 the t *of* Ephraim and Manasseh, 824

Jos 1: 4 Your t will extend from the desert 1473
11:22 No Anakites were left in Israelite t; 824
12: 1 whose t they took over east of the Jordan, 824
12: 4 And the t *of* Og king of Bashan, 1473
13: 3 of Egypt to the t *of* Ekron on the north, all 1473
13: 3 (the t of the five Philistine rulers in Gaza, NIH
13:11 the t *of* the people of Geshur and Maacah, 1473
13:16 The t from Aroer on the rim of 1473
13:25 The t *of* Jazer, all the towns of Gilead 1473
13:26 and from Mahanaim to the t of Debir; 1473
13:27 the t up to the end of the Sea 1473
13:30 The t extending from Mahanaim 1473
15: 1 extended down to the t *of* Edom, 1473
16: 2 over to the t *of* the Arkites in Ataroth, 1473
16: 3 the t *of* the Japhletites as far as the region 1473
16: 5 This was the t *of* Ephraim, clan by clan: 1473
17: 7 The t *of* Manasseh extended from Asher 1473
17:10 The t *of* Manasseh reached the sea 1473
18: 5 Judah is to remain in its t on the south and 1473
18: 5 the south and the house of Joseph in its t 1473
18:11 Their allotted t lay between the tribes 1473
19: 1 Their inheritance lay within the t *of* Judah. 5709
19: 9 inheritance within the t *of* Judah. 5709
19:12 to the t *of* Kisloth Tabor and went on 1473
19:18 Their t included: Jezreel, 1473
19:25 Their t included: Helkath, 1473
19:41 The t *of* their inheritance included: 1473
19:47 had difficulty taking possession of their t, 1473
21:41 the t *held by* the Israelites were forty-eight 299
Jdg 1: 3 "Come up with us into the t **allotted** 1598
1:18 each city with its t. 1473
11:18 They did not enter the t *of* Moab, 1473
11:20 did not trust Israel to pass through his t. 1473
1Sa 6: 1 in Philistine t seven months, 8441
6: 9 If it goes up to its own t, 1473
7:13 and did not invade Israelite t again. 1473
7:14 and Israel delivered the **neighboring** t from 1473
9: 4 Then he passed through the t *of* Benjamin, 824
27: 7 in Philistine t a year and four months. 8441
27:11 as long as he lived in Philistine t. 8441
30:14 and **the** t belonging to Judah and the Negev 889S
1Ki 9:19 and throughout all the t he ruled. 824
15:17 from leaving or entering the t of Asa king NIH
2Ki 6:23 from Aram stopped raiding Israel's t. 824
10:32 the Israelites throughout their t 1473
18: 8 as far as Gaza and its t. 1473
24: 7 the king of Babylon had taken all his t, 889S
1Ch 4:10 that you would bless me and enlarge my t! 1473
6:54 of their settlements **allotted** as their t 1473
6:66 as their t towns from the tribe of Ephraim. 1473
2Ch 8: 6 and throughout all the t he ruled. 824
16: 1 from leaving or entering the t of Asa king NIH
20:10 whose t you would not allow Israel 889S
34:33 from all the t belonging to the Israelites, 824
Jer 1: 1 one of the priests at Anathoth in the t 824
17:26 from the t *of* Benjamin and 824
32: 8 'Buy my field at Anathoth in the t 824
32:44 sealed and witnessed in the t *of* Benjamin, 824
33:13 in the t *of* Benjamin, in the villages 824
37:12 to leave the city to go to the t *of* Benjamin 824
Eze 16:27 against you and reduced your t; 2976
48: 2 it will border the t *of* Dan from east 1473
48: 3 it will border the t *of* Asher from east 1473
48: 4 it will border the t *of* Naphtali from east 1473
48: 5 it will border the t *of* Manasseh from east 1473
48: 6 it will border the t *of* Ephraim from east 1473
48: 7 it will border the t *of* Reuben from east 1473
48: 8 the t *of* Judah from east to west will be 1473
48:12 bordering the t *of* the Levites. 1473
48:13 "Alongside the t *of* the priests, 1473
48:24 it will border the t *of* Benjamin from east 1473
48:25 it will border the t *of* Simeon from east 1473
48:26 it will border the t *of* Issachar from east 1473
48:27 it will border the t *of* Zebulun from east 1473
2Co 10:16 work already done in another man's t. *2834*

TERROR (74) [TERRIBLE, TERRIBLY, TERRIFIED, TERRIFIES, TERRIFY, TERRIFYING, TERRORISTS, TERRORS]

Ge 35: 5 and the t *of* God fell upon the towns all 3150
Ex 15:16 t and dread will fall upon them. 399
23:27 "I will send my t ahead of you and throw 399
Lev 26:16 I will bring upon you **sudden** t, 988
Dt 2:25 the t and fear of you on all the nations 7065
11:25 the t and fear of you on the whole land, 7065
26: 8 with great t and with miraculous signs 4616
28:67 the t that will fill your hearts and the sights 7065
32:25 in their homes t will reign. 399
1Sa 11: 7 the t *of* the LORD fell on the people, 7065
28: 5 he was afraid; t **filled** his heart. 3006+4394
2Sa 17: 2 *I would* **strike** him **with** t, 3006
2Ch 14:14 the t *of* the LORD had fallen upon them. 7065
Job 9:34 so that his t would frighten me no more. 399
15:24 Distress and anguish **fill** him **with** t; 1286
39:20 striking t with his proud snorting? 399
Ps 9:20 Strike them with t, O LORD; 4616
31:13 there is t on every side; 4471
48: 5 and were astounded; they fled *in* t. 987
78:33 their days in futility and their years in t. 988
91: 5 You will not fear the t *of* night, 7065
Pr 21:15 to the righteous but t to evildoers. 4745
Isa 13: 8 T *will* **seize** *them,* pain and anguish 987
17:14 In the evening, **sudden** t! 1166
19:17 land of Judah will bring t to the Egyptians; 2505
21: 1 from the desert, from a land of t. 3707
Isa 22: 5 of tumult and trampling and t in the Valley 4428
24:17 T and pit and snare await you, 7065
24:18 Whoever flees at the sound of t will fall 7065
28:19 of this message will bring sheer t. 2317
31: 9 Their stronghold will fall because of t; 4471
33:18 In your thoughts you will ponder the former t: 399
44:11 *they will be* **brought down to** t and infamy. 7064
47:12 perhaps *you will* **cause** t. 6907
51:13 that *you* **live in** constant t every day 7064
54:14 T will be far removed; 4745
Jer 6:25 and there is t on every side. 4471
8:15 for a time of healing but there was only t. 1287
14:19 for a time of healing but there is only t. 1287
15: 8 down on them anguish and t. 988
17:17 Do not be a t to me; 4745
17:18 let them be terrified, but *keep* me from t. 3169
20: 4 a t to yourself and to all your friends; 4471
20:10 I hear many whispering, "T on every side! 4471
30: 5 Cries of fear are heard—t, not peace. 7065
32:21 and an outstretched arm and with great t. 4616
46: 5 and there is t on every side," 4471
48:43 T and pit and snare await you, 7065
48:44 "Whoever flees from the t will fall into 7065
49: 5 I will bring t on you from all those 7065
49:16 The t you inspire and the pride 9526
49:29 Men will shout to them, 'T on every side!' 4471
50: 2 put to shame, Marduk **filled with** t. 3169
50: 2 put to shame and her idols **filled with** t.' 3169
50:36 *They will be* **filled with** t. 3169
50:38 idols that will go mad with t. 399
La 3:47 We have suffered t and pitfalls, 7065
Eze 7:18 on sackcloth and be clothed with t. 7146
7:25 When t comes, they will seek peace, 7888
23:46 a mob against them and give them over to t 2400
26:16 Clothed with t, they will sit on the ground, 3010
26:17 you put your t on all who lived there. 3154
32:23 All who had spread t in the land of 3154
32:24 All who had spread t in the land of 3154
32:25 their t had spread in the land of the living, 3154
32:26 by the sword because they spread their t in 3154
32:27 the t *of* these warriors had stalked through 3154
32:30 the slain in disgrace despite the t caused 3154
32:32 I had him spread t in the land of the living, 3154
Da 10: 7 not see it, but such t overwhelmed them 3010
Am 6: 3 the evil day and bring near a reign of t. 2805
Lk 21:26 Men will faint from t, *5832*
Ro 13: 3 rulers **hold** no t for those who do right, *1639+5832*
Rev 11:11 and t struck those who saw them. *3489+5832*

TERRORISTS (1) [TERROR]

Ac 21:38 a revolt and led four thousand t *467+3836+4974*

TERRORS (14) [TERROR]

Job 6: 4 God's t are marshaled against me. 1243
13:21 and stop frightening me with your t. 399
18:11 T startle him on every side 1166
18:14 of his tent and marched off to the king of t. 1166
20:25 T will come over him; 399
24:17 they make friends with the t *of* darkness. 1166
27:20 T overtake him like a flood; 1166
30:15 T overwhelm me; my dignity is driven away 1166
Ps 55: 4 the t *of* death assail me. 399
73:19 completely swept away by t! 1166
88:15 I have suffered your t and am in despair. 399
88:16 your t have destroyed me. 1243
SS 3: 8 prepared for the t of the night. 7065
La 2:22 so you summoned *against* me t 4471

TERTIUS (1)

Ro 16:22 I, T, who wrote down this letter, *5470*

TERTULLUS (2)

Ac 24: 1 of the elders and a lawyer named T, *5472*
24: 2 T presented his case before Felix: *5472*

TEST (56) [TESTED, TESTER, TESTING, TESTINGS, TESTS]

Ex 16: 4 In this way *I will* t them 5814
17: 2 Why *do you* **put** the LORD **to the** t?" 5814
20:20 God has come to t you, 5814
Dt 6:16 *Do* not t the LORD your God as you did 5814
8: 2 and to t you in order to know what was 5814
8:16 to t you so that in the end it might go well 5814
Jdg 2:22 to t Israel and see whether they will keep 5814
3: 1 to t all those Israelites who had 5814
3: 4 They were left to t the Israelites 5814
6:39 *Allow me* one more t with the fleece. 5814
1Ki 10: 1 she came to t him with hard questions. 5814
1Ch 29:17 that you t the heart and are pleased 1043
2Ch 9: 1 to Jerusalem to t him with hard questions. 5814
32:31 to t him and to know everything that was 5814
Job 7:18 and t him every moment? 1043
12:11 the ear t words as the tongue tastes food? 1043
Ps 17: 3 though *you* t me, you will find nothing; 7671
26: 2 T me, O LORD, and try me, 1043
78:18 *They willfully* **put** God **to the** t 5814
78:41 Again and again, *they* **put** God **to the** t; 5814
78:56 But *they* **put** God **to the** t 5814
106:14 *they* **put** God **to the** t. 5814
139:23 t me and know my anxious thoughts. 1043
Ecc 2: 1 *I will* t you with pleasure 5814
Isa 7:12 *I will* not **put** the LORD **to the** t." 5814
Jer 6:27 that you may observe and t their ways. 1043
9: 7 "See, I will refine and t them, 1043
11:20 you who judge righteously and t the heart 1043
12: 3 you see me and t my thoughts about you. 1043
La 3:40 Let us examine our ways and t them, 2983
Da 1:12 "Please t your servants for ten days: 5814
Zec 13: 9 I will refine them like silver and t them 1043
Mal 3:10 T me in this," says the LORD Almighty, 1043
Mt 4: 7 *'Do* not **put** the Lord your God **to the** t.' " *1733*
19: 3 Some Pharisees came to him *to* t him. *4279*
Mk 8:11 *To* t him, they asked him for a sign *4279*
Lk 4:12 *'Do* not **put** the Lord your God **to the** t.' " *1733*
10:25 an expert in the law stood up *to* t Jesus. *1733*
Jn 6: 6 He asked this only *to* t him, *4279*
Ac 5: 9 could you agree *to* t the Spirit of the Lord? *4279*
15:10 why *do you try to* t God by putting on *4279*
Ro 12: 2 *to* t **and approve** what God's will is— *1507*
1Co 3:13 fire *will* t the quality of each man's work. *1507*
10: 9 *We should* not t the Lord, *1733*
2Co 2: 9 if you **would stand the** t and be obedient *1509*
8: 8 but *I want to* t the sincerity of your love *1507*
13: 5 whether you are in the faith; t yourselves. *1507*
13: 5 unless, of course, *you* **fail the** t? *99+1639*
13: 6 discover that we *have* not **failed the** t. *99+1639*
13: 7 see that we have **stood the** t but *1511*
Gal 6: 4 Each one *should* t his own actions. *1507*
1Th 5:21 T everything. Hold on to the good. *1507*
Jas 1:12 because when he has stood the t, *1511*
1Jn 4: 1 but t the spirits to see whether they are *1507*
Rev 2:10 will put some of you in prison to t *you,* *4279*
3:10 upon the whole world *to* t those who live *4279*

TESTATOR (KJV) See ONE WHO MADE IT

TESTED (29) [TEST]

Ge 22: 1 Some time later God t Abraham. 5814
42:15 And this is how *you will* **be** t: 1043
42:16 in prison, so that your words *may* **be** t to see 1043
Ex 15:25 and there *he* t them. 5814
17: 7 the Israelites quarreled and because they t 5814
Nu 14:22 who disobeyed and t me ten times— 5814
Dt 33: 8 *You* t him at Massah; 5814
Job 23:10 *when he has* t me, I will come forth as gold. 1043
28:27 he confirmed it and t it. 2983
34:36 that Job *might* **be** t to the utmost 1043
Ps 66:10 For *you,* O God, t us; 1043
81: 7 *I* t you at the waters of Meribah. 1043
95: 9 where your fathers t and tried me, 5814
119:140 Your promises *have* **been** thoroughly t, 7671
Pr 27:21 but man is t by the praise he receives. NIH
Ecc 7:23 All this *I* t by wisdom and I said, 5814
Isa 28:16 "See, I lay a stone in Zion, a t stone, 1046
48:10 *I have* t you in the furnace of affliction. 1047
Da 1:14 he agreed to this and t them for ten days. 5814
Mt 16: 1 and Sadducees came to Jesus and t him *4279*
22:35 t him with this question: *4279*
Mk 10: 2 Some Pharisees came and t him by asking, *4279*
Lk 11:16 Others t him by asking for a sign *4279*
Ac 20:19 *although* I *was severely* t by the plots of *4279*
Ro 16:10 Greet Apelles, t **and approved** in Christ. *1511*
1Ti 3:10 They *must* first **be** t; *1507*
Heb 3: 9 where your fathers t and tried me and *4279*
11:17 By faith Abraham, *when* God t him, *4279*
Rev 2: 2 *you have* t those who claim to be apostles *4279*

TESTER (1) [TEST]

Jer 6:27 a t **of metals** and my people the ore, 1031

TESTICLES (2)

Lev 21:20 or running sores or damaged t. 863
22:24 the LORD an animal whose t are bruised, NIH

TESTIFIED (14) [TESTIFY]

2Sa 1:16 Your own mouth t against you 6699
2Ch 24:19 and though *they* t against them, 6386
Mk 14:56 Many t **falsely** against him, *6018*
Jn 3:26 the one you t **about**— *3455*
5:33 "You have sent to John and *he has* t to *3455*
5:37 And the Father who sent me *has* himself t *3455*
13:21 Jesus was troubled in spirit and t, *3455*
Ac 6:13 They produced false witnesses, *who* t, *3306*
6:23 *When they had* t and proclaimed the word of *1371*
13:22 *He* t concerning him: *3455*
23:11 As *you have* t about me in Jerusalem, *1371*
1Co 15:15 for *we have* t about God that he raised *3455*
Heb 2: 4 God **also** t to it by signs, *5296*
2: 6 But there is a place where someone *has* t: *1371*

TESTIFIES (17) [TESTIFY]

Job 16: 8 my gauntness rises up and t against me. 6699
Isa 3: 9 The look on their faces t against them; 6699
Hos 5: 5 Israel's arrogance t against them; 6699
7:10 Israel's arrogance t against him, 6699
Jn 1:15 John t concerning him. *3455*
3:32 He t **to** what he has seen and heard, *3455*
5:32 There is another who t in my favor, *3455*
5:36 t that the Father has sent me. *3455*
8:18 I am one who t for myself; *3455*
19:35 and he t so that you also may believe. *NIG*
21:24 This is the disciple who t to these things *3455*
Ro 8:16 The Spirit himself t **with** our spirit *5210*
2Co 1:12 Our conscience t that we have conducted *3457*
Heb 10:15 The Holy Spirit also t to us **about** this. *3455*

1Jn 5: 6 And it is the Spirit who t, 3455
Rev 1: 2 who t to everything he saw— 3455
22:20 He who t to these things says, "Yes, 3455

TESTIFY (47) [TESTIFIED, TESTIFIES, TESTIFYING, TESTIMONY]

Ge 30:33 my honesty *will* t for me in the future, 6699
Lev 5: 1 to t regarding something he has seen 6332
Dt 8:19 *I* t against you today that you will surely 6386
31:21 this song *will* t against them, 4200+6332+6699
31:28 call heaven and earth to t against them. 6386
1Sa 12: 3 T against me in the presence of the LORD 6699
1Ki 21:10 and have *them* t that he has cursed 6386
Job 15: 6 your own lips t against you. 6699
Ps 50: 7 O Israel, and *I will* t against you: 6386
Pr 24:28 *Do* not t against your neighbor without cause, 2118+6332
29:24 he is put under oath and *dare* not t. 5583
Isa 59:12 and our sins t against us. 6699
Jer 14: 7 Although our sins t against us, O LORD, 6699
Am 3:13 "Hear this and t against the house 6386
Zep 3: 8 "for the day I will stand up to t. 6332
Mal 3: 5 I will be quick to t against sorcerers, 6332
Mt 23:31 So *you* t against yourselves that you are 3455
Lk 11:48 So *you* t that you approve of what 1639+3459
Jn 1: 7 as a witness to t concerning that light, 3455
1:34 have seen and *I* t that this is the Son of God. 3455
3:11 and *we* t to what we have seen, 3455
3:28 You yourselves *can* t that I said, 3455
5:31 I t about myself, my testimony is not valid. 3455
5:39 These are the Scriptures that t about me, 3455
7: 7 because I t that what it does is evil. 3455
8:14 "Even if I t on my own behalf, 3455
15:26 from the Father, he *will* t about me. 3455
15:27 And you also *must* t, 3455
18:23 Jesus replied, "t as to what is wrong. 3455
18:37 I came into the world, to t to the truth. 3455
Ac 4:33 power the apostles *continued to* t to 625+3457
10:42 to preach to the people and *to* t that he is 1371
10:43 All the prophets t about him 3455
22: 5 the high priest and all the Council *can* t. 3455
23:11 so you must also t in Rome." 3455
26: 5 have known me for a long time and can t, 3455
26:22 and so I stand here and t to small and great 3455
Ro 3:21 to which the Law and the Prophets t. 3455
10: 2 For *I can* t about them that they are zealous 3455
2Co 8: 3 For *I* t that they gave as much as they were 3455
Gal 4:15 *I can* t that, if you could have done so, 3455
Php 1: 8 God can t how I long for all of you with 3459
2Ti 1: 8 So do not be ashamed to t about our Lord, 3457
Jas 5: 3 Their corrosion *will* t against you 1639+3457
1Jn 1: 2 we have seen it and t to it, 3455
4:14 and t that the Father has sent his Son to be 3455
5: 7 For there are three that t: 3455

TESTIFYING (5) [TESTIFY]

Ac 18: 5 t to the Jews that Jesus was the Christ. 1371
20:24 the task of t to the gospel of God's grace. 1371
1Ti 6:13 who *while* t before Pontius Pilate made 3455
Heb 3: 5 t to what would be said in the future. 1650+3457
1Pe 5:12 and t that this is the true grace of God. 2148

TESTIMONY (113) [TESTIFY]

Ex 16:34 Aaron put the manna in front of the T, 6343
20:16 not give false t against your neighbor. 6332
23: 2 When *you* give t in a lawsuit, 6699
25:16 put in the ark the T, which I will give you. 6343
25:21 on top of the ark and put in the ark the T, 6343
25:22 that are over the ark of the T, 6343
26:33 the clasps and place the ark of the T behind 6343
26:34 Put the atonement cover on the ark of the T 6343
27:21 outside the curtain that is in front of the T, 6343
30: 6 the curtain that is before the ark of the T— 6343
30: 6 the atonement cover that is over the T— 6343
30:26 the Tent of Meeting, the ark of the T, 6343
30:36 of it to powder and place it in front of the T 6343
31: 7 the ark of the T with the atonement cover 6343
31:18 he gave him the two tablets of the T, 6343
32:15 the mountain with the two tablets of the T 6343
34:29 with the two tablets of the T in his hands, 6343
38:21 the tabernacle, the tabernacle of the T, 6343
39:35 the ark of the T with its poles and 6343
40: 3 the ark of the T in it and shield the ark with 6343
40: 5 of the T and put the curtain at the entrance 6343
40:20 He took the T and placed it in the ark, 6343
40:21 and shielded the ark of the T, 6343
Lev 16:13 the atonement cover above the T, 6343
24: 3 the curtain of the T in the Tent of Meeting, 6343
Nu 1:50 to be in charge of the tabernacle of the T— 6343
1:53 the tabernacle of the T so that wrath will 6343
1:53 for the care of the tabernacle of the T." 6343
4: 5 and cover the ark of the T with it. 6343
7:89 the atonement cover on the ark of the T. 6343
9:15 the Tent of the T, was set up, 6343
10:11 from above the tabernacle of the T. 6343
17: 4 in the Tent of Meeting in front of the T, 6343
17: 7 before the LORD in the Tent of the T. 6343
17: 8 of the T and saw that Aaron's staff, 6343
17:10 "Put back Aaron's staff in front of the T, 6343
18: 2 before the Tent of the T. 6343
35:30 be put to death as a murderer only on the t 7023
35:30 But no one is to be put to death *on the* t 6699
Dt 5:20 not give false t against your neighbor. 6332
17: 6 the t *of* two or three witnesses a man shall 7023
Dt 17: 6 no one shall be put to death on the t *of* only 7023
19:15 A matter must be established by the t *of* two 7023
19:18 giving false t against his brother, 6699
Jos 4:16 of the T to come up out of the Jordan." 6343
2Ch 24: 6 of Israel for the Tent of the T?" 6343
Pr 12:17 A truthful witness gives honest t, 5583
25:18 a sharp arrow is the man who gives false t 6332
Isa 8:16 Bind up the t and seal up the law 9496
8:20 To the law and to the t! 9496
29:21 with false t deprive the innocent of justice. NIH
Mt 8: 4 the gift Moses commanded, as a t to them." 3457
15:19 adultery, sexual immorality, theft, false t, 6019
18:16 by the t of two or three witnesses.' 5125
19:18 do not steal, *do* not give false t, 6018
24:14 in the whole world as a t to all nations, 3457
26:62 t that these men *are* bringing against you?" 2909
27:13 t *they are* bringing against you?" 2909
Mk 1:44 for your cleansing, as a t to them." 3457
6:11 when you leave, as a t against them." 3457
10:19 *do* not give false t, do not defraud, 6018
14:57 Then some stood up and gave this false t 6018
14:59 Yet even then their t did not agree. 3456
14:60 What *is* this t *that* these men *are* bringing against you?" 2909
Lk 5:14 for your cleansing, as a t to them." 3457
9: 5 you leave their town, as a t against them." 3457
18:20 do not steal, *do* not give false t, 6018
22:71 "Why do we need any more t? 3456
Jn 1:19 Now this was John's t when the Jews 3456
1:32 Then John gave this t: "I saw the Spirit 3455
2:25 He did not need man's t about man, 3455
3:11 but still you people do not accept our t. 3456
3:32 but no one accepts his t. 3456
4:39 in him because of the woman's t, 3455
5:31 "If I testify about myself, my t is not valid. 3456
5:32 and I know that *his* t about me is valid. 3455+3456+4005
5:34 Not that I accept human t; 3456
5:36 "I have t weightier than that of John. 3456
8:13 as your own witness; your t is not valid." 3456
8:14 my t is valid, for I know where I came from 3456
8:17 In your own Law it is written that the t 3456
19:35 The man who saw it *has* given t, 3455
19:35 and his t is true. 3456
21:24 We know that his t is true. 3456
Ac 7:44 the tabernacle *of* the T with them in 3457
14:17 Yet he has not left himself without t: 282
22:18 they will not accept your t about me.' 3456
1Co 1: 6 our t about Christ was confirmed in you. 3457
2: 1 as I proclaimed to you the t about God. 3457
2Co 13: 1 "Every matter must be established by the t 5125
2Th 1:10 because you believed our t to you. 3457
1Ti 2: 6 the t given in its proper time. 3457
Tit 1:13 This t is true. 3456
Heb 10:28 died without mercy on the t of two or three 3459
1Jn 5: 9 We accept man's t, but God's testimony 3456
5: 9 but God's t is greater because it is 3456
5: 9 because it is the t of God, 3456
5:10 in the Son of God has this t in his heart. 3456
5:10 the t God has given about his Son. 3456
5:11 this is the t: God has given us eternal life, 3456
3Jn 1:12 and you know that our t is true. 3456
Rev 1: 2 the word of God and the t of Jesus Christ. 3456
1: 9 of the word of God and the t of Jesus. 3456
6: 9 of God and the t they had maintained. 3456
11: 7 Now when they have finished their t, 3456
12:11 of the Lamb and by the word *of* their t; 3456
12:17 and hold to the t of Jesus. 3456
15: 5 the tabernacle *of* the T, was opened. 3457
17: 6 the blood *of* those who bore t to Jesus. 3459
19:10 and with your brothers who hold to the t 3456
19:10 For the t of Jesus is the spirit of prophecy." 3456
20: 4 of their t for Jesus and because of the word 3456
22:16 have sent my angel *to* give you this t for 3455

TESTING (5) [TEST]

Dt 13: 3 The LORD your God *is* t you to find out 5814
Eze 21:13 " '*T will* surely *come*. 1043
Lk 8:13 but in the time *of* t they fall away. 4280
Heb 3: 8 during the time *of* t in the desert, 4280
Jas 1: 3 the t of your faith develops perseverance. 1510

TESTINGS (1) [TEST]

Dt 4:34 by t, by miraculous signs and wonders, 4999

TESTS (4) [TEST]

Job 34: 3 the ear t words as the tongue tastes food. 1043
Pr 17: 3 but the LORD t the heart. 1043
Ecc 3:18 God t them so that they may see that 1405
1Th 2: 4 but God, who t our hearts. 1507

TETHER (1) [TETHERED]

Ge 49:11 *He will* t his donkey to a vine, 673

TETHERED (1) [TETHER]

2Ki 7:10 only t horses and donkeys, 673

TETRARCH (7)

Mt 14: 1 At that time Herod the t heard the reports 5490
Lk 3: 1 Herod t of Galilee, his brother Philip 5489
3: 1 of Galilee, his brother Philip t of Iturea 5489
3: 1 and Lysanias t of Abilene— 5489
3:19 when John rebuked Herod the t because 5490
Lk 9: 7 Now Herod the t heard about all that was going on. 5490
Ac 13: 1 up with Herod the t) and Saul. 5490

TEXT (4)

Est 3:14 of the t of the edict was to be issued as law 4181
4: 8 of the t *of* the edict for their annihilation, 4181
8:13 of the t of the edict was to be issued as law 4181
Jer 29: 1 This is the t *of* the letter that the prophet 1821

THADDAEUS (2)

Mt 10: 3 James son of Alphaeus, and T; 2497
Mk 3:18 Thomas, James son of Alphaeus, T, 2497

THAHASH (KJV) See TAHASH

THAMAH (KJV) See TEMAH

THAMAR (KJV) See TAMAR

THAN (535)

Ge 3: 1 Now the serpent was more crafty t any of 4946
4:13 "My punishment is more t I can bear. 4946
7:20 to a depth of more t twenty feet. 4946
18:28 number of the righteous is five less t 2893
19: 9 We'll treat you worse t them." 4946
25:23 one people will be stronger t the other, 4946
27:12 a curse on myself rather t a blessing." 2256+4202
28:17 This is none other t the house of God; 561+3954
29:19 that I give her to you t to some other man. 4946
29:30 and he loved Rachel more t Leah. 4946
37: 3 Now Israel loved Joseph more t any 4946
37: 4 that their father loved him more t any 4946
38:26 "She is more righteous t I, 4946
39: 9 No one is greater in this house t I am. 4946
41:40 to the throne will I be greater t you." 4946
48:19 his younger brother will be greater t he, 4946
49:12 His eyes will be darker t wine, 4946
49:12 his teeth whiter t milk. 4946
49:26 Your father's blessings are greater t 6584
49:26 t the bounty of the age-old hills. NIH
Ex 11: 6 worse *t* there has ever been or ever will AIT
14:12 for us to serve the Egyptians t to die in 4946
18:11 that the LORD is greater t all other gods, 4946
22:20 "Whoever sacrifices to any god other t the LORD must be destroyed. 963+1194+4200
30:15 not to give more t a half shekel and 4946
30:33 puts it on anyone other t a priest 2424
36: 5 "The people are bringing more t enough 4946
36: 7 what they already had *was* more *t* enough AIT
Lev 13: 3 and the sore appears to be more t skin deep, 4946
13: 4 to be more t skin deep and the hair in it has 4946
13:20 and if it appears to be more t skin deep and 4946
13:21 and it is not more t skin deep and has faded, 4946
13:25 and it appears to be more t skin deep, 4946
13:26 in the spot and if it is not more t skin deep 4946
13:30 and if it appears to be more t skin deep and 4946
13:31 it does not seem to be more t skin deep 4946
13:32 not appear to be more t skin deep, 4946
13:34 and appears to be no more t skin deep, 4946
14:37 that appear to be deeper t the surface of 4946
15:25 at a time other t her monthly period or has 4202
22:12 daughter marries anyone other t a priest, 2424
Nu 5:20 with a man other t your husband"— 1187+4946
11:32 No one gathered less t ten homers. 5070
12: 3 more humble t anyone else on the face of 4946
13:31 they are stronger t we are." 4946
14:12 into a nation greater and stronger t they." 4946
22:15 more numerous and more distinguished t 4946
24: 7 "Their king will be greater t Agag; 4946
Dt 1:28 people are stronger and taller t we are; 4946
3:11 and was more t thirteen feet long 564+9596
4:38 and stronger t you and to bring you 4946
7: 1 seven nations larger and stronger t you— 4946
7: 7 you were more numerous t other peoples, 4946
7:14 be blessed more t any other people; 4946
7:17 "These nations are stronger t we are. 4946
9: 1 nations greater and stronger t you, 4946
9:14 nation stronger and more numerous t they." 4946
11:23 nations larger and stronger t you. 4946
17:20 not consider himself better t his brothers 4946
20: 1 and chariots and an army greater t yours, 4946
25: 3 he must not give him more *t* forty lashes. AIT
25: 3 If he is flogged more t that, 6584
30: 5 prosperous and numerous t your fathers. 4946
Jos 4:18 No sooner had they set their feet on the dry ground t the waters 3869
10: 2 it was larger t Ai, 4946
10:11 the hailstones t were killed by the swords 4946
19: 9 Judah's portion was more t they needed. 4946
22:19 other t the altar of the LORD our God. 1187+4946
22:29 other t the altar of the LORD 963+4200+4946
Jdg 2:19 to ways even more corrupt t those 4946
6:27 he did it at night rather t in the daytime. 4946
7:12 Their camels could no more be counted t 3869
7:14 be nothing other t the sword of Gideon son 561
8: 2 the gleanings of Ephraim's grapes better t 4946
8:33 No sooner had Gideon died t 889+3869
11:25 Are you better t Balak son of Zippor, 4946
14:18 "What is sweeter t honey? 4946
14:18 What is stronger t a lion?" 4946
16:30 he killed many more when he died t 4946
18:19 priest rather t just one man's household?" 196

Ru 1:13 It is more bitter for me t for you, 4946
3:10 "This kindness is greater t 4946
3:12 there is a kinsman-redeemer nearer t I. 4946
4:15 and who is better to you t seven sons, 4946
1Sa 1: 8 Don't I mean more to you t ten sons?" 4946
2:29 Why do you honor your sons **more t** me 4946
9: 2 a head taller **t** any of the others. 4946
10:23 the people he was a head taller **t** any of 4946
15:22 To obey is better **t** sacrifice, 4946
15:22 and to heed is **better t** the fat of rams. 4946
15:28 one of your neighbors—to one better **t** you. 4946
18:25 **other** price for the bride **t** 3954
18:30 David met with **more** success **t** the rest 4946
24:17 "You are **more** righteous **t** I," he said. 4946
29: 4 **better** could he regain his master's favor **t** 4202
2Sa 1:23 They were swifter **t** eagles, 4946
1:23 they were stronger **t** lions. 4946
1:26 **more** wonderful **t** that of women. 4946
6:21 who chose me **rather t** your father 4946
6:22 I will become even **more** undignified **t** this, 4946
13:14 and since he was stronger **t** she, 4946
13:15 he hated her more **t** he had loved her. 4946
13:16 greater wrong **t** what you have already done 4946
17:14 "The advice of Hushai the Arkite is better **t** 4946
18: 8 and the forest claimed more lives that day **t** 4946
19: 7 for you **t** all the calamities that have come 4946
19:43 we have a **greater** claim on David **t** you 4946
19:43 of Judah responded **even more** harshly **t** 4946
20: 5 he took longer **t** the time the king had set 4946
20: 6 will do us **more** harm **t** Absalom did. 4946
23:19 not held in greater honor **t** the Three? 4946
23:23 He was held in **greater** honor **t** any of 4946
1Ki 1:37 to make his throne even greater **t** 4946
1:47 'May your God make Solomon's name
more famous **t** yours 4946
1:47 and his throne greater **t** yours!' 4946
2:32 were better men and **more** upright **t** he. 4946
4:30 Solomon's wisdom was greater **t** 4946
4:30 and greater **t** all the wisdom of Egypt. 4946
4:31 He was wiser **t** any other man, 4946
4:31 wiser **t** Heman, Calcol and Darda, NIH
10:23 in riches and wisdom **t** all the other kings 4946
12:10 My little finger is thicker **t** my father's waist 4946
14: 9 You have done **more** evil **t** all who lived 4946
14:22 jealous anger **more t** their fathers had done. 4946
16:22 Omri's followers **proved stronger** *t* those AIT
16:25 of the LORD and sinned **more t** all those 4946
16:30 **more** evil in the eyes of the LORD **t** 4946
16:33 to anger **t** did all the kings of Israel 4946
19: 4 I am no better **t** my ancestors." 4946
20:23 surely we will be stronger **t** they. 4946
20:25 Then surely we will be stronger **t** they." 4946
2Ki 5:12 better **t** any of the waters of Israel? 4946
6:16 with us are more **t** those who are 4946
21: 9 so that they did **more** evil **t** the nations 4946
21:11 He has done more evil **t** 4946
25:16 was **more t** could be weighed. 4202
25:28 gave him a seat of honor **higher t** 4946+6584
1Ch 4: 9 Jabez was **more** honorable **t** his brothers. 4946
11:25 He was held in **greater** honor **t** any of 4946
22: 3 and more bronze **t** could be weighed. 401
22: 4 also provided **more** cedar logs **t** could 401+4200
24: 4 among Eleazar's descendants **t** among 4946
2Ch 2: 5 because our God is greater **t** all other gods. 4946
9:12 gave her **more t** she had brought 963+4200+4946
9:22 in riches and wisdom **t** all the other kings 4946
10:10 My little finger is thicker **t** my father's waist 4946
11:21 of Absalom **more t** any of his other wives 4946
17: 4 and followed his commands **rather t** 2256+4202
20:25 **more** *t* they could take away. AIT
21:13 men who were better **t** you. 4946
25: 9 "The LORD can give you much **more t** that." 4946
29:34 **more** conscientious in consecrating
themselves **t** the priests 4946
32: 7 there is a greater power with us **t** with him. 4946
33: 9 so that they did **more** evil **t** the nations 4946
Ezr 9: 6 because our sins *are* **higher t** our heads
2025+4200+5087+8049
9:13 punished us less **t** our sins have **deserved** 4946
Ne 7: 2 and feared God **more t** most men do. 4946
Est 1:19 to someone else who is better **t** she. 4946
2:15 she asked for nothing **other t** what 561+3954
2:17 Now the king was attracted to Esther **more t** 4946
2:17 his favor and approval **more t** any of 4946
3: 1 a seat of honor **higher t** that of all the other
nobles. 4946+6584
6: 6 the king would rather honor **t** me?" 3463+4946
Job 3:21 who search for it **more t** for hidden treasure, 4946
4:17 'Can a mortal be **more** righteous **t** God? 4946
4:17 Can a man be **more** pure **t** his Maker? 4946
4:19 are crushed **more readily t** a moth! 4200+7156
7: 6 "My days are swifter **t** a weaver's shuttle, 4974
7:15 **rather t** this body of mine. 4946
8:12 they wither **more quickly t** grass. 4200+7156
9:25 "My days are swifter **t** a runner; 4974
11: 8 They are **higher** *t* the heavens— AIT
11: 8 They are deeper **t** the depths of the grave— 4946
11: 9 Their measure is longer **t** the earth 4946
11: 9 the earth and wider **t** the sea. 4974
11:12 a witless man can **no more** become wise **t** 2256
11:17 Life will be brighter **t** noonday, 4946
15:10 men even older **t** your father. 4946
23:12 words of his mouth **more t** my daily bread. 4946
30: 1 "But now they mock me, men younger **t** I, 4946
32: 2 for justifying himself **rather t** God. 4946
32: 4 to Job because they were older **t** he. 4946
33:12 for God is greater **t** man. 4946
Job 35:11 who teaches **more** to us **t** to the beasts of 4946
35:11 the beasts of the earth and makes us wiser **t** 4946
42:12 the latter part of Job's life **more t** the first. 4946
Ps 4: 7 You have filled my heart with **greater** joy **t** 4946
8: 5 a little lower **t** the heavenly beings 4946
19:10 They are **more** precious **t** gold, 4946
19:10 **t** much pure gold; 4946
19:10 they are sweeter **t** honey, 4946
19:10 **t** honey from the comb. NIH
37:16 Better the little that the righteous have **t** 4946
40:12 They are more **t** the hairs of my head, 4946
51: 7 wash me, and I will be whiter **t** snow. 4946
52: 3 You love evil **rather t** good, 4946
52: 3 falsehood **rather t** speaking the truth. 4946
55:21 his words are **more** soothing **t** oil, 4946
61: 2 lead me to the rock that is higher **t** I. 4946
63: 3 Because your love is better **t** life, 4946
69:31 This will please the LORD **more t** an ox, 4946
69:31 more **t** a bull with its horns and hoofs. NIH
76: 4 **more** majestic **t** mountains rich with game. 4946
78:29 They ate till they had **more t** enough, 4394
84:10 in your courts **t** a thousand elsewhere; 4946
84:10 the house of my God **t** dwell in the tents of 4946
87: 2 of Zion **more t** all the dwellings of Jacob. 4946
89: 7 he is **more** awesome **t** all who surround
him. 6584
93: 4 Mightier **t** the thunder of the great waters, 4946
93: 4 mightier **t** the breakers of the sea— NIH
108: 4 your love, **higher t** the heavens; 4946+6584
118: 8 It is better to take refuge in the LORD **t** 4946
118: 9 It is better to take refuge in the LORD **t** 4946
119:72 from your mouth is **more** precious to me **t** 4946
119:98 Your commands make me wiser **t** my
enemies, 4946
119:99 I have **more** insight **t** all my teachers, 4946
119:100 I have **more** understanding **t** the elders, 4946
119:103 sweeter **t** honey to my mouth! 4946
119:127 I love your commands **more t** gold, 4946
119:127 **more t** pure gold, 4946
130: 6 waits for the Lord **more t** watchmen wait 4946
130: 6 more **t** watchmen wait for the morning. NIH
135: 5 that our Lord is **greater t** all gods. 4946
Pr 3:14 for she is **more** profitable **t** silver 4946
3:14 and yields **better** returns **t** gold. 4946
3:15 She is **more** precious **t** rubies; 4946
5: 3 and her speech is smoother **t** oil; 4946
8:10 knowledge **rather t** choice gold, 4946
8:11 for wisdom is **more** precious **t** rubies, 4946
8:19 My fruit is better **t** fine gold; 4946
12: 9 a nobody and yet have a servant **t** pretend 4946
15:16 of the LORD **t** great wealth with turmoil. 4946
15:17 a meal of vegetables where there is love **t** 4946
16: 8 a little with righteousness **t** much gain 4946
16:16 How much better to get wisdom **t** gold, 4946
16:16 to choose understanding **rather t** silver! 4946
16:19 among the oppressed **t** to share plunder 4946
16:32 Better a patient man **t** a warrior, 4946
16:32 a man who controls his temper **t** one who 4946
17: 1 Better a dry crust with peace and quiet **t** 4946
17:10 of discernment **more t** a hundred lashes 4946
17:12 **Better** to meet a bear robbed of her cubs **t** 440
18:19 An offended brother is **more** unyielding **t** 4946
18:24 but there is a friend who sticks closer **t** 4946
19: 1 a poor man whose walk is blameless **t** 4946
19:22 better to be poor **t** a liar. 4946
21: 3 and just is **more** acceptable to the LORD **t** 4946
21: 9 Better to live on a corner of the roof **t** share 4946
21:19 to live in a desert **t** with a quarrelsome 4946
22: 1 good name is **more** desirable **t** great riches; 4946
22: 1 to be esteemed is better **t** silver or gold. 4946
25: 7 **t** for him to humiliate you before 4946
25:24 Better to live on a corner of the roof **t** share 4946
26:12 There is **more** hope for a fool **t** 4946
26:16 **t** seven men who answer discreetly. 4946
27: 3 but provocation by a fool is heavier **t** both. 4946
27: 5 Better is open rebuke **t** hidden love. 4946
27:10 a neighbor nearby **t** a brother far away. 4946
28: 6 a poor man whose walk is blameless **t** 4946
28:23 in the end gain **more** favor **t** he who has 4946
29:20 There is more hope for a fool **t** for him. 4946
31:10 She is worth far **more t** rubies. 4946
Ecc 1: 8 are wearisome, **more t** one can say. 4202
1:16 in wisdom **more t** anyone who has ruled 6584
2: 7 also owned more herds and flocks **t** anyone 4946
2: 9 by far **t** anyone in Jerusalem before me. 4946
2:12 What more can the king's successor do **t**
what has already been done? NIH
2:13 I saw that wisdom is better **t** folly, 4946
2:13 just as light is better **t** darkness. 4946
2:24 A man can do nothing better **t** to eat 8611
3:12 that there is nothing better for men **t** to 561+3954
3:22 that there is nothing better for a man **t** 889+4946
4: 2 are happier **t** the living, who are still alive. 4946
4: 3 better **t** both is he who has not yet been, 4946
4: 6 with tranquillity **t** two handfuls with toil 4946
4: 9 Two are better **t** one, 4946
4:13 Better a poor but wise youth **t** an old 4946
5: 1 near to listen **rather t** to offer the sacrifice 4946
5: 5 It is better not to vow **t** to make a vow and 4946
6: 3 I say that a stillborn child is better off **t** he. 4946
6: 5 it has **more** rest **t** does that man— 4946
6: 9 the eye sees **t** the roving of the appetite. 4946
6:10 with one who is stronger **t** he. 4946
7: 1 A good name is better **t** fine perfume, 4946
7: 1 the day of death **better t** the day of birth. 4946
7: 2 of mourning **t** to go to a house of feasting, 4946
7: 3 Sorrow is better **t** laughter, 4946
Ecc 7: 5 a wise man's rebuke **t** to listen to the song 4946
7: 8 end of a matter is better **t** its beginning, 4946
7: 8 and patience is better **t** pride. 4946
7:10 "Why were the old days better **t** these?" 4946
7:19 Wisdom makes one wise man **more**
powerful **t** ten rulers 4946
7:26 I find **more** bitter **t** death the woman who is 4946
8:15 a man under the sun **t** to eat and drink 561+3954
9: 4 even a live dog is better off **t** a dead lion! 4946
9:16 So I said, "Wisdom is better **t** strength." 4946
9:17 words of the wise are **more** to be heeded **t** 4946
9:18 Wisdom is better **t** weapons of war, 4946
SS 1: 2 for your love is **more** delightful **t** wine. 4946
1: 4 we will praise your love **more t** wine. 4946
4:10 **much more** pleasing is your love **t** 4946
4:10 the fragrance of your perfume **t** any spice! 4946
5: 9 How is your beloved **better t** others, 4946
5: 9 How is your beloved **better t** others, 4946
Isa 1:11 *"I* **have more t enough** *of* burnt offerings, 8425
5: 4 for my vineyard **t** I have done for it? 2256+4202
13:12 I will make man scarcer **t** pure gold, 4946
13:12 **more** rare **t** the gold of Ophir. 4946
32:10 **In little more t** a year you who feel 3427+6584
40:17 by him as worthless and **less t** nothing. 4946
40:24 **t** he blows on them and they wither, 1685+2256
41:24 But you are **less t** nothing 4946
54: 1 children of the desolate woman **t** of her who 4946
55: 9 "As the heavens are higher **t** the earth, 4946
55: 9 so are my ways higher **t** your ways 4946
55: 9 and my thoughts **t** your thoughts. 4946
56: 5 and a name better **t** sons and daughters; 4946
66: 8 **no sooner** is Zion in labor **t** she gives birth 1685
Jer 3:11 "Faithless Israel is **more** righteous **t**
unfaithful Judah. 4946
4:13 his horses are swifter **t** eagles. 4946
5: 3 They made their faces harder **t** stone 4946
7:26 and did **more** evil **t** their forefathers.' 4946
15: 8 I will make their widows **more** numerous **t** 4946
16:12 you have behaved **more** wickedly **t** your
fathers. 4946
31:11 from the hand of those stronger **t** they. 4946
46:23 They are **more** numerous **t** locusts, 4946
52:20 was **more t** could be weighed. 4202
52:32 and gave him a seat of honor higher **t** those 4200
La 3: 2 walk in darkness **rather t** light; 4202
4: 6 The punishment of my people is greater **t** 4946
4: 7 Their princes were brighter **t** snow 4946
4: 7 and whiter **t** milk, 4946
4: 7 their bodies **more** ruddy **t** rubies, 4946
4: 8 But now they are blacker **t** soot; 4946
4: 9 by the sword are better off **t** those who die 4946
4:19 Our pursuers were swifter **t** eagles in 4946
Eze 3: 9 like the hardest stone, harder **t** flint. 4946
5: 6 against my laws and decrees **more t** 4946
5: 7 You have been **more** unruly **t** the nations 4946
8:15 that are even **more** detestable **t** this." 4946
15: 2 of a vine **better t** that of a branch on any of 4946
16:47 you soon became **more** depraved **t** they. 4946
16:51 You have done **more** detestable things **t** they 4946
16:52 Because your sins were **more** vile **t** theirs, 4946
16:52 they appear **more** righteous **t** you. 4946
16:61 both those who are older **t** you 4946
23:11 and prostitution she was **more** depraved **t**
her sister. 4946
28: 3 Are you wiser **t** Daniel? 4946
31: 5 So it towered higher **t** all the trees of 4946
32:19 'Are you more favored **t** others? 4946
33:32 to them you are **nothing more t** one who
sings love songs 3869
34: 8 for themselves **rather t** for my flock, 4202
36:11 and will make you prosper **more t** before. 4946
42: 5 **more** space from them **t** from the rooms 4946
42: 6 so they were smaller in floor space **t** those 4946
Da 1:10 Why should he see you looking worse **t** 4946
1:15 and **better** nourished **t** any of 4946
1:20 he found them ten times **better t** all 6584
2:30 I have **greater** wisdom **t** other living men, 10427
2:43 **any more t** iron mixes with clay.
10168+10195+10341
3:19 furnace heated seven times hotter **t** usual 10542
3:28 to give up their lives **rather t** serve 10379
4:36 and became even greater **t** before. NIH
7:20 that looked **more** imposing **t** the others and 10427
8: 3 the horns was longer **t** the other but grew 4946
11: 2 who will be far richer **t** all the others. 4946
11: 5 commanders will become even stronger **t** he 6584
11:13 muster another army, larger **t** the first; 4946
Hos 2: 7 for then I was better off **t** now.' 4946
6: 6 acknowledgement of God **rather t** burnt 4946
Am 6: 2 Are they better off **t** your two kingdoms? 4946
6: 2 Is their land larger **t** yours? 4946
Jnh 1:13 for the sea grew even wilder **t** before. NIH
4: 3 for it is better for me to die **t** to live." 4946
4: 8 "It would be better for me to die **t** to live." 4946
4:11 But Nineveh has more **t** a hundred and 4946
Mic 7: 4 the most upright **worse t** a thorn hedge. 4946
Na 3: 8 Are you better **t** Thebes, 4946
3:16 till they are **more t** the stars of the sky, 4946
Hab 1: 8 Their horses are swifter **t** leopards, 4946
1: 8 fiercer **t** wolves at dusk. 4946
1:13 up those **more** righteous **t** themselves? 4946
Hag 2: 9 be greater **t** the glory of the former house,' 4946
Zec 12: 7 not be greater **t** that of Judah. 6584
Mt 3:11 me will come one who is more powerful *t* **I,** *AIT*
5:29 for you to lose one part of your body **t** *NIG*
5:30 of your body **t** for your whole body to go *NIG*
5:47 what are you doing more **t** others? *NIG*

Mt 6:25 Is not life **more** *important t* food, *AIT*
6:25 and the body more important **t** clothes? *NIG*
6:26 Are you not much more valuable **t they?** *899*
10:15 and Gomorrah on the day of judgment **t** for *2445*
10:31 you *are* **worth more t** many sparrows. *1422*
10:37 or mother **more t** me is not worthy of me; *5642*
10:37 or daughter **more t** me is not worthy of me; *5642*
11:9 Yes, I tell you, and **more t** a prophet. *4358*
11:11 not risen anyone **greater t** John the Baptist; *3505*
11:11 in the kingdom of heaven is **greater t** he. *3505*
11:22 and Sidon on the day of judgment **t** for you. *2445*
11:24 Sodom on the day of judgment **t** for you." *2445*
12:6 that **one greater t** the temple is here. *3505*
12:12 much more valuable is a man *t* a **sheep!** *AIT*
12:41 and now *one* **greater** *t* Jonah is here. *AIT*
12:42 and now *one* **greater** *t* Solomon is here. *AIT*
12:45 seven other spirits **more wicked t** itself, *4505*
12:45 the final condition of that man is **worse t** *5937*
18:8 or crippled **t** to have two hands or two feet *2445*
18:9 with one eye **t** to have two eyes and *2445*
18:13 he is happier about that one sheep **t** about *2445*
19:24 through the eye of a needle **t** for a rich man *2445*
21:36 **more** *t* the first time, *AIT*
26:53 my disposal **more** *t* twelve legions of angels? *AIT*
27:64 This last deception will be **worse t** *5937*
Mk 1:7 After me will come one **more powerful t** I, *2708*
9:3 whiter **t** anyone in the world could bleach *NIG*
9:43 to enter life maimed **t** with two hands to go *2445*
9:45 to enter life crippled **t** to have two feet and *2445*
9:47 to enter the kingdom of God with one eye **t** *2445*
10:25 through the eye of a needle **t** for a rich man *2445*
12:31 There is no commandment **greater t** these." *3505*
12:33 is **more important t** all burnt offerings *4358*
12:43 widow has put **more** into the treasury *t* *AIT*
14:5 It could have been sold for **more t** *2062*
Lk 3:13 "Don't collect any **more** *t* you are required *AIT*
3:16 But one **more powerful t** I will come, *2708*
7:26 Yes, I tell you, and **more t** a prophet. *4358*
7:28 of women there is no one **greater t** John; *3505*
7:28 in the kingdom of God is **greater t** he." *3505*
8:8 a hundred times more **t** was sown." *NIG*
10:12 be more bearable on that day for Sodom **t** *2445*
10:14 for Tyre and Sidon at the judgment **t** *2445*
11:26 seven other spirits **more wicked t** itself, *4505*
11:26 the final condition of that man is **worse t** *5937*
11:31 and now *one* **greater** *t* Solomon is here. *AIT*
11:32 and now *one* **greater** *t* Jonah is here. *AIT*
12:7 *you are* **worth more t** many sparrows. *1422*
12:23 Life is **more** *t* food, *AIT*
12:23 and the body more **t** clothes. *NIG*
12:24 how much **more** valuable you are **t** birds! *3437*
13:2 these Galileans were worse sinners **t** all *4123*
13:4 do you think they were more guilty **t** all *4123*
14:8 a **person more distinguished t** you *1952*
15:7 **more** rejoicing in heaven over one sinner who repents **t** over *2445*
16:8 **shrewd** in dealing with their own kind *t* *AIT*
16:17 and earth to disappear **t** for the least stroke *2445*
17:2 a millstone tied around his neck **t** for him *2445*
18:14 "I tell you that this man, **rather t** the other, *4123*
18:25 through the eye of a needle **t** for a rich man *2445*
21:3 "this poor widow has put in **more** *t* all *AIT*
Jn 1:50 You shall see **greater** *things* **t** that." *3505*
4:1 and baptizing more disciples **t** John, *2445*
4:12 Are you **greater t** our father Jacob, *3505*
5:20 even **greater** things **t** these. *3505*
5:36 "I have testimony **weightier t** that of John. *3505*
7:31 he do **more** miraculous signs *t* this man?" *AIT*
8:53 Are you **greater t** our father Abraham? *3505*
10:29 who has given them to me, is **greater t** all; *3505*
11:18 Bethany was less **t** two miles from *NIG*
11:50 people **t that** the whole nation perish." *2779+3590*
12:43 from men more **t** praise from God. *2472*
13:16 no servant is **greater t** his master, *3505*
13:16 nor is a messenger **greater t** the one who *3505*
14:12 He will do even **greater** things **t** these, *3505*
14:28 for the Father is **greater t** I. *3505*
15:13 **Greater** love has no one **t** this, that he lay *3505*
15:20 'No servant is **greater t** his master.' *3505*
16:12 to say to you, more **t** you can now bear. *NIG*
17:14 world **any more t** I am of the world. *2777+4024*
21:15 do you truly love me **more** *t* these?" *AIT*
Ac 4:19 in God's sight to obey you rather **t** God. *2445*
5:29 "We must obey God rather **t** men! *2445*
17:11 Bereans were **of more noble character t** *2302*
20:35 'It is more blessed to give **t** to receive.'" *2445*
23:13 **More t** forty men were involved *4498*
23:21 because **more t** forty of them are waiting *4498*
24:11 that no **more t** twelve days ago I went up *4498*
26:13 light from heaven, **brighter t** the sun, *3288+5642*
Ro 1:25 served created things **rather t** the Creator— *4123*
8:34 **more t that,** who was raised to life— *3437*
8:37 in all these things *we are* **more t conquerors** through him *5664*
12:3 of yourself **more** highly **t** you ought, *4123*
13:11 because our salvation is nearer now **t** *2445*
14:5 One man considers one day **more** sacred **t** another; *4123*
1Co 1:25 foolishness of God is **wiser** *t* man's wisdom, *AIT*
1:25 weakness of God is **stronger** *t* man's strength. *AIT*
3:11 For no one can lay any foundation other **t** *4123*
7:9 it is better to marry **t** to burn with passion. *2445*
9:12 anything **rather t** hinder the gospel *2671+3590*
9:15 I would rather die **t** have anyone deprive me *2445*
10:22 Are we **stronger t** he? *2708*
11:17 for your meetings do more harm **t** good. *NIG*
1Co 14:5 He who prophesies is greater **t** one who speaks in tongues, *2445*
14:18 that I speak in tongues **more t** all of you. *3437*
14:19 to instruct others **t** ten thousand words in *2445*
15:6 to **more t** five hundred of the brothers at *2062*
15:10 No, I worked **harder t** all of them— *4358*
15:15 **More t that,** we are then found to *2779*
15:19 we are to be **pitied more t** all men. *1795*
2Co 5:12 in what is seen **rather t** in what is in *2779+3590*
7:7 so that my joy was **greater t ever.** *3437*
10:8 building you up **rather t** pulling you *2779+4024*
11:4 a Jesus **other t** the Jesus we preached, *257*
12:6 no one will think **more** of me **t** is warranted *5642*
Gal 1:8 from heaven should preach a gospel **other t** *4123*
1:9 to you a gospel **other t** what you accepted, *4123*
4:27 children of the desolate woman **t** of *2445+3437*
Eph 3:8 I am *less t* the **least** of all God's people, *AIT*
3:20 to do immeasurably **more t** all we ask *5642*
4:10 the very one who ascended higher *t* **all** *AIT*
Php 2:3 in humility consider others **better t** yourselves. *5660*
Col 2:8 of this world **rather t** on Christ. *2779+4024*
1Ti 1:4 These promote controversies rather **t** God's work— *2445*
5:8 the faith and is **worse t** an unbeliever. *5937*
2Ti 3:4 lovers of pleasure rather **t** lovers of God— *2445*
Phm 1:16 but **better t** a slave, as a dear brother. *5642*
1:21 knowing that you will do even **more t** I ask. *5642*
Heb 2:7 You made him a little lower **t** the angels; *4123*
2:9 who was made a little lower **t** the angels, *4123*
3:3 worthy of greater honor **t** Moses, *4123*
3:3 the builder of a house has **greater** honor *t* *AIT*
4:12 Sharper **t** any double-edged sword, *5642*
6:16 by *someone* **greater t** themselves, *3505+3836*
9:23 with better sacrifices **t** these. *4123*
11:4 Abel offered God a better sacrifice **t** Cain *4123*
11:25 with the people of God rather **t** to enjoy *2445*
11:26 of Christ as *of* **greater** value **t** the treasures *3505*
12:24 that speaks a better word **t** the blood *4123*
1Pe 1:7 your faith—of **greater worth** *t* gold, *AIT*
3:17 to suffer for doing good **t** for doing evil. *2445*
2Pe 2:20 they are **worse off** at the end **t** *5937*
2:21 **t** to have known it and then to turn their *2445*
1Jn 3:20 For God is **greater t** our hearts, *3505*
4:4 because the one who is in you is greater **t** *2445*
3Jn 1:4 I have no **greater** joy **t** to hear *3504*
Rev 2:19 and that you are now doing **more** *t* you did *AIT*

THANK (34) [THANKED, THANKFUL, THANKFULNESS, THANKING, THANKS, THANKSGIVING]

Lev 7:12 with this **t** offering he is to offer cakes 9343
22:29 "When you sacrifice a **t** offering to 9343
Dt 24:13 Then *he will* **t** you, and it will be regarded 1385
1Ch 23:30 They were also to stand every morning to **t** 3344
2Ch 29:31 Come and bring sacrifices and **t offerings** 9343
29:31 assembly brought sacrifices and **t offerings,** 9343
33:16 fellowship offerings and **t offerings** on it, 9343
Ps 50:14 Sacrifice **t offerings** to God, 9343
50:23 He who sacrifices **t offerings** honors me, 9343
56:12 I will present my **t offerings** to you. 9343
107:22 Let them sacrifice **t** offerings and tell 9343
116:17 a **t** offering to you and call on the name of 9343
Jer 17:26 and **t offerings** to the house of the LORD. 9343
33:11 of those who bring **t offerings** to the house 9343
Da 2:23 I **t** and praise you, O God of my fathers: 10312
Am 4:5 Burn leavened bread as a **t offering** 9343
Lk 17:9 *Would he* **t** the servant because he did *2400+5921*
18:11 *I* **t** you that I am not like other men— *2373*
Jn 11:41 "Father, *I* **t** you that you have heard me. *2373*
Ro 1:8 *I* **t** my God through Jesus Christ for all *2373*
1Co 1:4 *I* always **t** God for you because *2373*
10:30 because of something I **t** God for? *2373*
14:18 *I* **t** God that I speak in tongues more than all *2373*
2Co 8:16 I **t** God, who put into the heart of Titus *5921*
Php 1:3 *I* **t** my God every time I remember you. *2373*
Col 1:3 *We* always **t** God, the Father of our Lord *2373*
1Th 1:2 *We* always **t** God for all of you, *2373*
2:13 And we also **t** God continually because, *2373*
3:9 How can we **t** God enough for you *2374*
2Th 1:3 We ought always *to* **t** God for you, *2373*
2:13 But we ought always *to* **t** God for you, *2373*
1Ti 1:12 *I* **t** Christ Jesus our Lord, *2400+5921*
2Ti 1:3 *I* **t** God, whom I serve, *2400+5921*
Phm 1:4 *I* always **t** my God as I remember you *2373*

THANKED (2) [THANK]

Lk 17:16 He threw himself at Jesus' feet and **t** him— *2373*
Ac 28:15 At the sight of these men Paul **t** God *2373*

THANKFUL (4) [THANK]

1Co 1:14 *I am* **t** that I did not baptize any of you *2373*
Col 3:15 you were called to peace. And be **t.** *2375*
4:2 to prayer, being watchful and **t.** *2374*
Heb 12:28 *let us be* **t,** and so worship God *2400+5921*

THANKFULNESS (3) [THANK]

Lev 7:12 "'If he offers it as an **expression of t,** 9343
1Co 10:30 If I take part in the meal *with* **t,** *5921*
Col 2:7 as you were taught, and overflowing with **t.** *2374*

THANKING (1) [THANK]

1Ch 25:3 using the harp in **t** and praising the LORD. 3344

THANKS (81) [THANK]

1Ch 16:4 to **give t,** and to praise the LORD, 3344
16:7 his associates *this* **psalm of t** to the LORD. 3344
16:8 **Give t** to the LORD, call on his name; 3344
16:34 **Give t** to the LORD, for he is good; 3344
16:35 that we *may* **give t** to your holy name, 3344
16:41 and designated by name to **give t** to 3344
29:13 Now, our God, we **give** you **t,** 3344
2Ch 5:13 to give praise and **t** to the LORD. 3344
7:3 they worshiped and **gave t** to the LORD, 3344
7:6 and which were used when he **gave t,** 2146
20:21 **"Give t** to the LORD, for his love endures 3344
31:2 to **give t** and to sing praises at the gates of 3344
Ne 12:31 I also assigned two large **choirs to give t.** 9343
12:40 The two **choirs that gave t** 9343
Ps 7:17 *I will* **give t** *to* the LORD because 3344
28:7 for joy and *I will* **give t** *to* him in song. 3344
30:12 *I will* **give** you **t** forever. 3344
35:18 *I will* **give** you **t** in the great assembly; 3344
75:1 *We* **give t** to you, O God, we give thanks, 3344
75:1 We give thanks to you, O God, *we* **give t,** 3344
100:T A psalm. For **giving t.** 9343
100:4 **give t** to him and praise his name. 3344
105:1 **Give t** to the LORD, call on his name; 3344
106:1 **Give t** to the LORD, for he is good; 3344
106:47 that we *may* **give t** to your holy name 3344
107:1 **Give t** to the LORD, for he is good; 3344
107:8 *Let them* **give t** to the LORD 3344
107:15 *Let them* **give t** to the LORD 3344
107:21 *Let them* **give t** to the LORD 3344
107:31 *Let them* **give t** to the LORD 3344
118:1 **Give t** to the LORD, for he is good; 3344
118:19 I will enter and **give t** *to* the LORD. 3344
118:21 *I will* **give** you **t,** for you answered me; 3344
118:28 You are my God, and *I will* **give** you **t;** 3344
118:29 **Give t** to the LORD, for he is good; 3344
119:62 to **give** you **t** for your righteous laws. 3344
136:1 **Give t** to the LORD, for he is good. 3344
136:2 **Give t** to the God of gods. 3344
136:3 **Give t** to the Lord of lords: 3344
136:26 **Give t** to the God of heaven. 3344
Isa 12:4 **"Give t** to the LORD, call on his name; 3344
Jer 33:11 saying, **"Give t** *to* the LORD Almighty, 3344
Da 6:10 and prayed, **giving t** to his God, 10312
Mt 14:19 *he* **gave t** and broke the loaves. *2328*
15:36 and *when he had* **given t,** *2373*
26:26 Jesus took bread, **gave t** and broke it, *2328*
26:27 **gave t** and offered it to them, saying, *2373*
Mk 6:41 *he* **gave t** and broke the loaves. *2328*
8:6 the seven loaves and **given t,** *2373*
8:7 *he* **gave t for** them also and told *2328*
14:22 Jesus took bread, **gave t** and broke it, *2328*
14:23 **gave t** and offered it to them, *2373*
Lk 2:38 *she* **gave t** to God and spoke about *469*
9:16 *he* **gave t** and broke them. *2328*
22:17 After taking the cup, *he* **gave t** and said, *2373*
22:19 And he took bread, **gave t** and broke it, *2373*
24:30 *he* took bread, **gave t,** broke it *2328*
Jn 6:11 Jesus then took the loaves, **gave t,** *2373*
6:23 the bread *after* the Lord *had* **given t.** *2373*
Ac 27:35 and **gave t** to God in front of them all. *2373*
Ro 1:21 neither glorified as God nor **gave t** to him, *2373*
6:17 But **t** be to God that, *5921*
7:25 **T** be to God—through Jesus Christ *5921*
14:6 eats to the Lord, for *he* **gives t** to God; *2373*
14:6 does so to the Lord and **gives t** to God. *2373*
1Co 10:16 for which *we* **give t** a participation in *2328*
11:24 and *when he had* **given t,** he broke it *2373*
14:17 You *may be* **giving t** well enough, *2373*
15:57 But **t** be to God! *5921*
2Co 1:11 Then many *will* **give t** on our behalf **for** *2373*
2:14 But **t** be to God, who always leads us in *5921*
9:12 also overflowing in many **expressions of t** *2374*
9:15 **T** be to God for his indescribable gift! *5921*
Eph 1:16 I have not stopped **giving t** for you, *2373*
5:20 always **giving t** to God the Father *2373*
Col 1:12 **giving t** to the Father, who has qualified you *2373*
3:17 **giving t** to God the Father through him. *2373*
1Th 5:18 **give t** in all circumstances, *2373*
Rev 4:9 honor and **t** to him who sits on the throne *2374*
7:12 and **t** and honor and power and strength be *2374*
11:17 *"We* **give t** to you, Lord God Almighty, *2373*

THANKSGIVING (25) [THANK]

Lev 7:13 of **t** he is to present an offering with cakes 9343
7:15 of **t** must be eaten on the day it is offered; 9343
Ezr 3:11 With praise and **t** they sang to the LORD: 3344
Ne 11:17 the director *who* **led in t** and prayer; 3344+9378
12:8 was in charge of the **songs of t.** 2117
12:24 stood opposite them to give praise and **t,** 3344
12:27 the dedication with **songs of t** and with 9343
12:46 and for the songs of praise and **t** to God. 3344
Ps 42:4 the house of God, with shouts of joy and **t** 9343
69:30 in song and glorify him with **t.** 9343
95:2 with **t** and extol him with music and song. 9343
100:4 Enter his gates with **t** and his courts 9343
147:7 Sing to the LORD with **t;** 9343
Isa 51:3 **t** and the sound of singing. 9343
Jer 30:19 From them will come **songs of t** and 9343
Jnh 2:9 I, with a song of **t,** will sacrifice to you. 9343
1Co 10:16 not the cup *of* **t** for which we give thanks *2330*
14:16 not understand say "Amen" to your **t,** *2374*
2Co 4:15 and more people may cause **t** to overflow *2374*
9:11 us your generosity will result in **t** to God. *2374*
Eph 5:4 which are out of place, but rather **t.** *2374*

Php 4: 6 with **t**, present your requests to God. *2374*
1Ti 2: 1 intercession and **t** be made for everyone— *2374*
4: 3 with **t** by those who believe and who know *2374*
4: 4 nothing is to be rejected if it is received with **t**, *2374*

THANKWORTHY (KJV) See COMMENDABLE

THARA (KJV) See TERAH

THARSHISH (KJV) See TRADING, TARSHISH

THAT (5758) [THAT'S] See Index of Articles Etc.

THAT'S (10) [BE, THAT]

Ge 42:21 **t why** this distress has come upon us." 4027+6584
Ex 5:17 Pharaoh said, "Lazy, **t** what you are— NIH
10:11 since **t** what you have been asking for." 2023
1Ki 1:45 **T** the noise you hear. 2085
2Ki 3:23 "**T** blood!" they said. "Those kings must 2296
9:12 "**T** not true!" NIH
Est 5:12 "And **t** not all," Haman added. NIH
Jer 37:14 "**T** not true!" NIH
Mt 27: 4 "**T your responsibility.**" *3972+5148*
Ac 24:25 "**T** enough for now! *NIG*

THAWING (1)

Job 6:16 by **t** ice and swollen with melting snow, NIH

THE (55728) See Index of Articles Etc.

THEATER (2)

Ac 19:29 and rushed as one man into the **t.** *2519*
19:31 begging him not to venture into the **t.** *2519*

THEBES (5)

Jer 46:25 to bring punishment on Amon god of **T,** 5530
Eze 30:14 to Zoan and inflict punishment on **T.** 5530
30:15 and cut off the hordes of **T.** 5530
30:16 **T** will be taken by storm; 5530
Na 3: 8 Are you better than **T**, situated on the Nile, 5531

THEBEZ (2)

Jdg 9:50 Next Abimelech went to **T** and besieged it 9324
2Sa 11:21 so that he died in **T?** 9324

THEFT (3) [THIEF]

Ex 22: 3 he must be sold to pay for his **t.** 1706
Mt 15:19 murder, adultery, sexual immorality, **t,** *3113*
Mk 7:21 come evil thoughts, sexual immorality, **t,** *3113*

THEFTS (1) [THIEF]

Rev 9:21 their sexual immorality or their **t.** *3092*

THEIR (3701) [THEY] See Index of Articles Etc.

THEIRS (21) [THEY] See Index of Articles Etc.

THELASAR (KJV) See TEL ASSAR

THEM (5162) [THEY] See Index of Articles Etc.

THEME (3)

Ps 22:25 the **t of** my **praise** in the great assembly; 9335
45: 1 a noble **t** as I recite my verses for the king; 1821
119:54 the **t of** my **song** wherever I lodge. 2369

THEMSELVES (236) [SELF, THEY] See Index of Articles Etc.

THEN (2001) See Index of Articles Etc.

THEOPHILUS (2)

Lk 1: 3 orderly account for you, most excellent **T,** *2541*
Ac 1: 1 In my former book, **T,** I wrote about all *2541*

THERE (1873) [THERE'S] See Index of Articles Etc.

THERE'S (1) [BE, THERE]

2Ki 4:25 **T** the Shunammite! 2137

THEREFORE (446)

Ge 32:32 **T** to this day the Israelites do not eat 4027+6584
Ex 6: 6 "**T,** say to the Israelites: 4027+4200
9:18 **T,** at this time tomorrow I will send 2180
20:11 **T** the LORD blessed the Sabbath day 4027+6584
Lev 11:45 **t** be holy, because I am holy. 2256
17:12 **T** I say to the Israelites, 4027+6584
20:25 " 'You must **t** make a distinction 2256
Nu 11:34 **T** the place was named Kibroth Hattaavah, 2256
25:12 **T** tell him I am making my covenant 4027+4200
Dt 4:15 **T** watch yourselves very carefully, 2256
5:15 **T** the LORD your God has commanded 4027+6584
7: 9 Know **t** that the LORD your God is God; 2256
7:11 **T,** take care to follow the commands, 2256
10:16 Circumcise your hearts, **t,** 2256
11: 8 Observe **t** all the commands I am giving you 2256
15:11 **T** I command you to be openhanded 4027+6584
28:48 **t** in hunger and thirst, in nakedness 2256
29:19 he invokes a blessing on himself and **t** NIH
29:27 **T** the LORD's anger burned 2256
32:52 **T,** you will see the land only from 3954
Jos 7:26 **T** that place has been called the Valley 4027+6584
Jdg 1:17 **T** it was called Hormah. 2256
2: 3 Now **t** I tell you that I will not drive them 2256
2:20 **T** the LORD was very angry with Israel 2256
1Sa 2:30 "**T** the LORD, the God of Israel, 4027+4200
3:14 **T,** I swore to the house of Eli, 4027+4200
14:38 Saul **t** said, "Come here, 2256
25: 8 **T** be favorable toward my young men, 2256
2Sa 6: 7 **t** God struck him down and he died there 2256
12:10 Now, **t,** the sword will never depart 2256
22:50 **T** I will praise you, O LORD, 4027+6584
1Ki 5: 5 **t,** to build a temple for the Name of 2256
13:22 **T** your body will not be buried in the tomb NIH
20:42 **T** it is your life for his life, 2256
22:19 "**T** hear the word of the LORD: 4027+4200
2Ki 1: 4 **T** this is what the LORD says: 4027+4200
1: 6 **T** you will not leave the bed 4027+4200
12: 7 **T** King Joash summoned Jehoiada 2256
17: 4 **T** Shalmaneser seized him and put him 2256
17:20 **T** the LORD rejected all the people 2256
19: 4 **T** pray for the remnant that still survives." 2256
19:32 "**T** this is what the LORD says 4027+4200
21:12 **T** this is what the LORD, 4027+4200
22:20 **T** I will gather you to your fathers, 4027+4200
1Ch 22: 5 **T** I will make preparations for it." 5528
2Ch 1:12 **t** wisdom and knowledge will be given you. NIH
2: 7 **t,** a man skilled to work in gold and silver, 6964
12: 5 **t,** I now abandon you to Shishak.' " 2256
18:18 "**T** hear the word of the LORD: 4027+4200
24: 6 **T** the king summoned Jehoiada 2256
28: 5 **T** the LORD his God handed him over to 2256
29: 8 **T,** the anger of the LORD has fallen 2256
32:25 **t** the LORD's wrath was on him and 2256
32:26 **t** the LORD's wrath did not come 2256
Ezr 9:12 **T,** do not give your daughters in marriage 6964
Ne 4:13 **T** I stationed some of the people behind 2256
6: 6 and **t** you are building the wall. 4027+6584
7:65 The governor, **t,** ordered them not 2256
9:17 **T** you did not desert them, 2256
9:32 "Now **t,** O our God, the great, 2256
13:15 **T** I warned them against selling food on 2256
Est 1:19 "**T,** if it pleases the king, NIH
3: 4 **T** they told Haman about it 2256
9:26 (**T** these days were called Purim, 4027+6584
Job 7:11 "**T** I will not keep silent; 1685
10: 1 **t** I will give free rein to my complaint NIH
17: 4 **t** you will not let them triumph. 4027+6584
32:10 "**T** I say: Listen to me; 4027+4200
37:24 **T,** men revere him, for does he 4027+4200
42: 6 **T** I despise myself and repent in dust 4027+6584
Ps 1: 5 **T** the wicked will not stand in 4027+6584
2:10 **T,** you kings, be wise; 6964
16: 9 **T** my heart is glad and my tongue 4027+4200
18:49 **T** I will praise you among the nations, 4027+6584
25: 8 **t** he instructs sinners in his ways. 4027+6584
32: 6 **T** let everyone who is godly pray to 2296+6584
42: 6 **t** I will remember you from the land of 4027+6584
45: 7 **t** God, your God, has set you 4027+6584
45:17 **t** the nations will praise you for ever 4027+6584
46: 2 **T** we will not fear, 4027+6584
73: 6 **T** pride is their necklace; 4027+4200
73:10 **T** their people turn to them and drink 4027+4200
106:40 **T** the LORD was angry with his people 2256
110: 7 **t** he will lift up his head. 4027+6584
116:10 I believed; **t** I said, "I am greatly afflicted." 3954
119:104 **t** I hate every wrong path. 4027+6584
119:119 **t** I love your statutes. 4027+4200
119:129 statutes are wonderful; **t** I obey them. 4027+6584
130: 4 **t** you are feared. 5100
Pr 4: 7 Wisdom is supreme; **t** get wisdom. NIH
6:15 **T** disaster will overtake him 4027+6584
Ecc 5: 7 **T** stand in awe of God. 3954
7:14 **T,** a man cannot discover 1826+6584+8611
Isa 1:24 **T** the Lord, the LORD Almighty, 4027+4200
3:17 **T** the Lord will bring sores on the heads of 2256
5:13 **T** my people will go into exile 4027+4200
5:14 **T** the grave enlarges its appetite 4027+4200
5:24 **T,** as tongues of fire lick up straw and 4027+4200
5:25 **T** the LORD's anger burns 4027+6584
7:14 **T** the Lord himself will give you a sign: 4027+4200
8: 7 **t** the Lord is about to bring against 4027+4200
9:17 **T** the Lord will take no pleasure in 4027+6584
10:16 **T,** the Lord, the LORD Almighty, 4027+4200
10:24 **T,** this is what the Lord, 4027+4200
13:13 **T** I will make the heavens tremble; 4027+6584
15: 4 **T** the armed men of Moab cry out, 4027+6584
16: 7 **T** the Moabites wail, 4027+4200
17:10 **T,** though you set out the finest plants 4027+6584
22: 4 **T** I said, "Turn away from me; 4027+6584
24: 6 **T** a curse consumes the earth; 4027+6584
24: 6 **T** earth's inhabitants are burned up, 4027+6584
24:15 **T** in the east give glory to the LORD; 4027+6584
25: 3 **T** strong peoples will honor you; 4027+6584
28:14 **T** hear the word of the LORD, 4027+4200
29:14 **T** once more I will astound these 4027+4200
29:22 **T** this is what the LORD, 4027+4200
30: 7 **T** I call her Rahab the Do-Nothing. 4027+4200
30:12 **T,** this is what the Holy One of Israel 4027+4200
30:16 **T** you will flee! 4027+6584
30:16 **T** your pursuers will be swift! 4027+6584
37: 4 **T** pray for the remnant that still survives." 2256
37:33 "**T** this is what the LORD says 4027+4200
48: 5 **T** I told you these things long ago; 2256
50: 7 **T** have I set my face like flint, 4027+6584
51:21 **T** hear this, you afflicted one, 4027+4200
52: 6 **T** my people will know my name; 4027+4200
52: 6 **t** in that day they will know 4027+4200
53:12 **T** I will give him a portion among 4027+4200
65:13 **T** this is what the Sovereign LORD 4027+4200
Jer 2: 9 "**T** I bring charges against you again," 4027+4200
3: 3 **T** the showers have been withheld, 2256
4:28 **T** the earth will mourn and 2296+6584
5: 6 **T** a lion from the forest will attack 4027+6584
5:14 **T** this is what the LORD God 4027+4200
6:18 **T** hear, O nations; 4027+4200
6:21 **T** this is what the LORD says: 4027+4200
7:14 **T,** what I did to Shiloh I will now do to 2256
7:20 " '**T** this is what the Sovereign LORD 4027+4200
7:28 **T** say to them, 2256
8:10 **T** I will give their wives to other men 4027+4200
9: 7 **T** this is what the LORD Almighty 4027+4200
9:15 **T,** this is what the LORD Almighty, 4027+4200
11:11 **T** this is what the LORD says: 4027+4200
11:21 "**T** this is what the LORD says about 4027+4200
11:22 **t** this is what the LORD Almighty says: 4027+4200
12: 8 She roars at me; **t** I hate her. 4027+6584
14:15 **T,** this is what the LORD says about 4027+4200
14:22 **T** our hope is in you, 2256
15:19 **T** this is what the LORD says: 4027+4200
16:21 "**T** I will teach them— 4027+4200
18:11 "Now **t** say to the people of Judah 2256
18:13 **T** this is what the LORD says: 4027+4200
22:18 **T** this is what the LORD says 4027+4200
23: 2 **T** this is what the LORD, 4027+4200
23:12 "**T** their path will become slippery; 4027+4200
23:15 **T,** this is what the LORD Almighty 4027+4200
23:30 "**T,**" declares the LORD, 4027+4200
23:39 **T,** I will surely forget you and 4027+4200
25: 8 **T** the LORD Almighty says this: 4027+4200
27:15 **T,** I will banish you and you will perish, 5100
28:16 **T,** this is what the LORD says: 4027+4200
29:20 **T,** hear the word of the LORD, 2256
29:28 **T** build houses and settle down; NIH
31:20 **T** my heart yearns for him; 4027+6584
32:28 **T,** this is what the LORD says: 4027+4200
34:17 "**T,** this is what the LORD says: 4027+4200
35:17 "**T,** this is what the LORD God 4027+4200
35:19 **T,** this is what the LORD Almighty, 4027+4200
36:30 **T,** this is what the LORD says 4027+4200
44: 6 **T,** my fierce anger was poured out; 2256
44:11 "**T,** this is what the LORD Almighty, 4027+4200
48:31 **T** I wail over Moab, for all Moab I cry 4027+6584
49:20 **T,** hear what the LORD has planned 4027+4200
50:18 **T** this is what the LORD Almighty, 4027+4200
50:30 **T,** her young men will fall in the 4027+4200
50:45 **T,** hear what the LORD has planned 4027+4200
51: 7 **t** they have now gone mad. 4027+6584
51:36 **T,** this is what the LORD says: 4027+4200
La 3:21 this I call to mind and **t** I have hope: 4027+6584
3:24 **t** I will wait for him." 4027+6584
Eze 5: 7 "**T** this is what the Sovereign LORD 4027+4200
5: 8 "**T** this is what the Sovereign LORD 4027+4200
5:10 **T** in your midst fathers will eat their children, 4027+4200
5:11 **T** as surely as I live, 4027+4200
7:20 **T** I will turn these into an unclean 4027+6584
8:18 **T** I will deal with them in anger; 1685+2256
11: 4 **T** prophesy against them; 4027+4200
11: 7 "**T** this is what the Sovereign LORD 4027+4200
11:16 "**T** say: 'This is what the Sovereign 4027+4200
11:17 "**T** say: 'This is what the Sovereign 4027+4200
12: 3 "**T,** son of man, pack your belongings 2256
12:28 "**T** say to them, 'This is what 4027+4200
13: 8 " '**T** this is what the Sovereign LORD 4027+4200
13:11 **t** tell those who cover it with whitewash NIH
13:13 " '**T** this is what the Sovereign LORD 4027+4200
13:20 " '**T** this is what the Sovereign LORD 4027+4200
13:23 **t** you will no longer see false visions 4027+4200
14: 4 **T** speak to them and tell them, 4027+4200
14: 6 "**T** say to the house of Israel, 4027+4200
15: 6 "**T** this is what the Sovereign LORD 4027+4200
16:35 " '**T,** you prostitute, hear the word of 4027+4200
16:37 **t** I am going to gather all your lovers, 4027+4200
16:50 **T** I did away with them as you have seen. 2256
17:19 " '**T** this is what the Sovereign LORD 4027+4200
18:30 "**T,** O house of Israel, I will judge you, 4027+4200
20:10 **T** I led them out of Egypt 2256
20:27 "**T,** son of man, speak to the people 4027+4200
20:30 "**T** say to the house of Israel: 4027+4200
21: 6 "**T** groan, son of man! 2256
21:12 **T** beat your breast. 4027+4200
21:24 "**T** this is what the Sovereign LORD 4027+4200
22: 4 **T** I will make you an object of scorn 4027+6584
22:19 **T** this is what the Sovereign LORD 4027+4200

Eze 23: 9 "T I handed her over to her lovers, 4027+4200
23:22 "T, Oholibah, this is what 4027+4200
23:35 "T this is what the Sovereign LORD 4027+4200
24: 9 " 'T this is what the Sovereign LORD 4027+4200
25: 4 t I am going to give you to the people 4027+4200
25: 7 t I will stretch out my hand against you 4027+4200
25: 9 t I will expose the flank of Moab, 4027+4200
25:13 t this is what the Sovereign LORD 4027+4200
25:16 t this is what the Sovereign LORD 4027+4200
26: 3 t this is what the Sovereign LORD 4027+4200
28: 6 " 'T this is what the Sovereign LORD 4027+4200
29: 8 " 'T this is what the Sovereign LORD 4027+4200
29:10 t I am against you and 4027+4200
29:19 T this is what the Sovereign LORD 4027+4200
30:22 T this is what the Sovereign LORD 4027+4200
31:10 " 'T this is what the Sovereign LORD 4027+4200
31:14 T no other trees by the waters are ever 5100
33:12 "T, son of man, say to your countrymen, 2256
33:25 T say to them, 'This is what 4027+4200
34: 7 " 'T, you shepherds, hear the word of 4027+4200
34: 9 t, O shepherds, hear the word of 4027+4200
34:20 " 'T this is what the Sovereign LORD 4027+4200
35: 6 t as surely as I live, 4027+4200
35:11 t as surely as I live, 4027+4200
36: 3 T prophesy and say, 'This is what 4027+4200
36: 4 t, O mountains of Israel, hear the word 4027+4200
36: 6 T prophesy concerning the land of Israel 4027+4200
36: 7 T this is what the Sovereign LORD 4027+4200
36:14 t you will no longer devour men 4027+4200
36:22 "T say to the house of Israel, 4027+4200
37:12 T prophesy and say to them: 4027+4200
38:14 "T, son of man, prophesy and say 4027+4200
39:25 "T this is what the Sovereign LORD 4027+4200
44:12 t I have sworn with uplifted hand 4027+6584
Da 3: 7 T, as soon as they heard 10180+10353+10619
3:29 T I decree that the people of any nation 10221
4:27 T, O king, be pleased to accept my advice: 10385
5:24 T he sent the hand that wrote 10008+10089
9:11 "T the curses and sworn judgments written 2256
9:23 T, consider the message and understand 2256
Hos 2: 6 T I will block her path with thornbushes; 4027+4200
2: 9 "T I will take away my grain 4027+4200
2:14 "T I am now going to allure her; 4027+4200
4:13 T your daughters turn to prostitution 4027+6584
6: 5 T I cut you in pieces with my prophets 4027+6584
10: 4 t lawsuits spring up like poisonous weeds 2256
13: 3 T they will be like the morning mist, 4027+4200
Am 3: 2 t I will punish you for all your sins." 4027+6584
3:11 T this is what the Sovereign LORD 4027+4200
4:12 "T this is what I will do to you, Israel, 4027+4200
5:11 T, though you have built stone mansions, 3610+4027+4200
5:13 T the prudent man keeps quiet 4027+4200
5:16 T this is what the Lord, 4027+4200
5:27 T I will send you into exile 2256
6: 7 T you will be among the first to go 4027+4200
7:17 "T this is what the LORD says: 4027+4200
Mic 1: 6 "T I will make Samaria a heap of rubble, 2256
1:14 T you will give parting gifts 4027+4200
2: 3 T, the LORD says: 4027+4200
2: 5 T you will have no one 4027+4200
3: 6 T night will come over you, 4027+4200
3:12 T because of you, 4027+4200
5: 3 T Israel will be abandoned until 4027+4200
6:13 T, I have begun to destroy you, 1685+2256
6:16 T I will give you over to ruin 5100
Hab 1: 4 T the law is paralyzed, 4027+6584
1:16 T he sacrifices to his net and 4027+6584
Zep 2: 9 T, as surely as I live," 4027+4200
3: 8 T wait for me," declares the LORD, 4027+4200
Hag 1:10 T, because of you the heavens have withheld their dew 4027+6584
Zec 1: 3 T tell the people: 2256
1:16 "T, this is what the LORD says: 4027+4200
8:19 T love truth and peace." 2256
10: 2 T the people wander like sheep 4027+6584
Mt 5:23 "T, if you are offering your gift at the altar *4036*
5:48 t, as your heavenly Father is perfect. *4036*
6:25 "T I tell you, do not worry about your life, *1328+4047*
6:34 T do not worry about tomorrow, *4036*
7:24 "T everyone who hears these words *4036*
9:38 Ask the Lord of the harvest, t, *4036*
10:16 T be as shrewd as snakes and as innocent *4036*
12:12 T it is lawful to do good on the Sabbath." *6063*
13:52 "T every teacher of the law *1328+4047*
18: 4 T, whoever humbles himself *4036*
18:23 "T, the kingdom of heaven is like *1328+4047*
19: 6 T what God has joined together, *4036*
21:40 "T, when the owner of the vineyard comes, *4036*
21:43 "T I tell you that the kingdom of God *1328+4047*
23:20 T, he who swears by the altar swears by it *4036*
23:34 T I am sending you prophets and wise *1328+4047*
24:42 "T keep watch, because you do not know *4036*
25:13 "T keep watch, because you do not know *4036*
28:19 T go and make disciples of all nations, *4036*
Mk 10: 9 T what God has joined together, *4036*
11:24 T I tell you, whatever you ask for *1328+4047*
13:35 "T keep watch because you do not know *4036*
Lk 1: 3 T, since I myself have carefully investigated everything *NIG*
7:47 T, I tell you, her many sins have been forgiven— *4005+5920*
8:18 T consider carefully how you listen. *4036*
10: 2 Ask the Lord of the harvest, t, *4036*
Lk 11:36 T, if your whole body is full of light, *4036*
11:50 T this generation will be held responsible *2671*
12:22 "T I tell you, do not worry about your life, *1328+4047*
23:16 T, I will punish him and then release him." *4036*
23:22 T I will have him punished and *4036*
Jn 7: 6 T Jesus told them, "The right time *4036*
9:15 T the Pharisees also asked him *4036*
10: 7 T Jesus said again, "I tell you the truth, *4036*
11:45 T many of the Jews who had come *4036*
11:54 T Jesus no longer moved about publicly *4036*
19:11 T the one who handed me over *1328+4047*
19:32 The soldiers t came and broke the legs of *4036*
Ac 1:21 T it is necessary to choose one of *4036*
2:26 T my heart is glad and my tongue *1328+4047*
2:36 "T let all Israel be assured of this: *4036*
5:38 T, in the present case I advise you: *2779*
7:43 T I will send you into exile' *2779*
13:38 "T, my brothers, I want you to know that *4036*
15:19 "It is my judgment, t, *1475*
15:27 T we are sending Judas and Silas *4036*
17:29 "T since we are God's offspring, *4036*
19:36 T, since these facts are undeniable, *4036*
20:26 T, I declare to you today that I am innocent *1484*
25:26 T I have brought him before all of you, *1475*
26: 3 T, I beg you to listen to me patiently. *1475*
28:28 "T I want you to know *4036*
Ro 1:24 T God gave them over in the sinful desires *1475*
2: 1 You, t, have no excuse, *1475*
3:20 T no one will be declared righteous *1484*
4:16 T, the promise comes by faith, *1328+4047*
5: 1 T, since we have been justified *4036*
5:12 T, just as sin entered the world *1328+4047*
6: 4 We were t buried with him *4036*
6:12 T do not let sin reign in your mortal body *4036*
8: 1 T, there is now no condemnation *726*
8:12 T, brothers, we have an obligation— *726+4036*
9:16 t, depend on man's desire or effort, *726+4036*
9:18 T God has mercy on whom he wants *726+4036*
11:22 Consider t the kindness and sternness *4036*
12: 1 T, I urge you, brothers, *4036*
13: 5 T, it is necessary to submit to the authorities *1475*
13:10 T love is the fulfillment of the law. *4036*
14:13 T let us stop passing judgment *4036*
14:19 Let us t make every effort to do *726+4036*
15: 9 T I will praise you among the Gentiles *1328+4047*
15:17 T I glory in Christ Jesus in my service *4036*
1Co 1: 7 T you do not lack any spiritual gift *6063*
1:31 T, as it is written: *2671*
4: 5 T judge nothing before the appointed time; *6063*
4:16 T I urge you to imitate me. *4036*
5: 8 T let us keep the Festival, *6063*
6: 4 T, if you have disputes about such matters, *4036*
6:20 T honor God with your body. *1314*
8:13 T, if what I eat causes my brother to fall *1478*
9:26 T I do not run like a man running aimlessly; *5523*
10:14 T, my dear friends, flee from idolatry. *1478*
11:27 T, whoever eats the bread or drinks the cup *6063*
12: 3 T I tell you that no one who is speaking by *1475*
14:39 T, my brothers, be eager to prophesy, *6063*
15:58 T, my dear brothers, stand firm. *6063*
2Co 2: 8 I urge you, t, to reaffirm your love for him. *1475*
3:12 T, since we have such a hope, *4036*
4: 1 T, since through God's mercy we have this ministry, *1328+4047*
4:13 It is written: "I believed; t I have spoken." *1475*
4:13 of faith we also believe and t speak, *1475*
4:16 T we do not lose heart. *1475*
5: 6 T we are always confident and know that *4036*
5:14 and t all died. *726*
5:17 T, if anyone is in Christ, *6063*
5:20 We are t Christ's ambassadors, *4036*
6:17 "T come out from them and be separate, *1475*
8:24 T show these men the proof of your love *4036*
12: 9 T I will boast all the more gladly *4036*
Gal 3:21 t, opposed to the promises of God? *4036*
4:31 T, brothers, we are not children of *1475*
6:10 T, as we have opportunity, *726+4036*
Eph 2:11 T, remember that formerly you who are Gentiles by birth *1475*
3:13 t, not to be discouraged because *1475*
4:25 T each of you must put off falsehood *1475*
5: 1 Be imitators of God, t, *4036*
5: 7 T do not be partners with them. *4036*
5:17 T do not be foolish, *1328+4047*
6:13 T put on the full armor of God, *1328+4047*
Php 2: 9 T God exalted him to the highest place *1475*
2:12 T, my dear friends, as you have always *6063*
2:23 t, to send him as soon as I see how things *4036*
2:28 T I am all the more eager to send him, *4036*
4: 1 T, my brothers, you whom I love and long *6063*
Col 2:16 T do not let anyone judge you *4036*
3: 5 t, whatever belongs to your earthly nature: *4036*
3:12 T, as God's chosen people, *4036*
1Th 1: 8 T we do not need to say anything about it, *6063*
3: 7 T, brothers, in all our distress *1328+4047*
4: 8 T, he who rejects this instruction does *5521*
4:18 T encourage each other with these words. *6063*
5:11 T encourage one another *1475*
2Th 1: 4 T, among God's churches we boast *6063*
2Ti 2:10 T I endure everything for the sake of *1328+4047*
Tit 1:13 T, rebuke them sharply, *162+1328+4005*
Phm 1: 8 T, although in Christ I could be bold *1475*
Heb 1: 9 t God, your God, has set you *1328+4047*
2: 1 We must pay more careful attention, t, *1328+4047*
3: 1 T, holy brothers, who share in *3854*
4: 1 T, since the promise of entering his rest *4036*
Heb 4: 7 T God again set a certain day, *NIG*
4:11 t, make every effort to enter that rest, *4036*
4:14 T, since we have a great high priest *4036*
6: 1 T let us leave the elementary teachings *1475*
7:25 T he is able to save completely *3854*
10: 5 T, when Christ came into the world, *1475*
10:19 T, brothers, since we have confidence *4036*
11:16 T God is not ashamed to be called their *1475*
12: 1 T, since we are surrounded by such *5521*
12:12 T, strengthen your feeble arms *1475*
12:28 T, since we are receiving a kingdom *1475*
13:15 t, let us continually offer to God a sacrifice *4036*
Jas 1:21 T, get rid of all moral filth and the evil *1475*
5:16 T confess your sins to each other and pray *4036*
1Pe 1:13 T, prepare your minds for action; *1475*
2: 1 T, rid yourselves of all malice *4036*
4: 1 T, since Christ suffered in his body, *4036*
4: 7 T be clear minded and self-controlled so *4036*
5: 6 Humble yourselves, t, *4036*
2Pe 1:10 T, my brothers, be all the more eager *1475*
3:17 T, dear friends, since you already know this, *4036*
1Jn 4: 5 They are from the world and t speak *1328+4047*
3Jn 1: 8 We ought t to show hospitality *4036*
Rev 1:19 "Write, t, what you have seen, *4036*
2:16 Repent t! Otherwise, I will soon come *4036*
3: 3 t, what you have received and heard; *4036*
7:15 T, "they are before the throne of God *1328+4047*
12:12 T rejoice, you heavens and you who *1328+4047*
18: 8 T in one day her plagues will overtake *1328+4047*

THESE (1120) [THIS] See Index of Articles Etc.

THESSALONIANS (3) [THESSALONICA]

Ac 17:11 of more noble character than the T, *1877+2553*
1Th 1: 1 the church *of* the T in God the Father and *2552*
2Th 1: 1 the church *of* the T in God our Father and *2552*

THESSALONICA (6) [THESSALONIANS]

Ac 17: 1 they came to T, where there was a Jewish *2553*
17:13 in T learned that Paul was preaching *2553*
20: 4 Aristarchus and Secundus **from T,** *2552*
27: 2 Aristarchus, a Macedonian **from T,** *2552*
Php 4:16 for even when I was in T, *2553*
2Ti 4:10 has deserted me and has gone to T. *2553*

THEUDAS (1)

Ac 5:36 Some time ago T appeared, *2554*

THEY (6563) [THEIR, THEIRS, THEM, THEMSELVES] See Index of Articles Etc.

THICK (28) [THICKER, THICKNESS]

Ge 15:12 a t and dreadful darkness came over him. 1524
Ex 19:16 with a t cloud over the mountain, 3878
20:21 while Moses approached the **t darkness** 6906
Jdg 7:12 settled in the valley, t as locusts. 8044
2Sa 18: 9 and as the mule went under the **t branches** 8449
1Ki 20:39 "Your servant went into the t *of* the battle, 7931
2Ki 8:15 But the next day he took a **t cloth,** 4802
Job 3: 6 That night—may **t darkness** seize it; 694
15:26 defiantly charging against him with a t, 6295
22:14 **T clouds** veil him, 6265
23:17 by the **t darkness** that covers my face. 694
38: 9 and wrapped it in **t darkness,** 6906
Ps 97: 2 Clouds and **t darkness** surround him; 6906
Isa 60: 2 the earth and **t darkness** is over the peoples, 6906
Jer 13:16 to **t darkness** and change it to deep gloom. 7516
51:58 "Babylon's t wall will be leveled 8146
52:21 each was four fingers t, and hollow. 6295
Eze 19:11 It towered high above the **t foliage,** 6291
31: 3 its top above the **t foliage.** 6291
31:10 lifting its top above the **t foliage,** 6291
31:14 lifting their tops above the **t foliage.** 6291
40: 5 it was one measuring rod t 8145
40: 7 between the alcoves were five cubits t. NIH
40: 9 and its jambs were two cubits t. NIH
41: 5 the wall of the temple; it was six cubits t, NIH
41: 9 of the side rooms was five cubits t. 8145
41:12 of the building was five cubits t all around, 8145
Rev 21:17 its wall and it was 144 cubits t, *NIG*

THICKER (2) [THICK]

1Ki 12:10 'My little finger *is* t than my father's waist. 6286
2Ch 10:10 'My little finger *is* t than my father's waist. 6286

THICKET (6) [THICKETS]

Ge 22:13 Abraham looked up and there in a t he saw 6019
Job 38:40 in their dens or lie in wait in a t? 6109
Ps 74: 5 like men wielding axes to cut through a t 6020
Hos 2:12 I will make them a t, 3623
Am 3: 4 a lion roar in the t when he has no prey? 3623
Zec 11: 3 the **lush** t *of* the Jordan is ruined! 1454

THICKETS (11) [THICKET]

1Sa 13: 6 they hid in caves and t, among the rocks, 2560
Isa 9:18 it sets the forest t ablaze, 6019
10:34 He will cut down the forest t with an ax; 6019
17: 9 will be like places abandoned to t 3091
21:13 who camp in the t of Arabia, 3623

Jer 4:29 Some go into the t; 6266
12: 5 how will you manage in the t *by* 1454
26:18 the temple hill a mound overgrown with t.' 3623
49:19 "Like a lion coming up from Jordan's t to 1454
50:44 Like a lion coming up from Jordan's t to 1454
Mic 3:12 the temple hill a mound overgrown with t. 3623

THICKNESS (2) [THICK]

1Ki 7:26 It was a handbreadth *in* t, 6295
2Ch 4: 5 It was a handbreadth *in* t, 6295

THIEF (23) [THEFT, THEFTS, THIEVES]

Ex 22: 2 "If a t is caught breaking in and is struck 1705
22: 3 "A t must certainly make restitution, NIH
22: 7 the t, if he is caught, must pay back 1705
22: 8 But if the t is not found, 1705
Job 24:14 in the night he steals forth like a t. 1705
Ps 50:18 When you see a t, you join with him; 1705
Pr 6:30 a t if he steals to satisfy his hunger 1705
29:24 The accomplice of a t is his own enemy; 1705
Jer 2:26 "As a t is disgraced when he is caught, 1705
Zec 5: 3 every t will be banished, 1704
5: 4 and it will enter the house of the t and 1705
Mt 24:43 at what time of night the t was coming, *3095*
Lk 12:33 no t comes near and no moth destroys. *3095*
12:39 at what hour the t was coming, *3095*
Jn 10: 1 by some other way, is a t and a robber. *3095*
10:10 t comes only to steal and kill and destroy; *3095*
12: 6 about the poor but because he was a t; *3095*
1Th 5: 2 of the Lord will come like a t in the night. *3095*
5: 4 that this day should surprise you like a t. *3095*
1Pe 4:15 not be as a murderer or t or any other kind *3095*
2Pe 3:10 But the day of the Lord will come like a t. *3095*
Rev 3: 3 if you do not wake up, I will come like a t, *3095*
16:15 "Behold, I come like a t! *3095*

THIEVES (11) [THIEF]

Job 30: 5 shouted at as if they were t. 1705
Isa 1:23 Your rulers are rebels, companions of t; 1705
Jer 48:27 Was she caught among t, 1705
49: 9 If t came during the night, 1705
Hos 7: 1 They practice deceit, t break into houses, 1705
Joel 2: 9 like t they enter through the windows. 1705
Ob 1: 5 "If t came to you, if robbers in the night— 1705
Mt 6:19 and where t break in and steal. *3095*
6:20 and where t do not break in and steal. *3095*
Jn 10: 8 All who ever came before me were t *3095*
1Co 6:10 nor t nor the greedy nor drunkards *3095*

THIGH (22) [THIGHS]

Ge 24: 2 "Put your hand under my t. 3751
24: 9 the t *of* his master Abraham and swore 3751
47:29 put your hand under my t and promise 3751
Ex 28:42 reaching from the waist to the t. 3751
29:22 kidneys with the fat on them, and the right t. 8797
29:27 the breast that was waved and the t 8797
Lev 7:32 the right t of your fellowship offerings to 8797
7:33 the right t as his share. 8797
7:34 the t that is presented and have given them 8797
8:25 both kidneys and their fat and the right t. 8797
8:26 on the fat portions and on the right t. 8797
9:21 Aaron waved the breasts and the right t 8797
10:14 the breast that was waved and the t 8797
10:15 The t that was presented and the breast 8797
Nu 5:21 and denounce you when he causes your t 3751
5:22 and your t wastes away." 3751
5:27 and her t waste away, 3751
6:20 with the breast that was waved and the t 8797
18:18 the wave offering and the right t are yours. 8797
Jdg 3:16 he strapped to his right t under his clothing. 3751
3:21 the sword from his right t and plunged it 3751
Rev 19:16 and on his t he has this name written: *3611*

THIGHS (2) [THIGH]

Job 40:17 the sinews of his t are close-knit. 7066
Da 2:32 its belly and t of bronze, 10334

THIMNATHAH (KJV) See TIMNAH

THIN (8)

Ge 41: 6 t and scorched by the east wind. 1987
41: 7 The t heads of grain swallowed up 1987
41:23 and t and scorched by the east wind. 1987
41:24 The t heads of grain swallowed up 1987
Ex 16:14 t flakes like frost on the ground appeared 1987
39: 3 They hammered out t **sheets** *of* gold 7063
Lev 13:30 and the hair in it is yellow and t, 1987
Ps 109:24 my body *is* t and gaunt. 3950

THING (148) [SOMETHING, THINGS]

Ge 1:21 and moving t with which the water teems, 5883
7:16 and female of every **living** t, 1414
7:21 Every **living** t that moved on the earth 1414
7:23 Every **living** t on the face of the earth 3685
18:25 Far be it from you to do such a t— 1821
19: 7 Don't **do** *this* **wicked** t. 8317
30:31 "But if you will do this *one* t for me, 1821
31:28 You have done a **foolish** *t.* AIT
32:19 the same t to Esau when you meet him. 1821
34: 7 a **disgraceful** t in Israel by lying 5576
34: 7 *t that should* not **be done.** AIT
34:14 They said to them, "We can't do such a t; 1821
Ge 39: 9 How then could I do such a **wicked** t 8288
44: 5 *This is a* **wicked** *t* you have done.' " AIT
44:17 "Far be it from me to do **such** *a t!* AIT
Ex 33:17 "I will do the very t you have asked, 1821
Lev 7:21 or any unclean, **detestable** *t*— AIT
11:46 every living t that moves in the water 5883
22: 5 or if he touches any **crawling** t 9238
22: 6 The one who touches **any such** t will 2257[S]
Dt 7:26 not bring a **detestable** t into your house 9359
9:21 Also I took that **sinful** t *of* yours, 2633
11: 6 and every **living** t that belonged to them. 3685
13:11 among you will do such an evil t again. 1821
13:14 that this **detestable** t has been done 9359
14: 3 Do not eat any **detestable** t. 9359
17: 4 that this **detestable** t has been done 9359
19:20 and never again will such an evil t be done 1821
22:21 She has done a **disgraceful** t in Israel 5576
27:15 a t **detestable** *to* the LORD, 9359
28:25 a t **of horror** to all the kingdoms on earth. 2400
28:37 a t **of horror** and an object of scorn 9014
Jos 6:21 with the sword every **living** t in it— 889[S]
7:15 and has done a **disgraceful** t in Israel!' " 5576
Jdg 6: 4 and did not spare a **living** t for Israel, 4695
13:19 the LORD did an **amazing** *t* while Manoah AIT
19:23 don't do this **disgraceful** t. 5576
19:24 don't do such a disgraceful t." 1821
19:30 "Such a t has never been seen or done, 2296[S]
20: 3 "Tell us how this **awful** t happened." 8288
1Sa 9:21 Why do you say such a t to me?" 1821
12:16 stand still and see this great t the LORD is 1821
12:17 an **evil** t you did in the eyes of the LORD 8288
24: 6 a t to my master, the LORD's anointed, 1821
25:30 for my master every **good** t he promised 3208
27: 1 The **best** *t* I can do is to escape to the land AIT
2Sa 3:13 But I demand one t of you: 1821
7:21 you have done this **great** t and 1525
11:11 surely as you live, I will not do such a t!" 1821
11:27 t David had done displeased the LORD. 1821
12: 6 because he did such a t and had no pity." 1821
12:12 but I will do this t in broad daylight 1821
13:12 **Such** *a t* should not be done in Israel! AIT
13:12 Don't do this **wicked** t. 5576
13:20 Don't take this t to heart." 1821
14:13 then have you devised a t like this against NIH
24: 3 the king want to do such a t?" 1821
24:10 *I have* **done a** very **foolish** t." 6118
1Ki 9: 8 the LORD done **such** *a t* to this land and AIT
12:30 And this t became a sin; 1821
22:12 other prophets were prophesying the **same** *t.* AIT
2Ki 2:10 "You have asked a **difficult** *t*," AIT
3:18 This *is an* **easy** *t* in the eyes of the LORD; AIT
5:13 prophet had told you to do *some* great t, 1821
5:16 whom I serve, I will not accept a t." NIH
5:18 forgive your servant for this one t: 1821
1Ch 17:19 you have done this **great** t 1525
21: 8 *I have* **done a** very **foolish** t." 6118
2Ch 7:21 the LORD done **such a** t to this land and 3970
16: 9 *You have* **done a foolish** t, 6118
18:11 other prophets were prophesying the **same** *t.* AIT
Ezr 10:13 because we have sinned greatly in this t. 1821
Ne 13: 7 about the **evil** t Eliashib had done 8288
13:17 "What is this wicked t you are doing— 1821
Est 7: 5 the man who has dared to do **such** *a t?"* AIT
8: 5 with favor and thinks it the right t to do, 1821
Job 28:21 from the eyes of every **living** t, 2645
39: 8 for his pasture and searches for any **green** t. 3728
Ps 16: 2 apart from you I have no **good** t." 3208
27: 4 **One** *t* I ask of the LORD, AIT
34:10 those who seek the LORD lack no **good** *t.* AIT
62:11 **One** *t* God has spoken, AIT
84:11 no **good** *t* does he withhold from those AIT
101: 3 I will set before my eyes no vile t. 1821
105:35 they ate up every **green** t in their land, 6912
145:16 and satisfy the desires of every **living** *t.* AIT
Ecc 7:11 is a **good** *t* and benefits those who see AIT
7:27 "Adding **one** *t* to another to discover AIT
12:14 including every **hidden** *t*, AIT
Isa 43:19 See, I am doing a **new** *t!* AIT
44:19 a **detestable** t from what is left? 9359
44:20 "Is not this t in my right hand a lie?" NIH
49: 6 "*It is* too **small** *a t for* you to AIT
52:11 Touch no **unclean** *t!* AIT
66: 8 Who has ever heard of such a t? 2296[S]
Jer 5:30 "A horrible and **shocking** t has happened in 9136
18:13 A most **horrible** t has been done 9137
22: 8 'Why has the LORD done **such a** t 3970
23:13 of Samaria I saw this **repulsive** t: 9524
31:22 The LORD will create a **new** *t* on earth— AIT
32:35 that they should do such a **detestable** t 9359
40:16 "Don't do such a t! 1821
44: 4 'Do not do this detestable t that I hate!' 1821
La 1:17 Jerusalem has become an **unclean** t 5614
Eze 7:19 and their gold will be an **unclean** t. 5614
7:20 I will turn these into an **unclean** t for them. 5614
Da 2:10 has ever asked such a t of any magician 10418
Hos 6:10 I have seen a **horrible** t in the house 9137
8: 8 she is among the nations like a worthless t. 3998
9:10 and became as vile as the t they **loved.** 171
Mal 2:11 A **detestable** t has been committed 9359
2:13 Another t you do: 2296[S]
Mt 19:16 what **good** *t* must I do to get eternal life?" *AIT*
20: 5 and the ninth hour and did the **same** t. *6058*
21:30 to the other son and said the **same** t. *6058*
22:26 **The same** t happened to the second *3931*
26:10 She has done a beautiful t to me. *2240*
26:44 prayed the third time, saying the same t. *3364*
Mk 10:21 "**One** *t* you lack," he said. *AIT*
Mk 14: 6 She has done a beautiful t to me. *2240*
14:39 he went away and prayed the same t. *3364*
Lk 2:15 "Let's go to Bethlehem and see this t *4839*
10:42 but only **one** *t* is needed. *AIT*
12:26 Since you cannot do this **very little** *t*, *AIT*
18:22 he said to him, "You still lack **one** *t.* *AIT*
Jn 1:41 The **first** *t* Andrew did was to find his *AIT*
9:25 **One** *t* I do know. I was blind but now I see!" *AIT*
Ac 4:17 to stop this t from spreading any further *NIG*
5: 4 What made you think of doing such a t? *4547*
19:32 Some were shouting *one* t, some another. *5516*
21:34 the crowd shouted **one** *t* and some another, *AIT*
24:21 unless it was this **one** *t* I shouted as I stood *AIT*
Ro 4: 6 David says **the same** t when he speaks *2749+2779*
1Co 7:37 this man also does **the right** t. *2822*
9: 8 Doesn't the Law say the same t? *NIG*
2Co 6:17 Touch no **unclean** *t*, and I will receive you." *AIT*
Gal 2:10 **the very** t I was eager to do. *899+4047*
3: 2 I would like to learn **just one** *t* from you: *AIT*
5: 6 The only t that counts is faith expressing itself through love. *NIG*
Php 1:18 The **important** t is that in every way, *4440*
3:13 But **one** *t* I do: Forgetting what is behind *AIT*
Phm 1: 6 *of* every **good** *t* we have in Christ. *AIT*
1:22 And **one** t **more:** Prepare a guest room *275*
Heb 10:29 who has treated as an **unholy** *t* the blood *AIT*
10:31 It is a **dreadful** *t* to fall into the hands of *AIT*
2Pe 3: 8 But do not forget this **one** *t*, dear friends: *AIT*
Rev 3:17 I have acquired wealth and do **not** need **a** t.' *4029*
16: 3 and every living t in the sea died. *6034*

THINGS (598) [THING]

Ge 20: 9 You have done t to me that should not 5126
24:10 taking with him all kinds of **good** t 3206
24:28 told her mother's household about these t. 1821
29:13 and there Jacob told him all these t. 1821
41:13 And *t* **turned out** exactly AIT
44: 7 "Why does my lord say such t? 1821
44:15 **find** t **out by divination?"** 5727+5727
45:23 ten donkeys loaded with the **best** t 3206
Ex 7:11 the Egyptian magicians also did the **same** *t* AIT
7:22 But the Egyptian magicians did the **same** *t* AIT
8: 7 But the magicians did the **same** *t* AIT
18: 9 the **good** t the LORD had done for Israel 3208
21:11 not provide her with these **three** *t*, AIT
35: 1 the t the LORD has commanded you 1821
Lev 2: 8 Bring the grain offering made of **these** *t* to AIT
5:15 in regard to any of the LORD's **holy** t, 7731
5:16 failed to do in regard to the **holy** t, 7731
6: 7 of **these** t he did that made him guilty." 3972[S]
9: 5 They took the t Moses commanded 889
10:19 but such *t* **as this** have happened to me. AIT
11:10 among all the **swarming** t or among all 9238
15:10 and whoever touches **any** *of the t* AIT
15:10 up *those* t must wash his clothes and bathe 4392[S]
15:31 separate from t **that make** them **unclean,** 3240
18:26 not do any of these **detestable** t, 9359
18:27 for all these t were done by the people 9359[S]
18:29 who does any of these **detestable** t— 9359
20:23 they did all **these** *t*, I abhorred them. AIT
26:23 of **these** *t* you do not accept my correction AIT
Nu 4: 4 the care of the **most holy** t. 7731+7731
4:15 not touch the **holy** t or they will die. 7731
4:15 The Kohathites are to carry **those** *t* that are AIT
4:19 near the **most holy** t, do this for them: 7731+7731
4:20 not go in to look at the **holy** t, 7731
4:26 to do all that needs to be done with **these** t. 2157[S]
4:32 each man the **specific** t he is to carry. 3998+5466
7: 9 to carry on their shoulders the **holy** t, 7731
10:21 the Kohathites set out, carrying the **holy** t. 5219
10:29 the LORD has promised **good** *t* to Israel." AIT
10:32 we will share with you whatever good t 2085[S]
14:28 I will do to you the **very** t I heard you say: 889+3869+4027
14:35 and I will surely do **these** *t* to this whole AIT
15:13 who is native-born must do **these** *t* AIT
16:28 the LORD has sent me to do all these t 5126
Dt 4: 9 the t your eyes have seen or let them slip 1821
4:19 and worshiping t the LORD your God has 4392[S]
4:30 in distress and all these t have happened 1821
4:34 the t the LORD your God did for you 889
4:35 You were shown these t so NIH
6:11 with all kinds of **good** t you did 3206
11: 3 and the t he **did** in the heart of Egypt, both 5126
11: 7 that saw all these great t the LORD has done. 5126
12:26 But take your **consecrated** t and 7731
12:31 all kinds of **detestable** t the LORD hates. 9359
13:17 None of those **condemned** t shall be found 3051
18:12 Anyone who does **these** *t* is detestable to AIT
20:18 to follow all the **detestable** t they do 9359
25:16 your God detests anyone who does **these** *t*, AIT
26:11 the **good** *t* the LORD your God has given AIT
29:29 The **secret** *t* belong to the LORD our God, AIT
29:29 but the *t* **revealed** belong to us and AIT
Jos 3: 5 for tomorrow the LORD will do **amazing** *t* AIT
6:18 But keep away from the **devoted** t, 3051
7: 1 unfaithfully in regard to the **devoted** t; 3051
7:11 They have taken some of the **devoted** t; 3051
7:15 He who is caught with the **devoted** t shall 3051
7:23 They took the t from the tent, 4392[S]
9: 1 of the Jordan heard about these t— NIH
22:20 the **devoted** t, did not wrath come upon 3051
24:26 And Joshua recorded these t in the Book of 1821
24:29 After these t, Joshua son of Nun, 1821
Jdg 2: 4 the angel of the LORD had spoken these t 1821
2: 7 the great t the LORD had done for Israel. 5126

Jdg 8:35 for all the **good t** he had done for them. 3208
13:23 nor shown us all **these** *t* or told us this." AIT
18: 8 **"How did you find t?"** 4537
1Sa 2:23 he said to them, "Why do you do such **t?** 1821
12:24 what **great t** *he has* **done** for you. 1540
16: 7 not look at the **t** man looks at. 889
17:22 David left his **t** with the keeper of supplies, 3998
18:26 When the attendants told David these **t,** 1821
21: 5 The men's **t** are holy even on missions 3998
25:37 his wife told him all these **t,** 1821
26:25 *you will* **do great t** and surely triumph. 6913+6913
2Sa 7:28 and you have promised these **good t** 3208
1Ki 2:15 But *t* **changed,** and the kingdom has gone AIT
7:47 Solomon left all these **t** unweighed, 3998
7:51 **t** his father David had **dedicated—** 7731
8:66 joyful and glad in heart for all the **good t** 3208
10: 7 But I did not believe these **t** until I came 1821
16: 7 provoking him to anger by the **t** he **did** 3338+5126
16:27 what he did and the **t** he achieved, 1476[S]
18:36 and have done all these **t** at your command. 1821
22:45 the **t** he achieved and his military exploits, 1476[S]
2Ki 5:24 the **t** from the servants and put them away NIH
7: 8 and took some **t** from it and hid them also. NIH
8: 4 about all the **great** *t* Elisha has done." AIT
9:11 the man and the **sort of t he says,"** 8490
17: 9 The Israelites secretly did **t** against 1821
17:11 They did wicked **t** that provoked the LORD 1821
17:15 the **t** the LORD had forbidden them to do. NIH
18:27 to say these **t,** and not to the men sitting on 1821
23:16 by the man of God who foretold these **t.** 1821
23:17 the altar of Bethel the very **t** you have done 1821
23:24 the other **detestable t** seen in Judah 9199
24: 3 Surely *these t* **happened** to Judah according AIT
1Ch 2: 7 by violating the ban on taking **devoted t.** 3051
17:26 You have promised these **good t** 3208
23:13 to consecrate the **most holy t,** 7731+7731
23:28 of all **sacred t** and the performance 7731
26:20 and the treasuries for the **dedicated t.** 7731
26:26 of all the treasuries for the **t** dedicated 7731[S]
26:28 the other **dedicated** *t* were in the care AIT
28:12 and for the treasuries for the **dedicated t.** 7731
29:12 you are the ruler of **all** *t.* AIT
29:17 All **these** *t* have I given willingly and AIT
2Ch 4: 6 In them the **t** to be *used for* the burnt 5126
4:18 All these **t** that Solomon made amounted 3998
5: 1 **t** his father David had **dedicated—** 7731
7:10 the **good t** the LORD had done for David 3208
27: 7 all his wars and the other **t** he **did,** 2006
28:21 Ahaz **took some of the t** from the temple 2745
31: 6 and a tithe of the **holy t** dedicated to 7731
31:12 a Levite, was in charge of **these** *t,* AIT
36: 8 Jehoiakim's reign, the **detestable t** he did 9359
Ezr 7: 1 After these **t,** during the reign of 1821
9: 1 After **these** *t* had been done, AIT
9:12 and eat the **good t** *of* the land and leave it 3206
Ne 1: 4 When I heard these **t,** I sat down and wept. 1821
4:14 After *I* **looked t over,** 8011
9:25 of houses filled with all kinds of **good t,** 3206
9:36 and the other **good t** it *produces.* 3206
13:18 Didn't your forefathers do *the* **same** *t,* AIT
Job 8: 2 "How long will you say **such** *t?* AIT
12: 3 Who does not know all **these** *t?* AIT
12:22 He reveals the **deep** *t* of darkness AIT
13:20 "Only grant me these **two** *t,* O God, AIT
13:26 For you write down **bitter t** against me 5353
16: 2 "I have heard **many** *t* like these; AIT
22:18 he who filled their houses with **good** *t,* AIT
28:11 and brings **hidden t** to light. 9502
31:23 fear of his splendor I could not do such **t.** NIH
33:29 "God does all **these** *t* to a man— AIT
37: 5 he does **great** *t* beyond our understanding. AIT
42: 2 "I know that you can do **all** *t;* AIT
42: 3 Surely I spoke of **t** I did not understand, NIH
42: 3 *t* too **wonderful** for me to know. AIT
42: 7 After the LORD had said these **t** to Job, 1821
Ps 15: 5 He who does **these** *t* will never be shaken. AIT
35:11 they question me on **t** I know nothing about. 889
40: 5 The **t** you **planned** for us 4742
42: 4 **These** *t* I remember as I pour out my soul: AIT
50:21 **These** *t* you have done and I kept silent; AIT
62:11 God has spoken, two **t** have I heard: 2306
65: 4 with the **good t** *of* your house, 3206
71:19 O God, you who have done **great** *t.* AIT
78: 2 I will utter **hidden t,** things from of old— 2648
78: 2 I will utter hidden things, **t** from of old— NIH
87: 3 **Glorious** *t* are said of you, O city of God: AIT
98: 1 for he has done **marvelous** *t;* AIT
103: 5 with **good** *t* so that your youth is renewed AIT
104:25 **living t** both large and small. 2651
104:28 they are satisfied with **good** *t.* AIT
106:21 who had done **great** *t* in Egypt, AIT
107: 9 and fills the hungry with **good** *t.* AIT
107:43 let him heed **these** *t* and consider AIT
118:15 LORD's right hand has done **mighty t!** 2657
118:16 the LORD's right hand has done **mighty t!"** 2657
119:18 Open my eyes that I may see **wonderful** *t* AIT
119:37 Turn my eyes away from **worthless t;** 8736
119:91 for **all** *t* serve you. AIT
126: 2 "The LORD has done **great** *t* for them." AIT
126: 3 The LORD has done **great** *t* for us, AIT
131: 1 with great matters or *t* too **wonderful** AIT
138: 2 above **all** *t* your name and your word. AIT
Pr 1:13 we will get all sorts of **valuable t** 2104+3701
6:16 There are six **t** the LORD hates, 2179[S]
8: 6 Listen, for I have **worthy** *t* to say; 5592
12:14 fruit of his lips a man is filled with **good** *t* AIT
13: 2 the fruit of his lips a man enjoys **good** *t,* AIT

Pr 14:17 A quick-tempered man does **foolish** *t,* AIT
23:33 and your mind imagine **confusing t.** 9337
30: 7 **"Two** *t* I ask of you, O LORD; AIT
30:15 "There are three **t** that are never satisfied, 2179[S]
30:18 "There are three **t** that are too amazing 2156[S]
30:21 "Under **three** *t* the earth trembles, AIT
30:24 "Four **t** on earth are small, 2156[S]
30:29 "There are three **t** that are stately 2156[S]
31:29 "Many women do **noble** *t,* AIT
Ecc 1: 8 All **t** are wearisome, more than one can say. 1821
1:14 I have seen all the **t** that are done under 5126
2:18 I hated all the **t** I had toiled for under 6662[S]
5: 8 do not be surprised at **such t;** 2914[S]
7:25 to search out wisdom and the **scheme of t** 3113
7:27 to another to discover the **scheme of t—** 3113
8: 1 Who knows the explanation of **t?** 1821
11: 5 the work of God, the Maker of **all** *t.* AIT
11: 9 that for all **these** *t* God will bring you AIT
Isa 12: 5 for he has done **glorious t;** 1455
25: 1 in perfect faithfulness you have done **marvelous t,** 7099
25: 1 *t* **planned** long ago. AIT
29:16 You turn **t** upside down, NIH
30:10 Tell us **pleasant** *t,* prophesy illusions. AIT
36:12 to say these **t,** and not to the men sitting on 1821
38:16 Lord, by **such t** men live; 2157[S]
41:22 Tell us what the **former** *t* were, AIT
41:22 Or declare to us the *t to* **come,** AIT
42: 9 See, the **former** *t* have taken place, AIT
42: 9 and **new** *t* I declare; AIT
42:16 These are the **t** I will do; 1821
42:20 You have seen **many** *t,* AIT
43: 9 and proclaimed to us the **former** *t?* AIT
43:18 "Forget the **former** *t;* AIT
44: 9 and the *t* they **treasure** are worthless. AIT
44:21 "Remember **these** *t,* O Jacob, AIT
44:24 I am the LORD, who has made **all** *t,* AIT
45: 7 I, the LORD, do all **these** *t.* AIT
45:11 Concerning **t to come,** do you question 910
46: 9 Remember the **former** *t,* those of long ago; AIT
47: 7 But you did not consider **these** *t* or reflect AIT
48: 3 I foretold the **former** *t* long ago, AIT
48: 5 Therefore I told you these **t** long ago; NIH
48: 6 You have heard these **t;** look at them all. NIH
48: 6 "From now on I will tell you of **new** *t,* AIT
48: 6 of **hidden** *t* unknown to you. AIT
48:14 Which of [the idols] has foretold **these** *t?* AIT
57: 6 In the light of **these** *t,* should I relent? AIT
59: 3 and your tongue mutters **wicked** *t.* AIT
63: 7 the many **good t** he has done for the house 3206
64: 3 you did **awesome** *t* that we did not expect, AIT
65:17 The **former** *t* will not be remembered, AIT
66: 2 Has not my hand made all **these** *t,* AIT
66: 8 Who has ever seen such **t?** 465[S]
66:17 of pigs and rats and other **abominable t—** 9211
Jer 7:10 safe to do all these **detestable t?** 9359
7:13 While you were doing all these **t,** 5126
10:16 for he is the Maker of **all** *t,* AIT
17: 9 The heart is deceitful above **all** *t* and AIT
20: 1 heard Jeremiah prophesying these **t,** 1821
25:13 that land all the **t** I have spoken against it, 1821
26:10 the officials of Judah heard about these **t,** 1821
26:12 and this city all the **t** you have heard. 1821
26:20 he prophesied the same **t** against this city 1821
27:21 says about the **t** that are left in the house of 3998
29:23 For they have done **outrageous t** in Israel; 5576
29:32 the **good** *t* I will do for my people, AIT
30:15 and many sins I have done **these** *t* to you. AIT
33: 3 and **unsearchable** *t* you do not know.' AIT
33: 9 on earth that hear of all the **good t** I do 3208
35: 7 you must never have any of these **t,** NIH
38: 4 by the **t** he is saying to them. 1821
44:22 and the **detestable t** you did, 9359
45: 5 Should you then seek **great** *t* for yourself? AIT
51:19 for he is the Maker of **all** *t,* AIT
La 3:36 would not the Lord see such **t?** NIH
3:38 that both calamities and **good** *t* come? AIT
5:17 because of **these** *t* our eyes grow dim AIT
Eze 3:20 The **righteous t** he did will not be 7407
8: 6 the utterly **detestable t** the house 9359
8: 6 **t** that will drive me far from my sanctuary? NIH
8: 6 **t** *that* are even more **detestable."** 9359
8: 9 and **detestable t** they are doing here." 9359
8:10 over the walls all kinds of **crawling t** 8254
8:13 **t** *that* are even more **detestable."** 9359
8:15 *t that* are even more **detestable** 9359
8:17 to do the **detestable t** they are doing here? 9359
9: 4 over all the **detestable t** that are done 9359
12: 7 During the day I brought out my **t** packed 3998
12:12 among them will put his **t** on his shoulder NIH
15: 3 they make pegs from it to hang **t** on? 3972+3998
16: 5 to do any of **these** *t* for you. AIT
16:16 *Such t should* **not happen,** AIT
16:30 when you do all **these** *t,* AIT
16:43 but enraged me with all **these** *t,* AIT
16:50 They were haughty and did **detestable t** 9359
16:51 You have done more **detestable t** than they, 9359
16:51 by all these **t** you have done. 9359[S]
17:12 'Do you not know what **these** *t* mean?' AIT
17:15 Will he who does **such** *t* escape? AIT
17:18 his hand in pledge and yet did all **these** *t,* AIT
18:10 or does any of **these other** *t* AIT
18:12 He does **detestable t.** 9359
18:13 he has done all these **detestable t,** 9359
18:14 he does not do such **t:** 2177
18:22 of the **righteous t** he has done, he will live. 7407
18:24 does the same **detestable t** the wicked man 9359

Eze 18:24 None of the **righteous t** he has done will 7407
22: 8 You have despised my **holy t** 7731
22:25 and **precious t** and make many widows 3702
22:26 to my law and profane my **holy t;** 7731
23:27 You will not look on **these** *t* with longing AIT
24:19 "Won't you tell us what **these** *t* have to do AIT
33:13 none of the **righteous t** he has done will 7407
33:26 rely on your sword, you do **detestable t,** 9359
33:29 of all the **detestable t** they have done.' 9359
35:12 the **contemptible t** you have said against 5542
36:22 that I am going to do these **t,** NIH
44: 8 your duty in regard to my **holy t,** 7731
44:13 as priests or come near any of my **holy t** 7731
Da 2: 9 to tell me misleading and wicked **t,** 10418
2:22 He reveals deep and **hidden** *t;* AIT
2:29 O king, your mind turned to **t** to come, 10408
2:40 and as iron breaks **t** to pieces, NIH
7:16 and gave me the interpretation of these **t:** 10418
11:36 above every god and will say **unheard-of** *t* AIT
12: 6 be before these **astonishing t** are fulfilled?" 7099
12: 7 all **these** *t* will be completed." AIT
Hos 8:12 I wrote for them the **many** *t of* my law, AIT
14: 9 He will realize **these** *t.* AIT
Joel 2:20 Surely he has done **great** *t.* AIT
2:21 Surely the LORD has done **great** *t.* AIT
Am 9:12 declares the LORD, who will do **these** *t.* AIT
Mic 2: 6 "Do not prophesy about **these** *t;* AIT
2: 7 Does he do **such** *t?"* AIT
Hag 2:13 with a dead body touches one of **these** *t,* AIT
2:15 how **t** were before one stone was laid NIH
Zec 3: 8 who are men **symbolic of t to come:** 4603
4:10 "Who despises the day of **small** *t?* AIT
8:12 I will give all **these** *t* as an inheritance to AIT
8:16 These are the **t** you are to do: 1821
Mal 3:13 "You *have* **said** harsh *t* against me," AIT
4: 3 of your feet on the day when I do these **t,"** NIH
Mt 6:32 For the pagans run after all **these** *t,* *AIT*
6:33 and all **these** *t* will be given to you as well. *AIT*
7:28 When Jesus had finished saying **these** *t,* *AIT*
11:25 because you have hidden **these** *t* from *AIT*
11:27 **"All** *t* have been committed to me *AIT*
12:35 The good man brings **good** *t* out of *AIT*
12:35 and the evil man brings **evil** *t* out of *AIT*
13: 3 he told them **many** *t* in parables, saying: *AIT*
13:34 Jesus spoke all **these** *t* to the crowd *AIT*
13:35 I will utter *t* **hidden** since the creation of *AIT*
13:51 "Have you understood all **these** *t?"* *AIT*
13:56 Where then did this man get all **these** *t?"* *AIT*
15:18 But **the** *t* that come out of the mouth come *AIT*
16:21 and suffer **many** *t* at the hands of the elders, *AIT*
16:23 you do not have in mind **the** *t* of God, *AIT*
16:23 but **the** *t* of men." *AIT*
17:11 Elijah comes and will restore **all** *t.* *AIT*
18: 7 because of **t that cause** people **to sin!** *4998*
18: 7 **Such t** must come, but woe to *3836+4998*[S]
19: 1 When Jesus had finished saying **these** *t,* *AIT*
19:26 but with God **all** *t* are possible." *AIT*
19:28 "I tell you the truth, at the renewal of all **t,** *NIG*
21:15 of the law saw the **wonderful** *t* he did and *AIT*
21:23 "By what authority are you doing **these** *t?"* *AIT*
21:24 by what authority I am doing **these** *t.* *AIT*
21:27 by what authority I am doing **these** *t.* *AIT*
24: 2 "Do you see all **these** *t?"* *AIT*
24: 6 Such **t** must happen, but the end is still *NIG*
24:33 Even so, when you see all **these** *t,* *AIT*
24:34 until all **these** *t* have happened. *AIT*
25:21 You have been faithful with a **few** *t;* *AIT*
25:21 I will put you in charge of **many** *t.* *AIT*
25:23 You have been faithful with a **few** *t;* *AIT*
25:23 I will put you in charge of **many** *t.* *AIT*
26: 1 When Jesus had finished saying all **these** *t,* *AIT*
Mk 2: 8 "Why are you thinking **these** *t?* *AIT*
4: 2 He taught them **many** *t* by parables, *AIT*
4:19 and the desires for **other** *t* come in and choke *AIT*
6: 2 "Where did this man get **these** *t?"* *AIT*
6:34 So he began teaching them **many** *t.* *AIT*
7:13 And you do **many** *t* like that." *AIT*
8:31 that the Son of Man must suffer **many** *t* and *AIT*
8:33 "You do not have in mind **the** *t* of God, *AIT*
8:33 but **the** *t* of men." *AIT*
9:12 Elijah does come first, and restores **all** *t.* *AIT*
10:27 **all** *t* are possible with God." *AIT*
11:28 "By what authority are you doing **these** *t?"* *AIT*
11:29 by what authority I am doing **these** *t.* *AIT*
11:33 by what authority I am doing **these** *t."* *AIT*
13: 4 when will **these** *t* happen? *AIT*
13: 7 Such **t** must happen, but the end is still *NIG*
13:29 Even so, when you see **these** *t* happening, *AIT*
13:30 until all **these** *t* have happened. *AIT*
14:16 and found **t** just as Jesus had told them. *NIG*
15: 3 The chief priests accused him of **many** *t.* *AIT*
15: 4 See **how many** *t* they are accusing you of." *AIT*
Lk 1: 1 an account of the **t that** have been fulfilled *4547*
1: 4 the certainty of the **t** you have been taught. *3364*
1:49 the Mighty One has done **great** *t* for me— *AIT*
1:53 He has filled the hungry *with* **good** *t* *AIT*
1:65 people were talking about all these **t.** *4839*
2:19 But Mary treasured up all these **t** *4839*
2:20 for **all the** *t* they had heard and seen, *AIT*
2:51 his mother treasured all these **t** in her heart. *4839*
3:19 and all the other **evil** *t* he had done, *AIT*
5:22 "Why are you thinking these **t** *NIG*
5:26 "We have seen **remarkable** *t* today." *AIT*
6:45 The good man brings good **t** out of *NIG*
6:45 and the evil man brings evil **t** out of *NIG*
7:18 John's disciples told him about all **these** *t.* *AIT*
9: 9 Who, then, is this I hear **such** *t* about?" *AIT*

Lk 9:22 "The Son of Man must suffer **many** *t* and AIT
9:52 a Samaritan village to get **t** ready for him; NIG
10:21 because you have hidden **these** *t* from AIT
10:22 "**All** *t* have been committed to me AIT
10:41 "you are worried and upset about **many** *t*, AIT
11:27 As Jesus was saying **these** *t*, AIT
11:45 when you say **these** *t*, you insult us also." AIT
12:19 "You have plenty of **good** *t* laid up AIT
12:21 be with anyone who stores up **t** for himself NIG
12:30 For the pagan world runs after all **such** *t*, AIT
12:31 and **these** *t* will be given to you as well. AIT
12:48 and does *t* **deserving** punishment will AIT
13:17 with all the **wonderful** *t* he was doing. AIT
16:25 in your lifetime you received your **good** *t*, AIT
16:25 while Lazarus received **bad** *t*, AIT
17:1 "**T that** cause people to sin are bound 3836
17:25 But first he must suffer **many** *t* and AIT
20:2 by what authority you are doing **these** *t*," AIT
20:8 by what authority I am doing **these** *t*." AIT
21:7 they asked, "when will **these** *t* happen? AIT
21:9 **These** *t* must happen first, AIT
21:28 When **these** *t* begin to take place, AIT
21:31 Even so, when you see **these** *t* happening, AIT
21:32 until **all** these *t* have happened. AIT
22:13 and found **t** just as Jesus had told them. NIG
22:65 they said **many other** insulting *t* to him. AIT
23:31 For if men do **these** *t* when the tree is green, AIT
23:49 stood at a distance, watching **these** *t*. AIT
24:9 they told all **these** *t* to the Eleven and to all AIT
24:15 and discussed these **t** with each other, NIG
24:18 not know **the** *t* **that** have happened there AIT
24:19 "**What** *t*?" he asked. "About Jesus AIT
24:26 Did not the Christ have to suffer **these** *t* and AIT
24:48 You are witnesses *of* **these** *t*. AIT
Jn 1:3 Through him **all** *t* were made; AIT
1:50 You shall see **greater** *t* **than** that." AIT
3:10 "and do you not understand **these** *t*? AIT
3:12 to you of **earthly t** and you do not believe; 2103
3:12 will you believe if I speak of **heavenly t?** 2230
5:16 Jesus was doing **these** *t* on the Sabbath, AIT
5:20 he will show him even greater **t** than these. 2240
7:4 Since you are doing **these** *t*, AIT
7:32 the crowd whispering **such** *t* about him. AIT
8:39 "then you would do the **t** Abraham did. 2240
8:40 Abraham did not do **such** *t*. AIT
8:41 You are doing the **t** your own father does." 2240
12:16 that **these** *t* had been written about him and AIT
12:16 about him and that they had done **these** *t* AIT
13:3 the Father had put **all** *t* under his power, AIT
13:17 Now that you know **these** *t*, AIT
14:12 He will do even greater *t* **than these,** AIT
14:26 will teach you **all** *t* and will remind you AIT
16:3 They will do **such** *t* because they have AIT
16:6 Because I have said **these** *t*, AIT
16:30 Now we can see that you know **all** *t* and AIT
16:33 "I have told you **these** *t*, AIT
17:13 I say **these** *t* while I am still in the world, AIT
19:36 **These** *t* happened so that the scripture AIT
20:18 she told them that he had said **these** *t* to her. AIT
21:17 He said, "Lord, you know **all** *t*; AIT
21:24 This is the disciple who testifies to **these** *t* AIT
21:25 Jesus did many **other** *t* as well. AIT
Ac 5:32 We are witnesses *of* these **t,** 4839
7:50 Has not my hand made all **these** *t*?' AIT
13:42 about these **t** on the next Sabbath. 4839
14:15 telling you to turn from these **worthless** *t* AIT
15:17 says the Lord, who does **these** *t*' AIT
15:29 You will do well to avoid **these** *t*. AIT
18:15 I will not be a judge *of* **such** *t*." AIT
24:9 asserting that **these** *t* were true. AIT
26:26 The king is familiar with **these** *t*, AIT
Ro 1:25 and served **created t** rather than the Creator 3232
1:32 that those who do **such** *t* deserve death, AIT
1:32 they not only continue to do **these** very *t* but AIT
2:1 you who pass judgment do the **same** *t*. AIT
2:2 against those who do **such** *t* is based AIT
2:3 judgment on them and yet do the **same** *t*, AIT
2:14 do by nature **t** required by the law, 3836
4:17 to the dead and calls **t** *that* are not as 3836
6:21 from **the** *t* you are now ashamed of? AIT
6:21 **Those** *t* result in death! AIT
8:28 And we know that in **all** *t* God works for AIT
8:32 graciously give us **all** *t*? AIT
8:37 in all **these** *t* we are more than conquerors AIT
10:5 "The man who does **these** *t* will live AIT
11:36 and through him and to him are **all t.** 3836+4246
14:22 So whatever you believe about these **t** keep NIG
1Co 1:27 But God chose the **foolish** *t* of the world AIT
1:27 God chose the **weak** *t* of the world to shame AIT
1:28 He chose the **lowly** *t* of this world and AIT
1:28 things of this world and the **despised** *t*— AIT
1:28 and **the** *t* **that** are not— AIT
1:28 to nullify **the** *t* **that** are, AIT
2:10 The Spirit searches **all** *t*, AIT
2:10 even the **deep** *t* of God. AIT
2:14 not accept **the** *t* **that** come from the Spirit AIT
2:15 about **all** *t*, but he himself is not subject AIT
3:7 but only God, who makes **t** grow. NIG
3:21 no more boasting about men! **All** *t* are yours, AIT
4:1 as those entrusted with the **secret** *t* of God. AIT
4:6 I have applied **these** *t* to myself and Apollos AIT
6:3 How much more the *t* **of this life!** AIT
7:31 those who use the **t** of the world, NIG
8:6 from whom **all t** came and 3836+4246
8:6 through whom **all** *t* came and AIT
9:15 in the hope that you will do **such t** for me. 4048
9:22 I have become **all** *t* to all men so that AIT
1Co 10:6 Now **these** *t* occurred as examples AIT
10:6 from setting our hearts on **evil** *t* AIT
10:11 **These** *t* happened to them as examples AIT
11:14 Does not the very nature of **t** teach you that NIG
14:7 in the case of **lifeless** *t* that make sounds, AIT
2Co 5:10 for **the** *t* done while in the body, AIT
9:8 so that in **all** *t* at all times, AIT
10:7 You are looking only on the surface of **t.** NIG
11:12 with us in **the** *t* they boast about. AIT
11:30 of **the** *t* that show my weakness. AIT
12:4 He heard **inexpressible** *t*, AIT
12:4 **t** that man is not permitted to tell. 4839
12:12 **The** *t* that mark an apostle— AIT
13:10 This is why I write **these** *t* AIT
Gal 3:12 man who does **these** *t* will live by them." AIT
4:24 **These** *t* may be taken figuratively, AIT
5:23 Against **such** *t* there is no law. AIT
6:6 in the word must share all **good** *t* with his AIT
Eph 1:10 to bring **all t** in heaven and on earth 3836+4246
1:22 And God placed **all** *t* under his feet AIT
3:9 hidden in God, who created **all t.** 3836+4246
4:15 we will in **all** *t* grow up into him who is AIT
5:6 for because of **such** *t* God's wrath comes AIT
Php 2:23 to send him as soon as I see how **t** go 3836
3:1 It is no trouble for me to write the **same t** 899
3:8 for whose sake I have lost **all** *t*. AIT
3:15 mature *should* **take such a view of t.** 5858
3:19 Their mind is on **earthly t.** 2103
4:8 think about **such** *t*. AIT
Col 1:16 For by him **all t** were created: 3836+4246
1:16 **t** in heaven and on earth, NIG
1:16 **all** *t* were created by him and for him. AIT
1:17 He is before **all** *t*, and in him all things AIT
1:17 and in him **all t** hold together. 3836+4246
1:20 to reconcile to himself **all t,** 3836+4246
1:20 whether **t** on earth or things in heaven, 3836
1:20 whether things on earth or **t** in heaven, 3836
2:17 These are a shadow *of* **the** *t* **that** were AIT
3:1 set your hearts on **t** above, 3836
3:2 Set your minds on **t** above, 3836
3:2 on things above, not on earthly **t.** 3836
3:8 rid yourselves of **all** such *t* as these: AIT
1Th 2:14 the **same** *t* those churches suffered from AIT
2Th 2:5 with you I used to tell you **these** *t*? AIT
3:4 and will continue to do the **t** we command. 4005
1Ti 4:1 and follow deceiving spirits and **t taught** 1436
4:6 If you point **these** *t* out to the brothers, AIT
4:8 but godliness has value for **all** *t*, AIT
4:11 Command and teach **these** *t*. AIT
5:13 and busybodies, saying **t** they ought not to. 3836
6:2 **These** are the *t* you are to teach and urge AIT
2Ti 2:2 And **the** *t* you have heard me say in AIT
2:14 Keep reminding them of **these** *t*. AIT
3:11 **what kinds of** *t* happened to me in Antioch, AIT
Tit 1:11 by teaching **t** they ought not to teach— 4005
1:15 To the pure, **all** *t* are pure, AIT
2:15 **These,** then, are the *t* you should teach. AIT
3:5 not because of righteous **t** we had done, 2240
3:8 And I want you to stress **these** *t*. AIT
3:8 **These** *t* are excellent and profitable AIT
Heb 1:2 whom he appointed heir *of* **all** *t*, AIT
1:3 sustaining **all t** by his powerful word. 3836+4246
6:9 we are confident of **better** *t* in your case— AIT
6:9 **t** that accompany salvation. NIG
6:18 by two unchangeable **t** in which it is 4547
7:13 He of whom **these** *t* are said belonged to AIT
9:5 But we cannot discuss **these** *t* in detail now. AIT
9:11 *of* the **good** *t* that are already here, AIT
9:23 for the copies of the **heavenly t** 1877+3836+4041
9:23 but the **heavenly** *t* themselves AIT
10:1 a shadow *of* the **good** *t* that are coming— AIT
11:7 when warned about **t** not yet seen, 3836
11:13 They did not receive **the t** promised; 3836
11:14 People who say **such** *t* show that they are AIT
12:27 what can be shaken—that is, **created t**— 4472
1Pe 1:12 of the *t* **that** have now been told you AIT
1:12 Even angels long to look into **these** *t*. AIT
1:18 not *with* **perishable** *t* such as silver or gold AIT
4:7 The end *of* **all** *t* is near. AIT
4:11 so that in **all** *t* God may be praised AIT
2Pe 1:10 For if you do **these** *t*, you will never fall, AIT
1:12 So I will always remind you of **these** *t*, AIT
1:15 be able to remember **these** *t*. AIT
3:16 His letters contain **some** *t* that are hard AIT
1Jn 2:26 I am writing **these** *t* to you about those who AIT
2:27 his anointing teaches you about **all** *t* AIT
5:13 I write **these** *t* to you who believe in AIT
Jude 1:10 and **what** *t* they do understand by instinct, AIT
1:10 these are the very **t** that destroy them. NIG
Rev 2:5 Repent and do the **t** you did at first. 2240
2:14 Nevertheless, I have a **few** *t* against you: AIT
4:11 for you created **all t,** and by your will 3836+4246
17:4 filled *with* **abominable** *t* and the filth AIT
18:15 The merchants who sold **these** *t* AIT
21:4 for the old order of **t** has passed away." NIG
22:6 the *t* **that** must soon take place." AIT
22:8 John, am the one who heard and saw **these** *t*. AIT
22:20 He who testifies to **these** *t* says, "Yes, AIT

THINK (87) [AFORETHOUGHT, THINKING, THINKS, THOUGHT, THOUGHTLESSLY, THOUGHTS]

Ge 16:6 "Do with her whatever you **t** best." 928+6524
Ex 14:3 Pharaoh *will* **t,** 'The Israelites are wandering 606
Jdg 9:17 and to **t** that my father fought for you, NIH
10:15 Do with us whatever you **t** best, 928+6524
19:30 **T** about it! Consider it! 4013+4200+8492
1Sa 18:23 "Do you **t** it is a small matter to become 928+6524
25:17 Now **t it over** and see what you can do, 3359
2Sa 10:3 "Do you **t** David is honoring your father 928+6524
13:32 "My lord *should* not **t** that they killed all 606
24:13 **t** *it* **over** and decide how I should answer 3359
1Ki 20:28 'Because the Arameans **t** the LORD is 606
2Ki 10:5 you do whatever you **t** best." 928+6524
1Ch 19:3 Do you **t** David is honoring your father 928+6524
Est 4:13 "*Do* not **t** that because you are in 1948
Job 4:3 **T** how you have instructed many, 2180
7:4 I lie down *I* **t,** 'How long before I get up?' 606
7:13 When *I* **t** my bed will comfort me 606
21:6 When *I* **t about** this, I am terrified; 2349
23:15 *when I* **t** of all this, I fear him. 1067
35:2 "*Do you* **t** this is just? 3108
41:32 *one would* **t** the deep had white hair. 3108
Ps 35:25 *Do* not *let them* **t,** "Aha, 606+928+4213
40:17 I am poor and needy; *may* the Lord **t** of me. 3108
63:6 *I* **t** of you through the watches of the night. 2047
144:3 the son of man that *you* **t** *of* him? 3108
Isa 29:15 who do their work in darkness and **t,** 606
44:19 No one **stops to t,** 448+4213+8740
Jer 15:15 **t** *of* how I suffer reproach for your sake. 3359
23:27 They **t** the dreams they tell one another will make my people forget my name, 3108
26:14 whatever you **t** is good and right. 928+6524
44:21 **t about** the incense burned in 4213+6584+6590
51:50 and **t** *on* Jerusalem." 4222+6584+6590
Eze 28:2 though *you* **t** you are as wise as a god. 4213+5989
28:6 " 'Because you **t** you are wise, 4222+5989
Zep 1:12 who **t,** 'The LORD will do nothing, 606+928+4222
Zec 7:10 In your hearts *do* not **t** evil of each other.' 3108
11:12 I told them, "If you **t** it best, 928+6524
Mt 3:9 And *do* not **t** you can say to yourselves, 1506
5:17 not **t** that I have come to abolish the Law 3787
6:7 for *they* **t** they will be heard because 1506
17:25 "What *do* you **t,** Simon?" 1506
18:12 "What *do* you **t?** If a man owns a hundred 1506
21:28 "What *do* you **t?** There was a man who had 1506
22:42 "What *do* you **t** about the Christ? 1506
26:53 *Do you* **t** I cannot call on my Father, 1506
26:66 What *do* you **t?"** 1506
Mk 14:64 heard the blasphemy. What *do* you **t?"** 5743
Lk 10:36 of these three *do* you **t** was a neighbor to 1506
12:51 *Do you* **t** I came to bring peace on earth? 1506
13:2 Jesus answered, "*Do you* **t** that these 1506
13:4 *do you* **t** they were more guilty than all 1506
Jn 5:39 study the Scriptures because you **t that** 1506
5:45 *do* not **t** I will accuse you before the Father. 1506
8:53 **Who do you t you are?"** 4472+4932+5515
11:56 "What *do* you **t?** Isn't he coming 1506
16:2 anyone who kills you *will* **t** he is offering 1506
Ac 5:4 What **made** you **t** of doing such a thing? 1877+2840+3836+5502
11:17 who was I to **t** that I could oppose God?" NIG
13:25 'Who *do you* **t** I am? 5706
15:38 but Paul *did* not **t it wise** to take him, 546
17:29 we should not **t that** the divine being is 3787
25:27 For I **t** it is unreasonable to send on 1506
26:28 "Do you **t** that in such a short time NIG
Ro 1:28 not **t it worthwhile** to retain the knowledge 1507
2:3 *do you* **t** you will escape God's judgment? 3357
12:3 *Do* not **t** of yourself more **highly** than 5672
12:3 but rather **t** of yourself with sober judgment, 5858
13:14 not **t about** how to gratify the desires 4472+4630
1Co 1:26 **t** of what you were when you were called. 1063
7:26 *I* **t** that it is good for you to remain 3787
7:40 and *I* **t that** I too have the Spirit of God. 1506
8:7 to idols that when they eat such food they **t** NIG
10:12 So, *if you* **t** you are standing firm, 1506
12:23 parts that *we* **t** are less honorable we treat 1506
2Co 10:2 toward some people who **t that** we live by 3357
11:5 But *I do* not **t** I am in the least inferior 3357
12:6 so no one *will* **t** more of me than is 3357
Php 2:25 But *I* **t** it is necessary to send back 2451
3:15 And if **on** some point *you* **t** differently, 5858
4:8 or praiseworthy—**t about** such things. 3357
1Ti 6:5 who **t that** godliness is a means to financial 3787
Heb 7:4 Just **t** how great he was: 2555
10:29 How much more severely *do you* **t** 1506
Jas 1:7 not **t** he will receive anything from 3887
4:5 Or *do you* **t** Scripture says without reason 1506
1Pe 4:4 *They* **t it strange** that you do not plunge 3826
2Pe 1:13 *I* **t** it is right to refresh your memory 2451

THINKING (33) [THINK]

Ex 2:14 *Are* you **t** *of* killing me as you killed 606
Dt 1:41 **t it easy** to go up into the hill country. 2103
1Sa 9:5 or my father will stop **t** about the donkeys NIH
10:2 now your father *has* **stopped t** *about* them 5759
15:32 Agag came to him confidently, **t,** 606
2Ki 7:12 **t,** 'They will surely come out, 606
2Ch 32:1 **t** to conquer them for himself. 606
Ne 6:9 They were all trying to frighten us, **t,** 606
Job 1:5 **t,** "Perhaps my children have sinned 606
21:27 "I know full well **what** you are **t,** 4742
Pr 23:7 for he is the kind of *man who is always* **t** 9132
Jer 37:9 Do not deceive yourselves, **t,** 606
Da 7:8 "While I was **t** about the horns, 10683
8:5 As I was **t** about this, suddenly a goat 1067
Mk 2:6 the law were sitting there, **t** to themselves, 1368
2:8 in his spirit that this was what *they were* **t** 1368
2:8 "Why *are you* **t** these things? 1368
Lk 2:44 **T** he was in their company, they traveled on 3787

Lk 5:21 and the teachers of the law began **t** *1368*
5:22 Jesus knew what they were **t** and asked, *1369*
5:22 "Why *are you* **t** these things in your hearts? *1368*
6: 8 But Jesus knew what they were **t** and said *1369*
24:37 and frightened, **t** they saw a ghost. *1506*
Jn 20:15 **T** he was the gardener, she said, "Sir, *1506*
Ac 10:19 *While* Peter *was still* **t** about the vision, *1445*
14:19 dragged him outside the city, **t** he was dead. *3787*
Ro 1:21 but their **t** became futile and their foolish *1369*
1Co 14:20 Brothers, stop **t** like children. *1181+3836+5856*
14:20 but *in* your **t** be adults. *5856*
2Co 12:19 *Have you been* **t** all along that we have been *1506*
Eph 4:17 as the Gentiles do, in the futility *of* their **t**. *3808*
Heb 11:15 If *they had been* **t** of the country *3648*
2Pe 3: 1 to stimulate you to wholesome **t**. *1379*

THINKS (11) [THINK]

Dt 29:19 and therefore **t**, "I will be safe, 606+928+4222
2Sa 16: 3 "He is staying in Jerusalem, because *he* **t**, 606
Est 8: 5 with favor and **t** *it* the **right** thing to do, 4178
Job 24:15 he **t**, 'No eye will see me,' 606
Lk 8:18 what *he* **t** he has will be taken from him." *1506*
1Co 3:18 of you **t** he is wise by the standards *1506*
7:36 If anyone **t** he is acting improperly toward *3787*
8: 2 The man who **t** he knows something does *1506*
14:37 If anybody **t** he is a prophet *1506*
Gal 6: 3 If anyone **t** he is something *1506*
Php 3: 4 If anyone else **t** he has reasons to put *1506*

THIRD (181) [THREE]

Ge 1:13 and there was morning—the **t** day. 8958
2:14 The name of the **t** river is the Tigris; 8958
22: 4 On the **t** day Abraham looked up and saw 8958
31:22 On the **t** day Laban was told 8958
32:19 the **t** and all the others who followed 8958
40:20 Now the **t** day was Pharaoh's birthday, 8958
42:18 On the **t** day, Joseph said to them, 8958
50:23 the **t generation** of Ephraim's children. 9000
Ex 19: 1 the **t** month after the Israelites left Egypt— 8958
19:11 and be ready by the **t** day, 8958
19:15 "Prepare yourselves for the **t** day. 8993
19:16 the morning of the **t** day there was thunder 8958
20: 5 of the fathers to the **t** and fourth generation 9000
25:35 and a **t** bud under the third pair— NIH
25:35 and a third bud under the **t** pair— NIH
28:19 in the **t** row a jacinth, an agate and 8958
34: 7 the fathers to the **t** and fourth generation." 9000
37:21 and a **t** bud under the third pair— NIH
37:21 and a third bud under the **t** pair— NIH
39:12 in the **t** row a jacinth, an agate and 8958
Lev 7:17 of the sacrifice left over till the **t** day must 8958
7:18 fellowship offering is eaten on the **t** day, 8958
19: 6 over until the **t** day must be burned up. 8958
19: 7 If any of it is eaten on the **t** day, 8958
Nu 2:24 They will set out **t**. 8958
7:24 On the **t** day, Eliab son of Helon, 8958
14:18 the fathers to the **t** and fourth generation.' 9000
15: 6 of an ephah of fine flour mixed with a **t** *of* 8958
15: 7 and a **t** *of* a hin of wine as a drink offering. 8958
19:12 on the **t** day and on the seventh day; 8958
19:12 But if he does not purify himself on the **t** 8958
19:19 to sprinkle the unclean person on the **t** 8958
28:14 with the ram, a **t** *of* a hin; 8958
29:20 " 'On the **t** day prepare eleven bulls, 8958
31:19 the **t** and seventh days you must purify 8958
Dt 5: 9 of the fathers to the **t** and fourth generation 9000
23: 8 The **t** generation of children born 8958
26:12 a tenth of all your produce in the **t** year, 8958
Jos 9:17 the Israelites set out and on the **t** day came 8958
17:11 with their surrounding settlements (the **t** in 8993
19:10 The **t** lot came up for Zebulun, 8958
Jdg 16:15 This is the **t** time you have made a fool 8993
20:30 up against the Benjamites on the **t** day 8958
1Sa 3: 8 The LORD called Samuel a **t** *time,* 8958
13:18 the **t** toward the borderland overlooking 285[s]
13:21 and a **t** *of* a shekel for sharpening forks 8993
17:13 the second, Abinadab; and the **t**, 8958
19:21 Saul sent men a **t** *time,* 8958
30: 1 and his men reached Ziklag on the **t** day. 8958
2Sa 1: 2 the **t** day a man arrived from Saul's camp, 8958
3: 3 the **t**, Absalom the son of Maacah daughter 8958
8: 2 and the **t** length was allowed to live. 4850[s]
18: 2 a **t** under the command of Joab, 8958
18: 2 a third under the command of Joab, a **t** 8958
18: 2 and a **t** under Ittai the Gittite. 8958
1Ki 3:18 The **t** day after my child was born, 8958
6: 6 and the **t** floor seven. 8958
6: 8 to the middle level and from there to the **t**. 8958
15:28 in the **t** year of Asa king of Judah 8993
15:33 In the **t** year of Asa king of Judah, 8993
18: 1 After a long time, in the **t** year, 8958
18:34 **"Do** *it* **a t time,"** he ordered, 8992
18:34 and *they* **did** *it* **the t time.** 8992
22: 2 the **t** year Jehoshaphat king of Judah went 8958
2Ki 1:13 the king sent a **t** captain with his fifty men. 8958
1:13 This **t** captain went up and fell 8958
11: 5 a **t** of you guarding the royal palace, 8958
11: 6 a **t** at the Sur Gate, and a third at the gate 8958
11: 6 and a **t** at the gate behind the guard, 8958
18: 1 In the **t** year of Hoshea son of Elah king 8993
19:29 But in the **t** year sow and reap, 8958
20: 5 On the **t** day from now you will go up to 8958
20: 8 up to the temple of the LORD on the **t** day 8958
1Ch 2:13 the second son was Abinadab, the **t** Shimea, 8958
3: 2 the **t**, Absalom the son of Maacah daughter 8958
1Ch 3:15 Jehoiakim the second son, Zedekiah the **t**, 8958
8: 1 Ashbel the second son, Aharah the **t**, 8958
8:39 Jeush the second son and Eliphelet the **t**. 8958
12: 9 the second in command, Eliab the **t**, 8958
23:19 Jahaziel the **t** and Jekameam the fourth. 8958
24: 8 the **t** to Harim, the fourth to Seorim, 8958
24:23 Jahaziel the **t** and Jekameam the fourth. 8958
25:10 the **t** to Zaccur, his sons and relatives, 12 8958
26: 2 Zebadiah the **t**, Jathniel the fourth, 8958
26: 4 Jehozabad the second, Joah the **t**, 8958
26:11 Tabaliah the **t** and Zechariah the fourth. 8958
27: 5 The **t** army commander, 8958
27: 5 third army commander, for the **t** month, 8958
2Ch 15:10 in the **t** month of the fifteenth year 8958
17: 7 In the **t** year of his reign he sent 8993
23: 4 A **t** of you priests and Levites 8958
23: 5 a **t** of you at the royal palace and a third at 8958
23: 5 a third of you at the royal palace and a **t** at 8958
27: 5 also in the second and **t** years. 8958
31: 7 They began doing this in the **t** month 8958
Ezr 6:15 The temple was completed on the **t** day of 10760
Ne 10:32 a **t** *of* a shekel each year for the service of 8958
Est 1: 3 in the **t** year of his reign he gave a banquet 8993
5: 1 On the **t** day Esther put on her royal robes 8958
8: 9 on the twenty-third day of the **t** month, 8958
Job 42:14 and the **t** Keren-Happuch. 8958
Isa 19:24 In that day Israel will be the **t**, 8958
37:30 But in the **t** year sow and reap, 8958
Jer 38:14 the **t** entrance to the temple of the LORD. 8958
Eze 5: 2 burn a **t** of the hair with fire inside the city. 8958
5: 2 a **t** and strike it with the sword all around 8958
5: 2 And scatter a **t** to the wind. 8958
5:12 A **t** *of* your *people* will die of the plague 8958
5:12 a **t** will fall by the sword outside your walls; 8958
5:12 a **t** I will scatter to the winds and pursue 8958
10:14 the **t** the face of a lion, 8958
31: 1 in the **t** month on the first day, 8958
42: 6 The rooms *on the* **t** *floor* had no pillars, 8992
46:14 with a **t** *of* a hin of oil to moisten the flour. 8958
Da 1: 1 In the **t** year of the reign of Jehoiakim king 8993
2:39 Next, a **t** kingdom, one of bronze, 10759
5: 7 made the **t highest** ruler in the kingdom." 10761
5:16 made the **t highest** ruler in the kingdom." 10761
5:29 and he was proclaimed the **t highest** ruler 10761
8: 1 In the **t** year of King Belshazzar's reign, 8993
10: 1 In the **t** year of Cyrus king of Persia, 8993
Hos 6: 2 on the **t** day he will restore us, 8958
Zec 6: 3 the **t** white, and the fourth dappled— 8958
13: 9 This **t** I will bring into the fire; 8958
Mt 16:21 and that he must be killed and *on* the **t** day *5569*
17:23 and *on* the **t** day he will be raised to life." *5569*
20: 3 "About the **t** hour he went out *5569*
20:19 *On* the **t** day he will be raised to life!" *5569*
21:35 killed another, and stoned a **t**. *NIG*
22:26 to the second and **t** brother, *5569*
26:44 and prayed the **t time,** *1666+5569*
27:64 the tomb to be made secure until the **t** day. *5569*
Mk 12:21 It was the same with the **t**. *5569*
14:41 Returning the **t time,** he said to them, *5568*
15:25 It was the **t** hour when they crucified him. *5569*
Lk 9:22 be killed and *on* the **t** day be raised to life." *5569*
12:38 even if he comes in the second or **t** watch *5569*
13:32 and *on* the **t** day I will reach my goal.' *5569*
18:33 *On* the **t** day he will rise again." *5569*
20:12 He sent still a **t**, and they wounded him *5569*
20:31 and then the **t** married her, *5569*
23:22 *For* the **t time** he spoke to them: "Why? *5568*
24: 7 and *on* the **t** day be raised again.' " *5569*
24:21 it is the **t** day since all this took place. *5569*
24:46 and rise from the dead *on* the **t** day, *5569*
Jn 2: 1 *On* the **t** day a wedding took place at Cana *5569*
21:14 the **t time** Jesus appeared to his disciples *5568*
21:17 The **t time** he said to him, *5568*
21:17 because Jesus asked him the **t time,** *5568*
Ac 10:40 from the dead on the **t** day and caused him *5569*
20: 9 the ground from the **t story** and was picked *5566*
27:19 *On* the **t** day, they threw the ship's tackle *5569*
1Co 12:28 **t** teachers, then workers of miracles, *5568*
15: 4 that he was raised *on* the **t** day according to *5569*
2Co 12: 2 who fourteen years ago was caught up to the **t** heaven. *5569*
12:14 Now I am ready to visit you *for* the **t time,** *5568*
13: 1 This will be my **t** visit to you. *5568*
Rev 4: 7 the **t** had a face like a man, *5569*
6: 5 When the Lamb opened the **t** seal, *5569*
6: 5 I heard the **t** living creature say, "Come!" *5569*
8: 7 A **t** of the earth was burned up, *5569*
8: 7 a **t** of the trees were burned up, *5569*
8: 8 A **t** of the sea turned into blood, *5569*
8: 9 a **t** of the living creatures in the sea died, *5569*
8: 9 and a **t** of the ships were destroyed. *5569*
8:10 The **t** angel sounded his trumpet, *5569*
8:10 fell from the sky on a **t** of the rivers and on *5569*
8:11 A **t** of the waters turned bitter, *5569*
8:12 and a **t** of the sun was struck, *5569*
8:12 a **t** of the moon, and a third of the stars, *5569*
8:12 a third of the moon, and a **t** of the stars, *5569*
8:12 so that a **t** of them turned dark. *5569*
8:12 A **t** of the day was without light, *5569*
8:12 and also a **t** of the night. *NIG*
9:15 and year were released to kill a **t** *5569*
9:18 A **t** of mankind was killed by *5569*
11:14 the **t** woe is coming soon. *5569*
12: 4 His tail swept a **t** of the stars out of the sky *5569*
14: 9 A **t** angel followed them and said in *5569*
16: 4 The **t** angel poured out his bowl on *5569*
21:19 the second sapphire, the **t** chalcedony, *5569*

THIRDS (1) [THREE]

1Sa 13:21 The price was **two t of a shekel** for 7088

THIRST (24) [THIRSTS, THIRSTY]

Ex 17: 3 and our children and livestock die of **t?"** 7533
Dt 28:48 therefore in hunger and **t**, 7533
Jdg 15:18 Must I now die of **t** and fall into the hands 7533
2Ch 32:11 to let you die of hunger and **t**. 7533
Ne 9:15 and in their **t** you brought them water from 7533
9:20 and you gave them water for their **t**. 7533
Job 24:11 they tread the winepresses, yet **suffer t**. 7532
Ps 69:21 in my food and gave me vinegar for my **t**. 7533
104:11 the wild donkeys quench their **t**. 7533
Isa 5:13 and their masses will be parched with **t**. 7533
29: 8 he awakens faint, with his **t** unquenched. 5883
41:17 their tongues are parched with **t**. 7533
48:21 not **t** when he led them through the deserts; 7532
49:10 They will neither hunger nor **t**, 7532
50: 2 their fish rot for lack of water and die of **t**. 7533
Jer 46:10 till *it has* **quenched its t** with blood. 8115
La 4: 4 Because of **t** the infant's tongue sticks to 7533
Hos 2: 3 and slay her with **t**. 7533
Am 8:11 not a famine of food or a **t** for water, 7533
8:13 strong young men will faint because of **t**. 7533
Mt 5: 6 Blessed are those who hunger and **t for** *1498*
Jn 4:14 the water I give him *will* never **t**. *1498*
2Co 11:27 and **t** and have often gone without food; *1499*
Rev 7:16 will they hunger; never again *will they* **t**. *1498*

THIRSTS (3) [THIRST]

Ps 42: 2 My soul **t** for God, for the living God. 7532
63: 1 my soul **t** for you, my body longs for you, 7532
143: 6 my soul **t** for you like a parched land. NIH

THIRSTY (33) [THIRST]

Ex 17: 3 But the people *were* **t** for water there, 7532
Dt 8:15 that **t** and waterless land, 7536
Jdg 4:19 *"I'm* **t,"** he said. 7532
15:18 Because *he was* very **t**, 7532
Ru 2: 9 And *whenever you are* **t**, 7532
2Sa 17:29 and tired and **t** in the desert." 7534
Job 5: 5 and the **t** pant after his wealth. 7534
Ps 107: 5 They were hungry and **t**, 7534
107: 9 for he satisfies the **t** and fills the 5883+8799
107:33 flowing springs into **t ground,** 7536
Pr 25:21 if he is **t**, give him water to drink. 7532
Isa 21:14 bring water for the **t**; 7534
29: 8 as when a **t** *man* dreams that he is drinking, 7534
32: 2 and the shadow of a great rock in a **t** land. 6546
32: 6 and from the **t** he withholds water. 7534
35: 7 the **t ground** bubbling springs. 7536
44: 3 For I will pour water on the **t** land, 7534
55: 1 "Come, all you *who* are **t**, 7534
65:13 my servants will drink, but you *will go* **t**; 7532
Eze 19:13 in the desert, in a dry and **t** land. 7533
Mt 25:35 *I was* **t** and you gave me something *1498*
25:37 or **t** and give you something to drink? *1498*
25:42 *I was* **t** and you gave me nothing to drink, *1498*
25:44 or **t** or a stranger or needing clothes or sick *1498*
Jn 4:13 who drinks this water *will be* **t** again, *1498*
4:15 give me this water so that *I* won't *get* **t** *1498*
6:35 he who believes in me *will* never *be* **t**. *1498*
7:37 "If anyone *is* **t**, let him come to me and *1498*
19:28 Jesus said, *"I am* **t."** *1498*
Ro 12:20 if *he is* **t**, give him something to drink. *1498*
1Co 4:11 To this very hour *we* go hungry and **t**, *1498*
Rev 21: 6 *To* him who *is* **t** I will give to drink *1498*
22:17 Whoever *is* **t**, let him come; *1498*

THIRTEEN (13) [THIRTEENTH, 13]

Ge 17:25 and his son Ishmael was **t**; 6926+8993
Nu 29:13 a burnt offering of **t** young bulls, 6925+8993
29:14 of the **t** bulls prepare a grain offering 6925+8993
Dt 3:11 of iron and was **more than t feet** long 564+9596
Jos 19: 6 **t** towns and their villages; 6926+8993
21: 4 the priest were allotted **t** towns 6926+8993
21: 6 of Gershon were allotted **t** towns from 6926+8993
21:19 **t**, together with their pasturelands. 6926+8993
21:33 towns of the Gershonite clans were **t**, 6926+8993
1Ki 7: 1 It took Solomon **t** years, however, 6926+8993
1Ch 6:60 Kohathite clans, were **t** in all. 6926+8993
6:62 were allotted **t** towns from the tribes 6926+8993
Eze 40:11 and its length was **t** cubits. 6926+8993

THIRTEENTH (11) [THIRTEEN]

Ge 14: 4 but in the **t** year they rebelled. 6926+8993
1Ch 24:13 the **t** to Huppah, 6925+8993
25:20 the **t** to Shubael, his sons and relatives, 6925+8993
Est 3:12 Then on the **t** day of the first month 6925+8993
3:13 the **t** day of the twelfth month, 6925+8993
8:12 was the **t** day of the twelfth month, 6925+8993
9: 1 On the **t** day of the twelfth month, 6925+8993
9:17 happened on the **t** day of the month 6925+8993
9:18 had assembled on the **t** and fourteenth, 6925+8993
Jer 1: 2 the LORD came to him in the **t** year of 6926+8993
25: 3 from the **t** year of Josiah son of Amon 6926+8993

THIRTIETH (1) [THIRTY]

Eze 1: 1 In the **t** year, in the fourth month on the 8993

THIRTY (95) [THIRTIETH, 30]

Ge 18:30 What if only **t** can be found there?" 8993

Ge 18:30 "I will not do it if I find **t** there." 8993
32:15 **t** female camels with their young, 8993
41:46 Joseph was **t** years old when he entered 8993
47: 9 of my pilgrimage are a hundred and **t**. 8993
Ex 21:32 the owner must pay **t** shekels of silver to 8993
26: 8 **t** cubits long and four cubits wide. 8993
36:15 **t** cubits long and four cubits wide. 8993
Lev 27: 4 set her value at **t** shekels. 8993
Nu 4: 3 Count all the men from **t** to fifty years 8993
4:23 Count all the men from **t** to fifty years 8993
4:30 Count all the men from **t** to fifty years 8993
4:35 from **t** to fifty years of age who came 8993
4:39 from **t** to fifty years of age who came 8993
4:43 from **t** to fifty years of age who came 8993
4:47 from **t** to fifty years of age who came to do 8993
7:13 plate weighing a hundred and **t** shekels, 8993
7:19 plate weighing a hundred and **t** shekels, 8993
7:25 plate weighing a hundred and **t** shekels, 8993
7:31 plate weighing a hundred and **t** shekels, 8993
7:37 plate weighing a hundred and **t** shekels, 8993
7:43 plate weighing a hundred and **t** shekels, 8993
7:49 plate weighing a hundred and **t** shekels, 8993
7:55 plate weighing a hundred and **t** shekels, 8993
7:61 plate weighing a hundred and **t** shekels, 8993
7:67 plate weighing a hundred and **t** shekels, 8993
7:73 plate weighing a hundred and **t** shekels, 8993
7:79 plate weighing a hundred and **t** shekels, 8993
7:85 plate weighed a hundred and **t** shekels, 8993
20:29 house of Israel mourned for him **t** days. 8993
Dt 34: 8 for Moses in the plains of Moab **t** days, 8993
Jos 8: 3 He chose **t** thousand of his best fighting 8993
Jdg 10: 4 He had **t** sons, who rode thirty donkeys. 8993
10: 4 He had thirty sons, who rode **t** donkeys. 8993
10: 4 They controlled **t** towns in Gilead, 8993
12: 9 He had **t** sons and thirty daughters. 8993
12: 9 He had thirty sons and **t** daughters. 8993
12: 9 for his sons he brought in **t** young women 8993
12:14 He had forty sons and **t** grandsons, 8993
14:11 he was given **t** companions. 8993
14:12 I will give you **t** linen garments 8993
14:12 linen garments and **t** sets of clothes. 8993
14:13 you must give me **t** linen garments 8993
14:13 linen garments and **t** sets of clothes." 8993
14:19 struck down **t** of their men, 8993
20:31 that about **t** men fell in the open field and 8993
20:39 casualties on the men of Israel (about **t**), 8993
1Sa 4:10 Israel lost **t** thousand foot soldiers. 8993
9:22 who were invited—about **t** in number. 8993
11: 8 and the men of Judah **t** thousand. 8993
13: 1 Saul was [**t**] years old when he became king 8993
2Sa 5: 4 David was **t** years old when he became king 8993
6: 1 chosen men, **t** thousand in all. 8993
23:13 of the **t** chief men came down to David at 8993
23:23 in greater honor than any of the **T**, 8993
23:24 Among the **T** were: 8993
1Ki 4:22 Solomon's daily provisions were **t** cors 8993
5:13 from all Israel—**t** thousand men. 8993
6: 2 twenty wide and **t** high. 8993
7: 2 fifty wide and **t** high, 8993
7: 6 a colonnade fifty cubits long and **t** wide. 8993
7:23 a line of **t** cubits to measure around it. 8993
2Ki 18:14 of silver and **t** talents of gold. 8993
1Ch 11:15 Three of the **t** chiefs came down to David 8993
11:25 in greater honor than any of the **T**, 8993
11:42 and the **t** with him, 8993
12: 4 a mighty man among the **T**, 8993
12: 4 who was a leader of the **T**; 8993
12:18 Spirit came upon Amasai, chief of the **T**, 8993
23: 3 The Levites **t** years old or more 8993
27: 6 a mighty man among the **T** and was over 8993
27: 6 among the Thirty and was over the **T**. 8993
2Ch 4: 2 a line of **t** cubits to measure around it. 8993
24:15 and he died at the age of a hundred and **t**. 8993
35: 7 a total of **t** thousand sheep and goats for 8993
Est 4:11 But **t** days have passed since I was called 8993
Pr 22:20 Have I not written **t** sayings for you, 8993
Jer 38:10 "Take **t** men from here with you 8993
Eze 40:17 there were **t** rooms along the pavement. 8993
41: 6 one above another, **t** on each level. 8993
46:22 forty cubits long and **t** cubits wide; 8993
Da 6: 7 to any god or man during the next **t** days, 10762
6:12 during the next **t** days anyone who prays 10762
Zec 5: 2 a flying scroll, **t feet** long 564+928+2021+6929
11:12 So they paid me **t** *pieces of* silver. 8993
11:13 the **t** *pieces of* silver and threw them into 8993
Mt 13: 8 sixty or **t** *times* what was sown. *5558*
13:23 sixty or **t** *times* what was sown." *5558*
26:15 So they counted out for him **t** silver coins. *5558*
27: 3 the **t** silver coins to the chief priests and *5558*
27: 9 "They took the **t** silver coins, *5558*
Mk 4: 8 grew and produced a crop, multiplying **t**, *5558*
4:20 **t**, sixty or even a hundred *times* what was sown." *5558*
Lk 3:23 Now Jesus himself was about **t** years old *5558*
Jn 2: 6 from **twenty to t gallons.** *1545+2445+3583+5552*

THIRTY-EIGHT (3) [THIRTY-EIGHTH]

Dt 2:14 **T** years passed from the time 2256+8993+9046
1Ch 23: 3 number of men was **t** thousand. 2256+8993+9046
Jn 5: 5 had been an invalid *for* **t** years. *2779+3893+5558*

THIRTY-EIGHTH (2) [THIRTY-EIGHT]

1Ki 16:29 the **t** year of Asa king of Judah, 2256+8993+9046
2Ki 15: 8 **t** year of Azariah king of Judah, 2256+8993+9046

THIRTY-FIFTH (1) [THIRTY-FIVE]

2Ch 15:19 was no more war until the **t** year 2256+2822+8993

THIRTY-FIRST (1)

1Ki 16:23 the **t** year of Asa king of Judah, 285+2256+8993

THIRTY-FIVE (3) [THIRTY-FIFTH, 35]

1Ki 22:42 Jehoshaphat was **t** years old 2256+2822+8993
2Ch 3:15 were **t** cubits long, each with 2256+2822+8993
20:31 He was **t** years old when he 2256+2822+8993

THIRTY-NINTH (3)

2Ki 15:13 **t** year of Uzziah king of Judah, 2256+8993+9596
15:17 **t** year of Azariah king of Judah, 2256+8993+9596
2Ch 16:12 In the **t** year of his reign Asa 2256+8993+9596

THIRTY-ONE (3)

Jos 12:24 **t** kings in all. 285+2256+8993
2Ki 22: 1 he reigned in Jerusalem **t** years. 285+2256+8993
2Ch 34: 1 he reigned in Jerusalem **t** years. 285+2256+8993

THIRTY-SECOND (2)

Ne 5:14 until his **t** year—twelve years— 2256+8993+9109
13: 6 for in the **t** year of Artaxerxes 2256+8993+9109

THIRTY-SEVEN (2) [THIRTY-SEVENTH]

Ge 25:17 Ishmael lived a hundred and **t** years 2256+8679+8993
2Sa 23:39 There were **t** in all. 2256+8679+8993

THIRTY-SEVENTH (3) [THIRTY-SEVEN]

2Ki 13:10 **t** year of Joash king of Judah, 2256+8679+8993
25:27 **t** year of the exile of Jehoiachin 2256+8679+8993
Jer 52:31 **t** year of the exile of Jehoiachin 2256+8679+8993

THIRTY-SIX (2) [THIRTY-SIXTH]

Jos 7: 5 who killed about **t** of them. 2256+8993+9252
2Ch 2: 2 and **t hundred** as foremen over them. 547+2256+4395+8993+9252

THIRTY-SIXTH (1) [THIRTY-SIX]

2Ch 16: 1 In the **t** year of Asa's reign 2256+8993+9252

THIRTY-THREE (7)

Ge 46:15 These sons and daughters of his were **t** in all. 2256+8993+8993
Lev 12: 4 must wait **t** days to be purified 2256+8993+8993
2Sa 5: 5 over all Israel and Judah **t** years. 2256+8993+8993
1Ki 2:11 seven years in Hebron and **t** in Jerusalem. 2256+8993+8993
5:16 **t hundred** foremen who supervised the project 547+2256+4395+8993+8993
1Ch 3: 4 David reigned in Jerusalem **t** years, 2256+8993+8993
29:27 seven in Hebron and **t** in Jerusalem. 2256+8993+8993

THIRTY-TWO (6) [32]

1Ki 20: 1 Accompanied by **t** kings with 2256+8993+9109
22:31 his **t** chariot commanders, 2256+8993+9109
2Ki 8:17 He was **t** years old when he 2256+8993+9109
1Ch 19: 7 They hired **t** thousand chariots 2256+8993+9109
2Ch 21: 5 Jehoram was **t** years old 2256+8993+9109
21:20 Jehoram was **t** years old 2256+8993+9109

THIS (3712) [THESE] See Index of Articles Etc.

THISTLE (4) [THISTLES]

2Ki 14: 9 "A **t** in Lebanon sent a message to a cedar 2560
14: 9 along and trampled the **t** underfoot. 2560
2Ch 25:18 "A **t** in Lebanon sent a message to a cedar 2560
25:18 along and trampled the **t** underfoot. 2560

THISTLES (4) [THISTLE]

Ge 3:18 It will produce thorns and **t** for you, 1998
Hos 10: 8 and **t** will grow up and cover their altars. 1998
Mt 7:16 grapes from thornbushes, or figs from **t**? *5560*
Heb 6: 8 that produces thorns and **t** is worthless *5560*

THOMAS (11)

Mt 10: 3 **T** and Matthew the tax collector; *2605*
Mk 3:18 **T**, James son of Alphaeus, Thaddaeus, *2605*
Lk 6:15 **T**, James son of Alphaeus, *2605*
Jn 11:16 Then **T** (called Didymus) said to the rest of *2605*
14: 5 **T** said to him, "Lord, we don't know where *2605*
20:24 Now **T** (called Didymus), one of the Twelve *2605*
20:26 and **T** was with them. *2605*
20:27 Then he said *to* **T**, "Put your finger here; *2605*
20:28 **T** said to him, "My Lord and my God!" *2605*
21: 2 **T** (called Didymus), Nathanael from Cana *2605*
Ac 1:13 Philip and **T**, Bartholomew and Matthew; *2605*

THONG (2) [THONGS]

Ge 14:23 not even a thread or the **t** *of* a sandal, 8579
Isa 5:27 not a sandal **t** is broken. 8579

THONGS (6) [THONG]

Jdg 16: 7 with seven fresh **t** that have not been dried, 3857
16: 8 of the Philistines brought her seven fresh **t** 3857
16: 9 But he snapped the **t** as easily as a piece 3857
Mk 1: 7 the **t** of whose sandals I am not worthy *2666*
Lk 3:16 the **t** of whose sandals I am not worthy *2666*
Jn 1:27 the **t** of whose sandals I am not worthy *2666*

THORN (2) [THORNBUSH, THORNBUSHES, THORNS]

Mic 7: 4 the most upright worse than a **t hedge.** 5004
2Co 12: 7 there was given me a **t** in my flesh, *5022*

THORNBUSH (5) [THORN]

Jdg 9:14 "Finally all the trees said to the **t**, 353
9:15 "The **t** said to the trees, 'If you really want 353
9:15 then let fire come out of the **t** and consume 353
Pr 26: 9 Like a **t** in a drunkard's hand is a proverb 2560
Isa 55:13 Instead of the **t** will grow the pine tree, 5848

THORNBUSHES (6) [THORN]

Ex 22: 6 "If a fire breaks out and spreads into **t** so 7764
Isa 7:19 on all the **t** and at all the water holes. 5848
33:12 like cut **t** they will be set ablaze." 7764
Hos 2: 6 Therefore I will block her path with **t**; 6106
Mt 7:16 Do people pick grapes from **t**, *180*
Lk 6:44 People do not pick figs from **t**, *180*

THORNS (43) [THORN]

Ge 3:18 It will produce **t** and thistles for you, 7764
Nu 33:55 barbs in your eyes and **t** in your sides. 7564
Jos 23:13 whips on your backs and **t** in your eyes, 7564
Jdg 2: 3 be [**t**] in your sides and their gods will be NIH
8: 7 I will tear your flesh with desert **t** 7764
8:16 by punishing them with desert **t** and briers. 7764
2Sa 23: 6 But evil men are all to be cast aside like **t**, 7764
23: 7 Whoever touches **t** uses a tool of iron or 2157[S]
Job 5: 5 taking it even from among **t**, 7553
Ps 58: 9 Before your pots can feel [the heat of] the **t** 353
118:12 but they died out as quickly as burning **t**; 7764
Pr 15:19 The way of the sluggard is blocked with **t**, 2537
22: 5 In the paths of the wicked lie **t** and snares, 7553
24:31 **t** had come up everywhere, 7853
Ecc 7: 6 Like the crackling of **t** under the pot, 6106
SS 2: 2 among **t** is my darling among the maidens. 2560
Isa 5: 6 and briers and **t** will grow there. 8885
7:23 there will be only briers and **t**. 8885
7:24 the land will be covered with briers and **t**. 8885
7:25 for fear of the briers and **t**; 8885
9:18 it consumes briers and **t**, 8885
10:17 a single day it will burn and consume his **t** 8885
27: 4 and **t** confronting me! 8885
32:13 a land overgrown with **t** and briers— 7764
34:13 **T** will overrun her citadels, 6106
Jer 4: 3 and do not sow among **t**. 7764
12:13 They will sow wheat but reap **t**; 7764
Eze 2: 6 though briers and **t** are all around you 6141
28:24 who are painful briers and sharp **t**. 7764
Hos 9: 6 and **t** will overrun their tents. 2560
10: 8 **T** and thistles will grow up 7764
Na 1:10 They will be entangled among **t** and drunk 6106
Mt 13: 7 Other seed fell among **t**, *180*
13:22 that fell among the **t** is the man who hears *180*
27:29 then twisted together a crown of **t** and set it *180*
Mk 4: 7 Other seed fell among **t**, *180*
4:18 Still others, like seed sown among **t**, *180*
15:17 then twisted together a crown **of t** and set it *181*
Lk 8: 7 Other seed fell among **t**, *180*
8:14 that fell among **t** stands for those who hear, *180*
Jn 19: 2 The soldiers twisted together a crown of **t** *180*
19: 5 the crown **of t** and the purple robe, *181*
Heb 6: 8 that produces **t** and thistles is worthless *180*

THOROUGH (3) [THOROUGHLY]

Dt 19:18 The judges must make a **t** investigation, 3512
Ac 12:19 Herod *had* a **t search made for** him *2118*
18:24 with a **t** knowledge of the Scriptures. *1543*

THOROUGHLY (11) [THOROUGH]

Ge 11: 3 make bricks and **bake** them **t.**" 4200+8596+8599
Dt 13:14 must inquire, probe and investigate it **t**. 3512
17: 4 then you must investigate it **t**. 3512
Jdg 15: 2 "I was so sure *you* **t hated** her," 8533+8533
Ps 119:140 Your promises have been **t** tested, 4394
Isa 1:25 *I will* **t purge away** your dross and remove 1342+2021+3869+7671
24:19 split asunder, the earth **is t shaken.** 4572+4572
Jer 6: 9 **glean** the remnant of Israel as **t** 6618+6618
20:11 They will fail and be **t** disgraced; 4394
Ac 22: 3 Under Gamaliel I was **t** trained in the law of our fathers *205+2848*
2Ti 3:17 so that the man of God may be **t** equipped *787*

THOSE (1368) [THAT] See Index of Articles Etc.

THOUGH (329) [ALTHOUGH]

Ge 8:21 **even t** every inclination of his heart is evil 3954
18:27 **t** I am nothing but dust and ashes, 2256
20:12 daughter of my father **t** not of my mother; 421

Ge 28:19 **t** the city used to be called Luz. 219
31:50 even **t** no one is with us, NIH
38:14 *t* Shelah *had* now **grown up,** AIT
39:10 And **t** she spoke to Joseph day after day, 3869
42:30 to us and treated us **as t** we were spying on 3869
44:18 **t** you are equal to Pharaoh himself. 3954
48:14 **t** he was the younger, 2256
48:14 **even t** Manasseh was the firstborn. 3954
Ex 3:2 that **t** the bush was on fire it did 2180
7:3 **and t** I multiply my miraculous signs 2256
13:17 **t** that was shorter. 3954
Lev 4:13 **even t** the community is unaware of 2256
5:2 **even t** he is unaware of it, 2256
5:3 **even t** he is unaware of it, 2256
5:4 **even t** he is unaware of it, 2256
5:17 **even t** he does not know it, 2256
11:4 The camel, **t** it chews the cud, 3954
11:5 The coney, **t** it chews the cud, 3954
11:6 The rabbit, **t** it chews the cud, 3954
11:7 **t** it has a split hoof completely divided, 3954
13:55 **even t** it has not spread, it is unclean. 2256
26:36 They will run as **t** fleeing from the sword, NIH
26:36 **even t** no one is pursuing them. 2256
26:37 They will stumble over one another **as t** 3869
26:37 **even t** no one is pursuing them. 2256
Nu 5:14 or if he is jealous and suspects her **even t** 2256
14:44 **t** neither Moses nor the ark of the LORD's 2256
Dt 18:8 **even t** he has received money from 963+4200
19:6 and kill him **even t** he is not deserving 2256
22:27 and **t** the betrothed girl screamed, NIH
29:19 **even t** I persist in going my own way." 3954
Jos 17:18 **t** the Canaanites have iron chariots and 3954
17:18 the Canaanites have iron chariots and **t** 3954
22:17 **even t** a plague fell on the community of 2256
Jdg 13:16 "**Even t** you detain me, 561
18:29 **t** the city used to be called Laish. 219
Ru 2:13 **t** I do not have the standing of one 2256
1Sa 12:12 **t** the LORD your God was your king. 2256
15:35 **t** Samuel mourned for him. 3954
20:20 as **t** I were shooting at a target. NIH
25:29 **Even t** someone is pursuing you 2256
2Sa 3:27 as **t** to speak with him privately. NIH
3:39 And today, **t** I am the anointed king, 2256
16:6 **t** all the troops and the special guard were 2256
19:14 over the hearts of all the men of Judah **as t** 3869
23:19 **even t** he was not included among them. 2256
1Ki 2:28 who had conspired with Adonijah **t** not 2256
9:8 **And t** this temple is now imposing, 2256
12:31 **even t** they were not Levites. 889
2Ki 4:39 **t** no one knew what they were. 3954
5:16 **And even t** Naaman urged him, he refused. 2256
17:12 **t** the LORD had said, 889
18:24 **even t** you are depending on Egypt 2256
25:4 **t** the Babylonians were surrounding 2256
1Ch 5:2 and **t** Judah was the strongest 3954
11:21 **even t** he was not included among them. 2256
17:17 on me **as t** I were the most exalted of men, 3869
2Ch 7:21 And **t** this temple is now so imposing, 889
16:12 **T** his disease was severe, 6330
24:19 **and t** they testified against them, 2256
Ezr 3:6 **t** the foundation of the LORD's temple 2256
9:9 **T** we are slaves, 3954
9:15 **t** because of it not one of us can stand 3954
Ne 5:5 as our countrymen and **t** our sons are NIH
6:1 **t** up to that time I had not set the doors in 1685
Est 4:16 **even t** it is against the law. 889
Job 2:3 **t** you incited me against him to ruin him 2256
6:14 **even t** he forsakes the fear of the Almighty. 2256
9:3 **T** one wished to dispute with him, 561
9:15 **T** I were innocent, I could not answer him; 561
10:7 **t** you know that I am not guilty and 6584
12:4 **t** I called upon God and he answered— NIH
12:4 **t** righteous and blameless! NIH
13:15 **T** he slay me, yet will I hope in him; 2176
15:27 "**T** his face is covered with fat 3954
19:7 "**T** I cry, 'I've been wronged!' 2176
19:7 **t** I call for help, there is no justice. NIH
19:16 **t** I beg him with my own mouth. NIH
20:6 **T** his pride reaches to the heavens 561
20:12 "**T** evil is sweet in his mouth 561
20:13 **t** he cannot bear to let it go and keeps it NIH
20:24 **T** he flees from an iron weapon, NIH
22:8 **t** you were a powerful man, owning land— 2256
24:22 **t** they become established, 2256
27:16 **T** he heaps up silver like dust and clothes 561
33:14 **t** man may not perceive it. NIH
40:23 he is secure, **t** the Jordan should surge 3954
Ps 17:3 **T** you probe my heart and examine me NIH
17:3 **t** you test me, you will find nothing; NIH
21:11 **T** they plot evil against you 3954
23:4 Even **t** I walk through the valley of 3954
25:11 forgive my iniquity, **t** it is great. 3954
27:3 **T** an army besiege me, 561
27:3 **t** war break out against me, 561
27:10 **T** my father and mother forsake me, 3954
31:12 I am forgotten by them **as t** I were dead; 3869
35:14 I went about mourning **as t** for my friend 3869
35:14 I bowed my head in grief **as t** weeping 3869
37:10 **t** you look for them, they will not be found. 2256
37:24 **t** he stumble, he will not fall, 3954
37:36 **t** I looked for him, he could not be found. 2256
44:17 **t** we had not forgotten you or been false 2256
46:2 **t** the earth give way and the mountains fall 928
46:3 **t** its waters roar and foam and NIH
49:11 **t** they had named lands after themselves. NIH
49:18 **T** while he lived he counted himself blessed 3954
55:18 **even t** many oppose me. 3954
Ps 62:10 **t** your riches increase, 3954
71:15 **t** I know not its measure. 3954
71:20 **T** you have made me see troubles, 889
77:19 **t** your footprints were not seen. 2256
78:9 The men of Ephraim, **t** armed with bows, NIH
90:6 **t** in the morning it springs up new, 2256
92:7 that **t** the wicked spring up like grass 928
95:9 **t** they had seen what I did. 1685
99:8 **t** you punished their misdeeds. 2256
119:23 **T** rulers sit together and slander me, 1685
119:61 **T** the wicked bind me with ropes, NIH
119:69 **T** the arrogant have smeared me with lies, NIH
119:83 **T** I am like a wineskin in the smoke, 3954
119:109 **T** I constantly take my life in my hands, NIH
119:141 **T** I am lowly and despised, NIH
138:6 **T** the LORD is on high, 3954
138:7 **T** I walk in the midst of trouble, 561
Pr 4:7 **T** it cost all you have, get understanding. 2256
6:31 **t** it costs him all the wealth of his house. NIH
19:7 **T** he pursues them with pleading, NIH
24:16 **for** *t* a righteous man falls seven times, AIT
26:25 **T** his speech is charming, 3954
27:22 **T** you grind a fool in a mortar, 561
28:1 The wicked man flees **t** no one pursues, 2256
29:19 **t** he understands, he will not respond. 3954
Ecc 4:12 **T** one may be overpowered, 561
6:5 **T** it never saw the sun or knew anything, 1685
8:6 **t** a man's misery weighs heavily upon him. 3954
Isa 1:18 "**T** your sins are like scarlet, 561
1:18 **t** they are red as crimson, 561
6:13 **And t** a tenth remains in the land, 2256
10:22 **T** your people, O Israel, 561+3954
17:10 *t you* **set out** the finest plants AIT
17:11 **t** on the day you set them out, NIH
26:10 **T** grace is shown to the wicked, NIH
28:28 **T** he drives the wheels of his threshing cart 2256
30:4 **T** they have officials in Zoan 3954
31:4 and **t** a whole band of shepherds is called 889
32:19 **T** hail flattens the forest and 2256
36:9 **even t** you are depending on Egypt 2256
40:15 the islands **as t** they were fine dust. 3869
41:12 **T** you search for your enemies, NIH
45:4 **t** you do not acknowledge me. 2256
45:5 **t** you have not acknowledged me, 2256
46:7 **T** one cries out to it, it does not answer; 677
48:10 See, I have refined you, **t** not as silver; 2256
49:15 **T** she may forget, I will not forget you! 1685
49:19 "**T** you were ruined and made desolate 3954
53:9 **t** he had done no violence, 6584
53:10 **t** the LORD makes his life a guilt offering, 561
54:10 **T** the mountains be shaken and the hills 3954
60:10 **T** in anger I struck you, 3954
63:16 **t** Abraham does not know us 3954
Jer 2:34 **t** you did not catch them breaking in. NIH
4:27 **t** I will not destroy it completely. 2256
6:14 They dress the wound of my people **as t** 6584
8:11 They dress the wound of my people **as t** 6584
10:2 **t** the nations are terrified by them. 3954
12:6 **t** they speak well of you. 3954
14:12 **t** they offer burnt offerings 3954
22:6 "**T** you are like Gilead to me, NIH
23:38 **t** I told you that you must not claim, 2256
25:4 **And t** the LORD has sent all his servants 2256
26:5 (**t** you have not listened), 2256
29:31 **even t** I did not send him, 2256
30:11 '**T** I completely destroy all the nations 3954
31:20 **T** I often speak against him, 3954
31:32 **t** I was a husband to them," 2256
32:25 **And t** the city will be handed over to 2256
32:33 **t** I taught them again and again, 2256
32:35 **t** I never commanded, 889
36:25 Even **t** Elnathan, Delaiah 2256
42:2 For as you now see, **t** we were once many, NIH
46:23 declares the LORD, "dense **t** it be. 3954
46:28 "**T** I completely destroy all the nations 3954
49:16 **T** you build your nest as high as 3954
51:5 **t** their land is full of guilt before 3954
52:7 **t** the Babylonians were surrounding 2256
La 3:32 **T** he brings grief, 561+3954
Eze 2:6 **t** briers and thorns are all around you 3954
2:6 **t** they are a rebellious house. 3954
3:9 **t** they are a rebellious house." 3954
3:26 **t** they are a rebellious house. 3954
7:14 **T** they blow the trumpet NIH
12:3 **t** they are a rebellious house. 3954
13:7 **t** I have not spoken? 2256
18:11 (**t** the father has done none of them): 2256
18:14 **and t** he sees them, 2256
28:2 **t** you think you are as wise as a god. 2256
32:27 **t** the terror of these warriors had stalked 3954
35:10 **even t** I the LORD was there, 2256
39:28 **t** I sent them into exile among the nations, 928
Da 5:22 **t** you knew all this. 10168+10353+10619
9:9 **even t** we have rebelled against him; 3954
11:33 **t** for a time they will fall by the sword or 2256
Hos 3:1 **t** she is loved by another and is NIH
3:1 **t** they turn to other gods and love 2256
4:15 "**T** you commit adultery, O Israel, 561
8:11 "**T** Ephraim built many altars 3954
13:15 **even t** he thrives among his brothers. 3954
Am 2:9 **t** he was tall as the cedars and strong as 889
5:11 **t** you have built stone mansions, NIH
5:11 **t** you have planted lush vineyards, NIH
5:19 **be as t** a man fled from a lion only to 889+3869
5:19 as **t** he entered his house NIH
5:22 Even **t** you bring me burnt offerings 561
5:22 **T** you bring choice fellowship offerings, 2256
Am 9:2 **T** they dig down to the depths of the grave, 561
9:2 **T** they climb up to the heavens, 561
9:3 **T** they hide themselves on the top 561
9:3 **T** they hide from me at the bottom of 561
9:4 **T** they are driven into exile 561
Ob 1:4 **T** you soar like the eagle 561
Jnh 4:10 **t** you did not tend it or make it grow, 889
Mic 5:2 **t** you are small among the clans of Judah, NIH
7:8 **T** I have fallen, I will rise. 3954
7:8 **T** I sit in darkness, 3954
Na 2:2 **t** destroyers have laid them waste 3954
Hab 2:3 **T** it linger, wait for it; 561
3:14 gloating **as t** about to devour 4017
3:17 **T** the fig tree does not bud 3954
3:17 **t** the olive crop fails and NIH
3:17 **t** there are no sheep in the pen and no cattle NIH
Zec 9:2 **t** they are very skillful. 3954
10:6 They will be as **t** I had not rejected them, 889
10:9 **T** I scatter them among the peoples, 2256
Mal 1:4 "*T we have* **been crushed,** AIT
2:12 **even t** he brings offerings to the LORD 2256
2:14 **t** she is your partner, 2256
Mt 7:11 If you, then, *t you* **are** evil, *AIT*
13:13 "*T* **seeing,** they do not see; *AIT*
13:13 *t* **hearing,** they do not hear or understand. *AIT*
13:32 **T** it is the smallest of all your seeds, *3525*
26:60 *t* many false witnesses **came forward.** *AIT*
Mk 4:27 **t** he does not know how. *NIG*
Lk 8:10 so that, " '*t* **seeing,** they may not see; *AIT*
8:10 *t* **hearing,** they may not understand.' *AIT*
8:29 and **t** he was chained hand and foot *NIG*
11:8 **t** he will not get up and give him *1623+2779*
11:13 If you then, *t you* **are** evil, *AIT*
18:4 'Even **t** I don't fear God or care about men, *1623*
Jn 1:10 **and t** the world was made through him, *2779*
2:9 **t** the servants who had drawn *1254*
6:71 who, **t** one of the Twelve, *1639*
7:22 (**t actually** it did not come from Moses, *4022*
8:55 **T** you do not know him, I know him. *2779*
10:38 But if I do it, even **t** you do not believe me, *1569*
10:41 "**T** John never performed a miraculous sign, *3525*
11:25 who believes in me will live, even **t** he dies; *1569*
13:10 And you are clean, **t** not every one of you." *247*
16:25 "**T** I have been speaking figuratively, *NIG*
17:25 **t** the world does not know you, *2779*
20:26 *T* the doors *were* **locked,** *AIT*
Ac 3:13 *t he had* **decided** to let him go. *AIT*
5:13 **even t** they were highly regarded by *247*
7:5 *t* at that time Abraham **had** no child. *AIT*
13:28 *T they* **found** no proper ground for a death *AIT*
16:37 *even t we* **are** Roman citizens, *AIT*
17:27 **t** he is not far from each one of us. *1145+2779*
18:25 *t he* **knew** only the baptism of John. *AIT*
19:37 *t they have* neither **robbed temples** nor *AIT*
28:4 for *t he* **escaped** from the sea, *AIT*
Ro 2:14 *t they do* not **have** *AIT*
2:25 as **t** you had not been circumcised. *NIG*
2:26 be regarded as **t** they were circumcised? *NIG*
2:27 even **t** you have the written code *NIG*
4:17 and calls things that are not as *t they* **were.** *AIT*
5:7 for a righteous man, **t** for *1142*
6:17 **t** you used to be slaves to sin, *NIG*
7:3 *even t she* **marries** another man. *AIT*
9:6 It is not as **t** God's word had failed. *4022*
9:27 "**T** the number of the Israelites be like *1569*
11:17 *t* a **wild olive shoot,** *AIT*
1Co 4:7 why do you boast **as t** you did not? *6055*
4:15 **Even t** you have ten thousand guardians in Christ, *1142+1569*
5:3 **Even t** I am not physically present, *1142+3525*
9:2 **Even t** I may not be an apostle to others, *1623*
9:19 *T I* **am** free and belong to no man, *AIT*
9:20 the law (*t I* myself **am** not under the law), *AIT*
9:21 the law (*t I* **am** not free from God's law *AIT*
11:5 it is **just as t** her head were shaved. *899+1651+2779+3836*
12:12 **t** it is made up of many parts; *2779*
12:12 and *t* all its parts **are** many, *AIT*
15:6 **t** some have fallen asleep. *1254*
2Co 3:7 because of its glory, **fading** *t it was,* *AIT*
4:16 **T** outwardly we are wasting away, *1623+2779*
5:16 **T** we once regarded Christ in this way, *1623+2779*
5:20 **as t** God were making his appeal *6055*
7:8 **T** I did regret it— *1623+2779*
7:12 So even **t** I wrote to you, *1623*
8:9 that *t he* **was** rich, yet for your sakes *AIT*
10:3 For *t we* **live** in the world, *AIT*
12:11 even **t** I am nothing. *1623*
13:7 but that you will do what is right even **t** *NIG*
Gal 2:3 *even t he* **was** a Greek. *AIT*
4:14 **Even t** my illness was a trial to you, *2779*
Php 3:4 **t** I myself have reasons for such confidence. *2788*
Col 2:5 For **t** I am absent from you in body, *1623*
2:20 why, **as t** you still belonged to it, *6055*
1Ti 1:13 *Even t I* **was** once a blasphemer and *AIT*
Heb 5:12 *t* by this time *you* **ought** to be teachers, *AIT*
6:9 Even **t** we speak like this, dear friends, *1623*
7:5 **even t** their brothers are descended *2788*
11:4 by faith he still speaks, *even t he is* **dead.** *AIT*
11:8 *t he did* not **know** where he was *AIT*
11:11 **even t** he was past age— *2779*
11:18 even **t** God had said to him, *NIG*
12:17 **t** he sought the blessing with tears. *2788*
1Pe 1:6 **t** now for a little while you may have had *1623*
1:7 which perishes even *t* **refined** by fire— *AIT*
1:8 *T* you *have* not **seen** him, you love him; *AIT*
1:8 *t you do* not **see** him now, you believe in him *AIT*

1Pe 2:12 *t they* **accuse** you of doing wrong, *AIT*
4:12 **as t** something strange were happening *6055*
2Pe 1:12 of these things, **even t** you know them *2788*
3Jn 1: 5 **even t** they are strangers to you. *2779*
Jude 1: 5 **T** you already **know** all this, *3857*
Rev 1:17 When I saw him, I fell at his feet **as t** dead. *6055*
3: 9 who claim to be Jews **t** they are not, *2779*

THOUGHT (94) [THINK]

Ge 18:12 So Sarah laughed to herself *as she* **t,** 606
19:14 But his sons-in-law **t** he was joking. 928+6524
21:16 for *she* **t,** "I cannot watch the boy die." 606
26: 7 He **t,** "The men of this place might kill me NIH
26: 9 *I* **t** I might lose my life on account of her." 606
27:42 with the **t** of killing you. NIH
28:16 When Jacob awoke from his sleep, *he* **t,** 606
31:31 *I* **t** you would take your daughters away 606
32: 8 *He* **t,** "If Esau comes and attacks 606
32:20 For *he* **t,** "I will pacify him 606
38:11 For *he* **t,** "He may die too, 606
38:15 Judah saw her, *he* **t** she was a prostitute, 3108
43:18 *They* **t,** "We were brought here because of 606
Ex 2:14 Then Moses was afraid and **t,** 606
3: 3 So Moses **t,** "I will go over and see 606
Dt 15: 9 Be careful not to harbor this wicked **t:** 1821
Jdg 16:20 He awoke from his sleep and **t,** 606
Ru 1:12 Even if *I* **t** there was still hope for me— 606
4: 4 I **t** I should bring the matter 606
1Sa 1:13 Eli **t** she was drunk 3108
13:12 *I* **t,** 'Now the Philistines will come down 606
16: 6 Samuel saw Eliab and **t,** 606
18: 8 *he* **t,** "but me with only thousands. 606
18:21 "I will give her to him," he **t,** 606
20:26 Saul said nothing that day, for *he* **t,** 606
27: 1 But David **t** to himself, "One of these days 606
27:11 for *he* **t,** "They might inform on us and say, 606
2Sa 4:10 and **t** he was bringing good news, 928+6524
5: 6 They **t,** "David cannot get in here." 606
10: 2 David **t,** "I will show kindness 606
12:18 for *they* **t,** "While the child was still living, 606
12:22 *I* **t,** 'Who knows? 606
14:15 Your servant **t,** 'I will speak to the king; 606
18:18 to himself, for *he* **t,** "I have no son to carry 606
1Ki 12:26 Jeroboam **t** to himself, "The kingdom will 606
18:27 Perhaps *he is* **deep in t,** or busy, 8488
22:32 they **t,** "Surely this is the king of Israel." 606
2Ki 5:11 "*I* **t** that he would surely come out 448+606+3276
20:19 For *he* **t,** "Will there not be peace 606
1Ch 19: 2 David **t,** "I will show kindness 606
2Ch 18:31 they **t,** "This is the king of Israel." 606
28:23 for *he* **t,** "Since the gods of the kings 606
Est 6: 6 Now Haman **t** to himself, "Who is there 606
Job 29:18 "*I* **t,** 'I will die in my own house, 606
32: 7 *I* **t,** 'Age should speak; 606
Ps 50:21 *you* **t** I was altogether like you. 1948
77: 5 *I* **t** *about* the former days, 3108
77:10 Then *I* **t,** "To this I will appeal: 606
106: 7 *they* **gave** no **t** *to* your miracles; 8505
109:16 For *he* never **t** *of* doing a kindness, 2349
Pr 5: 6 *She* **gives** no **t** *to* the way of life; 7143
14: 8 of the prudent is *to* **give t** *to* their ways, 1067
14:15 but a prudent man **gives t** to his steps. 1067
17:28 Even a fool **is t** wise if he keeps silent, 3108
21:29 but an upright man **gives t** *to* his ways. 1067
Ecc 1:16 I **t** to myself, "Look, I have grown and 1819
2: 1 I **t** in my heart, "Come now, I will test you 606
2:15 Then I **t** in my heart, "The fate of the fool 606
3:17 I **t** in my heart, "God will bring to judgment 606
3:18 I also **t,** "As for men, God tests them 606
Isa 29:16 as if the potter **were t** to be like the clay! 3108
39: 8 For *he* **t,** "There will be peace and security 606
65:20 at a hundred will be **t** a mere youth; NIH
Jer 3: 7 *I* **t** that after she had done all this she would 606
3:19 *I* **t** you would call me 'Father' and 606
5: 4 I **t,** "These are only the poor; 606
La 3:54 and *I* **t** I was about to be cut off. 606
4:20 *We* **t** that under his shadow we would live 606
Hag 1: 5 "**Give careful t** to your ways. 4222+8492
1: 7 "**Give careful t** to your ways. 4222+8492
2:15 " 'Now **give careful t** to this 4222+8492
2:18 **give careful t** to the day when 4222+8492
2:18 temple was laid. **Give careful t:** 4222+8492
Mk 5:28 because *she* **t,** "If I just touch his clothes, *3306*
6:49 saw him walking on the lake, *they* **t** he was
a ghost. *1506*
Lk 3:23 He was the son, so *it was* **t,** of Joseph, *3787*
12:17 *He* **t** to himself, 'What shall I do? *1368*
19:11 near Jerusalem and the people **t** that *1506*
Jn 8:56 Your father Abraham rejoiced at the **t** *NIG*
11:13 but his disciples **t** he meant natural sleep. *1506*
13:29 some **t** Jesus was telling him to buy *1506*
Ac 7:25 Moses **t that** his own people would realize *3787*
8:20 with you, because *you* **t** you could buy *3787*
8:22 for having such a **t** in your heart. *2154*
12: 9 *he* **t** he was seeing a vision. *1506*
16:27 and was about to kill himself *because he* **t** *3787*
27:13 *they* **t** they had obtained what they wanted; *1506*
1Co 1:10 be perfectly united in mind and **t.** *1191*
13:11 *I* **t** like a child, I reasoned like a child. *5858*
2Co 9: 5 So *I* **t** it necessary to urge the brothers *2451*
10: 5 and we take captive every **t** *3784*
1Th 2:17 for a short time (in person, not *in* **t**), *2840*
3: 1 *we* **t it best** to be left by ourselves *2305*
Heb 12:10 Our fathers disciplined us for a little while
as they **t** best; *1506*

THOUGHTLESSLY (1) [THINK]

Lev 5: 4 if a person **t** takes an oath 928+1051+4200+8557

THOUGHTS (47) [THINK]

Ge 6: 5 the **t** *of* his heart was only evil all the time. 4742
1Ch 28: 9 and understands every motive behind the **t.** 4742
Job 20: 2 "My **troubled t** prompt me to answer 8546
Ps 10: 4 in all his **t** there is no room for God. 4659
13: 2 must I wrestle with my **t** 928+5883+6783
55: 2 My **t** trouble me and I am distraught 8490
92: 5 O LORD, how profound your **t!** 4742
94:11 The LORD knows the **t** *of* man; 4742
139: 2 you perceive my **t** from afar. 8277
139:17 How precious to me are your **t,** O God! 8277
139:23 test me and know my **anxious t.** 8595
Pr 1:23 to you and made my **t** known to you. 1821
15:26 The LORD detests the **t** *of* the wicked, 4742
Ecc 2:12 Then I turned my **t** to consider wisdom, NIH
10:20 Do not revile the king even in your **t,** 4529
Isa 33:18 In your **t** you will ponder the former terror: 4213
55: 7 and the evil man his **t.** 4742
55: 8 "For my **t** are not your thoughts, 4742
55: 8 "For my thoughts are not your **t,** 4742
55: 9 and my **t** than your thoughts. 4742
55: 9 and my thoughts than your **t.** 4742
59: 7 Their **t** are evil thoughts; 4742
59: 7 Their thoughts are evil **t;** 4742
Jer 4:14 How long will you harbor wicked **t?** 4742
12: 3 you see me and test my **t** about you. 4213
Eze 38:10 On that day **t** will come into your mind 1821
Da 4:19 and his **t** terrified him. 10669
7:28 I, Daniel, was deeply troubled by my **t,** 10669
Am 4:13 creates the wind, and reveals his **t** to man, 8465
Mic 4:12 But they do not know the **t** *of* the LORD; 4742
Mt 9: 4 Knowing their **t,** Jesus said, *1927*
9: 4 "Why *do you* **entertain** evil **t** *1926*
12:25 Jesus knew their **t** and said to them, *1927*
15:19 For out of the heart come evil **t,** murder, *1369*
Mk 7:21 come evil **t,** sexual immorality, theft, *1369*
Lk 1:51 who are proud *in* their inmost **t.** *1379*
2:35 that the **t** of many hearts will be revealed. *1369*
9:47 Jesus, knowing their **t,** took a little child *1369*
11:17 Jesus knew their **t** and said to them: *1378*
Ro 2:15 and their **t** now accusing, *3361*
1Co 2:11 among men **knows** the **t** of a man except *3857*
2:11 In the same way no one **knows** the **t** *1182*
3:20 that the **t** of the wise are futile." *1369*
Eph 2: 3 and following its desires and **t.** *1379*
Heb 3: 1 **fix** *your* **t** on Jesus, the apostle and high *2917*
4:12 it judges the **t** and attitudes of the heart. *1927*
Jas 2: 4 and become judges *with* evil **t?** *1369*

THOUSAND (272) [THOUSANDS, 1000]

Ge 20:16 "I am giving your brother a **t** shekels 547
Ex 12:37 There were about six hundred **t** men 547
20: 6 to a **t** [generations] of those who love me 547
32:28 that day about three **t** of the people died. 547
Lev 26: 8 and a hundred of you will chase **ten t,** 8047
Nu 7:85 dishes weighed *two* **t** four hundred shekels, 547
11:21 "Here I am among six hundred **t** men 547
31: 4 into battle a **t** *men* from each of the tribes 547
31: 5 So twelve **t** men armed for battle, 547
31: 5 a **t** from each tribe, 547
31: 6 a **t** from each tribe, 547
35: 5 measure **three t feet** on the east side, 547+564
35: 5 *three* **t** on the south side, 547
35: 5 *three* **t** on the west and three thousand on 547
35: 5 three thousand on the west and *three* **t** on 547
Dt 1:11 a **t** times and bless you as he has promised! 547
5:10 to a **t** [generations] of those who love me 547
7: 9 to a **t** generations of those who love him 547
32:30 How could one man chase a **t,** 547
32:30 or two put **ten t** to flight, 8047
Jos 3: 4 of about a **t** yards between you and the ark; 547
4:13 About forty **t** armed for battle crossed over 547
7: 3 Send *two* or three **t** men to take it and do 547
7: 4 So about three **t** men went up; 547
8: 3 He chose thirty **t** of his best fighting men 547
8:12 about five **t** men and set them in ambush 547
8:25 Twelve **t** men and women fell that day— 547
23:10 One of you routs a **t,** 547
Jdg 1: 4 and they struck down ten **t** men at Bezek. 547
3:29 down about ten **t** Moabites, all vigorous 547
4: 6 'Go, take with you ten **t** men of Naphtali 547
4:10 Ten **t** men followed him, 547
4:14 followed by ten **t** men. 547
5: 8 or spear was seen among forty **t** in Israel. 547
7: 3 So twenty-two **t** men left, 547
7: 3 while ten **t** remained. 547
8:10 of about fifteen **t** men, all that were left of 547
8:10 and twenty **t** swordsmen had fallen. 547
9:49 about a **t** men and women, also died. 547
12: 6 Forty-two **t** Ephraimites were killed at 547
15:11 Then three **t** men from Judah went down to 547
15:15 he grabbed it and struck down a **t** men. 547
15:16 a donkey's jawbone I have killed a **t** men." 547
16:27 and on the roof were about three **t** men 547
20: 2 four hundred **t** soldiers armed with swords. 547
20:10 and a hundred from a **t,** 547
20:10 and a **t** from ten thousand, 547
20:10 and a thousand from **ten t,** 8047
20:15 mobilized twenty-six **t** swordsmen 547
20:17 mustered four hundred **t** swordsmen, 547
20:21 and cut down twenty-two **t** Israelites on 547
20:25 they cut down another eighteen **t** Israelites, 547
Jdg 20:34 Then ten **t** of Israel's finest men made 547
20:44 Eighteen **t** Benjamites fell, 547
20:45 the Israelites cut down five **t** men along 547
20:45 as Gidom and struck down *two* **t** more. 547
20:46 twenty-five **t** Benjamite swordsmen fell, 547
21:10 So the assembly sent twelve **t** fighting men 547
1Sa 4: 2 about four **t** of them on the battlefield. 547
4:10 Israel lost thirty **t** foot soldiers. 547
11: 8 the men of Israel numbered three hundred **t** 547
11: 8 and the men of Judah thirty **t.** 547
13: 2 Saul chose three **t** *men* from Israel; 547
13: 2 *two* **t** were with him at Micmash and in 547
13: 2 in the hill country of Bethel, and a **t** were 547
13: 5 with three **t** chariots, 547
13: 5 six **t** charioteers, and soldiers as numerous 547
15: 4 two hundred **t** foot soldiers 547
15: 4 and ten **t** men from Judah. 547
17: 5 of bronze weighing five **t** shekels; 547
18:13 and gave him command over a **t** *men,* 547
24: 2 So Saul took three **t** chosen men 547
25: 2 He had a **t** goats and three thousand sheep, 547
25: 2 He had a thousand goats and three **t** sheep, 547
26: 2 with his three **t** chosen men of Israel, 547
2Sa 6: 1 chosen men, thirty **t** in all. 547
8: 4 David captured a **t** of his chariots, 547
8: 4 of his chariots, seven **t** charioteers 547
8: 4 and twenty **t** foot soldiers. 547
8: 5 David struck down twenty-two **t** of them. 547
8:13 from striking down eighteen **t** Edomites in 547
10: 6 they hired twenty **t** Aramean foot soldiers 547
10: 6 well as the king of Maacah with a **t** men, 547
10: 6 and also twelve **t** men from Tob. 547
10:18 and forty **t** *of* their foot soldiers. 547
17: 1 "I would choose twelve **t** men 547
18: 3 but you are worth ten **t** of us. 547
18: 7 that day were great—twenty **t** men. 547
18:12 "Even if a **t** shekels were weighed out 547
19:17 With him were a **t** Benjamites, 547
24: 9 In Israel there were eight hundred **t**
able-bodied men who could handle 547
24: 9 and in Judah five hundred **t.** 547
24:15 and seventy **t** of the people from Dan 547
1Ki 3: 4 and Solomon offered a **t** burnt offerings on 547
4:26 Solomon had four **t** stalls 547
4:26 and twelve **t** horses. 547
4:32 He spoke three **t** proverbs 547
4:32 and his songs numbered a **t** and five. 547
5:11 and Solomon gave Hiram twenty **t** cors 547
5:11 to twenty **t** baths of pressed olive oil. 547
5:13 from all Israel—thirty **t** men. 547
5:14 to Lebanon in shifts of ten **t** a month, 547
5:15 Solomon had seventy **t** carriers 547
5:15 and eighty **t** stonecutters in the hills, 547
7:26 It held *two* **t** baths. 547
8:63 twenty-two **t** cattle and a hundred 547
8:63 a hundred and twenty **t** sheep and goats. 547
10:26 and twelve **t** horses, 547
12:21 a hundred and eighty **t** fighting men— 547
19:18 Yet I reserve seven **t** in Israel— 547
20:29 a hundred **t** casualties on the Aramean 547
20:30 where the wall collapsed on twenty-seven **t** 547
2Ki 3: 4 with a hundred **t** lambs and with the wool 547
3: 4 and with the wool of a hundred **t** rams. 547
5: 5 six **t** shekels of gold and ten sets 547
13: 7 ten chariots and ten **t** foot soldiers, 547
14: 7 the one who defeated ten **t** Edomites in 547
15:19 and Menahem gave him a **t** talents of silver 547
18:23 I will give you *two* **t** horses— 547
19:35 to death a hundred and eighty-five **t** men in 547
24:14 and artisans—a total of ten **t.** 547
24:16 the entire force of seven **t** fighting men, 547
24:16 and a **t** craftsmen and artisans. 547
1Ch 5:21 of the Hagrites—fifty **t** camels, 547
5:21 two hundred fifty **t** sheep 547
5:21 and *two* **t** donkeys. 547
5:21 also took one hundred **t** people captive, 547
12:14 and the greatest for a **t.** 547
12:20 leaders of **units of a t** in Manasseh. 547
15:25 of **units of a t** went to bring up the ark of 547
16:15 the word he commanded, for a **t** generations, 547
18: 4 David captured a **t** of his chariots, 547
18: 4 of his chariots, seven **t** charioteers 547
18: 4 and twenty **t** foot soldiers. 547
18: 5 David struck down twenty-two **t** of them. 547
18:12 down eighteen **t** Edomites in the Valley 547
19: 6 Hanun and the Ammonites sent a **t** talents 547
19: 7 They hired thirty-two **t** chariots 547
19:18 and David killed seven **t** of their charioteers 547
19:18 and forty **t** *of* their foot soldiers. 547
21: 5 In all Israel there were one million one
hundred **t** men who could handle 547
21: 5 including four hundred and seventy **t** 547
21:14 and seventy **t** men of Israel fell dead. 547
22:14 of the LORD a hundred **t** talents of gold, 547
23: 3 the total number of men was thirty-eight **t.** 547
23: 4 twenty-four **t** are to supervise the work of 547
23: 4 of the temple of the LORD and six **t** are to 547
23: 5 Four **t** are to be gatekeepers 547
23: 5 to be gatekeepers and four **t** are to praise 547
29: 4 three **t** talents of gold (gold of Ophir) 547
29: 4 and seven **t** talents of refined silver, 547
29: 7 on the temple of God five **t** talents 547
29: 7 and **ten t** darics of gold, 8052
29: 7 ten **t** talents of silver, 547
29: 7 **eighteen t** talents of bronze 547+2256+8052+9046
29: 7 of bronze and a hundred **t** talents of iron. 547
29:21 a **t** bulls, a thousand rams and 547

1Ch 29:21 a **t** rams and a thousand male lambs, 547
29:21 a thousand rams and a **t** male lambs, 547
2Ch 1: 6 of Meeting and offered a **t** burnt offerings 547
1:14 and twelve **t** horses, 547
2: 2 He conscripted seventy **t** men as carriers 547
2: 2 as carriers and eighty **t** as stonecutters in 547
2:10 twenty **t** cors of ground wheat, 547
2:10 twenty **t** cors of barley, 547
2:10 twenty **t** baths of wine 547
2:10 of wine and twenty **t** baths of olive oil." 547
4: 5 It held three **t** baths. 547
7: 5 a sacrifice of twenty-two **t** head of cattle 547
7: 5 of cattle and a hundred and twenty **t** sheep 547
9:25 Solomon had four **t** stalls for horses 547
9:25 and twelve **t** horses, 547
11: 1 a hundred and eighty **t** fighting men— 547
12: 3 and sixty **t** horsemen and 547
13: 3 of four hundred **t** able fighting men, 547
13: 3 with eight hundred **t** able troops. 547
13:17 so that there were five hundred **t** casualties 547
14: 8 Asa had an army of three hundred **t** men 547
14: 8 two hundred and eighty **t** from Benjamin, 547
15:11 of cattle and seven **t** sheep and goats from 547
17:11 seven **t** seven hundred rams 547
17:11 and seven **t** seven hundred goats. 547
25: 5 that there were three hundred **t** men ready 547
25: 6 a hundred **t** fighting men from Israel for 547
25:11 where he killed ten **t** men of Seir. 547
25:12 of Judah also captured ten **t** men alive, 547
25:13 They killed three **t** people 547
27: 5 ten **t** cors of wheat and ten thousand cors 547
27: 5 ten thousand cors of wheat and ten **t** cors 547
28: 6 a hundred and twenty **t** soldiers in Judah— 547
28: 8 from their kinsmen two hundred **t** wives, 547
29:33 to six hundred bulls and three **t** sheep 547
30:24 Hezekiah king of Judah provided a **t** bulls 547
30:24 a thousand bulls and seven **t** sheep 547
30:24 a **t** bulls and ten thousand sheep and goats. 547
30:24 a thousand bulls and ten **t** sheep and goats. 547
35: 7 a total of thirty **t** sheep and goats for 547
35: 7 and also three **t** cattle— 547
35: 9 provided five **t** Passover offerings 547
Est 3: 9 and I will put ten **t** talents of silver into 547
9:16 They killed seventy-five **t** of them but did 547
Job 1: 3 and he owned seven **t** sheep, 547
1: 3 three **t** camels, five hundred yoke of oxen 547
9: 3 not answer him one time out of a **t**. 547
33:23 as a mediator, one out of a **t**, 547
42:12 He had fourteen **t** sheep, 547
42:12 six **t** camels, a thousand yoke of oxen and 547
42:12 a **t** yoke of oxen and a thousand donkeys. 547
42:12 a thousand yoke of oxen and a **t** donkeys. 547
Ps 50:10 and the cattle on a **t** hills. 547
60: T and struck down twelve **T** Edomites in 547
84:10 in your courts than a **t** elsewhere; 547
90: 4 For a **t** years in your sight are like a day 547
91: 7 A **t** may fall at your side, 547
91: 7 **ten t** at your right hand, 8047
105: 8 the word he commanded, for a **t** generations, 547
Ecc 6: 6 if he lives a **t** years twice over but fails 547
7:28 I found one [upright] man among a **t**, 547
SS 4: 4 on it hang a **t** shields, 547
5:10 outstanding among **ten t**. 8047
8:11 Each was to bring for its fruit a **t** shekels 547
8:12 the **t** shekels are for you, O Solomon, 547
Isa 7:23 a **t** vines worth a thousand silver shekels, 547
7:23 a thousand vines worth a **t** silver shekels, 547
30:17 A **t** will flee at the threat of one; 547
36: 8 I will give you *two* **t** horses— 547
37:36 to death a hundred and eighty-five **t** men in 547
60:22 The least of you will become a **t**, 547
Eze 47: 3 he measured off a **t** cubits and then led me 547
47: 4 He measured off another **t** cubits 547
47: 4 He measured off another **t** and led me 547
47: 5 He measured off another **t**, 547
Da 5: 1 a **t** of his nobles and drank wine with them. 10038
7:10 **ten t** *times* ten thousand stood before him. 10649
7:10 ten thousand times **ten t** stood before him. 10649
Am 5: 3 "The city that marches out a **t** strong 547
Jnh 4:11 a **hundred and twenty t** people who cannot tell their right hand 6926+8052+9109
Mic 6: 7 with **ten t** rivers of oil? 8047
Mt 14:21 of those who ate was about **five t** men, *4295*
15:38 The number of those who ate was **four t**, *5483*
16: 9 the five loaves *for* the **five t**, *4295*
16:10 Or the seven loaves *for* the **four t**, *5483*
18:24 who owed him **ten t** talents was brought *3691*
Mk 5:13 The herd, about **two t** in number, *1493*
6:44 of the men who had eaten was **five t**. *4295*
8: 9 About **four t** *men* were present. *5483*
8:19 I broke the five loaves for the **five t**, *4295*
8:20 I broke the seven loaves for the **four t**, *5483*
Lk 9:14 (About **five t** men were there.) *4295*
14:31 with ten **t** *men* to oppose the one coming *5942*
14:31 against him with twenty **t**? *5942*
16: 7 " 'A **t bushels** of wheat,' he replied. *1669+3174*
Jn 6:10 the men sat down, about **five t** of them. *4295*
Ac 2:41 about **three t** were added to their number *5567*
4: 4 the number of men grew to about five **t**. *5942*
19:19 the total came to **fifty t** drachmas. *3689+4297*
21:38 a revolt and led **four t** terrorists out into *5483*
Ro 11: 4 for myself **seven t** who have not bowed *2233*
1Co 4:15 though you have **ten t** guardians in Christ, *3692*
10: 8 and in one day twenty-three **t** of them died. *5942*
14:19 to instruct others than **ten t** words in *3692*
2Pe 3: 8 With the Lord a day is like a **t** years, *5943*
3: 8 and a **t** years are like a day. *5943*
Rev 5:11 and **ten t** times ten thousand. *3689*
5:11 and ten thousand times **ten t**. *3689*
11:13 Seven **t** *people* were killed in *5942*
20: 2 or Satan, and bound him *for* a **t** years. *5943*
20: 3 until the **t** years were ended. *5943*
20: 4 to life and reigned with Christ a **t** years. *5943*
20: 5 to life until the **t** years were ended.) *5943*
20: 6 and will reign with him *for* a **t** years. *5943*
20: 7 When the **t** years are over, *5943*

THOUSANDS (53) [THOUSAND]

Ge 24:60 may you increase to **t** *upon* thousands; 547
24:60 may you increase to thousands upon **t**; 8047
Ex 18:21 and appoint them as officials over **t**, 547
18:25 officials over **t**, hundreds, fifties and tens. 547
34: 7 maintaining love to **t**, and forgiving 547
Nu 10:36 O LORD, to the countless **t** *of* Israel." 547
31:14 the commanders of **t** and commanders 547
31:48 the commanders of **t** and commanders 547
31:52 All the gold from the commanders of **t** 547
31:54 the commanders of **t** and commanders 547
Dt 1:15 as commanders of **t**, of hundreds, 547
33:17 Such are the **ten t** *of* Ephraim; 8047
33:17 such are the **t** *of* Manasseh." 547
1Sa 8:12 Some he will assign to be commanders of **t** 547
18: 7 "Saul has slain his **t**, 547
18: 7 and David his **tens of t**." 8047
18: 8 "They have credited David with **tens of t**," 8047
18: 8 he thought, "but me with only **t**. 547
21:11 " 'Saul has slain his **t**, 547
21:11 and David his **tens of t**'?" 8047
22: 7 of you commanders of **t** and commanders 547
29: 2 with their units of hundreds and **t**, 547
29: 5 " 'Saul has slain his **t**, 547
29: 5 and David his **tens of t**'?" 8047
2Sa 18: 1 and appointed over them commanders of **t** 547
18: 4 in units of hundreds and of **t**. 547
1Ch 13: 1 the commanders of **t** and commanders 547
26:26 of families who were the commanders of **t** 547
27: 1 heads of families, commanders of **t** 547
28: 1 the commanders of **t** and commanders 547
29: 6 the commanders of **t** and commanders 547
2Ch 1: 2 to the commanders of **t** and commanders 547
25: 5 to commanders of **t** and commanders 547
Ps 3: 6 not fear the **tens of t** drawn up against me 8047
68:17 chariots of God are **tens of t** and thousands 8052
68:17 are tens of thousands and **t** of thousands; 547
68:17 tens of thousands and thousands of **t**; 9099
119:72 to me than **t** *of pieces of* silver and gold. 547
144:13 Our sheep *will* **increase by t**, 545
144:13 *by* **tens of t** in our fields; 8045
Jer 32:18 to **t** but bring the punishment for 547
Da 7:10 **T** *upon* thousands attended him; 10038
7:10 Thousands upon **t** attended him; 10038
11:12 with pride and will slaughter **many t**, 8052
Mic 6: 7 Will the LORD be pleased with **t** *of* rams, 547
Lk 12: 1 when a crowd *of* **many t** had gathered, *3689*
Ac 21:20 how many **t** of Jews have believed, *3689*
Heb 12:22 You have come to **t upon thousands** *3689*
12:22 You have come to **thousands upon t** *3689*
Jude 1:14 the Lord is coming with **t upon thousands** *3689*
1:14 the Lord is coming with **thousands upon t** *3689*
Rev 5:11 many angels, numbering **t** upon thousands, *5942*
5:11 many angels, numbering thousands upon **t**, *5942*

THRASHING (2)

Job 41:25 they retreat before his **t**. 8691
Eze 32: 2 you are like a monster in the seas **t about** 1631

THREAD (3) [THREADS]

Ge 14:23 not even a **t** or the thong of a sandal, 2562
38:28 so the midwife took a **scarlet t** and tied it 9106
38:30 who had the **scarlet t** on his wrist, 9106

THREADS (1) [THREAD]

Jdg 16:12 the ropes off his arms as if they were **t**. 2562

THREAT (6) [THREATEN, THREATENED, THREATS]

Ezr 4:22 Why let this **t** grow, 10244
Ne 4: 9 a guard day and night to meet **this t**. 2157[S]
Ps 64: 1 protect my life from the **t** *of* the enemy. 7065
Pr 13: 8 but a poor man hears no **t**. 1722
Isa 30:17 A thousand will flee at the **t** *of* one; 1722
30:17 at the **t** *of* five you will all flee away, 1722

THREATEN (3) [THREAT]

Ps 73: 8 in their arrogance *they* **t** oppression. 1819
Eze 6:10 *I did* not **t** in vain to bring this calamity 1819
Eph 6: 9 Do not **t** them, since you know that *581*

THREATENED (6) [THREAT]

Ex 32:14 not bring on his people the disaster *he had* **t**. 1819
Jos 23:15 will bring on you all the evil he has **t**, 1821
Jer 27:13 with which the LORD *has* **t** any nation 1819
Jnh 1: 4 a violent storm arose that the ship **t** 3108
2: 5 The engulfing waters **t** me, 5883+6330
3:10 bring upon them the destruction *he had* **t**. 1819

THREATS (8) [THREAT]

Ps 10: 7 His mouth is full of curses and lies and **t**; 9412
55:11 **t** and lies never leave its streets. 9412
Jer 44:29 'so that you will know that my **t** of harm 1821
Zep 2: 8 who insulted my people and **made t** 1540
Ac 4:21 *After* **further t** they let them go. *4653*
4:29 consider their **t** and enable your servants *581*
9: 1 Saul was still breathing out murderous **t** *581*
1Pe 2:23 when he suffered, *he* **made** no **t**. *580*

THREE (393) [THIRD, THIRDS, THREE TAVERNS, THREE-DAY, THREE-PRONGED, THREE-TENTHS, THREE-YEAR-OLD, TWO-THIRDS]

Ge 6:10 Noah had **t** sons: Shem, Ham and Japheth. 8993
7:13 with his wife and the wives of his **t** sons, 8993
9:19 These were the **t** sons of Noah, 8993
15: 9 a goat and a ram, each **t years old**, 8992
18: 2 looked up and saw **t** men standing nearby. 8993
18: 6 "get **t** seahs of fine flour and knead it 8993
29: 2 with **t** flocks of sheep lying near it because 8993
29:34 because I have borne him **t** sons." 8993
34:25 **T** days later, while all of them were still 8958
38:24 About **t** months later Judah was told, 8993
40:10 and on the vine were **t** branches. 8993
40:12 "The **t** branches are three days. 8993
40:12 "The three branches are **t** days. 8993
40:13 Within **t** days Pharaoh will lift 8993
40:16 On my head were **t** baskets of bread. 8993
40:18 "The **t** baskets are three days. 8993
40:18 "The three baskets are **t** days. 8993
40:19 Within **t** days Pharaoh will lift off your head 8993
42:17 And he put them all in custody for **t** days. 8993
45:22 but to Benjamin he gave **t** hundred shekels 8993
Ex 2: 2 she hid him for **t** months. 8993
10:22 total darkness covered all Egypt for **t** days. 8993
10:23 or leave his place for **t** days. 8993
15:22 For **t** days they traveled in the desert 8993
21:11 not provide her with these **t** *things*, 8993
23:14 "**T** times a year you are to celebrate 8993
23:17 "**T** times a year all the men are to appear 8993
25:32 **t** on one side and three on the other. 8993
25:32 three on one side and **t** on the other. 8993
25:33 **T** cups shaped like almond flowers 8993
25:33 **t** on the next branch, 8993
27: 1 an altar of acacia wood, **t** cubits high; 8993
27:14 with **t** posts and three bases, 8993
27:14 with three posts and **t** bases, 8993
27:15 with **t** posts and three bases, 8993
27:15 with three posts and **t** bases. 8993
32:28 about **t** thousand of the people died. 8993
34:23 **T** times a year all your men are to appear 8993
34:24 up **t** times each year to appear before 8993
37:18 **t** on one side and three on the other. 8993
37:18 three on one side and **t** on the other. 8993
37:19 **T** cups shaped like almond flowers 8993
37:19 **t** on the next branch and the same 8993
38: 1 of acacia wood, **t** cubits high; 8993
38:14 with **t** posts and three bases, 8993
38:14 with three posts and **t** bases, 8993
38:15 with **t** posts and three bases, 8993
38:15 with three posts and **t** bases. 8993
Lev 19:23 For **t** years you are to consider it forbidden; 8993
25:21 that the land will yield enough for **t** years. 8993
27: 6 and that of a female at **t** shekels of silver. 8993
Nu 10:33 of the LORD and traveled for **t** days. 8993
10:33 during those **t** days to find them a place 8993
11:31 the camp to about **t feet** above the ground, 564
12: 4 to the Tent of Meeting, *all* **t** *of* you." 8993
12: 4 So the **t** *of* them came out. 8993
22:28 to you to make you beat me these **t** times?" 8993
22:32 "Why have you beaten your donkey these **t** times? 8993
22:33 and turned away from me these **t** times. 8993
24:10 but you have blessed them these **t** times. 8993
33: 8 and when they had traveled for **t** days in 8993
35: 5 measure **t thousand feet** on the east side, 547+564
35: 5 *t* **thousand** on the south side, AIT
35: 5 *t* **thousand** on the west and three thousand AIT
35: 5 three thousand on the west and *t* **thousand** AIT
35:14 Give **t** on this side of the Jordan and three 8993
35:14 and **t** in Canaan as cities of refuge. 8993
Dt 4:41 Moses set aside **t** cities east of the Jordan, 8993
14:28 At the end of every **t** years, 8993
16:16 **T** times a year all your men must appear 8993
17: 6 or **t** witnesses a man shall be put to death, 8993
19: 2 for yourselves **t** cities centrally located in 8993
19: 3 Build roads to them and **divide into t** parts 8992
19: 7 to set aside for yourselves **t** cities. 8993
19: 9 then you are to set aside **t** more cities. 8993
19:15 by the testimony of two or **t** witnesses. 8993
Jos 1:11 **T** days from now you will cross 8993
2:16 Hide yourselves there **t** days 8993
2:22 into the hills and stayed there **t** days, 8993
3: 2 After **t** days the officers went throughout 8993
7: 3 Send two or **t** thousand men to take it 8993
7: 4 So about **t** thousand men went up; 8993
9:16 **T** days after they made the treaty with 8993
15:14 From Hebron Caleb drove out the **t** Anakites— 8993
18: 4 Appoint **t** men from each tribe. 8993
21:32 with their pasturelands—**t** towns. 8993
Jdg 1:20 who drove from it the **t** sons of Anak. 8993
7: 6 **T** hundred men lapped with their hands 8993
7: 7 "With the **t** hundred men that lapped 8993
7: 8 to their tents but kept the **t** hundred, 8993
7:16 the **t** hundred men into three companies, 8993

Jdg 7:16 the three hundred men into t companies, 8993
7:20 The t companies blew the trumpets 8993
7:22 When the t hundred trumpets sounded, 8993
8: 4 Gideon and his t hundred men, 8993
9:22 Abimelech had governed Israel t years, 8993
9:43 into t companies and set an ambush in 8993
11:26 t hundred years Israel occupied Heshbon, 8993
14:14 For t days they could not give the answer. 8993
15: 4 So he went out and caught t hundred foxes 8993
15:11 Then t thousand men from Judah went 8993
16:27 and on the roof were about t thousand men 8993
19: 4 so he remained with him t days, 8993
1Sa 2:21 and gave birth to t sons and two daughters. 8993
9:20 As for the donkeys you lost t days ago, 8993
10: 3 T men going up to God 8993
10: 3 One will be carrying t young goats, 8993
10: 3 another t loaves of bread, 8993
11: 8 of Israel numbered t hundred thousand and 8993
11:11 Saul separated his men into t divisions; 8993
13: 2 Saul chose t thousand men from Israel; 8993
13: 5 with t thousand chariots, 8993
13:17 from the Philistine camp in t detachments. 8993
17:13 Jesse's t oldest sons had followed Saul to 8993
17:14 The t oldest followed Saul, 8993
20:20 I will shoot t arrows to the side of it, 8993
20:41 and bowed down before Jonathan t times, 8993
24: 2 So Saul took t thousand chosen men 8993
25: 2 a thousand goats and t thousand sheep, 8993
26: 2 with his t thousand chosen men of Israel, 8993
30:12 or drunk any water for t days 8993
30:12 for three days and t nights. 8993
30:13 when I became ill t days *ago*. 8993
31: 6 and his t sons and his armor-bearer 8993
31: 8 and his t sons fallen on Mount Gilboa. 8993
2Sa 2:18 The t sons of Zeruiah were there: 8993
2:31 But David's men had killed t hundred 8993
6:11 of Obed-Edom the Gittite for t months, 8993
13:38 he stayed there t years. 8993
14:27 T sons and a daughter were born 8993
18:14 So he took t javelins in his hand 8993
20: 4 of Judah to come to me within t days, 8993
21: 1 there was a famine for t successive years; 8993
21:16 spearhead weighed t hundred shekels 8993
23: 8 a Tahkemonite, was chief of the **T;** 8998
23: 9 As one of the t mighty men, 8993
23:13 t of the thirty chief men came down 8993
23:16 So the t mighty men broke through 8993
23:17 the exploits of the t mighty men. 8993
23:18 of Joab son of Zeruiah was chief of the **T.** 8998
23:18 He raised his spear against t hundred men, 8993
23:18 and so he became as famous as the **T.** 8993
23:19 not held in greater honor than the **T?** 8993
23:22 he too was as famous as the t mighty men. 8993
23:23 but he was not included among the **T.** 8993
24:12 I am giving you t *options*. 8993
24:13 upon you t years of famine in your land? 8993
24:13 Or t months of fleeing from your enemies 8993
24:13 Or t days of plague in your land? 8993
1Ki 2:39 But t years later, two of Shimei's slaves 8993
4:32 He spoke t thousand proverbs 8993
6:36 the inner courtyard of t courses 8993
7: 4 Its windows were placed high in sets of **t,** 8993
7: 5 they were in the front part in sets of **t,** 8993
7:12 by a wall of t courses of dressed stone 8993
7:25 Sea stood on twelve bulls, t facing north, 8993
7:25 three facing north, t facing west, 8993
7:25 t facing south and three facing east. 8993
7:25 three facing south and t facing east. 8993
7:27 four wide and t high. 8993
9:25 T times a year Solomon sacrificed burnt offerings 8993
10:17 He also made t hundred small shields 8993
10:17 with t minas of gold in each shield. 8993
10:22 Once every t years it returned, 8993
11: 3 of royal birth and t hundred concubines, 8993
12: 5 "Go away for t days and then come back 8993
12:12 T days later Jeroboam and all 8958
12:12 "Come back to me in t days." 8958
15: 2 and he reigned in Jerusalem t years. 8993
17:21 on the boy t times and cried to the LORD, 8993
22: 1 For t years there was no war 8993
2Ki 2:17 who searched for t days but did 8993
3:10 the LORD called us t kings together only 8993
3:13 the LORD who called us t kings together 8993
9:32 Two or t eunuchs looked down at him. 8993
11: 5 the t companies that are going on duty on NIH
13:18 He struck it t times and stopped 8993
13:19 But now you will defeat it only t times." 8993
13:25 T times Jehoash defeated him, 8993
17: 5 and laid siege to it for t years. 8993
18:10 At the end of t years the Assyrians took it. 8993
18:14 of Judah t hundred talents of silver 8993
23:31 and he reigned in Jerusalem t months. 8993
24: 1 Jehoiakim became his vassal for t years. 8993
24: 8 and he reigned in Jerusalem t months. 8993
25:18 in rank and the t doorkeepers. 8993
1Ch 2: 3 These t were born to him by 8993
2:16 Zeruiah's t sons were Abishai, 8993
3:23 and Azrikam—t in all. 8993
7: 6 T sons of Benjamin: 8993
10: 6 So Saul and his t sons died, 8993
11:11 he raised his spear against t hundred men, 8993
11:12 one of the t mighty men. 8993
11:15 T of the thirty chiefs came down to David 8993
11:18 So the T broke through the Philistine lines, 8993
11:19 the exploits of the t mighty men. 8993
11:20 the brother of Joab was chief of the **T.** 8993
1Ch 11:20 He raised his spear against t hundred men, 8993
11:20 and so he became as famous as the **T.** 8993
11:21 above the T and became their commander, 8993
11:24 he too was as famous as the t mighty men. 8993
11:25 but he was not included among the **T.** 8993
12:39 The men spent t days there with David, 8993
13:14 of Obed-Edom in his house for t months, 8993
21:10 I am giving you t *options*. 8993
21:12 t years of famine, three months 8993
21:12 t months of being swept away 8993
21:12 or t days of the sword of the LORD— 8993
23: 8 and Joel—t in all. 8993
23: 9 and Haran—t in all. 8993
23:23 and Jerimoth—t in all. 8993
25: 5 God gave Heman fourteen sons and t daughters. 8993
29: 4 t thousand talents of gold (gold of Ophir) 8993
2Ch 4: 4 Sea stood on twelve bulls, t facing north, 8993
4: 4 three facing north, t facing west, 8993
4: 4 t facing south and three facing east. 8993
4: 4 three facing south and t facing east. 8993
4: 5 It held t thousand baths. 8993
6:13 five cubits wide and t cubits high, 8993
8:13 New Moons and the t annual feasts— 8993
9:16 He also made t hundred small shields 8993
9:16 with t hundred bekas of gold 8993
9:21 Once every t years it returned, 8993
10: 5 "Come back to me in t days." 8993
10:12 T days later Jeroboam and all 8958
10:12 "Come back to me in t days." 8958
11:17 Rehoboam son of Solomon t years, 8993
13: 2 and he reigned in Jerusalem t years. 8993
14: 8 of t hundred thousand men from Judah, 8993
14: 9 with a vast army and t hundred chariots, 8993
20:25 so much plunder that it took t days 8993
25: 5 there were t hundred thousand men ready 8993
25:13 They killed t thousand people 8993
29:33 to six hundred bulls and t thousand sheep 8993
31:16 they distributed to the males t years old 8993
35: 7 and also t thousand cattle— 8993
35: 8 and t hundred cattle. 8993
36: 2 and he reigned in Jerusalem t months. 8993
36: 9 and he reigned in Jerusalem t months 8993
Ezr 6: 4 with t courses of large stones and one 10760
8:15 and we camped there t days. 8993
8:32 where we rested t days. 8993
10: 8 within t days would forfeit all his property, 8993
10: 9 Within the t days, all the men of Judah 8993
Ne 2:11 and after staying there t days 8993
Est 4:16 Do not eat or drink for t days, night or day. 8993
9:15 they put to death in Susa t hundred men, 8993
Job 1: 2 He had seven sons and t daughters, 8993
1: 3 t thousand camels, five hundred yoke 8993
1: 4 and they would invite their t sisters to eat 8993
1:17 "The Chaldeans formed t raiding parties 8993
2:11 When Job's t friends, Eliphaz the Temanite, 8993
32: 1 So these t men stopped answering Job, 8993
32: 3 He was also angry with the t friends, 8993
32: 5 that the t men had nothing more to say, 8993
33:29 to a man—twice, even t *times*— 8993
42:13 he also had seven sons and t daughters. 8993
Pr 30:15 "There are t things that are never satisfied, 8993
30:18 "There are t things that are too amazing 8993
30:21 "Under t *things* the earth trembles, 8993
30:29 "There are t things that are stately 8993
Ecc 4:12 A cord of t *strands* is not quickly broken. 8992
Isa 16:14 But now the LORD says: "Within t years, 8993
17: 6 or t olives on the topmost branches, 8993
20: 3 stripped and barefoot for t years, 8993
Jer 36:23 Whenever Jehudi had read t or four columns 8993
52:24 next in rank and the t doorkeepers. 8993
Eze 14:14 even if these t men—Noah, Daniel and Job 8993
14:16 even if these t men were in it, 8993
14:18 even if these t men were in it, 8993
21:14 Let the sword strike twice, even t *times*. 8958
40:10 the east gate were t alcoves on each side; 8993
40:10 the t had the same measurements, 8993
40:21 Its alcoves—t on each side— 8993
40:48 and its projecting walls were t cubits wide 8993
41: 6 The side rooms were on t levels, 8993
41:16 and galleries around the t *of* them— 8993
41:22 There was a wooden altar t cubits high 8993
42: 3 gallery faced gallery at the t *levels*. 8958
48:31 The t gates on the north side will be 8993
48:32 which is 4,500 cubits long, will be t gates: 8993
48:33 measures 4,500 cubits, will be t gates: 8993
48:34 which is 4,500 cubits long, will be t gates: 8993
Da 1: 5 They were to be trained for t years, 8993
3:23 and these t men, firmly tied, fell into 10760
3:24 "Weren't there t men that we tied up 10760
6: 2 with t administrators over them, 10760
6:10 T times a day he got down on his knees 10760
6:13 He still prays t times a day." 10760
7: 5 it had t ribs in its mouth between its teeth. 10760
7: 8 and t of the first horns were uprooted 10760
7:20 before which t of them fell— 10760
7:24 he will subdue t kings. 10760
10: 2 Daniel, mourned for t weeks. 8993
10: 3 at all until the t weeks were over. 8993
11: 2 T more kings will appear in Persia, 8993
Am 1: 3 "For t sins of Damascus, even for four, 8993
1: 6 "For t sins of Gaza, even for four, 8993
1: 9 "For t sins of Tyre, even for four, 8993
1:11 "For t sins of Edom, even for four, 8993
1:13 "For t sins of Ammon, even for four, 8993
2: 1 "For t sins of Moab, even for four, 8993
2: 4 "For t sins of Judah, even for four, 8993
Am 2: 6 "For t sins of Israel, even for four, 8993
4: 4 your tithes every t years. 8993
4: 7 when the harvest was still t months away. 8993
Jnh 1:17 inside the fish t days and three nights. 8993
1:17 inside the fish three days and t nights. 8993
3: 3 a visit required t days. 8993
Zec 11: 8 In one month I got rid of the t shepherds. 8993
Mt 12:40 For as Jonah was t days and three nights in *5552*
12:40 For as Jonah was three days and t nights in *5552*
12:40 Son of Man will be t days and three nights *5552*
12:40 Son of Man will be three days and t nights *5552*
15:32 with me t days and have nothing to eat. *5552*
17: 4 If you wish, I will put up t shelters— *5552*
18:16 by the testimony *of* two or t witnesses.' *5552*
18:20 where two or t come together in my name, *5552*
26:34 you will disown me **t times."** *5565*
26:61 the temple of God and rebuild it in t days.' " *5552*
26:75 you will disown me **t times."** *5565*
27:40 to destroy the temple and build it in t days, *5552*
27:63 'After t days I will rise again.' *5552*
Mk 8: 2 with me t days and have nothing to eat. *5552*
8:31 be killed and after t days rise again. *5552*
9: 5 Let us put up t shelters— *5552*
9:31 and after t days he will rise." *5552*
10:34 T days later he will rise." *5552*
14:30 rooster crows twice you yourself will disown me **t times."** *5565*
14:58 and in t days will build another, *5552*
14:72 crows twice you will disown me **t times."** *5565*
15:29 to destroy the temple and build it in t days, *5552*
Lk 1:56 about t months and then returned home. *5552*
2:46 After t days they found him in *5552*
4:25 the sky was shut for t and a half years *5552*
9:33 Let us put up t shelters— *5552*
10:36 *of* these t do you think was a neighbor to *5552*
11: 5 'Friend, lend me t loaves of bread, *5552*
12:52 t against two and two against three. *5552*
12:52 three against two and two against **t.** *5552*
13: 7 '*For* t years now I've been coming to look *5552*
22:34 you will deny **t times** that you know me." *5565*
22:61 you will disown me **t times."** *5565*
Jn 2:19 and I will raise it again in t days." *5552*
2:20 and you are going to raise it in t days?" *5552*
6:19 they had rowed **t or three and a half miles,** *1633+2445+4297+5084+5558*
6:19 they had rowed **three or t and a half miles,** *1633+2445+4297+5084+5558*
13:38 you will disown me **t times!** *5565*
Ac 2:41 and about **t thousand** were added *5567*
3: 1 time of prayer—at **t in the afternoon.** *1888*
5: 7 About t hours later his wife came in, *5552*
7:20 *For* t months he was cared for *5552*
9: 9 *For* t days he was blind, *5552*
10: 3 at about **t in the afternoon** he had a vision. *1888+2465+3836+6052*
10:16 This happened **t times,** *5565*
10:19 "Simon, t men are looking for you. *5552*
10:30 praying at this hour, at **t in the afternoon.** *1888*
11:10 This happened **t times,** *5565*
11:11 "Right then t men who had been sent to me *5552*
17: 2 on t Sabbath days he reasoned with them *5552*
19: 8 and spoke boldly there for t months, *5552*
20: 3 where he stayed t months. *5552*
20:31 *for* **t years** I never stopped warning each *5562*
25: 1 T days after arriving in the province, *5552*
28: 7 and *for* t days entertained us hospitably. *5552*
28:11 After t months we put out to sea in a ship *5552*
28:12 in at Syracuse and stayed there t days. *5552*
28:17 T days later he called together the leaders *5552*
1Co 13:13 now these t remain: faith, hope and love. *5552*
14:27 two—or at the most t—should speak, *5552*
14:29 Two or t prophets should speak, *5552*
2Co 11:25 **T times** I was beaten with rods, *5565*
11:25 **t times** I was shipwrecked, *5565*
12: 8 **T times** I pleaded with the Lord *5565*
13: 1 by the testimony of two or t witnesses." *5552*
Gal 1:18 Then after t years, I went up to Jerusalem *5552*
1Ti 5:19 unless it is brought by two or t witnesses. *5552*
Heb 10:28 on the testimony of two or t witnesses. *5552*
11:23 *for* **t months** after he was born, *5564*
Jas 5:17 not rain on the land *for* t and a half years. *5552*
1Jn 5: 7 For there are t that testify: *5552*
5: 8 and the t are in agreement. *5552*
Rev 6: 6 and t quarts of barley for a day's wages, *5552*
8:13 about to be sounded by the other t angels!" *5552*
9:18 of mankind was killed by the t plagues *5552*
11: 9 *For* t and a half days men from every *5552*
11:11 after the t and a half days a breath of life *5552*
16:13 I saw t evil spirits that looked like frogs; *5552*
16:19 The great city split into t parts, *5552*
21:13 There were t gates on the east, *5552*
21:13 t on the north, three on the south *5552*
21:13 t on the south and three on the west. *5552*
21:13 three on the south and t on the west. *5552*

THREE TAVERNS (1) [THREE]

Ac 28:15 Forum of Appius and the T to meet us. *5553*

THREE-DAY (4) [DAY, THREE]

Ge 30:36 he put a t journey between himself 3427+8993
Ex 3:18 Let us take a t journey into the desert 3427+8993
5: 3 let us take a t journey into the desert 3427+8993
8:27 We must take a t journey into the desert 3427+8993

THREE-PRONGED (1) [THREE]
1Sa 2:13 of the priest would come with a t fork 8993+9094

THREE-TENTHS (8) [TEN, THREE]
Lev 14:10 with t of an ephah of fine flour mixed 6928+8993
Nu 15: 9 offering of t of an ephah of fine flour 6928+8993
28:12 offering of t of an ephah of fine flour 6928+8993
28:20 offering of t of an ephah of fine flour 6928+8993
28:28 offering of t of an ephah of fine flour 6928+8993
29: 3 offering of t of an ephah of fine flour 6928+8993
29: 9 offering of t of an ephah of fine flour 6928+8993
29:14 offering of t of an ephah of fine flour 6928+8993

THREE-YEAR-OLD (1) [THREE, YEAR]
1Sa 1:24 young as he was, along with a t bull, 8992

THREESCORE (KJV) See SIXTY

THRESH (4) [THRESHED, THRESHER, THRESHES, THRESHING]
Isa 27:12 In that day the LORD *will* t from 2468
41:15 *You will* t the mountains and crush them, 1889
Hos 10:11 Ephraim is a trained heifer that loves to **t;** 1889
Mic 4:13 "Rise and **t,** O Daughter of Zion, 1889

THRESHED (4) [THRESH]
Ru 2:17 Then *she* t the barley she had gathered, 2468
Isa 28:27 Caraway **is** not t with a sledge, 1889
Am 1: 3 she t Gilead with sledges having iron teeth, 1889
Hab 3:12 the earth and in anger *you* t the nations. 1889

THRESHER (1) [THRESH]
1Co 9:10 the plowman plows and the t threshes, *262*

THRESHES (1) [THRESH]
1Co 9:10 the plowman plows and the thresher **t,** *NIG*

THRESHING (51) [THRESH]
Ge 50:10 When they reached the **t floor** *of* Atad, 1755
50:11 the mourning at the **t floor** *of* Atad, 1755
Lev 26: 5 Your t will continue until grape harvest 1912
Nu 15:20 as an offering from the **t floor.** 1755
18:27 to you as grain from the **t floor** or juice 1755
18:30 to you as the product of the **t floor** or 1755
Dt 15:14 your **t floor** and your winepress. 1755
16:13 of your **t floor** and your winepress. 1755
Jdg 6:11 where his son Gideon *was* t wheat in 2468
6:37 I will place a wool fleece on the **t floor.** 1755
Ru 3: 2 be winnowing barley on the **t floor.** 1755
3: 3 Then go down to the **t floor,** 1755
3: 6 So she went down to the **t floor** 1755
3:14 that a woman came to the **t floor."** 1755
1Sa 23: 1 and are looting the **t floors,"** 1755
2Sa 6: 6 When they came to the **t floor** *of* Nacon, 1755
24:16 at the **t floor** *of* Araunah the Jebusite. 1755
24:18 to the LORD on the **t floor** *of* Araunah 1755
24:21 "To buy your **t floor,"** David answered, 1755
24:22 and here are **t sledges** and ox yokes for 4617
24:24 So David bought the **t floor** and the oxen 1755
1Ki 22:10 at the **t floor** *by* the entrance of the gate 1755
2Ki 6:27 can I get help for you? From the **t floor?** 1755
13: 7 and made them like the dust at **t time.** 1889
1Ch 13: 9 When they came to the **t floor** *of* Kidon, 1755
21:15 then standing at the **t floor** *of* Araunah 1755
21:18 to the LORD on the **t floor** *of* Araunah 1755
21:20 While Araunah *was* t wheat, 1889
21:21 the **t floor** and bowed down before David 1755
21:22 of your **t floor** so I can build an altar to 1755
21:23 the **t sledges** for the wood, 4617
21:28 on the **t floor** *of* Araunah the Jebusite, 1755
2Ch 3: 1 on the **t floor** *of* Araunah the Jebusite, 1755
18: 9 at the **t floor** *by* the entrance to the gate 1755
Job 39:12 and gather it to your **t floor?** 1755
41:30 leaving a trail in the mud like a **t sledge.** 3023
Pr 20:26 he drives the *t* **wheel** over them. AIT
Isa 21:10 O my people, crushed on the **t floor,** 1755
28:28 so *one does* not **go on t** it forever. 1889+1889
28:28 Though he drives the wheels of his **t cart** 6322
41:15 "See, I will make you into a **t sledge,** 4617
Jer 50:11 a heifer **t grain** and neigh like stallions, 1889
51:33 like a **t floor** at the time it is trampled; 1755
Da 2:35 like chaff on a **t floor** *in* the summer. 10010
Hos 9: 1 wages of a prostitute at every **t floor.** 1755+1841
9: 2 **T floors** and winepresses will not feed 1755
13: 3 like chaff swirling from a **t floor,** 1755
Joel 2:24 The **t floors** will be filled with grain; 1755
Mic 4:12 like sheaves to the **t floor.** 1755
Mt 3:12 and he will clear his **t floor,** *272*
Lk 3:17 in his hand to clear his **t floor** and *272*

THRESHOLD (15) [THRESHOLDS]
Jdg 19:27 with her hands on the **t.** 6197
1Sa 5: 4 broken off and were lying on the **t;** 5159
5: 5 Dagon's temple at Ashdod step on the **t.** 5159
1Ki 14:17 as she stepped over the t *of* the house, 6197
Eze 9: 3 and moved to the t *of* the temple. 5159
10: 4 above the cherubim and moved to the t *of* 5159
10:18 over the t *of* the temple and stopped above 5159
40: 6 He climbed its steps and measured the t *of* 6197
40: 7 the t *of* the gate next to the portico facing 6197
Eze 41:16 beyond and including the t was covered 6197
43: 8 When they placed their t next 6197
43: 8 to my t and their doorposts 6197
46: 2 He is to worship at the t *of* the gateway 5159
47: 1 under the t *of* the temple toward the east 5159
Zep 1: 9 all who avoid stepping on the **t,** 5159

THRESHOLDS (5) [THRESHOLD]
1Ch 9:19 for guarding the t of the Tent just 6197
9:22 to be gatekeepers at the t numbered 212. 6197
Isa 6: 4 of their voices the doorposts and t shook 6197
Eze 41:16 the t and the narrow windows and galleries 6197
Am 9: 1 the tops of the pillars so that the t shake. 6197

THREW (70) [THROW]
Ge 33: 4 *he* **t** *his* **arms around** his neck 5877+6584
37:24 they took him and t him into the cistern. 8959
44:14 and *they* t *themselves* to the ground 5877
45:14 Then *he* **t** *his* **arms around** his 5877+6584+7418
46:29 *he* **t** *his* **arms around** his father 5877+6584+7418
50: 1 Joseph **t** *himself* upon his father and wept 5877
50:18 and **t** *themselves* **down** before him. 5877
Ex 4: 3 Moses **t** it on the ground and it became 8959
7:10 Aaron t his staff **down** in front of Pharaoh 8959
7:12 Each one **t down** his staff and it became 8959
14:24 the Egyptian army and t it **into confusion.** 2169
15: 7 the greatness of your majesty *you* **t down** 2238
15:25 *He* t it into the water, 8959
32:19 his anger burned and *he* t the tablets out 8959
32:24 and *I* t it into the fire, 8959
Dt 9:17 the two tablets and t them out of my hands, 8959
9:21 as fine as dust and t the dust into a stream 8959
Jos 10:10 The LORD **t** them **into confusion** 2169
10:27 from the trees and t them into the cave 8959
Jdg 8:25 each man t a ring from his plunder onto it. 8959
14:16 Then Samson's wife **t** herself on him, NIH
15:17 *he* **t away** the jawbone; 8959
1Sa 7:10 and **t** them **into** *such* **a panic** that 2169
2Sa 18:17 t him into a big pit in the forest and piled 8959
20:12 from the road into a field and t a garment 8959
20:22 the head of Sheba son of Bicri and t it 8959
1Ki 19:19 up to him and t his cloak around him. 8959
2Ki 2:21 and t the salt into it, saying, "This is what 8959
3:25 and each man t a stone *on* every good field 8959
6: 6 Elisha cut a stick and **t** it there, 8959
9:33 So *they* t her **down,** 9023
10:25 The guards and officers t the bodies **out** 8959
13:21 *they* t the man's body into Elisha's tomb. 8959
23:12 smashed them to pieces and t the rubble 8959
2Ch 25:12 took them to the top of a cliff and t them 8959
30:14 and t them into the Kidron Valley. 8959
33:15 and *he* t them out of the city. 8959
Ne 13: 8 and t all Tobiah's household goods out of 8959
Jer 36:23 a scribe's knife and t them into the firepot, 8959
41: 7 with him slaughtered them and t them into NIH
41: 9 Now the cistern where he t all the bodies 8959
La 3:53 to end my life in a pit and t stones at me; 3343
Eze 28:17 So *I* t you to the earth; 8959
Da 3:24 that *we* tied up and t into the fire?" 10667
6:16 and they brought Daniel and t him into 10667
8:10 **t** some of the starry host **down** to the earth 5877
Jnh 1: 5 And *they* t the cargo into the sea to lighten 3214
1:15 Then they took Jonah and t him overboard, 3214
Zec 11:13 the thirty pieces of silver and t them *into* 8959
Mt 13:48 the good fish in baskets, but t the bad away. *965*
21:39 So *they* took him and t him **out** of *1675*
27: 5 Judas t the money into the temple and left. *4849*
Mk 9:20 immediately t the boy **into a convulsion.** *5360*
11: 7 the colt to Jesus and t their cloaks **over** it, *2095*
12: 8 and t him out of the vineyard. *1675*
12:41 Many rich people t in large amounts. *965*
Lk 4:35 the demon t the man **down** before them all *4849*
9:42 the demon **t** him **to the ground** *4838*
15:20 **t his arms around** him *2093+2158+3836+5549*
17:16 *He* **t himself** at Jesus' feet *2093+4406+4725*
19:35 t their cloaks **on** the colt and put Jesus *2166*
20:12 and they wounded him and t him **out.** *1675*
20:15 So they t him out of the vineyard *1675*
Jn 9:34 And *they* t him out. *1675*
Ac 16:37 and t us into prison. *965*
20:10 went down, **t himself on** the young man *2158*
27:19 *they* t the ship's tackle **overboard** *4849*
Rev 14:19 and t them into the great winepress *965*
18:21 the size of a large millstone and t it into *965*
20: 3 *He* t him into the Abyss, *965*

THRICE (KJV) See THREE TIMES

THRIVE (11) [THRIVES, THRIVING]
Dt 31:20 and when they eat their fill and **t,** 2014
Job 8:11 *Can* reeds t without water? 8436
39: 4 Their young t and grow strong in 8049
Ps 72:16 *let it* t like the grass of the field. 6424
Pr 11:28 but the righteous *will* t like a green leaf. 7255
28:28 when the wicked perish, the righteous **t.** 8049
29: 2 When the righteous **t,** the people rejoice; 8049
29:16 When the wicked **t,** so does sin, 8049
Eze 17: 9 what the Sovereign LORD says: *Will it* **t?** 7503
17:10 Even if it is transplanted, *will it* **t?** 7503
Zec 9:17 Grain *will* **make** the young men **t,** 5649

THRIVES (1) [THRIVE]
Hos 13:15 even though he t among his brothers. 7229

THRIVING (1) [THRIVE]
Jer 11:16 a t olive tree with fruit beautiful in form. 8316

THROAT (4) [THROATS]
Ps 5: 9 Their t is an open grave; 1744
69: 3 calling for help; my t is parched. 1744
Pr 23: 2 and put a knife to your t if you are given 4350
Jer 2:25 until your feet are bare and your t is dry. 1744

THROATS (3) [THROAT]
Ps 115: 7 nor can they utter a sound with their **t.** 1744
Jer 4:10 when the sword is at our **t."** 5883
Ro 3:13 "Their t are open graves; *3296*

THROB (1)
Isa 60: 5 your heart *will* t and swell with joy; 7064

THROES (1)
2Sa 1: 9 I am in the **t of death,** but I'm still alive.' 8688

THRONE (170) [DETHRONED, ENTHRONED, ENTHRONES, THRONES]
Ge 41:40 to the t will I be greater than you." 4058
Ex 11: 5 Pharaoh, who sits on the **t,** 4058
12:29 Pharaoh, who sat on the **t,** 4058
17:16 "For hands were lifted up to the t *of* 4058
Dt 17:18 When he takes the t *of* his kingdom, 4058
1Sa 2: 8 with princes and has them inherit a t 4058
2Sa 3:10 of Saul and establish David's t over Israel 4058
7:13 establish the t *of* his kingdom forever. 4058
7:16 your t will be established forever.' " 4058
14: 9 and let the king and his t be without guilt." 4058
1Ki 1:13 and he will sit on my **t"?** 4058
1:17 and he will sit on my **t.'** 4058
1:20 from you who will sit on the t *of* my lord 4058
1:24 and that he will sit on your **t?** 4058
1:27 on the t *of* my lord the king after him?" 4058
1:30 and he will sit on my t in my place." 4058
1:35 and he is to come and sit on my t and reign 4058
1:37 to make his t even greater than the throne 4058
1:37 to make his throne even greater than the t 4058
1:46 Solomon has taken his seat on the royal **t.** 4058
1:47 and his t greater than yours!' 4058
1:48 to see a successor on my t today.' " 4058
2: 4 you will never fail to have a man on the t 4058
2:12 Solomon sat on the t *of* his father David, 4058
2:19 bowed down to her and sat down on his **t.** 4058
2:19 He had a t brought for the king's mother, 4058
2:24 the t *of* my father David and has founded 4058
2:33 his descendants, his house and his **t,** 4058
2:45 and David's t will remain secure before 4058
3: 6 a son to sit on his t this very day. 4058
5: 5 on the t in your place will build the temple 4058
7: 7 He built the t hall, the Hall of Justice, 4058
8:20 and now I sit on the t *of* Israel, 4058
8:25 a man to sit before me on the t *of* Israel, 4058
9: 5 I will establish your royal t over Israel 4058
9: 5 to have a man on the t *of* Israel.' 4058
10: 9 in you and placed you on the t *of* Israel. 4058
10:18 the king made a great t *inlaid with* ivory 4058
10:19 The t had six steps, 4058
16:11 to reign and was seated on the **t,** 4058
22:19 the LORD sitting on his t with all the host 4058
2Ki 10: 3 and set him on his father's **t.** 4058
10:30 on the t *of* Israel to the fourth generation." 4058
11:19 The king then took his place on the royal **t,** 4058
13:13 and Jeroboam succeeded him on the **t.** 4058
15:12 on the t *of* Israel to the fourth generation." 4058
1Ch 17:12 and I will establish his t forever. 4058
17:14 his t will be established forever.' " 4058
22:10 the t *of* his kingdom over Israel forever.' 4058
28: 5 on the t *of* the kingdom of the LORD 4058
29:23 So Solomon sat on the t *of* the LORD 4058
2Ch 6:10 and now I sit on the t *of* Israel, 4058
6:16 a man to sit before me on the t *of* Israel, 4058
7:18 I will establish your royal **t,** 4058
9: 8 and placed you on his t as king to rule for 4058
9:17 the king made a great t *inlaid with* ivory 4058
9:18 The t had six steps, 4058
18:18 the LORD sitting on his t with all the host 4058
23:20 and seated the king on the royal **t,** 4058
Est 1: 2 from his royal t in the citadel of Susa, 4058
5: 1 The king was sitting on his royal t in 4058
Ps 9: 4 you have sat on your **t,** 4058
9: 7 he has established his t for judgment. 4058
11: 4 the LORD is on his heavenly **t.** 4058
45: 6 Your **t,** O God, will last for ever and ever; 4058
47: 8 God is seated on his holy **t.** 4058
89: 4 make your t firm through all generations.' 4058
89:14 and justice are the foundation of your **t;** 4058
89:29 his t as long as the heavens endure. 4058
89:36 and his t endure before me like the sun; 4058
89:44 to his splendor and cast his t to the ground. 4058
93: 2 Your t was established long ago; 4058
94:20 Can a corrupt t be allied with you— 4058
97: 2 and justice are the foundation of his **t.** 4058
103:19 LORD has established his t in heaven, 4058
123: 1 to you *whose* t is in heaven. 3782
132:11 your own descendants I will place on your t 4058
132:12 then their sons will sit on your t for ever 4058
Pr 16:12 for a t is established through righteousness. 4058
20: 8 When a king sits on his t to judge, 4058
20:28 through love his t is made secure. 4058

Pr 25: 5 and his t will be established through 4058
29:14 his t will always be secure. 4058
Isa 6: 1 I saw the Lord seated on a t, 4058
9: 7 on David's t and over his kingdom, 4058
14:13 I will raise my t above the stars of God; 4058
16: 5 In love a t will be established; 4058
47: 1 sit on the ground without a t, 4058
63:15 from heaven and see from your **lofty** t, 2292
66: 1 "Heaven is my t, and the earth is my 4058
Jer 3:17 they will call Jerusalem The T *of* the LORD 4058
13:13 including the kings who sit on David's t, 4058
14:21 do not dishonor your glorious t. 4058
17:12 A glorious t, exalted from the beginning, 4058
17:25 then kings who sit on David's t will come 4058
22: 2 O king of Judah, you who sit on David's t— 4058
22: 4 then kings who sit on David's t will come 4058
22:30 none will sit of the t *of* David or rule 4058
29:16 about the king who sits on David's t 4058
33:17 a man to sit on the t *of* the house of Israel, 4058
33:21 a descendant to reign on his t. 4058
36:30 He will have no one to sit on the t 4058
43:10 of Babylon, and I will set his t 4058
49:38 I will set my t in Elam 4058
La 5:19 your t endures from generation 4058
Eze 1:26 over their heads was what looked like a t 4058
1:26 and high above on the t was a figure like 4058
10: 1 a t of sapphire above the expanse that was 4058
17:16 the king who **put** him **on** *the* t, 4887
28: 2 on the t *of* a god in the heart of the seas." 4632
43: 7 "Son of man, this is the place of my t and 4058
Da 4:36 and I was restored to my t and became 10424
5:20 from his royal t and stripped of his glory. 10372
7: 9 His t was flaming with fire, 10372
Jnh 3: 6 he rose from his t, took off his royal robes, 4058
Zec 6:13 with majesty and will sit and rule on his t. 4058
6:13 And he will be a priest on his t. 4058
Mt 5:34 either by heaven, for it is God's t; *2585*
19:28 when the Son of Man sits on his glorious t, *2585*
23:22 by God's t and by the one who sits on it. *2585*
25:31 he will sit on his t in heavenly glory. *2585*
Lk 1:32 The Lord God will give him the t *2585*
Ac 2:30 would place one of his descendants on his t. *2585*
7:49 " 'Heaven is my t, and the earth is my *2585*
12:21 sat on his t and delivered a public address *1037*
Heb 1: 8 But about the Son he says, "Your t, *2585*
4:16 Let us then approach the t of grace *2585*
8: 1 who sat down at the right hand *of* the t of *2585*
12: 2 sat down at the right hand *of* the t of God. *2585*
Rev 1: 4 and from the seven spirits before his t, *2585*
2:13 where Satan has his t. *2585*
3:21 I will give the right to sit with me on my t, *2585*
3:21 and sat down with my Father on his t. *2585*
4: 2 a t in heaven with someone sitting on it. *2585*
4: 3 resembling an emerald, encircled the t. *2585*
4: 4 the t were twenty-four other thrones, *2585*
4: 5 From the t came flashes of lightning, *2585*
4: 5 Before the t, seven lamps were blazing. *2585*
4: 6 t there was what looked like a sea of glass, *2585*
4: 6 In the center, around the t, *2585*
4: 9 honor and thanks to him who sits on the t *2585*
4:10 down before him who sits on the t, *2585*
4:10 They lay their crowns before the t and say: *2585*
5: 1 on the t a scroll with writing on both sides *2585*
5: 6 standing in the center *of* the t, *2585*
5: 7 the right hand of him who sat on the t. *2585*
5:11 the t and the living creatures and *2585*
5:13 "To him who sits on the t and to the Lamb *2585*
6:16 the face of him who sits on the t and from *2585*
7: 9 before the t and in front of the Lamb. *2585*
7:10 who sits on the t, and to the Lamb." *2585*
7:11 the angels were standing around the t and *2585*
7:11 They fell down on their faces before the t *2585*
7:15 the t of God and serve him day and night *2585*
7:15 and he who sits on the t will spread his tent *2585*
7:17 the center *of* the t will be their shepherd; *2585*
8: 3 on the golden altar before the t. *2585*
12: 5 child was snatched up to God and to his t. *2585*
13: 2 and his t and great authority. *2585*
14: 3 And they sang a new song before the t and *2585*
16:10 poured out his bowl on the t of the beast, *2585*
16:17 of the temple came a loud voice from the t, *2585*
19: 4 worshiped God, who was seated on the t. *2585*
19: 5 Then a voice came from the t, saying: *2585*
20:11 a great white t and him who was seated *2585*
20:12 great and small, standing before the t, *2585*
21: 3 And I heard a loud voice from the t saying, *2585*
21: 5 He who was seated on the t said, *2585*
22: 1 flowing from the t of God and of the Lamb *2585*
22: 3 The t of God and of the Lamb will be in *2585*

THRONES (17) [THRONE]

1Ki 22:10 on their t at the threshing floor by 4058
2Ch 18: 9 on their t at the threshing floor by 4058
Ps 122: 5 There the t for judgment stand, 4058
122: 5 the t of the house of David. 4058
Isa 14: 9 it makes them rise from their t— 4058
Jer 1:15 "Their kings will come and set up their t in 4058
13:18 "Come down from *your* t, 3782
Eze 26:16 down from their t and lay aside their robes 4058
Da 7: 9 "As I looked, "t were set in place, 10372
Hag 2:22 I will overturn royal t and shatter 4058
Mt 19:28 also sit on twelve t, *2585*
Lk 1:52 down rulers from their t but has lifted up *2585*
22:30 at my table in my kingdom and sit on t, *2585*
Col 1:16 and invisible, whether t or powers or rulers *2585*
Rev 4: 4 the throne were twenty-four other t, *2585*

Rev 11:16 who were seated on their t before God, *2585*
20: 4 I saw t on which were seated those who *2585*

THRONG (10) [THRONGED, THRONGS]

Job 21:33 and a countless t goes before him. NIH
Ps 42: 4 and thanksgiving among the festive t. 2162
55:14 as we walked with the t at the house 8094
68:27 there the **great** t *of* Judah's princes, 8086
109:30 in the **great** *t* I will praise him. AIT
Pr 7:26 her slain are a mighty t. 3972
Jer 31: 8 a great t will return. 7736
Eze 23:24 and wagons and with a t *of* people; 7736
32: 3 a great t *of* people I will cast my net 7736
Mic 2:12 the place *will* t with people. 2101

THRONGED (1) [THRONG]

Jer 5: 7 adultery and t *to* the houses of prostitutes. 1518

THRONGS (1) [THRONG]

Ps 35:18 among t of people I will praise you. 6786

THROUGH (740) [THROUGHOUT]

Ge 2:11 it **winds** t the entire land of Havilah, 6015
2:13 it **winds** t the entire land of Cush. 6015
3:17 t painful toil you will eat of it all the days 928
12: 3 all peoples on earth will be blessed t you." 928
12: 6 Abram traveled t the land as far as the site 928
13:17 walk t the length and breadth of the land, 4200
16: 2 perhaps I can build a family t her." 4946
18:18 all nations on earth will be blessed t him. 928
19:32 and preserve our family line t our father." 4946
19:34 we can preserve our family line t our father. 4946
21:12 because it is t Isaac that your offspring will 928
22:18 t your offspring all nations will be blessed, 928
26: 4 t your offspring all nations will be blessed, 928
28:14 All peoples on earth will be blessed t you 928
30: 3 that she can bear children for me and that t 4946
30:32 Let me go t all your flocks today 928
31:34 Laban **searched** t everything in the tent 5491
31:37 Now that *you have* **searched** t all my goods, 5491
47:17 And he brought them t that year with food 928
Ex 9:35 just as the LORD had said t Moses. 928+3338
12:12 "On that same night I will pass t Egypt 928
12:15 the first day t the seventh must be cut off 6330
12:23 When the LORD **goes** t the land to strike 6296
13:17 God did not lead them on the **road** *t* AIT
14: 4 But I will gain glory for myself t Pharaoh 928
14:16 the water so that the Israelites can go t 928+9348
14:17 And I will gain glory t Pharaoh 928
14:17 t his chariots and his horsemen. 928
14:18 that I am the LORD when I gain glory t 928
14:22 Israelites went t the sea on dry ground, 928+9348
14:29 Israelites went t the sea on dry ground, 928+9348
15:19 walked t the sea on dry ground. 928+9348
19:21 the people so *they do* not **force** *their* **way** t 2238
19:24 and the people *must* not **force** *their* **way** t 2238
32:27 Go back and forth t the camp from one end 928
35:29 the LORD t Moses had commanded 928+3338
Lev 8:36 the LORD commanded t Moses. 928+3338
10:11 the decrees the LORD has given them t 928+3338
22: 8 and so become unclean t it. 928
26: 6 and the sword will not pass t your country. 928
26:46 himself and the Israelites t Moses. 928+3338
Nu 4:37 to the LORD's command t Moses. 928+3338
4:45 to the LORD's command t Moses. 928+3338
4:49 At the LORD's command t Moses, 928+3338
9:23 accordance with his command t Moses. 928+3338
10:13 at the LORD's command t Moses. 928+3338
12: 2 "Has the LORD spoken only t Moses?" 928
12: 2 "Hasn't he also spoken t us?" 928
13:17 up t the Negev and on into the hill country. 928
13:22 up t the Negev and came to Hebron, 928
14: 7 "The land we passed t and explored 928
15:23 of the LORD's commands to you t him, 928+3338
15:23 and continuing t the generations to come— 4200
16:40 as the LORD directed him t Moses. 928+3338
20:17 Please let us pass t your country. 928
20:17 We will not go t any field or vineyard, 928
20:17 the right or to the left until *we have* **passed** t 6296
20:18 "You may not pass t here; 928
20:19 *We* only *want to* **pass** t on foot— 6296
20:20 they answered: *"You may* not **pass** t." 6296
20:21 Since Edom refused to let them go t 928
21:22 "Let us pass t your country. 928
21:22 the king's highway until *we have* **passed** t 6296
21:23 But Sihon would not let Israel pass t 928
25: 8 *He* **drove** the spear t both of them— 1991
25: 8 t the Israelite and into the woman's body. NIH
26: 5 t Hanoch, the Hanochite clan; NIH
26: 5 t Pallu, the Palluite clan; 4200
26: 6 t Hezron, the Hezronite clan; 4200
26: 6 t Carmi, the Carmite clan. 4200
26:12 t Nemuel, the Nemuelite clan; 4200
26:12 t Jamin, the Jaminite clan; 4200
26:12 t Jakin, the Jakinite clan; 4200
26:13 t Zerah, the Zerahite clan; 4200
26:13 t Shaul, the Shaulite clan. 4200
26:15 t Zephon, the Zephonite clan; 4200
26:15 t Haggi, the Haggite clan; 4200
26:15 t Shuni, the Shunite clan; 4200
26:16 t Ozni, the Oznite clan; 4200
26:16 t Eri, the Erite clan; 4200
26:17 t Arodi, the Arodite clan; 4200
26:17 t Areli, the Arelite clan. 4200
Nu 26:20 t Shelah, the Shelanite clan; 4200
26:20 t Perez, the Perezite clan; 4200
26:20 t Zerah, the Zerahite clan. 4200
26:21 t Hezron, the Hezronite clan; 4200
26:21 t Hamul, the Hamulite clan. 4200
26:23 t Tola, the Tolaite clan; NIH
26:23 t Puah, the Puite clan; 4200
26:24 t Jashub, the Jashubite clan; 4200
26:24 t Shimron, the Shimronite clan. 4200
26:26 t Sered, the Seredite clan; 4200
26:26 t Elon, the Elonite clan; 4200
26:26 t Jahleel, the Jahleelite clan. 4200
26:28 The descendants of Joseph by their clans t NIH
26:29 t Makir, the Makirite clan (Makir was 4200
26:29 t Gilead, the Gileadite clan. 4200
26:30 t Iezer, the Iezerite clan; NIH
26:30 t Helek, the Helekite clan; 4200
26:31 t Asriel, the Asrielite clan; NIH
26:31 t Shechem, the Shechemite clan; NIH
26:32 t Shemida, the Shemidaite clan; NIH
26:32 t Hepher, the Hepherite clan. NIH
26:35 t Shuthelah, the Shuthelahite clan; 4200
26:35 t Beker, the Bekerite clan; 4200
26:35 t Tahan, the Tahanite clan. 4200
26:36 t Eran, the Eranite clan. 4200
26:38 t Bela, the Belaite clan; 4200
26:38 t Ashbel, the Ashbelite clan; 4200
26:38 t Ahiram, the Ahiramite clan; 4200
26:39 t Shupham, the Shuphamite clan; 4200
26:39 t Hupham, the Huphamite clan. 4200
26:40 of Bela t Ard and Naaman were: NIH
26:40 t Ard, the Ardite clan; 4200
26:40 t Naaman, the Naamite clan. 4200
26:42 t Shuham, the Shuhamite clan. 4200
26:44 t Imnah, the Imnite clan; 4200
26:44 t Ishvi, the Ishvite clan; 4200
26:44 t Beriah, the Beriite clan; 4200
26:45 and t the descendants of Beriah: 4200
26:45 t Heber, the Heberite clan; 4200
26:45 t Malkiel, the Malkielite clan. 4200
26:48 t Jahzeel, the Jahzeelite clan; 4200
26:48 t Guni, the Gunite clan; 4200
26:49 t Jezer, the Jezerite clan; 4200
26:49 t Shillem, the Shillemite clan. 4200
26:57 t Gershon, the Gershonite clan; 4200
26:57 t Kohath, the Kohathite clan; 4200
26:57 t Merari, the Merarite clan. 4200
27:23 as the LORD instructed t Moses. 928+3338
31:23 that can withstand fire must be put t the fire, 928
31:23 must be put t that water. 928
33: 8 left Pi Hahiroth and passed t the sea 928+9348
36:13 and regulations the LORD gave t Moses 928+3338
Dt 1:19 **went** toward the hill country of the
Amorites *t* all that vast AIT
2: 4 to pass t the territory of your brothers 928
2: 7 He has watched over your **journey** *t* AIT
2:27 "Let us pass t your country. 928
2:28 Only *let us* **pass** t on foot— 6296
2:30 of Heshbon refused to let us pass t. 928
8:15 He led you t the vast and dreadful desert, 928
15:17 then take an awl and push it t his ear lobe 928
29: 5 the forty years that I led you t the desert, 928
29:16 and how we passed t the countries on 928+7931
Jos 1:11 "Go t the camp and tell the people, 928+7931
2:15 she let them down by a rope t the window, 1237
2:18 in the window t which you let us down, 928
14: 2 as the LORD had commanded t Moses. 928+3338
16: 1 from there t the desert into the hill country NIH
18: 9 So the men left and went t the land. 928
19:34 The boundary **ran** west *t* Aznoth Tabor AIT
20: 2 as I instructed you t Moses, 928+3338
21: 2 "The LORD commanded t Moses 928+3338
21: 8 as the LORD had commanded t Moses. 928+3338
22: 9 the command of the LORD t Moses. 928+3338
24:17 all the nations t which we traveled. 928+7931
Jdg 3: 4 which he had given their forefathers t 928+3338
4:21 drove the peg t his temple into the ground, 928
4:22 there lay Sisera with the tent peg t his temple 928
5:28 "T the window peered Sisera's mother; 1237
9:54 So his servant **ran** him t, and he died. 1991
11:16 Israel went t the desert to the Red Sea and 928
11:17 'Give us permission to go t your country,' 928
11:18 "Next they traveled t the desert, 928
11:19 'Let us pass t your country 928
11:20 did not trust Israel to pass t his territory. 928
11:29 **passed** t Mizpah of Gilead, 6296
Ru 4:12 T the offspring the LORD gives you 4946
1Sa 3:21 and there he revealed himself to Samuel t 928
9: 4 So he passed t the hill country of Ephraim 928
9: 4 of Ephraim and t the area around Shalisha, 928
9: 4 Then he passed t the territory of Benjamin, 928
19:12 So Michal let David down t a window, 1237
28:17 The LORD has done what he predicted t 928+3338
31: 4 "Draw your sword and **run** me t, 1991
31: 4 and **run** me t and abuse me." 1991
31:12 all their valiant men journeyed t the night 3972
2Sa 2:23 and the spear came out t his back. 4946
2:29 that night Abner and his men marched t 928
2:29 **continued** *t* the whole Bithron and came AIT
12:25 he sent word t Nathan the prophet 928+3338
20:14 Sheba passed t all the tribes of Israel 928
20:14 and t the entire region of the Berites, NIH
23: 2 "The Spirit of the LORD spoke t me; 928
23:16 So the three mighty men broke t 928
24: 5 and then went t Gad and on to Jazer. NIH
24: 8 After they had gone t the entire land, 928
24:19 as the LORD had commanded t Gad. 1821+3869

1Ki 6:12 I will fulfill **t** you the promise I gave 907
8:53 as you declared **t** your servant Moses 928+3338
8:56 of all the good promises he gave **t** 928+3338
12:15 to Jeroboam son of Nebat **t** Ahijah 928+3338
14:18 as the LORD had said **t** his servant 928+3338
15:29 of the LORD given **t** his servant Ahijah 928+3338
16: 7 of the LORD came **t** the prophet Jehu 928+3338
16:12 of the LORD spoken against Baasha **t** 928+3338
18: 5 "Go **t** the land to all the springs 928
22: 8 "There is still one man **t** whom we can 907+4946
22:28 the LORD has not spoken **t** me." 928
22:36 a cry spread **t** the army: 928
2Ki 1: 2 Now Ahaziah had fallen **t** the lattice 1237
3: 8 **"T** the Desert of Edom," he answered. 2006
3:11 we may inquire of the LORD **t** him?" 907+4946
3:26 to **break t** to the king of Edom, 1324
5: 1 because **t** him the LORD had given victory 928
8: 8 Consult the LORD **t** him; 907+4946
8:21 but he rose up and **broke t** by night; 5782
9:36 the word of the LORD that he spoke **t** 928+3338
10:10 The LORD has done what he promised **t** 928+3338
10:33 from Aroer by the Arnon Gorge **t** Gilead 2256
14:25 spoken **t** his servant Jonah son of 928+3338
17:13 The LORD warned Israel and Judah **t** 928+3338
17:13 that I delivered to you **t** my servants 928+3338
17:23 as he had warned **t** all his servants 928+3338
21:10 The LORD said **t** his servants 928+3338
25: 4 Then the city wall **was broken t,** 1324
25: 4 and the whole army fled at night **t** the gate 2006
1Ch 7:14 Asriel *was his* **descendant** *t* his Aramean AIT
10: 4 "Draw your sword and **run** me **t,** 1991
11: 3 as the LORD had promised **t** Samuel. 928+3338
11:18 So the Three broke **t** the Philistine lines, 928
25: 5 They were given him **t** the promises 928
26:12 the gatekeepers, **t** their chief men, 4200
26:21 who were Gershonites **t** Ladan 4200
26:25 His relatives **t** Eliezer: 4200
2Ch 10:15 to Jeroboam son of Nebat **t** Ahijah 928+3338
12: 7 wrath will not be poured out on Jerusalem **t**
Shishak. 928+3338
18: 7 "There is still one man **t** whom we can 907+4946
18:27 the LORD has not spoken **t** me." 928
21: 9 but he rose up and **broke t** by night. 5782
22: 7 **T** Ahaziah's visit to Joram, NIH
23:20 went into the palace **t** the Upper Gate 928+9348
29:25 this was commanded by the LORD **t** 928+3338
32: 4 the springs and the stream that flowed **t** 928+9348
33: 8 decrees and ordinances given **t** Moses." 928+3338
34:14 the LORD that had been given **t** Moses. 928+3338
35: 6 doing what the LORD commanded **t** 928+3338
36:15 to them **t** his messengers again and 928+3338
Ezr 2: 6 of Pahath-Moab (**t** the line of Jeshua 4200
2:16 of Ater (**t** Hezekiah) 98 4200
2:36 the descendants of Jedaiah (**t** the family 4200
2:40 the descendants of Jeshua and Kadmiel (**t** 4200
9:11 you gave **t** your servants the prophets 928+3338
Ne 2:13 By night I went out **t** the Valley Gate 928
2:14 not enough room for my mount to **get t;** 6296
2:15 and reentered **t** the Valley Gate. 928
7:11 of Pahath-Moab (**t** the line of Jeshua 4200
7:21 of Ater (**t** Hezekiah) 98 4200
7:39 the descendants of Jedaiah (**t** the family 4200
7:43 of Jeshua (**t** Kadmiel through the line 4200
7:43 of Jeshua (through Kadmiel **t** the line 4200
8:14 the LORD had commanded **t** Moses, 928+3338
9:11 so that they passed **t** it on dry ground, 928+9348
9:14 decrees and laws **t** your servant Moses. 928+3338
9:30 By your Spirit you admonished them **t** 928+3338
10:29 the Law of God given **t** Moses 928+3338
Est 6: 9 and lead him on the horse **t** the city streets, 928
6:11 and led him on horseback **t** the city streets, 928
Job 1: 7 "From roaming **t** the earth and going back 928
2: 2 "From roaming **t** the earth and going back 928
12:24 he sends them wandering **t** a trackless waste. 928
15:20 the ruthless **t** all the years stored up for him. NIH
22:13 Does he judge **t** such darkness? 1237
22:30 who will be delivered **t** the cleanness 928
28:10 He tunnels **t** the rock; 928
29: 3 and by his light **I walked** *t* darkness! AIT
30:14 *They* **advance** as *t* a gaping breach; AIT
37:11 *he* **scatters** his lightning *t* them. AIT
41: 2 a cord **t** his nose or pierce his jaw with 928
Ps 21: 5 **T** the victories you gave, his glory is great; 928
21: 7 **t** the unfailing love of the Most High 928
23: 4 I walk **t** the valley of the shadow of death, 928
32: 3 my bones wasted away **t** my groaning 928
33:11 the purposes of his heart **t** all generations. 4200
44: 5 **T** you we push back our enemies; 928
44: 5 **t** your name we trample our foes. 928
45:17 I will perpetuate your memory **t** all 928
63: 6 I think of you **t** the watches of the night. 928
66: 6 they passed **t** the waters on foot— 928
66:12 we went **t** fire and water, 928
68: 7 O God, when you marched **t** the wasteland, 928
72: 5 as long as the moon, **t all generations.** 1887+1887
72:17 All nations will be blessed **t** him, 928
74: 5 like men wielding axes to cut **t** a thicket 928
77:19 Your path led **t** the sea, 928
77:19 your way **t** the mighty waters, 928
78:13 He divided the sea and **led** them **t;** 6296
78:52 he led them like sheep **t** the desert. 928
84: 6 As they pass **t** the Valley of Baca, 928
85: 5 Will you prolong your anger **t** 4200
89: 1 I will make your faithfulness known **t** all 4200
89: 4 make your throne firm **t** all generations.' 4200
89:24 and **t** my name his horn will be exalted. 928
89:40 *You have* **broken t** all his walls 7287
Ps 100: 5 his faithfulness continues **t** all generations. 6330
102:12 your renown endures **t** all generations. 4200
102:24 your years go on **t** all generations. 928
106: 9 he led them **t** the depths as through 928
106: 9 he led them through the depths as **t** NIH
107:16 down gates of bronze and **cuts t** bars 1548
107:17 Some became fools **t** their rebellious ways 4946
118:20 This is the gate of the LORD **t** which 928
119:29 be gracious to me **t** your law. NIH
119:90 Your faithfulness continues **t** all generations 4200
119:148 My eyes **stay open** *t* the watches of AIT
135:13 your renown, O LORD, **t** all generations. 4200
136:14 and brought Israel **t** the midst of it, 928
136:16 to him who led his people **t** the desert, 928
145:13 your dominion endures **t** all generations. 928
Pr 7: 6 At the window of my house I looked out **t** 1237
9:11 For **t** me your days will be many, 928
11: 9 but **t** knowledge the righteous escape. 928
11:11 **T** the blessing of the upright 928
12: 3 A man cannot be established **t** wickedness, 928
16: 6 **T** love and faithfulness sin is atoned for; 928
16: 6 **t** the fear of the LORD a man avoids evil. 928
16:12 for a throne is established **t** righteousness. 928
20:28 **t** love his throne is made secure. 928
24: 3 and **t** understanding it is established; 928
24: 4 **t** knowledge its rooms are filled with rare 928
25: 5 throne will be established **t** righteousness. 928
25:15 **T** patience a ruler can be persuaded, 928
28:11 a poor man who has discernment **sees t** him. 2983
Ecc 5:14 or wealth lost **t** some misfortune, 928
6:12 the few and meaningless days *he* **passes t** 6913
10: 8 *whoever* **breaks t** a wall may be bitten by 7287
12: 3 those looking **t** the windows grow dim; 928
SS 2: 9 gazing **t** the windows, 4946
2: 9 peering **t** the lattice. 4946
3: 2 **t** its streets and squares; 928
5: 4 My lover thrust his hand **t** the latch-opening 4946
Isa 8: 8 **passing t** it and reaching up to the neck. 6296
8:21 they will roam **t** the land; 928
10:28 They enter Aiath; they pass **t** Migron; 928
13:15 Whoever is captured *will* **be thrust t;** 1991
13:20 be inhabited or lived in **t** all generations; 6330
20: 2 at that time the LORD spoke **t** Isaiah 928+3338
21: 1 Like whirlwinds **sweeping t** the southland, 928
23:16 **walk t** the city, O prostitute forgotten; 6015
28:19 by day and by night, *it will* **sweep t."** 6296
30: 6 **T** a land of hardship and distress, 928
34:10 no one will ever pass **t** it again. 928
38:10 the prime of my life must I go **t** the gates 928
41: 4 Who has done this and **carried** *it* **t,** 6913
43: 2 you pass **t** the waters, I will be with you; 928
43: 2 and when you pass **t** the rivers, 928
43: 2 you walk **t** the fire, you will not be burned; 1198
43:16 he who made a way **t** the sea, 928
43:16 a path **t** the mighty waters, 928
45: 2 down gates of bronze and **cut t** bars 1548
47: 2 bare your legs, and **wade t** the streams. 6296
48:21 not thirst when he led them **t** the deserts; 928
51: 8 my salvation **t** all generations." 4200
51: 9 **pierced** that monster **t?** 2726
60:15 with no *one* **traveling t,** 6296
62:10 **Pass t,** pass through the gates! 6296
62:10 Pass through, **pass t** the gates! 6296
63:11 where is he who brought them **t** the sea, 4946
63:13 who led them **t** the depths? 928
Jer 1: 3 and **t** the reign of Jehoiakim son of Josiah 928
2: 2 you loved me and followed me **t** the desert, 928
2: 2 **t** a land not sown. 928
2: 6 and led us **t** the barren wilderness, 928
2: 6 **t** a land of deserts and rifts, 928
5: 1 search **t** her squares. 928
5:10 "Go **t** her vineyards and ravage them, 928
7: 2 all you people of Judah who come **t** 928
9:21 Death has climbed in **t** our windows 928
17: 4 **T** your own **fault** you will lose 928
17:19 **t** which the kings of Judah go in and out; 928
17:20 in Jerusalem who come **t** these gates. 928
17:21 on the Sabbath day or bring it **t** the gates 928
17:24 and bring no load **t** the gates of this city on 928
17:25 on David's throne will come **t** the gates 928
17:27 as you come **t** the gates of Jerusalem on 928
22: 2 your officials and your people who come **t** 928
22: 4 on David's throne will come **t** the gates 928
23:27 just as their fathers forgot my name **t** 928
27: 3 and Sidon **t** the envoys who have come 928+3338
37: 2 to the words the LORD had spoken **t** 928+3338
39: 2 the city wall **was broken t.** 1324
39: 4 **t** the gate between the two walls, 928
39:11 orders about Jeremiah **t** Nebuzaradan 928+3338
39:16 about to fulfill my words against this city **t** 4200
50: 1 the LORD spoke **t** Jeremiah the prophet 928+3338
51:43 **t** which no man travels. 928
52: 7 Then the city wall **was broken t,** 1324
52: 7 at night **t** the gate between the two walls 2006
La 3:44 with a cloud so that no prayer *can* **get t.** 6296
4:14 Now they grope **t** the streets 928
Eze 5:17 Plague and bloodshed will sweep **t** you, 928
9: 5 "Follow him **t** the city and kill, 928
11: 5 but I know **what is going t** your mind. 5091
12: 5 dig **t** the wall and take your belongings out 928
12: 5 the wall and take your belongings out **t** it. 928
12: 7 Then in the evening I dug **t** the wall 928
12:12 hole will be dug in the wall for him to go **t.** 928
12:15 among the nations and scatter them **t** 928
14:15 "Or if I send wild beasts **t** that country 928
14:15 so that no *one can* **pass t** it because of 6296
14:19 and pour out my wrath upon it **t** bloodshed, 928
Eze 20:23 among the nations and scatter them **t** 928
20:26 I let them become defiled **t** their gifts— 928
22:15 the nations and scatter you **t** the countries; 928
26:10 a city whose walls *have* **been broken t.** 1324
28:16 **T** your widespread trade you were filled 928
29:11 No foot of man or animal will pass **t** it; 928
29:12 among the nations and scatter them **t** 928
30:23 among the nations and scatter them **t** 928
30:26 among the nations and scatter them **t** 928
32:27 of these warriors had stalked **t** the land of 928
36:19 and they were scattered **t** the countries; 928
36:23 I show myself holy **t** you before their eyes. 928
36:34 in the sight of all *who* **pass t** it. 6296
38:16 when I show myself holy **t** you 928
39:15 As they go **t** the land and one of them sees 928
39:27 I will show myself holy **t** them in the sight 928
40:28 Then he brought me into the inner court **t** 928
41: 7 up from the lowest floor to the top floor **t** 4200
43: 4 of the LORD entered the temple **t** 2006
44: 2 no one may enter **t** it. 928
44: 2 the God of Israel, has entered **t** it. 928
45:20 for anyone who sins unintentionally or **t** 4946
46: 2 to enter from the outside **t** the portico of 2006
46: 8 he is to go in **t** the portico of the gateway, 2006
46: 9 to return **t** the gate by which he entered, 2006
46:19 Then the man brought me **t** the entrance at 928
47: 2 He then brought me out **t** the north gate 2006
47: 3 a thousand cubits and then led me **t** water 928
47: 4 and led me **t** water that was knee-deep. 928
47: 4 and **led** me **t** water that was up to 6296
Da 2:28 Your dream and the **visions** *that passed t* AIT
2:30 and that you may understand what went **t** NIH
4: 5 the images and **visions** *that passed t* AIT
7: 1 and **visions** *passed t* his mind AIT
7:15 and the **visions** *that passed t* AIT
9:10 kept the laws he gave us **t** his servants 928+3338
11:21 and he will seize it **t** intrigue. 928
11:40 He will invade many countries and **sweep t** 6296
Hos 1: 2 When the LORD began to speak **t** Hosea, 928
12:10 many visions and told parables **t** them." 928+3338
13: 3 like smoke escaping **t** a window. 4946
Joel 2: 8 They plunge **t** defenses 1237
2: 9 like thieves they enter **t** the windows. 1237
3:20 be inhabited forever and Jerusalem **t** 4200
Am 4: 3 You will each go **straight** out **t** breaks in 5584
5: 6 or *he will* **sweep t** the house of Joseph like 7502
5:17 for I will pass **t** your midst," 928
8:11 "when I will send a famine **t** the land— 928
Ob 1:13 not march **t** the gates of my people in 928
Mic 2:13 they will break **t** the gate and go out. 6296
2:13 Their king *will* **pass t** before them, 6296
5: 5 and marches **t** our fortresses, 928
Na 2: 4 The chariots storm **t** the streets, 928
2: 4 rushing back and forth **t** the squares. 928
Hab 3:12 In wrath *you* **strode t** the earth and 7575
Zep 2:14 Their calls will echo **t** the windows, 928
3: 6 streets deserted, with no *one* **passing t.** 6296
Hag 1: 1 of the LORD came **t** the prophet Haggai 928+3338
1: 3 of the LORD came **t** the prophet Haggai: 928+3338
2: 1 of the LORD came **t** the prophet Haggai: 928+3338
Zec 7: 7 the words the LORD proclaimed **t** the 928+3338
7:12 by his Spirit **t** the earlier prophets. 928+3338
10:11 They will pass **t** the sea of trouble; 928
Mal 1: 1 word of the LORD to Israel **t** Malachi. 928+3338
Mt 1:18 to be with child **t** the Holy Spirit. *1666*
1:22 to fulfill what the Lord had said **t** the *1328*
2:15 so was fulfilled what the Lord had said **t** *1328*
2:17 Then what was said **t** the prophet Jeremiah *1328*
2:23 was fulfilled what was said **t** the prophets: *1328*
3: 3 This is he who was spoken of **t** the prophet *1328*
4:14 to fulfill what was said **t** the prophet Isaiah: *1328*
7:13 "Enter **t** the narrow gate. *1328*
7:13 and many enter **t** it. *1328*
8:17 This was to fulfill what was spoken **t** the *1328*
9:26 News of this spread **t** all that region. *1650*
9:35 Jesus **went t** all the towns and villages, *4310*
10:20 the Spirit of your Father speaking **t** you. *1877*
10:23 not finish going **t** the cities of Israel before *NIG*
12: 1 At that time Jesus went **t** the grainfields on *1328*
12:17 This was to fulfill what was spoken **t** the *1328*
12:43 *it* **goes t** arid places seeking rest and does *1451*
13:33 until *it* **worked all t the dough."** *2435*
13:35 So was fulfilled what was spoken **t** the *1328*
18: 7 but woe to the man **t** whom they come! *1328*
19:24 a camel *to* **go t** the eye of a needle than for *1451*
21: 4 to fulfill what was spoken **t** the prophet: *1328*
24:15 spoken of **t** the prophet Daniel— *1328*
Mk 2: 4 *after* **digging t** it, lowered the mat *2021*
2:23 One Sabbath Jesus was going **t** *1328*
7:31 the vicinity of Tyre and went **t** Sidon, *1328*
9:30 They left that place and passed **t** Galilee. *1328*
10:25 a camel *to* **go t** the eye of a needle than for *1451*
11:16 to carry merchandise **t** the temple courts. *1328*
Lk 1:70 (as he said **t** his holy prophets of long ago), *1328*
1:77 of salvation **t** the forgiveness of their sins, *1877*
4:14 about him spread **t** the whole countryside. *2848*
4:30 But he **walked right t** the crowd and went *1451*
5:19 and lowered him on his mat **t** the tiles into *1328*
6: 1 One Sabbath Jesus *was* **going t** *1388*
10:21 full of joy **t** the Holy Spirit, said, *1877*
11:24 *it* **goes t** arid places seeking rest and does *1451*
13:21 until *it* **worked all t the dough."** *2435*
13:22 Then Jesus **went t** the towns and villages, *1388*
13:24 "Make every effort to enter **t** the narrow *1328*
17: 1 but woe to that person **t** whom they come. *1328*
18:25 a camel to go **t** the eye of a needle than for *1328*
19: 1 Jesus entered Jericho and *was* **passing t.** *1451*

Lk 20:23 He saw t their duplicity and said to them, 2917
Jn 1: 3 T him all things were made; 1328
1: 7 so that t him all men might believe. 1328
1:10 and though the world was made t him, 1328
1:17 For the law was given t Moses; 1328
1:17 grace and truth came t Jesus Christ. 1328
3:17 but to save the world t him. 1328
3:21 that what he has done has been done t 1877
4: 4 Now he had to go t Samaria. 1451
7:14 Not until halfway t the Feast did Jesus go 3548
10: 9 whoever enters t me will be saved. 1328
11: 4 so that God's Son may be glorified t it." 1328
14: 6 No one comes to the Father except t me. 1328
17:10 And glory has come to me t them. 1877
17:20 also for those who will believe in me t 1328
Ac 1: 2 after giving instructions t the Holy Spirit to 1328
1:16 the Holy Spirit spoke long ago t the mouth 1328
2:22 which God did among you t him, 1328
3:16 It is Jesus' name and the faith that comes t 1328
3:18 how God fulfilled what he had foretold t 1328
3:21 he promised long ago t his holy prophets. 1328
3:25 'T your offspring all peoples on earth will 1877
4:25 the Holy Spirit t the mouth of your servant, AIT
4:30 signs and wonders t the name of your holy 1328
7:35 t the angel who appeared to him 5250+5931
7:53 into effect t angels but have not obeyed it." 1650
9:25 and lowered him in a basket t an opening 1328
10:36 the good news of peace t Jesus Christ, 1328
10:43 in him receives forgiveness of sins t 1328
11:14 He will bring you a message t which you 1877
11:28 stood up and t the Spirit predicted that 1328
12:10 opened for them by itself, and they went t it. 2002
13: 6 They traveled t the whole island 1451
13:38 to know that t Jesus the forgiveness 1328
13:39 T him everyone who believes is justified 1877
13:49 of the Lord spread t the whole region. 1328
14:22 "We must go t many hardships to enter 1328
14:24 After going t Pisidia, 1451
14:27 and reported all that God had done t them 3552
15: 3 as they traveled t Phoenicia and Samaria, 1451
15: 4 reported everything God had done t them. 3552
15:11 We believe it is t the grace of our Lord 1328
15:12 God had done among the Gentiles t them. 1328
15:41 He went t Syria and Cilicia, 1451
17: 1 When they had passed t Amphipolis 1476
19: 1 Paul took the road t the interior and arrived 1451
19:11 God did extraordinary miracles t Paul, 1328
19:21 passing t Macedonia and Achaia. 1451
20: 2 He traveled t that area, 1451
20: 3 he decided to go back t Macedonia. 1328
21: 4 T the Spirit they urged Paul not to go on 1328
21:19 among the Gentiles t his ministry. 1328
28:25 the truth to your forefathers when he said t 1328
Ro 1: 2 the gospel he promised beforehand t his 1328
1: 4 and who t the Spirit of holiness 2848
1: 5 T him and for his name's sake, 1328
1: 8 I thank my God t Jesus Christ for all 1328
2:16 when God will judge men's secrets t 1328
3:20 t the law we become conscious of sin. 1328
3:22 This righteousness from God comes t faith 1328
3:24 by his grace t the redemption that came 1328
3:25 atonement, t faith in his blood. 1328
3:30 and the uncircumcised t that same faith. 1328
4:13 It was not t law that Abraham 1328
4:13 but t the righteousness that comes by faith. 1328
4:20 Yet he did not waver t unbelief regarding AIT
5: 1 since we have been justified t faith, 1666
5: 1 with God t our Lord Jesus Christ, 1328
5: 2 t whom we have gained access by faith 1328
5: 9 be saved from God's wrath t him! 1328
5:10 we were reconciled to him t the death 1328
5:10 shall we be saved t his life! 1877
5:11 also rejoice in God t our Lord Jesus Christ, 1328
5:11 t whom we have now received reconciliation. 1328
5:12 just as sin entered the world t one man, 1328
5:12 and death t sin, and in this way death came 1328
5:17 death reigned t that one man, 1328
5:17 of the gift of righteousness reign in life t 1328
5:19 as t the disobedience of the one man 1328
5:19 so also t the obedience of the one man 1328
5:21 so also grace might reign t righteousness 1328
5:21 to bring eternal life t Jesus Christ our Lord. 1328
6: 4 with him t baptism into death in order that, 1328
6: 4 just as Christ was raised from the dead t 1328
7: 4 also died to the law t the body of Christ, 1328
7: 7 not have known what sin was except t 1328
7:11 and t the commandment put me to death. 1328
7:13 it produced death in me t what was good, 1328
7:13 so that t the commandment sin might 1328
7:25 Thanks be to God—t Jesus Christ our Lord! 1328
8: 2 because t Christ Jesus the law of the Spirit 1877
8:11 also give life to your mortal bodies t 1328
8:37 in all these things we are more than conquerors t him who loved us. 1328
9: 7 "It is t Isaac that your offspring will 1877
10:17 the message is heard t the word of Christ. 1328
11:36 and t him and to him are all things. 1328
15: 4 so that t endurance and the encouragement 1328
15:18 except what Christ has accomplished t me 1328
15:19 and miracles, t the power of the Spirit. 1877
15:24 while passing t and to have you assist me 1388
16:26 and made known t the prophetic writings 1328
16:27 to the only wise God be glory forever t 1328
1Co 1:21 For since in the wisdom of God the world t 1328
1:21 God was pleased t the foolishness of what 1328
3: 5 servants, t whom you came to believe— 1328
1Co 3:15 but only as one escaping t the flames. 1328
4:15 for in Christ Jesus I became your father t 1328
5: 6 Don't you know that a little yeast works t 2435
7:14 unbelieving husband has been sanctified t 1877
7:14 the unbelieving wife has been sanctified t 1877
8: 6 and there is but one Lord, Jesus Christ, t 1328
8: 6 whom all things came and t whom we live. 1328
10: 1 the cloud and that they all passed t the sea. 1451
12: 8 To one there is given t the Spirit 1328
14:21 "T men of strange tongues and through 1877
14:21 and t the lips of foreigners I will speak to 1877
15:21 For since death came t a man, 1328
15:21 the resurrection of the dead comes also t 1328
15:57 the victory t our Lord Jesus Christ. 1328
16: 5 After I go t Macedonia, 1451
16: 5 for I will be going t Macedonia. 1451
2Co 1: 5 so also t Christ our comfort overflows. 1328
1:20 And so t him the "Amen" is spoken by us 1328
2:14 and t us spreads everywhere the fragrance 1328
3: 4 Such confidence as this is ours t Christ 1328
4: 1 since t God's mercy we have this ministry, NIG
5:18 to himself t Christ and gave us the ministry 1328
5:20 though God were making his appeal t us. 1328
6: 8 t glory and dishonor, bad report 1328
8: 9 that you t his poverty might become rich. AIT
9:11 and t us your generosity will result 1328
11:33 window in the wall and slipped t his hands. 1767
12:17 Did I exploit you t any of the men I sent 1328
13: 3 that Christ is speaking t me. 1877
Gal 2:19 For t the law I died to the law so 1328
2:21 if righteousness could be gained t the law, 1328
3: 8 "All nations will be blessed t you." 1922
3:14 might come to the Gentiles t Christ Jesus, 1877
3:18 but God in his grace gave it to Abraham t 1328
3:19 The law was put into effect t angels by 1328
3:22 being given t faith in Jesus Christ, 1666
3:26 You are all sons of God t faith 1328
5: 5 But by faith we eagerly await t the Spirit AIT
5: 6 that counts is faith expressing itself t love. 1328
5: 9 "A little yeast works t the whole batch 2435
6:14 t which the world has been crucified to me, 1328
Eph 1: 5 as his sons t Jesus Christ, in accordance 1328
1: 7 In him we have redemption t his blood, 1328
2: 8 it is by grace you have been saved, t faith— 1328
2:13 brought near t the blood of Christ. 1877
2:16 to reconcile both of them to God t the cross, 1328
2:18 For t him we both have access to the Father 1328
3: 6 This mystery is that t the gospel 1328
3: 7 of God's grace given me t the working 2848
3:10 His intent was that now, t the church, 1328
3:12 and t faith in him we may approach God 1328
3:16 with power t his Spirit in your inner being, 1328
3:17 that Christ may dwell in your hearts t faith. 1328
4: 3 the unity of the Spirit t the bond of peace. 1877
4: 6 who is over all and t all and in all. 1328
5:26 cleansing her by the washing with water t 1877
Php 1:11 with the fruit of righteousness that comes t 1328
1:19 that t your prayers and the help given by 1328
1:26 so that t my being with you again your joy 1328
1:30 since you are going t the same struggle 2400
3: 9 but that which is t faith in Christ— 1328
4:13 I can do everything t him who gives me 1877
Col 1: 9 to fill you with the knowledge of his will t 1877
1:20 and t him to reconcile to himself all things, 1328
1:20 by making peace t his blood, 1328
1:22 by Christ's physical body t death 1328
2: 8 to it that no one takes you captive t hollow 1328
2:12 in baptism and raised with him t your faith 1328
3:17 giving thanks to God the Father t him. 1328
1Th 5: 9 to suffer wrath but to receive salvation t 1328
5:23 sanctify you t and through. 3911
5:23 sanctify you through and t. 3911
2Th 2:13 God chose you to be saved t the sanctifying 1877
2:13 work of the Spirit and t belief in the truth. NIG
2:14 He called you to this t our gospel, 1328
1Ti 2:15 But women will be saved t childbearing— 1328
4: 2 Such teachings come t hypocritical liars, 1877
4:14 which was given you t a prophetic message 1328
2Ti 1: 6 in you t the laying on of my hands. 1328
1:10 now been revealed t the appearing 1328
1:10 and immortality to light t the gospel. 1328
3:15 to make you wise for salvation t faith 1328
4:17 so that t me the message might 1328
Tit 1: 3 to light t the preaching entrusted to me by 1877
3: 5 He saved us t the washing of rebirth 1328
3: 6 on us generously t Jesus Christ our Savior, 1328
Heb 1: 1 In the past God spoke to our forefathers t 1877
1: 2 and t whom he made the universe. 1328
2:10 for whom and t whom everything exists, 1328
2:10 author of their salvation perfect t suffering. 1328
4: 7 when a long time later he spoke t David, 1877
4:14 great high priest who has gone t the heavens 1451
6:12 but to imitate those who t faith 1328
7: 9 paid the tenth t Abraham, 1328
7:11 If perfection could have been attained t 1328
7:25 those who come to God t him, 1328
9:11 he went t the greater and more perfect 1328
9:14 Christ, who t the eternal Spirit offered 1328
10:10 we have been made holy t the sacrifice of 1328
10:20 and living way opened for us t the curtain, 1328
11:18 "It is t Isaac that your offspring will 1877
11:29 By faith the people passed t the Red Sea as 1329
11:33 who t faith conquered kingdoms, 1328
13:12 to make the people holy t his own blood. 1328
13:15 T Jesus, therefore, let us continually offer 1328
13:20 who t the blood of the eternal covenant 1877
13:21 t Jesus Christ, to whom be glory for ever 1328
Jas 1:18 He chose to give us birth t the word AIT
1Pe 1: 2 t the sanctifying work of the Spirit, 1877
1: 3 into a living hope t the resurrection 1328
1: 5 who t faith are shielded by God's power 1328
1:21 T him you believe in God, 1328
1:23 t the living and enduring word of God. 1328
2: 5 acceptable to God t Jesus Christ. 1328
3:19 t whom also he went and preached to 1877
3:20 eight in all, were saved t water, 1407
4:11 so that in all things God may be praised t 1328
2Pe 1: 1 To those who t the righteousness 1877
1: 2 in abundance t the knowledge of God and 1877
1: 3 for life and godliness t our knowledge 1328
1: 4 T these he has given us his very great 1328
1: 4 so that t them you may participate in 1328
3: 2 by our Lord and Savior t your apostles. AIT
1Jn 4: 9 into the world that we might live t him. 1328
Jude 1:25 t Jesus Christ our Lord, before all ages, 1328
Rev 18:19 on the sea became rich t her wealth! 1666
22:14 of life and may go t the gates into the city. NIG

THROUGHLY (KJV) See ALL, PERFECTLY, REALLY, THOROUGHLY, VIGOROUSLY

THROUGHOUT (134) [THROUGH]

Ge 7: 3 various kinds alive t the earth. 3972+6584+7156
41:29 great abundance are coming t the land 928+3972
41:45 And Joseph went t the land of Egypt. 6584
41:46 from Pharaoh's presence and traveled t 928+3972
41:56 for the famine was severe t Egypt. 928
Ex 8:16 and t the land of Egypt 928+3972
8:17 dust t the land of Egypt became gnats. 928+3972
8:24 t Egypt the land was ruined by the flies. 928+3972
9: 9 on men and animals t the land." 928+3972
9:25 T Egypt hail struck everything in 928+3972
11: 4 'About midnight I will go t Egypt. 928+9348
11: 6 There will be loud wailing t Egypt— 928+3972
14:20 T the night the cloud brought darkness to AIT
36: 6 and they sent this word t the camp: 6296
Lev 6: 9 is to remain on the altar hearth t the night, 3972
25: 9 Day of Atonement sound the trumpet t 928+3972
25:10 the fiftieth year and proclaim liberty t 928
25:24 T the country that you hold as 928+3972
Nu 6: 6 T the period of his separation to the LORD 3972
6: 8 T the period of his separation 3972
15:21 T the generations to come you are 4200
15:38 'T the generations to come you are 4200
35:29 for you t the generations to come, 4200
Dt 28:40 You will have olive trees t your country 928+3972
28:52 They will lay siege to all the cities t 928+3972
28:52 They will besiege all the cities t the land 928+3972
Jos 3: 2 After three days the officers went t 928+7931
6:27 and his fame spread t the land. 928+3972
24: 3 the land beyond the River and led him t 928+3972
24:31 served the LORD t the lifetime of Joshua 3972
Jdg 2: 7 served the LORD t the lifetime of Joshua 3972
6:35 He sent messengers t Manasseh, 928+3972
7:22 men t the camp to turn on each other 928+3972
7:24 sent messengers t the hill country 928+3972
19:25 they raped her and abused her t the night, 3972
20:12 Israel sent men t the tribe of Benjamin, 928+3972
Ru 4:14 May he become famous t Israel! 928
1Sa 7:13 T Samuel's lifetime, the hand of 3972
11: 3 we can send messengers t Israel; 928+1473+3972
11: 7 the pieces by messengers t Israel, 928+1473+3972
13: 3 the trumpet blown t the land and said, 928+3972
31: 9 and they sent messengers t the land of 928+6017
2Sa 8:14 He put garrisons t Edom, 928+3972
15:10 Then Absalom sent secret messengers t 928+3972
19: 9 T the tribes of Israel, 928+3972
19:11 to his palace, since what is being said t 3972
24: 2 "Go t the tribes of Israel from Dan 928+3972
1Ki 1: 3 Then they searched t Israel for 928+1473+3972
9:19 in Lebanon and t all the territory he ruled. 928
15: 6 between Rehoboam and Jeroboam t 3972
15:16 between Asa and Baasha king of Israel t 3972
15:32 between Asa and Baasha king of Israel t 3972
18:20 So Ahab sent word t all Israel 928
2Ki 10:21 Then he sent word t Israel, 928+3972
10:32 Hazael overpowered the Israelites t 928+3972
13:22 Hazael king of Aram oppressed Israel t 3972
23:22 nor t the days of the kings of Israel and 3972
1Ch 5:10 of the Hagrites t the entire region east 6584
10: 9 and sent messengers t the land of 928+6017
13: 2 the rest of our brothers t the territories 928+3972
14:17 So David's fame spread t every land, 928
21: 4 and went t Israel and then came back 928+3972
27: 1 that were on duty month by month t 3972+4200
2Ch 8: 6 in Lebanon and t all the territory he ruled. 928
11:13 and Levites from all their districts t 928+3972
11:23 dispersing some of his sons t the 3972+4200
16: 9 the eyes of the LORD range t the earth 928+3972
17: 9 They taught t Judah, taking with them 928
17:19 in the fortified cities t Judah. 928+3972
23: 2 They went t Judah and gathered the Levites 6015
30: 5 They decided to send a proclamation t 928+3972
30: 6 couriers went t Israel and Judah 928+3972
31: 1 and the altars t Judah and Benjamin 3972+4946
31:20 This is what Hezekiah did t Judah, 928+3972
34: 7 and cut to pieces all the incense altars t 928+3972
36:22 to make a proclamation t his realm and 928+3972
Ezr 1: 1 to make a proclamation t his realm and 928+3972
10: 7 then issued t Judah and Jerusalem for all 928
Ne 8:15 and spread it t their towns and 928+3972

Est 1:20 Then when the king's edict is proclaimed t 928
2:18 He proclaimed a holiday t the provinces 4200
3:6 the Jews, t the whole kingdom of Xerxes. 928
9:4 his reputation spread t the provinces, 928+3972
9:20 Jews t the provinces of King Xerxes, 928+3972
10:1 King Xerxes imposed tribute t the empire, 6584
Job 1:10 his flocks and herds are spread t the land. 928
Ps 45:16 you will make them princes t the land. 928+3972
72:16 Let grain abound t the land; 928
90:1 you have been our dwelling place t all 928
105:31 and gnats t their country. 928+3972
105:32 with lightning t their land; 928
106:27 the nations and scatter them t the lands. 928
Jer 4:5 'Sound the trumpet t the land!' 928
15:13 because of all your sins t your country. 928+3972
17:3 because of sin t your country. 928+3972
23:15 of Jerusalem ungodliness has spread t 3972+4200
45:4 and uproot what I have planted, t the land. 3972
51:52 and t her land the wounded will groan. 928+3972
Eze 9:4 "Go t the city of Jerusalem and put 928+9348
9:7 they went out and began killing t the city. 928
14:17 'Let the sword pass t the land,' 928
30:13 and I will spread fear t the land. 928
39:14 Some will go t the land and, 928
Da 6:1 to appoint 120 satraps to rule t 10089+10353
6:25 men of every language t the land: 10089+10353
Zec 1:10 the LORD has sent to go t the earth." 928
1:11 "We have gone t the earth and found 928
4:10 which range t the earth.)" 928+3972
5:6 the iniquity of the people t the land." 928+3972
6:7 they were straining to go t the earth. 928
6:7 And he said, "Go t the earth!" 928
6:7 So they went t the earth. 928
Mt 4:23 Jesus went t Galilee, 1877+3910
26:13 wherever this gospel is preached t 1877+3910
Mk 1:39 So he traveled t Galilee, 1650+3910
6:55 *They* **ran** t that whole region and carried 4366
14:9 the gospel is preached t the world, 1650+3910
Lk 1:65 and t the hill country 1877+3910
4:25 there was a severe famine t the land. 2093+4246
4:37 spread t the surrounding area. 1650+4246
7:17 This news about Jesus spread t Judea 1877+3910
Ac 8:1 and all except the apostles were scattered t 2848
9:31 Then the church t Judea, 2848+3910
10:37 You know what has happened t Judea, 2848+3910
11:1 The apostles and the brothers t Judea heard 2848
16:6 and his companions **traveled** t the region 1451
18:23 **traveled** from place to place t the region 1451
19:27 who is worshiped t the province of Asia 3910
2Co 1:1 together with all the saints t Achaia: 1877+3910
Eph 3:21 be glory in the church and in Christ Jesus t 1650
Php 1:13 it has become clear t the whole palace guard 1877
1Th 4:10 do love all the brothers t Macedonia. 1877+3910
1Pe 1:1 strangers in the world, **scattered** t Pontus, 1402
5:9 because you know that your brothers t 1877

THROW (70) [THREW, THROWING, THROWN, THROWS]

Ge 27:40 t his yoke from **off** your neck." 7293
37:20 and t him into one of these cisterns and say 8959
37:22 T him into this cistern here in the desert, 8959
Ex 1:22 "Every boy that is born *you must* t into 8959
4:3 The LORD said, "T it on the ground." 8959
7:9 and t it **down** before Pharaoh,' 8959
22:31 torn by wild beasts; t it to the dogs. 8959
23:27 and t **into confusion** every nation you 2169
Lev 1:16 with its contents and t it to the east side of 8959
Nu 19:6 hyssop and scarlet wool and t them onto 8959
Jos 8:29 to take his body from the tree and t it **down** 8959
24:14 **T away** the gods your forefathers worshiped 6073
24:23 "**t away** the foreign gods that are among 6073
2Sa 11:21 a woman t an upper millstone on him from 8959
2Ki 9:25 up and t him on the field that belonged 8959
9:26 then, pick him up and t him on that plot, 8959
9:33 "**T** her **down!**" Jehu said. 9023
Job 18:7 his own schemes t him **down.** 8959
30:11 *they* t **off** restraint in my presence. 8938
Ps 2:3 they say, "and t **off** their fetters." 8959
17:11 with eyes alert, to t me to the ground. 5742
50:18 you t in your lot with adulterers. NIH
62:3 *Would* all of you t him **down—** 8357
Pr 1:14 t **in** your lot with us, and we will share 5877
Ecc 3:6 a time to keep and a time to **t away,** 8959
Isa 2:20 In that day men *will* **t away** to the rodents 8959
19:8 *those who* t nets on the waters will pine 7298
22:18 like a ball and t you into a large country. NIH
28:2 *he will* t it forcefully to the ground. 5663
30:22 *you will* t them **away** like a menstrual cloth 2430
Jer 7:29 Cut off your hair and t it **away;** 8959
16:13 So *I will* t you out of this land into 3214
22:7 up your fine cedar beams and t them into 5877
51:63 tie a stone to it and t it into the Euphrates. 8959
Eze 5:4 take a few of these and t them into the fire 8959
7:19 *They will* t their silver into the streets, 8959
26:12 and t your stones, timber and rubble 8492
32:4 *I will* t you on the land and hurl you on 5759
Da 3:20 Meshach and Abednego and t them into 10667
Hos 7:12 When they go, *I will* t my net over them; 7298
8:5 **T out** your calf-idol, O Samaria! 2396
Jnh 1:12 "Pick me up and t me into the sea," 3214
Zec 1:21 to terrify them and t **down** these horns of 3343
11:13 LORD said to me, "T it to the potter"— 8959
Mal 3:10 not t **open** the floodgates of heaven 7337
Mt 4:6 he said, "t yourself down. 965
5:29 causes you to sin, gouge it out and t it away. 965
5:30 causes you to sin, cut it off and t it away. 965
7:6 *do* not t your pearls to pigs. 965
13:42 *They will* t them into the fiery furnace, 965
13:50 and t them into the fiery furnace, 965
17:27 go to the lake and t out your line. 965
18:8 causes you to sin cut it off and t it away. 965
18:9 causes you to sin, gouge it out and t it away. 965
21:21 'Go, t *yourself* into the sea,' 965
22:13 'Tie him hand and foot, and t him **outside,** 1675
25:30 And t that worthless servant outside, 1675
Mk 11:23 'Go, t *yourself* into the sea,' 965
Lk 4:9 he said, "t yourself down from here. 965
4:29 in order to t him **down the cliff.** 2889
12:5 has power *to* t you into hell. 1833
12:58 and the officer t you into prison. 965
22:41 about a stone's t beyond them, 1074
Jn 8:7 *let him* be the first *to* t a stone at her." 965
21:6 "T your net on the right side of the boat 965
Ac 7:19 *to* t **out** their newborn babies so 1704
27:18 they began to t **the cargo overboard.** 1678
Heb 10:35 So *do* not **t away** your confidence; 610
12:1 *let us* t **off** everything that hinders and 700
Rev 18:19 *They will* t dust on their heads, 965

THROWING (11) [THROW]

Dt 7:23 t them **into** great **confusion** 2169+4539
1Sa 5:9 t it into a great panic. NIH
2Sa 16:13 and t stones at him and showering him 6232
Ezr 10:1 and t **himself down** before the house 5877
Mk 10:50 T his cloak **aside,** he jumped to his feet 610
Ac 16:20 and *are* t our city **into an uproar** 1752
22:4 arresting both men and women and t them 4140
22:23 and t **off** their cloaks and flinging dust 4849
27:38 they lightened the ship *by* t the grain into 1675
Gal 1:7 some people are t you **into confusion** 5429
5:10 one who *is* t you **into confusion** will pay 5429

THROWN (76) [THROW]

Lev 4:12 **where** the ashes are t, and burn it 9162
14:40 the contaminated stones be torn out and t 8959
2Sa 20:21 "His head will **be** t to you from the wall." 8959
1Ki 13:24 and his body was t **down** on the road, 8959
13:25 by saw the body t **down** there, 8959
13:28 and found the body t **down** on the road, 8959
2Ki 7:15 and equipment the Arameans *had* t **away** 8959
19:18 *They have* t their gods into the fire 5989
Ne 4:5 for *they have* t **insults** in the face of 4087
Job 16:11 over to evil men and t me into the clutches 3740
Ps 36:12 t **down,** not able to rise! 1890
102:10 for you have taken me up and t me **aside.** 8959
140:10 *may* they *be* t into the fire, into miry pits, 5877
141:6 their rulers *will* **be** t **down** from the cliffs, 9023
Isa 34:3 Their slain *will* **be** t **out,** 8959
37:19 They *have* t their gods into the fire 5989
Jer 14:16 be t **out** into the streets of Jerusalem 8959
22:19 and t outside the gates of Jerusalem." 8959
26:23 a sword and his body t into the burial place 8959
31:40 where dead bodies and ashes are t, NIH
36:30 be t **out** and exposed to the heat by day 8959
38:9 *They have* t him into a cistern, 8959
51:34 *he has* t us **into confusion,** 2169
Eze 11:7 The bodies *you have* t there are the meat 8492
15:4 And after *it* is t on the fire as fuel and 5989
16:5 Rather, *you* **were** t **out** into the open field, 8959
19:12 it was uprooted in fury and t to the ground. 8959
21:12 They are t to the sword along 4489
Da 3:6 down and worship *will* immediately **be** t 10667
3:11 not fall down and worship will **be** t into 10667
3:15 *you will* **be** t immediately into 10667
3:17 If we are t into the blazing furnace, NIH
3:21 were bound and t into the blazing furnace. 10667
6:7 O king, *shall* **be** t into the lions' den. 10667
6:12 O king, *would* **be** t into the lions' den?" 10667
6:24 brought in and t into the lions' den, 10667
7:11 its body destroyed and t into the blazing 10314
8:12 and truth *was* t to the ground. 8959
Joel 1:7 It has stripped off their bark and t it **away,** 8959
Na 2:6 The river gates *are* t **open** and 7337
Mt 3:10 be cut down and t into the fire. 965
5:13 except *to be* t out and trampled by men. 965
5:25 and *you may be* t into prison. 965
5:29 than for your whole body to *be* t into hell. 965
6:30 which is here today and tomorrow *is* t into 965
7:19 not bear good fruit is cut down and t into 965
8:12 subjects of the kingdom *will be* t outside, 1675
18:8 or two feet and *be* t into eternal fire. 965
18:9 to have two eyes and *be* t into the fire 965
18:30 *he* went off and *had* the man t into prison 965
24:2 every one *will be* **t down."** 2907
Mk 9:22 *"It has* often t him into fire or water 965
9:42 *be* t into the sea with a large millstone tied 965
9:45 to have two feet and *be* t into hell. 965
9:47 to have two eyes and *be* t into hell, 965
13:2 every one *will be* **t down."** 2907
Lk 3:9 be cut down and t into the fire." 965
12:28 and tomorrow *is* t into the fire, 965
13:28 but you yourselves t out. 1675
14:35 nor for the manure pile; it *is* t out. 965
17:2 be better for him *to be* t into the sea with 4849
21:6 every one of them *will be* **t down."** 2907
23:19 (Barabbas had been t into prison for 965
23:25 He released the man who *had been* t 965
Jn 9:35 Jesus heard that *they had* t him out, 1675
15:6 like a branch that is t away and withers; 965
15:6 branch that is t into the fire and burned. 965
Ac 16:23 they *were* t into prison, 965
17:8 and the city officials *were* **t into turmoil.** 5429
Rev 8:8 huge mountain, all ablaze, *was* t into the sea. 965
18:21 the great city of Babylon *will be* **t down,** 965
19:20 of them *were* t alive into the fiery lake 965
20:10 *was* t into the lake of burning sulfur, 965
20:10 the beast and the false prophet had been **t.** NIG
20:14 Then death and Hades *were* t into the lake 965
20:15 *he was* t into the lake of fire. 965

THROWS (6) [THROW]

Nu 35:20 or t something at him intentionally so 8959
35:22 or t something at him unintentionally 8959
Job 30:19 *He* t me into the mud, 3721
41:18 His snorting t **out flashes** *of* light; 2145
Mk 9:18 *it* t him **to the ground.** 4838
Lk 9:39 *it* t him **into convulsions** 5057

THRUSH (2)

Isa 38:14 I cried like a swift or t, 6315
Jer 8:7 the t observe the time of their migration. 6315

THRUST (15) [THRUSTING]

Dt 29:28 and t them into another land, 8959
1Sa 26:8 to the ground with one t of my spear; 7193
2Sa 2:16 and t his dagger into his opponent's side, NIH
2:23 so Abner t the butt of his spear 5782
1Ki 14:9 to anger and t me behind your back. 8959
2Ki 17:20 until *he* t them from his presence. 8959
24:20 and in the end he t them from his presence. 8959
Job 18:8 His feet t *him* into a net and he wanders 8938
24:4 *They* t the needy from the path 5742
SS 5:4 My lover t his hand through 8938
Isa 8:22 and *they will* **be** t *into* utter darkness. 5615
13:15 Whoever is captured *will* **be t through;** 1991
Jer 7:15 *I will* t you from my presence, 8959
52:3 and in the end he t them from his presence. 8959
Eze 23:35 Since you have forgotten me and t me 8959

THRUSTING (1) [THRUST]

Dt 6:19 **t out** all your enemies before you, 2074

THUMB (5) [THUMBS]

Lev 8:23 the t *of* his right hand and on the big toe 991
14:14 the t *of* his right hand and on the big toe 991
14:17 the t *of* his right hand and on the big toe 991
14:25 the t *of* his right hand and on the big toe 991
14:28 be cleansed, on the t *of* his right hand and 991

THUMBS (4) [THUMB]

Ex 29:20 on the t *of* their right hands, 991
Lev 8:24 on the t *of* their right hands and on 991
Jdg 1:6 and cut off his t and big toes. 984+3338
1:7 "Seventy kings with their t and big toes 984+3338

THUMMIM (5)

Ex 28:30 put the Urim and the T in the breastpiece, 9460
Lev 8:8 and put the Urim and T in the breastpiece. 9460
Dt 33:8 "Your T and Urim belong to the man 9460
Ezr 2:63 a priest ministering with the Urim and T. 9460
Ne 7:65 a priest ministering with the Urim and T. 9460

THUNDER (30) [THUNDERED, THUNDERING, THUNDERS]

Ex 9:23 the LORD sent t and hail, 7754
9:28 for we have had enough t and hail. 7754
9:29 t will stop and there will be no more hail, 7754
9:33 the t and hail stopped, 7754
9:34 that the rain and hail and t had stopped, 7754
19:16 On the morning of the third day there was t 7754
20:18 the t and lightning and heard the trumpet 7754
1Sa 2:10 *He will* t against them from heaven; 8306
7:10 that day the LORD thundered with loud t 7754
12:17 I will call upon the LORD to send t 7754
12:18 that same day the LORD sent t and rain. 7754
Job 26:14 then can understand the t *of* his power?" 8308
36:33 His t announces the coming storm; 8275
40:9 and *can* your voice t like his? 8306
Ps 77:17 the skies resounded with **t;** 7754
77:18 Your t was heard in the whirlwind, 8308
93:4 Mightier than the t *of* the great waters, 7754
104:7 at the sound of your t they took to flight; 8308
Isa 29:6 the LORD Almighty will come with t 8308
33:3 At the t *of* your voice, the peoples flee; 2162
Jer 25:30 *he will* t from his holy dwelling 5989+7754
Joel 3:16 The LORD will roar from Zion and t 5989+7754
Mk 3:17 Boanerges, which means Sons *of* **T);** 1103
Rev 4:5 lightning, rumblings and **peals of t.** 1103
6:1 four living creatures say in a voice like **t,** 1103
8:5 and there came **peals of t,** rumblings, 1103
11:19 lightning, rumblings, **peals of t,** 1103
14:2 and like a loud **peal of t.** 1103
16:18 **peals of** t and a severe earthquake. 1103
19:6 of rushing waters and like loud peals *of* **t,** 1103

THUNDERCLOUD (1) [CLOUD]

Ps 81:7 I answered you out of a **t;** 6260+8308

THUNDERED (5) [THUNDER]

Jdg 5:22 Then t the horses' hoofs— 2150
1Sa 7:10 that day the LORD t with loud thunder 8306

2Sa 22:14 The LORD t from heaven; 8306
Ps 18:13 The LORD t from heaven; 8306
Jn 12:29 that was there and heard it said it had t; 1103

THUNDERING (1) [THUNDER]

Rev 9: 9 and the sound of their wings was like the t 5889

THUNDERS (13) [THUNDER]

Job 36:29 how he t from his pavilion? 9583
37: 4 he t with his majestic voice. 8306
37: 5 God's voice t in marvelous ways; 8306
Ps 29: 3 the God of glory t, the LORD thunders over 8306
29: 3 the LORD t over the mighty waters. NIH
68:33 who t with mighty voice. 928+5989+7754
Jer 10:13 he t, the waters in the heavens roar; 5989+7754
51:16 he t, the waters in the heavens roar; 5989+7754
Joel 2:11 The LORD t at the head of his army; 5989+7754
Am 1: 2 "The LORD roars from Zion and t 5989+7754
Rev 10: 3 the voices of the seven t spoke. 1103
10: 4 the seven t spoke, I was about to write; 1103
10: 4 "Seal up what the seven t have said and do 1103

THUNDERSTORM (3) [STORM]

Job 28:26 decree for the rain and a path for the t, 2613+7754
38:25 torrents of rain, and a path for the t, 2613+7754
Isa 30:30 with cloudburst, t and hail. 2443

THUS (32)

Ge 2: 1 T the heavens and the earth were completed 2256
19:25 T he overthrew those cities and 2256
30:40 T he made separate flocks for himself 2256
41:43 T he put him in charge of the whole land 2256
Ex 28:30 T Aaron will always bear the means 2256
Lev 6: 4 when he t sins and becomes guilty, NIH
Nu 4:49 T they were counted, 2256
6: 9 t defiling the hair he has dedicated, 2256
Jdg 8:28 T Midian was subdued before the Israelites 2256
9:56 T God repaid the wickedness 2256
11:33 T Israel subdued Ammon. 2256
16:30 T he killed many more when he died than 2256
1Sa 7:12 "T far has the LORD helped us." 2178+6330
2Ki 23: 3 and all his soul, t confirming the words of 4200
Ezr 4:24 T the work on the house of God 10008+10089
Ps 73:15 If I had said, "I will speak t," 4017
78:54 T he brought them to the border 2256
128: 4 T is the man blessed who fears the LORD. 4027
Pr 2:20 T you will walk in the ways of good men 5100
SS 8:10 T I have become in his eyes 255
Eze 43:26 t they will dedicate it. 2256
Hos 10:15 T will it happen to you, O Bethel, 3970
Mt 1:17 T there were fourteen generations in all 4036
7:20 T, by their fruit you will recognize them 726+1145
15: 6 T you nullify the word of God for the sake 2779
Mk 7:13 T you nullify the word of God NIG
Jn 2:11 He t revealed his glory, 2779
4:37 T the saying 'One sows and another 1877+4047
7:43 T the people were divided because 4036
Gal 3:17 and t do away with the promise. 1650+3836
Eph 2:15 new man out of the two, t making peace, NIG
1Ti 5:12 T they bring judgment on themselves, NIG

THWART (1) [THWARTED, THWARTS]

Isa 14:27 Almighty has purposed, and who can t him? 7296

THWARTED (2) [THWART]

Job 42: 2 no plan of yours can be t. 1307
Isa 8:10 Devise your strategy, but it will be t; 7296

THWARTS (3) [THWART]

Job 5:12 He t the plans of the crafty, 7296
Ps 33:10 he t the purposes of the peoples. 5648
Pr 10: 3 but he t the craving of the wicked. 2074

THYATIRA (4)

Ac 16:14 a dealer in purple cloth from the city of T, 2587
Rev 1:11 to Ephesus, Smyrna, Pergamum, T, Sardis, 2587
2:18 "To the angel of the church in T write: 2587
2:24 Now I say to the rest of you in T, 2587

THYINE (KJV) See CITRON

TIARAS (1)

Isa 3:23 and the linen garments and t and shawls. 7566

TIBERIAS (3) [GALILEE]

Jn 6: 1 the Sea of Galilee (that is, the Sea of T), 5500
6:23 Then some boats from T landed near 5500
21: 1 to his disciples, by the Sea of T. 5500

TIBERIUS (1)

Lk 3: 1 the fifteenth year of the reign of T Caesar— 5501

TIBNI (3)

1Ki 16:21 half supported T son of Ginath for king, 9321
16:22 stronger than those of T son of Ginath. 9321
16:22 So T died and Omri became king. 9321

TIDAL (2)

Ge 14: 1 king of Elam and T king of Goiim 9331
14: 9 T king of Goiim, Amraphel king of Shinar 9331

TIDINGS (4)

Isa 40: 9 You who bring good t to Zion, 1413
40: 9 You who bring good t to Jerusalem, 1413
41:27 I gave to Jerusalem a messenger of good t. 1413
52: 7 who bring good t, who proclaim salvation, 1413

TIDY UP (Anglicized) See TAKE CARE

TIE (15) [TIED, TIES, TYING]

Ex 29: 9 Then t sashes on Aaron and his sons. 2520
Lev 16: 4 t the linen sash around 2520
Dt 6: 8 T them as symbols on your hands 8003
11:18 t them as symbols on your hands 8003
Jdg 15:12 "We've come to t you up and hand you 673
15:13 "We will only t you up and hand you 673+673
16: 5 so we may t him up and subdue him. 673
Job 41: 1 with a fishhook or t down his tongue with 9205
Jer 51:63 this scroll, t a stone to it and throw it into 8003
Eze 3:25 you, son of man, they will t with ropes; 5989+6584
4: 8 I will t you up with ropes so 5989
Da 3:20 of the strongest soldiers in his army to t up 10366
Mt 13:30 and t them in bundles to be burned; 1313
22:13 'T him hand and foot, 1313
23: 4 They t up heavy loads and put them 1297

TIED (25) [TIE]

Ge 38:28 so the midwife took a scarlet thread and t it 8003
Ex 28:28 The rings of the breastpiece are to be t to 8220
39:21 They t the rings of the breastpiece to 8220
Lev 8: 7 t the sash around him, 2520
8: 7 He also t the ephod to him 2520
8:13 t sashes around them and put headbands 2520
Jos 2:18 you have t this scarlet cord in the window 8003
2:21 And she t the scarlet cord in the window. 8003
Jdg 15: 4 and t them tail to tail in pairs. 7155
16: 6 and how you can be t up and subdued." 673
16: 8 and she t him with them. 673
16:10 Come now, tell me how you can be t." 673
16:12 So Delilah took new ropes and t him 673
16:13 Tell me how you can be t." 673
2Ki 5:23 t up the two talents of silver in two bags, 7443
Ps 109:19 like a belt t forever around him. 2520
Da 3:23 firmly t, fell into the blazing furnace. 10366
3:24 "Weren't there three men that we t up 10366
Mt 21: 2 and at once you will find a donkey t there, 1313
Mk 9:42 into the sea with a large millstone t around 4329
11: 2 you will find a colt t there, 1313
11: 4 a colt outside in the street, t at a doorway. 1313
Lk 17: 2 a millstone t around his neck than for him 4329
19:30 you will find a colt t there, 1313
Ac 21:11 t his own hands and feet with it and said, 1313

TIES (6) [TIE]

Jdg 16: 7 "If anyone t me with seven fresh thongs 673
16:11 "If anyone t me securely with new ropes 673+673
Job 12:18 and t a loincloth around their waist. 673
Hos 11: 4 cords of human kindness, with t of love; 6310
Mt 12:29 unless he first t up the strong man? 1313
Mk 3:27 unless he first t up the strong man. 1313

TIGHT (1) [TIGHTEN, TIGHTENED, TIGHTFISTED, TIGHTLY]

Jas 1:26 and yet does not keep a t rein on his tongue 5902

TIGHTEN (1) [TIGHT]

Jdg 16:13 and t it with the pin, I'll become as weak as 9546

TIGHTENED (1) [TIGHT]

Jdg 16:14 and t it with the pin. 9546

TIGHTFISTED (1) [FIST, TIGHT]

Dt 15: 7 or t toward your poor brother. 906+3338+7890

TIGHTLY (5) [TIGHT]

Jos 6: 1 Now Jericho was t shut up 2256+6037+6037
Job 41:15 has rows of shields t sealed together; 7639
41:23 The folds of his flesh are t joined; 1815
Isa 22:18 He will roll you up t like a ball 7571+7571+7572
Eze 27:24 with cords twisted and t knotted. 775

TIGLATH-PILESER (6) [PUL]

2Ki 15:29 T king of Assyria came and took Ijon, 9325
16: 7 Ahaz sent messengers to say to T king 9325
16:10 to Damascus to meet T king of Assyria. 9325
1Ch 5: 6 whom T king of Assyria took into exile. 9433
5:26 (that is, T king of Assyria), who took 9433
2Ch 28:20 T king of Assyria came to him, 9433

TIGRIS (2)

Ge 2:14 The name of the third river is the T; 2538
Da 10: 4 on the bank of the great river, the T, 2538

TIKVAH (2)

2Ki 22:14 who was the wife of Shallum son of T, 9537
Ezr 10:15 son of Asahel and Jahzeiah son of T, 9537

TIKVATH (KJV) See TOKHATH

TILES (1)

Lk 5:19 through the t into the middle of the crowd, 3041

TILGATHPILNESER (KJV) See TIGLATH-PILESER

TILL (137)

Ge 32: 4 with Laban and have remained there t now. 6330
32:24 and a man wrestled with him t daybreak. 6330
Ex 9:18 from the day it was founded t now. 6330
10: 6 the day they settled in this land t now.' " 6330
12:10 Do not leave any of it t morning; 6330
12:10 if some is left t morning, you must burn it. 6330
17:12 so that his hands remained steady t sunset. 6330
18:13 and they stood around him from morning t 6330
18:14 around you from morning t evening?" 6330
27:21 the LORD from evening t morning. 6330
29:34 or any bread is left over t morning, 6330
Lev 6: 9 on the altar hearth throughout the night, t 6330
7:15 he must leave none of it t morning. 6330
7:17 the sacrifice left over t the third day must 928
11:24 will be unclean t evening. 6330
11:25 and he will be unclean t evening. 6330
11:27 will be unclean t evening. 6330
11:28 and he will be unclean t evening. 6330
11:31 when they are dead will be unclean t 6330
11:32 Put it in water; it will be unclean t evening, 6330
11:39 the carcass will be unclean t evening. 6330
11:40 and he will be unclean t evening. 6330
11:40 and he will be unclean t evening. 6330
14:46 while it is closed up will be unclean t 6330
15: 5 and he will be unclean t evening. 6330
15: 6 and he will be unclean t evening. 6330
15: 7 and he will be unclean t evening. 6330
15: 8 and he will be unclean t evening. 6330
15:10 that were under him will be unclean t 6330
15:10 and he will be unclean t evening. 6330
15:11 and he will be unclean t evening. 6330
15:16 and he will be unclean t evening. 6330
15:17 and it will be unclean t evening. 6330
15:18 and they will be unclean t evening. 6330
15:19 will be unclean t evening. 6330
15:21 and he will be unclean t evening. 6330
15:22 and he will be unclean t evening. 6330
15:23 he will be unclean t evening. 6330
15:27 and he will be unclean t evening. 6330
17:15 he will be ceremonially unclean t evening; 6330
22: 6 will be unclean t evening. 6330
22:30 leave none of it t morning. 6330
24: 3 the LORD from evening t morning, 6330
Nu 9:12 not leave any of it t morning or break any 6330
9:15 From evening t morning the cloud above 6330
9:21 the cloud stayed only from evening t 6330
12:15 not move on t she was brought back. 6330
19: 7 he will be ceremonially unclean t evening. 6330
19: 8 and he too will be unclean t evening. 6330
19:10 and he too will be unclean t evening. 6330
19:21 the water of cleansing will be unclean t 6330
19:22 anyone who touches it becomes unclean t 6330
23:24 not rest t he devours his prey and drinks 6330
Dt 33:11 strike his foes t they rise no more." 4946
Jos 7: 6 remaining there t evening. 6330
10:13 t the nation avenged itself on its enemies, 6330
Jdg 19: 8 "Refresh yourself. Wait t afternoon!" 6330
Ru 2: 7 has worked steadily from morning t now, 6330
1Sa 1: 7 her rival provoked her t she wept 2256
14:36 the Philistines by night and plunder them t 6330
2Sa 1:12 and wept and fasted t evening for Saul 6330
10: 5 "Stay at Jericho t your beards have grown, 6330
19: 7 upon you from your youth t now." 6330
20: 3 They were kept in confinement t the day 6330
21:10 of the harvest t the rain poured down from 6330
22:38 I did not turn back t they were destroyed. 6330
23:10 the Philistines t his hand grew tired 3954+6330
1Ki 18:26 on the name of Baal from morning t noon. 6330
1Ch 19: 5 at Jericho t your beards have grown, 889+6330
Ne 4: 6 the wall t all of it reached half its height, 2256
4:21 the first light of dawn t the stars came out. 6330
8: 3 He read it aloud from daybreak t noon 6330
Job 7: 4 The night drags on, and I toss t dawn. 6330
14: 6 t he has put in his time like a hired man. 6330
14:12 t the heavens are no more, 6330
14:13 and conceal me t your anger has passed! 6330
19:10 He tears me down on every side t 2256
27: 5 t I die, I will not deny my integrity. 6330
39: 2 Do you count the months t they bear? NIH
39:10 Will he t the valleys behind you? 8440
Ps 18:37 I did not turn back t they were destroyed. 6330
59:13 consume them t they are no more. 2256
71:18 t I declare your power to the next generation 6330
72: 7 prosperity will abound t the moon is no 6330
73:17 t I entered the sanctuary of God; 6330
78:29 They ate t they had more than enough, 2256
84: 7 t each appears before God in Zion. NIH
94:13 t a pit is dug for the wicked. 6330
105:19 t what he foretold came to pass, 6330+6961
105:19 t the word of the LORD proved him true. NIH
123: 2 t he shows us his mercy. 6330+8611
132: 5 t I find a place for the LORD, 6330
Pr 4:16 For they cannot sleep t they do evil; 561+4202

Pr 4:16 of slumber **t** they make someone fall. 561+4202
4:18 shining ever brighter **t** the full light of day. 6330
7:18 Come, let's drink deep of love **t** morning; 6330
7:20 with money and will not be home **t** 4200
7:23 **t** an arrow pierces his liver, 6330
18:17 **t** another comes forward and questions him. 2256
28:17 by the guilt of murder will be a fugitive **t** 6330
SS 3:4 I held him and would not let him go **t** 6330+8611
Isa 5:8 to field **t** no space is left and you live alone 6330
5:11 at night *t* they *are* **inflamed** *with* wine. AIT
22:14 "**T** your dying *day* this sin will not 6330
23:10 **T** your land as along the Nile, 6268
30:17 **t** you are left like a flagstaff on a 561+6330
32:15 **t** the Spirit is poured upon us from on high, 6330
38:13 I waited patiently **t** dawn, 6330
42:4 or be discouraged **t** he establishes justice 6330
62:1 **t** her righteousness shines out like the dawn, 6330
62:7 give him no rest **t** he establishes Jerusalem 6330
Jer 3:25 from our youth **t** this day we have 6330
9:18 and wail over us **t** our eyes overflow 2256
27:11 that nation remain in its own land *to* **t** it 6268
36:2 to you in the reign of Josiah **t** now. 6330
46:10 The sword will devour **t** it is satisfied, 2256
46:10 **t** it has quenched its thirst with blood. 2256
47:6 'how long **t** you rest? 4202
52:11 put him in prison **t** the day of his death. 6330
52:34 **t** the day of his death. 6330
Eze 24:11 the empty pot on the coals **t** it becomes hot 5100
28:15 from the day you were created **t** 6330
39:19 you will eat fat **t** you are glutted 4200
39:19 and drink blood **t** you are drunk. 4200
Da 4:16 **t** seven times pass by for him. 10221
12:13 "As for you, go your way **t** the end. 4200
Hos 7:4 from the kneading of the dough **t** it rises. 6330
Am 1:8 **t** the last of the Philistines is dead," 2256
Na 3:16 **t** they are more than the stars of the sky, NIH
Hab 2:15 from the wineskin **t** they are drunk, 677+2256
Mt 12:20 **t** he leads justice to victory. *323+2401*
Jn 2:10 but you have saved the best **t** now." *2401*
Ac 28:23 From morning **t** evening he explained *2401*
1Co 4:5 wait **t** the Lord comes. *2401*
1Th 4:15 who are left **t** the coming of the Lord, *1650*
2Th 2:7 now holds it back will continue to do so **t** *2401*
Heb 3:14 to share in Christ if we hold firmly **t** *3588*

TILLAGE (KJV) See FARMED, FIELD, WORK

TILLED, TILLER, TILLEST, TILLETH (KJV) See CULTIVATED, PLOWED, WORK, WORKED, WORKS

TILON (1)

1Ch 4:20 Amnon, Rinnah, Ben-Hanan and **T.** 9400

TILTING (1)

Jer 1:13 a boiling pot, **t away from** the north," 4946+7156

TIMAEUS (1) [BARTIMEAUS]

Mk 10:46 Bartimaeus (that is, the Son *of* **T**), *5505*

TIMBER (12) [TIMBERS]

1Ki 5:6 that we have no one so skilled in felling **t** 6770
5:18 men of Gebal cut and prepared the **t** and 6770
15:22 stones and **t** Baasha had been using there. 6770
2Ki 12:12 They purchased **t** and dressed stone for 6770
22:6 Also have them purchase **t** and dressed 6770
2Ch 2:8 that your men are skilled in cutting **t** there. 6770
2:10 the woodsmen who cut the **t**, 6770
16:6 the stones and **t** Baasha had been using. 6770
34:11 and **t** for joists and beams for the buildings 6770
Ne 2:8 so he will give me **t** to make beams for 6770
Eze 26:12 your stones, **t** and rubble into the sea. 6770
Hag 1:8 Go up into the mountains and bring down **t** 6770

TIMBER (Anglicized) See also LUMBER

TIMBERS (5) [TIMBER]

Lev 14:45 its stones, **t** and all the plaster— 6770
Ezr 5:8 with large stones and placing the **t** in 10058
6:4 of large stones and one of **t**. 10058
Eze 27:5 They made all your **t** of pine trees 4283
Zec 5:4 both its **t** and its stones.'" 6770

TIMBREL (KJV) See TAMBOURINE

TIME (771) [TIMELY, TIMES]

Ge 4:3 In the course of **t** Cain brought some of 3427
4:26 **At that t** men began to call on the name of 255
6:5 of his heart was only evil all the **t.** 3427
6:9 blameless among the **people of** his **t**, 1887
8:12 but this **t** it did not return to him. NIH
10:25 because in his **t** the earth was divided; 3427
12:6 **At that t** the Canaanites were in the land. 255
13:7 also living in the land **at that t.** 255
14:1 At *this* **t** Amraphel king of Shinar, 3427
17:21 Sarah will bear to you by this **t** next year." 4595
18:10 surely return to you about this **t** next year, 6961
18:14 return to you at the appointed **t** next year 6961
19:23 **By the t** Lot reached Zoar, 2256
21:2 at the very **t** God had promised him. 4595
21:22 At that **t** Abimelech and Phicol 6961
21:34 in the land of the Philistines *for* a long **t.** 3427
22:1 **Some t later** God tested Abraham. 339+465+1821+2021+2021
22:15 called to Abraham from heaven a **second t** 9108
22:20 **Some t later** Abraham was told, 339+465+1821+2021+2021
24:11 the **t** the women go out to draw water. 6961
25:24 When the **t** came *for* her to give birth, 3427
26:1 besides the earlier famine of Abraham's **t—** 3427
26:8 When Isaac had been there a long **t**, 3427
26:15 that his father's servants had dug in the **t** 3427
26:18 the wells that had been dug in the **t** 3427
29:7 it is not **t** *for* the flocks to be gathered. 6961
29:21 My **t** is completed, 3427
29:35 "This **t** I will praise the LORD." 7193
30:20 This **t** my husband will treat me 7193
30:21 **Some t later** she gave birth to a daughter 339
34:19 **lost** no **t** in doing what they said, 336
37:9 and this **t** the sun and moon NIH
38:1 At that **t**, Judah left his brothers and went 6961
38:12 After a long **t** Judah's wife, 3427
38:27 When the **t** came *for* her to give birth, 6961
39:5 *the* **t** he put him in charge of his household 255
40:1 **Some t later,** the cupbearer and the baker 339+465+1821+2021+2021
40:4 After they had been in custody *for* **some t**, 3427
43:18 that was put back into our sacks the **first t.** 9378
43:20 down here the **first** to buy food. 9378
46:29 around his father and wept *for a* **long t.** 6388
47:29 When the **t** drew near *for* Israel to die, 3427
48:1 **Some t later** Joseph was told, "Your father is ill." 339+465+1821+2021+2021
50:3 for that was the **t** *required for* embalming. 3427
Ex 4:26 (**At that t** she said "bridegroom of blood," 255
8:9 leave to you the honor of **setting the t** 4200+5503
8:32 But this **t** also Pharaoh hardened his heart 7193
9:5 The LORD set a **t** and said, 4595
9:14 or this **t** I will send the full force 7193
9:18 at this **t** tomorrow I will send 6961
9:27 "This **t** I have sinned," he said to them. 7193
12:39 and *did* not **have t** to prepare food 3523+4538
12:40 the **length of t** the Israelite people lived 4632
13:10 at the **appointed t** year after year. 4595
21:19 the injured man for the **loss of** his **t** 8700
23:15 at the **appointed t** in the month of Abib, 4595
30:12 a ransom for his life **at the t** he is counted. 928
32:34 when the **t** comes for me to punish, 3427
34:18 at the **appointed t** *in* the month of Abib, 4595
Lev 14:2 at the **t** *of* his ceremonial cleansing, 3427
15:25 at a **t** other than her monthly period or has 6961
16:17 the Tent of Meeting **from the t** Aaron goes 928
19:10 **go over** your vineyard **a second t** 6618
25:29 **During that t** he may redeem it. 3427
25:50 to count the **t** from the year he sold himself NIH
26:34 the **t** *that* it lies desolate and you are in 3427
26:35 All the **t** that it lies desolate, 3427
Nu 3:1 of the family of Aaron and Moses at the **t** 3427
9:2 celebrate the Passover at the **appointed t.** 4595
9:3 Celebrate it at the **appointed t**, 4595
9:7 the other Israelites at the **appointed t?"** 4595
9:13 the LORD's offering at the **appointed t.** 4595
9:19 remained over the tabernacle a long **t**, 3427
10:13 They set out, this **first** *t*, AIT
14:15 If you put these people to death all at **one t**, 285
14:19 from the **t** they left Egypt until now." NIH
22:4 who was king of Moab at that **t**, 6961
28:2 that you present to me at the **appointed t** 4595
30:15 he nullifies them **some t after** he hears 339
Dt 1:9 At that **t** I said to you, 6961
1:16 And I charged your judges at that **t:** 6961
1:18 that **t** I told you everything you were to do. 6961
1:46 all the **t** you spent there. 3427
2:1 *For* a long **t** we made our way around 3427
2:14 from the **t** we left Kadesh Barnea 3427
2:34 At that **t** we took all his towns 6961
3:4 At that **t** we took all his cities. 6961
3:8 So at that **t** we took from these two kings 6961
3:12 Of the land that we took over at that **t**, 6961
3:18 I commanded you at that **t:** 6961
3:21 At that **t** I commanded Joshua: 6961
3:23 At that **t** I pleaded with the LORD: 6961
4:14 And the LORD directed me at that **t** 6961
4:25 **lived** in the land **a long t—** 3823
4:32 long before your **t**, from NIH
4:40 the LORD your God gives you *for* **all t.** 3427
5:5 that **t** I stood between the LORD and you 6961
9:20 but at that **t** I prayed for Aaron too. 6961
10:1 At that **t** the LORD said to me, 6961
10:8 that **t** the LORD set apart the tribe of Levi 6961
10:10 as I did the first **t**, 3427
10:10 the LORD listened to me at this **t** also. 7193
15:2 the LORD's **t for canceling debts** 9024
16:3 of your life you may remember the **t** 3427
16:9 from the **t** you begin to put the sickle to NIH
17:9 and to the judge who is in office at that **t.** 3427
17:20 and his descendants will reign a long **t** 3427
19:17 and the judges who are in office at the **t.** 3427
20:19 When you lay siege to a city *for* a long **t**, 3427
24:20 not **go over the branches a second t.** 339+6994
26:3 and say to the priest in office at the **t**, 3427
28:47 and gladly in the **t** of prosperity, NIH
32:35 In **due t** their foot will slip; 6961
34:8 the **t** *of* weeping and mourning was over. 3427
Jos 2:5 when it was **t** to close the city gate, NIH
Jos 5:2 At that **t** the LORD said to Joshua, 6961
6:9 **All this t** the trumpets were sounding. 2143
6:16 The seventh **t** around, 7193
6:26 that **t** Joshua pronounced this solemn oath: 6961
11:6 because by this **t** tomorrow I will hand all 6961
11:10 At that **t** Joshua turned back 6961
11:18 against all these kings *for* a long **t**. 3427
11:21 At that **t** Joshua went and destroyed 6961
14:10 for forty-five years since the **t** he said this 255
20:6 of the high priest who is serving at that **t.** 3427
22:3 *For* a long **t** now— 3427
23:1 After a long **t** had passed and 3427
24:7 Then you lived in the desert *for* a long **t.** 3427
Jdg 3:29 At that **t** they struck down about 6961
4:4 was leading Israel at that **t.** 6961
6:39 This **t** make the fleece dry and the ground NIH
10:1 **After the t** of Abimelech a man 339
11:4 **Some t later,** when the Ammonites 3427+4946
11:26 Why didn't you retake them during that **t?** 6961
12:6 Forty-two thousand Ephraimites were killed at that **t.** 6961
14:4 for at that **t** they were ruling over Israel.) 6961
14:8 **Some t later,** when he went back 3427+4946
15:1 Later on, at the **t** *of* wheat harvest, 3427
15:3 "This **t** I have a right to get even with 7193
16:4 **Some t later,** he fell in love with a 339+4027
16:15 This is the third **t** you have made a fool 7193
18:30 the tribe of Dan until the **t** *of* the captivity 3427
18:31 all the **t** the house of God was in Shiloh. 3427
20:25 This **t**, when the Benjamites came out 3427
21:14 So the Benjamites returned at that **t** 6961
21:24 At that **t** the Israelites left that place 6961
1Sa 1:20 So in the course of **t** Hannah conceived 3427
2:31 The **t** is coming when I will cut short 3427
3:8 The LORD called Samuel a **third** *t*, AIT
3:12 At that **t** I will carry out against Eli 3427
4:19 pregnant and **near the t of delivery.** 3528
7:2 It was a long **t**, twenty years in all, 3427
9:13 you should find him about this **t."** 3427
9:16 "About this **t** tomorrow I will send you 6961
9:24 from the **t** I said, 'I have invited guests.'" NIH
11:9 **'By the t** the sun is hot tomorrow, 3869
13:8 He waited seven days, the **t set** by Samuel; 4595
13:11 and that you did not come at the **set t**, 3427+4595
13:13 your kingdom over Israel for **all t.** 6409
14:18 (At that **t** it was with the Israelites.) 3427
14:35 it *was the* **first t** he had done this. 2725
17:12 in Saul's **t** he was old and well advanced 3427
18:9 that **t** on Saul kept a jealous eye on David. 3427
18:19 So when the **t** came *for* Merab, 6961
18:26 So before the **allotted t** elapsed, 3427
19:21 Saul sent men a **third** *t*, AIT
20:12 I will surely sound out my father by this **t** 6961
22:15 *Was* that day the **first t** I inquired of God 2725
25:7 "'Now I hear that *it is* **sheep-shearing t.** 1605
25:7 the whole **t** they were at Carmel nothing 3427
25:8 since we come at a festive **t.** 3427
25:15 and the whole **t** we were out in the fields 3427
25:16 the **t** we were herding our sheep near them. 3427
25:18 Abigail **lost no t.** 4554
26:10 either his **t** will come and he will die, 3427
2Sa 2:1 **In the course of t,** David inquired of 339+4027
2:11 The length of **t** David was king in Hebron 3427
3:1 and the house of David lasted a **long t.** 801
3:17 **"For some t** you have wanted to make David your king. 1685+1685+8997+9453
7:11 since the **t** I appointed leaders 3427
8:1 **In the course of t,** David defeated 339+4027
10:1 **In the course of t,** the king of 339+4027
11:1 at the **t** *when* kings go off to war, 6961
11:27 After the **t of mourning** was over, 65
13:1 **In the course of t,** Amnon son of David 339+4027
14:26 from **t** to time when it became too heavy 3427
14:26 to **t** when it became too heavy for him— 3427
14:29 he sent a second **t**, but he refused to come. 6388
15:1 **In the course of t,** Absalom 339+4027+4946
17:7 Ahithophel has given is not good this **t.** 7193
18:20 "You may take the news another **t**, 3427
20:5 he took longer than the **t** the king had set 4595
21:18 **In the course of t,** there was another 339+4027
21:18 **At that t** Sibbecai the Hushathite killed 255
23:13 During **harvest t**, three of the thirty chief 7907
23:14 **At that t** David was in the stronghold, 255
24:15 until the end of the **t** designated, 6961
1Ki 2:1 When the **t** drew near *for* David to die, 3427
2:38 Shimei stayed in Jerusalem *for* a long **t.** 3427
2:42 **At that t** you said to me, 2256
8:2 to King Solomon **at the t of** the festival in 928
8:40 so that they will fear you all the **t** they live 3427
8:61 obey his commands, as at this **t."** 3427
8:65 So Solomon observed the festival at that **t**, 6961
9:2 the LORD appeared to him a **second t**, 9108
11:29 About that **t** Jeroboam was going out 6961
14:1 that **t** Abijah son of Jeroboam became ill, 6961
16:9 Elah was in Tirzah at the **t**, NIH
16:34 In Ahab's **t**, Hiel of Bethel rebuilt Jericho. 3427
17:7 **Some t** later the brook dried up 3427
17:17 **Some t later** the son of the woman who owned the house 339+465+1821+2021+2021
18:1 After a long **t**, in the third year, 3427
18:29 prophesying **until the t for** the evening 6330
18:34 **"Do** *it* **a third t,"** he ordered. 8992
18:34 and *they* **did** *it* **the third t.** 8992
18:36 **At the t** of sacrifice, the prophet Elijah 928
18:44 The seventh **t** the servant reported, NIH
19:2 by this **t** tomorrow I do not make your life 6961
19:7 a **second t** and touched him and said, 9108

1Ki 20: 6 But about this **t** tomorrow I am going 6961
20: 9 servant will do all you demanded the **first** *t*, AIT
21: 1 **Some t later** there was an incident involving
a vineyard 339+465+1821+2021+2021
22:49 **At that t** Ahaziah son of Ahab said 255
2Ki 3: 6 at that **t** King Joram set out from Samaria 3427
3:20 about the **t** for offering the sacrifice, NIH
4:16 "About this **t** next year," Elisha said, 4595
4:17 about that same **t** she gave birth to a son, 4595
5:26 Is this the **t** to take money, 6961
6:10 **T and again** Elisha warned the king,
285+2256+4202+4202+9109
6:24 **Some t later,** Ben-Hadad king of Aram 339+4027
7: 1 About this **t** tomorrow, a seah of flour 6961
7:18 "About this **t** tomorrow, a seah of flour 6961
8:20 In the **t** *of* Jehoram, Edom rebelled 3427
8:22 Libnah revolted at the same **t.** 6961
10: 6 to me in Jezreel by this **t** tomorrow." 6961
10:36 The **t** that Jehu reigned over Israel 3427
12:17 **About this t** Hazael king of Aram went up 255
13: 3 *for* a long **t** he kept them under the power 3427
13: 7 and made them like the dust at **threshing t.** 1889
15:16 **At that t** Menahem, starting out from Tirzah 255
15:29 In the **t** *of* Pekah king of Israel, 3427
16: 6 that **t,** Rezin king of Aram recovered Elath 6961
18: 4 for up to that **t** the Israelites had been 3427
18:16 At this **t** Hezekiah king of Judah 6961
20:12 At that **t** Merodach-Baladan son of 6961
20:17 The **t** will surely come when everything 3427
24:10 that **t** the officers of Nebuchadnezzar king 6961
1Ch 1:19 because in his **t** the earth was divided; 3427
9:18 on the east, up to **the present t.** 2178
9:25 in their villages had to come from **t** to time 6961
9:25 in their villages had to come from time to **t** 6961
11:16 **At that t** David was in the stronghold, 255
15:13 did not bring it up the **first** *t* that AIT
17:10 since the **t** I appointed leaders over my 3427
18: 1 **In the course of t,** David defeated 339+4027
19: 1 **In the course of t,** Nahash king of 339+4027
20: 1 at the **t** *when* kings go off to war, 6961
20: 4 **In the course of t,** war broke out 339+4027
20: 4 **At that t** Sibbecai the Hushathite killed 255
21:28 At that **t,** when David saw that the LORD 6961
21:29 and the altar of burnt offering were at that **t** 6961
26:17 and **two at a t** at the storehouse. 9109+9109
28: 7 as is being done at this **t.'** 3427
29:22 Solomon son of David as king a **second t,** 9108
2Ch 5: 3 to the king **at the t of** the festival in 928
6:31 and walk in your ways all the **t** they live in 3427
7: 8 So Solomon observed the festival at that **t** 6961
11:17 of David and Solomon during **this t.** 8993+9102[S]
13:20 Jeroboam did not regain power during the **t** 3427
15: 3 a long **t** Israel was without the true God, 3427
15:11 At that **t** they sacrificed to the LORD 3427
16: 7 At that **t** Hanani the seer came to Asa king 6961
16:10 At the same **t** Asa brutally oppressed some 6961
21: 8 In the **t** *of* Jehoram, Edom rebelled 3427
21:10 Libnah revolted at the same **t,** 6961
21:19 **In the course of t,** 3427+3427+4200+4946
24: 4 **Some t later** Joash decided to restore 339+4027
25:27 From the **t** that Amaziah turned away 6961
28:16 At that **t** King Ahaz sent to the king 6961
28:22 In his **t** *of* trouble King Ahaz became 6961
30: 3 not been able to celebrate it at the regular **t** 6961
35:16 So at that **t** the entire service of the LORD 3427
35:17 celebrated the Passover at that **t** and 6961
35:21 It is not you I am attacking **at this t,** 2021+3427
36:21 all the **t** *of* its desolation it rested, 3427
Ezr 4: 2 since the **t** *of* Esarhaddon king of Assyria, 3427
5: 3 At that **t** Tattenai, governor of 10232
8:34 the entire weight was recorded at that **t.** 6961
9:12 a treaty of friendship with them at **any t,** 6409
10:14 a foreign woman come at a set **t,** 6961
Ne 2: 6 It pleased the king to send me; so I set a **t.** 2375
4:22 At that **t** I also said to the people, 6961
6: 1 that **t** I had not set the doors in the gates— 6961
6: 4 and each **t** I gave them the same answer. NIH
6: 5 Then, the fifth **t,** Sanballat sent his aide 7193
9:28 in your compassion you delivered them **t**
after time. 6961+8041
9:28 in your compassion you delivered them
time after t. 6961+8041
12:23 among the descendants of Levi up to the **t** 3427
12:44 that **t** men were appointed to be in charge 3427
13: 6 **Some t** later I asked his permission 3427
13:21 From that **t** on they no longer came on 6961
Est 1: 1 what happened during the **t** *of* Xerxes, 3427
1: 2 At that **t** King Xerxes reigned 3427
2:19 the virgins were assembled a **second t,** 9108
2:21 During the **t** Mordecai was sitting at 3427
4:14 For if you remain silent at this **t,** 6961
4:14 to royal position for such a **t** as this?" 6961
8:16 For the Jews it was a **t of happiness** and joy 245
9:22 as the **t** when the Jews got relief 3427
9:27 the way prescribed and at the **t appointed.** 2375
Job 9: 3 not answer him **one** *t* out of a thousand. AIT
14: 6 till he has put in his **t** like a hired man. 3427
14:13 If only you would set me a **t** and 2976
15:32 Before his **t** he will be paid in full, 3427
22:16 They were carried off before their **t,** 6961
39: 2 Do you know the **t** they give birth? 6961
Ps 21: 9 At the **t** *of* your appearing 6961
37:39 he is their stronghold in **t** *of* trouble. 6961
51: 5 sinful from the **t** my mother conceived me. NIH
69:13 O LORD, in the **t** *of* your favor; 6961
75: 2 You say, "I choose the **appointed t;** 4595
77: 8 Has his promise failed for **all t?** 1887+1887+2256
Ps 78:38 **T after time** he restrained his anger 8049
78:38 **Time after t** he restrained his anger 8049
102:13 for it is **t** to show favor to her; 6961
102:13 the **appointed t** has come. 4595
104:27 to give them their food at the **proper t.** 6961
119:126 It is **t** for you to act, O LORD; 6961
145:15 you give them their food at the **proper t.** 6961
Pr 20: 4 so at **harvest t** he looks but finds nothing. 7907
25:13 Like the coolness of snow at harvest **t** is 3427
Ecc 1:10 it was here **before** our **t.** 4200+4946+7156
3: 1 There is a **t** for everything, 2375
3: 2 a **t** to be born and a time to die, 6961
3: 2 a time to be born and a **t** to die, 6961
3: 2 a **t** to plant and a time to uproot, 6961
3: 2 a time to plant and a **t** to uproot, 6961
3: 3 a **t** to kill and a time to heal, 6961
3: 3 a time to kill and a **t** to heal, 6961
3: 3 a **t** to tear down and a time to build, 6961
3: 3 a time to tear down and a **t** to build, 6961
3: 4 a **t** to weep and a time to laugh, 6961
3: 4 a time to weep and a **t** to laugh, 6961
3: 4 a **t** to mourn and a time to dance, 6961
3: 4 a time to mourn and a **t** to dance, 6961
3: 5 a **t** to scatter stones and a time 6961
3: 5 to scatter stones and a **t** to gather them, 6961
3: 5 a **t** to embrace and a time to refrain, 6961
3: 5 a time to embrace and a **t** to refrain, 6961
3: 6 a **t** to search and a time to give up, 6961
3: 6 a time to search and a **t** to give up, 6961
3: 6 a **t** to keep and a time to throw away, 6961
3: 6 a time to keep and a **t** to throw away, 6961
3: 7 a **t** to tear and a time to mend, 6961
3: 7 a time to tear and a **t** to mend, 6961
3: 7 a **t** to be silent and a time to speak, 6961
3: 7 a time to be silent and a **t** to speak, 6961
3: 8 a **t** to love and a time to hate, 6961
3: 8 a time to love and a **t** to hate, 6961
3: 8 a **t** *for* war and a time for peace. 6961
3: 8 a time for war and a **t** *for* peace. 6961
3:11 He has made everything beautiful in its **t.** 6961
3:17 for there will be a **t** for every activity, 6961
3:17 a **t** for every deed." NIH
7:17 why die before your **t?** 6961
8: 5 and the wise heart will know the proper **t** 6961
8: 6 a proper **t** and procedure for every matter, 6961
8: 8 As no one is discharged in **t of war,** 4878
8: 9 There is a **t** when a man lords it over others 6961
8:12 a hundred crimes and still **lives a long t,** 799
9:11 but **t** and chance happen to them all. 6961
10:17 and whose princes eat at a *proper* **t**— 6961
Isa 7:17 on the house of your father a **t** unlike any 3427
9: 7 and righteousness from **that t on** 6964
11:11 a **second t** to reclaim the remnant that is left 9108
13:22 Her **t** is at hand, 6961
18: 7 At that **t** gifts will be brought to the LORD 6961
20: 2 that **t** the LORD spoke through Isaiah son 6961
23:15 At that **t** Tyre will be forgotten 3427
29:17 **In a very short t,** 4663+5071+6388
33: 2 our salvation in **t** *of* distress. 6961
39: 1 At that **t** Merodach-Baladan son 6961
39: 6 The **t** will surely come when everything 3427
42:14 "For a **long t** I have kept silent, 6409
42:23 to this or pay close attention in **t to come?** 294
48:16 at the **t** it happens, I am there," 6961
49: 8 "In the **t** *of* my favor I will answer you, 6961
59:21 of their descendants from **this t on** 6964
60:22 in its **t** I will do this swiftly." 6961
Jer 2:24 at **mating t** they will find her. 2544
3:17 that **t** they will call Jerusalem The Throne 6961
4:11 At that **t** this people and Jerusalem will 6961
7:25 From the **t** your forefathers left Egypt until 3427
8: 1 " 'At that **t,** declares the LORD, 6961
8: 7 the thrush observe the **t** *of* their migration. 6961
8:15 for a **t** *of* healing but there was only terror. 6961
10:18 "At this **t** I will hurl out those who live 7193
11: 7 From the **t** I brought your forefathers up 3427
11:14 not listen when they call to me in the **t** 6961
11:18 **at that t** he showed me what they were
doing. 255
13: 3 word of the LORD came to me a **second t:** 9108
14:19 for a **t** *of* healing but there is only terror. 6961
16:19 my refuge in **t** *of* distress, 3427
16:21 this **t** I will teach them my power 7193
18: 7 If **at any t** I announce that a nation 8092
18: 9 if **at another t** I announce that a nation 8092
18:23 deal with them in the **t** *of* your anger. 6961
25:33 At that **t** those slain by the LORD will 3427
25:34 For your **t** to be slaughtered has come; 3427
27: 7 and his son and his grandson until the **t** 6961
29:28 It will be a **long t.** 801
30: 7 It will be a **t** *of* trouble for Jacob, 6961
31: 1 "At that **t,"** declares the LORD, 6961
31:31 "The **t** is coming," declares the LORD, 3427
31:33 with the house of Israel after that **t,"** 3427
32:14 in a clay jar so they will last a long **t.** 3427
33: 1 of the LORD came to him a **second t:** 9108
33:15 " 'In those days and at that **t** I will make 6961
33:20 no longer come at their **appointed t,** 6961
35: 7 Then you will live a long **t** in the land 3427
36: 2 the **t** I began speaking to you in the reign 3427
36: 9 a **t of fasting** before the LORD 7427
37:16 where he remained a long **t.** 3427
39:10 at that **t** he gave them vineyards and fields. 3427
39:16 At that **t** they will be fulfilled 3427
44:17 **At that t** we had plenty of food 2256
46:21 the **t** *for* them to be punished. 6961
49: 8 disaster on Esau *at* the **t** I punish him. 6961
Jer 50: 4 "In those days, at that **t,"** 6961
50:20 In those days, at that **t,"** 6961
50:27 the **t** *for* them to be punished. 6961
50:31 the **t** *for* you to be punished. 6961
51: 6 It is **t** *for* the LORD's vengeance; 6961
51:13 the **t** *for* you to be cut off. 564
51:33 like a threshing floor at the **t** it is trampled; 6961
51:33 the **t** to harvest her will soon come." 6961
51:47 the **t** will surely come when I will punish 3427
Eze 4: 6 lie down again, **this t** on your right side, 9108
7: 7 The **t** has come, the day is near; 6961
7:12 The **t** has come, the day has arrived. 6961
11: 3 'Will it not soon be **t** to build houses? NIH
21:25 of Israel, whose day has come, whose **t** 6961
21:29 to be slain, whose day has come, whose **t** 6961
23:38 At that same **t** they defiled my sanctuary 3427
24:14 The **t** has come for me to act. NIH
24:27 At that **t** your mouth will be opened; 3427
30: 3 day of clouds, a **t** *of* doom *for* the nations. 6961
35: 5 over to the sword at the **t** *of* their calamity, 6961
35: 5 the **t** their punishment reached its climax, 6961
38:17 At that **t** they prophesied for years 3427
38:19 at that **t** there shall be a great earthquake in 3427
48:35 the name of the city from that **t** on will be: 3427
Da 1:18 of the **t** set by the king to bring them in, 3427
2: 8 "I am certain that you are trying to gain **t,** 10530
2:16 Daniel went in to the king and asked for **t,** 10232
2:35 the gold were broken to pieces at the **same** *t* AIT
2:44 "In the **t** of those kings, 10317
3: 8 At this **t** some astrologers came forward 10232
4:19 Belteshazzar) was greatly perplexed for a **t,** 10734
4:34 At the end of that **t,** I, Nebuchadnezzar, 10317
4:36 At the same **t** that my sanity was restored, 10232
5:11 In the **t** *of* your father he was found 10317
7:12 but were allowed to live for a **period of t.)**
10221+10232+10530
7:22 **t** came when they possessed the kingdom. 10232
7:25 be handed over to him for a **t,** times and 10530
7:25 over to him for a time, times and half a **t.** 10530
8:17 that the vision concerns the **t** *of* the end." 6961
8:19 tell you what will happen **later in** the **t** 344+928
8:19 vision concerns the **appointed t** *of* the end. 4595
9:21 came to me in swift flight about the **t** *of* 6961
10: 2 At that **t** I, Daniel, mourned for three weeks. 3427
10:14 for the vision concerns a **t** yet to come." 3427
11:24 but only for a **t.** 6961
11:27 an end will still come at the **appointed t.** 4595
11:29 "At the **appointed t** he will invade 4595
11:29 but this **t** the outcome will be different 340
11:33 *a t* they will fall by the sword or be burned 3427
11:35 and made spotless until the **t** *of* the end, 6961
11:35 for it will still come at the **appointed t.** 4595
11:36 until the **t** of wrath is completed, NIH
11:40 "At the **t** *of* the end the king of the South 6961
12: 1 "At that **t** Michael, the great prince 6961
12: 1 be a **t** *of* distress such as has not happened 6961
12: 1 But at that **t** your people— 6961
12: 4 and seal the words of the scroll until the **t** 6961
12: 7 "It will be for a **t,** times and half a time. 4595
12: 7 "It will be for a time, times and half a **t.** NIH
12: 9 up and sealed until the **t** *of* the end. 6961
12:11 the **t** *that* the daily sacrifice is abolished 6961
Hos 10:12 for it is **t** to seek the LORD, 6961
13:13 when the **t** arrives, he does not come 6961
Joel 3: 1 "In those days and at that **t,** 6961
Am 4: 2 "The **t** will surely come when you will 3427
8: 2 "The **t is ripe** for my people Israel; 995+7891
8:10 I will make **that t** like mourning for 2023[S]
Jnh 3: 1 of the LORD came to Jonah a **second t:** 9108
Mic 2: 3 for it will be a **t** *of* calamity. 6961
3: 4 At that **t** he will hide his face from them 6961
5: 3 be abandoned until the **t** when she who is 6961
7: 4 Now is the **t** of their confusion. NIH
Na 1: 9 trouble will not come a *second* **t.** 7193
Hab 2: 3 For the revelation awaits an **appointed t;** 4595
3: 2 in our **t** make them known; 9102
Zep 1:12 that **t** I will search Jerusalem with lamps 6961
2: 2 the **appointed t** arrives and that day sweeps 2976
3:19 At that **t** I will deal with all who oppressed 6961
3:20 At that **t** I will gather you; 6961
3:20 at that **t** I will bring you home. 6961
Hag 1: 2 "These people say, 'The **t** has not yet come 6961
1: 4 "Is it a **t** for you yourselves to be living 6961
2:20 the LORD came to Haggai a **second t** on 9108
Zec 8: 6 to the remnant of this people at that **t,** 3427
8:10 Before that **t** there were no wages for man 3427
Mal 3: 7 Ever since the **t** of your forefathers 3427
Mt 1:11 of Jeconiah and his brothers **at the t** of *2093*
2: 1 during the **t** of King Herod, *2465*
2: 7 and found out from them the exact **t** *5989*
2:16 with the **t** he had learned from the Magi. *5989*
4:17 From **that t on** Jesus began to preach, *5538*
7: 4 the **t** there is a plank in your own eye? *NIG*
8:29 to torture us before the appointed **t?"** *2789*
9:15 The **t** will come when the bridegroom will *2465*
10:19 At that **t** you will be given what to say, *6052*
11:25 At that **t** Jesus said, "I praise you, Father, *2789*
12: 1 that **t** Jesus went through the grainfields on *2789*
13:21 he has no root, he lasts **only a short t.** *4672*
13:30 At that **t** I will tell the harvesters: *2789*
14: 1 that **t** Herod the tetrarch heard the reports *2789*
16:21 From **that t on** Jesus began to explain *5538*
18: 1 At that **t** the disciples came to Jesus *6052*
21:34 When the harvest **t** approached, *2789*
21:36 other servants to them, more than the first **t,** *NIG*
21:41 his share of the crop at harvest **t."** *2789*
24:10 **At that t** many will turn away from *5538*

Mt 24:23 **At that t** if anyone says to you, 'Look, *5538*
24:25 See, *I have* **told** you **ahead of t.** *4625*
24:30 **"At that t** the sign of the Son of Man *5538*
24:43 of the house had known *at* what **t of night** *5871*
24:45 to give them their food at **the proper t?** *2789*
24:48 'My master *is* **staying away a long t,'** *5988*
25: 1 **"At that t** the kingdom of heaven will be *5538*
25: 5 The bridegroom *was* **a long t in coming,** *5988*
25:19 "After a long **t** the master of those servants *5989*
26:18 My appointed **t** is near. *2789*
26:42 He went away a **second t** and prayed, *1311+1666+4099*
26:44 once more and prayed the **third t,** *1666+5569*
26:55 At that **t** Jesus said to the crowd, *6052*
27:16 **At that t** they had a notorious prisoner, *5538*
Mk 1: 9 that **t** Jesus came from Nazareth in Galilee *2465*
1:15 "The **t** has come," he said. *2789*
2:20 the **t** will come when the bridegroom will *2465*
3: 1 **Another t** he went into the synagogue, *4099*
4:17 they have no root, they last **only a short t.** *4672*
6:21 Finally the opportune **t** came. *2465*
6:35 **By this t** it was late in the day, *2453*
12: 2 *At* harvest **t** he sent a servant to the tenants *2789*
13:11 Just say whatever is given you at the **t,** *6052*
13:21 **At that t** if anyone says to you, 'Look, *5538*
13:23 *I have* **told** you everything **ahead of t.** *4625*
13:26 **"At that t** men will see the Son of Man *5538*
13:33 You do not know when that **t** will come. *2789*
14: 7 and you can help them **any t** you want. *4020*
14:41 Returning the **third t,** he said to them, *5568*
14:72 the rooster crowed the **second t.** *1311+1666*
Lk 1: 5 In the **t** of Herod king of Judea there was *2465*
1:10 *when* the **t** for the burning of incense came, *6052*
1:20 which will come true at their **proper t."** *2789*
1:23 When his **t** of service was completed, *2465*
1:39 that **t** Mary got ready and hurried to a town *2465*
1:57 When it was **t** for Elizabeth to have her *5989*
2: 6 the **t** came for the baby to be born, *2465*
2:21 when *it was* **t** to circumcise him, *4398*
2:22 When the **t** of their purification according *2465*
4:13 he left him until an **opportune t.** *2789*
4:25 many widows in Israel in Elijah's **t,** *2465*
4:27 with leprosy **in the t of** Elisha the prophet, *2093*
5:35 the **t** will come when the bridegroom will *2465*
7:21 very **t** Jesus cured many who had diseases, *6052*
7:45 but this woman, **from the t** I entered, *608+4005*
8:13 but in the **t** of testing they fall away. *2789*
8:27 *For* a long **t** this man had not worn clothes *5989*
9:36 told no one at that **t** what they had seen. *2465*
9:51 As the **t** approached for him to be taken up *2465*
10:21 At that **t** Jesus, full of joy through the Holy *6052*
12:12 teach you at that **t** what you should say." *6052*
12:42 their food allowance at **the proper t?** *2789*
12:45 'My master *is* **taking a long t** in coming,' *5988*
12:56 how to interpret this present **t?** *2789*
13: 1 some present at that **t** who told Jesus about *2789*
13:31 At that **t** some Pharisees came to Jesus *6052*
14:17 *At* the **t** of the banquet he sent his servant *6052*
16:16 Since **that t,** the good news of the kingdom *5538*
16:22 **"The t came when** the beggar died *1181+1254*
17:22 "The **t** is coming when you will long to *2465*
18: 4 "For **some t** he refused. *5989*
19:44 you did not recognize the **t** of God's coming *2789*
20: 9 and went away *for* a long **t.** *5989*
20:10 *At* harvest **t** he sent a servant to the tenants *2789*
21: 6 the **t** will come when not one stone will *2465*
21: 8 claiming, 'I am he,' and, 'The **t** is near.' *2789*
21:22 the **t** of punishment in fulfillment of all *2465*
21:27 **At that t** they will see the Son of Man *5538*
23: 7 who was also in Jerusalem at that **t.** *2465*
23: 8 a long **t** he had been wanting to see him. *5989*
23:22 *For* the **third t** he spoke to them: "Why? *5568*
23:29 For the **t** will come when you will say, *2465*
Jn 2: 4 "My **t** has not yet come." *6052*
2:13 it was **almost t** for the Jewish Passover, *1584*
3: 4 a **second t** into his mother's womb to *1309*
3:22 where *he* **spent some t** with them, *1417*
4:21 a **t** is coming when you will worship *6052*
4:23 Yet a **t** is coming and has now come when *6052*
4:52 as to the **t** when his son got better, *6052*
4:53 the father realized that this was the exact **t** *6052*
5: 1 **Some t later,** Jesus went up to Jerusalem *3552+4047*
5: 6 he had been in this condition *for* a long **t,** *5989*
5:25 a **t** is coming and has now come when *6052*
5:28 for a **t** is coming when all who are *6052*
5:35 and you chose for a **t** to enjoy his light. *6052*
6: 1 **Some t after** this, Jesus crossed to the far *3552*
6:66 From this **t** many of his disciples turned *NIG*
7: 6 "The **right t** for me has not yet come; *2789*
7: 6 for you any **t** is right. *2789*
7: 8 for me the **right t** has not yet come." *2789*
7:30 because his **t** had not yet come. *6052*
7:33 "I am with you for only a short **t,** *5989*
7:39 **Up to that t** the Spirit had **not** been given, *4037*
8: 9 began to go away **one at a t,** *1651+1651+2848*
8:20 because his **t** had not yet come. *6052*
9:24 **A second t** they summoned the man *1311+1666*
11:39 **"by this t** there is a bad odor, *2453*
11:55 it was **almost t** for the Jewish Passover, *1584*
12:31 Now is the **t** for judgment on this world; *NIG*
12:42 Yet **at the same t** many even among *3940*
13: 1 the **t** had come for him to leave this world *6052*
14: 9 I have been among you such a long **t?** *5989*
16: 2 in fact, a **t** is coming when anyone who kills *6052*
16: 4 that when the **t** comes you will remember *6052*
16:21 to a child has pain because her **t** has come; *6052*
Jn 16:22 Now **is** *your* **t of grief,** *2400+3383*
16:25 a **t** is coming when I will no longer use this *6052*
16:32 "But a **t** is coming, and has come, *6052*
17: 1 "Father, the **t** has come. *6052*
18:39 to release to you one prisoner **at the t of** *1877*
19:27 From that **t** on, this disciple took her *6052*
21:14 the **third t** Jesus appeared to his disciples *5568*
21:17 The **third t** he said to him, "Simon *5568*
21:17 because Jesus asked him the **third t,** *5568*
Ac 1: 6 you at this **t** going to restore the kingdom *5989*
1:21 the men who have been with us the whole **t** *5989*
1:22 to the **t** when Jesus was taken up from us. *2465*
3: 1 up to the temple at the **t** of prayer— *6052*
3:21 the **t** comes for God to restore everything, *5989*
4:34 For from **t** to time those who owned lands *NIG*
4:34 For from time to **t** those who owned lands *NIG*
5:36 **Some t ago** Theudas appeared, claiming to be somebody, *2465+3836+4047+4574*
7: 5 though at that **t** Abraham had no child. *NIG*
7:17 "As the **t** drew near for God *5989*
7:20 "At that **t** Moses was born, *2789*
7:41 **That was the t** they made an idol in the form of a calf. *1697+1877+2465+3836*
7:45 It remained in the land until the **t** of David, *2465*
8: 9 Now **for some t** a man named Simon *4732*
8:11 because he had amazed them *for* a long **t** *5989*
9:31 Galilee and Samaria enjoyed a **t** of peace. *NIG*
9:37 About that **t** she became sick and died, *2465*
9:43 *for* some **t** with a tanner named Simon. *2465*
10:15 voice spoke to him a **second t,** *1311+1666+4099*
11: 9 voice spoke from heaven a **second t,** *1311+1666*
11:27 During this **t** some prophets came down *2465*
12: 1 It was about this **t** that King Herod *2789*
13:11 for a **t** you will be unable to see the light of *2789*
13:20 until the **t** of Samuel the prophet. *NIG*
14: 3 and Barnabas spent considerable **t** there, *5989*
14:28 And they stayed there **a long t** *3900+4024+5989*
15: 7 you know that **some t ago** God *608+792+2465*
15:33 After spending some **t** there, *5989*
15:36 Some **t** later Paul said to Barnabas, *2465*
17:21 **spent** *their* **t** doing nothing but talking about *2320*
18:18 Paul stayed on in Corinth *for* some **t.** *2465*
18:20 When they asked him *to* **spend** more **t** with them, *2093+3531+5989*
18:23 After spending some **t** in Antioch, *5989*
19:23 About that **t** there arose a great disturbance *2789*
20:16 to avoid **spending t** in the province of Asia, *1181+5990*
20:18 "You know how I lived the whole **t** I was *5989*
21: 5 But when our **t** was up, we left *2465*
21:38 the desert **some t ago?"** *2465+3836+4047+4574*
24:26 **At the same t** he was hoping that Paul *275*
26: 5 They have known me **for a long t** *540*
26:11 **Many a t** I went from one synagogue *4490*
26:28 in such **a short t** you can persuade me to be *3909*
26:29 Paul replied, **"Short t** or long— *1877+3900*
27: 9 Much **t** had been lost, *5989*
27:21 the men had gone a **long t** without food, *4498*
27:28 A short **t** later they took soundings again *NIG*
27:40 in the sea and **at the same t** untied the ropes *275*
28: 6 but after waiting **a long t** and seeing *2093+4498*
Ro 3:26 to demonstrate his justice at the present **t,** *2789*
5: 6 You see, **at just the right t,** *2789+2848*
5:14 from the **t** of Adam to the time of Moses, *NIG*
5:14 from the time of Adam to the **t** of Moses, *NIG*
6:21 What benefit did you reap **at that t** from *5538*
8:22 of childbirth right up to the **present t.** *3814*
9: 9 "At the appointed **t** I will return, *2789*
11: 5 at the present **t** there is a remnant chosen *2789*
11:30 Just as you who were **at one t** disobedient *4537*
13: 6 *who* **give** *their* **full t** to governing. *4674*
13:11 And do this, understanding the **present t.** *2789*
1Co 2: 7 God destined for our glory before **t** began. *172*
4: 5 judge nothing before the appointed **t;** *2789*
4: 5 **At that t** each will receive his praise *5538*
7: 5 by mutual consent and for a **t,** *2789*
7:29 What I mean, brothers, is that the **t** is short. *2789*
14:27 should speak, **one at a t,** *324+3538*
15: 6 five hundred of the brothers **at the same t,** *2384*
16: 7 I hope *to* **spend** some **t** with you, *2152+5989*
2Co 6: 2 he says, *"In* the **t** of my favor I heard you, *2789*
6: 2 I tell you, now is the **t** of God's favor, *2789*
8:14 At the present **t** your plenty will supply what they need, *2789*
12:14 Now I am ready to visit you *for* the **third t,** *5568*
13: 2 when I was with you the **second t.** *1309*
Gal 2: 1 again to Jerusalem, this **t** with Barnabas. *NIG*
4: 2 and trustees until the **t set** by his father. *4607*
4: 4 But when the **t** had fully come, *5989*
4:29 **At that t** the son born in the ordinary way *5538*
6: 9 the proper **t** we will reap a harvest if we do *2789*
Eph 2: 3 All of us also lived among them **at one t,** *4537*
2:12 remember that *at* that **t** you were separate *2789*
Php 1: 3 I thank my God every **t** I remember you. *NIG*
1Th 2:17 we were torn away from you for a short **t** *2789*
2Th 2: 6 so that he may be revealed at the proper **t.** *2789*
1Ti 2: 6 the testimony given *in* its proper **t.** *2789*
6:15 which God will bring about *in* his own **t—** *2789*
2Ti 1: 9 Christ Jesus before the **beginning of t,** *173+5989*
4: 3 For the **t** will come when men will not put *2789*
4: 6 and the **t** has come for my departure. *2789*
Tit 1: 2 promised before the **beginning of t,** *173+5989*
3: 3 **At one t** we too were foolish, disobedient, *4537*
3:10 and then warn him a **second** *t.* *AIT*
Heb 3: 8 during the **t** of testing in the desert, *2465*
4: 7 a long **t** later he spoke through David, *5989*
4:16 and find grace to help us in our **t of need.** *2322*
Heb 5:12 though by this **t** you ought to be teachers, *5989*
8: 8 "The **t** is coming, declares the Lord, *2465*
8:10 with the house of Israel after that **t,** *2465*
9: 9 This is an illustration for the present **t,** *2789*
9:10 external regulations applying until the **t** of *2789*
9:28 and he will appear a **second t,** *1311+1666*
10:12 this priest had offered **for all t** one sacrifice *1457+1650+3836*
10:13 **Since that t** he waits for his enemies *3370+3836*
10:16 covenant I will make with them after that **t,** *2465*
11:25 to enjoy the pleasures of sin *for* **a short t.** *4672*
11:32 I do not have **t** to tell about Gideon, Barak, *5989*
12:11 No discipline seems pleasant at the **t,** *4205*
12:26 **At that t** his voice shook the earth, *5538*
1Pe 1: 5 that is ready to be revealed in the last **t.** *2789*
1:11 the **t** and circumstances to which the Spirit *2789*
4: 3 For you have spent enough **t** in the past *5989*
4:17 For it is **t** for judgment to begin with *2789*
5: 6 that he may lift you up in **due t.** *2789*
2Pe 3: 6 also the world **of that t** was deluged *5538*
Rev 1: 3 because the **t** is near. *2789*
2:21 I have given her **t** to repent *5989*
3: 3 not know at what **t** I will come to you. *6052*
11: 6 not rain *during* the **t** they are prophesying; *2465*
11:18 The **t** has come for judging the dead, *2789*
12:12 because he knows that his **t** is short." *2789*
12:14 where she would be taken care of *for* a **t,** *2789*
12:14 for a time, times and half a **t,** *2789*
14:15 because the **t** to reap has come, *6052*
20: 3 After that, he must be set free *for* a short **t.** *5989*
22:10 because the **t** is near. *2789*

TIMELY (1) [TIME]

Pr 15:23 an apt reply–and how good is a **t** word! 928+6961

TIMES (183) [TIME]

Ge 4:15 he will suffer vengeance **seven** *t over."* AIT
4:24 If Cain is avenged **seven** *t,* AIT
4:24 then Lamech **seventy-seven** *t."* AIT
27:36 He has deceived me these *two* **t:** 7193
31: 7 by changing my wages ten **t.** 4951
31:41 and you changed my wages ten **t.** 4951
33: 3 and bowed down to the ground seven **t** 7193
43:34 Benjamin's portion was five **t** as much 3338
Ex 18:22 as judges for the people at all **t,** 6961
18:26 as judges for the people at all **t.** 6961
23:14 "Three **t** a year you are to celebrate 8079
23:17 "Three **t** a year all the men are to appear 7193
25:30 on this table to be before me **at all t.** 9458
34:23 Three **t** a year all your men are to appear 7193
34:24 when you go up three **t** each year to appear 7193
Lev 4: 6 the blood and sprinkle some of it seven **t** 7193
4:17 the LORD seven **t** in front of the curtain. 7193
8:11 some of the oil on the altar seven **t,** 7193
14: 7 Seven **t** he shall sprinkle the one to 7193
14:16 some of it before the LORD seven **t.** 7193
14:27 from his palm seven **t** before the LORD. 7193
14:51 and sprinkle the house seven **t.** 7193
16:14 of it with his finger seven **t** before 7193
16:19 of the blood on it with his finger seven **t** 7193
23: 4 to proclaim at their **appointed t:** 4595
25: 8 sabbaths of years—seven **t** seven years— 7193
26:18 punish you for your sins **seven** *t* over. AIT
26:21 I will multiply your afflictions **seven** *t* AIT
26:24 afflict you for your sins **seven** *t over.* AIT
26:28 punish you for your sins **seven** *t over.* AIT
Nu 10:10 Also at your **t** *of* rejoicing— 3427
14:22 but who disobeyed me and tested me ten **t—** 7193
19: 4 on his finger and sprinkle it seven **t** toward 7193
22:28 to you to make you beat me these three **t?"** 8079
22:32 "Why have you beaten your donkey these three **t?** 8079
22:33 and turned away from me these three **t.** 8079
24: 1 he did not resort to sorcery as **at other t,** 928+7193+7193
24:10 but you have blessed them these three **t.** 7193
Dt 1:11 increase you a thousand **t** and bless you 7193
16:16 Three **t** a year all your men must appear 7193
Jos 6: 4 march around the city seven **t,** 7193
6:15 and marched around the city seven **t** in 7193
6:15 on that day they circled the city seven **t.** 7193
Ru 4: 7 (Now in **earlier t** in Israel, 7156
1Sa 3:10 calling as at the other **t,** "Samuel! 7193
20:41 and bowed down before Jonathan three **t,** 7193
27: 8 (From **ancient t** these peoples had lived in 6409
2Sa 12: 6 He must pay for that lamb **four** *t over,* AIT
24: 3 multiply the troops a hundred **t** *over,* 7193
1Ki 9:25 Three **t** a year Solomon sacrificed burnt offerings 7193
17:21 on the boy three **t** and cried to the LORD, 7193
18:43 Seven **t** Elijah said, "Go back." 7193
22:16 "How many **t** must I make you swear 7193
2Ki 4:35 The boy sneezed seven **t** and opened his 7193
5:10 "Go, wash yourself seven **t** in the Jordan, 7193
5:14 and dipped himself in the Jordan seven **t,** 7193
13:18 He struck it three **t** and stopped. 7193
13:19 should have struck the ground five or six **t;** 7193
13:19 But now you will defeat it only three **t."** 7193
13:25 Three **t** Jehoash defeated him, 7193
1Ch 4:22 (These records are **from ancient t.)** 6972
9:20 **In earlier t** Phinehas son of Eleazar 4200+7156
12:32 who understood the **t** and knew what Israel 6961
21: 3 multiply his troops a hundred **t** *over.* 7193
2Ch 18:15 "How many **t** must I make you swear 7193
Ezr 4:15 a place of rebellion from ancient **t.** 10317

Ne 4:12 near them came and told us ten **t** *over,* 7193
6: 4 Four **t** they sent me the same message, 7193
10:34 of our God at set **t** each year a contribution 6961
13:31 for contributions of wood at designated **t,** 6961
Est 1:13 with the wise men who understood the **t** 6961
9:31 days of Purim at their **designated t,** 2375
9:31 and their descendants in regard to their **t** 1821
Job 19: 3 Ten **t** now you have reproached me; 7193
24: 1 the Almighty not set **t** for judgment? 6961
27:10 Will he call upon God at all **t?** 6961
33:29 to a man—twice, even **three** *t*— AIT
38:23 which I reserve for **t** *of* trouble, 6961
Ps 9: 9 a stronghold in **t** *of* trouble. 6961
10: 1 Why do you hide yourself in **t** *of* trouble? 6961
12: 6 in a furnace of clay, purified **seven** *t.* AIT
31:15 My **t** are in your hands; 6961
34: 1 I will extol the LORD at all **t;** 6961
37:19 In **t** *of* disaster they will not wither; 6961
41: 1 the LORD delivers him in **t** *of* trouble. 3427
59:16 my refuge in **t** *of* trouble. 3427
60: 3 You have shown your people **desperate t;** 7997
62: 8 Trust in him at all **t,** O people; 6961
79:12 into the laps of our neighbors **seven** *t* AIT
106:43 Many **t** he delivered them, 7193
119:20 with longing for your laws at all **t.** 6961
119:164 **Seven** *t* a day I praise you AIT
Pr 17:17 A friend loves at all **t,** 6961
24:10 If you falter in **t** *of* trouble, 3427
24:16 for though a righteous man falls **seven** *t,* AIT
25:19 a lame foot is reliance on the unfaithful in **t** 3427
Ecc 7:14 When **t** are good, be happy; 3427
7:14 but when **t** are bad, consider: 3427
7:22 many **t** you yourself have cursed others. 7193
9:12 by evil **t** that fall unexpectedly upon them. 6961
Isa 30:26 and the sunlight will be **seven** *t brighter,* AIT
33: 6 He will be the sure foundation for your **t,** 6961
46:10 from **ancient t,** what is still to come. 7710
64: 4 Since **ancient t** no one has heard, 6409
Jer 14: 8 O Hope of Israel, its Savior in **t** *of* distress, 6961
15:11 in **t** *of* disaster and times of distress. 6961
15:11 in times of disaster and **t** *of* distress. 6961
21: 2 perform wonders for us **as in t past** 3869+3972
28: 8 From **early t** the prophets who preceded 6409
46:26 Egypt will be inhabited as *in* **t** past," 3427
Eze 4:10 and eat it **at set t.** 4946+6330+6961+6961
4:11 water and drink it **at set t.** 4946+6330+6961+6961
21:14 Let the sword strike twice, even **three** *t.* AIT
Da 1:20 he found them ten **t** better than all 3338
2:21 He changes **t** and seasons; 10530
3:19 the furnace heated seven **t** hotter than usual 10248
4:16 till seven **t** pass by for him. 10530
4:23 until seven **t** pass by for him.' 10530
4:25 Seven **t** will pass by for you 10530
4:32 Seven **t** will pass by for you 10530
6:10 Three **t** a day he got down on his knees 10232
6:13 He still prays three **t** a day." 10232
7:10 **ten thousand** *t* ten thousand stood AIT
7:25 and try to change the **set t** and the laws. 10232
7:25 for a time, **t** and half a time. 10530
9:25 but in **t** of trouble. 6961
11:14 "In those **t** many will rise against the king 6961
12: 7 "It will be for a time, **t** and half a time. 4595
Am 4: 9 **"Many t** I struck your gardens 8049
5:13 the prudent man keeps quiet in such **t,** 6961
5:13 in such times, for the **t** are evil. 6961
Mic 5: 2 from of old, from ancient **t."** 3427
Na 1: 7 The LORD is good, a refuge in **t** *of* trouble. 3427
Mt 13: 8 **hundred,** sixty or thirty *t* what was sown. *AIT*
13:23 **hundred,** sixty or thirty *t* what was sown." *AIT*
16: 3 but you cannot interpret the signs *of* the **t.** *2789*
18:21 **how many t** shall I forgive my brother *4529*
18:21 Up to **seven t?"** *2232*
18:22 Jesus answered, "I tell you, not **seven t,** *2232*
18:22 not seven times, but **seventy-seven t.** *1574+2231*
19:29 for my sake will receive a **hundred t** as *1671*
26:34 you will disown me **three t."** *5565*
26:75 you will disown me **three t."** *5565*
Mk 4: 8 thirty, sixty, or even a **hundred** *t."* *AIT*
4:20 thirty, sixty or even a **hundred** *t* *AIT*
10:30 will fail to receive a **hundred t** as much *1671*
14:30 you yourself will disown me **three t."** *5565*
14:72 crows twice you will disown me **three t."** *5565*
Lk 8: 8 a **hundred t** more than was sown." *1671*
8:29 Many **t** it had seized him, *5989*
17: 4 If he sins against you **seven t** in a day, *2232*
17: 4 and **seven t** comes back to you and says, *2232*
18:30 to receive **many t as much** in this age and, *4491*
19: 8 I will pay back **four t** the amount." *5486*
21:24 be trampled on by the Gentiles until the **t** *2789*
22:34 you will deny **three t** that you know me." *5565*
22:61 you will disown me **three t."** *5565*
Jn 13:38 you will disown me **three t!** *5565*
Ac 1: 7 to know the **t** or dates the Father has set *5989*
3:19 **t** of refreshing may come from the Lord, *2789*
10:16 This happened **three t,** *5565*
11:10 This happened **three t,** *5565*
15:21 in every city from the earliest **t** and is read *1155*
17:26 and he determined the **t** set for them and *2789*
Ro 1:10 in my prayers **at all t;** *4121*
1:13 that I planned **many t** to come to you *4490*
2Co 9: 8 so that in all things **at all t,** *4121*
11:24 **Five t** I received from the Jews the forty *4294*
11:25 **Three t** I was beaten with rods, *5565*
11:25 **three t** I was shipwrecked, *5565*
12: 8 **Three t** I pleaded with the Lord *5565*
Eph 1:10 the **t** will have reached their fulfillment— *2789*
1Th 5: 1 about **t** and dates we do not need to write *5989*
2Th 3:16 Lord of peace himself give you peace at **all** *t* *AIT*
1Ti 4: 1 that in later **t** some will abandon the faith *2789*
2Ti 3: 1 There will be terrible **t** in the last days. *2789*
Heb 1: 1 through the prophets **at many t** and *4495*
9:26 to suffer **many t** since the creation of *4490*
10:33 **at other t** you stood side by side *1254+4047*
1Pe 1:20 was revealed in these last **t** for your sake. *5989*
Jude 1:18 "In the last **t** there will be scoffers *5989*
Rev 5:11 and ten thousand **t** ten thousand. *NIG*
12:14 for a time, **t** and half a time, *2789*

TIMID (2) [TIMIDITY]
2Co 10: 1 who am **"t"** when face to face with you, *5424*
1Th 5:14 warn those who are idle, encourage the **t,** *3901*

TIMIDITY (1) [TIMID]
2Ti 1: 7 For God did not give us a spirit *of* **t,** *1261*

TIMNA (6)
Ge 36:12 Eliphaz also had a concubine named **T,** 9465
36:22 **T** was Lotan's sister. 9465
36:40 to their clans and regions: **T,** 9465
1Ch 1:36 Gatam and Kenaz; *by* **T:** 9465
1:39 **T** was Lotan's sister. 9465
1:51 The chiefs of Edom were: **T,** Alvah, 9465

TIMNAH (11) [TIMNITE'S]
Ge 38:12 he went up to **T,** 9463
38:13 "Your father-in-law is on his way to **T** 9463
38:14 which is on the road to **T.** 9463
Jos 15:10 down to Beth Shemesh and crossed to **T.** 9463
15:57 Gibeah and **T**—ten towns and their villages. 9463
19:43 Elon, **T,** Ekron, 9463
Jdg 14: 1 Samson went down to **T** and saw there 9463
14: 2 "I have seen a Philistine woman in **T;** 9463
14: 5 to **T** together with his father and mother. 9463
14: 5 As they approached the vineyards of **T,** 9463
2Ch 28:18 as well as Soco, **T** and Gimzo, 9463

TIMNATH HERES (1) [HERES]
Jdg 2: 9 at **T** in the hill country of Ephraim, 9466

TIMNATH SERAH (2) [SERAH]
Jos 19:50 **T** in the hill country of Ephraim. 9467
24:30 at **T** in the hill country of Ephraim, 9467

TIMNITE'S (1) [TIMNAH]
Jdg 15: 6 they were told, "Samson, the **T** son-in-law, 9464

TIMON (1)
Ac 6: 5 also Philip, Procorus, Nicanor, **T,** *5511*

TIMOTHEUS (KJV) See TIMOTHY

TIMOTHY (25)
Ac 16: 1 where a disciple named **T** lived, *5510*
17:14 but Silas and **T** stayed at Berea. *5510*
17:15 then left with instructions for Silas and **T** *5510*
18: 5 When Silas and **T** came from Macedonia, *5510*
19:22 He sent two of his helpers, **T** and Erastus, *5510*
20: 4 Gaius from Derbe, **T** also, *5510*
Ro 16:21 **T,** my fellow worker, sends his greetings *5510*
1Co 4:17 For this reason I am sending to you **T,** *5510*
16:10 If **T** comes, see to it that he has nothing to *5510*
2Co 1: 1 and **T** our brother, To the church of God *5510*
1:19 among you by me and Silas and **T,** *5510*
Php 1: 1 Paul and **T,** servants of Christ Jesus, *5510*
2:19 in the Lord Jesus to send **T** to you soon, *5510*
2:22 But you know that **T** has proved himself, *899*[S]
Col 1: 1 and **T** our brother, *5510*
1Th 1: 1 and **T,** To the church of the Thessalonians *5510*
3: 2 We sent **T,** who is our brother *5510*
3: 6 But **T** has just now come to us from you *5510*
2Th 1: 1 and **T,** To the church of the Thessalonians *5510*
1Ti 1: 2 *To* **T** my true son in the faith: *5510*
1:18 **T,** my son, I give you this instruction *5510*
6:20 **T,** guard what has been entrusted *5510*
2Ti 1: 2 *To* **T,** my dear son: Grace, mercy and peace *5510*
Phm 1: 1 and **T** our brother, *5510*
Heb 13:23 that our brother **T** has been released. *5510*

TIN (4)
Nu 31:22 Gold, silver, bronze, iron, **t,** lead 974
Eze 22:18 all of them are the copper, **t,** 974
22:20 lead and **t** into a furnace to melt it with 974
27:12 iron, **t** and lead for your merchandise. 974

TINDER (1)
Isa 1:31 The mighty man will become **t** and his work 5861

TINGLE (3)
1Sa 3:11 the ears of everyone who hears of it **t.** 7509
2Ki 21:12 the ears of everyone who hears of it *will* **t.** 7509
Jer 19: 3 **make** the ears of everyone who hears of it **t.** 7509

TINKLING (KJV) See CLANGING

TIP (7)
Jdg 6:21 With the **t** *of* the staff that was in his hand, 7895
1Ki 6:24 ten cubits from wing **t** to wing tip. 7896
6:24 ten cubits from wing tip to wing **t.** 7896
Est 5: 2 So Esther approached and touched the **t** *of* 8031
Job 33: 2 words are **on the t** of my **tongue.** 928+2674+4383
38:37 Who *can* **t over** the water jars of the heavens 8886
Lk 16:24 and send Lazarus to dip the **t** of his finger *216*

TIPHSAH (3)
1Ki 4:24 from **T** to Gaza, and had peace on all sides. 9527
2Ki 15:16 attacked **T** and everyone in the city 9527
15:16 He sacked **T** and ripped open all NIH

TIRAS (2)
Ge 10: 2 Madai, Javan, Tubal, Meshech and **T.** 9410
1Ch 1: 5 Madai, Javan, Tubal, Meshech and **T.** 9410

TIRATHITES (1)
1Ch 2:55 the **T,** Shimeathites and Sucathites. 9571

TIRE (2) [TIRED]
Jer 2:24 that pursue her *need* not **t** *themselves;* 3615
2Th 3:13 brothers, never **t of** doing what is right. *1591*

TIRED (8) [TIRE]
Ex 17:12 When Moses' hands grew **t,** 3878
Jdg 16:16 after day until he *was* **t** to death. 7918
2Sa 17:29 "The people have become hungry and **t** 6546
23:10 the Philistines till his hand *grew* **t** and froze 3333
Isa 5:27 Not *one* of them grows **t** or stumbles, 6546
40:28 *He will* not *grow* **t** or weary, 3615
40:30 Even youths *grow* **t** and weary, 3615
Jn 4: 6 and Jesus, **t** as he was from the journey, *3159*

TIRES (KJV) See NECKLACES, TURBANS

TIRHAKAH (2)
2Ki 19: 9 Now Sennacherib received a report that **T,** 9555
Isa 37: 9 Now Sennacherib received a report that **T,** 9555

TIRHANAH (1)
1Ch 2:48 Maacah was the mother of Sheber and **T.** 9563

TIRIA (1)
1Ch 4:16 Ziph, Ziphah, **T** and Asarel. 9409

TIRSHATHA (KJV) See GOVERNOR

TIRZAH (18)
Nu 26:33 Noah, Hoglah, Milcah and **T.**) 9573
27: 1 Noah, Hoglah, Milcah and **T.** 9573
36:11 Mahlah, **T,** Hoglah, Milcah and Noah— 9573
Jos 12:24 the king of **T** one thirty-one kings in all. 9574
17: 3 Noah, Hoglah, Milcah and **T.** 9573
1Ki 14:17 got up and left and went to **T.** 9573
15:21 stopped building Ramah and withdrew to **T.** 9574
15:33 of Ahijah became king of all Israel in **T,** 9574
16: 6 with his fathers and was buried in **T.** 9574
16: 8 and he reigned in **T** two years. 9574
16: 9 Elah was in **T** at the time, 9574
16: 9 the man in charge of the palace at **T.** 9574
16:15 Zimri reigned in **T** seven days. 9574
16:17 from Gibbethon and laid siege to **T.** 9574
16:23 reigned twelve years, six of them in **T.** 9574
2Ki 15:14 Then Menahem son of Gadi went from **T** 9574
15:16 Menahem, starting out from **T,** attacked 9574
SS 6: 4 You are beautiful, my darling, as **T,** 9574

TISHBE (1) [TISHBITE]
1Ki 17: 1 Now Elijah the Tishbite, from **T** *in* Gilead, 9586

TISHBITE (6) [TISHBE]
1Ki 17: 1 Now Elijah the **T,** from Tishbe in Gilead, 9585
21:17 word of the LORD came to Elijah the **T:** 9585
21:28 word of the LORD came to Elijah the **T:** 9585
2Ki 1: 3 angel of the LORD said to Elijah the **T,** 9585
1: 8 The king said, "That was Elijah the **T."** 9585
9:36 through his servant Elijah the **T:** 9585

TITHE (15) [TEN]
Lev 27:30 " 'A **t** *of* everything from the land, 5130
27:31 If a man redeems any of his **t,** 5130
27:32 The entire **t** *of* the herd and flock— 5130
Nu 18:26 the **t** I give you as your inheritance, 5130
18:26 a tenth of that **t** as the LORD's offering. 5130
Dt 12:17 You must not eat in your own towns the **t** 5130
14:23 Eat the **t** *of* your grain, new wine and oil, 5130
14:24 and cannot carry **your t** (because the place 2257[S]
14:25 then exchange your **t** for silver, NIH
26:12 in the third year, the year of the **t,** 5130
2Ch 31: 5 brought a great amount, a **t** *of* everything. 5130
31: 6 a **t** *of* their herds and flocks and a tithe of 5130
31: 6 a tithe of their herds and flocks and a **t** *of* 5130
Ne 10:37 And we will bring a **t** *of* our crops to 5130
Mal 3:10 Bring the whole **t** into the storehouse, 5130

TITHES (16) [TEN]

Nu 18:21 the t in Israel as their inheritance in return 5130
18:24 to the Levites as their inheritance the t that 5130
18:28 the LORD from all the t you receive from 5130
18:28 From these t you must give the LORD's 5647S
Dt 12: 6 and sacrifices, your t and special gifts, 5130
12:11 and sacrifices, your t and special gifts, 5130
14:28 the t of that year's produce and store it 5130
2Ch 31:12 the contributions, t and dedicated gifts. 5130
Ne 10:37 for it is the Levites who collect *the* t 6923
10:38 the Levites when they receive *the* t, 6923
10:38 a tenth of the t up to the house of our God, 5130
12:44 for the contributions, firstfruits and t 5130
13: 5 and also the t *of* grain, new wine and oil 5130
13:12 All Judah brought the t *of* grain, 5130
Am 4: 4 your t every three years. 5130
Mal 3: 8 'How do we rob you?' "In t and offerings. 5130

TITIUS (1) [JUSTUS]

Ac 18: 7 went next door to the house *of* T Justus, *5517*

TITLE (3)

Isa 45: 4 and bestow *on* you a t of honor, 4033
Eph 1:21 and every t *that can be* given, *3950+3951*
Rev 17: 5 This t was written on her forehead: *3950*

TITTLE (KJV) See SMALLEST STROKE

TITUS (14)

2Co 2:13 because I did not find my brother T there. *5519*
7: 6 comforted us by the coming *of* T, *5519*
7:13 delighted to see how happy T was, *5519*
7:14 so our boasting about you to T has proved *5519*
8: 6 So we urged T, since he had earlier made a *5519*
8:16 into the heart *of* T the same concern I have *5519*
8:17 For T not only welcomed our appeal, *NIG*
8:23 for T, he is my partner and fellow worker *5519*
12:18 I urged T to go to you *5519*
12:18 T did not exploit you, did he? *5519*
Gal 2: 1 I took T along also. *5519*
2: 3 Yet not even T, who was with me, *5519*
2Ti 4:10 and T to Dalmatia. *5519*
Tit 1: 4 *To* T, my true son in our common faith: *5519*

TIZITE (1)

1Ch 11:45 Jediael son of Shimri, his brother Joha the T, 9407

TO (20933) [TOWARD] See Index of Articles Etc.

TO AND FRO (Anglicized) See BACK AND FORTH

TOAH (1)

1Ch 6:34 the son of Eliel, the son of T, 9346

TOB (4)

Jdg 11: 3 and settled in the land of T, 3204
11: 5 to get Jephthah from the land of T. 3204
2Sa 10: 6 and also twelve thousand men from T. 3204
10: 8 men of T and Maacah were by themselves 3204

TOB-ADONIJAH (1)

2Ch 17: 8 Jehonathan, Adonijah, Tobijah and T— 3207

TOBIAH (14) [TOBIAH'S]

Ezr 2:60 T and Nekoda 652 3209
Ne 2:10 When Sanballat the Horonite and T 3209
2:19 T the Ammonite official and Geshem 3209
4: 3 T the Ammonite, who was at his side, said, 3209
4: 7 But when Sanballat, T, the Arabs, 3209
6: 1 When word came to Sanballat, T, 3209
6:12 because T and Sanballat had hired him. 3209
6:14 Remember T and Sanballat, O my God, 3209
6:17 of Judah were sending many letters to T, 3209
6:17 and replies from T kept coming to them. 3209
6:19 And T sent letters to intimidate me. 3209
7:62 T and Nekoda 642 3209
13: 4 He was closely associated with T, 3209
13: 7 in providing T a room in the courts of 3209

TOBIAH'S (1) [TOBIAH]

Ne 13: 8 and threw all T household goods out of 3209

TOBIJAH (3)

2Ch 17: 8 Adonijah, T and Tob-Adonijah— 3210
Zec 6:10 from the exiles Heldai, T and Jedaiah, 3209
6:14 The crown will be given to Heldai, T, 3209

TOCHEN (KJV) See TOKEN

TODAY (212) [TODAY'S]

Ge 4:14 T you are driving me from the land, 2021+3427
19:37 he is the father of the Moabites of t. 2021+3427
19:38 he is the father of the Ammonites of t. 2021+3427
21:26 and I heard about it only t." 2021+3427
24:12 give me success t, 2021+3427
24:42 "When I came to the spring t, I said, 2021+3427
30:32 go through all your flocks t and 2021+3427
31:43 what can I do t about these daughters 2021+3427
31:48 a witness between you and me t." 2021+3427
40: 7 "Why are your faces so sad t?" 2021+3427
41: 9 T I am reminded of my shortcomings. 2021+3427
47:23 that I have bought you and your land t 2021+3427
47:26 still in force t— 2021+2021+2296+3427
Ex 2:18 "Why have you returned so early t?" 2021+3427
5:14 you quota of bricks yesterday or t, 2021+3427
13: 4 T, in the month of Abib, 2021+3427
14:13 deliverance the LORD will bring you t. 2021+3427
14:13 The Egyptians you see t you will never see again. 2021+3427
16:25 "Eat it t," Moses said, 2021+3427
16:25 "because t is a Sabbath to the LORD. 2021+3427
16:25 You will not find any of it on the ground t. 2021+3427
19:10 to the people and consecrate them t 2021+3427
32:29 You have been set apart to the LORD t, 2021+3427
34:11 Obey what I command you t. 2021+3427
Lev 8:34 What has been done t was commanded by the LORD 2021+2021+2296+3427
9: 4 For t the LORD will appear to you.' " 2021+3427
10:19 "T they sacrificed their sin offering 2021+3427
10:19 if I had eaten the sin offering t?" 2021+3427
Dt 1:10 so that t you are as many as the stars in 2021+3427
2:18 "T you are to pass by the region of Moab 2021+3427
4: 4 to the LORD your God are still alive t. 2021+3427
4: 8 of laws I am setting before you t? 2021+3427
4:38 your inheritance, as it is t. 2021+2021+2296+3427
4:40 commands, which I am giving you t, 2021+3427
5: 1 and laws I declare in your hearing t. 2021+3427
5: 3 with all of us who are alive here t. 2021+3427
5:24 T we have seen that a man can live even if God speaks 2021+2021+2296+3427
6: 6 I give you t are to be upon your hearts. 2021+3427
6:24 kept alive, as is the case t. 2021+2021+2296+3427
7:11 decrees and laws I give you t. 2021+3427
8: 1 every command I am giving you t, 2021+3427
8:18 he swore to your forefathers, as it is t. 2021+2021+2296+3427
8:19 I testify against you t that you will 2021+3427
9: 3 be assured t that the LORD your God is 2021+3427
10: 8 as they still do t. 2021+2021+2296+3427
10:13 I am giving you t for your own good? 2021+3427
10:15 above all the nations, as it is t. 2021+2021+2296+3427
11: 2 Remember t that your children were not the ones who saw 2021+3427
11: 8 the commands I am giving you t, 2021+3427
11:13 the commands I am giving you t— 2021+3427
11:26 I am setting before you t a blessing 2021+3427
11:27 that I am giving you t; 2021+3427
11:28 from the way that I command you t 2021+3427
11:32 and laws I am setting before you t. 2021+3427
12: 8 You are not to do as we do here t, 2021+3427
13:18 that I am giving you t 2021+3427
15: 5 to follow all these commands I am giving you t. 2021+3427
15:15 I give you this command t. 2021+3427
19: 9 you carefully follow all these laws I command you t— 2021+3427
20: 3 O Israel, t you are going into battle 2021+3427
26: 3 "I declare t to the LORD your God 2021+3427
27: 1 commands that I give you t. 2021+3427
27: 4 as I command you t, 2021+3427
27:10 and decrees that I give you t." 2021+3427
28: 1 follow all his commands I give you t, 2021+3427
28:14 any of the commands I give you t, 2021+3427
28:15 and decrees I am giving you t, 2021+3427
29:10 you are standing t in the presence of 2021+3427
29:15 who are standing here with us t in 2021+3427
29:15 but also with those who are not here t. 2021+3427
29:18 among you t whose heart turns away 2021+3427
30: 2 to everything I command you t, 2021+3427
30: 8 follow all his commands I am giving you t. 2021+3427
30:11 Now what I am commanding you t is 2021+3427
30:15 I set before you t life and prosperity, 2021+3427
30:16 For I command you t to love the LORD 2021+3427
Jos 3: 7 "T I will begin to exalt you in the eyes of all Israel, 2021+2021+2296+3427
5: 9 "T I have rolled away the reproach 2021+3427
7:25 The LORD will bring trouble on you t." 2021+2021+2296+3427
14:10 So here I am t, eighty-five years old! 2021+3427
14:11 strong t as the day Moses sent me out; 2021+3427
22:18 " 'If you rebel against the LORD t, 2021+3427
22:29 and turn away from him t by building 2021+3427
22:31 "T we know that the LORD is with us, 2021+3427
Jdg 9:18 (but t you have revolted against my 2021+3427
9:19 in good faith toward Jerub-Baal and his family t, 2021+2021+2296+3427
12: 3 why have you come up t to fight me?" 2021+2021+2296+3427
21: 3 one tribe be missing from Israel t?" 2021+3427
21: 6 "T one tribe is cut off from Israel," 2021+3427
Ru 2:19 "Where did you glean t? 2021+3427
2:19 of the man I worked with t is Boaz," 2021+3427
3:18 not rest until the matter is settled t." 2021+3427
4: 9 "T you are witnesses that I have bought from Naomi 2021+3427
4:10 T you are witnesses!" 2021+3427
1Sa 4: 3 the LORD bring defeat upon us t before 2021+3427
1Sa 9: 9 prophet of t used to be called a seer.) 2021+3427
9:12 he has just come to our town t, 2021+3427
9:19 for t you are to eat with me, 2021+3427
10: 2 When you leave me t, 2021+3427
11:13 Saul said, "No one shall be put to death t, 2021+2021+2296+3427
14:28 'Cursed be any man who eats food t!' 2021+3427
14:30 if the men had eaten t some of 2021+3427
14:38 let us find out what sin has been committed t. 2021+3427
14:45 for he did this t with God's help.". 2021+2021+2296+3427
15:28 torn the kingdom of Israel from you t 2021+3427
17:46 T I will give the carcasses 2021+2021+2296+3427
20:27 either yesterday or t?" 2021+3427
21: 5 How much more so t!" 2021+3427
22: 8 to lie in wait for me, as he does t." 2021+2021+2296+3427
22:13 and lies in wait for me, as he does t?" 2021+2021+2296+3427
24:19 for the way you treated me t. 2021+2021+2296+3427
25:32 who has sent you t to meet me. 2021+2021+2296+3427
26: 8 "T God has delivered your enemy 2021+3427
26:21 Because you considered my life precious t, 2021+2021+2296+3427
26:23 delivered you into my hands t, 2021+3427
26:24 as I valued your life t, 2021+2021+2296+3427
27:10 "Where did you go raiding t?" 2021+3427
28:18 the LORD has done this to you t. 2021+2021+2296+3427
2Sa 3:39 And t, though I am the anointed king, 2021+3427
6:20 "How the king of Israel has distinguished himself t, 2021+3427
14:22 "T your servant knows that 2021+3427
15:20 t shall I make you wander about 2021+3427
16: 3 'T the house of Israel will give me 2021+3427
16:12 repay me with good for the cursing I am receiving t." 2021+2021+2296+3427
18:20 "You are not the one to take the news t," 2021+2021+2296+3427
18:20 but you must not do so t, 2021+2021+2296+3427
18:31 The LORD has delivered you t 2021+3427
19: 5 "T you have humiliated all your men, 2021+3427
19: 6 You have made it clear t that 2021+3427
19: 6 be pleased if Absalom were alive t 2021+3427
19:20 but t I have come here as the first of 2021+3427
19:22 anyone be put to death in Israel t? 2021+3427
19:22 not know that t I am king over Israel?" 2021+3427
1Ki 1:25 T he has gone down and sacrificed 2021+3427
1:30 I will surely carry out t what I swore to you 2021+2021+2296+3427
1:48 to see a successor on my throne t.' " 2021+3427
1:51 to me t that he will not put his servant 2021+3427
2:24 Adonijah shall be put to death t!" 2021+3427
5: 7 "Praise be to the LORD t, 2021+3427
8: 8 and they are still there t. 2021+2021+2296+3427
8:24 fulfilled it—as it is t. 2021+2021+2296+3427
12: 7 "If t you will be a servant to these people 2021+3427
18:15 I will surely present myself to Ahab t. 2021+3427
18:36 let it be known t that you are God in Israel 2021+3427
20:13 I will give it into your hand t, 2021+3427
2Ki 2: 3 to take your master from you t?" 2021+3427
2: 5 to take your master from you t?" 2021+3427
4:23 "Why go to him t?" 2021+3427
6:28 Give up your son so we may eat him t, 2021+3427
6:31 of Shaphat remains on his shoulders t! 2021+3427
1Ch 29: 5 who is willing to consecrate himself t 2021+3427
2Ch 5: 9 and they are still there t. 2021+2021+2296+3427
6:15 fulfilled it—as it is t. 2021+2021+2296+3427
Ezr 9: 7 foreign kings, as it is t. 2021+2021+2296+3427
Ne 1:11 Give your servant success t 2021+3427
9:32 the days of the kings of Assyria until t. 2021+2021+2296+3427
9:36 "But see, we are slaves t, 2021+3427
Est 5: 4 come t to a banquet I have prepared 2021+3427
Job 23: 2 "Even t my complaint is bitter; 2021+3427
Ps 2: 7 t I have become your Father. 2021+3427
95: 7 T, if you hear his voice, 2021+3427
Pr 7:14 t I fulfilled my vows. 2021+3427
22:19 I teach you t, even you. 2021+3427
Isa 38:19 they praise you, as I am doing t; 2021+3427
48: 7 you have not heard of them before t. 3427
56:12 And tomorrow will be like t, 2296+3427
58: 4 as you do t and expect your voice to 2021+3427
Jer 1:10 t I appoint you over nations and kingdoms 2021+2021+2296+3427
1:18 T I have made you a fortified city, 2021+3427
11: 5 the land you possess t." 2021+2021+2296+3427
11: 7 up from Egypt until t, 2021+2021+2296+3427
25:18 and cursing, as they are t; 2021+2021+2296+3427
40: 4 But t I am freeing you from the chains 2021+3427
42:19 Be sure of this: I warn you t 2021+3427
42:21 I have told you t, but you still have 2021+3427
44: 2 T they lie deserted and in ruins 2021+2021+2296+3427
44: 6 desolate ruins they are t. 2021+2021+2296+3427
44:22 a desolate waste without inhabitants, as it is t. 2021+2021+2296+3427
Mt 6:11 Give us t our daily bread. *4958*
6:30 which is here t and tomorrow is thrown *4958*
16: 3 'T it will be stormy, *4958*
21:28 'Son, go and work t in the vineyard.' *4958*
27:19 for I have suffered a great deal t in a dream *4958*

Mk 14:30 "I tell you the truth," Jesus answered, "**t**— *4958*
Lk 2:11 **T** in the town of David a Savior has been *4958*
4:21 **T** this scripture is fulfilled in your hearing." *4958*
5:26 "We have seen remarkable things **t**." *4958*
12:28 the grass of the field, which is here **t**, *4958*
13:32 'I will drive out demons and heal people **t** *4958*
13:33 I must keep going **t** and tomorrow and *4958*
19: 5 I must stay at your house **t**." *4958*
19: 9 "**T** salvation has come to this house, *4958*
22:34 Peter, before the rooster crows **t**, *4958*
22:61 "Before the rooster crows **t**, *4958*
23:43 **t** you will be with me in paradise." *4958*
Ac 4: 9 to account **t** for an act of kindness shown *4958*
13:33 **t** I have become your Father.' *4958*
20:26 I declare to you **t** that I am innocent of the blood *1877+2465+3836+4958*
22: 3 as zealous for God as any of you are **t**. *4958*
24:21 of the dead that I am on trial before you **t**.' " *4958*
26: 2 to stand before you **t** as I make my defense *4958*
26: 6 that I am on trial **t**. *NIG*
26:29 listening to me **t** may become what I am, *4958*
Heb 1: 5 **t** I have become your Father"? *4958*
3: 7 So, as the Holy Spirit says: "**T**, if you hear *4958*
3:13 as long as it is called **T**, *4958*
3:15 As has just been said: "**T**, if you hear *4958*
4: 7 God again set a certain day, calling it **T**, *4958*
4: 7 "**T**, if you hear his voice, *4958*
5: 5 **t** I have become your Father." *4958*
13: 8 Jesus Christ is the same yesterday and **t** *4958*
Jas 4:13 "**T** or tomorrow we will go to this or *4958*

TODAY'S (1) [TODAY]

Ac 19:40 with rioting because *of* **t** events. *4958*

TOE (5) [TOES]

Lev 8:23 the thumb of his right hand and on the **big t** 991
14:14 the thumb of his right hand and on the **big t** 991
14:17 the thumb of his right hand and on the **big t** 991
14:25 the thumb of his right hand and on the **big t** 991
14:28 the thumb of his right hand and on the **big t** 991

TOES (8) [TOE]

Ex 29:20 and on the **big t** *of* their right feet. 991
Lev 8:24 of their right hands and on the **big t** 991
Jdg 1: 6 and cut off his thumbs and **big t**. 8079
1: 7 and **big t** cut off have picked up scraps 8079
2Sa 21:20 on each hand and six **t** on each foot— 720
1Ch 20: 6 on each hand and six **t** on each foot— NIH
Da 2:41 and **t** were partly of baked clay and partly 10064
2:42 As the **t** were partly iron and partly 10064+10655

TOGARMAH (2) [BETH TOGARMAH]

Ge 10: 3 Ashkenaz, Riphath and **T**. 9328
1Ch 1: 6 Ashkenaz, Riphath and **T**. 9328

TOGETHER (390) [ALTOGETHER]

Ge 3: 7 so *they* **sewed** fig leaves **t** 9529
7:13 **t with** his wife and the wives 2256
8:18 **t with** his sons and his wife 2256
11:31 and **t** they set out from Ur of the Chaldeans 907
13: 6 not support them while they stayed **t**, 3481
13: 6 so great that they were not able to stay **t**. 3481
14:16 **t with** the women and the other 1685+2256
22: 6 As the two of them went on **t**, 3481
22: 8 And the two of them went on **t**. 3481
22:19 and they set off **t** for Beersheba. 3481
29:22 So Laban **brought t** all the people of 665
36: 7 too great for them to remain **t**; 3481
50:14 Joseph returned to Egypt, **t with** his 2256
Ex 4:29 Moses and Aaron **brought t** all the elders 665
18: 5 **t with** Moses' sons and wife, 2256
19: 8 The people all responded **t**, 3481
26: 3 Join five of the curtains **t**, 295+448+851
26: 6 use them to fasten the curtains **t** so 295+448+851
26: 9 **Join** five of the curtains **t** 2489
26:11 in the loops *to* **fasten** the tent **t** as a unit. 2489
36:10 They joined five of the curtains **t** 285+285+448
36:13 to fasten the two sets of curtains **t** 285+285+448
36:18 to **fasten** the tent **t** as a unit. 2489
Lev 2: 2 **t with** all the incense, 6584
2:16 **t with** all the incense, 6584
6:15 **t with** all the incense on the grain offering, 2256
7:30 he is to bring the fat, **t with** the breast, 6584
9: 4 **t with** a grain offering mixed with oil. 2256
14: 6 **t with** the cedar wood, 2256
14:20 **t with** the grain offering, 2256
14:21 **t with** a tenth of an ephah 2256
14:24 **t with** the log of oil, 2256
14:31 **t with** the grain offering. 6584
23:13 **t with** its grain offering of two-tenths of 2256
23:18 **t with** their grain offerings 2256
23:20 **t with** the bread of the firstfruits. 6584
Nu 1:18 **called** the whole community **t** 7735
4: 9 **t with** its lamps, 2256
6:15 **t with** their grain offerings 2256
6:17 **t with** its grain offering and drink offering. 2256
6:20 the priest, **t with** the breast that was waved 6584
7:87 **t with** their grain offering. 2256
9:11 **t with** unleavened bread and bitter herbs. 6584
10: 2 use them for **calling** the community **t** 5246
11:24 *He* **brought t** seventy of their elders 665
14:35 which *has* **banded t** against me. 3585
16:11 and all your followers *have* **banded t**. 3585
20: 8 your brother Aaron **gather** the assembly **t**. 7735
Nu 20:10 He and Aaron **gathered** the assembly **t** 7735
21:16 "**Gather** the people **t** and 665
21:35 **t with** his sons and his whole army, 2256
24:10 *He* **struck** his hands **t** and said to him, 6215
27: 3 who **banded t** against the LORD, 3585
28: 5 **t with** a grain offering of a tenth of 2256
28: 9 **t with** its drink offering and a grain offering 2256
28:31 Prepare these **t with** their drink offerings, 2256
35: 7 forty-eight towns, **t with** their pasturelands. 2256
Dt 2:33 **t with** his sons and his whole army. 2256
3:12 hill country of Gilead, **t with** its towns. 2256
22:10 not plow with an ox and a donkey yoked **t**. 3481
22:11 clothes of wool and linen woven **t**. 3481
25: 5 If brothers are living **t** and one 3481
29:11 **t** with your children and your wives, NIH
Jos 4: 4 So Joshua **called t** the twelve men 7924
7:24 Then Joshua, **t with** all Israel, 6640
9: 2 *they* **came t** to make war against Joshua and Israel. 3481+7695
10:37 put it to the sword, **t with** its king, 2256
10:40 the mountain slopes, **t with** all their kings. 2256
11: 5 and made camp **t** at the Waters of Merom, 3481
15:46 vicinity of Ashdod, **t with** their villages; 2256
17:11 **t with** their surrounding settlements 2256
21:16 **t with** their pasturelands—nine towns 2256
21:18 **t with** their pasturelands—four towns. 2256
21:19 were thirteen, **t with** their pasturelands. 2256
21:22 **t with** their pasturelands—four towns. 2256
21:24 **t with** their pasturelands—four towns. 2256
21:25 **t with** their pasturelands—two towns. 2256
21:27 **t with** their pasturelands—two towns; 2256
21:29 **t with** their pasturelands—four towns; 2256
21:31 **t with** their pasturelands—four towns; 2256
21:32 **t with** their pasturelands—three towns. 2256
21:33 were thirteen, **t with** their pasturelands. 2256
21:35 **t with** their pasturelands—four towns; 2256
21:37 **t with** their pasturelands—four towns; 2256
21:39 **t with** their pasturelands—four towns in all. 2256
21:41 forty-eight in all, **t with** their pasturelands. 2256
Jdg 4:13 Sisera **gathered t** his nine hundred iron chariots 2410
6:16 strike down **all** the Midianites **t**." 285+408+3869
12: 4 Jephthah then **called t** the men of Gilead 7695
13:19 **t with** the grain offering, 2256
14: 5 to Timnah **t with** his father and mother. 2256
15: 5 **t with** the vineyards and olive groves. 2256+6330
16: 3 **t with** the two posts, and tore them loose, 2256
18:22 near Micah **were called t** and overtook 2410
19: 6 two of them sat down to eat and drink **t**. 3481
19: 8 So the two of them ate **t**. NIH
20:11 So all the men of Israel **got t** and united 665
20:14 From their towns they **came t** at Gibeah 665
Ru 1: 1 **t with** his wife and two sons, 2256
4:11 who **t** built up the house of Israel. 9109
1Sa 5: 8 So *they* **called t** all the rulers of 665+2256+8938
5:11 So *they* **called t** all the rulers of 665+2256+8938
6:15 **t with** the chest containing the gold objects, 2256
8: 4 of Israel **gathered t** and came to Samuel 7695
9:26 he and Samuel went outside **t**. 9109
11:11 so that no two of them were left **t**. 3480
14:32 and ate them, **t with** the blood. 6584
20:11 So they went there **t**. 9109
20:41 Then they kissed each other and wept **t**— 408+907+2084+8276
31: 6 and his armor-bearer and all his men died **t** 3481
2Sa 2:12 **t with** the men of Ish-Bosheth son of Saul, 2256
2:16 and they fell down **t**. 3481
6: 1 David again **brought t** out of Israel 665
19:41 across the Jordan, **t** with all his men?" 6640
20:14 *who* **gathered t** and followed him. 7735
21: 8 **t with** the five sons of Saul's daughter 2256
21: 9 All seven of them fell **t**; 3480
23:11 the Philistines **banded t** at 665+2021+2653+4200
1Ki 8: 2 the men of Israel **came t** to King Solomon 7735
22: 6 the king of Israel **brought t** the prophets— 7695
2Ki 2:11 As *they were* **walking along** and talking *t*, AIT
3:10 the LORD **called** us three kings **t** 7924
3:13 the LORD who **called** us three kings **t** 7924
9: 5 he found the army officers sitting **t**. NIH
9:25 Remember how you and I were riding **t** 7538
10:18 Jehu **brought** all the people **t** 7695
11:19 *t they* **brought** the king **down** AIT
23: 1 the king **called t** all the elders of Judah 665+2256+8938
25:26 **t with** the army officers, 2256
1Ch 6:33 the men who served, **t with** their sons. 2256
6:59 Beth Shemesh, **t with** their pasturelands. 2256
6:60 and Anathoth, **t with** their pasturelands. 2256
6:69 Gath Rimmon, **t with** their pasturelands. 2256
6:70 and Bileam, **t with** their pasturelands, 2256
6:71 also Ashtaroth, **t with** their pasturelands; 2256
6:73 and Anem, **t with** their pasturelands; 2256
6:75 and Rehob, **t with** their pasturelands; 2256
6:76 and Kiriathaim, **t with** their pasturelands. 2256
6:77 and Tabor, **t with** their pasturelands; 2256
6:79 and Mephaath, **t with** their pasturelands; 2256
6:81 and Jazer, **t with** their pasturelands. 2256
7:29 Megiddo and Dor, **t with** their villages. 2256
10: 6 and all his house died **t**. 3481
11: 1 All Israel **came t** to David at Hebron 7695
11:10 they, **t with** all Israel, 6640
12:34 1,000 officers, **t with** 37,000 men 6640
15: 4 He **called t** the descendants of Aaron 665
23: 2 *He* also **gathered t** all the leaders of Israel, 665
25: 1 David, **t with** the commanders of the army, 2256
28: 1 **t with** the palace officials, 6640
29:21 **t with** their drink offerings, 2256
1Ch 29:30 **t with** the details of his reign and power, 6640
2Ch 3:15 which [**t**] were thirty-five cubits long, NIH
5: 3 And all the men of Israel **came t** to the king 7735
18: 5 the king of Israel **brought t** the prophets— 7695
20: 4 The people of Judah **came t** to seek help 7695
21:17 **t with** his sons and wives. 1685+2256
24: 5 *He* **called t** the priests and Levites 7695
25: 5 Amaziah **called** the people of Judah **t** 7695
25:24 **t with** the palace treasures and the hostages, 2256
28:24 Ahaz **gathered t** the furnishings from 665
29:20 Hezekiah **gathered** the city officials **t** 665
29:35 **t with** the fat of the fellowship offerings 928
34:29 the king **called t** all the elders of Judah 665+2256+8938
36:10 **t with** articles of value from the temple of 6640
Ezr 3: 9 **joined t** in supervising those 285+3869+6641
4: 9 **t with** the rest of their associates— 10221
6:21 **t with** all who had separated themselves 2256
7:16 **t with** all the silver and gold 10221
7:17 **t with** their grain offerings 10221
8:19 **t with** Jeshaiah from the descendants 907
8:24 of the leading priests, **t with** Sherebiah, 4200
Ne 4: 8 They all plotted **t** to come and fight 3481
5: 7 So *I* **called t** a large meeting to deal 5989
6: 2 "Come, let us meet **t** in one of the villages 3481
6: 7 so come, let us confer **t**." 3481
9: 1 the Israelites **gathered t**, fasting and 665
10:28 of the Law of God, **t** with their wives NIH
12: 8 Mattaniah, who, **t with** his associates, 2256
12:28 The singers also **were brought t** from 665
12:38 **t with** half the people— 2256
12:40 so did I, **t with** half the officials, 6640
13:11 Then *I* **called** them **t** and stationed them 7695
13:15 **t with** wine, grapes, figs and all other 677+2256
Est 4:16 **gather t** all the Jews who are in Susa, 4043
5: 4 replied Esther, "let the king, **t with** Haman, 2256
5:10 **Calling t** his friends and Zeresh, 995+2256+8938
9:15 in Susa **came t** on the fourteenth day of 7735
10: 2 **t with** a full account of the greatness 2256
Job 2:11 from their homes and met **t** by agreement 3481
10:11 and **knit** me **t** with bones and sinews? 6115
16:10 strike my cheek in scorn and unite **t** against 3480
17:16 Will we descend **t** into the dust?" 3480
34: 4 let us learn **t** what is good. 1068
34:15 all mankind would perish **t** 3480
38: 7 while the morning stars sang **t** and all 3480
38:38 and the clods of earth **stick t**? 1815
40:13 Bury them all in the dust **t**; 3480
41:15 of shields tightly **sealed t**; 2597+6037
41:17 *they* **cling t** and cannot be parted. 4334
Ps 2: 2 the rulers gather **t** against the LORD and 3480
14: 3 they have **t** become corrupt; 3481
34: 3 let us exalt his name **t**. 3481
41: 7 All my enemies whisper **t** against me; 3480
48: 4 when they advanced **t**, 3481
53: 3 they have **t** become corrupt; 3481
62: 9 **t** they are only a breath. 3480
71:10 those who wait to kill me conspire **t**. 3481
83: 5 With one mind they plot **t**; 3481
85:10 Love and faithfulness **meet t**; 7008
94:21 *They* **band t** against the righteous 1518
98: 8 let the mountains sing **t** for joy; 3480
119:23 Though rulers **sit** *t* and slander me, AIT
122: 3 like a city that is closely compacted **t**. 3481
133: 1 when brothers live **t in unity**! 3480
139:13 *you* **knit** me **t** in my mother's womb. 6115
139:15 *I* **was woven t** in the depths of the earth, 8387
Pr 8:12 "I, wisdom, **dwell** *t with* prudence; AIT
30:27 yet they advance **t** in ranks; 3972
Ecc 4:11 if two **lie down** *t*, they will keep warm. AIT
Isa 1:18 "Come now, *let us* **reason t**," 3519
1:31 both will burn **t**, with no one to quench 3481
9:21 **t** they will turn against Judah. 3481
11: 6 the calf and the lion and the yearling **t**; 3481
11: 7 their young will lie down **t**, 3481
11:14 **t** they will plunder the people to the east. 3481
13: 4 like nations **massing t**! 665
16: 7 they wail **t** for Moab. 3972
19:23 Egyptians **and** Assyrians will worship **t**. 907
22: 3 All your leaders have fled **t**; 3480
22: 3 you who were caught were taken prisoner **t**, 3481
24:22 *They will* **be herded t** like prisoners 665+669
31: 3 both will perish **t**. 3481
31: 4 band of shepherds **is called t** against him, 7924
34:16 and his Spirit *will* **gather** them **t**. 7695
40: 5 and all mankind **t** will see it. 3481
41: 1 let us meet **t** at the place of judgment. 3481
41:19 the fir and the cypress **t**, 3481
43: 9 All the nations gather **t** and 3481
43:17 the army and reinforcements **t**, 3481
43:26 let us argue the matter **t**; 3480
44:11 *Let* them all **come t** and take their stand; 7695
45:16 they will go off into disgrace **t**. 3481
45:20 "**Gather t** and come; 7695
45:21 let them take counsel **t**. 3481
46: 2 They stoop and bow down **t**; 3481
48:13 when I summon them, they all stand up **t**. 3481
48:14 "**Come t**, all of you, and listen: 7695
52: 8 **t** they shout for joy. 3481
52: 9 Burst into songs of joy **t**, 3481
60:13 the pine, the fir and the cypress **t**, 3481
65:25 The wolf and the lamb will feed **t**, 285+3869
66:17 they will meet their end **t**," 3481
Jer 3:18 and **t** they will come from a northern land 3481
4: 5 Cry aloud and say: '**Gather t**! 665
6:11 and on the young men gathered **t**; 3481
6:12 **t with** their fields and their wives, 3481

Jer 8:14 "Why are we sitting here? **Gather t!** 665
17: 3 t with your high places, NIH
31:24 People will live t in Judah 3481
41: 1 While they were eating t there, 3481
42: 8 So *he* **called** t Johanan son of Kareah 7924
46:12 both will fall down t." 3481
46:21 They too will turn and flee t, 3481
48: 7 **t with** his priests and officials. 3481
49: 3 t with his priests and officials. NIH
50: 4 of Israel and the people of Judah t will go 3481
La 1:14 by his hands *they were* **woven t.** 8571
2: 8 t they wasted away. 3481
2:21 and old **lie** *t* in the dust of the streets; AIT
Eze 6:11 **Strike** your hands t and stamp your feet 5782
21:14 prophesy and strike your **hands t.** 448+4090+4090
21:17 I too will strike my **hands t,** 448+4090+4090
22:13 " '*I will* surely **strike** my hands t at 5782
33:30 your countrymen *are* **talking t** about you 1819
37: 7 a rattling sound, and the bones **came t,** 7928
37:17 Join them t into one stick so 285+285+448
39:17 'Assemble and come t from all around to 665
Da 5: 6 was so frightened that his knees knocked **t** 10154+10154+10378
11: 6 **t with** her royal escort and her father and 2256
Hos 7:12 I hear them **flocking t,** I will catch them. 6337
7:14 *They* **gather t** for grain and new wine 1591
8:10 *I will* now **gather them t.** 7695
Joel 2:16 **bring** t the elders, gather the children, 7695
Am 1:15 he and his officials **t,**" says the LORD. 3481
3: 3 Do two walk t unless they have agreed 3481
Mic 2:12 *I will* **surely bring** t the remnant 7695+7695
2:12 I will bring them t like sheep in a pen, 3480
7: 3 *they all* **conspire** *t.* AIT
Zep 2: 1 **Gather t,** gather together, O shameful 8006
2: 1 Gather together, **gather t,** O shameful 8006
Zec 7: 2 **t with** their men, to entreat the LORD. 2256
10: 5 **T** they will be like mighty men trampling 3481
Mt 1:18 but before they **came t,** *5302*
2: 4 *When* he *had* **called** t all the people's *5251*
13:30 Let both **grow t** until the harvest. *5277*
17:22 *When* they **came t** in Galilee, *5370*
18:20 two or three **come** t in my name, *1639+5251*
19: 6 Therefore what God *has* **joined t,** *5183*
20:25 Jesus **called** them t and said, *4673*
22:34 the Pharisees **got t.** *5251*
22:41 *While* the Pharisees *were* **gathered t,** *5251*
23:37 have longed to **gather** your children t, *2190*
27:29 then **twisted** t a crown of thorns and set it *4428*
Mk 10: 9 Therefore what God *has* **joined t,** *5183*
10:42 Jesus **called** them t and said, *4673*
10:46 **t with** a large crowd, were leaving the city, *2779*
14:53 elders and teachers of the law **came t.** *5302*
15:16 and **called** t the whole company *5157*
15:17 then **twisted** t a crown of thorns and set it *4428*
Lk 6:38 pressed down, **shaken t** and running over, *4888*
9: 1 When Jesus *had* **called** the Twelve **t,** *5157*
13:34 have longed to **gather** your children **t,** *2190*
15: 6 **calls** his friends and neighbors **t** *5157*
15: 9 **calls** her friends and neighbors **t** *5157*
15:13 the younger son **got** t all he had, *5251*
17:35 Two women will be grinding grain **t;** *899+2093+3836*
20: 1 **t with** the elders, came up to him. *5250*
22:55 of the courtyard and *had* **sat down t,** *5154*
22:66 **met t,** and Jesus was led before them. *5251*
23:13 Pilate **called** t the chief priests, *5157*
24:17 What are you discussing t as you walk *253+4639*
24:33 and those with them, **assembled t** *125*
Jn 4:36 the sower and the reaper may be glad **t.** *3938*
11:52 to **bring** them t and make them one. *5251*
18:20 at the temple, where all the Jews **come t.** *5302*
19: 2 The soldiers **twisted t** a crown of thorns *4428*
20:19 when the disciples were **t,** *3963*
21: 2 and two other disciples were **t.** *3938*
Ac 1: 6 So *when* they **met t,** they asked him, "Lord, *5302*
1:14 They all joined t constantly in prayer, *3924*
2: 1 they were all t in one place. *3938*
2: 6 a crowd **came** t in bewilderment, *5302*
2:44 All the believers were t and had *899+2093+3836*
2:46 Every day they continued to meet t in *3924*
2:46 They broke bread in their homes and ate t *3561*
4:15 the Sanhedrin and then conferred **t.** *253+4639*
4:24 they raised their voices t in prayer to God. *3924*
4:26 rulers gather t against the Lord *899+2093+3836*
4:27 Indeed Herod and Pontius Pilate **met** t with *5251*
5: 1 Ananias, **t with** his wife Sapphira, *5250*
5:12 And all the believers used to meet t *3924*
5:21 *they* **called** t the Sanhedrin— *5157*
6: 2 the Twelve **gathered** all the disciples t *4673*
10:24 and *had* **called** t his relatives *5157*
12:20 *they* now **joined** t and sought an audience *3924*
14: 5 Gentiles and Jews, **t with** their leaders, *5250*
14:27 *they* **gathered** the church t and reported all *5251*
15:30 where *they* **gathered** the church t *5251*
19:19 **brought** their scrolls t and burned them *5237*
19:25 He **called** them **t,** along with the workmen *5255*
20: 7 On the first day of the week we **came t** *5251*
27:17 **passed** ropes **under** the ship itself **to hold** it **t.** *5690*
28:17 Three days later he **called** t the leaders *5157*
Ro 3:12 they have t become worthless; *275*
15:32 **t** with you *be* **refreshed.** *5265*
1Co 1: 2 **t with** all those everywhere who call on *5250*
7: 5 Then **come** t again so that *899+1639+2093+3836*
11:18 I hear that *when* you **come** t as a church, *5302*
11:20 *When* you **come t,** it is not the Lord's Supper *5302*
11:33 then, my brothers, *when you* **come** t to eat, *5302*
1Co 11:34 *you* **meet** t it may not result in judgment. *5302*
14:23 So if the whole church **comes** t and everyone speaks *899+2093+3836+5302*
14:26 When you **come t,** everyone has a hymn, *5302*
2Co 1: 1 **t with** all the saints throughout Achaia: *5250*
6:14 Do not be **yoked** t with unbelievers. *2282*
Eph 1:10 **bring** all things in heaven and on earth **t under one head,** *368*
2:21 the whole building is **joined** t and rises *5274*
2:22 And in him you too *are being* **built t** *5325*
3: 6 the gospel the Gentiles are **heirs t with** *5169*
3: 6 **members t of one body,** and sharers *5362*
3: 6 and **sharers t in** the promise in Christ Jesus. *5212*
3:18 may have power, **t with** all the saints, *5250*
4:16 and **held** t by every supporting ligament, *5204*
Php 1: 1 **t with** the overseers and deacons: *5250*
Col 1:17 and in him all things **hold t.** *5319*
2:19 and **held** t by its ligaments and sinews, *5204*
3:14 **binds** them all t in perfect unity. *1639+5278*
1Th 4:17 and are left will be caught up t with them *275*
5:10 awake or asleep, we may live t with him. *275*
Heb 9:19 he took the blood of calves, **t with** water, *3552*
10:25 Let us not give up **meeting t,** *2191*
11:40 t with us would they be made perfect. *3590+6006*
Jas 2:22 his faith and his actions *were* **working t,** *5300*
1Pe 5:13 She who is in Babylon, **chosen t with** you, *5293*
3Jn 1: 8 so that we *may* **work** t for the truth. *1181+5301*
Rev 8: 4 *t with* **the prayers** of the saints, *AIT*
16:16 Then *they* **gathered** the kings t to the place *5251*
19:17 **gather** t for the great supper of God, *5251*
19:19 and their armies **gathered** t to make war *5251*

TOHU (1)

1Sa 1: 1 the son of Elihu, the son of **T,** 9375

TOIL (14) [TOILED, TOILING, TOILS, TOILSOME]

Ge 3:17 through **painful** t you will eat of it all 6779
5:29 and **painful** t *of* our hands caused by 6779
31:42 But God has seen my hardship and the t 3330
Dt 26: 7 and saw our misery, t and oppression. 6662
Jos 24:13 on which *you did* not t and cities you did 3333
Pr 5:10 and your t enrich another man's house. 6776
Ecc 2:22 a man get for all the t and anxious striving 6662
3: 9 What does the worker gain from his **t?** 6665
3:13 and find satisfaction in all his **t—** 6662
4: 6 with tranquillity than two handfuls with t 6662
4: 8 There was no end to his **t,** 6662
Isa 65:23 not t in vain or bear children doomed 3333
La 5:13 Young men t *at* the millstones; 5951
1Th 2: 9 brothers, our t and hardship; *3160*

TOILED (6) [TOIL]

Job 20:18 **What** he **t for** he must give back uneaten; 3334
Ps 105:44 they fell heir to **what** others had **t for—** 6662
Ecc 2:11 that my hands had done and what *I had* t 6661
2:18 I hated all the things I had **t for** under 6665
Isa 62: 8 the new wine for which *you have* **t;** 3333
2Co 11:27 I have labored and t and have often gone *3677*

TOILING (3) [TOIL]

Ps 127: 2 and stay up late, t for food to eat— 6776
Ecc 4: 8 "For whom am I **t,**" he asked, 6665
2Th 3: 8 and t so that we would not be a burden *3677*

TOILS (2) [TOIL]

Ecc 1: 3 all his labor at which *he* t under the sun? 6661
5:16 since *he* t for the wind? 6661

TOILSOME (3) [TOIL]

Ecc 2:20 to despair over all my t labor under 6662
5:18 and to find satisfaction in his t labor under 6662
9: 9 in life and in your t labor under the sun. 6665

TOKEN (1)

1Ch 4:32 Ain, Rimmon, **T** and Ashan— 9421

TOKHATH (1)

2Ch 34:22 who was the wife of Shallum son of **T,** 9534

TOLA (6) [TOLAITE]

Ge 46:13 **T,** Puah, Jashub and Shimron. 9356
Nu 26:23 through **T,** the Tolaite clan; 9356
Jdg 10: 1 **T** son of Puah, the son of Dodo, 9356
1Ch 7: 1 **T,** Puah, Jashub and Shimron—four in all. 9356
7: 2 The sons of **T:** 9356
7: 2 the descendants of **T** listed as fighting men 9356

TOLAD (1)

1Ch 4:29 Bilhah, Ezem, **T,** 9351

TOLAITE (1) [TOLA]

Nu 26:23 through Tola, the **T** clan; 9358

TOLD (451) [TELL]

Ge 3:11 he said, "Who **t** you that you were naked? 5583
9:22 and **t** his two brothers outside. 5583
12: 4 So Abram left, as the LORD *had* **t** him; 1819
16: 9 Then the angel of the LORD **t** her, 606
Ge 17:23 and circumcised them, as God **t** him. 1819
20: 8 *he* **t** them all that had happened, 265+928+1819
22: 3 for the place God *had* **t** him *about.* 606
22: 9 When they reached the place God *had* **t** him 606
22:20 Some time later Abraham **was t,** 5583
24:28 The girl ran and **t** her mother's household 5583
24:33 until *I have* **t** you what I have to say." 1819
24:66 Then the servant **t** Isaac all he had done. 6218
26:32 That day Isaac's servants came and **t** him 5583
27:19 I have done as *you* **t** me. 1819
27:42 Rebekah **was t** what her older son Esau had said, 5583
29:12 He *had* **t** Rachel that he was a relative 5583
29:12 So she ran and **t** her father. 5583
29:13 and there Jacob **t** him all these things. 6218
31:16 So do whatever God *has* **t** you." 606
31:22 On the third day Laban **was t** 5583
37: 5 and when *he* **t** it to his brothers, 5583
37: 9 and *he* **t** it to his brothers. 6218
37:10 When *he* **t** his father as well as his brothers, 6218
38:13 When Tamar **was t,** "Your father-in-law 5583
38:24 About three months later Judah **was t,** 5583
39: 8 "With me in charge," *he* **t** her, 606
39:17 Then *she* **t** him this story: 1819
39:19 the story his wife **t** him, 1819
40: 9 So the chief cupbearer **t** Joseph his dream. 6218
41: 8 Pharaoh **t** them his dreams, 6218
41:12 *We* **t** him our dreams, 6218
41:24 *I* **t** this to the magicians, 606
41:55 Then Pharaoh **t** all the Egyptians, 606
42:14 Joseph said to them, "It is just as *I* **t** you: 1819
42:29 *they* **t** him all that had happened to them. 5583
43:17 The man did as Joseph **t** him and took 606
43:27 "How is your aged father *you* **t** me *about?* 606
43:29 the one *you* **t** me *about?"* 606
44:23 But *you* **t** your servants, 606
44:24 *we* **t** him what my lord had said. 5583
45:26 *They* **t** him, "Joseph is still alive! 5583
45:27 *they* **t** him everything Joseph had said 1819
47: 1 Joseph went and **t** Pharaoh, 5583
48: 1 Some time later Joseph *was* **t,** 606
48: 2 When Jacob *was* **t,** "Your son Joseph 5583
Ex 1:17 not do what the king of Egypt *had* **t** them 1819
4:23 and *I* **t** you, "Let my son go, 606
4:28 Then Moses **t** Aaron everything 5583
4:30 and Aaron **t** them everything 1819
5:16 yet we *are* **t,** 'Make bricks!' 606
5:19 in trouble *when* they *were* **t,** 606
14: 5 of Egypt **was t** that the people had fled, 5583
16: 9 Then Moses **t** Aaron, "Say to the entire 606
16:17 The Israelites did as they were **t;** NIH
18: 8 Moses **t** his father-in-law *about* everything 6218
19: 9 Then Moses **t** the LORD what the people 5583
19:25 went down to the people and **t** them. 606
24: 3 and **t** the people all the LORD's words 6218
32:24 So *I* **t** them, 'Whoever has any gold 606
34:34 And when he came out and **t** 1819
Lev 21:24 So Moses **t** this to Aaron and his sons and 1819
Nu 4:49 each was assigned his work and **t** what NIH
9: 4 So Moses **t** the Israelites to celebrate 1819
11:24 and **t** the people what the LORD had said. 1819
11:27 A young man ran and **t** Moses, 5583
22: 7 *they* **t** him what Balak had said. 1819
26:65 LORD *had* **t** those Israelites they would 606
29:40 Moses **t** the Israelites all that the LORD 606
Dt 1:18 at that time *I* **t** you everything you were 7422
1:21 the God of your fathers, **t** you. 1819
1:43 So *I* **t** you, but you would not listen. 1819
9:12 Then the LORD **t** me, "Go down from here 606
10: 9 as the LORD your God **t** them.) 1819
17:16 for the LORD *has* **t** you, 606
32:48 On that same day the LORD **t** Moses, 1819
Jos 2: 2 The king of Jericho **was t,** "Look! 606
2:23 to Joshua son of Nun and **t** him everything 6218
3: 5 Joshua **t** the people, "Consecrate yourselves, 606
4: 8 as the LORD *had* **t** Joshua; 1819
7: 2 of Bethel, and **t** them, "Go up and spy out 606
9:24 "Your servants **were clearly t** how 5583+5583
10:17 When Joshua **was t** that the five kings 5583
Jdg 4:12 When *they* **t** Sisera that Barak son 5583
4:20 "Stand in the doorway of the tent," *he* **t** her. 606
6:13 that our fathers us **t** *about* when they said, 6218
6:27 and did as the LORD **t** him. 1819
6:29 *they were* **t,** "Gideon son of Joash did it." 606
7: 5 There the LORD **t** him, 606
7:17 "Watch me," *he* **t** them. 606
8:23 But Gideon **t** them, "I will not rule over you, 606
9: 7 When Jotham *was* **t** *about* this, 5583
13: 6 the woman went to her husband and **t** him, 606
13:13 "Your wife must do all that *I have* **t** her. 606
13:23 all these things or now **t** us this." 9048
14: 6 But *he* **t** neither his father 5583
14:16 but *you* haven't **t** me *the* **answer."** 5583
14:17 So on the seventh day *he* finally **t** her, 5583
15: 6 *they were* **t,** "Samson, the Timnite's 606
16: 2 people of Gaza *were* **t,** "Samson is here!" 606
16:15 a fool of me and haven't **t** me the secret 5583
16:17 So *he* **t** her everything. 5583
16:18 Delilah saw that *he had* **t** her everything, 5583
16:18 *he has* **t** me everything." 5583
18: 2 *They* **t** them, "Go, explore the land." 606
18: 4 *He* **t** them what Micah had done for him, 606
Ru 1:20 "Don't call me Naomi," *she* **t** them. 606
2: 9 *I have* **t** the men not to touch you. 7422
2:11 "I've **been t** all **about** what you have done 5583+5583
2:19 Then Ruth **t** her mother-in-law *about* 5583

Ru 3: 6 and did everything her mother-in-law **t** her 7422
3:16 *she* **t** her everything Boaz had done for her 5583
1Sa 1:23 Elkanah her husband **t** her. 606
3: 9 So Eli **t** Samuel, "Go and lie down, 606
3:13 For *I* **t** him that I would judge his family 5583
3:17 if you hide from me anything *he* **t** you." 1819
3:18 So Samuel **t** him everything, 5583
4:13 the town and **t** what had happened, 5583
4:16 He **t** Eli, "I have just come from 606
8: 7 And the LORD **t** him: "Listen to all that 606
8:10 Samuel **t** all the words of the LORD to 606
9:23 the one *I* **t** you to lay aside." 606
11: 9 *They* **t** the messengers who had come, 606
14:28 Then one of the soldiers **t** him, 6699
14:43 So Jonathan **t** him, "I merely tasted 5583
15:12 but he **was t,** "Saul has gone to Carmel. 5583
17:27 and **t** him, "This is what will be done for 606
18:20 and when *they* **t** Saul *about* it, 5583
18:24 Saul's servants **t** him what David had said, 5583
18:26 When the attendants **t** David these things, 5583
19: 1 Saul **t** his son Jonathan and all 1819
19: 7 So Jonathan called David and **t** him 5583
19:15 the men back to see David and **t** them, 606
19:17 Michal **t** him, "He said to me, 606
19:18 at Ramah and **t** him all that Saul had done 5583
19:21 Saul *was* **t** *about* it, and he sent more men, 5583
21: 2 *I have* **t** them to meet me at a certain place. 3359
22:21 He **t** David that Saul had killed the priests 5583
23: 1 When David *was* **t,** "Look, 5583
23: 7 Saul *was* **t** that David had gone to Keilah, 5583
23:13 When Saul **was t** that David had escaped 5583
23:25 and when David *was* **t** *about* it, 5583
24: 1 from pursuing the Philistines, he *was* **t,** 5583
24:18 now **t** me *of* the good you did to me; 5583
25:14 One of the servants **t** Nabal's wife Abigail: 5583
25:19 Then *she* **t** her servants, "Go on ahead; 606
25:36 So *she* **t** him nothing until daybreak. 5583
25:37 his wife **t** him all these things, 5583
27: 4 Saul **was t** that David had fled to Gath, 5583
28:21 in my hands and did what *you* **t** me to do. 1819
2Sa 2: 4 When David *was* **t** that it was the men 5583
3:23 he *was* **t** that Abner son of Ner had come to 5583
4:10 when a *man* **t** me, 'Saul is dead,' 5583
6:12 Now King David **was t,** "The LORD has 5583
10: 5 When David **was t** *about* this, 5583
10:17 When David **was t** *of* this, he gathered all 5583
11:10 When David *was* **t,** "Uriah did not go home, 5583
11:22 *he* **t** David everything Joab had sent him 5583
11:25 David **t** the messenger, "Say this to Joab: 606
13:34 The watchman went and **t** the king, 5583
14:33 So Joab went to the king and **t** him this. 5583
15:13 A messenger came and **t** David, 606
15:31 Now David *had been* **t,** "Ahithophel 5583
16:11 let him curse, for the LORD *has* **t** him to. 606
17:15 Hushai **t** Zadok and Abiathar, the priests, 606
17:18 But a young man saw them and **t** Absalom. 5583
18: 2 The king **t** the troops, 606
18:10 When one of the men saw this, *he* **t** Joab, 5583
18:11 Joab said to the man who *had* **t** him this, 5583
18:20 to take the news today," Joab **t** him. 606
19: 1 Joab **was t,** "The king is weeping 5583
19: 8 When the men *were* **t,** 5583
21:11 David **was t** what Aiah's daughter Rizpah, 5583
1Ki 1:23 And *they* **t** the king, "Nathan the prophet 5583
1:51 Then Solomon **was t,** "Adonijah is afraid 5583
2:29 King Solomon **was t** that Joab had fled to 5583
2:39 king of Gath, and Shimei *was* **t,** 5583
2:41 When Solomon **was t** that Shimei had gone 5583
5: 5 as the LORD **t** my father David, 1819
10: 7 Indeed, not even half **was t** me; 5583
11: 2 about which the LORD *had* **t** the Israelites, 606
13:11 whose sons came and **t** him all that 6218
13:11 *They* also **t** their father what he had said to 6218
13:17 I have been **t** by the word of the LORD: 1821
13:22 and drank water in the place where *he* **t** you 1819
14: 2 the one *who* **t** me I would be king 1819
14: 5 But the LORD *had* **t** Ahijah, 606
17: 5 So he did what the LORD had **t** him. 1821
17:15 She went away and did as Elijah had **t** her. 1821
18:16 So Obadiah went to meet Ahab and **t** him, 5583
18:43 look toward the sea," *he* **t** his servant, 606
19: 1 Ahab **t** Jezebel everything Elijah had done 5583
20:28 up and **t** the king of Israel, "This is what 606
22:34 The king **t** his chariot driver, 606
2Ki 1: 7 who came to meet you and **t** you this?" 1819
1:16 *He* **t** the king, "This is what the LORD says: 1819
4: 7 She went and **t** the man of God, 5583
4:17 just as Elisha *had* **t** her. 1819
4:19 His father **t** a servant, "Carry him to 606
4:27 from me and *has* not **t** me why." 5583
4:31 went back to meet Elisha and **t** him, 5583
5: 4 Naaman went to his master and **t** him what 5583
5:13 prophet *had* **t** you to do some great thing, 1819
5:14 as the man of God had **t** him, 1821
6:19 Elisha **t** them, "This is not the road 606
7:10 the city gatekeepers and **t** them, "We went 5583
8: 6 asked the woman about it, and *she* **t** him. 6218
8: 7 When the king **was t,** "The man of God 5583
8:14 "*He* **t** me that you would certainly recover." 606
9:12 Jehu said, "Here is what *he* **t** me: 606
9:36 They went back and **t** Jehu, who said, 5583
10: 8 When the messenger arrived, *he* **t** Jehu, 5583
13:18 Elisha **t** him, "Strike the ground." 606
18:25 The LORD *himself* **t** me to march against 606
18:37 **t** him what the field commander had said. 5583
19: 3 *They* **t** him, "This is what Hezekiah says: 606
1Ch 15:16 David **t** the leaders of the Levites 606
19: 5 someone came and **t** David about the men, 5583
19:17 When David **was t** *of* this, 5583
2Ch 9: 6 the greatness of your wisdom **was t** me; 5583
18:33 The king **t** the chariot driver, 606
19: 6 *He* **t** them, "Consider carefully what you do, 606
20: 2 Some men came and **t** Jehoshaphat, 5583
33:16 and **t** Judah to serve the LORD, 606
35:21 God *has* **t** me to hurry; 606
35:23 and he **t** his officers, "Take me away; 606
Ezr 5:15 and *he* **t** him, 'Take these articles and go 10042
8:17 *I* **t** them what to say to Iddo 928+7023+8492
8:22 because *we had* **t** the king, 606
Ne 2:12 *I had* not **t** anyone what my God had put 5583
2:18 *I* also **t** them *about* the gracious hand 5583
4:12 near them came and **t** us ten times over, 606
5: 7 *I* **t** them, "You are exacting usury 606
8: 1 *They* **t** Ezra the scribe to bring out 606
9:15 *you* **t** them to go in and take possession of 606
9:23 the land that *you* **t** their fathers to enter 606
Est 2:20 and nationality just as Mordecai *had* **t** her 7422
2:22 about the plot and **t** Queen Esther, 5583
3: 4 Therefore *they* **t** Haman *about* it 5583
3: 4 for *he had* **t** them he was a Jew. 5583
4: 4 Esther's maids and eunuchs came and **t** her 5583
4: 7 Mordecai **t** him everything 5583
4: 8 and he **t** him to urge her to go into NIH
6:13 and **t** Zeresh his wife and all his friends 6218
8: 1 for Esther *had* **t** how he was related to her. 5583
Job 37:20 *Should* he **be t** that I want to speak? 6218
42: 9 did what the LORD **t** them; 1819
Ps 22:30 future generations *will* **be t** about 6218
44: 1 our fathers *have* **t** us what you did 6218
52: T the Edomite had gone to Saul and **t** him: 5583
78: 3 what our fathers *have* **t** us. 6218
Isa 7: 2 Now the house of David **was t,** 5583
28:22 the LORD Almighty, *has* **t** *me of* 907+4946+9048
36:10 The LORD *himself* **t** me to march against 606
36:22 **t** him what the field commander had said. 5583
37: 3 *They* **t** him, "This is what Hezekiah says: 606
40:21 *Has it* not **been t** you from the beginning? 5583
41:26 Who **t** *of* this from the beginning, 5583
41:26 No *one* **t** *of* this, no one foretold it, 5583
48: 5 Therefore *I* **t** you these things long ago; 5583
52:15 For what they **were** not **t,** they will see, 6218
Jer 4:11 this people and Jerusalem *will* **be t,** 606
13: 5 as the LORD **t** me. 7422
13: 6 "Go now to Perath and get the belt *I* **t** you 7422
23:38 even though *I* **t** you that you must not claim, 606+4200+8938
26:18 *He* **t** all the people of Judah, 606
34: 6 the prophet **t** all this to Zedekiah king 1819
36: 5 Then Jeremiah **t** Baruch, "I am restricted; 7422
36: 8 Jeremiah the prophet **t** him to do; 7422
36:13 Micaiah **t** them everything he had heard 5583
38:27 and *he* **t** them everything the king had 5583
42:19 the LORD *has* **t** you, 'Do not go to Egypt.' 1819
42:21 *I have* **t** you today, but you still have not 5583
45: 1 the prophet **t** Baruch son of Neriah in 1819
Eze 11: 5 came upon me, and *he* **t** me to say: 606
11:25 and *I* **t** the exiles everything 1819
Da 1:10 but the official **t** Daniel, "I am afraid 606
4: 7 I **t** them the dream, 10042
4: 8 Daniel came into my presence and *I* **t** him 10042
7: 5 It *was* **t**, 'Get up and eat your fill of flesh!' 10042
7:16 "So *he* **t** me and gave me the interpretation 10042
Hos 3: 3 Then *I* **t** her, "You are to live with me 606
12:10 gave them many visions and **t parables** 1948
Jnh 1:10 because *he had already* **t** them so.) 5583
Hab 1: 5 would not believe, even if *you* **were t.** 6218
Zec 11:12 *I* **t** them, "If you think it best, 606
13: 3 because *you have* **t** lies in the LORD's name. 1819
Mt 8:22 But Jesus **t** him, "Follow me, 3306
9: 9 "Follow me," *he* **t** him, 3306
12:47 Someone **t** him, "Your mother 3306
13: 3 *he* **t** them many things in parables, saying: 3281
13:24 Jesus **t** them another parable: 3306+4192
13:31 *He* **t** them another parable: 3306+4192
13:33 *He* **t** them still another parable: 3281
14:12 Then *they* went and **t** Jesus. 550
15:35 *He* **t** the crowd to sit down on the ground. 4133
18:31 and went and **t** their master everything 1397
20: 4 *He* **t** them, 'You also go and work 3306
20:31 The crowd rebuked them and **t** them to NIG
22:13 "Then the king **t** the attendants, 3306
22:24 "Moses **t** us that if a man dies without 3306
24:25 See, *I have* **t** you **ahead of time.** 4625
26:13 what *she has done will* also *be* **t,** 3281
26:31 Then Jesus **t** them, "This very night 3306
28: 7 Now *I have* **t** you." 3306
28:16 the mountain where Jesus *had* **t** them to go. 5435
Mk 1:30 and *they* **t** Jesus about her. 3306
2:14 "Follow me," Jesus **t** him, 3306
3: 9 Because of the crowd *he* **t** his disciples 3306
3:32 and *they* **t** him, "Your mother and brothers 3306
4:11 *He* **t** them, "The secret of the kingdom 3306
5:16 Those who had seen it **t** the people 1455
5:16 and **t** about the pigs as well. NIG
5:33 trembling with fear, **t** him the whole truth. 3306
5:36 Jesus **t** the synagogue ruler, 3306
5:43 and **t** them to give her something to eat. 3306
7:27 the children eat all they want," *he* **t** her, 3306
7:29 *he* **t** her, "For such a reply, you may go; 3306
8: 6 *He* **t** the crowd to sit down on the ground. 4133
8: 7 also and **t** the disciples to distribute them. 3306
9:38 in your name and *we* **t** him **to stop,** 3266
10:32 and **t** them what was going to happen 3306
10:48 Many rebuked him and **t** him to be quiet, NIG
11: 6 They answered as Jesus *had* **t** them to, 3306
13:23 **t** you everything **ahead of time.** 4625
14: 9 what she has done *will* also *be* **t,** 3281
14:16 and found things just as Jesus *had* **t** them. 3306
14:27 "You will all fall away," Jesus **t** them, 3306
16: 7 There you will see him, just as *he* **t** you.'" 3306
16:10 She went and **t** those who had been 550
Lk 2:15 which the Lord *has* **t** us **about."** 1192
2:17 the word *concerning* what *had been* **t** them 3281
2:20 which were just as they *had been* **t.** 3281
3:13 "Don't collect any more than you are required to," he **t** them. 3306
5:36 *He* **t** them this parable: 3306
6:39 *He* also **t** them this parable: 3306
7:18 John's disciples **t** him about all these things. 550
8: 4 from town after town, *he* **t** this parable: 3306
8:20 Someone **t** him, "Your mother 550
8:36 Those who had seen it **t** the people how 550
8:39 So the man went away and **t** all over town 3062
8:47 *she* **t** why she had touched him and 550
8:55 Jesus **t** them to give her something to eat. 1411
9: 3 *He* **t** them: "Take nothing for the journey 3306
9:36 **t** no one at that time what they had seen. 550
10: 2 *He* **t** them, "The harvest is plentiful, 3306
10:37 Jesus **t** him, "Go and do likewise." 3306
12:16 And *he* **t** them this parable: 3306
13: 1 at that time *who* **t** Jesus about 550
13: 6 Then *he* **t** this parable: 3306
14: 7 *he* **t** them this parable: 3306
14:23 "Then the master **t** his servant, 3306
15: 3 Then Jesus **t** them this parable: 3306
16: 1 Jesus **t** his disciples: "There was a rich man 3306
16: 6 "The manager **t** him, 'Take your bill, 3306
16: 7 "*He* **t** him, 'Take your bill 3306
17: 9 because he did what *he was* **t to do?** 1411
17:10 you have done everything you *were* **t to do,** 1411
18: 1 Then Jesus **t** his disciples a parable 3306
18: 9 Jesus **t** this parable: 3306
18:31 Jesus took the Twelve aside and **t** them, 3306
18:37 *They* **t** him, "Jesus of Nazareth 550
18:39 the way rebuked him and **t** him to be quiet, NIG
19:32 and found it just as *he had* **t** them. 3306
21:29 *He* **t** them this parable: 3306
22:13 and found things just as Jesus *had* **t** them. 3306
24: 6 Remember how *he* **t** you, 3281
24: 9 *they* **t** all these things to the Eleven and 550
24:10 others with them *who* **t** this to the apostles. 3306
24:23 They came and **t** us that they had seen 3306
24:35 the two **t** what had happened on the way, 2007
24:44 "This is what *I* **t** you while I was still 3281
24:46 *He* **t** them, "This is what is written: 3306
Jn 1:33 who sent me to baptize with water **t** me, 3306
1:45 Philip found Nathanael and **t** him, 3306
1:50 "You believe because *I* **t** you I saw you 3306
2: 8 Then *he* **t** them, "Now draw some out 3306
4:16 *He* **t** her, "Go, call your husband 3306
4:29 see a man who **t** me everything I ever did. 3306
4:39 "*He* **t** me everything I ever did." 3306
4:48 Jesus **t** him, "you will never believe." 3306
5:12 "Who is this fellow who **t** you to pick it up 3306
5:15 The man went away and **t** the Jews 334
6:36 But as *I* **t** you, you have seen me 3306
6:65 "This is why *I* **t** you that no one can come 3306
7: 6 Therefore Jesus **t** them, "The right time 3306
8:24 *I* **t** you that you would die in your sins; 3306
8:40 a man who *has* **t** you the truth that I heard 3281
9: 7 *he* **t** him, "wash in the Pool of Siloam" 3306
9:11 *He* **t** me to go to Siloam and wash. 3306
9:27 "*I have* **t** you already and you did 3306
11:14 So then he **t** them plainly, 3306
11:27 "Yes, Lord," *she* **t** him, 3306
11:46 and **t** them what Jesus had done. 3306
12:22 Andrew and Philip in turn **t** Jesus. 3306
12:35 Then Jesus **t** them, "You are going to have 3306
12:50 what the Father *has* **t** me to say." 3306
13:27 about to do, do quickly," Jesus **t** him, 3306
13:33 and just as *I* **t** the Jews, so I tell you now: 3306
14: 2 if it were not so, *I* would *have* **t** you. 3306
14:29 *I have* **t** you now before it happens, 3306
15:11 *I have* **t** you this so that my joy may be 3281
16: 1 "All this *I have* **t** you so that you will 3281
16: 4 *I have* **t** you this, so that when the time 3281
16:33 "*I have* **t** you these things, 3281
18: 8 "*I* **t** you that I am he," Jesus answered. 3306
20:18 And she **t** them that he had said these things NIG
20:25 So the other disciples **t** him, 3306
20:29 Then Jesus **t** him, "Because you have seen 3306
21: 3 Simon Peter **t** them, and they said, 3306
Ac 5:21 the temple courts, *as they had been* **t,** 201
7:13 Joseph **t** his brothers *who he was,* 341
7:37 "This is that Moses who **t** the Israelites, 3306
7:40 *They* **t** Aaron, 'Make us gods who will go 3306
8:29 The Spirit **t** Philip, "Go to that chariot 3306
8:35 **t** him **the good news about** Jesus. 2294
9: 6 and you *will be* **t** what you must do." 3281
9:11 The Lord **t** him, "Go to the house of Judas NIG
9:27 *He* **t** them how Saul on his journey 1455
10: 8 He **t** them everything that had happened 2007
10:13 a voice **t him,** "Get up, Peter. 899+1181+4639
10:22 A holy angel **t** *him* to have you come 5976
11:12 The Spirit **t** me to have no hesitation 3306
11:13 *He* **t** us how he had seen an angel appear 550
12: 8 and follow me," the angel **t** him. 3306
12:15 "You're out of your mind," they **t** her. 3306
13:41 would never believe, even if someone **t** you. 1687
15: 3 *they* **t how** the Gentiles had been converted. 1687
16:36 The jailer **t** Paul, "The magistrates have 550

Ac 19: 4 *He* t the people to believe in the one 3306
22:10 *be* t all that you have been assigned to do.' 3281
23:16 *he* went into the barracks and t Paul. 550
25:16 "*I* t them that it is not the Roman custom 646
27:25 in God that it will happen just as *he* t me. 3281
Ro 9:12 she *was* t, "The older will serve 3306
15:21 "Those who *were* not t about him will see, 334
1Co 10:28 both for the sake of the man who t you and 3606
16: 1 Do what *I* t the Galatian churches to do. 1411
2Co 7: 7 *He* t us about your longing for me, 334
Php 3:18 as *I have* often t you before and 3306
Col 1: 8 who also t us **of** your love in the Spirit. 1317
1Th 3: 6 He has t us that you always have NIG
4: 6 as *we have* **already** t you and warned you. 4625
4:11 work with your hands, just as *we* t you, 4133
1Pe 1:12 of the things that *have* now *been* t you 334
2Pe 1:16 when *we* t you **about** the power 1192
3Jn 1: 6 They *have* t the church **about** your love. 3455
Rev 6:11 and they *were* t to wait a little longer, 3306
9: 4 They *were* t not to harm the grass of 3306
10:11 Then I *was* t, "You must prophesy again 3306
11: 1 a reed like a measuring rod and *was* t, 3306
22:10 Then *he* t me, "Do not seal up the words 3306

TOLERANCE (1) [TOLERATE]

Ro 2: 4 the riches *of* his kindness, t and patience, 496

TOLERATE (6) [TOLERANCE, TOLERATED]

Est 3: 8 not in the king's best interest to t them. 5663
Hab 1: 3 Why *do you* t wrong? 5564
1:13 you cannot t wrong. 5564
1:13 Why then *do you* t the treacherous? 5564
Rev 2: 2 I know that you cannot t wicked men, 1002
2:20 *You* t that woman Jezebel, 918

TOLERATED (1) [TOLERATE]

Est 3: 4 whether Mordecai's behavior *would be* t, 6641

TOLL (KJV) See TAXES

TOMB (64) [TOMBS]

Ge 23: 6 None of us will refuse you his t 7700
35:20 Over her t Jacob set up a pillar, 7690
35:20 and to this day that pillar marks Rachel's t. 7690
50: 5 bury me in the t I dug for myself in 7700
Jdg 8:32 and was buried in the t *of* his father Joash 7700
16:31 and Eshtaol in the t *of* Manoah his father. 7700
1Sa 10: 2 you will meet two men near Rachel's t, 7690
2Sa 2:32 and buried him in his father's t 7700
3:32 and the king wept aloud at Abner's t. 7700
4:12 of Ish-Bosheth and buried it in Abner's t 7700
17:23 So he died and was buried in his father's t. 7700
19:37 that I may die in my own town near the t 7700
21:14 of Saul and his son Jonathan in the t 7700
1Ki 13:22 not be buried in the t *of* your fathers.' " 7700
13:30 Then he laid the body in his own t, 7700
2Ki 9:28 and buried him with his fathers in his t in 7690
13:21 they threw the man's body into Elisha's t. 7700
23:17 the t *of* the man of God who came 7700
23:30 to Jerusalem and buried him in his own t. 7690
2Ch 16:14 in the t that he had cut out for himself in 7700
Job 21:32 and watch is kept over his t. 1539
Isa 14:18 lie in state, each in his own t. 1074
14:19 But you are cast out of your t like 7700
Mt 27:60 in his own new t that he had cut out of 3646
27:60 a big stone in front of the entrance *to* the t 3646
27:61 Mary were sitting there opposite the t. 5439
27:64 the t to be made secure until the third day. 5439
27:65 make the t as secure as you know how." NIG
27:66 and made the t secure by putting a seal on 5439
28: 1 and the other Mary went to look at the t. 5439
28: 2 going to the t, rolled back the stone NIG
28: 8 So the women hurried away from the t, 3646
Mk 6:29 and took his body and laid it in a t. 3646
15:46 and placed it in a t cut out of rock. 3646
15:46 a stone against the entrance *of* the t. 3646
16: 2 they were on their way to the t 3646
16: 3 from the entrance *of* the t?" 3646
16: 5 As they entered the t, 3646
16: 8 the women went out and fled from the t. 3646
Lk 23:53 in linen cloth and placed it in a t cut in 3645
23:55 and saw the t and how his body was laid 3646
24: 1 and went to the t. 3645
24: 2 the stone rolled away from the t, 3646
24: 9 When they came back from the t, 3646
24:12 Peter, however, got up and ran to the t. 3646
24:22 They went to the t early this morning 3646
24:24 of our companions went to the t 3646
Jn 11:17 that Lazarus had already been in the t 3646
11:31 supposing she was going to the t 3646
11:38 once more deeply moved, came to the t. 3646
12:17 when he called Lazarus from the t 3646
19:41 and in the garden a new t, 3646
19:42 of Preparation and since the t was nearby, 3646
20: 1 Mary Magdalene went to the t and saw 3646
20: 2 "They have taken the Lord out of the t, 3646
20: 3 and the other disciple started for the t. 3646
20: 4 and reached the t first. 3646
20: 6 arrived and went into the t. 3646
20: 8 who had reached the t first, 3646
20:11 but Mary stood outside the t crying. 3646
20:11 she bent over to look into the t 3646
Ac 2:29 and his t is here to this day. 3645
7:16 in the t that Abraham had bought from 3645
13:29 down from the tree and laid him in a t. 3646

TOMBS (20) [TOMB]

Ge 23: 6 Bury your dead in the choicest of our t. 7700
2Ki 23:16 he saw the t that were there on the hillside, 7700
2Ch 21:20 but not in the t *of* the kings. 7700
24:25 but not in the t *of* the kings. 7700
28:27 but he was not placed in the t *of* the kings 7700
32:33 where the t *of* David's descendants are. 7700
35:24 He was buried in the t *of* his fathers, 7700
Ne 3:16 made repairs up to a point opposite the t 7700
Ps 49:11 Their t will remain their houses forever, 7700
Mt 8:28 men coming from the t met him. 3646
23:27 You are like whitewashed t, 5439
23:29 You build t for the prophets and decorate 5439
27:52 The t broke open and the bodies 3646
27:53 They came out of the t, 3646
Mk 5: 2 an evil spirit came from the t to meet him. 3646
5: 3 This man lived in the t, 3645
5: 5 the t and in the hills he would cry out 3645
Lk 8:27 but had lived in the t. 3645
11:47 because you build t for the prophets, 3646
11:48 and you build their t. NIG

TOMBSTONE (1) [STONE]

2Ki 23:17 The king asked, "What is that t I see?" 7483

TOMORROW (58)

Ex 8:10 "T," Pharaoh said. 4737
8:23 This miraculous sign will occur t.' " 4737
8:29 and t the flies will leave Pharaoh 4737
9: 5 "T the LORD will do this in the land." 4737
9:18 at this time t I will send the worst hailstorm 4737
10: 4 I will bring locusts into your country t. 4737
16:23 'T is to be a day of rest, 4737
17: 9 T I will stand on top of the hill with 4737
19:10 and consecrate them today and t. 4737
32: 5 "T there will be a festival to the LORD." 4737
Nu 11:18 in preparation for t, 4737
14:25 turn back t and set out toward the desert 4737
16: 7 and t put fire and incense in them before 4737
16:16 to appear before the LORD t— 4737
Jos 3: 5 for t the LORD will do amazing things 4737
7:13 in preparation for t; 4737
11: 6 by this time t I will hand all of them over 4737
22:18 t he will be angry with the whole 4737
Jdg 19: 9 Early t morning you can get up and be 4737
20:28 for t I will give them into your hands." 4737
1Sa 9:16 "About this time t I will send you a man 4737
11: 9 'By the time the sun is hot t, 4737
11:10 "T we will surrender to you, 4737
19: 2 Be on your guard t morning; 2021[S]
19:11 t you'll be killed." 4737
20: 5 "Look, t is the New Moon festival, 4737
20: 5 until the evening of the **day after** t. 8958
20:12 by this time the day after t! 4737
20:18 "T is the New Moon festival. 4737
20:19 The **day after** t, toward evening, 8992
28:19 and t you and your sons will be with me. 4737
2Sa 11:12 and t I will send you back." 4737
1Ki 19: 2 if by this time t I do not make your life like 4737
20: 6 But about this time t I am going 4737
2Ki 6:28 and t we'll eat my son.' 4737
7: 1 About this time t, a seah of flour will sell 4737
7:18 "About this time t, a seah of flour will sell 4737
10: 6 and come to me in Jezreel by this time t." 4737
2Ch 20:16 T march down against them. 4737
20:17 Go out to face them t, 4737
Est 5: 8 let the king and Haman come t to 4737
5:12 along with the king t. 4737
9:13 to carry out this day's edict t also, 4737
Pr 3:28 "Come back later; I'll give it t"— 4737
27: 1 Do not boast about t, 3427+4737
Isa 22:13 you say, "for t we die!" 4737
56:12 t will be like today, or even far better." 4737
Mt 6:30 which is here today and t is thrown into 892
6:34 Therefore do not worry about t, 892+3836
6:34 for t will worry about itself. 892+3836
Lk 12:28 and t is thrown into the fire, 892
13:32 and heal people today and t, 892
13:33 I must keep going today and t and 892
Ac 23:20 to bring Paul before the Sanhedrin t on 892
25:22 He replied, "T you will hear him." 892
1Co 15:32 "Let us eat and drink, for t we die." 892
Jas 4:13 "Today or t we will go to this or that city, 892
4:14 you do not even know what will happen t. 892+3836

TONE (1)

Gal 4:20 could be with you now and change my t, 5889

TONGS (3)

1Ki 7:49 the gold floral work and lamps and t; 4920
2Ch 4:21 and lamps and t (they were solid gold); 4920
Isa 6: 6 which he had taken with t from the altar. 4920

TONGUE (93) [TONGUES]

Ex 4:10 I am slow of speech and t." 4383
2Sa 23: 2 his word was on my t. 4383
Est 1:22 in each people's t that every man should 4383
Job 5:21 be protected from the lash of the t, 4383
12:11 not the ear test words as the t tastes food? 2674
15: 5 you adopt the t *of* the crafty. 4383
20:12 in his mouth and he hides it under his t, 4383
27: 4 and my t will utter no deceit. 4383
33: 2 my words are **on the tip of** my t. 928+2674+4383
34: 3 For the ear tests words as the t tastes food. 2674
41: 1 a fishhook or tie down his t with a rope? 4383
Ps 5: 9 with their t they speak deceit. 4383
10: 7 trouble and evil are under his t. 4383
12: 3 all flattering lips and every boastful t 4383
15: 3 and has no slander on his t, 4383
16: 9 my heart is glad and my t rejoices; 3883
22:15 and my t sticks to the roof of my mouth; 4383
34:13 keep your t from evil and your lips 4383
35:28 My t will speak of your righteousness and 4383
37:30 and his t speaks what is just. 4383
39: 1 "I will watch my ways and keep my t 4383
39: 3 then I spoke with my t: 4383
45: 1 my t is the pen of a skillful writer. 4383
50:19 mouth for evil and harness your t to deceit. 4383
51:14 and my t will sing of your righteousness. 4383
52: 2 Your t plots destruction; 4383
52: 4 O you deceitful t! 4383
66:17 his praise was on my t. 4383
71:24 My t will tell of your righteous acts 4383
114: 1 house of Jacob from a people of **foreign** t, 4357
119:172 May my t sing of your word, 4383
120: 3 and what more besides, O deceitful t? 4383
137: 6 May my t cling to the roof of my mouth 4383
139: 4 a word is on my t you know it completely, 4383
Pr 6:17 a lying t, hands that shed innocent blood, 4383
6:24 from the smooth t *of* the wayward wife. 4383
10:19 but he who holds his t is wise. 8557
10:20 The t *of* the righteous is choice silver, 4383
10:31 but a perverse t will be cut out. 4383
11:12 but a man of understanding **holds** *his* t. 3087
12:18 but the t *of* the wise brings healing. 4383
12:19 but a lying t lasts only a moment. 4383
15: 2 The t *of* the wise commends knowledge, 4383
15: 4 The t that brings healing is a tree of life, 4383
15: 4 but a deceitful t crushes the spirit. 2023[S]
16: 1 from the LORD comes the reply of the t. 4383
17: 4 a liar pays attention to a malicious t. 4383
17:20 he whose t is deceitful falls into trouble. 4383
17:28 and discerning if he holds his t. 8557
18:21 The t has the power of life and death, 4383
21: 6 fortune made by a lying t is a fleeting vapor 4383
21:23 and his t keeps himself from calamity. 4383
25:15 and a gentle t can break a bone. 4383
25:23 so a sly t brings angry looks. 4383
26:28 A lying t hates those it hurts, 4383
28:23 more favor than he who has a flattering t. 4383
31:26 and faithful instruction is on her t. 4383
SS 4:11 milk and honey are under your t. 4383
Isa 30:27 and his t is a consuming fire. 4383
32: 4 the stammering t will be fluent and clear. 4383
33:19 with their strange, incomprehensible t. 4383
35: 6 and the mute t shout for joy. 4383
45:23 by me every t will swear. 4383
50: 4 an instructed t, to know the word 4383
54:17 you will refute every t that accuses you. 4383
57: 4 and stick out your t? 4383
59: 3 and your t mutters wicked things. 4383
Jer 9: 3 "They make ready their t like a bow, 4383
9: 8 Their t is a deadly arrow; 4383
La 4: 4 Because of thirst the infant's t sticks to 4383
Eze 3:26 I will make your t stick to the roof 4383
Mk 7:33 Then he spit and touched the man's t. 1185
7:35 his t was loosened and he began to speak 1185
Lk 1:64 and his t was loosed, 1185
16:24 the tip of his finger in water and cool my t, 1185
Ac 2:26 my heart is glad and my t rejoices; 1185
Ro 14:11 every t will confess to God.' " 1185
1Co 14: 2 *in* a t does not speak to men but to God. 1185
14: 4 He who speaks *in* a t edifies himself, 1185
14: 9 you speak intelligible words with your t, 1185
14:13 who speaks *in* a t should pray that he may 1185
14:14 For if I pray *in* a t, my spirit prays, 1185
14:19 words to instruct others than ten thousand words in a t. 1185
14:26 a revelation, a t or an interpretation. 1185
14:27 If anyone speaks *in* a t, two— 1185
Php 2:11 every t confess that Jesus Christ is Lord, 1185
Jas 1:26 and yet does not keep a tight rein on his t, 1185
3: 5 Likewise the t is a small part of the body, 1185
3: 6 The t also is a fire, 1185
3: 8 but no man can tame the t. 1185
3: 9 With **the** t we praise our Lord and Father, 899[S]
1Pe 3:10 and see good days must keep his t 1185
1Jn 3:18 not love *with* words or t but with actions 1185

TONGUES (45) [TONGUE]

Jdg 7: 5 who lap the water with their t like a dog 4383
Job 29:10 their t stuck to the roof of their mouths. 4383
Ps 12: 4 "We will triumph with our t; 4383
31:20 you keep them safe from accusing t. 4383
57: 4 whose t are sharp swords. 4383
64: 3 They sharpen their t like swords 4383
64: 8 He will turn their own t against them 4383
68:23 while the t *of* your dogs have their share." 4383
73: 9 and their t take possession of the earth. 4383
78:36 lying to him with their t; 4383
109: 2 they have spoken against me with lying t. 4383
120: 2 from lying lips and from deceitful t. 4383
126: 2 our t with songs of joy. 4383
140: 3 They make their t as sharp as a serpent's; 4383

Isa 5:24 as t *of* fire lick up straw and 4383
28:11 and strange t God will speak to this people, 4383
41:17 their t are parched with thirst. 4383
66:18 about to come and gather all nations and t, 4383
Jer 9: 5 They have taught their t to lie; 4383
18:18 with our t and pay no attention 4383
23:31 against the prophets who wag their own t 4383
Mic 6:12 and their t speak deceitfully. 4383
Zec 14:12 and their t will rot in their mouths. 4383
Mk 16:17 they will speak *in* new t; *1185*
Ac 2: 3 be t of fire that separated and came to rest *1185*
2: 4 *in* other t as the Spirit enabled them. *1185*
2:11 the wonders of God *in* our own t!" *1185*
10:46 For they heard them speaking *in* t *1185*
19: 6 and they spoke *in* t and prophesied. *1185*
Ro 3:13 their t practice deceit." *1185*
1Co 12:10 **speaking in** different kinds of t, *1185*
12:10 and to still another the interpretation *of* t. *1185*
12:28 *those* **speaking in** different kinds *of* t. *1185*
12:30 Do all speak *in* t? *1185*
13: 1 If I speak *in* the t of men and of angels, *1185*
13: 8 where there are t, they will be stilled; *1185*
14: 5 like every one of you to speak *in* t, *1185*
14: 5 one who speaks *in* t, unless he interprets, *1185*
14: 6 brothers, if I come to you and speak *in* t, *1185*
14:18 I thank God that I speak *in* t more than all *1185*
14:21 "Through *men of* **strange** t and through *2280*
14:22 T, then, are a sign, not for believers but *1185*
14:23 and everyone speaks *in* t, *1185*
14:39 and do not forbid speaking *in* t. *1185*
Rev 16:10 Men gnawed their t in agony *1185*

TONIGHT (13)

Ge 19: 5 are the men who came to you t? 2021+4326
19:34 Let's get him to drink wine again t, 2021+4326
30:15 "he can sleep with you t in return 2021+4326
Nu 22:19 Now stay here t as the others did, 2021+4326
Jos 2: 2 Israelites have come here t to spy out 2021+4326
4: 3 down at the place where you stay t." 2021+4326
Jdg 19: 6 "Please **stay** t and enjoy yourself." 4328
Ru 1:12 even if I had a husband t and then 2021+4326
3: 2 T he will be winnowing barley on 2021+4326
1Sa 19:11 "If you don't run for your life t, 2021+4326
2Sa 17: 1 and set out t in pursuit of David. 2021+4326
Mk 14:30 Jesus answered, "today—yes, t *3816+3836+4047*
Ac 23:23 spearmen to go to Caesarea at nine t. *3816*

TOO (258)

Ge 9: 5 **And** from each man, t, 2256
16:10 that they will be t numerous to count." 4946
18:14 Is anything t hard *for* the LORD? 4946
19:21 "Very well, I will grant this request t; 1685
24:14 'Drink, and I'll water your camels t'— 1685
24:19 "I'll draw water for your camels t, 1685
24:44 and I'll draw water for your camels t," 1685
24:46 'Drink, and I'll water your camels t.' 1685
26:16 you have become t powerful for us." 4394
27:31 He t prepared some tasty food 1685
27:34 to his father, "Bless me—me t, 1685
27:38 Bless me t, my father!" 1685
29:33 he gave me this one t." 1685
30: 3 for me and that through her I t can build 1685
30:15 Will you take my son's mandrakes t?" 1685
31:25 Laban and his relatives camped there t. NIH
33: 7 **and** they t bowed down. 2256
36: 7 Their possessions were t great *for* them 4946
38:11 For he thought, "He may die t, 1685
40:16 he said to Joseph, "I t had a dream: 677
44:29 from me t and harm comes to him, 1685
47:20 because the famine *was t* **severe** for them. AIT
48:11 God has allowed me to see your children t." 1685
48:19 He t will become a people, 1685
48:19 and he t will become great. 1685
Ex 1: 9 Israelites have become **much t numerous** for us. 2256+6786+8041
10:26 Our livestock t must go with us; 1685
12: 4 If any household is t small *for* a whole lamb 4946
16:18 he who gathered much *did* not **have t much,** 6369
16:18 he who gathered little did not **have t little.** 2893
18:18 The work is t heavy *for* you; 4946
23:29 and the wild animals t numerous *for* you. 6584
Lev 27: 8 If anyone making the vow is t poor to pay 4946
Nu 11:14 the burden is t heavy *for* me. 4946
11:23 *"Is* the LORD's arm **t short?** 7918
16: 3 "You have **gone t far!** 8041
16: 7 You Levites have **gone t far!"** 8041
16:10 now you are trying to get the priesthood t. 1685
16:34 "The earth is going to swallow us t!" 7153
19: 8 **and** he t will be unclean till evening. 2256
19:10 **and** he t will be unclean till evening. 2256
22: 6 because they are t powerful *for* me. 4946
24:24 but they t will come to ruin." 1685
27:13 you t will be gathered to your people, 1685
Dt 1: 9 "You *are* **t heavy a burden** for me **to carry** alone. 3523+4202+5951
1:17 Bring me any case t hard *for* you, 4946
2:11 they t were considered Rephaites, 677
2:20 t was considered a land of the Rephaites, 677
2:36 not one town was t strong *for* us. 4946
3:20 and they t have taken over the land that 1685
9:20 but at that time I prayed for Aaron t. 1685
12:21 to put his Name *is t* **far away** from you, AIT
14:24 But if that place is t distant 4946
17: 8 that are t difficult *for* you to judge— 4946
19: 6 overtake him if the distance *is t* **great,** AIT
Dt 20: 8 not become disheartened t." 3869
30:11 not t difficult *for* you or 4946
Jos 1:15 and until they t have taken possession of 1685
17:15 if the hill country of Ephraim *is t* **small** AIT
24:18 We t will serve the LORD, 1685
Jdg 1:33 **but** the Naphtalites t lived among 2256
1:35 they t were pressed into forced labor. 2256
3:31 He t saved Israel. 1685
6:35 so that they t went up to meet them. NIH
7: 2 "You have t many *men for* me 4946
7: 4 "There are still t many men. NIH
9:19 and may you be his, t! 1685
14: 9 he gave them some, **and** they t ate it. 2256
18:26 seeing that they were t strong *for* him, 4946
Ru 1:12 I am t old to have another husband. 4946
1Sa 19:21 and they prophesied t. 1685
22:17 because they t have sided with David. 1685
30:10 for two hundred men were t exhausted 4946
30:21 two hundred men who had been t exhausted 4946
31: 5 he t fell on his sword and died with him. 1685
2Sa 2: 6 and I t will show you the same favor 1685
3:39 these sons of Zeruiah are t strong *for* me. 4946
10:11 "If the Arameans are t strong *for* me, 4946
10:11 but if the Ammonites are t strong *for* you, 4946
12: 8 And if all this had been **t little,** 5071
13:36 The king, t, and all his servants wept 1685+2256
14:26 to time when it became t heavy *for* him— 6584
15:24 t, and all the Levites who were with him 1685
15:30 the people with him covered their heads t 2256
18:26 "He must be bringing good news, t." 1685
22:18 from my foes, who were t strong *for* me. 4946
23:22 he t was as famous as the three mighty men. 2256
1Ki 3: 8 t numerous to count or number. 4946
8:64 before the LORD was t small to hold 4946
10: 3 nothing was t hard *for* the king to explain 4946
12:28 "It is t much for you to go up to Jerusalem. 4946
13:18 "I t am a prophet, as you are. 1685
19: 7 for the journey is t much *for* you." 4946
19:10 and now they are trying to kill me t." NIH
19:14 and now they are trying to kill me t." NIH
20:23 That is why they were t strong *for* us. 4946
2Ki 2:17 But they persisted until he was t ashamed NIH
5:20 "My master *was* **t easy on** Naaman, 3104
6: 1 where we meet with you is t small *for* us. 4946
9:27 Jehu chased him, shouting, "Kill him t!" 1685
1Ch 8:32 They t lived near their relatives 677+2256
9:38 They t lived near their relatives 677+2256
10: 5 he t fell on his sword and died. 1685
11:24 he t was as famous as the three mighty men. 2256
19:12 "If the Arameans are t strong *for* me, 4946
19:12 but if the Ammonites are t strong *for* you, 4946
19:15 they t fled before his brother Abishai 1685
22:14 of bronze and iron t great to be weighed, 401
2Ch 9: 2 nothing was t hard *for* him to explain 4946
22: 3 He t walked in the ways of the house 1685
29:34 were **t few** to skin all the burnt offerings; 5071
Ezr 9: 6 "O my God, *I am t* **ashamed** and disgraced AIT
10: 1 They t wept bitterly. 3954
Ne 6: 9 "Their hands will get t weak *for* the work, 4946
13:27 you t are doing all this terrible wickedness 2256
Job 6:21 Now you t have proved to be of no help; 3954
32:10 I t will tell you what I know. 677
32:17 I t will have my say; 677
32:17 I t will tell what I know. 677
33: 6 I t have been taken from clay. 1685
42: 3 things t wonderful *for* me to know. 4946
Ps 18:17 from my foes, who were t strong *for* me. 4946
35:10 You rescue the poor from those t strong 4946
36: 2 in his own eyes *he* **flatters** himself *t much* AIT
38: 4 like a burden t heavy to bear. 4946
40: 5 they would be t many to declare. 4946
77: 4 I was t troubled to speak. 4202
87: 4 Philistia t, and Tyre, along with Cush— 2180
89: 5 O LORD, your faithfulness t, 677
105:24 he made them t numerous *for* their foes, 4946
120: 6 **T long** have I lived 8041
131: 1 with great matters or things t wonderful 4946
139: 6 Such knowledge is t wonderful *for* me, 4946
139: 6 t lofty for me to attain. NIH
142: 6 for they are t strong *for* me. 4946
Pr 20:19 so avoid a *man who* **talks t much.** 7331+8557
21:13 he t will cry out and not be answered. 1685
23:20 Do not join *those who* **drink t much** wine 6010
24: 7 Wisdom *is t* **high** for a fool; AIT
25:16 **t much** *of* it, and you will vomit. 8425
25:17 **t much** *of* you, and he will hate you. 8425
25:27 It is not good to eat **t much** honey, 8049
26:15 *he is t* **lazy** to bring it back to his mouth. AIT
30: 9 *I may* **have t much** and disown you and say, 8425
30:18 "There are three things that are t amazing 4946
Ecc 1:17 t, is a chasing after the wind. 1685
2:15 I said in my heart, "This t is meaningless." 1685
2:16 Like the fool, the wise man t must die! 375
2:19 This t is meaningless. 1685
2:21 This t is meaningless and 1685
2:23 This t is meaningless. 1685
2:24 This t, I see, is from the hand of God, 1685
2:26 This t is meaningless, 1685
4: 4 This t is meaningless, 1685
4: 8 This t is meaningless— 1685
4:16 This t is meaningless, 1685
5:10 This t is meaningless. 1685
5:16 This t is a grievous evil: 1685+2256
6: 9 This t is meaningless, 1685
7: 6 This t is meaningless. 1685+2256
8:10 Then t, I saw the wicked buried— 4027
8:10 This t is meaningless. 1685
Ecc 8:14 This t, I say, is meaningless. 1685
Isa 7: 8 be t shattered to be a people. 4946
28:20 The bed is t short to stretch out on, 4946
28:20 the blanket *t* **narrow** to wrap around you. AIT
31: 2 Yet he t is wise and can bring disaster; 1685
38:16 **and** my spirit finds life in them t. 2256
40:20 A *man t* **poor** *to* present such 6123
49: 6 "It is t small a thing for you to 4946
49:19 now you will be t small *for* your people, 4946
49:20 'This place is t small for us; NIH
50: 2 Was my arm t short to ransom you? 4946
59: 1 arm of the LORD is not t short to save, 4946
59: 1 nor his ear t dull to hear. 4946
63: 9 In all their distress he t was distressed, NIH
65: 5 for *I am t* **sacred** *for* you!' AIT
Jer 4:12 a wind t strong *for* that comes from me. 4946
5: 5 **But** with one accord they t had broken off 421
25:26 the king of Sheshach will drink it t. NIH
29: 6 in marriage, so that they t may have sons NIH
29: 7 because if it prospers, you t will prosper." NIH
32:17 Nothing is t hard *for* you. 4946
32:27 Is anything t hard *for* me? 4946
46:21 They t will turn and flee together, 1685
48: 2 You t, O Madmen, will be silenced; 1685
48: 7 you t will be taken captive, 1685
49:11 Your widows t can trust in me." 2256
Eze 16:28 in prostitution with the Assyrians t, 2256
21:17 I t will strike my hands together, 1685+2256
23:12 She t lusted after the Assyrians— NIH
23:13 I saw that she t defiled herself; NIH
24: 9 I, t, will pile the wood high. 1685
31:18 t, will be brought down with the trees NIH
32:28 "You t, O Pharaoh, will be broken 2256
Da 2:11 What the king asks is **t difficult.** 10330
4: 9 and no mystery is *t* **difficult** for you. AIT
Am 6: 9 they t will die. 2256
Na 3:11 You t will become drunk; 1685
Hab 1:13 Your eyes are t pure to look on evil; 4946
Zep 2:12 "You t, O Cushites, will be slain 1685
Zec 9: 2 and upon Hamath t, 1685
9: 5 Gaza will writhe in agony, **and** Ekron t, 2256
14:14 Judah t will fight at Jerusalem. 1685
Mt 2: 8 so that I t may go and worship him." *2779*
7: 1 "Do not judge, or you t will be judged. *NIG*
Mk 12:22 Last of all, the woman died t. *2779*
Lk 2:35 And a sword will pierce your own soul t." *2779*
3:21 Jesus was baptized t. *2779*
10:32 So t, a Levite, when he came to the place *2779*
13: 3 But unless you repent, you t will all perish. *3931*
13: 5 unless you repent, you t will all perish." *6058*
19: 9 because this man, t, is a son of Abraham. *2779*
20:32 Finally, the woman died t. *2779*
Jn 2:10 after the guests *have* **had t much to drink;** *3499*
5:17 **and** I, t, am working." *2779*
6:67 "You do not want to leave t, do you?" *2779*
7:52 They replied, "Are you from Galilee, t? *2779*
9:27 Do you want to become his disciples, t?" *2779*
9:40 Are we blind t?" *2779*
10:16 They t will listen to my voice, *2779*
14:21 **and** I t will love him and show myself *2779*
17:19 that they t may be truly sanctified. *2779*
Ac 2:13 *"They have* **had t much** wine." *1639+3551*
5:37 He t was killed, *2779*
14:15 We t are only men, human like you. *2779*
17:13 they went there t, agitating the crowds *2779*
26: 9 "I t was convinced that I ought to do all *4036*
Ro 3:29 Is he not the God of Gentiles t? *2779*
3:29 God of Gentiles too? Yes, of Gentiles t, *2779*
6: 4 we t may live a new life. *2779*
11: 5 So t, at the present time there is *2779*
11:31 so they t have now become disobedient *2779*
11:31 in order that they t may now receive mercy *2779*
16:13 who has been a mother to me, t. *2779*
1Co 7:40 and I think that I t have the Spirit of God. *2779*
9:11 is it t much if we reap a material harvest *NIG*
10:21 of the Lord and the cup of demons t; *NIG*
2Co 2: 5 not to **put it t severely.** *2096*
8:15 who gathered much *did* not **have t much,** *4429*
8:15 who gathered little *did* not **have t little."** *1782*
10:14 *We are* not **going t far** in our boasting, *5657*
11:18 I t will boast. *2779*
11:21 To my shame I admit that we were t weak *NIG*
Gal 2:16 **So** we, t, have put our faith in Christ Jesus *2779*
Eph 2:22 And in him you t are being built together *2779*
Php 2:18 you t should be glad and rejoice with me. *2779*
3:15 that t God will make clear to you. *2779*
Col 4: 3 And pray for us, t, *2779*
1Ti 5: 7 Give the people these instructions, t, *2779*
2Ti 2:10 that they t may obtain the salvation that is *2779*
4:15 You t should be on your guard *2779*
Tit 3: 3 At one time we t were foolish, disobedient, *2779*
Heb 2:14 he t shared in their humanity so that *4181*
Jas 5: 8 You t, be patient and stand firm, *2779*
2Pe 2:12 and like beasts they t will perish. *2779*
Rev 14:10 t, will drink of the wine of God's fury, *2779*
14:17 **and** he t had a sharp sickle. *2779*

TOOK (668) [TAKE]

Ge 2:15 The LORD God t the man and put him in 4374
2:21 *he* t one of the man's ribs and closed up 4374
3: 6 *she* t some and ate it. 4374
5:24 he was no more, because God t him **away.** 4374
8: 9 He reached out his hand and t the dove 4374
9:23 and Japheth t a garment and laid it 4374
11:31 Terah t his son Abram, 4374
12: 5 He t his wife Sarai, his nephew Lot, 4374

Ge 12:19 so that *I* t her to be my wife? 4374
15: 5 *He* t him outside and said, 3655
16: 3 Sarai his wife t her Egyptian maidservant 4374
17:23 that very day Abraham t his son Ishmael 4374
20: 2 king of Gerar sent for Sarah and t her. 4374
21:14 the next morning Abraham t some food 4374
22: 3 *He* t with him two of his servants 4374
22: 6 Abraham t the wood for the burnt offering 4374
22:10 Then he reached out his hand and t 4374
22:13 over and t the ram and sacrificed it as 4374
24:10 the servant t ten of his master's camels 4374
24:22 the man t **out** a gold nose ring weighing 4374
24:61 So the servant t Rebekah and left. 4374
24:65 So *she* t her veil and covered herself. 4374
25: 1 Abraham t another wife, 4374
27:15 Then Rebekah t the best clothes 4374
27:35 came deceitfully and t your blessing." 4374
27:36 *He* t my birthright, 4374
28:18 Early the next morning Jacob t 4374
29:23 *he* t his daughter Leah and gave her 4374
30: 9 *she* t her maidservant Zilpah and gave her 4374
30:15 that you t **away** my husband? 4374
30:37 however, t fresh-cut branches from poplar, 4374
31:16 that God t **away** from our father belongs 5911
31:36 Jacob was angry and t Laban **to task.** 8189
31:45 So Jacob t a stone and set it up as a pillar. 4374
31:46 So *they* t stones and piled them in a heap, 4374
31:53 So Jacob t **an oath** in the name of the Fear 8678
32:22 Jacob got up and t his two wives, 4374
34: 2 saw her, *he* t her and violated her. 4374
34:25 t their swords and attacked 4374
34:26 and t Dinah from Shechem's house 4374
36: 2 Esau t his wives from the women 4374
36: 6 Esau t his wives and sons and daughters 4374
37:24 *they* t him and threw him into the cistern. 4374
37:28 the Ishmaelites, *who* t him to Egypt. 995
37:32 t the ornamented robe **back** 995+2256+8938
38:14 *she* t **off** her widow's clothes, 6073
38:19 *she* t **off** her veil and put 6073
38:28 so the midwife t a scarlet thread and tied it 4374
39: 7 after a while his master's wife t **notice** 5951+6524
39:20 Joseph's master t him and put him in prison, 4374
40:11 and *I* t the grapes, squeezed them into 4374
41:42 Then Pharaoh t his signet ring 6073
43:15 the men t the gifts and double the amount 4374
43:17 The man did as Joseph told him and t 995
43:24 The steward t the men into Joseph's house, 995
46: 5 and Israel's sons t their father Jacob 5951
46: 6 *They* also t with them their livestock and 4374
46: 7 *He* t with him to Egypt his sons 995
48: 1 So *he* t his two sons Manasseh 4374
48:13 And Joseph t both of them, 4374
48:17 so *he* t **hold** *of* his father's hand to move it 9461
48:22 the ridge of land *I* t from the Amorites 4374
Ex 2: 9 So the woman t the baby and nursed him. 4374
2:10 *she* t him to Pharaoh's daughter 995
4: 4 and t **hold** of the snake and it turned back 2616
4: 6 and when *he* t it **out,** it was leprous, 3655
4: 7 and when *he* t it **out,** it was restored, 3655
4:20 So Moses t his wife and sons, 4374
4:20 And he t the staff of God in his hand. 4374
4:25 But Zipporah t a flint knife, 4374
9:10 So *they* t soot from a furnace and stood 4374
12:34 So the people t their dough before 5951
13:19 Moses t the bones of Joseph with him 4374
14: 6 and t his army with him. 4374
14: 7 *He* t six hundred of the best chariots, 4374
15:20 Aaron's sister, t a tambourine in her hand, 4374
17:12 *they* t a stone and put it under him 4374
18:13 The next day Moses t *his* **seat** to serve 3782
24: 6 Moses t half of the blood and put it 4374
24: 7 Then *he* t the Book of the Covenant 4374
24: 8 Moses then t the blood, 4374
32: 3 So all the people **t off** their earrings 7293
32: 4 *He* t what they handed him and made it into 4374
32:20 And *he* t the calf they had made 4374
40:20 *He* t the Testimony and placed it in the ark, 4374
Lev 8:10 Then Moses t the anointing oil 4374
8:15 Moses slaughtered the bull and t some of 4374
8:16 also t all the fat around the inner parts, 4374
8:23 the ram and t some of its blood and put it 4374
8:25 *He* t the fat, the fat tail, 4374
8:26 *he* t a cake of bread, and one made with oil, 4374
8:28 Then Moses t them from their hands 4374
8:29 He also t the breast— 4374
8:30 Then Moses t some of the anointing oil 4374
9: 5 *They* t the things Moses commanded to 4374
9:15 *He* t the goat for the people's sin offering 4374
9:17 **t a handful** of it and burned it 4090+4848
10: 1 and Abihu t their censers, put fire in them 4374
24:23 and *they* t the blasphemer outside 3655
Nu 1:17 Aaron t these men whose names had been given, 4374
7: 6 So Moses t the carts and oxen 4374
11:25 and *he* t of the Spirit that was on him 724
15:36 So the assembly t him outside the camp 3655
16:18 So each man t his censer, 4374
17: 9 and each man t his own staff. 4374
20: 9 So Moses t the staff from 4374
21:24 put him to the sword and t **over** his land 3769
21:35 And *they* t **possession** *of* his land. 3769
22:41 The next morning Balak t Balaam up 4374
23:14 So *he* t him *to* the field of Zophim on 4374
23:28 And Balak t Balaam *to* the top of Peor, 4374
25: 7 left the assembly, t a spear in his hand 4374
27:22 *He* t Joshua and had him stand 4374
31: 6 **t with** him articles from the sanctuary 928+3338

Nu 31: 9 t all the Midianite herds, flocks and goods **as plunder.** 1024
31:11 *They* t all the plunder and spoils, 4374
31:27 the soldiers who **t part in** the battle 3655+4200
31:32 the spoils that the soldiers t was 675,000 1024
Dt 1:15 So *I* t the leading men of your tribes, 4374
2:34 At that time *we* t all his towns 4334
3: 4 At that time *we* t all his cities. 4334
3: 8 So at that time *we* t from these two kings 4374
3:10 We t all the towns on the plateau, NIH
3:12 Of the land that *we* t **over** at that time, 3769
3:14 t the whole region of Argob as far as 4374
4:20 the LORD t you and brought you out of 4374
4:47 *They* t **possession** *of* his land and the land 3769
9:17 So *I* t the two tablets and threw them out 9530
9:21 Also *I* t that sinful thing of yours, 4374
29: 8 *We* t their land and gave it as 4374
32:37 are their gods, the rock *they* t **refuge** in, 2879
Jos 3: 6 So *they* t it **up** and went ahead of them. 5951
4: 8 *They* t twelve stones from the middle of 5951
6:12 and the priests t **up** the ark of the LORD. 5951
6:20 and *they* t the city. 4334
7: 1 of the tribe of Judah, t some of them. 4374
7:17 and *he* t the Zerahites. 4334
7:21 I coveted them and t them. 4374
7:23 *They* t the things from the tent, 4374
7:24 t Achan son of Zerah, the silver, the robe, 4374
8:23 But *they* t the king of Ai alive 9530
10: 5 up with all their troops and **t up positions** 2837
10: 9 Joshua t them by surprise. 448+995
10:27 the order and *they* t them **down** from 3718
10:28 That day Joshua t Makkedah. 4334
10:31 *he* **t up positions** against it and attacked it. 2837
10:32 and Joshua t it on the second day. 4334
10:34 *they* **t up positions** against it 2837
10:37 *They* t the city and put it to the sword, 4334
10:39 *They* t the city, its king and its villages, 4334
11:12 Joshua t all these royal cities 4334
11:16 So Joshua t this entire land: 4374
11:19 *who* t them all in battle. 4374
11:23 So Joshua t the entire land, 4374
12: 1 and whose territory *they* t **over** east of 3769
15:17 Othniel son of Kenaz, Caleb's brother, t it; 4334
19:47 so they went up and attacked Leshem, t it, 4334
21:43 and *they* t **possession** *of* it and settled there. 3769
24: 3 But *I* t your father Abraham from the land 4374
24: 8 and *you* t **possession** *of* their land. 3769
24:26 Then *he* t a large stone and set it up there 4374
Jdg 1: 8 of Judah attacked Jerusalem also and t it. 4334
1:13 Caleb's younger brother, t it; 4334
1:18 The men of Judah also t Gaza, 4334
1:19 *They* t **possession** *of* the hill country, 3769
3: 6 t their daughters **in marriage** 851+4200+4374
3:13 and *they* t **possession** *of* the City of Palms. 3769
3:25 *they* t a key and unlocked them. 4374
5: 6 travelers **t to** winding paths. 2143
6:27 So Gideon t ten of his servants and did as 4374
7: 5 So Gideon t the men **down** to the water. 3718
7: 8 *who* t **over** the provisions and trumpets of 4374
7:24 and *they* t the waters of the Jordan as far 4334
8:16 *He* t the elders of the town and taught 4374
8:21 and killed them, and t the ornaments 4374
9:34 and **t up concealed positions** 741
9:43 So *he* t his men, divided them into three 4374
9:48 He t an ax and cut off some branches, 4374
11:13 they t **away** my land from the Arnon to 4374
11:21 Israel t **over** all the land of the Amorites 3769
12: 3 *I* t my life in my hands and crossed over 8492
13:19 Then Manoah t a young goat, 4374
15: 1 Samson t a young goat and went 928
16: 3 up and t **hold** of the doors of the city gate, 296
16:12 So Delilah t new ropes and tied him 4374
16:13 Delilah t the seven braids of his head, NIH
16:21 gouged out his eyes and t him **down** 3718
17: 2 I have that silver with me; *I* t it." 4374
17: 4 and she t two hundred shekels of silver 4374
18:17 inside and t the carved image, 4374
18:18 into Micah's house and t the carved image, 4374
18:20 *He* t the ephod, the other household gods 4374
18:24 He replied, *"You* t the gods I made, 4374
18:27 Then they t what Micah had made, 4374
19: 1 of Ephraim t a concubine from Bethlehem 4374
19: 3 *She* t him **into** her father's house, 995
19:15 no one t them into his home for the night. 665
19:21 So *he* t him into his house 995
19:25 So the man t his concubine 2616
19:29 *he* t a knife and cut up his concubine, 4374
20: 2 of Israel t *their* **places** in the assembly of 3656
20: 6 *I* t my concubine, cut her into pieces 296
20:20 the Benjamites and **t up** battle **positions** 6885
20:22 and again **t up** *their* **positions** 6885
20:30 on the third day and **t up positions** 6885
20:33 from their places and **t up positions** 6885
21:12 and *they* t them to the camp at Shiloh 995
Ru 2:19 Blessed be the *man who* **t notice** *of* you!" 5795
4: 2 Boaz t ten of the elders of the town 4374
4: 7 one party **t off** his sandal and gave it to 8990
4:13 So Boaz t Ruth and she became his wife. 4374
4:16 Then Naomi t the child, 4374
1Sa 1:24 *she* t the boy with her, young as he was, 6590
2:19 a little robe and t it to him when she went 6590
5: 1 *they* t it from Ebenezer to Ashdod. 995
5: 3 *They* t Dagon and put him back 4374
6:10 *They* t two such cows and hitched them to 4374
6:15 The Levites t **down** the ark of the LORD, 3718
7: 1 of Kiriath Jearim came and t **up** the ark of 6590
7: 1 *They* t it to Abinadab's house on the hill 995

1Sa 7: 9 Then Samuel t a suckling lamb 4374
7:12 Then Samuel t a stone and set it up 4374
9:24 the cook t **up** the leg with what was on it 8123
10: 1 Then Samuel t a flask of oil and poured it 4374
11: 7 *He* t a pair of oxen, cut them into pieces, 4374
14:30 of the plunder *they* t from their enemies. 5162
14:52 *he* t him **into** his **service.** 665
15: 8 *He* t Agag king of the Amalekites alive, 9530
15:21 The soldiers t sheep and cattle from 4374
16:13 So Samuel t the horn of oil 4374
16:20 So Jesse t a donkey loaded with bread, 4374
17:16 and evening and t *his* **stand.** 3656
17:39 So he t them **off.** 6073
17:40 Then *he* t his staff in his hand, 4374
17:51 *He* t **hold** *of* the Philistine's sword 4374
17:54 David t the Philistine's head and brought it 4374
17:57 Abner t him and brought him before Saul, 4374
18: 4 Jonathan **t off** the robe he was wearing 7320
19: 5 *He* t his life in his hands when he killed 8492
19: 6 Saul listened to Jonathan and t *this* **oath:** 8678
19:13 Michal t an idol and laid it on the bed, 4374
20: 3 But David **t an oath** and said, 8678
21:12 David t these words to heart 8492
24: 2 So Saul t three thousand chosen men 4374
25:18 *She* t two hundred loaves of bread, 4374
26:12 So David t the spear and water jug 4374
27: 9 but t sheep and cattle, donkeys and camels, 4374
28:21 *I* t my life in my hands 8492
28:24 *She* t some flour, 4374
30:20 He t all the flocks and herds, 4374
31: 4 so Saul t his own sword and fell on it. 4374
31:12 *They* t **down** the bodies of Saul and his sons 4374
31:13 Then *they* t their bones and buried them 4374
2Sa 1:10 And *I* t the crown that was on his head 4374
1:11 the men with him t **hold** of their clothes 2616
1:17 David t **up** this **lament** concerning Saul and his son Jonathan, 7801+7806
2: 3 David also t the men who were with him, 6590
2:25 a group and t *their* **stand** on top of a hill. 6641
2:32 *They* t Asahel and buried him 5951
3:27 Joab t him **aside** into the gateway, 5742
3:35 but David **t an oath,** saying, 8678
3:36 All the people t **note** and were pleased; 5795
4:12 But *they* t the head of Ish-Bosheth 4374
5: 9 David then t **up residence** in the fortress 3782
5:13 David t more concubines and wives 4374
6: 6 Uzzah reached out and t **hold** of the ark 296
6:10 he t it **aside** *to* the house of Obed-Edom 5742
7: 8 I t you from the pasture and 4374
7:15 as *I* t it **away** from Saul, 6073
8: 1 and he t Metheg Ammah from the control 4374
8: 7 David t the gold shields that belonged to 4374
8: 8 King David t a great quantity of bronze. 4374
12: 4 *he* t the ewe lamb that belonged to 4374
12: 9 the Hittite with the sword and t his wife to 4374
12:10 because you despised me and t the wife 4374
12:30 *He* t the crown from the head 4374
12:30 t a great quantity of plunder **from** 3655
13: 8 *She* t some dough, kneaded it, 4374
13: 9 *she* t the pan and served him the bread, 4374
13:10 And Tamar t the bread she had prepared 4374
13:11 But when *she* t it to him to eat, 5602
15:29 t the ark of God **back** to Jerusalem 8740
17:19 His wife t a covering and spread it out over 4374
18: 6 the battle t **place** in the forest of Ephraim. 2118
18:14 So *he* t three javelins in his hand 4374
18:17 *They* t Absalom, threw him into a big pit in 4374
19: 8 king got up and t *his* **seat** in the gateway. 3782
20: 3 he t the ten concubines he had left 4374
20: 5 *he* t **longer** than the time the king had set 336
20: 9 Then Joab t Amasa by the beard 296
21: 8 But the king t Armoni and Mephibosheth, 4374
21:10 of Aiah t sackcloth and spread it out 4374
21:12 he went and t the bones of Saul 4374
21:20 *which* t **place** at Gath, 2118
22:17 down from on high and t **hold** *of* me; 4374
23:12 But Shammah t *his* **stand** in the middle of 3656
1Ki 1: 4 *she* t **care of** the king and 2118+6125
1:29 The king then **t an oath:** 8678
1:39 Zadok the priest t the horn of oil from 4374
1:50 went and t **hold** of the horns of the altar. 2616
2:28 of the LORD and t **hold** of the horns of 2616
3:20 up in the middle of the night and t my son 4374
7: 1 It t Solomon thirteen years, however, NIH
7:23 It t a line of thirty cubits to measure NIH
8: 3 the priests t **up** the ark, 5951
8:48 of their enemies who t them **captive,** 8647
11:24 where they settled and t **control.** 4887
11:30 and Ahijah t **hold** of the new cloak 9530
13:10 So *he* t another road and did not return by 2143
14:26 *He* t everything, including all 4374
15:18 then t all the silver and gold that was left 4374
17:19 *He* t him from her arms, 4374
18:26 *they* t the bull given them and prepared it. 4374
18:31 Elijah t twelve stones, 4374
19:21 *He* t his yoke of oxen 4374
20: 9 and t the answer **back** *to* Ben-Hadad. 8740
20:33 The men t *this* **as a good sign** 5727
20:34 the cities my father t from your father," 4374
21:13 So *they* t him outside the city 3655
2Ki 2: 8 Elijah t his cloak, rolled it up 4374
2:12 Then *he* t **hold** of his own clothes 2616
2:14 Then *he* t the cloak that had fallen 4374
3:26 *he* t with him seven hundred swordsmen 4374
3:27 Then *he* t his firstborn son, 4374
4:27 *she* t **hold** of his feet. 2616
4:37 Then *she* t her son and went out. 5951

2Ki 5: 6 that *he* t to the king of Israel read: 995
5:24 *he* t the things from the servants 4374
6: 7 Then the man reached out his hand and t it. 4374
7: 8 and entered another tent and t some things 5951
8:15 But the next day *he* t a thick cloth, 4374
9:13 and t their cloaks and spread them 4374
9:28 His servants t him **by chariot** to Jerusalem 8206
10: 7 these men t the princes and slaughtered 4374
10:14 So *they* t them alive and slaughtered them 9530
11: 2 t Joash son of Ahaziah and stole him away 4374
11: 9 Each one t his men— 4374
11:19 *He* t with him the commanders 4374
11:19 king then t *his* **place** on the royal throne, 3782
12: 9 Jehoiada the priest t a chest and bored 4374
12:18 of Judah t all the sacred objects dedicated 4374
13:18 "Take the arrows," and the king t them. 4374
14:14 *He* t all the gold and silver and all 4374
14:14 He also t hostages and returned to Samaria. NIH
14:21 Then all the people of Judah t Azariah, 4374
15:29 of Assyria came and t Ijon, 4374
15:29 He t Gilead and Galilee, NIH
16: 8 And Ahaz t the silver and gold found in 4374
16:17 King Ahaz t **away** the side panels 7915
16:18 *He* t **away** the Sabbath canopy 6015
17: 7 *All this* t **place** because 2118
17:24 *They* t **over** Samaria and lived in its towns. 3769
17:27 "Have one of the priests *you t* **captive** AIT
18:10 At the end of three years the Assyrians t it. 4334
21: 7 He t the carved Asherah pole he had made NIH
22:20 So *they* t her answer **back** *to* the king. 8740
23: 4 and t the ashes to Bethel. 5951
23: 6 *He* t the Asherah pole from the temple of 3655
23:30 And the people of the land t Jehoahaz son 4374
23:34 *he* t Jehoahaz and carried him off to Egypt, 4374
24:12 *he* t Jehoiachin **prisoner.** 4374
24:13 and t **away** all the gold articles 7915
24:15 Nebuchadnezzar t Jehoiachin **captive** 1655
24:15 *He* also t from Jerusalem to Babylon 1583+2143
25: 7 bound him with bronze shackles and t him 995
25:14 *They* also t **away** the pots, shovels, 4374
25:15 of the imperial guard t **away** the censers 4374
25:18 of the guard t **as prisoners** Seraiah 4374
25:19 *he* t the officer in charge of the fighting men 4374
25:19 also t the secretary who was chief officer NIH
25:20 Nebuzaradan the commander t them all 4374
25:24 Gedaliah t **an oath** to reassure them 8678
1Ch 5: 6 king of Assyria t **into exile.** 1655
5:21 t one hundred thousand people captive, NIH
5:26 t the Reubenites, the Gadites and the
half-tribe of Manasseh **into exile.** 1655
5:26 *He* t them to Halah, Habor, 995
7:15 Makir t a wife from among the Huppites 4374
9:30 the priests t **care of mixing** the spices. 5351+8379
10: 4 so Saul t his own sword and fell on it. 4374
10: 9 They stripped him and t his head 5951
10:12 all their valiant men went and t the bodies 5951
11: 7 David then t **up residence** in the fortress, 3782
11:14 But *they* t *their* **stand** in the middle of 3656
13:13 *he* t it **aside** to the house of Obed-Edom 5742
14: 3 In Jerusalem David t more wives 4374
17: 7 I t you from the pasture and 4374
17:13 as *I* t it **away** from your predecessor. 6073
18: 1 and *he* t Gath and its surrounding villages 4374
18: 7 David t the gold shields carried by 4374
18: 8 David t a great quantity of bronze, 4374
20: 2 David t the crown from the head 4374
20: 2 t a great quantity of plunder **from** 3655
20: 6 *which* t **place** at Gath, 2118
27:32 of Hacmoni t **care of** the king's sons. 6640
2Ch 2:17 Solomon t **a census** *of* all the aliens 6218
4: 2 It t a line of thirty cubits to measure NIH
5: 4 the Levites t **up** the ark, 5951
7: 6 The priests t their positions, 6641
11:23 and t many wives for them. 8626
12: 9 *He* t everything, including 4374
13:19 Abijah pursued Jeroboam and t from him 4334
14:10 and *they* t **up** battle **positions** in the Valley 6885
15: 8 of Oded the prophet, *he* t **courage.** 2616
15:14 *They* t **an oath** to the LORD 8678
16: 2 Asa then t the silver and gold **out** 3655
20:25 so much plunder that it t three days NIH
22:11 t Joash son of Ahaziah and stole him away 4374
23: 8 Each one t his men— 4374
23:20 *He* t with him the commanders 4374
25:12 t them to the top of a cliff and threw them 995
25:24 He t all the gold and silver and all NIH
26: 1 Then all the people of Judah t Uzziah, 4374
28: 5 t many of his people **as prisoners** 8647+8661
28: 8 The Israelites t **captive** 8647
28: 8 *They* also t a great deal of plunder, 1024
28:15 The men designated by name t the prisoners 2616
28:15 So *they* t them **back** to their fellow 995
28:21 Ahaz t **some of the things** from the temple 2745
28:24 from the temple of God and t them **away.** 7915
29:16 The Levites t it and carried it out to 7691
29:22 and the priests t the blood and sprinkled it 7691
30:16 Then *they* t **up** their regular positions 6584+6641
32:22 *He* t **care of** them on every side. 5633
33: 7 He t the carved image he had made NIH
33:11 *who* t Manasseh **prisoner,** 4334
33:11 bound him with bronze shackles and t him 2143
34:16 Then Shaphan t the book to the king 995
34:28 So *they* t her answer **back** *to* the king. 8740
35:24 So they t him out of his chariot, 6296
36: 1 And the people of the land t Jehoahaz son 4374
36: 4 But Neco t Eliakim's brother Jehoahaz 4374
36: 7 Nebuchadnezzar also t to Babylon articles 995
Ezr 3:10 t *their* **places** to praise the LORD, 6641
6: 5 which Nebuchadnezzar t from the temple 10485
7:28 I t **courage** and gathered leading men 2616
10: 5 And *they* t **the oath.** 8678
Ne 2: 1 *I* t the wine and gave it to the king. 5951
4:23 nor the guards with me t **off** our clothes; 7320
5:15 on the people and t forty shekels of silver 4374
9:22 *They* t **over** the country of Sihon king 3769
9:24 Their sons went in and t **possession** *of* 3769
9:25 *they* t **possession** *of* houses filled 3769
12:40 then t *their* **places** in the house of God; 6641
Est 3:10 So the king t his signet ring from his finger 6073
8: 2 The king t **off** his signet ring, 6073
9:27 the Jews t it upon themselves to establish 7691
Job 2: 8 Then Job t a piece of broken pottery 4374
29: 7 the city and t my seat in the public square, 3922
29:16 *I* t **up** the case of the stranger. 2983
Ps 18:16 He reached down from on high and t **hold** 4374
78:70 He chose David his servant and t him from 4374
80: 9 and *it* t **root** and filled the land. 9245+9247
104: 7 the sound of your thunder *they* t **to flight;** 2905
106:44 But *he* t **note** of their distress 8011
Pr 7:13 *She* t **hold** of him and kissed him and with 2616
7:20 *He* t his purse filled with money and will 4374
Ecc 2:10 My heart *t* **delight** in all my work, AIT
8: 2 I say, because you t an oath before God. NIH
SS 5: 7 *they* t away my cloak, 5951
Isa 33:18 Where is the *one who* t *the* **revenue?** 9202
41: 9 *I* t you from the ends of the earth, 2616
43:14 in the ships in which they t pride. NIH
44:14 or perhaps t a cypress or oak. 4374
53: 4 Surely he t **up** our infirmities 5951
Jer 13: 7 to Perath and dug up the belt and t it from 4374
25:17 So *I* t the cup from the LORD's hand 4374
26:10 and t *their* **places** at the entrance of 3782
26:23 They brought Uriah out of Egypt and t him 995
28: 3 of Babylon removed from here and t 995
28:10 Then the prophet Hananiah t the yoke off 4374
31:32 with their forefathers when *I* t them by 2616
32:11 *I* t the deed of purchase— 4374
32:23 They came in and t **possession** *of* it, 3769
34:11 and t **back** the slaves they had freed 8740
36:32 So Jeremiah t another scroll and gave it to 4374
38: 6 So *they* t Jeremiah and put him into 4374
38:11 So Ebed-Melech t the men with him 4374
38:11 *He* t some old rags and worn-out clothes 4374
39: 3 of the king of Babylon came and t **seats** in 3782
39: 5 and t him to Nebuchadnezzar king 6590
40: 9 t **an oath** to reassure them and their men. 8678
41:10 Ishmael son of Nethaniah t them **captive** 8647
41:12 *they* t all their men and went 4374
52:11 bound him with bronze shackles and t him 995
52:18 *They* also t **away** the pots, shovels, 4374
52:19 of the imperial guard t **away** the basins, 4374
52:24 of the guard t **as prisoners** Seraiah 4374
52:25 *he* t the officer in charge of the fighting men 4374
52:25 also t the secretary who was chief officer NIH
52:26 Nebuzaradan the commander t them all 4374
La 3:58 O Lord, *you* t **up** my case; 8189
Eze 3:14 The Spirit then lifted me up and t **me away,** 4374
3:21 he will surely live because *he* t **warning,** 2302
8: 3 a hand and t me by the hair of my head, 4374
8: 3 and in visions of God *he* t me to Jerusalem, 995
10: 7 *He* t **up** some of it and put it into the hands 5951
10: 7 *who* t it and went out. 4374
12: 7 *I* t my belongings **out** at dusk, 3655
16:16 *You* t some of your garments 4374
16:17 *You* also t the fine jewelry I gave you, 4374
16:18 And *you* t your embroidered clothes to put 4374
16:20 " 'And *you* t your sons and daughters 4374
17: 5 " '*He* t some of the seed of your land 4374
17:13 Then *he* t a member of the royal family 4374
18: 7 but returns **what** he t **in pledge** 2481
18:12 He does not return **what** he t **in pledge.** 2478
19: 5 *she* t another of her cubs and made him 4374
23:10 t **away** her sons and daughters 4374
25:12 Because Edom t **revenge** on the house 5933+5934
25:15 t **revenge** with malice in their hearts, 5933+5934
27: 5 *they* t a cedar from Lebanon to make 4374
33:15 gives back **what** he t **in pledge for a loan,** 2478
40: 1 the LORD was upon me and *he* t me there. 995
40: 2 In visions of God *he* t me to the land 995
40: 3 *He* t me there, and I saw a man 995
42: 5 the galleries t more **space** from them than 430
Da 1:16 So the guard t **away** their choice food and 5951
2:25 Arioch t Daniel to the king at once 10549
3:22 of the fire killed the soldiers who t **up** 10513
5:31 and Darius the Mede t **over** the kingdom, 10618
7: 9 and the Ancient of Days t *his* **seat.** 10338
8:11 *it* t **away** the daily sacrifice from him, 8123
11: 1 I t my **stand** to support and protect him.) 6641
Hos 13:11 and in my wrath *I* t him **away.** 4374
Joel 3: 5 For *you* t my silver and my gold 4374
Am 1: 6 Because she t **captive** whole communities 1655
7:14 and I also t **care of** sycamore-fig trees. 1179
7:15 the LORD t me from tending the flock 4374
Jnh 1:15 *they* t Jonah and threw him overboard, 5951
3: 6 rose from his throne, t **off** his royal robes, 6296
Zec 11: 7 Then *I* t two staffs and called one Favor 4374
11:10 *I* t my staff called Favor and broke it, 4374
11:13 So *I* t the thirty pieces of silver 4374
Mt 1:22 All this t **place** to fulfill what the Lord *1181*
1:24 and t Mary home as his wife. *4161*
2:14 t the child and his mother during the night *4161*
2:21 t the child and his mother and went to *4161*
4: 5 Then the devil t him to the holy city *4161*
4: 8 the devil t him to a very high mountain *4161*
Mt 8:17 "He t **up** our infirmities *3284*
9:25 *he* went in and t the girl by the hand, *3195*
13:31 which a man t and planted in his field. *3284*
13:33 a woman t and mixed into a large amount *3284*
13:57 And *they* t **offense** at him. *4997*
14:12 John's disciples came and t his body *149*
15:36 Then *he* t the seven loaves and the fish, *3284*
16:22 Peter t him **aside** and began to rebuke him. *4689*
17: 1 After six days Jesus t **with** him Peter, *4161*
18:27 The servant's master t **pity** on him, *5072*
20:17 *he* t the twelve disciples aside and said *4161*
21: 4 This t **place** to fulfill what was spoken *1181*
21:39 So they t him and threw him out of *3284*
24:39 until the flood came and t them all **away.** *149*
25: 1 be like ten virgins who t their lamps *3284*
25: 3 The foolish ones t their lamps but did *3284*
25: 4 t oil in jars along with their lamps. *3284*
26:26 While they were eating, Jesus t bread, *3284*
26:27 Then he t the cup, gave thanks and *3284*
26:37 t Peter and the two sons of Zebedee **along** *4161*
26:57 Those who had arrested Jesus t him *552*
27: 9 "*They* t the thirty silver coins, *3284*
27:24 he t water and washed his hands in front of *3284*
27:27 Then the governor's soldiers t Jesus into *4161*
27:30 and t the staff and struck him on *3284*
27:31 *they* t **off** the robe and put his own clothes *1694*
27:59 Joseph t the body, wrapped it in a clean *3284*
28:15 So the soldiers t the money and did *3284*
Mk 1:31 t her hand and helped her up. *3195*
2:12 t his mat and walked out in full view *149*
4:36 *they* t him **along,** just as he was, *4161*
5:40 *he* t the child's father and mother and *4161*
5:41 He t her by the hand and said to her, *3195*
6: 3 And *they* t **offense** at him. *4997*
6:29 John's disciples came and t his body *149*
7:33 he t him aside, **away from** the crowd, *655*
8:23 He t the blind man by the hand *2138*
8:32 Peter t him **aside** and began to rebuke him. *4689*
9: 2 Jesus t Peter, James and John **with** him *4161*
9:27 But Jesus t him by the hand and lifted him *3195*
9:36 He t a little child and had him stand *3284*
10:16 And he t the children **in his arms,** *1878*
10:32 Again he t the Twelve **aside** *4161*
12: 8 So they t him and killed him, *3284*
14:22 While they were eating, Jesus t bread, *3284*
14:23 Then he t the cup, gave thanks and *3284*
14:33 *He* t Peter, James and John along with him, *4161*
14:53 *They* t Jesus to the high priest, *552*
14:65 And the guards t him and beat him. *3284*
15:20 *they* t **off** the purple robe *1694*
15:46 t **down** the body, wrapped it in the linen, *2747*
Lk 2: 2 that t place while Quirinius was governor *NIG*
2:22 Joseph and Mary t him to Jerusalem *343*
2:28 Simeon t him in his arms and praised God, *1312*
4:29 and t him to the brow of the hill on which *72*
5:25 t what he had been lying on and went home *149*
8:54 But he t her by the hand and said, *3195*
9:10 Then *he* t them with him *4161*
9:28 after Jesus said this, *he* t Peter, John *4161*
9:47 t a little child and had him stand *2138*
10:33 and when he saw him, *he* t **pity** on him. *5072*
10:34 t him to an inn and took care of him. *72*
10:34 took him to an inn and t **care of** him. *2150*
10:35 The next day he t **out** two silver coins *1675*
13: 7 the man who t **care of the vineyard,** *307*
13:19 which a man t and planted in his garden. *3284*
13:21 a woman t and mixed into a large amount *3284*
18:31 Jesus t the Twelve **aside** and told them, *4161*
22:19 And he t bread, gave thanks and broke it, *3284*
22:20 after the supper he t the cup, saying, *NIG*
22:54 and t him **into** the house of the high priest. *1652*
23:48 to witness this sight saw what t **place,** *1181*
23:53 Then he t it **down,** wrapped it in a linen *2747*
24: 1 the *women* t the spices they had prepared *5770*
24:21 it is the third day since all this t **place.** *1181*
24:30 he t bread, gave thanks, *3284*
24:43 and he t it and ate it in their presence. *3284*
Jn 2: 1 the third day a wedding t **place** at Cana *1181*
4:50 The man t Jesus **at his word** *3364+4409*
5: 9 on which this t place was a Sabbath, *NIG*
6:11 Jesus then t the loaves, gave thanks, *3284*
11:41 So *they* t **away** the stone. *149*
12: 3 Then Mary t about a pint of pure nard, *3284*
12:13 *They* t palm branches and went out *3284*
13: 4 t **off** his outer clothing, *5502*
13:27 As soon as Judas t the bread, *NIG*
19: 1 Then Pilate t Jesus and had him flogged. *3284*
19:16 So the soldiers t **charge of** Jesus. *4161*
19:23 *they* t his clothes, dividing them into four *3284*
19:27 this disciple t her into his home. *3284*
19:38 he came and t the body **away.** *149*
21:13 t the bread and gave it to them, *3284*
Ac 4:13 and *they* t **note** that these men had been *2105*
7:21 Pharaoh's daughter t him and brought him *359*
7:45 with them when they t the land from *2959*
8:39 Spirit of the Lord **suddenly** t Philip **away,** *773*
9:25 But his followers t him by night *3284*
9:27 But Barnabas t him and brought him to *2138*
9:30 *they* t him **down** to Caesarea *2864*
9:41 *He* t her by the hand and helped her *1443*
13:20 All this t about 450 years. *NIG*
13:29 they t him **down** from the tree and laid him *2747*
15:39 Barnabas t Mark and sailed for Cyprus, *4161*
16:33 the jailer t them and washed their wounds; *4161*
17:19 Then they t him and brought him to *2138*
19: 1 Paul t **the road through** the interior *1451*
19: 9 *He* t the disciples with him *928*

Ac 20:12 The *people* **t** the young man home alive *72*
20:14 we **t** him **aboard** and went on to Mitylene. *377*
21:11 Coming over to us, *he* **t** Paul's belt, *149*
21:26 The next day Paul **t** the men *4161*
21:32 at once **t** some officers and soldiers and ran *4161*
23:18 So he **t** him to the commander. *72+4161*
23:19 The commander **t** the young man by *2138*
23:31 **t** Paul with them during the night *377*
27:18 **t** such **a** violent **battering from the storm** *5928*
27:28 They **t soundings** and found that *1075*
27:28 A short time later they **t soundings** again *1075*
27:35 he **t** some bread and gave thanks to God *3284*
1Co 11:23 on the night he was betrayed, **t** bread, *3284*
11:25 In the same way, after supper he **t** the cup, *NIG*
Gal 2: 1 *I* **t** Titus **along** also. *5221*
Php 3:12 that for which Christ Jesus **t hold of** *me*. *2898*
Col 2:14 *he* **t** it **away**, nailing it to the cross. *149*
Heb 8: 9 when I **t** them by the hand to lead them out *2138*
9:19 he **t** the blood of calves, *3284*
Rev 5: 7 and **t** the scroll from the right hand *3284*
8: 5 Then the angel **t** the censer, *3284*
10:10 *I* **t** the little scroll from the angel's hand *3284*

TOOL (9) [TOOLS]

Ex 20:25 for you will defile it if you use a **t** on it. 2995
32: 4 the shape of a calf, fashioning it with a **t**. 3032
Dt 27: 5 Do not use any **iron t** upon them. 1366
Jos 8:31 on which no **iron t** had been used. 1366
2Sa 23: 7 Whoever touches thorns uses a **t of iron** or 1366
1Ki 6: 7 chisel or any other iron **t** was heard at 3998
Job 19:24 they were inscribed with an iron **t** on lead, 6485
Isa 44:12 The blacksmith takes a **t** and works with it 5108
Jer 17: 1 "Judah's sin is engraved with an iron **t**, 6485

TOOLS (1) [TOOL]

Ge 4:22 who forged all kinds of **t** out of bronze 3086

TOOTH (11) [TEETH]

Ex 21:24 **t** for tooth, hand for hand, foot for foot, 9094
21:24 tooth for **t**, hand for hand, foot for foot, 9094
21:27 And if he knocks out the **t** *of* a manservant 9094
21:27 the servant go free to compensate for the **t**. 9094
Lev 24:20 eye for eye, **t** for tooth. 9094
24:20 eye for eye, tooth for **t**. 9094
Dt 19:21 life for life, eye for eye, **t** for tooth, 9094
19:21 life for life, eye for eye, tooth for **t**, 9094
Pr 25:19 Like a bad **t** or a lame foot is reliance on 9094
Mt 5:38 'Eye for eye, and **t** for tooth.' *3848*
5:38 'Eye for eye, and tooth for **t**.' *3848*

TOP (91) [TOPMOST, TOPS]

Ge 6:16 ark to within 18 inches of the **t**. 2025+4200+5087
22: 9 on the altar, on **t** of the wood. 5087
28:12 with its **t** reaching to heaven, 8031
28:18 and set it up as a pillar and poured oil on **t** 8031
40:17 the **t** basket were all kinds of baked goods 6609
47:31 and Israel worshiped as he leaned on the **t** 8031
Ex 12:22 and put some of the blood on the **t** and on 5485
12:23 he will see the blood on the **t** and sides of 5485
17: 9 Tomorrow I will stand on **t** *of* the hill with 8031
17:10 Aaron and Hur went to the **t** *of* the hill. 8031
19:20 the **t** *of* Mount Sinai and called Moses to 8031
19:20 and called Moses to the **t** *of* the mountain. 8031
24:17 like a consuming fire on **t** *of* the mountain. 8031
25:21 the cover on **t of** the ark 2025+4200+4946+5087
26:24 the bottom all the way to the **t**, and fitted 8031
30: 3 the **t** and all the sides and the horns 1511
34: 2 Present yourself to me there on **t** *of* 8031
36:29 the bottom all the way to the **t** and fitted 8031
37:26 They overlaid the **t** and all the sides and 1511
Lev 3: 5 the altar **on t of** the burnt offering that is 6584
4:35 the priest shall burn it on the altar **on t of** 6584
5:12 on the altar **on t of** the offerings made to 6584
8:28 on the altar **on t of** the burnt offering as 6584
9:14 and burned them **on t of** the burnt offering 6584
14:17 **on t of** the blood of the guilt offering. 6584
Nu 20:28 Aaron died there on **t** *of* the mountain. 8031
21:20 in Moab where the **t** *of* Pisgah overlooks 8031
23:14 to the field of Zophim on the **t** *of* Pisgah, 8031
23:28 And Balak took Balaam to the **t** *of* Peor, 8031
Dt 3:27 to the **t** *of* Pisgah and look west and north 8031
28:13 you will always be at the **t**, 2025+5087
28:35 the soles of your feet to the **t of** your **head.** 7721
34: 1 from the plains of Moab to the **t** *of* Pisgah, 8031
Jos 15: 8 the **t** *of* the hill west of the Hinnom Valley 8031
Jdg 6:26 of altar to the LORD your God on the **t** 8031
9: 7 up on the **t** *of* Mount Gerizim and shouted 8031
16: 3 to his shoulders and carried them to the **t** 8031
1Sa 26:13 over to the other side and stood on **t** *of* 8031
28:12 she cried out at the **t** of her voice and said 1524
2Sa 2:25 a group and took their stand on **t** *of* a hill. 8031
14:25 From the **t of** his **head** to the sole 7721
1Ki 7:17 the capitals on **t** *of* the pillars, 8031
7:18 to decorate the capitals on **t** *of* the pillars. 8031
7:19 on **t** *of* the pillars in the portico were in 8031
7:22 The capitals on **t** were in the shape 8031
7:25 Sea rested on **t** *of* them, 2025+4200+4946+5087
7:35 At the **t** *of* the stand there was 8031
7:35 panels were attached to the **t** *of* the stand. 8031
7:41 the two bowl-shaped capitals on **t** *of* 8031
7:41 the two bowl-shaped capitals on **t** *of* 8031
7:42 decorating the bowl-shaped capitals on **t** 7156
10:19 and its back had a rounded **t**. 8031
18:42 but Elijah climbed to the **t** *of* Carmel, 8031
2Ki 1: 9 who was sitting on the **t** *of* a hill, 8031
25:17 The bronze capital **on t of** one pillar 6584
2Ch 3:15 with a capital on **t** measuring five cubits. 8031
3:16 and put them on **t** *of* the pillars. 8031
4: 4 Sea rested on **t** *of* them, 2025+4200+4946+5087
4:12 the two bowl-shaped capitals on **t** *of* 8031
4:12 the two bowl-shaped capitals on **t** *of* 8031
4:13 decorating the bowl-shaped capitals on **t** 7156
25:12 to the **t** *of* a cliff and threw them down so 8031
Ne 12:31 the leaders of Judah go up on **t** of the wall. 6584
12:31 to proceed on **t** of the wall to the right, 6584
12:38 I followed them on **t** of the wall, 6584
Job 2: 7 the soles of his feet to the **t of** his **head.** 7721
Pr 23:34 lying on **t** *of* the rigging. 8031
SS 4: 8 from the **t** *of* Senir, the summit of Hermon, 8031
Isa 1: 6 the *t of* your **head** there is no soundness— AIT
Jer 52:22 The bronze capital **on t of** one pillar 6584
Eze 17: 3 Taking hold of the **t** *of* a cedar, 7550
17:22 I myself will take a shoot from the **very t** 8123
31: 3 its **t** above the thick foliage. 7550
31:10 lifting its **t** above the thick foliage, 7550
40:13 the gateway from the **t of the** *rear* **wall** 1511
40:13 of one alcove to the **t** *of* the opposite one; 1511
41: 7 to the **t** *floor* through the middle floor. 6609
43:12 on **t** *of* the mountain will be most holy. 8031
Da 4:11 and strong and its **t** touched the sky; 10660
4:20 with its **t** touching the sky, 10660
Am 1: 2 and the **t** *of* Carmel withers." 8031
9: 3 Though they hide themselves on the **t** 8031
Zec 4: 2 a solid gold lampstand with a bowl at the **t** 8031
Mt 27:51 curtain of the temple was torn in two from **t** *540*
Mk 5: 7 He shouted **at the t of** his voice, *3489*
15:38 curtain of the temple was torn in two from **t** *540*
Lk 4:33 cried out **at the t of** his **voice,** *3489+5889*
8:28 **shouting at the t of** *his* **voice,** *3306+3489+5889*
Jn 19:23 woven in one piece from **t** to bottom. *540*
Ac 7:57 yelling **at the t of** their **voices,** *3489+5889*
Heb 11:21 worshiped as he leaned on the **t** of his staff. *216*

TOPAZ (5)

Ex 28:17 a ruby, a **t** and a beryl; 7077
39:10 a ruby, a **t** and a beryl; 7077
Job 28:19 The **t** *of* Cush cannot compare with it; 7077
Eze 28:13 ruby, **t** and emerald, chrysolite, 7077
Rev 21:20 the ninth **t**, the tenth chrysoprase, *5535*

TOPHEL (1)

Dt 1: 1 opposite Suph, between Paran and **T**, 9523

TOPHETH (10)

2Ki 23:10 He desecrated **T**, which was in the Valley 9532
Isa 30:33 **T** has long been prepared; 9533
Jer 7:31 They have built the high places of **T** in 9532
7:32 when people will no longer call it **T** or 9532
7:32 the dead in **T** until there is no more room. 9532
19: 6 people will no longer call this place **T** 9532
19:11 the dead in **T** until there is no more room. 9532
19:12 I will make this city like **T**. 9532
19:13 of Judah will be defiled like this place, **T**— 9532
19:14 Jeremiah then returned from **T**, 9532

TOPMOST (3) [TOP, MOST]

Isa 17: 6 or three olives on the **t** branches, 8031
Eze 17: 4 he broke off its **t** shoot and carried it away 8031
17:22 a tender sprig from its **t** shoots and plant it 8031

TOPPLE (3)

Ps 62: 4 to **t** him from his lofty place; 5615
Isa 40:20 to set up an idol *that will* not **t**. 4572
41: 7 He nails down the idol so *it will* not **t**. 4572

TOPS (14) [TOP]

Ge 8: 5 on the first day of the tenth month the **t** *of* 8031
Ex 12: 7 of the blood and put it on the sides and **t** of 5485
36:38 the **t** *of* the posts and their bands with gold 8031
38:17 and their **t** were overlaid with silver; 8031
38:19 and their **t** were overlaid with silver. 8031
38:28 to overlay the **t** *of* the posts, 8031
Jdg 9:36 people are coming down from the **t** *of* 8031
2Sa 5:24 as you hear the sound of marching in the **t** 8031
1Ki 7:16 of cast bronze to set on the **t** *of* the pillars; 8031
1Ch 14:15 as you hear the sound of marching in the **t** 8031
Ps 72:16 on the **t** *of* the hills may it sway. 8031
Isa 14:14 I will ascend above the **t** *of* the clouds; 1195
Eze 31:14 lifting their **t** above the thick foliage. 7550
Am 9: 1 "Strike the **t of the pillars** so that 4117

TORCH (5) [TORCHES]

Ge 15:17 a blazing **t** appeared and passed between 4365
Jdg 15: 4 He then fastened a **t** to every pair of tails, 4365
Isa 62: 1 her salvation like a blazing **t**. 4365
Zec 12: 6 like a flaming **t** among sheaves. 4365
Rev 8:10 and a great star, blazing like a **t**, *3286*

TORCHES (9) [TORCH]

Jdg 7:16 in the hands of all of them, with **t** inside. 4365
7:20 the **t** in their left hands and holding 4365
15: 5 lit the **t** and let the foxes loose in 4365
Isa 50:11 and provide yourselves with **flaming t**, 2338
50:11 and of the **t** you have set ablaze. 2338
Eze 1:13 like burning coals of fire or like **t**. 4365
Da 10: 6 his eyes like flaming **t**, 4365
Na 2: 4 They look like **flaming t**; 4365
Jn 18: 3 They were carrying **t**, lanterns and weapons. *5749*

TORE (44) [TEAR]

Ge 37:29 that Joseph was not there, *he* **t** his clothes. 7973
37:34 Then Jacob **t** his clothes, 7973
44:13 At this, *they* **t** their clothes. 7973
Nu 14: 6 explored the land, **t** their clothes 7973
Jos 7: 6 Then Joshua **t** his clothes 7973
Jdg 11:35 *he* **t** his clothes and cried, "Oh! 7973
14: 6 that *he* **t** the lion **apart** with his bare hands 9117
16: 3 and **t** them **loose**, bar and all. 5825
1Sa 15:27 caught hold of the hem of his robe, and *it* **t**. 7973
2Sa 1:11 took hold of their clothes and **t** them. 7973
13:19 Tamar put ashes on her head and **t** 7973
13:31 **t** his clothes and lay down on the ground; 7973
1Ki 11:30 of the new cloak he was wearing and **t** it 7973
14: 8 *I* **t** the kingdom **away** from the house 7973
19:11 powerful wind **t** the mountains **apart** 7293
21:27 *he* **t** his clothes, put on sackcloth and 7973
2Ki 2:12 took hold of his own clothes and **t** them
apart. 4200+7973+7974+9109
5: 7 *he* **t** his robes and said, "Am I God? 7973
6:30 heard the woman's words, *he* **t** his robes. 7973
10:27 of Baal and **t down** the temple of Baal, 5997
11:14 Then Athaliah **t** her robes and called out, 7973
11:18 to the temple of Baal and **t** it **down.** 5997
17:21 *he* **t** Israel **away** from the house of David, 7973
19: 1 *he* **t** his clothes and put on sackcloth 7973
22:11 of the Book of the Law, *he* **t** his robes. 7973
22:19 *you* **t** your robes and wept in my presence, 7973
23: 7 *He* also **t down** the quarters of 5997
2Ch 23:13 Then Athaliah **t** her robes and shouted, 7973
23:17 to the temple of Baal and **t** it **down.** 5997
34: 7 *he* **t down** the altars and the Asherah poles 5997
34:19 the words of the Law, *he* **t** his robes. 7973
34:27 and **t** your robes and wept in my presence, 7973
Ezr 9: 3 When I heard this, *I* **t** my tunic and cloak, 7973
Est 4: 1 he **t** his clothes, put on sackcloth and ashes, 7973
Job 1:20 up and **t** his robe and shaved his head. 7973
2:12 and *they* **t** their robes and sprinkled dust 7973
Isa 22:10 and **t down** houses to strengthen the wall. 5997
37: 1 *he* **t** his clothes and put on sackcloth 7973
Jer 2:20 and **t off** your bonds; 5998
Eze 29: 7 and *you* **t open** their shoulders; 1324
Mt 26:65 Then the high priest **t** his clothes and said, *1396*
Mk 5: 4 but he **t** the chains **apart** and broke *1400*
14:63 The high priest **t** his clothes. *1396*
Ac 14:14 they **t** their clothes and rushed out into *1396*

TORMENT (13) [TORMENTED, TORMENTING, TORMENTORS]

Job 13:25 *Will you* **t** a windblown leaf? 6907
15:20 All his days the wicked man **suffers t**, 2655
19: 2 "How long *will you* **t** me and crush me 3324
Isa 50:11 You will lie down in **t**. 5107
La 1:20 I *am* **in t** within, 2813
2:11 I *am* **in t** within, 2813
Lk 16:23 In hell, where he was in **t**, *992*
16:28 they will not also come to this place *of* **t**.' *992*
2Co 12: 7 a messenger of Satan, to **t** me. *3139*
Rev 9:10 in their tails they had power *to* **t** people *92*
14:11 the smoke *of* their **t** rises for ever and ever. *990*
18:10 Terrified *at* her **t**, they will stand far off *990*
18:15 will stand far off, terrified *at* her **t**. *990*

TORMENTED (7) [TORMENT]

1Sa 16:14 and an evil spirit from the LORD **t** him. 1286
Pr 28:17 A man **t** by the guilt of murder will be 6943
Ac 5:16 bringing their sick and *those* **t** *4061*
2Pe 2: 8 *was* **t** in his righteous soul by *989*
Rev 11:10 these two prophets *had* **t** those who live *989*
14:10 *be* **t** with burning sulfur in the presence of *989*
20:10 *They will be* **t** day and night for ever *989*

TORMENTING (1) [TORMENT]

1Sa 16:15 "See, an evil spirit from God *is* **t** you. 1286

TORMENTORS (2) [TORMENT]

Ps 137: 3 our **t** demanded songs of joy; 9354
Isa 51:23 I will put it into the hands of your **t**, 3324

TORN (56) [TEAR]

Ge 31:39 did not bring you **animals t by wild beasts;** 3274
37:33 Joseph *has* **surely been t to pieces."** 3271+3271
44:28 *"He has* **surely been t to pieces."** 3271+3271
Ex 22:13 **was t to pieces by a wild animal,** 3271+3271
22:13 not be required to pay for the **t** animal. NIH
22:31 the meat of an **animal t** by wild **beasts;** 3274
Lev 7:24 or **t by wild animals** may be used 3274
13:45 an infectious disease must wear **t** clothes, 7268
14:40 that the contaminated stones *be* **t out** 2740
14:43 the house after the stones *have been* **t out** 2740
14:45 It *must be* **t down**— 5997
17:15 **t by wild animals** must wash his clothes 3274
22: 8 anything found dead or **t by wild animals,** 3274
22:24 are bruised, crushed, **t** or cut. 5998
Jdg 14: 6 with his bare hands as *he might have* **t** 9117
1Sa 4:12 his clothes **t** and dust on his head. 7973
15:28 "The LORD *has* **t** the kingdom of Israel 7973
28:17 The LORD *has* **t** the kingdom out 7973
2Sa 1: 2 with his clothes **t** and with dust on his head. 7973
13:31 his servants stood by with their clothes **t**. 7973

2Sa 15:32 his robe t and dust on his head. 7973
2Ki 5: 8 that the king of Israel *had* t his robes, 7973
5: 8 "Why *have you* t your robes? 7973
18:37 went to Hezekiah, with their clothes **t,** 7973
2Ch 34: 4 the altars of the Baals *were* **t down;** 5997
Ezr 9: 5 with my tunic and cloak **t,** 7973
Job 8:18 But when it *is* t from its spot, 1180
18:14 He **is t** from the security of his tent 5998
Ps 60: 2 You have shaken the land and t it **open;** 7204
124: 6 who has not let us be t by their teeth. 3272
Pr 2:22 and the unfaithful *will be* t from it. 5815
Isa 36:22 went to Hezekiah, with their clothes **t,** 7973
Jer 5: 5 broken off the yoke and **t off** the bonds. 5998
13:22 that your skirts *have* **been t off** 1655
18: 7 uprooted, **t down** and destroyed, 5997
33: 4 of Judah that *have* **been t down** to be used 5997
41: 5 t their clothes and cut themselves came 7973
50:15 her towers fall, her walls **are t down.** 2238
La 2: 2 in his wrath *he has* **t down** the strongholds 2238
Eze 4:14 anything found dead or **t by wild animals.** 3274
30: 4 and her foundations **t down.** 2238
44:31 found dead or **t by wild animals.** 3274
Da 7: 4 until its wings **were t off** and it was lifted 10440
Hos 6: 1 He *has* t us **to pieces** but he will heal us; 3271
Mt 27:51 the temple *was* t in two from top to bottom. *5387*
Mk 1:10 he saw heaven *being* **t open** and *5387*
15:38 the temple *was* t in two from top to bottom. *5387*
Lk 5:36 If he does, *he will have* t the new garment, *5387*
23:45 And the curtain of the temple *was* t in two. *5387*
Jn 21:11 but even with so many the net *was* not **t.** *5387*
Ac 21: 1 *After we had* t *ourselves* **away** from them, *685*
23:10 afraid Paul *would be* **t to pieces** by them. *1400*
Ro 11: 3 they have killed your prophets and **t down** *2940*
Gal 4:15 you would have **t out** your eyes *2021*
Php 1:23 *I am* t between the two: *5309*
1Th 2:17 *when* we *were* **t away from** you for a short *682*

TORRENT (6) [TORRENTS]

Ps 124: 4 the t would have swept over us, 5707
Isa 30:28 His breath is like a rushing **t,** 5707
Jer 47: 2 they will become an overflowing **t.** 5707
Lk 6:48 t struck that house but could not shake it, *4532*
6:49 The moment the t struck that house, *4532*
Rev 12:15 and **sweep** her **away with the t.** *4472+4533*

TORRENTS (8) [TORRENT]

2Sa 22: 5 the t *of* destruction overwhelmed me. 5707
Job 14:19 and t wash away the soil, 6207
38:25 Who cuts a channel for the **t of rain,** 8852
Ps 18: 4 the t *of* destruction overwhelmed me. 5707
Eze 13:11 Rain will come *in* **t,** 8851
13:13 and t *of* rain will fall with destructive fury. 8851
38:22 I will pour down t *of* rain, 8851
Hab 3:10 T *of* water swept by; 2443

TORTOISE (KJV) See GREAT LIZARD

TORTURE (5) [TORTURED]

Mt 8:29 "Have you come here *to* t us before *989*
Mk 5: 7 Swear to God that *you* won't t me!" *989*
Lk 8:28 I beg you, don't t *me*!" *989*
Rev 9: 5 but only to t them for five months. *989*
18: 7 Give her as much t and grief as the glory *990*

TORTURED (2) [TORTURE]

Mt 18:34 turned him over *to* the **jailers to be t,** *991*
Heb 11:35 Others *were* t and refused to be released, *5594*

TOSS (7) [TOSSED, TOSSES, TOSSING]

Ex 9: 8 and *have* Moses t it into the air in the 2450
Job 7: 4 The night drags on, and *I* t till dawn. 5611+8425
30:22 *you* t me **about** in the storm. 4570
Ps 60: 8 upon Edom *I* t my sandal; 8959
108: 9 upon Edom *I* t my sandal; 8959
Mt 15:26 the children's bread and t it to their dogs." *965*
Mk 7:27 the children's bread and t it to their dogs." *965*

TOSSED (3) [TOSS]

Ex 9:10 Moses t it into the air, 2450
Eph 4:14 be infants, **t back and forth by the waves,** *3115*
Jas 1: 6 a wave of the sea, blown and t by the wind. *4847*

TOSSES (2) [TOSS]

2Ki 19:21 The Daughter of Jerusalem t her head 5675
Isa 37:22 The Daughter of Jerusalem t her head 5675

TOSSING (2) [TOSS]

Isa 57:20 But the wicked are like the t sea, 1764
Lk 21:25 and perplexity at the roaring and t of *4893*

TOTAL (24) [TOTALED, TOTALLY]

Ex 10:22 and t **darkness** covered all Egypt for three days. 696+3125
38:24 The t *amount of* the gold from the wave 3972
38:26 twenty years old or more, a t *of* 603,550 4200
Nu 1:46 The t number was 603,550. 3972
3:39 The t number of Levites counted at 3972
3:43 The t number *of* firstborn males a month old 3972
4:37 This was the t *of* all those in the Kohathite 7212
4:41 This was the t *of those in the* 3972+7212
4:45 the t *of those in* the Merarite clans. 7212
7:87 The t *number of* animals for the burnt 3972
7:88 The t *number of* animals for the sacrifice 3972
26:51 **The t** number of the men of Israel 465[S]
Jos 15:32 a t *of* twenty-nine towns and their villages. 3972
1Sa 14:20 found the Philistines in t confusion, 1524+4394
2Ki 24:14 and artisans—a t of ten thousand. NIH
1Ch 23: 3 were counted, and the t number of men 1653
2Ch 3:11 The t **wingspan** *of* the cherubim 802+4053
26:12 The t number of family leaders over 3972
35: 7 a t of thirty thousand sheep and 3972+4200+5031
Ne 7:72 **The t** given by the rest of the people 889[S]
Job 20:26 t darkness lies in wait for his treasures. 3972
Jer 52:23 the t *number* of pomegranates above 3972
Eze 48:13 Its t length will be 25,000 cubits 3972
Ac 19:19 the t came to fifty thousand drachmas. *NIG*

TOTALED (2) [TOTAL]

Ne 11: 6 who lived in Jerusalem t 468 able men. 3972
11:18 The Levites in the holy city t 284. 3972

TOTALLY (25) [TOTAL]

Nu 16:30 if the LORD brings about **something t new,** 1375
21: 2 *we will* t **destroy** their cities." 3049
Dt 7: 2 then *you* **must destroy** them **t.** 3049+3049
Jos 10: 1 that Joshua had taken Ai and t **destroyed** it, 3049
10:28 to the sword and t **destroyed** everyone in it. 3049
10:35 to the sword and t **destroyed** everyone in it, 3049
10:37 *they* t **destroyed** it and everyone in it. 3049
10:39 Everyone in it *they* **t destroyed.** 3049
10:40 *He* **t destroyed** all who breathed, 3049
11:11 *They* **t destroyed** them, 3049
11:12 *He* **t destroyed** them, 3049
11:20 so that *he might* **destroy** them **t,** 3049
11:21 Joshua **t destroyed** them and their towns. 3049
Jdg 1:17 and *they* **t destroyed** the city. 3049
1Sa 15: 3 the Amalekites and **t destroy** everything 3049
15: 8 his people *he* **t destroyed** with the sword. 3049
15: 9 and weak *they* **t destroyed.** 3049
15:15 but *we* **t destroyed** the rest." 3049
2Ch 12:12 and he was not t destroyed. 3986
Isa 2:18 and the idols will t disappear. 4003
24: 3 laid waste and **t plundered.** 1024+1024
34: 2 *He will* **t destroy** them, 3049
34: 5 the people I have **t destroyed.** 3051
Am 9: 8 yet *I will* not **t destroy** the house of Jacob," 9012+9012
Zec 11:17 his right eye **t blinded!"** 3908+3908

TOTTER (1) [TOTTERING]

Jer 10: 4 with hammer and nails so *it will* not **t.** 7048

TOTTERING (1) [TOTTER]

Ps 62: 3 this leaning wall, this t fence? 1890

TOU (4)

2Sa 8: 9 When T king of Hamath heard 9497
8:10 who had been at war with **T.** 9497
1Ch 18: 9 When T king of Hamath heard 9495
18:10 who had been at war with **T.** 9495

TOUCH (40) [TOUCHED, TOUCHES, TOUCHING]

Ge 3: 3 and *you must* not t it, or you will die.'" 5595
20: 6 That is why I did not let you t her. 5595
27:21 "Come near so *I can* t you, my son, 4630
Ex 12:13 No destructive plague *will* t you 928+2118
19:12 not go up the mountain or t the foot of it. 5595
Lev 11: 8 not eat their meat or t their carcasses; 5595
12: 4 not t anything sacred or go to the sanctuary 5595
Nu 4:15 not t the holy things or they will die. 5595
16:26 *Do* not t anything belonging to them, 5595
Dt 14: 8 not to eat their meat or t their carcasses. 5595
28:56 that she would not venture *to* t the ground 3657
Jos 9:19 and we cannot t them now. 5595
Ru 2: 9 I have told the men not *to* t you. 5595
1Sa 24:12 but my hand *will* not t you. 928+2118
24:13 so my hand *will* not t you. 928+2118
2Sa 21:10 of the air t them by day or the wild animals 5663
1Ch 16:22 *"Do* not t my anointed ones; 5595
Job 6: 7 I refuse to t it; such food makes me ill. 5595
Ps 105:15 *"Do* not t my anointed ones; 5595
144: 5 t the mountains, so that they smoke. 5595
Isa 28:15 scourge sweeps by, *it* cannot t us, 995
52:11 T no unclean thing! 5595
Jer 13: 1 but *do* not **let** it t water." 928+995
14:15 'No sword or famine *will* t this land.' 928+2118
La 4:14 that no one dares *to* t their garments. 5595
4:15 "Away! Away! Don't t us!" 5595
Eze 9: 6 but *do* not t anyone who has the mark. 5602
Mt 9:21 She said to herself, "If *I* only t his cloak, *721*
14:36 to let the sick just t the edge of his cloak, *721*
Mk 3:10 with diseases were pushing forward to t him. *721*
5:28 "If *I* just t his clothes, I will be healed." *721*
6:56 to let *them* t even the edge of his cloak, *721*
8:22 a blind man and begged Jesus *to* t him. *721*
10:13 to Jesus to have him t them, *721*
Lk 6:19 and the people all tried *to* t him, *721*
18:15 bringing babies to Jesus to *have him* t them. *721*
24:39 T me and see; a ghost does not have flesh *6027*
2Co 6:17 T no unclean thing, and I will receive you." *721*
Col 2:21 "Do not handle! Do not taste! *Do* not **t!"?** *2566*
Heb 11:28 the destroyer of the firstborn *would* not t *2566*

TOUCHED (59) [TOUCH]

Ge 27:22 his father Isaac, *who* t him and said, 5491
32:25 *he* t the socket of Jacob's hip so 5595
32:32 socket of Jacob's hip *was* t near the tendon. 5595
Ex 4:25 son's foreskin and t [Moses'] feet with it. 5595
Nu 19:18 He must also sprinkle anyone *who has* t 5595
31:19 t anyone who was killed must stay outside 5595
Jos 3:15 the Jordan and their feet t the water's edge, 3188
16: 7 t Jericho and came out at the Jordan. 7003
19:11 to Maralah, t Dabbesheth, and extended to 7003
19:22 The boundary t Tabor, 7003
19:26 the boundary t Carmel and Shihor Libnath. 7003
19:27 t Zebulun and the Valley of Iphtah El, 7003
19:34 *It* t Zebulun on the south, 7003
Jdg 6:21 the angel of the LORD t the meat and 5595
1Sa 10:26 by valiant men whose hearts God *had* **t.** 5595
1Ki 6:27 The wing of one cherub t one wall, 5595
6:27 the wing of the other t the other wall, 5595
6:27 and their wings t each other in the middle 5595
19: 5 All at once an angel t him and said, 5595
19: 7 a second time and t him and said, 5595
2Ki 13:21 When the body t Elisha's bones, 5595
2Ch 3:11 the first cherub was five cubits long and t 5595
3:11 t the wing of the other cherub. 5595
3:12 and t the other temple wall, 5595
3:12 t the wing of the first cherub. 1816
Est 5: 2 So Esther approached and t the tip of 5595
Isa 6: 7 With it *he* t my mouth and said, "See, 5595
6: 7 "See, this *has* t your lips; 5595
Jer 1: 9 and t my mouth and said to me, 5595
Eze 1: 9 and their wings t one another. 2489
Da 4:11 The tree grew large and strong and its top t 10413
8:18 Then *he* t me and raised me to my feet. 5595
10: 3 no meat or wine t my lips; 448+995
10:10 A hand t me and set me trembling 5595
10:16 Then *one* who looked like a man t my lips, 5595
10:18 Again *the one* who looked like a man t me 5595
Mt 8: 3 Jesus reached out his hand and t the man. *721*
8:15 He t her hand and the fever left her, *721*
9:20 for twelve years came up behind him and t *721*
9:29 Then *he* t their eyes and said, *721*
14:36 and all who t him were healed. *721*
17: 7 But Jesus came and t them. *721*
20:34 had compassion on them and t their eyes. *721*
Mk 1:41 Jesus reached out his hand and t the man. *721*
5:27 behind him in the crowd and t his cloak, *721*
5:30 "Who t my clothes?" *721*
5:31 "and yet you can ask, 'Who t me?' " *721*
6:56 and all who t him were healed. *721*
7:33 Then *he* spit and t the man's tongue. *721*
Lk 5:13 Jesus reached out his hand and t the man. *721*
7:14 Then *he* went up and t the coffin, *721*
8:44 up behind him and t the edge of his cloak, *721*
8:45 "Who t me?" Jesus asked. *721*
8:46 But Jesus said, "Someone t me; *721*
8:47 she told why *she had* t him and *721*
22:51 And he t the man's ear and healed him. *721*
Ac 19:12 and aprons **that had** t him *608+3836+5999*
Heb 12:18 that can *be* t and that is burning with fire; *6027*
1Jn 1: 1 we have looked at and our hands *have* t— *6027*

TOUCHES (47) [TOUCH]

Ge 27:12 What if my father t me? 5491
Ex 19:12 Whoever t the mountain shall surely be put 5595
29:37 and whatever t it will be holy. 5595
30:29 and whatever t them will be holy. 5595
Lev 5: 2 person t anything ceremonially unclean— 5595
5: 3 " 'Or if *he* t human uncleanness— 5595
6:18 Whatever t them will become holy.' " 5595
6:27 Whatever t any of the flesh will become 5595
7:19 that t anything ceremonially unclean must 5595
7:21 If anyone t something unclean— 5595
11:24 whoever t their carcasses will be unclean 5595
11:26 whoever t [the carcass of] any of them will 5595
11:27 whoever t their carcasses will be unclean 5595
11:31 Whoever t them when they are dead will 5595
11:36 but *anyone who* t one of these carcasses 5595
11:39 anyone *who* t the carcass will be unclean 5595
15: 5 Anyone who t his bed must wash his clothes 5595
15: 7 " 'Whoever t the man who has 5595
15:10 and whoever t any of the things that were 5595
15:11 a discharge t without rinsing his hands 5595
15:12 'A clay pot that the man t must 5595
15:19 and anyone who t her will be unclean 5595
15:21 Whoever t her bed must wash his clothes 5595
15:22 Whoever t anything she sits 5595
15:23 when anyone t it, he will be unclean 5595
15:24 with her and her monthly flow t him, 2118+6584
15:27 Whoever t them will be unclean; 5595
22: 4 also be unclean if he t something defiled 5595
22: 5 or if he t any crawling thing 5595
22: 6 The one who t any such thing will 5595
Nu 19:11 "Whoever t the dead body of anyone will 5595
19:13 Whoever t the dead body of anyone 5595
19:16 open who t someone who has been killed 5595
19:16 or anyone who t a human bone or a grave, NIH
19:21 and anyone *who* t the water 5595
19:22 that an unclean person t becomes unclean, 5595
19:22 and anyone who t it becomes unclean 5595
2Sa 23: 7 Whoever t thorns uses a tool of iron or 5595
Job 20: 6 to the heavens and his head t the clouds, 5595
Ps 104:32 *who* t the mountains, and they smoke. 5595
Pr 6:29 no one who t her will go unpunished. 5595
Am 9: 5 he *who* t the earth and it melts, 5595
Hag 2:12 and that fold t some bread or stew, 5595

Hag 2:13 with a dead body t one of these things, 5595
Zec 2: 8 whoever t you touches the apple of his eye 5595
2: 8 whoever touches you t the apple of his eye 5595
Heb 12:20 "If even an animal t the mountain, *2566*

TOUCHING (4) [TOUCH]

Eze 1:11 *one* t the wing of another creature on 2489
Da 4:20 with its top t the sky, 10413
8: 5 the whole earth without t the ground. 5595
Lk 7:39 he would know who *is* t him *721*

TOW (KJV) See STRING, TINDER, WICK

TOWARD (229) [TO]

Ge 10:19 reached from Sidon t Gerar 995+2025+3870
10:19 and then t Sodom, Gomorrah, 995+2025+3870
10:30 they lived stretched from Mesha t 995+2025+3870
12: 8 From there he went on t the hills east 2025
12: 9 Abram set out and continued t the Negev. 2025
13:10 like the land of Egypt, t Zoar. 995+3870
13:11 the whole plain of the Jordan and set out t 4946
16:12 will live **in hostility** t all his brothers." 6584+7156
18:16 they looked down t Sodom, 6584+7156
18:22 The men turned away and went t Sodom, 2025
19:28 looked down t Sodom and Gomorrah, 6584+7156
19:28 t all the land of the plain, 6584+7156
24:11 it was t evening, the time the women go out 4200
25:18 the border of Egypt, as you go t Asshur. 2025
25:18 *they* **lived in hostility** t all their brothers. 5877+6584+7156
31: 2 And Jacob noticed that Laban's attitude t 6640
31: 5 "I see that your father's attitude t me is 448
34:21 "These men are friendly t us," they said. 907
48:13 Ephraim on his right t Israel's left hand 4946
48:13 on his left t Israel's right hand, 4946
49:13 his border will **extend** t Sidon. 6584
Ex 3:21 Egyptians **favorably disposed** t 928+2834+6524
9:22 "Stretch out your hand t the sky so 6584
9:23 Moses stretched out his staff t the sky, 6584
9:33 He spread out his hands t the LORD; 448
10:21 "Stretch out your hand t the sky so 6584
10:22 So Moses stretched out his hand t the sky, 6584
11: 3 Egyptians **favorably disposed** t 928+2834+6524
12:36 Egyptians **favorably disposed** t 928+2834+6524
13:18 **led** the people **around** *by* the desert road *t* AIT
14:27 The Egyptians were fleeing t it, 7925
16:10 they looked t the desert, 448
25:20 face each other, looking t the cover. 448
27:13 On the east end, t the sunrise, 2025
37: 9 faced each other, looking t the cover. 448
38:13 The east end, t the sunrise, 2025
Lev 9:22 Then Aaron lifted his hands t the people 448
26:21 " 'If you remain hostile t me and refuse 6640
26:23 but continue to be hostile t me, 6640
26:24 be hostile t you and will afflict you 6640
26:27 not listen to me but continue to be hostile t 6640
26:28 then in my anger I will be hostile t you, 6640
26:40 against me and their hostility t me, 6640
26:41 which made me hostile t them so 6640
Nu 2: 3 On the east, t the sunrise, 2025
3:38 of the tabernacle, t the sunrise, in front of 2025
6:26 the LORD turn his face t you and give you 448
12:10 Aaron turned t her and saw that she had 448
13:21 from the Desert of Zin as far as Rehob, t NIH
14:25 and **set out** *t* the desert along the route to AIT
14:40 Early the next morning they went up t 448
14:44 in their presumption they went up t 448
16:42 to Moses and Aaron and turned t the Tent 448
19: 4 and sprinkle it seven times t the front 448+5790
21:11 in the desert that faces Moab t the sunrise. 4946
21:33 and went up along the **road** *t* Bashan, AIT
24: 1 but turned his face t the desert. 448
34:15 on the east side of the Jordan of Jericho, t 2025
Dt 1:19 and went t the hill country of the Amorites 2006
1:40 turn around and set out t the desert along 2025
2: 1 and set out t the desert along the route to 2025
3: 1 and went up along the **road** *t* Bashan, AIT
11:30 west of the road, t the setting sun, NIH
15: 7 do not be hardhearted or tightfisted t 4946
15: 9 near," so that you do not show ill will t 928
15:11 be openhanded t your brothers and toward 4200
15:11 be openhanded toward your brothers and t 4200
32: 5 They have acted corruptly t him; 4200
Jos 1:15 the LORD gave you east of the Jordan t NIH
8:15 and they fled t the desert. 2006
8:18 "Hold out t Ai the javelin that is 448
8:18 So Joshua held out his javelin t Ai. 448
8:20 for the Israelites who *had been* **fleeing** *t* AIT
11:17 from Mount Halak, which **rises** *t* Seir, AIT
12: 7 which rises t Seir (their lands Joshua gave 2025
15: 9 From the hilltop the boundary headed t 448
15: 9 of Mount Ephron and **went down** *t* Baalah AIT
15:11 of Ekron, turned t Shikkeron, passed along 2025
15:21 the Negev t the boundary of Edom were: 448
19:12 It turned east from Sarid *t* the **sunrise** to AIT
19:13 it came out at Rimmon and **turned** *t* Neah. AIT
19:27 *It* then **turned** east *t* Beth Dagon, AIT
19:29 The boundary then **turned back** *t* Ramah AIT
19:29 **turned** *t* Hosah and came out at the sea in AIT
22:31 because you have not acted unfaithfully t 928
Jdg 7:22 The army fled to Beth Shittah t Zererah 2025
9:19 and in good faith t Jerub-Baal 6640
13:20 As the flame blazed up from the altar t 2025
14: 5 suddenly a young lion **came** roaring t him. 7925
15:14 the Philistines **came** t him shouting. 7925
Jdg 16:29 Then Samson **reached** t the two central 4369
19:10 the man left and went t Jebus (that is, 5790+6330
20:45 As they turned and fled t the desert to 2025
1Sa 6: 9 to its own territory, t Beth Shemesh, then NIH
6:12 cows went straight up t Beth Shemesh, 2006+6584
9:14 coming t them on his way up to 7925
13:17 One turned t Ophrah in the vicinity 448+2006
13:18 another t Beth Horon, 2006
13:18 and the third t the borderland overlooking 2006
14: 5 One cliff stood to the north t Micmash, 4578
14: 5 the other to the south t Geba. 4578
14: 8 over t the men and let them see us. 448
17:48 David **ran** quickly *t* the battle line AIT
20:12 If he is favorably disposed t you, 448
20:19 The day after tomorrow, **t evening,** 3718+4394
25: 8 Therefore *be* **favorable** t my young men, 928+2834+5162+6524
25:20 there were David and his men descending t 7925
2Sa 15: 6 in this way t all the Israelites who came to 4200
15:23 people moved on t the desert. 2006+6584+7156
20:17 He went t her, and she asked, 448
24: 6 and on to Dan Jaan and around t Sidon. 448
24: 7 Then *they* **went** *t* the fortress of Tyre AIT
24:20 and saw the king and his men coming t 6584
1Ki 7:25 and their hindquarters were t the center. 2025
8:22 **spread out** his hands *t* heaven AIT
8:29 May your eyes be open t this temple night 448
8:29 the prayer your servant prays t this place. 448
8:30 and of your people Israel when they pray t 448
8:35 and when they pray t this place 448
8:38 and spreading out his hands t this temple— 448
8:42 when he comes and prays t this temple, 448
8:44 the LORD t the city you have chosen and 2006
8:48 to you t the land you gave their fathers, 2006
8:48 t the city you have chosen and NIH
8:54 with his hands **spread out** *t* heaven. AIT
11:25 So Rezon ruled in Aram and was hostile t 928
13: 4 But the hand he stretched out t 6584
18:43 "Go and look t the sea," 2006
2Ki 5:21 When Naaman saw him running t him, 339
6:18 As the enemy came down t him, 448
10:12 Jehu then set out and **went** *t* Samaria. AIT
25: 4 They fled t the Arabah, 2006
1Ch 29: 7 They gave t the work on the temple 4200
2Ch 4: 4 and their hindquarters were t the center. 2025
6:13 of Israel and spread out his hands t heaven. 2025
6:20 May your eyes be open t this temple day 448
6:20 the prayer your servant prays t this place. 448
6:21 and of your people Israel when they pray t 448
6:26 and when they pray t this place 448
6:29 and spreading out his hands t this temple— 448
6:32 when he comes and prays t this temple, 448
6:34 to you t this city you have chosen and 2006
6:38 and pray t the land you gave their fathers, 2006
6:38 t the city you have chosen and toward NIH
6:38 toward the city you have chosen and t 4200
20:24 that overlooks the desert and looked t 448
Ezr 2:68 of the families gave freewill offerings t 4200
8:15 I assembled them at the canal that flows t 448
Ne 1: 7 We have acted very wickedly t you. 4200
2:13 the Valley Gate t the Jackal Well 448+7156
2:14 Then I moved on t the Fountain Gate and 448
3:26 a point opposite the Water Gate t the east 4200
12:31 t the Dung Gate. 4200
Job 10:17 against me and increase your anger t me; 6643
39:26 by your wisdom and spread his wings t 4200
Ps 5: 7 in reverence will I bow down t your holy 448
28: 2 I lift up my hands t your Most Holy Place. 448
74: 3 Turn your steps t these everlasting ruins, 4200
85: 4 and put away your displeasure t us. 6640
86:13 For great is your love t me; 6584
117: 2 For great is his love t us, 6584
119:36 Turn my heart t your statutes and not 448
119:36 toward your statutes and not t selfish gain. 448
119:80 May my heart be blameless t your decrees, 928
138: 2 I will bow down t your holy temple 448
145:13 and loving t all he has made. 928
145:17 and loving t all he has made. 928
Pr 24:11 hold back those staggering t slaughter. 4200
SS 7: 4 the tower of Lebanon looking t Damascus. 7156
Isa 8:22 Then they will look t the earth 448
11:13 nor Judah **hostile** *t* Ephraim. AIT
16: 8 which once reached Jazer and **spread** *t* AIT
Jer 3:12 Go, proclaim this message t the north: 2025
4:11 in the desert blows t my people, but not 2006
39: 4 and headed t the Arabah. 2006
50: 5 the way to Zion and turn their faces **t it.** 2178
52: 7 They fled t the Arabah, 2006
Eze 1:23 expanse their wings were stretched out one t 448
4: 3 and the city and turn your face t it. 448
4: 7 Turn your face t the siege of Jerusalem and 448
8: 5 "Son of man, look t the north." 2006
8:16 With their backs t the temple of 448
8:16 the temple of the LORD and their faces t 2025
17: 6 Its branches turned t him, 448
17: 7 The vine now sent out its roots t him from 6584
20:46 set your face t the south; 2006
39:11 in the valley of those who travel **east** *t* AIT
39:26 and all the unfaithfulness they showed t 928
41:19 of a man t the palm tree on one side and 448
41:19 and the face of a lion t the palm tree on 448
47: 1 under the threshold of the temple t the east 2025
47: 8 "This water flows t the eastern region 448
Da 3:19 and his attitude t them changed. 10542
4:34 Nebuchadnezzar, raised my eyes t heaven, 10378
6:10 where the windows opened t Jerusalem. 10458
8: 4 I watched the ram as he charged t the west 2025
Da 8: 6 He came t the two-horned ram I had seen 6330
8: 8 in its place four prominent horns grew up t 4200
8: 9 in power to the south and to the east and t 448
10:15 I bowed with my face t the ground 2025
11: 4 up and parceled out t the four winds 4200
11:19 he will turn back t the fortresses 4200
12: 7 lifted his right hand and his left hand t 448
Am 4: 3 and you will be cast out t Harmon," 2025
Jnh 2: 4 yet I will look again t your holy temple.' 448
Zec 6: 6 The one with the black horses is going t 448
6: 6 the one with the white horses t the west, 448
6: 6 one with the dappled horses t the south." 448
6: 8 Then he called to me, "Look, those going t 448
Mt 14:29 walked on the water and came t Jesus. *4639*
Lk 7:44 he turned t the woman and said to Simon, *4639*
12:21 up things for himself but is not rich t *1650*
Jn 1:29 The next day John saw Jesus coming t him *4639*
4:30 of the town and made their way t him. *4639*
6: 5 up and saw a great crowd coming t him, *4639*
17: 1 he looked t heaven and prayed: *1650*
20:16 She **turned** t him and cried out in Aramaic, *5138*
Ac 9:40 Turning t the dead woman, he said, *4639*
Ro 2: 4 God's kindness leads you t repentance? *1650*
1Co 7:36 If anyone thinks he is acting improperly t *2093*
2Co 10: 2 be t some people who think that we live by *2093*
Php 3:13 Forgetting what is behind and **straining** t *2085*
3:14 I press on t the goal to win the prize *2848*
Col 4: 5 Be wise in the way you act t outsiders; *4639*
Tit 3: 2 and to show true humility t all men. *4639*
Heb 10:24 how we may spur one another on t love *NIG*
Jas 4: 4 with the world is hatred *t* **God?** *AIT*
1Pe 3:21 but the pledge of a good conscience t God. *1650*
5: 5 yourselves with humility *t* **one another,** *AIT*

TOWEL (2)

Jn 13: 4 and wrapped a t around his waist. *3317*
13: 5 drying them *with* the t that was wrapped *3317*

TOWER (31) [TOWERED, TOWERING, TOWERS, WATCHTOWER, WATCHTOWERS]

Ge 11: 4 with a t that reaches to the heavens, 4463
11: 5 and the t that the men were building. 4463
Jdg 8: 9 I will tear down this **t.**" 4463
8:17 also pulled down the t *of* Peniel and killed 4463
9:46 the t *of* Shechem went into the stronghold 4463
9:49 So all the people in the t *of* Shechem, 4463
9:51 Inside the city, however, was a strong **t,** 4463
9:51 in and climbed up on the t roof. 4463
9:52 Abimelech went to the t and stormed it. 4463
9:52 But as he approached the entrance to the t 4463
2Ki 9:17 When the lookout standing on the t 4463
Ne 3: 1 building as far as the T *of* the Hundred, 4463
3: 1 and as far as the T *of* Hananel. 4463
3:11 and the T *of* the Ovens. 4463
3:25 the t projecting from the upper palace near 4463
3:26 toward the east and the projecting **t.** 4463
3:27 the great projecting t to the wall of Ophel. 4463
12:38 past the T *of* the Ovens to the Broad Wall, 4463
12:39 the T *of* Hananel and the Tower of the 4463
12:39 of Hananel and the T *of* the Hundred, 4463
Ps 61: 3 a strong t against the foe. 4463
Pr 18:10 The name of the LORD is a strong **t;** 4463
SS 4: 4 Your neck is like the t *of* David, 4463
7: 4 Your neck is like an ivory **t.** 4463
7: 4 Your nose is like the t *of* Lebanon looking 4463
Isa 2:15 for every lofty t and every fortified wall, 4463
Jer 31:38 be rebuilt for me from the T *of* Hananel to 4463
Eze 31:14 the waters *are ever to* t **proudly** on high, 1467
Zec 14:10 the T *of* Hananel to the royal winepresses. 4463
Lk 13: 4 Or those eighteen who died when the t *4788*
14:28 "Suppose one of you wants to build a **t.** *4788*

TOWERED (4) [TOWER]

Eze 19:11 *It* t high above the thick foliage, 1467
31: 3 it t on high, its top above the thick foliage. 1468
31: 5 So *it* t higher than all the trees of the field; 1467
31:10 Because *it* t on high, lifting its top above 1467

TOWERING (1) [TOWER]

Isa 2:14 the t mountains and all the high hills, 8123

TOWERS (19) [TOWER]

2Ch 14: 7 "and put walls around them, with **t,** 4463
26: 9 Uzziah built t in Jerusalem at the Corner 4463
26:10 He also built t in the desert 4463
26:15 for use on the t and on the corner defenses 4463
27: 4 and forts and t in the wooded areas. 4463
32: 5 of the wall and building t on it. 4463
Ps 48:12 go around her, count her **t,** 4463
SS 8: 9 we will build t *of* silver on her. 3227
8:10 I am a wall, and my breasts are like **t.** 4463
Isa 23:13 they raised up their **siege t,** 1032
29: 3 with t and set up my siege works 5164
30:25 the day of great slaughter, when the t fall, 4463
33:18 Where is the officer in charge of the **t?**" 4463
Jer 50:15 She surrenders, her t fall, 859
La 4:17 from our t we watched for a nation 7610
Eze 26: 4 the walls of Tyre and pull down her **t;** 4463
26: 9 against your walls and demolish your t 4463
27:11 men of Gammad were in your **t.** 4463
Zep 1:16 the fortified cities and against the corner **t.** 1469

TOWING (1)

Jn 21: 8 followed in the boat, **t** the net full of fish, *5359*

TOWN (177) [HOMETOWN, TOWNS, TOWNSMEN, TOWNSPEOPLE]

Ge 19:20 Look, here is a **t** near enough to run to, 6551
19:21 I will not overthrow the **t** you speak of. 6551
19:22 (That is why the **t** was called Zoar.) 6551
24:10 and made his way to the **t** *of* Nahor. 6551
24:11 down near the well outside the **t**; 6551
26:33 the name of the **t** has been Beersheba. 6551
Lev 14:40 into an unclean place outside the **t**. 6551
14:41 into an unclean place outside the **t**. 6551
14:45 and taken out of the **t** to an unclean place. 6551
14:53 in the open fields outside the **t**. 6551
25:33 that is, a house sold in any **t** they hold— 6551
Nu 20:16 a **t** on the edge of your territory. 6551
22:36 he went out to meet him at the Moabite **t** 6551
35: 4 fifteen hundred feet from the **t** wall. 6551
35: 5 Outside the **t**, measure three thousand feet 6551
35: 5 with the **t** in the center. 6551
Dt 2:36 and from the **t** in the gorge, 6551
2:36 not one **t** was too strong for us. 7953
13:13 and have led the people of their **t** astray, 6551
13:15 to the sword all who live in that **t**. 6551
13:16 **of the t** into the middle of the public square 2023S
13:16 the public square and completely burn the **t** 6551
16: 5 in any **t** the LORD your God gives you 9133
16:18 for each of your tribes in every **t** 9133
19:12 the elders of his **t** shall send for him, 6551
21: 3 of the **t** nearest the body shall take a heifer 6551
21: 6 Then all the elders of the **t** nearest 6551
21:19 to the elders at the gate of his **t**. 6551
21:21 the men of his **t** shall stone him to death. 6551
22:15 that she was a virgin to the **t** elders at 6551
22:17 the cloth before the elders of the **t**, 6551
22:21 and there the men of her **t** shall stone her 6551
22:23 in a **t** a virgin pledged to be married 6551
22:24 the gate of that **t** and stone them to death— 6551
22:24 because she was in a **t** and did not scream 6551
23:16 and in whatever **t** he chooses. 9133
25: 7 she shall go to the elders at the **t gate** 9133
25: 8 of his **t** shall summon him and talk to him. 6551
Jos 3:16 a **t** called Adam in the vicinity of Zarethan, 6551
13: 9 and from the **t** in the middle of the gorge, 6551
13:16 and from the **t** in the middle of the gorge, 6551
18: 9 **t** by town, in seven parts, NIH
18: 9 town by **t**, in seven parts, 6551
18:14 Kiriath Jearim), a **t** *of* the people of Judah. 6551
19:50 They gave him the **t** he asked for— 6551
19:50 And he built up the **t** and settled there. 6551
20: 6 in the **t** from which he fled." 6551
Jdg 6:27 of his family and the men of the **t**, 6551
6:28 the morning when the men of the **t** got up, 6551
6:30 The men of the **t** demanded of Joash, 6551
8:14 officials of Succoth, the elders of **the t**. 2023S
8:16 of the **t** and taught the men of Succoth 6551
8:17 of Peniel and killed the men of the **t**. 6551
8:27 which he placed in Ophrah, his **t**. 6551
12: 7 and was buried in a **t** *in* Gilead. 6551
14:18 on the seventh day the men of the **t** said 6551
17: 8 that **t** in search of some other place to stay. 6551
Ru 1:19 the whole **t** was stirred because of them, 6551
2:18 She carried it back to **t**, 6551
3:15 Then he went back to **t**. 6551
4: 1 Meanwhile Boaz went up to the **t gate** 9133
4: 2 Boaz took ten of the elders of the **t** 6551
4:10 his family or from the **t records**. 5226+9133
1Sa 1: 3 Year after year this man went up from his **t** 6551
4:13 the **t** and told what had happened, 6551
4:13 the whole **t** sent up a cry. 6551
8:22 "Everyone go back to his **t**." 6551
9: 6 "Look, in this **t** there is a man of God; 6551
9:10 So they set out for the **t** where the man 6551
9:11 As they were going up the hill to the **t**, 6551
9:12 he has just come to our **t** today, 6551
9:13 As soon as you enter the **t**, 6551
9:14 They went up to the **t**, 6551
9:25 down from the high place to the **t**, 6551
9:27 they were going down to the edge of the **t**, 6551
10: 5 As you approach the **t**, 6551
16: 4 of the **t** trembled when they met him. 6551
20:29 in the **t** and my brother has ordered me to 6551
20:40 "Go, carry them back to **t**." 6551
20:42 and Jonathan went back to the **t**. 6551
22:19 put to the sword Nob, the **t** *of* the priests, 6551
23: 7 by entering a **t** *with* gates and bars." 6551
23:10 to Keilah and destroy the **t** on account 6551
28: 3 and buried him in his own **t** of Ramah. 6551
2Sa 12: 1 "There were two men in a certain **t**, 6551
15: 2 "What **t** are you from?" 6551
19:37 that I may die in my own **t** near the tomb 6551
24: 5 south of the **t** in the gorge, 6551
1Ki 15:27 at Gibbethon, a Philistine **t**, while Nadab NIH
16:15 near Gibbethon, a Philistine **t**. 889S
17:10 When he came to the **t** gate, 6551
22:36 "Every man to his **t**; 6551
2Ki 2:19 "Look, our lord, this **t** is well situated, 6551
2:23 some youths came out of the **t** and jeered 6551
3:19 every fortified city and every major **t**. 6551
2Ch 14: 5 and incense altars in every **t** *in* Judah, 6551
20: 4 indeed, they came from every **t** *in* Judah 6551
28:25 In every **t** in Judah he built high places 6551
30:10 from **t** to town in Ephraim and Manasseh, 6551
30:10 from town to **t** in Ephraim and Manasseh, 6551
Ezr 2: 1 to Jerusalem and Judah, each to his own **t**, 6551
10:14 the elders and judges of **each t**, 2256+6551+6551
Ne 7: 6 to Jerusalem and Judah, each to his own **t**, 6551
Job 39: 7 He laughs at the commotion in the **t**; 7953
Ecc 10:15 he does not know the way to **t**. 6551
Isa 22: 2 O **t** full of commotion, 6551
25: 2 the fortified **t** a ruin, 7953
Jer 3:14 one from a **t** and two from a clan— 6551
4:29 of horsemen and archers every **t** takes 6551
48: 8 The destroyer will come against every **t**, 6551
48: 8 and not a **t** will escape. 6551
49:25 the **t** *in which* I delight? 7953
Eze 39:16 (Also a **t** called Hamonah will be there.) 6551
Am 4: 6 in every city and lack of bread in every **t**, 5226
4: 7 I sent rain on one **t**, but withheld it from 6551
4: 8 People staggered from **t** to town for water 6551
4: 8 People staggered from town to **t** for water 6551
5: 3 the **t** that marches out a hundred strong NIH
Mic 1:14 The **t** *of* Aczib will prove deceptive to 1074
Hab 2:12 bloodshed and establishes a **t** by crime! 7953
Mt 2:23 he went and lived in a **t** called Nazareth. *4484*
8:33 went into the **t** and reported all this, *4484*
8:34 Then the whole **t** went out to meet Jesus. *4484*
9: 1 crossed over and came to his own **t**. *4484*
10: 5 not go among the Gentiles or enter any **t** of *4484*
10:11 "Whatever **t** or village you enter, *4484*
10:14 when you leave that home or **t**. *4484*
10:15 on the day of judgment than *for* that **t**. *4484*
23:34 in your synagogues and pursue from **t** *4484*
23:34 and pursue from town to **t**. *4484*
Mk 1:33 The whole **t** gathered at the door, *4484*
1:45 Jesus could no longer enter a **t** openly *4484*
5:14 and reported this in the **t** and countryside, *4484*
6:10 stay there until you leave that **t**. *NIG*
Lk 1:26 the angel Gabriel to Nazareth, a **t** in Galilee, *4484*
1:39 that time Mary got ready and hurried to a **t** *4484*
2: 3 And everyone went to his own **t** to register. *4484*
2: 4 from the **t** of Nazareth in Galilee to Judea, *4484*
2: 4 to Bethlehem the **t** of David, *4484*
2:11 in the **t** of David a Savior has been born *4484*
2:39 they returned to Galilee to their own **t** *4484*
4:29 They got up, drove him out *of* the **t**, *4484*
4:29 of the hill on which the **t** was built, *4484*
4:31 he went down to Capernaum, a **t** in Galilee, *4484*
7:11 Jesus went to a **t** called Nain, *4484*
7:12 As he approached the **t** gate, *4484*
7:12 And a large crowd *from* the **t** was with her. *4484*
7:37 in that **t** learned that Jesus was eating at *4484*
8: 1 Jesus traveled about from one **t** and village *4484*
8: 4 and people were coming to Jesus from **t** *4484*
8: 4 coming to Jesus **from** town **after t**, *2848*
8:27 met by a demon-possessed man from the **t**. *4484*
8:34 and reported this in the **t** and countryside, *4484*
8:39 over **t** how much Jesus had done for him. *4484*
9: 4 stay there until you leave **that t**. *1696S*
9: 5 dust off your feet when you leave their **t**, *4484*
9:10 by themselves to a **t** called Bethsaida, *4484*
10: 1 of him to every **t** and place where he was *4484*
10: 8 "When you enter a **t** and are welcomed, *4484*
10:10 when you enter a **t** and are not welcomed, *4484*
10:11 of your **t** that sticks to our feet we wipe off *4484*
10:12 on that day for Sodom than *for* that **t**. *4484*
14:21 the streets and alleys *of* the **t** and bring in *4484*
18: 2 "In a certain **t** there was a judge *4484*
18: 3 a widow in that **t** who kept coming to him *4484*
23:51 He came from the Judean **t** of Arimathea *4484*
Jn 1:44 was from the **t** of Bethsaida. *4484*
4: 5 So he came to a **t** in Samaria called Sychar, *4484*
4: 8 disciples had gone into the **t** to buy food.) *4484*
4:28 the woman went back to the **t** and said to *4484*
4:30 They came out of the **t** and made their way *4484*
4:39 the Samaritans from that **t** believed in him *4484*
7:42 from Bethlehem, the **t** where David lived?" *3267*
Ac 16: 4 As they traveled **from t to town**, *3836+4484*
16: 4 As they traveled **from town to t**, *3836+4484*
27: 8 Fair Havens, near the **t** of Lasea. *4484*
Tit 1: 5 and appoint elders in every **t**, *4484*

TOWNCLERK (KJV) See CITY CLERK

TOWNS (299) [TOWN]

Ge 35: 5 terror of God fell upon the **t** all around them 6551
Lev 25:32 to redeem their houses in the Levitical **t**, 6551
25:33 the Jubilee, because the houses in the **t** *of* 6551
25:34 the pastureland belonging to their **t** must 6551
Nu 13:19 What kind of **t** do they live in? 6551
21: 3 They completely destroyed them and their **t**; 6551
31:10 the **t** where the Midianites had settled, 6551
35: 2 the Levites **t** to live in from the inheritance 6551
35: 2 And give them pasturelands around the **t**. 6551
35: 3 Then they will have **t** to live in 6551
35: 4 "The pasturelands around the **t** 6551
35: 5 as pastureland for the **t**. 6551
35: 6 of the **t** you give the Levites will be cities 6551
35: 6 In addition, give them forty-two other **t**. 6551
35: 7 you must give the Levites forty-eight **t**, 6551
35: 8 The **t** you give the Levites from the land 6551
35: 8 Take many **t** from a tribe that has many, 6551
35:11 select *some* **t** to be your cities of refuge, 6551
35:13 These six **t** you give will be your cities 6551
35:15 These six **t** will be a place of refuge 6551
Dt 1:22 we are to take and the **t** we will come to." 6551
2:34 At that time we took all his **t** 6551
2:35 from the **t** we had captured we carried off 6551
2:37 nor that around the **t** *in* the hills. 6551
3:10 We took all the **t** *on* the plateau, 6551
3:10 and Edrei, **t** *of* Og's kingdom in Bashan. 6551
3:12 hill country of Gilead, together with its **t**. 6551
3:19 in the **t** I have given you, 6551
12:12 and the Levites from your **t**, 9133
12:15 of your **t** and eat as much of the meat 9133
12:17 not eat in your own **t** the tithe of your grain 9133
12:18 and the Levites from your **t**— 9133
12:21 and in your own **t** you may eat as much 9133
13:12 of the **t** the LORD your God is giving you 6551
14:21 to an alien living in any of your **t**, 9133
14:27 do not neglect the Levites living in your **t**, 9133
14:28 that year's produce and store it in your **t**, 9133
14:29 the widows who live in your **t** may come 9133
15: 7 among your brothers in any of the **t** of 9133
15:22 You are to eat it in your own **t**. 9133
16:11 the Levites in your **t**, and the aliens, 9133
16:14 and the widows who live in your **t**. 9133
17: 2 or woman living among you in one of the **t** 9133
18: 6 from one of your **t** anywhere in Israel 9133
19: 1 and settled in their **t** and houses, 6551
21: 2 from the body to the neighboring **t**. 6551
24:14 or an alien living in one of your **t**. 9133
26:12 that they may eat in your **t** and be satisfied. 9133
31:12 and the aliens living in your **t**— 9133
Jos 11:21 Joshua totally destroyed them and their **t**. 6551
13:10 all the **t** *of* Sihon king of the Amorites, 6551
13:17 to Heshbon and all its **t** on the plateau, 6551
13:21 the **t** *on* the plateau and the entire realm 6551
13:23 These **t** and their villages were 6551
13:25 all the **t** *of* Gilead and half the Ammonite 6551
13:28 These **t** and their villages were 6551
13:30 the settlements of Jair in Bashan, sixty **t**, 6551
14: 4 of the land but only **t** to live in, 6551
15: 9 at the **t** *of* Mount Ephron and went down 6551
15:21 The southernmost **t** of the tribe of Judah in 6551
15:32 a total of twenty-nine **t** and their villages. 6551
15:36 fourteen **t** and their villages. 6551
15:41 sixteen **t** and their villages. 6551
15:44 nine **t** and their villages. 6551
15:51 eleven **t** and their villages. 6551
15:54 nine **t** and their villages. 6551
15:57 ten **t** and their villages. 6551
15:59 six **t** and their villages. 6551
15:60 two **t** and their villages. 6551
15:62 six **t** and their villages. 6551
16: 9 It also included all the **t** and their villages 6551
17: 9 There were **t** belonging to Ephraim lying 6551
17: 9 belonging to Ephraim lying among the **t** 6551
17:12 Manassites not able to occupy these **t**, 6551
18:24 twelve **t** and their villages. 6551
18:28 fourteen **t** and their villages. 6551
19: 6 thirteen **t** and their villages; 6551
19: 7 four **t** and their villages— 6551
19: 8 and all the villages around these **t** as far 6551
19:15 There were twelve **t** and their villages. 6551
19:16 These **t** and their villages were 6551
19:22 There were sixteen **t** and their villages. 6551
19:23 These **t** and their villages were 6551
19:30 There were twenty-two **t** and their villages. 6551
19:31 These **t** and their villages were 6551
19:38 There were nineteen **t** and their villages. 6551
19:39 These **t** and their villages were 6551
19:48 These **t** and their villages were 6551
21: 2 through Moses that you give us **t** to live in, 6551
21: 3 the following **t** and pasturelands out 6551
21: 4 of Aaron the priest were allotted thirteen **t** 6551
21: 5 of Kohath's descendants were allotted ten **t** 6551
21: 6 of Gershon were allotted thirteen **t** from 6551
21: 7 received twelve **t** from the tribes 6551
21: 8 the Israelites allotted to the Levites these **t** 6551
21: 9 and Simeon they allotted the following **t** 6551
21:10 (these **t** were assigned to the descendants NIH
21:16 nine **t** from these two tribes. 6551
21:18 with their pasturelands—four **t**. 6551
21:19 All the **t** *for* the priests, 6551
21:20 of the Levites were allotted **t** from the tribe 6551
21:22 with their pasturelands—four **t**. 6551
21:24 with their pasturelands—four **t**. 6551
21:25 with their pasturelands—two **t**. 6551
21:26 All these ten **t** and their pasturelands 6551
21:27 with their pasturelands—two **t**; 6551
21:29 with their pasturelands—four **t**; 6551
21:31 with their pasturelands—four **t**; 6551
21:32 with their pasturelands—three **t**. 6551
21:33 the **t** *of* the Gershonite clans were thirteen, 6551
21:35 with their pasturelands—four **t**; 6551
21:37 with their pasturelands—four **t**; 6551
21:39 with their pasturelands—four **t** in all. 6551
21:40 All the **t** allotted to the Merarite clans, 6551
21:41 The **t** *of* the Levites in the territory held by 6551
21:42 **Each** of these **t** had pasturelands 6551+6551
21:42 this was true for all these **t**. 6551
Jdg 10: 4 They controlled thirty **t** in Gilead, 6551
11:26 the surrounding settlements and all the **t** 6551
11:33 He devastated twenty **t** from Aroer to 6551
20:14 From their **t** they came together at Gibeah 6551
20:15 twenty-six thousand swordsmen from their **t** 6551
20:42 of Israel who came out of the **t** cut them 6551
20:48 to Benjamin and put all the **t** to the sword, 6551
20:48 All the **t** they came across they set on fire. 6551
21:23 and rebuilt the **t** and settled in them. 6551
1Sa 6:18 to the number of Philistine **t** belonging to 6551
6:18 the fortified **t** with their country villages. 6551
7:14 The **t** from Ekron to Gath that 6551
18: 6 from all the **t** *of* Israel to meet King Saul 6551
27: 5 be assigned to me in one of the country **t**, 6551

1Sa 30:29 the t *of* the Jerahmeelites and the Kenites; 6551
31: 7 they abandoned their t and fled. 6551
2Sa 2: 1 "Shall I go up to one of the t *of* Judah?" 6551
2: 3 and they settled in Hebron and its t. 6551
8: 8 t *that belonged to* Hadadezer, 6551
12:31 He did this to all the Ammonite t. 6551
24: 7 and all the t *of* the Hivites and Canaanites. 6551
1Ki 9:11 King Solomon gave twenty t in Galilee 6551
9:12 to see the t that Solomon had given him, 6551
9:13 of t are these you have given me, 6551
9:19 the t *for* his chariots and for his horses— 6551
12:17 for the Israelites who were living in the t 6551
13:32 the t *of* Samaria will certainly come true." 6551
15:20 the commanders of his forces against the t 6551
2Ki 3:25 They destroyed the t, 6551
13:25 of Hazael the t he had taken in battle 6551
13:25 and so he recovered the Israelite t. 6551
17: 6 the Habor River and in the t *of* the Medes. 6551
17: 9 built themselves high places in all their t. 6551
17:24 in the t *of* Samaria to replace the Israelites. 6551
17:24 They took over Samaria and lived in its t. 6551
17:26 the t *of* Samaria do not know what the god 6551
17:29 in the *several* t where they settled, 6551
18:11 on the Habor River and in t *of* the Medes. 6551
23: 5 to burn incense on the high places of the t 6551
23: 8 Josiah brought all the priests from the t 6551
23:19 that the kings of Israel had built in the t 6551
1Ch 2:22 who controlled twenty-three t in Gilead. 6551
2:23 with its surrounding settlements—sixty t.) 6551
4:31 These were their t until the reign of David. 6551
4:32 Token and Ashan—five t— 6551
4:33 and all the villages around these t as far 6551
6:60 These t, which were distributed among 6551
6:61 of Kohath's descendants were allotted ten t 6551
6:62 were allotted thirteen t from the tribes 6551
6:63 were allotted twelve t from the tribes 6551
6:64 the Levites these t and their pasturelands. 6551
6:65 they allotted the previously named t. 6551
6:66 as their territory t from the tribe of Ephraim. 6551
7:29 of Joseph son of Israel lived in these t. NIH
9: 2 in their own t were some Israelites, 6551
10: 7 they abandoned their t and fled. 6551
13: 2 and Levites who are with them in their t 6551
18: 8 t *that belonged to* Hadadezer, 6551
19: 7 the Ammonites were mustered from their t 6551
20: 3 David did this to all the Ammonite t. 6551
27:25 in the t, the villages and the watchtowers. 6551
2Ch 10:17 for the Israelites who were living in the t 6551
11: 5 in Jerusalem and built up t for defense 6551
13:19 and took from him the t of Bethel, 6551
14: 7 "Let us build up these t," he said to Judah, 6551
15: 8 and from the t he had captured in the hills 6551
16: 4 the commanders of his forces against the t 6551
17: 2 and put garrisons in Judah and in the t 6551
17: 7 and Micaiah to teach in the t *of* Judah. 6551
17: 9 to all the t *of* Judah and taught the people. 6551
17:13 and had large supplies in the t *of* Judah. 6551
23: 2 of Israelite families from all the t. 6551
24: 5 "Go to the t *of* Judah and collect 6551
25:13 in the war raided Judean t from Samaria 6551
26: 6 then rebuilt t near Ashdod and elsewhere 6551
27: 4 He built t in the Judean hills and forts 6551
28:18 the Philistines had raided t *in* the foothills 6551
31: 1 went out to the t *of* Judah, 6551
31: 1 to their own t and to their own property. 6551
31: 6 and Judah who lived in the t *of* Judah 6551
31:15 assisted him faithfully in the t *of* the priests, 6551
31:19 who lived on the farm lands around their t 6551
31:19 around their towns or in any other t, 6551
34: 6 In the t *of* Manasseh, Ephraim and Simeon, 6551
Ezr 2:59 The following came up from the t NIH
2:70 the temple servants settled in their own t, 6551
2:70 the rest of the Israelites settled in their t. 6551
3: 1 and the Israelites had settled in their t, 6551
10:14 Then let everyone in our t who has married 6551
Ne 7:61 The following came up from the t NIH
7:73 rest of the Israelites, settled in their own t. 6551
7:73 and the Israelites had settled in their t, 6551
8:15 throughout their t and in Jerusalem: 6551
10:37 the tithes in all the t *where* we work. 6551
11: 1 remaining nine were to stay in their own t. 6551
11: 3 of Solomon's servants lived in the t 6551
11: 3 each on his own property in the *various* t, 6551
11:20 were in all the t *of* Judah, 6551
12:44 the t they were to bring into the storerooms 6551
Job 15:28 he will inhabit ruined t and houses 6551
Isa 40: 9 say to the t *of* Judah, "Here is your God!" 6551
42:11 Let the desert and its t raise their voices; 6551
44:26 'It shall be inhabited,' of the t *of* Judah, 6551
Jer 1:15 and against all the t *of* Judah. 6551
2:15 his t are burned and deserted. 6551
2:28 For you have as many gods as you have t, 6551
4: 7 Your t will lie in ruins without inhabitant. 6551
4:26 all its t lay in ruins before the LORD, 6551
4:29 All the t are deserted; no one lives in them. 6551
5: 6 a leopard will lie in wait near their t to tear 6551
7:17 Do you not see what they are doing in the t 6551
7:34 the t *of* Judah and the streets of Jerusalem, 6551
9:11 the t *of* Judah so no one can live there." 6551
10:22 It will make the t *of* Judah desolate, 6551
11: 6 "Proclaim all these words in the t *of* Judah 6551
11:12 The t *of* Judah and the people 6551
11:13 You have as many gods as you have t, 6551
17:26 People will come from the t *of* Judah and 6551
20:16 the t the LORD overthrew without pity. 6551
22: 6 surely make you like a desert, like t 6551
25:18 and the t *of* Judah, its kings and officials, 6551
Jer 26: 2 of the t *of* Judah who come to worship in 6551
31:21 Return, O Virgin Israel, return to your t. 6551
31:23 in its t will once again use these words: 6551
31:24 will live together in Judah and all its t— 6551
32:44 in the t *of* Judah and in the towns of 6551
32:44 of Judah and in the t *of* the hill country, 6551
33:10 the t *of* Judah and the streets of Jerusalem 6551
33:12 in all its t there will again be pastures 6551
33:13 In the t *of* the hill country, 6551
33:13 the villages around Jerusalem and in the t 6551
34: 1 against Jerusalem and all its surrounding t, 6551
34:22 the t *of* Judah so no one can live there." 6551
36: 6 of Judah who come in from their t. 6551
36: 9 and those who had come from the t 6551
40: 5 king of Babylon has appointed over the t 6551
40:10 and live in the t you have taken over." 6551
44: 2 on Jerusalem and on all the t *of* Judah. 6551
44: 6 the t *of* Judah and the streets of Jerusalem 6551
44:17 and our officials did in the t *of* Judah and 6551
44:21 and think about the incense burned in the t 6551
47: 2 the t and those who live in them. 6551
48: 9 her t will become desolate, 6551
48:15 Moab will be destroyed and her t invaded; 6551
48:24 to all the t *of* Moab, far and near. 6551
48:28 Abandon your t and dwell among 6551
49: 1 Why do his people live in its t? 6551
49:13 and all its t will be in ruins forever." 6551
49:18 along with their neighboring t," NIH
50:32 a fire in her t that will consume all who are 6551
50:40 along with their neighboring t," declares NIH
51:43 Her t will be desolate, 6551
La 5:11 and virgins in the t *of* Judah. 6551
Eze 6: 6 the t will be laid waste and 6551
12:20 The inhabited t will be laid waste and 6551
19: 7 and devastated their t. 6551
25: 9 beginning at its frontier t— 6551
35: 4 I will turn your t into ruins and you will 6551
35: 9 your t will not be inhabited. 6551
36: 4 and the deserted t that have been plundered 6551
36:10 The t will be inhabited and 6551
36:33 I will resettle your t, 6551
39: 9 in the t *of* Israel will go out and use 6551
45: 5 as their possession for t to live in. 6551
Hos 8:14 Judah has fortified many t. 6551
13:10 Where are your rulers in all your t, 6551
Ob 1:20 in Sepharad will possess the t *of* the Negev. 6551
Zec 1:12 from Jerusalem and from the t *of* Judah, 6551
1:17 'My t will again overflow with prosperity, 6551
7: 7 when Jerusalem and its surrounding t were 6551
Mt 9:35 Jesus went through all the t and villages, *4484*
11: 1 on from there to teach and preach in the t *4484*
14:13 crowds followed him on foot from the t. *4484*
Mk 6:33 and ran on foot from all the t and got there *4484*
6:56 into villages, t or countryside— *4484*
Lk 4:43 of the kingdom of God *to* the other t also, *4484*
5:12 While Jesus was in one *of* the t, *4484*
13:22 Then Jesus went through the t and villages, *4484*
Ac 5:16 also *from* the t around Jerusalem, *4484*
8:40 in all the t until he reached Caesarea. *4484*
15:36 the brothers in all the t where we preached *4484*
Jude 1: 7 and the surrounding t gave themselves up *4484*

TOWNSMEN (2) [TOWN]

Ge 34:20 of their city to speak to their **fellow** t. 408+6551
Ru 3:11 All my **fellow** t know that you are 6639+9133

TOWNSPEOPLE (1) [TOWN]

Ge 24:13 the daughters of the t are coming out 408+6551

TRACE (2) [TRACED, TRACING]

Da 2:35 wind swept them away without leaving a t. 10087
Heb 7: 6 however, *did* not t *his* **descent** from Levi, *1156*

TRACED (1) [TRACE]

Ro 9: 5 and from them is t the human ancestry *NIG*

TRACHONITIS (KJV) See TRACONITIS

TRACING (1) [TRACE]

Ro 11:33 and his paths **beyond** t **out!** *453*

TRACK (2) [TRACKED, TRACKLESS, TRACKS]

1Sa 23:23 in the area, *I will* t him **down** among all 2924
Job 14:16 but not **keep** t **of** my sin. 9068

TRACKED (1) [TRACK]

Ps 17:11 *They have* t me **down,** they now surround me 892

TRACKLESS (2) [TRACK]

Job 12:24 them wandering through a t waste. 2006+4202
Ps 107:40 made them wander in a t waste. 2006+4202

TRACKS (1) [TRACK]

SS 1: 8 follow the t *of* the sheep 6811

TRACONITIS (1)

Lk 3: 1 his brother Philip tetrarch *of* Iturea and T, *5551*

TRACT (1) [TRACTS]

Jos 24:32 were buried at Shechem in the t *of* land 2754

TRACTS (1) [TRACT]

Jos 17: 5 consisted of ten t **of land** besides Gilead 824

TRADE (11) [TRADED, TRADERS, TRADES, TRADING]

Ge 34:10 Live in it, t *in* it, 6086
34:21 "Let them live in our land and t *in* it; 6086
42:34 and *you can* t *in* the land.' " 6086
2Ch 20:37 and were not able to set sail to t. 9576
Isa 23:17 as a prostitute and *will* **ply her** t with all 2388
Eze 27: 9 and their sailors came alongside to t 6842
28:16 Through your widespread t you were filled 8219
28:18 sins and dishonest t you have desecrated your sanctuaries. 8219
Zep 1:11 all **who** t **with** silver will be ruined. 5744
Ac 19:27 not only that our t will lose its good name, *3538*
Rev 18:22 No workman *of* any t will ever be found *5492*

TRADED (8) [TRADE]

Eze 27:13 " 'Greece, Tubal and Meshech t *with* you; 8217
27:15 " 'The men of Rhodes t *with* you, 8217
27:17 " 'Judah and Israel t **with** you; 8217
27:20 " 'Dedan t in saddle blankets *with* you. 8217
27:22 " 'The merchants of Sheba and Raamah t 8217
27:23 Asshur and Kilmad t *with* you. 8217
27:24 In your marketplace they t *with* you 8217
Joel 3: 3 for my people and t boys for prostitutes; 5989

TRADERS (6) [TRADE]

1Ki 10:15 and t and from all the Arabian kings and 8217
2Ch 9:14 revenues brought in by merchants and t. 6086
Job 41: 6 Will t barter for him? 2493
Isa 23: 8 whose t are renowned in the earth? 4048
Eze 17: 4 where he planted it in a city of t. 8217
1Ti 1:10 *for* **slave** t and liars and perjurers— *435*

TRADES (1) [TRADE]

Ac 19:25 along with the workmen in **related** t, *5525*[S]

TRADING (8) [TRADE]

1Ki 10:22 The king had a **fleet of** t **ships** at sea 639+9576
22:48 **fleet of** t **ships** to go to Ophir for gold, 641+9576
2Ch 9:21 a **fleet of** t **ships** manned by Hiram's men. 641+2143+9576
20:36 construct a **fleet of** t **ships.** 641+2143+4200+9576
Job 20:18 he will not enjoy the profit from his t. 9455
Pr 31:18 She sees that her t is profitable, 6087
Isa 2:16 for every t **ship** and every stately vessel. 641+9576
Eze 28: 5 in t you have increased your wealth, 8219

TRADITION (8) [TRADITIONS]

2Ch 35:25 a t in Israel and are written in the Laments. 2976
Mt 15: 2 "Why do your disciples break the t of *4142*
15: 3 of God for the sake of your t? *4142*
15: 6 the word of God for the sake of your t. *4142*
Mk 7: 3 holding to the t of the elders. *4142*
7: 5 according to the t of the elders instead *4142*
7:13 *by* your t that you have handed down. *4142*
Col 2: 8 on human t and the basic principles *4142*

TRADITIONS (5) [TRADITION]

Mic 6:16 and you have followed their t. 4600
Mk 7: 4 And they observe many other t, *4161*
7: 8 of God and are holding on to the t of men." *4142*
7: 9 of God in order to observe your own t! *4142*
Gal 1:14 extremely zealous for the t of my fathers. *4142*

TRAFFICK, TRAFFICKERS (KJV) See MERCHANTS, TRADE, TRADERS, TRADING

TRAFFICKED (1)

Isa 47:15 these you have labored with and t *with* 6086

TRAGEDY (1)

1Ki 17:20 *have you* **brought** t also upon this widow 8317

TRAIL (2)

Job 41:30 **leaving a** t in the mud like a threshing 8331
1Ti 5:24 the sins of others t **behind** them. *2051*

TRAIN (8) [TRAINED, TRAINING, TRAINS, WELL-TRAINED]

Ps 68:18 *you* **led** captives **in** *your* t; 8647
Pr 22: 6 T a child in the way he should go, 2852
Isa 2: 4 nor *will they* t *for* war anymore. 4340
6: 1 and the t **of** his **robe** filled the temple. 8767
Mic 4: 3 nor *will they* t *for* war anymore. 4340
Eph 4: 8 **led captives in his** t and gave gifts to *168+169*
1Ti 4: 7 rather, t yourself to be godly. *1214*
Tit 2: 4 Then *they can* t the younger women *5405*

TRAINED (13) [TRAIN]

Ge 14:14 the 318 **t men** born in his household 2849
1Ch 5:18 and *who* **were** *t for* battle. 4340
25: 7 all of *them* t and skilled *in* music for 4340
2Ch 2:14 *He is* t to work in gold and silver, 3359
26:13 an army of 307,500 *men* t *for* war, 6913
Da 1: 5 They *were* to *be* t for three years, 1540
Hos 7:15 I t them and strengthened them, 3579
10:11 Ephraim *is* a t heifer that loves to thresh; 4340
Lk 6:40 but everyone *who is* **fully** t will be *2936*
Ac 22: 3 Under Gamaliel *I was* thoroughly t in *4084*
2Co 11: 6 I may **not** be a t speaker, *2626*
Heb 5:14 who by constant use have t themselves *1214*
12:11 and peace *for* those who *have been* t by it. *1214*

TRAINING (4) [TRAIN]

1Co 9:25 competes in the games **goes into** strict **t.** *1603*
Eph 6: 4 bring them up in the t and instruction of *4082*
1Ti 4: 8 For physical t is of some value, *1215*
2Ti 3:16 rebuking, correcting and t in righteousness, *4082*

TRAINS (3) [TRAIN]

2Sa 22:35 *He* t my hands for battle; 4340
Ps 18:34 *He* t my hands for battle; 4340
144: 1 who t my hands for war, 4340

TRAITOR (5) [TREASON]

2Ki 17: 4 of Assyria discovered that Hoshea was a **t,** 8004
Isa 21: 2 The t betrays, the looter takes loot. 953
33: 1 Woe to you, O **t,** you who have not been 953
Lk 6:16 and Judas Iscariot, who became a **t.** *4595*
Jn 18: 5 Judas the t was standing there with them.) *4140*

TRAITORS (2) [TREASON]

Ps 59: 5 show no mercy to wicked **t.** 953
Mic 2: 4 He assigns our fields to **t.'** " 8745

TRAMPLE (21) [TRAMPLED, TRAMPLING]

Dt 33:29 and you *will* **t down** their high places." 2005
Job 39:15 that some wild animal *may* t them. 1889
Ps 7: 5 *let him* t my life to the ground 8252
44: 5 through your name *we* t our foes. 1008
60:12 and he *will* **t down** our enemies. 1008
91:13 *you will* t the great lion and the serpent. 8252
108:13 and he *will* **t down** our enemies. 1008
Isa 10: 6 to t them **down** like mud in the streets. 5330+8492
14:25 on my mountains *I will* t him **down.** 1008
26: 6 Feet **t it down**—the feet of the oppressed, 8252
Jer 12:10 and **t down** my field; 1008
Eze 26:11 hoofs of his horses *will* t all your streets; 8252
34:18 *Must you* also t the rest of your pasture 8252
Joel 3:13 **t the grapes,** for the winepress is full and 8097
Am 2: 7 They t on the heads of the poor as upon 8635
5:11 You t on the poor and force him 1424
8: 4 *you who* t the needy and do away with 8635
Mal 4: 3 Then *you will* **t down** the wicked; 6748
Mt 7: 6 If you do, *they may* t them under their feet, *2922*
Lk 10:19 I have given you authority *to* t on snakes *4251*
Rev 11: 2 *They will* **t on** the holy city for 42 months. *4251*

TRAMPLED (32) [TRAMPLE]

2Sa 22:43 and t them like mud in the streets. 8392
2Ki 7:17 and the people t him in the gateway, 8252
7:20 for the people t him in the gateway, 8252
9:33 and the horses as *they* t her **underfoot.** 8252
14: 9 and t the thistle **underfoot.** 8252
2Ch 25:18 and t the thistle **underfoot.** 8252
Isa 5: 5 I will break down its wall, and it will be **t.** 5330
14:19 Like a corpse **t underfoot,** 1008
16: 8 the nations *have* **t down** the choicest vines, 2150
25:10 but Moab *will* **be** t under him 1889
25:10 be trampled under him as straw **is t down** in 1889
28: 3 *will* **be** t underfoot. 8252
63: 3 *I* t them in my anger and trod them down 2005
63: 6 *I* t the nations in my anger; 1008
63:18 our enemies *have* **t down** your sanctuary. 1008
Jer 51:33 like a threshing floor at the time it *is* **t;** 2005
La 1:15 the Lord *has* t the Virgin Daughter 2005
3:16 *he has* t me in the dust. 4115
Eze 34:19 my flock feed on **what** you have t 5330+8079
Da 7: 7 and t underfoot whatever was left. 10672
7:19 and t underfoot whatever was left. 10672
8: 7 the goat knocked him to the ground and t 8252
8:10 of the starry host down to the earth and t 8252
8:13 and of the host that will be **t underfoot?"** 5330
Hos 5:11 Ephraim is oppressed, **t** in judgment, 8368
Mic 7:10 even now she will be **t underfoot** like mire 5330
Hab 3:15 *You* t the sea with your horses, 2005
Mt 5:13 except to be thrown out and t by men. *2922*
Lk 8: 5 *it was* **t on,** and the birds of the air ate it up. *2922*
21:24 Jerusalem will be **t on** by the Gentiles until *4251*
Heb 10:29 who *has* t the Son of God **under foot,** *2922*
Rev 14:20 They *were* t in the winepress outside *4251*

TRAMPLING (5) [TRAMPLE]

Isa 1:12 asked this of you, this t *of* my courts? 8252
22: 5 and t and terror in the Valley of Vision, 4431
Da 7:23 **t it down** and crushing it. 10165
Zec 10: 5 Together they will be like mighty men t 1008
Lk 12: 1 so that *they were* **t on** one another, *2922*

TRANCE (3)

Ac 10:10 he **fell into** a **t.** *1181+1749+2093*
11: 5 and in a t I saw a vision. *1749*
22:17 and was praying at the temple, I fell into a t *1749*

TRANQUILLITY (1)

Ecc 4: 6 handful with t than two handfuls with toil 5739

TRANS-EUPHRATES (17) [EUPHRATES]

Ezr 4:10 Samaria and elsewhere in **T.** 10191+10468+10526
4:11 your servants, the men of **T:** 10191+10468+10526
4:16 you will be left with nothing in **T.**
10002+10468+10526
4:17 Samaria and elsewhere in **T:** 10191+10468+10526
4:20 over the whole of **T,** 10191+10468+10526
5: 3 At that time Tattenai, governor of **T,**
10191+10468+10526
5: 6 that Tattenai, governor of **T,** 10191+10468+10526
5: 6 the officials of **T,** sent to King Darius.
10191+10468+10526
6: 6 Tattenai, governor of **T,** 10191+10468+10526
6: 8 from the revenues of **T,** 10191+10468+10526
6:13 Tattenai, governor of **T,** 10191+10468+10526
7:21 order all the treasurers of **T** 10191+10468+10526
7:25 to administer justice to all the people of **T—**
10191+10468+10526
8:36 and to the governors of **T,** 2021+5643+6298
Ne 2: 7 letters to the governors of **T,** 2021+5643+6298
2: 9 to the governors of **T** and gave them the
king's letters. 2021+5643+6298
3: 7 under the authority of the governor of **T.**
2021+5643+6298

TRANSACTION (1) [TRANSACTIONS]

Jer 32:25 with silver and **have the t witnessed.'** 6332+6386

TRANSACTIONS (1) [TRANSACTION]

Ru 4: 7 This was the **method of legalizing t** 9496

TRANSCENDS (1)

Php 4: 7 peace of God, which t all understanding, *5660*

TRANSFER (2) [TRANSFERRED]

Ru 4: 7 redemption and **t of property** 1821+3972+9455
2Sa 3:10 and t the kingdom from the house of Saul 6296

TRANSFERRED (1) [TRANSFER]

Ac 25: 3 to **have** Paul t to Jerusalem, *3569*

TRANSFIGURED (2)

Mt 17: 2 There *he was* t before them. *3565*
Mk 9: 2 There *he was* t before them. *3565*

TRANSFORM (1) [TRANSFORMED]

Php 3:21 *will* t our lowly bodies so that they will *3571*

TRANSFORMED (3) [TRANSFORM]

Job 28: 5 **is t** below as by fire; 2200
Ro 12: 2 but **be** t by the renewing of your mind. *3565*
2Co 3:18 *are being* **t into** his likeness *3565*

TRANSGRESSED (1) [TRANSGRESSION]

Da 9:11 All Israel *has* t your law and turned away, 6296

TRANSGRESSION (11) [TRANSGRESSED, TRANSGRESSIONS, TRANSGRESSORS]

Ps 19:13 will I be blameless, innocent of great **t.** 7322
Isa 53: 8 for the t *of* my people he was stricken. 7322
Da 9:24 and your holy city to finish **t,** 7322
Mic 1: 5 All this is because of Jacob's **t,** 7322
1: 5 What is Jacob's **t?** Is it not Samaria? 7322
3: 8 to declare to Jacob his **t,** to Israel his sin. 7322
6: 7 Shall I offer my firstborn for my **t,** 7322
7:18 the t of the remnant of his inheritance? 7322
Ro 4:15 And where there is no law there is no **t.** *4126*
11:11 Rather, *because of* their **t,** salvation has *4183*
11:12 But if their t means riches for the world, *4183*

TRANSGRESSIONS (15) [TRANSGRESSION]

Ps 32: 1 Blessed is he whose t are forgiven, 7322
32: 5 "I will confess my t to the LORD"— 7322
39: 8 Save me from all my **t;** 7322
51: 1 to your great compassion blot out my **t.** 7322
51: 3 For I know my **t,** 7322
65: 3 you forgave our **t.** 7322
103:12 so far has he removed our t from us. 7322
Isa 43:25 "I, even I, am he who blots out your **t,** 7322
50: 1 of your t your mother was sent away. 7322
53: 5 But he was pierced for our **t,** 7322
Mic 1:13 for the t *of* Israel were found in you. 7322
Ro 4: 7 "Blessed are they whose t are forgiven, *490*
Gal 3:19 It was added because of t until the Seed *4126*
Eph 2: 1 you were dead in *your* t and sins, *4183*
2: 5 with Christ even when we were dead *in* **t—** *4183*

TRANSGRESSORS (4) [TRANSGRESSION]

Ps 51:13 Then I will teach t your ways, 7321
Isa 53:12 and was numbered with the **t.** 7321
53:12 and made intercession for the **t.** 7321
Lk 22:37 'And he was numbered with the **t';** *491*

TRANSLATE (KJV) See TRANSFER

TRANSLATED (3)

Ezr 4:18 The letter you sent us has been read and t 10597
Jn 1:42 called Cephas" (which, when **t,** is Peter). *2257*
Ac 9:36 named Tabitha (which, *when* **t,** is Dorcas), *1450*

TRANSLATION (KJV) See TAKEN

TRANSPARENT (1)

Rev 21:21 of the city was of pure gold, like t glass. *1420*

TRANSPLANTED (1) [PLANT]

Eze 17:10 Even if *it* **is t,** will it thrive? 9278

TRANSPORT (1)

Ge 46: 5 in the carts that Pharaoh had sent to t him. 5951

TRAP (25) [TRAPPED, TRAPS]

1Sa 28: 9 Why *have* you **set a t** for my life to bring 5943
Job 18: 9 A t seizes him by the heel; 7062
18:10 a t lies in his path. 4892
40:24 or t him and pierce his nose? 4613
Ps 31: 4 Free me from the t that is set for me, 8407
69:22 may it become retribution and a **t.** 4613
Pr 20:25 a t *for* a man to dedicate something rashly 4613
28:10 along an evil path will fall into his own **t,** 8819
Ecc 7:26 a t and whose hands are chains. 3052
Isa 8:14 the people of Jerusalem he will be a t and 7062
Jer 9: 8 but in his heart he sets a t *for* him. 744
50:24 *I* **set a t** for you, O Babylon, 3704
Am 3: 5 Does a bird fall into a t *on* the ground 7062
3: 5 Does a t spring up from the earth 7062
Ob 1: 7 those who eat your bread will set a t 4650
Mt 22:15 and laid plans to t him in his words. *4074*
22:18 why *are you* **trying to t** me? *4279*
Mk 12:15 "Why *are you* **trying to t** me?" *4279*
Lk 20:26 unable *to* t him **in** what he had said there *2138*
21:34 will close on you unexpectedly like a **t.** *4075*
Jn 8: 6 They were using this question as a **t,** *4279*
Ro 11: 9 "May their table become a snare and a **t,** *2560*
1Ti 3: 7 not fall into disgrace and into the devil's **t.** *4075*
6: 9 to get rich fall into temptation and a t and *4075*
2Ti 2:26 to their senses and escape from the t of *4075*

TRAPPED (8) [TRAP]

Pr 6: 2 if *you have* **been** t by what you said, 3704
11: 6 but the unfaithful **are** t by evil desires. 4334
12:13 An evil man is t by his sinful talk, 4613
Ecc 9:12 or birds are taken in a snare, so men **are** t 3704
Isa 42:22 of them t in pits or hidden away in prisons. 7072
Jer 8: 9 they will be dismayed and **t.** 4334
Eze 19: 4 and *he* **was** t in their pit. 9530
19: 8 and *he* **was** t in their pit. 9530

TRAPS (6) [TRAP]

Jos 23:13 they will become snares and t for you, 4613
Ps 38:12 Those who seek my life **set** *their* **t,** 5943
140: 5 the cords of their net and have set t for me 4613
141: 9 from the t *set by* evildoers. 4613
Jer 5:26 and like those who set t to catch men. 5422
La 4:20 our very life breath, was caught in their **t.** 8827

TRAVAIL, TRAVAILED, TRAVAILEST, TRAVAILETH (KJV) See BIRTH, BURDEN, BUSINESS, HARDSHIP, HARDSHIPS, LABOR, MISFORTUNE, PAIN, PAINS, SUFFERING, TASK, TOIL

TRAVEL (9) [TRAVELED, TRAVELER, TRAVELERS, TRAVELING, TRAVELS]

Ex 13:21 so that they *could* t by day or night. 2143
Nu 20:17 *We will* **t along** the king's highway and 2143
21:22 *We will* t along the king's highway 2143
2Ch 15: 5 In those days it was not safe to **t about,**
995+2256+3655
Job 21:29 you never questioned *those who* **t?** 2006+6296
Pr 4:15 Avoid it, *do* not t on it; 6296
Eze 39:11 in the valley of those *who* t east toward 6296
Mt 23:15 *You* **t over** land and sea to win a single
convert, *4310*
Rev 18:17 "Every sea captain, and all who **t by ship,** *4434*

TRAVELED (36) [TRAVEL]

Ge 12: 6 Abram t through the land as far as the site 6296
41:46 Pharaoh's presence and t throughout Egypt. 6296
Ex 15:22 For three days *they* t in the desert 2143
Nu 10:12 **t from place to place** until the cloud came 5023
10:33 mountain of the LORD and t for three days. 2006

Nu 11:35 the people t *to* Hazeroth and stayed there. 5825
21: 4 *They* t from Mount Hor *along* the route to 5825
22: 1 Then the Israelites t to the plains of Moab 5825
33: 8 *they had* t for three days in the Desert 2006+2143
Dt 2: 8 and **t along** the desert road of Moab. 6296
10: 6 (The Israelites t from the wells of 5825
10: 7 From there *they* t *to* Gudgodah and on 5825
Jos 24:17 among all the nations through which *we* t. 6296
Jdg 11:18 "Next *they* t through the desert, 2143
2Sa 4: 7 *they* t all night by way of the Arabah. 2143
1Ki 19: 8 *he* t forty days and forty nights 2143
2Ki 5:19 After Naaman *had* t some distance, 2143
Isa 41: 3 by a path his feet *have* not t before. 995
Mk 1:39 So *he* t throughout Galilee, *2262*
Lk 2:44 *they* t on for a day. *2262*
8: 1 Jesus **t about** from one town and village *1476*
10:33 But a Samaritan, *as he* **t**, came where *3841*
17:11 Jesus **t along** the border between Samaria *1451*
Ac 8:36 As *they* t along the road, *4513*
8:40 however, appeared at Azotus and **t about,** *1451*
9:32 *As* Peter **t about the country,** *1328+1451+4246*
11:19 t as far as Phoenicia, Cyprus and Antioch, *1451*
13: 6 *They* **t through** the whole island *1451*
13:31 *by* those who *had* **t with** him from Galilee *5262*
15: 3 as they **t through** Phoenicia and Samaria, *1451*
16: 4 As *they* t from town to town, *1388*
16: 6 Paul and his companions t **throughout** *1451*
16:12 From there we t to Philippi, *NIG*
18:23 t from place to place **throughout** *1451*
20: 2 *He* **t through** that area, *1451*
28:15 and *they* t as far as the Forum of Appius *2262*

TRAVELER (5) [TRAVEL]

Jdg 19:17 he looked and saw the t in the city square, 782
2Sa 12: 4 "Now a t came to the rich man, 2144
12: 4 to prepare a meal for the t who had come 782
Job 31:32 for my door was always open to the t— 782
Jer 14: 8 like a t who stays only a night? 782

TRAVELERS (4) [TRAVEL]

Jdg 5: 6 t took to winding paths. 2143+5986
Isa 33: 8 no t are *on* the roads. 6296
Jer 9: 2 in the desert a lodging place for t, 782
Eze 39:11 It will block the way of t, 6296

TRAVELING (8) [TRAVEL]

Ex 14:19 who *had been* t in front of Israel's army, 2143
17: 1 **t from place to place** as the LORD 5023
1Ki 18:27 Perhaps he is deep in thought, or busy, or t. 2006
Job 6:19 the t **merchants** *of* Sheba look in hope. 2142
Isa 60:15 with no *one* **t through,** 6296
Lk 14:25 Large crowds *were* **t with** Jesus, *5233*
Ac 9: 7 The men **t with** Saul stood there speechless; *5321*
19:29 Paul's **t companions** from Macedonia, *5292*

TRAVELS (4) [TRAVEL]

Ex 40:36 In all the t *of* the Israelites, 5023
40:38 of all the house of Israel during all their **t.** 5023
Jer 2: 6 a land where no one t and no one lives?' 6296
51:43 through which no man **t.** 6296

TRAVERSING (KJV) See RUNNING

TRAYS (3)

Ex 25:38 Its wick trimmers and t are to be 4746
37:23 as well as its wick trimmers and **t,** 4746
Nu 4: 9 its wick trimmers and **t,** 4746

TREACHEROUS (7) [TREASON]

Ps 25: 3 be put to shame who *are* t without excuse. 953
Isa 24:16 Woe to me! The t betray! 953
24:16 With treachery the t betray!" 953
48: 8 Well do I know **how t** *you are;* 953+953
Hab 1:13 Why then do you tolerate the **t?** 953
Zep 3: 4 Her prophets are arrogant; they are t men. 956
2Ti 3: 4 **t,** rash, conceited, lovers of pleasure *4595*

TREACHEROUSLY (2) [TREASON]

Jdg 9:23 Shechem, who **acted t** against Abimelech. 953
Ac 7:19 He **dealt t with** our people and oppressed *2947*

TREACHERY (4) [TREASON]

Lev 26:40 their t against me and their hostility 5085+5086
2Ki 9:23 calling out to Ahaziah, **"T,** Ahaziah!" 5327
Isa 24:16 With t the treacherous betray!" 954
59:13 rebellion and t against the LORD, 3950

TREAD (5) [TREADING, TREADS, TROD, TRODDEN]

Job 24:11 *they* t the winepresses, yet suffer thirst. 2005
Ps 91:13 *You will* t upon the lion and the cobra; 2005
Jer 25:30 He will shout like *those who* t the grapes, 2005
Mic 7:19 *you will* t our sins **underfoot** 3899
Na 3:14 Work the clay, t the mortar, 8252

TREADING (7) [TREAD]

Dt 25: 4 an ox while it *is* **t out** *the* **grain.** 1889
Ne 13:15 in Judah t winepresses on the Sabbath 2005
Isa 41:25 as if *he were* a potter t the clay. 8252
Isa 63: 2 like those of *one* t the winepress? 2005
Am 9:13 and the planter by the *one* t grapes. 2005
1Co 9: 9 an ox *while it is* **t out the grain."** *262*
1Ti 5:18 the ox *while it is* **t out the grain,"** *262*

TREADS (7) [TREAD]

Job 9: 8 He alone stretches out the heavens and t on 2005
Isa 16:10 no *one* **t out** wine at the presses, 2005
41:25 *He* **t** *on* rulers as if they were mortar, 995
Jer 48:33 no *one* t them with shouts of joy. 2005
Am 4:13 and t the high places of the earth— 2005
Mic 1: 3 he comes down and t the high places of 2005
Rev 19:15 *He* t the winepress of the fury of the wrath *4251*

TREASON (4) [TRAITOR, TRAITORS, TREACHEROUS, TREACHEROUSLY, TREACHERY]

2Ki 11:14 Athaliah tore her robes and called out, **"T!** 8004
11:14 and called out, "Treason! **T!"** 8004
2Ch 23:13 Athaliah tore her robes and shouted, **"T!** 8004
23:13 and shouted, "Treason! **T!"** 8004

TREASURE (18) [TREASURED, TREASURER, TREASURERS, TREASURES, TREASURIES, TREASURY]

Ge 43:23 has given you t in your sacks; 4759
Job 3:21 who search for it more than for **hidden t,** 4759
20:20 he cannot save himself by his **t.** 2773
Pr 2: 4 for silver and search for it as for **hidden t,** 4759
15: 6 house of the righteous contains great **t,** 2890
Ecc 2: 8 and the t *of* kings and provinces. 6035
Isa 33: 6 the fear of the LORD is the key to this **t.** 238
44: 9 and the *things* they t are worthless. 2773
Da 1: 2 in Babylonia and put in the t house 238
Mt 6:21 your **t** is, there your heart will be also. *2565*
13:44 "The kingdom of heaven is like t hidden in *2565*
19:21 and you will have **t** in heaven. *2565*
Mk 10:21 and you will have **t** in heaven. *2565*
Lk 12:33 a **t** in heaven that will not be exhausted, *2565*
12:34 your **t** is, there your heart will be also. *2565*
18:22 and you will have **t** in heaven. *2565*
2Co 4: 7 But we have this **t** in jars of clay to show *2565*
1Ti 6:19 In this way *they will* **lay up t** *631*

TREASURED (11) [TREASURE]

Ex 19: 5 of all nations you will be my **t possession.** 6035
Dt 7: 6 the earth to be his people, his **t possession.** 6035
14: 2 chosen you to be his **t possession.** 6035
26:18 his **t possession** as he promised, 6035
Job 23:12 *I have* t the words of his mouth more than 7621
Ps 135: 4 Israel to be his **t possession.** 6035
Isa 64:11 and all *that* we t lies in ruins. 4718
Eze 7:22 and they will desecrate my **t place;** 7621
Mal 3:17 the day when I make up my **t possession.** 6035
Lk 2:19 But Mary **t up** all these things *5337*
2:51 his mother t all these things in her heart. *1413*

TREASURER (1) [TREASURE]

Ezr 1: 8 had them brought by Mithredath the **t,** 1601

TREASURERS (5) [TREASURE]

2Ki 12: 5 receive the money from one of the **t,** 4837
12: 7 Take no more money from your **t,** 4837
Ezr 7:21 the **t** of Trans-Euphrates to provide 10139
Da 3: 2 prefects, governors, advisers, **t,** judges, 10133
3: 3 prefects, governors, advisers, **t,** judges, 10133

TREASURES (44) [TREASURE]

Dt 33:19 on the **t hidden** *in* the sand." 3243+8561
1Ki 14:26 the t *of* the temple of the LORD and 238
14:26 the LORD and the t *of* the royal palace. 238
2Ki 20:13 and everything found among his **t.** 238
20:15 "There is nothing among my t that I did 238
24:13 the t *from* the temple of the LORD and 238
1Ch 29: 3 now give my **personal t** of gold and silver 6035
2Ch 12: 9 the t *of* the temple of the LORD and 238
12: 9 the LORD and the t *of* the royal palace. 238
25:24 together with the palace t and the hostages, 238
36:18 and the t *of* the LORD's temple and 238
36:18 the LORD's temple and the t *of* the king 238
Job 20:26 total darkness lies in wait for his **t.** 7621
28:10 his eyes see all its **t.** 3702
Pr 10: 2 Ill-gotten t are of no value, 238
24: 4 its rooms are filled with rare and beautiful **t.** 2104
Isa 2: 7 there is no end to their **t.** 238
10:13 I plundered their **t;** 6965
30: 6 their t on the humps of camels, 238
39: 2 and everything found among his **t.** 238
39: 4 "There is nothing among my t that I did 238
45: 3 I will give you the t *of* darkness, 238
Jer 15:13 Your wealth and your t I will give 238
17: 3 and all your t I will give away as plunder, 238
20: 5 all its valuables and all the t *of* the kings 238
50:37 A sword against her **t!** 238
51:13 who live by many waters and are rich in **t,** 238
La 1: 7 the t that were hers in days of old. 4719
1:10 The enemy laid hands on all her **t;** 4718
1:11 they barter their t for food 4718
Eze 22:25 they devour people, take t and precious 2890
Da 11:43 the t *of* gold and silver and all the riches 4819
Hos 9: 6 Their t of silver will be taken over 4718
Hos 13:15 will be plundered of all its **t.** 2775+3998
Joel 3: 5 and carried off my finest t to your temples. 4718
Ob 1: 6 will be ransacked, his **hidden t** pillaged! 5208
Mic 6:10 your ill-gotten t and the short ephah, 238
Na 2: 9 the wealth from all its **t!** 2775+3998
Mt 2:11 Then they opened their t and presented him *2565*
6:19 "Do not store up for yourselves t on earth, *2565*
6:20 But store up for yourselves t in heaven, *2565*
13:52 of his storeroom new t as well as old." *NIG*
Col 2: 3 in whom are hidden all the t of wisdom *2565*
Heb 11:26 as of greater value than the t of Egypt, *2565*

TREASURIES (20) [TREASURE]

1Ki 7:51 in the t *of* the LORD's temple. 238
15:18 the silver and gold that was left in the t *of* 238
2Ki 12:18 in the t *of* the temple of the LORD and of 238
14:14 in the temple of the LORD and in the t *of* 238
16: 8 the LORD and in the t *of* the royal palace 238
18:15 in the temple of the LORD and in the t *of* 238
1Ch 9:26 with the responsibility for the rooms and t 238
26:20 in charge of the t *of* the house of God and 238
26:20 the treasuries of the house of God and the t 238
26:22 They were in charge of the t *of* the temple 238
26:24 was the officer in charge of the **t.** 238
26:26 and his relatives were in charge of all the t 238
28:12 for the t *of* the temple of God and for 238
28:12 of the temple of God and for the t *for* 238
2Ch 5: 1 he placed them in the t *of* God's temple. 238
8:15 including that of the **t.** 238
16: 2 then took the silver and gold out of the t *of* 238
32:27 and he made t for his silver and gold and 238
Pr 8:21 and making their t full. 238
Eze 28: 4 and amassed gold and silver in your **t.** 238

TREASURY (19) [TREASURE]

Jos 6:19 sacred to the LORD and must go into his **t."** 238
6:24 the articles of bronze and iron into the t *of* 238
1Ch 29: 8 gave them to the t *of* the temple of the LORD 238
Ezr 2:69 According to their ability they gave to the t 238
6: 1 in the archives stored in the t at Babylon. 10148
6: 4 The costs are to be paid by the royal **t.** 10103
6: 8 to be fully paid out of the royal **t,** 10479
7:20 you may provide from the royal **t.** 10103+10148
Ne 7:70 The governor gave to the t 1,000 drachmas 238
7:71 the heads of the families gave to the t *for* 238
10:38 to the storerooms of the **t.** 238+1074
Est 3: 9 of silver into the royal t for the men 1709
4: 7 the royal t for the destruction of the Jews. 1709
Jer 38:11 with him and went to a room under the t in 238
Mt 27: 6 "It is against the law to put this into the **t,** *3168*
Mk 12:41 putting their money into the **temple t.** *1126*
12:43 poor widow has put more into the t than all *1126*
Lk 21: 1 the rich putting their gifts into the **temple t.** *1126*
Ac 8:27 an important official in charge of all the t *1125*

TREAT (31) [TREATED, TREATING, TREATMENT, TREATMENTS, TREATS]

Ge 19: 9 *We'll* t you **worse** than them." 8317
30:20 This time my husband *will* t me **with honor** 2290
Lev 22: 2 "Tell Aaron and his sons *to* **t with respect** 5692
Nu 10:29 Come with us and *we will* t you **well,** 3512
11:15 If this is how you *are going to* t me, 6913
14:11 *will* these people t me **with contempt?** 5540
25:17 **"T** the Midianites **as enemies** and kill them, 7675
Dt 20:15 how you *are to* t all the cities that are at 6913
21:14 You must not sell her or t her **as a slave,** 6683
Jos 2:14 *we will* t you kindly and faithfully when 6913
2Sa 19:43 So why *do you* t us **with contempt?** 7837
Job 6:26 t the words of a despairing man as wind? NIH
Ps 103:10 not t us as our sins deserve or repay us 6913
Jer 3:19 " 'How gladly *would I* t you like sons 8883
29:22 'The LORD t you like Zedekiah 8492
34:18 *I will* t *like* the calf they cut in two and 5989
Eze 15: 6 so *will I* t the people living in Jerusalem. 5989
35:11 *I will* t you in accordance with the anger 6913
35:15 that is how *I will* t you. 6913
Da 1:13 and t your servants in accordance 6913
Hos 11: 8 How *can I* t you like Admah? 5989
Na 3: 6 *I will* t you **with contempt** and make you 5571
Mt 18:17 the church, t *him* as you would a pagan or *1639*
18:35 how my heavenly Father *will* t each *4472*
Jn 15:21 *They will* t you this way because *1650+4472*
1Co 12:23 that we think are less honorable *we* **t with** *4363*
Gal 4:14 *you did* not t me **with contempt** or scorn. *2024*
Eph 6: 9 masters, t your slaves in the same way. *4472*
1Th 5:20 *do* not t prophecies **with contempt.** *2024*
1Ti 5: 1 **T** younger men as brothers, *NIG*
1Pe 3: 7 t them with respect as the weaker partner *671*

TREATED (38) [TREAT]

Ge 12:13 so that I *will be* **t well** for your sake and 3512
12:16 *He* t Abram **well** for her sake, 3512
26:29 but always t you well and sent you away 6913
34:31 *"Should he have* t our sister like a 6913
39:19 saying, "This is how your slave t me," 6913
42:30 to us and t us as though we were spying on 5989
Ex 5:15 "Why *have you* t your servants this way? 6913
18:11 to *those who had* t Israel **arrogantly."** 2326
Lev 19:34 The alien living with you *must be* t as one 2118
25:40 He is to be t **as** a hired worker or 3869
25:53 *to be* t as a man hired from year to 2118+6640
Nu 14:23 No one *who has* t me **with contempt** will ever see it. 5540
16:30 these men *have* t the LORD **with contempt."** 5540

Nu 25:18 because they **t** you **as enemies** 7675
Jdg 1:24 and *we will see that* you *are* **t** well." 6913
8: 1 "Why *have you* **t** us like this? 6913
9:16 and if *you have* **t** him as he deserves— 6913
1Sa 2:14 how *they* **t** all the Israelites who came 6913
6: 6 When *he* **t** them **harshly,** 6618
24:17 "You *have* **t** me well, 1694
24:17 but I *have* **t** you badly. 1694
24:19 for the way *you* **t** me today. 6913
1Ki 1:21 I and my son Solomon *will* **be t as** criminals 2118
1Ch 24:31 the oldest brother were **t the same as** 4200+6645
Ne 9:10 how **arrogantly** the Egyptians **t** them. 2326
La 2:20 Whom *have you ever* **t** like this? 6618
Eze 22: 7 **t** father and mother **with contempt;** 7837
Mt 21:36 and the tenants **t** them the same way. *4472*
Mk 12: 4 on the head and **t** him **shamefully.** *870*
Lk 2:48 "Son, why *have you* **t** us like this? *4472*
6:23 For that is how their fathers **t** the prophets. *4472*
6:26 how their fathers **t** the false prophets. *4472*
20:11 that one also they beat and **t shamefully** *869*
1Co 4:11 *we are* **brutally t,** we are homeless. *3139*
12:23 the parts that are unpresentable *are* **t with** *2400*
Heb 10:29 **who** *has* **t** as an unholy thing the blood of *2451*
10:33 by side *with* those who *were* so **t.** *418*
Rev 18:20 God has judged her for the **way** she **t** you.' *3210*[S]

TREATING (6) [TREAT]

Ge 18:25 **t** the righteous and the wicked alike. 2118
50:17 and the wrongs *they* **committed** *in t* you AIT
Lev 22: 9 **t** them **with contempt.** 2725
1Sa 2:17 **t** the LORD's offering **with contempt.** 5540
25:39 against Nabal for **t** me with contempt. NIH
Heb 12: 7 God *is* **t** you as sons. *4712*

TREATISE (KJV) See BOOK

TREATMENT (4) [TREAT]

1Sa 20:34 grieved at his father's **shameful t** *of* David. 4007
Isa 66: 4 so I also will choose **harsh t** *for* them 9500
1Co 12:24 our presentable parts need no **special t.** *5507*
Col 2:23 false humility and their **harsh t** of the body, *910*

TREATMENTS (3) [TREAT]

Est 2: 3 and let **beauty t** be given to them. 9475
2: 9 with her **beauty t** and special food. 9475
2:12 of **beauty t** prescribed for the women, 5299

TREATS (4) [TREAT]

Dt 24: 7 and **t** him **as a slave** or sells him, 6683
Job 39:16 *She* **t** her young **harshly,** 7996
41:27 Iron *he* **t** like straw and bronze like rotten 3108
Pr 27:11 answer *anyone who* **t** me **with contempt.** 3070

TREATY (31)

Ge 21:27 and the two men made a **t.** 1382
21:32 After the **t** had been made at Beersheba, 1382
26:28 Let us make a **t** with you 1382
Ex 34:12 to make a **t** with those who live in the land 1382
34:15 to make a **t** with those who live in the land; 1382
Dt 7: 2 Make no **t** with them, 1382
23: 6 not seek a **t of friendship** *with* them as long as you live. 2256+3208+8934
Jos 9: 6 make a **t** with us." 1382
9: 7 How then can we make a **t** with you?" 1382
9:11 "We are your servants; make a **t** with us." 1382
9:15 Then Joshua made a **t** of peace with them 1382
9:16 after they made the **t** with the Gibeonites, 1382
10: 1 Gibeon *had* **made a t of peace** with Israel 8966
11:19 not one city **made a t of peace** with the 8966
1Sa 11: 1 "Make a **t** with us, and we will be subject 1382
11: 2 *"I will* **make a t** with you only on the 4162
1Ki 5:12 and the two of them made a **t.** 1382
15:19 "Let there be a **t** between me and you," 1382
15:19 Now break your **t** with Baasha king 1382
20:34 "On the basis of a **t** I will set you free." 1382
20:34 So he made a **t** with him, and let him go. 1382
2Ch 16: 3 "Let there be a **t** between me and you," 1382
16: 3 Now break your **t** with Baasha king 1382
Ezr 9:12 Do not seek a **t of friendship** *with* them at any time, 2256+3208+8934
Isa 33: 8 The **t** is broken, its witnesses are despised, 1382
Eze 17:13 a member of the royal family and made a **t** 1382
17:14 surviving only by keeping his **t.** 1382
17:15 Will he break the **t** and yet escape? 1382
17:16 oath he despised and whose **t** he broke. 1382
Hos 12: 1 He makes a **t** with Assyria and sends 1382
Am 1: 9 disregarding a **t** *of* brotherhood, 1382

TREE (180) [TREES]

Ge 1:29 of the whole earth and every **t** that has fruit 6770
2: 9 the garden were the **t** *of* life and the tree of 6770
2: 9 the garden were the tree of life and the **t** *of* 6770
2:16 "You are free to eat from any **t** *in* 6770
2:17 the **t** *of* the knowledge of good and evil, 6770
3: 1 not eat from any **t** *in* the garden'?" 6770
3: 3 'You must not eat fruit from the **t** that is in 6770
3: 6 of the **t** was good for food and pleasing to 6770
3:11 from the **t** that I commanded you not 6770
3:12 she gave me some fruit from the **t,** 6770
3:17 from the **t** about which I commanded you, 6770
3:22 and take also from the **t** *of* life and eat, 6770
3:24 and forth to guard the way to the **t** *of* life. 6770
12: 6 as far as the site of the **great t** *of* Moreh 471
18: 4 wash your feet and rest under this **t.** 6770
18: 8 he stood near them under a **t.** 6770
21:33 Abraham planted a **tamarisk t** in Beersheba. 869
40:19 lift off your head and hang you on a **t.** 6770
Ex 9:25 in the fields and stripped every **t.** 6770
10: 5 including every **t** that is growing 6770
10:15 Nothing green remained on **t** or plant in all 6770
Lev 19:23 the land and plant any kind of fruit **t,** 6770
Dt 12: 2 the hills and under every spreading **t** where 6770
19: 5 and as he swings his ax to fell a **t,** 6770
21:22 to death and his body is hung on a **t,** 6770
21:23 not leave his body on the **t** overnight. 6770
21:23 who is hung on a **t** is under God's curse. NIH
22: 6 either in a **t** or on the ground, 6770
Jos 8:29 the king of Ai on a **t** and left him there 6770
8:29 the **t** and throw it down at the entrance of 6770
19:33 and the **large t** in Zaanannim, 471
Jdg 4:11 by the **great t** in Zaanannim near Kedesh. 471
9: 6 and Beth Millo gathered beside the **great t** 471
9: 8 They said to the **olive t,** 'Be our king.' 2339
9: 9 "But the **olive t** answered, 2339
9:10 "Next, the trees said to the **fig t,** 9300
9:11 "But the **fig t** replied, 9300
9:37 from the direction of the soothsayers' **t."** 471
1Sa 10: 3 on from there until you reach the **great t** 471
14: 2 under a **pomegranate t** in Migron. 8232
22: 6 was seated under the **tamarisk t** on the hill 869
31:13 and buried them under a **tamarisk t** 869
2Sa 18: 9 Absalom's head got caught in the **t.** 461
18:10 "I just saw Absalom hanging in an **oak t."** 461
18:14 while Absalom was still alive in the **oak t.** 461
1Ki 4:25 each man under his own vine and **fig t.** 9300
13:14 He found him sitting under an **oak t** 461
14:23 every high hill and under every spreading **t.** 6770
19: 4 He came to a **broom t,** sat down under it 8413
19: 5 he lay down under the **t** and fell asleep. 8413
2Ki 3:19 You will cut down every good **t,** 6770
3:25 the springs and cut down every good **t.** 6770
6: 5 As one of them was cutting down a **t,** 7771
16: 4 the hilltops and under every spreading **t.** 6770
17:10 every high hill and under every spreading **t.** 6770
18:31 of you will eat from his own vine and **fig t** 9300
1Ch 10:12 their bones under the **great t** in Jabesh, 461
2Ch 3: 5 **palm t** and chain **designs.** 9474
28: 4 the hilltops and under every spreading **t.** 6770
Ne 10:35 of our crops and of every fruit **t.** 6770
Job 14: 7 "At least there is hope for a **t:** 6770
15:33 like an **olive t** shedding its blossoms. 2339
19:10 he uproots my hope like a **t.** 6770
24:20 but are broken like a **t.** 6770
30: 4 and their food was the root of the **broom t.** 8413
Ps 1: 3 He is like a **t** planted by streams of water, 6770
37:35 and ruthless man flourishing like a **green t** 8316
52: 8 like an **olive t** flourishing in the house 2339
92:12 The righteous will flourish like a **palm t,** 9469
120: 4 with burning coals of the **broom t.** 8413
Pr 3:18 She is a **t** *of* life to those who embrace her; 6770
11:30 The fruit of the righteous is a **t** *of* life, 6770
13:12 but a longing fulfilled is a **t** *of* life. 6770
15: 4 tongue that brings healing is a **t** *of* life, 6770
27:18 He who tends a **fig t** will eat its fruit, 9300
Ecc 11: 3 a **t** falls to the south or to the north, 6770
12: 5 when the **almond t** blossoms and 9196
SS 2: 3 Like an **apple t** among the trees of 9515
2:13 The **fig t** forms its early fruit; 9300
4:14 with every kind of incense **t,** 6770
7: 8 I said, "I will climb the **palm t;** 9469
8: 5 Under the **apple t** I roused you; 9515
Isa 17: 6 as when an **olive t** is beaten, 2339
24:13 as when an **olive t** is beaten, 2339
34: 4 like shriveled figs from the **fig t.** 9300
36:16 of you will eat from his own vine and **fig t** 9300
55:13 of the thornbush will grow the **pine t,** 1360
56: 3 "I am only a dry **t."** 6770
57: 5 the oaks and under every spreading **t;** 6770
65:22 For as the days of a **t,** 6770
Jer 1:11 "I see the branch of an **almond t,"** I replied. 9196
2:20 and under every spreading **t** you lay down 6770
3: 6 and under every spreading **t** and has 6770
3:13 to foreign gods under every spreading **t,** 6770
8:13 There will be no figs on the **t,** 9300
10: 3 they cut a **t** out of the forest, 6770
11:16 The LORD called you a thriving **olive t** 2339
11:19 saying, "Let us destroy the **t** and its fruit; 6770
17: 8 He will be like a **t** planted by the water 6770
Eze 6:13 under every spreading **t** and every leafy oak 6770
17:24 the LORD bring down the tall **t** and make 6770
17:24 the tall tree and make the low **t** grow tall. 6770
17:24 the green **t** and make the dry tree flourish. 6770
17:24 the green tree and make the dry **t** flourish. 6770
20:28 and they saw any high hill or any leafy **t,** 6770
31: 8 no **t** in the garden of God could match 6770
31:13 the birds of the air settled on the fallen **t,** NIH
40:22 its portico and its **palm t decorations** had 9474
40:26 it had **palm t decorations** on the faces of 9474
41:19 toward the **palm t** on one side and the face 9474
41:19 and the face of a lion toward the **palm t** on 9474
Da 4:10 and there before me stood a **t** in the middle 10027
4:11 The **t** grew large and strong and its top 10027
4:14 'Cut down the **t** and trim off its branches; 10027
4:20 The **t** you saw, which grew large and 10027
4:22 O king, are **that t!** 10200[S]
4:23 'Cut down the **t** and destroy it, 10027
4:26 The command to leave the stump of the **t** 10027
Hos 9:10 like seeing the early fruit on the **fig t.** 9300
14: 6 His splendor will be like an **olive t,** 2339
Hos 14: 8 I am like a green **pine t;** 1360
Joel 1:12 vine is dried up and the **fig t** is withered; 9300
1:12 pomegranate, the palm and the **apple t**— 9515
2:22 the **fig t** and the vine yield their riches. 9300
Mic 4: 4 and under his own **fig t,** 9300
Hab 3:17 Though the **fig t** does not bud 9300
Hag 2:19 Until now, the vine and the **fig t,** 9300
2:19 the pomegranate and the olive **t** have 6770
Zec 3:10 to sit under his vine and **fig t,'** 9300
11: 2 Wail, O **pine t,** for the cedar has fallen; 1360
Mt 3:10 and every **t** that does not produce good fruit *1285*
7:17 Likewise every good **t** bears good fruit, *1285*
7:17 but a bad **t** bears bad fruit. *1285*
7:18 A good **t** cannot bear bad fruit, *1285*
7:18 and a bad **t** cannot bear good fruit. *1285*
7:19 Every **t** that does not bear good fruit is cut *1285*
12:33 "Make a **t** good and its fruit will be good, *1285*
12:33 or make a **t** bad and its fruit will be bad, *1285*
12:33 for a **t** is recognized by its fruit. *1285*
13:32 largest of garden plants and becomes a **t,** *1285*
21:19 Seeing a **fig t** by the road, *5190*
21:19 Immediately the **t** withered. *5190*
21:20 "How did the **fig t** wither so quickly?" *5190*
21:21 can you do what was done *to* the **fig t,** *5190*
24:32 "Now learn this lesson from the **fig t:** *5190*
Mk 11:13 Seeing in the distance a **fig t** in leaf, *5190*
11:14 Then he said *to* **the t,** "May no one ever *899*[S]
11:20 they saw the **fig t** withered from the roots. *5190*
11:21 The **fig t** you cursed has withered!" *5190*
13:28 "Now learn this lesson from the **fig t:** *5190*
Lk 3: 9 and every **t** that does not produce good fruit *1285*
6:43 "No good **t** bears bad fruit, *1285*
6:43 nor does a bad **t** bear good fruit. *1285*
6:44 Each **t** is recognized by its own fruit. *1285*
13: 6 "A man had a **fig t,** *5190*
13: 7 on this **fig t** and haven't found any. *5190*
13:19 It grew and became a **t,** *1285*
17: 6 you can say *to* this **mulberry t,** *5189*
19: 4 and climbed a **sycamore-fig t** to see him, *5191*
21:29 "Look at the **fig t** and all the trees. *5190*
23:31 if men do these things when the **t** is green, *3833*
Jn 1:48 under the **fig t** before Philip called you." *5190*
1:50 because I told you I saw you under the **fig t.** *5190*
Ac 5:30 whom you had killed by hanging him on a **t.** *3833*
10:39 They killed him by hanging him on a **t,** *3833*
13:29 down from the **t** and laid him in a tomb. *3833*
Ro 11:24 you were cut out of an **olive t that is wild** *66*
11:24 were grafted into a **cultivated olive t,** *2814*
11:24 be grafted into their own **olive t!** *1777*
Gal 3:13 "Cursed is everyone who is hung on a **t."** *3833*
Jas 3:12 My brothers, can a **fig t** bear olives, *5190*
1Pe 2:24 bore our sins in his body on the **t,** *3833*
Rev 2: 7 I will give the right to eat from the **t** of life, *3833*
6:13 *from* **a fig t** when shaken by a strong wind. *899*[S]
7: 1 on the land or on the sea or on any **t.** *1285*
9: 4 the grass of the earth or any plant or **t,** *1285*
22: 2 On each side of the river stood the **t** of life, *3833*
22: 2 And the leaves *of* the **t** are for the healing *3833*
22:14 that they may have the right to the **t** of life *3833*
22:19 from him his share in the **t** of life and in *3833*

TREES (137) [TREE]

Ge 1:11 and **t** on the land that bear fruit with seed 6770
1:12 and **t** bearing fruit with seed in it according 6770
2: 9 of **t** grow out of the ground— 6770
2: 9 **t** that were pleasing to the eye and good NIH
3: 2 "We may eat fruit from the **t** *in* the garden, 6770
3: 8 from the LORD God among the **t** *of* 6770
13:18 and went to live near the **great t** *of* Mamre 471
14:13 near the **great t** *of* Mamre the Amorite, 471
18: 1 the **great t** *of* Mamre while he was sitting 471
23:17 all the **t** within the borders of the field— 6770
30:37 and **plane t** and made white stripes 6895
Ex 10:15 in the fields and the fruit on the **t.** 6770
15:27 twelve springs and seventy **palm t,** 9469
Lev 23:40 to take choice fruit from the **t,** 6770
26: 4 the ground will yield its crops and the **t** *of* 6770
26:20 nor will the **t** *of* the land yield their fruit. 6770
27:30 from the soil or fruit from the **t,** belongs to 6770
Nu 13:20 Are there **t** on it or not? 6770
33: 9 twelve springs and seventy **palm t,** 9469
Dt 8: 8 vines and **fig t,** pomegranates, 9300
11:30 near the **great t** *of* Moreh, 471
20:19 not destroy its **t** by putting an ax to them, 6770
20:19 Are the **t** *of* the field people, 6770
20:20 down **t** that you know are not fruit trees 6770
20:20 that you know are not fruit **t** and use them 6770
24:20 When you beat the **olives from** your **t,** 2339
28:40 You will have **olive t** throughout your 2339
28:42 Swarms of locusts will take over all your **t** 6770
Jos 10:26 the kings and hung them on five **t,** 6770
10:26 and they were left hanging on the **t** 6770
10:27 from the **t** and threw them into the cave 6770
Jdg 9: 8 One day the **t** went out to anoint a king 6770
9: 9 to hold sway over the **t?'** 6770
9:10 "Next, the **t** said to the fig tree, 6770
9:11 to hold sway over the **t?'** 6770
9:12 **t** said to the vine, 'Come and be our king.' 6770
9:13 to hold sway over the **t?'** 6770
9:14 "Finally all the **t** said to the thornbush, 6770
9:15 "The thornbush said to the **t,** 6770
2Sa 5:23 and attack them in front of the **balsam t.** 1132
5:24 of marching in the tops of the **balsam t,** 1132
1Ki 6:29 **palm t** and open flowers. 9474
6:32 **palm t** and open flowers, 9474
6:32 the cherubim and **palm t** with beaten gold. 9474

1Ki 6:35 **palm t** and open flowers on them 9474
7:36 and **palm t** on the surfaces of the supports 9474
10:27 and cedar as plentiful as **sycamore-fig t** in 9204
2Ki 6:4 to the Jordan and began to cut down **t.** 6770
18:32 a land of **olive t** and honey. 2339+3658
1Ch 14:14 and attack them in front of the **balsam t.** 1132
14:15 of marching in the tops of the **balsam t,** 1132
16:33 Then the **t** *of* the forest will sing, 6770
27:28 in charge of the olive and **sycamore-fig t** in 9204
2Ch 1:15 and cedar as plentiful as **sycamore-fig t** in 9204
9:27 and cedar as plentiful as **sycamore-fig t** in 9204
Ne 8:15 and wild olive **t,** and from myrtles, palms 6770
8:15 palms and shade **t,** to make booths"— 6770
9:25 olive groves and fruit **t** in abundance. 6770
10:37 of the fruit of all our **t** and of our new wine 6770
Ps 74:5 to cut through a thicket of **t.** 6770
96:12 all the **t** *of* the forest will sing for joy; 6770
104:16 The **t** *of* the LORD are well watered, 6770
104:17 the stork has its home in the **pine t.** 1360
105:33 down their vines and **fig t** and shattered 9300
105:33 and shattered the **t** *of* their country. 6770
148:9 and all hills, fruit **t** and all cedars, 6770
Ecc 2:5 and parks and planted all kinds of fruit **t** 6770
2:6 to water groves of flourishing **t.** 6770
SS 2:3 the **t** *of* the forest is my lover among 6770
6:11 I went down to the grove of **nut t** to look 100
Isa 7:2 the **t** *of* the forest are shaken by the wind. 6770
9:10 the **fig t** have been felled, 9204
10:19 And the remaining **t** *of* his forests will be 6770
10:33 The **lofty t** will be felled, 7757+8123
14:8 the **pine t** and the cedars of Lebanon exult 1360
44:4 like **poplar t** by flowing streams. 6857
44:14 He let it grow among the **t** *of* the forest, 6770
44:23 you mountains, you forests and all your **t,** 6770
55:12 all the **t** *of* the field will clap their hands. 6770
Jer 5:17 devour your vines and **fig t.** 9300
6:6 "Cut down the **t** and build siege ramps 6785
7:20 on this place, on man and beast, on the **t** *of* 6770
17:2 and Asherah poles beside the spreading **t** 6770
46:22 like men who cut down **t.** 6770
Eze 15:2 of a branch on any of the **t** *in* the forest? 6770
15:6 the vine among the **t** *of* the forest as fuel 6770
17:24 All the **t** *of* the field will know that I 6770
20:47 and it will consume all your **t,** 6770
27:5 They made all your timbers of **pine t** 1360
31:4 and sent their channels to all the **t** *of* 6770
31:5 So it towered higher than all the **t** *of* 6770
31:8 nor could the **pine t** equal its boughs, 1360
31:8 the **plane t** compare with its branches— 6895
31:9 the envy of all the **t** *of* Eden in the garden 6770
31:14 Therefore no other **t** *by* the waters are ever 6770
31:14 No other **t** so well-watered are ever NIH
31:15 and all the **t** *of* the field withered away. 6770
31:16 Then all the **t** *of* Eden, 6770
31:16 all the **t** that were well-watered, NIH
31:18 of the **t** *of* Eden can be compared with you 6770
31:18 will be brought down with the **t** *of* Eden to 6770
34:27 The **t** *of* the field will yield their fruit and 6770
36:30 the fruit of the **t** and the crops of the field, 6770
40:16 walls were decorated with **palm t.** 9474
40:31 **palm t** decorated its jambs, 9474
40:34 **palm t** decorated the jambs on either side, 9474
40:37 **palm t** decorated the jambs on either side, 9474
41:18 were carved cherubim and **palm t.** 9474
41:18 **Palm t** alternated with cherubim. 9474
41:20 and **palm t** were carved on the wall of 9474
41:25 and **palm t** like those carved on the walls, 9474
41:26 with **palm t** carved on each side. 9474
47:7 I saw a great number of **t** on each side of 6770
47:12 Fruit **t** of all kinds will grow on both banks 6770
Hos 2:12 I will ruin her vines and her **fig t,** 9300
Joel 1:7 laid waste my vines and ruined my **fig t.** 9300
1:12 all the **t** *of* the field—are dried up. 6770
1:19 flames have burned up all the **t** *of* the field. 6770
2:22 The **t** are bearing their fruit; 6770
Am 4:9 Locusts devoured your fig and **olive t,** 2339
7:14 and I also took care of **sycamore-fig t.** 9204
Na 3:12 like **fig t** with their first ripe fruit; 9300
Zec 1:8 He was standing among the **myrtle t** in 2072
1:10 among the **myrtle t** explained, 2072
1:11 who was standing among the **myrtle t,** 2072
4:3 Also there are two **olive t** by it, 2339
4:11 "What are these two **olive t** on the right 2339
11:2 the stately **t** are ruined! NIH
Mt 3:10 The ax is already at the root *of* the **t,** *1285*
21:8 from the **t** and spread them on the road. *1285*
Mk 8:24 they look like **t** walking around." *1285*
Lk 3:9 The ax is already at the root *of* the **t,** *1285*
21:29 "Look at the fig tree and all the **t.** *1285*
Jude 1:12 autumn **t,** without fruit and uprooted— *1285*
Rev 7:3 the **t** until we put a seal on the foreheads of *1285*
8:7 a third *of* the **t** were burned up, *1285*
11:4 the two **olive t** and the two lampstands *1777*

TREMBLE (39) [TREMBLED, TREMBLES, TREMBLING]

Ex 15:14 The nations will hear and **t;** 8074
Dt 2:25 They will hear reports of you and *will* **t** 8074
1Ch 16:30 **T** before him, all the earth! 2655
Job 9:6 from its place and **makes** its pillars **t.** 7145
Ps 96:9 **t** before him, all the earth. 2655
99:1 The LORD reigns, *let* the nations **t;** 8074
114:7 **T,** O earth, at the presence of the Lord, 2655
Ecc 12:3 of the house **t,** and the strong men stoop, 2316
Isa 13:13 Therefore *I will* **make** the heavens **t;** 8074
14:16 who shook the earth and **made** kingdoms **t,** 8321
19:1 The idols of Egypt **t** before him, 5675
21:4 My heart falters, fear **makes** me **t;** 1286
23:11 over the sea and **made** its kingdoms **t.** 8074
32:10 a year you who feel secure *will* **t;** 8074
32:11 **T,** *you* complacent women; 3006
41:5 the ends of the earth **t.** 3006
44:8 *Do* not **t,** do not be afraid. 7064
64:1 that the mountains *would* **t** before you! 2362
66:5 you who **t** at his word: 3007
Jer 5:22 *"Should you* not **t** in my presence? 2655
23:9 heart is broken within me; all my bones **t.** 8173
33:9 and *will* **t** at the abundant prosperity 8074
49:21 At the sound of their fall the earth *will* **t;** 8321
50:46 of Babylon's capture the earth *will* **t;** 8321
Eze 7:27 the hands of the people of the land *will* **t.** 987
12:18 **t** as you eat your food, 8323
26:10 Your walls *will* **t** at the noise of the war 8321
26:15 the coastlands **t** at the sound of your fall, 8321
26:18 the coastlands **t** on the day of your fall; 3006
31:16 *I* **made** the nations **t** at the sound of its fall 8321
32:10 of them *will* **t** every moment for his life. 3006
38:20 the face of the earth *will* **t** at my presence. 8321
Joel 2:1 *Let* all who live in the land **t,** 8074
3:16 the earth and the sky *will* **t.** 8321
Am 3:6 *do* not the people **t?** 3006
8:8 *"Will* not the land **t** for this, 8074
Na 2:10 Hearts melt, knees give way, bodies **t,** 2714
Hab 2:7 Will they not wake up and **make** you **t?** 2316
3:6 he looked, and **made** the nations **t.** 6001

TREMBLED (16) [TREMBLE]

Ge 27:33 Isaac **t violently** 1524+3006+3010+4394+6330
Ex 19:16 Everyone in the camp **t.** 3006
19:18 the whole mountain **t** violently, 3006
20:18 saw the mountain in smoke, they **t** with fear. 5675
1Sa 16:4 of the town **t** when they met him. 3006
21:1 Ahimelech **t** when he met him, and asked, 3006
2Sa 22:8 "The earth **t** and quaked, 1723
22:8 *they* **t** because he was angry. 1723
Ezr 9:4 everyone *who* **t** at the words of the God of 3007
Ps 18:7 The earth **t** and quaked, 1723
18:7 *they* **t** because he was angry. 1723
77:18 the earth **t** and quaked. 8074
Isa 64:3 and the mountains **t** before you. 2362
Hos 13:1 When Ephraim spoke, men **t;** 8417
Hab 3:16 decay crept into my bones, and my legs **t.** 8074
Ac 7:32 Moses **t with fear** and did not dare to look. *1181+1958*

TREMBLES (13) [TREMBLE]

Jdg 7:3 'Anyone *who* **t** with fear may turn back 3007
Ps 97:4 the earth sees and **t.** 2655
104:32 and *it* **t,** who touches the mountains, 8283
119:120 My flesh **t** in fear of you; 6169
119:161 but my heart **t** at your word. 7064
Pr 30:21 "Under three things the earth **t,** 8074
Isa 10:29 Ramah **t;** Gibeah of Saul flees. 3006
66:2 and contrite in spirit, and **t** at my word. 3007
Jer 8:16 of their stallions the whole land **t.** 8321
10:10 When he is angry, the earth **t;** 8321
51:29 The land **t** and writhes, 8321
Joel 2:10 Before them the earth shakes, the sky **t,** 8321
Na 1:5 The earth **t** at his presence, 5951

TREMBLING (25) [TREMBLE]

Ge 42:28 and *they turned* to each other **t** and said, 3006
Ex 15:15 the leaders of Moab will be seized with **t,** 8284
2Sa 22:46 *they* **come t** from their strongholds. 3004
Job 4:14 fear and **t** seized me and made all my bones 8285
21:6 I am terrified; **t** seizes my body. 7146
Ps 2:11 the LORD with fear and rejoice with **t.** 8285
18:45 *they* **come t** from their strongholds. 3004
48:6 **T** seized them there, 8285
55:5 Fear and **t** have beset me; 8284
Isa 33:14 **t** grips the godless: 8285
Eze 26:16 **t** every moment, appalled at you. 3006
Da 10:10 and **set** me **t** on my hands and knees. 5675
10:11 And when he said this to me, I stood up **t.** 8283
Hos 3:5 *They will* **come t** to the LORD and 7064
11:10 his children *will* **come t** from the west. 3006
11:11 *They will* **come t** like birds from Egypt, 3006
Mic 7:17 *They will* **come t** out of their dens; 8074
Mk 5:33 came and fell at his feet and, **t** with fear, *5554*
16:8 **T** and bewildered, the women went out and
fled from the tomb. *899+2400+5571*
Lk 8:47 came **t** and fell at his feet. *5554*
Ac 16:29 and fell **t** before Paul and Silas. *1181+1958*
1Co 2:3 in weakness and fear, and with much **t.** *5571*
2Co 7:15 receiving him with fear and **t.** *5571*
Php 2:12 to work out your salvation with fear and **t,** *5571*
Heb 12:21 that Moses said, "I am **t** with fear." *1958*

TREMENDOUS (1)

Rev 16:18 has been on earth, so **t** was the quake. *3489+5496*

TRENCH (4)

1Ki 18:32 and he dug a **t** around it large enough 9498
18:35 down around the altar and even filled the **t.** 9498
18:38 and also licked up the water in the **t.** 9498
Da 9:25 It will be rebuilt with streets and a **t,** 3022

TRESPASS (5) [TRESPASSES]

Ro 5:15 But the gift is not like the **t.** *4183*
5:15 if the many died *by* the **t** of the one man, *4183*
5:17 For if, *by* the **t** of the one man, *4183*
5:18 as the result of one **t** was condemnation *4183*
5:20 so that the **t** might increase. *4183*

TRESPASSES (1) [TRESPASS]

Ro 5:16 but the gift followed many **t** and brought *4183*

TRESSES (1)

SS 7:5 the king is held captive by its **t.** 8111

TRIAL (19) [TRIALS]

Nu 35:12 of murder may not die before he stands **t** 5477
Jos 20:6 He is to stay in that city until he has stood **t** 5477
20:9 by the avenger of blood prior *to* **standing t** 6641
Ps 37:33 be condemned when **brought to t.** 9149
Mk 13:11 Whenever you are arrested and **brought to t,** *72*
Ac 12:4 to bring him out for public **t** after *NIG*
12:6 before Herod was to bring him to **t,** *NIG*
16:37 "They beat us publicly **without a t,** *185*
23:6 I **stand on t** because of my hope in *3212*
24:21 the dead that I *am* **on t** before you today.' " *3212*
25:9 to Jerusalem and **stand t** before me there *3212*
25:20 to go to Jerusalem and **stand t** there *3212*
26:6 that I am **on t** today. *2705+3212*
27:24 You must **stand t before** Caesar; *4225*
2Co 8:2 Out of the most **severe t,** *1509+2568*
Gal 4:14 Even though my illness was a **t** to you, *4280*
Jas 1:12 the man who perseveres *under* **t,** *4280*
1Pe 4:12 at the painful **t** you are suffering, *4280*
Rev 3:10 the hour *of* **t** that is going to come upon *4280*

TRIALS (8) [TRIAL]

Dt 7:19 You saw with your own eyes the great **t,** 4999
29:3 With your own eyes you saw those great **t,** 4999
Lk 22:28 those who have stood by me in my **t.** *4280*
1Th 3:3 that no one would be unsettled by these **t.** *2568*
2Th 1:4 the persecutions and **t** you are enduring. *2568*
Jas 1:2 whenever you face **t** of many kinds, *4280*
1Pe 1:6 have had to suffer grief in all kinds of **t.** *4280*
2Pe 2:9 Lord knows how to rescue godly men from **t** *4280*

TRIBAL (18) [TRIBE]

Ge 25:16 the names of the twelve **t** rulers according 569
Nu 4:18 the Kohathite **t** clans are not cut off from 8657
7:2 heads of families who were the **t** leaders 4751
25:15 Zur, a **t** chief of a Midianite family. 569
36:4 from the **t** inheritance of our forefathers." 4751
36:6 as long as they marry within the **t** clan 4751
36:7 the **t** land inherited from his forefathers. 4751
36:8 must marry someone in her father's **t** clan, 4751
Dt 1:15 of fifties and of tens and as **t** officials. 8657
Jos 11:23 to Israel according to their **t** divisions. 8657
12:7 of Israel according to their **t divisions—** 4713
14:1 the heads of the **t** clans of Israel allotted 4751
18:10 the Israelites according to their **t divisions.** 4713
19:51 the heads of the **t** clans of Israel assigned 4751
21:1 the heads of the other **t** families of Israel 4751
Eze 45:7 parallel to one of the **t** portions. NIH
48:8 to west will equal one of the **t** portions; NIH
48:21 of the **t** portions will belong to the prince, NIH

TRIBE (206) [HALF-TRIBE, TRIBAL, TRIBES]

Ex 31:2 the son of Hur, of the **t** *of* Judah, 4751
31:6 of the **t** *of* Dan, to help him. 4751
35:30 the son of Hur, of the **t** *of* Judah, 4751
35:34 of the **t** *of* Dan, the ability to teach others. 4751
38:22 the son of Hur, of the **t** *of* Judah, 4751
38:23 of the **t** *of* Dan—a craftsman 4751
Nu 1:4 One man from each **t,** 4751
1:21 number from the **t** *of* Reuben was 46,500. 4751
1:23 number from the **t** *of* Simeon was 59,300. 4751
1:25 The number from the **t** *of* Gad was 45,650. 4751
1:27 number from the **t** *of* Judah was 74,600. 4751
1:29 number from the **t** *of* Issachar was 54,400. 4751
1:31 number from the **t** *of* Zebulun was 57,400. 4751
1:33 number from the **t** *of* Ephraim was 40,500. 4751
1:35 from the **t** *of* Manasseh was 32,200. 4751
1:37 from the **t** *of* Benjamin was 35,400. 4751
1:39 The number from the **t** *of* Dan was 62,700. 4751
1:41 number from the **t** *of* Asher was 41,500. 4751
1:43 number from the **t** *of* Naphtali was 53,400. 4751
1:47 The families of the **t** *of* Levi, however, 4751
1:49 the **t** *of* Levi or include them in the census 4751
2:5 The **t** *of* Issachar will camp next to them. 4751
2:7 The **t** *of* Zebulun will be next. 4751
2:12 The **t** *of* Simeon will camp next to them. 4751
2:14 The **t** *of* Gad will be next. 4751
2:20 The **t** *of* Manasseh will be next to them. 4751
2:22 The **t** *of* Benjamin will be next. 4751
2:27 The **t** *of* Asher will camp next to them. 4751
2:29 The **t** *of* Naphtali will be next. 4751
3:6 the **t** *of* Levi and present them to Aaron 4751
7:12 of Amminadab of the **t** *of* Judah. 4751
10:15 over the division of the **t** *of* Issachar, 4751
10:16 of Helon was over the division of the **t** 4751
10:19 over the division of the **t** *of* Simeon, 4751
10:20 of Deuel was over the division of the **t** 4751
10:23 of Pedahzur was over the division of the **t** 4751
10:24 of Gideoni was over the division of the **t** 4751
10:26 of Ocran was over the division of the **t** 4751
10:27 over the division of the **t** *of* Naphtali. 4751

Nu 13: 2 From each ancestral t send one 4751
13: 4 from the t *of* Reuben, Shamma son of 4751
13: 5 from the t *of* Simeon, Shaphat son of Hori; 4751
13: 6 the t *of* Judah, Caleb son of Jephunneh; 4751
13: 7 from the t *of* Issachar, Igal son of Joseph; 4751
13: 8 the t *of* Ephraim, Hoshea son of Nun; 4751
13: 9 the t *of* Benjamin, Palti son of Raphu; 4751
13:10 the t *of* Zebulun, Gaddiel son of Sodi; 4751
13:11 from the t *of* Manasseh (a tribe of Joseph), 4751
13:11 from the tribe of Manasseh (a t *of* Joseph), 4751
13:12 the t *of* Dan, Ammiel son of Gemalli; 4751
13:13 the t *of* Asher, Sethur son of Michael; 4751
13:14 the t *of* Naphtali, Nahbi son of Vophsi; 4751
13:15 from the t *of* Gad, Geuel son of Maki. 4751
17: 3 for the head of each ancestral **t.** 1074
18: 2 from your ancestral t to join you 8657
24: 2 and saw Israel encamped t by tribe, NIH
24: 2 and saw Israel encamped tribe by **t,** 8657
26:55 according to the names for its ancestral **t.** 4751
31: 5 a thousand from each **t,** 4751
31: 6 a thousand from each **t,** 4751
34:14 because the families of the t *of* Reuben, 4751
34:14 the t *of* Gad and the half-tribe 4751
34:18 And appoint one leader from each t 4751
34:19 from the t *of* Judah; 4751
34:20 from the t *of* Simeon; 4751
34:21 from the t *of* Benjamin; 4751
34:22 the leader from the t *of* Dan; 4751
34:23 from the t *of* Manasseh son of Joseph; 4751
34:24 from the t *of* Ephraim son of Joseph; 4751
34:25 the leader from the t *of* Zebulun; 4751
34:26 the leader from the t *of* Issachar; 4751
34:27 the leader from the t *of* Asher; 4751
34:28 the leader from the t *of* Naphtali." 4751
35: 8 in proportion to the inheritance of each **t:** 2257^S
35: 8 Take many towns from a t that has many, 2257^S
36: 3 and added to that of the t they marry into. 4751
36: 4 to that of the t into which they marry, 4751
36: 5 "What the t *of* the descendants 4751
36: 7 No inheritance in Israel is to pass from t 4751
36: 7 in Israel is to pass from tribe to **t,** 4751
36: 8 in any Israelite t must marry someone 4751
36: 9 No inheritance may pass from t to tribe, 4751
36: 9 No inheritance may pass from tribe to **t,** 4751
36: 9 for each Israelite t is to keep 4751
36:12 in their father's clan and **t.** 4751
Dt 1:23 one man from each **t.** 8657
3:13 I gave to the half t *of* Manasseh. 8657
10: 8 that time the LORD set apart the t *of* Levi 8657
18: 1 indeed the whole t *of* Levi— 8657
29:18 man or woman, clan or t among you today 8657
Jos 3:12 one from each **t.** 8657
4: 2 one from each **t,** 8657
4: 4 one from each **t,** 8657
7: 1 of the t *of* Judah, took some of them. 4751
7:14 present yourselves t by tribe. NIH
7:14 present yourselves tribe by **t.** 8657
7:14 The t that the LORD takes shall come 8657
7:18 the son of Zerah, of the t *of* Judah, 4751
13: 7 among the nine tribes and half of the t 8657
13:14 to the t *of* Levi he gave no inheritance, 8657
13:15 This is what Moses had given to the t 4751
13:24 This is what Moses had given to the t 4751
13:33 But to the t of Levi, Moses had given no 8657
15: 1 The allotment for the t *of* Judah, 4751
15:20 This is the inheritance of the t *of* Judah, 4751
15:21 The southernmost towns of the t *of* Judah 4751
16: 8 the inheritance of the t *of* the Ephraimites, 4751
17: 1 the t *of* Manasseh as Joseph's firstborn, 4751
17: 6 the **t of Manasseh** received an inheritance 4985
18: 4 Appoint three men from each **t.** 8657
18:11 The lot came up for the t *of* Benjamin, 4751
18:21 The t *of* Benjamin, clan by clan, 4751
19: 1 The second lot came out for the t 4751
19: 8 the inheritance of the t *of* the Simeonites, 4751
19:23 the inheritance of the t *of* Issachar, 4751
19:24 The fifth lot came out for the t *of* Asher, 4751
19:31 the inheritance of the t *of* Asher, 4751
19:39 the inheritance of the t *of* Naphtali, 4751
19:40 The seventh lot came out for the t *of* Dan, 4751
19:48 the inheritance of the t *of* Dan, 4751
20: 8 in the desert on the plateau in the t *of* 4751
20: 8 Ramoth in Gilead in the t *of* Gad, 4751
20: 8 and Golan in Bashan in the t *of* Manasseh. 4751
21:17 the t *of* Benjamin they gave them Gibeon, 4751
21:20 the Levites were allotted towns from the t 4751
21:23 from the t *of* Dan they received Eltekeh, 4751
21:25 the t *of* Manasseh they received Taanach 4751
21:28 from the t *of* Issachar, Kishion, Daberath, 4751
21:30 from the t *of* Asher, Mishal, Abdon, 4751
21:32 the t *of* Naphtali, Kedesh in Galilee (a city 4751
21:34 from the t *of* Zebulun, Jokneam, Kartah, 4751
21:36 from the t *of* Reuben, Bezer, Jahaz, 4751
21:38 from the t *of* Gad, Ramoth in Gilead 4751
22: 7 the other half of **the t** Joshua gave land on 2257^S
Jdg 18: 1 the t *of* the Danites was seeking a place 8657
18:19 Isn't it better that you serve a t and clan 8657
18:30 the t *of* Dan until the time of the captivity 8657
20:12 of Israel sent men throughout the t 8657
21: 3 Why should one t be missing 8657
21: 6 "Today one t is cut off from Israel," 8657
21:17 "so that a t of Israel will not be wiped out. 8657
1Sa 9:21 a Benjamite, from the smallest t *of* Israel, 8657
9:21 of all the clans of the t *of* Benjamin? 8657
10:20 the t *of* Benjamin was chosen. 8657
10:21 he brought forward the t *of* Benjamin, 8657
2Sa 4: 2 the Beerothite from the t *of* Benjamin— 1201
1Ki 7:14 the t *of* Naphtali and whose father was 4751
8:16 not chosen a city in any t *of* Israel to have 8657
11:13 but will give him one t for the sake of David 8657
11:32 he will have one **t.** 8657
11:36 I will give one t to his son so that David 8657
12:20 the t *of* Judah remained loyal to the house 8657
12:21 the whole house of Judah and the t 8657
2Ki 17:18 Only the t *of* Judah was left, 8657
1Ch 6:60 the t *of* Benjamin they were given Gibeon, 4751
6:61 from the clans of half the t *of* Manasseh. 4751
6:62 from the part of the t *of* Manasseh that is 4751
6:66 as their territory towns from the t 4751
6:70 the t *of* Manasseh the Israelites gave Aner 4751
6:72 the t *of* Issachar they received Kedesh, 4751
6:74 from the t *of* Asher they received Mashal, 4751
6:76 the t *of* Naphtali they received Kedesh 4751
6:77 the t *of* Zebulun they received Jokneam, 4751
6:78 the t *of* Reuben across the Jordan east 4751
6:80 from the t *of* Gad they received Ramoth 4751
12: 2 kinsmen of Saul from the **t of Benjamin):** 1228
12:31 men of half the t *of* Manasseh, designated 4751
23:14 of God were counted as part of the **t** 8657
27:20 over half the t *of* Manasseh: 8657
2Ch 6: 5 not chosen a city in any t *of* Israel to have 8657
11:16 from every t *of* Israel who set their hearts 8657
19:11 the leader of the t *of* Judah, 1074
Est 2: 5 of Susa a Jew of the **t of Benjamin,** 408+3549
Job 30:12 On my right the t attacks; 7259
Ps 68:27 There is the little **t of Benjamin,** 1228
74: 2 the t *of* your inheritance, 8657
78:67 he did not choose the t *of* Ephraim; 8657
78:68 but he chose the t *of* Judah, 8657
Jer 10:16 including Israel, the t *of* his inheritance— 8657
51:19 including the t *of* his inheritance— 8657
Eze 47:23 In whatever t the alien settles, 8657
Lk 2:36 the daughter of Phanuel, of the t of Asher. *5876*
Ac 13:21 Saul son of Kish, of the t of Benjamin, *5876*
Ro 11: 1 of Abraham, *from* the t of Benjamin. *5876*
Php 3: 5 of the people of Israel, of the t of Benjamin, *5876*
Heb 7:13 things are said belonged to a different **t,** *5876*
7:13 and no one from **that** t has ever served at *4005^S*
7:14 to that t Moses said nothing about priests. *5876*
Rev 5: 5 See, the Lion of the t of Judah, *5876*
5: 9 from every t and language and people *5876*
7: 5 From the t of Judah 12,000 were sealed, *5876*
7: 5 were sealed, from the t of Reuben 12,000, *5876*
7: 5 from the t of Gad 12,000, *5876*
7: 6 from the t of Asher 12,000, *5876*
7: 6 from the t of Naphtali 12,000, *5876*
7: 6 from the t of Manasseh 12,000, *5876*
7: 7 from the t of Simeon 12,000, *5876*
7: 7 from the t of Levi 12,000, *5876*
7: 7 from the t of Issachar 12,000, *5876*
7: 8 from the t of Zebulun 12,000, *5876*
7: 8 from the t of Joseph 12,000, *5876*
7: 8 from the t of Benjamin 12,000. *5876*
7: 9 from every nation, **t,** people and language, *5876*
11: 9 and a half days men from every people, **t,** *5876*
13: 7 And he was given authority over every **t,** *5876*
14: 6 to every nation, **t,** language and people. *5876*

TRIBES (109) [TRIBE]

Ge 49:16 for his people as one of the t *of* Israel. 8657
49:28 All these are the twelve t *of* Israel, 8657
Ex 24: 4 representing the twelve t *of* Israel. 8657
28:21 a seal with the name of one of the twelve **t.** 8657
39:14 a seal with the name of one of the twelve **t.** 8657
Nu 1:16 the leaders of their ancestral **t.** 4751
10: 5 the t camping on the east are to set out. 4722
17: 2 from the leader of each of their ancestral **t.** 1074
17: 6 for the leader of each of their ancestral **t,** 1074
30: 1 Moses said to the heads of the t of Israel: 4751
31: 4 a thousand men from each of the t 4751
32:28 and to the family heads of the Israelite **t.** 4751
33:54 Distribute it according to your ancestral **t.** 4751
34:13 that it be given to the nine and a half **t,** 4751
34:15 and a half t have received their inheritance 4751
36: 3 they marry men from other Israelite **t;** 8657
Dt 1:13 and respected men from each of your **t,** 8657
1:15 So I took the leading men of your **t,** 8657
5:23 of your t and your elders came to me. 8657
12: 5 among all your t to put his Name there 8657
12:14 the LORD will choose in one of your **t,** 8657
16:18 for each of your t in every town 8657
18: 5 and their descendants out of all your t 8657
27:12 these t shall stand on Mount Gerizim NIH
27:13 And these t shall stand on Mount Ebal NIH
29:21 from all the t *of* Israel for disaster, 8657
31:28 Assemble before me all the elders of your t 8657
33: 5 along with the t *of* Israel. 8657
Jos 3:12 choose twelve men from the t *of* Israel, 8657
4: 5 to the number of the t *of* the Israelites, 8657
4: 8 to the number of the t *of* the Israelites, as 8657
7:16 Joshua had Israel come forward by **t,** 8657
12: 7 an inheritance to the t *of* Israel according 8657
13: 7 an inheritance among the nine t and half of 8657
14: 2 assigned by lot to the nine-and-a-half **t,** 4751
14: 3 the two-and-a-half t their inheritance east 4751
14: 4 for the sons of Joseph had become two t— 4751
18: 2 there were still seven Israelite t who had 8657
18:11 Their allotted territory lay between the t 1201
21: 4 thirteen towns from the t *of* Judah, 4751
21: 5 from the clans of the t *of* Ephraim, 4751
21: 6 from the clans of the t *of* Issachar, 4751
21: 7 received twelve towns from the t *of* Reuben, 4751
21: 9 the t *of* Judah and Simeon they allotted 4751
Jos 21:16 nine towns from these two **t.** 8657
22:14 one for each of the t *of* Israel, 4751
23: 4 as an inheritance for your t all the land of 8657
24: 1 Then Joshua assembled all the t *of* Israel 8657
Jdg 18: 1 into an inheritance among the t *of* Israel. 8657
20: 2 of the t *of* Israel took their places in 8657
20:10 of every hundred from all the t *of* Israel, 8657
20:12 The t *of* Israel sent men throughout 8657
21: 5 the t *of* Israel has failed to assemble before 8657
21: 8 of the t *of* Israel failed to assemble before 8657
21:15 LORD had made a gap in the t *of* Israel. 8657
21:24 and went home to their t and clans, 8657
1Sa 2:28 I chose your father out of all the t *of* Israel 8657
10:19 before the LORD by your t and clans." 8657
10:20 Samuel brought all the t *of* Israel near, 8657
15:17 not become the head of the t *of* Israel? 8657
2Sa 5: 1 All the t *of* Israel came to David at Hebron 8657
15: 2 "Your servant is from one of the t 8657
15:10 throughout the t *of* Israel to say, 8657
19: 9 Throughout the t *of* Israel, 8657
20:14 the t *of* Israel to Abel Beth Maacah and 8657
24: 2 "Go throughout the t *of* Israel from Dan 8657
1Ki 8: 1 the t and the chiefs of the Israelite families, 4751
11:31 of Solomon's hand and give you ten **t.** 8657
11:32 which I have chosen out of all the t 8657
11:35 from his son's hands and give you ten **t.** 8657
14:21 the t *of* Israel in which to put his Name. 8657
18:31 for each of the t descended from Jacob, 8657
2Ki 21: 7 which I have chosen out of all the t 8657
1Ch 6:62 were allotted thirteen towns from the t 4751
6:63 were allotted twelve towns from the t 4751
6:65 From the t *of* Judah, 4751
27:16 The officers over the t *of* Israel: 8657
27:22 These were the officers over the t 8657
28: 1 the officers over the **t,** 8657
29: 6 the officers of the t *of* Israel, 8657
2Ch 5: 2 the t and the chiefs of the Israelite families, 4751
12:13 the t *of* Israel in which to put his Name. 8657
33: 7 which I have chosen out of all the t 8657
Ezr 6:17 one for each of the t *of* Israel. 10694
Ps 72: 9 The **desert** t will bow before him 7470
78:55 he settled the t *of* Israel in their homes. 8657
105:37 and from among their t no one faltered. 8657
122: 4 That is where the t go up, 8657
122: 4 the t *of* the LORD, 8657
Isa 49: 6 to be my servant to restore the t *of* Jacob 8657
63:17 the t that are your inheritance. 8657
Eze 37:19 and of the Israelite t associated with him, 8657
45: 8 to possess the land according to their **t.** 8657
47:13 for an inheritance among the twelve t 8657
47:21 among yourselves according to the t 8657
47:22 to be allotted an inheritance among the t 8657
48: 1 "These are the **t,** listed by name: 8657
48:19 from all the t *of* Israel. 8657
48:23 "As for the rest of the **t:** 8657
48:29 to allot as an inheritance to the t *of* Israel, 8657
48:31 the city will be named after the t *of* Israel. 8657
Hos 5: 9 the t *of* Israel I proclaim what is certain. 8657
Zec 9: 1 and all the t *of* Israel are on the LORD— 8657
Mt 19:28 judging the twelve t of Israel. *5876*
Lk 22:30 judging the twelve t of Israel. *5876*
Ac 26: 7 the promise our **twelve** t are hoping to see *1559*
Jas 1: 1 the twelve t scattered among the nations: *5876*
Rev 7: 4 144,000 from all the t of Israel. *5876*
21:12 the names *of* the twelve t of Israel. *5876*

TRIBULATION (1)

Rev 7:14 they who have come out of the great **t;** *2568*

TRIBUTARIES, TRIBUTARY (KJV) See FORCED LABOR, FORCED LABORERS, SLAVE

TRIBUTE (27)

Nu 31:28 set apart as t for the LORD one out of every 4830
31:29 Take this t from their half share and give it NIH
31:37 of which the t for the LORD was 675; 4830
31:38 of which the t for the LORD was 72; 4830
31:39 of which the t for the LORD was 61; 4830
31:40 of which the t for the LORD was 32. 4830
31:41 Moses gave the t to Eleazar the priest as 4830
Jdg 3:15 sent him with t to Eglon king of Moab. 4966
3:17 He presented the t to Eglon king of Moab, 4966
3:18 After Ehud had presented the **t,** 4966
2Sa 8: 2 became subject to David and brought **t.** 4966
8: 6 became subject to him and brought **t.** 4966
1Ki 4:21 These countries brought t 4966
2Ki 17: 3 Shalmaneser's vassal and had paid him **t.** 4966
17: 4 he no longer paid t to the king of Assyria, 4966
1Ch 18: 2 they became subject to him and brought **t.** 4966
18: 6 became subject to him and brought **t.** 4966
2Ch 17:11 as **t,** and the Arabs brought him flocks: 5362
26: 8 The Ammonites brought t to Uzziah, 4966
Ezr 4:13 no more taxes, t or duty will be paid, 10107
4:20 and taxes, t and duty were paid to them. 10107
7:24 t or duty on any of the priests, Levites, 10107
Est 10: 1 King Xerxes imposed t throughout 4989
Ps 72:10 and of distant shores will bring t to him; 4966
89:22 No enemy *will* **subject** him **to t;** 5957
Isa 16: 1 Send lambs as t to the ruler of the land, NIH
Hos 10: 6 be carried to Assyria as t for the great king. 4966

TRICK (1) [TRICKERY, TRICKING]
1Th 2: 3 nor are we trying to **t** you. *1515*

TRICKERY (2) [TRICK]
Ac 13:10 You are full of all kinds of deceit and **t.** *4816*
2Co 12:16 crafty fellow that I am, I caught you *by* **t**! *1515*

TRICKING (1) [TRICK]
Ge 27:12 *to be* **t** him and would bring down a curse 9506

TRICKLETH (KJV) See FLOW

TRIED (44) [TRY]
Ge 37:21 *he* **t** *to* **rescue** him from their hands. AIT
Ex 2:15 Pharaoh heard of this, *he* **t** to kill Moses, 1335
8:18 when the magicians **t** to produce gnats 4027+6913
Dt 4:34 *Has* any god *ever* **t** to take for himself 5814
13: 5 *he has* **t** to **turn** you from the way AIT
13:10 because *he* **t** to turn you away from 1335
1Sa 17:39 on his sword over the tunic and **t** walking 3283
19:10 Saul **t** to pin him to the wall with his spear, 1335
2Sa 4: 8 your enemy, who **t to take** your life. 1335
21: 2 in his zeal for Israel and Judah *had* **t** 1335
1Ki 11:40 Solomon **t** to kill Jeroboam, 1335
Ps 73:16 When *I* **t** to understand all this, 3108
95: 9 where your fathers tested and **t** me, 1043
109: 7 When he **is t,** let him be found guilty, 9149
Ecc 2: 3 *I* **t** cheering myself with wine, 928+4213+9365
La 3:53 *They* **t** *to* **end** my life in a pit AIT
Eze 24:13 Because *I* **t** *to* **cleanse** you AIT
Da 6: 4 the satraps **t** to find grounds for charges 10114
Mt 3:14 But John **t** *to* **deter** him, saying, *AIT*
Lk 4:42 *they* **t** *to* **keep** him from leaving them. *AIT*
5:18 and **t** to take him into the house to lay him *2426*
6:19 and the people all **t** to touch him, *2426*
9: 9 And *he* **t** to see him. *2426*
9:49 in your name and *we* **t** *to* **stop** him, *AIT*
Jn 5:18 For this reason the Jews **t** all the harder *2426*
7:30 At this *they* **t** to seize him, *2426*
10:39 Again *they* **t** to seize him, *2426*
11: 8 "a short while ago the Jews **t** to stone you, *2426*
19:12 From then on, Pilate **t** to set Jesus free, *2426*
Ac 7:26 *He* **t** *to* **reconcile** them by saying, 'Men, *AIT*
9:26 *he* **t** to join the disciples, *4279*
9:29 but they **t** to kill him. *2217*
13: 8 and **t** to turn the proconsul from the faith. *2426*
16: 7 *they* **t** to enter Bithynia, *4279*
19:13 around driving out evil spirits **t** to invoke *2217*
24: 6 and even **t** to desecrate the temple; *4279*
25:10 where I ought *to be* **t.** *3212*
26:11 and *I* **t** *to* **force** them to blaspheme. *AIT*
26:21 in the temple courts and **t** to kill me. *4281*
28:23 and *t to* **convince** them about Jesus from *AIT*
Gal 1:13 the church of God and *t to* **destroy** it. *AIT*
1:23 the faith *he* once **t** *to* **destroy."** *4514*
Heb 3: 9 where your fathers tested and **t** me and *1508*
11:29 when Egyptians **t to do** so, they were drowned. *3284+4278*

TRIES (3) [TRY]
Job 34: 9 a man nothing when he *t to* **please** God.' AIT
Lk 17:33 Whoever **t** to keep his life will lose it, *2426*
Rev 11: 5 If anyone **t** to harm them, fire comes from *2527*

TRIFLING (1)
Ne 9:32 *do* not *let* all this hardship *seem* **t** 5070

TRIM (2) [TRIMMED, TRIMMERS]
Dt 21:12 and have her shave her head, **t** her nails 6913
Da 4:14 'Cut down the tree and **t off** its branches; 10635

TRIMMED (7) [TRIM]
2Sa 19:24 not taken care of his feet or **t** his mustache 6913
1Ki 6:36 and one course of **t** cedar **beams.** 4164
7: 2 of cedar columns supporting **t** cedar **beams.** 4164
7: 9 of high-grade stone cut to size and **t** with 1760
7:12 and one course of **t** cedar **beams,** 4164
Eze 44:20 **keep** *the* **hair** of their heads **t.** 4080+4080
Mt 25: 7 all the virgins woke up and **t** their lamps. *3175*

TRIMMERS (8) [TRIM]
Ex 25:38 Its **wick t** and trays are to be of pure gold. 4920
37:23 as well as its **wick t** and trays, of pure gold. 4920
Nu 4: 9 together with its lamps, its **wick t** and trays, 4920
1Ki 7:50 **wick t,** sprinkling bowls, 4662
2Ki 12:13 **wick t,** sprinkling bowls, 4662
25:14 also took away the pots, shovels, **wick t,** 4662
2Ch 4:22 the pure gold **wick t,** sprinkling bowls, 4662
Jer 52:18 shovels, **wick t,** sprinkling bowls, 4662

TRIP (1) [TRIPPING]
Ps 140: 4 men of violence who plan to **t** my feet. 1890

TRIPOLIS (1)
Ezr 4: 9 judges and officials over the **men from T,** 10305

TRIPPING (1) [TRIP]
Isa 3:16 **t along with mincing steps,** 2143+2256+3262

TRIUMPH (22) [TRIUMPHAL, TRIUMPHANT, TRIUMPHED, TRIUMPHING, TRIUMPHS]
Jdg 8: 9 "When I return in **t,** I will tear down this 8934
11:31 of my house to meet me when I return in **t** 8934
1Sa 26:25 you will do great things and **surely t."** 3523+3523
Job 17: 4 therefore *you will* not **let** them **t.** 8123
Ps 9:19 Arise, O LORD, *let* not man **t;** 6451
12: 4 *"We will* **t** with our tongues; 1504
13: 2 How long *will* my enemy **t** over me? 8123
25: 2 nor *let* my enemies **t** over me. 6636
41:11 for my enemy *does* not **t** over me. 8131
54: 7 and my eyes have looked in **t** on my foes. NIH
60: 6 *"In* **t** I will parcel out Shechem 6600
60: 8 over Philistia **I shout in t."** 8131
108: 7 *"In* **t** I will parcel out Shechem 6600
108: 9 over Philistia **I shout in t."** 8131
112: 8 in the end he will look in **t** on his foes. NIH
118: 7 I will look in **t** on my enemies. NIH
Pr 28:12 the righteous **t,** there is great elation; 6636
Isa 13: 3 those who rejoice in my **t.** 1452
42:13 the battle cry and *will* **t** over his enemies. 1504
Jer 9: 3 it is not by truth that *they* **t** in the land. 1504
51:14 and *they will* **shout in t** over you. 2116+6702
Mic 5: 9 be lifted up in **t** over your enemies, NIH

TRIUMPHAL (2) [TRIUMPH]
Isa 60:11 their kings **led in t procession.** 5627
2Co 2:14 God, who always **leads** us **in t procession** *2581*

TRIUMPHANT (1) [TRIUMPH]
Da 11:12 yet *he will* not *remain* **t.** 6451

TRIUMPHED (4) [TRIUMPH]
Dt 32:27 'Our hand *has* **t;** the LORD has not done 8123
1Sa 17:50 So David **t** over the Philistine with a sling 2616
La 1: 9 on my affliction, for the enemy *has* **t."** 1540
Rev 5: 5 the Root of David, *has* **t.** *3771*

TRIUMPHING (1) [TRIUMPH]
Col 2:15 spectacle of them, **t over** them by the cross. *2581*

TRIUMPHS (1) [TRIUMPH]
Jas 2:13 Mercy **t over** judgment! *2878*

TRIVIAL (3)
1Ki 16:31 not only **considered** *it* **t** to commit the sins 7837
Eze 8:17 *Is it a* **t** *matter* for the house of Judah 7837
1Co 6: 2 are you not competent to judge **t** cases? *1788*

TROAS (6)
Ac 16: 8 they passed by Mysia and went down to **T.** *5590*
16:11 From **T** we put out to sea *5590*
20: 5 on ahead and waited for us at **T.** *5590*
20: 6 and five days later joined the others at **T,** *5590*
2Co 2:12 Now when I went to **T** to preach the gospel *5590*
2Ti 4:13 bring the cloak that I left with Carpus at **T,** *5590*

TROD (2) [TREAD]
Job 22:15 to the old path that evil men *have* **t**? 2005
Isa 63: 3 in my anger and **t** them **down** in my wrath; 8252

TRODDEN (2) [TREAD]
Jdg 9:27 and gathered the grapes and **t** them, 2005
Isa 63: 3 *"I have* **t** the winepress alone; 2005

TRODE, TRODDEN (KJV) See also OVERRAN, TRAMPLED

TROOP (2) [TROOPS]
2Sa 22:30 With your help I can advance against a **t;** 1522
Ps 18:29 With your help I can advance against a **t;** 1522

TROOPS (68) [TROOP]
Ex 14: 9 and chariots, horsemen and **t**— 2657
Jos 10: 5 They moved up with all their **t** and took 4722
11: 4 with all their **t** and a large number 4722
Jdg 4: 7 and his **t** to the Kishon River and give him 2162
4:16 All the **t** *of* Sisera fell by the sword; 4722
8: 5 "Give my **t** some bread; 6639
8: 6 Why should we give bread to your **t**?" 7372
9:34 So Abimelech and all his **t** set out by night 6639
1Sa 13: 7 all the **t** with him were quaking with fear. 6639
14:24 So none of the **t** tasted food. 6639
18:13 and David led the **t** in their campaigns. 6639
2Sa 10: 9 so he selected some of the **best** *t* in Israel AIT
10:13 Then Joab and the **t** with him advanced 6639
12:28 of the **t** and besiege the city and capture it. 6639
16: 6 though all the **t** and the special guard were 6639
17: 8 he will not spend the night with the **t.** 6639
17: 9 If he should attack **your t** first, 2157[S]
17: 9 among the **t** who follow Absalom.' 6639
18: 2 David sent the **t** out— 6639
18: 2 The king told the **t,** 6639
18: 5 And all the **t** heard the king giving orders 6639
18:16 and the **t** stopped pursuing Israel, 6639
19: 2 because on that day the **t** heard it said, 6639
19:40 All the **t** *of* Judah and half the troops 6639
2Sa 19:40 of Judah and half the **t** *of* Israel had taken 6639
20:12 man saw that all the **t** came to a halt there. 6639
20:15 the **t** with Joab came and besieged Sheba 6639
23:10 The **t** returned to Eleazar, 6639
23:11 Israel's **t** fled from them. 6639
24: 3 "May the LORD your God multiply the **t** 6639
2Ki 9:17 in Jezreel saw Jehu's **t** approaching, 9180
9:17 he called out, "I see *some* **t** coming." 9180
11:15 who were in charge of the **t:** 2657
1Ch 11:13 the **t** fled from the Philistines. 6639
19: 7 as well as the king of Maacah with his **t,** 6639
19:10 so he selected some of the **best** *t* in Israel AIT
19:14 Then Joab and the **t** with him advanced 6639
21: 2 to Joab and the commanders of the **t,** 6639
21: 3 "May the LORD multiply his **t** a hundred 6639
2Ch 12: 3 and the innumerable **t** of Libyans, 6639
13: 3 with eight hundred thousand able **t.** 1475+2657
13:13 Jeroboam had sent **t** around to the rear, 4422
17: 2 He stationed **t** in all the fortified cities 2657
23:14 who were in charge of the **t,** 2657
25: 7 these **t** *from* Israel must not march 7372
25: 9 hundred talents I paid for these Israelite **t**?" 1522
25:10 So Amaziah dismissed the **t** who had come 1522
25:13 the **t** that Amaziah had sent back and 1201+1522
Job 19:12 His **t** advance in force; 1522
29:25 I dwelt as a king among his **t;** 1522
Ps 110: 3 Your **t** will be willing on your day of battle. 6639
SS 6: 4 majestic as **t with banners.** 1839
Eze 12:14 his staff and all his **t**— 111
17:21 All his fleeing **t** will fall by the sword, 111
38: 6 with all its **t,** and Beth Togarmah from 111
38: 6 from the far north with all its **t**— 111
38: 9 You and all your **t** and the many nations 111
38:22 on his **t** and on the many nations with him. 111
39: 4 and all your **t** and the nations with you. 111
Da 11:15 even their best **t** will not have the strength 6639
Mic 5: 1 **Marshal** *your* **t,** O city of troops, 1518
5: 1 Marshal your troops, O city of **t,** 1522
Na 2: 5 He summons his **picked t,** 129
3:13 Look at your **t**—they are all women! 6639
Ac 21:31 reached the commander *of* the **Roman t** *5061*
23:10 the **t** to go down and take him away *5128*
23:27 but I came with my **t** and rescued him, *5128*
Rev 9:16 *of* the mounted **t** was two hundred million. *5128*

TROPHIMUS (3)
Ac 20: 4 Tychicus and **T** from the province of Asia. *5576*
21:29 (They had previously seen **T** the Ephesian *5576*
2Ti 4:20 and I left **T** sick in Miletus. *5576*

TROUBLE (131) [TROUBLED, TROUBLEMAKER, TROUBLEMAKERS, TROUBLER, TROUBLES, TROUBLESOME, TROUBLING]
Ge 34:30 *"You have* **brought t** *on* me by making me 6579
41:51 because God has made me forget all my **t** 6662
43: 6 "Why *did you* **bring** *this* **t** on me 8317
Ex 5:19 they were in **t** when they were told, 8273
5:22 why *have you* **brought t** upon this people? 8317
5:23 *he has* **brought t** upon this people, 8317
Nu 11:11 "Why *have you* **brought** *this* **t** 8317
33:55 *They will* **give** you **t** in the land 7675
Jos 6:18 of Israel liable to destruction and **bring t** 6579
7:25 "Why *have you* **brought** *this* **t** *on* us? 6579
7:25 The LORD *will* **bring t** *on* you today." 6579
Jdg 10:14 Let them save you when you are in **t**!" 7650
11: 7 you come to me now, when you're *in* **t**?" 7639
1Sa 4: 7 "We're **in t**! Nothing like this has happened 208
14:29 "My father *has* **made t** *for* the country. 6579
20:19 the place where you hid when this **t** began, 5126
26:24 and deliver me from all **t."** 7650
2Sa 4: 9 who has delivered me out of all **t,** 7650
1Ki 1:29 who has delivered me out of every **t,** 7650
11:25 adding to the **t** caused by Hadad. 8288
18:18 *"I have* not **made t** *for* Israel," 6579
20: 7 "See how this man is looking for **t**! 8288
2Ki 4:13 *'You have* **gone to** all this **t** 3006+3010
14:10 for **t** and cause your own downfall and that 8288
1Ch 2: 7 who **brought t** *on* Israel by violating 6579
2Ch 25:19 for **t** and cause your own downfall and that 8288
28:20 but *he* **gave** him **t** instead of help. 7674
28:22 In his time of **t** King Ahaz became 7674
Ne 1: 3 in the province are in great **t** and disgrace. 8288
2:17 I said to them, "You see the **t** we are in: 8288
4: 8 against Jerusalem and stir up **t** against it. 9360
Job 2:10 we accept good from God, and not **t**?" 8273
3:10 of the womb on me to hide **t** from my eyes. 6662
4: 5 **t** comes to you, and you are discouraged; NIH
4: 8 and those who sow **t** reap it. 6662
5: 6 nor does **t** sprout from the ground. 6662
5: 7 to **t** as surely as sparks fly upward. 6662
11:16 You will surely forget your **t,** 6662
14: 1 of woman is of few days and full of **t.** 8075
15:35 They conceive **t** and give birth to evil; 6662
19:28 since the root of the **t** lies in him,' 1821
30:25 Have I not wept for *those* **in t**? 3427+7997
31:29 or gloated over the **t** that came to him— 8273
38:23 which I reserve for times of **t,** 7639
42:11 the **t** the LORD had brought upon him, 8288
Ps 7:14 with evil and conceives **t** gives birth 6662
7:16 The **t** he *causes* recoils on himself; 6662
9: 9 a stronghold in times of **t.** 1314
10: 1 Why do you hide yourself in times of **t**? 1314
10: 6 I'll always be happy and never have **t."** 8273

Ps 10: 7 **t** and evil are under his tongue. 6662
10:14 But you, O God, do see **t** and grief; 6662
22:11 for **t** is near and there is no one to help. 7650
27: 5 of **t** he will keep me safe in his dwelling; 8288
32: 7 from **t** and surround me with songs 7639
37:39 he is their stronghold in time of **t**. 7650
41: 1 the LORD delivers him in times of **t**. 8288
46: 1 an ever-present help in **t**. 7650
50:15 and call upon me in the day of **t**; 7650
55: 2 My thoughts **t** *me* and I am distraught 8113
59:16 my refuge in times of **t**. 7639
66:14 and my mouth spoke when I was in **t**. 7639
69:17 answer me quickly, for I am in **t**. 7639
86: 7 In the day of my **t** I will call to you, 7650
88: 3 For my soul is full of **t** and my life draws 8288
90:10 yet their span is but **t** and sorrow, 6662
90:15 for as many years as we have seen **t**. 8288
91:15 I will be with him in **t**, 7650
94:13 you grant him relief from days of **t**, 8273
106:32 and **t came** to Moses because of them; 8317
107: 6 they cried out to the LORD in their **t**, 7639
107:13 Then they cried to the LORD in their **t**, 7639
107:19 Then they cried to the LORD in their **t**, 7639
107:28 they cried out to the LORD in their **t**, 7639
116: 3 I was overcome by **t** and sorrow. 7650
119:143 **T** and distress have come upon me, 7639
138: 7 Though I walk in the midst of **t**, 7650
140: 9 with the **t** their lips have *caused*. 6662
142: 2 before him I tell my **t**. 7650
143:11 in your righteousness, bring me out of **t**. 7650
Pr 1:27 when distress and **t** overwhelm you. 7442
10:22 and he adds no **t** to it. 6776
11: 8 The righteous man is rescued from **t**, 7650
11:17 but a cruel man **brings t** *on* himself. 6579
11:29 *He who* **brings t** on his family will inherit 6579
12:13 but a righteous man escapes **t**. 7650
12:21 but the wicked have their fill of **t**. 8273
13:17 A wicked messenger falls into **t**, 8273
15: 6 the income of the wicked **brings** them **t**. 6579
15:27 A greedy man **brings t** *to* his family, 6579
17:20 he whose tongue is deceitful falls into **t**. 8288
19:23 Then one rests content, untouched by **t**. 8273
22: 8 He who sows wickedness reaps **t**, 224
24: 2 and their lips talk about **making t**. 6662
24:10 If you falter in times of **t**, 7650
25:19 on the unfaithful in times of **t**. 7650
28:14 but he who hardens his heart falls into **t**. 8288
Ecc 12: 1 the days of **t** come and the years approach 8288
Isa 59: 4 they conceive **t** and give birth to evil. 6662
Jer 2:27 yet when they are in **t**, they say, 8288
2:28 if they can save you when you are in **t**! 8288
20:18 to see **t** and sorrow and to end my days 6662
30: 7 It will be a time of **t** for Jacob, 7650
Eze 32: 9 *I will* **t** the hearts of many peoples 4087
Da 9:25 with streets and a trench, but in times of **t**. 7441
Ob 1:12 nor boast so much in the day of their **t**. 7650
1:14 over their survivors in the day of their **t**. 7650
Jnh 1: 8 who is responsible for making all this **t** 8288
Na 1: 7 The LORD is good, a refuge in times of **t**. 7650
1: 9 **t** will not come a second time. 7650
Zep 1:15 a day of **t** and ruin, 8739
Zec 10:11 They will pass through the sea of **t**; 7650
Mt 6:34 Each day has enough **t** of its own. *2798*
13:21 When **t** or persecution comes because of *2568*
28:14 we will satisfy him and keep you **out of t**." *291*
Mk 4:17 When **t** or persecution comes because of *2568*
Lk 7: 6 "Lord, don't **t** *yourself*, *5035*
Jn 16:33 In this world you will have **t**. *2568*
Ac 17: 6 "These men who *have* **caused t** all over *415*
Ro 2: 9 There will be **t** and distress for every human *2568*
8:35 Shall **t** or hardship or persecution *2568*
1Co 7:21 Don't *let it* **t** you—although if you can gain *3508*
2Co 1: 4 so that we can comfort those in any **t** with *2568*
Gal 6:17 Finally, let no one cause me **t**, *3160*
Php 1:17 that they can stir up **t** for me while I am *2568*
3: 1 It is no **t** for me to write the same things *3891*
2Th 1: 6 He will pay back **t** to those who trouble you *2568*
1: 6 He will pay back trouble *to* those who **t** you *2567*
1Ti 5:10 helping **those in t** and devoting herself *2567*
Heb 12:15 and that no bitter root grows up to **cause t** *1943*
Jas 5:13 *Is* any one of you *in* **t**? *2802*

TROUBLED (24) [TROUBLE]

Ge 41: 8 In the morning his mind *was* **t**, 7192
Nu 11:10 angry and Moses was **t**. 928+6524+8273
1Sa 1:15 "I am a woman who is **deeply t**. 7997+8120
15:11 Samuel *was* **t**, and he cried out to 3013
Job 20: 2 "My **t thoughts** prompt me to answer 8546
Ps 38:18 I confess my iniquity; *I am* **t** by my sin. 1793
77: 4 *I was* too **t** to speak, 7192
Isa 38:14 I am **t**; O Lord, come to my aid!" 6946
Jer 49:23 **t** like the restless sea. 3523+4202+9200
Da 2: 1 his mind *was* **t** and he could not sleep. 7192
7:15 "I, Daniel, *was* **t** in spirit, 10369
7:28 I, Daniel, *was* deeply **t** *by* my thoughts, 10097
Mt 26:37 and he began to be sorrowful and **t**. *86*
Mk 14:33 and he began to be deeply distressed and **t**. *86*
Lk 1:29 Mary *was* **greatly t** at his words *1410*
6:18 Those **t** by evil spirits were cured, *1943*
24:38 He said to them, "Why are you **t**, *5429*
Jn 11:33 he was deeply moved in spirit and **t**. *5429*
12:27 "Now my heart *is* **t**, and what shall I say? *5429*
13:21 Jesus *was* **t** in spirit and testified, *5429*
14: 1 "*Do* not *let* your hearts *be* **t**. *5429*
14:27 *Do* not *let* your hearts *be* **t** and do not *5429*
Ac 16:18 Finally Paul *became* so **t** that he turned *1387*
2Th 1: 7 and give relief *to* you who *are* **t**, and to us *2567*

TROUBLEMAKER (2) [TROUBLE]

2Sa 20: 1 Now a **t** named Sheba son of Bicri, 408+1175
Ac 24: 5 "We have found this man to be a **t**, *3369*

TROUBLEMAKERS (2) [TROUBLE]

1Sa 10:27 But *some* **t** said, "How can this fellow 1175+1201
30:22 and **t** among David's followers said, 1175

TROUBLER (1) [TROUBLE]

1Ki 18:17 "Is that you, you **t** *of* Israel?" 6579

TROUBLES (21) [TROUBLE]

Job 2:11 about all the **t** that had come upon him, 8288
Ps 25:17 The **t** *of* my heart have multiplied; 7650
25:22 Redeem Israel, O God, from all their **t**! 7650
34: 6 he saved him out of all his **t**. 7650
34:17 he delivers them from all their **t**. 7650
34:19 A righteous man may have many **t**, 8288
40:12 For **t** without number surround me; 8288
54: 7 For he has delivered me from all my **t**, 7650
71:20 Though you have made me see **t**, 7650
Ecc 11:10 from your heart and cast off the **t** 8288
Isa 22: 1 What **t** you now, that you have all gone up 4200
46: 7 it cannot save him from his **t**. 7650
65:16 For the past **t** will be forgotten and hidden 7650
Da 2: 3 "I have had a dream *that* **t** me and I want 7192
Ac 7:10 and rescued him from all his **t**. *2568*
1Co 7:28 But those who marry *will* face many **t** *2568*
2Co 1: 4 who comforts us in all our **t**, *2568*
4:17 and momentary **t** are achieving for us *2568*
6: 4 in **t**, hardships and distresses; *2568*
7: 4 in all our **t** my joy knows no bounds. *2568*
Php 4:14 Yet it was good of you to share *in* my **t**. *2568*

TROUBLESOME (1) [TROUBLE]

Ezr 4:15 a rebellious city, **t** *to* kings and provinces, 10472

TROUBLING (4) [TROUBLE]

2Sa 14: 5 The king asked her, **"What is t** you?" 4537
2Ch 15: 6 God *was* **t** them with every kind of distress. 2169
Est 4: 5 to find out what was **t** Mordecai and why. NIH
Ac 15:24 **t** your minds by what they said. *412*

TROUGH (3) [TROUGHS]

Ge 24:20 So she quickly emptied her jar into the **t**, 9216
Dt 28: 5 Your basket and your **kneading t** will 5400
28:17 Your basket and your **kneading t** will 5400

TROUGHS (5) [TROUGH]

Ge 30:38 peeled branches in all the watering **t**, 8110+9216
30:41 the branches in the **t** in front of the animals 8110
Ex 2:16 and they came to draw water and fill the **t** 8110
8: 3 and into your ovens and **kneading t**. 5400
12:34 on their shoulders in **kneading t** wrapped 5400

TROUSERS (1)

Da 3:21 So these men, wearing their robes, **t**, 10582

TRUCEBREAKERS (KJV) See UNFORGIVING

TRUDGE (1)

Isa 45:14 *they will* **t** behind you, coming over to you 2143

TRUE (117) [TRUTH]

Nu 11:23 or not what I say *will* **come t** *for* you." 7936
12: 7 But this is not **t** *of* my servant Moses; 4027
Dt 13:14 And if it is **t** and it has been proved 622
17: 4 If it is **t** and it has been proved 622
18:22 not take place or **come t**, that is a message 995
22:20 the charge is **t** and no proof of the girl's 622
Jos 7:20 Achan replied, "It is **t**! 593
21:42 this was **t** for all these towns. 4027
23:15 promise of the LORD your God *has* **come t**, 995
Jdg 13:17 when your word **comes t**?" 995
Ru 3:12 Although it is **t** that I am near of kin, 597
1Sa 9: 6 and everything he says **comes t**. 995+995
1Ki 8:26 your servant David my father **come t**. 586
10: 6 and your wisdom is **t**. 622
13:32 of Samaria *will* **certainly come t**." 2118+2118
2Ki 9:12 "That's **not t**!" they said. 9214
19:17 "It is **t**, O LORD, that the Assyrian kings 597
2Ch 6:17 you promised your servant David **come t**. 586
9: 5 and your wisdom is **t**. 622
15: 3 a long time Israel was without the **t** God, 622
Ne 6: 6 and Geshem says it is **t**— NIH
Est 2:23 report was investigated and **found to be t**, 5162
Job 5:27 "We have examined this, and it is **t**. 4027
9: 2 I know that this is **t**. 4027
11: 6 for **t wisdom** has two sides. 9370
19: 4 If it is **t** that I have gone astray, 597
Ps 33: 4 For the word of the LORD is **right and t**; 3838
105:19 till the word of the LORD **proved** him **t**. 7671
119:142 righteousness is everlasting and your law is **t**. 622
119:151 O LORD, and all your commands are **t**. 622
Ps 119:160 All your words are **t**; 622
144:15 Blessed are the people of whom *this* is **t**; 3970
Pr 8: 7 My mouth speaks *what* is **t**, 622
22:21 teaching you **t** and reliable words, 7999
Ecc 12:10 and what he wrote was upright and **t**. 622
Isa 37:18 "It is **t**, O LORD, that the Assyrian kings 597
43: 9 so that others may hear and say, "It is **t**." 622
Jer 10:10 But the LORD is the **t** God; 622
28: 9 the LORD only if his prediction **comes t**." 995
37:14 "That's **not t**!" Jeremiah said. 9214
40:16 you are saying about Ishmael is **not t**." 9214
42: 5 a **t** and faithful witness against us if we do 622
50: 7 sinned against the LORD, their **t** pasture, 7406
Eze 16:45 You are a **t** daughter of your mother, NIH
16:45 and you are a **t** sister of your sisters, NIH
33:33 "When all this **comes t**—and it surely will 995
Da 2:45 The dream is **t** and the interpretation 10327
3:14 said to them, **"Is it t**, Shadrach, 10190+10609
7:16 and asked him the **t meaning** of all this. 10327
7:19 to **know the t meaning** of the fourth beast, 10326
8:26 and mornings that has been given you is **t**, 622
10: 1 Its message was **t** and it concerned 622
Am 2:11 Is this not **t**, people of Israel?" 677
7: 7 by a wall that had been built **t to plumb**, 643
Mic 7:20 You will be **t** to Jacob, 622
Zec 7: 9 'Administer **t** justice; show mercy and 622
8:16 Speak the truth to each other, and render **t** 622
Mal 2: 6 **T** instruction was in his mouth 622
Lk 1:20 which *will* **come t** at their proper time." *4444*
16:11 who will trust you with **t** riches? *240*
24:34 and saying, **"It is t**! The Lord has risen *3953*
Jn 1: 9 The **t** light that gives light to every man *240*
1:47 he said of him, "Here is a **t** Israelite, *242*
4:18 What you have just said is quite **t**." *239*
4:23 the **t** worshipers will worship the Father *240*
4:37 'One sows and another reaps' is **t**. *240*
6:32 who gives you the **t** bread from heaven. *240*
7:28 but he who sent me is **t**. *240*
10:41 all that John said about this man was **t**." *239*
15: 1 "I am the **t** vine, and my Father is the *240*
17: 3 that they may know you, the only **t** God, *240*
19:35 and his testimony is **t**. *240*
21:24 We know that his testimony is **t**. *239*
Ac 7: 1 "Are these charges **t**?" *4048*
10:34 "I now realize **how t** it is that God does *237+2093*
11:23 to remain **t** to the Lord with all their hearts. *4606*
14:22 and encouraging them *to* **remain t to** *1844*
17:11 to see if what Paul said was **t**. *4048*
24: 9 asserting that these things were **t**. *4048*
25:11 against me by these Jews are not **t**, *NIG*
26:25 "What I am saying is **t** and reasonable. *237*
Ro 3: 4 Let God be **t**, and every man a liar. *239*
1Co 15:54 then the saying that is written *will* **come t**: *1181*
2Co 7:14 just as everything we said to you was **t**, *237+1877*
7:14 about you to Titus has proved to be **t** *237*
Eph 4:24 like God in **t** righteousness and holiness. *237*
Php 1:15 It is **t** that some preach Christ out of envy *NIG*
1:18 whether from false motives or **t**, *237*
4: 8 Finally, brothers, whatever is **t**, *239*
1Th 1: 9 from idols to serve the living and **t** God, *240*
1Ti 1: 2 To Timothy my **t** son in the faith: *1188*
2: 7 and a teacher of the **t** faith to the Gentiles. *237*
Tit 1: 4 my **t** son in our common faith: *1188*
1:13 This testimony is **t**. *239*
3: 2 and to show **t humility** toward all men. *4559*
Heb 8: 2 the **t** tabernacle set up by the Lord, *240*
9:24 that was only a copy *of* the **t** *one;* *240*
12: 8 illegitimate children and not **t** sons. *NIG*
1Pe 5:12 and testifying that this is the **t** grace *239*
2Pe 2:10 This is especially **t** of those who follow *NIG*
2:22 Of them the proverbs are **t**: *239*
1Jn 2: 8 and the **t** light is already shining. *240*
5:20 so that we may know *him* who is **t**. *240*
5:20 And we are in *him* who is **t**— *240*
5:20 He is the **t** God and eternal life. *240*
3Jn 1:12 and you know that our testimony is **t**. *239*
Rev 2:13 Yet *you* **remain t** to my name. *3195*
3: 7 the words of him who is holy and **t**, *240*
3:14 the faithful and **t** witness, *240*
6:10 "How long, Sovereign Lord, holy and **t**, *240*
15: 3 Just and **t** are your ways, King of the ages. *240*
16: 7 **t** and just are your judgments." *240*
19: 2 for **t** and just are his judgments. *240*
19: 9 he added, "These are the **t** words of God." *240*
19:11 whose rider is called Faithful and **T**. *240*
21: 5 for these words are trustworthy and **t**." *240*
22: 6 "These words are trustworthy and **t**. *240*

TRULY (11) [TRUTH]

Ps 116:16 O LORD, **t** I am your servant; 3954
Pr 11:19 The **t** righteous man attains life, 4026
Isa 10:20 will **t** rely on the LORD, the Holy One 622+928
45:15 **T** you are a God who hides himself, 434
Jer 28: 9 as one **t** sent by the LORD only if 622+928
Mt 14:33 saying, **"T** you are the Son of God." *242*
Jn 17:19 that they too may be **t** sanctified. *237+1877*
21:15 *do you* **t love** me more than these?" *26*
21:16 "Simon son of John, *do you* **t love** me?" *26*
1Ti 6:19 they may take hold of the life that is **t** life. *3953*
1Jn 2: 5 God's love is **t** made complete in him. *242*

TRUMP (KJV) See TRUMPET

TRUMPET (66) [TRUMPETERS, TRUMPETS]

Ex 19:16 over the mountain, and a very loud **t** blast. 8795

Ex 19:19 the sound of the t grew louder and louder. 8795
20:18 the thunder and lightning and heard the t 8795
Lev 23:24 a sacred assembly commemorated with t **blasts.** 9558
25: 9 the t sounded everywhere on the tenth day 8795+9558
25: 9 on the Day of Atonement sound the t 8795
Nu 10: 5 When a t **blast** is sounded, 9558
Jos 6:16 when the priests sounded the t blast, 8795
6:20 and at the sound of the t, 8795
Jdg 3:27 he blew a t in the hill country of Ephraim, 8795
6:34 and he blew a t, summoning the Abiezrites 8795
1Sa 13: 3 the t blown throughout the land and said, 8795
2Sa 2:28 So Joab blew the t, and all the men came 8795
18:16 Then Joab sounded the t, 8795
20: 1 He sounded the t and shouted, 8795
20:22 So he sounded the t, and his men dispersed 8795
1Ki 1:34 Blow the t and shout, 8795
1:39 the t and all the people shouted, 8795
1:41 On hearing the sound of the t, Joab asked, 8795
2Ki 9:13 Then they blew the t and shouted, 8795
Ne 4:18 the man who sounded the t stayed with me. 8795
4:20 Wherever you hear the sound of the t, 8795
Job 39:24 he cannot stand still when the t sounds. 8795
39:25 At the blast of the t he snorts, 'Aha!' 8795
Ps 150: 3 Praise him with the sounding of the t, 8795
Isa 18: 3 and when a t sounds, you will hear it. 8795
27:13 And in that day a great t will sound. 8795
58: 1 Raise your voice like a t. 8795
Jer 4: 5 'Sound the t throughout the land!' 8795
4:19 For I have heard the sound of the t; 8795
4:21 and hear the sound of the t? 8795
6: 1 Sound the t in Tekoa! 8795
6:17 'Listen to the sound of the t!' 8795
42:14 where we will not see war or hear the t or 8795
51:27 Blow the t among the nations! 8795
Eze 7:14 they blow the t and get everything ready, 9540
33: 3 against the land and blows the t to warn 8795
33: 4 the t but does not take warning and 8795
33: 5 the sound of the t but did not take warning, 8795
33: 6 and does not blow the t to warn the people 8795
Hos 5: 8 "Sound the t in Gibeah, 8795
8: 1 "Put the t to your lips! 8795
Joel 2: 1 Blow the t in Zion; sound the alarm 8795
2:15 Blow the t in Zion, declare a holy fast, 8795
Am 2: 2 amid war cries and the blast of the t. 8795
3: 6 When a t sounds in a city, 8795
Zep 1:16 a day of t and battle cry against 8795
Zec 9:14 The Sovereign LORD will sound the t; 8795
Mt 24:31 he will send his angels with a loud t **call,** *4894*
1Co 14: 8 Again, if the t does not sound a clear call, *4894*
15:52 in the twinkling of an eye, at the last t. *4894*
15:52 For the t *will* **sound,** the dead will be raised *4895*
1Th 4:16 the archangel and with the t **call** of God, *4894*
Heb 12:19 a t blast or to such a voice speaking words *4894*
Rev 1:10 I heard behind me a loud voice like a t, *4894*
4: 1 speaking to me like a t said, *4894*
8: 7 The first angel **sounded** *his* t, *4895*
8: 8 The second angel **sounded** *his* t, *4895*
8:10 The third angel **sounded** *his* t, *4895*
8:12 The fourth angel **sounded** *his* t, *4895*
8:13 because of the t blasts about to be sounded *4894*
9: 1 The fifth angel **sounded** *his* t, *4895*
9:13 The sixth angel **sounded** *his* t, *4895*
9:14 It said to the sixth angel who had the t, *4894*
10: 7 the seventh angel is about to **sound** *his* t, *4895*
11:15 The seventh angel **sounded** *his* t, *4895*

TRUMPETERS (5) [TRUMPET]

2Ki 11:14 The officers and the t were beside the king, 2956
2Ch 5:13 The t and singers joined in unison, 2955
23:13 The officers and the t were beside the king, 2956
29:28 while the singers sang and the t played. 2956
Rev 18:22 harpists and musicians, flute players and t, *4896*

TRUMPETS (53) [TRUMPET]

Nu 10: 2 "Make two t *of* hammered silver, 2956
10: 7 To gather the assembly, **blow** *the* t, 9546
10: 8 the priests, are to blow the t. 2956
10: 9 sound a blast on the t. 2956
10:10 to sound the t over your burnt offerings 2956
29: 1 It is a day for you to **sound the t.** 9558
31: 6 from the sanctuary and the t *for* signaling. 2956
Jos 6: 4 Have seven priests carry t *of* rams' horns 8795
6: 4 with the priests blowing the t. 8795
6: 5 hear them sound a long blast on the t, 3413+7967
6: 6 and have seven priests carry t in front 3413+8795
6: 8 the seven priests carrying the seven t 3413+8795
6: 8 blowing their t, and the ark of the LORD's 8795
6: 9 ahead of the priests who blew the t, 8795
6: 9 All this time the t were sounding. 8795
6:13 the seven t went forward, 3413+8795
6:13 the ark of the LORD and blowing the t. 8795
6:13 while the t kept sounding. 8795
6:20 When the t sounded, the people shouted, 8795
Jdg 7: 8 over the provisions and t *of* the others. 8795
7:16 he placed t and empty jars in the hands 8795
7:18 I and all who are with me blow our t, 8795
7:19 They blew their t and broke the jars 8795
7:20 The three companies blew the t 8795
7:20 in their right hands the t they were to blow, 8795
7:22 When the three hundred t sounded, 8795
2Sa 6:15 the LORD with shouts and the sound of t. 8795
15:10 "As soon as you hear the sound of the t, 8795
2Ki 11:14 of the land were rejoicing and blowing t. 2956
2Ki 12:13 t or any other articles of gold or silver for 2956
1Ch 13: 8 lyres, tambourines, cymbals and t. 2956
15:24 the priests were to blow t before the ark 2956
15:28 with the sounding of rams' horns and t, 2956
16: 6 to blow the t regularly before the ark of 2956
16:42 of the t and cymbals and for the playing of 2956
2Ch 5:12 accompanied by 120 priests sounding t. 2956
5:13 Accompanied by t, cymbals and other 2956
7: 6 the priests **blew** *their* t, and all the 2955
13:12 with their t will sound the battle cry 2956
13:14 The priests blew their t 2956
15:14 with shouting and with t and horns. 2956
20:28 of the LORD with harps and lutes and t. 2956
23:13 of the land were rejoicing and blowing t, 2956
29:26 and the priests with their t. 2956
29:27 by t and the instruments of David king 2956
Ezr 3:10 the priests in their vestments and with t, 2956
Ne 12:35 as well as some priests with t, 2956
12:41 Zechariah and Hananiah with their t— 2956
Ps 47: 5 the LORD amid the sounding of t. 8795
98: 6 with t and the blast of the ram's horn— 2956
Mt 6: 2 *do* not **announce** it **with** t, *4895*
Rev 8: 2 and to them were given seven t. *4894*
8: 6 the seven t prepared to sound them. *4894*

TRUST (89) [ENTRUST, ENTRUSTED, TRUSTED, TRUSTEES, TRUSTFULLY, TRUSTING, TRUSTS, TRUSTWORTHY]

Ex 14:31 feared the LORD and **put** *their* t in him 586
19: 9 with you and *will* always **put** *their* t 586
Nu 20:12 not t in me enough to honor me as holy in 586
Dt 1:32 you *did* not t in the LORD your God, 586
9:23 *You did* not t him or obey him. 586
28:52 fortified walls in which you t fall down. 1053
Jdg 11:20 *did* not t Israel to pass through his territory. 586
2Ki 17:14 who *did* not t in the LORD their God. 586
18:30 *Do* not **let** Hezekiah **persuade** you **to** t 1053
1Ch 9:22 to their positions of t by David and Samuel 575
Job 4:18 If God **places** no t in his servants, 586
15:15 If God **places** no t in his holy ones, 586
31:24 "If I have put my t in gold or said 4073
39:12 *Can you* t him to bring in your grain 586
Ps 4: 5 Offer right sacrifices and t in the LORD. 1053
9:10 Those who know your name *will* t in you, 1053
13: 5 But I t in your unfailing love; 1053
20: 7 Some t in chariots and some in horses, NIH
20: 7 we t in the name of the LORD our God. 2349
22: 4 In you our fathers **put** *their* t; 1053
22: 9 you **made** me t in you even at my mother's 1053
25: 2 in you *I* t, O my God. 1053
31: 6 I t in the LORD. 1053
31:14 But I t in you, O LORD; 1053
33:21 for *we* t in his holy name. 1053
37: 3 T in the LORD and do good; 1053
37: 5 t in him and he will do this: 1053
40: 3 Many will see and fear and **put** *their* t in 1053
40: 4 the man who makes the LORD his t, 4440
44: 6 *I do* not t in my bow, 1053
49: 6 those *who* t in their wealth and boast 1053
49:13 the fate of those who t in themselves, 4073
52: 8 *I* t in God's unfailing love for ever 1053
55:23 But as for me, *I* t in you. 1053
56: 3 When I am afraid, *I will* t in you. 1053
56: 4 In God, whose word I praise, in God *I* t; 1053
56:11 in God *I* t; I will not be afraid. 1053
62: 8 T in him at all times, O people; 1053
62:10 *Do* not t in extortion or take pride 1053
78: 7 Then they would put their t in God 4073
78:22 not believe in God or t in his deliverance. 1053
91: 2 my fortress, my God, in whom *I* t." 1053
115: 8 and so will all who t in them. 1053
115: 9 O house of Israel, t in the LORD— 1053
115:10 O house of Aaron, t in the LORD— 1053
115:11 *You* who fear him, t in the LORD— 1053
118: 8 to take refuge in the LORD than *to* t 1053
118: 9 to take refuge in the LORD than *to* t 1053
119:42 for *I* t in your word. 1053
125: 1 Those *who* t in the LORD are 1053
135:18 and so will all who t in them. 1053
143: 8 for *I have* **put** *my* t in you. 1053
146: 3 *Do* not **put** *your* t in princes, 1053
Pr 3: 5 T in the LORD with all your heart 1053
21:22 pulls down the stronghold in which they t. 4440
22:19 So that your t may be in the LORD, 4440
Isa 8:17 *I will* **put** *my* t in him. 7747
12: 2 *I will* t and not be afraid. 1053
26: 4 T in the LORD forever, for the LORD, 1053
30:15 in quietness and t is your strength, 1057
31: 1 *who* t in the multitude of their chariots and 1053
36:15 *Do* not **let** Hezekiah **persuade** you **to** t 1053
42:17 But those *who* t in idols, who say to images, 1053
50:10 t in the name of the LORD and rely 1053
Jer 2:37 for the LORD has rejected *those* you t; 4440
5:17 the fortified cities in which you t. 1053
7: 4 *Do* not t in deceptive words and say, 1053
7:14 the temple you t in, the place I gave to you 1053
9: 4 *do* not t your brothers. 1053
12: 6 *Do* not t them, though they speak well of 586
28:15 *have* **persuaded** this nation **to** t in lies. 1053
39:18 because *you* t in me, 1053
48: 7 Since you t in your deeds and riches, 1053
49: 4 you t in your riches and say, 1053
49:11 Your widows too *can* t in me." 1053
Mic 7: 5 *Do* not t a neighbor; 586
Na 1: 7 He cares for *those who* t in him, 2879
Zep 3: 2 *She does* not t in the LORD, 1053
3:12 *who* t in the name of the LORD. 2879
Lk 16:11 who *will* t you with true riches? *4409*
Jn 12:36 **Put** *your* t in the light while you have it, *4409*
14: 1 T in God; trust also in me. *4409*
14: 1 Trust in God; t also in me. *4409*
Ac 14:23 in whom *they had* **put** *their* t. *4409*
Ro 15:13 with all joy and peace as you t in him, *4409*
1Co 4: 2 those who **have been given a** t must prove *3874*
9:17 I am simply discharging the t committed *3873*
2Co 13: 6 And *I* t that you will discover *1827*
Heb 2:13 And again, "I *will* **put** *my* t in him." *1639+4275*

TRUSTED (27) [TRUST]

1Sa 27:12 Achish t David and said to himself, 586
2Ki 18: 5 Hezekiah t in the LORD, the God of Israel. 1053
1Ch 5:20 their prayers, because *they* t in him. 1053
Job 12:20 He silences the lips of t **advisers** 586
Ps 5: 9 Not a *word* from their mouth *can* **be** t; 3922
22: 4 *they* t and you delivered them. 1053
22: 5 in you *they* t and were not disappointed. 1053
26: 1 *I have* t in the LORD without wavering. 1053
41: 9 Even my close friend, whom *I* t, 1053
52: 7 but t in his great wealth and grew strong 1053
Pr 27: 6 Wounds from a friend *can* **be** t, 586
Isa 20: 5 Those who t **in** Cush and boasted 4438
25: 9 *we* t in him, and he saved us. 7747
25: 9 This is the LORD, *we* t in him; 7747
47:10 *You have* t in your wickedness 1053
Jer 13:25 you have forgotten me and t in false gods. 1053
38:22 those t **friends** *of* yours. 408+8934
48:13 was ashamed when they t in Bethel. 4440
Eze 16:15 " 'But *you* t in your beauty 1053
Da 3:28 *They* t in him and defied 10665
6:23 because *he had* t in his God. 10041
Lk 11:22 he takes away the armor in which the *man* t *4275*
16:10 "Whoever **can be** t with very little can also *4412*
16:10 with very little **can** also **be** t with much, *4412*
Ac 12:20 t **personal servant** of the king, *2093+3131+3836*
Tit 2:10 but to show that they can be fully t, *4411*
3: 8 so that those who *have* t in God may *4409*

TRUSTEES (1) [TRUST]

Gal 4: 2 He is subject to guardians and t until *3874*

TRUSTFULLY (1) [TRUST]

Pr 3:29 your neighbor, who lives t near you. 1055+4200

TRUSTING (4) [TRUST]

Job 15:31 not deceive himself *by* t what is worthless, 586
Ps 112: 7 his heart is steadfast, t in the LORD. 1053
Isa 2:22 **Stop** t **in** man, who has but a breath 2532+4946
Jer 7: 8 But look, you *are* t in deceptive words 1053

TRUSTS (24) [TRUST]

Job 8:14 What he t **in** is fragile; 4073
Ps 21: 7 For the king t in the LORD; 1053
22: 8 "*He* t in the LORD; let the LORD rescue him. 1670
28: 7 my heart t in him, and I am helped. 1053
32:10 love surrounds the *man who* t in him. 1053
84:12 blessed is the man *who* t in you. 1053
86: 2 save your servant who t in you. 1053
Pr 11:28 *Whoever* t in his riches will fall, 1053
16:20 and blessed is he *who* t in the LORD. 1053
28:25 but *he who* t in the LORD will prosper. 1053
28:26 *He who* t in himself is a fool, 1053
29:25 but *whoever* t in the LORD is kept safe. 1053
Isa 26: 3 mind is steadfast, because *he* t in you. 1053
28:16 the *one who* t will never be dismayed. 586
Jer 17: 5 "Cursed is the one who t in man, 1053
17: 7 blessed is the man who t in the LORD, 1053
Eze 33:13 but then he t in his righteousness 1053
Hab 2:18 For he who makes it t in his own creation; 1053
Mt 27:43 *He* t in God. Let God rescue him now *4275*
Ro 4: 5 but t God who justifies the wicked, *4409*
9:33 and the one who t in him will never be put *4409*
10:11 "Anyone who t in him will never be put *4409*
1Co 13: 7 It always protects, always t, always hopes, *4409*
1Pe 2: 6 and the one who t in him will never be put *4409*

TRUSTWORTHY (25) [TRUST]

Ex 18:21 t men who hate dishonest gain— 622
2Sa 7:28 Your words are t, and you have promised 622
Ne 13:13 because these men were considered t. 586
Ps 19: 7 The statutes of the LORD *are* t, 586
111: 7 all his precepts *are* t. 586
119:86 All your commands are t; 575
119:138 are righteous; they are fully t. 575
Pr 11:13 but a t *man* keeps a secret. 586+8120
13:17 but a t envoy brings healing. 574
25:13 of snow at harvest time is a t messenger 586
Da 2:45 dream is true and the interpretation *is* t." 10041
6: 4 because he *was* t and neither corrupt 10041
Lk 16:11 not been t in handling worldly wealth, *4412*
16:12 not been t with someone else's property, *4412*
19:17 'Because you have been t in a very small *4412*
1Co 7:25 as one who by the Lord's mercy is t. *4412*
1Ti 1:15 a t saying that deserves full acceptance: *4412*
3: 1 Here is a t saying: If anyone sets his heart *4412*
3:11 not malicious talkers but temperate and t *4412*
4: 9 a t saying that deserves full acceptance *4412*
2Ti 2:11 Here is a t saying: If we died with him *4412*
Tit 1: 9 to the t message as it has been taught, *4412*

Tit 3: 8 This is a t saying. And I want you to stress 4412
Rev 21: 5 for these words are t and true." 4412
22: 6 "These words are t and true. 4412

TRUTH (224) [TRUE, TRULY, TRUTHFUL, TRUTHFULLY, TRUTHFULNESS, TRUTHS]

Ge 42:16 be tested to see if you are telling the t. 622
1Ki 17:24 of the LORD from your mouth is the t." 622
22:16 to tell me nothing but the t in the name of 622
2Ch 18:15 to tell me nothing but the t in the name of 622
Ps 15: 2 who speaks the t from his heart 622
25: 5 guide me in your t and teach me, 622
26: 3 and I walk continually in your t. 622
31: 5 redeem me, O LORD, the God of t. 622
40:10 I do not conceal your love and your t from 622
40:11 and your t always protect me. 622
43: 3 Send forth your light and your t, 622
45: 4 in behalf of t, humility and righteousness; 622
51: 6 Surely you desire t in the inner parts; 622
52: 3 falsehood rather than speaking the t. 7406
86:11 O LORD, and I will walk in your t; 622
96:13 in righteousness and the peoples in his t. 575
119:30 I have chosen the way of t; 575
119:43 not snatch the word of t from my mouth, 622
145:18 to all who call on him in t. 622
Pr 16:13 they value a man who speaks the t. 3838
23:23 Buy the t and do not sell it; 622
Isa 45:19 I, the LORD, speak the t; 7406
48: 1 but not in t or righteousness— 622
59:14 t has stumbled in the streets, 622
59:15 T is nowhere to be found, 622
65:16 in the land will do so by the God of t; 589
65:16 in the land will swear by the God of t. 589
Jer 5: 1 who deals honestly and seeks the t, 575
5: 3 O LORD, do not your eyes look for t? 575
7:28 T has perished; it has vanished from 575
9: 3 it is not by t that they triumph in the land. 575
9: 5 and no one speaks the t. 622
26:15 for in t the LORD has sent me to you 622
Da 8:12 and t was thrown to the ground. 622
9:13 and giving attention to your t. 622
10:21 what is written in the Book of T. 622
11: 2 "Now then, I tell you the t: 622
Am 5:10 in court and despise him who tells the t. 9459
Zec 8: 3 Jerusalem will be called the City of T, 622
8:16 Speak the t to each other, 622
8:19 Therefore love t and peace." 622
Mt 5:18 I tell you the t, until heaven and earth 297
5:26 I tell you the t, you will not get out 297
6: 2 I tell you the t, they have received their 297
6: 5 I tell you the t, they have received their 297
6:16 I tell you the t, they have received their 297
8:10 "I tell you the t, I have not found anyone 297
10:15 I tell you the t, it will be more bearable 297
10:23 I tell you the t, you will not finish going 297
10:42 I tell you the t, he will certainly not lose his 297
11:11 I tell you the t: Among those born of women 297
13:17 For I tell you the t, many prophets and 297
16:28 I tell you the t, some who are standing here 297
17:20 I tell you the t, if you have faith 297
18: 3 And he said: "I tell you the t, 297
18:13 And if he finds it, I tell you the t, 297
18:18 "I tell you the t, whatever you bind on earth 297
19:23 Jesus said to his disciples, "I tell you the t, 297
19:28 Jesus said to them, "I tell you the t, 297
21:21 Jesus replied, "I tell you the t, 297
21:31 Jesus said to them, "I tell you the t, 297
22:16 the way of God in accordance with the t. 237
23:36 I tell you the t, all this will come 297
24: 2 "I tell you the t, not one stone here will be 297
24:34 I tell you the t, this generation will 297
24:47 I tell you the t, he will put him in charge 297
25:12 "But he replied, 'I tell you the t, 297
25:40 "The King will reply, 'I tell you the t, 297
25:45 "He will reply, 'I tell you the t, 297
26:13 I tell you the t, wherever this gospel 297
26:21 they were eating, he said, "I tell you the t, 297
26:34 "I tell you the t," Jesus answered, 297
Mk 3:28 I tell you the t, all the sins and blasphemies 297
5:33 trembling with fear, told him the whole t. 237
8:12 I tell you the t, no sign will be given to it." 297
9: 1 And he said to them, "I tell you the t, 297
9:41 I tell you the t, anyone who gives you a cup 297
10:15 I tell you the t, anyone who will not receive 297
10:29 "I tell you the t," Jesus replied, 297
11:23 "I tell you the t, if anyone says to this 297
12:14 the way of God in accordance with the t. 237
12:43 Jesus said, "I tell you the t, 297
13:30 I tell you the t, this generation will 297
14: 9 I tell you the t, wherever this gospel 297
14:18 he said, "I tell you the t, 297
14:25 "I tell you the t, I will not drink again 297
14:30 "I tell you the t," Jesus answered, "today— 297
Lk 4:24 "I tell you the t," he continued, 297
9:27 I tell you the t, some who are standing here 242
12:37 I tell you the t, he will dress himself to serve 297
12:44 I tell you the t, he will put him in charge 242
18:17 I tell you the t, anyone who will not receive 297
18:29 "I tell you the t," Jesus said to them, 297
20:21 the way of God in accordance with the t. 237
21: 3 "I tell you the t," he said, 242
21:32 "I tell you the t, this generation 297
23:43 Jesus answered him, "I tell you the t, 297
Jn 1:14 who came from the Father, full of grace and t 237
1:17 grace and t came through Jesus Christ. 237
1:51 He then added, "I tell you the t, 297
3: 3 In reply Jesus declared, "I tell you the t, 297
3: 5 Jesus answered, "I tell you the t, 297
3:11 I tell you the t, we speak of what we know, and testify to what we have seen, 297
3:21 whoever lives by the t comes into the light, 237
4:23 will worship the Father in spirit and t, 237
4:24 must worship in spirit and in t." 237
5:19 "I tell you the t, the Son can do nothing 297
5:24 "I tell you the t, whoever hears my word 297
5:25 I tell you the t, a time is coming 297
5:33 to John and he has testified to the t. 237
6:26 Jesus answered, "I tell you the t, 297
6:32 Jesus said to them, "I tell you the t, 297
6:47 I tell you the t, he who believes has eternal 297
6:53 Jesus said to them, "I tell you the t, 297
7:18 of the one who sent him is a man of t; 239
8:32 Then you will know the t, and the truth 237
8:32 and the t will set you free." 237
8:34 Jesus replied, "I tell you the t, 297
8:40 a man who has told you the t that I heard 237
8:44 not holding to the t, for there is no truth in 237
8:44 for there is no t in him. 237
8:45 because I tell the t, you do not believe me! 237
8:46 If I am telling the t, why don't you believe 237
8:51 I tell you the t, if anyone keeps my word, 297
8:58 "I tell you the t," Jesus answered, 297
10: 1 "I tell you the t, the man who does not enter 297
10: 7 Jesus said again, "I tell you the t, 297
12:24 I tell you the t, unless a kernel of wheat falls 297
13:16 I tell you the t, no servant is greater than 297
13:20 I tell you the t, whoever accepts anyone 297
13:21 "I tell you the t, one of you is going to betray 297
13:38 I tell you the t, before the rooster crows, 297
14: 6 "I am the way and the t and the life. 237
14:12 I tell you the t, anyone who has faith in me 297
14:17 the Spirit of t. The world cannot accept him, 237
15:26 Spirit of t who goes out from the Father, 237
16: 7 But I tell you the t: It is for your good 237
16:13 But when he, the Spirit of t, comes, 237
16:13 comes, he will guide you into all t. 237
16:20 I tell you the t, you will weep 297
16:23 I tell you the t, my Father will give you 297
17:17 Sanctify them by the t; your word is truth. 237
17:17 Sanctify them by the truth; your word is t. 237
18:23 if I spoke the t, why did you strike me?" 2822
18:37 I came into the world, to testify to the t. 237
18:37 Everyone on the side of t listens to me." 237
18:38 "What is t?" Pilate asked. 237
19:35 He knows that he tells the t, 239
21:18 I tell you the t, when you were younger 297
Ac 20:30 men will arise and distort the t 1406+3281
21:24 Then everybody will know there is no t 4029
21:34 not get at the t because of the uproar, 855+1182
24: 8 you will be able to learn the t 2105
28:25 "The Holy Spirit spoke the t to your 2822
Ro 1:18 and wickedness of men who suppress the t 237
1:25 They exchanged the t of God for a lie, 237
2: 2 judgment against those who do such things is based on t. 237
2: 8 and who reject the t and follow evil, 237
2:20 the embodiment of knowledge and t— 237
9: 1 I speak the t in Christ— 237
15: 8 a servant of the Jews on behalf of God's t, 237
1Co 5: 8 the bread of sincerity and t. 237
13: 6 not delight in evil but rejoices with the t. 237
2Co 4: 2 the t plainly we commend ourselves 237
11:10 As surely as the t of Christ is in me, 237
12: 6 because I would be speaking the t. 237
13: 8 For we cannot do anything against the t, 237
13: 8 but only for the t. 237
Gal 2: 5 the t of the gospel might remain with you. 237
2:14 that they were not acting in line with the t 237
4:16 become your enemy by telling you the t? 238
5: 7 on you and kept you from obeying the t? 237
Eph 1:13 in Christ when you heard the word of t, 237
4:15 Instead, speaking the t in love, 238
4:21 in accordance with the t that is in Jesus. 237
5: 9 in all goodness, righteousness and t) 237
6:14 the belt of t buckled around your waist, 237
Col 1: 5 about in the word of t, 237
1: 6 and understood God's grace in all its t. 237
2Th 2:10 because they refused to love the t and so 237
2:12 be condemned who have not believed the t 237
2:13 of the Spirit and through belief in the t. 237
1Ti 2: 4 and to come to a knowledge of the t. 237
2: 7 I am telling the t, I am not lying— 237
3:15 the pillar and foundation of the t. 237
4: 3 by those who believe and who know the t. 237
6: 5 of the t and who think that godliness is 237
2Ti 2:15 and who correctly handles the word of t. 237
2:18 who have wandered away from the t. 237
2:25 leading them to a knowledge of the t, 237
3: 7 but never able to acknowledge the t. 237
3: 8 so also these men oppose the t— 237
4: 4 They will turn their ears away from the t 237
Tit 1: 1 of God's elect and the knowledge of the t 237
1:14 to the commands of those who reject the t. 237
Heb 10:26 keep on sinning after we have received the knowledge of the t, 237
Jas 1:18 to give us birth through the word of t, 237
3:14 not boast about it or deny the t. 237+2848+6017
5:19 if one of you should wander from the t 237
1Pe 1:22 obeying the t so that you have sincere love 237
2Pe 1:12 and are firmly established in the t you 237
2: 2 and will bring the way of t into disrepute. 237
1Jn 1: 6 we lie and do not live by the t. 237
1: 8 we deceive ourselves and the t is not in us. 237
2: 4 is a liar, and the t is not in him. 237
2: 8 its t is seen in him and you, 239
2:20 and all of you know the t. NIG
2:21 write to you because you do not know the t, 237
2:21 and because no lie comes from the t. 237
3:18 or tongue but with actions and in t. 237
3:19 how we know that we belong to the t, 237
4: 6 the Spirit of t and the spirit of falsehood. 237
5: 6 because the Spirit is the t. 237
2Jn 1: 1 whom I love in the t— 237
1: 1 not I only, but also all who know the t— 237
1: 2 because of the t, which lives in us and will 237
1: 3 will be with us in t and love. 237
1: 4 of your children walking in the t, 237
3Jn 1: 1 whom I love in the t. 237
1: 3 tell about your faithfulness to the t and 237
1: 3 and how you continue to walk in the t. 237
1: 4 that my children are walking in the t. 237
1: 8 so that we may work together for the t. 237
1:12 and even by the t itself. 237

TRUTHFUL (8) [TRUTH]

Pr 12:17 A t witness gives honest testimony, 575
12:19 T lips endure forever, 622
12:22 but he delights in men who are t. 575
14: 5 A t witness does not deceive, 574
14:25 A t witness saves lives, 622
Jer 4: 2 if in a t, just and righteous way you swear, 622
Jn 3:33 has accepted it has certified that God is t. 239
2Co 6: 7 in t speech and in the power of God; 237

TRUTHFULLY (1) [TRUTH]

Eph 4:25 of you must put off falsehood and speak t 237

TRUTHFULNESS (1) [TRUTH]

Ro 3: 7 "If my falsehood enhances God's t and 237

TRUTHS (4) [TRUTH]

1Co 2:13 expressing spiritual t in spiritual words. NIG
1Ti 3: 9 They must keep hold of the deep t of 3696
4: 6 the t of the faith and of the good teaching 3364
Heb 5:12 the elementary t of God's word 794+3836+5122

TRY (23) [TRIED, TRIES, TRYING]

Nu 20:18 if you t, we will march out and attack you NIH
Jdg 19:13 let's t to reach Gibeah or Ramah AIT
Ru 3: 1 should I not t to find a home for you, 1335
1Sa 26:21 I will not t to harm you again. AIT
Job 17:10 "But come on, all of you, t again! 8740
Ps 26: 2 Test me, O LORD, and t me, 5814
Isa 7:13 Is it not enough to t the patience of men? 4206
7:13 Will you t the patience of my God also? 4206
22: 4 Do not t to console me over the destruction 237
Eze 7:26 They will t to get a vision from the prophet; 1335
Da 7:25 the Most High and oppress his saints and t 10503
11:26 king's provisions will t to destroy him; AIT
Zec 12: 3 All who t to move it will injure themselves. AIT
Mal 1: 8 T offering them to your governor! AIT
Lk 12:58 t hard to be reconciled to him on the way, 1443+2238
13:24 will t to enter and will not be able to. 2426
14:19 and I'm on my way to t them out. 1507
Ac 15:10 why do you t to test God by putting on AIT
1Co 10:33 as I t to please everybody in every way. 743
14:12 t to excel in gifts that build up the church. 2426
2Co 5:11 to fear the Lord, we t to persuade men. AIT
1Th 5:15 but always t to be kind to each other and 1503
Tit 2: 9 to t to please them, not to talk back to them, NIG

TRYING (41) [TRY]

Nu 16:10 now you are t to get the priesthood too. 1335
Jdg 6:31 Are you t to save him? AIT
1Sa 20: 1 that he is t to take my life?" 1335
2Sa 14:16 the hand of the man who is t to cut off AIT
16:11 my own flesh, is t to take my life. 1335
20:19 You are t to destroy a city that is a mother 1335
1Ki 19:10 and now they are t to kill me too." 1335
19:14 and now they are t to kill me too." 1335
2Ki 5: 7 he is t to pick a quarrel with me!" 628
Ne 6: 9 They were all t to frighten us, thinking, AIT
6:14 prophets who have been t to intimidate me. AIT
Isa 28: 9 "Who is it he is t to teach? AIT
Da 2: 8 "I am certain that you are t to gain time, AIT
8:15 watching the vision and t to understand it. 1335
Mt 2:20 for those who were t to take the child's 2426
22:18 why are you t to trap me? 4279
23:13 nor will you let those enter who are t to. NIG
Mk 12:15 "Why are you t to trap me?" 4279
Lk 19:47 and the leaders among the people were t 2426
Jn 5: 7 While I am t to get in, AIT
7:19 Why are you t to kill me?" 2426
7:20 "Who is t to kill you?" 2426
7:25 "Isn't this the man they are t to kill? 2426
Ac 17:18 "What is this babbler t to say?" 2527
18: 4 t to persuade Jews and Greeks. 4275
21:31 While they were t to kill him, 2426
Ro 11: 3 and they are t to kill me"? 2426+3836+6034
1Co 10:22 Are we t to arouse the Lord's jealousy? AIT
2Co 5:12 not t to commend ourselves to you again, AIT
10: 9 not want to seem to be t to frighten you NIG
Gal 1: 7 and are t to pervert the gospel of Christ. 2527
1:10 Am I now t to win the approval of men, 4275
1:10 Or am I t to please men? 2426

Gal 1:10 If *I were* still **t to please** men, *743*
3: 3 *are you* now *t to* **attain** *your* **goal** by human *AIT*
5: 4 You who *are t to be* **justified** by law *AIT*
6:12 *are t to* **compel** you to be circumcised. *AIT*
1Th 2: 3 nor are we t to trick you. *NIG*
2: 4 *We are* not **t to please** men but God, *743*
1Pe 1:11 **t to find out** the time and circumstances *2236*
1Jn 2:26 those who *are t to* **lead** you **astray.** *AIT*

TRYPHENA (1)

Ro 16:12 Greet T and Tryphosa, those women who *5586*

TRYPHOSA (1)

Ro 16:12 Greet Tryphena and T, those women who *5589*

TUBAL (8)

Ge 10: 2 Gomer, Magog, Madai, Javan, T, 9317
1Ch 1: 5 Gomer, Magog, Madai, Javan, T, 9317
Isa 66:19 and Lydians (famous as archers), to T 9317
Eze 27:13 " 'Greece, T and Meshech traded with you; 9317
32:26 "Meshech and T are there, 9317
38: 2 the chief prince of Meshech and T; 9317
38: 3 O Gog, chief prince of Meshech and T. 9317
39: 1 O Gog, chief prince of Meshech and T. 9317

TUBAL-CAIN (1) [TUBAL-CAIN'S]

Ge 4:22 Zillah also had a son, T, 9340

TUBAL-CAIN'S (1) [TUBAL-CAIN]

Ge 4:22 T sister was Naamah. 9340

TUBES (1)

Job 40:18 His bones are t *of* bronze, 692

TUCK (3) [TUCKED, TUCKING]

2Ki 4:29 **"T** your **cloak into** your **belt,** 2520+5516
9: 1 **"T** *your* **cloak into** your **belt,** 2520+5516
Eze 5: 3 a few strands of hair and t them **away** in 7443

TUCKED (1) [TUCK]

Ex 12:11 with your **cloak** t **into** your **belt,** 2520+5516

TUCKING (1) [TUCK]

1Ki 18:46 t his **cloak into** *his* **belt,** he ran ahead 5516+9113

TUMBLES (1) [TUMBLING]

Ge 49:17 the horse's heels so that its rider t backward. 5877

TUMBLEWEED (2) [WEED]

Ps 83:13 Make them like t, O my God, 1650
Isa 17:13 like chaff on the hills, like t before a gale. 1650

TUMBLING (1) [TUMBLES]

Jdg 7:13 "A round loaf of barley bread **came** t into 2200

TUMORS (8)

Dt 28:27 with the boils of Egypt and with t, 6754
1Sa 5: 6 upon them and afflicted them with t, 6754
5: 9 both young and old, with an outbreak of t. 6754
5:12 who did not die were afflicted with t, 6754
6: 4 "Five gold t and five gold rats, 6754
6: 5 of the t and of the rats that are destroying 6754
6:11 the gold rats and the models of the t. 3224
6:17 These are the gold t the Philistines sent as 3224

TUMULT (6)

1Sa 14:19 the t in the Philistine camp increased more 2162
Isa 22: 2 O city of t and revelry? 2159
22: 5 of t and trampling and terror in the Valley 4539
Jer 25:31 The t will resound to the ends of the earth, 8623
Eze 1:24 like the t of an army. 2167+7754
Am 2: 2 in **great** t amid war cries and the blast of 8623

TUNE (13) [TUNED]

Ps 9: T To [the t of] "The Death of the Son." NIH
22: T To [the t of] "The Doe of the Morning." NIH
45: T To [the t of] "Lilies." NIH
56: T To [the t of] "A Dove on Distant Oaks." NIH
57: T [To the t of] "Do Not Destroy." NIH
58: T [To the t of] "Do Not Destroy." NIH
58: 5 that will not heed the t *of* the charmer, 7754
59: T [To the t of] "Do Not Destroy." NIH
60: T To [the t of] "The Lily of the Covenant." NIH
69: T To [the t of] "Lilies." NIH
75: T [To the t of] "Do Not Destroy." NIH
80: T To [the t of] "The Lilies of the Covenant." NIH
1Co 14: 7 will anyone know what t is being played *NIG*

TUNED (1) [TUNE]

Job 30:31 My harp is **t to** mourning, 4200

TUNIC (16) [TUNICS]

Ex 28: 4 a breastpiece, an ephod, a robe, a woven t, 4189
28:39 the t *of* fine linen and make the turban 4189
29: 5 the garments and dress Aaron with the t, 4189
Lev 8: 7 He put the t on Aaron, 4189
Lev 16: 4 He is to put on the sacred linen t, 4189
1Sa 17:38 Then Saul dressed David in his own t. 4496
17:39 on his sword over the t and tried walking 4496
18: 4 along with his t, and even his sword, 4496
2Sa 20: 8 Joab was wearing his **military** t, 4230+4496
Ezr 9: 3 When I heard this, I tore my t and cloak, 955
9: 5 with my t and cloak torn, 955
Mt 5:40 someone wants to sue you and take your t, *5945*
10:10 or extra t, or sandals or a staff; *5945*
Mk 6: 9 Wear sandals but not an extra t. *5945*
Lk 6:29 do not stop him from taking your t. *5945*
9: 3 no bag, no bread, no money, no extra t. *5945*

TUNICS (7) [TUNIC]

Ex 28:40 Make t, sashes and headbands 4189
29: 8 Bring his sons and dress them in t 4189
39:27 they made t *of* fine linen— 4189
40:14 Bring his sons and dress them in t. 4189
Lev 8:13 put t on them, 4189
10: 5 they came and carried them, still in their t, 4189
Lk 3:11 "The man with two t should share *5945*

TUNNEL (1) [TUNNELS]

2Ki 20:20 and the t by which he brought water into 9498

TUNNELS (1) [TUNNEL]

Job 28:10 *He* t through the rock; 1324+3284

TURBAN (15) [TURBANS]

Ex 28: 4 a robe, a woven tunic, a t and a sash. 5200
28:37 Fasten a blue cord to it to attach it to the t; 5200
28:37 it is to be on the front of the t. 5200
28:39 of fine linen and make the t *of* fine linen. 5200
29: 6 Put the t on his head and attach 5200
29: 6 and attach the sacred diadem to the t. 5200
39:28 and the t *of* fine linen, 5200
39:31 a blue cord to it to attach it to the t, 5200
Lev 8: 9 Then he placed the t on Aaron's head 5200
16: 4 around him and put on the linen t. 5200
Job 29:14 justice was my robe and my t. 7565
Eze 21:26 Take off the t, remove the crown. 5200
24:17 Keep your t fastened and your sandals 6996
Zec 3: 5 Then I said, "Put a clean t on his head." 7565
3: 5 a clean t on his head and clothed him, 7565

TURBANS (4) [TURBAN]

Eze 23:15 around their waists and flowing t 3178
24:23 You will keep your t on your heads 6996
44:18 They are to wear linen t on their heads 6996
Da 3:21 trousers, t and other clothes, 10368

TURBULENT (1)

Ge 49: 4 T as the waters, you will no longer excel, 7070

TURMOIL (8)

2Ch 15: 5 the inhabitants of the lands were in great t. 4539
Job 3:17 There the wicked cease from t, 8075
3:26 I have no rest, but only t." 8075
Ps 65: 7 and the t *of* the nations. 2162
Pr 15:16 of the LORD than great wealth with t. 4539
Isa 14: 3 from suffering and t and cruel bondage, 8075
Eze 22: 5 O infamous city, full of t. 4539
Ac 17: 8 and the city officials *were* **thrown into** t. *5429*

TURN (327) [TURNED, TURNING, TURNS]

Ge 19: 2 "please **t aside** to your servant's house. 6073
24:49 tell me, so *I may know* which way *to* **t."** 7155
37:30 Where *can* I t *now?"* 995
Ex 7:19 and *they will* **t to** blood. 2118
14: 2 "Tell the Israelites *to* **t back** and encamp 8740
23:27 **make** all your enemies t their backs 448+5989
32: 8 *to* **t away** from what I commanded them 6073
32:12 **T** from your fierce anger; 8740
34:22 Feast of Ingathering at the t *of* the year. 9543
Lev 13:16 *Should* the raw flesh change and t white, 2200
19: 4 not t to idols or make gods of cast metal 7155
19:29 or the land *will* **t to prostitution** and 2388
19:31 not t to mediums or seek out spiritists, 7155
26:31 *I will* t your cities **into** ruins 5989
Nu 6:26 the LORD t his face toward you 5951
14:25 **t back** tomorrow and set out toward 7155
20:17 the king's highway and not t *to* the right 5742
21:22 not **t aside** into any field or vineyard, 5742
22:26 where there was no room to **t,** 5742
25: 4 that the LORD's fierce anger *may* **t away** 8740
27: 7 t their father's inheritance **over** to them. 6296
27: 8 t his inheritance **over** to his daughter. 6296
32:15 If *you* **t away** from following him, 8740
34: 5 where it *will* **t,** join the Wadi of Egypt 6015
Dt 1:40 **t around** and set out toward the desert 7155
2: 3 this hill country long enough; now t north. 7155
2:27 *we will* not **t aside** *to* the right or *to* 6073
5:32 *do* not **t aside** *to* the right or to the left. 6073
7: 4 for *they will* t your sons **away** from 6073
11:16 *to* **t away** and worship other gods and bow 6073
11:28 the LORD your God and t from the way 6073
13: 5 *he has tried* to t you from the way 5615
13:10 to t you **away** from the LORD your God, 5615
13:17 the LORD *will* t from his fierce anger; 8740
17:11 *Do* not **t aside** from what they tell you, 6073
17:20 and t from the law to the right or to 6073
23:14 among you anything indecent and t away 8740
Dt 28:14 *Do* not **t aside** from any of the commands 6073
28:24 t the rain of your country **into** dust 5989
30:10 of the Law and t to the LORD your God 8740
31:20 *they will* t to other gods 7155
31:29 *to* t from the way I have commanded you. 6073
Jos 1: 7 *do* not t from it to the right or to the left, 6073
7:12 *they* t their backs and run 7155
22:16 How could you **t away** from the LORD 8740
22:23 If we have built our own altar to **t away** 8740
22:29 and **t away** from him today by building 8740
23:12 "But if *you* **t away** and ally yourselves 8740+8740
24:20 *he will* t and bring disaster on you 8740
Jdg 1: 3 We **in** t will go with you into yours." 1685
7: 3 'Anyone who trembles with fear *may* **t back** 8740
7:22 **caused** the men throughout the camp **to t** 8492
14:17 She **in** t explained the riddle to her people. 2256
20:39 then the men of Israel *would* t in the battle. 2200
Ru 1:16 "Don't urge me to leave you or to **t back** 8740
1Sa 6:12 *they did* not t *to* the right or to the left. 6073
12:20 yet *do* not **t away** from the LORD, 6073
12:21 *Do* not **t away** after useless idols. 6073
22:17 "T and kill the priests of the LORD, 6015
22:18 "You t and strike down the priests." 6015
29: 4 or *he will* **t against** us during the fighting. 2118+4200+8477
29: 7 **T back** and go in peace; 8740
2Sa 1:22 the bow of Jonathan *did* not **t** back, 6047
2:21 **"T aside** to the right or to the left; 5742
14:19 no one can **t to the right** or to the left 3554
15:31 t Ahithophel's counsel **into foolishness."** 6118
22:37 so that my ankles *do* not **t.** 5048
22:38 *I did* not **t back** till they were destroyed. 8740
22:41 *You* **made** my enemies t their backs 5989
1Ki 8:33 *they* **t back** to you and confess your name, 8740
8:35 and confess your name and t from their sin 8740
8:48 and if *they* **t back** to you with all their heart 8740
8:58 *May he* t our hearts to him, 5742
9: 6 if you or your sons **t away** from me 8740+8740
11: 2 because *they will* surely t your hearts 5742
12:15 for this **t of events** was from the LORD, 6016
13:16 "I cannot **t back** and go with you, 8740
17: 3 t eastward and hide in the Kerith Ravine, 7155
2Ki 3: 3 *he did* not **t away** from them. 6073
10:29 not **t away** from the sins of Jeroboam son 6073
10:31 not **t away** from the sins of Jeroboam, 6073
13: 2 and *he did* not **t away** from them. 6073
13: 6 But *they did* not **t away** from the sins of 6073
13:11 the LORD and *did* not **t away** from any of 6073
14:24 the LORD and *did* not **t away** from any of 6073
15: 9 not **t away** from the sins of Jeroboam son 6073
15:18 not **t away** from the sins of Jeroboam son 6073
15:24 not **t away** from the sins of Jeroboam son 6073
15:28 not **t away** from the sins of Jeroboam son 6073
17:13 **"T** from your evil ways. 8740
17:22 of Jeroboam and *did* not **t away** from them 6073
23:26 not **t away** from the heat of his fierce anger, 8740
1Ch 12:23 to t Saul's kingdom **over** to him, 6015
2Ch 6:24 when *they* **t back** and confess your name, 8740
6:26 and confess your name and t from their sin 8740
6:38 and if *they* **t back** to you with all their heart 8740
7:14 and pray and seek my face and t 8740
7:19 "But if you **t away** and forsake the decrees 8740
10:15 for this **t of events** was from God, 5813
24:23 At the t *of* the year, the army of Aram 9543
29:10 that his fierce anger *will* **t away** from us. 8740
30: 8 that his fierce anger *will* **t away** from you. 8740
30: 9 not t his face from you if you return 6073
35:22 however, *would* not **t away** from him, 6015+7156
36:13 and hardened his heart and *would* not t to 8740
Ne 4: 4 **T** their insults **back** on their own heads. 8740
4:12 "Wherever *you* **t,** they will attack us." 8740
9:26 in order to t them **back** to you; 8740
9:35 not serve you or t from their evil ways. 8740
Est 2:12 a girl's t came to go in to King Xerxes, 9366
2:15 When the t came for Esther 9366
2:22 who **in** t reported it to the king, 2256
Job 3: 4 That day—*may it* **t to** darkness; 2118
5: 1 To which of the holy ones *will you* **t?** 7155
6:18 Caravans **t aside** *from* their routes; 4369
10: 8 Will you now t and destroy me? 6017
10: 9 *Will you* now t me to dust **again?** 8740
10:20 T away from me so I can have 8883
13: 9 Would it t out well if he examined you? NIH
13:16 Indeed, this will t out for my deliverance, NIH
17:12 These men t night into day; 8492
20:14 yet his food *will* t sour in his stomach; 2200
30:21 *You* t on me ruthlessly; 2200
33:17 to t man *from* wrongdoing and keep him 6073
33:30 to **t back** his soul from the pit, 8740
36:18 *do* not *let* a large bribe t you **aside.** 5742
Ps 4: 2 O men, will you t my glory **into** shame? 4200
6: 4 **T,** O LORD, and deliver me; 8740
6:10 *they will* **t back** in sudden disgrace. 8740
9: 3 My enemies **t** back; 8740
18:36 so that my ankles *do* not **t.** 5048
18:37 *I did* not **t back** till they were destroyed. 8740
18:40 *You* **made** my enemies **t** their backs 5989
21:12 for *you will* **make** them t their backs 8883
22:27 the ends of the earth will remember and t 8740
25:16 T to me and be gracious to me, 7155
27: 9 *do* not t your servant **away** in anger; 5742
27:12 *Do* not t me **over** to the desire of my foes, 5989
28: 1 *do* not **t a deaf ear** to me. 3087
31: 2 T your ear to me, 5742
34:14 T from evil and do good; 6073
37: 8 Refrain from anger and t **from** wrath; 6440
37:27 T from evil and do good; 6073

Ps 40: 4 to *those who* **t aside** *to* false gods. 8454
49: 4 *I will* **t** my ear to a proverb; 5742
51:13 and sinners *will* **t back** to you. 8740
56: 9 Then my enemies *will* **t** back when I call 8740
64: 8 He will **t** their own tongues against them NIH
69:16 in your great mercy **t** to me. 7155
70: 3 **t back** because of their shame. 8740
71: 2 **t** your ear to me and save me. 5742
73:10 Therefore their people **t** to them and drink 8740
74: 3 **T** your steps toward these everlasting ruins, 8123
78: 6 and they **in t** would tell their children. 7756
80:18 Then *we will* not **t away** from you; 6047
81:14 and **t** my hand against their foes! 8740
86:16 **T** to me and have mercy on me; 7155
88: 2 **t** your ear to my cry. 5742
90: 3 *You* **t** men **back** to dust, saying, 8740
102: 2 **T** your ear to me; when I call, 5742
119:36 **T** my heart toward your statutes and not 5742
119:37 **T** my eyes **away** from worthless things; 6296
119:51 but *I do* not **t** from your law. 5742
119:79 *May* those who fear you **t** to me, 8740
119:132 **T** to me and have mercy on me, 7155
125: 5 But those *who* **t** *to* crooked ways 5742
Pr 1:26 I **in t** will laugh at your disaster; 1685
4:15 **t** from it and go on your way. 8474
5: 7 *do* not **t aside** from what I say. 6073
7:25 not *let* your heart **t** to her ways or stray 8474
22: 6 and when he is old *he will* not **t** from it. 6073
24:18 and disapprove and **t** his wrath **away** 8740
29: 8 but wise men **t away** anger. 8740
SS 2:17 the shadows flee, **t**, my lover, and be like 6015
6: 1 Which way *did* your lover **t**, 7155
6: 5 **T** your eyes from me; they overwhelm me. 6015
Isa 1:25 *I will* **t** my hand against you; 8740
3:12 *they* **t** you *from* the path. 1182
6:10 with their hearts, and **t** and be healed." 8740
9:21 together they will **t** against Judah. NIH
14:23 *"I will* **t** her into a place for owls and 8492
14:27 and who *can* **t** it **back?** 8740
17: 7 and **t** their eyes to the Holy One of Israel. 8011
19:22 *They will* **t** to the LORD, 8740
22: 4 Therefore I said, **"T away** from me; 9120
28: 6 of strength to *those who* **t back** the battle at 8740
29:16 You **t** things **upside down,** 2201
30:21 Whether *you* **t to the right** or to the left, 3554
41:18 *I will* **t** the desert into pools of water, 8492
42:15 *I will* **t** rivers into islands and dry up 8492
42:16 *I will* **t** the darkness into light 8492
45:22 **"T** to me and be saved, 7155
49:11 *I will* **t** all my mountains into roads, 8492
50: 2 *I* **t** rivers **into** a desert; 8492
55: 7 *Let him* **t** to the LORD, 8740
56:11 they all **t** to their own way, 7155
58: 7 *to* **t away** from your own flesh and blood? 6623
Jer 2:21 then *did you* **t** against me **into** a corrupt, 2200
3:19 and not **t away** from following me. 8740
4:28 I have decided and *will* not **t back."** 8740
6: 8 or I *will* **t away** from you 3697
8: 5 Why does Jerusalem always **t away?** 5412
12:10 *they will* **t** my pleasant field into 5989
13:16 but *he will* **t** it to thick darkness 8492
15:19 *Let* this people **t** to you, 8740
15:19 but you *must* not **t** to them. 8740
17:13 *Those who* **t away** *from* you will be written 6073
18:11 So **t** from your evil ways, each one of you, 8740
18:20 in their behalf to **t** your wrath **away** 8740
21: 4 *I am about to* **t against** you the weapons 6015
23:20 The anger of the LORD *will* not **t back** 8740
25: 5 They said, **"T** now, each of you, 8740
26: 3 Perhaps they will listen and each *will* **t** 8740
30:24 not **t back** until he fully accomplishes 8740
31:13 *I will* **t** their mourning into gladness; 2200
31:39 to the hill of Gareb and then **t** to Goah. 6015
32:40 so that they *will* never **t away** from me. 6073
35:15 of *you must* **t** from your wicked ways 8740
36: 3 each of *them will* **t** from his wicked way; 8740
36: 7 and each *will* **t** from his wicked ways, 8740
44: 5 they *did* not **t** from their wickedness 8740
46:21 They too *will* **t** and flee together, 7155
47: 3 Fathers *will* not **t to help** their children; 7155
49: 8 **T** and flee, hide in deep caves, 7155
50: 5 the way to Zion and **t** their faces toward it. NIH
Eze 1: 9 *they did* not **t** as they moved. 6015
1:17 not **t about** as the creatures went. 6015
3:19 and *he does* not **t** from his wickedness or 8740
4: 3 between you and the city and **t** your face 3922
4: 7 **T** your face toward the siege of Jerusalem 3922
4: 8 so that *you* cannot **t** from one side to 2200
7:20 Therefore *I will* **t** these into an unclean 5989
7:22 *I will* **t** my face away from them, 6015
10:11 not **t about** as the cherubim went. 6015
13:22 the wicked not *to* **t** from their evil ways 8740
14: 6 **T** from your idols and renounce all your 8740
16:42 and my jealous anger *will* **t away** 6073
18:23 not pleased when they **t** from their ways 8740
18:30 **T away** from all your offenses; 8740
23:24 *I will* **t** you **over** to them for punishment, 5989
25: 5 *I will* **t** Rabbah into a pasture for camels 5989
33: 9 to **t** from his ways and he does not do so, 8740
33:11 rather that they **t** from their ways and live. 8740
33:11 from their ways and live. **T!** 8740
33:11 **T** from your evil ways! 8740
35: 4 *I will* **t** your towns **into** ruins 8492
38: 4 *I will* **t** you **around,** put hooks in your jaws 8740
38:12 and **t** my hand against the resettled ruins 8740
39: 2 *I will* **t** you **around** and drag you along. 8740
Da 9:16 **t away** your anger and your wrath 8740
Da 11:18 Then *he will* **t** his attention to 8740
11:18 and *will* **t** his insolence **back** upon him. 8740
11:19 *he will* **t back** toward the fortresses 8740
11:30 Then *he will* **t back** and vent his fury 8740
Hos 2: 3 **t** her into a parched land, 8883
3: 1 though they **t** to other gods and love 7155
4:13 Therefore your daughters **t to prostitution** 2388
4:14 when *they* **t to prostitution,** 2388
7:14 and new wine but **t away** from me. 6073
7:16 *They do* not **t** *to* the Most High; 8740
9:12 Woe to them when I **t away** from them! 6073
11: 7 My people are determined to **t from** me. 5412
11: 9 nor *will I* **t** and devastate Ephraim. 8740
Joel 2:14 *He may* **t** and have pity and leave behind 8740
Am 1: 3 *I will* not **t back** [my wrath]. 8740
1: 6 *I will* not **t back** [my wrath]. 8740
1: 8 *I will* **t** my hand against Ekron, 8740
1: 9 *I will* not **t back** [my wrath]. 8740
1:11 *I will* not **t back** [my wrath]. 8740
1:13 *I will* not **t back** [my wrath]. 8740
2: 1 *I will* not **t back** [my wrath]. 8740
2: 4 *I will* not **t back** [my wrath]. 8740
2: 6 *I will* not **t back** [my wrath]. 8740
5: 7 *You who* **t** justice into bitterness 2200
8: 3 songs in the temple *will* **t to wailing.** 3536
8:10 *I will* **t** your religious feasts into mourning 2200
Jnh 3: 9 with compassion **t** from his fierce anger so 8740
Mic 7:17 *they will* **t in fear** to the LORD our God 7064
Hab 2:16 Now it is your **t!** Drink and be exposed! NIH
Zep 1: 6 those *who* **t back** from following the LORD 6047
Hag 2:17 mildew and hail, yet you did not **t** to me,' NIH
Zec 1: 4 '**T** from your evil ways and your evil 8740
13: 7 *I will* **t** my hand against the little ones. 8740
Mal 4: 6 *He will* **t** the hearts of the fathers 8740
Mt 5:39 the right cheek, **t** to him the other also. *5138*
5:42 and *do* not **t away from** the one who wants *695*
7: 6 and then **t** and tear you to pieces. *5138*
10:35 *to* **t** " 'a man against his father, a daughter *1495*
13:15 understand with their hearts and **t,** *2188*
15:36 and they **in t** to the people. *NIG*
20:19 and *will* **t** him **over** to the Gentiles to *4140*
24:10 that time many *will* **t away** from the faith *4997*
Mk 4:12 otherwise they *might* **t** and be forgiven!' " *2188*
Lk 1:17 **t** the hearts of the fathers **to** their children *2188*
6:29 on one cheek, **t** to him the other also. *4218*
12:58 and the judge **t** you **over** to the officer, *4140*
Jn 2:16 **t** my Father's house **into** a market!" *4472*
12:22 Andrew and Philip **in t** told Jesus. *2779*
12:40 nor understand with their hearts, nor **t—** *5138*
16:20 but your grief *will* **t** to joy. *1181*
Ac 3:19 Repent, then, and **t** to God, *2188*
6: 3 *We will* **t** this responsibility **over to** them *2770*
13: 8 and tried *to* **t** the proconsul from the faith. *1406*
13:46 *we* now **t** to the Gentiles. *5138*
14:15 **t** from these worthless things **to** the living *2188*
20:21 *they must* **t** to God **in repentance** *3567*
21:21 among the Gentiles **to t away from** Moses, *686*
26:18 and **t** them from darkness to light, *2188*
26:20 I preached that they should repent and **t to** *2188*
28:27 understand with their hearts and **t,** *2188*
Ro 11:26 *he will* **t** godlessness **away from** Jacob. *695*
1Co 14:31 For you can all prophesy **in t** so *1651+2848*
15:23 But each in his own **t:** *5413*
2Co 7: 5 but we were harassed at every **t—** *NIG*
8:14 **in t** their plenty will supply what you need. *2779*
Php 1:19 to me **will t out** for my deliverance. *1650*
Col 4:16 that you **in t** read the letter from Laodicea. *2779*
1Ti 6:20 **T away from** godless chatter and *1762*
2Ti 2:19 the Lord *must* **t away from** wickedness." *923*
4: 4 *They will* **t** their ears **away from** the truth *695*
4: 4 from the truth and **t aside** to myths. *1762*
Heb 12:25 *if* we **t away from** him who warns us *695*
Jas 3: 3 *we* can **t** the whole animal. *3555*
1Pe 3:11 *He must* **t** from evil and do good; *1712*
2Pe 2:21 to have known it and then *to* **t their backs** *5715*
Rev 10: 9 *It will* **t** your stomach **sour,** *4393*
11: 6 *to* **t** the waters into blood and to strike *5138*

TURN, TURNED (Anglicized) See also HAND, HANDED

TURNED (262) [TURN]

Ge 9:23 Their faces were **t the other way** so 345
14: 7 *they* **t back** and went to En Mishpat (that is, 8740
18:22 The men **t** away and went toward Sodom, 7155
41:13 And *things* **t out** exactly as he interpreted 2118
42:24 *He* **t away** from them and began to weep, 6015
42:24 but then **t back** and spoke to them again. 8740
42:28 and *they* **t** to each other **trembling** AIT
Ex 4: 4 of the snake and *it* **t** *back* **into** a staff 2118+4200
7:23 Instead, he **t** and went into his palace, 7155
10: 6 Then Moses **t** and left Pharaoh. 7155
14:21 a strong east wind and **t** it into dry land. 8492
32:15 Moses **t** and went down the mountain with 7155
Lev 13: 3 the sore *has* **t** white and the sore appears to 2200
13: 4 and the hair in it *has* not **t** white, 2200
13:10 in the skin that *has* **t** the hair white and 2200
13:13 Since it *has* all **t** white, he is clean. 2200
13:17 and if the sores *have* **t** white, 2200
13:20 and the hair in it *has* **t** white, 2200
13:25 and if the hair in it *has* **t** white, 2200
Nu 12:10 Aaron **t** toward her and saw 7155
14:43 Because *you have* **t away** from the LORD, 8740
16:42 to Moses and Aaron and **t** toward the Tent 7155
20:21 Israel **t** away from them. 5742
Nu 21:33 Then *they* **t** and went up along the road 7155
22:23 she **t** off the road into a field. 5742
22:33 and **t away** from me these three times. 5742
22:33 If *she had* not **t away,** 5742
24: 1 but **t** his face toward the desert. 8883
25:11 *has* **t** my anger **away** from the Israelites; 8740
33: 7 They left Etham, **t back** to Pi Hahiroth, 8740
Dt 1:45 your weeping and **t a deaf ear** to you. 263+4202
2: 1 Then *we* **t back** and set out toward 7155
2: 8 *We* **t** from the Arabah road, 7155
3: 1 Next *we* **t** and went up along the road 7155
9:12 *They have* **t away** quickly from what 6073
9:15 So *I* **t** and went down from the mountain 7155
9:16 *You had* **t aside** quickly from the way that 6073
23: 5 to Balaam but **t** the curse into a blessing 2200
26:13 *I have* not **t aside** from your commands 6296
Jos 7:26 Then the LORD **t** from his fierce anger. 8740
8:20 the desert *had* **t back** against their pursuers. 2200
8:21 *they* **t around** and attacked the men of Ai. 8740
10:38 with him **t around** and attacked Debir. 8740
11:10 that time Joshua **t back** and captured Hazor 8740
15: 7 the Valley of Achor and **t** north to Gilgal, 7155
15:11 of Ekron, **t** toward Shikkeron, passed 9305
18:14 on the south the boundary **t** south along 9305
19:12 *It* **t** east from Sarid toward the sunrise to 8740
19:13 it came out at Rimmon and **t** *toward* Neah. 9305
19:27 *It* then **t** east *toward* Beth Dagon, 8740
19:29 The boundary then **t back** *toward* Ramah 8740
19:29 **t** *toward* Hosah and came out at the sea in 8740
Jdg 2:17 *they* quickly **t** from the way 6073
3:19 At the idols near Gilgal *he* himself **t back** 8740
6:14 The LORD **t** to him and said, 7155
14: 8 *he* **t aside** to look at the lion's carcass. 6073
18: 3 so *they* **t in** there and asked him, 6073
18:15 So *they* **t in** there and went to the house of 6073
18:21 *they* **t away** and left. 7155
18:23 the Danites **t** and said to Micah, 6015+7156
18:26 **t around** and went back home. 7155
20:40 the Benjamites **t** and saw the smoke of 7155
20:41 Then the men of Israel **t** *on* them, 2200
20:45 As *they* **t** and fled toward the desert to 7155
20:47 But six hundred men **t** and fled into 7155
Ru 2: 3 **As it t out,** she found herself working 5247+7936
3: 8 and *he* **t** and discovered a woman lying 4369
1Sa 8: 3 *They* **t aside** after dishonest gain 5742
9:20 **to** whom is all the desire of Israel **t,** 4200
10: 9 As Saul **t** to leave Samuel, 7155+8900
11: 7 and *they* **t out** as one man. 3655
13:17 One **t** toward Ophrah in the vicinity 7155
14:47 Wherever *he* **t,** he inflicted punishment 7155
15:11 because *he has* **t** away from me and has 8740
15:12 up a monument in his own honor and *has* **t** 6015
15:27 As Samuel **t** to leave, 6015
17:30 then **t** away to someone else and brought 6015
17:35 When *it* **t** on me, I seized it by its hair, 7756
17:51 that their hero was dead, *they* **t and ran.** 5674
22:18 Doeg the Edomite **t** and struck them down. 6015
25:12 David's men **t around** and went back. 2200
28:15 and God *has* **t away** from me. 6073
28:16 now that the LORD *has* **t away** from you 6073
2Sa 1: 7 When *he* **t** around and saw me, 7155
19: 2 victory that day *was* **t into** mourning, 2118+4200
22:23 *I have* not **t away** from his decrees. 6073
1Ki 6:34 each having two leaves *that* **t in sockets.** 1664
8:14 the king **t around** and blessed them. 6015
11: 4 his wives **t** his heart after other gods, 5742
11: 9 with Solomon because his heart *had* **t away** 5742
22:32 So *they* **t** to attack him, 6073
2Ki 2:24 *He* **t** around, looked at them and called 7155
4:35 Elisha **t away** and walked back and forth in 8740
5:12 So *he* **t** and went off in a rage. 7155
9:23 Joram **t about** and fled, 2200+3338
12:17 Then he **t** to attack Jerusalem. 7156+8492
19:25 you *have* **t** fortified cities **into** piles of stone. 8615
20: 2 Hezekiah **t** his face to the wall and prayed 6015
23:25 like him who **t** to the LORD as he did— 8740
1Ch 10:14 and **t** the kingdom **over** to David son 6015
21:20 he **t** and saw the angel; 8740
2Ch 6: 3 the king **t around** and blessed them. 6015
11: 4 of the LORD and **t back** from marching 8740
12:12 the LORD's anger **t** from him, 8740
13:14 Judah **t** and saw that they were being 7155
15: 4 But in their distress *they* **t** to the LORD, 8740
18:31 So *they* **t** to attack him, 6015
19: 4 of Ephraim and **t** them **back** to the LORD, 8740
20:10 so *they* **t away** from them and did not 6073
25:27 that Amaziah **t away** from following 6073
29: 6 *They* **t** their faces **away** from the LORD's 6015
29: 6 and **t** their backs on him. 5989
Ezr 10:14 of our God in this matter *is* **t away** 8740
Ne 2:15 *I* **t back** and reentered through 8740
9:29 Stubbornly *they* **t** their backs on you, 5989
13: 2 however, **t** the curse into a blessing.) 2200
Est 9: 1 but now **the tables were t** and the Jews got 2200
9:22 the month when their sorrow **was t** into joy 2200
Job 16:11 God *has* **t** me **over** to evil men 6037
19:19 those I love *have* **t** against me. 2200
31: 7 if my steps *have* **t** from the path, 5742
34:27 because *they* **t** from following him 6073
Ps 14: 3 All *have* **t aside,** 6073
18:22 *I have* not **t away** from his decrees. 6073
22:14 My heart *has* **t** to wax; 2118
30:11 *You* **t** my wailing into dancing; 2200
35: 4 *may* those who plot my ruin **be t** back 6047
40: 1 *he* **t** to me and heard my cry. 5742
40:14 *may* all who desire my ruin **be t** back 6047
44:18 Our hearts *had* not **t** back; 6047

Ps 53: 3 Everyone *has* **t away,** 6047
66: 6 *He* t the sea into dry land, 2200
70: 2 *may* all who desire my ruin **be t** back 6047
78: 9 **t back** on the day of battle; 2200
78:30 before *they* t from the food they craved, 2319
78:34 *they* eagerly t *to* him **again.** 8740
78:44 *He* t their rivers to blood; 2200
85: 3 You set aside all your wrath and t 8740
89:43 *You have* t **back** the edge of his sword 8740
105:25 whose hearts *he* t to hate his people, 2200
105:29 *He* t their waters into blood, 2200
105:32 *He* t their rain **into** hail, 5989
107:33 *He* t rivers into a desert, 8492
107:35 *He* t the desert into pools of water and 8492
114: 3 The sea looked and fled, the Jordan t back; 6015
114: 5 that you fled, O Jordan, that *you* t back, 6015
114: 8 who t the rock **into** a pool, 2200
116: 2 Because *he* t his ear to me, 5742
119:59 and *have* t my steps to your statutes. 8740
119:157 but *I have* not t from your statutes. 5742
129: 5 *May* all who hate Zion **be t** back in shame. 6047
Ecc 2:12 Then I t my thoughts to consider wisdom, 7155
7:25 So I t my mind to understand, 6015
Isa 1: 4 the Holy One of Israel and t *their* backs 2319
5:25 Yet for all this, his anger *is* not **t away,** 8740
7:25 become **places where** cattle are **t loose** 5448
9:12 Yet for all this, his anger *is* not **t away,** 8740
9:17 Yet for all this, his anger *is* not **t away,** 8740
9:21 Yet for all this, his anger *is* not **t away,** 8740
10: 4 Yet for all this, his anger *is* not **t away,** 8740
12: 1 your anger *has* **t away** and 8740
23:13 they stripped its fortresses bare and t it into 8492
29:17 *will* not Lebanon *be* t into a fertile field 8740
34: 9 Edom's streams *will* **be t** into pitch, 2200
37:26 to pass, that you *have* t fortified cities **into** 8615
38: 2 Hezekiah t his face to the wall and prayed 6015
42:17 *will* **be t** back in utter shame. 6047
53: 6 each of *us has* t to his own way; 7155
59: 8 *They have* t them *into* **crooked** roads; 6835
63:10 So *he* **t and became** their enemy 2200
Jer 2:27 *They have* t their backs to me and 7155
4: 8 of the LORD *has* not **t away** from us. 8740
5:23 *they have* **t aside** and gone away. 6073
6:12 Their houses *will* **be t over** to others, 6015
8: 5 Why then *have* these people **t away?** 8740
23:22 to my people and *would have* t them 8740
30: 6 every face t deathly pale? 2200
32:33 *They* t their backs to me and 7155
34:16 *you have* **t around** and profaned my name; 8740
39:14 *They* t him **over** to Gedaliah son 5989
40: 5 However, before Jeremiah **t to go,** 8740
41:14 at Mizpah **t** and went over to Johanan son 6015
49:24 *she has* t to flee and panic has gripped her; 7155
La 1:13 He spread a net for my feet and **t** me back. 8740
3: 3 *he has* t his hand against me again 2200
4: 6 in a moment without a hand t to help her. 2565
5: 2 Our inheritance *has* **been t over** to aliens, 2200
5:15 our dancing *has* t to mourning. 2200
Eze 6: 9 which *have* **t** away from me, 6073
17: 6 Its branches t toward him, 7155
21:16 then to the left, wherever your blade *is* **t.** 3585
23:17 she **t away** from them **in disgust.** 3697
23:18 **I t away** from her **in disgust,** 3697
23:18 just as I *had* **t away** from her sister. 5936
23:22 those you **t away** from **in disgust,** 5936
23:28 to those you **t away** from **in disgust.** 5936
42:19 Then *he* t to the west side and measured; 6015
Da 2: 5 into pieces and your houses **t into** piles 10682
2:29 O king, your mind t *to* things to come, 10513
3:29 be cut into pieces and their houses **be t into** 10702
5: 6 His face t pale and he was so frightened 10731
7:28 and my face t pale, 10731
9: 3 So *I* t to the Lord God and pleaded 5989+7156
9: 5 we *have* **t away** from your commands 6073
9:11 Israel has transgressed your law and **t away,** 6073
10: 8 my face t deathly pale and I was helpless. 2200
Hos 5: 3 *you have* now **t to prostitution;** 2388
5:13 then Ephraim t to Assyria, 2143
7: 8 Ephraim is a flat cake not **t over.** 2200
14: 4 for my anger *has* **t away** from them. 8740
Joel 2:31 The sun *will* **be t** to darkness and 2200
Am 6:12 But *you have* t justice into poison and 2200
Jnh 3:10 and how *they* t from their evil ways, 8740
Zep 3:15 *he has* **t back** your enemy. 7155
Hag 1: 9 but see, it t out to be little. NIH
Zec 7:11 stubbornly *they* t their backs and stopped 5989
8:10 for *I had* t every man against his neighbor. 8938
Mal 1: 3 *I have* t his mountains **into** a wasteland 8492
2: 6 and t many from sin. 8740
2: 8 But you *have* t from the way and 6073
3: 7 of your forefathers *you have* **t away** 6073
Mt 9:22 Jesus t and saw her. *5138*
16:23 Jesus t and said to Peter, "Get behind me, *5138*
18:34 In anger his master t him **over** to *4140*
Mk 5:30 He **t around** in the crowd and asked, *2188*
8:33 *when* Jesus t and looked at his disciples, *2188*
Lk 7:44 he t toward the woman and said to Simon, *5138*
9:55 But Jesus t and rebuked them, *5138*
10:23 *he* t to his disciples and said privately, *5138*
22:32 you *have* **t back,** strengthen your brothers." *2188*
22:61 The Lord t and looked straight at Peter. *5138*
23:28 Jesus t and said to them, *5138*
Jn 2: 9 the water *that had* **been t into** wine. *1181*
4:46 where *he had* t the water **into** wine. *4472*
6:66 From this time many of his disciples **t back** *599+1650+3836+3958*
9:17 Finally *they* t again to the blind man, *3306*
Jn 20:14 *she* **t around** and saw Jesus standing there, *1650+3836+3958+5138*
20:16 She **t toward** him and cried out *5138*
21:20 Peter t and saw that the disciple whom Jesus *2188*
Ac 2:20 *be* t to darkness and the moon to blood *3570*
7:39 they rejected him and in their hearts **t back** *5138*
7:42 But God **t away** and gave them over to *5138*
9:35 and Sharon saw him and **t to** the Lord. *2188*
11:21 a great number of people believed and **t to** *2188*
16:18 so troubled that he **t around** and said to *2188*
18:17 Then they all **t on** Sosthenes *2138*
Ro 3:12 All *have* **t away,** they have together become *1712*
1Th 1: 9 They tell how *you* t to God from idols *2188*
3: 4 And *it* **t out** that way, as you well know. *1181*
1Ti 1: 6 from these and t to meaningless talk. *846*
5:15 in fact already **t away** to follow Satan. *1762*
Heb 8: 9 and I **t away** from them, declares the Lord. *288*
11:34 whose weakness *was* **t to strength;** *1540*
Rev 1:12 *I* **t around** to see the voice *2188*
1:12 *when I* t I saw seven golden lampstands, *2188*
6:12 The sun t black like sackcloth made *1181*
6:12 the whole moon t blood red, *1181*
8: 8 A third of the sea **t into** blood, *1181*
8:11 A third of the waters t bitter, *1181+1650*
8:12 so that a third of them **t dark.** *5029*
10:10 but when I had eaten it, my stomach **t sour.** *4393*
16: 3 *it* **t into** blood like that of a dead man, *1181*

TURNING (33) [TURN]

Nu 31:16 and were the means of t the Israelites **away** 5086
Dt 31:18 of all their wickedness *in* t to other gods. 7155
Jos 22:18 And *are* you now **t away** from the LORD? 8740
23: 6 without **t aside** to the right or to the left. 6073
Jdg 8:20 **T** to Jether, his oldest son, he said, NIH
11: 8 "Nevertheless, *we are* t to you now; 8740
2Sa 2:19 t neither to the right nor to the left 5742
22:22 I have not done evil by **t from** my God. 4946
1Ki 18:37 and that you *are* t their hearts back again." 6015
2Ki 21:13 wiping it and t it upside down. 2200
22: 2 not **t aside** *to* the right or *to* the left. 6073
2Ch 34: 2 not **t aside** *to* the right or *to* the left. 6073
Job 23:11 I have kept to his way without **t aside.** 5742
36:21 Beware of t to evil, 7155
Ps 18:21 I have not done evil by **t from** my God. 4946
Pr 2: 2 t your ear to wisdom and 7992
13:14 t a man from the snares of death. 6073
13:19 but fools detest t from evil. 6073
14:27 t a man from the snares of death. 6073
Isa 59:13 t our backs *on* our God, 6047
Eze 1:12 they would go, without t as they went. 6015
10:11 without t as they went. 6015
29:16 a reminder of their sin in t to her for help. 7155
Da 9:13 of the LORD our God by t from our sins 8740
Hos 7:11 now calling to Egypt, now t *to* Assyria. 2143
Lk 7: 9 and t to the crowd following him, he said, *5138*
14:25 and t to them he said: *5138*
Jn 1:38 **T around,** Jesus saw them following *5138*
Ac 3:26 t each of you **from** your wicked ways." *695*
9:40 **T** toward the dead woman, he said, *2188*
15:19 for the Gentiles who *are* **t** to God. *2188*
Gal 1: 6 of Christ and are t to a different gospel— *NIG*
4: 9 how is it that *you are* t back **to** those weak *2188*

TURNS (40) [TURN]

Lev 20: 6 the person who t to mediums and spiritists 7155
Dt 29:18 among you today whose heart **t away** from 7155
30:17 your heart **t away** and you are not obedient, 7155
2Sa 22:29 the LORD t my darkness **into light.** 5585
2Ki 11: 6 who **take t** guarding the temple— 5005
Job 1: 4 *to* **take t** holding feasts in their homes, 2143+3427
23: 9 when *he* t *to* the south, I catch no glimpse 6493
Ps 18:28 my God t my darkness **into light.** 5585
Pr 15: 1 A gentle answer **t away** wrath, 8740
17: 8 wherever *he* t, he succeeds. 7155
26:14 As a door t on its hinges, 6015
26:14 so a sluggard t on his bed. NIH
28: 9 If *anyone* t a deaf ear to the law, 6073
Ecc 1: 6 wind blows to the south and t to the north; 6015
7: 7 Extortion t a wise man **into a fool,** 2147
Isa 24:11 all joy t **to gloom,** 6845
41: 2 *He* t them to dust *with* his sword, 5989
44:25 of the wise and t it **into nonsense,** 6118
Jer 8: 4 When *a man* **t away,** does he not return? 8740
17: 5 and whose heart **t away** from the LORD. 6073
23:14 so that no one t from his wickedness. 8740
48:39 How Moab t *her* back in shame! 7155
La 1: 8 she herself groans and t away. 8740
Eze 3:20 a righteous man t from his righteousness 8740
18:21 "But if a wicked man **t away** from all 8740
18:24 if a righteous man t from his righteousness 8740
18:26 If a righteous man t from his righteousness 8740
18:27 But if a wicked man **t away** from 8740
18:28 and **t away** from them, he will surely live; 8740
33:12 not cause him to fall when he t from it. 8740
33:14 but *he* then **t away** from his sin 8740
33:18 If a righteous man t from his righteousness 8740
33:19 a wicked man **t away** from his wickedness 8740
Joel 2: 6 every face **t pale.** 6999+7695
Am 4:13 *he who* t dawn to darkness, 6913
5: 8 *who* t blackness into dawn and darkens day 2200
Na 2: 8 they cry, but no *one* **t back.** 7155
2Co 3:16 But whenever *anyone* t to the Lord, *2188*
Heb 3:12 unbelieving heart that **t away from** *923*
Jas 5:20 Whoever t a sinner from the error of his way *2188*

TURQUOISE (6)

Ex 28:18 in the second row a t, a sapphire and 5876
39:11 in the second row a **t,** a sapphire and 5876
1Ch 29: 2 as well as onyx for the settings, **t,** 7037
Isa 54:11 I will build you with stones of t, 7037
Eze 27:16 they exchanged **t,** purple fabric, 5876
28:13 onyx and jasper, sapphire, t and beryl. 5876

TURTLE, TURTLEDOVE, TURTLES
(KJV) See DOVE, DOVES

TUSKS (1)

Eze 27:15 they paid you with ivory t and ebony. 7967

TUTORS (KJV) See GUARDIANS

TWAIN (KJV) See TWO

TWELFTH (23) [TWELVE]

Nu 7:78 On the t day Ahira son of Enan, 6925+9109
1Ki 19:19 and he himself was driving the t pair. 6925+9109
2Ki 8:25 In the t year of Joram son of Ahab 6926+9109
17: 1 In the t year of Ahaz king of Judah, 6926+9109
25:27 the twenty-seventh day of the t month. 6925+9109
1Ch 24:12 eleventh to Eliashib, the t to Jakim, 6925+9109
25:19 the t to Hashabiah, 6925+9109
27:15 The **t,** for the twelfth month, 6925+9109
27:15 The twelfth, for the t month, 6925+9109
2Ch 34: 3 In his t year he began to purge Judah 6926+9109
Ezr 8:31 the t day of the first month we set out 6925+9109
Est 3: 7 In the t year of King Xerxes, 6926+9109
3: 7 fell on the t month, the month of Adar. 6925+9109
3:13 the thirteenth day of the t month, 6925+9109
8:12 the thirteenth day of the t month, 6925+9109
9: 1 On the thirteenth day of the t month, 6925+9109
Jer 52:31 on the twenty-fifth day of the t month. 6925+9109
Eze 29: 1 in the tenth month on the t day, 6925+9109
32: 1 In the t year, in the twelfth month on 6926+9109
32: 1 in the t month on the first day, 6925+9109
32:17 In the t year, on the fifteenth day of 6926+9109
33:21 In the t year of our exile, 6926+9109
Rev 21:20 the eleventh jacinth, and the t amethyst. *1558*

TWELVE (146) [TWELFTH, 12, 12,000, 144,000]

Ge 14: 4 For t years they had been subject 6926+9109
17:20 He will be the father of t rulers, 6925+9109
25:16 the names of the t tribal rulers 6925+9109
35:22 Jacob had t sons: 6925+9109
42:13 "Your servants were t brothers, 6925+9109
42:32 We were t brothers, sons of one father. 6925+9109
49:28 All these are the t tribes of Israel, 6925+9109
Ex 15:27 where there were t springs and 6926+9109
24: 4 and set up t stone pillars representing 6926+9109
24: 4 the t tribes of Israel. 6925+9109
28:21 There are to be t stones, 6926+9109
28:21 with the name of one of the t tribes. 6925+9109
39:14 There were t stones, 6926+9109
39:14 with the name of one of the t tribes. 6925+9109
Lev 24: 5 "Take fine flour and bake t loaves 6926+9109
Nu 1:44 by Moses and Aaron and the t leaders 6925+9109
7: 3 six covered carts and t oxen— 6925+9109
7:84 when it was anointed: t silver plates, 6926+9109
7:84 t silver sprinkling bowls 6925+9109
7:84 and t gold dishes. 6926+9109
7:86 The t gold dishes filled with incense 6926+9109
7:87 burnt offering came to t young bulls, 6925+9109
7:87 t rams and twelve male lambs a year 6925+9109
7:87 rams and t male lambs a year old, 6925+9109
7:87 **T** male goats were used for 6925+9109
17: 2 Israelites and get t staffs from them, 6925+9109
17: 6 and their leaders gave him t staffs, 6925+9109
29:17 the second day prepare t young bulls, 6925+9109
31: 5 So t thousand men armed for battle, 6925+9109
33: 9 where there were t springs and 6926+9109
Dt 1:23 so I selected t of you, 6925+9109
Jos 3:12 choose t men from the tribes of Israel, 6925+9109
4: 2 Choose t men from among the people, 6925+9109
4: 3 take up t stones from the middle of the Jordan 6926+9109
4: 4 the t men he had appointed from 6925+9109
4: 8 They took t stones from the middle of 6926+9109
4: 9 the t stones that had been in the 6926+9109
4:20 at Gilgal the t stones they had taken 6926+9109
8:25 **T** thousand men and women fell that day— 6925+9109
18:24 t towns and their villages. 6926+9109
19:15 There were t towns and their villages. 6926+9109
21: 7 t towns from the tribes of Reuben, 6926+9109
21:40 were the rest of the Levites, were **t.** 6926+9109
Jdg 19:29 limb by limb, into t parts and sent 6925+9109
21:10 assembly sent t thousand fighting men 6925+9109
2Sa 2:15 t men for Benjamin and Ish-Bosheth 6925+9109
2:15 son of Saul, and t for David. 6925+9109
10: 6 and also t thousand men from Tob. 6925+9109
17: 1 "I would choose t thousand men 6925+9109
1Ki 4: 7 had t district governors over all Israel, 6925+9109
4:26 and t thousand horses. 6925+9109
7:15 each eighteen cubits high and t cubits 6926+9109
7:25 The Sea stood on t bulls, 6925+9109
7:44 the Sea and the t bulls under it; 6925+9109
10:20 T lions stood on the six steps, 6925+9109

1Ki 10:26 and t thousand horses, 6925+9109
11:30 and tore it into t pieces. 6925+9109
16:23 king of Israel, and he reigned t years, 6926+9109
18:31 Elijah took t stones, 6926+9109
19:19 He was plowing with t yoke of oxen, 6925+9109
2Ki 3: 1 king of Judah, and he reigned t years. 6926+9109
21: 1 Manasseh was t years old when 6926+9109
1Ch 6:63 were allotted t towns from the tribes 6926+9109
2Ch 1:14 and t thousand horses, 6925+9109
4: 4 The Sea stood on t bulls, 6925+9109
4:15 the Sea and the t bulls under it; 6925+9109
9:19 T lions stood on the six steps, 6925+9109
9:25 and t thousand horses, 6925+9109
12: 3 With t **hundred** chariots 547+2256+4395
33: 1 Manasseh was t years old when 6926+9109
Ezr 6:17 offering for all Israel, t male goats, 10573+10775
8:24 Then I set apart t of the leading priests, 6925+9109
8:35 t bulls for all Israel, ninety-six rams, 6925+9109
8:35 as a sin offering, t male goats. 6925+9109
Ne 5:14 until his thirty-second year—t years— 6926+9109
Est 2:12 she had to complete t months 6925+9109
Ps 60: T and struck down t thousand Edomites 6925+9109
Jer 52:20 the Sea and the t bronze bulls under it, 6925+9109
52:21 and t cubits in circumference; 6926+9109
Eze 40:49 and t cubits from front to back. 6926+9109
43:16 t cubits long and twelve cubits wide. 6926+9109
43:16 twelve cubits long and t cubits wide. 6926+9109
47:13 inheritance among the t tribes of Israel, 6925+9109
Da 4:29 T months later, as the king was 10573+10775
Mt 9:20 subject to bleeding *for* t years came up *1557*
10: 1 He called his t disciples to him *1557*
10: 2 These are the names *of* the t apostles: *1557*
10: 5 These t Jesus sent out with *1557*
11: 1 Jesus had finished instructing his t disciples, *1557*
14:20 and the disciples picked up t basketfuls *1557*
19:28 have followed me will also sit on t thrones, *1557*
19:28 judging the t tribes of Israel. *1557*
20:17 the t disciples aside and said to them, *1557*
26:14 Then one *of* the T—the one called Judas *1557*
26:20 Jesus was reclining at the table with the T. *1557*
26:47 Judas, one *of* the T, arrived. *1557*
26:53 at my disposal more than t legions *1557*
Mk 3:14 He appointed t—designating them apostles *1557*
3:16 These are the t he appointed: *1557*
4:10 the T and the others around him asked him *1557*
5:25 had been subject to bleeding *for* t years. *1557*
5:42 and walked around (she was t years old). *1557*
6: 7 Calling the T to him, he sent them out *1557*
6:43 up t basketfuls of broken pieces of bread *1557*
8:19 "T," they replied. *1557*
9:35 Sitting down, Jesus called the T and said, *1557*
10:32 the T aside and told them what was going *1557*
11:11 he went out to Bethany with the T. *1557*
14:10 Then Judas Iscariot, one *of* the T, *1557*
14:17 Jesus arrived with the T. *1557*
14:20 "It is one *of* the T," he replied, *1557*
14:43 Judas, one *of* the T, appeared. *1557*
Lk 2:42 When he was t years old, they went up *1557*
6:13 he called his disciples to him and chose t *1557*
8: 1 The T were with him, *1557*
8:42 a girl of about t, was dying. *1557*
8:43 had been subject to bleeding for t years, *1557*
9: 1 When Jesus had called the T together, *1557*
9:12 the afternoon the T came to him and said, *1557*
9:17 and the disciples picked up t basketfuls *1557*
18:31 Jesus took the T aside and told them, *1557*
22: 3 Judas, called Iscariot, one of the T. *1557*
22:30 judging the t tribes of Israel. *1557*
22:47 Judas, one *of* the T, was leading them. *1557*
Jn 6:13 So they gathered them and filled t baskets *1557*
6:67 Jesus asked the T. *1557*
6:70 "Have I not chosen you, the T? *1557*
6:71 though one of the T, was later to betray him *1557*
11: 9 "Are there not t hours of daylight? *1557*
20:24 Thomas (called Didymus), one of the T, *1557*
Ac 6: 2 So the T gathered all the disciples together *1557*
7: 8 Jacob became the father of the t patriarchs. *1557*
19: 7 There were about t men in all. *1557*
24:11 that no more than t days ago I went up *1557*
26: 7 This is the promise our t **tribes** are hoping *1559*
1Co 15: 5 he appeared to Peter, and then *to* the T. *1557*
Jas 1: 1 the t tribes scattered among the nations: *1557*
Rev 12: 1 moon under her feet and a crown *of* t stars *1557*
21:12 It had a great, high wall with t gates, *1557*
21:12 and with t angels at the gates. *1557*
21:12 the names *of* the t tribes of Israel. *1557*
21:14 The wall of the city had t foundations, *1557*
21:14 on them were the names *of* the t apostles *1557*
21:21 The t gates were twelve pearls, *1557*
21:21 The twelve gates were t pearls, *1557*
22: 2 bearing t crops of fruit, *1557*

TWENTIETH (9) [TWENTY]

Nu 10:11 On the t day of the second month of 6929
1Ki 15: 9 In the t year of Jeroboam king of Israel, 6929
2Ki 15:30 then succeeded him as king in the t year 6929
1Ch 24:16 nineteenth to Pethahiah, the t to Jehezkel, 6929
25:27 the t to Eliathah, his sons and relatives, 6929
Ezr 10: 9 And on the t day of the ninth month, 6929
Ne 1: 1 In the month of Kislev in the t year, 6929
2: 1 of Nisan in the t year of King Artaxerxes, 6929
5:14 from the t year of King Artaxerxes, 6929

TWENTY (125) [TWENTIETH, 20]

Ge 6: 3 his days will be a hundred and t years." 6929
7:20 to a depth of more than t **feet.** 564+2822+6926
18:31 what if only t can be found there?" 6929
18:31 He said, "For the sake of t, I will not 6929
31:38 "I have been with you for t years now. 6929
31:41 for the t years I was in your household. 6929
32:14 female goats and t male goats, 6929
32:14 two hundred ewes and t rams, 6929
32:15 t female donkeys and ten male donkeys. 6929
37:28 for t shekels *of* silver to the Ishmaelites, 6929
Ex 26:18 Make t frames for the south side of 6929
26:20 of the tabernacle, make t frames 6929
27:10 with t posts and twenty bronze bases and 6929
27:10 with twenty posts and t bronze bases and 6929
27:11 with t posts and twenty bronze bases and 6929
27:11 with twenty posts and t bronze bases and 6929
27:16 provide a curtain t cubits long, of blue, 6929
30:13 sanctuary shekel, which weighs t gerahs. 6929
30:14 those t years old or more, 6929
36:23 They made t frames for the south side of 6929
36:25 side of the tabernacle, they made t frames 6929
38:10 with t posts and twenty bronze bases, 6929
38:10 with twenty posts and t bronze bases, 6929
38:11 also a hundred cubits long and had t posts 6929
38:11 and had twenty posts and t bronze bases, 6929
38:18 It was t cubits long and, 6929
38:26 t years old or more, a total of 603,550 6929
Lev 27: 3 of a male between the ages of t and sixty 6929
27: 5 a person between the ages of five and t, 6929
27: 5 at t shekels and of a female at ten shekels. 6929
27:25 t gerahs to the shekel. 6929
Nu 1: 3 in Israel t years old or more who are able 6929
1:18 and the men t years old or more were listed 6929
1:20 the men t years old or more who were able 6929
1:22 the men t years old or more who were able 6929
1:24 the men t years old or more who were able 6929
1:26 the men t years old or more who were able 6929
1:28 the men t years old or more who were able 6929
1:30 the men t years old or more who were able 6929
1:32 the men t years old or more who were able 6929
1:34 the men t years old or more who were able 6929
1:36 the men t years old or more who were able 6929
1:38 the men t years old or more who were able 6929
1:40 the men t years old or more who were able 6929
1:42 the men t years old or more who were able 6929
1:45 All the Israelites t years old 6929
3:47 sanctuary shekel, which weighs t gerahs. 6929
7:86 dishes weighed a hundred and t shekels. 6929
11:19 or two days, or five, ten or t days, 6929
14:29 every one of you t years old of more 6929
18:16 sanctuary shekel, which weighs t gerahs. 6929
26: 2 all those t years old or more who are able 6929
26: 4 a census of the men t years old or more, 6929
32:11 of the men t years old or more who came 6929
Dt 31: 2 and t years old and I am no longer able 6929
34: 7 a hundred and t years old when he died, 6929
Jdg 4: 3 cruelly oppressed the Israelites for t years, 6929
8:10 and t thousand swordsmen had fallen. 6929
11:33 He devastated t towns from Aroer to 6929
15:20 Samson led Israel for t years in the days of 6929
16:31 He had led Israel t years. 6929
1Sa 7: 2 It was a long time, t years in all, 6929
14:14 and his armor-bearer killed some t men in 6929
2Sa 3:20 When Abner, who had t men with him, 6929
8: 4 and t thousand foot soldiers. 6929
9:10 (Now Ziba had fifteen sons and t servants.) 6929
10: 6 they hired t thousand Aramean foot soldiers 6929
18: 7 that day were great—t thousand men. 6929
19:17 and his fifteen sons and t servants. 6929
24: 8 at the end of nine months and t days. 6929
1Ki 4:23 t of pasture-fed cattle and a hundred sheep 6929
5:11 and Solomon gave Hiram t thousand cors 6929
5:11 to t thousand baths of pressed olive oil. 6929
6: 2 t wide and thirty high. 6929
6: 3 width of the temple, that is t cubits, 6929
6:16 He partitioned off t cubits at the rear of 6929
6:20 The inner sanctuary was t cubits long, 6929
6:20 t wide and twenty high. 6929
6:20 twenty wide and t high. 6929
8:63 a hundred and t thousand sheep and goats. 6929
9:10 At the end of t years, during which Solomon 6929
9:11 King Solomon gave t towns in Galilee 6929
2Ki 4:42 of God t loaves of barley bread baked from 6929
15:27 and he reigned t years. 6929
16: 2 Ahaz was t years old when he became king, 6929
1Ch 18: 4 and t thousand foot soldiers. 6929
23:24 the workers t years old or more who served 6929
23:27 from those t years old or more. 6929
27:23 not take the number of the men t years old 6929
2Ch 2:10 t thousand cors of ground wheat, 6929
2:10 t thousand cors of barley, 6929
2:10 t thousand baths of wine 6929
2:10 of wine and t thousand baths of olive oil." 6929
3: 3 and t cubits wide (using the cubit of 6929
3: 4 at the front of the temple was t cubits long 6929
3: 4 the width of the building and t cubits high. 6929
3: 8 t cubits long and twenty cubits wide. 6929
3: 8 twenty cubits long and t cubits wide. 6929
3:11 of the cherubim was t cubits. 6929
3:13 wings of these cherubim extended t cubits. 6929
4: 1 He made a bronze altar t cubits long, 6929
4: 1 t cubits wide and ten cubits high. 6929
7: 5 a hundred and t thousand sheep and goats. 6929
8: 1 At the end of t years, during which Solomon 6929
25: 5 He then mustered those t years old or more 6929
28: 1 Ahaz was t years old when he became king, 6929
28: 6 and t thousand soldiers in Judah— 6929
31:17 and likewise to the Levites t years old 6929
Ezr 3: 8 appointing Levites t years of age and older 6929
Eze 4:10 Weigh out t shekels of food to eat each day 6929
40:49 The portico was t cubits wide, 6929
41: 2 it was forty cubits long and t cubits wide. 6929
41: 4 of the inner sanctuary; it was t cubits, 6929
41: 4 and its width was t cubits across the end of 6929
41:10 was t cubits wide all around the temple. 6929
42: 3 in the section t cubits from the inner court 6929
45:12 The shekel is to consist of t gerahs. 6929
45:12 T shekels plus twenty-five shekels plus fifteen shekels equal one mina. 6929
Jnh 4:11 a **hundred and t thousand** people who cannot tell their right hand 6926+8052+9109
Hag 2:16 anyone came to a heap of t measures, 6929
2:16 to draw fifty measures, there were only t. 6929
Lk 14:31 one coming against him with t thousand? *1633*
Jn 2: 6 each holding from t **to thirty gallons.** *1545+2445+3583+5552*
Ac 1:15 (a group numbering about a hundred and t) *1633*
27:28 water was **a hundred and t feet deep.** *1633+3976*

TWENTY-EIGHT (4) [28]

Ex 26: 2 t cubits long and four cubits 2256+6929+9046
36: 9 t cubits long and four cubits 2256+6929+9046
2Ki 10:36 Israel in Samaria was t years. 2256+6929+9046
2Ch 11:21 t sons and sixty daughters. 2256+6929+9046

TWENTY-FIFTH (3) [TWENTY-FIVE]

Ne 6:15 So the wall was completed on the t of Elul, 2256+2822+6929
Jer 52:31 freed him from prison on the t day of the twelfth month. 2256+2822+6929
Eze 40: 1 In the t year of our exile, 2256+2822+6929

TWENTY-FIRST (4) [TWENTY-ONE]

Ex 12:18 until the evening of the t day. 285+2256+6929
1Ch 24:17 the t to Jakin, the twenty-second 285+2256+6929
25:28 the t to Hothir, his sons and 285+2256+6929
Hag 2: 1 the t day of the seventh month, 285+2256+6929

TWENTY-FIVE (23) [TWENTY-FIFTH]

Nu 8:24 Men t years old or more shall 2256+2822+6929
Jdg 20:46 On that day t thousand Benjamite swordsmen fell, 2256+2822+6929
1Ki 22:42 he reigned in Jerusalem t years. 2256+2822+6929
2Ki 14: 2 He was t years old when he 2256+2822+6929
15:33 He was t years old when he 2256+2822+6929
18: 2 He was t years old when he 2256+2822+6929
23:36 Jehoiakim was t years old when 2256+2822+6929
2Ch 20:31 he reigned in Jerusalem t years. 2256+2822+6929
25: 1 Amaziah was t years old when 2256+2822+6929
27: 1 Jotham was t years old when 2256+2822+6929
27: 8 He was t years old when he 2256+2822+6929
29: 1 Hezekiah was t years old when 2256+2822+6929
36: 5 Jehoiakim was t years old when 2256+2822+6929
Eze 8:16 were about t men. 2256+2822+6929
11: 1 entrance to the gate were t men, 2256+2822+6929
40:13 the distance was t cubits 2256+2822+6929
40:21 cubits long and t cubits wide. 2256+2822+6929
40:25 cubits long and t cubits wide. 2256+2822+6929
40:29 cubits long and t cubits wide. 2256+2822+6929
40:30 inner court were t cubits wide 2256+2822+6929
40:33 cubits long and t cubits wide. 2256+2822+6929
40:36 cubits long and t cubits wide. 2256+2822+6929
45:12 Twenty shekels plus t shekels plus fifteen shekels equal one mina. 2256+2822+6929

TWENTY-FOUR (11) [TWENTY-FOURTH]

Nu 7:88 the fellowship offering came to t oxen, 752+2256+6929
2Sa 21:20 six toes on each foot—t in all. 752+2256+6929
1Ki 15:33 and he reigned t years. 752+2256+6929
1Ch 20: 6 six toes on each foot—t in all. 752+2256+6929
23: 4 t thousand are to supervise the 752+2256+6929
Rev 4: 4 the throne were t other thrones, *1633+5475*
4: 4 and seated on them were t elders. *1633+5475*
4:10 the t elders fall down before him *1633+5475*
5: 8 the t elders fell down before the Lamb. *1633+5475*
11:16 And the t elders, who were seated *1633+5475*
19: 4 The t elders and the four living *1633+5475*

TWENTY-FOURTH (9) [TWENTY-FOUR]

1Ch 24:18 and the t to Maaziah. 752+2256+6929
25:31 the t to Romamti-Ezer, 752+2256+6929
Ne 9: 1 On the t day of the same month, 752+2256+6929
Da 10: 4 On the t day of the first month, 752+2256+6929
Hag 1:15 on the t day of the sixth month in 752+2256+6929
2:10 On the t day of the ninth month, 752+2256+6929
2:18 from this t day of the ninth month, 752+2256+6929
2:20 a second time on the t day of the 752+2256+6929
Zec 1: 7 the t day of the eleventh month, 752+2256+6929

TWENTY-NINE (5) [29]

Jos 15:32 of t towns and their villages. 2256+6929+9596
2Ki 14: 2 he reigned in Jerusalem t years. 2256+6929+9596
18: 2 he reigned in Jerusalem t years. 2256+6929+9596
2Ch 25: 1 he reigned in Jerusalem t years. 2256+6929+9596
29: 1 he reigned in Jerusalem t years. 2256+6929+9596

TWENTY-ONE (4) [TWENTY-FIRST]

2Ki 24:18 Zedekiah was t years old when 285+2256+6929
2Ch 36:11 Zedekiah was t years old when 285+2256+6929

Jer 52: 1 Zedekiah was t years old when 285+2256+6929
Da 10:13 the prince of the Persian kingdom resisted me t days. 285+2256+6929

TWENTY-SECOND (2) [TWENTY-TWO]

1Ch 24:17 to Jakin, the t to Gamul, 2256+6929+9109
25:29 the t to Giddalti, his sons and 2256+6929+9109

TWENTY-SEVEN (4) [TWENTY-SEVENTH]

Ge 23: 1 to be a hundred and t years old. 2256+6929+8679
1Ki 20:30 the wall collapsed on t thousand 2256+6929+8679
2Ki 25:17 Each pillar was t **feet** high. 564+6926+9046
1Ch 26:32 Jeriah had t **hundred** relatives, 547+2256+4395+8679

TWENTY-SEVENTH (6) [TWENTY-SEVEN]

Ge 8:14 the t day of the second month 2256+6929+8679
1Ki 16:10 killed him in the t year of Asa 2256+6929+8679
16:15 In the t year of Asa king of 2256+6929+8679
2Ki 15: 1 In the t year of Jeroboam king 2256+6929+8679
25:27 the t day of the twelfth month. 2256+6929+8679
Eze 29:17 In the t year, in the first month 2256+6929+8679

TWENTY-SIX (2) [TWENTY-SIXTH]

Jdg 20:15 Benjamites mobilized t thousand swordsmen 2256+6929+9252
2Ch 35: 8 gave the priests t **hundred** Passover offerings 547+2256+4395+9252

TWENTY-SIXTH (1) [TWENTY-SIX]

1Ki 16: 8 the t year of Asa king of Judah, 2256+6929+9252

TWENTY-THIRD (7) [TWENTY-THREE]

2Ki 12: 6 But by the t year of King Joash 2256+6929+8993
13: 1 In the t year of Joash son of 2256+6929+8993
1Ch 24:18 the t to Delaiah and 2256+6929+8993
25:30 the t to Mahazioth, 2256+6929+8993
2Ch 7:10 the t day of the seventh month 2256+6929+8993
Est 8: 9 on the t day of the third month, 2256+6929+8993
Jer 52:30 in his t year, 745 Jews taken 2256+6929+8993

TWENTY-THREE (7) [TWENTY-THIRD]

Nu 33:39 Aaron was a hundred and t years old when he died 2256+6929+8993
Jdg 10: 2 He led Israel t years; 2256+6929+8993
2Ki 23:31 Jehoahaz was t years old when 2256+6929+8993
1Ch 2:22 controlled t towns in Gilead. 2256+6929+8993
2Ch 36: 2 Jehoahaz was t years old when 2256+6929+8993
Jer 25: 3 *For* t years—from the thirteenth 2256+6929+8993
1Co 10: 8 in one day t thousand of them died. *1633+5552*

TWENTY-TWO (15) [TWENTY-SECOND, 22]

Jos 19:30 were t towns and their villages. 2256+6929+9109
Jdg 7: 3 So t thousand men left, 2256+6929+9109
10: 3 who led Israel t years. 2256+6929+9109
20:21 cut down t thousand Israelites 2256+6929+9109
2Sa 8: 5 David struck down t thousand 2256+6929+9109
1Ki 8:63 t thousand cattle and 2256+6929+9109
14:20 He reigned for t years and 2256+6929+9109
16:29 in Samaria over Israel t years. 2256+6929+9109
2Ki 8:26 Ahaziah was t years old when 2256+6929+9109
21:19 Amon was t years old when 2256+6929+9109
1Ch 18: 5 David struck down t thousand 2256+6929+9109
2Ch 7: 5 of t thousand head of cattle and 2256+6929+9109
13:21 fourteen wives and had t sons 2256+6929+9109
22: 2 Ahaziah was t years old when 2256+6929+9109
33:21 Amon was t years old when 2256+6929+9109

TWICE (21) [TWO]

Ge 43:10 we could have gone and returned **t."** 7193
Ex 16: 5 and that is to be **t as much** as they gather on 5467
16:22 On the sixth day, they gathered **t as much—** 5467
Nu 20:11 and struck the rock t with his staff. 7193
Dt 15:18 worth **t as much** as that of a hired hand. 5467
1Sa 18:11 But David eluded him **t.** 7193
26: 8 *I* won't **strike** him **t."** 9101
1Ki 11: 9 who had appeared to him **t.** 7193
Ne 13:20 or t the merchants and sellers of all kinds 9109
Job 33:29 "God does all these things to a man—**t,** 7193
40: 5 **t,** but I will say no more." 9109
42:10 and gave him t as much as he had before. 5467
Ecc 6: 6 if he lives a thousand years **t over** but fails 7193
Eze 21:14 *Let* the sword **strike t,** even three times. 4100
Zec 9:12 now I announce that I will restore **t as much** 5467
Mt 23:15 you make him **t as much** a son of hell *1486*
Mk 14:30 rooster crows t you yourself will disown me three times." *1489*
14:72 rooster crows t you will disown me three times." *1489*
Lk 18:12 I fast t a week and give a tenth of all I get.' *1489*
2Co 1:15 so that you might benefit **t.** *1311*
Jude 1:12 without fruit and uprooted—t dead. *1489*

TWIG (1) [TWIGS]

Hos 10: 7 and its king will float away like a t on 7913

TWIGS (4) [TWIG]

Isa 27:11 When its t are dry, they are broken off 7908
64: 2 fire sets t ablaze and causes water to boil, 2173
Mt 24:32 as its t get tender and its leaves come out, *3080*
Mk 13:28 as its t get tender and its leaves come out, *3080*

TWILIGHT (14) [LIGHT]

Ex 12: 6 Israel must slaughter them **at t.** 1068+2021+6847
16:12 **'At t** you will eat meat, 1068+2021+6847
29:39 the morning and the other **at t.** 1068+2021+6847
29:41 Sacrifice the other lamb **at t** 1068+2021+6847
30: 8 when he lights the lamps **at t** 1068+2021+6847
Lev 23: 5 LORD's Passover begins **at t** 1068+2021+6847
Nu 9: 3 **at t** on the fourteenth day of this month, 1068+2021+6847
9: 5 and they did so in the Desert of Sinai **at t** 1068+2021+6847
9:11 of the second month **at t.** 1068+2021+6847
28: 4 the morning and the other **at t,** 1068+2021+6847
28: 8 Prepare the second lamb **at t,** 1068+2021+6847
Pr 7: 9 at t, as the day was fading, as the dark 5974
Isa 21: 4 the t I longed for has become a horror 5974
59:10 At midday we stumble as if it were **t;** 5974

TWIN (6) [TWINS]

Ge 25:24 there were t *boys* in her womb. 9339
38:27 there were t *boys* in her womb. 9339
SS 4: 2 Each **has** *its* **t;** not one of them is alone. 9298
4: 5 like t fawns *of* a gazelle that browse 9339
6: 6 Each **has** its **t,** not one of them is alone. 9298
Ac 28:11 figurehead of the **t gods Castor and Pollux.** *1483*

TWINED (KJV) See TWISTED

TWINKLING (1)

1Co 15:52 in the t of an eye, at the last trumpet. *4846*

TWINS (2) [TWIN]

SS 7: 3 breasts are like two fawns, t *of* a gazelle. 9339
Ro 9:11 Yet, before the t were born or had done *NIG*

TWIST (1) [TWISTED, TWISTING, TWISTS]

Ps 56: 5 All day long *they* t my words; 6772

TWISTED (26) [TWIST]

Ex 26: 1 with ten curtains of **finely t** linen 8813
26:31 purple and scarlet yarn and **finely t** linen, 8813
26:36 and scarlet yarn and **finely t** linen— 8813
27: 9 and is to have curtains of **finely t** linen, 8813
27:16 and scarlet yarn and **finely t** linen— 8813
27:18 of **finely t** linen five cubits high, 8813
28: 6 and scarlet yarn, and of **finely t** linen— 8813
28: 8 and scarlet yarn, and with **finely t** linen. 8813
28:15 and scarlet yarn, and of **finely t** linen. 8813
36: 8 with ten curtains of **finely t** linen 8813
36:35 purple and scarlet yarn and **finely t** linen, 8813
36:37 and scarlet yarn and **finely t** linen— 8813
38: 9 and had curtains of **finely t** linen, 8813
38:16 the courtyard were of **finely t** linen. 8813
38:18 and scarlet yarn and **finely t** linen— 8813
39: 2 and scarlet yarn, and of **finely t** linen. 8813
39: 5 and scarlet yarn, and with **finely t** linen, 8813
39: 8 and scarlet yarn, and of **finely t** linen. 8813
39:24 and scarlet yarn and **finely t** linen around 8813
39:28 and the undergarments of **finely t** linen. 8813
39:29 The sash was of **finely t** linen and blue, 8813
Ecc 1:15 *What* **is t** cannot be straightened; 6430
Eze 27:24 and multicolored rugs with cords **t** 2502
Mt 27:29 then **t together** a crown of thorns and set it *4428*
Mk 15:17 then **t together** a crown of thorns and set it *4428*
Jn 19: 2 The soldiers **t together** a crown of thorns *4428*

TWISTING (1) [TWIST]

Pr 30:33 and as t the nose produces blood, 4790

TWISTS (3) [TWIST]

Ex 23: 8 a bribe blinds those who see and t the words 6156
Dt 16:19 a bribe blinds the eyes of the wise and t the 6156
Ps 29: 9 The voice of the LORD t the oaks 2655

TWO (621) [SECOND, TWICE, TWO-AND-A-HALF, TWO-DRACHMA, TWO-HORNED, TWO-TENTHS, TWO-THIRDS]

Ge 1:16 God made t great lights— 9109
4:19 Lamech married t women, 9109
6:19 into the ark t of all living creatures, 9109
6:20 T of every kind of bird, 9109
7: 2 and t of every kind of unclean animal, 9109
9:22 and told his t brothers outside. 9109
10:25 T sons were born to Eber: 9109
11:10 *T* **years** after the flood, AIT
13:11 The t men parted company: NIH
15:10 cut them in t and arranged the halves 9348
19: 1 The t angels arrived at Sodom in 9109
19: 8 I have t daughters who have never slept 9109
19:12 The t men said to Lot, NIH
19:15 and your t daughters who are here, 9109
19:16 the hands of his wife and of his t daughters 9109
19:30 and his t daughters left Zoar and settled in 9109
19:30 He and his t daughters lived in a cave. 9109
21:27 and the t men made a treaty. 9109
21:31 because the t men swore an oath there. 9109
22: 3 He took with him t *of* his servants 9109
22: 6 As the t *of* them went on together, 9109
22: 8 And the t *of* them went on together. 9109
24:22 and t gold bracelets weighing ten shekels. 9109
25:23 **"T** nations are in your womb, 9109
25:23 and t peoples from within you will 9109
27: 9 and bring me t choice young goats, 9109
27:36 He has deceived me these *t* **times:** AIT
29:16 Now Laban had t daughters; 9109
31:33 and into the tent of the t maidservants, 9109
31:37 and let them judge between the t *of* us. 9109
31:41 for you fourteen years for your t daughters 9109
32: 7 with him into t groups, 9109
32:10 but now I have become t groups. 9109
32:14 *t* **hundred** female goats and twenty male AIT
32:14 *t* **hundred** ewes and twenty rams, AIT
32:22 up and took his t wives, 9109
32:22 his t maidservants and his eleven sons 9109
33: 1 Rachel and the t maidservants. 9109
34:25 t *of* Jacob's sons, Simeon and Levi, 9109
40: 2 Pharaoh was angry with his t officials, 9109
40: 5 each *of* the t men— 9109
41: 1 When *t* **full years** had passed, AIT
41:32 to Pharaoh *in t* **forms** is that AIT
41:50 t sons were born to Joseph 9109
44:27 'You know that my wife bore me t *sons.* 9109
45: 6 *For* t **years** now there has been famine in AIT
46:27 the t sons who had been born to Joseph 9109
48: 1 So he took his t sons Manasseh 9109
48: 5 your t sons born to you in Egypt 9109
49:14 lying down between **t saddlebags.** 5478
Ex 2:13 and saw t Hebrews fighting. 9109
4: 9 if they do not believe these t signs or listen 9109
16:22 t omers for each person— 9109
16:29 the sixth day he gives you bread *for t* **days.** AIT
18: 3 and her t sons. 9109
18: 6 to you with your wife and her t sons." 9109
21:21 if the slave gets up after a day or **t,** 3427S
25:10 *t* and a half **cubits** long, AIT
25:12 with t rings on one side and two rings on 9109
25:12 with two rings on one side and t rings on 9109
25:17 *t* and a half **cubits** long, AIT
25:18 And make t cherubim out of hammered gold 9109
25:19 of one piece with the cover, at the t ends. 9109
25:22 the cover between the t cherubim that are 9109
25:23 *t* **cubits** long, a cubit wide and a cubit and AIT
26:17 with t projections set parallel to each other. 9109
26:19 t bases for each frame, 9109
26:21 t under each frame. 9109
26:23 and make t frames for the corners at 9109
26:24 At these t corners they must be double 9109
26:25 t under each frame. 9109
27: 7 be on t sides of the altar when it is carried. 9109
28: 7 to have t shoulder pieces attached to two 9109
28: 7 to have two shoulder pieces attached to t 9109
28: 9 "Take t onyx stones and engrave on them 9109
28:11 of the sons of Israel on the t stones the way 9109
28:14 and t braided chains of pure gold, 9109
28:23 Make t gold rings for it and fasten them 9109
28:23 for it and fasten them to t corners of 9109
28:24 the t gold chains to the rings at the corners 9109
28:25 of the chains to the t settings, 9109
28:26 Make t gold rings and attach them to 9109
28:26 the other t corners of the breastpiece on the 9109
28:27 Make t more gold rings and attach them to 9109
29: 1 a young bull and t rams without defect. 9109
29: 3 along with the bull and the t rams. 9109
29:38 regularly each day: t lambs a year old. 9109
30: 2 a cubit wide, and *t* **cubits** high— AIT
30: 4 Make t gold rings for the altar below 9109
30: 4 t on opposite sides—to hold the poles 9109
31:18 he gave him the t tablets of the Testimony, 9109
32:15 the t tablets of the Testimony in his hands. 9109
34: 1 "Chisel out t stone tablets like the first ones 9109
34: 4 So Moses chiseled out t stone tablets like 9109
34: 4 he carried the t stone tablets in his hands. 9109
34:29 the t tablets of the Testimony in his hands, 9109
36:13 to fasten the *t sets of* **curtains** together so AIT
36:22 with t projections set parallel to each other. 9109
36:24 t bases for each frame, 9109
36:26 t under each frame. 9109
36:28 and t frames were made for the corners of 9109
36:29 At these t corners the frames were double 9109
36:30 t under each frame. 9109
37: 1 *t* and a half **cubits** long, AIT
37: 3 with t rings on one side and two rings on 9109
37: 3 with two rings on one side and t rings on 9109
37: 6 *t* and a half **cubits** long AIT
37: 7 Then he made t cherubim out 9109
37: 8 the t ends he made them of one piece with 9109
37:10 *t* **cubits** long, a cubit wide, AIT
37:25 a cubit wide, and *t* **cubits** high— AIT
37:27 They made t gold rings below 9109
37:27 t on opposite sides—to hold the poles 9109
39: 4 which were attached to t *of* its corners, 9109
39:16 They made t gold filigree settings 9109
39:16 gold filigree settings and t gold rings, 9109
39:16 and fastened the rings to t *of* the corners of 9109
39:17 They fastened the t gold chains to the rings 9109
39:18 of the chains to the t settings, 9109
39:19 They made t gold rings and attached them 9109
39:19 the other t corners of the breastpiece on the 9109
39:20 Then they made t more gold rings 9109
Lev 5: 7 he is to bring t doves or two young pigeons 9109
5: 7 he is to bring two doves or t young pigeons 9109

Lev 5:11 If, however, he cannot afford t doves 9109
5:11 or t young pigeons, 9109
8: 2 the t rams and the basket containing 9109
12: 5 *for t* **weeks** the woman will be unclean, AIT
12: 8 to bring t doves or two young pigeons, 9109
12: 8 to bring two doves or t young pigeons, 9109
14: 4 the priest shall order that t live clean birds 9109
14:10 the eighth day he must bring t male lambs 9109
14:22 and t doves or two young pigeons, 9109
14:22 and two doves or t young pigeons, 9109
14:49 To purify the house he is to take t birds 9109
15:14 On the eighth day he must take t doves 9109
15:14 or t young pigeons and come before 9109
15:29 On the eighth day she must take t doves 9109
15:29 or t young pigeons and bring them to 9109
16: 1 the death of the t sons of Aaron who died 9109
16: 5 to take t male goats for a sin offering and 9109
16: 7 to take the t goats and present them before 9109
16: 8 He is to cast lots for the t goats— 9109
16:12 and t **handfuls** of finely ground 2908+4850
19:19 not plant your field with t **kinds** *of* seed. 3977
19:19 " 'Do not wear clothing woven of t **kinds** 3977
23:17 bring t loaves made of two-tenths of 9109
23:18 one young bull and t rams. 9109
23:19 for a sin offering and t lambs, 9109
23:20 to wave the t lambs before the LORD as 9109
24: 6 Set them in t rows, six in each row, 9109
Nu 6:10 on the eighth day he must bring t doves 9109
6:10 or t young pigeons to the priest at 9109
7: 3 from each leader and a cart from every t. 9109
7: 7 He gave t carts and four oxen to 9109
7:17 and t oxen, five rams, five male goats 9109
7:23 and t oxen, five rams, five male goats 9109
7:29 and t oxen, five rams, five male goats 9109
7:35 and t oxen, five rams, five male goats 9109
7:41 and t oxen, five rams, five male goats 9109
7:47 and t oxen, five rams, five male goats 9109
7:53 and t oxen, five rams, five male goats 9109
7:59 and t oxen, five rams, five male goats 9109
7:65 and t oxen, five rams, five male goats 9109
7:71 and t oxen, five rams, five male goats 9109
7:77 and t oxen, five rams, five male goats 9109
7:83 and t oxen, five rams, five male goats 9109
7:85 the silver dishes weighed *t* **thousand** four hundred shekels, AIT
7:89 to him from between the t cherubim above 9109
9:22 over the tabernacle *for t* **days** or a month or AIT
10: 2 "Make t trumpets of hammered silver, 9109
11:19 or *t* **days, or** five, ten or twenty days, AIT
11:26 However, t men, whose names were Eldad 9109
13:23 T of them carried it on a pole 9109
22:22 and his t servants were with him. 9109
22:24 in a narrow path between t vineyards, 2021[S]
23: 2 **the t of them** offered a bull 1189+1192+2256[S]
28: 3 t lambs a year old without defect, 9109
28: 9 make an offering of t lambs a year old 9109
28:11 a burnt offering of t young bulls, 9109
28:19 a burnt offering of t young bulls, 9109
28:27 Present a burnt offering of t young bulls, 9109
29:13 t rams and fourteen male lambs a year old, 9109
29:14 with each of the t rams, two-tenths; 9109
29:17 t rams and fourteen male lambs a year old, 9109
29:20 t rams and fourteen male lambs a year old, 9109
29:23 t rams and fourteen male lambs a year old, 9109
29:26 t rams and fourteen male lambs a year old, 9109
29:29 t rams and fourteen male lambs a year old, 9109
29:32 t rams and fourteen male lambs a year old, 9109
34:15 These t and a half tribes have received their inheritance on the east 9109
Dt 3: 8 So at that time we took from these t kings 9109
3:21 LORD your God has done to these t kings. 9109
4:13 and then wrote them on t stone tablets. 9109
4:47 the t Amorite kings east of the Jordan. 9109
5:22 on t stone tablets and gave them to me. 9109
9:10 The LORD gave me t stone tablets inscribed 9109
9:11 the LORD gave me the t stone tablets, 9109
9:15 t tablets of the covenant were in my hands. 9109
9:17 So I took the t tablets and threw them out 9109
10: 1 "Chisel out t stone tablets like the first ones 9109
10: 3 and chiseled out t stone tablets like 9109
10: 3 up on the mountain with the t tablets 9109
14: 6 a split hoof divided in t and that chews 9109
17: 6 of t or three witnesses a man shall be put 9109
19:15 by the testimony of t or three witnesses. 9109
19:17 the t men involved in the dispute 9109
21:15 If a man has t wives, and he loves one 9109
22: 9 not plant t **kinds** of seed in your vineyard; 3977
25:11 If t **men** are fighting and the wife of one 278+408+2256+5481
25:13 Do not have t **differing weights** 74+74+2256
25:14 Do not have t **differing measures** 406+406+2256
32:30 or t put ten thousand to flight, 9109
Jos 2: 1 of Nun secretly sent t spies from Shittim. 9109
2: 4 But the woman had taken the t men 9109
2:10 the t kings of the Amorites east of 9109
2:23 Then the t men started back. 9109
6:22 Joshua said to the t men who had spied out 9109
7: 3 Send *t* or three **thousand** men to take it AIT
7:21 *t* **hundred** shekels of silver and a wedge AIT
9:10 to the t kings of the Amorites east of 9109
14: 4 the sons of Joseph had become t tribes— 9109
15:60 and Rabbah—t towns and their villages. 9109
21:16 nine towns from these t tribes. 9109
21:25 with their pasturelands—t towns. 9109
21:27 with their pasturelands—t towns; 9109
24:12 also the t Amorite kings. 9109
Jdg 5:30 a girl or t for each man, 8169[S]
Jdg 7:25 also captured t *of* the Midianite leaders, 9109
8:12 the t kings of Midian, fled, 9109
9:44 Then t companies rushed upon those in 9109
11:37 "Give me t months to roam the hills 9109
11:38 And he let her go for t months. 9109
11:39 After the t months, she returned 9109
15:13 with t new ropes and led him up from 9109
16: 3 together with the t posts, 9109
16:28 on the Philistines for my t eyes." 9109
16:29 toward the t central pillars on which 9109
17: 4 and she took *t* **hundred** shekels of silver AIT
19: 3 He had with him his servant and t donkeys. 7538
19: 6 So the t *of* them sat down to eat 9109
19: 8 So the t *of* them ate together. 9109
19:10 with his t saddled donkeys 7538
20:45 and struck down *t* **thousand** more. AIT
Ru 1: 1 together with his wife and t sons, 9109
1: 2 and the names of his t sons were Mahlon 9109
1: 3 died, and she was left with her t sons. 9109
1: 5 and Naomi was left without her t sons 9109
1: 7 With her t daughters-in-law she left 9109
1: 8 Then Naomi said to her t daughters-in-law, 9109
1:19 So the t women went on until they came 9109
1Sa 1: 2 He had t wives; one was called Hannah 9109
1: 3 the t sons of Eli, were priests of the LORD 9109
2:21 to three sons and t daughters. 9109
2:34 " 'And what happens to your t sons, 9109
4: 4 And Eli's t sons, Hophni and Phinehas, 9109
4:11 and Eli's t sons, Hophni and Phinehas, 9109
4:17 Also your t sons, Hophni and Phinehas, 9109
6: 7 with t cows that have calved 9109
6:10 They took t such cows and hitched them to 9109
10: 2 you will meet t men near Rachel's tomb, 9109
10: 4 They will greet you and offer you t loaves 9109
11:11 so that no t of them were left together. 9109
13: 2 *t* **thousand** were with him at Micmash and AIT
13:21 was t **thirds of a shekel** for sharpening 7088
15: 4 *t* **hundred** thousand foot soldiers AIT
18:27 and killed *t* **hundred** Philistines. AIT
23:18 The t *of* them made a covenant before 9109
25:13 while *t* **hundred** stayed with the supplies. AIT
25:18 She took *t* **hundred** loaves of bread, AIT
25:18 t skins of wine, five dressed sheep, 9109
25:18 and *t* **hundred** cakes of pressed figs, AIT
27: 3 and David had his t wives: 9109
28: 8 at night he and t men went to the woman. 9109
30: 5 David's t wives had been captured— 9109
30:10 for *t* **hundred** men were too exhausted AIT
30:12 part of a cake of pressed figs and t cakes 9109
30:18 Amalekites had taken, including his t wives. 9109
30:21 *t* **hundred** men who had been too exhausted AIT
2Sa 1: 1 the Amalekites and stayed in Ziklag t days. 9109
2: 2 So David went up there with his t wives, 9109
2:10 and he reigned t years. 9109
4: 2 Saul's son had t men who were leaders 9109
8: 2 Every t lengths of them were put to death, 9109
12: 1 "There were t men in a certain town, 9109
13:23 *T* **years** later, when Absalom's sheepshearers AIT
14: 6 I your servant had t sons. 9109
14:26 and its weight was *t* **hundred** shekels by AIT
14:28 Absalom lived *t* **years** in Jerusalem AIT
15:11 *T* **hundred** men from Jerusalem AIT
15:27 and Abiathar take your t sons with you. 9109
15:36 Their t sons, Ahimaaz son of Zadok 9109
16: 1 and loaded with *t* **hundred** loaves of bread, AIT
17:18 So the t *of* them left quickly and went to 9109
17:21 the t climbed out of the well and went NIH
21: 8 the t sons of Aiah's daughter Rizpah, 9109
23:20 He struck down t *of* Moab's best men. 9109
1Ki 2: 5 to the t commanders of Israel's armies, 9109
2:32 of my father David he attacked t men 9109
2:39 t *of* Shimei's slaves ran off to Achish son 9109
3:16 Now t prostitutes came to the king 9109
3:18 was no one in the house but the t of us. 9109
3:25 the living child in t and give half to one 9109
3:26 **Cut** him **in t!"** 1615
5:12 and the t *of* them made a treaty. 9109
5:14 in Lebanon and t months at home. 9109
6:25 for the t cherubim were identical in size 9109
6:32 t olive wood doors he carved cherubim, 9109
6:34 He also made t pine doors, 9109
6:34 each having t leaves that turned in sockets. 9109
7:15 He cast t bronze pillars, 9109
7:16 also made t capitals of cast bronze to set 9109
7:18 in t rows encircling each network 9109
7:20 were the *t* **hundred** pomegranates AIT
7:24 in t rows in one piece with the Sea. 9109
7:26 It held *t* **thousand** baths. AIT
7:41 the t pillars; the two bowl-shaped capitals 9109
7:41 the t bowl-shaped capitals on top of 9109
7:41 the t *sets* of network decorating 9109
7:41 the t bowl-shaped capitals on top of 9109
7:42 for the t *sets* of network (two rows 9109
7:42 of network (t rows of pomegranates 9109
8: 9 the t stone tablets that Moses had placed 9109
9:10 Solomon built these t buildings— 9109
10:16 Solomon made *t* **hundred** large shields AIT
11:29 The t *of* them were alone out in 9109
12:28 the king made t golden calves. 9109
15:25 and he reigned over Israel *t* **years.** AIT
16: 8 and he reigned in Tirzah *t* **years.** AIT
16:21 people of Israel were split into t *factions;* 2942
16:24 for *t* **talents** *of* silver and built a city on AIT
18: 4 and hidden them in t caves, NIH
18:13 hundred of the LORD's prophets in t caves, NIH
18:21 "How long will you waver between t opinions? 9109
1Ki 18:23 Get t bulls for us. 9109
18:32 around it large enough to hold *t* **seahs** AIT
20:27 like t small flocks of goats, 9109
21:10 But seat t scoundrels opposite him 9109
21:13 Then t scoundrels came 9109
22:51 and he reigned over Israel *t* **years.** AIT
2Ki 1:14 the first t captains and all their men. 9109
2: 6 So the t *of* them walked on. 9109
2: 8 the t *of* them crossed over on dry ground. 9109
2:11 of fire appeared and separated the t 9109
2:24 Then t bears came out of the woods 9109
4: 1 to take my t boys as his slaves." 9109
4:33 on the t *of* them and prayed to the LORD. 9109
5:22 'T young men from the company of 9109
5:22 a talent of silver and t sets of clothing.' " 9109
5:23 "By all means, take *t* **talents,"** AIT
5:23 tied up the *t* **talents** of silver in two bags, AIT
5:23 tied up the two talents of silver in t bags, 9109
5:23 with t sets of clothing. 9109
5:23 He gave them to t *of* his servants, 9109
7: 1 a shekel and *t* **seahs** *of* barley for a shekel at AIT
7:14 they selected t chariots with their horses, 9109
7:16 and *t* **seahs** *of* barley sold for a shekel, AIT
7:18 a shekel and *t* **seahs** of barley for a shekel at AIT
9:32 T or three eunuchs looked down at him. 9109
10: 4 "If t kings could not resist him, 9109
10: 8 in t piles at the entrance of the city gate 9109
11: 7 and you who are in the other t companies 9109
15:23 and he reigned *t* **years.** AIT
17:16 and made for themselves t idols cast in 9109
18:23 I will give you *t* **thousand** horses— AIT
21:19 and he reigned in Jerusalem t years. 9109
23:12 in the t courts of the temple of the LORD. 9109
25: 4 through the gate between the *t* **walls** near AIT
25:16 The bronze from the t pillars, 9109
1Ch 1:19 T sons were born to Eber: 9109
4: 5 Ashhur the father of Tekoa had t wives, 9109
5:21 *t* **hundred** fifty thousand sheep AIT
5:21 and *t* **thousand** donkeys. AIT
11:22 He struck down t *of* Moab's best men. 9109
26:17 and t **at a time** at the storehouse. 9109+9109
26:18 there were four at the road and t at 9109
2Ch 3:15 In the front of the temple he made t pillars, 9109
4: 3 The bulls were cast in t rows in one piece 9109
4:12 the t pillars; the two bowl-shaped capitals 9109
4:12 the t bowl-shaped capitals on top of 9109
4:12 the t *sets* of network decorating 9109
4:12 the t bowl-shaped capitals on top of 9109
4:13 for the t *sets of* network (two rows 9109
4:13 of network (t rows of pomegranates 9109
5:10 the t tablets that Moses had placed in it 9109
8:10 *t* **hundred** and fifty officials supervising AIT
9:15 Solomon made *t* **hundred** large shields AIT
14: 8 and *t* **hundred** and eighty thousand AIT
24: 3 Jehoiada chose t wives for him, 9109
28: 8 their kinsmen *t* **hundred** thousand wives, AIT
29:32 hundred rams and *t* **hundred** male lambs— AIT
33:21 and he reigned in Jerusalem t years. 9109
Ezr 6:17 *t* **hundred** rams, four hundred male lambs AIT
8:27 and t fine articles of polished bronze, 9109
10:13 be taken care of in a day or t, 9109
Ne 11:16 t of the heads of the Levites, NIH
12:31 also assigned t large choirs to give thanks. 9109
12:40 The t choirs that gave thanks 9109
Est 2:21 t of the king's officers who guarded 9109
2:23 the t officials were hanged on a gallows. 9109
6: 2 t of the king's officers who guarded 9109
9:27 without fail observe these t days every year, 9109
Job 11: 6 for true wisdom has t **sides.** 4101
13:20 "Only grant me these t *things,* O God, 9109
42: 7 "I am angry with you and your t friends, 9109
Ps 62:11 t things have I heard: 9109
Pr 24:22 for those t will send sudden destruction 9109
30: 7 "T *things* I ask of you, O LORD; 9109
30:15 "The leech has t daughters. 'Give! Give!' 9109
Ecc 4: 6 with tranquillity than *t* **handfuls** with toil AIT
4: 9 T are better than one, 9109
4:11 t lie down together, they will keep warm. 9109
4:12 t can defend themselves. 9109
SS 4: 5 Your t breasts are like two fawns, 9109
4: 5 Your two breasts are like t fawns, 9109
7: 3 Your breasts are like t fawns, 9109
8:12 *t* **hundred** are for those who tend its fruit AIT
Isa 6: 2 With t wings they covered their faces, 9109
6: 2 with t they covered their feet, 9109
6: 2 and with t they were flying. 9109
7: 4 of these t smoldering stubs of firewood— 9109
7:16 of the t kings you dread will be laid waste. 9109
7:21 a young cow and t goats. 9109
17: 6 leaving t or three olives on 9109
22:11 You built a reservoir between the *t* **walls** AIT
36: 8 I will give you *t* **thousand** horses— AIT
Jer 2:13 "My people have committed t sins: 9109
3:14 one from a town and t from a clan— 9109
24: 1 the LORD showed me t baskets 9109
28: 3 Within *t* **years** I will bring back AIT
28:11 the neck of all the nations within *t* **years.' "** AIT
33:24 the t kingdoms he chose'? 9109
34:18 like the calf they cut in t and then walked 9109
39: 4 through the gate between the *t* **walls,** AIT
52: 7 through the gate between the *t* **walls** near AIT
52:20 The bronze from the t pillars, 9109
Eze 1:11 each had t wings, 9109
1:11 and t wings covering its body. 9109
1:23 and each had t wings covering its body. 9109
21:19 mark out t roads for the sword of the king 9109
21:21 at the junction of the t roads, 9109

Eze 23: 2 there were t women, daughters of the same 9109
35:10 "These t nations and countries will be ours 9109
37:22 and they will never again be t nations or 9109
37:22 or be divided into t kingdoms. 9109
40: 9 and its jambs were t cubits thick. 9109
40:39 In the portico of the gateway were t tables 9109
40:40 to the north gateway were t tables, 9109
40:40 on the other side of the steps were t tables. 9109
40:44 within the inner court, were t rooms, 9109
41: 3 each was t cubits wide. 9109
41:18 Each cherub had t faces: 9109
41:22 and t cubits square; 9109
41:24 Each door had t leaves— 9109
41:24 t hinged leaves for each door. 9109
43:14 up to the lower ledge it is t cubits high and 9109
45:15 be taken from every flock of *t* **hundred** AIT
47:13 with *t* **portions** for Joseph. AIT
Da 7: 4 from the ground so that it stood on *t* **feet** AIT
8: 3 before me was a ram with *t* **horns,** AIT
8: 7 striking the ram and shattering his t horns. 9109
11:27 The t kings, with their hearts bent on evil, 9109
12: 5 looked, and there before me stood t others, 9109
Hos 6: 2 After *t* **days** he will revive us; AIT
Am 1: 1 what he saw concerning Israel *t* **years** AIT
3: 3 Do t walk together unless they have agreed 9109
3:12 the lion's mouth only t leg bones or a piece 9109
6: 2 Are they better off than your t kingdoms? 465S
Zec 4: 3 Also there are t olive trees by it, 9109
4:11 "What are these t olive trees on the right 9109
4:12 "What are these t olive branches beside 9109
4:12 the t gold pipes that pour out golden oil?" 9109
4:14 "These are the t who are anointed to serve 9109
5: 9 and there before me were t women, 9109
6: 1 from between t mountains— 9109
6:13 And there will be harmony between the t.' 9109
11: 7 Then I took t staffs and called one Favor 9109
14: 4 and the Mount of Olives will be split in t 2942
Mt 2:16 and its vicinity who were **t years old** and *1453*
4:18 he saw t brothers, Simon called Peter *1545*
4:21 he saw t other brothers, James son of *1545*
5:41 to go one mile, go with him t miles. *1545*
6:24 "No one can serve t masters. *1545*
8:28 t demon-possessed men coming from *1545*
9:27 t blind men followed him, calling out, *1545*
10:29 Are not t sparrows sold for a penny? *1545*
14:17 five loaves of bread and t fish," *1545*
14:19 the five loaves and the t fish and looking *1545*
18: 8 or crippled than to have t hands or two feet *1545*
18: 8 or crippled than to have two hands or t feet *1545*
18: 9 to have t eyes and be thrown into the fire *1545*
18:15 just between **the t of you.** *899+2779+5148*
18:16 take one or t others along, *1545*
18:16 by the testimony *of* t or three witnesses.' *1545*
18:19 I tell you that if t of you on earth agree *1545*
18:20 t or three come together in my name, *1545*
19: 5 and the t will become one flesh'? *1545*
19: 6 So they are no longer t, but one. *1545*
20:21 that one of these t sons of mine may sit *1545*
20:24 they were indignant with the t brothers. *1545*
20:30 T blind men were sitting by the roadside, *1545*
21: 1 Jesus sent t disciples, *1545*
21:28 There was a man who had t sons. *1545*
21:31 of the t did what his father wanted?" *1545*
22:40 hang on these t commandments." *1545*
24:40 T *men* will be in the field; one will be taken *1545*
24:41 T women will be grinding with a hand mill; *1545*
25:15 to another t talents, *1545*
25:17 the one with the t talents gained two more. *1545*
25:17 the one with the two talents gained t more. *1545*
25:22 "The man with the t talents also came. *1545*
25:22 he said, 'you entrusted me with t talents; *1545*
25:22 see, I have gained t more.' *1545*
26: 2 the Passover is t days away— *1545*
26:37 and the t sons of Zebedee along with him, *1545*
26:60 Finally t came forward *1545*
27:21 of the t do you want me to release to you?" *1545*
27:38 T robbers were crucified with him, *1545*
27:51 the curtain of the temple was torn in t *1545*
Mk 5:13 The herd, about **t thousand** in number, *1493*
6: 7 he sent them out **t by two** *1545+1545*
6: 7 **two by t** and gave them authority *1545+1545*
6:38 they said, "Five—and t fish." *1545*
6:41 the five loaves and the t fish and looking *1545*
6:41 He also divided the t fish among them all. *1545*
9:43 to enter life maimed than with t hands *1545*
9:45 to enter life crippled than to have t feet and *1545*
9:47 of God with one eye than to have t eyes *1545*
10: 8 and the t will become one flesh.' *1545*
10: 8 So they are no longer t, but one. *1545*
11: 1 Jesus sent t of his disciples, *1545*
12:42 and put in t very small copper coins, *1545*
14: 1 Feast of Unleavened Bread were only t days away, *1545*
14:13 So he sent t of his disciples, telling them, *1545*
15:27 They crucified t robbers with him, *1545*
15:38 The curtain of the temple was torn in t *1545*
16:12 *to* t of them while they were walking in *1545*
Lk 2:24 "a pair of doves or t young pigeons." *1545*
3:11 "The man with t tunics should share *1545*
5: 2 he saw at the water's edge t boats, *1545*
7:18 Calling t of them, *1545*
7:41 "T men owed money to a certain *1545*
9:13 only five loaves of bread and t fish— *1545*
9:16 the five loaves and the t fish and looking *1545*
9:30 T men, Moses and Elijah, *1545*
9:32 they saw his glory and the t men standing *1545*
10: 1 sent them **t by two** ahead of him *324+1545+1545*
Lk 10: 1 sent them **two by t** ahead of him *324+1545+1545*
10:35 The next day he took out t silver coins *1545*
12: 6 Are not five sparrows sold *for* t pennies? *1545*
12:52 three against t and two against three. *1545*
12:52 three against two and t against three. *1545*
15:11 "There was a man who had t sons. *1545*
16:13 "No servant can serve t masters. *1545*
17:34 on that night t *people* will be in one bed; *1545*
17:35 T *women* will be grinding grain together; *1545*
18:10 "T men went up to the temple to pray, *1545*
19:29 he sent t of his disciples, saying to them, *1545*
21: 2 widow put in t very small copper coins. *1545*
22:38 "See, Lord, here are t swords." *1545*
23:32 T other men, both criminals, *1545*
23:45 And the curtain of the temple was torn **in t.** *3545*
24: 4 suddenly t men in clothes that gleamed *1545*
24:13 Now that same day t of them were going to *1545*
24:35 **the** t told what had happened on the way, *899S*
Jn 1:35 The next day John was there again with t *1545*
1:37 When the t disciples heard him say this, *1545*
1:40 of the t who heard what John had said *1545*
4:40 and he stayed t days. *1545*
4:43 After the t days he left for Galilee. *1545*
6: 9 five small barley loaves and t small fish, *1545*
8:17 that the testimony *of* t men is valid. *1545*
11: 6 he stayed where he was t more days. *1545*
11:18 Bethany was less than **t miles** from *1278+5084*
19:18 crucified him, and with him t others— *1545*
19:40 the t of them wrapped it, with the spices, *NIG*
20:12 and saw t angels in white, *1545*
21: 2 and t other disciples were together. *1545*
Ac 1:10 when suddenly t men dressed *1545*
1:23 So they proposed t *men:* *1545*
1:24 Show us which of these t you have chosen *1545*
7:26 upon **t Israelites** who were fighting. *899S*
7:29 he settled as a foreigner and had t sons. *1545*
9:38 they sent t men to him and urged him, *1545*
10: 7 Cornelius called t of his servants and *1545*
12: 6 Peter was sleeping between t soldiers, *1545*
12: 6 bound *with* t chains, and sentries stood *1545*
13: 4 The t of them, sent on their way *NIG*
15:22 *t* **men** who were leaders among the brothers. *AIT*
19:10 This went on for t years, *1545*
19:22 He sent t of his helpers, *1545*
19:34 in unison for about t hours: *1545*
21:33 and ordered him to be bound *with* t chains. *1545*
23:23 Then he called t of his centurions *1545*
23:23 a detachment of **t hundred** soldiers, *1357*
23:23 seventy horsemen and **t hundred** spearmen *1357*
24:27 When **t years** had passed, *1454*
28:30 For t whole **years** Paul stayed there *1454*
1Co 6:16 it is said, "The t will become one flesh." *1545*
14:27 If anyone speaks in a tongue, t— *1545*
14:29 T or three prophets should speak, *1545*
2Co 13: 1 by the testimony of t or three witnesses." *1545*
Gal 4:22 For it is written that Abraham had t sons, *1545*
4:24 for the women represent t covenants. *1545*
Eph 2:14 who has made the t one and has destroyed *317*
2:15 in himself one new man out of the t, *1545*
5:31 and the t will become one flesh." *1545*
Php 1:23 I am torn between the t: *1545*
1Ti 5:19 unless it is brought by t or three witnesses. *1545*
Heb 6:18 by t unchangeable things *1545*
10:28 on the testimony of t or three witnesses. *1545*
11:37 They were stoned; *they were* **sawed in t;** *4569*
Rev 9:12 t other woes are yet to come. *1545*
9:16 troops was **t hundred million.** *1490+3689*
11: 3 And I will give power *to* my t witnesses, *1545*
11: 4 the t olive trees and the two lampstands *1545*
11: 4 the t lampstands that stand before the Lord *1545*
11:10 these t prophets had tormented those who live on the earth. *1545*
12:14 The woman was given the t wings of *1545*
13:11 He had t horns like a lamb, *1545*
19:20 The t of them were thrown alive into the *1545*

TWO-AND-A-HALF (1) [HALF, TWO]

Jos 14: 3 the t tribes their inheritance east of the Jordan 2256+2942+9109

TWO-DRACHMA (1) [DRACHMAS, TWO]

Mt 17:24 the collectors of the t tax came to Peter *1440*

TWO-EDGED (KJV) See DOUBLE-EDGED

TWO-HORNED (2) [HORN, TWO]

Da 8: 6 the t ram I had seen standing 1251+2021+7967
8:20 t ram that you saw represents 1251+2021+7967

TWO-TENTHS (11) [TEN, TWO]

Lev 23:13 with its grain offering of t *of* an ephah 6928+9109
23:17 bring two loaves made of t *of* an ephah 6928+9109
24: 5 using t of an ephah for each loaf. 6928+9109
Nu 15: 6 a grain offering of t of an ephah 6928+9109
28: 9 and a grain offering of t of an ephah 6928+9109
28:12 a grain offering of t of an ephah 6928+9109
28:20 with the ram, t; 6928+9109
28:28 with the ram, t; 6928+9109
29: 3 with the ram, t; 6928+9109
29: 9 with the ram, t; 6928+9109
29:14 with each of the two rams, t; 6928+9109

TWO-THIRDS (1) [THREE, TWO]

Zec 13: 8 "t will be struck down and perish; 7023+9109

TYCHICUS (5)

Ac 20: 4 and T and Trophimus from the province *5608*
Eph 6:21 T, the dear brother and faithful servant in *5608*
Col 4: 7 T will tell you all the news about me. *5608*
2Ti 4:12 I sent T to Ephesus. *5608*
Tit 3:12 As soon as I send Artemas or T to you, *5608*

TYING (1) [TIE]

Pr 26: 8 Like t a stone in a sling is the giving of honor to a fool. 7674

TYPE (2)

1Ch 12:33 with **every** *t of* weapon, to help David AIT
12:37 armed with **every** *t of* weapon—120,000. AIT

TYRANNICAL (1) [TYRANNY]

Pr 28:16 A t ruler lacks judgment, 5131+8041

TYRANNUS (1)

Ac 19: 9 discussions daily in the lecture hall *of* T. *5598*

TYRANNY (1) [TYRANNICAL]

Isa 54:14 T will be far from you; 6945

TYRE (60) [TYRIANS]

Jos 19:29 and went to the fortified city of T, 7450
2Sa 5:11 Hiram king of T sent messengers to David, 7450
24: 7 toward the fortress of T and all the towns 7450
1Ki 5: 1 When Hiram king of T heard that Solomon 7450
7:13 Solomon sent to T and brought Huram, 7450
7:14 a man **of** T and a craftsman in bronze. 7660
9:11 towns in Galilee to Hiram king of T, 7450
9:12 when Hiram went from T to see the towns 7450
1Ch 14: 1 Hiram king of T sent messengers to David, 7450
2Ch 2: 3 sent this message to Hiram king of T: 7450
2:11 of T replied by letter to Solomon: 7450
2:14 from Dan and whose father was **from** T. 7660
Ezr 3: 7 and oil to the people of Sidon and T, 7660
Ne 13:16 **Men from** T who lived in Jerusalem 7660
Ps 45:12 The Daughter of T will come with a gift, 7450
83: 7 Philistia, with the people of T. 7450
87: 4 Philistia too, and T, along with Cush— 7450
Isa 23: 1 An oracle concerning T: 7450
23: 1 For T is destroyed and left without house NIH
23: 3 harvest of the Nile was the revenue of T, 2023S
23: 5 be in anguish at the report from T. 7450
23: 8 Who planned this against T, 7450
23:15 At that time T will be forgotten 7450
23:15 to T as in the song of the prostitute: 7450
23:17 the LORD will deal with T. 7450
Jer 25:22 all the kings of T and Sidon; 7450
27: 3 T and Sidon through the envoys 7450
47: 4 to cut off all survivors who could help T 7450
Eze 26: 2 because T has said of Jerusalem, 'Aha! 7450
26: 3 I am against you, O T, 7450
26: 4 They will destroy the walls of T and pull 7450
26: 7 to bring against T Nebuchadnezzar king 7450
26:15 the Sovereign LORD says to T: 7450
27: 2 take up a lament concerning T. 7450
27: 3 Say to T, situated at the gateway to the sea, 7450
27: 3 " 'You say, O T, "I am perfect in beauty." 7450
27: 8 your skilled men, O T, were aboard 7450
27:32 "Who was ever silenced like T, 7450
28: 2 "Son of man, say to the ruler of T, 7450
28:12 take up a lament concerning the king of T 7450
29:18 in a hard campaign against T; 7450
29:18 from the campaign he led against T. 7450
Hos 9:13 I have seen Ephraim, like T, 7450
Joel 3: 4 O T and Sidon and all you regions 7450
Am 1: 9 "For three sins of T, even for four, 7450
1:10 of T that will consume her fortresses." 7450
Zec 9: 2 which borders on it, and upon T and Sidon, 7450
9: 3 T has built herself a stronghold; 7450
Mt 11:21 in you had been performed in T and Sidon, *5602*
11:22 it will be more bearable *for* T and Sidon on *5602*
15:21 Jesus withdrew to the region *of* T *5602*
Mk 3: 8 the regions across the Jordan and around T *5602*
7:24 that place and went to the vicinity *of* T. *5602*
7:31 Then Jesus left the vicinity *of* T and went *5602*
Lk 6:17 and from the coast *of* T and Sidon, *5602*
10:13 in you had been performed in T and Sidon, *5602*
10:14 *for* T and Sidon at the judgment than *5602*
Ac 12:20 *with* the **people of** T and Sidon; *5601*
21: 3 We landed at T, where our ship was to *5602*
21: 7 We continued our voyage from T *5602*

TYRIANS (1) [TYRE]

1Ch 22: 4 and T had brought large numbers of them 7660

TYRUS (KJV) See TYRE

U

UCAL (1)
Pr 30: 1 man declared to Ithiel, to Ithiel and to U: 432

UEL (1)
Ezr 10:34 of Bani: Maadai, Amram, U, 198

UGLY (8)
Ge 41: 3 seven other cows, u and gaunt, 5260+8273
41: 4 the cows that were u and gaunt ate up 5260+8273
41:19 scrawny and very u and lean. 8273+9307
41:19 I had never seen such u cows in all the land 8278
41:20 u cows ate up the seven fat cows that came 8273
41:21 they looked just as u as before. 8273
41:27 The seven lean, u cows that came up 8273
Rev 16: 2 and u and painful sores broke out on 2805

ULAI (2)
Da 8: 2 in the vision I was beside the U Canal. 217
8:16 I heard a man's voice from the U calling, 217

ULAM (4)
1Ch 7:16 and his sons were U and Rakem. 220
7:17 The son of U: Bedan. 220
8:39 U his firstborn, Jeush the second son 220
8:40 of U were brave warriors who could handle 220

ULLA (1)
1Ch 7:39 The sons of U: Arah, Hanniel and Rizia. 6587

UMMAH (1)
Jos 19:30 U, Aphek and Rehob. 6646

UNABLE (12)
Lev 25:35 *is* u to support himself among you, 3338+4572
Jdg 1:19 but they were u to drive the people from 4202
Isa 46: 2 u to rescue the burden, 3523+4202
Eze 3:26 you will be silent and u to rebuke them, 4202
17:14 would be brought low, u to rise again, 1194
Da 6: 4 but *they were* u to do so. 10321+10379
Lk 1:22 signs to them but remained u to speak. 3273
20:26 *They were* u to trap him in what he 2710+4024
Jn 8:43 Because *you are* u to hear what I say. 1538+4024
21: 6 *they were* u to haul the net in because 2710+4033
Ac 13:11 *you will* be u to see the light of the sun 1063+3590
Heb 4:15 we do not have a high priest *who is* u 1538+3590

UNADVISEDLY (KJV) See RASH

UNAFRAID (1)
Ps 78:53 He guided them safely, so *they were* u 4202+7064

UNANSWERED (2)
Job 11: 2 "*Are* all these words *to* go u? 4202+6699
Ps 35:13 When my prayers returned to me u, 2668+8740

UNAPPROACHABLE (1)
1Ti 6:16 alone is immortal and who lives in u light, 717

UNASHAMED (1)
1Jn 2:28 and u before him at his coming. 159+3590

UNAUTHORIZED (4)
Lev 10: 1 and they offered u fire before the LORD, 2424
22:13 No u person, however, may eat any of it. 2424
Nu 3: 4 when they made an offering with u fire 2424
26:61 an offering before the LORD with u fire.) 2424

UNAWARE (9)
Lev 4:13 though the community *is* u *of* the matter, 4946+6524+6623
5: 2 even though he *is* u of *it*, 4946+6623
5: 3 even though he *is* u of *it*, 4946+6623
5: 4 even though he *is* u of *it*, 4946+6623
Ps 35:15 against me when *I was* u. 3359+4202
Pr 28:22 and *is* u that poverty awaits him. 3359+4202
Lk 2:43 but they *were* u of it. 1182+4024
Ro 1:13 I do not want you *to be* u, brothers, 51
2Co 2:11 For *we are* not u of his schemes. 51

UNAWARES (KJV) See ACCIDENTALLY, DECEIVED, SECRETLY, UNINTENTIONALLY, WITHOUT KNOWING

UNBELIEF (6) [UNBELIEVER, UNBELIEVERS, UNBELIEVING]
Mk 9:24 "I do believe; help me overcome my u!" 602
Ro 4:20 not waver *through* u regarding the promise 602
11:20 But they were broken off *because of* u, 602
11:23 And if they do not persist in u, 602
1Ti 1:13 because I acted in ignorance and u. 602
Heb 3:19 were not able to enter, because of their u. 602

UNBELIEVER (5) [UNBELIEF]
1Co 7:15 But if the u leaves, let him do so. 603
10:27 If some u invites you to a meal 603
14:24 But if an u or someone who does not 603
2Co 6:15 a believer have in common with an u? 603
1Ti 5: 8 the faith and is worse than an u. 603

UNBELIEVERS (8) [UNBELIEF]
Lk 12:46 to pieces and assign him a place with the u. 603
Ro 15:31 that I may be rescued from the u in Judea 578
1Co 6: 6 and this in front of u! 603
14:22 then, are a sign, not for believers but *for* u; 603
14:22 however, is for believers, not *for* u. 603
14:23 who do not understand or some u come in, 603
2Co 4: 4 god of this age has blinded the minds *of* u, 603
6:14 Do not be yoked together *with* u. 603

UNBELIEVING (7) [UNBELIEF]
Mt 17:17 "O u and perverse generation," 603
Mk 9:19 "O u generation," Jesus replied, 603
Lk 9:41 "O u and perverse generation," 603
1Co 7:14 For the u husband has been sanctified 603
7:14 and the u wife has been sanctified through 603
Heb 3:12 u heart that turns away from the living God. 602
Rev 21: 8 But the cowardly, the u, the vile, 603

UNBLAMEABLE (KJV) See BLAMELESS, WITHOUT BLEMISH

UNBLEMISHED (1)
Heb 9:14 through the eternal Spirit offered himself u 320

UNBORN (1) [BEAR]
Ps 22:31 proclaim his righteousness to a people yet u 3528

UNBOUND (1)
Da 3:25 walking around in the fire, u and unharmed, 10742

UNCEASING (2) [UNCEASINGLY]
Isa 14: 6 struck down peoples with u blows, 1194+6239
Ro 9: 2 I have great sorrow and u anguish in my 89

UNCEASINGLY (1) [UNCEASING]
La 3:49 My eyes will flow u, without relief, 1949+4202

UNCERTAIN (1)
1Ti 6:17 which is so u, but to put their hope in God, 84

UNCHANGEABLE (1) [UNCHANGED]
Heb 6:18 by two u things in which it is impossible 292

UNCHANGED (5) [UNCHANGEABLE, UNCHANGING]
Lev 13: 5 the sore *is* u and has not spread in the skin, 6641
13:23 But if the spot *is* u and has not spread, 6641+9393
13:28 spot *is* u and has not spread in the skin 6641+9393
13:37 If, however, in his judgment it *is* u 6641
Jer 48:11 tastes as she did, and her aroma *is* u. 4202+4614

UNCHANGING (1) [UNCHANGED]
Heb 6:17 Because God wanted to make the u nature 292

UNCHECKED (1)
Am 1:11 continually and his fury flamed u, 5905+9068

UNCIRCUMCISED (38) [UNCIRCUMCISION]
Ge 17:14 Any u male, who has not been circumcised 6888
Ex 12:48 No u *male* may eat of it. 6888
Lev 26:41 then when their u hearts are humbled 6888
Jos 5: 7 They were still u because they had 6888
Jdg 14: 3 Must you go to the u Philistines to get 6888
15:18 of thirst and fall into the hands of the u?" 6888
1Sa 14: 6 over to the outpost of those u *fellows*. 6888
17:26 Who is this u Philistine that he should defy 6888
17:36 this u Philistine will be like one of them, 6888
31: 4 or these u *fellows* will come and run me 6888
2Sa 1:20 lest the daughters of the u rejoice. 6888
1Ch 10: 4 or these u *fellows* will come and abuse me." 6888
Isa 52: 1 The u and defiled will not enter you again. 6888
Jer 9:26 For all these nations are really u, 6888
9:26 the whole house of Israel is u *in* heart." 6888
Eze 28:10 You will die the death of the u at the hands 6888
31:18 you will lie among the u, 6888
32:19 Go down and be laid among the u.' 6888
32:21 down and they lie with the u, 6888
32:24 the living went down u to the earth below. 6888
32:25 All of them are u, killed by the sword. 6888
32:26 All of them are u, killed by the sword 6888
32:27 with the other u warriors who have fallen, 6888
Eze 32:28 will be broken and will lie among the u, 6888
32:29 They lie with the u, 6888
32:30 They lie u with those killed by the sword 6888
32:32 and all his hordes will be laid among the u, 6888
44: 7 you brought foreigners u *in* heart and flesh 6888
44: 9 No foreigner u *in* heart and flesh is to enter 6888
Ac 7:51 stiff-necked people, with u hearts and ears! 598
11: 3 the house of u men and ate with them." 213+2400
Ro 3:30 the circumcised by faith and the u through 213
4: 9 only for the circumcised, or also for the u? 213
4:11 that he had by faith while he was still u. 213
1Co 7:18 *He should* not become u. 2177
7:18 *Was* a man u when he was called? 213+1877
Eph 2:11 and called "u" by those who call themselves 213
Col 3:11 circumcised or u, barbarian, Scythian, 213

UNCIRCUMCISION (4) [UNCIRCUMCISED]
1Co 7:19 Circumcision is nothing and u is nothing. 213
Gal 5: 6 neither circumcision nor u has any value. 213
6:15 Neither circumcision nor u means anything; 213
Col 2:13 and *in* the u of your sinful nature, 213

UNCLE (12) [UNCLE'S]
Lev 10: 4 sons of Aaron's u Uzziel, and said to them, 1856
20:20 he has dishonored his u. 1856
25:49 An u or a cousin or any blood relative 1856
1Sa 10:14 Now Saul's u asked him and his servant, 1856
10:15 Saul's u said, "Tell me what Samuel said 1856
10:16 not tell his u what Samuel had said about 1856
14:50 and Ner was Saul's u. 1856
2Ki 24:17 He made Mattaniah, Jehoiachin's u, king 1856
1Ch 27:32 Jonathan, David's u, was a counselor, 1856
2Ch 36:10 and he made Jehoiachin's u, Zedekiah, 278
Est 2:15 had adopted, the daughter of his u Abihail) 1856
Jer 32: 7 of Shallum your u is going to come to you 1856

UNCLE'S (1) [UNCLE]
Ge 29:10 of the well and watered his u sheep. 278+562

UNCLEAN (209) [UNCLEANNESS]
Ge 7: 2 and two of every kind of u animal, 3196+4202
7: 8 Pairs of clean and u animals, 401+3196
Lev 5: 2 person touches anything ceremonially u— 3238
5: 2 of u wild animals or of unclean livestock or 3238
5: 2 of unclean wild animals or of u livestock or 3238
5: 2 of unclean livestock or of u creatures 3238
5: 2 he *has become* u and is guilty. 3237
5: 3 anything that *would make him* u— 3237
7:19 touches anything ceremonially u must 3238
7:20 But if anyone who is u eats any meat of 3240
7:21 If anyone touches something u— 3238
7:21 whether human uncleanness or an u animal 3238
7:21 or an unclean animal or any u, detestable 3238
10:10 the common, between the u and the clean, 3238
11: 4 it is ceremonially u for you. 3238
11: 5 not have a split hoof; it is u for you. 3238
11: 6 not have a split hoof; it is u for you. 3238
11: 7 does not chew the cud; it is u for you. 3238
11: 8 they are u for you. 3238
11:24 " '*You will* make yourselves u by these; 3237
11:24 whoever touches their carcasses *will be* u 3237
11:25 and *he will be* u till evening. 3237
11:26 or that does not chew the cud is u for you; 3238
11:26 [the carcass of] any of them *will be* u. 3237
11:27 those that walk on their paws are u for you; 3238
11:27 whoever touches their carcasses *will be* u 3237
11:28 and *he will be* u till evening. 3237
11:28 They are u for you. 3238
11:29 these are u for you: the weasel, the rat, 3238
11:31 these are u for you. 3238
11:31 when they are dead *will be* u till evening. 3237
11:32 that article, whatever its use, *will be* u, 3237
11:32 Put it in water; *it will be* u till evening, 3237
11:33 everything in it *will be* u, 3237
11:34 but has water on it from such a pot *is* u, 3237
11:34 any liquid that could be drunk from it *is* u. 3237
11:35 of their carcasses falls on *becomes* u; 3237
11:35 They are u, and you are to regard them 3238
11:35 and you are to regard them as u. 3238
11:36 who touches one of these carcasses *is* u. 3237
11:38 it is u for you. 3238
11:39 anyone who touches the carcass *will be* u 3237
11:40 and *he will be* u till evening. 3237
11:40 and *he will be* u till evening. 3237
11:43 *Do* not make yourselves u by means of 3237
11:43 by means of them or be made u by them. 3237
11:44 *Do* not make yourselves u by any creature 3237
11:47 You must distinguish between the u and 3238
12: 2 *be* ceremonially u for seven days, 3237
12: 2 just as *she is* u during her monthly period. 3237
12: 5 for two weeks the woman *will be* u, 3237
13: 3 pronounce him ceremonially u. 3237
13: 8 he *shall* pronounce him u; 3237
13:11 and the priest *shall* pronounce him u. 3237
13:11 in isolation, because he is already u. 3238
13:14 raw flesh appears on him, *he will be* u. 3237
13:15 *he shall* pronounce him u. 3237
13:15 raw flesh is u; he has an infectious disease. 3238
13:20 the priest *shall* pronounce him u. 3237
13:22 the priest *shall* pronounce him u; 3237
13:25 The priest *shall* pronounce him u; 3237
13:27 the priest *shall* pronounce him u; 3237
13:30 the priest *shall* pronounce that person u; 3237

Lev 13:36 to look for yellow hair; the person is **u**. 3238
13:44 the man is diseased and is **u**. 3238
13:44 The priest *shall* **pronounce** him **u** 3237+3237
13:45 the lower part of his face and cry out, '**U**! 3238
13:45 and cry out, 'Unclean! **U**!' 3238
13:46 As long as he has the infection he **remains u**. 3237+3238
13:51 a destructive mildew; the article is **u**. 3238
13:55 even though it has not spread, it is **u**. 3238
13:59 for pronouncing them clean or **u**. 3237
14:36 in the house *will be* **pronounced u**. 3237
14:40 and thrown into an **u** place outside 3238
14:41 into an **u** place outside the town. 3238
14:44 a destructive mildew; the house is **u**. 3238
14:45 and taken out of the town to an **u** place. 3238
14:46 while it is closed up *will be* **u** till evening. 3237
14:57 to determine when something is clean or **u**. 3238
15: 2 a bodily discharge, the discharge is **u**. 3238
15: 3 it will make him **u**. 3240
15: 4 the man with a discharge lies on *will be* **u**, 3237
15: 4 and anything he sits on *will be* **u**. 3237
15: 5 and *he will be* **u** till evening. 3237
15: 6 and *he will be* **u** till evening. 3237
15: 7 and *he will be* **u** till evening. 3237
15: 8 and *he will be* **u** till evening. 3237
15: 9 the man sits on when riding *will be* **u**, 3237
15:10 of the things that were under him *will be* **u** 3237
15:10 and *he will be* **u** till evening. 3237
15:11 and *he will be* **u** till evening. 3237
15:16 and *he will be* **u** till evening. 3237
15:17 and *it will be* **u** till evening. 3237
15:18 and *they will be* **u** till evening. 3237
15:19 and anyone who touches her *will be* **u** 3237
15:20 on during her period *will be* **u**, 3237
15:20 and anything she sits on *will be* **u**. 3237
15:21 and *he will be* **u** till evening. 3237
15:22 and *he will be* **u** till evening. 3237
15:23 *he will be* **u** till evening. 3237
15:24 *he will be* **u** for seven days; 3237
15:24 any bed he lies on *will be* **u**. 3237
15:25 be **u** as long as she has the discharge, 3238
15:26 on while her discharge continues will be **u**, 3240
15:26 and anything she sits on will be **u**, 3238
15:27 Whoever touches them *will be* **u**; 3237
15:27 and *he will be* **u** till evening. 3237
15:31 separate from **things that make** them **u**, 3240
15:32 *anyone made* **u** by an emission of semen, 3237
15:33 with a *woman who is* **ceremonially u**. 3238
17:15 *he will be* **ceremonially u** till evening; 3237
20:25 a distinction between clean and **u** animals 3238
20:25 and unclean animals and between **u** 3238
20:25 those which I have set apart as **u** for you. 3237
21: 1 *must* not **make himself ceremonially u** 3237
21: 3 for her *he may* **make himself u**. 3237
21: 4 not **make himself u** for people related to him 3237
21:11 *He must* not **make himself u**, 3237
22: 3 of your descendants is **ceremonially u** and 3240
22: 4 also be **u** if he touches something defiled NIH
22: 5 any crawling thing that *makes* him **u**, 3237
22: 5 or any person who *makes* him **u**, 3237
22: 6 any such thing *will be* **u** till evening. 3237
22: 8 and so *become* **u** through it. 3237
27:11 a **ceremonially u** animal— 3238
27:27 If it is one of the **u** animals, 3238
Nu 5: 2 or who is **ceremonially u** because of 3238
6: 7 *must* not **make himself ceremonially u** 3237
9: 6 because they were **ceremonially u** 3238
9: 7 "We have become **u** because of 3238
9:10 of you or your descendants are **u** because of 3238
18:15 and every firstborn male of **u** animals. 3238
19: 7 he *will be* **ceremonially u** till evening. 3237
19: 8 and *he* too *will be* **u** till evening. 3237
19:10 and *he* too *will be* **u** till evening. 3237
19:11 of anyone *will be* **u** for seven days. 3237
19:13 he is **u**; his uncleanness remains on him. 3238
19:14 the tent and anyone who is in it *will be* **u** 3237
19:15 without a lid fastened on it will be **u**. 3238
19:16 *will be* **u** for seven days. 3237
19:17 "For the **u** *person,* put some ashes from 3238
19:19 the **u** *person* on the third and seventh days, 3238
19:20 a person who *is* **u** does not purify himself, 3237
19:20 not been sprinkled on him, and he is **u**. 3238
19:21 of cleansing *will be* **u** till evening. 3237
19:22 that an **u** *person* touches becomes unclean, 3238
19:22 that an unclean person touches *becomes* **u**, 3237
19:22 and anyone who touches it *becomes* **u** 3237
Dt 12:15 **ceremonially u** and the clean may eat it. 3238
12:22 the **ceremonially u** and the clean may eat. 3238
14: 7 they are **ceremonially u** for you. 3238
14: 8 pig is also **u**; although it has a split hoof, 3238
14:10 you may not eat it; for you it is **u**. 3238
14:19 All flying insects that swarm are **u** to you; 3238
15:22 **ceremonially u** and the clean may eat it, 3238
23:10 If one of your men is **u** because of 3196+4202
26:14 nor have I removed any of it while I was **u**, 3238
Jdg 13: 4 and that you do not eat anything **u**, 3238
13: 7 and do not eat anything **u**, 3240
13:14 nor eat anything **u**. 3240
1Sa 20:26 to David to make him **ceremonially u** 1194+3196
20:26 ceremonially unclean—surely he is **u**. 3196+4202
2Ch 23:19 no one who was in any way **u** might enter. 3238
29:16 of the LORD's temple everything **u** 3240
Ezr 2:62 so were excluded from the priesthood *as* **u**. 1458
6:21 the **u practices** *of* their Gentile neighbors 3240
Ne 7:64 so *were* excluded from the priesthood *as* **u**. 1458
Ecc 9: 2 the good and the bad, the clean and the **u**, 3238
Isa 6: 5 For I am a man of **u** lips, 3238
6: 5 and I live among a people of **u** lips, 3238
35: 8 The **u** will not journey on it; 3238
52:11 Touch no **u** *thing!* 3238
64: 6 All of us have become like one *who* is **u**, 3238
65: 4 and whose pots hold broth of **u meat;** 7002
Jer 13:27 How long *will you be* **u?**" 3197+4202
La 1: 8 and so has become **u**. 5765
1:17 Jerusalem has become an **u thing** 5614
4:15 "Go away! You are **u!**" 3238
Eze 4:14 No **u** meat has ever entered my mouth." 7002
7:19 and their gold will be an **u thing.** 5614
7:20 Therefore I will turn these into an **u thing** 5614
22:10 when they are **ceremonially u**. 3238
22:26 that there is no difference between the **u** 3238
44:23 to distinguish between the **u** and the clean. 3238
Hos 9: 3 Ephraim will return to Egypt and eat **u** food 3238
9: 4 all who eat them *will be* **u**. 3237
Mt 15:11 into a man's mouth *does* not **make** him '**u**,' *3124*
15:11 that *is* **what makes** him '**u**.' " *3124*
15:18 and these **make** a man '**u**.' *3124*
15:20 These are what **make** a man '**u**'; *3124*
15:20 unwashed hands does not **make** him '**u**.' " *3124*
23:27 of dead men's bones and everything **u**. *174*
Mk 7: 2 eating food *with* hands that were "**u**," *3123*
7: 5 of eating their food *with* '**u**' hands?" *3123*
7:15 a man can **make** him '**u**' by going into him. *3124*
7:15 of a man that **makes** him '**u**.' " *3124*
7:18 a man from the outside can **make** him '**u**'? *3124*
7:20 of a man is what **makes** him '**u**.' *3124*
7:23 from inside and **make** a man '**u**.' " *3124*
Ac 10:14 "I have never eaten anything impure or **u**." *176*
10:28 that I should not call any man impure or **u**. *176*
11: 8 or **u** has ever entered my mouth.' *176*
Ro 14:14 I am fully convinced that no food is **u** *3123*
14:14 But if anyone regards something as **u**, *3123*
14:14 then for him it is **u**. *3123*
1Co 7:14 Otherwise your children would be **u**, *176*
2Co 6:17 Touch no **u** *thing,* and I will receive you." *176*
Heb 9:13 who *are* **ceremonially u** sanctify them *3124*
Rev 18: 2 a haunt *for* every **u** and detestable bird. *176*

UNCLEANNESS (18) [UNCLEAN]

Lev 5: 3 " 'Or if he touches human **u**— 3240
7:21 whether human **u** or an unclean animal 3240
14:19 for the one to be cleansed from his **u**. 3240
15: 3 how his discharge will bring about **u**: 3240
15:30 the LORD for the **u** *of* her discharge. 3240
15:31 in their **u** for defiling my dwelling place, 3240
16:16 for the Most Holy Place because of the **u** 3240
16:16 among them in the midst of their **u**. 3240
16:19 to consecrate it from the **u** *of* the Israelites. 3240
18:19 to have sexual relations during the **u** 3240
22: 5 whatever the **u** may be. 3240
Nu 19:13 his **u** remains on him. 3240
2Sa 11: 4 (She had purified herself from her **u**.) 3240
Eze 22:15 and I will put an end to your **u**. 3240
36:17 like a **woman's monthly u** in my sight. 2021+3240+5614
36:29 I will save you from all your **u**. 3240
39:24 according to their **u** and their offenses, 3240
Jn 18:28 and to avoid **ceremonial u** the Jews did *3620*

UNCLOTHED (1)

2Co 5: 4 because we do not wish *to be* **u** but to *1694*

UNCOMELY (KJV) See IMPROPERLY, UNPRESENTABLE

UNCONCERNED (1)

Eze 16:49 were arrogant, overfed and **u**; 8932+9200

UNCONDEMNED (KJV) See HASN'T BEEN FOUND GUILTY, WITHOUT A TRIAL

UNCORRUPTIBLE (KJV) See IMMORTAL

UNCOVER (2) [UNCOVERED, UNCOVERS]

Ru 3: 4 Then go and **u** his feet and lie down. 1655
Jer 49:10 *I will* **u** his hiding places, 1655

UNCOVERED (12) [UNCOVER]

Ge 9:21 he became drunk and *lay* **u** inside his tent. 1655
44:16 God *has* **u** your servants' guilt. 5162
Lev 20:18 and she *has* also **u** it. 1655
Ru 3: 7 approached quietly, **u** his feet and lay down. 1655
Job 26: 6 before God; Destruction lies **u**. 401+4064
Isa 47: 3 be exposed and your shame **u**. 8011
57: 8 Forsaking me, *you* **u** your bed, 1655
Eze 16:57 before your wickedness **was u**. 1655
Hab 3: 9 *You* **u** your bow, you called for many 6423+6880
1Co 11: 5 *with* her head **u** dishonors her head— *184*
11:13 a woman to pray to God with her head **u**? *184*
Heb 4:13 Everything is **u** and laid bare before the *1218*

UNCOVERS (2) [UNCOVER]

Ex 21:33 "If a man **u** a pit or digs one and fails 7337
Isa 22: 6 charioteers and horses; Kir **u** the shield. 6867

UNCTION (KJV) See ANOINTING

UNCUT (2)

Jos 8:31 the Law of Moses—an altar of **u** stones, 8969
Job 8:12 While still growing and **u**, 4202+7786

UNDEFILED (KJV) See BLAMELESS, FAULTLESS, FLAWLESS, PERFECT, PURE, NEVER SPOIL

UNDENIABLE (1)

Ac 19:36 Therefore, since these facts are **u**, *394*

UNDEPENDABLE (1)

Job 6:15 brothers are as **u** as intermittent streams, 953

UNDER (370)

Ge 1: 7 and separated the water **u** the expanse 4946+9393
1: 9 "Let the water **u** the sky be gathered 4946+9393
4:11 Now you *are* **u a curse** and driven from 826
6:17 earth to destroy all life **u** the heavens, 4946+9393
7:19 and all the high mountains **u** 9393
17:18 Ishmael might live **u** your **blessing!**" 4200+7156
18: 4 then you may all wash your feet and rest **u** 9393
18: 8 While they ate, he stood near them **u** a tree. 9393
19: 8 for they have come **u** the protection 928
21:15 she put the boy **u** one of the bushes. 9393
24: 2 "Put your hand **u** my thigh. 9393
24: 9 So the servant put his hand **u** the thigh 9393
28:11 he put it **u** his **head** and lay down to sleep. 5265
28:18 the stone he had placed **u** his **head** and set it 5265
30:29 how your livestock has fared **u** my **care.** 907
35: 4 Jacob buried them **u** the oak at Shechem. 9393
35: 8 and was buried **u** the oak below Bethel. 9393
39:23 The warden paid no attention to anything **u** 928
41:35 that are coming and store up the grain **u** 9393
47:29 put your hand **u** my thigh and promise 9393
48: 6 be reckoned **u** the names of their brothers. 6584
Ex 6: 6 the LORD, and I will bring you out from **u** 9393
6: 7 who brought you out from **u** the yoke of 9393
17:12 a stone and put it **u** him and he sat on it. 9393
17:14 the memory of Amalek from **u** heaven." 9393
23: 5 of someone who hates you fallen down **u** 9393
24:10 **U** his feet was something like a pavement 9393
25:35 be **u** the first pair of branches extending 9393
25:35 a second bud **u** the second pair, 9393
25:35 and a third bud **u** the third pair— 9393
26:19 and make forty silver bases to go **u** them— 9393
26:19 one **u** each projection. 4200
26:21 and forty silver bases—two **u** each frame. 9393
26:25 two **u** each frame. 9393
27: 5 Put it **u** the ledge of the altar so 9393
36:24 and made forty silver bases to go **u** them— 9393
36:24 one **u** each projection. 4200
36:26 and forty silver bases—two **u** each frame. 9393
36:30 two **u** each frame. 9393
37:21 One bud was **u** the first pair 9393
37:21 a second bud **u** the second pair, 9393
37:21 and a third bud **u** the third pair— 9393
38: 4 to be **u** its ledge, halfway up the altar. 9393
38:21 the Levites **u** the direction of Ithamar son 928
Lev 15:10 the things that were **u** him will be unclean 9393
27:32 that passes **u** the shepherd's rod— 9393
Nu 1:52 in his own camp **u** his own standard. 6584
2: 2 each man **u** his standard with the banners 6584
2: 3 of Judah are to encamp **u** their standard. NIH
2:10 be the divisions of the camp of Reuben **u** NIH
2:17 each in his own place **u** his standard. 4200
2:18 be the divisions of the camp of Ephraim **u** NIH
2:25 be the divisions of the camp of Dan, **u** NIH
2:31 They will set out last, **u** their standards. 4200
2:34 is the way they encamped **u** their standards, 4200
4:27 is to be done **u** the direction of Aaron 6584
4:28 be **u** the direction of Ithamar son of Aaron, 928
4:33 of Meeting **u** the direction of Ithamar son 928
5:19 priest *shall* **put** the woman **u oath** 8678
5:21 to put the woman **u** this curse of the oath— 928
6:18 and put it in the fire that is **u** the sacrifice of 9393
7: 8 They were all **u** the direction 928
8:22 the Tent of Meeting **u** the **supervision** 4200+7156
10:14 of Judah went first, **u** their standard. 4200
10:18 of Reuben went next, **u** their standard. 4200
10:22 of Ephraim went next, **u** their standard. 4200
10:25 the divisions of the camp of Dan set out, **u** 4200
16:31 the ground **u** them split apart 9393
19: 2 and that *has* never **been u** a yoke. 6584+6590
22:27 she lay down **u** Balaam, 9393
30:10 a vow or obligates herself by a pledge **u** 928
31:49 "Your servants have counted the soldiers **u** 928
33: 1 by divisions **u** the leadership of Moses 928
Dt 2:25 and fear of you on all the nations **u** heaven. 9393
4:19 to all the nations **u** heaven. 9393
7:24 and you will wipe out their names from **u** 9393
9:14 and blot out their name from **u** heaven. 9393
12: 2 and on the hills and **u** every spreading tree 9393
21:23 who is hung on a tree is *u* God's **curse.** AIT
25:19 the memory of Amalek from **u** heaven. 9393
29:20 the LORD will blot out his name from **u** 9393
30: 4 to the **most distant land** *u* the heavens, AIT
Jos 2: 6 up to the roof and hidden them **u** the stalks 928
9:23 You *are* now **u a curse:** 826
18: 1 country **was brought u** their **control,** 3899
24:26 a large stone and set it up there **u** the oak 9393
Jdg 1: 7 and big toes cut off have picked up scraps **u** 9393
2:18 they groaned **u** those who oppressed 4946+7156

Jdg 3:16 which he strapped to his right thigh **u** 4946+9393
4: 5 She held court **u** the Palm of Deborah 9393
6:11 of the LORD came and sat down **u** the oak 9393
6:19 and offered them to him **u** the oak. 9393
9:29 If only this people were **u** my command! 928
9:31 **U cover** he sent messengers to Abimelech, 928+9564
Ru 2:12 **u** whose wings you have come to take 9393
1Sa 2:11 the boy ministered before the LORD **u** 907+7156
2:27 when they were in Egypt **u** Pharaoh? 1074+4200
3: 1 ministered before the LORD **u** Eli. 4200+7156
14: 2 of Gibeah **u** a pomegranate tree in Migron. 9393
14:24 **bound** the people **u an oath,** 457
14:28 **bound** the army **u a strict oath,** 8678+8678
22: 6 was seated **u** the tamarisk tree on the hill 9393
31:13 and buried them **u** a tamarisk tree at Jabesh, 9393
2Sa 10:10 He put the rest of the men **u** the command 928
11:16 So while Joab *had* the city **u siege,** 9068
18: 2 a third **u** the command of Joab, 928
18: 2 under the command of Joab, a third **u** 928+3338
18: 2 and a third **u** Ittai the Gittite. 928+3338
18: 9 and as the mule went **u** the thick branches 9393
20: 3 the palace and put them in a house **u guard.** 5466
20: 7 warriors went out **u the command of** 339
22:10 dark clouds were **u** his feet. 9393
22:48 who puts the nations **u** me, 9393
1Ki 4:25 each man **u** his own vine and fig tree. 9393
5: 3 until the LORD put his enemies **u** his feet. 9393
7:32 The four wheels were **u** the panels, 4946+9393
7:44 the Sea and the twelve bulls **u** it; 9393
13:14 He found him sitting **u** an oak tree 9393
14:23 and Asherah poles on every high hill and **u** 9393
19: 4 sat down **u** it and prayed that he might die. 9393
19: 5 Then he lay down **u** the tree and fell asleep. 9393
2Ki 9:13 and spread them **u** him on the bare steps. 9393
11: 4 a covenant with them and **put** them **u oath** 8678
13: 3 for a long time he kept them **u** the power 928
14:27 the name of Israel from **u** heaven, 9393
16: 4 on the hilltops and **u** every spreading tree. 9393
17: 7 from **u** the power of Pharaoh king of Egypt. 9393
17:10 and Asherah poles on every high hill and **u** 9393
25: 2 The city was kept **u** siege until 928
25:10 **u** the commander of the imperial guard, 889
1Ch 10:12 Then they buried their bones **u** the great tree 9393
12:32 with all their relatives **u** their command; 6584
17: 1 of the covenant of the LORD is **u** a tent." 9393
19:11 He put the rest of the men **u** the command 928
23:24 as they were registered **u** their names 928
23:32 **u** their brothers the descendants of Aaron, NIH
25: 2 of Asaph were **u** the supervision of Asaph, 6584
25: 2 who prophesied **u** the king's supervision. 6584
25: 3 **u** the supervision of their father Jeduthun, 6584
25: 6 All these men were **u** the supervision 6584
25: 6 and Heman were **u** the supervision of 6584
2Ch 4:15 the Sea and the twelve bulls **u** it; 9393
14: 5 and the kingdom was at peace **u** him. 4200+7156
17: 5 The LORD established the kingdom **u** 928
24:13 and the repairs progressed **u** them. 928+3338
26:11 the secretary and Maaseiah the officer **u** 6584
26:13 **U** their command was an army of 307,500 6584
28: 4 on the hilltops and **u** every spreading tree. 9393
31:13 Benaiah were supervisors **u** Conaniah 3338+4946
32:10 that you remain in Jerusalem **u** siege? 928
34: 4 **U** his **direction** the altars of the Baals 4200+7156
Ezr 4:14 *we are* **u obligation** *to* the palace 10419+10420
5: 8 and is making rapid progress **u** 10089
5:16 to the present *it has been* **u construction** 10111
6:14 the Jews continued to build and prosper **u** 10089
10: 5 **put** the leading priests and Levites and all Israel **u oath** 8678
Ne 3: 5 not put their shoulders to the **work** *u* AIT
3: 7 places **u** the authority of the governor 4200
3:17 the repairs were made by the Levites **u** NIH
3:18 by their countrymen **u** Binnui son NIH
6:18 many in Judah were **u oath** to him, 1251+8652
11:23 The singers were **u** the king's orders, 6584
12:42 The choirs sang **u** the direction NIH
Est 2: 3 Let them be placed **u** the care of Hegai, 448
2: 8 to the citadel of Susa and put **u** the care 448
Job 7:12 that you put me **u guard?** 5464+6584
20:12 in his mouth and he hides it **u** his tongue, 9393
26: 8 yet the clouds do not burst **u** their weight. 9393
28:24 the earth and sees everything **u** the heavens. 9393
35: 9 "Men cry out **u** a load of oppression; 4946
37:17 when the land lies hushed **u** the south wind, 4946
38:14 The earth takes shape like **clay** *u* a seal; AIT
40:21 **U** the lotus plants he lies, 9393
41:11 Everything **u** heaven belongs to me. 9393
Ps 8: 6 you put everything **u** his feet: 9393
10: 7 trouble and evil are **u** his tongue. 9393
10:10 they fall **u** his strength. 928
18: 9 dark clouds were **u** his feet. 9393
18:47 who subdues nations **u** me, 9393
47: 3 He subdued nations **u** us, 9393
47: 3 nations under us, peoples **u** our feet. 9393
56:12 I am **u** vows to you, O God; 6584
90: 9 All our days pass away **u** your wrath; 928
91: 4 and **u** his wings you will find refuge; 9393
95: 7 the flock **u** his **care.** 3338
144: 2 who subdues peoples **u** me. 9393
Pr 22:14 *he who is* **u** the LORD's **wrath** will fall 2404
22:27 your very bed will be snatched from **u** you. 9393
29:11 but a wise man keeps himself **u control.** 294+928
29:24 *he is* **put u oath** and dare not testify. 460+9048
30:21 "**U** three things the earth trembles, 9393
30:21 **u** four it cannot bear up: 9393
Ecc 1: 3 all his labor at which he toils **u** the sun? 9393

Ecc 1: 9 there is nothing new **u** the sun. 9393
1:13 explore by wisdom all that is done **u** the sun 9393
1:14 I have seen all the things that are done **u** 9393
2: 3 to see what was worthwhile for men to do **u** 9393
2:11 nothing was gained **u** the sun. 9393
2:17 that is done **u** the sun was grievous to me. 9393
2:18 I hated all the things I had toiled for **u** the 9393
2:19 and skill **u** the sun. 9393
2:20 to despair over all my toilsome labor **u** 9393
2:22 and anxious striving with which he labors **u** 9393
3: 1 and a season for every activity **u** heaven: 9393
3:16 And I saw something else **u** the sun: 9393
4: 1 the oppression that was taking place **u** 9393
4: 3 who has not seen the evil that is done **u** 9393
4: 7 Again I saw something meaningless **u** 9393
4:15 and walked **u** the sun followed the youth, 9393
5:13 I have seen a grievous evil **u** the sun: 9393
5:18 to find satisfaction in his toilsome labor **u** 9393
6: 1 I have seen another evil **u** the sun, 9393
6:12 Who can tell him what will happen **u** 9393
7: 6 Like the crackling of thorns **u** the pot, 9393
8: 9 as I applied my mind to everything done **u** 9393
8:15 a man **u** the sun than to eat and drink and 9393
8:15 the days of the life God has given him **u** 9393
8:17 No one can comprehend what goes on **u** 9393
9: 3 This is the evil in everything that happens **u** 9393
9: 6 a part in anything that happens **u** the sun. 9393
9: 9 that God has given you **u** the sun— 9393
9: 9 in life and in your toilsome labor **u** the sun. 9393
9:11 I have seen something else **u** the sun: 9393
9:13 also saw **u** the sun this example of wisdom 9393
10: 5 There is an evil I have seen **u** the sun, 9393
SS 2: 6 His left arm is **u** my head, 9393
4:11 milk and honey are **u** your tongue. 9393
8: 3 His left arm is **u** my head 9393
8: 5 **U** the apple tree I roused you; 9393
Isa 1: 8 like a city **u siege.** 7443
10:16 **u** his pomp a fire will be kindled like 9393
25:10 be trampled **u** him as straw is trampled 9393
34:15 for her young **u** the shadow of her wings; 928
57: 5 among the oaks and **u** every spreading tree; 9393
57: 5 in the ravines and **u** the overhanging crags. 9393
Jer 2:20 and **u** every spreading tree you lay down as 9393
3: 6 She has gone up on every high hill and **u** 9393
3:13 to foreign gods **u** every spreading tree, 9393
7:29 and abandoned this **generation** *that is u* AIT
10:11 from the earth and from **u** the heavens.' " 10757
10:17 you who live **u** siege. 928
27: 8 of Babylon or bow its neck **u** his yoke, 928
27:11 if any nation will bow its neck **u** the yoke 928
27:12 "Bow your neck **u** the yoke of the king 928
33:13 flocks will again pass **u** the hand of the one 6584
38:11 with him and went to a room **u** the treasury 9393
38:12 "Put these old rags and worn-out clothes **u** 9393
52: 5 The city was kept **u** siege until 928
52:14 The whole Babylonian army **u** the 907
52:20 the Sea and the twelve bronze bulls **u** it, 9393
La 3:66 and destroy them from **u** the heavens of 9393
4:20 that **u** his shadow we would live among 928
5:13 boys stagger **u** loads of wood. 928
Eze 1: 8 **U** their wings on their four sides 4946+9393
1:23 **U** the expanse their wings were stretched 9393
4: 3 It will be **u** siege, and you shall besiege it. 928
6:13 **u** every spreading tree and every leafy oak 9393
10: 8 (**U** the wings of the cherubim could 9393
10:21 and **u** their wings was what looked like 9393
17: 6 but its roots remained **u** it. 9393
17:13 made a treaty with him, putting him **u** oath. 928
20:37 I will take note of you as you pass **u** 9393
31: 6 all the beasts of the field gave birth **u** 9393
31:12 the nations of the earth came out **from** *u* AIT
32:27 whose swords were placed **u** their heads? 9393
46:23 with places for fire built all around **u** 4946+9393
47: 1 from **u** the threshold of the temple toward 9393
47: 1 down from **u** the south side of the temple, 9393
Da 4:12 **U** it the beasts of the field found shelter, 10757
4:14 Let the animals flee from **u** it and the birds 10757
7:27 of the kingdoms **u** the whole heaven will 10757
9:12 **U** the whole heaven nothing has ever been 9393
Hos 4:13 **u** oak, poplar and terebinth, 9393
8:10 to waste away **u** the oppression of 4946
Mic 4: 4 Every man will sit **u** his own vine and 9393
4: 4 under his own vine and **u** his own fig tree, 9393
Zec 3:10 of you will invite his neighbor to sit **u** 9393
Mal 1: 4 a people always **u the wrath** *of* the LORD. 2404
3: 9 You are **u** a curse—the whole nation 928
4: 3 be ashes **u** the soles of your feet on the day 9393
Mt 2:16 vicinity who were two years **old** and **u,** *3006*
5:15 Neither do people light a lamp and put it **u** *5679*
7: 6 you do, they may trample them **u** their feet, *1877*
8: 8 not deserve to have you come **u** my roof. *5679*
8: 9 For I myself am a man **u** authority, *5679*
8: 9 a man under authority, with soldiers **u** me. *5679*
22:44 at my right hand until I put your enemies **u** *5691*
23:37 as a hen gathers her chicks **u** her wings, *5679*
26:63 "*I* **charge** you **u oath** by the living God: *2019*
Mk 4:21 "Do you bring in a lamp to put it **u** a bowl *5679*
5:26 She had suffered a great deal **u** the care *5679*
7:28 "but even the dogs **u** the table eat *5691*
12:36 at my right hand until I put your enemies **u** *5691*
14:44 arrest him and lead him away **u guard."** *857*
Lk 7: 6 not deserve to have you come **u** my roof. *5679*
7: 8 For I myself am a man **u** authority, *5679*
7: 8 a man under authority, with soldiers **u** me. *5679*
8:16 hides it in a jar or puts it **u** a bed. *5691*
8:29 chained hand and foot and **kept u guard,** *5875*
11:33 where it will be hidden, or **u** a bowl. *5679*

Lk 13:34 as a hen gathers her chicks **u** her wings, *5679*
23: 7 that Jesus was **u** Herod's jurisdiction, *1666*
23:40 "since you are **u** the same sentence? *1877*
Jn 1:48 "I saw you while you were still **u** *5679*
1:50 because I told you I saw you **u** the fig tree. *5691*
13: 3 Father had put all things **u** his **power,** *1650+5931*
Ac 2: 5 from every nation **u** heaven. *5679*
4:12 for there is no other name **u** heaven given *5679*
7:45 our fathers **u** Joshua brought it with them *3552*
10:38 and healing all who *were* **u the power** of *2872*
22: 3 **U** Gamaliel I was thoroughly trained in the law of our fathers *3836+4123+4546*
23:35 Paul *be* **kept u guard** in Herod's palace. *5875*
24: 2 "We have enjoyed a long period of peace **u** *1328*
24:23 the centurion *to* **keep** Paul **u guard** but *5498*
27:17 *they* **passed** ropes **u** the ship itself **to hold it together.** *5690*
Ro 2:12 and all who sin **u** the law will be judged by *1877*
3: 9 that Jews and Gentiles alike are all **u** sin. *5679*
3:19 it says to those who are **u** the law, *1877*
4:10 **U what circumstances** was it credited? *4802*
6:14 because you are not **u** law, but under grace. *5679*
6:14 because you are not under law, but **u** grace. *5679*
6:15 because we are not **u** law but under grace? *5679*
6:15 because we are not under law but **u** grace? *5679*
16:20 of peace will soon crush Satan **u** your feet. *5679*
1Co 7:37 *who* **is u** no compulsion but has control *2400*
9:20 To those **u** the law I became like one under *5679*
9:20 To those under the law I became like one **u** *5679*
9:20 the law (though I myself am not **u** the law), *5679*
9:20 so as to win those **u** the law. *5679*
9:21 from God's law but am **u** Christ's **law),** *1937*
10: 1 that our forefathers were all **u** the cloud and *5679*
10:13 a way out so that you can **stand up u** it. *5722*
11:31 *we* would not **come u judgment.** *3212*
15:25 until he has put all his enemies **u** his feet. *5679*
15:27 For *he* "*has* **put** everything **u** his feet" *5718*
15:27 that "everything" *has been* **put u** him, *5718*
15:27 who **put** everything **u** Christ. *5718*
15:28 to him who **put** everything **u** him, *5718*
2Co 1: 8 *We were* **u** great **pressure,** *976*
9: 7 not reluctantly or **u** compulsion, *1666*
11:12 to **cut** the ground **from u** those who want *1716*
11:32 the governor *u* **King Aretas** had the city of *AIT*
Gal 3:10 All who rely on observing the law are **u** *5679*
3:25 we are no longer **u** the supervision of *5679*
4: 3 we were in slavery **u** the basic principles of *5679*
4: 4 born of a woman, born **u** law, *5679*
4: 5 to redeem those **u** law, *5679*
4:21 Tell me, you who want to be **u** the law, *5679*
5:18 you are led by the Spirit, you are not **u** law. *5679*
Eph 1:10 **bring** all things in heaven and on earth **together u one head,** *368*
1:22 And God **placed** all things **u** his feet *5718*
Php 2:10 in heaven and on earth and **u the earth,** *2973*
3:21 **bring** everything **u** his **control,** *5718*
Col 1:23 to every creature **u** heaven, *5679*
1Ti 3: 6 and fall **u** the same judgment as the devil. *1650*
6: 1 All who are **u** the yoke of slavery *5679*
Heb 2: 8 and **put** everything **u** his feet." *5718*
2: 8 In **putting** everything **u** him, *5718*
9:15 to set them free from the sins committed **u** *2093*
10:29 **trampled** the Son of God **u foot,** *2922*
Jas 1:12 the man who perseveres *u* **trial,** *AIT*
1Pe 2:19 *man* **bears up u** the pain of unjust suffering *5722*
5: 2 that is **u** your care, serving as overseers— *1877*
5: 6 therefore, **u** God's mighty hand, *5679*
1Jn 5:19 and that the whole world *is* **u the control** *3023*
Rev 4: 8 with eyes all around, even **u** his wings. *2277*
5: 3 on earth or **u** the earth could open the scroll *5691*
5:13 and on earth and **u** the earth and on the sea, *5691*
6: 9 I saw **u** the altar the souls of those who *5691*
12: 1 with the sun, with the moon **u** her feet and *5691*

UNDERFOOT (11) [FOOT]

2Ki 9:33 and the horses as *they* **trampled** her **u.** 8252
14: 9 and **trampled** the thistle **u.** 8252
2Ch 25:18 and **trampled** the thistle **u.** 8252
Isa 14:19 Like a corpse **trampled u,** 1008
28: 3 will be trampled **u.** 928+8079
La 3:34 To crush **u** all prisoners in the land, 8079+9393
Da 7: 7 and trampled **u** whatever was left. 10089+10655
7:19 and trampled **u** whatever was left. 10089+10655
8:13 and of the host that will be **trampled u?"** 5330
Mic 7:10 even now she will be **trampled u** like mire 5330
7:19 *you will* **tread** our sins **u** and hurl all our 3899

UNDERGARMENT (1) [GARMENT]

Jn 19:23 one for each of them, with the **u** remaining. *5945*

UNDERGARMENTS (5) [GARMENT]

Ex 28:42 "Make linen **u** as a covering for the body, 4829
39:28 and the **u** of finely twisted linen. 965+4829
Lev 6:10 with linen **u** next to his body, 4829
16: 4 with linen **u** next to his body; 4829
Eze 44:18 and linen **u** around their waists. 4829

UNDERGIRDING (KJV) See UNDER THE SHIP

UNDERGO (2) [UNDERGOES, UNDERGOING]

Ge 17:11 You *are to* **u circumcision,** 906+1414+4576+6889

Lk 12:50 But I have a **baptism** *to* **u**, *966+967*

UNDERGOES (1) [UNDERGO]

Heb 12: 8 (and everyone **u** discipline), *1181+3581*

UNDERGOING (1) [UNDERGO]

1Pe 5: 9 the world *are* **u** the same kind of sufferings. *2200*

UNDERGROWTH (2) [GROWTH]

Job 30: 7 among the bushes and huddled in the **u**. 3017
Isa 17: 9 be like places abandoned to thickets and **u**. 580

UNDERLINGS (2)

2Ki 19: 6 those words with which the **u** *of* the king 5853
Isa 37: 6 those words with which the **u** *of* the king 5853

UNDERMINE (1)

Job 15: 4 But you even **u** piety and hinder devotion 7296

UNDERNEATH (4) [BENEATH]

Dt 33:27 and **u** are the everlasting arms. 4946+9393
Jos 7:21 inside my tent, with the silver **u**." 9393
7:22 hidden in his tent, with the silver **u**. 9393
2Ki 6:30 there, **u**, he had sackcloth on his body. 1074+4946

UNDERSETTERS (KJV) See HANDLES, SUPPORTS

UNDERSIDES (1)

Job 41:30 His **u** are jagged potsherds, 9393

UNDERSTAND (124) [UNDERSTANDING, UNDERSTANDS, UNDERSTOOD]

Ge 11: 7 so *they will* not **u** each other." 9048
42:23 not realize that Joseph *could* **u** them, 9048
Dt 9: 6 **U**, then, that it is not because of your 3359
28:49 a nation whose language *you will* not **u**, 9048
32:29 If only they were wise and *would* **u** this 8505
1Sa 24:11 Now **u** and recognize that I am not guilty 3359
28: 1 *"You* **must u** that you and your men 3359+3359
2Ki 18:26 to your servants in Aramaic, since we **u** it. 9048
Ne 8: 2 and women and all who were able to **u**. 9048
8: 3 women and others *who could* **u**. 1067
8: 8 the people *could* **u** what was being read. 1067
10:28 and daughters who are able *to* **u**— 1067
Job 26:14 Who then *can* **u** the thunder of his power?" 1067
32: 9 not only the aged *who* **u** what is right. 1067
36:29 *Who can* **u** how he spreads out the clouds, 1067
38: 4 Tell me, if *you* **u**. 1069+3359
42: 3 Surely I spoke of things *I did* not **u**, 1067
Ps 14: 2 of men to see if there are *any who* **u**, 8505
53: 2 of men to see if there are *any who* **u**, 8505
73:16 When I tried to **u** all this, 3359
81: 5 where we heard a language *we did* not **u**. 3359
82: 5 "They know nothing, *they* **u** nothing. 1067
92: 6 man does not know, fools *do* not **u**, 1067
119:27 **Let** me **u** the teaching of your precepts; 1067
119:79 *those who* **u** your statutes. 3359
119:125 that *I may* **u** your statutes. 3359
Pr 2: 5 then *you will* **u** the fear of the LORD 1067
2: 9 Then *you will* **u** what is right and just 1067
20:24 How then *can* anyone **u** his own way? 1067
28: 5 Evil men *do* not **u** justice, 1067
28: 5 but those who seek the LORD **u** it fully. 1067
30:18 four *that I do* not **u**: 3359
Ecc 7:25 So I turned my mind to **u**, 3359
7:25 the scheme of things and to **u** the stupidity 3359
11: 5 so *you* cannot **u** the work of God, 3359
Isa 1: 3 my people *do* not **u**." 1067
6:10 **u** with their hearts, and turn and be healed." 1067
32: 4 The mind of the rash will know and **u**, 1067
36:11 to your servants in Aramaic, since we **u** it. 9048
41:20 may see and know, may consider and **u**, 8505
42:25 yet *they did* not **u**; 3359
43:10 that you may know and believe me and **u** 1067
44:18 They know nothing, *they* **u** nothing; 1067
44:18 and their minds closed so they cannot **u**. 8505
52:15 and what they have not heard, *they will* **u**. 1067
Jer 5:15 whose speech *you do* not **u**. 9048
9:12 What man is wise enough *to* **u** this? 1067
15:15 You **u**, O LORD; remember me and care for 3359
17: 9 and beyound cure. Who *can* **u** it? 3359
23:20 In days to come *you will* **u** it **clearly.** 1067+1069
30:24 In days to come *you will* **u** this. 1067
31:19 after I *came to* **u**, I beat my breast. 3359
Eze 3: 6 whose words *you* cannot **u**. 9048
12: 3 Perhaps *they will* **u**, 8011
Da 1: 4 well informed, **quick to u**, 1067+4529
1:17 And Daniel *could* **u** visions and dreams 1067
2:30 and that *you may* **u** what went through 10313
5:23 which cannot see or hear or **u**. 10313
8:15 was watching the vision and trying to **u** it, 1069
8:17 "**u** that the vision concerns the time of 1067
9:23 consider the message and **u** the vision: 1067
9:25 "Know and **u** this: 8505
12: 8 I heard, but *I did* not **u**. 1067
12:10 None of the wicked *will* **u**, 1067
12:10 but those who are wise *will* **u**. 1067
Hos 14: 9 Who is discerning? *He will* **u** them. 3359
Mic 4:12 *they do* not **u** his plan, 1067
Mt 13:13 though hearing, *they do* not hear or **u**. *5317*
13:15 **u** with their hearts and turn, *5317*
13:19 about the kingdom and *does* not **u** it, *5317*
15:10 the crowd to him and said, "Listen and **u**. *5317*
16: 9 *Do you* still not **u**? *3783*
16:11 How is it *you* don't **u** that I was not talking *3783*
24:15 the prophet Daniel—*let* the reader **u**— *3783*
24:43 But **u** this: If the owner of the house *1182*
Mk 4:13 "Don't *you* **u** this parable? *3857*
4:13 How then *will you* **u** any parable? *1182*
4:33 as much as they could **u**. *201*
7:14 "Listen to me, everyone, and **u** this. *5317*
8:17 Do you still not see or **u**? *5317*
8:21 He said to them, *"Do you* still not **u**?" *5317*
9:32 But they *did* **not u** what he meant *51*
13:14 it does not belong—*let* the reader **u**— *3783*
14:68 "I don't know or **u** what you're talking *2179*
Lk 2:50 they *did* not **u** what he was saying to them. *5317*
8:10 though hearing, *they may* not **u**.' *5317*
9:45 But they *did* **not u** what this meant. *51*
12:39 But **u** this: If the owner of the house *1182*
18:34 The disciples *did* not **u** any of this. *5317*
24:45 *so they could* **u** the Scriptures. *5317*
Jn 3:10 said Jesus, "and *do you* not **u** these things? *1182*
8:27 *They did* not **u** that he was telling them *1182*
10: 6 but they *did* not **u** what he was telling them. *1182*
10:38 that you may know and **u** that the Father is *1182*
12:16 At first his disciples *did* not **u** all this. *1182*
12:40 nor **u** with their hearts, nor turn— *3783*
13: 7 but later *you will* **u**." *1182*
13:12 *"Do you* **u** what I have done for you?" *1182*
16:18 *We* don't **u** what he is saying." *3857*
20: 9 not **u** from Scripture that Jesus had to rise *3857*
Ac 8:30 *"Do you* **u** what you are reading?" *1182*
22: 9 not **u** the voice of him who was speaking *201*
28:27 **u** with their hearts and turn, *5317*
Ro 7:15 *I do* not **u** what I do. *1182*
10:19 Again I ask: *Did* Israel not **u**? *1182*
15:21 and those who have not heard *will* **u**." *5317*
1Co 2:12 that *we may* **u** what God has freely given us. *3857*
2:14 and he cannot **u** them, *1182*
14:16 among **those who do not u** say "Amen" *2626*
14:23 **some who do not u** or some unbelievers *2626*
14:24 or **someone who does not u** come in *2626*
2Co 1:13 not write you anything you cannot read or **u**. *2105*
1:14 *you will* **come to u** fully that you can boast *2105*
Gal 3: 7 **U**, then, that those who believe are children *1182*
Eph 3: 4 *to* **u** my insight into the mystery of Christ, *3783*
5:17 but **u** what the Lord's will is. *5317*
Heb 11: 3 By faith *we* **u** that the universe was formed *3783*
2Pe 1:20 you must **u** that no prophecy of Scripture *1182*
2:12 men blaspheme in matters *they do* **not u**. *51*
3: 3 *you must* **u** that in the last days scoffers will *1182*
3: 9 in keeping his promise, as some **u** slowness. *2451*
3:16 contain some things that are **hard to u**, *1554*
Jude 1:10 against whatever *they do* not **u**; *3857*
1:10 and what things *they do* **u** by instinct, *2179*

UNDERSTANDING (115) [UNDERSTAND]

Dt 1:13 **u** and respected men from each of your 1067
4: 6 for this will show your wisdom and **u** to 1069
4: 6 this great nation is a wise and **u** people." 1067
32:21 angry by a nation that has **no u**. 5572
Jdg 13:18 you ask my name? It is **beyond u**." 7100
1Ki 4:29 a breadth of **u** as measureless as the sand 4213
1Ch 22:12 May the LORD give you discretion and **u** 1069
28:19 *he* **gave** me **u** *in* all the details of the plan." 8505
2Ch 30:22 who **showed** good **u** of the service of 8505+8507
Job 8:10 not bring forth words from their **u**? 4213
12:12 Does not long life bring **u**? 9312
12:13 counsel and **u** are his. 9312
17: 4 You have closed their minds to **u**; 8507
20: 3 and my **u** inspires me to reply. 1069
28:12 Where does **u** dwell? 1069
28:20 Where does **u** dwell? 1069
28:28 that is wisdom, and to shun evil is **u**.' " 1069
32: 8 breath of the Almighty, *that* **gives** him **u**. 1067
34:10 "So listen to me, you men of **u**. 4222
34:16 "If you have **u**, hear this; 1069
34:34 "Men of **u** declare, wise men who hear me 4222
36:26 How great is God—beyond *our* **u**! 3359
37: 5 he does great things beyond *our* **u**. 3359
38:36 with wisdom or gave **u** to the mind? 1069
Ps 32: 9 *which* **have** no **u** but must be controlled 1067
49: 3 the utterance from my heart will give **u**. 9312
49:20 A man who has riches without **u** is like 1067
111:10 all who follow his precepts have good **u**. 8507
119:34 **Give** me **u**, and I will keep your law 1067
119:73 **give** me **u** to learn your commands. 1067
119:100 *I* **have** more **u** than the elders, 1067
119:104 *I* **gain u** from your precepts; 1067
119:130 *it* **gives u** *to* the simple. 1067
119:144 **give** me **u** that I may live. 1067
119:169 **give** me **u** according to your word. 1067
136: 5 who by his **u** made the heavens, 9312
147: 5 his **u** has no limit. 9312
Pr 1: 2 for **u** words of insight; 1067
1: 6 for **u** proverbs and parables, 1067
2: 2 to wisdom and applying your heart to **u**, 9312
2: 3 you call out for insight and cry aloud for **u**, 9312
2: 6 from his mouth come knowledge and **u**. 9312
2:11 and **u** will guard you. 9312
3: 5 and lean not on your own **u**; 1069
3:13 the man who gains **u**, 9312
3:19 by **u** he set the heavens in place; 9312
4: 1 pay attention and gain **u**. 1069
4: 5 Get wisdom, get **u**; do not forget my words 1069
4: 7 Though it cost all you have, get **u**. 1069
7: 4 and call **u** your kinsman; 1069
8: 1 Does not **u** raise her voice? 9312
8: 5 you who are foolish, gain **u**. 4213
8:14 I have **u** and power. 1069
9: 6 walk in the way of **u**. 1069
9:10 and knowledge of the Holy One is **u**. 1069
10:23 but a man of **u** delights in wisdom. 9312
11:12 but a man of **u** holds his tongue. 9312
13:15 Good **u** wins favor, 8507
14:29 A patient man has great **u**, 9312
15:21 but a man of **u** keeps a straight course. 9312
15:32 but whoever heeds correction gains **u**. 4213
16:16 to choose **u** rather than silver! 1069
16:22 **U** is a fountain of life to those who have it, 8507
17:27 and a man of **u** is even-tempered. 9312
18: 2 in **u** but delights in airing his own opinions. 9312
19: 8 he who cherishes **u** prospers. 9312
20: 5 but a man of **u** draws them out. 9312
21:16 A man who strays from the path of **u** comes 8505
23:23 get wisdom, discipline and **u**. 1069
24: 3 and through **u** it is established; 9312
28: 2 a man of **u** and knowledge maintains order. 1067
30: 2 I do not have a man's **u**. 1069
Ecc 1:17 Then I applied myself to the **u** *of* wisdom, 3359
Isa 5:13 my people will go into exile for lack of **u**; 1981
6: 9 " 'Be ever hearing, but never **u**; 1067
10:13 and by my wisdom, because *I* **have u**. 1067
11: 2 the Spirit of wisdom and of **u**, 1069
27:11 For this is a people without **u**; 1069
28:19 The **u** *of* this message will bring sheer terror 1067
29:24 who are wayward in spirit will gain **u**; 1069
40:14 or showed him the path of **u**? 9312
40:28 and his **u** no one can fathom. 9312
44:19 no one has the knowledge or **u** to say, 9312
56:11 They are shepherds *who* lack **u**; 3359
Jer 3:15 who will lead you with knowledge and **u**. 8505
4:22 senseless children; they **have** no **u**. 1067
10:12 and stretched out the heavens by his **u**. 9312
51:15 and stretched out the heavens by his **u**. 9312
Eze 28: 4 and **u** you have gained wealth for yourself 9312
Da 1:17 and **u** of all kinds of literature and learning. 8505
1:20 In every matter of wisdom and **u** 1069
5:12 to have a keen mind and knowledge and **u**, 10684
8:27 appalled by the vision; it was beyond **u**. 1067
9:22 I have now come to give you insight and **u**. 1069
10: 1 The **u** *of* the message came to him in 1067
10:12 that you set your mind to **gain u** and 1067
Hos 4:11 old wine and new, which take away the **u** 4213
4:14 a people without **u** will come to ruin! 1067
Ob 1: 8 *men of* **u** in the mountains of Esau? 9312
Mt 13:14 " 'You will be ever hearing but never **u**; *5317*
Mk 4:12 and ever hearing but never **u**; *5317*
12:33 with all your **u** and with all your strength, *5304*
Lk 2:47 was amazed at his **u** and his answers. *5304*
Ac 28:26 "You will be ever hearing but never **u**; *5317*
Ro 10:19 make you angry by a nation that has **no u**." *852*
13:11 And do this, **u** the present time. *3857*
2Co 6: 6 in purity, **u**, patience and kindness; *1194*
Eph 1: 8 he lavished on us with all wisdom and **u**. *5860*
4:18 They are darkened *in* their **u** and separated *1379*
Php 4: 7 the peace of God, which transcends all **u**, *3808*
Col 1: 9 through all spiritual wisdom and **u**. *5304*
2: 2 the full riches *of* complete **u**, *5304*
Phm 1: 6 a **full u** of every good thing we have *2106*
Jas 3:13 Who is wise and **u** among you? *2184*
1Jn 5:20 of God has come and has given us **u**, *1379*

UNDERSTANDS (10) [UNDERSTAND]

Dt 29: 4 the LORD has not given you a mind that **u** 3359
1Ch 28: 9 and **u** every motive behind the thoughts. 1067
Job 28:23 God **u** the way to it and he alone knows 1067
Pr 29:19 though *he* **u**, he will not respond. 1067
Isa 57: 1 devout men are taken away, and no *one* **u** 1067
Jer 9:24 that *he* **u** and knows me, 8505
Mt 13:23 the man who hears the word and **u** it. *5317*
Ro 3:11 no one who **u**, no one who seeks God. *5317*
1Co 14: 2 Indeed, no one **u** him; he utters mysteries *201*
1Ti 6: 4 he is conceited and **u** nothing. *2179*

UNDERSTOOD (19) [UNDERSTAND]

1Ch 12:32 *who* **u** the times and knew what Israel 1069+3359
Ne 8:12 because *they* now **u** the words 1067
Est 1:13 he spoke with the wise men *who* **u** the times 3359
Job 13: 1 my ears have heard and **u** it. 1067
Ps 73:17 then *I* **u** their final destiny. 1067
Isa 40:13 Who *has* **u** the mind of the LORD, 9419
40:21 not **u** since the earth was founded? 1067
48: 8 You have neither heard nor **u**; 3359
Da 9: 2 I, Daniel, **u** from the Scriptures, 1067
Mt 13:51 *"Have you* **u** all these things?" *5317*
16:12 Then *they* **u** that he was not telling them *5317*
17:13 the disciples **u** that he was talking to them *5317*
Mk 6:52 for *they had* not **u** about the loaves; *5317*
Jn 1: 5 but the darkness *has* not **u** it. *2898*
13:28 but no one at the meal **u** why Jesus said this *1182*
Ro 1:20 *being* **u** from what has been made, *3783*
1Co 2: 8 None of the rulers of this age **u** it, *1182*
2Co 1:14 as *you have* **u** us in part, *2105*
Col 1: 6 the day you heard it and **u** God's grace *2105*

UNDERTAKEN (3) [UNDERTOOK]

1Ki 7:40 So Huram finished all the work *he had* **u** 6913
2Ch 4:11 So Huram finished the work *he had* **u** 6913

Lk 1: 1 Many *have* **u** to draw up an account of *2217*

UNDERTAKES (1) [UNDERTOOK]
Jos 6:26 the man who **u** to rebuild this city, Jericho: 7756

UNDERTOOK (4) [UNDERTAKEN, UNDERTAKES]
2Ki 18: 7 he was successful in whatever *he* **u.** 3655
2Ch 31:21 that *he* **u** in the service of God's temple and 2725
32:30 He succeeded in everything he **u.** 5126
Ecc 2: 4 *I* **u great** projects: I built houses for myself 1540

UNDESERVED (1)
Pr 26: 2 an **u** curse does not come to rest. 2855

UNDESIRABLE (1)
Jos 24:15 But if serving the LORD seems **u** to you, 8273

UNDETECTED (1)
Nu 5:13 from her husband and her impurity *is* **u** 6259

UNDIGNIFIED (1)
2Sa 6:22 *I will* **become** even more **u** than this, 7837

UNDISCIPLINED (1)
Pr 9:13 she is **u** and without knowledge. 7346

UNDISTURBED (2)
Job 12: 6 The tents of marauders *are* **u,** 8922
Isa 32:18 in secure homes, in **u** places of rest. 8633

UNDIVIDED (4)
1Ch 12:33 to help David with **u loyalty—**50,000 2256+4202+4213+4213
Ps 86:11 **give** me an **u** heart, that I may fear your 3479
Eze 11:19 an **u** heart and put a new spirit in them; 285
1Co 7:35 in a right way in **u** devotion to the Lord. *597*

UNDOING (2) [UNDONE]
2Ch 22: 4 they became his advisers, to his **u.** 5422
Pr 18: 7 A fool's mouth is his **u,** 4745

UNDONE (2) [UNDOING]
Jos 11:15 *he* **left** nothing **u** of all that the LORD 6073
Lk 11:42 the latter without **leaving** the former **u.** *4205*

UNDOUBTEDLY (1)
1Co 14:10 **U** there are all sorts of languages in *1623+5593*

UNDRESSED (KJV) See UNTENDED

UNDULY (1)
Pr 11:24 withholds **u,** but comes to poverty. 3841+4946

UNDYING (1)
Eph 6:24 love our Lord Jesus Christ with an **u** love. *914*

UNEATEN (1)
Job 20:18 he toiled for he must give back **u;** 1180+4202

UNENDING (1)
Jer 15:18 Why is my pain **u** and my wound grievous 5905

UNEQUALED (2)
Mt 24:21 great distress, **u** from the beginning of the world *1181+3888+4024*
Mk 13:19 be days of distress **u** from the beginning, *1181+3888+4024+5525*

UNEXPECTEDLY (2)
Ecc 9:12 so men are trapped by evil times that fall **u** 7328
Lk 21:34 and that day will close on you **u** like a trap. *167*

UNFADING (1)
1Pe 3: 4 the **u** beauty of a gentle and quiet spirit, *915*

UNFAILING (35)
Ex 15:13 "In your **u love** you will lead the people 2876
1Sa 20:14 But show me **u kindness** *like that of* 2876
2Sa 22:51 he shows **u kindness** to his anointed, 2876
Ps 6: 4 save me because of your **u love.** 2876
13: 5 But I trust in your **u love;** 2876
18:50 he shows **u kindness** to his anointed, 2876
21: 7 the **u love** *of* the Most High he will not 2876
31:16 save me in your **u love.** 2876
32:10 but the LORD's **u love** surrounds 2876
33: 5 the earth is full of his **u love.** 2876
33:18 on those whose hope is in his **u love,** 2876
33:22 May your **u love** rest upon us, O LORD, 2876
36: 7 How priceless is your **u love!** 2876
44:26 redeem us because of your **u love.** 2876
48: 9 O God, we meditate on your **u love.** 2876
51: 1 O God, according to your **u love;** 2876
52: 8 I trust in God's **u love** for ever and ever. 2876
77: 8 Has his **u love** vanished forever? 2876
85: 7 Show us your **u love,** O LORD, 2876
90:14 in the morning with your **u love,** 2876
107: 8 for his **u love** and his wonderful deeds 2876
107:15 for his **u love** and his wonderful deeds 2876
107:21 for his **u love** and his wonderful deeds 2876
107:31 for his **u love** and his wonderful deeds 2876
119:41 May your **u love** come to me, O LORD, 2876
119:76 May your **u love** be my comfort, 2876
130: 7 for with the LORD is **u love** and 2876
143: 8 the morning bring me word of your **u love,** 2876
143:12 In your **u love,** silence my enemies; 2876
147:11 who put their hope in his **u love.** 2876
Pr 19:22 What a man desires is **u love;** 2876
20: 6 Many a man claims to have **u love,** 2876
Isa 54:10 yet my **u love** for you will not be shaken 2876
La 3:32 so great is his **u love.** 2876
Hos 10:12 reap the fruit of **u love,** 2876

UNFAIR (1)
Mt 20:13 'Friend, *I am* not *being* **u** *to* you. *92*

UNFAITHFUL (50) [UNFAITHFULLY, UNFAITHFULNESS]
Lev 6: 2 "If anyone sins and *is* **u** to the LORD 5085+5086
Nu 5: 6 in any way and so *is* **u** to the LORD, 5085+5086
5:12 man's wife goes astray and *is* **u** to him 5085+5086
5:27 If she has defiled herself and *been* **u** 5085+5086
Dt 32:20 perverse generation, children who are **u.** 574+4202
Jdg 19: 2 But she *was* **u** to him. 2388
1Ch 5:25 But *they were* **u** to the God of their fathers 5085
10:13 Saul died because he was **u** to the LORD; 5085+5086
2Ch 12: 2 Because *they had been* **u** to the LORD, 5085
26:16 *He was* **u** to the LORD his God, 5085
26:18 Leave the sanctuary, for *you have been* **u;** 5085
28:19 and *had been* **most u** to the LORD. 5085+5086
28:22 Ahaz became even more **u** to the LORD. 5085
29: 6 Our fathers *were* **u;** they did evil 5085
30: 7 who *were* **u** to the LORD, 5085
36:14 and the people *became* **more and more u,** 5085+5086+8049
Ezr 10: 2 "We *have been* **u** to our God by marrying 5085
10:10 You *have been* **u;** you have married foreign 5085
Ne 1: 8 saying, 'If you *are* **u,** I will scatter you 5085
13:27 and *are being* **u** to our God by marrying 5085
Job 31:28 for *I would have been* **u** to God on high. 3950
Ps 73:27 you destroy all *who are* **u** to you. 2388
Pr 2:22 and the **u** will be torn from it. 953
11: 3 but the **u** are destroyed by their duplicity. 953
11: 6 but the **u** are trapped by evil desires. 953
13: 2 but the **u** have a craving for violence. 953
13:15 but the way of the **u** is hard. 953
21:18 and the **u** for the upright. 953
22:12 but he frustrates the words of the **u.** 953
23:28 and multiplies the **u** among men. 953
25:19 or a lame foot is reliance on the **u** in times 953
Jer 3: 7 and her **u** sister Judah saw it. 957
3: 8 that her **u** sister Judah had no fear; 953
3:10 her **u** sister Judah did not return to me 957
3:11 "Faithless Israel is more righteous than **u** Judah. 953
3:20 But like a woman **u** to her husband, 953
3:20 so *you have been* **u** to me, 953
5:11 the house of Judah *have been* **utterly u** 953+953
9: 2 they are all adulterers, a crowd of **u** *people.* 953
31:22 How long will you wander, O **u** daughter? 8745
49: 4 O **u** daughter, you trust in your riches 8745
Eze 14:13 if a country sins against me by *being* **u** 5085+5086
15: 8 desolate because *they have been* **u,** 5085+5086
17:20 upon him there because *he was* **u** to me. 5085
39:23 because *they were* **u** to me. 5085
Hos 2: 5 Their mother *has been* **u** and has conceived 2388
4:12 *they are* **u** to their God. 2388
5: 7 *They are* **u** to the LORD; 953
6: 7 *they were* **u** to me there. 953
9: 1 For *you have been* **u** to your God; 2388

UNFAITHFULLY (3) [UNFAITHFUL]
Jos 7: 1 But the Israelites **acted u** in regard to 5085+5086
22:20 *When* Achan son of Zerah **acted u** 5085+5086
22:31 because *you have* not **acted u** toward 5085

UNFAITHFULNESS (14) [UNFAITHFUL]
Nu 14:33 for forty years, suffering for your **u,** 2394
1Ch 9: 1 captive to Babylon because of their **u.** 5086
2Ch 29:19 articles that King Ahaz removed in his **u** 5086
33:19 as well as all his sins and **u,** 5086
Ezr 9: 2 and officials have led the way in this **u."** 5086
9: 4 around me because of this **u** *of* the exiles. 5086
10: 6 because he continued to mourn over the **u** 5086
Eze 18:24 Because of the **u** *he is* **guilty of** 5085+5086
39:26 and all the **u** *they* **showed** toward me 5085+5086
Da 9: 7 scattered us because of our **u** to you. 5085+5086
Hos 1: 2 an adulterous wife and children of **u,** 2393
2: 2 the adulterous look from her face and the **u** 5538
Mt 5:32 divorces his wife, except for **marital u,** *4518*
19: 9 divorces his wife, except for **marital u,** *4518*

UNFAMILIAR (1)
Isa 42:16 along **u** paths I will guide them; 3359+4202

UNFANNED (1)
Job 20:26 A fire **u** will consume him and devour 4202+5870

UNFAVORABLE (1)
Jer 42: 6 Whether it is favorable or **u,** we will obey 8273

UNFEELING (1)
Ps 119:70 Their hearts *are* callous and **u,** 3263

UNFEIGNED (KJV) See SINCERE

UNFILLED (1)
Jer 14: 3 They return with their jars **u;** 8200

UNFINISHED (1)
Tit 1: 5 you might straighten out what was left **u** *NIG*

UNFIT (1)
Tit 1:16 disobedient and **u** for doing anything good. *99*

UNFOLDING (1)
Ps 119:130 The **u** *of* your words gives light; 7340

UNFORGIVING (1)
2Ti 3: 3 **u,** slanderous, without self-control, brutal, *836*

UNFORMED (1)
Ps 139:16 your eyes saw my **u body.** 1677

UNFRIENDLY (1)
Pr 18: 1 An **u** *man* pursues selfish ends; 7233

UNFRUITFUL (3)
Mt 13:22 deceitfulness of wealth choke it, making it **u.** *182*
Mk 4:19 come in and choke the word, making it **u.** *182*
1Co 14:14 my spirit prays, but my mind is **u.** *182*

UNFULFILLED (1)
Eze 19: 5 " 'When she saw *her* **hope u,** 3498

UNFURLED (1)
Ps 60: 4 you have raised a banner to **be u** against 5824

UNGIRDED (KJV) See UNLOADED

UNGODLINESS (3) [UNGODLY]
Isa 32: 6 He practices **u** and spreads error concerning 2869
Jer 23:15 the prophets of Jerusalem **u** has spread 2870
Tit 2:12 to say "No" to **u** and worldly passions, *813*

UNGODLY (18) [UNGODLINESS]
Job 17: 8 the innocent are aroused against the **u.** 2868
Ps 35:16 Like the **u** they maliciously mocked; 2868
43: 1 plead my cause against an **u** nation; 2883+4202
Pr 11:31 how much more the **u** and the sinner! 8401
Isa 9:17 for everyone is **u** and wicked, 2868
Ro 5: 6 still powerless, Christ died for the **u.** *815*
1Co 6: 1 before the **u** for judgment instead of before *96*
1Ti 1: 9 the **u** and sinful, the unholy and irreligious; *815*
2Ti 2:16 in it will become more and more **u.** *813*
1Pe 4:18 what will become of the **u** and the sinner?" *815*
2Pe 2: 5 when he brought the flood on its **u** people, *815*
2: 6 of what is going to happen to the **u;** *815*
3: 7 day of judgment and destruction *of* **u** men. *815*
Jude 1:15 the **u** of all the ungodly acts they have done *815*
1:15 the ungodly of all the **u** acts they have done *813*
1:15 *they have* **done in the u way,** *814*
1:15 the harsh words **u** sinners have spoken *815*
1:18 there will be scoffers who will follow their own **u** desires." *813*

UNGRATEFUL (2)
Lk 6:35 because he is kind to the **u** and wicked. *940*
2Ti 3: 2 abusive, disobedient to their parents, **u,** *940*

UNHARMED (4)
1Sa 24:19 does he let him get away **u?** 3208
2Sa 17: 3 all the people will be **u."** 8934
Ps 55:18 He ransoms me **u** from the battle waged 928+8934
Da 3:25 in the fire, unbound and **u,** 10029+10244+10379

UNHEALTHY (1)
1Ti 6: 4 an **u** interest in controversies and quarrels *3796*

UNHEARD-OF (2)
Eze 7: 5 An **u** disaster is coming. 285
Da 11:36 above every god and will say **u** *things* 7098

UNHOLY (3)
1Ti 1: 9 the ungodly and sinful, the **u** and irreligious; *495*
2Ti 3: 2 disobedient to their parents, ungrateful, **u,** *495*
Heb 10:29 Who has treated as an **u** *thing* the blood of *3123*

UNICORN, UNICORNS (KJV) See WILD OX, WILD OXEN

UNIMPRESSIVE (1)
2Co 10:10 in person he is **u** and his speaking amounts *822*

UNINFORMED (1)
2Co 1: 8 We do not want you *to be* **u,** brothers, *51*

UNINTENTIONAL (1) [UNINTENTIONALLY]
Nu 15:26 all the people were involved in the **u wrong.** 8705

UNINTENTIONALLY (17) [UNINTENTIONAL]
Lev 4: 2 'When anyone sins **u** and does 928+8705
4:13 " 'If the whole Israelite community **sins u** 8706
4:22 leader sins **u** and does what is forbidden 928+8705
4:27 " 'If a member of the community sins **u** 928+8705
5:15 sins **u** in regard to any of the LORD's 928+8705
5:18 for the **wrong** *he has* **committed u,** 8704+8705
Nu 15:22 " 'Now if *you* **u** fail to keep any of these 8706
15:24 and if this is done **u** without 4200+8705
15:27 " 'But if just one person sins **u,** 928+8705
15:28 for the one who erred by sinning **u,** 928+8705
15:29 the same law applies to everyone *who* **sins u,** 928+6913+8705
35:22 or throws something at him **u** 928+4202+7402
Dt 4:42 if he *had* **u** killed his neighbor 928+1172+1981
19: 4 one who kills his neighbor **u,** 928+1172+1981
Jos 20: 3 kills a person accidentally and **u** 928+1172+1981
20: 5 because he killed his neighbor **u** 928+1172+1981
Eze 45:20 for anyone *who* **sins u** or through ignorance; 8706

UNION (3) [UNITE]
Zec 11: 7 and called one Favor and the other **U,** 2482
11:14 Then I broke my second staff called **U,** 2482
Mt 1:25 But *he had* no **u with** her until she gave birth to a son. *1182*

UNIQUE (2)
SS 6: 9 is **u,** the only daughter of her mother, 285
Zec 14: 7 It will be a **u** day, without daytime or 285

UNISON (2) [UNITE]
2Ch 5:13 The trumpeters and singers joined **in u,** 285+3869
Ac 19:34 they all shouted **in u** for about two hours: *1651*

UNIT (6) [UNITS]
Ex 26: 6 so that the tabernacle is **a u.** 285
26:11 the loops to fasten the tent together as **a u.** 285
36:13 so that the tabernacle was **a u.** 285
36:18 to fasten the tent together as **a u.** 285
1Sa 17:18 to the commander of their **u.** 548
1Co 12:12 The body is **a u,** though it is made up of *1651*

UNITE (4) [REUNITED, UNION, UNISON, UNITED, UNITES, UNITY]
1Ch 12:17 I *am ready to have* you **u** with me. 2118+3480+4200+4222
Job 16:10 in scorn and **u** together against me. 4848
Isa 14: 1 Aliens will join them and **u** with the house 6202
1Co 6:15 take the members of Christ and **u** them with a prostitute? *3517+4472*

UNITED (12) [UNITE]
Ge 2:24 and mother and *be* **u** to his wife, 1815
Jdg 20:11 So all the men of Israel got together and **u** 2492
Da 2:43 be a mixture and will not remain **u,** 10158+10180+10180+10554
Mt 19: 5 and mother and *be* **u to** his wife, *3140*
Mk 10: 7 and mother and *be* **u to** his wife, *4681*
Ac 18:12 a **u** attack on Paul and brought him *3924*
Ro 6: 5 If we have been **u** with him like this *5242*
6: 5 also be **u** with him in his resurrection. *NIG*
1Co 1:10 you may be **perfectly u** in mind *899+2936+3836*
Eph 5:31 and mother and *be* **u to** his wife, *4681*
Php 2: 1 encouragement from being **u with** Christ, *1877*
Col 2: 2 be encouraged in heart and **u** in love, *5204*

UNITES (2) [UNITE]
1Co 6:16 Do you not know that he who **u** *himself* *3140*
6:17 But he who **u** *himself* with the Lord is one *3140*

UNITS (13) [UNIT]
Nu 10:25 Finally, as the rear guard for all the **u,** 4722
31:48 officers who were over the **u** *of* the army— 548
1Sa 29: 2 with their **u of hundreds** and thousands, 4395
2Sa 18: 4 the men marched out in **u of hundreds** and 4395
2Ki 11: 4 for the commanders of **u of a hundred,** 4395
11: 9 The commanders of **u of a hundred** did just 4395
11:15 the commanders of **u of a hundred,** 4395
1Ch 12:20 leaders of **u of a thousand** in Manasseh. 547
15:25 of **u of a thousand** went to bring up the ark 547
2Ch 17:14 From Judah, commanders of **u of 1,000:** 547
23: 1 with the commanders of **u of a hundred:** 4395
23: 9 of **u of a hundred** the spears and the large 4395
2Ch 23:14 of **u of a hundred,** who were in charge of 4395

UNITY (7) [UNITE]
2Ch 30:12 of God was on the people to give them **u** 285
Ps 133: 1 when brothers live **together in u!** 3480
Jn 17:23 May they be brought to complete **u** to let *1651*
Ro 15: 5 give you a **spirit of u** among *899+3836+5858*
Eph 4: 3 to keep the **u** of the Spirit through the bond *1942*
4:13 until we all reach **u** in the faith and in *1942*
Col 3:14 which binds them all together in perfect **u.** *NIG*

UNIVERSE (5)
1Co 4: 9 have been made a spectacle *to* the whole **u,** *3180*
Eph 4:10 in order to fill the **whole u.)** *4246*
Php 2:15 in which you shine like stars in the **u** *3180*
Heb 1: 2 and through whom he made the **u.** *172*
11: 3 that the **u** was formed at God's command, *172*

UNJUST (19) [UNJUSTLY]
Job 6:29 Relent, do not be **u;** 6406
27: 7 my adversaries like the **u!** 6405
Ps 82: 2 the **u** and show partiality to the wicked? 6404
Isa 10: 1 Woe to those who make **u** laws, 224
Jer 17:11 the man who gains riches by **u** means. 4202+5477
Eze 18:25 Hear, O house of Israel: *Is* my way **u?** 4202+9419
18:25 Is it not your ways *that are* **u?** 4202+9419
18:29 *Are* my ways **u,** O house of Israel? 4202+9419
18:29 Is it not your ways *that are* **u?** 4202+9419
22:12 and excessive interest and **make u gain** 1298
22:13 at the **u gain** you have made and at 1299
22:27 and kill people to **make u gain.** 1298+1299
33:31 but their hearts are greedy for **u gain.** 1299
Hab 2: 9 Woe to him who builds his realm by **u** gain 8273
Lk 18: 6 Lord said, "Listen to what the **u** judge says. *94*
Ro 3: 5 That God is **u** in bringing his wrath on us? *96*
9:14 Is God **u?** Not at all! *94*
Heb 6:10 God is not **u;** he will not forget your work *96*
1Pe 2:19 a man bears up under the pain *of* **u** suffering *96*

UNJUSTLY (1) [UNJUST]
Jer 23:10 an evil course and use their power **u.** 4026+4202

UNKEMPT (3)
Lev 10: 6 *"Do* not *let* your hair *become* **u,** 7277
13:45 must wear torn clothes, let his hair be **u,** 7277
21:10 *must* not *let* his hair *become* **u** or tear his 7277

UNKNOWN (7)
Dt 28:36 to a nation **u** to you or to your fathers. 3359+4202
Isa 48: 6 of hidden things **u** *to you.* 3359+4202
Da 11:38 a god **u** *to* his fathers he will honor 3359+4202
Ac 17:23 with this inscription: TO AN U GOD. *58*
17:23 Now what you worship *as something* **u** *51*
2Co 6: 9 known, yet regarded as **u;** *51*
Gal 1:22 I was personally **u** to the churches of Judea *51*

UNLADE (KJV) See UNLOAD

UNLAWFUL (4)
Mt 12: 2 Your disciples are doing what is **u** on *2003+4024*
Mk 2:24 why are they doing what *is* **u** on *2003+4024*
Lk 6: 2 "Why are you doing what *is* **u** on *2003+4024*
Ac 16:21 advocating customs **u** for us Romans *2003+4024*

UNLEARNED (KJV) See IGNORANT, NOT UNDERSTAND, STUPID, UNSCHOOLED

UNLEASH (3) [UNLEASHED, UNLEASHES]
Job 40:11 **U** the fury of your wrath, 7046
Eze 7: 3 now upon you and *I will* **u** my anger 8938
13:13 In my wrath *I will* **u** a violent wind, 1324

UNLEASHED (2) [UNLEASH]
Ex 15: 7 *You* **u** your burning anger; 8938
Ps 78:49 *He* **u** against them his hot anger, his wrath, 8938

UNLEASHES (1) [UNLEASH]
Job 37: 3 *He* **u** his lightning beneath the whole heaven 9223

UNLEAVENED (29)
Ex 12:17 "Celebrate the **Feast of U Bread,** 5174
12:20 Wherever you live, you must eat **u bread."** 5174
12:39 they baked cakes of **u bread.** 5174
13: 7 Eat **u bread** during those seven days; 5174
23:15 "Celebrate the Feast of **U Bread;** 5174
34:18 "Celebrate the Feast of **U Bread.** 5174
Lev 23: 6 the LORD's Feast of **U Bread** begins; 5174
Nu 6:17 He is to present the basket of **u bread** and 5174
9:11 together with **u bread** and bitter herbs. 5174
Dt 16: 3 but for seven days eat **u bread,** 5174
16: 8 For six days eat **u bread** and on 5174
16:16 at the Feast of **U Bread,** the Feast of Weeks 5174
Jos 5:11 **u bread** and roasted grain. 5174
Jdg 6:20 "Take the meat and the **u bread,** 5174
6:21 the meat and the **u bread.** 5174
2Ki 23: 9 they ate **u bread** with their fellow priests. 5174
1Ch 23:29 the **u** wafers, the baking and the mixing, 5174
2Ch 8:13 the Feast of **U Bread,** the Feast of Weeks 5174
2Ch 30:13 the Feast of **U Bread** in the second month. 5174
30:21 the Feast of **U Bread** for seven days 5174
35:17 the Feast of **U Bread** for seven days. 5174
Ezr 6:22 with joy the Feast of **U Bread,** 5174
Mt 26:17 On the first day of the **Feast of U Bread,** *109*
Mk 14: 1 **Feast of U Bread** were only two days away, *109*
14:12 On the first day *of* the **Feast of U Bread,** *109*
Lk 22: 1 Now the Feast *of* **U Bread,** *109*
22: 7 Then came the day *of* **U Bread** on which *109*
Ac 12: 3 during the **Feast of U Bread.** *109*
20: 6 Philippi after the **Feast of U Bread,** *109+2465*

UNLESS (64)
Ge 32:26 "I will not let you go **u** you bless me." 561+3954
42:15 you will not leave this place **u** your 561+3954
43: 3 not see my face again **u** your brother is 1194
43: 5 not see my face again **u** your brother is 1194
44:23 '**U** your youngest brother comes down 561+4202
44:26 the man's face **u** our youngest brother is 401
Ex 3:19 that the king of Egypt will not let you go **u** 4202
33:16 with your people **u** you go with us? 2022+4202
Lev 22: 6 not eat any of the sacred offerings **u** 561+3954
Dt 32:30 **u** their Rock had sold them, 561+3954+4202
32:30 **u** the LORD had given them up? NIH
Jos 2:18 **u,** when we enter the land, 2180
2:18 **u** you have brought your father and mother, NIH
7:12 not be with you anymore **u** you destroy 561+4202
2Sa 3:13 Do not come into my presence **u** you bring Michal 561+3954+4200+7156
2Ki 4:24 don't slow down for me **u** I tell you." 561+3954
Est 2:14 not return to the king **u** he was pleased 561+3954
Ps 94:17 **U** the LORD had given me help, 4295
127: 1 **U** the LORD builds the house, 561+4202
127: 1 **U** the LORD watches over the city, 561+4202
Isa 1: 9 **U** the LORD Almighty had left us some survivors, 4295
La 5:22 **u** you have utterly rejected us and 561+3954
Da 6: 5 against this man Daniel **u** it has something 10386
Am 3: 3 two walk together **u** they have agreed 561+1194
Mt 5:20 that **u** your righteousness surpasses *1569+3590*
12:29 carry off his possessions **u** he first ties *1569+3590*
18: 3 **u** you change and become like little *1569+3590*
18:35 of you **u** you forgive your brother *1569+3590*
26:42 for this cup to be taken away **u** I drink *1569+3590*
Mk 3:27 carry off his possessions **u** he first ties *1569+3590*
7: 3 Pharisees and all the Jews do not eat **u** *1569+3590*
7: 4 from the marketplace they do not eat **u** *1569+3590*
Lk 9:13 **u** we go and buy food for all this *1623+3614*
13: 3 **u** you repent, you too will all perish. *1569+3590*
13: 5 **u** you repent, you too will all perish." *1569+3590*
Jn 3: 3 kingdom of God **u** he is born again." *1569+3590*
3: 5 of God **u** he is born of water and *1569+3590*
4:48 "**U** you people see miraculous signs *1569+3590*
6:44 **u** the Father who sent me draws him, *1569+3590*
6:53 **u** you eat the flesh of the Son of Man *1569+3590*
6:65 to me **u** the Father has enabled him." *1569+3590*
10:37 **u** I do what my Father does. *1623+4024*
12:24 **u** a kernel of wheat falls to the ground *1569+3590*
13: 8 Jesus answered, "**U** I wash you, *1569+3590*
15: 4 bear fruit **u** you remain in me. *1569+3590*
16: 7 **U** I go away, the Counselor will not *1569+3590*
20:25 "**U** I see the nail marks in his hands *1569+3590*
Ac 8:31 "**u** someone explains it to me?" *1569+3590*
15: 1 "**U** you are circumcised, *1569+3590*
24:21 **u** it was this one thing I shouted as I stood *2445*
27:31 "**U** these men stay with the ship, *1569+3590*
Ro 9:29 "**U** the Lord Almighty had left us descendants, *1623+3590*
10:15 how can they preach **u** they are sent? *1569+3590*
1Co 14: 5 **u** he interprets, so that the church may be edified. *1623+1760+3590*
14: 6 **u** I bring you some revelation or *1569+3590*
14: 7 **u** there is a distinction in the notes? *1569+3590*
14: 9 **U** you speak intelligible words *1569+3590*
15:36 What you sow does not come to life **u** *1569+3590*
2Co 13: 5 **u,** of course, you fail the test? *1623+3614*
1Ti 5: 9 on the list of widows **u** she is over sixty, *NIG*
5:19 an accusation against an elder **u** *1623+1760+3590*
2Ti 2: 5 **u** he competes according to the rules. *1569+3590*
Rev 2:22 **u** they repent of her ways. *1569+3590*
13:17 could buy or sell **u** he had the mark, *1623+3590*

UNLIKE (9)
Jdg 2:17 **U** their fathers, they quickly turned from the way 4027+4202+6913
2Ki 16: 2 **U** David his father, he did not do 3869+4202
2Ch 27: 2 but **u** him he did not enter the temple of NIH
28: 1 **U** David his father, he did not do 3869+4202
33:23 But **u** his father Manasseh, 3869+4202
Isa 7:17 on the house of your father a time **u** any 4202
Eze 16:31 you were **u** a prostitute, because you 3869+4202
2Co 2:17 **U** so many, we do not peddle the word *4024+6055*
Heb 7:27 **U** the other high priests, he does not need *6061*

UNLIMITED (1)
1Ti 1:16 Christ Jesus might display his **u** patience as *570*

UNLOAD (1) [UNLOADED]
Ac 21: 3 where our ship was to **u** its cargo. *711*

UNLOADED (1) [UNLOAD]
Ge 24:32 and the camels *were* **u.** 7337

UNLOCKED (1)
Jdg 3:25 they took a key and **u** them. 7337

UNLOOSE (KJV) See UNTIE

UNLOVED (2)
Dt 21:17 He must acknowledge the son of his **u** wife 8533
Pr 30:23 an **u** *woman* who is married, 8533

UNMARKED (1)
Lk 11:44 because you are like **u** graves, *83*

UNMARRIED (10)
Lev 21: 3 or an **u** sister who is dependent on him 1435
Ru 1:13 *Would you* **remain u** for them? 408+1194+2118+4200+4200+6328
Eze 44:25 brother or **u** sister, 408+2118+4200+4202
Ac 21: 9 He had four **u** daughters who prophesied. *4221*
1Co 7: 8 Now *to* the **u** and the widows I say: *23*
7: 8 It is good for them to stay **u**, as I am. *NIG*
7:11 she must remain **u** or else be reconciled *23*
7:27 *Are you* **u**? Do not look for a *608+1222+3395*
7:32 An **u** *man* is concerned about the Lord's *23*
7:34 An **u** woman or virgin is concerned about *23*

UNMINDFUL (1)
Job 39:15 **u** that a foot may crush them, 8894

UNMOVEABLE (KJV) See NOT MOVE, NOTHING MOVE

UNNATURAL (1)
Ro 1:26 Even their women exchanged natural relations for **u ones.** *3836+4123+5882*

UNNI (3)
1Ch 15:18 Zechariah, Jaaziel, Shemiramoth, Jehiel, **U**, 6716
15:20 Aziel, Shemiramoth, Jehiel, **U**, Eliab, 6716
Ne 12: 9 Bakbukiah and **U**, their associates, 6716

UNNOTICED (3)
1Sa 24: 4 David crept up **u** and cut off a 928+2021+4319
Job 4:20 **u**, they perish forever. 1172+4946+8492
Lk 8:47 the woman, seeing that *she could* not **go u**, *3291*

UNOCCUPIED (1)
Mt 12:44 When it arrives, it finds the house **u**, *5390*

UNPERFECT (KJV) See UNFORMED

UNPLOWED (3)
Ex 23:11 during the seventh year *let* the land **lie u** 9023
Jer 4: 3 "Break up your **u ground** and do not sow 5776
Hos 10:12 and break up your **u ground;** 5776

UNPREPARED (1)
2Co 9: 4 Macedonians come with me and find you **u**, *564*

UNPRESENTABLE (1)
1Co 12:23 that are **u** are treated with special modesty, *860*

UNPRODUCTIVE (4)
2Ki 2:19 but the water is bad and the land *is* **u**." 8897
2:21 will it cause death or **make** the land **u**.' " 8897
Tit 3:14 for daily necessities and not live **u** lives. *182*
2Pe 1: 8 being ineffective and **u** in your knowledge *182*

UNPROFITABLE (2)
Isa 30: 6 the humps of camels, to that **u** nation, 3603+4202
Tit 3: 9 because these are **u** and useless. *543*

UNPROTECTED (2)
Ge 42: 9 You have come to see where our land is **u**." 6872
42:12 You have come to see where our land is **u**." 6872

UNPUNISHED (19)
Ex 34: 7 Yet *he does* not **leave the guilty u;** 5927+5927
Nu 14:18 Yet *he does* not **leave the guilty u;** 5927+5927
Job 10:14 and *would* not **let** my offense **go u.** 5927
Pr 6:29 no one who touches her *will* **go u.** 5927
11:21 Be sure of this: The wicked *will* not **go u,** 5927
16: 5 Be sure of this: *They will* not **go u.** 5927
17: 5 whoever gloats over disaster *will* not **go u.** 5927
19: 5 A false witness *will* not **go u,** 5927
19: 9 A false witness *will* not **go u,** 5927
28:20 but one eager to get rich *will* not **go u.** 5927
Jer 25:29 and *will* you **indeed go u?** 5927+5927
25:29 *You will* not **go u,** 5927
30:11 *I will* not **let** you **go entirely u.'** 5927+5927
46:28 *I will* not **let** you **go entirely u."** 5927+5927
49:12 why *should* you **go u?** 5927+5927
49:12 *You will* not **go u,** but must drink it. 5927
Na 1: 3 the LORD *will* not **leave the guilty u.** 5927+5927
Zec 11: 5 Their buyers slaughter them and *go* **u.** 870+4202
Ro 3:25 **left** the sins committed beforehand **u**— *4217*

UNQUENCHABLE (3) [UNQUENCHED]
Jer 17:27 then I will kindle an **u** fire in the gates 3882+4202
Mt 3:12 and burning up the chaff *with* **u** fire." *812*
Lk 3:17 but he will burn up the chaff *with* **u** fire." *812*

UNQUENCHED (1) [UNQUENCHABLE]
Isa 29: 8 but he awakens faint, with his thirst **u.** 8799

UNREASONABLE (1) [UNREASONING]
Ac 25:27 For I think it is **u** to send on a prisoner *263*

UNREASONING (1) [UNREASONABLE]
Jude 1:10 by instinct, like **u** animals— *263*

UNREBUKEABLE (KJV) See BLAME

UNRELENTING (1)
Job 6:10 this consolation—my joy in **u** pain— 2798+4202

UNRELIABLE (1)
Ps 78:57 disloyal and faithless, as **u** as a faulty bow. 2200

UNREPENTANT (1)
Ro 2: 5 of your stubbornness and your **u** heart, *295*

UNREPROVEABLE (KJV) See FREE FROM ACCUSATION

UNREST (2)
Jer 50:34 but **u** to those who live in Babylon. 8074
Am 3: 9 the great **u** within her and the oppression 4539

UNRIGHTEOUS (4) [UNRIGHTEOUSNESS]
Zep 3: 5 yet the **u** know no shame. 6405
Mt 5:45 and sends rain on the righteous and the **u.** *96*
1Pe 3:18 Christ died for sins once for all, the righteous for the **u,** *96*
2Pe 2: 9 and to hold the **u** for the day of judgment, *96*

UNRIGHTEOUSNESS (3) [UNRIGHTEOUS]
Jer 22:13 "Woe to him who builds his palace by **u,** 4202+7406
Ro 3: 5 But if our **u** brings out God's righteousness *94*
1Jn 1: 9 forgive us our sins and purify us from all **u.** *94*

UNRIPE (1)
Job 15:33 be like a vine stripped of its **u grapes,** 1235

UNROLLED (1) [UNROLLING]
Eze 2:10 which *he* **u** before me. 7298

UNROLLING (1) [UNROLLED]
Lk 4:17 **U** it, he found the place where it is written: *408*

UNRULY (3)
Jer 31:18 'You disciplined me like an **u** calf, 4202+4340
Eze 5: 7 You *have been* more **u** than the nations 2171
Hos 11:12 And Judah *is* **u** against God, 8113

UNSANDALED (1)
Dt 25:10 in Israel as The Family of the **U.** 2740+5837

UNSATIABLE (KJV) See INSATIABLE

UNSATISFIED (1)
2Sa 1:22 the sword of Saul did not return **u.** 8200

UNSAVOURY (KJV) See SHREWD, TASTELESS

UNSCALABLE (1)
Pr 18:11 they imagine it an **u** wall. 8435

UNSCATHED (3)
Job 9: 4 Who has resisted him and *come out* **u**? 8966
Isa 41: 3 He pursues them and moves on **u,** 8934
Jer 43:12 around himself and depart from there **u.** 928+8934

UNSCHOOLED (1)
Ac 4:13 Peter and John and realized that they were **u,** *63*

UNSEALED (3)
Ne 6: 5 and in his hand was an **u** letter 7337
Jer 32:11 as well as the **u** *copy*— 1655
32:14 both the sealed and **u** *copies* of the deed 1655

UNSEARCHABLE (4)
Pr 25: 3 so the hearts of kings are **u.** 401+2984
Jer 33: 3 and tell you great and **u** *things* you do 1290
Ro 11:33 How **u** his judgments, *451*
Eph 3: 8 preach to the Gentiles the **u** riches of Christ, *453*

UNSEEMLY (KJV) See INDECENT, RUDE

UNSEEN (4)
Mt 6: 6 pray to your Father, who is **u.** *1877+3220+3836*
6:18 only to your Father, who is **u;** *1877+3224+3836*
2Co 4:18 not on what is seen, but on what *is* **u.** *1063+3590*
4:18 but what *is* **u** is eternal. *1063+3590*

UNSETTLED (2)
1Th 3: 3 so that no one *would be* **u** by these trials. *4883*
2Th 2: 2 not *to become* easily **u** or alarmed *4888*

UNSHARPENED (1)
Ecc 10:10 If the ax is dull and its edge **u,** 4202+7837

UNSHEATHED (1)
Eze 21: 4 my sword *will be* **u** against 3655+4946+9509

UNSHOD (KJV) See BARE

UNSHRUNK (2)
Mt 9:16 a patch *of* **u** cloth on an old garment, *47*
Mk 2:21 a patch *of* **u** cloth on an old garment. *47*

UNSKILFUL (KJV) See NOT ACQUAINTED

UNSPEAKABLE (KJV) See INDESCRIBABLE, INEXPRESSIBLE

UNSPIRITUAL (3)
Ro 7:14 but I am **u,** sold as a slave to sin. *4921*
Col 2:18 his **u** mind puffs him up with idle notions. *4922*
Jas 3:15 but is earthly, **u,** of the devil. *6035*

UNSPOTTED (KJV) See FROM BEING POLLUTED

UNSTABLE (3)
Jas 1: 8 he is a double-minded man, **u** in all he does. *190*
2Pe 2:14 never stop sinning; they seduce the **u;** *844+6034*
3:16 which ignorant and **u** *people* distort, *844*

UNSTOPPED (1)
Isa 35: 5 blind be opened and the ears of the deaf **u.** 7337

UNSTRUNG (1)
Job 30:11 that God *has* **u** my bow and afflicted me, 7337

UNSUCCESSFUL (1)
Dt 28:29 *You will be* **u** *in* everything you do; 4202+7503

UNSUITABLE (1) [UNSUITED]
Ac 27:12 Since the harbor was **u** to winter in, *460*

UNSUITED (1) [UNSUITABLE]
Pr 17: 7 Arrogant lips are **u** to a fool— 4202+5534

UNSUSPECTING (6)
Ge 34:25 took their swords and attacked the **u** city, 1055
Jdg 8:11 and Jogbehah and fell upon the **u** army. 1055
18: 7 like the Sidonians, **u** and secure. 9200
18:10 an **u** people and a spacious land 1053
18:27 against a peaceful and **u** people. 1053
Eze 38:11 I will attack a peaceful and **u** people— 1055+4200

UNSWERVING (1) [UNSWERVINGLY]
1Ch 28: 7 if *he is* **u** in carrying out my commands 2616

UNSWERVINGLY (1) [UNSWERVING]
Heb 10:23 Let us hold **u** to the hope we profess, *195*

UNTAKEN (KJV) See NOT REMOVED

UNTENDED (2)
Lev 25: 5 or harvest the grapes of your **u vines.** 5687
25:11 of itself or harvest the **u vines.** 5687

UNTHANKFUL (KJV) See UNGRATEFUL

UNTHINKABLE (1)
Job 34:12 It is **u** that God would do wrong, 597+4202

UNTIE (9) [UNTIED, UNTYING]
Isa 58: 6 the chains of injustice and **u** the cords of 6002
Mt 21: 2 **U** them and bring them to me. *3395*
Mk 1: 7 not worthy *to* stoop down and **u.** *3395*
11: 2 **U** it and bring it here. *3395*

Lk 3:16 of whose sandals I am not worthy *to* **u**. *3395*
13:15 of you on the Sabbath **u** his ox or donkey *3395*
19:30 **U** it and bring it here. *3395*
Jn 1:27 of whose sandals I am not worthy to **u**." *3395*
Ac 13:25 whose sandals I am not worthy *to* **u**.' *3395*

UNTIED (3) [UNTIE]

Job 39: 5 Who **u** his ropes? 7337
Mk 11: 4 tied at a doorway. As *they* **u** it, *3395*
Ac 27:40 same time **u** the ropes that held the rudders. *479*

UNTIL (414)

Ge 3:19 sweat of your brow you will eat your food **u** 6330
8: 5 The waters continued to recede **u** 6330
8: 7 and forth **u** the water had dried up from 6330
13: 3 the Negev he went from place to place **u** 6330
19:22 I cannot do anything **u** you reach it." 6330
24:19 **u** they have finished drinking." 561+6330
24:33 "I will not eat **u** I have told you what 561+6330
26:13 and his wealth continued to grow **u** 3954+6330
27:44 a while **u** your brother's fury subsides. 889+6330
28: 3 and increase your numbers **u** you become 2256
28:15 I will not leave you **u** I have done 889+6330
29: 8 "**u** all the flocks are gathered and 889+6330
33:14 **u** I come to my lord in Seir." 889+6330
34: 5 so he kept quiet about it **u** they came home. 6330
38:11 "Live as a widow in your father's house **u** 6330
38:17 "Will you give me something as a pledge **u** 6330
39:16 beside her **u** his master came home. 6330
49:10 **u** he comes to whom it belongs and 3954+6330
Ex 7:16 But **u** now you have not listened. 6330
10:15 They covered all the ground **u** it was black. 2256
10:26 and **u** we get there we will not know 6330
12: 6 of them **u** the fourteenth day of the month, 6330
12:18 from the evening of the fourteenth day **u** 6330
12:22 of you shall go out the door of his house **u** 6330
15:16 **u** your people pass by, O LORD, 6330
15:16 **u** the people you bought pass by. 6330
16:19 "No one is to keep any of it **u** morning." 6330
16:20 they kept part of it **u** morning, 6330
16:23 Save whatever is left and keep it **u** 6330
16:24 So they saved it **u** morning, 6330
16:35 **u** they came to a land that was settled; 6330
16:35 they ate manna **u** they reached the border 6330
23:18 of my festival offerings must not be kept **u** 6330
23:30 **u** you have increased enough 889+6330
24:14 "Wait here for us **u** we come back 889+6330
33: 8 watching Moses **u** he entered the tent. 6330
33:22 in the rock and cover you with my hand **u** 6330
34:25 from the Passover Feast remain **u** morning. 4200
34:34 he removed the veil **u** he came out. 6330
34:35 over his face **u** he went in to speak with 6330
40:37 **u** the day it lifted. 6330
Lev 8:33 to the Tent of Meeting for seven days, **u** 6330
12: 4 or go to the sanctuary **u** the days 6330
16:17 in the Most Holy Place **u** he comes out, 6330
19: 6 over **u** the third day must be burned up. 6330
22: 4 he may not eat the sacred offerings **u** 889+6330
23:14 **u** the very day you bring this offering 6330
23:32 the evening of the ninth day of the month **u** 6330
24:12 in custody **u** the will of the LORD should 4200
25:22 and will continue to eat from it **u** 6330
25:28 in the possession of the buyer **u** the Year 6330
25:40 he is to work for you **u** the Year of Jubilee. 6330
25:52 a few years remain **u** the Year of Jubilee, 6330
26: 5 threshing *will* **continue u** grape harvest 5952
26: 5 the grape harvest *will* **continue u** planting, 5952
27:18 that remain **u** the next Year of Jubilee, 6330
Nu 6: 5 be holy **u** the period of his separation to 6330
9: 8 "Wait **u** I find out what the LORD 2256
10:12 from place to place **u** the cloud came to rest 2256
11:20 **u** it comes out of your nostrils 889+6330
14:19 from the time they left Egypt **u** now." 6330
14:33 **u** the last of your bodies lies in the desert. 6330
20:17 the right or to the left **u** we have passed 889+6330
21:22 the king's highway **u** we have passed 889+6330
32:13 **u** the whole generation of those who 6330
32:17 **u** we have brought them to their 561+889+6330
32:18 We will not return to our homes **u** 6330
32:21 the LORD **u** he has driven his enemies out 6330
35:25 He must stay there **u** the death of the high 6330
35:28 of refuge **u** the death of the high priest; 6330
Dt 1:31 all the way you went **u** you reached 6330
2:14 from the time we left Kadesh Barnea **u** 889+6330
2:15 The LORD's hand was against them **u** 6330
2:29 **u** we cross the Jordan into the land 889+6330
3:20 **u** the LORD gives rest to your brothers 889+6330
7:20 among them **u** even the survivors who hide 6330
7:23 into great confusion **u** they are destroyed. 6330
9: 7 the day you left Egypt **u** you arrived here, 6330
11: 5 in the desert **u** you arrived at this place, 6330
16: 4 on the evening of the first day remain **u** 4200
20:20 to build siege works **u** the city at war 6330
22: 2 with you and keep it **u** he comes looking 6330
28:20 **u** you are destroyed and come to sudden 6330
28:21 with diseases **u** he has destroyed you from 6330
28:22 which will plague you **u** you perish. 6330
28:24 down from the skies **u** you are destroyed. 6330
28:45 They will pursue you and overtake you **u** 6330
28:48 He will put an iron yoke on your neck **u** 6330
28:51 the crops of your land **u** you are destroyed. 6330
28:51 or lambs of your flocks **u** you are ruined. 6330
28:52 to all the cities throughout your land **u** 6330
28:61 **u** you are destroyed. 6330
34: 8 **u** the time of weeping 2256
Jos 1:15 **u** the LORD gives them rest, 889+6330
1:15 and **u** they too have taken possession of NIH
2:16 Hide yourselves there three days **u** 6330
2:22 **u** the pursuers had searched all along 6330
3:17 by **u** the whole nation had completed 889+6330
4:10 in the middle of the Jordan **u** everything 6330
4:23 before you **u** you had crossed over. 6330
4:23 the Red Sea when he dried it up before us **u** 6330
5: 1 before the Israelites **u** we had crossed over, 6330
5: 6 about in the desert forty years **u** all 6330
5: 8 they remained where they were in camp **u** 6330
6:10 not say a word **u** the day I tell you to shout. 6330
7:13 You cannot stand against your enemies **u** 6330
8: 6 They will pursue us **u** we have lured them 6330
8:26 the hand that held out his javelin **u** 889+6330
8:29 of Ai on a tree and left him there **u** evening. 6330
10:26 and they were left hanging on the trees **u** 6330
10:33 **u** no survivors were left. 6330
11: 8 **u** no survivors were left. 6330
11:14 but all the people they put to the sword **u** 6330
20: 6 He is to stay in that city **u** he has stood trial 6330
20: 6 before the assembly and **u** the death of 6330
23: 8 as you have **u** now. 6330
23:13 **u** you perish from this good land, 6330
23:15 **u** he has destroyed you 6330
Jdg 3:11 **u** Othniel son of Kenaz died. 2256
4:24 Canaanite king, **u** they destroyed him. 889+6330
5: 7 Village life in Israel ceased, ceased **u** 6330+8611
6:18 Please do not go away **u** I come back 6330
6:18 the LORD said, "I will wait **u** you return." 6330
9:45 against the city **u** he had captured it 2256
13: 7 of God from birth **u** the day of his death.' " 6330
13:15 to stay **u** we prepare a young goat for you." 2256
15: 7 I **won't** stop **u** I get my revenge on you. 561+3954
16: 3 But Samson lay there only **u** the middle of 6330
16:13 Delilah then said to Samson, "**U** now, 6330
16:16 after day **u** he was tired to death. 2256
18:30 the tribe of Dan **u** the time of the captivity 6330
19:26 down at the door and lay there **u** daylight. 6330
20:23 up and wept before the LORD **u** evening, 6330
20:26 They fasted that day **u** evening 6330
21: 2 where they sat before God **u** evening, 6330
Ru 1:13 would you wait **u** they grew up? 889+6330
1:19 So the two women went on **u** they came 6330
2:17 So Ruth gleaned in the field **u** evening. 6330
2:21 'Stay with my workers **u** they finish 561+6330
2:23 to the servant girls of Boaz to glean **u** 6330
3: 3 but don't let him know you are there **u** 6330
3:13 Lie here **u** morning." 6330
3:14 So she lay at his feet **u** morning, 6330
3:18 **u** you find out what happens. 889+6330
3:18 not rest **u** the matter is settled today." 561+3954
1Sa 1:23 "Stay here **u** you have weaned him; 6330
1:23 and nursed her son **u** she had weaned him. 6330
3:15 down **u** morning and then opened the doors 6330
8: 8 the day I brought them up out of Egypt **u** 6330
9:13 The people will not begin eating **u** 6330
10: 3 on from there **u** you reach the great tree 2256
10: 8 but you must wait seven days **u** I come 6330
11:11 and slaughtered them **u** the heat of the day. 6330
12: 2 I have been your leader from my youth **u** 6330
14: 9 'Wait there **u** we come to you,' 6330
15:18 on them **u** you have wiped them out.' 6330
15:35 **U** the day Samuel died, 6330
16:11 we will not sit down **u** he arrives." 6330
19:23 along prophesying **u** he came to Naioth. 6330
20: 5 and hide in the field **u** the evening of 6330
22: 3 and mother come and stay with you **u** 889+6330
25:36 So she told him nothing **u** daybreak. 6330
29: 3 and from the day he left Saul **u** now, 6330
29: 6 From the day you came to me **u** now, 6330
29: 8 from the day I came to you **u** now? 6330
30: 4 So David and his men wept aloud **u** 889+6330
30:17 David fought them from dusk **u** the evening 6330
2Sa 2:27 the pursuit of their brothers **u** morning." 4946
15:24 and Abiathar offered sacrifices **u** all 6330
15:28 at the fords in the desert **u** word comes 6330
17:13 we will drag it down to the valley **u** not 889+6330
19:24 the king left **u** the day he returned safely. 6330
24:15 on Israel from that morning **u the end of** 6330
1Ki 3: 1 of David **u** he finished building his palace 6330
5: 3 for the Name of the LORD his God **u** 6330
10: 7 I did not believe these things **u** I came 889+6330
11:16 **u** they had destroyed all the men in Edom. 6330
11:40 and stayed there **u** Solomon's death. 6330
14:10 as one burns dung, **u** it is all gone. 6330
17:14 not run dry **u** the day the LORD gives rain 6330
18:28 as was their custom, **u** their blood flowed. 6330
18:29 **u the time for** the evening sacrifice. 6330
19: 8 he traveled forty days and forty nights **u** 6330
22:11 'With these you will gore the Arameans **u** 6330
22:27 and give him nothing but bread and water **u** 6330
2Ki 2:17 But they persisted **u** he was too ashamed 6330
3:24 the Israelites rose up and fought them **u** 2256
3:25 on every good field **u** it was covered. 2256
4:20 the boy sat on her lap **u** noon, 6330
7: 3 "Why stay here **u** we die? 6330
7: 9 If we wait **u** daylight, 6330
8: 6 from the day she left the country **u** now." 6330
8:11 with a fixed gaze **u** Hazael felt ashamed. 6330
10: 8 at the entrance of the city gate **u** morning." 6330
10:21 They crowded into the temple of Baal **u** 2256
15: 5 the king with leprosy **u** the day he died, 6330
17:20 **u** he thrust them from his presence. 889+6330
17:23 **u** the LORD removed them from his 889+6330
18:32 **u** I come and take you to a land 6330
20:17 that your fathers have stored up **u** this day, 6330
2Ki 21:15 came out of Egypt **u** this day." 6330
25: 2 The city was kept under siege **u** 6330
1Ch 4:31 These were their towns **u** the reign 6330
5:22 And they occupied the land **u** the exile. 6330
6:32 **u** Solomon built the temple of the LORD 6330
12:22 **u** he had a great army, 6330
12:29 remained loyal to Saul's house **u** then; 6330
28:20 or forsake you **u** all the work for the service 6330
2Ch 8:16 of the LORD was laid **u** its completion. 6330
9: 6 But I did not believe what they said **u** 889+6330
15:19 There was no more war **u** 6330
18:10 'With these you will gore the Arameans **u** 6330
18:26 and give him nothing but bread and water **u** 6330
18:34 up in his chariot facing the Arameans **u** 6330
21:15 **u** the disease causes your bowels 6330
24:10 dropping them into the chest **u** it was full. 6330
26:15 for he was greatly helped **u** he became 3954+6330
26:21 King Uzziah had leprosy **u** the day he died. 6330
29:28 All this continued **u** the sacrifice of 6330
29:34 so their kinsmen the Levites helped them **u** 6330
29:34 and **u** other priests had been consecrated, 6330
35:14 the burnt offerings and the fat portions **u** 6330
36:16 and scoffed at his prophets **u** the wrath of 6330
36:20 and his sons **u** the kingdom of Persia came 6330
36:21 all the time of its desolation it rested, **u** 6330
Ezr 2:63 not to eat any of the most sacred food **u** 6330
4:21 that this city will not be rebuilt **u** I so order. 10527
4:24 to a standstill **u** the second year of the reign 10527
5: 5 not stopped **u** a report could go to Darius 10527
8:29 Guard them carefully **u** you weigh them out 6330
9: 4 I sat there appalled **u** the evening sacrifice. 6330
9: 7 From the days of our forefathers **u** now, 6330
10:14 **u** the fierce anger of our God 6330
Ne 2: 7 they will provide me safe-conduct **u** 889+6330
5:14 **u** his thirty-second year— 6330
7: 3 gates of Jerusalem are not to be opened **u** 6330
7:65 of the most sacred food **u** there should be 6330
8:17 the days of Joshua son of Nun **u** that day, 6330
9:32 the days of the kings of Assyria **u** today. 6330
13:19 and not opened **u** the Sabbath was over. 6330
Ps 57: 1 of your wings **u** the disaster has passed. 6330
104:23 to his labor **u** evening. 6330
110: 1 at my right hand **u** I make your enemies 6330
SS 2: 7 or awaken love **u** it so desires. 6330+8611
2:17 **U** the day breaks and the shadows flee, 6330+8611
3: 5 or awaken love **u** it so desires. 6330+8611
4: 6 **U** the day breaks and the shadows flee, 6330+8611
8: 4 or awaken love **u** it so desires. 6330+8611
Isa 6:11 "**U** the cities lie ruined and 561+889+6330
6:11 **u** the houses are left deserted and 2256
6:12 **u** the LORD has sent everyone far away 2256
26:20 for a little while **u** his wrath has passed by. 6330
36:17 **u** I come and take you to a land 6330
39: 6 that your fathers have stored up **u** this day, 6330
Jer 2:25 Do not run **u** your feet are bare 4946
7:25 From the time your forefathers left Egypt **u** 6330
7:32 for they will bury the dead in Topheth **u** 4946
9:16 with the sword **u** I have destroyed them." 6330
11: 7 up from Egypt **u** today, 6330
19:11 They will bury the dead in Topheth **u** 4946
23:20 not turn back **u** he fully accomplishes 6330
24:10 against them **u** they are destroyed from 6330
25: 3 of Amon king of Judah **u** this very day— 6330
27: 7 and his son and his grandson **u** the time 6330
27: 8 **u** I destroy it by his hand. 6330
27:22 and there they will remain **u** the day I come 6330
30:24 not turn back **u** he fully accomplishes 6330
32: 5 where he will remain **u** I deal with him, 6330
32:31 From the day it was built **u** now, 6330
36:23 **u** the entire scroll was burned in the fire. 6330
37:21 from the street of the bakers each day **u** all 6330
38:28 in the courtyard of the guard **u** 6330
44:27 in Egypt will perish by sword and famine **u** 6330
49:37 the sword **u** I have made an end of them. 6330
52: 5 The city was kept under siege **u** 6330
La 3:50 **u** the LORD looks down from heaven 6330
Eze 4: 8 to the other **u** you have finished the days 6330
4:14 From my youth **u** I have never eaten 6330
21:27 It will not be restored **u** he comes 6330
24:13 you will not be clean again **u** my wrath 6330
34:21 the weak sheep with your horns **u** 889+6330
39:15 beside it **u** the gravediggers have buried it 6330
42:14 not to go into the outer court **u** they leave 2256
46: 2 but the gate will not be shut **u** evening. 6330
46:17 the servant may keep it **u** the year 6330
Da 1:21 And Daniel remained there **u** the first year 6330
4:22 your greatness has grown **u** it reaches 10221
4:23 **u** seven times pass by for him.' 10168+10527
4:25 by for you **u** you acknowledge that 10168+10527
4:32 by for you **u** you acknowledge that 10168+10527
4:33 **u** his hair grew like the feathers 10168+10527
5:21 **u** he acknowledged that the Most 10168+10527
6:14 to rescue Daniel and made every effort **u** 10527
7: 4 I watched **u** its wings were torn off 10168+10527
7:11 I kept looking **u** the beast was slain 10168+10527
7:22 **u** the Ancient of Days came 10168+10527
8:10 It grew **u** it reached the host of the heavens, 6330
9:25 and rebuild Jerusalem **u** the Anointed One, 6330
9:26 War will continue **u** the end, 6330
9:27 **u** the end that is decreed is poured out 6330
10: 3 at all **u** the three weeks were over. 6330
11:35 and made spotless **u** the time of the end, 6330
11:36 He will be successful **u** the time 6330
12: 1 from the beginning of nations **u** then. 6330
12: 4 close up and seal the words of the scroll **u** 6330
12: 9 the words are closed up and sealed **u** 6330
Hos 5:15 to my place **u** they admit their guilt. 889+6330

Hos 10:12 **u** he comes and showers righteousness 6330
Joel 2:26 You will have plenty to eat, **u** you are full, 2256
Mic 5: 3 be abandoned **u** the time when she who is 6330
7: 9 **u** he pleads my case 889+6330
Hag 2:19 **U** now, the vine and the fig tree, 6330
Mt 1:25 with her **u** she gave birth to a son. *2401+4005*
2: 9 in the east went ahead of them **u** it stopped *2401*
2:13 Stay there **u** I tell you, *323+2401*
2:15 where he stayed **u** the death of Herod. *2401*
5:18 **u** heaven and earth disappear, *323+2401*
5:18 by any means disappear from the Law **u** *323+2401*
5:26 get out **u** you have paid the last penny. *323+2401*
10:11 and stay at his house **u** you leave. *323+2401*
11:12 From the days of John the Baptist **u** now, *2401*
11:13 the Prophets and the Law prophesied **u** *2401*
13:30 Let both grow together **u** the harvest. *2401*
13:33 **u** it worked all through the dough." *2401+4005*
17: 9 **u** the Son of Man has been raised from *2401+4005*
18:30 the man thrown into prison **u** he could pay *2401*
18:34 **u** he should pay back all he owed. *2401+4005*
22:44 at my right hand **u** I put your enemies *323+2401*
23:39 you will not see me again **u** you say, *323+2401*
24:21 from the beginning of the world **u** now— *2401*
24:34 not pass away **u** all these things *323+2401*
24:39 about what would happen **u** the flood came *2401*
26:29 on **u** that day when I drink it anew with you *2401*
27:45 From the sixth hour **u** the ninth hour *2401*
27:64 the tomb to be made secure **u** the third day. *2401*
Mk 6:10 stay there **u** you leave that town. *323+2401*
9: 9 **u** the Son of Man had risen *1623+3590+4020*
12:36 at my right hand **u** I put your enemies *323+2401*
13:19 **u** now—and never to be equaled again. *2401*
13:30 not pass away **u** all these things *3588+4005*
14:25 of the vine **u** that day when I drink it anew *2401*
15:33 over the whole land **u** the ninth hour. *2401*
Lk 1:20 not able to speak **u** the day this happens, *948*
1:80 the desert **u** he appeared publicly to Israel. *2401*
2:37 then was a widow **u** she was eighty-four. *2401*
4:13 he left him **u** an opportune time. *948*
9: 4 stay there **u** you leave that town. *NIG*
12:50 how distressed I am **u** it is completed! *2401+4015*
12:59 not get out **u** you have paid the last penny." *2401*
13:21 **u** it worked all through the dough." *2401+4005*
13:35 you will not see me again **u** you say, *2401*
15: 4 and go after the lost sheep **u** he finds it? *2401*
15: 8 and search carefully **u** she finds it? *2401+4005*
16:16 and the Prophets were proclaimed **u** John. *3588*
19:13 he said, **'u** I come back.' *1877+4005*
20:43 **u** I make your enemies a footstool *2401*
21:24 trampled on by the Gentiles **u** the times *948+4005*
21:32 not pass away **u** all these things *323+2401*
22:16 not eat it again **u** it finds fulfillment *2401+4015*
22:18 the vine **u** the kingdom of God comes. *2401+4005*
23:44 and darkness came over the whole land **u** *2401*
24:49 **u** you have been clothed with power *2401+4005*
Jn 7:14 **Not u** halfway through the Feast *1254+2453*
8: 9 the older ones first, **u** only Jesus was left, *2779*
9:18 had received his sight **u** they sent for *2401+4015*
16:24 **U** now you have not asked for anything *2401*
21:22 "If I want him to remain alive **u** I return, *2401*
21:23 "If I want him to remain alive **u** I return, *2401*
Ac 1: 2 **u** the day he was taken up to heaven, *948*
2:35 **u** I make your enemies a footstool *323+2401*
3:21 in heaven **u** the time comes for God *948*
4: 3 they put them in jail **u** the next day. *1650*
7:45 It remained in the land **u** the time of David, *2401*
8:40 in all the towns **u** he reached Caesarea. *2401*
13: 6 They traveled through the whole island **u** *948*
13:20 God gave them judges **u** the time *2401*
20: 7 kept on talking **u** midnight. *3588*
20:11 After talking **u** daylight, he left. *948*
22:22 The crowd listened to Paul **u** he said this. *948*
23:12 to eat or drink **u** they had killed Paul. *2401+4005*
23:14 to eat anything **u** we have killed Paul. *2401+4005*
23:21 to eat or drink **u** they have killed him. *2401+4005*
25:21 I ordered him held **u** I could send him *2401+4005*
Ro 1:13 (but have been prevented from doing so **u** *948*
11:25 has experienced a hardening in part **u** *948+4005*
1Co 11:26 proclaim the Lord's death **u** he comes. *948+4005*
15:25 For he must reign **u** he has put all *948+4005*
16: 8 But I will stay on at Ephesus **u** Pentecost, *2401*
Gal 3:19 was added because of transgressions **u** *948+4005*
3:23 locked up **u** faith should be revealed. *1650*
4: 2 He is subject to guardians and trustees **u** *948*
4:19 pains of childbirth **u** Christ is formed *3588+4005*
Eph 1:14 a deposit guaranteeing our inheritance **u** *1650*
4:13 **u** we all reach unity in the faith and in *3588*
Php 1: 5 in the gospel from the first day **u** now, *948*
1: 6 on to completion **u** the day of Christ Jesus. *948*
1:10 be pure and blameless **u** the day of Christ, *1650*
2Th 2: 3 **u** the rebellion occurs and *1569+3590+4754*
1Ti 4:13 **U** I come, devote yourself to the public *2401*
6:14 without spot or blame **u** the appearing *3588*
2Ti 1:17 he searched hard for me **u** he found me. *2779*
Heb 1:13 at my right hand **u** I make your enemies *323+2401*
9:10 regulations applying **u** the time of the new *3588*
Jas 5: 7 then, brothers, **u** the Lord's coming. *2401*
1Pe 1: 5 by God's power **u** the coming of *1650*
2Pe 1:19 **u** the day dawns and the morning star *2401+4005*
Rev 2:25 hold on to what you have **u** I come *323+948+4005*
6:10 **u** *you* **judge** the inhabitants of the earth and avenge our blood?" *3212+4024*
6:11 **u** the number of their fellow servants *2401*
7: 3 the trees **u** we put a seal on the foreheads of *948*
15: 8 and no one could enter the temple **u** *948*
17:17 **u** God's words are fulfilled. *948*
20: 3 from deceiving the nations anymore **u** *948*
20: 5 (The rest of the dead did not come to life **u** *948*

UNTIMELY (KJV) See LATE, STILLBORN

UNTIRING (1)

Ps 77: 2 at night I stretched out **u** hands 4202+7028

UNTO (2)

Isa 53:12 because he poured out his life **u** death, 4200
Ac 11:18 even the Gentiles repentance **u** life." *1650*

UNTOUCHED (1)

Pr 19:23 Then one rests content, **u** *by* trouble. 1153+7212

UNTOWARD (KJV) See CORRUPT

UNTRAVELED (1)

Jer 9:10 They are desolate and **u**, 408+1172+4946+6296

UNTRUE (1)

Jos 24:27 It will be a witness against you if *you are* **u** 3950

UNTYING (4) [UNTIE]

Mk 11: 5 "What are you doing, **u** that colt?" *3395*
Lk 19:31 If anyone asks you, 'Why *are you* **u** it?' *3395*
19:33 *As* they *were* **u** the colt, *3395*
19:33 "Why *are you* **u** the colt?" *3395*

UNUSED (1)

Ex 23:11 seventh year let the land lie unplowed and **u** 5759

UNUSUAL (2)

Ac 28: 2 The islanders showed us **u** kindness. *4024+5593*
28: 6 a long time and seeing nothing **u** happen *876*

UNVEILED (1)

2Co 3:18 *who with* **u** faces all reflect the Lord's glory, *365*

UNWALLED (3)

Nu 13:19 Are they **u** or fortified? 4722
Dt 3: 5 and there were also a great many **u** villages. 7253
Eze 38:11 "I will invade a land of **u villages;** 7253

UNWASHED (2)

Mt 15:20 but eating *with* **u** hands does not make him *481*
Mk 7: 2 with hands that were "unclean," that is, **u.** *481*

UNWEIGHED (1)

1Ki 7:47 Solomon **left** all these things **u**, 5663

UNWHOLESOME (1)

Eph 4:29 not let any **u** talk come out of your mouths, *4911*

UNWILLING (9)

Ge 24: 5 if the woman *is* **u** to come back with me 14+4202
24: 8 If the woman *is* **u** to come back with you, 14+4202
Dt 1:26 But *you were* **u** to go up; 14+4202
Jdg 19:10 But, **u** to stay another night, 14+4202
1Sa 15: 9 These *they were* **u** to destroy completely, 14+4202
2Ki 13:23 To this day *he has been* **u** to destroy 14+4202
Isa 30: 9 children **u** to listen to the LORD's 14+4202
1Co 16:12 *He* was quite **u** to go now, *2525+4024*
Rev 2:21 repent of her immorality, but *she is* **u.** *2527+4024*

UNWISE (2)

Dt 32: 6 O foolish and **u** people? 2682+4202
Eph 5:15 how you live—not as **u** but as wise, *831*

UNWORTHY (4)

Ge 32:10 *I am* **u** of all the kindness 7781
Job 40: 4 *"I am* **u**—how can I reply to you? 7837
Lk 17:10 should say, 'We are **u** servants; *945*
1Co 11:27 of the Lord in an **u manner** will be guilty *397*

UNYIELDING (5)

Ex 7:14 "Pharaoh's heart is **u;** he refuses 3878
9: 7 Yet his heart *was* **u** and he would not let 3877
Pr 18:19 An offended brother is more **u** than NIH
SS 8: 6 its jealousy **u** as the grave. 7997
Eze 3: 8 But I will make you as **u** and hardened 2617+7156

UP (1905) [UPPER, UPWARD]

Ge 2: 5 and no plant of the field *had* yet **sprung u,** 7541
2: 6 but streams **came u** from the earth 6590
2:21 he took one of the man's ribs and **closed u** 6037
8: 7 until the water *had* **dried u** from the earth. 3312
8:13 the water *had* **dried u** from the earth. 2990
13: 1 So Abram **went u** from Egypt to the Negev, 6590
13:10 Lot looked **u** and saw that the whole plain 5951
13:14 **"Lift u** your eyes from where you are 5951
14: 8 and **drew u** their battle **lines** 6885
15: 5 **"Look u** at the heavens and count 5564
17:22 God **went u** from him. 6590
18: 2 Abraham looked **u** and saw three men 5951
18:16 When the men **got u** to leave, 7756
18:27 Then Abraham **spoke u** again: 6699
19: 1 *he* **got u** to meet them and bowed down 7756
19:27 **Early** the next morning Abraham **got u** 8899
19:33 of it when she lay down or when she **got u.** 7756
19:35 of it when she lay down or when she **got u.** 7756
20:18 the LORD *had* **closed u** every womb 6806+6806
21:18 **Lift** the boy **u** and take him by the hand, 5951
21:20 God was with the boy as *he* **grew u.** 1540
22: 3 **Early** the next morning Abraham **got u** 8899
22: 4 the third day Abraham looked **u** and saw 5951
22: 7 Isaac **spoke u** and said 606
22:13 Abraham looked **u** and there in 5951
24:16 filled her jar and **came u** again. 6590
24:54 When *they* **got u** the next morning, he said, 7756
24:63 and as he looked **u,** 5951
24:64 Rebekah also looked **u** and saw Isaac. 5951
25:27 The boys **grew u,** 1540
25:34 He ate and drank, and then **got u** and left. 7756
26:15 the Philistines **stopped u,** 6258
26:18 which the Philistines *had* **stopped u** 6258
26:23 From there *he* **went u** *to* Beersheba. 6590
27:19 Please sit **u** and eat some of my game so 7756
27:31 "My father, **sit u** and eat some of my game, 7756
28:18 and **set** it **u** *as* a pillar and poured oil on top 8492
28:22 and this stone that *I have* **set u** as 8492
31:10 a dream in which I looked **u** and saw that 5951
31:12 'Look **u** and see that all the male goats 5951
31:15 but *he has* **used u** what was paid for us. 430+430
31:23 and **caught u** *with* him in the hill country 1815
31:35 that I cannot **stand u** in your presence; 7756
31:45 Jacob took a stone and **set** it **u** as a pillar. 8123
31:51 and here is this pillar *I have* **set u** 3721
32:22 That night Jacob **got u** and took his 7756
33: 1 Jacob looked **u** and there was Esau, 5951
33: 5 Then Esau looked **u** and saw the women 5951
33:20 There *he* **set u** an altar 5893
35: 1 "Go **u** *to* Bethel and settle there, 6590
35: 3 Then come, *let us* **go u** *to* Bethel, 6590
35:13 Then God **went u** from him at the place 6590
35:14 Jacob **set u** a stone pillar at the place 5893
35:20 Over her tomb Jacob **set u** a pillar, 5893
37:25 they looked **u** and saw a caravan 5951
37:26 if we kill our brother and **cover u** 4059
37:28 his brothers pulled Joseph **u** out of 6590
38:11 until my son Shelah **grows u."** 1540
38:12 *he* **went u** to Timnah, 6590
38:14 *though* Shelah *had* now **grown u,** 1540
40:13 Within three days Pharaoh *will* **lift u** 5951
40:20 *He* **lifted u** the heads of 5951
41: 2 out of the river *there* **came u** seven cows, 6590
41: 3 **came u** out of the Nile and stood 6590
41: 4 the cows that were ugly and gaunt **ate u** 430
41: 4 Then Pharaoh **woke u.** 3699
41: 7 of grain **swallowed u** the seven healthy, 1180
41: 7 Then Pharaoh **woke u;** it had been a dream. 3699
41:18 out of the river *there* **came u** seven cows, 6590
41:19 After them, seven other cows **came u—** 6590
41:20 ugly cows **ate u** the seven fat cows 430
41:20 up the seven fat cows that came **u** first. NIH
41:21 Then *I* **woke u.** 3699
41:24 The thin heads of grain **swallowed u** 1180
41:27 that **came u** afterward are seven years, and 6590
41:35 that are coming and **store u** the grain under 7392
41:49 Joseph **stored u** huge quantities of grain, 7392
43:19 So *they* **went u** to Joseph's steward 5602
44: 4 and when *you* **catch u** *with* them, 5952
44: 6 When *he* **caught u** *with* them, 5952
44:18 Then Judah **went u** to him and said: 5602
44:30 whose life *is* **closely bound u** with 8003
45:25 So *they* **went u** out of Egypt and came 6590
46:31 *"I will* **go u** and speak to Pharaoh 6590
47:15 Our money *is* **used u."** 699
48: 2 Israel rallied his strength and **sat u** on 3782
49: 4 for *you* **went u** *onto* your father's bed, 6590
49:33 *he* **drew** his feet **u** into the bed, 665
50: 5 Now *let me* **go u** and bury my father; 6590
50: 6 Pharaoh said, **"Go u** and bury your father, 6590
50: 7 So Joseph **went u** to bury his father. 6590
50: 9 and horsemen also **went u** with him. 6590
50:24 surely come to your aid and **take** you **u** out 6590
50:25 and then *you must* **carry** my bones **u** 6590
Ex 2:11 One day, after Moses *had* **grown u,** 1540
2:17 but Moses **got u** and came to their rescue 7756
2:23 for help because of their slavery **went u** 6590
3: 2 the bush was on fire it *did* not **burn u.** 430
3: 3 why the bush *does* not **burn u."** 1277
3: 8 of the Egyptians and to **bring** them **u** out of 6590
3:17 *to* **bring** you **u** out of your misery in Egypt 6590
7:12 But Aaron's staff **swallowed u** their staffs. 1180
8: 3 They will come **u** into your palace 6590
8: 4 The frogs *will* **go u** on you 6590
8: 5 **make** frogs **come u** on the land of Egypt.' " 6590
8: 6 and the frogs **came u** and covered the land. 6590
8: 7 **made** frogs **come u** on the land of Egypt. 6590
8:20 **"Get u early** in the morning 8899
9:13 **"Get u early** in the morning, 8899
9:16 *I have* **raised** you **u** for this very purpose, 6641
10:19 *which* **caught u** the locusts and carried them 5951
12:30 the Egyptians **got u** during the night, 7756
12:31 Moses and Aaron and said, **"U!** 7756
12:38 Many other people **went u** with them, 6590
13:18 The Israelites **went u** out of Egypt armed 6590
13:19 then *you must* **carry** my bones **u** with you 6590
14:10 the Israelites looked **u,** 5951
15: 8 of your nostrils the waters **piled u.** 6890
17: 3 "Why *did you* **bring** us **u** out of Egypt 6590

Ex 17:11 As long as Moses **held u** his hands, 8123
17:12 Aaron and Hur **held** his hands **u—** 9461
17:16 "For hands were lifted **u** to the throne of NIH
19: 3 Then Moses **went u** to God, 6590
19:12 that you *do* not **go u** the mountain or touch 6590
19:13 a long blast *may* they **go u** to the mountain." 6590
19:18 The smoke **billowed u** *from* it like smoke 6590
19:20 So Moses **went u** 6590
19:23 "The people cannot **come u** Mount Sinai, 6590
19:24 "Go down and *bring* Aaron **u** with you. 6590
19:24 not force their way through to **come u** to 6590
20:26 And *do* not **go u** to my altar on steps, 6590
21:19 if the other **gets u** and walks around outside 7756
21:21 not to be punished if the slave **gets u** after 6641
21:29 but *has* not **kept** it **penned u** and it kills 9068
21:36 yet the owner *did* not **keep** it **penned u,** 9068
24: 1 he said to Moses, **"Come u** to the LORD, 6590
24: 2 And the people *may* not **come u** with him." 6590
24: 4 *He* **got u early** the next morning and built 8899
24: 4 and set **u** twelve stone pillars representing NIH
24: 9 and the seventy elders of Israel **went u** 6590
24:12 **"Come u** to me on the mountain 6590
24:13 and Moses **went u** on the mountain of God. 6590
24:15 When Moses **went u** on the mountain, 6590
24:18 the cloud as *he* **went** on **u** the mountain. 6590
25:37 "Then make its seven lamps and **set** them **u** 6590
26:30 **"Set u** the tabernacle according to 7756
27: 5 the ledge of the altar so that it is halfway **u** 6330
29:34 over till morning, **burn** it **u.** 836+928+2021+8596
32: 1 for this fellow Moses who **brought** us **u** out 6590
32: 4 O Israel, who **brought** you **u** out of Egypt." 6590
32: 6 down to eat and drink and **got u** to indulge 7756
32: 7 whom *you* **brought** you **u** out of Egypt, 6590
32: 8 O Israel, who **brought** you **u** out of Egypt.' 6590
32:23 for this fellow Moses who **brought** us **u** out 6590
32:30 But now *I will* **go u** to the LORD; 6590
33: 1 and the people *you* **brought u** out of Egypt, 6590
33: 1 and **go u** to the land I promised on oath 6590
33: 3 **Go u** to the land flowing with milk NIH
33:15 *do* not **send** us **u** from here. 6590
34: 2 and then **come u** on Mount Sinai. 6590
34: 4 the first ones and **went u** Mount Sinai early 6590
34:24 when you **go u** three times each year 6590
38: 4 to be under its ledge, halfway **u** the altar. 6330
40: 2 **"Set u** the tabernacle, 7756
40: 4 bring in the lampstand and **set u** its lamps. 6590
40: 8 **Set u** the courtyard around it and put 8492
40:17 So the tabernacle **was set u** on the first day 7756
40:18 When Moses **set u** the tabernacle, 7756
40:18 inserted the crossbars and **set u** the posts. 7756
40:25 and **set u** the lamps before the LORD, 6590
40:28 Then *he* **put u** the curtain at the entrance to 8492
40:33 Then Moses **set u** the courtyard around 7756
40:33 around the tabernacle and altar and **put u** 5989
Lev 5: 1 because *he does* not **speak u** when he hears 5583
7:17 third day *must* **be burned u.** 836+928+2021+8596
7:19 *it must* **be burned u.** 836+928+2021+8596
8:17 and its offal *he* **burned u** 836+928+2021+8596
8:32 **burn u** the rest of the meat 836+928+2021+8596
9:11 and the hide *he* **burned u** 836+928+2021+8596
10:16 and found that *it had* **been burned u,** 8596
11:25 Whoever **picks u** one of their carcasses 5951
11:28 Anyone *who* **picks u** their carcasses 5951
11:35 an oven or cooking pot *must* **be broken u.** 5997
11:40 Anyone *who* **picks u** the carcass 5951
11:45 I am the LORD who **brought** you **u** out 6590
13:52 *He must* **burn u** the clothing, 8596
13:52 article *must* **be burned u.** 836+928+2021+8596
14:38 of the house and **close** it **u** for seven days. 6037
14:46 into the house while it *is* **closed u** will 6037
15:10 whoever **picks u** those things must wash 5951
16:27 offal *are to be* **burned u.** 836+928+2021+8596
19: 6 third day *must* **be burned u.** 836+928+2021+8596
19:10 over your vineyard a second time or **pick u** 4377
21: 8 because they **offer u** the food of your God. 7928
23:16 Count off fifty days **u to** the day after 6330
25:50 from the year he sold himself **u to** the Year 6330
26: 1 " 'Do not make idols or **set u** an image or 7756
27:23 the priest will determine its value **u to** 6330
Nu 1:51 the tabernacle *is to be* **set u,** 2837
1:52 The Israelites *are to* **set u** their **tents** 2837
1:53 *to* **set u** their **tents** around the tabernacle of 2837
7: 1 When Moses finished **setting u** 7756
8: 2 'When you **set u** the seven lamps, 6590
8: 3 *he* **set u** the lamps so that they faced 6590
9:15 the Tent of the Testimony, *was* **set u,** 7756
10:21 *to be* **set u** before they arrived. 7756
10:35 Moses said, **"Rise u,** O LORD! 7756
11:28 **spoke u** and said, "Moses, my lord, 6699
13:17 **"Go u** through the Negev and on into 6590
13:21 So *they* **went u** and explored the land from 6590
13:22 *They* **went u** through the Negev and came 6590
13:30 *"We* **should go u** and take possession 6590+6590
13:31 But the men who *had* **gone u** with him said, 6590
14: 9 because we will **swallow** them **u.** 4312
14:13 **brought** these people **u** from among them. 6590
14:40 Early the next morning *they* **went u** toward 6590
14:40 *"We will* **go u** to the place 6590
14:42 *Do* not **go u,** because the LORD is not with 6590
14:44 in their presumption *they* **went u** toward 6590
16: 2 and **rose u** against Moses. 7756
16:13 Isn't it enough that *you have* **brought** us **u** 6590
16:25 Moses **got u** and went to Dathan 7756
16:39 by those *who had* **been burned u,** 8596
19: 9 "A man who is clean *shall* **gather u** 665
19:10 The *man who* **gathers u** the ashes of 665
20: 5 Why *did you* **bring** us **u** out of Egypt 6590
Nu 20:25 and his son Eleazar and **take** them **u** 6590
20:27 *They* **went u** Mount Hor in the sight of 6590
21: 5 "Why *have you* **brought** us **u** out of Egypt 6590
21: 8 "Make a snake and **put** it **u** on a pole; 8492
21: 9 So Moses made a bronze snake and **put** it **u** 8492
21:17 Israel sang this song: **"Spring u,** O well! 6590
21:29 *He has* **given u** his sons as fugitives 5989
21:33 Then they turned and **went u** *along* the road 6590
22: 4 "This horde *is* going to **lick u** everything 4308
22: 4 as an ox **licks u** the grass of the field." 4308
22:13 The next morning Balaam **got u** and said 7756
22:21 Balaam **got u** in the morning, 7756
22:41 The next morning Balak took Balaam **u** 6590
24:25 Then Balaam **got u** and returned home 7756
27:12 **"Go u** this mountain in the Abarim range 6590
32: 9 After *they* **went u** to the Valley of Eshcol 6590
32:11 or more who **came u** out of Egypt will see 6590
32:16 Then *they* **came u** to him and said, 5602
32:34 The Gadites **built u** Dibon, Ataroth, 1215
33:38 the priest **went u** Mount Hor, 6590
Dt 1:21 **Go u** and take possession of it as 6590
1:24 They left and **went u** into the hill country, 6590
1:26 But you were unwilling to **go u;** 6590
1:28 the cities are large, with walls **u to** the sky. 928
1:41 We *will* **go u** and fight, 6590
1:41 to **go u** into the hill country. 6590
1:42 "Tell them, *'Do* not **go u** and fight, 6590
1:43 and in your arrogance *you* **marched u** into 6590
2: 8 which comes **u** from Elath NIH
2:13 "Now **get u** and cross the Zered Valley." 7756
3: 1 and **went u** *along* the road toward Bashan, 6590
3:27 **Go u** *to* the top of Pisgah and look west 6590
4:19 when you look **u** to the sky and see the sun, 5951
5: 5 of the fire and *did* not **go u** the mountain.) 6590
6: 7 when you lie down and when you **get u.** 7756
7:24 No one *will be able to* **stand u** against you; 3656
9: 1 with large cities that have walls **u to** 928
9: 2 "Who *can* **stand u** against the Anakites?" 3656
9: 9 When I **went u** on the mountain to receive 6590
9:23 **"Go u** and take possession of the land 6590
10: 1 like the first ones and **come u** to me on 6590
10: 3 and *I* **went u** on the mountain with 6590
11: 6 of all Israel and **swallowed** them **u** 1180
11:19 when you lie down and when you **get u.** 7756
16:21 not **set u** any wooden Asherah pole beside 5749
18:15 The LORD your God *will* **raise u** for you 7756
18:18 *I will* **raise u** for them a prophet like you 7756
19:14 move your neighbor's boundary stone **set u** 1487
20: 1 who **brought** you **u** out of Egypt, 6590
20:10 When *you* **march u** to attack a city, 7928
23:13 and **cover u** your excrement. 2256+4059+8740
25: 9 his brother's widow *shall* **go u** to him in 5602
25: 9 not **build u** his brother's family line." 1215
27: 2 **set u** some large stones and coat them 7756
27: 4 **set u** these stones on Mount Ebal, 7756
27: 8 of this law on these stones you have set **u."** NIH
27:15 and **sets** it **u** in secret." 8492
28: 7 that the enemies who **rise u** against you will 7756
30:12 It is not **u** in heaven, NIH
32: 8 *he* **set u** boundaries for the peoples 5893
32:11 like an eagle *that* **stirs u** its nest and hovers 6424
32:30 unless the LORD *had* **given** them **u?** 6037
32:38 *Let them* **rise u** to help you! 7756
32:49 **"Go u** into the Abarim Range 6590
33:11 the loins of *those who* **rise u** *against* him; 7756
Jos 1: 5 *be able to* **stand u** against you all the days 3656
2: 5 *You may* **catch u** *with* them." 5952
2: 6 (But she *had* **taken** them **u** to the roof 6590
3: 8 she **went u** on the roof 6590
2:10 the LORD **dried u** the water of the Red Sea 3312
3: 6 **"Take u** the ark of the covenant and pass on 5951
3: 6 So *they* **took** it **u** and went ahead of them. 5951
3:13 be cut off and **stand u** in a heap." 6641
3:16 *It* **piled u** in a heap a great distance away, 7756
4: 3 *to* **take u** twelve stones from the middle of 5951
4: 5 of you *is to* **take u** a stone on his shoulder, 8123
4: 9 Joshua **set u** the twelve stones 7756
4:16 the Testimony *to* **come u** out of the Jordan." 6590
4:17 **"Come u** out of the Jordan." 6590
4:18 the priests **came u** out of the river carrying 6590
4:19 of the first month the people **went u** from 6590
4:20 And Joshua **set u** at Gilgal 7756
4:23 For the LORD your God **dried u** the Jordan 3312
4:23 to the Red Sea when *he* **dried** it **u** before us 3312
5: 1 the coast heard how the LORD *had* **dried u** 3312
5: 7 So *he* **raised u** their sons in their place, 7756
5:13 he looked **u** and saw a man standing 5951
5:13 Joshua **went u** to him and asked, 2143
6: 1 Now Jericho *was* **tightly shut u** 2256+6037+6037
6: 5 and the people *will* **go u,** 6590
6: 6 **"Take u** the ark of the covenant of 5951
6:12 Joshua **got u early** the next morning and 8899
6:12 the priests **took u** the ark of the LORD. 5951
6:15 *they* **got u** at daybreak and marched 8899
6:26 at the cost of his youngest *will he* **set u** 5893
7: 2 **"Go u** and spy out the region." 6590
7: 2 So the men **went u** and spied out Ai. 6590
7: 3 the people *will have to* **go u** *against* Ai. 6590
7: 4 So about three thousand men **went u;** 6590
7:10 The LORD said to Joshua, **"Stand u!** 7756
7:26 Over Achan *they* **heaped u** a large pile 7756
8: 1 and **go u** and attack Ai. 7756
8: 7 *to* **rise u** from ambush and take the city. 7756
8:11 **marched u** and approached the city 6590
8:11 *They* **set u camp** north of Ai, 2837
8:13 **had** the soldiers **take u** *their* **positions—** 8492
8:21 and that smoke *was* **going u** *from* the city, 6590
Jos 10: 4 **"Come u** and help me attack Gibeon," 6590
10: 5 They **moved u** with all their troops and took 6590
10: 5 up with all their troops and **took u positions** 2837
10: 6 **Come u** to us quickly and save us! 6590
10: 7 So Joshua **marched u** from Gilgal 6590
10:10 Israel pursued them along the road **going u** 5090
10:18 "Roll large rocks **u to** the mouth of 448
10:31 *he* **took u positions** against it 2837
10:33 of Gezer *had* **come u** to help Lachish, 6590
10:34 *they* **took u positions** against it 2837
10:36 Then Joshua and all Israel with him **went u** 6590
11:11 *he* **burned u** Hazor itself. 836+928+2021+8596
13:27 the territory **u to** the end of the Sea 6330
14: 8 but my brothers who **went u** with me made 6590
15: 3 past Hezron **u** to Addar and curved around 6590
15: 6 **went u** *to* Beth Hoglah and continued north 6590
15: 7 The boundary then **went u** to Debir from 6590
15: 8 Then it **ran u** the Valley of Ben Hinnom 6590
16: 1 and **went u** from there through the desert 6590
17:15 **go u** into the forest and clear land 6590
18: 1 of the Israelites gathered at Shiloh and **set u** 8905
18:11 The lot **came u** for the tribe of Benjamin, 6590
19:10 The third lot **came u** for Zebulun, 6590
19:12 and went on to Daberath and **u** *to* Japhia. 6590
19:47 so they **went u** and attacked Leshem, 6590
19:50 And *he* **built u** the town and settled there. 1215
22:17 **U to** this very day we have not cleansed 6330
24:17 **brought** us and our fathers **u** out of Egypt, 6590
24:25 at Shechem *he* **drew u** for them decrees 8492
24:26 Then he took a large stone and **set** it **u** there 7756
24:32 the Israelites *had* **brought u** from Egypt, 6590
Jdg 1: 1 be the first *to* **go u** and fight for us against 6590
1: 3 **"Come u** with us into the territory allotted 6590
1: 7 and big toes cut off *have* **picked u scraps** 4377
1:16 **went u** from the City of Palms with the men 6590
2: 1 of the LORD **went u** from Gilgal to Bokim 6590
2: 1 *"I* **brought** you **u** out of Egypt and led you 6590
2:10 another generation **grew u,** 7756
2:16 Then the LORD **raised u** judges, 7756
2:18 Whenever the LORD **raised u** a judge 7756
2:19 *They* refused *to* **give u** their evil practices 5877
3: 9 he **raised u** for them a deliverer, 7756
4:12 of Abinoam *had* **gone u** *to* Mount Tabor, 6590
4:19 gave him a drink, and **covered** him **u.** 4059
4:21 **picked u** a tent peg and a hammer 4374
5:12 **'Wake u,** wake up, Deborah! 6424
5:12 'Wake up, **wake u,** Deborah! 6424
5:12 **Wake u,** wake up, break out in song! 6424
5:12 Wake up, **wake u,** break out in song! 6424
6: 5 They **came u** with their livestock 6590
6: 8 I **brought** you **u** out of Egypt, 6590
6:13 not the LORD **bring** us **u** out of Egypt?' 6590
6:28 when the men of the town **got u,** 8899
6:35 so that *they* too **went u** to meet them. 6590
7: 9 **"Get u,** go down against the camp, 7756
7:15 the camp of Israel and called out, **"Get u!** 7756
8: 4 exhausted yet *keeping u* **the pursuit,** AIT
8: 8 From there *he* **went u** *to* Peniel and made 6590
8:11 Gideon **went u** *by* the route of 6590
8:33 *They* **set u** Baal-Berith as their god 8492
9: 7 *he* **climbed u** on the top of Mount Gerizim 2143
9: 9 *'Should I* **give u** my oil, 2532
9:11 fig tree replied, *'Should I* **give u** my fruit, 2532
9:13 *'Should I* **give u** my wine, 2532
9:31 and *are* **stirring u** the city against you. 7443
9:34 **took u concealed positions** 741
9:37 But Gaal **spoke u** again: 1819
9:48 he and all his men **went u** Mount Zalmon. 6590
9:51 They locked themselves in and **climbed u** 6590
11: 2 and when they *were* **grown u,** 1540
11:13 "When Israel **came u** out of Egypt, 6590
11:16 But when they **came u** out of Egypt, 6590
12: 3 why *have you* **come u** today to fight me?" 6590
13: 8 how *to* **bring u** the boy who is to be born." 6913
13:11 Manoah **got u** and followed his wife. 7756
13:20 As the flame **blazed u** from the altar 6590
14:19 *he* **went u** to his father's house. 6590
15: 5 *He* **burned u** the shocks and standing grain, 1277
15: 6 So the Philistines **went u** and burned her 6590
15: 9 The Philistines **went u** and camped 6590
15:12 "We've come to **tie** you **u** and hand you 673
15:13 *"We will* only **tie** you **u** and hand you 673+673
15:13 with two new ropes and **led** him **u** from 6590
15:19 God **opened u** the hollow place in Lehi, 1324
16: 3 Then *he* **got u** and took hold of the doors of 7756
16: 5 so *we may* **tie** him **u** and subdue him. 673
16: 6 and how *you can* **be tied u** and subdued." 673
16:14 from his sleep and **pulled u** the pin and 5825
18:12 On their way *they* **set u camp** 2837
18:30 the Danites **set u** for themselves the idols, 7756
19: 5 On the fourth day *they* **got u early** 8899
19: 7 And when the man **got u** to go, 7756
19: 9 **got u** to leave, his father-in-law, 7756
19: 9 **Early** tomorrow **morning** *you can* **get u** 8899
19:27 When her master **got u** in the morning 7756
19:28 He said to her, **"Get u;** let's go." 7756
19:29 he took a knife and **cut u** his concubine, 5983
19:30 the day the Israelites **came u** out of Egypt. 6590
20: 3 that the Israelites *had* **gone u** to Mizpah.) 6590
20: 7 **speak u** and give your verdict." 1821
20: 9 We'll go **u** against it as the lot directs. NIH
20:18 The Israelites **went u** *to* Bethel 6590
20:19 The next morning the Israelites **got u** 7756
20:20 and **took u** battle **positions** 6885
20:22 and again **took u** *their* **positions** 6885
20:23 The Israelites **went u** and wept before 6590
20:23 "Shall we **go u** again to battle against 5602

Jdg 20:23 **"Go u** against them." 6590
20:26 all the people, **went u** to Bethel, 6590
20:28 "Shall we **go u** again to battle 3655
20:30 They **went u** against the Benjamites on 6590
20:30 on the third day and **took u positions** 6885
20:33 from their places and **took u positions** 6885
20:38 with the ambush that they *should* **send u** 6590
20:40 the smoke of the whole city **going u** into 6590
Ru 1:13 would you wait until *they* **grew u?** 1540
2: 2 and **pick u** the leftover grain behind anyone 4377
2:15 As *she* **got u** to glean, 7756
2:16 and leave them for *her to* **pick u,** 4377
3:14 **got u** before anyone could be recognized; 7756
4: 1 Meanwhile Boaz **went u** *to* the town gate 6590
4:11 who together **built u** the house of Israel. 1215
1Sa 1: 3 after year this man **went u** from his town 6590
1: 7 Whenever Hannah **went u** to the house of 6590
1: 9 and drinking in Shiloh, Hannah **stood u.** 7756
1:21 the man Elkanah **went u** with all his family 6590
2: 6 he brings down to the grave and **raises u.** 6590
2:14 for himself whatever the fork **brought u.** 6590
2:16 *"Let* the fat *be* **burned u** first, 7787+7787
2:19 when she **went u** with her husband to offer 6590
2:21 the boy Samuel **grew u** in the presence of 1540
2:28 to **go u** to my altar, to burn incense, 6590
2:35 *I will* **raise u** for myself a faithful priest, 7756
3: 6 Samuel **got u** and went to Eli and said, 7756
3: 8 and Samuel **got u** and went to Eli and said, 7756
3:19 The LORD was with Samuel as he **grew u,** 1540
4:13 the whole town **sent u a cry.** 2410
5:12 and the outcry of the city **went u** *to* heaven. 6590
6: 7 take their calves away and **pen** them **u.** 1074+2025
6: 9 If *it* **goes u** to its own territory, 6590
6:10 and **penned u** their calves. 928+1074+2021+3973
6:12 Then the cows **went straight** *u* AIT
6:13 and when they looked **u** and saw the ark, 5951
6:14 The people **chopped u** the wood of the cart 1324
6:20 To whom *will* the ark **go u** from here?" 6590
6:21 Come down and **take** it **u** to your place." 6590
7: 1 the men of Kiriath Jearim came and **took u** 6590
7: 7 of the Philistines **came u** to attack them. 6590
7: 9 and **offered** it **u** as a whole burnt offering 6590
7:12 and **set** it **u** between Mizpah and Shen. 8492
8: 8 the day *I* **brought** them **u** out of Egypt 6590
9:11 As they *were* **going u** the hill to the town, 6590
9:13 before *he* **goes u** to the high place to eat. 6590
9:13 those who are invited will eat. **Go u** now; 6590
9:14 *They* **went u** *to* the town, 6590
9:14 coming toward them **on** *his* **way u** *to* 6590
9:19 **"Go u** ahead of me *to* the high place, 6590
9:24 the cook **took u** the leg with what was on it 8123
10: 3 Three men **going u** to God 6590
10:18 'I **brought** Israel **u** out of Egypt, 6590
11: 1 Nahash the Ammonite **went u** 6590
12: 6 **brought** your forefathers **u** 6590
13: 5 *They* **went u** and camped at Micmash, 6590
13: 9 And Saul **offered u** the burnt offering. 6590
13:15 Then Samuel left Gilgal and **went u** 6590
14: 9 we will stay where we are and not **go u** 6590
14:10 But if they say, **'Come u** to us,' 6590
14:10 'Come up to us,' *we will* **climb u,** 6590
14:12 **"Come u** to us and we'll teach you 6590
14:12 **"Climb u** after me; 6590
14:13 Jonathan **climbed u,** using his hands 6590
14:21 the Philistines and *had* **gone u** with them 6590
15: 2 when they waylaid them as they **came u** 6590
15: 6 to all the Israelites when they **came u** out 6590
15:12 **Early** in the morning Samuel **got u** 8899
15:12 There *he has* **set u** a monument 5893
15:34 Saul **went u** to his home in Gibeah of Saul. 6590
17: 2 **drew u** their battle **line** to meet 6885
17: 8 "Why do you come out and **line u** 6885
17:20 **loaded u** and set out, as Jesse had directed. 5951
17:21 Israel and the Philistines *were* **drawing u** 6885
17:30 and **brought u** the same matter, 606
19:15 **"Bring** him **u** to me in his bed so 6590
20:30 Saul's anger **flared u** at Jonathan 3013
20:34 Jonathan **got u** from the table 7756
20:38 The boy **picked u** the arrow and returned 4377
20:41 David **got u** from the south side 7756
23: 8 Saul **called u** all his forces for battle, 9048
23:19 The Ziphites **went u** to Saul at Gibeah 6590
23:29 And David **went u** from there and lived in 6590
24: 4 Then David **crept u** unnoticed and cut off 7756
24:22 and his men **went u** to the stronghold. 6590
25: 5 "Go **u** to Nabal at Carmel and greet him 6590
25:13 About four hundred men **went u** 6590
26:12 nor *did anyone* **wake u.** 7810
27: 1 Then Saul *will* **give u** searching 3286
27: 8 Now David and his men **went u** and raided 6590
28: 4 and came and **set u camp** at Shunem, 2837
28: 4 the Israelites and **set u camp** at Gilboa. 2837
28: 8 "and **bring u** for me the one I name." 6590
28:11 "Whom *shall I* **bring u** for you?" 6590
28:11 **"Bring u** Samuel," he said. 6590
28:13 "I see a spirit **coming u** out of the ground." 6590
28:14 "An old man wearing a robe *is* **coming u,"** 6590
28:15 disturbed me by **bringing** me **u?"** 6590
28:23 *He* **got u** from the ground and sat on 7756
28:25 That same night *they* **got u** and left. 7756
29: 9 *'He must* not **go u** with us into battle.' 6590
29:10 Now **get u early,** 8899
29:11 and his men **got u early** in the morning 8899
29:11 and the Philistines **went u** *to* Jezreel. 6590
2Sa 1:17 David **took u** this **lament** concerning Saul
and his son Jonathan, 7801+7806
2: 1 *"Shall I* **go u** to one of the towns 6590
2Sa 2: 1 The LORD said, **"Go u."** 6590
2: 2 So David **went u** there with his two wives, 6590
2:14 the young men **get u** and fight hand to hand 7756
2:15 So *they* **stood u** and were counted off— 7756
2:23 But Asahel refused to **give u** *the* **pursuit;** 6073
4: 4 His nurse **picked** him **u** and fled, 5951
5: 9 David then **took u residence** in the fortress 3782
5: 9 He **built u** the area around it, 1215
5:17 they **went u** in full force to search for him, 6590
5:22 the Philistines **came u** and spread out in 6590
5:23 and he answered, *"Do* not **go straight u,** 6590
6: 2 from Baalah of Judah to **bring u** from there 6590
6:12 So David went down and **brought u** the ark 6590
6:15 the entire house of Israel **brought u** the ark 6590
7: 6 **brought** the Israelites **u** out of Egypt 6590
7:12 *I will* **raise u** your offspring 7756
10: 8 The Ammonites came out and **drew u** 6885
11: 2 One evening David **got u** from his bed 7756
11:20 the king's anger *may* **flare u,** 6590
12: 3 and *it* **grew u** with him and his children. 1540
12:17 beside him to **get** him **u** from the ground, 7756
12:20 Then David **got u** from the ground. 7756
12:21 *you* **get u** and eat!" 7756
13:15 Amnon said to her, **"Get u** and get out!" 7756
13:29 Then all the king's sons **got u,** 7756
13:31 The king **stood u,** tore his clothes and lay 7756
13:34 Now the man standing watch looked **u** 5951
14: 7 Now the whole clan *has* **risen u** 7756
15: 2 He *would* **get u early** and stand by 8899
15:30 David *continued* **u** the Mount of Olives, 6590
15:30 and were weeping as *they* **went u.** 6590
17:16 with him *will* **be swallowed u.' "** 1180
18:17 and **piled u** a large heap of rocks over him. 5893
18:24 the watchman **went u** to the roof of 2143
18:28 *He has* **delivered u** the men who 6037
18:31 from all who **rose u** against you." 7756
18:32 the king and all who **rise u** to harm you be 7756
18:33 *He* **went u** to the room over the gateway 6590
19: 8 So the king **got u** and took his seat in 7756
19:34 *I should* **go u** *to* Jerusalem with the king? 6590
20:12 that everyone who came **u** to 6584
20:15 They built a siege ramp **u to** the city, 448
20:19 *to* **swallow u** the LORD's inheritance?" 1180
20:20 be it from me *to* **swallow u** or destroy! 1180
20:21 *has* **lifted u** his hand against the king, 5951
21:13 and exposed *were* **gathered u.** 665
23: 7 *they* **are burned u** where they lie."
836+928+2021+8596+8596
24:11 Before David **got u** the next morning, 7756
24:18 **"Go u** and build an altar to the LORD on 6590
24:19 So David **went u,** as the LORD had 6590
24:22 whatever pleases him and **offer** it **u.** 6590
1Ki 1:35 Then *you are* to **go u** with him, 6590
1:40 And all the people **went u** after him, 6590
1:45 From there *they have* **gone u** cheering, 6590
2:19 the king **stood u** to meet her, 7756
2:34 of Jehoiada **went u** and struck down Joab 6590
3:20 So *she* **got u** in the middle of the night 7756
3:21 *I* **got u** to nurse my son— 7756
6: 8 a stairway *led* **u** to the middle level and 6590
8: 1 to **bring u** the ark of the LORD's covenant 6590
8: 3 the priests **took u** the ark, 5951
8: 4 and *they* **brought u** the ark of the LORD 6590
8: 4 The priests and Levites **carried** them **u,** 6590
8:35 the heavens *are* **shut u** and there is no rain 6806
9:17 He built **u** Lower Beth Horon, NIH
9:24 After Pharaoh's daughter *had* **come u** from 6590
11:14 Then the LORD **raised u** against Solomon 7756
11:15 who *had* **gone u** to bury the dead, 6590
11:20 whom Tahpenes **brought u** in 1694
11:23 And God **raised u** against Solomon 7756
12: 8 the young men who *had* **grown u** with him 1540
12:10 The young men who *had* **grown u** 1540
12:24 *Do* not **go u** to fight against your brothers, 6590
12:25 From there he went out and **built u** Peniel. 1215
12:27 If these people **go u** to offer sacrifices at 6590
12:28 "It is too much for you *to* **go u** 6590
12:28 O Israel, who **brought** you **u** out of Egypt." 6590
12:29 One *he* **set u** in Bethel, 8492
12:33 the festival for the Israelites and **went u** to 6590
13: 4 toward the man **shriveled u,** 3312
13:29 the prophet **picked u** the body of the man 5951
14: 7 *'I* **raised** you **u** from among the people 8123
14:10 *I will* **burn u** the house of Jeroboam 1277
14:14 "The LORD *will* **raise u** for himself 7756
14:16 And *he will* **give** Israel **u** because of 5989
14:17 Then Jeroboam's wife **got u** and left 7756
14:22 **stirred u** his **jealous anger** more than 7861
14:23 They also **set u** for themselves high places, 1215
15: 4 a lamp in Jerusalem by **raising u** a son 7756
15:17 Baasha king of Israel **went u** against Judah 6590
15:22 With them King Asa **built u** Geba 1215
16: 2 *"I* **lifted** you **u** from the dust 8123
16:32 *He* **set u** an altar for Baal in the temple 7756
16:34 and *he* **set u** its gates at the cost 5893
17: 7 Some time later the brook **dried u** 3312
17:14 *be* **used u** and the jug of oil will not run dry 3983
17:16 of flour *was* not **used u** and the jug of oil 3983
17:23 Elijah **picked u** the child and carried him 4374
18:38 fell and **burned u** the sacrifice, 430
18:38 and also **licked u** the water in the trench. 4308
18:43 And *he* **went u** and looked. 6590
18:44 **'Hitch u** your chariot and go down before 673
19: 5 **"Get u** and eat." 7756
19: 7 **"Get u** and eat, 7756
19: 8 So *he* **got u** and ate and drank. 7756
19:19 Elijah **went u** to him and threw his cloak 6296
1Ki 20: 1 *he* **went u** and besieged Samaria 6590
20:26 and **went u** to Aphek to fight against Israel. 6590
20:28 of God **came u** and told the king of Israel, 5602
20:33 as a good sign and were quick *to* **pick u** 2715
20:33 Ahab **had** him **come u** into his chariot. 6590
20:34 *"You may* **set u** your own market areas 8492
21: 7 **Get u** and eat! Cheer up. 7756
21: 7 Get up and eat! **Cheer u.** 3512+4213
21:15 **"Get u** and take possession of the vineyard 7756
21:16 he **got u** and went down to take possession 7756
21:19 where dogs **licked u** Naboth's blood, 4379
21:19 dogs *will* **lick u** your blood— 4379
22:24 of Kenaanah **went u** and slapped Micaiah in 5602
22:29 and Jehoshaphat king of Judah **went u** 6590
22:35 the king was **propped u** in his chariot 6641
22:38 and the dogs **licked u** his blood, 4379
2Ki 1: 3 **"Go u** and meet the messengers of the king 6590
1: 9 The captain **went u** to Elijah, 6590
1:13 This third captain **went u** and fell 6590
1:15 So Elijah **got u** and went down with him to 7756
2: 1 *to* **take** Elijah **u** to heaven in a whirlwind, 6590
2: 5 at Jericho **went u** to Elisha and asked him, 5602
2: 8 **rolled** it **u** and struck the water with it. 1676
2:11 Elijah **went u** *to* heaven in a whirlwind. 6590
2:13 *He* **picked u** the cloak that had fallen 8123
2:16 of the LORD *has* **picked** him **u** and set him 5951
2:23 From there Elisha **went u** *to* Bethel. 6590
2:23 **"Go on u,** *you* baldhead!" 6590
2:23 **"Go on u,** *you* baldhead!" 6590
3:19 **stop u** all the springs, and ruin every good 6258
3:21 who could bear arms **was called u** 7590
3:22 When *they* **got u early** in the morning, 8899
3:24 the Israelites **rose u** and fought them 7756
3:25 *They* **stopped u** all the springs and cut 6258
4:11 *he* **went u** to his room and lay down there. 6073
4:20 After the servant *had* **lifted** him **u** 5951
4:21 *She* **went u** and laid him on the bed of 6590
4:30 So *he* **got u** and followed her. 7756
4:39 *he* **cut** them **u** into the pot of stew, 7114
5:23 **tied u** the two talents of silver in two bags, 7443
6: 8 "I will **set u** my **camp** in such and such 9381
6:15 of the man of God **got u** and went out early 7756
6:24 and **marched u** and laid siege to Samaria. 6590
6:28 **'Give u** your son so we may eat him today, 5989
6:29 **'Give u** your son so we may eat him,' 5989
7: 5 At dusk *they* **got u** and went to the camp of 7756
7: 7 So *they* **got u** and fled in the dusk 7756
7:12 The king **got u** in the night and said 7756
8: 7 "The man of God has come **all the way u** 6330
8:20 and **set u** its own **king.** 4887+4889
8:21 but he **rose u** and broke through by night; 7756
9: 6 Jehu **got u** and went into the house. 7756
9:21 **"Hitch u** my chariot," Joram ordered. 673
9:21 And when *it was* **hitched u,** 673
9:25 **"Pick** him **u** and throw him on the field 5951
9:26 then, **pick** him **u** and throw him on that plot, 5951
9:27 *he* **fled u** the road to Beth Haggan. 5674
9:27 in his chariot on the **way u** *to* Gur 5090
9:32 He looked **u** at the window and called out, 5951
10:15 and Jehu **helped** him **u** into the chariot. 6590
12:17 of Aram **went u** and attacked Gath 6590
13:21 the man came to life and **stood u** 7756
15:14 of Gadi went from Tirzah **u** *to* Samaria. 6590
16: 5 of Remaliah king of Israel **marched u** 6590
16: 7 **Come u** and save me out of the hand of 6590
16:13 *He* **offered u** his burnt offering 7787
17: 3 Shalmaneser king of Assyria **came u** 6590
17: 7 who *had* **brought** them **u** out of Egypt from 6590
17:10 *They* **set u** sacred stones and Asherah poles 5893
17:29 and **set** them **u** in the shrines the people 5663
17:36 who **brought** you **u** out of Egypt 6590
18: 4 for **u** to that time the Israelites had been 6330
18:17 They came **u** *to* Jerusalem and stopped at 6590
19:14 Then he **went u** *to* the temple of 6590
19:24 With the soles of my feet *I have* **dried u** all 2990
19:26 scorched before *it* **grows u.** 7756
19:35 When *the people* **got u** the next morning— 8899
20: 5 On the third day from now *you will* **go u** 6590
20: 8 and that *I will* **go u** *to* the temple of 6590
20:17 and all that your fathers *have* **stored u** 732
22: 4 **"Go u** to Hilkiah the high priest 6590
23: 2 He **went u** *to* the temple of the LORD 6590
23:29 of Egypt **went u** to the Euphrates River 6590
24:11 and Nebuchadnezzar *himself* **came u** to 993
25:13 The Babylonians **broke u** the bronze pillars, 8689
1Ch 5: 9 To the east they occupied the land **u to** 6330
5:26 So the God of Israel **stirred u** the spirit 6424
9:18 **u to** the present time. 6330
10:10 temple of their gods and **hung u** his head 9546
11: 6 Joab son of Zeruiah **went u** first, 6590
11: 7 David then **took u residence** in the fortress, 3782
11: 8 *He* **built u** the city around it, 1215
13: 6 to **bring u** from there the ark of God 6590
14: 8 they **went u** in full force to search for him, 6590
14:11 David and *his men* **went u** to Baal Perazim, 6590
14:14 *"Do* not go **straight u,** 6590
15: 3 to **bring u** the ark of the LORD to 6590
15:12 to consecrate yourselves and **bring u** 6590
15:13 did not bring it **u** the first time that NIH
15:14 in order to **bring u** the ark of the LORD, 6590
15:25 of a thousand went to **bring u** the ark of 6590
15:28 So all Israel **brought u** the ark of 6590
17: 5 a house from the day *I* **brought** Israel **u** out 6590
17:11 *I will* **raise u** your offspring 7756
19: 9 The Ammonites came out and **drew u** 6885
21: 1 Satan **rose u** against Israel and incited 6641
21:16 David looked **u** and saw the angel of 5951

1Ch 21:18 *to* **go u** and build an altar to the LORD on 6590
21:19 So David **went u** in obedience to the word 6590
2Ch 1: 4 Now David *had* **brought u** the ark of God 6590
1: 6 Solomon **went u** to the bronze altar before 6590
2:16 You *can* then **take** them **u** *to* Jerusalem." 6590
5: 2 to **bring u** the ark of the LORD's covenant 6590
5: 4 the Levites **took u** the ark, 5951
5: 5 and *they* **brought u** the ark and the Tent 6590
5: 5 priests, who were Levites, **carried** them **u;** 6590
6:26 the heavens *are* **shut u** and there is no rain 6806
7:13 "When *I* **shut u** the heavens so 6806
8: 4 also **built u** Tadmor in the desert and all 1215
8:11 **brought** Pharaoh's daughter **u** 6590
10: 8 the young men who *had* **grown u** with him 1540
10:10 The young men who *had* **grown u** 1540
11: 4 *Do* not **go u** to fight against your brothers. 6590
11: 5 Rehoboam lived in Jerusalem and **built u** 1215
13: 3 Jeroboam **drew u** *a* battle **line** 6885
14: 6 *He* **built u** the fortified cities of Judah, 1215
14: 7 *"Let us* **build u** these towns," 1215
14:10 and *they* **took u** battle **positions** 6885
15: 7 as for you, be strong and *do* not **give u,** 3338+8332
15:16 **broke** it **u** and burned it in 1990
16: 1 of Asa's reign Baasha king of Israel **went u** 6590
16: 6 With them *he* **built u** Geba and Mizpah. 1215
18:23 of Kenaanah **went u** and slapped Micaiah in 5602
18:28 and Jehoshaphat king of Judah **went u** 6590
18:34 and the king of Israel **propped** *himself* **u** 6641
20: 5 Then Jehoshaphat **stood u** in the assembly 6641
20:16 They *will be* **climbing u** by the Pass 6590
20:17 **Take u** *your* **positions;** 3656
20:19 from the Kohathites and Korahites **stood u** 7756
20:23 The men of Ammon and Moab **rose u** 6641
21: 8 and **set u** its own **king.** 4887+4889
21: 9 but *he* **rose u** and broke through by night. 7756
25:14 *He* **set** them **u** as his own gods, 6641
28:14 So the soldiers **gave u** the prisoners 6440
28:24 the doors of the LORD's temple and **set u** 6913
29:20 and **went u** *to* the temple of the LORD. 6590
30:16 *they* **took u** their regular positions 6584+6641
33:19 where he built high places and **set u** 6641
34:30 He **went u** *to* the temple of the LORD 6590
35:20 of Egypt **went u** to fight at Carchemish on 6590
36:17 *He* **brought u** against them the king of 6590
36:23 his God be with him, and *let him* **go u.'** " 6590
Ezr 1: 3 may his God be with him, and *let him* **go u** 6590
1: 5 to **go u** and build the house of the LORD 6590
1:11 along when the exiles **came u** from Babylon 6590
2: 1 the people of the province who **came u** 6590
2:59 The following **came u** from the towns 6590
4:12 that the Jews who **came u** to us 10513
6:11 and *he is to* **be lifted u** and impaled on it. 10238
7: 6 this Ezra **came u** from Babylon. 6590
7: 7 **came u** to Jerusalem in the seventh year 6590
7:22 **u to** a hundred talents of silver, 10527
7:28 from Israel to **go u** with me. 6590
8: 1 and those registered with them who **came u** 6590
9: 6 I am too ashamed and disgraced to **lift u** 8123
10: 4 **Rise u;** this matter is in your hands. 7756
10: 5 So Ezra **rose u** and put the leading priests 7756
10:10 Ezra the priest **stood u** and said to them, 7756
Ne 2:15 so *I* **went u** the valley by night, 6590
3:16 made repairs **u** to a point opposite 6330
3:26 on the hill of Ophel made repairs **u to** 6330
4: 3 if even a fox **climbed u** on it, 6590
4: 5 not **cover u** their guilt or blot out their sins 4059
4: 8 and fight against Jerusalem and **stir u** 6913
4:14 *I* **stood u** and said to the nobles, 7756
6: 1 though **u** to that time I had not set 6330
6: 8 you *are* just **making** it **u** out of your head." 968
7: 6 the people of the province who **came u** 6590
7:61 The following **came u** from the towns 6590
8: 2 which was **made u of** men and women 4946
8: 5 and as he opened it, the people all **stood u.** 6641
9: 5 **"Stand u** and praise the LORD your God, 7756
9:18 who **brought** you **u** out of Egypt,' 6590
10:38 **bring** a tenth of the tithes **u** 6590
12:23 the descendants of Levi **u to** the time 6330
12:31 **had** the leaders of Judah **go u** 6590
12:37 the Fountain Gate *they* **continued** directly **u** 6590
13:18 Now you *are* **stirring u more** wrath 3578
Est 2: 7 whom *he had* **brought u** 587
2:20 when he was **bringing** her **u.** 594
5: 3 Even **u to** half the kingdom, 6330
5: 6 **u to** half the kingdom, it will be granted." 6330
7: 2 **u to** half the kingdom, it will be granted." 6330
7: 7 The king **got u** in a rage, 7756
7: 9 who **spoke u** to help the king." 1819
10: 3 and **spoke u** *for* the welfare of all the Jews. 1819
Job 1:16 from the sky and **burned u** the sheep and 1277
1:20 Job **got u** and tore his robe 7756
4:21 **Are** not the cords of their tent **pulled u,** 5825
5:18 For he wounds, but *he* also **binds u;** 2502
6:18 *they* **go u** into the wasteland and perish. 6590
7: 4 'How long before *I* **get u?'** 7756
9:35 Then *I would* **speak u** without fear of him, 1819
11:15 then *you will* **lift u** your face 5951
14: 2 *He* **springs u** like a flower and withers 3655
14:17 My offenses *will* **be sealed u** in a bag; 3159
15:16 *who* **drinks u** evil like water! 9272
15:20 the ruthless through all the years **stored u** 7621
16: 8 my gauntness **rises u** and testifies 7756
17: 3 Who else *will* **put u security** *for* me? 3338+4200+9546
18:16 His roots **dry u** below 3312
20:15 God *will* **make** his stomach **vomit** them **u.** 3769
20:27 the earth *will* **rise u** against him. 7756
Job 21:19 'God **stores u** a man's punishment 7621
22:22 from his mouth and **lay u** his words 8492
22:26 in the Almighty and *will* **lift u** your face 5951
22:29 and you say, **'Lift them u!'** 1575
24:14 the murderer **rises u** and kills the poor 7756
24:24 they are brought low and **gathered u** 7890
26: 8 *He* **wraps u** the waters in his clouds, 7674
26:12 By his power *he* **churned u** the sea; 8088
27:16 Though *he* **heaps u** silver like dust 7392
27:17 what *he* **lays u** the righteous will wear, 3922
29:16 *I* **took u** the case of the stranger. 2983
30:13 *They* **break u** my road; 5995
30:20 *I* **stand u,** but you merely look at me. 6641
30:22 *You* **snatch** me **u** and drive me before 5951
30:28 *I* **stand u** in the assembly and cry for help. 7756
31:40 then *let* briers **come u** instead of wheat 3655
33:32 **speak u,** for I want you to be cleared. 1819
34:24 the mighty and **sets u** others in their place. 6641
35: 5 **Look u** *at* the heavens and see; 5564
36:27 *"He* **draws u** the drops of water, 1758
37:19 *we* cannot **draw u** our **case** because 6885
37:20 Would any man ask *to* **be swallowed u?** 1180
38: 8 "Who **shut u** the sea behind doors 6114
38:33 *Can you* **set u** [God's] dominion over 8492
39:24 In frenzied excitement *he* **eats u** the ground; 1686
41: 6 *Will they* **divide** him **u** among 2936
41:25 When he **rises u,** the mighty are terrified; 8420
41:31 and **stirs u** the sea like a pot of ointment. 8492
Ps 2:12 for his wrath *can* **flare u** in a moment. 1277
3: 1 How many **rise u** against me! 7756
3: 3 you bestow glory on me and **lift u** my head. 8123
3: 6 I will not fear the tens of thousands **drawn u** against me 8883
7: 6 **rise u** against the rage of my enemies. 5951
9:13 Have mercy and **lift** me **u** from the gates 8123
10:12 **Lift u** your hand, O God. 5951
16: 4 of blood or **take u** their names on my lips. 5951
17:10 *They* **close u** their callous hearts, 6037
17:13 **Rise u,** O LORD, confront them, 7756
17:14 and *they* **store u** wealth for their children. 5663
20: 5 and *will* **lift u** *our* **banners** in the name 1839
20: 8 but we **rise u** and stand firm. 7756
21: 9 the LORD *will* **swallow** them **u,** 1180
22:15 My strength *is* **dried u** like a potsherd, 3312
24: 4 who *does* not **lift u** his soul to an idol 5951
24: 7 **Lift u** your heads, O you gates; 5951
24: 7 **be lifted u,** *you* ancient doors, 5951
24: 9 **Lift u** your heads, O you gates; 5951
24: 9 **lift** them **u,** *you* ancient doors, 5951
25: 1 To you, O LORD, *I* **lift u** my soul; 5951
27:12 for false witnesses **rise u** against me, 7756
28: 2 as I **lift u** my hands 5951
28: 5 down and never **build** them **u** *again.* 1215
30: 3 *you* **brought** me **u** from the grave; 6590
31:19 which *you have* **stored u** for those who fear 7621
32: 5 to you and *did* not **cover u** my iniquity. 4059
35: 2 **Take u** shield and buckler; 2616
35:25 or say, *"We have* **swallowed** him **u."** 1180
39: 6 *he* **heaps u wealth,** 7392
41: 8 *he will* never **get u** *from* the place 7756
41: 9 *has* **lifted u** his heel against me. 1540
41:10 **raise** me **u,** that I may repay them. 7756
44:11 *You* **gave** us **u** to be devoured like sheep 5989
44:26 **Rise u** and help us; 7756
51:18 **build u** the walls of Jerusalem. 1215
52: 5 *He will* **snatch** you **u** and tear you 3149
59: 1 from *those who* **rise u** *against* me. 7756
63: 4 in your name *I will* **lift u** my hands. 5951
66: 7 *let* not the rebellious **rise u** against him. 8123
69: 1 for the waters have come **u to** my neck. 6330
69:15 or the depths **swallow** me **u** or 1180
71:20 of the earth you will again **bring** me **u.** 6590
73:10 to them and **drink u** waters in abundance. 5172
74: 4 *they* **set u** their standards as signs. 8492
74:15 It was you *who* **opened u** springs 1324
74:15 you **dried u** the ever flowing rivers. 3312
74:22 **Rise u,** O God, and defend your cause; 7756
75: 4 *'Do* not **lift u** your horns. 8123
75:10 horns of the righteous *will* **be lifted u.** 8123
76: 9 O God, **rose u** to judge, 7756
77:18 your lightning **lit u** the world; 239
78:38 and *did* not **stir u** his full wrath. 6424
78:60 the tent *he had* **set u** among men. 8905
80:15 the son *you have* **raised u** for yourself. 599
80:17 of man *you have* **raised u** for yourself. 599
81:10 who **brought** you **u** out of Egypt. 6590
82: 8 **Rise u,** O God, judge the earth, 7756
86: 4 for to you, O Lord, *I* **lift u** my soul. 5951
88:10 *Do* those who are dead **rise u** and praise 7756
89: 9 when its waves **mount u,** you still them. 5951
90: 6 though in the morning *it* **springs u** new, 7437
91:12 *they will* **lift** you **u** in their hands, 5951
92: 7 that though the wicked **spring u** like grass 7255
93: 3 The seas *have* **lifted u,** O LORD, 5951
93: 3 the seas *have* **lifted u** their voice; 5951
93: 3 seas *have* **lifted u** their pounding waves. 5951
94: 2 **Rise u,** O Judge of the earth; 5951
94:16 Who *will* **rise u** for me against the wicked? 7756
97: 4 His lightning **lights u** the world; 239
102:10 for *you have* **taken** me **u** and 5951
104:28 When you give it to them, *they* **gather** it **u;** 4377
105:30 which went **u** into the bedrooms NIH
105:35 *they* **ate u** every green thing in their land, 430
105:35 **ate u** the produce of their soil. 430
106: 9 He rebuked the Red Sea, and *it* **dried u;** 2990
106:17 The earth **opened u** and swallowed Dathan; 7337
106:30 But Phinehas **stood u** and intervened, 6641
Ps 107:25 and **stirred u** a tempest that lifted high 6641
107:26 *They* **mounted u** *to* the heavens and went 6590
110: 6 **heaping u** the dead and crushing the rulers 4848
110: 7 therefore *he will* **lift u** his head. 8123
116:13 *I will* **lift u** the cup of salvation and call 5951
118:27 join in the festal procession **u to** the horns 6330
119:48 *I* **lift u** my hands to your commands, 5951
121: 1 *I* **lift u** my eyes to the hills— 5951
122: 4 That is where the tribes **go u,** 6590
123: 1 *I* **lift u** my eyes to you, 5951
127: 2 In vain you rise early and **stay u** late, 3782
132:17 a horn grow for David and **set u** a lamp 6885
134: 2 **Lift u** your hands in the sanctuary 5951
139: 8 If *I* **go u** *to* the heavens, you are there; 6158
139:21 and abhor *those who* **rise u** *against* you? 7756
140: 2 in their hearts and **stir u** war every day. 1592
141: 2 may the **lifting u** *of* my hands be like 5368
141: 7 "As one plows and **breaks u** the earth, 1324
142: 1 **lift u** my voice to the LORD **for mercy.** 2858
143: 8 for to you *I* **lift u** my soul. 5951
145:14 and **lifts u** all who are bowed down. 2422
146: 8 the LORD **lifts u** those who are bowed 2422
147: 2 The LORD **builds u** Jerusalem; 1215
147: 3 brokenhearted and **binds u** their wounds. 2502
147:18 *he* **stirs u** his breezes, and the waters flow. 5959
148:14 *He has* **raised u** for his people a horn, 8123
Pr 2: 1 and **store u** my commands within you, 7621
3:35 but fools *he* **holds u** *to* shame. 8123
6: 1 *you have* **put u security** for your neighbor, 6842
6: 9 When *will you* **get u** from your sleep? 7756
6:14 *he* always **stirs u** dissension. 8938
6:19 and *a man who* **stirs u** dissension 8938
7: 1 keep my words and **store u** my commands 7621
10:12 Hatred **stirs u** dissension, 6424
10:14 Wise men **store u** knowledge, 7621
11:15 *He who* **puts u security** *for* another will 6842
12:25 but a kind word **cheers** him **u.** 8523
13:22 sinner's wealth **is stored u** for the righteous. 7621
15: 1 but a harsh word **stirs u** anger. 6590
15:18 A hot-tempered man **stirs u** dissension, 1741
16:28 A perverse man **stirs u** dissension, 8938
17:18 and **puts u security** for his neighbor. 6842+6859
17:22 but a crushed spirit **dries u** the bones. 3312
20:16 the garment of *one who* **puts u security** *for* 6842
20:17 but he **ends u** with a mouth full of gravel. 339
21:29 wicked man **puts u a bold front,** 928+6451+7156
22:15 Folly **is bound u** in the heart of a child, 8003
22:23 for the LORD *will* **take u** their case 8189
22:26 in pledge or **puts u security** *for* debts; 6842
22:28 not move an ancient boundary stone **set u** 6913
23: 8 *You will* **vomit u** the little you have eaten 7794
23:11 he *will* **take u** their case against you. 8189
23:35 *will I* **wake u** so I can find another drink?" 7810
24:31 thorns *had* **come u** everywhere, 6590
25: 7 to say to you, **"Come u** here," than for him 6590
27:13 the garment of one *who* **puts u security** *for* 6842
28:25 A greedy man **stirs u** dissension, 1741
29: 8 Mockers **stir u** a city, 7032
29:22 An angry man **stirs u** dissension, 1741
30: 4 Who *has* **gone u** *to* heaven 6590
30: 4 Who *has* **gathered u** the wind in the hollow 665
30: 4 Who *has* **wrapped u** the waters in his cloak? 7674
30:21 under four it cannot **bear u:** 5951
30:25 yet *they* **store u** their food in the summer; 3922
30:33 so **stirring u** anger produces strife." 4790
31: 8 **"Speak u** for those who cannot speak 7023+7337
31: 9 **Speak u** and judge fairly; 7023+7337
31:15 *She* **gets u** while it is still dark; 7756
Ecc 2:26 the task of gathering and **storing u wealth** 4043
3: 6 a time to search and a time to **give u,** 6
4:10 his friend *can* **help** him **u.** 7756
4:10 and has no one to **help** him **u!** 7756
8: 3 *Do* not **stand u** for a bad cause, 6641
12: 4 when *men* **rise u** at the sound of birds, 7756
SS 3: 2 *I will* **get u** now and go about the city, 7756
3: 6 Who is this **coming u** from the desert like 6590
4: 2 **coming u** from the washing. 6590
4:12 You are a garden **locked u,** my sister, 5835
6: 6 of sheep **coming u** from the washing. 6590
7:13 that *I have* **stored u** for you, my lover. 7621
8: 5 Who is this **coming u** from 6590
Isa 1: 2 "I reared children and **brought them u,** 8123
2: 3 *let us* **go u** to the mountain of the LORD 6590
2: 4 not **take u** sword against nation, 5951
3: 5 The young *will* **rise u** against the old, 8104
5: 2 *He* **dug** it **u** and cleared it of stones 6466
5:11 *who* **stay u late** at night 336
5:24 of fire **lick u** straw and as dry grass sinks 430
5:26 *He* **lifts u** a banner for the distant nations, 5951
7: 1 of Remaliah king of Israel **marched u** 6590
8: 8 through it and reaching **u to** the neck. 6330
8:16 **Bind u** the testimony and seal up the law 7674
8:16 Bind up the testimony and **seal u** the law 3159
10:15 As if a rod were to wield *him who* **lifts** it **u,** 8123
10:24 who beat you with a rod and **lift u** a club 5951
11: 1 A shoot *will* **come u** from the stump 3655
11:15 The LORD *will* **dry u** the gulf of 2990
11:15 *He will* **break** it **u** into seven streams so 5782
11:16 as there was for Israel when they **came u** 6590
13:17 See, I *will* **stir u** against them the Medes, 6424
14: 4 *you will* **take u** this taunt against the king 5951
14:22 *"I will* **rise u** against them," 7756
14:29 the root of that snake *will* **spring u** a viper, 3655
15: 2 Dibon **goes u** *to* its temple, 6590
15: 5 *They* **go u** the way to Luhith, 6590
15: 6 The waters of Nimrim are **dried u** and 5457

Isa 15: 7 the wealth they have acquired and **stored u** 7213
19: 2 *"I will* **stir u** Egyptian against Egyptian— 6056
19: 5 The waters of the river *will* **dry u,** 5980
19: 6 streams of Egypt will dwindle and **dry u.** 2990
21: 5 **Get u,** *you* officers, oil the shields! 7756
22: 1 that you *have* all **gone u** on the roofs, 6590
22: 6 Elam **takes u** the quiver, 5951
22: 9 *you* **stored u** water in the Lower Pool. 7695
22:18 *He will* **roll** you **u tightly** like a ball 7571+7571+7572
23: 4 I have neither reared sons nor **brought u** 8123
23:12 **"U,** cross over to Cyprus; 7756
23:13 *they* **raised u** their siege towers, 7756
23:16 **"Take u** a harp, walk through 4374
23:18 *they will* not **be stored u** or hoarded. 732
24: 4 The earth **dries u** and withers, 62
24: 6 Therefore earth's inhabitants *are* **burned u,** 3081
24: 7 The new wine **dries u** and the vine withers; 62
24:19 The earth **is broken u,** 8318+8318
24:22 *they will* **be shut u** in prison and 6037
25: 8 *he will* **swallow u** death forever. 1180
26:19 **wake u** and shout for joy. 7810
27:12 O Israelites, *will* **be gathered u** one by one. 4377
28:21 The LORD *will* **rise u** as he did 7756
28:24 *Does he keep on* **breaking u** and harrowing 7337
29: 3 I will encircle you with towers and **set u** 7756
29:13 of me is *made u only of* rules taught AIT
30:26 the LORD **binds u** the bruises of his people 2502
30:28 **rising u** to the neck. 2936
30:29 your hearts will rejoice as *when* people **go u** 2143
31: 2 *He will* **rise u** against the house of 7756
32: 7 he **makes u** evil schemes to destroy the poor 3619
32: 9 **rise u** and listen to me; 7756
33: 3 when you **rise u,** the nations scatter. 8129
33:10 will I be exalted; now *will I* **be lifted u.** 5951
33:20 its stakes *will* never *be* **pulled u,** 5825
34: 3 their dead bodies *will* **send u** a stench; 6590
34: 4 be dissolved and the sky **rolled u** like 1670
35: 9 nor *will* any ferocious beast **get u** *on* it; 6590
37:14 Then he **went u** *to* the temple of 6590
37:25 With the soles of my feet *I have* **dried u** all 2990
37:27 scorched before *it* **grows u.** 7756
37:36 When *the people* **got u** the next morning— 8899
38:12 Like a weaver *I have* **rolled u** my life, 7886
38:22 "What will be the sign that *I will* **go u** *to* 6590
39: 6 and all that your fathers *have* **stored u** 732
40: 4 Every valley *shall* **be raised u,** 5951
40: 9 **go u** on a high mountain. 6590
40: 9 **lift u** your voice with a shout, lift it up, 8123
40: 9 **lift it u,** do not be afraid; 8123
40:20 a skilled craftsman to **set u** an idol that will 3922
41: 2 "Who *has* **stirred u** one from the east, 6424
41:16 the wind *will* **pick** them **u,** 5951
41:25 *"I have* **stirred u** one from the north, 6424
42:13 like a warrior *he will* **stir u** his zeal; 6424
42:15 and hills and **dry u** all their vegetation; 3312
42:15 I will turn rivers into islands and **dry u** 3312
43: 6 I will say to the north, **'Give them u!'** 5989
43:19 Now *it* **springs u;** do you not perceive it? 7541
44: 4 *They will* **spring u** like grass in a meadow, 7541
44: 9 **Those who** would **speak u for** them 6332
44:27 'Be dry, and *I will* **dry u** your streams,' 3312
45: 8 *let* salvation **spring u,** 7238
45:13 I *will* **raise u** Cyrus in my righteousness: 6424
46: 7 *they* **set it u** in its place, and there it stands. 5663
47: 2 **Lift u** *your* skirts, bare your legs, 3106
47:14 the fire *will* **burn** them **u.** 8596
48:13 I summon them, *they all* **stand u** together. 6641
49: 7 "Kings will see you and **rise u,** 7756
49:11 and my highways *will be* **raised u.** 8123
49:18 **Lift u** your eyes and look around; 5951
49:21 Who **brought** these **u?** 1540
49:22 *I will* **lift u** my banner to the peoples; 8123
50: 2 By a mere rebuke *I* **dry u** the sea, 2990
50: 9 the moths *will* **eat** them **u.** 430
51: 6 **Lift u** your eyes to the heavens, 5951
51: 8 the moth *will* **eat** them **u** like a garment; 430
51:10 Was it not you who **dried u** the sea, 2990
51:15 *who* **churns u** the sea so that its waves roar 8088
51:17 **Rise u,** O Jerusalem, you who have drunk 7756
52: 2 **rise u,** sit enthroned, O Jerusalem. 7756
52: 8 Your watchmen **lift u** their voices; 5951
52:13 be raised and **lifted u** and highly exalted. 5951
53: 2 *He* **grew u** before him like a tender shoot, 6590
53: 4 Surely he **took u** our infirmities 5951
57: 7 there *you* **went u** to offer your sacrifices. 6590
57:14 **"Build u,** build up, prepare the road! 6148
57:14 "Build up, **build u,** prepare the road! 6148
57:20 whose waves **cast u** mire and mud. 1764
58:12 and *will* **raise u** the age-old foundations; 7756
60: 4 **"Lift u** your eyes and look about you: 5951
61: 1 He has sent me to **bind u** the brokenhearted, 2502
61:11 **makes** the sprout **come u** 3655
61:11 **make** righteousness and praise **spring u** 7541
62:10 **Build u,** build up the highway! 6148
62:10 Build up, **build u** the highway! 6148
63: 9 *he* **lifted** them **u** and carried them all 5747
64: 6 we all **shrivel u** like a leaf, 5570
66: 9 *"Do I* **close u** the womb when I bring 6806
Jer 1:15 and **set u** their thrones in the entrance of 5989
1:17 **Stand u** and say to them 7756
2: 6 who **brought** us **u** out of Egypt and led us 6590
3: 2 "Look **u** to the barren heights and see. 5951
3: 6 She *has* **gone u** on every high hill and 2143
4: 3 **"Break u** your unplowed ground and do 5774
4:29 *some* **climb u** among the rocks. 6590
Jer 5: 1 **"Go u and down** the streets of Jerusalem, 8763
6:22 a great nation *is being* **stirred u** from 6424
7:29 **take u** a lament on the barren heights, 5951
7:30 *They have* **set u** their detestable idols in 8492
8: 2 *They will* not **be gathered u** or buried, 665
8: 4 men fall down, *do they* not **get u?** 7756
9:10 for the mountains and take **u** a lament NIH
10:17 **Gather u** your belongings to leave the land, 665
10:20 now to pitch my tent or *to* **set u** my shelter. 7756
11: 7 **brought** your forefathers **u** from Egypt 6590
11:13 the altars *you have* **set u** to burn incense to 8492
13: 7 to Perath and **dug u** the belt and took it 2916
13:19 The cities in the Negev *will* **be shut u,** 6037
13:20 **Lift u** your eyes and see 5951
13:26 I *will* **pull u** your skirts over your face 3106
14: 2 and a cry **goes u** from Jerusalem. 6590
16:14 **brought** the Israelites **u** out of Egypt,' 6590
16:15 **brought** the Israelites **u** out of the land 6590
18: 9 that a nation or kingdom *is to be* **built u** 1215
18:15 in bypaths and on roads not **built u.** 6148
20: 9 a fire **shut u** in my bones. 6806
22: 7 and *they will* **cut u** your fine cedar beams 4162
22:20 **"Go u** *to* Lebanon and cry out, 6590
23: 5 *I will* **raise u** to David a righteous Branch, 7756
23: 7 **brought** the Israelites **u** out of Egypt,' 6590
23: 8 **brought** the descendants of Israel **u** 6590
24: 6 *I will* **build** them **u** and 1215
25:33 not be mourned or **gathered u** or buried, 665
26:10 *they* **went u** from the royal palace *to* 6590
29:15 "The LORD *has* **raised u** prophets for us 7756
30: 9 whom *I will* **raise u** for them. 7756
31: 4 *I will* **build** you **u** again and you will 1215
31: 4 Again *you will* **take u** your tambourines 6335
31: 6 'Come, *let us* **go u** *to* Zion, 6590
31:21 **"Set u** road signs; put up guideposts. 5893
31:21 "Set up road signs; **put u** guideposts. 8492
31:35 *who* **stirs u** the sea so that its waves roar— 8088
32:24 how the siege ramps *are* **built u** to take 995
32:34 *They* **set u** their abominable idols in 8492
36:28 which Jehoiakim king of Judah **burned u.** 8596
38:13 and *they* **pulled** him **u** with the ropes 5432
41: 2 and the ten men who were with him **got u** 7756
41:12 *They* **caught u** *with* him near the great pool 5162
42:10 *I will* **build** you **u** and 1215
46:11 **"Go u** *to* Gilead and get balm, 6590
46:16 They will say, **'Get u,** 7756
48: 5 *They* **go u** the way to Luhith, 6590
48:18 for he who destroys Moab *will* **come u** 6590
48:34 for even the waters of Nimrim are **dried u.** 5457
49:14 **Rise u** for battle!" 7756
49:19 a lion **coming u** from Jordan's thickets to 6590
50: 2 **lift u** a banner and proclaim it; 5951
50: 9 For I *will* **stir u** and bring against Babylon 6424
50: 9 *They will* **take u** *their* **positions** 6885
50:14 **"Take u** *your* **positions** around Babylon, 6885
50:26 **pile** her **u** like heaps of grain. 6148
50:32 and fall and no *one will* **help** her **u;** 7756
50:38 *They will* **dry u.** 3312
50:41 and many kings *are* **being stirred u** from 6424
50:44 Like a lion **coming u** from Jordan's thickets 6590
51: 1 "See, I *will* **stir u** the spirit of a destroyer 6424
51:11 "Sharpen the arrows, **take u** the shields! 4848
51:11 The LORD *has* **stirred u** the kings of 6424
51:12 **Lift u** a banner against the walls 5951
51:27 **"Lift u** a banner in the land! 5951
51:27 **send u** horses like a swarm of locusts. 6590
51:36 *I will* **dry u** her sea 2990
52:17 The Babylonians **broke u** the bronze pillars, 8689
La 2: 2 the Lord *has* **swallowed u** all the dwellings 1180
2: 5 *he has* **swallowed u** Israel. 1180
2: 5 *He has* **swallowed u** all her palaces 1180
2:16 *"We have* **swallowed** her **u.** 1180
2:19 **Lift u** your hands to him for the lives 5951
3:41 *Let us* **lift u** our hearts and our hands 5951
3:58 O Lord, *you* **took u** my case; 8189
5:12 Princes *have* **been hung u** by their hands; 9434
Eze 1:27 what appeared to be his waist **u** 2025+4200+5087
2: 1 **stand u** on your feet and I will speak 6641
3:12 Then the Spirit **lifted** me **u,** 5951
3:14 Spirit then **lifted** me **u** and took me away, 5951
3:22 **"Get u** and go out to the plain, 7756
3:23 So *I* **got u** and went out to the plain. 7756
4: 2 build a ramp **u to** it, 6584
4: 2 against it, build a ramp up to it, **set u** camps 5989
4: 8 *I will* **tie** you **u** *with* ropes so 5989
5: 1 take a set of scales and **divide u** the hair. 2745
5: 4 the fire and **burn** them **u.** 836+928+2021+8596
8: 2 from there **u** his appearance was 2025+4200+5087
8: 3 The Spirit **lifted** me **u** between earth 5951
9: 3 of Israel **went u** from above the cherubim, 6590
10: 7 *He* **took u** some of it and put it into 5951
11: 1 the Spirit **lifted** me **u** and brought me to 5951
11:23 of the LORD **went u** from within the city 6590
11:24 The Spirit **lifted** me **u** and brought me to 5951
11:24 Then the vision I had seen **went u** from me, 6590
13: 5 *You have* not **gone u** to the breaks in 6590
14: 3 these men *have* **set u** idols in their hearts 6590
14: 4 When any Israelite **sets u** idols in his heart 6590
14: 7 from me and **sets u** idols in his heart 6590
16: 7 *You* **grew u** and developed and became 8049
17: 9 a strong arm or many people to **pull it u** 5951
17:24 *I* **dry u** the green tree and make 3312
19: 1 **"Take u** a lament concerning the princes 5951
19: 3 *She* **brought u** one of her cubs, 6590
21:22 where he is to **set u** battering rams, 8492
22:30 for a man among them *who would* **build u** 1553
23: 8 not **give u** the prostitution she began 6440
Eze 23:22 I *will* **stir u** your lovers against you, 6424
23:24 *they will* **take u positions** against you 8492
24: 8 To **stir u** wrath and take revenge 6590
25: 4 *They will* **set u** their camps 3782
26: 3 like the sea **casting u** its waves. 6590
26: 8 *he will* **set u** siege works against you, 5989
26: 8 a ramp **u to** your walls and raise his shields 6584
26:17 Then *they will* **take u** a lament 5951
27: 2 **take u** a lament concerning Tyre. 5951
27:32 *they will* **take u a lament** concerning you: 7801
28:12 **take u** a lament concerning the king of Tyre 5951
29: 5 and not be gathered or **picked u.** 7695
30:12 *I will* **dry u** the streams of the Nile 3000+5989
30:21 *It has* not **been bound u** for healing or put 2502
32: 2 **take u** a lament concerning Pharaoh king 5951
32: 3 and *they will* **haul** you **u** in my net. 6590
34: 4 or healed the sick or **bound u** the injured. 2502
34:16 *I will* **bind u** the injured and strengthen 2502
37:10 to life and **stood u** on their feet— 6641
37:11 'Our bones *are* **dried u** 3312
37:12 to open your graves and **bring** you **u** 6590
37:13 when I open your graves and **bring** you **u** 6590
38: 9 and the many nations with you *will* **go u,** 6590
39: 9 the weapons for fuel and **burn** them **u—** 5956
39:15 *he will* **set u** a marker beside it until 1215
40:14 The measurement was **u to** the portico 448
40:22 Seven steps **led u** to it, 6590
40:26 Seven steps **led u** *to* it, 6590
40:31 and eight steps **led u** *to* it. 6590
40:34 and eight steps **led u** *to* it. 6590
40:37 and eight steps **led u** *to* it. 6590
41: 7 A stairway **went u** from the lowest floor to 6590
41:16 The floor, the wall **u to** the windows, 6330
43: 5 the Spirit **lifted** me **u** and brought me into 5951
43:14 From the gutter on the ground **u to** 6330
43:14 and from the smaller ledge **u to** 6330
45: 9 **Give u** your violence and oppression 6073
47: 4 and led me through **water** that was *u to* AIT
Da 2:21 *he* **sets u** kings and deposes them. 10624
2:44 the God of heaven *will* **set u** a kingdom 10624
3: 1 and **set it u** on the plain of Dura in 10624
3: 2 to the dedication of the image he *had* **set u.** 10624
3: 3 that King Nebuchadnezzar *had* **set u,** 10624
3: 5 that King Nebuchadnezzar *has* **set u.** 10624
3: 7 gold that King Nebuchadnezzar *had* **set u.** 10624
3:12 the image of gold *you have* **set u."** 10624
3:14 the image of gold *I have* **set u?** 10624
3:18 the image of gold *you have* **set u."** 10624
3:20 of the strongest soldiers in his army to **tie u** 10366
3:22 of the fire killed the soldiers who **took u** 10513
3:24 "Weren't there three men that we **tied u** 10366
3:28 *to* **give u** their lives rather than serve 10314
5:23 *you have* **set** *yourself* **u** against the Lord 10659
6:19 king **got u** and hurried to the lions' den. 10624
7: 2 the four winds of heaven **churning u** 10137
7: 3 **came u** out of the sea. 10513
7: 5 *It* **was raised u** on one of its sides, 10624
7: 5 **'Get u** and eat your fill of flesh!' 10624
7: 8 a little one, *which* **came u** among them; 10513
7:20 and about the other horn that **came u,** 10513
8: 3 I looked **u,** and there before me was a ram 5951
8: 3 the other but **grew u** later. 6590
8: 8 in its place four prominent horns **grew u** 6590
8:11 **set** *itself* **u to be** as **great** as the Prince 1540
8:26 but **seal u** the vision, 6258
8:27 Then *I* **got u** and went about 7756
9:24 to **seal u** vision and prophecy and to anoint 3159
9:27 [of the temple] he will set **u** an abomination NIH
10: 5 I looked **u** and there before me was 5951
10:11 to speak to you, and **stand u,** 6584+6641+6642
10:11 he said this to me, *I* **stood u** trembling. 6641
11: 2 *he will* **stir u** everyone against 6424
11: 4 his empire *will* **be broken u** 8689
11:15 and **build u** siege ramps and will capture 9161
11:25 a large army *he will* **stir u** his strength 6424
11:31 "His armed forces *will* **rise u** to desecrate 6641
11:31 Then *they will* **set u** the abomination 5989
12: 4 **close u** and seal the words of the scroll 6258
12: 9 because the words *are* **closed u** and sealed 6258
12:11 that causes desolation *is* **set u,** 5989
Hos 1:11 and *will* **come u** out of the land, 6590
2:15 as in the day she **came u** out of Egypt. 6590
4:15 *do* not **go u** *to* Beth Aven. 6590
6: 1 he has injured us but *he will* **bind u** 2502
8: 4 They **set u kings** without my consent; 4887
8: 7 foreigners *would* **swallow it u.** 1180
8: 8 Israel **is swallowed u;** 1180
8: 9 For they *have* **gone u** *to* Assyria like 6590
10: 4 therefore lawsuits **spring u** 7255
10: 8 Thorns and thistles *will* **grow u** 6590
10:11 and Jacob *must* **break u the ground.** 8440
10:12 and **break u** your unplowed ground; 5774
11: 8 "How *can I* **give** you **u,** Ephraim? 5989
12:13 a prophet *to* **bring** Israel **u** from Egypt, 6590
13:12 The guilt of Ephraim *is* **stored u,** 7674
13:15 his spring will fail and his well **dry u.** 2990
Joel 1: 5 **Wake u,** you drunkards, and weep! 7810
1:10 fields are ruined, the ground *is* **dried u;** 62
1:10 the new wine *is* **dried u,** the oil fails. 3312
1:12 vine *is* **dried u** and the fig tree is withered; 3312
1:12 of the field—*are* **dried u.** 3312
1:17 for the grain *has* **dried u.** 3312
1:19 the open pastures and flames *have* **burned u** 4265
1:20 of water *have* **dried u** and fire has devoured 3312
2: 5 like a mighty army **drawn u** *for* battle. 6885
2:20 its stench *will* **go u;** its smell will rise." 6590
3: 2 among the nations and **divided u** my land. 2745

Am 1: 2 the pastures of the shepherds dry u, 62
2:10 "I brought you u out of Egypt, 6590
2:11 I also raised u prophets from 7756
3: 1 the whole family I brought u out of Egypt: 6590
3: 5 Does a trap spring u from the earth 6590
4: 7 another had none and dried u. 3312
5: 1 this lament I take u concerning you: 5951
5: 2 with no one to lift her u." 7756
5:26 You have lifted u the shrine of your king, 5951
6: 8 I will deliver u the city and everything 6037
6:14 "I will stir u a nation against you, 7756
7: 1 and just as the second crop was coming u. 6590
7: 4 it dried u the great deep and devoured 430
7:17 be measured and divided u, 2745
8: 8 it will be stirred u and then sink like 1764
9: 2 Though they climb u to the heavens, 6590
9: 7 "Did I not bring Israel u from Egypt, 6590
Ob 1:21 Deliverers will go u on Mount Zion 6590
Jnh 1: 2 its wickedness has come u before me." 6590
1: 4 that the ship threatened to break u. 8689
1: 6 Get u and call on your god! 7756
1:12 "Pick me u and throw me into the sea," 5951
2: 6 But you brought my life u from the pit, 6590
3: 8 Let them give u their evil ways 4946+8740
4: 6 made it grow u over Jonah to give shade 6590
4:10 It sprang u overnight and died overnight. 2118
Mic 2: 4 my people's possession is divided u. 4614
2: 8 Lately my people have risen u like 7756
2:10 Get u, go away! 7756
2:13 One who breaks open the way will go u 6590
3: 3 who chop them u like meat for the pan, 7298
4: 2 let us go u to the mountain of 6590
4: 3 not take u sword against nation, 5951
5: 9 be lifted u in triumph over your enemies, 8123
6: 1 Listen to what the LORD says: "Stand u, 7756
6: 4 I brought you u out of Egypt 6590
6:14 You will store u but save nothing, 6047
7: 6 a daughter rises u against her mother, 7756
Na 1: 4 He rebukes the sea and dries it u; 3312
2:13 "I will burn u your chariots in smoke, 1277
Hab 1: 6 I am raising u the Babylonians, 7756
1:13 while the wicked swallow u those more 1180
1:15 pulls all of them u with hooks, 6590
1:15 he gathers them u in his dragnet; 665
2: 4 "See, he is puffed u; 6752
2: 6 " 'Woe to him who piles u stolen goods 8049
2: 7 not wake u and make you tremble? 3699
2:19 Or to lifeless stone, 'Wake u!' 6424
Zep 1:10 "a cry will go u from the Fish Gate, NIH
3: 8 "for the day I will stand u to testify. 7756
Hag 1: 8 Go u into the mountains and bring 6590
1:14 So the LORD stirred u the spirit 6424
Zec 1:18 Then I looked u— 5951
1:21 of the nations who lifted u their horns 5951
2: 1 Then I looked u— 5951
5: 5 "Look u and see what this is 5951
5: 9 Then I looked u— 5951
5: 9 and they lifted u the basket 5951
6: 1 I looked u again— 5951
7:11 and stopped u their ears. 3877+4946+9048
9: 3 she has heaped u silver like dust, 7392
10:11 and all the depths of the Nile will dry u. 3312
11:16 For I am going to raise u a shepherd over 7756
14:10 But Jerusalem will be raised u and remain 8027
14:16 that have attacked Jerusalem will go u 6590
14:17 not go u to Jerusalem to worship the King, 6590
14:18 If the Egyptian people do not go u 6590
14:18 on the nations that do not go u to celebrate 6590
14:19 the nations that do not go u to celebrate 6590
Mal 3:17 when I make u my treasured possession. 6913
Mt 1:24 When Joseph woke u, 1586
2:13 "Get u," he said, "take the child 1586
2:14 So he got u, took the child and his mother 1586
2:20 "Get u, take the child and his mother 1586
2:21 So he got u, took the child and his mother 1586
3: 9 of these stones God can raise u children 1586
3:12 into the barn and burning u the chaff 2876
3:16 he went u out of the water. 326
4: 6 and they will lift you u in their hands, 149
5: 1 he went u on a mountainside and sat down. 326
6:19 "Do not store u for yourselves treasures 2564
6:20 store u for yourselves treasures in heaven, 2564
7:12 for this sums u the Law and the Prophets. 1639
8:15 and she got u and began to wait on him. 1586
8:17 "He took u our infirmities 3284
8:24 a furious storm came u on the lake, 1181
8:26 Then he got u and rebuked the winds and 1586
9: 5 or to say, 'Get u and walk'? 1586
9: 6 Then he said to the paralytic, "Get u, 1586
9: 7 And the man got u and went home. 1586
9: 9 and Matthew got u and followed him. 482
9:19 Jesus got u and went with him, 1586
9:20 for twelve years came u behind him 4665
9:25 took the girl by the hand, and she got u. 1586
11:23 will you be lifted u to the skies? 5738
12:29 unless he first ties u the strong man? 1313
12:35 good things out of the good stored u in him, 2565
12:35 evil things out of the evil stored u in him. 2565
12:41 of Nineveh will stand u at the judgment 482
13: 4 and the birds came and ate it u. 2983
13: 5 It sprang u quickly, 1984
13: 6 But when the sun came u, 422
13: 7 which grew u and choked the plants. 326
13:28 to go and pull them u?' 5198
13:29 you may root u the wheat with them. 1748
13:40 "As the weeds are pulled u and burned in 5198
13:48 the fishermen pulled it u on the shore. 328
Mt 14:19 and the two fish and looking u to heaven, 329
14:20 and the disciples picked u twelve basketfuls 149
14:23 he went u on a mountainside by himself 326
15:13 will be pulled u by the roots. 1748
15:29 he went u on a mountainside and sat down. 326
15:37 the disciples picked u seven basketfuls 149
16:24 he must deny himself and take u his cross 149
17: 1 led them u a high mountain by themselves. 429
17: 4 If you wish, I will put u three shelters— 4472
17: 7 "Get u," he said. 1586
17: 8 When they looked u, 2048+3836+4057
17:17 How long shall I put u with you? 462
18:21 U to seven times?" 2401
19:16 Now a man came u to Jesus and asked, 4665
20:17 Now as Jesus was going u to Jerusalem, 326
20:18 "We are going u to Jerusalem, 326
21:19 he went u to it but found nothing 2093
23: 4 They tie u heavy loads and put them 1297
23:32 Fill u, then, the measure of the sin 4444
24: 1 when his disciples came u to him 4665
24:38 u to the day Noah entered the ark; 948
25: 7 the virgins woke u and trimmed their lamps. 1586
26:58 right u to the courtyard of the high priest. 2401
26:62 the high priest stood u and said to Jesus, 482
26:73 those standing there went u to Peter 4665
27: 6 The chief priests picked u the coins 3284
27:35 they divided u his clothes by casting lots. 1374
27:50 he gave u his spirit. 918
Mk 1:10 As Jesus was coming u out of the water, 326
1:31 took her hand and helped her u. 1586
1:35 while it was still dark, Jesus got u, 482
2: 9 or to say, 'Get u, take your mat and walk'? 1586
2:11 get u, take your mat and go home." 1586
2:12 He got u, took his mat and walked out 1586
2:14 and Levi got u and followed him. 482
3: 3 "Stand u in front of everyone." 1586
3:13 Jesus went u on a mountainside and called 326
3:27 unless he first ties u the strong man. 1313
4: 4 and the birds came and ate it u. 2983
4: 5 It sprang u quickly, 1984
4: 6 But when the sun came u, 422
4: 7 which grew u and choked the plants, 326
4: 8 It came u, grew and produced a crop, 326
4:27 Night and day, whether he sleeps or gets u, 1586
4:37 A furious squall came u, 1181
4:39 He got u, rebuked the wind and said to 1444
5:27 she came u behind him in the crowd NIG
5:41 "Little girl, I say to you, get u!"). 1586
5:42 Immediately the girl stood u and walked 482
6:23 u to half my kingdom." 2401
6:41 and the two fish and looking u to heaven, 329
6:43 and the disciples picked u twelve basketfuls 149
6:46 he went u on a mountainside to pray. 599
7:34 He looked u to heaven and with 329
8: 8 the disciples picked u seven basketfuls 149
8:19 many basketfuls of pieces did you pick u?" 149
8:20 many basketfuls of pieces did you pick u?" 149
8:24 He looked u and said, "I see people; 329
8:34 after me, he must deny himself and take u 149
9: 2 with him and led them u a high mountain, 1650
9: 5 Let us put u three shelters— 4472
9:19 How long shall I put u with you? 462
9:27 and he stood u. 482
10:17 a man ran u to him and fell on his knees 4708
10:32 were on their way u to Jerusalem, 326+1639
10:33 "We are going u to Jerusalem," he said, 326
10:49 So they called to the blind man, "Cheer u! 2510
14:57 Then some stood u and gave this false 482
14:60 Then the high priest stood u before them 482
15: 8 The crowd came u and asked Pilate to do 326
15:11 But the chief priests stirred u the crowd 411
15:24 Dividing u his clothes, 1374
15:41 Many other women who had come u with 5262
16: 4 But when they looked u, 329
16:18 they will pick u snakes with their hands; 149
16:19 he was taken u into heaven and he sat at 377
Lk 1: 1 to draw u an account of the things 421
1:52 from their thrones but has lifted u 5738
1:60 but his mother spoke u and said, 646
1:69 He has raised u a horn of salvation for us in 1586
2: 4 also went u from the town of Nazareth 326
2:19 But Mary treasured u all these things 5337
2:38 Coming u to them at that very moment, 2392
2:42 they went u to the Feast, 326
3: 8 of these stones God can raise u children 1586
3:17 but he will burn u the chaff 2876
3:20 He locked John u in prison. NIG
4: 5 The devil led him u to a high place 343
4:11 they will lift you u in their hands, 149
4:16 where he had been brought u, 5555
4:16 And he stood u to read. 482
4:20 Then he rolled u the scroll, 4771
4:29 They got u, drove him out of the town, 482
4:39 She got u at once and began to wait 482
5:11 So they pulled their boats u on shore, 2864
5:19 they went u on the roof and lowered him 326
5:23 or to say, 'Get u and walk'? 1586
5:24 get u, take your mat and go home." 1586
5:25 Immediately he stood u in front of them, 482
5:28 and Levi got u, left everything and followed 482
6: 8 "Get u and stand in front of everyone." 1586
6: 8 So he got u and stood there. 2705
6:45 out of the good stored u in his heart, 2565
6:45 out of the evil stored u in his heart. 2565
7:14 Then he went u and touched the coffin, 4665
7:14 He said, "Young man, I say to you, get u!" 1586
7:15 The dead man sat u and began to talk, 361
Lk 8: 5 and the birds of the air ate it u. 2983
8: 6 Some fell on rock, and when it came u, 5886
8: 7 which grew u with it and choked the plants. 5243
8: 8 It came u and yielded a crop, 5886
8:24 He got u and rebuked the wind and 1444
8:44 She came u behind him and touched 4665
8:54 by the hand and said, "My child, get u!" 1586
8:55 Her spirit returned, and at once she stood u. 482
9:16 and the two fish and looking u to heaven, 329
9:17 and the disciples picked u twelve basketfuls 149
9:23 after me, he must deny himself and take u 149
9:28 John and James with him and went u onto 326
9:33 Let us put u three shelters— 4472
9:41 with you and put u with you? 462
9:51 the time approached for him to be taken u 378
10:15 will you be lifted u to the skies? 5738
10:25 an expert in the law stood u to test Jesus. 482
11: 7 I can't get u and give you anything.' 482
11: 8 though he will not get u and give him 482
11: 8 because of the man's boldness he will get u 1586
11:22 the man trusted and divides u the spoils. 1344
11:32 of Nineveh will stand u at the judgment 482
12:19 "You have plenty of good things laid u 3023
12:21 with anyone who stores u things for himself 2564
13: 7 Why should it use u the soil?' 2934
13:11 over and could not straighten u at all. 376
13:13 and immediately she straightened u 494
13:25 the owner of the house gets u and closes 1586
14:10 'Friend, move u to a better place.' 542
14:33 not give u everything he has cannot 698
15:20 So he got u and went to his father. 482
16:23 he looked u and saw Abraham 2048+3836+4057
17:24 and lights u the sky from one end to 3290
17:27 marrying and being given in marriage u to 948
18: 1 they should always pray and not give u. 1591
18:10 "Two men went u to the temple to pray, 326
18:11 Pharisee stood u and prayed about himself: 2705
18:13 He would not even look u to heaven, 2048+3836+4057
18:31 "We are going u to Jerusalem, 326
19: 5 he looked u and said to him, "Zacchaeus, 329
19: 8 Zacchaeus stood u and said to the Lord, 2705
19:28 he went on ahead, going u to Jerusalem. 326
20: 1 together with the elders, came u to him. 2392
21: 1 As he looked u, Jesus saw the rich 329
21:14 make u your mind not to 1877+2840+3836+5502
21:28 stand u and lift up your heads, 376
21:28 stand up and lift u your heads, 2048
22:46 "Get u and pray so that you will not fall 482
22:47 he was still speaking a crowd came u, NIG
23: 5 "He stirs u the people all over Judea 411
23:34 they divided u his clothes by casting lots. 1374
23:36 The soldiers also came u and mocked him. 4665
24:12 Peter, however, got u and ran to the tomb. 482
24:15 Jesus himself came u and walked along 1581
24:33 They got u and returned at once 482
24:50 he lifted u his hands and blessed them. 2048
24:51 he left them and was taken u into heaven. 429
Jn 2:13 Jesus went u to Jerusalem. 326
3:14 as Moses lifted u the snake in the desert, 5738
3:14 so the Son of Man must be lifted u, 5738
4:14 in him a spring of water welling u 256
5: 1 Jesus went u to Jerusalem for a feast of 326
5: 8 Then Jesus said to him, "Get u! 1586
5: 8 Pick u your mat and walk." 149
5: 9 he picked u his mat and walked. 149
5:11 'Pick u your mat and walk.' " 149
5:12 to pick it u and walk?" 149
6: 3 Then Jesus went u on a mountainside 456
6: 5 When Jesus looked u and saw 2048+3836+4057
6: 8 Andrew, Simon Peter's brother, spoke u, NIG
6:39 but raise them u at the last day. 482
6:40 and I will raise him u at the last day." 482
6:44 and I will raise him u at the last day. 482
6:54 and I will raise him u at the last day. 482
7: 8 I am not yet going u to this Feast, 326
7:14 the Feast did Jesus go u to the temple courts 326
7:39 U to that time the Spirit had not been given 4037
8: 7 he straightened u and said to them, 376
8:10 Jesus straightened u and asked her, 376
8:28 "When you have lifted u the Son of Man, 5738
8:59 At this, they picked u stones to stone him, 149
10:17 lay down my life—only to take it u again. 3284
10:18 to lay it down and authority to take it u 3284
10:31 the Jews picked u stones to stone him, 1002
11:11 but I am going there to wake him u." 2030
11:29 she got u quickly and went to him. 1586
11:31 how quickly she got u and went out, 482
11:41 Then Jesus looked u and said, "Father, 539
11:49 who was high priest that year, spoke u, 3306
11:55 many went u from the country to Jerusalem 326
12:20 among those who went u to worship at 326
12:32 But I, when I am lifted u from the earth, 5738
12:34 The crowd spoke u, 646
12:34 'The Son of Man must be lifted u'? 5738
13: 4 so he got u from the meal, 1586
13:18 'He who shares my bread has lifted u 2048
15: 6 such branches are picked u, 5251
19: 3 and went u to him again and again, 4639
19:30 he bowed his head and gave u his spirit. 4140
20: 7 The cloth was folded u by itself, 1962
Ac 1: 2 until the day he was taken u to heaven, 377
1: 9 he was taken u before their very eyes, 2048
1:10 They were looking intently u into the sky NIG
1:15 In those days Peter stood u among 482
1:22 the time when Jesus was taken u from us. 377
2:14 Then Peter stood u with the Eleven, 2705

Ac 3: 1 One day Peter and John *were* **going u** to 326
3: 7 by the right hand, *he* **helped** him **u,** 1586
3:22 'The Lord your God *will* **raise u** for you 482
3:26 *When* God **raised u** his servant, 482
4: 1 the Sadducees **came u** to Peter and John 2392
5: 6 **wrapped u** his body, 5366
5:34 **stood u** in the Sanhedrin and ordered that 482
6:10 but they could not **stand u against** 468
6:12 So *they* **stirred u** the people and the elders 5167
7:21 and **brought** him **u** as her own son. 427
7:43 *You have* **lifted u** the shrine of Molech 377
7:55 looked **u** to heaven and saw the glory NIG
8:30 Then Philip **ran u to** the chariot and heard 4708
8:31 So he invited Philip *to* **come u** and sit 326
8:39 When *they* **came u** out of the water, 326
9: 6 "Now **get u** and go into the city, 482
9: 8 Saul **got u** from the ground, 1586
9:18 He **got u** and was baptized, 482
9:34 **Get u** and take care of your mat." 482
9:34 Immediately Aeneas **got u.** 482
9:40 he said, "Tabitha, **get u."** 482
9:40 and seeing Peter *she* **sat u.** 361
10: 4 *have* **come u** as a memorial offering 326
10: 9 Peter **went u** on the roof to pray. 326
10:13 Then a voice told him, **"Get u,** Peter. 482
10:20 So **get u** and go downstairs. 482
10:26 But Peter **made** him **get u.** 1586
10:26 **"Stand u,"** he said, "I am only 482
11: 2 So when Peter **went u** to Jerusalem, 326
11: 7 I heard a voice telling me, **'Get u,** Peter. 482
11:10 then *it was* all **pulled u** to heaven again. 413
11:28 **stood u** and through the Spirit predicted 482
12: 7 *He* struck Peter on the side and **woke** him **u.** 1586
12: 7 "Quick, **get u!"** he said, 482
13: 1 Manaen (who had been **brought u with** 5343
13:16 **Standing u,** Paul motioned with his hand 482
13:33 their children, *by* **raising u** Jesus. 482
13:50 **stirred u** persecution **against** Paul and 2074
14: 2 the Jews who refused to believe **stirred u** 2074
14:10 **"Stand u** on your feet!" 482+3981
14:10 the *man* **jumped u** and began to walk. 256
14:20 he **got u** and went back into the city. 482
15: 2 *to* **go u** to Jerusalem to see the apostles 326
15: 5 the party of the Pharisees **stood u** and said, 1985
15: 7 Peter **got u** and addressed them: 482
15:13 When they finished, James **spoke u:** 646
16:18 *She* **kept** this **u** for many days. 4472
16:27 The jailer **woke u,** and when he saw 1181+2031
17: 5 so *they* **rounded u** some bad characters 4689
17:13 agitating the crowds and **stirring** them **u.** 5429
17:22 Paul then **stood u** in the meeting of 2705
18:22 he **went u** and greeted the church and 326
19:39 If there is anything further *you* **want to bring u,** 2118
20: 9 from the third story and *was* **picked u** dead. 149
20:32 which can **build** you **u** and give you 3868
21: 5 But when our time was **u,** 1992
21:12 with Paul not *to* **go u** to Jerusalem. 326
21:14 *we* **gave u** and said, 2483
21:15 we got ready and **went u** to Jerusalem. 326
21:27 *They* **stirred u** the whole crowd 5177
21:33 The commander **came u** and arrested him 1581
22: 3 but **brought u** in this city. 427
22:10 " **'Get u,'** the Lord said, 482
22:16 **u,** be baptized and wash your sins away, 482
23: 9 of the law who were Pharisees **stood u** 482
24: 5 **stirring u** riots among the Jews all over 3075
24:11 that no more than twelve days ago *I* **went u** 326
24:12 **stirring u** a crowd in the synagogues 2180+4472
25: 1 Festus **went u** from Caesarea to Jerusalem, 326
25: 9 "Are you willing to **go u** to Jerusalem 326
25:18 *When* his accusers **got u** to speak, 2705
26:16 'Now **get u** and stand on your feet. 482
27:20 *we* finally **gave u** all hope of being saved. 4311
27:21 Paul **stood u** before them and said: 2705
27:22 But now I urge you *to* **keep u** your **courage,** 2313
27:25 So **keep u** *your* **courage,** men, 2313
28: 6 The people expected him to **swell u** 4399
28:13 The next day the south wind **came u,** 2104
Ro 2: 5 *you are* **storing u** wrath against yourself 2564
8:22 of childbirth **right u to** the present time. 948
8:32 but **gave** him **u** for us all— 4140
9:17 *"I* **raised** you **u** for this very purpose, 1995
10: 7 (that is, *to* **bring** Christ **u** from the dead). 343
13: 9 *are* **summed u** in this one rule: 368
13:11 for you *to* **wake u** from your slumber, 1586
14:13 **make u** *your* **mind** not to put any stumbling 3212
15: 2 for his good, to **build** him **u.** 3869
15:12 "The Root of Jesse will spring **u,** NIG
1Co 3:15 If it *is* **burned u,** he will suffer loss; 2876
4:13 **U to** this moment we have become 2401
7:37 and *who has* **made u** his mind not to marry 3212
8: 1 Knowledge **puffs u,** but love builds up. 5881
8: 1 Knowledge puffs up, but love **builds u.** 3868
9:12 *we* **put u with** anything rather than hinder 5095
10: 7 down to eat and drink and **got u** to indulge 482
10:13 a way out so that you can **stand u under** it. 5722
12:12 though *it is* **made u of** many parts; 2400
12:14 Now the body is not made **u** of one part but NIG
14:12 try to excel in gifts that **build u** the church. 3869
15:54 "Death *has been* **swallowed u** in victory." 2927
16: 2 in keeping with his income, saving it **u,** so NIG
2Co 2: 1 So *I* **made u** my **mind** that I would 3212
5: 4 what is mortal *may be* **swallowed u** by life. 2927
8: 2 and their extreme poverty **welled u** 4355
10: 5 *that* **sets** *itself* **u** against the knowledge 2048
10: 8 for **building** you **u** rather than pulling you 3869
2Co 11: 1 I hope *you will* **put u with** a little of my 462
11: 4 *you* **put u with** it easily enough. 462
11:19 *You* gladly **put u with** fools since you are 462
11:20 even **put u with** anyone who enslaves you 462
12: 2 *who* fourteen years ago *was* **caught u** 773
12: 4 *was* **caught u** to paradise. 773
12:14 not have *to* **save u** for their parents, 2564
13:10 the Lord gave me for **building** you **u,** 3869
Gal 1:11 not **something** that **man made u.** 476+2848
1:17 nor *did I* **go u** to Jerusalem 456
1:18 *I* **went u** to Jerusalem to get acquainted 456
2: 1 Fourteen years later *I* **went u** again 326
3:23 **locked u** until faith should be revealed. 5168
5:14 The entire law *is* **summed u** in a single 4444
6: 9 a harvest *if we do* not **give u.** 1725
Eph 2: 6 And God **raised** us **u with** Christ 5283
4:12 so that the body of Christ may be **built u** 3869
4:15 in all things **grow u** into him who is 889
4:16 grows and **builds** itself **u** in love, 3869
4:29 for **building** others **u** according 3869
5: 2 as Christ loved us **and** gave himself **u** for us 2779
5:14 This is why it is said: **"Wake u,** O sleeper, 1586
5:25 the church and **gave** himself **u** for her 4140
6: 4 **bring** them **u** in the training and instruction 1763
6:16 **take u** the shield of faith, 377
Php 1:17 supposing that they can **stir u** trouble 1586
2:30 to **make u for** the help you could 405
3:16 Only let us **live u** to what we have already 5123
Col 1: 5 the hope that is **stored u** for you in heaven 641
1:24 and *I* **fill u** in my flesh what is still lacking 499
2: 7 rooted and **built u** in him, 2224
2:18 and his unspiritual mind **puffs** him **u** 5881
1Th 2: 5 nor *did we* **put on a mask to cover u** greed 4733
2:16 **heap u** their sins **to the limit.** 405
4:17 and are left *will be* **caught u** together 773
5:11 and **build** each other **u,** 3868
2Th 2: 4 so that he **sets** *himself* **u** in God's temple, 2767
1Ti 2: 8 I want men everywhere to **lift u** holy hands 2048
3:16 *was* **taken u** in glory. 377
4: 6 **brought u** in the truths of the faith and of 1957
5:10 such as **bringing u children,** 5452
6:19 In this way *they will* **lay u treasure** 631
2Ti 4: 3 when *men will* not **put u with** 462
Heb 1:12 *You will* **roll** them **u** like a robe; 1813
5: 7 he **offered u** prayers and petitions 4712
8: 2 the true tabernacle **set u** by the Lord, 4381
9: 2 A tabernacle *was* **set u.** 2941
10:25 *Let us* not **give u** meeting together, 1593
11:24 By faith Moses, *when he had* **grown u** 1181+3489
12:15 that no bitter root grows **u** to cause trouble 539
Jas 4:10 and *he will* **lift** you **u.** 5738
5:15 the Lord *will* **raise** him **u.** 1586
1Pe 2: 2 that by it *you may* **grow u** in your salvation, 889
2:19 if a *man* **bears u under** the pain 5722
5: 6 that *he may* **lift** you **u** in due time. 5738
2Pe 2: 3 *with* stories they have **made u.** 4422
Jude 1: 7 **gave** themselves **u to sexual immorality** 1745
1:13 waves of the sea, **foaming u** their shame; 2072
1:20 **build** yourselves **u** in your most holy faith 2224
Rev 3: 2 **Wake u!** Strengthen what remains 1181+1213
3: 3 But if *you do* not **wake u,** 1213
4: 1 to me like a trumpet said, **"Come u** here, 326
6:14 The sky receded like a scroll, **rolling u,** 1813
7: 2 I saw another angel **coming u** from the east, 326
8: 4 **went u** before God from the angel's hand. 326
8: 7 A third of the earth *was* **burned u,** 2876
8: 7 a third of the trees *were* **burned u,** 2876
8: 7 and all the green grass *was* **burned u.** 2876
10: 4 **"Seal u** what the seven thunders have said 5381
11: 6 These men have power to shut **u** the sky so NIG
11: 7 the beast that **comes u** from the Abyss 326
11:12 from heaven saying to them, **"Come u** 326
11:12 And *they* **went u** to heaven in a cloud, 326
12: 5 And her child *was* **snatched u** to God and 773
13:14 He ordered them *to* **set u** an image 4472
16:12 its water *was* **dried u** to prepare the way 3830
17: 8 and will **come u** out of the Abyss and go 326
18: 5 for her sins *are* **piled u** to heaven, 3140
18:21 a mighty angel **picked u** a boulder the size 149
19: 3 The smoke from her **goes u** for ever 326
20:13 The sea **gave u** the dead that were in it, 1443
20:13 and death and Hades **gave u** the dead 1443
22:10 *"Do* not **seal u** the words of the prophecy 5381

UPBRAID, UPBRAIDED, UPBRAIDETH (KJV) See DENOUNCED, FINDING FAULT, REBUKED, TAUNTED

UPHARSIN (KJV) See PARSIN

UPHAZ (1)

Jer 10: 9 from Tarshish and gold from **U.** 233

UPHELD (4) [UPHOLD]

1Sa 25:39 who *has* **u** my cause against Nabal 8189
2Ch 20:20 the LORD your God and *you will* **be u;** 586
Ps 9: 4 For *you have* **u** my right and my cause; 6913
Isa 46: 3 whom I *have* **u** since you were conceived, 6673

UPHOLD (16) [UPHELD, UPHOLDING, UPHOLDS]

Dt 27:26 "Cursed is the man who *does* not **u** 7756
Dt 32:51 because *you did* not **u** my **holiness** among 7727
1Sa 24:15 May he consider my cause and **u** it; 8189
1Ki 8:45 and their plea, and **u** their cause. 6913
8:49 and their plea, and **u** their cause. 6913
8:59 that he *may* **u** the cause of his servant and 6913
2Ch 6:35 and their plea, and **u** their cause. 6913
6:39 and their pleas, and **u** their cause. 6913
9: 8 for Israel and his desire to **u** them forever, 6641
Ps 41:12 In my integrity *you* **u** me and set me 9461
119:117 **U** me, and I will be delivered; 6184
Isa 34: 8 a year of retribution, to **u** Zion's **cause.** 8189
41:10 *I will* **u** you with my righteous right hand. 9461
42: 1 "Here is my servant, whom *I* **u,** 9461
La 3:59 **U** my cause! 9149
Ro 3:31 Not at all! Rather, *we* **u** the law. 2705

UPHOLDING (1) [UPHOLD]

Isa 9: 7 and **u** it with justice and righteousness from 6184

UPHOLDS (6) [UPHOLD]

Ps 37:17 but the LORD **u** the righteous. 6164
37:24 for the LORD **u** him *with* his hand. 6164
63: 8 your right hand **u** me. 9461
140:12 for the poor and **u** the cause of the needy. NIH
145:14 The LORD **u** all those who fall and lifts 6164
146: 7 *He* **u** the cause of the oppressed 6913

UPHOLSTERED (1)

SS 3:10 Its seat was **u** with purple, its interior NIH

UPLIFTED (13) [LIFT]

Ex 6: 8 to the land **I swore with u** hand to give 5951
Nu 14:30 the land **I swore with u** hand to make your 5951
Ne 9:15 of the land *you had* **sworn with u** hand 5951
Ps 106:26 **swore** to them **with u** hand that he would 5951
Isa 19:16 the **u** hand that the LORD Almighty raises 9485
Eze 20: 5 the day I chose Israel, **I swore with u** hand 5951
20: 5 *With* **u** hand I said to them, "I am the LORD 5951
20:15 **with u** hand **I swore** to them in the desert 5951
20:23 **with u** hand **I swore** to them in the desert 5951
20:42 the land I *had* **sworn with u** hand to give 5951
36: 7 **I swear with u** hand that the nations 5951
44:12 therefore I *have* **sworn with u** hand 5951
47:14 Because **I swore with u** hand to give it 5951

UPON (351) See Index of Articles Etc.

UPPER (45) [UP]

Ge 6:16 make lower, middle and **u** *decks.* 8958
Dt 24: 6 not even the **u one—**as security for a debt, 8207
Jos 15:19 So Caleb gave her the **u** and lower springs. 6606
16: 5 in the east to **U** Beth Horon 6609
Jdg 1:15 Caleb gave her the **u** and lower springs. 6606
3:20 the **u room** *of* his summer palace and said, 6608
3:23 of the **u room** behind him and locked them. 6608
3:24 and found the doors of the **u room** locked. 6608
9:53 a woman dropped an **u** millstone on his 8207
2Sa 11:21 a woman throw an **u** millstone on him from 8207
1Ki 17:19 to the **u room** where he was staying, 6608
2Ki 1: 2 through the lattice of his **u room** in Samaria 6608
15:35 Jotham rebuilt the **U** Gate of the temple of 6609
18:17 and stopped at the aqueduct of the **U** Pool, 6609
23:12 on the roof near the **u room** *of* Ahaz, 6608
1Ch 7:24 who built Lower and **U** Beth Horon as well 6609
26:16 and the Shalleketh Gate on the **u** road fell 6590
28:11 its buildings, its storerooms, its **u parts,** 6608
2Ch 3: 9 He also overlaid the **u parts** with gold. 6608
8: 5 He rebuilt **U** Beth Horon 6609
23:20 through the **U** Gate and seated the king on 6609
27: 3 Jotham rebuilt the **U** Gate of the temple of 6609
32:30 It was Hezekiah who blocked the **u** outlet 6609
Ne 3:25 the tower projecting from the **u** palace near 6609
Est 9: 1 and the Jews **got the u hand** 8948
Ps 104: 3 beams of his **u chambers** on their waters. 6608
104:13 the mountains from his **u chambers;** 6608
Isa 7: 3 at the end of the aqueduct of the **U** Pool, 6609
11:11 from **U Egypt,** from Cush, from Elam, 7356
36: 2 at the aqueduct of the **U** Pool, 6609
Jer 20: 2 in the stocks at the **U** Gate of Benjamin at 6609
22:13 his **u rooms** by injustice, 6608
22:14 a great palace with spacious **u rooms.'** 6608
36:10 in the **u** courtyard at the entrance of 6609
44: 1 and Memphis—and in **U Egypt:** 824+7356
44:15 all the people living in Lower and **U Egypt,** 7356
Eze 9: 2 from the direction of the **u** gate, 6609
29:14 captivity and return them to **U Egypt,** 824+7356
30:14 I will lay waste **U Egypt,** 7356
42: 5 Now the **u** rooms were narrower, 6609
43:17 The **u** ledge also is square, NIH
43:20 on the four corners of the **u** ledge and all NIH
45:19 the **u** ledge of the altar and on the gateposts NIH
Mk 14:15 He will show you a large **u room,** 333
Lk 22:12 He will show you a large **u room,** 333

UPPERMOST (KJV) See HONOR, MOST IMPORTANT, TOP, TOPMOST

UPRAISED (6) [RISE]

Job 38:15 and their **u** arm is broken. 8123
Isa 5:25 anger is not turned away, his hand *is* still **u.** 5742
9:12 anger is not turned away, his hand *is* still **u.** 5742

Isa 9:17 anger is not turned away, his hand *is* still **u.** 5742
9:21 anger is not turned away, his hand *is* still **u.** 5742
10: 4 anger is not turned away, his hand *is* still **u.** 5742

UPRIGHT (67) [UPRIGHTLY, UPRIGHTNESS, UPRIGHTS]

Ge 37: 7 when suddenly my sheaf rose and **stood u,** 5893
Ex 26:15 "Make **u** frames of acacia wood for 6641
36:20 They made **u** frames of acacia wood for 6641
Dt 32: 4 God who does no wrong, **u** and just is he. 7404
1Ki 2:32 were better men and more **u** than he. 7404
3: 6 to you and righteous and **u** *in* heart. 3842
Job 1: 1 This man was blameless and **u;** 3838
1: 8 he is blameless and **u,** 3838
2: 3 he is blameless and **u,** 3838
4: 7 Where were the **u** ever destroyed? 3838
8: 6 if you are pure and **u,** 3838
17: 8 **U** *men* are appalled at this; 3838
23: 7 an **u** *man* could present his case before him, 3838
33: 3 My words come from an **u** heart; 3841
Ps 7:10 who saves the **u** *in* heart. 3838
11: 2 to shoot from the shadows at the **u** *in* heart. 3838
11: 7 **u** *men* will see his face. 3838
25: 8 Good and **u** is the LORD; 3838
32:11 sing, all you *who* are **u** *in* heart! 3838
33: 1 it is fitting for the **u** to praise him. 3838
36:10 your righteousness to the **u** *in* heart. 3838
37:14 to slay *those* whose ways are **u.** 3838
37:37 Consider the blameless, observe the **u;** 3838
49:14 The **u** will rule over them in the morning; 3838
64:10 let all the **u** *in* heart praise him! 3838
92:15 "The LORD is **u;** 3838
94:15 and all the **u** *in* heart will follow it. 3838
97:11 the righteous and joy on the **u** *in* heart. 3838
107:42 The **u** see and rejoice, 3838
111: 1 with all my heart in the council of the **u** and 3838
112: 2 the generation of the **u** will be blessed. 3838
112: 4 Even in darkness light dawns for the **u,** 3838
119: 7 an **u** heart as I learn your righteous laws. 3841
125: 4 to *those who* are **u** in heart. 3838
140:13 and the **u** will live before you. 3838
Pr 2: 7 He holds victory in store for the **u,** 3838
2:21 For the **u** will live in the land, 3838
3:32 but takes the **u** into his confidence. 3838
11: 3 The integrity of the **u** guides them, 3838
11: 6 The righteousness of the **u** delivers them, 3838
11:11 the blessing of the **u** a city is exalted, 3838
12: 6 but the speech of the **u** rescues them. 3838
14: 2 He whose walk is **u** fears the LORD, 3841
14: 9 but goodwill is found among the **u.** 3838
14:11 but the tent of the **u** will flourish. 3838
15: 8 but the prayer of the **u** pleases him. 3838
15:19 but the path of the **u** is a highway. 3838
16:17 The highway of the **u** avoids evil; 3838
21: 8 but the conduct of the innocent is **u.** 2341
21:18 and the unfaithful for the **u.** 3838
21:29 but an **u** *man* gives thought to his ways. 3838
28:10 the **u** along an evil path will fall 3838
29:10 a man of integrity and seek to kill the **u.** 3838
29:27 the wicked detest the **u.** 2006+3838
Ecc 7:28 I found one **[u]** man among a thousand, NIH
7:28 but not one **[u]** woman among them all. NIH
7:29 God made mankind **u,** but men have gone 3838
12:10 and what he wrote was **u** and true. 3841
Isa 26: 7 The path of the righteous is level; O **u** *One,* 3838
Mic 2: 7 do good to him whose ways are **u?** 3838
7: 2 not one **u** man remains. 3838
7: 4 the most **u** worse than a thorn hedge. 3838
Hab 2: 4 "See, he is puffed up; his desires *are* not **u** 3837
Lk 1: 6 Both of them were **u** in the sight of God, *1465*
23:50 member of the Council, a good and **u** man, *1465*
Tit 1: 8 who is self-controlled, **u,** holy and *1465*
2:12 **u** and godly *lives* in this present age, *1469*

UPRIGHTLY (3) [UPRIGHT]

Ps 58: 1 Do you judge **u** among men? 4797
75: 2 it is I who judge **u.** 4797
Isa 57: 2 Those who walk **u** enter into peace; 5791

UPRIGHTNESS (5) [UPRIGHT]

1Ki 9: 4 before me in integrity of heart and **u,** 3841
Ps 25:21 May integrity and **u** protect me, 3841
111: 8 done in faithfulness and **u.** 3838
Isa 26:10 even in a land of **u** they go on doing evil 5791
Mal 2: 6 He walked with me in peace and **u,** 4793

UPRIGHTS (3) [UPRIGHT]

1Ki 7:28 They had side panels attached to **u.** 8918
7:29 On the panels between the **u** were lions, 8918
7:29 and on the **u** as well. 8918

UPRISING (1) [RISE]

Mk 15: 7 who had committed murder in the **u.** *5087*

UPROAR (15)

1Sa 4: 6 Hearing the **u,** the Philistines asked, 7754+9558
4:14 "What is the meaning of this **u?"** 2162+7754
Ps 46: 6 Nations *are* in **u,** kingdoms fall; 2159
74:23 the **u** *of* your enemies, 8623
Isa 13: 4 Listen, an **u** *among* the kingdoms, 8623
17:12 Oh, the **u** *of* the peoples— 8623
25: 5 You silence the **u** *of* foreigners; 8623
66: 6 Hear that **u** from the city, 8623
Mt 27:24 but that instead an **u** was starting, *2573*
Ac 16:20 and *are* **throwing** our city **into an u** *1752*
19:29 Soon the whole city *was in* an **u.** *4398+5180*
20: 1 When the **u** had ended, *2573*
21:31 the whole city of Jerusalem *was* **in an u.** *5177*
21:34 not get at the truth because of the **u,** *2573*
23: 9 There was a great **u,** *3199*

UPROOT (14) [UPROOTED, UPROOTS]

1Ki 14:15 *He will* **u** Israel from this good land 6004
2Ch 7:20 then *I will* **u** Israel from my land, 6004
Ps 52: 5 *he will* **u** you from the land of the living. 9245
Ecc 3: 2 a time to plant and a time to **u,** 6827
Jer 1:10 over nations and kingdoms to **u** and tear 6004
12:14 I *will* **u** them from their lands 6004
12:14 from their lands and *I will* **u** the house 6004
12:15 But after I **u** them, I will again have 6004
12:17 *I will* **completely u** and destroy it," 6004+6004
24: 6 I will plant them and not **u** them. 6004
31:28 as I watched over them to **u** and tear down, 6004
42:10 I will plant you and not **u** you, 6004
45: 4 and **u** what I have planted, 6004
Mic 5:14 *I will* **u** from among you your Asherah 6004

UPROOTED (17) [UPROOT]

Dt 28:63 *You will* **be u** from the land 5815
29:28 and in great wrath the LORD **u** them 6004
Job 31: 8 and *may* my crops **be u.** 9245
31:12 *it would have* **u** my harvest. 9245
Ps 9: 6 *you have* **u** their cities; 6004
Pr 10:30 The righteous *will* never **be u,** 4572
12: 3 but the righteous cannot **be u.** 4572+9247
Jer 18: 7 that a nation or kingdom *is to be* **u,** 6004
31:40 city *will* never again **be u** or demolished." 6004
Eze 17: 9 *Will* it not *be* **u** and stripped of its fruit 5998+9247
19:12 *it* **was u** in fury and thrown to the ground. 6004
Da 7: 8 and three of the first horns **were u** before it. 10566
11: 4 his empire *will* **be u** and given to others. 6004
Am 9:15 *to* **be u** from the land I have given them," 6004
Zep 2: 4 Ashdod will be emptied and Ekron **u.** 6827
Lk 17: 6 *'Be* **u** and planted in the sea,' *1748*
Jude 1:12 autumn trees, without fruit and **u—** *1748*

UPROOTS (1) [UPROOT]

Job 19:10 *he* **u** my hope like a tree. 5825

UPSET (2)

2Sa 11:25 'Don't *let* this **u** you; 928+6524+8317
Lk 10:41 "you are worried and **u** about many things, *2571*

UPSIDE (2)

2Ki 21:13 wiping it and turning it **u down.** 6584+7156
Isa 29:16 You **turn** things **u down,** 2201

UPSTAIRS (6) [STAIRS]

Da 6:10 to his **u room** where the windows opened 10547
Ac 1:13 they went **u** to the **room** *5673*
9:37 and placed in an **u room.** *5673*
9:39 he arrived *he was* **taken u** to the room. *343*
20: 8 in the **u room** where we were meeting. *5673*
20:11 *he* **went u** again and broke bread and ate. *326*

UPSTREAM (1) [STREAM]

Jos 3:16 water from **u** stopped flowing. 2025+4200+5087

UPWARD (11) [UP]

Ex 25:20 to have their wings spread **u,** 2025+4200+5087
37: 9 The cherubim had their wings spread **u,** 2025+4200+5087
Job 5: 7 to trouble as surely as sparks fly **u.** 1467
Pr 15:24 path of life leads **u** for the wise 2025+4200+5087
Ecc 3:21 Who knows if the spirit of man rises **u** and 2025+4200+5087
Isa 8:21 become enraged, and, looking **u,** 2025+4200+5087
9:18 so that *it* **rolls u** *in* a column of smoke. 60
Eze 1:11 wings were spread out **u;** 2025+4200+4946+5087
10:15 Then the cherubim **rose u.** 8250
41: 7 rooms widened as one went **u.** 2025+4200+5087
43:15 and four horns **project u** from the hearth. 2025+4200+5087

UR (5)

Ge 11:28 Haran died in **U** *of* the Chaldeans, 243
11:31 from **U** *of* the Chaldeans to go to Canaan. 243
15: 7 of **U** *of* the Chaldeans to give you this land 243
1Ch 11:35 Eliphal son of **U,** 244
Ne 9: 7 and brought him out of **U** *of* the Chaldeans 243

URBANE (KJV) See URBANUS

URBANUS (1)

Ro 16: 9 Greet **U,** our fellow worker in Christ, *4042*

URGE (23) [URGED, URGENT, URGENTLY, URGING]

Ru 1:16 "Don't **u** me to leave you or to turn back 7003
Est 4: 8 to **u** her to go into the king's presence 7422
Ac 27:22 But now *I* **u** you to keep up your courage, *4147*
27:34 Now *I* **u** you to take some food. *4151*
Ro 12: 1 Therefore, *I* **u** you, brothers, *4151*
15:30 *I* **u** you, brothers, by our Lord Jesus Christ *4151*
16:17 *I* **u** you, brothers, to watch out *4151*
1Co 4:16 Therefore *I* **u** you to imitate me. *4151*
16:15 the service of the saints. *I* **u** you, brothers, *4151*
2Co 2: 8 *I* **u** you, therefore, to reaffirm your love *4151*
6: 1 As God's fellow workers *we* **u** you not *4151*
9: 5 So I thought it necessary *to* **u** the brothers *4151*
Eph 4: 1 I **u** you to live a life worthy of the calling *4151*
1Th 4: 1 and **u** you in the Lord Jesus to do this more *4151*
4:10 *we* **u** you, brothers, to do so more and more. *4151*
5:14 And *we* **u** you, brothers, warn those who *4151*
2Th 3:12 and **u** in the Lord Jesus Christ to settle *4151*
1Ti 2: 1 *I* **u,** then, first of all, that requests, prayers, *4151*
6: 2 These are the things *you are to* teach and **u** *4151*
Heb 13:19 *I* particularly **u** you to pray so that I may *4151*
13:22 *I* **u** you to bear with my word *4151*
1Pe 2:11 Dear friends, *I* **u** you, as aliens and strangers *4151*
Jude 1: 3 to write and **u** you to contend for the faith *4151*

URGED (27) [URGE]

Ge 19:15 With the coming of dawn, the angels **u** Lot, 237
Ex 12:33 The Egyptians **u** the people to hurry 2616
Jos 15:18 *she* **u** him to ask her father for a field. 6077
Jdg 1:14 *she* **u** him to ask her father for a field. 6077
1Sa 24:10 *Some* **u** me to kill you, but I spared you; 606
2Sa 3:35 and **u** David **to eat** something 1356
13:25 Although Absalom **u** him, he still refused 7287
13:27 But Absalom **u** him, so he sent with him 7287
1Ki 21:25 **u on** *by* Jezebel his wife. 6077
2Ki 4: 8 *who* **u** him to stay for a meal. 2616
5:16 even though Naaman **u** him, he refused. 7210
5:23 *He* **u** Gehazi to accept them, 7287
2Ch 18: 2 for him and the people with him and **u** him 6077
Jer 36:25 Delaiah and Gemariah **u** the king not 7003
Da 2:18 He **u** them to plead for mercy from the God NIH
Mt 15:23 So his disciples came to him and **u** him, *2263*
Lk 24:29 But *they* **u** him **strongly,** "Stay with us, *4128*
Jn 4:31 Meanwhile his disciples **u** him, "Rabbi, *2263*
4:40 *they* **u** him to stay with them, *2263*
Ac 9:38 they sent two men to him and **u** him, *4151*
13:43 and **u** them to continue in the grace of God. *4275*
21: 4 Through the Spirit they **u** Paul not to go on *3306*
27:33 Just before dawn Paul **u** them all to eat. *4151*
1Co 16:12 *I* strongly **u** him to go to you with *4151*
2Co 8: 6 So we **u** Titus, since he had earlier made *4151*
12:18 *I* **u** Titus to go to you and I sent *4151*
1Ti 1: 3 As *I* **u** you when I went into Macedonia, *4151*

URGENT (3) [URGE]

Nu 22:37 *"Did I* not **send** you an **u** summons? 8938+8938
1Sa 21: 8 because the king's business was **u."** 5722
Da 3:22 so **u** and the furnace so hot that the flames 10280

URGENTLY (3) [URGE]

Jnh 3: 8 Let everyone call **u** on God. 928+2622
Ac 25: 3 *They* **u requested** Festus, as a favor to *160+4151*
2Co 8: 4 they **u** pleaded with us for the privilege of sharing in this service *3552+4155+4498*

URGING (3) [URGE]

Ru 1:18 determined to go with her, she stopped **u** her. 1819
1Sa 28:23 But his men joined the woman *in* **u** him, 7287
1Th 2:12 comforting and **u** you to live lives worthy *3458*

URI (8)

Ex 31: 2 I have chosen Bezalel son of **U,** 247
35:30 the LORD has chosen Bezalel son of **U,** 247
38:22 (Bezalel son of **U,** the son of Hur, 247
1Ki 4:19 Geber son of **U**—in Gilead 788
1Ch 2:20 Hur was the father of **U,** 247
2:20 and **U** the father of Bezalel. 247
2Ch 1: 5 But the bronze altar that Bezalel son of **U,** 247
Ezr 10:24 Shallum, Telem and **U.** 247

URIAH (33) [URIAH'S]

2Sa 11: 3 the daughter of Eliam and the wife of **U** 249
11: 6 "Send me **U** the Hittite." 249
11: 7 When **U** came to him, 249
11: 8 Then David said to **U,** "Go down to your 249
11: 8 So **U** left the palace, 249
11: 9 But **U** slept at the entrance to the palace 249
11:10 David was told, **"U** did not go home," 249
11:11 **U** said to David, "The ark and Israel 249
11:12 So **U** remained in Jerusalem that day and 249
11:13 the evening **U** went out to sleep on his mat NIH
11:14 a letter to Joab and sent it with **U.** 249
11:15 "Put **U** in the front line where 249
11:16 he put **U** at a place where he knew 249
11:17 moreover, **U** the Hittite died. 249
11:21 'Also, your servant **U** the Hittite is dead.' " 249
11:24 your servant **U** the Hittite is dead." 249
12: 9 You struck down **U** the Hittite with 249
12:10 the wife of **U** the Hittite to be your own.' 249
23:39 and **U** the Hittite. 249
1Ki 15: 5 except in the case of **U** the Hittite. 249
2Ki 16:10 He saw an altar in Damascus and sent to **U** 249
16:11 So **U** the priest built an altar in accordance 249
16:15 King Ahaz then gave these orders to **U** 249
16:16 And **U** the priest did just as King Ahaz 249
1Ch 11:41 **U** the Hittite, Zabad son of Ahlai, 249
Ezr 8:33 into the hands of Meremoth son of **U,** 249
Ne 3: 4 Meremoth son of **U,** the son of Hakkoz, 249

Ne 3:21 Next to him, Meremoth son of U, 249
8: 4 Shema, Anaiah, U, Hilkiah and Maaseiah; 249
Isa 8: 2 in U the priest and Zechariah son 249
Jer 26:20 (Now U son of Shemaiah from Kiriath 250
26:21 But U heard of it and fled in fear to Egypt. 250
26:23 They brought U out of Egypt and took him 250

URIAH'S (3) [URIAH]

2Sa 11:26 U wife heard that her husband was dead, 249
12:15 the child that U wife had borne to David, 249
Mt 1: 6 Solomon, whose mother had been U wife, *4043*

URIAS, URIJAH (KJV) See URIAH

URIEL (4)

1Ch 6:24 U his son, Uzziah his son 248
15: 5 U the leader and 120 relatives; 248
15:11 and U, Asaiah, Joel, Shemaiah, 248
2Ch 13: 2 a daughter of U of Gibeah. 248

URIM (7)

Ex 28:30 the U and the Thummim in the breastpiece, 242
Lev 8: 8 the U and Thummim in the breastpiece. 242
Nu 27:21 by inquiring of the U before the LORD. 242
Dt 33: 8 and U belong to the man you favored. 242
1Sa 28: 6 not answer him by dreams or U or prophets. 242
Ezr 2:63 priest ministering with the U and Thummim. 242
Ne 7:65 priest ministering with the U and Thummim. 242

URINE (2)

2Ki 18:27 eat their own filth and drink their own u?" 8875
Isa 36:12 eat their own filth and drink their own u?" 8875

US (1431) [WE] See Index of Articles Etc.

USE (86) [USED, USEFUL, USELESS, USES, USING]

Ex 5:12 over Egypt to gather stubble to u for straw. NIH
10:26 *We have to* u some of them in worshiping 4374
10:26 not know what *we are to u to* worship AIT
20:25 for you will defile it if *you* u a tool on it. 5677
26: 6 and u them to fasten the curtains together 928
28: 5 *Have* them u gold, and blue, 4374
30:16 from the Israelites and u it for the service 5989
30:26 Then u it to anoint the Tent of Meeting, 928
Lev 11:32 article, whatever its u, will be unclean, 4856+6913
13:51 whatever its u, it is a destructive mildew; 6913
19:35 " '*Do* not u dishonest standards 6913
19:36 U honest scales and honest weights, 2118+4200
Nu 3:26 and everything related to their u. 6275
3:31 and everything related to their u. 6275
3:36 and everything related to their u, 6275
4:32 and everything related to their u. 6275
8:12 u the one for a sin offering to the LORD 6913
10: 2 and u them for calling the community 6913
19: 9 be kept by the Israelite community for u in 5466
Dt 14:26 *U* the silver *to* buy whatever you like: AIT
20:14 And *you may* u the plunder 430
20:20 and *u* them *to* build siege works until AIT
27: 5 *Do* not u any iron tool upon them. 5677
28:40 but *you will* not u the oil, 6057
Jdg 2:22 I will u them to test Israel 928
18:31 *to* u the idols Micah had made, 8492
19:24 and *you can* u them and do 6700
1Sa 8:16 donkeys he will take for his own u. 4856+6913
2Sa 5: 8 the Jebusites will have to u the water shaft 928
14: 2 and don't u any cosmetic lotions. 6057
1Ki 21: 2 "Let me have your vineyard *to* u for 2118
2Ki 16:15 But I *will* u the bronze altar 2118+4200
23:10 so no one *could u* it *to* sacrifice his son AIT
1Ch 5:18 *who could* u a bow, 2005
28:15 according to the u of each lampstand; 6275
2Ch 26:15 by skillful men for u on the towers and on 2118
Job 19: 5 above me and u my humiliation against me, 3519[S]
30: 2 Of what u was the strength of their hands 4200+4537
Ps 50:19 *You* u your mouth for evil 8938
102: 8 against me u my name as a curse. 928+8678
125: 3 righteous *might* u their hands to do evil. 8938
Pr 17:16 Of what u is money in the hand of a fool, 2296+4200+4537
24:28 or u your lips to deceive 928
Isa 7:20 that day the Lord will u a razor hired from 928
Jer 2:22 with soda and u an abundance *of* soap, 8049
2:25 But you said, *'It's* no u! 3286
18:12 But they will reply, *'It's* no u. 3286
23:10 an evil course and u their power unjustly. NIH
29:22 in Babylon *will* u this curse: 4374
31:23 in its towns *will* once again u these words: 606
Eze 4: 9 in a storage jar and u them to make bread 6913
5: 1 a sharp sword and u it as a barber's razor 4374
23:43 *let them* u her as a prostitute, 2388+9373
39: 9 and u the weapons for fuel 1277
39: 9 seven years *they will* u them for fuel. 836+1277
39:10 *they will* u the weapons for fuel. 836+1277
45:10 You *are to* u accurate scales, 2118
45:16 in this special gift for the u of the prince 4200
48:15 will be for the common u of the city, 2687
Am 2: 7 Father and son u the same girl and 448+2143
6: 6 by the bowlful and u the finest lotions, 5417
Mic 6:15 you will press olives but not u the oil 6057
Mt 7: 2 and with the measure *you* u, *3582[S]*
Mt 27: 7 to u the money to buy the potter's field as *NIG*
Mk 4:24 "With the measure *you* u, *3582[S]*
4:30 or what parable *shall we* u to describe it? *5502*
Lk 6:38 For with the measure *you* u, *3582[S]*
13: 7 Why *should it* u it up the soil?' *2934*
16: 9 u worldly wealth to gain friends *NIG*
Jn 16:25 no longer u this kind of language *3281*
Ac 5:26 They did not u force, *1040+3552*
Ro 9:21 noble purposes and some for common u? *NIG*
12: 6 let him u it in proportion to his faith. *NIG*
1Co 7:31 those who u the things of the world, *5968*
9:12 But *we did* not u this right. *5968*
9:18 so not make u of my rights in preaching it. *2974*
2Co 4: 2 *we do* not u deception, *1877+4111+4344*
13:10 not have to be harsh in *my* u of authority— *5968*
Gal 5:13 But do not u your freedom to indulge *NIG*
6:11 See what large letters I u as I write to you *NIG*
Col 2:22 These are all destined to perish *with* u, *712*
1Ti 5:23 and u a little wine because of your stomach *5968*
Heb 5:14 who by constant u have trained themselves *2011*
1Pe 2:16 *do* not *u* your freedom as a cover-up for evil *AIT*
4:10 Each one should u whatever gift he has received to serve others, *NIG*
2Jn 1:12 but I do not want to u paper and ink. *1328*

USED (115) [USE]

Ge 11: 3 They u brick instead of stone, 2118
28:19 the city u to be called Luz. 2021+4200+8037
31:15 but *he has* u up what was paid for us. 430+430
40:13 just as you u to do when you were 8037
41:36 to be u during the seven years of famine NIH
47:15 Our money *is* u up." 699
Ex 1:14 the Egyptians u them ruthlessly. 6268
25:27 to the rim to hold the poles *u in* carrying AIT
25:39 of pure gold *is to be* u *for* the lampstand 6913
27:19 All the other articles *u* in the service of AIT
30: 4 to hold the poles u to carry it. 928
33: 7 Now Moses *u to* take a tent and pitch it AIT
36:13 and u them to fasten the two sets 928
37:14 to the rim to hold the poles u in carrying NIH
37:27 to hold the poles u to carry it. 928
38:21 These are the amounts of the materials u NIH
38:24 of the gold from the wave offering u for all 6913
38:27 The 100 talents of silver *were* u to cast 2118
38:28 They u the 1,775 shekels to make the hooks 6913
38:30 They u it to make the bases for the entrance 928
40:31 and Moses and Aaron and his sons u it 4946
Lev 7:24 or torn by wild animals *may* be u 6913
16:10 to be u for making atonement by sending it 6584
18: 3 as they do in Egypt, where *you u to* live, AIT
Nu 3:31 of the sanctuary u *in* ministering, 928
4: 9 and all its jars for the oil u to supply it. 928
4:12 to take all the articles u for ministering in 928
4:14 the utensils u for ministering at the altar, 928
4:26 and all the equipment *u in* its service. AIT
6: 5 of separation no razor *may be* u on his head. 6296
7: 5 that they may be u *in* the work at the Tent 6268
7:87 Twelve male goats were u for 4200
Dt 2:10 (The Emites u to live there— 4200+7156
2:12 Horites u to live in Seir, 4200+7156
2:20 Rephaites, who u to live there; 4200+7156
3:13 *u to* be known as a land of the Rephaites. AIT
Jos 8:31 on which no iron tool *had been* u. 5677
14:15 (Hebron u to be called Kiriath Arba 4200+7156
Jdg 9: 4 and Abimelech u it to hire reckless 928
13: 5 No razor *may be* u on his head, 6590
16:11 new ropes that *have* never been u, 4856+6913
16:17 "No razor *has ever been* u on my head," 6590
18:29 the city u to be called Laish. 2021+4200+8037
1Sa 1:11 and no razor *will ever be* u on his head." 6590
9: 9 prophet of today u to be called a seer.) 4200+7156
17:39 because *he was* not u to them. 5814
17:39 "because *I am* not u to them." 5814
2Sa 14:26 *he* u to cut his hair from time to time 2118
15:32 where *people u to* worship God, AIT
20:18 continued, "Long ago *they* u to say, 1819+1819
1Ki 6: 7 only blocks dressed at the quarry were u, 1215
10:12 The king u the almugwood to make 6913
17:14 *be* u up and the jug of oil will not run dry 3983
17:16 For the jar of flour *was* not u up and the jug 3983
2Ki 3:11 He *u to* pour water on the hands AIT
10:27 and *people have* u it for a latrine to this day. 8492
12: 5 *be u to* repair whatever damage is found AIT
12:14 who u it to repair the temple 928
13:20 Now Moabite raiders *u to* enter AIT
21:13 the measuring line *u against* Samaria and AIT
21:13 and the plumb line *u against* the house AIT
25:14 the bronze articles u in the temple service. 928
1Ch 9:28 of them were in charge of the articles *u* AIT
18: 8 which Solomon u to make the bronze Sea, 928
23:26 the tabernacle or any of the articles u in 4200
28:13 for all the articles *to be u in* its service. AIT
28:14 the gold articles *to be u in* various kinds AIT
28:14 of silver for all the silver articles *to be u* AIT
2Ch 3: 6 And the gold he u was gold of Parvaim. NIH
4: 6 In them the things to be *u for* AIT
4: 6 but the Sea was to be u by the priests 4200
7: 6 for praising the LORD and which were u 928+3338
9:11 The king u the algumwood to make 6913
24: 7 of God and *had* u even its sacred objects for 6913
Ne 13: 5 with a large room formerly u to store 2118
Job 1: 4 His sons *u to* take turns holding feasts AIT
Ps 42: 4 how *I u to* go with the multitude, AIT
Ecc 8:10 *those who u to* come and go from AIT
Isa 1:21 righteousness *u to* dwell in her— AIT
9: 5 Every warrior's boot u in battle NIH
Isa 44:19 "Half of it *I* u for fuel; 836+1198+8596
Jer 23:38 You u the words, 'This is the oracle of 606
33: 4 be u against the siege ramps and the sword NIH
52:18 the bronze articles u in the temple service. 928
52:19 and bowls u for drink offerings— 4984
Eze 7:20 and u it to make their detestable idols 928
16:15 in your beauty and u your fame to become 6584
19:14 This is a lament and is to be u as a lament." 4200
45:15 These will be u for the grain offerings, NIH
Da 10: 3 and *I* u no lotions at all until 6057+6057
Hos 2: 8 silver and gold—which *they* u for Baal. 6913
12:13 The LORD u a prophet to bring Israel up 928
Am 9:11 and build it as it u to be, 3427+6409
Mic 1: 7 as wages of prostitutes *they will* again be u. 8740
Zec 9:15 be full like a bowl u for sprinkling 4670
Mt 16:12 not telling them to guard against the yeast u *NIG*
22:19 Show me the coin u for paying the tax." *NIG*
27:10 and they u them to buy the potter's field, *NIG*
Jn 2: 6 kind u by the Jews for ceremonial washing, *NIG*
5: 3 a great number of disabled people *u to* lie— *AIT*
9: 8 the same man who *u to* sit and beg?" *AIT*
10: 6 Jesus u this figure of speech, *3306*
12: 6 *u to* help himself to what was put into it. *AIT*
Ac 3:10 as the same man who *u to* sit begging at *AIT*
5:12 And all the believers *u to* meet together *AIT*
Ro 6:17 though *you u to* be slaves to sin, *AIT*
6:19 as *you u to* offer the parts of your body *AIT*
1Co 9:15 But I *have* not u any of these rights. *5968*
Gal 2:12 *he u to* eat with the Gentiles. *AIT*
Eph 2: 2 in which you u to live when you followed *4537*
Col 3: 7 You u to walk in these ways, *4537*
1Th 2: 5 You know *we* never u flattery, *1181*
2Th 2: 5 with you *I u to* tell you these things? *AIT*
Heb 9:21 both the tabernacle and everything u *NIG*
1Pe 3: 5 *u to* make themselves beautiful. *AIT*

USEFUL (9) [USE]

Eze 15: 3 wood taken from it to make anything u? 4856
15: 4 *is it* then u for anything? 7503
15: 5 not u for anything when it was whole, 6913
15: 5 into something u when the fire has burned 4856
Eph 4:28 doing something u with his own hands, *19*
2Ti 2:21 u to the Master and prepared to do any good *2378*
3:16 All Scripture is God-breathed and is u *6068*
Phm 1:11 he has become u both to you and to me. *2378*
Heb 6: 7 on it and that produces a crop u to those *2310*

USELESS (17) [USE]

1Sa 12:21 Do not turn away after u idols. 9332
12:21 nor can they rescue you, because they are u. 9332
25:21 David had just said, "It's been u 2021+4200+9214
Job 15: 3 Would he argue with u words, 4202+6122
Pr 1:17 How u to spread a net in full view of all 2855
Isa 30: 5 shame because of a people u to them, 3603+4202
30: 7 Egypt, whose help is utterly u. 2039+2256+8198
59: 6 Their cobwebs are u for clothing; 4202
Jer 13: 7 now it was ruined and completely u. 4202+7503
13:10 like this belt—completely u! 4202+7503
Mal 1:10 that you would not light u fires on my altar! 2855
1Co 15:14 our preaching is u and so is your faith. *3031*
1Th 3: 5 and our efforts might have been u. *3031*
Tit 3: 9 because these are unprofitable and u. *3469*
Phm 1:11 Formerly he was u to you, but now *947*
Heb 7:18 is set aside because it was weak and u *543*
Jas 2:20 evidence that faith without deeds is u? *734*

USES (8) [USE]

Ge 44: 5 from and also u for divination? 5727+5727
1Sa 23:23 the hiding places *he* u and come back to me 2461[S]
2Sa 23: 7 Whoever touches thorns u a tool of iron or 4848
Pr 17:27 man of knowledge u words with restraint, 3104
Isa 10:15 or the saw boast against *him who* u it? 5677
Eze 22: 6 of Israel who are in you u his power 4200
Hos 12: 7 The merchant u dishonest scales; 928+3338
1Ti 1: 8 that the law is good if one u it properly. *5968*

USHERS (1)

Pr 18:16 for the giver and u him into the presence of 5697

USING (18) [USE]

Ge 42:23 since he was u an interpreter. 1068
Lev 24: 5 u two-tenths of an ephah for each loaf. 2118
Jdg 6:26 U the wood of the Asherah pole 928
1Sa 14:13 Jonathan climbed up, u his hands and feet, 6584
1Ki 15:22 and timber Baasha *had been* u there. 1215[S]
1Ch 25: 3 of their father Jeduthun, who prophesied, u 928
2Ch 3: 3 and twenty cubits wide (u the cubit of 928
16: 6 the stones and timber Baasha *had been* u. 1215[S]
Isa 22: 3 they have been captured without u AIT
Jer 21: 4 that are in your hands, which you are u 928
Eze 4:12 u human excrement for fuel." 928
Mt 13:34 he did not say anything to them without u *NIG*
Mk 4:34 He did not say anything to them without u *NIG*
Jn 8: 6 They were u this question as a trap, *NIG*
Ac 7:25 that God was u him to rescue them, *1328+5931*
Ro 3: 5 *(I am* u a human argument.) *3306*
1Co 3:12 If any man builds on this foundation u gold, *NIG*
Rev 21:17 which the angel was u. *NIG*

USUAL (7) [USUALLY]

1Sa 3: 2 was lying down in his u place. NIH
17:23 from his lines and shouted his u defiance, 3869
21: 5 as u whenever I set out. 3869+8997+9453

2Sa 7:19 Is this your **u way of dealing** *with* man, 9368
Da 3:19 furnace heated seven times hotter than **u** 10255
Lk 22:39 Jesus went out **as u** to the *1621+2848+3836*
Ac 14: 1 At Iconium Paul and Barnabas went **as u** into the Jewish synagogue. *899+2848+3836*

USUALLY (5) [USUAL]

Nu 16:29 experience only **what u happens** *to* men, 7213
1Sa 18:10 David was playing the harp, **as** he **u did.** 928+3427+3427+3869
23:22 Find out where David *u* **goes** AIT
Eze 33:31 My people come to you, **as** they **u** do, 3869
Mk 15: 8 asked Pilate to do for them what he **u** did. *NIG*

USURER (KJV) See MONEYLENDER

USURP [AUTHORITY] (KJV) See HAVE [AUTHORITY]

USURY (8)

Ne 5: 7 "You are exacting **u** from your own 5391
5:10 But let the **exacting of u** stop! 5391
5:11 and also *the* **u** you *are* **charging** them— 5957
Ps 15: 5 who lends his money without **u** and does 5968
Eze 18: 8 not lend at **u** or take excessive interest. 5968
18:13 He lends at **u** and takes excessive interest. 5968
18:17 and takes no **u** or excessive interest. 5968
22:12 you take **u** and excessive interest 5968

UTENSILS (13)

Ex 27: 3 Make all its **u** of bronze— 3998
30:28 the altar of burnt offering and all its **u,** 3998
31: 9 of burnt offering and all its **u,** the basin 3998
35:16 its poles and all its **u;** 3998
38: 3 They made all its **u** *of* bronze— 3998
38:30 with its bronze grating and all its **u,** 3998
39:39 its poles and all its **u;** 3998
40:10 the altar of burnt offering and all its **u;** 3998
Lev 8:11 and all its **u** and the basin with its stand, 3998
Nu 4:14 to place on it all the **u** used for ministering 3998
7: 1 and consecrated the altar and all its **u.** 3998
2Ch 29:18 the altar of burnt offering with all its **u,** 3998
Eze 40:42 On them were placed the **u** for slaughtering 3998

UTHAI (2)

1Ch 9: 4 U son of Ammihud, 6433
Ezr 8:14 U and Zaccur, and with them 70 men. 6433

UTMOST (5)

2Ki 19:23 the **u heights** *of* Lebanon. 3752
Job 34:36 to the **u** for answering like a wicked man! 5905
Ps 48: 2 Like the **u heights** *of* Zaphon is Mount Zion 3752
Isa 14:13 on the **u heights** *of* the sacred mountain. 3752
37:24 the **u heights** *of* Lebanon. 3752

UTTER (19) [UTTERANCE, UTTERED, UTTERING, UTTERLY, UTTERS]

Nu 30: 6 after she makes a vow or after her lips **u** NIH
Dt 23:23 Whatever your lips **u** you must be sure 4604
Jdg 17: 2 and about which I heard you **u a curse—** 457
2Sa 12:14 *you have* **made** the enemies of the LORD **show u contempt,** 5540+5540
Job 26: 4 Who has helped *you* **u** these words? 5583
27: 4 and my tongue *will* **u** no deceit. 2047
Ps 31:11 I am the **u** contempt of my neighbors; 4394
59:12 For the curses and lies *they* **u,** 6218
78: 2 *I will* **u** hidden things, 5580
115: 7 nor *can they* **u a sound** with their throats. 2047
Pr 5:14 I have come to the brink of **u** ruin in 3972
Ecc 5: 2 do not be hasty in your heart to **u** anything 3655
Isa 8:22 and they will be thrust into **u darkness.** 696
42:17 will be turned back *in* **u shame.** 1017+1425
Jer 15:19 if *you* **u** worthy, not worthless, words, 3655
Eze 13: 9 and **u** lying **divinations.** 7876
14: 9 if the prophet is enticed *to* **u** a prophecy, 1819
Mt 13:35 *I will* **u** things hidden since the creation *2243*
Rev 13: 5 a mouth *to* **u** proud words and blasphemies *3281*

UTTERANCE (1) [UTTER]

Ps 49: 3 the **u** *from* my heart will give understanding 2050

UTTERED (11) [UTTER]

Nu 23: 7 Then Balaam **u** his oracle: 606+2256+5951
23:18 Then *he* **u** his oracle: 606+2256+5951
24: 3 and *he* **u** his oracle: 606+2256+5951
24:15 Then *he* **u** his oracle: 606+2256+5951
24:20 Then Balaam saw Amalek and **u** his oracle: 606+2256+5951
24:21 Then he saw the Kenites and **u** his oracle: 606+2256+5951
24:23 Then *he* **u** his oracle: 606+2256+5951
Jos 10:21 and no one **u a word** against the Israelites. 906+3076+4383
Ps 89:34 or alter **what** my lips have **u.** 4604
Isa 45:23 my mouth *has* **u** in all integrity a word 3655+4946
Eze 13: 7 and **u** lying divinations when you say, 606

UTTERING (1) [UTTER]

Isa 59:13 **u** lies our hearts have conceived. 2047

UTTERLY (20) [UTTER]

Dt 7:26 **U abhor** and detest it, 9210+9210
31:29 **sure to become u corrupt** 8845+8845
Ps 38: 8 I am feeble and **u** crushed; 4394+6330
119: 8 do not **u** forsake me. 4394+6330
Ecc 1: 2 says the Teacher. **"U meaningless!** 2039+2039
SS 8: 7 it *would be* **u scorned.** 996+996
Isa 6:12 and the land is **u** forsaken. 8041
30: 7 whose help is **u useless.** 2039+2256+8198
41:24 and your works are **u** worthless; 4946
60:12 it *will be* **u ruined.** 2990+2990
Jer 5:11 house of Judah *have been* **u unfaithful** 953+953
La 5:22 unless *you have* **u rejected** us 4415+4415
Eze 8: 6 the **u** detestable things the house of Israel 1524
20:13 and they **u** desecrated my Sabbaths. 4394
Ob 1: 2 you will be **u** despised. 4394
Mic 2: 4 *'We are* **u ruined;** 8720+8720
Hab 1: 5 and watch—and *be* **u amazed.** 9449+9449
Zep 2:13 leaving Nineveh **u desolate** and dry as 9039
Ac 2: 7 **U amazed,** they asked: *2014+2513*
Ro 7:13 commandment sin might become **u** sinful. *5651*

UTTERMOST (KJV) See COMPLETELY, DISTANT, EDGE, EDGES, EXTREME, FAR, FARTHEST, MOUTH, OUTER, SOUTHERNMOST, TIP, WESTERN

UTTERS (2) [UTTER]

Ps 37:30 The mouth of the righteous man **u** wisdom, 2047
1Co 14: 2 *he* **u** mysteries with his spirit. *3281*

UZ (8)

Ge 10:23 U, Hul, Gether and Meshech. 6419
22:21 U the firstborn, Buz his brother, Kemuel 6419
36:28 The sons of Dishan: U and Aran. 6419
1Ch 1:17 U, Hul, Gether and Meshech. 6419
1:42 The sons of Dishan: U and Aran. 6419
Job 1: 1 In the land of U there lived a man 6420
Jer 25:20 all the kings of U; 824+6420
La 4:21 you who live in the land of U. 6420

UZAI (1)

Ne 3:25 and Palal son of U worked opposite 206

UZAL (3)

Ge 10:27 Hadoram, U, Diklah, 207
1Ch 1:21 Hadoram, U, Diklah, 207
Eze 27:19 from U bought your merchandise; 207

UZZA (5)

2Ki 21:18 in his palace garden, the garden of U. 6438
21:26 in his grave in the garden of U. 6438
1Ch 8: 7 and who was the father of U and Ahihud. 6438
Ezr 2:49 U, Paseah, Besai, 6438
Ne 7:51 Gazzam, U, Paseah, 6438

UZZAH (9)

2Sa 6: 3 U and Ahio, sons of Abinadab, 6438
6: 6 U reached out and took hold of the ark 6438
6: 7 against U because of his irreverent act; 6446
6: 8 LORD's wrath had broken out against U, 6446
1Ch 6:29 Libni his son, Shimei his son, U his son, 6446
13: 7 with U and Ahio guiding it. 6438
13: 9 U reached out his hand to steady the ark, 6438
13:10 The LORD's anger burned against U, 6438
13:11 LORD's wrath had broken out against U, 6438

UZZEN SHEERAH (1)

1Ch 7:24 and Upper Beth Horon as well as U. 267

UZZI (12)

1Ch 6: 5 Bukki the father of U, 6454
6: 6 U the father of Zerahiah, 6454
6:51 Bukki his son, U his son, Zerahiah his son, 6454
7: 2 The sons of Tola: U, Rephaiah, Jeriel, 6454
7: 3 The son of U: Izrahiah. 6454
7: 7 The sons of Bela: Ezbon, U, Uzziel, 6454
9: 8 Elah son of U, the son of Micri; 6454
Ezr 7: 4 the son of U, the son of Bukki, 6454
Ne 11:22 of the Levites in Jerusalem was U son 6454
11:22 U was one of Asaph's descendants, NIH
12:19 of Joiarib's, Mattenai; of Jedaiah's, U; 6454
12:42 U, Jehohanan, Malkijah, Elam and Ezer. 6454

UZZIA (1)

1Ch 11:44 U the Ashterathite, Shama and Jeiel 6455

UZZIAH (28) [AZARIAH, UZZIAH'S]

2Ki 15:13 in the thirty-ninth year of U king of Judah, 6459
15:30 in the twentieth year of Jotham son of U. 6459
15:32 Jotham son of U king of Judah began 6460
15:34 just as his father U had done. 6460
1Ch 6:24 Uriel his son, U his son and Shaul his son. 6459
27:25 of U was in charge of the storehouses in 6460
2Ch 26: 1 Then all the people of Judah took U, 6460
26: 3 U was sixteen years old when 6460
26: 8 The Ammonites brought tribute to U, 6460
26: 9 U built towers in Jerusalem at 6460
26:11 U had a well-trained army, 6460
26:14 U provided shields, spears, helmets, 6460
26:16 But after U became powerful, his pride led 2257[S]
26:18 U, to burn incense to the LORD. 6460
26:19 U, who had a censer in his hand ready 6460
26:21 King U had leprosy until the day he died. 6460
26:23 U rested with his fathers and was buried 6460
27: 2 just as his father U had done, 6460
Ezr 10:21 Maaseiah, Elijah, Shemaiah, Jehiel and U. 6459
Ne 11: 4 Athaiah son of U, the son of Zechariah, 6459
Isa 1: 1 of Amoz saw during the reigns of U, 6460
6: 1 In the year that King U died, 6460
7: 1 When Ahaz son of Jotham, the son of U, 6460
Hos 1: 1 of U, Jotham, Ahaz and Hezekiah, kings 6459
Am 1: 1 the earthquake, when U was king of Judah 6459
Zec 14: 5 from the earthquake in the days of U king 6459
Mt 1: 8 Jehoram the father of U, *3852*
1: 9 U the father of Jotham, *3852*

UZZIAH'S (1) [UZZIAH]

2Ch 26:22 The other events of U reign, 6460

UZZIEL (16) [UZZIELITES]

Ex 6:18 Kohath were Amram, Izhar, Hebron and U. 6457
6:22 The sons of U were Mishael, 6457
Lev 10: 4 sons of Aaron's uncle U, and said to them, 6457
Nu 3:19 Amram, Izhar, Hebron and U. 6457
3:30 the Kohathite clans was Elizaphan son of U. 6457
1Ch 4:42 Neariah, Rephaiah and U, the sons of Ishi, 6457
6: 2 Amram, Izhar, Hebron and U. 6457
6:18 Amram, Izhar, Hebron and U. 6457
7: 7 The sons of Bela: Ezbon, Uzzi, U, 6457
15:10 from the descendants of U, 6457
23:12 Amram, Izhar, Hebron and U—four in all. 6457
23:20 The sons of U: Micah the first 6457
24:24 The son of U: Micah; 6457
25: 4 Bukkiah, Mattaniah, U, 6457
2Ch 29:14 of Jeduthun, Shemaiah and U. 6457
Ne 3: 8 U son of Harhaiah, one of the goldsmiths, 6457

UZZIELITES (2) [UZZIEL]

Nu 3:27 Izharites, Hebronites and U; 6458
1Ch 26:23 the Izharites, the Hebronites and the U: 6458

V

VAGABOND, VAGABONDS (KJV) See WANDERER, WANDERING BEGGARS

VAIL, VAILS (KJV) See VEIL, VEILS

VAIN (33)

Lev 26:16 You will plant seed **in v,** 4200+8198
26:20 Your strength will be spent **in v,** 4200+8198
Job 3: 9 for daylight **in v** and not see the first rays 401
9:29 why should I struggle **in v?** 2039
24: 1 Why must those who know him look **in v** 4202
39:16 she cares not that her labor was **in v,** 4200+8198
Ps 2: 1 and the peoples plot **in v?** 8198
33:17 A horse is a **v hope** for deliverance; 9214
39: 6 He bustles about, but only **in v;** 2039
73:13 Surely **in v** have I kept my heart pure; 8198
73:13 **in v** have I washed my hands in innocence. NIH
119:118 for their deceitfulness is **in v.** 9214
127: 1 Unless the LORD builds the house, its builders labor **in v.** 8736
127: 1 the watchmen stand guard **in v.** 8736
127: 2 **In v** you rise early and stay up late, 8736
Isa 45:19 to Jacob's descendants, 'Seek me **in v.'** 9332
49: 4 I have spent my strength **in v** and 2039
65:23 not toil **in v** or bear children doomed 4200+8198
Jer 2:30 **"In v** I punished your people; 2021+4200+8736
4:30 You adorn yourself **in v.** 2021+4200+8736
6:29 but the refining goes on **in v;** 2021+4200+8736
46:11 But you multiply remedies **in v;** 2021+4200+8736
La 4:17 our eyes failed, looking **in v** for help; 2039
Eze 6:10 not threaten **in v** to bring this calamity 448+2855
Zec 10: 2 they give comfort **in v.** 2039
Mt 15: 9 They worship me **in v;** *3472*
Mk 7: 7 They worship me **in v;** *3472*
Ac 4:25 the nations rage and the peoples plot **in v?** *3031*
1Co 15: 2 Otherwise, you have believed **in v.** *1632*
15:58 that your labor in the Lord is not **in v.** *3031*
2Co 6: 1 not to receive God's grace **in v.** *3031*
Gal 2: 2 that I was running or had run my race **in v.** *3031*
Php 2: 3 of selfish ambition or **v conceit,** *3029*

VAIZATHA (1)

Est 9: 9 Parmashta, Arisai, Aridai and V, 2262

VALE (KJV) See FOOTHILLS, VALLEY

VALIANT (11) [VALIANTLY]

Jdg 20:44 all of them v **fighters.** 408+2657
20:46 all of them v **fighters.** 408+2657
1Sa 10:26 by v *men* whose hearts God had touched. 2657
31:12 all their v men journeyed through the night 2657
2Sa 23:20 was a v **fighter** from Kabzeel, 408+1201+2657
2Ki 5: 1 He was a v **soldier,** but he had leprosy. 1475+2657
1Ch 10:12 all their v men went and took the bodies 2657
11:22 was a v **fighter** from Kabzeel, 408+1201+2657
2Ch 17:17 From Benjamin: Eliada, a v **soldier,** 1475+2657
Ps 76: 5 **V men** lie plundered, 52+4213
Jer 48:14 'We are warriors, men v in battle'? 2657

VALIANTLY (1) [VALIANT]

1Sa 14:48 He fought v and defeated the Amalekites, 2657

VALID (6)

2Sa 15: 3 "Look, your claims are v and proper, 3202
Jn 5:31 my testimony is not v. *239*
5:32 I know that his testimony about me is v. *239*
8:13 as your own witness; your testimony is not v. *239*
8:14 my testimony is v, for I know where I came *239*
8:17 that the testimony of two men is v. *239*

VALLEY (146) [VALLEYS]

Ge 14: 3 All these latter kings joined forces in the V 6677
14: 8 up their battle lines in the V *of* Siddim 6677
14:10 Now the V *of* Siddim was full of tar pits, 6677
14:17 came out to meet him in the V *of* Shaveh 6677
14:17 Valley of Shaveh (that is, the King's V). 6677
26:17 in the V *of* Gerar and settled there. 5707
26:19 in the v and discovered a well 5707
37:14 he sent him off from the V *of* Hebron. 6677
Nu 13:23 When they reached the V *of* Eshcol, 5707
13:24 the V *of* Eshcol because of the cluster 5707
21:12 on and camped in the Zered V. 5707
21:20 and from Bamoth to the v in Moab where 1628
32: 9 up to the V *of* Eshcol and viewed the land, 5707
Dt 1:24 came to the V *of* Eshcol and explored it. 5707
2:13 "Now get up and cross the Zered V." 5707
2:13 So we crossed the v. 5707
2:14 until we crossed the Zered V. 5707
3:29 So we stayed in the v near Beth Peor. 1628
4:46 in the v near Beth Peor east of the Jordan, 1628
21: 4 to a v that has not been plowed or planted 5707
21: 4 in the v they are to break the heifer's neck. 5707
21: 6 the heifer whose neck was broken in the v, 5707
34: 3 the whole region from the V *of* Jericho, 1326
34: 6 in the v opposite Beth Peor, 1628
Jos 7:24 to the V *of* Achor. 6677
7:26 Therefore that place has been called the V 6677
8:11 with the v between them and the city. 1628
8:13 That night Joshua went into the v. 6677
10:12 O moon, over the V *of* Aijalon." 6677
11: 8 and to the V *of* Mizpah on the east, 1326
11:17 the V *of* Lebanon below Mount Hermon. 1326
12: 7 in the V *of* Lebanon to Mount Halak, 1326
13:19 Sibmah, Zereth Shahar on the hill in the v, 6677
13:27 and in the v, Beth Haram, Beth Nimrah, 6677
15: 7 the V *of* Achor and turned north to Gilgal, 6677
15: 8 Then it ran up the V *of* Ben Hinnom along 1628
15: 8 to the top of the hill west of the Hinnom V 1628
15: 8 at the northern end of the V *of* Rephaim. 6677
17:16 and its settlements and those in the V 6677
18:16 of the hill facing the V *of* Ben Hinnom, 1628
18:16 north of the V *of* Rephaim. 6677
18:16 the Hinnom V along the southern slope of 1628
19:14 and ended at the V *of* Iphtah El. 1628
19:27 touched Zebulun and the V *of* Iphtah El, 1628
Jdg 5:15 rushing after him into the v. 6677
6:33 the Jordan and camped in the V *of* Jezreel. 6677
7: 1 of Midian was north of them in the v near 6677
7: 8 camp of Midian lay below him in the v. 6677
7:12 other eastern peoples had settled in the v, 6677
16: 4 in the V *of* Sorek whose name was Delilah. 5707
18:28 The city was in a v near Beth Rehob. 6677
1Sa 6:13 in the v, and when they looked up and saw 6677
13:18 toward the borderland overlooking the V 1628
17: 2 the V *of* Elah and drew up their battle line 6677
17: 3 with the v between them. 1628
17:19 with Saul and all the men of Israel in the V 6677
21: 9 whom you killed in the V *of* Elah, is here; 6677
31: 7 the v and those across the Jordan saw that 6677
2Sa 5:18 and spread out in the V *of* Rephaim; 6677
5:22 up and spread out in the V *of* Rephaim; 6677
8:13 eighteen thousand Edomites in the V *of* Salt. 1628
15:23 The king also crossed the Kidron V, 5707
17:13 and we will drag it down to the v until not 5707
18:18 in the King's V as a monument to himself, 6677
23:13 of Philistines was encamped in the V 6677
1Ki 2:37 The day you leave and cross the Kidron V, 5707
15:13 down and burned it in the Kidron V. 5707
18:40 to the Kishon V and slaughtered there. 5707
2Ki 2:16 down on some mountain or in some v." 1628
3:16 Make this v full of ditches. 5707
3:17 yet this v will be filled with water, 5707
14: 7 the V *of* Salt and captured Sela in battle, 1628
23: 4 the Kidron V and took the ashes to Bethel. NIH
23: 6 to the Kidron V outside Jerusalem 5707
23:10 which was in the V *of* Ben Hinnom, 1628
23:12 and threw the rubble into the Kidron V. 5707
1Ch 4:39 the v in search of pasture for their flocks. 1628
10: 7 When all the Israelites in the v saw that 6677
11:15 of Philistines was encamped in the V 6677
1Ch 14: 9 come and raided the V *of* Rephaim; 6677
14:13 Once more the Philistines raided the v; 6677
18:12 eighteen thousand Edomites in the V *of* Salt. 1628
2Ch 14:10 up battle positions in the V *of* Zephathah 1628
15:16 broke it up and burned it in the Kidron V. 5707
20:26 On the fourth day they assembled in the V 6677
20:26 This is why it is called the V *of* Beracah 6677
25:11 and led his army to the V *of* Salt, 1628
26: 9 at the V Gate and at the angle of the wall, 1628
28: 3 burned sacrifices in the V *of* Ben Hinnom 1628
29:16 and carried it out to the Kidron V. 5707
30:14 and threw them into the Kidron V. 5707
33: 6 He sacrificed his sons in the fire in the V 1628
33:14 west of the Gihon spring in the v, 5707
Ne 2:13 through the V Gate toward the Jackal Well 1628
2:15 so I went up the v by night, 5707
2:15 and reentered through the V Gate. 1628
3:13 The V Gate was repaired by Hanun and 1628
11:30 from Beersheba to the V *of* Hinnom. 1628
11:35 and in the V *of* the Craftsmen. 1628
Job 21:33 The soil in the v is sweet to him; 5707
Ps 23: 4 though I walk through the v *of* the shadow 1628
60: T twelve thousand Edomites in the V *of* Salt. 1628
60: 6 and measure off the V *of* Succoth. 6677
84: 6 As they pass through the V *of* Baca, 6677
108: 7 and measure off the V *of* Succoth. 6677
Pr 30:17 will be pecked out by the ravens of the v, 5707
SS 6:11 to look at the new growth in the v, 5707
Isa 17: 5 when a man gleans heads of grain in the V 6677
22: 1 An oracle concerning the V *of* Vision: 1628
22: 5 of tumult and trampling and terror in the V 1628
28: 1 set on the head of a fertile v— 1628
28: 4 set on the head of a fertile v, 1628
28:21 he will rouse himself as in the V 6677
40: 4 Every v shall be raised up, 1628
65:10 the V *of* Achor a resting place for herds, 6677
Jer 2:23 See how you behaved in the v; 1628
7:31 in the V *of* Ben Hinnom to burn their sons 1628
7:32 Topheth or the V *of* Ben Hinnom, 1628
7:32 Ben Hinnom, but the V *of* Slaughter, 1628
19: 2 and go out to the V *of* Ben Hinnom, 1628
19: 6 Topheth or the V *of* Ben Hinnom, 1628
19: 6 Ben Hinnom, but the V *of* Slaughter. 1628
21:13 above this v on the rocky plateau, declares 6677
31:40 The whole v *where* dead bodies 6677
31:40 the terraces out to the Kidron V on the east 5707
32:35 They built high places for Baal in the V 1628
48: 8 The v will be ruined and 6677
Eze 37: 1 and set me in the middle of a v; 1326
37: 2 a great many bones on the floor of the v, 1326
39:11 in the v *of* those who travel east toward 1628
39:11 So it will be called the V *of* Hamon Gog. 1628
39:15 the gravediggers have buried it in the V 1628
Hos 1: 5 that day I will break Israel's bow in the V 6677
2:15 will make the V *of* Achor a door of hope. 6677
Joel 3: 2 down to the V *of* Jehoshaphat. 6677
3:12 let them advance into the V *of* Jehoshaphat, 6677
3:14 multitudes in the v *of* decision! 6677
3:14 day of the LORD is near in the v *of* decision. 6677
3:18 of the LORD's house and will water the v 5707
Am 1: 5 in the V *of* Aven and the one who holds 1326
6:14 the way from Lebo Hamath to the v *of* 5707
Mic 1: 6 into the v and lay bare her foundations. 1628
Zec 14: 4 forming a great v, with half of the mountain 1628
14: 5 You will flee by my mountain v, 1628
Lk 3: 5 Every v shall be filled in, *5754*
Jn 18: 1 and crossed the Kidron V. *5929*

VALLEYS (26) [VALLEY]

Nu 14:25 and Canaanites are living in the v, 6677
24: 6 "Like v they spread out, 5707
Dt 8: 7 with springs flowing in the v and hills; 1326
11:11 a land of mountains and v that drinks rain 1326
2Sa 22:16 The v *of* the sea were exposed and 692
1Ki 18: 5 through the land to all the springs and v. 5707
20:28 a god of the hills and not a god of the v, 6677
1Ch 12:15 put to flight everyone living in the v, 6677
27:29 in charge of the herds in the v. 6677
Job 39:10 Will he till the v behind you? 6677
Ps 18:15 The v *of* the sea were exposed and 692
65:13 with flocks and the v are mantled 6677
104: 8 they went down into the v, 1326
SS 2: 1 I am a rose of Sharon, a lily of the v. 6677
Isa 22: 7 Your choicest v are full of chariots, 6677
41:18 and springs within the v. 1326
Jer 49: 4 Why do you boast of your v, 6677
49: 4 boast of your v so fruitful? 6677
Eze 6: 3 mountains and hills, to the ravines and v: 1628
7:16 moaning like doves of the v, 1628
31:12 on the mountains and in all the v; 1628
32: 5 and fill the v with your remains. 1628
35: 8 and in your v and in all your ravines. 1628
36: 4 mountains and hills, to the ravines and v, 1628
36: 6 mountains and hills, to the ravines and v: 1628
Mic 1: 4 and the v split apart, like wax before 6677

VALOUR (KJV) See ABLE, BRAVE, CAPABLE, FIGHTERS, FIGHTING MEN, STANDING, STRONG, VALIANT, WARRIOR

VALUABLE (8) [VALUE]

2Ch 32:23 for the LORD and v **gifts** for Hezekiah king 4458
Ezr 1: 6 and with v **gifts,** in addition to all the 4458
Pr 1:13 we will get all sorts of v **things** 2104+3701
Da 11: 8 their metal images and their v articles 2775
Mt 6:26 *Are* you not much **more v than** they? *1422*
12:12 How much more v *is* a man than a sheep! *1422*
Lk 12:24 And how much more v you *are* than birds! *1422*
Jas 5: 7 to yield its v crop and how patient he is for *5508*

VALUABLES (2) [VALUE]

2Ch 32:27 spices, shields and all kinds of v. 2775
Jer 20: 5 all its v and all the treasures of the kings 3702

VALUE (58) [VALUABLE, VALUABLES, VALUED, VALUES]

Lev 5:15 one without defect and of the **proper** v 6886
5:16 add a fifth of **the** v to that and give it all to 2257S
5:18 one without defect and of the **proper** v. 6886
6: 5 of **the** v to it and give it all to the owner on 2257S
6: 6 one without defect and of the **proper** v. 6886
22:14 the offering and add a fifth of **the** v to it. 2257S
25:27 *he is to* **determine the** v *for* the years 3108
27: 3 the v *of* a male between the ages of twenty 6886
27: 4 set her v at thirty shekels. 6886
27: 5 set the v *of* a male at twenty shekels and 6886
27: 6 the v *of* a male at five shekels of silver and 6886
27: 7 set the v *of* a male at fifteen shekels and of 6886
27: 8 who *will* **set** *the* v *for* him according 6885
27:12 Whatever v the priest then sets, 6886
27:13 he must add a fifth to its v. 6886
27:14 Whatever v the priest then **sets,** 6885
27:15 he must add a fifth to its v, 4084+6886
27:16 its v is to be set according to the amount 6886
27:17 the v that has been set remains. 6886
27:18 the priest will determine the v according to 4084
27:18 and its **set** v will be reduced. 6886
27:19 he must add a fifth to its v, 4084+6886
27:23 the priest will determine its v up to 4831+6886
27:23 and the man must pay its v on that day 6886
27:25 Every v is to be set according to 6886
27:27 he may buy it back at its **set** v, 6886
27:27 adding a fifth of **the** v to it. 2257S
27:27 it is to be sold at its **set** v. 6886
27:31 he must add a fifth of **the** v to it. 2257S
1Sa 26:24 so *may* the LORD v my life and 928+1540+6524
1Ki 10:21 silver was considered of **little** v 4202+4399
20: 6 They will seize everything you v 4718+6524
2Ch 9:20 because silver was considered of **little** v 4399
20:25 and clothing and also articles of v— 2776
21: 3 of silver and gold and **articles of** v, 4458
36:10 together with articles of v *from* the temple 2775
36:19 and destroyed everything of v there. 4718
Job 15: 3 with speeches that **have** no v? 3603
Pr 10: 2 Ill-gotten treasures *are* **of** no v, 3603
10:20 the heart of the wicked is **of little** v. 3869+5071
16:13 *they* v a man who speaks the truth. 170
31:11 in her and lacks nothing of v. 8965
Eze 7:11 no wealth, nothing *of* v. 5625
Hab 2:18 **"Of** what v *is* an idol, 3603
Mt 13:46 When he found one *of* **great** v, *4501*
Ac 19:19 When they calculated the v of the scrolls, *5507*
Ro 2:25 Circumcision *has* v if you observe the law, *6067*
3: 1 or what v is there in circumcision? *6066*
4:14 faith *has* **no** v and the promise is worthless, *3033*
Gal 5: 2 Christ *will be of* no v *to* you at all. *6067*
5: 6 circumcision nor uncircumcision *has* any v. *2710*
Col 2:23 but they lack any v in restraining sensual *5507*
1Ti 4: 8 For physical training is of some v, *6068*
4: 8 but godliness has v for all things, *6068*
2Ti 2:14 it is of no v, and only ruins those who *5978*
Heb 4: 2 message they heard *was of* no v to them, *6067*
11:26 as *of* greater v than the treasures of Egypt, *4458*
13: 9 which *are* of no v to those who eat them. *6067*

VALUED (4) [VALUE]

1Sa 26:24 As surely as I v your life today, 928+1540+6524
Ezr 8:27 20 bowls of gold v **at** 1,000 darics, 4200
Lk 7: 2 servant, whom his master v **highly,** *1639+1952*
16:15 is **highly** v among men is detestable *3836+5734*

VALUES (1) [VALUE]

Lev 27: 2 persons to the LORD by giving **equivalent** v, 6886

VANIAH (1)

Ezr 10:36 V, Meremoth, Eliashib, 2264

VANISH (14) [VANISHED, VANISHES]

Job 6:17 and in the heat v from their channels. 1980
Ps 37:20 *they will* v—vanish like smoke. 3983
37:20 they will vanish—v like smoke. 3983
58: 7 *Let them* v like water that flows away; 4416
102: 3 For my days v like smoke; 3983
104:35 But *may* sinners v from the earth and 9462
Isa 11:13 Ephraim's jealousy *will* v, 6073
16: 4 the aggressor *will* v from the land. 9462
29:14 the intelligence of the intelligent *will* v." 6259
29:20 The ruthless *will* v, the mockers will 699
34:12 all her princes will v **away.** 700
51: 6 the heavens *will* v like smoke, 4872
Jer 18:14 of Lebanon *ever* v from its rocky slopes? 6440
31:36 "Only if these decrees v from my sight," 4631

VANISHED (5) [VANISH]

Ps 12: 1 the faithful *have* v from among men. 7182

Ps 77: 8 *Has* his unfailing love v forever? 699
Ecc 9: 6 and their jealousy *have* long since v; 6
Jer 7:28 *it has* v from their lips. 4162
Rev 18:14 All your riches and splendor *have* v, *660*

VANISHES (3) [VANISH]
Job 7: 9 As a cloud v and is gone, 3983
30:15 my safety v like a cloud. 6296
Jas 4:14 that appears for a little while and then v. *906*

VANITIES, VANITY (KJV) See BREATH, DECEIT, DELUSIONS, DESTRUCTION, DISHONEST, EMPTY, EVIL, FALSE, FALSEHOOD, FALSELY, FLEETING, FRUSTRATION, FUTILE, FUTILITY, LIES, MEANINGLESS, NO MEANING, WORTHLESS IDOLS

VAPOR (1)
Pr 21: 6 by a lying tongue is a fleeting v and 2039

VAPOUR (KJV) See MIST

VARIABLENESS (KJV) See CHANGE

VARIANCE (KJV) See AGAINST, DISCORD

VARIED (1) [VARIOUS]
Eze 17: 3 and full plumage *of* v **colors** came 8391

VARIOUS (25) [VARIED]
Ge 1:11 according to their v **kinds."** 4786
7: 3 to keep their v **kinds** alive throughout 2446
Jdg 2:12 They followed and worshiped v gods of 337
1Ch 18: 8 the pillars and v bronze articles. NIH
28:14 be used in v **kinds of service,** 2256+6275+6275
28:14 be used in v **kinds of service:** 2256+6275+6275
29: 2 turquoise, stones of v **colors,** 8391
2Ch 8:14 by divisions for the v **gates,** 2256+9133+9133
16:14 with spices and v blended perfumes, 2385
31:16 to perform the daily duties of their *v* **tasks,** AIT
32:28 and he made stalls for v kinds of cattle, 3972
Ne 11: 3 each on his own property in the *v* **towns,** AIT
Est 3:12 governors of the v **provinces** 2256+4519+4519
3:12 and the nobles of the v **peoples.** 2256+6639+6639
Eze 13:18 and make veils of v lengths for their heads 3972
Mt 4:24 to him all who were ill *with* v diseases, *4476*
24: 7 be famines and earthquakes **in** v places. *2848*
Mk 1:34 Jesus healed many who had v diseases. *4476*
13: 8 There will be earthquakes **in** v places, *2848*
Lk 4:40 to Jesus all who had v **kinds** of sickness, *4476*
21:11 famines and pestilences **in** v places, *2848*
Heb 1: 1 the prophets at many times and **in** v **ways,** *4502*
2: 4 by signs, wonders and v miracles, *4476*
9:10 and drink and v ceremonial washings— *1427*
1Pe 4:10 administering God's grace in its v forms. *4476*

VASHNI (KJV) See SECOND

VASHTI (10)
Est 1: 9 Queen **V** also gave a banquet for the women 2267
1:11 to bring before him Queen **V**, 2267
1:12 Queen **V** refused to come. 2267
1:15 what must be done to Queen **V?"** 2267
1:16 "Queen **V** has done wrong, 2267
1:17 'King Xerxes commanded Queen **V** to 2267
1:19 that **V** is never again to enter the presence 2267
2: 1 he remembered **V** and what she had done 2267
2: 4 pleases the king be queen instead of **V."** 2267
2:17 and made her queen instead of **V.** 2267

VASSAL (3) [VASSALS]
2Ki 16: 7 "I am your servant and v. 1201
17: 3 Hoshea, who had been Shalmaneser's v 6269
24: 1 Jehoiakim became his v for three years. 6269

VASSALS (2) [VASSAL]
2Sa 10:19 the kings who were v *of* Hadadezer saw 6269
1Ch 19:19 When the v *of* Hadadezer saw that 6269

VAST (25)
Ge 2: 1 were completed in all their v **array.** 7372
Dt 1:19 through all that v and dreadful desert 1524
2: 7 over your journey through this v desert. 1524
8:15 through the v and dreadful desert, 1524
1Ki 8:65 a v assembly, people from Lebo Hamath to 1524
20:13 'Do you see this v army? 1524
20:28 I will deliver this v army into your hands, 1524
2Ch 7: 8 v assembly, people from Lebo Hamath 1524+4394
13: 8 You are indeed a v army and have 8041
14: 9 a v army and three hundred chariots, 547+547
14:11 we have come against this v **army.** 2162
20: 2 "A v army is coming against you 8041
20:12 For we have no power to face this v army 8041
20:15 or discouraged because of this v army. 8041
20:24 the desert and looked toward the v **army,** 2162
2Ch 32: 7 of the king of Assyria and the v army 3972
Est 1: 4 a full 180 days he displayed the v wealth 3883
1:20 throughout all his v realm, 8041
5:11 Haman boasted to them about his v wealth, 3883
Job 9: 4 His wisdom is profound, his power is v. 579
38:18 Have you comprehended the v **expanses** *of* 8144
Ps 104:25 There is the sea, v and spacious, 1524
139:17 How v *is* the sum of them! 6793
Eze 26:19 over you and its v waters cover you, 8041
37:10 up on their feet—a v army. 1524+4394+4394

VAT (1) [VATS]
Hag 2:16 went to a **wine** v to draw fifty measures, 3676

VATS (5) [VAT]
Ex 22:29 from your granaries or your v. 1964
1Ch 27:27 produce of the vineyards for the wine v. 238
Pr 3:10 and your v will brim over with new wine. 3676
Joel 2:24 the v will overflow with new wine and oil. 3676
3:13 the winepress is full and the v overflow— 3676

VAULTED (2) [VAULT]
Job 22:14 as he goes about in the v heavens.' 2553
Jer 37:16 Jeremiah was put into a v **cell** in 2844

VAULTS (1) [VAULTED]
Dt 32:34 kept this in reserve and sealed it in my v? 238

VAUNT, VAUNTETH (KJV) See BOAST

VAUNTS (1)
Job 15:25 at God and v **himself** against the Almighty, 1504

VEGETABLE (2) [VEGETABLES]
Dt 11:10 and irrigated it by foot as in a v garden. 3763
1Ki 21: 2 your vineyard to use for a v garden, 3763

VEGETABLES (4) [VEGETABLE]
Pr 15:17 Better a meal of v where there is love than 3763
Da 1:12 Give us nothing but v to eat and water 2447
1:16 they were to drink and gave them v instead. 2448
Ro 14: 2 whose faith is weak, eats only v. *3303*

VEGETATION (6)
Ge 1:11 Then God said, "Let the land produce v: 2013
1:12 The land produced v: 2013
19:25 and also the v *in* the land. 7542
Dt 29:23 nothing sprouting, no v growing on it. 6912
Isa 15: 6 the v is gone and nothing green is left. 2013
42:15 and hills and dry up all their v; 6912

VEHEMENT (KJV) See LONGING, MIGHTY, SCORCHING

VEHEMENTLY (1)
Lk 23:10 teachers of the law were standing there, v accusing him. *2364*

VEIL (16) [VEILED, VEILS]
Ge 24:65 So she took her v and covered herself. 7581
38:14 with a v to disguise herself, 7581
38:19 she took off her v and put 7581
Ex 34:33 he put a v over his face. 5003
34:34 he removed the v until he came out. 5003
34:35 the v back over his face until he went in 5003
Job 22:14 Thick clouds v him, 6260
SS 4: 1 Your eyes behind your v are doves. 7539
4: 3 Your temples behind your v are like 7539
6: 7 Your temples behind your v are like 7539
Isa 47: 2 take off your v. 7539
La 3:65 Put a v *over* their hearts, 4485
2Co 3:13 who would put a v over his face to keep *2820*
3:14 for to this day the same v remains when *2820*
3:15 when Moses is read, a v covers their hearts. *2820*
3:16 turns to the Lord, the v is taken away. *2820*

VEILED (3) [VEIL]
SS 1: 7 Why should I be like a v *woman* beside 6486
2Co 4: 3 And even if our gospel is v, *2821*
4: 3 it is v to those who are perishing. *2821*

VEILS (3) [VEIL]
Isa 3:19 the earrings and bracelets and v, 8304
Eze 13:18 and make v of various lengths 5029
13:21 I will tear off your v and save my people 5029

VEIN (KJV) See MINE

VENGEANCE (33) [AVENGE, AVENGED, AVENGER, AVENGES, AVENGING, REVENGE]
Ge 4:15 *he will* **suffer** v seven times over." 5933
Nu 31: 2 **"Take** v on the Midianites *for* 5933+5935
31: 3 and to carry out the LORD's v on them. 5935
Dt 32:41 *I will* **take** v on my adversaries 5934+8740
32:43 *he will* **take** v on his enemies 5934+8740
Ps 149: 7 to inflict v on the nations and punishment 5935
Isa 34: 8 For the LORD has a day of v, 5934
35: 4 your God will come, he will come with v; 5934
47: 3 I will take v; I will spare no one." 5934
59:17 on the garments of v and wrapped himself 5934
61: 2 of the LORD's favor and the day of v 5934
63: 4 For the day of v was in my heart, 5934
Jer 11:20 let me see your v upon them, 5935
20:12 let me see your v upon them, 5935
46:10 a day of v, for vengeance on his foes. 5935
46:10 a day of vengeance, for v on his foes. 5933
50:15 Since this is the v *of* the LORD, 5935
50:15 **take** v on her; do to her as she has done 5933
50:28 how the LORD our God has taken v, 5935
50:28 God has taken vengeance, v *for* his temple. 5935
51: 6 It is time for the LORD's v; 5935
51:11 The LORD will take v, 5935
51:11 LORD will take vengeance, v *for* his temple. 5935
La 3:60 You have seen the depth of their v, 5935
Eze 16:38 upon you the **blood** v *of* my wrath 1947
25:14 I will take v on Edom by the hand 5935
25:14 they will know my v, declares the Sovereign 5935
25:15 the Philistines acted in v and took revenge 5935
25:17 I will carry out great v on them 5935
25:17 when I take v on them.' " 5935
Mic 5:15 I will take v in anger and wrath upon 5934
Na 1: 2 the LORD **takes** v and is filled with wrath. 5933
1: 2 The LORD **takes** v on his foes 5933

VENISON (KJV) See GAME, WILD GAME

VENOM (5) [VENOMOUS]
Dt 32:24 the v *of* vipers that glide in the dust. 2779
32:33 Their wine is the v *of* serpents, 2779
Job 20:14 it will become the v *of* serpents 5355
Ps 58: 4 Their v is like the venom of a snake, 2779
58: 4 Their venom is like the v *of* a snake, 2779

VENOMOUS (4) [VENOM]
Nu 21: 6 the LORD sent v snakes among them; 8597
Dt 8:15 with its v snakes and scorpions, 8597
Isa 14:29 its fruit will be a darting, v **serpent.** 8597
Jer 8:17 "See, I will send v **snakes** among you, 5729

VENT (5)
Job 15:13 so that *you* v your rage against God 8740
20:23 God *will* v his burning anger against him 8938
Pr 29:11 A fool **gives** full v **to** his anger, 3655
La 4:11 LORD *has* **given full** v *to* his wrath; 3983
Da 11:30 and v *his* **fury** against the holy covenant. 2404

VENTURE (4) [VENTURES]
Dt 28:56 that *she would* not v to touch the ground 5814
Jer 5: 6 to tear to pieces any who v **out,** 3655
Ac 19:31 sent him a message begging him not *to* v *1443*
Ro 15:18 *I will* not v to speak of anything except *5528*

VENTURES (1) [VENTURE]
Job 4: 2 "If *someone* v a word with you, 5814

VERDANT (1)
SS 1:16 And our bed is v. 8316

VERDICT (6)
Dt 17: 9 of them and they will give you the **v.** 1821+5477
Jdg 20: 7 speak up and give your **v."** 6783
1Ki 3:28 all Israel heard the v the king had given, 5477
2Ch 19: 6 is with you whenever you give a **v.** 1821+5477
Da 4:17 the holy ones declare the **v,** 10690
Jn 3:19 This is the **v:** Light has come into the world, *3213*

VERIFIED (1) [VERIFY]
Ge 42:20 that your words *may* **be** v and that you may 586

VERIFY (1) [VERIFIED]
Ac 24:11 You can easily v that no more than twelve *2105*

VERILY (KJV) See TRUTH

VERITY (KJV) See FAITHFUL

VERMILION (KJV) See RED

VERSED (1)
Ezr 7: 6 a teacher **well** v in the Law of Moses, 4542

VERSES (1)
Ps 45: 1 a noble theme as I recite my v for the king; 5126

VERY (297)
Ge 1:31 God saw all that he had made, and it was v good. 4394
4: 5 So Cain was v angry, 4394
7:13 On that v day Noah and his sons, Shem, 6795
12:14 that she was a v beautiful woman. 4394
13: 2 Abram had become v wealthy in livestock 4394
15: 1 I am your shield, your v great reward." 4394

Ge 17: 6 I will make you v fruitful; 928+4394+4394
17:23 that v day Abraham took his son Ishmael 6795
18: 5 **"V well,"** they answered, "do as you say." 4027
19:20 Let me flee to it—it is v **small,** isn't it? AIT
19:21 He said to him, **"V well,** 2180
20: 8 they were v **much** afraid. 4394
21: 2 at the v time God had promised him. NIH
24:16 The girl was v beautiful, a virgin; 4394
26:13 to grow until he became v wealthy. 4394
30:15 **"V well,"** Rachel said, 4027+4200
37:13 **"V well,"** he replied. 2180
41:19 scrawny and v ugly and lean. 4394
44:10 **"V well,** then," he said, 1685
50: 9 It was a v large company. 4394
Ex 8:28 but *you* **must** not go v **far.** 8178+8178
9:16 I have raised you up for this v purpose, 2296
10:19 the wind to a v strong west wind, 4394
12:17 because it was on this v day 6795
12:41 At the end of the 430 years, to the v day, 6795
12:51 And on that v day the LORD brought 6795
19: 1 the Israelites left Egypt—on the v day— 2296
19:16 and a v loud trumpet blast. 4394
33:17 "I will do the v thing you have asked, 2296
Lev 19: 9 do not reap to the v edges of your field 3983
23:14 until the v day you bring this offering 6795
23:22 do not reap to the v edges of your field 3983
Nu 12: 3 (Now Moses was a v humble man, 4394
13:28 and the cities are fortified and v large. 4394
14:28 you the v **things** I heard you say: 889+3869+4027
16:15 Then Moses became v angry and said to 4394
22:22 But God *was* v **angry** when he went, 678+3013
32: 1 who had v large herds and flocks, 4394+6786
Dt 1:30 did for your in Egypt, before your v eyes, NIH
2: 4 They will be afraid of you, but be v careful. 4394
2:25 **This** v day I will begin to put the terror 2296
4:11 while it blazed with fire to the v heavens, 4213
4:15 Therefore watch yourselves v carefully, 4394
4:34 for you in Egypt before your v eyes? NIH
13: 6 If your v **own brother,** 278+562+1201+3870
24: 8 In cases of leprous diseases be v careful 4394
27: 8 And you shall write v clearly all the words 3512
30:14 No, the word is v near you; 4394
Jos 1: 7 Be strong and v courageous. 4394
5:11 The day after the Passover, that v day, 6795
8: 4 Don't go v far from it. 4394
9: 9 a v distant country because of the fame of 4394
9:13 worn out by the v long journey." 4394
10: 2 and his people were v **much** alarmed at this, 4394
13: 1 the LORD said to him, "You *are* v **old,** 928+995+2021+2416+3427
13: 1 and there are still v large areas of land to 4394
17:17 "You are numerous and v powerful. 1524
22: 3 For a long time now—to **this** v day— 2296
22: 5 But be v careful to keep the commandment 4394
22:17 Up to **this** v day we have not cleansed 2296
23: 6 "Be v strong; be careful to obey 4394
23:11 be v careful to love the LORD your God. 4394
Jdg 2:20 LORD *was* v **angry** with Israel and said, 678+3013
3:17 Eglon king of Moab, who was a v fat man. 4394
4: 9 **"V well,"** Deborah said, *"I will* **go** 2143+2143
5:18 The people of Zebulun risked their v lives; NIH
9:30 he *was* v **angry.** 678+3013
13: 6 like an angel of God, v awesome. 4394
15:18 Because he was v thirsty, 4394
18: 9 We have seen that the land is v good. 4394
Ru 1:20 the Almighty has made my life v bitter. 4394
1Sa 2:17 This sin of the young men was v great in 4394
2:22 Now Eli, who was v old, 4394
4:10 The slaughter was v great; 4394
4:16 I fled from it **this** v day." 2021
5:11 God's hand was v heavy upon it. 4394
16:21 Saul liked him v **much,** 4394
18: 8 Saul was v angry; this refrain galled him. 4394
19: 1 But Jonathan was v fond of David 4394
20: 3 "Your father **knows** v **well** 3359+3359
20: 7 If he says, **'V well,'** 3202
21:12 and was v **much** afraid of Achish king 4394
23:22 They tell me he *is* v **crafty.** 6891+6891
25: 2 property there at Carmel, was v wealthy. 4394
25:15 Yet these men were v good to us. 4394
25:36 He was in high spirits and v drunk. 4394+6330
28: 2 Achish replied, **"V well,** 4027+4200
2Sa 1:26 you were v dear to me. 4394
2:17 The battle that day was v fierce, 4394+6330
3: 8 Abner was v angry because 4394
3: 8 **This** v day I am loyal to the house 2021
7:24 as **your** v **own forever,** 3870+4200
11: 2 The woman was v beautiful, 4394
12: 2 a v large number of sheep and cattle, 4394
12:11 Before your v eyes I will take your wives NIH
13: 3 Jonadab was a v shrewd man. 4394
13:36 too, and all his servants wept v bitterly. 4394
14:21 The king said to Joab, **"V well,** 2180+5528
19:32 Now Barzillai was a v old man, 4394
19:32 for he was a v wealthy man. 4394
24:10 I have done a v foolish thing." 4394
1Ki 1: 4 The girl was v beautiful; 4394+6330
1: 6 also v handsome and was born next 4394
2:18 **"V well,"** Bathsheba replied, 3202
3: 6 a son to sit on his throne **this** v day. 2296
4:29 gave Solomon wisdom and v great insight, 4394
10: 2 at Jerusalem with a v great caravan— 4394
16:16 over Israel **that** v day there in the camp. 2085
19:10 *"I have been* v **zealous** for the LORD 7861+7861
19:14 *"I have been* v **zealous** for the LORD 7861+7861
2Ki 6:12 the v words you speak in your bedroom." NIH
17:18 So the LORD was v angry with Israel 4394
2Ki 23:17 of Bethel the v things you have done to it." 465
1Ch 17:22 You made your people Israel **your** v **own** forever, 3870+4200
21: 8 I have done a v foolish thing." 4394
21:13 for his mercy is v great; 4394
23:17 of Rehabiah were v numerous. 2025+4200+5087
26: 6 because they were v **capable men.** 1475+2657
2Ch 9: 1 Arriving with a v great caravan— 4394
11:12 and made them v strong. 2221+4394
20:19 God of Israel, with v loud voice. 2025+4200+5087
21:15 will be v ill with a lingering disease of 8041
26: 8 because he had become v powerful. 2025+4200+5087+6330
30:13 A v large crowd of people assembled 4394
32:27 Hezekiah had v great riches and honor, 4394
32:29 for God had given him v great riches. 4394
Ne 1: 7 *We have* **acted** v **wickedly** toward you 2472+2472
2: 2 I was v much afraid, 4394
2:10 they *were* v much **disturbed** 8288+8317
4: 7 they were v angry. 4394
5: 6 and these charges, I was v angry. 4394
8:17 And their joy was v great. 4394
Est 1:18 **This** v day the Persian and Median women 2296
Job 1:12 The LORD said to Satan, **"V well, then,** 2180
2: 6 The LORD said to Satan, **"V well, then,** 2180
10: 1 "I loathe my v life; NIH
32: 2 *became* v **angry** with Job for 678+3013
33: 8 I heard the v words— 7754
33:20 so that his v **being** finds food repulsive 2652
Ps 37:32 for the righteous, seeking their v lives; NIH
38: 6 I am bowed down and brought v low; 4394+6330
75: 8 of the earth drink it down to its v dregs. NIH
77:16 the v depths were convulsed. 677
78:21 the LORD heard them, *he was* v **angry;** 6297
78:59 When God heard them, *he was* v **angry;** 6297
78:62 *he was* v **angry** with his inheritance. 6297
89:38 *you have been* v **angry** with your anointed 6297
102:14 her v dust moves them to pity. NIH
104: 1 O LORD my God, you are v great; 4394
105:24 The LORD made his people v fruitful; 4394
119:112 set on keeping your decrees **to the** v **end.** 4200+6409+6813
146: 4 on **that** v day their plans come to nothing. 2085
Pr 6:26 and the adulteress preys upon your v life. 3701
22:27 your v bed will be snatched from under you. NIH
Isa 10:25 **V soon** my anger against you will end 4663+5071+6388
16:14 her survivors will be v **few** and feeble. 4663+5071
24: 6 and v **few** are left. 632+4663
25:12 down to the ground, to the v dust. NIH
28:11 **V well then,** with foreign lips 3954
29:17 **In a** v **short time,** will not 4663+5071+6388
47: 6 Even on the aged you laid a v heavy yoke. 4394
65: 3 to my v face, offering sacrifices in gardens NIH
Jer 20:15 *who* **made** him v **glad,** saying, 8523+8523
24: 2 One basket had v good figs, 4394
24: 2 the other basket had v poor figs, 4394
24: 3 "The good ones are v good, 4394
25: 3 of Amon king of Judah until **this** v day— 2296
27:16 not listen to the prophets who say, **'V soon** 4559
28:16 This v year you are going to die, NIH
29:21 put them to death before your v eyes. NIH
44:28 of Judah from Egypt will be v **few,** 5031+5493
La 4:20 The LORD's anointed, our v life breath, NIH
Eze 2: 3 in revolt against me to this v day. 6795
4:15 **"V well,"** he said, "I will let you bake your 8011
16:13 You became v beautiful and rose 928+4394+4394
16:34 You are the v **opposite,** for you give 2201
17:22 I myself will take a shoot from the v **top** 8123
23:39 On the v day they sacrificed their children 2085
24: 2 record this date, this v date, 6795
24: 2 has laid siege to Jerusalem this v day. 6795
25:12 the house of Judah and *became* v **guilty** 870+870
37: 2 bones that were v dry. 4394
40: 1 on that v day the hand of the LORD was 6795
40: 2 of Israel and set me on a v high mountain, 4394
Da 3:15 and worship the image I made, v good. NIH
5:30 That v night Belshazzar, king of the NIH
7: 7 terrifying and frightening and v powerful. 10339
8: 8 The goat became v great, 4394+6330
8:24 *He will become* v **strong,** 3946+6793
11:25 with a large and v powerful army, 4394+6330
Hos 12: 8 Ephraim boasts, "I am v rich; 421
Joel 1:16 the food been cut off before our v eyes— NIH
Am 7:10 a conspiracy against you in the v heart NIH
Jnh 2: 3 into the v heart of the seas, NIH
3: 3 Now Nineveh was a v important city— 466+4200
4: 6 and Jonah was v happy about the vine. 1524
Mic 1: 9 It has reached the v gate of my people, NIH
Zep 3:20 restore your fortunes before your v eyes," NIH
Zec 1: 2 "The LORD *was* v **angry** with your forefathers. 7911+7912
1:14 'I am v jealous for Jerusalem and Zion, 1524
1:15 but I am v angry with the nations 1524
7:12 So the LORD Almighty was v angry. 1524
8: 2 "I am v jealous for Zion; 1524
9: 2 though they are v skillful. 4394
Mt 4: 8 the devil took him to a v high mountain *3336*
8:13 And his servant was healed at **that** v hour. *1697*
10:30 the v hairs of your head are all numbered. *NIG*
15:28 her daughter was healed from that v hour. *NIG*
21: 8 A *v* **large** crowd spread their cloaks on *AIT*
26: 7 an alabaster jar *of* v **expensive** perfume, *988*
26:22 They were v sad and began to say *5379*
26:31 **"This** v night you will all fall away *4047*
26:34 **"this** v night, before the rooster crows, *4047*
28:15 among the Jews to this v **day.** *2465+4958*
Mt 28:20 with you always, to the v **end** of the age." *5333*
Mk 1:35 V early in the morning, *3336*
6:35 they said, "and it's already v **late.** *4498+6052*
9:35 he must be the v last, and the servant of all." *4246*
12:42 and put in two v small copper coins, *NIG*
14: 3 an alabaster jar *of* v **expensive** perfume, *4500*
15: 1 **V early in the morning,** *2317+4745*
16: 2 V early on the first day of the week, *3336*
16: 4 they saw that the stone, which was v large, *5379*
Lk 2:36 She was v old; she had lived with her *4498*
2:38 Coming up to them *at* **that** v moment, *899*
7:21 At that v time Jesus cured many *NIG*
9:25 and yet lose or forfeit his v self? *NIG*
9:32 Peter and his companions were v **sleepy** *976+5678*
12: 7 the v hairs of your head are all numbered. *NIG*
12:20 **This** v night your life will be demanded *4047*
12:26 Since you cannot do this v **little** *thing,* *1788*
16:10 trusted with v **little** can also be trusted *1788*
16:10 dishonest with v **little** will also be dishonest *1788*
18:23 When he heard this, he became v **sad,** *4337*
19:17 have been trustworthy in a v **small** *matter,* *1788*
21: 2 widow put in two v small copper coins. *NIG*
24: 1 v **early in the morning,** *960+3986*
Jn 5:17 is always at his work to **this** v **day,** *785*
5:36 the v work that the Father has given me *NIG*
10:36 the Father set apart as his v own and sent *NIG*
12:27 **for this** v **reason** I came to this hour. *1328+4047*
12:48 **that** v word which I spoke will condemn him at the last day. *1697*
Ac 1: 9 he was taken up **before their** v **eyes,** *899+1063*
8:35 that v passage of Scripture and told him *NIG*
15: 3 This news made all the brothers v glad. *3489*
17:22 that in every way you are v **religious.** *1273*
22: 2 they became v quiet. *3437*
22:13 *at* **that** v moment I was able to see him. *899*
25:10 as you yourself know v **well.** *2822*
26:22 But I have had God's help to **this** v day, *4047*
27:14 **Before** v **long,** a wind of *3552+4024+4498*
Ro 1:32 they not only continue to do these v things *NIG*
3: 2 they have been entrusted with the v words *NIG*
5: 7 **V rarely** will anyone die for a righteous *3660*
7:10 that the v commandment that was intended *NIG*
9:17 "I raised you up for this v purpose, *899*
9:26 in the v place where it was said to them, *NIG*
11: 8 that they could not hear, to this v **day.** *2465+4958*
14: 9 For **this** v **reason,** Christ died and *1650+4047*
16: 6 Greet Mary, who worked v **hard** for you. *4498*
16:12 another woman who has worked v hard in *4498*
1Co 4: 3 I **care** v **little** if I am judged by you or by any human court; *1639+1650+1788*
4:11 To **this** v hour we go hungry and thirsty, *785*
4:19 But I will come to you v **soon,** *5441*
6: 7 The v fact that you have lawsuits *NIG*
11:14 not the v nature of things teach you that if *899*
2Co 3:12 since we have such a hope, we are v bold. *4498*
5: 5 for this v purpose and has given us *899*
12:15 So I will v **gladly** spend for you everything *2452*
Gal 2:10 **the** v **thing** I was eager to do. *899+4047*
3: 1 Before your v eyes Jesus Christ was clearly portrayed as crucified. *NIG*
Eph 4:10 He who descended is **the** v **one** who ascended higher than all *899*
5:15 Be v **careful,** then, how you live— *209*
6:22 I am sending him to you for this v purpose, *899*
Php 2: 6 Who, being in v nature God, *NIG*
2: 7 taking the v nature of a servant, *NIG*
1Th 5: 2 for you know v **well** that the day of the Lord *209*
1Ti 1:16 **for that** v **reason** I was shown mercy *1328+4047*
2Ti 1:18 You know v **well** in how many ways *1019*
3: 9 But *they will* **not get** v **far** *2093+4498+4621*
Tit 2:14 for himself a people that are **his** v **own,** *4342*
Phm 1:12 I am sending him—who is my v **heart—** *5073*
1:16 He is v dear to me but even dearer to you, *3436*
1:19 to mention that you owe me **your** v **self.** *4932*
Heb 6:11 to show this same diligence to the v end, *NIG*
6:17 of his purpose v clear to the heirs *4358*
10:37 For in just a v little **while,** *2285+4012+4012*
Jas 3: 4 a v **small** rudder wherever the pilot wants *1788*
1Pe 4:11 as one speaking the v words of God. *NIG*
2Pe 1: 4 Through these he has given us his v **great** *3492*
1: 5 **For this** v **reason,** make every effort to *899+4047*
Jude 1: 3 although I was v eager to write to you *4246*
1: 8 In the v same way, these dreamers pollute *3530*
1:10 these are the v things that destroy them. *NIG*
Rev 9:15 ready for this v hour and day and month *NIG*
11:13 that v hour there was a severe earthquake *NIG*
21:11 like that of a v **precious** jewel, *5508*

VESSEL (1) [VESSELS]

Isa 2:16 for every trading ship and every stately v. 8500

VESSELS (3) [VESSEL]

Isa 22:24 all its lesser v, from the bowls to all the jars. 3998
52:11 you who carry the v *of* the LORD. 3998
66:20 of the LORD in ceremonially clean v. 3998

VESTMENTS (1) [VESTMENT]

Ezr 3:10 the priests *in their* v and with trumpets, 4252

VESTRY (KJV) See WARDROBE

VESTURE (KJV) See CLOAK, CLOTHING, ROBE

VETERAN (1)
Eze 27: 9 V craftsmen of Gebal were on board 2418

VEX, VEXATION, VEXED (KJV) See AFFLICTED, CHASING, CONFUSION, ENEMIES, ENEMY, FRUSTRATED, HOSTILE, MISTREAT, MISTREATED, PERSECUTE, PUNISHMENT, RIVAL, SHATTERED, TERRIFIES, TIRED, TORMENT, TREMBLE, TROUBLE, TROUBLING

VEXED (2)
Ps 78:41 *they* v the Holy One of Israel. 9345
112:10 The wicked man will see and *be* v, 4087

VIAL, VIALS (KJV) See FLASK, BOWL, BOWLS

VICINITY (14)
Dt 11:30 in the Arabah **in the** v **of** Gilgal. 4578
Jos 3:16 a town called Adam in the v *of* Zarethan, 7396
15:46 all that were in the v *of* Ashdod, 3338
Jdg 11:33 from Aroer **to the** v **of** Minnith, 995+3870+6330
20:43 and easily overran them in the v *of* Gibeah 5790
1Sa 5: 6 upon the people of Ashdod and its v; 1473
13:17 One turned toward Ophrah in the v 824
2Ki 15:16 and everyone in the city and its v, 1473
Mt 2:16 and its v who were two years old and *3990*
15:22 A Canaanite woman from that v came *3990*
15:39 the boat and went to the v of Magadan. *3990*
Mk 7:24 Jesus left that place and went to the v *3990*
7:31 Then Jesus left the v of Tyre and went *3990*
Lk 24:50 he had led them out to the v **of** Bethany, *4639*

VICIOUSLY (1)
Jdg 15: 8 *He* **attacked** them v and slaughtered many 3751+5782+6584+8797

VICTIM (2) [VICTIMS]
Ps 10:14 The v commits himself to you; 2724
Hab 2: 7 Then you will become their v. 5468

VICTIMS (10) [VICTIM]
Nu 23:24 and drinks the blood of his v." 2728
31: 8 Among their v were Evi, Rekem, Zur, 2728
Job 29:17 and snatched the v from their teeth. 3272
Ps 10: 8 watching in secret for his v. 2724
10:10 His v are crushed, they collapse; 2724
Pr 7:26 Many are the v she has brought down; 2728
Eze 34:29 and they will no longer be v *of* famine in 665
Da 7: 7 it crushed and devoured its v NIH
7:19 the beast that crushed and devoured its v NIH
Na 3: 1 full of plunder, never without v! 3272

VICTOR'S (1) [VICTORY]
2Ti 2: 5 not **receive the** v **crown** unless he competes *5110*

VICTORIES (5) [VICTORY]
2Sa 22:51 He gives his king great v; 3802
Ps 18:50 He gives his king great v; 3802
21: 1 How great is his joy in the v you give! 3802
21: 5 Through the v you gave, his glory is great; 3802
44: 4 who decrees v *for* Jacob. 3802

VICTORIOUS (9) [VICTORY]
1Ki 22:12 "Attack Ramoth Gilead and *be* v," 7503
22:15 "Attack and *be* v," he answered, 7503
2Ch 13:18 men of Judah *were* v because they relied on 599
18:11 "Attack Ramoth Gilead and *be* v," 7503
18:14 "Attack and *be* v," he answered, 7503
Ps 20: 5 when you are v and will lift up our banners 3802
Da 11: 7 he will fight against them and *be* v. 2616
Hab 3: 8 with your horses and your v chariots? 3802
Rev 15: 2 those who *had been* v over the beast *3771*

VICTORIOUSLY (1) [VICTORY]
Ps 45: 4 In your majesty ride forth v in behalf 7503

VICTORY (40) [VICTOR'S, VICTORIES, VICTORIOUS, VICTORIOUSLY]
Ex 32:18 Moses replied: "It is not the sound of v, 1476
Dt 20: 4 against your enemies to **give** you v." 3828
Jos 10:10 who defeated them in a great v at Gibeon. 4804
Jdg 12: 3 LORD **gave** me the v *over* them. 928+3338+5989
15:18 "You have given your servant this great v. 9591
1Sa 19: 5 The LORD won a great v for all Israel, 9591
2Sa 8: 6 The LORD **gave** David v wherever he went. 3828
8:10 to greet him and congratulate him on *his* v 5782
8:14 The LORD **gave** David v wherever he went. 3828
19: 2 the whole army the v that day was turned 9591
22:36 You give me your shield of v; 3829
23:10 The LORD brought about a great v 9591
23:12 and the LORD brought about a great v. 9591
2Ki 5: 1 through him the LORD had given v 9591
13:17 "The LORD's arrow of v, 9591
13:17 the arrow of v over Aram!" 9591
14:10 Glory in your v, but stay at home! NIH
1Ch 11:14 the LORD **brought about** a great v. 3828+9591
18: 6 LORD **gave** David v everywhere he went. 3828
18:10 to greet him and congratulate him on *his* v 5782
18:13 LORD **gave** David v everywhere he went. 3828
Job 12:16 To him belong strength and v; 9370
Ps 18:35 You give me your shield of v, 3829
44: 3 nor *did* their arm **bring** them v; 3828
44: 6 my sword *does* not **bring** me v; 3828
44: 7 but *you* **give** us v over our enemies, 3828
60:12 With God we will gain the v, 2657
108:13 With God we will gain the v, 2657
118:15 and v resound in the tents of the righteous: 3802
129: 2 but *they have* not **gained the** v over me. 3523
144:10 to the One who gives v to kings, 9591
Pr 2: 7 He holds v in store for the upright, 9370
11:14 but many advisers make v sure. 9591
21:31 but v rests with the LORD. 9591
24: 6 and for v many advisers. 9591
Mt 12:20 till he leads justice to v. *3777*
1Co 15:54 "Death has been swallowed up in v." *3777*
15:55 "Where, O death, is your v? *3777*
15:57 the v through our Lord Jesus Christ. *3777*
1Jn 5: 4 This is the v that has overcome the world, *3772*

VICTUAL, VICTUALS (KJV) See FOOD, PROVISIONS

VIEW (18) [VIEWED, VIEWPOINT, VIEWS]
Nu 23: 9 from the heights *I* v them. 8800
33: 3 They marched out boldly in **full** v *of* all 6524
Dt 32:49 across from Jericho, and v Canaan, 8011
Ne 9:38 **"In** v **of** all this, we are making a binding 928
Ps 48:13 v her citadels, that you may tell of them to 7170
68:24 Your procession *has* **come into** v, O God, 8011
Pr 1:17 to spread a net in **full** v *of* all the birds! 6524
5:21 man's ways are **in full** v *of* the LORD, 5790+6524
17:24 A discerning man keeps wisdom **in** v, 907+7156
Isa 33:17 the king in his beauty and v a land 8011
Mk 2:12 took his mat and walked out **in full** v **of** *1869*
Ro 12: 1 I urge you, brothers, **in** v **of** God's mercy, *1328*
1Co 9: 8 merely **from** a **human point of** v? *476+2848*
2Co 5:16 no one **from a worldly point of** v. *2848+4922*
Gal 5:10 in the Lord that *you will* **take** no other v. *5858*
Php 3:15 mature *should* **take such a** v **of things.** *5858*
2Ti 4: 1 and in v of his appearing and his kingdom, *NIG*
Rev 13:13 down from heaven to earth **in full** v of men. *1967*

VIEWED (2) [VIEW]
Nu 32: 9 up to the Valley of Eshcol and v the land, 8011
Ps 102:19 from heaven *he* v the earth, 5564

VIEWPOINT (1) [VIEW]
1Jn 4: 5 and therefore speak from the v of the world, *NIG*

VIEWS (2) [VIEW]
Job 28:24 for he v the ends of the earth 5564
Ac 28:22 But we want to hear what *your* v **are,** *5858*

VIGIL (3)
Ex 12:42 Because the LORD kept v that night 9081
12:42 on this night all the Israelites are to keep v 9081
Isa 65: 4 and spend their nights **keeping secret** v; 5915

VIGILANT (KJV) See ALERT, TEMPERATE

VIGOR (7) [VIGOROUS, VIGOROUSLY]
Job 5:26 You will come to the grave in **full** v, 3995
18: 7 The v *of* his step is weakened; 226
20:11 The **youthful** v that fills his bones will lie 6596
21:23 One man dies in full v, 6795
30: 2 since their v had gone from them? 3995
Pr 31: 3 your v on those who ruin kings. 2006
Ecc 11:10 for youth and v are meaningless. 8841

VIGOROUS (4) [VIGOR]
Ex 1:19 are v and give birth before the midwives 2650
Jos 14:11 as v to go out to battle now as I was then. 3946
Jdg 3:29 all v and strong; not a man escaped. 9045
Ps 38:19 Many are those who are my v enemies; 2645

VIGOROUSLY (4) [VIGOR]
Pr 31:17 She sets about her work v; 928+6437
Jer 50:34 *He will* v **defend** their cause so 8189+8189
Ac 18:28 For he v refuted the Jews in public debate, *2364*
23: 9 Pharisees stood up and **argued** v. *1372*

VILE (26) [VILENESS, VILEST]
Jdg 19:23 "No, my friends, don't *be so* v. 8317
2Ki 23:13 Ashtoreth the v **goddess** *of* the Sidonians, 9199
23:13 for Chemosh the v **god** *of* Moab, 9199
Est 7: 6 and enemy is this v Haman." 8273
Job 15:16 how much less man, *who is* v and corrupt, 9493
Ps 12: 8 when *what* is v is honored among men. 2359
14: 1 They are corrupt, their deeds *are* v; 9493
15: 4 a v *man* but honors those who fear 4415
41: 8 "A v disease has beset him; 1175
53: 1 They are corrupt, and *their* ways *are* v; 9493
101: 3 I will set before my eyes no v thing. 1175
Jer 16:18 with the lifeless forms of their v **images** 9199
Eze 5:11 with all your v **images** and detestable 9199
7:20 to make their detestable idols and v **images.** 9199
11:18 return to it and remove all its v **images** 9199
11:21 to their v **images** and detestable idols, 9199
16:52 Because your sins *were* more v than theirs, 9493
20: 7 of the v **images** you have set your eyes on, 9199
20: 8 of the v **images** they had set their eyes on, 9199
20:30 and lust after their v **images?** 9199
37:23 and v **images** or with any of their offenses, 9199
Hos 9:10 to that shameful idol and became as v as 9199
Na 1:14 I will prepare your grave, for *you are* v." 7837
Rev 21: 8 But the cowardly, the unbelieving, the v, *1009*
22:11 let him who *is* v continue to be vile; *4865*
22:11 *let* him who is vile continue *to be* v; *4862*

VILENESS (2) [VILE]
Jdg 20:10 for all this v done in Israel." 5576
Isa 9:17 ungodly and wicked, every mouth speaks v. 5576

VILEST (2) [VILE]
1Ki 21:26 *He* **behaved in the** v **manner** by 4394+9493
Hos 1: 2 the land *is* **guilty of the** v **adultery** 2388+2388

VILLAGE (22) [VILLAGES]
Jdg 5: 7 V **life** in Israel ceased, ceased until I, 7251
Mt 10:11 "Whatever town or v you enter, *3267*
21: 2 "Go to the v ahead of you, *3267*
Mk 6: 6 around teaching **from** v **to village.** *3241+3267*
6: 6 around teaching **from village to** v. *3241+3267*
8:23 by the hand and led him outside the v. *3267*
8:26 saying, "Don't go into the v." *3267*
11: 2 "Go to the v ahead of you, *3267*
Lk 5:17 who had come from every v of Galilee and *3267*
8: 1 Jesus traveled about from one town and v *3267*
9: 6 out and went **from** v **to village,** *2848+3267+3836*
9: 6 out and went **from village to** v, *2848+3267+3836*
9:52 a Samaritan v to get things ready for him; *3267*
9:56 and they went to another v. *3267*
10:38 came to a v where a woman named Martha *3267*
17:12 As he was going into a v, *3267*
19:30 "Go to the v ahead of you, *3267*
24:13 of them were going to a v called Emmaus, *3267*
24:28 the v to which they were going, *3267*
Jn 11: 1 the v of Mary and her sister Martha. *3267*
11:30 Now Jesus had not yet entered the v, *3267*
11:54 near the desert, to a v called Ephraim, *4484*

VILLAGES (87) [VILLAGE]
Lev 25:31 in v without walls around them are to 2958
Dt 2:23 the Avvites who lived in v as far as Gaza, 2958
3: 5 there were also a great many unwalled v. 6551
Jos 10:37 its v and everyone in it. 6551
10:39 They took the city, its king and its v, 6551
13:23 and their v were the inheritance of 2958
13:28 and their v were the inheritance of 2958
15:32 a total of twenty-nine towns and their v. 2958
15:36 fourteen towns and their v. 2958
15:41 sixteen towns and their v. 2958
15:44 nine towns and their v. 2958
15:45 with its surrounding settlements and v; 2958
15:46 together with their v; 2958
15:47 its surrounding settlements and v; 2958
15:47 and Gaza, its settlements and v, 2958
15:51 eleven towns and their v. 2958
15:54 nine towns and their v. 2958
15:57 ten towns and their v. 2958
15:59 six towns and their v. 2958
15:60 two towns and their v. 2958
15:62 six towns and their v. 2958
16: 9 It also included all the towns and their v 2958
18:24 twelve towns and their v. 2958
18:28 fourteen towns and their v. 2958
19: 6 thirteen towns and their v; 2958
19: 7 four towns and their v— 2958
19: 8 and all the v around these towns as far 2958
19:15 There were twelve towns and their v. 2958
19:16 and their v were the inheritance 2958
19:22 There were sixteen towns and their v. 2958
19:23 and their v were the inheritance of the tribe 2958
19:30 There were twenty-two towns and their v. 2958
19:31 and their v were the inheritance of the tribe 2958
19:38 There were nineteen towns and their v. 2958
19:39 and their v were the inheritance of the tribe 2958
19:48 and their v were the inheritance of the tribe 2958
21:12 and v *around* the city they had given 2958
1Sa 6:18 the fortified towns with their country v. 4108
1Ch 4:32 Their **surrounding** v were Etam, Ain, 2958
4:33 the v around these towns as far as Baalath. 2958
5:16 in Bashan and its **outlying** v, 1426
6:56 the fields and v *around* the city were given 2958
7:28 included Bethel and its **surrounding** v, 1426
7:28 Gezer and its v to the west, 1426
7:28 and Shechem and its v all the way 1426
7:28 the way to Ayyah and its v. 1426
7:29 Megiddo and Dor, together with their v. 1426
8:12 and Lod with its **surrounding** v), 1426
9:16 who lived in the v *of* the Netophathites. 2958
9:22 registered by genealogy in their v. 2958
9:25 in their v had to come from time to time 2958
18: 1 and its **surrounding** v from the control of 1426
27:25 in the towns, the v and the watchtowers. 4107

2Ch 8: 2 the v that Hiram had given him, 6551
13:19 with their **surrounding** v. 1426
14:14 They destroyed all the v around Gerar, 6551
14:14 They plundered all these v, 6551
28:18 and Gimzo, with their **surrounding** v. 1426
32:29 He built v and acquired great numbers 6551
Ne 6: 2 "Come, let us meet together in one of the v 4099
11:25 As for the v with their fields, 2958
11:25 in Jekabzeel and its v, 2958
11:30 Adullam and their v, 2958
12:28 from the v *of* the Netophathites, 2958
12:29 for the singers had built v for themselves 2958
Est 9:19 why rural Jews—those living in v— 6551+7252
Ps 10: 8 He lies in wait near the v; 2958
48:11 the v *of* Judah are glad because 1426
97: 8 and rejoices and the v *of* Judah are glad 1426
SS 7:11 let us spend the night in the v. 4107
Jer 17:26 of Judah and the v around Jerusalem, NIH
19:15 the v around it every disaster I pronounced 6551
32:44 in the v around Jerusalem, in the towns of NIH
33:13 in the v around Jerusalem and in the towns NIH
49: 2 and its **surrounding** v will be set on fire. 1426
Eze 30:18 and her v will go into captivity. 1426
38:11 "I will invade a land of **unwalled** v; 7253
38:13 of Tarshish and all her v will say to you, 4099
Mt 9:35 Jesus went through all the towns and v, *3267*
14:15 to the v and buy themselves some food." *3267*
Mk 1:38 to the nearby v—so I can preach there also. *3268*
6:36 and v and buy themselves something *3267*
6:56 into v, towns or countryside— *3267*
8:27 Jesus and his disciples went on to the v *3267*
Lk 9:12 to the surrounding v and countryside *3267*
13:22 Then Jesus went through the towns and v, *3267*
Ac 8:25 preaching the gospel in many Samaritan v. *3267*

VILLAIN (1)

Pr 6:12 A scoundrel and v, who goes about with 224

VINDICATE (6) [VINDICATED, VINDICATES, VINDICATION]

1Sa 24:15 *may he* v me by delivering me from your 9149
Ps 26: 1 V me, O LORD, for I have led a blameless 9149
35:24 V me in your righteousness, 9149
43: 1 V me, O God, and plead my cause against 9149
54: 1 v me by your might. 1906
135:14 For the LORD *will* v his people 1906

VINDICATED (6) [VINDICATE]

Ge 20:16 *you* **are** completely v." 3519
30: 6 Then Rachel said, "God *has* v me; 1906
Job 11: 2 *Is* this talker *to be* v? 7405
13:18 I have prepared my case, I know I *will be* v. 7405
Jer 51:10 " 'The LORD *has* v us; 3655+7407
1Ti 3:16 He appeared in a body, *was* v by the Spirit, *1467*

VINDICATES (1) [VINDICATE]

Isa 50: 8 *He who* v me is near. 7405

VINDICATION (4) [VINDICATE]

Ps 17: 2 May my v come from you; 5477
24: 5 from the LORD and v from God his Savior. 7407
35:27 May those who delight in my v shout 7406
Isa 54:17 and this is their v from me," 7407

VINE (53) [VINES, VINEYARD, VINEYARDS, VINTAGE]

Ge 40: 9 "In my dream I saw a v in front of me, 1728
40:10 and on the v were three branches. 1728
49:11 He will tether his donkey to a v, 1728
49:22 "Joseph is a **fruitful** v, 1201+7238
49:22 a **fruitful** v near a spring, 1201+7238
Dt 32:32 Their v comes from the vine of Sodom and 1728
32:32 from the v *of* Sodom and from the fields 1728
Jdg 9:12 "Then the trees said to the v, 1728
9:13 "But the v answered, 1728
1Ki 4:25 each man under his own v and fig tree. 1728
2Ki 4:39 to gather herbs and found a wild v. 1728
18:31 of you will eat from his own v and fig tree 1728
Job 15:33 be like a v stripped of its unripe grapes, 1728
Ps 80: 8 You brought a v out of Egypt; 1728
80:14 Watch over this v, 1728
80:16 Your v is cut down, it is burned with fire; NIH
128: 3 be like a fruitful v within your house, 1728
SS 7: 8 your breasts be like the clusters of the v, 1728
Isa 24: 7 The new wine dries up and the v withers; 1728
34: 4 like withered leaves from the v, 1728
36:16 of you will eat from his own v and fig tree 1728
Jer 2:21 like a **choice** v of sound and reliable stock. 8603
2:21 against me into a corrupt, wild v? 1728
6: 9 the remnant of Israel as thoroughly as a v; 1728
8:13 There will be no grapes on the v. 1728
Eze 15: 2 how is the wood of a v better than that 1728
15: 6 As I have given the wood of the v among 1728
17: 6 and became a low, spreading v. 1728
17: 6 So it became a v and produced branches 1728
17: 7 The v now sent out its roots toward him 1728
17: 8 bear fruit and become a splendid v.' 1728
19:10 a v in your vineyard planted by the water; 1728
Hos 10: 1 Israel was a spreading v; 1728
14: 7 He will blossom like a v, 1728
Joel 1:11 Despair, you farmers, wail, you v **growers;** 4144
1:12 v is dried up and the fig tree is withered; 1728
Joel 2:22 the fig tree and the v yield their riches. 1728
Jnh 4: 6 a v and made it grow up over Jonah 7813
4: 6 and Jonah was very happy about the v. 7813
4: 7 which chewed the v so that it withered. 7813
4: 9 a right to be angry about the v?" 7813
4:10 "You have been concerned about this v, 7813
Mic 4: 4 Every man will sit under his own v and 1728
Hag 2:19 Until now, the v and the fig tree, 1728
Zec 3:10 to sit under his v and fig tree,' 1728
8:12 the v will yield its fruit, 1728
Mt 26:29 not drink of this fruit *of* the v from now on *306*
Mk 14:25 *of* the v until that day when I drink it anew *306*
Lk 22:18 *of* the v until the kingdom of God comes." *306*
Jn 15: 1 "I am the true v, and my Father is the *306*
15: 4 bear fruit by itself; it must remain in the v. *306*
15: 5 "I am the v; you are the branches. *306*
Rev 14:18 the clusters of grapes *from* the earth's v, *306*

VINEDRESSERS (KJV) See VINE GROWERS, WORK THE VINEYARDS

VINEGAR (9)

Nu 6: 3 and must not drink v *made from* wine or 2810
Ru 2:14 Have some bread and dip it in the **wine** v." 2810
Ps 69:21 They put gall in my food and gave me v 2810
Pr 10:26 As v to the teeth and smoke to the eyes, 2810
25:20 or like v poured on soda, 2810
Mt 27:48 He filled it *with* **wine** v, put it on a stick, *3954*
Mk 15:36 One man ran, filled a sponge *with* **wine** v, *3954*
Lk 23:36 They offered him **wine** v *3954*
Jn 19:29 A jar *of* **wine** v was there, *3954*

VINES (23) [VINE]

Lev 25: 5 or harvest the grapes of your **untended** v. 5687
25:11 of itself or harvest the **untended** v. 5687
Dt 8: 8 v and fig trees, pomegranates, 1728
24:21 *do* not **go over the** v **again.** 339+6618
Ps 78:47 He destroyed their v with hail 1728
105:33 down their v and fig trees and shattered 1728
SS 2:13 the blossoming v spread their fragrance. 1728
6:11 to see if the v had budded or 1728
7:12 the vineyards to see if the v have budded, 1728
Isa 5: 2 of stones and planted it with the **choicest** v. 8603
7:23 where there were a thousand v worth 1728
16: 8 of Heshbon wither, the v *of* Sibmah also. 1728
16: 8 nations have trampled down the **choicest** v, 8602
16: 9 as Jazer weeps, for the v *of* Sibmah. 1728
17:10 the finest plants and plant imported v, 2367
32:12 for the pleasant fields, for the fruitful v 1728
Jer 5:17 devour your v and fig trees. 1728
48:32 as Jazer weeps, O v *of* Sibmah. 1728
Hos 2:12 I will ruin her v and her fig trees, 1728
Joel 1: 7 It has laid waste my v and ruined my fig 1728
Na 2: 2 and have ruined their v. 2367
Hab 3:17 not bud and there are no grapes on the v, 1728
Mal 3:11 the v in your fields will not cast their fruit," 1728

VINEYARD (69) [VINE]

Ge 9:20 a man of the soil, proceeded to plant a v. 4142
Ex 22: 5 a man grazes his livestock in a field or v 4142
22: 5 from the best of his own field or v. 4142
23:11 the same with your v and your olive grove. 4142
Lev 19:10 not go over your v a second time or pick 4142
Nu 20:17 We will not go through any field or v, 4142
21:22 We will not turn aside into any field or v, 4142
Dt 20: 6 Has anyone planted a v and not begun 4142
22: 9 Do not plant two kinds of seed in your v; 4142
22: 9 but also the fruit of the v will be defiled. 4142
23:24 If you enter your neighbor's v, 4142
24:21 When you harvest the grapes in your v, 4142
28:30 You will plant a v, but you will not even 4142
1Ki 21: 1 a v belonging to Naboth the Jezreelite. 4142
21: 1 **The** v was in Jezreel, close to the palace 889S
21: 2 "Let me have your v to use for 4142
21: 2 In exchange I will give you a better v or, 4142
21: 6 'Sell me your v; or if you prefer, 4142
21: 6 I will give you another v in its place.' 4142
21: 6 But he said, 'I will not give you my v.' " 4142
21: 7 I'll get you the v *of* Naboth the Jezreelite." 4142
21:15 up and take possession of the v *of* Naboth 4142
21:16 down to take possession of Naboth's v. 4142
21:18 He is now in Naboth's v, 4142
Pr 24:30 past the v *of* the man who lacks judgment; 4142
31:16 out of her earnings she plants a v. 4142
SS 1: 6 my own v I have neglected. 4142
8:11 Solomon had a v in Baal Hamon; 4142
8:11 he let out his v to tenants. 4142
8:12 But my own v is mine to give; 4142
Isa 1: 8 Daughter of Zion is left like a shelter in a v, 4142
3:14 "It is you who have ruined my v; 4142
5: 1 for the one I love a song about his v: 4142
5: 1 My loved one had a v on a fertile hillside. 4142
5: 3 judge between me and my v. 4142
5: 4 for my v than I have done for it? 4142
5: 5 what I am going to do to my v: 4142
5: 7 The v *of* the LORD Almighty is the house of Israel, 4142
5:10 A ten-acre v will produce only a bath 4142
27: 2 In that day—"Sing about a fruitful v: 4142
Jer 12:10 Many shepherds will ruin my v 4142
Eze 19:10 like a vine in your v planted by the water; 4142
Mic 7: 1 summer fruit at the gleaning of the v; 1292
Mt 20: 1 the morning to hire men to work in his v. *308*
20: 2 for the day and sent them into his v. *308*
Mt 20: 4 'You also go and work in my v, *308*
20: 7 'You also go and work in my v.' *308*
20: 8 the owner *of* the v said to his foreman, *308*
21:28 'Son, go and work today in the v.' *308*
21:33 There was a landowner who planted a v. *308*
21:33 Then he rented **the** v to some farmers *899S*
21:39 and threw him out *of* the v and killed him. *308*
21:40 when the owner *of* the v comes, *308*
21:41 "and he will rent the v to other tenants, *308*
Mk 12: 1 "A man planted a v. *308*
12: 1 Then he rented **the** v to some farmers *899S*
12: 2 from them some of the fruit *of* the v. *308*
12: 8 and threw him out of the v. *308*
12: 9 "What then will the owner *of* the v do? *308*
12: 9 and kill those tenants and give the v *308*
Lk 13: 6 "A man had a fig tree, planted in his v, *308*
13: 7 he said to the man who **took care of the** v, *307*
20: 9 this parable: "A man planted a v, *308*
20:10 would give him some of the fruit *of* the v. *308*
20:13 the owner *of* the v said, 'What shall I do? *308*
20:15 So they threw him out *of* the v *308*
20:15 then will the owner *of* the v do to them? *308*
20:16 and kill those tenants and give the v *308*
1Co 9: 7 a v and does not eat of its grapes? *308*

VINEYARDS (54) [VINE]

Lev 25: 3 and for six years prune your v 4142
25: 4 Do not sow your fields or prune your v. 4142
Nu 16:14 or given us an inheritance of fields and v. 4142
22:24 in a narrow path between two v, 4142
Dt 6:11 and v and olive groves you did not plant— 4142
28:39 You will plant v and cultivate them 4142
Jos 24:13 in them and eat from v and olive groves 4142
Jdg 14: 5 As they approached the v *of* Timnah, 4142
15: 5 together with the v and olive groves. 4142
21:20 saying, "Go and hide in the v 4142
21:21 then rush from the v and each of you seize 4142
1Sa 8:14 He will take the best of your fields and v 4142
22: 7 of Jesse give all of you fields and v? 4142
2Ki 5:26 or to accept clothes, olive groves, v, 4142
18:32 a land of bread and v, a land of olive trees 4142
19:29 plant v and eat their fruit. 4142
25:12 the poorest people of the land to **work** *the* v 4144
1Ch 27:27 the Ramathite was in charge of the v. 4142
27:27 of the produce of the v for the wine vats. 4142
2Ch 26:10 **working** his **fields and** v in the hills 4144
Ne 5: 3 our v and our homes to get grain during 4142
5: 4 to pay the king's tax on our fields and v. 4142
5: 5 because our fields and our v belong to 4142
5:11 v, olive groves and houses, 4142
9:25 of good things, wells already dug, v, 4142
Job 24: 6 the fields and glean in the v *of* the wicked. 4142
24:18 so that no one goes to the v. 4142
Ps 107:37 They sowed fields and planted v 4142
Ecc 2: 4 I built houses for myself and planted v. 4142
SS 1: 6 with me and made me take care of the v; 4142
1:14 of henna blossoms from the v *of* En Gedi. 4142
2:15 the little foxes that ruin the v, 4142
2:15 our v that are in bloom. 4142
7:12 to the v to see if the vines have budded, 4142
Isa 16:10 no one sings or shouts in the v; 4142
36:17 and new wine, a land of bread and v. 4142
37:30 plant v and eat their fruit. 4142
61: 5 foreigners will work your fields and v. 4144
65:21 they will plant v and eat their fruit. 4142
Jer 5:10 "Go through her v and ravage them, 9224
31: 5 Again you will plant v on the hills 4142
32:15 Houses, fields and v will again be bought 4142
35: 7 sow seed or plant v; 4142
35: 9 or built houses to live in or had v, 4142
39:10 and at that time he gave them v and fields. 4142
52:16 the poorest people of the land to **work** the v 4144
Eze 28:26 and will build houses and plant v; 4142
Hos 2:15 There I will give her back her v, 4142
Am 4: 9 "Many times I struck your gardens and v, 4142
5:11 though you have planted lush v, 4142
5:17 There will be wailing in all the v, 4142
9:14 They will plant v and drink their wine; 4142
Mic 1: 6 a place for planting v. 4142
Zep 1:13 they will plant v but not drink the wine. 4142

VINTAGE (1) [VINE]

1Sa 8:15 and of your v and give it to his officials 4142

VIOL, VIOLS (KJV) See HARPS

VIOLATE (6) [VIOLATED, VIOLATES, VIOLATING, VIOLATION]

Lev 26:15 and so v my covenant, 7296
Jos 23:16 If you v the covenant of the LORD your God 6296
Ps 89:31 if *they* v my decrees and fail to keep my 2725
89:34 *I will* not v my covenant or alter what 2725
Eze 22:10 in you are *those who* v **women** during their 6700
Ac 23: 3 yet you yourself v **the law** by commanding *4174*

VIOLATED (12) [VIOLATE]

Ge 34: 2 saw her, he took her and v her. 2256+6700+8886
Dt 22:24 the man because *he* v another man's wife. 6700
22:29 He must marry the girl, for *he has* v her. 6700
Jos 7:11 Israel has sinned; *they have* v my covenant, 6296
7:15 *He has* v the covenant of the LORD 6296
Jdg 2:20 "Because this nation *has* v the covenant 6296
1Sa 15:24 *I* v the LORD's command 6296

2Ki 18:12 but *had* v his covenant—all that Moses 6296
Isa 24: 5 the laws, v the statutes and broken 2736
Jer 34:18 The men who *have* v my covenant 6296
Da 11:32 With flattery he will corrupt *those who have* v the covenant, 8399
Mal 2: 8 *you have* v the covenant with Levi," 8845

VIOLATES (2) [VIOLATE]

Ps 55:20 attacks his friends; *he* v his covenant. 2725
Eze 22:11 and another v his sister, his own father's 6700

VIOLATING (1) [VIOLATE]

1Ch 2: 7 who brought trouble on Israel *by* v **the ban** 5085

VIOLATION (3) [VIOLATE]

Lev 5:15 "When a person **commits a** v 5085+5086
Dt 17: 2 the LORD your God in v *of* his covenant, 6296
Heb 2: 2 by angels was binding, and every v *4126*

VIOLENCE (53) [VIOLENT]

Ge 6:11 in God's sight and was full of v. 2805
6:13 the earth is filled with v because of them. 2805
49: 5 their swords are weapons of v. 2805
1Ch 12:17 when my hands are free from v, 2805
Job 16:17 yet my hands have been free of v 2805
Ps 7: 9 to an end the v *of* the wicked and make 8273
7:16 his v comes down on his own head. 2805
11: 5 and those who love v his soul hates. 2805
27:12 rise up against me, breathing out v. 2805
55: 9 for I see v and strife in the city. 2805
58: 2 and your hands mete out v on the earth. 2805
72:14 He will rescue them from oppression and v, 2805
73: 6 they clothe themselves with v. 2805
74:20 haunts of v fill the dark places of the land. 2805
140: 1 protect me from men of v, 2805
140: 4 from men of v who plan to trip my feet. 2805
140:11 may disaster hunt down men of v. 2805
Pr 4:17 bread of wickedness and drink the wine of v 2805
10: 6 v overwhelms the mouth of the wicked. 2805
10:11 v overwhelms the mouth of the wicked. 2805
13: 2 but the unfaithful have a craving for v. 2805
21: 7 The v *of* the wicked will drag them away, 8719
24: 2 for their hearts plot v, and their lips talk 8719
26: 6 Like cutting off one's feet or drinking v is 2805
Isa 42:25 his burning anger, the v *of* war. 6449
53: 9 though he had done no v, 2805
59: 6 and acts of v are in their hands. 2805
60:18 No longer will v be heard in your land, 2805
Jer 6: 7 V and destruction resound in her; 2805
20: 8 I cry out proclaiming v and destruction. 2805
22: 3 Do no wrong or v *to* the alien, 2803
51:35 the v done to our flesh be upon Babylon," 2805
51:46 of v in the land and of ruler against ruler. 2805
Eze 7:11 V has grown into a rod to punish 2805
7:23 full of bloodshed and the city is full of v. 2805
8:17 Must they also fill the land with v 2805
12:19 in it because of the v *of* all who live there. 2805
22:26 Her priests **do** v *to* my law 2803
28:16 Through your widespread trade you were filled with v, 2805
45: 9 Give up your v and oppression 2805
Hos 12: 1 and multiplies lies and v. 8719
Joel 3:19 because of v *done to* the people of Judah, 2805
Ob 1:10 of the v *against* your brother Jacob, 2805
Jnh 3: 8 give up their evil ways and their v. 2805
Hab 1: 2 Or cry out to you, **"V!"** 2805
1: 3 Destruction and v are before me; 2805
1: 9 they all come bent on v. 2805
2:17 The v you have done to Lebanon 2805
Zep 1: 9 the temple of their gods with v and deceit. 2805
3: 4 Her priests profane the sanctuary and **do** v 2803
Mal 2:16 a man's covering himself with v as well as 2805
Ac 21:35 the v of the mob was so great he had to *1040*
Rev 18:21 "With such v the great city of Babylon will *3996*

VIOLENT (23) [VIOLENCE, VIOLENTLY]

2Sa 22: 3 from v *men* you save me. 2805
22:49 from v men you rescued me. 2805
Ps 17: 4 I have kept myself from the ways of the v. 7265
18:48 from v men you rescued me. 2805
Pr 3:31 Do not envy a v man or choose any 2805
16:29 A v man entices his neighbor 2805
Eze 13:11 and v **winds** will burst forth. 6194+8120
13:13 In my wrath I will unleash a v **wind,** 6194+8120
18:10 "Suppose he has a v son, 7265
28: 8 and you will die a v death in the heart of 2728
Da 11:14 v men *among* your own people will rebel 7265
Am 1:14 amid v **winds** on a stormy day. 6193
Jnh 1: 4 a v storm arose that the ship threatened 1524
Mic 6:12 Her rich men *are* v; 2805+4848
Mt 8:28 They were so v that no one could pass *3336+5901*
28: 2 There was a v earthquake, *3489*
Ac 2: 2 the blowing of a v wind came from heaven *1042*
16:26 Suddenly there was such a v earthquake *3489*
23:10 The dispute became so v that *4498*
27:18 We took **such** a v battering from the storm *5380*
1Ti 1:13 a blasphemer and a persecutor and a v **man,** *5616*
3: 3 not v but gentle, not quarrelsome, *4438*
Tit 1: 7 not v, not pursuing dishonest gain. *4438*

VIOLENTLY (4) [VIOLENT]

Ge 27:33 Isaac **trembled** v 1524+3006+3010+4394+6330
Ex 19:18 the whole mountain trembled v, 4394
Mk 1:26 The evil spirit **shook** the man v and came *5057*
9:26 shrieked, convulsed him v and came out. *4498*

VIPER (4) [VIPER'S, VIPERS]

Ge 49:17 a v along the path, that bites the horse's 9159
Pr 23:32 like a snake and poisons like a v. 7626
Isa 14:29 the root of that snake will spring up a v, 7625
Ac 28: 3 a v, driven out by the heat, *2399*

VIPER'S (1) [VIPER]

Isa 11: 8 young child put his hand into the v nest. 7626

VIPERS (9) [VIPER]

Dt 32:24 the venom of v that glide in the dust. NIH
Ps 140: 3 the poison of v is on their lips. 6582
Isa 59: 5 the eggs of v and spin a spider's web. 7626
Jer 8:17 v that cannot be charmed, 7626
Mt 3: 7 "You brood *of* v! Who warned you to flee *2399*
12:34 You brood *of* v, how can you who are evil *2399*
23:33 You brood *of* v! How will you escape *2399*
Lk 3: 7 "You brood *of* v! Who warned you to flee *2399*
Ro 3:13 "The poison *of* v is on their lips." *835*

VIRGIN (41) [VIRGIN'S, VIRGINITY, VIRGINS]

Ge 24:16 The girl was very beautiful, a v; 1435
Ex 22:16 "If a man seduces a v who is not pledged 1435
Lev 21:13 " 'The woman he marries must **be a** v. 928+1436
21:14 but only a v from his own people, 1435
Dt 22:15 mother shall bring **proof that** she was **a** v 1436
22:17 'I did not find your daughter **to be a** v.' 1436
22:19 because this man has given an Israelite v 1435
22:23 a v pledged to be married and he sleeps 1435
22:28 a v who is not pledged to be married 1435
Jdg 11:39 And she *was a* v. 408+3359+4202
19:24 Look, here is my v daughter, 1435
21:11 every woman *who is* **not a** v." 2351+3359+5435
2Sa 13: 2 his sister Tamar, for she was a v, 1435
13:18 the kind of garment the v daughters of 1435
1Ki 1: 2 a young v to attend the king and take care 1435
2Ki 19:21 " 'The V Daughter of Zion despises you 1435
Ps 45:14 her v companions follow her 1435
Isa 7:14 The v will be with child and will give birth 6625
23:12 O V Daughter of Sidon, now crushed! 1435
37:22 "The V Daughter of Zion despises 1435
47: 1 sit in the dust, V Daughter of Babylon; 1435
Jer 14:17 for my v daughter—my people— 1435
18:13 A most horrible thing has been done by V Israel. 1435
31: 4 and you will be rebuilt, O V Israel. 1435
31:21 Return, O V Israel, return to your towns. 1435
46:11 O V Daughter of Egypt. 1435
La 1:15 the Lord has trampled the V Daughter 1435
2:13 O V Daughter of Zion? 1435
Eze 23: 3 and their v bosoms caressed. 1436
23: 8 slept with her, caressed her v bosom 1435
Joel 1: 8 a v in sackcloth grieving for the husband 1435
Am 5: 2 "Fallen is V Israel, never to rise again, 1435
Mt 1:23 "The v will be with child and will give birth *4221*
Lk 1:27 to a v pledged to be married to a man *4221*
1:34 Mary asked the angel, "since I am a v?" *NIG*
1Co 7:28 and if a v marries, she has not sinned. *4221*
7:34 or v is concerned about the Lord's affairs: *4221*
7:36 toward the v he is engaged to, *4221*
7:37 made up his mind not to marry the v— *4221*
7:38 So then, he who marries the v does right, *4221*
2Co 11: 2 that I might present you as a pure v to him. *4221*

VIRGIN'S (1) [VIRGIN]

Lk 1:27 The v name was Mary. *4221*

VIRGINITY (3) [VIRGIN]

Dt 22:14 I did not find **proof of** her v," 1436
22:17 But here is **proof of** my daughter's v." 1436
22:20 and no **proof of** the girl's v can be found, 1436

VIRGINS (11) [VIRGIN]

Ex 22:17 he must still pay the bride-price for v. 1435
Est 2: 2 be made for beautiful young v for the king. 1435
2:17 and approval more than any of the other v. 1435
2:19 When the v were assembled a second time, 1435
SS 6: 8 and v beyond number; 6625
La 5:11 and v in the towns of Judah. 1435
Eze 44:22 they may marry only v of Israelite descent 1435
Mt 25: 1 be like ten v who took their lamps *4221*
25: 7 all the v woke up and trimmed their lamps. *4221*
25:10 The v who were ready went in with him to *NIG*
1Co 7:25 Now about v: I have no command from the *4221*

VIRTUE (KJV) See EXCELLENT, GOODNESS, POWER

VIRTUES (1)

Col 3:14 And over all these v put on love, *NIG*

VISAGE (KJV) See APPEARANCE, ATTITUDE

VISIBLE (8)

Ge 8: 5 the tops of the mountains *became* v. 8011
Da 4:11 it was v to the ends of the earth. 10257
4:20 touching the sky, v to the whole earth, 10257
Mt 24:27 as lightning that comes from the east *is* v *5743*
Eph 5:13 everything exposed by the light *becomes* v, *5746*
5:14 for it is light that **makes** everything v. *5746*
Col 1:16 v and invisible, whether thrones or powers *3971*
Heb 11: 3 was not made out of what was v. *5743*

VISION (70) [VISIONS]

Ge 15: 1 word of the LORD came to Abram in a v: 4690
46: 2 And God spoke to Israel in a v *at* night 5261
Nu 24: 4 who sees a v *from* the Almighty, 4690
24:16 who sees a v *from* the Almighty, 4690
1Sa 3:15 He was afraid to tell Eli the v, 5261
2Ch 32:32 and his acts of devotion are written in the v 2606
Job 20: 8 banished like a v *of* the night. 2612
33:15 In a dream, in a v *of* the night, 2612
Ps 89:19 Once you spoke in a v, 2606
Isa 1: 1 The v concerning Judah and Jerusalem 2606
21: 2 A dire v has been shown to me: 2607
22: 1 An oracle concerning the Valley of V: 2612
22: 5 and terror in the Valley of V, 2612
29: 7 with a v *in* the night— 2606
29:11 For you this whole v is nothing 2607
Eze 7:13 the v concerning the whole crowd will not 2606
7:26 They will try to get a v from the prophet; 2606
8: 4 as in the v I had seen in the plain. 5260
11:24 to the exiles in Babylonia in the v given by 5260
11:24 Then the v I had seen went up from me, 5260
12:22 'The days go by and every v comes 2606
12:23 'The days are near when every v will 2606
12:27 'The v he sees is for many years from now, 2606
43: 3 The v I saw was like the vision I had seen 5260
43: 3 The vision I saw was like the v I had seen 5260
Da 2:19 the mystery was revealed to Daniel in a v. 10256
2:45 *the* v of the rock cut out of a mountain, but 10255
7: 2 Daniel said: "In my v at night I looked, 10256
7: 7 "After that, in my v *at* night I looked, 10256
7:13 "In my v *at* night I looked, 10256
8: 1 I, Daniel, had a v, after the one that 2606
8: 2 In my v I saw myself in the citadel of Susa 2606
8: 2 in the v I was beside the Ulai Canal. 2606
8:13 "How long will it take for the v to be 2606
8:13 the v concerning the daily sacrifice, NIH
8:15 watching the v and trying to understand it, 2606
8:16 tell this man the meaning of the v." 5260
8:17 "understand that the v concerns the time of 2606
8:19 v concerns the appointed time of the end. NIH
8:26 "The v *of* the evenings and mornings 5260
8:26 but seal up the v, for it concerns the 2606
8:27 I was appalled by the v; 5260
9:21 the man I had seen in the earlier v, 2606
9:23 the message and understand the v: 5260
9:24 to seal up v and prophecy and to anoint 2606
10: 1 of the message came to him in a v. 5260
10: 7 I, Daniel, was the only one who saw the v; 5261
10: 8 So I was left alone, gazing at this great v; 5261
10:14 for the v concerns a time yet to come." 2606
10:16 overcome with anguish because of the v, 5261
11:14 people will rebel in fulfillment of the v, 2606
Ob 1: 1 The v *of* Obadiah. 2606
Mic 1: 1 the v *he* **saw** concerning Samaria and 2600
Na 1: 1 The book of the v *of* Nahum the Elkoshite. 2606
Zec 1: 8 During the night *I* **had a** v— 8011
13: 4 prophet will be ashamed of his prophetic v. 2612
Lk 1:22 They realized he had seen a v in *3965*
24:23 and told us that they had seen a v of angels, *3965*
Ac 9:10 The Lord called to him in a v, "Ananias!" *3969*
9:12 In a v he has seen a man named Ananias *3969*
10: 3 at about three in the afternoon he had a v. *3969*
10:17 wondering about the meaning of the v, *3969+3972*
10:19 While Peter was still thinking about the v, *3969*
11: 5 and in a trance I saw a v. *3969*
12: 9 he thought he was seeing a v. *3969*
16: 9 Paul **had a** v of a man of Macedonia *3969+3972*
16:10 After Paul had seen the v, *3969*
18: 9 One night the Lord spoke to Paul in a v: *3969*
26:19 not disobedient *to* the v from heaven. *3965*
Rev 9:17 The horses and riders I saw in my v looked *3970*

VISIONS (37) [VISION]

Nu 12: 6 I reveal myself to him in v, 5261
1Sa 3: 1 there were not many v. 2606
2Ch 9:29 the Shilonite and in the v *of* Iddo the seer 2608
Job 7:14 with dreams and terrify me with v, 2612
Isa 28: 7 they stagger when **seeing** v, 8015
30:10 They say to the seers, **"See** no *more* v!" 8011
30:10 and to the prophets, **"Give** us no *more* v 2600
Jer 14:14 They are prophesying to you false v, 2606
23:16 They speak v *from* their own minds, 2606
La 2: 9 and her prophets no longer find v from 2606
2:14 *The* v of your prophets were false 2600
Eze 1: 1 heavens were opened and I saw v *of* God. 5261
8: 3 and in v *of* God he took me to Jerusalem, 5261
12:24 be no more false v or flattering divinations 2606
13: 6 *Their* v *are* false and their divinations a lie. 2600
13: 7 Have you not seen false v and uttered 4690
13: 8 Because of your false words and lying v, 2600
13: 9 be against the prophets who see false v 2600
13:16 Jerusalem and **saw** v *of* peace for her 2600+2606
13:23 therefore *you will* no longer **see** false v 2600
21:29 Despite false v concerning you 2600
22:28 for them by false v and lying divinations. 2600

Eze 40: 2 In v of God he took me to the land of Israel 5261
43: 3 and like the v I had seen by the Kebar River, 5261
Da 1:17 And Daniel could understand v and dreams 2606
2:28 and the v that passed through your mind 10256
4: 5 and v that passed through my mind 10256
4:10 the v I saw while lying in my bed: 10256
4:13 "In the v I saw while lying in my bed, 10256
7: 1 and v passed through his mind 10256
7:15 and the v that passed through my mind 10256
Hos 12:10 gave them many v and told parables 2606
Joel 2:28 your young men will see v. 2612
Mic 3: 6 night will come over you, without v, 2606
Zec 10: 2 diviners see v that lie; 2600
Ac 2:17 your young men will see v, 3970
2Co 12: 1 go on to v and revelations from the Lord. 3965

VISIT (26) [VISITED, VISITOR, VISITORS, VISITS]

Ge 34: 1 went out to v the women of the land. 8011
Jdg 15: 1 a young goat and went to v his wife. 7212
2Ch 18: 2 Some years later he went down to v Ahab NIH
22: 7 Through Ahaziah's v to Joram, 995
Jnh 3: 3 a v required three days. 4544
Mt 25:36 I was in prison and you came to v me.' NIG
25:39 or in prison and go to v you?' NIG
Jn 11:45 many of the Jews who had come to v Mary, NIG
Ac 7:12 he sent our fathers on their first v. NIG
7:13 On their **second** v, Joseph told his brothers AIT
7:23 he decided to v his fellow Israelites. 2170
9:32 he went to v the saints in Lydda. NIG
10:28 a Jew to associate with a Gentile or v him. 4665
15:36 "Let us go back and v the brothers in all 2170
19:21 he said, "I must v Rome also." 3972
Ro 15:24 I hope to v you while passing through and 2517
15:28 I will go to Spain and v you **on the way.** 1328
1Co 16: 7 now and make only a passing v; NIG
2Co 1:15 I planned to v you first so 2262
1:16 I planned to v you **on** my **way** to Macedonia 1451
2: 1 that I would not **make** another painful v 2262
9: 5 urge the brothers to v you **in advance** 1650+4601
12:14 I am ready to v you for the third time, 2262
13: 1 This will be my third v to you. 2262
1Th 2: 1 that our v to you was not a failure. 1658
2Jn 1:12 to v you and talk with you face to face, 1181

VISITATION (KJV) See PUNISH, JUDGMENT

VISITED (2) [VISIT]

Jn 4:46 Once more he v Cana in Galilee, 1650+2262
19:39 man who earlier had v Jesus at night. 2262+4639

VISITOR (1) [VISIT]

Lk 24:18 "Are you only a v **to** Jerusalem and 4228

VISITORS (1) [VISIT]

Ac 2:10 parts of Libya near Cyrene; v **from** Rome 2111

VISITS (2) [VISIT]

Mic 7: 4 watchmen has come, the day God v you. 7213
1Pe 2:12 and glorify God on the day he v us. 2175

VOCATION (KJV) See CALLING

VOICE (198) [VOICES]

Ge 27:22 "The v is the voice of Jacob, 7754
27:22 "The voice is the v of Jacob, 7754
Ex 15:26 "If you listen carefully to the v of the LORD 7754
19:19 and the v of God answered him. 7754
24: 3 they responded with one v, 7754
Nu 7:89 he heard the v speaking to him from 7754
Dt 4:12 but saw no form; there was only a v. 7754
4:33 the v of God speaking out of fire, 7754
4:36 From heaven he made you hear his v 7754
5:22 a loud v to your whole assembly there on 7754
5:23 When you heard the v out of the darkness, 7754
5:24 and we have heard his v from the fire. 7754
5:25 the v of the LORD our God any longer. 7754
5:26 For what mortal man has ever heard the v 7754
18:16 not hear the v of the LORD our God 7754
26: 7 LORD heard our v and saw our misery, 7754
27:14 to all the people of Israel in a loud v: 7754
30:20 listen to his v, and hold fast to him. 7754
Jdg 5:11 the v of the singers at the watering places. 7754
18: 3 they recognized the v of the young Levite; 7754
1Sa 1:13 and her lips were moving but her v was 7754
15:22 and sacrifices as much as in obeying the v 7754
24:16 "Is that your v, David my son?" 7754
26:17 Saul recognized David's v and said, 7754
26:17 "Is that your v, David my son?" 7754
28:12 she cried out at the top of her v and said 7754
2Sa 22: 7 From his temple he heard my v; 7754
22:14 the v of the Most High resounded. 7754
1Ki 8:55 the whole assembly of Israel in a loud v, 7754
19:13 Then a v said to him, "What are you doing 7754
2Ki 19:22 Against whom have you raised your v 7754
2Ch 5:13 and singers joined in unison, as with one v, 7754
20:19 the God of Israel, with very loud v. 7754
Ezr 10:12 whole assembly responded with a loud v: 7754
Job 4:16 and I heard a hushed v: 7754
37: 2 Listen to the roar of his v, 7754
37: 4 he thunders with his majestic v. 7754
37: 4 his v resounds, he holds nothing back. 7754
37: 5 God's v thunders in marvelous ways; 7754
38:34 "Can you raise your v to the clouds 7754
40: 9 and can your v thunder like his? 7754
Ps 5: 3 In the morning, O LORD, you hear my v; 7754
18: 6 From his temple he heard my v; 7754
18:13 the v of the Most High resounded. 7754
19: 3 or language where their v is not heard. 7754
19: 4 Their v goes out into all the earth, 7754
27: 7 Hear my v when I call, O LORD; 7754
29: 3 The v of the LORD is over the waters; 7754
29: 4 The v of the LORD is powerful; 7754
29: 4 the v of the LORD is majestic. 7754
29: 5 The v of the LORD breaks the cedars; 7754
29: 7 The v of the LORD strikes with flashes 7754
29: 8 The v of the LORD shakes the desert; 7754
29: 9 The v of the LORD twists the oaks 7754
46: 6 he lifts his v, the earth melts. 7754
55: 3 at the v of the enemy, at the stares of 7754
55:17 and he hears my v. 7754
64: 1 Hear me, O God, as I v my complaint; 7754
66:19 surely listened and heard my v in prayer. 7754
68:33 who thunders with mighty v. 7754
93: 3 O LORD, the seas have lifted up their v; 7754
95: 7 Today, if you hear his v, 7754
116: 1 I love the LORD, for he heard my v; 7754
119:149 Hear my v in accordance with your love; 7754
130: 2 O Lord, hear my v. 7754
141: 1 Hear my v when I call to you. 7754
142: 1 I lift up my v to the LORD for mercy. 7754
Pr 1:20 she raises her v in the public squares; 7754
8: 1 Does not understanding raise her v? 7754
8: 4 I raise my v to all mankind. 7754
SS 2:14 show me your face, let me hear your v; 7754
2:14 for your v is sweet, and your face is lovely. 7754
8:13 let me hear your v! 7754
Isa 6: 8 Then I heard the v of the Lord saying, 7754
28:23 Listen and hear my v; 7754
29: 4 Your v will come ghostlike from the earth; 7754
30:21 your ears will hear a v behind you, saying, 1821
30:30 will cause men to hear his majestic v 7754
30:31 The v of the LORD will shatter Assyria; 7754
33: 3 At the thunder of your v, the peoples flee; 7754
37:23 Against whom have you raised your v 7754
40: 3 A v of one calling: "In the desert prepare 7754
40: 6 A v says, "Cry out." 7754
40: 9 lift up your v with a shout, lift it up, 7754
42: 2 or raise his v in the streets. 7754
58: 1 Raise your v like a trumpet. 7754
58: 4 and expect your v to be heard on high. 7754
Jer 4:15 A v is announcing from Dan, 7754
22:20 let your v be heard in Bashan, 7754
31:15 "A v is heard in Ramah, mourning and 7754
31:16 "Restrain your v from weeping 7754
Eze 1:24 like the v of the Almighty, 7754
1:25 Then there came a v from above 7754
1:28 and I heard the v of one speaking. 7754
9: 1 Then I heard him call out in a loud v, 7754
10: 5 the v of God Almighty when he speaks. 7754
11:13 I fell facedown and cried out in a loud v, 7754
27:30 They will raise their v and cry bitterly 7754
33:32 a beautiful v and plays an instrument well, 7754
43: 2 His v was like the roar of rushing waters, 7754
Da 4:14 He called in a **loud** v. AIT
4:31 on his lips when a v came from heaven, 10631
6:20 he called to Daniel in an anguished v, 10631
8:16 I heard a man's v from the Ulai calling, 7754
10: 6 and his v like the sound of a multitude. 1821
Hag 1:12 the v of the LORD their God and 7754
Mt 2:18 "A v is heard in Ramah, Rachel weeping 5889
3: 3 "A v of one calling in the desert, 5889
3:17 And a v from heaven said, 5889
12:19 no one will hear his v in the streets. 5889
17: 5 and a v from the cloud said, 5889
27:46 the ninth hour Jesus cried out in a loud v, 5889
27:50 Jesus had cried out again in a loud v, 5889
Mk 1: 3 "a v of one calling in the desert, 5889
1:11 And a v came from heaven: 5889
5: 7 He shouted at the top of his v, 5889
9: 7 and a v came from the cloud: 5889
15:34 the ninth hour Jesus cried out in a loud v, 5889
Lk 1:42 In a loud v she exclaimed: 3199
3: 4 "A v of one calling in the desert, 5889
3:22 And a v came from heaven: 5889
4:33 cried out **at the top of** his v, 3489+5889
8:28 **shouting at the top of** his v, 3306+3489+5889
9:35 A v came from the cloud, saying, 5889
9:36 When the v had spoken, 5889
17:13 and **called out in a loud** v, 149+5889
17:15 came back, praising God in a loud v. 5889
23:18 **With one** v they cried out, 4101
23:46 Jesus called out with a loud v, "Father, 5889
Jn 1:23 "I am the v of one calling in the desert, 5889
3:29 of joy when he hears the bridegroom's v. 5889
5:25 now come when the dead will hear the v of 5889
5:28 who are in their graves will hear his v 5889
5:37 You have never heard his v nor seen his 5889
7:37 Jesus stood and said in **a loud** v, 3189
10: 3 and the sheep listen to his v. 5889
10: 4 sheep follow him because they know his v. 5889
10: 5 they do not recognize a stranger's v." 5889
10:16 They too will listen to my v, 5889
10:27 My sheep listen to my v; I know them, 5889
11:43 Jesus called in a loud v, "Lazarus, 5889
12:28 Then a v came from heaven, 5889
12:30 Jesus said, "This v was for your benefit, 5889
Ac 2:14 raised his v and addressed the crowd: 5889
7:31 to look more closely, he heard the Lord's v: 5889
9: 4 to the ground and heard a v say to him, 5889
10:13 Then a v told him, "Get up, Peter. 5889
10:15 The v spoke to him a second time, 5889
11: 7 Then I heard a v telling me, 'Get up, Peter. 5889
11: 9 "The v spoke from heaven a second time, 5889
12:14 When she recognized Peter's v, 5889
12:22 They shouted, "This is the v of a god, 5889
22: 7 to the ground and heard a v say to me, 5889
22: 9 the v of him who was speaking to me. 5889
26:14 and I heard a v saying to me in Aramaic, 5889
Ro 10:18 "Their v has gone out into all the earth, 5782
1Th 4:16 with the v of the archangel and with 5889
Heb 3: 7 "Today, if you hear his v, 5889
3:15 "Today, if you hear his v, 5889
4: 7 "Today, if you hear his v, 5889
12:19 or to such a v speaking words 5889
12:26 At that time his v shook the earth, 5889
2Pe 1:17 the Father when the v came to him from 5889
1:18 We ourselves heard this v that came 5889
2:16 who spoke with a man's v and restrained 5889
Rev 1:10 I heard behind me a loud v like a trumpet, 5889
1:12 around to see the v that was speaking 5889
1:15 his v was like the sound of rushing waters. 5889
3:20 If anyone hears my v and opens the door, 5889
4: 1 And the v I had first heard speaking to me 5889
5: 2 a mighty angel proclaiming in a loud v, 5889
5:11 I looked and heard the v of many angels, 5889
5:12 In a loud v they sang: "Worthy is the Lamb 5889
6: 1 of the four living creatures say in a v 5889
6: 6 Then I heard what sounded like a v among 5889
6: 7 the v of the fourth living creature say, 5889
6:10 They called out in a loud v, "How long, 5889
7: 2 He called out in a loud v to 5889
7:10 And they cried out in a loud v: 5889
8:13 in midair call out in a loud v: 5889
9:13 and I heard a v coming from the horns of 5889
10: 4 but I heard a v from heaven say, 5889
10: 8 the v that I had heard from heaven spoke 5889
11:12 a loud v from heaven saying to them, 5889
12:10 Then I heard a loud v in heaven say: 5889
14: 7 He said in a loud v, "Fear God 5889
14: 9 and said in a loud v: "If anyone worships 5889
14:13 Then I heard a v from heaven say, "Write: 5889
14:15 in a loud v to him who was sitting on 5889
14:18 came from the altar and called in a loud v 5889
16: 1 a loud v from the temple saying to 5889
16:17 the temple came a loud v from the throne, 5889
18: 2 With a mighty v he shouted: "Fallen! 5889
18: 4 Then I heard another v from heaven say: 5889
18:23 The v of bridegroom and bride will never 5889
19: 5 Then a v came from the throne, saying: 5889
19:17 who cried in a loud v to all the birds flying 5889
21: 3 I heard a loud v from the throne saying, 5889

VOICES (26) [VOICE]

Nu 14: 1 the people of the community raised their v 7754
Jos 6:10 do not raise your v, do not say a word 7754
Jdg 21: 2 raising their v and weeping bitterly. 7754
2Sa 19:35 the v of men and women singers? 7754
2Ch 5:13 they raised their v in praise to the LORD 7754
Ne 9: 4 with loud v to the LORD their God. 7754
Job 29:10 the v of the nobles were hushed, 7754
Isa 6: 4 At the sound of their v the doorposts 7924
15: 4 their v are heard all the way to Jahaz. 7754
24:14 They raise their v, they shout for joy; 7754
42:11 Let the desert and its towns raise their v; NIH
52: 8 Your watchmen lift up their v; 7754
Jer 7:34 the v of bride and bridegroom in the towns 7754
16: 9 the sounds of joy and gladness and to the v 7754
25:10 the v of bride and bridegroom, 7754
33:11 the v of bride and bridegroom, 7754
33:11 the v of those who bring thank offerings to 7754
51:55 the roar of their v will resound, 7754
Da 5:10 hearing the v of the king and his nobles, 10418
Na 2:13 The v of your messengers will no longer 7754
Lk 19:37 to praise God in loud v for all the miracles 5889
Ac 4:24 they raised their v together in prayer 5889
7:57 yelling **at the top of** their v, 3489+5889
22:22 Then they raised their v and shouted, 5889
Rev 10: 3 the v of the seven thunders spoke. 5889
11:15 and there were loud v in heaven, 5889

VOID (KJV) See BROKEN, CLEAR, EMPTY, LACKED, LACKING, LACKS, NO VALUE, NULLIFIES, NULLIFY, PLUNDERED, RENOUNCED, WITHOUT

VOLUME (KJV) See SCROLL

VOLUNTARILY (4) [VOLUNTEERS]

2Ki 12: 4 and the money brought v to the temple. 408+4213+6584+6590
2Ch 35: 8 officials also contributed v to the people and 5607
1Co 9:17 If I preach v, I have a reward; 1776
9:17 if **not** v, I am simply discharging the trust 220

VOLUNTEERED (3) [VOLUNTEERS]

1Ch 12:38 All these were fighting men who **v to serve** 6370
2Ch 17:16 who v **himself for** the **service** of the LORD, 5605
Ne 11: 2 The people commended all the men who v 5605

VOLUNTEERS (1) [VOLUNTARILY, VOLUNTEERED]

Jdg 5: 9 with the **willing** v among the people. 5605

VOMIT (11) [VOMITED]

Lev 18:28 it *will* v you **out** as it vomited out 7794
20:22 I am bringing to live *may* not v you **out.** 7794
Job 20:15 God *will* **make** his stomach v them **up.** 3769
Pr 23: 8 *You will* v **up** the little you have eaten 7794
25:16 too much of it, and *you will* v. 7794
26:11 As a dog returns to its v, 7683
Isa 19:14 as a drunkard staggers around in his v. 7795
28: 8 All the tables are covered with v and 7795
Jer 25:27 Drink, get drunk and v, 7794
48:26 Let Moab wallow in her v; 7795
2Pe 2:22 "A dog returns to its v," and, *2000*

VOMITED (3) [VOMIT]

Lev 18:25 and the land v **out** its inhabitants. 7794
18:28 as *it* v **out** the nations that were before you. 7794
Jnh 2:10 and *it* v Jonah onto dry land. 7794

VOPHSI (1)

Nu 13:14 from the tribe of Naphtali, Nahbi son of V; 2265

VOTE (1)

Ac 26:10 I cast my v against them. *6029*

VOUCH (1)

Col 4:13 *I* v for him that he is working hard for you *3455*

VOW (42) [VOWED, VOWS]

Ge 28:20 Then Jacob **made a** v, saying, 5623+5624
31:13 and where *you* **made a** v to me. 5623+5624
Lev 7:16 the result of a v or is a freewill offering, 5624
22:18 either to fulfill a v or as a freewill offering, 5624
22:21 to the LORD to **fulfill a special** v or 5624+7098
22:23 it will not be accepted in fulfillment of a v. 5624
27: 2 'If anyone **makes a special** v 5624+7098
27: 8 If anyone making the v is too poor to pay NIH
27: 8 to what the *man* **making** *the* v can afford. 5623
Nu 6: 2 or woman *wants* to **make a special** v, 5623+7098
6: 2 to make a special vow, a v *of* separation to 5624
6: 5 of his v *of* separation no razor may be used 5624
6:21 He must fulfill the v *he has* **made,** 5623+5624
15: 8 for a **special** v or a fellowship offering 5624+7098
21: 2 Then Israel **made** *this* v to the LORD: 5623+5624
29:39 to *what* you v and your freewill offerings, 5624
30: 2 a man **makes a** v to the LORD or takes 5623+5624
30: 3 in her father's house **makes a** v to 5623+5624
30: 4 and her father hears about her v or pledge 5624
30: 6 after she makes a v or after her lips utter 5624
30: 8 the v that obligates her or the rash promise 5624
30: 9 "Any v or obligation taken by a widow 5624
30:10 a woman living with her husband **makes a** v 5623
30:13 may confirm or nullify any v she makes 5624
Dt 23:18 house of the LORD your God to pay any v, 5624
23:21 If *you* **make a** v to the LORD your God 5623+5624
23:22 But if you refrain from **making a** v, 5623
23:23 because *you* **made** *your* v freely to the LORD 5623
Jdg 11:30 And Jephthah **made a** v to the LORD: 5623+5624
11:35 because I *have* **made a** v to the LORD 7023+7198
1Sa 1:11 And *she* **made a** v, saying, 5623+5624
1:21 sacrifice to the LORD and to fulfill his v, 5624
2Sa 15: 7 and fulfill a v *I* **made** to the LORD. 5623+5624
15: 8 *I* **made** *this* v: 'If the LORD takes me 5623+5624
Ps 132: 2 and **made a** v to the Mighty One of Jacob: 5623
Ecc 5: 4 When *you* **make a** v to God, 5623+5624
5: 4 He has no pleasure in fools; fulfill *your* v. 5623
5: 5 It is better not *to* v than to make a vow and 5623
5: 5 than *to* **make a** v and not fulfill it. 5623
5: 6 "**My** v was a mistake." 2085[S]
Ac 18:18 at Cenchrea because of a v he had taken. *2376*
21:23 four men with us who have made a v. *2376*

VOWED (9) [VOW]

Lev 23:38 whatever you have v and all the freewill 5624
27: 9 " 'If what he v is an animal NIH
27:11 If what he v is a ceremonially unclean NIH
Dt 12: 6 *what* you have v to give and your freewill 5624
12:11 all the choice possessions you *have* v 5623+5624
12:17 or whatever you *have* v to give, 5623+5624
12:26 and whatever you have v to give, 5624
Jdg 11:39 father and he did to her as he *had* v. 5623+5624
Jnh 2: 9 What *I have* v I will make good. 5623

VOWS (30) [VOW]

Nu 6:21 the law of the Nazirite who v his offering 5623
15: 3 for **special** v or freewill offerings 5624+7098
30: 4 then all her v and every pledge by which 5624
30: 5 none of her v or the pledges by which she 5624
30: 7 then her v or the pledges by which she 5624
30:11 then all her v or the pledges by which she 5624
30:12 then none of the v or pledges that came 5624
30:14 then he confirms all her v or the pledges 5624
2Ki 12: 4 the money received from **personal** v 5883+6886
Job 22:27 and you will fulfill your v. 5624
Ps 22:25 before those who fear you will I fulfill my v. 5624
50:14 fulfill your v to the Most High, 5624
56:12 I am under v *to* you, O God; 5624
61: 5 For you have heard my v, O God; 5624
61: 8 to your name and fulfill my v day after day. 5624
65: 1 to you our v will be fulfilled. 5624
66:13 with burnt offerings and fulfill my v to you 5624
66:14 v my lips promised and my mouth spoke 889[S]
76:11 **Make** v to the LORD your God and fulfill 5623
116:14 I will fulfill my v to the LORD 5624
116:18 I will fulfill my v to the LORD 5624
Pr 7:14 today I fulfilled my v. 5624
20:25 rashly and only later to consider his v. 5624
31: 2 O son of my womb, O son of my v, 5624
Isa 19:21 *they will* **make** v to the LORD 5623+5624
Jer 44:25 'We will certainly carry out the v *we* **made** 5623+5624
44:25 do what you promised! Keep your v! 5624
Jnh 1:16 sacrifice to the LORD and **made** v to 5623+5624
Na 1:15 O Judah, and fulfill your v. 5624
Mal 1:14 acceptable male in his flock and v **to give** it, 5623

VOYAGE (2)

Ac 21: 7 We continued our v from Tyre and landed *4452*
27:10 I can see that our v is going to be disastrous *4452*

VULGAR (1)

2Sa 6:20 of his servants as any v *fellow* would!" 8199

VULTURE (6) [VULTURES]

Lev 11:13 the eagle, the v, the black vulture, 7272
11:13 the eagle, the vulture, the **black** v, 6465
Dt 14:12 the eagle, the v, the black vulture, 7272
14:12 the eagle, the vulture, the **black** v, 6465
Mic 1:16 make yourselves as bald as the v, 5979
Hab 1: 8 They fly like a v swooping to devour; 5979

VULTURES (4) [VULTURE]

Job 15:23 He wanders about—food for v; 370
Pr 30:17 will be eaten by the v. 1201+5979
Mt 24:28 there is a carcass, there the v will gather. *108*
Lk 17:37 there is a dead body, there the v will gather." *108*

W

WADE (1)

Isa 47: 2 bare your legs, and w **through** the streams. 6296

WADI (9)

Nu 34: 5 join the W *of* Egypt and end at the Sea. 5707
Jos 15: 4 along to Azmon and joined the W *of* Egypt, 5707
15:47 and villages, as far as the W *of* Egypt and 5707
1Ki 8:65 from Lebo Hamath to the W *of* Egypt. 5707
2Ki 24: 7 the W *of* Egypt to the Euphrates River. 5707
2Ch 7: 8 from Lebo Hamath to the W *of* Egypt. 5707
Isa 27:12 the flowing Euphrates to the W *of* Egypt, 5707
Eze 47:19 along the W [of Egypt] to the Great Sea. 5711
48:28 along the W [of Egypt] to the Great Sea. 5711

WAFER (3) [WAFERS]

Ex 29:23 and a cake made with oil, and a w. 8386
Lev 8:26 and one made with oil, and a w; 8386
Nu 6:19 and a cake and a w from the basket, 8386

WAFERS (6) [WAFER]

Ex 16:31 like coriander seed and tasted like w made 7613
29: 2 cakes mixed with oil, and w spread with oil. 8386
Lev 2: 4 w *made* without yeast and spread with oil. 8386
7:12 w made without yeast and spread with oil, 8386
Nu 6:15 flour mixed with oil, and w spread with oil. 8386
1Ch 23:29 for the grain offerings, the unleavened w, 8386

WAG (1)

Jer 23:31 the prophets who w their own tongues and 4374

WAGE (7) [WAGED, WAGES, WAGING]

Jos 11:20 to w war *against* Israel, 7925
Pr 20:18 if *you* w war, obtain guidance. 6913
Isa 19:10 and all the w earners will be sick at heart. 8512
41:12 Those who w war against you will be NIH
Da 11:25 The king of the South *will* w **war** with a large and 1741+2021+4200+4878
Mic 3: 5 they prepare to w war against him. NIH
2Co 10: 3 *we do* not w **war** as the world does. *5129*

WAGED (5) [WAGE]

Jos 11:18 Joshua w war against all these kings for 6913
1Ki 5: 3 w **against** my father David **from all sides,** 6015
1Ch 5:10 During Saul's reign *they* w war against 6913
5:19 *They* w war against the Hagrites, Jetur, 6913
Ps 55:18 He ransoms me unharmed from the battle w NIH

WAGES (35) [WAGE]

Ge 29:15 Tell me what your w should be." 5382
30:28 He added, "Name your w, 8510
30:32 They will be my w. 8510
30:33 you check on the w you *have paid* me. 8510
31: 7 by changing my w ten times. 5382
31: 8 he said, 'The speckled ones will be your w,' 8510
31: 8 he said, 'The streaked ones will be your w,' 8510
31:41 and you changed my w ten times. 5382
Lev 19:13 hold back the w *of* a hired man overnight. 7190
Nu 18:31 for it is your w for your work at the Tent 8510
Dt 24:15 Pay him his w each day before sunset, 8510
1Ki 5: 6 *for* your men whatever w you set. 8510
Job 7: 2 or a hired man waiting eagerly for his w, 7189
Pr 10:16 The w *of* the righteous bring them life, 7190
11:18 The wicked man earns deceptive w, 7190
Hos 9: 1 you love the **w of a prostitute** 924
Mic 1: 7 Since she gathered her gifts from the w 924
1: 7 as the w *of* prostitutes they will again be used 924
Hag 1: 6 You **earn** w, only to put them in a purse with holes in it." 8509+8509
Zec 8:10 that time there were no w *for* man or beast. 8510
Mal 3: 5 who defraud laborers of their w, 8510
Mt 20: 8 'Call the workers and pay them their w, *3635*
Mk 6:37 take **eight months of a man's w!** *1324+1357*
14: 5 have been sold for more than a year's w *NIG*
Lk 10: 7 for the worker deserves his w. *3635*
Jn 4:36 Even now the reaper draws his w, *3635*
6: 7 **"Eight months'** w would not buy *1324+1357*
12: 5 **the money** given to the poor? It was **worth a year's w."** *1324+5559*
Ro 4: 4 his w are not credited to him as a gift, *3635*
6:23 For the w of sin is death, but the gift of God *4072*
1Ti 5:18 and "The worker deserves his w." *3635*
Jas 5: 4 The w you failed to pay the workmen *3635*
2Pe 2:15 who loved the w of wickedness. *3635*
Rev 6: 6 saying, "A quart of wheat *for* **a day's** w, *1324*
6: 6 and three quarts of barley *for* **a day's** w, *1324*

WAGGING (KJV) See SHAKING

WAGING (4) [WAGE]

Jdg 11:27 but you are doing me wrong by w **war** 4309
Pr 24: 6 for w war you need guidance, 6913
Da 7:21 this horn *was* w war against the saints 10522
Ro 7:23 w **war against** the law of my mind *529*

WAGON (KJV) See CART

WAGONS (3)

Isa 66:20 on horses, in chariots and w, 7369
Eze 23:24 chariots and w and with a throng of people; 1649
26:10 w and chariots when he enters your gates 1649

WAHEB (1)

Nu 21:14 "...W in Suphah and the ravines, 2259

WAIL (40) [WAILED, WAILING, WAILS]

Isa 13: 6 W, for the day of the LORD is near; 3536
14:31 W, O gate! Howl, O city! 3536
15: 3 and in the public squares they all w, 3536
16: 7 Therefore the Moabites w, 3536
16: 7 they w together for Moab. 3536
22:12 called you on that day to weep and to w, 5027
23: 1 W, O ships of Tarshish! 3536
23: 6 w, you people of the island. 3536
23:14 W, *you* ships of Tarshish; 3536
65:14 from anguish of heart and w in brokenness 3536
Jer 4: 8 So put on sackcloth, lament and w, 3536
9:10 and w for the mountains and take up 5631
9:18 Let them come quickly and w over us 5631+5951
9:20 Teach your daughters how to w; 5631
14: 2 *they* w for the land, 7722
25:34 Weep and w, *you* shepherds; 2410
47: 2 all who dwell in the land *will* w 3536
48:20 W and cry out! 3536
48:31 Therefore *I* w over Moab, 3536
48:39 How *they* w! How Moab turns her back 3536
49: 3 "W, O Heshbon, for Ai is destroyed! 3536
51: 8 W over her! Get balm for her pain; 3536
Eze 21:12 Cry out and w, son of man, 3536
27:32 As they w and mourn over you, 5760
30: 2 " 'W and say, "Alas for that day!" 3536
32:18 w for the hordes of Egypt and consign to 5629
Hos 7:14 not cry out to me from their hearts but w 3536
Joel 1: 5 W, all you drinkers of wine; 3536
1: 5 w because of the new wine, NIH
1:11 Despair, you farmers, w, you vine growers; 3536
1:13 w, you who minister before the altar. 3536
Am 5:16 to weep and the mourners to w. 5027
Mic 1: 8 Because of this I will weep and w; 3536
Zep 1:11 W, you who live in the market district; 3536
Zec 11: 2 W, O pine tree, for the cedar has fallen; 3536
11: 2 W, oaks of Bashan; 3536
11: 3 Listen to the w *of* the shepherds; 3538
Mal 2:13 and w because he no longer pays attention 651
Jas 4: 9 Grieve, mourn and w. *3081*
5: 1 and w because of the misery that is coming *3909*

WAILED (3) [WAIL]

Nu 11:18 The LORD heard you when *you* w, 1134
11:20 who is among you, and *have* w before him, 1134
Lk 23:27 women who mourned and w **for** him. *2577*

WAILING (24) [WAIL]

Ex 11: 6 There will be loud w throughout Egypt— 7591
12:30 and there was loud w in Egypt, 7591
Nu 11: 4 and again the Israelites *started* w and said, 1134
11:10 Moses heard the people of every family w, 1134
11:13 *They keep* w to me, 'Give us meat to eat!' 1134
2Sa 13:36 the king's sons came in, w loudly. 1134
Est 4: 1 w loudly and bitterly. 2410+2411
4: 3 with fasting, weeping and **w.** 5027
Job 30:31 and my flute to the sound of **w.** 1134
Ps 30:11 You turned my w into dancing; 5027
Isa 15: 8 their w reaches as far as Eglaim, 3538
Jer 6:26 mourn with bitter w as for an only son, 5027
9:17 Call for the w *women* to come; 7801
9:19 The sound of w is heard from Zion: 5631
20:16 May he hear w in the morning, 2411
25:36 the w *of* the leaders of the flock, 3538
Am 5:16 "There will be w in all the streets and cries 5027
5:17 There will be w in all the vineyards, 5027
8: 3 "the songs in the temple *will* **turn to w.** 3536
Zep 1:10 w from the New Quarter, 3538
Mk 5:38 with people crying and w loudly. *226*
5:39 "Why all this commotion and **w?** *3081*
Lk 8:52 all the people *were* w and mourning for her. *3081*
8:52 "Stop **w,"** Jesus said. *3081*

WAILS (1) [WAIL]

Isa 15: 2 Moab w over Nebo and Medeba. 3536

WAIST (24) [WAISTS]

Ex 28:42 reaching from the w to the thigh. 5516
2Sa 20: 8 and strapped over it at his w was a belt with 5516
1Ki 2: 5 that blood stained the belt around his w and 5516
12:10 'My little finger is thicker than my father's **w.** 5516
2Ki 1: 8 and with a leather belt around his **w."** 5516
2Ch 10:10 'My little finger is thicker than my father's **w.** 5516
Job 12:18 by kings and ties a loincloth around their **w.** 5516
15:27 with fat and his w bulges with flesh, 4072
SS 7: 2 Your w is a mound of wheat encircled 1061
Isa 5:27 not a belt is loosened at the **w,** 2743
11: 5 and faithfulness the sash around his **w.** 2743
Jer 13: 1 a linen belt and put it around your **w,** 5516
13: 2 and put it around my **w.** 5516
13: 4 and are wearing around your **w,** 5516
13:11 For as a belt is bound around a man's **w,** 5516
48:37 and every w is covered with sackcloth. 5516
Eze 1:27 his w up he looked like glowing metal, 5516
8: 2 to be his w down he was like fire, 5516
47: 4 through water that was up to the **w.** 5516
Da 10: 5 with a belt of the finest gold around his **w.** 5516
Mt 3: 4 and he had a leather belt around his **w.** *4019*
Mk 1: 6 with a leather belt around his **w,** *4019*
Jn 13: 4 **wrapped** a towel **around** his **w.** *1346*
Eph 6:14 the belt of truth **buckled around** your **w,** *4322*

WAISTBAND (8)

Ex 28: 8 Its skillfully woven w is to be like it— 3109
28:27 to the seam just above the w *of* the ephod. 3109
28:28 connecting it to the **w,** 3109
29: 5 the ephod on him by its skillfully woven **w.** 3109
39: 5 Its skillfully woven w was like it— 3109
39:20 to the seam just above the w *of* the ephod. 3109
39:21 to the w so that the breastpiece would 3109
Lev 8: 7 ephod to him by its **skillfully woven w;** 3109

WAISTS (5) [WAIST]

1Ki 20:31 around our w and ropes around our heads. 5516
20:32 Wearing sackcloth around their w and ropes 5516
Isa 32:11 put sackcloth around your **w.** 2743
Eze 23:15 belts around their w and flowing turbans 5516
44:18 and linen undergarments around their **w.** 5516

WAIT (92) [AWAIT, AWAITS, WAITED, WAITING, WAITS]

Ex 7:15 **W** on the bank of the Nile to meet him, 5893
24:14 **"W** here for us until we come back to you. 3782
Lev 12: 4 Then the woman *must* w thirty-three days 3782
12: 5 *she must* w sixty-six days to be purified 3782
Nu 9: 8 **"W** until I find out what the LORD 6641
Dt 19:11 if a man hates his neighbor and **lies in w** 741
Jos 8: 9 of ambush and **lay in w** between Bethel 3782
18: 3 "How long *will* you w before you begin 8332
Jdg 6:18 LORD said, "I *will* w until you return." 3782
9:32 and your men should come and **lie in w** in 741
16: 2 So they surrounded the place and **lay in w** 741
19: 8 **W** till afternoon!" 4538
Ru 1:13 *would you* w until they grew up? 8432
3:18 Then Naomi said, **"W,** my daughter, 3782
1Sa 10: 8 but *you must* w seven days until I come 3498
14: 9 **'W** there until we come to you,' 1957
20:19 and w by the stone Ezel. 3782
22: 8 incited my servant to **lie in w** for me, 741
22:13 against me and **lies in w** for me, 741
2Sa 15:28 I *will* w at the fords in the desert 4538
18:14 *"I'm not going to* w like this for you." 3498
18:30 The king said, "Stand aside and w here." 3656
2Ki 6:33 Why *should I* w for the LORD any longer?" 3498
7: 9 If *we* w until daylight, 2675
Job 3: 9 *may it* w for daylight in vain and not see 7747
14:14 the days of my hard service *I will* **w for** 3498
20:26 total darkness **lies in w** for his treasures. 3243
32:16 *Must I* **w,** now that they are silent, 3498
35:14 before him and *you must* w for him, 2565
38:40 when they crouch in their dens or lie in w in 743
Ps 5: 3 requests before you and **w in expectation.** 7595
10: 8 He lies in w *near* the villages; 4422
10: 9 *He* **lies in** w like a lion in cover; 741
10: 9 *he* **lies in** w to catch the helpless; 741
27:14 **W** for the LORD; 7747
27:14 and take heart and w for the LORD. 7747
33:20 We **w in hope** for the LORD; 2675
37: 7 Be still before the LORD and **w patiently** 2565
37:32 The wicked **lie in w** for the righteous, 7595
37:34 **W** for the LORD and keep his way. 7747
38:15 *I* w for you, O LORD; 3498
59: 3 See how *they* **lie in w** for me! 741
71:10 *those who* **w to kill** me conspire 5883+9068
106:13 and *did* not w for his counsel. 2675
119:84 **How long must** your servant **w?** 3427+3869+4537
119:166 *I* w for your salvation, O LORD, 8432
130: 5 *I* **w for** the LORD, my soul waits, 7747
130: 6 waits for the Lord more than watchmen w NIH
130: 6 more than watchmen w for the morning. NIH
Pr 1:11 *let's* **lie in w** for someone's blood, 741
1:18 These men **lie in w** for their own blood; 741
12: 6 words of the wicked **lie in w** *for* blood, 741
20:22 **W** for the LORD, and he will deliver you. 7747
23:28 Like a bandit she **lies in w,** 741
24:15 *Do* not **lie in w** like an outlaw against 741
Isa 8:17 *I will* w for the LORD, 2675
26: 8 the way of your laws, *we* **w for** you; 7747
30:18 Blessed are all *who* w for him! 2675
51: 5 The islands will look to me and **w in hope** 3498
64: 4 who acts on behalf of *those who* w for him. 2675
Jer 5: 6 a leopard *will* **lie in w** near their towns 9193
5:26 are wicked men *who* **lie in w** 8800
La 3:10 Like a bear **lying in w,** 741
3:24 therefore *I will* w for him." 3498
3:26 to w quietly for the salvation of the LORD. 3497
4:19 and **lay in w** for us in the desert. 741
Eze 44:26 After he is cleansed, *he must* w seven days. 6218
Hos 12: 6 and w for your God always. 7747
Ob 1:14 *You should* not w at the crossroads to cut 6641
Mic 5: 7 not w for man or linger for mankind. 7747
7: 2 All men **lie in w** to shed blood; 741
7: 7 *I* w for God my Savior; 3498
Hab 2: 3 Though it linger, w for it; 2675
3:16 *I will* **w patiently** for the day of calamity 5663
Zep 3: 8 Therefore w for me," declares the LORD, 2675
Mt 8:15 and she got up and *began to* **w on** him. *1354*
Mk 1:31 The fever left her and *she began to* **w on** *1354*
Lk 4:39 *She* got up at once and *began to* **w on** them. *1354*
12:37 at the table and *will* come and **w on** them. *1354*
17: 8 get yourself ready and **w on** me while I eat *1354*
Jn 18:16 but Peter **had to w** outside at the door. *2705*
Ac 1: 4 but **w for** the gift my Father promised, *4338*
6: 2 of the word of God *in order to* **w on** tables. *1354*
Ro 8:23 *as we* **w eagerly for** our adoption as sons, *587*
8:25 we do not yet have, *we* **w for** it patiently. *587*
1Co 1: 7 *as you* **eagerly w for** our Lord Jesus Christ *587*
4: 5 w till the Lord comes. *NIG*
11:33 come together to eat, **w for** each other. *1683*
1Th 1:10 and *to* **w for** his Son from heaven, *388*
Tit 2:13 *while we* **w for** the blessed hope— *4657*
Jude 1:21 in God's love *as* you **w for** the mercy *4657*
Rev 6:11 and they were told to w a little longer, *399*

WAITED (16) [WAIT]

Ge 8:10 *He* w seven more days and again sent out 3498
8:12 *He* w seven more days and sent 3498
Jdg 3:25 *They* w to the point of embarrassment, 3498
3:26 While they **w,** Ehud got away. 4538
1Sa 13: 8 *He* w seven days, the time set by Samuel; 3498
25: 9 Then *they* **w.** 5663
1Ki 1: 4 she took care of the king and **w on** him, 9250
Job 29:23 *They* w for me as for showers and drank 3498
32: 4 Now Elihu *had* w before speaking to Job 2675
32:11 *I* w while you spoke, 3498
Ps 40: 1 *I* **w patiently for** the LORD; 7747+7747
Isa 38:13 *I* **w patiently** till dawn, 8750
La 2:16 This is the day *we have* **w for;** 7747
Jnh 4: 5 and w to see what would happen to the city. 6330
Ac 20: 5 These men went on ahead and **w for us** *3531*
1Pe 3:20 when God w patiently in the days of Noah *587*

WAITING (26) [WAIT]

Ex 5:20 they found Moses and Aaron w to meet 5893
2Sa 16: 1 steward of Mephibosheth, w to meet him. NIH
1Ki 20:38 **stood** by the road **w** for the king. 6641
Job 7: 2 or a hired man **w eagerly** *for* his wages, 7747
29:21 **w in silence** for my counsel. 1957
Ps 119:95 The wicked *are* w to destroy me, 7747
Pr 8:34 at my doors, w *at* my doorway. 9068
Jer 3: 2 By the roadside *you* **sat** w for lovers, 3782
20:10 All my friends *are* w *for* me to slip, saying, 9068
Mic 1:12 w for relief, because disaster has come from NIH
Mk 15:43 who was himself **w for** the kingdom *4657*
Lk 1:21 the people were **w for** Zechariah *4659*
2:25 *He was* **w for** the consolation of Israel, *4657*
3:15 The people *were* **w expectantly** *4659*
11:54 w to catch him in something he might say. *1910*
12:36 like men **w for** their master to return from *4657*
23:51 and he *was* **w for** the kingdom of God. *4657*
Jn 7: 1 from Judea because the Jews there *were* w *2426*
Ac 17:16 *While* Paul *was* **w for** them in Athens, *1683*
22:16 And now what *are you* **w for?** *3516*
23:21 forty of them *are* **w in ambush for** him. *1910*
23:21 **w for** your consent to their request." *4657*
28: 6 but *after* w a long time and seeing nothing *4659*
1Co 11:21 ahead without w for anybody else. *NIG*
Heb 6:15 And so *after* **w patiently,** *3428*
9:28 to bring salvation *to* those who *are* **w for** *587*

WAITS (7) [WAIT]

Ps 130: 5 I wait for the LORD, my soul **w,** 7747
130: 6 My soul w for the Lord more than NIH
Da 12:12 Blessed is the *one who* **w for** and reaches 2675
Jn 3:29 The friend who attends the bridegroom w *2705*
Ro 8:19 The creation w in eager expectation for *587*
Heb 10:13 Since that time *he* w for his enemies to *1683*
Jas 5: 7 See how the farmer **w for** the land *1683*

WAKE (17) [AWAKE, AWAKEN, AWAKENED, AWAKENS, AWAKES, AWOKE, WAKENED, WAKENS, WAKES, WOKE]

Jdg 5:12 **'W up,** wake up, Deborah! 6424
5:12 'Wake up, **w up,** Deborah! 6424
5:12 **W up,** wake up, break out in song! 6424
5:12 Wake up, **w up,** break out in song! 6424
1Sa 26:12 nor *did anyone* **w up.** 7810
Job 41:32 Behind him he leaves a glistening **w;** 5985
Ps 3: 5 *I* w again, because the LORD sustains me. 7810
Pr 23:35 *will I* **w up** so I can find another drink?" 7810
Isa 26:19 **w up** and shout for joy. 7810
Joel 1: 5 **W up,** you drunkards, and weep! 7810
Hab 2: 7 *Will they* not **w up** and make you tremble? 3699
2:19 Or to lifeless stone, **'W up!'** 6424
Jn 11:11 but I am going there to **w** him **up."** *2030*
Ro 13:11 for you *to* **w up** from your slumber, *1586*
Eph 5:14 This is why it is said: **"W up,** O sleeper, *1586*
Rev 3: 2 **W up!** Strengthen what remains *1181+1213*
3: 3 But if *you do* not **w up,** *1213*

WAKENED (2) [WAKE]

Zec 4: 1 who talked with me returned and w me, 6424
4: 1 as a man **is** w from his sleep. 6424

WAKENS (2) [WAKE]

Isa 50: 4 *He* w me morning by morning, 6424
50: 4 w my ear to listen like one being taught. 6424

WAKES (1) [WAKE]

Ps 78:65 as a man **w from** *the* **stupor** of wine. 8130

WALK (137) [WALKED, WALKING, WALKS]

Ge 13:17 w through the length and breadth of the land 2143
17: 1 w before me and be blameless. 2143
Ex 17: 5 **"W on** ahead of the people. 6296
Lev 11:20 " 'All flying insects that w on all fours are 2143
11:21 some winged creatures that w on all fours 2143
11:27 Of all the animals that w on all fours, 2143
11:27 *that* w on their paws are unclean for you; 2143
26:12 *I will* w among you and be your God, 2143
26:13 the bars of your yoke and **enabled** you **to w** 2143
Nu 11:31 as far as a day's w in any direction. 2006
Dt 5:33 **W** in all the way that the LORD your God 2143
6: 7 at home and when you w along the road, 2143
10:12 to w in all his ways, to love him, 2143
11:19 at home and when you w along the road, 2143
11:22 the LORD your God, to w in all his ways 2143
19: 9 the LORD your God and to w always 2143
26:17 and that you *will* w in his ways, 2143
28: 9 of the LORD your God and w in his ways. 2143
30:16 love the LORD your God, to w in his ways, 2143
Jos 22: 5 to w in all his ways, to obey his commands, 2143
Jdg 2:22 and w in it as their forefathers did." 2143
5:10 and *you who* w along the road, 2143
1Sa 8: 3 But his sons *did* not w in his ways. 2143
8: 5 and your sons *do* not w in your ways; 2143
2Sa 3:31 and put on sackcloth and **w in mourning** 6199
1Ki 2: 3 **W** in his ways, and keep his decrees 2143
2: 4 how they live, and if they w faithfully 2143
3:14 if *you* w in my ways and obey my statutes 2143
8:25 to w before me as you have done.' 2143
8:58 to w in all his ways and to keep 2143
9: 4 if *you* w before me in integrity of heart 2143
11:38 If you do whatever I command you and w 2143
2Ki 21:22 and *did* not w in the way of the LORD. 2143
2Ch 6:16 in all they do to w before me according 2143
6:31 and w in your ways all the time they live in 2143
7:17 *you* w before me as David your father did, 2143
Ne 5: 9 Shouldn't *you* w in the fear of our God 2143
Ps 1: 1 not w in the counsel of the wicked or stand 2143
15: 2 *He whose* w *is* blameless 2143
23: 4 Even though *I* w through the valley of 2143
26: 3 and *I* **w continually** in your truth. 2143
48:12 **W about** Zion, go around her, 6015
56:13 that I *may* w before God in the light of life. 2143
82: 5 *They* **w about** in darkness; 2143
84:11 from those *whose* w is blameless. 2143
86:11 O LORD, and *I will* w in your truth; 2143
89:15 *who* w in the light of your presence, 2143
101: 2 *I will* w in my house with blameless heart. 2143
101: 6 *he whose* w *is* blameless will 928+2006+2143
115: 7 but cannot feel, feet, but *they* cannot **w;** 2143
116: 9 that *I may* w before the LORD in the land 2143
119: 1 who w according to the law of the LORD. 2143

Ps 119: 3 They do nothing wrong; *they* w in his ways. 2143
119:45 *I will* w **about** in freedom, 2143
128: 1 who fear the LORD, who w in his ways. 2143
138: 7 Though *I* w in the midst of trouble, 2143
142: 3 where *I* w men have hidden a snare for me. 2143
Pr 2: 7 he is a shield to *those whose* w is blameless, 2143
2:13 leave the straight paths to w in dark ways, 2143
2:20 Thus *you will* w in the ways of good men 2143
4:12 you w, your steps will not be hampered; 2143
4:14 of the wicked or w in the way of evil men. 886
6:22 When you w, they will guide you; 2143
6:28 Can a man w on hot coals without 2143
8:20 *I* w in the way of righteousness, 2143
9: 6 w in the way of understanding. 886
14: 2 *He* whose w is upright fears the LORD, 2143
19: 1 a poor man whose w is blameless than 2143
28: 6 a poor man *whose* w *is* blameless than 2143
28:18 *He whose* w is blameless is kept safe, 2143
Isa 2: 3 so that *we may* w in his paths." 2143
2: 5 *let us* w in the light of the LORD. 2143
23:16 w **through** the city, O prostitute forgotten; 6015
30:21 "This is the way; w in it." 2143
35: 8 it will be for those *who* w *in* that Way; 2143
35: 9 But only the redeemed *will* w there, 2143
38:15 *I will* w **humbly** all my years because 1844
40:31 *they will* w and not be faint. 2143
42: 5 and life to those *who* w on it: 2143
43: 2 When *you* w through the fire, 2143
50:11 w in the light of your fires and of 2143
51:23 'Fall prostrate that *we may* w **over** you.' 6296
57: 2 *Those who* w uprightly enter into peace; 2143
59: 9 for brightness, but *we* w in deep shadows. 2143
65: 2 who w *in* ways not good, 2143
Jer 6:16 ask where the good way is, and w in it, 2143
6:16 But you said, *'We will* not w in it.' 2143
6:25 not go out to the fields or w on the roads, 2143
7:23 W in all the ways I command you, 2143
10: 5 they must be carried because *they* cannot w. 7575
18:15 They *made* them w *in* bypaths and on roads 2143
La 3: 2 He has driven me away and **made** me w 2143
4:18 so we *could* not w in our streets. 2143
Eze 36:12 *I will* **cause** people, my people Israel, **to** w 2143
Da 4:37 those *who* w in pride he is able to humble. 10207
Hos 11: 3 It was I *who* **taught** Ephraim **to** w, 8078
14: 9 the righteous w in them, but the rebellious 2143
Am 3: 3 *Do* two w together unless they have agreed 2143
Mic 2: 3 *You will* no longer w proudly, 2143
4: 2 so that *we may* w in his paths." 2143
4: 5 the nations *may* w in the name of their gods; 2143
4: 5 we *will* w in the name of the LORD 2143
6: 8 and to love mercy and *to* w humbly 2143
Zep 1:17 the people and *they will* w like blind men, 2143
Zec 3: 7 'If *you will* w in my ways 2143
10:12 in the LORD and in his name *they will* w," 2143
Mt 9: 5 or to say, 'Get up and w'? *4344*
11: 5 The blind receive sight, the lame w, *4344*
Mk 2: 9 or to say, 'Get up, take your mat and w'? *4344*
12:38 They like *to* w **around** in flowing robes and *4344*
Lk 5:23 or to say, 'Get up and w'? *4344*
7:22 The blind receive sight, the lame w, *4344*
11:44 which men w over without knowing it." *4344*
20:46 like *to* w **around** in flowing robes and love *4344*
24:17 you discussing together *as you* w **along**?" *4344*
Jn 5: 8 Pick up your mat and w." *4344*
5:11 'Pick up your mat and w.' " *4344*
5:12 to pick it up and w?" *4344*
8:12 follows me *will* never w in darkness, *4344*
12:35 W while you have the light, *4344*
Ac 1:12 a **Sabbath day's** w **from** the city.
1584+2400+3847+4879
3: 6 In the name of Jesus Christ of Nazareth, w." *4344*
3: 8 He jumped to his feet and *began to* w. *4344*
3:12 or godliness we had made this man w? *4344*
14:10 At that, the *man* jumped up and *began to* w. *4344*
Ro 4:12 not only are circumcised but who also w in *5123*
2Co 6:16 "I will live with them and w **among** them, *1853*
Col 3: 7 You used to w in these ways, *4344*
1Jn 1: 6 fellowship with him yet w in the darkness, *4344*
1: 7 But if *we* w in the light, as he is in the light, *4344*
2: 6 claims to live in him must w as Jesus did. *4344*
2Jn 1: 6 that *we* w in obedience to his commands. *4344*
1: 6 his command is that *you* w in love. *4344*
3Jn 1: 3 to the truth and how you *continue to* w in *4344*
Rev 3: 4 *They will* w with me, dressed in white, *4344*
9:20 idols that cannot see or hear or w. *4344*
21:24 The nations *will* w by its light, *4344*

WALKED (60) [WALK]

Ge 5:22 Enoch w with God 300 years 2143
5:24 Enoch w with God; then he was no more, 2143
6: 9 and he w with God. 2143
9:23 then *they* w *in* backward 2143
18:16 and Abraham w **along** with them 2143
24:40 'The LORD, before whom *I have* w, 2143
48:15 my fathers Abraham and Isaac w, 2143
Ex 15:19 Israelites w through the sea on dry ground. 2143
Jos 14: 9 'The land on which your feet *have* w will 2005
Jdg 2:17 from the way in which their fathers *had* w, 2143
1Sa 19:23 and *he* w **along** prophesying until 2143+2143
2Sa 3:31 King David *himself* w behind the bier. 2143
11: 2 up from his bed and w **around** on the roof 2143
1Ki 11:33 and *have* not w in my ways, 2143
16: 2 but *you* w in the ways of Jeroboam 2143
16:26 *He* w in all the ways of Jeroboam son 2143
22:43 In everything *he* w in the ways of his father 2143
22:52 because *he* w in the ways of his father 2143
2Ki 2: 6 So the two of them w **on.** 2143
4:35 Elisha turned away and w back and forth in 2143
8:18 *He* w in the ways of the kings of Israel, 2143
8:27 *He* w in the ways of the house of Ahab 2143
16: 3 *He* w in the ways of the kings of Israel and 2143
20: 3 how *I have* w before you faithfully and 2143
21:21 *He* w in all the ways of his father; 2143
22: 2 and w in all the ways of his father David, 2143
2Ch 17: 3 because in his early years *he* w in the ways 2143
20:32 *He* w in the ways of his father Asa and did 2143
21: 6 *He* w in the ways of the kings of Israel, 2143
21:12 *'You have* not w in the ways of your father 2143
21:13 But *you have* w in the ways of the kings 2143
22: 3 He too w in the ways of the house of Ahab, 2143
27: 6 because he w steadfastly before the LORD 2006
28: 2 *He* w in the ways of the kings of Israel and 2143
34: 2 in the eyes of the LORD and w in the ways 2143
Est 2:11 Every day he w **back and forth** near 2143
Job 29: 3 and by his light *I* w *through* darkness! 2143
31: 5 "If *I have* w in falsehood 2143
38:16 of the sea or w in the recesses of the deep? 2143
Ps 55:14 *as we* w with the throng at the house 2143
Ecc 4:15 and w under the sun followed the youth, 2143
Isa 38: 3 how *I have* w before you faithfully and 2143
51:23 like a street to *be* w **over.**" 6296
Jer 34:18 like the calf they cut in two and then w 6296
34:19 who w between the pieces of the calf, 6296
Eze 16:47 *You* not only w in their ways 2143
28:14 *you* w among the fiery stones. 2143
Mal 2: 6 *He* w with me in peace and uprightness, 2143
Mt 14:29 w on the water and came toward Jesus. *4344*
Mk 1:16 *As* Jesus w **beside** the Sea of Galilee, *4135*
2:12 took his mat and w **out** in full view *2002*
2:14 *As he* w **along,** he saw Levi son of *4135*
2:23 and as his disciples w **along,** *3847+4472*
5:42 and w around (she was twelve years old). *4344*
Lk 4:30 But he w **right through** the crowd and went *1451*
24:15 Jesus himself came up and w **along with** *5233*
Jn 5: 9 he picked up his mat and w. *4344*
Ac 12:10 When *they had* w the length of one street, *4601*
14: 8 who was lame from birth and *had* never w. *4344*
17:23 For *as I* w **around** and looked carefully *1451*

WALKING (36) [WALK]

Ge 3: 8 the sound of the LORD God *as he was* w in 2143
Ex 2: 5 her attendants *were* w along the river bank. 2143
Dt 8: 6 w in his ways and revering him. 2143
1Sa 17:39 over the tunic and tried w **around,** 2143
2Sa 6: 4 and Ahio *was* w in front of it. 2143
1Ki 3: 3 the LORD by w according to the statutes 2143
15:26 w in the ways of his father and in his sin, 2143
15:34 w in the ways of Jeroboam and in his sin, 2143
16:19 in the eyes of the LORD and w in the ways 2143
18: 7 As Obadiah was w **along,** Elijah met him.
928+2006+2021
2Ki 2:11 were w **along** and talking *together,* 2143+2143
2:23 As he *was* w along the road, 6590
2Ch 11:17 w in the ways of David and Solomon 2143
Pr 7: 8 w **along** *in* the direction of her house 7575
Isa 3:16 w **along** with outstretched necks, 2143
9: 2 The people w in darkness have seen 2143
26: 8 Yes, LORD, w in the way of your laws, NIH
Da 3:25 I see four men w **around** in the fire, 10207
4:29 as the king was w on the roof of the royal 10207
Mt 4:18 *As* Jesus *was* w beside the Sea of Galilee, *4344*
14:25 Jesus went out to them, w on the lake. *4344*
14:26 When the disciples saw him w on the lake, *4344*
15:31 the lame w and the blind seeing. *4344*
24: 1 and *was* w **away** when his disciples came *4513*
Mk 6:48 he went out to them, w on the lake. *4344*
6:49 but when they saw him w on the lake, *4344*
8:24 they look like trees w **around."** *4344*
11:27 and *while* Jesus *was* w in the temple courts, *4344*
16:12 of them *while they were* w in the country. *4344*
Lk 9:57 *As* they *were* w along the road, *4513*
Jn 6:19 w on the water; and they were terrified. *4344*
10:23 the temple area w in Solomon's Colonnade. *4344*
Ac 3: 8 w and jumping, and praising God. *4344*
3: 9 all the people saw him w and praising God, *4344*
2Jn 1: 4 to find some of your children w in the truth, *4344*
3Jn 1: 4 to hear that my children *are* w in the truth. *4344*

WALKS (15) [WALK]

Ex 21:19 if the other gets up and w **around** outside 2143
Lev 11:42 whether it moves on its belly or w 2143
Pr 10: 9 The man of integrity w securely, 2143
13:20 *He who* w with the wise grows wise, 2143
28:26 but *he who* w in wisdom is kept safe. 2143
Ecc 2:14 while the fool w in the darkness; 2143
10: 3 Even as *he* w along the road, 2143
Isa 33:15 *He who* w righteously 2143
50:10 Let *him* who w *in* the dark, 2143
59: 8 no one *who* w in them will know peace. 2005
Jn 11: 9 A man who w by day will not stumble, *4344*
11:10 It is when he w by night that he stumbles, *4344*
12:35 The man who w in the dark does not know *4344*
1Jn 2:11 the darkness and w **around** in the darkness; *4344*
Rev 2: 1 and w among the seven golden lampstands: *4344*

WALL (169) [WALLED, WALLS]

Ge 49:22 whose branches climb over a w. 8803
Ex 14:22 a w *of* water on their right and on their left. 2570
14:29 a w *of* water on their right and on their left. 2570
15: 8 The surging waters stood firm like a w; 5603
Lev 11:30 the w **lizard,** the skink and the chameleon. 4321
Lev 14:37 to be deeper than the surface of the w, 7815
Nu 22:25 she pressed close to the w, 7815
35: 4 fifteen hundred feet from the town w. 7815
Jos 2:15 house she lived in was part of the city w. 2570
6: 5 then the w *of* the city will collapse and 2570
6:20 a loud shout, the w collapsed; 2570
1Sa 18:11 saying to himself, "I'll pin David to the w." 7815
19:10 Saul tried to pin him to the w with his spear, 7815
19:10 as Saul drove the spear into the w. 7815
20:25 He sat in his customary place by the w, 7815
25:16 Night and day they were a w around us all 2570
31:10 and fastened his body to the w 2570
31:12 the bodies of Saul and his sons from the w 2570
2Sa 11:20 know they would shoot arrows from the w? 2570
11:21 an upper millstone on him from the w, 2570
11:21 Why did you get so close to the w?' 2570
11:24 at your servants from the w, 2570
18:24 up to the roof of the gateway by the w. 2570
20:15 they were battering the w to bring it down, 2570
20:21 His head will be thrown to you from the w." 2570
22:30 with my God I can scale a w. 8803
1Ki 3: 1 and the w around Jerusalem. 2570
6:27 The wing of one cherub touched one w, 7815
6:27 the wing of the other touched the other w, 7815
7:12 The great courtyard was surrounded by a w NIH
9:15 the supporting terraces, the w *of* Jerusalem, 2570
11:27 and had filled in the **gap in the** w *of* the city 7288
20:30 the w collapsed on twenty-seven thousand 2570
21:23 'Dogs will devour Jezebel by the w 2658
2Ki 3:27 and offered him as a sacrifice on the **city** w. 2570
6:26 the king of Israel was passing by on the w, 2570
6:30 As he went along the w, the people looked, 2570
9:33 of her blood spattered the w and the horses 7815
14:13 the w *of* Jerusalem from the Ephraim Gate 2570
18:26 in the hearing of the people on the w." 2570
18:27 and not to the men sitting on the w— 2570
20: 2 to the w and prayed to the LORD, 7815
25: 4 Then the city w was broken through, NIH
1Ch 11: 8 terraces to the **surrounding** *w,* AIT
2Ch 3:11 and touched the temple w, 7815
3:12 and touched the other temple w, 7815
25:23 the w *of* Jerusalem from the Ephraim Gate 2570
26: 9 the Valley Gate and at the **angle of the** w, 5243
27: 3 and did extensive work on the w *at* the hill 2570
32: 5 sections of the w and building towers on it. 2570
32: 5 He built another w outside that one 2570
32:18 the people of Jerusalem who were on the w, 2570
33:14 Afterward he rebuilt the outer w of the City 2570
36:19 to God's temple and broke down the w 2570
Ezr 9: 9 a w **of protection** in Judah and Jerusalem. 1555
Ne 1: 3 The w *of* Jerusalem is broken down, 2570
2: 8 the citadel by the temple and for the city w 2570
2:15 up the valley by night, examining the w. 2570
2:17 Come, let us rebuild the w *of* Jerusalem, 2570
3: 8 as far as the Broad W. 2570
3:13 also repaired five hundred yards of the w 2570
3:15 also repaired the w *of* the Pool of Siloam, 2570
3:27 from the great projecting tower to the w 2570
4: 1 that we were rebuilding the w, 2570
4: 2 *Will they* **restore** their w? 6441
4: 3 he would break down their w *of* stones!" 2570
4: 6 the w till all of it reached half its height, 2570
4:10 that we cannot rebuild the w." 2570
4:13 the people behind the lowest points of the w 2570
4:15 we all returned to the w, 2570
4:17 who were building the w. 2570
4:19 from each other along the w. 2570
5:16 I devoted myself to the work on this w. 2570
6: 1 of our enemies that I had rebuilt the w and 2570
6: 6 and therefore you are building the w. 2570
6:15 So the w was completed on the twenty-fifth 2570
7: 1 After the w had been rebuilt and I had set 2570
12:27 At the dedication of the w *of* Jerusalem, 2570
12:30 purified the people, the gates and the w. 2570
12:31 the leaders of Judah go up on top of the w. 2570
12:31 to proceed on top of the w to the right, 2570
12:37 the w and passed above the house of David 2570
12:38 I followed them on top of the w, 2570
12:38 the Tower of the Ovens to the Broad W, 2570
13:21 "Why do you spend the night by the w? 2570
Ps 18:29 with my God I can scale a w. 8803
62: 3 this leaning w, this tottering fence? 7815
78:13 he made the water stand firm like a w. 5603
Pr 18:11 they imagine it an unscalable w. 2570
24:31 and the stone w was in ruins. 1555
Ecc 10: 8 whoever breaks through a w may be bitten 1555
SS 2: 9 There he stands behind our w, 4185
8: 9 If she is a w, we will build towers of silver 2570
8:10 I am a w, and my breasts are like towers. 2570
Isa 2:15 for every lofty tower and every fortified w, 2570
5: 5 I will break down its w, 1555
22:10 and tore down houses to strengthen the w. 2570
25: 4 like a storm driving against a w 7815
30:13 this sin will become for you like a high w, 2570
36:11 in the hearing of the people on the w." 2570
36:12 and not to the men sitting on the w— 2570
38: 2 to the w and prayed to the LORD, 7815
59:10 Like the blind we grope along the w, 7815
Jer 1:18 an iron pillar and a bronze w to stand 2570
15:20 I will make you a w to this people, 2570
15:20 a fortified w of bronze; NIH
21: 4 who are outside the w besieging you. 2570
39: 2 the city w was broken through. NIH
51:44 And the w *of* Babylon will fall. 2570
51:58 "Babylon's thick w will be leveled 2570
52: 7 Then the city w was broken through, NIH
La 2: 8 The LORD determined to tear down the w 2570

La 2:18 O w *of* the Daughter of Zion, 2570
Eze 4: 3 as an iron **w** between you and the city 7815
8: 7 I looked, and I saw a hole in the **w.** 7815
8: 8 "Son of man, now dig into the **w.**" 7815
8: 8 I dug into the **w** and saw a doorway there. 7815
12: 5 through the **w** and take your belongings out 7815
12: 7 Then in the evening I dug through the **w** 7815
12:12 and a hole will be dug in the **w** for him 7815
13: 5 You have not gone up to the breaks in the **w** 1555
13:10 and because, when a **flimsy w** is built, 2666
13:12 When the **w** collapses, 7815
13:14 I will tear down the **w** you have covered 7815
13:15 So I will spend my wrath against the **w** and 7815
13:15 "The **w** is gone and so are those who 7815
22:30 up the **w** and stand before me in the gap 1555
23:14 She saw men portrayed on a **w,** 7815
38:20 the cliffs will crumble and every **w** will fall 2570
40: 5 I saw a **w** completely surrounding 2570
40: 5 He measured the **w;** 1230
40:12 of each alcove was a **w** one cubit high, 1473
40:13 from the **top of the** *rear* **w** 1511
40:40 the outside **w** of the portico of the gateway, 4190
40:43 were attached to the **w** all around. 1074
41: 5 Then he measured the **w** *of* the temple; 7815
41: 6 the **w** of the temple to serve as supports for 7815
41: 6 the supports were not inserted into the **w** *of* 7815
41: 9 The outer **w** of the side rooms 7815
41:12 The **w** *of* the building was five cubits thick 7815
41:16 The floor, the **w** up to the windows, NIH
41:20 and palm trees were carved on the **w** *of* 7815
42: 1 and opposite the **outer w** on the north side. 1230
42: 7 There was an outer **w** parallel to the rooms 1555
42:10 along the length of the **w** *of* the outer court, 1555
42:10 and opposite the **outer w,** 1230
42:12 to the corresponding **w** extending eastward, 1556
42:20 It had a **w** around it, 2570
43: 8 with only a **w** between me and them, 7815
Da 5: 5 and wrote on the plaster of the **w,** 10376
Hos 2: 6 *I will* **w** her **in** so that she cannot find 1553+1555
Joel 2: 9 they run along the **w.** 2570
Am 4: 3 straight out through **breaks in the w,** 7288
5:19 and rested his hand on the **w** only to have 7815
7: 7 by a **w** that had been built true to plumb, 2570
Na 2: 5 They dash to the **city w;** 2570
3: 8 The river was her defense, the waters her **w.** 2570
Hab 2:11 The stones of the **w** will cry out, 7815
Zec 2: 5 And I myself will be a **w** *of* fire around it,' 2570
Mt 21:33 He put a **w** around it, *5850*
Mk 12: 1 He put a **w** around it, *5850*
Ac 9:25 in a basket through an opening in the **w.** *5446*
23: 3 "God will strike you, *you* whitewashed **w!** *5526*
2Co 11:33 in the **w** and slipped through his hands. *5446*
Eph 2:14 the **dividing w** of hostility, *3546*
Rev 21:12 It had a great, high **w** with twelve gates, *5446*
21:14 The **w** of the city had twelve foundations, *5446*
21:17 He measured its **w** and it was 144 cubits *5446*
21:18 The **w** was made of jasper, *5446*

WALLED (4) [WALL]

Lev 25:29 " 'If a man sells a house in a **w** city, 2570
25:30 the house in the **w** city shall belong
permanently to the buyer 2257+2570+4200
1Ki 4:13 Argob in Bashan and its sixty large **w** cities 2570
La 3: 7 *He has* **w** me in so I cannot escape; 1553

WALLOW (1) [WALLOWING]

Jer 48:26 *Let* Moab **w** in her vomit; 6216

WALLOWING (2) [WALLOW]

2Sa 20:12 Amasa **lay w** in his blood in the middle of 1670
2Pe 2:22 "A sow that is washed goes back to her **w** in *3243*

WALLS (98) [WALL]

Lev 14:37 He is to examine the mildew on the **w,** 7815
14:39 If the mildew has spread on the **w,** 7815
14:41 the inside **w** of the house scraped and NIH
25:31 houses in villages without **w** around them 2570
Nu 22:24 two vineyards, with **w** on both sides. 1555
Dt 1:28 the cities are large, with **w** up to the sky. 1290
3: 5 All these cities were fortified with high **w** 2570
9: 1 with large cities that have **w** up to the sky. 1290
28:52 until the high fortified **w** in which you trust 2570
1Ki 4:33 to the hyssop that grows out of **w.** 7815
6: 5 Against the **w** of the main hall 7815
6: 6 be inserted into the temple **w.** 7815
6:15 He lined its interior **w** with cedar boards, 7815
6:29 On the **w** all around the temple, 7815
2Ki 25: 4 at night through the gate between the *two* **w** 2570
25:10 broke down the **w** around Jerusalem. 2570
1Ch 29: 4 for the overlaying of the **w** *of* the buildings, 7815
2Ch 3: 7 **w** and doors of the temple with gold, 7815
3: 7 and he carved cherubim on the **w.** 7815
8: 5 with **w** and with gates and bars, 2570
14: 7 he said to Judah, "and put **w** around them, 2570
26: 6 the Philistines and broke down the **w** 2570
Ezr 4:12 They are restoring the **w** and repairing 10703
4:13 if this city is built and its **w** are restored, 10703
4:16 if this city is built and its **w** are restored, 10703
5: 8 and placing the timbers in the **w.** 10376
Ne 2:13 examining the **w** *of* Jerusalem, 2570
4: 7 the repairs to Jerusalem's **w** had gone ahead 2570
Ps 51:18 build up the **w** *of* Jerusalem. 2570
55:10 Day and night they prowl about on its **w;** 2570
80:12 Why have you broken down its **w** so 1555
89:40 You have broken through all his **w** 1556
122: 7 May there be peace within your **w** 2658
144:14 There will be no **breaching of w,** 7288
Pr 25:28 Like a city whose **w** are broken down is 2570
SS 5: 7 those watchmen of the **w!** 2570
Isa 22: 5 a day of battering down **w** and of crying out 7815
22:11 You built a reservoir between the *two* **w** for 2570
25:12 He will bring down your high fortified **w** 2570
26: 1 God makes salvation its **w** and ramparts. 2570
49:16 your **w** are ever before me. 2570
54:12 and all your **w** of precious stones. 1473
56: 5 within my temple and its **w** a memorial and 2570
58:12 **Repairer of** Broken **W,** 1553
60:10 "Foreigners will rebuild your **w,** 2570
60:18 but you will call your **w** Salvation 2570
62: 6 I have posted watchmen on your **w,** 2570
Jer 1:15 against all her surrounding **w** and against all 2570
39: 4 through the gate between the *two* **w,** 2570
39: 8 and broke down the **w** *of* Jerusalem. 2570
49: 3 rush here and there inside the **w,** 1555
49:27 "I will set fire to the **w** *of* Damascus; 2570
50:15 her towers fall, her **w** are torn down. 2570
51:12 Lift up a banner against the **w** *of* Babylon! 2570
52: 7 at night through the gate between the *two* **w** 2570
52:14 of the imperial guard broke down all the **w** 2570
La 2: 7 over to the enemy the **w** *of* her palaces; 2570
2: 8 He made ramparts and **w** lament; 2570
Eze 5:12 by the sword **outside** your **w;** 6017
8:10 and I saw portrayed all over the **w** all kinds 7815
26: 4 They will destroy the **w** *of* Tyre and pull 2570
26: 8 to your **w** and raise his shields against you. NIH
26: 9 against your **w** and demolish your towers 2570
26:10 Your **w** will tremble at the noise of 2570
26:10 a city whose **w** have been broken through. NIH
26:12 down your **w** and demolish your fine houses 2570
27:10 and helmets on your **w,** NIH
27:11 Men of Arvad and Helech manned your **w** 2570
27:11 They hung their shields around your **w;** 2570
33:30 by the **w** and at the doors of the houses, 7815
38:11 of them living without **w** and without gates 2570
40: 7 and the projecting **w** between NIH
40:10 of the **projecting w** on each side had 382
40:14 the faces of the **projecting w** all around the 382
40:16 The alcoves and the **projecting w** inside 382
40:16 of the **projecting w** were decorated 382
40:21 its **projecting w** and its portico had 382
40:26 the faces of the **projecting w** on each side. 382
40:29 its **projecting w** and its portico had 382
40:33 its **projecting w** and its portico had 382
40:36 its **projecting w** and its portico, 382
40:48 and its **projecting w** were three cubits wide 4190
41: 2 and the **projecting w** on each side 4190
41: 3 and the projecting **w** on each side NIH
41:13 with its **w** were also a hundred cubits long. 7815
41:17 and on the **w** at regular intervals all around 7815
41:25 and palm trees like those carved on the **w,** 7815
Joel 2: 7 they scale **w** like soldiers. 2570
Am 1: 7 I will send fire upon the **w** *of* Gaza 2570
1:10 I will send fire upon the **w** *of* Tyre 2570
1:14 I will set fire to the **w** *of* Rabbah 2570
Mic 7:11 The day for building your **w** will come, 1556
Na 3:17 like swarms of locusts that settle in the **w** on 1556
Zec 2: 4 'Jerusalem will be a **city without w** because 7252
Lk 19:44 you and the children within your **w.** *NIG*
Heb 11:30 By faith the **w** of Jericho fell, *5446*
Rev 21:15 to measure the city, its gates and its **w.** *5446*
21:19 the city **w** were decorated with every kind *5446*

WANDER (17) [WANDERED, WANDERER, WANDERERS, WANDERING, WANDERS]

Ge 20:13 And when God **had** me **w** from my father's 9494
Nu 32:13 *he* **made** them **w** in the desert forty years, 5675
2Sa 15:20 today *shall I* **make** you **w about** with us, 5675
2Ki 21: 8 I will not again **make** the feet of the
Israelites **w** from the land 5653
Job 38:41 when its young cry out to God and **w about** 9494
Ps 59:11 In your might **make** them **w about,** 5675
59:15 They **w about** for food and howl if 5675
107:40 **made** them **w** in a trackless waste. 9494
Pr 17:24 but a fool's eyes **w** to the ends of the earth. NIH
Isa 63:17 *do you* **make** us **w** from your ways 9494
Jer 14:10 "They greatly love to **w;** 5675
31:22 How long *will you* **w,** 2811
La 4:15 When they flee and **w about,** 5675
Am 8:12 from sea to sea and **w** from north to east, 8763
Zec 10: 2 *the people* **w** like sheep oppressed for lack 5825
Mt 18:13 about the ninety-nine that *did* not **w off.** *4414*
Jas 5:19 if one of you *should* **w** from the truth *4414*

WANDERED (14) [WANDER]

Ge 21:14 She went on her way and **w** in the desert 9494
1Ch 16:20 *they* **w** from nation to nation, 2143
Ps 105:13 *they* **w** from nation to nation, 2143
107: 4 *Some* **w** in desert wastelands, 9494
Jer 50: 6 *They* **w** over mountain and hill 2143
Eze 34: 6 My sheep **w** over all the mountains and 8706
44:10 when Israel went astray and who **w** from me 9494
Mt 18:12 and go to look for the one that **w off?** *4414*
1Ti 1: 6 Some *have* **w away from** these and turned *1762*
6:10 eager for money, *have* **w from** the faith *675*
6:21 and in so doing *have* **w** from the faith. *846*
2Ti 2:18 who *have* **w away** from the truth. *846*
Heb 11:38 *They* **w** in deserts and mountains, *4414*
2Pe 2:15 and **w off** to follow the way of Balaam son *4414*

WANDERER (3) [WANDER]

Ge 4:12 You will be a restless **w** on the earth." 5653
4:14 I will be a restless **w** on the earth, 5653
Isa 58: 7 and to provide the poor **w** with shelter— 5291

WANDERERS (1) [WANDER]

Hos 9:17 they will be **w** among the nations. 5610

WANDERING (10) [WANDER]

Ge 37:15 a man found him **w around** in the fields 9494
Ex 14: 3 **w around** the land **in confusion,** 1003
23: 4 across your enemy's ox or donkey **w off,** 9494
Dt 26: 5 "My father *was* a **w** Aramean, 6
Job 12:24 *he* **sends** them **w** through a trackless waste. 9494
Ps 109:10 *May* his children *be* **w** beggars; 5675
La 1: 7 her affliction and **w** Jerusalem remembers 5291
3:19 I remember my affliction and my **w,** 5291
Hos 8: 9 up to Assyria like a wild donkey **w alone.** 969
Jude 1:13 **w** stars, for whom the blackest darkness *4417*

WANDERS (3) [WANDER]

Job 15:23 He **w about**—food for vultures; 5610
18: 8 His feet thrust him into a net and *he* **w** into 2143
Mt 18:12 and one of them **w away,** *4414*

WANE (1)

Isa 60:20 and your moon *will* **w** no more; 665

WANT (175) [WANTED, WANTING, WANTS]

Ge 24: 3 *I* **w** you **to swear** by the LORD, 8678
29:21 and *I* **w** *to* **lie with** her." AIT
42:36 and now *you* **w** *to* **take** Benjamin. AIT
Ex 16: 8 **all** the bread you **w** in the morning, 8425
16:23 So bake what *you* **w** *to* **bake** AIT
16:23 to bake and boil what *you* **w** *to* **boil.** AIT
21: 5 and children and *do* not **w** *to* **go** free,' AIT
Lev 26: 5 you will eat **all** the food you **w** 8427
Nu 16:13 And now *you* also **w** *to* **lord it** over us? AIT
20:19 *We* only **w** *to* **pass through** on foot— AIT
Dt 12:15 and eat as much of the meat as you **w,** 205
12:20 then you may eat as much of it as you **w.** 205
12:21 you may eat as much of them as you **w.** 205
15:16 *"I do* not **w** *to* **leave** you," AIT
23:24 you may eat **all** the grapes you **w,** 8427
25: 7 man *does* not **w** to marry his brother's wife, 2911
25: 8 *"I do* not **w** to marry her," 2911
Jdg 9:15 you really **w** *to* **anoint** me king over you, AIT
1Sa 2:16 and then take whatever you **w,"** 203
8:19 "We **w** a king over us. 2118[S]
12:12 'No, we **w** a king to rule over us'— NIH
20: 4 "Whatever you **w** me to do, I'll do for you." 606
21: 9 If *you* **w** it, take it; 4374
2Sa 14:32 Now then, *I* **w** *to* **see** the king's face, AIT
18:22 "My son, why *do* you **w** *to* **go?** AIT
18:23 He said, "Come what may, *I* **w** *to* **run."** AIT
20:19 Why *do you* **w** *to* **swallow up** AIT
21: 4 "What *do* you **w** me to do for you?" 606
24: 3 But why *does* my lord the king **w** to do such 2911
1Ki 1:16 "What is it you **w?"** 4200
3: 5 "Ask for whatever you **w** me to give you." NIH
5: 8 and will do all you **w** in providing the cedar 2914
11:22 "What have you lacked here that you **w** 1335
1Ch 21: 3 Why *does* my lord **w to do** this? 1335
2Ch 1: 7 "Ask for whatever you **w** me to give you." NIH
Ne 2: 4 The king said to me, "What is it you **w?"** 1335
Job 24:16 *they* **w** nothing **to do with** the light. 3359
30: 3 Haggard from **w** and hunger, 2895
33:32 speak up, for *I* **w** you to be cleared. 2911
37:20 Should he be told that *I* **w** *to* **speak?** AIT
Ps 23: 1 The LORD is my shepherd, *I shall* not *be*
in w. 2893
71:13 may *those who* **w to** harm me be covered 1335
Jer 40: 4 but if you do **not w** to, then don't come.
928+6524+8273
42:22 and plague in the place where *you* **w** to go 2911
Eze 20:32 " 'You say, *"We w to* **be** like the nations, AIT
36:32 *I w* you *to* **know** that I am not doing this AIT
Da 2: 3 a dream that troubles me and I **w** NIH
3:18 But even if he does not, we *w* you *to* **know,** AIT
Mt 1:19 did not **w** to expose her to public disgrace *2527*
8:29 **"What do** you **w with** us, *2779+5515*
12:38 *we* **w** to see a miraculous sign from you." *2527*
13:28 *'Do you* **w** us to go and pull them up?' *2527*
15:32 *I do* not **w** to send them away hungry, *2527*
19:17 If *you* **w** to enter life, *2527*
19:21 Jesus answered, "If *you* **w** to be perfect, go, *2527*
20:14 *I* **w** to give the man who was hired last *2527*
20:15 to do what *I* **w** with my own money? *2527*
20:21 "What is it *you* **w?"** *2527*
20:32 "What *do you* **w** me to do for you?" *2527*
20:33 "Lord," they answered, "we **w** our sight." *2671*
26:17 "Where *do you* **w** us to make preparations *2527*
27:17 "Which one *do you* **w** me to release to you: *2527*
27:21 of the two *do you* **w** me to release to you?" *2527*
Mk 1:24 **"What do** you **w with** us, Jesus *2779+5515*
5: 7 **"What do** you **w with** me, Jesus, *2779+5515*
6:22 "Ask me for anything *you* **w,** *2527*
6:25 *"I* **w** you to give me right now the head *2527*
6:26 *he did* not **w** to refuse her. *2527*
7:24 a house and *did* not **w** anyone to know it; *2527*
7:27 "First let the children **eat all they w,"** *5963*
9:30 not **w** anyone to know where they were, *2527*
10:35 *"we* **w** you to do for us whatever we ask." *2527*

Mk 10:36 "What *do you* w me to do for you?" *2527*
10:51 "What *do you* w me to do for you?" *2527*
10:51 The blind man said, "Rabbi, I w to see." *2671*
14: 7 and you can help them any time *you* w. *2527*
14:12 "Where *do you* w us to go *2527*
15: 9 *"Do you* w me to release to you the king of *2527*
Lk 4: 6 and I can give it to anyone *I* w **to.** *2527*
4:34 **What do** you w **with** us, Jesus *2779+5515*
8:28 **"What do** you w **with** me, Jesus, *2779+5515*
9:54 *do you* w us to call fire down from heaven *2527*
16:26 those who w to go from here to you cannot, *2527*
18:41 "What *do you* w me to do for you?" *2527*
18:41 "Lord, I w to see," he replied. *2671*
19:14 *'We* don't w this man to be our king.' *2527*
19:27 of mine who *did* not w me to be king *2527*
22: 9 "Where *do you* w us to prepare for it?" *2527*
Jn 1:38 "What *do you* **w?"** *2426*
4:27 But no one asked, "What *do you* **w?"** *2426*
5: 6 he asked him, *"Do you* w to get well?" *2527*
6:67 "You *do* not w to leave too, do you?" *2527*
8:44 and *you* w to carry out your father's desire. *2527*
9:27 Why *do you* w to hear it again? *2527*
9:27 *Do you* w to become his disciples, too?" *2527*
17:24 *I* w those you have given me to be with me *2527*
18: 4 "Who is it *you* **w?"** *2426*
18: 7 Again he asked them, "Who is it *you* **w?"** *2426*
18:39 *Do you* w me to release 'the king of the *1089*
19:31 Because the Jews did not w the bodies left *NIG*
21:18 and lead you where *you do* not w to go." *2527*
21:22 "If *I* w him to remain alive until I return, *2527*
21:23 "If *I* w him to remain alive until I return, *2527*
Ac 7:26 why do you w to hurt each other?' *NIG*
7:28 *Do* you w to kill me as you killed *2527*
13:22 he will do everything I w him to do.' *2525*
13:38 *I* w you to know that through Jesus *1639*
16:37 now *do they* w *to* **get rid of** us quietly? *AIT*
17:20 and *we* w to know what they mean." *1089*
17:32 *"We* w *to* **hear** you again on this subject." *AIT*
19:39 there is anything further *you* **w to bring up,** *2118*
23:19 "What is it *you* w to tell me?" *2400*
28:22 But *we* w to hear what your views are, *546*
28:28 "Therefore *I* w you *to* **know** that God's *AIT*
Ro 1:13 *I do* not w you to be unaware, brothers, *2527*
7:15 For what *I* w to do I do not do, *2527*
7:16 And if I *do* not w to do, *2527*
7:19 For what I do is not the good *I* w to do; *2527*
7:19 no, the evil *I do* not w to do— *2527*
7:20 Now if I do what *I do* not w to do, *2527*
7:21 I w to do good, evil is right there with me. *2527*
11:25 not w you to be ignorant of this mystery, *2527*
13: 3 *Do you* w to be free from fear of the one *2527*
16:19 but *I* w you to be wise about what is good, *2527*
1Co 4: 8 Already *you* **have all you w!** *1639+3170*
7:28 and I w to spare you this. *NIG*
10: 1 *I do* not w you to be ignorant of the fact, *2527*
10:20 not w you to be participants with demons. *2527*
10:27 invites you to a meal and *you* w to go, *2527*
11: 3 Now *I* w you to realize that the head *2527*
12: 1 brothers, *I do* not w you to be ignorant. *2527*
14:35 If *they* w to inquire about something, *2527*
15: 1 *I* w *to* **remind** you **of** the gospel I preached *AIT*
16: 7 *I do* not w to see you now and make only *2527*
2Co 1: 8 *We do* not w you to be uninformed, *2527*
8: 1 *we* w you *to* **know about** the grace that God *AIT*
8: 8 but *I* w *to* **test** the sincerity of your love *AIT*
8:20 *We* w *to* **avoid** any criticism of the way we *AIT*
10: 9 not w to seem to be trying to frighten you *2671*
10:16 not w *to* **boast about** work already done *AIT*
11:12 from under those who w an opportunity to *2527*
12:14 what *I* w is not your possessions but you. *2426*
12:20 when I come I may not find you as *I* w you *2527*
12:20 and you may not find me as *you* w me *2527*
Gal 1:11 *I* w you *to* **know,** brothers, that the gospel *AIT*
4:17 What *they* w is to alienate you [from us], *2527*
4:21 Tell me, you who w to be under the law, *2527*
5:17 so that you do not do what *you* **w.** *2527*
6:12 Those who w to make a good impression *2527*
6:13 yet *they* w you to be circumcised *2527*
Php 1:12 Now *I* w you to know, brothers, *1089*
3:10 I w *to* **know** Christ and the power of his *AIT*
4:12 whether living in plenty or **in w.** *5728*
Col 2: 1 *I* w you to know how much I am struggling *2527*
1Th 4:13 *we do* not w you to be ignorant *2527*
1Ti 1: 7 *They* w to be teachers of the law, *2527*
2: 8 *I* w men everywhere to lift up holy hands *1089*
2: 9 I also w women to dress modestly, *NIG*
5:11 their dedication to Christ, *they* w to marry. *2527*
6: 9 People who w to get rich fall into temptation *1089*
2Ti 4: 3 to say **what** their itching ears **w to hear.** *198*
Tit 3: 8 And *I* w you to stress these things, *1089*
Phm 1:14 not w to do anything without your consent, *2527*
Heb 6:11 *We* w each of you to show this same *2121*
6:12 We do not w you to become lazy, *2671*
13:23 I *w you to* **know** that our brother Timothy *AIT*
Jas 2:20 *do you* w evidence that faith without deeds *2527*
4: 2 *You* w something but don't get it. *2121*
4: 2 but you cannot have what you w. *NIG*
2Pe 3: 2 I w *you to* **recall** the words spoken in the *AIT*
2Jn 1:12 but *I do* not w to use paper and ink. *1089*
3Jn 1:10 He also stops those who w to do so *1089*
1:13 but *I do* not w to do so with pen and ink. *2527*
Jude 1: 5 *I* w to remind you that the Lord delivered *1089*
Rev 11: 6 every kind of plague as often as *they* **w.** *2527*

WANTED (53) [WANT]

Ex 4:19 men who **w to kill** you are dead." 906+1335+5883
16: 3 and ate **all** the food we w, 8427
Ru 2:14 She ate **all** *she* w and had some left over. 8425
2Sa 3:17 "For some time *you have* **w to make** David your king. 1335+4200
3:19 house of Benjamin **w to do.** 928+3202+6524
1Ki 5:10 with all the cedar and pine logs he w, 2914
9:11 with all the cedar and pine and gold he w. 2914
13:33 Anyone *who* w to become a priest 2913
Est 2:13 Anything *she* w was given her to take 606
Ps 35:25 "Aha, **just what** we **w!"** 5883
71:24 for *those who* **w to** harm me have been put 1335
Ecc 2: 3 *I w to* **see** what was worthwhile for men AIT
Jer 49: 9 they not steal only **as much as** they **w?** 1896
Da 5:19 Those the king **w to** put to death, 10605
5:19 those *he* **w to** spare, he spared; 10605
5:19 those *he* **w to** promote, he promoted; 10605
5:19 and those *he* **w to** humble, he humbled. 10605
7:19 "Then *I* w to know the true meaning of 10605
7:20 I also w to know about the ten horns NIH
Ob 1: 5 they not steal only **as much as** they **w?** 1896
Jnh 4: 8 He w to die, and said, 906+5883+8626
Mt 14: 5 Herod w to kill John, *2527*
18:23 the kingdom of heaven is like a king who w *2527*
21:31 "Which of the two did what his father **w?"** *2525*
Mk 3:13 and called to him those he **w;** *2527*
6:19 a grudge against John and w to kill him. *2527*
Lk 10:24 and kings w to see what you see but did *2527*
10:29 But he w to justify himself, *2527*
19: 3 *He* w to see who Jesus was, *2426*
Jn 6:11 to those who were seated as much as *they* **w.** *2527*
7:44 Some w to seize him, *2527*
16:19 Jesus saw that *they* w to ask him about this, *2527*
18:28 *w to be able to* **eat** the Passover. *AIT*
21:18 and went where *you* **w;** *2527*
Ac 5:33 were furious and w to put them to death. *1089*
10:10 He became hungry and w something to eat, *2527*
13: 7 for Barnabas and Saul because he w to hear *2118*
14:13 to the city gates because *he* and the crowd w *2527*
15:37 Barnabas w to take John, also called Mark, *1089*
16: 3 Paul w to take him along on the journey, *2527*
18:27 When Apollos w to go to Achaia, *1089*
19:30 Paul w to appear before the crowd, *1089*
22:30 *since* the commander w to find out *1089*
23:28 *I* w to know why they were accusing him, *1089*
24:27 Felix w to grant a favor to the Jews, *2527*
27:13 they thought they had obtained what they **w;** *4606*
27:38 When *they had* **eaten as much as** *they* **w,** *3170*
27:43 But the centurion w to spare Paul's life *1089*
28:18 They examined me and w to release me, *1089*
1Co 12:18 every one of them, just as *he* w them to be. *2527*
1Th 2:18 For *we* w to come to you— *2527*
Heb 6:17 Because God w to make the unchanging *1089*
12:17 *when he* w to inherit this blessing, *2527*

WANTING (10) [WANT]

Da 5:27 been weighed on the scales and found **w.** 10276
Mt 12:46 stood outside, w to speak to him. *2426*
12:47 standing outside, w to speak to you." *2426*
Mk 15:15 **W** to satisfy the crowd, Pilate released *1089*
Lk 8:20 standing outside, w to see you." *2527*
23: 8 for a long time he had been w to see him. *2527*
23:20 **W** to release Jesus, Pilate appealed to them *2527*
Ac 23:15 the pretext of w more accurate information *3516*
23:20 the pretext of w more accurate information *3516*
2Pe 3: 9 patient with you, not w anyone to perish, *1089*

WANTON (2)

Isa 47: 8 "Now then, listen, you w *creature,* 6349
Na 3: 4 all because of the w **lust** *of* a harlot, 2393

WANTS (36) [WANT]

Ge 19: 9 now *he w to* **play the judge!** AIT
43:18 He w to attack us and overpower us NIH
Ex 12:48 *who w to* **celebrate** the LORD's Passover AIT
Nu 6: 2 *w to* **make a special vow,** AIT
9:14 *who w to* **celebrate** the LORD's Passover AIT
Ru 3:13 and in the morning if *he w to* **redeem,** good; AIT
1Sa 18:25 'The king w no other price for 2914
Jer 22:28 broken pot, an object no one **w?** 2914
48:38 like a jar that no one **w,"** 2914
Eze 46: 7 the lambs as much as he **w to give,** 3338+5952
Mt 5:40 someone w to sue you and take your tunic, *2527*
5:42 and do not turn away from the one who w *2527*
16:25 For whoever w to save his life will lose it, *2527*
20:26 whoever w to become great among you *2527*
20:27 whoever w to be first must be your slave— *2527*
27:43 Let God rescue him now if *he* w him, *2527*
Mk 8:35 For whoever w to save his life will lose it, *2527*
9:35 "If anyone w to be first, he must be *2527*
10:43 whoever w to become great among you *2527*
10:44 whoever w to be first must be slave of all. *2527*
Lk 5:39 no one after drinking old wine w the new, *2527*
9:24 For whoever w to save his life will lose it, *2527*
12:47 not do what his master w will be beaten *2525*
13:31 Herod w to kill you." *2527*
14:28 "Suppose one of you w to build a tower. *2527*
Jn 7: 4 No one who w to become a public figure *2426*
Ro 9:18 Therefore God has mercy on whom *he* w *2527*
9:18 and he hardens whom *he* w to harden. *2527*
1Co 7:36 he should do as *he* **w.** *2527*
11:16 If anyone w to be contentious about this, *1506*
1Ti 2: 4 who w all men to be saved and to come to *2527*
2Ti 2: 4 he w to please his commanding officer. *2671*
3:12 everyone who w to live a godly life *2527*
Jas 3: 4 by a very small rudder wherever the pilot w *1089*
1Pe 5: 2 you are willing, as God w you to be; *NIG*
Rev 11: 5 how anyone who w to harm them must die. *2527*

WAR (134) [WARFARE, WARRIOR, WARRIOR'S, WARRIORS, WARS]

Ge 14: 2 **went to** w *against* Bera king of 4878+6913
31:26 carried off my daughters like captives in w. 2995
Ex 1:10 if w breaks out, will join our enemies, 4878
13:17 For God said, "If they face w, 4878
17:16 at w against the Amalekites from generation 4878
32:17 "There is the sound of w in the camp." 4878
Nu 31: 3 to w against the Midianites and to carry out 7372
32: 6 "Shall your countrymen go to w 4878
Dt 2: 5 *Do* not **provoke** them **to w,** 1741
2: 9 the Moabites or provoke them to w, 4878
2:19 do not harass them or **provoke** them **to w,** 1741
4:34 by miraculous signs and wonders, by w, 4878
20: 1 to w against your enemies and see horses 4878
20:20 to build siege works until the city **at w** 4878+6913
21:10 When you go to w against your enemies 4878
24: 5 not be sent to w or have any other duty laid 7372
Jos 4:13 the LORD to the plains of Jericho for w. 4878
6:10 *"Do* not **give a w cry,** 8131
9: 2 came together to **make** w against Joshua 4309
11:18 Joshua waged w against all these kings for 4878
11:20 to wage w against Israel, 4878
11:23 Then the land had rest from **w.** 4878
14:15 Then the land had rest from **w.** 4878
22:12 of Israel gathered at Shiloh to go to w 7372
22:33 about going to w against them to devastate 7372
Jdg 3:10 he became Israel's judge and went to **w.** 4878
5: 8 chose new gods, w came to the city gates, 4311
11: 4 when the Ammonites **made** w on Israel, 4309
11:27 but you are doing me wrong by **waging w** 4309
21:22 we did not get wives for them during the w, 4878
1Sa 8:12 to make weapons of w and equipment 4878
14:52 All the days of Saul there was bitter w with 4878
15:18 **make** w on them until you have wiped them 4309
17: 1 the Philistines gathered their forces for w 4878
17:13 oldest sons had followed Saul to the **w:** 4878
17:20 to its battle positions, shouting the **w cry.** 4878
19: 8 Once more w broke out, 4878
2Sa 1:27 The weapons of w have perished!" 4878
3: 1 The w between the house of Saul and 4878
3: 6 During the w between the house of Saul and 4878
8:10 who had been **at w with** Tou. 408+4878
11: 1 at the time when kings **go off to w,** 3655
11: 7 the soldiers were and how the w was going. 4878
1Ki 8:44 your people go to w against their enemies, 4878
12:21 to **make** w against the house of Israel and 4309
15: 6 There was w between Rehoboam and 4878
15: 7 There was w between Abijah and Jeroboam. 4878
15:16 There was w between Asa and Baasha king 4878
15:32 There was w between Asa and Baasha king 4878
20:18 if they have come out for w, 4878
22: 1 For three years there was no w 4878
22: 6 "Shall I go to w against Ramoth Gilead, 4878
22:15 shall we go to w against Ramoth Gilead, 4878
2Ki 6: 8 the king of Aram was **at** w with Israel. 4309
8:28 Ahaziah went with Joram son of Ahab to w 4878
13:12 including *his* w against Amaziah king 4309
14:15 including *his* w against Amaziah king 4309
24:16 fighting men, strong and fit for w, 4878
1Ch 5:10 During Saul's reign they waged w against 4878
5:19 They waged w against the Hagrites, Jetur, 4878
7:11 fighting men ready to go out to w. 4878
18:10 who had been **at w with** Tou. 408+4878
20: 1 at the time when kings go off to w, NIH
20: 4 w broke out with the Philistines, at Gezer. 4878
2Ch 6:34 your people go to w against their enemies, 4878
11: 1 to **make** w against Israel and to regain 4309
13: 2 There was w between Abijah and Jeroboam. 4878
14: 6 at w with him during those years, 4878
15:19 There was no more w until the thirty-fifth 4878
16: 9 and from now on you will be at **w."** 4878
17:10 that *they did* not **make** w with Jehoshaphat. 4309
18: 3 we will join you in the **w."** 4878
18: 5 "Shall we go to w against Ramoth Gilead, 4878
18:14 shall we go to w against Ramoth Gilead, 4878
20: 1 with some of the Meunites came to make w 4878
22: 5 with Joram son of Ahab king of Israel to w 4878
25:13 in the w raided Judean towns from Samaria 4878
26: 6 *to* w against the Philistines and broke down 4309
26:13 an army of 307,500 men trained for w, 4878
27: 5 Jotham **made** w on the king of the 4309
28:12 those who were arriving from the w. 7372
32: 2 that he intended to *make* w on Jerusalem, 4878
35:21 but the house with which I am **at w.** 4878
Job 38:23 for days of w and battle? 7930
Ps 27: 3 though w break out against me, 4878
55:21 yet w is *in* his heart; 7930
68:30 Scatter the nations who delight in **w.** 7930
76: 3 and the swords, the weapons of w. 4878
120: 7 but when I speak, they are for w. 4878
140: 2 in their hearts and stir up w every day. 4878
144: 1 who trains my hands for w, 7930
Pr 20:18 if you wage **w,** obtain guidance. 4878
24: 6 for waging w you need guidance, 4878
Ecc 3: 8 a time for w and a time for peace. 4878
8: 8 As no one is discharged in **time of w,** 4878
9:18 Wisdom is better than weapons of w, 7930
Isa 2: 4 nor will they train for w anymore. 4878
8: 9 **Raise the w cry,** *you* nations, 8131
13: 4 Almighty is mustering an army for w. 4878
41:12 Those who wage w *against* you will be 4878
42:25 his burning anger, the violence of w. 4878

Jer 4:16 raising a w **cry** against the cities of Judah. 7754
21: 4 about to turn against you the weapons of w 4878
28: 8 and me have prophesied **w,** 4878
42:14 where we will not see w or hear the trumpet 4878
51:20 "You are my w **club,** 5151
Eze 17:17 be of no help to him in **w,** 4878
26:10 at the noise of the w **horses,** 7304
27:14 w **horses** and mules for your merchandise. 7304
32:27 down to the grave with their weapons of **w,** 4878
38: 8 a land that has recovered from **w,** 2995
39: 9 the w **clubs** and spears. 3338+5234
Da 7:21 this horn was waging w against the saints 10639
9:26 **W** will continue until the end, 4878
10: 1 and it concerned a great **w.** 7372
11:10 His sons *will* **prepare for** w and assemble 1741
11:25 The king of the South *will* **wage** w with a large and 1741+2021+4200+4878
Hos 10: 9 Did not w overtake the evildoers in Gibeah? 4878
Joel 3: 9 among the nations: Prepare for **w!** 4878
Am 1:14 will consume her fortresses amid w **cries** 9558
2: 2 in great tumult amid w **cries** and the blast of 9558
Mic 3: 5 they prepare to wage w against him. 4878
4: 3 nor will they train for w anymore. 4878
Lk 14:31 "Or suppose a king is about *to* **go** to w 4483+5202
Ro 7:23 **waging** w **against** the law of my mind *529*
2Co 10: 3 *we do* not **wage** w as the world does. *5129*
1Pe 2:11 sinful desires, which w against your soul. *5129*
Rev 12: 7 And there was w in heaven. *4483*
12:17 the woman and went off to make w against *4483*
13: 4 Who can **make** w against him?" *4482*
13: 7 He was given power to make w against *4483*
17:14 They *will* **make** w against the Lamb, *4482*
19:11 With justice *he* judges and **makes w.** *4482*
19:19 to make w against the rider on the horse *4483*

WAR-HORSES (2) [HORSE]

Hos 14: 3 we will not mount **w.** 6061
Zec 9:10 from Ephraim and the w from Jerusalem, 6061

WARD (3)

2Sa 5: 6 even the blind and the lame *can* w you **off."** 6073
Isa 47:11 that you cannot w **off with a ransom;** 4105
La 2:14 not expose your sin to w **off** your captivity. 8740

WARDEN (3)

Ge 39:21 him favor in the eyes of the prison **w.** 8569
39:22 the w put Joseph in charge of all those held 8569
39:23 The w paid no attention to anything 8569

WARDER (Anglicized) See WARDEN

WARDROBE (3)

2Ki 10:22 And Jehu said to the keeper of the **w,** 4921
22:14 the son of Harhas, keeper of the **w.** 955
2Ch 34:22 the son of Hasrah, keeper of the **w.** 955

WARES (9)

2Ki 8: 9 a gift forty camel-loads of all the **finest** w 3206
Eze 27: 9 came alongside to trade for your **w.** 5114
27:13 and articles of bronze for your **w.** 5114
27:17 honey, oil and balm for your **w.** 5114
27:19 cassia and calamus for your **w.** 5114
27:25 of Tarshish serve as carriers for your **w.** 5114
27:27 Your wealth, merchandise and **w,** 5114
27:33 and your w you enriched the kings of 5114
27:34 your w and all your company have gone 5114

WARFARE (4) [WAR]

Jdg 3: 2 to teach w to the descendants of 4878
1Ki 14:30 There was continual w between Rehoboam 4878
2Ch 12:15 There was continual w *between* Rehoboam 4878
Isa 27: 8 By w and exile you contend with her— 6009

WARM (12) [LUKEWARM, WARMED, WARMING, WARMLY, WARMS]

Jos 9:12 of ours was w when we packed it at home 2768
1Ki 1: 1 not *keep* w even when they put covers 2801
1: 2 so that our lord the king *may keep* **w."** 2801
2Ki 4:34 the boy's body *grew* **w.** 2801
Job 39:14 on the ground and **lets** them w in the sand, 2801
Ecc 4:11 if two lie down together, they will *keep* **w.** 2801
4:11 But how *can one keep* w alone? 2801
Isa 44:16 *I am* **w;** I see the fire." 2801
47:14 Here are no coals to w anyone; 2801
Hag 1: 6 You put on clothes, but *are* not **w.** 2801
Jn 18:18 around a fire they had made to **keep w.** *2548*
Jas 2:16 I wish you well; *keep* w and well fed," *2548*

WARMED (1) [WARM]

Mk 14:54 There he sat with the guards and w *himself* *2548*

WARMING (4) [WARM]

Job 31:20 for w him with the fleece from my sheep, 2801
Mk 14:67 When she saw Peter w *himself,* *2548*
Jn 18:18 also was standing with them, w *himself.* *2548*
18:25 As Simon Peter stood w *himself,* *2548*

WARMLY (2) [WARM]

Ac 21:17 at Jerusalem, the brothers received us **w.** *830*
1Co 16:19 Aquila and Priscilla greet you w in the Lord, *4498*

WARMS (2) [WARM]

Isa 44:15 some of it he takes and w *himself,* 2801
44:16 *He* also w *himself* and says, "Ah! 2801

WARN (24) [WARNED, WARNING, WARNINGS, WARNS]

Ex 19:21 "Go down and w the people so they do 6386
Nu 24:14 *let me* w you of what this people will do 3619
1Sa 8: 9 but w them **solemnly** and 6386+6386
1Ki 2:42 make you swear by the LORD and w you, 6386
2Ch 19:10 *to* w them not to sin against the LORD; 2302
Ps 81: 8 O my people, and *I will* w you— 6386
Jer 42:19 Be sure of this: *I* w you today 6386
Eze 3:18 not w him or speak out to dissuade him 2302
3:19 But if you *do* w the wicked man and he does 2302
3:20 *you did* not w him, he will die for his sin. 2302
3:21 But if you *do* w the righteous man not to sin 2302
33: 3 and blows the trumpet *to* w the people 2302
33: 6 not blow the trumpet *to* w the people and 2302
33: 9 But if you *do* w the wicked man to turn 2302
Lk 16:28 *Let him* w them, so that they will not *1371*
Ac 4:17 *we must* w these men to speak no longer *580*
1Co 4:14 but *to* w you, as my dear children. *3805*
Gal 5:21 *I* w you, as I did before, *4625*
1Th 5:14 we urge you, brothers, w those who are idle, *3805*
2Th 3:15 as an enemy, but w him as a brother. *3805*
2Ti 2:14 **W** them before God against quarreling *1371*
Tit 3:10 **W** a divisive person once, *3804*
3:10 and then w him a second time. *NIG*
Rev 22:18 I w everyone who hears the words of *3455*

WARNED (36) [WARN]

Ge 43: 3 "The man w us **solemnly,** 6386+6386
Ex 19:23 because *you* yourself w us, 6386
21:29 habit of goring and the owner *has* **been** w 6386
Nu 16:26 *He* w the assembly, "Move back from 1819
1Sa 19: 2 and w him, "My father Saul is looking for 5583
19:11 But Michal, David's wife, w him, 5583
2Sa 2:22 Again Abner w Asahel, "Stop chasing me! 606
1Ki 13:26 as the word of the LORD *had* w him." 1819
2Ki 6:10 Time and again Elisha w the king, 2302
17:13 The LORD w Israel and Judah through all 6386
17:23 as *he had* w through all his servants 1819
Ne 9:29 *"You* w them to return to your law, 6386
13:15 *I* w them *against* selling food on that day. 6386
13:21 But *I* w them and said, 6386
Ps 2:10 **be w,** *you* rulers of the earth. 3579
19:11 By them **is** your servant **w;** 2302
Ecc 12:12 **Be w,** my son, *of* anything in addition 2302
Jer 11: 7 *I* w them again and again, saying, 6386+6386
18: 8 and if that nation *I* w repents of its evil, 1819
22:21 *I* w you when you felt secure, but you said, 1819
Mt 2:12 And *having been* w in a dream not *5976*
2:22 *Having been* w in a dream, *5976*
3: 7 Who w you to flee from the coming wrath? *5683*
9:30 Jesus w them **sternly,** "See that no one *1839*
16:20 Then *he* w his disciples not to tell anyone *2203*
Mk 8:15 "Be careful," Jesus w them. *1403*
8:30 Jesus w them not to tell anyone about him. *2203*
Lk 3: 7 Who w you to flee from the coming wrath? *5683*
9:21 Jesus **strictly** w them not to tell this *2203+4133*
Jn 16: 4 time comes you will remember that I w you. *3306*
Ac 2:40 With many other words *he* w them; *1371*
27: 9 So Paul w them, *4147*
1Th 4: 6 as we have already told you and w you. *1371*
Heb 8: 5 This is why Moses *was* w when he was *5976*
11: 7 *when* w about things not yet seen, *5976*
12:25 when they refused him who w them *5976*

WARNING (20) [WARN]

Nu 26:10 And they served as a w **sign.** 5812
2Ki 10:24 had posted eighty men outside with *this* **w:** 606
Ecc 4:13 who no longer knows how to **take w.** 2302
Isa 8:11 w me not to follow the way of this people. 3579
Jer 6: 8 **Take w,** O Jerusalem, or I will turn away 3579
6:10 To whom can I speak and **give w?** 6386
Eze 3:17 the word I speak and **give** them w from me. 2302
3:21 he will surely live because *he* **took w,** 2302
5:15 a w and an object of horror to the nations 4592
23:48 all women *may* **take** w and not imitate you. 3579
33: 4 but *does* not **take** w and the sword comes 2302
33: 5 the sound of the trumpet but *did* not **take w,** 2302
33: 5 If he *had* **taken w,** he would have saved 2302
33: 7 the word I speak and **give** them w from me. 2302
Mt 8:24 **Without w,** a furious storm came up on *2627*
12:16 w them not to tell who he was. *2203*
Mk 1:43 sent him away at once *with* a **strong w:** *1839*
Ac 20:31 that for three years I never stopped w each *3805*
2Co 13: 2 **already gave** you a w when I was with you *4625*
1Ti 5:20 so that the others may take w. *5832*

WARNINGS (4) [WARN]

2Ki 17:15 and the w *he had* **given** them. 6343+6386
Ne 9:34 commands or the w *you* **gave** them. 6343+6386
Job 33:16 in their ears and terrify them with **w,** 4592
1Co 10:11 as examples and were written down as w *3804*

WARNS (2) [WARN]

Ac 20:23 that in every city the Holy Spirit w me *1371*
Heb 12:25 if we turn away from him who w us *NIG*

WARP (KJV) See WOVEN

WARPED (3)

Dt 32: 5 but a w and crooked generation. 6836
Pr 12: 8 but *men with* w minds are despised. 6390
Tit 3:11 be sure that such a man *is* w and sinful; *1750*

WARRANTED (1)

2Co 12: 6 so no one will think more of me than is w *NIG*

WARRIOR (21) [WAR]

Ge 10: 8 who grew to be a **mighty** w on the earth. 1475
Ex 15: 3 The LORD is a **w;** the LORD is his name. 408+4878
Jdg 6:12 "The LORD is with you, mighty **w."** 1475
11: 1 Jephthah the Gileadite was a **mighty w.** 1475+2657
1Sa 16:18 He is a brave man and a **w.** 408+4878
1Ch 1:10 who grew to be a **mighty** w on earth. 1475
12:28 a **brave** young **w,** with 22 officers 1475+2657
28: 3 you are a w and have shed blood.' 408+4878
2Ch 28: 7 Zicri, an Ephraimite **w,** killed Maaseiah 1475
Job 16:14 he rushes at me like a **w.** 1475
Ps 33:16 no w escapes by his great strength. 1475
89:19 "I have bestowed strength on a **w;** 1475
127: 4 of a w are sons born in one's youth. 1475
Pr 16:32 Better a patient man than a **w,** 1475
Isa 3: 2 the hero and the **w,** the judge and prophet, 408+4878
42:13 like a w he will stir up his zeal; 408+4878
Jer 14: 9 like a w powerless to save? 1475
20:11 But the LORD is with me like a mighty **w;** 6883
46:12 *One* w will stumble over another; 1475
Am 2:14 and the w will not save his life. 1475
Zep 1:14 the shouting of the w there. 1475

WARRIOR'S (4) [WAR]

2Sa 18:11 give you ten shekels of silver and a w **belt."** 2514
Ps 120: 4 He will punish you with a w sharp arrows, 1475
Isa 9: 5 Every w boot used in battle 6008
Zec 9:13 O Greece, and make you like a w sword. 1475

WARRIORS (47) [WAR]

Jdg 5:11 the righteous acts of his w in Israel. 7251
18: 2 So the Danites sent five w from Zorah 1201+2657
1Sa 2: 4 "The bows of the w are broken, 1475
2Sa 20: 7 Pelethites and all the **mighty** w went out 1475
1Ch 5:24 They were brave **w,** famous men, 1475
7:40 **brave** w and outstanding leaders. 1475+2657
8:40 The sons of Ulam were **brave** w who 1475+2657
12: 1 among the w who helped him in battle; 1475
12: 8 They were **brave w,** 1475+2657
12:21 for all of them were **brave w,** 1475+2657
12:25 men of Simeon, w ready for battle— 1475+2657
12:30 **brave w,** famous in their own clans— 1475+2657
28: 1 the mighty men and all the **brave w.** 1475+2657
Ps 76: 5 not one of the w can lift his hands. 408+2657
SS 3: 7 escorted by sixty **w,** the noblest of Israel, 1475
4: 4 all of them shields of **w.** 1475
Isa 3:25 men will fall by the sword, your w in battle. 1476
10:16 a wasting disease upon his **sturdy** *w;* AIT
13: 3 I have summoned my w 1475
21:17 the w *of* Kedar, will be few." 1475
49:24 Can plunder be taken from **w,** 1475
49:25 "Yes, captives will be taken from **w,** 1475
Jer 5:16 all of them are **mighty w.** 1475
46: 5 they are retreating, their w are defeated. 1475
46: 9 O charioteers! March on, O **w**— 1475
46:15 Why will your w be laid low? 52
48:14 "How can you say, 'We are **w,** 1475
48:41 the hearts of Moab's w will be like the heart 1475
49:22 the hearts of Edom's w will be like the heart 1475
50: 9 Their arrows will be like skilled w who do 1475
50:36 A sword against her **w!** 1475
51:30 Babylon's w have stopped fighting; 1475
51:56 her w will be captured, 1475
51:57 her governors, officers and w as well; 1475
La 1:15 Lord has rejected all the w in my midst; 52
Eze 23: 5 after her lovers, the Assyrians—**w** 7940
23:12 governors and commanders, w in full dress, 7940
32:27 the other uncircumcised w who have fallen, 1475
32:27 of those w had stalked through the land of 1475
Hos 10:13 on your own strength and on your many **w,** 1475
Joel 2: 7 They charge like **w;** they scale walls 1475
3: 9 Prepare for war! Rouse the **w!** 1475
3:11 Bring down your **w,** O LORD! 1475
Am 2:16 the bravest w will flee naked on that day," 1475
Ob 1: 9 Your **w,** O Teman, will be terrified, 1475
Na 2: 3 the w are clad in scarlet. 408+2657
Hab 3:14 when his w stormed out to scatter us, 7250

WARS (12) [WAR]

Nu 21:14 the Book of the **W** *of* the LORD says: 4878
Jdg 3: 1 not experienced any of the w *in* Canaan 4878
1Ki 5: 3 "You know that because of the w waged 4878
14:19 Jeroboam's reign, *his* w and how he ruled, 4309
1Ch 22: 8 shed much blood and have fought many **w.** 4878
2Ch 27: 7 including all his w and the other things 4878
Ps 46: 9 He makes w cease to the ends of the earth; 4878
Mt 24: 6 You will hear *of* w and rumors of wars, *4483*
24: 6 You will hear of wars and rumors *of* **w,** *4483*
Mk 13: 7 When you hear *of* w and rumors of wars, *4483*
13: 7 When you hear of wars and rumors *of* **w,** *4483*
Lk 21: 9 When you hear *of* w and revolutions, *4483*

WARTS (1)

Lev 22:22 or **anything with** w or festering 3301

WAS (4158) [BE] See Index of Articles Etc.

WASH (79) [WASHED, WASHERMAN'S, WASHING, WASHINGS, WHITEWASH, WHITEWASHED]

Ge 18: 4 and then *you may all* w your feet and rest 8175
19: 2 *You can* w your feet and spend the night and 8175
24:32 water for him and his men to w their feet. 8175
43:24 *to* w their feet and provided fodder 8175
49:11 *he will* w his garments in wine, 3891
Ex 19:10 *Have them* w their clothes 3891
29: 4 the Tent of Meeting and w them with water. 8175
29:17 the ram into pieces and w the inner parts 8175
30:19 and his sons *are to* w their hands and feet 8175
30:20 *they shall* w *with* water so that they will 8175
30:21 *they shall* w their hands and feet so 8175
40:12 the Tent of Meeting and w them with water. 8175
40:31 and his sons used it *to* w their hands 8175
Lev 1: 9 *to* w the inner parts and the legs with water, 8175
1:13 *to* w the inner parts and the legs with water, 8175
6:27 *you must* w it in a holy place. 3891
11:25 of their carcasses *must* w his clothes, 3891
11:28 up their carcasses *must* w his clothes, 3891
11:40 of the carcass *must* w his clothes, 3891
11:40 up the carcass *must* w his clothes, 3891
13: 6 The man *must* w his clothes, 3891
13:34 *He must* w his clothes, and he will be clean. 3891
14: 8 to be cleansed *must* w his clothes, 3891
14: 9 *He must* w his clothes and bathe himself 3891
14:47 or eats in the house *must* w his clothes. 3891
15: 5 who touches his bed *must* w his clothes 3891
15: 6 with a discharge sat on *must* w his clothes 3891
15: 7 a discharge *must* w his clothes and bathe 3891
15: 8 that person *must* w his clothes and bathe 3891
15:10 up those things *must* w his clothes 3891
15:11 with water *must* w his clothes and bathe 3891
15:13 *he must* w his clothes and bathe himself 3891
15:21 Whoever touches her bed *must* w his clothes 3891
15:22 on *must* w his clothes and bathe 3891
15:27 *he must* w his clothes and bathe with water, 3891
16:26 the goat as a scapegoat *must* w his clothes 3891
16:28 The man who burns them *must* w his clothes 3891
17:15 or torn by wild animals *must* w his clothes 3891
17:16 *he does* not w his clothes and bathe himself, 3891
Nu 5:23 and then w them **off** into the bitter water. 4681
8: 7 and w their clothes, and so purify 3891
19: 7 the priest *must* w his clothes 3891
19: 8 also w his clothes and bathe with water, 3891
19:10 of the heifer *must* also w his clothes, 3891
19:19 person being cleansed *must* w his clothes 3891
19:21 of cleansing *must* also w his clothes, 3891
31:24 the seventh day w your clothes and you will 3891
Dt 21: 6 nearest the body *shall* w their hands over 8175
23:11 as evening approaches *he is to* w *himself,* 8175
Ru 3: 3 W and perfume yourself, 8175
1Sa 25:41 and w the feet of my master's servants." 8175
2Sa 11: 8 "Go down to your house and w your feet." 8175
2Ki 5:10 "Go, w *yourself* seven times in the Jordan, 8175
5:12 Couldn't *I* w in them and be cleansed?" 8175
5:13 when he tells you, **'W** and be cleansed'!" 8175
Job 14:19 and torrents w **away** the soil, 8851
Ps 26: 6 *I* w my hands in innocence, 8175
51: 2 W **away** all my iniquity and cleanse me 3891
51: 7 w me, and I will be whiter than snow. 3891
SS 8: 7 rivers cannot w it **away.** 8851
Isa 1:16 w and make yourselves clean. 8175
4: 4 The Lord *will* w **away** the filth of 8175
Jer 2:22 Although *you* w *yourself* with soda 3891
4:14 w the evil from your heart and be saved. 3891
Mt 6:17 put oil on your head and w your face, *3782*
15: 2 *They* don't w their hands before they eat!" *3782*
Mk 7: 4 they do not eat unless *they* w. *966*
Lk 11:38 that Jesus *did* not first w before the meal, *966*
Jn 9: 7 "w in the Pool of Siloam" *3782*
9:11 He told me to go to Siloam and w. *3782*
13: 5 a basin and began *to* w his disciples' feet, *3782*
13: 6 "Lord, *are you going to* w my feet?" *3782*
13: 8 said Peter, *"you shall* never w my feet." *3782*
13: 8 Jesus answered, "Unless *I* w you, *3782*
13:10 a bath needs only *to* w his feet; *3782*
13:14 you also should w one another's feet. *3782*
Ac 22:16 Get up, be baptized and w your sins **away,** *666*
Jas 4: 8 W your hands, you sinners, *2751*
Rev 22:14 "Blessed are those who w their robes, *4459*

WASHBASIN (2)

Ps 60: 8 Moab is my w, upon Edom I toss 6105+8176
108: 9 Moab is my w, upon Edom I toss 6105+8176

WASHED (36) [WASH]

Ge 43:31 After *he had* w his face, he came out and, 8175
Ex 19:14 and *they* w their clothes. 3891
40:32 *They* w whenever they entered the Tent 8175
Lev 8: 6 and his sons forward and w them 8175
8:21 *He* w the inner parts and the legs with water 8175
9:14 *He* w the inner parts and the legs and 8175
13:54 that the contaminated article *be* w. 3891
13:55 After the affected article *has* **been** w, 3891
13:56 after the article *has* **been** w, 3891
13:58 that *has been* w and is rid of the mildew, 3891
Lev 13:58 *must* **be** w again, and it will be clean." 3891
15:17 that has semen on it *must* **be** w with water, 3891
Nu 8:21 purified themselves and w their clothes. 3891
Jdg 19:21 After *they had* w their feet, 8175
2Sa 12:20 After *he had* w, put on lotions 8175
19:24 or w his clothes from the day the king left 3891
1Ki 22:38 *They* w the chariot at a pool in Samaria 8851
Job 9:30 if *I* w **myself** with soap and my hands 8175
22:16 their foundations w **away** *by* a flood. 3668
Ps 73:13 in vain *have I* w my hands in innocence. 8175
SS 5: 3 *I have* w my feet—must I soil them again? 8175
5:12 w in milk, mounted like jewels. 8175
Eze 16: 4 nor **were** *you* w with water 8175
16: 9 " 'I bathed you with water and w the blood 8851
40:38 where the burnt offerings *were* w. 1866
Mt 27:24 he took water and w his hands in front of *672*
Jn 9: 7 man went and w, and came home seeing. *3782*
9:11 So *I* went and w, and then I could see." *3782*
9:15 the man replied, "and *I* w, and now I see." *3782*
13:14 I, your Lord and Teacher, *have* w your feet, *3782*
Ac 9:37 and her body *was* w and placed in *3374*
16:33 the jailer took them and w their wounds; *3374*
1Co 6:11 But *you were* w, you were sanctified, *666*
Heb 10:22 a guilty conscience and *having* our bodies w *3374*
2Pe 2:22 *that is* w goes back to her wallowing in *3374*
Rev 7:14 they *have* w their robes and made them *4459*

WASHERMAN'S (3) [WASH]

2Ki 18:17 on the road to the **W** Field. 3891
Isa 7: 3 on the road to the **W** Field. 3891
36: 2 on the road to the **W** Field, 3891

WASHING (16) [WASH]

Ex 30:18 with its bronze stand, for w. 8175
40:30 and the altar and put water in it for w, 8175
2Ch 4: 6 then made ten basins for w and placed five 8175
4: 6 the Sea was to be used by the priests for w. 8175
Job 9:30 with soap and my hands with w **soda,** 1342
SS 4: 2 sheep just shorn, coming up from the w. 8177
6: 6 like a flock of sheep coming up from the w. 8177
Mk 7: 3 *give* their hands a ceremonial w, *3782*
7: 4 such as the w of cups, pitchers and kettles.) *968*
Lk 5: 2 the fishermen, who *were* w their nets. *4459*
Jn 2: 6 kind used by the Jews for **ceremonial** w, *2752*
3:25 over the matter of **ceremonial** w. *2752*
13:12 When *he had finished* w their feet, *3782*
Eph 5:26 cleansing her *by* the w with water through *3373*
1Ti 5:10 showing hospitality, w the feet of the saints, *3782*
Tit 3: 5 through the w of rebirth and renewal by *3373*

WASHINGS (1) [WASH]

Heb 9:10 food and drink and various **ceremonial** w— *968*

WASHPOT (KJV) See WASHBASIN

WASN'T (4) [BE, NOT]

Ge 30:15 But she said to her, **"W** it **enough** 5071
1Ki 3:21 I saw that *it* w the son I had borne." 2118+4202
Jn 12: 5 "Why w this perfume sold and *4024*
Ac 5: 4 it was sold, w the money at your disposal? *5639*

WASTE (73) [WASTED, WASTES, WASTING]

Lev 26:31 into ruins and **lay** w your sanctuaries, 9037
26:32 I *will* **lay** w the land, 9037
26:33 Your land will be **laid** w, 9039
26:39 Those of you who are left *will* w **away** in 5245
26:39 of their fathers' sins *they will* w **away.** 5245
Nu 5:21 *to* w **away** and your abdomen to swell. 5877
5:27 and her thigh w **away,** 5877
Dt 29:23 The whole land will be a **burning** w *of* salt 8599
32:10 in a barren and howling w. 3810
Jdg 16:24 the *one who* **laid** w our land 2990
2Ki 19:17 Assyrian kings *have* **laid** w these nations 2990
22:19 they would become accursed and **laid** w, 9014
1Ch 20: 1 *He* **laid** w the land of the Ammonites 8845
Job 12:24 them wandering through a trackless w. 9332
Ps 107:34 and fruitful land into a **salt** w, 4877
107:40 made them wander in a trackless w. 9332
112:10 he will gnash his teeth and w **away;** 5022
Isa 1: 7 **laid** w as when overthrown by strangers. 9039
6:13 it will again be **laid** w. 1278
7:16 of the two kings you dread *will* **be laid** w. 6440
10:18 the fat of his body *will* w **away.** 8135
17: 4 the fat of his body *will* w **away.** 8135
24: 1 the LORD *is going to* **lay** w the earth 1327
24: 3 The earth *will* **be completely laid** w 1327+1327
24:16 But I said, "I w **away,** I waste away! 8140
24:16 But I said, "I waste away, I w **away!** 8140
37:18 Assyrian kings *have* **laid** w all these peoples 2990
42:15 *I will* **lay** w the mountains and hills 2990
49:17 *those who* **laid** you w depart 2238+2256+2990
49:19 and made desolate and your land laid w, 2233
64: 7 and **made** us w **away** because of our sins. 4570
Jer 2:15 They have laid w his land; 9014
4: 7 He has left his place to lay w your land. 9014
9:11 and I will lay w the towns of Judah 9039
9:12 Why has the land been ruined and **laid** w 5898
12:11 the whole land *will be* **laid** w 9037
18:16 Their land will be laid w, 9014
25:37 The peaceful meadows *will* **be laid** w 1959
32:43 It is a **desolate** w, without men or animals, 9039
33:10 It is a **desolate** w, without men or animals. 2992
34:22 And I will lay w the towns of Judah 9039
Jer 44:22 and a desolate w without inhabitants, 9014
46:19 for Memphis will be **laid** w and lie in ruins 9014
48: 9 Put salt on Moab, for *she will be* **laid** w; 5898+5898
50: 3 the north will attack her and lay w her land. 9014
51:29 to lay w the land of Babylon so 9014
La 2: 6 *He has* **laid** w his dwelling like a garden; 2803
4: 9 *they* w **away** for lack of food from the field. 2307
Eze 4:17 at the sight of each other and *will* w **away** 5245
6: 6 *be* **laid** w and the high places demolished, 2990
6: 6 your altars *will be* **laid** w and devastated, 2990
6:14 a desolate w from the desert to Diblah— 5457
12:20 The inhabited towns *will be* **laid** w and 2990
24:23 but *will* w **away** because of your sins 5245
25: 3 over the land of Israel when *it* **was laid** w 9037
25:13 I will lay it w, and from Teman to Dedan 2999
29:10 the land of Egypt a ruin and a desolate w 2997
30:12 by the hand of foreigners *I will* **lay** w 9037
30:14 *I will* **lay** w Upper Egypt, 9037
33:28 I will make the land a desolate **w,** 5457
33:29 when I have made the land a desolate w 5457
35: 3 against you and make you a desolate **w.** 5457
35: 7 I will make Mount Seir a desolate w 9039
35:12 *"They have been* **laid** w 9037
36:35 "This land that **was laid** w has become like 9037
Hos 4: 3 and all who live in it w **away;** 581
5: 9 be **laid** w on the day of reckoning. 9014
8:10 to w **away** under the oppression of 5071
Joel 1: 7 It has laid w my vines and ruined 9014
2: 3 a desert w—nothing escapes them. 9039
3:19 Egypt will be desolate, Edom a desert w, 9039
Na 2: 2 though destroyers *have* **laid** them w 1327
Mt 26: 8 "Why this w?" they asked. *724*
Mk 14: 4 "Why this w of perfume? *724+1181*

WASTED (7) [WASTE]

Ge 47:13 and Canaan w **away** because of the famine. 3532
Ps 32: 3 my bones w **away** through my groaning 1162
106:43 on rebellion and *they* w **away** in their sin. 4812
Pr 23: 8 and *will have* w your compliments. 8845
La 2: 8 together *they* w **away.** 581
Jn 6:12 Let nothing *be* w." *660*
Gal 4:11 that somehow I have w my efforts on you. *1632*

WASTELAND (21) [LAND]

Nu 21:20 where the top of Pisgah overlooks the w. 3810
23:28 to the top of Peor, overlooking the w. 3810
2Sa 2:24 near Giah on the way to the w *of* Gibeon. 4497
Job 6:18 they go up into the w and perish. 9332
24: 5 the w provides food for their children. 6858
38:27 a desolate w and make it sprout with grass? 5409
39: 6 I gave him the w as his home, 6858
Ps 68: 7 O God, when you marched through the w, 3810
78:40 in the desert and grieved him in the w! 3810
106:14 in the w they put God to the test. 3810
Isa 5: 6 I will make it a w, neither pruned nor 1429
32:14 and watchtower will become a w forever, 5118
41:19 I will set pines in the w, 6858
43:19 a way in the desert and streams in the w. 3810
43:20 in the desert and streams in the w, 3810
Jer 12:10 turn my pleasant field into a desolate w. 4497
12:11 It will be made a w, 9039
25:11 a desolate w, and these nations will serve 9014
Eze 29: 9 Egypt will become a desolate w. 2999
Zep 2: 9 a place of weeds and salt pits, a w forever. 9039
Mal 1: 3 and I have turned his mountains into a w 9039

WASTELANDS (4) [LAND]

Job 30: 3 they roamed the parched land in desolate w 5409
Ps 107: 4 Some wandered in desert w, 3810
Isa 51: 3 her w like the garden of the LORD. 6858
Jer 17: 6 He will be like a bush in the w; 6858

WASTES (5) [WASTE]

Nu 5:22 and your thigh w **away."** 5877
Job 13:28 "So man w **away** like something rotten, 1162
33:21 His flesh w **away** to nothing, and his bones, 3983
Isa 10:18 as *when* a sick man w **away.** 5022
33: 9 The land mourns and w **away,** 581

WASTING (8) [WASTE]

Lev 26:16 upon you sudden terror, w **diseases** and 8831
Dt 28:22 The LORD will strike you with w **disease,** 8831
32:24 I will send w famine against them, 4642
Ps 106:15 but sent a w **disease** upon them. 8137
Isa 10:16 a w **disease** upon his sturdy warriors; 8137
Eze 33:10 and we *are* w **away** because of them. 5245
Lk 16: 1 was accused of w his possessions. *1399*
2Co 4:16 Though outwardly we *are* w **away,** *1425*

WATCH (88) [WATCHED, WATCHER, WATCHES, WATCHFUL, WATCHING, WATCHMAN, WATCHMEN]

Ge 21:16 for she thought, *"I* cannot w the boy die." 8011
28:15 and *will* w **over** you wherever you go, 9068
28:20 "If God will be with me and *will* w **over** 9068
31:49 *May* the LORD **keep** w between you and me 7595
Ex 14:24 During **last** w **of the night** 874+1332
Dt 4: 9 and w yourselves closely so that you do 9068
4:15 Therefore w yourselves very **carefully,** 9068
Jdg 7:17 **"W** me," he told them. "Follow my lead. 8011
7:19 the camp at the beginning of the middle w, 874

Jdg 21:21 and w. When the girls of Shiloh come out 8011
Ru 2: 9 W the field where the men are harvesting, 928+6524
1Sa 11:11 during the **last w of the night** 874+1332+2021
17:28 you came down only to w the battle." 8011
19:11 Saul sent men to David's house to w it and 9068
2Sa 13: 5 in my sight so *I may* w her and then eat it 8011
13:34 Now the man **standing** w looked up 7595
1Ki 2: 4 'If your descendants w how they live, 9068
2Ch 23: 4 on the Sabbath are to **keep** w *at* the doors, 8788
Ne 11:19 who **kept** w at the gates—172 men. 9068
Job 13:27 *you* **keep close** w **on** all my paths 9068
21:32 and w *is* **kept** over his tomb. 9193
33:11 *he* **keeps close** w *on* all my paths.' 9068
39: 1 *Do you* w when the doe bears her fawn? 9068
Ps 32: 8 I will counsel you and w over you. 6524
39: 1 *"I will* w my ways and keep my tongue 9068
56: 6 They conspire, they lurk, *they* w my steps, 9068
59: T *to* w David's house in order to kill him. 9068
59: 9 O my Strength, *I* w for you; 9068
66: 7 his eyes w the nations— 7595
80:14 **W over** this vine, 7212
90: 4 or like a w in the night. 874
121: 7 *he will* w **over** your life; 9068
121: 8 the LORD *will* w **over** your coming 9068
141: 3 keep w over the door of my lips. 5917
Pr 4: 6 love her, and *she will* w **over** you. 5915
6:22 when you sleep, *they will* w over you; 9068
15: 3 **keeping** w *on* the wicked and the good. 7595
22:12 eyes of the LORD **keep** w **over** knowledge, 5915
Isa 27: 3 **w over** it; I water it continually. 5915
Jer 24: 6 My eyes *will* w **over** them for their good, 6584+8492
31:10 and *will* w **over** his flock like a shepherd.' 9068
31:28 *I will* w over them to build and to plant," 9193
48:19 Stand by the road and w, 7595
Eze 12: 3 as they w, set out and go from 4200+6524
12: 4 During the daytime, while they w, 4200+6524
12: 5 While they w, dig through the wall 4200+6524
Da 7:11 *to* w because of the boastful words 10255
Mic 7: 7 But as for me, *I* w **in hope** for the LORD, 7595
Na 2: 1 Guard the fortress, w the road, 7595
Hab 1: 5 "Look at the nations and w— 5564
2: 1 at my w and station myself on the ramparts; 5466
Zec 9: 8 for now I *am* **keeping** w. 928+6524+8011
Mt 7:15 **"W out** for false prophets. *4668*
14:25 the fourth w of the night Jesus went out *5871*
24: 4 **"W out** that no one deceives you. *1063*
24:42 "Therefore **keep** w, because you do *1213*
24:43 the thief was coming, *he* would *have* **kept** w *1213*
25:13 "Therefore **keep** w, because you do *1213*
26:38 Stay here and **keep** w with me." *1213*
26:40 "Could you men not **keep** w with me *1213*
26:41 **"W** and pray so that you will not fall *1213*
27:36 sitting down, *they* **kept** w **over** him there. *5498*
Mk 6:48 About the fourth w of the night he went out *5871*
8:15 **"W out** for the yeast of the Pharisees and *1063*
12:38 **"W out** for the teachers of the law. *1063*
13: 5 **"W out** that no one deceives you. *1063*
13:34 and tells the one at the door to **keep** w. *1213*
13:35 Therefore **keep** w because you do not know *1213*
13:37 What I say to you, I say to everyone: **'W!'** " *1213*
14:34 "Stay here and **keep** w." *1213*
14:37 Could you not **keep** w for one hour? *1213*
14:38 **W** and pray so that you will not fall *1213*
Lk 2: 8 **keeping** w over their flocks at night. *5871+5875*
12:15 Then he said to them, **"W out!** *3972*
12:38 in the second or third w **of the night.** *5871*
17: 3 So w yourselves. *4668*
20:20 **Keeping a close** w on him, they sent spies, *4190*
21: 8 **"W out** that you are not deceived. *1063*
21:36 *Be* always **on the** w, and pray that *70*
Ac 9:24 Day and night *they* **kept close** w **on** *4190*
20:28 **Keep** w **over** yourselves and all the flock *4668*
Ro 16:17 *to* w **out for** those who cause divisions *5023*
Gal 5:15 w **out** or you will be destroyed *1063*
6: 1 w yourself, or you also may be tempted. *5023*
Php 3: 2 **W out for** those dogs, those men who *1063*
1Ti 4:16 **W** your life and doctrine **closely.** *2091*
Heb 13:17 They **keep** w over you as men who must give an account. *70*
2Jn 1: 8 **W out** that you do not lose what *1063+4932*

WATCHED (31) [WATCH]

Ge 24:21 the man w her **closely** to learn whether or 8617
Ex 2:11 to where his own people were and w them 8011
3:16 *I have* w **over** you **and** *have* **seen** 7212+7212
Dt 2: 7 *He has* w **over** your journey 3359
33: 9 but *he* w **over** your word 9068
Jos 4:11 to the other side while the people w. 4200+7156
Jdg 13:19 while Manoah and his wife w: 8011
1Sa 17:55 As Saul w David going out to meet 8011
2Sa 6:16 Michal daughter of Saul w from a window. 9207
1Ch 15:29 Michal daughter of Saul w from a window. 9207
Job 10:12 and in your providence w **over** my spirit. 9068
29: 2 for the days when God w **over** me, 9068
Jer 31:28 as *I* w over them to uproot and tear down, 9193
La 4:17 from our towers *we* w for a nation that could 7595
Eze 10: 2 And as I w, he went in. 4200+6524
10:19 I w, the cherubim spread their wings 4200+6524
12: 7 on my shoulders while they w. 4200+6524
Da 5: 5 The king w the hand as it wrote. 10255
7: 4 I w until its wings were torn off 10255
7:21 *As* I w, this horn was waging war against 10255
8: 4 *I* w the ram as he charged toward the west 8011
Mt 26:16 From then on Judas w **for** an opportunity *2426*
Mk 3: 2 *they* w him **closely** to see if he would heal *4190*
12:41 and w the crowd putting their money into *2555*
14:11 *he* w **for** an opportunity to hand him over. *2426*
Lk 6: 7 *they* w him **closely** to see if he would heal *4190*
14: 1 he was *being* **carefully** w. *4190*
22: 6 and w **for** an opportunity to hand Jesus *2426*
Rev 6: 1 *I* w as the Lamb opened the first of the *3972*
6:12 *I* w as he opened the sixth seal. *3972*
8:13 As *I* w, I heard an eagle that was flying *3972*

WATCHER (1) [WATCH]

Job 7:20 what have I done to you, O w *of* men? 5915

WATCHES (16) [WATCH]

Nu 19: 5 While he w, the heifer is to be burned— 6524
Job 24:15 The eye of the adulterer w *for* dusk; 9068
Ps 1: 6 LORD **w over** the way of the righteous, 3359
33:14 from his dwelling place *he* w all who live 8708
63: 6 I think of you through the **w of the night.** 874
119:148 through the **w of the night,** 874
121: 3 *he who* **w over** you will not slumber; 9068
121: 4 *he who* **w over** Israel will neither slumber 9068
121: 5 The LORD **w over** you— 9068
127: 1 Unless the LORD **w over** the city, 9068
145:20 The LORD **w over** all who love him, 9068
146: 9 The LORD **w over** the alien and sustains 9068
Pr 31:27 *She* **w over** the affairs of her household 7595
Ecc 11: 4 *Whoever* w the wind will not plant; 9068
La 2:19 as the **w of the night** begin; 874
4:16 he no longer **w over** them. 5564

WATCHFUL (2) [WATCH]

Zec 12: 4 *"I will* **keep** a w eye over the house 7219
Col 4: 2 Devote yourselves to prayer, *being* w and *1213*

WATCHING (29) [WATCH]

Ge 30:31 I will go on tending your flocks and **w over** 9068
Ex 33: 8 w Moses until he entered the tent. 5564
Dt 28:32 and you will wear out your eyes w 8011
Jdg 16:27 men and women w Samson perform. 8011
1Sa 4:13 w, because his heart feared for the ark of 7595
6: 9 but *keep* w it. If it goes up to its own 8011
25:21 all *my* **w over** this fellow's property in 9068
2Ki 2:15 prophets from Jericho, who *were* w, said, 8011
Ezr 5: 5 the eye of their God was w over the elders NIH
Job 10:14 If I sinned, *you would be* w me 9068
Ps 10: 8 w in secret for his victims. 6524
Pr 8:34 listens to me, w daily at my doors, 9193
Jer 1:12 for I *am* w to see that my word is fulfilled." 9193
7:11 But I *have been* **w!** 8011
19:10 the jar while those who go with you are **w,** 6524
43: 9 "While the Jews are w, take some large 6524
44:27 I *am* w over them for harm, not for good; 9193
Eze 12: 4 Then in the evening, while they are **w,** 4200+6524
12: 6 they are w and carry them out at dusk. 4200+6524
28:18 the ground in the sight of all *who were* **w.** 8011
Da 2:34 While you were w, a rock was cut out, 10255
8:15 *was* w the vision and trying to understand it, 8011
Zec 11:11 of the flock who *were* w me knew it was 9068
Mt 27:55 Many women were there, w from a distance. *2555*
Mk 15:40 Some women were w from a distance. *2555*
Lk 12:37 those servants whose master finds them w *1213*
23:35 The people stood w, and the rulers even *2555*
23:49 stood at a distance, w these things. *3972*
Jn 7:11 Now at the Feast the Jews *were* **w for** him *2426*

WATCHMAN (16) [WATCH]

2Sa 13:34 The w went and told the king, 7595
18:24 the w went up to the roof of the gateway by 7595
18:25 The w called out to the king and reported it. 7595
18:26 Then the w saw another man running, 7595
18:27 The w said, "It seems to me that the first 7595
Job 27:18 like a hut made by a **w.** 5915
Isa 21:11 Someone calls to me from Seir, **"W,** 9068
21:11 **W,** what is left of the night?" 9068
21:12 The w replies, "Morning is coming, 9068
Eze 3:17 I have made you a w for the house of Israel; 7595
33: 2 of their men and make him their w, 7595
33: 6 if the w sees the sword coming and does 7595
33: 6 I will hold the w accountable for his blood.' 7595
33: 7 I have made you a w for the house of Israel; 7595
Hos 9: 8 along with my God, *is* the w *over* Ephraim, 7595
Jn 10: 3 The w opens the gate for him, *2601*

WATCHMEN (13) [WATCH]

Ps 127: 1 the w stand guard in vain. 9068
130: 6 more than w wait for the morning, 9068
130: 6 more than w wait for the morning. 9068
SS 3: 3 The w found me as they made their rounds 9068
5: 7 The w found me as they made their rounds 9068
5: 7 those w *of* the walls! 9068
Isa 52: 8 Your w lift up their voices; 7595
56:10 Israel's w are blind, 7595
62: 6 I have posted w on your walls, O Jerusalem; 9068
Jer 6:17 I appointed w over you and said, 7595
31: 6 when w cry out on the hills of Ephraim, 5915
51:12 Reinforce the guard, station the w, 9068
Mic 7: 4 The day of your w has come, 7595

WATCHTOWER (8) [TOWER]

2Ki 17: 9 From w to fortified city they built 4463+5915
18: 8 From w to fortified city, he defeated 4463+5915
Isa 5: 2 He built a w in it and cut out a winepress 4463
21: 8 "Day after day, my lord, I stand on the **w;** 5205
32:14 and w will become a wasteland forever, 1044
Mic 4: 8 As for you, O w *of* the flock, 4463
Mt 21:33 dug a winepress in it and built a w. *4788*
Mk 12: 1 dug a pit for the winepress and built a **w.** *4788*

WATCHTOWERS (1) [TOWER]

1Ch 27:25 in the towns, the villages and the w. 4463

WATER (482) [WATER'S, WATERCOURSE, WATERED, WATERFALLS, WATERING, WATERLESS, WATERS, WATERY, WELL-WATERED]

Ge 1: 6 the waters to separate w from water." 4784
1: 6 the waters to separate water from **w."** 4784
1: 7 and separated the w under the expanse from 4784
1: 7 the water under the expanse from the w 4784
1: 9 "Let the w under the sky be gathered 4784
1:20 "Let the w teem with living creatures, 4784
1:21 and moving thing with which the w teems, 4784
1:22 and increase in number and fill the w in 4784
7:18 and the ark floated on the surface of the **w.** 4784
8: 3 The w receded steadily from the earth. 4784
8: 3 the hundred and fifty days the w had gone 4784
8: 7 until the w had dried up from the earth. 4784
8: 8 to see if the w had receded from the surface 4784
8: 9 because there was w over all the surface of 4784
8:11 Then Noah knew that the w had receded 4784
8:13 the w had dried up from the earth. 4784
18: 4 Let a little w be brought, 4784
21:14 and a skin of w and gave them to Hagar. 4784
21:15 When the w in the skin was gone, 4784
21:19 and she saw a well of **w.** 4784
21:19 and filled the skin with w and gave the boy 4784
21:25 of w that Abimelech's servants had seized. 4784
24:11 the time the *women* go out *to* **draw w.** 8612
24:13 the townspeople are coming out to draw **w.** 4784
24:14 'Drink, and *I'll* w your camels too'— 9197
24:17 "Please give me a little w from your jar." 4784
24:19 she said, *"I'll* **draw** w for your camels too, 8612
24:20 ran back to the well to **draw** *more* **w,** 8612
24:32 w for him and his men to wash their feet. 4784
24:43 if a maiden comes out to **draw** w and I say 8612
24:43 to her, "Please let me drink a little w 4784
24:44 and *I'll* **draw** w for your camels too," 8612
24:45 She went down to the spring and **drew w,** 8612
24:46 'Drink, and *I'll* w your camels too.' 9197
26:19 and discovered a well of fresh w there. 4784
26:20 "The w is ours!" 4784
26:32 They said, "We've found **w!"** 4784
29: 3 from the well's mouth and w the sheep. 9197
29: 7 **W** the sheep and take them back 9197
29: 8 Then *we will* w the sheep." 9197
37:24 the cistern was empty; there was no w in it. 4784
43:24 gave them w to wash their feet 4784
Ex 2:10 saying, "I drew him out of the **w."** 4784
2:16 and they came *to* **draw** w and fill 1926
2:16 and fill the troughs to w their father's flock. 9197
2:19 **drew** w for us and watered the flock." 1926+1926
4: 9 take some w *from* the Nile and pour it on 4784
4: 9 The w you take from the river will become 4784
7:15 in the morning as he goes out to the **w.** 4784
7:17 in my hand I will strike the w of the Nile, 4784
7:18 not be able to drink its **w.'** " 4784
7:20 and his officials and struck the w of 4784
7:20 and all the w was changed into blood. 4784
7:21 that the Egyptians could not drink its **w.** 4784
7:24 along the Nile to get drinking **w,** 4784
7:24 they could not drink the w *of* the river. 4784
8:20 and confront Pharaoh as he goes to the w 4784
12: 9 Do not eat the meat raw or cooked in **w,** 4784
14:16 to divide **the** w so that the Israelites can go 2084S
14:22 a wall of w on their right and on their left. 4784
14:28 The w flowed back and covered the chariots 4784
14:29 a wall of w on their right and on their left. 4784
15:22 in the desert without finding **w.** 4784
15:23 not drink its w because it was bitter. 4784
15:25 He threw it into the **w,** 4784
15:25 and the w became sweet. 4784
15:27 and they camped there near the **w.** 4784
17: 1 but there was no w for the people to drink. 4784
17: 2 "Give us w to drink." 4784
17: 3 But the people were thirsty for w there, 4784
17: 6 and w will come out of it for the people 4784
23:25 and his blessing will be on your food and **w.** 4784
29: 4 the Tent of Meeting and wash them with **w.** 4784
30:18 and the altar, and put w in it. 4784
30:19 to wash their hands and feet with w from it. NIH
30:20 they shall wash with w so that they will 4784
32:20 to powder, scattered it on the w and made 4784
34:28 without eating bread or drinking **w.** 4784
40: 7 the Tent of Meeting and the altar and put w 4784
40:12 the Tent of Meeting and wash them with **w.** 4784
40:30 the Tent of Meeting and the altar and put w 4784
Lev 1: 9 to wash the inner parts and the legs with **w,** 4784
1:13 to wash the inner parts and the legs with **w,** 4784
6:28 the pot is to be scoured and rinsed with **w.** 4784
8: 6 and washed them with **w.** 4784
8:21 the legs with w and burned the whole ram 4784
11: 9 the creatures living in the w of the seas and 4784
11:10 among all the other living creatures in the w 4784
11:12 the w that does not have fins and scales 4784
11:32 Put it in **w;** it will be unclean till evening, 4784

Lev 11:34 Any food that could be eaten but has w on it 4784
11:36 or a cistern for collecting w remains clean, 4784
11:38 But if w has been put on the seed and 4784
11:46 the w and every creature that moves about 4784
14: 5 that one of the birds be killed over fresh w 4784
14: 6 of the bird that was killed over the fresh w. 4784
14: 8 shave off all his hair and bathe with w; 4784
14: 9 and bathe himself with w, 4784
14:50 He shall kill one of the birds over fresh w in 4784
14:51 the blood of the dead bird and the fresh w, 4784
14:52 the fresh w, the live bird, the cedar wood, 4784
15: 5 must wash his clothes and bathe with w, 4784
15: 6 must wash his clothes and bathe with w, 4784
15: 7 must wash his clothes and bathe with w, 4784
15: 8 must wash his clothes and bathe with w, 4784
15:10 must wash his clothes and bathe with w, 4784
15:11 with w must wash his clothes and bathe 4784
15:11 must wash his clothes and bathe with w, 4784
15:12 any wooden article is to be rinsed with w. 4784
15:13 and bathe himself with fresh w, 4784
15:16 he must bathe his whole body with w, 4784
15:17 on it must be washed with w, 4784
15:18 both must bathe with w, 4784
15:21 must wash his clothes and bathe with w, 4784
15:22 must wash his clothes and bathe with w, 4784
15:27 he must wash his clothes and bathe with w, 4784
16: 4 so he must bathe himself with w 4784
16:24 He shall bathe himself with w in 4784
16:26 and bathe himself with w; 4784
16:28 and bathe himself with w; 4784
17:15 must wash his clothes and bathe with w, 4784
22: 6 unless he has bathed himself with w. 4784
Nu 5:17 Then he shall take some holy w in a clay jar 4784
5:17 from the tabernacle floor into the w. 4784
5:18 while he himself holds the bitter w 4784
5:19 may this bitter w that brings a curse 4784
5:22 May this w that brings a curse enter 4784
5:23 and then wash them off into the bitter w. 4784
5:24 He shall have the woman drink the bitter w 4784
5:24 and this w will enter her 4784
5:26 he is to have the woman drink the w. 4784
5:27 when she is made to drink the w that brings 4784
8: 7 Sprinkle the w *of* cleansing on them; 4784
19: 7 and bathe himself with w. 4784
19: 8 also wash his clothes and bathe with w, 4784
19: 9 by the Israelite community for use in the w 4784
19:12 He must purify himself with the w on NIH
19:13 the w *of* cleansing has not been sprinkled 4784
19:17 into a jar and pour fresh w over them. 4784
19:18 dip it in the w and sprinkle the tent and all 4784
19:19 must wash his clothes and bathe with w, 4784
19:20 The w *of* cleansing has not been sprinkled 4784
19:21 "The man who sprinkles the w 4784
19:21 the w *of* cleansing will be unclean 4784
20: 2 Now there was no w for the community, 4784
20: 5 And there is no w to drink!" 4784
20: 8 before their eyes and it will pour out its w. 4784
20: 8 You will bring w out of the rock for 4784
20:10 must we bring you w out of this rock?" 4784
20:11 W gushed out, and the community 4784
20:17 or drink w *from* any well. 4784
20:19 if we or our livestock drink any of your w, 4784
21: 5 There is no w! 4784
21:16 the people together and I will give them w." 4784
21:22 or drink w *from* any well. 4784
24: 7 W will flow from their buckets; 4784
24: 7 their seed will have abundant w. 4784
31:23 also be purified with the w *of* cleansing. 4784
31:23 withstand fire must be put through that w. 4784
33:14 where there was no w for the people 4784
Dt 2: 6 for the food you eat and the w you drink.'" 4784
2:28 to eat and w to drink for their price in silver. 4784
8: 7 a land with streams and pools of w, 4784
8:15 He brought you w out of hard rock. 4784
9: 9 I ate no bread and drank no w. 4784
9:18 I ate no bread and drank no w, 4784
10: 7 a land with streams of w. 4784
12:16 pour it out on the ground like w. 4784
12:24 pour it out on the ground like w. 4784
14: 9 Of all the creatures living in the w, 4784
15:23 pour it out on the ground like w. 4784
23: 4 to meet you with bread and w on your way 4784
29:11 who chop your wood and carry your w. 4784
Jos 2:10 the LORD dried up the w *of* the Red Sea 4784
3:16 the w from upstream stopped flowing. 4784
3:16 while the w flowing down to the Sea of NIH
7: 5 of the people melted and became like w. 4784
9:21 but let them be woodcutters and w carriers 4784
9:23 as woodcutters and w carriers for the house 4784
9:27 the Gibeonites woodcutters and w carriers 4784
15:19 give me also springs of w." 4784
Jdg 1:15 give me also springs of w." 4784
4:19 "Please give me some w." 4784
5: 4 the clouds poured down w. 4784
5:25 He asked for w, and she gave him milk; 4784
6:38 wrung out the dew—a bowlful of w. 4784
7: 4 Take them down to the w. 4784
7: 5 So Gideon took the men down to the w. 4784
7: 5 the w with their tongues like a dog 4784
15:19 and w came out of it. 4784
Ru 2: 9 a drink from the w jars the men have filled." NIH
1Sa 7: 6 they drew w and poured it out before 4784
9:11 they met some girls coming out to draw w, 4784
25:11 Why should I take my bread and w, 4784
26:11 the spear and w jug that are near his head, 4784
26:12 the spear and w jug near Saul's head, 4784
26:16 Where are the king's spear and w jug 4784
1Sa 30:11 They gave him w to drink and food to eat— 4784
30:12 not eaten any food or drunk *any* w 4784
2Sa 5: 8 the Jebusites will have to use the w **shaft** 7562
12:27 against Rabbah and taken its w **supply.** 4784
14:14 Like w spilled on the ground, 4784
23:15 David longed for w and said, "Oh, NIH
23:15 that someone would get me a drink of w 4784
23:16 drew w from the well near the gate 4784
1Ki 13: 8 nor would I eat bread or drink w here. 4784
13: 9 not eat bread or drink w or return by 4784
13:16 nor can I eat bread or drink w with you 4784
13:17 not eat bread or drink w there or return by 4784
13:18 so that he may eat bread and drink w.'" 4784
13:22 and drank w in the place where he told you 4784
14:15 that it will be like a reed swaying in the w. 4784
17:10 a little w in a jar so I may have a drink?" 4784
18: 4 and had supplied them with food and w.) 4784
18:13 and supplied them with food and w. 4784
18:33 "Fill four large jars with w and pour it on 4784
18:35 The w ran down around the altar and 4784
18:38 and also licked up the w in the trench. 4784
19: 6 bread baked over hot coals, and a jar of w. 4784
22:27 but bread and w until I return safely.'" 4784
2Ki 2: 8 rolled it up and struck the w with it. 4784
2: 8 The w divided to the right and to the left, NIH
2:14 that had fallen from him and struck the w 4784
2:14 When he struck the w, it divided 4784
2:19 the w is bad and the land is unproductive." 4784
2:21 'I have healed this w. 4784
2:22 the w has remained wholesome to this day, 4784
3: 9 the army had no more w for themselves or 4784
3:11 He used to pour w on the hands of Elijah." 4784
3:17 yet this valley will be filled with w, 4784
3:20 w flowing from the direction of Edom! 4784
3:20 And the land was filled with w. 4784
3:22 the sun was shining on the w. 4784
3:22 the w looked red—like blood. 4784
6: 5 the iron axhead fell into the w. 4784
6:22 and w before them so that they may eat 4784
8:15 in w and spread it over the king's face, 4784
18:31 from his own vine and fig tree and drink w 4784
19:24 in foreign lands and drunk the w there. 4784
20:20 and the tunnel by which he brought w into 4784
1Ch 11:17 David longed for w and said, "Oh, NIH
11:17 that someone would get me a drink of w 4784
11:18 drew w from the well near the gate 4784
2Ch 18:26 but bread and w until I return safely.'" 4784
32: 3 and military staff about blocking off the w 4784
32: 4 of Assyria come and find plenty of w?" 4784
32:30 Gihon spring and channeled **the** w down 4392S
Ezr 10: 6 he ate no food and drank no w, 4784
Ne 3:26 a point opposite the W Gate toward the east 4784
4:23 even when he went for w. 4784
8: 1 as one man in the square before the W Gate. 4784
8: 3 as he faced the square before the W Gate in 4784
8:16 and in the square by the W Gate and the one 4784
9:15 and in their thirst you brought them w from 4784
9:20 and you gave them w for their thirst. 4784
12:37 above the house of David to the W Gate on 4784
13: 2 and w but had hired Balaam to call a curse 4784
Job 3:24 my groans pour out like w. 4784
5:10 he sends w upon the countryside. 4784
6:19 The caravans of Tema look for w, 4564S
8:11 Can reeds thrive without w? 4784
14: 9 of w it will bud and put forth shoots like 4784
14:11 As w disappears from the sea or 4784
14:19 as w wears away stones and torrents wash 4784
15:16 who drinks up evil like w! 4784
22: 7 You gave no w to the weary 4784
22:11 and why a flood of w covers you. 4784
24:18 "Yet they are foam on the surface of the w; 4784
29:19 My roots will reach to the w, 4784
34: 7 who drinks scorn like w? 4784
36:27 "He draws up the drops of w, 4784
37:13 or to w his earth and show his love. NIH
38:26 to w a land where no man lives, 4763
38:34 and cover yourself with a flood of w? 4784
38:37 Who can tip over the w **jars** *of* the heavens 5574
Ps 1: 3 He is like a tree planted by streams of w, 4784
22:14 I am poured out like w, 4784
42: 1 As the deer pants for streams of w, 4784
58: 7 Let them vanish like w that flows away; 4784
63: 1 in a dry and weary land where there is no w. 4784
65: 9 You care for the land and w it; 8796
65: 9 with w to provide the people with grain, 4784
66:12 we went through fire and w, 4784
77:17 The clouds poured down w, 4784
78:13 he made the w stand firm like a wall. 4784
78:15 the desert and **gave** them w as abundant as 9197
78:16 of a rocky crag and made w flow down 4784
78:20 When he struck the rock, w gushed out, 4784
79: 3 They have poured out blood like w all 4784
104:10 He makes springs pour w into the ravines; NIH
104:11 *They* **give** w *to* all the beasts of the field; 9197
105:41 He opened the rock, and w gushed out; 4784
107:35 He turned the desert into pools of w and 4784
109:18 it entered into his body like w, 4784
114: 8 the hard rock into springs of w. 4784
Pr 5:15 Drink w from your own cistern, 4784
5:15 **running** w from your own well. 5689
5:16 your streams of w in the public squares? 4784
8:24 there were no springs abounding with w; 4784
9:17 "Stolen w is sweet; food eaten in secret 4784
25:21 if he is thirsty, give him w to drink. 4784
25:25 Like cold w to a weary soul is good news 4784
27:19 As w reflects a face, so a man's heart 4784
30:16 which is never satisfied with w, and fire, 4784
Ecc 2: 6 to w groves of flourishing trees. 9197
11: 3 If clouds are full of w, they pour rain NIH
SS 4:15 a well of flowing w streaming down 4784
5:12 His eyes are like doves by the w streams, 4784
Isa 1:22 your choice wine is diluted with w. 4784
1:30 like a garden without w. 4784
3: 1 all supplies of food and all supplies of w, 4784
7:19 the thornbushes and at all the w **holes.** 5635
12: 3 With joy you will draw w from the wells 4784
18: 2 by sea in papyrus boats over the w. 4784
19: 8 who throw nets on the w will pine away. 4784
21:14 bring w for the thirsty; 4784
22: 9 you stored up w *in* the Lower Pool. 4784
22:11 a reservoir between the two walls for the w 4784
27: 3 *I* w it continually. 9197
28:17 and w will overflow your hiding place. 4784
30:14 a hearth or scooping w out of a cistern." 4784
30:20 and the w *of* affliction, your teachers will 4784
30:25 of w will flow on every high mountain 4784
32: 2 of w in the desert and the shadow of 4784
32: 6 and from the thirsty he withholds w. 5482
33:16 and w will not fail him. 4784
35: 6 W will gush forth in the wilderness 4784
36:16 from his own vine and fig tree and drink w 4784
37:25 in foreign lands and drunk the w there. 4784
41:17 "The poor and needy search for w, 4784
41:18 I will turn the desert into pools of w, 4784
43:20 because I provide w in the desert 4784
44: 3 For I will pour w on the thirsty land, 4784
44:12 he drinks no w and grows faint. 4784
48:21 he made w flow for them from the rock; 4784
48:21 he split the rock and w gushed out. 4784
49:10 and lead them beside springs of w. 4784
50: 2 their fish rot for lack of w and die of thirst. 4784
64: 2 fire sets twigs ablaze and causes w to boil, 4784
Jer 2:13 have forsaken me, the spring of living w, 4784
2:13 broken cisterns that cannot hold w. 4784
2:18 Now why go to Egypt to drink w *from* 4784
2:18 And why go to Assyria to drink w *from* 4784
6: 7 As a well pours out its w, 4784
8:14 to perish and given us poisoned w to drink, 4784
9: 1 a **spring of** w and my eyes a fountain 4784
9:15 and drink poisoned w. 4784
9:18 with tears and w streams from our eyelids. 4784
13: 1 but do not let it touch w." 4784
14: 3 The nobles send their servants for w; 4784
14: 3 they go to the cisterns but find no w. 4784
17: 8 the w that sends out its roots by the stream. 4784
17:13 forsaken the LORD, the spring of living w. 4784
23:15 and drink poisoned w, 4784
31: 9 I will lead them beside streams of w on 4784
38: 6 it had no w in it, only mud, 4784
La 2:19 pour out your heart like w in the presence of 4784
5: 4 We must buy the w we drink; 4784
Eze 4:11 Also measure out a sixth of a hin of w 4784
4:16 in anxiety and drink rationed w in despair, 4784
4:17 for food and w will be scarce. 4784
7:17 and every knee will become as weak as w. 4784
12:18 and shudder in fear as you drink your w. 4784
12:19 in anxiety and drink their w in despair, 4784
16: 4 nor were you washed with w 4784
16: 9 with w and washed the blood from you 4784
17: 5 He planted it like a willow by abundant w, 4784
17: 7 and stretched out its branches to him for w. 9197
17: 8 in good soil by abundant w so 4784
19:10 a vine in your vineyard planted by the w; 4784
19:10 and full of branches because of abundant w. 4784
21: 7 and every knee become as weak as w.' 4784
24: 3 put it on and pour w into it. 4784
32: 2 about in your streams, churning the w 4784
34:18 Is it not enough for you to drink clear w? 4784
36:25 I will sprinkle clean w on you, 4784
47: 1 and I saw w coming out from under 4784
47: 1 The w was coming down from under 4784
47: 2 and the w was flowing from the south side. 4784
47: 3 then led me through w that was ankle-deep. 4784
47: 4 and led me through w that was knee-deep. 4784
47: 4 and led me through w that was *up to* 4784
47: 5 the w had risen and was deep enough 4784
47: 8 "This w flows toward the eastern region 4784
47: 8 into the Sea, the w there becomes fresh. 4784
47: 9 because this w flows there and makes 4784
47: 9 and makes the salt w fresh; NIH
47:12 the w from the sanctuary flows to them. 4784
Da 1:12 Give us nothing but vegetables to eat and w 4784
Hos 2: 5 who give me my food and my w, 4784
5:10 on them like a flood of w. 4784
6: 3 like the spring rains *that* w the earth." 3722
Joel 1:20 of w have dried up and fire has devoured 4784
3:18 all the ravines of Judah will run with w. 4784
3:18 the LORD's house and *will* w the valley 9197
Am 4: 8 People staggered from town to town for w 4784
8:11 not a famine of food or a thirst for w, 4784
Mic 1: 4 like w rushing down a slope. 4784
Na 2: 8 and its w is draining away. 4784
3: 8 situated on the Nile, with w around her? 4784
3:14 Draw w *for* the siege, 4784
Hab 3:10 Torrents of w swept by; 4784
Zec 14: 8 On that day living w will flow out 4784
Mt 3:11 "I baptize you with w for repentance. *5623*
3:16 he went up out *of* the w. *5623*
8:32 into the lake and died in the w. *5623*
10:42 **gives** even a cup of cold w to one of these *4540*
14:28 "tell me to come to you on the w." *5623*
14:29 walked on the w and came toward Jesus. *5623*
17:15 He often falls into the fire or into the w. *5623*
27:24 he took w and washed his hands in front of *5623*

Mk 1: 8 I baptize you *with* w, 5623
1:10 As Jesus was coming up out *of* the w, 5623
9:22 "It has often thrown him into fire or w 5623
9:41 a cup *of* w in my name because you belong 5623
14:13 a man carrying a jar *of* w will meet you. 5623
Lk 3:16 "I baptize you *with* w. 5623
5: 4 he said to Simon, "Put out into deep w, NIG
7:44 You did not give me any w for my feet, 5623
8:25 He commands even the winds and the w, 5623
13:15 from the stall and lead it out *to* **give** it w? 4540
16:24 of his finger *in* w and cool my tongue, 5623
22:10 a man carrying a jar *of* w will meet you. 5623
Jn 1:26 "I baptize with w," John replied, 5623
1:31 but the reason I came baptizing with w was 5623
1:33 to baptize with w told me, 5623
2: 6 Nearby stood six stone w **jars,** 5620
2: 7 "Fill the jars *with* w"; 5623
2: 9 and the master of the banquet tasted the w 5623
2: 9 the servants who had drawn the w knew. 5623
3: 5 of God unless he is born of w and the Spirit. 5623
3:23 because there was plenty of w, 5623
4: 7 When a Samaritan woman came to draw w, 5623
4:10 and he would have given you living w." 5623
4:11 Where can you get this living w? 5623
4:13 "Everyone who drinks this w will 5623
4:14 the w I give him will never thirst. 5623
4:14 the w I give him will become in him 5623
4:14 a spring *of* w welling up to eternal life." 5623
4:15 give me this w so that I won't get thirsty 5623
4:15 and have to keep coming here *to* **draw** w." 533
4:28 Then, leaving her w **jar,** 5620
4:46 where he had turned the w into wine. 5623
5: 7 into the pool when the w is stirred. 5623
6:19 walking on the w; and they were terrified. 2498
7:38 streams *of* living w will flow from within him." 5623
13: 5 he poured w into a basin and began to wash 5623
19:34 bringing a sudden flow of blood and w. 5623
21: 7 and jumped into the w. 2498
Ac 1: 5 For John baptized *with* w, 5623
8:36 they came to some w and the eunuch said, 5623
8:36 and the eunuch said, "Look, here is w. 5623
8:38 down into the w and Philip baptized him. 5623
8:39 When they came up out of the w, 5623
10:47 these people from being baptized with w? 5623
11:16 'John baptized *with* w, 5623
27:28 the w was a hundred and twenty feet deep. NIG
Eph 5:26 by the washing *with* w through the word, 5623
1Ti 5:23 Stop **drinking only** w, and use a little wine 5621
Heb 9:19 together with w, scarlet wool and branches 5623
10:22 and having our bodies washed *with* pure w. 5623
Jas 3:11 Can both **fresh** w and salt water flow from 1184
3:11 Can both fresh water and **salt** w flow from 4395
3:12 Neither can a salt spring produce fresh w. 5623
1Pe 3:20 eight in all, were saved through w, 5623
3:21 this w symbolizes baptism that now saves NIG
2Pe 2:17 These men are springs **without** w 536
3: 5 the earth was formed out of w and by water. 5623
3: 5 the earth was formed out of water and by w. 5623
1Jn 5: 6 This is the one who came by w and blood— 5623
5: 6 He did not come by w only, 5623
5: 6 but by w and blood. 5623
5: 8 the Spirit, the w and the blood; 5623
Rev 7:17 he will lead them to springs *of* living w. 5623
8:10 a third of the rivers and on the springs *of* w 5623
12:15 Then from his mouth the serpent spewed w 5623
14: 7 the earth, the sea and the springs *of* w." 5623
16: 4 on the rivers and springs *of* w, 5623
16:12 and its w was dried up to prepare the way 5623
21: 6 without cost from the spring *of* the w of life. 5623
22: 1 angel showed me the river *of* the w of life, 5623
22:17 let him take the free gift *of* the w of life. 5623

WATER'S (3) [WATER]

Jos 3:15 and their feet touched the w edge, 4784
Mk 4: 1 along the shore at the w **edge.** 2498
Lk 5: 2 he saw at the w edge two boats, 3349

WATERCOURSE (1) [WATER]

Pr 21: 1 directs it like a w wherever he pleases. 4784+7104

WATERED (10) [WATER]

Ge 2: 6 up from the earth and w the whole surface 9197
13:10 the whole plain of the Jordan *was* **well** w, 5482
24:46 So I drank, and *she* w the camels also. 9197
29: 2 because the flocks *were* w from that well. 9197
29:10 of the well and w his uncle's sheep. 9197
Ex 2:17 and came to their rescue and w their flock. 9197
2:19 He even drew water for us and w the flock." 9197
Dt 29:19 This will bring disaster on the w **land** 8116
Ps 104:16 The trees of the LORD *are* **well** w, 8425
1Co 3: 6 I planted the seed, Apollos w it, 4540

WATERFALLS (1) [WATER]

Ps 42: 7 Deep calls to deep in the roar of your w; 7562

WATERFLOOD (KJV) See FLOODWATERS

WATERING (5) [WATER]

Ge 2:10 A river w the garden flowed from Eden; 9197
30:38 the peeled branches in all the w troughs, 4784
Jdg 5:11 the voice of the singers at the w **places.** 5393
Ps 72: 6 like showers w the earth. 2449
Isa 55:10 to it without w the earth and making it bud 8115

WATERLESS (2) [WATER]

Dt 8:15 that thirsty and w land, 401+4784
Zec 9:11 I will free your prisoners from the w pit. 401+4784

WATERPOT, WATERPOTS (KJV) See JARS, WATER JAR

WATERS (165) [WATER]

Ge 1: 2 the Spirit of God was hovering over the w. 4784
1: 6 an expanse between the w to separate water 4784
1:10 and the gathered w he called "seas." 4784
7: 7 the ark to escape the w *of* the flood. 4784
7:17 as the w increased they lifted the ark high 4784
7:18 The w rose and increased greatly on 4784
7:20 The w rose and covered the mountains to 4784
7:24 The w flooded the earth for a hundred 4784
8: 1 a wind over the earth, and the w receded. 4784
8: 5 The w continued to recede until 4784
9:11 Never again will all life be cut off by the w 4784
9:15 the w become a flood to destroy all life. 4784
49: 4 Turbulent as the w, you will no longer excel 4784
Ex 7:19 and stretch out your hand over the w 4784
8: 6 So Aaron stretched out his hand over the w 4784
14:21 The w were divided, 4784
14:26 the sea so that the w may flow back over 4784
15: 5 The **deep** w have covered them; 9333
15: 8 By the blast of your nostrils the w piled up. 4784
15: 8 The surging w stood firm like a wall; NIH
15: 8 the **deep** w congealed in the heart of the sea. 9333
15:10 They sank like lead in the mighty w. 4784
15:19 the LORD brought the w *of* the sea back 4784
20: 4 or on the earth beneath or in the w below. 4784
Nu 20:13 These were the w of Meribah, 4784
20:24 against my command at the w *of* Meribah. 4784
24: 6 like cedars beside the w. 4784
27:14 for when the community rebelled at the w 4784
27:14 (These were the w *of* Meribah Kadesh, 4784
Dt 4:18 along the ground or any fish in the w below. 4784
5: 8 or on the earth beneath or in the w below. 4784
11: 4 how he overwhelmed them with the w *of* 4784
32:51 of the Israelites at the w *of* Meribah Kadesh 4784
33: 8 you contended with him at the w 4784
33:13 above and with the **deep** w that lie below; 9333
Jos 3: 8 the edge of the Jordan's w, go and stand 4784
3:13 its w flowing downstream will be cut off 4784
4: 7 the w *of* the Jordan were cut off. 4784
4:18 the w *of* the Jordan returned to their place 4784
11: 5 made camp together at the W *of* Merom, 4784
11: 7 against them suddenly at the W *of* Merom 4784
15: 7 along to the w *of* En Shemesh and came out 4784
15: 9 toward the spring of the w *of* Nephtoah, 4784
16: 1 east of the w *of* Jericho, 4784
18:15 at the spring of the w *of* Nephtoah. 4784
Jdg 5:19 of Canaan fought at Taanach by the w 4784
7:24 down against the Midianites and seize the w 4784
7:24 the w of the Jordan as far as Beth Barah. 4784
2Sa 5:20 "As w break out, the LORD has broken out 4784
22:17 he drew me out of deep w. 4784
2Ki 5:12 better than any of the w *of* Israel? 4784
1Ch 14:11 "As w break out, God has broken out 4784
Ne 9:11 like a stone into mighty w. 4784
Job 11:16 recalling it only as w gone by. 4784
12:15 If he holds back the w, there is drought; 4784
20:28 rushing w on the day of God's wrath. NIH
26: 5 those beneath the w and all that live 4784
26: 8 He wraps up the w in his clouds, 4784
26:10 of the w for a boundary between light 4784
28:25 of the wind and measured out the w, 4784
37:10 and the broad w become frozen. 4784
38:30 when the w become hard as stone, 4784
Ps 18:16 he drew me out of deep w. 4784
23: 2 he leads me beside quiet w, 4784
24: 2 upon the seas and established it upon the w. 5643
29: 3 The voice of the LORD is over the w; 4784
29: 3 the LORD thunders over the mighty w. 4784
32: 6 the mighty w rise, they will not reach him. 4784
33: 7 He gathers the w *of* the sea into jars; 4784
46: 3 though its w roar and foam and 4784
66: 6 they passed through the w on foot— 5643
69: 1 O God, for the w have come up to my neck. 4784
69: 2 I have come into the deep w; 4784
69:14 from those who hate me, from the deep w. 4784
73:10 to them and drink up w *in* abundance. 4784
74:13 the heads of the monster in the w. 4784
77:16 The w saw you, O God, the waters saw you 4784
77:16 O God, the w saw you and writhed; 4784
77:19 your way through the mighty w, 4784
81: 7 I tested you at the w *of* Meribah. 4784
93: 4 Mightier than the thunder of the great w, 4784
104: 3 the beams of his upper chambers on their w. 4784
104: 6 the w stood above the mountains. 4784
104: 7 But at your rebuke the w fled, NIH
104:12 The birds of the air nest by **the** w; 2157
104:13 *He* w the mountains 9197
105:29 He turned their w into blood, 4784
106:11 The w covered their adversaries; 4784
106:32 the w *of* Meribah they angered the LORD, 4784
107:23 they were merchants on the mighty w. 4784
124: 5 the raging w would have swept us away. 4784
136: 6 who spread out the earth upon the w, 4784
144: 7 and rescue me from the mighty w, 4784
147:18 he stirs up his breezes, and the w flow. 4784
148: 4 you highest heavens and you w above 4784
Pr 8:29 so the w would not overstep his command, 4784
18: 4 The words of a man's mouth are deep w, 4784
20: 5 The purposes of a man's heart are deep w, 4784
30: 4 Who has wrapped up the w in his cloak? 4784
Ecc 11: 1 Cast your bread upon the w, 4784
SS 8: 7 Many w cannot quench love; 4784
Isa 8: 6 the gently flowing w *of* Shiloah 4784
10:26 and he will raise his staff over the w, 3542
11: 9 the knowledge of the LORD as the w cover 4784
15: 6 The w *of* Nimrim are dried up and 4784
15: 9 Dimon's w are full of blood, 4784
17:12 they roar like the roaring of great w! 4784
17:13 the peoples roar like the roar of surging w, 4784
19: 5 The w of the river will dry up, 4784
23: 3 the great w came the grain of the Shihor; 4784
40:12 Who has measured the w in the hollow 4784
43: 2 you pass through the w, I will be with you; 4784
43:16 a path through the mighty w, 4784
51:10 the w *of* the great deep, 4784
54: 9 that the w *of* Noah would never again cover 4784
55: 1 all you who are thirsty, come to the w; 4784
58:11 like a spring whose w never fail. 4784
63:12 who divided the w before them, 4784
Jer 10:13 he thunders, the w in the heavens roar; 4784
18:14 Do its cool w from distant sources ever 4784
46: 7 like rivers of surging w? 4784
46: 8 like rivers of surging w. 4784
47: 2 "See how the w are rising in the north; 4784
48:34 for even the w *of* Nimrim are dried up. 4784
50:38 A drought on her w! 4784
51:13 You who live by many w and are rich 4784
51:16 he thunders, the w in the heavens roar; 4784
51:55 Waves [of enemies] will rage like great w; 4784
La 3:54 the w closed over my head, 4784
Eze 1:24 like the roar of rushing w, 4784
26:19 over you and its vast w cover you, 4784
27:34 by the sea in the depths of the w; 4784
31: 4 The w nourished it, 4784
31: 5 spreading because of abundant w. 4784
31: 7 for its roots went down to abundant w. 4784
31:14 by the w are ever to tower proudly on high, 4784
31:15 and its abundant w were restrained. 4784
32:13 beside abundant w no longer to be stirred 4784
32:14 Then I will let her w settle 4784
43: 2 His voice was like the roar of rushing w, 4784
47:19 as far as the w *of* Meribah Kadesh, 4784
48:28 of Gad will run south from Tamar to the w 4784
Da 12: 6 who was above the w *of* the river, 4784
12: 7 who was above the w *of* the river, 4784
Hos 10: 7 like a twig on the surface of the w. 4784
Am 5: 8 the w *of* the sea and pours them out over 4784
9: 6 the w *of* the sea and pours them out over 4784
Jnh 2: 5 The engulfing w threatened me, 4784
Na 3: 8 The river was her defense, the w her wall. 4784
Hab 2:14 glory of the LORD, as the w cover the sea. 4784
3:15 with your horses, churning the great w. 4784
Lk 8:24 up and rebuked the wind and the raging w; 5623
Jn 6:18 and the w grew rough. 2498
1Co 3: 7 he who plants nor he who w is anything, 4540
3: 8 and the man who w have one purpose, 4540
2Pe 3: 6 By **these** w also the world of that time 4005S
Rev 1:15 his voice was like the sound *of* rushing w. 5623
8:11 A third *of* the w turned bitter, 5623
8:11 from the w that had become bitter. 5623
11: 6 the w into blood and to strike the earth 5623
14: 2 from heaven like the roar *of* rushing w and 5623
16: 5 I heard the angel in charge *of* the w say: 5623
17: 1 the great prostitute, who sits on many w. 5623
17:15 Then the angel said to me, "The w you saw, 5623
19: 6 of rushing w and like loud peals of thunder, 5623

WATERSPOUTS (KJV) See WATERFALLS

WATERY (1) [WATER]

Isa 44:27 who says to the w **deep,** 'Be dry, 7425

WAVE (37) [WAVED, WAVES, WAVY]

Ex 29:24 the hands of Aaron and his sons and w them 5677
29:24 before the LORD as a w **offering.** 9485
29:26 w it before the LORD as a wave offering, 5677
29:26 wave it before the LORD as a w **offering,** 9485
35:22 as a w **offering** to the LORD. 9485
38:24 of the gold from the w **offering** used for all 9485
38:29 the w **offering** was 70 talents and 2,400 9485
Lev 7:30 with the breast, and w the breast before 5677
7:30 before the LORD as a w **offering.** 9485
8:27 before the LORD as a w **offering.** 9485
8:29 before the LORD as a w **offering,** 9485
9:21 before the LORD as a w **offering,** 9485
10:15 before the LORD as a w **offering.** 9485
14:12 *he shall* w them before the LORD as 5677
14:12 before the LORD as a w **offering.** 9485
14:24 and w them before the LORD as 5677
14:24 before the LORD as a w **offering.** 9485
23:11 *to* w the sheaf before the LORD so it will 5677
23:11 the priest *is to* w it on the day after 5677
23:12 On the day you w the sheaf, 5677
23:15 the sheaf of the w **offering,** 9485
23:17 as a w **offering** of firstfruits to the LORD. 9485
23:20 *to* w the two lambs before the LORD as 5677
23:20 before the LORD as a w **offering,** 9485
Nu 5:25 w it before the LORD and bring it to 5677
6:20 The priest *shall* then w them before 5677

Nu 6:20 before the LORD as a w **offering;** 9485
8:11 before the LORD as a w **offering** from 9485
8:13 and then present them as a w **offering** to 9485
8:15 and presented them as a w **offering,** 9485
8:21 Then Aaron presented them as a w **offering** 9485
18:11 from the gifts of all the w **offerings** *of* 9485
18:18 the w **offering** and the right thigh are yours. 9485
2Ki 5:11 w his hand over the spot and cure me 5677
Job 10:17 your forces come against me w **upon wave.** 2722
10:17 your forces come against me **wave upon** w. 2722
Jas 1:6 he who doubts is like a w of the sea, *3114*

WAVED (10) [WAVE]

Ex 29:27 the breast that **was** w and the thigh 5677+9485
Lev 7:34 the breast that is w and the thigh 9485
8:27 the hands of Aaron and his sons and w them 5677
8:29 w it before the LORD as a wave offering, 5677
9:21 Aaron w the breasts and the right thigh 5677
10:14 that was w and the thigh that was presented. 9485
10:15 the breast that was w must be brought with 9485
10:15 *be* w before the LORD as a wave offering. 5677
14:21 a guilt offering to be w to make atonement 9485
Nu 6:20 that was w and the thigh that was presented. 9485

WAVER (2) [WAVERING]

1Ki 18:21 How long *will* you w between two opinions? 7174
Ro 4:20 Yet *he did* not w through unbelief regarding *1359*

WAVERING (1) [WAVER]

Ps 26:1 I have trusted in the LORD without w. 5048

WAVES (29) [WAVE]

2Sa 22:5 "The w *of* death swirled about me; 5403
Job 9:8 the heavens and treads on the w *of* the sea. 1195
38:11 here is where your proud w halt'? 1644
Ps 42:7 all your w and breakers have swept 5403
65:7 the roaring of their w, 1644
88:7 you have overwhelmed me with all your w. 5403
89:9 when its w mount up, you still them. 1644
93:3 the seas have lifted up their **pounding** w. 1922
107:25 up a tempest that lifted high the w. 1644
107:29 the w *of* the sea were hushed. 1644
Isa 48:18 your righteousness like the w *of* the sea. 1644
51:15 who churns up the sea so that its w roar— 1644
57:20 whose w cast up mire and mud. 4784
Jer 5:22 The w may roll, but they cannot prevail; 1644
31:35 who stirs up the sea so that its w roar— 1644
51:42 its roaring w will cover her. 1644
51:55 W *[of* enemies] will rage like great waters; 1644
Eze 26:3 like the sea casting up its w. 1644
Jnh 2:3 all your w and breakers swept over me. 1644
Hab 3:10 the deep roared and lifted its w on high. 3338
Mt 8:24 so that the w swept over the boat. *3246*
8:26 he got up and rebuked the winds and the w, *2498*
8:27 Even the winds and the w obey him!" *2498*
14:24 by the w because the wind was against it. *3246*
Mk 4:37 and the w broke over the boat, *3246*
4:39 rebuked the wind and said *to* the w, *2498*
4:41 Even the wind and the w obey him!" *2498*
Eph 4:14 **tossed back and forth by the** w, *3115*
Jude 1:13 They are wild w of the sea, *3246*

WAVY (1) [WAVE]

SS 5:11 his hair is w and black as a raven. 9446

WAX (4)

Ps 22:14 My heart has turned to w; 1880
68:2 as w melts before the fire, 1880
97:5 mountains melt like w before the LORD, 1880
Mic 1:4 like w before the fire, 1880

WAY (595) [AWAY, WAYS]

Ge 3:24 and forth to guard the w *to* the tree of life. 2006
9:23 Their faces were **turned the other** w so 345
12:20 and *they* **sent** him **on** his w, 906+8938
18:5 can be refreshed and then **go on** *your* w— 6296
18:16 with them to **see** them **on** their w. 8938
18:19 the w *of* the LORD by doing what is right 2006
19:2 then go on your w early in the morning." 2006
19:9 "Get out of our w," they replied. 2134
21:14 *She* **went on** *her* w and wandered in 2143
24:1 and the LORD had blessed him in **every** w. 3972
24:10 for Aram Naharaim and **made** *his* w to 2143
24:49 if not, tell me, so I may know **which** w to
turn." 196+3545+6584+6584+8520
24:50 we can say nothing to you **one** w or 8273[S]
24:54 **"Send** me **on** my w to my master." 8938
24:56 **Send** me **on** my w so I may go 8938
24:59 *they* **sent** their sister Rebekah **on** her w, 8938
26:31 Then Isaac **sent** them **on** their w, 8938
27:9 **just the** w he likes it. 889+3869
27:14 **just the** w his father liked it. 889+3869
28:5 Then Isaac **sent** Jacob **on** *his* w, 8938
30:25 **"Send** me **on** my w so I can go back 8938
30:26 and *I will* **be on** *my* w. 2143
30:43 **In this** w the man grew exceedingly
prosperous 2256
32:1 Jacob also went on his w, 2006
33:12 *"Let us* **be on** *our* w; 2143+2256+5825
33:16 that day Esau started on his w back to Seir. 2006
35:19 and was buried on the w to Ephrath (that is, 2006
37:25 and *they* **were on** *their* w to take them down 2143
38:13 "Your father-in-law **is on** *his* w to Timnah 6590
41:43 and men shouted before him, **"Make** w!" 91
44:3 the men **were sent on** *their* w 8938
45:24 "Don't quarrel on the w!" 2006
48:7 of Canaan while we were still on the w, 2006
Ex 2:12 Glancing **this** w and that and seeing no one, AIT
3:9 the w the Egyptians are oppressing them. 4316[S]
4:14 He *is* already **on** *his* w to meet you, 3655
4:24 At a lodging place on the w, 2006
5:15 Why have you treated your servants **this** w? 3907
13:21 in a pillar of cloud to guide them on their w 2006
16:4 **In this** w I will test them 5100
18:8 the w and how the LORD had saved them. 2006
18:20 the w to live and the duties they are 2006
18:27 **sent** his father-in-law **on** *his* w, 8938
19:21 not **force** *their* w **through** to see the LORD 2238
19:24 the people *must* not **force** *their* w **through** 2238
23:20 ahead of you to guard you along the w and 2006
23:28 and Hittites **out of** your w. 4200+4946+7156
26:17 the frames of the tabernacle **in this** w. 4027
26:24 the bottom **all the** w **to** the top, and fitted 6584
28:11 of the sons of Israel on the two stones the w 5126
29:9 **In this** w you shall ordain Aaron 2256
33:3 and I might destroy you on the w." 2006
36:22 the frames of the tabernacle **in this** w. 4027
36:29 the bottom **all the** w **to** the top and fitted 448
Lev 4:20 **In this** w the priest will make atonement 2256
4:26 **In this** w the priest will make atonement for 2256
4:31 **In this** w the priest will make atonement 2256
4:35 **In this** w the priest will make atonement 2256
5:5 he must confess in **what** *w* he has sinned AIT
5:10 in the **prescribed** w and make atonement 5477
5:13 **In this** w the priest will make atonement 2256
5:18 **In this** w the priest will make atonement 2256
6:7 **In this** w the priest will make atonement 2256
9:16 and offered it in the **prescribed** w. 5477
12:8 **In this** w the priest will make atonement 2256
14:31 **In this** w the priest will make atonement 2256
14:53 **In this** w he will make atonement for 2256
15:15 **In this** w he will make atonement before 2256
15:30 **In this** w he will make atonement for her 2256
16:16 **In this** w he will make atonement for 2256
19:5 sacrifice it **in such a** w **that** it will be 4200
19:25 **In this** w your harvest will be increased. 4200
22:29 sacrifice it **in such a** w **that** it will be 4200
Nu 2:34 **that is the** w they encamped 4027
2:34 and **that is the** w they set out, 4027
5:6 in **any** *w* and so is unfaithful to the LORD, AIT
8:14 **In this** w you are to set the Levites apart 2256
14:45 and beat them down **all the** w **to** Hormah. 6330
15:13 native-born must do these things **in this** w 3970
18:28 **In this** w you also will present an offering 4027
21:4 But the people grew impatient on the w; 2006
21:30 Heshbon is destroyed **all the** w **to** Dibon. 6330
24:25 and Balak went his own w. 2006
28:24 In this w prepare the food for 3869
Dt 1:31 all the w you went until you reached 2006
1:33 and to show you the w you should go. 2006
1:44 and beat you down from Seir **all the** w **to** 6330
2:1 For a long time *we* **made** *our* w **around** 6015
2:3 "You *have* **made** *your* w **around** 6015
4:7 near them the w the LORD our God is 3869
5:33 Walk in all the w that the LORD your God 2006
8:2 how the LORD your God led you all the w 2006
9:16 the w that the LORD had commanded you. 2006
10:11 "and lead the people on their w, 5023
11:28 the LORD your God and turn from the w 2006
12:4 the LORD your God **in** their w. 4027
12:31 the LORD your God **in** their w, 4027
13:5 he has tried to turn you from the w 2006
16:17 a gift in proportion to **the** w 889[S]
17:16 "You are not to go back that w again." 2006
20:3 be terrified or **give** w **to panic** before them. 6907
23:4 to meet you with bread and water on your w 2006
24:9 your God did to Miriam along the w 2006
25:17 along the w when you came out of Egypt. 2006
29:16 through the countries **on the** w here. 6296
29:19 **persist** in going **my own** w." 4213+9244
31:29 to turn from the w I have commanded you. 2006
32:6 Is **this** *the* w you repay the LORD, AIT
Jos 2:5 I don't know **which** w they went. 625+2025
2:16 and then go on your w." 2006
3:4 Then you will know which w to go, 2006
3:4 since you have never been this w before. 2006
5:4 in the desert on the w after leaving Egypt. 2006
5:7 not been circumcised on the w. 2006
9:22 'We live a **long** w from you,' 4394+8158
10:10 and cut them down **all the** w **to** Azekah 6330
11:8 pursued them **all the** w **to** Greater Sidon, 6330
18:8 As the men started **on** *their* w to map out 2143
23:5 The LORD your God himself will drive
them out of your w. 7156
23:14 "Now I am about to go the w *of* all 2006
Jdg 2:17 the w in which their fathers had walked, 2006
2:17 w of obedience to the LORD's commands. NIH
2:22 and see whether they will keep the w *of* 2006
3:18 *he* **sent on** their w the men 8938
4:6 of Naphtali and Zebulun and **lead the** w 5432
4:9 because of the w you are going about this, 2006
6:4 the land and ruined the crops **all the** w **to** 6330
9:40 **all the** w **to** the entrance to the gate. 6330
11:13 **all the** w **to** the Jordan. 6330
17:8 **On** his w he came to Micah's house in 2006+6913
18:7 they lived a **long** w from the Sidonians 8158
18:12 **On** *their* w they set up camp 6590
18:26 So the Danites went their w, and Micah, 2006
18:28 to rescue them because they lived a **long** w 8158
Jdg 19:9 get up and be on your w home." 2006
19:18 "We *are* **on** our w from Bethlehem in Judah 6296
19:27 and stepped out to continue on his w, 2006
20:36 men of Israel had given w before Benjamin, 5226
1Sa 1:18 Then she went her w and ate something, 2006
6:6 so *they could* **go on** *their* w? 2143
6:8 Send it **on** *its* w, 2143
6:12 **keeping** on the road and lowing **all the** w;
2143+2143
7:11 along the w to a point below Beth Car. NIH
9:6 Perhaps he will tell us what w to take." 2006
9:8 so that he will tell us what w to take." 2006
9:14 toward them **on** *his* w **up** *to* the high place. 6590
9:26 and *I will* **send** you **on** *your* w." 8938
12:23 I will teach you the w that is good and right. 2006
15:7 **all the** w from Havilah **to** Shur, 995
16:1 Fill your horn with oil and **be on** *your* w; 2143
19:24 He lay **that** w all that day and night. 6873[S]
24:3 He came to the sheep pens along the w; 2006
24:7 And Saul left the cave and went his w. 2006
24:19 for **the** w you treated me today. 889[S]
26:25 So David went on his w, 2006
28:22 and have the strength to go on your w." 2006
30:2 carried them off as they went on their w. 2006
2Sa 2:24 on the w *to* the wasteland of Gibeon. 2006
3:16 weeping behind her **all the** w to Bahurim. 2143
4:7 they traveled all night **by** w **of** the Arabah. 2006
5:25 **all the** w from Gibeon **to** Gezer. 995+6330
7:19 Is this your **usual** w **of dealing** *with* man, 9368
12:21 "Why are you acting this w? 1821
13:30 While they were on their w, 2006
15:6 in this w toward all the Israelites who came 1821
18:23 *by* w *of* the plain and outran the Cushite. 2006
19:31 to **send** him **on** his w from there. 8938
19:36 why should the king reward me in this w? 1692[S]
20:2 by their king **all the** w **from** the Jordan 4946
22:31 "As for God, his w is perfect; 2006
22:33 with strength and makes my w perfect. 2006
1Ki 2:2 "I am about to go the w *of* all the earth," 2006
5:10 **In this** w Hiram kept Solomon supplied 2256
6:33 **In the same** w he made four-sided jambs 4027
7:37 This is the w he made the ten stands. 3869
8:23 your servants who continue wholeheartedly
in your w. 4200+7156
8:36 Teach them the right w to live, 2006
11:29 the prophet of Shiloh met him on the w, 2006
13:9 or return by the w you came.' " 2006
13:10 not return by the w he had come to Bethel. 2006
13:12 "Which w did he go?" 2006
13:17 or return by the w you came.' " 2006
13:24 As *he* **went on** *his* w, 2143
18:46 he ran ahead of Ahab **all the** w **to** Jezreel.
995+3870+6330
19:15 "Go back the w you came, 2006
22:24 **"Which** w did the spirit from the LORD 361+2296
2Ki 2:1 and Elisha **were on** *their* w from Gilgal. 2143
3:22 To the Moabites **across the** w, 4946+5584
4:9 that this man who often comes our w is NIH
8:7 "The man of God has come **all the** w **up** 6330
9:15 Jehu said, "If this is the w you feel, NIH
9:27 in his chariot on the w **up** *to* Gur 5090
10:15 who *was on his* w to **meet** him. AIT
11:19 entering *by* w *of* the gate of the guards. 2006
19:28 I will make you return by the w you came.' 2006
19:33 By the w that he came he will return; 2006
21:22 and did not walk in the w *of* the LORD. 2006
1Ch 7:28 and Shechem and its villages **all the** w **to** 6330
14:16 **all the** w from Gibeon **to** 6330
15:13 about how to do it in the **prescribed** w." 5477
23:31 and in the w **prescribed** for them. 5477
2Ch 6:14 your servants who continue wholeheartedly
in your w. 4200+7156
6:27 Teach them the right w to live, 2006
18:23 **"Which** w did the spirit from the LORD go
361+2006+2021+2296
23:19 who was in any w unclean might enter. 1821
29:25 and lyres in the w **prescribed** *by* David 5184
Ezr 7:27 of the LORD in Jerusalem **in** this w 3869
8:31 from enemies and bandits along the w. 2006
9:2 and officials *have* **led the** w 2118+3338+8037
Ne 5:13 **"In this** w may God shake out of his house 3970
9:12 of fire to give them light on the w they were 2006
9:19 by night to shine on the w they were to take. 2006
11:30 **all the** w from Beersheba **to** the Valley 6330
Est 1:8 was allowed to **drink in** his **own** w, 9276
1:18 to all the king's nobles in the same w. NIH
3:6 for a w to destroy all Mordecai's people, NIH
9:27 **in the** w prescribed and at the time 3869
Job 3:23 to a man whose w is hidden, 2006
8:15 He leans on his web, but *it* **gives** w; 4202+6641
19:8 He has blocked my w so I cannot pass; 784
22:21 in this w prosperity will come to you. NIH
23:10 But he knows the w that I take; 2006
23:11 I have kept to his w without turning aside. 2006
28:23 the w *to* it and he alone knows 2006
29:25 the w *for* them and sat as their chief; 2006
32:3 because they had found no w **to refute** Job, 5101
33:14 For God does speak—now **one** w, 285+928
36:31 **This is the** w he governs the nations 928+4392
38:19 "What is the w to the abode of light? 2006
38:24 What is the w to the place where 2006
38:35 the lightning bolts **on** *their* w? 2143
Ps 1:1 or stand in the w *of* sinners or sit in the seat 2006
1:6 LORD watches over the w *of* the righteous, 2006
1:6 but the w *of* the wicked will perish. 2006
2:12 be angry and you be destroyed *in* your w, 2006
5:8 make straight your w before me. 2006

Ps 18:30 As for God, his w is perfect; 2006
18:32 with strength and makes my w perfect. 2006
25:9 in what is right and teaches them his **w.** 2006
25:12 He will instruct him in the w chosen 2006
27:11 Teach me your **w,** O LORD; 2006
32:8 and teach you in the w you should go; 2006
37:5 Commit your w to the LORD; 2006
37:23 If the LORD delights in a man's **w,** 2006
37:34 Wait for the LORD and keep his **w.** 2006
46:2 the earth **give w** and the mountains fall into 4614
50:23 the w so that I may show him the salvation 2006
77:19 your w through the mighty waters, 8666
85:13 before him and prepares the w *for* his steps. 2006
86:11 Teach me your **w,** O LORD, 2006
107:4 finding no w *to* a city 2006
107:7 He led them by a straight w to a city 2006
109:24 My knees **give w** from fasting; 4173
110:7 He will drink from a brook beside the **w;** 2006
119:9 How can a young man keep his w pure? 784
119:30 I have chosen the w *of* truth; 2006
139:24 See if there is any offensive w in me, 2006
139:24 and lead me in the w everlasting. 2006
142:3 it is you who know my **w.** 5986
143:8 Show me the w I should go, 2006
Pr 2:8 and protects the w *of* his faithful ones. 2006
3:23 Then you will go on your w in safety, 2006
4:11 I guide you in the w *of* wisdom and 2006
4:14 of the wicked or walk in the w *of* evil men. 2006
4:15 turn from it and **go on** *your* **w.** 6296
4:19 the w *of* the wicked is like deep darkness; 2006
5:6 She gives no thought to the w *of* life; 784
6:23 corrections of discipline are the w *to* life, 2006
8:2 On the heights along the **w,** 2006
8:20 I walk in the w *of* righteousness, 784
9:6 walk in the w *of* understanding. 2006
9:15 who go straight on their **w.** 784
10:17 He who heeds discipline shows the w 784
10:29 The w *of* the LORD is a refuge for 2006
11:5 the blameless makes a straight w *for* them, 2006
12:15 The w *of* a fool seems right to him, 2006
12:26 but the w *of* the wicked leads them astray. 2006
12:28 In the w *of* righteousness there is life; 784
13:15 but the w *of* the unfaithful is hard. 2006
14:12 There is a w that seems right to a man, 2006
15:9 The LORD detests the w *of* the wicked 2006
15:19 w *of* the sluggard is blocked with thorns, 2006
16:17 he who guards his w guards his life. 2006
16:25 There is a w that seems right to a man, 2006
18:16 A gift **opens the w** for the giver 8143
19:2 nor to be hasty and **miss the w.** 2627
20:24 then can anyone understand his own **w?** 2006
21:8 The w *of* the guilty is devious, 2006
22:6 a child **in the w** he **should go,** 2006+6584+7023
25:26 a righteous man *who* **gives** w to the wicked. 4572
30:19 the w *of* an eagle in the sky, 2006
30:19 the w *of* a snake on a rock, 2006
30:19 the w *of* a ship on the high seas, 2006
30:19 and the w *of* a man with a maiden. 2006
30:20 "This is the w *of* an adulteress: 2006
Ecc 10:15 he does not know the w to town. 2143
SS 6:1 **Which w** did your lover turn, 625+2025
Isa 8:11 not to follow the w *of* this people. 2006
9:1 *by* the w *of* the sea, along the Jordan— 2006
15:4 their voices are heard **all the w to** Jahaz. 6330
15:5 They go up the w *to* Luhith, 5090
22:25 peg driven into the firm place *will* **give w;** 4631
26:7 you make the w *of* the righteous smooth. 5047
26:8 LORD, walking in the w *of* your laws, 784
28:26 and teaches him the **right w.** 5477
30:11 Leave this w, get off this path, 2006
30:21 saying, "This is the w; walk in it." 2006
35:3 steady the knees *that* **give w;** 4173
35:8 it will be called the **W** *of* Holiness. 2006
35:8 it will be for those who walk in that **W;** 2006
37:29 I will make you return by the w you came. 2006
37:34 By the w that he came he will return; 2006
40:3 "In the desert prepare the w *for* the LORD; 2006
40:14 and who taught him the right **w?** 784
40:27 O Israel, "My w is hidden from the LORD; 2006
43:16 he who made a w through the sea, 2006
43:19 I am making a w in the desert and streams 2006
48:17 who directs you in the w you should go. 2006
51:5 my salvation *is* **on the w,** 3655
53:6 each of us has turned to his own **w;** 2006
55:7 Let the wicked forsake his w and 2006
56:11 they all turn to their own **w,** 2006
57:14 the obstacles out of the w *of* my people." 2006
58:13 if you honor it by not going your own w 2006
59:8 The w *of* peace they do not know; 2006
59:10 **feeling** *our* w like men without eyes. 1779
62:10 Prepare the w *for* the people. 2006
Jer 2:17 when he led you in the **w?** 2006
4:2 just and **righteous** *w* you swear, AIT
5:4 for they do not know the w *of* the LORD, 2006
5:5 surely they know the w *of* the LORD, 2006
5:31 and my people love it **this w.** 4027
6:16 ask where the good w is, and walk in it, 2006
12:1 Why does the w *of* the wicked prosper? 2006
13:9 **In the same w** I will ruin the pride of Judah 3970
21:8 See, I am setting before you the w *of* life 2006
21:8 before you the way of life and the w 2006
22:21 This has been your w from your youth; 2006
26:3 and each will turn from his evil **w.** 2006
28:11 '**In the same w** will I break the yoke of 3970
28:11 At this, the prophet Jeremiah went on his **w.** 2006
36:3 each of them will turn from his wicked **w;** 2006
39:4 the city at night *by* w *of* the king's garden, 2006
Jer 41:17 near Bethlehem *on their* w to Egypt 2143
48:5 They go up the w *to* Luhith, 5090
50:5 the w to Zion and turn their faces toward it. 2006
La 2:15 All who pass your w clap their hands 2006
3:9 He has barred my w with blocks of stone; 2006
Eze 4:13 "**In this** w the people will eat defiled food 3970
18:25 you say, 'The w *of* the Lord is not just.' 2006
18:25 Hear, O house of Israel: Is my w unjust? 2006
18:29 'The w *of* the Lord is not just.' 2006
20:30 the w your fathers did and lust after 2006
23:13 both of them went the same **w.** 2006
23:31 You have gone the w *of* your sister; 2006
32:6 with your flowing blood **all the w to** 448
33:17 'The w *of* the Lord is not just.' 2006
33:17 But it is their w that is not just. 2006
33:20 you say, 'The w *of* the Lord is not just.' 2006
39:11 It *will* **block the w** *of* travelers, 2888
44:3 to enter by w *of* the portico of the gateway 2006
44:3 of the gateway and go out the same **w.**" 2006
44:4 the man brought me *by* w *of* the north gate 2006
46:8 and he is to come out the same **w.** 2006
Da 1:8 for permission not to defile himself this **w.** NIH
3:29 for no other god can save **in** this **w.**" 10341
5:6 and his legs **gave w.** 10742
12:9 He replied, "**Go** *your* **w,** Daniel, 2143
12:13 "As for you, **go** *your* w till the end. 2143
Hos 2:6 in so that she cannot find her **w.** 5986
Am 6:14 the w from Lebo Hamath to the valley of NIH
Mic 2:13 One who breaks open the w will go up NIH
Na 1:3 His w is in the whirlwind and the storm, 2006
2:5 yet they stumble on their **w.** 2142
2:10 Hearts melt, knees **give w,** bodies tremble, 7211
Mal 2:8 But you have turned from the w and 2006
3:1 who will prepare the w before me. 2006
Mt 2:9 *they* **went on** *their* **w,** 4513
3:3 'Prepare the w for the Lord, 3847
4:15 the w to the sea, along the Jordan, 3847
5:12 **in the same w** they persecuted the prophets 4048
5:16 **In the same w,** let your light shine before 4048
5:25 Do it while you are still with him on the **w,** 3847
7:2 For in **the same w** you judge others, 3210[S]
8:28 so violent that no one could pass that **w.** 3847
11:10 who will prepare your w before you.' 3847
15:32 or they may collapse on the **w.**" 3847
17:12 **In the same w** the Son of Man is 2779+4048
18:14 **In the same w** your Father in heaven is 4048
19:8 But it was not **this w** from the beginning. 4048
19:12 eunuchs because they were born **that w;** 4048
19:12 others *were* **made that w** by men; 2335+2336[S]
21:18 *as he was* **on his w back** to the city, 2056
21:32 to you to show you the w of righteousness, 3847
21:36 and the tenants treated them **the same w.** 6058
21:46 *They* **looked for a w** to arrest him, 2426
22:16 of integrity and that you teach the w of God 3847
23:28 **In the same w,** on the outside you appear 4048
25:10 *while* they *were* **on their w** to buy the oil, 599
26:4 to arrest Jesus *in* some **sly w** and kill him. 1515
26:54 that say it must happen **in this w?**" 4048
27:41 **In the same w** the chief priests, 3931
27:44 **In the same w** the robbers who were 899
28:11 *While* the women *were* **on** *their* **w,** 4513
Mk 1:2 ahead of you, who will prepare your w"— 3847
1:3 'Prepare the w for the Lord, 3847
7:9 a **fine w** of setting aside the commands 2822
8:3 home hungry, they will collapse on the **w,** 3847
8:27 On the w he asked them, 3847
9:34 on the w they had argued about who was 3847
10:17 As Jesus started on his **w,** 3847
10:32 They were on their w up to Jerusalem, 3847
10:32 with Jesus leading the **w,** NIG
11:18 and began looking for a w to kill him, 4802
12:12 Then *they* **looked for a w** to arrest him 2426
12:14 the w of God in accordance with the truth. 3847
14:1 for **some** sly w to arrest Jesus and kill him. 4802
15:21 was passing by on his w in from 2262
15:31 **In the same w** the chief priests and 3931
16:2 *they were* **on their** w to the tomb 2262
Lk 1:76 on before the Lord to prepare the w for him, 3847
3:4 'Prepare the w for the Lord, 3847
4:30 through the crowd and **went on** *his* **w.** 4513
5:19 When they could not find a w to do this 4481
7:27 who will prepare your w before you.' 3847
7:29 acknowledged that God's w was right, NIG
8:14 **on** *their* w they are choked by life's worries, 4513
8:42 As Jesus *was* **on** *his* **w,** 5632
10:38 As Jesus and his disciples *were* **on** *their* **w,** 4513
12:58 try hard to be reconciled to him on the **w,** 3847
13:2 because they suffered this **w?** NIG
13:22 teaching as he made his w to Jerusalem. 4512
14:19 and I'm **on** *my* w to try them out. 4513
14:32 the other is still a **long w off** and will ask 4522
14:33 **In the same w,** any of you who does not 4048
15:7 I tell you that **in the same** w there will 4048
15:10 **In the same w,** I tell you, there is rejoicing 4048
15:20 "But while he was still a **long w off,** 3426
16:16 and everyone *is* **forcing** *his* w into it. 1041
17:11 Now on his w to Jerusalem, 4513
18:39 Those who **led the w** rebuked him 4575
19:4 since Jesus was coming that **w.** NIG
19:48 Yet they could not find **any w** to do it, 3836+5515
20:19 chief priests **looked for a w** to arrest him 2426
20:21 but teach the w of God in accordance with 3847
20:31 and **in the same w** the seven died, 6058
22:2 looking for **some** w to get rid of Jesus, 3836+4802
22:20 **In the same w,** after supper he took the cup, 6058
23:5 in Galilee and has come all the w here." NIG
23:26 *who was* **on** *his* w in from the country, 2262
Lk 24:35 the two told what had happened on the **w,** 3847
Jn 1:23 'Make straight the w for the Lord.'" 3847
4:30 and **made their** w toward him. 2262
4:51 *While* he *was* still **on the w,** 2849
7:46 "No one ever spoke **the w** this man does," 4048
10:1 but climbs in by some **other w,** 249
12:12 for the Feast heard that Jesus *was* **on his w** 2262
14:4 the w to the place where I am going." 3847
14:5 so how can we know the **w?"** 3847
14:6 "I am the w and the truth and the life. 3847
15:21 They will treat you this w because NIG
18:22 "Is **this the w** you answer the high priest?" 4048
21:1 It happened **this w:** 4048
Ac 1:11 will come back **in the same w** you have
seen him go into heaven." 4005+5573
7:6 God spoke to him **in this w:** 4048
8:27 and on his w he met an Ethiopian eunuch, NIG
8:28 and **on** *his* **w home** was sitting 5715
8:39 but went *on* his w rejoicing. 3847
9:2 he found any there who belonged to the **W,** 3847
13:4 **sent on** *their* w by the Holy Spirit, 1734
14:16 he let all nations go their own **w.** 3847
15:3 The church **sent** *them* **on** *their* **w,** 4636
16:17 who are telling you the w to be saved." 3847
17:22 I see that in **every** *w* you are very religious. AIT
18:25 He had been instructed in the w of the Lord, 3847
18:26 to their home and explained to him the w 3847
19:9 to believe and publicly maligned the **W.** 3847
19:20 **In this** w the word of the Lord spread 4048
19:23 a great disturbance about the **W.** 3847
21:5 *we* left and **continued on** *our* **w.** 4513
21:11 '**In this** w the Jews of Jerusalem will bind 4048
22:4 the followers of this **W** to their death, 3847
24:3 Everywhere and *in* **every** *w,* AIT
24:14 of our fathers as a follower of the **W,** 3847
24:22 Felix, who was well acquainted with the **W,** 3847
25:3 an ambush to kill him along the **w.** 3847
26:4 the w I have **lived** ever since I was a child, 1052
27:15 so we **gave** w to it and were driven along. 2113
27:44 **In this** w everyone reached land in safety. 4048
Ro 1:10 by God's will the w *may be* **opened for** me 2338
1:27 **In the same** w the men also abandoned 3931
3:2 Much in every **w!** 5573
3:17 and the w of peace they do not know." 3847
5:12 and **in this** w death came to all men, 4048
6:11 **In the same w,** count yourselves dead to sin 4048
7:6 from the law so that we serve in the **new w** 2786
7:6 and not in the **old** w of the written code. 4095
8:26 **In the same w,** the Spirit helps us 6058
10:5 Moses describes in this w the righteousness NIG
14:13 or obstacle in your brother's **w.** NIG
14:18 in **this** *w* is pleasing to God and approved AIT
15:19 from Jerusalem **all the w** around **to** Illyricum 3588
15:25 *I am* **on** *my* w to Jerusalem in the service of 4513
15:28 go to Spain and **visit** you **on the w.** 1328
16:2 in the Lord **in a w worthy** of the saints and 547
16:17 and put obstacles in your w that are NIG
1Co 1:5 in him you have been enriched in **every** *w*— AIT
2:11 **In the same** w no one knows the thoughts
of God except the Spirit of God. 2779+4048
4:17 He will remind you of my **w of life** 3847
7:4 **In the same w,** the husband's body does not 3931
7:35 a **right** *w* in undivided devotion to the Lord. AIT
8:12 you sin against your brothers **in this w** 4048
9:14 **In the same w,** the Lord has commanded 4048
9:24 Run **in such a w** as to get the prize. 4048
10:13 also provide a **w out** so that you can stand 1676
10:33 as I try to please everybody *in* **every** *w.* AIT
11:25 **In the same w,** after supper he took the cup, 6058
12:31 now I will show you the most excellent **w.** 3847
14:1 Follow the w of love and eagerly desire NIG
14:40 be done in a fitting and **orderly w.** 2848+5423
16:11 **Send** him **on** his w in peace 4636
2Co 1:16 planned to **visit** you **on** *my* w to Macedonia 1451
1:16 to *have you* **send** me **on** my w to Judea. 4636
5:16 we once regarded Christ **in this w,** 2848+4922[S]
6:4 of God we commend ourselves in **every** *w:* AIT
7:9 and so were **not** harmed in **any w** by us 3594
8:20 of the w we administer this liberal gift. NIG
9:11 be made rich in **every** *w* so that you can AIT
11:6 made this perfectly clear to you in **every** *w.* AIT
11:9 from being a burden to you in **any** *w* AIT
11:18 many are boasting **in the w** the world **does,** 2848
Gal 1:13 heard of my previous **w of life** in Judaism, 419
4:23 was born **in the ordinary w;** 2848+4922
4:29 the son born **in the ordinary w** 2848+4922
5:12 go the whole w and emasculate themselves! NIG
6:2 **in this** w you will fulfill the law of Christ. 4048
Eph 1:23 of him who fills everything in **every** *w.* AIT
4:20 did not come to know Christ **that w.** 4048
4:22 with regard to your former **w of life,** 419
5:28 **In this same w,** husbands ought to 2779+4048
6:9 masters, treat your slaves in the **same w.** 899
Php 1:7 It is right for me to feel **this** w about all 4047
1:18 The important thing is that *in* every **w,** 5573
1:20 I eagerly expect and hope that I will in **no w** 4029
1:28 in **any** w by those who oppose you. 3594
Col 1:10 of the Lord and may please him in **every** *w:* AIT
4:5 Be wise in the w you act toward outsiders; NIG
1Th 2:16 In **this** w they always heap up their sins to 3836
3:4 And it turned out **that w,** as you well know. 2777
3:5 I was afraid that **in some** w the tempter 4803
3:11 and our Lord Jesus clear the w for us 3847
4:4 to control his own body in a w that is holy NIG
2Th 2:3 Don't let anyone deceive you **in any w,**
2848+3594+5573
2:7 to do so till he is taken out of the **w.** 3545

2Th 3:16 give you peace at all times and in every **w**. 5573
1Ti 3:11 **In the same w**, their wives are to be 6058
5:25 **In the same w**, good deeds are obvious, 6058
6:19 In this **w** they will lay up treasure NIG
2Ti 3: 6 the kind who **worm** *their* **w** into homes 1905
3:10 know all about my teaching, my **w of life**, 73
Tit 2: 3 to be reverent in the **w** they **live**, 2949
2:10 that in **every** *w* they will make the teaching AIT
3:13 to **help** Zenas the lawyer and Apollos **on** *their* **w** 4636
Heb 2:17 to be made like his brothers in **every** *w*, AIT
4:15 tempted in **every** *w*, just as we are— AIT
9: 8 that the **w** into the Most Holy Place had not 3847
9:21 **In the same w**, he sprinkled with blood 3931
9:25 **the w** the high priest enters the Most Holy 6061
10:20 a new and living **w** opened for us through 3847
13: 7 *of* their **w of life** and imitate their faith. 419
13:18 and desire to live honorably in **every** *w*. AIT
Jas 1:11 **In the same w**, the rich man will fade away 4048
2:17 **In the same w**, faith by itself, 4048
2:25 **In the same w**, was not even Rahab 3931
5:20 the error *of* his **w** will save him from death 3847
1Pe 1:18 the empty **w of life** handed down to you 419
3: 1 Wives, **in the same w** be submissive 3931
3: 5 For **this is the w** the holy women of the 4048
3: 6 if you do what is right and do not **give w** 4766
3: 7 Husbands, **in the same w** be considerate 3931
5: 5 Young men, **in the same w** be submissive 3931
2Pe 2: 2 and will bring the **w** of truth into disrepute. 3847
2:15 the straight **w** and wandered off to follow 3847
2:15 to follow the **w** of Balaam son of Beor, 3847
2:21 not to have known the **w** of righteousness, 3847
3:11 everything will be destroyed **in** this **w**, 4048
3:16 He writes **the same w** in all his letters, 2779+6055
1Jn 4:17 In **this** *w*, love is made complete among us AIT
3Jn 1: 6 **send** them **on their w** in a manner worthy 4636
Jude 1: 7 In a similar **w**, Sodom and Gomorrah 5573
1: 8 **In the** very **same w**, these dreamers pollute 3931
1:11 They have taken the **w** of Cain; 3847
1:15 acts *they have* **done in** the **ungodly w**, 814
Rev 16:12 to prepare the **w** for the kings from the East. 3847
18:20 judged her for the **w** she **treated** you.' " 3210S

WAYFARING (KJV) See TRAVELER, WALK

WAYLAID (1) [WAYLAY]

1Sa 15: 2 when *they* **w** them as they came up from Egypt. 928+2006+2021+8492

WAYLAY (2) [WAYLAID]

Pr 1:11 *let's* **w** some harmless soul; 7621
1:18 *they* **w** only themselves! 7621

WAYMARKS (KJV) See ROAD SIGNS

WAYS (229) [WAY]

Ge 6:12 the people on earth had corrupted their **w**. 2006
Ex 33:13 teach me your **w** so I may know you 2006
Lev 5: 5 " 'When anyone is guilty in any of **these** *w*, AIT
18:24 not defile yourselves in any of **these** *w*, AIT
25:54 if he is not redeemed in any of **these** *w*, AIT
Dt 8: 6 walking in his **w** and revering him. 2006
10:12 to walk in all his **w**, to love him, 2006
11:22 the LORD your God, to walk in all his **w** 2006
18: 9 do not learn to imitate the **detestable w** *of* 9359
19: 9 and to walk always in his **w**— 2006
26:17 and that you will walk in his **w**, 2006
28: 9 of the LORD your God and walk in his **w**. 2006
30:16 love the LORD your God, to walk in his **w**, 2006
32: 4 his works are perfect, and all his **w** are just. 2006
Jos 22: 5 to walk in all his **w**, to obey his commands, 2006
Jdg 2:19 to **w** even more corrupt than those NIH
2:19 up their evil practices and stubborn **w**. 2006
1Sa 8: 3 But his sons did not walk in his **w**. 2006
8: 5 and your sons do not walk in your **w**; 2006
2Sa 14:14 he devises **w** so that a banished person may 4742
22:22 For I have kept the **w** *of* the LORD; 2006
1Ki 2: 3 Walk in his **w**, and keep his decrees 2006
3:14 if you walk in my **w** and obey my statutes 2006
8:58 in all his **w** and to keep the commands, 2006
11:33 and have not walked in my **w**, 2006
11:38 in my **w** and do what is right in my eyes 2006
13:33 this, Jeroboam did not change his evil **w**, 2006
15:26 walking in the **w** *of* his father and in his sin, 2006
15:34 in the **w** *of* Jeroboam and in his sin, 2006
16: 2 but you walked in the **w** *of* Jeroboam 2006
16:19 and walking in the **w** *of* Jeroboam and in 2006
16:26 in all the **w** *of* Jeroboam son of Nebat and 2006
22:43 in the **w** *of* his father Asa and did not stray 2006
22:52 because he walked in the **w** *of* his father 2006
22:52 and mother and in the **w** *of* Jeroboam son 2006
2Ki 8:18 He walked in the **w** *of* the kings of Israel, 2006
8:27 the **w** *of* the house of Ahab and did evil in 2006
16: 3 He walked in the **w** *of* the kings of Israel 2006
16: 3 following the **detestable w** *of* the nations 9359
17:13 "Turn from your evil **w**. 2006
21:21 He walked in all the **w** of his father; 2006
22: 2 and walked in all the **w** *of* his father David, 2006
2Ch 6:31 and walk in your **w** all the time they live in 2006
7:14 and turn from their wicked **w**, 2006
11:17 walking in the **w** *of* David and Solomon 2006
17: 3 in the **w** his father David had followed. 2006
17: 6 His heart was devoted to the **w** *of* 2006
20:32 in the **w** *of* his father Asa and did not stray 2006
2Ch 21: 6 He walked in the **w** *of* the kings of Israel, 2006
21:12 in the **w** *of* your father Jehoshaphat or 2006
21:13 But you have walked in the **w** *of* the kings 2006
22: 3 He too walked in the **w** *of* the house 2006
28: 2 He walked in the **w** *of* the kings of Israel 2006
28: 3 following the **detestable w** *of* the nations 9359
28:26 The other events of his reign and all his **w**, 2006
34: 2 the eyes of the LORD and walked in the **w** 2006
Ne 9:35 not serve you or turn from their evil **w**. 5095
Est 5:11 and all **the w** the king had honored him and 889S
Job 4: 6 and your blameless **w** your hope? 2006
13:15 I will surely defend my **w** to his face. 2006
17: 9 the righteous will hold to their **w**, 2006
21:14 We have no desire to know your **w**. 2006
22: 3 if your **w** were blameless? 2006
22:28 and light will shine on your **w**. 2006
24:13 who do not know its **w** or stay in its paths. 2006
24:23 but his eyes are on their **w**. 2006
27:11 **the w** of the Almighty I will not conceal. 889S
31: 4 not see my **w** and count my every step? 2006
34:21 "His eyes are on the **w** *of* men; 2006
34:27 and had no regard for any of his **w**. 2006
36:23 Who has prescribed his **w** for him, 2006
37: 5 God's voice thunders *in* **marvelous** *w*; AIT
Ps 10: 5 His **w** are always prosperous; 2006
17: 4 I have kept myself from the **w** *of* the violent. 784
18:21 For I have kept the **w** *of* the LORD; 2006
25: 4 Show me your **w**, O LORD, 784
25: 7 of my youth and my **rebellious** *w*; AIT
25: 8 therefore he instructs sinners in his **w**. 2006
25:10 the **w** *of* the LORD are loving and faithful 784
37: 7 do not fret when men succeed in their **w**, 2006
37:14 to slay those whose **w** are upright. 2006
39: 1 "I will watch my **w** and keep my tongue 2006
51:13 Then I will teach transgressors your **w**, 2006
53: 1 They are corrupt, and their **w** are vile; 6404
55:19 men who never change their **w** NIH
67: 2 that your **w** may be known on earth, 2006
77:13 Your **w**, O God, are holy. 2006
81:13 if Israel would follow my **w**, 2006
91:11 concerning you to guard you in all your **w**; 2006
95:10 and they have not known my **w**." 2006
103: 7 He made known his **w** to Moses, 2006
107:17 became fools through their rebellious **w** 2006
119: 1 Blessed are they whose **w** are blameless, 2006
119: 3 They do nothing wrong; they walk in his **w**. 2006
119: 5 that my **w** were steadfast in obeying 2006
119:15 on your precepts and consider your **w**. 784
119:26 I recounted my **w** and you answered me; 2006
119:29 Keep me from deceitful **w**; 2006
119:59 I have considered my **w** 2006
119:168 for all my **w** are known to you. 2006
125: 5 those who turn to **crooked w** the LORD 6824
128: 1 who fear the LORD, who walk in his **w**. 2006
138: 5 May they sing of the **w** *of* the LORD, 2006
139: 3 you are familiar with all my **w**. 2006
145:17 The LORD is righteous in all his **w** 2006
146: 9 but he frustrates the **w** *of* the wicked. 2006
Pr 1:22 "How long will you simple ones love your **simple w**? 7344
1:31 They will eat the fruit of their **w** and 2006
2:12 Wisdom will save you from the **w** 2006
2:13 the straight paths to walk in dark **w**, 2006
2:15 and who are devious in their **w**. 5047
2:20 Thus you will walk in the **w** *of* good men 2006
3: 6 in all your **w** acknowledge him, 2006
3:17 Her **w** are pleasant ways, 2006
3:17 Her ways are pleasant **w**, 2006
3:31 a violent man or choose any of his **w**, 2006
4:26 for your feet and take only **w** that are firm. 2006
5:21 a man's **w** are in full view of the LORD, 2006
6: 6 consider its **w** and be wise! 2006
7:25 Do not let your heart turn to her **w** or stray 2006
8:32 blessed are those who keep my **w**. 2006
9: 6 Leave your **simple w** and you will live; 7344
11:20 in those whose **w** are blameless. 2006
14: 2 but he whose **w** are devious despises him. 2006
14: 8 of the prudent is to give thought to their **w**, 2006
14:14 faithless will be fully repaid for their **w**, 2006
16: 2 All a man's **w** seem innocent to him, 2006
16: 7 a man's **w** are pleasing to the LORD, 2006
19:16 he who is contemptuous of his **w** will die. 2006
21: 2 All a man's **w** seem right to him, 2006
21:29 but an upright man gives thought to his **w**. 2006
22:25 or you may learn his **w** 784
23:26 and let your eyes keep to my **w**, 2006
28: 6 a rich man whose **w** are perverse. 2006
28:18 he whose **w** are perverse will suddenly fall. 2006
Ecc 11: 9 Follow the **w** *of* your heart 2006
Isa 2: 3 He will teach us his **w**, 2006
42:16 the blind by **w** they have not known, 2006
42:24 For they would not follow his **w**; 2006
45:13 I will make all his **w** straight. 2006
55: 8 neither are your **w** my ways," 2006
55: 8 neither are your ways my **w**," 2006
55: 9 so are my **w** higher than your ways 2006
55: 9 so are my ways higher than your **w** 2006
57:10 You were wearied by all your **w**, 2006
57:17 yet he kept on in his willful **w**. 2006
57:18 I have seen his **w**, but I will heal him; 2006
58: 2 they seem eager to know my **w**, 2006
59: 7 ruin and destruction mark their **w**. 5019
63:17 from your **w** and harden our hearts so we do 2006
64: 5 who gladly do right, who remember your **w**. 2006
65: 2 who walk in **w** not good, 2006
66: 3 They have chosen their own **w**, 2006
Jer 2:33 the worst of women can learn from your **w**. 2006
Jer 2:36 you go about so much, changing your **w**? 2006
3:21 because they have perverted their **w** 2006
6:27 that you may observe and test their **w**. 2006
7: 3 Reform your **w** and your actions, 2006
7: 5 If you really change your **w** 2006
7:23 Walk in all the **w** I command you, 2006
10: 2 not learn the **w** *of* the nations or be terrified 2006
12:16 the **w** *of* my people and swear by my name, 2006
15: 7 for they have not changed their **w**. 2006
16:17 My eyes are on all their **w**; 2006
18:11 So turn from your evil **w**, each one of you, 2006
18:11 and reform your **w** and your actions.' 2006
18:15 which made them stumble in their **w** and in 2006
23:22 from their evil **w** and from their evil deeds. 2006
25: 5 from your evil **w** and your evil practices, 2006
26:13 Now reform your **w** and your actions 2006
32:19 Your eyes are open to all the **w** *of* men; 2006
35:15 "Each of you must turn from your wicked **w** 2006
36: 7 and each will turn from his wicked **w**, 2006
La 3:40 Let us examine our **w** and test them, 2006
Eze 3:18 or speak out to dissuade him from his evil **w** 2006
3:19 or from his evil **w**, he will die for his sin; 2006
13:22 the wicked not to turn from their evil **w** and 2006
16:47 You not only walked in their **w** 2006
16:47 in all your **w** you soon became more depraved than they. 2006
16:61 Then you will remember your **w** and 2006
18:23 not pleased when they turn from their **w** 2006
18:25 Is it not your **w** that are unjust? 2006
18:29 Are my **w** unjust, O house of Israel? 2006
18:29 Is it not your **w** that are unjust? 2006
18:30 each one according to his **w**, 2006
20:44 to your evil **w** and your corrupt practices, 2006
28:15 in your **w** from the day you were created 2006
33: 8 not speak out to dissuade him from his **w**, 2006
33: 9 to turn from his **w** and he does not do so, 2006
33:11 rather that they turn from their **w** and live. 2006
33:11 Turn from your evil **w**! 2006
33:20 each of you according to his own **w**." 2006
36:31 Then you will remember your evil **w** 2006
Da 4:37 and all his **w** are just. 10068
5:23 in his hand your life and all your **w**. 10068
Hos 4: 9 for their **w** and repay them for their deeds. 2006
4:18 their rulers dearly love **shameful w**. 7830
12: 2 according to his **w** and repay him according 2006
14: 9 The **w** *of* the LORD are right; 2006
Jnh 3: 8 give up their evil **w** and their violence. 2006
3:10 and how they turned from their evil **w**, 2006
Mic 2: 7 to *him whose* **w** are upright? 2143
4: 2 He will teach us his **w**, 2006
Hab 3: 6 His **w** are eternal. 2142
Hag 1: 5 "Give careful thought to your **w**. 2006
1: 7 "Give careful thought to your **w**. 2006
Zec 1: 4 from your evil **w** and your evil practices.' 2006
1: 6 to us what our **w** and practices deserve, 2006
3: 7 in my **w** and keep my requirements, 2006
Mal 2: 9 because you have not followed my **w** 2006
Lk 3: 5 the rough **w** smooth. 3847
Ac 3:26 by turning each of you from your **wicked w**. 4504
13:10 Will you never stop perverting the right **w** 3847
18:13 the people to worship God in **w** contrary to NIG
28:10 *in* **many** *w* and when we were ready to sail, AIT
Ro 1:30 they invent **w** of doing evil; NIG
3:16 ruin and misery mark their **w**, 3847
1Co 13:11 I became a man, I put **childish** *w* behind me. AIT
2Co 4: 2 we have renounced secret and shameful **w**; NIG
8:22 to us in **many** *w* that he is zealous, AIT
Eph 2: 2 when you followed the **w** of this world and 172
Col 3: 7 You used to walk in **these** *w*, AIT
2Ti 1:18 in **how many** *w* he helped me in Ephesus. AIT
Heb 1: 1 at many times and **in various w**, 4502
3:10 and they have not known my **w**.' 3847
Jas 3: 2 We all stumble in **many** *w*. AIT
2Pe 2: 2 Many will follow their **shameful** *w* AIT
Rev 2:22 unless they repent of her **w**. 2240
15: 3 Just and true are your **w**, King of the ages. 3847

WAYSIDE (KJV) See ALONG MY PATH, SIDE OF ROAD

WAYWARD (8) [WAYWARDNESS]

Ps 58: 3 from the womb *they are* **w** and speak lies. 9494
Pr 2:16 from the **w** *wife* with her seductive words, 5799
6:24 from the smooth tongue of the **w** *wife*. 5799
7: 5 from the **w** *wife* with her seductive words. 5799
20:16 hold it in pledge if he does it for a **w** *woman*. 5799
23:27 for a prostitute is a deep pit and a **w** *wife* is 5799
27:13 hold it in pledge if he does it for a **w** *woman*. 5799
Isa 29:24 *who are* **w** *in* spirit will gain understanding; 9494

WAYWARDNESS (2) [WAYWARD]

Pr 1:32 For the **w** *of* the simple will kill them, 5412
Hos 14: 4 "I will heal their **w** and love them freely, 5412

WE (1884) [OUR, OURS, OURSELVES, US, WE'LL, WE'RE, WE'VE] See Index of Articles Etc.

WE'LL (13) [BE, WE]

Ge 19: 9 *W* **treat** you **worse** than them." AIT
34:16 *W* **settle** among you and become one people AIT

Ge 34:17 *w* **take** our sister and go." AIT
37:20 Then *w* **see** what comes of his dreams." AIT
Jdg 8:25 *"W be* **glad to give** them." AIT
16: 2 saying, "At dawn *w* **kill** him." AIT
20: 9 But now this is what *w* **do** to Gibeah: AIT
20: 9 **W** go up against it as the lot directs. NIH
20:10 *W* **take** ten men out of every hundred AIT
1Sa 14:12 "Come up to us and *w* **teach** you a lesson." AIT
2Ki 6:28 and tomorrow *w* **eat** my son.' AIT
7: 4 If we say, *'W* **go into** the city'— AIT
Jn 21: 3 and they said, **"W** go with you." *1609*

WE'RE (6) [BE, WE]

Ge 29: 4 **"W** from Haran," they replied. 636
Jdg 12: 1 *W going to* **burn down** your house AIT
1Sa 4: 7 **"W** in trouble! Nothing like this has 5646
2Ki 7: 9 they said to each other, **"W** not doing right. 636
Mt 8:25 "Lord, save us! *W going to* **drown!"** *AIT*
Lk 8:24 "Master, Master, *w going to* **drown!"** *AIT*

WE'VE (3) [HAS, WE]

Ge 26:32 They said, *"W* **found** water!" AIT
Jdg 15:12 *"W* **come** to tie you up and hand you over to AIT
Lk 5: 5 *w* worked hard all night and haven't **caught** *AIT*

WEAK (65) [WEAKENED, WEAKENING, WEAKER, WEAKEST, WEAKLING, WEAKNESS, WEAKNESSES]

Ge 27: 1 When Isaac was old and his eyes *were so* **w** 3908
29:17 Leah had **w** eyes, but Rachel was lovely 8205
30:42 but if the animals *were* **w,** 6494
30:42 So the **w** animals went to Laban and 6488
Nu 13:18 the people who live there are strong or **w,** 8333
Dt 34: 7 his eyes *were* not **w** nor his strength gone. 3908
Jdg 16: 7 I'll become as **w** as any other man." 2703
16:11 I'll become as **w** as any other man." 2703
16:13 I'll become as **w** as any other man." 2703
16:17 I would become as **w** as any other man." 2703
1Sa 3: 2 whose eyes were becoming *so* **w** 3910
15: 9 and **w** they totally destroyed. 5022
2Sa 3:39 though I am the anointed king, I am **w,** 8205
17: 2 I would attack him while he is weary and **w.** 3338+8333
2Ch 28:15 All *those who were* **w** they put on donkeys. 4173
Ne 6: 9 "Their hands *will get* too **w** for the work, 8332
Ps 6: 7 My eyes *grow* **w** with sorrow; 6949
10: 2 the wicked man hunts down the **w,** 6714
12: 5 the oppression of the **w** and the groaning of 6714
31: 9 my eyes *grow* **w** with sorrow, 6949
31:10 and my bones *grow* **w.** 6949
34:10 The lions *may grow* **w** and hungry, 8133
41: 1 Blessed is he who has regard for the **w;** 1924
72:13 on the **w** and the needy and save the needy 1924
82: 3 Defend the cause of the **w** and fatherless; 1924
82: 4 Rescue the **w** and needy; 1924
Isa 14:10 "You also *have become* **w,** as we are; 2703
38:14 My eyes *grew* **w** as I looked to the heavens. 1937
40:29 and increases the power of the **w.** 226+401
Eze 7:17 and every knee *will become as* **w as** water. 2143
21: 7 and every knee *become as* **w as** water.' 2143
29:15 *I will* **make** it *so* **w** that it will never again 5070
34: 4 You have not strengthened the **w** or healed 2703
34:16 up the injured and strengthen the **w,** 2703
34:21 butting all the **w** sheep with your horns 2703
Mt 26:41 The spirit is willing, but the body is **w."** *822*
Mk 14:38 The spirit is willing, but the body is **w."** *822*
Ac 20:35 of hard work we must help the **w,** *820*
Ro 6:19 I put this in human terms because you are **w** *819*
14: 1 Accept him whose faith *is* **w,** *820*
14: 2 whose faith *is* **w,** eats only vegetables. *820*
15: 1 to bear with the failings *of* the **w** and not *105*
1Co 1:27 God chose the **w** *things* of the world *822*
4:10 We are **w,** but you are strong! *822*
8: 7 and since their conscience is **w,** it is defiled. *822*
8: 9 not become a stumbling block *to* the **w.** *822*
8:10 with a **w** conscience sees you who have this knowledge eating *822*
8:11 So this **w** brother, for whom Christ died, *820*
8:12 in this way and wound their **w** conscience, *820*
9:22 *To* the **w** I became weak, to win the weak. *822*
9:22 To the weak I became **w,** to win the weak. *822*
9:22 To the weak I became weak, to win the **w.** *822*
11:30 That is why many among you are **w** *822*
2Co 11:21 To my shame I admit that we *were* too **w** *820*
11:29 Who *is* **w,** and I do not feel weak? *820*
11:29 Who is weak, and *I do not* **feel w?** *820*
12:10 For when *I am* **w,** then I am strong. *820*
13: 3 He *is* not **w** in dealing with you, *820*
13: 4 Likewise, we *are* **w** in him, *820*
13: 9 We are glad whenever we *are* **w** *820*
Gal 4: 9 to those **w** and miserable principles? *822*
1Th 5:14 help the **w,** be patient with everyone. *822*
Heb 7:18 because it was **w** and useless *822*
7:28 as high priests men who are **w;** *819*
12:12 strengthen your feeble arms and **w** knees. *4168*

WEAK-WILLED (2) [WILL]

Eze 16:30 'How **w** you are, declares the Sovereign 581+4226
2Ti 3: 6 into homes and gain control over **w women,** *1220*

WEAKENED (2) [WEAK]

Job 18: 7 The vigor of his step *is* **w;** 7674
Ro 8: 3 in that *it was* **w** by the sinful nature, *820*

WEAKENING (1) [WEAK]

Ro 4:19 Without **w** in his faith, he faced the fact *820*

WEAKER (4) [WEAK]

2Sa 3: 1 while the house of Saul **grew w and weaker.** 1924+2143+2256
3: 1 while the house of Saul **grew weaker and w.** 1924+2143+2256
1Co 12:22 body that seem to be **w** are indispensable, *822*
1Pe 3: 7 and treat them with respect as the **w** partner *822*

WEAKEST (1) [WEAK]

Jdg 6:15 My clan is the **w** in Manasseh, 1924

WEAKLING (1) [WEAK]

Joel 3:10 Let the **w** say, "I am strong!" 2766

WEAKNESS (10) [WEAK]

La 1: 6 in **w** they have fled before the pursuer. 3946+4202
Ro 8:26 the Spirit helps us *in* our **w.** *819*
1Co 1:25 **w** of God is stronger than man's strength. *822*
2: 3 I came to you in **w** and fear, *819*
15:43 it is sown in **w,** it is raised in power; *819*
2Co 11:30 I will boast of the things that show my **w.** *819*
12: 9 for my power is made perfect in **w."** *819*
13: 4 For to be sure, he was crucified in **w,** *819*
Heb 5: 2 since he himself is subject to **w.** *819*
11:34 whose **w** was turned to strength; *819*

WEAKNESSES (4) [WEAK]

2Co 12: 5 not boast about myself, except about my **w.** *819*
12: 9 I will boast all the more gladly about my **w,** *819*
12:10 is why, for Christ's sake, I delight in **w,** *819*
Heb 4:15 who is unable to sympathize with our **w,** *819*

WEALTH (117) [WEALTHY]

Ge 26:13 and his **w** continued to grow until 1541
31: 1 and has gained all this **w** 3883
31:16 Surely all the **w** that God took away 6948
34:29 They carried off all their **w** 2657
Dt 8:17 of my hands have produced this **w** for me." 2657
8:18 the ability to produce **w,** 2657
Jos 22: 8 "Return to your homes with your great **w**— 5794
1Sa 2: 7 The LORD sends poverty and **w;** 6947
17:25 The king *will* **give** great **w** *to* 6947+6948
1Ki 3:11 and not for long life or **w** for yourself, 6948
10: 7 in wisdom and **w** you have far exceeded 3202
1Ch 29:12 **W** and honor come from you; 6948
29:28 having enjoyed long life, **w** and honor. 6948
2Ch 1:11 and you have not asked for **w,** 6948
1:12 And I will also give you **w,** 6948
17: 5 so that he had great **w** and honor. 6948
18: 1 Now Jehoshaphat had great **w** and honor, 6948
Est 1: 4 the vast **w** *of* his kingdom and the splendor 6948
5:11 Haman boasted to them about his vast **w,** 6948
Job 5: 5 and the thirsty pant after his **w.** 2657
6:22 pay a ransom for me from your **w,** 3946
15:29 He will no longer be rich and his **w** will 2657
20:10 his own hands must give back his **w.** 226
22:20 and fire devours their **w.'** 3856
31:25 if I have rejoiced over my great **w,** 2657
36:19 Would your **w** or even all your mighty 8782
Ps 17:14 and they store up **w** for their children. 3856
37:16 the little that the righteous have than the **w** 2162
39: 6 *he* **heaps up w,** not knowing who will get it. 7392
39:11 you consume their **w** like a moth— 2773
45:12 men of **w** will seek your favor. 6938
49: 6 in their **w** and boast of their great riches? 2657
49:10 the senseless alike perish and leave their **w** 2657
52: 7 but trusted in his great **w** and grew strong 6948
73:12 always carefree, they increase in **w.** 2657
112: 3 **W** and riches are in his house, 2104
Pr 3: 9 Honor the LORD with your **w,** 2104
5:10 lest strangers feast on your **w** 3946
6:31 though it costs him all the **w** *of* his house. 2104
8:18 enduring **w** and prosperity. 2104
8:21 bestowing **w** *on* those who love me 3780
10: 4 but diligent hands **bring w.** 6947
10:15 The **w** *of* the rich is their fortified city, 2104
10:22 The blessing of the LORD **brings w,** 6947
11: 4 **W** is worthless in the day of wrath, 2104
11:16 but ruthless men gain only **w.** 6948
13: 7 another pretends to be poor, yet has great **w.** 2104
13:22 a sinner's **w** is stored up for the righteous. 2657
14:24 The **w** *of* the wise is their crown, 6948
15:16 of the LORD than great **w** with turmoil. 238
18:11 The **w** *of* the rich is their fortified city; 2104
19: 4 **W** brings many friends, 2104
19:14 Houses and **w** are inherited from parents, 2104
22: 4 of the LORD bring **w** and honor and life. 6948
22:16 to increase his **w** and he who gives gifts to NIH
28: 8 who increases his **w** by exorbitant interest 2104
29: 3 a companion of prostitutes squanders his **w.** 2104
Ecc 2:26 of gathering and **storing up w** to hand it 4043
4: 8 yet his eyes were not content with his **w.** 6948
5:10 whoever loves **w** is never satisfied 2162
5:13 **w** hoarded to the harm of its owner, 6948
5:14 or **w** lost through some misfortune, 6948
5:19 God gives any man **w** and possessions, 6948
6: 2 God gives a man **w,** 6948
9:11 or **w** to the brilliant or favor to the learned; 6948
SS 8: 7 If one were to give all the **w** *of* his house 2104
Isa 8: 4 the **w** *of* Damascus and the plunder 2657
10:14 my hand reached for the **w** *of* the nations; 2657
15: 7 So the **w** they have acquired and stored 3860
60: 5 the **w** *on* the seas will be brought to you, 2162
60:11 men may bring you the **w** *of* the nations— 2657
61: 6 You will feed on the **w** *of* nations, 2657
66:12 and the **w** *of* nations like a flooding stream; 3883
Jer 15:13 Your **w** and your treasures I will give 2657
17: 3 and your **w** and all your treasures I will give 2657
20: 5 I will hand over to their enemies all the **w** 2890
48:36 The **w** they acquired is gone. 3860
Eze 7:11 no **w,** nothing of value. 2155
16:36 Because you poured out your **w** 5733
26:12 They will plunder your **w** 2657
27:12 with you because of your great **w of goods;** 2104
27:18 and great **w of goods,** 2104
27:27 Your **w,** merchandise and wares, 2104
27:33 with your great **w** and your wares 2104
28: 4 and understanding you have gained **w** 2657
28: 5 in trading you have increased your **w,** 2657
28: 5 of your **w** your heart has grown proud. 2657
29:19 and he will carry off its **w.** 2162
30: 4 her **w** will be carried away 2162
Da 11: 2 When he has gained power by his **w,** 6948
11:24 loot and **w** among his followers. 8214
11:28 to his own country with great **w,** 8214
Hos 12: 8 With all my **w** they will not find 3330
Ob 1:11 while strangers carried off his **w** 2657
1:13 nor seize their **w** in the day of their disaster. 2657
Mic 4:13 their **w** to the Lord of all the earth. 2657
Na 2: 9 the **w** from all its treasures! 3883
Zep 1:13 Their **w** will be plundered, 2657
Zec 14:14 The **w** *of* all the surrounding nations will 2657
Mt 13:22 and the deceitfulness *of* **w** choke it, *4458*
19:22 he went away sad, because he had great **w.** *3228*
Mk 4:19 *of* **w** and the desires for other things come *4458*
10:22 He went away sad, because he had great **w.** *3228*
12:44 They all gave out *of* their **w;** *4355*
Lk 15:13 and there squandered his **w** in wild living. *4045*
16: 9 use worldly **w** to gain friends *3440*
16:11 not been trustworthy in handling worldly **w,** *3440*
18:23 because he was a *man of* great **w.** *4454*
21: 4 these people gave their gifts out of their **w;** *4355*
1Ti 6:17 not to be arrogant nor to put their hope in **w,** *4458*
Jas 5: 2 Your **w** has rotted, and moths have eaten *4458*
5: 3 *You have* **hoarded w** in the last days. *2564*
Rev 3:17 *I have* **acquired w** and do not need a thing.' *4456*
5:12 and **w** and wisdom and strength and honor *4458*
18:15 and **gained** their **w** from her *4456*
18:17 In one hour such great **w** has been brought *4458*
18:19 on the sea became rich through her **w!** *5509*

WEALTHY (10) [WEALTH]

Ge 13: 2 Abram *had become* very **w** in livestock and 3877
24:35 and *he has become* **w.** 1540
26:13 to grow until *he became* very **w.** 1540
1Sa 25: 2 had property there at Carmel, was very **w.** 1524
2Sa 19:32 for he was a very **w** man. 1524
2Ki 15:20 Every **w** man had to contribute fifty shekels 2657
Job 27:19 He lies down **w,** but will do so no more; 6938
Hos 12: 8 "I am very rich; I have become **w.** 226
Hab 2: 6 up stolen goods and **makes** himself **w** 3877
Lk 19: 2 he was a chief tax collector and was **w.** *4454*

WEANED (10)

Ge 21: 8 The child grew and **was w,** 1694
21: 8 and on the day Isaac **was w** Abraham held 1694
1Sa 1:22 "After the boy **is w,** 1694
1:23 "Stay here until you *have* **w** him; 1694
1:23 and nursed her son until she *had* **w** him. 1694
1:24 After he *was* **w,** she took the boy with her, 1694
Ps 131: 2 like a **w** *child* with its mother, 1694
131: 2 like a **w** *child* is my soul within me. 1694
Isa 28: 9 To *children* **w** from their milk, 1694
Hos 1: 8 After *she had* **w** Lo-Ruhamah, 1694

WEAPON (15) [WEAPONS]

1Sa 21: 8 I haven't brought my sword or any *other* **w,** 3998
1Ki 20:35 "Strike me with your **w,"** NIH
2Ki 11: 8 each man with his **w** in his hand. 3998
11:11 The guards, each with his **w** in his hand, 3998
1Ch 12:33 with every type of **w,** to help David 3998+4878
12:37 armed with every type of **w**— 3998+4878+7372
2Ch 23:10 each with his **w** in his hand, 8939
Ne 4:17 with one hand and held a **w** in the other, 8939
4:23 had his **w,** even when he went for water. 8939
Job 20:24 Though he flees from an iron **w,** 5977
Isa 54:16 into flame and forges a **w** fit for its work. 3998
54:17 no **w** forged against you will prevail, 3998
Jer 51:20 "You are my war club, my **w** *for* battle— 3998
Eze 9: 1 each with a **w** in his hand." 3998+5424
9: 2 each with a deadly **w** in his hand. 3998

WEAPONS (30) [WEAPON]

Ge 27: 3 Now then, get your **w**— 3998
49: 5 their swords are **w** *of* violence. 3998
Dt 1:41 So every one of you put on his **w,** 3998+4878
1Sa 8:12 to make **w** *of* war and equipment 3998
17:54 he put the Philistine's **w** in his own tent. 3998
20:40 Jonathan gave his **w** to the boy and said, 3998
2Sa 1:27 The **w** *of* war have perished!" 3998
2:21 of the young men and strip him of his **w."** 2723
1Ki 10:25 robes, **w** and spices, and horses and mules. 5977
2Ki 10: 2 chariots and horses, fortified city and **w,** 5977

2Ch 9:24 w and spices, and horses and mules. 5977
23: 7 each man with his w in his hand. 3998
32: 5 also made large numbers of w and shields. 8939
Ps 7:13 He has prepared his deadly w; 3998
76: 3 the shields and the swords, the w of war. NIH
Ecc 9:18 Wisdom is better than w *of* war, 3998
Isa 13: 5 the LORD and the w *of* his wrath— 3998
22: 8 And you looked in that day to the w *in* 5977
Jer 21: 4 I am about to turn against you the w *of* war 3998
22: 7 each man with his w, 3998
50:25 and brought out the w *of* his wrath, 3998
Eze 23:24 They will come against you with w, 2210
26: 9 and demolish your towers with his w. 2995
32:27 who went down to the grave with their w 3998
39: 9 the towns of Israel will go out and use the w 5977
39:10 because they will use the w for fuel. 5977
Jn 18: 3 They were carrying torches, lanterns and w. *3960*
2Co 6: 7 with w of righteousness in the right hand *3960*
10: 4 The w we **fight with** are not the *3836+3960+5127*
10: 4 we fight with are not the w of the world. *NIG*

WEAR (45) [WEARING, WEARS, WORE, WORN, WORN-OUT]

Ge 28:20 give me food to eat and clothes to w 4252
Ex 18:18 *will* **only** w *yourselves* **out.** 5570+5570
28:35 Aaron *must* w *it* when he ministers. 2118+6584
28:43 sons *must* w *them* whenever they enter 2118+6584
29:30 in the Holy Place *is to* w them seven days. 4252
Lev 13:45 an infectious disease *must* w torn clothes, 2118
19:19 " '*Do* not w clothing woven of two kinds 6590
21:10 on his head and who has been ordained to w 4252
Dt 8: 4 not w **out** and your feet did not swell 1162
22: 5 A woman *must* not w men's clothing, 2118+6584
22: 5 nor a man w women's clothing, 4252
22:11 *Do* not w **clothes** of wool and linen woven 4252
22:12 on the four corners of the cloak *you* w. 4059
28:32 and you *will* w **out** your eyes watching 3983
29: 5 your clothes *did* not w **out,** 1162
Jdg 8:24 custom of the Ishmaelites to w gold earrings 4200
1Sa 2:28 and to w an ephod in my presence. 5951
1Ki 22:30 but you w your royal robes." 4252
2Ch 18:29 but you w your royal robes." 4252
Ne 9:21 their clothes *did* not w **out** 1162
Job 27:17 what he lays up the righteous *will* w, 4252
31:36 Surely *I would* w it on my shoulder, 5951
Ps 102:26 they *will* all w **out** like a garment. 1162
Pr 23: 4 *Do* not w *yourself* **out** to get rich; 3333
Isa 15: 3 In the streets *they* w sackcloth; 2520
49:18 "*you will* w them all as ornaments; 4252
50: 9 They *will* all w **out** like a garment; 1162
51: 6 like smoke, the earth *will* w **out** like 1162
Jer 12:13 *they will* w **themselves out** 2703
Eze 44:17 *they are to* w linen clothes; 4252
44:17 they *must* not w any woolen garment 6584+6590
44:18 *They are to* w linen turbans on their heads 2118
44:18 not w anything that makes them perspire. 2520
Am 8:10 **make** all of you w sackcloth 5516+6584+6590
Mt 6:25 or about your body, what *you will* w. *1907*
6:31 or 'What *shall we* w?' *4314*
11: 8 who w fine clothes are in kings' palaces. *5841*
Mk 6: 9 W sandals but not an extra tunic. *5686*
Lk 7:25 those who w expensive clothes and indulge *1877*
12:22 or about your body, what *you will* w. *1907*
12:33 purses for yourselves *that will* not w **out,** *4096*
18: 5 so that *she* won't eventually w **me out** *5724*
Heb 1:11 *they will* all w **out** like a garment. *4096*
Rev 3:18 and white clothes to w, so you can cover *4314*
19: 8 bright and clean, was given her to w." *4314*

WEARIED (6) [WEARY]

Isa 43:22 *you have* not w *yourselves* for me, 3333
43:23 nor w you with demands for incense. 3333
43:24 with your sins and w me with your offenses. 3333
57:10 *You were* w by all your ways, 3333
Mal 2:17 *You have* w the LORD with your words. 3333
2:17 "How *have we* w him?" 3333

WEARIES (2) [WEARY]

Ecc 10:15 A fool's work w him; 3333
12:12 and much study w the body. 3331

WEARING (32) [WEAR]

Ge 37:23 the richly ornamented robe he was w— 6584
Ex 32: 2 your sons and your daughters are w, 265+928
Dt 21:13 the clothes she was w when captured. 6584
Ru 3:15 the shawl you are w and hold it out." 6584
1Sa 2:18 before the LORD—a boy w a linen ephod. 2520
14: 3 Ahijah, *who was* w an ephod. 5951
18: 4 the robe he was w and gave it to David, 6584
28:14 "An old man w a robe is coming up," 6486
2Sa 6:14 David, w a linen ephod, danced before 2520
13:18 She was w a richly ornamented robe, 6584
13:19 and tore the ornamented robe she was w. 6584
20: 8 Joab *was* w his military tunic, 2520
1Ki 11:29 met him on the way, w a new cloak. 4059
11:30 of the new cloak he was w and tore it 6584
20:32 W sackcloth around their waists and ropes 2520
2Ki 19: 2 and the leading priests, *all* w sackcloth, 4059
Ne 9: 1 fasting and w sackcloth and having dust 928
Est 1:11 Queen Vashti, w her royal crown, 928
8:15 the king's presence w royal garments 928
SS 3: 8 all of them w the sword, 296
3:11 and look at King Solomon w the crown, 928
Isa 37: 2 and the leading priests, *all* w sackcloth, 4059
Jer 13: 4 "Take the belt you bought and are w **around** your waist, 6584
Da 3:21 So these men, w their robes, trousers, 10089
Mt 22:11 who *was* not w wedding clothes. *1907*
Mk 14:51 w **nothing** but a linen garment, *1218+2093+4314*
Jn 19: 5 When Jesus came out w the crown of thorns *5841*
Ac 12:21 Herod, w his royal robes, sat on his throne *1907*
Jas 2: 2 comes into your meeting w **a gold ring** *5993*
2: 3 special attention to the man w fine clothes *5841*
1Pe 3: 3 and the w of gold jewelry and fine clothes. *4324*
Rev 7: 9 *They were* w white robes *4314*

WEARISOME (1) [WEARY]

Ecc 1: 8 All things are w, more than one can say. 3335

WEARS (3) [WEAR]

Job 14:19 as water w **away** stones and torrents wash 8835
Ps 119:139 My zeal w me **out,** for my enemies ignore 7551
Isa 16:12 at her high place, *she* only w **herself out;** 4206

WEARY (29) [WEARIED, WEARIES, WEARISOME]

Dt 25:18 When you were w and worn out, 6546
28:65 an anxious mind, eyes w **with longing,** 4001
Jos 7: 3 to take it and *do* not w all the people, 3333
2Sa 17: 2 I would attack him while he is w and weak. 3335
Job 3:17 and there the w are at rest. 3329+3946
22: 7 You gave no water to the w and 6546
31:16 or *let* the eyes of the widow **grow** w, 3983
Ps 63: 1 in a dry and w land where there is no water. 6546
68: 9 you refreshed your w inheritance. 4206
119:28 My soul *is* w with sorrow; 1941
Pr 25:25 to a w soul is good news from a distant land. 6546
Isa 1:14 *I am* w *of* bearing them. 4206
28:12 "This is the resting place, let the w rest"; 6546
40:28 He will not grow tired or w, 3333
40:29 He gives strength to the w and 3617
40:30 Even youths grow tired and w, 3333
40:31 they will run and not *grow* w, 3333
46: 1 are burdensome, a burden for the w. 6546
50: 4 to know the word that sustains the w. 3617
Jer 6:11 *they* w **themselves** *with* sinning. 4206
20: 9 *I am* w *of* holding it in; indeed, I cannot. 4206
31:25 I will refresh the w and satisfy 5883+6546
La 5: 5 *we are* w and find no rest. 3333
Zec 11: 8 and I **grew** w of them 7918
Mt 11:28 "Come to me, all you who *are* w and *3159*
Ac 24: 4 But in order not to w you further, *1601*
Gal 6: 9 *Let us* not **become** w in doing good, *1591*
Heb 12: 3 so that *you will* not **grow** w and lose heart. *2827*
Rev 2: 3 for my name, and *have* not **grown** w. *3159*

WEASEL (1)

Lev 11:29 the w, the rat, any kind of great lizard, 2700

WEATHER (1)

Mt 16: 2 'It will be **fair** w, for the sky is red,' *2304*

WEAVE (2) [INTERWOVEN, WEAVER, WEAVER'S, WEAVERS, WEAVING, WOVE, WOVEN]

Ex 28:39 "W the tunic of fine linen and make 8687
Jdg 16:13 "If *you* w the seven braids of my head into 755

WEAVER (3) [WEAVE]

Ex 39:22 entirely of blue cloth—the work of a w— 755
39:27 tunics of fine linen—the work of a w— 755
Isa 38:12 Like a w I have rolled up my life, 755

WEAVER'S (5) [WEAVE]

1Sa 17: 7 His spear shaft was like a w rod, 755
2Sa 21:19 who had a spear with a shaft like a w rod. 755
1Ch 11:23 the Egyptian had a spear like a w rod 755
20: 5 who had a spear with a shaft like a w rod. 755
Job 7: 6 "My days are swifter than a w **shuttle,** 756

WEAVERS (2) [WEAVE]

Ex 35:35 and scarlet yarn and fine linen, and w— 755
Isa 19: 9 the w *of* fine linen will lose hope. 755

WEAVING (1) [WEAVE]

2Ki 23: 7 and where women **did** w for Asherah. 755+1428

WEB (3) [COBWEBS]

Job 8:14 what he relies on is a spider's w. 1074
8:15 He leans on his w, but it gives way; 1074
Isa 59: 5 the eggs of vipers and spin a spider's w. 7770

WEDDING (19)

Jdg 14:20 friend who *had* **attended** him **at** his w. 8287
1Ki 9:16 and then gave it as a w **gift** to his daughter, 8933
Ps 45: T A maskil. A w song. 3353
78:63 and their maidens **had** no w **songs;** 2146
SS 3:11 crowned him on the day of his w, 3164
Jer 2:32 a bride her w **ornaments?** 8005
Mt 22: 2 like a king who prepared a w **banquet** *1141*
22: 4 Come to the w **banquet.'** *1141*
22: 8 'The w **banquet** is ready, *1141*
22:10 and the w **hall** was filled with guests. *1141*
22:11 a man there who was not wearing w clothes. *1141*
22:12 how did you get in here without w clothes?' *1141*
25:10 went in with him to the w **banquet.** *1141*
Lk 12:36 for their master to return from a w **banquet,** *1141*
14: 8 "When someone invites you to a w **feast,** *1141*
Jn 2: 1 On the third day a w took place at Cana *1141*
2: 2 had also been invited to the w. *1141*
Rev 19: 7 For the w of the Lamb has come, *1141*
19: 9 Blessed are those who are invited to the w supper of the Lamb! *1141*

WEDGE (2)

Jos 7:21 and a w *of* gold weighing fifty shekels, 4383
7:24 the gold w, his sons and daughters, 4383

[BREAK] WEDLOCK (KJV) See COMMIT ADULTERY

WEED (1) [SEAWEED, TUMBLEWEED, WEEDS]

Mt 13:41 and *they will* w out of his kingdom *5198*

WEEDS (12) [WEED]

Job 31:40 instead of wheat and w instead of barley." 947
Pr 24:31 the ground was covered with w, 3017
Hos 10: 4 up like **poisonous** w in a plowed field. 8032
Zep 2: 9 place of w and salt pits, a wasteland forever. 3017
Mt 13:25 his enemy came and sowed w among *2429*
13:26 then the w also appeared. *2429*
13:27 Where then did the w come from?' *2429*
13:29 'because while you are pulling the w, *2429*
13:30 the w and tie them in bundles to be burned; *2429*
13:36 to us the parable *of* the w in the field." *2429*
13:38 The w are the sons of the evil one, *2429*
13:40 the w are pulled up and burned in the fire, *2429*

WEEK (14) [WEEKS]

Ge 29:27 Finish this daughter's **bridal** w; 8651
29:28 He finished the w *with* Leah, 8651
Mt 28: 1 at dawn on the first day *of* the w, *4879*
Mk 16: 2 Very early on the first day *of* the w, *4879*
16: 9 Jesus rose early on the first **day of the** w, *4879*
Lk 18:12 I fast twice a w and give a tenth of all I get.' *4879*
24: 1 On the first day *of* the w, *4879*
Jn 19:14 the day of Preparation of Passover W, *NIG*
20: 1 Early on the first day *of* the w, *4879*
20:19 On the evening of that first day *of* the w, *4879*
20:26 **A** w **later** his disciples were in *2465+3552+3893*
Ac 20: 7 On the first day of the w we came together *4879*
28:14 to spend a w with them. *2231+2465*
1Co 16: 2 On the first day *of* every w, *4879*

WEEKS (11) [WEEK]

Ex 34:22 the Feast of W with the firstfruits of 8651
Lev 12: 5 *for two* w the woman will be unclean, 8651
23:15 count off seven full w. 8701
Nu 28:26 of new grain during the **Feast of** W, 8651
Dt 16: 9 Count off seven w from the time you begin 8651
16:10 the Feast of W to the LORD your God 8651
16:16 Feast of Unleavened Bread, the Feast of W 8651
2Ch 8:13 Feast of Unleavened Bread, the Feast of W 8651
Jer 5:24 who assures us of the regular w *of* harvest.' 8651
Da 10: 2 I, Daniel, mourned *for* three w. 3427+8651
10: 3 at all until the three w were over. 3427+8651

WEEP (48) [WEEPING, WEEPS, WEPT]

Ge 23: 2 to mourn for Sarah and to w *over* her. 1134
29:11 Jacob kissed Rachel and *began to* w aloud. 1134
42:24 He turned away from them and *began to* w, 1134
43:30 and looked for a place to w. 1134
Jdg 11:37 to roam the hills and w with my friends, 1134
1Sa 30: 4 until they had no strength left to w. 1134
2Sa 1:24 "O daughters of Israel, w for Saul, 1134
2Ki 8:11 Then the man of God *began to* w. 1134
Ne 8: 9 Do not mourn or w." 1134
Job 2:12 *they began to* w aloud, 1134
27:15 and their widows *will* not w *for* them. 1134
Ps 69:10 When *I* w and fast, I must endure scorn; 1134
78:64 and their widows *could* not w. 1134
Ecc 3: 4 a time to w and a time to laugh, 1134
Isa 15: 2 to its high places to w; 1140
16: 9 So *I* w, as Jazer weeps, 1134
22: 4 "Turn away from me; let me w bitterly. 1140
22:12 called you on that day to w and to wail, 1140
30:19 *you will* w *no more.* 1134+1134
33: 7 the envoys of peace w bitterly. 1134
Jer 9: 1 *I would* w day and night *for* the slain 1134
9:10 *I will* w and wail for the mountains 1140+5951
13:17 *I will* w in secret because of your pride; 1134
13:17 my eyes *will* w **bitterly,** 1963+1963
22:10 not w for the dead [king] or mourn his loss; 1134
22:10 w **bitterly** for him who is exiled, 1134+1134
25:34 W and wail, you shepherds; 3536
48:32 *I* w for you, as Jazer weeps, 1134
La 1:16 "This is why I w and my eyes overflow 1134
Eze 24:16 Yet do not lament or w or shed any tears. 1134
24:23 not mourn or w but will waste away 1134
27:31 *They will* w over you with anguish of soul 1134
Joel 1: 5 Wake up, you drunkards, and w! 1134
2:17 w between the temple porch and the altar. 1134
Am 5:16 The farmers will be summoned to w and 65

Mic 1: 8 Because of this *I will* w and wail; 6199
1:10 Tell it not in Gath; w not **at all.** 1134+1134
Mal 2:13 *You* w and wail because he no longer 1140
Lk 6:21 Blessed are you who w now, *3081*
6:25 for *you will* mourn and w. *3081*
23:28 "Daughters of Jerusalem, *do* not w for me; *3081*
23:28 w for yourselves and for your children. *3081*
Jn 16:20 you *will* w and mourn while the world *3081*
Jas 5: 1 w and wail because of the misery *3081*
Rev 5: 5 one of the elders said to me, *"Do* not w! *3081*
18: 9 *they will* w and mourn over her. *3081*
18:11 of the earth *will* w and mourn over her *3081*
18:15 *They will* w and mourn *3081*

WEEPING (56) [WEEP]

Ge 45:14 and Benjamin embraced him, w. 1134
Nu 25: 6 of Israel while they *were* w at the entrance 1134
Dt 1:45 to your w and turned a deaf ear to you. 7754
34: 8 until the time of w and mourning was over. 1140
Jdg 20:26 and there they sat w before the LORD. 1134
21: 2 raising their voices and w bitterly. 1134+1140
1Sa 1: 8 "Hannah, why *are you* w? 1134
11: 5 Why *are they* w?" 1134
2Sa 3:16 w behind her all the way to Bahurim. 1134
13:19 and went away, w **aloud** as she went. 2410
15:30 up the Mount of Olives, w as he went; 1134
15:30 and *were* w as they went up. 1134
19: 1 "The king *is* w and mourning 1134
2Ki 8:12 "Why *is* my lord w?" 1134
Ezr 3:13 of the shouts of joy from the sound of w, 1140
10: 1 w and throwing himself down before 1134
Ne 8: 9 the people *had been* w as they listened to 1134
Est 4: 3 with fasting, w and wailing. 1140
8: 3 falling at his feet and w. 1134
Job 16:16 My face is red with w, 1140
Ps 6: 6 all night long I flood my bed with w NIH
6: 8 for the LORD has heard my w. 1140
30: 5 w may remain for a night, 1140
35:14 I bowed my head in grief as though w 63
39:12 be not deaf to my w. 1965
126: 6 He who goes out w, carrying seed to sow, 1134
Isa 15: 3 they all wail, prostrate with w. 1140
15: 5 They go up the way to Luhith, w as they go; 1140
65:19 the sound of w and of crying will be heard 1140
Jer 3:21 the w and pleading of the people of Israel, 1140
31: 9 They will come with w; 1140
31:15 heard in Ramah, mourning and great w, 1140
31:15 Rachel w for her children and refusing to 1134
31:16 "Restrain your voice from w and your eyes 1140
41: 6 from Mizpah to meet them, w as he went. 1134
48: 5 way to Luhith, w **bitterly** as they go; 1140+1140
La 2:11 My eyes fail from w, 1965
Joel 2:12 with fasting and w and mourning." 1140
Am 8:10 into mourning and all your singing into w. 7806
Zec 12:11 that day the w in Jerusalem will be great, 5027
12:11 like the w *of* Hadad Rimmon in the plain 5027
Mt 2:18 heard in Ramah, w and great mourning, *3088*
2:18 Rachel w **for** her children and refusing to *3081*
8:12 there will be w and gnashing of teeth." *3088*
13:42 where there will be w and gnashing of teeth. *3088*
13:50 where there will be w and gnashing of teeth. *3088*
22:13 where there will be w and gnashing of teeth. *3088*
24:51 where there will be w and gnashing of teeth. *3088*
25:30 where there will be w and gnashing of teeth. *3088*
Mk 16:10 with him and who were mourning and w. *3081*
Lk 7:38 and as she stood behind him at his feet w, *3081*
13:28 "There will be w there, and gnashing *3088+3836*
Jn 11:33 When Jesus saw her w, *3081*
11:33 Jews who had come along with her also w, *3081*
Ac 21:13 *are you* w and breaking my heart? *3081+4472*
Rev 18:19 and *with* w and mourning cry out: " 'Woe! *3081*

WEEPS (3) [WEEP]

Isa 16: 9 So I weep, as Jazer w, 1140
Jer 48:32 I weep for you, as Jazer w, 1140
La 1: 2 **Bitterly** *she* w at night, 1134+1134

WEIGH (7) [OUTWEIGH, OUTWEIGHS, WEIGHED, WEIGHING, WEIGHS, WEIGHT, WEIGHTIER, WEIGHTS, WEIGHTY]

2Sa 14:26 *he would* w it, and its weight was 9202
Ezr 8:29 Guard them carefully until *you* w them **out** 9202
Job 31: 6 *let* God w me in honest scales 9202
Isa 46: 6 from their bags and w **out** silver on scales; 9202
Eze 4:10 **W out** twenty shekels of food to eat each 5484
33:10 "Our offenses and sins w us **down,** 6584
1Co 14:29 others *should* w **carefully** what is said. *1359*

WEIGHED (31) [WEIGH]

Ge 23:16 and w **out** for him the price he had named 9202
Nu 7:85 Each silver plate w a hundred and thirty NIH
7:85 silver dishes w two thousand four hundred NIH
7:86 filled with incense w ten shekels each, NIH
7:86 the gold dishes w a hundred and twenty NIH
31:52 as a gift to the LORD w 16,750 shekels. 2118
1Sa 2: 3 and by him deeds **are** w. 9419
17: 7 and its iron point w six hundred shekels. NIH
2Sa 18:12 "Even if a thousand shekels *were* w **out** 9202
21:16 bronze spearhead w three hundred shekels 5486
2Ki 25:16 was more than could be w. 5486
1Ch 22: 3 and more bronze than could be w. 5486
22:14 of bronze and iron too great to be w, 5486
2Ch 3: 9 The gold nails w fifty shekels. 5486
Ezr 8:25 and *I* w **out** to them the offering of silver 9202
8:26 *I* w **out** to them 650 talents of silver, 9202
8:30 and sacred articles that had been w **out** to 5486
8:33 *we* w **out** the silver and gold and 9202
Job 6: 2 "If only my anguish *could* **be** w 9202+9202
28:15 nor *can* its price **be** w *in* silver. 9202
Ps 62: 9 if w on a balance, they are nothing; 6590
Pr 16: 2 but motives are w *by* the LORD. 9419
Isa 40:12 or w the mountains on the scales and 9202
Jer 6:11 and the old, *those* w **down** *with* years. 4849
32: 9 and w **out** for him seventeen shekels 9202
32:10 and w **out** the silver on the scales. 9202
52:20 was more than could be w. 5486
La 3: 7 *he has* w me **down** *with* chains. 3877
Da 5:27 *You have* **been** w on the scales 10769
Lk 21:34 or your hearts *will be* w **down** with *976*
Ac 27:13 so they w **anchor** and sailed along the shore *149*

WEIGHING (42) [WEIGH]

Ge 24:22 the man took out a gold nose ring w a beka 5486
24:22 a beka and two gold bracelets w ten shekels. 5486
Nu 3:50 of the Israelites he collected silver w 1,365 NIH
7:13 silver plate w a hundred and thirty shekels 5486
7:13 silver sprinkling bowl w seventy shekels, NIH
7:14 one gold dish w ten shekels, filled with NIH
7:19 silver plate w a hundred and thirty shekels 5486
7:19 silver sprinkling bowl w seventy shekels, NIH
7:20 one gold dish w ten shekels, filled with NIH
7:25 silver plate w a hundred and thirty shekels 5486
7:25 silver sprinkling bowl w seventy shekels, NIH
7:26 one gold dish w ten shekels, filled with NIH
7:31 silver plate w a hundred and thirty shekels 5486
7:31 silver sprinkling bowl w seventy shekels, NIH
7:32 one gold dish w ten shekels, filled with NIH
7:37 silver plate w a hundred and thirty shekels 5486
7:37 silver sprinkling bowl w seventy shekels, NIH
7:38 one gold dish w ten shekels, filled with NIH
7:43 silver plate w a hundred and thirty shekels 5486
7:43 silver sprinkling bowl w seventy shekels, NIH
7:44 one gold dish w ten shekels, filled with NIH
7:49 silver plate w a hundred and thirty shekels 5486
7:49 silver sprinkling bowl w seventy shekels, NIH
7:50 one gold dish w ten shekels, filled with NIH
7:55 silver plate w a hundred and thirty shekels 5486
7:55 silver sprinkling bowl w seventy shekels, NIH
7:56 one gold dish w ten shekels, filled with NIH
7:61 silver plate w a hundred and thirty shekels 5486
7:61 silver sprinkling bowl w seventy shekels, NIH
7:62 one gold dish w ten shekels, filled with NIH
7:67 silver plate w a hundred and thirty shekels 5486
7:67 silver sprinkling bowl w seventy shekels, NIH
7:68 one gold dish w ten shekels, filled with NIH
7:73 silver plate w a hundred and thirty shekels 5486
7:73 silver sprinkling bowl w seventy shekels, NIH
7:74 one gold dish w ten shekels, filled with NIH
7:79 silver plate w a hundred and thirty shekels 5486
7:79 silver sprinkling bowl w seventy shekels, NIH
7:80 one gold dish w ten shekels, filled with NIH
Jos 7:21 and a wedge of gold w fifty shekels, 5486
1Sa 17: 5 armor of bronze w five thousand shekels; 5486
Ezr 8:26 silver articles w 100 talents, NIH

WEIGHS (10) [WEIGH]

Ex 30:13 sanctuary shekel, which w twenty gerahs. 9203
Nu 3:47 sanctuary shekel, which w twenty gerahs. NIH
18:16 sanctuary shekel, which w twenty gerahs. NIH
Pr 12:25 An anxious heart w a man **down,** 8817
15:28 The heart of the righteous w its answers, 2047
21: 2 but the LORD w the heart. 9419
24:12 does not he *who* w the heart perceive it? 9419
Ecc 6: 1 and it w **heavily** on men: 8041
8: 6 a man's misery w **heavily** upon him. 8041
Isa 40:15 *he* w the islands as though they were 5747

WEIGHT (27) [WEIGH]

Ge 23:16 **according to the** w **current** among the 6296
43:21 the **exact** w—in the mouth of his sack. 5486
Lev 19:35 when measuring length, w or quantity. 5486
26:26 and they will dole out the bread by w. 5486
Jdg 8:26 The w *of* the gold rings he asked for came 5486
2Sa 12:30 its w was a **talent** of gold, 5486
14:26 and its w was two hundred shekels by NIH
1Ki 7:47 the w *of* the bronze was not determined. 5486
10:14 The w *of* the gold that Solomon received 5486
1Ch 20: 2 its w was found to be a talent of gold, 5486
28:14 the w of gold for all the gold articles to 5486
28:14 and the w of silver for all the silver articles 5486
28:15 the w of gold for the gold lampstands 5486
28:15 the w *for* each lampstand and its lamps; 5486
28:15 and the w of silver for each silver lampstand 5486
28:16 the w of gold for each table 5486
28:16 the w of silver for the silver tables; NIH
28:17 the w of pure gold for the forks, NIH
28:17 the w of gold for each gold dish; 5486
28:17 the w of silver for each silver dish; 5486
28:18 and the w of the refined gold for the altar 5486
2Ch 4:18 the w *of* the bronze was not determined. 5486
9:13 The w *of* the gold that Solomon received 5486
Ezr 8:34 accounted for by number and w, 5486
8:34 and the entire w was recorded at that time. 5486
Job 26: 8 yet the clouds do not burst under their w. NIH
La 4: 2 sons of Zion, once **worth their** w in gold, 6131

WEIGHTIER (1) [WEIGH]

Jn 5:36 "I have testimony w **than** that of John. *3505*

WEIGHTS (8) [WEIGH]

Lev 19:36 Use honest scales and honest w, 74
Dt 25:13 Do not have **two differing** w in your bag— 74+74+2256
25:15 You must have accurate and honest w 74
Pr 11: 1 but accurate w are his delight. 74
16:11 all the w *in* the bag are of his making. 74
20:10 **Differing** w and differing measures 74+74+2256
20:23 The LORD detests **differing** w, 74+74+2256
Mic 6:11 with a bag of false w? 74

WEIGHTY (1) [WEIGH]

2Co 10:10 some say, "His letters are w and forceful, *987*

WELCOME (15) [WELCOMED, WELCOMES]

Jdg 19:20 "You are w at my house," the old man said. 8934
Mt 10:14 If anyone *will* not w you or listen *1312*
Mk 6:11 if any place *will* not w you or listen to you, *1312*
9:37 and whoever welcomes me *does* not w me *1312*
Lk 9: 5 If people *do* not w you, *1312*
9:53 but the *people* there *did* not w him, *1312*
16: 4 *people will* w me into their houses.' *1312*
Ac 18:27 and wrote to the disciples there *to* w him. *622*
Php 2:29 **W** him in the Lord with great joy, *4657*
Col 4:10 if he comes to you, w him.) *1312*
Phm 1:17 w him as you would welcome me. *4689*
1:17 welcome him as you would w me. *NIG*
2Pe 1:11 and you will receive a rich w **into** *1658*
2Jn 1:10 not take him into your house or w him *3306+5897*
3Jn 1:10 he refuses to w the brothers. *2110*

WELCOMED (19) [WELCOME]

Jdg 19: 3 her father saw him, he gladly w him. 7925
Ps 21: 3 *You* w him *with* rich blessings and placed 7709
Lk 8:40 Now when Jesus returned, a crowd w him, *622*
9:11 He w them and spoke to them about *622*
10: 8 "When you enter a town and *are* w, *1312*
10:10 But when you enter a town and *are* not w, *1312*
16: 9 you *will be* w into eternal dwellings. *1312*
19: 6 So he came down at once and w him gladly. *5685*
Jn 4:45 arrived in Galilee, the Galileans w him. *1312*
Ac 15: 4 *they were* w by the church and the apostles *4138*
17: 7 and Jason *has* w them **into** *his* **house.** *5685*
28: 2 a fire and w us all because it was raining *4689*
28: 7 He w us to his home and *346*
28:30 in his own rented house and w all who came *622*
2Co 8:17 For Titus not only w our appeal, *1312*
Gal 4:14 *you* w me as if I were an angel of God, *1312*
1Th 1: 6 *you* w the message with the joy given by *1312*
Heb 11:13 *they* only saw them and w them from *832*
11:31 *because she* w the spies, *1312+1645+3552*

WELCOMES (11) [WELCOME]

Mt 18: 5 "And whoever w a little child like this *1312*
18: 5 a little child like this in my name w me. *1312*
Mk 9:37 "Whoever w one of these little children *1312*
9:37 of these little children in my name w me; *1312*
9:37 and whoever w me does not welcome me *1312*
Lk 9:48 "Whoever w this little child in my name *1312*
9:48 child in my name w me; *1312*
9:48 and whoever w me welcomes the one who *1312*
9:48 welcomes me w the one who sent me. *1312*
15: 2 "This man w sinners and eats with them." *4657*
2Jn 1:11 who w him shares in his wicked work. *3306+5897*

WELDING (1)

Isa 41: 7 He says of the w, "It is good." 1817

WELFARE (3)

Ne 2:10 had come to promote the w of the Israelites. 3208
Est 10: 3 and spoke up for the w of all the Jews. 8934
Php 2:20 who takes a genuine interest in your w. *NIG*

WELL (302) [WELL'S, WELLED, WELLING, WELLS]

Ge 12:13 so that I *will be* **treated** w for your sake 3512
12:16 *He* **treated** Abram w for her sake, 3512
13:10 plain of the Jordan *was* w **watered,** 5482
14: 7 **as** w **as** the Amorites who were living 1685+2256
16:14 the w was called Beer Lahai Roi; 931
18: 5 **"Very** w," they answered, "do as you say." 4027
18:11 and Sarah were already old and w **advanced** 995
19:21 He said to him, **"Very** w, 2180
21:19 Then God opened her eyes and she saw a w 931
21:25 complained to Abimelech about a w *of* water 931
21:30 from my hand as a witness that I dug this w. 931
24: 1 Abraham was now old and w **advanced** 995
24:11 had the camels kneel down near the w 931+4784
24:20 ran back to the w to draw more water, 931
24:25 **as** w **as** room for you to spend the night." 1685
26:10 **might** w **have** slept with your wife, 3869+5071
26:19 and discovered a w *of* fresh water there. 931
26:20 So he named the w Esek, 931
26:21 Then they dug another w, 931
26:22 He moved on from there and dug another w, 931
26:25 and there his servants dug a w. 931

Ge 26:29 but always treated you w and sent you away 3202
26:32 and told him about the w they had dug. 931
29: 2 There he saw a w in the field, 931
29: 2 the flocks were watered from that w. 931
29: 2 over the mouth of the w was large. 931
29: 3 to its place over the mouth of the w. 931
29: 6 Then Jacob asked them, "Is he **w?"** 8934
29: 8 rolled away from the mouth of the w. 931
29:10 the stone away from the mouth of the w 931
30:15 **"Very w,"** Rachel said, "he can sleep 4027+4200
32: 7 and the flocks and herds **and** camels **as w.** 2256
36: 6 **as w as** his livestock and all his other 2256
37:10 When he told his father **as w as** his brothers, 2256
37:13 **"Very w,"** he replied. 2180
37:14 "Go and see if all is w *with* your brothers 8934
40:14 But when *all* **goes** w with you, 3512
43:28 Your servant our father is still alive and **w."** 8934
44:10 **"Very w,** then," he said, 1685
47:19 we and our land **as w?** 1685
Ex 2:15 in Midian, where he sat down by a **w.** 931
4:14 I know he *can* **speak w.** 1819+1819
4:18 Jethro said, "Go, and I **wish** you w." 4200+8934
11: 5 **and** all the firstborn of the cattle **as w.** 2256
12:29 **and** the firstborn of all the livestock **as w.** 2256
12:38 **as w as** large droves of livestock, 2256
23:12 **and** the alien **as w,** 2256
25:29 **as w as** its pitchers and bowls for 2256
37:23 **as w as** its wick trimmers and trays, 2256
Lev 4:11 **as w as** the head and legs, 6584
21:22 **as w as** the holy food; 2256
25: 7 **as w as** for your livestock and 2256
Nu 3:37 **as w as** the posts of 2256
4:32 **as w as** the posts of 2256
10:29 Come with us and *we will* **treat** you **w,** 3512
20:17 or drink water from any **w.** 931
21:16 the w where the LORD said to Moses, 931
21:17 Israel sang this song: "Spring up, O **w!** 931
21:18 the w that the princes dug, that the nobles of 931
21:22 or drink water from any **w.** 931
22:38 **"W,** I have come to you now," 2180
31:10 **as w as** all their camps. 2256
31:20 Purify every garment **as w as** 2256
32:38 **as w as** Nebo and Baal Meon 2256
Dt 4:40 that *it may* **go** w with you and your children 3512
5:16 that you may live long and that *it may* **go w** 3512
5:29 so that *it might* **go** w with them 3512
6: 3 and be careful to obey so that *it may* **go w** 3512
6:18 that *it may* **go** w with you and you may go 3512
7:18 **remember** w what the LORD your God did to Pharaoh 2349+2349
8:16 to test you so that in the end *it might* **go w** 3512
12:25 that *it may* **go** w with you and your children 3512
12:28 so that *it may* always **go w** with you 3512
15:16 and your family and *is* **w off** with you, 3201
19:13 so that *it may* **go w** with you. 3201
22: 7 so that *it may* **go w** with you 3512
29:19 on the watered land **as w as** the dry. 907
Jos 13: 1 Joshua was old and **w advanced** in years, 995
17:18 but the forested hill country **as w.** 3954
23: 1 by then old and **w advanced** in years, 995
23: 2 "I am old and **w advanced** in years. 995
Jdg 1:24 and we will see that you are treated **w."** 2876
4: 9 **"Very w,"** Deborah said, *"I will* **go** 2143+2143
Ru 3: 1 where you *will be* **w provided for?** 3512
1Sa 16:17 "Find someone who plays w and bring him 3512
16:18 He speaks w and is a fine-looking man. 1067
17:12 in Saul's time he was old and **w advanced** 995
18: 5 and Saul's officers **as w.** 1685
18:30 and his name *became* **w known.** 3700+4394
19: 4 Jonathan spoke w of David to Saul 3202
20: 3 "Your father **knows very w** 3359+3359
20: 7 If he says, **'Very w,'** 3202
24:17 "You have treated me **w,** 3208
24:19 May the LORD reward you w for the way 3208
28: 2 Achish replied, **"Very w,** 4027+4200
2Sa 3:26 they brought him back from the **w** *of* Sirah. 1014
10: 6 **as w as** the king of Maacah with 2256
11:25 sword devours one **as w as** another. 2256+3869
14: 7 then we will get rid of the heir **as w.'** 1685
14:21 said to Joab, **"Very w,** I will do it. 2180+5528
17:18 He had a w in his courtyard, 931
17:19 and spread it out over the opening of the w 931
17:21 of the w and went to inform King David. 931
18:28 Ahimaaz called out to the king, **"All is w!"** 8934
23:15 from the w near the gate *of* Bethlehem!" 1014
23:16 from the w near the gate *of* Bethlehem 1014
1Ki 1: 1 When King David was old and **w advanced** 995
2:18 **"Very w,"** Bathsheba replied, 3202
2:22 *as w* **request** the kingdom for him— AIT
4:13 as w as the district of Argob in Bashan NIH
4:23 **as w as** deer, gazelles, roebucks 963+4200+4946
5:16 **as w as** thirty-three hundred foremen who supervised the project 963+4200+4946
7:29 and on the uprights **as w.** 4027
8:18 *you* **did** w to have this in your heart. 3201
9:19 **as w as** all his store cities and the towns 2256
11:28 Solomon saw **how w** the young man did 3954
2Ki 2:19 "Look, our lord, this town is w situated, 3202
3:25 **and** attacked it **as w.** 2256
4:14 **"W,** she has no son and her husband is old." 66
10:11 **as w as** all his chief men, 2256
10:14 and slaughtered them by the w 1014
10:30 "Because *you have* **done w** 3201
17: 8 **as w as** the practices that the kings 2256
25:24 and *it will* **go w** with you." 3512
1Ch 2:23 as w as Kenath with its surrounding NIH
7:24 Upper Beth Horon **as w as** Uzzen Sheerah. 2256
9:29 **as w as** the flour and wine, and the oil, 2256
11:17 from the w near the gate *of* Bethlehem!" 1014
11:18 from the w near the gate *of* Bethlehem 1014
19: 7 **as w as** the king of Maacah with his troops, 2256
22:15 stonecutters, masons and carpenters, **as w as** 2256
23: 2 **as w as** the priests and Levites. 2256
25: 8 teacher **as w as** student, 6640
28:13 **as w as** for all the articles to be used 2256
29: 2 **as w as** onyx for the settings, turquoise, 2256
29:24 **as w as** all of King David's sons, 1685+2256
2Ch 6: 8 *you* **did** w to have this in your heart. 3201
8: 6 **as w as** Baalath and all his store cities, 2256
9: 3 **as w as** the palace he had built, 2256
19:11 may the LORD be with those who do **w."** 3202
21: 3 **as w as** fortified cities in Judah, 6640
28:18 Aijalon and Gederoth, **as w as** Soco, 2256
33:15 **as w as** all the altars he had built on 2256
33:19 **as w as** all his sins and unfaithfulness, 2256
Ezr 3: 5 **as w as** those brought as freewill offerings 2256
7: 6 a teacher **w versed** in the Law of Moses, 4542
7:16 **as w as** the freewill offerings of the people 10554
8:28 "You **as w as** these articles are consecrated 2256
Ne 2:13 the Valley Gate toward the Jackal **W** and 6524
5:17 **as w as** those who came to us from 2256
12:22 **as w as** those of the priests, 2256
12:35 **as w as** some priests with trumpets, 2256
12:41 **as w as** the priests— 2256
13: 5 **as w as** the contributions for the priests. 2256
Job 1:12 The LORD said to Satan, **"Very w, then,** 2180
2: 6 The LORD said to Satan, **"Very w, then,** 2180
12: 3 But I have a mind **as w as** you; 4017
13: 9 Would it turn out w if he examined you? 3202
15:21 when all seems **w,** marauders attack him. 8934
16:12 *All* was w with me, but he shattered me; 8929
21:24 his body **w nourished,** 2692+4848
21:27 "I know **full** w what you are thinking, 2176
29:11 Whoever heard me **spoke w of** me, 887
Ps 48:13 **consider** w her ramparts, 4213+8883
104:16 The trees of the LORD *are* **w watered,** 8425
109:21 deal w with me for your name's sake; NIH
139:14 I know that **full w.** 4394
141: 6 that my words *were* **w** spoken. 5838
Pr 4:13 **guard** it **w,** for it is your life. 5915
5: 1 **listen** w to my words of insight, 265+5742
5:15 running water from your own **w.** 931
23: 1 **note** w what is before you, 1067+1067
23:27 and a wayward wife is a narrow **w.** 931
24:25 But *it will* **go** w with those who convict 5838
25:26 Like a muddied spring or a polluted w is 5227
Ecc 2: 8 and a harem as **w—** NIH
7:14 God has made the one **as w as** the other. 4200+6645
8:13 it will not go w with them, 3202
11: 6 or whether both will do equally **w.** 3202
12: 6 or the wheel broken at the **w,** 1014
SS 4:15 a **w** *of* flowing water streaming down 931
Isa 3:10 Tell the righteous it will be w with them, 3202
5: 2 and cut out a winepress **as w.** 1685
23:16 play the harp **w,** sing many a song, 3512
28:11 **Very w then,** with foreign lips and 3954
48: 8 **W** do I know how treacherous you are; 3954
Jer 6: 7 As a w pours out its water, 931
7:23 that *it may* **go w** with you. 3512
12: 6 though they speak w of you. 3208
12:16 if *they* **learn** w the ways of my people 4340+4340
22:15 so all went w with him. 3202
22:16 and so all went **w.** 3202
31:13 young men and old **as w.** 3481
32:11 **as w as** the unsealed copy— 2256
38: 4 left in this city, **as w as** all the people, 2256
38:20 Then *it will* **go w** with you, 3512
40: 9 and *it will* **go w** with you. 3512
41: 3 **as w as** the Babylonian soldiers who were 2256
42: 6 so that *it will* **go w** with us, 3512
44:17 and were **w off** and suffered no harm. 3202
50:33 and the people of Judah **as w.** 3481
51:57 her governors, officers and warriors **as w;** 2256
La 3:20 *I* **w remember** them, 2349+2349
Eze 4:15 **"Very w,"** he said, "I will let you bake 8011
16:37 those you loved **as w as** those you hated. 6584
18: 4 the father **as w as** the son— 3869
24:10 **Cook** the meat **w,** mixing in the spices; 9462
24:25 and their sons and daughters **as w—** 2256
30:22 the good arm **as w as** the broken one, 2256
33:32 a beautiful voice and plays an instrument **w,** 3512
40:19 a hundred cubits on the east side **as w as** on 2256
41:16 as w as the thresholds and NIH
45: 4 a place for their houses **as w as** a holy place 2256
Da 1: 4 **w informed,** quick to understand, 1981+3359
Hos 13:15 his spring will fail and his w dry up. 5078
Jnh 4:11 **and** many cattle **as w.** 2256
Zec 8:12 "The seed will **grow w,** 8934
12: 2 will be besieged **as w as** Jerusalem. 1685+2256
Mal 2:16 with violence as w as with his garment," NIH
Mt 3:17 whom I love; with him *I am* **w pleased."** *2305*
5:40 let him have your cloak **as w.** *2779*
6:33 all these things will be given to you as w. *NIG*
13:52 of his storeroom new treasures **as w as** old." *2779*
15:31 the mute speaking, the crippled **made w,** *5618*
17: 5 whom I love; with him *I am* **w pleased.** *2305*
25:21 "His master replied, **'W done,** *2292*
25:23 "His master replied, **'W done,** *2292*
25:27 **W then,** you should have put my money *4036*
Mk 1:11 whom I love; with you *I am* **w pleased."** *2305*
5:16 and told about the pigs as w. *NIG*
6:14 for Jesus' name had become **w known.** *5745*
7:37 "He has done everything **w,"** they said. *2822*
8: 7 They had a few small fish **as w;** *2779*
12:32 **"W said,** teacher," the man replied. *2822*
16:18 hands on sick people, and they will get **w."** *2822*
Lk 1: 7 and they were both **w along** in years. *4581*
1:18 I am an old man and my wife is **w along** *4581*
3:22 whom I love; with you *I am* **w pleased."** *2305*
4:22 All **spoke w of** him and were amazed at *3455*
6:25 Woe to you who *are* **w fed** now, *1855*
6:26 Woe to you when all men speak w of you, *2822*
6:48 could not shake it, because it was **w** built. *2822*
7:10 to the house and found the servant **w.** *5617*
12:31 and these things will be given to you as **w.** *NIG*
14: 5 an ox that falls into a w on the Sabbath day, *5853*
17:19 your faith *has* **made** you **w."** *5392*
19:17 **" 'W done,** my good servant!' *2301*
20:39 the teachers of the law responded, **"W** said, *2822*
Jn 3:26 **w,** he is baptizing, and everyone is going *3972*
4: 6 Jacob's w was there, and Jesus, *4380*
4: 6 from the journey, sat down by the **w.** *4380*
4:11 nothing to draw with and the w is deep. *5853*
4:12 gave us the w and drank from it himself, *5853*
5: 6 he asked him, "Do you want to get **w?"** *5618*
5:11 "The man who made me w said to me, *5618*
5:14 "See, you are w again. *5618*
5:15 that it was Jesus who had made him **w.** *5618*
12:10 priests made plans to kill Lazarus **as w,** *2779*
13: 9 but my hands and my head **as w!"** *2779*
14: 7 you would know my Father **as w.** *2779*
15:23 He who hates me hates my Father **as w.** *2779*
20: 7 **as w as** the burial cloth that had been *2779*
21:25 Jesus did many other things **as w.** *NIG*
Ac 6: 9 Jews of Cyrene and Alexandria **as w as** *2779*
10:12 **as w as** reptiles of the earth and birds of *2779*
10:28 "You *are* **w aware** that it is against our law *2179*
15:29 You will do w to avoid these things. *2292*
16: 2 at Lystra and Iconium **spoke w of** him. *3455*
17:17 **as w as** in the marketplace day by day *2779*
24:22 Felix, who was w acquainted with the Way, *209*
25:10 as you yourself know **very w.** *2822*
26: 3 so because you are **w acquainted with** all *1195*
1Co 4: 9 to angels **as w as** to men. *2779*
14:17 You may be giving thanks w enough, *2822*
2Co 7:14 to Titus has proved to be true as **w.** *NIG*
12:15 **and** expend myself **as w.** *2779*
Eph 6: 3 "that it may go w with you and *2292*
Php 4:12 whether **w fed** or hungry, *5963*
1Th 2: 8 the gospel of God but our lives **as w,** *2779*
3: 3 You know quite w that we were destined *NIG*
3: 4 And it turned out that way, as you w know. *NIG*
5: 2 you know **very** w that the day of the Lord *209*
2Th 1: 7 to you who are troubled, and to us as **w.** *NIG*
1Ti 3: 4 He must manage his own family w and *2822*
3:12 manage his children and his household **w.** *2822*
3:13 Those who have served w gain *2822*
5:10 and *is* **w known** for her good deeds, *3455*
5:17 of the church w are worthy of double honor, *2822*
2Ti 1:18 You know **very w** in how many ways *1019*
Heb 5: 3 own sins, **as w as** for the sins of the people. *2777*
11: 4 *when* God **spoke w of** his offerings. *3455*
Jas 2:16 **"Go, I wish you w;** *1645+1877+5632*
2:16 I wish you well; *keep* warm and **w fed,"** *5963*
5:15 offered in faith *will* **make** the sick person **w** *5392*
2Pe 1:17 whom I love; with him I *am* **w pleased."** *2305*
1:19 and *you* will do w to pay attention to it, *2822*
1Jn 5: 1 the father loves his child **as w.** *2779*
3Jn 1: 2 and that all *may* **go w** with you, *2338*
1: 2 even as your soul **is getting along w.** *2338*
1: 6 You will do w to send them on their way in *2822*
1:12 Demetrius *is* **w spoken of** by everyone— *3455*
1:12 We also **speak w of** him, *3455*

WELL'S (1) [WELL]

Ge 29: 3 the stone away from the w mouth and water 931

WELL-BEING (4)

Ezr 6:10 and pray for the **w** *of* the king and his sons. 10261
Ps 35:27 who delights in the **w** *of* his servant." 8934
119:122 Ensure your servant's **w;** 3202
Jer 14:11 "Do not pray for the **w** of this people. 3208

WELL-BUILT (1) [BUILD]

Ge 39: 6 Now Joseph was w and handsome, 3637+9307

WELL-DRESSED (1) [DRESS]

Isa 3:24 instead of **w hair,** baldness; 5126+5250

WELL-FED (1) [FEED]

Jer 5: 8 They are w, lusty stallions, each neighing 8889

WELL-KNEADED (1) [KNEAD]

Lev 7:12 cakes of fine flour w and mixed with oil. 8057

WELL-KNOWN (1) [KNOW]

Nu 16: 2 250 Israelite men, w community leaders 408+9005

WELL-MIXED (1) [MIX]

Lev 6:21 bring it w and present the grain offering 8057

WELL-NOURISHED (1) [NOURISH]

Ne 9:25 They ate to the full and *were* **w;** 9042

WELL-NURTURED (1) [NURTURED]

Ps 144:12 our sons in their youth will be like **w** plants, 1540

WELL-TO-DO (1)

2Ki 4: 8 And a **w** woman was there, who urged him 1524

WELL-TRAINED (1) [TRAIN]

2Ch 26:11 Uzziah had a **w** army, ready to go out 4878+6913

WELL-WATERED (6) [WATER]

Job 8:16 He is like a **w plant** in the sunshine, 8183
Isa 58:11 You will be like a **w** garden, 8116
Jer 31:12 They will be like a **w** garden, 8116
Eze 31:14 No other trees *so* **w** are ever to reach 4784+9272
31:16 all the trees *that were* **w**, 4784+9272
45:15 of two hundred from the **w** pastures 5482

WELLBELOVED (KJV) See DEAR FRIEND, LOVE, LOVED ONE

WELLED (1) [WELL]

2Co 8: 2 extreme poverty **w up** in rich generosity. *4355*

WELLING (1) [WELL]

Jn 4:14 a spring of water **w up** to eternal life." *256*

WELLPLEASING (KJV) See PLEASING

WELLS (8) [WELL]

Ge 26:15 the **w** that his father's servants had dug 931
26:18 Isaac reopened the **w** that had been dug 931+4784
Dt 6:11 **w** you did not dig, and vineyards 1014
10: 6 from the **w** *of* the Jaakanites to Moserah. 931
2Ki 19:24 I *have* **dug w** in foreign lands and drunk 7769
Ne 9:25 **w** already dug, vineyards, olive groves 1014
Isa 12: 3 With joy you will draw water from the **w** *of* salvation. 5078
37:25 I *have* **dug w** in foreign lands and drunk 7769

WELLSPRING (1) [SPRING]

Pr 4:23 guard your heart, for it is the **w** *of* life. 9362

WELTS (1)

Isa 1: 6 only wounds and **w** and open sores, 2467

WEN (KJV) See WARTS

WENCH (KJV) See SERVANT GIRL

WENT (1232) [GO]

Ge 4:16 So Cain **w out** from the LORD's presence 3655
6: 4 the sons of God **w** to the daughters of men 995
10:11 From that land *he* **w** *to* Assyria, 3655
12: 4 and Lot **w** with him. 2143
12: 8 From there *he* **w on** toward the hills east 6980
12:10 and Abram **w down** to Egypt to live there 3718
13: 1 So Abram **w up** from Egypt to the Negev, 6590
13: 1 and Lot **w** with him. NIH
13: 3 From the Negev *he* **w** from place to place 2143
13:18 and **w** to live near the great trees of Mamre 995
14: 2 **w to war** *against* Bera king of Sodom, 4878+6913
14: 5 with him **w out** and defeated the Rephaites 995
14: 7 Then they turned back and **w** to En Mishpat 995
14:11 then *they* **w away.** 2143
14:14 in his household and **w in pursuit** as far 8103
14:24 that belongs to the men who **w** with me— 2143
17:22 God **w up** from him. 6590
18:22 The men turned away and **w** toward Sodom, 2143
19: 6 Lot **w** outside to meet them and shut 3655
19:14 So Lot **w out** and spoke to his sons-in-law, 3655
19:33 the older daughter **w in** and lay with him. 995
19:35 the younger daughter **w** and lay with him. 7756
21:14 *She* **w on** *her* **way** and wandered 2143
21:16 Then *she* **w off** and sat down nearby, 2143
21:19 So *she* **w** and filled the skin with water 2143
22: 6 As the two of them **w on** together, 2143
22: 8 And the two of them **w on** together. 2143
22:13 He **w over** and took the ram 2143
23: 2 and Abraham **w** to mourn for Sarah and 995
24:16 *She* **w down** to the spring, 3718
24:30 *he* **w** *out* to the man 995
24:32 So the man **w** to the house, 995
24:45 *She* **w down** to the spring and drew water, 3718
24:61 and mounted their camels and **w** back with 2143
24:63 He **w out** to the field one evening 3655
25:22 So *she* **w** to inquire of the LORD. 2143
26: 1 Isaac **w** to Abimelech king of the Philistines 2143
26:23 From there *he* **w up** *to* Beersheba. 6590
27:14 So *he* **w** and got them and brought them 2143
27:18 *He* **w** to his father and said, "My father." 995
27:22 Jacob **w close** to his father Isaac, 5602
27:27 So *he* **w** to him and kissed him. 5602
28: 5 and *he* **w** to Paddan Aram, 2143
28: 9 so he **w** to Ishmael and married Mahalath, 2143
29:10 he **w over** and rolled the stone away from 5602
30:14 Reuben **w out** into the fields 2143
30:16 Leah **w out** to meet him. 3655
30:42 So the weak animals **w** to Laban and 2118
31:33 So Laban **w** into Jacob's tent and 995
32: 1 Jacob also **w** on his way, 2143
32: 6 they said, "*We* **w** to your brother Esau, 995
32:21 So Jacob's gifts **w on** ahead of him, 6296
33: 3 *He* himself **w on** ahead and bowed down to 6296
33:17 Jacob, however, **w** to Succoth, 5825
34: 1 **w out** to visit the women of the land. 3655
34: 6 Then Shechem's father Hamor **w out** 3655
34:20 So Hamor and his son Shechem **w** to 995
34:24 the *men who* **w out** *of* the city gate agreed 3655
35:13 Then God **w up** from him at the place 6590
35:22 Reuben **w in** and slept with his father's 2143
37:17 So Joseph **w** after his brothers 2143
37:30 *He* **w back** to his brothers and said, 8740
38: 1 Judah left his brothers and **w down** to stay 3718
38:11 So Tamar **w** to live in her father's house. 2143
38:12 *he* **w up** to Timnah, 6590
38:12 his friend Hirah the Adullamite **w** with him. NIH
38:16 *he* **w over** to her by the roadside and said, 5742
38:22 So *he* **w back** to Judah and said, 8740
39:11 One day *he* **w** into the house to attend 995
41:45 And Joseph **w** throughout the land of Egypt. 3655
41:46 And Joseph **w out** from Pharaoh's presence 3655
42: 3 of Joseph's brothers **w down** to buy grain 3718
42: 5 So Israel's sons were among those *who* **w** 995
43:19 So *they* **w up** to Joseph's steward and spoke 5602
43:30 *He* **w** into his private room and wept there. 995
44:18 Then Judah **w up** to him and said: 5602
44:24 When *we* **w back** to your servant my father, 6590
44:28 One of them **w away** from me, and I said, 3655
45:25 So *they* **w up** out of Egypt and came 6590
46: 6 and Jacob and all his offspring **w** to Egypt. 995
46: 8 (Jacob and his descendants) who **w** to Egypt: 995
46:26 All those who **w** to Egypt with Jacob— 995
46:27 which **w** to Egypt, were seventy in all. 995
46:29 and **w** to Goshen to meet his father Israel. 6590
47: 1 Joseph **w** and told Pharaoh, 995
47:10 Then Jacob blessed Pharaoh and **w out** 3655
49: 4 for *you* **w up** *onto* your father's bed, 6590
50: 7 So Joseph **w up** to bury his father. 6590
50: 9 Chariots and horsemen also **w up** with him. 6590
Ex 1: 1 of Israel who **w** to Egypt with Jacob, each 995
2: 5 Pharaoh's daughter **w down** to the Nile 3718
2: 8 And the girl **w** and got the baby's mother. 2143
2:11 *he* **w out** to where his own people were 3655
2:13 The next day *he* **w out** and saw 3655
2:15 but Moses fled from Pharaoh and **w** to live NIH
2:23 cry for help because of their slavery **w up** 6590
4:18 Then Moses **w** back to Jethro 2143
5: 1 Afterward Moses and Aaron **w** to Pharaoh 995
5:10 the foremen **w out** and said to the people, 3655
5:15 Then the Israelite foremen **w** and appealed 995
5:23 Ever since *I* **w** to Pharaoh to speak 995
7:10 and Aaron **w** to Pharaoh and did just as 995
7:23 Instead, he turned and **w** into his palace, 995
9:33 Moses left Pharaoh and **w** out of the city. NIH
10: 3 So Moses and Aaron **w** to Pharaoh and said 995
12:38 Many other people **w up** with them, 6590
13:18 The Israelites **w up** out of Egypt armed 6590
13:21 By day the LORD **w** ahead of them in 2143
14:19 withdrew and **w** behind them. 2143
14:20 so neither **w near** the other all night long. 7928
14:22 Israelites **w** through the sea on dry ground, 995
14:27 and at daybreak the sea **w back** to its place. 8740
14:29 Israelites **w** through the sea on dry ground, 2143
15:19 chariots and horsemen **w** into the sea, 995
15:22 the Red Sea and *they* **w** into the Desert 3655
16:27 some of the people **w out** on the seventh day 3655
17:10 Aaron and Hur **w** *to* the top of the hill. 6590
18: 7 So Moses **w out** to meet his father-in-law 3655
18: 7 They greeted each other and then **w** into 995
19: 3 Then Moses **w up** to God, 6590
19: 7 So Moses **w back** and summoned the elders 995
19:20 the top of the mountain. So Moses **w up** 6590
19:25 Moses **w down** to the people and told them. 3718
24: 3 When Moses **w** and told the people all 995
24: 9 and the seventy elders of Israel **w up** 6590
24:13 and Moses **w up** on the mountain of God. 6590
24:15 When Moses **w up** on the mountain, 6590
24:18 Moses entered the cloud as *he* **w** on **up** 6590
32:15 Moses turned and **w down** the mountain 3718
32:31 So Moses **w back** to the LORD and said, 8740
33: 8 And whenever Moses **w out** to the tent, 3655
33: 9 As Moses **w** into the tent, 995
34: 4 the first ones and **w up** Mount Sinai early in 6590
34:35 over his face until he **w in** to speak with 995
Lev 9:23 and Aaron then **w** into the Tent of Meeting. 995
24:10 and an Egyptian father **w out** among 3655
Nu 10:14 The divisions of the camp of Judah **w** first, 5825
10:18 divisions of the camp of Reuben **w** next, 5825
10:22 divisions of the camp of Ephraim **w** next, 5825
10:33 the covenant of the LORD **w** before them 5825
11: 8 The people **w around** gathering it, 8763
11:24 So Moses **w out** and told the people what 3655
11:31 Now a wind **w out** from the LORD 5825
11:32 and all the next day the people **w out** 7756
13:21 So *they* **w up** and explored the land from 6590
13:22 *They* **w up** through the Negev and came 6590
13:27 "*We* **w** into the land to which you sent us, 995
14:24 I will bring him into the land *he* **w** to, 995
14:38 Of the men who **w** to explore the land, 2143
14:40 Early the next morning *they* **w up** toward 6590
14:44 in their presumption *they* **w up** toward 6590
16:25 Moses got up and **w** to Dathan and Abiram, 2143
16:33 They **w down** alive into the grave, 3718
16:43 Then Moses and Aaron **w** to the front of 995
20: 6 Moses and Aaron **w** from the assembly to 995
Nu 20:15 Our forefathers **w down** into Egypt, 3718
20:27 *They* **w up** Mount Hor in the sight of 6590
21:18 Then they **w** from the desert to Mattanah, NIH
21:28 "Fire **w out** from Heshbon, 3655
21:33 Then they turned and **w up** *along* the road 6590
22:21 saddled his donkey and **w** with the princes 2143
22:22 But God was very angry when he **w**, 2143
22:35 So Balaam **w** with the princes of Balak. 2143
22:36 *he* **w out** to meet him at the Moabite town 3655
22:39 Balaam **w** with Balak *to* Kiriath Huzoth. 2143
23: 3 Then *he* **w off** *to* a barren height. 2143
23: 6 So *he* **w back** to him and found him 8740
23:17 So *he* **w** to him and found him standing 995
24:25 and Balak **w** his own way. 2143
31:13 of the community **w** to meet them outside 3655
31:48 and commanders of hundreds—**w** to Moses 7928
32: 9 After *they* **w up** to the Valley of Eshcol 6590
32:39 of Makir son of Manasseh **w** to Gilead, 2143
33: 9 They left Marah and **w** to Elim, 995
33:38 the priest **w up** Mount Hor, 6590
Dt 1:19 from Horeb and **w** toward the hill country 2143
1:24 They left and **w up** into the hill country, 6590
1:31 all the way *you* **w** until you reached this 2143
1:33 who **w** ahead of you on your journey, 2143
2: 8 So *we* **w on** past our brothers 6296
3: 1 and **w up** *along* the road toward Bashan, 6590
9: 9 When I **w up** on the mountain to receive 6590
9:15 So I turned and **w down** from the mountain 3718
10: 3 and *I* **w up** on the mountain with the two 6590
10:22 Your forefathers *who* **w down** AIT
26: 5 *he* **w down** into Egypt with a few people 3718
29:26 *They* **w off** and worshiped other gods 2143
31: 1 Then Moses **w out** and spoke these words 2143
Jos 2: 1 So *they* **w** and entered the house of 2143
2: 5 I don't know which way they **w.** 2143
2: 8 she **w up** on the roof 6590
2:22 *they* **w** into the hills and stayed there 995
2:23 *They* **w down** out of the hills, 3718
3: 1 the Israelites set out from Shittim and **w** to 995
3: 2 After three days the officers **w** throughout 6296
3: 6 So they took it up and **w** ahead of them. 2143
3:14 the ark of the covenant **w** ahead of them. NIH
4:19 of the first month the people **w up** from 6590
5:13 Joshua **w up** to him and asked, 2143
6: 1 No *one* **w out** and no one came in. 3655
6: 8 **w forward,** blowing their trumpets, 6296
6:13 carrying the seven trumpets **w forward,** 2143
6:13 The armed men **w** ahead of them and 2143
6:23 the spying **w in** and brought out Rahab, 995
7: 2 So the men **w up** and spied out Ai. 6590
7: 4 So about three thousand men **w up;** 6590
8: 9 and *they* **w** to the place of ambush and lay 2143
8:13 That night Joshua **w** into the valley. 2143
8:17 the city open and **w in pursuit** *of* Israel. 8103
9: 4 *They* **w** as a delegation whose donkeys 2143
9: 6 Then *they* **w** to Joshua in the camp at Gilgal 2143
10:36 Then Joshua and all Israel with him **w up** 6590
11:21 At that time Joshua **w** and destroyed 995
14: 8 but my brothers who **w up** with me made 6590
15: 3 continued on to Zin and **w over** to the south 6590
15: 6 **w up** *to* Beth Hoglah and continued north 6590
15: 7 The boundary then **w up** to Debir from 6590
15: 9 Mount Ephron and **w down** *toward* Baalah 9305
15:11 It **w** to the northern slope of Ekron, 3655
16: 1 and **w up** from there through the desert into 6590
16: 2 *It* **w on** from Bethel (that is, Luz), 3655
16: 5 of their inheritance **w** from Ataroth Addar 2118
16: 7 Then *it* **w down** from Janoah to Ataroth 3718
16: 8 the border **w** west to the Kanah Ravine 2143
17: 4 *They* **w** to Eleazar the priest, 7928
18: 9 So the men left and **w** through the land. 6296
18:13 and **w down** *to* Ataroth Addar on the hill 3718
18:16 The boundary **w down** to the foot of 3718
18:17 It then curved north, **w** *to* En Shemesh, 3655
18:19 then **w** to the northern slope of Beth Hoglah 6296
19:10 The boundary of their inheritance **w** as far 2118
19:12 of Kisloth Tabor and **w on** to Daberath and 3655
19:14 There the boundary **w around** on the north 6015
19:27 and **w** north to Beth Emek and Neiel, NIH
19:28 It **w** to Abdon, Rehob, Hammon and Kanah, NIH
19:29 then turned back toward Ramah and **w** to NIH
19:33 Their boundary **w** from Heleph and 2118
19:47 so they **w up** and attacked Leshem, took it, 6590
22: 6 and *they* **w** to their homes. 2143
22:15 When *they* **w** to Gilead— 995
24: 4 but Jacob and his sons **w down** *to* Egypt. 3718
Jdg 1: 3 So the Simeonites **w** with them. 2143
1: 9 the men of Judah **w down** to fight against 3718
1:16 **w up** from the City of Palms with the men 6590
1:17 Then the men of Judah **w** with 2143
1:26 He then **w** *to* the land of the Hittites, 2143
2: 1 The angel of the LORD **w up** from Gilgal 6590
2: 6 they **w** to take possession of the land, 2143
2:15 Whenever Israel **w out** to fight, 3655
3:10 that he became Israel's judge and **w** to war. 3655
3:23 Then Ehud **w out** to the porch; 3655
3:27 Israelites **w down** with him from the hills, 3718
4: 9 So Deborah **w** with Barak to Kedesh, 2143
4:10 and Deborah also **w** with him. 6590
4:14 So Barak **w down** Mount Tabor, 3718
4:18 Jael **w out** to meet Sisera and said to him, 3655
4:21 up a tent peg and a hammer and **w** quietly 995
4:22 and Jael **w out** to meet him. 3655
4:22 So *he* **w** in *with* her, and there lay Sisera 995
5: 4 "O LORD, when you **w out** from Seir, 3655
5:11 "Then the people of the LORD **w down** to 3718
6:19 Gideon **w in,** prepared a young goat, 995

Jdg 6:35 so that *they* too **w up** to meet them. 6590
7:11 So he and Purah his servant **w down** to 3718
8: 1 Why didn't you call us when *you* **w** 2143
8: 8 From there *he* **w up** *to* Peniel and made 6590
8:11 Gideon **w up** *by* the route of the nomads 6590
8:29 Jerub-Baal son of Joash **w back** home 2143
9: 1 of Jerub-Baal **w** to his mother's brothers 2143
9: 5 *He* **w** *to* his father's home in Ophrah and 995
9: 8 the trees **w out** to anoint a king 2143+2143
9:42 The next day the people of Shechem **w out** 3655
9:46 the tower of Shechem **w** into the stronghold 995
9:48 he and all his men **w up** Mount Zalmon. 6590
9:50 Next Abimelech **w** to Thebez 2143
9:52 Abimelech **w** to the tower and stormed it. 995
9:55 that Abimelech was dead, they **w** home. 2143
11: 5 the elders of Gilead **w** to get Jephthah from 2143
11:11 So Jephthah **w** with the elders of Gilead, 2143
11:16 Israel **w** through the desert to the Red Sea 2143
11:32 Jephthah **w** over to fight the Ammonites, 6296
11:38 She and the girls **w** into the hills and wept 2143
13: 6 the woman **w** to her husband and told him, 995
14: 1 Samson **w down** to Timnah and saw there 3718
14: 5 Samson **w down** to Timnah together 3718
14: 7 *he* **w down** and talked with the woman, 3718
14: 8 when *he* **w back** to marry her, 8740
14: 9 with his hands and ate as *he* **w along.** 2143+2143
14:10 Now his father **w down** to see the woman. 3718
14:19 *He* **w down** *to* Ashkelon, 3718
14:19 *he* **w up** *to* his father's house. 6590
15: 1 a young goat and **w** *to* **visit** his wife. AIT
15: 4 So he **w out** and caught three hundred foxes 2143
15: 6 So the Philistines **w up** and burned her 6590
15: 8 Then *he* **w down** and stayed in a cave in 3718
15: 9 The Philistines **w up** and camped in Judah, 6590
15:11 from Judah **w down** to the cave in the rock 3718
16: 1 One day Samson **w** to Gaza, 2143
16: 1 *He* **w in to spend the night with** her. 448+995
16: 5 The rulers of the Philistines **w** to her 6590
16:31 and his father's whole family **w down** 3718
18:13 From there *they* **w on** *to* the hill country 6296
18:15 So they turned in there and **w** to the house 995
18:17 The five men who had spied out the land **w** 995
18:18 When these men **w into** Micah's house 995
18:20 and the carved image and **w** along with 995
18:24 and my priest, and **w away.** 2143
18:26 So the Danites **w** their way, and Micah, 2143
18:26 turned around and **w back** home. 8740
18:27 and his priest, and **w on** to Laish, 995
19: 2 and **w** back to her father's house NIH
19: 3 her husband **w** to her to persuade her 2143
19:10 the man left and **w** toward Jebus (that is, 995
19:14 So *they* **w on,** and the sun set 6296
19:15 *They* **w** and sat in the city square, 995
19:23 The owner of the house **w outside** and said 3655
19:26 At daybreak the woman **w back** *to* 995
20:18 The Israelites **w up** *to* Bethel and inquired 6590
20:20 of Israel **w out** to fight the Benjamites 3655
20:23 The Israelites **w up** and wept before 6590
20:26 the Israelites, all the people, **w up** to Bethel, 6590
20:30 They **w up** against the Benjamites on 6590
20:48 of Israel **w back** to Benjamin and put all 8740
21: 2 The people **w** *to* Bethel, 995
21:24 the Israelites left that place and **w** home 3655
Ru 1: 1 **w** to live for a while in the country 2143
1: 2 And *they* **w** *to* Moab and lived there. 995
1:19 So the two women **w on** until they came 2143
1:21 I **w away** full, but the LORD has brought me 2143
2: 3 So *she* **w** out and began to glean in 2143
2: 7 *She* **w into** the field and has worked 995
3: 6 So *she* **w down** *to* the threshing floor 3718
3: 7 *he* **w over** to lie down at the far end of 995
3:15 Then *he* **w back** *to* town. 995
4: 1 Meanwhile Boaz **w up** *to* the town gate 6590
4: 1 So *he* **w over** and sat down. 6073
4:13 Then *he* **w** to her, and the LORD enabled her 995
1Sa 1: 3 Year after year this man **w up** from his town 6590
1: 7 This **w on** year after year. 6913
1: 7 Whenever Hannah **w up** to the house of 6590
1:18 Then she **w** her way and ate something, 2143
1:19 the LORD and then **w** back to their home 995
1:21 the man Elkanah **w up** with all his family 6590
2:11 Then Elkanah **w** home to Ramah, 2143
2:19 when she **w up** with her husband to offer 6590
3: 5 So *he* **w** and lay down. 2143
3: 6 And Samuel got up and **w** to Eli and said, 2143
3: 8 and Samuel got up and **w** to Eli and said, 2143
3: 9 So Samuel **w** and lay down in his place. 2143
4: 1 Now the Israelites **w out** to fight against 3655
4:12 a Benjamite ran from the battle line and **w** 995
4:19 *she* **w into labor** and gave birth, 4156
5:12 and the outcry of the city **w up** *to* heaven. 6590
6:12 cows **w straight** *up* toward Beth Shemesh, 3837
7:16 to year *he* **w** on a circuit from Bethel 2143
7:17 But he always **w back** to Ramah, 9588
9: 4 *They* **w on** into the district of Shaalim, 6296
9: 9 if a man **w** to inquire of God, he would say, 2143
9:14 *They* **w up** *to* the town, 6590
9:26 he and Samuel **w** outside together. 3655
10:13 *he* **w** *to* the high place. 995
10:14 *we* **w** to Samuel." 995
10:26 Saul also **w** to his home in Gibeah, 2143
11: 1 Nahash the Ammonite **w up** and besieged 6590
11: 9 When the messengers **w** and reported this to 995
11:15 the people **w** *to* Gilgal and confirmed Saul 2143
13: 5 *They* **w up** and camped at Micmash, 6590
13:10 and Saul **w out** to greet him. 3655
13:15 Then Samuel left Gilgal and **w up** to Gibeah 6590
1Sa 13:17 Raiding parties **w out** from the Philistine 3655
13:20 So all Israel **w down** *to* the Philistines 3718
14:20 Then Saul and all his men assembled and **w** 995
14:21 up with them to their camp **w over** to 2118+6017
14:26 When they **w** into the woods, 995
15: 5 Saul **w** to the city of Amalek and set an 995
15:12 Samuel got up and **w to meet** Saul, 7925
15:20 "*I* **w** on the mission the LORD assigned me. 2143
15:31 So Samuel **w back** with Saul, 8740
15:34 Saul **w up** to his home in Gibeah of Saul. 6590
16:13 Samuel then **w** to Ramah. 2143
17: 7 His shield bearer **w** ahead of him. 2143
17:15 but David **w** back and **forth** from Saul 2143
17:35 *I* **w** after it, struck it and rescued the sheep 3655
18:27 David and his men **w** out and killed 2143
19: 8 and David **w out** and fought the Philistines. 3655
19:18 *he* **w** to Samuel at Ramah and told him all 995
19:18 and Samuel **w** to Naioth and stayed there. 2143
19:22 for Ramah and **w** to the great cistern 995
19:23 So Saul **w** to Naioth at Ramah. 2143
20: 1 from Naioth at Ramah and **w** to Jonathan 995
20:11 So *they* **w** there together. 3655
20:35 In the morning Jonathan **w out** *to* the field 3655
20:42 and Jonathan **w back** *to* the town. 995
21: 1 David **w** to Nob, to Ahimelech the priest. 995
21:10 from Saul and **w** to Achish king of Gath. 995
22: 1 *they* **w down** to him there. 3718
22: 3 From there David **w** *to* Mizpah in Moab 2143
22: 5 So David left and **w** *to* the forest of Hereth. 995
23: 5 So David and his men **w** *to* Keilah, 2143
23:16 And Saul's son Jonathan **w** to David 2143
23:18 Then Jonathan **w** home, 2143
23:19 The Ziphites **w up** to Saul at Gibeah 6590
23:24 So they set out and **w** to Ziph ahead of Saul. 2143
23:25 *he* **w down** *to* the rock and stayed in 3718
23:25 **w** *into* the Desert of Maon **in pursuit** 8103
23:28 of David and **w** to meet the Philistines. 2143
23:29 And David **w up** from there and lived in 6590
24: 3 and Saul **w in** to relieve himself. 995
24: 7 And Saul left the cave and **w** his way. 2143
24: 8 Then David **w out** of the cave 3655
24:22 and his men **w up** to the stronghold. 6590
25:12 David's men turned around and **w back.** 8740
25:13 About four hundred men **w up** with David, 6590
25:36 When Abigail **w** to Nabal, 995
25:40 His servants **w** to Carmel and said 995
25:42 **w** with David's messengers 2143
26: 1 The Ziphites **w** to Saul at Gibeah and said, 995
26: 2 So Saul **w down** to the Desert of Ziph, 3718
26: 5 and **w** to the place where Saul had camped. 995
26: 7 David and Abishai **w** to the army by night, 995
26:25 So David **w** on his way, 2143
27: 2 and **w over** to Achish son of Maoch king 6296
27: 8 and his men **w up** and raided the Geshurites, 6590
28: 8 at night he and two men **w** to the woman. 995
29:11 and the Philistines **w up** *to* Jezreel. 6590
30: 2 but carried them off as *they* **w** on their way. 2143
30:24 to be the same as that of him *who* **w down** 3718
31:12 from the wall of Beth Shan and **w** to Jabesh, 995
2Sa 2: 2 So David **w up** there with his two wives, 6590
2:12 left Mahanaim and **w** to Gibeon. NIH
2:13 Joab son of Zeruiah and David's men **w out** 3655
3:16 Her husband, however, **w** with her, 2143
3:16 So *he* **w back.** 8740
3:19 Then he **w** to Hebron to tell David 2143
3:21 David sent Abner away, and *he* **w** in peace. 2143
3:24 So Joab **w** to the king and said, 995
4: 6 They **w** into the inner part of the house as if 995
5:17 they **w up** in full force to search for him, 6590
5:17 but David heard about it and **w down** to 3718
5:20 So David **w** to Baal Perazim, 995
6:12 So David **w down** and brought up the ark 2143
6:19 And all the people **w** to their homes. 2143
7:18 King David **w in** and sat before the LORD, 995
7:23 the one nation on earth that God **w out** 2143
8: 3 when he **w** to restore his control along 2143
8: 6 LORD gave David victory wherever *he* **w.** 2143
8:14 LORD gave David victory wherever *he* **w.** 2143
10:14 fled before Abishai and **w inside** the city. 995
10:16 *they* **w** *to* Helam, with Shobach 995
10:17 crossed the Jordan and **w** to Helam. 995
11: 4 Then *she* **w back** home. 8740
11:13 the evening Uriah **w out** to sleep on his mat 3655
12:16 He fasted and **w into** his house and spent 995
12:20 *he* **w into** the house of the LORD 995
12:20 Then *he* **w** to his own house, 995
12:24 and *he* **w** to her and lay with her. 995
12:29 So David mustered the entire army and **w** 2143
13: 8 So Tamar **w** *to* the house of her brother 2143
13:19 She put her hand on her head and **w away,** 2143
13:19 weeping aloud *as she* **w.** 2143
13:24 Absalom **w** to the king and said, 995
13:34 The watchman **w** and told the king, 995
13:37 Absalom fled and **w** to Talmai son 2143
13:38 After Absalom fled and **w** *to* Geshur, 2143
14: 4 When the woman from Tekoa **w** to the king, 995
14:23 Then Joab **w** to Geshur 2143
14:24 So Absalom **w** to his own house and did 6015
14:33 So Joab **w** to the king and told him this. 995
15: 9 So *he* **w** to Hebron. 2143
15:11 invited as guests and **w** quite innocently, 2143
15:30 up the Mount of Olives, weeping as *he* **w**; 6590
15:30 and were weeping as *they* **w up.** 6590
16:13 cursing as *he* **w** and throwing stones at him 2143
16:16 **w** to Absalom and said to him, 995
17:18 left quickly and **w** to the house of a man 995
17:21 out of the well and **w** to inform King David. 2143
2Sa 17:24 David **w** to Mahanaim, 995
18: 9 and *as* the mule **w** under the thick branches 995
18:24 the watchman **w up** to the roof of 2143
18:33 *He* **w up** to the room over the gateway 6590
18:33 As he **w,** he said: "O my son Absalom! 2143
19: 5 Joab **w** into the house to the king and said, 995
19:15 the king returned and **w** as far as the Jordan. 995
19:24 also **w down** to meet the king. 3718
20: 5 But when Amasa **w** to summon Judah, 2143
20: 7 and all the mighty warriors **w out** under 3655
20:13 all the men **w on** with Joab 6296
20:17 *He* **w** toward her, and she asked, 7928
20:22 Then the woman **w** to all the people 995
20:22 And Joab **w back** to the king in Jerusalem. 8740
21:12 he **w** and took the bones of Saul 2143
21:15 David **w down** with his men to fight against 3718
23:17 "Is it not the blood of men who **w** at the risk 2143
23:20 He also **w down** into a pit on a snowy day 3718
23:21 Benaiah **w** against him with a club. 3718
24: 5 and then **w** through Gad and on to Jazer. NIH
24: 6 *They* **w** to Gilead and the region 995
24: 7 Then *they* **w** *toward* the fortress of Tyre 995
24: 7 *they* **w on** to Beersheba in the Negev 3655
24:13 So Gad **w** to David and said to him, 995
24:18 that day Gad **w** to David and said to him, 995
24:19 David **w up,** as the LORD had commanded 6590
24:20 he **w out** and bowed down before the king 3655
1Ki 1:15 So Bathsheba **w** to see the aged king 995
1:23 So *he* **w** before the king and bowed 995
1:38 and the Pelethites **w down** and put Solomon 3718
1:40 And all the people **w up** after him, 6590
1:50 **w** and took hold of the horns of the altar. 2143
2: 8 down bitter curses on me the day I **w** 2143
2:13 **w** to Bathsheba, Solomon's mother. 995
2:19 When Bathsheba **w** to King Solomon 995
2:34 So Benaiah son of Jehoiada **w up** and struck 6590
2:40 he saddled his donkey and **w** to Achish 2143
2:40 So Shimei **w away** and brought 2143
2:46 and *he* **w out** and struck Shimei down 3655
3: 4 The king **w** to Gibeon to offer sacrifices, 2143
8:66 They blessed the king and then **w** home, 2143
9:12 when Hiram **w** from Tyre to see the towns 3655
10:16 six hundred bekas of gold **w** 6590
11:18 They set out from Midian and **w** *to* Paran. 995
11:18 *they* **w** *to* Egypt, to Pharaoh king of Egypt, 995
11:24 the rebels **w** *to* Damascus, 2143
12: 1 Rehoboam **w** *to* Shechem, 2143
12: 3 and he and the whole assembly of Israel **w** 995
12: 5 So the people **w away.** 2143
12:16 So the Israelites **w** home. 2143
12:24 the word of the LORD and **w home** again, 2143
12:25 From there *he* **w out** and built up Peniel. 3655
12:30 the people **w** even as far as Dan to worship 2143
12:33 the festival for the Israelites and **w up** to 6590
13:24 As *he* **w on** *his* **way,** 2143
13:25 and *they* **w** and reported it in the city where 995
13:28 Then *he* **w out** and found the body thrown 2143
14: 4 So Jeroboam's wife did what he said and **w** 2143
14:17 Then Jeroboam's wife got up and left and **w** 995
14:28 the king **w** *to* the LORD's temple, 995
15:17 Baasha king of Israel **w up** against Judah 6590
16:18 *he* **w** into the citadel of the royal palace 995
17: 5 *He* **w** to the Kerith Ravine, 2143
17:10 So *he* **w** to Zarephath. 2143
17:15 *She* **w away** and did as Elijah had told her. 2143
18: 2 So Elijah **w** to present himself to Ahab. 2143
18:16 So Obadiah **w** to meet Ahab and told him, 2143
18:16 and Ahab **w** to meet Elijah. 2143
18:21 Elijah **w** before the people and said, 5602
18:42 So Ahab **w off** to eat and drink, 6590
18:43 And *he* **w up** and looked. 6590
19: 4 *he* himself **w** a day's journey into the desert. 2143
19: 9 There *he* **w** into a cave and spent the night. 995
19:13 he pulled his cloak over his face and **w out** 3655
19:19 So Elijah **w** from there and found Elisha 2143
19:19 Elijah **w up** to him and threw his cloak 6296
19:21 So Elisha left him and **w back.** 8740
20: 1 *he* **w up** and besieged Samaria 6590
20:17 of the provincial commanders **w out** first. 3655
20:26 and **w up** to Aphek to fight against Israel. 6590
20:32 *they* **w** to the king of Israel and said, 995
20:36 And after the man **w** away, 2143
20:38 the prophet **w** and stood by the road waiting 2143
20:39 "Your servant **w** into the thick of the battle, 3655
20:43 king of Israel **w** to his palace in Samaria. 2143
21: 4 So Ahab **w** home, sullen and angry 995
21:16 he got up and **w down** to take possession 3718
21:27 He lay in sackcloth and **w around** meekly. 2143
22: 2 of Judah **w down** to see the king of Israel. 3718
22:24 of Kenaanah **w up** and slapped Micaiah in 5602
22:24 the LORD go when he **w** from me to speak NIH
22:29 and Jehoshaphat king of Judah **w up** 6590
22:30 the king of Israel disguised himself and **w** 995
2Ki 1: 4 So Elijah **w.** 2143
1: 9 The captain **w up** to Elijah, 6590
1:13 This third captain **w up** and fell on his knees 6590
1:15 So Elijah got up and **w down** with him to 3718
2: 2 So *they* **w down** *to* Bethel. 3718
2: 4 So *they* **w** *to* Jericho. 995
2: 5 at Jericho **w up** to Elisha and asked him, 5602
2: 7 Fifty men of the company of the prophets **w** 2143
2:11 and Elijah **w up** *to* heaven in a whirlwind. 6590
2:13 that had fallen from Elijah and **w back** 8740
2:15 And *they* **w** to meet him and bowed to 995
2:21 Then *he* **w out** to the spring and threw 3655
2:23 From there Elisha **w up** *to* Bethel. 6590
2:25 And *he* **w on** to Mount Carmel and 2143

2Ki 3:12 and the king of Edom **w down** to him. 3718
4: 7 *She* w and told the man of God, and he said, 995
4: 8 One day Elisha w to Shunem. 6296
4:11 *he* **w up** to his room and lay down there. 6073
4:18 and one day *he* **w out** to his father, 3655
4:21 *She* **w up** and laid him on the bed of 6590
4:21 then shut the door and **w out.** 3655
4:31 Gehazi **w on** ahead and laid the staff on 6296
4:31 Gehazi **w back** to meet Elisha and told him, 8740
4:33 *He* **w in,** shut the door on the two of them 995
4:37 Then she took her son and **w out.** 3655
4:39 of them **w out** into the fields to gather herbs 3655
5: 4 Naaman w to his master and told him what 995
5: 9 So Naaman w with his horses and chariots 995
5:11 But Naaman **w away** angry and said, 2143
5:12 So he turned and **w off** in a rage. 2143
5:13 Naaman's servants w to him and said, 5602
5:14 So *he* **w down** and dipped himself in 3718
5:15 Then Naaman and all his attendants **w back** 8740
5:25 he **w in** and stood before his master Elisha. 995
5:27 Then Gehazi w from Elisha's presence 3655
6: 4 And *he* w with them. 2143
6: 4 *They* w to the Jordan and began to cut 995
6:14 *They* w by night and surrounded the city. 995
6:15 of the man of God got up and **w out** early 3655
6:30 As he w along the wall, the people looked, 6296
7: 5 At dusk they got up and w to the camp of 995
7: 8 gold and clothes, and **w off** and hid them. 2143
7:10 So *they* w and called out to the city 995
7:10 "*We* w into the Aramean camp and not 995
7:16 the people **w out** and plundered the camp 3655
8: 2 She and her family **w away** and stayed in 2143
8: 3 the land of the Philistines and w to the king 3655
8: 7 Elisha w *to* Damascus, 995
8: 9 Hazael w to meet Elisha, 2143
8: 9 *He* **w in** and stood before him, and said, 995
8:21 So Jehoram w to Zair with all his chariots. 6296
8:28 Ahaziah w with Joram son of Ahab to war 2143
8:29 king of Judah **w down** to Jezreel to see 3718
9: 4 the prophet, w *to* Ramoth Gilead, 2143
9: 6 Jehu got up and w into the house. 995
9:11 When Jehu **w out** to his fellow officers, 3655
9:30 Then Jehu w to Jezreel. 995
9:34 Jehu **w in** and ate and drank. 995
9:35 But when *they* **w out** to bury her, 2143
9:36 *They* **w back** and told Jehu, who said, 8740
10: 9 The next morning Jehu **w out.** 3655
10:12 Jehu then set out and w *toward* Samaria. 2143
10:23 of Recab **w into** the temple of Baal. 995
10:24 So *they* w in to make sacrifices 995
11:13 *she* w to the people at the temple of 995
11:18 All the people of the land w *to* the temple 995
11:19 from the temple of the LORD and **w into** 995
12:17 About this time Hazael king of Aram **w up** 6590
13:14 Jehoash king of Israel **w down** to see him 3718
14:13 Then Jehoash w *to* Jerusalem and broke 995
15:14 Then Menahem son of Gadi w from Tirzah 995
16:10 Then King Ahaz w *to* Damascus 2143
18:18 and Joah son of Asaph the recorder **w out** 3655
18:37 and Joah son of Asaph the recorder w 995
19: 1 and put on sackcloth and **w into** the temple 995
19:14 Then he **w up** *to* the temple of the LORD 6590
19:35 That night the angel of the LORD **w out** 3655
20: 1 of Amoz w to him and said, "This is what 995
20:14 Then Isaiah the prophet w to King Hezekiah 995
22: 9 Then Shaphan the secretary w to the king 995
22:14 Shaphan and Asaiah w to speak to 2143
23: 2 He **w up** *to* the temple of the LORD with 6590
23:20 Then *he* **w back** *to* Jerusalem. 8740
23:29 of Egypt **w up** to the Euphrates River 6590
25:21 So Judah **w into captivity,** 1655
1Ch 4:39 and *they* w to the outskirts of Gedor to 2143
7:21 when *they* **w down** to seize their livestock. 3718
10:12 all their valiant men w and took the bodies 7756
11: 6 Joab son of Zeruiah **w up** first, 6590
11:19 the blood of these men who w at the risk NIH
11:22 He also **w down** into a pit on a snowy day 3718
11:23 Benaiah w against him with a club. 3718
12:17 David **w out** to meet them and said to them, 3655
12:19 of Manasseh defected to David when he w 995
12:20 When David w to Ziklag, 2143
13: 6 and all the Israelites with him w to Baalah 6590
14: 8 they **w up** in full force to search for him, 6590
14: 8 but David heard about it and **w out** 3655
14:11 David and *his men* **w up** to Baal Perazim, 6590
15:25 of units of a thousand w to bring up the ark 2143
17:16 King David **w in** and sat before the LORD, 995
17:21 the one nation on earth whose God **w out** 2143
18: 3 when he w to establish his control along 2143
18: 6 LORD gave David victory everywhere *he* **w.** 2143
18:13 LORD gave David victory everywhere *he* **w.** 2143
19:15 before his brother Abishai and w inside 995
19:15 So Joab **w back** *to* Jerusalem. 995
20: 1 of the Ammonites and w *to* Rabbah 995
21: 4 and w throughout Israel and then came back 2143
21:11 So Gad w to David and said to him, 995
21:19 So David **w up** in obedience to the word 6590
2Ch 1: 3 and the whole assembly w to the high place 2143
1: 6 Solomon **w up** to the bronze altar before 6590
1:13 Then Solomon w *to* Jerusalem from 995
8: 3 then w *to* Hamath Zobah and captured it. 2143
8:17 Then Solomon w to Ezion Geber and Elath 2143
9:15 six hundred bekas of hammered gold w 6590
10: 1 Rehoboam w to Shechem, 2143
10: 3 and all Israel w to Rehoboam and said 995
10: 5 So the people **w away.** 2143
10:16 So all the Israelites w home. 2143
2Ch 12:11 the king w *to* the LORD's temple, 995
12:11 the guards w with him, bearing the shields, 995
13: 3 Abijah **w into** battle with a force 673
14:10 Asa **w out** to meet him, 3655
15: 2 *He* **w out** to meet Asa and said to him, 3655
16: 1 of Asa's reign Baasha king of Israel **w up** 6590
17: 9 *they* **w around** to all the towns of Judah 6015
18: 2 Some years later *he* **w down** to visit Ahab 3718
18:23 of Kenaanah **w up** and slapped Micaiah in 5602
18:23 the LORD go when he w from me to speak NIH
18:28 and Jehoshaphat king of Judah **w up** 6590
18:29 the king of Israel disguised himself and w 995
19: 2 **w out** to meet him and said to the king, 3655
19: 4 and *he* **w out** again among the people 3655
20:21 the splendor of his holiness as they **w out** at 3655
20:25 and his men w to carry off their plunder, 995
20:28 *They* **entered** Jerusalem and w to the temple 995
21: 9 So Jehoram w there with his officers 6296
22: 5 He also followed their counsel when *he* w 2143
22: 6 king of Judah **w down** to Jezreel to see 3718
22: 7 *he* **w out** with Joram to meet Jehu son 3655
22: 9 *He* then **w in search of** Ahaziah, 1335
23: 2 *They* **w throughout** Judah and gathered 6015
23:12 *she* w to them at the temple of the LORD. 995
23:17 All the people w *to* the temple of Baal 995
23:20 *They* **w into** the palace through 995
26: 6 *He* w to war against the Philistines 3655
28: 9 and *he* **w out** to meet the army 3655
29:15 *they* **w in** to purify the temple of the LORD, 995
29:16 The priests w into the sanctuary of the LORD 995
29:18 *they* w in to King Hezekiah and reported: 995
29:20 and **w up** *to* the temple of the LORD. 6590
30: 6 couriers w throughout Israel and Judah 2143
30:10 The couriers w from town to town 6296
30:11 and Zebulun humbled themselves and w 995
31: 1 the Israelites who were there **w out** to 3655
31: 5 As soon as the order **w out,** 7287
32:21 And when *he* **w into** the temple of his god, 995
34: 7 Then *he* **w back** to Jerusalem. 8740
34: 9 *They* w to Hilkiah the high priest 995
34:22 the king had sent with him w to speak to 2143
34:30 He **w up** *to* the temple of the LORD with 6590
35:20 of Egypt **w up** to fight at Carchemish on 6590
35:22 but w to fight him on the plain of Megiddo. 995
Ezr 4:23 *they* w immediately to the Jews 10016
5: 3 and Shethar-Bozenai and their associates w 10085
5: 8 The king should know that *we* w to 10016
10: 6 of God and w to the room of Jehohanan son 2143
Ne 2: 9 So *I* w to the governors of Trans-Euphrates 995
2:11 *I* w to Jerusalem, and after staying there 995
2:13 By night *I* **w out** through the Valley Gate 3655
2:15 so *I* **w up** the valley by night, 6590
3: 1 and his fellow priests **w to work** and rebuilt 7756
4:23 even when he w for water. NIH
6:10 One day I w *to* the house of Shemaiah son 995
8:12 Then all the people **w away** to eat and drink 2143
8:16 So the people **w out** and brought back 3655
9:24 Their sons **w in** and took possession of 995
Est 3:15 the couriers **w out,** and the edict was issued 3655
4: 1 and **w out** into the city, 3655
4: 2 But *he* w only as far as the king's gate, 995
4: 6 So Hathach **w out** to Mordecai in 3655
4: 9 Hathach **w back** and reported 995
4:17 So Mordecai **w away** and carried out all 6296
5: 5 So the king and Haman w to the banquet 995
5: 9 Haman **w out** that day happy and 3655
5:10 Haman restrained himself and w home. 995
7: 1 and Haman w to dine with Queen Esther, 995
7: 7 and w out into the palace garden. NIH
8:17 wherever the edict of the king **w,** 5595
Job 1:12 Then Satan **w out** from the presence of 3655
2: 7 So Satan **w out** from the presence of 3655
29: 7 "When I w *to* the gate of the city 3655
Ps 35:14 *I* **w about** mourning as though 2143
66:12 *we* w through fire and water, 995
68: 7 When you **w out** before your people, 3655
81: 5 for Joseph when he **w out** against Egypt, 3655
104: 8 *they* **w down** *into* the valleys, 3718
105:30 which w up into the bedrooms NIH
107:23 *Others* **w out** *on* the sea in ships; 3718
107:26 up to the heavens and **w down** *to* the depths; 3718
119:67 Before I was afflicted I **w astray,** 8704
Pr 24:30 I w past the field of the sluggard, 6296
SS 6:11 *I* **w down** to the grove of nut trees to look at 3718
Isa 8: 3 Then *I* w to the prophetess 7928
16: 8 Their shoots spread out and **w as far as** 6296
36: 3 and Joah son of Asaph the recorder **w out** 3655
36:22 and Joah son of Asaph the recorder w to 995
37: 1 and put on sackcloth and **w into** the temple 995
37:14 Then he **w up** *to* the temple of the LORD 6590
37:36 the angel of the LORD **w out** and put 3655
38: 1 of Amoz w to him and said, "This is what 995
38: 8 So the sunlight **w back** the ten steps 8740
39: 3 Then Isaiah the prophet w to King Hezekiah 995
52: 4 "At first my people **w down** *to* Egypt 3718
57: 7 there *you* **w up** to offer your sacrifices. 6590
57: 9 *You* w to Molech with olive oil 8801
Jer 1: 3 when the people of Jerusalem **w into exile.** 1655
3: 8 she also **w out** and committed adultery. 2143
7:24 *They* w backward and not forward. 2118
13: 5 So *I* w and hid it at Perath, 2143
13: 7 So *I* w to Perath and dug up the belt 2143
18: 3 So *I* **w down** *to* the potter's house, 3718
22:15 so all w well with him. NIH
22:16 and so all w well. NIH
26:10 *they* **w up** from the royal palace *to* 6590
28: 4 and all the other exiles from Judah who w 995
Jer 28:11 At this, the prophet Jeremiah **w on** his way. 2143
35: 3 So *I* w *to* **get** Jaazaniah son of Jeremiah, AIT
36:12 *he* **w down** to the secretary's room in 3718
36:14 So Baruch son of Neriah w to them with 995
36:20 *they* w to the king in the courtyard 995
38: 8 Ebed-Melech **w out** of the palace and said 3655
38:11 the men with him and w to a room under 995
40: 6 So Jeremiah w to Gedaliah son of Ahikam 995
41: 6 of Nethaniah **w out** from Mizpah 3655
41: 6 to meet them, weeping *as he* **w.** 2143+2143
41: 7 When they w into the city, 995
41:12 and w to fight Ishmael son of Nethaniah. 2143
41:14 and **w over** to Johanan son of Kareah. 2143
41:17 And *they* **w on,** stopping at Geruth Kimham 2143
43: 7 in disobedience to the LORD and w as far 995
51:59 when he w *to* Babylon with Zedekiah king 2143
52:27 So Judah **w into captivity,** 1655
Eze 1: 9 Each one w straight ahead; 2143
1:12 Each one w straight ahead. 2143
1:12 they would go, without turning as they **w.** 2143
1:17 not turn about as the creatures **w.** 2143
3:14 and *I* w in bitterness and in the anger 2143
3:23 So I got up and **w out** to the plain. 3655
8:10 So *I* **w in** and looked, 995
9: 3 of Israel **w up** from above the cherubim, 6590
9: 7 So *they* **w out** and began killing throughout 3655
10: 2 And as I watched, *he* **w in.** 995
10: 3 of the temple when the man **w in,** 995
10: 6 the man **w in** and stood beside a wheel. 995
10: 7 who took it and **w out.** 3655
10:11 not turn about as the cherubim **w.** 2143
10:11 The cherubim w *in* whatever direction 2143
10:11 without turning as they **w.** 2143
10:19 and as they **w,** the wheels went with them. 3655
10:19 and as they went, the wheels **w** with them. NIH
10:22 Each one w straight ahead, 2143
11:23 The glory of the LORD **w up** from within 6590
11:24 Then the vision I had seen **w up** from me, 6590
17:12 'The king of Babylon w *to* Jerusalem 995
23:13 both of them w the same way. NIH
25: 3 the people of Judah when *they* w into exile, 2143
27:33 When your merchandise **w out** on the seas, 3655
31: 7 for its roots w *down* to abundant waters. 2118
32:24 **w down** uncircumcised to the earth 3718
32:27 who **w down** *to* the grave 3718
32:30 *they* **w down** with the slain in disgrace 3718
36:20 And wherever *they* w among the nations 995
39:23 that the people of Israel **w into exile** 1655
40: 6 Then *he* w to the gate facing east. 995
41: 3 Then *he* w into the inner sanctuary 995
41: 7 so that the rooms widened as one w upward. NIH
41: 7 A stairway **w up** from the lowest floor to 6590
44:10 " 'The Levites who **w far** from me 8178
44:10 when Israel **w astray** and who wandered 9494
44:15 the Israelites **w astray** from me, are to come 9494
47: 3 the man w eastward with a measuring line 3655
48:11 when the Israelites **w astray.** 9494
Da 2:16 Daniel **w in** *to* the king and asked for time, 10549
2:24 Then Daniel w to Arioch, 10549
2:30 and that you may understand what w NIH
6: 6 and the satraps **w as a group** to the king 10656
6:10 *he* w home to his upstairs room where 10549
6:11 Then these men **w as a group** 10656
6:12 So *they* w *to* the king and spoke to him 10638
6:15 the men **w as a group** to the king and said 10656
8:27 I got up and **w about** the king's business. 6913
Hos 2:13 and w after her lovers, but me she forgot," 2143
11: 2 the further they w from me. 2143
Jnh 1: 3 *He* **w down** *to* Joppa, 3718
1: 3 *he* **w aboard** and sailed for Tarshish 928+3718
1: 6 The captain w to him and said, 7928
3: 3 the word of the LORD and w to Nineveh. 2143
4: 5 Jonah **w out** and sat down at a place east of 3655
Na 2:11 where the lion and lioness **w,** and the cubs, 2143
3:10 Yet she was taken captive and w into exile. 2143
Hab 3: 5 Plague w before him; 2143
Hag 2:16 *When anyone* w to a wine vat 995
Zec 6: 7 When the powerful horses **w out,** 3655
6: 7 So *they* w throughout the earth. 2143
Mt 2: 9 *they* **w on** *their* **way,** *4513*
2: 9 the star they had seen in the east **w ahead of** *4575*
2:21 and his mother and **w to** the land of Israel. *1656*
2:23 he w and lived in a town called Nazareth. *2262*
3: 5 People **w out** to him from Jerusalem *1744*
3:16 *he* **w up** out of the water. *326*
4:13 he w and lived in Capernaum, *2262*
4:23 Jesus w throughout Galilee, *4310*
5: 1 *he* **w up** on a mountainside and sat down. *326*
8:25 The disciples w and woke him, saying, *4665*
8:32 So they came out and w into the pigs, *599*
8:33 w into the town and reported all this, *599*
8:34 Then the whole town **w out** to meet Jesus. *2002*
9: 7 And the man got up and w home. *599*
9: 9 *As* Jesus **w on** from there, *4135*
9:19 Jesus got up and **w with** him, *199*
9:25 he **w in** and took the girl by the hand, *1656*
9:27 *As* Jesus **w on** from there, *4135*
9:31 But they **w out** and spread the news *2002*
9:35 Jesus **w through** all the towns and villages, *4310*
11: 1 *he* **w on** from there to teach and preach in *3553*
12: 1 that time Jesus w through the grainfields on *4513*
12: 9 *he* w into their synagogue, *2262*
12:14 But the Pharisees **w out** and plotted *2002*
13: 1 That same day Jesus **w out of** the house *2002*
13: 3 "A farmer **w out** to sow his seed. *2002*
13:25 sowed weeds among the wheat, and **w away.** *599*
13:36 Then *he* left the crowd and **w** into the house. *2262*

Mt 13:44 in his joy **w** and sold all he had and bought *5632*
13:46 he **w away** and sold everything he had *599*
14:12 Then they **w** and told Jesus. *2262*
14:23 *he* **w up** on a mountainside by himself *326*
14:25 the fourth watch of the night Jesus **w out** *599*
15:29 Jesus left there and **w** along the Sea *2262*
15:29 he **w up** on a mountainside and sat down. *326*
15:39 the boat and **w** to the vicinity of Magadan. *2262*
16:4 Jesus then left them and **w away.** *599*
16:5 *When they* **w** across the lake, *2262*
18:28 "But *when* that servant **w out,** *2002*
18:30 he **w off** and had the man thrown *599*
18:31 and **w** and told their master everything *2262*
19:1 he left Galilee and **w** into the region *2262*
19:15 *he* **w** on from there. *4513*
19:22 *he* **w away** sad, because he had great wealth. *599*
20:1 like a landowner who **w out** early in *2002*
20:3 "About the third hour he **w out** *2002*
20:5 So they **w.** *599*
20:5 "He **w out** again about the sixth hour and *2002*
20:6 About the eleventh hour he **w out** *2002*
21:6 The disciples **w** and did as Jesus had *4513*
21:9 The crowds that **w ahead of** him and those *4575*
21:17 And *he* left them and **w out of** the city *2002*
21:19 *he* **w** up to it but found nothing *2262*
21:28 *He* **w to** the first and said, 'Son, *4665*
21:29 but later he changed his mind and **w.** *599*
21:30 "Then the father **w to** the other son and said *4665*
21:33 and **w away on a journey.** *623*
22:5 "But *they* paid no attention and **w off—** *599*
22:10 So the servants **w out** into the streets *2002*
22:15 Then the Pharisees **w out** and laid plans *4513*
22:22 So *they* left him and **w away.** *599*
25:1 and **w out** to meet the bridegroom. *2002*
25:10 The virgins who were ready **w in** with him *1656*
25:15 Then *he* **w on** *his* **journey.** *623*
25:16 the five talents **w** at once and put his money *4513*
25:18 man who had received the one talent **w off,** *599*
25:25 and **w out** and hid your talent in the ground. *599*
26:14 Judas Iscariot—**w** to the chief priests *4513*
26:30 *they* **w out** to the Mount of Olives. *2002*
26:36 Then Jesus **w** with his disciples to *2262*
26:42 He **w away** a second time and prayed, *599*
26:44 So he left them and **w away** once more *599*
26:71 Then *he* **w out** to the gateway, *2002*
26:73 those standing there **w up to** Peter and said, *4665*
26:75 And *he* **w** outside and wept bitterly. *2002*
27:5 Then he **w away** and hanged himself. *599*
27:53 and after Jesus' resurrection *they* **w into** *1656*
27:60 of the entrance to the tomb and **w away.** *599*
27:62 chief priests and the Pharisees **w** to Pilate. *5251*
27:66 So they **w** and made the tomb secure *4513*
28:1 and the other Mary **w** to look at the tomb. *2262*
28:11 of the guards **w** into the city and reported to *2262*
28:16 Then the eleven disciples **w** to Galilee, *4513*
Mk 1:5 the people of Jerusalem **w out** to him. *1744*
1:14 Jesus **w** into Galilee, *2262*
1:21 *They* **w to** Capernaum, *1660*
1:21 Jesus **w into** the synagogue and began *1656*
1:29 *they* **w** with James and John to the home *2262*
1:31 So *he* **w to** her, took her hand and *4665*
1:35 left the house and **w off** to a solitary place, *599*
1:36 Simon and his companions *w* **to look for** *AIT*
1:45 Instead he **w out** and began to talk freely, *2002*
2:13 Once again Jesus **w out** beside the lake. *2002*
3:1 Another time *he* **w into** the synagogue, *1656*
3:6 Then the Pharisees **w out** and began to plot *2002*
3:13 Jesus **w up** on a mountainside and called *326*
3:21 *they* **w** to take charge of him, for they said, *2002*
4:3 "Listen! A farmer **w out** to sow his seed. *2002*
5:1 *They* **w** across the lake to the region of *2262*
5:13 evil spirits came out and **w into** the pigs. *1656*
5:14 the *people* **w out** to see what had happened. *2262*
5:20 So the *man* **w away** and began to tell in *599*
5:24 So Jesus **w** with him. *599*
5:39 He **w in** and said to them, *1656*
5:40 and **w in** where the child was. *1660*
6:1 Jesus left there and **w** to his hometown, *2262*
6:6 Then Jesus **w around** teaching from village *4310*
6:12 They **w out** and preached *2002*
6:24 She **w out** and said to her mother, *2002*
6:27 The man **w,** beheaded John in the prison, *599*
6:32 So *they* **w away** by themselves in a boat to *599*
6:46 *he* **w up** on a mountainside to pray. *599*
6:48 the fourth watch of the night *he* **w out** *2262*
6:56 And wherever *he* **w—into** villages, *1660*
7:20 *He* **w on:** "What comes out of a *3306*
7:24 Jesus left that place and **w** to the vicinity *599*
7:30 She **w** home and found her child lying on *599*
7:31 Then Jesus left the vicinity of Tyre and **w** *2262*
8:10 *he* got into the boat with his disciples and **w** *2262*
8:27 Jesus and his disciples **w on** to the villages *2002*
10:1 and **w** into the region of Judea and across *2262*
10:22 *He* **w away** sad, because he had great wealth. *599*
11:4 *They* **w** and found a colt outside in *599*
11:9 Those who **w ahead** and those who followed *4575*
11:11 Jesus entered Jerusalem and **w** to the temple. *NIG*
11:11 *he* **w out** to Bethany with the Twelve. *2002*
11:13 *he* **w** to find out if it had any fruit. *2262*
11:19 When evening came, *they* **w** out of the city. *1744*
11:20 In the morning, *as they* **w along,** *4182*
12:1 and **w away on a journey.** *623*
12:12 so *they* left him and **w away.** *599*
14:10 **w** to the chief priests to betray Jesus *599*
14:16 **w** into the city and found things just *2262*
14:26 *they* **w out** to the Mount of Olives. *2002*
14:32 *They* **w** to a place called Gethsemane, *2262*
Mk 14:39 Once more he **w away** and prayed *599*
14:68 he said, and **w out** into the entryway. *2002+2032*
15:43 **w** boldly to Pilate and asked for Jesus' body *1656*
16:8 the women **w out** and fled from the tomb. *2002*
16:10 She **w** and told those who had been *4513*
16:20 disciples **w out** and preached everywhere, *2002*
Lk 1:28 The angel **w** to her and said, "Greetings, *1656*
2:3 everyone **w** to his own town to register. *4513*
2:4 also **w up** from the town of Nazareth *326*
2:5 He **w** there to register with Mary, *NIG*
2:27 *he* **w** into the temple courts. *2262*
2:41 Every year his parents **w** to Jerusalem for *4513*
2:42 they **w up** to the Feast, *326*
2:45 *they* **w back** to Jerusalem to look for him. *5715*
2:51 Then *he* **w down** to Nazareth with them *2849*
3:3 *He* **w** into all the country around the Jordan, *2262*
4:16 *He* **w** to Nazareth, *2262*
4:16 the Sabbath day *he* **w into** the synagogue, *1656*
4:30 through the crowd and **w on** *his* **way.** *4513*
4:31 Then *he* **w down** to Capernaum, *2982*
4:38 Jesus left the synagogue and **w to** the home *1656*
4:42 At daybreak Jesus **w out** to a solitary place. *4513*
5:19 *they* **w up** on the roof and lowered him *326*
5:25 on and **w** home praising God. *599*
5:27 Jesus **w out** and saw a tax collector by *2002*
6:6 On another Sabbath he **w into** the synagogue *1656*
6:12 of those days Jesus **w out** to a mountainside *2002*
6:17 He **w down** with them and stood on *2849*
7:6 So Jesus **w** with them. *4513*
7:11 Jesus **w** to a town called Nain, *4513*
7:11 and a large crowd **w along with** him. *5233*
7:13 *his* **heart w out** to her and he said, *5072*
7:14 Then he **w up** and touched the coffin, *4665*
7:36 so *he* **w to** the Pharisee's house and reclined *1656*
8:5 "A farmer **w out** to sow his seed. *2002*
8:24 The disciples **w** and woke him, saying, *4665*
8:33 came out of the man, *they* **w into** the pigs, *1656*
8:35 the *people* **w out** to see what had happened. *2002*
8:39 So the man **w away** and told all over town *599*
9:6 *they* set out and **w** from village to village, *1451*
9:28 with him and **w up** onto a mountain to pray. *326*
9:52 *who* **w into** a Samaritan village *1656+4513*
9:56 and *they* **w** to another village. *4513*
10:30 beat him and **w away,** *599*
10:34 *He* **w to** him and bandaged his wounds, *4665*
11:37 so he **w in** and reclined at the table. *1656*
13:6 and *he* **w** to look for fruit on it, *2262*
13:22 Jesus **w through** the towns and villages, *1388*
14:1 when Jesus **w** to eat in the house of *2262*
15:15 So he **w** and hired himself out to a citizen of *4513*
15:20 So *he* got up and **w** to his father. *2262*
15:28 So his father **w out** and pleaded with him. *2002*
17:14 And as they **w,** they were cleansed. *5632*
18:10 "Two men **w up** to the temple to pray, *326*
18:14 **w** home justified before God. *2849*
19:11 he **w on** to tell them a parable, *4707*
19:12 "A man of noble birth **w** to a distant country *4513*
19:28 After Jesus had said this, *he* **w** on ahead, *4513*
19:32 Those who were sent ahead **w** *599*
19:36 *As* he **w along,** people spread their cloaks *4513*
20:9 *He* **w on** to tell the people this parable: *806*
20:9 some farmers and **w away** for a long time. *623*
21:37 each evening he **w out** to spend the night *2002*
22:4 And Judas **w** to the chief priests and *599*
22:39 Jesus **w out** as usual to the Mount *2002+4513*
22:45 When he rose from prayer and **w back** to *2262*
22:62 And he **w** outside and wept bitterly. *2002*
23:48 *they* beat their breasts and **w away.** *5715*
23:56 Then they *w* **home** and prepared spices *AIT*
24:1 the spices they had prepared and **w** to *2262*
24:12 and *he* **w away,** wondering to himself *599*
24:22 *They* **w** to the tomb early this morning *1181*
24:24 Then some of our companions **w** to *599*
24:29 So *he* **w in** to stay with them. *1656*
Jn 1:39 So *they* **w** and saw where he was staying, *2262*
2:12 After this *he* **w down** to Capernaum *2849*
2:13 Jesus **w up** to Jerusalem. *326*
3:22 Jesus and his disciples **w out** into *2262*
4:3 he left Judea and **w back** once more *599*
4:28 the woman **w back** to the town and said to *599*
4:47 *he* **w** to him and begged him to come *599*
5:1 Jesus **w up** to Jerusalem for a feast of *326*
5:15 The man **w away** and told the Jews *599*
6:3 Then Jesus **w up** on a mountainside and sat *456*
6:16 his disciples **w down** to the lake, *2849*
6:24 they got into the boats and **w** to Capernaum *2262*
6:65 *He w on to* **say,** "This is why I told you *AIT*
7:1 After this, Jesus **w around** in Galilee, *4344*
7:10 his brothers had left for the Feast, he **w** also, *326*
7:45 temple guards **w back** to the chief priests *2262*
7:53 Then each **w** to his own home. *4513*
8:1 But Jesus **w** to the Mount of Olives. *4513*
9:1 *As he* **w along,** he saw a man blind *4135*
9:7 man **w** and washed, and came home seeing. *599*
9:11 So *I* **w** and washed, and then I could see." *599*
10:40 Then Jesus **w** back across the Jordan to *599*
11:11 After he had said this, he **w** on to tell them, *NIG*
11:20 *she* **w out to meet** him, *5636*
11:28 *she* **w back** and called her sister Mary aside. *599*
11:29 she got up quickly and **w** to him. *2262*
11:31 noticed how quickly she got up and **w out,** *2002*
11:46 But some of them **w** to the Pharisees *599*
11:55 many **w up** from the country to Jerusalem *326*
12:13 They took palm branches and **w out** *2002*
12:18 this miraculous sign, **w out to meet** him. *5636*
12:20 who **w up** to worship at the Feast. *326*
12:22 Philip **w** to tell Andrew; *2262*
Jn 13:30 as Judas had taken the bread, *he* **w out.** *2002*
18:1 and he and his disciples **w into** it. *1656*
18:4 **w out** and asked them, *2002*
18:15 *he* **w with** Jesus **into** the high priest's *5291*
18:33 Pilate then **w** back **inside** the palace, *1656*
18:38 With this *he* **w out** again to the Jews *2002*
19:3 and **w** up to him *again and again,* *2262*
19:9 and *he* **w** back **inside** the palace. *1656*
19:17 *he* **w out** to the place of the Skull *2002*
20:1 Mary Magdalene **w** to the tomb and saw *2262*
20:6 arrived and **w into** the tomb. *1656*
20:8 reached the tomb first, also **w inside.** *1656*
20:10 Then the disciples **w back** to their homes, *599*
20:18 Mary Magdalene **w** to the disciples with *2262*
21:3 So *they* **w out** and got into the boat, *2002*
21:18 and **w** where you wanted; *4344*
Ac 1:13 *they* **w** upstairs to the room *326*
1:21 the whole time the Lord Jesus **w in** and out *1656*
3:8 Then *he* **w** with them **into** the temple courts, *1656*
4:23 Peter and John **w back** to their own people *2262*
5:22 So they **w back** and reported, *418*
5:26 the captain **w** with his officers and brought *599*
7:15 Then Jacob **w down** to Egypt, *2849*
7:24 so he **w to** *his* **defense** and avenged him *310*
7:31 *As* he **w over** to look more closely, *4665*
8:4 the word wherever *they* **w.** *1451*
8:5 Philip **w down** to a city in Samaria *2982*
8:38 Then both Philip and the eunuch **w down** *2849*
8:39 but **w** on his way rejoicing. *4513*
9:1 *He* **w to** the high priest *4665*
9:17 Then Ananias **w** to the house and entered it. *599*
9:32 he **w** to visit the saints in Lydda. *2982*
9:39 Peter **w with** them, and when he arrived *5302*
10:9 Peter **w up** on the roof to pray. *326*
10:21 Peter **w down** and said to the men, *2849*
10:23 some of the brothers from Joppa **w along.** *5302*
10:27 Peter **w inside** and found a large gathering *1656*
10:38 and how he **w around** doing good *1451*
11:2 So when Peter **w up** to Jerusalem, *326*
11:3 *You* **w into** the house of uncircumcised men *1656*
11:12 These six brothers also **w** with me, *2262*
11:20 **w** to Antioch and began to speak to Greeks *2262*
11:25 Then Barnabas **w** to Tarsus to look for Saul, *2002*
12:10 and *they* **w through** it. *2002*
12:12 *he* **w** to the house of Mary the mother *2262*
12:19 Then Herod **w** from Judea to Caesarea *2982*
13:4 **w down** to Seleucia and sailed from there *2982*
13:14 Perga they **w on** to Pisidian Antioch. *1451+4134*
13:51 in protest against them and **w** to Iconium. *2262*
14:1 **w** as usual **into** the Jewish synagogue. *1656*
14:20 *he* got up and **w** back **into** the city. *1656*
14:25 *they* **w down** to Attalia. *2849*
15:24 We have heard that some **w out from** us *2002*
15:30 The men were sent off and **w down** *2982*
15:41 *He* **w through** Syria and Cilicia, *1451*
16:8 they passed by Mysia and **w down** to Troas. *2849*
16:13 On the Sabbath *we* **w** outside the city gate to *2002*
16:40 *they* **w** to Lydia's house, *1656*
17:2 Paul **w into** the synagogue, *1656*
17:10 they **w** to the Jewish synagogue. *583*
17:13 *they* **w** there too, agitating the crowds *2262*
18:1 this, Paul left Athens and **w** to Corinth. *2262*
18:2 Paul **w** to see them, *4665*
18:7 Paul left the synagogue and **w** next door **to** *1656*
18:19 *He* himself **w into** the synagogue *1656*
18:22 he **w up** and greeted the church and *326*
18:22 up and greeted the church and then **w down** *2849*
19:10 This **w on** for two years, *1181*
19:13 Some Jews who **w around** driving out *4320*
20:5 These men **w on ahead** and waited for us *4601*
20:10 Paul **w down,** threw himself on *2849*
20:11 *he* **w upstairs** again and broke bread and *326*
20:13 We **w on ahead** to the ship and sailed *4601*
20:14 *we* took him aboard and **w on** to Mitylene. *2262*
21:1 The next day *we* **w** to Rhodes and *2262*
21:2 **w on board** and set sail. *2094*
21:6 *we* **w** aboard the ship, *326*
21:15 *we* got ready and **w up** to Jerusalem. *326*
21:18 The next day Paul and the rest of us **w** *1655*
21:26 Then *he* **w to** the temple to give notice of *1655*
22:5 and **w** there to bring these people *4513*
22:19 that I **w** from one synagogue to another *1639*
22:26 *he* **w to** the commander and reported it. *4665*
22:27 The commander **w to** Paul and asked, *4665*
23:14 They **w to** the chief priests and elders *4665*
23:16 he **w into** the barracks and told Paul. *1656*
24:1 the high priest Ananias **w down** to Caesarea *2849*
24:11 that no more than twelve days ago *I* **w up** *326*
25:1 Festus **w up** from Caesarea to Jerusalem, *326*
25:6 *he* **w down** to Caesarea, *2849*
25:15 *When* I **w** to Jerusalem, *1181*
26:11 a time I **w** from one synagogue to another *NIG*
26:11 I even **w** to foreign cities to persecute them. *NIG*
28:8 Paul **w in** to see him and, after prayer, *1656*
2Co 2:12 Now *when I* **w** to Troas to preach the gospel *2262*
2:13 So *I* said good-by to them and **w on** *2002*
Gal 1:17 but *I* **w** immediately into Arabia *599*
1:18 *I* **w up** to Jerusalem to get acquainted *456*
1:21 Later *I* **w** to Syria and Cilicia. *2262*
2:1 Fourteen years later *I* **w up** again *326*
2:2 *I* **w** in response to a revelation and set *326*
1Ti 1:3 As I urged you *when I* **w** into Macedonia, *4513*
Heb 6:20 who **w before** us, has entered on our behalf. *4596*
9:11 he **w** through the greater and more perfect *NIG*
11:8 obeyed and **w,** even though he did not know *2002*
11:37 *They* **w about** in sheepskins and goatskins, *4320*
1Pe 3:19 through whom also he **w** and preached to *4513*

1Jn 2:19 *They* **w out from** us, but they did not *2002*
3Jn 1: 7 for the sake of the Name that *they* **w out,** *2002*
Rev 8: 4 **w up** before God from the angel's hand. *326*
10: 9 So *I* w to the angel and asked him *599*
11:12 And *they* **w up** to heaven in a cloud, *326*
12:17 the woman and **w off** to make war against *599*
16: 2 The first angel w and poured out his bowl *599*

WEPT (53) [WEEP]

Ge 27:38 Then Esau w aloud. 1134
33: 4 and kissed him. And *they* **w.** 1134
37:35 So his father w *for* him. 1134
43:30 He went into his private room and w there. 1134
45: 2 And he **w so loudly** 906+928+1140+5989+7754
45:14 around his brother Benjamin and w, 1134
45:15 he kissed all his brothers and w over them. 1134
46:29 he threw his arms around his father and w 1134
50: 1 Joseph threw himself upon his father and w 1134
50:17 When their message came to him, Joseph **w.** 1134
Nu 14: 1 community raised their voices and **w aloud.** 1134
Dt 1:45 You came back and w before the LORD, 1134
Jdg 2: 4 the people **w** aloud, 1134
11:38 She and the girls went into the hills and w 1134
20:23 up and w before the LORD until evening, 1134
Ru 1: 9 Then she kissed them and *they* w aloud 1134
1:14 At this *they* w again. 1134
1Sa 1: 7 her rival provoked her till *she* w and 1134
1:10 Hannah **w much** and prayed to 1134+1134
11: 4 they all w aloud. 1134
20:41 they kissed each other and w together— 1134
20:41 but David w the most. NIH
24:16 And he w aloud. 1134
30: 4 So David and his men w aloud 1134
2Sa 1:12 They mourned and w and fasted till evening 1134
3:32 and the king w aloud at Abner's tomb. 1134
3:32 All the people w also. 1134
3:34 And all the people w over him again. 1134
12:21 While the child was alive, you fasted and w, 1134
12:22 I fasted and w. 1134
13:36 and all his servants w very bitterly. 1134+1140
15:23 The whole countryside w aloud as all 1134
18:33 up to the room over the gateway and w. 1134
2Ki 13:14 of Israel went down to see him and w 1134
20: 3 And Hezekiah w bitterly. 1134+1140
22:19 you tore your robes and w in my presence, 1134
2Ch 34:27 and tore your robes and w in my presence, 1134
Ezr 3:12 w aloud when they saw the foundation 1134
10: 1 They too w **bitterly.** 1134+1135+2221
Ne 1: 4 I sat down and w. 1134
Job 30:25 *Have I* not w for those in trouble? 1134
Ps 137: 1 By the rivers of Babylon we sat and w 1134
Isa 38: 3 And Hezekiah w bitterly. 1134+1140
Hos 12: 4 *he* w and begged for his favor. 1134
Mt 26:75 And he went outside and w bitterly. *3081*
Mk 14:72 And *he* broke down and w. *3081*
Lk 19:41 and saw the city, *he* w over it *3081*
22:62 And *he* went outside and w bitterly. *3081*
Jn 11:35 Jesus w. *1233*
20:11 As *she* w, she bent over to look into *3081*
Ac 20:37 *They* all w as they embraced *1181+2653+3088*
Rev 5: 4 *I* **w and wept** because no one *3081+4498*
5: 4 *I* **wept and** w because no one *3081+4498*

WERE (2530) [BE] See Index of Articles Etc.

WEREN'T (1) [BE, NOT]

Da 3:24 **"W** there three men that we tied up 10379

WEST (96) [NORTHWEST, SOUTHWEST, WESTERN, WESTWARD]

Ge 12: 8 with Bethel on the w and Ai on the east. 3542
13:14 and look north and south, east and **w.** 2025+3542
28:14 you will spread out to the w and to the east, 3542
Ex 10:19 the wind to a very strong w wind, 3542
26:22 that is, the w end of the tabernacle, 2025+3542
26:27 and five for the frames on the w, 3542
27:12 "The w end of the courtyard shall 3542
36:27 that is, the w end *of* the tabernacle, 2025+3542
36:32 and five for the frames on the w, 3542
38:12 The w end was fifty cubits wide 3542
Nu 2:18 On the w will be the divisions of the camp 3542
3:23 Gershonite clans were to camp on the w, 3542
34: 6 This will be your boundary on the **w.** 3542
35: 5 three thousand on the w and three thousand 3542
Dt 3:27 top of Pisgah and look w and north 2025+3542
11:30 w *of* the road, toward the setting sun, 339
Jos 1: 4 to the Great Sea **on the w.** 2021+4427+9087
5: 1 all the Amorite kings w *of* the Jordan 2025+3542
8: 9 to the w of Ai— 3542
8:12 to the w of the city. 3542
8:13 of the city and the ambush to the w of it. 3542
9: 1 all the kings w *of* the Jordan heard 928+6298
11: 2 and in Naphoth Dor on the w; 3542
11: 3 to the Canaanites in the east and **w;** 3542
12: 7 on the w side of the Jordan, from Baal Gad 3542
15: 8 top of the hill w *of* the Hinnom Valley 2025+3542
15:46 w of Ekron, all that were in the vicinity 3542
16: 8 border went w to the Kanah Ravine 2025+3542
18:12 slope of Jericho and headed w 2025+3542
18:15 at the outskirts of Kiriath Jearim on the w, 3542
19:11 Going w it ran to Maralah, 2025+3542
19:26 On the w the boundary touched Carmel 3542
19:34 The boundary ran w through Aznoth 2025+3542
19:34 Asher on the w and the Jordan on the east. 3542
Jos 22: 7 gave land on the w side of the Jordan 2025+3542
23: 4 the Jordan and the Great Sea in the **w.** 4427+9087
Jdg 18:12 This is why the place w *of* Kiriath Jearim 339
20:33 of its place on the w *of* Gibeah. 5115
2Sa 13:34 and saw many people on the road w *of* him, 339
1Ki 4:24 For he ruled over all the kingdoms w *of* 6298
7:25 three facing north, three facing w, 2025+3542
1Ch 7:28 Gezer and its villages to the w, 5115
9:24 four sides: east, **w,** north and south. 2025+3542
12:15 to the east and to the **w.** 5115
26:16 for the W Gate and the Shalleketh Gate on 5115
26:18 As for the court to the w, 5115
26:30 Israel w of the Jordan for all the work 4946+6298
2Ch 4: 4 three facing north, three facing w, 2025+3542
32:30 and channeled the water down to the w *side* 5115
33:14 w of the Gihon spring in the valley, 2025+5115
Job 18:20 *Men of the* w are appalled at his fate; 340
23: 8 if I go to the **w,** I do not find him. 294
Ps 75: 6 the east or the w or from the desert can exalt 5115
103:12 as far as the east is from the w, 5115
107: 3 from east and **w,** from north and south. 5115
Isa 9:12 from the w have devoured Israel 294
11:14 down on the slopes of Philistia to the **w;** 3542
24:14 the w they acclaim the LORD's majesty. 3542
43: 5 from the east and gather you from the **w.** 5115
49:12 some from the north, some from the w, 3542
59:19 From the **w,** men will fear the name of 5115
Eze 41:12 on the w side was seventy cubits wide. 3542
42:19 Then he turned to the w side and measured; 3542
45: 7 the w side and eastward from the east side, 3542
47:20 "On the w side, the Great Sea will be the 3542
47:20 This will be the w boundary. 3542
48: 1 from the east side to the w *side.* 3542
48: 2 the territory of Dan from east to **w.** 2025+3542
48: 3 the territory of Asher from east to **w.** 2025+3542
48: 4 territory of Naphtali from east to **w.** 2025+3542
48: 5 territory of Manasseh from east to **w.** 2025+3542
48: 6 territory of Ephraim from east to **w.** 2025+3542
48: 7 the territory of Reuben from east to **w.** 2025+3542
48: 8 the territory of Judah from east to w 2025+3542
48: 8 its length from east to w will equal 2025+3542
48:10 10,000 cubits wide on the w *side,* 3542
48:16 and the w side 4,500 cubits. 2025+3542
48:17 and 250 cubits on the w. 3542
48:18 and 10,000 cubits on the w *side.* 3542
48:23 from the east side to the w side. 2025+3542
48:24 territory of Benjamin from east to **w.** 2025+3542
48:25 territory of Simeon from east to w. 2025+3542
48:26 territory of Issachar from east to **w.** 2025+3542
48:27 territory of Zebulun from east to **w.** 2025+3542
48:34 "On the w side, which is 4,500 cubits long, 3542
Da 8: 4 toward the w and the north and the south. 3542
8: 5 between his eyes came from the w, 5115
Hos 11:10 his children will come trembling from the w 3542
Zec 6: 6 the one with the white horses toward the w, 339
8: 7 the countries of the east and the **w.** 4427+9087
14: 4 be split in two from east to w, 3542
Mt 8:11 from the east and the w, *1553*
24:27 from the east is visible even in the w, *1553*
Lk 12:54 "When you see a cloud rising in the w, *1553*
13:29 People will come from east and w and north *1553*
Rev 21:13 three on the south and three on the w. *1553*

WESTERN (26) [WEST]

Nu 34: 6 " 'Your w boundary will be the coast of 3542
Dt 1: 7 in the mountains, in the w **foothills,** 9169
3:17 Its w border was the Jordan 2025+4667[S]
11:24 and from the Euphrates River to the w sea. 340
34: 2 all the land of Judah as far as the w sea, 340
Jos 9: 1 the w **foothills,** and along the entire coast 9169
10:40 the w **foothills** and the mountain slopes, 9169
11: 2 in the w **foothills** and in Naphoth Dor on 9169
11:16 whole region of Goshen, the w **foothills,** 9169
12: 8 the w **foothills,** the Arabah, 9169
15:12 The w boundary is the coastline of 3542
15:33 In the w **foothills:** Eshtaol, Zorah, 9169
18:14 the boundary turned south along the w side 3542
18:14 This was the w side. 3542
Jdg 1: 9 the Negev and the w **foothills.** 9169
1Ch 27:28 and sycamore-fig trees in the w **foothills.** 9169
Jer 17:26 of Benjamin and the w **foothills,** 9169
32:44 of the w **foothills** and of the Negev, 9169
33:13 of the w **foothills** and of the Negev, 9169
Eze 45: 7 the w to the eastern border parallel to one of 3542
46:19 and showed me a place at the w end. 2025+3542
48:21 25,000 cubits to the w border. 2025+3542
Da 11:30 Ships of the w **coastlands** will oppose him, 4183
Joel 2:20 and those in the rear into the w sea. 340
Zec 7: 7 and the w **foothills** were settled?' " 9169
14: 8 half to the eastern sea and half to the w sea, 340

WESTWARD (4) [WEST]

Jos 15:10 curved w from Baalah to Mount Seir, 2025+3542
16: 3 descended w to the territory of 2025+3542
Eze 45: 7 It will **extend** w from the west side 2025+3542
48:21 and w from the 25,000 cubits to 2025+3542

WET (3)

Job 31:38 and all its furrows *are* **w with tears,** 1134
Lk 7:38 she began *to* w his feet with her tears. *1101*
7:44 but she w my feet with her tears *1101*

WHALE, WHALE'S, WHALES (KJV)

See CREATURES, HUGE FISH, MONSTER

WHAT (2501) [SOMEWHAT, WHAT'S, WHATEVER]

Ge 2:19 to the man to see w he would name them; 4537
3:13 **"W** is this you have done?" 4537
4: 7 If *you* **do w is right,** 3512
4: 7 But if *you do* not **do w is right,** 3512
4:10 The LORD said, **"W** have you done? 4537
9:24 and found out w his youngest son had done 889
12:11 "I know w a beautiful woman you are. 3954
12:18 **"W** have you done to me?" 4537
14:24 but w my men have eaten and the share 889
15: 2 w can you give me since I remain childless 4537
16: 2 Abram agreed to w Sarai **said.** 7754
18:17 "Shall I hide from Abraham w I am about 889
18:19 of the LORD by doing *w* is **right** and just, AIT
18:19 for Abraham w he has promised him." 889
18:21 down and see if *w they have* **done** is as bad AIT
18:24 **W if** there are fifty righteous people in 218
18:28 **w if** the number of the righteous is five less 218
18:29 **"W if** only forty are found there?" 218
18:30 **W if** only thirty can be found there?" 218
18:31 **w if** only twenty can be found there?" 218
18:32 **W if** only ten can be found there?" 218
19: 8 and you can do w you like with them. 3869
20: 9 **"W** have you done to us? 4537
20:10 **"W** was your reason for doing this?" 4537
21: 1 LORD did for Sarah w he had promised. 889+3869
21:17 **"W is the matter,** Hagar? 3871+4200+4537
21:29 **W is the meaning** of these seven ewe 2179+4537
23:15 but w is that between me and you? 4537
24: 5 **"W if** the woman is unwilling to come back 218
24:30 and had heard Rebekah tell w the man said 3907
24:33 until I have told you w I **have to say."** 1821
24:39 **'W if** the woman will not come back 218
24:52 When Abraham's servant heard w they **said,** 1821
25:32 **"W** *good* is the birthright to me?" 4200+4537
26:10 **"W** is this you have done to us? 4537
27: 8 my son, listen carefully and do w I tell you: 889
27:12 **W if** my father touches me? 218
27:13 Just do w I say; go and get them for me." 928
27:37 So w can I possibly do for you, my son?" 4537
27:42 w her older son Esau had **said,** 1821
27:43 Now then, my son, do w I **say:** 7754
27:45 with you and forgets w you did to him, 889
28:15 until I have done w I have promised you." 889
29:15 Tell me w your wages should be." 4537
29:25 **"W** is this you have done to me? 4537
30:11 Then Leah said, **"W** good fortune!" 928
30:31 **"W** shall I give you?" 4537
31: 1 from w belonged to our father." 889
31: 2 attitude toward him was not w it had been. 3869
31: 5 attitude toward me is not w it was before, 3869
31:15 but he has used up w was **paid** *for* us. 4084
31:26 Laban said to Jacob, **"W** have you done? 4537
31:36 **"W** is my crime?" 4537
31:36 **"W** sin have I committed 4537
31:37 w have you found that belongs 4537
31:43 Yet w can I do today about these daughters 4537
32: 4 **This is** w you are to say to my master Esau: 3907
32:13 w he had with him he selected a gift 995+2021[S]
32:27 The man asked him, **"W** is your name?" 4537
33: 8 **"W** do you mean by all these droves I met?" 4769
33: 9 Keep w you have for yourself." 889
34: 7 as soon as they heard w had happened. NIH
34:19 lost no time in doing w they said, 2021[S]
37: 8 because of his dream and w he had **said.** 1821
37:10 **"W** is this dream you had? 4537
37:15 **"W** are you looking for?" 4537
37:20 Then we'll see w comes of his dreams." 4537
37:26 **"W** will we gain if we kill our brother 4537
38:10 W he did was wicked in the LORD's sight 889
38:16 w will you give me to sleep with you?" 4537
38:18 He said, **"W** pledge should I give you?" 4537
38:23 Then Judah said, "Let her keep w she has, NIH
40:12 "This is *w* it **means,"** Joseph said to him. AIT
40:18 "This is *w* it **means,"** Joseph said. AIT
41:25 God has revealed to Pharaoh w he is about 889
41:28 God has shown Pharaoh w he is about 889
41:55 "Go to Joseph and do w he tells you." 889
42:28 **"W** is this that God has done to us?" 4537
44:15 **"W** is this you have done? 4537
44:16 **"W** can we say to my lord?" 4537
44:16 **"W** can we say? 4537
44:24 we told him w my lord had **said.** 1821
45: 9 **'This is** w your son Joseph says: 3907
45:23 And this is w he sent to his father: 3869
46:33 **'W** is your occupation?' 4537
47: 3 **"W** is your occupation?" 4537
49: 1 around so I can tell you w will happen 889
49:28 and this is w their father said to them 889
50:15 **"W if** Joseph holds a grudge against us 4273
50:17 **'This is** w you are to say to Joseph: 3907
50:20 to accomplish w is now being done, 3869
Ex 1:17 did not do w the king of Egypt had told 889+3869
2: 4 at a distance to see w would happen to him. 4537
2:14 **"W** I did must have become known." 1821+2021[S]
3:13 and they ask me, **'W** is his name?' 4537
3:13 Then w shall I tell them?" 4537
3:14 **This is** w you are to say to the Israelites: 3907
3:16 over you and have seen w has been done 2021
4: 1 **"W if** they do not believe me or listen 2176
4: 2 **"W** is that in your hand?" 4537
4:12 I will help you speak and will teach you w 889
4:14 **"W about** your brother, Aaron 2022+4202
4:15 of you speak and will teach you w to do. 889
4:22 say to Pharaoh, **'This is** w the LORD says: 3907

Ex 5: 1 **"This is** w the LORD, the God of Israel, 3907
5:10 **"This is** w Pharaoh says: 3907
5:17 Pharaoh said, "Lazy, that's w you are— NIH
6: 1 "Now you will see w I will do to Pharaoh: 889
7:17 **This is** w the LORD says: 3907
8: 1 **'This is** w the LORD says: 3907
8:13 And the LORD did w Moses asked. 3869
8:20 **'This is** w the LORD says: 3907
8:31 and the LORD did w Moses asked: 3869
9: 1 **This is** w the LORD, the God of the Hebrews 3907
9:13 **This is** w the LORD, the God of the Hebrews 3907
10: 3 **This is** w the LORD, the God of the Hebrews 3907
10: 5 They will devour w little you have left after 2021
10:11 since that's *w* you have been asking for." AIT
10:26 not know w we are to use to worship 4537
11: 4 So Moses said, **"This is** w the LORD says: 3907
12: 4 of lamb needed **in accordance with** *w* each AIT
12:26 'W does this ceremony mean to you?' 4537
12:28 The Israelites did **just** w 889+3869+4027
12:36 **gave** them w they **asked for;** 8626
12:50 All the Israelites did **just** w 889+3869+4027
13: 8 'I do this because of w the LORD did 2296
13:14 'W does this **mean?'** 4537
14: 5 "W have we done? 4537
14:11 W have you done to us by bringing us out 4537
15:24 saying, "W are we to drink?" 4537
15:26 of the LORD your God and do w is right 2021
16: 5 to prepare w they bring in, 889
16:15 they said to each other, "W is it?" 4943
16:15 For they did not know w it was. 4537
16:16 This is w the LORD has commanded: 1821+2021[S]
16:23 "This is w the LORD commanded: 889
16:23 So bake w you want to bake 889
16:23 to bake and boil w you want to boil. 889
16:32 "This is w the LORD has commanded: 1821+2021[S]
17: 4 "W am I to do with these people? 4537
18:14 "W is this you are doing for the people? 4537
18:17 "W you are doing is not good. 1821+2021[S]
19: 3 **"This is** w you are to say to the house 3907
19: 3 to say to the house of Jacob and w you are NIH
19: 4 'You yourselves have seen w I did to Egypt, 889
19: 9 told the LORD w the people had **said.** 1821
22:27 W *else* will he sleep in? 4537
23:11 the wild animals may eat w they **leave.** AIT
23:21 Pay attention to him and listen to w he **says.** 7754
23:22 If you listen carefully to w he **says** 7754
26:13 w is left will hang over the sides of 2021
29: 1 This is w you are to do to consecrate 1821+2021[S]
29:38 "This is w you are to offer on 889
32: 1 we don't know w has happened to him." 4537
32: 4 He took w they handed him and made it NIH
32: 8 to turn away from w I commanded 2006+2021[S]
32:21 "W did these people do to you, 4537
32:23 we don't know w has happened to him.' 4537
32:27 Then he said to them, **"This is** w the LORD, 3907
32:31 w a great sin these people have committed! NIH
32:35 of w they did with the calf Aaron had made. 889
33: 5 and I will decide w to do with you.' " 4537
33:16 W else will distinguish me and your people NIH
34:11 Obey w I command you today. 889
34:34 the Israelites w he had been commanded, 889
35: 4 "This is w the LORD has commanded: 1821+2021[S]
35: 5 From w you have, take an offering NIH
35:25 and brought w she had **spun—** 4757
36: 7 w they already had was more than enough 2021+4856[S]
40: 4 Bring in the table and set out w **belongs** 6886
Lev 3:14 From w he offers he is to make this offering 5647
4: 2 and does w is forbidden in any of 889
4:13 and does w is forbidden in any of 889
4:22 and does w is forbidden in any of 889
4:27 and does w is forbidden in any of 889
5: 5 he must confess in w *way* he has sinned 889
5:16 for w he has failed to do in regard to 889
5:17 a person sins and does w is forbidden in any 889
6: 4 he must return w he has stolen or taken 889
6: 4 or w was entrusted to him, 889
8: 5 "This is w the LORD has commanded to 1821[S]
8:34 W has been done today was commanded by the LORD 889+3869
8:35 and do w the LORD **requires,** so you will 5466
8:35 for **that is** w I have been commanded." 4027
9: 6 "This is w the LORD has commanded 1821+2021[S]
10: 3 "This is w the LORD spoke of 889
17: 2 'This is w the LORD has commanded: 1821+2021[S]
19: 8 because he has desecrated w is **holy** *to* 7731
20:12 W they have done is a perversion; NIH
20:13 both of them have done w is **detestable.** 9359
25: 5 Do not reap w **grows of itself** or harvest 6206
25:11 not sow and do not reap w **grows of itself** 6206
25:12 eat only w **is taken** directly from the fields. 9311
25:16 because w he is really selling you is NIH
25:20 "W will we eat in the seventh year if we do 4537
25:25 redeem w his countryman has **sold.** 4928
25:28 w he **sold** will remain in the possession of 4928
27: 8 to w the man making the vow can afford. 889
27: 9 " 'If w he vowed is an animal NIH
27:11 If w he vowed is a ceremonially unclean NIH
27:12 that *is w it will* **be.** AIT
Nu 4:19 and w he is **to carry.** 5362
4:49 and told w **to carry.** 5362
5:10 but w he gives to the priest will belong to 889
9: 8 until I find out w the LORD commands 4537
11:11 W have I done to displease you 4200+4537
11:23 or not *w* I **say** will come true for you." AIT
11:24 told the people w the LORD had **said.** 1821
13:18 See w the land is **like** 4537
Nu 13:19 W *kind of* land do they live in? 4537
13:19 W *kind of* towns do they live in? 4537
14:34 **know** w **it is like** to have me against you.' 3359
15:34 it was not clear w should be done to him. 4537
16:29 and experience only w **usually happens** 7213
20:14 **"This is** w your brother Israel says: 3907
21:34 Do to him w you did to Sihon king of 889+3869
22: 7 they told him w Balak had **said.** 1821
22:16 **"This is** w Balak son of Zippor says: 3907
22:19 and I will find out w else 4537
22:20 but do only w I tell you." 1821+2021[S]
22:28 "W have I done to you 4537
22:35 but speak only w I tell you." 1821+2021[S]
22:38 I must speak only w God puts 1821+2021[S]
23:11 "W have you done to me? 4537
23:12 not speak w the LORD puts in my mouth?" 889
23:17 Balak asked him, "W did the LORD say?" 4537
23:23 'See w God has done!' 4537
24:13 and I must say only w the LORD says'? 889
24:14 let me warn you *of* w this people will do 889
26:55 W each group inherits will be according to NIH
27: 7 "*W* Zelophehad's daughters *are* **saying** AIT
29:39 to *w* you **vow** and your freewill offerings, AIT
30: 1 "This is w the LORD commands: 1821+2021[S]
31:16 from the LORD in w **happened** *at* Peor, 1821
32: 8 **This is** w your fathers did when I sent them 3907
32:24 but do w you have promised." 2021
32:31 "Your servants will do w the LORD has said. 4027
33:56 I will do to you w I plan to do to them. 889+3869
36: 5 "W the tribe of the descendants NIH
36: 6 This is w the LORD commands 1821+2021[S]
Dt 1:14 "W you propose to do is good." 1821+2021[S]
1:34 When the LORD heard w you **said,** 1821+7754
3: 2 Do to him w you did to Sihon king of 889+3869
3:24 For w god is there in heaven or 4769
4: 2 Do not add to w I command you 1821+2021[S]
4: 3 with your own eyes w the LORD did 889
4: 7 W other nation is so great as 4769
4: 8 And w other nation is so great as 4769
5:26 For w mortal man has ever heard the voice 4769
5:28 "I have heard w this people said 1821+7754[S]
5:32 So be careful to do w the LORD 889+3869
6:18 Do w is right and good in the LORD's 2021[S]
6:20 "W **is the meaning of** the stipulations, 4537
7: 5 **This is** w you are to do to them: 3907
7:18 remember well w the LORD your God did 889
8: 2 and to test you in order to know w was 889
9: 5 to accomplish w he swore 1821+2021[S]
9:12 from w I commanded them 2006+2021[S]
9:18 doing w was evil in the LORD's sight and 2021[S]
10: 4 on these tablets w he had written before, 3869
10:12 w does the LORD your God ask of you but 4537
11: 4 w he did to the Egyptian army, 889
11: 5 not your children who saw w he did for you 889
11: 6 and w he did to Dathan and Abiram, 889
12: 6 *w* you have **vowed** to give AIT
12:25 because you will be doing w is right in 2021
12:28 be doing w is good and right in the eyes of 2021
13:18 and doing w is right in his eyes. 2021
17:11 Do not turn aside from w they tell you, 1821+2021[S]
18:16 For this is w you asked of the LORD 889
18:17 "W they say is good. 889
18:22 If w a prophet proclaims in the name of 889
21: 9 since you have done w is right in the eyes 2021
24: 8 You must follow carefully w I have commanded them. 889+3869
24: 9 Remember w the LORD your God did 889
24:10 *w* he is **offering as a pledge.** AIT
24:20 Leave w remains for the alien, NIH
24:21 Leave w remains for the alien, NIH
25: 9 **"This is** w is done to the man who will 3970
25:17 Remember w the Amalekites did to you 889
28:33 that you do not know will eat w your land NIH
30:11 Now w I am commanding you today is not too difficult 2021+2021+2296+5184[S]
31: 4 And the LORD will do to them w he did 889+3869
31:21 I know w they are disposed to do, 889
31:29 w your hands have **made."** 5126
32:20 he said, "and see w their end will be; 4537
32:21 They made me jealous by w is no god NIH
32:29 and discern w their end will be! NIH
34: 9 the Israelites listened to him and did w 889+3869
Jos 2:10 and w you did to Sihon and Og, 889
2:14 "If you don't tell w we are doing, 2296
2:20 But if you tell w we are doing, 2296
4: 6 'W do these stones **mean?'** 4537
4:21 'W do these stones **mean?'** 4537
4:23 to the Jordan **just** w he had done to 889+3869
5:14 "W message does my Lord have 4537
7: 8 O Lord, w can I say, 4537
7: 9 W then will you do for your own great name?" 4537
7:10 W are you doing down on your face? 4200+4537
7:13 **this is** w the LORD, the God of Israel, says: 3907
7:19 Tell me w you have done; 4537
7:20 This is w I have done: 3869
8: 8 Do w the LORD has commanded. 3869
8:31 according to w is written in the Book of 2021
9: 3 people of Gibeon heard w Joshua had done 889
9:20 This is w we will do to them: NIH
9:27 And that is w they are to this day. NIH
10:25 **This is** w the LORD will do to all 3970
13:15 This is w Moses had given to the tribe NIH
13:24 This is w Moses had given to the tribe NIH
13:29 This is w Moses had given to the half-tribe NIH
14: 6 You know w the LORD said to Moses 1821+2021[S]
Jos 15:18 Caleb asked her, "W can I do for you?" 4537
22:24 'W do you have to do with the LORD, 4537
22:30 heard w Reuben, Gad and Manasseh 1821+2021[S]
24: 2 **"This is** w the LORD, the God of Israel, 3907
24: 5 I afflicted the Egyptians by w I did there, 889
24: 7 You saw with your own eyes w I did to 889
Jdg 1: 7 God has paid me back for w I did to them." 889+3869+4027
1:14 Caleb asked her, "W can I do for you?" 4537
2:10 LORD nor w he had done for Israel. 2021+5126[S]
6: 8 **"This is** w the LORD, the God of Israel, 3907
6:38 And that *is w* **happened.** AIT
7:11 and listen to w they are saying. 4537
8: 2 "W have I accomplished compared to you? 4537
8: 3 W was I able to do compared to you?" 4537
8:18 "W kind of men did you kill at Tabor?" 407
9:30 w Gaal son of Ebed **said,** 1821
9:48 Do w you have seen me do!" 4537
11:12 "W do you have against us 4537
11:15 **"This is** w Jephthah says: 3907
11:23 w right have you to take it over? NIH
11:24 not take w your god Chemosh gives you? 889
13:12 w is to be the rule for the boy's life 4537
13:17 "W is your name, 4769
14: 6 nor his mother w he had done. 889
14:18 "W is sweeter than honey? 4537
14:18 W is stronger than a lion?" 4537
15:11 W have you done to us?" 4537
15:11 did to them w they did to me." 889+3869+4027
18: 3 W are you doing in this place? 4537
18: 4 He told them w Micah had done for him, 2256+2296+2297+3869+3869
18:14 Now you know w to do." 4537
18:18 the priest said to them, "W are you doing?" 4537
18:24 W else do I have? 4537
18:27 Then they took w Micah had made, 889
19:30 Tell us w to do!" NIH
20: 9 But now this is w we'll do to Gibeah: 1821+2021[S]
20:10 it can give them w they **deserve for** 3869
20:12 "W *about* this awful crime 4537
21:11 "This is w you are to do," they said. 1821+2021[S]
21:23 So **that is** w the Benjamites did. 4027
Ru 2:11 "I've been told all about w you have done 889
2:12 the LORD repay you for w you have **done.** 7189
2:18 also brought out and gave her w she had left 889
3: 4 He will tell you w to do." 889
3:18 my daughter, until you find out w happens. 375
1Sa 1:17 of Israel grant you w you have asked 8924[S]
1:23 "Do w seems best to you," 2021
1:27 LORD has granted me w I asked of him. 8629[S]
2:27 **"This is** w the LORD says: 3907
2:34 " 'And w happens to your two sons, 889
2:35 who will do according to w is in my heart 889
3:17 "W was it he said to you?" 4537
3:18 let him do w is good in his eyes." 2021
4:13 the town and told w had happened, NIH
4:14 "W **is the meaning** *of* this uproar?" 4537
4:16 Eli asked, "W happened, my son?" 4537
5: 7 the men of Ashdod saw w was happening, 3954
5: 8 "W shall we do with the ark of the god 4537
6: 2 "W shall we do with the ark of the LORD? 4537
6: 4 "W guilt offering should we send to him?" 4537
8: 9 w the king who will reign over them will **do."** 5477[S]
8:11 w the king who will reign over you will **do:** 5477[S]
9: 6 Perhaps he will tell us w way to take." 889
9: 7 "If we go, w can we give the man? 4537
9: 7 W do we have?" 4537
9: 8 so that he will tell us w way to take." 5646[S]
9:24 with w was on it and set it in front of Saul. 2021
9:24 "Here is w has been kept for you. 2021
10: 2 "W shall I do about my son?" ' 4537
10: 8 until I come to you and tell you w you are 889
10:11 "W is this that has happened to the son 4537
10:15 "Tell me w Samuel said to you." 4537
10:16 not tell his uncle w Samuel had said about 1821[S]
10:18 **"This is** w the LORD, the God of Israel, 3907
11: 5 he asked, "W **is wrong** with the people? 4537
11: 5 w the men of Jabesh had **said.** 1821
11: 7 **"This is** w will be done to the oxen 3907
12:17 And you will realize w an evil thing you did 8041
12:24 consider w great things he has done for you. 889
13:11 "W have you done?" 4537
14:38 find out w sin has been committed 928+4537
14:40 "Do w seems best to you," the men replied. 2021
14:43 "Tell me w you have done." 4537
15: 2 **This is** w the LORD Almighty says: 3907
15: 2 'I will punish the Amalekites for w they did 889
15:14 "W then is this bleating of sheep 4537
15:14 W is this lowing of cattle that I hear?" NIH
15:16 "Let me tell you w the LORD said 889
15:21 the best of w was devoted to God, 2021
16: 3 and I will show you w to do. 889
16: 4 Samuel did w the LORD said. 889
17:26 "W will be done for the man who 4537
17:27 to him w they had been saying 3869
17:27 **"This is** w will be done for the man who 3907
17:29 "Now w have I done?" 4537
17:31 W David said was overheard and 1821+2021[S]
18: 8 W more can he get but the kingdom?" NIH
18:18 w is my family or my father's clan in Israel, 4769
18:24 Saul's servants told him w David had said, 465+1821+2021+2021[S]
19: 3 about you and will tell you w I find out." 4537
19: 4 w he has **done** has benefited you greatly. 5126
20: 1 "W have I done? 4537
20: 1 W is my crime? 4537

1Sa 20:32 **W** has he done?" 4537
21: 3 Now then, **w** do you have on hand? 4537
22: 3 with you until I learn **w** God will do 4537
25:17 Now think it over and see **w** you can do, 4537
25:24 **w** your servant has to **say.** 1821
25:35 from her hand **w** she had brought him 889
26:16 **W** you have done is not good. 1821+2021+2021+2296S
26:18 **W** have I done, 4537
26:18 and **w** wrong am I guilty of? 4537
27:11 **'This is w** David did.' " 3907
28: 2 for yourself **w** your servant can do." 889
28: 9 "Surely you know **w** Saul has done. 889
28:13 **W** do you see?" 4537
28:14 **"W** does he look like?" 4537
28:15 So I have called on you to tell me **w** to do." 4537
28:17 The LORD has done **w** he predicted 889+3869
28:21 in my hands and did **w** you told me to do. 1821S
29: 3 **"W about** these Hebrews?" 4537
29: 8 "But **w** have I done?" 4537
29: 8 **"W** have you found against your servant 4537
30:23 not do that with **w** the LORD has given us. 889
30:24 Who will listen to **w** you **say?** 1821
31:11 the people of Jabesh Gilead heard of **w** 889
2Sa 1: 4 **"W** happened?" David asked. 4537
1: 7 and I said, **'W can I do?'** 2180
3: 8 of **w** Ish-Bosheth **said** and he answered, 1821
3: 9 for David **w** the LORD promised him 889+3869
3:24 **"W** have you done? 4537
7: 5 **'This is w** the LORD says: 3907
7: 8 **'This is w** the LORD Almighty says: 3907
7:18 O Sovereign LORD, and **w** is my family, 4769
7:20 **"W** more can David say to you? 4537
8:15 doing **w** was just and right NIH
9: 8 **"W** is your servant, 4537
10:12 The LORD will do **w** is good in his sight." 2021
12: 7 **This is w** the LORD, the God of Israel, 3907
12: 9 the LORD by doing **w** is evil in his eyes? 2021
12:11 **"This is w** the LORD says: 3907
13:13 **W about** me? 2256
13:13 **And w about** you? 2256
13:16 greater wrong than **w** you have already done 337S
13:29 to Amnon **w** Absalom had ordered. 889+3869
14: 5 The king asked her, **"W is troubling** you?" 4537
14:15 perhaps he will do **w** his servant **asks.** 1821
14:18 the answer *to* **w** I am going to ask you." 889
15: 2 **"W** town are you from?" 361
16:10 **"W** do you and I have in common, 4537
16:20 **W** should we do?" 4537
17: 5 so we can hear **w** he has to say." 4537
17: 6 Should we do **w** he **says?** 1821
18:11 **"W!** You saw him? 2180
18:21 "Go, tell the king **w** you have seen." 889
18:22 again said to Joab, **"Come w may,** 2118+4537
18:23 said, **"Come w may,** I want to run." 2118+4537
18:29 your servant, but I don't know **w** it was." 4537
19:11 to his palace, since **w** is being **said** 1821
19:22 **"W** do you and I have in common, 4537
19:28 So **w** right do I have to make any more 4537
19:35 Can I tell the difference between **w** is good NIH
19:35 between what is good and **w** is not? NIH
19:35 Can your servant taste **w** he eats and drinks? 889
20:17 **w** your servant *has to* **say."** 1821
21: 3 **"W** shall I do for you? 4537
21: 4 **"W** do you want me to do for you?" 4537
21:11 David was told **w** Aiah's daughter Rizpah, 889
24:10 "I have sinned greatly *in* **w** I have done 889
24:12 **'This is w** the LORD says: 3907
24:17 **W** have they done? 4537
1Ki 1:14 I will come in and confirm **w** you have **said.** 1821
1:16 **"W** is it you want?" 4537
1:30 surely carry out today **w** I swore to you 889+3869
2: 3 **w** the LORD your God **requires:** 5466
2: 5 "Now you yourself know **w** Joab son 889
2: 5 **w** he did to the two commanders 889
2: 9 you will know **w** to do to him. 889
2:38 **"W** you **say** is good. 1821
2:42 **'W** you **say** is good. 1821
3:12 I will do **w** you have asked. 3869
3:13 I will give you **w** you have not asked for— 889
8:15 his own hand has fulfilled **w** he promised 889
8:32 down on his own head **w** he has **done.** 2006
9:13 **"W** kind of towns are these you have given 4537
10:13 besides **w** he had given her out of his royal 889
11:22 **"W** have you lacked here that you want 4537
11:31 for **this is w** the LORD, the God of Israel, 3907
11:33 nor done **w** is right in my eyes, 2021
11:38 in my ways and do **w** is right in my eyes 2021
12: 9 He asked them, **"W** is your advice? 4537
12:16 **"W** share do we have in David, 4537
12:16 **w** part in Jesse's son? NIH
12:24 **'This is w** the LORD says: 3907
13: 2 **This is w** the LORD says: 3907
13: 4 When King Jeroboam heard **w** the man 1821S
13:11 also told their father **w** he had said to 1821+2021S
13:21 **"This is w** the LORD says: 3907
14: 3 He will tell you **w** will happen to the boy." 4537
14: 4 So Jeroboam's wife did **w** he said and went 4027
14: 7 Go, tell Jeroboam that **this is w** the LORD, 3907
14: 8 doing only **w** was right in my eyes. 2021
14:14 This is the day! **W?** Yes, even now. 4537
15: 5 For David had done **w** was right in the eyes 2021
15:11 Asa did **w** was right in the eyes of the LORD 2021
16: 5 **w** he did and his achievements, 889
16:27 **w** he did and the things he achieved, 889
17: 5 So he did **w** the LORD had told him. 3869
17:13 for me from **w** you have and bring it to me, 9004S
1Ki 17:14 **this is w** the LORD, the God of Israel, says: 3907
17:18 **"W** do you have against me, man of God? 4537
18: 9 **"W** have I done wrong," asked Obadiah, 4537
18:13 **w** I did while Jezebel was killing 889
18:24 all the people said, **"W** you say is good." 2021
19: 9 **W are you doing** here, Elijah? 3870+4200+4537
19:13 a voice said to him, **"W are you doing** here, 3870+4200+4537
19:20 **"W** have I done to you?" 4537
20: 2 saying, **"This is w** Ben-Hadad says: 3907
20: 5 **"This is w** Ben-Hadad says: 3907
20:13 **"This is w** the LORD says: 3907
20:14 **"This is w** the LORD says: 3907
20:22 "Strengthen your position and see **w** must 889
20:28 **"This is w** the LORD says: 3907
20:42 **"This is w** the LORD says: 3907
21:19 Say to him, **'This is w** the LORD says: 3907
21:19 say to him, **'This is w** the LORD says: 3907
22:11 **"This is w** the LORD says: 3907
22:14 I can tell him only **w** the LORD tells me." 889
22:22 **" 'By w means?'** 928+4537
22:27 **'This is w** the king says: 3907
22:43 he did **w** was right in the eyes of 2021
2Ki 1: 4 Therefore **this is w** the LORD says: 3907
1: 6 **"This is w** the LORD says: 3907
1: 7 **"W** kind of man was it who came 4537
1:11 "Man of God, **this is w** the king says, 3907
1:16 **"This is w** the LORD says: 3907
1:18 events of Ahaziah's reign, and **w** he did, 889
2: 9 **w** can I do for you before I am taken 4537
2:21 saying, **"This is w** the LORD says: 3907
3: 8 **"By w** route shall we attack?" 361+2296
3:10 **"W!"** exclaimed the king of Israel. 177
3:13 **"W** do we have to do with each other? 4537
3:16 **"This is w** the LORD says: 3907
3:17 For **this is w** the LORD says: 3907
4: 2 Tell me, **w** do you have in your house?" 4537
4: 7 You and your sons can live on **w** is left." 2021
4:13 Now **w** can be done for you? 4537
4:14 **"W** can be done for her?" 4537
4:39 though no one knew **w** they were. NIH
4:43 For **this is w** the LORD says: 3907
5: 4 and told him **w** the girl from Israel had said. 2256+2296+2296+3869+3869
5:20 by not accepting from him **w** he brought. 889
6:15 "Oh, my lord, **w** shall we do?" 377
7: 1 **This is w** the LORD says: 3907
7:12 "I will tell you **w** the Arameans have done 889
7:13 let us send them to find out **w** happened." NIH
7:14 "Go and find out **w** has happened." NIH
7:20 And that is exactly *w* **happened** to him, AIT
8:14 **"W** did Elisha say to you?" 4537
9: 3 **'This is w** the LORD says: 3907
9: 6 **"This is w** the LORD, the God of Israel, 3907
9:12 Jehu said, **"Here is w** he told me: 2256+2296+2296+3869+3869
9:12 **'This is w** the LORD says: 3907
9:18 **"This is w** the king says: 3907
9:18 **"W** do you have to do with peace?" 4537
9:19 **"This is w** the king says: 3907
9:19 **"W** do you have to do with peace? 4537
9:27 of Judah saw **w** had happened, NIH
10:10 The LORD has done **w** he promised 889
10:30 in accomplishing **w** is right in my eyes 2021
11: 5 saying, "This is **w** you are to do: 1821+2021S
12: 2 Joash did **w** was right in the eyes of 2021
14: 3 He did **w** was right in the eyes of 2021
14: 6 in accordance with **w** is written in the Book 2021
14:15 **w** he did and his achievements, 889
15: 3 He did **w** was right in the eyes of the LORD, 2021
15:34 He did **w** was right in the eyes of the LORD, 2021
15:36 events of Jotham's reign, and **w** he did, 889
16: 2 he did not do **w** was right in the eyes of 2021
16:19 events of the reign of Ahaz, and **w** he did, 889
17:26 **w** the god of that country **requires.** 5477
17:26 the people do not know **w** he **requires."** 5477
17:27 **w** the god of the land **requires."** 5477
18: 3 He did **w** was right in the eyes of the LORD, 2021
18:19 **" 'This is w** the great king, 3907
18:19 On **w** are you basing this confidence 4537
18:29 **This is w** the king says: 3907
18:31 **This is w** the king of Assyria says: 3907
18:37 **w** the field commander had **said.** 1821
19: 3 They told him, **"This is w** Hezekiah says: 3907
19: 6 **'This is w** the LORD says: 3907
19: 6 Do not be afraid of **w** you have heard— 889
19:11 Surely you have heard **w** the kings 889
19:20 **"This is w** the LORD, the God of Israel, 3907
19:29 "This year you will eat **w grows by itself,** 6206
19:29 and the second year **w springs from** *that.* 6084
19:32 "Therefore **this is w** the LORD says 3907
20: 1 **"This is w** the LORD says: 3907
20: 3 and have done **w** is good in your eyes." 2021
20: 5 **'This is w** the LORD, 3907
20: 8 **"W** will be the sign that the LORD will heal 4537
20: 9 the LORD will do **w** he has promised: 1821+2021S
20:14 **"W** did those men say, 4537
20:15 **"W** did they see in your palace?" 4537
21:12 Therefore **this is w** the LORD, 3907
21:25 other events of Amon's reign, and **w** he did, 889
22: 2 He did **w** was right in the eyes of 2021
22:13 and for all Judah about **w** is **written** 1821
22:15 She said to them, **"This is w** the LORD, 3907
22:16 **'This is w** the LORD says: 3907
22:18 **'This is w** the LORD, the God of Israel, 3907
22:19 when you heard **w** I have spoken 889
23:17 **"W** is that tombstone I see?" 4537
1Ch 12:32 the times and knew **w** Israel should do— 4537
16: 8 among the nations **w** he has **done.** 6613
17: 4 **'This is w** the LORD says: 3907
17: 7 **'This is w** the LORD Almighty says: 3907
17:16 O LORD God, and **w** is my family, 4769
17:18 **"W** more can David say to you 4537
18:14 doing *w* was **just** and right AIT
19:13 The LORD will do **w** is good in his sight." 2021
21:10 **'This is w** the LORD says: 3907
21:11 **"This is w** the LORD says: 3907
21:17 **W** have they done? 4537
21:24 I will not take for the LORD **w** is yours, 889
29:14 and we have given you only **w** comes NIH
2Ch 6: 4 with his hands has fulfilled **w** he promised 889
6:23 down on his own head **w** he has **done.** 2006
8:14 because **this was w** David the man 4027
9: 6 not believe **w** they **said** until I came and saw 1821
10: 9 He asked them, **"W** is your advice? 4537
10:16 **"W** share do we have in David, 4537
10:16 **w** part in Jesse's son? NIH
11: 4 **'This is w** the LORD says: 3907
12: 5 **"This is w** the LORD says, 3907
13: 9 a priest of **w** are not gods. NIH
13:22 **w** he **did** and what he said, 2006
13:22 what he did and **w** he **said,** 1821
14: 2 Asa did **w** was good and right in the eyes of 2021
18:10 and he declared, **"This is w** the LORD says: 3907
18:13 I can tell him only **w** my God says." 889
18:20 **" 'By w means?'** 928+4537
18:26 **'This is w** the king says: 3907
19: 6 "Consider carefully **w** you do, 4537
20:12 We do not know **w** to do, 4537
20:15 **This is w** the LORD says to you: 3907
20:32 he did **w** was right in the eyes of 2021
20:37 the LORD will destroy **w** you have **made."** 5126
21:12 **"This is w** the LORD, 3907
23: 4 Now this is **w** you are to do: 1821+2021S
23: 6 guard *w* the LORD has **assigned** to them. AIT
24: 2 Joash did **w** was right in the eyes of the LORD 2021
24:20 **"This is w** God says: 3907
25: 2 He did **w** was right in the eyes of 2021
25: 4 but acted in accordance with **w** is written in 2021
25: 9 "But **w** about the hundred talents I paid 4537
26: 4 He did **w** was right in the eyes of the LORD, 2021
27: 2 He did **w** was right in the eyes of the LORD, 2021
28: 1 he did not do **w** was right in the eyes of 2021
29: 2 He did **w** was right in the eyes of the LORD, 2021
29:36 at **w** God had brought about for his people, 2021
30: 5 according to **w** was written. 2021
30:12 **w** the king and his officials had **ordered,** 5184
30:18 contrary to **w** was written. 2021
31:20 This is **w** Hezekiah did throughout Judah, 3869
31:20 doing **w** was good and right and faithful 2021
32: 8 **w** Hezekiah the king of Judah **said.** 1821
32:10 **This is w** Sennacherib king of Assyria says: 3907
32:10 On **w** are you basing your confidence, 4537
32:13 not know **w** I and my fathers have done 4537
34: 2 He did **w** was right in the eyes of 2021
34:21 and Judah about **w** is **written** *in* this book 1821
34:23 She said to them, **"This is w** the LORD, 3907
34:24 **'This is w** the LORD says: 3907
34:26 **'This is w** the LORD, the God of Israel, 3907
34:27 before God when you heard **w** he **spoke** 1821
35: 6 doing **w** the LORD commanded 3869
35:21 **"W** quarrel is there between you and me, 4537
35:22 He would not listen to **w** Neco had **said** 1821
35:26 to **w** is written in the Law of the LORD— 2021
36:23 **"This is w** Cyrus king of Persia says: 3907
Ezr 1: 2 **"This is w** Cyrus king of Persia says: 3907
3: 2 in accordance with **w** is written in the Law 2021
3: 4 Then in accordance with **w** is written, 2021
5: 4 **"W** are the names of the men constructing 10426
6: 8 I hereby decree **w** you are to do 10378+10408
6:18 to **w** is **written** *in* the Book of Moses. 10375
8:17 I told them **w** to say to Iddo 1821S
9:10 now, O our God, **w** can we say after this? 4537
9:13 **"W** has happened to us is a result 3972S
10: 5 under oath to do **w** had been suggested. 3869
Ne 2: 4 king said to me, **"W** is it you want?" 4537+6584
2:12 I had not told anyone **w** my God had put 4537
2:16 where I had gone or **w** I was doing, 4537
2:18 upon me and **w** the king had said to me. 1821S
2:19 **"W** is this you are doing?" 4537
4: 2 he said, **"W** are those feeble Jews doing? 4537
4: 3 said, **"W** they are building— 889
5: 9 **"W** you are doing is not right. 1821+2021S
5:12 an oath to do **w** they had promised. 3869
6: 8 "Nothing like **w** you are saying is happening; 465+1821+2021+2021S
6:14 O my God, because of **w** they have done; 465
6:19 and then telling him **w** I **said.** 1821
7: 5 This is **w** I found written there: NIH
8: 8 people could understand **w** was being read. 2021
9:28 they again did **w** was evil in your sight. NIH
13:14 not blot out **w** I have so faithfully done for 889
13:17 **"W** is this wicked thing you are doing— 4537
Est 1: 1 *This is w* **happened** during the time AIT
1: 8 to serve each man **w** he wished. 3869
1:15 **w** must be done to Queen Vashti?" 4537
2: 1 he remembered Vashti and **w** she had done 889
2: 1 and **w** he had decreed about her. 889
2:11 how Esther was and **w** was happening 4537
2:15 she asked for nothing other than **w** Hegai, 889
4: 5 to find out **w** was troubling Mordecai 4537
4: 9 and reported to Esther **w** Mordecai had **said.** 1821
5: 3 the king asked, **"W** is it, Queen Esther? 4537

Est	5: 3	**W** is your request?	4537
	5: 5	"so that we may do **w** Esther **asks."**	1821
	5: 6	"Now **w** is your petition?	4537
	5: 6	And **w** is your request?	4537
	6: 3	**"W** honor and recognition has Mordecai received for this?"	4537
	6: 6	**"W** should be done for the man	4537
	6: 9	**'This is w** is done for the man	3970
	6:11	**"This is w** is done for the man	3970
	7: 2	"Queen Esther, **w** is your petition?	4537
	7: 2	**W** is your request?	4537
	9: 5	and they did **w** they pleased	3869
	9:12	**W** have they done in the rest of	4537
	9:12	Now **w** is your petition?	4537
	9:12	**W** is your request?	4537
	9:23	doing **w** Mordecai had written to them.	889
	9:26	in this letter and because of **w** they had seen	4537
	9:26	of what they had seen and **w** had happened	4537
Job	2:10	In all this, Job did not sin in **w** he **said.**	8557
	3:25	**W** I feared has come upon me;	7065[S]
	3:25	**w** I dreaded has happened to me.	889
	4:16	It stopped, but I could not tell **w** it was.	5260[S]
	6: 8	that God would grant *w* I **hope** *for,*	AIT
	6:11	**"W** strength do I have,	4537
	6:11	**W** prospects, that I should be patient?	4537
	6:25	But **w** do your arguments prove?	4537
	6:26	Do you mean to correct **w** I **say,**	4863
	7:17	**"W** is man that you make so much of him,	4537
	7:20	If I have sinned, **w** have I done to you,	4537
	8: 3	Does the Almighty pervert *w* is **right?**	AIT
	8: 8	**w** their fathers **learned,**	2984
	8:14	**W** he trusts in is fragile;	889
	8:14	**w** he **relies on** is a spider's web.	4440
	9:12	Who can say to him, **'W** are you doing?'	4537
	10: 2	but tell me **w** charges you have against me.	4537
	10:13	"But this is **w** you concealed in your heart,	NIH
	11: 8	**w** can you do?	4537
	11: 8	**w** can you know?	4537
	12:14	**W** he tears down cannot be rebuilt;	NIH
	13: 2	**W** you know, I also know;	3869
	13:13	then let come to me **w** may.	4537
	13:17	let your ears take in **w** I **say.**	289
	14: 4	Who can bring *w* is **pure** from the impure?	AIT
	15: 9	**W** do you know that we do not know?	4537
	15: 9	**W** insights do you have that we do	NIH
	15:14	**"W** is man, that he could be pure,	4537
	15:17	let me tell you **w** I have seen,	2296
	15:18	**w** wise men have declared,	889
	15:31	by trusting **w** is worthless,	2021
	16: 3	**W** ails you that you keep on arguing?	4537
	20:18	**W** he **toiled for** he must give back uneaten;	3334
	20:26	and devour *w* is **left** in his tent.	AIT
	21:15	**W** would we gain by praying to him?'	4537
	21:21	For **w** does he care about the family	4537
	21:27	"I know full well **w** you are **thinking,**	4742
	21:31	Who repays him for **w** he has done?	2085
	22: 3	**W** pleasure would it give the Almighty	NIH
	22: 3	**W** would he gain if your ways were blameless?	NIH
	22:13	Yet you say, **'W** does God know?	4537
	22:17	**W** can the Almighty do to us?'	4537
	22:28	**W** you decide on will be done,	608[S]
	23: 5	I would find out **w** he would answer me,	4863[S]
	23: 5	and consider **w** he would say.	4537
	26: 3	**W** advice you have offered to one	4537
	26: 3	And **w** great insight you have displayed!	NIH
	27: 8	**w** hope has the godless when he is cut off,	4537
	27:17	**w** he lays up the righteous will wear,	NIH
	30: 2	**Of w use** was the strength of their hands	4200+4537
	31: 2	For **w** is man's lot from God above,	4537
	31: 8	then may others eat **w** I have sown,	NIH
	31:14	**w** will I do when God confronts me?	4537
	31:14	**W** will I answer when called to account?	4537
	32: 6	not daring to tell you **w** I **know.**	1976
	32: 9	the aged who understand *w* is **right.**	AIT
	32:10	I too will tell you **w** I **know.**	1976
	32:17	I too will tell **w** I **know.**	1976
	33: 3	my lips sincerely speak **w** I **know.**	1981
	33:23	to tell a man **w** is **right** *for* him,	AIT
	33:27	'I sinned, and perverted **w** was **right,**	AIT
	33:27	but I *did* not **get w** I **deserved.**	8750
	34: 4	Let us discern for ourselves *w* is **right;**	AIT
	34: 4	let us learn together **w** is good.	4537
	34: 7	**W** man is like Job, who drinks scorn	4769
	34:11	He repays a man for **w** he has **done;**	7189
	34:11	brings upon him **w** his conduct **deserves.**	3869
	34:16	listen to **w** I say.	7754[S]
	34:32	Teach me **w** I cannot see;	NIH
	34:33	so tell me **w** you know.	4537
	35: 3	Yet you ask him, **'W** profit is it to me,	4537
	35: 3	and **w** do I gain by not sinning?'	4537
	35: 6	your sins are many, **w** does that do to him?	4537
	35: 7	If you are righteous, **w** do you give to him,	4537
	35: 7	or **w** does he receive from your hand?	4537
	36: 9	he tells them **w** they have **done—**	7189
	37:19	"Tell us **w** we should say to him;	4537
	38: 6	On **w** were its footings set,	4537
	38:19	**"W** is the way to the abode of light?	361+2296
	38:24	**W** is the way to the place where	361+2296
	40:16	**W** strength he has in his loins,	2180
	40:16	**w** power in the muscles of his belly!	NIH
	42: 7	you have not spoken of me *w* is **right,**	AIT
	42: 8	You have not spoken of me *w* is **right,**	AIT
	42: 9	did **w** the LORD told them;	889+3869
Ps	8: 4	**w** is man that you are mindful of him,	4537
	9:11	proclaim among the nations **w** he has **done.**	6613
	11: 3	**w** can the righteous do?"	4537
	12: 8	when *w* is **vile** is honored among men.	AIT
	15: 2	and who does *w* is **righteous,**	AIT
	17: 2	may your eyes see *w* is **right.**	AIT
	24: 4	to an idol or swear by *w* is **false.**	AIT
	25: 9	in **w** is right and teaches them his way.	2021
	27: 4	this is **w** I seek: that I may dwell in the	NIH
	28: 4	upon them **w** their hands have **done**	5126
	28: 4	and bring back upon them **w** they **deserve.**	1691
	28: 5	**w** his hands have **done,**	5126
	30: 9	**"W** gain is there in my destruction,	4537
	35:25	"Aha, **just w** we **wanted!"**	5883
	36: 4	and does not reject *w* is **wrong.**	AIT
	37:30	and his tongue speaks *w* is **just.**	AIT
	38:20	when I pursue *w* is **good.**	AIT
	39: 7	"But now, Lord, **w** do I look for?	4537
	44: 1	our fathers have told us **w** you did	7189[S]
	50:16	**"W right have you** to recite my laws	3870+4200+4537
	51: 4	have I sinned and done **w** is evil	2021
	52: 9	for *w you have* **done;**	AIT
	56: 4	**W** can mortal man do to me?	4537
	56:11	**W** can man do to me?	4537
	59: 7	See **w** they spew from their mouths—	NIH
	62:12	according to **w** he has **done.**	5126
	64: 9	and ponder **w** he has **done.**	5126
	66: 5	Come and see **w** God has **done,**	5149
	66:16	let me tell you **w** he has done for me.	889
	69: 4	I am forced to restore **w** I did not steal.	889
	73:12	This is **w** the wicked are like—	NIH
	77:13	**W** god is so great as our God?	4769
	78: 3	**w** we have heard and known,	889
	78: 3	**w** our fathers have told us.	NIH
	78:11	They forgot **w** he had **done,**	6613
	78:29	for he had given them **w** they **craved.**	9294
	85: 8	I will listen to **w** God the LORD will say;	4537
	85:12	The LORD will indeed give **w** is good,	2021
	89:34	**w** my lips have **uttered.**	4604
	89:47	For **w** futility you have created all men!	4537
	89:48	**W** man can live and not see death,	4769
	94: 2	pay back to the proud **w** they **deserve.**	1691
	95: 9	though they had seen **w** I **did.**	7189
	99: 4	in Jacob you have done *w* is **just** and right.	AIT
	105: 1	among the nations **w** he has **done.**	6613
	105:19	till **w** he **foretold** came to pass,	1821
	105:44	**w** others had **toiled for—**	6662
	106: 3	who constantly do *w* is **right.**	AIT
	106:13	But they soon forgot **w** he had **done** and did	5126
	106:15	So he gave them **w** they **asked for,**	8629
	106:39	They defiled themselves by **w** they **did;**	5126
	118: 6	**W** can man do to me?	4537
	118:17	**w** the LORD has **done.**	5126
	119:68	You are good, and *w you* **do** *is* **good;**	AIT
	119:121	I have done *w* is **righteous** and just;	AIT
	120: 3	**W** will he do to you,	4537
	120: 3	and **w** more besides, O deceitful tongue?	4537
	137: 7	**w** the Edomites did on the day Jerusalem	NIH
	137: 8	for **w** you have done to us—	1691[S]
	141: 4	Let not my heart be drawn to **w** is evil,	1821[S]
	143: 5	**w** your hands have **done.**	5126
	144: 3	O LORD, **w** is man that you care for him,	4537
Pr	1: 3	*doing w* is **right** and just and fair;	AIT
	2: 9	Then you will understand *w* is **right** and just	AIT
	4:10	Listen, my son, accept **w** I **say,**	609
	4:19	do not know **w** makes them stumble.	928+4537
	4:20	My son, pay attention to **w** I **say;**	1821
	5: 7	do not turn aside from **w** I **say.**	609+7023
	6: 2	if you have been trapped by **w** you **said,**	609+7023
	7:24	pay attention to **w** I **say.**	609+7023
	8: 6	I open my lips to speak *w* is **right.**	AIT
	8: 7	My mouth speaks *w* is **true,**	AIT
	8:19	*w* I **yield** surpasses choice silver.	AIT
	10:24	*W* the wicked **dreads** will overtake him;	AIT
	10:24	*w* the righteous **desire** will be granted.	AIT
	10:32	lips of the righteous know *w* is **fitting,**	AIT
	10:32	the mouth of the wicked only *w* is **perverse.**	AIT
	13: 5	The righteous hate **w** is false,	1821[S]
	14:22	But those who plan *w* is **good** find love	AIT
	17:16	**Of w use** is money in the hand of a fool,	2296+4200+4537
	18:22	a wife finds *w* is **good** and receives favor	AIT
	19:17	and he will reward him for **w** he has **done.**	1691
	19:22	*W* a man **desires** is unfailing love;	AIT
	21: 3	To do *w* is **right** and just is more acceptable	AIT
	21: 7	for they refuse to do *w* is **right.**	AIT
	22:17	apply your heart to **w** I **teach,**	1981
	23: 1	note well **w** is before you,	889
	23:16	when your lips speak *w* is **right.**	AIT
	24:12	according to **w** he has **done?**	7189
	24:22	who knows **w** calamities they can bring?	NIH
	24:29	I'll pay that man back for **w** he did."	3869
	24:32	to **w** I observed and learned a lesson	NIH
	24:32	and learned a lesson from **w** I saw:	NIH
	25: 7	**W** you have seen with your eyes	889
	25: 8	for **w** will you do in the end	4537
	27: 1	you do not know **w** a day may bring forth.	4537
	27: 7	to the hungry even *w* is **bitter** tastes sweet.	AIT
	30: 4	**W** is his name, and the name of his son?	4537
	31: 5	lest they drink and forget **w** the law decrees,	NIH
Ecc	1: 3	**W** does man gain from all his labor	4537
	1: 9	**W** has been will be again,	4537
	1: 9	**w** has been done will be done again;	4537
	1:13	**W** a heavy burden God has laid on men!	2085
	1:15	*W* **is twisted** cannot be straightened;	AIT
	1:15	*w* **is lacking** cannot be counted.	AIT
	2: 1	with pleasure to find out *w* is **good."**	AIT
	2: 2	And **w** does pleasure accomplish?"	4537
	2: 3	to see **w** was worthwhile for men	361+2296
	2:11	that my hands had done and **w** I had toiled	6662[S]
	2:12	**W more** can the king's successor do	3954+4537
	2:12	successor do than **w** has already been done?	889
	2:15	**W** then do I gain by being wise?"	4200+4537
	2:22	**W** does a man get for all the toil	4537
	3: 9	**W** does the worker gain from his toil?	4537
	3:11	they cannot fathom **w** God has done	2021+5126[S]
	3:15	and **w** will be has been before;	889
	3:22	For who can bring him to see **w** will happen	4537
	5: 6	be angry at **w** you **say** and destroy the work	7754
	5:11	And **w** benefit are they to the owner except	4537
	5:16	so he departs, and **w** does he gain,	4537
	6: 8	**W** advantage has a wise man over a fool?	4537
	6: 8	**W** does a poor man gain by knowing how	4537
	6: 9	Better **w** the eye **sees** than the roving of	5260
	6:10	and **w** man is has been known;	889
	6:12	For who knows **w** is good for a man in life,	4537
	6:12	Who can tell him **w** will happen under	4537
	7:13	Consider **w** God has **done:**	5126
	7:13	Who can straighten **w** he has made crooked?	889
	7:20	on earth who does *w* is **right** and never sins.	AIT
	7:27	"this is **w** I have discovered:	NIH
	8: 4	who can say to him, **"W** are you doing?"	4537
	8: 7	who can tell him **w** is to come?	889+3869
	8:14	righteous men who get **w** the wicked **deserve,**	3869+5126
	8:14	wicked men who get **w** the righteous **deserve.**	3869+5126
	8:17	No one can comprehend **w** goes on	2021+5126[S]
	9: 1	the wise and **w** they **do** are in God's hands,	6271
	9: 7	for it is now that God favors **w** you **do.**	5126
	10:14	No one knows **w** is coming—	4537
	10:14	who can tell him **w** will happen after him?	889
	10:20	a bird on the wing may report **w** you **say.**	1821
	11: 2	for you do not know **w** disaster may come	4537
	12:10	and **w** he wrote was upright and true.	1821[S]
SS	5: 8	if you find my lover, **w** will you tell him?	4537
	8: 8	**W** shall we do for our sister for the day	4537
Isa	1:11	sacrifices—**w** are they to me?"	4200+4537
	2: 1	This is **w** Isaiah son of Amoz saw	889
	2: 8	to **w** their fingers have made.	889
	2:22	Of **w** account is he?	4537
	3:11	**w** their hands have **done.**	1691
	3:15	**W** do you mean by crushing my people	4537
	5: 4	**W** more could have been done	4537
	5: 5	Now I will tell you **w** I am going to do	889
	7: 7	Yet **this is w** the Sovereign LORD says:	3907
	8:12	do not fear **w** they **fear,** and do not dread it.	AIT
	10: 3	**W** will you do on the day of reckoning,	4537
	10: 7	But this is not **w** he intends,	4027
	10: 7	this is not **w** he has in mind;	4027
	10:24	Therefore, **this is w** the Lord,	3907
	11: 3	He will not judge by **w** he **sees** *with* his eyes	5260
	11: 3	or decide by **w** he **hears** *with* his ears;	5461
	12: 4	among the nations **w** he has **done,**	6613
	14:32	**W** answer shall be given to the envoys of	4537
	18: 4	**This is w** the LORD says to me:	3907
	19:12	Let them show you and make known **w**	4537
	19:17	of **w** the LORD Almighty is planning	889
	20: 6	'See **w** has **happened** *to* those we relied on,	3907
	21: 3	I am staggered by *w* I **hear,**	AIT
	21: 3	I am bewildered by *w* I **see.**	AIT
	21: 6	**This is w** the Lord says to me:	3907
	21: 6	a lookout and have him report **w** he sees.	889
	21:10	I tell you **w** I have heard from	889
	21:11	"Watchman, **w** is left of the night?	4537
	21:11	Watchman, **w** is left of the night?"	4537
	21:16	**This is w** the Lord says to me:	3907
	22: 1	**W** troubles you now,	4537
	22:15	**This is w** the Lord, the LORD Almighty,	3907
	22:16	**W are you doing** here	3870+4200+4537
	22:22	**w** he opens no one can shut,	NIH
	22:22	and **w** he shuts no one can open.	NIH
	28:16	So **this is w** the Sovereign LORD says:	3907
	28:23	pay attention and hear **w** I **say.**	614
	29:16	Shall *w* is **formed** say to him who formed it,	AIT
	29:22	Therefore **this is w** the LORD,	3907
	30:10	"Give us no more visions of *w* is **right!**	AIT
	30:12	**this is w** the Holy One of Israel says:	3907
	30:15	**This is w** the Sovereign LORD,	3907
	31: 4	**This is w** the LORD says to me:	3907
	32: 9	hear **w** I **have to say!**	614
	33:13	You who are far away, hear **w** I have done;	889
	33:15	and speaks *w* is **right,** who rejects gain	AIT
	36: 4	"Tell Hezekiah, " **'This is w** the great king,	3907
	36: 4	On **w** are you basing this confidence	4537
	36:14	**This is w** the king says:	3907
	36:16	**This is w** the king of Assyria says:	3907
	36:22	told him **w** the field commander had **said.**	1821
	37: 3	They told him, **"This is w** Hezekiah says:	3907
	37: 6	**'This is w** the LORD says:	3907
	37: 6	Do not be afraid of **w** you have heard—	889
	37:11	Surely you have heard **w** the kings	889
	37:21	**"This is w** the LORD, the God of Israel,	3907
	37:30	"This year you will eat **w grows by itself,**	6206
	37:30	and the second year **w springs from** *that.*	8826
	37:33	"Therefore **this is w** the LORD says	3907
	38: 1	**"This is w** the LORD says:	3907
	38: 3	and have done **w** is good in your eyes."	2021
	38: 5	**'This is w** the LORD,	3907
	38: 7	that the LORD will do **w** he has promised:	1821+2021+2021+2296[S]
	38:15	But **w** can I say?	4537
	38:22	**"W** will be the sign that I will go up to	4537
	39: 2	the envoys gladly and showed them **w** was	NIH
	39: 3	**"W** did those men say,	4537

Isa 39: 4 **“W** did they see in your palace?” 4537
40: 6 And I said, **“W** shall I cry?” 4537
40:18 W image will you compare him to? 4537
41:22 to tell us **w** is going to happen. 889
41:22 Tell us **w** the former things were, 4537
41:23 tell us **w** the future holds, 2021
42: 5 **This is w** God the LORD says— 3907
43: 1 But now, **this is w** the LORD says— 3907
43:14 **This is w** the LORD says— 3907
43:16 **This is w** the LORD says— 3907
44: 2 **This is w** the LORD says— 3907
44: 6 **“This is w** the LORD says— 3907
44: 7 and lay out before me **w** has **happened** 2023[S]
44: 7 and *w is yet to* **come—** AIT
44: 7 yes, let him foretell **w** will come. 889
44:19 a detestable thing from *w* is **left?** AIT
44:24 **“This is w** the LORD says— 3907
45: 1 **“This is w** the LORD says to his anointed, 3907
45: 9 **‘W** are you making?’ 4537
45:10 **‘W** have you begotten?’ 4537
45:10 **‘W** have you brought to birth?’ 4537
45:11 **“This is w** the LORD says— 3907
45:14 **This is w** the LORD says: 3907
45:18 For **this is w** the LORD says— 3907
45:19 I declare *w* is **right.** AIT
45:21 Declare **w** is to be, present it— NIH
46:10 from ancient times, **w** is still to come. 889
46:11 **W** I have said, that will I bring about; NIH
46:11 **w** I have planned, that will I do. NIH
47: 7 or reflect on **w might happen.** 344
47:13 let them save you from **w** is coming 889
48:17 **This is w** the LORD says— 3907
48:17 who teaches you *w is* **best** for you, AIT
49: 4 Yet *w* is **due** me is in the LORD's hand, AIT
49: 7 **This is w** the LORD says— 3907
49: 8 **This is w** the LORD says: 3907
49:22 **This is w** the Sovereign LORD says: 3907
49:25 But **this is w** the LORD says: 3907
50: 1 **This is w** the LORD says: 3907
50:11 **This is w** you shall receive from my hand: 2296
51: 7 “Hear me, you who know *w* is **right,** AIT
51:22 **This is w** your Sovereign LORD says, 3907
52: 3 For **this is w** the LORD says: 3907
52: 4 For **this is w** the Sovereign LORD says: 3907
52: 5 “And now **w** do I have here?” 4537
52:15 For **w** they were not told, they will see, 889
52:15 they will see, and **w** they have not heard, 889
55: 2 Why spend money on *w* is not **bread,** AIT
55: 2 and your labor on *w* does not **satisfy?** AIT
55: 2 Listen, listen to me, and eat *w* is **good,** AIT
55:11 to me empty, but will accomplish **w** I desire 889
56: 1 **This is w** the LORD says: 3907
56: 1 “Maintain justice and do *w* is **right,** AIT
56: 4 For **this is w** the LORD says: 3907
56: 4 who choose **w** pleases me and hold fast 889
57:15 For **this is w** the high and lofty One says— 3907
58: 2 as if they were a nation that does *w* is **right** AIT
58: 5 Is that **w** you call a fast, NIH
59: 6 with **w** they **make.** 5126
59:18 According to **w** they have **done,** 1692
65: 8 **This is w** the LORD says: 3907
65:12 in my sight and chose **w** displeases me.” 889
65:13 Therefore **this is w** the Sovereign LORD says 3907
65:18 and rejoice forever in **w** I will create, 889
66: 1 **This is w** the LORD says: 3907
66: 4 and will bring upon them *w* they **dread.** AIT
66: 4 in my sight and chose **w** displeases me.” 889
66:12 For **this is w** the LORD says: 3907
Jer 1:11 **“W** do you see, Jeremiah?” 4537
1:13 **“W** do you see?” 4537
1:16 worshiping **w** their hands have **made.** 5126
2: 5 **This is w** the LORD says: 3907
2: 5 **“W** fault did your fathers find in me, 4537
2:23 consider **w** you have done. 4537
3: 6 “Have you seen **w** faithless Israel has done? 889
4: 3 **This is w** the LORD says to the men 3907
4:27 **This is w** the LORD says: 3907
4:30 **W** are you doing, O devastated one? 4537
5:13 so let **w** they say be done to them.” NIH
5:14 Therefore **this is w** 3907
5:31 But **w** will you do in the end? 4537
6: 6 **This is w** the LORD Almighty says: 3907
6: 9 **This is w** the LORD Almighty says: 3907
6:16 **This is w** the LORD says: 3907
6:18 O witnesses, **w** will happen to them. 889
6:20 **W do I care about** 2296+3276+4200+4200+4537
6:21 Therefore **this is w** the LORD says: 3907
6:22 **This is w** the LORD says: 3907
7: 3 **This is w** the LORD Almighty, 3907
7:12 and see **w** I did to it because of 889
7:14 **w** I did to Shiloh I will now do to 889+3869
7:17 not see **w** they are doing in the towns 4537
7:20 “ ‘Therefore **this is w** the Sovereign LORD 3907
7:21 “ **‘This is w** the LORD Almighty, 3907
8: 4 “Say to them, **‘This is w** the LORD says: 3907
8: 6 but they do not say *w* is **right.** AIT
8: 6 saying, **“W** have I done?” 4537
8: 9 **w kind** *of* wisdom do they have? 4537
8:13 **W** I have given them will be taken NIH
9: 7 Therefore **this is w** the LORD Almighty says 3907
9: 7 and test them, for **w else** can I do because 375
9:12 **W** man is wise enough to understand this? 4769
9:15 Therefore, **this is w** the LORD Almighty, 3907
9:17 **This is w** the LORD Almighty says: 3907
9:22 Say, **“This is w** the LORD declares: 3907
9:23 **This is w** the LORD says: 3907
10: 1 Hear **w** the LORD says to you, 1821+2021[S]
Jer 10: 2 **This is w** the LORD says: 3907
10: 9 **W** the craftsman and goldsmith have **made** 5126
10:18 For **this is w** the LORD says: 3907
11: 3 Tell them that **this is w** the LORD, 3907
11:11 Therefore **this is w** the LORD says: 3907
11:15 **“W is** my beloved **doing** in my temple 4200+4537
11:18 that time he showed me **w** they were **doing.** 5095
11:21 “Therefore **this is w** the LORD says about 3907
11:22 therefore **this is w** the LORD Almighty says: 3907
12: 4 “He will not see **w happens** *to* us.” 344
12:14 **This is w** the LORD says: 3907
13: 1 **This is w** the LORD said to me: 3907
13: 9 **“This is w** the LORD says: 3907
13:12 **‘This is w** the LORD, the God of Israel, 3907
13:13 then tell them, **‘This is w** the LORD says: 3907
13:21 **W** will you say when [the LORD] sets 4537
14:10 **This is w** the LORD says about this people: 3907
14:15 **this is w** the LORD says about 3907
15: 2 tell them, **‘This is w** the LORD says: 3907
15: 4 of the earth because of **w** Manasseh son 889
15:19 Therefore **this is w** the LORD says: 3907
16: 3 For **this is w** the LORD says about the sons 3907
16: 5 For **this is w** the LORD says: 3907
16: 9 For **this is w** the LORD Almighty, 3907
16:10 **W** wrong have we done? 4537
16:10 **W** sin have we committed against 4537
17: 5 **This is w** the LORD says: 3907
17:10 according to **w** his deeds **deserve.”** 7262
17:16 **W passes** my lips is open before you. 4604
17:19 **This is w** the LORD said to me: 3907
17:21 **This is w** the LORD says: 3907
18:11 **‘This is w** the LORD says: Look! 3907
18:13 Therefore **this is w** the LORD says: 3907
18:19 **w** my accusers are **saying!** 7754
19: 1 **This is w** the LORD says: 3907
19: 3 **This is w** the LORD Almighty, 3907
19:11 **‘This is w** the LORD Almighty says: 3907
19:12 **This is w** I will do to this place and 4027
19:15 **“This is w** the LORD Almighty, the God 3907
20: 4 For **this is w** the LORD says: 3907
21: 4 **‘This is w** the LORD, the God 3907
21: 8 tell the people, **‘This is w** the LORD says: 3907
21:12 **this is w** the LORD says: 3907
22: 1 **This is w** the LORD says: 3907
22: 3 **This is w** the LORD says: 3907
22: 3 Do *w* is **just** and right. AIT
22: 6 For **this is w** the LORD says about 3907
22:11 For **this is w** the LORD says 3907
22:15 He did *w* was **right** and just, AIT
22:16 Is that not **w** it means to know me?” NIH
22:18 Therefore **this is w** the LORD says 3907
22:30 **This is w** the LORD says: 3907
23: 2 Therefore **this is w** the LORD, 3907
23: 5 and do *w* is **just** and right in the land. AIT
23:15 **this is w** the LORD Almighty says 3907
23:16 **This is w** the LORD Almighty says: 3907
23:16 not listen to **w** the prophets are prophesying 1821[S]
23:25 “I have heard **w** the prophets say 889
23:28 For **w** has straw to do with grain?” 4537
23:33 ask you, **‘W** is the oracle of the LORD?’ 4537
23:33 say to them, **‘W** oracle?’ 4537
23:35 **This is w** each of you keeps on saying 3907
23:35 **‘W** is the LORD's answer?’ 4537
23:35 or **‘W** has the LORD spoken?’ 4537
23:37 **This is w** you keep saying to a prophet: 3907
23:37 **‘W** is the LORD's answer to you?’ 4537
23:37 or **‘W** has the LORD spoken?’ 4537
23:38 **this is w** the LORD says: 3907
24: 3 Then the LORD asked me, **“W** do you see, 4537
24: 5 **“This is w** the LORD, the God 3907
25: 6 **w** your hands have **made.** 5126
25: 7 **w** your hands have **made,** 5126
25:15 **This is w** the LORD, the God of Israel, 3907
25:27 tell them, **‘This is w** the LORD Almighty, 3907
25:28 **‘This is w** the LORD Almighty says: 3907
25:32 **This is w** the LORD Almighty says: “Look! 3907
26: 2 **“This is w** the LORD says: 3907
26: 4 Say to them, **‘This is w** the LORD says: 3907
26:18 **‘This is w** the LORD Almighty says: 3907
27: 2 **This is w** the LORD said to me: 3907
27: 4 **‘This is w** the LORD Almighty, 3907
27:16 **“This is w** the LORD says: 3907
27:19 For **this is w** the LORD Almighty says 3907
27:21 **this is w** the LORD Almighty, 3907
28: 2 **“This is w** the LORD Almighty, the God 3907
28: 7 listen to **w** I have to say 1821+2021+2021+2206[S]
28:11 **“This is w** the LORD says: 3907
28:13 **‘This is w** the LORD says: 3907
28:14 **This is w** the LORD Almighty, 3907
28:16 Therefore, **this is w** the LORD says: 3907
29: 4 **This is w** the LORD Almighty, the God 3907
29: 5 plant gardens and eat *w* they **produce.** AIT
29: 8 Yes, **this is w** the LORD Almighty, 3907
29:10 **This is w** the LORD says: 3907
29:16 but **this is w** the LORD says about 3907
29:17 **this is w** the LORD Almighty says: 3907
29:21 **This is w** the LORD Almighty, 3907
29:25 **“This is w** the LORD Almighty, the God 3907
29:28 plant gardens and eat *w* they **produce.’ ”** AIT
29:31 **‘This is w** the LORD says about Shemaiah 3907
29:32 **this is w** the LORD says: 3907
30: 2 **“This is w** the LORD, the God of Israel, 3907
30: 5 **“This is w** the LORD says: 3907
30:12 **“This is w** the LORD says: 3907
30:18 **“This is w** the LORD says: 3907
31: 2 **This is w** the LORD says: 3907
31: 7 **This is w** the LORD says: 3907
Jer 31:15 **This is w** the LORD says: 3907
31:16 **This is w** the LORD says: 3907
31:23 **This is w** the LORD Almighty, 3907
31:35 **This is w** the LORD says, 3907
31:37 **This is w** the LORD says: 3907
32: 3 You say, **‘This is w** the LORD says: 3907
32:14 **‘This is w** the LORD Almighty, the God 3907
32:15 For **this is w** the LORD Almighty, 3907
32:23 they did not do **w** you commanded them 3972[S]
32:24 **W** you said has happened, as you now see. 889
32:28 Therefore, **this is w** the LORD says: 3907
32:30 **w** their hands have **made,** 5126
32:36 but **this is w** the LORD, the God of Israel, 3907
32:42 **“This is w** the LORD says: 3907
33: 2 **“This is w** the LORD says, he who made 3907
33: 4 For **this is w** the LORD, the God of Israel, 3907
33:10 **“This is w** the LORD says: 3907
33:12 **“This is w** the LORD Almighty says: 3907
33:15 he will do *w* is **just** and right in the land. AIT
33:17 For **this is w** the LORD says: 3907
33:20 **“This is w** the LORD says: 3907
33:25 **This is w** the LORD says: 3907
34: 2 **“This is w** the LORD, the God 3907
34: 2 **‘This is w** the LORD says: 3907
34: 4 **This is w** the LORD says concerning you: 3907
34:13 **“This is w** the LORD, the God 3907
34:15 Recently you repented and did *w* is **right** AIT
34:17 “Therefore, **this is w** the LORD says: 3907
35:13 **“This is w** the LORD Almighty, the God 3907
35:17 **this is w** the LORD God Almighty, 3907
35:18 **“This is w** the LORD Almighty, 3907
35:19 Therefore, **this is w** the LORD Almighty, 3907
36:29 **‘This is w** the LORD says: 3907
36:30 **this is w** the LORD says 3907
37: 7 **“This is w** the LORD, the God 3907
37: 9 **“This is w** the LORD says: 3907
37:18 **“W** crime have I committed against you 4537
38: 1 heard **w** Jeremiah was telling all 1821+2021[S]
38: 2 **“This is w** the LORD says: 3907
38: 3 And **this is w** the LORD says: 3907
38:17 **“This is w** the LORD God Almighty, 3907
38:20 “Obey the LORD by doing **w** I tell you. 889
38:21 is **w** the LORD has revealed to me: 1821+2021[S]
38:25 ‘Tell us **w** you said to the king and what 4537
38:25 ‘Tell us what you said to the king and **w** 4537
39:16 **‘This is w** the LORD Almighty, 3907
40:16 *W* you *are* **saying** about Ishmael is not true.” AIT
42: 3 we should go and **w** we should do.” 1821+2021[S]
42: 9 He said to them, **“This is w** the LORD, 3907
42:15 **This is w** the LORD Almighty, 3907
42:18 **This is w** the LORD Almighty, 3907
43:10 **‘This is w** the LORD Almighty, 3907
44: 2 **“This is w** the LORD Almighty, the God 3907
44: 7 “Now **this is w** the LORD God Almighty, 3907
44: 8 to anger with **w** your hands have **made,** 5126
44:11 “Therefore, **this is w** the LORD Almighty, 3907
44:25 **This is w** the LORD Almighty, 3907
44:25 shown by your actions **w** you promised NIH
44:25 “Go ahead then, do **w** you **promised!** 5624
44:30 **This is w** the LORD says: 3907
45: 1 This is **w** Jeremiah the prophet told Baruch 1821[S]
45: 2 **“This is w** the LORD, the God 3907
45: 4 **‘This is w** the LORD says: 3907
45: 4 I will overthrow **w** I have built 889
45: 4 and uproot **w** I have planted, 889
46: 5 **W** do I see? They are terrified, 4508
47: 2 **This is w** the LORD says: 3907
48: 1 **This is w** the LORD Almighty, 3907
48:19 ask them, **‘W** has happened?’ 4537
48:40 **This is w** the LORD says: “Look! 3907
49: 1 **This is w** the LORD says: 3907
49: 7 **This is w** the LORD Almighty says: 3907
49:12 **This is w** the LORD says: 3907
49:19 And **w** shepherd can stand against me?” 4769
49:20 hear **w** the LORD has planned 889
49:20 **w** he has purposed against those who live 889
49:28 **This is w** the LORD says: 3907
49:35 **This is w** the LORD Almighty says: 3907
50:18 Therefore **this is w** the LORD Almighty, 3907
50:33 **This is w** the LORD Almighty says: 3907
50:44 And **w** shepherd can stand against me? 2296+4769
50:45 hear **w** the LORD has planned 889
50:45 **w** he has purposed against the land of 889
51: 1 **This is w** the LORD says: 3907
51: 6 he will pay her **w** she **deserves.** 1691
51:10 tell in Zion **w** the LORD our God has **done.’** 5126
51:33 **This is w** the LORD Almighty, 3907
51:36 Therefore, **this is w** the LORD says: 3907
51:41 **W** a horror Babylon will be among 375
51:44 make him spew out **w** he has **swallowed.** 1183
51:58 **This is w** the LORD Almighty says: 3907
La 1:21 they rejoice at **w** you have done. NIH
2:13 **W** can I say for you? 4537
2:13 With **w** can I compare you, 4537
2:13 To **w** can I liken you, 4537
2:17 The LORD has done **w** he planned; 889
3:17 I have forgotten **w** prosperity is. NIH
3:51 **W I see** brings grief to my soul because 6524
3:62 *w* my enemies **whisper** and mutter AIT
3:64 Pay them back **w** they **deserve,** O LORD, 1691
3:64 for **w** their hands have **done.** 5126
5: 1 O LORD, **w** has happened to us; 4537
Eze 1: 5 and in the fire was *w* **looked like** AIT
1:22 of the living creatures was *w* **looked like** AIT
1:26 over their heads was **w** looked like a throne NIH
1:27 I saw that from *w* **appeared** to be his waist AIT
2: 4 **‘This is w** the Sovereign LORD says.’ 3907

Eze 2: 6 be afraid of w they say or terrified by them, 1821
2: 8 you, son of man, listen to w I say to you. 889
2: 8 open your mouth and eat w I give you." 889
3: 1 eat w is before you, eat this scroll; 889
3:11 'This is w the Sovereign LORD says,' 3907
3:27 'This is w the Sovereign LORD says.' 3907
5: 5 "This is w the Sovereign LORD says: 3907
5: 7 "Therefore this is w the Sovereign LORD 3907
5: 8 "Therefore this is w the Sovereign LORD 3907
5: 9 I will do to you w I have never done 889+4017
6: 3 This is w the Sovereign LORD says to 3907
6: 6 and w you have made wiped out. 5126
6:11 " 'This is w the Sovereign LORD says: 3907
7: 2 this is w the Sovereign LORD says to 3907
7: 5 "This is w the Sovereign LORD says: 3907
8: 2 From *w* appeared to be his waist AIT
8: 3 He stretched out *w* looked like a hand AIT
8: 6 do you see w they are doing— 4537
8:12 have you seen w the elders of the house 889
9:10 on their own heads w they have done." 2006
10: 8 be seen *w* looked like the hands of a man.) AIT
10:21 and under their wings was *w* looked like AIT
11: 5 "This is w the LORD says: 3907
11: 5 That is w you are saying, O house of Israel, 4027
11: 5 but I know w is going through your mind. 5091
11: 7 "Therefore this is w the Sovereign LORD 3907
11: 8 and the sword is w I will bring against you, NIH
11:16 'This is w the Sovereign LORD says: 3907
11:17 'This is w the Sovereign LORD says: 3907
11:21 down on their own heads w they have done, 2006
12: 9 'W are you doing?' 4537
12:10 'This is w the Sovereign LORD says: 3907
12:19 'This is w the Sovereign LORD says 3907
12:22 w is this proverb you have in the land 4537
12:23 'This is w the Sovereign LORD says: 3907
12:25 But I the LORD will speak w I will, 889
12:28 'This is w the Sovereign LORD says: 3907
13: 3 This is w the Sovereign LORD says: 3907
13: 8 " 'Therefore this is w the Sovereign LORD 3907
13:13 " 'Therefore this is w the Sovereign LORD 3907
13:18 'This is w the Sovereign LORD says: 3907
13:20 " 'Therefore this is w the Sovereign LORD 3907
14: 4 'This is w the Sovereign LORD says: 3907
14: 6 'This is w the Sovereign LORD says: 3907
14:21 "For this is w the Sovereign LORD says: 3907
15: 6 "Therefore this is w the Sovereign LORD 3907
16: 3 'This is w the Sovereign LORD says 3907
16:19 *That is w* happened, AIT
16:36 This is w the Sovereign LORD says: 3907
16:43 down on your head w you have done, 2006
16:48 and her daughters never did w you 889+3869
16:55 will return to *w* they were before; AIT
16:55 will return to *w* you were before. AIT
16:59 " 'This is w the Sovereign LORD says: 3907
17: 3 'This is w the Sovereign LORD says: 3907
17: 9 'This is w the Sovereign LORD says: 3907
17:12 'Do you not know w these things mean?' 4537
17:19 " 'Therefore this is w the Sovereign LORD 3907
17:22 " 'This is w the Sovereign LORD says: 3907
18: 2 "W do you people mean 4013+4200+4537
18: 5 a righteous man who does *w* is just AIT
18: 7 but returns w he took in pledge 2481
18:12 does not return w he took in pledge. 2478
18:18 robbed his brother and did w was wrong 889
18:19 Since the son has done *w* is just and right AIT
18:21 and keeps all my decrees and does *w* is just AIT
18:27 and does *w* is just and right, AIT
19: 2 " 'W a lioness was your mother among 4537
20: 3 'This is w the Sovereign LORD says: 3907
20: 5 'This is w the Sovereign LORD says: 3907
20: 9 the sake of my name I did w would keep it NIH
20:14 the sake of my name I did w would keep it NIH
20:22 the sake of my name I did w would keep it NIH
20:27 'This is w the Sovereign LORD says: 3907
20:29 W is this high place you go to?' " 4537
20:30 'This is w the Sovereign LORD says: 3907
20:32 But w you have in mind will never happen. 2021
20:39 this is w the Sovereign LORD says: 3907
20:47 This is w the Sovereign LORD says: 3907
21: 3 'This is w the LORD says: 3907
21: 9 prophesy and say, 'This is w the Lord says: 3907
21:13 And w if the scepter [of Judah], 4537
21:24 "Therefore this is w the Sovereign LORD 3907
21:26 this is w the Sovereign LORD says: 3907
21:28 'This is w the Sovereign LORD says about 3907
22: 3 'This is w the Sovereign LORD says: 3907
22:19 Therefore this is w the Sovereign LORD 3907
22:28 'This is w the Sovereign LORD says'— 3907
23:22 this is w the Sovereign LORD says: 3907
23:28 "For this is w the Sovereign LORD says: 3907
23:32 "This is w the Sovereign LORD says: 3907
23:35 "Therefore this is w the Sovereign LORD 3907
23:39 That is w they did in my house. 3907
23:46 "This is w the Sovereign LORD says: 3907
24: 3 'This is w the Sovereign LORD says: 3907
24: 6 " 'For this is w the Sovereign LORD says: 3907
24: 9 " 'Therefore this is w the Sovereign LORD 3907
24:19 "Won't you tell us w these things have 4537
24:21 'This is w the Sovereign LORD says: 3907
25: 3 This is w the Sovereign LORD says: 3907
25: 6 For this is w the Sovereign LORD says: 3907
25: 8 "This is w the Sovereign LORD says: 3907
25:12 "This is w the Sovereign LORD says: 3907
25:13 therefore this is w the Sovereign LORD 3907
25:15 "This is w the Sovereign LORD says: 3907
25:16 therefore this is w the Sovereign LORD says: 3907
26: 3 therefore this is w the Sovereign LORD says: 3907

Eze 26: 7 "For this is w the Sovereign LORD says: 3907
26:15 "This is w the Sovereign LORD says 3907
26:19 "This is w the Sovereign LORD says: 3907
27: 3 'This is w the Sovereign LORD says: 3907
28: 2 'This is w the Sovereign LORD says: 3907
28: 6 " 'Therefore this is w the Sovereign LORD 3907
28:12 'This is w the Sovereign LORD says: 3907
28:22 'This is w the Sovereign LORD says: 3907
28:25 " 'This is w the Sovereign LORD says: 3907
29: 3 'This is w the Sovereign LORD says: 3907
29: 8 " 'Therefore this is w the Sovereign LORD 3907
29:13 " 'Yet this is w the Sovereign LORD says: 3907
29:19 Therefore this is w the Sovereign LORD 3907
30: 2 'This is w the Sovereign LORD says: 3907
30: 6 " 'This is w the LORD says: 3907
30:10 " 'This is w the Sovereign LORD says: 3907
30:13 " 'This is w the Sovereign LORD says: 3907
30:22 Therefore this is w the Sovereign LORD 3907
31:10 " 'Therefore this is w the Sovereign LORD 3907
31:15 " 'This is w the Sovereign LORD says: 3907
32: 3 " 'This is w the Sovereign LORD says: 3907
32:11 " 'For this is w the Sovereign LORD says: 3907
33:10 'This is w you are saying: 4027
33:14 from his sin and does *w* is just and right— AIT
33:15 w he took in pledge for a loan, 2478
33:15 returns w he has stolen, 1611
33:16 He has done *w* is just and right; AIT
33:19 from his wickedness and does *w* is just AIT
33:25 'This is w the Sovereign LORD says: 3907
33:27 'This is w the Sovereign LORD says: 3907
34: 2 'This is w the Sovereign LORD says: 3907
34:10 This is w the Sovereign LORD says: 3907
34:11 " 'For this is w the Sovereign LORD says: 3907
34:17 this is w the Sovereign LORD says: 3907
34:19 flock feed on w you have trampled 5330+8079
34:19 and drink w you have muddied 5343
34:20 " 'Therefore this is w the Sovereign LORD 3907
35: 3 'This is w the Sovereign LORD says: 3907
35:14 This is w the Sovereign LORD says: 3907
36: 2 This is w the Sovereign LORD says: 3907
36: 3 'This is w the Sovereign LORD says: 3907
36: 4 This is w the Sovereign LORD says to 3907
36: 5 this is w the Sovereign LORD says: 3907
36: 6 'This is w the Sovereign LORD says: 3907
36: 7 Therefore this is w the Sovereign LORD 3907
36:13 " 'This is w the Sovereign LORD says: 3907
36:22 'This is w the Sovereign LORD says: 3907
36:33 " 'This is w the Sovereign LORD says: 3907
36:36 the LORD have rebuilt w was destroyed 2021
36:36 and have replanted w was desolate. 2021
36:37 "This is w the Sovereign LORD says: 3907
37: 5 This is w the Sovereign LORD says 3907
37: 9 'This is w the Sovereign LORD says: 3907
37:12 'This is w the Sovereign LORD says: 3907
37:18 'Won't you tell us w you mean by this?' 4537
37:19 'This is w the Sovereign LORD says: 3907
37:21 'This is w the Sovereign LORD says: 3907
38: 3 'This is w the Sovereign LORD says: 3907
38:10 " 'This is w the Sovereign LORD says: 3907
38:14 'This is w the Sovereign LORD says: 3907
38:17 " 'This is w the Sovereign LORD says: 3907
38:18 *This is w will* happen in that day: AIT
39: 1 'This is w the Sovereign LORD says: 3907
39:17 this is w the Sovereign LORD says: 3907
39:25 "Therefore this is w the Sovereign LORD 3907
42:15 When he had finished measuring w was NIH
43:18 this is w the Sovereign LORD says: 3907
44: 6 'This is w the Sovereign LORD says: 3907
44: 9 This is w the Sovereign LORD says: 3907
45: 9 " 'This is w the Sovereign LORD says: 3907
45: 9 and oppression and do *w* is just and right. AIT
45:18 " 'This is w the Sovereign LORD says: 3907
46: 1 " 'This is w the Sovereign LORD says: 3907
46:16 " 'This is w the Sovereign LORD says: 3907
47:13 This is w the Sovereign LORD says: 3907
48:18 W remains of the area, 2021
48:21 "W remains on both sides of the area 2021
Da 1:13 in accordance with w you see." 889
2: 2 to tell him *w* he had dreamed. AIT
2: 3 and I want to know w it means." 3359
2: 5 "This is w I have firmly decided: NIH
2: 5 not tell me w my dream was and interpret it, NIH
2: 8 that this is w I have firmly decided: NIH
2:10 a man on earth who can do w the king asks! 10418
2:11 W the king asks is too difficult. 10002+10418[S]
2:22 he knows w lies in darkness, 10408
2:23 you have made known to me w we asked 10168
2:25 who can tell the king w his dream means." AIT
2:26 "Are you able to tell me w I saw 10168
2:28 He has shown King Nebuchadnezzar w will happen 10408
2:29 revealer of mysteries showed you w is going to happen. 10408
2:30 and that you may understand w went NIH
2:45 the king w will take place in the future. 10408
3: 4 "This is w you are commanded to do, NIH
3:15 Then w god will be able to rescue you 10426
4:18 Now, Belteshazzar, tell me *w* it means, AIT
4:27 Renounce your sins by doing *w* is right, AIT
4:31 "This is w is decreed for you, NIH
4:33 Immediately w had been said 10418
4:35 "W have you done?" 10408
5: 7 and tells me *w* it means will be clothed AIT
5: 8 the writing or tell the king *w* it meant. AIT
5:12 and he will tell you w the writing means." AIT
5:15 to read this writing and tell me *w* it means, AIT
5:16 and tell me *w* it means, AIT

Da 5:17 for the king and tell him *w* it means. AIT
5:26 "This is *w* these words mean: AIT
8:19 "I am going to tell you w will happen later 889
9:12 like w has been done to Jerusalem. 889
10:14 to you w will happen to your people in 889
10:21 but first I will tell you w is written in 2021
11:24 and will achieve w neither his fathers 889
11:29 be different from w it was before. NIH
11:36 for *w has* been determined must take place. AIT
12: 8 w will the outcome of all this be?" 4537
Hos 5: 9 the tribes of Israel I proclaim *w is* certain. AIT
6: 4 "W can I do with you, Ephraim? 4537
6: 4 W can I do with you, Judah? 4537
8: 3 But Israel has rejected w is good; NIH
9: 5 W will you do on the day of your appointed 4537
9:14 w will you give them? 4537
10: 3 if we had a king, w could he do for us?" 4537
14: 3 to w our own hands have made, 5126
14: 8 O Ephraim, w more have I to do with idols? 4537
Joel 1: 4 *W* the locust swarm has left AIT
1: 4 *w* the great locusts have left AIT
1: 4 *w* the young locusts have left AIT
3: 4 "Now w have you against me, 4537
3: 4 on your own heads w you have done. 1691
3: 7 on your own heads w you have done. 1691
Am 1: 1 w he saw concerning Israel two years 889
1: 3 This is w the LORD says: 3907
1: 6 This is w the LORD says: 3907
1: 9 This is w the LORD says: 3907
1:11 This is w the LORD says: 3907
1:13 This is w the LORD says: 3907
2: 1 This is w the LORD says: 3907
2: 4 This is w the LORD says: 3907
2: 6 This is w the LORD says: 3907
3:11 Therefore this is w the Sovereign LORD 3907
3:12 This is w the LORD says: 3907
4: 5 you Israelites, for this is w you love to do," 4027
4:12 "Therefore this is w I will do to you, Israel, 3907
5: 3 This is w the Sovereign LORD says: 3907
5: 4 This is w the LORD says to the house 3907
5:16 Therefore this is w the Lord, 3907
7: 1 This is w the Sovereign LORD showed me: 3907
7: 4 This is w the Sovereign LORD showed me: 3907
7: 7 This is w he showed me: 3907
7: 8 LORD asked me, "W do you see, Amos?" 4537
7:11 For this is w Amos is saying: 3907
7:17 "Therefore this is w the LORD says: 3907
8: 1 This is w the Sovereign LORD showed me: 3907
8: 2 "W do you see, Amos?" 4537
Ob 1: 1 This is w the Sovereign LORD says 3907
1: 5 Oh, w a disaster awaits you— 375
Jnh 1: 8 W do you do? Where do you come from? 4537
1: 8 W is your country? 4537
1: 8 From w people are you?" 2296
1:10 "W have you done?" 4537
1:11 "W should we do to you to make the sea 4537
2: 9 W I have vowed I will make good. 889
3:10 When God saw w they did and 5126
4: 2 is this not w I said when I was still at home? 1821
4: 5 and waited to see w would happen to 4537
Mic 1: 5 W is Jacob's transgression? 4769
1: 5 W is Judah's high place? 4769
3: 5 This is w the LORD says: 3907
6: 1 Listen to w the LORD says: 889
6: 1 let the hills hear w you have to say. 7754
6: 3 "My people, w have I done to you? 4537
6: 5 remember w Balak king of Moab counseled 4537
6: 5 of Moab counseled and w Balaam son 4537
6: 6 With w shall I come before the LORD 4537
6: 8 He has showed you, O man, w is good. 4537
6: 8 And w does the LORD require of you? 4537
6:14 because w you save I will give to the sword. 889
7: 1 W misery is mine! 518
7: 3 the powerful dictate w they desire— NIH
Na 1:12 This is w the LORD says: 3907
Hab 2: 1 I will look to see w he will say to me, 4537
2: 1 w answer I am to give to this complaint. 4537
2:18 "Of w value is an idol, 4537
Zep 2: 3 you who do w he commands. 889
2:10 This is w they will get in return NIH
2:15 W a ruin she has become, 375
Hag 1: 2 This is w the LORD Almighty says: 3907
1: 5 Now this is w the LORD Almighty says: 3907
1: 7 This is w the LORD Almighty says: 3907
1: 9 W you brought home, I blew away. NIH
2: 5 'This is w I covenanted with you 889
2: 6 "This is w the LORD Almighty says: 3907
2:11 "This is w the LORD Almighty says: 3907
2:11 'Ask the priests w the law says: NIH
Zec 1: 3 This is w the LORD Almighty says: 3907
1: 4 This is w the LORD Almighty says: 3907
1: 6 w our ways and practices deserve, 3869
1: 9 I asked, "W are these, my lord?" 4537
1: 9 "I will show you w they are." 4537
1:14 This is w the LORD Almighty says: 3907
1:16 "Therefore, this is w the LORD says: 3907
1:17 This is w the LORD Almighty says: 3907
1:19 to me, "W are these?" 4537
1:21 I asked, "W are these coming to do?" 4537
2: 8 For this is w the LORD Almighty says: 3907
3: 7 "This is w the LORD Almighty says: 3907
4: 2 He asked me, "W do you see?" 4537
4: 4 "W are these, my lord?" 4537
4: 5 "Do you not know w these are?" 4537
4: 7 "W are you, O mighty mountain? 4769
4:11 "W are these two olive trees on the right 4537
4:12 "W are these two olive branches beside 4537

Zec 4:13 He replied, "Do you not know w these are?" 4537
5: 2 He asked me, "W do you see?" 4537
5: 3 for according to w it says on one side, NIH
5: 3 and according to w it says on the other, NIH
5: 5 up and see w this is that is appearing." 4537
5: 6 I asked, "W is it?" 4537
6: 4 "W are these, my lord?" 4537
6:12 Tell him this is w the LORD Almighty says: 3907
7: 9 "This is w the LORD Almighty says: 3907
8: 2 This is w the LORD Almighty says: 3907
8: 3 This is w the LORD says: 3907
8: 4 This is w the LORD Almighty says: 3907
8: 6 This is w the LORD Almighty says: 3907
8: 7 This is w the LORD Almighty says: 3907
8: 9 This is w the LORD Almighty says: 3907
8:14 This is w the LORD Almighty says: 3907
8:19 This is w the LORD Almighty says: 3907
8:20 This is w the LORD Almighty says: 3907
8:23 This is w the LORD Almighty says: 3907
11: 4 This is w the LORD my God says: 3907
13: 6 'W are these wounds on your body?' 4537
Mal 1: 4 But this is w the LORD Almighty says: 3907
1:13 And you say, 'W a burden!' 4537
3:13 you ask, 'W have we said against you?' 4537
3:14 W did we gain by carrying out his 4537
Mt 1:20 because w is conceived in her is from 3836
1:22 to fulfill w the Lord had said through 3836
1:24 he did w the angel of the Lord had 6055
2: 5 "for this is w the prophet has written: 4048
2:15 so was fulfilled w the Lord had said through 3836
2:17 Then w was said through the prophet 3836
2:23 So was fulfilled w was said through 3836
4:14 to fulfill w was said through 3836
5:46 w reward will you get? 5515
5:47 w are you doing more than others? 5515
6: 3 know w your right hand is doing, 5515
6: 4 your Father, who sees w is done in secret, NIG
6: 6 your Father, who sees w is done in secret, NIG
6: 8 for your Father knows w you need 4005
6:18 your Father, who sees w is done in secret, NIG
6:25 w you will eat or drink; 5515
6:25 or about your body, w you will wear. 5515
6:31 So do not worry, saying, 'W shall we eat?' 5515
6:31 or 'W shall we drink?' 5515
6:31 or 'W shall we wear?' 5515
7: 6 "Do not give dogs w is sacred; 3836
7:12 do to others w you would have them do to you, 1569+4012
8:17 This was to fulfill w was spoken through 3836
8:27 "W kind of *man* is this? 4534
8:29 "W do you want with us, 2779+5515
8:33 including w had happened to 3836
9:13 But go and learn w this means: 5515
10:19 not worry about w to say or how to say it. 5515
10:19 At that time you will be given w to say, 5515
10:27 W I tell you in the dark, 4005
10:27 w is whispered in your ear, 4005
11: 2 John heard in prison w Christ was doing, 3836
11: 4 "Go back and report to John w you hear 4005
11: 7 "W did you go out into the desert to see? 5515
11: 8 If not, w did you go out to see? 5515
11: 9 Then w did you go out to see? 5515
11:16 "*To* w can I compare this generation? 5515
12: 2 Your disciples are doing w is unlawful on 4005
12: 3 "Haven't you read w David did when he 5515
12: 7 If you had known w these words mean, 5515
12:17 This was to fulfill w was spoken through 3836
13: 8 a hundred, sixty or thirty times w was sown. NIG
13:12 even w he has will be taken from him. 4005
13:17 and righteous men longed to see w you see 4005
13:17 and to hear w you hear but did not hear it. 4005
13:18 then to w the parable of the sower means: NIG
13:19 and snatches away w was sown in his heart. 3836
13:23 sixty or thirty times w was sown." NIG
13:35 So was fulfilled w was spoken through 3836
14:13 When Jesus heard w had happened, NIG
15:11 W goes into a man's mouth does 3836
15:11 but w comes out of his mouth, 3836
15:11 that is w makes him 'unclean.' " 3124
15:20 These are w make a man 'unclean'; 3836
16:15 "But w about you?" NIG
16:26 W good will it be for a man if he gains 5515
16:26 w can a man give in exchange for his soul? 5515
16:27 according to w he has done. 3836
17: 9 "Don't tell anyone w you have seen, 3836
17:25 "W do you think, Simon?" 5515
18:12 "W do you think? 5515
18:28 'Pay back w you owe me!' 1623+5516
18:31 the other servants saw w had happened, 3836
19: 6 Therefore w God has joined together, 4005
19:16 w good thing must I do to get eternal life?" 5515
19:17 "Why do you ask me about w is good?" 3836
19:20 "W do I still lack?" 5515
19:27 W then will there be for us?" 5515
20:15 to do w I want with my own money? 4005
20:21 "W is it you want?" 5515
20:22 "You don't know w you are asking," 5515
20:32 "W do you want me to do for you?" 5515
21: 4 to fulfill w was spoken through the prophet: 3836
21:16 "Do you hear w these children are saying?" 5515
21:21 only can you do w was done to the fig tree, 3836
21:23 By w authority are you doing these things?" 4481
21:24 by w authority I am doing these things. 4481
21:27 by w authority I am doing these things. 4481
21:28 "W do you think? 5515
21:31 "Which of the two did w his father wanted?" NIG
21:40 w will he do to those tenants?" 5515
Mt 22:17 Tell us then, w is your opinion? 5515
22:21 "Give to Caesar w is Caesar's, 3836
22:21 and to God w is God's." 3836
22:31 have you not read w God said to you, 3306+3836[S]
22:42 "W do you think about the Christ? 5515
23: 3 But do not do w they do, NIG
23: 3 for they do not practice w they preach. NIG
24: 3 and w will be the sign of your coming and 5515
24:39 about w would happen until the flood came NIG
24:42 not know *on* w day your Lord will come. 4481
24:43 of the house had known *at* w time of night 4481
25:25 See, here is w belongs to you.' 3836
25:29 even w he has will be taken from him. 4005
26:13 w she has done will also be told, 4005
26:15 "W are you willing to give me if I hand him 5515
26:50 replied, "Friend, do w you came for." 2093+4005
26:62 W is this testimony that these men 5515
26:66 W do you think?" 5515
26:70 "I don't know w you're talking about," 5515
27: 4 "W is that to us?" 5515
27: 9 Then w was spoken by Jeremiah 3836
27:22 "W shall I do, then, with Jesus 5515
27:23 W crime has he committed?" 5515
Mk 1:24 "W do you want with us, Jesus 2779+5515
1:27 that they asked each other, "W is this? 5515
2: 8 that this was w they were thinking NIG
2:24 why are they doing w is unlawful on 4005
2:25 "Have you never read w David did when he 5515
4:20 sixty or even a hundred times w was sown." NIG
4:24 "Consider carefully w you hear," 5515
4:25 even w he has will be taken from him." 4005
4:26 "This is w the kingdom of God is like. 4048
4:30 "W shall we say the kingdom of God is 4802
4:30 w parable shall we use to describe it? 1877+5515
5: 7 "W do you want with me, Jesus, 2779+5515
5: 9 Then Jesus asked him, "W is your name?" 5515
5:14 the people went out to see w had happened. 5515
5:16 told the people w had happened to 4802
5:33 woman, knowing w had happened to her, 4005
5:36 Ignoring w they said, Jesus told 3364+3836[S]
6:24 "W shall I ask for?" 5515
7:15 it is w comes out of a man that makes him 3836
7:20 "W comes out of a man is what makes him 3836
7:20 of a man is w makes him 'unclean.' NIG
8:29 "But w about you?" NIG
8:36 W good is it for a man to gain the whole 5515
8:37 w can a man give in exchange for his soul? 5515
9: 6 (He did not know w to say, 5515
9: 9 to tell anyone w they had seen until the Son 4005
9:10 discussing w "rising from the dead" meant. 5515
9:16 "W are you arguing with them about?" 5515
9:32 not understand w he meant and were afraid NIG
9:33 "W were you arguing about on the road?" 5515
10: 3 "W did Moses command you?" he replied. 5515
10: 9 Therefore w God has joined together, 4005
10:17 "w must I do to inherit eternal life?" 5515
10:32 and told them w was going to happen 3836
10:36 "W do you want me to do for you?" 5515
10:38 "You don't know w you are asking," 5515
10:51 "W do you want me to do for you?" 5515
11: 5 "W are you doing, untying that colt?" 5515
11:23 but believes that w he says will happen, 4005
11:28 By w authority are you doing these things?" 4481
11:29 by w authority I am doing these things. 4481
11:33 by w authority I am doing these things." 4481
12: 9 "W then will the owner of the vineyard do? 5515
12:17 "Give to Caesar w is Caesar's and 3836
12:17 and to God w is God's." 3836
13: 1 W massive stones! 4534
13: 1 W magnificent buildings!" 4534
13: 4 And w will be the sign that they are all 5515
13:11 do not worry beforehand about w to say. 5515
13:37 W I say to you, I say to everyone: 4005
14: 8 She did w she could. 4005
14: 9 w she has done will also be told, 4005
14:36 Yet not w I will, but what you will." 5515
14:36 Yet not what I will, but w you will." 5515
14:40 They did not know w to say to him. 5515
14:60 W is this testimony that these men 5515
14:64 W do you think?" 5515
14:68 or understand w you're talking about," 5515
15: 8 to do for them w he usually did. NIG
15:12 "W shall I do, then, with the one you call 5515
15:14 W crime has he committed?" 5515
15:24 they cast lots to see w each would get. 5515
Lk 1:29 at his words and wondered w kind of 4534
1:45 Blessed is she who has believed that w 3836
1:62 to find out w he would like to name 5515
1:66 asking, "W then is this child going to be?" 5515
2:17 the word *concerning* w had been told them 3836
2:18 and all who heard it were amazed at w 3836
2:24 to offer a sacrifice in keeping with w is said 3836
2:27 for him w the custom of the Law required, NIG
2:33 and mother marveled at w was said 3836
2:50 not understand w he was saying to them. 4005
3:10 "W should we do then?" the crowd asked. 5515
3:12 "Teacher," they asked, "w should we do?" 5515
3:14 "And w should we do?" 5515
4:23 Do here in your hometown w we have heard 4012
4:34 W do you want with us, Jesus 2779+5515
4:36 "W is this teaching? 5515
5:22 Jesus knew w they were thinking and asked, NIG
5:25 took w he had been lying on 4005
6: 2 "Why are you doing w is unlawful on 4005
6: 3 "Have you never read w David did when he 4005
6: 4 he ate w is lawful only for priests to eat. 4005
6: 8 But Jesus knew w they were thinking 3836
Lk 6:11 to discuss with one another w they might do 5515
6:30 and if anyone takes w belongs to you, 3836
6:32 w credit is that to you? 4481
6:33 w credit is that to you? 4481
6:34 w credit is that to you? 4481
6:46 'Lord, Lord,' and do not do w I say? 4005
6:47 I will show you w he is like who comes 5515
7:22 to John w you have seen and heard: 4005
7:24 "W did you go out into the desert to see? 5515
7:25 If not, w did you go out to see? 5515
7:26 But w did you go out to see? 5515
7:31 "*To* w, then, can I compare the people 5515
7:31 W are they like? 5515
7:39 and w kind of woman she is— 4534
8: 9 disciples asked him w this parable meant. 5515
8:18 w he thinks he has will be taken from him." 4005
8:28 "W do you want with me, Jesus, 2779+5515
8:30 Jesus asked him, "W is your name?" 5515
8:34 the pigs saw w had happened, 3836
8:35 the people went out to see w had happened. 3836
8:56 not to tell anyone w had happened. 3836
9:10 they reported to Jesus w they had done. 4012
9:20 "But w about you?" NIG
9:25 W good is it for a man to gain the whole 5515
9:33 (He did not know w he was saying.) 4005
9:36 told no one at that time w they had seen. 4005
9:44 "Listen carefully to w I am about NIG
9:45 But they did not understand w this meant. 3836
10: 8 eat w is set before you. 3836
10:23 "Blessed are the eyes that see w you see. 4005
10:24 and kings wanted to see w you see but did 4005
10:24 and to hear w you hear but did not hear it." 4005
10:25 "w must I do to inherit eternal life?" 5515
10:26 "W is written in the Law?" 5515
10:39 at the Lord's feet listening to w he said. 3836
10:42 Mary has chosen w is better, 3535[S]
11:41 But give w is inside [the dish] to the poor, 3836
11:48 that you approve of w your forefathers did; NIG
12: 3 W you have said in the dark will be heard in 4012
12: 3 and w you have whispered in the ear in 4005
12:11 defend yourselves or w you will say, 5515
12:12 at that time w you should say." 4005
12:17 He thought to himself, 'W shall I do? 5515
12:18 "Then he said, 'This is w I'll do. NIG
12:20 Then who will get w you have prepared 4005
12:22 not worry about your life, w you will eat; 5515
12:22 or about your body, w you will wear. 5515
12:29 And do not set your heart on w you will eat 5515
12:39 of the house had known *at* w hour 4481
12:47 not do w his master wants will be beaten NIG
12:57 judge for yourselves w is right? 3836
13:16 free on the Sabbath day from w bound her?" 3836
13:18 "W is the kingdom of God like? 5515
13:18 W shall I compare it *to?* 5515
13:20 "W shall I compare the kingdom 5515
14:22 'w you ordered has been done, 4005
15:26 and asked him w was going on. 323+4047+5515
16: 2 'W is this I hear about you? 5515
16: 3 'W shall I do now? 5515
16: 4 I know w I'll do so that, 5515
16:15 W is highly valued among men is detestable 4022
16:21 to eat w fell from the rich man's table. 3836
17: 9 the servant because he did w he was told 3836
18: 6 "Listen to w the unjust judge says. 5515
18:18 w must I do to inherit eternal life?" 5515
18:27 "W is impossible with men is possible 3836
18:34 they did not know w he was talking about. 3836
18:36 he asked w was happening. 5515
18:41 "W do you want me to do for you?" 5515
19:10 to seek and to save w was lost." 3836
19:15 in order to find out w they had gained 5515
19:21 You take out w you did not put in 4005
19:21 not put in and reap w you did not sow.' 4005
19:22 taking out w I did not put in, 4005
19:22 and reaping w I did not sow? 4005
19:26 even w he has will be taken away. 4005
19:42 on this day w would bring you peace— 3836
20: 2 by w authority you are doing these things," 4481
20: 8 by w authority I am doing these things." 4481
20:13 owner of the vineyard said, 'W shall I do? 5515
20:15 "W then will the owner of the vineyard do 5515
20:17 w is the meaning of that which is written: 5515
20:21 that you speak and teach w is right, 3987
20:25 "Then give to Caesar w is Caesar's 3836
20:25 and to God w is God's. 3836
20:26 to trap him in w he had said there in public. 4839
21: 6 for w you see here, the time will come when 4005
21: 7 And w will be the sign that they are about 5515
21:26 apprehensive *of* w is coming on the world, 3836
22:37 w is written about me is reaching its fulfillment." 3836
22:49 When Jesus' followers saw w was going 3836
22:60 I don't know w you're talking about!" 4005
23: 8 From w he had heard about him, 3836
23:22 W crime has this man committed? 5515
23:31 w will happen when it is dry?" 5515
23:34 for they do not know w they are doing." 5515
23:41 for we are getting w our deeds deserve. 4005
23:47 The centurion, seeing w had happened, 3836
23:48 to witness this sight saw w took place, 3836
24:12 wondering to himself w had happened. 3836
24:17 "W are you discussing together 5515
24:19 "W *things?*" he asked. "About Jesus 4481
24:21 And w is more, it is the third day 247+1145+2779+4047+4246+5250
24:27 *he* explained to them w *was* said in all 1450
24:35 the two told w had happened on the way, 3836

Lk 24:44 "This is w I told you while I was still *4005*
24:46 He told them, **"This is** w is written: *4048*
24:49 to send you w my Father has promised; *3836*
Jn 1:22 **W** do you say about yourself?" *5515*
1:38 **"W** do you want?" *5515*
1:40 of the two who heard w John had said *NIG*
2:18 **"W** miraculous sign can you show us *5515*
2:22 his disciples recalled w he had said. *4047*
2:25 for he knew w was in a man. *5515*
3:11 I tell you the truth, we speak of w we know, *4005*
3:11 and we testify to w we have seen, *4005*
3:21 that w he has done has been done *3836*
3:27 "A man can receive only w is given him *4005*
3:32 He testifies to w he has seen and heard, *4005*
4:18 **W** you have just said is quite true." *4047*
4:22 You Samaritans worship w you do *4005*
4:22 we worship w we do know, *4005*
4:27 But no one asked, **"W** do you want?" *5515*
4:38 to reap w you have not worked for. *4005*
4:42 because of w you said; *NIG*
5:19 can do only w he sees his Father doing, *323+5516*
5:47 But since you do not believe w he wrote, *3836*
5:47 how are you going to believe w I say?" *3836*
6:6 for he already had in mind w he was going *5515*
6:28 **"W** must we do to do *5515*
6:30 **"W** miraculous sign then will you give *5515*
6:30 **W** will you do? *5515*
6:62 **W** if you see the Son of Man ascend to *NIG*
7:7 because I testify that w it does is evil. *3836*
7:36 **W** did he mean when he said, *5515*
7:51 to find out w he is doing?" *5515*
8:5 Now w do you say?" *5515*
8:25 Just w I have been claiming all along," *4005+5516*
8:26 w I have heard from him I tell the world." *4005*
8:28 but speak just w the Father has taught me. *NIG*
8:29 for I always do w pleases him." *3836*
8:38 I am telling you w I have seen in *4005*
8:38 you do w you have heard from your father." *4005*
8:43 Because you are unable to hear w I say. *NIG*
8:47 He who belongs to God hears w God says. *3836*
9:17 **"W** have you to say about him?" *5515*
9:26 Then they asked him, **"W** did he do to you? *5515*
9:40 with him heard him say this and asked, **"W?** *NIG*
10:6 not understand w he was telling them. *4005*
10:36 w about the one whom the Father set apart *NIG*
10:37 unless I do w my Father does. *2240+3836*[S]
11:45 and had seen w Jesus did, *4005*
11:46 and told them w Jesus had done. *4005*
11:47 **"W** are we accomplishing?" *5515*
11:56 **"W** do you think? *5515*
12:6 he used to help himself to w was put into it. *3836*
12:27 my heart is troubled, and w shall I say? *5515*
12:49 the Father who sent me commanded me w *5515*
12:50 So whatever I say is **just w** *2777*
13:7 "You do not realize now w I am doing, *4005*
13:12 "Do you understand w I have done *5515*
13:13 and rightly so, for that is w I am. *NIG*
13:27 **"W** you are about to do, do quickly," *4005*
13:29 to buy w was needed for the Feast, *4005*
14:12 in me will do w I have been doing. *4005*
14:15 you love me, you will obey w I command. *NIG*
14:31 I do exactly w my Father has commanded
me. *2777*
15:14 You are my friends if you do w I command. *4005*
15:24 not done among them w no one else did, *4005*
15:25 this is to fulfill w is written in their Law: *3836*
16:13 he will speak only w he hears, *4012*
16:13 and he will tell you w is yet to come. *3836*
16:14 from w is mine and making it known *3836*
16:15 from w is mine and make it known to you. *3836*
16:17 **"W** does he mean by saying, *5515*
16:18 **"W** does he mean by 'a little while'? *4036+5515*
16:18 We don't understand w he is saying." *5515*
16:19 Are you asking one another w **I meant** *4047+4309*
18:21 Surely they know w I said." *4005*
18:23 Jesus replied, "testify as to w is wrong. *3836*
18:29 **"W** charges are you bringing *5515*
18:35 **W** is it you have done?" *5515*
18:38 **"W** is truth?" Pilate asked. *5515*
19:22 Pilate answered, **"W** I have written, *4005*
19:24 So this is w the soldiers did. *NIG*
21:21 he asked, "Lord, w about him?" *5515*
21:22 w is that to you? *5515*
21:23 w is that to you?" *5515*
Ac 2:3 They saw w **seemed to be** tongues of fire *6059*
2:12 **"W** does this mean?" *5515*
2:14 listen carefully to w I say. *3836*
2:16 this is w was spoken by the prophet Joel: *3836*
2:31 **Seeing w was ahead,** he spoke of the *4632*
2:33 and has poured out w you now see and hear. *4005*
2:37 "Brothers, w shall we do?" *5515*
3:6 but w I have I give you. *4005*
3:10 and amazement at w had happened to him. *3836*
3:18 how God fulfilled w he had foretold *4005*
4:7 w power or what name did you do *4481*
4:7 or w name did you do this?" *4481*
4:16 **"W** are we going to do with these men?" *5515*
4:20 about w we have seen and heard." *4005*
4:21 for w had happened. *3836*
4:28 They did w your power *4012*
5:4 **W** made you think of doing such a thing? *5515*
5:5 fear seized all who heard w had happened. *NIG*
5:7 not knowing w had happened. *3836*
5:24 wondering w would come of this. *5515*
5:35 of Israel, consider carefully w you intend *5515*
7:40 we don't know w has happened to him!' *5515*
7:41 in honor of w their hands had made. *NIG*

Ac 7:42 This agrees with *w is* **written** in the book *AIT*
7:49 **W kind of** house will you build for me? *4481*
8:6 they all paid close attention *to w* he **said.** *AIT*
8:30 "Do you understand w you are reading?" *4005*
9:6 and you will be told w you must do." *4005+5515*
10:1 in w was known as the Italian Regiment. *3836*
10:4 **"W** is it, Lord?" he asked. *5515*
10:22 so that he could hear w you have to say." *NIG*
10:35 and do w **is right.** *1466*
10:37 You know w has happened *3836*
11:16 Then I remembered w the Lord had said: *NIG*
12:9 but he had no idea that w *3836*
12:18 the soldiers as to w had become of Peter. *5515*
13:8 that is w his name means) opposed them *NIG*
13:12 When the proconsul saw w had happened, *3836*
13:32 **W** God promised our fathers *3836*
13:40 that w the prophets have said does *3836*
13:45 against w Paul was saying. *3836*
13:47 For **this is** w the Lord has commanded us: *4048*
14:11 When the crowd saw w Paul had done, *4005*
15:24 troubling your minds *by w they* **said.** *3364*
15:27 by word of mouth w **we are writing.** *899+3836*[S]
16:30 "Sirs, w must I do to be saved?" *5515*
17:11 to see if w **Paul said** was true. *4047*[S]
17:18 **"W** is this babbler trying to say?" *5515*
17:19 "May we know w this new teaching is *5515*
17:20 and we want to know w they mean." *5515*
17:23 Now w you worship as something unknown *4005*
19:3 "Then w baptism did you receive?" *1650+5515*
20:22 not knowing w will happen to me there. *3836*
20:38 **W** grieved them most was his statement *NIG*
21:19 and reported in detail w God had done *4005*
21:22 **W shall we do?** *1639+4036+5515*
21:23 so do w we tell you. *4005*
21:33 he asked who he was and w he had done. *5515*
22:10 " 'W shall I do, Lord?' *5515*
22:15 to all men *of* w you have seen and heard. *4005*
22:16 And now w are you waiting for? *5515*
22:26 **"W** are you going to do?" *5515*
23:9 **"W if** a spirit or an angel has spoken *1623*
23:19 **"W** is it you want to tell me?" *5515*
23:34 and asked w province he was from. *4481*
24:20 are here should state w crime they found *5515*
26:6 in w God has promised our fathers that I am *NIG*
26:10 And that is just w I did in Jerusalem. *4005*
26:16 and as a witness *of* w you have seen of me *4005*
26:16 of me and w I will show you. *4005*
26:22 I am saying nothing beyond w the prophets *4005*
26:25 **"W** I am saying is true and reasonable. *247*
26:29 to me today may become w I am, *3961+5525*
27:11 instead of listening to w Paul said, *3836*
27:13 thought they had obtained w they wanted; *NIG*
28:22 But we want to hear w your views are, *4005*
28:24 Some were convinced *by w he* said, *3836*
Ro 1:19 since w may be known about God is plain *3836*
1:20 being understood *from* w has been made, *3836*
1:28 to do w ought not to be done. *3836*
2:6 to each person according to w he has done." *3836*
2:18 of w is superior because you are instructed *3836*
3:1 **W** advantage, then, is there in being a Jew, *5515*
3:1 or w value is there in circumcision? *5515*
3:3 **W** if some did not have faith? *5515*
3:5 w shall we say? That God is unjust in *5515*
3:9 **W** shall we conclude then? *5515*
3:27 On w principle? On that of observing *4481*
4:1 **W** then shall we say that Abraham, *5515*
4:3 **W** does the Scripture say? *5515*
4:10 **Under w circumstances** was it credited? *4802*
4:21 to do w he had promised. *4005*
6:1 **W** shall we say, then? *5515*
6:15 **W** then? Shall we sin because we are not *5515*
6:21 **W** benefit did you reap at that time from *5515*
7:6 But now, by dying to w once bound us, *4005*
7:7 **W** shall we say, then? Is the law sin? *5515*
7:7 not have known w **sin was** except through *281*
7:7 not have known w **coveting** really **was** if *2123*
7:13 in me through w was good, *3836*
7:15 I do not understand w I do. *4005*
7:15 For w I want to do I do not do, *4005*
7:15 but w I hate I do. *4005*
7:16 And if I do w I do not want to do, *3836*
7:18 For I have the desire to do w is good, *NIG*
7:19 For w I do is not the good I want to do; *4005*
7:20 Now if I do w I do not want to do, *4005*
7:24 **W** a wretched man I am! *NIG*
8:3 For w the law was powerless to do in *NIG*
8:5 the sinful nature have their minds set on w *3836*
8:5 with the Spirit have their minds set on w *3836*
8:24 Who hopes for w he already has? *4005*
8:25 But if we hope for w we do not yet have, *4005*
8:26 We do not know w we ought to pray for, *5515*
8:31 **W,** then, shall we say in response to this? *5515*
9:14 **W** then shall we say? Is God unjust? *5515*
9:20 "Shall w is formed say to him who formed *3836*
9:22 **W** if God, choosing to show his wrath *NIG*
9:23 **W** if he did this to make the riches *NIG*
9:30 **W** then shall we say? *5515*
10:8 But w does it say? "The word is near you; *5515*
11:2 Don't you know w the Scripture says in *5515*
11:4 And w was God's answer to him? *5515*
11:7 **W** then? What Israel sought so earnestly *5515*
11:7 **W** Israel sought so earnestly it did *4005*
11:15 w will their acceptance be but life from *5515*
12:2 to test and approve w God's will is— *5515*
12:9 Hate w is evil; cling to what is good. *3836*
12:9 Hate what is evil; cling *to* w is good. *3836*
12:17 to do w is right in the eyes of everybody. *NIG*

Ro 13:2 against w God has instituted, *3836*
13:3 do w is right and he will commend you. *3836*
13:7 Give everyone w you owe him: *3836*
14:15 brother is distressed because of w *you* **eat,** *1109*
14:16 not allow w you consider good to be spoken *3836*
14:19 therefore make every effort to do w leads *3836*
14:22 not condemn himself by w he approves. *4005*
15:18 anything except w Christ has accomplished *4005*
15:18 the Gentiles to obey God by w I have said *NIG*
16:19 but I want you to be wise about w is good, *3836*
16:19 and innocent about w is evil. *3836*
1Co 1:12 **W** I mean is this: One of you says, *NIG*
1:21 through the foolishness *of* w **was preached** *3060*
1:26 think of w you were when you were called. *NIG*
2:9 no mind has conceived w God has prepared *4005*
2:12 may understand w God has freely given us. *3836*
2:13 This is w we speak, *4005*
3:5 **W,** after all, is Apollos? *5515*
3:5 And w is Paul? Only servants, *5515*
3:13 his work will be shown for w it is, *NIG*
3:14 If w he has built survives, *2240+3836+5516*[S]
4:5 He will bring to light w is hidden *3836*
4:6 "Do not go beyond w is written." *4005*
4:7 **W** do you have that you did not receive? *5515*
4:17 with w I teach everywhere in every church. *NIG*
4:19 but w power they have. *3836*
4:21 **W** do you prefer? Shall I come to you with *5515*
5:12 **W business is it of mine** to judge *1609+5515*
6:11 And that is w some of you were. *NIG*
7:19 Keeping God's commands is w counts. *NIG*
7:29 **W** I mean, brothers, is that the time is short. *4047*
8:10 be emboldened to eat w has been sacrificed *3836*
8:13 if w I **eat** causes my brother to fall into sin, *1109*
9:13 the altar share in w is offered on the altar? *NIG*
9:18 **W** then is my reward? *5515*
10:13 No temptation has seized you except w is
common to man. *NIG*
10:13 be tempted beyond w you can bear. *4005*
10:15 judge for yourselves w I say. *4005*
11:22 **W** shall I say to you? *5515*
11:23 from the Lord w I also passed on to you: *4005*
14:6 w good will I be to you, *5515*
14:7 will anyone know w tune is being played *3836*
14:9 how will anyone know w you are saying? *3836*
14:11 the meaning of w someone is saying, *3836*
14:13 that he may interpret w he says. *NIG*
14:15 So w shall I do? I will pray with my spirit, *5515*
14:16 since he does not know w you are saying? *5515*
14:26 **W** then shall we say, brothers? *5515*
14:29 the others should weigh carefully w is said. *NIG*
14:37 let him acknowledge that w I am writing *4005*
15:3 For w I received I passed on to you as *4005*
15:10 But by the grace of God I am w I am, *4005*
15:11 then, it was I or they, **this is** w we preach, *4048*
15:11 and **this is** w you believed. *4048*
15:29 w will those do who are baptized for *5515*
15:32 for merely human reasons, w have I gained? *5515*
15:35 *With* w **kind of** body will they come?" *4481*
15:36 **W** you sow does not come to life *4005*
16:1 Do w I told the Galatian churches to do. *6061*
16:17 they have supplied w was lacking from you. *3836*
2Co 1:22 guaranteeing w is to come. *NIG*
2:10 And w I have forgiven— *4005*
3:10 For w was glorious has no glory now *3836*
3:11 And if w was fading away came with glory, *3836*
4:18 So we fix our eyes not on w is seen, *3836*
4:18 but on w is unseen. *3836*
4:18 For w is seen is temporary, *3836*
4:18 but w is unseen is eternal. *3836*
5:4 w is mortal may be swallowed up by life. *3836*
5:5 guaranteeing w is to come. *NIG*
5:10 that each one may receive w is due him for *3836*
5:11 then, we know w it is to fear the Lord, *NIG*
5:11 *W we are is* **plain** to God, *AIT*
5:12 in w is seen rather than in what is in *NIG*
5:12 in what is seen rather than in w is in *NIG*
6:14 For w do righteousness and wickedness *5515*
6:14 w fellowship can light have with darkness? *5515*
6:15 **W** harmony is there between Christ *5515*
6:15 **W** does a believer have in common with *5515*
6:16 **W** agreement is there between the temple *5515*
7:11 See w this godly sorrow has produced *4531*
7:11 w earnestness, what eagerness *NIG*
7:11 w eagerness to clear yourselves, *NIG*
7:11 w indignation, what alarm, what longing, *NIG*
7:11 what indignation, w alarm, what longing, *NIG*
7:11 what indignation, what alarm, w longing, *NIG*
7:11 what alarm, what longing, w concern, *NIG*
7:11 w readiness to see justice done. *NIG*
8:10 And here is my advice about w is best *NIG*
8:12 is acceptable according to w one has, *1569+4005*
8:12 not according to w he does not have. *4005*
8:14 your plenty will supply w they need, *NIG*
8:14 in turn their plenty will supply w you need. *NIG*
8:19 **W is more,** he was chosen by the churches
247+1254+2779+3667+4024
8:21 For we are taking pains to do w is right, *NIG*
9:7 Each *man* should give w he has decided *2777*
10:11 Such people should realize that w we are *3888*
11:9 from Macedonia supplied w I needed. *3836*
11:12 And I will keep on doing w I am doing *NIG*
11:15 Their end will be *w* their **actions deserve.** *AIT*
11:21 **W** anyone else dares to boast about— *NIG*
12:6 of me than is warranted by w I do or say. *4005*
12:14 w I want is not your possessions but you. *NIG*
13:7 the test but that you will do w is right even *3836*
Gal 1:9 to you a gospel other than w you accepted, *4005*

Gal 1:20 that w I am writing you is no lie. 4005
2:18 If I rebuild w I destroyed, 4005
3: 2 or by believing w you **heard?** 198
3: 5 or because you believe w you **heard?** 198
3:17 W I mean is this: The law, NIG
3:19 W, then, was the purpose of the law? 5515
3:22 so that w was promised, 3836
4: 1 W I am saying is that as long as the heir is NIG
4:15 W has happened to all your joy? 4544
4:17 W they want is to alienate you [from us], NIG
4:21 are you not aware of w the law says? NIG
4:30 But w does the Scripture say? 5515
5:17 For the sinful nature desires w is contrary to NIG
5:17 the Spirit w is contrary to the sinful nature. NIG
5:17 so that you do not do w you want. 1569+4005
6: 7 A man reaps w he sows. 1569+4005
6:11 See w **large** letters I use as I write to you 4383
6:15 w counts is a new creation. NIG
Eph 4: 9 (W does "he ascended" mean except that he 5515
4:29 but only w is helpful for building others up 5516
5:10 and find out w pleases the Lord. 5515
5:12 to mention w the disobedient do in secret. NIG
5:17 but understand w the Lord's will is. 5515
6:21 also may know how I am and w I am doing. 5515
Php 1:10 be able to discern w **is best** and 1422+3836
1:12 that w **has happened to** me has really served to advance the gospel. 2848+3836
1:18 But w **does it matter?** 1142+5515
1:19 w has happened to me will turn out 4047
1:22 Yet w shall I choose? 5515
3: 8 **W is more,** I consider everything 247+3529
3:13 Forgetting w is behind and straining NIG
3:13 behind and straining toward w is ahead, NIG
3:16 up to w we have already attained. 4005
4:12 I know w it is to be in need, NIG
4:12 and I know w it is to have plenty. NIG
4:17 but I am looking for w may be credited 3836
Col 1:24 Now I rejoice in w was suffered for you, 3836
1:24 up in my flesh w **is still lacking** in regard 5729
2:16 not let anyone judge you by w you eat NIG
2:18 into great detail about w he has seen, 4005
4: 1 provide your slaves with w is right and fair, 3836
1Th 1: 9 for they themselves report w **kind of** 3961
2:19 For w is our hope, our joy, 5515
3:10 and supply w is lacking in your faith. 3836
4: 2 For you know w instructions we gave you 5515
2Th 2: 6 And now you know w is holding him back, 3836
3:13 you, brothers, never tire of **doing w is right.** 2818
1Ti 1: 7 but they do not know w they are talking 4005
1: 7 about or w they so confidently affirm. 5515
6:20 **w has been entrusted to** *your* **care.** 4146
6:20 *of* w is falsely called knowledge, 3836
2Ti 1:12 that he is able to guard w I have entrusted 3836
1:13 W you heard from me, keep as the pattern 4005
2: 7 Reflect on w I am saying, 4005
3:11 **w kinds of** *things* happened to me 3888
3:14 continue in w you have learned 4005
4: 3 to say w their itching ears want to hear. 198
4:14 The Lord will repay him for w he has done. 3836
Tit 1: 5 might straighten out w was left unfinished 3836
1: 8 hospitable, **one who loves w is good,** 5787
2: 1 You must teach w is in accord 4005
2: 3 but to **teach w is good.** 2815
2: 7 an example by doing w is good. NIG
2:14 eager to do w is good. NIG
3: 8 to devote themselves to doing w is good, NIG
3:14 to devote themselves to doing w is good, NIG
Phm 1: 8 order you to do w **you ought to do,** 465+3836
Heb 2: 1 therefore, to w we have heard, 3836
2: 6 **"W** is man that you are mindful of him, 5515
3: 5 testifying *to* w would be said in the future. 3836
3: 9 and for forty years saw w I did. NIG
5: 8 he learned obedience from w he suffered 4005
6:12 patience inherit w **has been promised.** 2039+3836
6:15 Abraham received w **was promised.** 2039+3836
6:16 the oath confirms w is said and puts an end NIG
6:17 to the heirs *of* w **was promised,** 2039+3836
7:15 And w we have said is even more clear NIG
8: 1 The point of w we are saying is this: 3836
8: 5 a copy and shadow *of* w is in heaven. 3836
8:13 w is obsolete and aging will soon disappear. 3836
10:36 you will receive w he has promised. 3836
11: 1 Now faith is being sure *of* w we **hope for** AIT
11: 1 hope for and certain *of* w we do not see. 4547
11: 2 This is w the ancients were commended for. NIG
11: 3 so that w is seen was not made out 3836
11: 3 not made out of w was visible. NIG
11:32 And w more shall I say? 5515
11:33 and gained w **was promised;** 2039
11:39 none of them received w **had been promised.** 2039+3836
12: 7 For w son is not disciplined by his father? 5515
12:20 they could not bear w was commanded: 3836
12:27 the removing *of* w can be shaken— 3836
12:27 so that w cannot be shaken may remain. 3836
13: 5 of money and be content *with* w you have, 3836
13: 6 W can man do to me?" 5515
13:21 and may he work in us w is pleasing to him, 3836
Jas 1:22 Do w it says. NIG
1:23 to the word but does not do w it says is like 4047
1:24 and immediately forgets w he looks like. 3961
1:25 not forgetting *w he has* **heard,** but doing it AIT
1:25 he will be blessed in w he does. 3836
2:14 W good is it, my brothers, 5515
2:16 about his physical needs, w good is it? 5515
2:18 and I will show you my faith by w I do. NIG
2:21 for w **he did** when he offered his son Isaac 2240

Jas 2:22 his faith was made complete by w **he did.** 2240
2:24 that a person is justified by w **he does** and 2240
2:25 for w **she did** when she gave lodging to 2240
3: 2 If anyone is never at fault in w he **says,** 3364
3: 5 Consider w **a great** forest is set on fire by 2462
4: 1 **W causes** fights and quarrels among you? 4470
4: 2 but you cannot have w you want. NIG
4: 3 that you may spend w you get NIG
4:14 not even know w **will happen** 3836+4481
4:14 W is your life? You are a mist NIG
5:11 of Job's perseverance and have seen w NIG
1Pe 2: 8 which is also w they were destined for. 4005
3: 6 You are her daughters *if you* **do w is right** 16
3:14 But even if you should suffer for w **is right,** 1466
3:14 "Do not fear w they fear; 3836
4: 3 in the past doing w pagans choose to do— NIG
4:17 and if it begins with us, w will the outcome 5515
4:18 w will become of the ungodly and 4544
2Pe 2: 6 *w is* **going to happen** to the ungodly; AIT
3:11 **w kind of** *people* ought you to be? 4534
1Jn 1: 3 We proclaim to you w we have seen 4005
2: 4 but does not do w he commands is a liar, 3836
2:16 the boasting of w **he has and does—** 1050
2:24 See that w you have heard from the 4005
2:25 this is w he promised us—even eternal life. 4005
2:29 everyone who does w **is right** has been born 1466
3: 1 And that is w we are! NIG
3: 2 w we will be has not yet been made known. 5515
3: 7 He who does w **is right** is righteous, 1466
3: 8 He who does w **is sinful** is of the devil, 281
3:10 Anyone who does not do w **is right** is not 1466
3:16 This is how we know w love is: NIG
3:22 and do w pleases him. 3836
5:15 we know that we have w we asked of him. 4005
2Jn 1: 8 that you do not lose w you have worked for, 4005
3Jn 1: 5 you are faithful in w you are doing for 4005
1:10 I will call attention to w he is doing, 4005
1:11 do not imitate w is evil but what is good. 3836
1:11 do not imitate what is evil but w is good. 3836
1:11 Anyone who **does w is good** is from God. 16
1:11 who **does w is evil** has not seen God. 2803
Jude 1:10 w *things* they do understand by instinct, 4012
1:17 remember w the apostles of our Lord NIG
Rev 1: 1 show his servants w must soon take place. 4005
1: 3 and take to heart w is written in it, 3836
1:11 "Write on a scroll w you see and send it to 4005
1:19 "Write, therefore, w you have seen, 4005
1:19 w is now and what will take place later. 4005
1:19 what is now and w will take place later. 4005
2: 7 let him hear w the Spirit says to 5515
2:10 not be afraid of w you are about to suffer. 4005
2:11 him hear w the Spirit says to the churches. 5515
2:17 him hear w the Spirit says to the churches. 5515
2:25 Only hold on to w you have until I come. 4005
2:29 him hear w the Spirit says to the churches. 5515
3: 2 Strengthen w remains and is about to die, 3836
3: 3 therefore, w you have received and heard; 4802
3: 3 not know at w time I will come to you. 4481
3: 6 him hear w the Spirit says to the churches. 5515
3: 7 W he opens no one can shut, NIG
3: 7 and w he shuts no one can open. NIG
3:11 Hold on to w you have, 4005
3:13 him hear w the Spirit says to the churches. 5515
3:22 him hear w the Spirit says to the churches. 5515
4: 1 and I will show you w must take place 4005
4: 6 Also before the throne there was w looked NIG
6: 6 Then I heard w sounded like a voice among NIG
10: 4 up w the seven thunders have said and do 4005
15: 2 And I saw w looked like a sea NIG
16:11 they refused to repent of w they had done. 3836
18: 6 pay her back double for w she has done. 3836
19: 1 After this I heard w **sounded like** the roar of 6055
19: 6 I heard w sounded like a great multitude, NIG
20:12 according to w they had done as recorded in 3836
20:13 according to w he had done. 3836
21:27 nor will anyone who does w **is shameful** 1007
22:12 to everyone according to w he has done. 3836

WHAT'S (6) [WHAT]

Jdg 18:23 **"W the matter** with you 4537
18:24 **'W the matter** with you?' " 4537
1Sa 4: 6 **"W** all this shouting in the Hebrew camp?" 4537
1Ki 1:41 **"W the meaning of** all the noise in the city? 4508
2Ki 6:28 Then he asked her, **"W the matter?"** 4537
Mk 6: 2 **"W** this wisdom that has been given him, 5313

WHATEVER (182) [WHAT]

Ge 2:19 w the man called each living creature, 889+3972
16: 6 "Do with her w you think best." 2021
21:12 Listen to w Sarah tells you, 889+3972
31:16 So do w God has told you." 889+3972
31:39 from me for w **was stolen** *by* day or night. AIT
34:11 and I will give you w you ask. 889
34:12 and I'll pay w you ask me. 889+3869
39:23 and gave him success in w he did. 889
Ex 16:23 Save w is left and keep it until morning.' " 3972
21:22 fined w the woman's husband demands 889+3869
21:30 by paying w is demanded. 889+3869+3972
27:19 w their function, including all the tent pegs 3972
28:38 w their gifts may be. 3972
29:37 and w touches it will be holy. 3972
30:29 and w touches them will be holy. 3972
Lev 6: 5 or w it was he swore falsely about. 889+3972
6:18 W touches them will become holy.' " 889+3972
6:27 W touches any of the flesh will become 889+3972

Lev 11:32 that article, w its use, will be unclean, 889
13:51 w its use, it is a destructive mildew; 889+3972
13:57 w has the mildew must be burned with fire. 889
16:16 w their sins have been. 3972
22: 5 w the uncleanness may be. 3972
23:38 to your gifts and w you have vowed and all 3972
24:19 w he has done must be done to him: 889+3869+4027
25: 6 W the land yields during the sabbath year NIH
25: 7 W the land produces may be eaten. 3972
27:12 W value the priest then sets, 3869
27:14 W value the priest then sets, 889+3869
Nu 6:21 in addition to w *else* he can afford. 889
10:32 we will share with you w good things 889
18:11 *w* is **set aside** *from* the gifts of all AIT
18:19 W is set aside from the holy offerings 3972
22:17 and do w you say. 889+3972
23: 3 W he reveals to me I will tell you." 1821+4537
23:26 tell you I must do w the LORD says?" 889+3972
31:23 And w cannot withstand fire must be 889+3972
33:54 W falls to them by lot will be theirs. 889
Dt 5:27 tell us w the LORD our God tells you. 889+3972
12:17 or w you have vowed to give, 3972
12:26 and w you have vowed to give, 889
14:26 Use the silver to buy w you like: 889+3972
15: 8 and freely lend him w he needs. 1896
23:16 and in w town he chooses. 285S
23:23 W your lips utter you must be sure to 889+3869
Jos 1:16 W you have commanded us we will do, 889+3972
1:18 w you may command them, 889+3972
7:12 unless you destroy w among you is devoted 2021
9:25 Do to us w seems good and right to you." 3869
Jdg 9:33 do w your hand finds to do." 889+3869
10:15 Do with us w you think best, 3869+3972
11:24 w the LORD our God has given us, 889+3972
11:31 w comes out of the door of my house 2021+3655S
18:10 a land that lacks **nothing w."** 401+1821+3972
19:20 "Let me supply w you need. 3972
19:24 and do to them w you wish. 2021
Ru 3: 5 "I will do w you say," Ruth answered. 889+3972
1Sa 2:14 and the priest would take for himself w 889+3972
2:16 and then take w you want," 889+3869
10: 7 do w your hand finds to do, 889
11:10 can do to us w seems good to you." 3869+3972
14:36 "Do w seems best to you," they replied. 3972
18: 5 W Saul sent him to do, 889+928+3972
20: 4 **"W** you want me to do, I'll do for you." 4537
21: 3 or w you can find." 2021
25: 8 and your son David w you can find 889
2Sa 7: 3 **"W** you have in mind, go ahead and do 889+3972
9:11 "Your servant will do w my lord the king commands 889+3869+3972+4027
15:15 "Your servants are ready to do w our lord the king chooses." 889+3869+3972
15:26 let him do to me w seems good to him." 889+3869
18: 4 "I will do w seems best to you." 889
19:18 over and to do w he wished. 2021
19:27 so do w pleases you. 2021
19:37 Do for him w pleases you." 889
19:38 and I will do for him w pleases you. 2021
24:22 the king take w pleases him and offer it up. 2021
1Ki 3: 5 "Ask for w you want me to give you." 4537
5: 6 for your men w wages you set. 889+3869+3972
8:37 w disaster or disease may come, 3972
8:43 do w the foreigner asks of you, 889+3869+3972
9:19 w he desired to build in Jerusalem, 889
11:38 If you do w I command you and walk 889+3972
21: 2 if you prefer, I will pay you *w* it is **worth."** AIT
2Ki 10: 5 you do w you think best." 2021
12: 5 repair w damage is found in the temple. 889+3972
18: 7 he was successful in w he undertook. 889+3972
18:14 and I will pay w you demand of me." 889
1Ch 17: 2 **"W** you have in mind, do it, 889+3972
21:23 Let my lord the king do w pleases him. 2021
2Ch 1: 7 "Ask for w you want me to give you." 4537
6:28 w disaster or disease may come, 3972
6:33 do w the foreigner asks of you, 889+3869+3972
8: 6 w he desired to build in Jerusalem, 3972
Ezr 6: 9 W is needed—young bulls, 10408
7:18 then do w seems best with the rest 10168+10408
7:21 to provide with diligence w Ezra 10168+10353
7:23 W the God of heaven has prescribed, 10168+10353
Job 23:13 He does w he pleases. NIH
37:12 the whole earth to do w he commands 889+3972
Ps 1: 3 W he does prospers. 889+3972
115: 3 he does w pleases him. 889+3972
135: 6 The LORD does w pleases him, 889+3972
Pr 16: 3 Commit to the LORD w you **do,** 5126
Ecc 3:15 W is has already been, 4537
6:10 W exists has already been named, 4537
7:24 W wisdom may be, it is far off 4537
8: 3 for he will do w he pleases. 889+3972
9:10 W your hand finds to do, 889+3972
11: 9 the ways of your heart and *w* your eyes **see,** AIT
Jer 1: 7 and say w I command you. 889+3972
1:17 up and say to them w I command you. 889+3972
26:14 do with me w you think is good and right. 3869
39:12 but do for him w he asks." 889+3869+4027
Eze 10:11 The cherubim went in w direction 889
12:25 you rebellious house, I will fulfill *w I* **say,** AIT
12:28 w I say will be fulfilled, 889
47:23 In w tribe the alien settles, 2021
Da 7: 7 and trampled underfoot *w* was **left.** AIT
7:19 and trampled underfoot *w* was **left.** AIT
8:24 and will succeed in w he does. NIH
Na 1: 9 W they plot against the LORD 4537
Hag 1:11 the oil and w the ground produces, 889

Hag 2:14 'W they do and whatever they offer there is 3972
2:14 and w they offer there is defiled. 889
Mt 10:11 "W town or village you enter, 323+1650+4005
14: 7 with an oath to give her w she asked. *1569+4005*
15: 5 'W help you might otherwise have *1569+4005*
15:17 that w enters the mouth goes into *3836+4246*
16:19 w you bind on earth will be bound *1569+4005*
16:19 w you loose on earth will be loosed *1569+4005*
18:18 w you bind on earth will be bound *1569+4012*
18:18 w you loose on earth will be loosed *1569+4012*
20: 4 and I will pay you w is right.' *1569+4005*
21:22 will receive w you ask for in prayer." *4012+4246*
25:40 w you did for one of the least *2093+4012*
25:45 w you did not do for one of the least *2093+4012*
Mk 4:22 For w is hidden is meant to be disclosed, *1569*
4:22 and w is concealed is meant to *NIG*
6:23 "W you ask I will give you, *1569+4005+5516*
7:11 'W help you might otherwise have *1569+4005*
10:35 "we want you to do for us w we ask." *1569+4005*
11:24 w you ask for in prayer, *4012+4246*
13:11 Just say w is given you at the time, *1569+4005*
Lk 9: 4 W house you enter, *323+1650+4005*
10: 7 eating and drinking w they **give** you, *3836*
Jn 2: 5 "Do w he tells you." *323+4005+5516*
5:19 w the Father does the Son also does. *4005*
11:22 even now God will give you w you ask. *323+4012*
12:50 So w I say is just what the Father *4005*
14:13 And I will do w you ask in my name, *323+4005*
15: 7 ask w you wish, and it will be given *1569+4005*
15:16 the Father will give you w you ask in my name. *323+4005+5516*
16:23 my Father will give you w you ask in my name. *323+5516*
Ac 18:17 But Gallio showed **no** concern w. *4029*
Ro 2: 1 for at w *point* you judge the other, *4005*
3:19 Now we know that w the law says, *4012*
13: 9 w other commandment there may be, *1623+5516*
14:22 So w you believe about these things keep *4005*
1Co 10:27 eat w is put before you without raising *4246*
10:31 So whether you eat or drink or w you do, *5516*
Gal 2: 6 w they were makes no difference to me; *3961*
Eph 6: 8 reward everyone for w good he does, *1569+5516*
Php 1:27 **W happens**, conduct yourselves in *3668*
3: 7 But w was to my profit I now consider loss *4015*
4: 8 Finally, brothers, w is true, *4012*
4: 8 brothers, whatever is true, w is noble, *4012*
4: 8 whatever is noble, w is right, *4012*
4: 8 w is pure, whatever is lovely, *4012*
4: 8 w is lovely, whatever is admirable— *4012*
4: 8 whatever is lovely, w is admirable— *4012*
4: 9 W you have learned or received or heard *4005*
4:11 to be content w the circumstances. *4005*
Col 3: 5 therefore, w belongs to your earthly nature: *NIG*
3:13 forgive w grievances you may have *1569+5516*
3:17 w you do, whether in word or deed, *1569+5516*
3:23 W you do, work at it with all your heart, *1569+4005*
1Ti 1:10 w else is contrary to the sound doctrine *1623+5516*
Tit 3: 1 to be obedient, to be ready to do w is good, *4246*
1Pe 4:10 Each one should use w gift he has received *NIG*
2Pe 2:19 for a man is a slave *to* w has mastered him. *4005*
1Jn 5:15 that he hears us—w we ask— *1569+4005*
Jude 1:10 against w they do not understand; *4012*

WHEAT (46)

Ge 30:14 During w harvest, Reuben went out into 2636
Ex 9:32 The w and spelt, however, were not 2636
29: 2 And from fine w flour, without yeast, 2636
34:22 with the firstfruits of the w harvest, 2636
Dt 8: 8 a land with w and barley, vines 2636
32:14 of Bashan and the finest kernels of **w.** 2636
Jdg 6:11 where his son Gideon was threshing w in 2636
15: 1 Later on, at the time of w harvest, 2636
Ru 2:23 the barley and w harvests were finished. 2636
1Sa 6:13 of Beth Shemesh were harvesting their w in 2636
12:17 Is it not w harvest now? 2636
2Sa 4: 6 of the house as if to get *some* **w,** 2636
17:28 They also brought w and barley, 2636
1Ki 5:11 of w as food for his household, 2636
1Ch 21:20 While Araunah was threshing **w,** 2636
21:23 and the w for the grain offering. 2636
2Ch 2:10 twenty thousand cors of ground **w,** 2636
2:15 "Now let my lord send his servants the w 2636
27: 5 of w and ten thousand cors of barley. 2636
Ezr 6: 9 and **w,** salt, wine and oil, 10272
7:22 a hundred cors of **w,** 10272
Job 31:40 then let briers come up instead of w 2636
Ps 81:16 But you would be fed with the finest of **w;** 2636
147:14 and satisfies you with the finest of **w.** 2636
SS 7: 2 Your waist is a mound of w encircled 2636
Isa 28:25 Does he not plant w in its place, 2636
Jer 12:13 They will sow w but reap thorns; 2636
41: 8 We have w and barley, oil and honey, 2636
Eze 4: 9 "Take w and barley, beans and lentils, 2636
27:17 they exchanged w *from* Minnith 2636
45:13 an ephah from each homer of w and a sixth 2636
Joel 1:11 grieve for the w and the barley, 2636
Am 8: 5 Sabbath be ended that we may market **w?"** 1339
8: 6 selling even the sweepings with the w. 1339
Mt 3:12 gathering his w into the barn and burning *4992*
13:25 and sowed weeds among the **w,** *4992*
13:26 When the w sprouted and formed heads, *5965*
13:29 you may root up the w with them. *4992*
13:30 the w and bring it into my barn.' " *4992*
Lk 3:17 and to gather the w into his barn, *4992*
16: 7 " 'A thousand bushels *of* **w,**' he replied. *4992*
Lk 22:31 Simon, Satan has asked to sift you as **w.** *4992*
Jn 12:24 a kernel *of* w falls to the ground and dies, *4992*
1Co 15:37 perhaps *of* w or of something else. *4992*
Rev 6: 6 saying, "A quart *of* w for a day's wages, *4992*
18:13 of wine and olive oil, of fine flour and **w;** *4992*

WHEEL (12) [WHEELS]

1Ki 7:32 The diameter of each w was a cubit and 236
22:34 **"W around** and get me out of the 2200+3338
2Ch 18:33 **"W around** and get me out of the 2200+3338
Pr 20:26 he drives the *threshing* w over them. 236
Ecc 12: 6 or the w broken at the well, 1649
Jer 18: 3 and I saw him working at the **w.** 78
Eze 1:15 a w on the ground beside each creature 236
1:16 to be made like a w intersecting a wheel. 236
1:16 to be made like a wheel intersecting a **w.** 236
10: 6 the man went in and stood beside a **w.** 236
10:10 each was like a w intersecting a wheel. 236
10:10 each was like a wheel intersecting a **w.** 236

WHEELS (32) [WHEEL]

Ex 14:25 He made the w *of* their chariots come off so 236
1Ki 7:30 Each stand had four bronze w 236
7:32 The four w were under the panels, 236
7:32 axles of the w were attached to the stand. 236
7:33 The w were made like chariot wheels; 236
7:33 The wheels were made like chariot **w;** 236
Isa 5:28 their **chariot** w like a whirlwind. 1649
28:28 the w *of* his threshing cart over it, 1651
Jer 47: 3 and the rumble of their **w.** 1649
Eze 1:16 the appearance and structure of the **w:** 236
1:17 w did not turn about as the creatures went. NIH
1:19 the w beside them moved; 236
1:19 from the ground, the w also rose. 236
1:20 and the w would rise along with them, 236
1:20 spirit of the living creatures was in the **w.** 236
1:21 the w rose along with them, 236
1:21 spirit of the living creatures was in the **w.** 236
3:13 against each other and the sound of the w 236
10: 2 "Go in among the w beneath the cherubim. 1649
10: 6 "Take fire from among the **w,** 1649
10: 9 and I saw beside the cherubim four **w,** 236
10: 9 the w sparkled like chrysolite. 236
10:11 w did not turn about as the cherubim went. NIH
10:12 as were their four **w.** 236
10:13 the w being called "the whirling wheels." 236
10:13 the wheels being called "the **whirling w."** 1649
10:16 the w beside them moved; 236
10:16 the w did not leave their side. 236
10:19 and as they went, the w went with them. 236
11:22 Then the cherubim, with the w beside them, 236
Da 7: 9 and its w were all ablaze. 10143
Na 3: 2 The crack of whips, the clatter of **w,** 236

WHELP, WHELPS (KJV) See CUB, CUBS

WHEN (2816) [WHENEVER] See Index of Articles Etc.

WHENCE (KJV) See WHERE, WHICH

WHENEVER (72) [WHEN]

Ge 9:14 W I bring clouds over the earth and 928
9:16 W the rainbow appears in the clouds, 2256
30:33 w you check on the wages you have paid me 3954
30:41 W the stronger females were in heat, 928+3972
38: 9 so w he lay with his brother's wife, 561
Ex 17:11 but w he lowered his hands, 889+3869
18:16 W they have a dispute, it is brought to me, 3954
28:29 "W Aaron enters the Holy Place, 928
28:30 over Aaron's heart w he enters the presence 928
28:43 and his sons must wear them w they enter 928
30:20 W they enter the Tent of Meeting, 928
33: 8 And w Moses went out to the tent, 3869
33:10 W the people saw the pillar of cloud 2256
34:34 But w he entered the LORD's presence 928
40:32 They washed w they entered the Tent 928
40:36 w the cloud lifted from above the tabernacle 928
Lev 10: 9 or other fermented drink w you go into 928
13:14 But w raw flesh appears on him, 928+3427
16: 2 not to come w he chooses into 928+3972+6961
Nu 1:51 W the tabernacle is to move, 928
1:51 and w the tabernacle is to be set up, 928
9:17 W the cloud lifted from above the 4200+7023
9:21 w the cloud lifted, they set out. 2256
10:35 W the ark set out, Moses said, "Rise up, 928
10:36 W it came to rest, he said, "Return, 928
15:14 w an alien or anyone else living 3954
Dt 4: 7 the LORD our God is near us w we pray 928+3972
Jdg 2:15 W Israel went out to fight, 889+928+3972
2:18 W the LORD raised up a judge for them, 3954
6: 3 W the Israelites planted their crops, 561
12: 5 and w a survivor of Ephraim said, 3954
Ru 2: 9 And *w you are* **thirsty,** AIT
1Sa 1: 4 W the day came for Elkanah to sacrifice, 2256
1: 7 W Hannah went up to the house of 1896+4946
2:13 the people that w anyone offered a sacrifice NIH
14:52 **and** w Saul saw a mighty or brave man, 2256
16:23 W the spirit from God came upon Saul, 928
21: 5 as usual w I set out. 928
23:20 come down w it pleases you to do so, 3972
27: 9 W David attacked an area, 2256
2Sa 14:26 W he cut the hair of his head— 928
15: 2 W anyone came with a complaint to 2256
15: 5 w anyone approached him to bow down 928
1Ki 8:52 may you listen to them w they cry out 928+3972
14:28 W the king went to the LORD's temple, 1896+4946
18:10 And w a nation or kingdom claimed you NIH
2Ki 4: 8 So w he came by, he stopped there 1896+4946
4:10 Then he can stay there w he comes to us." 928
12:10 W they saw that there was a large amount 3869
1Ch 23:31 and w burnt offerings were presented 3972+4200
2Ch 12:11 W the king went to the LORD's temple, 1896+4946
19: 6 who is with you w you give a verdict. 928
24:11 W the chest was brought in 928+6961
Ps 41: 6 W one comes to see me, he speaks falsely, 561
78:34 W God slew them, they would seek him; 561
Jer 20: 8 W I speak, I cry out proclaiming violence 1896+3954+4946
36:23 W Jehudi had read three or four columns of 3869
48:27 in scorn w you speak of her? 1896+4946
Hos 6:11 "W I would restore the fortunes of my 928
7: 1 w I would heal Israel, 3869
Mk 3:11 W the evil spirits saw him, they fell down *4020*
6:10 W you enter a house, stay there until *1569+3963*
9:18 W it seizes him, it throws him to *1569+3963*
13:11 W you are arrested and brought to trial, *4020*
1Co 11:25 do this, w you drink it, *1569+4006*
11:26 For w you eat this bread and drink *1569+4006*
2Co 3:16 But w anyone turns to the Lord, *1569+2471*
13: 9 We are glad w we are weak *4020*
Eph 6:19 Pray also for me, that w I open my mouth, *NIG*
Jas 1: 2 w you face trials of many kinds, *4020*
1Jn 3:20 w our hearts condemn us. *1569*
Rev 4: 9 W the living creatures give glory, *4020*

WHERE (697) [ELSEWHERE, SOMEWHERE, WHEREVER]

Ge 2:11 the entire land of Havilah, w there is gold. 9004
3: 9 But the LORD God called to the man, **"W** 361
4: 9 **"W** is your brother Abel?" 361
10:11 w he built Nineveh, Rehoboth Ir, NIH
10:30 The **region** w they **lived** stretched 4632
13: 3 to the place between Bethel and Ai w 9004
13: 4 and w he had first built an altar. 9004
13:14 from w you are and look north 2021+5226[S]
13:18 w he built an altar to the LORD. 9004
16: 8 servant of Sarai, w have you come from, 361
16: 8 and w are you going?" 625+2025
17: 8 w you are now an alien, 824[S]
18: 9 **"W** is your wife Sarah?" 372
19: 5 **"W** are the men who came to you tonight? 372
19:27 the place w he had stood before the LORD. 9004
19:29 the catastrophe that overthrew the cities w 889
21:23 and the country w you are living as an alien 889
22: 7 "but w is the lamb for the burnt offering?" 372
26: 2 live in the land w I tell you to live. 889
28: 4 that you may take possession of the **land** *w* AIT
29: 4 "My brothers, w are you from?" 402
31: 4 to come out to the fields w his flocks were. NIH
31:13 w you anointed a pillar and 9004
31:13 a pillar and w you made a vow to me. 9004
32:17 and w are you going, 625+2025
33:17 w he built a place for himself NIH
33:19 the plot of ground w he pitched his tent. 9004
34:27 upon the dead bodies and looted the city w 889
35: 3 w I will build an altar to God, 9004
35:13 Then God went up from him at the place w 889
35:14 a stone pillar at the place w God had talked 889
35:15 Jacob called the place w God had talked 9004
35:27 Hebron), w Abraham and Isaac had stayed. 9004
36: 7 the **land** *w* they were staying could AIT
37: 1 in the **land** *w* his father had stayed, AIT
37:16 Can you tell me w they are 407
37:30 W can I turn now?" 625+2025
38:21 **"W** is the shrine prostitute who was beside 372
39:20 and put him in prison, the place w 889
40: 3 in the same prison w Joseph was confined. 9004
42: 7 **"W** do you come from?" 402
42: 9 to see w our land is unprotected." NIH
42:12 to see w our land is unprotected." NIH
42:27 At the **place** w **they stopped for the night** 4869
43:21 at the **place** w **we stopped for the night** 4869
47:30 of Egypt and bury me w they are buried." 928
Ex 2:11 he went out to w his own people were AIT
2:15 in Midian, w he sat down by a well. NIH
2:20 "And w is he?" he asked his daughters. 361
3: 5 for the place w you are standing is holy 889
6: 4 Canaan, w they **lived** as aliens. 4472
8:21 and even the ground w they are. 889
8:22 land of Goshen, w my people live; 889
9:26 land of Goshen, w the Israelites were. 889
10:23 in the **places** w they **lived.** 4632
12: 7 and tops of the doorframes of the houses w 889
12:13 be a sign for you on the houses w you are; 9004
15:27 w there were twelve springs and seventy 9004
16:29 to stay w he is on the seventh day; 9393
18: 5 w he was camped near the mountain 9004
20:21 the thick darkness w God was. 9004
25:26 four corners, w the four legs are. 889
30: 6 Testimony—w I will meet with you. 2025+9004
30:36 of Meeting—w I will meet with you. 2025+9004
33:21 a place near me w you may stand on a rock. NIH
34:12 a treaty with those who live in the land w 889
37:13 four corners, w the four legs were. 889
Lev 1:16 side of the altar, w the ashes are. 5226[S]
4:12 w the ashes are **thrown,** 9162
4:24 the place w the burnt offering is slaughtered 889
4:33 for a sin offering at the place w 889

Ex 7: 2 to be slaughtered in the place w 889
13:19 and in the place w the boil was, NIH
13:20 that has broken out w the boil was. 928
14:13 the lamb in the holy place w the sin offering 889
18: 3 w you used to live, 889
18: 3 w I am bringing you. 2025+9004
20:22 the land w I am bringing you to live 2025+9004
21:11 not enter a place w there is a dead body. NIH
Nu 5: 3 w I dwell among them." 889
10:31 You know w we should camp in the desert, NIH
11:13 W can I get meat for all these people? 402+4946
13:22 w Ahiman, Sheshai and Talmai, 9004
17: 4 w I meet with you. 2025+9004
18: 4 and no one else may come near w you are. NIH
20:13 w the Israelites quarreled with the LORD 889
20:13 and w he showed himself holy among them. NIH
21:16 the well w the LORD said to Moses, 889
21:20 and from Bamoth to the valley in Moab w NIH
22:26 a narrow place w there was no room to turn, 889
23:13 to another place w you can see them; 889
31:10 the towns w the Midianites had settled, 928
33: 9 w there were twelve springs 396+928[S]
33:14 w there was no water for the people 9004
33:38 w he died on the first day of the fifth month 9004
33:55 They will give you trouble in the land w 889
34: 5 w it will turn, join the Wadi of Egypt 6801[S]
35:33 " 'Do not pollute the land w you are. 889
35:34 the land w you live and where I dwell, 889
35:34 Do not defile the land where you live and w 889
Dt 1:28 W can we go? 625+2025
3:21 the same to all the kingdoms over there w 889
8: 9 a land w bread will not be scarce 889
8: 9 a land w the rocks are iron 889
11:10 w you planted your seed and irrigated it 889
11:24 Every place w you set your foot will 889
12: 2 the hills and under every spreading tree w 9004
12:21 If the place w the LORD your God chooses 889
14:24 the place w the LORD will choose 9004
18: 6 of your towns anywhere in Israel w 9004
21: 4 or planted and w there is a flowing stream. NIH
23:12 camp w you can go to relieve yourself. 2025+9004
28:37 the nations w the LORD will drive you. 2025+9004
30: 3 gather you again from all the nations w 2025+9004
31:14 w I will commission him." NIH
32:37 He will say: "Now w are their gods, 361
33:28 w the heavens drop dew. NIH
34: 6 but to this day no one knows w his grave is. NIH
Jos 1: 3 I will give you every place w 889
2: 4 but I did not know w they had come from. 402
3: 1 w they camped before crossing over. 9004
4: 3 of the Jordan from right w the priests stood 2296
4: 3 with you and put them down at the place w 889
4: 8 w they put them down. 9004
4: 9 the spot w the priests who carried the ark of NIH
5: 8 they remained w they were in camp 9393
5:15 for the place w you are standing is holy." 889
8:24 and in the desert w they had chased them, 889
9: 8 "Who are you and w do you come from?" 402
10:27 the trees and threw them into the cave w 9004
22:19 w the LORD's tabernacle stands, 9004
22:33 to devastate the country w the Reubenites 889
Jdg 1:26 w he built a city and called it Luz, NIH
4:10 w he summoned Zebulun and 2025+7730[S]
5:27 w he sank, there he fell—dead. 889+928
6:11 w his son Gideon was threshing wheat in NIH
6:13 W are all his wonders 372
9:38 Zebul said to him, "W is your big talk now, 372
11: 3 w a group of adventurers gathered NIH
13: 6 I didn't ask him w he came from, 361
16: 1 w he saw a prostitute. 9004
16:26 "Put me w I can feel the pillars that support NIH
17: 9 Micah asked him, "W are you from?" 402
18: 1 a place of their own w they might settle, NIH
18: 2 w they spent the night. 9004
18: 7 w they saw that the people were living NIH
19:17 the old man asked, "W are you going? 625+2025
19:17 W did you come from?" 402
19:18 in the hill country of Ephraim w I live. 4946+9004
19:26 to the house w her master was staying, 9004
20:22 again took up their positions w 928+2021+5226[S]
20:47 w they stayed four months. 928+6152+8234[S]
21: 2 w they sat before God until evening, 9004
Ru 1: 7 the place w she had been living and 2025+9004
1:16 W you go I will go, 889
1:16 and w you stay I will stay. 889
1:17 W you die I will die, 889
2: 9 Watch the field w the men are harvesting, 889
2:19 "W did you glean today? 407
2:19 W did you work? 625+2025
3: 1 w you will be well provided for? 889
3: 4 note the place w he is lying. 9004
1Sa 1: 3 at Shiloh, w Hophni and Phinehas, 9004
3: 3 w the ark of God was. 9004
7:17 w his home was, 9004
9:10 So they set out for the town w the man 9004
9:18 "Would you please tell me w 361+2296
10: 5 w there is a Philistine outpost. 889
10:14 "W have you been?" 625
14: 9 we will stay w we are and not go up 9393
19: 3 and stand with my father in the field w 9004
19:22 And he asked, "W are Samuel and David?" 407
20:19 go to the place w you hid 9004
20:37 to the place w Jonathan's arrow had fallen, 889
23:22 Find out w David usually goes 5226[S]
25:11 give it to men coming from who knows w?" 361
26: 5 Then David set out and went to the place w 9004
26: 5 He saw w Saul and Abner son of Ner, 2021+5226[S]
1Sa 26:16 W are the king's spear and water jug 361
27:10 "W did you go raiding today?" 625
30: 9 w some stayed behind, 2256
30:13 and w do you come from?" 361
30:31 and to those in all the other places w David 9004
31:12 w they burned them. 9004
2Sa 1: 3 "W have you come from?" 361
1:13 "W are you from?" 361
2: 1 David asked, "W shall I go?" 625+2025
2:23 to the place w Asahel had fallen and died. 9004
9: 4 "W is he?" 407
11:15 in the front line w the fighting is fiercest. NIH
11:16 he put Uriah at a place w he knew 9004
13:13 W could I get rid of my disgrace? 625+2025
15:20 when I do not know w I am going?
889+2143+2143+6584
15:32 w people used to worship God, 9004
16: 3 "W is your master's grandson?" 372
17:20 "W are Ahimaaz and Jonathan?" 372
19:17 rushed to the Jordan, w the king was. 4200+7156[S]
21:12 w the Philistines had hung them 9004
23: 7 they are burned up w they lie." 928
23:11 the Philistines banded together at a place w 9004
1Ki 1:15 to see the aged king in his room, w Abishag NIH
7: 7 the Hall of Justice, w he was to judge, 9004
8: 9 w the LORD made a covenant with 889
8:47 the land w they are held captive, and repent 9004
8:54 w he had been kneeling NIH
11:24 w they settled and took control. 928+2023[S]
11:36 the city w I chose to put my Name. 9004
12: 2 w he had fled from King Solomon), 889
13:22 and drank water in the place w he told you 889
13:25 and they went and reported it in the city w 889
13:31 in the grave w the man of God is buried; 889
17:19 to the upper room w he was staying, 9004
18:10 not a nation or kingdom w my master has 9004
18:12 I don't know w the Spirit of the LORD 889
20:30 w the wall collapsed NIH
21:18 w he has gone to take possession of it. 9004
21:19 the place w dogs licked up Naboth's blood, 889
22:38 a pool in Samaria (w the prostitutes bathed), NIH
2Ki 2: 7 the place w Elijah and Elisha had stopped at NIH
2:14 "W now is the LORD, the God of Elijah?" 372
5:25 "W have you been, Gehazi?" 402+4946
6: 1 the place w we meet with you is too small 9004
6: 2 w each of us can get a pole; 4946+9004
6: 6 The man of God asked, "W did it fall?" 625+2025
6:13 "Go, find out w he is," the king ordered, 378
6:27 w can I get help for you? 402+4946
11:16 as she reached the place *w* the horses enter AIT
14: 6 of Moses w the LORD commanded: 889
17:29 in the several towns w they settled, 9004
18:34 W are the gods of Hamath and Arpad? 372
18:34 W are the gods of Sepharvaim, 372
19:13 W is the king of Hamath, the king of Arpad, 361
19:27 " 'But I know *w* you stay and AIT
20:14 and w did they come from?" 402
23: 7 of the LORD and w women did weaving 9004
23: 8 w the priests had burned incense. 2025+9004
25: 6 w sentence was pronounced on him. NIH
1Ch 3: 4 w he reigned seven years and six months. 9004
5:26 w they are to this day. NIH
11:13 At a place w there was a field full of barley, NIH
2Ch 3: 1 Mount Moriah, w the LORD had appeared 889
5:10 w the LORD made a covenant with 889
6:37 the land w they are held captive, and repent 9004
6:38 and soul in the land of their captivity w 889
10: 2 w he had fled from King Solomon), 889
20:26 w they praised the LORD. 9004
25: 4 w the LORD commanded: 889
25:11 w he killed ten thousand men of Seir. NIH
32:33 and was buried on the hill *w* the tombs AIT
33:19 and the sites w he built high places and set 889
35:24 and brought him to Jerusalem, w he died. NIH
Ezr 1: 4 the people of any place w survivors may 9004
8:32 w we rested three days. 9004
Ne 2: 3 when the city w my fathers are buried lies 1074[S]
2: 5 the city in Judah w my fathers are buried so NIH
2:16 officials did not know w I had gone or 625+2025
9: 3 They stood w they were and read 6584+6642[S]
10:37 the tithes in all the towns *w* we work. AIT
10:39 and oil to the storerooms w the articles for 9004
10:39 the articles for the sanctuary are kept and w NIH
12:27 from w they lived and were brought 5226
Est 7: 5 W is the man who has dared to do such 361+2296
7: 8 on the couch w Esther was reclining. 889
Job 1: 7 "W have you come from?" 402
2: 2 "W have you come from?" 361
4: 7 W were the upright ever destroyed? 407
6:24 show me w I have been wrong. 4537
8:11 Can papyrus grow tall w there is no marsh? 928
10:22 w even the light is like darkness." NIH
15:28 and houses w no one lives, 4200+4564[S]
17:15 w then is my hope? 372
18:19 no survivor w once he lived. 928
20: 7 those who have seen him will say, 'W 361
21:28 You say, 'W now is the great man's house, 372
21:28 the tents w wicked men lived?' NIH
23: 3 If only I knew w to find him; NIH
28: 1 "There is a mine for silver and a place w NIH
28: 4 Far from w people dwell he cuts a shaft, 6640
28:12 "But w can wisdom be found? 402+4946
28:12 W does understanding dwell? 361+2296
28:20 "W then does wisdom come from? 402
28:20 W does understanding dwell? 361+2296
28:23 to it and he alone knows w it dwells, 5226
34:22 no deep shadow, w evildoers can hide. 9004
Job 34:26 punishes them for their wickedness w 928+5226[S]
35:10 But no one says, 'W is God my Maker, 372
38: 4 "W were you when I laid 407
38:11 here is w your proud waves halt'? NIH
38:19 And w does darkness reside? 361+2296
38:24 to the place w the lightning is dispersed, NIH
38:24 the place w the east winds are scattered over NIH
38:26 to water a land w no man lives, NIH
39:30 and w the slain are, there is he." 889+928
40:12 crush the wicked w they stand. 9393
Ps 19: 3 or language w their voice is not heard. NIH
26: 8 I love the house w you live, O LORD, 5061
26: 8 O LORD, the place w your glory dwells. 5438
41: 8 he will never get up from the place w 889
42: 3 "W is your God?" 372
42:10 "W is your God?" 372
43: 3 to the place w you dwell. 5438
46: 4 w the Most High dwells. 5438
50: 1 the rising of the sun to the place w it sets. 4427
53: 5 w there was nothing to dread. NIH
63: 1 in a dry and weary land w there is no water. NIH
65: 8 w morning dawns and evening fades 4604
68:16 at the mountain w God chooses to reign, NIH
68:16 w the LORD himself will dwell forever? NIH
69: 2 w there is no foothold. NIH
74: 2 Mount Zion, w you dwelt. 928+2257[S]
74: 4 Your foes roared in the place w you met 4595
74: 8 place w God was worshiped 4595
79:10 "W is their God?" 372
81: 5 w we heard a language we did NIH
84: 3 w she may have her young— 889
89:49 w is your former great love, 372
95: 9 w your fathers tested and tried me, 889
107: 4 to a city w they could settle. 4632
107: 7 a straight way to a city w they could settle. 4632
107:36 and they founded a city w they could settle. 4632
113: 3 the rising of the sun to the place w it sets, 4427
115: 2 Why do the nations say, "W is their God?" 372
121: 1 w does my help come from? 402
122: 4 That is w the tribes go up, 9004
139: 7 W can I go from your Spirit? 625+2025
139: 7 W can I flee from your presence? 625+2025
142: 3 the path w I walk men have hidden a snare 2306
Pr 8: 2 w the paths meet, she takes her stand; NIH
14: 4 W there are no oxen, the manger is empty, 928
15:17 a meal of vegetables w there is love than 9004
29:18 W there is no revelation, 928
31:23 w he takes his seat among the elders of 928
Ecc 1: 5 and hurries back to w it rises. 5226[S]
8:10 and receive praise in the city w 889
9:10 for in the grave, w you are going, 2025+9004
11: 3 in the place w it falls, there will it lie. 8611
SS 1: 7 w you graze your flock and 377
1: 7 and w you rest your sheep at midday. 377
6: 1 W has your lover gone, 625+2025
Isa 7:23 in every place w there were 9004
7:25 places w cattle are turned loose 5448
7:25 and w sheep run. 5330
10: 3 W will you leave your riches? 625+2025
19:12 W are your wise men now? 361
29: 1 Ariel, Ariel, the city *w* David settled! AIT
33:18 "W is that chief officer? 372
33:18 W is the one who took the revenue? 372
33:18 W is the officer in charge of the towers?" 372
35: 7 In the haunts w jackals once lay, 8070
36:19 W are the gods of Hamath and Arpad? 372
36:19 W are the gods of Sepharvaim? 372
37:13 W is the king of Hamath, the king of Arpad, 372
37:28 "But I know *w* you stay and AIT
39: 3 and w did they come from?" 402
42:11 let the settlements w Kedar lives rejoice. NIH
49:21 w have they come from?' " 407
50: 1 "W is your mother's certificate of divorce
361+2296
51:13 For w is the wrath of the oppressor? 372
63:11 w is he who brought them through the sea, 372
63:11 W is he who set his Holy Spirit 372
63:15 W are your zeal and your might? 372
64:11 w our fathers praised you, 889
66: 1 W is the house you will build for me? 361+2296
66: 1 W will my resting place be? 361+2296
Jer 2: 6 They did not ask, 'W is the LORD, 372
2: 6 a land w no one travels and no one lives?' 9004
2: 8 The priests did not ask, 'W is the LORD?' 372
2:28 W then are the gods you made 372
3: 2 Is there *any place* w you have 407
6:16 ask w the good way is, and walk in it, 361+2296
7:12 the place in Shiloh w I first made a dwelling 9004
13: 7 from the place w I had hidden it, 2025+9004
13:20 W is the flock that was entrusted to you, 372
15: 2 And if they ask you, 'W shall we go?' 625+2025
16: 5 not enter a house *w there* is a funeral meal; AIT
16: 8 "And do not enter a house *w there* is feasting AIT
16:15 north and out of all the countries w 2025+9004
17: 6 in a salt land w no one lives. NIH
17:15 "W is the word of the LORD? 372
19:13 all the houses w they burned incense on 889
19:14 w the LORD had sent him to prophesy, 9004
22:12 in the place w they have led him captive; 9004
22:26 w neither of you was born, 9004
23: 3 of all the countries w I have driven them 9004
23: 3 w they will be fruitful and increase NIH
23: 8 of the north and out of all the countries w 9004
29:14 and places w I have banished you," 9004
29:18 among all the nations w I drive them. 9004
31: 9 on a level path w they will not stumble 928+2023[S]
31:40 The whole valley *w* dead bodies and AIT

Jer 32: 5 w he will remain until I deal with him, 9004
32:29 with the houses w the people provoked me 889
32:37 surely gather them from all the lands w 9004
34:16 and female slaves you had set free to go w NIH
35: 7 Then you will live a long time in the land w 9004
36:12 w all the officials were sitting: 9004
36:19 Don't let anyone know w you are." 407
37:16 w he remained a long time. 9004
37:17 w he asked him privately, NIH
37:19 W are your prophets who prophesied 372
38: 9 w he will starve to death 9393
39: 5 w he pronounced sentence on him. NIH
40:12 the countries w they had been scattered. 9004
41: 9 Now the cistern w he threw all the bodies of 9004
42: 3 that the LORD your God will tell us w 2006+2021^S
42:14 w we will not see war or hear the trumpet or 889
42:22 the sword, famine and plague in the place w 9004
43: 5 in the land of Judah from all the nations w 9004
44: 8 w you have come to live? 9004
49:36 not be a nation w Elam's exiles do not go. 9004
51:37 a place w no one lives. NIH
51:43 and desert land, a land w no one lives, 928+2177^S
52: 9 w he pronounced sentence on him. NIH
52:11 w he put him in prison till the day NIH
La 2:12 "W is bread and wine?" 372
Eze 3:15 And **there,** *w* they were living, AIT
4:13 among the nations w I will drive them." 9004
6: 9 Then in the nations w they have been 9004
6:13 places w they offered fragrant incense 9004
8: 3 w the idol that provokes to jealousy stood. 9004
9: 3 w it had been, 889
11:16 for them in the countries w they have gone.' 9004
11:17 and bring you back from the countries w 889
12: 3 and go from w you are to another place. 5226^S
12:16 so that in the nations w they go 9004
13:12 "W is the whitewash you covered it with?" 372
16:16 w you carried on your prostitution. 2157+6584^S
17: 4 w he planted it in a city of traders. NIH
17: 7 toward him from the **plot** *w* it was planted AIT
17:10 wither away in the **plot** *w* it grew?' " AIT
20:34 the countries w you have been scattered— 889
20:38 of the **land** *w* they are living, AIT
20:41 the countries w you have been scattered, 889
21:19 Make a signpost w the road branches off to 928
21:22 w he is to set up battering rams, NIH
21:30 In the place w you were created, 889
24: 7 w the dust would cover it. NIH
28:25 the nations w they have been scattered, 889
29:13 the nations w they were scattered. 2025+9004
34:12 from all the places w they were scattered on 9004
36:21 Israel profaned among the nations w 2025+9004
36:22 among the nations w you have gone. 9004
37:21 I will take the Israelites out of the nations w 9004
37:25 the land w your fathers lived. 889
40:38 w the burnt offerings were washed. 9004
42:13 w the priests who approach 9004
43: 7 This is w I will live among 9004
44:19 into the outer court w 2021+2021+2667+2958^S
46:20 "This is the place w the priests will cook 9004
46:24 the kitchens w those who minister at 9004
47: 8 w it enters the Sea. NIH
47: 9 w the river flows everything will live. 2025+9004
Da 6:10 to his upstairs room w the windows opened NIH
8:17 near the **place** w I was **standing,** 6642
9: 7 in all the countries w you have scattered us 9004
Hos 1:10 In the place w it was said to them, 889
4:13 w the shade is pleasant. 3954
13:10 W is your king, that he may save you? 180+686
13:10 W are your rulers in all your towns, NIH
13:14 W, O death, are your plagues? 180
13:14 W, O grave, is your destruction? 180
Joel 2:17 'W is their God?' " 372
Am 3: 5 Does a bird fall into a trap on the ground w 2256
Jnh 1: 3 w he found a ship bound for that port. NIH
1: 5 w he lay down and fell into a deep sleep. NIH
1: 8 W do you come from? 402
Mic 7:10 "W is the LORD your God?" 361
Na 2:11 W now is the lions' den, 372
2:11 the **place** w they **fed** their young, 5337
2:11 w the lion and lioness went, and the cubs, 9004
3: 7 W can I find anyone to comfort you?" 402+4946
3:17 and no one knows **w.** 361+5226
Hab 3: 4 w his power was hidden. 9004
Zep 2: 6 *w* the Kerethites **dwell,** AIT
3:19 and honor in every **land** *w* they were put AIT
Zec 1: 5 W are your forefathers now? 372
2: 2 I asked, "W are you going?" 625+2025
5:10 "W are they taking the basket?" 625+2025
7:14 w they were strangers. 889
Mal 1: 6 If I am a father, w is the honor due me? 372
1: 6 If I am a master, w is the respect due me?" 372
2:17 with them" or "W is the God of justice?" 372
Mt 2: 2 "W is the one who has been born king of *4544*
2: 4 he asked them w the Christ was to be born. *4544*
2: 9 of them until it stopped over **the place w** *4023*
2:15 w he stayed until the death of Herod. *1695*
3: 7 the Pharisees and Sadducees coming **to w** *2093*
6:19 w moth and rust destroy, *3963*
6:19 and w thieves break in and steal. *3963*
6:20 w moth and rust do not destroy, *3963*
6:20 and w thieves do not break in and steal. *3963*
6:21 For w your treasure is, *3963*
8:12 w there will be weeping and gnashing *1695*
13: 5 w it did not have much soil. *3963*
13: 8 w it produced a crop— *NIG*
13:27 W then did the weeds come **from?'** *4470*
13:42 w there will be weeping and gnashing *1695*
Mt 13:50 w there will be weeping and gnashing *1695*
13:54 "W did this man get this wisdom *4470*
13:56 W then did this man get all these things?" *4470*
15:33 "W could we get enough bread *4470*
18:20 w two or three come together in my name, *4023*
21:17 w he spent the night. *1695*
21:25 w did it come **from?** *4470*
22:13 w there will be weeping and gnashing *1695*
24:51 w there will be weeping and gnashing *1695*
25:24 harvesting w you have not sown *3963*
25:24 where you have not sown and gathering w *3854*
25:26 that I harvest w I have not sown and gather *3963*
25:26 where I have not sown and gather w I have *3854*
25:30 w there will be weeping and gnashing *1695*
26:17 "W do you want us to make preparations *4544*
26:57 w the teachers of the law and *3963*
26:71 w another girl saw him and said to *NIG*
28: 6 Come and see the place w he lay. *3963*
28:16 the mountain w Jesus had told them to go. *4023*
Mk 1:35 the house and went off to a solitary place, w *1695*
4: 5 w it did not have much soil. *3963*
4:15 w the word is sown. *3963*
5:40 and went in w the child was. *3963*
6: 2 "W did this man get these things?" *4470*
8: 4 His disciples answered, "But w *4470*
9: 2 w they were all alone. *NIG*
9:30 not want anyone to know w they were, *NIG*
9:43 w the fire never goes out. *NIG*
9:48 w " 'their worm does not die, *3963*
12:41 **place w the offerings were put** *1126*
13:14 that causes desolation' standing w it does *3963*
14:12 "W do you want us to go *4544*
14:14 W is my guest room, *4544*
14:14 Where is my guest room, w I may eat *3963*
15:47 the mother of Joses saw w he was laid. *4544*
16: 6 See the place w they laid him. *3963*
Lk 1:40 w she entered Zechariah's home *2779*
4: 2 w for forty days he was tempted by *NIG*
4:16 w he had been brought up, *4023*
4:17 he found the place w it is written: *4023*
4:42 for him and when they came **to w** he was, *2401*
8:25 "W is your faith?" *4544*
10: 1 of him to every town and place w he was *4023*
10:33 as he traveled, came w the man was; *2848*
10:38 he came to a village w a woman *1254*
11:33 and puts it in a place w it will be hidden, *NIG*
12:33 w no thief comes near *3963*
12:34 For w your treasure is, *3963*
13:25 'I don't know you or w you come **from.'** *4470*
13:27 'I don't know you or w you come **from.** *4470*
16:23 In hell, w he was in torment, *NIG*
17:17 W are the other nine? *4544*
17:37 "W, Lord?" they asked. *4544*
17:37 He replied, "W there is a dead body, *3963*
19:37 near the **place w the road goes down** *2853*
20: 7 "We don't know w it was **from."** *4470*
22: 9 "W do you want us to prepare for it?" *4544*
22:11 W is the guest room, *4544*
22:11 the guest room, w I may eat the Passover *3963*
Jn 1:28 w John was baptizing. *3963*
1:38 "w are you staying?" *4544*
1:39 So they went and saw w he was staying, *4544*
2: 9 w it had come **from,** *4470*
3: 8 but you cannot tell w it comes from or *4470*
3: 8 where it comes from or w it is going. *4544*
3:22 w he spent some time with them, *1695*
4:11 W can you get this living water? *4470*
4:20 that the place w we must worship is *3963*
4:46 w he had turned the water into wine. *3963*
6: 5 "W shall we buy bread for these people *4470*
6:17 w they got into a boat and set off across *2779*
6:21 the shore w they were heading. *1650+4005*
6:23 the place w the people had eaten the bread *3963*
6:62 What if you see the Son of Man ascend to w *3963*
7:11 "W is that man?" *4544*
7:27 But we know w this man is **from;** *4470*
7:27 no one will know w he is **from."** *4470*
7:28 you know me, and you know w I am **from.** *4470*
7:34 and w I am, you cannot come." *3963*
7:35 "W does this man intend to go *4544*
7:35 Will he go w our people live scattered *1650*
7:36 but you will not find me,' and 'W I am, *3963*
7:42 the town w David lived?" *3963*
8: 2 w all the people gathered around him, *2779*
8:10 up and asked her, "Woman, w are they? *4544*
8:14 for I know w I came **from** and *4470*
8:14 where I came from and w I am going. *4544*
8:14 But you have no idea w I come **from** or *4470*
8:14 where I come from or w I am going. *4544*
8:19 Then they asked him, "W is your father?" *4544*
8:20 **place w the offerings were put.** *1126*
8:21 W I go, you cannot come." *3963*
8:22 Is that why he says, 'W I go, *3963*
9:12 "W is this man?" *4544*
9:29 we don't even know w he comes **from."** *4470*
9:30 You don't know w he comes **from,** *4470*
10:40 to the place w John had been baptizing in *3963*
11: 6 stayed w he was two more days. *1877+4005+5536*
11:30 was still at the place w Martha had met him. *3963*
11:32 When Mary reached **the place** w Jesus was *3963*
11:34 "W have you laid him?" *4544*
11:54 w he stayed with his disciples. *1695*
11:57 that if anyone found out w Jesus was, *4544*
12: 1 Jesus arrived at Bethany, w Lazarus lived, *3963*
12:26 and w I am, my servant also will be. *3963*
12:35 in the dark does not know w he is going. *4544*
13:33 W I am going, you cannot come. *3963*
Jn 13:36 "Lord, w are you going?" *4544*
13:36 Jesus replied, "W I am going, *3963*
14: 3 to be with me that you also may be w I am. *3963*
14: 4 the way to the place w I am going." *3963*
14: 5 "Lord, we don't know w you are going, *4544*
16: 5 'W are you going?' *4544*
16:10 w you can see me no longer; *2779*
17:24 given me to be with me w I am, *3963*
18:20 w all the Jews come together. *3963*
19: 9 "W do you come **from?"** *4470*
19:20 for the place w Jesus was crucified was near *3963*
19:41 At the place w Jesus was crucified, *3963*
20: 2 and we don't know w they have put him!" *4544*
20:12 seated w Jesus' body had been, *3963*
20:13 "and I don't know w they have put him." *4544*
20:15 tell me w you have put him, *4544*
20:25 put my finger w the nails were, *1650+3836+5596*^S
21:18 and went w you wanted; *3963*
21:18 and lead you w you do not want to go." *3963*
Ac 1:13 to the room w they were staying. *4023*
1:25 which Judas left to go w he belongs." *1650+5536*
2: 2 from heaven and filled the whole house w *4023*
3: 2 w he was put every day to beg *NIG*
4:31 w they were meeting was shaken. *1877+4005*
7: 4 God sent him to this land w you are *1650+4005*
7:15 w he and our fathers died. *2779*
7:29 w he settled as a foreigner *4023*
7:33 the place w you are standing is holy *2093+4005*
7:49 Or w will my resting place be? *5515*
10:17 the men sent by Cornelius found out w *NIG*
11: 5 and it came down **to w** I was. *948*
11:11 stopped at the house w I was staying. *1877+4005*
12:12 w many people had gathered *4023*
13:13 w John left them to return to Jerusalem. *1254*
14: 7 w they continued to preach the good news. *1695*
14:26 w they had been committed to the grace *3854*
15:30 w they gathered the church together *2779*
15:35 w they and many others taught *NIG*
15:36 in all the towns w we preached *1877+4005*
16: 1 w a disciple named Timothy lived, *2779*
16:13 w we expected to find a place of prayer. *4023*
16:40 w they met with the brothers *NIG*
17: 1 w there was a Jewish synagogue. *3963*
17:19 w they said to him, *NIG*
17:26 and the exact places w they should live. *NIG*
18:19 w Paul left Priscilla and Aquila. *1695*
20: 3 w he stayed three months. *NIG*
20: 6 w we stayed seven days. *3963*
20: 8 in the upstairs room w we were meeting. *4023*
20:13 w we were going to take Paul aboard. *1696*
21: 3 w our ship was to unload its cargo. *1698*
21: 7 w we greeted the brothers and stayed *NIG*
21:16 w we were to stay. *4005+4123*
25: 2 w the chief priests and Jewish leaders *NIG*
25:10 w I ought to be tried. *4023*
27:39 w they decided to run the ship aground *1650+4005*
28:23 to the **place** w *he* was **staying.** *3825*
Ro 3:27 W, then, is boasting? It is excluded. *4544*
4:15 w there is no law there is no transgression. *4023*
5:20 But w sin increased, grace increased *4023*
9:26 that in the very place w it was said to them, *4023*
15:20 the gospel w Christ was not known, *3963*
1Co 1:20 W is the wise man? *4544*
1:20 W is the scholar? *4544*
1:20 W is the philosopher of this age? *4544*
12:17 w would the sense of hearing be? *4544*
12:17 w would the sense of smell be? *4544*
12:19 w would the body be? *4544*
13: 8 But w there are prophecies, they will cease; *1664*
13: 8 w there are tongues, they will be stilled; *1664*
13: 8 w there is knowledge, it will pass away. *1664*
15:55 "W, O death, is your victory? *4544*
15:55 W, O death, is your sting?" *4544*
2Co 3:17 and w the Spirit of the Lord is, *4023*
Col 3: 1 w Christ is seated at the right hand of God. *4023*
Heb 2: 6 there is **a place** w someone has testified: *4543*
3: 9 w your fathers tested and tried me and *4023*
6:20 w Jesus, who went before us, has entered *3963*
10:18 And w these have been forgiven, *3963*
11: 8 though he did not know w he was going. *4544*
Jas 3:16 For w you have envy and selfish ambition, *3963*
2Pe 3: 4 "W is this 'coming' he promised? *4544*
1Jn 2:11 he does not know w he is going, *4544*
Rev 2:13 I know w you live— *4544*
2:13 w Satan has his throne. *3963*
2:13 in your city—w Satan lives. *3963*
7:13 w did they come **from?"** *4470*
11: 8 w also their Lord was crucified. *3963*
12: 6 w she might be taken care of for 1,260 days. *3963*
12:14 w she would be taken care of for a time, *3963*
17:15 "The waters you saw, w the prostitute sits, *4023*
18:19 w all who had ships on the sea *1877+4005*
20:10 w the beast and the false prophet *3963*

WHEREVER (68) [WHERE]

Ge 20:15 live w you like." 928
28:15 and will watch over you w you go, 889+928+3972
30:30 LORD has blessed you w I have been. 4200+8079
35: 3 with me w I have gone." 889+928+2006+2021
Ex 5:11 get your own straw w you can find it, 889+4946
12:20 W you live, you must eat unleavened 928+3972
20:24 W I cause my name to be honored, 889+928+2021+3972+5226
Lev 3:17 for the generations to come, w you live: 928+3972
7:26 And w you live, you must not eat 928+3972
23: 3 w you live, it is a Sabbath to the LORD. 928+3972

Lev 23:14 for the generations to come, w you live. 928+3972
23:17 From *w* you **live,** AIT
23:21 for the generations to come, w you live. 928+3972
23:31 for the generations to come, w you live. 928+3972
Nu 9:17 w the cloud settled, the Israelites encamped. 889+928+5226
35:29 the generations to come, w you live. 928+3972
Dt 11:25 of you on the whole land, w you go. 889
21:14 let her go w she wishes. 4200
23:16 Let him live among you w he likes and 889+928+2021+5226
30:1 and you take them to heart w 889+2025+9004
Jos 1:7 you may be successful w you go. 889+928+3972
1:9 be with you w you go." 889+928+3972
1:16 and w you send us we will go. 448+889+3972
1Sa 14:47 W he turned, he inflicted punishment 889+928+3972
2Sa 7:7 W I have moved with all the Israelites, 889+928+3972
7:9 I have been with you w you have gone, 889+928+3972
8:6 The LORD gave David victory w he went. 889+928+3972
8:14 The LORD gave David victory w he went. 889+928+3972
15:21 w my lord the king may be, 889+928+5226
17:12 we will attack him w he may be found, 285+889+928+2021+5226
1Ki 2:3 in all you do and w you go, 889+3972+9004
8:44 w you send them, 889+928+2006+2021
2Ki 8:1 and stay for a while w you can, 889+928
11:8 Stay close to the king w he **goes."** 928+928+995+2256+3655
1Ch 17:6 W I have moved with all the Israelites, 889+928+3972
17:8 I have been with you w you have gone, 889+928+3972
2Ch 6:34 w you send them, 889+928+2006+2021
23:7 Stay close to the king w he **goes."** 928+928+995+2256+3655
Ne 4:12 "W you turn, they will attack us." 2021+3972+4946+5226
4:20 W you hear the sound of the trumpet, 889+928+5226
Est 8:17 w the edict of the king went, 889+5226S
Ps 119:54 the theme of my song w I lodge. 928
Pr 17:8 w he turns, he succeeds. 448+889+3972
21:1 he directs it like a watercourse w he pleases. 889+3972+6584
Jer 8:3 W I banish them, 928+2021+3972+5226
24:9 w I banish them. 889+928+2021+3972+5226
40:4 lies before you; go w you please." 2025+9004
45:5 but w you go I will let you escape 889+2021+3972+5226+6584
Eze 1:12 W the spirit would go, they would go, 2025+9004
1:20 W the spirit would go, they would go, 9004
6:6 W you live, the towns will be laid waste 928+3972
6:14 to Diblah—w they live. 928+3972
21:16 then to the left, w your blade is turned. 625+2025
36:20 And w they went among 889
47:9 living creatures will live w 448+889+3972
Da 2:38 W they live, he has made you ruler over them all. 10089+10168+10353
Mt 8:19 "Teacher, I will follow you w you go." *1569+3963*
24:28 W there is a carcass, *1569+3963*
26:13 w this gospel is preached throughout *1569+3963*
Mk 6:55 the sick on mats to w they heard he was. *3963*
6:56 And w he went—into villages, *323+3963*
14:9 w the gospel is preached throughout *1569+3963*
Lk 9:57 "I will follow you w you go." *1569+3963*
Jn 3:8 The wind blows w it pleases. *3963*
Ac 8:4 preached the word w they went. *NIG*
1Co 16:6 can help me on my journey, w I go. *1569+4023*
Jas 3:4 a very small rudder w the pilot wants to go. *3963*
Rev 14:4 They follow the Lamb w he goes. *323+3963*

WHET (KJV) See SHARPEN

WHETHER (120)

Ge 17:13 *W* born in your household **or** AIT
24:21 the man watched her closely to learn w or 2022
27:21 to know w you really are my son Esau 2022
31:32 see for yourself w there is anything 4537
37:32 Examine it to see w it is your son's 561+4202
42:33 how I will know w you are honest men: 3954
Ex 12:19 w he is an alien or native-born. 928
13:2 w man or animal." 928
16:4 see w they will follow my instructions. 561+2022+4202
19:13 W man or animal, 561
22:4 w ox or donkey or sheep— 4946
22:8 to determine w he has laid his hands on 561+4202
34:19 w from herd or flock. NIH
Lev 3:1 w male or female, 561
5:2 w the carcasses of unclean wild animals or 196
5:4 w good **or** evil— 196
7:10 w mixed with oil **or** 2256
7:21 w human uncleanness **or** 196
11:10 w among all the swarming things **or** 2256
11:32 w it is made of wood, cloth, hide **or** 196
11:42 w it moves on its belly **or** 2256
13:55 w the mildew has affected one side **or** 196
15:3 W it continues flowing from his body **or** 196
15:23 W it is the bed or anything she was sitting 561
16:29 w native-born **or** an alien living 2256
Lev 17:15 " 'Anyone, w native-born or alien, 928
18:9 w she was born in the same home **or** 196
24:16 W an alien or native-born, 3869
27:26 w an ox or a sheep, it is the LORD's. 561
27:28 w man or animal or family land— 4946
27:30 w grain from the soil or fruit from the trees, 4946
Nu 3:13 w man or animal. 4946
4:27 w carrying or doing other work, 4200
8:17 w man or animal, is mine. 928
9:21 W by day or by night, 196
9:22 W the cloud stayed over the tabernacle 196
11:23 now see w or not what I say will come true 2022
13:18 and w the people who live there are strong 2022
15:3 w burnt offerings **or** sacrifices, 196
15:29 w he is a native-born Israelite **or** 2256
15:30 w native-born **or** alien, 2256
18:9 w grain **or** sin or guilt offerings, 2256
31:28 w persons, cattle, donkeys, sheep or goats. 4946
31:30 select one out of every fifty, w persons, 4946
Dt 1:16 w the case is between brother Israelites **or** 2256
4:16 w formed like a man **or** 196
8:2 w or not you would keep his commands. 2022
13:3 to find out w you love him 2022
13:7 the peoples around you, w near **or** far, 196
17:8 w bloodshed, lawsuits or assaults— 1068
23:19 w on money or food or anything else NIH
24:14 w he is a brother Israelite **or** 196
Jos 24:15 w the gods your forefathers served beyond 561
Jdg 2:22 to test Israel and see w they will keep 2022
3:4 the Israelites to see w they would obey 2022
18:5 to learn w our journey will be successful." 2022
Ru 3:10 after the younger men, w rich or poor. 561
1Sa 14:6 w by many **or** by few." 196
2Sa 15:21 w it means life or death, 561
1Ki 16:11 w relative or friend. 2256
2Ki 14:26 w slave or free, was suffering; 700+2256
2Ch 15:13 were to be put to death, w small or great, 4946
19:10 w bloodshed or other concerns of the law, 1068
20:9 w the sword of judgment, **or** 2256
Est 3:4 to see w Mordecai's behavior would 2022
Ps 58:9 w they be green or dry— 4017
Pr 20:11 by w his conduct is pure and right. 561
Ecc 2:19 And who knows w he will be a wise man or 2022
5:12 w he eats little or much, 561
9:1 no man knows w love or hate awaits him. 1685
11:3 W a tree falls to the south or to the north, 561
11:6 which will succeed, w this or that, 2022
11:6 or w both will do equally well. 561
12:14 w it is good or evil. 561
Isa 7:11 w in the deepest depths **or** 196
30:21 W you turn to the right or to the left, 3954
41:23 Do something, w good or bad, 677
Jer 24:8 w they remain in this land **or** live in Egypt. 2256
42:6 W it is favorable or unfavorable, 561
Eze 2:5 And w they listen or fail to listen— 561
2:7 w they listen or fail to listen, 561
3:11 w they listen or fail to listen." 561
46:12 w a burnt offering **or** fellowship offerings 196
Mk 4:27 Night and day, w he sleeps or gets up, *2779*
13:35 w in the evening, or at midnight, *2445*
Lk 14:31 not first sit down and consider w he is able *1623*
Jn 7:17 he will find out w my teaching comes *4538*
7:17 from God or w I speak on my own. *NIG*
9:25 "W he is a sinner **or not,** *1623*
Ac 4:19 for yourselves w it is right in God's sight *1623*
9:2 belonged to the Way, w men or women, *5445*
Ro 6:16 w you are slaves to sin, *2486*
14:8 So, w we live or die, we belong to the Lord. *1569*
1Co 3:22 w Paul or Apollos or Cephas or the world *1664*
7:16 wife, w you will save your husband? *1623*
7:16 husband, w you will save your wife? *1623*
8:5 w in heaven or on earth *1664*
10:31 So w you eat or drink or whatever you do, *1664*
10:32 Do not cause anyone to stumble, w Jews, *2779*
12:13 w Jews or Greeks, slave or free— *1664*
15:11 W, then, it was I or they, *1664*
2Co 5:9 w we are at home in the body or away *1664*
5:10 done while in the body, w good or bad. *1664*
12:2 W it was in the body or out of the body I do *1664*
12:3 w in the body or apart from the body I do *1664*
13:5 Examine yourselves to see w you are in *1623*
Eph 6:8 w he is slave or free. *1664*
Php 1:7 for w I am in chains or defending *NIG*
1:18 w from false motives or true, *1664*
1:20 w by life or by death. *1664*
1:27 w I come and see you or only hear *1664*
4:12 w well fed or hungry, *2779*
4:12 w living in plenty or in want. *2779*
Col 1:16 w thrones or powers or rulers or authorities; *1664*
1:20 w things on earth or things in heaven, *1664*
3:17 And whatever you do, w in word or deed, *NIG*
1Th 5:10 w we are awake or asleep, *1664*
2Th 2:15 w by word of mouth or by letter. *1664*
1Pe 2:13 w to the king, as the supreme authority, *1664*
1Jn 4:1 test the spirits to see w they are from God, *1623*

WHICH (707) [WHAT] See Index of Articles Etc.

WHILE (428) [AWHILE, MEANWHILE]

Ge 2:21 and w he was sleeping, 2256
4:8 And w they were in the field, 928
11:28 W his father Terah was **still alive,** 6584+7156
12:10 **live** there **for a w** because the famine 1591
13:6 not support them w they stayed together, 4200
Ge 13:12 w Lot lived among the cities of the plain 2256
18:1 to Abraham near the great trees of Mamre w 2256
18:8 W they ate, he stood near them under a tree. 2256
20:1 **For a w** *he* **stayed** in Gerar, 1591
21:21 W he was living in the Desert of Paran, 2256
22:5 the donkey w I and the boy go over there. 2256
25:6 But w he was still living, 928
25:27 w Jacob was a quiet man, 2256
26:3 **Stay** in this land **for a w,** 1591
27:44 Stay with him **for a w** 285+3427
29:9 W he was **still** talking with them, 6388
30:36 w Jacob continued to tend the rest 2256
33:14 w I move along slowly at the pace of 2256
34:25 w all of them were still in pain, 928
35:16 W they were still some distance 2256
35:22 W Israel was living in that region, 928
36:24 in the desert w he was grazing the donkeys 928
37:7 w your sheaves gathered around mine 2256
39:7 and **after a w** his master's wife took notice 339+465+1821+2021+2021
39:20 **But** w Joseph was there in the prison, 2256
42:19 w the rest of you go and take grain back 2256
48:7 in the land of Canaan w we were still on 928
Ex 16:10 W Aaron was speaking to the whole 3869
18:14 w all these people stand around you 2256
20:21 w Moses approached the thick darkness 2256
22:10 *w* no *one is* **looking,** AIT
22:14 *w* the owner **is not** AIT
33:9 w the LORD spoke with Moses. 2256
Lev 14:46 house w it is closed up will be unclean 3427+3972
15:26 w her discharge **continues** 3427+3972
18:18 and have sexual relations with her w 928
25:22 W you plant during the eighth year, 2256
26:43 and will enjoy its sabbaths w it lies desolate 928
Nu 5:18 w he himself holds the bitter water 2256
5:19 and become impure w **married to** 9393
5:20 But if you have gone astray w **married to** 9393
5:29 and defiles herself w **married to** 9393
11:33 w the meat was **still** between their teeth 6388
15:32 W the Israelites were in the desert, 2256
18:21 in return for the work they do w serving at NIH
19:5 W he watches, the heifer is to be burned— 4200
23:3 "Stay here beside your offering w I go 2256
23:15 "Stay here beside your offering w I meet 2256
25:1 W Israel was staying in Shittim, 2256
25:6 and the whole assembly of Israel w 2256
32:6 "Shall your countrymen go to war w 2256
Dt 4:11 near and stood at the foot of the mountain w 2256
5:23 w the mountain was ablaze with fire, 2256
9:15 from the mountain w it was ablaze with fire. 2256
22:21 in Israel by being promiscuous w still NIH
25:4 Do not muzzle an ox w it is treading out 928
26:14 I have not eaten any of the sacred portion w 928
26:14 nor have I removed any of it w 928
31:27 the LORD w I am still alive and with you, 928
32:42 w my sword devours flesh: 2256
Jos 3:16 w the water flowing down to the Sea of 2256
3:17 w all Israel passed by until 2256
4:11 and the priests came to the other side w NIH
5:10 *w* **camped** at Gilgal on the plains of Jericho, AIT
6:13 w the trumpets kept sounding. 2256
9:22 w actually you live near us? 2256
14:10 w Israel moved about in the desert. 889
Jdg 3:20 then approached him w he was sitting alone 2256
3:26 W they waited, Ehud got away. 6330
4:21 and a hammer and went quietly to him w 2256
7:3 w ten thousand remained. 2256
7:21 W each man held his position around 2256
9:27 W they were eating and drinking, 2256
13:9 to the woman w she was out in the field; 2256
13:19 the LORD did an amazing thing w Manoah 2256
13:25 the Spirit of the LORD began to stir him w NIH
16:13 So *w he was* **sleeping,** AIT
16:25 W they were in high spirits, they shouted, 3869
16:30 when he died than w he lived. 928
18:17 and the cast idol w the priest and 2256
19:22 *W* they *were* **enjoying** themselves, AIT
20:32 W the Benjamites were saying, 2256
21:23 W the girls were dancing, 4946
Ru 1:1 to **live for a w** in the country of Moab. 1591
1Sa 2:13 a sacrifice and w the meat was being boiled, 3869
7:10 W Samuel was sacrificing 2256
13:16 w the Philistines camped at Micmash. 2256
14:19 W Saul was talking to the priest, 6330
18:10 w David was playing the harp, 2256
19:9 W David was playing the harp, 2256
21:13 and w he was in their hands he acted like NIH
23:15 W David was at Horesh in the Desert 2256
25:4 W David was in the desert, 2256
25:13 w two hundred stayed with the supplies. 2256
28:4 w Saul gathered all the Israelites and set 2256
2Sa 3:1 w the house of Saul grew weaker 2256
3:35 and urged David to eat something w 928
4:5 the day w he was taking his noonday rest. 2256
4:7 into the house w he was lying on the bed 2256
5:2 In the past, w Saul was king over us, 928
6:15 w he and the entire house of Israel brought 2256
7:2 w the ark of God remains in a tent." 2256
10:8 w the Arameans of Zobah and Rehob and 2256
11:16 So w Joab had the city under siege, 928
12:18 "W the child was still living, 928
12:21 W the child was alive, you fasted and wept, 6288
12:22 He answered, "W the child was still alive, 928
13:30 W they were on their way, 2256
15:8 W your servant was living at Geshur 928
15:12 W Absalom was offering sacrifices, 928
16:13 along the road w Shimei was going along 2256

2Sa 17: 2 I would attack him w he is weary and weak. 2256
18: 4 the gate w all the men marched out in units 2256
18: 9 w the mule he was riding kept on going. 2256
18:14 w Absalom was still alive 6388
18:24 W David was sitting between the inner 2256
20: 8 W they were at the great rock in Gibeon, NIH
20:15 W they were battering the wall to bring it 2256
23:13 w a band of Philistines was encamped in 2256
24:13 from your enemies w they pursue you? 2256
1Ki 1:14 W you are still there talking to the king, 6388
1:22 W she was still speaking with the king, 6388
3:17 I had a baby w she was there with me. NIH
3:20 the night and took my son from my side w 2256
3:23 w that one says, 'No! Your son is dead 2256
6: 7 at the temple site w it was being built. 928
6:27 w the wing of the other touched 2256
8:14 W the whole assembly of Israel was 2256
11:21 W he was in Egypt, 2256
13:20 W they were sitting at the table, 2256
15:27 w Nadab and all Israel were besieging it. 2256
18: 4 W Jezebel was killing off the LORD's 928
18:13 what I did w Jezebel was killing 928
19: 4 w he himself went a day's journey into 2256
20:12 Ben-Hadad heard this message w he and 3869
20:16 They set out at noon w Ben-Hadad and 2256
20:27 w the Arameans covered the countryside. 2256
20:40 W your servant was busy here and there, 2256
2Ki 3:15 W the harpist was playing, 3869
4:38 W the company of the prophets was 2256
6:33 W he was still talking to them, 6388
8: 1 and stay for a w wherever you can, 1591
11: 3 at the temple of the LORD for six years w 2256
13:21 w some Israelites were burying AIT
17:41 Even w these people were worshiping 2256
19:37 w he was worshiping in the temple AIT
23:29 W Josiah was king, 928+3427
24:11 to the city w his officers were besieging it. 2256
1Ch 11: 2 In the past, even w Saul was king, 928
11: 8 w Joab restored the rest of the city. 2256
11:15 w a band of Philistines was encamped in 2256
12: 1 w he was banished from the presence 6388
17: 1 w the ark of the covenant of the LORD is 2256
19: 7 w the Ammonites were mustered 2256
19: 9 w the kings who had come were 2256
21:20 W Araunah was threshing wheat, 2256
2Ch 3:11 w its other wing, also five cubits long, 2256
6: 3 W the whole assembly of Israel was 2256
13:13 so that w he was in front of Judah AIT
22: 8 W Jehu was executing judgment on 3869
22: 9 and his men captured him w he was hiding 2256
22:12 for six years w Athaliah ruled the land. 2256
25:16 W he was still speaking, 928
26:19 W he was raging at the priests 928
28:18 w the Philistines had raided towns in 2256
29:19 in his unfaithfulness w he was king. 928
29:28 w the singers sang and 2256
30:21 w the Levites and priests sang to 2256
34: 3 w he was still young, 6388
34:14 W they were bringing out the money 928
35:11 w the Levites skinned the animals. 2256
Ezr 3:12 w many others shouted for joy. 2256
10: 1 W Ezra was praying and confessing, 3869
10: 6 W he was there, he ate no food NIH
Ne 1: 1 w I was in the citadel of Susa, 2256
4:16 w the other half were equipped with spears, 2256
6: 3 the work stop w I leave it and go down 889+3869
7: 3 W the gatekeepers are still on duty, 6330
8: 7 the Law w the people were standing there. 2256
9:33 you have acted faithfully, w we did wrong. 2256
9:35 Even w they were in their kingdom, NIH
11: 1 w the remaining nine were to stay 2256
11: 4 w other people from both Judah 2256
13: 6 But w all this was going on, 928
Est 6:14 W they were still talking with him, 6388
7: 8 even molest the queen w she is with me in NIH
Job 1:16 W he was still speaking, 6388
1:17 W he was still speaking, 6388
1:18 W he was still speaking, 6330
8:12 W still growing and uncut, 6388
10: 3 w you smile on the schemes of the wicked? 2256
21: 3 Bear with me w I speak, 2256
24:24 For a little w they are exalted, 5071
32:11 I waited w you spoke, 4200
32:11 w you were searching for words, 6330
38: 7 w the morning stars sang together and all 928
Ps 32: 6 to you w you may be found; 4200+6961
37:10 A little w, and the wicked will 5071+6388
41: 6 w his heart gathers slander; AIT
42: 3 w men say to me all day long, 928
49:18 w he lived he counted himself blessed— 928
63:11 w the mouths of liars will be silenced. 3954
68:13 Even w you sleep among the campfires, 561
68:23 in the blood of your foes, w the tongues NIH
78:30 even w it was still in their mouths, 6388
137: 4 of the LORD w in a foreign land? NIH
141:10 w I pass by in safety. 6330
Pr 31:15 She gets up w it is still dark; 928
Ecc 2:14 w the fool walks in the darkness; 2256
3:12 for men than to be happy and do good w 928
7:28 w I was still searching but not finding— 6388
9: 3 and there is madness in their hearts w 928
10: 6 w the rich occupy the low ones. 2256
10: 7 w princes go on foot like slaves. 2256
11: 9 Be happy, young man, w you are young, 928
SS 1:12 W the king was at his table, 6330+8611
Isa 22: 3 having fled w the enemy was still far away. NIH
26:20 a little w until his wrath has passed by. 5071+8092
Isa 37:38 w he was worshiping in the temple AIT
55: 6 Seek the LORD w he may be found; 928
55: 6 call on him w he is near. 928
63:18 For a little w your people possessed 5203
65:24 w they are still speaking I will hear. 6388
Jer 7:13 W you were doing all these things, 3610
15: 9 Her sun will set w it is still day; 928
19:10 "Then break the jar w those who go 4200
33: 1 W Jeremiah was still confined 6388
34: 1 W Nebuchadnezzar king of Babylon 2256
34: 7 w the army of the king of Babylon 2256
36: 4 and w Jeremiah dictated all the words NIH
38: 7 W the king was sitting in 2256
39:15 W Jeremiah had been confined in 928
41: 1 W they were eating together there, 2256
43: 9 "W the Jews are watching, 4200
51:39 But w they are aroused, 928
La 1:19 and my elders perished in the city w 3954
3:27 for a man to bear the yoke w he is young. 928
Eze 1: 1 w I was among the exiles by 2256
8: 1 w I was sitting in my house and the elders AIT
9: 8 W they were killing and I was left alone, 3869
10:19 W I watched, the cherubim spread their wings NIH
11:16 yet for a little w I have been a sanctuary 5071
12: 4 During the daytime, w they watch, NIH
12: 4 Then in the evening, w they are watching, NIH
12: 5 W they watch, dig through the wall NIH
12: 7 carrying them on my shoulders w NIH
23: 5 in prostitution w she was still mine; NIH
35:14 W the whole earth rejoices, 3869
42: 8 W the row of rooms on the side next to 3954
43: 6 W the man was standing beside me, 2256
44: 7 desecrating my temple w you offered me 928
44:17 not wear any woolen garment w ministering 928
Da 2:34 W you were watching, a rock 10168+10527
2:49 w Daniel himself remained at 10221
4:10 the visions I saw w lying in my bed: NIH
4:13 "In the visions I saw w lying in my bed, NIH
4:23 w its roots remain in the ground. NIH
5: 2 W Belshazzar was drinking his wine, 10089
7: 8 "W I was thinking about the horns, AIT
8:15 W I, Daniel, was watching the vision 928
8:18 W he was speaking to me, 928
9:20 W I was speaking and praying, 6388
9:21 w I was still in prayer, 6388
10:15 W he was saying this to me, 928
Ob 1:11 On the day you stood aloof w 928+3427
Hab 1:13 Why are you silent w the wicked swallow 928
Hag 1: 4 w this house remains a ruin?" 2256
1: 9 w each of you is busy with his own house. 2256
2: 6 'In a little w I will once more shake 5071
Zec 3: 5 w the angel of the LORD stood by. 2256
14:12 Their flesh will rot w they are still standing 2256
Mt 5:25 Do it w you are still with him 2401+4015
9:10 W Jesus was having dinner AIT
9:15 mourn w he is still with them? 2093+4012
9:18 W he was saying this, AIT
9:32 W they were going out, AIT
12:46 W Jesus was still talking AIT
13: 2 w all the people stood on the shore. 2779
13:25 w everyone was sleeping, AIT
13:29 'because w you are pulling the weeds, AIT
14:22 w he dismissed the crowd. 2401+4005
17: 5 W he was still speaking, AIT
21: 8 w others cut branches from the trees 1254
21:23 and, w he was teaching, AIT
22:41 W the Pharisees were gathered together, AIT
25:10 w they were on their way AIT
26: 6 W Jesus was in Bethany in the home of AIT
26:21 And w they were eating, he said, AIT
26:26 W they were eating, Jesus took bread, AIT
26:36 "Sit here w I go over there and pray." 2401+4005
26:47 W he was still speaking, AIT
26:73 After a little w, those standing there AIT
27:19 W Pilate was sitting on the judge's seat, AIT
27:63 "we remember that w he was still alive 2285
28:11 W the women were on their way, AIT
28:13 and stole him away w we were asleep.' AIT
Mk 1:35 w it was still dark, Jesus got up, 1939
2:15 W Jesus was having dinner at Levi's house, NIG
2:19 bridegroom fast w he is with them? 1877+4005
4: 1 w all the people were along the shore at 2779
5:21 a large crowd gathered around him w 2779
5:35 W Jesus was still speaking, AIT
6:45 w he dismissed the crowd. 2401
10:32 w those who followed were afraid. 1254
11: 8 w others spread branches they had cut in 1254
11:27 w Jesus was walking in the temple courts, AIT
12:35 W Jesus was teaching in the temple courts, AIT
14: 3 W he was in Bethany, AIT
14:18 W they were reclining at the table eating, AIT
14:22 W they were eating, Jesus took bread, AIT
14:32 "Sit here w I pray." 2401
14:66 W Peter was below in the courtyard, AIT
14:70 After a little w, those standing near AIT
16:12 of them w they were walking in the country. AIT
Lk 2: 2 w Quirinius was governor AIT
2: 6 W they were there, 1639+1877+3836
2:43 w his parents were returning home, 1877
5:12 W Jesus was in one of the towns, 1877
5:34 bridegroom fast w he is with them? 1877+4005
8: 4 W a large crowd was gathering AIT
8:13 They believe for a w, 2789
8:49 W Jesus was still speaking, AIT
9:34 W he was speaking, AIT
9:42 w the boy was coming, AIT
Lk 9:43 W everyone was marveling AIT
14:32 he will send a delegation w the other is still AIT
15:20 "But w he was still a long way off, AIT
16:25 w Lazarus received bad things, 2779
17: 8 get yourself ready and wait on me w I eat 2401
19:11 W they were listening AIT
20:45 W all the people were listening, AIT
22:47 W he was still speaking AIT
24: 4 W they were wondering about this, 1877+3836
24: 6 w he was still with you in Galilee: AIT
24:32 not our hearts burning within us w he talked 6055
24:36 W they were still talking about AIT
24:41 w they still did not believe AIT
24:44 "This is what I told you w I was still AIT
24:51 W he was blessing them, 1877+3836
Jn 1:48 "I saw you w you were still under AIT
2:23 Now w he was in Jerusalem at 6055
4:51 W he was still on the way, AIT
5: 7 W I am trying to get in, 1877+4005
6:59 He said this w teaching in the synagogue AIT
8:20 He spoke these words w teaching in AIT
9: 5 W I am in the world, 4020
11: 8 "a short w ago the Jews tried to stone you, 3814
12: 2 w Lazarus was among those reclining at 1254
12:25 w the man who hates his life 2779
12:35 to have the light just a little w longer. 5989
12:35 Walk w you have the light, 6055
12:36 Put your trust in the light w you have it, 6055
14:25 "All this I have spoken w still with you. AIT
15: 2 in me that bears no fruit, w every branch 2779
16:16 "In a little w you will see me no more, 3625
16:16 then after a little w you will see me." 3625
16:17 'In a little w you will see me no more, 3625
16:17 then after a little w you will see me,' 3625
16:18 "What does he mean by 'a little w'? 3625
16:19 'In a little w you will see me no more, 3625
16:19 then after a little w you will see me'? 3625
16:20 and mourn w the world rejoices. 1254
17:12 W I was with them, 4021
17:13 I say these things w I am still in the world, NIG
20: 1 w it was still dark, AIT
Ac 1: 4 w he was eating with them, AIT
3:11 W the beggar held on to AIT
4: 1 John w they were speaking to the people. AIT
5:34 the men be put outside for a little w. 1099
7: 2 to our father Abraham w he was still AIT
7:59 W they were stoning him, Stephen prayed, AIT
9:39 that Dorcas had made w she was still AIT
10:10 w the meal was being prepared, AIT
10:17 W Peter was wondering about the meaning 6055
10:19 W Peter was still thinking AIT
10:44 W Peter was still speaking AIT
12:19 to Caesarea and stayed there a w. 1417
13: 2 W they were worshiping the Lord and AIT
17:16 W Paul was waiting for them AIT
18:12 W Gallio was proconsul of Achaia, AIT
19: 1 W Apollos was at Corinth, 1877+3836
19:22 w he stayed in the province of Asia NIG
21:31 W they were trying to kill him, AIT
23:32 w they returned to the barracks. NIG
26:31 and w talking with one another, they said, AIT
Ro 4:11 he had by faith w he was still uncircumcised 1877
5: 8 W we were still sinners, Christ died for us. AIT
7: 3 w her husband is still alive, AIT
15:24 I hope to visit you w passing through and AIT
15:24 after I have enjoyed your company for a w. 3538
1Co 2: 2 For I resolved to know nothing w I was with you except NIG
9: 9 an ox w it is treading out the grain." AIT
12:24 w our presentable parts need no special treatment. 1254
14:24 in w everybody is prophesying, 1254
16:10 that he has nothing to fear w he is with you, NIG
2Co 3:13 w the radiance was fading away. AIT
5: 4 For w we are in this tent, AIT
5:10 for the things done w in the body, NIG
7: 8 but only for a little w— 6052
8:13 be relieved w you are hard pressed, NIG
13: 2 I now repeat it w absent: AIT
Gal 2:17 "If, w we seek to be justified in Christ, AIT
Eph 4:26 Do not let the sun go down w you are still angry, NIG
Php 1:17 that they can stir up trouble for me w I am NIG
1Th 2: 9 burden to anyone w we preached the gospel AIT
5: 3 W people are saying, "Peace and safety," 4020
1Ti 5: 6 for pleasure is dead even w she lives. AIT
5:18 w it is treading out the grain," AIT
6:13 and of Christ Jesus, who w testifying AIT
2Ti 3:13 w evil men and impostors will go from bad NIG
Tit 2:13 w we wait for the blessed hope— AIT
Phm 1:10 who became my son w I was in chains. 1877
1:13 in helping me w I am in chains for 1877
1:15 was separated from you for a little w 4639+6052
Heb 9:17 it never takes effect w who made is living. 4021
10:37 For in just a very little w, 2285+4012+4012
11:36 w still others were chained and put NIG
12:10 Our fathers disciplined us for a little w 2465
Jas 1:11 the rich man will fade away even w he goes 1877
4:14 You are a mist that appears for a little w 3900
1Pe 1: 6 for a little w you may have had to suffer 3900
3:20 w the ark was being built. AIT
5:10 after you have suffered a little w, 3900
2Pe 2: 9 w continuing their punishment. AIT
2:13 reveling in their pleasures w they feast with AIT
2:19 w they themselves are slaves of depravity— AIT
Rev 11:12 w their enemies looked on. 2779
17:10 he must remain for a little w. 3900

WHIP (4) [WHIPS]
Pr 26: 3 A w for the horse, a halter for the donkey, 8765
Isa 10:26 with a w, as when he struck down Midian at 8765
Jn 2:15 So he made a w out of cords, *5848*
1Co 4:21 Shall I come to you with a w, *4811*

WHIPS (6) [WHIP]
Jos 23:13 w on your backs and thorns in your eyes, 8849
1Ki 12:11 My father scourged you with w; 8765
12:14 My father scourged you with w; 8765
2Ch 10:11 My father scourged you with w; 8765
10:14 My father scourged you with w; 8765
Na 3: 2 The crack of w, the clatter of wheels, 8765

WHIRLING (1)
Eze 10:13 the wheels being called "the w **wheels.**" 1649

WHIRLWIND (13) [WIND]
2Ki 2: 1 about to take Elijah up to heaven in a w, 6194
2:11 and Elijah went up to heaven in a w. 6194
Ps 77:18 Your thunder was heard in the w, 1649
Pr 1:27 when disaster sweeps over you like a w, 6070
Isa 5:28 their chariot wheels like a w. 6070
40:24 and a w sweeps them away like chaff. 6194
66:15 and his chariots are like a w; 6070
Jer 4:13 his chariots come like a w, 6070
23:19 a w swirling down on the heads of 6193
Hos 4:19 A w will sweep them away, 8120
8: 7 "They sow the wind and reap the w. 6070
Na 1: 3 His way is in the w and the storm, 6070
Zec 7:14 *'I* **scattered** them **with a** w among the 6192

WHIRLWINDS (1) [WIND]
Isa 21: 1 Like w sweeping through the southland, 6070

WHIRRING (1)
Isa 18: 1 Woe to the land of w wings along the rivers 7527

WHISPER (9) [WHISPERED, WHISPERING]
1Ki 19:12 And after the fire came a gentle w. 1960+7754
Job 4:12 my ears caught a w of it. 9066
26:14 how faint the w we hear of him! 1821
Ps 41: 7 All my enemies w together against me; 4317
107:29 He stilled the storm to a w; 1960
Isa 8:19 and spiritists, who w and mutter, 7627
26:16 *they could* **barely** w **a prayer.** 4318+7440
29: 4 out of the dust your speech *will* w. 7627
La 3:62 *what* my enemies w and mutter against me 8557

WHISPERED (2) [WHISPER]
Mt 10:27 what *is* w in your ear, *201*[S]
Lk 12: 3 and what *you have* w in the ear in *3281*

WHISPERING (4) [WHISPER]
2Sa 12:19 that his servants *were* w **among themselves** 4317
Jer 20:10 I hear many w, "Terror on every side! 1804
Jn 7:12 Among the crowds there was widespread w *1198*
7:32 the crowd w such things about him. *1197*

WHISTLE (1) [WHISTLES, WHISTLING]
Isa 7:18 that day the LORD *will* w for flies from 9239

WHISTLES (1) [WHISTLE]
Isa 5:26 *he* w for those at the ends of the earth. 9239

WHISTLING (1) [WHISTLE]
Jdg 5:16 the campfires to hear the w *for* the flocks? 9241

WHIT (KJV) See ALL, EVERY, EVERYTHING, IN THE LEAST

WHITE (61) [REDDISH-WHITE, WHITER]
Ge 30:35 or spotted female goats (all that had w 4237
30:37 and plane trees and made w stripes on them 4237
30:37 the bark and exposing the w inner *wood* of 4237
Ex 16:31 It was w like coriander seed and tasted 4237
Lev 11:18 the w **owl,** the desert owl, the osprey, 9492
13: 3 and if the hair in the sore has turned w and 4237
13: 4 the spot on his skin is w **but does not appear** 4237
13: 4 and the hair in it has not turned w, 4237
13:10 a w swelling in the skin that has turned 4237
13:10 in the skin that has turned the hair w and 4237
13:13 Since it has all turned w, he is clean. 4237
13:16 Should the raw flesh change and turn w, 4237
13:17 and if the sores have turned w, 4237
13:19 a w swelling or reddish-white spot appears, 4237
13:20 and the hair in it has turned w, 4237
13:21 there is no w hair in it and it is 4237
13:24 and a reddish-white or w spot appears in 4237
13:25 and if the hair in it has turned w, 4237
13:26 the priest examines it and there is no w hair 4237
13:38 a man or woman has w spots on the skin, 4237
13:39 and if the spots are dull w, 4237
Dt 14:16 the little owl, the great owl, the w **owl,** 9492
Jdg 5:10 "You who ride on w donkeys, 7467
2Ki 5:27 and he was leprous, as w as snow. NIH
Est 1: 6 garden had hangings of w and blue linen, 2580
1: 6 with cords of w **linen** and purple material 1009
8:15 royal garments of blue and w, 2580
Job 6: 6 or is there flavor in the w *of* an egg? 8202
41:32 one would think the deep had w **hair.** 8484
Ecc 9: 8 Always be clothed in w, 4237
Isa 1:18 *they shall be* as w as snow; 4235
Da 7: 9 His clothing was as w as snow; 10254
7: 9 the hair of his head was w like wool. 10490
Joel 1: 7 **leaving** their branches w. 4235
Zec 1: 8 Behind him were red, brown and w horses. 4237
6: 3 the third w, and the fourth dappled— 4237
6: 6 the one with the w horses toward the west, 4237
Mt 5:36 you cannot make even one hair w or black. *3328*
17: 2 and his clothes became as w as the light. *3328*
28: 3 and his clothes were w as snow. *3328*
Mk 9: 3 His clothes became dazzling w, *3328+3336*
16: 5 a young man dressed in a w robe sitting on *3328*
Jn 20:12 and saw two angels in w, *3328*
Ac 1:10 when suddenly two men dressed in w stood *3328*
Rev 1:14 His head and hair were w like wool, *3328*
1:14 white like wool, as w as snow, *3328*
2:17 a w stone with a new name written on it, *3328*
3: 4 They will walk with me, dressed in w, *3328*
3: 5 overcomes will, like them, be dressed in w. *3328*
3:18 and w clothes to wear, so you can cover *3328*
4: 4 in w and had crowns of gold on their heads. *3328*
6: 2 and there before me was a w horse! *3328*
6:11 Then each of them was given a w robe, *3328*
7: 9 They were wearing w robes *3328*
7:13 "These in w robes—who are they, *3328*
7:14 and **made** them w in the blood of the Lamb. *3326*
14:14 and there before me was a w cloud, *3328*
19:11 and there before me was a w horse, *3328*
19:14 riding on w horses and dressed in fine linen, *3328*
19:14 on white horses and dressed in fine linen, w *3328*
20:11 a great w throne and him who was seated *3328*

WHITER (4) [WHITE]
Ge 49:12 his teeth w than milk. 4237
Ps 51: 7 wash me, and *I will be* w than snow. 4235
La 4: 7 brighter than snow and w than milk, 7458
Mk 9: 3 w than anyone in the world could bleach *NIG*

WHITEWASH (6) [WASH]
Eze 13:10 they cover it with w, 9521
13:11 therefore tell those who cover it with w 9521
13:12 "Where is the w you covered it with?" 3225
13:14 the wall you have covered with w 9521
13:15 and against those who covered it with w. 9521
22:28 Her prophets w these deeds for them 3212+9521

WHITEWASHED (3) [WASH]
Eze 13:15 "The wall is gone and so are those *who* w it, 3212
Mt 23:27 You are like w tombs, *3154*
Ac 23: 3 "God will strike you, *you* w wall! *3154*

WHITHER (KJV) See WHERE, WHICH

WHITHERSOEVER (KJV) See EVERYWHERE, WHENEVER, WHEREVER

WHO (5081) [WHOEVER, WHOM, WHOSE] See Index of Articles Etc.

WHOEVER (191) [WHO]
Ge 4:14 and w finds me will kill me." 3972
9: 6 "*W* **sheds** the blood of man, AIT
12: 3 and *w* **curses** you I will curse; AIT
44:10 W is found to have it will become my slave; 889
Ex 12:15 for w eats anything with yeast in it from 3972
12:19 And w eats anything with yeast in it must 3972
19:12 W touches the mountain shall surely be put 3972
22:20 "*W* **sacrifices** to any god other than AIT
30:33 W makes perfume like it 408+889
30:33 like it and w puts it on anyone other than 889
30:38 W makes any like it 408+889
31:14 w does any work on that day must 3972
31:15 W does any work on the Sabbath day must 3972
32:24 So I told them, 'W has any gold jewelry, 4769
32:26 "W is for the LORD, come to me." 4769
32:33 "W has sinned against me I will blot out 4769
35: 2 W does any work on it must be put to death. 3972
Lev 11:24 W touches their carcasses will be unclean 3972
11:25 W picks up one of their carcasses 3972
11:26 w touches [the carcass of] any of them will 3972
11:27 w touches their carcasses will be unclean 3972
11:31 W touches them when they are dead will 3972
15: 6 W sits on anything that the man with 2021
15: 7 " 'W touches the man who has 2021
15:10 and w touches any of the things that were 3972
15:10 w picks up those things must wash 2021
15:21 W touches her bed must wash his clothes 3972
15:22 W touches anything she sits 3972
15:27 W touches them will be unclean; 3972
19: 8 *W* **eats** it will be held responsible AIT
24:21 *W* **kills** an animal must make restitution, AIT
24:21 but *w* **kills** a man must be put to death. AIT
Nu 19:11 "W touches the dead body of anyone will 2021
19:13 W touches the dead body of anyone 3972
Jos 1:18 W rebels against your word and 408+889+3972
Jdg 6:31 W fights for him shall be put to death 889
Jdg 10:18 "W will launch the attack against 408+2021+4769
2Sa 17: 9 w hears about it will say, 2021
20:11 "W favors Joab, and whoever is for 889+4769
20:11 favors Joab, and w is for David, 889+4769
23: 7 W touches thorns uses a tool of iron or 408
1Ch 11: 6 "W leads the attack on the Jebusites 3972
2Ch 13: 9 W comes to consecrate himself with 3972
Ezr 7:26 W does not obey the law of your God 10168+10353
Job 29:11 W heard me spoke well of me, 265[S]
Ps 34:12 W of you loves life and desires 408+2021+4769
101: 5 *W* **slanders** his neighbor in secret, AIT
101: 5 w has haughty eyes and a proud heart, NIH
107:43 W is wise, let him heed these things 4769
Pr 1:33 but *w* **listens** to me will live in safety and AIT
6:32 w does so destroys himself. 2085
8:35 For *w* **finds** me finds life and receives favor AIT
8:36 But *w* **fails to find** me harms himself; AIT
9: 7 "*W* **corrects** a mocker invites insult; AIT
9: 7 *w* **rebukes** a wicked man incurs abuse. AIT
10:17 *W* **ignores** correction leads others astray. AIT
10:18 and *w* **spreads** slander is a fool. AIT
11:15 but *w* **refuses** to strike hands in pledge AIT
11:28 *W* **trusts** in his riches will fall, AIT
12: 1 *W* **loves** discipline loves knowledge, AIT
13:18 but *w* **heeds** correction is honored. AIT
14:31 but *w is* **kind** *to* the needy honors God. AIT
15: 5 but *w* **heeds** correction shows prudence. AIT
15:32 but *w* **heeds** correction gains understanding. AIT
16:20 *W* **gives heed** to instruction prospers, AIT
17: 5 *w* **gloats** over disaster will not go unpunished AIT
17: 9 *w* **repeats** the matter separates close friends. AIT
20: 1 w is led astray by them is not wise. 3972
21:17 *w* **loves** wine and oil will never be rich. AIT
21:28 w listens to him will be destroyed forever. 408
24:24 *W* **says** to the guilty, "You are innocent"— AIT
28:13 *w* **confesses** and renounces them finds mercy AIT
29: 5 W flatters his neighbor is spreading a net 1505[S]
29:25 but *w* **trusts** in the LORD is kept safe. AIT
Ecc 5:10 *W* **loves** money never has money enough; AIT
5:10 w loves wealth is never satisfied 4769
8: 5 *W* **obeys** his command will come AIT
10: 8 *W* **digs** a pit may fall into it; AIT
10: 8 *w* **breaks through** a wall may be bitten by AIT
10: 9 *W* **quarries** stones may be injured by them; AIT
10: 9 *w* **splits** logs may be endangered by them. AIT
11: 4 *W* **watches** the wind will not plant; AIT
11: 4 *w* **looks** at the clouds will not reap. AIT
Isa 13:15 W is captured will be thrust through; 3972
24:18 W flees at the sound of terror will fall into 2021
24:18 w climbs out of the pit will be caught in 2021
54:15 w attacks you will surrender to you. 4769
59: 5 W eats their eggs will die, 2021
59:15 and *w* **shuns** evil becomes a prey. AIT
65:16 W invokes a blessing in the land will do so 889
66: 3 But *w* **sacrifices** a bull is like one who kills AIT
66: 3 and *w* **offers** a lamb, AIT
66: 3 *w* **makes** a grain **offering** AIT
66: 3 and *w* **burns memorial** incense, AIT
Jer 21: 9 W stays in this city will die by the sword, 2021
21: 9 But w goes out and surrenders to 2021
31:30 w eats sour grapes— 132+2021+3972
38: 2 'W stays in this city will die by the sword, 2021
38: 2 w goes over to the Babylonians will live. 2021
48:44 "W flees from the terror will fall into a pit, 2021
48:44 w climbs out of the pit will be caught in 2021
50: 7 W found them devoured them; 3972
Eze 3:27 W will listen let him listen, 2021
3:27 and w will refuse let him refuse; 2021
46: 9 w enters by the north gate to worship is 2021
46: 9 and w enters by the south gate is to go out 2021
Da 3: 6 W does not fall down and worship 10168+10426
3:11 w does not fall down and worship 10168+10426
5: 7 "W reads this writing 10050+10168+10353
Zec 2: 8 for w touches you touches the apple 2021[S]
Mal 2:12 As for the man who does this, w **he may be,** 2256+6424+6699
Mt 5:19 but w practices and teaches these *323+4005*
10:32 "W acknowledges me before men, *4015+4246*
10:33 But w disowns me before men, *323+4015*
10:39 W finds his life will lose it, *3836*
10:39 and w loses his life for my sake will find it. *3836*
12:50 For w does the will of my Father *323+4015*
13:12 W has will be given more, *4015*
13:12 W does not have, even what he has *4015*
16:25 w wants to save his life will lose it, *1569+4005*
16:25 but w loses his life for me will find it. *323+4005*
18: 4 w humbles himself like this child is *4015*
18: 5 And w welcomes a little child like this *1569+4005*
20:26 w wants to become great among you *1569+4005*
20:27 w wants to be first must be your slave *323+4005*
23:12 For w exalts himself will be humbled, *4015*
23:12 and w humbles himself will be exalted. *4015*
25:29 W does not have, even what he has *3836*
Mk 3:29 w blasphemes against the Holy Spirit *323+4005*
3:35 W does God's will is my brother and *323+4005*
4:25 W has will be given more; *4005*
4:25 w does not have, even what he has *4005*
8:35 w wants to save his life will lose it, *1569+4005*
8:35 but w loses his life for me and for *323+4005*
9:37 W welcomes one of these little children *323+4005*
9:37 w welcomes me does not welcome me *323+4005*
9:40 for w is not against us is for us. *4005*
10:43 w wants to become great among you *323+4005*
10:44 w wants to be first must be slave of all. *323+4005*
16:16 W believes and is baptized will be saved, *3836*
16:16 but w does not believe will be condemned. *3836*

Lk 8:18 W has will be given more; *323+4005*
8:18 w does not have, even what he thinks *323+4005*
9:24 For w wants to save his life will lose it, *323+4005*
9:24 but w loses his life for me will save it. *323+4005*
9:48 "W welcomes this little child *1569+4005*
9:48 and w welcomes me welcomes *323+4005*
9:50 "for w is not against you is for you." *4005*
12: 8 w acknowledges me before men, *323+4005*
16:10 "W can be trusted with very little can also *3836*
16:10 and w is dishonest with very little will also *3836*
17:33 W tries to keep his life will lose it, *1569+4005*
17:33 and w loses his life will preserve it. *323+4005*
Jn 3:16 that w believes in him shall not perish *3836+4246*
3:18 W believes in him is not condemned, *3836*
3:18 but w does not believe stands condemned *3836*
3:21 w lives by the truth comes into the light, *3836*
3:36 W believes in the Son has eternal life, *3836*
3:36 but w rejects the Son will not see life, *3836*
4:14 but w drinks the water I give him will never thirst. *323+4005*
5:24 w hears my word and believes him who *3836*
6:37 and w comes to me I will never drive away. *3836*
6:54 W eats my flesh and drinks my blood *3836*
6:56 W eats my flesh and drinks my blood *3836*
7:38 W believes in me, as the Scripture has said, *3836*
8:12 W follows me will never walk in darkness, *3836*
10: 9 w enters through me will be saved. *1569+5516*
11:26 w lives and believes in me will never die. *3836+4246*
12:26 W serves me must follow me; *1569+5516*
13:20 w accepts anyone I send accepts me; *323+3836*
13:20 w accepts me accepts the one who sent me." *3836*
14:21 W has my commands and obeys them, *3836*
1Co 11:27 w eats the bread or drinks the cup of *323+4005*
2Co 9: 6 W sows sparingly will also reap sparingly, *3836*
9: 6 and w sows generously will also reap *3836*
Gal 5:10 will pay the penalty, w he may be. *1569+4015*
Jas 2:10 For w keeps the whole law and yet stumbles *4015*
5:20 W turns a sinner from the error of his way *3836*
1Pe 3:10 "W would love life and see good days *3836*
1Jn 2: 6 W claims to live in him must walk as Jesus *3836*
2:10 W loves his brother lives in the light, *3836*
2:11 But w hates his brother is in the darkness *3836*
2:23 w acknowledges the Son has the Father *3836*
4: 6 and w knows God listens to us; *3836*
4: 6 but w is not from God does not listen to us. *4005*
4: 8 W does not love does not know God, *3836*
4:16 W lives in love lives in God, *3836*
4:21 W loves God must also love his brother. *3836*
2Jn 1: 9 w continues in the teaching has both *3836*
Rev 22:17 W is thirsty, let him come; *3836*
22:17 and w wishes, let him take the free gift of *3836*

WHOLE (393) [WHOLLY, WHOLEHEARTED, WHOLEHEARTEDLY]

Ge 1:29 of the w earth and every tree that has fruit 3972
2: 6 up from the earth and watered the w surface 3972
7: 1 "Go into the ark, you and your w family, 3972
11: 1 Now the w world had one language and 3972
11: 4 be scattered over the face of the w earth." 3972
11: 9 the language of the w world. 3972
11: 9 over the face of the w earth. 3972
13: 9 Is not the w land before you? 3972
13:10 the w plain of the Jordan was well watered, 3972
13:11 the w plain of the Jordan and set out toward 3972
14: 7 and they conquered the w territory of 3972
17: 8 The w land of Canaan, 3972
18:26 I will spare the w place for their sake." 3972
18:28 Will you destroy the w city because 3972
25:25 and his w *body* was like a hairy garment; 3972
29:14 with him for a **w month,** 2544+3427
41:41 "I hereby put you in charge of the w land 3972
41:43 Thus he put him in charge of the w land 3972
41:54 but in the w land of Egypt there was food. 3972
41:56 the famine had spread over the w country, 3972
47:13 no food, however, in the w region 3972
Ex 8: 2 I will plague your w country with frogs. 3972
9: 9 It will become fine dust over the w land 3972
12: 3 Tell the w community of Israel that on 3972
12: 4 If any household is too small for a *w* **lamb,** AIT
12:47 w community of Israel must celebrate it. 3972
16: 1 The w Israelite community set out 3972
16: 2 the w community grumbled against Moses 3972
16:10 to the w Israelite community, 3972
17: 1 The w Israelite community set out from 3972
19: 5 Although the w earth is mine, 3972
19:18 the w mountain trembled violently, 3972
22: 6 of grain or standing grain or the *w* **field,** AIT
35: 1 Moses assembled the w Israelite community 3972
35: 4 Moses said to the w Israelite community, 3972
35:20 Then the w Israelite community withdrew 3972
Lev 4:13 w Israelite community sins unintentionally 3972
8:21 the w ram on the altar as a burnt offering, 3972
10: 6 be angry with the w community. 3972
13:13 and if the disease has covered his w body, 3972
15:16 he must bathe his w body with water, 3972
16:17 his household and the w community 3972
Nu 1: 2 of the w Israelite community by their clans 3972
1:18 and they called the w community together 3972
3: 7 for the w community at the Tent of Meeting 3972
8: 7 then have them shave their w bodies 3972
8: 9 and assemble the w Israelite community. 3972
8:20 Aaron and the w Israelite community did 3972
10: 3 the w community is to assemble before you 3972
11:20 but for a w month—until it comes out of 3427
11:21 give them meat to eat for a w month!' 3427

Nu 13:26 and the w Israelite community at Kadesh in 3972
13:26 the w assembly and showed them the fruit 3972
14: 2 and the w assembly said to them, 3972
14: 5 of the w Israelite assembly gathered there. 3972
14:10 the w assembly talked about stoning them. 3972
14:21 as the glory of the LORD fills the w earth, 3972
14:35 to this w wicked community, 3972
14:36 the w community grumble against him 3972
15:24 the w community is to offer a young bull 3972
15:25 for the w Israelite community, 3972
15:26 The w Israelite community and 3972
15:33 to Moses and Aaron and the w assembly, 3972
15:35 The w assembly must stone him outside 3972
16: 3 The w community is holy, 3972
16:41 the w Israelite community grumbled 3972
20: 1 the w Israelite community arrived at 3972
20:22 The w Israelite community set out 3972
20:27 in the sight of the w community. 3972
20:29 w community learned that Aaron had died, 3972
21:33 and his w army marched out to meet them 3972
21:34 with his w army and his land. 3972
21:35 together with his sons and his w army, 3972
25: 6 of Moses and the w assembly of Israel 3972
26: 2 of the w Israelite community by families— 3972
27: 2 the leaders and the w assembly, and said, 3972
27:20 so the w Israelite community will obey him. 3972
27:22 the priest and the w assembly. 3972
32:13 the w generation of those who had done evil 3972
32:33 the w land with its cities and the territory NIH
Dt 2:33 together with his sons and his w army. 3972
3: 1 with his w army marched out to meet us 3972
3: 2 over to you with his w army and his land. 3972
3: 4 the w region of Argob, 3972
3:13 (The w region of Argob in Bashan used to 3972
3:14 the w region of Argob as far as the border 3972
5:22 in a loud voice to your w assembly there on 3972
6:22 and Pharaoh and his w household. 3972
11: 3 king of Egypt and to his w country; 3972
11:25 the terror and fear of you on the w land, 3972
13:16 and all its plunder as a **w burnt offering** to 4003
18: 1 indeed the w tribe of Levi— 3972
19: 8 and gives you the w land he promised them, 3972
29:23 The w land will be a burning waste of salt 3972
31:30 in the hearing of the w assembly of Israel: 3972
33:10 and **w burnt offerings** on your altar. 4003
34: 1 There the LORD showed him the w land— 3972
34: 3 and the **w region** *from* the Valley of Jericho, 3971
34:11 and to all his officials and to his w land. 3972
Jos 2: 3 they have come to spy out the w land." 3972
2:24 "The LORD has surely given the w land 3972
3:17 the w nation had completed the crossing 3972
4: 1 When the w nation had finished crossing 3972
5: 8 after the w nation had been circumcised, 3972
6:24 they burned the w city and everything in it, NIH
8: 1 Take the w army with you, 3972
8: 3 and the w army moved out to attack Ai. 3972
8:35 that Joshua did not read to the w assembly 3972
9:18 The w assembly grumbled against 3972
9:24 the w land and to wipe out all its inhabitants 3972
10:21 The w army then returned safely to Joshua 3972
10:40 So Joshua subdued the w region, 3972
10:41 and from the w region of Goshen to Gibeon. 3972
11: 7 and his w army came against them suddenly 3972
11:16 all the Negev, the w region of Goshen, 3972
13: 9 and included the w plateau of Medeba as far 3972
13:12 the w kingdom of Og in Bashan, 3972
13:16 and the w plateau past Medeba 3972
18: 1 The w assembly of the Israelites gathered 3972
22:12 the w assembly of Israel gathered at Shiloh 3972
22:16 "The w assembly of the LORD says: 3972
22:18 be angry with the w community of Israel. 3972
22:20 did not wrath come upon the w community 3972
Jdg 1:25 but spared the man and his w family. 3972
2:10 After that w generation had been gathered 3972
7:14 and the w camp into his hands." 3972
9:29 'Call out your w army!'" 8049
14:17 She cried the w seven days of the feast. NIH
16:31 and his father's w family went down 3972
20:37 spread out and put the w city to the sword. 3972
20:40 and saw the smoke of the w city going up 4003
21:13 Then the w assembly sent an offer of peace 3972
Ru 1:19 the w town was stirred because of them, 3972
1Sa 1:28 For his w life he will be given over to 3972
4:13 the w town sent up a cry. 3972
7: 3 And Samuel said to the w house of Israel, 3972
7: 9 and offered it up as a w burnt offering to 4003
13:19 a blacksmith could be found in the w land 3972
14:15 Then panic struck the w army— 3972
17:46 the w world will know that there is a God 3972
19: 7 and told him the w conversation. 3972
20: 6 sacrifice is being made there for his w clan.' 3972
22:11 of Ahitub and his father's w family, 3972
22:15 knows nothing at all about this w affair." 3972
22:16 you and your father's w family." 3972
22:22 for the death of your father's w family. 3972
25: 7 and the w time they were at Carmel nothing 3972
25:15 and the w time we were out in the fields 3972
25:17 over our master and his w household. 3972
2Sa 2:29 continued through the w Bithron and came 3972
3:19 and the w house of Benjamin wanted to do. 3972
6: 5 and the w house of Israel were celebrating 3972
6:19 to each person in the w crowd of Israelites, 3972
11: 1 the king's men and the w Israelite army. 3972
14: 7 the w clan has risen up against your servant; 3972
15:23 The w countryside wept aloud as all 3972
18: 8 battle spread out over the w countryside, 3972
19: 2 the w army the victory that day was turned 3972

2Sa 19:20 the first of the w house of Joseph to come 3972
1Ki 6:22 So he overlaid the w interior with gold. 3972
8:14 the w assembly of Israel was standing there, 3972
8:22 of the LORD in front of the w assembly 3972
8:55 the w assembly of Israel in a loud voice, 3972
10:24 The w world sought audience with Solomon 3972
11:13 Yet I will not tear the w kingdom from him, 3972
11:28 he put him in charge of the w labor force of 3972
11:34 " 'But I will not take the w kingdom out 3972
12: 3 the w assembly of Israel went to Rehoboam 3972
12:21 he mustered the w house of Judah and 3972
12:23 to the w house of Judah and Benjamin, 3972
15:29 he killed Jeroboam's w family. 3972
16:11 he killed off Baasha's w family. 3972
16:12 So Zimri destroyed the w family of Baasha, 3972
2Ki 7:15 and they found the w road strewn with 3972
9: 8 The w house of Ahab will perish. 3972
11: 1 to destroy the w royal family. 3972
21: 8 and will keep the w Law 3972
25: 1 against Jerusalem with his w army. 3972
25: 4 the w army fled at night through the gate 3972
25:10 The w Babylonian army, 3972
1Ch 11:10 to extend it over **the w land,** as 3776S
13: 2 He then said to the w assembly of Israel, 3972
13: 4 The w assembly agreed to do this, 3972
28: 4 chose me from my w family to be king 3972
29: 1 Then King David said to the w assembly: 3972
29:10 in the presence of the w assembly, 3972
29:20 Then David said to the w assembly, 3972
2Ch 1: 3 and the w assembly went to the high place 3972
6: 3 the w assembly of Israel was standing there, 3972
6:12 of the LORD in front of the w assembly 3972
6:13 and then knelt down before the w assembly 3972
15: 8 the w land of Judah and Benjamin and from 3972
22:10 she proceeded to destroy the w royal family 3972
23: 3 the w assembly made a covenant with 3972
29:28 The w assembly bowed in worship, 3972
30: 2 and the w assembly in Jerusalem decided 3972
30: 4 both to the king and to the w assembly. 3972
30:23 The w assembly then agreed to celebrate 3972
31:18 and daughters of the w community listed 3972
Ezr 2:64 The w company numbered 42,360, 3972
4:20 over the w *of* Trans-Euphrates, 10353
10:12 The w assembly responded with 3972
10:14 Let our officials act for the w assembly. 3972
Ne 5:13 At this the w assembly said, "Amen," 3972
7:66 The w company numbered 42,360, 3972
8:17 The w company that had returned 3972
Est 3: 6 throughout the w kingdom of Xerxes. 3972
Job 17: 7 my w frame is but a shadow. 3972
34:13 Who put him in charge of the w world? 3972
37: 3 the w heaven and sends it to the ends of 3972
37:12 around over the face of the **w earth** 824+9315
Ps 35:10 My w being will exclaim, "Who is like you, 3972
48: 2 the joy of the w earth. 3972
51:19 w burnt offerings to delight you; 4003
72:19 may the w earth be filled with his glory. 3972
110: 6 and crushing the rulers of the w earth. 8041
Pr 1:12 and w, like those who go down to the pit; 9459
4:22 and health to a man's w body. 3972
5:14 the brink of utter ruin in the midst of the w **assembly."** 2256+6337+7736
8:31 rejoicing in his **w world** and 824+9315
Ecc 12:13 for this is the w [duty] *of* man. 3972
Isa 1: 5 Your w head is injured, 3972
1: 5 your w heart afflicted. 3972
6: 3 the w earth is full of his glory." 3972
10:23 the destruction decreed upon the w land. 3972
13: 5 to destroy the w country. 3972
14:26 This is the plan determined for the w world; 3972
28:22 the destruction decreed against the w land. 3972
29:11 For you this w vision is nothing 3972
31: 4 a **w band** *of* shepherds is called together 4850
Jer 1:18 a bronze wall to stand against the w land— 3972
4:20 the w land lies in ruins. 3972
4:27 "The w land will be ruined, 3972
8:16 of their stallions the w land trembles. 3972
9:26 even the w house of Israel is uncircumcised 3972
12:11 the w land will be laid waste 3972
13:11 the w house of Israel and the whole house 3972
13:11 of Israel and the w house of Judah to me,' 3972
15:10 with whom the w land strives and contends! 3972
25:11 This w country will become a desolate 3972
31:40 The w valley where dead bodies 3972
35: 3 the w family of the Recabites. 3972
39: 1 with his w army and laid siege to it. 3972
40: 4 Look, the w country lies before you; 3972
44:28 the w remnant of Judah who came to live 3972
50:23 and shattered is the hammer of the w earth! 3972
51: 7 she made the w earth drunk. 3972
51:25 you who destroy the w earth," 3972
51:41 the boast of the w earth seized! 3972
51:47 her w land will be disgraced 3972
52: 4 against Jerusalem with his w army. 3972
52: 7 and the w army fled. 3972
52:14 The w Babylonian army under 3972
La 2:15 the joy of the w earth?" 3972
Eze 3: 7 w house of Israel is hardened and obstinate. 3972
5: 4 A fire will spread from there to the w house 3972
7:12 for wrath is upon the w crowd. 3972
7:13 the vision concerning the w crowd will not 3972
7:14 for my wrath is upon the w crowd. 3972
11:15 and the w house of Israel— 3972
12:10 and the w house of Israel who are there.' 3972
15: 5 not useful for anything when it was w, 9459
32:22 "Assyria is there with her w army; 3972
34: 6 They were scattered over the w earth, 3972

Eze 35:14 w earth rejoices, I will make you desolate. 3972
36:10 even the w house of Israel. 3972
37:11 these bones are the w house of Israel. 3972
38: 4 and bring you out with your w army— 3972
41:19 They were carved all around the w temple. 3972
43:11 its w design and all its regulations and laws. 3972
45: 6 it will belong to the w house of Israel. 3972
Da 1:20 and enchanters in his w kingdom. 3972
2:35 a huge mountain and filled the w earth. 10353
2:39 one of bronze, will rule over the w earth. 10353
4:20 visible to the w earth, 10353
6: 3 to set him over the w kingdom. 10353
7:23 and will devour the w earth, 10353
7:27 under the w heaven will be handed over to 10353
8: 5 the w earth without touching the ground. 3972
9:12 the w heaven nothing has ever been done 3972
Am 1: 6 Because she took captive w communities 8969
1: 9 Because she sold w communities 8969
3: 1 the w family I brought up out of Egypt: 3972
8: 8 The w land will rise like the Nile; 3972
9: 5 the w land rises like the Nile, 3972
Hab 1: 6 across the w earth to seize dwelling places 5303
Zep 1:18 In the fire of his jealousy the w world will 3972
3: 8 The w world will be consumed by the fire 3972
Hag 1:12 and the w remnant of the people obeyed 3972
1:14 the spirit of the w remnant of the people. 3972
Zec 1:11 and found the w world at rest and in peace." 3972
5: 3 the curse that is going out over the w land; 3972
6: 5 in the presence of the Lord of the w world. 3972
13: 8 In the w land," declares the LORD, 3972
14: 9 The LORD will be king over the w earth. 3972
14:10 The w land, from Geba to Rimmon, 3972
Mal 3: 9 the w nation *of* you— 3972
3:10 Bring the w tithe into the storehouse, 3972
Mt 3: 5 and all Judea and the w region of *4246*
5:29 for your w body to be thrown into hell. *3910*
5:30 of your body than for your w body to go *3910*
6:22 your w body will be full of light. *3910*
6:23 your w body will be full of darkness. *3910*
8:32 the w herd rushed down the steep bank into *4246*
8:34 Then the w town went out to meet Jesus. *4246*
16:26 be for a man if he gains the w world, *3910*
21:10 the w city was stirred and asked, *4246*
24:14 in the w world as a testimony to all nations, *3910*
26:59 and the w Sanhedrin were looking *3910*
27:27 the Praetorium and gathered the w company *3910*
Mk 1: 5 The w Judean countryside and all *4246*
1:28 spread quickly over the w region *3910+4116*
1:33 The w town gathered at the door, *3910*
5:33 trembling with fear, told him the w truth. *4246*
6:55 that w region and carried the sick on mats *3910*
8:36 for a man to gain the w world, *3910*
11:18 the w crowd was amazed at his teaching. *4246*
14:55 the w Sanhedrin were looking for evidence *3910*
15: 1 the teachers of the law and the w Sanhedrin, *3910*
15:16 and called together the w company *3910*
15:33 over the w land until the ninth hour. *3910*
Lk 4:14 through the w countryside. *3910*
9:25 for a man to gain the w world, *3910*
11:34 your w body also is full of light. *3910*
11:36 Therefore, if your w body is full of light, *3910*
15:14 there was a severe famine **in** that w country, *2848*
19:37 the w crowd of disciples began joyfully *570*
21:35 on the face *of* the w earth. *4246*
23: 1 w assembly rose and led him off to Pilate. *570*
23:44 and darkness came over the w land until *3910*
Jn 7:23 for healing the w man on the Sabbath? *3910*
11:50 the people than that the w nation perish." *3910*
12:19 Look how the w world has gone after him!" *NIG*
13:10 his w body is clean. *3910*
21:25 that even the w world would not have room *899*
Ac 1:21 the men who have been with us the w time *4246*
2: 2 the w house where they were sitting. *3910*
5:11 the w church and all who heard *3910*
6: 5 This proposal pleased the w group. *4246*
7:14 for his father Jacob and his w family, *4246*
11:26 So *for* a w year Barnabas and Saul met with *3910*
13: 6 the w island until they came to Paphos. *3910*
13:44 the next Sabbath almost the w city gathered *4246*
13:49 of the Lord spread through the w region. *3910*
15:12 The w assembly became silent *4246*
15:22 the apostles and elders, with the w church, *3910*
16:34 believe in God—he and his w **family.** *4109*
17:26 that they should inhabit the w earth; *4246*
19:26 and *in* practically the w province of Asia. *4246*
19:29 Soon the w city was in an uproar. *NIG*
20:18 "You know how I lived the w time I was *4246*
20:27 not hesitated to proclaim to you the w will *4246*
21:27 stirred up the w crowd and seized him, *4246*
21:30 The w city was aroused, *3910*
21:31 the w city of Jerusalem was in an uproar. *3910*
25:24 The w Jewish community has petitioned me *570*
28:30 For two w years Paul stayed there *3910*
Ro 1: 9 whom I serve with my w heart in preaching *NIG*
3:19 and the w world held accountable to God. *4246*
8:22 that the w creation has been groaning as in *4246*
11:16 then the w batch is holy; *NIG*
16:23 and the w church here enjoy, *3910*
1Co 4: 9 a spectacle to the w universe, *NIG*
5: 6 that a little yeast works through the w batch *3910*
12:17 If the w body were an eye, *3910*
12:17 If the w body were an ear, *3910*
14:23 So if the w church comes together *3910*
Gal 3:22 the Scripture declares that the **w world** is *4246*
4: 1 although he owns **the w** *estate.* *4246*
5: 3 that he is obligated to obey the w law. *3910*
5: 9 "A little yeast works through the w batch *3910*
Gal 5:12 go the w way and emasculate themselves! *NIG*
Eph 2:21 the w building is joined together and rises *4246*
3:15 from whom his w family in heaven and *4246*
4:10 in order to fill the **w universe.)** *4246*
4:13 to the w measure of the fullness of Christ. *NIG*
4:16 From him the w body, joined and held *4246*
Php 1:13 the w palace guard and to everyone else *3910*
Col 2:19 from whom the w body, supported and held *4246*
1Th 5:23 May your w spirit, soul and body *3908*
Tit 1:11 because they are ruining w households *3910*
Jas 2:10 For whoever keeps the w law and *3910*
3: 2 able to keep his w body in check. *3910*
3: 3 we can turn the w animal. *3910*
3: 6 It corrupts the w person, *3910*
3: 6 sets the w course of his life on fire, *NIG*
1Jn 2: 2 for ours but also for the sins *of* the w world. *3910*
5:19 w world is under the control of the evil one. *3910*
Rev 3:10 upon the w world to test those who live on *3910*
6:12 the w moon turned blood red, *3910*
12: 9 or Satan, who leads the w world astray. *3910*
13: 3 The w world was astonished and followed *3910*
16:14 and they go out to the kings *of* the w world, *3910*

WHOLEHEARTED (4) [HEART, WHOLE]

2Ki 20: 3 you faithfully and with w **devotion** 4222+8969
1Ch 28: 9 w **devotion** and with a willing mind, 4213+8969
29:19 give my son Solomon the w **devotion** 4222+8969
Isa 38: 3 you faithfully and with w **devotion** 4213+8969

WHOLEHEARTEDLY (16) [HEART, WHOLE]

Nu 14:24 a different spirit and follows me w, 4848
32:11 'Because *they have* not followed me w, 4848
32:12 for *they* followed the LORD w.' 4848
Dt 1:36 because *he* followed the LORD w." 4848
Jos 14: 8 however, followed the LORD my God w. 4848
14: 9 *you have* followed the LORD my God w.' 4848
14:14 followed the LORD, the God of Israel, w. 4848
1Ki 8:23 your servants who continue w 928+3972+4213
1Ch 29: 9 given freely and w to the LORD. 928+4213+8969
2Ch 6:14 your servants who continue w 928+3972+4213
15:15 oath because they had sworn it w. 928+3972+4222
19: 9 "You must serve faithfully and w 928+4222+8969
25: 2 the eyes of the LORD, but not w. 928+4222+8969
31:21 he sought his God and worked w. 928+3972+4222
Ro 6:17 you w obeyed the form of teaching *1666+2840*
Eph 6: 7 Serve w, as if you were serving the Lord, *2334+3552*

WHOLESOME (2)

2Ki 2:22 And the water *has remained* w to this day, 8324
2Pe 3: 1 as reminders to stimulate you to w thinking. *1637*

WHOLLY (3) [WHOLE]

Nu 3: 9 *who are to* **be given** w to him. 5989+5989
8:16 Israelites *who are to* **be given** w to me. 5989+5989
1Ti 4:15 in these matters; **give yourself** w to them, *3509*

WHOM (394) [WHO] See Index of Articles Etc.

WHOMSOEVER (KJV) See ANY, ANYONE, EVERYONE, ONE, WHATEVER, WHOEVER, WHOM

WHORE, WHORE'S, WHORES (KJV) See PROMISCUOUS, PROSTITUTE, PROSTITUTES, PROSTITUTION, UNFAITHFUL

WHOREDOM (KJV) See UNFAITHFULNESS, ADULTERY, PROSTITUTION

WHOREMONGER, WHOREMONGERS (KJV) See IMMORAL, SEXUALLY IMMORAL

WHOSO, WHOSOEVER (KJV) See ANYONE, MAN, WHO, WHOEVER

WHOSE (278) [WHO] See Index of Articles Etc.

WHY (550)

Ge 4: 6 LORD said to Cain, "**W** are you angry? 4200+4537
4: 6 W is your face downcast? 4200+4537
10: 9 **that is w** it is said, "Like Nimrod, 4027+6584
11: 9 **That is w** it was called Babel— 4027+6584
12:18 "**W** didn't you tell me she was your wife? 4200+4537
12:19 W did you say, 'She is my sister,' 4200+4537
16:14 **That is w** the well was called Beer Lahai Roi; 4027+6584
18:13 "**W** did Sarah laugh and say, 4200+4537
19:22 (**That is w** the town was called Zoar.) 4027+6584
20: 6 **That is w** I did not let you touch her. 4027+6584
24:31 "**W** are you standing out here? 4200+4537
25:22 and she said, "**W** is this happening to me?" 561+4027+4200+4537
25:30 (**That is w** he was also called Edom.) 4027+6584
26: 9 **W** did you say, 'She is my sister'?" 375
26:27 Isaac asked them, "**W** have you come to me 4508
27:45 **W** should I lose both of you in one day?" 4200+4537
29:25 **W** have you deceived me?" 4200+4537
31:27 **W** did you run off secretly and 4200+4537
31:27 **W** didn't you tell me, NIH
31:30 But **w** did you steal my gods?" 4200+4537
31:48 **That is w** it was called Galeed. 4027+6584
32:29 he replied, "**W** do you ask my name?" 4200+4537
33:15 "**But w** do that?" 4200+4537
33:17 **That is w** the place is called Succoth. 4027+6584
40: 7 "**W** are your faces so sad today?" 4508
42: 1 "**W** do you just keep looking 4200+4537
42:21 **that's w** this distress has come upon us." 4027+6584
43: 6 "**W** did you bring this trouble on me 4200+4537
44: 4 '**W** have you repaid good with evil? 4200+4537
44: 7 "**W** does my lord say such things? 4200+4537
44: 8 So **w** would we steal silver or gold 375
47:15 **W** should we die before your eyes? 4200+4537
47:19 **W** should we perish before your eyes 4200+4537
47:22 **That is w** they did not sell their land. 4027+6584
50:11 **That is w** that place near 4027+6584
Ex 1:18 "**W** have you done this? 4508
1:18 **W** have you let the boys live?" NIH
2:13 "**W** are you hitting your fellow Hebrew?" 4200+4537
2:18 "**W** have you returned so early today?" 4508
2:20 "**W** did you leave him? 4200+4537
3: 3 **w** the bush does not burn up." 4508
5: 4 **w** are you taking the people away 4200+4537
5: 8 lazy; **that is w** they are crying out, 4027+6584
5:14 "**W** didn't you meet your quota 4508
5:15 "**W** have you treated your servants this way? 4200+4537
5:17 **That is w** you keep saying, 4027+6584
5:22 **w** have you brought trouble 4200+4537
5:22 Is this **w** you sent me? 4200+4537
6:12 **w** would Pharaoh listen to me, 375
6:30 **w** would Pharaoh listen to me?" 375
13:15 **This is w** I sacrifice to the LORD 4027+6584
14:15 "**W** are you crying out to me? 4537
15:23 (**That is w** the place is called Marah.) 4027+6584
16:29 **that is w** on sixth day he gives you 4027+6584
17: 2 Moses replied, "**W** do you quarrel with me? 4537
17: 2 **W** do you put the LORD to the test?" 4537
17: 3 "**W** did you bring us up out of Egypt 4200+4537
18:14 **W** do you alone sit as judge, 4508
32:11 "**w** should your anger burn 4200+4537
32:12 **W** should the Egyptians say, 4200+4537
Lev 10:17 "**W** didn't you eat the sin offering in 4508
17:14 **That is w** I have said to the Israelites, 2256
Nu 9: 7 **w** should we be kept from presenting 4200+4537
11:11 "**W** have you brought this trouble 4200+4537
11:12 **W** do you tell me to carry them in my arms, 3954
11:20 saying, "**W** did we ever leave Egypt?" 4200+4537
12: 8 **W** then were you not afraid to speak 4508
14: 3 **W** is the LORD bringing us to this land 4200+4537
14:41 "**W** are you disobeying the LORD's 4200+4537
16: 3 **W** then do you set yourselves above 4508
18:24 **That is w** I said concerning them: 4027+6584
20: 4 **W** did you bring the LORD's 4200+4537
20: 5 **W** did you bring us up out of Egypt 4200+4537
21: 5 "**W** have you brought us up out of Egypt to this terrible place? 4200+4537
21:14 **That is w** the Book of the Wars of 4027+6584
21:27 **That is w** the poets say: 4027+6584
22:32 "**W** have you beaten your donkey 4537+6584
22:37 **W** didn't you come to me? 4200+4537
27: 4 **W** should our father's name disappear 4200+4537
32: 7 **W** do you discourage the Israelites 4200+4537
Dt 5:25 But now, **w** should we die? 4200+4537
10: 9 **That is w** the Levites have no share 4027+6584
15:15 **That is w** I give you this command 4027+6584
19: 7 **This is w** I command you to set aside 4027+6584
24:18 **That is w** I command you to do this. 4027+6584
24:22 **That is w** I command you to do this. 4027+6584
29:24 **W** has the LORD done this to this land? 4537+6584
29:24 **W** this fierce, burning anger?" 4537
Jos 5: 4 Now this is **w** he did so: 1821
7: 7 **w** did you ever bring this people 4200+4537
7:12 **That is w** the Israelites cannot stand 2256
7:25 "**W** have you brought this trouble on us? 4537
9:22 "**W** did you deceive us by saying, 4200+4537
9:24 **and that is w** we did this. 2256
17:14 "**W** have you given us only one allotment 4508
22:26 "**That is w** we said, 'Let us get ready 2256
Jdg 2: 2 **W** have you done this? 4537
5:16 **W** did you stay among the campfires 4200+4537
5:17 And Dan, **w** did he linger by the ships? 4200+4537
5:28 '**W** is his chariot so long in coming? 4508
5:28 **W** is the clatter of his chariots delayed?' 4508
6:13 **w** has all this happened to us? 4200+4537
8: 1 "**W** have you treated us like this? 4537
8: 1 **W** didn't you call us when you went NIH
8: 6 **W** should we give bread to your troops?" 3954
8:15 **W** should we give bread to your exhausted 3954
9:28 **W** should we serve Abimelech? 4508
11: 7 **W** do you come to me now, 4508

Jdg 11:26 W didn't you retake them during that time? 4508
12: 1 "W did you go to fight the Ammonites 4508
12: 3 w have you come up today to fight me?" 4200+4537
13:18 He replied, "W do you ask my name? 4200+4537
14:16 "so *w should I* **explain** it to you?" AIT
15:10 "W have you come to fight us?" 4200+4537
18: 3 W are you here?" 4537
18:12 **This is** w the place west 4027+6584
21: 3 cried, "w has this happened to Israel? 4200+4537
21: 3 W should one tribe be missing NIH
Ru 1:11 W would you come with me? 4200+4537
1:21 W call me Naomi? 4200+4537
2:10 "W have I found such favor in your eyes 4508
1Sa 1: 8 "Hannah, w are you weeping? 4200+4537
1: 8 W don't you eat? 4200+4537
1: 8 W are you downhearted? 4200+4537
2:23 to them, "W do you do such things? 4200+4537
2:29 W do you scorn my sacrifice and 4200+4537
2:29 W do you honor your sons more than me NIH
4: 3 "W did the LORD bring defeat 4200+4537
5: 5 **That is** w to this day neither 4027+6584
6: 3 know w his hand has not been lifted 4200+4537
6: 6 W do you harden your hearts as 4200+4537
9:21 W do you say such a thing to me?" 4200+4537
11: 5 W are they weeping?" 3954
14:28 **That is** w the men are faint." 2256
15:19 W did you not obey the LORD? 4200+4537
15:19 W did you pounce on the plunder NIH
17: 8 "W do you come out and line up 4200+4537
17:28 "W have you come down here? 4200+4537
19: 5 W then would you do wrong to 4200+4537
19:17 "W did you deceive me like this 4200+4537
19:17 W should I kill you?' " 4200+4537
19:24 **This is** w people say, 4027+6584
20: 2 W would he hide this from me? 4508
20: 8 W hand me over to your father?" 4200+4537
20:27 "W hasn't the son of Jesse come to 4508
20:29 **That is** w he has not come to 4027+6584
20:32 "W should he be put to death? 4200+4537
21: 1 and asked, "W are you alone? 4508
21: 1 W is no one with you?" NIH
21:14 W bring him to me? 4200+4537
22: 8 **Is that** w you have all conspired 3954
22:13 "W have you conspired against me, 4200+4537
23:28 **That is** w they call this place Sela Hammahlekoth. 4027+6584
24: 9 "W do you listen when men say, 4200+4537
25:11 W should I take my bread and water, NIH
26:15 W didn't you guard your lord 4200+4537
26:18 "W is my lord pursuing his servant? 4200+4537
27: 5 W should your servant live in the 4200+4537
28: 9 W have you set a trap for my life 4200+4537
28:12 "W have you deceived me? 4200+4537
28:15 "W have you disturbed me 4200+4537
28:16 Samuel said, "W do you consult me, 4200+4537
29: 8 W can't I go and fight against the enemies 3954
2Sa 1:14 "W were you not afraid to lift your hand 375
2:22 W should I strike you down? 4200+4537
3: 7 "W did you sleep with my father's 4508
3:24 W did you let him go? 4200+4537
5: 8 **That is** w they say, 4027+6584
7: 7 "W have you not built me a house 4200+4537
11:10 W didn't you go home?" 4508
11:20 'W did you get so close to the city to fight? 4508
11:21 W did you get so close to the wall?' 4200+4537
12: 9 W did you despise the word of the LORD 4508
12:21 "W are you acting this way? 4537
12:23 now that he is dead, w should I fast? 4200+4537
13: 4 He asked Amnon, "W do you, 4508
13:26 "W should he go with you?" 4200+4537
14:13 "W then have you devised a thing 4200+4537
14:31 "W have your servants set my field 4200+4537
14:32 W have I come from Geshur? 4200+4537
15:19 "W should you come along with us? 4200+4537
16: 2 "W have you brought these?" 4537
16: 9 W should this dead dog curse my lord 4200+4537
16:10 who can ask, 'W do you do this?' " 4508
16:17 W didn't you go with your friend?" 4200+4537
18:11 W didn't you strike him to the ground 4508
18:22 "My son, w do you want to go? 4200+4537
19:10 So w do you say nothing about 4200+4537
19:11 'W should you be the last to bring 4200+4537
19:12 w should you be the last to bring back 4200+4537
19:25 "W didn't you go with me, 4200+4537
19:29 The king said to him, "W say more? 4200+4537
19:35 W should your servant be an added 4200+4537
19:36 w should the king reward me 4200+4537
19:41 "W did our brothers, the men of Judah, 4508
19:42 W are you angry about it? 4200+4537
19:43 So w do you treat us with contempt? 4508
20:19 W do you want to swallow up 4200+4537
24: 3 But w does my lord the king want 4200+4537
24:21 "W has my lord the king come 4508
1Ki 1: 6 "W do you behave as you do?" 4508
1:13 W then has Adonijah become king?' 4508
2:22 "W do you request Abishag 4200+4537
2:43 W then did you not keep your oath to 4508
9: 8 'W has the LORD done such a thing 4537+6584
9: 9 **that is** w the LORD brought all this disaster on them.' " 4027+6584
14: 6 W this pretense? 4200+4537
20:23 **That is** w they were too strong for us. 4027+6584
21: 5 "W are you so sullen? 4537
21: 5 W won't you eat?" NIH
2Ki 1: 5 he asked them, "W have you come back?" 4537
4:23 "W go to him today?" 4508
2Ki 4:27 from me and has not told me w." NIH
5: 7 W does this fellow send someone to me to 3954
5: 8 "W have you torn your robes? 4200+4537
6:33 W should I wait for the LORD 4537
7: 3 "W stay here until we die? 4537
8:12 "W is my lord weeping?" 4508
9:11 W did this madman come to you?" 4508
12: 7 "W aren't you repairing the damage done to 4508
14:10 W ask for trouble 4200+4537
1Ch 17: 6 "W have you not built me a house 4200+4537
21: 3 W does my lord want to do this? 4200+4537
21: 3 W should he bring guilt on Israel?" 4200+4537
2Ch 7:21 'W has the LORD done such a thing 928+4537
7:22 **that is** w he brought all this disaster 4027+6584
20:26 **This is** w it is called the Valley of Beracah 4027+6584
24: 6 "W haven't you required the Levites 4508
24:20 'W do you disobey the LORD's 4200+4537
25:15 "W do you consult this people's gods, 4200+4537
25:16 W be struck down?" 4200+4537
25:19 W ask for trouble 4200+4537
29: 9 **This is** w our fathers have fallen by 2180
29: 9 and w our sons and daughters and 2296+6584
32: 4 "W should the kings of Assyria come 4200+4537
Ezr 4:15 **That is** w this city was destroyed. 10180+10542
4:22 W let this threat grow, 10378+10408
7:23 W should there be wrath against 10378+10408
Ne 2: 2 "W does your face look so sad 4508
2: 3 W should my face not look sad when 4508
6: 3 W should the work stop while I leave 4200+4537
13:11 "W is the house of God neglected?" 4508
13:21 "W do you spend the night by the wall? 4508
Est 3: 3 "W do you disobey the king's command?" 4508
4: 5 what was troubling Mordecai and **w.** 4537+6584
9:19 **That is** w rural Jews— 4027+6584
Job 3:11 "W did I not perish at birth, 4200+4537
3:12 W were there knees to receive me 4508
3:16 Or w was I not hidden in the ground like NIH
3:20 "W is light given to those in misery, 4200+4537
3:23 W is life given to a man whose way NIH
7:20 W have you made me your target? 4200+4537
7:21 W do you not pardon my offenses 4537
9:22 It is all the same; **that is** w I say, 4027+6584
9:29 w should I struggle in vain? 4200+4537
10:18 "W then did you bring me out of the womb? 4200+4537
13:14 W do I put myself in jeopardy 4537+6584
13:24 W do you hide your face 4200+4537
15:12 W has your heart carried you away, 4537
15:12 and w do your eyes flash, 4537
18: 3 W are we regarded as cattle 4508
19:22 W do you pursue me as God does? 4200+4537
21: 4 W should I not be impatient? 4508
21: 7 W do the wicked live on, 4508
22:10 **That is** w snares are all around you, 4027+6584
22:10 w sudden peril terrifies you, NIH
22:11 w it is so dark you cannot see, NIH
22:11 and w a flood of water covers you. NIH
23:15 **That is** w I am terrified before him; 4027+6584
24: 1 "W does the Almighty not set times 4508
24: 1 W must those who know him look in vain NIH
27:12 W then this meaningless talk? 4200+4537
32: 6 **that is** w I was fearful, 4027+6584
33:13 W do you complain to him 4508
Ps 2: 1 W do the nations conspire and 4200+4537
10: 1 W, O LORD, do you stand far off? 4200+4537
10: 1 *W do you* **hide** *yourself* in times AIT
10:13 W does the wicked man revile God? 4537+6584
10:13 W does he say to himself, NIH
22: 1 my God, w have you forsaken me? 4200+4537
22: 1 W are you so far from saving me, NIH
42: 5 W are you downcast, O my soul? 4537
42: 5 W so disturbed within me? NIH
42: 9 "W have you forgotten me? 4200+4537
42: 9 W must I go about mourning, 4200+4537
42:11 W are you downcast, O my soul? 4537
42:11 W so disturbed within me? 4537
43: 2 W have you rejected me? 4200+4537
43: 2 W must I go about mourning, 4200+4537
43: 5 W are you downcast, O my soul? 4537
43: 5 W so disturbed within me? 4537
44:23 W do you sleep? 4200+4537
44:24 W do you hide your face 4200+4537
49: 5 W should I fear when evil days come, 4200+4537
52: 1 W do you boast of evil, you mighty man? 4537
52: 1 W do you boast all day long, NIH
68:16 W gaze in envy, O rugged mountains, 4200+4537
74: 1 W have you rejected us forever, 4200+4537
74: 1 W does your anger smolder against NIH
74:11 W do you hold back your hand, 4200+4537
79:10 W should the nations say, 4200+4537
80:12 W have you broken down its walls so 4200+4537
88:14 W, O LORD, do you reject me 4200+4537
114: 5 W was it, O sea, that you fled, O Jordan, 4537
115: 2 W do the nations say, 4200+4537
Pr 5:20 W be captivated, my son, by an adulteress? 4200+4537
5:20 W embrace the bosom of another man's NIH
Ecc 4: 8 w am I depriving myself of enjoyment?" NIH
5: 6 W should God be angry at 4200+4537
7:10 "W were the old days better than these?" 4537
7:16 be overwise—w destroy yourself? 4200+4537
7:17 w die before your time? 4200+4537
SS 1: 7 W should I be like a veiled 4200+4537+8611
6:13 W would you gaze on the Shulammite as 4537
Isa 1: 5 W should you be beaten anymore? 4537+6584
1: 5 W do you persist in rebellion? NIH
Isa 5: 4 w did it yield only bad? 4508
8:19 W consult the dead on behalf of the living? NIH
40:27 W do you say, O Jacob, and complain, 4200+4537
50: 2 When I came, w was there no one? 4508
50: 2 I called, w was there no one to answer? NIH
55: 2 W spend money on what is not bread, 4200+4537
58: 3 'W have we fasted,' they say, 4200+4537
58: 3 W have we humbled ourselves, NIH
63: 2 W are your garments red, 4508
63:17 W, O LORD, do you make us wander 4200+4537
Jer 2:14 W then has he become plunder? 4508
2:18 Now w go to Egypt to drink water from 4537
2:18 And w go to Assyria to drink water from 4537
2:29 "W do you bring charges against me? 4200+4537
2:31 W do my people say, 'We are free to roam; 4508
2:36 W do you go about so much, 4537
4:30 W dress yourself in scarlet and put 3954
4:30 W shade your eyes with paint? 3954
5: 7 "W should I forgive you? 361+2296+4200
5:19 'W has the LORD our God done all this 4537+9393
8: 5 W then have these people turned away? 4508
8: 5 W does Jerusalem always turn away? NIH
8:14 "W are we sitting here? 4537+6584
8:19 "W have they provoked me to anger 4508
8:22 W then is there no healing for the wound 4508
9:12 W has the land been ruined and 4537+6584
12: 1 W does the way of the wicked prosper? 4508
12: 1 W do all the faithless live at ease? NIH
13:22 "W has this happened to me?"— 4508
14: 8 w are you like a stranger in the land, 4200+4537
14: 9 W are you like a man taken by surprise, 4200+4537
14:19 W have you afflicted us so that we cannot 4508
15:18 W is my pain unending 4200+4537
16:10 'W has the LORD decreed such 4537+6584
20:18 W did I ever come out of the womb 4200+4537
22: 8 'W has the LORD done such a thing 4537+6584
22:28 W will he and his children be hurled out, 4508
26: 9 W do you prophesy in the LORD's name 4508
27:13 W will you and your people die by 4200+4537
27:17 W should this city become a ruin? 4200+4537
29:27 w have you not reprimanded Jeremiah 4200+4537
30: 6 Then w do I see every strong man 4508
30:15 W do you cry out over your wound, 4537
32: 3 saying, "W do you prophesy as you do? 4508
36:29 that scroll and said, "W did you write on it 4508
40:15 W should he take your life and 4200+4537
44: 7 W bring such great disaster on 4200+4537
44: 8 W provoke me to anger NIH
46:15 W will your warriors be laid low? 4508
49: 1 W then has Molech taken possession 4508
49: 1 W do his people live in its towns? NIH
49: 4 W do you boast of your valleys, 4537
49:12 w should you go unpunished? NIH
49:25 W has the city of renown 375
La 1:16 "**This is** w I weep and my eyes 465+6584
3:39 W should any living man complain 4537
5:20 W do you always forget us? 4200+4537
5:20 W do you forsake us so long? NIH
Eze 18:19 'W does the son not share the guilt 4508
18:31 W will you die, O house of Israel? 4200+4537
21: 7 they ask you, 'W are you groaning?' 4537+6584
33:11 W will you die, O house of Israel?' 4200+4537
40: 4 for **that is** w you have been brought here. 5100
Da 1:10 W should he see you looking worse 4200+4537
2:15 "W did the king issue such a harsh decree?" 10408+10542
10:20 "Do you know w I have come to you? 4200+4537
Joel 2:17 W should they say among the peoples, 4200+4537
Am 5:18 W do you long for the day of the LORD? 4200+4537
Jnh 4: 2 **That is** w I was so quick to flee 4027+6584
Mic 4: 9 W do you now cry aloud— 4200+4537
Hab 1: 3 W do you make me look at injustice? 4200+4537
1: 3 W do you tolerate wrong? NIH
1:13 W then do you tolerate the treacherous? 4200+4537
1:13 W are you silent while the wicked swallow NIH
Hag 1: 9 you brought home, I blew away. **W?"** 3610+4537
Mal 2:10 W do we profane the covenant 4508
2:14 You ask, "**W?"** 4537+6584
2:15 And w one? 4537
Mt 6:28 "And w do you worry about clothes? *5515*
7: 3 "W do you look at the speck of sawdust *5515*
8:26 "You of little faith, w are you so afraid?" *5515*
9: 4 "W do you entertain evil thoughts *2672*
9:11 "W does your teacher eat with tax collectors *1328+5515*
13:10 "W do you speak to the people *1328+5515*
13:13 **This is** w I speak to them in parables: *1328+4047*
14: 2 **That is** w miraculous powers are at work *1328+4047*
14:31 he said, "w did you doubt?" *1650+5515*
15: 2 "W do your disciples break the tradition of the elders? *1328+5515*
15: 3 "And w do you break the command of God *1328+5515*
16: 8 w are you talking among yourselves *5515*
17:10 "W then do the teachers of the law say *5515*
17:19 "W couldn't we drive it out?" *1328+5515*
19: 7 "W then," they asked, "did Moses command *5515*
19:17 "W do you ask me about what is good?" *5515*
20: 6 'W have you been standing here all day *5515*
21:25 'Then w didn't you believe him?' *1328+5515*
22:18 w are you trying to trap me? *5515*
26: 8 "W this waste?" *1650+5515*

Mt 26:10 “**W** are you bothering this woman? *5515*
26:65 **W** do we need any more witnesses? *5515*
27: 8 **That is w** it has been called the Field *1475*
27:23 “**W**? What crime has he committed?” *1142*
27:46 my God, **w** have you forsaken me?” *2672*
Mk 1:38 **That is w** I have come.” *1650+4047*
2: 7 “**W** does this fellow talk like that? *5515*
2: 8 “**W** are you thinking these things? *5515*
2:16 “**W** does he eat with tax collectors *4022*
2:24 **w** are they doing what is unlawful on *5515*
4:40 “**W** are you so afraid? *5515*
5:35 “**W** bother the teacher any more?” *5515*
5:39 “**W** all this commotion and wailing? *5515*
6:14 and **that is w** miraculous powers are *1328+4047*
7: 5 “**W** don't your disciples live according to
the tradition of the elders *1328+5515*
8:12 “**W** does this generation ask for *5515*
8:17 “**W** are you talking about having no bread? *5515*
9:11 “**W** do the teachers of the law say *NIG*
9:12 **W** then is it written that the Son of Man *4802*
9:28 “**W** couldn't we drive it out?” *NIG*
10:18 “**W** do you call me good?” *5515*
11: 3 If anyone asks you, ‘**W** are you doing this?’ *5515*
11:31 ‘Then **w** didn't you believe him?’ *1328+5515*
12:15 “**W** are you trying to trap me?” *5515*
14: 4 “**W** this waste of perfume? *1650+5515*
14: 6 “**W** are you bothering her? *5515*
14:63 “**W** do we need any more witnesses?” *5515*
15:14 “**W**? What crime has he committed?” *1142*
15:34 my God, **w** have you forsaken me?” *1650+5515*
Lk 1:21 for Zechariah and **wondering w** he stayed *2513*
1:43 But **w** am I so favored, *4470*
2:48 “Son, **w** have you treated us like this? *5515*
2:49 “**W** were you searching for me?” *4022+5515*
4:43 because **that is w** I was sent.” *2093+4047*
5:22 “**W** are you thinking these things *5515*
5:30 “**W** do you eat and drink with tax collectors
1328+5515
6: 2 “**W** are you doing what is unlawful on *5515*
6:41 “**W** do you look at the speck of sawdust *5515*
6:46 “**W** do you call me, ‘Lord, Lord,’ *5515*
7: 7 **That is w** I did not even consider myself *1475*
8:47 she told **w** she had touched him *162+1328+4005*
12:26 **w** do you worry about the rest? *5515*
12:57 “**W** don't you judge for yourselves *5515*
13: 7 **W** should it use up the soil?’ *2672*
18:19 “**W** do you call me good?” *5515*
19:23 **W** then didn't you put my money *1328+5515*
19:31 asks you, ‘**W** are you untying it?’ *1328+5515*
19:33 “**W** are you untying the colt?” *5515*
20: 5 will ask, ‘**W** didn't you believe him?’ *1328+5515*
22:46 “**W** are you sleeping?” *5515*
22:71 “**W** do we need any more testimony? *5515*
23:22 For the third time he spoke to them: “**W**? *1142*
24: 5 “**W** do you look for the living among *5515*
24:38 He said to them, “**W** are you troubled, *5515*
24:38 and **w** do doubts rise in your minds? *1328+5515*
Jn 1:25 “**W** then do you baptize if you are not *5515*
2: 4 “Dear woman, **w do** you **involve** me?” *2779+5515*
4:27 or “**W** are you talking with her?” *5515*
6:65 “**This is w** I told you that no one can *1328+4047*
7:19 **W** are you trying to kill me?” *5515*
7:23 **w** are you angry with me for healing *NIG*
7:45 “**W** didn't you bring him in?” *1328+5515*
8:22 **Is that w** he says, ‘Where I go, *4022*
8:43 **W** is my language not clear to you? *1328+5515*
8:46 **w** don't you believe me? *1328+5515*
9:23 **That was w** his parents said, *1328+4047*
9:27 **W** do you want to hear it again? *5515*
10:20 **W** listen to him?” *5515*
10:36 **W** then do you accuse me of blasphemy *NIG*
12: 5 “**W** wasn't this perfume sold and *1328+5515*
13:11 **that was w** he said not every one was clean.
1328+4047
13:28 at the meal understood **w** Jesus said this *5515*
13:37 “Lord, **w** can't I follow you now? *1328+5515*
14:22 **w** do you intend to show yourself to us and *5515*
15:19 **That is w** the world hates you. *1328+4047*
16:15 **That is w** I said the Spirit will take *1328+4047*
18:21 **W** question me? *5515*
18:23 if I spoke the truth, **w** did you strike me?” *5515*
20:13 “Woman, **w** are you crying?” *5515*
20:15 “Woman,” he said, “**w** are you crying? *5515*
Ac 1:11 “**w** do you stand here looking into the sky? *5515*
3:12 “Men of Israel, **w** does this surprise you? *5515*
3:12 **W** do you stare at us as if by our own power *5515*
4:25 “ ‘**W** do the nations rage and *2672*
7:26 **w** do you want to hurt each other?’ *2672*
8:36 **W** shouldn't I be baptized?” *5515*
9: 4 “Saul, Saul, **w** do you persecute me? *5515*
10:21 **W** have you come?” *5515*
10:29 May I ask **w** you sent for me?” *3364+5515*
14:15 **w** are you doing this? *5515*
15:10 **w** do you try to test God by putting on *5515*
19:32 not even know **w** they were there. *1915+5515*
21:13 “**W** are you weeping *5515*
22: 7 **W** do you persecute me?’ *5515*
22:24 **w** the people were shouting *162+1328+4005*
22:30 find out exactly **w** Paul was being accused *5515*
23:28 know **w** they were accusing him, *162+1328+4005*
26: 8 **W** should any of you consider it incredible *5515*
26:14 ‘Saul, Saul, **w** do you persecute me? *5515*
26:21 That is **w** the Jews seized me in *1915*
Ro 1:15 **That is w** I am so eager to preach the gospel *4048*
3: 7 **w** am I still condemned as a sinner?” *5515*
3: 8 **W** not say—as we are being slanderously *NIG*
4:22 **This is w** “it was credited to him *1475*
9:19 “Then **w** does God still blame us? *5515*
9:20 ‘**W** did you make me like this?’ ” *5515*
9:32 **W** not? Because they pursued it *1328+5515*
13: 6 **This is** also **w** you pay taxes, *1328+4047*
14:10 You, then, **w** do you judge your brother? *5515*
14:10 Or **w** do you look down on your brother? *5515*
15:22 **This is w** I have often been hindered *1475*
1Co 4: 7 **w** do you boast as though you did not? *5515*
6: 7 **W** not rather be wronged? *1328+5515*
6: 7 **W** not rather be cheated? *1328+5515*
10:29 For **w** should my freedom be judged *2672*
10:30 **w** am I denounced because of something *5515*
11:30 **That is w** many among you are weak *1328+4047*
15:29 **w** are people baptized for them? *5515*
15:30 us, **w** do we endanger ourselves every hour? *5515*
2Co 11:11 **W**? Because I do not love you? *1328+5515*
12:10 **That is w**, for Christ's sake, *1475*
13:10 **This is w** I write these things *1328+4047*
Gal 5:11 **w** am I still being persecuted? *5515*
Eph 4: 8 **This is w** it says: “When he ascended *1475*
5:14 **This is w** it is said: “Wake up, O sleeper, *1475*
Col 2:20 **w**, as though you still belonged to it, *5515*
2Ti 1:12 **That is w** I am suffering as I am. *162+1328+4005*
Heb 3:10 **That is w** I was angry with that generation, *1475*
5: 3 **This is w** he has to offer sacrifices *899+1328*
7:11 **w** was there still need for another priest *5515*
8: 5 **This is w** Moses was warned when he was *2777*
9:18 **This is w** even the first covenant was not *3854*
Jas 4: 6 **That is w** Scripture says: “God opposes *1475*
4:14 **W**, you do not even know what will happen *NIG*
1Jn 3:12 And **w** did he murder him? *5515+5920*
Rev 17: 7 said to me: “**W** are you astonished? *1328+5515*

WICK (11)

Ex 25:38 Its **w trimmers** and trays are to be 4920
37:23 as well as its **w trimmers** and trays, 4920
Nu 4: 9 its **w trimmers** and trays, 4920
1Ki 7:50 **w trimmers**, sprinkling bowls, 4662
2Ki 12:13 **w trimmers**, sprinkling bowls, 4662
25:14 the pots, shovels, **w trimmers**, dishes and 4662
2Ch 4:22 the pure gold **w trimmers**, 4662
Isa 42: 3 and a smoldering **w** he will not snuff out. 7325
43:17 extinguished, snuffed out like a **w**: 7325
Jer 52:18 shovels, **w trimmers**, sprinkling bowls, 4662
Mt 12:20 and a smoldering **w** he will not snuff out, *3351*

WICKED (363) [OVERWICKED, WICKEDLY, WICKEDNESS]

Ge 13:13 of Sodom were **w** and were sinning greatly 8273
18:23 sweep away the righteous with the **w**? 8401
18:25 to kill the righteous with the **w**, 8401
18:25 treating the righteous and the **w** alike. 8401
19: 7 Don't **do** *this* **w thing.** 8317
38: 7 was **w** in the LORD's sight; 8273
38:10 What he did *was* **w** in the LORD's sight; 8317
39: 9 How then could I do such a **w thing** and sin 8288
44: 5 *This is a* **w** *thing* you have done.' ” 8317
Ex 23: 1 a **w** *man* by being a malicious witness. 8401
Lev 20:14 both a woman and her mother, it is **w**. 2365
Nu 14:27 “How long will this **w** community grumble 8273
14:35 to this whole **w** community, 8273
16:26 “Move back from the tents of these **w** men! 8401
Dt 13:13 that **w** men have arisen among you 1175+1201
15: 9 Be careful not to harbor this **w** thought: 1175
Jdg 19:22 the **w** men of the city surrounded 1175+1201
20:13 Now surrender those **w** men of Gibeah 1175+1201
1Sa 1:16 Do not take your servant for a **w** woman; 1175
2: 9 but the **w** will be silenced in darkness. 8401
2:12 Eli's sons were **w** men; 1175
2:23 the people about these **w** deeds of yours. 8273
15:18 and completely destroy those **w people,** 2629
17:28 and how **w** your heart is; 8278
25:17 He is such a **w** man that no one can talk 1175
25:25 pay no attention to that **w** man Nabal. 1175
2Sa 3:34 You fell as one falls before **w** men.” 6406
4:11 when **w** men have killed an innocent man 8401
7:10 **W** people will not oppress them anymore, 6406
13:12 Don't do this **w thing.** 5576
13:13 You would be like one of the **w fools** 5572
2Ki 17:11 They did **w** things that provoked 8273
1Ch 2: 3 was **w** in the LORD's sight; 8273
17: 9 **W** people will not oppress them anymore, 6406
2Ch 7:14 and turn from their **w** ways, 8273
19: 2 the **w** and love those who hate the LORD? 8401
24: 7 of that **w** *woman* Athaliah had broken into 5360
Ezr 4:12 rebuilding that rebellious and **w** city. 10090
Ne 13:17 “What is this **w** thing you are doing— 8273
Job 3:17 There the **w** cease from turmoil, 8401
8:22 and the tents of the **w** will be no more.” 8401
9:22 ‘He destroys both the blameless and the **w**.’ 8401
9:24 When a land falls into the hands of the **w**, 8401
10: 3 while you smile on the schemes of the **w**? 8401
11:20 But the eyes of the **w** will fail, 8401
15:20 All his days the **w** *man* suffers torment, 8401
16:11 and thrown me into the clutches of the **w**. 8401
18: 5 “The lamp of the **w** is snuffed out; 8401
20: 5 that the mirth of the **w** is brief, 8401
20:29 Such is the fate God allots the **w**, 8401
21: 7 Why do the **w** live on, 8401
21:16 so I stand aloof from the counsel of the **w**. 8401
21:17 how often is the lamp of the **w** snuffed out? 8401
21:28 the tents where **w** *men* lived?' 8401
22:18 so I stand aloof from the counsel of the **w**. 8401
24: 6 and glean in the vineyards of the **w**. 8401
27: 7 “May my enemies be like the **w**, 8401
27:13 “Here is the fate God allots to the **w**, 8401
29:17 the fangs of the **w** and snatched the victims 6405
31: 3 Is it not ruin for the **w**, 6405
34: 8 he associates with **w** men. 8400
34:18 and to nobles, ‘You are **w**,’ 8401
34:36 to the utmost for answering like a **w** man! 224
35:12 because of the arrogance of the **w**. 8273
36: 6 He does not keep the **w** alive but gives 8401
36:17 you are laden with the judgment due the **w**; 8401
38:13 the earth by the edges and shake the **w** out 8401
38:15 The **w** are denied their light, 8401
40:12 crush the **w** where they stand. 8401
Ps 1: 1 of the **w** or stand in the way of sinners or sit 8401
1: 4 Not so the **w**! They are like chaff 8401
1: 5 the **w** will not stand in the judgment, 8401
1: 6 but the way of the **w** will perish. 8401
3: 7 break the teeth of the **w**. 8401
5: 4 with you the **w** cannot dwell. 8273
7: 9 to an end the violence of the **w** and make 8401
9: 5 the nations and destroyed the **w**; 8401
9:16 the **w** are ensnared by the work 8401
9:17 The **w** return to the grave, 8401
10: 2 In his arrogance the **w** *man* hunts down 8401
10: 4 In his pride the **w** does not seek him; 8401
10:13 Why does the **w** *man* revile God? 8401
10:15 Break the arm of the **w** and evil man; 8401
11: 2 For look, the **w** bend their bows; 8401
11: 5 but the **w** and those who love violence 8401
11: 6 On the **w** he will rain fiery coals 8401
12: 8 The **w** freely strut about 8401
17: 9 from the **w** who assail me, 8401
17:13 rescue me from the **w** by your sword. 8401
21:11 and devise **w schemes,** they cannot succeed; 4659
26: 5 of evildoers and refuse to sit with the **w**. 8401
26:10 in whose hands are **w schemes,** 2365
28: 3 Do not drag me away with the **w**, 8401
31:17 but let the **w** be put to shame and lie silent 8401
32:10 Many are the woes of the **w**, 8401
34:21 Evil will slay the **w**; 8401
36: 1 concerning the sinfulness of the **w**: 8401
36: 3 The words of his mouth are **w** and deceitful; 224
36:11 nor the hand of the **w** drive me away. 8401
37: 7 when they carry out their **w schemes.** 4659
37:10 A little while, and the **w** will be no more; 8401
37:12 The **w** plot against the righteous 8401
37:13 but the Lord laughs at **the w**, 2257[S]
37:14 The **w** draw the sword and bend the bow 8401
37:16 the wealth of many **w**; 8401
37:17 for the power of the **w** will be broken, 8401
37:20 But the **w** will perish: 8401
37:21 The **w** borrow and do not repay, 8401
37:28 but the offspring of the **w** will be cut off; 8401
37:32 The **w** lie in wait for the righteous, 8401
37:34 when the **w** are cut off, you will see it. 8401
37:35 a **w** and ruthless man flourishing like 8401
37:38 the future of the **w** will be cut off. 8401
37:40 he delivers them from the **w** 8401
39: 1 a muzzle on my mouth as long as the **w** are 8401
43: 1 rescue me from deceitful and **w** men. 6406
49: 5 when **w** deceivers surround me— 6411
50:16 But to the **w**, God says: 8401
55: 3 at the stares of the **w**; 8401
55: 9 Confuse the **w**, O Lord, NIH
55:23 down **the w** into the pit of corruption; 4392[S]
58: 3 Even from birth the **w** go astray; 8401
58: 9 **the w** will be swept away. 5647[S]
58:10 they bathe their feet in the blood of the **w**. 8401
59: 5 show no mercy to **w** traitors. 224
64: 2 Hide me from the conspiracy of the **w**, 8317
68: 2 may the **w** perish before God. 8401
71: 4 O my God, from the hand of the **w**, 8401
73: 3 when I saw the prosperity of the **w**. 8401
73:12 This is what the **w** are like— 8401
75: 4 and to the **w**, ‘Do not lift up your horns. 8401
75: 8 and all the **w** *of* the earth drink it down 8401
75:10 I will cut off the horns of all the **w**, 8401
82: 2 the unjust and show partiality to the **w**? 8401
82: 4 deliver them from the hand of the **w**. 8401
84:10 of my God than dwell in the tents of the **w**. 8400
89:22 no **w** man will oppress him. 6406
91: 8 and see the punishment of the **w**. 8401
92: 7 that though the **w** spring up like grass 8401
92:11 my ears have heard the rout of my **w** foes. 8317
94: 3 How long will the **w**, O LORD, 8401
94: 3 O LORD, how long will the **w** be jubilant? 8401
94:13 till a pit is dug for the **w**. 8401
94:16 Who will rise up for me against the **w**? 8317
97:10 and delivers them from the hand of the **w**. 8401
101: 8 Every morning I will put to silence all the **w** 8401
104:35 from the earth and the **w** be no more. 8401
106:18 a flame consumed the **w**. 8401
106:29 the LORD to anger by their **w deeds,** 5095
107:42 but all the **w** shut their mouths. 6406
109: 2 for **w** and deceitful men have opened their
mouths against me; 8401
112:10 The **w** *man* will see and be vexed, 8401
112:10 the longings of the **w** will come to nothing. 8401
119:53 Indignation grips me because of the **w**, 8401
119:61 Though the **w** bind me with ropes, 8401
119:95 The **w** are waiting to destroy me, 8401
119:110 The **w** have set a snare for me, 8401
119:119 the **w** *of* the earth you discard like dross; 8401
119:150 Those who devise **w schemes** are near, 2365
119:155 Salvation is far from the **w**, 8401
125: 3 the **w** will not remain over the land allotted 8400
129: 4 he has cut me free from the cords of the **w**. 8401
139:19 If only you would slay the **w**, O God! 8401

Ps 140: 4 Keep me, O LORD, from the hands of the w; 8401
140: 8 do not grant the w their desires, O LORD; 8401
141: 4 in w deeds with men who are evildoers; 8400
141: 6 and the w will learn that my words were NIH
141:10 Let the w fall into their own nets, 8401
145:20 but all the w he will destroy. 8401
146: 9 but he frustrates the ways of the w. 8401
147: 6 the humble but casts the w to the ground. 8401
Pr 2:12 will save you from the ways of w *men,* 8273
2:22 but the w will be cut off from the land, 8401
3:25 or of the ruin that overtakes the w, 8401
3:33 LORD's curse is on the house of the w, 8401
4:14 Do not set foot on the path of the w or walk 8401
4:19 But the way of the w is like deep darkness; 8401
5:22 The evil deeds of a w *man* ensnare him; 8401
6:18 a heart that devises w schemes, 224
9: 7 whoever rebukes a w *man* incurs abuse. 8401
10: 3 but he thwarts the craving of the w. 8401
10: 6 violence overwhelms the mouth of the w. 8401
10: 7 but the name of the w will rot. 8401
10:11 violence overwhelms the mouth of the w. 8401
10:16 income of the w brings them punishment. 8401
10:20 but the heart of the w is of little value. 8401
10:24 What the w dreads will overtake him; 8401
10:25 the storm has swept by, the w are gone, 8401
10:27 but the years of the w are cut short. 8401
10:28 but the hopes of the w come to nothing. 8401
10:30 but the w will not remain in the land. 8401
10:32 the mouth of the w only what is perverse. 8401
11: 5 but the w are brought down by their own 8401
11: 7 When a w man dies, his hope perishes; 8401
11: 8 and it comes on the w instead. 8401
11:10 when the w perish, there are shouts of joy. 8401
11:11 but by the mouth of the w it is destroyed. 8401
11:18 The w *man* earns deceptive wages, 8401
11:21 The w will not go unpunished, 8273
11:23 but the hope of the w only in wrath. 8401
12: 5 but the advice of the w is deceitful. 8401
12: 6 The words of the w lie in wait for blood, 8401
12: 7 W *men* are overthrown and are no more, 8401
12:10 but the kindest acts of the w are cruel. 8401
12:12 The w desire the plunder of evil men, 8401
12:21 but the w have their fill of trouble. 8401
12:26 but the way of the w leads them astray. 8401
13: 5 but the w bring shame and disgrace. 8401
13: 9 but the lamp of the w is snuffed out. 8401
13:17 A w messenger falls into trouble, 8401
13:25 but the stomach of the w goes hungry. 8401
14:11 The house of the w will be destroyed, 8401
14:19 and the w at the gates of the righteous. 8401
14:32 calamity comes, the w are brought down, 8401
15: 3 keeping watch on the w and the good. 8273
15: 6 the income of the w brings them trouble. 8401
15: 8 The LORD detests the sacrifice of the w, 8401
15: 9 The LORD detests the way of the w 8401
15:26 The LORD detests the thoughts of the w, 8273
15:28 but the mouth of the w gushes evil. 8401
15:29 The LORD is far from the w but he hears 8401
16: 4 even the w for a day of disaster. 8401
17: 4 A w *man* listens to evil lips; 8317
17:23 A w *man* accepts a bribe in secret to pervert 8401
18: 5 be partial to the w or to deprive the innocent 8401
19:28 and the mouth of the w gulps down evil. 8401
20:26 A wise king winnows out the w; 8401
21: 4 a proud heart, the lamp of the w, are sin! 8401
21: 7 The violence of the w will drag them away, 8401
21:10 The w man craves evil; 8401
21:12 of the house of the w and brings the wicked 8401
21:12 of the house of the wicked and brings the w 8401
21:18 The w become a ransom for the righteous, 8401
21:27 The sacrifice of the w is detestable— 8401
21:29 A w man puts up a bold front, 8401
22: 5 In the paths of the w lie thorns and snares, 6836
24: 1 Do not envy w men, 8288
24:16 but the w are brought down by calamity. 8401
24:19 because of evil men or be envious of the w, 8401
24:20 and the lamp of the w will be snuffed out. 8401
25: 5 remove the w from the king's presence, 8401
25:26 a righteous man who gives way to the w. 8401
28: 1 The w *man* flees though no one pursues, 8401
28: 4 Those who forsake the law praise the w, 8401
28:12 the w rise to power, men go into hiding. 8401
28:15 or a charging bear is a w *man* ruling over 8401
28:28 the w rise to power, people go into hiding; 8401
28:28 but when **the** w perish, the righteous thrive. 4392[S]
29: 2 when the w rule, the people groan. 8401
29: 7 but the w have no such concern. 8401
29:12 all his officials become w. 8401
29:16 When the w thrive, so does sin, 8401
29:27 the w detest the upright. 8401
Ecc 3:17 to judgment both the righteous and the w, 8401
7:15 and a w *man* living long in his wickedness. 8401
8:10 Then too, I saw the w buried— 8401
8:12 a w *man* commits a hundred crimes 2627
8:13 Yet because the w do not fear God, 8401
8:14 righteous men who get what the w deserve, 8401
8:14 w *men* who get what the righteous deserve. 8401
9: 2 common destiny—the righteous and the w, 8401
10:13 at the end they are w madness— 8273
Isa 3:11 Woe to the w! Disaster is upon them! 8401
9:17 for everyone is ungodly and w, 8317
11: 4 the breath of his lips he will slay the w. 8401
13:11 the w for their sins. 8401
14: 5 The LORD has broken the rod of the w, 8401
14:20 of the w will never be mentioned again. 8317
26:10 Though grace is shown to the w, 8401
31: 2 He will rise up against the house of the w, 8317

Isa 32: 7 The scoundrel's methods are w, 8273
35: 8 w **fools** will not go about on it. 211
48:22 says the LORD, "for the w." 8401
53: 9 He was assigned a grave with the w, 8401
55: 7 Let the w forsake his way and 8401
57:20 But the w are like the tossing sea, 8401
57:21 says my God, "for the w." 8401
58: 4 and in striking each other with w fists. 8400
59: 3 and your tongue mutters w *things.* 6406
Jer 4:14 How long will you harbor w thoughts? 224
5:26 "Among my people are w *men* who lie 8401
6:29 the w are not purged out. 8273
12: 1 Why does the way of the w prosper? 8401
12: 4 Because those who live in it are w, 8288
12:14 "As for all my w neighbors who seize 8273
13:10 These w people, who refuse to listen 8273
15:21 "I will save you from the hands of the w 8273
20:13 of the needy from the hands of the w. 8317
23:19 down on the heads of the w. 8401
25:31 on all mankind and put the w to the sword,' 8401
30:23 down on the heads of the w. 8401
35:15 from your w ways and reform your actions; 8288
36: 3 each of them will turn from his w way; 8288
36: 7 and each will turn from his w ways, 8288
44:22 could no longer endure your w actions 8278
Eze 3:18 When I say to a w *man,* 8401
3:18 that w *man* will die for his sin, 8401
3:19 But if you do warn the w *man* and he does 8401
6:11 because of all the w and detestable practices 8288
7:21 as plunder to foreigners and as loot to the w 8401
7:24 I will bring the *most* w *of* the nations 8273
8: 9 "Go in and see the w and detestable things 8273
11: 2 and giving w advice in this city. 8273
13:22 the w not to turn from their evil ways and 8401
14: 3 in their hearts and put w stumbling blocks 6411
14: 4 in his heart and puts a w stumbling block 6411
14: 7 in his heart and puts a w stumbling block 6411
18:20 and the wickedness of the w will be charged 8401
18:21 "But if a w *man* turns away from all 8401
18:23 I take any pleasure in the death of the w? 8401
18:24 the same detestable things the w *man* does, 8401
18:27 But if a w *man* turns away from 8401
21: 3 from you both the righteous and the w. 8401
21: 4 to cut off the righteous and the w, 8401
21:25 " 'O profane and w prince of Israel, 8401
21:29 it will be laid on the necks of the w who are 8401
33: 8 When I say to the w, 'O wicked man, 8401
33: 8 When I say to the wicked, 'O w *man,* 8401
33: 8 that w *man* will die for his sin, 8401
33: 9 warn the w *man* to turn from his ways 8401
33:11 I take no pleasure in the death of the w, 8401
33:12 of the w *man* will not cause him to fall 8401
33:14 And if I say to the w *man,* 8401
33:19 if a w *man* turns away from his wickedness 8401
36:31 remember your evil ways and w deeds, 3202+4202
Da 2: 9 to tell me misleading and w things, 10705
8:23 when rebels have become completely w, NIH
9: 5 *We have been* w and have rebelled; 8399
12:10 but the w will continue to be wicked. 8401
12:10 but the wicked *will continue to be* w. 8399
12:10 None of the w will understand, 8401
Hos 6: 8 Gilead is a city of **w men,** 224
12:11 Is Gilead w? Its people are worthless! 224
Mic 6:10 Am I still to forget, O w house, 8401
Na 1:15 No more will the w invade you; 1175
Hab 1: 4 The w hem in the righteous, 8401
1:13 Why are you silent while the w swallow 8401
1:15 The w foe pulls all of them up with hooks, NIH
Zep 1: 3 The w will have only heaps of rubble 8401
Mal 1: 4 They will be called the W Land, 8402
3:18 between the righteous and the w, 8401
4: 3 Then you will trample down the w; 8401
Mt 12:39 "A w and adulterous generation asks for *4505*
12:45 seven other spirits **more w than** itself, *4505*
12:45 is how it will be *with* this w generation." *4505*
13:49 The angels will come and separate the w *4505*
16: 4 A w and adulterous generation looks for *4505*
18:32 'You w servant,' he said, *4505*
24:48 But suppose that servant is w and says *2805*
25:26 "His master replied, '*You* w, lazy servant! *4505*
Lk 6:35 because he is kind to the ungrateful and w. *4505*
11:26 takes seven other spirits **more w than** itself, *4505*
11:29 Jesus said, "This is a w generation. *4505*
19:22 by your own words, *you* w servant! *4505*
Ac 2:23 and you, with the help *of* w *men,* *491*
3:26 by turning each of you from your **w ways."** *4504*
24:15 *of* both the righteous and the w. *96*
Ro 4: 5 not work but trusts God who justifies the w, *815*
1Co 5:13 "Expel the w *man* from among you." *4505*
6: 9 Do you not know that the w will not inherit *96*
2Th 3: 2 And pray that we may be delivered from w *876*
2Jn 1:11 who welcomes him shares *in* his w work. *4505*
Rev 2: 2 I know that you cannot tolerate w *men,* *2805*

WICKEDLY (7) [WICKED]

1Ki 8:47 we have done wrong, *we have* **acted** w'; 8399
2Ch 6:37 we have done wrong and **acted** w'; 8399
Ne 1: 7 *We have* **acted very** w toward you. 2472+2472
Job 13: 7 Will you speak w on God's behalf? 6406
Ps 106: 6 we have done wrong and **acted** w. 8399
Jer 16:12 you have behaved more w than your fathers. 8317
38: 9 these men *have* **acted** w in all they have 8317

WICKEDNESS (112) [WICKED]

Ge 6: 5 The LORD saw how great man's w on 8288

Ex 34: 7 and forgiving w, rebellion and sin. 6411
34: 9 forgive our w and our sin, and take us as 6411
Lev 16:21 of the live goat and confess over it all the w 6411
18:17 they are her close relatives. That is w. 2365
19:29 to prostitution and be filled with w. 2365
20:14 so that no w will be among you. 2365
Dt 9: 4 on account of the w *of* these nations that 8402
9: 5 but on account of the w *of* these nations, 8402
9:27 their w and their sin. 8400
31:18 on that day because of all their w in turning 8288
Jdg 9:56 the w that Abimelech had done to his father 8288
9:57 the men of Shechem pay for all their w. 8288
2Ch 20:35 Israel, who *was* **guilty of** w. 8399
28:19 for *he had* **promoted** w in Judah 7277
Ne 9: 2 and confessed their sins and the w 6411
13:27 that you too are doing all this terrible w 8288
Job 6:30 Is there any w on my lips? 6406
22: 5 Is not your w great? 8288
22:23 If you remove w far from your tent 6406
27: 4 my lips will not speak w, 6406
34:26 for their w where everyone can see them, 8401
35: 8 Your w affects only a man like yourself, 8400
35:15 and he does not take the least notice of w. 7317
Ps 10:15 call him to account for his w that would not 8400
45: 7 You love righteousness and hate w; 8400
92:15 he is my Rock, and there is no w in him." 6406
94:23 for their sins and destroy them for their w; 8288
107:34 because of the w *of* those who lived there. 8288
Pr 4:17 They eat the bread of w and drink the wine 8400
8: 7 for my lips detest w. 8400
11: 5 wicked are brought down by their own w. 8402
12: 3 A man cannot be established through w, 8400
13: 6 but w overthrows the sinner. 8402
18: 3 When w comes, so does contempt, 8401
22: 8 He who sows w reaps trouble, 6406
26:26 but his w will be exposed in the assembly. 8288
Ecc 3:16 w was there, in the place of justice— 8400
3:16 in the place of justice—w was there. 8400
7:15 and a wicked man living long in his w. 8288
7:25 the stupidity of w and the madness of folly. 8400
8: 8 so w will not release those who practice it. 8400
Isa 5:18 and w as with cart ropes, 10258
9:18 Surely w burns like a fire; 8402
47:10 You have trusted in your w and have said, 8288
Jer 1:16 because of their w in forsaking me, 8288
2:19 Your w will punish you; 8288
3: 2 the land with your prostitution and w. 8288
6: 7 so she pours out her w. 8288
7:12 to it because of the w *of* my people Israel. 8288
8: 6 No one repents of his w, saying, 8288
11:15 you engage in your w, then you rejoice." 8288
14:10 now remember their w and punish them 6411
14:20 we acknowledge our w and the guilt 8400
16:18 I will repay them double for their w 6411
22:22 and disgraced because of all your w. 8288
23:11 even in my temple I find their w," 8288
23:14 so that no one turns from his w. 8288
31:34 "For I will forgive their w 6411
33: 5 from this city because of all its w. 8288
36: 3 then I will forgive their w and their sin." 6411
36:31 and his attendants for their w; 6411
44: 5 from their w or stop burning incense 8288
44: 9 the w committed *by* your fathers and by 8288
44: 9 and the w committed *by* you and your wives 8288
La 1:22 "Let all their w come before you; 8288
4:22 he will punish your sin and expose your w. 2633
Eze 3:19 not turn from his w or from his evil ways, 8400
5: 6 in her w she has rebelled against my laws 8402
7:11 Violence has grown into a rod to punish w; 8400
16:23 In addition to all your other w, 8288
16:57 before your w was uncovered. 8288
18:20 and the w *of* the wicked will be charged 8402
18:27 from the w he has committed 8402
28:15 the day you were created till w was found 6406
31:11 for him to deal with according to its w. 8400
33:12 the w *of* the wicked man will not cause him 8402
33:19 And if a wicked man turns away from his w 8402
Da 4:27 and your w by being kind to the oppressed. 10532
9:24 to put an end to sin, to atone for w, 6411
Hos 4: 8 on the sins of my people and relish their w. 6411
7: 3 "They delight the king with their w, 8288
8:13 Now he will remember their w 6411
9: 9 God will remember their w and punish them 6411
9:15 of all their w in Gilgal, I hated them there. 8288
10: 8 The high places of w will be destroyed— 224
10:13 But you have planted w, 8400
10:15 O Bethel, because your **w is great.** 8288+8288
Joel 3:13 so great is their **w!"** 8288
Jnh 1: 2 because its w has come up before me." 8288
Mic 3:10 and Jerusalem with w. 6406
Na 1:11 against the LORD and counsels w. 1175
Hab 3:13 You crushed the leader of the land of w, 8401
Zec 5: 8 He said, "This is w," 8402
Mt 23:28 the inside you are full *of* hypocrisy and w. *490*
24:12 Because of the increase of w, *490*
Lk 11:39 but inside you are full of greed and w. *4504*
Ac 1:18 (With the reward he got *for* his w, *94*
8:22 Repent of this w and pray to the Lord. *2798*
Ro 1:18 the godlessness and w of men who suppress *94*
1:18 of men who suppress the truth by their w, *94*
1:29 have become filled with every kind of w, *94*
6:13 *of* w, but rather offer yourselves to God, *94*
6:19 and *to* **ever-increasing** w, *490+490+1650+3836*
1Co 5: 8 the old yeast, the yeast *of* malice and w, *4504*
2Co 6:14 For what do righteousness and w have *490*
2Th 2:12 the truth but have delighted *in* w. *94*
2Ti 2:19 name of the Lord must turn away from w." *94*

Tit 2:14 for us to redeem us from all **w** and to purify *490*
Heb 1: 9 You have loved righteousness and hated **w**; *490*
8:12 For I will forgive their **w** and will remember *94*
2Pe 2:15 son of Beor, who loved the wages *of* **w**. *94*

WIDE (105) [WIDELY, WIDENED, WIDER, WIDTH]

Ge 6:15 75 feet **w** and 45 feet high. 8145
Ex 25:10 a cubit and a half **w**, 8145
25:17 a half cubits long and a cubit and a half **w**. 8145
25:23 a cubit **w** and a cubit and a half high. 8145
25:25 make a rim around it a **handbreadth** *w* AIT
26: 2 twenty-eight cubits long and four cubits **w**. 8145
26: 8 thirty cubits long and four cubits **w**. 8145
26:16 be ten cubits long and a cubit and a half **w**, 8145
27: 1 five cubits long and five cubits **w**. 8145
27:12 of the courtyard shall be fifty cubits **w** 8145
27:13 the courtyard shall also be fifty cubits **w**. 8145
27:18 be a hundred cubits long and fifty cubits **w**, 8145
28:16 be square—a span long and a span **w**— **8145**
30: 2 a cubit long and a cubit **w**, 8145
36: 9 twenty-eight cubits long and four cubits **w**. 8145
36:15 thirty cubits long and four cubits **w**. 8145
36:21 and a cubit and a half **w**, 8145
37: 1 a cubit and a half **w**, 8145
37: 6 a half cubits long and a cubit and a half **w**. 8145
37:10 two cubits long, a cubit **w**, 8145
37:12 a handbreadth **w** and put a gold molding on NIH
37:25 It was square, a cubit long and a cubit **w**, 8145
38: 1 five cubits long and five cubits **w**. 8145
38:12 The west end was fifty cubits **w** NIH
38:13 toward the sunrise, was also fifty cubits **w**. NIH
39: 9 It was square—a span long and a span **w**— 8145
Dt 3:11 thirteen feet long and six feet **w**. 8145
1Sa 26:13 there was a **w** space between them. 8041
1Ki 6: 2 twenty **w** and thirty high. 8145
6: 6 The lowest floor was five cubits **w**, 8145
6:20 twenty **w** and twenty high. 8145
7: 2 fifty **w** and thirty high, 8145
7: 6 a colonnade fifty cubits long and thirty **w**. 8145
7:27 four **w** and three high. 8145
1Ch 13: 2 let us send word **far and w** to the rest 7287
2Ch 3: 3 and twenty cubits **w** (using the cubit of 8145
3: 8 twenty cubits long and twenty cubits **w**. 8145
4: 1 twenty cubits **w** and ten cubits high. 8145
6:13 five cubits **w** and three cubits high, 8145
26:15 fame spread **far and w**, 4200+4946+6330+8158
Ezr 6: 3 to be ninety feet high and ninety feet **w**, 10603
Ps 22:13 Roaring lions tearing their prey **open** their mouths **w** against me. 7198
81:10 **Open w** your mouth and I will fill it. 8143
Isa 18: 2 people feared **far and w**, 2085+2134+2256+4946
18: 7 people feared **far and w**, 2085+2134+2256+4946
30:33 Its fire pit has been made deep and **w**, 8143
45: 8 *Let* the earth **open w**, let salvation spring up 7337
54: 2 **stretch** your tent curtains **w**, 5742
57: 8 you climbed into it and **opened** it **w**; 8143
La 2:16 All your enemies **open** their mouths **w** 7198
3:46 our enemies *have* **opened** their mouths **w** 7198
Eze 40: 7 one rod long and one rod **w**, 8145
40:18 the sides of the gateways and was as **w** NIH
40:21 and twenty-five cubits **w**. 8145
40:25 and twenty-five cubits **w**. 8145
40:29 and twenty-five cubits **w**. 8145
40:30 the inner court were twenty-five cubits **w** 802
40:33 and twenty-five cubits **w**. 8145
40:36 and twenty-five cubits **w**. 8145
40:42 a cubit and a half **w** and a cubit high. 8145
40:47 hundred cubits long and a hundred cubits **w**. 8145
40:48 they were five cubits **w** on either side. NIH
40:48 and its projecting walls were three cubits **w** NIH
40:49 The portico was twenty cubits **w**, 802
41: 2 The entrance was ten cubits **w**, 8145
41: 2 on each side of it were five cubits **w**. NIH
41: 2 and twenty cubits **w**. 8145
41: 3 each was two cubits **w**. NIH
41: 3 The entrance was six cubits **w**, NIH
41: 3 on each side of it were seven cubits **w**. 8145
41: 5 around the temple was four cubits **w**. 8145
41:10 the [priests'] rooms was twenty cubits **w** all 8145
41:11 the open area was five cubits **w** all around. 8145
41:12 on the west side was seventy cubits **w**. 8145
42: 2 a hundred cubits long and fifty cubits **w**. 8145
42: 4 an inner passageway ten cubits **w** and 8145
42:20 and five hundred cubits **w**, 8145
43:13 Its gutter is a cubit deep and a cubit **w**, 8145
43:14 and a cubit **w**, 8145
43:14 and a cubit **w**. 8145
43:16 twelve cubits long and twelve cubits **w**. 8145
43:17 fourteen cubits long and fourteen cubits **w**, 8145
45: 1 25,000 cubits long and 20,000 cubits **w**; 8145
45: 3 cubits long and 10,000 cubits **w**. 8145
45: 5 10,000 cubits **w** will belong to the Levites, 8145
45: 6 5,000 cubits **w** and 25,000 cubits long, 8145
46:22 forty cubits long and thirty cubits **w**; 8145
48: 8 It will be 25,000 cubits **w**, 8145
48: 9 cubits long and 10,000 cubits **w**. 8145
48:10 10,000 cubits **w** on the west side, 8145
48:10 10,000 cubits **w** on the east side and 8145
48:13 25,000 cubits long and 10,000 cubits **w**. 8145
48:15 5,000 cubits **w** and 25,000 cubits long, 8145
Da 3: 1 ninety feet high and nine feet **w**, 10603
Mic 4: 3 for strong nations **far and w**. 6330+8158
Na 3:13 your land *are* **w open** to your enemies; 7337+7337
Zec 2: 2 to find out how **w** and how long it is." 8145
5: 2 thirty feet long and fifteen feet **w**." 8145
Mt 7:13 For **w** is the gate and broad is the road *4426*
23: 5 *They* **make** their phylacteries **w** *4425*
2Co 6:11 and **opened w** our hearts to you. *4425*
6:13 **open w** *your* hearts also. *4425*
Eph 3:18 how **w** and long and high and deep is *4424*
Rev 21:16 like a square, as long as it was **w**. *4424*
21:16 and as **w** and high as it is long. *4424*

WIDELY (3) [WIDE]

Ne 4:19 and we are **w** separated from each other 8158
Mt 28:15 And this story *has been* **w circulated** *1424*
Ac 19:20 In this way the word of the Lord **spread w** *889*

WIDENED (1) [WIDE]

Eze 41: 7 so that the rooms **w** as one went upward. 8145

WIDENESS (KJV) See WIDE

WIDER (2) [WIDE]

Job 11: 9 longer than the earth and **w** than the sea. 8146
Eze 41: 7 the temple *were* **w** at each successive level. 8143

WIDESPREAD (2) [SPREAD]

Eze 28:16 your **w** trade you were filled with violence, 8044
Jn 7:12 Among the crowds there was **w** whispering *4498*

WIDOW (58) [WIDOW'S, WIDOWHOOD, WIDOWS, WIDOWS']

Ge 38:11 "Live *as* a **w** in your father's house 530
Ex 22:22 "Do not take advantage of a **w** or an orphan. 530
Lev 21:14 He must not marry a **w**, a divorced woman, 530
22:13 But if a priest's daughter becomes a **w** 530
Nu 30: 9 by a **w** or divorced woman will be binding 530
Dt 10:18 the cause of the fatherless and the **w**, 530
24:17 or take the cloak of the **w** as a pledge. 530
24:19 the alien, the fatherless and the **w**, 530
24:20 the alien, the fatherless and the **w**. 530
24:21 the alien, the fatherless and the **w**. 530
25: 5 **w** must not marry outside the family. 851+4637
25: 9 his **brother's w** shall go up to him in 3304
26:12 the alien, the fatherless and the **w**, 530
26:13 the alien, the fatherless and the **w**, 530
27:19 the alien, the fatherless or the **w**." 530
Ru 4: 5 you acquire the dead man's **w**, 851
4:10 the Moabitess, Mahlon's **w**, as my wife, 851
1Sa 27: 3 and Abigail of Carmel, the **w** *of* Nabal. 851
30: 5 Abigail, the **w** *of* Nabal of Carmel. 851
2Sa 2: 2 Abigail, the **w** *of* Nabal of Carmel. 851
3: 3 Kileab the son of Abigail the **w** *of* Nabal 851
14: 5 She said, "I am indeed a **w**; 530
1Ki 7:14 whose mother was a **w** from the tribe 530
11:26 and his mother was a **w** named Zeruah. 530
17: 9 a **w** in that place to supply you with food." 530
17:10 a **w** was there gathering sticks. 530
17:20 also upon this **w** I am staying with, 530
Job 24:21 and to the **w** show no kindness. 530
31:16 or let the eyes of the **w** grow weary, 530
31:18 and from my birth I guided the **w**— 5626[S]
Ps 94: 6 They slay the **w** and the alien; 530
109: 9 be fatherless and his wife a **w**. 530
146: 9 and sustains the fatherless and the **w**, 530
Isa 1:17 plead the case of the **w**. 530
47: 8 be a **w** or suffer the loss of children.' 530
Jer 7: 6 or the **w** and do not shed innocent blood 530
22: 3 to the alien, the fatherless or the **w**, 530
La 1: 1 How like a **w** is she, 530
Eze 22: 7 and mistreated the fatherless and the **w**. 530
Zec 7:10 Do not oppress the **w** or the fatherless, 530
Mt 22:24 the **w** and have children for him. *899+1222*
Mk 12:19 the **w** and have children for his brother. *1222*
12:21 The second one married **the w**, *899*[S]
12:42 But a poor **w** came and put in two *5939*
12:43 this poor **w** has put more into the treasury *5939*
Lk 2:37 and then was a **w** until she was eighty-four. *5939*
4:26 but to a **w** in Zarephath *1222+5939*
7:12 the only son of his mother, and she was a **w**. *5939*
18: 3 a **w** in that town who kept coming to him *5939*
18: 5 yet because this **w** keeps bothering me, *5939*
20:28 the **w** and have children for his brother. *1222*
21: 2 He also saw a poor **w** put in two *5939*
21: 3 "this poor **w** has put in more than all *5939*
1Ti 5: 4 But if a **w** has children or grandchildren, *5939*
5: 5 The **w** who is really in need *5939*
5: 6 the **w** who lives for pleasure is dead even *NIG*
5: 9 No **w** may be put on the list of widows *5939*
Rev 18: 7 I am not a **w**, and I will never mourn.' *5939*

WIDOW'S (6) [WIDOW]

Ge 38:14 she took off her **w** clothes, 531
38:19 and put on her **w** clothes again. 531
Job 24: 3 the orphan's donkey and take the **w** ox 530
29:13 I made the **w** heart sing. 530
Pr 15:25 but he keeps the **w** boundaries intact. 530
Isa 1:23 the **w** case does not come before them. 530

WIDOWHOOD (2) [WIDOW]

Isa 47: 9 loss of children and **w**. 529
54: 4 remember no more the reproach of your **w**. 531

WIDOWS (31) [WIDOW]

Ex 22:24 your wives will become **w** and your children 530
Dt 14:29 and the **w** who live in your towns may come 530
16:11 the fatherless and the **w** living among you. 530
16:14 the aliens, the fatherless and the **w** who live 530
2Sa 20: 3 till the day of their death, living as **w**. 531
Job 22: 9 And you sent **w** away empty-handed 530
27:15 and their **w** will not weep for them. 530
Ps 68: 5 A father to the fatherless, a defender of **w**, 530
78:64 and their **w** could not weep. 530
Isa 9:17 nor will he pity the fatherless and **w**, 530
10: 2 making **w** their prey and robbing 530
Jer 15: 8 I will make their **w** more numerous than 530
18:21 Let their wives be made childless and **w**; 530
49:11 Your **w** too can trust in me." 530
La 5: 3 orphans and fatherless, our mothers like **w**. 530
Eze 22:25 and precious things and make many **w** 530
44:22 They must not marry **w** or divorced women; 530
44:22 of Israelite descent or **w** of priests. 530
Mal 3: 5 who oppress the **w** and the fatherless, 530
Lk 4:25 I assure you that there were many **w** *5939*
Ac 6: 1 because their **w** were being overlooked in *5939*
9:39 All the **w** stood around him, *5939*
9:41 and the **w** and presented her to them alive. *5939*
1Co 7: 8 Now *to* the unmarried and the **w** I say: *5939*
1Ti 5: 3 to those **w** who are really in need. *5939*
5: 9 on the list of **w** unless she is over sixty, *NIG*
5:11 younger **w**, do not put them on such a list. *5939*
5:14 So I counsel younger **w** to marry, *NIG*
5:16 If any woman who is a believer has **w** *5939*
5:16 the church can help those **w** who are really *5939*
Jas 1:27 to look after orphans and **w** in their distress *5939*

WIDOWS' (2) [WIDOW]

Mk 12:40 They devour **w'** houses and for a show *5939*
Lk 20:47 They devour **w'** houses and for a show *5939*

WIDTH (11) [WIDE]

1Ki 6: 3 of the temple extended the **w** *of* the temple, 8145
2Ch 3: 4 across the **w** *of* the building 8145
3: 8 corresponding to the **w** *of* the temple— 8145
Eze 40:11 Then he measured the **w** *of* the entrance to 8145
40:20 the length and **w** *of* the gate facing north, 8145
40:48 The **w** *of* the entrance was fourteen cubits 8145
41: 1 **w** *of* the jambs was six cubits on each side. 8145
41: 4 and its **w** was twenty cubits across the end 8145
41:14 The **w** *of* the temple courtyard on the east, 8145
42:11 they had the same length and **w**, 8145
48:13 25,000 cubits and its **w** 10,000 cubits. 8145

WIELD (1) [WIELDING]

Isa 10:15 As if a rod *were to* **w** him who lifts it up, 5677

WIELDING (1) [WIELD]

Ps 74: 5 behaved like *men* **w** axes 995+2025+4200+5087

WIFE (333) [WIFE'S, WIVES, WIVES']

Ge 2:24 and mother and be united to his **w**, 851
2:25 The man and his **w** were both naked, 851
3: 8 Then the man and his **w** heard the sound of 851
3:17 "Because you listened to your **w** and ate 851
3:20 Adam named his **w** Eve, 851
3:21 for Adam and his **w** and clothed them. 851
4: 1 Adam lay with his **w** Eve, 851
4:17 Cain lay with his **w**, 851
4:25 Adam lay with his **w** again, 851
6:18 and your **w** and your sons' wives with you. 851
7: 7 and his **w** and his sons' wives entered 851
7:13 with his **w** and the wives of his three sons, 851
8:16 and your **w** and your sons and their wives. 851
8:18 with his sons and his **w** and his sons' wives. 851
11:29 The name of Abram's **w** was Sarai, 851
11:29 and the name of Nahor's **w** was Milcah; 851
11:31 Sarai, the **w** *of* his son Abram, 851
12: 5 He took his **w** Sarai, his nephew Lot, 851
12:11 he said to his **w** Sarai, 851
12:12 they will say, 'This is his **w**.' 851
12:17 because of Abram's **w** Sarai. 851
12:18 "Why didn't you tell me she was your **w**? 851
12:19 so that I took her to be my **w**? 851
12:19 Now then, here is your **w**. 851
12:20 with his **w** and everything he had. 851
13: 1 with his **w** and everything he had, 851
16: 1 Now Sarai, Abram's **w**, had borne him no 851
16: 3 Sarai his **w** took her Egyptian maidservant 851
16: 3 and gave her to her husband to be his **w**. 851
17:15 "As for Sarai your **w**, 851
17:19 "Yes, but your **w** Sarah will bear you a son, 851
18: 9 "Where is your **w** Sarah?" 851
18:10 and Sarah your **w** will have a son." 851
19:15 your **w** and your two daughters who are 851
19:16 the hands of his **w** and of his two daughters 851
19:26 But Lot's **w** looked back, 851
20: 2 and there Abraham said of his **w** Sarah, 851
20: 7 Now return the man's **w**, 851
20:11 and they will kill me because of my **w**.' 851
20:12 and she became my **w**. 851
20:14 and he returned Sarah his **w** to him. 851
20:17 Abimelech, his **w** and his slave girls 851
20:18 because of Abraham's **w** Sarah. 851
21:21 his mother got a **w** for him from Egypt. 851
23: 3 Then Abraham rose from beside his **dead** *w* AIT
23:19 Afterward Abraham buried his **w** Sarah in 851
24: 3 not get a **w** for my son from the daughters 851
24: 4 my own relatives and get a **w** for my son 851
24: 7 that you can get a **w** for my son from there. 851

Ge 24:15 the w *of* Abraham's brother Nahor. 851
24:36 My master's w Sarah has borne him a son 851
24:37 not get a w for my son from the daughters 851
24:38 and get a w for my son.' 851
24:40 a w for my son from my own clan and 851
24:51 let her become the w of your master's son, 851
24:67 So she became his w, and he loved her; 851
25: 1 Abraham took another w, 851
25:10 Abraham was buried with his w Sarah. 851
25:21 prayed to the LORD on behalf of his w, 851
25:21 and his w Rebekah became pregnant. 851
26: 7 men of that place asked him about his w, 851
26: 7 he was afraid to say, "She is my w." 851
26: 8 and saw Isaac caressing his w Rebekah. 851
26: 9 "She is really your w! 851
26:10 the men might well have slept with your w, 851
26:11 or his w shall surely be put to death." 851
27:46 If Jacob takes a w from among the women 851
28: 2 Take a w for yourself there, 851
28: 6 to Paddan Aram to take a w from there, 851
29:21 Then Jacob said to Laban, "Give me my w. 851
29:28 gave him his daughter Rachel to be his w. 851
30: 4 So she gave him her servant Bilhah as a w. 851
30: 9 and gave her to Jacob as a w. 851
34: 4 "Get me this girl as my w." 851
34: 8 Please give her to him as his w. 851
34:12 Only give me the girl as my w." 851
36:10 Eliphaz, the son of Esau's w Adah, 851
36:10 and Reuel, the son of Esau's w Basemath. 851
36:12 These were grandsons of Esau's w Adah. 851
36:13 grandson's of Esau's w Basemath. 851
36:14 The sons of Esau's w Oholibamah daughter 851
36:17 they were grandsons of Esau's w Basemath. 851
36:18 The sons of Esau's w Oholibamah: 851
36:18 from Esau's w Oholibamah daughter 851
38: 6 Judah got a w for Er, his firstborn, 851
38: 8 with your brother's w and fulfill your duty 851
38: 9 so whenever he lay with his brother's w, 851
38:12 After a long time Judah's w, 851
38:14 she had not been given to him as his w. 851
39: 7 a while his master's w took notice of Joseph 851
39: 9 because you are his w. 851
39:19 his master heard the story his w told him, 851
41:45 of Potiphera, priest of On, to be his w. 851
44:27 'You know that my w bore me two sons. 851
46:19 The sons of Jacob's w Rachel: 851
49:31 and his w Sarah were buried, 851
49:31 there Isaac and his w Rebekah were buried, 851
Ex 4:20 So Moses took his w and sons, 851
18: 2 After Moses had sent away his w Zipporah, 851
18: 5 together with Moses' sons and w, 851
18: 6 to you with your w and her two sons." 851
20:17 You shall not covet your neighbor's w, 851
21: 3 but if he has a w when he comes, 851
21: 4 a w and she bears him sons or daughters, 851
21: 5 'I love my master and my w and children 851
22:16 and she shall be his w. 851
Lev 18: 8 sexual relations with your father's w; 851
18:11 with the daughter of your father's w, 851
18:14 by approaching his w to have sexual relations 851
18:15 She is your son's w; 851
18:16 sexual relations with your brother's w; 851
18:18 not take your wife's sister as a **rival** w 7675
18:18 with her while **your** w is living. 2023S
18:20 sexual relations with your neighbor's w 851
20:10 commits adultery with another man's w 851
20:10 with the w *of* his neighbor— 851
20:11 " 'If a man sleeps with his father's w, 851
20:21 " 'If a man marries his brother's w, 851
Nu 5:12 'If a man's w goes astray and is unfaithful 851
5:14 and he suspects his w and she is impure— 851
5:15 then he is to take his w to the priest. 851
5:30 over a man because he suspects his w. 851
12: 1 against Moses because of his Cushite w, 851
26:59 the name of Amram's w was Jochebed, 851
30:16 relationships between a man and his w, 851
Dt 5:21 "You shall not covet your neighbor's w. 851
13: 6 or your son or daughter, or the w you love, 851
21:11 you may take her as your w. 851
21:13 and be her husband and she shall be your w. 851
21:15 but the firstborn is the son of the w he does NIH
21:16 of the firstborn to the son of the w he loves NIH
21:16 the son of the w he does not love. NIH
21:17 the son of his unloved w as the firstborn NIH
22:13 If a man takes a w and, after lying with her, 851
22:19 She shall continue to be his w; 851
22:22 found sleeping with another man's w, 851+1249
22:24 because he violated another man's w. 851
22:30 A man is not to marry his father's w; 851
24: 2 and she becomes the w of another man, NIH
24: 5 bring happiness to the w he has married. 851
25: 7 does not want to marry his **brother's** w, 3304
25:11 If two men are fighting and the w *of* one 851
27:20 the man who sleeps with his father's w, 851
28:54 or the w he loves or his surviving children, 851
Jdg 4: 4 Deborah, a prophetess, the w *of* Lappidoth, 851
4:17 the w *of* Heber the Kenite, 851
4:21 But Jael, Heber's w, picked up a tent peg 851
5:24 the w *of* Heber the Kenite, 851
11: 2 Gilead's w also bore him sons, 851
13: 2 a w who was sterile and remained childless. 851
13:11 Manoah got up and followed his w. 851
13:11 "Are you the one who talked to my w?" 851
13:13 "Your w must do all that I have told her. 851
13:19 while Manoah and his w watched: 851
13:20 and his w fell with their faces to the ground. 851
13:21 show himself again to Manoah and his w, 851
Jdg 13:22 "We are doomed to die!" he said to his w. 851
13:23 But his w answered, 851
14: 2 now get her for me as my w." 851
14: 3 the uncircumcised Philistines to get a w?" 851
14:15 On the fourth day, they said to Samson's w, 851
14:16 Then Samson's w threw herself on him, 851
14:20 And Samson's w was given to 851
15: 1 a young goat and went to visit his w. 851
15: 6 because his w was given to his friend." 851
21:18 be anyone who gives a w to a Benjamite.' 851
21:21 of you seize a w from the girls of Shiloh 851
21:23 and carried her off to be his w. 851
Ru 1: 1 together with his w and two sons, 851
4:10 the Moabitess, Mahlon's widow, as my w, 851
4:13 So Boaz took Ruth and she became his w. 851
1Sa 1: 4 to his w Peninnah and to all her sons 851
1:19 Elkanah lay with Hannah his w, 851
2:20 Eli would bless Elkanah and his w, saying, 851
4:19 His daughter-in-law, the w *of* Phinehas, 851
19:11 But Michal, David's w, warned him, 851
25:14 One of the servants told Nabal's w Abigail: 851
25:37 his w told him all these things, 851
25:39 asking her to **become** his w. 851+4200+4374
25:40 to you to take you to become his w." 851
25:42 with David's messengers and became his w. 851
25:44 David's w, to Paltiel son of Laish, 851
30:22 each man may take his w and children 851
2Sa 3: 5 Ithream the son of David's w Eglah. 851
3:14 demanding, "Give me my w, Michal, 851
11: 3 the daughter of Eliam and the w *of* Uriah 851
11:11 to eat and drink and lie with my w? 851
11:26 Uriah's w heard that her husband was dead, 851
11:27 and she became his w and bore him a son. 851
12: 9 the Hittite with the sword and took his w to 851
12:10 the w *of* Uriah the Hittite to be your own.' 851
12:15 the child that Uriah's w had borne to David, 851
12:24 Then David comforted his w Bathsheba, 851
17:19 His w took a covering and spread it out over 851
1Ki 2:17 Abishag the Shunammite as my w." 851
9:16 wedding gift to his daughter, Solomon's w. 851
11:19 that he gave him a sister of his own w, 851
14: 2 and Jeroboam said to his w, 851
14: 2 be recognized as the w *of* Jeroboam. 851
14: 4 So Jeroboam's w did what he said and went 851
14: 5 "Jeroboam's w is coming to ask you 851
14: 6 he said, "Come in, w *of* Jeroboam. 851
14:17 Then Jeroboam's w got up and left 851
21: 5 His w Jezebel came in and asked him, 851
21: 7 Jezebel his w said, "Is this how you act 851
21:25 urged on by Jezebel his w. 851
2Ki 4: 1 The w of a man from the company of 851
5: 2 and she served Naaman's w. 851
22:14 who was the w *of* Shallum son of Tikvah, 851
1Ch 2:18 of Hezron had children by his w Azubah 851
2:24 the w *of* Hezron bore him Ashhur the father 851
2:26 Jerahmeel had another w, 851
2:29 Abishur's w was named Abihail, 851
3: 3 and the sixth, Ithream, by his w Eglah. 851
4:18 (His Judean w gave birth to Jered the father 851
4:19 The sons of Hodiah's w, 851
7:15 Makir took a w from among the Huppites 851
7:16 Makir's w Maacah gave birth to a son 851
7:23 Then he lay with his w again, 851
8: 9 By his w Hodesh he had Jobab, Zibia, 851
2Ch 8:11 "My w must not live in the palace 851
22:11 the daughter of King Jehoram and w *of* 851
34:22 who was the w *of* Shallum son of Tokhath, 851
Est 5:10 his friends and Zeresh, his w, 851
5:14 His w Zeresh and all his friends said to him, 851
6:13 and told Zeresh his w and all his friends 851
6:13 His advisers and his w Zeresh said to him, 851
Job 2: 9 His w said to him, "Are you still holding on 851
19:17 My breath is offensive to my w; 851
31:10 then may my w grind another man's grain, 851
Ps 109: 9 May his children be fatherless and his w 851
128: 3 Your w will be like a fruitful vine 851
Pr 2:16 the **wayward** *w* with her seductive words, AIT
5:18 and may you rejoice in the w *of* your youth. 851
5:20 the bosom of **another** *man's w?* AIT
6:24 from the smooth tongue of the **wayward** *w.* AIT
6:29 So is he who sleeps with another man's w; 851
7: 5 the **wayward** *w* with her seductive words. AIT
12: 4 A w *of* noble character is her husband's crown, 851
12: 4 a disgraceful w is like decay in his bones. NIH
18:22 a w finds what is good and receives favor 851
19:13 a quarrelsome w is like a constant dripping. 851
19:14 but a prudent w is from the LORD. 851
21: 9 a house with a quarrelsome w. 851
21:19 with a quarrelsome and ill-tempered w. 851
23:27 and a **wayward** *w* is a narrow well. AIT
25:24 a house with a quarrelsome w. 851
27:15 A quarrelsome w is like a constant dripping 851
31:10 A w *of* noble character who can find? 851
Ecc 9: 9 Enjoy life with your w, whom you love, 851
Isa 54: 6 as if you were a w deserted and distressed 851
54: 6 a w *who married* young, only to be rejected, 851
Jer 3: 1 "If a man divorces his w and she leaves him 851
5: 8 each neighing for another man's w. 851
6:11 both husband and w will be caught in it, 851
Eze 16:32 " 'You adulterous w! You prefer strangers 851
18: 6 He does not defile his neighbor's w or lie 851
18:11 He defiles his neighbor's w. 851
18:15 He does not defile his neighbor's w. 851
22:11 a detestable offense with his neighbor's w, 851
24:18 and in the evening my w died. 851
33:26 and each of you defiles his neighbor's w. 851
Hos 1: 2 to yourself an adulterous w and children 851
2: 2 rebuke her, for she is not my w, 851
3: 1 "Go, show your love to your w again, 851
12:12 Israel served to get a w, 851
Am 7:17 " 'Your w will become a prostitute in 851
Mal 2:14 between you and the w *of* your youth, 851
2:14 the w *of* your marriage covenant. 851
2:15 do not break faith with the w *of* your youth. 851
Mt 1: 6 whose mother had been Uriah's w, *3836*
1:20 not be afraid to take Mary home as your w, *1222*
1:24 and took Mary home as his w. *1222*
5:31 'Anyone who divorces his w must give her *1222*
5:32 I tell you that anyone who divorces his w, *1222*
14: 3 Herodias, his brother Philip's w, *1222*
18:25 that he and his w and his children and all *1222*
19: 3 to divorce his w for any and every reason?" *1222*
19: 5 and mother and be united to his w, *1222*
19: 7 "did Moses command that a man give his w *NIG*
19: 9 I tell you that anyone who divorces his w, *1222*
19:10 the situation between a husband and w, *1222*
22:25 he left his w to his brother. *1222*
22:28 whose w will she be of the seven, *1222*
27:19 his w sent him this message: *1222*
Mk 6:17 Herodias, his brother Philip's w, *1222*
6:18 not lawful for you to have your brother's w. *1222*
10: 2 "Is it lawful for a man to divorce his w?" *1222*
10: 7 and mother and be united to his w, *1222*
10:11 "Anyone who divorces his w *1222*
12:19 that if a man's brother dies and leaves a w *1222*
12:23 At the resurrection whose w will she be, *1222*
Lk 1: 5 his w Elizabeth was also a descendant *1222*
1:13 Your w Elizabeth will bear you a son, *1222*
1:18 I am an old man and my w is well along *1222*
1:24 After this his w Elizabeth became pregnant *1222*
3:19 because of Herodias, his brother's w, *1222*
8: 3 Joanna the w of Cuza, the manager *1222*
14:26 his w and children, his brothers *1222*
16:18 "Anyone who divorces his w *1222*
17:32 Remember Lot's w! *1222*
18:29 "no one who has left home or w or brothers *1222*
20:28 if a man's brother dies and **leaves** a w *1222+2400*
20:33 at the resurrection whose w will she be, *1222*
Jn 19:25 his mother's sister, Mary **the** w of Clopas, *3836*
Ac 5: 1 Ananias, together with his w Sapphira, *1222*
5: 7 About three hours later his w came in, *1222*
18: 2 from Italy with his w Priscilla, *1222*
24:24 Felix came with his w Drusilla, *1222*
1Co 5: 1 A man has his father's w. *1222*
7: 2 each man should have his own w, *1222*
7: 3 should fulfill his marital duty *to* his w, *1222*
7: 3 and likewise the w to her husband. *1222*
7: 4 not belong to him alone but also to his w. *1222*
7:10 A w must not separate from her husband. *1222*
7:11 And a husband must not divorce his w. *1222*
7:12 If any brother has a w who is not a believer *1222*
7:14 For the unbelieving husband has been sanctified through his w, *1222*
7:14 and the unbelieving w has been sanctified *1222*
7:16 How do you know, w, *1222*
7:16 husband, whether you will save your w? *1222*
7:27 Do not look for a w. *1222*
7:33 how he can please his w— *1222*
9: 5 the right to take a **believing** w along *80+1222*
Eph 5:23 the husband is the head *of* the w as Christ is *1222*
5:28 He who loves his w loves himself. *1222*
5:31 and mother and be united to his w, *1222*
5:33 also must love his w as he loves himself, *1222*
5:33 and the w must respect her husband. *1222*
1Ti 3: 2 the husband *of* but one w, temperate, *1222*
3:12 A deacon must be the husband *of* but one w *1222*
Tit 1: 6 blameless, the husband *of* but one w, *1222*
Rev 21: 9 the bride, the w of the Lamb." *1222*

WIFE'S (11) [WIFE]

Ge 36:39 and his w name was Mehetabel daughter 851
Lev 18:18 " 'Do not take your w sister as a rival wife 851
Jdg 15: 1 He said, "I'm going to my w room." 851
Ru 1: 2 Elimelech, his w name Naomi, 851
1Sa 14:50 His w name was Ahinoam daughter 851
25: 3 and his w name was Abigail. 851
1Ch 1:50 and his w name was Mehetabel daughter 851
8:29 His w name was Maacah, 851
9:35 His w name was Maacah, 851
Ac 5: 2 With his w full knowledge he kept back part *1222*
1Co 7: 4 The w body does not belong to her alone *1222*

WILD (98) [WILDER, WILDERNESS, WILDS]

Ge 1:24 and w animals, each according to its kind." 824
1:25 the w animals according to their kinds, 824
3: 1 the w animals the LORD God had made. 8441
3:14 the livestock and all the w animals! 8441
7:14 with them every w **animal** according 2651
7:21 birds, livestock, w **animals,** 2651
8: 1 the w **animals** and the livestock that were 2651
9:10 the livestock and all the w animals, 824
16:12 He will be a w **donkey** of a man; 7230
25:28 Isaac, who had a taste for w **game,** 7473
27: 3 to the open country to hunt *some* w **game** 7473
31:39 not bring you **animals torn by** w **beasts;** 3274
Ex 22:13 *it* **was torn to pieces by a** w **animal,** 3271+3271
22:31 of an animal torn by w beasts; 928+2021+8441
23:11 and the w animals may eat what they leave. 8441
23:29 and the w animals too numerous for you. 8441
32:25 Moses saw that the people *were* **running** w 7277
Lev 5: 2 whether the carcasses of unclean w **animals** 2651

Lev 7:24 or **torn by w animals** may be used 3274
17:15 or **torn by w animals** must wash his clothes 3274
22: 8 found dead or **torn by w animals,** 3274
25: 7 as for your livestock and the w **animals** 2651
26:22 I will send w animals against you, 8441
Nu 23:22 they have the strength of a w **ox.** 8028
24: 8 they have the strength of a w **ox.** 8028
Dt 7:22 or the w animals will multiply around you. 8441
14: 5 the gazelle, the roe deer, the w **goat,** 735
32:24 against them the fangs of w **beasts,** 989
33:17 his horns are the horns of a w **ox.** 8028
1Sa 24: 2 and his men near the Crags of the **W Goats.** 3604
2Sa 2:18 Asahel was as fleet-footed as a w gazelle. 928+2021+8441
17: 8 as a w bear robbed of her cubs. 928+2021+8441
21:10 the air touch them by day or the w animals 8441
2Ki 4:39 to gather herbs and found a w vine. 8441
14: 9 Then a w beast in Lebanon came along 8441
2Ch 25:18 Then a w beast in Lebanon came along 8441
Ne 8:15 and w **olive** trees, and from myrtles, palms 9043
Job 5:23 the w animals will be at peace with you. 8441
6: 5 Does a w **donkey** bray when it has grass, 7230
11:12 a w **donkey's** colt can be born a man. 7230
24: 5 Like w **donkeys** in the desert, 7230
39: 5 "Who let the w **donkey** go free? 7230
39: 9 "Will the w **ox** consent to serve you? 8028
39:15 that some w animal may trample them. 8441
40:20 and all the w animals play nearby. 8441
Ps 22:21 save me from the horns of the w **oxen.** 8028
29: 6 Sirion like a young w **ox.** 8028
74:19 over the life of your dove to w **beasts;** 2651
92:10 exalted my horn like that of a w **ox;** 8028
104:11 the w **donkeys** quench their thirst. 7230
104:18 The high mountains belong to the w **goats;** 3604
148:10 w **animals** and all cattle, 2651
Isa 13:21 and there the w **goats** will leap about. 8538
18: 6 of prey and to the w animals; 824
18: 6 the w animals all winter. 824
34: 7 And the w **oxen** will fall with them, 8028
34:14 and w **goats** will bleat to each other; 8538
43:20 The w animals honor me, 8441
Jer 2:21 against me into a corrupt, w vine? 5799
2:24 a w **donkey** accustomed to the desert, 7241
12: 9 Go and gather all the w beasts; 8441
14: 6 **W donkeys** stand on the barren heights 7230
27: 6 I will make even the w animals subject 8441
28:14 give him control over the w animals.' " 8441
Eze 4:14 found dead or **torn by w animals.** 3274
5:17 I will send famine and w beasts against you, 8273
14:15 "Or if I send w beasts through that country 8273
14:21 and famine and w beasts and plague— 8273
33:27 the country I will give to the w **animals** to 2651
34: 5 they became food for all the w animals. 8441
34: 8 and has become food for all the w animals, 8441
34:25 the land of w beasts so that they may live in 8273
34:28 nor will w animals devour them. 824
39: 4 of carrion birds and to the w animals. 8441
39:17 to every kind of bird and all the w animals: 8441
44:31 found dead or **torn by w animals.** 3274
Da 4:23 let him live like the w animals, 10119
4:25 and will live with the w animals; 10119
4:32 and will live with the w animals; 10119
5:21 the w **donkeys** and ate grass like cattle; 10570
Hos 2:12 and w animals will devour them. 8441
8: 9 like a w **donkey** wandering alone. 7230
13: 8 a w animal will tear them apart. 8441
Joel 1:20 Even the w animals pant for you; 8441
2:22 Be not afraid, O w animals, 8442
Zep 2:15 a lair for w **beasts!** 2651
Mt 3: 4 His food was locusts and w honey. *67*
Mk 1: 6 and he ate locusts and w honey. *67*
1:13 He was with the w **animals,** *2563*
Lk 15:13 and there squandered his wealth in w living. *862*
Ac 11: 6 w **beasts,** reptiles, and birds of the air. *2563*
Ro 11:17 and you, *though* a w **olive shoot,** *66*
11:24 **olive tree that is w** *66*
1Co 15:32 If *I* **fought w beasts** in Ephesus *2562*
Tit 1: 6 and are not open to the charge of being w *861*
Jas 1:10 because he will pass away like a w flower. *5965*
Jude 1:13 They are w waves of the sea, *67*
Rev 6: 8 and by the w **beasts** of the earth. *2563*

WILDER (1) [WILD]

Jnh 1:13 sea **grew even** w than before. 2143+2256+6192

WILDERNESS (5) [WILD]

Isa 35: 1 the w will rejoice and blossom. 6858
35: 6 Water will gush forth in the w and streams 4497
40: 3 make straight in the w a highway 6858
Jer 2: 6 of Egypt and led us through the **barren** w, 4497
50:12 a w, a dry land, a desert. 4497

WILDS (1) [WILD]

Job 39: 4 and grow strong in the w; 1340

WILL (166 of 10192) [FREEWILL, WEAK-WILLED, WILLFUL, WILLFULLY, WILLING, WILLINGLY, WILLINGNESS, WILLS, WON'T] See Index of Articles Etc. for an Exhaustive Listing (See Introduction, page xi)

Ge 15: 2 the **one who** w **inherit** my estate 1201+5479
23:13 "Listen to me, if you w. 4273
24:42 God of my master Abraham, if you w, 3780
24:49 if you w show kindness and faithfulness 3780
27:33 and indeed *he* w be blessed!" 2118
27:46 my **life** w **not be worth living."** 2644+4200+4537
43: 4 If you w send our brother along with us, 3780
43: 5 But if you w **not** send him, 401
45: 6 the next five years **there** w **not be** plowing 401
Ex 9: 9 and festering boils w break out on men 2118
18:15 the people come to me to **seek** God's w. 2011
Lev 24:12 until the w *of* the LORD should be made clear to them. 6584+7023
25:46 *You can* w them to your children 5706
Dt 10:10 *It was* not his w to destroy you. 14
11:17 and he will shut the heavens so that *it* w 2118
15: 9 *do* not **show ill** w toward your needy brother 6524+8317
25: 7 *He* w not fulfill the duty of a brother-in-law 14
28:26 **there** w **be no** one to frighten them away. 401
28:34 The sights you see w drive you mad. 2118
28:66 You w live in constant suspense, 2118
33:21 he carried out the LORD's **righteous** w, 7407
Jdg 6:36 "If you w save Israel by my hand 3780
Ru 4:15 *He* w renew your life and sustain you 2118
1Sa 2:25 for *it was* the LORD's w to put them 2911
23:11 And the LORD said, *"He* w." 3718[S]
23:12 And the LORD said, *"They* w." 6037[S]
2Sa 5:24 because **that** w **mean** the LORD has gone 255
7:21 sake of your word and according to your w, 4213
15:14 or none of us w escape from Absalom. 2118
2Ki 6: 3 "I w," Elisha replied. 2143[S]
1Ch 13: 2 if it is the w *of* the LORD our God, 4946
14:15 **because that** w **mean** God has gone out 3954
17:19 of your servant and according to your w, 4213
Ezr 4:16 you w **be left with** nothing 10029+10378
7:18 in accordance with the w *of* your God. 10668
10:11 the God of your fathers, and do his w. 8356
Job 5: 1 "Call **if you** w, but who will answer you? 5528
Ps 40: 8 I desire to do your w, O my God; 8356
103:21 you his servants who do his w. 8356
143:10 Teach me to do your w, 8356
144:14 **There** w **be no** breaching of walls, 401
Isa 5:24 so their roots w decay and their flowers 2118
8: 8 Its outspread wings w cover the breadth 2118
9: 7 and peace **there** w **be no** end. 401
29: 2 *she* w mourn and lament, 2118
30:29 And you w sing as on the night you 2118
34:12 all her princes w vanish away. 2118
47:12 Perhaps *you* w succeed, 3523
53:10 the LORD's w to crush him and cause him 2911
53:10 the w *of* the LORD will prosper in his hand. 2914
Jer 7:33 **there** w **be no** one to frighten them away. 401
8:13 **There** w **be no** grapes on the vine. 401
8:13 **There** w **be no** figs on the tree, 401
13:19 and **there** w **be no** one to open them. 401
14:16 **There** w **be no** one to bury them 401
29: 7 because if it prospers, you too w prosper." 2118
30: 7 **None** w **be** like it. 401+4946
31: 6 **There** w **be** a day when watchmen cry out 3780
42:17 not *one* of them w survive or escape 2118
44:14 in Egypt w escape or survive to return to 2118
50:20 but **there** w **be none,** 401
51: 2 *they* w oppose her on every side in the day 2118
Eze 7:25 they will seek peace, but **there** w **be none.** 401
12:25 But I the LORD will speak what *I* w, 1819+1821[S]
18:13 Will such a man live? *He* w not! 2649[S]
33:33 When all this comes true—and *it* surely w— 995[S]
Da 11:42 Egypt w not escape. 2118
Mic 5:12 and you w no longer cast spells. 2118
Zec 2: 9 so that their slaves w plunder them. 2118
Mt 6:10 your w be done on earth as it is in heaven. *2525*
7:21 the w of my Father who is in heaven. *2525*
10:29 apart from the w of your Father. NIG
12:50 the w of my Father in heaven is my brother *2525*
21:29 " *'I* w not,' he answered, *2527*
24: 6 You w hear of wars and rumors of wars, *3516*
26:39 Yet not as I w, but as you will." *2527*
26:39 Yet not as I will, but as you **w."** *NIG*
26:42 may your w be done." *2525*
Mk 3:35 Whoever does God's w is my brother *2525*
14:36 Yet not what I w, but what you will." *2527*
14:36 Yet not what I will, but what you **w."** *NIG*
Lk 1:33 his kingdom w never end." *1639*
12:47 "That servant who knows his master's w *2525*
22:42 yet not my w, but yours be done." *2525*
23:25 and surrendered Jesus *to* their w. *2525*
Jn 1:13 nor of human decision or a husband's w, *2525*
4:34 "is to do the w of him who sent me and *2525*
6: 9 but **how far** w **they go** among *1639+4047+5515*
6:38 down from heaven not to do my w but to do *2525*
6:38 but to do the w of him who sent me. *2525*
6:39 And this is the w of him who sent me, *2525*
6:40 For my Father's w is that everyone who *2525*
7:17 If anyone chooses to do God's **w,** *2525*
7:35 **W** he go where our people live scattered *3516*
9:31 He listens to the godly man who does his w. *2525*
19:24 "Let's decide by lot who w get it." *1639*
Ac 4:28 your power and w had decided beforehand *1087*
17:31 when *he* w judge the world with justice by *3516*
18:15 I w not be a judge of such things." *1089*
18:21 "I will come back *if it is* God's **w."** *2527*
19:27 w be robbed of her divine majesty." *3516*
20:27 to proclaim to you the whole w of God. *1087*
21:14 "The Lord's w be done." *2525*
22:14 of our fathers has chosen you to know his w *2525*
23: 3 Then Paul said to him, "God w strike you, *3516*
24:15 that there w be a resurrection of both *3516*
Ro 1:10 by God's w the way may be opened for me *2525*
2:18 if you know his w and approve of what *2525*
4:24 to whom God w credit righteousness— *3516*
8:13 according to the sinful nature, *you* w die; *3516*
8:18 not worth comparing with the glory that w *3516*
8:20 but by the w of the one who subjected it, *NIG*
9:19 For who resists his **w?"** *1088*
12: 2 **Then** you w **be able** to test and *1650+3836*
12: 2 to test and approve what God's w is— *2525*
12: 2 his good, pleasing and perfect **w.** *NIG*
15:12 Isaiah says, "The Root of Jesse w spring up, *1639*
15:32 that by God's w I may come to you with joy *2525*
1Co 1: 1 an apostle of Christ Jesus by the w of God, *2525*
7:37 but has control over his own w, *2525*
2Co 1: 1 an apostle of Christ Jesus by the w of God, *2525*
8: 5 and then to us in keeping with God's **w.** *2525*
Gal 1: 4 according to the w of our God and Father, *2525*
Eph 1: 1 an apostle of Christ Jesus by the w of God, *2525*
1: 5 in accordance with his pleasure and **w—** *2525*
1: 9 *of* his w according to his good pleasure, *2525*
1:11 in conformity with the purpose *of* his **w,** *2525*
5:17 but understand what the Lord's w is. *2525*
6: 6 doing the w of God from your heart. *2525*
Php 1:19 to me w **turn out** for my deliverance. *1650*
2:13 for it is God who works in you *to* w and *2527*
Col 1: 1 an apostle of Christ Jesus by the w of God, *2525*
1: 9 to fill you with the knowledge *of* his w *2525*
4:12 that you may stand firm in all the w of God, *2525*
1Th 4: 3 It is God's w that you should be sanctified: *2525*
5:18 for this is God's w for you in Christ Jesus. *2525*
2Th 3:10 "If a man w not work, he shall not eat." *2527*
2Ti 1: 1 an apostle of Christ Jesus by the w of God, *2525*
2:26 who has taken them captive to do his **w.** *2525*
4: 1 who w judge the living and the dead, *3516*
Heb 1:14 to serve those who w inherit salvation? *3516*
2: 4 distributed according to his **w.** *2526*
9:16 In the case of a w, it is necessary *1347*
9:17 w is in force only when somebody has died; *1347*
10: 7 I have come to do your **w,** O God.' " *2525*
10: 9 "Here I am, I have come to do your **w."** *2525*
10:10 And by that w, we have been made holy *2525*
10:27 of raging fire that w consume the enemies *3516*
10:36 so that when you have done the w of God, *2525*
13:21 with everything good for doing his w, *2525*
Jas 4:15 you ought to say, "If it is the Lord's **w,** *2527*
1Pe 2:15 For it is God's w that by doing good *2525*
3:17 It is better, if it is God's w, to suffer for *2525*
4: 2 but rather *for* the w of God. *2525*
4:19 those who suffer according to God's w *2525*
2Pe 1:12 So *I* w always remind you of these things, *3516*
1:21 For prophecy never had its origin *in* the w *2525*
1Jn 2:17 man who does the w of God lives forever. *2525*
5:14 that if we ask anything according to his w, *2525*
Rev 1:19 what is now and what w take place later. *3516*
2:10 the devil w put some of you in prison *3516*
2:26 To him who overcomes and does my w to *2240*
4:11 and by your w they were created *2525*
12: 5 who w rule all the nations with *3516*
17: 8 and w come up out of the Abyss and go *3516*

WILLFUL (3) [WILL]

Ps 19:13 Keep your servant also from w **sins;** 2294
Isa 10:12 for the w **pride** *of* his heart and 1542+7262
57:17 yet he kept on in his w ways. 4213

WILLFULLY (1) [WILL]

Ps 78:18 They w put God to the test by 928+4222

WILLING (57) [WILL]

Ge 23: 8 "If you are w to let me bury my dead, 5883
Ex 10:27 and *he was* not w to let them go. 14
35: 5 Everyone who is w is to bring to 4213+5618
35:21 and everyone who *was* w 5605+8120
35:22 All who were w, men and women 4213+5618
35:26 And all the women who *were* w and 4213+5951
35:29 and women who *were* w brought to 4213+5605
36: 2 who *was* w to come and do the work. 4213+5951
Dt 29:20 LORD *will* never *be* w to forgive him; 14
Jdg 5: 9 with the w **volunteers** among the people. 5605
Ru 3:13 But if *he is* not w, as surely as the LORD 2911
1Sa 22:17 not w to raise a hand to strike the priests of 14
2Sa 6:10 He *was* not w to take the ark of the LORD 14
2Ki 8:19 the LORD *was* not w to destroy Judah. 14
24: 4 and the LORD *was* not w to forgive. 14
1Ch 19:19 not w to help the Ammonites anymore. 14
28: 9 wholehearted devotion and with a w mind, 2913
28:21 and every w *man* skilled in any craft 5618
29: 5 who *is* w to consecrate himself today to 5605
29: 9 The people rejoiced at the w **response** 5605
2Ch 21: 7 the LORD *was* not w to destroy the house 14
29:31 whose hearts were w brought burnt offerings 5618
Job 6: 9 that God *would be* w to crush me, 3283
Ps 51:12 of your salvation and grant me a w spirit, 5618
110: 3 Your troops will be w on your day of battle. 5607
119:108 O LORD, the w praise *of* my mouth, 5607
Pr 11:26 but blessing crowns *him who is* w *to* **sell.** AIT
19:18 *do* not **be a** w **party** to his death. 5883+5951
Isa 1:19 If *you are* w and obedient, 14
Eze 3: 7 the house of Israel *is* not w to listen to you 14
3: 7 to you because they *are* not w to listen 14
Da 3:28 the king's command and *were* w *to* **give up** AIT
Mt 8: 2 if *you are* w, you can make me clean." *2527*
8: 3 *"I am* **w,"** he said. *2527*
11:14 And if *you are* w to accept it, *2527*
18:14 not w that any of these little ones should *2525*

Mt 23: 4 but they themselves *are* not w to lift a finger *2527*
23:37 but *you were* not w. *2527*
26:15 "What *are you* w to give me if I hand him *2527*
26:41 The spirit is w, but the body is weak." *4609*
Mk 1:40 "If *you are* w, you can make me clean." *2527*
1:41 "*I am* w," he said. *2527*
14:38 The spirit is w, but the body is weak." *4609*
Lk 5:12 if *you are* w, you can make me clean." *2527*
5:13 "*I am* w," he said. *2527*
13:34 but *you were* not w! *2527*
22:42 if *you are* w, take this cup from me; *1089*
Jn 6:21 Then *they were* w to take him into the boat, *2527*
Ac 25: 9 "*Are you* w to go up to Jerusalem *2527*
25:20 *be* w to go to Jerusalem and stand trial there *1089*
26: 5 and can testify, if *they are* w, *2527*
Ro 12:16 but be w **to associate** with people *5270*
1Co 4:19 come to you very soon, if the Lord *is* w, *2527*
7:12 a wife who is not a believer and she *is* w *5306*
7:13 a husband who is not a believer and he *is* w *5306*
1Ti 6:18 and to be generous and w to share. *NIG*
1Pe 5: 2 because you must, but *because* you are w, *1731*

WILLINGLY (5) [WILL]

Jdg 5: 2 when the people w **offer themselves—** 5605
1Ch 29: 6 in charge of the king's work **gave** w. 5605
29:17 All these things *have* I **given** w and 5605
29:17 w your people who are here *have* **given** 5605
La 3:33 he does not w bring affliction or grief 4213+4946

WILLINGNESS (2) [WILL]

2Co 8:11 that your eager w to do it may be matched *2527*
8:12 For if the w is there, the gift is acceptable *4608*

WILLOW (1)

Eze 17: 5 He planted it like a w by abundant water, 7628

WILLOWS (KJV) See POPLAR

WILLS (1) [WILL]

Dt 21:16 when he w his property *to* his sons, 5706

WILY (1)

Job 5:13 and the schemes of the w are swept away. 7349

WIN (14) [WINNING, WINS, WON]

Pr 3: 4 Then *you will* w favor and a good name in 5162
Jer 5:28 not plead the case of the fatherless *to* w it, 7503
Mt 23:15 over land and sea *to* w a single convert, *4472*
1Co 9:19 slave to everyone, to w as many as possible. *3045*
9:20 I became like a Jew, to w the Jews. *3045*
9:20 so as to w those under the law. *3045*
9:21 so as to w those not having the law. *3045*
9:22 To the weak I became weak, to w the weak. *3045*
Gal 1:10 now **trying to** w **the approval of** men, *4275*
4:17 Those people are zealous to w you over, *NIG*
Eph 6: 6 not only to w their **favor** when their eye is *473*
Php 3:14 I press on toward the goal to w the prize *NIG*
Col 3:22 when their eye is on you and to w their **favor**, *473*
1Th 4:12 so that your daily life may w **the respect** *2361*

WIND (125) [WINDBLOWN, WINDING, WINDS, WINDSTORM, WOUND]

Ge 8: 1 and he sent a w over the earth, 8120
41: 6 thin and scorched by the **east** w. 7708
41:23 and thin and scorched by the **east** w. 7708
41:27 heads of grain scorched by the **east** w: 7708
Ex 10:13 and the LORD made an east w blow across 8120
10:13 By morning the w had brought the locusts; 8120
10:19 And the LORD changed the w to NIH
10:19 the wind to a very strong west w, 8120
14:21 a strong east w and turned it into dry land. 8120
Nu 11:31 Now a w went out from the LORD 8120
2Sa 22:11 he soared on the wings of the w. 8120
1Ki 18:45 the sky grew black with clouds, the w rose, 8120
19:11 and powerful w tore the mountains apart 8120
19:11 but the LORD was not in the w. 8120
19:11 After the w there was an earthquake, 8120
2Ki 3:17 You will see neither w nor rain, 8120
Job 1:19 when suddenly a mighty w swept in from 8120
6:26 treat the words of a despairing man as w? 8120
8: 2 Your words are a blustering w. 8120
15: 2 or fill his belly with the **hot east** w? 7708
21:18 How often are they like straw before the w, 8120
27:21 The **east** w carries him off, and he is gone; 7708
28:25 When he established the force of the w 8120
30:15 my dignity is driven away as by the w, 8120
30:22 snatch me up and drive me before the w; 8120
37:17 the land lies hushed under the **south** w, 1999
37:21 the skies after the w has swept them clean. 8120
Ps 1: 4 They are like chaff that the w blows away. 8120
11: 6 a scorching w will be their lot. 8120
18:10 he soared on the wings of the w. 8120
18:42 I beat them as fine as dust borne on the w; 8120
35: 5 May they be like chaff before the w, 8120
48: 7 of Tarshish shattered by an east w. 8120
68: 2 As smoke is blown away by the w, NIH
78:26 the **east** w from the heavens and led forth 7708
78:26 from the heavens and led forth the **south** w 9402
83:13 O my God, like chaff before the w. 8120
103:16 the w blows over it and it is gone, 8120
104: 3 and rides on the wings of the w. 8120
135: 7 and brings out the w from his storehouses. 8120
Pr 11:29 trouble on his family will inherit only w, 8120
25:14 and w without rain is a man who boasts 8120
25:23 As a north w brings rain, 8120
27:16 like restraining the w or grasping oil with 8120
30: 4 Who has gathered up the w in the hollow 8120
Ecc 1: 6 w blows to the south and turns to the north; 8120
1:14 meaningless, a chasing after the w. 8120
1:17 too, is a chasing after the w. 8120
2:11 meaningless, a chasing after the w; 8120
2:17 meaningless, a chasing after the w. 8120
2:26 meaningless, a chasing after the w. 8120
4: 4 meaningless, a chasing after the w. 8120
4: 6 with toil and chasing after the w. 8120
4:16 meaningless, a chasing after the w. 8120
5:16 since he toils for the w? 8120
6: 9 meaningless, a chasing after the w. 8120
8: 8 No man has power over the w to contain it; 8120
11: 4 Whoever watches the w will not plant; 8120
11: 5 As you do not know the path of the w, 8120
SS 4:16 Awake, **north** w, and come, south wind! 7600
4:16 Awake, north wind, and come, **south** w! 9402
Isa 7: 2 the trees of the forest are shaken by the w. 8120
11:15 with a scorching w he will sweep his hand 8120
17:13 driven before the w like chaff on the hills, 8120
24:20 it sways like a hut in the w; NIH
26:18 we writhed in pain, but we gave birth to w. 8120
27: 8 as on a day the **east** w blows. 7708
28: 2 Like a hailstorm and a destructive w, 8551
32: 2 like a shelter from the w and a refuge from 8120
41:16 the w will pick them up, 8120
41:29 their images are but w and confusion. 8120
57:13 The w will carry all of them off, 8120
64: 6 and like the w our sins sweep us away. 8120
Jer 2:24 sniffing the w in her craving— 8120
4:11 "A scorching w *from* the barren heights in 8120
4:12 a w too strong for that comes from me. 8120
5:13 The prophets are but w and the word is not 8120
10:13 and brings out the w from his storehouses. 8120
13:24 like chaff driven by the desert w. 8120
18:17 Like a w *from* the east, 8120
22:22 The w will drive all your shepherds away, 8120
30:23 a driving w swirling down on the heads of 6193
51:16 and brings out the w from his storehouses. 8120
Eze 5: 2 And scatter a third to the w. 8120
13:13 In my wrath I will unleash a **violent** w 6194+8120
17:10 when the east w strikes it— 8120
19:12 The east w made it shrivel, 8120
27:26 But the east w will break you to pieces in 8120
Da 2:35 The w swept them away without leaving 10658
Hos 8: 7 "They sow the w and reap the whirlwind. 8120
12: 1 Ephraim feeds on the w; 8120
12: 1 the **east** w all day and multiplies lies 7708
13:15 An east w *from* the LORD will come, 8120
Am 4:13 He who forms the mountains, creates the w, 8120
Jnh 1: 4 Then the LORD sent a great w on the sea, 8120
4: 8 God provided a scorching east w, 8120
Hab 1: 9 a **desert** w and gather prisoners like sand. 7708
1:11 they sweep past like the w and go on— 8120
Zec 5: 9 with the w in their wings! 8120
Mt 11: 7 A reed swayed by the w? *449*
14:24 by the waves because the w was against it. *449*
14:30 But when he saw the w, he was afraid and, *449*
14:32 climbed into the boat, the w died down. *449*
Mk 4:39 rebuked the w and said to the waves, *449*
4:39 w died down and it was completely calm. *449*
4:41 Even the w and the waves obey him!" *449*
6:48 because the w was against them. *449*
6:51 and the w died down. *449*
Lk 7:24 A reed swayed by the w? *449*
8:24 up and rebuked the w and the raging waters; *449*
12:55 And when the south w **blows**, you say, *4463*
Jn 3: 8 The w blows wherever it pleases. *4460*
6:18 A strong w was blowing and *449*
Ac 2: 2 blowing *of* a violent w came from heaven *4466*
27: 7 the w did not allow us to hold our course, *449*
27:13 When a gentle **south** w began to blow, *3803*
27:14 Before very long, a w of hurricane force, *449*
27:15 by the storm and could not head into the w; *449*
27:40 Then they hoisted the foresail *to* the w *4463*
28:13 The next day the **south** w came up, *3803*
Eph 4:14 blown here and there *by* every w of teaching *449*
Jas 1: 6 wave of the sea, **blown** and tossed **by the** w. *448*
Jude 1:12 clouds without rain, blown along by the w; *449*
Rev 6:13 from a fig tree when shaken by a strong w. *449*
7: 1 the four winds of the earth to prevent any w *449*

WINDBLOWN (3) [WIND, BLOW]

Lev 26:36 the sound of a w leaf will put them to flight. 5622
Job 13:25 Will you torment a w leaf? 5622
Isa 41: 2 to w chaff with his bow. 5622

WINDING (1) [WIND]

Jdg 5: 6 travelers took to w paths. 6824

WINDOW (16) [WINDOWS]

Ge 8: 6 Noah opened the w he had made *in* the ark 2707
26: 8 of the Philistines looked down from a w 2707
Jos 2:15 she let them down by a rope through the w, 2707
2:18 in the w through which you let us down, 2707
2:21 And she tied the scarlet cord in the w. 2707
Jdg 5:28 "Through the w she peered Sisera's mother; 2707
1Sa 19:12 So Michal let David down through a w, 2707
2Sa 6:16 Michal daughter of Saul watched from a w. 2707
2Ki 9:30 arranged her hair and looked out of a w. 2707
2Ki 9:32 He looked up at the w and called out, 2707
13:17 "Open the east w," he said, and he opened 2707
1Ch 15:29 Michal daughter of Saul watched from a w. 2707
Pr 7: 6 At the w *of* my house I looked out through 2707
Hos 13: 3 like smoke escaping through a w. 748
Ac 20: 9 in a w was a young man named Eutychus, *2600*
2Co 11:33 in a basket from a w in the wall and slipped *2600*

WINDOWS (13) [WINDOW]

1Ki 6: 4 He made narrow clerestory w in the temple. 2707
7: 4 Its w were **placed high** in sets of three, 9209
Ecc 12: 3 and those looking through the w grow dim; 748
SS 2: 9 gazing through the w, 2707
Jer 9:21 Death has climbed in through our w 2707
22:14 So he makes large w in it, 2707
Eze 41:16 the narrow w and galleries around the three 2707
41:16 The floor, the wall up to the w, 2707
41:16 and the w were covered. 2707
41:26 the sidewalls of the portico were narrow w 2707
Da 6:10 to his upstairs room where the w opened 10348
Joel 2: 9 like thieves they enter through the w. 2707
Zep 2:14 Their calls will echo through the w, 2707

WINDS (31) [WIND]

Ge 2:11 it w **through** the entire land of Havilah, 6015
2:13 it w **through** the entire land of Cush. 6015
Job 37: 9 the cold from the **driving** w. 4668
38:24 or the place where the **east** w are scattered 7708
Ps 104: 4 He makes w his messengers, 8120
148: 8 stormy w that do his bidding, 8120
Jer 49:32 to the w those who are in distant places 8120
49:36 I will bring against Elam the four w from 8120
49:36 I will scatter them to the four w, 8120
Eze 5:10 and will scatter all your survivors to the w. 8120
5:12 and a third I will scatter to the w and pursue 8120
12:14 to the w all those around him— 8120
13:11 and **violent** w will burst forth. 6194+8120
17:21 and the survivors will be scattered to the w. 8120
37: 9 Come from the four w, O breath, 8120
Da 7: 2 and there before me were the four w 10658
8: 8 up toward the four w *of* heaven. 8120
11: 4 up and parceled out toward the four w 8120
Am 1:14 amid **violent** w on a stormy day. 6193
Zec 2: 6 "for I have scattered you to the four w 8120
Mt 7:25 and the w blew and beat against that house; *449*
7:27 and the w blew and beat against that house, *449*
8:26 he got up and rebuked the w and the waves, *449*
8:27 Even the w and the waves obey him!" *449*
24:31 they will gather his elect from the four w, *449*
Mk 13:27 and gather his elect from the four w, *449*
Lk 8:25 He commands even the w and the water, *449*
Ac 27: 4 of Cyprus because the w were against us. *449*
Heb 1: 7 "He makes his angels w, his servants *4460*
Jas 3: 4 are so large and are driven by strong w, *449*
Rev 7: 1 the four w of the earth to prevent any wind *449*

WINDSTORM (2) [STORM, WIND]

Isa 29: 6 with w and tempest and flames of a 6070
Eze 1: 4 I saw a w coming out of the north— 6194+8120

WINDY (KJV) See TEMPEST

WINE (234) [WINES]

Ge 9:21 When he drank some of its w, 3516
9:24 When Noah awoke from his w 3516
14:18 king of Salem brought out bread and w. 3516
19:32 Let's get our father to drink w and then lie 3516
19:33 That night they got their father to drink w, 3516
19:34 Let's get him to drink w again tonight, 3516
19:35 So they got their father to drink w that night 3516
27:25 and he brought *some* w and he drank. 3516
27:28 an abundance of grain and **new** w. 9408
27:37 I have sustained him with grain and **new** w. 9408
49:11 he will wash his garments in w, 3516
49:12 His eyes will be darker than w, 3516
Ex 29:40 a quarter of a hin of w as a drink offering. 3516
Lev 10: 9 "You and your sons are not to drink w 3516
23:13 its drink offering of a quarter of a hin of w. 3516
Nu 6: 3 from w and other fermented drink and must 3516
6: 3 and must not drink vinegar made from w or 3516
6:20 After that, the Nazirite may drink w. 3516
15: 5 a quarter of a hin of w as a drink offering. 3516
15: 7 and a third of a hin of w as a drink offering. 3516
15:10 bring half a hin of w as a drink offering. 3516
18:12 and all the finest **new** w and grain they give 9408
28:14 to be a drink offering of half a hin of w; 3516
Dt 7:13 your grain, **new** w and oil— 9408
11:14 gather in your grain, **new** w and oil. 9408
12:17 the tithe of your grain and **new** w and oil, 9408
14:23 Eat the tithe of your grain, **new** w and oil, 9408
14:26 cattle, sheep, w or other fermented drink, 3516
18: 4 firstfruits of your grain, **new** w and oil, 9408
28:39 but you will not drink the w or gather 3516
28:51 They will leave you no grain, **new** w or oil, 9408
29: 6 and drank no w or other fermented drink. 3516
32:33 Their w is the venom of serpents, 3516
32:38 and drank the w *of* their drink offerings? 3516
33:28 in a land of grain and **new** w, 9408
Jdg 9:13 the vine answered, 'Should I give up my w, 9408
13: 4 Now see to it that you drink no w 3516
13: 7 drink no w or other fermented drink and do 3516
13:14 nor drink any w or other fermented drink 3516
19:19 bread and w for ourselves you servants— 3516
Ru 2:14 and dip it in the w **vinegar**." 2810

1Sa 1:14 Get rid of your **w.**" 3516
1:15 I have not been drinking **w** or beer; 3516
1:24 an ephah of flour and a skin of **w,** 3516
10:3 and another a skin of **w.** 3516
16:20 a skin of **w** and a young goat and sent them 3516
25:18 two skins of **w,** five dressed sheep, 3516
2Sa 13:28 in high spirits from drinking **w** and I say 3516
16:1 a hundred cakes of figs and a skin of **w.** 3516
16:2 and the **w** is to refresh those who become 3516
2Ki 18:32 a land of grain and **new w,** 9408
1Ch 9:29 as well as the flour and **w,** and the oil, 3516
12:40 raisin cakes, **w,** oil, cattle and sheep, 3516
27:27 the produce of the vineyards for the **w** vats. 3516
2Ch 2:10 of **w** and twenty thousand baths 3516
2:15 and the olive oil and **w** he promised, 3516
11:11 with supplies of food, olive oil and **w.** 3516
31:5 of their grain, **new w,** oil and honey and all 9408
32:28 harvest of grain, **new w** and oil; 9408
Ezr 6:9 and wheat, salt, **w** and oil, 10271
7:22 a hundred baths of **w,** a hundred baths of 10271
Ne 2:1 when **w** was brought for him, 3516
2:1 I took the **w** and gave it to the king. 3516
5:11 the money, grain, **new w** and oil." 9408
5:15 from them in addition to food and **w.** 3516
5:18 and every ten days an abundant supply of **w** 3516
10:37 of the fruit of all our trees and of our **new w** 9408
10:39 **new w** and oil to the storerooms where 9408
13:5 **new w** and oil prescribed for the Levites, 9408
13:12 **new w** and oil into the storerooms. 9408
13:15 together with **w,** grapes, figs 3516
Est 1:7 **W** *was* **served** in goblets of gold, 9197
1:7 and the royal **w** was abundant, 3516
1:8 the king instructed all the **w stewards** 1074+8042
1:10 King Xerxes was in high spirits from **w,** 3516
5:6 As they were drinking **w,** 3516
7:2 as they were drinking **w** on that second day, 3516
7:7 left his **w** and went out into 3516
Job 1:13 and daughters were feasting and drinking **w** 3516
1:18 and daughters were feasting and drinking **w** 3516
32:19 inside I am like bottled-up **w,** 3516
Ps 4:7 when their grain and **new w** abound. 9408
60:3 you have given us **w** that makes us stagger. 3516
75:8 a cup full of foaming **w** mixed with spices; 3516
78:65 as a man wakes from the stupor of **w.** 3516
104:15 **w** that gladdens the heart of man, 3516
Pr 3:10 and your vats will brim over with **new w.** 9408
4:17 of wickedness and drink the **w** *of* violence. 3516
9:2 prepared her meat and mixed her **w;** 3516
9:5 eat my food and drink the **w** I have mixed. 3516
20:1 **W** is a mocker and beer a brawler; 3516
21:17 whoever loves **w** and oil will never be rich. 3516
23:20 Do not join those who drink too much **w** 3516
23:30 Those who linger over **w,** 3516
23:30 who go to sample **bowls of mixed w.** 4932
23:31 Do not gaze at **w** when it is red, 3516
31:4 O Lemuel—not for kings to drink **w,** 3516
31:6 **w** to those who are in anguish; 3516
Ecc 2:3 I tried cheering myself with **w,** 3516
9:7 and drink your **w** with a joyful heart, 3516
10:19 and **w** makes life merry, 3516
SS 1:2 for your love is more delightful than **w.** 3516
1:4 we will praise your love more than **w.** 3516
4:10 much more pleasing is your love than **w,** 3516
5:1 I have drunk my **w** and my milk. 3516
7:2 that never lacks **blended w.** 4641
7:9 and your mouth like the best **w.** 3516
7:9 May the **w** go straight to my lover, NIH
8:2 I would give you spiced **w** to drink, 3516
Isa 1:22 your **choice w** is diluted with water. 6011
5:10 vineyard will produce only a bath of **w,** NIH
5:11 at night till they are inflamed with **w.** 3516
5:12 tambourines and flutes and **w,** 3516
5:22 Woe to those who are heroes at drinking **w** 3516
16:10 no one treads out **w** at the presses, 3516
22:13 eating of meat and drinking of **w!** 3516
24:7 The **new w** dries up and the vine withers; 9408
24:9 No longer do they drink **w** with a song; 3516
24:11 In the streets they cry out for **w;** 3516
25:6 a banquet of **aged w**—the best of meats 9069
28:1 the pride of those laid low by **w!** 3516
28:7 also stagger from **w** and reel from beer: 3516
28:7 from beer and are befuddled with **w;** 3516
29:9 be drunk, but not from **w,** stagger, 3516
36:17 a land of grain and **new w,** 9408
49:26 be drunk on their own blood, as with **w.** 6747
51:21 made drunk, but not with **w.** 3516
55:1 buy **w** and milk without money and 3516
56:12 "Come," each one cries, "let me get **w!** 3516
62:8 the **new w** for which you have toiled; 9408
65:11 and fill **bowls of mixed w** for Destiny, 4932
Jer 13:12 Every wineskin should be filled with **w.**' 3516
13:12 every wineskin should be filled with **w?**' 3516
23:9 like a man overcome by **w,** 3516
25:15 the **w** of my wrath and make all the nations 3516
31:12 the grain, the **new w** and the oil, 9408
35:2 of the house of the LORD and give them **w** 3516
35:5 Then I set bowls full of **w** and some cups 3516
35:5 and said to them, "Drink *some* **w.**" 3516
35:6 But they replied, "We do not drink **w,** 3516
35:6 nor your descendants must ever drink **w.** 3516
35:8 and daughters have ever drunk **w** 3516
35:14 to drink **w** and this command has been kept. 3516
35:14 To this day they do not drink **w,** NIH
40:10 but you are to harvest the **w,** 3516
40:12 And they harvested an abundance of **w** 3516
48:11 like **w** left on its dregs, NIH
48:33 I have stopped the flow of **w** from 3516
Jer 51:7 The nations drank her **w;** 3516
La 2:12 "Where is bread and **w?**" 3516
Eze 27:18 in **w** *from* Helbon and wool from Zahar. 3516
44:21 to drink **w** when he enters the inner court. 3516
Da 1:5 of food and **w** from the king's table. 3516
1:8 to defile himself with the royal food and **w,** 3516
1:16 and the **w** they were to drink 3516
5:1 for a thousand of his nobles and drank **w** 10271
5:2 While Belshazzar was drinking his **w,** 10271
5:4 As they drank the **w,** they praised the gods 10271
5:23 and your concubines drank **w** from them. 10271
10:3 no meat or **w** touched my lips; 3516
Hos 2:8 who gave her the grain, the **new w** and oil, 9408
2:9 and my **new w** when it is ready. 9408
2:22 respond to the grain, the **new w** and oil, 9408
4:11 to prostitution, to **old w** and new, 3516
7:5 the princes become inflamed with **w,** 3516
7:14 for grain and **new w** but turn away from me. 9408
9:2 the **new w** will fail them. 9408
9:4 not pour out **w offerings** to the LORD, 3516
14:7 his fame will be like the **w** *from* Lebanon. 3516
Joel 1:5 Wail, all you drinkers of **w;** 3516
1:5 wail because of the **new w,** 6747
1:10 grain is destroyed, the **new w** is dried up, 9408
2:19 "I am sending you grain, **new w** and oil, 9408
2:24 the vats will overflow with **new w** and oil. 9408
3:3 they sold girls for **w** that they might drink. 3516
3:18 "In that day the mountains will drip **new w,** 6747
Am 2:8 the house of their god they drink **w** *taken* 3516
2:12 the Nazirites drink **w** and commanded 3516
5:11 you will not drink their **w.** 3516
6:6 You drink **w** by the bowlful and use 3516
9:13 **New w** will drip from the mountains 6747
9:14 will plant vineyards and drink their **w;** 3516
Mic 2:11 'I will prophesy for you plenty of **w** 3516
6:15 you will crush grapes but not drink the **w.** 3516
Na 1:10 among thorns and drunk from their **w;** 6011
Hab 2:5 indeed, **w** betrays him; 3516
Zep 1:12 who are like **w** left on its dregs, who think, NIH
1:13 will plant vineyards but not drink the **w.** 3516
Hag 1:11 on the grain, the **new w,** the oil 9408
2:12 some **w,** oil or other food, 3516
2:16 to a **w vat** to draw fifty measures, 3676
Zec 9:15 They will drink and roar as with **w;** 3516
9:17 and **new w** the young women. 9408
10:7 and their hearts will be glad as with **w.** 3516
Mt 9:17 Neither do men pour new **w** into old *3885*
9:17 the **w** will run out and the wineskins will *3885*
9:17 No, they pour new **w** into new wineskins, *3885*
27:34 There they offered Jesus **w** to drink, *3885*
27:48 He filled it *with* **w vinegar,** *3954*
Mk 2:22 no one pours new **w** into old wineskins. *3885*
2:22 If he does, the **w** will burst the skins, *3885*
2:22 both the **w** and the wineskins will be ruined. *3885*
2:22 No, he pours new **w** into new wineskins." *3885*
15:23 Then they offered him **w** mixed with myrrh, *3885*
15:36 filled a sponge *with* **w vinegar,** *3954*
Lk 1:15 to take **w** or other fermented drink, *3885*
5:37 no one pours new **w** into old wineskins. *3885*
5:37 If he does, the new **w** will burst the skins, *3885*
5:37 **the w** will run out and the wineskins will *899S*
5:38 new **w** must be poured into new wineskins. *3885*
5:39 no one after drinking old **w** wants the new, *NIG*
7:33 nor drinking **w,** and you say, 'He has *3885*
10:34 bandaged his wounds, pouring on oil and **w.** *3885*
23:36 They offered him **w vinegar** *3954*
Jn 2:3 When the **w** was gone, *3885*
2:3 "They have no more **w.**" *3885*
2:9 the water that had been turned into **w.** *3885*
2:10 the choice **w** first and then the cheaper wine *3885*
2:10 the choice wine first and then the cheaper **w** *NIG*
4:46 where he had turned the water into **w.** *3885*
19:29 A jar *of* **w vinegar** was there, *3954*
Ac 2:13 "They have had too much **w.**" *1183*
Ro 14:21 to eat meat or drink **w** or to do anything else *3885*
Eph 5:18 Do not get drunk *on* **w,** *3885*
1Ti 3:8 sincere, not indulging *in* much **w,** *3885*
5:23 and use a little **w** because of your stomach *3885*
Tit 2:3 not to be slanderers or addicted *to* much **w,** *3885*
Rev 6:6 and do not damage the oil and the **w!**" *3885*
14:8 the maddening **w** of her adulteries." *3885*
14:10 too, will drink of the **w** of God's fury, *3885*
16:19 and gave her the cup filled *with* the **w** of *3885*
17:2 of the earth were intoxicated with the **w** *3885*
18:3 the nations have drunk the maddening **w** *3885*
18:13 myrrh and frankincense, of **w** and olive oil, *3885*

WINEBIBBER, WINEBIBBERS (KJV)
See DRUNKARD, DRUNKARDS

WINEFAT (KJV) See WINEPRESS

WINEPRESS (17) [WINEPRESSES]

Nu 18:27 the threshing floor or juice from the **w.** 3676
18:30 the product of the threshing floor or the **w.** 3676
Dt 15:14 your threshing floor and your **w.** 3676
16:13 of your threshing floor and your **w.** 3676
Jdg 6:11 in a **w** to keep it from the Midianites. 1780
7:25 and Zeeb at the **w** *of* Zeeb. 3676
2Ki 6:27 From the threshing floor? From the **w?**" 3676
Isa 5:2 He built a watchtower in it and cut out a **w** 3676
63:2 like those of one treading the **w?** 1780
63:3 "I have trodden the **w** alone; 7053
La 1:15 In his **w** the Lord has trampled 1780
Joel 3:13 for the **w** is full and the vats overflow— 1780
Mt 21:33 dug a **w** in it and built a watchtower. *3332*
Mk 12:1 dug a **pit for the w** and built a watchtower. *5700*
Rev 14:19 into the great **w** of God's wrath. *3332*
14:20 They were trampled in the **w** outside *3332*
19:15 He treads the **w** of the fury of *3332+3836+3885*

WINEPRESSES (4) [WINEPRESS]

Ne 13:15 In those days I saw men in Judah treading **w** 1780
Job 24:11 they tread the **w,** yet suffer thirst. 3676
Hos 9:2 Threshing floors and **w** will not feed 3676
Zec 14:10 from the Tower of Hananel to the royal **w.** 3676

WINES (1) [WINE]

Isa 25:6 the best of meats and the finest of **w.** 9069

WINESKIN (4) [WINESKINS]

Ps 119:83 Though I am like a **w** in the smoke, 5532
Jer 13:12 Every **w** should be filled with wine.' 5574
13:12 that every **w** should be filled with wine?' 5574
Hab 2:15 pouring it from the **w** till they are drunk, 2827

WINESKINS (12) [WINESKIN]

Jos 9:4 with worn-out sacks and old **w,** 3516+5532
9:13 And these **w** that we filled were new, 3516+5532
Job 32:19 like new **w** ready to burst. 199
Mt 9:17 Neither do men pour new wine into old **w.** *829*
9:17 the wine will run out and the **w** will *829*
9:17 No, they pour new wine into new **w,** *829*
Mk 2:22 And no one pours new wine into old **w.** *829*
2:22 and both the wine and the **w** will be ruined. *829*
2:22 No, he pours new wine into new **w.**" *829*
Lk 5:37 And no one pours new wine into old **w.** *829*
5:37 the wine will run out and the **w** will *829*
5:38 No, new wine must be poured into new **w.** *829*

WING (16) [WINGED, WINGS, WINGSPAN]

1Ki 6:24 **w** *of* the first cherub was five cubits long, 4053
6:24 and the other **w** five cubits— 4053
6:24 ten cubits from **w** tip to wing tip. 4053
6:24 ten cubits from wing tip to **w** tip. 4053
6:27 The **w** *of* one cherub touched one wall, 4053
6:27 the **w** *of* the other touched the other wall, 4053
2Ch 3:11 **w** *of* the first cherub was five cubits long 4053
3:11 while its other **w,** also five cubits long, 4053
3:11 touched the **w** *of* the other cherub. 4053
3:12 Similarly one **w** *of* the second cherub 4053
3:12 and its other **w,** also five cubits long, 4053
3:12 touched the **w** *of* the first cherub. 4053
Ecc 10:20 and a **bird on the w** may report what you say. 1251+4053
Isa 10:14 not one flapped a **w,** or opened its mouth 4053
Eze 1:11 one touching the **w** of another creature on NIH
Da 9:27 And on a **w** *[of* the temple] he will set up 4053

WINGED (4) [WING]

Ge 1:21 and every **w** bird according to its kind. 4053
Lev 11:21 some **w** creatures that walk on all fours 6416
11:23 But all other **w** creatures that have four 6416
Dt 14:20 any **w creature** that is clean you may eat. 6416

WINGS (73) [WING]

Ge 7:14 according to its kind, everything with **w.** 4053
Ex 19:4 on eagles' **w** and brought you to myself. 4053
25:20 to have their **w** spread upward, 4053
37:9 The cherubim had their **w** spread upward, 4053
Lev 1:17 He shall tear it open by the **w,** 4053
Dt 32:11 that spreads its **w** to catch them 4053
Ru 2:12 under whose **w** you have come to take refuge." 4053
2Sa 22:11 he soared on the **w** *of* the wind. 4053
1Ki 6:27 with their **w** spread out. 4053
6:27 and their **w** touched each other in 4053
8:6 and put it beneath the **w** *of* the cherubim. 4053
8:7 The cherubim spread their **w** over the place 4053
1Ch 28:18 that spread their **w** and shelter the ark of NIH
2Ch 3:13 **w** *of* these cherubim extended twenty cubits. 4053
5:7 and put it beneath the **w** *of* the cherubim. 4053
5:8 The cherubim spread their **w** over the place 4053
Job 39:13 "The **w** *of* the ostrich flap joyfully, 4053
39:26 by your wisdom and spread his **w** toward 4053
Ps 17:8 hide me in the shadow of your **w** 4053
18:10 he soared on the **w** *of* the wind. 4053
36:7 in the shadow of your **w.** 4053
55:6 I said, "Oh, that I had the **w** of a dove! 88
57:1 I will take refuge in the shadow of your **w** 4053
61:4 and take refuge in the shelter of your **w.** 4053
63:7 I sing in the shadow of your **w.** 4053
68:13 **w** *of* [my] dove are sheathed with silver, 4053
91:4 and under his **w** you will find refuge; 4053
104:3 his chariot and rides on the **w** *of* the wind. 4053
139:9 If I rise on the **w** *of* the dawn, 4053
Pr 23:5 for they will surely sprout **w** and fly off to 4053
Isa 6:2 Above him were seraphs, each with six **w:** 4053
6:2 With two **w** they covered their faces, NIH
8:8 Its outspread **w** will cover the breadth 4053
18:1 to the land of whirring **w** along the rivers 4053
34:15 for her young under the shadow of her **w;** NIH
40:31 They will soar on **w** like eagles; 88
Jer 48:40 spreading its **w** over Moab. 4053
49:22 spreading its **w** over Bozrah. 4053
Eze 1:6 but each of them had four faces and four **w.** 4053

Eze 1: 8 Under their w on their four sides they had 4053
1: 8 All four of them had faces and w, 4053
1: 9 and their w touched one another. 4053
1:11 Their w were spread out upward; 4053
1:11 each had two w, NIH
1:11 and two w covering its body. NIH
1:23 the expanse their w were stretched out one 4053
1:23 and each had two w covering its body. NIH
1:24 I heard the sound of their w, 4053
1:24 When they stood still, they lowered their w. 4053
1:25 as they stood with lowered w. 4053
3:13 of the w *of* the living creatures brushing 4053
10: 5 The sound of the w *of* the cherubim could 4053
10: 8 (Under the w of the cherubim could 4053
10:12 their hands and their w, 4053
10:16 when the cherubim spread their w to rise 4053
10:19 the cherubim spread their w and rose from 4053
10:21 Each had four faces and four w, 4053
10:21 and under their w was what looked like 4053
11:22 the wheels beside them, spread their w, and 4053
17: 3 A great eagle with powerful w, 4053
17: 7 with powerful w and full plumage. 4053
Da 7: 4 and it had the w of an eagle. 10149
7: 4 until its w were torn off and it was lifted 10149
7: 6 on its back it had four w like those of a bird. 10149
Zec 5: 9 with the wind in their w! 4053
5: 9 They had w like those of a stork, 4053
Mal 4: 2 will rise with healing in its w. 4053
Mt 23:37 as a hen gathers her chicks under her w, *4763*
Lk 13:34 as a hen gathers her chicks under her w, *4763*
Rev 4: 8 Each of the four living creatures had six w *4763*
4: 8 with eyes all around, even under his w. *NIG*
9: 9 the sound *of* their w was like the thundering *4763*
12:14 The woman was given the two w of *4763*

WINGSPAN (1) [WING]

2Ch 3:11 The **total** w *of* the cherubim was twenty 802+4053

WINK (1) [WINKS]

Ps 35:19 without reason **maliciously** w the eye. 7975

WINKS (3) [WINK]

Pr 6:13 *who* w with his eye, signals with his feet 7975
10:10 *He who* w **maliciously** causes grief, 6524+7975
16:30 *He who* w *with* his eye is plotting perversity 6781

WINNING (2) [WIN]

Ex 17:11 As long as Moses held up his hands, the Israelites *were* w, 1504
17:11 lowered his hands, the Amalekites *were* w. 1504

WINNOW (4) [WINNOWING, WINNOWS]

Isa 41:16 *You will* w them, the wind will pick them up 2430
Jer 4:11 but not to w or cleanse; 2430
15: 7 *I will* w them with a winnowing fork at 2430
51: 2 I will send foreigners to Babylon *to* w her 2430

WINNOWED (KJV) See SPREAD OUT

WINNOWING (4) [WINNOW]

Ru 3: 2 *be* w barley *on* the threshing floor. 2430
Jer 15: 7 with a w **fork** at the city gates of the land. 4665
Mt 3:12 His w **fork** is in his hand, *4768*
Lk 3:17 His w **fork** is in his hand *4768*

WINNOWS (2) [WINNOW]

Pr 20: 8 *he* w **out** all evil with his eyes. 2430
20:26 A wise king w **out** the wicked; 2430

WINS (2) [WIN]

Pr 11:30 and *he who* w souls is wise. 4374
13:15 Good understanding w favor, 5989

WINTER (16) [WINTERED]

Ge 8:22 cold and heat, summer and w, 3074
Ps 74:17 you made both summer and w. 3074
SS 2:11 The w is past; the rains are over and gone. 6255
Isa 18: 6 the wild animals **all** w. 3069
Jer 36:22 and the king was sitting in the w apartment, 3074
Hos 6: 3 he will come to us like the w **rains,** 1773
Am 3:15 the w house along with the summer house; 3074
Zec 14: 8 in summer and in w. 3074
Mt 24:20 Pray that your flight will not take place in w *5930*
Mk 13:18 Pray that this will not take place in w, *5930*
Jn 10:22 Feast of Dedication at Jerusalem. It was w, *5930*
Ac 27:12 Since the harbor was unsuitable to w **in,** *4200*
27:12 hoping to reach Phoenix and w there. *4199*
1Co 16: 6 or even **spend the** w, *4199*
2Ti 4:21 Do your best to get here before w. *5930*
Tit 3:12 because I have decided *to* w there. *4199*

WINTERED (1) [WINTER]

Ac 28:11 to sea in a ship *that had* w in the island. *4199*

WIPE (14) [WIPED, WIPES, WIPING]

Ge 6: 7 So the LORD said, *"I will* w mankind, 4681
7: 4 and *I will* w from the face of the earth 4681
Ex 23:23 and *I will* w them **out.** 3948
32:12 and to w them off the face of the earth 3983
Dt 7:24 and *you will* w **out** their names from 6
12: 3 and w **out** their names from those places. 6
Jos 7: 9 and w **out** our name from the earth. 4162
9:24 to w **out** all its inhabitants from before you. 9012
1Sa 24:21 or w **out** my name from my father's family. 9012
2Ki 21:13 *I will* w **out** Jerusalem as one wipes a dish, 4681
Isa 25: 8 The Sovereign LORD *will* w **away** 4681
Lk 10:11 that sticks to our feet *we* w **off against** you. *669*
Rev 7:17 God *will* w **away** every tear **from** their eyes. *1981*
21: 4 *He will* w every tear **from** their eyes. *1981*

WIPED (15) [WIPE]

Ge 7:23 on the face of the earth *was* w **out;** 4681
7:23 the ground and the birds of the air *were* w 4681
Ex 9:15 with a plague *that would have* w *you* off 3948
Jdg 21:17 "so that a tribe of Israel *will* not **be** w **out.** 4681
1Sa 15:18 on them until you *have* w them **out.'** 3983
Ps 119:87 *They* almost w me from the earth, 3983
Pr 6:33 and his shame *will* never **be** w **away;** 4681
Isa 26:14 *you* w **out** all memory of them. 6
Eze 6: 6 and what you have made w **out.** 4681
Zep 1:11 all your merchants *will* **be** w **out,** 1950
Lk 7:38 Then *she* w them with her hair, *1726*
7:44 with her tears and w them with her hair. *1726*
Jn 11: 2 on the Lord and w his feet with her hair. *1726*
12: 3 on Jesus' feet and w his feet with her hair. *1726*
Ac 3:19 so that your sins *may be* w **out,** *1981*

WIPES (2) [WIPE]

2Ki 21:13 I will wipe out Jerusalem as *one* w a dish, 4681
Pr 30:20 She eats and w her mouth and says, 4681

WIPING (1) [WIPE]

2Ki 21:13 w it and turning it upside down. 4681

WIRES (KJV) See STRANDS

WISDOM (218) [WISE]

Ge 3: 6 and also desirable for **gaining** w, 8505
Ex 28: 3 skilled men to whom I have given w 2683+8120
Dt 4: 6 for this will show your w and understanding 2683
34: 9 son of Nun was filled with the spirit of w 2683
2Sa 14:20 My lord has w like that of an angel 2682
1Ki 2: 6 Deal with him according to your w, 2683
2: 9 You are a man of w; 2682
3:28 because they saw that he had w *from* God 2683
4:29 God gave Solomon w and very great insight 2683
4:30 Solomon's w was greater than the wisdom 2683
4:30 Solomon's wisdom was greater than the w 2683
4:30 and greater than all the w *of* Egypt. 2683
4:34 nations came to listen to Solomon's w, 2683
4:34 who had heard of his w. 2683
5:12 The LORD gave Solomon w, just as he 2683
10: 4 queen of Sheba saw all the w *of* Solomon 2683
10: 6 about your achievements and your w is true. 2683
10: 7 in w and wealth you have far exceeded 2683
10: 8 before you and hear your w! 2683
10:23 and w than all the other kings of the earth. 2683
10:24 with Solomon to hear the w God had put 2683
11:41 all he did and the w he displayed— 2683
2Ch 1:10 Give me w and knowledge, 2683
1:11 for w and knowledge to govern my people 2683
1:12 w and knowledge will be given you. 2683
9: 3 the queen of Sheba saw the w *of* Solomon, 2683
9: 5 about your achievements and your w is true. 2683
9: 6 half the greatness of your w was told me; 2683
9: 7 before you and hear your w! 2683
9:22 and w than all the other kings of the earth. 2683
9:23 with Solomon to hear the w God had put 2683
Ezr 7:25 in accordance with the w *of* your God, 10266
Job 4:21 so that they die without w?' 2683
9: 4 His w is profound, his power is vast. 2682
11: 6 and disclose to you the secrets of w, 2683
11: 6 for **true** w has two sides. 9370
12: 2 and w will die with you! 2683
12:12 Is not w found among the aged? 2683
12:13 "To God belong w and power; 2683
13: 5 For you, that would be w. 2683
15: 8 Do you limit w to yourself? 2683
26: 3 advice you have offered to one without w! 2683
26:12 by his w he cut Rahab to pieces. 9312
28:12 "But where can w be found? 2683
28:18 the price of w is beyond rubies. 2683
28:20 "Where then does w come from? 2683
28:27 then he looked at w and appraised it; 2023S
28:28 is w, and to shun evil is understanding.' " 2683
32: 7 advanced years should teach w.' 2683
32:13 Do not say, 'We have found w; 2683
33:33 be silent, and I will teach you w." 2683
38:36 with w or gave understanding to the mind? 2683
38:37 Who has the w to count the clouds? 2683
39:17 for God did not endow her with w 2683
39:26 "Does the hawk take flight by your w 1069
Ps 37:30 The mouth of the righteous man utters w, 2683
49: 3 My mouth will speak *words of* w; 2684
51: 6 you teach me w in the inmost place. 2683
90:12 that we may gain a heart of w. 2683
104:24 In w you made them all; 2683
105:22 as he pleased and **teach** his elders w. 2681
111:10 The fear of the LORD is the beginning of w; 2683
Pr 1: 2 for attaining w and discipline; 2683
1: 7 but fools despise w and discipline. 2683
1:20 W calls aloud in the street, 2684
2: 2 to w and applying your heart 2683
2: 6 For the LORD gives w, 2683
2:10 For w will enter your heart, 2683
2:12 W will save you from the ways NIH
3:13 Blessed is the man who finds w, 2683
3:19 By w the LORD laid the earth's foundations, 2683
4: 5 Get w, get understanding; 2683
4: 6 Do not forsake w, and she will protect you; 2023S
4: 7 W is supreme; therefore get wisdom. 2683
4: 7 Wisdom is supreme; therefore get w. 2683
4:11 I guide you in the way of w and lead you 2683
5: 1 My son, pay attention to my w, 2683
7: 4 Say to w, "You are my sister," 2683
8: 1 Does not w call out? 2683
8:11 for w is more precious than rubies, 2683
8:12 "I, w, dwell together with prudence; 2683
9: 1 W has built her house; 2684
9:10 fear of the LORD is the beginning of w, 2683
9:12 If you are wise, *your* w will reward you; 2681
10:13 W is found on the lips of the discerning, 2683
10:23 but a man of understanding delights in w. 2683
10:31 The mouth of the righteous brings forth w, 2683
11: 2 but with humility comes w. 2683
12: 8 A man is praised according to his w, 8507
13:10 but w is found in those who take advice. 2683
14: 6 The mocker seeks w and finds none, 2683
14: 8 The w *of* the prudent is to give thought 2683
14:33 W reposes in the heart of the discerning and 2683
15:33 The fear of the LORD teaches a man w, 2683
16:16 How much better to get w than gold, 2683
17:16 since he has no desire to get w? 2683
17:24 A discerning man keeps w in view, 2683
18: 4 but the fountain of w is a bubbling brook. 2683
19: 8 He who gets w loves his own soul; 4213
19:11 A man's w gives him patience; 8507
21:11 a mocker is punished, the simple *gain* w; 2681
21:30 There is no w, no insight, 2683
23: 4 have the w to show restraint. 1069
23: 9 for he will scorn the w *of* your words. 8507
23:23 get w, discipline and understanding. 2683
24: 3 By w a house is built, 2683
24: 7 W is too high for a fool; 2684
24:14 Know also that w is sweet to your soul; 2683
28:26 but he who walks in w is kept safe. 2683
29: 3 A man who loves w brings joy to his father, 2683
29:15 The rod of correction imparts w, 2683
30: 3 I have not learned w, 2683
31:26 She speaks with w, and faithful instruction 2683
Ecc 1:13 to study and to explore by w all that is done 2683
1:16 in w more than anyone who has ruled 2683
1:16 I have experienced much of w 2683
1:17 I applied myself to the understanding of w, 2683
1:18 For with much w comes much sorrow; 2683
2: 3 my mind still guiding me with w. 2683
2: 9 In all this my w stayed with me. 2683
2:12 Then I turned my thoughts to consider w, 2683
2:13 I saw that w is better than folly, 2683
2:21 For a man may do his work with w, 2683
2:26 To the man who pleases him, God gives w, 2683
7:11 W, like an inheritance, is a good thing 2683
7:12 W is a shelter as money is a shelter, 2683
7:12 that w preserves the life of its possessor. 2683
7:19 W makes one wise man more powerful than ten rulers 2683
7:23 All this I tested by w and I said, 2683
7:24 Whatever w may be, it is far off 8611S
7:25 to search out w and the scheme of things 2683
8: 1 W brightens a man's face 2683
8:16 When I applied my mind to know w and 2683
9:10 nor planning nor knowledge nor w. 2683
9:13 I also saw under the sun this example of w 2683
9:15 and he saved the city by his w. 2683
9:16 So I said, **"W is better than strength."** 2683
9:16 But the poor man's w is despised, 2683
9:18 W is better than weapons of war, 2683
10: 1 so a little folly outweighs w and honor. 2683
Isa 10:13 of my hand I have done this, and by my w, 2683
11: 2 the Spirit of w and of understanding, 2683
28:29 wonderful in counsel and magnificent in w. 9370
29:14 the w *of* the wise will perish, 2683
33: 6 of salvation and w and knowledge; 2683
47:10 Your w and knowledge mislead you 2683
Jer 8: 9 what kind of w do they have? 2683
9:23 "Let not the wise man boast of his w or 2683
10:12 by his w and stretched out the heavens 2683
49: 7 "Is there no longer w in Teman? 2683
49: 7 Has their w decayed? 2683
51:15 by his w and stretched out the heavens 2683
Eze 28: 4 By your w and understanding you have gained wealth 2683
28: 7 their swords against your beauty and w 2683
28:12 full of w and perfect in beauty. 2683
28:17 and you corrupted your w because 2683
Da 1:20 In every matter of w and understanding 2683
2:14 Daniel spoke to him with w and tact. 10539
2:20 w and power are his. 10266
2:21 He gives w to the wise and knowledge to 10266
2:23 You have given me w and power, 10266
2:30 I have greater w than other living men, 10266
5:11 and intelligence and w like that of the gods. 10266
5:14 insight, intelligence and outstanding w. 10266
Hos 13:13 but he is a child without w; 2682
Mic 6: 9 and to fear your name is w— 9370
Mt 11:19 But w is proved right by her actions." *5053*
12:42 ends of the earth to listen to Solomon's w, *5053*
13:54 "Where did this man get this w *5053*
Mk 6: 2 "What's this w that has been given him, *5053*
Lk 1:17 the disobedient to the w of the righteous— *5860*

Lk 2:40 he was filled *with* w, 5053
2:52 And Jesus grew *in* w and stature, 5053
7:35 But w is proved right by all her children." 5053
11:31 ends of the earth to listen to Solomon's w, 5053
11:49 Because of this, God in his w said, 5053
21:15 For I will give you words and w that none 5053
Ac 6: 3 known to be full of the Spirit and w. 5053
6:10 but they could not stand up against his w or 5053
7:10 He gave Joseph w and enabled him to gain 5053
7:22 educated in all the w of the Egyptians 5053
Ro 11:33 the riches *of* the w and knowledge of God! 5053
1Co 1:17 not with words *of* human w, 5053
1:19 "I will destroy the w of the wise; 5053
1:20 not God made foolish the w of the world? 5053
1:21 For since in the w of God the world 5053
1:21 the world through its w did not know him, 5053
1:22 and Greeks look for w, 5053
1:24 Christ the power of God and the w of God. 5053
1:25 foolishness of God is wiser than man's w, NIG
1:30 who has become for us w from God— 5053
2: 1 I did not come with eloquence or **superior** w 5053+5667
2: 5 that your faith might not rest on men's w, 5053
2: 6 speak a message of w among the mature, 5053
2: 6 the w of this age or of the rulers of this age, 5053
2: 7 No, we speak of God's secret w, 5053
2: 7 secret wisdom, a w that has been hidden NIG
2:13 not in words taught us *by* human w but 5053
3:19 For the w of this world is foolishness 5053
12: 8 through the Spirit the message *of* w, 5053
2Co 1:12 so not according to worldly w but according 5053
Eph 1: 8 on us with all w and understanding. 5053
1:17 the Spirit *of* w and revelation, 5053
3:10 the manifold w of God should 5053
Col 1: 9 through all spiritual w and understanding. 5053
1:28 and teaching everyone with all w, 5053
2: 3 in whom are hidden all the treasures *of* w 5053
2:23 indeed have an appearance *of* w, 5053
3:16 and admonish one another with all w, 5053
Jas 1: 5 If any of you lacks w, he should ask God, 5053
3:13 in the humility that comes *from* w. 5053
3:15 Such "w" does not come down from heaven 5053
3:17 But the w that comes from heaven is first 5053
2Pe 3:15 with the w that God gave him. 5053
Rev 5:12 and wealth and w and strength and honor 5053
7:12 and w and thanks and honor and power 5053
13:18 This calls for w. 5053
17: 9 "This calls for a mind with w. 5053

WISE (186) [OVERWISE, WISELY, WISDOM, WISER, WISEST]

Ge 41: 8 so he sent for all the magicians and w *men* 2682
41:33 for a discerning and w man and put him 2682
41:39 there is no one so discerning and w as you. 2682
Ex 7:11 then summoned w *men* and sorcerers, and 2682
Dt 1:13 Choose *some* w, understanding 2682
1:15 w and respected men, and appointed them 2682
4: 6 a w and understanding people." 2682
16:19 the w and twists the words of the righteous. 2682
32:29 If only *they were* w and would understand 2681
2Sa 14: 2 and had a w woman brought from there. 2682
20:16 a w woman called from the city, 2682
20:22 to all the people with her w **advice,** 2683
1Ki 3:12 I will give you a w and discerning heart, 2682
5: 7 a w son to rule over this great nation." 2682
1Ch 26:14 for his son Zechariah, a w counselor, and 8507
2Ch 2:12 He has given King David a w son, 2682
Est 1:13 with the w *men* who understood the times 2682
Job 5:13 He catches the w in their craftiness, 2682
11:12 a witless man *can* no more **become** w than 4220
15: 2 "Would a w *man* answer with empty notions 2682
15:18 what w *men* have declared, 2682
17:10 I will not find a w *man* among you. 2682
22: 2 Can even a w *man* benefit him? 8505
32: 9 It is not only the old *who are* w, 2681
34: 2 "Hear my words, you w *men;* 2682
34:34 w men who hear me say to me, 2682
37:24 for does he not have regard for all the w 2682
Ps 2:10 Therefore, *you* kings, *be* w; 8505
19: 7 trustworthy, **making** w the simple. 2681
36: 3 he has ceased to *be* w and to do good. 8505
49:10 For all can see that w *men* die; 2682
94: 8 you fools, when *will you become* w? 8505
107:43 Whoever is w, let him heed these things 2682
Pr 1: 5 let the w listen and add to their learning, 2682
1: 6 the sayings and riddles of the w. 2682
3: 7 Do not be w in your own eyes; 2682
3:35 The w inherit honor, 2682
6: 6 consider its ways and *be* w! 2681
8:33 Listen to my instruction and *be* w; 2681
9: 8 rebuke a w *man* and he will love you. 2682
9: 9 Instruct a w *man* and he will be wiser still; 2682
9:12 If *you are* w, your wisdom will reward you; 2681
10: 1 A w son brings joy to his father, 2682
10: 5 who gathers crops in summer *is* a w son, 8505
10: 8 The w *in* heart accept commands, 2682
10:14 W *men* store up knowledge, 2682
10:19 but he who holds his tongue *is* w. 8505
11:29 and the fool will be servant to the w. 2682+4213
11:30 and he who wins souls is w. 2682
12:15 but a w *man* listens to advice. 2682
12:18 but the tongue of the w brings healing. 2682
13: 1 A w son heeds his father's instruction, 2682
13:14 The teaching of the w is a fountain of life, 2682
13:20 He who walks with the w grows wise, 2682
13:20 He who walks with the wise *grows* w, 2681
Pr 14: 1 The w woman builds her house, 2682
14: 3 but the lips of the w protect them. 2682
14:16 A w *man* fears the LORD and shuns evil, 2682
14:24 The wealth of the w is their crown, 2682
14:35 A king delights in a w servant, 8505
15: 2 The tongue of the w commends knowledge, 2682
15: 7 The lips of the w spread knowledge; 2682
15:12 he will not consult the w. 2682
15:20 A w son brings joy to his father, 2682
15:24 for the w to keep him from going down to 8505
15:31 be at home among the w. 2682
16:14 but a w man will appease it. 2682
16:21 The w *in* heart are called discerning, 2682
16:23 A w *man's* heart guides his mouth, 2682
17: 2 A w servant will rule over a disgraceful son, 8505
17:28 Even a fool is thought w if he keeps silent, 2682
18:15 the ears of the w seek it out. 2682
19:20 and in the end *you will be* w. 2681
20: 1 whoever is led astray by them *is* not w. 2681
20:26 A w king winnows out the wicked; 2682
21:11 when a w *man* is instructed, 2682
21:20 the house of the w are stores of choice food 2682
21:22 A w *man* attacks the city of the mighty 2682
22:17 and listen to the sayings of the w; 2682
23:15 My son, if your heart *is* w, 2681
23:19 Listen, my son, and *be* w, 2681
23:24 he who has a w son delights in him. 2682
24: 5 A w man has great power, 2682
24:23 These also are sayings of the w: 2682
25:12 a w *man's* rebuke to a listening ear. 2682
26: 5 or he will be w in his own eyes. 2682
26:12 Do you see a man w in his own eyes? 2682
27:11 *Be* w, my son, and bring joy to my heart; 2681
28:11 A rich man may be w in his own eyes, 2682
29: 8 but w *men* turn away anger. 2682
29: 9 If a w man goes to court with a fool, 2682
29:11 but a w *man* keeps himself under control. 2682
30:24 yet they *are* **extremely** w: 2681+2682
Ecc 2:14 The w *man* has eyes in his head, 2682
2:15 What then do I gain *by being* w?" 2681
2:16 For the w *man,* like the fool, 2682
2:16 Like the fool, the w *man* too must die! 2682
2:19 And who knows whether he will be a w *man* 2682
4:13 Better a poor but w youth than an old 2682
6: 8 What advantage has a w *man* over a fool? 2682
7: 4 heart of the w is in the house of mourning, 2682
7: 5 a w *man's* rebuke than to listen to the song 2682
7: 7 Extortion turns a w *man* into a fool, 2682
7:10 For it is not w to ask such questions. 2683
7:19 Wisdom makes one w *man* more powerful than ten rulers 2682
7:23 *"I am determined to be* w"— 2681
8: 1 Who is like the w *man?* 2682
8: 5 and the w heart will know the proper time 2682
8:17 Even if a w *man* claims he knows, 2682
9: 1 the w and what they do are in God's hands, 2682
9:11 to the w or wealth to the brilliant or favor to 2682
9:15 there lived in that city a man poor but w, 2682
9:17 the w are more to be heeded than the shouts 2682
10: 2 The heart of the w inclines to the right, 2682
10:12 Words from a w *man's* mouth are gracious, 2682
12: 9 Not only was the Teacher w, 2682
12:11 The words of the w are like goads, 2682
Isa 5:21 Woe to *those who* are w in their own eyes 2682
19:11 w counselors of Pharaoh give senseless advice. 2682
19:11 "I am one of the w *men,* 2682
19:12 Where are your w *men* now? 2682
29:14 the wisdom of the w will perish, 2682
31: 2 Yet he too is w and can bring disaster; 2682
44:25 who overthrows the learning of the w 2682
Jer 8: 8 " 'How can you say, "We are w, 2682
8: 9 The w will be put to shame; 2682
9:12 What man is w *enough* to understand this? 2682
9:23 "Let not the w *man* boast of his wisdom or 2682
10: 7 Among all the w *men of* the nations and 2682
18:18 nor will counsel from the w, 2682
50:35 and against her officials and w *men!* 2682
51:57 I will make her officials and w *men* drunk, 2682
Eze 28: 2 though you think you are as w as a god. 4213
28: 6 " 'Because you think you are w, NIH
28: 6 you think you are wise, as w as a god, 4213
Da 2:12 the execution of all the w *men of* Babylon. 10265
2:13 decree was issued to put the w *men* to death 10265
2:14 had gone out to put to death the w *men* 10265
2:18 not be executed with the rest of the w *men* 10265
2:21 He gives wisdom to the w and knowledge 10265
2:24 king had appointed to execute the w *men* 10265
2:24 "Do not execute the w *men of* Babylon. 10265
2:27 Daniel replied, "No w *man,* enchanter, 10265
2:48 and placed him in charge of all its w *men.* 10265
4: 6 the w *men of* Babylon be brought before me 10265
4:18 the w *men in* my kingdom can interpret it 10265
5: 7 to be brought and said to these w *men* 10265
5: 8 Then all the king's w *men* came in, 10265
5:15 The w *men* and enchanters were brought 10265
11:33 "Those *who are* w will instruct many, 8505
11:35 Some of the w will stumble, 8505
12: 3 Those *who are* w will shine like 8505
12:10 but those *who are* w will understand. 8505
Hos 14: 9 Who is w? He will realize these things. 2682
Ob 1: 8 "will I not destroy the w *men* of Edom, 2682
Mt 7:24 a w man who built his house on the rock. 5861
11:25 hidden these things from the w and learned, 5055
23:34 prophets and w *men* and teachers. 5055
24:45 "Who then is the faithful and w servant, 5861
25: 2 Five of them were foolish and five were w. 5861
Mt 25: 4 The w, however, took oil in jars along 5861
25: 8 The foolish ones said *to* the w, 5861
Lk 10:21 from the w and learned, 5055
12:42 "Who then is the faithful and w manager, 5861
Ac 15:38 but Paul *did* not **think it** w to take him, 546
Ro 1:14 both *to* the w and the foolish. 5055
1:22 Although they claimed to be w, 5055
16:19 but I want you to be w about what is good, 5055
16:27 *to* the only w God be glory forever 5055
1Co 1:19 "I will destroy the wisdom *of* the w; 5055
1:20 Where is the w *man?* 5055
1:26 Not many of you were w by human standards; 5055
1:27 foolish things of the world to shame the w; 5055
2: 4 and my preaching were not with w 5053
3:18 of you thinks he is w by the standards 5055
3:18 become a "fool" so that he may become w. 5055
3:19 "He catches the w in their craftiness"; 5055
3:20 that the thoughts *of* the w are futile." 5055
4:10 but you are so w in Christ! 5861
6: 5 that there is nobody among you w enough 5055
2Co 10:12 *they are* not w. 5317
11:19 put up with fools since you are so w! 5861
Eph 5:15 how you live—not as unwise but as w, 5055
Col 4: 5 Be w in the way you act toward outsiders; 5053
2Ti 3:15 which are able *to* **make** you w for salvation 5054
Jas 3:13 Who is w and understanding among you? 5055

WISELY (4) [WISE]

2Ch 11:23 *He* **acted** w, dispersing some of his sons 1067
Isa 52:13 See, my servant *will* **act** w; 8505
Jer 23: 5 a King who will reign w and do what is just 8505
Mk 12:34 When Jesus saw that he had answered w, 3807

WISER (8) [WISE]

1Ki 4:31 *He was* w than any other man, 2681
4:31 w than Heman, Calcol and Darda, NIH
Job 35:11 and **makes** us w than the birds of the air?' 2681
Ps 119:98 commands **make** me w than my enemies, 2681
Pr 9: 9 Instruct a wise man and *he will be* w still; 2681
26:16 The sluggard is w in his own eyes than 2682
Eze 28: 3 Are you w than Daniel? 2682
1Co 1:25 foolishness of God is w *than* man's wisdom, 5055

WISEST (1) [WISE]

Jdg 5:29 The w *of* her ladies answer her; 2682

WISH (22) [WISHED, WISHES, WISHING]

Ex 4:18 Jethro said, "Go, and I w you **well.**" 4200+8934
Nu 11:29 **I** w *that* all the LORD's people were 4769+5989
Dt 14:26 other fermented drink, or anything you w. 8626
Jdg 19:24 and do to them whatever you w. 928+3202+6524
1Sa 24: 4 for you to deal with as you w.' " 928+3512+6524
1Ki 5: 9 to grant my w by providing food 2914
Ezr 7:13 *who* w to go to Jerusalem with you, may go. 10461
Job 10:18 *I* w *I had* **died** before any eye saw me. AIT
11: 5 **Oh, how I** w that God would speak, 4769+5989
Mt 17: 4 If *you* w, I will put up three shelters— 2527
Lk 12:49 and how *I* w it were already kindled! 2527
Jn 15: 7 ask whatever *you* w, and it will be given 2527
Ro 9: 3 For *I could* w that I myself were cursed 2377
1Co 4: 8 **How I** w **that** you really had become kings 4054
7: 7 *I* w **that** all men were as I am. 2527
2Co 5: 4 because *we do* not w to be unclothed but to 2527
Gal 4: 9 *Do you* w to be enslaved by them all over 2527
4:20 how *I* w I could be with you now 2527
5:12 **I** w they would go the whole way 4054
Phm 1:20 *I do* w, brother, *that I may have* some **benefit** AIT
Jas 2:16 **"Go, I** w **you well;** 1645+1877+5632
Rev 3:15 **I** w you were either one or the other! 4054

WISHED (6) [WISH]

2Sa 19:18 over and to do whatever he w. 928+3202+6524
Est 1: 8 to serve each man what he w. 8356
Job 9: 3 Though *one* w to dispute with him, 2911
Jer 34:16 slaves you had set free to go where they w. 5883
Mt 17:12 but have done to him everything *they* w. 2527
Mk 9:13 they have done to him everything *they* w, 2527

WISHES (9) [WISH]

Lev 27:13 If the owner *w to* **redeem** the animal, AIT
27:19 who dedicates the field *w to* **redeem** it, AIT
Dt 21:14 let her go wherever she w. 5883
Da 4:17 and gives them to anyone *he* w and sets 10605
4:25 of men and gives them to anyone *he* w. 10605
4:32 of men and gives them to anyone *he* w." 10605
5:21 of men and sets over them anyone *he* w. 10605
1Co 7:39 she is free to marry anyone *she* w, 2527
Rev 22:17 and whoever w, let him take the free gift of 2527

WISHING (1) [WISH]

Ac 25: 9 Festus, w to do the Jews a favor, 2527

WIST (KJV) See AWARE, IDEA, KNOW, REALIZE

WIT (KJV) See KNOW, LEARN, SEE, THAT IS

WITCH (KJV) See SORCERESS, SORCERY

WITCHCRAFT (6) [BEWITCHED]

Dt 18:10 interprets omens, **engages in w**, 4175
2Ki 9:22 and w *of* your mother Jezebel abound?" 4176
2Ch 33: 6 practiced sorcery, divination and w, 4175
Mic 5:12 I will destroy your w and you will no longer 4176
Na 3: 4 by her prostitution and peoples by her w. 4176
Gal 5:20 idolatry and w; hatred, *5758*

WITH (5912) See Index of Articles Etc.

WITHDRAW (13) [WITHDRAWN, WITHDRAWS, WITHDREW]

Lev 26:25 When *you* w into your cities, 665
1Sa 14:19 So Saul said to the priest, "**W** your hand." 665
2Sa 11:15 Then w from him so he will be struck down 8740
20:21 and *I'll* w from the city." 2143
24:16 "Enough! **W** your hand." 8332
1Ki 15:19 with Baasha king of Israel so *he will* w 6590
2Ki 18:14 "I have done wrong. **W** from me, 8740
1Ch 21:15 "Enough! **W** your hand." 8332
2Ch 16: 3 with Baasha king of Israel so *he will* w 6590
Job 13:21 **W** your hand **far** from me, 8178
Jer 21: 2 as in times past so that *he will* w from us." 6590
Eze 5:11 *I* myself *will* w *my* **favor;** 1757
Ac 4:15 So they ordered them *to* w from *599*

WITHDRAWN (5) [WITHDRAW]

Jer 16: 5 because *I have* w my blessing, 665
34:21 which *has* w from you. 6590
37:11 the Babylonian army *had* w from Jerusalem 6590
La 2: 3 *He has* w his right hand 294+8740
Hos 5: 6 *he has* w *himself* from them. 2740

WITHDRAWS (1) [WITHDRAW]

2Sa 17:13 If *he* w into a city, then all Israel will bring 665

WITHDREW (30) [WITHDRAW]

Ex 14:19 w and went behind them. 5825
35:20 Then the whole Israelite community w 3655
1Sa 14:46 and they w to their own land. 2143
1Ki 8:10 When the priests w from the Holy Place, 3655
15:21 he stopped building Ramah and w 3782
16:17 Then Omri and all the Israelites with him w 6590
2Ki 3:27 *they* w and returned to their own land. 5825
12:18 *who* then w from Jerusalem. 6590
15:20 So the king of Assyria w and stayed in 8740
19: 8 *he* w and found the king fighting 8740
19:36 king of Assyria broke camp and **w.** 2143
2Ch 5:11 The priests then w from the Holy Place. 3655
24:25 When the Arameans **w,** 2143+4946
32:21 So *he* w to his own land in disgrace. 8740
Ezr 10: 6 Then Ezra w from before the house of God 7756
Job 34:14 If it were his intention and *he* w his spirit 665
Isa 37: 8 *he* w and found the king fighting 8740
37:37 king of Assyria broke camp and **w.** 2143
Jer 37: 5 *they* w from Jerusalem. 6590
Mt 2:22 *he* w to the district of Galilee, *432*
12:15 Aware of this, Jesus w from that place. *432*
14:13 *he* w by boat privately to a solitary *432+1696*
15:21 Jesus w to the region of Tyre and Sidon. *432*
Mk 3: 7 Jesus w with his disciples to the lake, *432*
Lk 5:16 Jesus *often* w to lonely places and prayed. *1639+5723*
9:10 Then he took them with him and *they* w *5723*
22:41 He w about a stone's throw beyond them, *685*
Jn 6:15 w again to a mountain by himself. *432*
11:54 Instead *he* w to a region near the desert, *599*
Ac 22:29 about to question him w immediately. *923*

WITHER (18) [WITHERED, WITHERS]

Job 8:12 *they* w more quickly than grass. 3312
15:30 a flame *will* w his shoots, 3312
18:16 dry up below and his branches w above. 4908
Ps 1: 3 fruit in season and whose leaf *does* not w. 5570
37: 2 for like the grass *they will* soon w, 4908
37:19 In times of disaster *they will* not **w;** 3312
102:11 I **w away** like grass. 3312
Isa 16: 8 The fields of Heshbon **w,** 581
19: 6 The reeds and rushes *will* **w,** 7857
40:24 than he blows on them and *they* **w,** 3312
Jer 8:13 and their leaves *will* **w.** 5570
Eze 17: 9 All its new growth *will* **w.** 3312
17:10 *Will it* not **w completely** when 3312+3312
17:10 **w away** in the plot where it grew?' " 3312
47:12 Their leaves *will* not **w,** 5570
Na 1: 4 Bashan and Carmel w and the blossoms 581
Zec 9: 5 and Ekron too, for her hope *will* **w.** 3312
Mt 21:20 "How *did* the fig tree w so quickly?" *3830*

WITHERED (20) [WITHER]

Ge 41:23 w and thin and scorched by the east wind. 7568
Ps 90: 6 by evening it is dry and w. 3312
102: 4 My heart is blighted and w like grass; 3312
Isa 15: 6 of Nimrim are dried up and the grass *is* **w;** 3312
34: 4 the starry host will fall like w leaves from 5570
Jer 12: 4 and the grass in every field *be* **w?** 3312
23:10 and the pastures in the desert *are* w. 3312
Eze 19:12 its strong branches w and fire consumed 3312
31:15 and all the trees of the field **w away.** 6634
Hos 9:16 Ephraim is blighted, their root *is* **w,** 3312
Joel 1:12 The vine is dried up and the fig tree *is* **w;** 581
1:12 Surely the joy of mankind *is* **w away.** 3312
Jnh 4: 7 which chewed the vine so that *it* **w.** 3312
Zec 11:17 *May* his arm *be* **completely** w, 3312+3312
Mt 13: 6 and *they* w because they had no root. *3830*
21:19 Immediately the tree **w.** *3830*
Mk 4: 6 and *they* w because they had no root. *3830*
11:20 they saw the fig tree w from the roots. *3830*
11:21 The fig tree you cursed *has* **w!"** *3830*
Lk 8: 6 the plants w because they had no moisture. *3830*

WITHERS (14) [WITHER]

Job 8:19 Surely its life **w away,** 5376
14: 2 He springs up like a flower and **w away;** 4908
Ps 129: 6 which w before it can grow; 3312
Isa 24: 4 The earth dries up and w, 5570
24: 4 the world languishes and w, 5570
24: 7 The new wine dries up and the vine w; 581
33: 9 Lebanon is ashamed and **w;** 7857
40: 7 The grass w and the flowers fall, 3312
40: 8 The grass w and the flowers fall, 3312
Eze 17: 9 and stripped of its fruit so that *it* **w?** 3312
Am 1: 2 and the top of Carmel **w."** 3312
Jn 15: 6 like a branch that is thrown away and **w;** *3830*
Jas 1:11 For the sun rises with scorching heat and w *3830*
1Pe 1:24 the grass w and the flowers fall, *3830*

WITHHELD (14) [WITHHOLD]

Ge 22:12 because *you have* not w from me your son, 3104
22:16 you have done this and *have* not w your son, 3104
39: 9 My master *has* w nothing from me except 3104
Job 22: 7 the weary and *you* w food from the hungry, 4979
Ps 21: 2 of his heart and *have* not w the request 4979
66:20 not rejected my prayer or w his love NIH
77: 9 *Has he* in anger w his compassion?" 7890
Isa 63:15 Your tenderness and compassion **are** w 706
Jer 3: 3 Therefore the showers *have* **been w,** 4979
Eze 20:22 *I* w my hand, and for the sake of my name 8740
Joel 1:13 the grain offerings and drink offerings *are* w 4979
Am 4: 7 "I also w rain from you when the harvest 4979
4: 7 but w it from another. 4202+4763[S]
Hag 1:10 of you the heavens *have* w their dew 3973

WITHHOLD (8) [WITHHELD, WITHHOLDING, WITHHOLDS]

Ne 9:20 not w your manna from their mouths, 4979
Ps 40:11 *Do* not w your mercy from me, O LORD; 3973
84:11 no good thing *does he* w from those whose 4979
Pr 3:27 *Do* not w good from those who deserve it, 4979
23:13 *Do* not w discipline from a child; 4979
Isa 10: 2 and w justice *from* the oppressed 1608
La 2: 8 and *did* not w his hand from destroying. 8740
Zec 1:12 how long will you w mercy from Jerusalem 4202

WITHHOLDING (2) [WITHHOLD]

2Co 6:12 We *are* not w our affection from *you,* *5102*
6:12 but *you are* w yours from us. *5102*

WITHHOLDS (5) [WITHHOLD]

Dt 27:19 "Cursed is the man *who* w justice from 5742
Pr 11:24 *another* w unduly, but comes to poverty. 3104
Isa 32: 6 and *from* the thirsty *he* w water. 2893
Eze 18: 8 *He* w his hand from doing wrong 8740
18:17 *He* w his hand from sin and takes no usury 8740

WITHIN (113) [IN]

Ge 6:16 and finish the ark **to** w 18 inches of the top. 448
10: 5 into their territories by their clans w 928
10:32 to their lines of descent, w their nations. 928
23:17 and all the trees w the borders of the field— 928
25:22 The babies jostled each other w her, 928+7931
25:23 two peoples from w you will be separated; 5055
33:18 and camped w **sight of** the city. 907+7156
40:13 **W** three days Pharaoh will lift up 928+6388
40:19 **W** three days Pharaoh will lift off 928+6388
Ex 3: 2 to him in flames of fire from w a bush. 9348
3: 4 God called to him from w the bush, 9348
13: 7 nor shall any yeast be seen anywhere w 928
20:10 nor the alien w your gates. 928
24:16 the LORD called to Moses from w the cloud. 9348
Nu 36: 6 as long as they marry w the tribal clan 4200
36:12 They married w the clans of 4946
Dt 5:14 nor the alien w your gates, 928
Jos 16: 9 were set aside for the Ephraimites w 928+9348
17:11 **W** Issachar and Asher, 928
19: 1 Their inheritance lay w the territory 928+9348
19: 9 Simeonites received their inheritance w 928+9348
Jdg 14:12 the answer *w* the seven **days** *of* the feast, AIT
17: 7 who had been living w the clan of Judah, 4946
2Sa 20: 4 of Judah to come to me *w* three **days,** AIT
1Ki 6:16 from floor to ceiling to form w the temple 4946
6:19 the inner sanctuary w the temple to set 928+9348
9:18 and Tadmor in the desert, w his land, 928
2Ki 7:11 and it was reported w the palace. 7163
Ezr 10: 8 Anyone who failed to appear w three days 4200
10: 9 **W** the three days, all the men of Judah 4200
Job 19:27 How my heart yearns w me! 928+2668
20:14 it will become the venom of serpents w 928+7931
27: 3 as long as I have life w me, 928
31:15 the same one form us both w our mothers? 928
32:18 and the spirit w me compels me; 1061
Ps 22:14 it has melted away w me. 928+5055+9348
36: 1 An oracle is w my heart concerning 928+7931
39: 3 My heart grew hot w me, 928+7931
40: 8 your law is w my heart." 928+9348
40:12 and my heart **fails** *w* me. AIT
42: 5 Why so disturbed w me? 6584
42: 6 My soul is downcast w me; 6584
42:11 Why so disturbed w me? 6584
43: 5 Why so disturbed w me? 6584
45:13 All glorious is the princess w [her chamber]; 7163
46: 5 God is w her, she will not fall; 928+7931
48: 9 **W** your temple, O God, we meditate 928+7931
51:10 and renew a steadfast spirit w me. 928+7931
55: 4 My heart is in anguish w me; 928+7931
55:10 malice and abuse are w it. 928+7931
94:19 When anxiety was great w me, 928+7931
109:22 and my heart is wounded w me. 928+7931
122: 7 be peace w your walls and security 928
122: 7 be peace within your walls and security w 928
122: 8 I will say, "Peace be w you." 928
128: 3 Your wife will be like a fruitful vine w 928+3752
131: 2 like a weaned child is my soul w me. 6584
142: 3 When my spirit grows faint w me, 6584
143: 4 So my spirit grows faint w me; 6584
143: 4 my heart w me is dismayed. 928+9348
147:13 your gates and blesses your people w 928+7931
Pr 2: 1 and store up my commands w you, 907
4:21 keep them w your heart; 928+9348
7: 1 and store up my commands w you. 907
Ecc 4:14 or he may have been born in poverty w 928
Isa 7: 8 **W** sixty-five years Ephraim will 928+6388
13: 9 the land desolate and destroy the sinners w 4946
16:14 But now the LORD says: "**W** three years, 928
19: 1 hearts of the Egyptians melt w them. 928+7931
21:16 "**W** one year, as a servant bound 928+6388
41:18 and springs w the valleys. 928+9348
56: 5 to them I will give w my temple 928
60:18 nor ruin or destruction w your borders, 928
Jer 4:19 My heart pounds w me, 4200
8:18 my heart is faint w me. 6584
23: 9 My heart is broken w me; 928+7931
28: 3 **W** two years I will bring back 928+6388
28:11 off the neck of all the nations w two 928+6388
51:47 and her slain will all lie fallen w her. 928+9348
La 1:20 I am in torment **w,** 928+7931
2:11 I am in torment **w,** 5055
3:20 and my soul is downcast w me. 6584
4:13 shed w her the blood of the righteous. 928+7931
Eze 11:23 The glory of the LORD went up from w 9348
22:25 is a conspiracy of her princes w her 928+9348
22:25 and make many widows w her. 928+9348
22:27 Her officials w her are 928+7931
28:22 O Sidon, and I will gain glory w you. 928+9348
28:22 on her and show myself holy w her. 928
28:23 The slain will fall w her, 928+9348
30: 6 to Aswan they will fall by the sword w her, 928
32:21 From w the grave the mighty leaders 9348
40:44 Outside the inner gate, w the inner court, 928
Hos 11: 8 My heart is changed w me; 6584
Am 3: 9 see the great unrest w her and 928+9348
Zep 3: 5 The LORD w her is righteous; 928+7931
3:12 I will leave w you the meek and 928+7931
Zec 2: 5 'and I will be its glory **w.'** 928+9348
12: 1 and who forms the spirit of man w him, 928+7931
Mt 6:23 If then the light w you is darkness, *1877*
Mk 7:21 For **from w,** out of men's hearts, *2277*
Lk 11:35 then, that the light w you is not darkness. *1877*
17:21 because the kingdom of God is w you." *1955*
19:44 you and the children w your walls. *1877*
24:32 not our hearts burning w us while he talked *1877*
Jn 7:38 streams of living water will flow from w *3120*
17:13 the full measure of my joy w them. *1877*
Ro 7:23 of the law of sin at work w my members. *1877*
1Co 2:11 of a man except the man's spirit w him? *1877*
2Co 7: 5 conflicts on the outside, fears **w.** *2277*
Eph 3:20 according to his power that *is* **at work** w us, *1919*
Jas 4: 1 your desires that battle w you? *1877+3517+3836*
Rev 11:19 and w his temple was seen the ark *1877*

WITHOUT (375)

Ge 19: 3 baking **bread w yeast,** and they ate. 5174
24:21 **W saying a word,** the man watched her 3087
41:44 but w your word no one will lift hand 1187
Ex 12: 5 must be year-old males **w defect,** 9459
12: 8 and **bread made w yeast.** 5174
12:15 to eat **bread made w yeast.** 5174
12:18 to eat **bread made w yeast,** 5174
12:30 for there was not a house w someone dead. 401
12:39 The dough was w yeast 4202
13: 6 For seven days eat **bread made w yeast** and 5174
15:22 For three days they traveled in the desert w 4202
21: 2 he shall go free, **w paying anything.** 2855
21:11 is to go free, **w any payment** of money. 401+2855
23:15 for seven days eat **bread made w yeast,** 5174
29: 1 Take a young bull and two rams **w defect.** 9459
29: 2 And from fine wheat flour, **w yeast,** 5174
29:23 From the basket of **bread made w yeast,** 5174
34:18 For seven days eat **bread made w yeast,** 5174
34:28 the LORD forty days and forty nights w 4202
Lev 1: 3 he is to offer a male **w defect.** 9459
1:10 he is to offer a male **w defect.** 9459
2: 4 cakes made **w yeast** and mixed with oil, 5174
2: 4 or wafers made **w yeast** and spread with oil. 5174
2: 5 of fine flour mixed with oil, and **w yeast.** 5174
2:11 to the LORD must be made w yeast, 4202
3: 1 before the LORD an animal **w defect.** 9459
3: 6 he is to offer a male or female **w defect.** 9459
4: 3 a young bull **w defect** as a sin offering for 9459
4:23 as his offering a male goat **w defect.** 9459

Lev 4:28 a female goat **w defect.** 9459
4:32 he is to bring a female **w defect.** 9459
5:15 one **w defect** and of the proper value 9459
5:18 one **w defect** and of the proper value. 9459
6:6 one **w defect** and of the proper value. 9459
6:16 but it is to be eaten **w yeast** in a holy place; 5174
7:12 of **bread made w yeast** and mixed with oil, 5174
7:12 wafers **made w yeast** and spread with oil, 5174
8:2 the basket containing **bread made w yeast,** 5174
8:26 from the basket of **bread made w yeast,** 5174
9:2 *both* **w defect,** and present them before 9459
9:3 both a year old and **w defect—** 9459
10:12 and eat it **prepared w yeast** beside the altar, 5174
14:10 each **w defect,** along with three-tenths of 9459
15:11 a discharge touches **w** rinsing his hands 4202
22:19 you must present a male **w defect** from 9459
22:21 be **w defect** or blemish to be acceptable. 9459
23:6 you must eat **bread made w yeast.** 5174
23:12 to the LORD a lamb a year old **w defect,** 9459
23:18 each a year old and **w defect,** 9459
25:31 in villages **w** walls around them are to 401
26:43 while it lies desolate **w** them. 4946
Nu 6:14 a year-old male lamb **w defect** for 9459
6:14 a year-old ewe lamb **w defect** for 9459
6:14 a ram **w defect** for a fellowship offering, 9459
6:15 and a basket of **bread made w yeast—** 5174
6:19 both **made w yeast.** 5174
15:24 **w** the community **being aware** 4946+6524
19:2 a red heifer **w defect** or blemish and 9459
19:15 and every open container **w** a lid fastened 401
27:17 not be like sheep **w** a shepherd." 401
28:3 two lambs a year old **w defect,** 9459
28:9 of two lambs a year old **w defect,** 9459
28:11 seven male lambs a year old, *all* **w defect.** 9459
28:17 for seven days eat **bread made w yeast.** 5174
28:19 seven male lambs a year old, *all* **w defect.** 9459
28:31 Be sure the animals are **w defect.** 9459
29:2 male lambs a year old, *all* **w defect.** 9459
29:8 male lambs a year old, *all* **w defect.** 9459
29:13 male lambs a year old, *all* **w defect.** 9459
29:17 male lambs a year old, *all* **w defect.** 9459
29:20 male lambs a year old, *all* **w defect.** 9459
29:23 male lambs a year old, *all* **w defect.** 9459
29:26 male lambs a year old, *all* **w defect.** 9459
29:29 male lambs a year old, *all* **w defect.** 9459
29:32 male lambs a year old, *all* **w defect.** 9459
29:36 male lambs a year old, *all* **w defect.** 9459
35:22 if **w** hostility someone suddenly shoves 928+4202
35:23 or, **w** seeing him, drops a stone on him 928+4202
35:27 the avenger of blood may kill the accused **w** 401
Dt 4:42 he had unintentionally killed his neighbor **w** 4202
7:14 nor any of your livestock **w young.** 6829
15:10 to him and do so **w** a grudging heart; 4202
19:4 unintentionally, **w** malice aforethought. 4202
19:6 to his neighbor **w** malice aforethought. 4202
25:5 and one of them dies **w** a son, 401
28:50 a fierce-looking nation **w** respect for the old 4202
32:28 They are a nation **w** sense, 6
Jos 2:22 along the road and returned **w** finding them. 4202
11:20 exterminating them **w** mercy, 1194
20:5 unintentionally and **w** malice aforethought. 4202
23:6 **w** turning aside to the right or to the left. 1194
Jdg 6:19 an ephah of flour he made **bread w yeast.** 5174
12:1 the Ammonites **w** calling us to go with you? 4202
Ru 1:5 and Naomi was left **w** her two sons 4946
4:14 not **left** you **w** a kinsman-redeemer. 8697
1Sa 9:2 impressive young man **w equal** 401+3202+4946
17:50 **w** a sword in his hand he struck down 401
20:2 great or small, **w** confiding in me. 4202
28:24 kneaded it and baked **bread w yeast.** 5174
2Sa 3:29 *May* Joab's house never **be w** 4162+4946
14:9 and let the king and his throne **be w guilt."** 5929
14:28 Absalom lived two years in Jerusalem **w** 4202
17:16 **cross over w fail,** or the king 6296+6296
20:10 **W** being stabbed again, Amasa died. 4202
1Ki 1:11 has become king **w** our lord David's 4202
1:27 the king has done **w** letting his servants 4202
2:32 because **w** the knowledge of my father 4202
22:17 on the hills like sheep **w** a shepherd, 401
2Ki 18:25 attack and destroy this place **w** word 1187+4946
1Ch 2:30 Seled died **w** children. 4202
2:32 Jether died **w** children. 4202
23:22 Eleazar died **w** having sons: 4202
29:15 on earth are like a shadow, **w** hope. 401
2Ch 15:3 a long time Israel was **w** the true God, 4200+4202
15:3 **w** a priest to teach and without 4200+4202
15:3 a priest to teach and **w** the law. 4200+4202
18:16 on the hills like sheep **w** a shepherd, 401
Ezr 6:9 must be given them daily **w** fail 10379
7:22 baths of olive oil, and salt **w** limit. 10379
Est 4:11 in the inner court **w** being summoned 4202
9:27 and all who join them should **w** 4202
Job 2:3 against him to ruin him **w any reason."** 2855
4:21 so that they die **w** wisdom?' 4202
5:4 crushed in court **w** a defender. 401
6:6 Is tasteless food eaten **w** salt, 1172+4946
7:6 and they come to an end **w** hope. 700+928
8:11 Can reeds thrive **w** water? 1172
9:5 He moves mountains **w** their knowing it 4202
9:25 they fly away **w** a glimpse of joy. 4202
9:35 Then I would speak up **w** fear of him, 4202
11:15 then you will lift up your face **w** shame; 4946
11:15 you will stand firm and **w** fear. 4202
16:13 **W** pity, he pierces my kidneys 4202
23:11 I have kept to his way **w** turning aside. 4202
26:3 What advice you have offered to one **w** 4202
27:22 against him **w** mercy as he flees headlong 4202
Job 30:13 **w** anyone's helping them. 4202
31:19 or a needy man **w** a garment, 401
31:39 if I have devoured its yield **w** payment 1172
33:9 'I am pure and **w** sin; 1172
34:20 the mighty are removed **w** human hand. 4202
34:24 **W** inquiry he shatters the mighty and sets 4202
34:35 'Job speaks **w** knowledge; 928+4202
35:16 **w** knowledge he multiplies words." 928+1172
36:12 they will perish by the sword and die **w** 1172+3869
38:2 that darkens my counsel with words **w** 1172
41:33 a creature **w** fear. 1172+4200
42:3 that obscures my counsel **w** knowledge?' 1172
Ps 7:4 with me or **w cause** have robbed my foe— 8200
15:5 who lends his money **w** usury and does 928+4202
25:3 to shame who are treacherous **w excuse.** 8200
26:1 I have trusted in the LORD **w** wavering. 4202
35:7 for me **w cause** and without cause dug a pit 2855
35:7 without cause and **w cause** dug a pit for me, 2855
35:15 They slandered me **w** ceasing. 4202
35:19 over me who are my enemies **w cause;** 9214
35:19 who hate me **w reason** maliciously wink 2855
38:19 those who hate me **w reason** are numerous. 9214
40:12 For troubles **w** number surround me; 401+6330
49:20 A man who has riches **w** understanding is 4202
54:3 men **w** regard for God. 4202
64:4 they shoot at him suddenly, **w** fear. 4202
69:4 Those who hate me **w reason** outnumber 2855
69:4 many are my enemies **w cause,** 9214
86:14 men **w** regard for you. 4202
88:4 I am like a man **w** strength. 401
105:34 the locusts came, grasshoppers **w** number; 401
109:3 they attack me **w cause.** 2855
119:51 The arrogant mock me **w restraint,** 4394+6330
119:78 be put to shame for wronging me **w cause;** 9214
119:86 help me, for men persecute me **w cause.** 9214
119:161 Rulers persecute me **w cause,** 2855
Pr 1:33 and be at ease, **w** fear of harm." 4946
6:15 will suddenly be destroyed—**w** remedy. 401
6:27 into his lap **w** his clothes being burned? 4202
6:28 on hot coals **w** his feet being scorched? 4202
9:13 she is undisciplined and **w** knowledge. 1153
14:28 but **w** subjects a prince is ruined. 700+928
19:2 not good to have zeal **w** knowledge, 928+4202
20:9 I am clean and **w** sin"? 4946
21:26 but the righteous give **w** sparing. 4202
24:28 not testify against your neighbor **w cause,** 2855
25:14 and wind **w** rain is a man who boasts 401
26:20 **W** wood a fire goes out; 700+928
26:20 **w** gossip a quarrel dies down. 401+928
29:1 be destroyed—**w** remedy. 401
Ecc 2:25 for **w** him, who can eat or 2575+4946
6:4 It comes **w meaning,** it departs in darkness, 928+2021+2039
Isa 1:30 like a garden **w** water. 401+4200
5:9 the fine mansions left **w** occupants. 401+4946
5:14 and opens its mouth **w** limit; 1172+4200
6:11 the cities lie ruined and **w** inhabitant, 401+4946
13:14 like sheep **w** a shepherd, 401
22:3 they have been captured **w** *using* the bow. 4946
23:1 For Tyre is destroyed and left **w** house 4946
27:11 For this is a people **w** understanding; 4202
28:8 with vomit and there is not a spot **w** filth. 1172
30:2 who go down to Egypt **w** consulting me; 4202
36:10 and destroy this land **w** the LORD? 1187+4946
47:1 sit on the ground **w** a throne, 401
52:3 and **w** money you will be redeemed." 928+4202
55:1 buy wine and milk **w** money and 928+4202
55:1 and milk without money and **w** cost. 928+4202
55:10 do not return to it **w** watering the earth 561+3954
56:2 who keeps the Sabbath **w** desecrating it, 4946
56:6 all who keep the Sabbath **w** desecrating it 4946
59:10 feeling our way like men **w** eyes. 401
Jer 2:32 Yet my people have forgotten me, days **w** 401
4:6 Flee for safety **w** delay! 440
4:7 towns will lie in ruins **w** inhabitant. 401+4946
10:14 Everyone is senseless and **w** knowledge; 4946
14:17 with tears night and day **w** ceasing; 440
15:13 I will give as plunder, **w** charge. 928+4202
20:16 like the towns the LORD overthrew **w** pity. 4202
32:43 a desolate waste, **w** men or animals, 401+4946
33:10 a desolate waste, **w** men or animals. 401+4946
33:12 desolate and **w** men or animals— 401+4946
44:7 and so leave yourselves **w** a remnant? 1194
44:22 and a desolate waste **w** inhabitants, 401+4946
46:5 They flee in haste **w** looking back, 4202
46:19 laid waste and lie in ruins **w** inhabitant. 401+4946
50:42 they are cruel and **w** mercy; 4202
51:17 "Every man is senseless and **w** knowledge; 4946
La 2:2 **W** pity the Lord has swallowed up all 4202
2:17 He has overthrown you **w** pity, 4202
2:21 you have slaughtered them **w** pity. 4202
3:11 and mangled me and left me **w help.** 9037
3:43 you have slain **w** pity. 4202
3:49 My eyes will flow unceasingly, **w** relief, 401+4946
3:52 my enemies **w cause** hunted me like a bird. 2855
4:6 in a moment **w** a hand turned to help her. 4202
Eze 1:12 they would go, **w** turning as they went. 4202
9:5 **w** showing pity or compassion. 440
10:11 **w** turning as they went. 4202
12:25 and it shall be fulfilled **w** delay. 4202
14:23 that I have done nothing in it **w cause,** 2855
24:6 Empty it piece by piece **w** casting lots 4202
35:13 and spoke against me **w restraint,** 6984
38:11 all of them living **w** walls and without 401+928
38:11 all of them living without walls and **w** gates 401
43:22 a male goat **w defect** for a sin offering, 9459
43:23 and a ram from the flock, both **w defect.** 9459
Eze 43:25 and a ram from the flock, *both* **w defect.** 9459
45:18 to take a young bull **w defect** and purify 9459
45:21 you shall eat **bread made w yeast.** 5174
45:23 and seven rams **w defect** as a burnt offering 9459
46:4 be six male lambs and a ram, *all* **w defect.** 9459
46:6 six lambs and a ram, *all* **w defect.** 9459
46:13 to provide a year-old lamb **w defect** for 9459
Da 1:4 young men **w** any physical defect, 401
2:35 The wind swept them away **w** leaving 10379
6:18 to his palace and spent the night **w eating** 10297
6:18 and spent the night without eating and **w** 10379
8:5 the whole earth **w** touching the ground. 401
11:14 in fulfillment of the vision, but **w success.** 4173
Hos 3:4 the Israelites will live many days **w** king 401
3:4 **w** sacrifice or sacred stones, 401
3:4 **w** ephod or idol. 401
4:14 a people **w** understanding will come to ruin! 4202
8:4 They set up kings **w** my consent; 4202
8:4 they choose princes **w** my approval. 4202
13:13 but he is a child **w** wisdom; 4202
Joel 1:6 invaded my land, powerful and **w** number; 401
2:8 through defenses **w** breaking ranks. 4202
Am 3:7 the Sovereign LORD does nothing **w** 561+3954
5:20 pitch-dark, **w** a ray of brightness? 4202
Mic 2:8 from those who pass by **w a care,** 1055
3:6 **w** visions, and darkness, without divination. 4946
3:6 without visions, and darkness, **w** divination. 4946
Na 3:1 full of lies, full of plunder, never **w** victims! 4631
3:3 piles of dead, bodies **w** number, 401
Hab 1:17 destroying nations **w** mercy? 4202
Zec 2:4 'Jerusalem will be a **city w walls** because 7252
14:7 **w** daytime or nighttime— 4202
Mt 8:24 **W warning,** a furious storm came up on *2627*
9:36 like sheep **w** a shepherd. *2400+3590*
13:34 not say anything to them **w** using a parable. *6006*
13:57 in his own house is a prophet **w honor."** *872*
22:12 in here **w** wedding clothes?' *2400+3590*
22:24 that if a man dies **w** having children, *3590*
23:23 **w** neglecting the former. *3590*
Mk 1:20 **W delay** he called them, *2317*
4:34 not say anything to them **w** using a parable. *6006*
6:4 in his own house is a prophet **w honor."** *872*
6:34 they were like sheep **w** a shepherd. *2400+3590*
12:20 The first one married and died **w** leaving *4024*
Lk 1:74 and to enable us to serve him **w fear** *925*
4:35 down before them all and came out **w** *3594*
6:35 lend to them **w** expecting to get **anything** *3594*
6:49 a man who built a house on the ground **w** *6006*
11:42 the latter **w** leaving the former undone. *3590*
11:44 which men walk over **w** knowing it." *4024*
22:35 "When I sent you **w** purse, bag or sandals, *868*
Jn 1:3 **w** him nothing was made *6006*
3:34 for God gives the Spirit **w** limit. *1666+4024*
7:15 "How did this man get such learning **w** *3590*
7:51 "Does our law condemn anyone **w** *1569+3590*
8:7 "If any one of you is **w sin,** *387*
15:25 'They hated me **w reason.'** *1562*
16:29 "Now you are speaking clearly and **w** *4029*
Ac 10:29 I came **w raising any objection.** *395*
12:11 "Now I know **w a doubt** that the Lord *242*
12:14 so overjoyed she ran back **w** opening it *4024*
14:17 Yet he has not left himself **w testimony:** *282*
15:24 some went out from us **w** our authorization *4024*
16:37 "They beat us publicly **w a trial,** *185*
25:27 on a prisoner **w** specifying the charges *3590*
27:21 After the men had gone a long time **w food,** *826*
27:33 in constant suspense and have gone **w food** *827*
28:31 and **w hindrance** he preached the kingdom *219*
Ro 1:20 so that men are **w excuse.** *406*
4:19 **W** weakening in his faith, *3590*
10:14 how can they hear **w** someone preaching *6006*
14:1 **w** passing judgment on disputable matters. *1650+3590*
1Co 2:14 The man **w the Spirit** does not accept *6035*
4:8 You have become kings—and that **w** us! *6006*
5:7 that you may be a new batch **w yeast—** *109*
5:8 but with **bread w yeast,** *109*
10:25 Eat anything sold in the meat market **w** *3594*
10:27 eat whatever is put before you **w** *3594*
11:21 ahead **w** waiting for anybody else. *NIG*
11:29 drinks **w** recognizing the body of the Lord *3590*
14:10 yet none of them is **w meaning.** *936*
15:10 and his grace to me was not **w effect.** *3031*
2Co 11:27 and **have** often **gone w sleep;** *71+1877*
11:27 and thirst **and have** often **gone w food;** *3763*
Gal 6:4 **w** comparing himself to somebody *2779+4024*
Eph 2:12 **w** hope and without God in the world. *2400+3590*
2:12 without hope and **w God** in the world. *117*
5:27 **w** stain or wrinkle or any other blemish, *2400+3590*
Php 1:28 **w** being frightened in any way *3590*
2:14 Do everything **w** complaining or arguing, *6006*
2:15 children of God **w fault** in a crooked *320*
Col 1:22 **w blemish** and free from accusation— *320*
2Th 3:8 did we eat anyone's food **w paying for it.** *1562*
1Ti 2:8 in prayer, **w** anger or disputing. *6006*
5:21 to keep these instructions **w** partiality, *6006*
6:14 to keep this command **w spot** or blame until *834*
2Ti 3:3 **w love,** unforgiving, slanderous, *845*
3:3 unforgiving, slanderous, **w self-control,** *203*
Phm 1:14 not want to do anything **w** your consent, *6006*
Heb 4:15 just as we are—yet was **w** sin. *6006*
7:3 **W father** or mother, without genealogy, *574*
7:3 Without father or mother, **w genealogy,** *37*
7:3 **w** beginning of days or end of life, *3612*
7:7 **w** doubt the lesser person is blessed by *4246+6006*
7:20 And it was not **w** an oath! *6006*

Heb 7:20 Others became priests w any oath, *6006*
9: 7 and never w blood, which he offered for *6006*
9:18 the first covenant was not put into effect w *6006*
9:22 and w the shedding of blood there is no *6006*
10:28 died w mercy on the testimony of two or *6006*
11: 6 And w faith it is impossible to please God, *6006*
12:14 w holiness no one will see the Lord. *6006*
13: 2 have entertained angels w **knowing** it. *3291*
Jas 1: 5 gives generously to all w finding fault, *2779+3590*
2:13 because judgment w **mercy** will be shown *447*
2:15 Suppose a brother or sister is w **clothes** *1218*
2:18 Show me your faith w deeds, *6006*
2:20 do you want evidence that faith w deeds *6006*
2:26 As the body w the spirit is dead, *6006*
2:26 so faith w deeds is dead. *6006*
4: 5 Or do you think Scripture says w **reason** *3036*
1Pe 1:19 a lamb w **blemish** or defect. *320*
3: 1 be won over w words by the behavior *459*
4: 9 Offer hospitality to one another w grumbling *459*
2Pe 2:16 by a donkey—a beast w **speech—** *936*
2:17 These men are springs w **water** *536*
1Jn 1: 8 If we claim to be w **sin,** we deceive *281+4024*
Jude 1:12 eating with you w **the slightest qualm—** *925*
1:12 They are clouds w **rain,** blown along *536*
1:12 autumn trees, w **fruit** and uprooted— *182*
1:24 before his glorious presence w **fault** and *320*
Rev 8:12 A third of the day *was* w **light,** *3590+5743*
21: 6 to drink w **cost** from the spring of the water *1562*

WITHS (KJV) See THONGS

WITHSTAND (8) [WITHSTOOD]

Nu 31:23 *can* w fire must be put through the fire, 928+995
31:23 And whatever cannot w fire must be put 928+995
Jos 10: 8 Not one of them *will be able to* w you." 928+6641+7156
23: 9 no one *has been able to* w you. 928+6641+7156
2Ch 20: 6 and no one *can* w you. 3656+6640
Ps 147:17 Who *can* w his icy blast? 4200+6641+7156
La 1:14 He has handed me over to those I cannot w. 7756
Na 1: 6 Who *can* w his indignation? 4200+6641+7156

WITHSTOOD (1) [WITHSTAND]

Jos 21:44 Not one of their enemies w them; 928+6641+7156

WITLESS (1) [WITS']

Job 11:12 But a w man can no more become wise than 5554

WITNESS (64) [EYEWITNESSES, WITNESSED, WITNESSES]

Ge 21:30 from my hand as a w that I dug this well." 6338
31:44 and let it serve as a w between us." 6332
31:48 a w between you and me today." 6332
31:50 remember that God is a w between you 6332
31:52 This heap is a w, and this pillar is a witness, 6332
31:52 This heap is a witness, and this pillar is a w, 6338
Ex 23: 1 a wicked man by being a malicious w. 6332
Nu 5:13 (since there is no w against her and she has 6332
35:30 to death on the testimony of only one **w.** 6332
Dt 17: 6 to death on the testimony of only one **w.** 6332
19:15 One w is not enough to convict 6332
19:16 If a malicious w takes the stand to accuse 6332
19:18 and if the w proves to be a liar, 6332
31:19 so that it may be a w for me against them. 6332
31:26 There it will remain as a w against you. 6332
Jos 22:27 a w between us and you and the generations 6332
22:28 but as a w between us and you.' 6332
22:34 A W Between Us that the LORD is God. 6332
24:27 "This stone will be a w against us. 6338
24:27 It will be a w against you if you are untrue 6338
Jdg 11:10 "The LORD is our **w;** 1068+9048
1Sa 6:18 is a w to this day in the field of Joshua 6332
12: 5 "The LORD is w against you, 6332
12: 5 and also his anointed is w this day, 6332
12: 5 "He is **w,"** they said. 6332
20:23 LORD is w between you and me forever." NIH
20:42 'The LORD is w between you and me, NIH
Job 16: 8 and it has become a **w;** 6332
16:19 my w is in heaven; my advocate is on high. 6332
Ps 89:37 the faithful w in the sky." 6332
Pr 6:19 a false w who pours out lies and 6332
12:17 A truthful w gives honest testimony, NIH
12:17 but a false w tells lies. 6332
14: 5 A truthful w does not deceive, 6332
14: 5 but a false w pours out lies. 6332
14:25 A truthful w saves lives, 6332
14:25 but a false w is deceitful. 7032
19: 5 A false w will not go unpunished, 6332
19: 9 A false w will not go unpunished, 6332
19:28 A corrupt w mocks at justice, 6332
21:28 A false w will perish, 6332
Isa 19:20 be a sign and w to the LORD Almighty in 6332
30: 8 days to come it may be an everlasting **w.** 6332
55: 4 See, I have made him a w *to* the peoples, 6332
Jer 29:23 I know it and am a w to it," 6332
42: 5 be a true and faithful w against us if we do 6332
Mic 1: 2 the Sovereign LORD may w against you, 6332
Mal 2:14 the LORD *is* **acting as** *the* w between you 6386
Lk 23:48 to w this sight saw what took place, *NIG*
Jn 1: 7 as a w to testify concerning that light, *3456*
1: 8 he came only as a w to the light. *3455*
8:13 "Here you are, **appearing** as your own **w;** *3455*
8:18 my other w is the Father, who sent me." *3455*
Ac 1:22 For one of these must become a w with us *3459*
22:15 be his w to all men of what you have seen *3459*
26:16 a servant and as a w of what you have seen *3459*
Ro 1: 9 is my w how constantly I remember you *3459*
2:15 their consciences also **bearing w,** *5210*
2Co 1:23 I call God as my w that it was in order to *3459*
1Th 2: 5 God is our **w.** *3459*
1Pe 5: 1 a fellow elder, a w of Christ's sufferings *3459*
Rev 1: 5 Jesus Christ, who is the faithful **w,** *3459*
2:13 my faithful **w,** who was put to death *3459*
3:14 the Amen, the faithful and true **w,** *3459*

WITNESSED (3) [WITNESS]

Jer 32:10 I signed and sealed the deed, **had** it w, 6332+6386
32:25 and **have the transaction w.' "** 6332+6386
32:44 and w in the territory of Benjamin, 6332+6386

WITNESSES (48) [WITNESS]

Nu 35:30 as a murderer only on the testimony of **w.** 6332
Dt 4:26 *I* **call** heaven and earth **as** w against you 6386
17: 6 the testimony of two or three w a man shall 6332
17: 7 of the w must be the first in putting him 6332
19:15 by the testimony of two or three **w.** 6332
30:19 *I* **call** heaven and earth **as** w against you 6386
Jos 24:22 "You are w against yourselves 6332
24:22 "Yes, we are **w,"** they replied. 6332
Ru 4: 9 "Today you are w that I have bought 6332
4:10 Today you are **w!"** 6332
4:11 and all those at the gate said, "We are **w.** 6332
Job 10:17 You bring new w against me 6332
Ps 27:12 for false w rise up against me, 6332
35:11 Ruthless w come forward; 6332
Isa 8: 2 **call in** Uriah the priest and Zechariah son of Jeberekiah **as** reliable w 6332+6386
33: 8 The treaty is broken, its w are despised, 6332
43: 9 bring in their w to prove they were right, 6332
43:10 "You are my **w,"** declares the LORD, 6332
43:12 You are my **w,"** declares the LORD, 6332
44: 8 You are my **w.** 6332
Jer 6:18 observe, O **w,** what will happen to them. 6338
32:12 of the w who had signed the deed and of all 6332
Mt 10:18 be brought before governors and kings as w *3457*
18:16 by the testimony *of* two or three **w.'** *3459*
26:60 though many **false** w came forward. *6019*
26:65 Why do we need any more **w?** *3459*
Mk 13: 9 before governors and kings as w to them. *3457*
14:63 "Why do we need any more **w?"** *3459*
Lk 21:13 This will result in your being w to them. *3457*
24:48 You are w of these things. *3459*
Ac 1: 8 and you will be my w in Jerusalem, *3459*
2:32 and we are all w of the fact. *3459*
3:15 We are w of this. *3459*
5:32 We are w of these things, *3459*
6:13 They produced false **w,** who testified, *3459*
7:58 the w laid their clothes at the feet of *3459*
10:39 "We are w of everything he did in *3459*
10:41 but *by* w whom God had already chosen— *3459*
13:31 They are now his w to our people. *3459*
1Co 15:15 we are then found to be **false** w about God, *6020*
2Co 13: 1 by the testimony of two or three **w."** *3459*
1Th 2:10 You are **w,** and so is God, of how holy, *3459*
1Ti 5:19 unless it is brought by two or three **w.** *3459*
6:12 in the presence *of* many **w.** *3459*
2Ti 2: 2 of many **w** entrust to reliable men who will *3459*
Heb 10:28 on the testimony of two or three **w.** *NIG*
12: 1 surrounded by such a great cloud *of* **w,** *3459*
Rev 11: 3 And I will give power *to* my two **w,** *3459*

WITS' (1) [WITLESS]

Ps 107:27 they *were* **at** their **w' end.** 1182+2683+3972

WITTY (KJV) See DISCRETION

WIVES (113) [WIFE]

Ge 4:23 Lamech said to his **w,** "Adah and Zillah, 851
4:23 w *of* Lamech, hear my words. 851
6:18 and your wife and your sons' w with you. 851
7: 7 and his wife and his sons' w entered the ark 851
7:13 with his wife and the w *of* his three sons, 851
8:16 and your wife and your sons and their **w.** 851
8:18 with his sons and his wife and his sons' **w.** 851
28: 9 in addition to the w he already had. 851
30:26 Give me my w and children, 851
31:17 Jacob put his children and his w on camels, 851
31:50 or if you take any w besides my daughters, 851
32:22 That night Jacob got up and took his two **w,** 851
36: 2 Esau took his w from the women 851
36: 6 Esau took his w and sons and daughters 851
37: 2 his father's **w,** and he brought their father 851
45:19 from Egypt for your children and your **w,** 851
46: 5 and their children and their w in the carts 851
46:26 not counting his sons' **w—** 851
Ex 22:24 your w will become widows 851
32: 2 "Take off the gold earrings that your **w,** 851
34:16 **choose** some of their daughters **as w** 4374
Nu 14: 3 Our w and children will be taken 851
16:27 and were standing with their **w,** 851
32:26 Our children and **w,** our flocks and herds 851
Dt 3:19 However, your **w,** your children 851
17:17 He must not take many **w,** 851
21:15 If a man has two **w,** and he loves one but 851
29:11 together with your children and your **w,** 851
Jos 1:14 Your **w,** your children and your livestock 851
Jdg 8:30 seventy sons of his own, for he had many **w.** 851
Jdg 12: 9 **brought in** thirty young women **as w** 995
21: 7 can we provide w for those who are left, 851
21:16 how shall we provide w for 851
21:18 We can't give them our daughters as **w,** 851
21:22 we did not get w *for* them during the war, 851
1Sa 1: 2 He had two **w;** one was called Hannah 851
25:43 and they both were his **w.** 851
27: 3 and David had his two **w:** 851
30: 3 they found it destroyed by fire and their w 851
30: 5 David's two w had been captured— 851
30:18 Amalekites had taken, including his two **w.** 851
2Sa 2: 2 So David went up there with his two **w,** 851
5:13 David took more concubines and w 851
12: 8 and your master's w into your arms. 851
12:11 Before your very eyes I will take your w 851
12:11 he will lie with your w in broad daylight. 851
19: 5 and the lives of your w and concubines. 851
1Ki 11: 3 He had seven hundred w of royal birth 851
11: 3 and his w led him astray. 851
11: 4 his w turned his heart after other gods, 851
11: 8 He did the same for all his foreign **w,** 851
20: 3 the best of your w and children are mine.' " 851
20: 5 your w and your children. 851
20: 7 When he sent for my w and my children, 851
2Ki 24:15 his **w,** his officials and the leading men of 851
1Ch 4: 5 Ashhur the father of Tekoa had two **w,** 851
4:17 One of Mered's w gave birth to Miriam, NIH
7: 4 for they had many w and children. 851
8: 8 after he had divorced his w Hushim 851
14: 3 In Jerusalem David took more w 851
2Ch 11:21 of Absalom more than any of his other w 851
11:21 he had eighteen w and sixty concubines, 851
11:23 and took many w for them. 851
13:21 He married fourteen w and had 851
20:13 with their w and children and little ones, 851
21:14 your w and everything that is yours, 851
21:17 together with his sons and **w.** 851
24: 3 Jehoiada chose two w for him, 851
28: 8 their kinsmen two hundred thousand **w,** 851
29: 9 and daughters and our w are in captivity. 851
31:18 They included all the little ones, the **w,** 851
Ezr 9: 2 **taken** some of their daughters **as w** 5951
10:11 around you and from your foreign **w."** 851
10:19 in pledge to put away their **w,** 851
10:44 and some of them had children by these **w.** 851
Ne 4:14 your w and your homes." 851
5: 1 the men and their w raised a great outcry 851
10:28 of the Law of God, together with their w 851
Isa 13:16 be looted and their w ravished. 851
Jer 6:12 together with their fields and their **w,** 851
8:10 Therefore I will give their w to other men 851
14:16 be no one to bury them or their **w,** 851
18:21 Let their w be made childless and widows; 851
29: 6 find w for your sons and give your 851
29:23 committed adultery with their neighbors' w 851
35: 8 Neither we nor our w nor our sons 851
38:23 "All your w and children will be brought 851
44: 9 by you and your w in the land of Judah and 851
44:15 that their w were burning incense 851
44:25 You and your w have shown by your actions 851
Da 5: 2 his w and his concubines might drink 10699
5: 3 his w and his concubines drank from them. 10699
5:23 your w and your concubines drank wine 10699
6:24 along with their w and children. 10493
Zec 12:12 with their w by themselves: NIH
12:12 the clan of the house of David and their **w,** 851
12:12 the clan of the house of Nathan and their **w,** 851
12:13 the clan of the house of Levi and their **w,** 851
12:13 the clan of Shimei and their **w,** 851
12:14 and all the rest of the clans and their **w.** 851
Mt 19: 8 "Moses permitted you to divorce your w *1222*
Ac 21: 5 All the disciples and their w and children *1222*
1Co 7:29 From now on those who have w should live *1222*
Eph 5:22 **W,** submit to your husbands as to the Lord. *1222*
5:24 so also w should submit to their husbands *1222*
5:25 Husbands, love your **w,** just as Christ *1222*
5:28 to love their w as their own bodies. *1222*
Col 3:18 **W,** submit to your husbands, as is fitting *1222*
3:19 love your w and do not be harsh with them. *1222*
1Ti 3:11 their w are to be women worthy of respect, *1222*
1Pe 3: 1 **W,** in the same way be submissive *1222*
3: 1 without words by the behavior *of* their **w,** *1222*
3: 7 be considerate as you live with your **w,** *1221*

WIVES' (1) [WIFE]

1Ti 4: 7 with godless myths and **old w' tales;** *1212*

WIZARD (KJV) See SPIRITIST

WOE (102) [WOES]

Nu 21:29 **W** to you, O Moab! 208
1Sa 4: 8 **W** to us! Who will deliver us 208
Job 10:15 If I am guilty—**w** to me! 518
Ps 120: 5 **W** to me that I dwell in Meshech, 210
Pr 23:29 Who has **w?** Who has sorrow? 208
Ecc 10:16 **W** to you, O land whose king was a servant 365
Isa 3: 9 **W** to them! They have brought disaster 208
3:11 **W** to the wicked! Disaster is upon them! 208
5: 8 **W** *to* you who add house to house 2098
5:11 **W** to those who rise early in the morning 2098
5:18 **W** *to* those who draw sin along with cords 2098
5:20 **W** *to* those who call evil good 2098
5:21 **W** *to* those who are wise in their own eyes 2098
5:22 **W** *to* those who are heroes at drinking wine 2098
6: 5 **"W** to me!" I cried. "I am ruined! 208

Isa 10: 1 W *to* those who make unjust laws, 2098
10: 5 "W *to* the Assyrian, the rod of my anger, 2098
18: 1 W *to* the land of whirring wings along 2098
24:16 "I waste away! I waste away! W to me! 208
28: 1 W *to* that wreath, the pride of Ephraim's 2098
29: 1 W *to* you, Ariel, Ariel, 2098
29:15 W *to* those who go to great depths 2098
30: 1 "W *to* the obstinate children," 2098
31: 1 W *to* those who go down to Egypt for help, 2098
33: 1 W *to* you, O destroyer, 2098
33: 1 W to you, O traitor, NIH
45: 9 "W *to* him who quarrels with his Maker, 2098
45:10 W *to* him who says to his father, 2098
Jer 4:13 W to us! We are ruined! 208
10:19 W to me because of my injury! 208
13:27 W to you, O Jerusalem! 208
22:13 "W *to* him who builds his palace 2098
23: 1 "W *to* the shepherds who are destroying 2098
45: 3 You said, 'W to me! 208
48: 1 "W to Nebo, for it will be ruined. 2098
48:46 W to you, O Moab! 208
50:27 W to them! For their day has come, 2098
La 5:16 W to us, for we have sinned! 208
Eze 2:10 words of lament and mourning and w. 2113
13: 3 W to the foolish prophets who follow their 2098
13:18 W to the women who sew magic charms 2098
16:23 " 'W! Woe to you, declares the Sovereign 208
16:23 W to you, declares the Sovereign LORD. 208
24: 6 " 'W *to* the city of bloodshed, 208
24: 9 " 'W *to* the city of bloodshed! 208
34: 2 W *to* the shepherds of Israel 2098
Hos 7:13 W to them, because they have strayed 208
9:12 W to them when I turn away from them! 208
Am 5:18 W to you who long for the day of 2098
6: 1 W to you who are complacent in Zion, 2098
Mic 2: 1 W to those who plan iniquity, 2098
Na 3: 1 W to the city of blood, full of lies, 2098
Hab 2: 6 " 'W to him who piles up stolen goods 2098
2: 9 "W to him who builds his realm 2098
2:12 "W to him who builds a city with bloodshed 2098
2:15 "W to him who gives drink 2098
2:19 W to him who says to wood, 'Come to life!' 2098
Zep 2: 5 W to you who live by the sea, 2098
3: 1 W to the city of oppressors, 2098
Zec 11:17 "W to the worthless shepherd, 2098
Mt 11:21 "W to you, Korazin! *4026*
11:21 W to you, Bethsaida! *4026*
18: 7 "W to the world because of the things *4026*
18: 7 but w to the man through whom they come! *4026*
23:13 "W to you, teachers of the law *4026*
23:15 "W to you, teachers of the law *4026*
23:16 "W to you, blind guides! *4026*
23:23 "W to you, teachers of the law *4026*
23:25 "W to you, teachers of the law *4026*
23:27 "W to you, teachers of the law *4026*
23:29 "W to you, teachers of the law *4026*
26:24 w to that man who betrays the Son of Man! *4026*
Mk 14:21 w to that man who betrays the Son of Man! *4026*
Lk 6:24 "But w to you who are rich, *4026*
6:25 W to you who are well fed now, *4026*
6:25 W to you who laugh now, *4026*
6:26 W to you when all men speak well of you, *4026*
10:13 "W to you, Korazin! *4026*
10:13 W to you, Bethsaida! *4026*
11:42 "W to you Pharisees, *4026*
11:43 "W to you Pharisees, *4026*
11:44 "W to you, because you are *4026*
11:46 "And you experts in the law, w to you, *4026*
11:47 "W to you, because you build tombs for *4026*
11:52 "W to you experts in the law, *4026*
17: 1 w to that person through whom they come. *4026*
22:22 but w to that man who betrays him." *4026*
1Co 9:16 W to me if I do not preach the gospel! *4026*
Jude 1:11 W to them! They have taken the way of *4026*
Rev 8:13 in a loud voice: "W! Woe! Woe to *4026*
8:13 in a loud voice: "Woe! W! Woe to *4026*
8:13 Woe! W to the inhabitants of the earth, *4026*
9:12 The first w is past; *4026*
11:14 The second w has passed; *4026*
11:14 the third w is coming soon. *4026*
12:12 But w to the earth and the sea, *4026*
18:10 they will stand far off and cry: " 'W! *4026*
18:10 W, O great city, O Babylon, city of power! *4026*
18:16 and cry out: " 'W! Woe, O great city, *4026*
18:16 W, O great city, dressed in fine linen, *4026*
18:19 cry out: " 'W! Woe, O great city, *4026*
18:19 W, O great city, where all who had ships *4026*

WOES (2) [WOE]

Ps 32:10 Many are the w of the wicked, 4799
Rev 9:12 two other w are yet to come. *4026*

WOKE (10) [WAKE]

Ge 41: 4 Then Pharaoh w **up.** 3699
41: 7 Then Pharaoh w **up;** it had been a dream. 3699
41:21 Then *I* w **up.** 3699
Mt 1:24 *When* Joseph w **up,** he did what the angel *1586*
8:25 The disciples went and w him, saying, *1586*
25: 7 the virgins w **up** and trimmed their lamps. *1586*
Mk 4:38 The disciples w him and said to him, *1586*
Lk 8:24 The disciples went and w him, saying, *1444*
Ac 12: 7 *He* struck Peter on the side and w him **up.** *1586*
16:27 The jailer w **up,** and when he saw *1181+2031*

WOLF (6) [WOLVES]

Ge 49:27 "Benjamin is a ravenous w; 2269
Isa 11: 6 The w will live with the lamb, 2269
65:25 The w and the lamb will feed together, 2269
Jer 5: 6 a w *from* the desert will ravage them, 2269
Jn 10:12 So when he sees the w coming, *3380*
10:12 Then the w attacks the flock and scatters it. *3380*

WOLVES (7) [WOLF]

Eze 22:27 within her are like w tearing their prey; 2269
Hab 1: 8 fiercer than w *at* dusk. 2269
Zep 3: 3 her rulers are evening w, 2269
Mt 7:15 but inwardly they are ferocious w. *3380*
10:16 I am sending you out like sheep among w. *3380*
Lk 10: 3 I am sending you out like lambs among w. *3380*
Ac 20:29 savage w will come in among you and will *3380*

WOMAN (353) [WOMAN'S, WOMEN, WOMEN'S]

Ge 2:22 Then the LORD God made a w from 851
2:23 she shall be called 'w,' 851
3: 1 He said to the w, "Did God really say, 851
3: 2 The w said to the serpent, 851
3: 4 the serpent said to the w. 851
3: 6 the w saw that the fruit of the tree was good 851
3:12 "The w you put here with me— 851
3:13 Then the LORD God said to the w, 851
3:13 The w said, "The serpent deceived me, 851
3:15 I will put enmity between you and the w, 851
3:16 To the w he said, "I will greatly increase 851
12:11 "I know what a beautiful w you are. 851
12:14 that she was a very beautiful w. 851
20: 3 as dead because of the w you have taken; 851
20: 3 she *is a* **married** *w*." AIT
21:10 "Get rid of that **slave** w and her son, 563
24: 5 if the w is unwilling to come back with me 851
24: 8 If the w is unwilling to come back with you, 851
24:39 if the w will not come back with me?' 851
28: 1 "Do not marry a Canaanite w. 1426
28: 6 "Do not marry a Canaanite w," 1426
38:20 in order to get his pledge back from the w, 851
46:10 Zohar and Shaul the son of a Canaanite *w*. AIT
Ex 2: 1 of the house of Levi married a Levite w, 1426
2: 9 So the w took the baby and nursed him. 851
3:22 *Every* w is to ask her neighbor 851
3:22 and *any* w **living** *in* her house for articles AIT
6:15 Zohar and Shaul the son of a **Canaanite** *w*. AIT
21: 4 the w and her children shall belong 851
21:10 If he marries **another** *w*, AIT
21:22 "If men who are fighting hit a pregnant w 851
21:28 "If a bull gores a man or a w to death, 851
21:29 penned up and it kills a man or w, 851
35:25 Every skilled w spun with her hands 851
36: 6 or w is to make anything else as an offering 851
Lev 12: 2 'A w who becomes pregnant and gives birth 851
12: 4 Then the w must wait thirty-three days to NIH
12: 5 for two weeks the w will be unclean, NIH
12: 7 the regulations for the *w who* **gives birth** to AIT
13:29 "If a man or w has a sore on the head or on 851
13:38 a man or w has white spots on the skin, 851
15:18 a man lies with a w and there is an emission 851
15:19 " 'When a w has her regular flow of blood, 851
15:25 a w has a discharge of blood for many days 851
15:33 *w* in her **monthly period,** AIT
15:33 for a man or a w with a discharge, 5922
15:33 *w who is* **ceremonially unclean.** AIT
18:17 not have sexual relations with both a w 851
18:19 not approach a w to have sexual relations 851
18:22 not lie with a man as one lies with a w; 851
18:23 A w must not present herself to an animal 851
19:20 with a w who is a slave girl promised 851
20:11 **the man and the** w must be put to death; 2157[S]
20:13 a man lies with a man as one lies with a w, 851
20:14 a man marries both a w and her mother, 851
20:16 " 'If a w approaches an animal 851
20:16 kill both the w and the animal. 851
20:18 with a w during her monthly period 851
20:27 " 'A man or w who is a medium or spiritist 851
21:13 " 'The w he marries must be a virgin. 851
21:14 He must not marry a widow, a **divorced** *w*, AIT
21:14 or a *w* **defiled** *by* prostitution, AIT
24:11 the Israelite w blasphemed the Name with 851
Nu 3:12 the first male offspring of every Israelite w. NIH
5: 6 a man or w wrongs another in any way and 851
5:18 After the priest has had the w stand before 851
5:19 the priest shall put the w under oath and say 851
5:21 the priest is to put the w under this curse of 851
5:22 " 'Then the w is to say, "Amen. 851
5:24 He shall have the w drink the bitter water 851
5:26 he is to have the w drink the water. 851
5:28 the w has not defiled herself and is free 851
5:29 is the law of jealousy when a w goes astray 851
5:31 w will bear the consequences of her sin.' " 851
6: 2 'If a man or w wants to make a special vow, 851
8:16 first male offspring from every Israelite w. 8167
25: 6 to his family a **Midianite** *w* right before AIT
25:14 who was killed with the **Midianite** *w* AIT
25:15 the name of the Midianite w who was put AIT
25:18 the *w who* **was killed** when the plague came AIT
30: 3 "When a young w still living in her father's 851
30: 9 by a widow or **divorced** *w* will be binding AIT
30:10 a w living with her husband makes a vow NIH
31:17 And kill every w who has slept with a man, 851
Dt 4:16 whether formed like a man or a w, 5922
15:12 If a fellow Hebrew, a man or a w, 6303[S]
17: 2 or w living among you in one of the towns 851
17: 5 the man or w who has done this evil deed 851
20: 7 Has anyone become pledged to a w and 851
21:11 the captives a beautiful w and are attracted 851
22: 5 A w must not wear men's clothing, 851
22:14 a bad name, saying, "I married this w, 851
22:22 who slept with her and the w must die. 851
23:17 or w is to become a shrine prostitute. 1426
24: 1 a w who becomes displeasing to him 851
28:30 You will be pledged to be married to a w, 851
28:56 most gentle and **sensitive** *w* among you— AIT
29:18 Make sure there is no man or w, 851
Jos 2: 4 w had taken the two men and hidden them. 851
Jdg 4: 9 for the LORD will hand Sisera over to a w." 851
9:53 a w dropped an upper millstone on his head 851
9:54 so that they can't say, 'A w killed him.' " 851
11: 2 "because you are the son of another w." 851
13: 6 the w went to her husband and told him, 851
13: 9 and the angel of God came again to the w 851
13:10 The w hurried to tell her husband, 851
13:24 The w gave birth to a boy 851
14: 1 and saw there a young Philistine w. 851
14: 2 "I have seen a Philistine w in Timnah; 851
14: 3 an acceptable w among your relatives or 851
14: 7 Then he went down and talked with the w, 851
14:10 Now his father went down to see the w. 851
16: 4 he fell in love with a w in the Valley 851
19:26 At daybreak the w went back to the house 851
20: 4 the Levite, the husband of the murdered w, 851
21:11 "Kill every male and every w who is not 851
Ru 2: 5 "Whose **young** w is that?" 5855
3: 8 and he turned and discovered a w lying 851
3:11 that you are a w *of* noble character. 851
3:14 "Don't let it be known that a w came to 851
4:11 May the LORD make the w who is coming 851
4:12 the LORD gives you by this **young** w, 5855
1Sa 1:15 "I am a w who is deeply troubled. 851
1:16 Do not take your servant for a wicked w; 1426
1:23 So the w stayed at home and nursed her son 851
1:26 the w who stood here beside you praying to 851
2:20 the LORD give you children by this w 851
20:30 "You son of a **perverse** and rebellious *w!* AIT
25: 3 She was an intelligent and beautiful w, 851
27: 9 he did not leave a man or w alive, 851
27:11 not leave a man or w alive to be brought 851
28: 7 "Find me a w who is a medium, 851
28: 8 and at night he and two men went to the w. 851
28: 9 But the w said to him, 851
28:11 w asked, "Whom shall I bring up for you?" 851
28:12 When the w saw Samuel, 851
28:13 The w said, "I see a spirit coming up out of 851
28:21 When the w came to Saul and saw 851
28:23 But his men joined the w in urging him, 851
28:24 The w had a fattened calf at the house, 851
2Sa 3: 8 of an offense involving this w! 851
11: 2 From the roof he saw a w bathing. 851
11: 2 The w was very beautiful, 851
11: 5 The w conceived and sent word to David, 851
11:21 Didn't a w throw an upper millstone on him 851
13:17 "Get *this* w out of here and bolt the door 2296
13:20 her brother Absalom's house, a **desolate** *w*. AIT
14: 2 and had a wise w brought from there. 851
14: 2 like a w who has spent many days grieving 851
14: 4 When the w from Tekoa went to the king, 851
14: 8 The king said to the w, "Go home, 851
14: 9 But the w from Tekoa said to him, 851
14:12 Then the w said, 851
14:13 The w said, "Why then have you devised 851
14:18 Then the king said to the w, 851
14:18 "Let my lord the king speak," the w said. 851
14:19 The w answered, "As surely as you live, 851
14:27 and she became a beautiful w. 851
17:20 Absalom's men came to the w at the house, 851
17:20 The w answered them, 851
20:16 a wise w called from the city, 851
20:21 The w said to Joab, 851
20:22 Then the w went to all the people 851
1Ki 3:17 this w and I live in the same house. 851
3:18 this w also had a baby. 851
3:22 The other w said, "No! The living one is my 851
3:26 The w whose son was alive was filled 851
3:27 "Give the living baby to **the first** w. 2023[S]
17:15 for Elijah and for **the** w and her family. 2085[S]
17:17 of the w who owned the house became ill. 851
17:24 Then the w said to Elijah, 851
2Ki 4: 8 And a well-to-do w was there, 851
4:17 But the w became pregnant, 851
6:26 a w cried to him, "Help me, 851
6:28 She answered, "This w said to me, 851
8: 1 to the w whose son he had restored to life, 851
8: 2 The w proceeded to do as the man 851
8: 5 the w whose son Elisha had brought back 851
8: 5 Gehazi said, "This is the w, 851
8: 6 The king asked the w about it, 851
9:34 "Take care of that **cursed** *w*," he said, AIT
1Ch 2: 3 three were born to him by a **Canaanite** *w*. AIT
16: 3 cake of raisins to each Israelite man and w. 851
2Ch 15:13 whether small or great, man or w. 851
24: 7 of that **wicked** *w* Athaliah had broken into AIT
24:26 son of Shimeath an **Ammonite** *w*, AIT
24:26 son of Shimrith a **Moabite** *w*. AIT
36:17 and spared neither young man nor **young** w, 1435
Ezr 10:14 a foreign w come at a set time, 851
Est 4:11 for any man or w who approaches the king 851
Job 2:10 "You are talking like a **foolish** *w*. AIT
14: 1 "Man born of w is of few days and full 851

Job 15:14 that he could be pure, or one born of w, 851
24:21 They prey on the barren and **childless** w, AIT
25:4 How can one born of w be pure? 851
31:9 "If my heart has been enticed by a w, 851
Ps 48:6 pain like that of a w **in labor.** AIT
113:9 He settles the **barren** w in her home as a happy mother AIT
Pr 6:24 keeping you from the immoral w, 851
7:10 Then out came a w to meet him, 851
9:13 The w Folly is loud; 851
11:16 A kindhearted w gains respect, 851
11:22 a beautiful w who shows no discretion. 851
14:1 The wise w builds her house, 851
20:16 in pledge if he does it for a **wayward** w. AIT
27:13 in pledge if he does it for a **wayward** w. AIT
30:23 an **unloved** w who is married, AIT
31:30 a w who fears the LORD is to be praised. 851
Ecc 7:26 I find more bitter than death the w who is 851
7:28 but not one [upright] w among them all. 851
SS 1:7 Why should I be like a **veiled** w beside AIT
Isa 13:8 they will writhe like a w **in labor.** AIT
21:3 pangs seize me, like those of a w **in labor;** AIT
26:17 As a w **with child** and about AIT
42:14 But now, like a w **in childbirth,** I cry out, AIT
54:1 O **barren** w, you who never bore a child; AIT
54:1 of the **desolate** w than of her who has AIT
Jer 3:20 But like a w unfaithful to her husband, 851
4:31 I hear a cry as of a w **in labor,** AIT
6:24 pain like that of a w **in labor.** AIT
13:21 not pain grip you like that of a w in labor? 851
22:23 pain like that of a w **in labor!** AIT
30:6 on his stomach like a w **in labor,** AIT
31:22 a w will surround a man." 5922
48:19 Ask the man fleeing and the w **escaping,** AIT
48:41 be like the heart of a w in labor. 851
49:22 be like the heart of a w in labor. 851
49:24 pain like that of a w **in labor.** AIT
50:43 pain like that of a w **in labor.** AIT
51:22 with you I shatter man and w, 851
Eze 18:6 or lie with a w during her period. 851
23:42 on the arms of **the w and her sister** 2177[S]
Hos 13:13 Pains as of a w **in childbirth** come to him, AIT
Mic 4:9 pain seizes you like that of a w **in labor?** AIT
4:10 O Daughter of Zion, like a w **in labor,** AIT
Zec 5:7 and there in the basket sat a w! 851
Mt 5:28 who looks at a w lustfully has already committed adultery 1222
5:32 the **divorced** w commits adultery. AIT
9:20 then a w who had been subject to bleeding 1222
9:22 And the w was healed from that moment. 1222
13:33 that a w took and mixed into a large amount 1222
15:22 A Canaanite w from that vicinity came 1222
15:25 The w came and knelt before him. NIG
15:28 Jesus answered, **"W,** you have great faith! 1222
19:9 and marries **another** w commits adultery." AIT
22:27 Finally, the w died. 1222
26:7 a w came to him with an alabaster jar 1222
26:10 "Why are you bothering this w? 1222
Mk 5:25 And a w was there who had been subject 1222
5:33 Then the w, knowing what had happened 1222
7:25 a w whose little daughter was possessed by 1222
7:26 The w was a Greek, 1222
10:11 and marries **another** w commits adultery AIT
12:22 Last of all, the w died too. 1222
14:3 a w came with an alabaster jar 1222
Lk 7:37 When a w who had lived a sinful life in 1222
7:39 and what kind of w she is— 1222
7:44 he turned toward the w and said to Simon, 1222
7:44 "Do you see this w? 1222
7:45 You did not give me a kiss, but **this** w, AIT
7:50 Jesus said to the w, "Your faith has saved 1222
8:43 And a w was there who had been subject 1222
8:47 Then the w, seeing that she could not go 1222
10:38 a w named Martha opened her home to him. 1222
11:27 a w in the crowd called out, 1222
13:11 and a w was there who had been crippled by 1222
13:12 **"W,** you are set free from your infirmity." 1222
13:16 Then should not **this** w, AIT
13:21 that a w took and mixed into a large amount 1222
15:8 a w has ten silver coins and loses one. 1222
16:18 and marries **another** w commits adultery, AIT
16:18 who marries a **divorced** w commits adultery. AIT
20:29 The first one **married a** w and died childless. 1222+3284
20:32 Finally, the w died too. 1222
22:57 **"W,** I don't know him," he said. 1222
Jn 2:4 **"Dear** w, why do you involve me?" 1222
4:7 When a Samaritan w came to draw water, 1222
4:9 The Samaritan w said to him, 1222
4:9 "You are a Jew and I am a Samaritan w. 1222
4:11 the w said, "you have nothing to draw with 1222
4:15 The w said to him, "Sir, give me this water 1222
4:19 the w said, "I can see that you are a prophet. 1222
4:21 Jesus declared, "Believe me, w, 1222
4:25 The w said, "I know that Messiah" 1222
4:27 to find him talking with a w. 1222
4:28 the w went back to the town and said to 1222
4:42 They said to the w, 1222
8:3 and the Pharisees brought in a w caught 1222
8:4 this w was caught in the act of adultery. 1222
8:9 with the w still standing there. 1222
8:10 Jesus straightened up and asked her, **"W,** 1222
16:21 A w giving birth to a child has pain 1222
19:26 he said to his mother, **"Dear** w, 1222
20:13 They asked her, **"W,** why are you crying?" 1222
20:15 **"W,"** he said, "why are you crying? 1222
Ac 9:40 Turning toward the **dead** w, he said, AIT
16:14 of those listening was a w named Lydia, 1222
17:34 also a w named Damaris, 1222
Ro 7:2 a married w is bound to her husband as long 1222
16:12 **another** w **who** has worked very hard in AIT
1Co 7:2 and **each** w her own husband. AIT
7:13 if a w has a husband who is not a believer 1222
7:15 or w is not bound in such circumstances; 80
7:34 An unmarried w or virgin is concerned 1222
7:34 a **married** w is concerned about the affairs AIT
7:39 A w is bound to her husband as long as he 1222
11:3 and the head of the w is man, 1222
11:5 And every w who prays or prophesies 1222
11:6 If a w does not cover her head, 1222
11:6 if it is a disgrace for a w to have her hair cut 1222
11:7 but the w is the glory of man. 1222
11:8 For man did not come from w, 1222
11:8 but w from man; 1222
11:9 neither was man created for w, 1222
11:9 but w for man. 1222
11:10 the w ought to have a sign of authority 1222
11:11 however, w is not independent of man, 1222
11:11 nor is man independent of w. 1222
11:12 For as w came from man, 1222
11:12 so also man is born of w. 1222
11:13 Is it proper for a w to pray to God 1222
11:15 but that if a w has long hair, 1222
14:35 for it is disgraceful for a w to speak in 1222
Gal 4:4 God sent his Son, born of a w, 1222
4:22 one by the **slave** w and the other by 4087
4:22 and the other by the **free** w. AIT
4:23 the **slave** w was born in the ordinary way; 4087
4:23 by the **free** w was born as the result of AIT
4:27 For it is written: "Be glad, O **barren** w, 5096
4:27 of the **desolate** w than of her who has AIT
4:30 "Get rid of the **slave** w and her son, 4087
4:31 we are not children of the **slave** w, 4087
4:31 but of the **free** w. AIT
1Th 5:3 as labor pains on a **pregnant** w, 1143+1877+2400
1Ti 2:11 A w should learn in quietness and full 1222
2:12 not permit a w to teach or to have authority 1222
2:14 it was the w who was deceived and became 1222
5:16 If **any** w who is a believer has widows AIT
Rev 2:20 You tolerate that w Jezebel, 1222
12:1 a w clothed with the sun, 1222
12:4 The dragon stood in front of the w who was 1222
12:6 The w fled into the desert to a place 1222
12:13 the w who had given birth to the male child. 1222
12:14 The w was given the two wings of a great 1222
12:15 to overtake the w and sweep her away with 1222
12:16 the earth helped the w by opening its mouth 1222
12:17 at the w and went off to make war against 1222
17:3 There I saw a w sitting on a scarlet beast 1222
17:4 The w was dressed in purple and scarlet, 1222
17:6 I saw that the w was drunk with the blood 1222
17:7 I will explain to you the mystery of the w 1222
17:9 seven hills on which the w sits. 1222
17:18 The w you saw is the great city that rules 1222

WOMAN'S (9) [WOMAN]

Ge 21:10 for that **slave** w son will never share in 563
Ex 21:22 be fined whatever the w husband demands 851
Nu 25:8 through the Israelite and into the w body. 851
1Ki 3:19 the night this w son died because she lay 851
2Ki 6:30 When the king heard the w words, 851
Eze 36:17 Their conduct was like a w **monthly uncleanness** 2021+3240+5614
Jn 4:39 in him because of the w testimony, 1222
Gal 4:30 for the **slave** w son will never share in 4087
4:30 in the inheritance with the **free** w son." AIT

WOMB (56) [WOMBS]

Ge 20:18 up every w in Abimelech's household 8167
25:23 "Two nations are in your w, 1061
25:24 there were twin boys in her w. 1061
29:31 he opened her w, but Rachel was barren. 8167
30:22 he listened to her and opened her w. 8167
38:27 there were twin boys in her w. 1061
49:25 blessings of the breast and w. 8167
Ex 13:2 of every w among the Israelites belongs 8167
13:12 to the LORD the first offspring of every w. 8167
13:15 the first male offspring of every w 8167
34:19 first offspring of every w belongs to me, 8167
Nu 12:12 stillborn infant from its mother's w 8167
18:15 The first offspring of every w, 8167
Dt 7:13 He will bless the fruit of your w, 1061
28:4 The fruit of your w will be blessed, 1061
28:11 in the fruit of your w, the young of your 1061
28:18 The fruit of your w will be cursed, 1061
28:53 you will eat the fruit of the w, 1061
28:57 from her w and the children she bears. 1068+8079
30:9 of your hands and in the fruit of your w, 1061
1Sa 1:5 and the LORD had closed her w. 8167
1:6 And because the LORD had closed her w, 8167
Job 1:21 "Naked I came from my mother's w, 1061
3:10 for it did not shut the doors of the w on me 1061
3:11 and die as I came from the w? 1061
10:18 "Why then did you bring me out of the w? 8167
10:19 or had been carried straight from the w to 1061
15:35 their w fashions deceit." 1061
24:20 w forgets them, the worm feasts on them; 8167
31:15 not he who made me in the w make them? 1061
38:8 when it burst forth from the w, 8167
38:29 From whose w comes the ice? 1061
Ps 22:9 Yet you brought me out of the w; 1061
22:10 from my mother's w you have been my God 1061
58:3 the w they are wayward and speak lies. 1061
71:6 you brought me forth from my mother's w. 5055
110:3 the w of the dawn you will receive the dew 8167[S]
139:13 you knit me together in my mother's w. 1061
Pr 30:16 the barren w, land, which is never satisfied 8167
31:2 O son of my w, O son of my vows, 1061
Ecc 5:15 Naked a man comes from his mother's w, 1061
11:5 or how the body is formed in a mother's w, 1061
Isa 44:2 who made you, who formed you in the w, 1061
44:24 your Redeemer, who formed you in the w: 1061
49:5 the w to be his servant to bring Jacob back 1061
66:9 up the w when I bring to delivery?" NIH
Jer 1:5 "Before I formed you in the w I knew you, 1061
20:17 For he did not kill me in the w, 8167
20:17 her w enlarged forever. 8167
20:18 of the w to see trouble and sorrow and 8167
Hos 12:3 In the w he grasped his brother's heel; 1061
13:13 not come to the **opening of the w.** 1201+5402
Lk 1:41 the baby leaped in her w, 3120
1:44 the baby in my w leaped for joy. 3120
Jn 3:4 second time into his mother's w to be born! 3120
Ro 4:19 and that Sarah's w was also dead. 3616

WOMBS (2) [WOMB]

Hos 9:14 Give them w that miscarry and breasts 8167
Lk 23:29 the w that never bore and the breasts 3120

WOMEN (228) [WOMAN]

Ge 4:19 Lamech married two w, 851
14:16 together with the w and the other people. 851
24:11 the time the w go out to **draw water.** AIT
27:46 with living because of these Hittite w. 1426
27:46 If Jacob takes a wife from among the w 1426
27:46 from Hittite w like these, 1426
28:8 the Canaanite w were to his father Isaac; 1426
30:13 The w will call me happy." 1426
31:43 "The w are my daughters, 1426
33:5 Esau looked up and saw the w and children. 851
34:1 went out to visit the w of the land. 1426
34:29 and all their w and children, 851
36:2 Esau took his wives from the w of Canaan: 1426
Ex 1:16 the **Hebrew** w in childbirth and observe AIT
1:19 **"Hebrew** w are not like Egyptian women; AIT
1:19 "Hebrew women are not like Egyptian w; 851
2:7 the Hebrew w to nurse the baby for you?" 851
10:10 along with your w **and children!** 3251
10:24 your w **and children** may go with you; 3251
11:2 Tell the people that men and w alike are 851
12:37 besides w **and children.** 3251
15:20 and all the w followed her, 851
35:22 All who were willing, men and w alike, 851
35:26 And all the w who were willing and had 851
35:29 men and w who were willing brought to 851
38:8 the w who **served** at the entrance to the Tent AIT
Lev 21:7 not marry w defiled by prostitution 851
26:26 ten w will be able to bake your bread 851
Nu 25:1 in sexual immorality with Moabite w, 1426
31:9 the Midianite w and children and took all 851
31:15 "Have you allowed all the w to live?" 5922
31:35 w who had never slept with a man. 851
32:16 and cities for our w **and children.** 3251
32:17 Meanwhile our w **and children** will live 3251
32:24 Build cities for your w **and children,** 3251
Dt 2:34 men, w and children. 851
3:6 men, w and children. 851
7:14 none of your men or w will be **childless,** AIT
20:14 As for the w, the children, 851
31:12 men, w and children, and the aliens living 851
32:25 Young men and **young** w will perish, 1435
Jos 6:21 men and w, young and old, cattle, 851
8:25 Twelve thousand men and w fell that day— 851
8:35 including the w and children, 851
Jdg 5:24 "Most blessed of w be Jael, 851
5:24 most blessed of tent-dwelling w. 851
9:49 about a thousand men and w, also died. 851
9:51 to which all the men and w— 851
11:40 that each year the **young** w of Israel go out 1426
12:9 for his sons he brought in thirty **young** w 1426
16:27 the temple was crowded with men and w; 851
16:27 men and w watching Samson perform. 851
21:10 including the w and children. 851
21:12 young w who had never slept with a man, 1435
21:14 and were given the w of Jabesh Gilead 851
21:16 "With the w of Benjamin destroyed, 851
Ru 1:4 They married **Moabite** w, AIT
1:19 So the two w went on until they came 2157[S]
1:19 and the w **exclaimed,** "Can this be Naomi?" AIT
4:14 The w said to Naomi: "Praise be to the 851
4:17 w **living** there said, "Naomi has a son." AIT
1Sa 2:22 the w who served at the entrance to the Tent 851
4:20 As she was dying, the w **attending** her said, AIT
15:3 Do not spare them; put to death men and w, 851
15:33 "As your sword has made w childless, 851
15:33 so will your mother be childless among w." 851
18:6 the w came out from all the towns of Israel 851
21:4 the men have kept themselves from w." 851
21:5 "Indeed w have been kept from us, 851
22:19 with its men and w, its children and infants, 851
30:2 the w and all who were in it, 851
2Sa 1:26 more wonderful than that of w. 851
6:19 crowd of Israelites, both men and w. 851
19:35 the voices of men and w singers? 8876[S]
1Ki 11:1 Solomon, however, loved many foreign w 851
2Ki 8:12 and rip open their **pregnant** w." AIT
15:16 and ripped open all the **pregnant** w. AIT

2Ki 23: 7 and where w did weaving for Asherah. 851
2Ch 28:10 And now you intend to make the men and w 9148
35:25 the men and w singers commemorate Josiah 8876[S]
Ezr 2:65 and they also had 200 men and w singers. 8876[S]
10: 1 men, w and children— 851
10: 2 by marrying foreign w from the peoples 851
10: 3 to send away all these w and their children, 851
10:10 you have married foreign w, 851
10:17 the men who had married foreign w. 851
10:18 the following had married foreign w: 851
10:44 All these had married foreign w, 851
Ne 7:67 and they also had 245 men and w singers. 8876[S]
8: 2 and w and all who were able to understand. 851
8: 3 w and others who could understand. 851
12:43 The w and children also rejoiced. 851
13:23 of Judah who had married w from Ashdod, 851
13:26 but even he was led into sin by foreign w. 851
13:27 to our God by marrying foreign w?" 851
Est 1: 9 Queen Vashti also gave a banquet for the w 851
1:17 conduct will become known to all the w, 851
1:18 Median **w of the nobility** who have heard 8576
1:20 all the w will respect their husbands, 851
2: 3 who is in charge of the w; 851
2:12 of beauty treatments prescribed for the w, 851
2:17 to Esther more than to any of the other w, 851
3:13 young and old, w and little children— 851
8:11 that might attack them and their w 851
Job 42:15 Nowhere in all the land were there found w 851
Ps 45: 9 of kings are among your **honored** *w;* AIT
Pr 31: 3 do not spend your strength on w, 851
31:29 "Many w do noble things, 1426
Ecc 2: 8 I acquired men and w singers, 8876[S]
SS 1: 8 If you do not know, most beautiful of w, 851
5: 9 better than others, most beautiful of w? 851
6: 1 has your lover gone, most beautiful of w? 851
Isa 3:12 w rule over them. 851
3:16 "The w *of* Zion are haughty, 1426
3:17 on the heads of the w *of* Zion; 1426
4: 1 that day seven w will take hold of one man 851
4: 4 The Lord will wash away the filth of the w 1426
16: 2 the w *of* Moab at the fords of the Arnon. 1426
19:16 In that day the Egyptians will be like w. 851
27:11 and w come and make fires with them. 851
32: 9 You w who are so complacent, 851
32:11 Tremble, you **complacent** *w;* AIT
Jer 2:33 the **worst** *of w* can learn from your ways. AIT
7:18 and the w knead the dough and make cakes 851
9:17 Call for the **wailing** *w* to come; AIT
9:20 Now, O w, hear the word of the LORD; 851
16: 3 and about the w who are their mothers and 3528[S]
31: 8 expectant mothers and *w* **in labor;** AIT
38:22 All the w left in the palace of the king 851
38:22 Those *w will* **say** to you: AIT
40: 7 w and children who were the poorest in 851
41:16 the soldiers, w, children and court officials 851
43: 6 led away all the men, w and children and 851
44: 7 by cutting off from Judah the men and w, 851
44:15 along with all the w who were present— 851
44:19 The w added, "When we burned incense to NIH
44:20 both men and w, who were answering him, 851
44:24 the people, including the w, "Hear the word 851
50:37 They will become w. 851
51:30 they have become like w. 851
La 2:10 **young** w *of* Jerusalem have bowed their 1435
2:20 Should w eat their offspring, 851
3:51 to my soul because of all the w *of* my city. 1426
4:10 With their own hands compassionate w
have cooked their own children, 851
5:11 W have been ravished in Zion, 851
Eze 8:14 I saw w sitting there, mourning for Tammuz. 851
9: 6 young men and maidens, w and children, 851
13:18 Woe to *the w who* **sew** magic charms AIT
16:38 the punishment of *w who* **commit adultery** AIT
16:41 punishment on you in the sight of many w. 851
22:10 in you are *those who* **violate** w 6700
23: 2 there were two w, daughters of the same 851
23:10 She became a byword among w, 851
23:44 so they slept with those lewd w, 851
23:45 the punishment of *w who* **commit adultery** AIT
23:48 all w may take warning and not imitate you. 851
44:22 not marry widows or **divorced** *w;* AIT
Da 11:37 of his fathers or for the one desired by w, 851
Hos 13:16 their **pregnant** w ripped open." 2230
Joel 2:29 Even on my servants, both men and w, 9148
Am 1:13 Because he ripped open the **pregnant** w 2226
4: 1 you *w who* **oppress** the poor and crush AIT
8:13 "the lovely **young** w *and* strong young men 1435
Mic 2: 9 You drive the w *of* my people 851
Na 3:13 Look at your troops—they are all w! 851
Zec 5: 9 and there before me were two w, 851
8: 4 and w of ripe old age will sit in the streets 2418[S]
9:17 and new wine the **young** w. 1435
14: 2 the houses ransacked, and the w raped. 851
Mt 11:11 Among those born *of* w there has *1222*
14:21 besides w and children. *1222*
15:38 besides w and children. *1222*
24:19 *for* **pregnant** w and nursing *1143+1877+2400*
24:41 Two *w will be* **grinding** with a hand mill; *AIT*
27:55 w were there, watching from a distance. *1222*
28: 5 The angel said *to* the w, "Do not be afraid, *1222*
28: 8 So the w hurried away from the tomb, *NIG*
28:11 While **the** w were on their way, *899[S]*
Mk 13:17 *for* **pregnant** w and nursing *1143+1877+2400*
15:40 Some w were watching from a distance. *1222*
15:41 In Galilee **these** *w* had followed him *AIT*
15:41 **Many other** *w* who had come up with him *AIT*
16: 8 the w went out and fled from the tomb. *NIG*
Lk 1:42 "Blessed are you among w, *1222*
7:28 *of* w there is no one greater than John; *1222*
8: 2 and also some w who had been cured *1222*
8: 3 **These** *w* were helping to support them out *AIT*
17:35 **Two** *w* will be grinding grain together; *AIT*
21:23 *for* **pregnant** w and nursing *1143+1877+2400*
23:27 including w who mourned and wailed *1222*
23:29 'Blessed are the **barren** w, *5096*
23:49 the w who had followed him from Galilee, *1222*
23:55 The w who had come with Jesus *1222*
24: 1 the *w* **took** the spices they had prepared *AIT*
24: 5 the *w* **bowed down** with their faces to *AIT*
24:11 But they did not believe **the** w, *899[S]*
24:22 In addition, some of our w amazed us. *1222*
24:24 the tomb and found it just as the w had said, *1222*
Jn 8: 5 Moses commanded us to stone **such** *w.* *AIT*
Ac 1:14 with the w and Mary the mother of Jesus, *1222*
2:18 Even on my servants, both men and w, *NIG*
5:14 and w believed in the Lord and were added *1222*
8: 3 he dragged off men and w and put them *1222*
8:12 they were baptized, both men and w. *1222*
9: 2 belonged to the Way, whether men or w, *1222*
13:50 the God-fearing w of high standing and *1222*
16:13 to speak *to* the w who had gathered there. *1222*
17: 4 and not a few prominent w. *1222*
17:12 as did also a number of prominent Greek w *1222*
22: 4 and w and throwing them into prison, *1222*
Ro 1:26 Even their w exchanged natural relations *2559*
1:27 also abandoned natural relations *with* w *2559*
16:12 **those** w **who** work hard in the Lord. *AIT*
1Co 14:34 w should remain silent in the churches. *1222*
Gal 4:24 for **the** w represent two covenants. *4047[S]*
Php 4: 3 help **these** *w* who have contended at my
side in the cause of the gospel, *AIT*
1Ti 2: 9 I also want w to dress modestly, *1222*
2:10 *for* w who profess to worship God. *1222*
2:15 But w will be saved through childbearing— *NIG*
3:11 their wives are to be w worthy of respect, *NIG*
5: 2 **older** *w* as mothers, and younger women *AIT*
5: 2 **younger** *w* as sisters, with absolute purity. *AIT*
2Ti 3: 6 and gain control over **weak-willed** w, *1220*
Tit 2: 3 teach the **older** *w* to be reverent in *AIT*
2: 4 the **younger** *w* to love their husbands *AIT*
Heb 11:35 W received back their dead, *1222*
1Pe 3: 5 the holy w of the past who put their hope *1222*
Rev 14: 4 not defile themselves with w, *1222*

WOMEN'S (2) [WOMAN]

Dt 22: 5 nor a man wear w clothing, 851
Rev 9: 8 Their hair was like w hair, *1222*

WOMENSERVANTS (KJV) See MAIDSERVANTS, FEMALE SLAVES

WON (11) [WIN]

Ge 30: 8 struggle with my sister, and *I have* w." 3523
1Sa 19: 5 The LORD w a great victory for all Israel, 6913
2Sa 19:14 *He* w **over** the hearts of all the men of Judah 5742
Est 2: 9 pleased him and w his favor. 4200+5951+7156
2:15 And Esther w the favor of 928+5951+6524
2:17 *she* w his favor and approval 4200+5951+7156
Ps 44: 3 not by their sword that *they* w the land, 3769
Mt 18:15 *you have* w your brother **over.** *3045*
Ac 14:19 and Iconium and w the crowd **over.** *4275*
14:21 and w a large number of **disciples.** *3411*
1Pe 3: 1 *be* w **over** without words by the behavior *3045*

WON'T (22) [NOT, WILL]

Ge 34:23 W their livestock, their property 4202
Jdg 4: 8 but if you don't go with me, I w go." 4202
15: 7 I w stop **until** I get my revenge on you." 561+3954
15:12 to me that you w kill me yourselves." 7153
16:15 'I love you,' when you w confide in me? 401
19:12 We w go into an alien city, 4202
1Sa 2:15 he w accept boiled meat from you, 4202
26: 8 I w strike him twice." 4202
2Sa 13: 4 W you tell me?" 4202
15:35 W the priests Zadok and Abiathar be there 4202
18: 3 they w care about us. 4202
18: 3 Even if half of us die, they w care; 4202
1Ki 14: 2 so you w be recognized as the wife 4202
21: 5 Why w you eat?" 401
2Ki 6: 3 *"W you* please **come** with your servants?" AIT
Ps 10:13 "He w call me to account"? 4202
Eze 24:19 "W you tell us what these things have to do 4202
37:18 'W you tell us what you mean by this?' 4202
Mk 5: 7 Swear to God that you w torture me!" *3590*
Lk 18: 5 so that she w eventually wear me out *3590*
Jn 4:15 give me this water so that I w get thirsty *3590*
1Co 8:10 w he be emboldened to eat *4049*

WONDER (12) [WONDERED, WONDERFUL, WONDERFULLY, WONDERING, WONDERS, WONDROUS]

Dt 13: 1 announces to you a miraculous sign or w, 4603
13: 2 or w of which he has spoken takes place, 4603
28:46 a w to you and your descendants forever. 4603
Job 6: 3 **no** w my words have been impetuous. 4027+6584
Ps 17: 7 **Show** *the* w *of* your great love, 7098
SS 1: 3 **No** w the maidens love you! 4027+6584
Isa 29:14 astound these people with w upon wonder; 7098
29:14 astound these people with wonder upon w; 7099
Mk 9:15 *they were* **overwhelmed with** w and ran *1701*
Ac 3:10 and they were filled *with* w and amazement *2502*
13:41 "Look, you scoffers, w and perish, *2513*
2Co 11:14 And no w, for Satan himself masquerades *2512*

WONDERED (2) [WONDER]

Lk 1:29 and w what kind of greeting this might be. *1368*
1:66 Everyone who heard this w **about** it, *1877+2840+3836+5502*

WONDERFUL (24) [WONDER]

2Sa 1:26 Your love for me *was* w, 7098
1:26 more w than that of women. NIH
1Ch 16: 9 sing praise to him; tell of all his w *acts.* 7098
Job 42: 3 *things* too w for me to know. 7098
Ps 26: 7 and telling of all your w *deeds.* 7098
31:21 for *he* **showed** his w love to me 7098
75: 1 men tell of your w *deeds.* 7098
105: 2 tell of all his w *acts.* 7098
107: 8 for his unfailing love and his w *deeds* 7098
107:15 for his unfailing love and his w *deeds* 7098
107:21 for his unfailing love and his w *deeds* 7098
107:24 his w *deeds* in the deep. 7098
107:31 for his unfailing love and his w *deeds* 7098
119:18 Open my eyes that I may see w *things* 7098
119:129 Your statutes are w; therefore I obey them. 7099
131: 1 with great matters or *things* too w for me. 7098
139: 6 Such knowledge is too w for me, 7100
139:14 your works **are** w, I know that full well. 7098
145: 5 and I will meditate on your w *works.* 7098
Isa 9: 6 And he will be called W Counselor, 7099
28:29 w *in* counsel and magnificent in wisdom. 7098
Mt 21:15 teachers of the law saw the w *things* he did *2514*
Lk 13:17 delighted with all the w *things* he was doing *1902*
1Pe 2: 9 called you out of darkness into his w light. *2515*

WONDERFULLY (1) [WONDER]

Ps 139:14 because *I* **am** fearfully and w **made;** 7098

WONDERING (6) [WONDER]

Lk 1:21 and w **why** he stayed so long in the temple. *2513*
3:15 and *were* all w in their hearts *1368*
24: 4 While they *were* w about this, *679*
24:12 w to himself what had happened. *2513*
Ac 5:24 w what would come of this. *NIG*
10:17 While Peter *was* w **about** the meaning of *1389*

WONDERS (62) [WONDER]

Ex 3:20 and strike the Egyptians with all the w 7098
4:21 before Pharaoh all the w I have given you 4603
7: 3 my miraculous signs and w in Egypt, 4603
11: 9 so that my w may be multiplied in Egypt." 4603
11:10 Moses and Aaron performed all these w 4603
15:11 awesome in glory, working w? 7099
34:10 Before all your people I will do w never 7098
Dt 4:34 by testings, by miraculous signs and w, 4603
6:22 the LORD sent miraculous signs and w— 4603
7:19 the miraculous signs and w, 4603
10:21 **awesome** w you saw with your own eyes. 3707
26: 8 and with miraculous signs and w. 4603
29: 3 those miraculous signs and great w. 4603
34:11 who did all those miraculous signs and w 4603
Jdg 6:13 Where are all his w that our fathers told us 7098
2Sa 7:23 and **awesome** w by driving out nations 3707
1Ch 16:12 Remember the w he has done, his miracles, 7098
17:21 and **awesome** w by driving out nations from 3707
Ne 9:10 You sent miraculous signs and w 4603
Job 5: 9 He performs w that cannot be fathomed, 1524
9:10 He performs w that cannot be fathomed, 1524
37:14 stop and consider God's w. 7098
37:16 *those* w *of* him who is perfect in knowledge? 5140
Ps 9: 1 I will tell of all your w. 7098
40: 5 O LORD my God, are the w you have done. 7098
65: 8 Those living far away fear your w; 253
78: 4 his power, and the w he has done. 7098
78:11 the w he had shown them. 7098
78:32 in spite of his w, they did not believe. 7098
78:43 his w in the region of Zoan. 4603
88:10 Do you show your w to the dead? 7099
88:12 Are your w known in the place of darkness, 7099
89: 5 The heavens praise your w, 7099
105: 5 Remember the w he has done, his miracles, 7098
105:27 his w in the land of Ham. 4603
111: 4 He has caused his w to be remembered; 7098
119:27 then I will meditate on your w. 7098
135: 9 He sent his signs and w into your midst, 4603
136: 4 to him who alone does great w, 7098
Jer 21: 2 Perhaps the LORD will perform w for us 7098
32:20 and w in Egypt and have continued them 4603
32:21 Israel out of Egypt with signs and w, 4603
Da 4: 2 to tell you about the miraculous signs and w 10763
4: 3 How great are his signs, how mighty his w! 10763
6:27 he performs signs and w in the heavens 10763
Joel 2:26 your God, who has worked w for you; 7098
2:30 I will show w in the heavens and on 4603
Mic 7:15 I will show them my w." 7098
Jn 4:48 "Unless you people see miraculous signs
and w," *5469*
Ac 2:11 we hear them declaring the w of God *3483*
2:19 I will show w in the heaven above and signs *5469*
2:22 by God to you *by* miracles, w and signs, *5469*
2:43 Everyone was filled with awe, and many w *5469*
4:30 to heal and perform miraculous signs and w *5469*
5:12 miraculous signs and w among the people. *5469*

Ac 6: 8 did great w and miraculous signs among *5469*
7:36 and did w and miraculous signs in Egypt, *5469*
14: 3 to do miraculous signs and w. *5469*
15:12 the miraculous signs and w God had done *5469*
2Co 12:12 mark an apostle—signs, w and miracles— *5469*
2Th 2: 9 kinds of counterfeit miracles, signs and w, *5469*
Heb 2: 4 God also testified to it by signs, w and *5469*

WONDROUS (1) [WONDER]

Rev 12: 1 A great and w **sign** appeared in heaven: *4956*

WONT (KJV) See CUSTOM, EXPECTED, HABIT, USUAL

WOOD (121) [BRUSHWOOD, WOODCUTTERS, WOODED, WOODEN, WOODPILE, WOODS, WOODSMAN, WOODSMEN, WOODWORK]

Ge 6:14 So make yourself an ark of cypress w; 6770
22: 3 he had cut *enough* w *for* the burnt offering, 6770
22: 6 Abraham took the w *for* the burnt offering 6770
22: 7 "The fire and w are here," Isaac said, 6770
22: 9 an altar there and arranged the w on it. 6770
22: 9 on the altar, on top of the w. 6770
30:37 the bark and exposing the **white** inner *w* of AIT
Ex 15:25 and the LORD showed him a **piece of w.** 6770
25: 5 and hides of sea cows; acacia w; 6770
25:10 "Have them make a chest of acacia w— 6770
25:13 of acacia w and overlay them with gold. 6770
25:23 "Make a table of acacia w— 6770
25:28 Make the poles of acacia w, 6770
26:15 "Make upright frames of acacia w for 6770
26:26 "Also make crossbars of acacia w: 6770
26:32 of **acacia** w overlaid with gold and standing 8847
26:37 and five posts of **acacia** w overlaid 8847
27: 1 "Build an altar of acacia w, 6770
27: 6 of acacia w for the altar and overlay them 6770
30: 1 an altar of acacia w for burning incense. 6770
30: 5 of acacia w and overlay them with gold. 6770
31: 5 to cut and set stones, to work in w, 6770
35: 7 and hides of sea cows; acacia w; 6770
35:24 and everyone who had acacia w for any part 6770
35:33 to work in w and to engage in all kinds 6770
36:20 They made upright frames of acacia w for 6770
36:31 They also made crossbars of acacia w: 6770
36:36 They made four posts of **acacia** w for it 8847
37: 1 Bezalel made the ark of acacia w— 6770
37: 4 of acacia w and overlaid them with gold. 6770
37:10 They made the table of acacia w— 6770
37:15 of acacia w and were overlaid with gold. 6770
37:25 the altar of incense out of acacia w. 6770
37:28 of acacia w and overlaid them with gold. 6770
38: 1 the altar of burnt offering of acacia w, 6770
38: 6 of acacia w and overlaid them with bronze. 6770
Lev 1: 7 to put fire on the altar and arrange w on 6770
1: 8 on the burning w that is on the altar. 6770
1:12 on the burning w that is on the altar. 6770
1:17 then the priest shall burn it on the w that is 6770
3: 5 the burnt offering that is on the burning w, 6770
4:12 and burn it in a w fire on the ash heap. 6770
11:32 will be unclean, whether it is made of w, 6770
14: 4 that two live clean birds and *some* cedar w, 6770
14: 6 together with the cedar w, 6770
14:49 to take two birds and *some* cedar w, 6770
14:51 Then he is to take the cedar w, the hyssop, 6770
14:52 the cedar w, the hyssop and the scarlet yarn. 6770
Nu 15:32 man was found gathering w on the Sabbath 6770
15:33 Those who found him gathering w brought 6770
19: 6 The priest is to take *some* cedar w, 6770
31:20 everything made of goat hair or w." 6770
Dt 4:28 worship man-made gods of w and stone, 6770
10: 3 So I made the ark out of acacia w 6770
19: 5 into the forest with his neighbor to cut w, 6770
28:36 other gods, gods of w and stone. 6770
28:64 other gods—gods of w and stone, 6770
29:11 in your camps who chop your w 6770
29:17 and idols of w and stone, 6770
Jdg 6:26 the w *of* the Asherah pole that you cut 6770
1Sa 6:14 up the w *of* the cart and sacrificed the cows 6770
2Sa 24:22 and ox yokes for the w. 6770
1Ki 6:23 a pair of cherubim of olive w, 6770
6:31 of olive w with five-sided jambs. 6770
6:32 the two olive w doors he carved cherubim, 6770
6:33 of olive w for the entrance to the main hall. 6770
18:23 and put it on the w but not set fire to it. 6770
18:23 and put it on the w but not set fire to it. 6770
18:33 He arranged the w, 6770
18:33 cut the bull into pieces and laid it on the w. 6770
18:33 and pour it on the offering and on the w." 6770
18:38 the w, the stones and the soil, 6770
2Ki 19:18 they were not gods but only w and stone, 6770
1Ch 21:23 the threshing sledges for the w, 6770
22:14 and w and stone. 6770
29: 2 iron for the iron and w for the wood, 6770
29: 2 iron for the iron and wood for the w, 6770
2Ch 2:14 bronze and iron, stone and w, 6770
Ne 10:34 a contribution of w to burn on the altar of 6770
13:31 I also made provision for contributions of w 6770
Job 41:27 like straw and bronze like rotten w. 6770
Pr 26:20 Without w a fire goes out; 6770
26:21 As charcoal to embers and as w to fire, 6770
SS 3: 9 he made it of w *from* Lebanon. 6770
Isa 10:15 or a club brandish him who is not w! 6770
30:33 with an abundance of fire and w; 6770
37:19 they were not gods but only w and stone, 6770
40:20 an offering selects w that will not rot. 6770
44:16 Half of **the** w he burns in the fire; 2257[S]
44:19 Shall I bow down to a block of w?" 6770
45:20 those who carry about idols of w, 6770
60:17 Instead of w I will bring you bronze, 6770
Jer 2:27 They say to w, 'You are my father,' 6770
3: 9 and committed adultery with stone and w. 6770
5:14 a fire and these people the w it consumes. 6770
7:18 The children gather w, 6770
La 5: 4 our w can be had only at a price. 6770
5:13 boys stagger under **loads of w.** 6770
Eze 15: 2 the w *of a* vine better than that of a branch 6770
15: 3 Is w ever taken from it to make anything 6770
15: 6 As I have given the w *of* the vine among 6770
20:32 who serve w and stone." 6770
24: 5 **Pile** w beneath it *for* the bones; 1883
24: 9 I, too, will pile the w high. 4509
24:10 So heap on the w and kindle the fire. 6770
27: 6 of **cypress** w from the coasts 9309
37:16 take a **stick of** w and write on it, 6770
37:16 Then take another **stick of** w, 6770
37:19 making them a single **stick of** w, 6770
39:10 not need to gather w from the fields or cut it 6770
41:16 the threshold was covered with w. 6770
41:22 its corners, its base and its sides were of w. 6770
Da 5: 4 of bronze, iron, w and stone. 10058
5:23 of bronze, iron, w and stone, 10058
Hos 4:12 and are answered by a **stick of** w. 5234
Hab 2:19 Woe to him who says to w, 'Come to life!' 6770
1Co 3:12 silver, costly stones, w, hay or straw, *3833*
2Ti 2:20 but also of w and clay; some are for noble *3832*
Rev 9:20 silver, bronze, stone and w— *3832*
18:12 every sort of citron w, *3833*
18:12 costly w, bronze, iron and marble; *3833*

WOODCUTTERS (3) [WOOD]

Jos 9:21 but let them be w and water carriers 2634+6770
9:23 as w and water carriers for the house 2634+6770
9:27 the Gibeonites w and water carriers 2634+6770

WOODED (1) [WOOD]

2Ch 27: 4 and forts and towers in the w **areas.** 3091

WOODEN (13) [WOOD]

Ex 7:19 even in the w *buckets* and stone jars." 6770
Lev 15:12 and any w article is to be rinsed with water. 6770
Nu 35:18 Or if anyone has a w object in his hand 6770
Dt 10: 1 Also make a w chest. 6770
16:21 Do not set up any w Asherah pole beside 6770
Ne 8: 4 on a high w platform built for the occasion. 6770
Isa 48: 5 my w image and metal god ordained them.' NIH
Jer 10: 8 they are taught by worthless w idols. 6770
28:13 You have broken a w yoke, 6770
Eze 41:22 There was a w altar three cubits high 6770
41:25 and there was a w overhang on the front of 6770
Hos 4:12 They consult a w **idol** and are answered by 6770
10: 6 Israel will be ashamed of its w **idols.** 6785

WOODPILE (1) [WOOD]

Zec 12: 6 the leaders of Judah like a firepot in a w, 6770

WOODS (3) [WOOD]

1Sa 14:25 The entire army entered the w, 3623
14:26 When they went into the w, 3623
2Ki 2:24 the w and mauled forty-two of the youths. 3623

WOODSMAN (1) [WOOD, MAN]

Isa 14: 8 no *w* comes *to* **cut** us **down."** AIT

WOODSMEN (1) [WOOD, MAN]

2Ch 2:10 your servants, the w who cut the timber, 2634

WOODWORK (1) [WOOD]

Hab 2:11 and the beams of the w will echo it. 6770

WOOF (KJV) See KNITTED

WOOING (1)

Job 36:16 *"He is* w you from the jaws of distress to 6077

WOOL (18) [WOOLEN]

Lev 13:48 or knitted material of linen or w, any leather 7547
13:52 the woven or knitted material of w or linen, 7547
Nu 19: 6 hyssop and **scarlet** w and throw them 9106+9357
Dt 18: 4 the first w **from** *the* **shearing** *of* your sheep, 1600
22:11 clothes of w and linen woven together. 7547
Jdg 6:37 a w fleece on the threshing floor. 7547
2Ki 3: 4 a hundred thousand lambs and with the w of 7547
Ps 147:16 He spreads the snow like w and scatters 7547
Pr 31:13 She selects w and flax and works 7547
Isa 1:18 they shall be like w. 7547
51: 8 the worm will devour them like w. 7547
Eze 27:18 in wine from Helbon and w *from* Zahar. 7547
34: 3 clothe yourselves with the w and slaughter 7547
Da 7: 9 the hair of his head was white like w. 10556
Hos 2: 5 my w and my linen, my oil and my drink.' 7547
2: 9 I will take back my w and my linen, 7547
Heb 9:19 scarlet w and branches of hyssop, *2250*
Rev 1:14 His head and hair were white like w, *2250*

WOOLEN (3) [WOOL]

Lev 13:47 with mildew—any w or linen clothing, 7547
13:59 concerning contamination by mildew in w 7547
Eze 44:17 not wear any w **garment** while ministering 7547

WOOLLEN (KJV) See WOOL, WOOLEN

WORD (569) [BYWORD, WORDS]

Ge 15: 1 the w *of* the LORD came to Abram in 1821
15: 4 Then the w *of* the LORD came to him: 1821
24:21 **Without saying a** w, the man watched her 3087
27:45 *I'll* **send** w *for* you to come back 8938
31: 4 So Jacob **sent** w to Rachel and 2256+7924+8938
37: 4 hated him and could not **speak** a kind *w* AIT
37:14 and bring w back to me." 1821
41:44 without your w no one will lift hand or foot NIH
44:18 let your servant speak a w to my lord. 1821
50:16 So *they* **sent** w to Joseph, saying, 7422
Ex 9:20 Those officials of Pharaoh who feared the w 1821
9:21 the w *of* the LORD left their slaves 1821
18: 6 Jethro *had* **sent** w to him, 606
36: 6 and they sent this w throughout the camp: 7754
Nu 3:16 as he was commanded by the w *of* the LORD 7023
3:51 as he was commanded by the w *of* the LORD 7023
15:31 the LORD's w and broken his commands, 1821
30: 2 he must not break his w but must do 1821
Dt 5: 5 to declare to you the w of the LORD, 1821
8: 3 but on every **w that comes from** the mouth 4604
30:14 No, the w is very near you; 1821
33: 9 over your w and guarded your covenant. 614
Jos 1:18 Whoever rebels against your w and does 7023
6:10 not say a w until the day I tell you to shout. 1821
8:35 not a w of all that Moses had commanded 1821
10: 6 then sent w to Joshua in the camp at Gilgal: 606
10:21 no one **uttered a** w against the Israelites.
906+3076+4383
11: 1 *he* **sent** w to Jobab king of Madon, 8938
Jdg 11:36 *"you have* **given** your w to the LORD.
906+7023+7198
12: 6 he could not pronounce the w correctly, NIH
13:17 honor you when your w comes true?" 1821
16:18 she sent w to the rulers of the Philistines, 7924
18:19 **Don't say a w.** 3338+6584+7023+8492
1Sa 1:23 only may the LORD make good his **w."** 1821
3: 1 In those days the w *of* the LORD was rare; 1821
3: 7 w *of* the LORD had not yet been revealed 1821
3:21 revealed himself to Samuel through his **w.** 1821
4: 1 And Samuel's w came to all Israel. 1821
14:39 But not one of the men **said a w.** 6699
15:10 Then the w *of* the LORD came to Samuel: 1821
15:23 you have rejected the w *of* the LORD, 1821
15:26 You have rejected the w *of* the LORD, 1821
16:22 Then Saul **sent** w to Jesse, saying, 8938
19:19 **W came** to Saul: 5583
20:12 *will I* not **send** you w and let you know? 8938
25:12 When they arrived, they reported every **w.** 1821
25:39 Then David **sent** w to Abigail, 8938
2Sa 3:11 Ish-Bosheth did not dare to say another w 1821
7: 4 the w *of* the LORD came to Nathan, 1821
7:21 sake of your w and according to your will, 1821
11: 5 The woman conceived and **sent** w to David,
2256+5583+8938
11: 6 So David **sent** *this* w to Joab: 8938
12: 9 Why did you despise the w *of* the LORD 1821
12:25 *he* **sent** w through Nathan the prophet 8938
13: 7 David sent w to Tamar at the palace: 606
13:22 Absalom never **said a** w to Amnon, 1819
14:12 "Let your servant speak a w to my lord 1821
14:17 the w *of* my lord the king bring me rest, 1821
14:32 "Look, *I* **sent** w to you and said, 8938
15:28 until w comes from you to inform me." 1821
19:14 *They* **sent** w to the king, "Return, 8938
22:31 the w *of* the LORD is flawless. 614
23: 2 his w was on my tongue. 4863
24: 4 The king's w, however, overruled Joab 1821
24:11 the w *of* the LORD had come to Gad 1821
1Ki 2:27 the w the LORD had spoken at Shiloh 1821
5: 8 So Hiram sent w to Solomon: 606
6:11 The w *of* the LORD came to Solomon: 1821
8:26 And now, O God of Israel, let your w 1821
8:56 Not one w has failed of all the good 1821
12:15 to fulfill the w the LORD had spoken 1821
12:22 But this w *of* God came to Shemaiah 1821
12:24 the w *of* the LORD and went home again, 1821
13: 1 By the w *of* the LORD a man of God came 1821
13: 2 He cried out against the altar by the w *of* 1821
13: 5 by the man of God by the w *of* the LORD. 1821
13: 9 I was commanded by the w *of* the LORD: 1821
13:17 I have been told by the w *of* the LORD: 1821
13:18 an angel said to me by the w *of* the LORD: 1821
13:20 the w *of* the LORD came to the old prophet 1821
13:21 'You have defied the w *of* the LORD and 7023
13:26 "It is the man of God who defied the w *of* 7023
13:26 as the w *of* the LORD had warned him." 1821
13:32 For the message he declared by the w *of* 1821
15:29 according to the w *of* the LORD given 1821
16: 1 Then the w *of* the LORD came to Jehu son 1821
16: 7 the w *of* the LORD came through the prophet 1821
16:12 the w *of* the LORD spoken against Baasha 1821
16:34 the w *of* the LORD spoken by Joshua son 1821
17: 1 in the next few years except at my w." 1821
17: 2 Then the w *of* the LORD came to Elijah: 1821
17: 8 Then the w *of* the LORD came to him: 1821

1Ki 17:16 with the w *of* the LORD spoken by Elijah. 1821
17:24 that you are a man of God and that the w *of* 1821
18: 1 the w *of* the LORD came to Elijah: 1821
18:20 So Ahab **sent** w throughout all Israel 8938
18:31 to whom the w *of* the LORD had come, 1821
19: 9 And the w *of* the LORD came to him: 1821
20:33 and were quick to pick up his **w.** 2023S
20:35 By the w *of* the LORD one of the sons of 1821
21:14 Then they sent w to Jezebel: 606
21:17 Then the w *of* the LORD came to Elijah 1821
21:28 Then the w *of* the LORD came to Elijah 1821
22:13 Let your w agree with theirs, 1821
22:19 "Therefore hear the w *of* the LORD: 1821
22:38 as the w *of* the LORD had declared. 1821
2Ki 1:17 the w *of* the LORD that Elijah had spoken. 1821
2:22 according to the w Elisha had spoken. 1821
3:12 "The w *of* the LORD is with him." 1821
4:44 according to the w *of* the LORD. 1821
6: 9 of God sent w to the king of Israel: 606
7: 1 Elisha said, "Hear the w *of* the LORD. 1821
9:26 in accordance with the w *of* the LORD." 1821
9:36 "This is the w *of* the LORD that he spoke 1821
10:10 that not a w the LORD has spoken against 1821
10:17 according to the w *of* the LORD spoken 1821
10:21 Then he **sent** w throughout Israel, 8938
14:25 in accordance with the w *of* the LORD, 1821
15:12 So the w *of* the LORD spoken 1821
18:25 to attack and destroy this place without w NIH
18:28 "Hear the w *of* the great king, 1821
19: 9 to Hezekiah *with this* w: 606
19:21 This is the w that the LORD has spoken 1821
20: 4 the w *of* the LORD came to him: 1821
20:16 "Hear the w *of* the LORD: 1821
20:19 The w *of* the LORD you have spoken is good 1821
23:16 the w *of* the LORD proclaimed by the man 1821
24: 2 with the w *of* the LORD proclaimed 1821
1Ch 10:13 he did not keep the w *of* the LORD and 1821
13: 2 *let us* **send** w far and wide to the rest 8938
15:15 in accordance with the w *of* the LORD. 1821
16:15 the w he commanded, 1821
17: 3 That night the w *of* God came to Nathan, 1821
21: 4 The king's w, however, overruled Joab; 1821
21:19 to the w that Gad had spoken in the name of 1821
22: 8 But this w *of* the LORD came to me: 1821
2Ch 6:17 now, O LORD, God of Israel, let your w 1821
10:15 to fulfill the w the LORD had spoken 1821
11: 2 But this w *of* the LORD came to Shemaiah 1821
12: 7 this w *of* the LORD came to Shemaiah: 1821
18:12 Let your w agree with theirs, 1821
18:18 "Therefore hear the w *of* the LORD: 1821
29:15 following the w *of* the LORD. 1821
30: 1 Hezekiah **sent** w to all Israel and Judah and 8938
30:12 following the w *of* the LORD. 1821
34:21 because our fathers have not kept the w *of* 1821
36:12 who **spoke the** w *of* the LORD. 4946+7023
36:15 **sent** w to them through his messengers 8938
36:21 the w *of* the LORD spoken by Jeremiah. 1821
36:22 the w *of* the LORD spoken by Jeremiah, 1821
Ezr 1: 1 the w *of* the LORD spoken by Jeremiah, 1821
Ne 6: 1 When w **came** to Sanballat, Tobiah, 9048
8:15 and that they should proclaim this w 7754
Est 7: 8 As soon as the w left the king's mouth, 1821
9:26 days were called Purim, from the w pur.) 9005
Job 2:13 No one said a w to him, 1821
4: 2 "If someone ventures a w with you, 1821
4:12 "A w was secretly brought to me, 1821
Ps 5: 9 Not a w from their mouth *can* **be trusted;** AIT
17: 4 the w *of* your lips I have kept myself from 1821
18:30 the w *of* the LORD is flawless. 614
33: 4 For the w *of* the LORD is right and true; 1821
33: 6 By the w *of* the LORD were the heavens 1821
52: 4 You love every harmful w, 1821
56: 4 In God, whose w I praise, in God I trust; 1821
56:10 In God, whose w I praise, in the LORD, 1821
56:10 in the LORD, whose w I praise— 1821
68:11 The Lord announced the w, 608
103:20 who do his bidding, who obey his w. 1821
105: 8 the w he commanded, 1821
105:19 till the w *of* the LORD proved him true. 614
107:20 He sent forth his w and healed them; 1821
119: 9 By living according to your w. 1821
119:11 I have hidden your w in my heart 614
119:16 I will not neglect your w. 1821
119:17 I will obey your w. 1821
119:25 preserve my life according to your w. 1821
119:28 strengthen me according to your w. 1821
119:37 preserve my life according to your w. 1821
119:42 for I trust in your w. 1821
119:43 not snatch the w *of* truth from my mouth, 1821
119:49 Remember your w to your servant, 1821
119:65 to your servant according to your w, 1821
119:67 but now I obey your w. 614
119:74 for I have put my hope in your w. 1821
119:81 but I have put my hope in your w. 1821
119:89 Your w, O LORD, is eternal; 1821
119:101 so that I might obey your w. 1821
119:105 Your w is a lamp to my feet and a light 1821
119:107 O LORD, according to your w. 1821
119:114 I have put my hope in your w. 1821
119:133 Direct my footsteps according to your w; 614
119:147 I have put my hope in your w. 1821
119:158 for they do not obey your w. 614
119:161 but my heart trembles at your w. 1821
119:169 give me understanding according to your w. 1821
119:172 May my tongue sing of your w, 614
130: 5 my soul waits, and in his w I put my hope. 1821
138: 2 above all things your name and your w. 614
Ps 139: 4 Before a w is on my tongue you know it 4863
143: 8 *Let* the morning **bring** me w of your 9048
147:15 his w runs swiftly. 1821
147:18 He sends his w and melts them; 1821
147:19 He has revealed his w to Jacob, 1821
Pr 12:25 but a kind w cheers him up. 1821
15: 1 but a harsh w stirs up anger. 1821
15:23 and how good is a timely w! 1821
25:11 A w aptly spoken is like apples of gold 1821
30: 5 "Every w *of* God is flawless; 614
Ecc 7:21 Do not pay attention to every w people say, 1821
8: 4 Since a king's w is supreme, 1821
Isa 1:10 Hear the w *of* the LORD, 1821
2: 3 the w *of* the LORD from Jerusalem. 1821
5:24 and spurned the w *of* the Holy One of Israel. 614
8:20 If they do not speak according to this w, 1821
16:13 the w the LORD has already spoken 1821
23: 1 the land of Cyprus w *has* **come** to them. 1655
23: 5 When w comes to Egypt, 9051
24: 3 The LORD has spoken this w. 1821
28:13 the w *of* the LORD to them will become: 1821
28:14 Therefore hear the w *of* the LORD, 1821
29:21 those who with a w make a man out to 1821
37: 9 messengers to Hezekiah *with this* w: 606
37:22 the w the LORD has spoken against him: 1821
38: 4 Then the w *of* the LORD came to Isaiah: 1821
39: 5 "Hear the w *of* the LORD Almighty: 1821
39: 8 The w *of* the LORD you have spoken is good 1821
40: 8 but the w *of* our God stands forever." 1821
45:23 in all integrity a w that will not be revoked: 1821
50: 4 to know the w that sustains the weary. 1821
50:10 the LORD and obeys the w *of* his servant? 7754
55:11 so is my w that goes out from my mouth: 1821
66: 2 and trembles at my w. 1821
66: 5 Hear the w *of* the LORD, 1821
66: 5 you who tremble at his w: 1821
Jer 1: 2 The w *of* the LORD came to him 1821
1: 4 The w *of* the LORD came to me, saying, 1821
1:11 The w *of* the LORD came to me: 1821
1:12 to see that my w is fulfilled." 1821
1:13 The w *of* the LORD came to me again: 1821
2: 1 The w *of* the LORD came to me: 1821
2: 4 Hear the w *of* the LORD, 1821
2:31 consider the w *of* the LORD: 1821
5:13 The prophets are but wind and the w is not 1825
6:10 The w *of* the LORD is offensive to them; 1821
7: 1 This is the w that came to Jeremiah from 1821
7: 2 " 'Hear the w *of* the LORD, 1821
8: 9 they have rejected the w *of* the LORD, 1821
9:20 Now, O women, hear the w *of* the LORD; 1821
11: 1 This is the w that came to Jeremiah from 1821
13: 3 w *of* the LORD came to me a second time: 1821
13: 8 Then the w *of* the LORD came to me: 1821
14: 1 This is the w *of* the LORD to Jeremiah 1821
14:17 "Speak this w to them: 1821
16: 1 Then the w *of* the LORD came to me: 1821
17:15 "Where is the w *of* the LORD? 1821
17:20 Say to them, 'Hear the w *of* the LORD, 1821
18: 1 This is the w that came to Jeremiah from 1821
18: 5 Then the w *of* the LORD came to me: 1821
18:18 nor the w from the prophets. 1821
19: 3 'Hear the w *of* the LORD, 1821
20: 8 the w *of* the LORD has brought me insult 1821
20: 9 his w is in my heart like a fire, NIH
21: 1 The w came to Jeremiah from the LORD 1821
21:11 'Hear the w *of* the LORD; 1821
22: 2 'Hear the w *of* the LORD, O king 1821
22:29 land, land, hear the w *of* the LORD! 1821
23:18 of the LORD to see or to hear his w? 1821
23:18 Who has listened and heard his w? 1821
23:28 the one who has my w speak it faithfully. 1821
23:29 "Is not my w like fire," 1821
23:36 every man's own w becomes his oracle 1821
24: 4 Then the w *of* the LORD came to me: 1821
25: 1 The w came to Jeremiah concerning all 1821
25: 3 the w *of* the LORD has come to me 1821
26: 1 this w came from the LORD: 1821
26: 2 everything I command you; do not omit a w. 1821
27: 1 this w came to Jeremiah from the LORD: 1821
27: 3 Then **send** w to the kings of Edom, Moab, 8938
27:18 If they are prophets and have the w *of* 1821
28:12 the w *of* the LORD came to Jeremiah: 1821
29:20 Therefore, hear the w *of* the LORD, 1821
29:30 the w *of* the LORD came to Jeremiah: 1821
30: 1 This is the w that came to Jeremiah from 1821
31:10 "Hear the w *of* the LORD, O nations; 1821
32: 1 This is the w that came to Jeremiah from 1821
32: 6 "The w *of* the LORD came to me: 1821
32: 8 "I knew that this was the w *of* the LORD; 1821
32:26 the w *of* the LORD came to Jeremiah: 1821
33: 1 the w *of* the LORD came to him 1821
33:19 The w *of* the LORD came to Jeremiah: 1821
33:23 The w *of* the LORD came to Jeremiah: 1821
34: 1 this w came to Jeremiah from the LORD: 1821
34: 8 The w came to Jeremiah from the LORD 1821
34:12 the w *of* the LORD came to Jeremiah: 1821
35: 1 This is the w that came to Jeremiah from 1821
35:12 w *of* the LORD came to Jeremiah, saying: 1821
36: 1 this w came to Jeremiah from the LORD: 1821
36:27 the w *of* the LORD came to Jeremiah: 1821
37: 6 the w *of* the LORD came to Jeremiah 1821
37:17 "Is there any w from the LORD?" 1821
39:15 the w *of* the LORD came to him: 1821
40: 1 The w came to Jeremiah from the LORD 1821
42: 7 Ten days later the w *of* the LORD came 1821
42:15 then hear the w *of* the LORD, 1821
43: 8 In Tahpanhes the w *of* the LORD came 1821
Jer 44: 1 This w came to Jeremiah concerning all 1821
44:24 "Hear the w *of* the LORD, 1821
44:26 But hear the w *of* the LORD, 1821
44:28 in Egypt will know whose w will stand— 1821
46: 1 the w *of* the LORD that came to Jeremiah 1821
47: 1 the w *of* the LORD that came to Jeremiah 1821
49:34 the w *of* the LORD that came to Jeremiah 1821
50: 1 the w the LORD spoke through Jeremiah 1821
La 2:17 he has fulfilled his w, 614
Eze 1: 3 w *of* the LORD came to Ezekiel the priest, 1821
3:16 of seven days the w *of* the LORD came 1821
3:17 the w I speak and give them warning 1821
6: 1 The w *of* the LORD came to me: 1821
6: 3 hear the w *of* the Sovereign LORD. 1821
7: 1 The w *of* the LORD came to me: 1821
9:11 the writing kit at his side brought back w, 1821
11:14 The w *of* the LORD came to me: 1821
12: 1 The w *of* the LORD came to me: 1821
12: 8 In the morning the w *of* the LORD came 1821
12:17 The w *of* the LORD came to me: 1821
12:21 The w *of* the LORD came to me: 1821
12:26 The w *of* the LORD came to me: 1821
13: 1 The w *of* the LORD came to me: 1821
13: 2 'Hear the w *of* the LORD! 1821
14: 2 Then the w *of* the LORD came to me: 1821
14:12 The w *of* the LORD came to me: 1821
15: 1 The w *of* the LORD came to me: 1821
16: 1 The w *of* the LORD came to me: 1821
16:35 you prostitute, hear the w *of* the LORD! 1821
17: 1 The w *of* the LORD came to me: 1821
17:11 Then the w *of* the LORD came to me: 1821
18: 1 The w *of* the LORD came to me: 1821
20: 2 Then the w *of* the LORD came to me: 1821
20:45 The w *of* the LORD came to me: 1821
20:47 'Hear the w *of* the LORD. 1821
21: 1 The w *of* the LORD came to me: 1821
21: 8 The w *of* the LORD came to me: 1821
21:18 The w *of* the LORD came to me: 1821
22: 1 The w *of* the LORD came to me: 1821
22:17 Then the w *of* the LORD came to me: 1821
22:23 Again the w *of* the LORD came to me: 1821
23: 1 The w *of* the LORD came to me: 1821
24: 1 the w *of* the LORD came to me: 1821
24:15 The w *of* the LORD came to me: 1821
24:20 "The w *of* the LORD came to me: 1821
25: 1 The w *of* the LORD came to me: 1821
25: 3 'Hear the w *of* the Sovereign LORD. 1821
26: 1 the w *of* the LORD came to me: 1821
27: 1 The w *of* the LORD came to me: 1821
28: 1 The w *of* the LORD came to me: 1821
28:11 The w *of* the LORD came to me: 1821
28:20 The w *of* the LORD came to me: 1821
29: 1 the w *of* the LORD came to me: 1821
29:17 the w *of* the LORD came to me: 1821
30: 1 The w *of* the LORD came to me: 1821
30:20 the w *of* the LORD came to me: 1821
31: 1 the w *of* the LORD came to me: 1821
32: 1 the w *of* the LORD came to me: 1821
32:17 the w *of* the LORD came to me: 1821
33: 1 The w *of* the LORD came to me: 1821
33: 7 the w I speak and give them warning 1821
33:23 Then the w *of* the LORD came to me: 1821
34: 1 The w *of* the LORD came to me: 1821
34: 7 you shepherds, hear the w *of* the LORD: 1821
34: 9 O shepherds, hear the w *of* the LORD: 1821
35: 1 The w *of* the LORD came to me: 1821
36: 1 hear the w *of* the LORD. 1821
36: 4 hear the w *of* the Sovereign LORD: 1821
36:16 Again the w *of* the LORD came to me: 1821
37: 4 'Dry bones, hear the w *of* the LORD! 1821
37:15 The w *of* the LORD came to me: 1821
38: 1 The w *of* the LORD came to me: 1821
Da 9: 2 to the w *of* the LORD given to Jeremiah 1821
Hos 1: 1 The w *of* the LORD that came to Hosea 1821
4: 1 Hear the w *of* the LORD, you Israelites, 1821
Joel 1: 1 The w *of* the LORD that came to Joel son of 1821
Am 3: 1 Hear this w the LORD has spoken 1821
4: 1 Hear this w, you cows of Bashan 1821
5: 1 Hear this w, O house of Israel, 1821
7:16 Now then, hear the w *of* the LORD. 1821
8:12 searching for the w *of* the LORD, 1821
Jnh 1: 1 The w *of* the LORD came to Jonah son of 1821
3: 1 Then the w *of* the LORD came to Jonah 1821
3: 3 the w *of* the LORD and went to Nineveh. 1821
Mic 1: 1 The w *of* the LORD that came to Micah 1821
4: 2 the w *of* the LORD from Jerusalem. 1821
Zep 1: 1 The w *of* the LORD that came to Zephaniah 1821
2: 5 the w *of* the LORD is against you, 1821
Hag 1: 1 the w *of* the LORD came through the prophet 1821
1: 3 Then the w *of* the LORD came through 1821
2: 1 the w *of* the LORD came through the prophet 1821
2:10 the w *of* the LORD came to the prophet 1821
2:20 The w *of* the LORD came to Haggai 1821
Zec 1: 1 the w *of* the LORD came to the prophet 1821
1: 7 the w *of* the LORD came to the prophet 1821
1:14 to me said, "Proclaim this w: 606
4: 6 "This is the w *of* the LORD to Zerubbabel: 1821
4: 8 Then the w *of* the LORD came to me: 1821
6: 9 The w *of* the LORD came to me: 1821
7: 1 the w *of* the LORD came to Zechariah on 1821
7: 4 **the** w *of* the LORD Almighty came to me: 1821
7: 8 w *of* the LORD came again to Zechariah: 1821
8: 1 the w *of* the LORD Almighty came to me. 1821
8:18 the w *of* the LORD Almighty came to me. 1821
9: 1 The w *of* the LORD is against the land of 1821
11:11 knew it was the w *of* the LORD. 1821
12: 1 the w *of* the LORD concerning Israel. 1821

Mal 1: 1 w of the LORD to Israel through Malachi. 1821
Mt 4: 4 but on every w that comes from the mouth 4839
8: 8 But just say the w, and my servant will be 3364
8:16 the spirits with a w and healed all the sick. 3364
12:32 Anyone who speaks a w against the Son 3364
12:36 for every careless w they have spoken. 4839
13:20 on rocky places is the man who hears the w 3364
13:21 or persecution comes because of the w, 3364
13:22 the thorns is the man who hears the w, 3364
13:23 the man who hears the w and understands it. 3364
14:35 they sent w to all the surrounding country. 690
15: 6 the w of God for the sake of your tradition. 3364
15:23 Jesus did not answer a w. 3364
19:11 "Not everyone can accept this w, 3364
22:46 No one could say a w in reply, 3364
26:75 Peter remembered the w Jesus had spoken: 4839
Mk 2: 2 and he preached the w to them. 3364
4:14 The farmer sows the w. 3364
4:15 along the path, where the w is sown. 3364
4:15 and takes away the w that was sown 3364
4:16 hear the w and at once receive it with joy. 3364
4:17 or persecution comes because of the w, 3364
4:18 like seed sown among thorns, hear the w; 3364
4:19 for other things come in and choke the w, 3364
4:20 hear the w, accept it, and produce a crop— 3364
4:33 parables Jesus spoke the w to them, 3364
7:13 the w of God by your tradition 3364
14:72 the w Jesus had spoken to him: 4839
16:20 with them and confirmed his w by the signs 3364
Lk 1: 2 eyewitnesses and servants of the w. 3364
2:17 the w concerning what had been told them 4839
3: 2 the w of God came to John son of Zechariah 4839
5: 1 around him and listening to the w of God, 3364
7: 7 say the w, and my servant will be healed. 3364
8:11 The seed is the w of God. 3364
8:12 then the devil comes and takes away the w 3364
8:13 on the rock are the ones who receive the w 3364
8:15 who hear the w, retain it, 3364
8:21 and brothers are those who hear God's w 3364
11:28 "Blessed rather are those who hear the w 3364
12:10 And everyone who speaks a w against 3364
22:61 the w the Lord had spoken to him: 4839
24:19 powerful in w and deed before God and all 3364
Jn 1: 1 In the beginning was the W, 3364
1: 1 and the W was with God, 3364
1: 1 and the W was God. 3364
1:14 The W became flesh and made his dwelling 3364
4:50 took Jesus at his w and departed. 3364+4409
5:24 whoever hears my w and believes him who 3364
5:38 nor does his w dwell in you, 3364
7:26 and they are not saying a w to him. 3306+4029
8:37 because you have no room for my w. 3364
8:51 I tell you the truth, if anyone keeps my w, 3364
8:52 yet you say that if anyone keeps your w, 3364
8:55 but I do know him and keep his w. 3364
9: 7 in the Pool of Siloam" (this w means Sent). NIG
10:35 to whom the w of God came— 3364
11: 3 So the sisters sent w to Jesus, "Lord, 3306
12:17 from the dead continued to spread the w. 3455
12:38 to fulfill the w of Isaiah the prophet: 3364
12:48 very w which I spoke will condemn him 3364
15: 3 because of the w I have spoken to you. 3364
17: 6 to me and they have obeyed your w. 3364
17:14 I have given them your w and 3364
17:17 Sanctify them by the truth; your w is truth. 3364
Ac 4:29 and enable your servants to speak your w 3364
4:31 with the Holy Spirit and spoke the w 3364
6: 2 of the w of God in order to wait on tables. 3364
6: 4 to prayer and the ministry of the w." 3364
6: 7 So the w of God spread. 3364
8: 4 preached the w wherever they went. 3364
8:14 that Samaria had accepted the w of God, 3364
8:25 and proclaimed the w of the Lord, 3364
11: 1 the Gentiles also had received the w of God. 3364
12:24 w of God continued to increase and spread. 3364
13: 5 the w of God in the Jewish synagogues. 3364
13: 7 and Saul because he wanted to hear the w 3364
13:15 the synagogue rulers sent w to them, saying, NIG
13:44 the whole city gathered to hear the w of 3364
13:46 "We had to speak the w of God to you first. 3364
13:48 they were glad and honored the w of 3364
13:49 The w of the Lord spread through 3364
14:25 and when they had preached the w in Perga, 3364
15:27 by w of mouth what we are writing. 3364
15:35 and many others taught and preached the w 3364
15:36 in all the towns where we preached the w of 3364
16: 6 by the Holy Spirit from preaching the w in 3364
16:32 Then they spoke the w of the Lord to him 3364
17:13 that Paul was preaching the w of God 3364
18:11 teaching them the w of God. 3364
19:10 in the province of Asia heard the w of 3364
19:20 In this way the w of the Lord spread widely 3364
20:32 "Now I commit you to God and to the w 3364
Ro 9: 6 It is not as though God's w had failed. 3364
10: 8 "The w is near you; it is in your mouth 4839
10: 8 that is, the w of faith we are proclaiming: 4839
10:17 message is heard through the w of Christ. 4839
1Co 14: 6 or prophecy or w of instruction? NIG
14:26 everyone has a hymn, or a w of instruction, NIG
14:36 Did the w of God originate with you? 3364
15: 2 you hold firmly to the w I preached to you. 3364
2Co 2:17 we do not peddle the w of God for profit. 3364
4: 2 nor do we distort the w of God. 3364
Gal 6: 6 in the w must share all good things with 3364
Eph 1:13 in Christ when you heard the w of truth, 3364
5:26 by the washing with water through the w, 4839
6:17 sword of the Spirit, which is the w of God. 4839
Php 1:14 to speak the w of God more courageously 3364
2:16 as you hold out the w of life— 3364
Col 1: 5 that you have already heard about in the w 3364
1:25 to you the w of God in its fullness— 3364
3:16 Let the w of Christ dwell in you richly 3364
3:17 whatever you do, whether in w or deed, 3364
1Th 2:13 when you received the w of God, 3364
2:13 you accepted it not as the w of men, 3364
2:13 but as it actually is, the w of God, 3364
4:15 According to the Lord's own w, 3364
2Th 2:15 whether by w of mouth or by letter. 3364
2:17 in every good deed and w. 3364
1Ti 4: 5 because it is consecrated by the w of God 3364
2Ti 2: 9 But God's w is not chained. 3364
2:15 and who correctly handles the w of truth. 3364
4: 2 Preach the W; be prepared 3364
Tit 1: 3 at his appointed season he brought his w 3364
2: 5 so that no one will malign the w of God. 3364
Heb 1: 3 sustaining all things by his powerful w. 4839
4:12 For the w of God is living and active. 3364
5:12 the elementary truths of God's w all 3364
6: 5 who have tasted the goodness of the w 4839
12: 5 that w of encouragement that addresses you NIG
12:19 that no further w be spoken to them, 3364+4707
12:24 that speaks a better w than the blood NIG
13: 7 who spoke the w of God to you. 3364
13:22 to bear with my w of exhortation, 3364
Jas 1:18 He chose to give us birth through the w 3364
1:21 and humbly accept the w planted in you, 3364
1:22 Do not merely listen to the w, 3364
1:23 to the w but does not do what it says is like 3364
1Pe 1:23 through the living and enduring w of God. 3364
1:25 but the w of the Lord stands forever." 4839
1:25 And this is the w that was preached to you. 4839
3: 1 if any of them do not believe the w, 3364
2Pe 1:19 the w of the prophets made more certain, 3364
3: 5 by God's w the heavens existed and 3364
3: 7 By the same w the present heavens 3364
1Jn 1: 1 this we proclaim concerning the W of life. 3364
1:10 be a liar and his w has no place in our lives. 3364
2: 5 But if anyone obeys his w, 3364
2:14 and the w of God lives in you, 3364
Rev 1: 2 w of God and the testimony of Jesus Christ. 3364
1: 9 of the w of God and the testimony of Jesus. 3364
3: 8 yet you have kept my w and have 3364
6: 9 because of the w of God and 3364
12:11 the Lamb and by the w of their testimony; 3364
19:13 and his name is the W of God. 3364
20: 4 for Jesus and because of the w of God. 3364

WORDS (424) [WORD]

Ge 4:23 wives of Lamech, hear my w. 614
27:34 When Esau heard his father's w, 1821
42:16 in prison, so that your w may be tested 1821
42:20 so that your w may be verified and 1821
44: 6 he repeated these w to them. 1821
Ex 4:15 You shall speak to him and put w 1821
19: 6 the w you are to speak to the Israelites." 1821
19: 7 of the people and set before them all the w 1821
20: 1 And God spoke all these w: 1821
23: 8 and twists the w of the righteous. 1821
24: 3 the people all the LORD's w and laws, 1821
24: 8 with you in accordance with all these w." 1821
33: 4 When the people heard these distressing w, 1821
34: 1 on them the w that were on the first tablets, 1821
34:27 "Write down these w, 1821
34:27 for in accordance with these w I have made 1821
34:28 on the tablets the w of the covenant— 1821
Nu 12: 6 "Listen to my w: 1821
24: 4 the oracle of one who hears the w of God, 609
24:16 the oracle of one who hears the w of God, 609
Dt 1: 1 These are the w Moses spoke to all Israel in 1821
4:10 the people before me to hear my w so 1821
4:12 You heard the sound of w but saw no form; 1821
4:36 and you heard his w from out of the fire. 1821
10: 2 I will write on the tablets the w that were on 1821
11:18 Fix these w of mine in your hearts 1821
13: 3 you must not listen to the w of that prophet 1821
16:19 the wise and twists the w of the righteous. 1821
17:19 and follow carefully all the w of this law 1821
18:18 I will put my w in his mouth, 1821
18:19 not listen to my w that the prophet speaks 1821
27: 3 the w of this law when you have crossed 1821
27: 8 And you shall write very clearly all the w 1821
27:26 the w of this law by carrying them out." 1821
28:58 not carefully follow all the w of this law, 1821
29:19 a person hears the w of this oath, 1821
29:29 that we may follow all the w of this law. 1821
31: 1 Then Moses went out and spoke these w 1821
31:12 and follow carefully all the w of this law. 1821
31:24 in a book the w of this law from beginning 1821
31:28 so that I can speak these w in their hearing 1821
31:30 the w of this song from beginning to end in 1821
32: 1 hear, O earth, the w of my mouth. 609
32: 2 like rain and my w descend like dew, 614
32:44 with Joshua son of Nun and spoke all the w 1821
32:45 When Moses finished reciting all these w 1821
32:46 to heart all the w I have solemnly declared 1821
32:46 to obey carefully all the w of this law. 1821
32:47 They are not just idle w for you— 1821
Jos 1:18 and does not obey your w, 1821
3: 9 and listen to the w of the LORD your God. 1821
8:34 Joshua read all the w of the law— 1821
24:27 It has heard all the w the LORD has said 609
Jdg 11:11 And he repeated all his w before 1821
13:12 "When your w are fulfilled, 1821
1Sa 3:19 and he let none of his w fall to the ground. 1821
8:10 Samuel told all the w of the LORD to 1821
11: 6 When Saul heard their w, 1821
17:11 On hearing the Philistine's w, 1821
18:23 They repeated these w to David. 1821
21:12 David took these w to heart 1821
24: 7 With these w David rebuked his men 1821
25:35 I have heard your w and granted your 7754
26:19 the king listen to his servant's w. 1821
28:20 filled with fear because of Samuel's w. 1821
2Sa 7:17 to David all the w of this entire revelation. 1821
7:28 Your w are trustworthy, 1821
14: 3 go to the king and speak these w to him." 1821
14: 3 And Joab put the w in her mouth. 1821
14:19 and who put all these w into the mouth 1821
22: 1 to the LORD the w of this song when 1821
23: 1 These are the last w of David: 1821
1Ki 8:59 And may these w of mine, 1821
21:27 When Ahab heard these w, 1821
22:28 he added, "Mark my w, all you people!" 9048
2Ki 6:12 tells the king of Israel the very w you speak 1821
6:30 When the king heard the woman's w, 1821
18:20 but you speak only empty w. 1821+8557
19: 4 the LORD your God will hear all the w of 1821
19: 4 for the w the LORD your God has heard. 1821
19: 6 those w with which the underlings of 1821
19:16 to the w Sennacherib has sent to insult 1821
22:11 the king heard the w of the Book of the Law 1821
22:13 because our fathers have not obeyed the w 1821
22:18 says concerning the w you heard: 1821
23: 2 in their hearing all the w of the Book of 1821
23: 3 the w of the covenant written in this book. 1821
1Ch 17:15 to David all the w of this entire revelation. 1821
2Ch 11: 4 the w of the LORD and turned back 1821
15: 8 When Asa heard these w and the prophecy 1821
18:27 he added, "Mark my w, all you people!" 9048
29:30 the Levites to praise the LORD with the w 1821
32: 6 and encouraged them with these w: 606
33:18 to his God and the w the seers spoke to him 1821
34:19 When the king heard the w of the Law, 1821
34:26 says concerning the w you heard: 1821
34:30 in their hearing all the w of the Book of 1821
34:31 the w of the covenant written in this book. 1821
36:16 despised his w and scoffed at his prophets 1821
Ezr 9: 4 Then everyone who trembled at the w of 1821
Ne 1: 1 The w of Nehemiah son of Hacaliah: 1821
8: 9 as they listened to the w of the Law. 1821
8:12 the w that had been made known to them. 1821
8:13 the scribe to give attention to the w of 1821
Est 4:12 Esther's w were reported to Mordecai, 1821
9:30 w of goodwill and assurance— 1821
Job 4: 4 Your w have supported those who stumbled 4863
6: 3 no wonder my w have been impetuous. 1821
6:10 I had not denied the w of the Holy One. 609
6:25 How painful are honest w! 609
6:26 treat the w of a despairing man as wind? 609
8: 2 Your w are a blustering wind. 609+7023
8:10 not bring forth w from their understanding? 4863
9:14 How can I find w to argue with him? 1821
11: 2 "Are all these w to go unanswered? 1821
12:11 not the ear test w as the tongue tastes food? 4863
13:17 Listen carefully to my w; 4863
15: 3 Would he argue with useless w, 1821
15:11 w spoken gently to you? 1821
15:13 and pour out such w from your mouth? 4863
19: 2 and crush me with w? 4863
19:23 "Oh, that my w were recorded, 4863
21: 2 "Listen carefully to my w; 4863
22:22 and lay up his w in your heart. 609
23:12 I have treasured the w of his mouth more 609
24:25 who can prove me false and reduce my w 4863
26: 4 Who has helped you utter these w? 4863
29:22 my w fell gently on their ears. 4863
29:23 for me as for showers and drank in my w as NIH
31:40 The w of Job are ended. 1821
32:11 while you were searching for w, 4863
32:14 But Job has not marshaled his w against me, 4863
32:15 no more to say; w have failed them. 4863
32:18 For I am full of w, 4863
33: 1 "But now, Job, listen to my w; 4863
33: 2 my w are on the tip of my tongue. 1819
33: 3 My w come from an upright heart; 609
33: 8 I heard the very w— 4863
33:13 to him that he answers none of man's w? 1821
34: 2 "Hear my w, you wise men; 4863
34: 3 For the ear tests w as the tongue tastes food. 4863
34:35 without knowledge; his w lack insight.' 1821
34:37 and multiplies his w against God." 609
35:16 without knowledge he multiplies w." 4863
36: 4 Be assured that my w are not false; 4863
38: 2 that darkens my counsel with w 4863
41: 3 speak to you with gentle w? 1819
Ps 5: 1 Give ear to my w, O LORD, 609
12: 6 And the w of the LORD are flawless, 614
18: T He sang to the LORD the w of this song 1821
19: 4 their w to the ends of the world. 4863
19:14 May the w of my mouth and the meditation 609
22: 1 so far from the w of my groaning? 1821
36: 3 w of his mouth are wicked and deceitful; 1821
49: 3 My mouth will speak w of wisdom; AIT
50:17 You hate my instruction and cast my w 1821
54: 2 listen to the w of my mouth. 609
55:21 his w are more soothing than oil, 1821
56: 5 All day long they twist my w; 1821
59:12 sins of their mouths, for the w of their lips, 1821
64: 3 and aim their w like deadly arrows. 1821
78: 1 listen to the w of my mouth. 609

Ps 94: 4 They pour out arrogant w; 1819
105:28 for had they not rebelled against his w? 1821
106:33 and **rash w came** from Moses' lips. 1051
107:11 for they had rebelled against the w *of* God 609
109: 3 With w *of* hatred they surround me; 1821
119:57 I have promised to obey your w. 1821
119:103 How sweet are your w to my taste, 614
119:130 The unfolding of your w gives light; 1821
119:139 for my enemies ignore your w. 1821
119:160 All your w are true; 1821
138: 4 when they hear the w *of* your mouth. 609
141: 6 that my w were well spoken. 609
Pr 1: 2 for understanding w *of* insight; 609
2: 1 if you accept my w and store 609
2:12 from men *whose* w are perverse, 1819
2:16 the wayward wife with her seductive w, 609
4: 4 "Lay hold of my w with all your heart; 1821
4: 5 do not forget my w or swerve from 609+7023
4:20 listen closely to my w. 609
5: 1 listen well to my w **of insight,** 9312
6: 2 ensnared by the w *of* your mouth, 609
7: 1 keep my w and store up my commands 609
7: 5 the wayward wife with her seductive w. 609
7:21 With **persuasive** w she led him astray; 4375
8: 8 All the w *of* my mouth are just; 609
10:19 When w are many, sin is not absent, 1821
12: 6 The w *of* the wicked lie in wait for blood, 1821
12:18 **Reckless** w pierce like a sword, 1051
16:21 and pleasant w promote instruction. 8557
16:24 Pleasant w are a honeycomb, 609
17:27 A man of knowledge uses w with restraint, 609
18: 4 The w *of* a man's mouth are deep waters, 1821
18: 8 The w *of* a gossip are like choice morsels; 1821
19:27 you will stray from the w *of* knowledge. 609
22:12 but he frustrates the w *of* the unfaithful. 1821
22:21 teaching you true and reliable w, 609
23: 9 for he will scorn the wisdom of your w. 4863
23:12 and your ears to w *of* knowledge. 609
26:22 The w *of* a gossip are like choice morsels; 1821
29:19 A servant cannot be corrected by mere w; 1821
30: 6 Do not add to his w, 1821
Ecc 1: 1 The w *of* the Teacher, son of David, 1821
5: 2 so let your w be few. 1821
5: 3 the speech of a fool when there are many w. 1821
5: 7 and many w are meaningless. 1821
6:11 The more the w, the less the meaning, 1821
9:16 and his w are no longer heeded. 1821
9:17 The quiet w *of* the wise are more to 1821
10:12 W *from* a wise man's mouth are gracious, 1821
10:13 At the beginning his w are folly; 1821+7023
10:14 and the fool multiplies w. 1821
10:20 because a bird of the air may carry your w, 7754
12:10 Teacher searched to find just the right w, 1821
12:11 The w *of* the wise are like goads, 1821
Isa 3: 8 their w and deeds are against the LORD, 4383
29:11 but w sealed *in* a scroll. 1821
29:18 In that day the deaf will hear the w *of* 1821
31: 2 he does not take back his w. 1821
36: 5 but you speak only **empty** w. 1821+8557
36:13 "Hear the w *of* the great king, 1821
37: 4 that the LORD your God will hear the w 1821
37: 4 for the w the LORD your God has heard. 1821
37: 6 those w with which the underlings of 1821
37:17 to all the w Sennacherib has sent to insult 1821
41:26 no one heard *any* w *from* you. 609
44:26 who carries out the w *of* his servants 1821
51:16 I have put my w in your mouth 1821
58:13 not doing as you please or speaking idle w, 1821
59:21 and my w that I have put in your mouth will 1821
Jer 1: 1 The w *of* Jeremiah son of Hilkiah, 1821
1: 9 "Now, I have put my w in your mouth. 1821
5:14 "Because the people have spoken these w, 1821
5:14 I will make my w in your mouth a fire 1821
6:19 because they have not listened to my w 1821
7: 4 Do not trust in deceptive w and say, 1821
7: 8 in deceptive w that are worthless. 1821
9:20 open your ears to the w *of* his mouth. 1821
11: 6 "Proclaim all these w in the towns of Judah 1821
11:10 who refused to listen to my w. 1821
13:10 who refuse to listen to my w, 1821
15:16 When your w came, I ate them; 1821
15:19 if you utter worthy, not worthless, w, NIH
19: 2 There proclaim the w I tell you, 1821
19:15 and would not listen to my w.' " 1821
23: 9 because of the LORD and his holy w. 1821
23:22 they would have proclaimed my w 1821
23:30 from one another w supposedly *from* me. 1821
23:36 and so you distort the w *of* the living God, 1821
23:38 You used the w, 'This is the oracle of 1821
25: 8 "Because you have not listened to my w, 1821
25:30 "Now prophesy all these w against them 1821
26: 5 if you do not listen to the w *of* my servants 1821
26: 7 the people heard Jeremiah speak these w in 1821
26:15 to you to speak all these w in your hearing." 1821
26:21 and officials heard his w, 1821
27:14 not listen to the w *of* the prophets who say 1821
28: 6 the w you have prophesied by bringing 1821
29:19 For they have not listened to my w," 1821
29:19 "w that I sent to them again and again NIH
30: 2 in a book all the w I have spoken to you. 1821
30: 4 the w the LORD spoke concerning Israel 1821
31:23 in its towns will once again use these w: 1821
35:13 not learn a lesson and obey my w?' 1821
36: 2 and write on it all the w I have spoken 1821
36: 4 and while Jeremiah dictated all the w 1821
36: 6 and read to the people from the scroll the w 1821
36: 8 at the LORD's temple he read the w *of* 1821
36:10 at the LORD's temple the w *of* Jeremiah 1821
36:11 the w *of* the LORD from the scroll, 1821
36:16 When they heard all these w, 1821
36:16 "We must report all these w to the king." 1821
36:18 "he dictated all these w to me, 1821
36:24 who heard all these w showed no fear, 1821
36:27 the king burned the scroll containing the w 1821
36:28 on it all the w that were on the first scroll, 1821
36:32 Baruch wrote on it all the w *of* the scroll 1821
36:32 And many similar w were added to them. 1821
37: 2 of the land paid any attention to the w 1821
39:16 I am about to fulfill my w against this city 1821
43: 1 the w *of* the LORD their God— 1821
45: 1 a scroll the w Jeremiah was then dictating: 1821
51:61 see that you read all these w aloud. 1821
51:64 The w *of* Jeremiah end here. 1821
Eze 2: 6 do not be afraid of them or their w. 1821
2: 7 You must speak my w to them, 1821
2:10 both sides of it were written w *of* lament 4180
3: 4 the house of Israel and speak my w to them. 1821
3: 6 whose w you cannot understand. 1821
3:10 and take to heart all the w I speak to you. 1821
12:28 None of my w will be delayed any longer; 1821
13: 6 yet they expect their w to be fulfilled. 1821
13: 8 Because of your false w and lying visions, 1819
33:31 and sit before you to listen to your w, 1821
33:32 for they hear your w but do not put them 1821
Da 4:31 The w were still on his lips when 10418
5:26 "This is *what* these w mean: 10418
7:11 of the boastful w the horn was speaking. 10418
9:12 You have fulfilled the w spoken against us 1821
10:11 consider carefully the w I am about to speak 1821
10:12 your w were heard, and I have come 1821
12: 4 up and seal the w of the scroll until the time 1821
12: 9 the w are closed up and sealed until the time 1821
Hos 6: 5 I killed you with the w *of* my mouth; 609
7:16 by the sword because of their insolent w. 4383
14: 2 Take w with you and return to the LORD. 1821
Am 1: 1 The w *of* Amos, one of the shepherds 1821
7:10 The land cannot bear all his w. 1821
8:11 a famine of hearing the w *of* the LORD. 1821
Mic 2: 7 "Do not my w do good to him whose ways 1821
7: 5 in your embrace be careful of your w. 7023+7339
Zec 1: 6 But did not my w and my decrees, 1821
1:13 the LORD spoke kind and comforting w to 1821
7: 7 Are these not the w the LORD proclaimed 1821
7:12 to the w that the LORD Almighty had sent 1821
8: 9 "You who now hear these w spoken by 1821
Mal 2:17 You have wearied the LORD with your w. 1821
Mt 6: 7 be heard because of their **many** w. *4494*
7:24 "Therefore everyone who hears these w *3364*
7:26 But everyone who hears these w of mine *3364*
10:14 not welcome you or listen to your w, *3364*
12: 7 If you had known what these w mean, *NIG*
12:37 For by your w you will be acquitted, *3364*
12:37 and by your w you will be condemned." *3364*
22:15 and laid plans to trap him in his w. *3364*
24:35 but my w will never pass away. *3364*
Mk 8:38 If anyone is ashamed of me and my w *3364*
10:24 The disciples were amazed at his w. *3364*
12:13 to Jesus to catch him *in* his w. *3364*
13:31 but my w will never pass away. *3364*
Lk 1:20 because you did not believe my w, *3364*
1:29 Mary was greatly troubled at his w *3364*
3: 4 As is written in the book *of* the w of Isaiah *3364*
3:18 And with many other w John exhorted *NIG*
4:22 and were amazed at the gracious w *3364*
6:47 and hears my w and puts them into practice. *3364*
6:49 But the one who hears my w and does *NIG*
7:29 when they heard Jesus' w, *NIG*
9:26 If anyone is ashamed of me and my w, *3364*
19:22 'I will judge you by your own w, *5125*
19:48 because all the people hung on his w. *NIG*
21:15 For I will give you w and wisdom that none *5125*
21:33 but my w will never pass away. *3364*
24: 8 Then they remembered his w. *4839*
24:11 their w seemed to them like nonsense. *4839*
Jn 1:23 John replied in the w of Isaiah the prophet, *NIG*
2:22 Then they believed the Scripture and the w *3364*
3:34 the one whom God has sent speaks the w *4839*
4:41 of his w many more became believers. *3364*
6:63 The w I have spoken to you are spirit *4839*
6:68 You have the w of eternal life. *4839*
7:40 On hearing his w, some of the people said, *3364*
8:20 He spoke these w while teaching in *4839*
10:19 At these w the Jews were again divided *3364*
12:47 for the person who hears my w but does *4839*
12:48 and does not accept my w; *4839*
14:10 The w I say to you are not just my own. *4839*
14:24 These w you hear are not my own; *3364*
15: 7 you remain in me and my w remain in you, *4839*
15:20 Remember the w I spoke to you: *3364*
17: 8 the w you gave me and they accepted them. *4839*
18: 9 that the w he had spoken would be fulfilled: *3364*
18:32 the w Jesus had spoken indicating the kind *3364*
Ac 2:40 *With* many other w he warned them; *3364*
6:11 "We have heard Stephen speak w *4839*
7:35 Moses whom they had rejected **with the** w, *3306*
7:38 and he received living w to pass on to us. *3359*
10:44 While Peter was still speaking these w, *4839*
13:27 yet in condemning him they fulfilled the w *5889*
13:34 never to decay, is stated **in these** w: *4048*
14:18 Even *with* these w, they had difficulty *3306*
15:15 The w of the prophets are in agreement *3364*
18:15 about w and names and your own law— *3364*
20: 2 speaking many w of encouragement to *3364*
20:35 the w the Lord Jesus himself said: *3364*
Ac 22:14 and to see the Righteous One and to hear w *5889*
Ro 3: 2 they have been entrusted with the very w *3359*
4:23 The w "it was credited to him" were written *NIG*
8:26 for us with groans *that* w **cannot express.** *227*
9: 8 **In other** w, it is not the natural *1639+4047*
10:18 their w to the ends of the world." *4839*
1Co 1:17 not with w of human wisdom, *3364*
2: 4 not with wise and persuasive w, *3364*
2:13 not in w taught us by human wisdom but *3364*
2:13 but in w taught by the Spirit, *NIG*
2:13 expressing spiritual truths in spiritual w. *NIG*
14: 9 you speak intelligible w with your tongue, *3364*
14:19 I would rather speak five intelligible w to *3364*
14:19 to instruct others than ten thousand w in *3364*
Gal 5: 2 **Mark my** w! I, Paul, tell you *3972*
Eph 5: 6 Let no one deceive you *with* empty w, *3364*
6:19 w may be given me so that I will fearlessly *3364*
1Th 1: 5 our gospel came to you not simply with w, *3364*
4:18 encourage each other with these w. *3364*
1Ti 6: 4 and **quarrels about** w that result in envy, *3363*
2Ti 2:14 before God against **quarreling about** w; *3362*
Heb 4: 4 about the seventh day **in these** w: *4048*
12:19 or to such a voice speaking w *4839*
12:27 The w "once more" indicate the removing *NIG*
1Pe 3: 1 without w by the behavior of their wives, *3364*
4:11 he should do it as one speaking the very w *3359*
2Pe 2:18 For *they* **mouth** empty, boastful w *5779*
3: 2 I want you to recall the w spoken in the past *4839*
1Jn 3:18 not love *with* w or tongue but with actions *3364*
Jude 1:15 the **harsh** w ungodly sinners have spoken *AIT*
Rev 1: 3 the one who reads the w of this prophecy, *3364*
2: 1 These are the w **of** him who holds *3306*
2: 8 These are the w **of** him who is the First and *3306*
2:12 These are the w **of** him who has the sharp, *3306*
2:18 These are the w **of** the Son of God, *3306*
3: 1 the w *of* him who holds the seven spirits *3306*
3: 7 These are the w **of** him who is holy *3306*
3:14 These are the w **of** the Amen, *3306*
13: 5 a mouth to utter proud w and blasphemies *NIG*
17:17 until God's w are fulfilled. *3364*
19: 9 he added, "These are the true w of God." *3364*
21: 5 for these w are trustworthy and true." *3364*
22: 6 "These w are trustworthy and true. *3364*
22: 7 the w of the prophecy in this book." *3364*
22: 9 and of all who keep the w of this book. *3364*
22:10 up the w of the prophecy of this book, *3364*
22:18 I warn everyone who hears the w of *3364*
22:19 And if anyone takes w away from this book *3364*

WORE (11) [WEAR]

Jos 9: 5 on their feet and w old clothes. 6584
1Sa 17: 5 and w a coat of scale armor of bronze 4229
17: 6 on his legs he w bronze greaves, NIH
22:18 That day he killed eighty-five men *who* w 5951
2Sa 13:18 the virgin daughters of the king w. 4252
1Ch 15:27 David also w a linen ephod. 6584
Ne 4:18 of the builders w his sword at his side 673
Ps 109:18 *He* w cursing as his garment; 4252
Mk 1: 6 John w **clothing** made of camel's hair, *1639+1907*
Rev 9: 7 On their heads they w something like crowns *NIG*
15: 6 and w golden sashes around their chests *4322*

WORK (394) [HARDWORKING, METALWORKER, WORKED, WORKER, WORKERS, WORKING, WORKMAN, WORKMAN'S, WORKMANSHIP, WORKMEN, WORKS]

Ge 2: 2 God had finished the w he had been doing; 4856
2: 2 on the seventh day he rested from all his w. 4856
2: 3 from all the w of creating that he had done. 4856
2: 5 on the earth and there was no man to w 6268
2:15 in the Garden of Eden to w it and take care 6268
3:23 from the Garden of Eden to w the ground 6268
4:12 When *you* w the ground, 6268
29:15 *should you* w **for** me for nothing? 6268
29:18 *"I'll* w **for** you seven years in return 6268
29:27 in return for another seven years of w." 6275
30:26 You know how much w I've done for you." 6275
Ex 1:14 in brick and mortar and with all kinds of w 6275
5: 4 Get back to your w!" 6026
5: 9 Make the w harder for the men so 6275
5:11 but your w will not be reduced at all.' " 6275
5:13 the w *required of* you for each day, 5126
5:18 Now get *to* w. 6268
12:16 Do no w at all on these days, 4856
18:18 The w is too heavy for you; 1821
20: 9 Six days you shall labor and do all your w, 4856
20:10 On it you shall not do any w, neither you, 4856
23:12 "Six days do your w, 5126
23:12 but on the seventh day **do not** w, 8697
26:36 the w *of* an embroiderer. 5126
27:16 the w *of* an embroiderer— 5126
28: 6 the w *of* a skilled craftsman. 5126
28:15 the w *of* a skilled craftsman. 5126
28:39 The sash is to be the w *of* an embroiderer. 5126
30:25 a fragrant blend, the w *of* a perfumer. 5126
30:35 the w *of* a perfumer. 5126
31: 4 to make artistic designs for w in gold, 6913
31: 5 to cut and set stones, to w *in* wood, 3098
31:14 whoever does any w on that day must 4856
31:15 For six days, w is to be done, 4856
31:15 Whoever does any w on the Sabbath day 4856
31:17 on the seventh day *he* **abstained from** w 8697
32:16 The tablets were the w *of* God; 5126

Ex 34:10 will see how awesome is the w that I, 5126
35: 2 For six days, w is to be done, 4856
35: 2 Whoever does any w on it must be put 4856
35:21 an offering to the LORD for the w *on* 4856
35:24 for any part of the w brought it. 6275
35:29 the LORD freewill offerings for all the w 4856
35:32 to make artistic designs for w in gold, 6913
35:33 to w *in* wood and to engage in all kinds 3098
35:35 with skill to do all kinds of w *as* craftsmen, 4856
36: 1 how to carry out all the w *of* constructing 4856
36: 1 the sanctuary *are to* **do** *the* w just as 6913
36: 2 and who was willing to come and do the **w.** 4856
36: 3 the Israelites had brought to carry out the w 4856
36: 4 the w *on* the sanctuary left their work 4856
36: 4 the work on the sanctuary left their w 4856
36: 5 the w the LORD commanded to be done." 4856
36: 7 more than enough to do all the **w.** 4856
36:37 the w *of* an embroiderer; 5126
37:29 the w *of* a perfumer. 5126
38:18 the w *of* an embroiderer. 5126
38:24 from the wave offering used for all the w *on* 4856
39: 3 the w *of* a skilled craftsman. 5126
39: 8 the w *of* a skilled craftsman. 5126
39:22 the w *of* a weaver— 5126
39:27 the w *of* a weaver— 5126
39:29 the w *of* an embroiderer— 5126
39:32 So all the w *on* the tabernacle, 6275
39:42 The Israelites had done all the w just as 6275
39:43 the w and saw that they had done it just as 4856
40:33 And so Moses finished the **w.** 4856
Lev 16:29 deny yourselves and not do any **w—** 4856
23: 3 'There are six days when *you may* **w,** 4856+6913
23: 3 You are not to do any **w;** 4856
23: 7 sacred assembly and do no **regular w.** 4856+6275
23: 8 sacred assembly and do no **regular w.** 4856+6275
23:21 sacred assembly and do no **regular w.** 4856+6275
23:25 Do no **regular w,** 4856+6275
23:28 Do no w on that day, 4856
23:30 among his people anyone who does any w 4856
23:31 You shall do no w at all. 4856
23:35 a sacred assembly; do no **regular w.** 4856+6275
23:36 closing assembly; do no **regular w.** 4856+6275
25:39 *do* not **make** him w as a slave. 6268
25:40 *he is to* w for you until the Year of Jubilee. 6268
Nu 3: 7 at the Tent of Meeting by doing the w *of* 6275
3: 8 of the Israelites by doing the w *of* 6275
4: 3 to serve in the w in the Tent of Meeting. 4856
4: 4 "This is the w *of* the Kohathites in the Tent 6275
4:19 and assign to each man his w and what he is 6275
4:23 serve in the w at the Tent of Meeting. 6268+6275
4:24 of the Gershonite clans *as* they w 6268
4:27 whether carrying or **doing** other **w,** 6275
4:30 serve in the w *at* the Tent of Meeting. 6268+6275
4:33 the service of the Merarite clans as they w 6275
4:35 to serve in the w in the Tent of Meeting, 6275
4:39 to serve in the w at the Tent of Meeting, 6275
4:43 to serve in the w at the Tent of Meeting, 6275
4:47 to do the w *of* serving and carrying the Tent 6275
4:49 each was assigned his w and told what 6275
7: 5 that they may be used in the w *at* the Tent 6275
7: 5 to the Levites as each man's w requires." 6275
7: 7 to the Gershonites, as their w required, 6275
7: 8 to the Merarites, as their w required. 6275
8:11 so that they may be ready to do the w *of* 6275
8:15 they are to come to **do** *their* w at the Tent 6268
8:19 as gifts to Aaron and his sons to do the w at 6275
8:22 to do their w at the Tent of Meeting under 6275
8:24 to take part in the w *at* the Tent of Meeting, 6275
8:25 from their regular service and w no longer. 6268
8:26 but they themselves must not do the **w.** 6275
16: 9 and brought you near himself to do the w *at* 6275
18: 4 all the w *at* the Tent— 6275
18: 6 dedicated to the LORD to do the w *at* 6275
18:21 in return for the w they do while serving at 6275
18:23 to do the w *at* the Tent of Meeting and bear 6275
18:31 for it is your wages for your w at the Tent 6275
28:18 sacred assembly and do no **regular w.** 4856+6275
28:25 sacred assembly and do no **regular w.** 4856+6275
28:26 sacred assembly and do no **regular w.** 4856+6275
29: 1 sacred assembly and do no **regular w.** 4856+6275
29: 7 You must deny yourselves and do no w. 4856
29:12 sacred assembly and do no **regular w.** 4856+6275
29:35 an assembly and do no **regular w.** 4856+6275
Dt 2: 7 blessed you in all the w *of* your hands. 5126
5:13 Six days you shall labor and do all your **w,** 4856
5:14 On it you shall not do any **w,** neither you, 4856
14:29 bless you in all the w *of* your hands. 5126+6913
15:10 will bless you in all your w and 5126
15:19 **put** the firstborn of your oxen **to w,** 6268
16: 8 to the LORD your God and do no **w.** 4856
16:15 in all your harvest and in all the w 5126
20:11 be subject to forced labor and *shall* **w for** 6268
24:19 in all the w *of* your hands. 5126
27:15 the w *of* the craftsman's hands— 5126
28:12 on your land in season and to bless all the w 5126
30: 9 in all the w *of* your hands and in the fruit 5126
33:11 and be pleased with the w *of* his hands. 7189
Jdg 13:12 to be the rule for the boy's life and **w?"** 5126
19:16 came in from his w in the fields. 5126
Ru 2:19 Where *did you* **w?** 6913
2Sa 12:31 and *he* **made** them w at brickmaking. 6296
1Ki 5: 6 My men *will* w with yours, 2118
7:14 and experienced in all kinds of bronze **w.** 4856
7:14 to King Solomon and did all the w *assigned* 4856
7:22 And so the w *on* the pillars was completed. 4856
7:29 and bulls were wreaths of hammered **w.** 5126
7:40 the w he had undertaken for King Solomon 4856
1Ki 7:49 the gold **floral** w and lamps and tongs; 7258
7:51 When all the w King Solomon had done for 4856
9:23 supervising the men who did the **w.** 4856
11:28 how well the young man did his **w,** 4856
2Ki 12:11 to the men appointed to supervise the w on 4856
22: 5 to the men appointed to supervise the w on 4856
25:12 of the land to w *the* **vineyards** and fields. 4144
1Ch 9:33 because they were responsible for the w day 4856
22:15 as well as men skilled in every kind of w 4856
22:16 begin *the* **w,** and the LORD be with you." 6913
23: 4 twenty-four thousand are to supervise the w 4856
26: 8 with the strength to do the **w—** 6275
26:30 in Israel west of the Jordan for all the w *of* 4856
28:10 Be strong and **do** *the* **w."** 6913
28:13 and for all the w *of* serving in the temple of 4856
28:20 "Be strong and courageous, and **do** the **w.** 6913
28:20 or forsake you until all the w *for* the service 4856
28:21 and Levites are ready for all the w *on* 6275
28:21 in any craft will help you in all the **w.** 4856
29: 2 gold for the **gold** *w,* silver for the silver, AIT
29: 5 for the **gold** *w* and the silver work, AIT
29: 5 for the gold work and the **silver** *w,* AIT
29: 5 for all the w to be done by the craftsmen. 4856
29: 6 in charge of the king's w gave willingly. 4856
29: 7 They gave toward the w *on* the temple 6275
2Ch 2: 7 a man skilled to w in gold and silver, 6913
2: 7 to w in Judah and Jerusalem NIH
2: 8 My men will w with yours NIH
2:14 He is trained to w in gold and silver, 6913
2:14 He will w with your craftsmen and NIH
4:11 So Huram finished the w he had undertaken 4856
4:21 the gold **floral** w and lamps 7258
5: 1 the w Solomon had done for the temple of 4856
8: 9 not make slaves of the Israelites for his **w;** 4856
8:16 All Solomon's w was carried out, 4856
15: 7 for your w will be rewarded." 7190
16: 5 and abandoned his **w.** 4856
24:12 the men who carried out the w required for 4856
24:13 The men in charge of the w were diligent, 4856
27: 3 the LORD and **did** extensive w on the wall 1215
29:12 Then these Levites **set to w:** 7756
32:19 the w *of* men's hands. 5126
34:10 to supervise the w on the LORD's temple. 4856
34:12 The men did the w faithfully. 4856
Ezr 2:69 to the treasury for this w 61,000 drachmas 4856
3: 8 the captivity to Jerusalem) began the **w,** NIH
4: 5 to w against them and frustrate their plans NIH
4:21 Now issue an order to these men to **stop w,** 10098
4:24 Thus the w *on* the house of God 10525
5: 2 **set to w** to rebuild the house 10221+10624+10742
5: 8 The w is being carried on with diligence 10525
6: 7 Do not interfere with the w *on* this temple 10525
6: 8 so that the w will not stop. NIH
6:22 that he assisted them in the w *on* the house 4856
Ne 2:16 or any others who would be doing the **w.** 4856
2:18 So they began this **good w.** 3208
3: 1 and his fellow priests **went to** w and rebuilt 7756
3: 5 to the w *under* their supervisors. 6275
4:11 and will kill them and put an end to the **w."** 4856
4:15 returned to the wall, each to his own **w.** 4856
4:16 half of my men did the **w,** 4856
4:17 Those who carried materials did their w 4856
4:19 "The w is extensive and spread out, 4856
4:21 the w with half the men holding spears, 4856
5:16 I devoted myself to the w *on* this wall. 4856
5:16 All my men were assembled there for the **w;** 4856
6: 3 the w stop while I leave it and go down 4856
6: 9 "Their hands will get too weak for the **w,** 4856
6:16 that this w had been done with the help 4856
7:70 of the families contributed to the **w.** 4856
7:71 to the treasury for the w 20,000 drachmas 4856
10:37 the tithes in all the towns where we **w.** 6275
11:12 who carried on w for the temple— 4856
11:16 of the outside w of the house of God; 4856
Job 1:10 You have blessed the w *of* his hands, 5126
10: 3 to spurn the w *of* your hands, 3330
23: 9 he **is at w** in the north, I do not see him; 6913
34:19 for they are all the w *of* his hands? 5126
36:24 Remember to extol his **w,** 7189
37: 7 that all men he has made may know his **w,** NIH
39:11 Will you leave your **heavy** w to him? 3330
Ps 8: 3 your heavens, the w *of* your fingers, 5126
9:16 the wicked are ensnared by the w 7189
19: 1 the skies proclaim the w *of* his hands. 5126
28: 4 for their deeds and for their evil **w;** 5095
55:11 Destructive forces are at w in the city; NIH
90:17 establish the w *of* our hands for us— 5126
90:17 yes, establish the w *of* our hands. 5126
102:25 and the heavens are the w *of* your hands. 5126
104:13 the earth is satisfied by the fruit of his **w.** 5126
104:23 Then man goes out to his **w,** 7189
Pr 12:14 surely as the w *of* his hands rewards him. 1691
14:23 All **hard** w brings a profit, 6776
18: 9 in his w is brother to one who destroys. 4856
21:25 because his hands refuse to **w.** 6913
22:29 Do you see a man skilled in his **w?** 4856
24:27 Finish your outdoor w and 4856
31:17 *She* **sets about** her w vigorously; 2520+5516
Ecc 2:10 My heart took delight in all my **w,** 6662
2:17 because the w that is done under the sun 5126
2:19 the w into which I have poured my effort 6662
2:21 For a man may do his w with wisdom, 6662
2:23 All his days his w is pain and grief; 6721
2:24 and drink and find satisfaction in his **w.** 6662
3:22 for a man than to enjoy his **w,** 5126
4: 9 because they have a good return for their **w:** 6662
5: 6 be angry at what you say and destroy the w 5126
Ecc 5:19 to accept his lot and be happy in his **w—** 6662
8:15 Then joy will accompany him in his w all 6662
10:15 A fool's w wearies him; 6662
11: 5 so you cannot understand the w *of* God, 5126
SS 7: 1 the w *of* a craftsman's hands. 5126
Isa 1:31 man will become tinder and his w a spark; 7189
2: 8 they bow down to the w *of* their hands, 5126
5:12 no respect for the w *of* his hands. 5126
5:19 let him hasten his w so we may see it. 5126
10:12 When the Lord has finished all his w 5126
17: 8 not look to the altars, the w *of* their hands, 5126
19: 9 *Those who* w *with* combed flax will despair, 6268
28:21 to do his w, his strange work, 5126
28:21 to do his work, his strange **w,** 5126
29:15 who do their w in darkness and think, 5126
29:23 the w *of* my hands, 5126
30:24 and donkeys *that* w the soil will eat fodder 6268
45: 9 Does your w say, 'He has no hands'? 7189
45:11 or give me orders about the w *of* my hands? 7189
54:16 into flame and forges a weapon fit for its **w.** 5126
54:16 the destroyer to **w havoc;** 2472
60:21 shoot I have planted, the w *of* my hands, 5126
61: 5 foreigners will w your **fields** 438
64: 8 we are all the w *of* your hand. 5126
Jer 17:22 of your houses or do any w on the Sabbath, 4856
17:24 the Sabbath day holy by not doing any w 4856
22:13 **making** his countrymen w for nothing, 6268
25:14 to their deeds and the w *of* their hands." 5126
31:16 for your w will be rewarded," 7190
48:10 on him who is lax in doing the LORD's **w!** 4856
50:25 for the Sovereign LORD Almighty has w 4856
52:16 of the land to w the **vineyards** and fields. 4144
La 4: 2 the w *of* a potter's hands! 5126
Eze 27:14 of Beth Togarmah exchanged w **horses,** 6061
27:16 purple fabric, **embroidered w,** fine linen, 8391
27:24 **embroidered** w and multicolored rugs 8391
44:14 of the temple and all the w that is to be done 6275
Hos 13: 2 all of them the w *of* craftsmen. 5126
Mic 5:13 you will no longer bow down to the w 5126
Na 3:14 **W** the clay, tread the mortar, 995
Hag 1:14 to w on the house of the LORD Almighty, 4856
2: 4 'and **w.** For I am with you,' 6913
2:17 I struck all the w *of* your hands with blight, 5126
Mt 14: 2 That is why miraculous powers *are* **at w in** *1919*
20: 1 to hire **men to** w in his vineyard. *2239*
20: 4 'You also go and w in my vineyard, *NIG*
20: 7 'You also go and w in my vineyard.' *NIG*
20:12 the burden of the w and the heat of the day.' *NIG*
20:13 Didn't you agree to w for a denarius? *NIG*
21:28 'Son, go and w today in the vineyard.' *2237*
25:16 **put** his money to w and gained five more. *2237*
Mk 6:14 that is why miraculous powers *are* **at w in** *1919*
Lk 10:40 that my sister has left me *to* **do the w** *1354*
13:14 There are six days for **w.** *1256+1877+2237+4005*
19:13 **'Put** this money **to w,'** he said, *4549*
Jn 4:34 of him who sent me and to finish his **w.** *2240*
4:38 Others *have done the* **hard w,** *3159*
5:17 "My Father is always **at** his w to this very *2237*
5:36 For the very w that the Father has given me *2240*
6:27 *Do* not w **for** food that spoils, but for *2237*
6:29 Jesus answered, "The w of God is this: *2240*
9: 3 the w of God might be displayed in his life. *2240*
9: 4 we must do the w of him who sent me. *2240*
9: 4 Night is coming, when no one can **w.** *2237*
14:10 living in me, who is doing his **w.** *2240*
17: 4 on earth by completing the w you gave me *2240*
Ac 13: 2 for the w to which I have called them." *2240*
13:25 As John was completing his **w,** he said: *1536*
14:26 of God for the w they had now completed. *2240*
15:38 and had not continued with them in the **w.** *2240*
20:35 that by this kind of **hard** w we must help *3159*
Ro 4: 5 not w but trusts God who justifies *2237*
7: 5 by the law *were* **at w in** our bodies, *1919*
7:21 So I find this law at **w:** *NIG*
7:23 but I see another law at w in the members *NIG*
7:23 of the law of sin **at w** within my members. *1639*
14:20 Do not destroy the w of God for the sake *2240*
15:23 now that there is no more place for me to w *NIG*
16:12 those women who w **hard** in the Lord. *3159*
1Co 3:13 his w will be shown for what it is, *2240*
3:13 fire will test the quality of each man's **w.** *2240*
4:12 *We* w **hard** with our own hands. *2237+3159*
9: 1 Are you not the result of my w in the Lord? *2240*
9: 6 and Barnabas who must w **for a living?** *2237*
9:13 Don't you know that those who w in *2237*
12:11 the w of one and the same Spirit, *1919*
12:29 Do all w **miracles?** *1539*
15:58 Always give yourselves fully to the w of *2240*
16: 9 a great door for **effective** w has opened *1921*
16:10 for he is carrying on the w of the Lord, *2240*
16:16 and *to* everyone who **joins in the w,** *5300*
2Co 1:24 but *we* **w with** you for your joy, *1639+5301*
4:12 So then, death *is* **at w in** us, *1919*
4:12 but life is at w in you. *NIG*
6: 5 in **hard w,** sleepless nights and hunger; *3160*
8:11 Now finish the **w,** so that your eager *4472*
9: 8 you will abound in every good **w.** *2240*
10:15 beyond our limits by boasting of w done *3160*
10:16 not want to boast about w **already done** *2289*
Gal 2: 8 *at* **w in** the ministry of Peter as an apostle *1919*
2: 8 *was* also **at w in** my ministry as an apostle *1919*
3: 5 and w miracles **among** you *1919*
Eph 2: 2 now **at w in** those who are disobedient. *1919*
3:20 according to his power that *is* **at w within** *1919*
4:16 as each part does its **w.** *1918*
4:28 but *must* **w,** doing something useful *3159*
Php 1: 6 who began a good w in you will carry it on *2240*

Php 2:12 *continue to* w **out** your salvation *2981*
2:22 with me in the w of the gospel. *NIG*
2:30 because he almost died for the w of Christ, *2240*
Col 1:10 bearing fruit in every good w, *2240*
3:23 Whatever you do, w at it with all your heart, *2237*
4:17 that you complete the w you have received *1355*
1Th 1:3 before our God and Father your w produced *2240*
2:13 which *is* **at** w **in** you who believe. *1919*
4:11 to mind your own business and *to* w *2237*
5:12 to respect those who w **hard** among you, *3159*
5:13 highest regard in love because of their w. *2240*
2Th 2:7 power of lawlessness *is* already **at** w; *1919*
2:9 in accordance with the w of Satan displayed *1918*
2:13 through the sanctifying w of the Spirit and *NIG*
3:10 "If a man will not w, he shall not eat." *2237*
1Ti 1:4 These promote controversies rather than God's w— *3873*
5:17 especially those whose w is preaching *3159*
2Ti 2:21 the Master and prepared to do any good w. *2240*
3:17 be thoroughly equipped for every good w. *2240*
4:5 endure hardship, do the w of an evangelist, *2240*
Tit 1:7 an overseer is **entrusted with** God's w, *3874*
Heb 1:10 and the heavens are the w of your hands. *2240*
4:3 And yet his w has been finished since *2240*
4:4 the seventh day God rested from all his w." *2240*
4:10 also rests from his own w, *2240*
6:10 he will not forget your w and *2240*
13:17 Obey them so that **their** w will be a joy, *4047S*
13:21 and *may he* w in us what is pleasing to him, *4472*
Jas 1:4 Perseverance must finish its w so *2240*
1Pe 1:2 through the sanctifying *w of* the **Spirit,** *AIT*
1:17 Father who judges each man's w impartially, *2240*
1Jn 3:8 God appeared was to destroy the devil's w. *2240*
2Jn 1:11 who welcomes him shares *in* his wicked w. *2240*
3Jn 1:8 that *we may* w **together** for the truth. *1181+5301*
Rev 2:2 your **hard** w and your perseverance. *3160*
9:20 by these plagues still did not repent of the w *2240*

WORKED (44) [WORK]

Ge 4:2 Now Abel kept flocks, and Cain w the soil. 6268
29:30 And *he* w for Laban another seven years. 6268
30:29 "You know how *I have* w **for** you and 6268
31:6 You know that *I've* w **for** your father 6268
31:41 *I* w **for** you fourteen years 6268
Ex 1:13 and w them ruthlessly. 6268
26:1 with cherubim w *into* them *by* a skilled 5126
26:31 with cherubim w *into* it *by* a skilled 5126
36:8 with cherubim w *into* them *by* a skilled 5126
36:35 with cherubim w *into* it *by* a skilled 5126
39:3 and cut strands to *be* w into the blue, purple 6913
Dt 21:3 that *has* never **been** w and has never worn 6268
Ru 2:7 and *has* w *steadily* from morning till now, 6641
2:19 of the man *I* w with today is Boaz," 6913
2Ki 12:11 With it they paid those who w on the temple 6913
1Ch 4:23 they stayed there and w for the king. 4856
2Ch 3:14 and fine linen, with cherubim w into it. 6590
25:20 for God so w that he might hand them over 4946
31:21 he sought his God and w wholeheartedly. 6913
32:5 Then *he* w **hard** repairing all the broken 2616
Ne 3:25 and Palal son of Uzai w opposite the angle NIH
4:6 for the people w with all their heart. 6913
4:18 wore his sword at his side as *he* w. 1215
Est 10:3 because *he* w **for** the good of his people 2011
Ps 98:1 and his holy arm *have* w **salvation** 3828
Ecc 2:21 to someone who *has* not w for it. 6661
Isa 59:16 so his own arm w **salvation** for him, 3828
63:5 so my own arm w **salvation** for me, 3828
Eze 23:29 and take away everything you have w *for.* 3330
Joel 2:26 who *has* w wonders for you; 6913
Mt 13:33 until *it* w all **through the dough."** *2435*
20:12 men who were hired last w only one hour,' *4472*
Mk 16:20 and the Lord w **with** them and confirmed *5300*
Lk 5:5 "Master, we've w **hard** all night *3159*
13:21 until *it* w all **through the dough."** *2435*
Jn 4:38 I sent you to reap what you *have* not w **for.** *3159*
Ac 18:3 he stayed and w with them. *2237*
Ro 16:6 Greet Mary, who w very hard for you. *3159*
16:12 another woman who *has* w very **hard** in *3159*
1Co 15:10 No, *I* w harder than all of them— *3159*
2Co 11:23 I have w much harder, *3160*
1Th 2:9 *we* w night and day in order not to be *2237*
2Th 3:8 On the contrary, *we* w night and day, *2237*
2Jn 1:8 that you do not lose what *you have* w **for,** *2237*

WORKER (14) [WORK]

Ex 12:45 but a temporary resident and a **hired** w may 8502
Lev 22:10 nor may the guest of a priest or his **hired** w 8502
25:6 the **hired** w and temporary resident who 8502
25:40 treated as a **hired** w or a temporary resident 8502
Ecc 3:9 What does the w gain from his toil? 6913
Mt 10:10 for the w is worth his keep. *2239*
Lk 10:7 for the w deserves his wages. *2239*
Ro 16:9 Greet Urbanus, our **fellow** w in Christ, *5301*
16:21 Timothy, my **fellow** w, sends his greetings *5301*
2Co 8:23 Titus, he is my partner and **fellow** w *5301*
Php 2:25 my brother, **fellow** w and fellow soldier, *5301*
1Th 3:2 who is our brother and God's **fellow** w *5301*
1Ti 5:18 and "The w deserves his wages." *2239*
Phm 1:1 *To* Philemon our dear friend and **fellow** w, *5301*

WORKERS (30) [WORK]

Ru 2:21 'Stay with my w until they finish 5853
2Ki 12:15 they gave the money to pay the w, 4856+6913
22:5 have these men pay the w who repair 4856+6913
22:9 and have entrusted it to the w 4856+6913
1Ch 4:21 clans of the linen w at Beth Ashbea, 1074+6275
23:24 the w twenty years old or more who 4856+6913
27:26 in charge of the field w who farmed 4856+6913
2Ch 24:12 w *in* iron and bronze to repair the temple. 3093
34:10 the w who repaired and restored the temple. 6913
34:13 supervised all the w from job to job. 4856+6913
34:17 to the supervisors and w." 4856+6913
Ezr 7:24 temple servants or other w *at* this house 10586
Isa 19:10 The w **in cloth** will be dejected, 9271
58:3 you do as you please and exploit all your w. 6774
Jer 10:9 blue and purple— all made by **skilled** *w.* AIT
Eze 48:18 Its produce will supply food for the w *of* 6268
48:19 The w *from* the city who farm it will come 6268
Mt 9:37 "The harvest is plentiful but the w are few. *2239*
9:38 to send out w into his harvest field." *2239*
20:8 'Call the w and pay them their wages, *2239*
20:9 "The w who were hired about *NIG*
Lk 10:2 "The harvest is plentiful, but the w are few. *2239*
10:2 to send out w into his harvest field. *2239*
Ro 16:3 and Aquila, my **fellow** w in Christ Jesus. *5301*
1Co 3:9 For we are God's **fellow** w; *5301*
12:28 third teachers, then w **of miracles,** *1539*
2Co 6:1 As God's **fellow** w we urge you not *5300*
Php 4:3 and the rest *of* my **fellow** w, *5301*
Col 4:11 the only Jews among my **fellow** w for *5301*
Phm 1:24 Demas and Luke, my **fellow** w. *5301*

WORKING (19) [WORK]

Ex 5:5 and you are stopping them from w." 6026
5:9 so that *they keep* w and pay no attention 6913
15:11 awesome in glory, w wonders? 6913
Ru 2:3 she found herself w in a field belonging NIH
2:19 the one at whose place *she had been* w. 6913
2Ch 2:18 foremen over them to **keep** the people w. 6268
26:10 He had people w his **fields and vineyards** 4144
Ezr 3:9 in supervising *those* w *on* the house of God. 6913
Ne 10:31 Every seventh year we will forgo w the land NIH
Ecc 9:10 there is neither w nor planning 5126
Jer 18:3 and I saw him w at the wheel. 4856+6913
Eze 46:1 is to be shut on the six w days, 5126
Jn 5:17 his work to this very day, and I, too, *am* w." *2237*
1Co 12:6 There are different kinds *of* w, *1920*
Eph 1:19 power is like the w of his mighty strength, *1918*
3:7 of God's grace given me through the w *1918*
Col 3:23 as w for the Lord, not for men, *NIG*
4:13 I vouch for him that *he* is w hard for you *4506*
Jas 2:22 and his actions *were* w **together,** *5300*

WORKMAN (2) [MAN, WORK]

2Ti 2:15 a w who does not need to be ashamed *2239*
Rev 18:22 No w of any trade will ever be found *5493*

WORKMAN'S (1) [MAN, WORK]

Jdg 5:26 her right hand for the w hammer. 6664

WORKMANSHIP (1) [WORK]

Eph 2:10 For we are God's w, created in Christ Jesus *4473*

WORKMEN (8) [MAN, WORK]

Ex 36:8 the w made the tabernacle with ten 4856+6913
1Ki 5:16 supervised the project and directed the w. 928+2021+4856+6913
2Ki 12:14 it was paid to the w, who used it 4856+6913
1Ch 22:15 You have many w: stonecutters, 4856+6913
Ne 4:22 as guards by night and w by day." 4856
Ac 19:25 along with the w in related trades, and said: *2239*
2Co 11:13 such men are false apostles, deceitful w, *2239*
Jas 5:4 the w who mowed your fields are crying out *2239*

WORKS (67) [WORK]

Dt 3:24 the deeds and **mighty** w you do? 1476
20:20 not fruit trees and use them to build **siege** w 5189
32:4 He is the Rock, his w are perfect, 7189
2Ki 25:1 the city and built **siege** w all around it. 1911
Job 26:14 And these are but the outer fringe of his w; 2006
40:19 He ranks first among the w *of* God, 2006
Ps 8:6 You made him ruler over the w *of* your 5126
28:5 Since they show no regard for the w *of* 7190
46:8 Come and see the w *of* the LORD, 5149
64:9 they will proclaim the w *of* God and ponder 7189
66:5 how awesome his w in man's behalf! 6613
77:12 I will meditate on all your w 7189
92:4 I sing for joy at the w *of* your hands. 5126
92:5 How great are your w, O LORD, 5126
103:6 The LORD w righteousness and justice 6913
103:22 all his w everywhere in his dominion. 5126
104:24 How many are your w, O LORD! 5126
104:31 may the LORD rejoice in his w— 5126
107:22 and tell of his w with songs of joy. 5126
107:24 They saw the w *of* the LORD, 5126
111:2 Great are the w *of* the LORD; 5126
111:6 the power of his w, 5126
111:7 The w *of* his hands are faithful and just; 5126
138:8 do not abandon the w *of* your hands. 5126
139:14 your w are wonderful, I know that full well. 5126
143:5 I meditate on all your w 7189
145:4 One generation will commend your w 5126
145:5 and I will meditate on your **wonderful** *w.* AIT
145:6 of the power of your **awesome** w, 3707
Pr 8:22 as the first of his w, before his deeds of old; 2006
12:11 *He who* w his land will have abundant food, 6268
16:4 The LORD w **out** everything 7188
16:26 The laborer's appetite w for him; 6661
26:28 and a flattering mouth w ruin. 6913
28:19 *He who* w his land will have abundant food, 6268
31:13 and flax and w with eager hands. 6913
31:31 let her w bring her praise at the city gate. 5126
Isa 29:3 and set up my **siege** w against you. 5193
41:24 and your w are utterly worthless; 7189
44:12 The blacksmith takes a tool and w with it in 7188
57:12 expose your righteousness and your w, 5126
65:22 my chosen ones will long enjoy the w 5126
Jer 11:15 in my temple *as* she w **out** her evil schemes 6913
52:4 the city and built **siege** w all around it. 1911
Eze 4:2 Then lay siege to it: Erect **siege** w against it, 1911
17:17 and **siege** w erected to destroy many lives. 1911
21:22 to build a ramp and to erect **siege** w. 1911
26:8 he will set up **siege** w against you, 1911
Jn 6:28 must we do to do the w God requires?" *2240*
7:18 but he who w **for** the honor of the one who *2426*
Ro 4:2 If, in fact, Abraham was justified by w, *2240*
4:4 Now *when* a man w, his wages are not *2237*
4:6 God credits righteousness apart from w: *2240*
8:28 And we know that in all things God w for *5300*
9:12 not by w but by him who calls— *2240*
9:32 not by faith but as if it were by w. *2240*
11:6 And if by grace, then it is no longer by w; *2240*
16:23 who is the city's **director of public** w, *3874*
1Co 5:6 Don't you know that a little yeast w **through** the whole batch *2435*
12:6 but the same God w all of them in all men. *1919*
Gal 5:9 "A little yeast w **through** the whole batch *2435*
Eph 1:11 *of* him who w **out** everything in conformity *1919*
2:9 not by w, so that no one can boast. *2240*
2:10 created in Christ Jesus to do good w, *2240*
4:12 to prepare God's people for w of service, *2240*
Php 2:13 for it is God who w **in** you to will and to act *1919*
Col 1:29 his energy, which so powerfully w **in** me. *1919*

WORLD (261) [WORLD'S, WORLDLY]

Ge 11:1 Now the whole w had one language and 824
11:9 the language of the whole w. 824
41:57 because the famine was severe in all the w. 824
Ex 34:10 before done in any nation in all the w. 824
1Sa 2:8 upon them he has set the w. 9315
17:46 the whole w will know that there is a God 824
1Ki 4:34 sent by all the kings of the w, 824
8:53 of the w to be your own inheritance, 824
10:24 The whole w sought audience 824
2Ki 5:15 that there is no God in all the w except 824
1Ch 16:30 The w is firmly established; 9315
2Ch 32:19 about the gods of the other peoples of the w 824
Job 18:18 into darkness and is banished from the w. 9315
34:13 Who put him in charge of the whole w? 9315
Ps 9:8 He will judge the w in righteousness; 9315
17:14 of this w whose reward is in this life. 2698
19:4 their words to the ends of the w. 9315
24:1 the w, and all who live in it; 9315
33:8 let all the people of the w revere him. 9315
49:1 listen, all who live in this w, 2698
50:12 for the w is mine, and all that is in it. 9315
77:18 your lightning lit up the w; 9315
89:11 you founded the w and all that is in it. 9315
90:2 or you brought forth the earth and the w, 9315
93:1 The w is firmly established; 9315
96:10 The w is firmly established, 9315
96:13 He will judge the w in righteousness and 9315
97:4 His lightning lights up the w; 9315
98:7 the w, and all who live in it. 9315
98:9 He will judge the w in righteousness and 9315
Pr 8:23 from the beginning, before the w began. 824
8:26 or its fields or any of the dust of the w. 9315
8:31 rejoicing in his **whole** w and delighting 824+9315
Isa 12:5 let this be known to all the w. 824
13:11 I will punish the w for its evil, 9315
14:9 all those who were leaders in the w; 824
14:17 the man who made the w a desert, 9315
14:26 the plan determined for the whole w; 824
18:3 All you people of the w, 9315
24:4 the w languishes and withers, 9315
26:9 the people of the w learn righteousness. 9315
26:18 we have not given birth to people of the w. 9315
27:6 and blossom and fill all the w with fruit. 9315
34:1 Let the earth hear, and all that is in it, the w, 9315
38:11 or be with those who now dwell in **this** w. 2535
40:23 and reduces the rulers of this w to nothing 824
Jer 10:12 he founded the w by his wisdom and 9315
51:15 he founded the w by his wisdom and 9315
Eze 20:32 like the peoples of the w, 824
Da 4:1 who live in all the w: 10075
Na 1:5 the w and all who live in it. 9315
Zep 1:18 In the fire of his jealousy the whole w will 824
3:8 The whole w will be consumed by the fire 824
Zec 1:11 and found the whole w at rest and in peace." 824
6:5 in the presence of the Lord of the whole w. 824
Mt 4:8 and showed him all the kingdoms *of* the w *3180*
5:14 "You are the light *of* the w. *3180*
13:35 since the creation *of* the w." *3180*
13:38 The field is the w, *3180*
16:26 if he gains the whole w, yet forfeits his soul? *3180*
18:7 "Woe *to* the w because of the things *3180*
24:14 in the whole w as a testimony to all nations, *3876*
24:21 from the beginning *of* the w until now— *3180*
25:34 for you since the creation *of* the w. *3180*
26:13 the w, what she has done will also be told, *3180*
Mk 8:36 to gain the whole w, yet forfeits his soul? *3180*
9:3 than anyone in the w could bleach them. *1178*
13:19 when God created the w, until now— *3232*
14:9 the gospel is preached throughout the w, *3180*

Mk 16:15 into all the w and preach the good news *3180*
Lk 2: 1 be taken of the entire **Roman** w. *3876*
4: 5 in an instant all the kingdoms *of* the w. *3876*
9:25 for a man to gain the whole w, *3180*
11:50 shed since the beginning *of* the w, *3180*
12:30 For the pagan w runs after all such things, *3180*
16: 8 For the people *of* this w are more shrewd *172*
21:26 apprehensive of what is coming on the w, *3876*
Jn 1: 9 to every man was coming into the w. *3180*
1:10 He was in the w, and though the world was *3180*
1:10 and though the w was made through him, *3180*
1:10 the w did not recognize him. *3180*
1:29 who takes away the sin *of* the w! *3180*
3:16 the w that he gave his one and only Son, *3180*
3:17 For God did not send his Son into the w *3180*
3:17 into the world to condemn the w, *3180*
3:17 but to save the w through him. *3180*
3:19 Light has come into the w, *3180*
4:42 that this man really is the Savior *of* the w." *3180*
6:14 the Prophet who is to come into the w." *3180*
6:33 down from heaven and gives life *to* the w." *3180*
6:51 which I will give for the life *of* the w." *3180*
7: 4 doing these things, show yourself *to* the w." *3180*
7: 7 The w cannot hate you, but it hates me *3180*
8:12 he said, "I am the light *of* the w. *3180*
8:23 You are of this w; I am not of this world. *3180*
8:23 You are of this world; I am not of this w. *3180*
8:26 what I have heard from him I tell the w." *3180*
9: 5 I am in the w, I am the light of the world." *3180*
9: 5 I am in the world, I am the light *of* the w." *3180*
9:39 "For judgment I have come into this w, *3180*
10:36 as his very own and sent into the w? *3180*
11:27 who was to come into the w." *3180*
12:19 Look how the whole w has gone after him!" *3180*
12:25 in this w will keep it for eternal life. *3180*
12:31 Now is the time for judgment *on* this w; *3180*
12:31 now the prince *of* this w will be driven out. *3180*
12:46 I have come into the w as a light, *3180*
12:47 I did not come to judge the w, but to save it. *3180*
13: 1 for him to leave this w and go to the Father. *3180*
13: 1 Having loved his own who were in the w, *3180*
14:17 The w cannot accept him, *3180*
14:19 Before long, the w will not see me anymore, *3180*
14:22 to show yourself to us and not *to* the w?" *3180*
14:27 I do not give to you as the w gives. *3180*
14:30 for the prince *of* this w is coming. *3180*
14:31 the w must learn that I love the Father and *3180*
15:18 "If the w hates you, keep in mind that *3180*
15:19 If you belonged to the w, it would love you *3180*
15:19 As it is, you do not belong to the w, *3180*
15:19 but I have chosen you out of the w. *3180*
15:19 That is why the w hates you. *3180*
16: 8 he will convict the w of guilt in regard *3180*
16:11 the prince *of* this w now stands condemned. *3180*
16:20 and mourn while the w rejoices. *3180*
16:21 of her joy that a child is born into the w. *3180*
16:28 I came from the Father and entered the w; *3180*
16:28 now I am leaving the w and going back to *3180*
16:33 In this w you will have trouble. *3180*
16:33 I have overcome the w." *3180*
17: 5 with you before the w began. *3180*
17: 6 to those whom you gave me out of the w. *3180*
17: 9 I am not praying for the w, *3180*
17:11 I will remain in the w no longer, *3180*
17:11 but they are still in the w, *3180*
17:13 I say these things while I am still in the w, *3180*
17:14 and the w has hated them, *3180*
17:14 for they are not of the w any more than I am *3180*
17:14 of the world any more than I am of the w. *3180*
17:15 not that you take them out of the w but *3180*
17:16 They are not of the w, *3180*
17:18 As you sent me into the w, *3180*
17:18 I have sent them into the w. *3180*
17:21 the w may believe that you have sent me. *3180*
17:23 to complete unity to let the w know *3180*
17:24 before the creation *of* the w. *3180*
17:25 though the w does not know you, *3180*
18:20 "I have spoken openly *to* the w," *3180*
18:36 Jesus said, "My kingdom is not of this w. *3180*
18:37 and for this I came into the w, *3180*
21:25 that even the whole w would not have room *3180*
Ac 11:28 would spread over the entire **Roman** w. *3876*
17: 6 *over* the w have now come here, *3876*
17:24 "The God who made the w and everything *3180*
17:31 a day when he will judge the w with justice *3876*
19:27 throughout the province of Asia and the w, *3876*
19:35 "Men of Ephesus, doesn't **all the** w know *476+1639+4005+5515*
24: 5 up riots among the Jews all over the w. *3876*
Ro 1: 8 your faith is being reported all over the w. *3180*
1:20 since the creation *of* the w God's invisible *3180*
3: 6 how could God judge the w? *3180*
3:19 and the whole w held accountable to God. *3180*
4:13 the promise that he would be heir *of* the w, *3180*
5:12 just as sin entered the w through one man, *3180*
5:13 before the law was given, sin was in the w. *3180*
10:18 their words to the ends *of* the w." *3876*
11:12 their transgression means riches *for* the w, *3180*
11:15 their rejection is the reconciliation *of* the w, *3180*
12: 2 conform any longer to the pattern of this w, *172*
1Co 1:20 God made foolish the wisdom *of* the w? *3180*
1:21 the w through its wisdom did not know him, *3180*
1:27 But God chose the foolish things *of* the w *3180*
1:27 God chose the weak things *of* the w *3180*
1:28 He chose the lowly things *of* this w and *3180*
2:12 We have not received the spirit *of* the w but *3180*
3:19 For the wisdom *of* this w is foolishness *3180*
1Co 3:22 whether Paul or Apollos or Cephas or the w *3180*
4:13 scum of the earth, the refuse *of* **the w.** *4246S*
5:10 the people *of* this w who are immoral, *3180*
5:10 In that case you would have to leave this w. *3180*
6: 2 not know that the saints will judge the w? *3180*
6: 2 And if you are to judge the w, *3180*
7:31 those who use the things of the w, *3180*
7:31 this w in its present form is passing away. *3180*
7:33 about the affairs *of* this w— *3180*
7:34 about the affairs *of* this w— *3180*
8: 4 in the w and that there is no God but one. *3180*
11:32 that we will not be condemned with the w. *3180*
14:10 there are all sorts of languages in the w, *3180*
2Co 1:12 that we have conducted ourselves in the w, *3180*
5:19 that God was reconciling the w to himself *3180*
10: 2 that we live by the standards of **this w.** *4922*
10: 3 For though we live in **the w,** *4922*
10: 3 we do not wage war as **the w** does. *4922*
10: 4 with are not the weapons **of the w.** *4920*
11:18 many are boasting in the way the w does, *4922*
Gal 3:22 the Scripture declares that the **whole w** is *4246*
4: 3 under the basic principles *of* the w. *3180*
6:14 which the w has been crucified to me, *3180*
6:14 crucified to me, and I *to* the w. *3180*
Eph 1: 4 the w to be holy and blameless in his sight. *3180*
2: 2 *of* this w and of the ruler of the kingdom of *3180*
2:12 without hope and without God in the w. *3180*
6:12 against the **powers of** this dark w *3179*
Col 1: 6 All over the w this gospel is bearing fruit *3180*
2: 8 the basic principles *of* this w rather than *3180*
2:20 to the basic principles *of* this w, *3180*
1Ti 1:15 Christ Jesus came into the w to save sinners *3180*
3:16 was believed on in the w, was taken up in *3180*
6: 7 For we brought nothing into the w, *3180*
6:17 in this present w not to be arrogant nor *172*
2Ti 4:10 for Demas, because he loved this w, *172*
Heb 1: 6 when God brings his firstborn into the w, *3876*
2: 5 not to angels that he has subjected the w *3876*
4: 3 since the creation *of* the w. *3180*
9:26 since the creation *of* the w. *3180*
10: 5 when Christ came into the w, he said: *3180*
11: 7 the w and became heir of the righteousness *3180*
11:38 the w was not worthy of them. *3180*
Jas 1:27 from being polluted by the w. *3180*
2: 5 *in* the eyes of the w to be rich in faith and *3180*
3: 6 a w of evil among the parts of the body. *3180*
4: 4 that friendship *with* the w is hatred *3180*
4: 4 to be a friend *of* the w becomes an enemy *3180*
1Pe 1: 1 To God's elect, strangers in the w, *NIG*
1:20 He was chosen before the creation *of* the w, *3180*
2:11 I urge you, as aliens and strangers in the w, *NIG*
5: 9 the w are undergoing the same kind *3180*
2Pe 1: 4 and escape the corruption in the w caused *3180*
2: 5 not spare the ancient w when he brought *3180*
2:20 If they have escaped the corruption *of* the w *3180*
3: 6 also the w of that time was deluged *3180*
1Jn 2: 2 but also for the sins *of* the whole w. *3180*
2:15 Do not love the w or anything in the world. *3180*
2:15 Do not love the world or anything in the w. *3180*
2:15 If anyone loves the w, the love of the Father *3180*
2:16 For everything in the w—the cravings of *3180*
2:16 comes not from the Father but from the w. *3180*
2:17 The w and its desires pass away, *3180*
3: 1 The reason the w does not know us is *3180*
3:13 my brothers, if the w hates you. *3180*
4: 1 false prophets have gone out into the w. *3180*
4: 3 and even now is already in the w. *3180*
4: 4 is greater than the one who is in the w. *3180*
4: 5 They are from the w and therefore speak *3180*
4: 5 from the viewpoint *of* the w, *3180*
4: 5 and the w listens to them. *3180*
4: 9 and only Son into the w that we might live *3180*
4:14 to be the Savior *of* the w. *3180*
4:17 because in this w we are like him. *3180*
5: 4 for everyone born of God overcomes the w. *3180*
5: 4 This is the victory that has overcome the w, *3180*
5: 5 Who is it that overcomes the w? *3180*
5:19 whole w is under the control of the evil one. *3180*
2Jn 1: 7 have gone out into the w. *3180*
Rev 3:10 upon the whole w to test those who live on *3876*
11:15 the w has become the kingdom of our Lord *3180*
12: 9 or Satan, who leads the whole w astray. *3876*
13: 3 The whole w was astonished and followed *1178*
13: 8 that was slain from the creation *of* the w. *3180*
16:14 they go out to the kings *of* the whole w, *3876*
17: 8 *of* the w will be astonished when they see *3180*

WORLD'S (3) [WORLD]

La 4:12 did not believe, nor did any of the w people, 9315
Jn 11: 9 will not stumble, for he sees by this w light. *3180*
Rev 18:23 Your merchants were the w great men. *1178*

WORLDLY (10) [WORLD]

Lk 16: 9 use w wealth to gain friends for yourselves, *94*
16:11 not been trustworthy in handling w wealth, *96*
1Co 3: 1 I could not address you as spiritual but as w *4921*
3: 3 You are still w. For since there is jealousy *4920*
3: 3 and quarreling among you, are you not w? *4920*
2Co 1:12 so not according to w wisdom but according *4920*
1:17 Or do I make my plans in a w **manner** so *4922*
5:16 regard no one **from a w point of view.** *2848+4922*
7:10 but w sorrow brings death. *3180+3836*
Tit 2:12 to say "No" to ungodliness and w passions, *3176*

WORM (10) [WORMS]

Job 17:14 and to the w, 'My mother' or 'My sister,' 8231
24:20 womb forgets them, the w feasts on them; 8231
25: 6 a son of man, who is only a w!" 9357
Ps 22: 6 But I am a w and not a man, 9357
Isa 41:14 Do not be afraid, O w Jacob, O little Israel, 9357
51: 8 the w will devour them like wool. 6182
66:24 their w will not die, nor will their fire 9357
Jnh 4: 7 But at dawn the next day God provided a w, 9357
Mk 9:48 where " 'their w does not die, and the fire *5038*
2Ti 3: 6 the kind who w *their* **way** into homes *1905*

WORMS (5) [WORM]

Dt 28:39 gather the grapes, because w will eat them. 9357
Job 7: 5 My body is clothed with w and scabs, 8231
21:26 and w cover them both. 8231
Isa 14:11 spread out beneath you and w cover you. 9357
Ac 12:23 and he was **eaten by** w and died. *5037*

WORMWOOD (1)

Rev 8:11 the name of the star is **W.** *952*

WORN (19) [WEAR]

Ge 18:12 "After I *am* w **out** and my master is old, 1162
Ex 35:19 the woven garments w for ministering in NIH
39:26 the hem of the robe to be w for ministering, NIH
39:41 and the woven garments w for ministering NIH
Dt 21: 3 been worked and *has* never w a yoke 928+5432
25:18 When you were weary and w **out,** 3335
Jos 9: 5 The men put w and patched sandals 1165
9:13 And our clothes and sandals *are* w **out** by 1162
Jdg 8: 5 my troops some bread; they are w **out,** 6546
8:26 purple garments w *by* the kings of Midian 6584
Est 6: 8 have them bring a royal robe the king *has* w 4252
Job 16: 7 Surely, O God, *you have* w me **out;** 4206
Ps 6: 6 *I am* w **out** from groaning; 3333
69: 3 *I am* w **out** calling for help; 3333
Isa 47:13 counsel you have received *has only* w *you* **out!** 4206
Jer 12: 5 with men on foot and *they have* w you **out,** 4206
45: 3 *I am* w **out** with groaning 3333
Eze 23:43 I said about the *one* w **out** *by* adultery, 1165
Lk 8:27 For a long time this man *had* not w clothes *1907*

WORN-OUT (3) [WEAR]

Jos 9: 4 with w sacks and old wineskins, 1165
Jer 38:11 and w clothes from there and let them down 1170
38:12 and w clothes under your arms to pad NIH

WORRIED (2) [WORRY]

1Sa 10: 2 thinking about them and *is* w about you. 1793
Lk 10:41 *"you are* w and upset about many things, *3534*

WORRIES (4) [WORRY]

Jer 17: 8 *It* **has** no w in a year of drought 1793
Mt 13:22 but the w of this life and the deceitfulness *3533*
Mk 4:19 but the w of this life, the deceitfulness *3533*
Lk 8:14 on their way they are choked by life's w, *3533*

WORRY (13) [WORRIED, WORRIES, WORRYING]

1Sa 9:20 *do* not w about them;. 906+4213+8492
Mt 6:25 I tell you, *do* not w **about** your life, *3534*
6:28 "And why *do you* w about clothes? *3534*
6:31 So *do* not w, saying, 'What shall we eat?' *3534*
6:34 Therefore *do* not w about tomorrow, *3534*
6:34 for tomorrow *will* w **about** itself. *3534*
10:19 *do* not w **about** what to say or how to say it. *3534*
Mk 13:11 *do* not w **beforehand about** what to say. *4628*
Lk 12:11 *do* not w **about** how you will defend *3534*
12:22 *do* not w **about** your life, what you will eat; *3534*
12:26 why *do you* w about the rest? *3534*
12:29 eat or drink; *do* not w **about** it. *3577*
21:14 make up your mind not *to* w **beforehand** *4627*

WORRYING (3) [WORRY]

1Sa 9: 5 about the donkeys and *start* w about us." 1793
Mt 6:27 Who of you *by* w can add a single hour *3534*
Lk 12:25 Who of you *by* w can add a single hour *3534*

WORSE (22) [WORST]

Ge 19: 9 *We'll* **treat** you w than them." 8317
Ex 11: 6 w *than* there has ever been or ever will 4017+4202
2Sa 19: 7 be w for you than all the calamities 8273
1Ki 17:17 **He grew** w **and worse,** 2118+2617+2716+4394
17:17 **He grew worse and** w, 2118+2617+2716+4394
Pr 17: 7 **how much** w lying lips to a ruler! 677+3954
19:10 **how much** w for a slave to rule over princes! 677+3954
Eze 14:21 **How much** w will it be when I send 677+3954
Da 1:10 Why should he see you **looking** w than 2407
Mic 7: 4 the most upright w **than** a thorn hedge. 4946
Mt 9:16 away from the garment, making the tear **w.** *5937*
12:45 the final condition of that man is **w than** *5937*
27:64 This last deception will be **w than** the first." *5937*
Mk 2:21 pull away from the old, making the tear **w.** *5937*
5:26 yet instead of getting better she grew **w.** *5937*
Lk 11:26 the final condition of that man is **w than** *5937*
13: 2 that these Galileans were w sinners than all *NIG*
Jn 5:14 Stop sinning or something w may happen *5937*

1Co 8: 8 *we are* no **w** if we do not eat, *5728*
1Ti 5: 8 the faith and is **w than** an unbeliever. *5937*
2Ti 3:13 and impostors will go **from bad to w,** *2093+3836+5937*
2Pe 2:20 **w off** at the end **than** they were at the *5937*

WORSHIP (158) [WORSHIPED, WORSHIPER, WORSHIPERS, WORSHIPING, WORSHIPS]

Ge 22: 5 *We will* **w** and then we will come back 2556
Ex 3:12 *you will* **w** God on this mountain." 6268
4:23 "Let my son go, so *he may* **w** me." 6268
7:16 so that *they may* **w** me in the desert. 6268
8: 1 Let my people go, so that *they may* **w** me. 6268
8:20 Let my people go, so that *they may* **w** me. 6268
9: 1 "Let my people go, so that *they may* **w** me." 6268
9:13 Let my people go, so that *they may* **w** me, 6268
10: 3 Let my people go, so that *they may* **w** me. 6268
10: 7 so that *they may* **w** the LORD their God. 6268
10: 8 "Go, **w** the LORD your God," he said. 6268
10:11 Have only the men go; and **w** the LORD, 6268
10:24 and said, "Go, **w** the LORD. 6268
10:26 not know what *we are to use to* **w** 6268
12:31 Go, **w** the LORD as you have requested. 6268
20: 5 You shall not bow down to them or **w** them; 6268
23:24 not bow down before their gods or **w** them 6268
23:25 **W** the LORD your God, 6268
23:33 the **w** *of* their gods will certainly be a snare 6268
24: 1 *You are to* **w** at a distance, 2556
34:14 *Do* not **w** any other god, for the LORD, 2556
Dt 4:28 There *you will* **w** man-made gods of wood 6268
5: 9 You shall not bow down to them or **w** them; 6268
8:19 and follow other gods and **w** and bow down 6268
11:16 and **w** other gods and bow down to them. 6268
12: 2 nations you are dispossessing **w** their gods, 6268
12: 4 not **w** the LORD your God in their way. 6913
12:31 not **w** the LORD your God in their way, 6913
13: 2 you have not known) "and *let us* **w** them," 6268
13: 6 and **w** other gods" (gods that neither you 6268
13:13 and **w** other gods" (gods you have not 6268
28:36 There *you will* **w** other gods, 6268
28:64 There *you will* **w** other gods— 6268
29:18 the LORD our God to go and **w** the gods 6268
30:17 to bow down to other gods and **w** them, 6268
31:20 they will turn to other gods and **w** them, 6268
Jos 22:27 we *will* **w** the LORD at his sanctuary 6268+6275
Jdg 6:10 *do* not **w** the gods of the Amorites, 3707
1Sa 1: 3 to **w** and sacrifice to the LORD Almighty 2556
15:25 so that *I may* **w** the LORD." 2556
15:30 so that *I may* **w** the LORD your God." 2556
2Sa 15: 8 *I will* **w** the LORD in Hebron.' " 6268
15:32 where *people used to* **w** God, 2556
1Ki 1:47 And the king **bowed in w** on his bed 2556
9: 6 and go off to serve other gods and **w** them, 2556
12:30 people went even as far as Dan to **w** 4200+7156
16:31 and began to serve Baal and **w** him. 2556
2Ki 10:28 So Jehu destroyed **Baal w** in Israel. 1251
10:29 the **w** of the golden calves at Bethel NIH
17:25 *they did* not **w** the LORD; 3707
17:28 and taught them how *to* **w** the LORD. 3707
17:34 They neither **w** the LORD nor adhere to 3710
17:35 not **w** any other gods or bow down to them, 3707
17:36 is the one *you must* **w.** 3707
17:37 *Do* not **w** other gods. 3707
17:38 and *do* not **w** other gods. 3707
17:39 Rather, **w** the LORD your God; 3707
18:22 *"You must* **w** before this altar in Jerusalem" 2556
1Ch 16:29 **w** the LORD in the splendor of his holiness. 2556
2Ch 7:19 and go off to serve other gods and **w** them, 2556
20:18 of Judah and Jerusalem fell down in **w** 2556
29:28 The whole assembly **bowed in w,** 2556
32:12 *'You must* **w** before one altar 2556
Ezr 7:19 to you for **w** *in* the temple of your God. 10587
Ne 9: 6 and the multitudes of heaven **w** you. 2556
Job 1:20 Then he fell to the ground *in* **w** 2556
Ps 22:29 All the rich of the earth will feast and **w;** 2556
29: 2 **w** the LORD in the splendor of his holiness. 2556
86: 9 the nations you have made will come and **w** 2556
95: 6 Come, let us bow down *in* **w,** 2556
96: 9 **W** the LORD in the splendor 2556
97: 7 All *who* **w** images are put to shame, 6268
97: 7 **w** him, all *you* gods! 2556
99: 5 the LORD our God and **w** at his footstool; 2556
99: 9 Exalt the LORD our God and **w** 2556
100: 2 **W** the LORD with gladness; 6268
102:22 the kingdoms assemble to **w** the LORD. 6268
132: 7 *let us* **w** at his footstool— 2556
Isa 2:20 and idols of gold, which they made to **w.** 2556
19:21 *They will* **w** *with* sacrifices 6268
19:23 and Assyrians *will* **w** together. 6268
27:13 in Egypt will come and **w** the LORD on 2556
29:13 Their **w** *of* me is made up only 3707
36: 7 *"You must* **w** before this altar"? 2556
46: 6 and they bow down and **w** it. 2556
56: 6 and to **w** him, all who keep the Sabbath 6269
Jer 7: 2 through these gates to **w** the LORD. 2556
13:10 to serve and **w** them, will be like this belt— 2556
23:27 fathers forgot my name through **Baal w.** 1251
25: 6 not follow other gods to serve and **w** them; 2556
26: 2 of the towns of Judah who come to **w** *in* 2556
Eze 46: 2 *He is to* **w** at the threshold of the gateway 2556
46: 3 of the land *are to* **w** in the presence of 2556
46: 9 whoever enters by the north gate to **w** is 2556
Da 3: 5 must fall down and **w** the image of gold 10504
3: 6 down and **w** will immediately be thrown 10504
Da 3:10 all kinds of music must fall down and **w** 10504
3:11 **w** will be thrown into a blazing furnace. 10504
3:12 nor **w** the image of gold you have set up." 10504
3:14 or **w** the image of gold I have set up? 10504
3:15 to fall down and **w** the image I made, 10504
3:15 But if *you do* not **w** it, 10504
3:18 or **w** the image of gold you have set up." 10504
3:28 or **w** any god except their own God. 10504
7:27 and all rulers *will* **w** and obey him.' 10586
Hos 13: 1 But he became guilty of **Baal w** and died. 1251
Jnh 1: 9 "I am a Hebrew and I **w** the LORD, 3707
Zep 1: 5 **bow down** on the roofs **to w** the starry host, 2556
2:11 The nations on every shore *will* **w** him, 2556
Zec 14:16 go up year after year to **w** the King, 2556
14:17 of the earth do not go up to Jerusalem to **w** 2556
Mt 2: 2 in the east and have come *to* **w** him." *4686*
2: 8 so that I too *may* go and **w** him." *4686*
4: 9 "if *you will* bow down and **w** me." *4686*
4:10 For it is written: '**W** the Lord your God, *4686*
15: 9 *They* **w** me in vain; their teachings are but *4936*
Mk 7: 7 *They* **w** me in vain; their teachings are but *4936*
Lk 4: 7 So if you **w** me, it will all be yours." *4686*
4: 8 '**W** the Lord your God and serve him *4686*
Jn 4:20 the place where we must **w** is in Jerusalem." *4686*
4:21 when *you will* **w** the Father neither *4686*
4:22 You Samaritans **w** what you do not know; *4686*
4:22 we **w** what we do know, *4686*
4:23 now come when the true worshipers *will* **w** *4686*
4:24 and his worshipers must **w** in spirit and *4686*
12:20 among those who went up to **w** at the Feast. *4686*
Ac 7: 7 of that country and **w** me in this place.' *3302*
7:42 over *to* the **w** of the heavenly bodies. *3302*
7:43 the idols you made *to* **w.** *4686*
8:27 This man had gone to Jerusalem *to* **w,** *4686*
13:16 of Israel and you Gentiles who **w** God, *5828*
17:23 and looked carefully at your **objects of w,** *4934*
17:23 Now what *you* **w** as something unknown *2355*
18:13 "is persuading the people *to* **w** God in ways *4936*
24:11 I went up to Jerusalem *to* **w.** *4686*
24:14 I admit that *I* **w** the God of our fathers as *3302*
Ro 9: 4 the **temple w** and the promises. *3301*
12: 1 this is your spiritual **act of w.** *3301*
1Co 14:25 So *he will* fall down and **w** God, *4686*
Php 3: 3 we who **w** by the Spirit of God, *3302*
Col 2:18 the **w** of angels disqualify you for the prize. *2579*
2:23 their **self-imposed w,** their false humility *1615*
1Ti 2:10 for women who profess to **w God.** *2537*
Heb 1: 6 he says, *"Let* all God's angels **w** him." *4686*
9: 1 the first covenant had regulations *for* **w** and *3301*
10: 1 make perfect those who draw near to **w.** *NIG*
12:28 and so **w** God acceptably with reverence *3302*
Rev 4:10 and **w** him who lives for ever and ever. *4686*
13: 8 All inhabitants of the earth *will* **w** *4686*
13:12 and made the earth and its inhabitants **w** *4686*
13:15 all who **refused to w** the image to *3590+4686*
14: 7 **W** him who made the heavens, the earth, *4686*
14:11 for those who **w** the beast and his image, *4686*
15: 4 All nations will come and **w** before you, *4686*
19:10 At this I fell at his feet *to* **w** him. *4686*
19:10 to the testimony of Jesus. **W** God! *4686*
22: 8 I fell down *to* **w** at the feet of the angel *4686*
22: 9 who keep the words of this book. **W** God!" *4686*

WORSHIPED (65) [WORSHIP]

Ge 24:26 the man bowed down and **w** the LORD, 2556
24:48 and I bowed down and **w** the LORD. 2556
47:31 Israel **w** *as he* **leaned** on the top of his staff. 2556
Ex 4:31 they bowed down and **w.** 2556
12:27 Then the people bowed down and **w.** 2556
33:10 they all stood and **w,** 2556
34: 8 Moses bowed to the ground at once and **w.** 2556
Dt 17: 3 contrary to my command *has* **w** other gods, 6268
29:26 and **w** other gods and bowed down to them, 6268
Jos 24: 2 lived beyond the River and **w** other gods. 6268
24:14 Throw away the gods your forefathers **w** 6268
Jdg 2:12 They followed and **w** various gods of 2556
2:17 to other gods and **w** them. 2556
7:15 the dream and its interpretation, *he* **w** God. 2556
1Sa 1:19 the next morning they arose and **w** before 2556
1:28 And *he* **w** the LORD there. 2556
15:31 and Saul **w** the LORD. 2556
2Sa 12:20 into the house of the LORD and **w.** 2556
1Ki 11:33 **w** Ashtoreth the goddess of the Sidonians, 2556
18:12 Yet I your servant *have* **w** the LORD 3707
22:53 and **w** Baal and provoked the LORD, 2556
2Ki 17: 7 *They* **w** other gods 3707
17:12 *They* **w** idols, though the LORD had said, 6268
17:16 all the starry hosts, and *they* **w** Baal. 6268
17:32 *They* **w** the LORD, but they also appointed 3710
17:33 *They* **w** the LORD, but they also served 3710
21: 3 down to all the starry hosts and **w** them. 6268
21:21 *he* **w** the idols his father had worshiped, 6268
21:21 he worshiped the idols his father *had* **w,** 6268
2Ch 7: 3 and *they* **w** and gave thanks to the LORD, 2556
24:18 and **w** Asherah poles and idols. 6268
29:29 present with him knelt down and **w.** 2556
29:30 with gladness and bowed their heads and **w.** 2556
33: 3 down to all the starry hosts and **w** them. 6268
33:22 Amon **w** and offered sacrifices to all 6268
Ne 8: 6 Then they bowed down and **w** the LORD 2556
Ps 74: 8 every **place where** God was **w** in the land. 4595
106:19 made a calf and **w** an idol cast from metal. 2556
106:36 *They* **w** their idols, which became a snare 6268
Jer 8: 2 they have followed and consulted and **w.** 2556
16:11 followed other gods and served and **w** them. 2556
22: 9 and *have* **w** and served other gods.' " 2556
Da 3: 7 and men of every language fell down and **w** 10504
7:14 nations and men of every language **w** him. 10586
Mt 2:11 and *they* bowed down and **w** him. *4686*
14:33 Then those who were in the boat **w** him, *4686*
28: 9 clasped his feet and **w** him. *4686*
28:17 When they saw him, *they* **w** him; *4686*
Lk 2:37 She never left the temple but **w** night *3302*
24:52 Then they **w** him and returned to Jerusalem *4686*
Jn 4:20 Our fathers **w** on this mountain, *4686*
9:38 "Lord, I believe," and *he* **w** him. *4686*
Ac 19:27 who *is* **w** throughout the province of Asia *4936*
Ro 1:25 and **w** and served created things rather than *4933*
2Th 2: 4 over everything that is called God or is **w,** *4934*
Heb 11:21 and **w** as he leaned on the top of his staff. *4686*
Rev 5:14 "Amen," and the elders fell down and **w.** *4686*
7:11 on their faces before the throne and **w** God, *4686*
11:16 fell on their faces and **w** God, *4686*
13: 4 *Men* **w** the dragon because he had given *4686*
13: 4 and *they* also **w** the beast and asked, *4686*
16: 2 the mark of the beast and **w** his image. *4686*
19: 4 four living creatures fell down and **w** God, *4686*
19:20 the mark of the beast and **w** his image. *4686*
20: 4 They *had* not **w** the beast or his image *4686*

WORSHIPER (3) [WORSHIP]

Ac 16:14 who was a **w of** God. *4936*
18: 7 the house of Titius Justus, a **w of** God. *4936*
Heb 9: 9 not able to clear the conscience of the **w.** *3302*

WORSHIPERS (7) [WORSHIP]

Zep 3:10 From beyond the rivers of Cush my **w,** 6985
Lk 1:10 all the **assembled w** were praying outside. *3295+3836+4436*
Jn 4:23 the true **w** will worship the Father in spirit *4687*
4:23 for they are the kind of **w** the Father seeks. *4686*
4:24 his **w** must worship in spirit and in truth." *4686*
Heb 10: 2 For the **w** would have been cleansed once *3302*
Rev 11: 1 and count the **w** there. *4686*

WORSHIPING (19) [WORSHIP]

Ex 10:26 We have to use some of them in **w** 6268
Nu 25: 3 So Israel **joined in w** the Baal of Peor. 7537
25: 5 *of* your men who *have* **joined in w** the Baal 7537
Dt 4:19 into bowing down to them and **w** things 6268
12:31 because in **w** their gods, they do all kinds of NIH
20:18 detestable things they do in **w** their gods, NIH
Jdg 2:19 other gods and serving and **w** them. 2556
8:27 prostituted themselves *by* **w** it there, 339
1Ki 9: 9 embraced other gods, **w** and serving them— 2556
2Ki 17:41 while these people were **w** the LORD, 3710
19:37 *while* he *was* **w** in the temple of his god 2556
2Ch 7:22 embraced other gods, **w** and serving them— 2556
28: 2 and also made cast idols for **w** the Baals. NIH
Ne 9: 3 and *in* **w** the LORD their God. 2556
Isa 37:38 he *was* **w** in the temple of his god Nisroch, 2556
Jer 1:16 and *in* **w** what their hands have made. 2556
44: 3 by **w** other gods that neither they nor you 6268
Ac 13: 2 *While* they *were* **w** the Lord and fasting, *3310*
Rev 9:20 *they did* not stop **w** demons, *4686*

WORSHIPS (4) [WORSHIP]

Isa 44:15 But he also fashions a god and **w** it; 2556
44:17 he bows down to it and **w.** 2556
66: 3 like *one who* **w** an idol. 1385
Rev 14: 9 "If anyone **w** the beast and his image *4686*

WORST (6) [WORSE]

Ex 9:18 the **w** hailstorm that has ever fallen 3878+4394
9:24 the **w** storm in all the land of Egypt 3878+4394
Ps 41: 7 they imagine the **w** for me, saying, 8288
Jer 2:33 the **w** *of women* can learn from your ways. 8273
1Ti 1:15 to save sinners—of whom I am the **w.** *4755*
1:16 shown mercy so that in me, the **w** of sinners, *4755*

WORTH (18) [WORTHLESS, WORTHWHILE, WORTHY]

Ge 23:15 the land is **w** four hundred shekels of silver, NIH
27:46 my **life will not be w living."** 2644+4200+4537
Dt 15:18 to you these six years has been **w** twice 8510
2Sa 18: 3 but you are **w** ten thousand *of* us. 4017
1Ki 21: 2 I will pay you *whatever* it is **w."** 4697
Job 28:13 Man does not comprehend its **w;** 6886
Pr 31:10 She is **w** far more than rubies. 4836
Isa 7:23 where there were a thousand vines **w** 928
La 4: 2 once **w their weight** in gold, 6131
Mt 10:10 for the worker is **w** his keep. *545*
10:31 you *are* **w more than** many sparrows. *1422*
Mk 12:42 **w** only a fraction of a penny. *NIG*
Lk 12: 7 *you are* **w more than** many sparrows. *1422*
Jn 12: 5 **the money** given to the poor? It was **w a year's wages."** *1324+5559*
Ac 20:24 I consider my life **w** nothing to me, *5508*
Ro 8:18 not **w** comparing with the glory that will *545*
1Pe 1: 7 your faith—of **greater w** *than* gold, *4501*
3: 4 which is of **great w** in God's sight. *4500*

WORTHIES (KJV) See PICKED TROOPS

WORTHILY (KJV) See HAVE STANDING

WORTHLESS (43) [WORTH]

Ge 41:27 so are the seven w heads of grain scorched 8199
Dt 32:21 and angered me with their w **idols.** 2039
1Ki 16:13 the God of Israel, to anger by their w **idols.** 2039
16:26 the God of Israel, to anger by their w **idols.** 2039
2Ki 17:15 They followed w **idols** and 2039
17:15 and *themselves became* w. 2038
2Ch 13: 7 Some w scoundrels gathered around him 8199
Job 13: 4 you are w physicians, all of you! 496
15:31 not deceive himself by trusting what is w, 8736
34:18 'You are w,' and to nobles, 1175
Ps 31: 6 I hate those who cling to w **idols;** 2039+8736
60:11 for the help of man is w. 8736
108:12 for the help of man is w. 8736
119:37 Turn my eyes away from w **things;** 8736
Pr 11: 4 Wealth *is* w in the day of wrath, 3603+4202
Isa 40:17 by him as w and less than nothing. 9332
41:24 and your works are utterly w; 703
44: 9 and the things they treasure *are* w. 1153+3603
Jer 2: 5 They followed w **idols** and became 2039
2: 5 and *became* w *themselves.* 2038
2: 8 prophesied by Baal, following w **idols.** 3603+4202
2:11 But my people have exchanged their Glory for w **idols.** 3603+4202
7: 8 in deceptive words *that are* w. 1194+3603
8:19 with their w foreign **idols?"** 2039
10: 3 For the customs of the peoples are w; 2039
10: 8 they are taught by w wooden **idols.** 2039
10:15 They are w, the objects of mockery; 2039
14:22 of the w **idols** *of* the nations bring rain? 2039
15:19 if you utter worthy, not w, words, 2361
16:19 w **idols** that did them no good. 2039
18:15 they burn incense to w **idols,** 8736
51:18 They are w, the objects of mockery; 2039
La 2:14 visions of your prophets were false and w; 9522
Hos 8: 8 she is among the nations like a w thing. 401+2914
12:11 Is Gilead wicked? Its people are w! 8736
Jnh 2: 8 who cling to w idols forfeit the grace 2039
Zec 11:17 "Woe to the w shepherd, 496
Mt 25:30 And throw that w servant outside, *945*
Ac 14:15 telling you to turn from these w *things* to *3469*
Ro 3:12 *they have* together **become w;** *946*
4:14 faith has no value and the promise *is* w, *2934*
Heb 6: 8 that produces thorns and thistles is w and is *99*
Jas 1:26 he deceives himself and his religion is w. *3469*

WORTHWHILE (2) [WORTH]

Ecc 2: 3 I wanted to see what was w for men to do 3202
Ro 1:28 not **think it** w to retain the knowledge *1507*

WORTHY (49) [WORTH]

2Sa 22: 4 I call to the LORD, *who is* w **of praise,** 2146
1Ki 1:42 A w man like you must be bringing good 2657
1:52 "If he shows himself to be a w man, 2657
2Ki 10: 3 the best and most w of your master's sons 3838
1Ch 16:25 great is the LORD and most w **of praise;** 2146
Job 28:18 Coral and jasper *are* not w **of mention;** 2349
Ps 18: 3 I call to the LORD, *who is* w **of praise,** 2146
48: 1 Great is the LORD, and most w **of praise,** 2146
96: 4 great is the LORD and most w **of praise;** 2146
145: 3 Great is the LORD and most w **of praise;** 2146
Pr 8: 6 Listen, for I have w **things** to say; 5592
Jer 15:19 if you utter w, not worthless, words, 3701
Mt 10:11 search for some w *person* there and stay *545*
10:37 or mother more than me is not w of me; *545*
10:37 or daughter more than me is not w of me; *545*
10:38 not take his cross and follow me is not w *545*
26:66 "He is w of death," they answered. *1944*
Mk 1: 7 of whose sandals I am not w to stoop down *2653*
14:64 They all condemned him as w of death. *1944*
Lk 3:16 the thongs of whose sandals I am not w *2653*
7: 7 not even **consider** myself w to come to you. *546*
15:19 I am no longer w to be called your son; *545*
15:21 I am no longer w to be called your son.' *545*
20:35 those who *are* **considered w of** taking part *2921*
Jn 1:27 the thongs of whose sandals I am not w *545*
Ac 5:41 rejoicing because *they had been* **counted** w *2921*
13:25 whose sandals I am not w to untie.' *545*
13:46 not consider yourselves w of eternal life, *545*
Ro 16: 2 in the Lord **in a way** w of the saints and *547*
Eph 4: 1 a life w of the calling you have received. *547*
Php 1:27 in **a manner** w of the gospel of Christ. *547*
Col 1:10 a life w of the Lord and may please him *547*
1Th 2:12 comforting and urging you to live lives w *547*
2Th 1: 5 and as a result you *will be* **counted** w of *2921*
1:11 our God *may* **count** you w of his calling, *546*
1Ti 3: 8 likewise, are to be men w **of respect,** *4948*
3:11 their wives are to be women w **of respect,** *4948*
5:17 of the church well *are* w of double honor, *546*
6: 1 of slavery should consider their masters w *545*
Tit 2: 2 temperate, w **of respect,** self-controlled, *4948*
Heb 3: 3 Jesus *has been* **found** w of greater honor *546*
11:38 the world was not w of them. *545*
3Jn 1: 6 to send them on their way in a **manner** w *547*
Rev 3: 4 dressed in white, for they are w. *545*
4:11 "You are w, our Lord and God, *545*
5: 2 "Who is w to break the seals and open *545*
5: 4 because no one was found who was w *545*
5: 9 "You are w to take the scroll and *545*
5:12 In a loud voice they sang: "W is the Lamb, *545*

WOT, WOTTETH (KJV) See CONCERN, KNOW

WOULD (679) [WOULDN'T]

Ge 2:19 to the man to see what *he* w **name** them; AIT
3:20 she w **become** the mother of all the living. AIT
4:15 so that no one who found him w **kill** him. AIT
9:23 that *they* w not **see** their father's nakedness. AIT
21: 7 "Who w *have* **said** to Abraham AIT
21: 7 to Abraham that Sarah w **nurse** children? AIT
26:10 and *you* w *have* **brought** guilt upon us." AIT
27:12 *I* w **appear** to be tricking him AIT
27:12 and w **bring down** a curse on myself AIT
29: 3 the shepherds w **roll** the stone away from AIT
29: 3 Then *they* w **return** the stone to its place AIT
30:38 that they w be directly in front of the flocks NIH
30:41 Jacob w **place** the branches in the troughs AIT
30:41 in front of the animals so they w **mate** near AIT
30:42 *he* w not **place** them there. AIT
31:31 I thought you w take your daughters away 7153
31:42 w surely *have* **sent** me **away** AIT
34:14 That w be a disgrace to us. NIH
38: 9 Onan knew that the offspring w not **be** his; AIT
42:21 but *we* w not **listen;** AIT
43: 7 How were we to know *he* w **say,** AIT
44: 8 So why w *we* **steal** silver or gold AIT
44:34 not let me see the misery that w **come upon** AIT
Ex 2: 4 at a distance to see what w **happen** to him. AIT
6:12 why w Pharaoh **listen** *to* me, AIT
6:30 why w Pharaoh **listen** to me?" AIT
7:13 and *he* w not **listen** to them, AIT
7:22 *he* w not **listen** to Moses and Aaron, AIT
8:15 he hardened his heart and w not **listen** AIT
8:19 and *he* w not **listen,** AIT
8:26 But Moses said, "That w not *be* **right.** AIT
8:26 the LORD our God w be detestable to NIH
8:32 and w not **let** the people **go.** AIT
9: 7 and *he* w not **let** the people **go.** AIT
9:12 and *he* w not **listen** to Moses and Aaron, AIT
9:15 with a plague *that* w *have* **wiped** *you* off AIT
9:35 and *he* w not **let** the Israelites **go,** AIT
10:20 and *he* w not **let** the Israelites **go.** AIT
11:10 and *he* w not **let** the Israelites **go** AIT
14:12 It w have been better for us to serve NIH
23:29 because the land w **become** desolate and AIT
33: 7 Anyone inquiring of the LORD w **go** to AIT
33: 9 the pillar of cloud w **come down** and stay at AIT
33:11 The LORD w **speak** to Moses face to face, AIT
33:11 Then Moses w **return** to the camp, AIT
34:35 Moses w **put** the veil **back** over his face AIT
38: 7 into the rings so they w be on the sides of NIH
39:21 so that the breastpiece w not **swing out** from AIT
39:23 so that *it* w not **tear.** AIT
40:36 from above the tabernacle, *they* w **set out;** AIT
Lev 5: 3 anything that w *make him* **unclean—** AIT
10:19 W the LORD *have been* **pleased** AIT
18: 8 that w dishonor your father. NIH
18:10 that w dishonor you. NIH
18:16 that w dishonor your brother. NIH
20:19 for *that* w **dishonor** a close relative; AIT
20:19 w *be* **held responsible.** AIT
25:35 as you w an alien or a temporary resident, NIH
26:13 of Egypt so that you w no longer **be** slaves AIT
Nu 9:20 at the LORD's command *they* w **encamp,** AIT
9:20 and then at his command *they* w **set out.** AIT
9:22 the Israelites w **remain in camp** and AIT
9:22 but when it lifted, *they* w **set out.** AIT
11:22 *W* they **have enough** if flocks AIT
11:22 *W* they **have enough** if all the fish in AIT
11:29 that the LORD w **put** his Spirit on them!" AIT
12:14 w *she* not *have* **been in disgrace** AIT
14:31 for your children that you said w *be* **taken** AIT
16:40 *he* w **become** like Korah and his followers. AIT
21:23 But Sihon w not **let** Israel pass through AIT
22:29 *I* w **kill** you right now." AIT
22:33 *I* w certainly *have* **killed** you by now, AIT
22:33 but *I* w *have* **spared** her." AIT
24:11 w **reward** you **handsomely,** AIT
26:65 told those Israelites *they* w **surely die** AIT
32:16 *"We* w *like to* **build** pens here AIT
Dt 1: 8 of the land that the LORD swore *he* w **give** AIT
1:39 little ones that you said w **be** taken captive, AIT
1:43 So I told you, but *you* w not **listen.** AIT
3:26 with me and w not **listen** to me. AIT
4:21 and he solemnly swore that I w not **cross** AIT
5:29 that their hearts w *be* **inclined** to fear me AIT
8: 2 whether or not *you* w **keep** his commands. AIT
9:25 the LORD had said *he* w **destroy** you. AIT
12:20 *"I* w **like** some meat," AIT
12:22 Eat them as you w gazelle or deer. 430[S]
17: 1 for that w be detestable to him. NIH
23: 5 the LORD your God w not listen 14
24: 4 That w be detestable in the eyes of NIH
24: 6 w *be* **taking** a man's livelihood **as security.** AIT
28:56 that *she* w not **venture** to touch the ground AIT
32:26 I said *I* w **scatter** them AIT
32:29 and w **understand** this AIT
Jos 5: 6 to them that they w not **see** the land AIT
9:27 at the place the LORD w **choose.** AIT
24:10 But *I* w not listen to Balaam, 14
Jdg 2:17 Yet *they* w not **listen** to their judges AIT
3: 4 the Israelites to see whether *they* w **obey** AIT
8:19 *I* w not **kill** you." AIT
9:29 Then *I* w **get rid** of him. AIT
9:29 *I* w **say** to Abimelech, AIT
11:17 but the king of Edom w not **listen.** AIT
11:38 and wept because she w never marry. NIH
13:15 *"We* w *like* you *to* **stay** until AIT
13:23 *he* w not *have* **accepted** a burnt offering AIT
Jdg 14:18 *you* w not *have* **solved** my riddle." AIT
15: 1 But her father w not **let** him go in. AIT
16:17 my strength w **leave** me, AIT
16:17 and *I* w **become** as weak as any other man." AIT
19:25 But the men w not listen to him. 14
20:13 But the Benjamites w not listen 14
20:39 then the men of Israel w **turn** in the battle. AIT
Ru 1: 7 that w **take** them **back** to the land of Judah. AIT
1:11 Why w *you* **come** with me? AIT
1:13 w *you* **wait** until they grew up? AIT
1:13 *W you* **remain unmarried** AIT
1Sa 1: 4 *he* w **give** portions of the meat AIT
1: 7 till she w**e**pt and w not **eat.** AIT
1: 8 Elkanah her husband w **say** to her, "Hannah, AIT
2:13 the priest w **come** with a three-pronged fork AIT
2:14 *He* w **plunge** it into the pan or kettle AIT
2:14 and the priest w **take** for himself whatever AIT
2:15 the servant of the priest w **come** and say to AIT
2:16 the servant w then **answer,** "No, AIT
2:20 Eli w **bless** Elkanah and his wife, saying, AIT
2:20 Then *they* w **go** home. AIT
2:30 and your father's house w **minister** AIT
3:13 that I w **judge** his family forever because of AIT
9: 9 if a man went to inquire of God, *he* w **say,** AIT
9:18 *"W you* please **tell** me where AIT
13:13 he w *have* **established** your kingdom AIT
14:30 How much better it w have been if NIH
14:30 *W* not the slaughter of the Philistines *have been* even **greater?"** AIT
16:23 David w **take** his harp and play. AIT
16:23 Then **relief** w **come** to Saul; AIT
16:23 he w **feel better,** and the evil spirit AIT
16:23 and the evil spirit w **leave** him. AIT
19: 5 then w *you* **do wrong** to an innocent man AIT
20: 2 Why w he **hide** this from me? AIT
22: 3 *"W you let* my father and mother **come** AIT
22:22 I knew *he* w **be sure to tell** Saul. AIT
25:34 belonging to Nabal w *have* **been left alive** AIT
26:23 but *I* w not lay a hand on the LORD's 14
27:10 David w **say,** "Against the Negev of Judah" AIT
29: 6 and I w be pleased to have you serve NIH
31: 4 was terrified and w not do it; 14
2Sa 2:21 But Asahel w not stop chasing him. 14
2:27 the men w *have* **continued** the pursuit AIT
6:20 his servants as any vulgar fellow **w!"** 1655+1655[S]
11:20 Didn't you know *they* w **shoot arrows** from AIT
12: 8 w *have* **given** you **even more.** AIT
12:17 and *he* w not **eat** any food with them. AIT
12:18 we spoke to David but *he* w not **listen** AIT
13: 5 **'I w like** my sister Tamar to come 5528
13: 6 **"I w like** my sister Tamar to come 5528
13:13 *You* w **be** like one of the wicked fools AIT
13:16 "Sending me away w be a greater wrong NIH
13:25 *we* w only *be a* **burden** to you." AIT
14: 7 *They* w **put out** the only burning coal AIT
14:26 *he* w **weigh** it, and its weight was AIT
14:32 It w be better for me if I were still there!" ' NIH
15: 2 He w **get up early** and stand by the side of AIT
15: 2 Absalom w **call out** to him, AIT
15: 2 *He* w **answer,** "Your servant is from one of AIT
15: 3 Then Absalom w **say** to him, "Look, AIT
15: 4 And Absalom w **add,** AIT
15: 4 and *I* w **see that** he **gets justice."** AIT
15: 5 Absalom w **reach out** his hand, AIT
17: 1 *"I* w **choose** twelve thousand men AIT
17: 2 *I* w **attack** him while he is weary AIT
17: 2 *I* w **strike** him **with terror,** AIT
17: 2 *I* w **strike down** only the king AIT
18: 3 *It* w **be** better now for you AIT
18:11 Then I w have had to give you ten shekels NIH
18:12 *I* w not **lift** my hand against the king's son. AIT
18:13 *you* w *have* **kept** *your* **distance** AIT
19: 6 I see that you w be pleased NIH
21:16 said he w **kill** David. AIT
23:15 "Oh, that someone w **get** me **a drink** AIT
23:17 And David w not drink it. 14
1Ki 6: 6 so that nothing w *be* **inserted** into the temple AIT
8:12 "The LORD has said that he w **dwell** in AIT
12: 6 w you **advise** me to answer these people?" AIT
13: 8 *I* w not **go** with you, AIT
13: 8 nor w *I* **eat** bread or drink water here. AIT
14: 2 the one who told me I w be king NIH
17:10 *"W you* **bring** me a little water in a jar AIT
2Ki 3:14 *I* w not **look** at you or even notice you. AIT
5: 3 "If only my master w see the prophet who is NIH
5: 3 *He* w **cure** him of his leprosy." AIT
5:11 "I thought that *he* w **surely come out** to me AIT
5:13 w *you* not *have* **done** it? AIT
6:22 *"W* you **kill** men you have captured AIT
8:14 "He told me that *you* w **certainly recover."** AIT
11:17 and the king and people that *they* w **be** AIT
12: 8 that *they* w not **collect** any more money AIT
12: 8 from the people and that they w not **repair** AIT
13:19 then *you* w *have* **defeated** Aram AIT
14:11 Amaziah, however, w not **listen,** AIT
14:27 not said he w **blot out** the name of Israel AIT
17:14 But *they* w not **listen** and were AIT
17:40 They w not **listen,** however, AIT
22:19 that they w **become** accursed and laid waste, AIT
1Ch 4:10 *you* w **bless** me and enlarge my territory! AIT
9:27 *They* w **spend the night** stationed around AIT
10: 4 But his armor-bearer was terrified and w 14
11:17 "Oh, that someone w **get** me **a drink** AIT
11:19 David w not drink it. 14
22:11 the LORD your God, as he said you w. NIH
2Ch 6: 1 "The LORD has said that he w **dwell** in AIT
6:20 you said you w **put** your Name there. AIT

2Ch 10: 6 "How *w you* **advise** me to answer AIT
15:13 All who *w* not **seek** the LORD, AIT
20:10 whose territory *you w* not **allow** Israel AIT
23:16 that he and the people and the king *w* **be** AIT
24:11 the chief priest *w* **come** and empty the chest AIT
24:19 *they w* not **listen.** AIT
25:20 Amaziah, however, *w* not **listen,** AIT
31:16 all who *w* **enter** the temple of the LORD AIT
35:22 however, *w* not **turn away** from him, AIT
35:22 *He w* not **listen** to what Neco had said AIT
36:13 and hardened his heart and *w* not **turn** to AIT
Ezr 3: 7 so that they *w* **bring** cedar logs by sea AIT
9:14 *W you* not *be* **angry** AIT
10: 8 within three days *w* **forfeit** all his property, AIT
10: 8 *w* himself **be expelled** AIT
Ne 2:16 or officials or any others *who w be* **doing** AIT
3: 5 but their nobles *w* not **put** their shoulders to AIT
4: 3 *he w* **break down** their wall of stones!" AIT
6:13 to intimidate me so that *I w* **commit a sin** AIT
6:13 they *w* **give** me a bad name to discredit me. AIT
Est 1:17 but *she w* not **come.'** AIT
2:13 And this is how she *w* **go** to the king: AIT
2:14 In the evening she *w* **go** there and in AIT
2:14 *She w* not **return** to the king AIT
3: 2 But Mordecai *w* not **kneel down** AIT
3: 4 whether Mordecai's behavior *w be* **tolerated,** AIT
3: 5 that Mordecai *w* not **kneel down** AIT
3:14 the people of every nationality so they *w* **be** AIT
4: 4 but *he w* not **accept** them. AIT
6: 6 that the king *w* **rather** honor than me?" AIT
7: 4 *I w have kept* **quiet,** AIT
7: 4 no such distress *w* **justify** disturbing AIT
8:13 of every nationality so that the Jews *w* **be** AIT
Job 1: 4 and *they w* **invite** their three sisters to eat AIT
1: 5 Job *w* **send** and have them purified. AIT
1: 5 the morning *he w* **sacrifice** a burnt offering AIT
3:13 For now *I w be* **lying down** in peace; AIT
3:13 *I w be* **asleep** and at rest AIT
5: 8 "But if it were I, *I w* **appeal** to God; AIT
5: 8 *I w* **lay** my cause before him. AIT
6: 3 *It w* surely **outweigh** the sand of the seas— AIT
6: 8 that God *w* **grant** what I hope for, AIT
6: 9 that God *w be* **willing** to crush me, AIT
6:10 Then I *w* still **have** this consolation— AIT
6:27 *You w* even **cast** lots for the fatherless AIT
6:28 *W I* **lie** to your face? AIT
7:16 I despise my life; *I w* not **live** forever. AIT
9:16 I do not believe *he w* **give** me **a hearing.** AIT
9:17 He *w* **crush** me with a storm AIT
9:18 *He w* not **let** me regain my breath AIT
9:18 but *w* **overwhelm** me *with* misery. AIT
9:20 I were innocent, my mouth *w* **condemn** me; AIT
9:20 *it w* **pronounce** me **guilty.** AIT
9:31 *you w* **plunge** me into a slime pit so that AIT
9:31 so that even my clothes *w* **detest** me. AIT
9:34 so that his terror *w* **frighten** me no more. AIT
9:35 Then *I w* **speak up** without fear of him, AIT
10:14 *you w be* **watching** me and would AIT
10:14 *w* not **let** my offense **go unpunished.** AIT
11: 5 Oh, how I wish that God *w* **speak,** AIT
11: 5 that *he w* **open** his lips against you AIT
13: 5 If only *you w be* **altogether silent!** AIT
13: 5 For you, *that w* **be** wisdom. AIT
13: 9 **W** it turn out well if he examined you? NIH
13:10 *He w* **surely rebuke** you AIT
13:11 *W* not his splendor **terrify** AIT
13:11 *W* not the dread of him **fall** AIT
13:16 no godless man *w dare* **come** before him! AIT
14:13 "If only *you w* **hide** me in the grave AIT
14:13 If only *you w* **set** me a time and AIT
15: 2 "*W* a wise man **answer** with empty notions AIT
15: 3 *W* **he argue** with useless words, AIT
16: 5 But my mouth *w* **encourage** you; AIT
16: 5 comfort from my lips *w* **bring** you **relief.** AIT
19: 5 If indeed *you w* **exalt** *yourselves* AIT
21:15 What *w we* **gain** by praying to him?' AIT
21:27 the schemes by which *you w* **wrong** me. AIT
22: 3 What pleasure **w** it give the Almighty NIH
22: 3 What **w** he gain if your ways were NIH
23: 4 *I w* **state** my case before him AIT
23: 5 *I w* **find out** what he would answer me, AIT
23: 5 I would find out what *he w* **answer** me, AIT
23: 5 and consider what *he w* **say.** AIT
23: 6 *W he* **oppose** me with great power? AIT
23: 6 No, he *w* not **press charges** against me. AIT
23: 7 *I w be* **delivered** forever from my judge. AIT
30: 1 whose fathers *I w have* **disdained** to put AIT
31:11 **w** have been shameful, a sin to be judged. NIH
31:12 *it w have* **uprooted** my harvest. AIT
31:18 from my youth I reared him as **w** a father, NIH
31:28 then these also **w** be sins to be judged, NIH
31:28 for *I w have been* **unfaithful** AIT
31:34 that I kept silent and *w* not **go** outside AIT
31:36 Surely *I w* **wear** it on my shoulder, AIT
31:36 *I w* **put it on** like a crown. AIT
31:37 *I w* **give** him an account of my every step; AIT
31:37 like a prince *I w* **approach** him.)— AIT
32:22 my Maker *w* soon **take** me **away.** AIT
34:12 It is unthinkable that God *w* **do wrong,** AIT
34:12 that the Almighty *w* **pervert** justice. AIT
34:15 all mankind *w* **perish** together AIT
34:15 and man *w* **return** to the dust. AIT
35: 4 "I *w like to* **reply** *to* you and AIT
36:19 *W* your wealth or even all your mighty efforts **sustain** you AIT
36:19 so you **w** not be in distress? NIH
37:20 *W* any man **ask** to be swallowed up? AIT

Job 40: 8 "*W you* **discredit** my justice? AIT
40: 8 *W you* **condemn** me to justify yourself? AIT
41:13 Who *w* **approach** him with a bridle? AIT
41:32 *one w* **think** the deep had white hair. AIT
Ps 10:15 wickedness that *w* not *be* **found out.** AIT
14: 7 that salvation for Israel **w** come out of Zion! NIH
38:12 *those who* **w** harm me talk of my ruin; 2011
39: 9 I was silent; *I w* not **open** my mouth, AIT
40: 5 *they w be* too **many** to declare. AIT
44:21 *w* not God *have* **discovered** AIT
50:12 If I were hungry *I w* not **tell** you, AIT
51:16 not delight in sacrifice, or *I w* **bring** it; AIT
53: 6 that salvation for Israel **w** come out of Zion! NIH
55: 6 *I w* **fly away** and be at rest— AIT
55: 7 *I w* flee **far away** and stay in the desert; AIT
55: 8 *I w* **hurry** *to* my place of shelter, AIT
62: 3 *W* all of you **throw** him **down—** AIT
66:18 the Lord *w* not *have* **listened;** AIT
73:15 *I w have* **betrayed** your children. AIT
78: 6 so the next generation *w* **know** them, AIT
78: 6 and *they* in turn *w* **tell** their children. AIT
78: 7 Then *they w* **put** their trust in God AIT
78: 7 in God and *w* not **forget** his deeds AIT
78: 7 but *w* **keep** his commands. AIT
78: 8 *They w* not **be like** their forefathers— AIT
78:34 Whenever God slew them, *they w* **seek** him; AIT
78:36 *they w* **flatter** him with their mouths, AIT
81: 8 if *you w but* **listen** to me, O Israel! AIT
81:11 "But my people *w* not **listen** to me; AIT
81:11 Israel *w* not **submit** to me. AIT
81:13 "If my people *w but* **listen** to me, AIT
81:13 if Israel *w* **follow** my ways, AIT
81:14 how quickly *w I* **subdue** their enemies AIT
81:15 Those who hate the LORD *w* **cringe** AIT
81:15 and their punishment *w* **last** forever. AIT
81:16 But you *w be* **fed** with the finest of wheat; AIT
81:16 with honey from the rock *I w* **satisfy** you." AIT
84:10 *I* **w rather be** a doorkeeper in the house 1047
94:17 *I w* soon *have* **dwelt in** the silence AIT
106:23 So he said *he w* **destroy** them— AIT
106:26 that he *w* **make** them **fall** in the desert, AIT
119: 6 Then *I w* not **be put to shame** AIT
119:92 *I w have* **perished** in my affliction. AIT
124: 3 *they w have* **swallowed** us alive; AIT
124: 4 the flood *w have* **engulfed** us, AIT
124: 4 the torrent *w have* **swept** over us, AIT
124: 5 the raging waters *w have* **swept** us **away.** AIT
139:18 *they w* **outnumber** the grains of sand. AIT
139:19 If only *you w* **slay** the wicked, O God! AIT
Pr 1:23 *I w have* **poured out** my heart to you AIT
1:25 and *w* not **accept** my rebuke, AIT
1:30 since *they w* not **accept** my advice AIT
5:13 *I w* not **obey** my teachers or listen AIT
8:29 so the waters *w* not **overstep** his command, AIT
SS 3: 4 and *w* not **let** him **go** till I had brought him AIT
6:13 Why *w you* **gaze** on the Shulammite as on AIT
8: 1 Then, if I found you outside, *I w* **kiss** you, AIT
8: 1 I would kiss you, and no *one w* **despise** me. AIT
8: 2 *I w* **lead** you and bring you AIT
8: 2 *I w* **give** you spiced wine **to drink,** AIT
8: 7 *it w be* **utterly scorned.** AIT
Isa 1: 9 *we w have* **become** like Sodom, AIT
1: 9 *we w have* **been like** Gomorrah. AIT
14:17 and *w* not *let* his captives **go** AIT
16:14 a servant bound by contract **w** count them, NIH
21:12 If *you w* **ask,** then ask; AIT
21:16 as a servant bound by contract **w** count it, NIH
27: 4 *I w* **march** against them in battle; AIT
27: 4 *I w* **set** them all **on fire.** AIT
28:12 but *they* **w** not listen. 14
30:15 but *you w* **have** none of it. 14
42:24 For *they* **w** not follow his ways; 14
44: 9 Those who **w** speak up for them are blind; NIH
48:18 your peace *w have* **been** like a river, AIT
48:19 Your descendants *w have* **been** like the sand, AIT
48:19 their name *w* never **be cut off** AIT
54: 9 the waters of Noah *w* never again **cover** AIT
57:10 but *you w* not **say,** 'It is hopeless,' AIT
57:16 the spirit of man *w grow* **faint** before me— AIT
64: 1 *you w* **rend** the heavens and come down, AIT
64: 1 that the mountains *w* **tremble** before you! AIT
Jer 3: 1 *W* not the land *be* **completely defiled?** AIT
3: 1 *w* you now **return** to me?" AIT
3: 7 that after she had done all this *she w* **return** AIT
3:19 " 'How gladly *w I* **treat** you like sons AIT
3:19 I thought *you w* **call** me 'Father' and AIT
9: 1 *I w* **weep** day and night *for* the slain AIT
12: 1 Yet *I w* **speak** with you about your justice: AIT
15: 1 my heart **w** not go out to this people. NIH
17:23 and *w* not **listen** or respond to discipline. AIT
19:15 and *w* not **listen** *to* my words.' " AIT
22:24 *I w* still **pull** you **off.** AIT
23:22 *they w have* **proclaimed** my words AIT
23:22 to my people and *w have* **turned** them AIT
30:14 as an enemy **w** and punished you as would NIH
30:14 as an enemy would and punished you as **w** NIH
32:33 they *w* not **listen** or respond to discipline. AIT
34:10 that they *w* **free** their male and female AIT
36:25 *he w* not **listen** to them. AIT
36:29 that the king of Babylon *w* **certainly come** AIT
37:10 *they w* **come out** and burn this city down." AIT
37:14 But Irijah *w* not **listen** to him; AIT
38:15 *you w* not **listen** to me." AIT
40: 3 he has done just as he said he **w.** NIH
44:17 will certainly do everything we said we **w:** NIH
49: 9 *w they* not **leave** a few grapes? AIT
49: 9 *w they* not **steal** only as much as they wanted AIT

Jer 51: 9 " '*We w have* **healed** Babylon, AIT
51:60 the disasters that *w* **come** upon Babylon— AIT
La 3:30 to *one who w* **strike** him, AIT
3:36 *w* not the Lord **see** such things? AIT
4:20 that under his shadow *we w* **live** among AIT
Eze 1:12 Wherever the spirit *w* **go,** they would go, AIT
1:12 Wherever the spirit would go, *they w* **go,** AIT
1:17 *they w* **go** in any one of the four directions AIT
1:20 Wherever the spirit *w* **go,** they would go, AIT
1:20 Wherever the spirit would go, *they w* **go,** AIT
1:20 and the wheels *w* **rise** along with them, AIT
3: 6 they *w have* **listened** to you. AIT
4:12 Eat the food as you **w** a barley cake; NIH
10:11 *they w* **go** in any one of the four directions AIT
14:16 They alone *w* **be saved,** AIT
14:16 but the land *w* **be** desolate. AIT
14:18 They alone *w* **be saved.** AIT
14:20 They *w* **save** only themselves AIT
16:56 You **w** not even mention your sister Sodom NIH
17: 8 so that *it w* **produce** branches, AIT
17:14 so that the kingdom *w* **be** brought low, AIT
20: 6 to them that *I w* **bring** them **out** of Egypt AIT
20: 8 " 'But they rebelled against me and **w** 14
20: 8 So I said *I w* **pour out** my wrath on them AIT
20: 9 the sake of my name I did what **w** keep it NIH
20:12 so they *w* **know** that I the LORD made them AIT
20:13 So I said *I w* **pour out** my wrath on them AIT
20:14 the sake of my name I did what **w** keep it NIH
20:15 to them in the desert that I *w* not **bring** them AIT
20:21 So I said *I w* **pour out** my wrath on them AIT
20:22 the sake of my name I did what **w** keep it NIH
20:23 to them in the desert that I *w* **disperse** them AIT
20:26 so *they w* **know** that I am the LORD.' AIT
22:30 a man among them *who w* **build up** the wall AIT
22:30 so *I w* not *have to* **destroy** it, AIT
24: 7 where the dust *w* **cover** it. AIT
24: 8 so that it *w* not **be covered.** AIT
24:13 to cleanse you but *you w* not *be* **cleansed** AIT
33: 5 *he w have* **saved** himself. AIT
38:17 for years that *I w* **bring** you against them. AIT
Da 1:10 king **w** then have my head because of you." NIH
6:12 O king, *w* **be thrown** into the lions' den?" AIT
9: 2 of Jerusalem *w* **last** seventy years. AIT
Hos 6:11 "Whenever I *w* **restore** the fortunes AIT
7: 1 whenever I *w* **heal** Israel, AIT
8: 7 foreigners *w* **swallow** it **up.** AIT
Ob 1: 5 *w they* not **steal** only as much as they wanted AIT
1: 5 *w they* not **leave** a few grapes? AIT
Jnh 4: 5 and waited to see what *w* **happen** to the city. AIT
4: 8 "It **w** be better for me to die than to live." NIH
Mic 2:11 *he w* **be** just the prophet for this people! AIT
Hab 1: 5 in your days that *you w* not **believe,** AIT
Zep 3: 7 her dwelling *w* not **be cut off,** AIT
Zec 1: 4 But *they w* not **listen** or pay attention AIT
7:12 as hard as flint and *w* not **listen** *to* the law AIT
7:13 so when they called, *I w* not **listen,'** AIT
Mal 1: 8 *W he be* **pleased with** you? AIT
1: 8 *W he* **accept** you?" AIT
1:10 that one of you *w* **shut** the temple doors, AIT
1:10 so that *you w* not **light** useless **fires** AIT
Mt 7:12 to others what *you* **w** have them do to you, *2527*
8:13 It will be done just as you believed it **w."** *NIG*
11:21 they **w** have repented long ago in sackcloth *323*
11:23 it **w** have remained to this day. *323*
12: 7 you **w** not have condemned the innocent. *323*
13:15 and turn, and *I w* **heal** them.' *AIT*
16:24 "If anyone **w** come after me, *2527*
18: 6 *it w be* **better** for him to have *AIT*
18:17 to the church, treat him as you **w** a pagan or *NIG*
23:30 we **w** not have taken part with them *323*
24:22 no one *w* **survive,** *AIT*
24:39 about what **w** happen until the flood came *NIG*
24:43 the thief was coming, he **w** have kept watch *323*
24:43 and **w** not have let his house be broken into. *323*
25:27 when I returned I **w** have received it back *323*
26:24 *It w* **be** better for him if he had not been *AIT*
26:25 Then Judas, the one who *w* **betray** him, *AIT*
26:54 But how then *w* the Scriptures *be* **fulfilled** *AIT*
Mk 1:34 but *he w* not **let** the demons speak *AIT*
3: 2 to see if *he w* **heal** him on the Sabbath. *AIT*
5: 5 and in the hills *he* **w** cry out and cut himself *1639*
6:37 **w** take eight months of a man's wages! *NIG*
8:34 "If anyone **w** come after me, *2527*
9:42 *it w* **be** better for him to be thrown into *AIT*
11:16 and *w* not **allow** anyone to carry *AIT*
13:20 no one **w** survive. *323*
14:21 It **w** be better for him if he had not been *NIG*
15:24 they cast lots to see what each *w* **get.** *AIT*
Lk 1:62 to find out what he **w** like to name the child. *323*
2:26 to him by the Holy Spirit that he *w* not **die** *AIT*
4:41 and *w* not **allow** them to speak, *AIT*
6: 7 to see if *he w* **heal** on the Sabbath. *AIT*
6:31 Do to others as *you* **w** have them do to you. *2527*
7:39 he **w** know who is touching him *323*
9:23 "If anyone **w** come after me, *2527*
9:46 the disciples as to which of them *w* **be** *AIT*
10:13 they **w** have repented long ago, *323*
12:39 he **w** not have let his house be broken into. *323*
17: 2 *It w be* **better** for him to be thrown into *AIT*
17: 7 *W he* **say** to the servant when he comes in *AIT*
17: 8 *W he* not rather **say,** 'Prepare my supper, *AIT*
17: 9 *W he* **thank** the servant because he did *AIT*
17:20 when the kingdom of God *w* **come,** *AIT*
18:13 *He* **w** not even look up to heaven, *2527*
19:42 on this day what **w** bring you peace— *NIG*
20:10 to the tenants so *they w* **give** him some of *AIT*
22:23 which of them it might be who **w** do this. *3516*

Lk 22:68 and if I asked you, *you* w not **answer.** *AIT*
Jn 1:33 I *w* not *have* **known** him, *AIT*
2:24 But Jesus *w* not **entrust** himself to them, *AIT*
4:10 you w have asked him and *323*
4:10 and he **w** have given you living water." *323*
5:46 If you believed Moses, you **w** believe me, *323*
6: 7 "Eight months' wages **w** not buy enough *NIG*
6:64 not believe and who *w* **betray** him. *AIT*
7:13 But no one *w* **say** anything publicly *AIT*
8:19 you knew me, you **w** know my Father also." *323*
8:24 I told you that *you w* **die** in your sins; *AIT*
8:39 "then *you* **w do** the things Abraham did. *AIT*
8:42 "If God were your Father, you **w** love me, *323*
8:55 If I said I did not, *I w* **be** a liar like you, *AIT*
9:22 the Christ *w* **be** put out of the synagogue. *AIT*
9:41 you w not be guilty of sin; *323*
11:21 my brother **w** not have died. *323*
11:32 my brother **w** not have died." *323*
11:40 *you w* **see** the glory of God?" *AIT*
11:51 that year he prophesied that Jesus **w** die for *3516*
12:21 "Sir," they said, *"we w* **like** to see Jesus." *AIT*
12:37 *they* still *w* not **believe** in him. *AIT*
12:40 nor turn—and *I w* **heal** them." *AIT*
12:42 the Pharisees *they w* not **confess** their faith *AIT*
12:42 for fear *they w* **be** put out of the synagogue; *AIT*
14: 2 if it were not so, I **w** have told you. *323*
14: 7 *you w* **know** my Father as well. *AIT*
14:28 you **w** be glad that I am going to the Father, *323*
15:19 it **w** love you as its own. *323*
15:22 *they w* not **be guilty of sin.** *AIT*
15:24 *they w* not **be guilty of sin.** *AIT*
17:12 so that Scripture *w be* **fulfilled.** *AIT*
18: 9 the words he had spoken *w be* **fulfilled:** *AIT*
18:14 the Jews that *it w be* **good** if one man died *AIT*
18:30 "we **w** not have handed him over to you." *323*
18:32 death he was going to die *w be* **fulfilled.** *AIT*
18:36 my servants **w** fight to prevent my arrest by *323*
19:11 *"You w* **have** no power over me if it were *AIT*
19:28 and so that the Scripture *w be* **fulfilled,** *AIT*
19:36 so that the scripture *w be* **fulfilled:** *AIT*
21:19 of death by which Peter *w* **glorify** God. *AIT*
21:23 the brothers that this disciple *w* not **die.** *AIT*
21:23 But Jesus did not say that *he w* not **die;** *AIT*
21:25 world *w* not **have room for** the books *AIT*
21:25 for the books that *w be* **written.** *AIT*
Ac 2:30 that he **w** place one of his descendants *NIG*
3:18 saying that his Christ *w* **suffer.** *AIT*
5:24 wondering what **w** come of this. *323*
5:26 they feared that the people *w* **stone** them. *AIT*
6: 2 *"It w* not **be** right for us to neglect *AIT*
7: 5 and his descendants after him *w* **possess** *AIT*
7:19 so that they *w* **die.** *AIT*
7:25 that his own people *w* **realize** that God *AIT*
11:28 that a severe famine **w** spread over *3516*
13:41 in your days that *you w* never **believe,** *AIT*
16: 7 the Spirit of Jesus *w* not **allow** them to. *AIT*
17:27 that men **w** seek him and perhaps reach out *NIG*
18:14 it **w** be reasonable for me to listen to you. *323*
19:13 *They w* **say,** "In the name of Jesus, *AIT*
19:30 but the disciples *w* not **let** him. *AIT*
19:40 In that case *we w* not *be* **able** to account *AIT*
20:20 to preach anything that *w be* **helpful** *AIT*
20:38 that *they* **w** never see his face again. *3516*
21:14 *When* he *w* not **be dissuaded,** *AIT*
21:26 of purification *w* **end** and the offering would *AIT*
21:26 the **offering** *w be* **made** for each of them. *AIT*
23:10 was afraid Paul *w be* **torn to pieces** *AIT*
24: 4 *I w* **request that** you be kind enough *AIT*
24:26 that Paul *w* **offer** him a bribe, *AIT*
25:20 if *he w be* **willing** to go to Jerusalem *AIT*
25:22 *"I w* **like** to hear this man myself." *AIT*
26:22 the prophets and Moses said **w** happen— *3516*
26:23 that the Christ **w** suffer and, *NIG*
26:23 **w** proclaim light to his own people and to *3516*
27: 1 When it was decided that we *w* **sail** *AIT*
27:17 that *they w* **run aground** on the sandbars *AIT*
27:21 you **w** have spared yourselves this damage *NIG*
27:29 that *we w be* **dashed** against the rocks, *AIT*
27:41 The bow stuck fast and **w not move,** *810+3531*
28:24 but others *w* not **believe.** *AIT*
28:27 and turn, and *I w* **heal** them.' *AIT*
Ro 4:13 the promise that he *w be* **heir** of the world, *AIT*
7: 7 *I w* not *have* **known** what sin was except *AIT*
7: 7 For *I w* not *have* **known** what coveting really was *AIT*
9:29 we **w** have become like Sodom, *323*
9:29 we **w** have been like Gomorrah." *323*
11: 6 if it were, grace *w* no longer **be** grace. *AIT*
15:20 so that *I w* not *be* **building** on someone else's *AIT*
1Co 2: 8 they **w** not have crucified the Lord of glory. *323*
5:10 In that case *you w* **have** to leave this world. *AIT*
7:14 Otherwise your children *w* **be** unclean, *AIT*
7:32 *I w* **like** you to be free from concern. *AIT*
9:15 I *w* rather **die** than have anyone deprive me *AIT*
11:31 we **w** not come under judgment. *323*
12:15 *w* not for that reason **cease to be** part of *AIT*
12:16 *w* not for that reason **cease to be** part of *AIT*
12:17 where **w** the sense of hearing be? *NIG*
12:17 where **w** the sense of smell be? *NIG*
12:19 where **w** the body be? *NIG*
14: 5 *I w* **like** every one of you to speak *AIT*
14: 5 but I **w** rather have you prophesy. *NIG*
14:19 *I w* **rather** speak five intelligible words *2527*
2Co 2: 1 that I **w** not make another painful visit *NIG*
2: 3 that you **w** all share my joy. *NIG*
2: 9 if you *w* **stand the test** and be obedient *1509*
3:13 who *w* **put** a veil over his face to keep *AIT*
2Co 5: 8 and *w* **prefer** to be away from the body and *AIT*
7: 3 that *we w* **live** or die with you. *AIT*
9: 3 you may be ready, as I said you **w** be. *NIG*
9: 4 *w be* **ashamed of** having been so confident. *AIT*
10:14 as **w** be the case if we had not come to you, *NIG*
11:16 then receive me just as you **w** a fool, *1569*
11:17 I am not talking as the Lord **w,** *NIG*
12: 6 *I w* not **be** a fool, *AIT*
12: 6 because *I w be* **speaking** the truth. *AIT*
Gal 1:10 I **w** not be a servant of Christ. *323*
3: 2 *I w* **like** to learn just one thing from you: *AIT*
3: 8 The Scripture foresaw that God *w* **justify** *AIT*
3:21 then righteousness **w** certainly have come *323*
4:15 *w have* torn out your eyes and **given** *AIT*
5:12 *w* go the whole way and **emasculate** *AIT*
Eph 6: 5 just as you **w** obey Christ. *NIG*
1Th 3: 3 that no one *w be* **unsettled** by these trials. *AIT*
3: 4 we kept telling you that *we* **w** be persecuted. *3516*
2Th 3: 8 *we w* not **be a burden** to any of you. *AIT*
1Ti 1:16 an example *for* those who **w** believe on him *3516*
Phm 1:13 *I w have* **liked** to keep him with me so *AIT*
1:17 welcome him as you **w** welcome me. *NIG*
Heb 3: 5 *to* what *w be* **said** *in the future.* *AIT*
3:18 that they **w** never enter his rest if not *NIG*
4: 8 God **w** not have spoken later *323*
8: 4 If he were on earth, he **w** not be a priest, *323*
8: 7 no place **w** have been sought for another. *323*
9:26 Then Christ *w have* **had** to suffer many times *AIT*
10: 2 **w** they not have stopped being offered? *323*
10: 2 the worshipers *w have been* **cleansed** once *AIT*
10: 2 **w** no longer have felt guilty for their sins. *NIG*
11: 8 to go to a place *he w* **later** receive *AIT*
11:15 they **w** have had opportunity to return. *323*
11:28 the destroyer of the firstborn *w* not **touch** *AIT*
11:40 together with us *w they be* **made perfect.** *5457*
13:17 for that **w** be of no advantage to you. *NIG*
Jas 5:17 He prayed earnestly that *it w* not **rain,** *AIT*
1Pe 1:11 Christ and the glories **that w follow.** *3552+4047*
3:10 "Whoever **w** love life and see good days *2527*
2Pe 2:21 *It w have been* better for them not to have *1639*
1Jn 2:19 they **w** have remained with us; *323*
Rev 12:14 *she w be* **taken care of** for a time, times and *AIT*

WOULDN'T (5) [NOT, WOULD]

Ge 38:26 since I **w** give her to my son Shelah." 4202
42:22 not to sin against the boy? But you **w** listen! 4202
Nu 14: 3 **W** it be better for us to go back to Egypt?" 4202
Jdg 12: 3 When I saw that you **w** help, 401
1Sa 20: 9 determined to harm you, **w** I tell you?" 4202

WOUND (21) [WIND, WINDING, WINDS, WOUNDED, WOUNDING, WOUNDS]

Ex 21:25 **w** for wound, bruise for bruise. 7206
21:25 wound for **w,** bruise for bruise. 7206
1Ki 22:35 from his **w** ran onto the floor of the chariot, 4804
Job 34: 6 his arrow inflicts an **incurable w.'** 631
Ps 69:26 For they persecute those you **w** and talk 5782
Jer 6:14 the **w** *of* my people as though it were 8691
8:11 the **w** *of* my people as though it were 8691
8:22 Why then is there no **healing for** the **w** 776
10:19 My **w** is incurable! 4804
14:17 has suffered a grievous **w,** a crushing blow. 8691
15:18 and my **w** grievous and incurable? 4804
30:12 " 'Your **w** is incurable, 8691
30:15 Why do you cry out over your **w,** 8691
La 2:13 Your **w** is as deep as the sea. 8691
Da 6:23 no **w** was found on him, 10244
Mic 1: 9 For her **w** is incurable; it has come to Judah. 4804
Na 3:19 Nothing can heal your **w;** 8691
1Co 8:12 in this way and **w** their weak conscience, *5597*
Rev 13: 3 of the beast seemed *to have* **had** a fatal **w,** *5377*
13: 3 but the fatal **w** had been healed. *4435*
13:12 whose fatal **w** had been healed. *4435*

WOUNDED (24) [WOUND]

Dt 32:39 *I have* **w** and I will heal, 4730
Jdg 9:40 and many fell **w** in the flight— 2728
1Sa 31: 3 they **w** *him* critically. 2655
1Ki 20:37 So the man struck him and **w** him. 7205
22:34 get me out of the fighting. *I've* **been w."** 2703
2Ki 8:28 The Arameans **w** Joram; 5782
8:29 son of Ahab because he *had been* **w.** 2703
9:27 They **w** him in his chariot on the way up NIH
1Ch 10: 3 when the archers overtook him, they **w** *him.* 2655
2Ch 18:33 get me out of the fighting. *I've* **been w."** 2703
22: 5 The Arameans **w** Joram; 5782
22: 6 son of Ahab because he *had been* **w.** 2703
24:25 they left Joash severely **w.** 4708
35:23 "Take me away; *I am* badly **w."** 2703
Job 24:12 and the souls of the **w** cry out for help. 2728
Ps 109:22 and my heart *is* **w** within me. 2726
Jer 37:10 and only **w** men were left in their tents, 1991
51: 4 in Babylon, **fatally w** in her streets. 1991
51:52 and throughout her land the **w** will groan. 2728
La 2:12 as they faint like **w** *men* in the streets of 2728
Eze 26:15 at the sound of your fall, when the **w** groan 2728
30:24 before him like a **mortally w man.** 2728
Lk 20:12 and they **w** him and threw him out. *5547*
Rev 13:14 in honor of the beast who *was* **w** *2400+3836+4435*

WOUNDING (1) [WOUND]

Ge 4:23 I have killed a man for **w** me, 7206

WOUNDS (27) [WOUND]

2Ki 8:29 the **w** the Arameans had inflicted on him 4804
9:15 the **w** the Arameans had inflicted on him in 4804
18:21 a man's hand and **w** him if he leans on it! 928+995
2Ch 22: 6 the **w** they had inflicted on him at Ramoth 4804
Job 5:18 For he **w,** but he also binds up; 3872
9:17 a storm and multiply my **w** for no reason. 7206
Ps 38: 5 My **w** fester and are loathsome because 2467
38:11 companions avoid me because of my **w;** 5596
147: 3 the brokenhearted and binds up their **w.** 6780
Pr 20:30 Blows and **w** cleanse away evil, 7206
26:10 an archer *who* **w** at random is he who hires 2726
27: 6 **W** *from* a friend can be trusted, 7206
Isa 1: 6 only **w** and welts and open sores, 7206
30:26 of his people and heals the **w** he inflicted. 4731
36: 6 a man's hand and **w** him if he leans on it! 928+995
53: 5 and by his **w** we are healed. 2467
Jer 6: 7 her sickness and **w** are ever before me. 4804
19: 8 and will scoff because of all its **w.** 4804
30:17 restore you to health and heal your **w,'** 4804
49:17 and will scoff because of all its **w.** 4804
50:13 be horrified and scoff because of all her **w.** 4804
Hos 6: 1 he has injured us but he will bind up our **w.** NIH
Zec 13: 6 'What are these **w** on your body?' 4804
13: 6 'The **w** *I* **was given** at the house 5782
Lk 10:34 He went to him and bandaged his **w,** *5546*
Ac 16:33 the jailer took them and washed their **w;** *4435*
1Pe 2:24 *by* his **w** you have been healed. *3698*

WOVE (1) [WEAVE]

Jdg 16:13 braids of his head, **w** them into the fabric 755

WOVEN (24) [WEAVE]

Ex 28: 4 a breastpiece, an ephod, a robe, a **w** tunic, 9587
28: 8 Its **skillfully w** waistband is to be 682
28:32 a **w** edge like a collar around this 755+5126
29: 5 on him by its skillfully **w** waistband. NIH
31:10 and also the **w** garments, 8573
35:19 the **w** garments worn for ministering in 8573
39: 1 and scarlet yarn they made **w** garments 8573
39: 5 Its **skillfully w** waistband was like it— 682
39:41 and the **w** garments worn for ministering in 8573
Lev 8: 7 ephod to him by its **skillfully w waistband;** 3109
13:48 any **w** or knitted material of linen or wool, 9274
13:49 or leather, or **w** or knitted material, 9274
13:51 or the **w** or knitted material, or the leather, 9274
13:52 the **w** or knitted material of wool or linen, 9274
13:53 or the **w** or knitted material, 9274
13:56 or the leather, or the **w** or knitted material. 9274
13:57 or in the **w** or knitted material, 9274
13:58 The clothing, or the **w** or knitted material, 9274
13:59 **w** or knitted material, or any leather article, 9274
19:19 **w** of two kinds of **material.** 9122
Dt 22:11 of wool and linen **w** together. 9122
Ps 139:15 *I* **was w together** in the depths of the earth, 8387
La 1:14 by his hands *they were* **w together.** 8571
Jn 19:23 **w** in one piece from top to bottom. *5733*

WRAP (5) [WRAPPED, WRAPS]

Nu 4:10 Then *they are to* **w** it and all its accessories 5989
4:12 **w** them in a blue cloth, cover that with 5989
Isa 28:20 the blanket too narrow *to* **w around** *you.* 4043
Jer 43:12 so *will he* **w** Egypt **around himself** 6486
Ac 12: 8 **"W** your cloak **around** *you* and follow me," *4314*

WRAPPED (20) [WRAP]

Ex 12:34 in kneading troughs **w** in clothing. 7674
1Sa 21: 9 it *is* **w** in a cloth behind the ephod. 4286
Job 38: 9 when I made the clouds its garment and **w** it 3157
Ps 109:19 May it be like a cloak **w** about him, 6486
109:29 with disgrace and **w** *in* shame as in a cloak. 6486
Pr 30: 4 Who *has* **w up** the waters in his cloak? 7674
Isa 59:17 the garments of vengeance and **w himself** 6486
Eze 16: 4 rubbed with salt or **w in cloths.** 3156+3156
Jnh 2: 5 seaweed *was* **w around** my head. 2502
Mt 27:59 **w** it in a clean linen cloth, *1962*
Mk 15:46 took down the body, **w** it **in** the linen, *1912*
Lk 2: 7 *She* **w** him **in cloths** and placed him in *5058*
2:12 a baby **w in cloths** and lying in a manger." *5058*
23:53 **w** it in linen cloth and placed it in a tomb *1962*
Jn 11:44 his hands and feet **w** with strips of linen, *1313*
13: 4 **w** a towel **around** his **waist.** *1346*
13: 5 with the towel that was **w around** *him.* *1346*
19:40 Taking Jesus' body, the two of *them* **w** it, *1313*
21: 7 *he* **w** his outer garment **around** him *1346*
Ac 5: 6 young men came forward, **w up** his body, *5366*

WRAPS (3) [WRAP]

Job 26: 8 *He* **w up** the waters in his clouds, 7674
Ps 104: 2 *He* **w himself** *in* light as with a garment; 6486
Jer 43:12 **w** his garment **around him,** 6486

WRATH (197)

Nu 1:53 of the Testimony so that **w** will not fall on 7912
16:46 **W** has come out from the LORD; 7912
18: 5 that **w** will not fall on the Israelites again. 7912
Dt 9: 8 At Horeb *you* **aroused** the LORD's **w** 7911
9:19 I feared the anger and **w** of the LORD, 2779
29:20 his **w** and zeal will burn against that man. 678
29:28 and in great **w** the LORD uprooted them 7912
32:22 For a fire has been kindled by my **w,** 678
Jos 9:20 We will let them live, so that **w** will not fall 7912

Jos 22:20 did not w come upon the whole community 7912
1Sa 28:18 the LORD or carry out his fierce w against 678
2Sa 6: 8 because the LORD's w had broken out 7288
1Ch 13:11 because the LORD's w had broken out 7288
27:24 W came on Israel on account of this 7912
2Ch 12: 7 My w will not be poured out on Jerusalem 2779
19: 2 the w of the LORD is upon you. 7912
19:10 otherwise his w will come on you 7912
32:25 therefore the LORD's w was on him and 7912
32:26 the LORD's w did not come upon them 7912
36:16 and scoffed at his prophets until the w *of* 2779
Ezr 7:23 Why should there be w against the realm of 10634
Ne 13:18 up more w against Israel by desecrating 3019
Job 19:29 for w will bring punishment by the sword, 2779
20:28 rushing waters on the day of God's w. 678
21:20 let him drink of the w *of* the Almighty. 2779
21:30 that he is delivered from the day of w? 6301
40:11 Unleash the fury of your w, 678
Ps 2: 5 in his anger and terrifies them in his w, 3019
2:12 for his w can flare up in a moment. 678
6: 1 in your anger or discipline me in your w. 2779
7:11 a God *who* **expresses** his w every day. 2404
21: 9 In his w the LORD will swallow them up, 678
37: 8 Refrain from anger and turn from w; 2779
38: 1 in your anger or discipline me in your w. 2779
38: 3 of your w there is no health in my body; 2405
59:13 consume them in w, consume them till 2779
69:24 Pour out your w on them; 2405
76:10 your w *against* men brings you praise, 2779
76:10 and the survivors of your w are restrained. 2779
78:21 and his w rose against Israel, 678
78:38 and did not stir up his full w. 2779
78:49 his w, indignation and hostility— 6301
79: 6 Pour out your w on the nations that do 2779
85: 3 You set aside all your w and turned 6301
88: 7 Your w lies heavily upon me; 2779
88:16 Your w has swept over me; 3019
89:46 How long will your w burn like fire? 2779
90: 9 All our days pass away under your w; 6301
90:11 For your w is as great as the fear 6301
102:10 because of your **great** w, 2256+2405+7912
106:23 stood in the breach before him to keep his w 2779
110: 5 he will crush kings on the day of his w. 678
Pr 11: 4 Wealth is worthless in the day of w, 6301
11:23 but the hope of the wicked only in w. 6301
14:35 but a shameful servant incurs his w. 6301
15: 1 A gentle answer turns away w, 2779
16:14 A king's w is a messenger of death, 2779
20: 2 A king's w is like the roar of a lion; 399
21:14 bribe concealed in the cloak pacifies great w 2779
22:14 *he who is* **under** the LORD's w will fall 2404
24:18 and disapprove and turn his w away 678
Isa 9:19 the w *of* the LORD Almighty the land will 6301
10: 5 in whose hand is the club of my w! 2405
10:25 against you will end and my w will 678
13: 3 my warriors to carry out my w— 678
13: 5 the LORD and the weapons of his w— 2405
13: 9 a cruel day, with w and fierce anger— 6301
13:13 the earth will shake from its place at the w 6301
26:20 for a little while until his w has passed by. 2405
30:27 his lips are full of w, 2405
34: 2 his w is upon all their armies. 2779
48: 9 For my own name's sake I delay my w; 678
51:13 because of the w *of* the oppressor, 2779
51:13 For where is the w *of* the oppressor? 2779
51:17 the hand of the LORD the cup of his w, 2779
51:20 with the w *of* the LORD and the rebuke 2779
51:22 from that cup, the goblet of my w, 2779
59:18 so will he repay w to his enemies 2779
63: 3 in my anger and trod them down in my w; 2779
63: 5 and my own w sustained me. 2779
63: 6 in my w I made them drunk 2779
Jer 3: 5 Will your w continue forever?' NIH
4: 4 or my w will break out and burn like fire 2779
6:11 But I am full of the w *of* the LORD, 2779
7:20 and my w will be poured out on this place, 2779
7:29 this generation that is under his w. 6301
10:10 the nations cannot endure his w. 2405
10:25 Pour out your w on the nations that do 2779
18:20 in their behalf to turn your w away 2779
21: 5 a mighty arm in anger and fury and great w. 7912
21:12 or my w will break out and burn like fire 2779
23:19 the storm of the LORD will burst out in w, 2779
25:15 the wine of my w and make all the nations 2779
30:23 the storm of the LORD will burst out in w, 2779
32:31 and w that I must remove it from my sight. 2779
32:37 in my furious anger and great w; 7912
33: 5 of the men I will slay in my anger and w. 2779
36: 7 and w pronounced against this people by 2779
42:18 'As my anger and w have been poured out 2779
42:18 in Jerusalem, so will my w be poured out 2779
50:25 and brought out the weapons of his w, 2405
La 2: 2 in his w he has torn down the strongholds of 6301
2: 4 he has poured out his w like fire on the tent 2779
3: 1 affliction by the rod of his w. 6301
4:11 The LORD has given full vent to his w; 2779
Eze 5:13 "Then my anger will cease and my w 2779
5:13 And when I have spent my w upon them, 2779
5:15 in anger and in w and with stinging rebuke. 2779
6:12 So will I spend my w upon them. 2779
7: 8 I am about to pour out my w on you 2779
7:12 for w is upon the whole crowd. 3019
7:14 for my w is upon the whole crowd. 3019
7:19 to save them in the day of the LORD's w. 6301
9: 8 in this outpouring of your w on Jerusalem?" 2779
13:13 In my w I will unleash a violent wind, 2779
13:15 So I will spend my w against the wall and 2779
Eze 14:19 a plague into that land and pour out my w 2779
16:38 upon you the blood vengeance of my w 2779
16:42 Then my w against you will subside 2779
20: 8 So I said I would pour out my w on them 2779
20:13 So I said I would pour out my w on them 2779
20:21 So I said I would pour out my w on them 2779
20:33 an outstretched arm and with outpoured w. 2779
20:34 an outstretched arm and with outpoured w. 2779
21:17 and my w will subside. 2779
21:31 I will pour out my w upon you 2405
22:20 so will I gather you in my anger and my w 2779
22:21 and I will blow on you with my fiery w, 6301
22:22 that I the LORD have poured out my w 2779
22:24 or showers in the day of w.' 2405
22:31 So I will pour out my w on them 2405
24: 8 up w and take revenge I put her blood on 2779
24:13 you will not be clean again until my w 2779
25:14 in accordance with my anger and my w; 2779
25:17 on them and punish them in my w. 2779
30:15 I will pour out my w on Pelusium, 2779
36: 6 in my jealous w because you have suffered 2779
36:18 So I poured out my w on them 2779
38:19 In my zeal and fiery w I declare that at 6301
Da 8:19 what will happen later in the time of w, 2405
9:16 turn away your anger and your w 2779
11:36 until the time of w is completed, 2405
Hos 5:10 I will pour out my w on them like a flood 6301
11: 9 I will not come in w. 6552
13:11 and in my w I took him away. 6301
Am 1: 3 even for four, I will not turn back **[my w]**. 5647S
1: 6 even for four, I will not turn back **[my w]**. 5647S
1: 9 even for four, I will not turn back **[my w]**. 5647S
1:11 even for four, I will not turn back **[my w]**. 5647S
1:13 even for four, I will not turn back **[my w]**. 5647S
2: 1 even for four, I will not turn back **[my w]**. 5647S
2: 4 even for four, I will not turn back **[my w]**. 5647S
2: 6 even for four, I will not turn back **[my w]**. 5647S
Mic 5:15 I will take vengeance in anger and w upon 2779
7: 9 I will bear the LORD's w, 2408
Na 1: 2 takes vengeance and is filled with w. 2779
1: 2 and **maintains** *his* w against his enemies. 5757
1: 6 His w is poured out like fire; 2779
Hab 3: 2 in w remember mercy. 8075
3: 8 Was your w against the streams? 678
3:12 In w you strode through the earth and 2405
Zep 1:15 That day will be a day of w, 6301
1:18 to save them on the day of the LORD's w. 6301
2: 2 the day of the LORD's w comes upon you. 678
3: 8 the kingdoms and to pour out my w 2405
Mal 1: 4 a people always **under the** w *of* the LORD. 2404
Mt 3: 7 warned you to flee from the coming w? *3973*
Lk 3: 7 warned you to flee from the coming w? *3973*
21:23 in the land and w against this people. *3973*
Jn 3:36 for God's w remains on him." *3973*
Ro 1:18 The w of God is being revealed *3973*
2: 5 you are storing up w against yourself for *3973*
2: 5 against yourself for the day *of* God's w, *3973*
2: 8 there will be w and anger. *3973*
3: 5 That God is unjust in bringing his w on us? *3973*
4:15 because law brings w. *3973*
5: 9 be saved from God's w through him! *3973*
9:22 to show his w and make his power known, *3973*
9:22 with great patience the objects *of* his w— *3973*
12:19 my friends, but leave room *for* God's w, *3973*
13: 4 of w to bring punishment on the wrongdoer. *3973*
Eph 2: 3 we were by nature objects *of* w. *3973*
5: 6 for because of such things God's w comes *3973*
Col 3: 6 Because of these, the w of God is coming. *3973*
1Th 1:10 Jesus, who rescues us from the coming w. *3973*
2:16 The w of God has come upon them at last. *3973*
5: 9 For God did not appoint us to suffer w but *3973*
Rev 6:16 on the throne and from the w of the Lamb! *3973*
6:17 For the great day *of* their w has come, *3973*
11:18 nations were angry; and your w has come. *3973*
14:10 poured full strength into the cup *of* his w. *3973*
14:19 into the great winepress *of* God's w. *2596*
15: 1 because with them God's w is completed. *2596*
15: 7 seven golden bowls filled *with* the w of God *2596*
16: 1 the seven bowls *of* God's w on the earth." *2596*
16:19 with the wine of the fury *of* his w. *3973*
19:15 He treads the winepress of the fury *of* the w *3973*

WREATH (3) [WREATHS]

Isa 28: 1 that w, the pride of Ephraim's drunkards, 6498
28: 3 That w, the pride of Ephraim's drunkards, 6498
28: 5 a beautiful w for the remnant of his people. 6498

WREATHS (4) [WREATH]

1Ki 7:29 and bulls were w *of* hammered work. 4324
7:30 cast with w on each side. 4324
7:36 in every available space, with w all around. 4324
Ac 14:13 and w to the city gates because he and *5098*

WRECKED (2) [SHIPWRECK, SHIPWRECKED]

1Ki 22:48 they **were** w at Ezion Geber. 8689
2Ch 20:37 The ships **were** w and were not able 8689

WRENCHED (2)

Ge 32:25 so that his hip *was* w as he wrestled with 3697
Eze 29: 7 you broke and their backs *were* w. 5048

WREST (KJV) See DENY, DISTORT, PERVERT, TWIST

WRESTLE (1) [WRESTLED, WRESTLING]

Ps 13: 2 How long *must I* w *with* my thoughts 8883

WRESTLED (2) [WRESTLE]

Ge 32:24 and a man w with him till daybreak. 84
32:25 so that his hip was wrenched as he w with 84

WRESTLING (1) [WRESTLE]

Col 4:12 He is always w in prayer for you, *76*

WRETCHED (6) [WRETCHES]

Jdg 11:35 You have made me miserable and w, 6579
Pr 15:15 All the days of the oppressed are w, 8273
Hab 3:14 as though about to devour the w who were 6714
Mt 21:41 "He will bring those wretches to a w end," *2809*
Ro 7:24 What a w man I am! *5417*
Rev 3:17 But you do not realize that you are w, *5417*

WRETCHES (1) [WRETCHED]

Mt 21:41 "He will bring those w to a wretched end," *2805*

WRING (2)

Lev 1:15 w **off** the head and burn it on the altar; 4916
5: 8 *He is to* w its head from its neck, 4916

WRINKLE (1)

Eph 5:27 without stain or w or any other blemish, *4869*

WRIST (2) [WRISTS]

Ge 38:28 a scarlet thread and tied it on his w and said, 3338
38:30 who had the scarlet thread on his w, 3338

WRISTS (3) [WRIST]

Jer 40: 4 freeing you from the chains on your w. 3338
Eze 13:18 who sew magic charms on all their w 723+3338
Ac 12: 7 he said, and the chains fell off Peter's w. *5931*

WRITE (86) [WRITER, WRITES, WRITING, WRITINGS, WRITTEN, WROTE]

Ex 17:14 "W this on a scroll as something to 4180
34: 1 and *I will* w on them the words that were 4180
34:27 "W **down** these words, 4180
Nu 5:23 " 'The priest *is to* w these curses on 4180
17: 2 W the name of each man on his staff. 4180
17: 3 On the staff of Levi w Aaron's name, 4180
Dt 6: 9 W them on the doorframes of your houses 4180
10: 2 *I will* w on the tablets the words that were 4180
11:20 W them on the doorframes of your houses 4180
17:18 *he is to* w for himself on a scroll a copy 4180
27: 3 W on them all the words of this law 4180
27: 8 And *you shall* w very clearly all the words 4180
31:19 "Now w **down** for yourselves this song 4180
Jos 18: 4 a survey of the land and *to* w **a description** 4180
18: 8 a survey of the land and w **a description** 4180
Ezr 5:10 so that *we could* w **down** the names 10374
Est 8: 8 Now w another decree in the king's name 4180
Job 13:26 For *you* w **down** bitter things against me 4180
Ps 87: 6 The LORD *will* w in the register of 6218
Pr 3: 3 w them on the tablet of your heart. 4180
7: 3 w them on the tablet of your heart. 4180
Isa 8: 1 "Take a large scroll and w on it with 4180
10:19 be so few that a child *could* w them **down.** 4180
30: 8 Go now, w it on a tablet for them, 4180
44: 5 still another *will* w *on* his hand, 4180
Jer 30: 2 'W in a book all the words I have spoken 4180
31:33 "I will put my law in their minds and w it 4180
36: 2 and w on it all the words I have spoken 4180
36:17 "Tell us, how *did you come to* w all this? 4180
36:28 and w on it all the words that were on 4180
36:29 that scroll and said, "Why *did you* w on it 4180
Eze 37:16 take a stick of wood and w on it, 4180
37:16 and w on it, 'Ephraim's stick, 4180
43:11 W these **down** before them so that they may 4180
Hab 2: 2 "W **down** the revelation and make it plain 4180
Mk 10: 4 "Moses permitted a man *to* w a certificate *1211*
Lk 1: 3 to me *to* w **an** orderly **account** for you, *1211*
Jn 8: 6 But Jesus bent down and *started to* w on *2863*
19:21 "*Do* not w 'The King of the Jews,' *1211*
Ac 15:20 Instead *we should* w to them, *2182*
25:26 But I have nothing definite *to* w *1211*
25:26 investigation I may have something *to* w. *1211*
1Co 16:21 I, Paul, w this greeting in my own hand. *NIG*
2Co 1:13 not w you anything you cannot read *1211*
9: 1 *to* w to you about this service to the saints. *1211*
13:10 This is why *I* w these things *1211*
Gal 6:11 See what large letters I use as *I* w to you *1211*
Php 3: 1 It is no trouble for me *to* w the same things *1211*
Col 4:18 I, Paul, w this greeting in my own hand. *NIG*
1Th 4: 9 about brotherly love we do not need *to* w *1211*
5: 1 about times and dates we do not need *to* w *1211*
2Th 3:17 *I*, Paul, w this greeting in my own hand, *1211*
3:17 This is how I w. *NIG*
Phm 1:21 Confident of your obedience, *I* w to you, *1211*
Heb 8:10 in their minds and w them **on** their hearts. *2108*
10:16 and *I will* w them **on** their minds." *2108*
1Jn 1: 4 We w this to make our joy complete. *1211*
2: 1 *I* w this to you so that you will not sin. *1211*
2:12 *I* w to you, dear children, *1211*

1Jn 2:13 *I* **w** to you, fathers, *1211*
2:13 *I* **w** to you, young men, *1211*
2:13 *I* **w** to you, dear children, *1211*
2:14 *I* **w** to you, fathers, *1211*
2:14 *I* **w** to you, young men, *1211*
2:21 *I do* not **w** to you because you do not know *1211*
5:13 *I* **w** these things to you who believe in *1211*
2Jn 1:12 I have much *to* **w** to you, *1211*
3Jn 1:13 I have much *to* **w** you, *1211*
Jude 1:3 *to* **w** to you about the salvation we share, *1211*
1:3 I felt I had *to* **w** and urge you to contend for *1211*
Rev 1:11 **"W** on a scroll what you see and send it to *1211*
1:19 **"W,** therefore, what you have seen, *1211*
2:1 "To the angel of the church in Ephesus **w:** *1211*
2:8 "To the angel of the church in Smyrna **w:** *1211*
2:12 the angel of the church in Pergamum **w:** *1211*
2:18 "To the angel of the church in Thyatira **w:** *1211*
3:1 "To the angel of the church in Sardis **w:** *1211*
3:7 the angel of the church in Philadelphia **w:** *1211*
3:12 *I will* **w** on him the name of my God and *1211*
3:12 and I will also **w** on him my new name. *NIG*
3:14 "To the angel of the church in Laodicea **w:** *1211*
10:4 the seven thunders spoke, I was about to **w;** *1211*
10:4 and *do* not **w** it **down."** *1211*
14:13 Then I heard a voice from heaven say, **"W:** *1211*
19:9 Then the angel said to me, **"W:** *1211*
21:5 Then he said, **"W** this **down,** *1211*

WRITER (1) [WRITE]

Ps 45:1 my tongue is the pen of a skillful **w.** 6221

WRITES (3) [WRITE]

Dt 24:1 and *he* **w** her a certificate of divorce, 4180
24:3 and **w** her a certificate of divorce, 4180
2Pe 3:16 He **w** the same way in all his letters, *NIG*

WRITHE (6) [WRITHED, WRITHES]

Isa 13:8 *they will* **w** like a woman in labor. 2655
Jer 4:19 *I* **w in pain.** Oh, the agony of my heart! 2655
Eze 30:16 Pelusium *will* **w in agony.** 2655+2655
Mic 1:12 Those who live in Maroth **w in pain,** 2655
4:10 **W** in agony, O Daughter of Zion, 2655
Zec 9:5 Gaza *will* **w in agony,** and Ekron too, 2655+4394

WRITHED (3) [WRITHE]

Ps 77:16 O God, the waters saw you and **w;** 2655
Isa 26:18 We were with child, *we* **w in pain,** 2655
Hab 3:10 the mountains saw you and **w.** 2655

WRITHES (2) [WRITHE]

Isa 26:17 to give birth **w** and cries out in her pain, 2655
Jer 51:29 The land trembles and **w,** 2655

WRITING (35) [WRITE]

Ex 32:16 the **w** was the writing of God, 4844
32:16 the writing was the **w** *of* God, 4844
Dt 31:24 After Moses finished **w** in a book the words 4180
1Ch 28:19 in **w** from the hand of the LORD upon me, 4181
2Ch 36:22 throughout his realm and to put it in **w:** 4844
Ezr 1:1 throughout his realm and to put it in **w:** 4844
Ne 9:38 **putting** it **in w,** and our leaders, 4180
Job 31:35 *let* my accuser **put** *his* indictment **in w.** 4180
Isa 38:9 A **w** of Hezekiah king of Judah 4844
Eze 9:2 a man clothed in linen who had a **w** kit 6221
9:3 the man clothed in linen who had the **w** kit 6221
9:11 the **w kit** at his side brought back word, 7879
Da 5:7 "Whoever reads this **w** and tells me what 10375
5:8 read the **w** or tell the king what it meant. 10375
5:12 and he will tell you what the **w** means." NIH
5:15 to read this **w** and tell me what it means, 10375
5:16 If you can read this **w** and tell me what 10375
5:17 I will read the **w** for the king 10375
6:8 issue the decree and **put it in w** 10375+10673
6:9 So King Darius **put** the decree **in w.** 10375+10673
6:13 O king, or to the decree *you* **put in w.** 10673
Lk 1:63 He asked for a **w tablet,** *4400*
Ac 15:27 to confirm by word of mouth **what we are w.** *899+3836[S]*
1Co 4:14 *I am* not **w** this to shame you, *1211*
5:11 now *I am* **w** you that you must not associate *1211*
9:15 And *I am* not **w** this in the hope *1211*
14:37 let him acknowledge that what *I am* **w** *1211*
Gal 1:20 before God that what *I am* **w** you is no lie. *1211*
1Ti 3:14 *I am* **w** you these instructions so that, *1211*
Phm 1:19 I, Paul, *am* **w** this with my own hand. *1211*
1Jn 2:7 not **w** you a new command but an old one, *1211*
2:8 Yet *I am* **w** you a new command; *1211*
2:26 *I am* **w** these things to you about those *1211*
2Jn 1:5 I am not **w** you a new command *1211*
Rev 5:1 a scroll **with w** on both sides and sealed *1211*

WRITINGS (2) [WRITE]

Mt 26:56 the **w** of the prophets might be fulfilled." *1210*
Ro 16:26 through the prophetic **w** by the command of *1210*

WRITTEN (257) [WRITE]

Ge 5:1 This is the **w** account of Adam's line. 6219
Ex 24:12 with the law and commands *I have* **w** 4180
32:32 then blot me out of the book *you have* **w."** 4180
Dt 10:4 on these tablets what he had **w** before, 4844
28:58 which *are* **w** in this book, 4180
29:20 the curses **w** in this book will fall upon him, 4180
29:21 the curses of the covenant **w** in this Book of 4180
29:27 so that he brought on it all the curses **w** 4180
30:10 that *are* **w** in this Book of the Law and turn 4180
Jos 1:8 you may be careful to do everything **w** in it. 4180
8:31 according to what *is* **w** in the Book of 4180
8:32 the Law of Moses, which *he had* **w.** 4180
8:34 just as it *is* **w** in the Book of the Law. 4180
10:13 as it *is* **w** in the Book of Jashar. 4180
18:6 After you *have* **w descriptions** *of* 4180
23:6 to obey all that *is* **w** in the Book of the Law 4180
2Sa 1:18 of the bow (*it is* **w** in the Book of Jashar): 4180
1Ki 2:3 as **w** in the Law of Moses, 4180
11:41 not **w** in the book of the annals of Solomon? 4180
14:19 *are* **w** in the book of the annals of the kings 4180
14:29 not **w** in the book of the annals of the kings 4180
15:7 not **w** in the book of the annals of the kings 4180
15:23 not **w** in the book of the annals of the kings 4180
15:31 not **w** in the book of the annals of the kings 4180
16:5 not **w** in the book of the annals of the kings 4180
16:14 not **w** in the book of the annals of the kings 4180
16:20 not **w** in the book of the annals of the kings 4180
16:27 not **w** in the book of the annals of the kings 4180
21:11 as Jezebel directed in the letters she *had* **w** 4180
22:39 not **w** in the book of the annals of the kings 4180
22:45 not **w** in the book of the annals of the kings 4180
2Ki 1:18 not **w** in the book of the annals of the kings 4180
8:23 not **w** in the book of the annals of the kings 4180
10:34 not **w** in the book of the annals of the kings 4180
12:19 not **w** in the book of the annals of the kings 4180
13:8 not **w** in the book of the annals of the kings 4180
13:12 not **w** in the book of the annals of the kings 4180
14:6 in accordance with what *is* **w** in the Book 4180
14:15 not **w** in the book of the annals of the kings 4180
14:18 not **w** in the book of the annals of the kings 4180
14:28 not **w** in the book of the annals of the kings 4180
15:6 not **w** in the book of the annals of the kings 4180
15:11 *are* **w** in the book of the annals of the kings 4180
15:15 *are* **w** in the book of the annals of the kings 4180
15:21 not **w** in the book of the annals of the kings 4180
15:26 *are* **w** in the book of the annals of the kings 4180
15:31 *are* **w** in the book of the annals of the kings 4180
15:36 not **w** in the book of the annals of the kings 4180
16:19 not **w** in the book of the annals of the kings 4180
20:20 not **w** in the book of the annals of the kings 4180
21:17 not **w** in the book of the annals of the kings 4180
21:25 not **w** in the book of the annals of the kings 4180
22:13 the people and for all Judah about **what** is **w** 1821
22:13 with all that *is* **w** there concerning us." 4180
22:16 and its people, according to everything **w** 1821
23:3 the words of the covenant **w** in this book. 4180
23:21 as *it is* **w** in this Book of the Covenant." 4180
23:24 the requirements of the law **w** in the book 4180
23:28 not **w** in the book of the annals of the kings 4180
24:5 not **w** in the book of the annals of the kings 4180
1Ch 16:40 in accordance with everything **w** in the Law 4180
29:29 *are* **w** in the records of Samuel the seer, 4180
2Ch 9:29 not **w** in the records of Nathan the prophet, 4180
12:15 *are* they not **w** in the records of Shemaiah 4180
13:22 *are* **w** in the annotations of the prophet Iddo. 4180
16:11 *are* **w** in the book of the kings of Judah 4180
20:34 *are* **w** in the annals of Jehu son of Hanani, 4180
23:18 of the LORD as **w** in the Law of Moses, 4180
24:27 of God *are* **w** in the annotations on the book 4180
25:4 in accordance with what *is* **w** in the Law, in 4180
25:26 not **w** in the book of the kings of Judah 4180
27:7 *are* **w** in the book of the kings of Israel 4180
28:26 *are* **w** in the book of the kings of Judah 4180
30:5 in large numbers according to what *was* **w.** 4180
30:18 contrary to what *was* **w.** 4180
31:3 New Moons and appointed feasts as **w** in 4180
32:32 and his acts of devotion *are* **w** in the vision 4180
33:18 are **w** in the annals of the kings of Israel. NIH
33:19 all *are* **w** in the records of the seers. 4180
34:21 and Judah about **what** is **w** in this book 1821
34:21 not acted in accordance with all that *is* **w** 4180
34:24 the curses **w** in the book that has been read 4180
34:31 the words of the covenant **w** in this book. 4180
35:4 the **directions w** *by* David king of Israel and 4181
35:12 as *is* **w** in the Book of Moses. 4180
35:25 These became a tradition in Israel and *are* **w** 4180
35:26 to what *is* **w** in the Law of the LORD— 4180
35:27 *are* **w** in the book of the kings of Israel 4180
36:8 *are* **w** in the book of the kings of Israel 4180
Ezr 3:2 in accordance with what *is* **w** in the Law 4180
3:4 Then in accordance with what *is* **w,** 4180
4:7 The letter *was* **w** in Aramaic script and in 4180
5:5 a report could go to Darius and his **w reply** 10496
6:2 and this **was w** on it: 10374
6:18 to **what** is **w** *in* the Book of Moses. 10375
Ne 6:6 in which *was* **w:** "It is reported 4180
7:5 This is what I found **w** there: 4180
8:14 They found **w** in the Law, 4180
8:15 to make booths"—as it *is* **w.** 4180
10:34 as it *is* **w** in the Law. 4180
10:36 "As it *is* also **w** in the Law, 4180
13:1 and there it was found **w** that no Ammonite 4180
Est 1:19 let him issue a royal decree and *let it* **be w** 4180
3:12 *These* **were w** in the name of King Xerxes 4180
8:5 *let an* **order be w** overruling the dispatches 4180
8:8 for no document **w** in the king's name 4180
8:9 These orders were **w** in the script NIH
9:23 doing what Mordecai *had* **w** to them. 4180
9:25 he issued **w** orders that the evil scheme 6219
9:26 Because of everything **w** *in* this letter and 1821
9:32 and *it* **was w down** in the records. 4180
10:2 not **w** in the book of the annals of the kings 4180
Job 19:23 that *they* **were w** on a scroll, 2980
Ps 40:7 *it is* **w** about me in the scroll. 4180
102:18 *Let* this **be w** for a future generation, 4180
139:16 for me **were w** in your book before one 4180
149:9 to carry out the sentence **w** against them. 4180
Pr 22:20 *Have I* not **w** thirty sayings for you, 4180
Isa 65:6 "See, *it stands* **w** before me: 4180
Jer 17:13 Those who turn away from you *will* **be w** 4180
25:13 all that *are* **w** in this book and prophesied 4180
36:27 that Baruch *had* **w** at Jeremiah's dictation, 4180
45:1 after Baruch *had* **w** on a scroll 4180
51:60 Jeremiah *had* **w** on a scroll *about* all 4180
Eze 2:10 of it *were* **w** words of lament and mourning 4180
37:20 before their eyes the sticks *you have* **w** on 4180
Da 5:25 "This is the inscription that **was w:** 10673
9:11 the curses and sworn judgments **w** in 4180
9:13 Just as *it is* **w** in the Law of Moses, 4180
10:21 but first I will tell you what *is* **w** in 8398
12:1 everyone whose name is found **w** in 4180
Mal 3:16 of remembrance **was w** in his presence 4180
Mt 2:5 "for this is what the prophet *has* **w:** *1211*
4:4 Jesus answered, *"It is* **w:** 'Man does not *1211*
4:6 For *it is* **w:** " 'He will command *1211*
4:7 Jesus answered him, *"It is* also **w:** *1211*
4:10 For *it is* **w:** 'Worship the Lord your God, *1211*
11:10 This is the one about whom *it is* **w:** *1211*
21:13 *"It is* **w,"** he said to them, *1211*
26:24 Son of Man will go just as *it is* **w** about him. *1211*
26:31 for *it is* **w:** " 'I will strike the shepherd, *1211*
27:37 Above his head they placed the **w** charge *1211*
Mk 1:2 *It is* **w** in Isaiah the prophet: *1211*
7:6 as *it is* **w:** " 'These people honor me with *1211*
9:12 Why then *is it* **w** that the Son of Man *1211*
9:13 just as *it is* **w** about him." *1211*
11:17 as he taught them, he said, *"Is it* not **w:** *1211*
14:21 of Man will go just as *it is* **w** about him. *1211*
14:27 Jesus told them, "for *it is* **w:** *1211*
15:26 The **w notice** of the charge *2107*
Lk 2:23 (as *it is* **w** in the Law of the Lord, *1211*
3:4 As *is* **w** in the book of the words of Isaiah *1211*
4:4 Jesus answered, *"It is* **w:** 'Man does not *1211*
4:8 Jesus answered, *"It is* **w:** 'Worship the Lord *1211*
4:10 For *it is* **w:** " 'He will command *1211*
4:17 he found the place where it is **w:** *1211*
7:27 This is the one about whom *it is* **w:** *1211*
10:20 rejoice that your names *are* **w in** heaven." *1582*
10:26 "What *is* **w** in the Law?" *1211*
18:31 and everything that *is* **w** by the prophets *1211*
19:46 *"It is* **w,"** he said to them, *1211*
20:17 what is the meaning of that which *is* **w:** *1211*
21:22 in fulfillment of all that *has been* **w.** *1211*
22:37 It *is* **w:** 'And he was numbered with the *1211*
22:37 what is **w** about me is reaching its fulfillment." *NIG*
23:38 There was a **w notice** above him, *2107*
24:44 be fulfilled that *is* **w** about me in the Law *1211*
24:46 He told them, "This is what *is* **w:** *1211*
Jn 2:17 His disciples remembered that it is **w:** *1211*
6:31 as *it is* **w:** 'He gave them bread from heaven *1211*
6:45 It is **w** in the Prophets: *1211*
8:17 In your own Law *it is* **w** that *1211*
10:34 "Is it not **w** in your Law, *1211*
12:14 young donkey and sat upon it, as it is **w,** *1211*
12:16 that these things had been **w** about him and *1211*
15:25 But this is to fulfill what *is* **w** in their Law: *1211*
19:20 and the sign was **w** in Aramaic, *1211*
19:22 Pilate answered, "What *I have* **w,** *1211*
19:22 "What I have written, *I have* **w."** *1211*
20:31 But these *are* **w** that you may believe *1211*
21:25 If every one of them *were* **w down,** *1211*
21:25 for the books that *would be* **w.** *1211*
Ac 1:20 said Peter, *"it is* **w** in the book of Psalms, *1211*
7:42 with *what is* **w** in the book of the prophets: *1211*
13:29 When they had carried out all that *was* **w** *1211*
13:33 As *it is* **w** in the second Psalm: *1211*
15:15 in agreement with this, as *it is* **w:** *1211*
21:25 we *have* **w** to them our decision *2182*
23:5 for *it is* **w:** 'Do not speak evil about *1211*
24:14 with the Law and that *is* **w** in the Prophets, *1211*
Ro 1:17 just as *it is* **w:** "The righteous will live *1211*
2:15 that the requirements of the law are **w** *1209*
2:24 As *it is* **w:** "God's name is blasphemed *1211*
2:27 you have the **w** code and circumcision, *1207*
2:29 by the Spirit, not *by* the **w** code. *1207*
3:4 As *it is* **w:** "So that you may be proved *1211*
3:10 As *it is* **w:** "There is no one righteous *1211*
4:17 As *it is* **w:** "I have made you a father of *1211*
4:23 The words "it was credited to him" *were* **w** *1211*
7:6 and not in the old way *of* the **w code.** *1207*
8:36 As *it is* **w:** "For your sake we face death *1211*
9:13 Just as *it is* **w:** "Jacob I loved, but Esau *1211*
9:33 As *it is* **w:** "See, I lay in Zion a stone *1211*
10:15 As *it is* **w,** "How beautiful are the feet *1211*
11:8 as *it is* **w:** "God gave them a spirit of *1211*
11:26 And so all Israel will be saved, as *it is* **w:** *1211*
12:19 for *it is* **w:** "It is mine to avenge; *1211*
14:11 *It is* **w:** " 'As surely as I live,' *1211*
15:3 as *it is* **w:** "The insults of those who insult *1211*
15:4 For everything that *was* **w in the past** *4592*
15:4 that was written in the past *was* **w** *1211*
15:9 as *it is* **w:** "Therefore I will praise you *1211*
15:15 *I have* **w** you quite boldly on some points, *1211*
15:21 Rather, as *it is* **w:** "Those who were not *1211*
1Co 1:19 For *it is* **w:** "I will destroy the wisdom of *1211*
1:31 Therefore, as *it is* **w:** "Let him who boasts *1211*
2:9 However, as *it is* **w:** "No eye has seen, *1211*
3:19 As *it is* **w:** "He catches the wise *1211*
4:6 "Do not go beyond what *is* **w."** *1211*

1Co 5: 9 *I have* **w** you in my letter not to associate *1211*
9: 9 For *it is* **w** in the Law of Moses: *1211*
9:10 Yes, *this was* **w** for us, *1211*
10: 7 as *it is* **w**: "The people sat down to eat *1211*
10:11 as examples and *were* **w down** as warnings *1211*
14:21 In the Law *it is* **w**: "Through men of *1211*
15:45 So *it is* **w**: "The first Adam became a *1211*
15:54 then the saying that *is* **w** will come true: *1211*
2Co 3: 2 **w on** our hearts, known and read by *1582*
3: 3 **w** not with ink but with the Spirit of *1582*
4:13 *It is* **w**: "I believed; *1211*
8:15 as *it is* **w**: "He who gathered much *1211*
9: 9 As *it is* **w**: "He has scattered abroad his gifts *1211*
Gal 3:10 for *it is* **w**: "Cursed is everyone who *1211*
3:10 to do everything **w** in the Book of the Law." *1211*
3:13 for *it is* **w**: "Cursed is everyone who is hung *1211*
4:22 For *it is* **w** that Abraham had two sons, *1211*
4:27 For *it is* **w**: "Be glad, O barren woman, *1211*
Eph 3: 3 as *I have* **already w** briefly. *4592*
Col 2:14 the **w code,** with its regulations, that was *5934*
Heb 10: 7 *it is* **w** about me in the scroll— *1211*
12:23 whose names *are* **w** in heaven. *616*
13:22 for *I have* **w** you only a short letter. *2182*
1Pe 1:16 for *it is* **w**: "Be holy, because I am holy." *1211*
5:12 *I have* **w** to you briefly, *1211*
2Pe 3: 1 *I have* **w** both of them as reminders *1211*
Jude 1: 4 men whose condemnation **was w about** *4592*
Rev 1: 3 and take to heart what *is* **w** in it, *1211*
2:17 a white stone with a new name **w** on it, *1211*
13: 8 not *been* **w** in the book of life belonging to *1211*
14: 1 and his Father's name **w** on their foreheads. *1211*
17: 5 This title *was* **w** on her forehead: *1211*
17: 8 of the earth whose names *have* not *been* **w** *1211*
19:12 He has a name **w** on him that no one knows *1211*
19:16 and on his thigh he has this name **w**: *1211*
20:15 If anyone's name was not found **w** in *1211*
21:12 On the gates *were* **w** the names of *2108*
21:27 but only those whose names *are* **w** in *1211*

WRONG (101) [WRONGDOER, WRONGDOING, WRONGDOINGS, WRONGED, WRONGING, WRONGS]

Ge 16: 5 responsible for the **w** I am *suffering*. 2805
Ex 2:13 He asked the **one in the w,** 8401
9:27 and I and my people are **in the w.** 8401
23: 2 "Do not follow the crowd in *doing* **w.** 8288
Lev 5:18 **w** *he has* **committed unintentionally,** 8704+8705
Nu 5: 7 He must make full restitution for his **w,** 871
5: 8 to whom restitution can be made for the **w,** 871
15:25 to the LORD for their **w** an offering made 8705
15:26 were involved in the **unintentional w.** 8705
Dt 32: 4 A faithful God who does no **w,** 6404
Jdg 11:27 but you are doing me **w** by waging war 8288
1Sa 11: 5 and he asked, **"What is w** with the people? 4537
19: 4 *"Let* not the king **do w** to his servant David; 2627
19: 5 then *would you* **do w** to an innocent man 2627
25:39 He has kept his servant from doing **w** 8288
26:18 and what **w** am I guilty of? 8288
2Sa 7:14 When he **does w,** I will punish him 6390
13:16 greater **w** than what you have already done 8288
19:19 how your servant **did w** on the day my lord 6390
24:17 "I am the one who has sinned and **done w.** 6390
1Ki 2:44 "You know in your heart all the **w** you did 8288
3: 9 and to distinguish between right and **w.** 8273
8:47 *we have* **done w,** we have acted wickedly'; 6390
18: 9 "What *have I* **done w,"** asked Obadiah, 2627
2Ki 18:14 *"I have* **done w.** Withdraw from me, 2627
1Ch 21:17 I am the one who has sinned and **done w.** 8317+8317
2Ch 6:37 *we have* **done w** and acted wickedly'; 6390
22: 3 for his mother encouraged him in **doing w.** 8399
Ne 9:33 you have acted faithfully, while we **did w.** 8399
Est 1:16 "Queen Vashti *has* **done w,** 6390
Job 6:24 show me where *I have been* **w.** 8706
21:27 the schemes by which *you would* **w** me. 2803
31: 3 disaster for those who do **w?** 224
32:12 But not *one* of you *has* **proved** Job **w;** 3519
34:10 from the Almighty to do **w.** 6404
34:12 It is unthinkable that God *would* **do w,** 8399
34:32 if I have done **w,** I will not do so again.' 6404
36:23 or said to him, 'You have done **w'?** 6406
Ps 5: 5 you hate all who do **w.** 224
15: 3 who does his neighbor no **w** 8288
36: 4 and does not reject *what* is **w.** 8273
37: 1 or be envious of those who do **w;** 6406
59: 4 I have done no **w,** yet they are ready to 6411
106: 6 *we have* **done w** and acted wickedly. 6390
119: 3 They do nothing **w;** they walk in his ways. 6406
119:104 therefore I hate every **w** path. 9214
119:128 I hate every **w** path. 9214
Pr 2:14 in doing **w** and rejoice in the perverseness 8273
20:22 Do not say, "I'll pay you back for this **w!"** 8273
28:21 yet a man *will* **do w** for a piece of bread. 7321
28:24 or mother and says, "It's not **w"**— 7322
30:20 'I've done nothing **w.'** 224
Ecc 5: 1 who do not know that they do **w.** 8273
8:11 the people are filled with schemes to do **w.** 8273
Isa 1:16 evil deeds out of my sight! Stop **doing w,** 8317
7:15 when he knows enough to reject the **w** 8273
7:16 the boy knows enough to reject the **w** 8273
Jer 16:10 What **w** have we done? 6411
22: 3 **Do** no **w** or violence to the alien, 3561
51:24 in Babylonia for all the **w** they have done 8288
La 3:59 O LORD, the **w** *done to* me. 6432
Eze 18: 8 He withholds his hand from **doing w** 6404
18:18 robbed his brother and did what was **w** 3202+4202
Da 6:22 Nor have I ever done any **w** before you, 10242
9: 5 we have sinned and **done w.** 6390
9:15 we have sinned, *we have* **done w.** 8399
Hab 1: 3 Why do you tolerate **w?** 6662
1:13 you cannot tolerate **w.** 6662
Zep 3: 5 LORD within her is righteous; he does no **w.** 6406
3:13 The remnant of Israel will do no **w;** 6406
Mal 1: 8 blind animals for sacrifice, is that not **w?** 8273
1: 8 or diseased animals, is that not **w?** 8273
Lk 23:41 But this man has done nothing **w."** *876*
Jn 18:23 "If I said something **w,"** Jesus replied, *2809*
18:23 Jesus replied, "testify as to what *is* **w.** *2805*
Ac 23: 9 "We find nothing **w** with this man," *2805*
25: 5 if he has done anything **w."** *876*
25: 8 *"I have* **done** nothing **w** against the law of *279*
25:10 *I have* not **done** any **w** to the Jews, *92*
Ro 13: 3 but *for* those who do **w.** *2805*
13: 4 But if you do **w,** be afraid, *2805*
14:20 but it is **w** for a man to eat anything *2805*
1Co 6: 8 Instead, *you* yourselves cheat and **do w,** *92*
2Co 7:12 not on account of the one who **did** the **w** or *92*
12:13 Forgive me this **w!** *94*
13: 7 to God that you will not do anything **w.** *2805*
Gal 2:11 because he was **clearly in the w.** *2861*
4:12 *You have* **done** me no **w.** *92*
Col 3:25 Anyone who **does w** will be repaid *92*
3:25 will be repaid for *his* **w,** *92*
1Th 4: 6 in this matter no one should **w** his brother *5648*
5:15 that nobody pays back **w** for wrong, *2805*
5:15 that nobody pays back wrong for **w,** *2805*
Phm 1:18 If *he has* **done** you any **w** or owes you *92*
Heb 8: 7 For if there had been **nothing w with** *289*
Jas 4: 3 because you ask with **w** motives, *2809*
1Pe 2:12 though they accuse you of **doing w,** *2804*
2:14 by him to punish *those who* **do w** and *2804*
2:20 a beating *for* **doing w** and endure it? *279*
Rev 22:11 Let him who **does w** continue to do wrong; *92*
22:11 *Let* him who does wrong continue *to* **do w;** *92*

WRONGDOER (1) [WRONG]

Ro 13: 4 wrath to bring punishment *on* the **w.** *2805+4556*

WRONGDOING (12) [WRONG]

Lev 5:19 *he has been* **guilty of w** against the LORD 870+870
Nu 5:31 The husband will be innocent of any **w,** 6411
1Sa 24:11 and recognize that I am not guilty of **w** 8288
25:28 Let no **w** be found in you as long 8288
25:39 and has brought Nabal's **w** down on his own 8288
1Ki 2:44 Now the LORD will repay you for your **w.** 8288
Job 1:22 Job did not sin by charging God with **w.** 9524
24:12 But God charges no one with **w.** 9524
33:17 to turn man from **w** and keep him 5126
Pr 16:12 Kings detest **w,** for a throne is 6913+8400
2Pe 2:16 he was rebuked *for* his **w** by a donkey— *4175*
1Jn 5:17 All **w** is sin, and there is sin that *94*

WRONGDOINGS (1) [WRONG]

Jer 5:25 Your **w** have kept these away; 6411

WRONGED (11) [WRONG]

Ge 20: 9 How *have I* **w** you that you have brought 2627
Nu 5: 7 to it and give it all to the person *he has* **w.** 870
16:15 nor *have I* **w** any of them." 8317
Jdg 11:27 I *have* not **w** you, but you are doing me 2627
1Sa 19: 4 *he has* not **w** you, and what he has done 2627
20: 1 How have I **w** your father, 2633
24:11 *I have* not **w** you, but you are hunting me 2627
Job 19: 6 that God *has* **w** me and drawn his net 6430
19: 7 "Though I cry, 'I've been **w!'** 2805
1Co 6: 7 Why not rather *be* **w?** *92*
2Co 7: 2 *We have* **w** no one, we have corrupted no one *92*

WRONGING (1) [WRONG]

Ps 119:78 May the arrogant be put to shame for **w** me 6430

WRONGS (10) [WRONG]

Ge 50:15 and pays us back for all the **w** we did 8288
50:17 and the **w** they committed in treating you 2633
Nu 5: 6 man or woman **w** another in any way 2633+6913
1Sa 24:12 the LORD **avenge** *the* **w** you have done 5933
1Ki 8:31 a man **w** his neighbor and is required to take 2627
2Ch 6:22 a man **w** his neighbor and is required to take 2627
Job 13:23 How many **w** and sins have I committed? 6411
Pr 10:12 but love covers over all **w.** 7322
Zep 3:11 to shame for all the **w** you *have* done to me, 7321
1Co 13: 5 it keeps no record of **w.** *2805*

WROTE (59) [WRITE]

Ex 24: 4 Moses then **w down** everything the LORD 4180
34:28 And *he* **w** on the tablets the words of 4180
Dt 4:13 and then **w** them on two stone tablets. 4180
5:22 Then he **w** them on two stone tablets 4180
10: 4 The LORD **w** on these tablets 4180
31: 9 So Moses **w down** this law and gave it to 4180
31:22 So Moses **w down** this song that day 4180
Jos 18: 9 *They* **w** its **description** on a scroll, 4180
Jdg 8:14 the young man **w down** for him the names 4180
1Sa 10:25 *He* **w** them **down** on a scroll and deposited 4180
2Sa 11:14 In the morning David **w** a letter to Joab 4180
11:15 In it *he* **w,** "Put Uriah in the front line 4180
1Ki 21: 8 So *she* **w** letters in Ahab's name, 4180
21: 9 In those letters *she* **w**: 4180
2Ki 10: 1 So Jehu **w** letters and sent them to Samaria: 4180
10: 6 Then Jehu **w** them a second letter, saying, 4180
17:37 the laws and commands *he* **w** for you. 4180
2Ch 30: 1 also **w** letters to Ephraim and Manasseh, 4180
32:17 king also **w** letters insulting the LORD, 4180
Ezr 4: 7 of his associates **w** a letter to Artaxerxes. 4180
4: 8 the secretary **w** a letter against Jerusalem 10374
Est 3:12 *They* **w out** in the script of each province 4180
8: 5 devised and **w** to destroy the Jews in all 4180
8: 9 *They* **w out** all Mordecai's orders to 4180
8:10 Mordecai **w** in the name of King Xerxes, 4180
9:22 He **w** them to observe the days as days NIH
9:29 **w** with full authority to confirm 4180
Ecc 12:10 and what *he* **w** was upright and true. 4180
Jer 36: 4 Baruch **w** them on the scroll. 4180
36: 6 words of the LORD that *you* **w** as I dictated. 4180
36:18 and I **w** them in ink on the scroll." 4180
36:32 Baruch **w** on it all the words of the scroll 4180
Da 5: 5 a human hand appeared and **w** on the plaster 10374
5: 5 The king watched the hand as *it* **w.** 10374
5:24 Therefore he sent the hand that **w** 10673
6:25 Then King Darius **w** to all the peoples, 10374
7: 1 *He* **w down** the substance of his dream. 10374
Hos 8:12 *I* **w** for them the many things of my law, 4180
Mk 10: 5 that Moses **w** you this law," *1211*
12:19 "Moses **w** for us that if a man's brother dies *1211*
Lk 1:63 and to everyone's astonishment *he* **w,** *1211*
20:28 "Moses **w** for us that if a man's brother dies *1211*
Jn 1:45 "We have found the one Moses **w about** in *1211*
1:45 and about whom the prophets also **w**— *NIG*
5:46 you would believe me, for he **w** about me. *1211*
5:47 But since you do not believe what he **w,** *1207*
8: 8 Again he stooped down and **w** on *1211*
21:24 to these things and who **w** them **down.** *1211*
Ac 1: 1 *I* **w** about all that Jesus began to do and *4472*
18:27 the brothers encouraged him and **w** to *1211*
23:25 *He* **w** a letter as follows: *1211*
Ro 16:22 I, Tertius, who **w down** this letter, *1211*
1Co 7: 1 Now for the matters *you* **w** about: *1211*
2Co 2: 3 *I* **w** as I did so that when I came I should *1211*
2: 4 For *I* **w** you out of great distress *1211*
2: 9 The reason *I* **w** you was to see *1211*
7:12 So even though *I* **w** to you, *1211*
2Pe 3:15 as our dear brother Paul also **w** you with *1211*
3Jn 1: 9 *I* **w** to the church, but Diotrephes, *1211*

WROUGHT (1)

Eze 27:19 they exchanged **w** iron, cassia and calamus 6936

WRUNG (1)

Jdg 6:38 he squeezed the fleece and **w out** the dew— 5172

X

XERXES (31)

Ezr 4: 6 At the beginning of the reign of **X,** 347
Est 1: 1 during the time of **X,** the Xerxes who ruled 347
1: 1 the **X** who ruled over 127 provinces 347
1: 2 At that time King **X** reigned from his royal 347
1: 9 the women in the royal palace of King **X.** 347
1:10 King **X** was in high spirits from wine, 347
1:15 not obeyed the command of King **X** that 347
1:16 the peoples of all the provinces of King **X.** 347
1:17 'King **X** commanded Queen Vashti to 347
1:19 never again to enter the presence of King **X.** 347
2: 1 when the anger of King **X** had subsided, 347
2:12 a girl's turn came to go in to King **X,** 347
2:16 taken to King **X** in the royal residence in 347
2:21 and conspired to assassinate King **X.** 347
3: 1 King **X** honored Haman son of Hammedatha 347
3: 6 throughout the whole kingdom of **X.** 347
3: 7 In the twelfth year of King **X,** 347
3: 8 Then Haman said to King **X,** 347
3:12 in the name of King **X** *himself* and sealed 347
6: 2 who had conspired to assassinate King **X.** 347
7: 5 King **X** asked Queen Esther, "Who is he? 347
8: 1 That same day King **X** gave Queen Esther 347
8: 7 King **X** replied to Queen Esther and 347
8:10 Mordecai wrote in the name of King **X,** 347
8:12 of King **X** was the thirteenth day of 347
9: 2 in their cities in all the provinces of King **X** 347
9:20 throughout the provinces of King **X,** 347
9:30 in the 127 provinces of the kingdom of **X**— 347
10: 1 King **X** imposed tribute throughout 347
10: 3 the Jew was second in rank to King **X,** 347
Da 9: 1 In the first year of Darius son of **X** (a Mede 347

Y

YAHWEH See †LORD

YARDS (3)

Jos 3: 4 But keep a distance of about a thousand y 564
Ne 3:13 also repaired **five hundred** y of the wall 547+564
Jn 21: 8 about a **hundred** y. *1357+4388*

YARN (34)

Ex 25: 4 purple and **scarlet** y and fine linen; 9106+9357
26: 1 purple and **scarlet** y, 9106+9357
26:31 and **scarlet** y and finely twisted linen, 9106+9357
26:36 and **scarlet** y and finely twisted linen 9106+9357
27:16 and **scarlet** y and finely twisted linen 9106+9357
28: 5 purple and **scarlet** y, and fine linen. 9106+9357
28: 6 and of blue, purple and **scarlet** y, 9106+9357
28: 8 and with blue, purple and **scarlet** y, 9106+9357
28:15 and of blue, purple and **scarlet** y, 9106+9357
28:33 **scarlet** y around the hem of the robe, 9106+9357
35: 6 purple and **scarlet** y and fine linen; 9106+9357
35:23 purple or **scarlet** y or fine linen, 9106+9357
35:25 blue, purple or **scarlet** y or fine linen. 9106+9357
35:35 purple and **scarlet** y and fine linen, 9106+9357
36: 8 purple and **scarlet** y, 9106+9357
36:35 and **scarlet** y and finely twisted linen, 9106+9357
36:37 and **scarlet** y and finely twisted linen 9106+9357
38:18 and **scarlet** y and finely twisted linen 9106+9357
38:23 purple and **scarlet** y and fine linen.) 9106+9357
39: 1 **scarlet** y they made woven garments 9106+9357
39: 2 and of blue, purple and **scarlet** y, 9106+9357
39: 3 purple and **scarlet** y and fine linen— 9106+9357
39: 5 and with blue, purple and **scarlet** y, 9106+9357
39: 8 and of blue, purple and **scarlet** y, 9106+9357
39:24 and **scarlet** y and finely twisted linen 9106+9357
39:29 purple and **scarlet** y— 9106+9357
Lev 14: 4 **scarlet** y and hyssop be brought for 9106+9357
14: 6 the **scarlet** y and the hyssop, 9106+9357
14:49 **scarlet** y and hyssop. 9106+9357
14:51 hyssop, the **scarlet** y and the live bird, 9106+9357
14:52 the hyssop and the **scarlet** y. 9106+9357
2Ch 2: 7 and in purple, crimson and **blue** y, 9418
2:14 and with purple and **blue** and crimson y 9418
3:14 **blue,** purple and crimson y 9418

YAUDI (1)

2Ki 14:28 and Hamath, which had belonged to **Y**, 3373

YEA (KJV) See YES

YEAR (350) [YEAR-OLD, YEAR'S, YEARLING, YEARLY, YEARS]

Ge 7:11 In the six hundredth y of Noah's life, 9102
8:13 month of Noah's six hundred and first y, 9102
14: 4 but in the thirteenth y they rebelled. 9102
14: 5 In the fourteenth y, Kedorlaomer and 9102
17:21 will bear to you by this time next y." 9102
18:10 surely return to you about this time **next** y, 2645
18:14 to you at the appointed time **next** y 2645
26:12 and the same y reaped a hundredfold, 9102
47:17 through that y with food in exchange 9102
47:18 When that y was over, 9102
47:18 they came to him the following y and said, 9102
Ex 12: 2 the first month of your y. 9102
13:10 at the appointed time y after year. 3427
13:10 at the appointed time year after y. 3427
21: 2 But in the seventh y, he shall go free, NIH
23:11 the seventh y let the land lie unplowed NIH
23:14 a y you are to celebrate a festival to me. 9102
23:16 the Feast of Ingathering at the end of the y, 9102
23:17 "Three times a y all the men are to appear 9102
23:29 But I will not drive them out in a single y, 9102
29:38 regularly each day: two lambs a y old. 9102
30:10 Once a y Aaron shall make atonement 9102
34:22 the Feast of Ingathering at the turn of the y. 9102
34:23 Three times a y all your men are to appear 9102
34:24 up three times each y to appear before 9102
40:17 of the first month in the second y. 9102
Lev 9: 3 both a y old and without defect— 9102
14:10 and one ewe lamb a y old, 9102
16:34 Atonement is to be made once a y for all 9102
19:24 In the fourth y all its fruit will be holy, 9102
19:25 But in the fifth y you may eat its fruit. 9102
23:12 the LORD a lamb a y old without defect, 9102
23:18 each a y old and without defect, 9102
23:19 each a y old, for a fellowship offering. 9102
23:41 to the LORD for seven days each y. 9102
25: 4 the seventh y the land is to have a sabbath 9102
25: 5 The land is to have a y *of* rest. 9102
25: 6 during the sabbath y will be food for you— NIH
25:10 the fiftieth y and proclaim liberty 9102
25:11 The fiftieth y shall be a jubilee for you; 9102
25:13 " 'In this **Y** *of* Jubilee everyone is to return 9102
25:20 "What will we eat in the seventh y if we do 9102
25:21 the sixth y that the land will yield enough 9102
Lev 25:22 While you plant during the eighth y, 9102
25:22 until the harvest of the ninth y comes in. 9102
25:28 in the possession of the buyer until the **Y** 9102
25:29 he retains the right of redemption a full y 9102
25:30 not redeemed before a full y has passed, 9102
25:40 he is to work for you until the **Y** *of* Jubilee. 9102
25:50 to count the time from the y he sold himself 9102
25:50 from the year he sold himself up to the **Y** 9102
25:52 a few years remain until the **Y** *of* Jubilee, 9102
25:53 to be treated as a man hired from y to year; 9102
25:53 to be treated as a man hired from year to y; 9102
25:54 and his children are to be released in the **Y** 9102
27:17 If he dedicates his field during the **Y** 9102
27:18 that remain until the next **Y** *of* Jubilee, 9102
27:23 determine its value up to the **Y** *of* Jubilee, 9102
27:24 In the **Y** *of* Jubilee the field will revert to 9102
Nu 1: 1 of the second y after the Israelites came out 9102
7:15 one ram and one male lamb a y old, 9102
7:17 and five male lambs a y old, 9102
7:21 one ram and one male lamb a y old, 9102
7:23 and five male lambs a y old, 9102
7:27 one ram and one male lamb a y old, 9102
7:29 and five male lambs a y old, 9102
7:33 one ram and one male lamb a y old, 9102
7:35 and five male lambs a y old, 9102
7:39 one ram and one male lamb a y old, 9102
7:41 and five male lambs a y old, 9102
7:45 one ram and one male lamb a y old, 9102
7:47 and five male lambs a y old, 9102
7:51 one ram and one male lamb a y old, 9102
7:53 and five male lambs a y old, 9102
7:57 one ram and one male lamb a y old, 9102
7:59 and five male lambs a y old, 9102
7:63 one ram and one male lamb a y old, 9102
7:65 and five male lambs a y old, 9102
7:69 one ram and one male lamb a y old, 9102
7:71 and five male lambs a y old, 9102
7:75 one ram and one male lamb a y old, 9102
7:77 and five male lambs a y old, 9102
7:81 one ram and one male lamb a y old, 9102
7:83 and five male lambs a y old, 9102
7:87 twelve rams and twelve male lambs a y old, 9102
7:88 and sixty male lambs a y old. 9102
9: 1 the second y after they came out of Egypt. 9102
9:22 a month or a y, the Israelites would remain 3427
10:11 of the second month of the second y, 9102
14:34 forty years—one y for each of the forty days 9102
28: 3 two lambs a y old without defect, 9102
28: 9 make an offering of two lambs a y old 9102
28:11 one ram and seven male lambs a y old, 9102
28:14 to be made at each new moon during the y. 9102
28:19 one ram and seven male lambs a y old, 9102
28:27 a y old as an aroma pleasing to the LORD. 9102
29: 2 one ram and seven male lambs a y old, 9102
29: 8 one ram and seven male lambs a y old, 9102
29:13 two rams and fourteen male lambs a y old, 9102
29:17 two rams and fourteen male lambs a y old, 9102
29:20 two rams and fourteen male lambs a y old, 9102
29:23 two rams and fourteen male lambs a y old, 9102
29:26 two rams and fourteen male lambs a y old, 9102
29:29 two rams and fourteen male lambs a y old, 9102
29:32 two rams and fourteen male lambs a y old, 9102
29:36 one ram and seven male lambs a y old, 9102
33:38 of the fortieth y after the Israelites came out 9102
36: 4 the **Y of Jubilee** for the Israelites comes, 3413
Dt 1: 3 In the fortieth y, on the first day of 9102
11:12 on it from the beginning of the y to its end. 9102
14:22 of all that your fields produce **each** y. 9102+9102
15: 9 "The seventh y, the year for canceling 9102
15: 9 the y *for* canceling debts, is near," 9102
15:12 in the seventh y you must let him go free. 9102
15:20 **Each** y you and your family are to eat them 928+9102+9102
16:16 Three times a y all your men must appear 9102
24: 5 *For* one y he is to be free to stay at home 9102
26:12 a tenth of all your produce in the third y, 9102
26:12 in the third year, the y *of* the tithe, 9102
31:10 in the y *for* canceling debts, 9102
Jos 5:12 that y they ate of the produce of Canaan. 9102
Jdg 10: 8 who that y shattered and crushed them. 9102
11:40 that **each** y the young women of Israel go out for four days 2025+3427+3427+4946
17:10 you ten shekels of silver a y, 2021+3427+4200
1Sa 1: 3 **Y** after year this man went up 3427
1: 3 after y this man went up from his town 3427
1: 7 This went on y after year. 9102
1: 7 This went on year after y. 9102
2:19 **Each** y his mother made him a little robe 2025+3427+3427+4946
7:16 From y to year he went on a circuit 9102
7:16 to y he went on a circuit from Bethel 9102
27: 7 in Philistine territory a y and four months. 3427
29: 3 He has already been with me for **over a** y, 196+2296+2296+3427+9102
1Ki 4: 7 to provide supplies for one month in the y. 9102
5:11 Solomon continued to do this for Hiram y 9102
5:11 to do this for Hiram year after y. 9102
6: 1 In the four hundred and eightieth y after 9102
6: 1 the fourth y of Solomon's reign over Israel, 9102
6:37 of the LORD was laid in the fourth y, 9102
6:38 In the eleventh y in the month of Bul, 9102
9:25 a y Solomon sacrificed burnt offerings 9102
10:25 **Y** after year, everyone who came brought 9102
10:25 Year after y, everyone who came brought 9102
14:25 In the fifth y of King Rehoboam, 9102
15: 1 In the eighteenth y of the reign 9102
15: 9 the twentieth y of Jeroboam king of Israel, 9102
1Ki 15:25 in the second y of Asa king of Judah, 9102
15:28 in the third y of Asa king of Judah 9102
15:33 In the third y of Asa king of Judah, 9102
16: 8 In the twenty-sixth y of Asa king of Judah, 9102
16:10 the twenty-seventh y of Asa king of Judah. 9102
16:15 the twenty-seventh y of Asa king of Judah, 9102
16:23 In the thirty-first y of Asa king of Judah, 9102
16:29 In the thirty-eighth y of Asa king of Judah, 9102
18: 1 After a long time, in the third y, 9102
22: 2 the third y Jehoshaphat king of Judah went 9102
22:41 of Asa became king of Judah in the fourth y 9102
22:51 in the seventeenth y of Jehoshaphat king 9102
2Ki 1:17 as king in the second y of Jehoram son 9102
3: 1 in the eighteenth y of Jehoshaphat king 9102
4:16 "About this time **next** y," Elisha said, 2645+6961
4:17 and the **next** y about that same time 2645+6961
8:16 In the fifth y of Joram son of Ahab king 9102
8:25 In the twelfth y of Joram son of Ahab king 9102
8:26 and he reigned in Jerusalem one y. 9102
9:29 (In the eleventh y of Joram son of Ahab, 9102
11: 4 In the seventh y Jehoiada sent for 9102
12: 1 In the seventh y of Jehu, 9102
12: 6 But by the twenty-third y of King Joash 9102
13: 1 In the twenty-third y of Joash son 9102
13:10 the thirty-seventh y of Joash king of Judah, 9102
14: 1 In the second y of Jehoash son of Jehoahaz 9102
14:23 In the fifteenth y of Amaziah son of Joash 9102
15: 1 In the twenty-seventh y of Jeroboam king 9102
15: 8 In the thirty-eighth y of Azariah king 9102
15:13 of Jabesh became king in the thirty-ninth y 9102
15:17 the thirty-ninth y of Azariah king of Judah, 9102
15:23 In the fiftieth y of Azariah king of Judah, 9102
15:27 the fifty-second y of Azariah king of Judah, 9102
15:30 in the twentieth y of Jotham son of Uzziah. 9102
15:32 In the second y of Pekah son of Remaliah 9102
16: 1 In the seventeenth y of Pekah son of 9102
17: 1 In the twelfth y of Ahaz king of Judah, 9102
17: 4 as he had done y by year. 9102
17: 4 as he had done year by y. 9102
17: 6 In the ninth y of Hoshea, the king of 9102
18: 1 In the third y of Hoshea son of Elah king 9102
18: 9 In King Hezekiah's fourth y, 9102
18: 9 the seventh y of Hoshea son of Elah king 9102
18:10 Samaria was captured in Hezekiah's sixth y, 9102
18:10 which was the ninth y of Hoshea king 9102
18:13 the fourteenth y of King Hezekiah's reign, 9102
19:29 "This y you will eat what grows by itself, 9102
19:29 and the second y what springs from that. 9102
19:29 But in the third y sow and reap, 9102
22: 3 In the eighteenth y of his reign, 9102
23:23 But in the eighteenth y of King Josiah, 9102
24:12 In the eighth y of the reign of the king 9102
25: 1 So in the ninth y of Zedekiah's reign, 9102
25: 2 until the eleventh y of King Zedekiah. 9102
25: 8 in the nineteenth y of Nebuchadnezzar king 9102
25:27 In the thirty-seventh y of the exile 9102
25:27 in the y Evil-Merodach became king 9102
1Ch 26:31 In the fortieth y of David's reign 9102
27: 1 on duty month by month throughout the y. 9102
2Ch 3: 2 of the second month in the fourth y 9102
9:24 **Y** after year, everyone who came brought 9102
9:24 Year after y, everyone who came brought 9102
12: 2 of Egypt attacked Jerusalem in the fifth y 9102
13: 1 the eighteenth y of the reign of Jeroboam, 9102
15:10 in the third month of the fifteenth y 9102
15:19 until the thirty-fifth y of Asa's reign. 9102
16: 1 In the thirty-sixth y of Asa's reign 9102
16:12 In the thirty-ninth y*of* his reign Asa 9102
16:13 in the forty-first y *of* his reign Asa died 9102
17: 7 In the third y*of* his reign he sent 9102
21:19 at the end of the second y, 3427
22: 2 and he reigned in Jerusalem one y. 9102
23: 1 the seventh y Jehoiada showed his strength. 9102
24:23 At the turn of the y, the army of Aram 9102
27: 5 That y the Ammonites paid him 9102
29: 3 In the first month of the first y of his reign, 9102
34: 3 In the eighth y *of* his reign, 9102
34: 3 In his twelfth y he began to purge Judah 9102
34: 8 In the eighteenth y *of* Josiah's reign, 9102
35:19 in the eighteenth y of Josiah's reign. 9102
36:22 In the first y of Cyrus king of Persia, 9102
Ezr 1: 1 In the first y of Cyrus king of Persia, 9102
3: 8 the second y after their arrival at the house 9102
4:24 to a standstill until the second y of the reign 10732
5:13 in the first y of Cyrus king of Babylon, 10732
6: 3 In the first y of King Cyrus, the king issued 10732
6:15 in the sixth y of the reign of King Darius. 10732
7: 7 also came up to Jerusalem in the seventh y 9102
7: 8 the fifth month of the seventh y of the king. 9102
Ne 1: 1 In the month of Kislev in the twentieth y, 9102
2: 1 In the month of Nisan in the twentieth y 9102
5:14 from the twentieth y of King Artaxerxes, 9102
5:14 until his thirty-second y— 9102
10:31 Every seventh y we will forgo working 9102
10:32 a shekel each y for the service of the house 9102
10:34 to the house of our God at set times **each** y a contribution 928+9102+9102
10:35 of the LORD **each** y the firstfruits 928+9102+9102
13: 6 in the thirty-second y of Artaxerxes king 9102
Est 1: 3 in the third y of his reign he gave a banquet 9102
2:16 in the seventh y of his reign. 9102
3: 7 In the twelfth y of King Xerxes, 9102
9:27 without fail observe these two days every y, 9102
Job 3: 6 not be included among the days of the y nor 9102
Ps 65:11 You crown the y with your bounty, 9102
Isa 6: 1 In the y *that* King Uzziah died, 9102
14:28 This oracle came in the y King Ahaz died: 9102

Isa 20: 1 In the **y** that the supreme commander, 9102
21:16 "Within *one* **y**, as a servant bound 9102
29: 1 Add **y** to year and let your cycle 9102
29: 1 to **y** and let your cycle of festivals go on. 9102
32:10 a **y** you who feel secure will tremble; 9102
34: 8 a **y** *of* retribution, to uphold Zion's cause. 9102
36: 1 the fourteenth **y** of King Hezekiah's reign, 9102
37:30 "This **y** you will eat what grows by itself, 9102
37:30 and the second **y** what springs from that. 9102
37:30 But in the third **y** sow and reap, 9102
61: 2 the **y** *of* the LORD's favor and the day 9102
63: 4 and the **y** *of* my redemption has come. 9102
Jer 1: 2 in the thirteenth **y** of the reign of Josiah son 9102
1: 3 down to the fifth month of the eleventh **y** 9102
11:23 of Anathoth in the **y** *of* their punishment.' " 9102
17: 8 a **y** *of* drought and never fails to bear fruit." 9102
23:12 on them in the **y** they are punished," 9102
25: 1 of Judah in the fourth **y** of Jehoiakim son 9102
25: 1 the first **y** of Nebuchadnezzar king 9102
25: 3 the thirteenth **y** of Josiah son of Amon king 9102
28: 1 In the fifth month of that same **y**, 9102
28: 1 the fourth **y**, early in the reign of Zedekiah 9102
28:16 This very **y** you are going to die, 9102
28:17 In the seventh month of that same **y**, 9102
32: 1 the LORD in the tenth **y** of Zedekiah king 9102
32: 1 the eighteenth **y** of Nebuchadnezzar. 9102
34:14 'Every seventh **y** each of you must free any 9102
36: 1 In the fourth **y** of Jehoiakim son of Josiah 9102
36: 9 the fifth **y** of Jehoiakim son of Josiah king 9102
39: 1 In the ninth **y** of Zedekiah king of Judah, 9102
39: 2 the fourth month of Zedekiah's eleventh **y**, 9102
45: 1 of Neriah in the fourth **y** of Jehoiakim son 9102
46: 2 of Babylon in the fourth **y** of Jehoiakim son 9102
48:44 upon Moab the **y** *of* her punishment," 9102
51:46 one rumor comes this **y**, another the next, 9102
51:59 with Zedekiah king of Judah in the fourth **y** 9102
52: 4 So in the ninth **y** of Zedekiah's reign, 9102
52: 5 until the eleventh **y** of King Zedekiah. 9102
52:12 in the nineteenth **y** of Nebuchadnezzar king 9102
52:28 in the seventh **y**, 3,023 Jews; 9102
52:29 in Nebuchadnezzar's eighteenth **y**, 9102
52:30 in his twenty-third **y**, 745 Jews taken 9102
52:31 In the thirty-seventh **y** of the exile 9102
52:31 in the **y** Evil-Merodach became king 9102
Eze 1: 1 In the thirtieth **y**, in the fourth month 9102
1: 2 the fifth **y** of the exile of King Jehoiachin— 9102
4: 6 assigned you 40 days, a day for each **y**. 9102
8: 1 In the sixth **y**, in the sixth month 9102
20: 1 In the seventh **y**, in th fifth month 9102
24: 1 In the ninth **y**, in the tenth month 9102
26: 1 In the eleventh **y**, on the first day of 9102
29: 1 In the tenth **y**, in the tenth month on 9102
29:17 In the twenty-seventh **y**, 9102
30:20 In the eleventh **y**, in the first month on 9102
31: 1 In the eleventh **y**, in the third month on 9102
32: 1 In the twelfth **y**, in the twelfth month on 9102
32:17 In the twelfth **y**, on the fifteenth day of 9102
33:21 In the twelfth **y** of our exile, 9102
40: 1 In the twenty-fifth **y** of our exile, 9102
40: 1 at the beginning of the **y**, 9102
40: 1 the fourteenth **y** after the fall of the city— 9102
46:17 the servant may keep it until the **y** 9102
Da 1: 1 In the third **y** of the reign of Jehoiakim king 9102
1:21 And Daniel remained there until the first **y** 9102
2: 1 In the second **y** of his reign, 9102
7: 1 the first **y** of Belshazzar king of Babylon, 10732
8: 1 In the third **y** of King Belshazzar's reign, 9102
9: 1 the first **y** of Darius son of Xerxes (a Mede 9102
9: 2 in the first **y** *of* his reign, 9102
10: 1 In the third **y** of Cyrus king of Persia, 9102
11: 1 And in the first **y** of Darius the Mede, 9102
Mic 6: 6 with burnt offerings, with calves a **y** old? 9102
Hag 1: 1 In the second **y** of King Darius, 9102
1:15 of the sixth month in the second **y** 9102
2:10 in the second **y** of Darius, 9102
Zec 1: 1 the eighth month of the second **y** of Darius, 9102
1: 7 in the second **y** of Darius, 9102
7: 1 In the fourth **y** of King Darius, 9102
14:16 that have attacked Jerusalem will go up **y** 9102
14:16 up year after **y** to worship the King, 9102
Lk 2:41 Every **y** his parents went to Jerusalem for *2291*
3: 1 In the fifteenth **y** of the reign of Tiberius *2291*
4:19 to proclaim the **y** of the Lord's favor." *1929*
13: 8 'leave it alone *for* one more **y**, *2291*
13: 9 If it bears fruit next **y**, fine! *NIG*
Jn 11:49 who was high priest that **y**, spoke up, *1929*
11:51 that **y** he prophesied that Jesus would die *1929*
18:13 Caiaphas, the high priest that **y**. *1929*
Ac 11:26 *for* a whole **y** Barnabas and Saul met with *1929*
18:11 So Paul stayed *for* a **y** and a half, *1929*
2Co 8:10 **Last y** you were the first not only to give *4373*
9: 2 that since **last y** you in Achaia were ready *4373*
Heb 9: 7 the inner room, and that only once a **y**, *1929*
9:25 the Most Holy Place every **y** with blood *1929*
10: 1 same sacrifices repeated endlessly **y after year,** *1929+2848*
10: 1 repeated endlessly **year after y**, *1929+2848*
Jas 4:13 go to this or that city, spend a **y** there, *1929*
Rev 9:15 and day and month and **y** were released *1929*

YEAR'S (4) [YEAR]

Lev 26:10 You will still be eating **last y harvest** 3823+3824
Dt 14:28 of that **y** produce and store it in your towns, 9102
Mk 14: 5 have been sold for more than a **y** wages *NIG*
Jn 12: 5 and **the money** given to the poor? It was **worth a y wages."** *1324+5559*

YEAR-OLD (7) [YEAR]

Ex 12: 5 animals you choose must be **y** males 1201+9102
Lev 12: 6 a **y** lamb for a burnt offering 1201+9102
Nu 6:12 a **y** male lamb as a guilt offering. 1201+9102
6:14 a **y** male lamb without defect for 1201+9102
6:14 for a burnt offering, a **y** ewe lamb 1426+9102
15:27 a **y** *female* goat for a sin offering. 1426+9102
Eze 46:13 a **y** lamb without defect for a burnt 1201+9102

YEARLING (1) [YEAR]

Isa 11: 6 the calf and the lion and the **y** together; 5309

YEARLY (3) [YEAR]

1Ki 10:14 the gold that Solomon received **y** was 666 talents, 285+928+9102
2Ch 9:13 the gold that Solomon received **y** was 666 talents, 285+928+9102
Hos 2:11 her **y festivals,** her New Moons, 2504

YEARNS (4)

Job 19:27 How my heart **y** within me! 3983
Ps 84: 2 My soul **y**, even faints, for the courts of 4083
Isa 26: 9 My soul **y for** you in the night; 203
Jer 31:20 Therefore my heart **y** for him; 2159

YEARS (507) [YEAR]

Ge 1:14 as signs to mark seasons and days and **y**, 9102
5: 3 When Adam had lived 130 **y**, 9102
5: 4 Adam lived 800 **y** and had other sons 9102
5: 5 Altogether, Adam lived 930 **y**, 9102
5: 6 When Seth had lived 105 **y**, 9102
5: 7 Seth lived 807 **y** and had other sons 9102
5: 8 Altogether, Seth lived 912 **y**, 9102
5: 9 When Enosh had lived 90 **y**, 9102
5:10 Enosh lived 815 **y** and had other sons 9102
5:11 Altogether, Enosh lived 905 **y**, 9102
5:12 When Kenan had lived 70 **y**, 9102
5:13 Kenan lived 840 **y** and had other sons 9102
5:14 Altogether, Kenan lived 910 **y**, 9102
5:15 When Mahalalel had lived 65 **y**, 9102
5:16 Mahalalel lived 830 **y** and had other sons 9102
5:17 Altogether, Mahalalel lived 895 **y**, 9102
5:18 When Jared had lived 162 **y**, 9102
5:19 Jared lived 800 **y** and had other sons 9102
5:20 Altogether, Jared lived 962 **y**, 9102
5:21 When Enoch had lived 65 **y**, 9102
5:22 with God 300 **y** and had other sons 9102
5:23 Altogether, Enoch lived 365 **y**. 9102
5:25 When Methuselah had lived 187 **y**, 9102
5:26 Methuselah lived 782 **y** and had other sons 9102
5:27 Altogether, Methuselah lived 969 **y**, 9102
5:28 Lamech had lived 182 **y**, he had a son. 9102
5:30 Lamech lived 595 **y** and had other sons 9102
5:31 Altogether, Lamech lived 777 **y**, 9102
5:32 After Noah was 500 **y** old, 9102
6: 3 his days will be a hundred and twenty **y."** 9102
7: 6 Noah was six hundred **y** old when 9102
9:28 After the flood Noah lived 350 **y**. 9102
9:29 Altogether, Noah lived 950 **y**, 9102
11:10 *Two* **y** after the flood, when Shem was 100 9102
11:10 when Shem was 100 **y** old, 9102
11:11 Shem lived 500 **y** and had other sons 9102
11:12 When Arphaxad had lived 35 **y**, 9102
11:13 Arphaxad lived 403 **y** and had other sons 9102
11:14 When Shelah had lived 30 **y**, 9102
11:15 Shelah lived 403 **y** and had other sons 9102
11:16 When Eber had lived 34 **y**, 9102
11:17 Eber lived 430 **y** and had other sons 9102
11:18 When Peleg had lived 30 **y**, 9102
11:19 Peleg lived 209 **y** and had other sons 9102
11:20 When Reu had lived 32 **y**, 9102
11:21 Reu lived 207 **y** and had other sons 9102
11:22 When Serug had lived 30 **y**, 9102
11:23 Serug lived 200 **y** and had other sons 9102
11:24 When Nahor had lived 29 **y**, 9102
11:25 Nahor lived 119 **y** and had other sons 9102
11:26 After Terah had lived 70 **y**, 9102
11:32 Terah lived 205 **y**, and he died in Haran. 9102
12: 4 Abram was seventy-five **y** old when he set 9102
14: 4 For twelve **y** they had been subject 9102
15: 9 a goat and a ram, each **three y old,** 8992
15:13 be enslaved and mistreated four hundred **y**. 9102
16: 3 Abram had been living in Canaan ten **y**, 9102
16:16 Abram was eighty-six **y** old when Hagar 9102
17: 1 When Abram was ninety-nine **y** old, 9102
17:17 a son be born to a man a hundred **y** old? 9102
17:24 Abraham was ninety-nine **y** old 9102
18:11 already old and well advanced in **y**, 3427
21: 5 Abraham was a hundred **y** old 9102
23: 1 to be a hundred and twenty-seven **y** *old*. 9102
24: 1 now old and well advanced in **y**, 3427
25: 7 Abraham lived a hundred and seventy-five **y** 9102
25: 8 an old man and full of **y**; NIH
25:17 Ishmael lived a hundred and thirty-seven **y**. 9102
25:20 and Isaac was forty **y** old when he married 9102
25:26 Isaac was sixty **y** old when Rebekah gave 9102
26:34 When Esau was forty **y** old, 9102
29:18 "I'll work for you seven **y** in return 9102
29:20 So Jacob served seven **y** to get Rachel, 9102
29:27 in return for another seven **y** *of* work." 9102
29:30 And he worked for Laban another seven **y**. 9102
31:38 "I have been with you for twenty **y** now. 9102
31:41 for the twenty **y** I was in your household. 9102
31:41 for you fourteen **y** for your two daughters 9102
Ge 31:41 two daughters and six **y** for your flocks, 9102
35:28 Isaac lived a hundred and eighty **y**. 9102
35:29 gathered to his people, old and full of **y**. 3427
41: 1 When *two* **full y** had passed, 3427+9102
41:26 The seven good cows are seven **y**, 9102
41:26 the seven good heads of grain are seven **y**; 9102
41:27 that came up afterward are seven **y**, and 9102
41:27 They are seven **y** *of* famine. 9102
41:29 Seven **y** *of* great abundance are coming 9102
41:30 but seven **y** *of* famine will follow them. 9102
41:34 of Egypt during the seven **y** *of* abundance. 9102
41:35 of these good **y** that are coming and store 9102
41:36 to be used during the seven **y** *of* famine 9102
41:46 Joseph was thirty **y** old when he entered 9102
41:47 During the seven **y** *of* abundance 9102
41:48 in those seven **y** of abundance in Egypt 9102
41:50 Before the **y** *of* famine came, 9102
41:53 The seven **y** *of* abundance in Egypt came 9102
41:54 and the seven **y** *of* famine began, 9102
45: 6 *For two* **y** now there has been famine in 9102
45: 6 *for* the next five **y** there will not be plowing 9102
45:11 because five **y** *of* famine are still to come. 9102
47: 9 "The **y** *of* my pilgrimage are a hundred 3427+9102
47: 9 My **y** have been few and difficult, 3427+9102
47: 9 the **y** of the pilgrimage of my fathers." 3427+9102
47:28 Jacob lived in Egypt seventeen **y**, 9102
47:28 and the **y** *of* his life were a hundred 3427+9102
50:22 He lived a hundred and ten **y** 9102
Ex 6:16 Levi lived 137 **y**. 9102
6:18 Kohath lived 133 **y**. 9102
6:20 Amram lived 137 **y**. 9102
7: 7 Moses was eighty **y** old and Aaron 9102
12:40 Israelite people lived in Egypt was 430 **y**. 9102
12:41 At the end of the 430 **y**, to the very day, 9102
16:35 The Israelites ate manna forty **y**, 9102
21: 2 he is to serve you *for* six **y**. 9102
23:10 *"For* six **y** you are to sow your fields 9102
30:14 those twenty **y** old or more, 9102
38:26 twenty **y** old or more, a total of 603,550 9102
Lev 19:23 *For* three **y** you are to consider it forbidden; 9102
25: 3 *For* six **y** sow your fields, 9102
25: 3 and *for* six **y** prune your vineyards 9102
25: 8 " 'Count off seven sabbaths of **y**— 9102
25: 8 seven times seven **y**—so that the seven 9102
25: 8 of **y** amount to a period of forty-nine years. 9102
25: 8 of years amount to a period of forty-nine **y**. 9102
25:15 on the basis of the number of **y** since 9102
25:15 to you on the basis of the number of **y** *left* 9102
25:16 When the **y** are many, 9102
25:16 and when the **y** are few, 9102
25:21 that the land will yield enough for three **y**. 9102
25:27 he is to determine the value for the **y** 9102
25:50 to a hired man for that number of **y**. 9102
25:51 If many **y** remain, he must pay for 9102
25:52 a few **y** remain until the Year of Jubilee, 9102
26:34 the land will enjoy its sabbath **y** all the time NIH
27: 6 a person between one month and five **y**, 9102
27: 7 If it is a person sixty **y** old or more, 9102
27:18 according to the number of **y** that remain 9102
Nu 1: 3 in Israel twenty **y** old or more who are able 9102
1:18 the men twenty **y** old or more were listed 9102
1:20 All the men twenty **y** old or more 9102
1:22 All the men twenty **y** old or more 9102
1:24 All the men twenty **y** old or more 9102
1:26 All the men twenty **y** old or more 9102
1:28 All the men twenty **y** old or more 9102
1:30 All the men twenty **y** old or more 9102
1:32 All the men twenty **y** old or more 9102
1:34 All the men twenty **y** old or more 9102
1:36 All the men twenty **y** old or more 9102
1:38 All the men twenty **y** old or more 9102
1:40 All the men twenty **y** old or more 9102
1:42 All the men twenty **y** old or more 9102
1:45 All the Israelites twenty **y** old or more 9102
4: 3 Count all the men from thirty to fifty **y** 9102
4:23 Count all the men from thirty to fifty **y** 9102
4:30 Count all the men from thirty to fifty **y** 9102
4:35 from thirty to fifty **y** of age who came 9102
4:39 from thirty to fifty **y** of age who came 9102
4:43 from thirty to fifty **y** of age who came 9102
4:47 from thirty to fifty **y** of age who came to do 9102
8:24 Men twenty-five **y** old or more shall come 9102
13:22 (Hebron had been built seven **y** before 9102
14:29 every one of you twenty **y** old or more 9102
14:33 be shepherds here *for* forty **y**, 9102
14:34 *For* forty **y**—one year for each of the forty 9102
20:15 and we lived there many **y**. 3427
26: 2 all those twenty **y** old or more who are able 9102
26: 4 a census of the men twenty **y** old or more, 9102
32:11 of the men twenty **y** old or more who came 9102
32:13 he made them wander in the desert forty **y**, 9102
33:39 and twenty-three **y** old when he died 9102
Dt 2: 7 forty **y** the LORD your God has been with you, 9102
2:14 Thirty-eight **y** passed from the time we left 9102
8: 2 the way in the desert these forty **y**, 9102
8: 4 not swell *during* these forty **y**. 9102
14:28 At the end of every three **y**, 9102
15: 1 of every seven **y** you must cancel debts. 9102
15:12 sells himself to you and serves you six **y**, 9102
15:18 to you these six **y** has been worth twice 9102
29: 5 the forty **y** that I led you through the desert, 9102
30:20 he will give you **many y** in the land 802+3427
31: 2 and twenty **y** old and I am no longer able 9102
31:10 "At the end of every seven **y**, 9102
34: 7 a hundred and twenty **y** old when he died, 9102
Jos 5: 6 moved about in the desert forty **y** until all 9102

Jos 13: 1 Joshua was old and well advanced in y, 3427
14: 7 I was forty y old when Moses the servant of 9102
14: 10 he has kept me alive *for* forty-five y since 9102
14: 10 So here I am today, eighty-five y old! 9102
23: 1 Joshua, by then old and well advanced in y, 3427
23: 2 "I am old and well advanced in y. 3427
Jdg 3: 8 the Israelites were subject *for* eight y. 9102
3: 11 So the land had peace *for* forty y, 9102
3: 14 to Eglon king of Moab *for* eighteen y. 9102
3: 30 and the land had peace *for* eighty y. 9102
4: 3 oppressed the Israelites *for* twenty y, 9102
5: 31 Then the land had peace forty y. 9102
6: 1 *for* seven y he gave them into the hands of 9102
6: 25 your father's herd, the one seven y old. 9102
8: 28 the land enjoyed peace forty y. 9102
9: 22 Abimelech had governed Israel three y, 9102
10: 2 He led Israel twenty-three y; 9102
10: 3 who led Israel twenty-two y. 9102
10: 8 *For* eighteen y they oppressed all 9102
11: 26 three hundred y Israel occupied Heshbon, 9102
12: 7 Jephthah led Israel six y. 9102
12: 9 Ibzan led Israel seven y. 9102
12: 11 Elon the Zebulunite led Israel ten y. 9102
12: 14 He led Israel eight y. 9102
13: 1 into the hands of the Philistines *for* forty y. 9102
15: 20 Samson led Israel *for* twenty y in the days 9102
16: 31 He had led Israel twenty y. 9102
Ru 1: 4 After they had lived there about ten y, 9102
1Sa 4: 15 who was ninety-eight y old 9102
4: 18 He had led Israel forty y. 9102
7: 2 It was a long time, twenty y in all, 9102
13: 1 Saul was [thirty] y old when he became king 9102
13: 1 and he reigned over Israel [forty-]two y. 9102
17: 12 and well advanced in y. NIH
2Sa 2: 10 Ish-Bosheth son of Saul was forty y old 9102
2: 10 and he reigned two y. 9102
2: 11 of Judah was seven y and six months. 9102
4: 4 He was five y old when the news 9102
5: 4 David was thirty y old when he became 9102
5: 4 and he reigned forty y. 9102
5: 5 In Hebron he reigned over Judah seven y 9102
5: 5 over all Israel and Judah thirty-three y. 9102
13: 23 *Two* y later, when Absalom's sheepshearers were at Baal Hazor 3427+9102
13: 38 he stayed there three y. 9102
14: 28 Absalom lived *two* y in Jerusalem 3427+9102
15: 7 At the end of four y, Absalom said 9102
19: 32 a very old man, eighty y of age. 9102
19: 34 "How many more y will I live, 9102
19: 35 I am now eighty y old. 9102
21: 1 a famine *for* three **successive** y; 339+9102+9102
24: 13 upon you three y of famine in your land? 9102
1Ki 1: 1 David was old and well advanced in y, 3427
2: 11 He had reigned forty y over Israel— 9102
2: 11 seven y in Hebron and thirty-three 9102
2: 39 But three y later, two of Shimei's slaves 9102
6: 38 He had spent seven y building it. 9102
7: 1 It took Solomon thirteen y, however, 9102
9: 10 At the end of twenty y, 9102
10: 22 Once every three y it returned, 9102
11: 42 in Jerusalem over all Israel forty y. 9102
14: 20 He reigned *for* twenty-two y and 9102
14: 21 He was forty-one y old when he became 9102
14: 21 and he reigned seventeen y in Jerusalem, 9102
15: 2 and he reigned in Jerusalem three y. 9102
15: 10 and he reigned in Jerusalem forty-one y. 9102
15: 25 and he reigned over Israel *two* y. 9102
15: 33 and he reigned twenty-four y. 9102
16: 8 and he reigned in Tirzah *two* y. 9102
16: 23 and he reigned twelve y, 9102
16: 29 in Samaria over Israel twenty-two y. 9102
17: 1 *in* the next few y except at my word." 9102
22: 1 *For* three y there was no war 9102
22: 42 Jehoshaphat was thirty-five y old 9102
22: 42 and he reigned in Jerusalem twenty-five y. 9102
22: 51 and he reigned over Israel *two* y. 9102
2Ki 3: 1 and he reigned twelve y. 9102
8: 1 a famine in the land that will last seven y." 9102
8: 2 in the land of the Philistines seven y. 9102
8: 3 the seven y she came back from the land of 9102
8: 17 He was thirty-two y old when he became 9102
8: 17 and he reigned in Jerusalem eight y. 9102
8: 26 Ahaziah was twenty-two y old 9102
10: 36 over Israel in Samaria was twenty-eight y. 9102
11: 3 the LORD *for* six y while Athaliah ruled 9102
11: 21 Joash was seven y old when he began 9102
12: 1 and he reigned in Jerusalem forty y. 9102
12: 2 in the eyes of the LORD all the y Jehoiada 3427
13: 1 and he reigned seventeen y. 9102
13: 10 and he reigned sixteen y. 9102
14: 2 He was twenty-five y old when he became 9102
14: 2 and he reigned in Jerusalem twenty-nine y. 9102
14: 17 *for* fifteen y after the death of Jehoash son 9102
14: 21 took Azariah, who was sixteen y old, 9102
14: 23 and he reigned forty-one y. 9102
15: 2 He was sixteen y old when he became king, 9102
15: 2 and he reigned in Jerusalem fifty-two y. 9102
15: 17 and he reigned in Samaria ten y. 9102
15: 23 and he reigned *two* y. 9102
15: 27 and he reigned twenty y. 9102
15: 33 He was twenty-five y old when he became 9102
15: 33 and he reigned in Jerusalem sixteen y. 9102
16: 2 Ahaz was twenty y old when he became 9102
16: 2 and he reigned in Jerusalem sixteen y. 9102
17: 1 and he reigned nine y. 9102
17: 5 and laid siege to it *for* three y. 9102
18: 2 He was twenty-five y old when he became 9102
2Ki 18: 2 and he reigned in Jerusalem twenty-nine y. 9102
18: 10 At the end of three y the Assyrians took it. 9102
20: 6 I will add fifteen y to your life. 9102
21: 1 Manasseh was twelve y old when he became 9102
21: 1 and he reigned in Jerusalem fifty-five y. 9102
21: 19 Amon was twenty-two y old 9102
21: 19 and he reigned in Jerusalem two y. 9102
22: 1 Josiah was eight y old when he became 9102
22: 1 and he reigned in Jerusalem thirty-one y. 9102
23: 31 Jehoahaz was twenty-three y old 9102
23: 36 Jehoiakim was twenty-five y old 9102
23: 36 and he reigned in Jerusalem eleven y. 9102
24: 1 Jehoiakim became his vassal *for* three y. 9102
24: 8 Jehoiachin was eighteen y old 9102
24: 18 Zedekiah was twenty-one y old 9102
24: 18 and he reigned in Jerusalem eleven y. 9102
1Ch 2: 21 married her when he was sixty y old), 9102
3: 4 where he reigned seven y and six months. 9102
3: 4 David reigned in Jerusalem thirty-three y, 9102
21: 12 three y of famine, three months 9102
23: 1 When David was old and full of y, 3427
23: 3 The Levites thirty y old or more 9102
23: 24 that is, the workers twenty y old or more 9102
23: 27 from those twenty y old or more. 9102
27: 23 the number of the men twenty y old or less, 9102
29: 27 He ruled over Israel forty y— 9102
2Ch 8: 1 At the end of twenty y, 9102
9: 21 Once every three y it returned, 9102
9: 30 in Jerusalem over all Israel forty y. 9102
11: 17 Rehoboam son of Solomon three y, 9102
12: 13 He was forty-one y old when he became 9102
12: 13 and he reigned seventeen y in Jerusalem, 9102
13: 2 and he reigned in Jerusalem three y. 9102
14: 1 the country was at peace *for* ten y. 9102
14: 6 No one was at war with him during those y, 9102
17: 3 because in his early y he walked in NIH
18: 2 **Some y later** he went down to 4200+7891+9102
20: 31 He was thirty-five y old when he became 9102
20: 31 and he reigned in Jerusalem twenty-five y. 9102
21: 5 Jehoram was thirty-two y old 9102
21: 5 and he reigned in Jerusalem eight y. 9102
21: 20 Jehoram was thirty-two y old NIH
21: 20 and he reigned in Jerusalem eight y. 9102
22: 2 Ahaziah was twenty-two y old 9102
22: 12 with them at the temple of God *for* six y 9102
24: 1 Joash was seven y old when he became 9102
24: 1 and he reigned in Jerusalem forty y. 9102
24: 2 the LORD all the y *of* Jehoiada the priest. 3427
24: 15 Now Jehoiada was old and full of y, 3427
25: 1 Amaziah was twenty-five y old 9102
25: 1 and he reigned in Jerusalem twenty-nine y. 9102
25: 5 then mustered those twenty y old or more 9102
25: 25 *for* fifteen y after the death of Jehoash son 9102
26: 1 who was sixteen y old, 9102
26: 3 Uzziah was sixteen y old when he became 9102
26: 3 and he reigned in Jerusalem fifty-two y. 9102
27: 1 Jotham was twenty-five y old 9102
27: 1 and he reigned in Jerusalem sixteen y. 9102
27: 5 also in the second and third y. 9102
27: 8 He was twenty-five y old when he became 9102
27: 8 and he reigned in Jerusalem sixteen y. 9102
28: 1 Ahaz was twenty y old when he became 9102
28: 1 and he reigned in Jerusalem sixteen y. 9102
29: 1 Hezekiah was twenty-five y old 9102
29: 1 and he reigned in Jerusalem twenty-nine y. 9102
31: 16 they distributed to the males three y old 9102
31: 17 and likewise to the Levites twenty y old 9102
33: 1 Manasseh was twelve y old 9102
33: 1 and he reigned in Jerusalem fifty-five y. 9102
33: 21 Amon was twenty-two y old 9102
33: 21 and he reigned in Jerusalem two y. 9102
34: 1 Josiah was eight y old when he became 9102
34: 1 and he reigned in Jerusalem thirty-one y. 9102
36: 2 Jehoahaz was twenty-three y old 9102
36: 5 Jehoiakim was twenty-five y old 9102
36: 5 and he reigned in Jerusalem eleven y. 9102
36: 9 Jehoiachin was eighteen y old 9102
36: 11 Zedekiah was twenty-one y old 9102
36: 11 and he reigned in Jerusalem eleven y. 9102
36: 21 the seventy y were completed in fulfillment 9102
Ezr 3: 8 appointing Levites twenty y of age 9102
5: 11 the temple that was built many y ago, 10732
Ne 5: 14 until his thirty-second year—twelve y— 9102
9: 21 *For* forty y you sustained them in 9102
9: 30 *For* many y you were patient with them. 9102
Job 10: 5 like those of a mortal or your y like those 9102
15: 20 the ruthless through all the y stored up 9102
16: 22 a few y will pass before I go on the journey 9102
21: 13 They spend their y in prosperity and go 3427
32: 6 "I am young in y, and you are old; 3427
32: 7 advanced y should teach wisdom.' 9102
36: 11 in prosperity and their y in contentment. 9102
36: 26 The number of his y is past finding out. 9102
38: 21 You have lived so many y! 3427
42: 16 After this, Job lived a hundred and forty y; 9102
42: 17 And so he died, old and full of y. 3427
Ps 31: 10 My life is consumed by anguish and my y 9102
39: 5 the **span of** my y is as nothing before you. 2698
61: 6 his y for many generations. 9102
77: 5 the former days, the y *of* long ago; 9102
77: 10 the y *of* the right hand of the Most High." 9102
78: 33 So he ended their days in futility and their y 9102
90: 4 a thousand y in your sight are like a day 9102
90: 9 we finish our y with a moan. 9102
90: 10 The length of our days is seventy y— 9102
90: 15 *for* as many y as we have seen trouble. 9102
95: 10 forty y I was angry with that generation; 9102
Ps 102: 24 your y go on through all generations. 9102
102: 27 and your y will never end. 9102
Pr 3: 2 will prolong your life **many** y 2256+3427+9102
4: 10 and the y *of* your life will be many. 9102
5: 9 to others and your y to one who is cruel, 9102
9: 11 and y will be added to your life. 9102
10: 27 but the y *of* the wicked are cut short. 9102
Ecc 6: 3 a hundred children and live many y; 9102
6: 6 if he lives a thousand y twice over but fails 9102
11: 8 However many y a man may live, 9102
12: 1 and the y approach when you will say, 9102
Isa 7: 8 Within sixty-five y Ephraim will 9102
16: 14 But now the LORD says: "Within three y, 9102
20: 3 has gone stripped and barefoot *for* three y, 9102
23: 15 Tyre will be forgotten *for* seventy y, 9102
23: 15 But at the end of these seventy y, 9102
23: 17 At the end of seventy y, 9102
38: 5 I will add fifteen y to your life. 9102
38: 10 and be robbed of the rest of my y?" 9102
38: 15 I will walk humbly all my y because 9102
65: 20 or an old man who does not live out his y; 3427
Jer 6: 11 and the old, those weighed down with y. 3427
25: 3 For twenty-three y—from the thirteenth 9102
25: 11 serve the king of Babylon seventy y. 9102
25: 12 "But when the seventy y are fulfilled, 9102
28: 3 Within *two* y I will bring back 3427+9102
28: 11 neck of all the nations within *two* y.' 3427+9102
29: 10 seventy y are completed for Babylon, 9102
34: 14 After he has served you six y, 9102
52: 1 Zedekiah was twenty-one y old 9102
52: 1 and he reigned in Jerusalem eleven y. 9102
Eze 4: 5 the same number of days as the y 9102
12: 27 vision he sees is for many y from now, 3427
22: 4 and the end of your y has come. 9102
29: 11 no one will live there *for* forty y. 9102
29: 12 and her cities will lie desolate forty y 9102
29: 13 of forty y I will gather the Egyptians from 9102
38: 8 In future y you will invade a land 9102
38: 17 *for* y that I would bring you against them. 9102
39: 9 *For* seven y they will use them for fuel. 9102
Da 1: 5 They were to be trained *for* three y, 9102
9: 2 that the desolation of Jerusalem would last seventy y. 9102
11: 6 After *some* y, they will become allies. 9102
11: 8 *For some* y he will leave the king of 9102
11: 13 and after *several* y, 2021+6961+9102
11: 20 In a few y, however, he will be destroyed, 3427
Joel 2: 25 for the y the locusts have eaten— 9102
Am 1: 1 what he saw concerning Israel *two* y before 9102
2: 10 and I led you forty y in the desert 9102
4: 4 your tithes every three y. 3427
5: 25 and offerings forty y in the desert, 9102
Zec 1: 12 you have been angry with these seventy y?" 9102
7: 3 as I have done for so many y?" 9102
7: 5 and seventh months for the past seventy y, 9102
Mal 3: 4 as in days gone by, as in former y. 9102
Mt 2: 16 and its vicinity who were **two y old** and *1453*
9: 20 bleeding *for* twelve y came up behind him *2291*
Mk 5: 25 subject to bleeding *for* twelve y. *2291*
5: 42 and walked around (she was twelve y old). *2291*
Lk 1: 7 and they were both well along in y. *2465*
1: 18 an old man and my wife is well along in y." *2465*
2: 36 she had lived with her husband seven y *2291*
2: 42 When he was twelve **y old,** *2291*
3: 23 Now Jesus himself was about thirty y **old** *2291*
4: 25 when the sky was shut for three and a half y *2291*
8: 43 subject to bleeding for twelve y, *2291*
12: 19 of good things laid up for many y. *2291*
13: 7 '*For* three y now I've been coming to look *2291*
13: 11 crippled by a spirit *for* eighteen y. *2291*
13: 16 Satan has kept bound *for* eighteen long y, *2291*
15: 29 *All* these y I've been slaving for you *2291*
Jn 2: 20 "It has taken forty-six y to build this temple *2291*
5: 5 an invalid *for* thirty-eight y. *2291*
8: 57 "You are not yet fifty **y old,"** *2291*
Ac 4: 22 miraculously healed was over forty y old. *2291*
7: 6 be enslaved and mistreated four hundred y. *2291*
7: 23 "When Moses *was* **forty** y old, *5478*
7: 30 "After forty y had passed, *2291*
7: 36 at the Red Sea and *for* forty y in the desert. *2291*
7: 42 and offerings forty y in the desert, *2291*
9: 33 a paralytic who had been bedridden for eight y. *2291*
13: 18 he endured their conduct *for* about **forty** y *5478*
13: 20 All this took about 450 y. *2291*
13: 21 of the tribe of Benjamin, who ruled forty y. *2291*
19: 10 This went on for two y, *2291*
20: 31 *for* **three** y I never stopped warning each *5562*
24: 10 for a number *of* y you have been a judge *2291*
24: 17 "After an absence *of* several y, *2291*
24: 27 When **two** y had passed, *1454*
28: 30 For **two** whole y Paul stayed there *1454*
Ro 4: 19 since he was about a **hundred y old—** *1670*
15: 23 I have been longing for many y to see you, *2291*
1Co 7: 36 and if she is **getting along in** y *5644*
2Co 12: 2 in Christ who fourteen y ago was caught up *2291*
Gal 1: 18 Then after three y, I went up to Jerusalem *2291*
2: 1 Fourteen y later I went up again *2291*
3: 17 The law, introduced 430 y later, *2291*
4: 10 and months and seasons and y! *1929*
Heb 1: 12 and your y will never end." *2291*
3: 9 and tried me and *for* forty y saw what I did. *2291*
3: 17 And with whom was he angry *for* forty y? *2291*
Jas 5: 17 not rain on the land *for* three and a half y. *1929*
2Pe 3: 8 With the Lord a day is like a thousand y, *2291*
3: 8 and a thousand y are like a day. *2291*
Rev 20: 2 or Satan, and bound him *for* a thousand y. *2291*

Rev 20: 3 until the thousand y were ended. *2291*
20: 4 and reigned with Christ a thousand **y.** *2291*
20: 5 to life until the thousand y were ended.) *2291*
20: 6 and will reign with him *for* a thousand **y.** *2291*
20: 7 When the thousand y are over, *2291*

YEAST (58)

Ge 19: 3 baking **bread without y,** and they ate. 5174
Ex 12: 8 and **bread made without y.** 5174
12:15 you are to eat **bread made without y.** 5174
12:15 On the first day remove the y from your 8419
12:15 whoever eats **anything with y in it** 2809
12:18 to eat **bread made without y,** 5174
12:19 For seven days no y is to be found 8419
12:19 whoever eats **anything with y in it** 4721
12:20 Eat nothing **made with y.** 4721
12:34 before *the* y *was* **added,** 2806
12:39 without y because they had been driven out 2806
13: 3 Eat nothing **containing y.** 2809
13: 6 For seven days eat **bread made without y** 5174
13: 7 nothing **with y in it** is to be seen 2809
13: 7 to be seen among you, nor shall *any* y 8419
23:15 for seven days eat **bread made without y,** 5174
23:18 along with **anything containing y.** 2809
29: 2 And from fine wheat flour, **without y,** 5174
29:23 From the basket of **bread made without y,** 5174
34:18 For seven days eat **bread made without y,** 5174
34:25 along with **anything containing y,** 2809
Lev 2: 4 cakes made **without** y and mixed with oil, 5174
2: 4 wafers made **without** y and spread with oil. 5174
2: 5 of fine flour mixed with oil, and **without y.** 5174
2:11 to the LORD must be made without **y,** 2809
2:11 to burn any y or honey in an offering made 8419
6:16 it is to be eaten **without** y in a holy place; 5174
6:17 It must not be baked with **y;** 2809
7:12 **bread made without** y and mixed with oil, 5174
7:12 wafers **made without** y and spread with oil, 5174
7:13 offering with cakes of bread **made with y.** 2809
8: 2 basket containing **bread made without y,** 5174
8:26 from the basket of **bread made without y,** 5174
10:12 by fire and eat it **prepared without** y beside 5174
23: 6 you must eat **bread made without y.** 5174
23:17 of an ephah of fine flour, baked with **y,** as 2809
Nu 6:15 and a basket of **bread made without y—** 5174
6:19 both **made without y.** 5174
28:17 for seven days eat **bread made without y.** 5174
Dt 16: 3 Do not eat it with **bread made with y,** 2809
16: 4 Let no y be found in your possession 8419
Jdg 6:19 an ephah of flour he made **bread without y.** 5174
1Sa 28:24 kneaded it and baked **bread without y.** 5174
Eze 45:21 you shall eat **bread made without y.** 5174
Mt 13:33 like y that a woman took and mixed into *2434*
16: 6 on your guard against the y of the Pharisees *2434*
16:11 on your guard against the y of the Pharisees *2434*
16:12 not telling them to guard against the y used *2434*
Mk 8:15 the y of the Pharisees and that of Herod." *2434*
Lk 12: 1 "Be on your guard against the y of *2434*
13:21 like y that a woman took and mixed into *2434*
1Co 5: 6 a little y works through the whole batch *2434*
5: 7 of the old y that you may be a new batch *2434*
5: 7 that you may be a new batch **without y—** *109*
5: 8 let us keep the Festival, not with the old y, *2434*
5: 8 the y of malice and wickedness, *2434*
5: 8 but with **bread without y,** *109*
Gal 5: 9 "A little y works through the whole batch *2434*

YELLING (1) [YELL]

Ac 7:57 y at the top of their voices, they all rushed *3189*

YELLOW (4)

Lev 13:30 in it is y and thin, the priest shall pronounce 7411
13:32 and there is no y hair in it and it does 7411
13:36 the priest does not need to look for y hair; 7411
Rev 9:17 fiery red, dark blue, and **y as sulfur.** *2523*

YES (97)

Ge 17:19 **"Y, but** your wife Sarah will bear you 66
18:15 But he said, **"Y,** you did laugh." 3954+4202
20: 6 Then God said to him in the dream, **"Y,** 1685
22: 7 **"Y,** my son?" Abraham replied. 2180
27:18 **"Y,** my son," he answered. 2180
29: 5 **"Y,** we know him," they answered. NIH
29: 6 **"Y,** he is," they said, 8934S
Ex 2: 8 **"Y,** go," she answered. NIH
Jos 2: 4 She said, **"Y,** the men came to me, 4026
24:22 **"Y,** we are witnesses," they replied. NIH
Jdg 5:15 **y,** Issachar was with Barak, 4027
1Sa 10:22 And the LORD said, **"Y,** he has hidden 2180
16: 5 Samuel replied, **"Y,** in peace; NIH
22:12 **"Y,** my lord," he answered. 2180
26:17 David replied, **"Y** it is, my lord the king." NIH
2Sa 12:19 **"Y,"** they replied, "he is dead." NIH
14:19 from anything my lord the king says. **Y,** 3954
1Ki 2:13 He answered, **"Y,** peacefully." NIH
2:22 **y,** for him and for Abiathar the priest 2256
14:14 This is the day! What? **Y,** even now. NIH
18: 8 **"Y,"** he replied. 638S
20:33 **"Y,** your brother Ben-Hadad!" NIH
21:19 dogs will lick up your blood—**y,** yours!' " 1685
2Ki 2: 3 **"Y,** I know," Elisha replied, 1685
2: 5 **"Y,** I know," he replied, 1685
7:13 **y,** they will only be like all these 2180
Ps 77:11 **y,** I will remember your miracles 3954
90:17 **y,** establish the work of our hands. 2256
Ecc 11: 2 Give portions to seven, **y** to eight, 1685+2256
Isa 26: 8 **Y,** LORD, walking in the way of your laws, 677
27: 5 let them make peace with me, **y,** NIH
32:13 **y,** mourn for all houses of merriment and 3954
43:13 **Y,** and from ancient days I am he. NIH
44: 7 **y,** let him foretell what will come. 2256
48: 7 So you cannot say, **'Y,** I knew of them.' 2180
48:15 I, even I, have spoken; **y,** I have called him. 677
49:25 **"Y,** captives will be taken from warriors, 1685
52: 6 I who foretold it. **Y,** it is I." 2180
57: 6 **Y,** to them you have poured out drink 1685
63: 7 **y,** the many good things he has done for 2256
Jer 3:22 **"Y,** we will come to you, 2180
16:20 **Y,** but they are not gods!" NIH
23:31 **Y,"** declares the LORD, 2180
27:21 **y,** this is what the LORD Almighty, 3954
29: 8 **Y,** this is what the LORD Almighty, 3954
29:17 **y,** this is what the LORD Almighty says: NIH
36:18 **"Y,"** Baruch replied, "he dictated all these NIH
37:17 **"Y,"** Jeremiah replied, "you will be handed 3780
Da 7:18 possess it forever—**y,** for ever and ever.' 10221
Hag 2:13 **"Y,"** the priests replied, NIH
Mal 2: 2 **Y,** I have already cursed them, 1685+2256
Mt 5:37 Simply let your **'Y'** be 'Yes,' *3721*
5:37 Simply let your 'Yes' be **'Y,'** *3721*
9:28 **"Y,** Lord," they replied. *3721*
11: 9 **Y,** I tell you, and more than a prophet. *3721*
11:26 **Y,** Father, for this was your good pleasure. *3721*
13:51 **"Y,"** they replied. *3721*
15:27 **"Y,** Lord," she said, "but even the dogs eat *3721*
17:25 **"Y,** he does," he replied. *3721*
21:16 **"Y,"** replied Jesus, "have you never read, *3721*
26:25 Jesus answered, **"Y,** it is you." *NIG*
26:64 **"Y,** it is as you say," Jesus replied. *NIG*
27:11 **"Y,** it is as you say," Jesus replied. *NIG*
Mk 7:28 **"Y,** Lord," she replied, *3721*
14:30 today—**y,** tonight—before the rooster crows *NIG*
15: 2 **"Y,** it is as you say," Jesus replied. *NIG*
Lk 7:26 **Y,** I tell you, and more than a prophet. *3721*
10:21 **Y,** Father, for this was your good pleasure. *3721*
11:51 **Y,** I tell you, this generation will be held *3721*
12: 5 **Y,** I tell you, fear him. *3721*
14:26 **y,** even his own life— *2285+5445*
22:37 **Y,** what is written about me is reaching *1142*
23: 3 **"Y,** it is as you say," Jesus replied. *NIG*
Jn 5:20 **Y,** to your amazement he will show him *NIG*
7:28 cried out, **"Y,** you know me, *NIG*
11:27 **"Y,** Lord," she told him, *3721*
21:15 **"Y,** Lord," he said, "you know that I love *3721*
21:16 He answered, **"Y,** Lord, *3721*
Ac 5: 8 **"Y,"** she said, "that is the price." *3721*
9:10 **"Y,** Lord," he answered. *1609+2627*
22:27 **"Y,** I am," he answered. *3721*
Ro 3:29 the God of Gentiles too? **Y,** of Gentiles too, *3721*
1Co 1:16 **(Y,** I also baptized the household *1254*
9:10 **Y,** this was written for us, *1142*
2Co 1:17 **"Y,** yes" and "No, no"? *3721*
1:17 "Yes, **y"** and "No, no"? *3721*
1:18 our message to you is not **"Y"** and "No." *3721*
1:19 was not **"Y"** and "No," *3721*
1:19 but in him it has always been **"Y."** *3721*
1:20 they are **"Y"** in Christ. *3721*
Php 1:18 **Y,** and I will continue to rejoice, *247*
4: 3 **Y,** and I ask you, loyal yokefellow, *3721*
Jas 5:12 Let your **"Y"** be yes, and your "No," no, *3721*
5:12 Let your "Yes" be **y,** and your "No," no, *3721*
Rev 14:13 **"Y,"** says the Spirit, "they will rest *3721*
16: 7 And I heard the altar respond: **"Y,** *3721*
22:20 He who testifies to these things says, **"Y,** *3721*

YESTERDAY (8)

Ex 5:14 meet your quota of bricks y or today, 9453
1Sa 20:27 come to the meal, either y or today?" 9453
2Sa 15:20 You came only **y.** 9453
2Ki 9:26 **'Y** I saw the blood of Naboth and the blood 621
Job 8: 9 for we were born only y and know nothing, 9453
Jn 4:52 "The fever left him y at the seventh hour." *2396*
Ac 7:28 to kill me as you killed the Egyptian **y?'** *2396*
Heb 13: 8 Jesus Christ is the same y and today *2396*

YESTERNIGHT (KJV) See LAST NIGHT

YET (404)

Ge 2: 5 **no** shrub of the field had y appeared 3270
2: 5 **no** plant of the field had y sprung up 3270+3972
15:16 for the sin of the Amorites has not y 2178+6330
21: 7 **Y** I have borne him a son in his old age." 3954
31: 7 y your father has cheated me 2256
31:43 **Y** what can I do today 2256
32:30 **and** y my life was spared." 2256
Ex 5:16 y we are told, 'Make bricks!' 2256
5:18 y you must produce your full quota 2256
7:13 **Y** Pharaoh's heart became hard 2256
9: 7 **Y** his heart was unyielding and he would 2256
10: 7 Do you **not** y realize that Egypt is ruined?" 3270
10:23 **Y** all the Israelites had light in the places 2256
21:36 y the owner did not keep it penned up, 2256
34: 7 **Y** he does not leave the guilty unpunished; 2256
Lev 19:20 **Y** they are not to be put to death, NIH
21:23 y because of his defect, 421
22: 3 ceremonially unclean **and** y comes near 2256
22:13 y has no children, 2256
26:44 **Y** in spite of this, when they are in the 677+2256
Nu 11:26 **Y** the Spirit **also** rested on them, 2256
14:18 **Y** he does not leave the guilty unpunished; 2256
24:22 y you Kenites will be destroyed 561+3954
Dt 1:39 your children who do not y know good 2021+3427
10:15 **Y** the LORD set his affection on your 8370
12: 9 not y reached the resting place and 6330+6964
34: 7 y his eyes were not weak NIH
Jos 3:15 **Y** as soon as the priests who carried 2256
11:13 **Y** Israel did not burn any of the cities built 8370
17:12 **Y** the Manassites were not able 2256
18: 2 not *y* **received** their inheritance. AIT
Jdg 2: 2 **Y** you have disobeyed me. 2256
2:17 **Y** they would not listen to their judges 1685+2256
8: 4 exhausted y keeping up the pursuit, 2256
18: 1 they had not y come into an inheritance 2021+2021+2085+3427+6330
1Sa 3: 3 The lamp of God had **not** y gone out, 3270
3: 7 Now Samuel did **not** y know the LORD: 3270
3: 7 of the LORD had **not** y been revealed 3270
10:22 "Has the man come here **y?"** 6388
12:20 y do not turn away from the LORD, 421
12:25 **Y** if you persist in doing evil, 2256
14:26 y no one put his hand to his mouth, 2256
20: 3 **Y** as surely as the LORD lives and 219
22:17 y they did not tell me." 2256
25:15 **Y** these men were very good to us. 2256
2Sa 3: 8 **Y** now you accuse me of an offense 2256
1Ki 3: 2 a temple had not y been built for the Name of the LORD. 2021+2021+2156+3427+6330
8:28 **Y** give attention to your servant's prayer 2256
11:13 **Y** I will not tear the whole kingdom 8370
18:12 **Y** I your servant have worshiped 2256
19:18 **Y** I reserve seven thousand in Israel— 2256
22: 3 that Ramoth Gilead belongs to us **and y** 2256
2Ki 2:10 **"y if** you see me when I am taken 561
3:17 y this valley will be filled with water, 2256
10:31 **Y** Jehu was not careful to keep the law of 2256
14: 6 **Y** he did not put the sons of the assassins 2256
1Ch 28: 4 **"Y** the LORD, the God of Israel, 2256
2Ch 6:19 **Y** give attention to your servant's prayer 2256
13: 6 **Y** Jeroboam son of Nebat, 2256
16: 8 **Y** when you relied on the LORD, 2256
25: 4 **Y** he did not put their sons to death, 2256
30:18 y they ate the Passover, 3954
Ezr 3: 6 **the foundation** of the LORD's temple *had* not *y* **been laid.** AIT
5:16 under construction but is **not** *y* finished." AIT
9:13 of our evil deeds and our great guilt, and **y,** 3954
Ne 2:16 because as y I had said nothing to the Jews 4027
5: 5 y we have to subject our sons 2256
7: 4 and the houses had **not** *y* been rebuilt. AIT
9:30 **Y** they paid no attention, 2256
Est 3: 6 **Y** having learned who Mordecai's people 3954
Job 1:18 y another messenger came and said, 2256
4:10 y the teeth of the great lions are broken. 2256
5: 7 **Y** man is born to trouble as surely 3954
8:21 He will y fill your mouth with laughter 6330
11:13 **"Y if** you devote your heart to him 561
13:15 Though he slay me, y will I hope in him; NIH
14: 9 y at the scent of water it will bud NIH
16: 6 **"Y if** I speak, my pain is not relieved; 561
16:17 y my hands have been free of violence 6584
19:26 y in my flesh I will see God; 2256
20:14 y his food will turn sour in his stomach; NIH
21:14 **Y** they say to God, 'Leave us alone! 2256
21:17 **"Y** how often is the lamp of the wicked NIH
22:13 **Y** you say, 'What does God know? 2256
22:18 **Y** it was he who filled their houses 2256
23:17 **Y** I am not silenced by the darkness, 3954
24:11 they tread the winepresses, y suffer thirst. 2256
24:18 **"Y** they are foam on the surface of NIH
26: 8 y the clouds do not burst 2256
30:26 **Y** when I hoped for good, evil came; 3954
32: 3 **and y** had condemned him. 2256
33:10 **Y** God has found fault with me; 2176
33:23 **"Y if** there is an angel on his side as 561
34:29 **Y** he is over man and nation alike, 2256
35: 3 **Y** you ask him, 'What profit is it to me, 3954
39:18 **Y** when she spreads her feathers to run, 3869
40:19 y his Maker can approach him NIH
Ps 22: 3 **Y** you are enthroned as the Holy One; 2256
22: 9 **Y** you brought me out of the womb; 3954
22:31 his righteousness to a people y **unborn—** 3528
31:22 **Y** you heard my cry for mercy 434
35:13 **Y** when they were ill, 2256
37:25 y I have never seen the righteous forsaken 2256
40:17 **Y** I am poor and needy; 2256
42: 5 for I will y praise him, 6388
42:11 for I will y praise him, 6388
43: 5 for I will y praise him, 6388
44:22 **Y** for your sake we face death all day long; 3954
55:21 y war is in his heart; 2256
55:21 y they are drawn swords. 2256
59: 4 y they are ready to attack me. NIH
70: 5 **Y** I am poor and needy; 2256
73:23 **Y** I am always with you; 2256
78: 6 even the children *y to* **be born,** AIT
78:23 **Y** he gave a command to the skies above 2256
78:38 **Y** he was merciful; 2256
90:10 y their span is but trouble and sorrow, 2256
102:18 that a people **not y created** may praise 1343
106: 8 **Y** he saved them for his name's sake, 2256
119:151 **Y** you are near, O LORD, NIH
141: 5 **Y** my prayer is ever against the deeds 3954
Pr 6: 8 y it stores its provisions in summer NIH
6:31 **Y** if he is caught, he must pay sevenfold, 2256
11:24 One man gives freely, y gains even more; 2256
12: 9 a nobody **and y** have a servant than pretend 2256
13: 7 One man pretends to be rich, y has nothing; 2256

Pr 13: 7 pretends to be poor, y has great wealth. 2256
19: 3 y his heart rages against the LORD. 2256
28:21 y a man will do wrong for a piece of bread. 2256
30:12 those who are pure in their own eyes **and** y 2256
30:24 y they are extremely wise: 2256
30:25 y they store up their food in the summer; 2256
30:26 y they make their home in the crags; 2256
30:27 y they advance together in ranks; 2256
30:28 y it is found in kings' palaces. 2256
Ecc 1: 7 y the sea is never full. 2256
1:11 and even those who are y **to come** will not 340
2:11 Y when I surveyed all that my hands 2256
2:19 Y he will have control over all the work 2256
3:11 y they cannot fathom what God has done 889+1172+4946
4: 3 better than both is he who has not y been, 6362
4: 8 y his eyes were not content with his wealth. 1685
6: 3 y no matter how long he lives, 2256
6: 7 y his appetite is never satisfied. 1685+2256
8:13 Y because the wicked do not fear God, 2256
SS 1: 5 Dark am I, y lovely, 2256
8: 8 and her breasts are **not** y grown. AIT
Isa 5:25 Y for all this, his anger is not turned away, NIH
7: 7 Y this is what the Sovereign LORD says: NIH
9:12 Y for all this, his anger is not turned away, NIH
9:17 Y for all this, his anger is not turned away, NIH
9:21 Y for all this, his anger is not turned away, NIH
10: 4 Y for all this, his anger is not turned away, NIH
17: 6 Y some gleanings will remain, 2256
17:11 y the harvest will be as nothing in the day NIH
21:12 and come back y again." NIH
23:18 Y her profit and her earnings will 2256
29: 2 Y I will besiege Ariel; 2256
30:18 Y the LORD longs to be gracious to you; 4027+4200
31: 2 Y he too is wise and can bring disaster; 2256
42:25 y they did not understand; 2256
43:22 "Y you have not called upon me, O Jacob, 2256
44: 7 and *what is y to* **come**— AIT
49: 4 Y what is due me is in the LORD's hand, 434
49:20 during your bereavement will y say 6388
53: 4 y we considered him stricken by God, 2256
53: 7 y he did not open his mouth; 2256
53:10 Y it was the LORD's will to crush him 2256
54:10 y my unfailing love for you will not 2256
57:17 y he kept on in his willful ways. 2256
58: 3 "Y on the day of your fasting, 2176
63:10 Y they rebelled and grieved his Holy Spirit. 2256
64: 8 Y, O LORD, you are our Father. 2256+6964
65: 8 there is y some good in it,' 3954
66: 5 Y they will be put to shame. 2256
66: 8 Y no sooner is Zion in labor than 3954
Jer 2:11 (Y they are not gods at all.) 2256
2:27 y when they are in trouble, they say, 2256
2:32 Y my people have forgotten me, 2256
2:34 Y in spite of all this 3954
3: 3 Y you have the brazen look of a prostitute; 2256
3: 8 Y I saw that her unfaithful sister Judah had 2256
5: 7 y they committed adultery and thronged to 2256
5:18 "Y even in those days," 2256
10:19 Y I said to myself, "This is my sickness, 2256
12: 1 Y I would speak with you 421
12: 3 Y you know me, O LORD; 2256
14:15 I did not send them, y they are saying, 2256
15:10 y everyone curses me. NIH
17:23 Y they did not listen or pay attention; 2256
18:15 Y my people have forgotten me; 3954
18:20 Y they have dug a pit for me. 3954
23:21 y they have run with their message; 2256
23:21 y they have prophesied. 2256
23:31 prophets who wag their own tongues **and** y 2256
23:32 y I did not send or appoint them. 2256
28:15 y you have persuaded this nation to trust 2256
33:10 Y in the towns of Judah and the streets NIH
34: 4 " 'Y hear the promise of the LORD, 421
35:14 y you have not obeyed me. 2256
37: 4 for he had **not** y been put in prison. AIT
48:47 "Y I will restore the fortunes of Moab 2256
49: 6 "Y afterward, I will restore the fortunes of 2256
49:39 "Y I will restore the fortunes of Elam 2256
50:34 Y their Redeemer is strong; NIH
La 1:18 y I rebelled against his command. 3954
3:21 Y this I call to mind and NIH
3:29 there **may** y be hope. 218
Eze 5: 6 Y in her wickedness she has rebelled 2256
11:16 and scattered them among the countries, **y** 2256
13: 6 y they expect their words to be fulfilled. 2256
14:22 Y there will be some survivors— 2256
15: 7 the fire *will* y **consume** them. AIT
16:60 Y I will remember the covenant I made 2256
17:15 Will he break the treaty **and** y escape? 2256
17:18 in pledge **and** y did all these things, 2256
18:19 "Y you ask, 'Why does the son not share 2256
18:25 "Y you say, 'The way of the Lord is 2256
18:29 Y the house of Israel says, 2256
20:13 " 'Y the people of Israel rebelled 2256
20:17 Y I looked on them with pity and did 2256
20:38 y they will not enter the land of Israel. 2256
23:11 y in her lust and prostitution she was 2256
23:19 Y she became more and more promiscuous 2256
24:16 Y do not lament or weep or shed any tears. 2256
29:13 " 'Y this is what the Sovereign LORD says: 3954
29:18 Y he and his army got no reward from 2256
31:18 Y you, too, will be brought down with 2256
33:17 "Y your countrymen say, 2256
33:20 Y, O house of Israel, you say, 2256
33:24 y he possessed the land. 2256
Eze 36:20 **and** y they had to leave his land.' 2256
44:14 Y I will put them in charge of the duties of 2256
Da 2:41 y it will have some of the strength of iron 10221
8:25 Y he will be destroyed, NIH
9:13 y we have not sought the favor of the LORD 2256
9:14 y we have not obeyed him. 2256
10:14 for the vision concerns a time y **to come."** 6388
11:12 y he will not remain triumphant. 2256
11:20 y not in anger or in battle. 2256
11:45 Y he will come to his end, 2256
Hos 1: 7 Y I will show love to the house of Judah; 2256
1:10 "Y the Israelites will be like the sand on 2256
9: 8 y snares await him on all his paths, NIH
Am 4: 4 go to Gilgal and sin y **more.** 8049
4: 6 y you have not returned to me," 2256
4: 8 y you have not returned to me," 2256
4: 9 y you have not returned to me," 2256
4:10 y you have not returned to me," 2256
4:11 y you have not returned to me," 2256
9: 8 y I will not totally destroy the house 700+3954
Jnh 2: 4 y I will look again toward your holy temple 421
3: 9 God may y relent and with compassion turn NIH
Mic 3:11 Y they lean upon the LORD and say, 2256
Na 2: 5 y they stumble on their way. NIH
3:10 Y she was taken captive and went 1685
Hab 3:16 Y I will wait patiently for the day 889
3:18 y I will rejoice in the LORD, 2256
Zep 3: 5 y the unrighteous know no shame. 2256
Hag 1: 2 not y **come** for the LORD's house to AIT
2:17 mildew and hail, y you did not turn to me,' 2256
2:19 Is there y any seed left in the barn? 6388
Zec 8:20 the inhabitants of many cities will y come, 6388
10: 9 y in distant lands they will remember me. 2256
13: 8 y one-third will be left in it. 2256
Mal 1: 2 "Y I have loved Jacob, 2256
3: 8 "Will a man rob God? Y you rob me. 3954
3:13 "Y you ask, 'What have we said 2256
Mt 6:26 **and** y your heavenly Father feeds them. *2779*
6:29 Y I tell you that not even Solomon *1254*
7:25 against that house; y it did not fall, *2779*
10:29 Y not one of them will fall to the ground *2779*
11:11 y he who is least in the kingdom *1254*
12: 5 in the temple desecrate the day **and** y *2779*
13:32 y when it grows, it is the largest of *1254*
16:26 gains the whole world, y forfeits his soul? *1254*
26:39 Y not as I will, but as you will." *4440*
28: 8 afraid y filled with joy, *2779*
Mk 1:45 Y the people still came to him *2779*
4:32 Y when planted, it grows and becomes *2779*
5:26 y instead of getting better she grew worse. *247*
5:31 his disciples answered, **"and** y you can ask, *2779*
6:20 y he liked to listen to him. *2779*
7:24 y he could not keep his presence secret. *2779*
8:36 to gain the whole world, y forfeit his soul? *2779*
14:36 Y not what I will, but what you will." *247*
14:59 Y even then their testimony did not agree. *NIG*
Lk 4:26 Y Elijah was not sent to any of them, *2779*
4:27 y not one of them was cleansed— *2779*
5:15 Y the news about him spread all the more, *1254*
7:28 y the one who is least in the kingdom *1254*
9:25 **and** y lose or forfeit his very self? *1254*
10:11 Y be sure of this: *4440*
11: 8 y because of the man's boldness he will get *1145*
12: 6 Y not one of them is forgotten by God. *2779*
12:24 no storeroom or barn; y God feeds them. *2779*
12:27 Y I tell you, not even Solomon *1254*
15:29 Y you never gave me **even** a young goat *2779*
18: 5 y because this widow keeps bothering me, *1145*
19:48 Y they could not find any way to do it, *2779*
22:42 y not my will, but yours be done." *4440*
23:53 one in which no one had y been laid. *4024+4037*
Jn 1:12 Y to all who received him, *1254*
2: 4 "My time has **not** y come." *4037*
4:23 Y a time is coming and has now come *247*
5:40 y you refuse to come to me to have life. *2779*
5:44 y make no effort to obtain the praise *2779*
6:17 and Jesus had **not** y joined them. *4037*
6:49 the manna in the desert, y they died. *2779*
6:64 Y there are some of you who do *247*
6:70 Y one of you is a devil!" *2779*
7: 6 "The right time for me has **not** y come; *4037*
7: 8 I am **not** y going up to this Feast, *4037*
7: 8 for me the right time has **not** y come." *4037*
7:19 Y not one of you keeps the law. *2779*
7:22 Y, because Moses gave you circumcision *NIG*
7:30 because his time had **not** y come. *4037*
7:39 since Jesus had **not** y been glorified. *4031*
8:20 Y no one seized him, *2779*
8:20 because his time had **not** y come. *4037*
8:37 Y you are ready to kill me, *247*
8:45 Y because I tell the truth, *1254*
8:52 y you say that if anyone keeps your word, *2779*
8:57 "You are **not** y fifty years old," *4037*
9:30 y he opened my eyes. *2779*
11: 6 Y when he heard that Lazarus was sick, *4036*
11: 8 and y you are going back there?" *4099*
11:30 Now Jesus had **not** y entered the village, *4037*
12:42 Y at the same time many even among *3530*
15:24 **and** y they have hated both me *2779*
16: 5 y none of you asks me, *2779*
16:13 and he will tell you what is y to come. *NIG*
16:32 Y I am not alone, for my Father is with me. *2779*
20:17 for I have **not** y returned to the Father. *4037*
20:29 blessed are those who have not seen **and** y *2779*
Ac 2:34 **and** y he said, " 'The Lord said to my Lord: *1254*
5:28 "Y you have filled Jerusalem *2779*
8:16 the Holy Spirit had **not** y come upon any *4031*
Ac 9:22 Y Saul grew more and more powerful *1254*
13:27 y in condemning him they fulfilled *2779*
14:17 Y he has not left himself without testimony: *2792*
23: 3 y you yourself violate the law *2779*
Ro 2: 3 on them **and** y do the same things, *2779*
2:27 not circumcised physically and y obeys *NIG*
4:20 Y he did not waver through unbelief *1254*
8:10 y your spirit is alive because *1254*
8:25 But if we hope for what we do not y have, *NIG*
9:11 **Y, before** the twins were born *3609*
1Co 3: 2 for you were **not** y ready for it. *4037*
8: 2 who thinks he knows something does **not** y *4037*
8: 6 y for us there is but one God, the Father, *247*
9:16 Y when I preach the gospel, I cannot boast, *1142*
14:10 y none of them is without meaning. *2779*
15:10 y not I, but the grace of God that was *1254*
2Co 4:16 y inwardly we are being renewed day *247*
6: 8 genuine, y regarded as impostors; *2779*
6: 9 known, y regarded as unknown; *2779*
6: 9 dying, and y we live on; *2627*
6: 9 beaten, **and** y not killed; *2779*
6:10 sorrowful, y always rejoicing; *1254*
6:10 poor, y making many rich; *1254*
6:10 nothing, **and** y possessing everything. *2779*
7: 9 y now I am happy, *NIG*
8: 9 y for your sakes he became poor, *NIG*
12:16 **Y,** crafty fellow that I am, *247*
13: 4 y he lives by God's power. *247*
13: 4 y by God's power we will live with him *247*
Gal 2: 3 Y not even Titus, who was with me, *247*
2:14 y you live like a Gentile and not like a Jew. *NIG*
6:13 y they want you to be circumcised *247*
Php 1:22 Y what shall I choose? *2779*
3:13 not consider myself y to have taken hold *NIG*
4:14 Y it was good of you to share *4440*
1Th 4:10 Y we urge you, brothers, *1254*
2Th 3:15 Y do not regard him as an enemy, *2779*
2Ti 1:12 Y I am not ashamed, *247*
3:11 Y the Lord rescued me from all of them. *2779*
Phm 1: 9 y I appeal to you on the basis of love. *NIG*
Heb 2: 8 Y at present we do **not** see everything *4037*
4: 3 **And** y his work has been finished since *2792*
4:15 just as we are—y was without sin. *NIG*
7: 6 y he collected a tenth from Abraham *NIG*
9: 8 the way into the Most Holy Place had **not** y *3609*
11: 7 when warned about things **not** y seen, *3596*
11:39 for their faith, y none of them received *NIG*
12: 4 you have **not** y resisted to the point *4037*
Jas 1:26 If anyone considers himself religious and y *NIG*
2:10 For whoever keeps the whole law **and** y *1254*
2Pe 2:11 y **even** angels, although they are stronger *3963*
1Jn 1: 6 If we claim to have fellowship with him y *2779*
2: 8 Y I am writing you a new command; *4099*
3: 2 be has **not** y been made known. *4037*
4:20 "I love God," y hates his brother, *2779*
Jude 1:10 Y these men speak abusively against *1254*
Rev 2: 4 Y I hold this against you: *247*
2: 9 and your poverty—y you are rich! *247*
2:13 Y you remain true to my name. *2779*
3: 4 Y you have a few people in Sardis who *247*
3: 8 y you have kept my word and have *2779*
9:12 two other woes are y to come. *3552+4047*
13:14 wounded by the sword **and** y lived. *2779*
17: 8 now is not, and y will come. *NIG*
17:10 one is, the other has **not** y come; *4037*
17:12 "The ten horns you saw are ten kings who have **not** y received a kingdom, *4037*

YIELD (25) [YIELDED, YIELDING, YIELDS]

Ge 4:12 *it will* no longer y its crops for you. 5989
Lev 25:19 Then the land *will* y its fruit, 5989
25:21 that the land *will* y enough for three years. 6913
26: 4 the ground *will* y its crops and the trees of 5989
26:20 because your soil *will* not y its crops, 5989
26:20 nor *will* the trees of the land y their fruit. 5989
Dt 11:17 not rain and the ground *will* y no produce, 5989
13: 8 *do* not y to him or listen to him. 14
33:14 and the finest the moon can **y;** 1765
Jos 24:23 that are among you and y your hearts to 5742
2Sa 1:21 nor **fields** *that* y offerings [of grain]. AIT
Job 31:39 if I have devoured its y without payment 3946
Ps 67: 6 Then the land *will* y its harvest, and God, 5989
85:12 and our land *will* y its harvest. 5989
Pr 8:19 *what* I y surpasses choice silver. 9311
Isa 5: 4 why *did it* y only bad? 6913
48:11 *I will* not y my glory to another. 5989
Eze 34:27 The trees of the field *will* y their fruit and 5989
34:27 and the ground *will* y its crops; 5989
36:37 Once again *I will* y **to the plea** of 2011
Hos 8: 7 Were it to y grain, 6913
9:16 their root is withered, *they* y no fruit. 6913
Joel 2:22 the fig tree and the vine y their riches. 5989
Zec 8:12 the vine *will* y its fruit, 5989
Jas 5: 7 to y its valuable crop and how patient he is *NIG*

YIELDED (3) [YIELD]

Ps 107:37 and planted vineyards *that* y a fruitful 6913
Isa 5: 2 but *it* y only bad fruit. 6913
Lk 8: 8 It came up and y a crop, *4472*

YIELDING (3) [YIELD]

SS 5:13 like beds of spice y perfume. 1540
Mt 13:23 He produces a crop, y a hundred, *4472*
Rev 22: 2 twelve crops of fruit, y its fruit every month. *625*

YIELDS (5) [YIELD]
Lev 25: 6 the land y during the sabbath year will NIH
Ps 1: 3 which y its fruit in season 5989
Pr 3:14 and y better **returns** than gold. 9311
14:24 but the folly of fools y folly. NIH
Isa 55:10 that *it* y seed for the sower and bread for 5989

YOKE (61) [YOKED, YOKEFELLOW, YOKES]
Ge 27:40 you will throw his y from off your neck." 6585
Ex 6: 6 and I will bring you out from under the y 6026
6: 7 who brought you out from under the y *of* 6026
Lev 26:13 the bars of your y and enabled you to walk 6585
Nu 19: 2 and that has never been under a **y.** 6585
Dt 21: 3 and has never worn a y 6585
28:48 He will put an iron y on your neck 6585
1Ki 12: 4 "Your father put a heavy y *on* us, 6585
12: 4 the harsh labor and the heavy y he put 6585
12: 9 'Lighten the y your father put on us'?" 6585
12:10 'Your father put a heavy y *on* us, 6585
12:10 but make our y lighter'— NIH
12:11 My father laid on you a heavy **y;** 6585
12:14 "My father made your y heavy; 6585
19:19 He was plowing with twelve **y of oxen,** 7538
19:21 He took his y *of* oxen 7538
2Ch 10: 4 "Your father put a heavy y *on* us, 6585
10: 4 the harsh labor and the heavy y he put 6585
10: 9 'Lighten the y your father put on us'?" 6585
10:10 'Your father put a heavy y *on* us, 6585
10:10 but make our y lighter'— NIH
10:11 My father laid on you a heavy **y;** 6585
10:14 "My father made your y heavy; 6585
Job 1: 3 five hundred y *of* oxen 7538
42:12 a thousand y *of* oxen and 7538
Isa 9: 4 the y *that* burdens them, 6585
10:27 their y from your neck; 6585
10:27 the y will be broken 6585
14:25 His y will be taken from my people, 6585
47: 6 Even on the aged you laid a very heavy **y.** 6585
58: 6 of injustice and untie the cords of the **y,** 4574
58: 6 the oppressed free and break every **y?** 4574
58: 9 "If you do away with the y of oppression, 4574
Jer 2:20 "Long ago you broke off your y 6585
5: 5 the y and torn off the bonds. 6585
27: 2 a y *out* **of straps** and crossbars and put it 4593
27: 8 of Babylon or bow its neck under his **y,** 6585
27:11 the y *of* the king of Babylon and serve him, 6585
27:12 "Bow your neck under the y *of* the king 6585
28: 2 'I will break the y *of* the king of Babylon. 6585
28: 4 I will break the y *of* the king of Babylon.' " 6585
28:10 the y off the neck of the prophet Jeremiah 4574
28:11 'In the same way will I break the y 6585
28:12 the prophet Hananiah had broken the y off 4574
28:13 You have broken a wooden **y,** 4574
28:13 but in its place you will get a y *of* iron. 4574
28:14 an iron y on the necks of all these nations 6585
30: 8 'I will break the y off their necks 6585
La 1:14 "My sins have been bound into a **y;** 6585
3:27 for a man to bear the y while he is young. 6585
Eze 30:18 be the day at Tahpanhes when I break the y 4574
34:27 of their y and rescue them from the hands 6585
Hos 10:11 so I *will* **put a** y on her fair neck. 6296
11: 4 I lifted the y from their neck and bent down 6585
Na 1:13 Now I will break their y from your neck 4573
Mt 11:29 Take my y upon you and learn from me, *2433*
11:30 For my y is easy and my burden is light." *2433*
Lk 14:19 'I have just bought five y of oxen, *2414*
Ac 15:10 by putting on the necks of the disciples a y *2433*
Gal 5: 1 not let yourselves be burdened again *by* a y *2433*
1Ti 6: 1 All who are under the y of slavery *2433*

YOKED (4) [YOKE]
Dt 22:10 with an ox and a donkey y together. NIH
1Sa 6: 7 have calved and *have* never *been* **y.** 6585+6590
Ps 106:28 *They* y **themselves** to the Baal of Peor 7537
2Co 6:14 Do not be **y together** with unbelievers. *2282*

YOKEFELLOW (1) [YOKE]
Php 4: 3 Yes, and I ask you, loyal y, *5187*

YOKES (1) [YOKE]
2Sa 24:22 and here are threshing sledges and ox y for 3998

YONDER (KJV) See OTHER, SOME DISTANCE AWAY, THERE

YOU (13727) [YOU'LL, YOU'RE, YOU'VE, YOUR, YOURS, YOURSELF, YOURSELVES] See Index of Articles Etc.

YOU'LL (1) [BE, YOU]
1Sa 19:11 run for your life tonight, tomorrow y be killed." 911

YOU'RE (9) [BE, YOU]
Jdg 4:22 "I will show you the man y looking for." 911
11: 7 come to me now, when y in trouble?" 4013
1Sa 26:15 David said, "**Y** a man, aren't you? 911
Mt 26:70 "I don't know what y **talking about,"** *AIT*
Mk 14:68 "I don't know or understand what y talking *5148*
Mk 14:71 "I don't know this man y **talking about."** *AIT*
Lk 22:60 I don't know what y **talking about!"** *AIT*
Ac 10:21 "I'm the one y **looking for.** *AIT*
12:15 *"Y* **out of** *your* **mind,"** they told her. *AIT*

YOU'VE (4) [HAVE, YOU]
Ge 31:26 "What have you done? *Y* **deceived** me, AIT
31:26 and *y* **carried off** my daughters AIT
Jdg 14:16 *Y* **given** my people a riddle, AIT
15: 7 "Since *y* **acted** like this, AIT

YOUNG (292) [YOUNGER, YOUNGEST, YOUTH, YOUTHFUL, YOUTHS]
Ge 4:23 a **y man** for injuring me. 3529
15: 9 along with a dove and a **y pigeon."** 1578
19: 4 both y and old—surrounded the house. 5853
19:11 y and old, with blindness so that they could 7785
27: 9 and bring me two choice **y goats,** 1531+6436
30:39 And they **bore** y that were streaked 3528
30:40 the y **of the flock** by themselves, 4166
31: 8 then all the flocks gave birth to **speckled** *y;* AIT
31: 8 then all the flocks bore **streaked** *y.* AIT
32:15 thirty female camels with their **y,** 1201
33:13 the ewes and cows *that are* **nursing** *their* **y.** 6402
34:19 The **y man,** who was the most honored 5853
37: 2 Joseph, a **y man** of seventeen, 5853
38:17 "I'll send you a **y goat** from my flock, 1531+6436
38:20 Judah sent the **y goat** by his friend 1531+6436
38:23 After all, I did send her this **y goat,** 1531
41:12 Now a y Hebrew was there with us, 5853
44:20 there is a **y** son born to him in his old age. 7783
Ex 10: 9 "We will go with our y and old, 5853
23:19 "Do not cook a **y goat** in its mother's milk. 1531
24: 5 Then he sent y Israelite **men,** 5853
24: 5 sacrificed **y bulls** as fellowship offerings 7228
29: 1 Take a y bull and two rams without defect. 1201
33:11 but his y aide Joshua son of Nun did 5853
34:26 not cook a **y goat** in its mother's milk." 1531
Lev 1: 5 to slaughter the y bull before the LORD, 1201
1:14 he is to offer a dove or a y pigeon. 1201
4: 3 a y bull without defect as a sin offering for 1201
4:14 a y bull as a sin offering and present it 1201
5: 7 he is to bring two doves or two y pigeons to 1201
5:11 cannot afford two doves or two y pigeons, 1201
12: 6 and a y pigeon or a dove for a sin offering. 1201
12: 8 she is to bring two doves or two y pigeons, 1201
14:22 and two doves or two y pigeons, 1201
14:30 the doves or the y pigeons, 1201
15:14 or two y pigeons and come before 1201
15:29 or two y pigeons and bring them to 1201
16: 3 with a y bull for a sin offering and a ram 1201
22:28 a cow or a sheep and its y on the same day. 1201
23:18 one y bull and two rams. 1201
Nu 6:10 or two y pigeons to the priest at 1201
7:15 one y bull, one ram and one male lamb 1201
7:21 one y bull, one ram and one male lamb 1201
7:27 one y bull, one ram and one male lamb 1201
7:33 one y bull, one ram and one male lamb 1201
7:39 one y bull, one ram and one male lamb 1201
7:45 one y bull, one ram and one male lamb 1201
7:51 one y bull, one ram and one male lamb 1201
7:57 one y bull, one ram and one male lamb 1201
7:63 one y bull, one ram and one male lamb 1201
7:69 one y bull, one ram and one male lamb 1201
7:75 one y bull, one ram and one male lamb 1201
7:81 one y bull, one ram and one male lamb 1201
7:87 the burnt offering came to twelve **y bulls,** 7228
8: 8 a y bull with its grain offering 1201
8: 8 to take a second y bull for a sin offering. 1201
11:27 A **y man** ran and told Moses, 5853
15: 8 a y bull as a burnt offering or sacrifice, 1201
15:11 Each bull or ram, each lamb or **y goat,** 6436
15:24 the whole community is to offer a y bull for 1201
28:11 the LORD a burnt offering of two y bulls, 1201
28:19 a burnt offering of two y bulls, 1201
28:27 Present a burnt offering of two y bulls, 1201
29: 2 prepare a burnt offering of one y bull, 1201
29: 8 the LORD a burnt offering of one y bull, 1201
29:13 a burnt offering of thirteen y bulls, 1201
29:17 the second day prepare twelve y bulls, 1201
30: 3 "When a y woman still living in her father's 5830
30:16 and his y daughter still living in his house. 5830
Dt 7:14 nor any of your livestock **without y.** 6829
14:21 Do not cook a **y goat** in its mother's milk. 1531
22: 6 the mother is sitting on the y or on the eggs, 711
22: 6 do not take the mother with the **y.** 1201
22: 7 You may take the **y,** 1201
28: 4 of your land and the y *of* your livestock— 7262
28:11 of your womb, the y *of* your livestock and 7262
28:50 without respect for the old or pity for the **y.** 5853
28:51 They will devour the y *of* your livestock 7262
30: 9 the y *of* your livestock and the crops 7262
32:11 that stirs up its nest and hovers over its **y,** 1578
32:25 **Y men** and young women will perish, 1033
32:25 Young men and **y women** will perish, 1435
Jos 6:21 men and women, y and old, cattle, 5853
6:23 So the **y men** who had done the spying went 5853
Jdg 6:19 Gideon went in, prepared a **y goat,** 1531+6436
8:14 a y man of Succoth and questioned him, 5853
8:14 the y man wrote down for him the names of NIH
11:40 that each year the **y women** *of* Israel go out 1426
12: 9 for his sons he brought in thirty **y women** 1426
13:15 until we prepare a **y goat** for you." 1531+6436
13:19 Then Manoah took a **y goat,** 1531+6436
14: 1 and saw there a y Philistine woman. 1426
Jdg 14: 5 a **y lion** came roaring toward him. 787+4097
14: 6 as he might have torn a **y goat.** 1531
15: 1 a **y goat** and went to visit his wife. 1531+6436
17: 7 A y Levite from Bethlehem in Judah, 5853
17:11 the **y man** was to him like one of his sons. 5853
17:12 and the **y man** became his priest and lived 5853
18: 3 they recognized the voice of the y Levite; 5853
18:15 the house of the y Levite at Micah's place 5853
19:19 your maidservant, and the **y man** with us. 5853
21:12 in Jabesh Gilead four hundred **y** women who had never slept with a man, 5855
Ru 2: 5 "Whose **y woman** is that?" 5855
4:12 the LORD gives you by this **y woman,** 5855
1Sa 1:24 she took the boy with her, **y** as he was, 5853
2:17 This sin of the **y men** was very great in 5853
5: 9 both y and old, with an outbreak of tumors. 7785
9: 2 an impressive **y man** without equal among 1033
10: 3 One will be carrying three **y goats,** 1531
14: 1 of Saul said to the **y man** bearing his armor, 5853
14: 6 Jonathan said to his y armor-bearer, 5853
16:20 a skin of wine and a **y goat** 1531+6436
17:55 "Abner, whose son is that **y man?"** 5853
17:56 "Find out whose son this **y man** is." 6624
17:58 "Whose son are you, **y man?"** 5853
25: 5 So he sent ten **y men** and said to them, 5853
25: 8 Therefore be favorable toward my **y men,** 5853
26:22 of your **y men** come over and get it. 5853
30: 2 all who were in it, both y and old. 7785
30:17 except four hundred y men who rode off 5853
30:19 Nothing was missing: y or old, boy or girl, 7785
2Sa 1: 5 to the **y man** who brought him the report, 5853
1: 6 the **y man** said, "and there was Saul, 5853
1:13 David said to the **y man** who brought him 5853
2:14 of the **y men** get up and fight hand to hand 5853
2:21 of the **y men** and strip him of his weapons." 5853
9:12 Mephibosheth had a **y** son named Mica, 7783
14:21 Go, bring back the **y man** Absalom." 5853
17:18 But a **y man** saw them and told Absalom. 5853
18: 5 with the **y man** Absalom for my sake." 5853
18:12 'Protect the **y man** Absalom for my sake.' 5853
18:29 "Is the **y man** Absalom safe?" 5853
18:32 "Is the **y man** Absalom safe?" 5853
18:32 up to harm you be like that **y man."** 5853
1Ki 1: 2 a y virgin to attend the king and take care 5855
11:28 how well the **y man** did his work, 5853
12: 8 and consulted the **y men** who had grown up 3529
12:10 The **y men** who had grown up 3529
12:14 he followed the advice of the **y men** 3529
20:14 'The **y officers** *of* the provincial 5853
20:15 So Ahab summoned the **y officers** *of* 5853
20:17 The **y officers** *of* the provincial 5853
20:19 The **y officers** *of* the provincial 5853
2Ki 3:21 so every man, **y and old,** 2025+2256+5087
5: 2 and had taken captive a y girl from Israel, 7783
5:14 and became clean like that of a y boy. 7785
5:22 'Two **y men** from the company of 5853
8:12 kill their **y men** with the sword, 1033
9: 4 **y man,** the prophet, went to Ramoth Gilead. 5853
1Ch 12:28 a brave y warrior, with 22 officers 5853
22: 5 "My son Solomon is y and inexperienced, 5853
25: 8 **Y** and old alike, teacher as well as student, 7785
26:13 according to their families, y and old alike. 7785
29: 1 God has chosen, is y and inexperienced. 5853
2Ch 10: 8 and consulted the **y men** who had grown up 3529
10:10 The **y men** who had grown up with him 3529
10:14 he followed the advice of the **y men** 3529
13: 7 of Solomon when he was y and indecisive 5853
13: 9 with a y bull and seven rams may become 1201
31:15 their divisions, old and y alike. 7783
34: 3 while he was still **y,** he began to seek the 5853
36:17 who killed their **y men** with the sword in 1033
36:17 spared neither **y man** nor young woman, 1033
36:17 spared neither young man nor **y woman,** 1435
Ezr 6: 9 Whatever is needed—y bulls, rams, 10120
Est 2: 2 be made for beautiful y virgins for the king. 5855
3:13 y and old, women and little children— 5853
Job 29: 8 the **y men** saw me and stepped aside and 5853
32: 6 "I am y in years, and you are old; 7582
38:41 when its y cry out to God and wander about 3529
39: 3 They crouch down and bring forth their **y;** 3529
39: 4 Their y thrive and grow strong in the wilds; 1201
39:16 She treats her y harshly, 1201
39:30 His **y ones** feast on blood, 711
Ps 29: 6 Sirion like a y wild ox. 1201
37:25 I was y and now I am old, 5853
78:31 cutting down the **y men** *of* Israel. 1033
78:63 Fire consumed their **y men,** 1033
84: 3 where she may have her **y—** 711
89:19 I have exalted a **y man** from among 1033
119: 9 How can a **y man** keep his way pure? 5853
147: 9 and for the y ravens when they call. 1201
148:12 **y men** and maidens, old men and children. 1033
Pr 1: 4 knowledge and discretion to the **y—** 5853
7: 7 I noticed among the **y men,** 1201
20:29 The glory of **y men** is their strength, 1033
Ecc 11: 9 Be happy, **y man,** while you are young, 1033
11: 9 Be happy, young man, while you are **y,** 3531
SS 1: 8 of the sheep and graze your **y goats** by 1537
2: 3 of the forest is my lover among the **y men.** 1201
2: 9 My lover is like a gazelle or a **y stag.** 385+6762
2:17 and be like a gazelle or like a **y stag** on 385+6762
8: 8 We have a y sister, 7783
8:14 a **y stag** on the spice-laden mountains. 385+6762
Isa 3: 5 The y will rise up against the old, 5853
5:29 they roar like **y lions;** 4097
7:21 man will keep alive a **y cow** and 1330+6320
9:17 the Lord will take no pleasure in the **y men,** 1033

Isa 11: 7 their y will lie down together, 3529
11: 8 y child put his hand into the viper's nest. 1694
13:18 Their bows will strike down the y men; 5853
20: 4 y and old, with buttocks bared— 5853
31: 8 before the sword and their y men will be put 1033
33: 4 O nations, is harvested as by y locusts; 2885
34:15 and care for *her* y under the shadow 1842
40:11 he gently leads *those that* have y. 6402
40:30 and y men stumble and fall; 1033
54: 6 a wife who married y, only to be rejected," 5830
60: 6 y camels *of* Midian and Ephah. 1145
62: 5 As a y man marries a maiden, 1033
Jer 6:11 and on the y men gathered together; 1033
9:21 the children from the streets and the y men 1033
11:22 Their y men will die by the sword, 1033
15: 8 against the mothers of their y men; 1033
18:21 their y men slain by the sword in battle. 1033
31:12 the y *of* the flocks and herds. 1201
31:13 y men and old as well. 1033
48:15 her finest y men will go down in 1033
49:20 The y *of* the flock will be dragged away; 7582
49:26 Surely, her y men will fall in the streets; 1033
50:27 Kill all her y bulls; 7228
50:30 Therefore, her y men will fall in the streets; 1033
50:45 The y *of* the flock will be dragged away; 7582
51: 3 Do not spare her y men; 1033
51:22 with you I shatter y man and maiden, 1033
51:38 Her people all roar like y lions, 4097
La 1:15 an army against me to crush my y men. 1033
1:18 y men and maidens have gone into exile. 1033
2:10 y women *of* Jerusalem have bowed their heads to the ground. 1435
2:21 "Y and old lie together in the dust of 5853
2:21 my y men and maidens have fallen by 1033
3:27 for a man to bear the yoke while he is y. 5830
4: 3 jackals offer their breasts to nurse their y, 1594
5:13 Y men toil at the millstones; 1033
5:14 the y men have stopped their music. 1033
Eze 9: 6 Slaughter old men, y men and maidens, 1033
19: 2 among the y lions and reared her cubs. 4097
23: 6 all of them handsome y men, 1033
23:12 mounted horsemen, all handsome y men. 1033
23:21 and your y breasts fondled. 5830
23:23 the Assyrians with them, handsome y men, 1033
30:17 The y men *of* Heliopolis and Bubastis 1033
43:19 You are to give a y bull as a sin offering to 1201
43:23 to offer a y bull and a ram from the flock. 1201
43:25 you are also to provide a y bull and a ram 1201
45:18 to take a y bull without defect and purify 1201
46: 6 of the New Moon he is to offer a y bull, 1201
Da 1: 4 y men without any physical defect, 3529
1:10 the other y men your age? 3529
1:13 that of the y men who eat the royal food, 3529
1:15 of the y men who ate the royal food. 3529
1:17 To these four y men God gave knowledge 3529
Hos 14: 6 his y shoots will grow. 3438
Joel 1: 4 the y locusts have eaten; 3540
1: 4 what the y locusts have left other locusts 3540
2:25 the great locust and the y locust, 3540
2:28 your y men will see visions. 1033
Am 2:11 and Nazirites from among your y men. 1033
4:10 I killed your y men with the sword, 1033
8:13 "In that day "the lovely y women 1435
8:13 and strong y men will faint because 1033
Mic 5: 8 like a y lion among flocks of sheep, 4097
Na 2:11 the place where they fed their y, 4097
2:13 and the sword will devour your y lions. 4097
Zec 2: 4 "Run, tell that y man, 5853
9:17 Grain will make the y men thrive, 1033
9:17 and new wine the y women. 1435
11:16 or seek the y, or heal the injured, 5853
Mt 19:20 "All these I have kept," the y man said. *3734*
19:22 When the y man heard this, *3734*
Mk 14:51 A y man, wearing nothing but a linen *3734*
16: 5 a y man dressed in a white robe sitting on *3734*
Lk 2:24 "a pair of doves or two y pigeons." *3801*
7:14 He said, "Y man, I say to you, get up!" *3734*
15:29 Yet you never gave me even a y goat *2253*
Jn 12:14 Jesus found a y donkey and sat upon it, *3942*
Ac 2:17 your y men will see visions, *3734*
5: 6 Then the y *men* came forward, *3742*
5:10 Then the y men came in and, *3734*
7:58 at the feet *of* a y man named Saul. *3733*
20: 9 in a window was a y man named Eutychus, *3733*
20:10 went down, threw himself on the y man *899S*
20:12 The people took the y man home alive *4090*
23:17 "Take this y man to the commander; *3733*
23:18 for me and asked me to bring this y man *3734*
23:19 commander took the y man by the hand, *899S*
23:22 The commander dismissed the y man *3734*
1Ti 4:12 look down on you because you are y, *3744*
Tit 2: 6 encourage the y *men* to be self-controlled. *3742*
1Pe 5: 5 Y *men*, in the same way be submissive *3742*
1Jn 2:13 I write to you, y men, *3734*
2:14 I write to you, y men, *3734*

YOUNGER (31) [YOUNG]

Ge 19:31 One day the older daughter said to the y, 7582
19:34 the older daughter said to the y, 7582
19:35 and the y *daughter* went and lay with him. 7582
19:38 The y *daughter* also had a son, 7582
25:23 and the older will serve the y." 7582
27:15 and put them on her y son Jacob. 7783
27:42 she sent for her y son Jacob and said 7783
29:16 and the name of the y was Rachel. 7783
29:18 in return for your y daughter Rachel." 7783
29:26 not our custom here to give the y *daughter* 7582
29:27 then we will give you the y one also, 2296S
48:14 on Ephraim's head, though he was the y, 7582
48:19 his y brother will be greater than he, 7785
Jdg 1:13 Othniel son of Kenaz, Caleb's y brother, 7785
3: 9 Othniel son of Kenaz, Caleb's y brother, 7785
15: 2 Isn't her y sister more attractive? 7783
Ru 3:10 You have not run after the y men, 1033
1Sa 14:49 and that of the y was Michal. 7783
Job 30: 1 they mock me, *men* y than I, 3427+4200+7582
Eze 16:46 and your y sister, who lived to the south 7783
16:61 and those *who* are y. 7783
Mk 15:40 the mother of James the y and of Joses, *3625*
Lk 15:12 The y *one* said to his father, 'Father, *3742*
15:13 the y son got together all he had, *3742*
Jn 21:18 when you were y you dressed yourself *3742*
Ro 9:12 she was told, "The older will serve the y." *1781*
1Ti 5: 1 Treat y *men* as brothers, *3742*
5: 2 and y *women* as sisters, with absolute purity. *3742*
5:11 y widows, do not put them on such a list. *3742*
5:14 So I counsel y widows to marry, *3742*
Tit 2: 4 the y *women* to love their husbands *3742*

YOUNGEST (22) [YOUNG]

Ge 9:24 and found out what his y son had done 7783
42:13 The y is now with our father, 7785
42:15 unless your y brother comes here. 7785
42:20 But you must bring your y brother to me, 7785
42:32 and the y is now with our father in Canaan.' 7785
42:34 But bring your y brother to me 7785
43:29 he asked, "Is this your y brother, 7785
43:33 from the firstborn to the y; 7582
44: 2 in the mouth of the y *one's* sack, 7785
44:12 with the oldest and ending with the y. 7785
44:23 your y brother comes down with you, 7785
44:26 Only if our y brother is with us will we go. 7785
44:26 see the man's face unless our y brother is 7785
Jos 6:26 at the cost of his y will he set up its gates." 7582
Jdg 9: 5 But Jotham, the y son of Jerub-Baal, 7785
1Sa 16:11 "There is still the y," Jesse answered, 7783
17:14 David was the y. 7783
1Ki 16:34 up its gates at the cost of his y *son* Segub, 7582
1Ch 24:31 the same as those of the y. 7783
2Ch 21:17 a son was left to him except Ahaziah, the y. 7785
22: 1 Jehoram's y son, king in his place, 7785
Lk 22:26 greatest among you should be like the y, *3742*

YOUR (6631) [YOU] See Index of Articles Etc.

YOURS (86) [YOU] See Index of Articles Etc.

YOURSELF (191) [SELF, YOU] See Index of Articles Etc.

YOURSELVES (213) [SELF, YOU] See Index of Articles Etc.

YOUTH (56) [YOUNG]

Lev 22:13 to live in her father's house as in her y, 5830
Nu 11:28 who had been Moses' aide since y, 1036
1Sa 12: 2 I have been your leader from my y 5830
17:33 and he has been a fighting man from his y." 5830
2Sa 19: 7 that have come upon you from your y 5830
1Ki 18:12 worshiped the LORD since my y. 5830
Job 13:26 and make me inherit the sins of my y. 5830
31:18 from my y I reared him as would a father, 5830
33:25 it is restored as in the days of his y. 6596
36:14 They die in their y, 5854
Ps 25: 7 the sins of my y and my rebellious ways; 5830
71: 5 my confidence since my y. 5830
71:17 Since my y, O God, you have taught me, 5830
88:15 From my y I have been afflicted and close 5854
89:45 You have cut short the days of his y; 6596
103: 5 with good things so that your y is renewed 5830
110: 3 you will receive the dew of your y. 3531
127: 4 of a warrior are sons born in one's y. 5830
129: 1 They have greatly oppressed me from my y 5830
129: 2 they have greatly oppressed me from my y, 5830
144:12 in their y will be like well-nurtured plants, 5830
Pr 2:17 who has left the partner of her y 5830
5:18 and may you rejoice in the wife of your y. 5830
7: 7 a y who lacked judgment. 5853
29:21 If a man pampers his servant from y, 5854
Ecc 4:13 Better a poor but wise y than an old but 3529
4:14 The y may have come from prison to NIH
4:15 and walked under the sun followed the y, 3529
11: 9 give you joy in the days of your y. 1035
11:10 for y and vigor are meaningless. 3531
12: 1 Remember your Creator in the days of your y, 1035
Isa 54: 4 the shame of your y and remember no more 6596
65:20 dies at a hundred will be thought a *mere* y; 5853
Jer 2: 2 " 'I remember the devotion of your y, 5830
3: 4 'My Father, my friend from my y, 5830
3:24 From our y shameful gods have consumed 5830
3:25 from our y till this day we have not obeyed 5830
22:21 This has been your way from your y; 5830
31:19 because I bore the disgrace of my y.' 5830
32:30 but evil in my sight from their y; 5831
48:11 "Moab has been at rest from y, 5830
51:22 with you I shatter old man and y, 5853
Eze 4:14 From my y until now I have never eaten 5830
16:22 you did not remember the days of your y, 5830
16:43 you did not remember the days of your y 5830
16:60 I made with you in the days of your y, 5830
23: 3 engaging in prostitution from their y. 5830
23: 8 when during her y men slept with her, 5830
23:19 as she recalled the days of her y, 5830
23:21 So you longed for the lewdness of your y, 5830
Hos 2:15 There she will sing as in the days of her y, 5830
Joel 1: 8 grieving for the husband of her y. 5830
Zec 13: 5 land has been my livelihood since my y.' 5830
Mal 2:14 between you and the wife of your y, 5830
2:15 do not break faith with the wife of your y. 5830
2Ti 2:22 Flee the evil desires of y, *3754*

YOUTHFUL (1) [YOUNG]

Job 20:11 The y vigor that fills his bones will lie with 6596

YOUTHS (4) [YOUNG]

2Ki 2:23 *some* y came out of the town and jeered at him. 5853+7783
2:24 of the woods and mauled forty-two of the y. 3529
Isa 3:12 Y oppress my people, women rule over 6620
40:30 Even y grow tired and weary, 5853

Z

ZAANAIM (KJV) See ZAANANNIM

ZAANAN (1)

Mic 1:11 Those who live in Z will not come out. 7367

ZAANANNIM (2)

Jos 19:33 from Heleph and the large tree in Z, 7588
Jdg 4:11 and pitched his tent by the great tree in Z 7588

ZAAVAN (2)

Ge 36:27 The sons of Ezer: Bilhan, Z and Akan. 2401
1Ch 1:42 The sons of Ezer: Bilhan, Z and Akan. 2401

ZABAD (8)

1Ch 2:36 Nathan the father of Z, 2274
2:37 Z the father of Ephlal, 2274
7:21 Z his son and Shuthelah his son. 2274
11:41 Uriah the Hittite, Z son of Ahlai, 2274
2Ch 24:26 Those who conspired against him were Z, 2274
Ezr 10:27 Eliashib, Mattaniah, Jeremoth, Z and Aziza. 2274
10:33 Mattenai, Mattattah, Z, Eliphelet, Jeremai, 2274
10:43 Jeiel, Mattithiah, Z, Zebina, Jaddai, 2274

ZABBAI (2)

Ezr 10:28 Jehohanan, Hananiah, Z and Athlai. 2287
Ne 3:20 son of Z zealously repaired another section, 2287

ZABBUD (KJV) See ZACCUR

ZABDI (3)

1Ch 8:19 Jakim, Zicri, Z, 2275
27:27 Z the Shiphmite was in charge of 2275
Ne 11:17 the son of Z, the son of Asaph, 2275

ZABDIEL (2)

1Ch 27: 2 was Jashobeam son of Z. 2276
Ne 11:14 Their chief officer was Z son 2276

ZABUD (1)

1Ki 4: 5 Z son of Nathan— 2280

ZABULON (KJV) See ZEBULUN

ZACCAI (2)

Ezr 2: 9 of Z 760 2347
Ne 7:14 of Z 760 2347

ZACCHAEUS (3)

Lk 19: 2 A man was there by the name *of* Z; *2405*
19: 5 he looked up and said to him, "Z, *2405*
19: 8 But Z stood up and said to the Lord, "Look, *2405*

ZACCHUR (KJV) See ZACCUR

ZACCUR (10)

Nu 13: 4 the tribe of Reuben, Shammua son of Z; 2346
1Ch 4:26 Z his son and Shimei his son. 2346
24:27 Beno, Shoham, Z and Ibri. 2346
25: 2 Z, Joseph, Nethaniah and Asarelah. 2346
25:10 the third to Z, his sons and relatives, 12 2346

Ezr 8:14 Uthai and **Z**, and with them 70 men. 2346
Ne 3: 2 and **Z** son of Imri built next to them. 2346
10:12 **Z**, Sherebiah, Shebaniah, 2346
12:35 the son of Micaiah, the son of **Z**, 2346
13:13 the storerooms and made Hanan son of **Z**, 2346

ZACHARIAH, ZACHARIAS (KJV) See ZECHARIAH

ZACHER (KJV) See ZEKER

ZADOK (53) [ZADOKITES]
2Sa 8:17 **Z** son of Ahitub and Ahimelech son 7401
15:24 **Z** was there, too, and all the Levites 7401
15:25 Then the king said to **Z**, 7401
15:27 The king also said to **Z** the priest, 7401
15:29 So **Z** and Abiathar took the ark of God back 7401
15:35 Won't the priests **Z** and Abiathar be there 7401
15:36 Ahimaaz son of **Z** and Jonathan son 7401
17:15 Hushai told **Z** and Abiathar, the priests, 7401
18:19 Now Ahimaaz son of **Z** said, 7401
18:22 Ahimaaz son of **Z** again said to Joab, 7401
18:27 the first one runs like Ahimaaz son of **Z**." 7401
19:11 King David sent this message to **Z** 7401
20:25 **Z** and Abiathar were priests; 7401
1Ki 1: 8 But **Z** the priest, Benaiah son of Jehoiada, 7401
1:26 But me your servant, and **Z** the priest, 7401
1:32 King David said, "Call in **Z** the priest, 7401
1:34 There have **Z** the priest and Nathan 7401
1:38 So **Z** the priest, Nathan the prophet, 7401
1:39 **Z** the priest took the horn of oil from 7401
1:44 The king has sent with him **Z** the priest, 7401
1:45 and **Z** the priest and Nathan 7401
2:35 and replaced Abiathar with **Z** the priest. 7401
4: 2 Azariah son of **Z**—the priest; 7401
4: 4 **Z** and Abiathar—priests; 7401
2Ki 15:33 mother's name was Jerusha daughter of **Z**. 7401
1Ch 6: 8 Ahitub the father of **Z**, 7401
6: 8 **Z** the father of Ahimaaz, 7401
6:12 Ahitub the father of **Z**, 7401
6:12 **Z** the father of Shallum, 7401
6:53 **Z** his son and Ahimaaz his son. 7401
9:11 the son of Meshullam, the son of **Z**, 7401
12:28 and **Z**, a brave young warrior, 7401
15:11 Then David summoned **Z** and Abiathar 7401
16:39 David left **Z** the priest and his fellow priests 7401
18:16 **Z** son of Ahitub and Ahimelech son 7401
24: 3 of **Z** a descendant of Eleazar and Ahimelech 7401
24: 6 **Z** the priest, Ahimelech son of Abiathar and 7401
24:31 in the presence of King David and of **Z**, 7401
27:17 of Kemuel; over Aaron: **Z**; 7401
29:22 the LORD to be ruler and **Z** to be priest. 7401
2Ch 27: 1 mother's name was Jerusha daughter of **Z**. 7401
31:10 from the family of **Z**, answered, 7401
Ezr 7: 2 the son of **Z**, the son of Ahitub, 7401
Ne 3: 4 to him **Z** son of Baana also made repairs. 7401
3:29 Next to them, **Z** son 7401
10:21 Meshezabel, **Z**, Jaddua, 7401
11:11 the son of Meshullam, the son of **Z**, 7401
13:13 I put Shelemiah the priest, **Z** the scribe, 7401
Eze 40:46 These are the sons of **Z**, 7401
43:19 who are Levites, of the family of **Z**, 7401
44:15 who are Levites and descendants of **Z** 7401
Mt 1:14 Azor the father of **Z**, *4882*
1:14 **Z** the father of Akim, *4882*

ZADOKITES (1) [ZADOK]
Eze 48:11 the **Z**, who were faithful in serving me 1201+7401

ZAHAM (1)
2Ch 11:19 She bore him sons: Jeush, Shemariah and **Z**. 2300

ZAHAR (1)
Eze 27:18 in wine from Helbon and wool from **Z**. 7466

ZAIR (1)
2Ki 8:21 So Jehoram went to **Z** with all his chariots. 7583

ZALAPH (1)
Ne 3:30 the sixth son of **Z**, repaired another section. 7523

ZALMON (3)
Jdg 9:48 he and all his men went up Mount **Z**. 7515
2Sa 23:28 **Z** the Ahohite, Maharai the Netophathite, 7514
Ps 68:14 it was like snow fallen on **Z**. 7515

ZALMONAH (2)
Nu 33:41 They left Mount Hor and camped at **Z**. 7517
33:42 They left **Z** and camped at Punon. 7517

ZALMUNNA (10)
Jdg 8: 5 and I am still pursuing Zebah and **Z**, 7518
8: 6 hands of Zebah and **Z** in your possession? 7518
8: 7 when the LORD has given Zebah and **Z** 7518
8:10 Now Zebah and **Z** were in Karkor with 7518
8:12 Zebah and **Z**, the two kings of Midian, fled, 7518
8:15 "Here are Zebah and **Z**, 7518
8:15 hands of Zebah and **Z** in your possession? 7518
8:18 Then he asked Zebah and **Z**, 7518
Jdg 8:21 Zebah and **Z** said, "Come, do it yourself. 7518
Ps 83:11 all their princes like Zebah and **Z**, 7518

ZAMZUMMITES (1)
Dt 2:20 but the Ammonites called them **Z**. 2368

ZANOAH (5)
Jos 15:34 **Z**, En Gannim, Tappuah, Enam, 2391
15:56 Jezreel, Jokdeam, **Z**, 2391
1Ch 4:18 and Jekuthiel the father of **Z**.) 2392
Ne 3:13 by Hanun and the residents of **Z**. 2391
11:30 **Z**, Adullam and their villages, in Lachish 2391

ZAPHENATH-PANEAH (1)
Ge 41:45 Pharaoh gave Joseph the name **Z** 7624

ZAPHON (3)
Jos 13:27 Succoth and **Z** with the rest of the realm 7601
Jdg 12: 1 crossed over to **Z** and said to Jephthah, 7601
Ps 48: 2 Like the utmost heights of **Z** is Mount Zion, 7601

ZARA, ZARAH (KJV) See ZERAH

ZAREAH (KJV) See ZORAH

ZAREATHITES (KJV) See ZORATHITES

ZARED (KJV) See ZERED

ZAREPHATH (4)
1Ki 17: 9 "Go at once to **Z** of Sidon and stay there. 7673
17:10 So he went to **Z**. 7673
Ob 1:20 will possess [the land] as far as **Z**; 7673
Lk 4:26 but to a widow in **Z** in the region of Sidon. *4919*

ZARETHAN (4)
Jos 3:16 at a town called Adam in the vicinity of **Z**, 7681
1Ki 4:12 in all of Beth Shan next to **Z** below Jezreel, 7681
7:46 of the Jordan between Succoth and **Z**. 7681
2Ch 4:17 of the Jordan between Succoth and **Z**. 7681

ZARETHSHAHAR (KJV) See ZERETH SHAHAR

ZARTANAH, ZARTHAN (KJV) See ZARETHAN

ZATTU (5)
Ezr 2: 8 of **Z** 945 2456
8: 5 of the descendants of **Z**, Shecaniah son NIH
10:27 From the descendants of **Z**: Elioenai, 2456
Ne 7:13 of **Z** 845 2456
10:14 Parosh, Pahath-Moab, Elam, **Z**, Bani, 2456

ZAVAN (KJV) See ZAAVAN

ZAZA (1)
1Ch 2:33 The sons of Jonathan: Peleth and **Z**. 2321

ZEAL (21) [ZEALOUS, ZEALOUSLY]
Nu 25:11 so that in my **z** I did not put an end to them. 7863
Dt 29:20 his wrath and **z** will burn against that man. 7863
2Sa 21: 2 but Saul in his **z** for Israel and Judah 7861
2Ki 10:16 with me and see my **z** for the LORD." 7863
19:31 The **z** *of* the LORD Almighty will accomplish this. 7863
Ps 69: 9 for **z** *for* your house consumes me, 7863
119:139 My **z** wears me out, 7863
Pr 19: 2 It is not good to have **z** without knowledge, 5883
Isa 9: 7 **z** *of* the LORD Almighty will accomplish this. 7863
26:11 Let them see your **z** *for* your people and 7863
37:32 The **z** *of* the LORD Almighty will accomplish this. 7863
42:13 like a warrior he will stir up his **z**; 7863
59:17 of vengeance and wrapped himself in **z** as 7863
63:15 Where are your **z** and your might? 7863
Eze 5:13 that I the LORD have spoken in my **z**. 7863
36: 5 In my burning **z** I have spoken against 7863
38:19 In my **z** and fiery wrath I declare that at 7863
Jn 2:17 "**Z** for your house will consume me." *2419*
Ro 10: 2 but their **z** is not based on knowledge. *NIG*
12:11 Never be lacking *in* **z**, *5082*
Php 3: 6 as for **z**, persecuting the church; *2419*

ZEALOT (4)
Mt 10: 4 Simon the **Z** and Judas Iscariot, *2831*
Mk 3:18 of Alphaeus, Thaddaeus, Simon the **Z** *2831*
Lk 6:15 Simon who was called the **Z**, *2421*
Ac 1:13 James son of Alphaeus and Simon the **Z**, *2421*

ZEALOUS (14) [ZEAL]
Nu 25:11 as **z** as I am for my honor among them, 7861+7863
25:13 because *he was* **z** for the honor of his God 7861
1Ki 19:10 *"I have been* **very z** for the LORD God 7861+7861
1Ki 19:14 *"I have been* **very z** for the LORD God 7861+7861
Pr 23:17 but always *be* **z** for the fear of the LORD. NIH
Eze 39:25 and *I will be* **z** for my holy name. 7861
Ac 21:20 and all of them are **z** for the law. *2421*
22: 3 in the law of our fathers and was just as **z** *2421*
Ro 10: 2 For I can testify about them that they are **z** *2419*
2Co 8:22 to us in many ways that he is **z**, *5080*
Gal 1:14 of my own age and was extremely **z for** *2421*
4:17 *Those people are* **z** to win you over, *2420*
4:17 so that *you may be* **z for** them. *2420*
4:18 It is fine *to be* **z**, provided the purpose is good, *2420*

ZEALOUSLY (1) [ZEAL]
Ne 3:20 son of Zabbai **z** repaired another section, 3013

ZEBADIAH (9)
1Ch 8:15 **Z**, Arad, Eder, 2277
8:17 **Z**, Meshullam, Hizki, Heber, 2277
12: 7 and **Z** the sons of Jeroham from Gedor. 2277
26: 2 **Z** the third, Jathniel the fourth, 2278
27: 7 his son **Z** was his successor. 2277
2Ch 17: 8 Shemaiah, Nethaniah, **Z**, Asahel, 2278
19:11 and **Z** son of Ishmael, 2278
Ezr 8: 8 **Z** son of Michael, and with him 80 men; 2277
10:20 of Immer: Hanani and **Z**. 2277

ZEBAH (10)
Jdg 8: 5 and I am still pursuing **Z** and Zalmunna, 2286
8: 6 have the hands of **Z** and Zalmunna in your possession? 2286
8: 7 the LORD has given **Z** and Zalmunna 2286
8:10 Now **Z** and Zalmunna were in Karkor with 2286
8:12 **Z** and Zalmunna, the two kings of Midian, 2286
8:15 "Here are **Z** and Zalmunna, 2286
8:15 have the hands of **Z** and Zalmunna in your possession? 2286
8:18 Then he asked **Z** and Zalmunna, 2286
8:21 **Z** and Zalmunna said, "Come, 2286
Ps 83:11 all their princes like **Z** and Zalmunna, 2286

ZEBAIM (KJV) See POKERETH HAZZEBAIM

ZEBEDEE (10) [ZEBEDEE'S]
Mt 4:21 James son *of* **Z** and his brother John. *2411*
4:21 They were in a boat with their father **Z**, *2411*
10: 2 James son *of* **Z**, and his brother John; *2411*
26:37 He took Peter and the two sons *of* **Z** along *2411*
Mk 1:19 he saw James son *of* **Z** and his brother John *2411*
1:20 and they left their father **Z** in the boat with *2411*
3:17 *of* **Z** and his brother John (to them he gave *2411*
10:35 Then James and John, the sons *of* **Z**, *2411*
Lk 5:10 the sons *of* **Z**, Simon's partners. *2411*
Jn 21: 2 the sons *of* **Z**, and two other disciples *2411*

ZEBEDEE'S (2) [ZEBEDEE]
Mt 20:20 the mother *of* **Z** sons came to Jesus with her sons *2411*
27:56 and the mother *of* **Z** sons. *2411*

ZEBIDAH (1)
2Ki 23:36 His mother's name was **Z** daughter of 2288

ZEBINA (1)
Ezr 10:43 Jeiel, Mattithiah, Zabad, **Z**, Jaddai, 2289

ZEBOIIM (5)
Ge 10:19 Gomorrah, Admah and **Z**, as far as Lasha. 7375
14: 2 Shemeber king of **Z**, 7375
14: 8 the king of **Z** and the king of Bela, 7375
Dt 29:23 Admah and **Z**, which the LORD overthrew 7375
Hos 11: 8 How can I make you like **Z**? 7375

ZEBOIM (2)
1Sa 13:18 the Valley of **Z** facing the desert. 7391
Ne 11:34 in Hadid, **Z** and Neballat, 7391

ZEBUDAH (KJV) See ZEBIDAH

ZEBUL (6)
Jdg 9:28 and isn't **Z** his deputy? 2291
9:30 When **Z** the governor of the city heard 2291
9:36 When Gaal saw them, he said to **Z**, "Look, 2291
9:36 **Z** replied, "You mistake the shadows of 2291
9:38 **Z** said to him, "Where is your big talk now, 2291
9:41 and **Z** drove Gaal and his brothers out 2291

ZEBULONITE (KJV) See ZEBULUNITE

ZEBULUN (49) [ZEBULUNITE]
Ge 30:20 So she named him **Z**. 2282
35:23 Simeon, Levi, Judah, Issachar and **Z**. 2282
46:14 The sons of **Z**: Sered, Elon and Jahleel. 2282
49:13 "**Z** will live by the seashore and become 2282
Ex 1: 3 Issachar, **Z** and Benjamin; 2282
Nu 1: 9 from **Z**, Eliab son of Helon; 2282
1:30 From the descendants of **Z**: 2282

Nu 1:31 The number from the tribe of Z was 57,400. 2282
2: 7 The tribe of Z will be next. 2282
2: 7 The leader of the people of Z is Eliab son 2282
7:24 the leader of the people of Z, 2282
10:16 over the division of the tribe of Z. 1201+2282
13:10 from the tribe of Z, Gaddiel son of Sodi; 2282
26:26 The descendants of Z by their clans were: 2282
26:27 These were the clans of Z; 2283
34:25 the leader from the tribe of Z; 1201+2282
Dt 27:13 Reuben, Gad, Asher, Z, Dan and Naphtali. 2282
33:18 About Z he said: "Rejoice, Zebulun, 2282
33:18 "Rejoice, Z, in your going out, and you, 2282
Jos 19:10 The third lot came up for Z, clan by 1201+2282
19:16 villages were the inheritance of Z, 1201+2282
19:27 touched Z and the Valley of Iphtah El, 2282
19:34 It touched Z on the south, 2282
21: 7 from the tribes of Reuben, Gad and Z. 2282
21:34 from the tribe of Z, Jokneam, Kartah, 2282
Jdg 1:30 Neither did Z drive out the Canaanites 2282
4: 6 Z and lead the way to Mount Tabor. 1201+2282
4:10 where he summoned Z and Naphtali. 2282
5:14 from Z those who bear a commander's staff. 2282
5:18 The people of Z risked their very lives; 2282
6:35 and also into Asher, Z and Naphtali, 2282
12:12 and was buried in Aijalon in the land of Z. 2282
1Ch 2: 1 Reuben, Simeon, Levi, Judah, Issachar, Z, 2282
6:63 from the tribes of Reuben, Gad and Z. 2282
6:77 From the tribe of Z they received Jokneam, 2282
12:33 men of Z, experienced soldiers prepared 2282
12:40 Z and Naphtali came bringing food 2282
27:19 over Z: Ishmaiah son of Obadiah; 2282
2Ch 30:10 as far as Z, but the people scorned and 2282
30:11 Manasseh and Z humbled themselves 2282
30:18 Issachar and Z had not purified themselves, 2282
Ps 68:27 and there the princes of Z and of Naphtali. 2282
Isa 9: 1 past he humbled the land of Z and the land 2282
Eze 48:26 "Z will have one portion; 2282
48:27 it will border the territory of Z from east 2282
48:33 the gate of Issachar and the gate of Z. 2282
Mt 4:13 by the lake in the area *of* Z and Naphtali— *2404*
4:15 "Land *of* Z and land of Naphtali, the way to *2404*
Rev 7: 8 from the tribe *of* Z 12,000, *2404*

ZEBULUNITE (1) [ZEBULUN]

Jdg 12:11 After him, Elon the Z led Israel ten years. 2283

ZECHARIAH (53) [ZECHARIAH'S]

2Ki 14:29 And Z his son succeeded him as king. 2357
15: 8 Z son of Jeroboam became king of Israel 2357
15:10 Shallum son of Jabesh conspired against Z. 2257S
18: 2 mother's name was Abijah daughter of Z. 2357
1Ch 5: 7 Jeiel the chief, Z, 2358
9:21 Z son of Meshelemiah was the gatekeeper at 2357
9:37 Gedor, Ahio, Z and Mikloth. 2357
15:18 Z, Jaaziel, Shemiramoth, Jehiel, Unni, 2358
15:20 Z, Aziel, Shemiramoth, 2357
15:24 Shebaniah, Joshaphat, Nethanel, Amasai, Z, 2358
16: 5 Z second, then Jeiel, Shemiramoth, Jehiel, 2357
24:25 from the sons of Isshiah: Z. 2357
26: 2 Meshelemiah had sons: Z the firstborn, 2358
26:11 Tabaliah the third and Z the fourth. 2358
26:14 Then lots were cast for his son Z, 2358
27:21 of Manasseh in Gilead: Iddo son of Z; 2358
2Ch 17: 7 Z, Nethanel and Micaiah to teach in 2357
20:14 of the LORD came upon Jahaziel son of Z, 2358
21: 2 Z, Azariahu, Michael and Shephatiah. 2358
24:20 Then the Spirit of God came upon Z son 2357
26: 5 He sought God during the days of Z, 2358
29: 1 mother's name was Abijah daughter of Z. 2358
29:13 the descendants of Asaph, Z and Mattaniah; 2358
34:12 and Z and Meshullam, 2357
35: 8 Z and Jehiel, the administrators of God's 2358
Ezr 5: 1 Now Haggai the prophet and Z the prophet, 10230
6:14 the preaching of Haggai the prophet and Z, 10230
8: 3 of the descendants of Parosh, Z, 2357
8:11 Z son of Bebai, and with him 28 men; 2357
8:16 Jarib, Elnathan, Nathan, Z and Meshullam, 2357
10:26 Mattaniah, Z, Jehiel, Abdi, 2357
Ne 8: 4 Hashum, Hashbaddanah, Z and Meshullam. 2357
11: 4 Athaiah son of Uzziah, the son of Z, 2357
11: 5 the son of Z, a descendant of Shelah. 2357
11:12 the son of Z, the son of Pashhur, 2357
12:16 of Iddo's, Z; of Ginnethon's, Meshullam; 2357
12:35 and also Z son of Jonathan, 2357
12:41 Z and Hananiah with their trumpets— 2357
Isa 8: 2 And I will call in Uriah the priest and Z son 2358
Zec 1: 1 came to the prophet Z son of Berekiah, 2357
1: 7 word of the LORD came to the prophet Z 2357
7: 1 the word the LORD came to Z on the fourth 2357
7: 8 the word of the LORD came again to Z: 2357
Mt 23:35 blood of righteous Abel to the blood *of* Z *2408*
Lk 1: 5 there was a priest named Z, who belonged *2408*
1:12 When Z saw him, he was startled *2408*
1:13 the angel said to him, "Do not be afraid, Z; *2408*
1:18 Z asked the angel, "How can I be sure *2408*
1:21 for Z and wondering why he stayed so long *2408*
1:59 to name him after his father Z, *2408*
1:67 His father Z was filled with the Holy Spirit *2408*
3: 2 of God came to John son *of* Z in the desert. *2408*
11:51 from the blood of Abel to the blood *of* Z, *2408*

ZECHARIAH'S (4) [ZECHARIAH]

2Ki 15:11 The other events of Z reign are written in 2357
2Ch 24:22 kindness Z father Jehoiada had shown him 2257S
Lk 1: 8 Once when Z division was on duty *899S*
Lk 1:40 she entered Z home and greeted Elizabeth. *2408*

ZEDAD (2)

Nu 34: 8 Then the boundary will go to Z, 7398
Eze 47:15 by the Hethlon road past Lebo Hamath to Z, 7398

ZEDEKIAH (60) [ZEDEKIAH'S]

1Ki 22:11 Z son of Kenaanah had made iron horns 7408
22:24 Then Z son of Kenaanah went up 7409
2Ki 24:17 in his place and changed his name to Z. 7409
24:18 Z was twenty-one years old 7409
24:20 Z rebelled against the king of Babylon. 7409
25: 2 until the eleventh year of King Z. 7409
25: 7 They killed the sons of Z before his eyes. 7409
1Ch 3:15 Jehoiakim the second son, Z the third, 7409
3:16 Jehoiachin his son, and Z. 7408
2Ch 18:10 Z son of Kenaanah had made iron horns, 7409
18:23 Then Z son of Kenaanah went up 7409
36:10 and he made Jehoiachin's uncle, Z, 7409
36:11 Z was twenty-one years old 7409
Ne 10: 1 the son of Hacaliah. Z, 7408
Jer 1: 3 the fifth month of the eleventh year of Z son 7409
21: 1 when King Z sent to him Pashhur son 7409
21: 3 But Jeremiah answered them, "Tell Z, 7409
21: 7 I will hand over Z king of Judah, 7409
24: 8 'so will I deal with Z king of Judah, 7409
27: 1 the reign of Z son of Josiah king of Judah, 7409
27: 3 to Jerusalem to Z king of Judah. 7409
27:12 I gave the same message to Z king of Judah. 7408
28: 1 early in the reign of Z king of Judah, 7408
29: 3 whom Z king of Judah sent to King 7408
29:21 says about Ahab son of Kolaiah and Z son 7409
29:22 'The LORD treat you like Z and Ahab, 7409
32: 1 from the LORD in the tenth year of Z king 7409
32: 3 Z king of Judah had imprisoned him there, 7409
32: 4 Z king of Judah will not escape out of 7409
32: 5 He will take Z to Babylon, 7409
34: 2 Go to Z king of Judah and tell him, 7409
34: 4 O Z king of Judah. 7409
34: 6 the prophet told all this to Z king of Judah, 7409
34: 8 after King Z had made a covenant with all 7409
34:21 "I will hand Z king of Judah and his 7409
36:12 of Acbor, Gemariah son of Shaphan, Z son 7409
37: 1 Z son of Josiah was made king of Judah 7409
37: 3 King Z, however, sent Jehucal son 7409
37:17 Then King Z sent for him 7409
37:18 Then Jeremiah said to King Z, 7409
37:21 King Z then gave orders for Jeremiah to 7409
38: 5 "He is in your hands," King Z answered. 7409
38:14 Then King Z sent for Jeremiah the prophet 7409
38:15 Jeremiah said to Z, "If I give you an answer, 7409
38:16 King Z swore this oath secretly to Jeremiah: 7409
38:17 Then Jeremiah said to Z, "This is what 7409
38:19 King Z said to Jeremiah, "I am afraid 7409
38:24 Then Z said to Jeremiah, "Do not let anyone 7409
39: 1 In the ninth year of Z king of Judah, 7409
39: 4 When Z king of Judah and all the soldiers 7409
39: 5 and overtook Z in the plains of Jericho. 7409
39: 6 sons of Z before his eyes and also killed all 7409
44:30 just as I handed Z king of Judah over 7409
49:34 early in the reign of Z king of Judah: 7408
51:59 with Z king of Judah in the fourth year 7409
52: 1 Z was twenty-one years old 7409
52: 3 Z rebelled against the king of Babylon. 7409
52: 5 until the eleventh year of King Z. 7409
52: 8 but the Babylonian army pursued King Z 7409
52:10 of Babylon slaughtered the sons of Z 7409

ZEDEKIAH'S (5) [ZEDEKIAH]

2Ki 25: 1 So in the ninth year of Z reign, 2257S
Jer 39: 2 the fourth month of Z eleventh year, 4200+7409
39: 7 Then he put out Z eyes and bound him 7409
52: 4 So in the ninth year of Z reign, 2257S
52:11 Then he put out Z eyes, 7409

ZEEB (6)

Jdg 7:25 of the Midianite leaders, Oreb and Z. 2270
7:25 and Z at the winepress of Zeeb. 2270
7:25 and Zeeb at the winepress of Z. 2270
7:25 and brought the heads of Oreb and Z 2270
8: 3 God gave Oreb and Z, 2270
Ps 83:11 Make their nobles like Oreb and Z, 2270

ZEKER (1)

1Ch 8:31 Gedor, Ahio, Z 2353

ZELA (1)

2Sa 21:14 in the tomb of Saul's father Kish, at Z 7522

ZELAH (1)

Jos 18:28 Z, Haeleph, the Jebusite city 7522

ZELEK (2)

2Sa 23:37 Z the Ammonite, Naharai the Beerothite, 7530
1Ch 11:39 Z the Ammonite, Naharai the Berothite, 7530

ZELOPHEHAD (5) [ZELOPHEHAD'S]

Nu 26:33 (Z son of Hepher had no sons; 7524
27: 1 The daughters of Z son of Hepher, 7524
36: 2 to give the inheritance of our brother Z 7524
Jos 17: 3 Now Z son of Hepher, the son of Gilead, 7524
1Ch 7:15 Another descendant was named Z, 7524

ZELOPHEHAD'S (4) [ZELOPHEHAD]

Nu 27: 7 "What Z daughters are saying is right. 7524
36: 6 the LORD commands for Z daughters: 7524
36:10 So Z daughters did as the LORD commanded 7524
36:11 Z daughters—Mahlah, Tirzah, Hoglah, 7524

ZELOTES (KJV) See ZEALOT

ZELZAH (1)

1Sa 10: 2 at Z on the border of Benjamin. 7525

ZEMARAIM (2)

Jos 18:22 Beth Arabah, Z, Bethel, 7549
2Ch 13: 4 Abijah stood on Mount Z, 7549

ZEMARITES (2)

Ge 10:18 Arvadites, Z and Hamathites. 7548
1Ch 1:16 Arvadites, Z and Hamathites. 7548

ZEMIRAH (1)

1Ch 7: 8 Z, Joash, Eliezer, Elioenai, Omri, Jeremoth, 2371

ZENAN (1)

Jos 15:37 Z, Hadashah, Migdal Gad, 7569

ZENAS (1)

Tit 3:13 Do everything you can to help Z the lawyer *2424*

ZEPHANIAH (11)

2Ki 25:18 Z the priest next in rank and 7623
1Ch 6:36 the son of Azariah, the son of Z, 7622
Jer 21: 1 and the priest Z son of Maaseiah. 7622
29:25 to Z son of Maaseiah the priest, 7622
29:25 You said to Z, NIH
29:29 Z the priest, however, read the letter 7622
37: 3 the priest Z son of Maaseiah to Jeremiah 7623
52:24 Z the priest next in rank and 7622
Zep 1: 1 The word of the LORD that came to Z son 7622
Zec 6:10 to the house of Josiah son of Z. 7622
6:14 Jedaiah and Hen son of Z as a memorial in 7622

ZEPHATH (1)

Jdg 1:17 and attacked the Canaanites living in Z, 7634

ZEPHATHAH (1)

2Ch 14:10 took up battle positions in the Valley of Z 7635

ZEPHO (3)

Ge 36:11 Teman, Omar, Z, Gatam and Kenaz. 7598
36:15 Chiefs Teman, Omar, Z, Kenaz, 7598
1Ch 1:36 Teman, Omar, Z, Gatam and Kenaz; 7598

ZEPHON (2) [BAAL ZEPHON, ZEPHONITE]

Ge 46:16 The sons of Gad: Z, Haggi, Shuni, Ezbon, 7602
Nu 26:15 through Z, the Zephonite clan; 7602

ZEPHONITE (1) [ZEPHON]

Nu 26:15 through Zephon, the Z clan; 7604

ZER (1)

Jos 19:35 The fortified cities were Ziddim, Z, 7643

ZERAH (21) [ZERAHITE, ZERAHITES]

Ge 36:13 Nahath, Z, Shammah and Mizzah. 2438
36:17 Chiefs Nahath, Z, Shammah and Mizzah. 2438
36:33 Jobab son of Z from Bozrah succeeded him 2438
38:30 came out and he was given the name Z. 2438
46:12 and Z (but Er and Onan had died in the land 2438
Nu 26:13 through Z, the Zerahite clan; 2438
26:20 through Z, the Zerahite clan. 2438
Jos 7: 1 the son of Z, of the tribe of Judah, 2438
7:18 the son of Z, of the tribe of Judah, 2438
7:24 took Achan son of Z, the silver, the robe, 2438
22:20 of Z acted unfaithfully regarding 2438
1Ch 1:37 Nahath, Z, Shammah and Mizzah. 2438
1:44 Jobab son of Z from Bozrah succeeded him 2438
2: 4 bore him Perez and Z. 2438
2: 6 The sons of Z: Zimri, Ethan, 2438
4:24 Nemuel, Jamin, Jarib, Z and Shaul; 2438
6:21 Z his son and Jeatherai his son. 2438
6:41 the son of Z, the son of Adaiah, 2438
2Ch 14: 9 Z the Cushite marched out against them 2438
Ne 11:24 one of the descendants of Z son of Judah, 2438
Mt 1: 3 Judah the father of Perez and Z, *2406*

ZERAHIAH (5)

1Ch 6: 6 Uzzi the father of Z, 2440
6: 6 Z the father of Meraioth, 2440
6:51 Bukki his son, Uzzi his son, Z his son, 2440
Ezr 7: 4 the son of Z, the son of Uzzi, 2440
8: 4 Eliehoenai son of Z, and with him 200 men; 2440

ZERAHITE (4) [ZERAH]

Nu 26:13 through Zerah, the Z clan; 2439

Nu 26:20 through Zerah, the **Z** clan. 2439
1Ch 27:11 was Sibbecai the Hushathite, a **Z.** 2439
27:13 was Maharai the Netophathite, a **Z.** 2439

ZERAHITES (3) [ZERAH]

Jos 7:17 Judah came forward, and he took the **Z.** 2439
7:17 the clan of the **Z** come forward by families, 2439
1Ch 9:6 Of the **Z:** Jeuel. 1201+2438

ZERED (3)

Nu 21:12 on and camped in the **Z** Valley. 2429
Dt 2:13 "Now get up and cross the **Z** Valley." 2429
2:14 until we crossed the **Z** Valley. 2429

ZEREDAH (1)

1Ki 11:26 an Ephraimite from **Z,** and his mother was 7649

ZEREDATHAH (KJV) See ZARETHAN

ZERERAH (1)

Jdg 7:22 to Beth Shittah toward **Z** as far as the border 7678

ZERESH (4)

Est 5:10 Calling together his friends and **Z,** his wife, 2454
5:14 His wife **Z** and all his friends said to him, 2454
6:13 and told **Z** his wife and all his friends 2454
6:13 His advisers and his wife **Z** said to him, 2454

ZERETH (1) [ZERETH SHAHAR]

1Ch 4:7 The sons of Helah: **Z,** Zohar, Ethnan, 7679

ZERETH SHAHAR (1) [ZERETH]

Jos 13:19 Sibmah, **Z** on the hill in the valley, 7680

ZERI (1)

1Ch 25:3 Gedaliah, **Z,** Jeshaiah, Shimei, 7662

ZEROR (1)

1Sa 9:1 the son of **Z,** the son of Becorath, 7657

ZERUAH (1)

1Ki 11:26 and his mother was a widow named **Z.** 7654

ZERUBBABEL (25)

1Ch 3:19 The sons of Pedaiah: **Z** and Shimei. 2428
3:19 The sons of **Z:** Meshullam and Hananiah. 2428
Ezr 2:2 in company with **Z,** Jeshua, Nehemiah, 2428
3:2 and his fellow priests and **Z** son of Shealtiel 2428
3:8 **Z** son of Shealtiel, Jeshua son of Jozadak 2428
4:2 to **Z** and to the heads of the families 2428
4:3 But **Z,** Jeshua and the rest of the heads of 2428
5:2 Then **Z** son of Shealtiel and Jeshua son 10239
Ne 7:7 in company with **Z,** Jeshua, Nehemiah, 2428
12:1 with **Z** son of Shealtiel and with Jeshua: 2428
12:47 So in the days of **Z** and of Nehemiah, 2428
Hag 1:1 the prophet Haggai to **Z** son of Shealtiel, 2428
1:12 Then **Z** son of Shealtiel, Joshua son of 2428
1:14 So the LORD stirred up the spirit of **Z** son 2428
2:2 "Speak to **Z** son of Shealtiel, 2428
2:4 now be strong, O **Z,'** declares the LORD. 2428
2:21 "Tell **Z** governor of Judah that I will shake 2428
2:23 my servant **Z** son of Shealtiel,' 2428
Zec 4:6 "This is the word of the LORD to **Z:** 2428
4:7 Before **Z** you will become level ground. 2428
4:9 of **Z** have laid the foundation of this temple; 2428
4:10 the plumb line in the hand of **Z.** 2428
Mt 1:12 Shealtiel the father of **Z,** *2431*
1:13 **Z** the father of Abiud, *2431*
Lk 3:27 the son *of* **Z,** the son of Shealtiel, *2431*

ZERUIAH (25) [ZERUIAH'S]

1Sa 26:6 the Hittite and Abishai son of **Z,** 7653
2Sa 2:13 Joab son of **Z** and David's men went out 7653
2:18 The three sons of **Z** were there: 7653
3:39 and these sons of **Z** are too strong for me. 7653
8:16 Joab son of **Z** was over the army; 7653
14:1 of **Z** knew that the king's heart longed 7653
16:9 Then Abishai son of **Z** said to the king, 7653
16:10 you and I have in common, you sons of **Z?** 7653
17:25 the daughter of Nahash and sister of **Z** 7653
18:2 under Joab's brother Abishai son of **Z,** 7653
19:21 Then Abishai son of **Z** said, 7653
19:22 you and I have in common, you sons of **Z?** 7653
21:17 Abishai son of **Z** came to David's rescue; 7653
23:18 the brother of Joab son of **Z** was chief of 7653
23:37 the armor-bearer of Joab son of **Z,** 7653
1Ki 1:7 Adonijah conferred with Joab son of **Z** and 7653
2:5 know what Joab son of **Z** did to me— 7653
2:22 for Abiathar the priest and Joab son of **Z!"** 7653
1Ch 2:16 Their sisters were **Z** and Abigail. 7653
11:6 Joab son of **Z** went up first, 7653
11:39 the armor-bearer of Joab son of **Z,** 7653
18:12 Abishai son of **Z** struck down 7653
18:15 Joab son of **Z** was over the army; 7653
26:28 Abner son of Ner and Joab son of **Z,** 7653
27:24 Joab son of **Z** began to count the men 7653

ZERUIAH'S (1) [ZERUIAH]

1Ch 2:16 **Z** three sons were Abishai, Joab and Asahel. 7653

ZETHAM (2)

1Ch 23:8 Jehiel the first, **Z** and Joel—three in all. 2457
26:22 the sons of Jehieli, **Z** and his brother Joel. 2457

ZETHAN (1)

1Ch 7:10 Jeush, Benjamin, Ehud, Kenaanah, **Z,** 2340

ZETHAR (1)

Est 1:10 Harbona, Bigtha, Abagtha, **Z** and Carcas— 2458

ZEUS (2)

Ac 14:12 Barnabas they called **Z,** and Paul *2416*
14:13 The priest *of* **Z,** whose temple was *2416*

ZIA (1)

1Ch 5:13 Jorai, Jacan, **Z** and Eber—seven in all. 2333

ZIBA (16) [ZIBA'S]

2Sa 9:2 a servant of Saul's household named **Z.** 7471
9:2 and the king said to him, "Are you **Z?"** 7471
9:3 **Z** answered the king, "There is still a son 7471
9:4 **Z** answered, "He is at the house 7471
9:9 Then the king summoned **Z,** Saul's servant, 7471
9:10 **Z** had fifteen sons and twenty servants.) 7471
9:11 Then **Z** said to the king, 7471
16:1 there was **Z,** the steward of Mephibosheth, 7471
16:2 The king asked **Z,** "Why have you brought 7471
16:2 **Z** answered, "The donkeys are for 7471
16:3 **Z** said to him, "He is staying in Jerusalem, 7471
16:4 Then the king said to **Z,** 7471
16:4 "I humbly bow," **Z** said. 7471
19:17 with **Z,** the steward of Saul's household, 7471
19:26 But **Z** my servant betrayed me. NIH
19:29 I order you and **Z** to divide the fields." 7471

ZIBA'S (1) [ZIBA]

2Sa 9:12 the members of **Z** household were servants 7471

ZIBEON (8)

Ge 36:2 and granddaughter of **Z** the Hivite— 7390
36:14 and granddaughter of **Z,** whom she bore 7390
36:20 Lotan, Shobal, **Z,** Anah, 7390
36:24 The sons of **Z:** Aiah and Anah. 7390
36:24 was grazing the donkeys of his father **Z.** 7390
36:29 Lotan, Shobal, **Z,** Anah, 7390
1Ch 1:38 The sons of Seir: Lotan, Shobal, **Z,** Anah, 7390
1:40 The sons of **Z:** Aiah and Anah. 7390

ZIBIA (1)

1Ch 8:9 By his wife Hodesh he had Jobab, **Z,** 7384

ZIBIAH (2)

2Ki 12:1 His mother's name was **Z;** 7385
2Ch 24:1 His mother's name was **Z;** 7385

ZICHRI (KJV) See ZICRI

ZICRI (12)

Ex 6:21 of Izhar were Korah, Nepheg and **Z.** 2356
1Ch 8:19 Jakim, **Z,** Zabdi, 2356
8:23 Abdon, **Z,** Hanan, 2356
8:27 Elijah and **Z** were the sons of Jeroham. 2356
9:15 the son of **Z,** the son of Asaph; 2356
26:25 **Z** his son and Shelomith his son. 2356
27:16 Eliezer son of **Z;** 2356
2Ch 17:16 Amasiah son of **Z,** who volunteered himself 2356
23:1 and Elishaphat son of **Z.** 2356
28:7 **Z,** an Ephraimite warrior, killed Maaseiah 2356
Ne 11:9 Joel son of **Z** was their chief officer, 2356
12:17 of Abijah's, **Z;** of Miniamin's 2356

ZIDDIM (1)

Jos 19:35 The fortified cities were **Z,** Zer, Hammath, 7403

ZIDKIJAH (KJV) See ZEDEKIAH

ZIDON, ZIDONIANS (KJV) See SIDON, SIDONIANS

ZIF (KJV) See ZIV

ZIHA (3)

Ezr 2:43 the descendants of **Z,** Hasupha, Tabbaoth, 7484
Ne 7:46 the descendants of **Z,** Hasupha, Tabbaoth, 7484
11:21 and **Z** and Gishpa were in charge of them. 7484

ZIKLAG (15)

Jos 15:31 **Z,** Madmannah, Sansannah, 7637
19:5 **Z,** Beth Marcaboth, Hazar Susah, 7637
1Sa 27:6 So on that day Achish gave him **Z,** 7637
30:1 and his men reached **Z** on the third day. 7637
30:1 the Amalekites had raided the Negev and **Z.** 7637
1Sa 30:1 They had attacked **Z** and burned it, 7637
30:3 When David and his men came to **Z,** 2021+6551[S]
30:14 And we burned **Z."** 7637
30:26 When David arrived in **Z,** 7637
2Sa 1:1 the Amalekites and stayed in **Z** two days. 7637
4:10 I seized him and put him to death in **Z.** 7637
1Ch 4:30 Bethuel, Hormah, **Z,** 7637
12:1 to David at **Z,** while he was banished from 7637
12:20 When David went to **Z,** 7637
Ne 11:28 in **Z,** in Meconah and its settlements, 7637

ZILLAH (3)

Ge 4:19 one named Adah and the other **Z.** 7500
4:22 **Z** also had a son, Tubal-Cain, 7500
4:23 Lamech said to his wives, "Adah and **Z,** 7500

ZILLETHAI (2)

1Ch 8:20 Elienai, **Z,** Eliel, 7531
12:20 Jediael, Michael, Jozabad, Elihu and **Z,** 7531

ZILPAH (7)

Ge 29:24 And Laban gave his servant girl **Z** 2364
30:9 she took her maidservant **Z** and gave her 2364
30:10 Leah's servant **Z** bore Jacob a son. 2364
30:12 Leah's servant **Z** bore Jacob a second son. 2364
35:26 The sons of Leah's maidservant **Z:** 2364
37:2 the sons of Bilhah and the sons of **Z,** 2364
46:18 These were the children born to Jacob by **Z,** 2364

ZILTHAI (KJV) See ZILLETHAI

ZIMMAH (3)

1Ch 6:20 Libni his son, Jehath his son, **Z** his son, 2366
6:42 the son of **Z,** the son of Shimei, 2366
2Ch 29:12 Joah son of **Z** and Eden son of Joah; 2366

ZIMRAN (2)

Ge 25:2 She bore him **Z,** Jokshan, Medan, Midian, 2383
1Ch 1:32 **Z,** Jokshan, Medan, Midian, 2383

ZIMRI (17) [ZIMRI'S]

Nu 25:14 the Midianite woman was **Z** son of Salu, 2381
Jos 7:1 Achan son of Carmi, the son of **Z,** 2381
7:17 came forward by families, and **Z** was taken. 2381
7:18 and Achan son of Carmi, the son of **Z,** 2381
1Ki 16:9 **Z,** one of his officials, who had command 2381
16:10 **Z** came in, struck him down and killed him 2381
16:12 So **Z** destroyed the whole family of Baasha, 2381
16:15 **Z** reigned in Tirzah seven days. 2381
16:16 in the camp heard that **Z** had plotted against 2381
16:18 When **Z** saw that the city was taken, 2381
2Ki 9:31 she asked, "Have you come in peace, **Z,** 2381
1Ch 2:6 **Z,** Ethan, Heman, Calcol and Darda— 2381
8:36 Azmaveth and **Z,** and Zimri was the father 2381
8:36 and **Z** was the father of Moza. 2381
9:42 Azmaveth and **Z,** and Zimri was the father 2381
9:42 and **Z** was the father of Moza. 2381
Jer 25:25 all the kings of **Z,** Elam and Media; 2382

ZIMRI'S (1) [ZIMRI]

1Ki 16:20 As for the other events of **Z** reign, 2381

ZIN (10)

Nu 13:21 and explored the land from the Desert of **Z** 7554
20:1 community arrived at the Desert of **Z,** 7554
27:14 rebelled at the waters in the Desert of **Z,** 7554
27:14 Meribah Kadesh, in the Desert of **Z.)** 7554
33:36 camped at Kadesh, in the Desert of **Z.** 7554
34:3 the Desert of **Z** along the border of Edom. 7554
34:4 on to **Z** and go south of Kadesh Barnea. 7554
Dt 32:51 of Meribah Kadesh in the Desert of **Z** and 7554
Jos 15:1 to the Desert of **Z** in the extreme south. 7554
15:3 continued on to **Z** and went over to 7554

ZION (163) [ZION'S]

2Sa 5:7 David captured the fortress of **Z,** 7482
1Ki 8:1 the ark of the LORD's covenant from **Z,** 7482
2Ki 19:21 " 'The Virgin Daughter of **Z** despises you 7482
19:31 and out of Mount **Z** a band of survivors. 7482
1Ch 11:5 David captured the fortress of **Z,** 7482
2Ch 5:2 the ark of the LORD's covenant from **Z,** 7482
Ps 2:6 "I have installed my King on **Z,** 7482
9:11 Sing praises to the LORD, enthroned in **Z;** 7482
9:14 praises in the gates of the Daughter of **Z** 7482
14:7 for Israel would come out of **Z!** 7482
20:2 the sanctuary and grant you support from **Z.** 7482
48:2 the utmost heights of Zaphon is Mount **Z,** 7482
48:11 Mount **Z** rejoices, the villages of Judah 7482
48:12 Walk about **Z,** go around her, 7482
50:2 From **Z,** perfect in beauty, God shines forth. 7482
51:18 In your good pleasure make **Z** prosper; 7482
53:6 salvation for Israel would come out of **Z!** 7482
65:1 Praise awaits you, O God, in **Z;** 7482
69:35 for God will save **Z** and rebuild the cities 7482
74:2 Mount **Z,** where you dwelt. 7482
76:2 His tent is in Salem, his dwelling place in **Z.** 7482
78:68 Mount **Z,** which he loved. 7482
84:7 till each appears before God in **Z.** 7482
87:2 of **Z** more than all the dwellings of Jacob. 7482
87:4 and will say, 'This one was born **in Z.'** " 9004[S]

Ps 87: 5 Indeed, of Z it will be said, 7482
87: 6 "This one was born **in Z.**" 9004[S]
97: 8 **Z** hears and rejoices and the villages 7482
99: 2 Great is the LORD in **Z;** 7482
102:13 You will arise and have compassion on **Z,** 7482
102:16 For the LORD will rebuild **Z** and appear 7482
102:21 be declared in **Z** and his praise in Jerusalem 7482
110: 2 The LORD will extend your mighty scepter from **Z;** 7482
125: 1 who trust in the LORD are like Mount **Z,** 7482
126: 1 the LORD brought back the captives to **Z,** 7482
128: 5 the LORD bless you from **Z** all the days 7482
129: 5 May all who hate **Z** be turned back 7482
132:13 For the LORD has chosen **Z,** 7482
133: 3 of Hermon were falling on Mount **Z.** 7482
134: 3 May the LORD, the Maker of heaven and earth, bless you from **Z.** 7482
135:21 Praise be to the LORD from **Z,** 7482
137: 1 and wept when we remembered **Z.** 7482
137: 3 they said, "Sing us one of the songs of **Z!**" 7482
146:10 The LORD reigns forever, your God, O **Z,** 7482
147:12 praise your God, O **Z,** 7482
149: 2 let the people of **Z** be glad in their King. 7482
SS 3:11 Come out, you daughters of **Z,** 7482
Isa 1: 8 The Daughter of **Z** is left like a shelter in 7482
1:27 **Z** will be redeemed with justice, 7482
2: 3 The law will go out from **Z,** 7482
3:16 "The women of **Z** are haughty, 7482
3:17 on the heads of the women of **Z;** 7482
3:26 The gates of **Z** will lament and mourn; 2023[S]
4: 3 Those who are left in **Z,** 7482
4: 4 the filth of the women of **Z;** 7482
4: 5 the LORD will create over all of Mount **Z** 7482
8:18 Almighty, who dwells on Mount **Z.** 7482
10:12 against Mount **Z** and Jerusalem, 7482
10:24 "O my people who live in **Z,** 7482
10:32 at the mount of the Daughter of **Z,** 7482
12: 6 Shout aloud and sing for joy, people of **Z,** 7482
14:32 "The LORD has established **Z,** 7482
16: 1 to the mount of the Daughter of **Z.** 7482
18: 7 the gifts will be brought to Mount **Z,** 7482
24:23 the LORD Almighty will reign on Mount **Z** 7482
28:16 "See, I lay a stone in **Z,** a tested stone, 7482
29: 8 of all the nations that fight against Mount **Z.** 7482
30:19 O people of **Z,** who live in Jerusalem, 7482
31: 4 to do battle on Mount **Z** and on its heights. 7482
31: 9 declares the LORD, whose fire is in **Z,** 7482
33: 5 he will fill **Z** with justice and righteousness. 7482
33:14 The sinners in **Z** are terrified; 7482
33:20 Look upon **Z,** the city of our festivals; 7482
33:24 No one living in **Z** will say, "I am ill"; NIH
35:10 They will enter **Z** with singing; 7482
37:22 "The Virgin Daughter of **Z** despises 7482
37:32 and out of Mount **Z** a band of survivors. 7482
40: 9 You who bring good tidings to **Z,** 7482
41:27 I was the first to tell **Z,** 'Look, 7482
46:13 I will grant salvation to **Z,** 7482
49:14 But **Z** said, "The LORD has forsaken me, 7482
51: 3 The LORD will surely comfort **Z** 7482
51:11 They will enter **Z** with singing; 7482
51:16 and who say to **Z,** 'You are my people.' " 7482
52: 1 awake, O **Z,** clothe yourself with strength. 7482
52: 2 O captive Daughter of **Z.** 7482
52: 7 who proclaim salvation, who say to **Z,** 7482
52: 8 When the LORD returns to **Z,** 7482
59:20 "The Redeemer will come to **Z,** 7482
60:14 **Z** *of* the Holy One of Israel. 7482
61: 3 and provide for those who grieve in **Z—** 7482
62:11 "Say to the Daughter of **Z,** 'See, 7482
64:10 even **Z** is a desert, Jerusalem a desolation. 7482
66: 8 Yet no sooner is **Z** in labor 7482
Jer 3:14 and bring you to **Z.** 7482
4: 6 Raise the signal to go to **Z!** 7482
4:31 cry of the Daughter of **Z** gasping for breath, 7482
6: 2 I will destroy the Daughter of **Z,** 7482
6:23 to attack you, O Daughter of **Z.**" 7482
8:19 "Is the LORD not in **Z?** 7482
9:19 The sound of wailing is heard from **Z:** 7482
14:19 Do you despise **Z?** 7482
26:18 " '**Z** will be plowed like a field, 7482
30:17 **Z** for whom no one cares.' 7482
31: 6 let us go up to **Z,** to the LORD our God.' " 7482
31:12 and shout for joy on the heights of **Z;** 7482
50: 5 the way to **Z** and turn their faces toward it. 7482
50:28 and refugees from Babylon declaring in **Z** 7482
51:10 in **Z** what the LORD our God has done.' 7482
51:24 for all the wrong they have done in **Z,**" 7482
51:35 say the inhabitants of **Z.** 7482
La 1: 4 The roads to **Z** mourn, 7482
1: 6 has departed from the Daughter of **Z.** 7482
1:17 **Z** stretches out her hands, 7482
2: 1 the Lord has covered the Daughter of **Z** 7482
2: 4 like fire on the tent of the Daughter of **Z.** 7482
2: 6 has made **Z** forget her appointed feasts 7482
2: 8 down the wall around the Daughter of **Z.** 7482
2:10 of the Daughter of **Z** sit on the ground 7482
2:13 O Virgin Daughter of **Z?** 7482
2:18 O wall of the Daughter of **Z,** 7482
4: 2 How the precious sons of **Z,** 7482
4:11 a fire in **Z** that consumed her foundations. 7482
4:22 O Daughter of **Z,** your punishment will end; 7482
5:11 Women have been ravished in **Z,** 7482
5:18 for Mount **Z,** which lies desolate, 7482
Joel 2: 1 Blow the trumpet in **Z;** sound the alarm 7482
2:15 Blow the trumpet in **Z,** declare a holy fast, 7482
2:23 Be glad, O people of **Z,** rejoice in the LORD 7482
2:32 for on Mount **Z** and in Jerusalem there will 7482
Joel 3:16 The LORD will roar from **Z** and thunder 7482
3:17 the LORD your God, dwell in **Z,** 7482
3:21 The LORD dwells in **Z!** 7482
Am 1: 2 "The LORD roars from **Z** and thunders 7482
6: 1 Woe to you who are complacent in **Z,** 7482
Ob 1:17 But on Mount **Z** will be deliverance; 7482
1:21 Deliverers will go up on Mount **Z** to govern 7482
Mic 1:13 the beginning of sin to the Daughter of **Z,** 7482
3:10 who build **Z** with bloodshed, 7482
3:12 **Z** will be plowed like a field, 7482
4: 2 The law will go out from **Z,** 7482
4: 7 The LORD will rule over them in Mount **Z** 7482
4: 8 O stronghold of the Daughter of **Z,** 7482
4:10 Writhe in agony, O Daughter of **Z,** 7482
4:11 let our eyes gloat over **Z!**" 7482
4:13 "Rise and thresh, O Daughter of **Z,** 7482
Zep 3:14 Sing, O Daughter of **Z;** 7482
3:16 O **Z;** do not let your hands hang limp. 7482
Zec 1:14 'I am very jealous for Jerusalem and **Z,** 7482
1:17 and the LORD will again comfort **Z** 7482
2: 7 "Come, O **Z!** Escape, you who live in 7482
2:10 "Shout and be glad, O Daughter of **Z.** 7482
8: 2 "I am very jealous for **Z;** 7482
8: 3 "I will return to **Z** and dwell in Jerusalem. 7482
9: 9 Rejoice greatly, O Daughter of **Z!** 7482
9:13 I will rouse your sons, O **Z,** 7482
Mt 21: 5 "Say to the Daughter *of* **Z,** *4994*
Jn 12:15 "Do not be afraid, O Daughter *of* **Z;** *4994*
Ro 9:33 I lay in **Z** a stone that causes men to stumble *4994*
11:26 "The deliverer will come from **Z;** *4994*
Heb 12:22 But you have come to Mount **Z,** *4994*
1Pe 2: 6 "See, I lay a stone in **Z,** *4994*
Rev 14: 1 was the Lamb, standing on Mount **Z,** *4994*

ZION'S (2) [ZION]

Isa 34: 8 a year of retribution, to uphold **Z** cause. 7482
62: 1 For **Z** sake I will not keep silent, 7482

ZIOR (1)

Jos 15:54 Kiriath Arba (that is, Hebron) and **Z—** 7486

ZIPH (9) [ZIPHITES]

Jos 15:24 **Z,** Telem, Bealoth, 2334
15:55 Maon, Carmel, **Z,** Juttah, 2334
1Sa 23:14 and in the hills of the Desert of **Z.** 2334
23:15 David was at Horesh in the Desert of **Z,** 2334
23:24 So they set out and went to **Z** ahead of Saul. 2334
26: 2 So Saul went down to the Desert of **Z,** 2334
1Ch 2:42 his firstborn, who was the father of **Z,** 2335
4:16 **Z,** Ziphah, Tiria and Asarel. 2335
2Ch 11: 8 Gath, Mareshah, **Z,** 2334

ZIPHAH (1)

1Ch 4:16 Ziph, **Z,** Tiria and Asarel. 2336

ZIPHITES (3) [ZIPH]

1Sa 23:19 The **Z** went up to Saul at Gibeah and said, 2337
26: 1 The **Z** went to Saul at Gibeah and said, 2337
Ps 54: T When the **Z** had gone to Saul and said, 2337

ZIPHRON (1)

Nu 34: 9 continue to **Z** and end at Hazar Enan. 2412

ZIPPOR (7)

Nu 22: 2 son of **Z** saw all that Israel had done to 7607
22: 4 So Balak son of **Z,** who was king of Moab 7607
22:10 Balaam said to God, "Balak son of **Z,** 7607
22:16 "This is what Balak son of **Z** says: 7607
23:18 and listen; hear me, son of **Z.** 7607
Jos 24: 9 When Balak son of **Z,** the king of Moab, 7607
Jdg 11:25 Are you better than Balak son of **Z,** 7607

ZIPPORAH (4)

Ex 2:21 who gave his daughter **Z** to Moses 7631
2:22 **Z** gave birth to a son, and Moses named him NIH
4:25 But **Z** took a flint knife, 7631
18: 2 After Moses had sent away his wife **Z,** 7631

ZITHER (4)

Da 3: 5 **z,** lyre, harp, pipes and all kinds of music, 10630
3: 7 flute, **z,** lyre, harp and all kinds of music, 10630
3:10 of the horn, flute, **z,** lyre, harp, pipes 10630
3:15 **z,** lyre, harp, pipes and all kinds of music, 10630

ZITHRI (KJV) See SITHRI

ZIV (2)

1Ki 6: 1 in the month of **Z,** the second month, 2304
6:37 in the fourth year, in the month of **Z.** 2304

ZIZ (1)

2Ch 20:16 They will be climbing up by the Pass of **Z,** 7489

ZIZA (4)

1Ch 4:37 and **Z** son of Shiphi, the son of Allon, 2330
23:10 sons of Shimei: Jahath, **Z,** Jeush and Beriah. 2330
23:11 Jahath was the first and **Z** the second, 2331
2Ch 11:20 Attai, **Z** and Shelomith. 2330

ZOAN (7)

Nu 13:22 (Hebron had been built seven years before **Z** 7586
Ps 78:12 in the land of Egypt, in the region of **Z.** 7586
78:43 his wonders in the region of **Z.** 7586
Isa 19:11 The officials of **Z** are nothing but fools; 7586
19:13 The officials of **Z** have become fools, 7586
30: 4 in **Z** and their envoys have arrived in Hanes, 7586
Eze 30:14 to **Z** and inflict punishment on Thebes. 7586

ZOAR (10) [BELA]

Ge 13:10 like the land of Egypt, toward **Z.** 7593
14: 2 and the king of Bela (that is, **Z**). 7593
14: 8 the king of Bela (that is, **Z**) marched out 7593
19:22 (That is why the town was called **Z.**) 7593
19:23 By the time Lot reached **Z,** 7593
19:30 Lot and his two daughters left **Z** and settled 7593
19:30 for he was afraid to stay in **Z.** 7593
Dt 34: 3 the City of Palms, as far as **Z.** 7593
Isa 15: 5 her fugitives flee as far as **Z,** 7593
Jer 48:34 from **Z** as far as Horonaim 7593

ZOBAH (13) [ARAM ZOBAH, HAMATH ZOBAH]

1Sa 14:47 Edom, the kings of **Z,** and the Philistines. 7420
2Sa 8: 3 of **Z,** when he went to restore his control 7420
8: 5 to help Hadadezer king of **Z,** 7420
8:12 from Hadadezer son of Rehob, king of **Z.** 7420
10: 6 foot soldiers from Beth Rehob and **Z,** 7419
10: 8 the Arameans of **Z** and Rehob and the men 7419
23:36 Igal son of Nathan from **Z,** the son of Hagri, 7420
1Ki 11:23 from his master, Hadadezer king of **Z.** 7420
11:24 when David destroyed the forces [of **Z**]; NIH
1Ch 18: 3 David fought Hadadezer king of **Z,** 7420
18: 5 to help Hadadezer king of **Z,** 7420
18: 9 the entire army of Hadadezer king of **Z,** 7420
19: 6 Aram Naharaim, Aram Maacah and **Z.** 7420

ZOHAR (5)

Ge 23: 8 to me and intercede with Ephron son of **Z** 7468
25: 9 in the field of Ephron son of **Z** the Hittite, 7468
46:10 **Z** and Shaul the son of a Canaanite woman. 7468
Ex 6:15 **Z** and Shaul the son of a Canaanite woman. 7468
1Ch 4: 7 The sons of Helah: Zereth, **Z,** Ethnan, 7468

ZOHELETH (1)

1Ki 1: 9 cattle and fattened calves at the Stone of **Z** 2325

ZOHETH (1)

1Ch 4:20 The descendants of Ishi: **Z** and Ben-Zoheth. 2311

ZOPHAH (2)

1Ch 7:35 **Z,** Imna, Shelesh and Amal. 7432
7:36 The sons of **Z:** Suah, Harnepher, 7432

ZOPHAI (1)

1Ch 6:26 Elkanah his son, **Z** his son, Nahath his son, 7433

ZOPHAR (4)

Job 2:11 Bildad the Shuhite and **Z** the Naamathite, 7436
11: 1 Then **Z** the Naamathite replied: 7436
20: 1 Then **Z** the Naamathite replied: 7436
42: 9 and **Z** the Naamathite did what the LORD 7436

ZOPHIM (1)

Nu 23:14 So he took him to the field of **Z** on the top 7614

ZORAH (10)

Jos 15:33 In the western foothills: Eshtaol, **Z,** Ashnah, 7666
19:41 **Z,** Eshtaol, Ir Shemesh, 7666
Jdg 13: 2 A certain man of **Z,** named Manoah, 7666
13:25 in Mahaneh Dan, between **Z** and Eshtaol. 7666
16:31 and buried him between **Z** and Eshtaol in 7666
18: 2 So the Danites sent five warriors from **Z** 7666
18: 8 When they returned to **Z** and Eshtaol, 7666
18:11 armed for battle, set out from **Z** and Eshtaol. 7666
2Ch 11:10 **Z,** Aijalon and Hebron. 7666
Ne 11:29 in En Rimmon, in **Z,** in Jarmuth, 7666

ZORATHITES (2)

1Ch 2:53 From these descended the **Z** and Eshtaolites. 7670
4: 2 These were the clans of the **Z.** 7670

ZORITES (1)

1Ch 2:54 half the Manahathites, the **Z,** 7668

ZOBEBAH (KJV) See HAZZOBEBAH

ZOREAH (KJV) See ZORAH

ZOROBABEL (KJV) See ZERUBBABEL

ZUAR (5)

Nu 1: 8 from Issachar, Nethanel son of **Z;** 7428
2: 5 the people of Issachar is Nethanel son of **Z.** 7428
7:18 On the second day Nethanel son of **Z,** 7428
7:23 This was the offering of Nethanel son of **Z.** 7428

Nu 10:15 Nethanel son of **Z** was over the division of 7428

ZUPH (3) [ZUPHITE]
1Sa 1: 1 the son of Tohu, the son of **Z**, 7431
9: 5 When they reached the district of **Z**, 7431
1Ch 6:35 the son of **Z**, the son of Elkanah, 7431

ZUPHITE (1) [ZUPH]
1Sa 1: 1 a **Z** from the hill country of Ephraim, 7434

ZUR (5) [BETH ZUR]
Nu 25:15 put to death was Cozbi daughter of **Z**, 7448
31: 8 Among their victims were Evi, Rekem, **Z**, 7448
Jos 13:21 Evi, Rekem, **Z**, Hur and Reba— 7448
1Ch 8:30 followed by **Z**, Kish, Baal, Ner, Nadab, 7448
9:36 followed by **Z**, Kish, Baal, Ner, Nadab, 7448

ZURIEL (1)
Nu 3:35 the families of the Merarite clans was **Z** son 7452

ZURISHADDAI (5)
Nu 1: 6 from Simeon, Shelumiel son of **Z**; 7453
2:12 the people of Simeon is Shelumiel son of **Z**. 7453
7:36 On the fifth day Shelumiel son of **Z**, 7453
7:41 This was the offering of Shelumiel son of **Z**. 7453
10:19 Shelumiel son of **Z** was over the division of 7453

ZUZIMS (KJV) See ZUZITES

ZUZITES (1)
Ge 14: 5 the **Z** in Ham, the Emites in Shaveh 2309

NUMERALS

12 (24) [TWELVE]
1Ch 25: 9 to Joseph, his sons and relatives, **12** 6925+9109
25: 9 he and his relatives and sons, **12** 6925+9109
25:10 to Zaccur, his sons and relatives, **12** 6925+9109
25:11 to Izri, his sons and relatives, **12** 6925+9109
25:12 Nethaniah, his sons and relatives, **12** 6925+9109
25:13 to Bukkiah, his sons and relatives, **12** 6925+9109
25:14 to Jesarelah, his sons and relatives, **12** 6925+9109
25:15 to Jeshaiah, his sons and relatives, **12** 6925+9109
25:16 Mattaniah, his sons and relatives, **12** 6925+9109
25:17 to Shimei, his sons and relatives, **12** 6925+9109
25:18 to Azarel, his sons and relatives, **12** 6925+9109
25:19 Hashabiah, his sons and relatives, **12** 6925+9109
25:20 to Shubael, his sons and relatives, **12** 6925+9109
25:21 Mattithiah, his sons and relatives, **12** 6925+9109
25:22 to Jerimoth, his sons and relatives, **12** 6925+9109
25:23 Hananiah, his sons and relatives, **12** 6925+9109
25:24 his sons and relatives, **12** 6925+9109
25:25 to Hanani, his sons and relatives, **12** 6925+9109
25:26 to Mallothi, his sons and relatives, **12** 6925+9109
25:27 to Eliathah, his sons and relatives, **12** 6925+9109
25:28 to Hothir, his sons and relatives, **12** 6925+9109
25:29 to Giddalti, his sons and relatives, **12** 6925+9109
25:30 Mahazioth, his sons and relatives, **12** 6925+9109
25:31 his sons and relatives, **12** 6925+9109

13 (1) [THIRTEEN]
1Ch 26:11 and relatives of Hosah were **13** in all. 6925+8993

18 (3) [EIGHTEEN]
Ge 6:16 finish the ark to within **18 inches** of the top. 564
1Ch 26: 9 who were able men—**18** in all. 6925+9046
Ezr 8:18 sons and brothers, **18** *men;* 6925+9046

20 (2) [TWENTY]
Ezr 8:19 and his brothers and nephews, **20** *men.* 6929
8:27 **20** bowls of gold valued at 1,000 darics, 6929

22 (1) [TWENTY TWO]
1Ch 12:28 with **22** officers from his family; 2256+6929+9109

28 (1) [TWENTY-EIGHT]
Ezr 8:11 of Bebai, and with him **28** men; 2256+6929+9046

29 (3) [TWENTY-NINE]
Ge 11:24 When Nahor had lived **29** years, 2256+6929+9596
Ex 38:24 on the sanctuary was **29** talents 2256+6929+9596
Ezr 1: 9 silver pans **29** 2256+6929+9596

30 (5) [THIRTY]
Ge 11:14 When Shelah had lived **30** years, 8993
11:18 When Peleg had lived **30** years, 8993
11:22 When Serug had lived **30** years, 8993
Ezr 1: 9 gold dishes **30** silver dishes 1,000 8993
1:10 gold bowls **30** matching silver bowls 410 8993

32 (3) [THIRTY-TWO]
Ge 11:20 When Reu had lived **32** years, 2256+8993+9109
Nu 31:40 16,000 people, of which the tribute for the LORD was **32.** 2256+8993+9109
1Ki 20:16 Ben-Hadad and the **32** kings 2256+8993+9109

34 (1)
Ge 11:16 When Eber had lived **34** years, 752+2256+8993

35 (1) [THIRTY-FIVE]
Ge 11:12 Arphaxad had lived **35** years, 2256+2822+8993

40 (1) [FORTY]
Eze 4: 6 I have assigned you **40** days, a day for each 752

42 (3) [FORTY-TWO]
Ezr 2:24 of Azmaveth **42** 752+2256+9109
Ne 7:28 of Beth Azmaveth **42** 752+2256+9109
Rev 11: 2 They will trample on the holy city *for* **42** months. *1545+5477*

45 (1) [FORTY-FIVE]
Ge 6:15 75 feet wide and **45 feet** high. 564+8993

50 (3) [FIFTY]
Ezr 8: 6 Ebed son of Jonathan, and with him **50** men; 2822
Ne 7:70 **50** bowls and 530 garments for priests. 2822
Eze 45: 2 with **50** cubits around it for open land. 2822

52 (2) [FIFTY-TWO]
Ezr 2:29 of Nebo **52** 2256+2822+9109
Ne 7:33 of the other Nebo **52** 2256+2822+9109

56 (1)
Ezr 2:22 of Netophah **56** 2256+2822+9252

60 (1) [SIXTY]
Ezr 8:13 Jeuel and Shemaiah, and with them **60** men; 9252

61 (1)
Nu 31:39 the tribute for the LORD was **61;** 285+2256+9252

62 (1) [SIXTY-TWO]
1Ch 26: 8 of Obed-Edom, **62** in all. 2256+9109+9252

65 (2) [SIXTY-FIVE]
Ge 5:15 Mahalalel had lived **65** years, 2256+2822+9252
5:21 Enoch had lived **65** years, 2256+2822+9252

67 (1)
Ne 7:72 and **67** garments for priests. 2256+8679+9252

70 (5) [SEVENTY]
Ge 5:12 When Kenan had lived **70** years, 8679
11:26 After Terah had lived **70** years, 8679
Ex 38:29 the wave offering was **70** talents and 2,400 8679
Ezr 8: 7 son of Athaliah, and with him **70** men; 8679
8:14 Uthai and Zaccur, and with them **70** men. 8679

72 (1) [SEVENTY-TWO]
Nu 31:38 tribute for the LORD was **72;** 2256+8679+9109

74 (2)
Ezr 2:40 through the line of Hodaviah) **74** 752+2256+8679
Ne 7:43 through the line of Hodaviah) **74** 752+2256+8679

75 (1) [SEVENTY-FIVE]
Ge 6:15 **75 feet** wide and 45 feet high. 564+2822

80 (2) [EIGHTY]
1Ch 15: 9 Eliel the leader and **80** relatives; 9046
Ezr 8: 8 and with him **80** men; 9046

90 (1) [NINETY]
Ge 5: 9 When Enosh had lived **90** years, 9596

95 (2)
Ezr 2:20 of Gibbar **95** 2256+2822+9596
Ne 7:25 of Gibeon **95** 2256+2822+9596

98 (2) [NINETY-EIGHT]
Ezr 2:16 of Ater (through Hezekiah) **98** 2256+9046+9596
Ne 7:21 of Ater (through Hezekiah) **98** 2256+9046+9596

100 (8) [HUNDRED]
Ge 11:10 when Shem was **100** years old, 4395
Ex 38:25 the census was **100** talents and 4395
38:27 The **100** talents of silver were used to cast 4395
38:27 **100** bases from the 100 talents, 4395
38:27 100 bases from the **100** talents, 4395
Ezr 2:69 minas of silver and **100** priestly garments. 4395
8:26 silver articles weighing **100** talents, 4395
8:26 **100** talents of gold, 4395

105 (1)
Ge 5: 6 When Seth had lived **105** years, 2256+2822+4395

110 (1)
Ezr 8:12 and with him **110** men; 2256+4395+6927

112 (3)
1Ch 15:10 Amminadab the leader and **112** relatives. 2256+4395+6925+9109
Ezr 2:18 of Jorah **112** 2256+4395+6925+9109
Ne 7:24 of Hariph **112** 4395+6925+9109

119 (1)
Ge 11:25 Nahor lived **119** years 2256+4395+6926+9596

120 (6)
1Ki 9:14 Now Hiram had sent to the king **120** talents of gold. 2256+4395+6929
10:10 And she gave the king **120** talents of gold, 2256+4395+6929
1Ch 15: 5 Uriel the leader and **120** relatives; 2256+4395+6929
2Ch 5:12 **120** priests sounding trumpets. 2256+4395+6929
9: 9 Then she gave the king **120** talents of gold, 2256+4395+6929
Da 6: 1 appoint **120** satraps to rule 10221+10395+10574

122 (2)
Ezr 2:27 of Micmash **122** 2256+4395+6929+9109
Ne 7:31 of Micmash **122** 2256+2256+4395+6929+9109

123 (2)
Ezr 2:21 men of Bethlehem **123** 2256+4395+6929+8993
Ne 7:32 of Bethel and Ai **123** 2256+4395+6929+8993

127 (3)
Est 1: 1 Xerxes who ruled over **127** provinces 2256+2256+4395+6929+8679
8: 9 satraps, governors and nobles of the **127** provinces 2256+2256+4395+6929+8679
9:30 sent letters to all the Jews in the **127** provinces 2256+2256+4395+6929+8679

128 (4)
Ezr 2:23 of Anathoth **128** 2256+4395+6929+9046
2:41 The singers: the descendants of Asaph **128** 2256+4395+6929+9046
Ne 7:27 of Anathoth **128** 2256+4395+6929+9046
11:14 were able men—**128.** 2256+4395+6929+9046

130 (2)
Ge 5: 3 Adam had lived **130** years, 2256+4395+8993
1Ch 15: 7 Joel the leader and **130** relatives 2256+4395+8993

133 (1)
Ex 6:18 Kohath lived **133** years. 2256+2256+4395+8993+8993

137 (2)
Ex 6:16 Levi lived **137** years. 2256+2256+4395+8679+8993
6:20 Amram lived **137** years. 2256+2256+4395+8679+8993

138 (1)
Ne 7:45 Hatita and Shobai **138** 2256+4395+8993+9046

139 (1)
Ezr 2:42 Hatita and Shobai **139** 2256+4395+8993+9596

144 (1)
Rev 21:17 and it was **144** cubits thick, *1669+5475+5477*

148 (1)
Ne 7:44 The singers: the descendants of Asaph **148** 752+2256+4395+9046

150 (2)
1Ch 8:40 sons and grandsons—**150** in all. 2256+2822+4395
Ezr 8: 3 were registered **150** men; 2256+2822+4395

153 (1)
Jn 21:11 It was full of large fish, **153,** *1669+4299+5552*

156 (1)
Ezr 2:30 of Magbish **156** 2256+2822+4395+9252

160 (1)
Ezr 8:10 and with him **160** men; 2256+4395+9252

162 (1)
Ge 5:18 When Jared had lived **162** years, 2256+2256+4395+9109+9252

172 (1)
Ne 11:19 at the gates—**172** men. 2256+4395+8679+9109

180 (1)
Est 1: 4 a full **180** days he displayed the vast wealth of his kingdom 2256+4395+9046

182 (1)
Ge 5:28 Lamech had lived **182** years, he had a son. 2256+2256+4395+9046+9109

187 (1)
Ge 5:25 When Methuselah had lived **187** years, 2256+2256+4395+8679+9046

188 (1)
Ne 7:26 the men of Bethlehem and Netophah **188** 2256+4395+9046+9046

200 (5)
Ge 11:23 Serug lived **200** years and had other sons 4395
1Ch 12:32 **200** chiefs, with all their relatives 4395
15: 8 Shemaiah the leader and **200** relatives; 4395
Ezr 2:65 also had **200** men and women singers. 4395
8: 4 and with him **200** men; 4395

205 (1)
Ge 11:32 Terah lived **205** years, 2256+2822+4395

207 (1)
Ge 11:21 Reu lived **207** years 2256+4395+8679

209 (1)
Ge 11:19 Peleg lived **209** years 2256+4395+9596

212 (1)
1Ch 9:22 gatekeepers at the thresholds numbered **212.** 2256+4395+6925+9109

218 (1)
Ezr 8: 9 and with him **218** men; 2256+4395+6925+9046

220 (2)
1Ch 15: 6 Asaiah the leader and **220** relatives; 2256+4395+6929
Ezr 8:20 **220** of the temple servants— 2256+4395+6929

223 (2)
Ezr 2:19 of Hashum **223** 2256+4395+6929+8993
2:28 of Bethel and Ai **223** 2256+4395+6929+8993

232 (1)
1Ki 20:15 of the provincial commanders, **232** men. 2256+4395+8993+9109

242 (1)
Ne 11:13 heads of families—**242** 752+2256+4395+9109

245 (3)
Ezr 2:66 had 736 horses, **245** mules, 752+2256+2822+4395
Ne 7:67 and they also had **245** men and women singers. 752+2256+2256+2822+4395
7:68 There were 736 horses, **245** mules, NIH

250 (10)
Ex 30:23 (that is, **250** shekels) 2256+2822+4395
30:23 **250** shekels of fragrant cane, 2256+2822+4395
Nu 16: 2 were **250** Israelite men, 2256+2822+4395
16:17 **250** censers in all— 2256+2822+4395
16:35 the **250** men who were offering 2256+2822+4395
26:10 the fire devoured the **250** men. 2256+2822+4395
Eze 48:17 the city will be **250** cubits on 2256+2822+4395
48:17 **250** cubits on the south, 2256+2822+4395
48:17 **250** cubits on the east, 2256+2822+4395
48:17 and **250** cubits on the west. 2256+2822+4395

273 (1)
Nu 3:46 To redeem the **273** firstborn Israelites who exceed 2256+2256+4395+8679+8993

276 (1)
Ac 27:37 Altogether there were **276** of us *1357+1573+1971*

284 (1)
Ne 11:18 The Levites in the holy city totaled **284.** 752+2256+4395+9046

288 (1)
1Ch 25: 7 they numbered **288.** 2256+4395+9046+9046

300 (2)
Ge 5:22 Enoch walked with God **300** years 4395+8993
Ezr 8: 5 and with him **300** men; 4395+8993

318 (1)
Ge 14:14 the **318** trained men born in his household 2256+4395+6925+8993+9046

320 (2)
Ezr 2:32 of Harim **320** 2256+4395+6929+8993
Ne 7:35 of Harim **320** 2256+4395+6929+8993

323 (1)
Ezr 2:17 of Bezai **323** 2256+4395+6929+8993+8993

324 (1)
Ne 7:23 of Bezai **324** 752+2256+4395+6929+8993

328 (1)
Ne 7:22 of Hashum **328** 2256+4395+6929+8993+9046

345 (2)
Ezr 2:34 of Jericho **345** 752+2256+2822+4395+8993
Ne 7:36 of Jericho **345** 752+2256+2822+4395+8993

350 (1)
Ge 9:28 After the flood Noah lived **350** years. 2256+2822+4395+8993

365 (1)
Ge 5:23 Altogether, Enoch lived **365** years. 2256+2256+2822+4395+8993+9252

372 (2)
Ezr 2: 4 of Shephatiah **372** 2256+4395+8679+8993+9109
Ne 7: 9 of Shephatiah **372** 2256+4395+8679+8993+9109

390 (2)
Eze 4: 5 So for **390** days you will bear the sin of the house of Israel. 2256+4395+8993+9596
4: 9 You are to eat it during the **390** days you lie on your side. 2256+4395+8993+9596

392 (2)
Ezr 2:58 of the servants of Solomon **392** 2256+4395+8993+9109+9596
Ne 7:60 of the servants of Solomon **392** 2256+4395+8993+9109+9596

403 (2)
Ge 11:13 Arphaxad lived **403** years 752+2256+4395+8993
11:15 Shelah lived **403** years 752+2256+4395+8993

410 (1)
Ezr 1:10 matching silver bowls **410** 752+2256+4395+6927

420 (1)
1Ki 9:28 **420** talents of gold, 752+2256+4395+6929

430 (4)
Ge 11:17 Eber lived **430** years 752+2256+4395+8993
Ex 12:40 the Israelite people lived in Egypt was **430** years. 752+2256+4395+8993
12:41 At the end of the **430** years, 752+2256+4395+8993
Gal 3:17 The law, introduced **430** years later, *2779+5484+5558*

435 (2)
Ezr 2:67 **435** camels and 752+2256+2822+4395+8993
Ne 7:69 **435** camels and 752+2256+2822+4395+8993

450 (2)
Ge 6:15 The ark is to be **450 feet** long, 564+4395+8993
Ac 13:20 All this took about **450** years. *2779+4299+5484*

454 (1)
Ezr 2:15 of Adin **454** 752+752+2256+2822+4395

468 (1)
Ne 11: 6 totaled **468** able men. 752+2256+4395+9046+9252

500 (5)
Ge 5:32 After Noah was **500** years old, 2822+4395
11:11 Shem lived **500** years and 2822+4395
Ex 30:23 **500** shekels of liquid myrrh, 2822+4395
30:24 **500** shekels of cassia— 2822+4395
Eze 45: 2 a section **500** cubits square 2822+4395

530 (1)
Ne 7:70 **530** garments for priests. 2256+2822+4395+8993

550 (1)
1Ki 9:23 **550** officials supervising 2256+2822+2822+4395

595 (1)
Ge 5:30 Lamech lived **595** years and 2256+2256+2822+2822+4395+9596

621 (2)
Ezr 2:26 and Geba **621** 285+2256+4395+6929+9252
Ne 7:30 and Geba **621** 285+2256+4395+6929+9252

623 (1)
Ezr 2:11 of Bebai **623** 2256+4395+6929+8993+9252

628 (1)
Ne 7:16 of Bebai **628** 2256+4395+6929+9046+9252

642 (2)
Ezr 2:10 of Bani **642** 752+2256+4395+9109+9252
Ne 7:62 Nekoda **642** 752+2256+2256+4395+9109+9252

648 (1)
Ne 7:15 of Binnui **648** 752+2256+4395+9046+9252

650 (1)
Ezr 8:26 I weighed out to them **650** talents of silver, 2256+2822+4395+9252

652 (2)
Ezr 2:60 and Nekoda **652** 2256+2822+4395+9109+9252
Ne 7:10 of Arah **652** 2256+2822+4395+9109+9252

655 (1)
Ne 7:20 of Adin **655** 2256+2822+2822+4395+9252

666 (4)
1Ki 10:14 Solomon received yearly was **666** talents, 2256+4395+9252+9252+9252
2Ch 9:13 Solomon received yearly was **666** talents, 2256+2256+4395+9252+9252+9252
Ezr 2:13 of Adonikam **666** 2256+4395+9252+9252+9252
Rev 13:18 His number is **666.** *1971+1980+2008*

667 (1)
Ne 7:18 of Adonikam **667** 2256+4395+8679+9252+9252

675 (1)
Nu 31:37 of which the tribute for the LORD was **675;** 2256+2822+4395+8679+9252

690 (1)
1Ch 9: 6 The people from Judah numbered **690.** 2256+4395+9252+9596

721 (1)
Ne 7:37 of Lod, Hadid and Ono **721** 285+2256+2256+4395+6929+8679

725 (1)
Ezr 2:33 of Lod, Hadid and Ono **725** 2256+2822+4395+6929+8679

730 (1)
Ex 38:24 and **730** shekels, 2256+4395+8679+8993

736 (2)
Ezr 2:66 had **736** horses, 2256+4395+8679+8993+9252
Ne 7:68 There were **736** horses, 245 mules, NIH

743 (2)
Ezr 2:25 Beeroth **743** 752+2256+2256+4395+8679+8993
Ne 7:29 Beeroth **743** 752+2256+4395+8679+8993

745 (1)
Jer 52:30 **745** Jews taken into exile by Nebuzaradan 752+2256+2822+4395+8679

760 (2)
Ezr 2: 9 of Zaccai **760** 2256+4395+8679+9252
Ne 7:14 of Zaccai **760** 2256+4395+8679+9252

775 (1)
Ezr 2: 5 of Arah **775** 2256+2822+4395+8679+8679

777 (1)
Ge 5:31 Altogether, Lamech lived **777** years, 2256+2256+4395+8679+8679+8679

782 (1)
Ge 5:26 Methuselah lived **782** years 2256+2256+4395+8679+9046+9109

800 (2)
Ge 5: 4 Adam lived **800** years and had other 4395+9046
5:19 Jared lived **800** years and had other 4395+9046

807 (1)
Ge 5: 7 Seth lived **807** years 2256+4395+8679+9046

815 (1)
Ge 5:10 Enosh lived **815** years and had other sons 2256+2822+4395+6926+9046

822 (1)
Ne 11:12 who carried on work for the temple—**822** men; 2256+4395+6929+9046+9109

830 (1)
Ge 5:16 Mahalalel lived **830** years 2256+4395+8993+9046

832 (1)
Jer 52:29 **832** people from Jerusalem; 2256+4395+8993+9046+9109

840 (1)
Ge 5:13 Kenan lived **840** years 752+2256+4395+9046

845 (1)
Ne 7:13 of Zattu **845** 752+2256+2822+4395+9046

895 (1)
Ge 5:17 Altogether, Mahalalel lived **895** years, 2256+2256+2822+4395+9046+9596

905 (1)
Ge 5:11 Enosh lived **905** years, 2256+2822+4395+9596

910 (1)
Ge 5:14 Kenan lived **910** years, 2256+4395+6924+9596

912 (1)
Ge 5:8 Altogether, Seth lived **912** years, 2256+4395+6926+9109+9596

928 (1)
Ne 11:8 Sallai—**928** men. 2256+4395+6929+9046+9596

930 (1)
Ge 5:5 Adam lived **930** years, 2256+4395+8993+9596

945 (1)
Ezr 2:8 of Zattu **945** 752+2256+2256+2822+4395+9596

950 (1)
Ge 9:29 Noah lived **950** years, 2256+2822+4395+9596

956 (1)
1Ch 9:9 as listed in their genealogy, numbered **956.** 2256+2256+2822+4395+9252+9596

962 (1)
Ge 5:20 Altogether, Jared lived **962** years, 2256+2256+4395+9109+9252+9596

969 (1)
Ge 5:27 Altogether, Methuselah lived **969** years, 2256+2256+4395+9252+9596+9596

973 (2)
Ezr 2:36 (through the family of Jeshua) **973** 2256+4395+8679+8993+9596
Ne 7:39 (through the family of Jeshua) **973** 2256+4395+8679+8993+9596

1,000 (6) [THOUSAND]
1Ch 12:34 men of Naphtali—**1,000** officers, 547
2Ch 17:14 From Judah, commanders of **units of 1,000:** 547
Ezr 1:9 gold dishes 30 silver dishes **1,000** 547
1:10 other articles **1,000** 547
8:27 20 bowls of gold valued at **1,000** 547
Ne 7:70 The governor gave to the treasury **1,000** 547

1,017 (2)
Ezr 2:39 of Harim **1,017** 547+2256+6925+8679
Ne 7:42 of Harim **1,017** 547+6925+8679

1,052 (2)
Ezr 2:37 of Immer **1,052** 547+2256+2822+9109
Ne 7:40 of Immer **1,052** 547+2256+2822+9109

1,222 (1)
Ezr 2:12 of Azgad **1,222** 547+2256+4395+6929+9109

1,247 (2)
Ezr 2:38 of Pashhur **1,247** 547+752+2256+4395+8679
Ne 7:41 of Pashhur **1,247** 547+752+2256+4395+8679

1,254 (4)
Ezr 2:7 of Elam **1,254** 547+752+2256+2822+4395
2:31 the other Elam **1,254** 547+752+2256+2822+4395
Ne 7:12 of Elam **1,254** 547+752+2256+2822+4395
7:34 the other Elam **1,254** 547+752+2256+2822+4395

1,260 (2)
Rev 11:3 and they will prophesy *for* **1,260** days, *1357+2008+5943*
12:6 where she might be taken care of *for* **1,260** *1357+2008+5943*

1,290 (1)
Da 12:11 there will be **1,290** days. 547+2256+4395+9596

1,335 (1)
Da 12:12 who waits for and reaches the end of the **1,335** days. 547+2256+2822+4395+8993+8993

1,365 (1)
Nu 3:50 he collected silver weighing **1,365** shekels, 547+2256+2256+2256+2822+4395+8993+9252

1,600 (1)
Rev 14:20 as high as the horses' bridles for a distance of **1,600** stadia. *1980+5943*

1,760 (1)
1Ch 9:13 who were heads of families, numbered **1,760.** 547+2256+2256+4395+8679+9252

1,775 (2)
Ex 38:25 100 talents and **1,775** shekels, 547+2256+2256+2256+2822+4395+8679+8679
38:28 They used the **1,775** shekels to make hooks 547+2256+2256+2256+2822+4395+8679+8679

2,000 (1)
Ne 7:72 **2,000** minas of silver and 67 garments 547

2,056 (1)
Ezr 2:14 of Bigvai **2,056** 547+2256+2822+9252

2,067 (1)
Ne 7:19 of Bigvai **2,067** 547+2256+8679+9252

2,172 (2)
Ezr 2:3 the descendants of Parosh **2,172** 547+2256+4395+8679+9109
Ne 7:8 the descendants of Parosh **2,172** 547+2256+2256+4395+8679+9109

2,200 (1)
Ne 7:71 and **2,200** minas of silver. 547+2256+4395

2,300 (1)
Da 8:14 "It will take **2,300** evenings and mornings; 547+2256+4395+8993

2,322 (1)
Ne 7:17 of Azgad **2,322** 547+2256+4395+6929+8993+9109

2,400 (1)
Ex 38:29 the wave offering was 70 talents and **2,400** shekels. 547+752+2256+4395

2,600 (1)
2Ch 26:12 fighting men was **2,600.** 547+2256+4395+9252

2,630 (1)
Nu 4:40 counted by their clans and families, were **2,630.** 547+2256+2256+4395+8993+9252

2,750 (1)
Nu 4:36 counted by clans, were **2,750.** 547+2256+2822+4395+8679

2,812 (1)
Ezr 2:6 (through the line of Jeshua and Joab) **2,812** 547+2256+4395+6925+9046+9109

2,818 (1)
Ne 7:11 (through the line of Jeshua and Joab) **2,818** 547+2256+4395+6925+9046+9046

3,000 (1)
1Ch 12:29 of Benjamin, Saul's kinsmen—**3,000,** 547+8993

3,023 (1)
Jer 52:28 in the seventh year, **3,023** Jews; 547+2256+2256+6929+8993+8993

3,200 (1)
Nu 4:44 counted by their clans, were **3,200.** 547+2256+4395+8993

3,600 (1)
2Ch 2:18 with **3,600** foremen over them 547+2256+4395+8993+9252

3,630 (1)
Ezr 2:35 of Senaah **3,630** 547+2256+2256+4395+8993+8993+9252

3,700 (1)
1Ch 12:27 with **3,700** men, 547+2256+4395+8679+8993

3,930 (1)
Ne 7:38 Senaah **3,930** 547+2256+4395+8993+8993+9596

4,500 (8)
Eze 48:16 the north side **4,500** cubits, 547+752+2256+2822+4395
48:16 the south side **4,500** cubits, 547+752+2256+2822+4395
48:16 the east side **4,500** cubits, 547+752+2256+2822+4395
48:16 and the west side **4,500** cubits. 547+752+2256+2822+4395
48:30 is **4,500** cubits long, 547+752+2256+2822+4395
48:32 "On the east side, which is **4,500** cubits long 547+752+2256+2822+4395
48:33 "On the south side, which measures **4,500** 547+752+2256+2822+4395
48:34 "On the west side, which is **4,500** cubits long 547+752+2256+2822+4395

4,600 (2)
1Ch 12:26 men of Levi—**4,600,** 547+752+2256+4395+9252
Jer 52:30 **4,600** people in all. 547+752+2256+4395+9252

5,000 (3)
Ezr 2:69 **5,000** minas of silver and 100 priestly 547+2822
Eze 45:6 as its property an area **5,000** cubits wide 547+2822
48:15 "The remaining area, **5,000** cubits wide 547+2822

5,400 (1)
Ezr 1:11 **5,400** articles of gold 547+752+2256+2822+4395

6,200 (1)
Nu 3:34 were counted was **6,200.** 547+2256+4395+9252

6,720 (2)
Ezr 2:67 435 camels and **6,720** donkeys. 547+2256+4395+6929+8679+9252
Ne 7:69 435 camels and **6,720** donkeys. 547+2256+4395+6929+8679+9252

6,800 (1)
1Ch 12:24 of Judah, carrying shield and spear **6,800** armed for battle; 547+2256+4395+9046+9252

7,000 (1)
1Ki 20:15 the rest of the Israelites, **7,000** 547+8679

7,100 (1)
1Ch 12:25 ready for battle—**7,100;** 547+2256+4395+8679

7,337 (2)
Ezr 2:65 besides their **7,337** menservants and 547+2256+4395+8679+8679+8993+8993
Ne 7:67 besides their **7,337** menservants and 547+2256+4395+8679+8679+8993+8993

7,500 (1)
Nu 3:22 a month old or more who were counted was **7,500.** 547+2256+2822+4395+8679

8,580 (1)
Nu 4:48 numbered **8,580.** 547+2256+2256+2822+4395+9046+9046

8,600 (1)
Nu 3:28 the males a month old or more was **8,600.** 547+2256+4395+9046+9252

10,000 (9)
Eze 45:3 cubits long and **10,000** cubits wide. 547+6930
45:5 cubits long and **10,000** cubits wide 547+6930
48:9 cubits long and **10,000** cubits wide. 547+6930
48:10 **10,000** cubits wide on the west side, 547+6930
48:10 **10,000** cubits wide on the east side, 547+6930
48:13 cubits long and **10,000** cubits wide. 547+6930
48:13 cubits and its width **10,000** cubits. 547+6930
48:18 will be **10,000** cubits on the east side 547+6930
48:18 and **10,000** cubits on the west side 547+6930

12,000 (13)
Rev 7:5 From the tribe of Judah **12,000** *1557+5942*
7:5 from the tribe of Reuben **12,000,** *1557+5942*
7:5 from the tribe of Gad **12,000,** *1557+5942*

Rev 7: 6 from the tribe of Asher **12,000**, *1557+5942*
7: 6 from the tribe of Naphtali **12,000**, *1557+5942*
7: 6 from the tribe of Manasseh **12,000**, *1557+5942*
7: 7 from the tribe of Simeon **12,000**, *1557+5942*
7: 7 from the tribe of Levi **12,000**, *1557+5942*
7: 7 from the tribe of Issachar **12,000**, *1557+5942*
7: 8 from the tribe of Zebulun **12,000**, *1557+5942*
7: 8 from the tribe of Joseph **12,000**, *1557+5942*
7: 8 from the tribe of Benjamin **12,000**. *1557+5942*
21:16 and found it to be **12,000** stadia *1557+5942*

14,700 (1)
Nu 16:49 But **14,700** people died from the plague, 547+752+2256+4395+6925+8679

16,000 (2)
Nu 31:40 **16,000** people, of which the tribute for the LORD was 32. 547+6925+9252
31:46 and **16,000** people. 547+6925+9252

16,750 (1)
Nu 31:52 a gift to the LORD weighed **16,750** shekels. 547+2256+2822+4395+6925+8679+9252

17,200 (1)
1Ch 7:11 There were **17,200** fighting men ready to go 547+2256+4395+6925+8679

18,000 (2)
1Ch 12:31 and make David king—**18,000**; 547+6925+9046
Eze 48:35 all around will be **18,000** cubits. 547+6925+9046

20,000 (3)
Ne 7:71 to the treasury for the work **20,000** 8052+9109
7:72 by the rest of the people was **20,000** 8052+9109
Eze 45: 1 cubits long and **20,000** cubits wide; 547+6929

20,200 (1)
1Ch 7: 9 and **20,200** fighting men. 547+2256+4395+6929

20,800 (1)
1Ch 12:30 famous in their own clans—**20,800**; 547+2256+4395+6929+9046

22,000 (1)
Nu 3:39 every male a month old or more, was **22,000**. 547+2256+6929+9109

22,034 (1)
1Ch 7: 7 Their genealogical record listed **22,034** 547+752+2256+2256+2256+6929+8993+9109

22,200 (1)
Nu 26:14 clans of Simeon, there were **22,200** men. 547+2256+2256+4395+6929+9109

22,273 (1)
Nu 3:43 listed by name, was **22,273**. 547+2256+2256+4395+6929+8679+8993+9109

22,600 (1)
1Ch 7: 2 in their genealogy numbered **22,600**. 547+2256+2256+4395+6929+9109+9252

23,000 (1)
Nu 26:62 a month old or more numbered **23,000**. 547+2256+6929+8993

24,000 (14)
Nu 25: 9 those who died in the plague numbered **24,000**. 547+752+2256+6929
1Ch 27: 1 Each division consisted of **24,000** men. 547+752+2256+6929
27: 2 **24,000** men in his division. 547+752+2256+6929
27: 4 **24,000** men in his division. 547+752+2256+6929
27: 5 **24,000** men in his division. 547+752+2256+6929
27: 7 **24,000** men in his division. 547+752+2256+6929
27: 8 **24,000** men in his division. 547+752+2256+6929
27: 9 **24,000** men in his division. 547+752+2256+6929
27:10 **24,000** men in his division. 547+752+2256+6929
27:11 **24,000** men in his division. 547+752+2256+6929
27:12 **24,000** men in his division. 547+752+2256+6929
27:13 **24,000** men in his division. 547+752+2256+6929
27:14 **24,000** men in his division. 547+752+2256+6929
27:15 **24,000** men in his division. 547+752+2256+6929

25,000 (14)
Eze 45: 1 **25,000** cubits long and 20,000 cubits wide; 547+2256+2822+6929
45: 3 measure off a section **25,000** cubits long 547+2256+2822+6929
45: 5 An area **25,000** cubits long 547+2256+2822+6929
45: 6 and **25,000** cubits long, 547+2256+2822+6929
48: 8 It will be **25,000** cubits wide, 547+2256+2822+6929
48: 9 offer to the LORD will be **25,000** cubits 547+2256+2822+6929
48:10 It will be **25,000** long on the north side, 547+2256+2822+6929
48:10 and **25,000** long on the south side. 547+2256+2822+6929
48:13 the Levites will have an allotment **25,000** long and 547+2256+2822+6929
48:13 Its total length will be **25,000** cubits 547+2256+2822+6929
48:15 and **25,000** cubits long, 547+2256+2822+6929
48:20 The entire portion will be a square, **25,000** on each side. 547+2256+2822+6929
48:21 It will extend eastward from the **25,000** 547+2256+2822+6929
48:21 and westward from the **25,000** cubits 547+2256+2822+6929

25,100 (1)
Jdg 20:35 that day the Israelites struck down **25,100** Benjamites, 547+2256+2256+2822+4395+6929

26,000 (1)
1Ch 7:40 as listed in their genealogy, was **26,000**. 547+2256+6929+9252

28,600 (1)
1Ch 12:35 men of Dan, ready for battle—**28,600**; 547+2256+2256+4395+6929+9046+9252

30,500 (2)
Nu 31:39 **30,500** donkeys, 547+2256+2822+4395+8993
31:45 **30,500** donkeys 547+2256+2822+4395+8993

32,000 (1)
Nu 31:35 and **32,000** women who had never slept with a man. 547+2256+8993+9109

32,200 (2)
Nu 1:35 from the tribe of Manasseh was **32,200**. 547+2256+2256+4395+8993+9109
2:21 His division numbers **32,200**. 547+2256+2256+4395+8993+9109

32,500 (1)
Nu 26:37 those numbered were **32,500**. 547+2256+2256+2822+4395+8993+9109

35,400 (2)
Nu 1:37 from the tribe of Benjamin was **35,400**. 547+752+2256+2256+2822+4395+8993
2:23 His division numbers **35,400**. 547+752+2256+2256+2822+4395+8993

36,000 (3)
Nu 31:38 **36,000** cattle, 547+2256+8993+9252
31:44 **36,000** cattle, 547+2256+8993+9252
1Ch 7: 4 they had **36,000** men ready for battle, 547+2256+8993+9252

37,000 (1)
1Ch 12:34 1,000 officers, together with **37,000** 547+2256+8679+8993

40,000 (1)
1Ch 12:36 experienced soldiers prepared for battle—**40,000**; 547+752

40,500 (3)
Nu 1:33 from the tribe of Ephraim was **40,500**. 547+752+2256+2822+4395
2:19 His division numbers **40,500**. 547+752+2256+2822+4395
26:18 clans of Gad; those numbered were **40,500**. 547+752+2256+2822+4395

41,500 (2)
Nu 1:41 The number from the tribe of Asher was **41,500**. 285+547+752+2256+2256+2822+4395
2:28 His division numbers **41,500**. 285+547+752+2256+2256+2822+4395

42,360 (2)
Ezr 2:64 The whole company numbered **42,360**, 547+752+4395+8052+8993+9252
Ne 7:66 The whole company numbered **42,360**, 547+752+2256+4395+8052+8993+9252

43,730 (1)
Nu 26: 7 those numbered were **43,730**. 547+752+2256+2256+2256+4395+8679+8993+8993

44,760 (1)
1Ch 5:18 and the half-tribe of Manasseh had **44,760** 547+752+752+2256+2256+2256+4395+8679+9252

45,400 (1)
Nu 26:50 of Naphtali; those numbered were **45,400**. 547+752+752+2256+2256+2822+4395

45,600 (1)
Nu 26:41 of Benjamin; those numbered were **45,600**. 547+752+2256+2256+2822+4395+9252

45,650 (2)
Nu 1:25 from the tribe of Gad was **45,650**. 547+752+2256+2256+2256+2822+2822+4395+9252
2:15 His division numbers **45,650**. 547+752+2256+2256+2256+2822+2822+4395+9252

46,500 (2)
Nu 1:21 from the tribe of Reuben was **46,500**. 547+752+2256+2256+2822+4395+9252
2:11 His division numbers **46,500**. 547+752+2256+2256+2822+4395+9252

50,000 (1)
1Ch 12:33 with undivided loyalty—**50,000**; 547+2822

52,700 (1)
Nu 26:34 those numbered were **52,700**. 547+2256+2256+2822+4395+8679+9109

53,400 (3)
Nu 1:43 from the tribe of Naphtali was **53,400**. 547+752+2256+2256+2822+4395+8993
2:30 His division numbers **53,400**. 547+752+2256+2256+2822+4395+8993
26:47 those numbered were **53,400**. 547+752+2256+2256+2822+4395+8993

54,400 (2)
Nu 1:29 from the tribe of Issachar was **54,400**. 547+752+752+2256+2256+2822+4395
2: 6 His division numbers **54,400**. 547+752+752+2256+2256+2822+4395

57,400 (2)
Nu 1:31 from the tribe of Zebulun was **57,400**. 547+752+2256+2256+2822+4395+8679
2: 8 His division numbers **57,400**. 547+752+2256+2256+2822+4395+8679

59,300 (2)
Nu 1:23 from the tribe of Simeon was **59,300**. 547+2256+2256+2822+4395+8993+9596
2:13 His division numbers **59,300**. 547+2256+2256+2822+4395+8993+9596

60,500 (1)
Nu 26:27 those numbered were **60,500**. 547+2256+2822+4395+9252

61,000 (2)
Nu 31:34 **61,000** donkeys 285+547+2256+9252
Ezr 2:69 for this work **61,000** drachmas of gold, 547+2256+8052+9252

62,700 (2)
Nu 1:39 number from the tribe of Dan was **62,700**. 547+2256+2256+4395+8679+9109+9252
2:26 His division numbers **62,700**. 547+2256+2256+4395+8679+9109+9252

64,300 (1)
Nu 26:25 those numbered were **64,300**. 547+752+2256+2256+4395+8993+9252

64,400 (1)
Nu 26:43 and those numbered were **64,400**. 547+752+752+2256+2256+4395+9252

70,000 (1)
2Ch 2:18 He assigned **70,000** of them 547+8679

72,000 (1)
Nu 31:33 **72,000** cattle, 547+2256+8679+9109

74,600 (2)
Nu 1:27 number from the tribe of Judah was **74,600**. 547+752+2256+2256+4395+8679+9252
2: 4 His division numbers **74,600**. 547+752+2256+2256+4395+8679+9252

76,500 (1)
Nu 26:22 of Judah; those numbered were **76,500**. 547+2256+2256+2822+4395+8679+9252

80,000 (1)
2Ch 2:18 and **80,000** to be stonecutters 547+9046

87,000 (1)

1Ch 7: 5 of Issachar, as listed in their genealogy, were **87,000** 547+2256+8679+9046

108,100 (1)

Nu 2:24 to their divisions, number **108,100.** 547+547+2256+2256+4395+4395+9046

120,000 (1)

1Ch 12:37 of Manasseh, armed with every type of weapon—**120,000.** 547+2256+4395+6929

144,000 (3)

Rev 7: 4 **144,000** from all the tribes of Israel. *1669+5475+5477+5942*
14: 1 and with him **144,000** who had his name *1669+5475+5477+5942*
14: 3 could learn the song except the **144,000** *1669+5475+5477+5942*

151,450 (1)

Nu 2:16 to their divisions, number **151,450.** 285+547+547+752+2256+2256 +2256+2256+2822+2822+4395+4395

153,600 (1)

2Ch 2:17 and they were found to be **153,600.** 547+547+2256+2256+2256 +2822+4395+4395+8993+9252

157,600 (1)

Nu 2:31 to the camp of Dan number **157,600.** 547+547+2256+2256+2256 +2822+4395+4395+8679+9252

180,000 (1)

2Ch 17:18 with **180,000** men armed for battle. 547+2256+4395+9046

186,400 (1)

Nu 2: 9 to their divisions, number **186,400.** 547+547+547+752+2256 +2256+2256+4395+4395+9046+9252

200,000 (2)

2Ch 17:16 the service of the LORD, with **200,000.** 547+4395
17:17 Eliada, a valiant soldier, with **200,000** 547+4395

280,000 (1)

2Ch 17:15 Jehohanan the commander, with **280,000;** 547+2256+4395+9046

300,000 (1)

2Ch 17:14 Adnah the commander, with **300,000** 547+4395+8993

307,500 (1)

2Ch 26:13 an army of **307,500** 547+547+2256+2256 +2822+4395+4395+8679+8993

337,500 (2)

Nu 31:36 who fought in the battle was: **337,500** sheep, 547+547+547+2256+2256+2256 +2822+4395+4395+8679+8993+8993
31:43 the community's half—was **337,500** sheep, 547+547+547+2256+2256 +2822+4395+4395+8679+8993+8993

601,730 (1)

Nu 26:51 The total number of the men of Israel was **601,730.** 547+547+2256+2256 +4395+4395+8679+8993+9252

603,550 (3)

Ex 38:26 a total of **603,550** men. 547+547+2256+2256+2256 +2822+2822+4395+4395+8993+9252
Nu 1:46 The total number was **603,550.** 547+547+2256+2256+2256 +2822+2822+4395+4395+8993+9252
2:32 by their divisions, number **603,550.** 547+547+2256+2256+2256 +2822+2822+4395+4395+8993+9252

675,000 (1)

Nu 31:32 spoils that the soldiers took was **675,000** sheep, 547+547+547+2256+2256 +2822+4395+8679+9252

INDEX OF ARTICLES, CONJUNCTIONS, PARTICLES, PREPOSITIONS, AND PRONOUNS

A (9144)

Ge 2:7, 8, 10, 18, 21, 22, 24; **3:**24; **4:**1, 11, 12, 14, 15, 17, 22, 23[2], 25, 26; **5:**3, 28; **6:**3, 9, 16[2]; **7:**2[2], 20, 24; **8:**1, 7, 8, 11; **9:**11[2], 12, 15, 20[2], 23; **10:**8, 9[2]; **11:**1, 2, 4[3]; **12:**2[2], 10[2], 11, 14; **14:**13, 20, 23[2]; **15:**1, 3, 4, 9[5], 12[2], 13, 15, 17[2], 18; **16:**2, 7, 11, 12[2], 15; **17:**5, 12, 16, 17[4], 19, 20, 27; **18:**4, 7[2], 8, 10, 13, 14, 18, 25; **19:**3, 8, 20, 26, 28, 30, 37, 38; **20:**1, 3[2], 5, 6, 7, 16; **21:**2, 5, 7, 8, 13, 14, 16, 18, 19[2], 21, 25, 27, 30, 33, 34; **22:**2, 12, 13[3], 15, 20; **23:**1, 4[2], 6, 9, 20; **24:**3, 4, 7, 14[2], 16, 17, 18, 19, 21, 22[2], 29, 31, 36, 37, 38, 40[2], 43[2], 45; **25:**7, 8, 17, 25, 27[3], 28; **26:**1, 3, 8[2], 12, 19, 25, 28[2], 30, 35; **27:**11[2], 12[2], 27, 34, 41, 44, 46; **28:**1, 2, 3, 6[2], 11, 12[2], 18, 20, 22[2]; **29:**2, 9, 12[2], 14, 15, 20, 22, 32, 33, 34, 35; **30:**3, 4, 5, 6, 7, 8, 9, 10, 12, 17, 19, 20, 21, 23, 36; **31:**10, 13[2], 24, 28, 44[2], 45[2], 46, 48, 50, 52[2], 54[2]; **32:**13, 18, 24; **33:**17, 19; **34:**7[2], 14[3], 30, 31; **35:**11[2], 14[2], 20, 28; **36:**6, 12; **37:**2[2], 3, 4, 5, 15, 20, 22, 25, 31; **38:**1, 2, 3, 4, 6, 8, 11, 12, 14, 15, 17[2], 23, 24, 25, 28; **39:**7, 9; **40:**5[2], 9, 15, 16[2], 19, 20; **41:**1, 5[2], 7, 11[2], 12[2], 15[2], 22, 33, 34, 42, 43; **42:**7; **43:**2, 11[3], 12, 30; **44:**5, 15, 17, 18, 19[2], 20, 25; **45:**7[2]; **46:**2, 3, 10, 29; **47:**9, 22, 24, 26[2], 28; **48:**4, 7, 19[2]; **49:**9[3], 11, 13, 14, 17[2], 19, 20, 21, 22[4], 27, 30; **50:**3, 9, 10, 11, 13, 15, 22, 26[2]; **Ex 1:**8, 16[2]; **2:**1[2], 2[2], 3, 4, 11, 15, 16, 22[2]; **3:**2, 8[2], 17, 18, 19; **4:**2, 3, 4, 20, 24, 25[2]; **5:**1, 3, 21[2]; **6:**8, 15; **7:**9[2], 10, 12, 15; **8:**23, 27, 31; **9:**3, 4, 5, 8, 10, 15, 19, 24; **10:**7, 9, 14, 19[2], 26; **11:**7[2]; **12:**3, 4, 13, 14[3], 16, 17, 22, 24, 30, 45[2]; **13:**3, 5, 6, 9[2], 13, 14, 16[2], 21[2]; **14:**21, 22, 29; **15:**3, 5, 8, 16, 20, 25[3]; **16:**13, 23[2], 25, 33, 35; **17:**12, 14; **18:**3, 12, 16; **19:**6[2], 9, 13[2], 16[2], 18; **20:**5, 6, 10, 18, 21, 25; **21:**2, 3, 4, 7[2], 9, 12, 13, 14, 18, 20[3], 21, 22, 26[2], 27, 28[3], 29, 31, 32, 33[3], 35; **22:**1[2], 2, 3, 5[2], 6, 7, 9[3], 10[3], 13, 14, 16[2], 18, 22, 25, 26; **23:**1[2], 2, 3, 7, 8[2], 14[2], 17, 18, 19, 26, 29, 32, 33; **24:**1, 10, 14, 17; **25:**8, 10[6], 11, 17[3], 23[4], 24, 25[3], 31, 35[2], 39; **26:**1, 6, 11, 13, 14[2], 16[2], 24, 31[2], 36; **27:**2, 4[3], 9[2], 11, 16, 18, 21; **28:**4[5], 6, 11[2], 12, 14, 15[2], 16[2], 17[3], 18[2], 19, 20[2], 21, 22, 29, 32[2], 36[2], 37, 42, 43; **29:**1, 3, 9, 14, 18[2], 23[3], 24, 25, 26, 31, 36[2], 38, 40[6], 41; **30:**2[2], 3, 9, 10, 12[2], 13, 15, 16, 18, 21, 24, 25[3], 33, 35[2]; **31:**13, 15, 16, 17; **32:**4[2], 5, 8, 9, 10, 11, 25, 27, 30, 31, 35; **33:**3, 3[3], 7, 11, 21[2], 22; **34:**9, 10, 12[2], 14, 15, 20, 23, 25, 26, 27, 33; **35:**2, 3, 22; **36:**8, 13, 18, 19[2], 21[2], 29, 35, 37; **37:**1[5], 2, 6[3], 10[3], 11, 12[3], 21[2], 25[2], 26, 29; **38:**2, 4[2], 9, 11, 23, 26[2]; **39:**3, 6, 8, 9[2], 10[3], 11[2], 12, 13[2], 14, 15, 22, 23[2], 27, 30, 31; **40:**15; **Lev 1:**3[2], 9, 10[2], 13, 14[3], 17; **2:**1, 2[2], 3, 4, 5, 6, 7, 10, 12, 14, 15; **3:**1, 3, 6[2], 7, 9, 12, 16, 17; **4:**3[2], 10, 12[2], 14[2], 22, 23, 24, 27, 28, 32[2], 33; **5:**1[2], 2, 4, 6[3], 7[4], 9, 10, 11[3], 12[3], 15[5], 16[2], 17, 18[2], 19; **6:**5, 6[2], 11, 15, 16, 20[2], 21, 23, 26, 27[2], 28, 29; **7:**5, 6[2], 8, 9[2], 11, 14, 16[2], 29, 30, 32; **8:**21[2], 26[2], 27, 28, 29; **9:**2[2], 3[6], 4[3], 8, 15, 17, 21; **10:**9, 13, 14, 15; **11:**3, 4[2], 5, 6, 7, 26, 33, 34, 36[2], 37, 38; **12:**2[2], 5, 6[6], 7[2], 8[3]; **13:**2[4], 6, 10, 11, 18, 19, 23, 24[2], 28[2], 29[2], 38, 39, 40, 41, 42, 49, 51; **14:**5, 10[2], 12[2], 21[4], 22[2], 24, 31[2], 34[2], 44, 50, 55, 56[3]; **15:**2, 4, 6, 7, 11, 12, 13, 15[2], 16, 18[2], 19, 24, 25[4], 30[2], 32[2], 33[6]; **16:**3[4], 5[3], 9, 10, 12, 21, 22, 24, 26, 29, 31[2], 34[2]; **17:**3[2], 7, 8, 11; **18:**17, 18, 19, 22[2], 23[2]; **19:**5[2], 10, 13, 14, 18, 20[3], 21[2], 29; **20:**10, 11, 12[2], 13[3], 14[2], 15, 16, 17[2], 18[2], 19, 20, 21, 24, 25, 27[2]; **21:**1, 2, 9[2], 11[2], 13, 14[4], 17, 19, 21; **22:**4[3], 10[7], 11[3], 12[2], 13[2], 14[2], 18[4], 19, 20, 21[3], 23[3], 25, 27[3], 28[2], 29[2]; **23:**3[3], 7, 8, 10, 12[3], 13[3], 14, 17, 18[2], 19[3], 20[2], 21[2], 24[2], 27, 31, 32, 35, 36, 39[2], 41[2]; **24:**3, 7, 8, 9[2], 10, 11, 17, 21; **25:**2, 4[2], 5, 8, 10, 11, 12, 21, 24, 26, 29[4], 30, 33, 35, 37, 39, 40[2], 47[2], 49, 50, 51, 52, 53; **26:**1[2], 8[2], 25, 36; **27:**2, 3, 4, 5[3], 6[3], 7[3], 10[4], 11, 13, 14, 15, 16[2], 19, 21, 22[2], 26, 27, 28, 30, 31[2], 33; **Nu 1:**2; **3:**15, 22, 28, 34, 39, 40[2], 43; **4:**2, 6, 7, 8, 9, 10[2], 11, 12[2], 13, 14, 20, 22; **5:**2[2], 6, 9, 12, 15[3], 17, 18, 19, 20, 22, 23, 24, 26[2], 27, 29, 30; **6:**2[4], 4, 6, 11[2], 12[2], 14[6], 15, 17, 19[3], 20; **7:**3, 13[2], 15[2], 16, 17[2], 19[2], 21[2], 22, 23[2], 25[2], 27[2], 28, 29[2], 31[2], 33[2], 34, 35[2], 37[2], 39[2], 40, 41[2], 43[2], 45[2], 46, 47[2], 49[2], 51[2], 52, 53[2], 55[2], 57[2], 58, 59[2], 61[2], 63[2], 64, 65[2], 67[2], 69[2], 70, 71[2], 73[2], 75[2], 76, 77[2], 79[2], 81[2], 82, 83[2], 85, 86, 87, 88; **8:**8[3], 11, 12[2], 13, 15, 21; **9:**6, 7, 10[2], 13[2], 19, 20, 22[2]; **10:**5, 6, 8, 9, 10, 33; **11:**8[3], 12, 20, 21, 27, 31[2], 33; **12:**1, 3, 5, 6, 12; **13:**11, 23[3], 32; **14:**4, 8, 12[2], 14[2], 24, 36, 37; **15:**2, 4[4], 5[3], 6[4], 7[3], 8[4], 9[2], 10[2], 15, 19, 20, 24[4], 25, 27[2], 29, 32, 38; **16:**3, 13, 14, 15, 29, 38, 40; **17:**10; **18:**6, 7, 16, 17[2], 23, 26; **19:**2[3], 9[2], 10, 14[2], 15, 16[4], 17, 18[4], 20, 21; **20:**16, 20; **21:**8[2], 9[3], 28; **22:**5, 6, 11[2], 12, 17, 23[2], 24, 26, 29[2], 32; **23:**2[2], 3, 4[2], 5, 9, 13, 14[2], 16, 19[2], 20, 22, 24[2], 30[2]; **24:**4, 6, 8, 9[2], 16, 17[2], 19, 21; **25:**6, 7, 13[2], 14, 15[2], 18[2]; **26:**2, 4, 10, 46, 54[4], 59, 62; **27:**8, 11, 16, 17, 18; **28:**3[2], 5[4], 6, 7[2], 9[2], 11[2], 12[2], 13[4], 14[6], 15, 17, 18, 19[2], 20, 22, 25, 26, 27[2], 28; **29:**1[2], 2[2], 3, 5, 6, 7, 8[2], 9, 11, 12[2], 13[2], 14, 16, 17, 19, 20, 22, 23, 25, 26, 28, 29, 31, 32, 34, 36[2], 38; **30:**2[3], 3[3], 6[2], 9, 10[3], 16[2]; **31:**4, 5, 6, 16, 17, 18, 35, 52, 54; **32:**14, 41; **33:**39, 54[4]; **34:**7, 10, 13, 15; **35:**6, 8, 11, 12, 15, 16[2], 17[2], 18[2], 21, 23, 30[2], 31[2], 32[2]; **Dt 1:**9, 11, 22, 25, 31, 33, 35, 44, 45; **2:**1, 9, 10, 19, 20, 21; **3:**5, 13, 14; **4:**6, 12, 16[2], 24[2], 25, 27, 31, 34, 42; **5:**2, 9, 10, 14, 15, 22, 24; **6:**3, 10, 15, 21; **7:**6, 8, 9, 16, 21, 26; **8:**5, 7[2], 8, 9[2]; **9:**3, 6, 12, 13, 14, 16, 21, 26; **10:**1, 7; **11:**9, 10, 11, 12, 26[2]; **12:**11; **13:**1[2], 16[2]; **14:**2, 6, 7[2], 8, 21[3], 22, 23; **15:**3, 7, 10, 12[3], 18[2], 21; **16:**2, 6, 10, 11, 16, 17, 19[2], 22; **17:**1, 2, 6, 14, 15[2], 18[4], 20; **18:**3[2], 6, 11, 13, 18, 20[2], 21, 22[2]; **19:**3, 5[2], 6, 11, 15[2], 16[3], 18[2]; **20:**5, 6, 7, 10, 15, 19[2]; **21:**1[2], 3[2], 4[2], 11, 13, 14, 15, 17, 18[2], 20[2], 22[3], 23; **22:**5[2], 6[2], 7, 8[2], 10, 13[2], 14, 15, 17, 19[2], 21, 22, 23[3], 24, 25[2], 28[2], 30; **23:**2, 4, 5, 6, 10, 12, 13, 15, 17, 18[2], 20[2], 21, 22, 25; **24:**1[3], 3, 5, 6[3], 7[2], 10[2], 13, 14[2], 17, 19, 20; **25:**1, 5[2], 7[2]; **26:**2[2], 5[3], 8, 9, 12, 15, 19; **27:**3, 14, 15, 25; **28:**8, 25, 29, 30[3], 32, 33, 36, 37, 46[2], 49[2], 50, 65, 68; **29:**4, 12[2], 19[2], 23; **31:**2, 15, 19, 24, 26; **32:**4, 5, 10[2], 20, 21[2], 22, 28, 30, 52; **33:**17[2], 20, 22, 28, 29; **34:**7; **Jos 2:**1, 9, 12, 15, 19; **3:**4[2], 13, 16[3]; **4:**5, 6, 7; **5:**6, 13[2]; **6:**5[2], 10[2], 20, 23; **7:**3, 15, 21[2], 26; **8:**14, 17, 28[2], 29[2], 35; **9:**4[2], 6[2], 7, 9, 11, 15, 22, 23; **10:**1, 10, 13, 14[3], 20, 21; **11:**4[2], 18, 19; **14:**7; **15:**13, 18, 19, 32; **17:**14; **18:**4[2], 7, 8[2], 9, 14; **20:**3, 4; **21:**13, 21, 27, 32, 38; **22:**3, 8, 14, 17, 25, 27, 28, 34; **23:**1, 10; **24:**7, 9, 13, 19[2], 25, 26, 27[2], 29, 32; **Jdg 1:**14, 15, 24, 26; **2:**2, 3, 8, 18; **3:**9, 15[2], 16[3], 17, 19, 20, 25, 27, 29; **4:**2, 4, 9, 16, 18, 19[2], 21[2]; **5:**7, 8, 14, 25, 30; **6:**4, 8, 11, 17, 19[3], 26[2], 31, 34, 37, 38; **7:**5, 13[4], 20; **8:**10[2], 14, 16, 18, 20, 25[2], 27, 31, 32; **9:**8, 18, 27, 37, 44, 49, 51, 53, 54; **10:**1; **11:**1[2], 3, 30, 31, 35, 39; **12:**2, 5, 7; **13:**2[2], 3, 5[2], 6, 7[2], 15, 16, 19[2], 23, 24; **14:**1, 2, 3, 5, 6, 8, 10, 12, 16, 18; **15:**1, 3, 4, 8, 15[3], 16[3]; **16:**1, 4, 9[2], 10, 13, 15, 17, 19, 23; **17:**1, 2, 3[2], 4, 5, 7, 9[2], 10; **18:**1, 7, 10[2], 14[2], 19[2], 27, 28[2]; **19:**1[3], 18, 24, 29, 30; **20:**10[3], 16[2], 34, 37, 38; **21:**1, 5, 11, 12, 15, 17, 18[2], 21, 22; **Ru 1:**1[3], 12; **2:**1[2], 3, 7, 9, 10, 11; **3:**1, 2, 8, 9, 11, 12, 14; **4:**13, 14, 17; **1Sa 1:**1[2], 5, 9, 11[2], 15, 16, 20, 24[2]; **2:**3, 8, 13[2], 18[2], 19, 24, 25[2], 27, 34, 35, 36[2]; **3:**8, 20; **4:**5, 7, 12, 13, 20; **5:**9; **6:**3, 7, 8[2], 14[2], 17, 18; **7:**2, 9[2], 10, 11, 12, 16; **8:**5, 6, 10, 15, 17, 19, 20, 22; **9:**1[2], 2[2], 6, 8[2], 9[2], 12, 16, 21[2], 27; **10:**1, 3, 5[2], 6, 10, 12[2], 19, 23, 25; **11:**1, 2, 7, 15; **12:**1, 2, 3, 12, 13, 17, 19; **13:**2, 4, 14, 19, 21[3], 22[2], 23; **14:**2, 3, 4, 12, 15, 28, 29, 33, 39, 43, 45, 52; **15:**12, 18, 29; **16:**2, 12, 18[4], 20[3]; **17:**4, 5[2], 6, 7, 8[2], 10, 20, 33[2], 34[3], 38[2], 42, 43, 46, 49, 50[3], 52; **18:**3, 5, 9, 10, 13, 17, 21[2], 23[2], 25; **19:**2, 5, 12, 13, 20, 21; **20:**3, 8, 16, 20, 21, 29, 30, 35; **21:**2[2], 8[2], 9, 13; **22:**8, 13, 17, 20; **23:**7, 17, 18, 27; **24:**3, 4, 5, 6, 14[2], 19; **25:**2[2], 3, 8, 16, 17, 18, 20, 28, 29, 36[2], 37, 42; **26:**9, 11, 12, 13, 15, 20[2], 21, 23; **27:**5, 7, 9, 11; **28:**7[2], 8, 9, 13, 14, 24; **29:**3; **30:**11, 12, 25, 26; **31:**13; **2Sa 1:**2; **2:**18, 25[2], 28; **3:**1, 7, 8, 14, 20, 21, 22[2], 29[2], 38[2]; **4:**4, 10; **5:**3, 11; **6:**3, 13[2], 14, 16, 19[3]; **7:**2[2], 5, 6[2], 7, 10[2], 11, 13, 23[2], 27; **8:**2, 4[2], 8; **9:**2, 3, 8, 12; **10:**2, 6[2]; **11:**2, 8, 10, 11, 14, 16, 18, 21, 27; **12:**1, 2, 3, 4[2], 6, 24, 30[2]; **13:**2, 3[2], 12, 16, 18, 20, 22, 25; **14:**2[2], 5, 6, 12, 13, 14, 25, 27[2], 29; **15:**1, 2[2], 4, 7, 13, 17, 19, 27, 33; **16:**1[5], 5, 8, 21, 22; **17:**8, 9[2], 10[2], 13[2], 16, 17, 18[3], 19, 25; **18:**2[3], 9, 11, 12, 17[2], 18[2], 21, 22, 24, 27; **19:**7, 17, 28, 32[2], 36, 43; **20:**1[2], 3, 8[2], 12[3], 15, 16, 19[2], 21; **21:**1, 2, 9, 10, 15, 16, 19[3], 20; **22:**20, 30[2], 31, 34, 35; **23:**4, 7[2], 8, 10, 11[2], 12, 13, 15, 20[4], 21[3]; **24:**1, 3[2], 9, 10, 15; **1Ki 1:**2, 3[2], 42, 48, 52[2]; **2:**1, 2, 4, 9, 19, 24, 36, 38; **3:**2, 4, 5, 6, 7, 8, 9, 12, 14, 15[2], 17, 18, 24[2]; **4:**5, 23, 29, 32; **5:**3, 5, 7, 12, 14, 17; **6:**5, 8, 23; **7:**2, 3, 6[2], 8, 9, 12, 14[3], 17, 23, 24, 26[3], 30, 31[3], 32[2], 35[2]; **8:**9, 12, 13[2], 16[2], 17, 18, 21, 25, 31, 38, 41, 47, 55, 63[2], 65; **9:**2, 5, 7, 8, 13, 16, 25; **10:**2, 18, 19[2], 22, 25, 29[3]; **11:**7[2], 17, 18, 19, 20, 24, 26, 28, 29, 36, 38; **12:**4, 7[2], 10, 11, 21, 30, 32, 33; **13:**1, 2, 3, 7, 11, 18, 24, 33; **14:**3, 7, 14, 15; **15:**4[2], 13, 19[2], 27; **16:**11, 15, 24; **17:**9, 10[4], 11, 12[6], 13, 24; **18:**1, 3, 4, 10[2], 13, 27, 32, 34, 41, 44[2], 45; **19:**2, 4[2], 6[2], 7, 9, 11, 12[2], 13; **20:**10, 13, 28[2], 29, 33, 34[2], 36[2], 39[2], 42; **21:**1, 2[2], 9[2], 12[2], 19, 25; **22:**7, 17, 21, 22, 23, 36, 38, 47, 48; **2Ki 1:**6, 8[3], 9[2], 10, 12, 13; **2:**1, 7, 9, 10, 11[2], 20, 24; **3:**4[2], 9, 15, 25, 27; **4:**1, 2, 3, 6, 8[2], 9, 10[5], 13, 16, 17, 19, 22, 28, 38, 39, 42, 43; **5:**1[2], 2, 5, 7, 8, 10, 12, 14, 15, 16, 17, 22; **6:**2[2], 5, 6, 8, 14, 23, 25[4], 26, 32; **7:**1[3], 5, 6, 9, 10[2], 16[3], 18[3]; **8:**1[2], 8, 9, 11, 13[2], 15, 18, 19, 26; **9:**1, 5, 17, 19, 20, 30, 34; **10:**2, 6, 10, 18, 19, 27; **11:**2, 4[2], 5, 6[2], 9, 12, 15, 17[2]; **12:**9[2], 10; **13:**3, 5, 15, 21[2]; **14:**9[4], 13; **15:**5, 19; **16:**8, 10, 17; **17:**4, 21, 35; **18:**17, 21[2], 23, 32[4]; **19:**3, 7[2], 9, 20, 30, 31[2], 32, 35; **20:**7, 10, 12, 14; **21:**13; **22:**10; **23:**25, 30, 33[3]; **24:**14, 16; **25:**17[2], 28, 30; **1Ch 1:**10; **2:**3; **4:**33; **5:**2, 6, 18; **6:**57, 67; **7:**15, 16, 23; **9:**4, 14, 31; **10:**13; **11:**3, 11, 13[2], 14, 15, 17, 22[4], 23[4]; **12:**4[2], 14[3], 20, 22, 28; **13:**7; **14:**1; **15:**1[2], 25, 27[2], 29; **16:**3[3], 15, 17; **17:**1[2], 4, 5, 6, 9[2], 10, 12, 21[2], 25; **18:**4[2], 8; **19:**2, 6[2]; **20:**2[2], 5[3], 6; **21:**1, 3, 5, 8, 14, 16, 24; **22:**3, 6, 7, 8, 9[2], 10, 14[2]; **24:**3[2], 4, 6; **26:**14, 17[4], 24, 31; **27:**3, 6, 11, 12, 13, 18, 32[3]; **28:**2[2], 3[2], 9, 10[2]; **29:**7, 15, 16, 21[3], 22, 28; **2Ch 1:**4, 6, 9, 11, 17[3]; **2:**1[2], 3, 4[2], 6[3], 7, 12[3], 13, 17; **3:**10, 15, 16; **4:**1, 2, 3, 5[3], 8; **5:**10, 13; **6:**1, 2[2], 5[2], 7, 8, 13, 16, 22, 29, 32, 36, 37; **7:**5[2], 8, 12, 13, 18, 20, 21; **9:**1, 17, 18[2], 21, 24; **10:**4, 7, 10, 11; **11:**1; **13:**2, 3[2], 5, 8, 9[2]; **14:**9, 13[2]; **15:**3[2], 12, 16; **16:**3, 8, 9, 12, 14[2]; **17:**17; **18:**6, 16, 20, 21, 22; **19:**6; **20:**2, 3, 8, 14, 25, 36; **21:**6, 7, 12, 14, 15, 17; **22:**2, 9, 11; **23:**1[2], 3, 4, 5[2], 9, 11, 14, 16; **24:**8, 9, 11[2], 15, 24[2], 26; **25:**6[2], 7, 10, 12, 15, 18[4], 23; **26:**11, 13, 19, 21, 23; **27:**5; **28:**6, 8, 9[2]; **29:**10, 21, 24, 32; **30:**5, 13, 24[3]; **31:**5[2], 6[2], 12; **32:**4, 7, 24; **33:**11; **34:**18; **35:**5, 7, 18, 25; **36:**3[3], 4, 22, 23; **Ezr 1:**1, 2; **2:**61[2], 63; **3:**11; **4:**1, 3, 7, 8, 11, 15[3], 19[3], 24; **5:**1, 5, 6, 11, 13, 14, 17[2]; **6:**2, 3[2], 11[2], 12, 14, 17[2]; **7:**6, 11[2], 12, 21, 22[4], **8:**18, 20, 21[2], 28, 35[2]; **9:**8[4], 9, 11, 12, 13[2], 15; **10:**1, 3, 7, 12, 13, 14[2], 19[2]; **Ne 1:**9; **2:**6, 8, 12; **3:**9, 12, 16[2], 19, 26; **4:**2, 3, 4, 9, 17; **5:**1, 7, 13, 15, 17; **6:**1, 3, 7, 11, 13[2]; **7:**2, 63[2], 65; **8:**4, 11; **9:**3, 8, 10, 11, 12[2], 17[2], 18, 29, 31, 38; **10:**29, 32[2], 34, 37, 38[2]; **11:**4, 5; **13:**2[2], 5, 7, 13; **Est 1:**3, 4, 5, 6, 9, 19; **2:**2, 5, 7, 12, 17, 18[2], 19, 23; **3:**1, 4, 6, 7, 8, 9, 13, 14; **4:**8, 14; **5:**4, 14; **6:**8[3]; **7:**5, 7, 9; **8:**13, 15[3], 16; **9:**17, 18, 19[2], 22; **10:**2; **Job 1:**1, 3, 5[2], 8, 10, 12, 14, 19; **2:**3, 4, 8, 10, 12, 13; **3:**3, 5, 16, 23; **4:**2, 12[2], 15, 16[2], 17[2], 19; **5:**2, 3, 4, 23; **6:**5, 14, 22, 26; **7:**1, 2[2], 6, 7, 9, 20; **8:**2, 9, 14, 16, 17[2], 20; **9:**2, 3, 16, 17, 19[2], 23, 24, 25[2], 31, 32; **10:**4, 5[2], 16, 20; **11:**10, 12[3], 20; **12:**3, 4[2], 18, 24; **13:**25, 28; **14:**2[2], 3, 6, 7, 9, 11, 13, 14, 17, 18[2]; **15:**2, 24, 26, 30, 33; **16:**8, 14, 21[2], 22; **17:**5, 6[2], 7, 10; **18:**8, 9[2], 10[2]; **19:**10, 12, 15, 23; **20:**3, 5, 8[2], 24, 26, 28; **21:**11, 18, 19, 33; **22:**2[2], 8, 11, 16; **24:**9, 14, 20, 23, 24; **25:**4, 6[3]; **26:**10; **27:**13, 18[3], 20[2]; **28:**1[2], 4, 22, 26[2]; **29:**16, 25; **30:**8, 9, 14, 15, 24[2], 29[3]; **31:**1[4], 9, 11, 12, 13, 18, 19[2], 27, 30, 36, 37; **32:**8; **33:**15[2], 19[2], 23[3], 24, 25, 29; **34:**6, 9, 11, 30, 31, 36; **35:**8, 9; **36:**2, 16, 18, 22; **37:**6, 18; **38:**3, 5, 14[2], 25[2], 26[2], 27, 28, 34, 40; **39:**7, 10, 15, 17, 19, 20, 28[2]; **40:**7, 17; **41:**1[2], 2[2], 5[3], 8, 11, 13, 20[2], 24, 29[2], 30[2], 31[2], 32, 33; **42:**8, 11[2], 12[2], 16; **Ps 1:**3; **2:**12; **3:**T, 3; **4:**T; **5:**T, 4, 9, 12; **6:**T; **7:**T[2], 2, 11[2], 15; **8:**T, 5; **9:**T, 9[2]; **10:**9; **11:**1, 6; **12:**T, 6; **13:**T; **15:**T, 4, 5; **16:**T, 6; **17:**T, 12[2]; **18:**19, 29[2], 30, 33, 34; **19:**T, 4, 5[2]; **20:**T; **21:**T, 3, 9; **22:**T, 6[2], 15, 16, 31; **23:**T, 5; **24:**T, 4; **26:**1, 11; **27:**5, 11; **28:**1, 8; **29:**T, 6[2]; **30:**T[2], 5[3]; **31:**T, 2, 8, 11, 21; **32:**T; **33:**3, 17[2]; **34:**19; **35:**7; **36:**4; **37:**10, 23, 35[2], 37; **38:**T[2], 4, 13[2], 14; **39:**T, 1, 5[2], 6, 11[2], 12; **40:**T, 2[2], 3[2]; **41:**T, 8; **42:**T, 8; **44:**T, 12, 13, 14, 19, 20; **45:**T[2], 1[2], 6, 12; **46:**T, 4; **47:**T, 7; **48:**T[2], 6; **49:**T, 4, 7, 8, 16, 20; **50:**T, 3[2], 5, 9, 10, 18; **51:**T, 10[2], 12, 17[2]; **52:**T, 1, 2; **53:**T; **54:**T, 6; **55:**T, 6, 12, 13; **56:**T[2]; **57:**T, 6[2]; **58:**T, 4[2], 8[2], 11; **59:**T; **60:**T, 4; **61:**3; **62:**T, 3, 9[4]; **63:**T, 1; **64:**T, 6; **65:**T[2]; **66:**T[2], 12; **67:**T[2]; **68:**T[2], 5[2], 6, 20; **69:**8, 22[2], 31; **70:**T; **71:**7; **72:**6; **73:**T, 20, 22; **74:**T, 5;

75:T^2, 6, 8; 76:T^2; 77:T, 20; 78:T, 8, 13, 16, 19, 23, 39, 49, 50, 52, 57, 65; 79:T; 80:T, 1, 6, 8; 81:4, 5^2, 7; 82:T; 83:T^2, 4, 14; 84:T, 3^3, 6, 10^2, 11; 85:T; 86:T, 14, 15, 17; 87:T^2; 88:T^3, 4, 17; 89:T, 3, 19^3, 45; 90:T, 4^3, 9, 12; 91:7, 12; 92:T^2, 10, 12^2; 94:13, 16, 20; 95:10; 96:1; 98:T, 1; 99:8; 100:T; 101:T, 2, 5; 102:T, 6, 7^2, 8, 18^2, 26; 103:13, 15; 104:2^2, 6, 9, 18; 105:8, 10, 17^2, 39^3, 41; 106:9, 15, 18, 19, 20, 29, 36; 107:4, 7^2, 25, 29, 33, 34, 36, 37, 40; 108:T^2; 109:T, 4, 9, 11, 16, 17, 19^2, 23, 29; 110:T, 1, 4, 7; 112:6; 113:9; 114:1, 8; 115:7; 116:17; 119:9, 19, 63, 83, 96, 105^2, 110, 164, 176; 120:T, 4, 7; 121:T; 122:T, 3; 123:T, 2; 124:T, 7; 125:T; 126:T; 127:T, 3^2, 4; 128:T, 3; 129:T; 130:T, 3; 131:T, 2^2; 132:T, 2, 5^2, 11, 17^2; 133:T; 134:T; 136:12; 137:4; 139:T, 4; 140:T, 3, 5; 141:T, 3, 5^2; 142:T^2, 3; 143:T, 6; 144:4^2, 9, 12; 145:T; 147:10; 148:6, 14; 149:1, 6; Pr 1:3, 9^2, 14, 17, 27^2; 2:7; 3:4, 12, 18, 30, 31, 32; 4:1, 3, 9^2, 22; 5:4, 8, 19^2, 21, 22; 6:5^2, 10^3, 11, 12^2, 17, 18, 19^2, 23^2, 26, 27, 28, 30, 32, 34; 7:7, 10^2, 13, 19, 22^2, 23^2, 26, 27; 9:7^2, 8^2, 9^2, 12, 14; 10:1^2, 4, 5^2, 7, 8, 10, 11, 13, 14, 18, 23^2, 26, 29, 31; 11:5, 7, 11, 12^2, 13^4, 14, 16, 17^2, 18, 22^3, 25, 28, 30; 12:2^2, 3, 4^2, 8, 9^2, 10, 13, 14, 15^2, 16^2, 17^2, 18, 19^2, 23, 25^2, 26; 13:1^2, 2^2, 8^2, 12^2, 13, 14^2, 16, 17^2, 19, 20, 22^2, 23; 14:3^2, 5^2, 7, 12^2, 15^2, 16^2, 17^2, 23, 25^2, 26^2, 27^2, 28^3, 29^2, 30, 32, 34^2, 35^3; 15:1^2, 4^2, 5, 12, 13, 14, 15, 16, 17^2, 18^3, 19, 20^2, 21^3, 23^2, 27, 30, 31, 33; 16:2, 4, 6, 7, 8, 9, 10, 12, 13, 14^3, 15^2, 18^2, 22, 23, 24, 25^2, 27^2, 28^2, 29^2, 31^2, 32^4; 17:1^2, 2^2, 4^3, 6, 7^2, 8^2, 10^4, 11, 12^2, 13, 14^3, 16, 17^2, 18, 19^2, 20, 21^3, 22^2, 23^2, 24^2, 25, 27^2, 28; 18:2, 4^2, 6^2, 7^2, 8^2, 10, 12, 14^2, 16, 19^2, 20, 22, 23^2, 24^3; 19:1^2, 3, 4, 5, 6^2, 7, 9, 10^2, 11, 12^2, 13^3, 14, 18, 19, 21, 22^2, 25^2, 26, 28; 20:1^2, 2^2, 3, 4, 5^2, 6^2, 7, 8, 11, 15, 16^2, 17^2, 19^3, 20, 24, 25^2, 26, 27, 28; 21:1, 2, 4, 6^4, 9^3, 11^2, 13, 14^2, 16, 18, 19^2, 20, 22, 28, 29^2; 22:1, 3, 6, 9, 11, 13, 14, 15, 24, 26, 29; 23:1, 2, 5, 6, 9, 13, 18, 24^2, 27^4, 28, 32^2; 24:3, 5^2, 7, 8, 9, 14, 15, 16, 26, 32, 33^3, 34; 25:2^2, 6, 7, 9, 11, 12^2, 13, 14, 15^3, 18^3, 19^2, 20^3, 23^2, 24^3, 25^2, 26^3, 28^2; 26:1, 2^2, 3^3, 4, 5, 6^2, 7^3, 8^3, 9^4, 10, 11^2, 12^2, 13^2, 14^2, 17^3, 18, 19, 20^2, 21, 22^2, 23, 24, 27^4, 28^2; 27:1, 3^2, 6, 8^2, 10^2, 13^2, 14^2, 15^3, 18, 19^2, 22^3, 24, 26; 28:1, 2^2, 3^2, 6^2, 7^2, 9, 10, 11^2, 15^4, 16^2, 17^2, 20, 21^2, 22, 23^2, 25, 26; 29:1, 3^2, 4^2, 5, 6, 8, 9^2, 10, 11^2, 12, 14, 15, 19, 20^2, 21, 22, 23^2, 24, 25, 26; 30:2, 5, 6, 10, 17^2, 19^5, 22^2, 23, 28, 30, 31^3; 31:10, 16^2, 30; Ecc 1:13, 14, 17; 2:8, 11, 17, 19^2, 21^2, 22, 24, 26; 3:1^2, 2^4, 3^4, 4^4, 5^4, 6^4, 7^4, 8^4, 17^2, 22; 4:4, 8^2, 9, 12, 13, 16; 5:3^2, 4, 5, 6, 8^2, 12^2, 13, 14, 15, 16^2, 18, 19; 6:2^3, 3^3, 6, 8^3, 9, 12^2; 7:1, 2^2, 3, 5, 7^3, 8, 11, 12^2, 14, 15^2, 17, 19, 20, 26^2, 28; 8:1, 3^2, 4, 6^2, 9^2, 11, 12^3, 13, 15, 17; 9:2, 4^2, 6, 7, 12^2, 14^3, 15, 17; 10:1^2, 4, 5, 8^3, 11, 12^2, 15, 16, 17, 18, 19, 20^2; 11:3, 5, 8; SS 1:7, 9, 13, 14; 2:1^2, 2, 9^2, 17^2; 3:6; 4:1, 2, 3^2, 4, 5, 12^3, 15^2; 5:11; 6:5, 6, 7; 7:1, 2^2, 3; 8:1, 6^3, 8, 9^2, 10, 11^2, 14^2; Isa 1:4^2, 8^5, 14, 21, 30, 31; 2:12, 22; 3:6^2, 24^3; 4:4^2, 5^3, 6^2; 5:1^3, 2^3, 6, 10^3, 23, 26, 27^2, 28; 6:1, 5^2, 6, 13; 7:8, 11, 14^2, 17, 20, 21^2, 23^2; 8:1, 3, 14^5, 19; 9:2^2, 6^2, 8, 14, 18^2; 10:6^2, 13, 14^2, 15^2, 16^3, 17^3, 18, 19, 21^2, 22, 24^2, 26; 11:1^2, 6, 10, 11, 12, 15, 16; 13:2^2, 4^2, 8, 9, 14^2; 14:17, 19^2, 21, 23, 29^2, 31^2; 15:1^2, 9; 16:3, 5^2, 11, 14; 17:1^2, 5^2, 13; 18:2^2, 3^2, 4, 5, 7^2; 19:1, 4^2, 11, 14^2, 19, 20^2, 22, 23, 24; 20:3; 21:1, 2, 3, 4, 6, 9^3, 16; 22:5^2, 11, 16, 18^2, 21, 23^3; 23:10, 13^2, 15, 16^2, 17; 24:6, 9, 18^2, 20^2, 22; 25:2^3, 4^6, 5, 6^2, 11; 26:1, 10, 16, 17, 20; 27:2, 8, 11, 13; 28:1, 2^4, 4^2, 5^2, 6^2, 8, 10^2, 13^2, 15^2, 16^4, 24, 27^4; 29:6, 7^2, 8^2, 10, 11, 17^3, 21^2; 30:5, 6, 8^2, 13, 14^3, 17^5, 18, 21, 22, 27, 28^2, 29, 33; 31:4^3, 8^2; 32:1, 2^4, 10, 13, 14^2, 15^2; 33:4, 6, 11, 17, 20^2, 21; 34:3, 4, 6^2, 8^2, 12, 13^2; 35:6, 7, 8; 36:2, 6^2, 8, 17^3; 37:3, 7^2, 9, 21, 31, 32^2, 33, 36; 38:9, 12^2, 13, 14^2, 21; 39:1, 3; 40:3^2, 4, 6, 9^2, 11, 12^2, 15^2, 19^2, 20^2, 22^2, 24; 41:3, 15, 16, 25, 27; 42:3^2, 6^2, 10, 13^3, 14^2, 22; 43:16^2, 17, 19^2; 44:4, 10, 12, 13^3, 14^2, 15^2, 17, 19^2, 20^2, 22; 45:4, 9, 13, 15, 19, 21^2, 23; 46:1, 6^2, 11^3; 47:1, 6, 8, 9^2, 11^3; 48:8, 18; 49:2^2, 6^2, 8, 15, 18; 50:2^2, 9; 51:4, 6, 8, 10, 20, 23; 53:2^2, 3, 7^2, 9, 10, 12; 54:1^2, 6^2, 7, 8^2, 16; 55:4^2; 56:3, 5^2, 7; 57:3, 4, 7, 8, 13, 15; 58:1, 2, 5^5, 11^3, 13; 59:5, 14, 15, 17, 19; 60:22^2; 61:3^4, 7^2, 9, 10^4, 11; 62:1, 2, 3^2, 5^3, 10; 63:13, 14, 18; 64:6, 10^3; 65:1, 3, 5, 8, 10^2, 11, 15, 16, 17, 18^2, 20^4, 22, 23; 66:3^5, 7, 8^5, 12^2, 13, 15, 19; Jer 1:5, 6, 7, 13, 18^2; 2:2^2, 6^3, 7, 11, 14^2, 20, 21^2, 23, 24, 26, 30, 31^2, 32^2; 3:1^2, 2, 3, 14^2, 18, 19, 20, 21, 23; 4:2, 7^2, 11, 12, 13, 15, 16^3, 17, 20, 26, 31^3; 5:6^3, 9, 14, 15^2, 19, 22, 29, 30; 6:7, 9, 20, 22, 24, 25, 27; 7:11, 12, 29; 8:4, 6, 15, 19; 9:1^2, 2^2, 3, 4^2, 8^2, 9, 10, 11^2, 12, 20; 10:3^2, 5^2, 14, 22^2, 23; 11:5, 9, 11, 16^2, 19, 23; 12:1, 6, 8, 9, 10, 11; 13:1, 2, 3, 4, 11^2, 21; 14:2, 8^3, 9^2, 17^2, 18, 19; 15:7, 8, 10, 11, 12, 14^2, 18^2, 20^2; 16:5^2, 7^3, 8, 10, 13; 17:1, 4, 6^2, 8^2, 10, 11^2, 12, 17, 21, 22; 18:7, 9, 11^2, 13, 17, 20, 22^2; 19:1^2, 3, 4; 20:4, 9^2, 11, 15^2, 16; 21:5, 6, 14; 22:5, 6, 8, 14, 15, 19, 23, 24, 28^2, 30; 23:5^2, 9^2, 14, 19, 23^2, 25^2, 28, 29^2, 33^2, 34^2, 37; 24:7, 9^2; 25:11, 18, 29, 32, 38; 26:2, 18^3, 19, 23; 27:2, 4, 17; 28:13^2; 29:11, 23, 26, 27, 28, 31; 30:2, 6^2, 7, 10, 23; 31:6, 8, 9, 10, 12, 15, 22^3, 31, 32, 34^2, 36; 32:14^2, 21, 22, 35, 43; 33:1, 10, 15, 17, 18, 21, 24; 34:5^2, 8, 9, 13, 15; 35:7, 13, 19; 36:2, 6, 9, 22, 23, 26; 37:15, 16^3; 38:7, 9, 11; 39:3^2, 13^2; 40:5, 11, 16; 41:7, 8; 42:2, 5, 20; 43:12; 44:7, 14, 15, 22; 45:1; 46:10, 17, 20^2, 22, 27; 48:6, 8, 10^2, 28^2, 36^2, 38, 41, 42, 44^2, 45^2; 49:2, 9, 13, 14, 19^2, 22, 24, 30, 31^2, 33^2, 36; 50:2, 3, 11, 12^3, 17, 24, 32, 35, 36^2, 37^2, 38^2, 41, 43, 44^2; 51:1, 7, 12, 14, 17, 25, 26^2, 27^3, 33, 34, 37^3, 39, 41, 43^2, 50, 54, 56^2, 60, 63; 52:22, 23, 32, 34; La 1:1^2, 13, 14; 2:3, 4, 6, 7, 8, 18, 22; 3:10^2, 27, 35, 36, 44, 52, 53, 65; 4:2, 6^2, 8, 11, 17; 5:4; Eze 1:4, 5, 7, 8, 10^2, 15, 16^2, 25, 26^3, 28^2; 2:3, 5^2, 6, 9^2; 3:5, 9, 12, 13, 17, 18, 20^2, 26, 27; 4:1, 2, 3, 6, 9, 11^2, 12; 5:1^3, 2^3, 3, 4^2, 12^3, 14^2, 15^3; 6:3, 14; 7:11, 26; 8:2^2, 3, 7, 8, 11^2, 17; 9:1^2, 2^3, 4; 10:1, 3, 6, 8, 10^2, 14^3, 21; 11:3, 11, 13, 16^2, 19^2; 12:2^2, 3, 6, 11, 12, 16; 13:6, 10, 13, 19; 14:4^2, 7^2, 8, 9, 13, 17, 19; 15:2^2; 16:3, 7, 8, 11, 12^2, 13, 15, 24^2, 29, 30, 31, 33, 40, 41, 45^3; 17:2, 3^2, 4^2, 5, 6^2, 8, 9, 13^2, 15, 22^4, 23; 18:5, 6, 7, 10, 13, 14, 16^2, 21, 24, 26, 27, 31^2; 19:1, 2, 3, 5, 6, 9, 10, 11, 13, 14^3; 20:6^2, 12, 15, 20, 33, 34; 21:9^2, 14^2, 19, 22, 23, 27^3, 28^2; 22:4^2, 11, 18, 20^2, 22, 24, 25^2, 30; 23:7, 10, 14, 19, 24, 27, 32, 41, 42, 43, 44, 46; 24:3, 5, 24, 26, 27; 25:4, 5^2, 10; 26:4, 5, 7, 8, 10, 14^2, 17^2, 19, 21; 27:2, 5^2, 32, 36; 28:2^5, 6, 8, 9^3, 12, 14, 17, 18, 19, 23; 29:6, 8, 9, 10^2, 14, 16^2, 18, 20, 21; 30:3^2, 4, 13, 21^2, 24; 31:3, 14; 32:2^3, 3, 7, 25; 33:2, 7, 15, 18, 19, 21, 27, 28, 29, 32, 33; 34:8, 12^2, 14^2, 25, 29; 35:3, 7; 36:17, 26^3; 37:1, 2, 7^2, 10, 16, 19, 26; 38:4, 8, 9^2, 11^2, 15^2, 16, 19, 21; 39:11, 13, 15^2, 16; 40:2^2, 3^3, 5^3, 12, 17, 19, 23^2, 24, 27^2, 38^2, 42^5, 43, 47^2, 49; 41:7, 8, 13^2, 14, 15, 19^2, 21, 22, 25; 42:2, 4, 8, 11, 12, 20; 43:8, 13^5, 14^2, 17^4, 19^2, 22^2, 23^2, 24, 25^4; 44:25^2, 27, 30; 45:1^2, 2, 3, 4^2, 11^4, 13^2, 14^3, 18, 21, 22^2, 23^3, 24^2; 46:4, 5, 6^2, 7^2, 11^3, 12^2, 13^2, 14^5, 15, 16, 17, 19, 23; 47:3^2, 5^2, 7, 20; 48:8, 12^2, 20^2; Da 1:5; 2:3, 10^2, 15, 19, 25, 28, 31, 34, 35^3, 39, 40, 41, 43, 44, 45^2, 47, 48; 3:6, 10, 11, 15, 25, 27; 4:5, 10, 13^2, 14, 16, 19, 23^2, 31, 33; 5:1^2, 5, 7, 11, 12, 16, 29; 6:6, 10, 11, 12, 13, 15, 17, 26; 7:1, 4^3, 5^2, 6^2, 7, 8^3, 10, 12, 13, 20, 23, 25^2; 8:1, 3, 5^2, 13, 15, 16, 18, 23^2; 9:1, 15^2, 25, 26, 27^2; 10:1^3, 5^2, 6, 9, 10, 14, 16, 18; 11:2, 3, 10, 11^2, 13, 15, 17, 18, 20^2, 21, 22, 23, 24, 25^2, 33, 34, 38^2, 39^2, 40^2, 44; 12:1, 7^2; Hos 1:3, 6; 2:3^2, 12, 15, 18; 3:2^2, 3; 4:1, 4^2, 12^3, 14, 16^2, 19; 5:1^2, 4, 10, 12, 14^2; 6:8, 9, 10, 11; 7:6, 8, 11, 16; 8:6, 8, 9; 9:1, 7^2, 11, 13; 10:1, 3, 4, 7, 11^2; 11:1, 10; 12:1, 2, 3, 11, 12, 13^2; 13:3^2, 7^2, 8^3, 10, 11, 13^2; 14:5^2, 6, 7, 8; Joel 1:6^3, 8, 14^2; 2:2^3, 3^2, 5^3, 14, 15^2, 17, 20; 3:8, 16^2, 18, 19; Am 1:9, 11, 14; 2:6, 13; 3:4, 5^3, 6^3, 12^2; 4:5, 11; 5:3^3, 6, 19^4, 20, 24^2; 6:3, 10, 14; 7:7^2, 8^2, 10^2, 14^3, 17^2; 8:1, 2, 6, 10, 11^4; 9:9^2; Ob 1:1, 5^2, 7, 18^2; Jnh 1:3, 4^2, 5, 9, 16, 17; 2:9; 3:1, 3^2, 5, 7; 4:2^2, 5^2, 6, 7, 8, 9, 11; Mic 1:4, 6^2, 8, 15; 2:2^2, 3, 8, 11, 12^2; 3:11^2, 12^3; 4:7^2, 9, 10; 5:1^2, 8^2; 6:2^2, 6, 11^2; 7:2, 4^2, 5^2, 6^4, 14, 17, 18; Na 1:2, 7, 9, 14; 2:8; 3:4, 6, 17; Hab 1:7^2, 8, 9; 2:2, 12^2, 18; 3:1, 19; Zep 1:7, 10^2, 15^5, 16, 18; 2:6, 9^2, 15^2; 3:18^2; Hag 1:4^2, 6, 9, 11; 2:6, 12, 13^2, 16^2, 20; Zec 1:8^4, 15; 2:1^2, 4, 5; 3:2, 5^2, 7, 9; 4:1, 2^2; 5:1, 2, 6, 7, 9, 11; 6:11, 13, 14; 7:14; 8:13; 9:3, 9^3, 13, 15, 16; 10:2, 3; 11:15, 16; 12:2, 4, 6^3, 10^2; 13:1, 4, 5^2; 14:1, 4, 7^2, 15, 21; Mal 1:3, 4, 6^4, 13, 14^2; 2:2, 5, 7, 11^2, 16; 3:2^2, 3, 8, 9, 12, 16, 17; 4:1^3, 6; Mt 1:1, 19, 20, 21, 23, 25; 2:6, 8, 12, 13, 18, 19, 22, 23^2; 3:3, 4, 16, 17; 4:6, 8, 16^2, 18, 21; 5:1, 14^2, 15^2, 18, 28, 31; 6:27; 7:4, 9, 10^2, 14, 17, 18^2, 24, 26, 27; 8:2, 4, 5, 9, 14, 16, 19, 24, 30; 9:1, 2^2, 9, 12, 16, 18, 20, 32, 36; 10:10, 21, 24^2, 29, 34, 35^3, 36, 41^6, 42; 11:7, 8, 9^2, 17, 18, 19^3; 12:10^3, 11^2, 12^2, 20^2, 22, 29, 32, 33^3, 38, 39^2, 40, 43; 13:2, 3, 8^2, 21, 23^2, 24, 31^2, 32, 33^2, 34, 44^2, 45, 47, 52, 57; 14:5, 8, 11, 13, 14, 15, 23, 24, 26; 15:5^2, 11, 14^3, 18, 20, 22, 23, 29, 33, 34; 16:1, 4^2, 23, 26^2; 17:1, 5^2, 14, 20, 27; 18:2, 5, 6, 12^2, 17^2, 23, 24, 28; 19:3, 5, 7^2, 10, 16, 23, 24^3, 29; 20:1, 2, 9, 10, 13, 20, 28, 29; 21:2, 5^3, 8, 13^2, 19, 26, 28, 33^6, 35, 41, 43, 46^2; 22:2^2, 11, 16, 19, 23, 24, 46; 23:4, 15^2, 23, 24^2, 37; 24:14, 28, 31, 41, 48, 50, 51; 25:5, 14^2, 18, 19, 21, 23, 24, 32, 35, 38, 43, 44; 26:5, 6, 7, 9, 10, 18, 30, 36, 39, 42, 47, 48, 55, 58, 69, 73, 74; 27:7, 14, 15, 16, 19^2, 28, 29^2, 32, 33, 46, 48^2, 50, 55, 57^2, 59, 60, 65, 66; 28:2, 12^2; Mk 1:3, 4, 6, 10, 11, 16, 19^2, 23, 26, 27, 30, 35, 40, 43, 44, 45^2; 2:1, 3, 13, 17, 21; 3:1^2, 2, 7, 9, 13, 20^2, 24, 25, 27, 32, 34; 4:1, 3, 8^2, 17, 20^2, 21^3, 26, 31, 34, 37, 38; 5:2, 3, 6, 11, 21, 24, 25, 26, 38; 6:4, 5, 8, 10, 11, 15, 19, 20, 21, 25, 28, 29, 31^2, 32^2, 34^2, 35, 37, 46, 49; 7:3, 9, 11^2, 15^2, 18, 20, 23, 24, 25, 26, 29, 32, 34; 8:3, 7, 11, 12, 22, 36, 37; 9:2, 7^2, 14, 17^2, 20, 25, 26, 36, 38, 39, 41, 42; 10:2, 4^2, 7, 15, 17, 20, 25^3, 30, 45, 46^2; 11:2, 4^2, 13, 17^2, 18, 32; 12:1^6, 2, 6, 12, 14, 15, 18, 19^2, 28, 40, 42^3; 13:12, 34; 14:3^2, 5, 6, 13^2, 15, 26, 32, 35, 43, 44, 48, 51^2, 54, 70^2; 15:1, 6, 7, 17^2, 19, 21, 34, 36^2, 37, 40, 43, 46^2; 16:5^2, 12; Lk 1:5^2, 13, 14, 17, 22, 26, 27^3, 31, 34, 36, 39, 42, 57, 63, 69, 76; 2:1^2, 5, 7^2, 11, 12^3, 13, 24^2, 25, 32, 34, 35, 36, 37, 44; 3:3, 4, 22^2; 4:5, 11, 25^2, 26, 31, 33^2, 38, 42; 5:3, 4, 6, 8, 12, 14, 18^2, 19, 27, 29^2, 31, 36^2; 6:6, 7, 12, 16, 17^3, 38, 39^3, 40, 43, 48^3, 49^3; 7:2, 8, 11^2, 12^3, 16, 24, 25, 26^2, 32, 33, 34^3, 37^2, 39^2, 41, 45; 8:4, 5, 8^2, 13, 15^2, 16^4, 22, 23, 27^3, 32, 40, 41^2, 42, 43; 9:5, 10, 12, 25, 28, 29, 34, 35, 37, 38, 39, 42, 47, 49, 52, 57; 10:4, 5, 6, 8, 10, 30, 31, 32, 33, 36, 38^2, 39; 11:1, 5, 6^2, 11^2, 12, 14, 16, 17, 21, 24, 27, 29^2, 30, 33^3, 36, 37, 42; 12:1, 10, 14, 15, 16^2, 25, 33, 36, 45, 46^2, 50, 54; 13:6^2, 10, 11^2, 16, 19^3, 21^2, 23, 34; 14:1, 2, 5^2, 8^2, 10, 12, 13, 16^2, 18, 24, 28, 31, 32^2; 15:4, 8^2, 11, 13, 14, 15, 20, 22, 23, 29; 16:1, 7, 17, 18, 19, 20, 26; 17:2, 4, 6, 7, 12^2, 13, 15, 16, 37; 18:1, 2^2, 3, 10^2, 12^2, 13^2, 17, 18, 21, 23, 25^3, 35; 19:2^2, 3, 4, 7, 9, 11, 12^2, 14, 17, 20, 21, 22, 30, 46^2; 20:3, 6, 9^3, 10, 12, 19, 20, 24, 27, 28^2, 29, 43, 47; 21:2, 18, 27, 34; 22:10^2, 12, 24, 29, 36^3, 41, 47, 48, 52, 53, 54, 55, 56, 58, 59; 23:2, 4, 6, 8, 27, 38, 46, 47, 49, 50^3, 53; 24:13, 18, 19, 23, 37, 39, 42; Jn 1:6, 7, 8, 13, 30, 32, 47; 2:1, 12, 15, 16, 25; 3:1^2, 2, 4^2, 25, 27; 4:5, 7^2, 9^3, 10, 14, 19, 21, 23, 27, 29, 44, 46; 5:1, 2, 3, 6, 9, 25, 28, 35^2; 6:2, 3, 5, 7, 9, 15, 17, 18, 19, 50, 60, 70; 7:4, 12, 18, 22, 23, 24, 26, 30, 33, 37, 44, 49, 52; 8:3, 6^2, 7, 9, 34, 35^2, 40, 44^2, 48, 49, 55; 9:1, 14, 16, 17, 24^2, 25, 32; 10:1^2, 5^2, 13, 21^3, 33, 41; 11:1, 8, 9, 38^2, 39, 43, 44, 47, 54^2; 12:2, 3, 5, 6, 9, 14, 15, 21, 24^2, 28, 35, 44, 46, 48; 13:4, 5, 10^2, 16, 22, 33, 34; 14:2, 3, 9; 15:5, 6, 15; 16:2^2, 16^2, 17^2, 18, 19^2, 21^3, 25, 32; 18:3, 10, 18, 26, 27, 30, 35, 37^2, 38, 40; 19:2^2, 4, 6, 7, 11, 12, 13, 19, 29^3, 31, 34^2, 38, 39, 41^2; 20:26; 21:8, 9; Ac 1:3, 5, 9, 12, 15^2, 18, 22; 2:2^2, 6, 22, 30, 35; 3:2, 14, 22; 4:9, 36, 37; 5:1^2, 4, 15, 30, 34^3, 37; 6:5^2, 7, 8; 7:5, 6, 9, 11, 16, 29, 30, 37, 41^2, 46, 52, 58; 8:1, 5, 9, 11, 22, 32^2; 9:3, 4, 10^2, 11, 12^2, 25, 26, 31, 33^2, 36, 43; 10:1^2, 3, 4, 5, 7, 10, 11, 13, 15, 22^2, 26, 27, 28^2, 30, 32, 39, 48; 11:5^3, 7, 9, 14, 21, 24^2, 26, 28; 12:7, 9, 11, 13, 19^2, 20, 21, 22^2; 13:6, 10, 11, 15, 21, 22, 28, 29, 47; 14:1, 5, 8, 21, 28; 15:7, 10, 14, 39; 16:1^4, 3, 9^2, 12, 13, 14^3, 15, 16^3, 26, 34, 37; 17:1, 4^2, 5^2, 12, 18, 19, 31, 34^4; 18:2^2, 3, 7, 9, 11^2, 12, 14, 15, 18, 24^4, 27; 19:2, 4, 14, 16, 19, 22, 23, 24, 25, 31, 33, 34, 38, 39; 20:3, 9^3, 16; 21:2, 7, 10^2, 16, 23, 38, 39^2; 22:3, 6, 7, 12^2, 17, 25, 26, 27, 28^2, 29; 23:6^2, 7, 9^2, 12, 14, 23, 25, 27, 30; 24:1, 2, 5^2, 10^2, 12, 14^2, 15, 24, 26, 27; 25:3, 9, 13, 14^2, 19, 20, 26, 27; 26:4, 5^2, 11, 13, 14, 16^2, 18, 26, 28^2; 27:1, 2^2, 8, 12, 13, 14, 16, 18, 21, 28^2, 34, 39^2, 41; 28:2, 3^2, 4, 6^2, 11, 14, 16, 23; Ro 1:1, 3, 13, 17^2, 25, 28; 2:3, 14, 17, 19^2, 20, 27, 28^2, 29^3; 3:1, 4, 5, 7, 21, 25, 28; 4:4^2, 11, 17, 19; 5:7^2, 14^2; 6:4; 7:1, 2, 14, 23, 24, 25^2; 8:3, 15^2; 9:9, 30, 31, 33^2; 10:19^2, 21; 11:1, 5, 8, 9^4, 17, 24, 25, 30, 31; 12:6; 14:17, 20; 15:5, 8, 16, 24, 26; 16:1, 2^2, 13, 16; 1Co 1:23; 2:4, 6, 7, 11; 3:10, 18; 4:2, 9, 20, 21^2; 5:1^2, 6, 7, 11^5; 6:1, 5, 15, 16, 18, 19, 20; 7:1, 5, 6^2, 10, 11, 12^2, 13^3, 15, 18^2, 21, 22^2, 23, 25, 27^2, 28, 33, 34, 35, 39; 8:9, 10; 9:5, 6, 7^3, 8, 11, 17, 19, 20, 24^2, 25^2, 26^2; 10:13, 16^2, 19, 21, 27; 11:6^3, 7, 10, 13, 14^2, 15^2, 18, 28, 30; 12:12, 15, 27; 13:1^2, 2, 11^5, 12^2; 14:2, 4, 7, 8, 11^2, 13, 14, 19, 22, 24, 26^4, 27^2, 30, 33, 35, 37, 40; 15:21^2, 37, 38, 44^4, 45^2, 51, 52; 16:2, 7, 9, 20, 22; 2Co 1:10, 17, 22; 2:12, 16; 3:3, 6, 12, 13, 15; 5:1, 5, 16, 17; 6:13, 15, 18; 7:3, 8; 8:6; 9:5, 7; 10:13; 11:1, 2^2, 4^3, 6, 7, 9^2, 16^3, 17, 21, 25^2, 33^2; 12:2, 5, 6, 7^2, 11, 13, 14, 16; 13:2, 12; Gal 1:6, 8, 9, 10; 2:2, 3, 5, 14^3, 16, 18; 3:10, 13^2, 15, 18^2, 19, 20, 21, 22; 4:1^2, 4, 7^3, 14, 23, 27; 5:1, 7, 9, 14; 6:1, 7, 9, 12, 15; Eph 1:13, 14; 2:21, 22; 3:7; 4:1^2, 19, 27; 5:2^2, 3, 5, 27, 31, 32; 6:2; Php 1:6, 13, 27, 28; 2:7, 8^2, 15, 17, 20, 22; 3:1, 5^2, 8, 9, 15, 20; 4:17, 18; Col 1:7, 10, 23; 2:11, 15, 16^3, 17, 18; 3:24; 4:1, 3, 7^2, 11, 12; 1Th 1:7; 2:1, 5, 6, 7, 9, 11, 17; 4:4, 7, 11, 16; 5:2, 3, 4, 8^2, 26; 2Th 1:5; 2:11; 3:8, 9, 10, 15; 1Ti 1:5^3, 13^3, 15, 19; 2:4, 6, 7^2, 11, 12^2, 14; 3:1^2, 3, 6, 7, 9, 12, 16; 4:2, 6, 9, 14; 5:4, 11, 16, 23; 6:5, 9, 10, 19; 2Ti 1:3, 7^2, 9, 11^2; 2:3, 4, 6, 9, 11, 15, 20, 21, 22, 25; 3:5, 12; 4:3, 6, 14; Tit 1:1, 2, 6; 2:14; 3:8, 10^2, 11; Phm 1:1, 6, 9, 15, 16^5, 17, 22; Heb 1:11, 12^2, 13; 2:3, 6, 7, 9, 17; 3:3, 5, 6, 12; 4:7^2, 9, 14, 15; 5:5, 6, 8; 6:7, 20; 7:2, 3, 4, 5, 6, 12^2, 13, 16^2, 17, 19, 21^2, 22, 24, 26; 8:1, 4, 5^2, 8, 11^2; 9:2, 3, 7, 10, 11, 13, 15^2, 16, 17, 24^2, 28; 10:1, 5, 20, 21, 22^2, 27, 29, 31, 32, 37; 11:4^2, 8, 9^2, 11, 13, 14, 16^3, 17, 25, 35; 12:1, 6, 10, 11, 16, 18, 19^2, 24^2, 28, 29; 13:11, 15, 17^2, 18, 22; Jas 1:1, 6, 8, 10, 18, 23^2, 26; 2:2^3, 3, 11, 14, 15, 24, 25; 3:2, 4, 5^3, 6^2, 8, 12^3, 18; 4:4, 13, 14^2; 5:16, 17^2, 20^2; 1Pe 1:3, 6, 17, 19; 2:5^2, 6^2, 8^2, 9^4, 10, 16, 19, 20; 3:4, 9, 16, 20, 21; 4:2, 8, 15^2, 16; 5:1^2, 8, 10, 12, 14; 2Pe 1:1^2, 11, 19^2; 2:5, 7, 16^3, 17, 19^2, 22^2; 3:8^4, 10^2, 13^2; 1Jn 1:10; 2:4, 7, 8, 22; 3:10, 15; 4:20; 5:10, 16^2; 2Jn 1:5; 3Jn 1:6; Jude 1:1^2, 4, 7, 9; Rev 1:6, 10^2, 11, 13^3, 15, 16; 2:9, 14, 17^2, 20, 22; 3:1, 3, 4, 12, 17; 4:1^2, 2, 3, 6, 7^4; 5:1, 2^2, 6, 8, 9, 10, 12; 6:1, 2^4, 4^2, 5^2, 6^4, 8^2, 10, 11^2, 12, 13^2, 14; 7:2, 3, 9, 10; 8:3, 7^2, 8^2, 9^2, 10^3, 11, 12^6, 13; 9:1, 2, 5^2, 13, 15, 18; 10:1^2, 2, 3^2, 4; 11:1^2, 9, 11^2, 12^2, 13^2, 19; 12:1^3, 4, 5^2, 6, 10, 14^3, 15; 13:1^2, 2^4, 3, 5, 11^2, 16; 14:2^2, 3, 7, 8, 9^2, 13, 14^4, 15, 17, 18, 20; 15:2; 16:1, 3, 15, 17, 18, 21; 17:3^3, 4, 9, 10, 12; 18:2^4, 6, 7, 18, 21^3, 22, 23; 19:1, 5, 6, 10, 11, 12, 13, 15, 17; 20:1, 2, 3, 4, 6, 11; 21:1^2, 2, 3, 10, 11^2, 12, 15, 16, 21, 22; 22:5, 9.

AM (1125)

See also the selected listing for "I AM" in the Main Concordance.

Ge 4:9; 6:7, 13^2, 17; 9:12; 13:17; 15:1, 7; 16:5; 17:1; 18:12, 13, 17, 27; 20:16; 22:1, 11; 23:4; 24:3, 13, 24, 34, 43; 25:32; 26:24^2; 27:1, 2, 19, 24, 32; 28:13, 15, 20; 29:33; 30:2, 13; 31:11, 13; 32:5, 10, 11, 20; 34:12; 35:11; 37:13; 38:25; 39:9; 41:9, 44; 43:14^2; 45:3, 4, 12; 46:2, 3, 30; 48:4, 21; 49:29; 50:5, 19, 24; Ex 3:4, 6, 7, 10, 11, 14^3, 15; 4:10; 6:2, 6, 7, 8, 29; 7:5, 17; 8:22; 10:2; 12:12; 14:4, 18; 15:26; 16:12; 17:4; 18:6; 19:9; 20:2, 5; 22:27; 23:20; 29:46^2; 31:13; 33:17; 34:10; Lev 11:44^2, 45^2; 14:34; 18:2, 3, 4, 5, 6, 21, 24, 30; 19:2, 3, 4, 10, 12, 14, 16, 18, 25, 28, 30, 31, 32, 34, 36, 37; 20:7, 8, 22, 23, 24, 26; 21:8, 12, 15, 23; 22:2, 3, 8, 9, 16, 30, 31, 32, 33; 23:10, 22, 43; 24:22; 25:2, 17, 38, 55; 26:1, 2, 13, 44, 45; Nu 3:13, 41, 45; 10:10, 30; 11:21; 13:2; 15:2, 18, 41^2; 18:7, 20; 22:30, 37; 24:14; 25:11, 12; Dt 4:1, 8, 40; 5:6, 9, 31; 8:1, 11; 10:13; 11:8, 13, 22, 26, 27, 32; 12:28; 13:18; 15:5; 28:15; 29:6, 14; 30:8, 11; 31:2^2, 27; 32:39, 49, 52; Jos 1:2; 3:7; 14:10, 11; 23:2, 14; Jdg 6:10, 14, 15; 7:9; 8:5; 9:2; 13:11; 18:4; 19:18; Ru 1:11, 12; 3:9, 12; 4:4; 1Sa 1:15, 26; 3:4, 5, 6, 8, 11, 16; 9:19, 21; 12:2, 7; 14:7; 15:1, 11; 16:1, 22; 17:8, 39, 43, 58; 18:18; 20:5, 8; 21:15; 22:22; 23:4; 24:11; 26:18; 28:15; 30:13; 2Sa 1:9, 13; 3:8^2, 39^2; 7:2, 18; 11:5; 12:11; 14:5, 18, 32; 15:20, 26^2; 16:12; 19:22, 26, 35; 20:17; 22:4; 24:12, 14, 17; 1Ki 2:2; 3:7; 11:31; 13:14, 18; 14:10; 15:19; 16:3; 17:12, 20; 18:22, 36; 19:4, 10, 14; 20:6, 13, 28; 21:21; 22:4; 2Ki 1:10, 12; 2:9, 10; 3:7; 5:6, 7; 10:15^2, 19, 24; 16:7; 19:7; 21:12; 22:16, 20; 1Ch 12:17; 17:1, 16; 21:10, 13, 17; 29:14; 2Ch 2:4, 5, 6, 13; 16:3; 18:3; 34:24, 28; 35:21^2, 23; Ezr 9:6; Ne 6:3; Job 1:15, 16, 17, 19; 7:12; 9:21, 29; 10:7, 15^3; 11:4; 12:3; 13:2; 19:10, 17, 20; 20:2; 21:6; 23:15, 17; 30:19; 31:6; 32:6, 18, 19; 33:2, 6, 9^2; 34:5, 6^3, 31; 40:4; 42:7; Ps 6:2, 6; 18:3; 22:2, 6, 14; 25:16; 27:13; 28:7; 31:9, 11^2, 12, 22; 35:3; 37:25; 38:6, 8, 13, 17, 18; 39:10, 13; 40:7, 17; 46:10; 50:7; 52:8; 55:2; 56:3, 12; 57:4; 69:3, 4, 8, 12, 17, 19, 29; 70:5; 71:9, 18; 73:23; 81:10; 86:1, 2; 88:4^2, 5, 8, 15; 102:2, 5, 6; 109:4, 22, 23, 25; 116:10, 16^2; 119:19, 25, 63, 83, 94, 125, 141; 120:7; 139:14, 18; 142:6; 143:12; Pr 20:9; 30:2; Ecc 4:8^2; 7:23; SS 1:5, 6^2; 2:1, 5, 16; 5:8; 6:3; 8:10; Isa 1:14; 5:5; 6:5^2, 8; 8:18; 19:11; 21:3^2; 27:4; 33:24; 37:7; 38:14, 19; 41:4, 10^2, 13; 42:8; 43:3, 5, 10, 11, 12, 13, 15, 19^2, 25; 44:6^2, 16, 24; 45:3, 5, 6, 18, 22; 46:4^2, 9^2, 13; 47:8, 10; 48:12^3, 16, 17; 49:5, 23, 26; 51:12, 15; 56:3; 58:9; 60:16, 22; 65:1^2, 5; 66:18; Jer 1:6, 7, 8, 12, 15, 19; 2:23, 35; 3:12, 14; 4:6, 31; 5:15; 6:11, 19; 7:19; 8:21; 9:24; 13:13; 15:20; 18:11; 19:3, 15; 20:7, 9; 21:4, 8, 13; 23:9, 23, 30, 31, 32; 24:7; 25:29^2; 26:14; 28:16; 29:23; 30:11; 31:9; 32:3, 27, 28; 34:2, 22; 35:17; 36:5; 37:14; 38:14, 19; 39:16; 40:4; 42:10, 11; 44:11, 27, 30; 45:3; 46:25, 28; 50:31; 51:25; La 1:11, 20^3; 2:11; 3:1; Eze 2:3, 4; 3:3; 5:8;

6:3, 7, 10, 13, 14; **7:**4, 8, 27; **11:**10, 12; **12:**11, 15, 16, 20, 23; **13:**8, 9, 14, 20, 21, 23; **14:**8; **15:**7; **16:**37, 62; **18:**23; **20:**5, 7, 19, 20, 26, 31, 38, 42, 44, 47; **21:**3, 4; **22:**16, 26; **23:**28, 49; **24:**16, 21, 24, 27; **25:**4, 5, 7, 11, 16, 17; **26:**3, 6, 7; **27:**3; **28:**2, 7, 9, 22[2], 23, 24, 26; **29:**3, 6, 9, 10, 16, 19, 21; **30:**8, 19, 22, 25, 26; **32:**15; **33:**29; **34:**10, 27, 30, 31; **35:**3, 4, 9, 15; **36:**9, 11, 22, 23, 32, 38; **37:**6, 12, 13, 19; **38:**3, 23; **39:**1, 6, 7, 13, 17, 19, 22, 28; **40:**4; **44:**28; **Da 1:**10; **2:**8; **8:**19; **10:**11, 16[2]; **Hos 1:**9; **2:**2, 14; **5:**12; **11:**9; **12:**8, 9; **13:**4; **14:**8; **Joel 2:**19, 27[2]; **3:**7, 10; **Am 7:**8; **Jnh 1:**9; **4:**9; **Mic 2:**3; **3:**8; **6:**10; **7:**1; **Na 2:**13; **3:**5; **Hab 1:**5, 6; **2:**1; **Zep 2:**15; **Hag 1:**13; **2:**4; **Zec 1:**14, 15; **2:**10; **3:**8; **8:**2[2], 21; **9:**8; **10:**6; **11:**5, 16; **12:**2; **13:**5[2]; **Mal 1:**6[2], 10, 14; **Mt 3:**11, 17; **8:**3, 9; **9:**28; **10:**16; **11:**29; **16:**15; **17:**5; **18:**20; **20:**13, 15, 22; **21:**24, 27; **22:**32; **23:**34; **24:**5; **26:**18, 55, 61; **27:**24, 43; **28:**20; **Mk 1:**7, 11, 41; **8:**27, 29; **10:**38, 39; **11:**29, 33; **12:**26; **13:**6; **14:**48, 62; **Lk 1:**18, 19, 34, 38, 43; **3:**16, 22; **5:**8, 13; **7:**8; **9:**18, 20, 44; **10:**3; **12:**50; **15:**17, 19, 21; **16:**24; **18:**11; **19:**22; **20:**8; **21:**8; **22:**27, 33, 52, 58, 70; **24:**49; **Jn 1:**20, 21, 23, 27; **3:**28[2]; **4:**9, 26; **5:**7, 17, 36; **6:**35, 41, 48, 51; **7:**8, 28[2], 29, 33, 34, 36; **8:**12, 14[2], 16, 18, 21, 23[2], 24, 28, 38, 42, 46, 49, 50, 58; **9:**5[2], 9; **10:**7, 9, 11, 14, 36; **11:**11, 15, 25; **12:**26, 32; **13:**7, 13, 18, 19[2], 33, 36; **14:**2, 3, 4, 6, 10, 11, 12, 20[2], 28[3]; **15:**1, 5; **16:**5, 7, 10, 17, 26, 28, 32; **17:**9, 11, 13[2], 14, 16, 21, 24; **18:**5, 6, 8, 17, 25, 35, 37; **19:**4, 28; **20:**17, 21; **Ac 7:**32; **9:**5; **10:**26; **13:**25[3], 41; **17:**3, 23; **18:**6, 10; **20:**22, 26; **21:**13, 39; **22:**3, 8, 27; **23:**6; **24:**21; **25:**4, 10, 11; **26:**6, 15, 17, 22, 25[2], 26, 29; **27:**23; **28:**20; **Ro 1:**14, 15, 16; **3:**5, 7; **7:**1, 14, 24, 25; **8:**38; **9:**1; **11:**1, 3, 13[2]; **14:**14; **15:**14, 25; **16:**19; **1Co 1:**14; **4:**3, 14, 17; **5:**3[2], 4, 11; **7:**7, 8, 35; **9:**1[2], 2, 15, 16, 17, 19, 20, 21[2]; **10:**30, 33; **12:**15, 16; **13:**1, 2, 12; **14:**11, 37; **15:**9, 10[2]; **16:**10, 11; **2Co 7:**4, 9, 16; **8:**8; **9:**3; **10:**1; **11:**2, 3, 5, 12, 17, 21, 22[3], 23[2], 31; **12:**10[2], 11[2], 14, 16, 20, 21; **13:**10; **Gal 1:**6, 10[2], 20; **2:**18; **4:**1, 18, 19, 20; **5:**10, 11[2]; **Eph 3:**8; **5:**32; **6:**20, 21[2], 22; **Php 1:**7, 13, 16, 17, 22, 23; **2:**17[2], 24, 28; **4:**11[2], 17[2], 18; **Col 2:**1, 5[2]; **4:**3, 8; **1Ti 1:**15; **2:**7[2]; **3:**14, 15; **2Ti 1:**5, 12[4]; **2:**7, 9; **4:**6; **Phm 1:**12, 13, 19; **Heb 2:**13; **10:**7, 9; **12:**21; **1Pe 1:**16; **2Pe 1:**17; **1Jn 2:**7, 8, 26; **5:**16; **2Jn 1:**5; **Rev 1:**8, 17, 18[2]; **2:**23; **3:**11, 16, 17, 20; **18:**7; **19:**10; **21:**5, 6; **22:**7, 8, 9, 12, 13, 16, 20.

AN (1185)

Ge 1:6; **4:**3; **6:**13, 14; **8:**20; **9:**5[3]; **12:**7, 8; **13:**4, 18; **14:**22; **16:**1; **17:**7, 8[2], 13, 19; **19:**9; **20:**4; **21:**20, 23, 31; **22:**9; **23:**4; **24:**9, 37; **25:**8, 33; **26:**25, 31; **27:**2, 28; **28:**4; **31:**53; **33:**20; **35:**1, 3, 7; **39:**1; **41:**53; **42:**22, 23; **43:**16; **44:**20; **48:**4; **50:**5, 25; **Ex 2:**11, 19, 22; **6:**6; **9:**19; **10:**13; **12:**19, 48; **13:**19; **16:**16, 32, 33, 36[2]; **17:**15; **18:**3; **20:**4, 24, 25; **21:**6, 33; **22:**1, 9, 10, 11, 14, 19, 21, 22, 31; **23:**7, 9, 20, 22; **24:**4; **25:**2, 17; **26:**36; **27:**1, 16; **28:**4, 18, 19[2], 20, 32, 39; **29:**18, 25, 40, 41; **30:**1, 13, 14, 20; **32:**4, 5, 8; **33:**2; **35:**5[2], 21, 24[2]; **36:**6[2], 37; **38:**18, 23; **39:**11, 12[2], 13, 23, 29, 30; **Lev 1:**2[2], 9[2], 13[2], 17[2]; **2:**2[2], 4, 9[2], 11, 12, 16; **3:**1[2], 5[2], 6, 11, 16; **4:**31; **5:**4, 11[2]; **6:**15, 20, 21; **7:**5, 9, 12, 13, 14, 21, 24, 25[2]; **8:**21, 28[2]; **9:**4; **11:**35, 39; **13:**2, 3, 8, 9, 15, 20, 25[2], 27, 30[2], 42, 43, 45; **14:**10, 21, 32, 40, 41, 45, 54; **15:**16, 18, 32; **16:**29; **17:**3, 4, 6, 12; **18:**23[2]; **19:**24, 33, 36[2]; **20:**15, 16, 21, 24; **21:**3; **22:**4[2], 18[2], 22, 23, 24, 27; **23:**8, 13[2], 16, 17, 18[2], 25, 27, 36; **24:**5, 7, 10[3], 16, 21; **25:**35, 47, 49; **26:**1; **27:**9[3], 11, 26[2]; **Nu 3:**4; **5:**2, 15[2]; **7:**3; **9:**14; **10:**9; **11:**12; **15:**3, 4, 6, 7, 9, 10[2], 13[2], 14[3], 19, 20, 24, 25, 29; **16:**14, 21, 45; **17:**10; **18:**17[3], 19, 24, 28; **19:**22; **20:**16; **22:**4, 37; **25:**6, 11; **26:**53, 61; **27:**7; **28:**2, 5, 6, 8[2], 9[2], 12[2], 13[2], 19, 20, 24, 26, 27, 28; **29:**2, 3, 8, 9, 13[4], 14, 35, 36[2]; **30:**2; **31:**50; **34:**2, 13, 17; **35:**16; **36:**2; **Dt 1:**16; **4:**16[2], 23, 34; **5:**8, 15; **9:**16; **12:**10; **13:**11; **14:**21; **15:**17, 21; **16:**2, 8; **17:**1; **19:**3, 20; **20:**1, 10, 16, 19; **21:**8, 23; **22:**10, 19; **23:**7[3]; **24:**4, 14; **25:**4, 19; **26:**1, 8; **27:**5[2], 15[2], 25; **28:**37, 48, 49, 65; **29:**8, 12; **32:**11; **Jos 8:**2, 4, 14, 30, 31; **9:**18; **10:**2, 9; **11:**23; **12:**7; **13:**6, 7; **14:**1, 3; **17:**4[2], 6, 14; **19:**49; **22:**10, 16, 19, 26, 29; **23:**4; **24:**20; **Jdg 3:**31; **6:**19, 24; **8:**24, 27; **9:**23, 43, 48, 53; **11:**34; **12:**5; **13:**6, 19; **14:**3, 4; **17:**5; **18:**1, 10, 14; **19:**12, 16; **20:**29; **21:**1, 4, 7, 13; **Ru 2:**17; **1Sa 1:**1, 24; **2:**28, 31, 32; **4:**18; **5:**9; **7:**17; **9:**2; **12:**17; **14:**3, 14[2], 24, 35; **15:**5; **16:**14, 15; **17:**12; **18:**10; **19:**5, 9, 13; **20:**3, 6, 36; **25:**3; **26:**19; **27:**9; **28:**14; **29:**3, 9; **30:**11, 13[2]; **2Sa 1:**8, 13[2]; **3:**8, 12, 13, 35; **4:**11, 12; **11:**21; **14:**8, 17, 20; **15:**19; **17:**8, 25; **18:**10; **19:**27, 35; **23:**5; **24:**18, 21, 25; **1Ki 1:**29; **3:**1, 25; **6:**16; **7:**6, 31; **8:**31, 33, 36, 37; **9:**7; **11:**14, 26; **13:**1, 14, 18; **14:**5, 21, 31; **15:**22; **16:**32, 33; **18:**32; **19:**5, 11; **20:**25, 30; **21:**1; **22:**25; **2Ki 3:**11, 18; **6:**15; **8:**6; **9:**2; **10:**20; **12:**15; **16:**10, 11; **17:**16; **19:**32; **21:**3; **23:**11; **25:**8, 24; **1Ch 2:**34; **11:**23; **16:**17, 29; **21:**15, 18, 22, 26; **27:**10, 14; **28:**8; **2Ch 6:**22, 24, 27; **7:**9, 20; **12:**13; **13:**6; **14:**8; **15:**14; **18:**24; **20:**11, 35, 37; **21:**18; **24:**26; **25:**16; **26:**13; **28:**7; **29:**8; **30:**7; **32:**21; **36:**13; **Ezr 4:**6, 19, 21; **6:**1; **9:**12; **Ne 4:**11; **5:**12, 18; **6:**5; **8:**18; **9:**18, 31; **10:**29; **13:**25; **Est 8:**3, 5; **9:**14; **Job 3:**16; **6:**5, 6; **7:**6, 19; **15:**33; **18:**21; **19:**15, 24; **20:**16, 24; **21:**21; **22:**8; **23:**7; **28:**3; **31:**37; **33:**3, 23; **34:**6, 20; **40:**9, 15; **41:**4; **42:**15; **Ps 2:**9; **5:**9; **7:**9; **24:**4; **27:**3; **36:**1; **39:**12; **43:**1; **46:**1; **48:**7; **52:**8; **55:**12; **66:**15; **69:**8, 31; **78:**55; **81:**4, 9; **83:**5; **86:**11; **89:**44; **96:**8; **102:**T, 6; **105:**10, 23; **106:**19, 20; **109:**6[2], 23, 25; **119:**7, 106; **132:**2, 11; **135:**12[2]; **136:**21, 22; **145:**13; **Pr 3:**22; **4:**3; **5:**3, 20; **6:**11, 15; **7:**22, 23; **12:**13, 16, 25; **13:**22; **14:**4[2]; **15:**23; **16:**10; **17:**9, 11, 26; **18:**1, 11, 19; **19:**11; **20:**21; **21:**29; **22:**14, 28; **23:**5, 10; **24:**15, 26, 34; **25:**12[2]; **26:**2, 10, 23; **27:**6; **28:**10; **29:**6, 22, 26; **30:**1, 19, 20, 23; **31:**1; **Ecc 4:**13; **7:**11; **8:**2; **10:**5; **SS 2:**3; **4:**13; **7:**4; **Isa 1:**30; **5:**10; **8:**1; **10:**7, 34; **13:**1, 4[2], 11; **14:**4; **15:**1; **16:**4, 10; **17:**1, 6; **18:**2, 7; **19:**1, 19; **21:**1[2], 2, 11, 13, 16; **22:**1; **23:**1, 11; **24:**13; **27:**10; **28:**15[2]; **29:**2, 5, 20; **30:**1, 6, 8, 13, 33; **33:**19, 23; **37:**33; **38:**12, 13; **40:**19, 20[2]; **44:**10, 12, 13, 15; **45:**17; **50:**4; **55:**3, 13; **56:**5; **59:**5; **61:**8; **65:**2, 16, 20[2]; **66:**3, 20; **Jer 1:**11, 18; **2:**22; **3:**18; **4:**20; **5:**15, 16, 22; **6:**22, 26; **7:**34; **16:**9; **17:**1, 27; **18:**16; **19:**8; **21:**5; **22:**28; **23:**10; **24:**9[2]; **25:**9[2], 18; **26:**6; **28:**14; **29:**18; **30:**14, 17; **31:**3, 18; **32:**21, 40; **38:**7, 15; **40:**9, 12; **42:**18; **44:**8, 12, 22; **47:**2; **48:**2, 26, 35, 39[2], 40; **49:**13, 14, 17, 19, 22, 37; **50:**5, 9, 41, 44; **51:**12, 34, 37; **La 1:**15, 17; **2:**4, 5, 7; **5:**10; **Eze 1:**4, 10[2], 22, 24; **4:**3[2]; **5:**2, 15; **7:**5, 19, 20, 24; **10:**14; **11:**19; **12:**23; **14:**8; **16:**3, 10, 45, 60; **17:**2; **20:**17, 33, 34; **21:**21; **22:**4, 15; **23:**41, 48; **26:**13; **30:**10, 13, 18; **33:**28, 32; **35:**5; **37:**26; **38:**10; **42:**4, 7, 9; **45:**1, 5, 6, 10[2], 13[2], 24[2]; **46:**5, 11[2], 14; **47:**13, 22[2]; **48:**13, 29; **Da 2:**31, 44, 46; **3:**1; **4:**3, 16, 33, 34; **5:**21, 26; **6:**7, 20; **7:**4, 14, 27; **9:**16, 23, 24, 27[2]; **11:**6, 10, 17, 18, 22, 23, 27; **Hos 1:**2, 4; **3:**1; **7:**4, 6, 7; **8:**1, 3; **11:**6; **13:**15; **14:**6; **Joel 2:**17, 19; **Am 3:**11, 12; **8:**10; **Ob 1:**1; **Jnh 1:**14; **Mic 1:**8; **2:**8; **Na 1:**1, 8[2], 9; **2:**1; **Hab 2:**3, 18[2]; **Zec 3:**9; **8:**12, 13, 23; **9:**8; **11:**17; **12:**3, 10; **Mal 1:**1, 14; **Mt 1:**20; **2:**13, 19; **5:**32, 39; **9:**16; **12:**43; **13:**12, 28; **14:**7; **22:**35; **24:**44, 50; **25:**29; **26:**7, 16, 72; **27:**24; **28:**2; **Mk 1:**23; **2:**4, 21; **3:**29, 30; **5:**2; **6:**9, 23, 27; **7:**25; **14:**3, 11; **Lk 1:**1, 3, 11, 18; **2:**9; **4:**5, 13, 33; **5:**36; **7:**37; **9:**46; **10:**25, 34; **11:**12, 24; **12:**14, 40, 46; **14:**5; **16:**2; **19:**43; **22:**6, 43, 59; **23:**11, 19; **Jn 1:**22; **3:**25; **5:**5; **12:**3, 29; **13:**15; **18:**1; **Ac 4:**9, 16; **5:**19; **6:**15; **7:**24, 30, 41; **8:**26, 27[2]; **9:**25, 37; **10:**3; **11:**13; **12:**7, 20, 23; **13:**7[2], 10; **16:**20; **17:**23[2], 29; **19:**29; **20:**32; **21:**31; **23:**9, 12, 21; **24:**17; **25:**3, 16; **27:**6, 23, 30; **28:**7, 11; **Ro 1:**1; **2:**20; **4:**4; **7:**3[2]; **8:**12; **11:**1, 24; **13:**4; **14:**12; **15:**16; **1Co 1:**1; **3:**10; **5:**11; **7:**32, 34; **8:**4, 7, 10; **9:**1, 2, 9; **10:**19[2]; **11:**27; **12:**16, 17[2]; **14:**24, 26; **15:**9, 52; **2Co 1:**1; **4:**17; **5:**1, 12; **6:**15; **8:**23; **11:**12, 14; **12:**12; **Gal 1:**1, 8; **2:**8[2]; **3:**15; **4:**7, 13, 14; **Eph 1:**1; **5:**5; **6:**20, 24; **Php 4:**18; **Col 1:**1; **2:**23; **3:**24; **2Th 3:**15; **1Ti 1:**1, 16; **2:**7; **3:**1, 13; **4:**12; **5:**1, 8, 19[2]; **6:**4; **2Ti 1:**1, 11; **2:**5, 21; **4:**5; **Tit 1:**1, 6, 7; **2:**7; **Phm 1:**9; **Heb 5:**13; **6:**16, 17, 19; **7:**16, 20, 21; **9:**1, 9; **10:**3, 29; **11:**7; **12:**20; **13:**10, 14, 17; **Jas 3:**4; **4:**4; **5:**10; **1Pe 1:**1, 4, 8; **2:**21; **3:**15; **2Pe 2:**6, 14; **1Jn 2:**7, 20; **4:**10; **Jude 1:**7; **Rev 2:**7, 11, 17, 27, 29; **3:**6, 8, 13, 22; **4:**3, 7; **8:**1, 5, 13; **11:**19; **12:**3, 5; **13:**9, 14; **17:**11; **19:**15, 17; **20:**1.

AND (29600)

Ge 1:1, 2[2], 3[2], 4, 5[3], 6, 7[2], 8[2], 9[3], 10[2], 11[2], 12[2], 13[2], 14[4], 15[2], 16, 18[3], 19[2], 20[2], 21[4], 22[4], 23[2], 24[3], 25[2], 26[3], 27, 28[5], 29, 30[4], 31[3]; **2:**1, 3[2], 4[2], 5[3], 6, 7[2], 8, 9[4], 12, 14, 15[2], 16, 17, 19[2], 20, 21[2], 22, 23, 24[3], 25[2]; **3:**3, 5[2], 6[4], 7[2], 8[2], 10, 11, 12, 13, 14[2], 15[5], 16, 17, 18[2], 19, 21[2], 22[5], 24[2]; **4:**1[2], 2, 4, 5[2], 8[2], 11, 14[2], 16, 17[3], 18[3], 19, 20, 21, 22, 23, 25[2], 26; **5:**2[3], 3, 4[2], 5, 7[3], 8, 10[3], 11, 13[3], 14, 16[3], 17, 19[3], 20, 22[3], 26[3], 27, 29[2], 30[2], 31, 32; **6:**1, 2, 3, 4[2], 5, 6, 7[3], 9, 10, 11, 13, 14[2], 15, 16[3], 18[4], 19, 20, 21[2]; **7:**1, 2[3], 3[2], 4[2], 5, 7[4], 8[2], 9[2], 10, 11, 12[2], 13[3], 14, 15, 16, 17, 18[2], 19, 20, 21, 23[4], 24; **8:**1[4], 2[2], 3, 4, 5, 7[3], 9[2], 10, 12, 13[2], 16[3], 17[3], 18[2], 19[2], 20[2], 21[2], 22[4]; **9:**1[3], 2[3], 3, 5[2], 7[2], 8, 9, 10[2], 12[3], 13[2], 14, 15[2], 16[2], 17, 18, 19, 21, 22, 23[3], 24, 27, 29; **10:**1, 2, 3, 4, 6, 7[2], 10, 12[2], 14, 15, 18, 19[3], 20[2], 22, 23, 24, 29, 31[2]; **11:**1, 2, 3[2], 4, 5, 7, 8, 11[3], 13[3], 15[3], 17[3], 19[3], 21[3], 23[3], 25[3], 26, 27[2], 29[3], 31[2], 32; **12:**1[2], 2[2], 3[2], 4, 5[3], 7, 8[3], 9, 10, 13, 15[2], 16[5], 17, 19, 20[2]; **13:**1[2], 2[2], 3, 4, 5[2], 7[3], 8[2], 10[2], 11, 12, 13, 14[3], 15, 17, 18; **14:**1, 2, 5[2], 6, 7[2], 8[2], 9, 10[3], 11[2], 12, 13[2], 14, 15, 16[3], 17, 18, 19[2], 20, 21, 22[2], 24[2]; **15:**2, 3, 5[2], 6, 9[2], 10, 12[2], 13[2], 14, 15, 17[2], 18, 21; **16:**3, 4, 5[2], 8[2], 9, 11, 12[2], 14, 15; **17:**1[2], 2[2], 3, 6, 7[3], 8[2], 9, 10, 11[2], 16, 17, 18, 19, 20[3], 23[2], 25, 26, 27; **18:**2[2], 4[2], 5, 6[2], 7[2], 8[3], 10, 11[3], 12, 13, 14, 15, 16, 18[2], 19[2], 20[2], 21, 22, 23, 24, 25, 27, 33; **19:**1[2], 2[2], 3[2], 4, 6, 7, 8, 9[3], 10[2], 11, 14[2], 15, 16[3], 17, 19[2], 20, 24, 25[2], 26, 27, 28[2], 29, 30[3], 31, 32[2], 33[2], 34[2], 35[2], 37, 38; **20:**1[2], 2[2], 3, 5[2], 6, 7[3], 8, 9[2], 10, 11, 12, 13, 14[5], 15, 17[2]; **21:**1, 2, 6, 7, 8[2], 10[2], 12, 14[4], 16[2], 17[2], 18, 19[3], 20, 22, 23, 26, 27[3], 29, 32, 33, 34; **22:**2, 3[2], 4, 5[2], 6[3], 7[2], 8, 9[2], 10, 13[3], 14, 16[2], 17[2], 18, 19[2], 22, 24; **23:**1, 2[2], 3, 4, 7, 8, 9, 10, 11, 13, 15, 16, 17[2], 20; **24:**1[2], 3, 4[2], 7[3], 9, 10[2], 12, 13, 14[2], 16, 17, 18[2], 20, 22, 25[2], 26, 27, 28, 29, 30[3], 31, 32[4], 35[6], 36, 37[2], 38[2], 40[2], 43, 44[2], 45[2], 46[3], 47, 48[2], 49[2], 50, 51[2], 53[4], 54[3], 55, 57, 58, 59[2], 60[2], 61[4], 63, 64, 65[2], 67[3]; **25:**2, 3[2], 4, 6, 7, 8[3], 9, 15, 16[2], 17[3], 18, 20[2], 21, 22, 23[2], 25, 27, 34[4]; **26:**1, 2, 3[4], 4[2], 5[2], 8, 9, 10, 12, 13, 14[2], 17[2], 18, 19, 20, 22[3], 24[2], 25[2], 26, 27, 28, 29[2], 30[2], 31, 32, 33, 34, 35; **27:**1[2], 2, 3[2], 4, 5, 7, 8, 9, 11, 12, 13, 14[3], 15, 16, 17, 18, 19, 22, 25[3], 26, 27[2], 28[2], 29[3], 30, 31[2], 33[4], 34[2], 35, 36, 37[3], 40, 42, 45; **28:**1[2], 3[2], 4, 5[2], 6[2], 7[3], 9[2], 10, 11, 12[2], 13[3], 14[4], 15[2], 16, 17, 18[2], 20[3], 22[2]; **29:**1, 3, 6, 7, 8, 10[3], 11, 12[2], 13[3], 14, 16, 17, 18, 21, 22, 23[2], 24, 28[2], 30[2], 32, 33, 34, 35; **30:**2, 3, 5[2], 6, 7, 8, 9, 14, 17[2], 19, 21, 22, 23[2], 24, 26[2], 28, 29, 30, 31, 32[2], 33, 35[3], 36, 37[3], 38, 39, 40[2], 42, 43[5]; **31:**1, 2, 3[2], 4, 8, 9, 10, 12[2], 13[2], 14, 16, 17, 18, 21, 23, 24, 25[2], 26, 27[3], 28, 32, 33[2], 34[2], 36, 37[2], 38, 39, 40[2], 41[2], 42[3], 43, 44[2], 45, 46[2], 47, 48, 49, 50, 51[2], 52[3], 53, 54, 55[3]; **32:**1, 4, 5[3], 6[2], 7[4], 8, 9[2], 10, 11[2], 12, 13, 14[2], 15[3], 16[2], 17[3], 18, 19, 20, 22[3], 24, 28[2], 30, 31; **33:**1[2], 2[4], 3, 4[3], 5[2], 6[2], 7[4], 11[2], 13[2], 14, 17, 18, 20; **34:**2, 3[2], 4, 7, 9, 10, 11[2], 12[2], 13, 16[2], 17, 18, 20, 21[7], 23[2], 24[2], 25[2], 26[3], 27, 28[4], 29[2], 30[5]; **35:**1[2], 2[3], 3, 4[2], 5, 6, 7, 8, 9, 11[4], 12[2], 14, 16, 17, 19, 20, 21, 22[7], 23, 24, 25, 26, 27, 28, 29[5]; **36:**2[2], 3, 5[2], 6[6], 10, 11, 13, 14[2], 16, 17, 18, 19, 21, 22, 23, 24, 25, 26, 27, 28, 30, 39, 40, 43; **37:**2[2], 3, 4, 5, 7[2], 8[2], 9[4], 10[4], 13, 14[3], 15, 17, 18, 20[2], 22, 24[2], 25[3], 26, 27[2], 28, 29, 30, 31, 32, 33, 34, 35; **38:**1, 2, 3, 4[2], 5, 6, 8, 12, 14, 16[2], 18[4], 19, 22, 24[2], 25[3], 26[2], 28[2], 29[2], 30; **39:**2[2], 3, 4[2], 5[2], 6, 7[2], 9, 10, 11, 12[2], 13, 15, 18, 20, 21, 22, 23; **40:**1, 2, 3, 4, 5[2], 10[2], 11[2], 13[2], 14[2], 15, 19[2], 20[2]; **41:**2[2], 3[2], 4[2], 5[2], 6, 8, 10[2], 11, 12, 13[2], 14[2], 15, 18[2], 19[2], 22, 23[2], 25, 26[2], 27, 30, 32, 33[3], 35, 37, 39, 40, 42[2], 43, 45[2], 46[2], 48, 51[2], 52, 54, 55, 56, 57; **42:**2[2], 7, 9, 13, 15, 17, 18, 19, 20, 24[3], 25, 26, 27, 28[2], 30, 32, 33[2], 34, 35, 36[2], 37, 38; **43:**2, 4, 7, 8[4], 9, 10, 11[4], 13, 14[2], 15[3], 16, 17, 18[3], 19, 21, 24, 26, 27, 28[2], 29[2], 30[2], 31, 32, 33, 34; **44:**1, 2, 4, 5, 9, 11, 12[2], 13, 14[2], 16, 18, 20[4], 22, 25, 28[2], 29, 30, 33; **45:**1, 2[2], 5[2], 6[2], 7, 8, 9, 10[4], 11[2], 12, 13[2], 14[2], 15[2], 16, 17, 18[3], 19[3], 21, 22, 23[4], 24, 25, 27, 28[2]; **46:**1, 2[2], 4[2], 5[3], 6[3], 7[3], 8, 9, 10, 11, 12[3], 13, 14, 15, 16, 17[2], 19, 20, 21, 24, 29[2], 31[4], 32[3], 33; **47:**1[5], 2, 4, 5, 6[3], 7, 9[4], 10, 11[2], 12[2], 13, 14[2], 15[2], 17[4], 18[3], 19[5], 20, 21, 22, 23, 24[3], 27[2], 28[2], 29[3], 30, 31; **48:**1, 2, 3, 4[3], 5[2], 10[3], 11, 12, 13[3], 14[2], 15[2], 16[3], 19[3], 20[2], 21, 22[2]; **49:**1, 2, 4, 5, 6, 7[2], 9, 10, 13, 15[2], 25, 28, 31[3], 32, 33; **50:**1[2], 3, 5[2], 6, 7, 8[4], 9, 10[2], 13, 14, 15, 17, 18, 21[3], 22, 23, 24[2], 25[3], 26[2]; **Ex 1:**2, 3, 4[2], 6[7], 7[2], 10[2], 11[2], 12, 13, 14[2], 15, 16, 17, 18, 19, 20[2], 21; **2:**2[2], 3[3], 5[2], 6[2], 7, 8[2], 9[3], 10, 11, 12[3], 13, 14[2], 15, 16[2], 17[3], 19, 20, 22, 23[3], 24[3], 25; **3:**1[2], 3, 4, 6, 7, 8[4], 9[2], 11, 12[2], 13[2], 15, 16[4], 17[3], 18[2], 20, 21, 22[5]; **4:**1, 3[2], 4[3], 5, 6, 7, 9, 10, 12, 14[2], 15[2], 16[2], 18[2], 20[3], 23, 24, 25, 27, 28, 29, 30, 31[4]; **5:**1[2], 2[2], 4, 5, 6, 7, 8, 9, 10[2], 11, 14, 15, 17, 20, 21[4], 22, 23; **6:**3, 5, 6[3], 7, 8[2], 9, 13[3], 14[2], 15, 16, 17, 18, 19, 20, 21, 22, 23[4], 24, 25, 26, 27; **7:**1, 2, 3[2], 4, 5[2], 6, 7, 8, 9[2], 10[4], 11[2], 12, 13, 15, 17, 18, 19[5], 20[4], 21, 22[2], 23[2], 24; **8:**1, 3[5], 4[2], 5[3], 6[2], 8[4], 9[3], 11[2], 12, 13[2], 14, 15[2], 16[2], 17[3], 18[2], 19, 20[2], 21[3], 23, 24[3], 25[2], 26, 29[3], 30, 31[3], 32; **9:**1, 2, 3[5], 4, 5, 6, 7[2], 8[2], 9[2], 10[3], 11, 12[2], 13, 14[2], 15[2], 16, 17, 19[4], 20, 21, 22[2], 23[2], 24[2], 25[2], 27[3], 28, 29, 30, 31[2], 32, 33[3], 34[3], 35; **10:**1, 2[3], 3[2], 6[3], 8, 9[4], 10, 11[2], 12[2], 13[2], 14, 15, 16[3], 17, 18, 19[2], 20, 22, 24[3], 25, 26, 27; **11:**1[2], 2[2], 3[2], 5, 7, 8[2], 10[2]; **12:**1, 5, 7[2], 8, 9, 11, 12[3], 13, 16, 19, 21[3], 22[2], 23[4], 24, 26, 27[2], 28, 29, 30[3], 31[3], 32[3], 33, 34, 35[3], 36, 37, 38, 39, 43, 45, 49, 50, 51; **13:**5[2], 6, 9, 11[2], 15[2], 16[2], 17, 19, 21; **14:**2[2], 4[4], 5[3], 6, 9[3], 10[2], 13, 16, 17[3], 18, 19[2], 20[2], 21[2], 22[2], 23[3], 24[2], 25, 26[2], 27[2], 28[2], 29, 30, 31[3]; **15:**1[2], 2[3], 4, 9, 10, 12, 14, 16, 17, 18, 19, 20[2], 21, 22, 25[4], 26[2], 27[2]; **16:**1[2], 2, 3, 4[2], 5, 6, 7, 8, 10, 12, 13[2], 18[2], 20, 21, 22[2], 23[2], 24, 28, 31, 32, 33; **17:**2, 3[3], 5[2], 6, 7[3], 8, 9, 10[2], 12[3], 14, 15; **18:**1[3], 3, 4, 5, 6, 7[3], 8[3], 10[2], 12[2], 13, 16[3], 18, 19[3], 20[3], 21[2], 23[2], 24, 25[2], 27; **19:**2, 3[3], 4[2], 5, 6, 7[2], 9, 10[3], 11, 12, 14, 16[2], 17, 19[3], 20, 21[3], 23, 24[2], 25; **20:**1, 5, 6, 9, 11[3], 12, 18[3], 19[2], 24[5], 26; **21:**4[3], 5[3], 6, 10, 12, 14[2], 16, 18[2], 19[2], 20, 22[2], 26, 27, 28, 29[3], 32, 33[2], 34, 35[3], 36; **22:**1[2], 2, 5[2], 6, 7, 10, 11, 13, 14, 16[2], 23, 24[2], 30; **23:**3, 7, 8, 10, 11[3], 12[3], 20, 21, 22[2], 23[3], 24, 25[2], 26, 27[2], 28, 29, 31[2]; **24:**1[3], 2, 3[2], 4[2], 5[2], 6[2], 7, 8, 9[3], 10, 11[2], 12[3], 13, 14[2], 16[2], 18[2]; **25:**3, 4[2], 5, 6, 7[3], 8, 9, 10[4], 11[2], 12[2], 13, 17[3], 18, 19, 21, 22, 23[2], 24, 25, 26, 28, 29[3], 31[3], 32, 33[2], 34[2], 35, 36, 37, 38, 39; **26:**1[2], 2, 3, 4, 5, 6, 8, 9, 10, 11, 14, 16[2], 19, 21, 23, 24, 25, 27, 29, 31[2], 32, 33, 35, 36[2], 37[2]; **27:**1, 2[2], 3[2], 4, 6, 9, 10[3], 11[4], 12[2], 14, 15[2], 16[3], 17[2], 18[2], 19, 21; **28:**1[2], 2, 4[2], 5[3], 6[3], 8[4], 9, 10, 12, 14[2], 15[3], 16[2], 17, 18, 19, 20, 23, 25, 26, 27, 30, 33, 34, 35, 36, 38, 39, 40[2], 41[2], 43[3]; **29:**1, 2[3], 3[2], 4[2], 5[2], 6, 7, 8, 9[3], 10[2], 12[2], 13[2], 14[2], 15[2], 16[2], 17[3], 19[2], 20[3], 21[8], 22, 23[2], 24[2], 25, 26, 27[2], 28, 29, 30, 31, 32[2], 33, 34, 35, 36, 37[2], 39, 40, 41, 42, 43, 44[3], 45; **30:**2[2], 3[3], 5, 9, 15, 16, 18[2], 19[2], 21[2], 24, 27[2], 28[2], 29, 30[2], 32[2], 33, 34[2], 35[3], 36; **31:**3[2], 4, 5[2], 7, 8[2], 9, 10[2], 11[2], 13, 17[4]; **32:**1, 2[2], 3, 4, 5, 6[4], 8[3], 9, 10, 11, 12[2], 13[3], 14, 15[2], 19[3], 20[3], 24[2], 25[2], 26[2], 27[3], 28, 29[2], 31, 34, 35; **33:**1[3], 2[2], 3[2], 4, 5, 7, 8[2], 9, 10, 12, 13, 14, 16[2], 17[2], 19[3], 20, 22, 23; **34:**1, 2, 3, 4[2], 5[2], 6[3], 7[4], 8, 9[2], 11, 13, 15[2], 16[2], 21, 22, 24[2], 25, 27, 28[2], 30[2], 31[2], 32, 34[2]; **35:**1, 5, 6[2], 7, 8, 9[3], 10, 11[2], 12[2], 13[2], 14, 15, 16, 17[2], 18[2], 19, 21[4], 22[3], 24, 25, 26[2], 27[2], 28[3], 29, 31[2], 32, 33[2], 34[2], 35[4]; **36:**1[2], 2[4], 3, 5, 6[2], 8[2], 9, 10, 11, 12, 13, 15, 16, 17, 19, 21[2], 24, 26, 28, 29, 30, 32, 34, 35[2], 36[2], 37[2], 38[3]; **37:**1[4], 2[2], 3[2], 4, 5, 6[3], 8, 10[2], 11, 12, 13, 15, 16[4], 17[3], 18, 19[2], 20[2], 21, 22, 23, 24, 25[2], 26[3], 28, 29; **38:**1, 2[2], 3, 6, 8, 9, 10[3], 11[3], 12[3], 14, 15[2], 17[2], 18[3], 19[3], 20, 23[4], 24, 25, 27, 28, 29, 30, 31[3]; **39:**1, 2[3], 3[3], 5[4], 6, 8[3], 9[2], 10, 11, 12, 13, 16[2], 18, 19, 20, 23, 24[2], 25[2], 26, 27, 28[2], 29[2], 30, 33[2], 34, 35, 36, 37[2], 38, 39, 40[3], 41[2], 43; **40:**3, 4[2], 5, 7[2], 8, 9[4], 10[2], 11[2], 12[2], 13, 14, 18, 19, 20[2], 21[2], 23, 25, 27, 29[2], 30[2], 31[4], 33[3], 34, 35, 38; **Lev 1:**1, 2, 4, 5[2], 6, 7, 8, 9[2], 11, 12[2], 13[3], 15, 16, 17; **2:**2[3], 3, 4[2], 5, 6, 7, 9, 10, 15, 16; **3:**1, 2, 4, 8, 10, 13, 15; **4:**2, 4, 5, 6, 9, 11[3], 12, 13, 14, 15, 17, 19, 20[2], 21, 22, 24, 25[2], 26, 27, 29, 30[2], 31[2], 33, 34[2], 35[2]; **5:**2, 6[2], 7, 9, 10[2], 12, 13, 15[2], 16[2], 17[2], 18[2]; **6:**2, 3, 4, 5, 6[2], 7, 9[2], 10[2], 11[2], 12[2], 15[2], 16, 17, 20[2], 21, 22, 25, 27, 28; **7:**2, 3, 4, 7, 10, 12[4], 21, 26, 30, 31, 33, 34[3], 35, 37; **8:**2[2], 3, 4, 6[2], 7, 8[2], 9, 10[3], 11[2], 12, 13, 14[2], 15[2], 16[3], 17[2], 18[2], 19, 20[2], 21[2], 22[2], 23[3], 24[2], 25[2], 26[3], 27[2], 28, 29, 30[8], 31[3], 32, 35[2], 36; **9:**1[2], 2[2], 3[2], 4[2], 5[2], 7[5], 8, 9[2], 10, 11, 12, 13, 14[2], 15[2], 16, 17, 18[2], 19[2], 20, 21, 22[3], 23[2], 24[4]; **10:**1[3], 2[2], 4[2], 5, 6[4], 9, 10[2], 11, 12[3], 13, 14[4], 15[2], 16[3], 19; **11:**1, 3, 7, 9[2], 10, 11[2], 12, 13, 19, 25, 28, 30, 32[2], 33, 34, 35, 38, 40[2], 44, 46, 47[2]; **12:**2, 6, 7, 8[2]; **13:**1, 3[2], 4, 5[2], 6[3], 8, 10[2], 11, 12, 13, 16, 17, 18, 19, 20[2], 21[2], 23[2], 24, 25[2], 26[3], 27, 28[2], 30[3], 31, 32[3], 33, 34[3], 36, 37[2], 39, 40, 41, 43, 44, 45, 49[2], 50, 51, 55, 57, 58[2]; **14:**3, 4[2], 6[2], 7, 8, 9[3], 10[2], 11, 12, 13, 14[2], 16, 17, 18, 19, 20[3], 21, 22[2], 24, 25[3], 27, 28, 31, 32, 33, 34, 35, 36, 37, 38, 40, 41, 42[2], 43[2], 44[2], 45[2], 48, 49[2], 51[3], 52, 53, 56, 57; **15:**1, 2, 4, 5[2], 6[2], 7[2], 8[2], 10[3], 11[2], 12, 13[2], 14[2], 15, 16, 17, 18[2], 19, 20, 21[2], 22[2], 24, 26, 27[2], 28, 29, 30, 33; **16:**3, 4, 5, 6, 7, 8, 9, 11[2], 12[2], 13, 14, 15[3], 16, 17, 18[3], 19, 20, 21[3], 22, 23[2], 24[4], 26, 27[2], 28, 29, 31, 32, 33[4], 34; **17:**2[3], 4, 5, 6, 7, 9, 10, 11, 13, 15[2], 16; **18:**2, 3, 4, 5, 17, 18, 20, 23, 25, 26[2], 27, 28, 30[2]; **19:**2, 3[2], 7, 10, 12, 22, 23, 29, 30, 32, 36[2], 37[2]; **20:**3[2], 4, 5[3], 6[2], 7, 8, 9, 10, 11, 14[2], 15, 16, 17[2], 18[2], 22[2], 24, 25[3], 26; **21:**1, 4, 6, 10, 23, 24[2]; **22:**2, 3, 7, 8, 9, 13, 14, 16, 18[3], 25[3], 28, 31, 33; **23:**2, 7, 8[2], 10[2], 13, 16, 18[3], 19, 21, 22, 27[2], 32, 34, 36[2], 37[2], 38[3], 39, 40[3]; **24:**5, 7, 9, 10[3], 14, 22, 23[2]; **25:**2, 3[2], 6[3], 7, 10[2], 11, 12, 15, 16, 18[2], 19[2], 22, 23[2], 25[2], 26, 27, 28, 30, 31, 33, 35, 38, 39, 41[3], 44, 45[2], 46, 47[2], 50, 52, 54; **26:**1, 2, 3, 4[2], 5[3], 6[3], 7, 8[2], 9[3], 11, 12[2], 13, 14, 15[4], 16[2], 17, 19[2], 21, 22[2], 24, 25[2], 26, 28, 29, 30[2], 31[2], 33[3], 34[2], 36, 40[2], 41, 42[3], 43[2], 46[2]; **27:**2, 3, 4, 5[2], 6[2], 7, 10, 15, 18, 19, 23, 28, 32, 33[2]; **Nu 1:**2, 3, 17, 18[3], 19, 20, 22[2], 24, 26, 28, 30, 32, 34, 36, 38, 40, 42, 44[2], 50[3], 51; **2:**1, 17, 34[2]; **3:**1, 2[2], 4[2], 6, 7, 9, 10, 15, 17, 18, 19, 20, 21, 25, 26[3], 27, 31, 33, 36, 37, 38[2], 39, 40, 41, 45, 48, 51; **4:**1, 2, 5[3], 6, 7[3], 8, 9[3], 10[2], 11[2], 12, 13, 14[2], 15[3], 16[3], 17, 19[4], 22, 24, 25, 26[2], 27, 29, 31, 32, 34[2], 37, 38, 40, 41, 42, 45, 46[2], 47, 49; **5:**3, 6, 7[2], 8, 12[2], 13[3], 14[4], 16, 17, 18, 19[3], 20, 21[2], 22, 23, 24[2], 25, 26, 27[4], 28[2], 29, 30; **6:**2, 3[2], 11, 12, 15[3],

8, 9[2], 10, 11, 12, 13, 14, 15[2], 17, 18[2], 19, 20, 21[2], 22, 23, 24[3], 25[3], 26[2], 27[2], 28[2], 29, 34[2]; **18:**1, 3[2], 4, 5, 6[2], 7, 8[3], 10[2], 11, 12, 15[2], 17, 18[2], 19[2], 22[2], 23[2], 25[2], 26[2], 27; **19:**1, 2, 6[2], 8, 9[2], 10, 12[3], 15, 16[2], 17[2], 18, 19, 20, 21, 22, 25, 26[4], 27[2], 28, 29[2], 33, 35[2], 36, 38[2]; **20:**1[2], 2, 4[3], 5, 6, 7, 9[2], 10, 11[2], 12, 13, 14, 15[2], 19, 20, 21[2], 22, 23, 24, 28, 29, 30, 31, 32[2], 34, 36, 37; **21:**1[2], 2, 3, 5[4], 6, 7[2], 8, 11[3], 12, 13, 14, 15, 16[2], 18[2], 19, 20, 24, 25, 26[2], 27, 28[4], 29, 30[2], 32[3], 33[3], 34[2], 38, 40; **22:**1, 3, 4[2], 5[2], 7, 10, 12, 13[2], 14[2], 15, 16[2], 17, 18, 19, 20[2], 22, 23[2], 24, 26, 27, 30[3]; **23:**1, 6, 7[2], 8, 9[2], 10[2], 11, 12, 14[2], 15, 16, 17, 18, 19, 22, 23[2], 27[2], 31, 33, 34; **24:**1[2], 2, 3, 6, 13, 14, 15[2], 16, 17, 19, 23, 24, 25[2], 26; **25:**2[2], 4, 5, 6[2], 9, 13, 15[2], 16, 17, 19, 20, 23[3], 24[2], 26; **26:**1, 3[2], 4, 5, 6, 7, 10[2], 11, 12, 13, 14, 16[3], 17, 18[3], 20[4], 21, 22[4], 23[2], 25, 26, 30[3], 31; **27:**1, 2, 3, 4, 5, 6, 7, 8, 9, 10[3], 11, 12[2], 13, 15[2], 17, 20, 21[2], 23, 24[2], 28[3], 29, 31, 32, 33, 35[2], 36, 40[2], 41[3], 42, 43[2]; **28:**2[2], 3, 5, 6[2], 7, 8[3], 9, 10, 11, 12, 13[2], 14, 15[3], 17, 18, 20, 21, 23[4], 25, 26, 27[3], 28, 30, 31[2]; **Ro 1:**1, 4, 5[2], 6, 7[3], 10, 12, 14[2], 18, 20, 21, 23[4], 25[2], 27[2], 29[2], 30; **2:**3, 4, 5, 7, 8[3], 9, 10, 12, 15, 17, 18, 20, 27[2], 28, 29; **3:**4[2], 7, 8, 9, 14, 16, 17, 19, 21, 23, 24, 26, 30; **4:**3, 11, 12, 13, 14, 15, 16, 17, 18, 19, 20, 25; **5:**2, 4, 5, 12[2], 15, 16[2], 17; **6:**13, 18, 19, 22[2]; **7:**3, 6, 9, 11, 12[2], 16, 23; **8:**2, 3, 6, 9, 11, 15, 17, 21, 27, 28, 30, 34; **9:**2, 3, 4, 5, 9, 10, 15, 17, 18, 21, 22, 25, 26, 28, 33[2]; **10:**1, 3, 8, 9, 10[3], 12[2], 14[2], 15, 17, 20, 21; **11:**3[2], 4, 6, 8, 9[3], 10, 12, 14, 17[2], 20, 22, 23, 24, 26, 27, 29, 33[2], 36[2]; **12:**1, 2[2], 4, 5, 14; **13:**2, 3, 9, 11, 12, 13[3], 14; **14:**3, 4, 6[2], 7, 8, 9[2], 17[2], 18, 19, 22, 23; **15:**1, 4, 5, 6[2], 11[2], 12, 13, 14, 18, 19, 21, 23, 24, 26, 27, 28[2], 30, 31, 32; **16:**2, 3, 7[2], 9, 10, 12, 13, 14, 15[3], 17, 18, 19, 21, 23[2], 25, 26[2]; **1Co 1:**1, 2[2], 3[2], 5, 10[2], 14, 22, 23, 24[2], 25, 28[2], 30; **2:**2, 3[2], 4[2], 7, 14; **3:**3, 4, 5, 8[2], 10, 13, 16, 17, 20, 23[2]; **4:**1, 5, 6, 7, 8, 11, 19, 21; **5:**1, 2[2], 3, 4[2], 5, 8[2], 10; **6:**2, 6, 8[2], 11[2], 13[2], 14, 15; **7:**2, 3, 5, 8, 11, 12, 13[2], 14, 17, 19, 28[2], 34[2], 36[2], 37, 40; **8:**4, 5, 6[3], 7, 8, 12; **9:**4, 5[2], 6, 7[2], 10, 13, 15, 18, 19, 27; **10:**1, 2, 4[2], 7[2], 8, 9, 10[2], 11, 13, 16, 20, 21[2], 26, 27, 28; **11:**2, 3[2], 5, 6, 7, 10, 18, 22[2], 24[2], 26, 27, 28, 29[2], 30[2], 34; **12:**2, 3, 10, 11[2], 12, 13, 16, 21, 23[2], 24, 27, 28[2], 31; **13:**1, 2[3], 3, 9, 13[2]; **14:**1, 3, 6, 11, 21, 23[2], 24, 25[2], 27, 28[2], 29, 30, 31, 39, 40; **15:**1, 5[7], 8, 9, 10, 11, 14[2], 17, 24, 30, 32, 34, 38, 39, 40[2], 41[2], 46, 48, 49, 50, 52, 53, 54, 56; **16:**3, 7, 9, 15, 16[2], 17, 18, 19[2]; **2Co 1:**1, 2[2], 3[2], 6, 7, 10, 12[2], 13, 16[2], 17, 18, 19[3], 20, 21, 22; **2:**4[2], 7, 9, 10, 12, 13, 14, 15, 16; **3:**2, 11, 17, 18; **4:**2, 3, 5, 7, 13, 14, 15, 17; **5:**4, 5, 6, 8[2], 11, 14, 15[2], 18, 19; **6:**2, 4, 5[2], 6[2], 7[2], 8[2], 9[2], 10, 11, 14, 15, 16[4], 17[2], 18[2]; **7:**1, 7, 9, 10, 14, 15[2]; **8:**1, 2, 3, 5[2], 7, 10, 15, 17, 18, 19, 22, 23[2], 24; **9:**2[2], 4, 5, 6, 8, 10[3], 11, 13[2], 14; **10:**1, 5[2], 6, 10[2], 12; **11:**3, 4, 9[3], 12, 14, 23[2], 25, 26, 27[5], 29[2], 31, 33, **12:**1, 3, 12, 14, 15, 18[2], 19, 20[2], 21[3]; **13:**6, 9, 11[2], 14[2]; **Gal 1:**1, 2, 3[2], 4, 5, 6, 7, 13, 14, 15, 17, 18, 21, 24; **2:**2, 4, 9[3], 12, 14, 15, 16, 20[2]; **3:**5, 6, 8, 16[3], 17, 29; **4:**2, 7, 9, 10[3], 15, 18[2], 20, 22, 24, 25, 26, 27, 30; **5:**1, 7, 12, 15, 16, 17, 19, 20, 21[2], 23, 24, 26; **6:**2, 14, 16; **Eph 1:**2[2], 3, 4, 5, 8, 9, 10, 13, 15, 17, 19, 20, 21[3], 22[2]; **2:**1, 2, 3[2], 6[2], 8, 11, 12[2], 14, 15, 16, 17[2], 19[2], 20, 21, 22; **3:**5, 6, 9, 10, 12[2], 15, 17[2], 18[3], 19, 21[2]; **4:**2, 4, 6[3], 8, 11[2], 13[2], 14[5], 16[2], 17, 18, 21, 24[2], 25, 27, 30, 31[2], 32; **5:**2[3], 5, 9, 10, 14, 19[2], 25, 27[2], 29, 31[3], 32, 33; **6:**2, 3, 4, 5[2], 9[3], 10, 12[2], 13, 15, 17, 18[3], 21[2], 22, 23[2]; **Php 1:**1[2], 2[2], 7, 9[3], 10[2], 11, 13, 14, 15, 18[2], 19, 20, 21, 23, 25[2], 27, 28, 30; **2:**1, 2, 8[2], 9, 10[2], 11, 12, 13, 15[2], 17[2], 18, 24, 25, 26, 27[2], 28, 29; **3:**1, 3, 9[2], 10[2], 11, 13, 15, 17, 18, 19, 20; **4:**1[2], 2, 3[2], 6, 7[2], 9, 12[2], 15, 16, 18, 19, 20[2]; **Col 1:**1, 2[2], 4, 5[2], 6[2], 8, 9[2], 10[2], 11[2], 13, 16[3], 17, 18[2], 20, 21, 22, 23[3], 24, 26, 28; **2:**1[2], 2, 3, 5[2], 7[2], 8[2], 10[2], 12, 13, 14, 15[2], 18[2], 19[2], 22, 23; **3:**3, 5, 8, 10, 11, 12[?], 13, 14, 15, 16[3], 17, 19, 22[3], 25; **4:**1, 2, 3, 7, 8, 9, 11, 12[2], 13[2], 14, 15[2], 16; **1Th 1:**1[3], 3[2], 5, 6, 7[2], 8, 9, 10; **2:**2, 9[2], 10[2], 12[2], 13, 15[3], 18, 20; **3:**2[2], 4, 5, 6[3], 7, 10[2], 11[2], 12[2], 13[2]; **4:**1[2], 4, 6[2], 10[2], 11, 12, 14[2], 16[2], 17[2]; **5:**1, 3[2], 5, 6, 7, 8[2], 11, 12, 14, 15, 23[2], 24; **2Th 1:**1[2], 2[2], 3[3], 4[2], 5, 7[2], 8, 9[2], 10, 11[2], 12[2]; **2:**1, 3, 4, 6, 8[2], 9, 10[2], 12, 13, 15, 16[3], 17[2]; **3:**1, 2[2], 3[2], 4, 5, 6, 8[2], 12[2], 13, 16; **1Ti 1:**1, 2[2], 4, 5[2], 6, 9[3], 10[4], 13[3], 14, 16, 17[2], 19[2], 20; **2:**1, 2[3], 3, 4, 5[2], 7[3], 9, 11, 14[2], 15; **3:**4, 6, 7, 8, 10, 11, 12[2], 13, 15; **4:**1[2], 3[2], 4, 5, 6, 7, 8, 10[3], 11, 12, 13, 16[2]; **5:**2, 4[2], 5[4], 8[2], 10[2], 13[3], 14, 16, 17, 18, 21[3], 22, 23[2], 25; **6:**1, 2[2], 3[2], 4[2], 5[2], 7, 8, 9[4], 10, 11[2], 13, 15[2], 16[2], 18[2], 20, 21; **2Ti 1:**2[2], 3, 5[2], 7, 9[2], 10[2], 11[3], 12, 13, 15, 16; **2:**2, 14, 15, 16, 17, 18, 19, 20[3], 21, 22[2], 23, 24, 26[2]; **3:**6[2], 8, 11, 13[2], 14, 15, 16[2]; **4:**1[4], 2[3], 4, 6, 8, 10[2], 11, 13, 17[3], 18[2], 19[2], 20, 21[2]; **Tit 1:**1[2], 2, 3, 4[2], 5, 6[2], 8, 9, 10, 11, 14, 15[2], 16; **2:**2[2], 4, 5[2], 8, 10, 12[3], 13, 14, 15; **3:**1, 2[2], 3[4], 4, 5, 8[2], 9[4], 10, 11, 13[2], 14; **Phm 1:**1[2], 2, 3[2], 5, 7, 8, 9, 11, 14, 16, 22, 24[2]; **Heb 1:**1, 2, 3, 5, 6, 8[2], 9, 10, 12; **2:**2[2], 4[2], 7, 8, 9, 10, 11, 13[3], 14, 15, 17[2]; **3:**1, 6[2], 9[2], 10[2], 16, 17, 18; **4:**3, 4, 5, 6, 12[4], 13, 16; **5:**1[2], 2, 6, 7[3], 9, 10; **6:**1[2], 2, 3, 5, 6, 7, 8[2], 10[2], 12, 14, 15, 16[2], 19; **7:**1[2], 2, 6, 7, 13, 14, 15, 18, 19, 20, 21, 27; **8:**2, 3[2], 5, 6, 8[2], 9, 10[2], 12, 13[2]; **9:**1, 2, 4[2], 7[3], 9, 10[2], 11, 12, 13[2], 19[3], 21, 22, 25, 27, 28; **10:**2, 4, 5, 6, 8[2], 10, 11[2], 16, 17, 18, 20, 21, 22, 24[2], 25, 27, 29, 30, 33, 34[2], 37, 38, 39[2]; **11:**1, 4, 6[2], 7, 8, 9, 10, 11, 12[3], 13[3], 17, 19, 20, 21, 22, 23, 28, 32[2], 33, 34[3], 35, 36[2], 37[2], 38[3]; **12:**1[2], 2[2], 3, 5[2], 6, 8[2], 9[2], 11, 12, 14, 15[2], 18[2], 24, 28[2]; **13:**3, 4[2], 5, 7, 8[2], 12, 16[2], 17, 18, 21[2], 24; **Jas 1:**1, 4, 5, 6[2], 11[2], 14, 15, 17, 19, 21[2], 22, 24[2], 25, 26[2], 27[3]; **2:**2[2], 3, 4, 5, 9, 10, 12, 15, 16, 18, 19, 22[2], 23[3], 24, 25; **3:**4, 6, 7[2], 9[2], 10, 11, 13, 14, 16[2], 17[2]; **4:**1, 2[2], 7, 8[2], 9[2], 10, 11, 12[2], 13, 14, 15, 16, 17; **5:**1, 2, 3[2], 5, 6, 7[2], 8, 11[2], 12, 14, 15, 16[2], 17[2], 18[2], 19, 20; **1Pe 1:**1, 2[2], 3, 4, 7[2], 8[3], 10, 11[2], 21[3], 23, 24[2], 25; **2:**1[2], 4, 6[2], 8[2], 11, 12, 14, 18, 20[2], 22, 24, 25; **3:**2, 3[2], 4, 6[2], 7[2], 8, 10[2], 11[2], 12, 15, 19, 21, 22[2]; **4:**3, 4, 5, 7, 11[2], 14, 17, 18[2], 19; **5:**1, 4, 8, 10[3], 11, 12, 13; **2Pe 1:**1[2], 2[2], 3[2], 4[2], 5, 6[3], 7[2], 8, 9[2], 10, 11[2], 12, 15, 16, 17, 19[3]; **2:**2, 3, 5, 6[2], 7, 8, 9, 10[2], 11, 12[2], 13, 15, 16, 17, 18, 20[3], 21, 22; **3:**2[2], 3, 5[2], 6, 7[2], 8, 10[2], 11, 12[2], 13, 14, 16, 17, 18[3]; **1Jn 1:**1, 2[3], 3[3], 5, 6, 7, 8, 9[3], 10; **2:**2, 4, 8[2], 10, 11, 14[2], 16[2], 17, 18, 20, 21, 22, 24, 25, 27[2], 28[2]; **3:**1, 2, 5, 10, 12[3], 15, 16, 17, 18, 19, 20, 22[2], 23[2], 24[2]; **4:**3, 4, 5[2], 6[2], 7, 9, 10, 12, 13, 14[2], 15, 16[3], 21; **5:**1, 2, 3, 6[3], 8[2], 11[2], 15, 16, 17, 18, 19, 20[3]; **2Jn 1:**1[2], 2, 3[3], 5, 6, 7, 9[2], 10, 12[2]; **3Jn 1:**2, 3[2], 10, 12[2], 13, 14; **Jude 1:**1[2], 2, 3, 4[2], 6, 7[3], 8, 10, 12, 15[2], 16[2], 19, 20, 23, 24[2], 25[2]; **Rev 1:**2, 3[2], 4[4], 5[3], 6[5], 7[2], 8[3], 9[4], 10, 11[2], 12, 13[2], 14[2], 15, 16, 17[2], 18[4], 19, 20[2]; **2:**1, 2[2], 3[2], 5[2], 8[2], 9[2], 10[2], 14, 16, 18, 19[3], 20, 22, 23[2], 24, 26; **3:**1, 2, 3[3], 5, 7[2], 8, 9[2], 12[2], 14, 17[2], 18[2], 19[2], 20[4], 21; **4:**1[3], 2, 3[2], 4[2], 5, 6[2], 8[4], 9[3], 10[3], 11[5]; **5:**1, 2[2], 4, 5, 6[2], 7, 8[3], 9[6], 10[2], 11[4], 12[6], 13[9], 14[2]; **6:**2[3], 4, 5, 6[3], 8[4], 9, 10[2], 11[2], 13, 14[2], 15[3], 16[3], 17; **7:**2, 9[4], 10[2], 11[3], 12[7], 13, 14[2], 15[3], 17; **8:**2[2], 3, 5[3], 7[4], 8, 9, 10[2], 11, 12[3]; **9:**1, 2, 3[2], 5, 7, 8, 9[2], 10[2], 11, 13, 15[4], 17[4], 18, 19, 20[2]; **10:**1, 2, 3, 4[2], 5, 6[7], 8, 9[2], 10, 11; **11:**1[4], 3[2], 4, 5, 6[2], 7[2], 8, 9[3], 10, 11[3], 12, 13[3], 15[4], 16[2], 17[2], 18[6], 19[3]; **12:**1[2], 2, 3[2], 4, 5[2], 7[4], 8, 9, 10[4], 11, 12[2], 14, 15, 16, 17[2]; **13:**1[4], 2[3], 3, 4[2], 5[2], 6[3], 7[3], 10, 12[2], 13[2], 14, 15, 16[3]; **14:**1[3], 2[2], 3[3], 4[2], 6[2], 7[2], 8, 9[3], 10, 11[3], 12, 14[3], 15[2], 16, 17, 18[2], 19, 20; **15:**1, 2[4], 3[4], 4[2], 5, 6, 7, 8[3]; **16:**2[4], 3[2], 4[2], 5, 6[2], 7[2], 8, 9[2], 10, 11[2], 12, 13, 14, 15[2], 17, 18, 19[2], 20, 21; **17:**1, 2, 3[2], 4[4], 5, 7[2], 8[3], 11[2], 13[2], 14[3], 15, 16[3]; **18:**1, 2[2], 3, 5, 7[3], 8, 9[2], 10, 11, 12[4], 13[8], 14, 15[2], 16[4], 17[2], 19[2], 20[2], 21[2], 22[2], 23, 24[2]; **19:**1[2], 2, 3[2], 4[3], 5, 6, 7[3], 8, 9, 10, 11[3], 12, 13, 14[2], 16[2], 17, 18[5], 19[3], 20[2], 21; **20:**1[2], 2, 3[7], 4[4], 6[3], 8[2], 9[2], 10[4], 11[3], 12[3], 13[3], 14; **21:**1[3], 3[4], 5, 6[2], 7[2], 8, 9, 10[3], 11, 12, 13, 14, 15, 16[3], 17, 18, 20, 22, 23, 24, 26; **22:**1, 2, 3[2], 4, 5[2], 6, 8[3], 9[2], 11, 12, 13[3], 14, 15[2], 16[2], 17[3], 19[2].

ARE (3890)

Ge 2:12, 16; **3:**9, 14, 19; **4:**6, 11, 14; **6:**15, 19, 21; **9:**2; **10:**20, 31, 32; **12:**11, 13; **13:**8, 14; **16:**5, 8, 11, 13; **17:**8, 10, 11, 12, 15; **18:**24, 29; **19:**5, 13, 15; **20:**3, 16[2]; **21:**23; **22:**7; **23:**6, 8; **24:**13, 23, 31[2], 47; **25:**13, 16, 23; **26:**29; **27:**21, 22, 24, 32, 41; **28:**13; **29:**4, 8, 14, 15; **31:**12, 43[3], 49; **32:**4, 6, 17, 18[2], 19; **33:**5[2], 13[3]; **34:**21, 22, 30; **36:**10; **37:**13, 15, 16; **38:**25; **39:**9; **40:**7, 12, 18; **41:**25, 26[2], 27[3], 29, 35, 40; **42:**9, 11[2], 14, 16[3], 19, 21, 31[2], 33, 34, 38; **43:**16; **44:**16, 18; **45:**11, 19; **46:**8, 30, 32, 34; **47:**1, 3, 8, 9, 30; **48:**5, 8, 9; **49:**3, 5[2], 9, 26, 28; **50:**11, 17, 18; **Ex 1:**1, 19[2]; **2:**13, 14; **3:**5, 9, 14, 18; **4:**18, 19, 25; **5:**4, 5[2], 7, 8[2], 16[3], 17, 19; **6:**5; **7:**2; **8:**21, 26; **9:**27; **10:**9, 10, 26; **11:**2; **12:**4[2], 7, 8, 11, 13, 14, 15, 18, 42, 43; **13:**4, 5, 12; **14:**2, 3, 15; **15:**4, 24; **16:**4, 5, 7, 8[2], 26; **17:**4; **18:**14, 17, 20; **19:**3[2], 6[2]; **21:**1[2], 22, 23, 35; **22:**7, 9, 31; **23:**10, 14, 17; **24:**1, 14; **25:**2, 3[2], 15[2], 20[2], 22, 26, 27, 32, 33, 34, 38; **26:**2, 8; **27:**2, 7, 14, 15, 17, 19, 21; **28:**3, 4[3], 21, 28, 34; **29:**1, 28, 32, 33[2], 38; **30:**14, 15[2], 19, 32; **31:**11, 16; **32:**2, 4, 8, 9, 22; **33:**3, 5, 13, 16; **34:**12, 23; **35:**1, 10[2]; **36:**1, 5; **38:**21; **Lev 1:**7, 16; **2:**11, 12; **3:**5; **4:**12, 13, 15; **6:**9, 14[2], 16, 20, 25; **7:**1, 11, 32, 37; **8:**31, 33; **10:**9; **11:**2, 4, 8, 10, 11, 13[3], 20, 21, 23, 27, 28, 29, 31[2], 35[2], 37, 39, 42, 46; **12:**4, 6, 7; **13:**39, 59; **14:**2, 13, 32, 42, 54, 57; **15:**32; **16:**4, 27; **17:**5; **18:**17; **19:**20, 23; **20:**2, 26, 27; **21:**6, 7; **22:**7, 9, 24, 25; **23:**2[2], 3[2], 4[2], 20, 21, 24, 32, 37[2], 38, 40, 42; **24:**9, 14, 22; **25:**15, 16[4], 23, 31[2], 33, 41, 42, 44, 50, 54, 55; **26:**3, 34, 36, 39, 41, 44, 46; **27:**34; **Nu 1:**3[2], 5[2], 50[2], 51, 52, 53[2]; **2:**2, 3, 32; **3:**7, 8, 9[2], 12, 13[2], 40, 45; **4:**5, 6, 7, 8, 9, 10, 11, 12, 13, 14[2], 15[3], 18, 19, 25, 26, 27, 28; **5:**10; **6:**20, 23; **8:**2, 8, 10[2], 14, 15, 16[2], 26; **9:**10[2], 11[2]; **10:**3, 4, 5, 6, 8, 10, 29; **11:**15, 16, 27, 29; **13:**4, 16, 18, 19, 20, 28[2], 31[2], 32; **14:**14, 25, 41; **15:**21, 38; **16:**6, 10, 16, 17, 37; **17:**12[2], 13; **18:**1[2], 3[2], 4[2], 5, 9, 16, 17, 18, 23; **20:**16; **21:**29; **22:**6[3], 9, 12, 34; **24:**4, 5, 16; **26:**2, 63; **27:**7; **28:**3, 31; **29:**6[2]; **30:**16; **31:**26, 30; **32:**4, 14, 17; **33:**1; **34:**17[2], 19, 29; **35:**8, 29, 33; **36:**13; **Dt 1:**1, 9, 10, 22, 28[3]; **2:**4, 6, 18; **3:**21, 27; **4:**4, 5, 14[2], 20, 22, 26, 30, 45; **5:**3, 22, 31; **6:**1[2], 6, 11, 25; **7:**1, 5, 6, 12, 17[2], 23, 25; **8:**9, 10, 12; **9:**1, 2, 5, 6, 13, 29; **10:**2, 5, 19[2]; **11:**8, 10, 11, 12, 21, 29[2], 30, 31[2]; **12:**1, 2, 5, 8, 11, 18[2], 29; **14:**1, 2, 4, 7, 8, 19, 21; **15:**5, 20, 22; **17:**8, 9, 16, 18; **18:**1[2], 4; **19:**9, 17; **20:**2, 3, 15[2], 19, 20; **21:**4, 11, 14; **22:**28; **23:**9, 20; **24:**8, 11, 19; **25:**1, 5, 11; **26:**18[2]; **27:**9; **28:**10, 20, 21, 24, 45, 51[2], 58, 61, 63; **29:**1, 10, 12, 15[2]; **30:**10, 16, 17[2], 18; **31:**13, 16[2], 21, 27, 29; **32:**4[2], 5, 17, 20[2], 21, 28, 32, 37, 47[3]; **33:**3, 17[3], 27, 29; **Jos 1:**14; **2:**9, 14, 20, 24; **3:**3[2]; **4:**7, 9; **5:**13, 15; **6:**17[2], 19; **7:**3, 10, 21; **8:**4, 6, 7; **9:**8[2], 11, 13[2], 23, 25, 27; **10:**25, 27; **11:**6; **12:**1, 7; **13:**1[2], 14; **14:**1; **15:**12; **16:**10; **17:**2, 14, 15, 17, 18; **18:**5; **19:**51; **20:**4; **22:**18; **23:**8; **24:**15, 19, 22[2], 23, 27; **Jdg 1:**24; **3:**1; **4:**9; **5:**30; **6:**13, 23, 31[2]; **7:**4, 10, 11, 18; **8:**5, 15; **9:**9, 31, 36, 37; **10:**4, 14; **11:**2[2], 8, 25, 27; **12:**4, 5; **13:**3[2], 11, 12, 22; **15:**11; **16:**9, 12, 14, 20; **17:**9; **18:**3[2], 18; **19:**12, 17, 18, 20; **20:**32, 39; **21:**7, 11, 16, 22; **Ru 2:**9[2]; **3:**3, 9[2], 11, 15; **4:**9, 10, 11; **1Sa 1:**8[2]; **2:**3, 4[2], 8; **4:**8, 17; **6:**5, 8, 17; **7:**3; **8:**5, 7, 8; **9:**13, 19; **10:**7, 8; **11:**5; **12:**2, 21; **14:**9, 11, 28, 33, 38; **16:**3, 11; **17:**8, 18, 19, 28, 33[2], 58; **19:**3, 22; **20:**2, 21[2], 22; **21:**1, 5[2]; **23:**1[2], 3, 27; **24:**11, 14, 17; **25:**10; **26:**11, 14, 16; **28:**12, 15; **2Sa 1:**4, 5, 8, 13; **3:**25, 28, 39; **5:**1, 8, 14; **6:**2; **7:**5, 12, 22, 28[2]; **9:**2, 10; **10:**11[3]; **11:**11[2]; **12:**7, 13, 21; **13:**33, 35; **14:**2; **15:**2, 3, 13, 15, 19, 36; **16:**2[2], 8; **17:**8, 10, 20; **18:**3[2], 20; **19:**3, 12, 13[2], 42; **20:**9, 17, 19[2]; **22:**23, 28, 29, 44; **23:**1, 6[2], 7, 8; **24:**2, 17, 22[2]; **1Ki 1:**14, 20, 25, 35; **2:**9, 39; **4:**8; **5:**9; **6:**12; **8:**8, 19, 25, 35, 47, 51; **9:**13; **11:**41; **12:**28; **13:**14, 18; **14:**5, 19, 29; **15:**7, 23, 31; **16:**5, 14, 20, 27; **17:**24; **18:**9, 25, 36, 37[2]; **19:**9, 10, 13, 14; **20:**3[2], 4, 17, 23, 31; **21:**5; **22:**3, 4, 11, 13, 39, 45; **2Ki 1:**3, 4, 6[2], 16, 18; **3:**7; **4:**26; **5:**12; **6:**9, 16[3], 19; **7:**9, 12, 13[2]; **8:**23; **9:**7; **10:**2, 5, 6, 9, 13[2], 15, 23, 34; **11:**5[3], 7[2]; **12:**19; **13:**8, 12; **14:**10, 15, 18, 28; **15:**6, 11, 15, 21, 26, 31, 36; **16:**7, 19; **17:**23, 26; **18:**19, 20, 21, 22, 24, 34[2]; **19:**15, 19, 26[2]; **20:**1, 20; **21:**17, 25; **22:**7; **23:**28; **24:**5; **1Ch 2:**55; **4:**22; **5:**26; **6:**17, 19, 31, 33; **11:**1; **12:**17, 18[2], 23; **13:**2; **14:**4; **15:**12[2]; **16:**14, 26, 27; **17:**4, 11, 26; **19:**12[3]; **21:**2, 3, 17; **22:**8, 13; **23:**4[2], 5[2]; **28:**3[2], 21; **29:**11, 12[2], 14, 15[2], 17[2], 29; **2Ch 1:**9; **2:**8; **5:**9; **6:**9, 16, 26, 37; **7:**14; **8:**11; **9:**29; **12:**15; **13:**8, 9, 10, 11, 22; **14:**11; **15:**2; **16:**9, 11; **18:**3, 10, 12; **19:**6, 10; **20:**6[2], 10, 11, 12, 34[2]; **23:**4[3], 5, 6[2], 7; **24:**27; **25:**19, 26; **26:**22; **27:**7; **28:**26; **29:**9, 19; **30:**6; **32:**10, 32, 33; **33:**18, 19; **34:**16; **35:**25, 27; **36:**8; **Ezr 1:**4; **2:**1; **4:**12[2], 13, 14[2], 16; **5:**4, 8, 11[2]; **6:**4, 5[2], 8[2]; **7:**14, 15, 24, 25; **8:**1, 28[2]; **9:**6, 9, 11, 15[3]; **10:**12, 13; **Ne 1:**3[2], 8, 9, 10; **2:**2, 3, 5, 17, 19[2]; **4:**2[2], 3, 4, 19; **5:**2, 3, 5[3], 7, 8, 9, 10, 11; **6:**6[3], 8[2], 10[2]; **7:**3[2], 6; **9:**6, 7, 8, 13[2], 17, 31, 36, 37, 38[2]; **10:**28, 38, 39[2]; **11:**3, **13:**17, 18, 25[2], 27[2]; **Est 3:**8; **4:**13, 16; **10:**2; **Job 1:**10, 19; **2:**9, 10; **3:**8, 17, 19, 22; **4:**5[2], 9, 10, 11, 19[2], 20, 21; **5:**4, 11, 13; **6:**4[2], 15, 20, 21, 25; **7:**1, 6; **8:**2, 6, 9; **9:**12, 25; **10:**5, 20; **11:**2, 4, 8[2]; **12:**2, 5, 6[2], 13, 16; **13:**4, 12[2]; **14:**5, 12, 21[2]; **15:**7, 10, 11, 15; **16:**2; **17:**1, 8[2], 11[2], 14; **18:**3, 20[2]; **19:**13; **21:**9, 18, 27; **22:**5, 10, 12, 20, 29; **24:**8, 13, 18, 20[2], 23, 24[4]; **25:**5; **26:**5, 14; **27:**5; **28:**18; **31:**24, 38, 40; **32:**6, 9, 15, 16; **33:**2, 12; **34:**18[2], 19, 20[2], 21, 25; **35:**6, 7; **36:**4, 8, 17; **38:**15, 24, 35; **39:**3, 30; **40:**17, 18; **41:**17, 18, 23[2], 25, 28, 30, 34[2]; **Ps 1:**4; **2:**7, 12; **3:**1, 2, 3; **4:**4, 6; **5:**4; **6:**2; **8:**4; **9:**15, 16, 20; **10:**2, 5[2], 7, 10, 14; **11:**3; **12:**1, 6; **14:**1[2], 2, 5; **16:**2, 3[2]; **17:**12; **18:**22, 27, 43; **19:**7, 8[2], 9, 10[2]; **20:**1, 5, 8; **22:**1, 3[2], 14; **23:**4; **25:**3, 5, 6, 7, 10, 15; **26:**10[2]; **31:**3, 4, 14, 15; **32:**1[2], 7, 10, 11; **33:**18; **34:**5[2], 15[2], 18; **35:**19; **36:**3; **37:**14, 18, 26, 34; **38:**5, 19[3]; **39:**1, 9; **40:**5, 12, 17; **41:**11; **42:**5, 11; **43:**2, 5; **44:**4, 22, 25; **45:**2, 8, 9, 14, 15; **46:**6; **48:**11; **49:**14; **50:**8, 11; **51:**4, 17; **52:**1; **53:**1[2], 2; **54:**3; **55:**10, 11, 21[2]; **56:**2, 5, 8; **57:**4[2]; **58:**3, 10, 11; **59:**4, 9, 13, 16, 17; **62:**9[4], 11, 12; **63:**1, 7; **64:**6; **65:**4[2], 9, 12, 13[2]; **66:**3; **68:**13, 15[2], 17, 25[2], 35; **69:**4, 19; **70:**5; **71:**3, 7, 18; **73:**1, 4, 5[2], 12, 19, 27[2]; **74:**9[2], 12; **76:**4, 7[2], 10; **77:**13, 14; **79:**4, 8; **82:**5, 6[2], 8; **83:**2, 18; **84:**4[2], 5; **86:**2, 5, 10[2], 14, 15; **87:**3, 7; **88:**5, 9, 10, 12; **89:**8, 11, 14, 15, 17, 26; **90:**2, 4, 5, 7; **92:**5, 8; **93:**2; **94:**4, 11; **95:**4, 7, 10; **96:**5, 6[2]; **97:**2, 7, 8, 9[2], 12; **100:**3[2]; **102:**11, 14, 25; **103:**11, 14[2], 15; **104:**1[2], 16, 18, 24, 28, 29, 30; **105:**7; **106:**3; **110:**4; **111:**2[2], 3, 7[2], 8; **112:**3; **115:**4; **116:**11; **118:**28[2]; **119:**1[2], 2, 4, 21, 24[2], 39, 54, 57, 68, 70, 75, 86, 95, 96, 98, 103, 111[2], 114, 129, 137[2], 138[2], 143, 144, 150[2], 151[2], 157, 160[2], 168, 172; **120:**7; **122:**2; **125:**1, 4[2]; **126:**3; **127:**3, 4; **128:**1; **130:**4; **131:**1; **135:**15; **139:**3, 8[2], 14, 17; **140:**6; **141:**4, 8; **142:**5, 6; **143:**10; **144:**4, 8[2], 11[2], 15[2]; **145:**14; **146:**8; **Pr 1:**16; **2:**12, 15[2]; **3:**16, 17[2]; **4:**16, 22, 26; **5:**6, 11, 21; **6:**16[2], 18, 23[2], 33; **7:**4, 26[2]; **8:**5[2], 8, 9[2], 14, 15, 18, 32; **9:**4, 12[2], 16, 18[2]; **10:**2, 19, 25, 27; **11:**1, 3, 5, 6, 10, 20, 21; **12:**5, 7[2], 8, 10, 22; **13:**4; **14:**2, 4, 18, 20, 32; **15:**3, 15, 26; **16:**2, 7, 11[2], 21, 24; **17:**6[2], 7; **18:**4, 7, 8, 10, 19; **19:**1, 7, 14, 21, 29; **20:**5, 7, 15, 24; **21:**4, 20; **22:**10, 22; **23:**2, 5; **24:**4, 9, 16, 23, 24; **25:**1, 3[2], 28; **26:**22, 23; **27:**20[2]; **28:**1, 6, 9, 18; **30:**11, 12[2], 13[2], 14[2], 15[2], 18[2], 24[2], 25, 26, 29[2]; **31:**6[2], 8, 17, 21; **Ecc 1:**8, 11, 14[2]; **3:**18; **4:**2[2], 9; **5:**2, 3[2], 7, 8, 11; **6:**7; **7:**14[2], 26; **8:**4, 11, 12; **9:**1, 2, 3, 10, 12[3], 16, 17; **10:**6, 12, 13[2], 17, 18; **11:**3, 9, 10; **12:**3, 4, 5, 11; **SS 1:**4, 10, 15[2], 16, 17[2]; **2:**11, 15; **4:**1[2], 2, 3[2], 5, 7, 11, 12[2], 13, 15; **5:**12, 13[2], 14, 15; **6:**4, 6, 7; **7:**1, 3, 4, 6, 12; **8:**8, 10, 12[2]; **Isa 1:**7, 11, 15, 18[2], 19, 23; **2:**6; **3:**8, 16; **4:**3[2]; **5:**7, 11, 21, 22, 25, 28[2]; **6:**11, 13; **7:**2, 25; **8:**13[3], 18, 21; **9:**15[2], 16[2]; **10:**8; **13:**15; **14:**7, 10, 11, 15, 19[2], 21; **15:**4[2], 6, 9; **16:**2, 6, 10; **17:**14; **19:**11, 12, 13; **22:**7[2], 8, 16; **23:**8[2], 9; **24:**6[2], 13, 18; **25:**1; **26:**8, 14; **27:**11[2]; **28:**7, 8; **29:**13, 24; **30:**1, 9, 17, 18, 27; **31:**3[2]; **32:**7, 9; **33:**8[3], 13[2], 14; **36:**4, 5, 6, 7, 9, 19[2]; **37:**16, 20, 27[2]; **38:**1; **40:**6, 7, 15[2], 17[2], 22, 24[2]; **41:**9, 17, 23, 24[2], 27, 29[2]; **42:**7, 16, 17, 20; **43:**1, 4, 8[2], 10, 12; **44:**8, 9[4], 11, 17, 18, 21[2]; **45:**9, 15, 20, 24; **46:**1[3], 12; **47:**14[2]; **48:**1, 7, 8; **49:**3, 16; **51:**12[2], 16, 20; **52:**7; **53:**5; **54:**1; **55:**1, 8[2], 9[2]; **56:**10[2], 11[2]; **57:**1[2], 4[2], 6[2], 20; **59:**3, 6[3], 7[2], 10, 12[2]; **60:**4, 8, 9, 21; **61:**9; **63:**2, 8, 15[2], 16[2], 17, 19; **64:**6, 8[4], 9; **65:**5, 24; **66:**15; **Jer 2:**11, 15, 23, 25, 27[2], 28[2], 31, 33; **3:**22; **4:**13[2], 20, 22[3], 29, 30; **5:**2, 4[2], 7, 8, 13, 16[2], 26, 27; **6:**7, 10, 13, 15, 20, 23[2], 28[2], 29, 30; **7:**8[2], 10, 17, 19[2], 32; **8:**8, 10, 12[2], 14, 20, 21; **9:**2, 10[2], 19[2], 25[2], 26; **10:**2, 3, 6, 8[2], 14, 15, 20[3], 21; **11:**13, 21; **12:**1, 2, 4[2]; **13:**4, 20, 23; **14:**4, 8, 9[2], 14[2], 15[2], 16, 22; **15:**5, 15; **16:**3[2], 14, 17[2], 20; **17:**8, 14, 17, 24; **18:**6, 19; **19:**6, 10; **20:**10; **21:**4[3], 9; **22:**4, 6, 17, 20, 23; **23:**1, 5, 7, 10, 11, 12, 14[2], 16; **24:**3[2], 8, 10; **25:**12, 13, 18, 23; **26:**19; **27:**5, 14, 15, 16, 18, 19, 21; **28:**16; **29:**9, 10, 17, 21, 22; **30:**3, 4, 5, 17; **31:**15, 18, 27, 29, 38, 40; **32:**19[3], 24[2], 29, 36; **33:**10, 14, 18, 21, 24; **35:**7; **36:**7, 19; **37:**13, 19; **38:**4, 16, 22; **40:**10, 15, 16; **42:**2, 6, 15, 17; **43:**2, 9; **44:**6, 27; **46:**5[3], 21, 23; **47:**2; **48:**5, 12, 14, 33[3], 34, 46[2]; **49:**2, 23[2], 32; **50:**7, 11, 15, 32, 33, 41, 42[2]; **51:**13, 17, 18, 20, 30[2], 39, 46, 51, 52; **La 1:**2, 4, 5, 6, 16, 22; **2:**9, 11; **3:**22, 23, 31, 48; **4:**1, 2, 5, 8[2], 9, 14[2], 15, 16; **5:**5[2], 7, 12, 14, 17, 22; **Eze 2:**4, 5, 6[2], 7; **3:**5, 7, 8, 9, 26, 27; **4:**4, 9; **6:**8; **7:**15; **8:**6[2], 9, 12, 13, 15, 17; **9:**4, 8; **11:**2[2], 3, 5, 7, 15[3], 21; **12:**2[2], 3[2], 4, 6, 9, 10, 23; **13:**2, 4, 6, 15; **16:**30, 34[2], 45[2], 57, 61[2]; **17:**17; **18:**2, 25, 29[2]; **20:**38, 49; **21:**7, 12, 29; **22:**5[2], 6, 9[2], 10[3], 18[2], 24, 27; **23:**25[2], 45; **26:**17, 18; **27:**25, 34, 35[2]; **28:**2[2], 3, 6, 19, 24; **30:**8; **31:**14[3]; **32:**2[2], 19, 23[2], 24, 25[2], 26[2], 29, 30; **33:**10[2], 24[2], 27, 30, 31, 32; **34:**30, 31; **36:**20, 35; **37:**11[3]; **38:**14, 17; **39:**19[2]; **40:**46[2]; **42:**13, 14[4]; **43:**11, 13, 19[2], 20, 21, 22, 23, 24[2], 25[2], 26, 27; **44:**13, 15[3], 16[2], 17, 18, 19[3], 20, 23, 24[3], 28, 30; **45:**1, 6, 10, 11, 13, 14, 18, 20[2], 21; **46:**2, 3, 13, 14, 24; **47:**13[2], 14, 21, 22[3], 23; **48:**1, 8, 9, 29; **Da 2:**8, 20, 26, 28, 37, 38; **3:**4, 12, 15, 17; **4:**3, 10, 22, 35, 37; **5:**13, 16; **7:**17, 24; **9:**7[2], 8, 18, 23, 24; **10:**11; **11:**33, 34; **12:**3, 6, 9, 10; **Hos 1:**9, 10; **2:**4, 23[2]; **3:**3; **4:**3, 4, 6, 12[2], 16, 18; **5:**2, 7, 10; **7:**1, 2, 4, 6, 7, 16; **8:**6; **9:**7[3], 14, 15; **11:**7; **12:**11; **13:**9[2], 10, 12, 14; **14:**9; **Joel 1:**9[2], 10, 12, 13, 17[2], 18; **2:**6, 10, 11[2], 22[2], 26; **3:**4[2]; **Am 5:**12, 13; **6:**1, 2, 9; **8:**11; **9:**1, 4, 7, 8, 13; **Ob 1:**20[2]; **Jnh 1:**8; **4:**2; **Mic 1:**2; **2:**4, 7; **4:**11; **5:**2[2]; **6:**12[2]; **7:**3, 6; **Na 1:**3, 6, 12, 14[2]; **2:**3[4], 6; **3:**8, 12[2], 13[2], 16, 17, 18; **Hab 1:**3, 7[2], 8, 12, 13[2]; **2:**4, 8, 15; **3:**6, 17[2]; **Zep 1:**12[2]; **3:**3[2], 4[2], 6[2], 18; **Hag 1:**6; **Zec 1:**5, 9[2], 10, 19[2], 21[2]; **2:**2; **3:**8, 9; **4:**3, 4, 5, 7, 10, 11, 12, 13, 14[2]; **5:**10; **6:**4, 5, 15; **7:**7; **8:**16[2]; **9:**1, 2, 7; **10:**2; **11:**2, 3, 9; **12:**3, 5; **13:**6, 9; **14:**12; **Mal 2:**15, 17; **3:**1, 6, 7, 9[2]; **Mt 1:**21; **2:**6, 18, 20; **4:**3, 6; **5:**3, 4, 5, 6, 7, 8, 9, 10[2], 11, 13, 14, 23, 25, 46, 47; **6:**16, 18, 22, 23, 26; **7:**11, 15; **8:**2, 26; **9:**2, 5, 17, 37; **10:**2, 23, 29, 30, 31; **11:**3, 5[2], 8, 14, 16, 28; **12:**2, 5, 34, 47, 48, 49; **13:**16, 29, 38, 39, 40; **14:**2, 33; **15:**8, 9, 14, 16, 20; **16:**8, 16, 17, 18, 23, 28; **17:**26; **19:**6, 12, 26, 30[2]; **20:**15, 18, 22; **21:**13, 16, 23, 26, 31; **22:**14[2], 16[2], 18, 29; **23:**4, 8[2], 10, 13, 15, 25, 27[2], 28,

AS (4006)

AT (2217)

BE (5161)

7:20; 8:33; 9:9, 11^{2}; 10:7, 9, 24, 30, 31; 11:21, 25, 29; 12:3^{2}, 9^{2}; 13:7^{2}; 14:11, 14, 26, 33; 15:31; 16:5, 19; 17:11; 18:5; 19:2, 7, 18, 20, 22; 20:20, 21; 21:13, 17, 25, 28; 22:1, 8, 9, 13, 19, 26, 27; 23:15, 17, 18, 19, 25, 34; 24:8, 14, 19, 20; 25:5, 15; 26:4, 5, 26^{2}; 27:6, 11, 14, 18, 23; 28:8, 11, 17, 20; 29:1, 6, 14, 19, 25; 30:17^{2}, 28; 31:30; Ecc 1:9^{2}, 11, 15^{2}; 2:1, 16^{2}, 19; 3:2, 7, 12, 14, 15, 17; 4:12; 5:2^{3}, 6, 8, 19; 7:9, 14, 16^{2}, 17^{2}, 23, 24; 8:3, 15; 9:8, 17; 10:8, 9^{2}; 11:6, 8, 9; 12:12; SS 1:7; 2:17; 6:8; 7:8; 8:7, 14; Isa 1:5, 18^{2}, 20, 26, 27, 28, 29^{2}, 30; 2:2^{2}, 9, 11^{2}, 12, 17^{2}; 3:6, 10, 11, 24; 4:1, 2^{2}, 3, 5, 6; 5:5^{2}, 13, 15, 16, 30; 6:9^{2}, 10, 13^{2}; 7:4^{2}, 8^{2}, 14, 16, 23, 24; 8:4, 9^{3}, 10, 14^{3}, 15^{2}, 22; 9:1, 5^{2}, 6^{2}, 7, 19^{2}, 20^{2}; 10:16, 19, 22, 24, 25, 27^{2}, 33^{2}; 11:5, 9, 10, 13^{2}, 14, 16; 12:2, 5; 13:10, 15, 16^{2}, 19, 20, 22; 14:20, 24, 25, 29, 32; 16:4, 5, 14^{2}; 17:1, 2, 3, 5, 9^{2}, 11; 18:6, 7^{2}; 19:5, 7, 10^{2}, 16, 17, 18, 19, 20, 23, 24, 25; 20:5; 21:7, 17; 22:14, 19, 21, 23, 25^{2}; 23:2, 4, 5, 11, 15, 16, 18^{2}; 24:2, 3, 13, 18, 22^{3}, 23; 25:2, 9, 10; 26:1, 11; 27:9^{4}, 12; 28:3, 4, 5, 6, 13, 16, 18^{2}, 28; 29:2, 7, 8, 9^{3}, 16, 17, 20, 21, 22; 30:3, 5, 8, 14, 16, 18, 19, 20, 23, 26, 32; 31:8; 32:2, 3, 4, 5^{2}, 14, 17^{2}, 20; 33:1^{2}, 2^{2}, 6, 10^{2}, 12^{2}, 16^{2}, 20^{2}, 21^{2}, 23, 24; 34:3^{2}, 4, 7^{2}, 9, 10, 12, 16; 35:1, 2, 4, 5, 8^{3}, 9^{2}; 36:15; 37:4, 6, 10, 11, 30; 38:10, 11, 22; 39:6^{2}, 7^{2}, 8; 40:4, 5, 9, 31; 41:1, 6, 10, 11^{2}, 12, 14, 23; 42:4, 6, 17; 43:2^{2}, 5, 10; 44:2, 8, 11^{2}, 26^{2}, 27, 28^{2}; 45:1, 14, 16, 17^{2}, 18^{2}, 21, 22, 23, 24, 25; 46:5, 13; 47:1, 3, 5, 8; 48:11, 14, 19; 49:5, 6, 8, 9, 11, 19^{2}, 23^{2}, 24, 25, 26; 50:7^{2}; 51:3, 7, 14, 23; 52:3, 11, 12, 13; 53:11; 54:4^{2}, 6, 9, 10^{4}, 13^{2}, 14^{3}, 15; 55:6, 12, 13^{2}; 56:1, 5, 7^{2}, 12; 57:1, 14, 16; 58:4, 8, 11, 12; 59:15; 60:5^{2}, 7^{2}, 11, 12, 16, 18, 19^{3}, 20, 21; 61:3, 6^{2}, 7, 9; 62:2, 3, 4^{2}, 6, 12^{2}; 63:7, 8, 12; 64:5, 9; 65:13, 16, 17, 18^{2}, 19, 20^{3}, 22, 23, 25; 66:1, 5^{2}, 8^{2}, 10, 11, 12, 13, 14^{2}, 16, 21, 24^{2}; Jer 1:8, 14, 17; 2:12, 36, 37; 3:1, 5, 12, 16^{3}; 4:2, 9^{2}, 11, 14, 27; 5:13; 6:6, 11, 12, 15; 7:20^{2}, 23^{2}, 33; 8:1, 2^{3}, 9^{2}, 12, 13^{3}, 17; 10:2, 5, 18; 11:4^{2}, 16, 19, 23; 12:3, 4, 11^{2}, 12, 16; 13:10, 11, 12^{2}, 15, 17, 19^{3}, 26, 27; 14:16^{2}, 19; 15:9, 18, 19; 16:4^{2}, 6; 17:6, 8, 11, 13^{2}, 14^{2}, 15, 17, 18^{2}, 21, 25; 18:7, 9, 16^{2}, 18, 20, 21^{2}, 22, 23; 19:8, 11, 13; 20:6, 10, 11^{2}, 14^{2}, 15, 16; 21:10; 22:9, 20, 22, 28; 23:3, 4^{2}, 6^{2}, 12, 40; 24:2, 3, 7^{2}, 8; 25:14, 33^{3}, 34^{2}, 37; 26:9^{2}, 11, 15, 16, 18, 24; 27:16, 18, 22; 28:9; 29:14, 17, 26, 28; 30:7^{4}, 10, 16^{2}, 18, 19^{2}, 20^{2}, 21^{2}, 22^{2}; 31:1^{2}, 4, 6, 8, 12, 13, 14, 15, 16, 30, 32, 33^{2}, 36, 37^{2}, 38, 40^{2}; 32:4, 15, 24, 25, 36, 38^{2}, 43, 44^{2}; 33:4, 5, 9, 10, 12, 16^{2}, 21; 34:3; 36:30; 37:17, 21; 38:3, 4, 17^{2}, 18, 20, 22, 23^{3}; 39:16, 17, 18; 40:9, 15; 42:5, 11^{2}, 14, 18^{2}, 19, 22; 44:28, 29; 46:15, 19, 21, 23^{2}, 24, 26, 27; 47:5, 6; 48:1^{3}, 2^{2}, 4, 7, 8, 9, 13, 15, 26, 28, 41^{2}, 42, 44; 49:2, 5, 10, 13, 17, 20, 22, 26, 29^{2}, 32, 36; 50:2^{3}, 5, 8, 9^{2}, 10, 12^{3}, 13^{3}, 19, 20^{3}, 27, 30, 31, 36, 37, 39, 45; 51:6, 8^{2}, 9, 13, 26^{2}, 35^{2}, 37, 41^{2}, 43, 46, 47, 56^{2}, 58, 62; 52:20; La 2:20; 3:29, 30, 54, 65; 4:21^{3}; 5:4; Eze 1:16, 27; 2:6^{3}; 3:9, 12, 20, 25, 26; 4:3^{2}, 17^{2}; 5:13, 15; 6:4^{2}, 6^{2}; 7:11, 13, 15, 16, 18^{3}, 19^{2}, 24, 25, 26, 27; 8:2; 10:5, 8; 11:3, 11^{2}, 20^{3}; 12:11, 12, 13, 19, 20^{2}, 23, 24, 25, 28^{2}; 13:6, 9^{2}, 14^{2}; 14:10, 11^{2}, 16^{2}, 18, 21, 22^{3}, 23; 15:5; 16:13, 42, 52, 54, 61, 63; 17:9, 14, 17, 20, 21; 18:13^{2}, 20^{2}, 22, 24, 30; 19:14; 20:19, 20, 32, 47^{2}, 48; 21:4, 11^{2}, 15, 24, 26^{3}, 27, 29^{2}, 32^{3}; 22:14, 21, 22; 23:25, 29, 33; 24:8, 10, 11, 13^{2}, 14, 24, 27^{3}; 25:10; 26:6, 10, 13, 14, 21^{3}; 27:36; 28:9, 19; 29:5, 14, 15, 16^{2}; 30:4, 7, 11, 13, 16^{2}, 18^{2}; 31:2, 18^{2}; 32:6, 10, 12, 13, 19, 20, 28, 31, 32; 33:4, 5, 6, 12, 13, 16, 27; 34:10, 14, 22, 23, 24^{2}, 26, 27, 28, 29; 35:4, 9, 10, 15; 36:9, 10, 11, 12, 25, 27, 28^{2}, 32, 33, 34, 38; 37:22^{3}, 23^{2}, 24^{2}, 25, 26, 27^{3}; 38:5, 7, 8, 9, 18, 19, 20, 21; 39:7, 11^{2}, 12, 13, 14, 16, 25; 43:10, 11, 12, 18, 22; 44:2, 14, 28^{2}; 45:1, 2, 3, 4^{2}, 8, 11^{2}, 15^{2}, 17; 46:1^{2}, 2, 4, 5^{2}, 10, 11, 12^{2}, 15, 16, 18; 47:9, 10^{2}, 11, 15, 17, 18, 19, 20^{2}, 22; 48:1, 8^{3}, 9, 10^{3}, 11, 12, 13, 15^{2}, 17, 18, 20, 21, 29, 30, 31^{2}, 32, 33, 34, 35^{2}; Da 1:5; 2:18, 20, 40, 41, 42, 43, 44^{2}, 46; 3:6, 11, 15^{2}, 28, 29^{2}; 4:6, 15, 16^{2}, 23, 25^{2}, 26, 27^{2}, 32; 5:7^{3}, 10, 16^{2}; 6:7, 8^{2}, 12^{2}, 15, 17, 26; 7:14, 23, 25, 26, 27^{2}; 8:11, 13^{2}, 14, 25; 9:25^{2}, 26; 10:12, 19^{3}; 11:2, 4^{2}, 6, 7, 11, 12, 15, 16, 19, 20, 21, 22^{2}, 25, 26, 28, 29, 33, 35, 36, 41; 12:1^{2}, 6, 7^{2}, 8, 10^{2}, 11; Hos 1:10^{3}, 11^{2}; 2:17; 3:3^{2}; 4:9; 5:9, 14; 7:16; 8:5, 6; 9:1, 4^{3}, 6, 17; 10:6^{3}, 8, 10, 14, 15; 12:11; 13:3, 15, 16; 14:5, 6, 7; Joel 2:2, 18, 21^{2}, 22, 23, 24, 26, 27, 31, 32^{2}; 3:12, 15, 16, 17, 19, 20; Am 3:12, 14, 15^{2}; 4:2, 3; 5:5, 14, 16^{2}, 17, 18, 19, 20; 6:7; 7:9^{2}, 17; 8:5^{2}, 8; 9:11, 13, 15; Ob 1:2, 6, 9^{2}, 10^{2}, 15, 16, 17^{2}, 18^{3}, 21; Jnh 2:8; 3:4, 8; 4:4, 8, 9, 11; Mic 1:7^{3}; 2:3, 7, 11; 3:7, 12; 4:1^{2}, 8, 10, 11; 5:2, 3, 5, 7, 8, 9^{2}; 6:7, 14^{2}; 7:5, 8, 10^{2}, 16, 17, 20; Na 1:10^{2}, 12, 15; 2:7, 13; Hab 1:5; 2:14, 16^{2}, 20; 3:18; Zep 1:7, 11^{2}, 13, 14, 15, 17, 18^{2}; 2:3, 4^{2}, 5, 6, 11, 12, 14^{2}; 3:6, 7, 8, 11^{2}, 13, 14; Hag 1:2, 4, 8, 9; 2:4^{3}, 9; Zec 1:4, 16^{2}; 2:4, 5^{2}, 10, 11, 13; 5:3^{2}, 11; 6:13^{3}, 14; 8:3^{2}, 5, 8^{2}, 9^{2}, 13^{3}, 15; 9:4, 5, 7, 10, 15, 17; 10:5, 6, 7^{2}, 8, 10, 11^{2}; 11:9, 17; 12:2, 7, 8^{2}, 11; 13:1, 2, 4, 7, 8^{2}; 14:1, 2^{2}, 4, 6, 7^{2}, 9^{2}, 10, 11^{3}, 13, 14, 19, 20^{2}, 21^{2}; Mal 1:4, 8, 9, 11^{3}, 14; 2:3, 9, 12; 3:2, 4, 5, 10, 12, 17; 4:1^{2}, 3; Mt 1:18^{2}, 20, 23; 2:4, 6, 18, 23; 3:10, 13, 14, 15; 4:1; 5:4, 6, 7, 9, 12, 13^{2}, 14, 19^{2}, 21, 22^{2}, 24, 25, 29, 37, 45, 48; 6:1^{2}, 2, 4, 5^{2}, 7, 8, 9, 10, 18, 21, 22, 23, 24, 33; 7:1, 2^{2}, 7^{2}, 8; 8:3, 8, 12^{2}, 13; 9:15, 17, 21, 29; 10:15, 16, 17, 18, 19, 20, 22, 25, 26^{3}, 28^{2}, 31, 36; 11:22, 23, 24; 12:23, 25, 27, 31^{2}, 32^{2}, 33^{2}, 37^{2}, 39, 40, 45; 13:12^{2}, 14^{2}, 30, 40, 42, 49, 50; 14:9, 27; 15:4, 13; 16:2, 3, 4, 6^{2}, 11, 19^{2}, 21^{2}, 26; 17:4, 7, 11, 20, 22, 23; 18:6^{2}, 8, 9, 14, 16, 18^{2}, 19, 25, 26, 29, 34; 19:5, 21, 25, 27, 30^{2}; 20:16^{2}, 18, 19^{2}, 26, 27^{2}, 28, 31; 21:13, 21, 43, 44^{2}; 22:13, 28, 30^{2}, 45; 23:7, 8, 10, 11, 12^{2}, 26; 24:2^{2}, 3, 7, 9^{3}, 13, 14, 19, 21^{2}, 22, 27, 29^{2}, 37, 39, 40^{2}, 41^{2}, 43, 44, 46, 51; 25:1, 9, 14, 29^{2}, 30, 32; 26:2^{2}, 5, 13, 24, 31, 37, 39, 42^{2}, 54, 56; 27:25, 26, 58, 64^{2}; 28:5, 10; Mk 1:25, 41; 2:20, 22; 3:14, 28, 29; 4:12^{2}, 22^{2}, 24, 25^{2}, 39; 5:23, 28, 34, 36; 6:20, 50; 7:10, 34; 8:12, 15, 31^{2}, 38; 9:5, 12^{2}, 31, 35^{2}, 42^{2}, 45, 47, 49, 50; 10:7, 26, 31, 33, 38, 39, 43, 44^{2}, 45, 48; 11:17, 23, 24; 12:7, 23, 25^{2}, 37, 38, 40; 13:2^{2}, 4^{2}, 7, 8, 9^{2}, 10, 13, 17, 19^{2}, 23, 24, 25, 33^{2}; 14:9, 21, 27, 33, 49; 15:15; 16:6, 16^{2}; Lk 1:13, 14, 15^{2}, 18, 20, 27, 29, 30, 31, 32^{2}, 34, 35^{2}, 36, 38, 45, 54, 60, 66, 68, 76; 2:1, 5, 6, 10^{2}, 12, 23, 34^{2}, 35, 49; 3:5, 7, 9, 12, 14, 15; 4:7, 35; 5:10, 13, 15, 35, 37, 38; 6:18, 21, 34, 35^{2}, 36, 37^{3}, 38^{3}, 40; 7:7; 8:12, 17^{2}, 18^{2}, 50^{2}; 9:22^{3}, 26, 33, 44, 46, 51; 10:11, 12, 14, 15, 31, 40, 42; 11:2, 9^{2}, 10, 17, 19, 29, 30, 33, 36, 41, 50, 51; 12:1, 2^{2}, 3^{2}, 4, 7, 9, 10^{2}, 15, 19, 20, 21, 31, 32, 33, 34, 35, 37, 38, 39, 40, 43, 47, 48^{3}, 52, 53, 55, 58; 13:14, 16, 23, 24, 28, 30^{2}; 14:10, 11^{2}, 12, 14^{2}, 23, 26, 27, 33, 34; 15:7, 14, 19, 21, 32; 16:2, 9, 10^{3}, 13, 31; 17:2^{2}, 6, 24, 25, 26, 30, 34^{2}, 35^{2}; 18:14^{2}, 26, 31, 32, 39, 40; 19:7, 14, 26^{2}, 27, 46; 20:14, 16, 18^{2}, 20, 33, 35, 44, 46, 47; 21:6^{2}, 7, 9, 11, 12, 15, 16, 23^{2}, 24^{2}, 25^{2}, 26, 34^{2}, 36^{3}; 22:7, 23, 24, 26^{2}, 37, 42, 69; 23:2, 23, 32, 43; 24:7^{3}, 20, 36, 44, 47; Jn 1:31, 42; 3:4^{2}, 7^{2}, 9, 14, 20, 21, 23; 4:13, 29, 36; 5:24, 28, 29, 34; 6:12, 20, 35, 45; 7:23^{2}; 8:7, 24, 28, 33, 36, 55; 9:3, 22, 41; 10:9, 16, 33, 35; 11:4; 12:15, 23, 26, 31, 34, 42; 13:17, 33; 14:1, 3^{2}, 8, 16, 17, 21, 27^{2}, 28; 15:2, 7, 8, 11^{2}, 22, 24; 16:24, 32; 17:11, 12, 19, 21^{2}, 22, 23, 24, 26^{2}; 18:9, 14, 28, 32; 19:7, 12, 16, 21, 24, 28, 31, 36^{2}; 20:19, 21, 26; 21:25; Ac 1:5, 8, 16, 20^{2}; 2:3, 20, 21, 25, 36, 38; 3:13, 14, 19, 23, 25; 4:12; 5:27, 34, 36, 39; 6:2, 3; 7:6^{2}, 35, 49; 8:36; 9:6, 17; 10:23, 40, 48; 11:14, 16; 12:4, 15, 17, 19; 13:11^{2}, 39; 14:9; 15:1, 5; 16:17, 22, 30, 31, 36; 17:17, 18; 18:6, 9^{2}, 14, 15; 19:27^{2}, 36, 39, 40; 20:10, 20, 28, 31; 21:13, 14^{2}, 26, 33, 34, 35; 22:5, 10, 15, 16, 24^{2}; 23:3, 10, 24, 30, 35; 24:4, 5, 8, 15, 19; 25:6, 10, 15, 17, 20, 21; 26:28; 27:10, 17, 22^{2}, 24, 29, 31; 28:4, 26^{2}; Ro 1:1, 4, 7, 10, 12, 13, 19, 22, 28; 2:5, 8, 9, 12, 13, 26; 3:4^{2}, 19, 20, 26; 4:11, 13, 16^{2}, 18; 5:9, 10, 19; 6:5, 6^{2}, 14, 17^{2}; 7:13, 25; 8:3, 4, 18, 19, 21, 29^{2}, 31, 36, 39; 9:7, 17, 26, 27^{2}, 33; 10:1, 4, 9, 11, 13; 11:6, 10^{2}, 15, 19, 20^{2}, 22, 23, 24, 25^{2}, 26, 36; 12:2^{2}, 9, 10, 11, 12, 16^{3}, 17, 21; 13:3, 4, 9; 14:5, 9, 16; 15:16, 20, 31^{2}, 32, 33; 16:19, 20, 27; 1Co 1:1, 2, 7, 8, 10^{2}, 17; 3:8, 10, 13^{2}, 15; 4:8; 5:5, 7; 6:7^{2}, 9, 12; 7:11, 14, 18, 32, 34; 8:9, 10; 9:2, 27; 10:1, 7, 12, 13, 20, 29, 33; 11:16, 19, 27, 32; 12:1, 3, 15, 16, 17^{2}, 18, 19, 22, 25; 13:8; 14:5, 6, 9, 17, 20^{2}, 24^{2}, 25, 26, 31, 34, 38, 39, 40; 15:9, 15, 19, 22, 26, 28^{2}, 33, 37, 42, 51, 52^{2}, 57; 16:2, 5, 13^{3}, 22, 23; 2Co 1:3, 8; 2:3, 7, 9, 14; 3:8; 4:10, 11; 5:2, 3, 4^{3}, 8, 20, 21; 6:3, 14, 16^{2}, 17, 18^{2}; 7:11, 14; 8:11, 13^{2}, 14; 9:3^{2}, 4, 5, 11^{2}, 15; 10:2^{2}, 6, 8, 9, 11, 14; 11:3, 6, 12, 15, 31; 12:1, 6^{2}, 14, 16, 20^{3}, 21; 13:1^{2}, 4, 10, 11^{2}, 14; Gal 1:5, 8, 9, 10; 2:2, 3, 6, 9, 16^{2}, 17, 21; 3:8, 22, 23, 24; 4:9, 17, 18^{2}, 20, 21, 24^{2}, 27; 5:1, 2^{2}, 3, 4, 10, 13, 15; 6:1, 7^{2}, 12, 13, 18; Eph 1:3, 4, 5, 10, 12, 18, 21, 22; 3:4, 10, 13, 19, 21; 4:2^{2}, 11^{4}, 12, 14, 23, 24, 32; 5:1, 3, 4, 5, 7, 15, 17, 18, 21; 6:10, 13, 18, 19; Php 1:10^{2}, 20^{2}, 23, 28^{2}; 2:5, 6, 18, 19, 28; 3:9, 21; 4:5, 6, 9, 11, 12, 17, 20, 23; Col 2:2; 3:15, 19, 25; 4:5, 6, 18; 1Th 2:4, 9, 16; 3:1, 3, 4, 13; 4:3, 7, 12, 13, 17^{2}; 5:6^{2}, 8, 14, 15, 16, 23, 28; 2Th 1:5, 9, 10^{2}, 12; 2:4, 6, 8, 9, 10, 12, 13; 3:1, 2, 8, 16, 18; 1Ti 1:7, 17, 20; 2:1, 4, 12, 15; 3:2, 6, 8, 10, 11, 12; 4:3, 4, 6, 7, 15; 5:7, 9, 16, 20, 22, 25; 6:1, 8, 16, 17, 18^{2}, 21; 2Ti 1:4, 8; 2:1, 2, 6, 15, 21, 24; 3:1, 2, 9, 12, 17; 4:2, 15, 16, 17, 18, 22^{2}; Tit 1:6, 7, 8, 11, 13; 2:2, 3^{2}, 5^{4}, 6, 8^{2}, 9, 10; 3:1^{3}, 2, 8, 11, 15; Phm 1:6, 8, 14, 22, 25; Heb 1:5^{2}, 8, 12; 2:17; 3:5, 13; 4:1^{2}; 5:4, 10, 12; 6:6, 8, 18; 7:8, 12; 8:4, 9, 10^{2}; 9:22, 23; 10:8, 13, 29, 35, 38; 11:5, 16, 18, 24, 25, 35, 40; 12:13, 14, 18, 19, 20, 27^{2}, 28^{2}; 13:4, 5, 6, 9^{2}, 17^{2}, 19, 21, 25; Jas 1:4, 5, 13, 16, 18, 19, 25; 2:5, 12, 13; 3:1^{2}, 10; 4:4; 5:7, 8, 9, 12^{2}, 15, 16; 1Pe 1:2, 3, 5, 7, 13^{2}, 15, 16; 2:5, 6; 3:1^{2}, 4, 7, 8^{2}, 14, 15, 16; 4:6, 7, 11^{2}, 12, 13, 15, 16, 17, 18; 5:1, 2^{2}, 5, 8, 11; 2Pe 1:2, 10, 15; 2:1, 4, 12, 13; 3:10^{2}, 11^{2}, 14, 17^{2}, 18; 1Jn 1:8, 10; 2:9, 28; 3:1, 2^{2}, 12, 13, 17; 4:14; 5:10; 2Jn 1:2, 3, 8, 12; 3Jn 1:9; Jude 1:2, 18, 22, 25; Rev 1:6^{2}, 7, 17; 2:2, 10^{2}, 11; 3:5, 9, 19; 5:10, 13; 6:11; 7:12, 17; 8:13; 10:6, 7, 9; 12:6, 14; 13:10^{2}, 15; 14:10; 16:15, 20; 17:8, 14; 18:8, 14, 21^{2}, 22^{3}, 23; 19:7; 20:3, 6, 7, 10; 21:3^{3}, 4, 7^{2}, 8, 16, 25^{2}, 26; 22:3^{2}, 4, 5, 11^{2}, 21.

BEEN (890)

Ge 2:2; 3:23; 8:2; 13:3; 14:4, 14; 16:3; 17:14; 18:8, 27, 31; 21:32; 26:8, 18, 33; 29:8; 30:30; 31:2, 5, 12, 38, 42; 32:4; 33:11; 34:5, 13, 27; 35:3; 37:3, 33; 38:14, 21, 22; 39:1, 14; 40:4; 41:7, 32; 42:28; 43:33; 44:28; 45:6; 46:27; 47:9; 48:15; Ex 3:16; 4:10; 9:19; 10:11, 14; 11:6; 12:39; 14:12, 19; 21:29; 32:8, 29; 33:12; 34:34; Lev 5:19; 8:34, 35; 10:13, 14, 16, 19; 11:38; 13:55, 56, 58; 14:3, 43, 48; 16:16; 19:20^{2}; 21:10, 12; 27:17; Nu 1:17; 5:13, 27; 11:28; 12:14; 13:22; 14:14; 15:28; 16:2, 39; 19:2, 13, 16, 18, 20; 22:30; 35:33; Dt 2:7; 4:32; 9:7, 24; 12:30; 13:14^{2}; 14:24; 15:2, 18; 17:4^{3}; 18:21; 21:3, 4; 23:1; 24:4; 30:4; 31:27; 32:22; Jos 3:4; 4:9; 5:5, 7, 8, 9; 7:7, 8, 12, 26; 8:14, 20, 24, 31; 10:14, 17, 27; 11:10; 22:22; 23:9, 14; 24:20, 33; Jdg 2:10; 9:16; 16:7, 8, 11, 13, 17^{2}, 22; 17:7; 19:2, 18, 30; 20:37; 21:14; Ru 1:7; 2:11, 19; 3:2; 1Sa 1:15, 16; 3:7; 4:9, 17, 19, 22; 5:4; 6:1, 3, 7; 9:20, 24; 10:2, 14, 16; 12:2; 14:21, 30^{2}, 38; 17:25, 27, 33, 34; 20:13; 21:5, 6; 22:6; 25:21, 34; 29:3, 6, 9; 30:5, 21; 2Sa 3:6; 5:17; 7:6, 9; 8:10; 10:15, 19; 12:8; 13:20, 32; 15:11, 31; 17:9, 23; 20:13; 21:5, 13; 22:24; 1Ki 3:2, 12, 15; 5:1^{2}; 8:33, 54; 10:12, 20; 11:4; 12:19; 13:17; 14:6, 8; 15:3, 22; 17:7; 19:10, 14; 21:14, 15; 22:34; 2Ki 5:25; 8:22, 29; 9:14; 11:20; 12:10, 11; 13:7, 23; 16:18; 17:3, 28, 33; 18:4, 35; 22:4, 13; 23:2, 22; 1Ch 7:23; 9:19, 22; 14:2, 8; 17:8, 27; 18:10; 19:16, 19; 2Ch 6:24; 9:9, 11, 19; 10:19; 12:2; 16:6; 18:33; 21:10; 22:6, 8; 23:21; 25:24; 26:18^{2}; 28:19; 29:34^{3}; 30:3, 5, 26; 32:14, 15; 34:9, 14^{2}, 16, 21, 24, 30; 35:3, 18; Ezr 3:6; 4:2, 18, 19; 5:16; 8:30; 9:1, 7^{2}, 8; 10:2, 5, 10; Ne 1:3; 2:1, 3, 13^{2}, 17; 5:5; 6:13, 14, 16; 7:1, 4, 5; 8:9, 12; 9:33; 12:46; 13:4, 10; Est 2:6, 8; 4:1, 8; 6:3; 7:4^{2}; 8:5; 9:1; Job 6:3, 13, 20, 24; 7:3^{2}; 10:19; 16:17; 19:7, 26; 20:4; 31:7^{2}, 9, 11, 28; 33:6; 38:17; Ps 13:6; 18:23; 22:10; 27:9; 42:3; 44:17; 45:2; 60:1; 61:3; 71:5, 24; 73:14^{2}; 88:15; 89:38, 50; 90:1; 92:10; 116:7; 119:56, 92, 140; 124:1, 2, 7; 141:7; Pr 6:2; Ecc 1:9^{2}; 2:12; 3:15^{2}; 4:3, 14; 6:10^{2}; 12:13; Isa 1:9; 5:4; 9:10; 10:22; 14:8, 11, 12; 16:9; 21:2; 22:3; 23:4; 25:4; 27:7; 30:33^{3}; 33:1^{2}; 36:20; 38:12; 40:2^{2}, 21; 42:14, 22; 48:8, 18, 19; 49:5; 50:5; 52:5; 53:1; 57:11^{2}; 60:15; 61:4; 63:19; 64:11; Jer 2:10, 31; 3:2, 3, 20; 5:11; 7:11; 9:12^{2}; 11:19; 13:22; 18:13; 21:12; 22:3, 21; 31:18, 26; 32:43; 33:4; 35:14; 37:4; 39:15; 40:7, 12; 41:1; 42:18; 43:5; 44:18; 48:11; 49:25; 50:6; 51:5, 51, 60; La 1:14, 20; 3:17; 5:2, 11, 12; Eze 2:3, 5; 5:7; 6:9^{2}; 9:3; 11:16, 17; 15:8; 17:8; 18:19; 20:34, 41; 22:16; 23:17; 24:12, 18; 26:10; 28:25; 29:6; 30:21; 33:24, 33; 34:8; 35:12^{2}; 36:4, 23; 38:8^{2}; 40:4, 17; 44:19; Da 2:30; 4:31, 33; 5:3, 27; 6:10, 20; 7:12; 8:26; 9:5, 11, 12^{2}, 26; 10:11; 11:21, 36; 12:7; Hos 2:5; 5:1; 9:1; 14:1; Joel 1:5, 16, 17; Am 2:4; 3:5; 7:1, 7; Ob 1:16; Jnh 2:4; 4:10; Mic 7:2; Zep 3:19; Zec 1:12; 8:13; 11:2; 13:5; Mal 1:4; 2:11; Mt 1:6; 2:2, 12, 16, 22; 4:12; 5:31; 9:20, 25, 33^{2}; 10:25; 11:12, 20, 21, 23, 27; 13:11, 52; 14:4; 15:32; 17:9; 19:11; 20:6, 23; 22:3, 4^{2}; 23:35; 24:22; 25:21, 23; 26:9, 24; 27:8, 64; 28:15, 18; Mk 4:11; 5:4, 15, 18, 25; 6:2, 14, 16, 18; 8:2; 9:21; 10:40; 14:5, 21; 16:4, 10; Lk 1:1, 4, 13, 19, 48; 2:11, 17, 20, 21, 22, 26, 48; 4:6, 16; 5:25; 7:20, 29, 30, 47^{2}; 8:2, 10, 29, 36, 43, 47; 9:7; 10:13, 22; 11:14, 50; 12:32, 48^{2}; 13:7, 11; 14:8, 17, 22; 15:29; 16:11, 12, 26; 17:20; 19:17; 21:22; 22:22; 23:8, 12, 19, 25, 53; 24:49; Jn 1:3, 24; 2:2, 9; 3:21; 4:45; 5:5, 6, 10; 6:22; 7:39^{2}; 8:25, 33; 9:13, 18, 24; 10:40; 11:13, 17, 21, 31, 32, 39; 12:16, 38; 14:9, 12; 15:27; 16:25; 17:12; 19:32, 41; 20:1, 7, 12; Ac 1:11, 21; 3:20; 4:13, 14; 5:21, 41; 7:44; 8:4, 16; 9:33; 10:45; 11:11, 19; 12:20; 13:1, 26; 14:26; 15:3, 10, 18, 21; 16:6, 23; 18:25; 19:21; 21:10, 21; 22:10, 25; 24:10; 26:32; 27:9, 33; 28:28; Ro 1:13, 20^{2}; 2:25; 3:2, 21; 4:9, 11, 18; 5:1, 9, 10; 6:5, 7, 13, 18, 22; 7:6; 8:22, 28; 9:29; 11:17^{2}, 34; 13:1; 15:20, 22, 23; 16:2, 7, 13; 1Co 1:5; 2:7; 4:2, 9; 5:2, 7; 6:7; 7:14^{2}; 8:7, 10; 10:28; 15:12, 13, 14, 16, 17, 20, 27, 54^{2}; 2Co 1:19; 3:14; 7:13; 9:2, 4; 11:23^{3}, 26^{2}, 27; 12:11, 16, 19^{3}; Gal 2:7^{2}, 20; 3:15, 21; 5:4, 11; 6:14; Eph 1:11; 2:5, 8, 13; 3:5; 4:7, 28; Php 1:14, 29; 3:12; 4:10; Col 1:6, 23, 26; 2:10, 12; 3:1; 4:16; 1Th 2:2, 6; 3:5; 4:9; 1Ti 4:2; 5:9; 6:5, 20; 2Ti 1:5, 10; Tit 1:9; 3:7; Heb 3:3, 15; 4:3, 15; 6:4, 12; 7:11, 23, 28; 8:7^{2}; 9:6, 8; 10:2, 10, 18; 11:15, 39; 12:11; 13:23; Jas 2:13; 3:7, 9; 1Pe 1:2, 12, 23; 2:24; 2Pe 1:9; 2:3^{2}, 21; 1Jn 2:12, 29; 3:2, 8, 9; 4:7; Jude 1:1, 11, 13; Rev 5:6; 6:9, 11; 7:2; 9:15; 11:2; 12:10, 13; 13:3, 8, 12; 14:3, 10; 15:2, 4; 16:18; 17:8; 18:17, 19, 24; 20:4^{2}, 10; 22:8.

BUT (3983)

Ge 2:6, 17, 20; 3:3, 9; 4:4, 5, 7^{2}, 15; 6:8, 18; 8:1, 9, 12; 9:4, 23; 11:5, 31; 12:12, 17; 13:6; 14:4, 22, 24; 15:2, 4, 8, 11, 14; 16:1; 17:19, 21; 18:15, 22, 27, 30, 32; 19:3, 8, 10, 14, 18, 19, 22, 26; 20:3, 7; 21:9, 12, 26; 22:7, 11; 23:15; 24:4, 33, 38, 55, 56; 25:6, 28, 33; 26:20, 21, 29; 27:11, 22, 35, 40; 29:17, 20, 23, 31; 30:15, 27, 30, 31, 40, 42; 31:5, 15, 29, 30, 32, 33, 34, 35, 42; 32:10, 12, 21, 26, 28, 29; 33:4, 9, 13, 15; 34:8, 17, 22, 31; 35:10, 18; 37:11, 18, 22, 35; 38:7, 9, 20, 23, 29; 39:8, 12, 14, 18, 20; 40:8, 14, 17, 22; 41:8, 15, 16, 21, 24, 30, 44, 54; 42:4, 7, 13, 20, 21, 22, 24, 31, 34^{2}, 38; 43:3, 5, 21; 44:7, 17, 23, 26; 45:3, 7, 8, 22, 27; 46:12; 47:24, 30; 48:14, 19, 21; 49:19, 24; 50:19, 20, 24; Ex 1:7, 12, 16, 22; 2:3, 15, 17; 3:11, 19; 4:9, 13, 17, 21, 23, 25; 5:4, 8, 11, 16; 6:3, 9, 12, 30; 7:3, 12, 16, 22; 8:7, 15, 18, 19, 22, 26, 28, 32; 9:4, 6, 12, 16, 21, 30; 10:8, 20, 25, 27; 11:7, 10, 12; 12:9, 45; 13:13; 14:4, 29; 15:10, 19; 16:3, 8, 20, 26, 27; 17:1, 3, 11; 18:21, 22, 26; 19:24; 20:6, 10, 11, 19; 21:2, 3, 5, 13, 14, 18, 21, 22, 23, 28, 29; 22:3^{2}, 8, 12, 15, 30; 23:11, 12, 29; 24:2, 11; 29:14, 33; 31:15; 32:11, 30, 32^{2}; 33:3, 11, 12, 20, 23; 34:20, 21, 31, 34; 35:2; 40:37; Lev 2:12; 4:11; 6:16, 28, 30; 7:6, 16, 20, 24, 31; 8:17; 9:19; 10:6, 14, 19; 11:4, 10, 23, 34, 36, 38; 13:4, 7, 14, 21, 23, 26, 28, 31, 35, 42, 53, 57; 14:8, 48; 16:10; 17:16; 18:26; 19:14, 15, 18, 20, 25; 20:24; 21:14; 22:11, 13, 23; 23:3, 25; 24:21; 25:4, 17, 23, 26, 28, 31, 34, 36, 43, 46; 26:14, 23, 26, 27, 40, 45; 27:18, 28; Nu 4:15, 20; 5:8, 10, 20, 31; 7:9; 8:25, 26; 9:6, 7, 13, 22; 10:7, 31; 11:6^{2}, 20, 21, 25, 26, 29, 33; 12:7; 13:28, 31; 14:9, 10, 12, 22, 24, 32, 41; 15:27, 30; 16:10, 12, 22, 30, 42, 47, 49; 17:8; 18:3, 7, 15, 17; 19:7, 12, 20; 20:12, 16, 18; 21:4, 23, 24, 30; 22:12, 18, 20, 22, 33, 35, 38; 23:11^{3}, 13; 24:1, 10, 11, 14, 17^{2}, 18, 20, 24; 25:9; 26:19, 61; 27:3; 30:2, 4, 5, 7, 8, 11, 12, 14; 31:18, 23; 32:17, 23, 24, 27, 30, 32; 33:55; 35:8, 22, 26, 30; Dt 1:12, 26, 38, 40, 42, 43, 45; 2:4, 11, 12, 20, 30, 35, 37; 3:7, 16, 18, 26, 28; 4:2, 4, 12, 20, 22, 26, 29; 5:3, 10, 14, 25, 31; 6:21, 23; 7:8, 10, 15, 18, 23; 8:3, 18; 9:3, 5, 19, 20, 23, 29; 10:12; 11:7, 11; 12:5, 10, 16, 23, 26, 27, 29; 14:10, 12, 20, 21, 24; 15:3, 6^{2}, 16, 23; 16:3; 17:6; 18:14, 20; 19:11; 21:15^{2}; 22:1, 7, 9, 14, 16, 17, 25; 23:5, 11, 20, 22, 24, 25; 25:3; 26:6; 28:7, 12, 25, 30^{3}, 31, 33, 38, 39, 40, 41, 43, 44^{2}, 62, 68; 29:4, 7, 15, 29; 30:17; 32:5, 27; 33:9; 34:4, 6; Jos 1:12, 14; 2:4^{2}, 6, 20; 3:4; 5:5, 12, 14; 6:10, 18, 24, 25; 7:1, 4; 8:9, 14, 20, 23, 27; 9:7, 8, 12, 13, 14, 18, 19, 21; 10:19, 20, 33; 11:14; 13:13, 14, 33; 14:3, 4, 8, 12; 16:10; 17:3, 8, 9, 13, 17, 18; 18:2; 19:47; 21:12; 22:3, 5, 19, 26, 28; 23:8, 12, 15; 24:3, 4, 7, 8, 10, 11, 15^{2}, 21; Jdg 1:6, 19, 25, 27, 28, 29, 30, 33, 35; 2:2, 17, 19; 3:9, 25; 4:8, 9, 16, 21; 5:19, 31; 6:10, 13^{2}, 15, 23, 27, 31; 7:4^{2}, 8; 8:2, 6, 8, 12, 20, 23; 9:5, 9, 11, 13, 15, 18, 20, 37, 52; 10:13, 15^{2}; 11:16, 17, 27, 34, 37; 13:3, 7, 9, 16, 23; 14:3, 6, 9, 16; 15:1; 16:3, 9, 12, 20, 22; 19:2, 5, 10, 15, 24, 25, 28; 20:9, 13, 22, 40, 42, 47; 21:14, 19; Ru 1:11, 14, 16, 17, 21; 3:3, 13, 14; 4:4; 1Sa 1:2, 5, 11, 13; 2:4, 5^{2}, 9, 11, 15^{2}, 18, 25, 30^{2}; 3:5, 16; 4:19, 20; 5:4, 9; 6:3, 7, 9^{2}, 19; 7:10, 17; 8:3, 6, 7, 9, 19; 9:4^{3}, 6, 21, 27; 10:8, 14, 16, 19, 21, 27^{2}; 11:2, 13; 12:9, 10, 12, 15, 20, 24; 13:8, 14; 14:1, 10, 27, 36, 37, 39, 45; 15:9^{2}, 12, 14, 15, 20, 22, 26, 30, 33, 34;

BY (2431)

FOR (7282)

FROM (5013)

20[2], 21, 22[2], 24, 25, 27, 28, 29; 25:2, 3, 4; 26:1, 23, 29[2], 30; 27:15; 28:4[3], 19; 29:10, 12, 14[2], 16, 29; 2Ch 1:4, 13[2], 16[3], 17; 2:8, 14[2], 16; 4:2; 5:2, 9[3], 11; 6:21, 23, 25, 26, 27, 30, 32, 33, 35, 39; 7:1, 8, 14[2], 20; 8:7, 11, 15, 16; 9:10, 26, 28[2], 29; 10:2[2], 15; 11:4, 13, 16; 12:3, 12, 15; 13:19; 14:8[2]; 15:8[2], 9[2], 11, 16, 17; 16:1, 3, 6, 7, 9, 11, 12[2]; 17:6, 14, 17; 18:23[2], 31; 19:4, 10; 20:2[2], 4[2], 10[3], 19, 23[2], 32, 34; 21:12; 22:6, 11[2]; 23:2, 10, 20; 24:1, 5, 6; 25:1, 6, 7, 10, 13, 14, 15, 23, 26, 27[2]; 26:3, 21, 22; 28:8, 12, 15, 21[3], 24, 26; 29:5, 6, 10, 12[3], 13[2], 14[2]; 30:5, 6[3], 8, 9, 10, 18, 25[2]; 31:3, 10; 32:3, 8, 11, 13, 14[2], 15[2], 17[2], 22[2], 23; 33:15; 34:9[2], 12[2], 13, 18, 30, 33; 35:7, 22, 27; 36:7, 10, 18, 20; Ezr 1:7, 11; 2:1, 59[2], 61, 62; 3:7, 8, 13; 4:9, 11, 12, 15; 5:14[2], 16; 6:5, 6, 8, 11, 21[2]; 7:6, 9, 16, 20, 28; 8:1, 18, 19, 22, 31[2], 35; 9:1, 3, 5, 7, 11; 10:2, 6, 8, 11[2], 14, 16, 18, 19, 20, 21, 22, 24[2], 25, 26, 27, 28, 29, 30, 31, 33, 34, 38, 43; Ne 1:2, 9; 3:7, 15, 19, 20, 21, 22, 24, 25, 27; 4:2, 5, 16, 19, 21; 5:7, 12, 14, 15, 17; 6:17; 7:6, 61[2], 63, 64; 8:3, 8, 15[2], 17[2], 18[2]; 9:2, 3, 5, 13, 15[2], 20, 27[2], 28, 32, 35; 10:28, 31, 38; 11:4[2], 7, 10, 15, 30, 31; 12:27, 28[2], 29[2], 44; 13:3, 16, 21, 23, 28; Est 1:1, 2, 5, 7, 10, 20; 2:6, 9, 13; 3:8, 10; 4:14; 7:8; 8:2, 9; 9:16, 22, 26; Job 1:7[2], 12, 16, 19, 21; 2:2[2], 7[2], 10, 11, 12; 3:10, 11, 17, 19; 4:2; 5:4, 5, 6[2], 15[2], 19, 20[2], 21; 6:13, 17, 18, 22, 23[2]; 7:19; 8:10, 18, 19; 9:6, 34; 10:7, 19, 20; 13:20, 21; 14:4, 6, 11, 12, 18; 15:13, 18; 16:5; 18:4, 14, 17, 18[2]; 19:9, 13[2]; 20:4, 18, 20, 24; 21:9, 16, 30[2]; 22:6, 7, 18, 22, 23; 23:7, 12; 24:4, 9, 12; 26:4; 27:13, 22; 28:2[2], 4[2], 5, 6, 20, 21[2]; 29:9, 17; 30:2, 3, 5; 31:2[2], 7, 18[2], 20, 22, 23; 33:3, 6, 9, 17[2], 18[2], 24, 28, 30; 34:10[2], 27, 30[2]; 35:7, 9; 36:3, 16[2], 20, 25, 29; 37:1, 2, 7, 9[2]; 38:8, 29[2]; 39:22, 25, 29[2]; 41:19, 20[2], 21; Ps 3:T, 4, 8; 4:1; 5:9; 6:5, 6, 8; 7:1, 7; 8:2; 9:13; 10:5, 8, 16; 11:2; 12:1, 5, 7; 13:1; 14:2; 15:2; 16:2; 17:1, 2, 4, 7, 9[2], 13, 14[2]; 18:T[2], 3, 6, 8[2], 13, 15, 16, 17[2], 21, 22, 23, 43, 45, 48[2]; 19:5, 6, 10, 13; 20:2[2], 6; 21:10[2]; 22:1[2], 10[2], 11, 20[2], 21[2], 24, 25; 24:5[2]; 25:6, 15, 17, 22; 27:9; 30:3[2]; 31:4, 11, 15[2], 20[2], 22; 32:7; 33:13, 14, 19; 34:4, 13[2], 14, 16, 17, 19; 35:10[2], 17[2], 22; 36:8; 37:8[2], 27, 39, 40; 38:9, 10, 21; 39:1, 8, 10, 13; 40:10, 11; 41:3, 8, 13; 42:6[2]; 43:1; 44:12, 18; 45:8; 49:3, 14, 15; 50:1, 2, 9[2]; 51:2, 5, 9, 11[2], 14; 52:5[2]; 53:2; 54:7; 55:8, 12, 18; 56:13[2]; 57:T, 3; 58:3[2]; 59:1[2], 2[2], 7[2]; 60:6; 61:2; 62:1, 4, 5; 64:1, 2[2], 4; 66:9, 20; 68:10, 17, 18[2], 20[2], 22[2], 31; 69:5, 14[3], 17; 71:4[2], 6[2], 12, 20; 72:8[2], 13, 14, 15; 73:5, 7, 27; 74:11, 12; 75:6[2]; 76:8; 77:4; 78:2, 4, 14, 26, 30, 42, 44, 50, 65[2], 70, 71; 79:13; 80:13, 14, 18; 81:6[2], 16; 82:4; 84:7, 11; 85:3, 11[2]; 86:13; 88:5, 8, 14, 15, 18; 89:19, 33, 48; 90:2; 91:3[2]; 93:2; 94:12, 13; 97:10; 99:7; 101:4, 8; 102:2, 19[2]; 103:4, 12[2], 17; 104:13, 14, 21, 35; 105:13[2], 37; 106:10[2], 19, 23, 33, 47, 48; 107:2, 3[3], 6, 13, 19, 20; 108:7; 109:10, 13, 15, 17, 24, 31; 110:2, 3, 7; 113:3, 7[2]; 114:1; 116:8[3], 16; 118:26; 119:10, 13, 19, 21, 22, 29, 37, 43, 51, 72, 87, 101, 102, 104, 110, 115, 118, 134, 136, 150, 152, 155, 157; 120:2[2]; 121:1, 2, 7; 123:4[2]; 127:3[2]; 128:5; 129:1, 2, 4; 130:8; 134:3; 135:7[2], 21; 136:11, 24; 138:6; 139:2, 7[2], 15, 19; 140:1[2], 4[2]; 141:6, 9[2]; 142:6, 7; 143:7, 9; 144:7[3], 10, 11; 148:1, 7; Pr 2:6, 12[2], 16[2], 22[2]; 3:26, 27; 4:5, 15, 24[2], 27; 5:7, 8, 15[2]; 6:5[2], 9, 24[2]; 7:5[2], 16; 8:23[2], 35; 9:3; 10:2; 11:4, 7, 8; 12:2, 14; 13:2, 14, 19; 14:4, 7, 27; 15:24, 29; 16:1, 11, 33; 18:20[2], 22; 19:14[2], 27; 21:10, 16, 23; 22:5, 6, 15, 27; 23:13, 14; 24:13, 18, 32; 25:4, 5, 25; 27:6, 8[2], 9, 22, 25; 29:21, 26; 30:8, 14[2]; 31:14; Ecc 1:3, 7; 2:24; 3:9, 11, 14, 20; 4:4, 14; 5:9[2], 15[2]; 8:10; 10:5, 12; 11:10; 12:7; SS 1:14; 3:6[2], 9; 4:1, 2, 8[5], 15; 6:5[2], 6; 8:5; Isa 1:6, 15, 19, 24; 2:3[2], 6, 10, 19, 21; 3:1, 12, 14; 4:4, 6[2]; 6:6; 7:17, 18[2], 20; 8:17, 18; 9:7, 12[2], 14; 10:2, 3, 27[2]; 11:1[2], 11[8], 12, 16[2]; 12:3; 13:5[2], 6, 13; 14:3, 9, 12, 22, 25[2], 29, 31; 16:1, 2, 4[2], 5, 10; 17:3[2]; 18:4, 7[2]; 19:23; 20:2[2], 6; 21:1[2], 10[2], 11, 15[4]; 22:4, 19[2], 24; 23:1, 5; 24:11, 14, 16; 25:4[2], 8[2]; 27:12; 28:7[4], 9[2], 29; 29:4[2], 9[2], 13, 15; 30:14, 23, 27; 31:1; 32:2[2], 6, 15; 33:15[2]; 34:4[2], 6, 10, 17; 36:2, 16[2], 18, 19, 20[2]; 37:14, 20, 30; 38:6, 12[2], 17; 39:3[3]; 40:2, 21, 27; 41:2, 4, 9[2], 25[2], 26[2]; 42:7[2], 10, 11; 43:5[2], 6[2], 11, 13; 44:6, 17, 19; 45:5, 6, 19, 20, 21[2]; 46:6, 7[2], 10[2], 11[2], 12; 47:13, 14; 48:1, 6, 8[2], 9, 16, 19, 20, 21; 49:1, 12[4], 17, 21, 24[2], 25[2]; 50:6, 11; 51:1[2], 4, 17, 22; 52:2, 11[2]; 53:3, 8; 54:8, 14, 17; 55:10, 11; 56:2, 3; 57:1; 58:7, 13[2]; 59:2[2], 9, 19[2], 21[4]; 60:4, 6, 9; 61:1; 63:1[2], 3, 15[3], 16, 17, 19; 64:7; 65:9[2], 14, 16; 66:6[2], 20, 23[2]; Jer 1:13, 14; 2:5, 18[2], 33; 3:4, 14[2], 18, 19, 24, 25; 4:6, 8, 11, 12, 14, 15[2], 16; 5:6[2]; 6:1, 8, 13, 20[2], 22[2]; 7:1, 15, 25, 28; 8:1, 10, 13, 16, 19; 9:2, 3, 18, 19, 21[2]; 10:9[2], 11[2], 13[2], 20, 22; 11:1, 7[2], 19; 12:2, 12, 14[2]; 13:7, 14, 18[2], 20; 14:2; 15:1, 12, 21[2]; 16:5, 16, 17[2], 19; 17:5, 12, 13, 16, 18[2], 26[3]; 18:1, 4, 11, 14[2], 17, 18[2], 20, 22, 23; 19:1, 14; 20:3, 13; 21:1, 2, 12; 22:3, 8, 11, 20, 21; 23:14, 15, 16[2], 22[2], 30[2]; 24:1, 5[2], 8, 10; 25:3, 5, 10, 15, 17, 28, 30[2], 32[2], 33; 26:1, 3, 10, 20; 27:1, 10, 16[2], 20; 28:1, 3, 4, 6, 8, 16; 29:1[2], 2, 4, 14[3], 20, 22, 27; 30:1, 3, 10, 19, 21; 31:8[2], 11, 16[3], 23, 34, 36, 38, 39; 32:1, 9, 30, 31[2], 37, 40; 33:5, 7, 8, 15; 34:1, 3, 8, 21; 35:1, 15; 36:1, 2, 3, 6[2], 7, 8, 9, 10[2], 11, 13, 14, 21, 29; 37:5, 11, 17, 21; 38:10, 11, 14, 18, 23, 25; 40:1[2], 4, 12; 41:5, 6, 15, 16[3]; 42:1, 4, 8, 11; 43:5, 12; 44:5, 7, 12[2], 26, 28; 46:16, 20, 27; 47:4; 48:3, 10, 11[2], 12, 18, 33[2], 34[2], 44, 45[2]; 49:5, 7, 14, 16, 19[2], 32, 36; 50:3, 9[2], 16, 26, 28, 39, 41[2], 44[2]; 51:6, 16[2], 26, 45, 54[2]; 52:1, 3, 8, 20, 27, 29, 31; La 1:6, 13; 2:1, 8, 9, 11, 19; 3:11, 13, 18, 38, 48, 50, 55, 66; 4:9, 17; 5:8, 10, 14, 15, 16, 19; Eze 1:19, 21, 25, 27[2]; 3:17, 18, 19[2], 20; 4:8, 14; 5:4; 6:9, 14; 7:22, 26; 8:2[2], 6; 9:2, 3; 10:2, 4, 6[2], 16, 18, 19; 11:15, 17[2], 19, 23, 24; 12:3, 16, 27; 13:20, 21, 22, 23; 14:6, 7, 8, 9, 11; 15:3[2]; 16:9, 33, 37, 42; 17:7, 22[2]; 18:8, 17, 21, 23, 24, 26, 27, 28, 30; 19:8, 14; 20:9, 14, 22, 34[2], 41[2], 47; 21:3[2], 4, 5, 14, 19; 22:12; 23:3, 17, 18[2], 22[2], 28, 40, 42[2]; 24:13, 16; 25:7[2], 13; 26:7, 16; 27:5[2], 6[2], 7[2], 17, 18[2], 19; 28:3, 15, 16[2], 18, 25; 29:4, 10, 13, 14, 18; 30:6, 9, 22; 31:12; 32:13, 21; 33:7, 8, 9, 11[2], 12, 14, 18, 19, 21, 30; 34:10[2], 12, 13[2], 27; 35:7; 36:3, 24, 25[2], 26, 29, 33; 37:9, 12, 13, 21, 23; 38:6, 8[3], 12, 15; 39:2, 3[2], 10[2], 17, 18, 22, 23, 24, 25, 27[2], 29; 40:13[2], 15, 19, 23, 27, 49; 41:7, 11, 20; 42:3, 5[2], 9, 20; 43:2, 6, 9, 14[2], 15, 23, 25, 27; 44:10[2], 15; 45:7[3], 13[2], 14, 15[2]; 46:2, 16, 17, 18; 47:1[2], 2, 10, 12, 15, 17, 19; 48:1, 2, 3, 4, 5, 6, 7, 8[2], 12, 19[2], 21[2], 23, 24, 25, 26, 27, 28, 35; Da 1:2, 3, 5, 6; 2:6, 18, 25; 3:15, 17[2]; 4:3, 12, 13, 14[2], 16, 23, 25, 31[2], 32, 33, 34; 5:2[2], 3[2], 13, 20, 21, 23[2]; 6:13, 20, 23, 27; 7:3, 4, 7, 10, 17, 19, 23, 24[2]; 8:4, 5, 7, 11, 16, 22; 9:2, 5, 13, 16, 25; 11:7, 26, 29, 41, 44; 12:1, 11; Hos 1:2; 2:2[2], 12, 17, 18; 4:6; 5:3, 6; 7:4, 13, 14[2]; 8:6; 9:6, 12; 10:5; 11:2, 4, 7, 10, 11[2]; 12:13; 13:2, 3, 14[2], 15[2]; 14:4, 7, 8; Joel 1:5, 9, 13, 15, 16; 2:7, 13, 20; 3:6, 11, 16[2]; Am 1:2[2]; 2:11[2]; 3:5, 12; 4:7[2], 8, 11; 5:19; 6:2, 14; 7:11, 15, 17; 8:12[2]; 9:2[2], 3, 7[3], 8, 13[2], 15; Ob 1:1, 4, 18, 19[2], 20; Jnh 1:3[2], 8[2], 10; 2:1, 2, 4, 6, 9; 3:5, 6, 9, 10; 4:2, 11; Mic 1:2, 3, 7, 11, 12, 16; 2:3, 4, 8[2], 9[2]; 3:2[2], 4, 7; 4:2[2], 7; 5:2[2], 6, 7, 10, 13, 14; 6:4, 5; 7:2, 12[4]; Na 1:10, 11, 13; 2:9; 3:7, 11; Hab 1:8, 12; 2:15, 16; 3:3[2], 4, 13; Zep 1:2, 3, 4, 6, 10[3]; 3:10, 11, 18; Hag 2:15, 18[2], 19; Zec 1:4, 12[2]; 2:6, 13; 3:2; 4:1; 6:1, 5, 10[2], 12; 8:7, 23; 9:7[2], 10[4], 11; 10:4[4], 10[2]; 11:6; 13:1, 2[2]; 14:2, 4, 5, 8, 10[3], 16; Mal 1:9, 10, 11, 13; 2:3, 6, 7, 8, 12, 13; 3:7, 11; 4:2; Mt 1:17[3], 20, 21; 2:1, 7, 16; 3:5, 7, 13, 17; 4:4, 10, 17, 21, 25; 5:18, 37, 42[2]; 6:1, 13; 7:5, 16[2], 23; 8:1, 11, 28, 30; 9:9, 15, 16, 22, 27; 10:27, 29; 11:1, 12, 25, 29; 12:9, 15, 38, 42; 13:12, 27, 49, 53; 14:2, 13, 24; 15:1, 5, 8, 18, 22[2], 27, 28; 16:1, 21; 17:5, 9, 18, 20, 25[3], 26; 18:35; 19:8, 15; 20:23; 21:8, 11, 16, 25[4], 26, 43; 22:46; 23:34, 35; 24:10, 21, 27, 29, 31[2], 32; 25:28, 29, 32[2], 41; 26:16, 27, 29, 39, 47; 27:32, 40, 42, 45, 51, 55[2], 57, 64; 28:2, 7, 8; Mk 1:9, 11, 45; 2:20, 21; 3:7, 8, 9, 22; 4:25; 5:2, 6, 29, 30, 34, 35; 6:6, 14, 16, 33; 7:1, 4, 6, 11, 18, 21, 23, 33; 8:11; 9:7, 9, 10, 21; 11:14, 20, 30[2], 31, 32; 12:2, 34[2]; 13:19, 25, 27[2], 28; 14:23, 35, 36, 43; 15:21[2], 30, 32, 38, 40, 45; 16:3, 8; Lk 1:2, 3, 15, 48, 50, 52, 71[2], 74, 78; 2:4; 3:7, 22; 4:1, 9, 22, 38, 42; 5:3[2], 8, 10, 17[2], 35, 36[2]; 6:17[3], 19, 29, 34, 42, 44[2]; 7:6, 12, 45; 8:1, 2, 4, 12, 18, 26, 27, 35, 38, 46, 49; 9:6, 7, 35, 37, 45, 54; 10:7, 18, 21, 30, 42; 11:16, 31, 51; 12:3, 20, 36, 48[2], 52; 13:12, 15, 16, 25, 27[2], 29; 14:2; 16:21, 26[2], 30, 31; 17:7, 24, 29; 18:34; 19:24, 42; 20:4[2], 5, 6, 7, 35; 21:11, 26; 22:42, 43, 45[2], 69, 71; 23:8, 26[2], 49, 51, 55; 24:2, 9, 13, 16, 31, 46, 49; Jn 1:6, 14, 16, 32, 44, 46; 2:6, 9, 15, 22; 3:2, 8, 13, 27, 31[4]; 4:6, 12, 22, 39, 47, 54; 5:24, 41, 44[2]; 6:23, 31, 32[2], 33, 34, 38, 41, 42, 45, 46, 50, 51, 58, 64, 66; 7:1, 16, 17, 22[2], 27[2], 28, 29, 38, 41, 42[2], 52; 8:14[2], 23[2], 26, 38, 40, 42, 44, 59; 9:1, 16, 29, 30, 33; 10:5, 18[2], 32; 11:1, 18, 37, 53, 55; 12:1, 9, 17[2], 21, 27, 28, 32, 34, 36, 43[2]; 13:3, 4; 14:7; 15:5, 15, 26[2], 27; 16:14, 15, 27, 28, 30; 17:7, 8, 15; 18:3, 28, 36; 19:9, 11, 12, 23, 27; 20:1, 7, 9[2]; 21:2, 8, 14; Ac 1:9, 11, 12[2], 22[2]; 2:2, 5, 10, 24[2], 33, 40; 3:2[2], 5, 15, 19, 22, 23, 24, 26; 4:10, 15, 17, 34[2], 36; 5:16, 30, 39, 42; 6:3, 5, 9; 7:10, 16, 37, 45; 8:3, 26, 33; 9:3, 8, 11, 14, 18; 10:22, 23, 35, 40, 41, 47; 11:5, 9, 11, 20, 27; 12:11[2], 19, 25; 13:4, 8, 13, 14, 15, 23, 29, 30, 31, 34, 37, 39[2], 50, 51; 14:8, 15, 17, 18, 19, 26; 15:1, 7, 14, 20[4], 21, 24, 29[4]; 16:4, 6, 11, 12, 14, 39; 17:2, 3, 5, 26, 27, 31; 18:2, 5, 6, 16, 21, 23[2], 28; 19:25, 29, 35; 20:4[4], 6, 9, 15, 17, 18, 20, 30; 21:1[2], 7, 10, 16[2], 21, 25[4], 27, 30[2], 39; 22:5, 6, 14, 19; 23:10, 34[2]; 24:19; 25:1, 7; 26:4, 11, 13, 17[2], 18[2], 19, 23; 27:2[2], 4, 14, 18, 21, 29, 30[2], 34, 42, 43; 28:4[2], 8, 13, 21[2], 23[3]; Ro 1:4, 5[2], 7[2], 13, 17[2], 18, 20; 2:12[2], 29[2]; 3:21[2], 22, 28; 4:6, 24; 5:9, 14; 6:4, 7, 9, 13, 18, 20, 21, 22; 7:2, 3, 4, 6, 8, 9, 24; 8:2, 11[2], 21, 35, 39; 9:3, 5, 6, 24[2]; 10:3, 7, 9, 17; 11:1, 15, 17, 26[2], 36; 13:3, 11; 14:23[2]; 15:19, 22, 31; 16:2, 17; 1Co 1:3, 11, 30; 2:12, 14; 4:5, 6, 7; 5:13; 6:14, 18, 19; 7:7, 10, 25, 29, 32; 8:6; 9:8, 11, 12, 13, 14, 21; 10:4, 6, 14; 11:8[2], 12[2], 23; 15:12, 15, 20, 41, 47, 48, 49; 16:17; 2Co 1:2, 4, 10, 12, 16; 2:17; 3:1, 3, 5, 13, 18; 4:7[2], 14; 5:1, 6, 8, 9, 16[2], 18; 6:12[2], 17; 7:1; 11:3, 4[2], 8, 9[2], 12, 24, 26[5], 33; 12:1, 3, 7, 8; Gal 1:1[2], 3, 4, 8, 12[2], 15; 2:12[2]; 3:2, 13, 15; 4:1, 17, 24; 5:4[2], 7, 8; 6:8[2]; Eph 1:2, 20; 2:8, 12[2]; 3:15; 4:16, 18; 5:14; 6:6, 15, 23; Php 1:2, 5, 18; 2:1[2], 17; 3:9[2], 11, 20; 4:9, 15, 18; Col 1:2, 5, 7, 13, 18, 21, 22, 23; 2:5, 12, 19; 3:8, 24; 4:16; 1Th 1:8, 9, 10[3]; 2:3, 6[2], 13, 14[2], 16, 17; 3:6; 4:16; 2Th 1:2, 7, 9[2]; 2:2, 13; 3:2, 3, 6[2]; 1Ti 1:2, 5, 6; 4:3; 5:13; 6:2, 10, 11, 20, 21; 2Ti 1:2, 13, 18; 2:8[2], 18, 19, 21, 26; 3:11, 13, 14, 15; 4:4, 17, 18; Tit 1:4; 2:10, 14; Phm 1:3, 15, 20; Heb 3:12; 4:4, 10[2], 13; 5:1, 7, 8, 14; 6:1; 7:1, 5[2], 6[2], 13, 14, 23, 26; 8:9, 11; 9:14, 15; 10:22; 11:5, 12, 13, 19, 22; 12:3, 25[2]; 13:5, 10, 20, 24; Jas 1:7, 17[2], 27; 3:11, 13, 15, 17; 4:1, 7; 5:19, 20[2]; 1Pe 1:3, 12, 18[2], 21, 22; 2:11; 3:3, 10[2], 11, 21; 2Pe 1:8, 9, 17[2], 18, 21; 2:9, 18; 3:17; 1Jn 1:1, 5, 7, 9; 2:13, 14, 16[2], 19, 20, 21, 24, 27; 3:8, 11, 14, 22; 4:1, 2, 3, 4, 5[2], 6[2], 7; 5:21; 2Jn 1:3[2], 5, 6; 3Jn 1:7, 11; Jude 1:14, 23, 24; Rev 1:4[2], 5[3]; 2:5[2], 7, 27; 3:5, 10, 12, 18; 4:5; 5:7, 9; 6:4, 13, 14, 16[2]; 7:1, 2, 4, 5[3], 6[3], 7[3], 8[3], 9, 13, 17; 8:4, 5, 10, 11; 9:1, 2[3], 13; 10:1, 4, 8, 10; 11:5, 7, 9, 11, 12; 12:11, 15; 13:8, 13; 14:2, 3, 4, 13[3], 18[2]; 15:8[2]; 16:1, 12, 17, 21; 17:8; 18:1, 3, 4, 6, 14, 15, 17; 19:3, 5; 20:3, 7, 9, 11; 21:2, 3, 4, 6, 10; 22:1, 19[2].

HAD (2791)

See also the selected listing for "HAD" in the Main Concordance.

Ge 1:31; 2:2[2], 3, 5[3], 8[2], 19, 22; 3:1, 23; 4:22, 26; 5:3[2], 4, 6, 7, 9, 10, 12, 13, 15, 16, 18, 19, 21, 22, 25, 26, 28[2], 30; 6:4, 5, 6, 10, 12[2]; 7:9, 14, 16, 22; 8:2[2], 3, 6, 7, 8, 11, 13; 9:24; 10:1; 11:1, 11, 12, 13, 14, 15, 16, 17, 18, 19, 20, 21, 22, 23, 24, 25, 26, 30; 12:1, 4, 5[2], 7, 20; 13:1, 2, 3, 4, 5, 14; 14:4, 13, 14; 15:17[2]; 16:1[2], 3, 15; 17:22; 18:8, 33; 19:4, 17, 23, 27, 29, 37, 38; 20:4, 8, 13, 18; 21:1[2], 2, 9, 25, 32; 22:3[2], 9, 24; 23:10, 16, 18; 24:1, 2, 11, 15, 16, 19, 21, 22, 29, 30[2], 48, 62, 66; 25:10, 28; 26:8, 14, 15, 18[3], 26, 32; 27:15, 17, 30, 41, 42; 28:6[2], 7[2], 9, 11, 12, 18; 29:12, 14, 16, 17; 30:8, 9, 30, 35; 31:2, 10, 18, 19, 21, 22, 25, 32, 34, 42, 54; 32:10, 13, 23; 34:1, 5, 7[3], 13, 27; 35:4, 13, 14, 15, 16, 22, 27; 36:6, 12; 37:1, 3, 5, 6, 8, 9[2], 10, 12; 38:12, 14[2], 15, 30; 39:1[2], 5, 6, 13[2]; 40:4, 5[2], 8, 16[2], 22; 41:1[2], 5, 7, 11[2], 14, 15, 19, 21, 43, 54, 56; 42:24, 29; 43:2[2], 6, 10, 25, 26, 31, 33; 44:4, 24; 45:4, 16, 21, 27[2]; 46:5, 6, 12, 18, 25, 27, 29; 47:22; 49:33; 50:4, 12, 13, 14; Ex 1:17; 2:11, 16; 3:4; 4:19, 28[2], 30, 31; 5:13; 7:13, 20, 22; 8:12, 15, 19; 9:7, 12, 24, 28, 31, 34, 35; 10:13, 14, 23; 11:1, 9; 12:36, 39[2], 50; 13:19[2]; 14:5, 6, 19, 25, 28; 16:1, 3; 17:10; 18:1[2], 2, 6, 8[3], 9, 11; 19:7, 9, 14; 21:29, 36; 24:4; 32:14, 20, 25, 35; 33:5; 34:4, 29, 32, 34; 35:23, 24, 25, 26, 29; 36:2, 3, 7; 37:9; 38:9, 11, 12, 17, 26; 39:42[2], 43[2]; 40:35; Lev 10:16, 19; 19:20; 21:10; 23:43; Nu 1:17, 48; 3:4; 5:4, 18; 7:11; 8:4; 11:3, 4, 18, 24[2], 26, 28, 34; 12:1, 10, 14; 13:22, 31, 32; 14:2, 6, 36; 16:2, 19, 27, 39[2], 47, 49, 50; 17:8[2]; 20:3, 29; 21:26[2], 32; 22:2, 7, 29, 33; 23:30; 26:33[2], 46, 65; 27:4, 11, 22; 31:10, 21, 35, 53; 32:1, 9, 13; 33:4[2], 8; Dt 1:3, 4[2]; 2:1, 14[2], 15, 16, 22, 30, 35; 3:6; 4:25, 42[2]; 8:3, 16; 9:9, 16[4], 18, 21, 25, 28; 10:4[2], 5, 10; 25:18; 29:1, 26; 32:17, 30[2]; 34:5, 9[2]; Jos 2:4[2], 6[2], 7, 16, 22, 23; 3:17; 4:1, 4, 8, 9[2], 10[2], 11, 12, 14, 18, 20, 23[3]; 5:1[3], 5[2], 6[5], 7, 8; 6:8, 10, 11, 22, 23, 25; 7:7, 16, 17, 18, 24, 25; 8:12, 13, 14, 20[3], 21, 24[3], 26, 27, 31[2], 32, 33, 35; 9:3, 18, 24; 10:1[3], 16, 17, 24[2], 27, 28, 30, 32, 33, 35, 39, 40; 11:9, 10, 12, 20, 23[2]; 12:1; 13:8[3], 12[3], 15, 21, 22, 24, 29, 32, 33; 14:2, 3[2], 4, 5, 15; 17:1, 3, 8, 11; 18:2, 21; 19:47, 49, 50; 21:3, 8, 12, 42, 43, 44; 22:7, 9, 11, 30; 23:1[2]; 24:31[2], 32, 33; Jdg 1:19, 20; 2:4, 6, 7[2], 10[2], 12, 15, 17, 18, 23; 3:1, 2[2], 4, 11, 16, 18[2], 24, 30; 4:3[2], 11, 12; 5:31; 7:12, 13, 19; 8:8, 10, 19, 30[2], 33, 34, 35; 9:22, 24, 27, 35, 45, 47, 56; 10:4; 11:34, 39; 12:4, 9, 14; 13:2, 23; 14:6, 9, 18, 19, 20; 16:8, 18, 20, 22, 31; 17:5, 6, 7; 18:1[2], 4, 7, 14, 17, 22, 27, 28, 31; 19:1, 2, 3, 21[2]; 20:3, 22, 30, 36[2], 37, 38, 39, 41; 21:1, 5, 8, 12, 14, 15, 25; Ru 1:4, 6, 7, 12; 2:1, 14, 17, 18[3], 19; 3:7, 16; 4:1; 1Sa 1:2[3], 5, 6, 9, 23, 25; 2:5, 12; 3:3, 7; 4:6, 13, 18, 19; 5:1, 4, 9, 11; 6:1, 19[2]; 7:6, 7, 14; 9:2, 15; 10:11, 16[2], 26; 11:5, 9; 13:3, 13, 19, 22[2], 23; 14:3, 21[2], 22, 24, 27[2], 30, 31, 35, 47, 48; 15:35; 16:8, 9, 10, 12, 14; 17:5, 12, 13, 20, 25, 27; 18:1, 6, 10, 12, 14, 24; 19:18[2]; 20:9, 17, 35, 37, 41; 21:6; 22:6, 21; 23:6, 7, 13, 15; 25:2[2], 21, 34, 35, 43, 44; 26:3, 4, 5[2], 12; 27:3[2], 4, 8; 28:3[2], 20, 24; 30:1[2], 2, 4, 5, 12, 16, 18, 19, 21, 31; 31:7[2], 11; 2Sa 1:10, 12, 16; 2:4, 8, 23, 27, 31; 3:6, 7[2], 15, 20, 22[2], 23[3], 30, 37; 4:1, 2, 4, 7; 5:3, 12[2], 17, 18; 6:8, 13, 17, 18, 23; 7:1; 8:9, 10, 11[2]; 9:5, 10, 12; 10:6, 15, 16, 19; 11:4, 16, 22, 27[2]; 12:2, 3[2], 4[2], 6, 8, 15[2], 20; 13:3, 10, 15, 22, 24, 29, 34; 14:2, 6; 15:11[2], 18, 24, 31; 16:1[2]; 17:14, 18, 21, 22, 23, 25[2]; 18:11[2], 13, 18, 33; 19:8, 15, 24, 32, 40; 20:3, 5, 13; 21:2[2], 8[2], 11, 12[2], 13, 19; 23:21; 24:8, 10, 11, 19; 1Ki 1:4, 6; 2:11, 19, 27, 28, 29, 41[2]; 3:2, 10, 15, 17, 18, 21, 28[2]; 4:7[2], 15, 24, 26, 34; 5:1[2], 12, 15; 6:1, 38; 7:5, 8, 28, 30[2], 31, 34, 40, 46, 51[2]; 8:3, 5, 9, 17, 54[2], 66; 9:1[3], 2, 11, 12, 14, 16[2], 24[2], 25; 10:2, 4, 13, 19[2], 20, 22, 24, 26; 11:2, 3, 4, 6, 9[2], 10, 15[2], 16, 17, 23, 27[2]; 12:1, 2, 6, 8, 10, 12, 15, 20, 24, 32[2], 33; 13:10, 11[2], 12, 13, 20, 21, 23[2], 26[2], 28; 14:5, 18, 21, 22, 24, 26; 15:3[2], 5[2], 11, 12, 13, 15, 22, 26, 30[2], 34; 16:7, 9, 13[2], 16, 19[3], 26; 17:5, 7, 15; 18:3, 4[2], 5, 26, 31, 40; 19:1[2], 4; 20:17, 33, 42; 21:4, 11, 15; 22:3, 11, 13, 31, 38, 53; 2Ki 1:2, 17[2]; 2:7, 9, 13, 14, 22; 3:2[2], 3, 4, 9, 21[2], 26; 4:17, 20, 44; 5:1[2], 2[2], 4, 8, 13, 14, 19; 6:15, 18, 23, 29, 30; 7:6, 8, 15, 16, 17[2], 18, 19[2]; 8:1[2], 4, 5[2], 18, 19, 27, 29[2]; 9:14, 15[2], 16, 21, 27, 29; 10:16, 24, 25, 29, 30, 31; 11:4, 10, 15, 20; 12:6, 10, 11, 18; 13:2, 5, 6, 7[2], 11, 16, 23, 25; 14:3, 5, 24, 26, 27, 28; 15:3, 5, 9[2], 18, 20, 24, 28, 34; 16:3, 11, 16, 18; 17:3[2], 4[2], 7[2], 8[2], 11[2], 12, 15[4], 19, 23, 28, 29, 33; 18:3, 4[2], 6, 12[2], 16, 36, 37; 19:8; 20:4, 8, 11, 12; 21:2, 3[2], 4, 7[2], 9, 16, 20, 21, 24; 23:2, 8, 11, 12[2], 13, 15, 16, 18, 19[3], 22, 24, 26, 32, 37; 24:3, 4, 7, 9, 13[2], 19; 25:3, 11, 16, 21, 22, 23; 1Ch 2:4, 18, 21, 26, 34[2]; 4:5, 9, 18, 27, 40, 43; 5:9, 18, 25; 6:49; 7:4[2], 15, 23; 8:8, 9, 11, 38, 40; 9:19, 22, 25, 27[2], 44; 10:7[2], 11; 11:3[2], 6, 10, 23; 12:22, 23, 29, 39; 13:10, 11, 14; 14:2[2], 8, 9, 12; 15:1, 3, 15, 26; 16:1, 2, 40; 18:9, 10, 11[2]; 19:6, 9, 16[2], 19; 20:5; 21:19, 28, 29; 22:4, 7; 23:17, 22, 25; 24:2, 19, 28; 26:2, 4, 5, 6, 9, 10[2], 12[2], 32; 27:23; 28:2, 12; 29:8, 9, 25; 2Ch 1:3, 4[3], 5, 12, 14; 2:17; 3:1; 4:11, 17; 5:1[2], 4, 6, 10, 11; 6:7, 13[2]; 7:6, 7, 9, 10, 11[3]; 8:2, 4, 8, 11, 12, 14; 9:1, 3, 9, 11, 12, 18, 19, 21, 23, 25; 10:1, 2, 6, 8, 10, 12, 15; 11:14, 15, 21; 12:1, 2, 5, 9, 13, 14; 13:13, 21; 14:8, 14; 15:8, 9[2], 11, 15, 16, 18; 16:6, 14; 17:2, 3, 5, 13; 18:1, 10, 12, 30; 20:24, 27, 29, 30, 33; 21:3[2], 6, 7[2], 10, 11[3], 19; 22:1, 4, 6[2], 7, 8; 23:8, 9, 14, 18[2], 21; 24:3, 7[2], 9, 14, 16, 22, 24[2]; 25:3, 10, 13[2], 24; 26:4, 8, 10[2], 11, 19, 20[2], 21[2], 23; 27:2; 28:3, 6, 17, 18, 19[3], 23; 29:2, 15[2], 24, 34[3], 36; 30:3[3], 5, 12, 17[2], 18, 25[2], 26; 31:1[2], 10; 32:1, 2, 27, 29, 31; 33:2, 3, 4, 7[2], 9, 15, 22[2], 25; 34:4, 9[2], 11, 13, 14[2], 22, 30, 32, 33; 35:3, 10, 16, 18[2], 20, 22, 24; 36:13, 14, 15; Ezr 1:5, 7[2], 8; 2:1, 61, 65, 66; 3:1, 6, 8, 12; 4:20; 5:14[2]; 6:13, 20, 21[2], 22; 7:6[2], 9, 10, 11; 8:20, 22, 25, 30, 35; 9:1; 10:5, 9, 17, 18, 44[2]; Ne 2:1, 9, 10, 12[2], 13[2], 16[2], 18; 4:7, 15, 23; 5:4, 12, 13; 6:1[2], 12[3], 13, 16, 18; 7:1[2], 4, 5, 6, 63, 67, 73; 8:1, 9, 12, 14, 17[2]; 9:2, 15, 26; 11:16; 12:29, 30, 31, 43, 46; 13:2[2], 4, 5, 6, 7, 10[2], 23; Est 1:6, 14; 2:1[3], 6, 7[4], 8[2], 10[2], 12, 15, 20[3]; 3:2, 4; 4:1, 7[2], 8, 9; 5:5, 11[2], 14; 6:2[2], 4[2], 13, 14; 7:4, 7, 9, 10; 8:1, 2, 3, 17; 9:1, 3, 18, 23[2], 24[2], 25, 26[2], 31[2]; 10:2; Job 1:2, 3, 5; 2:11; 3:15; 6:10, 20; 10:18, 19[2]; 28:17; 29:12, 22; 30:2; 31:13, 21, 25, 31, 32, 35; 32:3[2], 4, 5; 34:27; 41:32; 42:5, 7, 10[2], 11[2], 12, 13; Ps 44:17, 18[2], 20; 49:11; 51:T; 52:T; 54:T; 55:6; 56:T; 57:T; 59:T; 66:18; 73:2[2], 15; 78:11[2], 29[2], 54, 60, 63; 94:17; 95:9; 105:26, 28, 38, 44; 106:13, 21, 23, 34; 107:11; 119:92; 124:1, 2; Pr 1:23; 24:31; Ecc 2:7, 11[2], 18; 4:2, 8; SS 3:4[2]; 5:6; 6:11; 8:11; Isa 1:9; 5:1; 6:6; 22:9; 36:21, 22; 37:8; 38:8, 21, 22; 39:1; 48:18; 53:2, 9; Jer 2:21; 3:7, 8; 4:25; 5:5; 9:2; 11:8, 19[2]; 13:7; 15:17; 16:15; 18:8, 10; 19:14; 20:2; 23:8, 22, 25[2]; 24:2[2]; 26:8, 23; 28:12; 29:1, 2; 31:26; 32:3, 8, 10, 12, 16, 22; 34:8, 11, 16; 35:9; 36:4, 9, 13, 23, 26, 27, 32; 37:2, 4, 5, 11, 15[2], 17;

HAS (2407)

See also the selected listing for "HAS" in the Main Concordance.

HAVE (4313)

See also the selected listing for "HAVE" in the Main Concordance.

11[3], 12; **6:**2, 5[3], 6[2], 8, 10[2], 11, 15[3], 16[2], 18, 24[2], 26[2], 33, 34[2], 37[3], 38[2], 39; **7:**12[2], 16, 18, 19, 20[2], 22[2]; **9:**6; **10:**10, 16; **12:**5, 7; **13:**8, 10, 11; **14:**7, 11; **16:**9; **18:**16; **19:**3[2]; **20:**8[2], 12, 17, 20[2], 37[2]; **21:**12, 13[3]; **24:**20; **25:**16[3], 19; **26:**18[2]; **28:**9, 11, 23; **29:**9, 18, 19, 31; **30:**6; **31:**10; **32:**13; **33:**7; **34:**15, 17[2], 21[2], 25[2], 27; **Ezr 4:**2, 3, 12; **6:**12; **7:**15, 20, 24; **9:**1, 2[3], 7, 10, 11, 13[3]; **10:**2, 10[2], 13; **Ne 1:**3, 6, 7[2], 9; **2:**3, 7, 8, 17, 20; **4:**5, 22; **5:**4, 5[2], 8, 19; **6:**7, 14[2]; **7:**3; **8:**10; **9:**8, 33[2], 37; **10:**34; **13:**14; **Est 1:**15, 18; **4:**11, 14; **5:**4, 14[2]; **6:**8, 10[2]; **7:**3, 4[2]; **8:**7[2]; **9:**12[2], 21; **Job 1:**5[2], 7, 8, 10[2]; **2:**2, 3; **3:**26[2]; **4:**3[2], 4[2], 8; **5:**3, 16, 23, 27; **6:**3, 8, 10, 11, 12, 13, 14, 21, 22, 24; **7:**1, 3[2], 16, 20[4]; **9:**21; **10:**2, 4, 20; **12:**3, 4, 5; **13:**1[2], 18, 23; **14:**5[2], 15; **15:**3, 9[2], 17, 18; **16:**2, 7[2], 8, 15, 17; **17:**4, 7, 11; **19:**3, 4, 14[2], 19, 20, 21[2]; **20:**7, 20; **21:**3, 14, 29[2]; **22:**15; **23:**11[2], 12[2]; **24:**2, 7, 19, 22; **26:**2[2], 3[2]; **27:**3, 12, 14; **30:**1, 9, 25, 29; **31:**5, 7[2], 8, 9, 11, 12, 13, 16, 17, 19, 21, 24, 25, 26, 28, 29, 30, 31, 33, 39; **32:**13, 15[2], 17; **33:**6, 8, 24, 32; **34:**16, 32; **36:**9[2], 17, 23, 24; **37:**24; **38:**12, 16, 17[2], 18, 21, 22, 28; **40:**5, 9; **42:**5, 7, 8; **Ps 2:**6, 7; **4:**7; **5:**10; **7:**3, 4[2]; **8:**1, 2, 3; **9:**4[2], 5[2], 6, 10, 13, 15[3]; **10:**6; **12:**1; **13:**2, 4; **14:**3[2]; **16:**2, 5[2], 6[2], 8, 11; **17:**3, 4, 5[2], 11, 14; **18:**21[2], 22, 23[2], 43[2]; **21:**2[2], 5, 6; **22:**1, 10, 16[2]; **25:**17, 19; **26:**1[2]; **27:**9; **28:**1, 4, 5; **31:**1, 8[2], 12, 17, 19; **32:**9; **34:**19; **35:**21, 22, 25; **37:**16, 25, 35; **38:**2, 3, 14; **39:**5; **40:**5, 6, 7, 12; **41:**4[2], 10; **42:**3, 7, 9; **43:**2; **44:**1[2], 9, 10, 11, 13, 14, 21; **45:**2; **48:**8[2]; **50:**9, 16, 21; **51:**1, 4, 8; **52:**9; **53:**3; **54:**7; **55:**5, 19; **56:**13; **57:**1[2], 6; **59:**4; **60:**1[2], 2, 3[2], 4, 10; **61:**3, 5[2]; **62:**11; **63:**2; **64:**6; **65:**9; **66:**18; **68:**23, 28; **69:**1, 2; **71:**1, 5, 6, 7, 14, 17, 19, 20, 23, 24; **72:**12; **73:**4, 11, 13[2], 14[2], 15, 25, 28; **74:**1, 18, 20; **78:**3[2]; **79:**1[3], 2, 3, 7, 12; **80:**5[2], 6, 12, 15, 17; **81:**9; **84:**3, 5; **86:**3, 9, 13, 16, 17; **88:**6, 7, 8[2], 15[2], 16, 17, 18; **89:**3[2], 15, 19[2], 20[2], 34, 35, 38[3], 39[2], 40, 41, 42[2], 43[2], 44, 45[2], 47, 51[2]; **90:**1, 8, 10, 13, 15[2]; **92:**10[2], 11[2]; **93:**3[3]; **94:**17; **95:**10; **98:**1, 3; **99:**4[2]; **101:**4; **102:**7, 10, 13; **106:**6[2]; **108:**11; **109:**2[2], 27; **111:**10; **112:**7, 8; **115:**5, 6, 7; **116:**8, 16; **118:**21; **119:**4, 11, 30[2], 32, 43, 45, 49, 53, 57, 58, 59[2], 69, 74, 75, 81, 87, 92, 93, 94, 99, 100, 101, 102[2], 106, 107, 110[2], 114, 117, 121, 132, 138, 140, 143, 147, 153, 157, 165, 173, 176[2]; **120:**6; **123:**3[3], 4; **124:**3, 4[2], 5, 7[2]; **129:**1, 2[2], 3; **131:**2; **132:**14; **135:**14, 16, 17; **137:**8; **138:**2; **139:**1, 5, 22; **140:**5[3], 9; **141:**7, 9; **142:**3, 4; **143:**5, 8; **145:**10; **Pr 1:**23; **3:**25, 28; **4:**7; **5:**14; **6:**1[2], 2, 3; **7:**14, 15, 16, 17; **8:**6, 9, 14; **9:**5; **12:**9[2], 11, 21; **13:**2; **14:**20, 32; **16:**22; **17:**21; **19:**2, 19; **20:**6, 9, 13; **22:**2, 11, 18, 20; **23:**4, 8[2]; **25:**7; **27:**27; **28:**19[2]; **29:**7, 13; **30:**2, 3[2], 9, 27, 32[2]; **Ecc 1:**14, 16[2]; **2:**19[2]; **3:**10, 19; **4:**1[2], 9, 14[2]; **5:**13; **6:**1, 3; **7:**15, 22, 27, 29[2]; **9:**5, 6[2], 11; **10:**5, 7; **SS 1:**6; **3:**3; **4:**9[2]; **5:**1[4], 3[2]; **7:**12[2], 13; **8:**8, 10; **Isa 1:**2, 4[2], 9[2], 11[2], 14, 29[2]; **2:**6, 8; **3:**6, 7[2], 9, 11, 14; **5:**4[2], 12[2], 24; **6:**5; **7:**5, 22; **8:**20; **9:**2, 3, 4, 10[2], 12, 13[2]; **10:**13[2], 27; **12:**1; **13:**3[2], 17, 18; **14:**1, 8, 10[2], 12[2], 20, 24[2]; **15:**7; **16:**6, 8, 9, 10; **17:**8[2], 10[2]; **19:**13[2]; **21:**6, 10; **22:**1, 3[2], 11; **23:**2, 4[2], 7, 10, 13; **24:**5; **25:**1, 2, 4; **26:**1, 12[2], 13, 15[4], 18[2]; **28:**15[3]; **29:**20; **30:**4[2], 12, 15; **31:**6, 7; **32:**9; **33:**1[2], 13; **34:**5, 12; **36:**5, 10, 12, 19; **37:**6[2], 7, 11[2], 16, 18, 19, 21, 23[2], 24[5], 25[2], 26[3]; **38:**3[2], 5, 12, 17; **39:**6, 8; **40:**11, 21[2], 28; **41:**3, 5, 8, 9[2], 25; **42:**6, 9, 14[2], 16, 20[2], 22[2], 24; **43:**1[2], 8[2], 10, 12, 22[2], 23[2], 24[2]; **44:**1, 2, 21, 22[2]; **45:**5, 8, 10[2], 19[2], 23, 24; **46:**3[2], 4, 11[2]; **47:**10[2], 12, 13, 15; **48:**6, 7, 8, 10[2], 12, 15[2], 16, 18, 19; **49:**4[2], 6, 13, 15, 16, 21; **50:**5[2], 7, 11; **51:**7, 16, 17[2], 19, 20, 22; **52:**5[2], 15; **53:**6; **54:**8, 9, 14, 16; **55:**1, 4, 7; **56:**11; **57:**6, 7, 8, 11[4], 16, 18; **58:**3[4], 5, 6; **59:**2[2], 3, 8, 13, 18, 21; **60:**15, 21; **61:**4; **62:**6, 8; **63:**3, 18, 19[2]; **64:**6, 7, 10; **65:**2; **66:**3, 5, 19; **Jer 1:**9, 12, 16, 18; **2:**11, 13[3], 15[3], 16, 17, 19, 23[2], 27, 28[2], 29, 31, 32, 35; **3:**1, 2[2], 3[3], 4, 6, 13[3], 16, 20, 21[2], 24, 25[2]; **4:**4, 10[2], 18, 19[2], 22, 28[2]; **5:**7, 11, 12, 14, 19, 21[2], 23[2], 25[2], 27, 28[2]; **6:**15, 19[2], 24, 27; **7:**9, 11, 30[3], 31; **8:**2[2], 5, 6[2], 8, 9[2], 12, 13, 14, 16, 19; **9:**5, 10, 13[2], 14[2], 16[2]; **10:**9, 14, 25[2]; **11:**10[3], 13[3], 17, 20; **12:**2[2], 4, 5[2], 6[2], 15; **13:**11, 22, 25[2], 27; **14:**7, 14, 18, 19[2], 20; **15:**5, 6, 7, 10; **16:**2, 5, 10[2], 12, 13, 18[2]; **17:**4, 13, 16[2]; **18:**15, 20, 22[2]; **19:**4[3], 5; **20:**6, 12; **21:**10, 12; **22:**9[2], 12, 15[2], 19, 21; **23:**2[3], 3, 14, 17, 21[2], 22[2], 25; **25:**3[2], 4, 6, 7[3], 8, 13, 35; **26:**3, 4, 5[2], 11, 12; **27:**3, 15, 18; **28:**6, 7, 8, 13, 15, 16; **29:**6[2], 7, 8, 9, 11, 14, 19[2], 20, 23[3], 27, 32; **30:**2, 10, 14[2], 15, 18; **31:**3[2], 18[2], 20, 29, 37; **32:**17, 20[2], 25, 30[3], 32[2], 42[2]; **33:**4, 8, 17, 18, 21, 24, 25, 26; **34:**16[2], 17[2], 18[2]; **35:**7, 8[2], 10[2], 11, 14[2], 15[2], 16[2], 18[3], 19; **36:**2, 14, 30, 31; **37:**18[2]; **38:**9[3], 19, 22; **40:**10; **41:**8; **42:**4[2], 10, 12, 18, 21[2]; **43:**10; **44:**3, 8[2], 9, 10[2], 14, 16, 18[2], 23[3], 25; **45:**4[2]; **46:**27; **48:**29, 33, 38; **49:**14, 16, 23, 24, 37; **50:**6[2], 10, 17, 21; **51:**5, 7, 9, 17, 24, 30[2], 49, 50, 51[2], 62; **La 1:**2[2], 3, 5[2], 6, 8, 14[2], 18, 20, 21[4], 22; **2:**7, 9, 10[2], 16[3], 20[2], 21[3]; **3:**17[2], 21, 37, 42[2], 43[2], 44, 45, 46, 47, 59, 60, 61, 64; **4:**3, 10; **5:**3, 11, 12, 14, 16, 22; **Eze 2:**3; **3:**6, 17, 19, 21; **4:**5, 6[2], 8, 14[2]; **5:**5, 7[3], 9, 11, 13[2], 15, 17; **6:**6, 9[5]; **8:**12, 17; **9:**10, 11; **11:**6, 7, 12[2], 15, 16[2], 17, 21; **12:**2, 6, 11, 22; **13:**3, 5, 7[2], 14, 19[4]; **14:**3, 5, 9, 22[2], 23; **15:**6, 7, 8; **16:**43, 48, 50, 51[3], 52[2], 54, 59, 63; **17:**21, 24; **18:**31; **20:**3, 7, 32, 34, 41, 43[2], 48; **21:**5, 15, 17, 23, 24[2], 32; **22:**4[5], 7[2], 8, 12, 13[2], 14, 16, 19, 22, 30, 31; **23:**29, 30, 31, 34, 35, 37, 38; **24:**14[2], 19, 22; **25:**6; **26:**2, 5, 10, 14; **27:**34, 36; **28:**4, 5, 10, 18, 19, 24, 25; **29:**6, 20; **30:**12, 21; **32:**9, 21, 22, 27; **33:**5, 7, 9, 29[2]; **34:**4[3], 15, 19[2], 21, 24; **35:**10, 12[4]; **36:**2, 4, 5, 6, 22[2], 23, 36[3]; **37:**14[2], 20, 21, 24; **38:**13[2]; **39:**5, 8, 15, 25, 27[2]; **40:**4, 45, 46; **43:**11, 23; **44:**12, 19, 28; **45:**7, 9; **47:**22[2]; **48:**1, 2, 3, 4, 5, 6, 7, 13, 16, 23, 24, 25, 26, 27; **Da 1:**10; **2:**3, 5[2], 8, 9, 23[3], 25, 30, 41; **3:**10, 12[2], 14, 18; **4:**22, 30, 35; **5:**7, 11, 12, 14[2], 16[2], 22, 23, 27; **6:**7, 22[2]; **8:**22, 23; **9:**5[4], 6, 7, 8, 9, 10, 11[2], 12, 13, 14, 15[2], 16, 22, 23, 26[2]; **10:**11, 12, 14, 19, 20; **11:**4, 15, 16, 32; **Hos 4:**6[2], 10[2]; **5:**1, 3; **6:**7, 10; **7:**13[2]; **8:**1, 9, 10, 11; **9:**1, 9, 13, 17; **10:**3, 9[2], 13[4]; **12:**8; **13:**14, 16; **14:**1, 3, 8; **Joel 1:**4[5], 17, 18, 19, 20; **2:**4, 14, 25, 26; **3:**4[3], 7, 21; **Am 2:**4[3]; **3:**2, 3; **4:**6, 8, 9, 10, 11; **5:**3[2], 6, 11[2], 15, 19, 22, 26; **6:**12; **8:**7; **9:**15; **Ob 1:**1, 15; **Jnh 1:**10, 14; **2:**4, 9; **4:**4, 9, 10; **Mic 2:**5, 8; **3:**4; **4:**6, 9; **5:**15; **6:**1, 3[2], 13, 16[2]; **7:**2, 8, 9, 19; **Na 1:**12[2], 14; **2:**2[2]; **3:**16; **Hab 1:**12[2], 14[2]; **2:**8[3], 10, 17[3]; **3:**2; **Zep 1:**3, 17; **2:**8; **3:**6[2], 8, 11, 19; **Hag 1:**6[4], 10; **2:**19, 23; **Zec 1:**11, 12, 21; **2:**6, 8; **3:**4, 7, 9; **4:**9; **6:**8, 10; **7:**3; **8:**13, 15, 23; **10:**6; **11:**6; **12:**10; **13:**3; **14:**16, 17, 18; **Mal 1:**2[3], 3[2], 4, 6, 7; **2:**2[2], 4, 8[3], 9[3], 10, 14, 17[2]; **3:**3, 7[2], 10, 13[2], 14; **Mt 2:**2; **3:**9; **4:**16; **5:**17[2], 21, 26, 27, 33[2], 38, 40, 43; **6:**1, 2, 5, 12, 16; **7:**12; **8:**8, 10, 20[2], 29; **9:**13, 27; **10:**8[2], 21, 34, 35; **11:**5, 21, 23, 25, 27; **12:**7, 18, 36[2]; **13:**5, 12[2], 15, 51; **14:**4, 17; **15:**5, 22, 28, 32[3], 34; **16:**23; **17:**9, 12, 15, 20[2]; **18:**6, 8, 9, 15, 33; **19:**12, 20, 21, 27, 28; **20:**6, 12[2], 15, 23, 30, 31; **21:**16[2], 21, 42; **22:**4[3], 24, 31; **23:**7, 8, 9, 10, 23[2], 30, 37; **24:**25, 34, 43[2]; **25:**20, 21, 22, 23, 24[2], 26[2], 27[2], 29[2]; **26:**9, 11[2], 32, 35, 55, 65; **27:**4[2], 19[2], 20, 46; **28:**7, 20; **Mk 1:**24, 38; **2:**12, 17, 19, 25; **3:**9, 15; **4:**5, 17, 25, 40; **6:**17, 18, 31, 38, 39; **7:**8, 9, 11, 13; **8:**2[3], 3, 5, 16, 18, 33; **9:**13, 45, 47, 50; **10:**13, 20, 21[2], 28, 40, 47, 48; **11:**17, 22, 24; **12:**19, 26, 39; **13:**12, 23, 30; **14:**5, 7[2], 28, 31, 48, 64; **15:**11, 34; **Lk 1:**1[2], 3, 4, 19, 30, 36, 38, 57; **2:**29, 30, 31, 48[2]; **3:**8; **4:**23, 34; **5:**26, 32, 36; **6:**3, 24, 31; **7:**4, 6, 9, 22[2], 36, 40, 43, 47; **8:**13, 18; **9:**13, 14, 35, 58[2]; **10:**13, 19, 21, 22, 28, 35; **11:**6, 42, 52[3]; **12:**3[2], 17, 19, 20, 24, 37, 39, 49, 50, 59; **13:**34; **14:**8, 9, 18, 19; **15:**6, 9, 17, 18, 21, 23, 31; **16:**11, 12, 24, 28, 29; **17:**6, 10[2], 13; **18:**13, 15, 21, 22[2], 28, 38, 39; **19:**8, 12, 17, 20, 23, 46; **20:**28, 46; **21:**32; **22:**15, 28, 32[2], 36[2], 52, 71; **23:**2, 14[2], 22[2]; **24:**18, 25, 26, 39[2], 41, 49; **Jn 1:**14, 16, 33, 34, 41, 45; **2:**3, 10[2]; **3:**11, 12, 15, 16; **4:**10[2], 11, 15, 17[2], 18[3], 32, 33, 38[3], 42; **5:**7, 26, 29[2], 33, 36, 37, 40, 42, 43; **6:**7, 10, 36, 38, 40, 53, 63, 68, 70; **7:**26; **8:**6, 12, 14, 25, 26[2], 28, 33, 37, 38[2], 41, 42, 57; **9:**17, 27, 37, 39; **10:**10[3], 16, 18, 32, 34; **11:**21, 32, 34, 37, 41; **12:**8[2], 28, 34, 35[2], 36, 46; **13:**8, 12, 14, 15[2], 18, 26, 34; **14:**2, 7, 9, 12, 25, 26, 29; **15:**3, 9, 10, 11, 12, 15[2], 19, 22, 24[2], 27; **16:**1, 3, 4, 6, 12, 24, 25, 27[2], 30, 33[4]; **17:**2, 3, 4, 6[2], 7, 9, 10[2], 13, 14, 18, 21, 22, 23[2], 24[2], 25, 26[2]; **18:**9, 20, 30, 31, 35; **19:**7, 10, 11, 15, 22[2], 31, 37; **20:**2[2], 13[2], 15[2], 17, 18, 25, 29[4], 31; **21:**10, 12, 25; **Ac 1:**4, 11, 21, 24; **2:**13, 28; **3:**6[2], 24[2]; **4:**16, 20; **5:**3[2], 4, 28; **6:**11, 14; **7:**34[3], 43, 52, 53[2]; **8:**21, 24; **9:**13; **10:**4, 14, 20, 21, 22[3], 47[2]; **11:**12; **13:**2, 15, 22, 28, 33, 40, 47; **14:**11; **15:**10, 18, 24, 26; **16:**36; **17:**6[2], 28[2]; **18:**10; **19:**2, 21, 37[2], 38; **20:**20[2], 21[2], 25, 27, 33, 34; **21:**20, 21, 22, 23, 24, 25; **22:**10, 15; **23:**1, 11, 14[2], 20, 21[2], 22; **24:**2, 5, 10, 15, 19; **25:**3, 8, 10, 12, 26[3]; **26:**1, 4, 5, 11, 16[2], 22, 32; **27:**21[2], 25, 33[2]; **28:**17, 20, 21[2], 27; **Ro 1:**13[3], 20, 29; **2:**1, 14[2], 20, 25, 27; **3:**2, 3, 9, 12[2], 23, 26; **4:**9, 11, 17; **5:**1[2], 2, 9, 11; **6:**5, 13, 18[2], 22[2]; **7:**6, 7[2], 18; **8:**5[2], 9, 12, 23, 25, 28; **9:**2, 9, 15[4], 18, 21, 29[2], 30; **10:**14[2], 21; **11:**3, 4[2], 17[2], 30, 31, 32; **12:**4, 6; **13:**1; **15:**3, 4, 15, 18, 19, 21, 22, 23, 24[2], 27, 28[3]; **16:**7, 17; **1Co 1:**5, 11; **2:**8, 12, 16; **3:**8; **4:**2, 6, 7, 8[3], 9, 13, 15[2], 18, 19; **5:**2[2], 3, 9, 10; **6:**4, 7[2], 19; **7:**2, 25, 28, 29, 40; **8:**10; **9:**1, 4, 5, 11, 12[2], 15[2], 17, 22, 27; **10:**21; **11:**6[2], 10, 16, 17, 19[2], 22[2], 30; **12:**25, 30; **13:**1, 2[3], 3; **14:**5, 12; **15:**1, 2, 6, 15, 18, 19, 20, 32, 39[2], 49; **16:**2, 15, 17; **2Co 1:**4, 10, 12[2], 14, 16; **2:**2, 10[2]; **3:**12; **4:**1, 2, 7, 13; **5:**1; **6:**11, 14[2], 15; **7:**1, 2[3], 3[2], 4, 11, 14, 16; **8:**10, 12, 15[2], 16; **9:**2, 13; **10:**2, 4; **11:**6[2], 9, 23, 26[2], 27[5]; **12:**11[2], 14, 15, 16, 19[3], 21[3]; **13:**6, 7[2], 10; **Gal 1:**9, 13; **2:**4, 16, 20; **3:**4, 9, 21, 27; **4:**11, 12, 15[2], 16, 27; **5:**4[2], 24; **6:**10; **Eph 1:**7, 10, 16; **2:**5, 8, 13, 18; **3:**2, 3, 18; **4:**1, 19, 28; **5:**11; **6:**13; **Php 1:**7, 14, 20, 30; **2:**1, 12, 20, 28; **3:**4[2], 8, 12[2], 13, 16, 18; **4:**3, 9, 10[2], 11, 12[2], 18[2]; **Col 1:**4[2], 5, 9, 11, 14, 18, 19, 23, 25; **2:**1, 2, 10, 23; **3:**1, 9, 10, 13; **4:**1, 10, 11, 17; **1Th 2:**6; **3:**5[2], 6, 9; **4:**6, 9, 13, 14, 15; **5:**27; **2Th 1:**10; **2:**2, 12[2]; **3:**4, 9; **1Ti 1:**6, 19[2], 20; **2:**12; **3:**7, 13; **4:**2, 6, 7, 10; **5:**12, 14, 15; **6:**2, 5, 8, 10, 21[2]; **2Ti 1:**5, 9, 12[2]; **2:**2, 18, 23; **3:**5, 14[2], 15; **4:**7[3], 8; **Tit 2:**8; **3:**8, 10, 12, 13; **Phm 1:**6[2], 7, 13, 15, 20; **Heb 1:**5, 9; **2:**1, 14; **3:**10, 14; **4:**1, 2, 3, 8, 14, 15[2]; **5:**5, 11, 14; **6:**4[3], 5, 10[2], 18, 19; **7:**11, 15, 23; **8:**1, 3, 7; **9:**26; **10:**2[3], 7, 9, 10, 18, 19, 21, 26, 36; **11:**15, 32; **12:**4, 5, 9, 11, 18, 22[2], 23; **13:**2, 5, 10[2], 14, 18, 22; **Jas 2:**4, 6, 11, 14, 18[2]; **3:**7, 9, 16; **4:**2[2]; **5:**2, 3, 4, 5[2], 6, 11[3]; **1Pe 1:**2, 6, 7, 8, 12[2], 22[2], 23; **2:**3, 10, 24, 25; **3:**15; **4:**3, 5; **5:**10, 12; **2Pe 1:**1, 9, 12, 19; **2:**3, 13, 15, 20, 21[3]; **3:**1; **1Jn 1:**1[4], 2, 3[2], 5, 6, 7, 10; **2:**1, 3, 7[2], 12, 13[3], 14[2], 18[2], 19, 20, 24; **3:**14, 21; **4:**1, 3, 4, 14, 17; **5:**12[2], 13, 14, 15; **2Jn 1:**5, 6, 7, 8, 9, 12; **3Jn 1:**3, 4, 6, 9, 13; **Jude 1:**1, 4, 11[3], 15[2], 19; **Rev 1:**19; **2:**2[2], 3[3], 4, 5, 6, 14[2], 15, 20, 21, 24, 25, 27; **3:**1, 2, 3, 4[2], 8[4], 9, 10, 11, 17; **4:**11; **5:**10; **7:**14[2]; **9:**4; **10:**4; **11:**6[2], 7, 17[2]; **12:**10; **13:**3, 8; **15:**4; **16:**5, 6[2]; **17:**8, 10, 12, 13; **18:**3, 14, 24; **20:**6; **22:**14, 16.

HE (9660)

Ge 1:4, 5, 10, 16, 27[2], 31; **2:**2[2], 3[2], 8[2], 19[2], 21[2], 22[2]; **3:**1, 6, 8, 10, 11, 15, 16[2], 17, 22, 23, 24[2]; **4:**5, 9, 15, 17, 20, 21, 26; **5:**1, 2[2], 3[2], 5, 6, 7, 8, 9, 10, 11, 12, 13, 14, 15, 16, 17, 18, 19, 20, 21, 22, 24, 25, 26, 27, 28, 29[2], 31, 32; **6:**3, 6, 9; **8:**1, 6, 8, 9, 10, 12, 20; **9:**21[2], 25[2], 26, 29; **10:**9, 11[2]; **11:**10, 11, 12, 13, 14, 15, 16, 17, 18, 19, 20, 21, 22, 23, 24, 25, 26, 32; **12:**4, 5, 7, 8[2], 11[2], 16, 18, 20; **13:**1, 3[2], 4, 18; **14:**12, 14, 15, 16, 18, 19; **15:**5[2], 6, 7, 10; **16:**4, 8, 12[2]; **17:**14, 17, 20, 22, 24; **18:**1, 2[2], 3, 6, 7, 8[2], 9, 15, 19[2], 28, 29[2], 30[2], 31, 32[2], 33; **19:**1[2], 2, 3[2], 9, 13, 14[2], 16, 21, 25, 27, 28[2], 29[2], 30[2], 33, 35, 37, 38; **20:**1, 4, 5[2], 7[2], 8, 13, 14, 16; **21:**1[2], 13, 14, 17, 20[2], 21, 30, 33; **22:**1[2], 3[3], 5, 6, 9, 10, 11, 12, 13[2]; **23:**3, 8, 9, 10, 11, 13, 16; **24:**2[2], 7, 10, 11, 12, 15, 23, 29, 30[2], 31, 33, 34, 35[2], 36[2], 40, 52, 53, 54[2], 56, 62, 63[3], 65, 66, 67[2]; **25:**5, 6[2], 8, 17[2], 20, 26, 30[2], 33, 34; **26:**7[3], 13, 14, 18, 20, 21, 22[2], 23, 25, 33, 34; **27:**1[3], 9, 10[2], 14, 18[2], 20, 23[2], 24[2], 25[4], 27[2], 31[2], 32, 33, 34, 35, 36[4], 41; **28:**4, 5, 6[2], 9[2], 11[3], 12[2], 13, 16, 17, 18, 19; **29:**2, 5, 6[2], 7, 9, 10, 12[2], 13[2], 23, 28, 30[2], 31, 33, 34; **30:**6, 14, 15, 16, 22, 28, 31, 35[2], 36, 38, 40, 42; **31:**5, 8[2], 12, 15[3], 18[2], 20, 21[3], 23, 32, 33[3], 35, 36, 42, 46, 49, 54, 55; **32:**2[2], 4, 6, 8, 11, 13[3], 16, 17, 18, 19, 20[2], 21, 23[2], 25[3], 27, 29[2], 31[2]; **33:**1, 2, 3[2], 4, 5, 8, 17, 18, 19[2], 20; **34:**2, 3, 5, 19, 31; **35:**7[3], 10, 13, 14[2], 29; **36:**6, 24; **37:**2, 3[2], 5, 6, 8, 9[3], 10, 13, 14[2], 16, 18, 21[2], 23, 27, 29, 30, 33, 35[2]; **38:**2, 9[2], 10[2], 11[2], 12, 15, 16, 17, 18[2], 20, 21, 22, 26, 29[2], 30; **39:**2[2], 3, 4[2], 5[2], 6[4], 8[4], 10, 11, 12, 13, 14, 15[2], 18, 19, 21, 22, 23; **40:**4, 6, 7, 9, 16, 20[2], 21[2], 22, 23; **41:**1, 5, 8, 10, 12, 13, 14[3], 16, 25, 28, 42, 43[2], 46, 48, 49, 52, 55; **42:**1, 2, 4, 7[3], 9, 12, 17, 21[2], 23, 24[2], 27, 28, 38; **43:**7[2], 14, 16, 18, 23[2], 27[3], 29[3], 30, 31[2]; **44:**2, 6[2], 9, 10, 20, 22, 28, 31; **45:**1[2], 2, 4, 8, 14, 15, 21, 22[2], 23, 24[2], 26[2], 27; **46:**1[2], 2, 3, 7, 29; **47:**2, 14, 17[2], 22, 29, 30, 31[2]; **48:**1, 3, 8, 10, 14[2], 15, 16, 17[2], 19[3], 20[2]; **49:**9, 10, 11[2], 15[2], 19, 20, 27[2], 28, 29, 33; **50:**6, 12, 16, 21, 22, 24, 26; **Ex 1:**9, 21; **2:**2, 6, 10, 11[2], 12, 13[2], 15[2], 18, 19, 20[2], 24; **3:**1, 4, 6[2], 20; **4:**2, 3, 6, 7[2], 14[4], 16[2], 20, 21, 23, 27, 28, 30; **5:**3, 23; **6:**1[2], 13, 29; **7:**4, 13, 14, 15, 20, 22, 23; **8:**12, 15, 19, 20, 27; **9:**7, 12, 27, 33, 34[2], 35; **10:**8, 20, 27; **11:**1[3], 10; **12:**19, 23[2], 25, 27, 48; **13:**5, 11, 19; **14:**4, 6, 7, 8, 25; **15:**1[2], 2[2], 4, 21[2], 25[2], 26; **16:**7, 8[2], 9, 16, 18[3], 21, 23, 29[2]; **17:**7, 11, 12, 16; **18:**4[2], 5, 10, 11, 14, 24, 25; **19:**13[2], 14, 15, 24; **20:**11; **21:**2[2], 3[4], 6[2], 8[3], 9[2], 10[2], 11, 13[2], 16, 18, 19[2], 20, 21, 26, 27[2], 30, 34; **22:**1, 2, 3[3], 4, 5, 7, 8, 12, 13[2], 14, 16, 17, 27[3]; **23:**21[2], 22; **24:**1, 4, 5, 6, 7, 14, 18[2]; **28:**3, 29, 30, 35[4], 38; **29:**21; **30:**7, 8[2], 12; **31:**17, 18; **32:**4, 5, 11, 12, 14, 17, 19, 20[2], 21, 26, 27, 29; **33:**8, 20; **34:**4, 6, 7[2], 9, 28, 29[2], 31, 32, 33, 34[5], 35; **35:**31, 34, 35; **37:**2, 3, 4, 5, 6, 7, 8[2]; **40:**13, 18, 19, 20, 21, 24, 28, 29, 30; **Lev 1:**1, 3[2], 4, 5, 6, 9, 10, 11, 12, 13, 14, 16, 17; **2:**1, 9; **3:**1[2], 2, 3, 4, 6[2], 7[2], 8, 9, 10, 12, 13, 14[2], 15; **4:**3[2], 4[2], 6, 7, 8, 9, 12, 17, 18[2], 19, 20, 21[2], 22, 23[3], 24, 26[3], 27, 28[4], 29, 31[2], 32[2], 33, 35[3]; **5:**1[4], 2[2], 3[4], 4[3], 5[2], 6[2], 7[2], 8[2], 10[2], 11[3], 12, 13[2], 15, 16[3], 17[2], 18[3], 19; **6:**2, 3[3], 4[4], 5[3], 6, 7[2], 11, 20; **7:**12[2], 13, 14, 15, 16, 30[2], 38; **8:**7[2], 8, 9, 11, 12, 13, 14, 15[3], 17, 18, 20, 21, 22, 24, 25, 26[2], 27, 29, 30; **9:**2, 9[2], 10, 11, 12[2], 13, 14, 15[2], 16, 17, 18[2], 22; **10:**3, 16, 20; **11:**25, 28, 40[2]; **12:**7; **13:**2, 3, 5[2], 6, 7[2], 8, 9, 11[2], 13[2], 14, 15[2], 16, 17, 19, 33, 34[2], 35, 37, 40, 41[2], 42, 46[4], 51, 52, 54[2], 56; **14:**2, 6, 7[2], 8[3], 9[4], 10, 12, 13, 20, 21[2], 22, 23, 25, 28[2], 30, 36, 37, 40, 41, 48, 49, 50, 51, 52, 53[2]; **15:**4, 5, 6, 7, 8, 10, 11, 13[3], 14, 15, 16[2], 21, 22, 23, 24[2], 27[2], 30; **16:**2[2], 4[4], 5, 7, 8, 11, 12, 13[2], 14[2], 15[3], 16[2], 17, 18[2], 19, 20, 21[2], 23[3], 24[2], 25, 26, 28, 32; **17:**4, 15[2], 16[2]; **19:**8, 22; **20:**3, 9[2], 11, 14, 15, 17, 18, 20, 21; **21:**3, 4, 11[2], 12, 13, 14, 15, 21[2], 22, 23; **22:**4[4], 5, 6[2], 7[2], 8, 14; **23:**11; **24:**15, 16[2], 17, 19, 20[2]; **25:**15, 16, 26, 27[4], 28[3], 29[2], 35, 40[2], 41[2], 48[2], 49[2], 50[2], 51, 52, 53, 54[2]; **27:**8, 9, 10[2], 11, 13, 15, 17, 18, 19, 20[2], 22, 24, 27[2], 29, 31, 33[2]; **Nu 1:**1, 19; **3:**16, 32, 50, 51; **4:**16, 19, 32; **5:**7[3], 10, 14[2], 15[3], 17, 18[2], 21, 24, 26, 30; **6:**3[2], 4[2], 5[2], 6, 7, 8, 9[2], 10, 11[2], 12[2], 13, 14, 17, 18[2], 21[3]; **7:**1[2], 7, 8, 19, 89[2]; **8:**3; **9:**1, 13; **10:**30, 36; **11:**1, 2, 11, 24, 25, 33; **12:**1, 2, 5, 6, 7, 8, 9, 11; **13:**17; **14:**8, 16[2], 18[2], 24, 43; **15:**13, 14, 27, 28, 29, 31; **16:**4, 5[4], 10, 26, 31, 39, 40, 48; **19:**5, 7[2], 8, 10, 12[4], 13, 18, 19[2], 20[3]; **20:**9, 10, 13, 16, 24, 26; **21:**1, 9, 23[3], 29; **22:**22, 25, 27, 30, 31[2], 36, 41; **23:**3[2], 6, 7, 12, 14[2], 17, 18, 19[4], 20, 24; **24:**1, 3, 10, 15, 17, 20, 21, 23; **25:**7, 8, 11, 13[2]; **26:**33; **27:**3[2], 4, 9, 10, 11, 21[2], 22, 23; **30:**2[2], 5, 8[2], 12, 14[3], 15[3]; **31:**15; **32:**10, 13, 15, 21, 29; **33:**38, 39; **35:**12, 16[2], 17[3], 18[3], 19[2], 20, 21[4], 23[3], 25[2], 26, 28, 31; **36:**2; **Dt 1:**4, 8, 11, 27, 30, 34, 36[3], 38, 45; **2:**7, 15, 22, 30; **3:**20, 28; **4:**10, 13[2], 21, 23, 31[2], 36[2], 37[2], 42[2]; **5:**5, 22[2]; **6:**10, 15, 17, 23[2], 25; **7:**8[2], 9, 10[2], 12, 13[3], 15[2], 24; **8:**3, 10, 15[2], 16, 18[2]; **9:**3[2], 5, 8, 19, 23, 25, 28[3]; **10:**4[2], 15, 18, 21[2]; **11:**3[2], 4[2], 5, 6, 17, 25; **12:**8, 10, 20; **13:**2[2], 5[2], 10, 17[2]; **14:**21, 23; **15:**2[2], 4, 6, 8, 9, 16, 17, 20; **16:**1, 6, 11, 16; **17:**15, 17[2], 18[2], 19[2], 20; **18:**2, 6, 7, 8[2], 18; **19:**1, 5, 6[2], 8[2], 15, 19; **20:**3, 5, 6, 7; **21:**15[2], 16[4], 17[2], 20[2]; **22:**2[2], 3, 16, 17, 19[2], 23, 24, 29[5], 30; **23:**7, 10, 11[2], 14, 16[2]; **24:**1[2], 3, 5[3], 10, 13[2], 14, 15[2]; **25:**3[2], 7, 8, 19; **26:**5, 9, 18, 19[4]; **27:**20; **28:**8, 9, 11, 21, 44[2], 45, 48[2], 54, 55[3], 60; **29:**1, 13[3], 19, 25[2], 26, 27; **30:**3, 5[2], 9, 20[2]; **31:**3, 4[2], 6, 8, 11, 25; **32:**4[2], 6, 7, 8[2], 10[3], 13[2], 15[2], 19, 20, 36, 37, 39, 43[2], 46; **33:**2[3], 5, 7[2], 8, 9[3], 10[2], 12[2], 13, 17[2], 18, 20[2], 21[2], 22, 23[2], 24, 27, 29; **34:**6, 7; **Jos 1:**15, 17; **2:**1; **3:**10; **4:**4, 21, 23[2], 24; **5:**4, 6, 7, 13, 14; **6:**7, 11, 26[2]; **7:**15[2], 17[2], 24; **8:**3, 10, 14[2], 19, 26, 29, 31, 32, 33; **9:**9, 10, 27; **10:**1, 2, 4, 18, 24, 28[4], 30[3], 31, 32[2], 40[2]; **11:**1, 9, 11, 12, 15, 17, 20, 23; **12:**2, 3, 5; **13:**8, 14[2], 32, 33; **14:**10[2], 12, 14; **15:**15; **18:**10; **19:**50[2]; **20:**4[2], 5, 6[4]; **21:**43, 44; **22:**4, 7, 18, 20, 22; **23:**5, 10, 15[3], 16[2]; **24:**1, 7[2], 9, 10, 17, 18, 19[3], 20[2], 25, 26, 27; **Jdg 1:**7, 25, 26[2]; **2:**10, 14, 15, 18, 21, 23; **3:**2, 4, 8, 9, 10, 15, 16, 17, 18, 19, 20, 23, 24[2], 25, 26, 27[2], 28, 31; **4:**3, 10, 18, 19, 20, 21[2], 22; **5:**17, 25, 27[7]; **6:**1, 8, 12, 19[2], 22, 27[2], 30[2], 31, 32, 34, 35, 38; **7:**4[2], 11, 13, 15[2], 16, 17; **8:**2, 5, 8, 9, 12, 14, 16, 17, 18, 20[2], 24, 26, 27, 30[2], 31, 35; **9:**3, 5, 7, 16, 18, 21[2], 28, 30, 31, 36, 43[3], 45[2], 48[4], 52, 54[2]; **10:**1, 2[2], 3, 4, 5, 7[2], 16; **11:**11, 17, 20, 25, 29[2], 33, 34, 35[2], 38[2], 39[2]; **12:**5, 6[2], 9[3], 14[2]; **13:**5, 6[3], 7, 11[3], 18, 22, 23, 24, 25; **14:**2[2], 6[4], 7[2], 8[2], 9[6], 11[2], 14, 16, 17, 19[2]; **15:**1, 2, 4[2], 5, 8[2], 10, 11, 14, 15, 17[2], 18[2], 19; **16:**1[2], 3[2], 4, 9, 11, 12, 13[2], 14, 16, 17[2], 18[2], 20[2], 25, 30[4], 31; **17:**3, 4, 5, 6, 8, 9; **18:**4[2], 20, 24; **19:**3[2], 4, 5, 7, 8, 13, 17, 18, 21, 28, 29[2]; **21:**25; **Ru 2:**14, 20[2], 21; **3:**2, 3, 4[3], 7, 8, 9, 10, 13[2], 14, 15[3], 17; **4:**1[2], 3, 4, 8, 13, 14, 15, 17; **1Sa 1:**2, 4, 5[2], 22, 24[2], 28[2]; **2:**6, 7[2], 8[3], 9, 10[2], 14, 15, 23, 35; **3:**2, 5[2], 9, 13[2], 15, 17[2], 18, 19[2], 21; **4:**13, 15, 16, 18[4]; **5:**6, 9; **6:**5, 6; **7:**3, 8, 9, 12, 16, 17[3]; **8:**1, 6, 11[2], 12, 13, 14, 15, 16, 17, 21; **9:**2, 4[2], 6[3], 8[2], 9, 12[2], 13[3], 16, 17, 26; **10:**2, 10, 13, 14, 16[2], 21[2], 22, 23[2], 25; **11:**5, 6, 7; **12:**5, 9, 11, 24; **13:**1[2], 2, 8, 9, 10, 13; **14:**1, 3, 27[2], 33, 34, 35, 39, 45[3], 47[3], 48, 52; **15:**6, 8[2], 11[2], 12[2], 18, 23, 29[3], 35[2]; **16:**4, 5, 11[3], 12[3], 16, 18[2], 23; **17:**4, 5, 6, 9, 12, 20, 23, 25[2], 26, 28, 30, 33, 36, 38, 39[3], 40, 42[3], 43, 44, 47, 49[2], 50, 51[3], 54, 55; **18:**1, 3, 4, 8[2], 10[2], 11, 13, 14[2], 15[2], 16, 20, 21, 26, 27[2], 29; **19:**4[2], 5[2], 7, 8, 9, 12, 14, 17[2], 18[2], 20, 21, 22[2], 23[2], 24[2]; **20:**1, 2, 3[2], 7[3], 12, 13, 17[2], 25, 26[2], 29[2], 30, 31, 32[2], 34[2], 35, 36[2], 38; **21:**1, 7, 11, 13[3], 14; **22:**2, 4, 7, 8, 10, 12, 13[2], 17, 18, 19, 21, 22; **23:**2, 5, 6, 7, 9, 11, 13, 15, 17, 22, 23[2], 25[2]; **24:**1, 3, 4, 6[2], 9, 10, 15[2], 16, 17, 19; **25:**2[2], 4, 5, 14, 17, 21, 25, 28, 29, 30, 36[2], 37, 38, 39[2]; **26:**3, 4, 5, 10[3], 14, 18, 19; **27:**4, 9[2], 11[3], 12[2]; **28:**5, 6, 8[2], 9, 11, 14[3], 15, 17, 20, 21, 23[3]; **29:**3[2], 4[4], 9; **30:**8, 12[2], 13, 15, 16, 20, 21, 23, 26, 27; **31:**5; **2Sa 1:**2[2], 3, 4, 7[2], 8, 9, 10[2], 13, 15[2]; **2:**1, 5, 9, 10[2], 19[2], 20, 23[2]; **3:**8, 11, 16, 19, 21, 22, 23[2], 24, 25, 27, 28, 30; **4:**1, 4[2], 5, 7, 10; **5:**4[2], 5[2], 9, 10, 13, 20[2], 23,

HER (1669)

HERSELF (45)

HIM (5427)

HIMSELF (430)

HIS (7165)

42^2, 43; **21:**4, 5, 7, 8, 19, 25, 27, 29^3; **22:**3, 9, 19^3, 20, 22, 31, 34^3, 35^2, 36^2, 38, 40^2, 42, 43, 45, 46, 50^3, 52, 53; **2Ki 1:**2, 8, 9, 10, 11, 12, 13^2; **2:**8, 12; **3:**2^2, 27; **4:**1^2, 11, 12, 18, 19^3, 20, 25, 27, 32, 35, 37, 38, 39, 43; **5:**1, 3, 4, 6, 7^2, 8, 9, 11^2, 14, 15, 23, 25, 26; **6:**7, 8, 10, 11, 12, 17, 24, 30^2, 31, 32^2; **7:**12, 13, 17; **8:**14, 16, 19^2, 21^3, 24^2, 26, 29; **9:**2, 3, 11, 16, 21, 24^3, 25^2, 26, 27, 28^3, 36; **10:**3, 10, 11^3, 15, 16, 19^2, 24, 31, 34, 35^2; **11:**2, 3, 8^2, 9, 11^2, 19; **12:**1, 18, 20, 21^2; **13:**3, 8, 9^2, 12^2, 13, 16, 21, 23^2, 24, 25; **14:**2, 3^2, 5^2, 6, 12, 15^2, 16^2, 20, 21, 22, 25, 28, 29^2; **15:**2, 3, 7^2, 9, 18, 19^2, 22^2, 25, 33, 34, 38^3; **16:**2^2, 3, 13^3, 15, 20^2; **17:**13, 15, 18, 20, 23^2; **18:**2, 3, 12, 17^3, 31^2, 33, 35; **19:**1, 4, 7, 19, 37^3; **20:**2, 13^5, 20, 21^2; **21:**1, 3, 6, 7, 10, 11, 18^3, 19, 20, 21^2, 22, 23, 24^2, 26^2; **22:**1, 2, 3, 11; **23:**3^3, 10, 18^2, 25^3, 26, 30^3, 31, 32, 34, 36, 37; **24:**1^2, 2, 3, 6^2, 7^2, 8, 9, 11, 12^4, 15^2, 17^2, 18, 20; **25:**1, 5, 7^2, 19, 29^2; **1Ch 1:**13, 19^2, 46, 50^2; **2:**13, 18, 25, 35^2, 42^2; **3:**3, 9^2, 10^3, 11^3, 12^3, 13^3, 14^2, 16, 17, 22; **4:**9^2, 10, 18, 25^2, 26^3, 27; **5:**1^3, 2, 4^3, 5^3, 6; **6:**20^3, 21^4, 22^3, 23^3, 24^4, 26^3, 27^4, 29^3, 30^3, 39, 44, 49, 50^3, 51^3, 52^3, 53^2; **7:**14^2, 15, 16^2, 18, 20^4, 21^2, 22, 23^2, 24, 25^4, 26^3, 27^2, 35; **8:**1, 8, 9, 10, 29, 30, 37^3, 39^2; **9:**5, 19^2, 35, 36, 43^3; **10:**2^2, 4^3, 5, 6^2, 7, 8, 9^2, 10^2, 12; **11:**10, 11, 20, 23^2, 25, 45; **12:**8, 16, 18, 19^2, 21, 28; **13:**1, 9, 10, 14^2; **14:**2^2, 11; **15:**17, 22; **16:**7, 8, 9, 10, 11^2, 12, 13^2, 14, 15, 23, 24^2, 27, 29^2, 34, 37, 38, 39, 41, 43^2; **17:**1, 11, 12, 13, 14, 23; **18:**3, 4, 10^2, 14; **19:**1, 2^3, 3, 7, 11, 13, 15, 17^2; **20:**3, 8; **21:**3, 13, 16, 20, 21, 27; **22:**5, 6, 9^3, 10^2, 17, 18; **23:**1, 13^2, 25; **24:**21; **25:**3, 4, 9^2, 10, 11, 12, 13, 14, 15, 16, 17, 18, 19, 20, 21, 22, 23, 24, 25, 26, 27, 28, 29, 30, 31; **26:**6, 7, 10, 14, 15, 22, 25^6, 26, 28, 29, 30; **27:**2, 4^2, 5, 6^2, 7^3, 8, 9, 10, 11, 12, 13, 14, 15; **28:**1, 2, 6, 7, 11, 12, 20; **29:**23, 28, 30; **2Ch 1:**1^2, 8; **2:**11, 15, 17; **3:**1, 2; **5:**1, 13; **6:**4^2, 7, 12, 13, 19, 22, 23^2, 29^2, 30; **7:**3, 6, 10, 11; **8:**1, 6^3, 8, 9^4, 14, 18; **9:**4^2, 8^2, 23, 31^3; **10:**6^2, 18; **11:**12, 14, 15, 21, 22, 23; **12:**13^2, 14, 16^2; **13:**2, 5, 6, 12, 17; **14:**1^3, 2, 4, 11, 13^2; **15:**9, 16, 17, 18; **16:**2, 4, 5, 12^4, 13^2, 14; **17:**1, 2, 3^2, 4^2, 5, 6, 7^2; **18:**8, 18^3, 19, 21, 30, 33^2, 34; **19:**1, 10; **20:**18, 20, 21^2, 25, 30, 31, 32; **21:**1^2, 3, 4^2, 7, 9^3, 10, 17, 19^4; **22:**1, 2, 3, 4^3, 6, 9^2, 11; **23:**1, 7^2, 8, 10^2, 11, 13; **24:**1, 16, 22, 25^2, 27^2; **25:**1, 3^2, 4, 11^2, 14, 17, 22, 28; **26:**1, 2, 3, 4, 8, 10, 13, 15, 16^3, 19^2, 20, 21, 23^2; **27:**1, 2, 6, 7, 9^2; **28:**1, 3, 5^2, 13, 22, 23, 25, 26^2, 27^2; **29:**1, 2, 3, 10, 19, 25, 30, 36; **30:**2, 6, 8, 9, 12, 19^2, 27; **31:**3, 8^2, 10, 12, 13, 20, 21; **32:**3, 9^2, 14, 15, 16, 17, 21^3, 26, 27^2, 31, 32, 33^2; **33:**3, 6, 7, 10, 11, 12^3, 13^3, 18^2, 19^3, 20^3, 22, 23^2, 24, 25^2; **34:**2, 3^3, 4, 8, 19, 31^4; **35:**3, 4, 8, 9, 23, 24^2, 26; **36:**1, 5, 7, 8, 12, 13, 15^3, 16^3, 18, 20, 22, 23^2; **Ezr 1:**1, 3^2, 7; **2:**1; **3:**2^2, 9^2, 11; **4:**7; **5:**5, 17; **6:**10, 11^2, 12; **7:**6, 9^2, 14, 15, 23, 28^2; **8:**17, 19, 22, 25^2; **9:**8; **10:**8, 11, 18; **Ne 1:**5^2; **2:**1, 5, 20; **3:**1, 10, 12, 17, 23, 28, 29, 30; **4:**2, 3, 15, 18^2, 22, 23; **5:**13, 14; **6:**5^2, 10, 11, 18, 19; **7:**6; **8:**4^2; **9:**8^2, 10^2, 32; **11:**3, 8, 13, 14, 17, 20; **12:**8, 36, 45; **13:**6, 26, 30; **Est 1:**2, 3^2, 4^2, 8, 20, 21, 22; **2:**3, 7, 9, 15, 16, 17, 18; **3:**10^2, 12; **4:**1, 4, 11; **5:**1, 2, 9, 10^2, 11^2, 14^2; **6:**1, 3, 5, 12, 13^4; **7:**7^3; **8:**2, 3, 7, 8; **9:**4, 25^2; **10:**2, 3^2; **Job 1:**4, 10^3, 20^2; **2:**3, 4, 5, 6, 7^2, 9, 13; **3:**1^2, 19; **4:**9, 17, 18^2; **5:**3, 4, 5^2, 18; **6:**9, 14; **7:**1, 2, 10^2; **8:**15; **9:**4^2, 5, 13^2, 33, 34; **11:**5; **12:**10, 13, 16; **13:**11, 15; **14:**5, 6, 10, 20, 21, 22; **15:**2, 15^2, 20, 21, 25, 27^2, 29^2, 30, 32^2; **16:**9^3, 12, 13, 21; **17:**5^2; **18:**5, 6, 7^2, 8, 10, 11, 13^2, 14, 15^2, 16^2, 19, 20; **19:**6, 11^2, 12; **20:**6^2, 7, 9, 10^3, 11, 12^2, 13, 14^2, 15, 18, 20^2, 21, 22, 23^3, 25^2, 26^2, 27, 28; **21:**17, 19, 20^2, 21, 24^2, 31^2, 32; **22:**22^2; **23:**2, 3, 7, 11^2, 12^2, 14; **24:**15, 22, 23; **25:**3^2, 5; **26:**8, 9, 11, 12^2, 13^2, 14^2; **27:**1, 8, 9, 14^2, 17, 19, 21, 23; **28:**10; **29:**1, 3^2, 25; **30:**18, 24; **31:**2, 20, 23, 30, 31, 35; **32:**1, 5, 12, 14; **33:**10, 18^2, 19, 20^2, 21^2, 22^2, 23, 25^2, 26, 30; **34:**6, 11, 14^2, 19, 21, 27, 29, 35, 37^3; **35:**15, 16; **36:**5, 7, 22, 23, 24, 26, 29, 30, 32, 33; **37:**2^2, 3, 4^3, 7^2, 11, 12, 13^2, 15, 23; **39:**5, 6^2, 8, 11, 19^2, 20, 21, 23, 26, 27, 28, 29^2, 30; **40:**9, 16^2, 17^2, 18^2, 19^2, 23, 24; **41:**1, 2^2, 7^2, 12^3, 13, 14^2, 15, 18^2, 19, 20, 21^2, 22, 23, 24, 25, 30, 33; **42:**8, 10, 11^2, 16; **Ps 1:**2^2; **2:**2, 5^2, 12; **3:**T, 4; **7:**11, 12^2, 13^2, 16^2, 17; **8:**6; **9:**7, 16; **10:**2, 3, 4^2, 5^2, 7^2, 8, 9, 10^2, 11, 15, 16; **11:**4^3, 5, 7; **12:**2; **14:**1, 7; **15:**2, 3^3, 4, 5; **18:**T, 6^2, 8^2, 9, 11^2, 12, 14, 22^2, 24, 30, 50^3; **19:**1, 5^2, 12; **20:**6^3; **21:**1, 2^2, 3, 5, 9^2; **22:**24^2, 31; **23:**3; **24:**3, 4, 5; **25:**8, 9, 10, 13^2, 14; **27:**4, 5^2, 6, 8; **28:**5, 8^2; **29:**2^2, 9, 11^2; **30:**4^2, 5^2; **31:**21, 23; **33:**5, 6, 11, 12, 14, 16^2, 18, 21; **34:**1, 3, 6, 9, 15, 20, 22; **35:**9, 27; **36:**1, 2^2, 3, 4; **37:**23, 24, 28, 30, 31^3, 34; **38:**13; **40:**4; **41:**2^2, 3^2, 5, 6, 9; **42:**8^2; **46:**6; **47:**8; **48:**1; **49:**12, 16, 17, 19; **50:**4, 6; **52:**7^2; **53:**1, 6; **55:**20^2, 21^3; **57:**2, 3^2; **60:**6; **61:**6; **62:**4; **66:**2^2, 5, 7^2, 8, 17, 20; **67:**1; **68:**1^2, 4^2, 5, 17, 21, 35; **69:**33, 36^2; **72:**7, 9, 14, 17, 19^2; **76:**1, 2^2, 5; **77:**7, 8^2, 9; **78:**4, 7^2, 10, 20, 21^2, 22, 26, 32, 37, 38^2, 42, 43^2, 49^2, 50, 52, 54^2, 56, 58, 61^2, 62^2, 66, 69, 70, 71^2; **79:**7; **85:**8^2, 9^2, 13; **87:**1; **89:**23^2, 24, 25^2, 29^2, 30, 36^2, 39, 40^2, 41, 42^2, 43, 44^2, 45; **91:**4^3, 11; **94:**14^2; **95:**4, 5^2, 7^3; **96:**2^2, 3^2, 6, 8^2, 9, 13; **97:**2, 3, 4, 6^2, 10, 12; **98:**1^2, 2^2, 3^2; **99:**5, 6^2, 7, 9; **100:**3^3, 4^3, 5^2; **101:**5; **102:**T, 16, 19, 21; **103:**1, 2, 7^2, 9, 11, 13, 15, 17, 18^2, 19^2, 20^3, 21^3, 22^2; **104:**3^2, 4^2, 13^2, 15^2, 23^2, 31; **105:**1, 2, 3, 4^2, 5, 6^2, 7, 8, 18^2, 21, 22^2, 24, 25^2, 26, 27^2, 28, 42^2, 43^2, 45^2; **106:**1, 2, 8^2, 12^2, 13, 23^2, 24, 40^2, 45^2; **107:**1, 8^2, 15^2, 20, 21^2, 22, 24, 31^2; **108:**7; **109:**6, 7, 8^2, 9^2, 10, 11, 12, 13, 14^2, 18^3, 31; **110:**4, 5, 7; **111:**3^2, 4, 5, 6^2, 7^2, 9^3, 10; **112:**1, 2, 3^2, 5, 7, 8^2, 9^3, 10; **113:**4; **114:**2; **116:**2, 12, 14, 15, 18; **117:**2; **118:**1, 2, 3, 4, 27, 29; **119:**2, 3, 9; **123:**2; **125:**2; **128:**1; **129:**7^2; **130:**5; **132:**7^2, 13, 18^2; **133:**2, 3; **135:**3, 4^2, 7, 9^2, 12, 14^2; **136:**1, 2, 3, 4, 5^2, 6, 7, 8, 9, 10, 11, 12, 13, 14, 15^2, 16^2, 17, 18, 19, 20, 21, 22^2, 23, 24, 25, 26; **138:**8; **144:**4, 10; **145:**3, 13, 17, 21; **146:**5; **147:**5, 10^2, 11, 15^2, 17^2, 18^2, 19^2, 20; **148:**2^2, 8, 13^2, 14^3; **149:**1, 3, 4, 9; **150:**1^2, 2^2; **Pr 2:**6, 8; **3:**11, 20, 31, 32; **5:**21, 22, 23; **6:**13^3, 14, 27^2, 28, 30, 31, 33^2; **7:**20, 23^2; **8:**22^2, 29, 30^2, 31; **9:**9; **10:**1^2, 18, 19; **11:**1, 7^2, 9^2, 12^2, 19, 28, 29; **12:**4, 8, 10, 11, 13, 14^2, 16, 23, 27^2; **13:**1, 2, 3^2, 8, 16, 22, 24; **14:**3, 7, 14, 15, 21, 26, 35; **15:**5, 20^2, 27; **16:**4, 7, 9^3, 10, 11, 15, 17^2, 23^2, 26, 27, 29, 30^2, 32; **17:**12, 13, 18, 25, 28; **18:**2, 6, 7^3, 9, 12, 13^2, 17, 20^2; **19:**3^2, 7^2, 8, 11, 12, 13, 16^2, 18, 24^2, 26^2; **20:**2, 7, 8^2, 11^2, 14, 20^2, 24, 25, 27, 28; **21:**10, 13, 23^2, 24, 25, 29; **22:**5, 8, 9, 11, 16, 25, 29; **23:**3, 6, 7, 14; **24:**15, 18; **25:**5, 13, 18, 22; **26:**4, 5^2, 11, 12, 14, 15^2, 16, 17, 19, 24^2, 25^2, 26^2; **27:**8, 9, 14, 18, 22; **28:**7, 8, 9, 10, 11, 13, 14, 19^2, 24, 27; **29:**3^2, 5^2, 6, 11, 12, 14, 15, 21, 24; **30:**4^4, 6, 10, 31; **31:**1, 23; **Ecc 1:**3; **2:**14, 21, 23^3, 24; **3:**9, 13, 22^2; **4:**4, 5, 8^3, 10, 14; **5:**10, 11, 15^3, 17, 18^2, 19^2, 20; **6:**2, 3, 6, 7^2; **7:**14, 15^2; **8:**5, 8, 9, 15, 16, 17; **9:**12, 15, 16; **10:**12, 13, 18; **12:**5, 13; **SS 1:**2, 4, 12; **2:**3^2, 4, 6^2, 16; **3:**8^2, 11^3; **4:**16; **5:**4, 6, 11^2, 12, 13^2, 14^2, 15^2, 16; **6:**2; **7:**10; **8:**3^2, 7, 10, 11; **Isa 1:**3^2, 31; **2:**3^2, 10, 19, 21, 22; **3:**6^2, 8, 13, 14; **5:**1, 7, 12, 16^2, 19, 25^4; **6:**1, 3, 6; **7:**2; **8:**7, 11, 17; **9:**6, 7^2, 12^2, 17^2, 19, 20, 21^2; **10:**4^2, 7, 12^3, 16^2, 17^2, 18, 19, 26; **11:**1, 3^2, 4^2, 5^2, 8, 10, 11^2, 15, 16; **12:**4^2; **13:**5, 13, 14^2, 20^2; **14:**4, 17, 18, 21, 25^2, 27, 32; **17:**4, 5; **19:**14; **22:**22, 23, 24; **23:**11; **25:**4, 8, 9, 11; **26:**20, 21; **27:**1^2, 8, 9; **28:**1, 4^2, 5, 9, 21^4, 26, 28^2; **29:**8^2; **30:**26, 27^2, 28, 30^2, 31, 32^2; **31:**2, 3, 4; **32:**6; **33:**15^3, 16, 17; **34:**2, 16^2, 17; **36:**2, 16^2, 18, 20; **37:**1, 4, 7, 20, 38^3; **38:**2, 9; **39:**1, 2^5; **40:**10^3, 11^3, 12^2, 13, 26, 28; **41:**2^3, 3, 6; **42:**2, 4, 10, 12, 13^2, 21^2, 24^2, 25; **44:**5, 11, 12^2, 13, 16^3, 17, 23, 26^2; **45:**1, 9, 10^2, 13; **46:**7; **47:**4, 15; **48:**2, 14^2, 15, 16, 20; **49:**2^2, 5, 13^2; **50:**10^2; **51:**15, 17, 22; **52:**9, 10, 14^2; **53:**2, 5, 6, 7^2, 8, 9^2, 10^4, 11^2, 12; **54:**5; **55:**7^2; **56:**2, 3, 11; **57:**1, 13, 17^2, 18; **59:**1, 2, 4, 16^2, 17^2, 18^2, 19; **60:**2; **61:**3, 10; **62:**5, 8^2, 11^2; **63:**1^2, 7, 9^2, 10, 11^4, 12; **65:**15, 20; **66:**5, 6, 14^3, 15^3, 16; **Jer 1:**9; **2:**3, 15^2; **3:**1; **4:**7^2, 13^2, 26; **6:**3; **7:**29; **8:**6^2; **9:**8^3, 20, 23^3; **10:**3, 10, 12^3, 13, 14^2, 16^2, 23^2, 25; **11:**19; **12:**15^2; **13:**23; **16:**6, 12; **17:**5, 10^2, 11; **18:**4, 12; **20:**9^2; **21:**7, 9, 12; **22:**3, 7, 10^2, 11, 13^3, 18, 28, 30^2; **23:**6, 9, 14, 18^2, 20, 28, 34, 35, 36; **24:**8; **25:**4, 12, 19^3, 30^2, 38; **26:**3, 19, 21^2, 23; **27:**7^3, 8^2, 12; **28:**9, 11; **29:**32; **30:**6^2, 18, 24; **31:**10, 30^2, 34^2, 35; **32:**4, 19^2; **33:**2, 11, 21, 26; **34:**1, 3, 9, 15, 21; **35:**3^2, 14, 18; **36:**3, 7, 14, 24, 30, 31^2; **37:**2, 12; **38:**2, 27; **39:**1, 6, 14^2; **41:**9, 15; **42:**11; **43:**10^2, 12; **44:**23^3, 30^3; **46:**10, 17, 26; **48:**7, 10; **49:**1, 3, 10^2; **50:**16^3, 17, 18, 19^2, 25^2, 28, 34, 43; **51:**3^2, 9, 11^2, 12^2, 15^3, 16, 17^2, 19^2, 31, 34, 59; **52:**1, 3, 4, 8, 10, 11, 25, 30, 33^2, 34; **La 1:**12, 14, 15, 17^2, 18; **2:**1^3, 2, 3, 4^3, 6^3, 7^2, 8, 17; **3:**1, 3, 12^2, 13, 22, 29, 30, 32, 35, 39; **4:**11^2, 20; **Eze 1:**27; **3:**12, 18^4, 19^3, 20^3; **7:**13, 16; **8:**2^2, 11, 12; **9:**1, 2^2, 3, 11; **10:**7; **12:**12^3, 14^2; **14:**4^3, 7^2; **16:**15; **17:**14, 15, 17, 18, 19, 21; **18:**6, 7, 8, 11, 13^2, 14, 15, 16, 17^2, 18^4, 19, 24, 26, 27, 30; **19:**7, 9; **21:**21, 22; **22:**6, 11^4; **26:**8, 9^2, 10, 11; **29:**18^2, 19, 20^2; **30:**11, 22^2, 24; **31:**2, 18; **32:**10, 31^2, 32; **33:**4^3, 5^2, 6^2, 8^3, 9^2, 12, 13, 14, 18, 19, 20, 26; **34:**12; **36:**20; **38:**21, 22; **39:**11; **40:**3; **43:**2^2; **44:**25; **45:**8; **46:**2^2, 12^2, 16^3, 17^4, 18^3; **47:**3, 23; **Da 1:**2^3, 3, 20; **2:**1^2, 7, 13, 17^2, 18, 20, 24, 25; **3:**19, 20, 24^2, 28^2; **4:**3^4, 16, 19, 31, 33^3, 34^2, 35, 37; **5:**1, 2^5, 3^3, 6^3, 7, 9^2, 10, 20^3, 21, 22, 23^2, 29; **6:**3, 4, 5, 10^3, 12, 17^2, 18, 22^2, 23, 26^2; **7:**1^3, 9^4, 13, 14^2, 25, 26, 27; **8:**4, 5, 7^2, 8^2, 11, 21, 22, 24, 25; **9:**2, 4^2, 10, 20; **10:**5, 6^5; **11:**2, 4^3, 5^2, 6, 7, 9, 10^2, 17^2, 18^3, 19, 20, 24^3, 25, 26, 28^3, 30, 31, 37, 38, 41, 42, 45^2; **12:**7^2; **Hos 3:**5; **5:**13^2; **6:**2; **7:**9^2, 10; **8:**14; **9:**8^2; **10:**1^3; **11:**10; **12:**2^2, 3, 4, 5, 14^3; **13:**12, 15^4; **14:**5, 6^3, 7^2; **Joel 2:**11^3, 16, 18^2; **3:**16; **Am 1:**11^3, 13, 15; **2:**4, 9^2, 14, 15^2; **3:**4, 7^2; **4:**2, 13^2; **5:**8, 19^2; **6:**8; **7:**7, 10; **9:**6^2; **Ob 1:**6, 11^2, 12; **Jnh 1:**5; **2:**1; **3:**6^2, 7, 9; **4:**6^2; **Mic 1:**2, 3; **2:**2^2; **3:**4, 8^2; **4:**2^2, 4^2, 12; **5:**3, 4^3; **6:**2; **7:**2, 6^2, 9, 18; **Na 1:**2^3, 3^2, 5, 6^3, 8; **2:**3, 5, 12^4; **3:**19; **Hab 1:**15^2, 16^3, 17; **2:**4^2, 9^2, 15, 18, 20; **3:**3^2, 4^3, 5, 6, 14^3; **Zep 1:**18; **2:**13; **3:**5, 17; **Hag 1:**9; **2:**12, 22; **Zec 1:**21; **2:**1, 8, 12, 13; **3:**1, 4, 5^2, 10^2; **4:**1, 9; **5:**4; **6:**12, 13^2; **7:**12; **8:**4, 10^3, 23; **9:**10, 14, 16^2; **10:**3, 12; **11:**6^2, 17^4; **13:**3^2, 4; **14:**4, 9; **Mal 1:**3^2, 6^2, 14; **2:**6^2, 7, 15, 16; **3:**1, 2, 14, 16^2, 17; **Mt 1:**2, 11, 18, 21, 24; **2:**2, 11, 13, 14, 20, 21, 22; **3:**4^2, 12^4; **4:**6, 18, 21; **5:**1, 22^2, 28, 31, 32, 35, 45; **6:**27, 29, 33^2; **7:**9, 24, 26, 28; **8:**3^2, 13, 20, 23; **9:**1, 10, 11, 19, 20, 21, 37, 38; **10:**1, 2^2, 10, 11, 21, 24^2, 25^3, 35, 36, 37^2, 38, 39^2, 42; **11:**1, 2, 20; **12:**1, 3, 4, 19, 21, 26, 29^2, 46, 49; **13:**3, 19, 24, 25, 31, 36, 41^2, 44, 52, 54, 55^2, 56, 57^2; **14:**2, 3, 9^2, 11, 12, 31, 36; **15:**4, 5, 6, 11, 23, 30, 32, 33; **16:**13, 20, 21, 24^2, 25^2, 26^2, 27^2, 28; **17:**2^2, 24; **18:**6, 15, 23, 25^2, 26, 28, 29^2, 34; **19:**3, 5^2, 7, 9, 13, 15, 23, 28; **20:**1, 2, 8, 28, 29; **21:**18, 29, 31, 34^2, 35, 37, 38, 41; **22:**2, 3, 5^2, 6, 7, 8, 15, 24, 25^2, 33, 45; **23:**1, 16, 18; **24:**1^2, 17, 18, 31^2, 43, 45, 47, 49; **25:**14^2, 15^2, 16, 18, 21, 23, 26, 31^2, 33^2, 34, 41^2; **26:**1, 7, 23, 26, 36, 39, 40, 51^2, 65, 67; **27:**19, 24, 25, 29^2, 31, 35, 37, 38^2, 50, 55, 60, 64; **28:**3^2, 7, 8, 9, 13; **Mk 1:**6, 7, 16, 19, 22, 36, 40, 41; **2:**8, 12, 15, 16, 23, 25, 26; **3:**5, 7, 9, 17, 20, 21^2, 26, 27^2; **4:**2, 3, 34, 35, 40; **5:**4, 6, 7, 15, 22, 27, 28, 31, 33; **6:**1^2, 3, 4^3, 5, 8, 17, 21^2, 22, 26^2, 28, 29, 35, 41, 45, 56; **7:**2, 10, 11, 12, 17, 19^3, 24, 25, 32, 33, 35; **8:**1, 4, 6, 10, 23, 25^3, 27, 33, 34^2, 35^2, 36, 37, 38; **9:**3, 18, 27, 28, 31, 36, 41, 42; **10:**1, 2, 7^2, 11, 16^2, 17^2, 23, 24, 45, 46, 50^2, 52; **11:**1, 14, 18, 23; **12:**13, 19, 37, 43; **13:**1, 12, 15, 16, 27^2, 34^3; **14:**3, 13, 22, 32, 37, 47^2, 52, 63; **15:**20, 21, 24, 27^2, 37, 39, 41; **16:**7, 20; **Lk 1:**5, 14, 23, 24, 25, 29, 32, 33, 48, 49, 50, 51, 54, 55, 59, 60, 62, 63, 64^2, 67, 68, 69, 70, 72, 77; **2:**3, 14, 28, 34, 41, 43, 47^2, 48^2, 51; **3:**1, 17^4, 19, 23; **4:**10, 16, 22, 24, 30, 32^2, 33, 40; **5:**9, 12, 13, 19, 27, 29, 30; **6:**1, 3, 4, 10, 13, 14, 17, 20, 40^2, 45^4; **7:**2, 3, 11, 12, 13, 15, 16, 38^2; **8:**5, 9, 22, 25, 28^2, 29, 35, 41, 42^2, 44, 47; **9:**14, 18, 23, 24^2, 25, 26, 29^2, 31, 32^2, 42, 43, 58, 62; **10:**2, 7, 23, 30, 34^2, 38; **11:**1^2, 8, 18, 21^2, 49; **12:**1, 15, 22, 25, 27, 31, 39, 42, 44, 47^2; **13:**6, 13, 15, 17, 19, 22; **14:**12, 17, 21^2, 23, 26^4, 27; **15:**5, 6, 12^2, 13, 15, 16, 17, 20^4, 22^3, 28, 29; **16:**1^2, 5, 16, 18, 20, 21, 23, 24; **17:**1, 2, 11, 22, 24, 31^2, 33^2; **18:**1, 7, 13, 43; **19:**13, 14, 17, 19, 22, 24, 29, 48; **20:**26, 28, 44, 45; **21:**5; **22:**14, 39, 44, 50, 71; **23:**5, 11, 26, 33^2, 34, 46, 55; **24:**8, 23, 26, 40, 47, 50; **Jn 1:**6, 11^2, 12, 14^2, 16, 35, 41; **2:**2, 5, 11^3, 12^2, 17, 21, 22, 23; **3:**4, 16, 17, 20, 22, 32, 35; **4:**2, 5, 8, 12^2, 24, 27, 31, 33, 34, 36, 41, 44, 47, 50, 51^2, 52, 53; **5:**9, 17, 18, 19, 28, 32, 35, 37^2, 38, 43; **6:**3, 8, 12, 16, 22, 24, 27, 52, 53, 60, 61, 66; **7:**1, 5, 10, 18, 30, 40, 53; **8:**6, 20, 27, 44, 55; **9:**2^2, 3^2, 8, 15, 18, 21, 22, 23, 27, 31; **10:**2, 3^2, 4^3, 11, 36; **11:**2, 7, 12, 13^2, 17, 32, 44^2, 51, 53, 54; **12:**3, 4, 12, 16, 25^2, 50; **13:**1^2, 3, 4^2, 5, 10^2, 12^2, 16, 18, 22; **14:**10; **15:**10, 13^2, 15, 20; **16:**13, 17, 32; **18:**1^2, 2, 10, 17, 19^2, 25; **19:**2, 17, 23, 25^2, 26^2, 27, 30^2, 33, 35, 36; **20:**20, 23, 25^2, 26, 30, 31; **21:**1, 7, 14, 24; **Ac 1:**3, 7, 14, 18^3, 20^2, 22; **2:**6, 8, 14, 29, 30^2, 31, 41; **3:**5, 8, 13, 18, 21, 23, 26; **4:**26, 32^2; **5:**1, 2, 6, 7, 10, 17, 21, 26, 31, 36, 37, 40; **6:**10, 15; **7:**4, 5, 8, 10^2, 13, 14^2, 17, 20, 23, 24, 25, 60; **8:**1, 11, 27, 28^2, 32, 33^3, 39; **9:**3, 8, 12^2, 17, 19, 25, 27, 40; **10:**2, 7^2, 22, 23, 24, 25, 43; **11:**13, 29; **12:**11, 15, 17, 21^2; **13:**8, 13, 16, 19, 25, 31, 36^3; **14:**3, 8; **15:**14; **16:**3, 6, 27, 32, 33, 34^2; **17:**2, 7, 28; **18:**2, 6, 8, 18; **19:**6, 22, 38; **20:**10, 28, 32, 38^2; **21:**11, 19, 32; **22:**14^2, 15, 16; **23:**15, 23, 26, 30; **24:**2, 23^2, 24; **25:**8, 12, 16, 18, 21, 25, 26; **26:**1^2, 23, 26; **27:**3^2, 34; **28:**3, 4, 7, 8^2, 30; **Ro 1:**2, 3^2, 4, 5, 9, 20; **2:**4, 5, 18; **3:**5, 7, 20, 24, 25^3, 26; **4:**4, 5, 13, 19^2, 20; **5:**5, 8, 9, 10^2; **6:**3, 5^2; **8:**3, 11, 17^2, 28, 29, 32; **9:**7, 19, 22^3, 23^2, 28; **11:**1, 2, 22, 29, 33^2, 34; **12:**2, 6, 20; **13:**8; **14:**4, 5, 23; **15:**2^2, 9, 10; **16:**13, 15, 21, 23; **1Co 1:**4, 9; **2:**10; **3:**5, 8, 13, 14; **4:**5; **5:**1, 5; **6:**14, 18^2; **7:**2, 3^2, 4, 7, 11, 14, 33, 34, 37^3; **9:**7; **10:**24; **11:**4^2, 7; **14:**2, 25; **15:**10, 23, 25^2, 27; **16:**2, 11; **2Co 1:**22^2; **2:**11; **3:**13, 18; **4:**6, 11, 14; **5:**20; **7:**7, 13, 15; **8:**9, 17, 18, 22; **9:**7, 9^2, 15; **10:**10^2; **11:**15, 33; **Gal 1:**15, 16; **2:**11, 13; **3:**5, 16, 18; **4:**2, 4, 6, 23^2; **6:**4, 5, 6, 8; **Eph 1:**4, 5^2, 6, 7, 9^2, 11, 12, 14, 18, 19^2, 20, 22, 23; **2:**4, 7^2, 15^2, 22; **3:**7, 10, 11, 15, 16^2, 20; **4:**8, 25, 28; **5:**23, 28, 29, 30, 31^2, 33; **6:**10; **Php 2:**1, 13, 21, 22, 30; **3:**10^3, 21^2; **4:**19; **Col 1:**9, 11, 19, 20, 22, 24, 29; **2:**18; **3:**25; **4:**10; **1Th 1:**10; **2:**2, 11, 12; **3:**13; **4:**4, 6, 8; **2Th 1:**7, 9, 10, 11^2; **2:**8^2, 16; **1Ti 1:**12, 16; **3:**1, 4^2, 5, 12^2; **5:**8^2, 18; **6:**15; **2Ti 1:**8, 9; **2:**4, 19, 26; **4:**1^2, 8, 18; **Tit 1:**3^2; **2:**14; **3:**5, 7; **Heb 1:**2, 3^2, 5, 6, 7^2; **2:**4, 8, 14, 17; **3:**6, 7, 15, 18; **4:**1, 3, 4, 7, 10^2; **5:**3, 7; **6:**10, 13, 17; **7:**2, 6, 10, 16, 21, 27; **8:**11^2; **9:**12, 25; **10:**11, 13^2, 20, 30; **11:**4, 7^2, 8, 9, 17, 21, 22^2, 26; **12:**7, 10, 16, 26; **13:**12, 15, 21; **Jas 1:**9, 10, 11, 14, 23, 26^2; **2:**16, 21, 22^3; **3:**2, 6, 13; **4:**11; **5:**20; **1Pe 1:**2, 3; **2:**9, 21, 22, 24^2; **3:**10^2, 12; **4:**1^2, 2, 13; **5:**10; **2Pe 1:**3^2, 4, 9, 16; **2:**8, 16; **3:**9, 13, 16^2; **1Jn 1:**3, 7, 10; **2:**3, 5, 9, 10, 11, 12, 16, 27, 28; **3:**10, 12^3, 15, 16, 17, 19, 22, 23^2, 24; **4:**9^2, 10, 12, 13, 14, 20^2, 21; **5:**1, 2, 3^2, 9, 10^2, 11, 14, 16, 20; **2Jn 1:**6^2, 11; **Jude 1:**5, 14, 24; **Rev 1:**1^3, 4, 5, 6, 13^2, 14^2, 15^2, 16^3, 17^2; **2:**1, 13; **3:**5^3, 21; **4:**8; **6:**5; **7:**15^2; **8:**7, 8, 10, 12; **9:**1, 13; **10:**1^3, 2^3, 5, 7^2; **11:**15^2, 19^2; **12:**3, 4, 5, 7^2, 9, 10, 12, 15, 16; **13:**1, 2^2, 5, 6^3, 12, 16^2, 17, 18; **14:**1^2, 7, 9^2, 10, 11^2, 14^2, 16, 19; **15:**2^2, 8; **16:**2^2, 3, 4, 8, 10^2, 12, 15, 17, 19; **17:**8, 11, 14, 17; **18:**1; **19:**2^2, 5, 7, 10, 12^2, 13, 15, 16^2, 19, 20^2; **20:**1, 4^2, 7, 11; **21:**3, 7; **22:**3, 4^2, 6^2, 19.

I (8747)

See also selected listing of "I AM" in the Main Concordance.

Ge 1:29, 30; **2:**18; **3:**10^4, 11, 12, 13, 15, 16, 17; **4:**1, 9^2, 13, 14^2, 23; **6:**7^4, 13^2, 17, 18; **7:**1, 4^3; **8:**21^3; **9:**3^2, 5^3, 9, 11, 12, 13, 14, 15, 16, 17; **12:**1, 2^3, 3^2, 7, 11, 13, 19; **13:**15, 16, 17; **14:**22, 23^2, 24; **15:**1, 2, 7, 8^2, 14, 18; **16:**2, 5^2, 10, 13; **17:**1, 2, 5, 6^2, 7, 8^2, 16^2, 19, 20^4, 21; **18:**3, 10, 12^2, 13^2, 14, 15, 17^2, 19, 21^2, 26^2, 27^2, 28^2, 29, 30^2, 31^2, 32; **19:**8, 19, 21^2, 22, 34; **20:**5, 6^3, 9, 11, 13, 16; **21:**7, 13, 16, 18, 23, 24, 26^2, 30; **22:**1, 2, 5, 11, 12, 16, 17; **23:**4^2, 11^3, 13^2; **24:**3^2, 5, 7, 13, 14^3, 24, 31, 33^3, 34, 37, 39, 40, 42^3, 43^2, 45^2, 46, 47^2, 48^2, 49, 56, 58; **25:**32; **26:**2, 3^3, 4, 9^2, 24^3; **27:**1, 2, 4^3, 6, 7^2, 8, 9, 12, 13, 19^2, 21, 24, 25, 32, 33^2, 37^3, 41, 43, 45; **28:**13^2, 15^5, 16, 20, 21, 22^2; **29:**19, 21, 25^2, 33, 34, 35; **30:**2, 3, 8^2, 13, 16, 20, 25, 26^2, 27^2, 28, 29, 30^3, 31^2; **31:**3, 5, 10^2, 11^2, 12, 13, 27, 29, 31^2, 35, 36, 38^2, 39^2, 41^2, 43, 44, 51, 52; **32:**4, 5^3, 9, 10^4, 11^2, 12, 20^3, 26, 30; **33:**8, 9, 10, 11^2, 13, 14^2; **34:**11, 12, 30; **35:**3^2, 11, 12^3; **37:**6, 9, 10, 13, 17, 30, 35; **38:**18, 22, 23, 25, 26^2; **39:**9^2, 14, 18; **40:**9, 11, 15^2, 16; **41:**9, 13, 15^2, 16, 17, 19, 21, 22, 24, 28, 40, 41, 44; **42:**2, 14, 18, 22, 33, 34^2, 37^2; **43:**9^3, 14^2, 23; **44:**21, 28^2, 30, 32^3, 34; **45:**3, 4, 11, 12, 18, 28^2; **46:**2, 3^2, 4^2, 30^2, 31; **47:**16, 23, 29, 30^2; **48:**4^3, 5, 7^2, 9, 11, 19^2, 21, 22^2; **49:**1, 7, 18, 29, 31; **50:**4, 5^3, 17, 19, 21, 24; **Ex 2:**7, 9, 10, 14, 22; **3:**3, 4, 6, 7^3, 8, 9, 10, 11^2, 12^2, 13^2, 14^3, 15, 16, 17, 19, 20^2, 21; **4:**10^2, 11, 12, 14, 15, 18, 21^2, 23^2; **5:**2^3, 10, 23; **6:**1, 2, 3^2, 4, 5^2, 6^4, 7^3, 8^4, 12, 29^2, 30; **7:**1, 2, 3^2, 4^2, 5^2, 17^2; **8:**2, 8, 9, 21, 22^2, 23, 28, 29^2; **9:**14, 15, 16^2, 18, 27^2, 28, 29^2, 30; **10:**1^2, 2^3, 4, 10, 16, 29; **11:**1, 4, 8; **12:**12^3, 13^3, 17; **13:**8^2, 15; **14:**4^3, 17^2, 18^2; **15:**1, 2^2, 9^5, 26^3; **16:**4^2, 12^2, 32^2; **17:**4, 6, 9, 14; **18:**3, 6, 11, 16, 19; **19:**4^2, 9; **20:**2, 5, 22, 24^2; **21:**5, 13; **22:**23, 24, 27^2; **23:**7, 13, 15, 20^2, 22^2, 23, 25, 26, 27^2, 28, 29, 30, 31^2; **24:**12^2; **25:**8, 9, 16, 21, 22; **28:**3; **29:**35, 42, 43, 44, 45, 46^3; **30:**6, 36; **31:**2, 3, 6^3, 11, 13; **32:**8, 9, 10^2, 13^3, 18, 24^2, 30^2, 33, 34^2; **33:**1^2, 2, 3^2, 5^3, 12, 13, 14, 17^3, 19^6, 22^2, 23; **34:**1, 9, 10^3, 11^2, 18, 24, 27; **Lev 6:**17; **7:**34; **8:**31, 35; **10:**3^2, 13, 18, 19; **11:**44^2, 45^2; **14:**34^2, 35; **16:**2; **17:**10, 11, 12, 14; **18:**2, 3, 4, 5, 6, 21, 24, 25, 30; **19:**2, 3, 4, 10, 12, 14, 16, 18, 25, 28, 30, 31, 32, 34, 36, 37; **20:**3^2, 5, 6^2, 7, 8, 22, 23^2, 24^3, 25, 26^2; **21:**8^2, 12, 15, 23; **22:**2, 3, 8, 9, 16, 30, 31, 32^2, 33; **23:**10, 22, 30, 43^3; **24:**22; **25:**2, 17, 21, 38, 42, 55^2; **26:**1, 2, 4, 6^2, 9^2, 11^2, 12, 13^2, 16^2, 17, 18, 19, 21, 22, 24, 25^2, 26, 28^2, 30^2, 31^2, 32, 33, 36, 41, 42^2, 44^2, 45^3; **Nu 3:**12, 13^3, 41, 45; **5:**3; **6:**27; **8:**16, 17^2, 18, 19; **9:**8; **10:**10, 29, 30^2; **11:**11, 12^2, 13, 14, 15, 17^2, 21^2, 23, 29; **12:**6^2, 8; **13:**2; **14:**11, 12^2, 20, 21, 22, 23, 24, 27, 28^3, 30, 31, 35^2; **15:**2, 18, 41^2; **16:**15^2, 21, 45; **17:**4, 5^2; **18:**6, 7, 8^2, 11, 12, 19, 20, 21, 24^2, 26; **20:**12, 24; **21:**16, 34; **22:**6^2, 8, 11, 17, 18, 19, 20, 28, 29^2, 30^2, 32, 33^2, 34^3, 35, 37^2, 38^3; **23:**3^2, 4^2, 8^2, 9^3, 11, 12, 15, 20^2, 26^2; **24:**10, 11^2, 12, 13^2, 14, 17^2; **25:**11^2, 12; **27:**12; **32:**8, 11; **33:**53, 56^2; **35:**34^2; **Dt 1:**8, 9, 12, 13, 15, 16, 17, 18, 20, 23, 29, 35, 36, 39, 42, 43; **2:**5^2, 9^2, 19^2, 24, 25, 26, 31; **3:**2, 12, 13, 15, 16, 18, 19^2, 20, 21, 23; **4:**1, 2^2, 5, 8, 21, 22^2, 26, 40; **5:**1, 5, 6, 9, 28, 31^2; **6:**2, 6; **7:**11; **8:**1, 11, 19; **9:**9^3, 12, 13, 14^2, 15, 16^2, 17, 18^2, 19, 20, 21^2, 23, 24, 25, 26; **10:**2, 3^2, 5^2, 10^2, 11, 13; **11:**8, 13, 14, 15, 22, 26, 27, 28, 32; **12:**11, 14, 20, 21, 28, 32;

25; **8**:18, 38; **9**:1[2], 2, 3[2], 9, 13[2], 15[4], 17[2], 25[2], 33; **10**:2, 18, 19[3], 20[2], 21; **11**:1[2], 3, 4, 11, 13[3], 14, 19, 25, 27; **12**:1, 3, 19; **14**:11, 14; **15**:8, 9[2], 14, 15, 17, 18[2], 19, 20, 22, 23, 24[4], 25, 28[2], 29[3], 30, 31, 32; **16**:1, 2, 4, 7, 8, 17, 19[2], 22, 23; **1Co 1**:4, 10, 12[5], 14[2], 16[3], 19[2]; **2**:1[3], 2[2], 3; **3**:1, 2, 4[2], 6, 10; **4**:3[3], 6, 8, 14, 15, 16, 17[3], 18, 19[2], 21; **5**:3[4], 4, 9, 11; **6**:5, 12, 15; **7**:6, 7[2], 8[2], 10[2], 12[2], 17, 25[2], 26, 28, 29, 32, 35, 40[2]; **8**:13[3]; **9**:1[3], 2[2], 6, 8, 15[3], 16[4], 17[3], 18, 19[2], 20[3], 21[2], 22[3], 23[2], 26[2], 27[3]; **10**:1, 15[2], 19, 20, 29, 30[3], 33[2]; **11**:1, 2[2], 3, 17, 18[2], 22[2], 23[2], 34[2]; **12**:1, 3, 15[2], 16[2], 21[2], 31; **13**:1[2], 2[3], 3[3], 11[6], 12[3]; **14**:5[2], 6[3], 11[2], 14, 15[5], 18[2], 19, 21, 37; **15**:1[2], 2, 3[2], 9[2], 10[4], 11, 31[3], 32[2], 34, 50, 51; **16**:1, 2, 3[2], 5[3], 6[2], 7[2], 8, 10, 11, 12, 15, 17, 21; **2Co 1**:13, 15[2], 16, 17[4], 23[2]; **2**:1[2], 2[2], 3[5], 4, 8, 9, 10[3], 12, 13[3]; **4**:13[2]; **5**:8, 11; **6**:2[3], 13, 16[2], 17, 18; **7**:3[2], 4[3], 8[4], 9, 12, 14, 16[2]; **8**:3, 8[2], 16[2]; **9**:2[2], 3[2], 5; **10**:1[2], 2[4], 8[2], 9; **11**:1, 2[3], 3, 5[2], 6[2], 8, 9[4], 11[2], 12[2], 16[2], 17, 18, 21[3], 22[3], 23[3], 24, 25[4], 26[2], 27[3], 28, 29[2], 30[2], 31, 33; **12**:1[2], 2[2], 3[2], 5[2], 6[5], 8, 9, 10[3], 11[4], 13, 14[3], 15[3], 16[3], 17[2], 18[2], 20[5], 21[3]; **13**:2[4], 6, 10[4]; **Gal 1**:6, 9, 10[4], 11[2], 12[3], 13, 14, 16[2], 17[3], 18, 19, 20[2], 21, 22; **2**:1[2], 2[4], 7, 10, 11, 14[2], 18[4], 19[2], 20[4], 21; **3**:2, 17; **4**:1, 11[2], 12[2], 13, 14[2], 15, 16, 18, 19, 20[3]; **5**:2, 3, 10, 11[2], 12, 16, 21[2]; **6**:11[2], 14[2], 17; **Eph 1**:15, 16, 17, 18; **3**:1, 3, 7, 8, 13, 14, 16, 17; **4**:1, 17; **5**:32; **6**:19[2], 20[3], 21[2], 22; **Php 1**:3[2], 4, 7[2], 8, 12, 13, 16, 17, 18[2], 19, 20[2], 22[3], 23[2], 24, 25[3], 27[2], 30[2]; **2**:16[2], 17[2], 19[3], 20, 23[2], 24[2], 25, 28[2]; **3**:4[2], 7, 8[4], 10, 12[2], 13[2], 14, 18; **4**:1, 2[2], 3, 4, 10, 11[3], 12[3], 13, 15, 16[2], 17[2], 18[3]; **Col 1**:23, 24[2], 25, 29; **2**:1[2], 4, 5[2]; **4**:3, 4[2], 8, 13, 18; **1Th 2**:18; **3**:5[3]; **5**:27; **2Th 2**:5[2]; **3**:17[2]; **1Ti 1**:3[2], 12, 13[3], 15, 16, 18, 20; **2**:1, 7[3], 8, 9, 12; **3**:14[2], 15; **4**:13; **5**:14, 21; **6**:13; **2Ti 1**:3[3], 4[2], 5[2], 6, 11, 12[6]; **2**:7, 9, 10; **3**:11; **4**:1, 6, 7[3], 12, 13, 17, 20; **Tit 1**:5[2]; **3**:8, 12[2]; **Phm 1**:4[2], 5, 6, 8, 9[2], 10[2], 12, 13[2], 14, 19[2], 20[2], 21[2], 22; **Heb 1**:5[2], 13; **2**:12[2], 13[2]; **3**:9, 10[2], 11; **4**:3; **5**:5; **6**:14; **8**:8, 9[3], 10[3], 12; **10**:7[3], 9[2], 16[3], 17, 30, 38; **11**:32[2]; **12**:21, 26; **13**:5[2], 6, 19[2], 22[2], 23[2]; **Jas 2**:16, 18[3]; **1Pe 1**:16; **2**:6, 11; **5**:1, 12[2]; **2Pe 1**:12, 13[2], 14[2], 15, 17[2]; **3**:1, 2; **1Jn 2**:1, 4, 7, 8, 12, 13[3], 14[2], 21, 26; **4**:20; **5**:13, 16[2]; **2Jn 1**:1[2], 5[2], 12[3]; **3Jn 1**:1, 2, 4, 9, 10[2], 13[2], 14; **Jude 1**:3[3], 5; **Rev 1**:8, 9, 10[2], 12[3], 17[3], 18[4]; **2**:2[2], 4, 5, 6, 7, 9[2], 10[2], 13, 14, 16, 17[2], 19, 20, 21, 22[2], 23[3], 24[2], 25, 26, 27, 28; **3**:1, 2, 3[2], 5, 8[3], 9[3], 10, 11, 12[3], 15[2], 16, 17[2], 18, 19[2], 20[3], 21[2]; **4**:1[3], 2; **5**:1, 2, 4, 6, 11, 13; **6**:1[2], 2, 3, 5[2], 6, 7, 8, 9, 12; **7**:1, 2, 4, 9, 14; **8**:2, 13[2]; **9**:1, 13, 16, 17; **10**:1, 4[2], 5, 8, 9, 10[2], 11; **11**:1, 3; **12**:10; **13**:1, 2, 11; **14**:1, 2[2], 6, 13, 14; **15**:1, 2, 5; **16**:1, 5, 7, 13, 15; **17**:1, 3, 6[3], 7; **18**:1, 4, 7[3]; **19**:1, 6, 10[2], 11, 17, 19; **20**:1, 4[2], 11, 12; **21**:1, 2, 3, 5, 6[2], 7, 9, 22; **22**:7, 8[3], 9, 12[2], 13, 16[2], 18, 20.

I'LL (38)

Ge 13:9[2]; **19**:19; **24**:14, 19, 44, 46; **27**:45; **29**:18; **30**:1; **33**:12; **34**:12; **38**:17; **Jdg 16**:7, 11, 13, 20; **17**:10; **1Sa 2**:16; **17**:44, 46; **18**:11; **19**:3; **20**:4; **25**:19; **26**:6; **2Sa 20**:21; **1Ki 21**:7; **Ps 10**:6; **Pr 3**:28; **20**:22; **24**:29[2]; **Mk 6**:22; **Lk 12**:18, 19; **13**:8; **16**:4.

I'M (24)

Ge 16:8; **25**:30; **27**:11, 46; **31**:35; **37**:16; **45**:28; **Jos 14**:11; **Jdg 4**:19; **15**:1; **17**:9[2]; **1Sa 18**:23; **2Sa 1**:9; **13**:4; **18**:14; **20**:17; **Est 5**:12; **Pr 23**:35; **Lk 14**:19; **16**:3[2]; **Jn 21**:3; **Ac 10**:21.

IN (11277)

Ge 1:1, 11, 12, 14, 15, 17, 22[2], 26[2], 27[2], 28, 29, 30; **2**:1, 8[2], 9, 15, 16; **3**:1, 2, 3, 8[2], 10, 16; **4**:3, 8, 16, 20, 25; **5**:1, 3[2], 29; **6**:1, 4, 8, 11, 14, 16, 17; **7**:1, 11, 15, 16[2], 22, 23; **8**:1, 6, 9[2], 11[2], 17, 21; **9**:1, 4, 6, 7, 13, 14, 16, 23, 27; **10**:10, 20, 25, 30, 31; **11**:2, 28[2], 32; **12**:5, 6, 10; **13**:2[2], 7, 12; **14**:3, 4, 5[4], 6, 7, 8, 12, 14[2], 17; **15**:1, 3, 10[2], 13, 15, 16; **16**:3, 5, 6, 7, 12; **17**:12, 13[2], 14, 23[2], 27[2]; **18**:1, 3, 9, 11, 24[2], 26; **19**:1[2], 2[2], 12, 17, 19[2], 25[2], 30[3], 33, 34; **20**:1, 3, 6, 9, 11, 18; **21**:2, 7, 10, 14, 15, 20, 21, 22, 33, 34; **22**:4, 13, 17, 19; **23**:2, 6, 10, 11[2], 13, 16, 17[2], 18, 19[3], 20; **24**:1[2], 2[2], 23, 36, 37, 45, 47, 62, 65; **25**:9[2], 13, 18[2], 23, 24, 29; **26**:1[2], 2, 3, 4, 6, 12, 15, 17, 18, 19, 22, 29, 31; **27**:7, 15, 30, 43, 45; **28**:9, 12, 16; **29**:2, 17, 18[2], 26, 27; **30**:2, 15, 16, 27, 33[2], 35, 38[3], 39, 41[3], 43; **31**:10[2], 11, 14, 18[2], 23, 24, 25, 26, 32, 34, 35, 37, 40, 41, 46, 53, 54; **32**:3, 5, 7, 16, 17[2], 21; **33**:2[2], 8, 10, 14, 15, 18; **34**:5, 7[2], 10[3], 11, 19, 21[2], 24, 25, 28[2], 29, 30[2]; **35**:3, 4, 6, 11, 17, 22[2], 26, 27; **36**:5, 6, 8, 9, 16, 17, 20, 21, 24, 30, 31, 35, 43; **37**:1, 3, 7, 11, 15, 18, 22, 24, 31, 35, 36; **38**:7, 10, 11[2], 18, 20, 27; **39**:2, 3, 4[2], 5[3], 6[2], 8[2], 9, 12, 13, 14, 20[2], 21, 22[2], 23; **40**:3[3], 4, 5, 7[2], 9[2], 11[2], 13, 15, 17, 20, 22; **41**:8, 10, 17, 19, 22, 30, 31, 32, 33, 35, 36, 38, 40, 41, 42, 43[2], 44, 48[5], 52, 53, 54[2], 57; **42**:1, 2, 5, 13, 16, 17, 19, 25, 27, 28, 29, 32, 34, 35, 38; **43**:1, 11, 21, 22, 23, 33[2]; **44**:1, 2, 12, 14[2], 17, 20, 29, 31, 33; **45**:6, 10, 13, 25, 26; **46**:2, 5, 6, 12, 15[2], 18, 20, 22, 25, 27[2], 28, 31, 33, 34; **47**:1, 4[2], 6[3], 7, 11[2], 13, 14[2], 16, 17[2], 19[2], 20, 24, 25[2], 26[2], 27[3], 28, 29[2]; **48**:3, 5, 6, 7, 20; **49**:1, 3[2], 6, 7[2], 11[2], 27[2], 29[2], 30[2], 32; **50**:2, 4, 5[2], 8, 13[2], 17, 19, 22, 26[2]; **Ex 1**:5[2], 8, 14[3], 16; **2**:3, 12, 13, 15, 21, 22, 23; **3**:2, 7, 16, 17, 22; **4**:2, 4, 10, 15, 17, 18, 19, 20; **5**:1, 6, 19, 21, 23; **6**:28; **7**:3, 10, 15[2], 16, 17, 18, 19[2], 20, 21[2]; **8**:9, 11, 13[3], 20, 22, 25, 26, 28; **9**:3, 5, 8, 13, 14, 16, 19[3], 21, 22, 24, 25[2], 27[2], 29, 31; **10**:5, 6, 12, 14[2], 15[2], 19, 23, 26; **11**:3, 5, 9; **12**:1, 4, 9, 11[2], 15, 18, 19[2], 22, 27, 29[2], 30, 34[2], 40, 48[2]; **13**:4, 5, 7, 14, 15, 21[2], 22; **14**:3[2], 11, 12[2], 17, 19[2], 31[2]; **15**:4, 6, 7, 8, 10, 11[2], 13[2], 17, 20, 22, 26; **16**:2, 3, 4, 5, 6, 7, 8[2], 10, 12, 13, 16, 24, 29, 32, 33, 34; **17**:5, 6, 9; **18**:3, 5, 9, 12; **19**:1, 2[2], 9[2], 11, 16, 18; **20**:4[3], 11[2], 12, 18; **21**:2, 26; **22**:2, 4, 5[2], 9, 13, 21, 27; **23**:2[2], 3, 6, 9, 12, 15[2], 16[2], 19, 21, 26, 29, 31, 33; **24**:6, 8, 14; **25**:15, 16, 21, 27, 35, 37; **26**:4[2], 10[2], 11, 17, 34; **27**:19, 21[2]; **28**:3, 10, 11, 17, 18, 19, 20[2], 30, 32, 38, 43; **29**:3[2], 8, 9, 11, 24, 29, 30, 31, 32, 39, 41; **30**:6, 18, 34, 36[2]; **31**:3, 4, 5[2], 17; **32**:1, 4, 5, 6, 8, 12, 13, 15, 17, 20; **33**:19[2], 22[2]; **34**:2, 3, 4[2], 5, 6[2], 9, 10[2], 12, 15, 18[2], 26, 27, 29, 35; **35**:3, 19, 31, 32, 33[2], 35; **36**:11[2], 17[2], 22; **37**:14, 21; **38**:23, 25; **39**:1, 6, 10, 11, 12, 13[2], 23, 41; **40**:3, 4[2], 5, 6, 7, 9, 13, 14, 17, 18, 20, 22, 24, 26[2], 30, 36, 38[2]; **Lev 2**:4, 7, 11, 14; **3**:8, 13; **4**:2, 6, 7, 12, 13, 17, 18, 20, 22, 26, 27, 31, 35; **5**:4[2], 5[2], 10, 13[2], 15[2], 16, 17, 18; **6**:2, 5, 7, 14, 16[2], 20[2], 21, 25, 26[2], 27, 28[2], 29, 30; **7**:2, 6[2], 9[2], 38; **8**:8, 10, 27; **9**:16, 17; **10**:1, 3, 5, 13, 14, 17, 18; **11**:9, 10[2], 12, 32, 33, 46; **12**:8; **13**:3, 4[2], 5[2], 6, 7, 8, 10[2], 11, 19, 20, 21[2], 22, 24, 25[2], 26[2], 27, 28, 30, 31[2], 32, 33, 34, 35, 36, 37[2], 49, 51, 52, 53, 57[3], 59; **14**:5, 7, 13, 15, 16, 17, 18, 28, 29, 31, 34[2], 35, 36[3], 43, 44, 47, 50, 53[2], 55[2]; **15**:15, 25, 30, 31, 33; **16**:2[2], 15, 16[2], 17[3], 21, 22, 24; **17**:3, 4, 5, 11; **18**:3[2], 9, 24, 27; **19**:5, 14, 17[2], 24, 25[2], 26, 32, 33, 34; **20**:2, 5, 14; **21**:9; **22**:11, 13[2], 18, 19, 23, 24, 29; **23**:38[2], 41, 42[2], 43; **24**:3, 6[2], 9, 10, 12; **25**:4, 7, 13, 18, 19, 20, 21, 22, 28[2], 29, 30[2], 31[2], 32, 33[3], 45, 49, 54[2]; **26**:1, 4, 5[2], 6, 16, 20, 22, 23, 26, 27, 28, 31, 33, 34, 35, 36, 39, 44[2], 45; **27**:21, 24; **Nu 1**:1[2], 3[2], 19, 20, 22, 24, 26, 28, 30, 32, 34, 36, 38, 40, 42, 45, 49, 50, 52; **2**:17[3], 32; **3**:4, 12, 13[2], 14, 31, 38, 41[2], 45[2]; **4**:3[2], 4, 5, 6, 8, 10, 11, 12[2], 14, 15, 16[2], 20, 23, 26, 30, 35[2], 37[2], 39, 41, 43, 45; **5**:6, 13, 17, 18; **6**:9, 11, 18, 19, 21[2]; **7**:2, 5; **8**:2, 13, 14, 16, 17[2], 18[2], 24, 26; **9**:1[2], 3, 5, 14, 18, 21, 22, 23; **10**:9, 12, 14, 18, 22, 25, 31; **11**:1, 5, 8[3], 12, 15, 18[2], 22, 25, 26[2], 27, 31[2]; **12**:5, 6[2], 7, 8, 14[2], 16; **13**:19[2], 22, 26, 29[2], 32, 33; **14**:2[2], 5, 11[2], 14, 16, 18, 19, 22[2], 25, 29[2], 31, 32, 33, 35, 44, 45; **15**:11, 13, 26, 32, 34; **16**:5, 7, 13, 17[2], 18, 19, 42, 46, 49; **17**:4[2], 7, 10; **18**:7, 8, 11, 13, 14, 20, 21[2], 28, 32; **19**:3, 9[2], 14[2], 16, 18; **20**:1, 2, 10, 12[2], 27; **21**:1, 5, 11[2], 12, 13, 14, 20, 31, 33, 34; **22**:5, 21, 22, 23[2], 24, 26, 29, 30, 31, 34, 38; **23**:5, 12, 16, 21[2]; **24**:8, 14, 21; **25**:1[2], 3, 4, 5, 7, 9, 11, 18; **26**:2, 19, 59, 64, 65; **27**:3, 11, 12, 14[2], 17[2], 18, 19, 21; **28**:4, 8, 10, 23, 24[2], 31; **29**:6, 11, 16, 19, 22, 25, 28, 31, 34, 38, 39; **30**:3, 16; **31**:16, 27, 28, 36; **32**:5, 13[2], 14, 15, 17, 26, 30; **33**:1, 2, 3, 8, 11, 15, 36, 40, 47, 53, 55[3]; **34**:29; **35**:2, 3, 5, 6, 7, 8, 14, 17, 18, 21, 28; **36**:7, 8[2], 12; **Dt 1**:1[2], 3, 4[2], 5, 7[4], 8, 10, 17, 27, 30, 31, 32[2], 33[2], 43, 44, 46; **2**:4, 6, 7, 8, 12[3], 21, 22[2], 23[2], 24, 25, 28, 29[2], 30, 32, 36, 37[2]; **3**:1, 2, 4, 10, 11, 13, 17, 19, 24, 29; **4**:1, 5, 10, 14, 17, 18, 22, 23, 25[2], 30[2], 34, 39, 40, 43[3], 46[3]; **5**:1, 8[3], 15, 16, 22, 31, 33[2]; **6**:1, 3, 13, 18[2], 20, 21, 23; **7**:5, 13, 15, 25; **8**:2[3], 5, 6, 7, 16[2]; **9**:1, 5, 7, 15, 16, 18, 21, 28; **10**:2, 3, 5, 8, 12, 14, 19, 20, 22[2]; **11**:3, 5, 6, 8, 9, 10, 14[2], 15, 18, 21, 22, 30[3]; **12**:1[2], 3, 4, 7[2], 10[2], 14, 15, 17, 18[2], 19, 21, 25, 28, 29, 31[3]; **13**:9, 12, 15, 17, 18; **14**:6, 9, 21[2], 23, 26, 27, 28, 29[2]; **15**:4, 7, 10[2], 11[2], 12, 15, 18, 20, 22; **16**:1, 3, 4[2], 5, 6[2], 7, 10, 11, 12, 14, 15[2], 17, 18; **17**:1, 2[3], 4, 7, 9, 14, 20; **18**:5, 6[2], 7[2], 8, 10[2], 18, 19, 20[2], 22; **19**:1, 2, 6, 9, 10, 11, 14[2], 17[3]; **20**:5, 6, 7, 11, 12, 13, 14, 16, 18; **21**:1[2], 4, 5, 6, 9, 13, 16; **22**:6, 9, 16, 21[2], 23, 24, 25, 27; **23**:4, 7, 14, 16, 20[2], 24; **24**:4, 8, 12, 13[2], 14, 18, 19[2], 21, 22; **25**:2, 3, 7, 8, 9[2], 10, 13, 14, 15, 19; **26**:1, 2, 3, 4, 11, 12[2], 14, 17, 19; **27**:7, 14, 15; **28**:3[2], 6, 7, 8, 9, 11[2], 12, 16[2], 19, 20[2], 25, 29[2], 30, 38, 47, 48[2], 52, 57[2], 58, 61, 62[2], 63, 66, 67[2], 68; **29**:1[2], 2, 9, 10, 11, 12, 15, 16, 19, 20, 21, 22, 23, 27, 28[2]; **30**:9[4], 10, 12, 14[2], 16[2], 18, 20; **31**:7, 10, 11, 12, 13, 15, 18, 24, 28, 29[2], 30; **32**:10[2], 24, 25[2], 28, 34[2], 35, 37, 41, 44, 47, 49, 51[2]; **33**:3, 12, 16, 17, 18[2], 19, 24, 26, 28[2]; **34**:5, 6[2], 8, 10, 11, 12; **Jos 1**:8, 11, 14; **2**:7, 9[2], 11, 15, 18, 19, 21, 24; **3**:1, 7, 8, 13[2], 16[2], 17; **4**:6, 9, 10, 12, 14, 21; **5**:4, 5, 6, 7, 8, 13[2], 14; **6**:1, 4, 5, 6, 15, 17[2], 20, 21, 22, 23[2], 24; **7**:1, 13, 14, 15, 21[2], 22; **8**:9, 11, 12, 13, 14[2], 17[2], 18, 19, 20, 22, 24[3], 26, 31, 32, 33[2], 34; **9**:1[2], 6, 9, 10, 11, 25; **10**:6, 10, 12, 13[2], 16, 17, 21, 28, 30, 32, 35, 37[2], 39, 42; **11**:2[4], 3[3], 11, 17, 19[2], 22[2]; **12**:2, 4, 7, 22, 23[2], 24; **13**:1, 3, 9, 10, 12[2], 16, 19, 21, 22[2], 27, 30, 31, 32; **14**:1, 4, 10; **15**:1, 13[2], 15, 16, 17, 19, 21, 33, 46, 48, 61, 63; **16**:2, 5, 10; **17**:11, 12, 15, 16[3]; **18**:5[2], 6, 8, 9[2], 10[2], 19; **19**:8, 29, 33, 47, 50, 51; **20**:4, 6[2], 7[4], 8[6]; **21**:2[2], 6, 11, 21, 27, 32, 38, 39, 41[2]; **22**:2, 4, 5, 7, 9[2], 10, 16, 22, 25, 27[2], 31, 32; **23**:1, 2, 4, 6, 13; **24**:7, 13, 14, 15, 18, 26, 30[2], 32, 33; **Jdg 1**:3, 9, 10, 11, 12, 13, 15, 16, 17, 21, 27, 29, 30, 31, 33[2], 35; **2**:3, 9[2], 11, 14, 15, 17, 22; **3**:1, 3, 6, 7, 12, 20, 22[2], 24, 27; **4**:1, 2[2], 5, 6, 11, 18, 20, 22[2]; **5**:2, 6[2], 7[2], 8, 11, 12, 14, 15, 16, 17, 25, 28, 31; **6**:1, 2, 10, 11[2], 14, 15[2], 17, 19[3], 21, 24, 27, 28, 33; **7**:1[2], 2, 8, 12, 16, 19, 20[2]; **8**:6, 9, 10, 15, 27, 31, 32[2]; **9**:1, 5, 6, 15, 16, 19, 24, 25, 26, 27, 32[2], 33, 34, 40, 41, 43, 44, 46, 49, 51; **10**:1[2], 2, 4, 5, 6, 8, 9, 14, 17, 18; **11**:2, 3, 7, 8, 11, 19, 21, 31, 34; **12**:2, 3, 7[2], 9[2], 10, 12[2], 15[2]; **13**:1, 9, 20, 25; **14**:2, 6, 8, 17, 19; **15**:1, 4, 5, 8[2], 9, 11, 14, 19[2], 20; **16**:1, 2, 4[2], 9, 12, 15, 18, 21, 25, 30, 31; **17**:4, 6, 7, 8[2], 9, 12; **18**:1[2], 3[2], 6, 7, 12, 15, 19, 21, 28, 31; **19**:1[4], 2, 13, 14, 15, 16[3], 17, 18[3], 20, 27[2]; **20**:1, 2, 4, 6, 10[2], 15[2], 27, 31, 37, 39[2], 42, 43; **21**:1, 7, 12[2], 15, 19, 20, 21, 23, 25; **Ru 1**:1[4], 6, 9, 19, 22; **2**:2, 3[2], 7, 8, 10, 13, 14, 17, 22; **3**:7, 8, 13; **4**:4[3], 5, 7[3], 10, 11[2], 15, 16; **1Sa 1**:6, 9, 10, 13, 17, 18, 20; **2**:1[3], 9, 13, 17, 21, 26[2], 27, 28, 31, 32[2], 33, 35, 36; **3**:1, 2, 3, 9, 11, 18; **4**:6, 7, 8; **5**:3; **6**:1, 8, 13, 18, 20; **7**:2, 10, 16; **8**:3, 5, 11, 18; **9**:6, 7, 9, 18, 19[2], 22, 24; **10**:6, 10[2], 26; **11**:6, 15; **12**:3, 5, 8, 17, 18, 25; **13**:2[2], 6[2], 15, 16[2], 17[2], 19, 22; **14**:2, 3, 6, 7, 11, 14[2], 15[2], 16[2], 19, 20, 22[2], 24, 27, 33, 34, 45; **15**:5, 12[2], 14, 17, 19, 21, 22[2], 24, 34; **16**:4, 5, 8, 12, 13[2], 22; **17**:1, 2, 12[3], 19, 20, 24, 25[2], 28, 38, 39, 40[3], 41, 45, 46, 50, 54; **18**:1, 5, 10[2], 13, 14, 16, 17, 18, 19, 20, 27; **19**:3, 5, 9[2], 11, 15, 16, 19, 22, 24; **20**:2, 3, 5, 24, 25, 29[2], 34, 35, 42[2]; **21**:9[2], 11, 13[2], 15; **22**:2[2], 3, 4, 5, 6, 8, 13, 14; **23**:3, 13, 14[2], 15, 16, 19, 23, 24[2], 25[2], 26, 29; **24**:1, 3[2], 10, 11, 20; **25**:1, 2[2], 3, 4, 5, 9, 15, 21, 28, 29, 35, 36[2], 37; **26**:3, 7, 15, 19, 20; **27**:1, 3, 5[3], 7, 8, 11; **28**:1[2], 3, 7, 15, 21, 23; **29**:1, 3, 5, 6[2], 7, 9, 10, 11; **30**:2, 6[2], 8, 11, 26, 27, 28, 29, 30, 31; **31**:9, 10; **2Sa 1**:1, 9, 18, 20[2], 23[2], 24, 25; **2**:1, 3, 11, 14, 16, 22, 26, 32; **3**:2, 5, 6, 19, 21, 22[2], 23, 27, 30, 31[2], 32, 37, 38; **4**:1, 4, 5, 6, 7, 10, 11, 12[2]; **5**:2, 5[2], 6[2], 9, 13, 17, 18, 22, 23, 24[2]; **6**:1, 4, 10, 11, 16, 17, 18, 19, 20, 22[2]; **7**:1, 2[2], 3, 5, 6, 18, 19, 29; **8**:1, 6, 10, 13; **9**:3, 4, 10, 13[2]; **10**:1, 4, 6, 8[2], 9[2], 12; **11**:1[2], 11[2], 12, 13, 14, 15[2], 17, 21, 23; **12**:1, 3, 9, 11, 12[2]; **13**:1[2], 4, 5, 6, 8, 10, 12, 13, 15, 20, 28, 34, 36; **14**:2[2], 3, 6, 8, 17, 19, 20, 22, 25[2], 28, 29, 33; **15**:1, 4, 6, 8[2], 9, 10, 14, 25, 27, 28, 34, 35; **16**:2, 3, 4, 8[2], 10, 21, 22, 23; **17**:1, 9, 14, 16, 18[2], 23[3], 25, 26, 29; **18**:4, 6, 9[2], 10, 12, 13, 14[2], 17, 18; **19**:3, 8[2], 10, 13, 22[2], 32, 33, 36, 37, 43; **20**:1[2], 3[3], 8[2], 10, 12[2], 15, 19[2], 22, 24; **21**:2, 4, 5, 14[3], 18, 19, 20[2], 22; **22**:3, 7, 19, 20, 25, 31, 41, 43; **23**:3[2], 5, 8, 12, 13, 14, 19, 21, 23[2], 29, 39; **24**:5, 7, 9[2], 10, 13[2], 14, 25; **1Ki 1**:1, 13, 14, 15, 28, 30, 32, 35, 41, 42, 47, 49, 50, 52; **2**:3[3], 5[2], 6, 9, 10, 11[2], 21, 26, 34, 35, 36, 38, 39, 40, 44, 46; **3**:5, 6, 7, 11, 13, 14, 17, 18, 20, 21, 25, 26, 28; **4**:4, 5, 6[2], 7, 8, 9, 10, 11, 12[2], 13[3], 14, 15, 16[2], 17, 18, 19, 25, 27; **5**:5, 6, 8, 9, 10, 11, 14[3], 15; **6**:1[3], 4, 5, 7, 17, 23, 25, 27, 29, 33, 34, 37[2], 38[3]; **7**:4, 5[2], 6[2], 8[2], 14[2], 18, 19[2], 20, 22, 23, 24[2], 26, 36, 37[2], 40, 46[2], 48, 49, 51[2]; **8**:2, 4, 6, 8, 9[2], 12, 16, 17, 18[2], 21, 22, 23[2], 25, 28, 31, 33, 37, 40, 47[2], 48, 55, 58, 64, 65, 66; **9**:4, 11, 18, 19[2], 21, 23, 26, 27; **10**:5, 6, 7, 9, 10, 17[2], 21[2], 23, 24, 26[2], 27[2]; **11**:2, 6, 15, 16, 19, 20, 21, 25, 27[2], 28, 29, 33[2], 36, 38[2], 41, 42, 43; **12**:2, 12, 16[2], 17, 18, 19, 21, 25, 27, 29[2], 32[2]; **13**:11, 16, 19, 22[2], 25, 30, 31, 32[2]; **14**:4, 6, 8, 10, 11[2], 12, 13[2], 15, 19, 21[3], 22, 24[2], 25, 29, 31; **15**:1, 2, 4, 5[2], 7, 8, 9, 10, 11, 13, 18[2], 20, 22, 23[2], 24, 25, 26[3], 28, 31, 33[2], 34[3]; **16**:2, 4[2], 5, 6, 7, 8[2], 9[3], 10[2], 12, 14, 15[2], 16[2], 19[3], 20, 23[2], 25, 26[2], 27, 28, 29[2], 30, 32[2], 34[2]; **17**:1[2], 3, 6[2], 7, 9, 10, 12[2], 16; **18**:1, 2, 3[2], 4[2], 6[2], 13[2], 27, 30, 32, 36, 38; **19**:3, 11[3], 12, 18; **20**:10, 12, 15, 16, 20, 29, 30, 34[2], 43; **21**:1, 2, 5, 6, 8[2], 9[2], 11[2], 12, 18[2], 19, 20, 21, 24[2], 25, 26, 27, 29[2]; **22**:2, 10, 16, 17, 22[2], 23, 24, 25, 27, 30, 35, 38, 39, 41, 42, 43[3], 45, 47, 50, 51[2], 52[3]; **2Ki 1**:2, 3, 6, 16, 17, 18; **2**:1, 11, 16, 18, 20, 24; **3**:1[2], 2, 18, 22, 25; **4**:2, 10, 15, 16, 25, 27, 29, 33, 35, 37, 38, 40, 41; **5**:1, 3, 8, 10, 12[2], 14, 15[2], 18, 19, 23, 24, 25; **6**:8, 10, 12[2], 13, 25, 32; **7**:7, 12[2], 13, 15, 17[2], 20; **8**:1, 2, 9, 10, 15, 16, 17, 18[2], 20, 22, 23, 24, 25, 26, 27[2], 29; **9**:8, 15[2], 17[2], 18[2], 19[2], 21, 22, 24, 25, 26, 27, 28[2], 29, 31, 34, 37; **10**:1, 6, 7[2], 8, 11, 15, 16, 19, 20, 24[2], 25, 28, 30[3], 32, 33, 34, 35, 36; **11**:2, 4, 5, 7, 8, 10, 11, 15[2], 18; **12**:1[2], 2, 4, 5, 9, 10, 18, 19, 21; **13**:1[2], 2, 5, 6[2], 8, 9, 10[2], 11[2], 12, 13, 16, 25; **14**:1, 2, 3[2], 5, 6[2], 7[2], 9[4], 10, 11, 14[2], 15, 16, 18, 19, 20[2], 21, 23[2], 24, 25, 26, 28; **15**:1, 2, 3, 5, 6, 7, 8[2], 9, 10, 11, 13[2], 14, 15, 16, 17[2], 18, 20, 21, 23[2], 24, 25, 26, 27[2], 28, 29, 30, 31, 32, 33, 34, 36, 37, 38; **16**:1, 2[2], 3[2], 8[2], 10, 11, 18, 19, 20; **17**:1[2], 2, 4, 6[4], 9, 13, 14, 16, 17[2], 22, 23, 24[2], 26, 28, 29[2], 31, 32, 33, 34, 40; **18**:1, 2, 3, 5, 7, 9, 10, 11[3], 13, 15[2], 22, 26[3], 28, 30, 36; **19**:7, 12, 22, 24, 25, 26, 28[2], 29, 35, 37; **20**:1[2], 3, 13[3], 15[2], 17, 18, 19, 20; **21**:1, 2, 4[2], 5, 6[2], 7[3], 15, 16, 17, 18, 19, 20, 21, 22, 23, 24, 25, 26[2]; **22**:1, 2[2], 3, 8, 9, 10, 13[2], 14[2], 16, 19, 20; **23**:2[2], 3[2], 4[2], 7, 9, 10[2], 11, 12, 16, 19, 21, 23[2], 24[3], 25, 28, 29, 30[3], 31, 32, 33[3], 34, 35, 36, 37; **24**:2, 3, 5, 8, 9, 12, 17, 18, 19, 20; **25**:1, 3, 5, 8, 11, 14, 18, 19[4], 21, 22, 24, 25, 27[2], 28; **1Ch 1**:19, 43, 46; **2**:3, 4, 6, 22, 24, 35; **3**:1, 4[2], 8, 22, 23, 24; **4**:9, 22, 28, 39, 41[3]; **5**:1[2], 8, 9, 11, 12, 13, 16[2], 17, 20[2], 23; **6**:10[2], 31[2], 32, 49[3], 55, 60, 62, 67, 71, 76, 78, 80; **7**:1, 2, 5[2], 7, 23, 29, 40; **8**:6, 8, 13, 28[2], 29, 32, 40; **9**:1[2], 2, 3, 9, 11, 13, 16, 20[2], 22, 23, 25, 26, 28[3], 32, 33, 34[2], 35, 38; **10**:7, 10[2], 12; **11**:2, 5, 7, 11, 14, 15, 16, 23, 25[2], 31; **12**:1, 8[2], 9, 15[2], 16, 17, 20, 21, 30, 38, 40; **13**:2, 5, 13, 14; **14**:3, 8, 12, 14, 15[2]; **15**:1, 3, 13[2], 14, 15, 18, 22, 27[2], 29; **16**:2, 10, 14, 19[2], 27, 29, 32[2], 35, 39, 40[2]; **17**:1[2], 2, 4, 5, 16, 17, 27; **18**:1, 6, 10, 12, 13; **19**:1, 2, 4, 6, 9[2], 10[2], 13, 17; **20**:1[3], 4, 5, 6[2], 8; **21**:5[2], 6, 7, 12, 13, 16[2], 19[2], 29; **22**:2, 5, 7, 8, 12, 15, 16; **23**:8, 9, 10, 12, 13, 23, 24, 25, 26, 28[2], 29, 30, 31[2]; **24**:6, 31; **25**:3[2], 7; **26**:6, 8, 9, 11, 12, 20, 22, 24, 26, 27, 28, 30, 31[3], 32; **27**:1, 2[2], 4[2], 5, 6, 7, 8, 9, 10, 11, 12, 13, 14, 15, 21, 23, 24, 25[4], 26, 27[2], 28[3], 29[4], 30[2], 31[2]; **28**:1[2], 2, 7, 8[2], 12, 13[2], 14[2], 19[2], 21[2]; **29**:2, 3, 6, 8, 10, 11, 12, 15, 18, 21, 22, 23, 25, 27[2], 29; **2Ch 1**:2, 3, 4, 5[2], 6, 8, 14[2], 15[2]; **2**:2, 3, 7[4], 8, 14[2], 16, 17, 18; **3**:1, 2, 10, 15, 17; **4**:2, 3[2], 5, 6, 7, 8, 11, 17[2], 19, 20; **5**:1[2], 3, 5, 7, 9, 10[2], 12, 13[2]; **6**:1, 5, 7, 8[2], 11, 12, 13, 14[2], 16, 19, 22, 24, 28, 31[2], 37[2], 38, 40, 41; **7**:7, 10, 11[4], 15; **8**:2, 4[2], 6[2], 8, 11, 12, 14, 15; **9**:4[2], 5, 8, 11, 14, 16[2], 20[2], 22, 23, 25[2], 27[2], 29[3], 30, 31; **10**:2, 5, 12, 16[2], 17, 18, 19; **11**:1, 3, 5[2], 10, 11, 12, 17, 21, 22; **12**:2, 5, 12, 13[3], 15, 16; **13**:1, 2, 4, 8, 13, 21, 22; **14**:1[2], 2, 5[2], 10, 11; **15**:4, 5[2], 8[2], 10, 16; **16**:1, 2, 10, 11, 12[3], 13, 14[3]; **17**:2[3], 3[2], 7[2], 12, 13[2], 19; **18**:2, 3, 9, 15, 16, 21[2], 22, 23, 24, 26, 29, 34; **19**:1, 3, 4, 5[2], 8[2], 9, 10[2], 11[2]; **20**:2, 4, 5[2], 6[2], 8[2], 9[2], 14, 15, 16, 18, 20[3], 26, 31, 32[2], 34[2]; **21**:1, 3, 5, 6[2], 8, 10, 12, 13, 17, 19[3], 20[3]; **22**:1, 2, 3[2], 4, 6, 9[3], 11; **23**:1, 5, 7, 9, 10, 14, 17, 18[3], 19; **24**:1, 2, 6, 9[2], 11, 12, 13, 14, 16[2], 21, 23, 25[3], 27; **25**:1, 2, 3, 4[3], 8, 10, 13, 18[4], 21, 24[2], 26, 27, 28; **26**:1, 3, 4, 5, 7, 9, 10[5], 15, 17, 19[3], 21, 23; **27**:1, 2, 4[2], 5, 7[2], 8, 9; **28**:1[2], 2, 3[2], 6[2], 7, 9, 12, 14, 18[2], 19, 22, 24, 25[2], 26, 27[2]; **29**:1, 2, 3, 4[2], 6, 9, 15, 16, 18, 19[2], 25[2], 28, 34, 35; **30**:1, 2[2], 3, 5, 10, 12, 13[2], 14, 16, 17, 21, 25, 26[2]; **31**:1, 3, 4, 6[2], 7[2], 11, 12[3], 13, 14, 15, 16[2], 17, 18[2], 19[2], 21[3]; **32**:6, 10, 18[2], 20, 21[2], 24, 30, 31[2], 32[2]; **33**:1, 2, 4[2], 5, 6[3], 7[3], 11, 12, 14[3], 15, 18[2], 19, 20, 21, 22, 24, 25; **34**:1, 2[2], 3[2], 6[2], 8, 12, 15, 17, 18, 21[4], 22[2], 24[2], 27, 28, 30[2], 31[2], 32[2], 33; **35**:1, 2, 3, 4, 5, 10[2], 12, 13, 15, 18, 19, 20[2], 22, 24[2], 25[3], 26, 27; **36**:1[2], 2, 3, 5[2], 7, 8, 9[2], 10, 11, 12, 13, 14, 17, 21, 22[3], 23; **Ezr 1**:1[3], 2, 3[2], 4, 5, 6, 7, 11; **2**:2, 68, 70[2]; **3**:1[2], 2[2], 4, 8[2], 9, 10; **4**:3, 7[3], 10[2], 15[2], 16, 17[2], 18, 23, 24; **5**:1[2], 2, 8, 13, 14[2], 15[2], 16, 17[4]; **6**:1[2], 2[2], 3[2], 5[4], 8, 9, 12, 15, 18[3], 21, 22; **7**:6, 7, 8[2], 9, 10, 11, 13, 14, 15, 16, 17, 18, 19, 25, 27[2]; **8**:17[2], 29[2], 30, 32, 33; **9**:2, 8[3], 9[3], 12, 15[2]; **10**:2, 3, 4, 7, 8, 9[2], 13[2], 14[2], 19; **Ne 1**:1[3], 3[2], 11[2]; **2**:1[3], 3, 5[2], 7, 12, 17[3], 20; **3**:1, 3, 6, 13, 14, 15, 23, 28; **4**:2[2], 4, 5, 10, 17; **5**:2, 7, 9, 13, 14, 15, 18; **6**:1[2], 2, 5, 6, 7[2], 10[2], 15, 17, 18; **7**:1, 2, 4, 7, 73[2]; **8**:1, 3, 7, 14[2], 15, 16[3], 17, 18; **9**:2, 3[2], 6, 9, 15[3], 17[3], 19, 21, 23, 24[2], 25[2], 26, 27, 28[2], 31, 32, 33, 35[2], 36, 37, 38[2]; **10**:30, 34, 36, 37; **11**:1[3], 2, 3[3], 4, 6, 11, 17, 18, 20, 21, 22, 24, 25[3], 26[3], 27[2], 28[2], 29[3], 30[2], 31, 32, 33, 34, 35[2], 36; **12**:7, 8, 9, 12, 22[2], 23, 26[2], 38, 40, 43,

IS (7214)

4:2[2], 3; **Mic 1:**3, 5[5], 9, 11[2], 15; **2:**1, 4, 7, 10[3]; **3:**5, 7, 9, 11; **5:**1, 3; **6:**2, 8, 9[2], 10; **7:**1[2], 4[2], 10, 18; **Na 1:**2[2], 3[2], 6, 7, 12; **2:**5, 7, 8[2], 9, 10, 11; **3:**7, 19; **Hab 1:**3, 4[2], 11, 15, 17; **2:**4, 5[3], 13, 16[2], 18, 19[2], 20; **3:**19; **Zep 1:**7, 14; **2:**5, 10, 15[2]; **3:**5, 15, 17[2]; **Hag 1:**2, 4, 5, 7, 9; **2:**3, 5, 6, 8[2], 11, 14[2], 19; **Zec 1:**3, 4, 14, 16, 17; **2:**2, 8; **3:**2, 7; **4:**1, 6; **5:**3[2], 5[2], 6[3], 8, 11; **6:**6, 12[3], 13; **7:**9, 14; **8:**2, 3, 4, 6, 7, 9, 14, 19, 20, 23[2]; **9:**1; **10:**1, 5; **11:**3, 4; **12:**1, 5; **13:**7, 9; **14:**1, 12; **Mal 1:**4, 5, 6[3], 7, 8[2], 12[2], 14[2]; **2:**1, 7, 14[3], 17[2]; **3:**14; **4:**1[2]; **Mt 1:**16, 18, 20[2]; **2:**2, 5, 13, 18; **3:**2, 3, 10, 11, 12, 15, 17; **4:**4, 6, 7, 10, 17; **5:**3, 10, 12, 13, 18, 22[2], 25, 29, 30, 34, 35[2], 48; **6:**3, 4, 6[2], 9, 10, 18[2], 21, 22, 23[2], 25, 30[3]; **7:**4, 6, 13[2], 14, 19, 21, 24, 26; **8:**27; **9:**3, 5, 12, 14, 15, 24, 34, 37; **10:**2, 7, 10, 13[2], 24, 25, 26, 27, 37[2], 38, 41[2], 42; **11:**5, 6, 10[2], 11[2], 14, 19[2], 30[2]; **12:**2, 6, 8, 10, 12[2], 18, 24, 26, 30[2], 33, 41, 42, 45[2], 48, 50; **13:**13, 14, 19, 20, 22, 23, 24, 31, 32[2], 33, 37, 38, 39[2], 44, 45, 47, 49, 52, 57; **14:**2[2], 4, 15, 27; **15:**5, 6, 11, 22, 26, 28; **16:**2, 3, 7, 11, 13, 27; **17:**4, 5, 12, 15, 22; **18:**1, 4, 8, 9, 13, 14, 23, 35; **19:**3, 10[2], 17[3], 23, 24, 26; **20:**1, 4, 21, 23; **21:**9, 10, 11, 13, 38, 42; **22:**2, 4, 8, 17[2], 20, 21[2], 23, 32, 36, 38, 39, 42, 43; **23:**5, 9, 16, 17, 18, 19, 38, 39; **24:**6, 23[2], 26[2], 27, 28, 32, 33, 39, 45, 48[2], 50; **25:**25; **26:**2, 13, 18, 24, 25, 26, 28[2], 31, 38, 39, 41[2], 42, 45[2], 48, 62, 64, 66; **27:**4, 6[2], 8, 11, 17, 22, 24, 37; **28:**6, 7; **Mk 1:**2, 15, 27, 37, 38; **2:**9, 17, 18, 19, 24, 26, 28; **3:**4, 21, 22[2], 24, 25, 26, 29, 35; **4:**11, 15, 22[4], 26[2], 29, 30, 31[2], 41; **5:**9[2], 23, 35, 39; **6:**4, 14, 15[2], 18, 35, 50; **7:**2, 6, 11[2], 15, 20, 27; **8:**16, 36, 38; **9:**5, 7, 12, 13, 17, 23, 31, 40[2], 43, 45, 47, 48, 50; **10:**2, 18, 23, 24, 25, 27, 40, 46; **11:**9, 10, 17; **12:**7, 11, 14, 16, 17[2], 18, 27, 28, 29[2], 31[2], 32[2], 33, 35[2]; **13:**7, 11[2], 21[2], 28, 29; **14:**9, 14, 18, 20, 21, 22, 24[2], 27, 34, 36, 38[2], 41, 44, 60, 69; **15:**2, 16, 42; **16:**6, 7, 16; **Lk 1:**15, 18, 28, 36[2], 37, 42, 45, 49, 60, 61, 63, 66; **2:**11, 23[2], 24, 34; **3:**4, 9, 17; **4:**4, 8, 10, 17, 18, 21, 24, 36, 43; **5:**21, 23, 31, 34, 39; **6:**2, 4, 5, 9, 20, 23[2], 26, 32, 33, 34, 35, 36, 40[2], 44, 47, 48, 49; **7:**7, 22, 23, 27[2], 28[3], 34, 35, 39[3], 49; **8:**11[2], 17, 25[2], 26, 30, 49, 52; **9:**9, 25, 26, 33, 35, 38, 39, 44, 48[2], 49, 50[2], 62; **10:**2, 6, 8, 9, 11, 22[2], 26, 29, 42[2]; **11:**7, 8, 15, 18, 23[2], 26, 27, 29, 31, 32, 34[3], 35, 36, 41; **12:**1, 2, 6, 18, 21[2], 23, 28[3], 34, 42, 45, 46, 50, 55, 56, 57; **13:**18, 19, 21, 35[2]; **14:**3, 15, 17, 22, 29, 31[2], 32[2], 34, 35[2]; **15:**10, 24[2], 31, 32[2]; **16:**2, 3, 9, 10, 15[2], 16[2], 17, 25; **17:**21[3], 22, 23[2], 30, 31, 37; **18:**19, 24, 25, 27[2], 31, 37; **19:**9, 20, 38, 42, 46; **20:**14, 17[2], 21, 22, 25[2], 27, 38, 41[2]; **21:**8, 20, 22, 26, 28, 30, 31, 36; **22:**11, 19, 20[2], 21[2], 27[4], 37[3], 38, 53, 59; **23:**3, 31[2], 35, 38; **24:**6, 21[2], 29[2], 34, 39, 44[2], 46[2]; **Jn 1:**18, 27, 30, 33, 34, 41, 42, 47[2]; **2:**17; **3:**3, 4, 5, 8[2], 18, 19, 26[2], 27, 29[3], 31[3], 33; **4:**10, 11, 18[3], 20, 21, 22, 23, 24, 25, 34, 37, 42; **5:**2[3], 7, 10, 12, 17, 21, 25, 27, 28, 30, 31, 32[2], 45; **6:**1, 9, 14[2], 20, 29, 31, 32[2], 33, 39, 40, 42, 45, 46, 50, 51, 55[2], 58, 60, 65, 70; **7:**6, 7, 11, 12, 16, 18[2], 20, 26[2], 27[2], 28, 37, 40, 41, 49, 51; **8:**7, 13, 14, 17[2], 18, 19, 22, 26, 29, 34, 39, 40, 41, 43, 44[2], 47, 50[2], 54; **9:**4[2], 12, 16, 17, 19[3], 20, 21, 23, 24, 25, 30, 36, 37; **10:**1, 2, 12, 13, 17, 20, 29, 34, 38; **11:**3, 4, 10, 14, 28[2], 39, 47, 50; **12:**13[2], 14, 15, 19, 27, 31, 34, 35, 48, 50; **13:**10, 13, 16[2], 18, 21, 25, 26, 31[2], 32; **14:**10[3], 11, 21, 28, 30; **15:**1, 6[2], 8, 12, 17, 19[2], 20, 25[2]; **16:**2[2], 7, 13, 14, 15[3], 18, 21[2], 22, 25, 32[2]; **17:**3, 10[2], 15, 17, 20; **18:**4, 7, 22, 23, 34, 35, 36[2], 38, 39; **19:**5, 11, 13, 14, 17, 24, 26, 27, 30, 35; **20:**15, 31; **21:**7[2], 20, 22, 23, 24[2]; **Ac 1:**7, 19, 20, 21; **2:**8, 16, 25, 26, 29, 39; **3:**16, 18; **4:**10, 11, 12[2], 19; **5:**3, 8[2], 32, 38, 39, 42; **7:**33, 35, 37, 42, 49[2]; **8:**10, 21, 32, 34, 36; **9:**11, 15, 20, 22, 26; **10:**4, 5, 6[2], 22[2], 28, 32[2], 34, 35, 36, 42; **11:**13; **12:**14, 22; **13:**8, 10, 11, 25, 26, 33, 34, 35, 38, 39, 47; **15:**11, 15, 19, 21; **17:**3, 7, 18, 19, 24, 25, 27, 29; **18:**10, 13, 21; **19:**2, 4, 27[2], 28, 34, 35, 39, 40[2]; **20:**35; **21:**24, 28; **22:**25, 26; **23:**5, 8, 19, 27; **24:**5, 14, 21; **25:**4, 14, 16, 27; **26:**6, 7[2], 10, 14, 21, 24, 25, 26, 31; **27:**10; **28:**20; **Ro 1:**8, 9, 12, 15, 16, 17[3], 18, 19, 25; **2:**2, 13[2], 18, 24[2], 27, 28[3], 29[4]; **3:**1[2], 4, 5, 8, 10[2], 11, 12, 13, 18, 22, 27[2], 28, 29[2], 30; **4:**5, 8, 9, 11, 12, 14, 15[2], 16, 17[2], 22; **5:**11, 13[2], 15, 16; **6:**22, 23[2]; **7:**2[3], 3[4], 7, 8, 12[2], 13, 14, 16, 17[3], 18[2], 19, 20[2], 21; **8:**1, 6[2], 7, 10[3], 11, 12, 24[2], 31, 33, 34[3], 36, 39; **9:**4, 5[2], 6, 7, 8[2], 13, 14, 20, 25, 29, 30, 33; **10:**1, 2, 4, 5, 6[2], 7, 8[3], 9, 10[2], 12[2], 15, 17; **11:**5, 6, 8, 15, 16[3], 23, 24, 26, 27, 28[2]; **12:**1, 2, 6, 7[2], 8[4], 9[2], 17, 18, 19[2], 20[2]; **13:**1, 2, 3, 4[2], 5, 6, 10, 11, 12[2]; **14:**1, 2, 4, 11, 14[3], 15, 17, 18, 20[2], 21, 22, 23[3]; **15:**3, 9, 21, 22, 23; **16:**19[2], 23, 25; **1Co 1:**9, 12, 13, 18[2], 19, 20[3], 25[2], 30[2], 31; **2:**9, 12, 13, 15; **3:**3, 5[2], 7, 10, 11, 13, 15, 17, 18, 19[2], 23; **4:**2, 4[2], 5, 6, 17, 19, 20; **5:**1[2], 4, 6, 11, 12; **6:**5[2], 11, 12[3], 13, 16[2], 17, 19[2]; **7:**1, 2, 8, 9, 12[2], 13[2], 14, 15, 17, 19[3], 22[2], 25, 26, 29[2], 31, 32, 33, 34[3], 36[4], 37, 39[2], 40[2]; **8:**3, 4[2], 6[2], 7[2], 11; **9:**3, 6, 9[4], 11, 13, 18; **10:**7, 13[2], 16[2], 17, 19[2], 23[4], 26, 27; **11:**3[3], 5, 6, 7[2], 11[2], 12, 13, 14, 15[2], 20, 24[2], 25, 30, 34; **12:**3[2], 7, 8, 12[3], 14, 20, 26, 27; **13:**4[3], 5[3], 8, 13; **14:**5, 7[2], 9, 10, 11[2], 12, 14, 17, 21, 22, 24[2], 25, 28, 29, 30, 33, 35, 37[2]; **15:**11[2], 12[2], 13, 14[2], 17, 26, 27, 29, 39, 40[2], 42[3], 43[4], 44[4], 45, 48, 54, 55[2], 56[2], 58; **16:**10[2]; **2Co 1:**6[2], 7, 12, 18[2], 20, 21, 22, 24; **2:**2, 6, 16; **3:**4, 9[2], 11, 14[2], 15, 16, 17[3], 18; **4:**3[2], 4, 7, 12[2], 13, 15[2], 18[6]; **5:**1, 4, 5[2], 10, 11[3], 12[2], 13[2], 17[2], 18; **6:**2[2], 15, 16; **7:**15; **8:**10[2], 12[2], 13, 15, 17, 18, 19, 21, 22, 23; **9:**1, 8, 9, 12[2]; **10:**6, 7, 10, 15, 18[2]; **11:**10, 15, 29[2], 31; **12:**1, 4, 6, 9[2], 10, 14, 19; **13:**3[3], 5, 7, 9, 10; **Gal 1:**7, 9, 11, 20, 23; **2:**14, 16; **3:**10[2], 11, 12, 13[3], 15, 16, 17, 20, 21, 22, 28; **4:**1[3], 2, 9, 17, 18[2], 19, 22, 24[2], 25, 26[3], 27, 29; **5:**1, 3, 6, 10, 14, 17[2], 22, 23; **6:**1, 3[2], 12, 15; **Eph 1:**14, 19, 23; **2:**2, 4, 5, 8[2], 14, 21; **3:**3, 6, 18, 20[2]; **4:**4, 6, 8, 10, 15[2], 18, 21, 22, 29; **5:**5, 12, 14[3], 17, 23[3], 32; **6:**1, 2, 6, 8, 9[3], 12, 17; **Php 1:**7, 9, 10, 15, 18[2], 21[2], 23, 24, 28; **2:**9, 11, 13, 25[2], 26; **3:**1[2], 3, 8, 9[2], 13[2], 19[4], 20; **4:**1, 5, 8[7], 12[2]; **Col 1:**5, 6, 7, 15, 17, 18[2], 23, 24[2], 26, 27; **2:**2, 5, 10, 17; **3:**1, 3, 4, 5, 6, 10, 11[3], 18, 22, 24, 25; **4:**1, 7, 9[3], 11, 12[2], 13, 16; **1Th 2:**5, 10, 13[2], 19[2]; **3:**2, 10; **4:**3, 4; **5:**18, 24; **2Th 1:**3[2], 5[2], 6, 7; **2:**3, 4[2], 6, 7[2]; **3:**3, 6, 13, 17[2]; **1Ti 1:**4, 5, 8, 9, 10, 15; **2:**3, 5; **3:**1, 10, 15, 16; **4:**4[3], 5, 8, 9, 10; **5:**4, 5, 6, 8, 9, 10, 16, 17, 18, 19; **6:**4, 5, 6, 10, 16, 17, 19, 20; **2Ti 1:**1, 6, 12[2]; **2:**1, 8, 9, 10, 11, 14; **3:**8, 16[2]; **4:**8, 11[2]; **Tit 1:**7, 8[2], 13, 15; **2:**1, 3, 7, 14; **3:**1, 8[2], 11[2], 14; **Phm 1:**12, 16; **Heb 1:**3, 4; **2:**5, 6[2], 8, 11, 14, 16, 18; **3:**4[2], 6, 10, 13; **4:**12, 13[2], 15; **5:**1[2], 2[2], 3, 11, 13, 14; **6:**4, 7, 8[2], 10, 16, 18; **7:**5, 7, 8[2], 12, 14, 15, 17, 18, 19, 25, 26; **8:**1, 3, 5[3], 6[4], 8, 10, 13; **9:**9, 11[2], 15, 16, 17[2], 18, 20, 22, 25, 27; **10:**1, 4, 7, 16, 18, 20, 23, 26, 30, 31, 37; **11:**1, 2, 3, 4, 6, 10, 16, 18, 27; **12:**7[2], 16[2], 18, 27, 29; **13:**6, 8, 9, 14, 16, 21; **Jas 1:**6, 8, 10, 11, 12, 13, 14[2], 15, 17, 21, 23, 26, 27; **2:**6, 10, 14, 15, 16, 17[2], 19, 20, 24, 26[2]; **3:**2[2], 5[2], 6[2], 8, 13, 15, 17; **4:**4, 6, 12[2], 14, 15, 16[2]; **5:**1, 7, 8, 9, 11, 13[2], 14, 16; **1Pe 1:**5, 7, 13, 15, 16, 24, 25; **2:**3, 7, 8, 15, 19[2], 20[2]; **3:**4, 5, 6, 12, 13, 14, 17[2], 22; **4:**1, 5, 6, 7, 13, 17, 18; **5:**2, 12, 13; **2Pe 1:**9, 13, 17; **2:**6, 9, 10, 13, 17, 19, 22; **3:**1, 4, 8, 9[2]; **1Jn 1:**3, 5[3], 7, 8, 9; **2:**2, 4[2], 5[2], 7, 8[3], 9, 10, 11[2], 13, 14, 15, 18[4], 22[4], 25, 27, 29[2]; **3:**1[3], 2, 3, 4, 5, 7[3], 8[2], 9, 10[4], 11, 15, 16[2], 19, 20, 23, 24; **4:**2[2], 3[4], 4[3], 6[2], 8, 9, 10, 12, 15, 16, 17, 18[2], 20; **5:**1[2], 2, 3, 4, 5[2], 6[3], 9[2], 11[2], 14, 16, 17[2], 19, 20[3]; **2Jn 1:**6[2], 7; **3Jn 1:**2, 10, 11[5], 12[2]; **Jude 1:**14, 24; **Rev 1:**2, 3[3], 4[2], 5, 7, 8[2], 19, 20; **2:**7, 8, 21; **3:**2, 7, 10, 12; **4:**8[3]; **5:**2, 5, 12, 13; **8:**11; **9:**11, 12, 13; **10:**6[3], 7, 8; **11:**5, 8, 14, 17; **12:**12[2]; **13:**4, 10[2], 17, 18[2]; **14:**8, 11, 15; **15:**1, 5; **16:**15, 16, 17; **17:**8[2], 10, 11[3], 14, 18; **18:**2, 8, 14; **19:**10, 11, 13[2]; **20:**2, 5, 12, 14; **21:**3, 6[2], 8, 16, 23, 27; **22:**7, 10, 11[2], 12, 17.

ISN'T (32)

Ge 19:20; **27:**36; **37:**30; **44:**5, 31; **Nu 16:**9, 13; **Jdg 9:**28[2]; **14:**3; **15:**2; **18:**19; **1Sa 20:**37; **21:**11[2]; **29:**5; **2Sa 11:**3; **14:**19; **2Ki 9:**18, 20; **18:**22; **Isa 36:**7; **Eze 20:**49; **Mt 13:**55[2]; **Mk 6:**3[2]; **Lk 4:**22; **Jn 7:**25; **9:**8; **11:**56; **Ac 9:**21.

IT (5147)

Ge 1:7[2], 9, 10, 11[2], 12[2], 15, 18, 21, 24, 25, 28, 29, 30[2], 31; **2:**3[2], 10, 11, 13, 14, 15[2], 17, 18; **3:**3, 5, 6[2], 12, 17[2], 18, 19; **4:**7[2], 12, 17; **6:**14[2], 15, 16, 17, 21; **8:**7, 9[2], 12, 17, 20; **9:**4, 7, 13, 16, 23; **10:**9; **11:**9; **13:**17; **15:**6, 7, 8; **16:**7, 14; **17:**11; **18:**6, 7[2], 24[2], 25[2], 28, 29, 30, 31, 32; **19:**13, 20[4], 22, 33, 35; **21:**11, 12, 24, 26; **22:**6, 9, 13, 14[2]; **23:**9, 11[2], 13, 17, 20; **24:**11, 14, 57; **26:**21, 22[2], 33; **27:**4, 5, 9, 10, 14, 18, 20, 25, 31, 33[3]; **28:**11, 12, 13, 16, 18[2]; **29:**2, 7, 26, 32; **30:**15, 34; **31:**2, 5, 32, 37, 41, 44, 45, 47[2], 48, 49; **32:**26, 30; **33:**11, 20; **34:**5, 10[3], 21; **35:**7, 8, 14[2], 22; **37:**5, 7, 9, 24, 32[2], 33[2]; **38:**5, 17, 28; **40:**10[2], 12, 18; **41:**7, 15[3], 16, 24, 26, 28, 31, 32, 42, 48[2], 49[2], 51, 52; **42:**14, 28; **43:**10, 11, 12, 21; **44:**7, 9, 10[2], 11, 17; **45:**2, 5, 8, 12; **47:**14, 24, 26[2]; **48:**14, 17; **49:**4, 10, 32; **50:**9, 20; **Ex 1:**16[2]; **2:**3[3], 5, 6; **3:**2, 12; **4:**3[4], 4[2], 6[2], 7[3], 9, 11, 13, 16, 17, 25; **5:**11; **6:**8, 26, 27; **7:**5, 9[2], 10, 12, 17; **8:**10; **9:**6, 8, 9, 10, 18, 24[2], 25, 26; **10:**5, 15; **12:**7, 9, 10[2], 11[3], 14, 15, 17, 19, 22, 27, 34, 43, 44, 45, 46, 47, 48; **13:**3, 7, 11, 13, 16; **14:**11, 12, 21, 24, 27; **15:**7, 23, 25; **16:**6, 8, 15[4], 18, 19, 20[2], 21, 23, 24[3], 25[2], 26, 27, 31, 32, 33[2], 34; **17:**6, 12[2], 14, 15; **18:**16, 18, 22; **19:**12, 18[2], 23; **20:**8, 10, 11, 24, 25[3], 26; **21:**13[2], 26, 29[2], 33[2], 35, 36[2]; **22:**1[2], 3, 6, 10, 13, 14, 26, 31; **23:**4, 5[2], 9, 11; **24:**6, 7, 8, 15; **25:**11[2], 12, 14, 24[2], 25, 31[2], 37[2]; **26:**13, 31, 32, 35; **27:**1, 4, 5[2], 7, 8, 19; **28:**7[2], 8, 15, 16, 17, 23, 28, 32, 35, 36, 37[3], 38[2]; **29:**3, 7, 11, 12[2], 14, 16[2], 18, 20[2], 21, 26[2], 28, 34[3], 36[3], 37[2]; **30:**2[2], 3, 4, 9, 10, 16[2], 18[2], 19, 25, 26, 32[3], 33[2], 35, 36[3], 37, 38; **31:**7, 14[2], 16, 17; **32:**4[2], 8[2], 12, 13, 18[3], 20[4], 24[2]; **33:**1, 7[2]; **34:**20; **35:**2, 12, 24[2]; **36:**33, 35, 36; **37:**2[2], 3, 5, 11[2], 12, 17[2], 25[2], 26, 27; **38:**1, 7[2], 18, 30; **39:**4, 5, 8, 9, 10, 21, 23, 30, 31[2], 43; **40:**3, 4, 7, 8, 9[3], 10, 20[2], 23, 27, 29, 30, 31, 35, 37; **Lev 1:**3[2], 4, 5, 6, 9[2], 11, 12, 13[3], 15[2], 16, 17[4]; **2:**1[2], 2, 3, 4, 5, 6[3], 7, 8[2], 9, 10, 15[2]; **3:**2, 5, 7, 8, 12, 13; **4:**4, 5, 6, 12, 14, 17, 19[2], 21, 24[2], 25, 29, 30, 31, 33, 34, 35; **5:**2, 3[2], 4[2], 8, 9, 11[2], 12[4], 15, 16, 17, 19; **6:**3, 5[3], 12[2], 13, 14, 16[3], 17[3], 18[2], 20, 21[2], 22[2], 23, 25, 26[3], 27, 28, 29[2], 30; **7:**5, 6[3], 9, 12, 14, 15[2], 16, 18[5], 19[2], 24, 29; **8:**7, 9, 10, 15[3], 16, 23, 29, 31[2]; **9:**9, 12, 15[2], 16, 17[2], 18, 24; **10:**12[2], 13[2], 16, 17[2]; **11:**4[2], 5[2], 6[2], 7[2], 32[4], 33, 34[2], 38[2], 41, 42[2]; **13:**3, 4, 6, 8, 11, 12, 13, 18, 20[4], 21[3], 22[2], 23, 25[4], 26[2], 27[2], 28[2], 30[3], 31[2], 32[2], 34, 37[2], 39, 42, 49, 51[2], 52, 53, 54, 55[4], 56, 57[2], 58; **14:**6, 12, 13, 14, 15, 16, 20, 25, 37, 38, 44[2], 45, 46, 48, 53; **15:**3[2], 17[2], 23[2]; **16:**9, 10, 14[2], 15[3], 18[2], 19[3], 21, 22, 31[2], 34; **17:**3, 4[2], 9[2], 11[2], 13, 14; **18:**23[2], 25, 28[2]; **19:**5[2], 6[2], 7[2], 8, 23[2], 26; **20:**14, 16, 17, 18, 21, 24; **21:**12; **22:**8, 10, 13, 14, 19, 20, 21, 23, 27[2], 29[2], 30[2]; **23:**3, 11[2], 28, 32, 34, 36, 41; **24:**9[3]; **25:**10, 12, 22, 26[2], 27[2], 28, 29, 30[2], 34, 53; **26:**1, 10, 16, 34, 35[3], 43; **27:**4, 5, 6, 7, 10[2], 12, 14, 15, 16, 19, 20[2], 21[2], 24[2], 26, 27[5], 30, 31; **Nu 1:**50[3], 51[3]; **2:**2; **4:**5, 7[2], 9, 10[2], 13, 14[2], 16; **5:**7[2], 15[3], 22, 25[2], 26, 27; **6:**18; **7:**1[2], 84, 88; **8:**4; **9:**3, 11, 12, 15, 16[3], 21, 22; **10:**17, 29, 36; **11:**8[6], 17, 18, 19, 20[2], 31, 33; **13:**19, 20[3], 23, 27, 30, 32; **14:**3, 8, 13, 14, 23, 24, 34, 36; **15:**7, 10, 20, 24, 25, 34; **16:**9, 11, 13[2], 17[2], 18, 28, 42, 46; **18:**10[3], 11, 13, 19, 23[2], 30, 31[2], 32; **19:**3[2], 4, 8, 9, 14, 15, 18, 22; **20:**5, 8, 19; **21:**8[2], 9, 17, 27, 28; **22:**25; **23:**20, 23, 27; **24:**1; **27:**11, 13; **28:**24; **29:**1; **30:**5, 7, 8, 11, 14; **31:**23[2], 29, 54; **32:**39, 42; **33:**53, 54; **34:**4, 5, 13; **35:**33; **36:**9; **Dt 1:**2, 17, 21, 24, 25[2], 36, 37, 38[2], 39[2], 41; **2:**19, 24; **3:**9, 11, 14, 18; **4:**2, 5, 11, 32, 38[2], 40; **5:**3, 12, 14, 16, 29; **6:**3, 18; **7:**8, 25[3], 26[3]; **8:**16, 18[2]; **9:**2, 4, 5, 6, 15, 21[3]; **10:**10, 14, 15; **11:**5, 7, 10, 12[2], 17, 31; **12:**15[2], 16, 20, 24, 25[2], 28, 32[2]; **13:**4, 12, 14[3], 15, 16; **14:**8[2], 10, 21[3], 28; **15:**2, 17, 18, 21, 22[3], 23; **16:**3, 7[2]; **17:**1, 4[3], 14[2], 19[2]; **19:**6, 13; **20:**5[2], 6[2], 9, 11, 13[2], 19[2]; **21:**1, 7, 21; **22:**1[2], 2[4], 3, 4[2], 7; **23:**21[2]; **24:**1, 3, 13[2], 15, 19[2]; **25:**1, 4; **26:**1[2], 4, 12, 13, 14[2]; **27:**6, 15; **28:**24, 30, 31, 38, 55, 63[2], 67[2]; **29:**8, 22, 23[2], 25, 27, 28; **30:**5, 12[4], 13[4], 14[2]; **31:**7, 9, 13, 19[3], 21, 22, 26[2]; **32:**22, 34, 35, 41; **33:**3; **34:**4[3]; **Jos 1:**7, 8[2]; **2:**5, 11, 21; **3:**3[2], 4, 6, 16; **4:**7, 23; **6:**6, 11, 17, 18, 21, 24; **7:**3, 13, 19, 20, 22; **8:**4, 7, 8[2], 11, 13, 19[2], 24, 28, 29[2], 31[2], 33, 34; **9:**12[2], 15; **10:**1, 2, 4, 5, 13, 14, 18, 28, 29, 30, 31[2], 32[2], 34[2], 35[3], 36, 37[4], 39; **11:**11, 15, 20, 23; **13:**3, 7, 8, 9, 11; **15:**3, 4, 7, 8[2], 10, 11, 17; **16:**2, 6[2], 7, 9; **17:**18; **18:**4, 7, 8, 13, 16, 17, 18, 19; **19:**2, 11, 12, 13[2], 27, 28, 34, 47[4]; **21:**42, 43; **22:**23, 24, 27, 29; **23:**3; **24:**12, 16, 17, 26, 27[2]; **Jdg 1:**5, 8[2], 13, 17, 20, 26; **2:**22; **3:**18, 21, 22; **5:**31; **6:**5[2], 11, 17, 18, 22, 24[2], 25, 27, 28, 29, 30; **7:**9, 13; **8:**4, 21, 24, 25, 27[2]; **9:**4, 45[2], 49, 50[2], 52[2]; **11:**13, 22, 23, 31; **13:**4, 16[7], 18, 19, 21; **14:**8, 9, 13, 16[2]; **15:**15, 19[2]; **16:**9, 13, 14, 22, 30; **17:**2, 3; **18:**2, 9, 19, 29; **19:**30[3]; **20:**9, 10, 28; **Ru 1:**13, 17; **2:**3, 14, 17, 18, 22; **3:**12, 13, 14, 15[3], 16; **4:**4[4], 6[3], 7, 8; **1Sa 2:**9, 13, 14, 16[2], 19, 24, 25, 30; **3:**11, 17[3]; **4:**3, 16; **5:**1, 2, 9[2], 11[3]; **6:**2, 3, 8[3], 9[5], 11, 14, 21; **7:**1, 2, 6, 7, 9, 12[2]; **8:**7, 15, 21; **9:**8, 14, 24[3]; **10:**1, 12, 25; **11:**12; **12:**3, 6, 15, 17, 23; **13:**3; **14:**15, 17, 18, 27, 30, 33, 34[2], 35, 39, 44; **15:**27, 28; **16:**2; **17:**23, 35[6], 47, 49, 51, 54; **18:**4, 5, 11, 20, 23; **19:**5, 11, 13[2], 21; **20:**13, 20; **21:**6, 9[5]; **22:**1; **23:**20, 25; **24:**15; **25:**7, 11, 17, 22; **26:**12, 17, 19, 22; **27:**6; **28:**14, 17, 24, 25; **29:**10; **30:**1, 2, 3, 7, 27; **31:**4[2]; **2Sa 1:**18, 20[2]; **2:**4, 14, 20; **3:**9, 12, 18, 26, 35[2]; **4:**7, 12; **5:**9[2], 17; **6:**3, 4[2], 10, 17[2], 21; **7:**3, 15, 21, 29; **10:**3[2]; **11:**14, 15, 25; **12:**3[4], 4, 12, 28[2], 29, 30[2]; **13:**2, 5, 8[2], 10, 11, 35; **14:**19, 21, 26[2], 30, 32; **15:**21, 25; **16:**12; **17:**9, 13[2], 18, 19[3]; **18:**3, 18[2], 25, 27, 29; **19:**2, 6, 13, 19, 26, 42; **20:**8[2], 10, 15[2], 18, 20[2], 22; **21:**1[2], 10; **22:**9, 33; **23:**12, 16[3], 17[3]; **24:**3, 13, 22, 24; **1Ki 1:**11, 16, 18, 36, 41, 45; **2:**14, 15, 16, 20, 23; **3:**15, 21; **4:**27; **6:**7, 9[2], 14, 38; **7:**1, 3, 6, 7, 23[2], 24, 26[2], 31, 44; **8:**4, 6, 9, 17, 18, 24[2], 65; **9:**16[2], 21; **10:**20, 22; **11:**11, 12[2], 30; **12:**11, 14, 28; **13:**3, 4, 6, 13, 24, 25, 26[2], 28, 29[2]; **14:**8, 10, 15; **15:**13, 18, 27; **16:**7, 24, 31; **17:**11, 12, 13; **18:**7, 23[5], 25, 26, 32, 33[2], 34[4], 36; **19:**2, 4, 13, 21; **20:**1, 6, 10, 11, 13, 14, 39, 40, 42; **21:**2[2], 18, 29; **22:**3, 6, 12, 15, 22; **2Ki 1:**3, 6, 7, 16; **2:**3, 5, 8[2], 10, 14[2], 20[2], 21[2]; **3:**13, 20, 25[3]; **4:**4, 10, 27, 40[2], 41[2], 42, 43, 44; **5:**13; **6:**5, 6[2], 7[2], 31, 32; **7:**2[2], 7, 8, 9, 11, 18, 19[2]; **8:**6, 15[2]; **9:**21, 26, 30; **10:**9, 20, 21, 24, 26, 27; **11:**18; **12:**5, 7, 9, 10, 11, 14[2], 16, 17; **13:**16, 17, 18, 19[2]; **14:**7[2], 22; **16:**8, 9, 11, 12[2], 14, 17[2]; **17:**5, 26, 39; **18:**4[2], 9, 10, 16, 21, 25, 26, 27; **19:**4, 14[2], 17, 22, 25[3], 26, 32[2], 34; **20:**7, 9, 10[2], 11; **21:**7, 12, 13[2]; **22:**5, 8[2], 9, 10; **23:**6[2], 10, 15, 16, 17[2], 18, 21; **24:**10, 11, 20; **25:**1, 24; **1Ch 4:**14; **6:**10; **9:**27[2]; **10:**4[2]; **11:**7, 8, 10, 14, 18[3], 19[2]; **12:**15[2], 17, 19; **13:**2[2], 3, 4, 7, 13; **14:**8; **15:**1, 3, 12, 13[3], 22; **16:**1[2], 17, 19, 30, 32; **17:**2, 13, 24, 27[3]; **19:**3; **20:**1[2], 2[2]; **21:**15, 17, 22, 23, 30; **22:**5, 7; **28:**2[2], 8; **29:**16[2]; **2Ch 1:**4[2], 6; **2:**4; **3:**1, 5[2], 14; **4:**2[2], 3, 5[2], 15; **5:**5, 7, 10; **6:**7, 8, 13, 15[2]; **7:**2, 20; **8:**3, 8; **9:**18, 19, 21; **10:**11, 14; **15:**5, 15, 16[2]; **16:**2; **18:**5, 11, 21; **20:**2, 7, 8[2], 25[2], 26; **21:**17; **23:**17; **24:**5, 10, 11, 12, 13, 14, 23; **26:**2, 18; **28:**9; **29:**16[3], 22, 36; **30:**3, 5; **32:**5, 12, 30; **33:**7, 14, 16; **34:**10, 15, 17, 18, 32; **35:**3, 21; **36:**21, 22; **Ezr 1:**1; **3:**2, 3; **4:**3, 14, 19; **5:**8, 16, 17; **6:**2, 3, 11, 12[2], 13, 21; **7:**23, 27; **9:**7, 11, 12, 15; **10:**3, 4, 13; **Ne 2:**1, 4, 5[2], 6, 7, 19, 20; **3:**1, 13, 14, 15[2], 21; **4:**3, 6, 8, 11, 15; **5:**12, 15; **6:**1, 3, 6[2], 8, 9; **7:**4, 5; **8:**3, 5, 8, 15[2], 17; **9:**5, 6, 11, 36, 38[2]; **10:**1, 34, 36, 37; **13:**1, 15, 26; **Est 1:**13, 19[2]; **2:**4, 22; **3:**4, 8, 9, 10; **4:**2, 8, 16; **5:**3[2], 4, 6[2], 8, 14; **6:**2; **7:**2[2], 3, 9[2]; **8:**2, 5[2], 8, 16; **9:**12[2], 13, 17, 18, 27, 32; **Job 1:**7, 19; **2:**2, 8; **3:**3, 4[3], 5[2], 6[2], 7, 9, 10, 21; **4:**5, 8, 12, 16[2]; **5:**5, 8, 27[3]; **6:**3, 5[2], 7; **8:**15[3], 17, 18[2]; **9:**5, 7, 19[2], 20, 22, 24[2], 35; **10:**3; **11:**16; **12:**8; **13:**1, 9; **14:**7[2], 9, 21[2]; **16:**6, 8; **17:**16; **18:**13; **19:**4; **20:**4, 12, 13[2], 14, 25; **21:**19[2]; **22:**3, 4, 8, 11, 18; **26:**9; **27:**6, 21, 22, 23; **28:**7, 8, 13, 14[2], 15, 16, 17[2], 19[2], 21, 22, 23[2], 27[3]; **29:**24; **31:**3, 12[2], 17, 22, 36[2]; **32:**8, 9; **33:**14, 25; **34:**9, 10, 12, 14; **35:**3, 13; **36:**25[2], 32; **37:**3, 21; **38:**5, 8, 9, 10, 13[2], 26, 27; **39:**12, 29; **41:**8; **Ps 7:**15, **10:**14[2]; **15:**4; **17:**1; **18:**8, 32; **19:**6; **21:**4; **22:**14, 31; **24:**1[2], 2[2]; **25:**11; **30:**9; **33:**1, 9[2], 17; **34:**14; **35:**21; **37:**8, 29, 34; **39:**6; **40:**7; **41:**6; **44:**3[2], 21; **48:**2; **50:**1, 12; **51:**16; **52:**2; **54:**6; **55:**10, 12, 13; **57:**6; **58:**8; **59:**13; **60:**2[2], 10; **65:**9[3], 10; **68:**10, 11, 14, 30; **69:**22, 35, 36; **72:**16[2], 17; **73:**16, 28; **74:**11, 13, 14, 15, 17; **75:**2, 3, 7, 8[2]; **78:**30; **80:**8, 9[2], 11, 13[2], 16; **81:**5, 10; **84:**6[2]; **86:**17; **87:**5; **89:**11, 37; **90:**6[2], 13; **91:**7; **92:**1; **93:**1; **94:**15; **95:**5; **96:**10, 11; **98:**7[2]; **100:**3; **102:**13; **103:**16[3]; **104:**5, 6, 10, 20, 28[2], 32; **105:**10, 12, 41; **106:**9, 17; **107:**30; **108:**11; **109:**17[2], 18, 19, 27[2]; **113:**3; **114:**5; **115:**17, 18; **118:**8, 9, 23, 24; **119:**34, 71, 89, 90, 97, 106, 126, 130; **126:**2; **129:**6, 7; **132:**6[2], 13, 14; **133:**1, 2, 3; **136:**14; **137:**7[2]; **139:**4; **141:**5[3]; **142:**3; **147:**1; **Pr 1:**19[2]; **2:**4[2], 16, 21, 22; **3:**27[2], 28[2]; **4:**7, 13[3], 15[3], 23; **5:**6; **6:**7, 8, 31, 35; **7:**23; **8:**33; **10:**22, 29; **11:**8, 11, 27; **13:**11, 13, 23; **14:**12, 26; **16:**14, 15, 22, 25, 31; **17:**8, 26; **18:**5, 10, 11, 15, 21; **19:**2, 10, 11, 19, 21, 24; **20:**3, 16[2], 25, 27; **21:**1, 15; **22:**3, 6, 14, 15, 18; **23:**23, 31[3], 32, 35; **24:**3, 12[2], 13, 14, 25; **25:**2, 7, 10, 16, 27[2]; **26:**15, 27[2], 28; **27:**12, 13[2], 14; **28:**2, 5, 8; **29:**4, 26; **30:**10, 21, 28; **31:**4, 15, 16, 21; **Ecc 1:**5, 6, 10[2]; **2:**17, 21, 26; **3:**14[3]; **5:**4, 5[2], 18; **6:**1, 4[2], 5[2]; **7:**2, 5, 10, 18, 24[2]; **8:**8[2], 9, 12, 13, 17[2]; **9:**2[2], 7, 10, 14[4]; **10:**8, 11; **11:**1, 3[2], 7; **12:**7[2], 14; **SS 2:**7; **3:**5, 7, 9; **4:**4; **5:**3; **6:**12; **8:**4, 6, 7[2]; **Isa 2:**2[2]; **3:**9, 10, 14; **4:**6; **5:**2[5], 4[2], 5[2], 6[2], 14, 19[3], 29, 30; **6:**7, 13; **7:**1, 6[3], 7[2], 13; **8:**1, 7, 8[2], 10[2], 12; **9:**7, 8, 9, 18[3]; **10:**15[3], 17, 18; **11:**15; **13:**6, 9; **14:**9[2], 24[2], 27, 30; **16:**5, 12; **17:**5; **18:**3[2]; **19:**20; **20:**1; **21:**16; **22:**11[2], 25[2]; **23:**9, 13[2], 15; **24:**1, 2, 13, 20[3]; **25:**2, 11; **26:**5[2], 6, 11; **27:**3[4]; **28:**2, 4[3], 9, 10, 15, 18, 19[3], 28[3]; **29:**7, 8, 11, 16; **30:**8[3], 14, 15, 21, 33[2]; **31:**5[4]; **33:**4, 21, 22; **34:**1[2], 5, 6, 10[3], 11, 16, 17; **35:**2[3], 8[4], 9; **36:**6, 10, 11, 12; **37:**4, 9, 14[2], 18, 23, 26[3], 27, 33[2], 35; **38:**8[2], 17, 21; **40:**5, 9, 14, 19[3], 21; **41:**4, 5, 7[2], 20, 26; **42:**5[2], 10, 21, 24, 25[3]; **43:**9, 13, 19[2]; **44:**7, 8, 12[2], 13[4], 14[2], 15[4], 16, 17[2], 19, 25, 26, 28; **45:**8[3], 12[2], 18[3], 21[3]; **46:**6[2], 7[8], 8[2], 13; **47:**11; **48:**9, 16, 20[2]; **49:**6; **50:**9; **51:**9, 10, 23; **52:**6[3], 8, 11; **53:**10; **54:**14, 15, 16[2]; **55:**10[3], 11[2]; **56:**2[2], 6; **57:**1, 8[2], 10, 11, 14; **58:**1, 3, 5, 7, 13; **59:**10, 11; **60:**12; **62:**9[3]; **63:**1; **65:**6[2], 8[2], 19, 20; **66:**6; **Jer 2:**19; **3:**7, 16[2]; **4:**4, 16, 18[2], 23, 27; **5:**14, 20, 22[2], 28, 31; **6:**6, 8, 10, 11[3], 14, 16[2]; **7:**12, 20, 23, 28, 29, 30, 31, 32; **8:**8, 11, 16; **9:**3, 8, 12, 13, 21; **10:**3, 4[3], 19, 22, 23; **11:**16, 18; **12:**4, 11, 17; **13:**1[2], 2, 4, 5, 7[3], 16[2], 22; **14:**21, 22; **15:**9; **16:**11; **17:**4, 6, 8[2], 9, 11, 15, 21, 24; **18:**4[2], 8, 10[2]; **19:**3, 4, 5, 8, 15; **20:**5[2], 9; **21:**10[2], 12; **22:**14[3], 15, 16; **23:**20, 28; **25:**12, 13, 15, 16, 17, 26, 28;

IT'S (20)

ITS (1008)

ITSELF (53)

MAY (1231)

ME (4015)

MY (4597)

MYSELF (153)

NOT (5888)

O (978)

OF (25210)

6, 13, 14, 19, 21, 23, 25, 27^2, 28, 29, 30, 31^2; **5:**1, 2, 8, 9, 11, 16, 19, 20, 21, 22; **6:**2, 10, 12, 14, 16, 17, 18; **Eph 1:**1^2, 3, 4, 6, 7^2, 9, 11^2, 12, 13^2, 14^2, 17^2, 18^2, 19, 23; **2:**2^4, 3^3, 4, 7, 8, 11, 12, 13, 14, 15, 16, 19, 20; **3:**1^2, 2, 4, 6, 7^3, 8^2, 9, 10, 13, 16, 18, 19^2; **4:**1, 3^2, 6, 7, 12^2, 13^4, 14^2, 17, 18^3, 19, 21, 22, 23, 25^2, 29, 30^2, 31^2; **5:**1, 2, 3^4, 4, 5^3, 6, 8, 9, 11, 16, 20, 21, 23^3, 30, 33; **6:**4, 5, 6^2, 11, 12^2, 13^2, 14^2, 15, 16^2, 17^3, 18, 19; **Php 1:**1, 4, 5, 6^2, 7^2, 8^2, 9, 10, 11^2, 14^3, 15^2, 16, 17, 18, 19, 25^2, 26, 27^3, 29; **2:**3, 4^2, 5, 7, 10, 11, 15, 16^2, 17, 21, 22, 25, 26, 30; **3:**2, 3, 5^5, 7, 8, 9, 10^2, 12^2, 13, 15^2, 17, 18^2; **4:**3^3, 7, 9, 12, 14, 15^2, 23; **Col 1:**1^2, 3, 4^2, 5, 7, 8, 9, 10^2, 12^2, 13^2, 14, 15, 18, 21, 23, 24, 25, 27^2; **2:**2^2, 3, 8, 9, 11^2, 12, 13, 15, 17, 18, 20, 23^2; **3:**1, 6^2, 8, 10, 15^2, 16, 17, 22; **4:**3, 5, 6, 9, 10, 11, 12^3, 16; **1Th 1:**1, 2, 6^3, 9; **2:**2^2, 6, 8, 9, 10, 11, 12, 13^3, 14, 16, 17, 19; **3:**2, 6, 7, 9^2, 13; **4:**2, 4, 6, 12, 13, 15, 16^2; **5:**2, 5^2, 8, 13, 22, 23^2, 28; **2Th 1:**1, 3, 5^2, 8, 9^2, 11^2, 12^2; **2:**1, 2, 3, 7^2, 8^2, 9^3, 10, 13, 14, 15; **3:**1, 6, 8, 13, 14, 16^2, 18; **1Ti 1:**1^3, 5, 7, 11, 14, 15, 16; **2:**1, 4, 7; **3:**2, 3, 5, 8, 9^2, 11, 12, 15^2, 16; **4:**5, 6^3, 8, 10^2, 13, 14; **5:**4, 9, 10^2, 13, 17^2, 21^2, 22^2, 23, 24^4; **6:**1^2, 3, 5^2, 7, 10^3, 11, 12^3, 13^2, 14, 15^2, 19, 20; **2Ti 1:**1^3, 5, 6^2, 7^4, 8^2, 9^3, 10, 11, 13, 14, 15, 16^2; **2:**2, 3, 6, 9, 10, 14^2, 15, 18, 19, 20^2, 22^2, 25, 26; **3:**2^2, 3, 4^2, 5, 6, 8, 9, 10, 11^2, 14, 17; **4:**1^3, 2, 3, 5^2, 8, 14, 19; **Tit 1:**1^4, 2^2, 3, 6^2, 10, 11, 12, 14; **2:**2, 5, 8, 11, 13; **3:**3, 4, 5^3, 7; **Phm 1:**1, 6, 7, 9^2, 21, 25; **Heb 1:**2, 3^3, 5, 7^2, 8, 9, 10^2, 13; **2:**4, 6^2, 9, 10, 11, 12, 14, 15, 17; **3:**3^2, 4, 6, 8, 12, 13, 16, 19; **4:**1^3, 2, 3, 6, 9, 11, 12^2, 13, 14, 16^2; **5:**3, 5, 6, 7^2, 9, 10, 12; **6:**1^2, 2^2, 5^3, 6, 7, 8, 9, 11, 17^2, 18, 20; **7:**1^3, 2^4, 3^3, 4, 5, 10, 11^3, 12^2, 13, 16^3, 17, 22^2, 23, 27; **8:**1^3, 5, 6, 8^2, 9, 10, 11; **9:**4^4, 5, 9, 10^2, 11^2, 12^2, 13^2, 14, 15, 16^2, 19^3, 20, 22, 23, 24, 26^3, 28; **10:**1, 3, 4, 10^2, 12, 19, 21, 22, 25, 26, 27^3, 28^2, 29^3, 31, 32, 34, 36, 39^2; **11:**1^2, 3, 4, 7, 9, 14, 15, 21^2, 22, 23, 24, 25^2, 26^3, 28^3, 30, 33, 34^2, 38, 39; **12:**1, 2^3, 4, 5^2, 9, 11, 15, 17, 22^2, 23^3, 24^2, 27; **13:**5, 7^3, 9^2, 11, 15^2, 17, 20^3, 22; **Jas 1:**1^2, 2, 3, 5, 6, 12, 17, 18^3, 19, 21; **2:**5, 7, 10^2, 16; **3:**1, 3, 5, 6^3, 7^2, 8, 10, 15, 17^2, 18; **4:**4^2; **5:**1, 4^2, 5, 10^3, 11^2, 13^2, 14^3, 16, 19, 20^2; **1Pe 1:**1, 2^2, 3^2, 5, 6, 7, 9^2, 10, 11^2, 12, 18, 19, 20, 23^3, 24, 25; **2:**1^2, 9^2, 10, 12, 15, 16, 17, 19^2, 25; **3:**1^2, 2, 3, 4^3, 5, 7^2, 8, 12^2, 16, 20, 21^3; **4:**2^2, 4, 7, 8, 11, 13, 14^4, 15, 17^2, 18; **5:**1, 2, 4, 5, 9, 10, 12^2, 14^2; **2Pe 1:**1^2, 2^2, 3, 8, 11, 12, 13, 16^2, 19, 20, 21; **2:**2, 5, 6^2, 7, 9, 10^2, 11, 12, 13, 14, 15^3, 18, 19, 20, 21, 22; **3:**1, 3, 4, 5, 6, 7^2, 10, 11, 12^2, 13, 16, 17, 18; **1Jn 1:**1, 7; **2:**2, 12, 14, 15, 16^3, 17, 19, 20, 29; **3:**1, 2, 8^2, 9^2, 10^3, 17, 23; **4:**2, 3, 5, 6^2, 7, 13, 14, 15, 17; **5:**1, 2, 4, 5, 9, 10, 12, 13^2, 15, 18^2, 19^2, 20; **2Jn 1:**2, 4, 9, 13; **3Jn 1:**6, 7, 10, 12^2; **Jude 1:**1^2, 4, 5, 6, 7^2, 9, 11, 13, 14, 15^2, 17, 21; **Rev 1:**1, 2^2, 3, 4, 5^2, 7^2, 9^4, 13, 15, 16, 18, 20^3; **2:**1^2, 6, 7^2, 8^2, 9^2, 10^4, 12^2, 13, 14, 15, 16, 17, 18^3, 20, 21, 22^2, 23, 24; **3:**1^4, 2, 5, 7^3, 9^2, 10, 12^5, 14^3, 16; **4:**3, 4, 5^3, 6, 8; **5:**1, 5^4, 6^2, 7, 8^2, 11; **6:**1^2, 5, 6^2, 7, 8^2, 9^3, 10, 11^2, 12, 15^2, 16^2, 17; **7:**1^2, 2, 3^2, 4^2, 5^3, 6^3, 7^3, 8^3, 9, 13, 14^2, 15, 17^2; **8:**3, 4^2, 5^2, 7^2, 8, 9^2, 10^2, 11^2, 12^6, 13^2; **9:**1, 3^3, 4^2, 5^2, 7, 9^3, 11, 13, 15, 16, 17^3, 18^3, 19, 20^4, 21; **10:**3^2, 7, 8; **11:**1, 4, 6, 8, 10, 11, 13^2, 15^3, 19^3; **12:**1, 4^3, 6, 10^3, 11^2, 14^3, 16, 17^2; **13:**1^2, 2^2, 3^2, 8^3, 10, 11, 12, 13, 14^4, 15, 17^2, 18; **14:**2^3, 7^2, 8, 10^5, 11^2, 12, 14^2, 15^2, 17, 18^2, 19, 20^2; **15:**2^2, 3^4, 5, 6, 7^2, 8^2; **16:**1, 2, 3, 4, 5, 6, 9, 10, 11^3, 13^6, 14^3, 17, 18^2, 19^3, 21^3; **17:**1^2, 2^3, 4, 5^3, 6^2, 7^2, 8^4, 14^2, 18; **18:**3^3, 4^2, 9^2, 10, 11, 12^4, 13^5, 18, 21^2, 22^3, 23^2, 24^3; **19:**1, 2, 6^2, 7, 8, 9^2, 10^3, 13, 14, 15^4, 16^2, 17, 18^3, 19, 20^3, 21^3; **20:**1, 4^4, 5, 6^2, 8, 9^2, 10, 12, 14^2, 15^2; **21:**2, 3, 4, 6^2, 8, 9^3, 10, 11^2, 12^2, 14^3, 15, 18^2, 19^2, 21^3, 23, 24, 26, 27; **22:**1^4, 2^7, 3^2, 5^2, 6^2, 7, 8, 9^2, 10^2, 14, 16, 17^2, 18^2, 19^2, 21.

OH (37)

Ex 32:31; Dt 5:29; 32:3; 33:7; Jdg 11:35; 2Sa 23:15; 1Ki 13:30; 2Ki 6:5, 15; 1Ch 4:10; 11:17; Job 6:8; 11:5; 19:23; 29:4; 31:35; 34:36; Ps 14:7; 53:6; 55:6; 119:5, 97; SS 1:15, 16; 4:1; Isa 17:12^2; 64:1, 9; Jer 4:19^2; 9:1, 2; Eze 21:15; Ob 1:5; Mal 1:10; Ro 11:33.

ON (4658)

For "ON" as a proper name see the Main Concordance.

Ge 1:11, 15, 17, 22, 28, 29, 30; **2:**2, 3, 5^2; **3:**14, 24; **4:**4, 5, 12, 14, 15, 26; **6:**1, 4, 5, 6, 12, 17^2; **7:**4, 6, 10, 11^2, 12, 13, 17, 18^2, 19, 21, 22, 23; **8:**4^2, 5, 17, 19, 20; **9:**7, 10, 16, 17; **10:**8; **12:**3, 8^4, 17, 20; **13:**4; **15:**11, 18; **17:**23, 26; **18:**5, 16, 18; **19:**2, 9, 24; **20:**1; **21:**8, 14^2; **22:**2, 4, 6^2, 8, 9^3, 12, 14, 17, 18; **23:**8; **24:**7, 15, 27, 30, 42, 45, 47, 48, 54, 56, 59; **25:**21; **26:**4, 7, 9, 22, 25, 31; **27:**12, 13, 15; **28:**5, 12^2, 13, 14, 18, 20; **29:**1; **30:**25, 26, 31, 33, 35, 37; **31:**17, 22, 34; **32:**1, 20, 21; **33:**3, 12, 14, 16; **34:**8, 15, 22, 30; **35:**14^2, 16, 19, 21; **36:**37; **37:**17, 22, 25, 27, 34; **38:**9, 13, 14, 19, 28, 30; **39:**5; **40:**10, 16, 17, 19; **41:**3, 5, 17, 22, 42, 45, 50; **42:**18, 26, 30, 38; **43:**6; **44:**3; **45:**7, 24; **46:**20, 34; **47:**31; **48:**2, 7, 13^2, 14^2, 17, 18; **49:**8, 26^2; **50:**23, 24; **Ex 1:**16; **2:**25; **3:**2, 12, 22; **4:**3^2, 9^2, 14, 20, 24; **7:**4, 15; **8:**3, 4, 5, 7, 12, 18, 21^2, 22; **9:**3^3, 9, 10, 11^2, 18, 19, 22^2, 23, 33; **10:**10, 15^2; **11:**1^2, 5; **12:**3, 7, 11, 12^2, 13, 15, 16^3, 17, 22^2, 23, 29, 34, 37, 42, 51; **13:**6, 8, 9^3, 11, 16^2, 17, 20, 21; **14:**15, 16, 22^3, 29^3, 30; **15:**9, 17, 19, 26^2; **16:**1, 5^2, 14^2, 22, 25, 26, 27, 29^2, 30; **17:**5, 9, 12^3, 14; **18:**27; **19:**1, 4, 11^2, 13, 16, 18; **20:**4, 10, 11, 24, 25, 26^2; **22:**8, 11, 30; **23:**12, 13, 25; **24:**6, 8, 12, 13, 15, 16^2, 17, 18^2; **25:**7, 12^2, 14, 19^2, 21, 25, 30, 32^2, 33^2, 34, 37, 40; **26:**5^2, 13, 26, 27^2, 30, 32^2, 34, 35^2; **27:**7, 8, 10, 11, 13, 14, 15; **28:**9, 10^2, 11, 12^2, 17, 26, 27, 29, 36^2, 37, 38^2, 41; **29:**5, 6, 7, 9^2, 10, 12, 13^2, 15, 16, 18, 19, 20^4, 21^3, 22, 25, 38; **30:**4, 7, 9^2, 10, 12, 32, 33; **31:**7, 14, 15, 17, 18; **32:**12, 14, 15, 16, 20; **33:**1, 3, 4, 16, 19^2, 21; **34:**1^2, 2^2, 3, 21, 28, 32; **35:**2, 3, 9, 21, 27; **36:**4, 12^2, 31, 32^2; **37:**3^2, 5, 8^2, 12, 18^2, 19^2, 20, 27; **38:**7, 10, 11, 12, 14, 15, 17, 24; **39:**7, 10, 19, 20, 30^2, 32; **40:**2, 4, 17, 22, 23, 24, 27, 29; **Lev 1:**4^2, 5, 7^2, 8^2, 9, 11, 12^2, 13, 15^2, 17^3; **2:**1^2, 2, 5, 6, 9, 12, 15; **3:**2^2, 4, 5^3, 8^2, 10, 11, 13^2, 15, 16; **4:**3, 4, 7, 9, 10, 12, 15, 18, 19, 24, 25, 26, 29, 30, 31, 33, 34, 35^2; **5:**11, 12^2; **6:**5, 9^2, 10^2, 11, 12^3, 13, 15^2, 20, 21, 27; **7:**2, 4, 5, 9, 15, 16^2, 18, 31, 35, 36, 38^2; **8:**7^3, 8, 9^2, 11, 12, 13^2, 14, 15, 16, 18, 19, 21, 22, 23^3, 24^4, 26^2, 28^2, 30^2; **9:**1, 9, 10, 12, 13, 14^2, 17, 18, 20^2, 24; **10:**7; **11:**2, 20, 21^2, 27^2, 29, 32, 34, 35, 37, 38^2, 41, 42^4, 44, 46; **12:**3; **13:**2, 3, 4, 5, 6, 14, 18, 24, 27, 29^2, 32, 34, 38, 39, 42^2, 43, 44, 51; **14:**9, 10, 14^3, 17^4, 18, 20, 23, 25^3, 28^4, 29, 31, 37, 39^2; **15:**4^2, 6^2, 8, 9, 14, 17, 20^2, 22, 23, 24, 26^2, 29; **16:**2, 4^3, 13, 14, 15, 18, 19, 21^2, 22, 23, 24, 25, 29, 30, 32; **17:**11; **19:**5, 6^2, 7, 28; **20:**9, 11, 12, 13, 16, 27; **21:**3, 10; **22:**19, 20, 22, 25, 27, 28, 29; **23:**5, 6, 7, 8, 11^2, 12, 21, 24, 28, 29, 30, 34, 36, 40; **24:**4, 6, 8, 14; **25:**1, 9^2, 15^2, 50; **26:**9, 30, 46; **27:**23, 34; **Nu 1:**1, 18, 53; **2:**3, 10, 18, 25; **3:**1, 23, 29, 35, 38; **4:**7^2, 10, 12, 14; **5:**15^3, 23, 26; **6:**5, 7^2, 9, 10, 27; **7:**9, 12, 18, 24, 30, 36, 42, 48, 54, 60, 66, 72, 78, 89; **8:**3, 7, 10, 12, 19; **9:**3, 5, 6^2, 10, 11, 13, 15; **10:**5, 6, 9, 11; **11:**9, 11^2, 12, 17^2, 21, 25^3, 26, 29; **12:**3, 15; **13:**17, 20, 23; **14:**16, 23; **15:**31, 32, 38^2; **16:**1; **17:**2, 3; **18:**5, 17, 22; **19:**4, 12^3, 13^2, 15, 19^2, 20; **20:**16, 19, 26, 28^2; **21:**4, 8, 9, 10, 12, 16; **22:**6, 11, 12, 17, 22, 23, 24, 26, 36; **23:**2, 4, 14^2, 30; **26:**3, 53, 63; **27:**18, 23; **28:**9, 11, 16, 17, 18, 25, 26; **29:**1, 7, 12, 17, 20, 23, 26, 29, 32, 35; **30:**9, 14; **31:**2, 3, 12, 19, 24; **32:**11, 19^2, 32; **33:**3, 4, 6, 37, 38, 39, 44, 48, 49, 50; **34:**3, 4, 6, 9, 11, 12, 15; **35:**1, 5^4, 14, 23, 30^2, 32, 33; **36:**11, 13; **Dt 1:**3, 33, 36, 41; **2:**5, 8, 25, 27, 28, 36, 37; **3:**10, 24; **4:**13, 17, 32, 36, 39, 48; **5:**4, 8, 14, 21, 22^2; **6:**7, 8^2, 9^2, 18, 23; **7:**6, 7, 15^2, 16, 25; **8:**1, 3^2; **9:**4, 5, 9^2, 10^3; **10:**1, 2^2, 3, 4^3, 7, 10, 11, 15; **11:**4, 12, 14, 18^2, 20^2, 25, 29^2; **12:**2^2, 16, 24, 27; **13:**17^2; **14:**2; **15:**23; **16:**4, 6, 8; **17:**6^2, 18; **18:**1, 16; **19:**8; **21:**22, 23^2; **22:**4, 6^3, 8, 12; **23:**14^2, 16; **24:**5, 15; **25:**16, 7, 18; **26:**15; **27:**3, 4, 6, 8, 11, 12, 13, 18; **28:**1, 8^2, 9, 10, 12, 20, 25, 48, 53, 54, 55, 57, 59, 61, 68; **29:**5, 16, 19^2, 22, 23, 27; **30:**3, 7; **31:**17^2, 18, 20, 21, 23; **32:**2^2, 11, 13, 36, 41, 43, 48, 50^2; **33:**1, 10, 16^2, 19^2, 26^2; **34:**4, 9; **Jos 1:**4, 8; **2:**6, 7, 8, 9, 11, 16, 17, 19^3; **3:**6, 17^2; **4:**5, 18, 19^2, 22; **5:**4, 7, 10^2; **6:**4, 5, 14, 15^2, 18; **7:**5, 6, 7, 10, 25^2; **8:**4, 5, 8, 19, 22, 29, 30, 31^2, 32, 33; **9:**5, 12, 17, 20; **10:**11^2, 12, 13, 24^2, 26^2, 29, 31, 32, 34; **11:**2, 4, 8, 13; **12:**2, 7; **13:**3^2, 9, 16, 17, 19, 21; **14:**9^2; **15:**3; **16:**2, 3, 6^2; **17:**8, 10^4; **18:**5^2, 7, 8, 9, 12, 13, 14, 15, 18, 20^2; **19:**12, 14, 26, 27, 34^3; **20:**8^2; **21:**44; **22:**4, 7, 11^2, 17, 23, 27; **23:**13, 15; **24:**9, 13, 17, 20, 25; **Jdg 1:**8; **2:**18; **3:**18; **4:**15, 17, 23; **5:**1, 10^2, 17, 18, 21; **6:**4, 20, 26, 28, 37^2; **7:**6, 12, 22; **8:**26, 34; **9:**5, 7, 18, 24^2, 25, 46, 49, 51, 52, 53, 57; **10:**8; **11:**4, 16, 18; **12:**14; **13:**5, 19; **14:**15, 16, 17, 18; **15:**1, 7, 14; **16:**13, 17, 19, 22, 27, 28, 29^3, 30; **17:**8; **18:**9, 12, 13, 27; **19:**5, 8, 9, 12, 14, 18, 22, 27^2, 28; **20:**21, 30, 31^2, 33, 34, 35, 36, 39, 41, 43, 46, 48; **Ru 1:**7, 19; **2:**1; **3:**2, 3, 15; **4:**5; **1Sa 1:**7, 9, 11, 12, 14; **2:**29, 34; **4:**2, 12, 13; **5:**3^2, 4^3, 5; **6:**6, 8^2, 9, 11, 12, 15^2, 18; **7:**1, 6, 9, 16; **9:**4, 14, 24, 25, 26^2, 27; **10:**1, 2, 3, 25; **11:**2^2, 7; **12:**11; **13:**5, 22; **14:**1, 2, 4, 22, 23, 24, 25, 32^2, 47^2; **15:**12, 18^2, 19, 20; **16:**1, 13; **17:**5, 6^2, 11, 32, 35, 38^2, 39, 49^2; **18:**9^2, 25; **19:**2, 13; **20:**21, 31, 34; **21:**3, 4, 5, 6, 13, 15; **22:**6; **23:**5, 10, 17, 19, 26^2; **24:**9; **25:**13^3, 18, 19, 24, 31, 39, 42; **26:**1, 3, 9, 11, 13, 23, 25; **27:**6, 11; **28:**8, 15, 20, 22, 23; **30:**1, 2, 17; **31:**1, 4, 5, 8; **2Sa 1:**2^2, 6^2, 10^2, 16, 19, 25; **2:**13^2, 21, 23, 24, 25; **3:**8, 9, 12, 29, 31, 37; **4:**7, 11; **5:**2, 8; **6:**2, 3^2, 4; **7:**23; **8:**2, 10; **10:**7; **11:**2, 13, 21; **12:**16, 18, 20, 30; **13:**2, 19^2, 30, 31, 34^2; **14:**7, 9^2, 14, 30^2, 31; **15:**12, 22^2, 23, 32; **16:**2, 6, 22; **17:**11, 12^2, 14; **18:**9, 18; **19:**2, 13, 19, 23, 26, 31, 43; **20:**10^2, 13; **21:**1, 9, 10^2, 12, 20^2; **22:**11, 17, 28, 34; **23:**2, 4, 20; **24:**5, 6, 7, 15, 18^2, 21, 24, 25; **1Ki 1:**4, 13, 17, 20^2, 24, 27, 30, 33, 35, 38, 41, 44, 46, 47, 48; **2:**4, 5, 8, 12, 19, 24, 33^2, 34, 37, 42; **3:**3, 4, 6, 19; **4:**20, 24, 29; **5:**1, 4, 5; **6:**8, 29, 32, 35; **7:**3, 9, 16, 17, 18, 19, 20, 22^2, 25^2, 29^2, 30^2, 31, 34, 36^2, 38, 39^3, 41^2, 42, 48, 49^2; **8:**20, 23, 25, 27, 32, 36, 64, 66; **9:**5, 9, 16, 25, 26; **10:**2, 5, 9, 19, 20; **11:**7, 29; **12:**4^2, 9, 10, 11, 31, 32^2, 33^2; **13:**2^2, 3, 24^3, 28, 29, 32; **14:**10, 11, 23, 27; **16:**4, 11, 18, 24; **17:**14, 19, 21; **18:**1, 19, 20, 23^2, 24^2, 25, 26, 33^3, 45; **19:**11; **20:**11, 20, 21, 23, 25, 29^2, 30, 34; **21:**4, 8, 21, 24, 25, 27, 29; **22:**10, 17, 19^3, 25; **2Ki 1:**4, 6, 9, 13, 16; **2:**1, 6, 8, 13, 15, 16, 23^2, 24, 25; **3:**11, 21, 22, 25, 27; **4:**7, 10, 13, 20, 21, 24, 29, 31^2, 32, 33, 34, 35, 38; **5:**11, 18, 20; **6:**10^2, 11, 26, 30, 31; **7:**2, 17; **8:**29; **9:**3, 6, 10, 13, 15, 17, 25, 26^2, 27, 32, 36, 37; **10:**3, 6, 15, 30; **11:**5^2, 9^2, 12, 19; **12:**9, 11^2, 20; **13:**13, 16, 21; **15:**12, 19; **16:**4, 12, 13, 14, 15^2, 17; **17:**6, 10; **18:**11, 17, 19, 20, 21^3, 22, 23, 24, 26, 27; **19:**1, 10, 19, 23, 26; **20:**5, 8, 11; **21:**12; **22:**5, 16, 20; **23:**5^2, 8, 12, 13, 16^2, 20^2, 33; **24:**10; **25:**1, 6, 8, 17, 27; **1Ch 1:**10, 48; **2:**7^2; **5:**16; **6:**49^2; **9:**2, 18, 24, 32; **10:**1, 4, 5, 8; **11:**2, 6, 22; **12:**40; **13:**7, 10; **15:**15; **16:**8, 40; **17:**17, 21; **18:**10; **19:**8; **20:**2, 6^2; **21:**3, 14, 17, 18, 22, 24, 26^2, 28, 29; **22:**8, 9, 18; **23:**29, 31; **26:**16, 17^3; **27:**1, 24^2; **28:**5, 8, 21; **29:**7, 15, 23, 25; **2Ch 1:**6; **2:**4; **3:**1^2, 2, 7, 13, 15, 16; **4:**4^2, 6^2, 7^2, 8^2, 10, 12^2, 13, 19; **5:**12; **6:**10, 13, 14, 16, 18, 23, 27; **7:**3, 9, 10, 22; **8:**12, 17; **9:**1, 4, 8, 18, 19; **10:**4^2, 9, 10, 11; **11:**16; **12:**7, 10, 14; **13:**4, 11^2, 17, 18^2; **14:**7, 11; **15:**15; **16:**7^2, 8, 9, 14; **17:**10; **18:**9, 16, 18^3, 24; **19:**3, 10; **20:**1, 24, 26, 30, 33; **21:**11; **22:**6, 8; **23:**4^2, 6, 8^2, 11, 15, 20; **24:**24, 27; **26:**15^2, 16, 19, 20; **27:**3, 5; **28:**4, 5, 11, 13, 15; **29:**4, 6, 8, 17^2, 21, 22^3, 23, 24, 27; **30:**12, 15, 19; **31:**3, 19; **32:**2, 5, 10, 12, 18, 22, 23, 25^2, 33; **33:**15, 16; **34:**5, 10, 21, 24, 25, 28^2; **35:**1, 3, 16, 20, 22; **36:**3, 15^2; **Ezr 2:**68; **3:**2, 3^2, 6, 9; **4:**4, 24; **5:**8, 15; **6:**2, 7^2, 11, 15, 19, 22; **7:**6, 9^3, 17, 24, 28; **8:**18, 22^2, 31^2, 33; **9:**5; **10:**9, 16; **Ne 2:**12, 14; **3:**26; **4:**3, 4, 16; **5:**4, 15, 16, 18; **6:**2, 3, 15; **7:**3; **8:**2, 4^3, 13, 16, 18; **9:**1^2, 4, 6, 11, 12, 13, 19^2, 29; **10:**31^3, 33^2, 34; **11:**3, 12, 20, 21; **12:**31^2, 37^2, 38, 43; **13:**1, 2, 6, 15^4, 16, 19^2, 21^3, 25; **Est 1:**6^2, 10; **2:**17, 23; **3:**7, 12, 13, 15; **4:**1, 4; **5:**1^3, 14; **6:**4, 8, 9, 11; **7:**2, 8, 9, 10; **8:**6, 7, 9, 13^2, 14; **9:**1^2, 10, 13, 15^2, 16, 17^2, 18^2, 25; **Job 1:**8, 12, 17, 19; **2:**1, 3, 9, 12, 13; **3:**10; **4:**13, 15^2; **5:**10, 11; **6:**2, 22, 30; **7:**1, 4; **8:**6, 9, 14, 15; **9:**8, 26; **10:**3; **12:**18, 21; **13:**7, 11, 27^2; **14:**3; **15:**8, 10; **16:**3, 9, 13, 19, 21, 22; **17:**2, 10; **18:**10, 11; **19:**10, 21, 23, 24; **20:**4, 9, 28; **21:**3, 7; **22:**8, 28^2; **24:**18, 20, 21, 23; **26:**10; **28:**8; **29:**14, 19, 22; **30:**12, 21, 24; **31:**2, 28, 36^2; **33:**2, 11, 15, 19, 23, 30; **34:**21, 33; **36:**25, 28; **37:**6; **38:**6, 35; **39:**11, 14, 27, 28, 30; **40:**15; **41:**5, 8, 33, 34; **Ps 1:**2; **2:**6; **3:**3, 6, 7, 8; **4:**4; **7:**3, 7, 16^2; **9:**4; **11:**4, 6; **13:**3; **14:**2, 4; **15:**1, 3^2; **16:**4; **17:**6; **18:**10, 16, 33, 42; **21:**3, 5, 8; **25:**15; **26:**12; **31:**11, 13, 16, 19; **33:**2, 14, 18^2; **34:**1, 15; **35:**11, 13, 17; **36:**4, 8; **39:**1; **40:**2; **41:**3, 4, 10; **44:**16; **46:**8; **47:**8; **48:**9; **49:**9, 14; **50:**10, 16; **51:**1, 19; **53:**2, 4; **54:**5, 7; **55:**10, 22; **56:**T, 7, 8; **57:**1^2; **58:**2; **59:**4; **62:**7, 9, 10; **63:**6; **66:**6, 11, 17; **67:**2; **68:**4, 14, 18, 21; **69:**9, 11, 24; **71:**6; **72:**6, 13, 16; **73:**18; **74:**3; **77:**12; **78:**9, 27^2, 32; **79:**6^3; **80:**13, 17, 18; **81:**3; **83:**10; **84:**5, 9; **86:**3, 16; **87:**1; **89:**19; **90:**13; **93:**4; **94:**15, 20; **95:**11; **97:**3, 11; **99:**6^2; **101:**6; **102:**7, 13, 19, 24; **103:**13^2; **104:**3^2, 5; **105:**1, 16, 38; **106:**43; **107:**23^2, 40; **109:**12, 17; **110:**3, 5; **112:**8; **113:**5, 6; **116:**2, 4, 13, 17; **118:**7, 11; **119:**15, 19, 23, 27, 30, 48, 78, 97, 99, 112, 132, 148, 158; **120:**1; **123:**3^2; **124:**1, 2; **129:**6; **132:**11, 12, 18; **133:**2^3, 3; **135:**6, 14; **137:**2, 7; **138:**6; **139:**4, 9^2; **140:**3; **141:**5, 8; **143:**5, 10; **144:**7, 9; **145:**5, 9, 18^2; **146:**4; **147:**7, 8; **148:**11; **149:**5, 7^2; **Pr 1:**15; **3:**3, 5, 23, 33; **4:**9, 13, 14, 15^2; **5:**10; **6:**11, 28; **7:**3^2, 19; **8:**2, 16, 21, 27; **9:**14, 15; **10:**13; **11:**8, 17, 29, 31; **14:**7; **15:**3, 14; **16:**26, 30; **17:**11; **19:**12, 15; **20:**8; **21:**9; **22:**18; **23:**10, 19, 20, 34^2; **24:**26, 34; **25:**19, 20^2, 22, 24; **26:**14^2, 27; **27:**15; **30:**19^2, 24; **31:**3^2, 26; **Ecc 1:**6, 13; **3:**10; **4:**1; **5:**2, 11, 20; **6:**1; **7:**20; **8:**14, 16, 17; **9:**1; **10:**7^2, 20; **SS 2:**12, 14, 17; **3:**1, 11; **4:**4, 16; **5:**3, 5, 15; **6:**13^3; **8:**5, 6, 9, 14; **Isa 1:**4, 24; **3:**9, 16, 17, 26; **5:**1, 6; **6:**1; **7:**3, 17^3, 19; **8:**1, 8, 18, 19; **9:**2, 6, 7^2, 8, 11, 20^3, 21^2; **10:**3, 20^2; **11:**2, 9, 14^2; **12:**4; **13:**2, 4, 18^2; **14:**1, 3, 13^2, 25; **15:**3, 5; **16:**5; **17:**6^2, 11^2, 13; **18:**3^2, 4, 6; **19:**1, 8, 24; **20:**6^2; **21:**7^2, 8, 9, 10; **22:**1, 12^2, 16, 22, 24, 25; **23:**3, 9, 17; **24:**13, 21, 23; **25:**6, 7, 10; **26:**5, 10; **27:**4, 8, 11, 13; **28:**1, 4, 10^2, 13^2, 20, 24, 28; **29:**1; **30:**6^2, 8^2, 12^2, 16^2, 17^2, 25, 29, 32; **31:**1, 4^2; **32:**15; **33:**4, 5, 8, 16; **34:**5; **35:**8^2, 9; **36:**2, 4, 5, 6^3, 7, 8, 9, 11, 12; **37:**1, 10, 20, 24, 27; **38:**8, 11; **40:**7, 9, 12, 15, 24, 31; **41:**3, 7, 18, 25^2; **42:**1, 4, 5, 25; **43:**18, 24; **44:**3^4, 5, 20; **45:**4, 9; **46:**6; **47:**1, 6, 7, 9, 12, 15; **48:**2, 6; **49:**9, 10, 13, 15, 16, 18, 22, 26; **50:**10; **51:**3, 5, 13; **52:**1, 2, 7; **53:**6; **54:**8, 10; **55:**2^2, 6, 7; **56:**7; **57:**7, 8, 17, 19; **58:**3, 4, 5, 13, 14^2; **59:**4, 13, 17^3, 21^2; **60:**4, 5, 7, 19; **61:**1, 3, 6; **62:**6^2; **63:**6; **64:**4, 7; **65:**1, 3, 7^2, 25; **66:**12^2, 20^2; **Jer 1:**14, 16; **2:**17, 20, 34, 35, 37; **3:**6, 12, 21, 23; **4:**8, 30; **5:**9, 29; **6:**11^2, 19, 23, 25^2, 26, 29; **7:**20^4, 29; **8:**2, 13^2; **9:**9, 22, 24; **10:**18, 25^3; **11:**8, 11, 16, 23; **12:**2, 5; **13:**13, 16, 27; **14:**6, 16; **15:**5, 6^2, 7, 8, 15, 17; **16:**4, 16, 17; **17:**1^2, 2, 5, 18, 21, 22, 24^2, 25^2, 27; **18:**8, 15; **19:**3, 9, 13, 15; **20:**10^2; **21:**13; **22:**2, 4^2, 17^3, 24, 30; **23:**2^2, 12, 19, 35; **25:**26, 29^2, 30^2, 31, 33; **26:**3, 15^3, 19; **27:**2, 5; **28:**11, 14; **29:**16; **30:**6, 18^2, 23; **31:**5, 6, 9, 12, 22, 29, 30, 33, 40; **32:**10, 29^2, 42; **33:**9, 17, 21, 22, 26; **35:**17^2; **36:**2, 3, 4, 6, 18, 28^2, 29, 30, 31, 32; **39:**2, 5, 17; **40:**4; **41:**17^2; **42:**10, 12, 17, 18^2; **44:**2^2, 7, 8, 11; **45:**1, 5; **46:**2, 4^2, 5, 9, 10, 25^5; **47:**5; **48:**5, 9, 10^2, 11, 18, 32, 35, 38, 47; **49:**2, 3, 5, 8, 29, 32; **50:**6, 15^2, 19^2, 38, 42; **51:**2, 3, 30, 32, 35, 50, 58, 60; **52:**4, 9, 12, 22, 23, 31; **La 1:**9, 10, 12^2, 13; **2:**4, 7, 10^3, 11, 22; **3:**28, 55, 65; **4:**5, 8; **Eze 1:**1, 2, 8, 10^2, 11, 15, 26, 28; **2:**1, 10; **4:**1, 4^2, 6, 9; **5:**8, 10, 11, 15; **6:**10, 13^2; **7:**4, 8, 9, 18; **8:**1, 18; **9:**4, 8, 10^2; **10:**3; **11:**9, 10, 11, 21; **12:**6, 7, 12; **13:**5, 18; **15:**2, 3, 4; **16:**4, 5^2, 9, 10, 11, 12^3, 14, 15, 16, 18, 41, 43, 61; **17:**16, 19, 22, 23; **18:**2, 13; **19:**9, 14; **20:**1, 5, 6, 7, 8^2, 13, 17, 21, 40; **21:**14, 29; **22:**3, 9, 21, 30, 31^2; **23:**10, 14, 15, 18, 23, 24, 27, 37, 39, 40, 41^2, 42^2, 45; **24:**1, 3^2, 7^2, 8, 10, 11, 17, 23^2, 25, 26; **25:**11, 12, 14, 17^2; **26:**1, 6, 8, 16, 17^2, 18; **27:**3, 4, 9, 10, 11, 27^2, 29, 30, 31, 33; **28:**2, 13, 14, 17, 18, 22, 23, 26; **29:**1, 5, 7, 17, 21; **30:**9^2, 14, 15, 19, 20; **31:**1, 3, 10, 12, 13, 14, 15; **32:**1, 4^4, 5, 10, 17, 27; **33:**4, 5, 21, 26; **34:**6, 12, 13, 14, 18, 19; **35:**8; **36:**9, 11, 18, 25, 33; **37:**2, 8, 10, 16^2, 20, 22; **38:**10, 15, 20, 21, 22^3; **39:**4, 6^2, 11, 14, 17, 25, 29; **40:**1^2, 2^2, 10^2, 19^2, 21, 23, 26^2, 27, 32, 34, 37, 39^2, 40, 41^3, 42, 48^2, 49; **41:**1, 2, 3, 6^2, 11^2, 12, 14, 15, 17, 19^2, 20, 25^3, 26^2; **42:**1, 4, 5, 6^2, 8^2, 9, 10, 11^2, 12, 14, 20; **43:**12, 14, 20^2, 22, 24, 27^2; **44:**18, 19, 27, 30; **45:**18, 19^3, 20, 21, 22, 25; **46:**1^3, 3, 4, 6, 12; **47:**7, 12, 15, 16^2, 18, 19, 20; **48:**10^4, 17^4, 18^3, 20, 21, 30, 31, 32, 33, 34, 35; **Da 2:**10, 28, 34, 35, 48; **3:**1, 27; **4:**12, 29, 31; **5:**5, 27; **6:**10, 23, 27; **7:**1, 4, 5, 6, 20, 23; **8:**7, 10; **9:**11, 17, 27^2; **10:**4^2, 10; **11:**10, 27; **12:**5^2; **Hos 1:**10; **2:**3, 8; **4:**8, 13^2; **5:**1, 8, 9, 10, 11; **6:**2, 3, 9; **7:**5, 7; **9:**5^2, 8, 10; **10:**7, 8, 11, 12, 13^2, 14; **12:**1, 11; **13:**12; **Joel 1:**13; **2:**1, 18, 28, 29, 30, 32^2; **3:**4, 7, 12; **Am 1:**14^2; **2:**7, 8, 16; **3:**5, 9, 12^2, 14; **4:**1, 7; **5:**9, 11, 15, 19, 24; **6:**1, 4^3, 5^2, 12; **9:**1, 3, 6, 8; **Ob 1:**3, 11, 12, 13, 16, 17, 18, 21; **Jnh 1:**4, 6, 7; **3:**4, 5, 8; **4:**8; **Mic 1:**11; **2:**1; **5:**1, 7; **6:**15; **7:**16, 17, 19, 20; **Na 1:**2, 15; **2:**3^2, 5, 13; **3:**8, 17, 18; **Hab 1:**9, 11, 13, 17; **2:**1, 2, 6, 9, 15; **3:**1, 10, 16, 17, 19^2; **Zep 1:**5, 8, 9^2, 10, 12, 14, 17, 18; **2:**2, 3, 11, 14; **3:**8, 9, 11^2, 16; **Hag 1:**1, 6, 11^4, 14, 15; **2:**1, 10, 15^2, 18, 19, 20, 23; **Zec 1:**7; **3:**4, 5^2, 9^2; **4:**2, 3^2, 11; **5:**3^2; **6:**11, 13^2; **7:**1; **9:**1, 2, 4, 9^2, 16; **10:**6; **11:**6, 11; **12:**3, 4, 6, 8, 9, 10^2, 11; **13:**1, 2, 4^2, 6, 9; **14:**4^2, 6, 8, 9, 12, 13, 18^2, 20^2, 21; **Mal 1:**7, 10; **2:**3, 6; **4:**1, 3; **Mt 2:**9, 11; **3:**16; **4:**4^2, 5, 16, 17, 21; **5:**1, 14, 15, 25, 39, 45^2; **6:**2, 5, 7, 10, 17, 19; **7:**22, 24, 25, 26; **8:**15, 24; **9:**2, 6, 9, 12, 16, 18, 27^2, 36; **10:**13, 15, 17, 18; **11:**1, 6, 22, 24; **12:**1, 2, 5, 9, 10, 11, 12, 18, 36; **13:**2, 5, 8, 20, 23, 48, 53; **14:**6, 8, 11, 13, 14, 19, 22, 23, 25, 26, 28, 29; **15:**22, 29, 32, 35; **16:**6, 11, 18, 19^2, 21^2; **17:**15, 23; **18:**10, 12, 18^2, 19, 26, 27, 33^2; **19:**13, 15^2, 28^2; **20:**8, 19, 30, 31, 34; **21:**1, 5^2, 7^2, 8^2, 18, 19, 33, 44^2; **22:**26, 40, 46; **23:**4, 5, 9, 18, 20, 22, 27^2, 28^2, 35; **24:**2, 3, 17, 20, 30, 42, 50; **25:**10, 14, 15, 27, 31, 33^2, 34, 41; **26:**7, 12, 16, 17, 29, 31, 33, 53, 64, 74; **27:**9, 19, 25^2, 28, 29, 30^2, 31, 38^2, 44, 48, 66; **28:**1, 2, 11, 18; **Mk 1:**10, 31, 40; **2:**4, 10, 17, 20, 21, 24; **3:**2, 4, 13; **4:**1, 5, 8, 11, 16, 20, 21, 26, 38; **5:**4, 6,

11, 19, 23; 6:5, 21, 25, 28, 29, 33, 34, 37, 39, 45, 46, 47, 48, 49, 55; 7:8, 20, 30, 32; 8:3, 6, 23^2, 25, 27^2; 9:22, 33, 34; 10:16, 17^2, 32, 34, 47, 48, 49; 11:7, 8, 15; 12:1, 4, 34, 44; 13:2, 3, 9^2, 15, 23, 33; 14:3, 8, 12, 62, 71; 15:17^2, 19^3, 20, 21, 27^2, 32, 36; 16:2^2, 5, 9, 18; Lk 1:8, 17, 48, 59, 76, 79; 2:14^2, 21, 44; 3:22; 4:4, 9, 16, 18, 20, 29, 30, 31, 39, 40, 44; 5:10, 11, 18, 19^2, 24, 25, 33, 36; 6:2, 6, 7, 9, 17, 29, 48, 49; 7:23, 38, 46^2; 8:5, 6, 8, 13, 14, 15, 16, 23, 32, 42; 9:7, 22, 52; 10:4, 6, 12, 19, 25, 31, 32, 33, 34^2, 37, 38; 11:6, 33, 36; 12:1^2, 15, 29, 37, 46, 49, 51, 52, 58; 13:4, 6, 7, 10, 13, 14^3, 15, 16, 32; 14:3, 5, 19; 15:5, 22^3, 26; 16:24; 17:8, 11, 13, 30, 31^2, 34; 18:8, 9, 13, 32, 33, 38, 39; 19:11, 23, 28, 35^2, 36, 42, 43, 44, 48; 20:9, 18^2, 20, 24; 21:4, 6, 12^2, 24, 25, 26, 34, 35, 36, 37; 22:7, 21, 29^2, 30, 40, 53, 69; 23:6, 26^2, 30, 33^2, 56; 24:1, 7, 32, 35, 46, 49; Jn 1:28, 32, 33, 51; 2:1; 3:26, 36; 4:20, 21, 51; 5:9, 16, 45; 6:2, 3, 19, 22, 25, 27, 34, 57, 58, 60, 65; 7:17, 18, 22, 23^2, 28, 30, 37, 40, 44, 49; 8:6, 7, 8, 14, 15, 28, 42; 9:6^2, 11, 14, 15; 10:4; 11:2, 11, 17, 48, 51, 53; 12:3, 11, 12, 15, 31; 13:12; 14:7, 11, 20, 30; 16:13, 26; 17:4; 18:1, 16, 37; 19:2, 12, 13, 18, 27, 29, 31, 37; 20:1, 17, 19, 22; 21:4, 6, 9; Ac 1:4, 8; 2:3, 17, 18, 19, 21, 24, 30^2; 3:11, 24, 25; 4:23; 5:15^2, 22, 24, 30; 6:2, 6; 7:12, 13, 38^2, 60; 8:1, 17, 18, 19, 27, 28, 39; 9:3, 11, 12, 14, 17^2, 21, 24, 27, 40; 10:9^2, 39, 40, 44, 45; 11:15^2; 12:7, 8, 12, 16, 20, 21^2; 13:3, 4, 14^2, 42, 44; 14:10, 27; 15:3, 10, 21; 16:3, 11, 13; 17:2, 10, 32; 18:6^2, 9, 12, 17, 18, 27; 19:5, 6^2, 10, 16; 20:5, 7^2, 9^2, 10, 13^2, 14, 15, 31; 21:2, 3, 4, 5^2, 40; 22:16; 23:2, 6, 15, 20, 32; 24:21, 25; 25:9, 20, 27; 26:6, 10, 12, 13, 16; 27:6, 12, 17, 19, 26, 27, 37, 44^2; 28:1, 3^2, 8, 9, 13, 23; Ro 2:1, 2, 3, 15, 16, 17; 3:5, 13, 27^3; 6:1; 7:19; 8:5^2; 9:7, 15^2, 16^2, 18, 28; 10:2, 12, 13, 14; 11:28^2, 32; 12:18, 20^2; 13:2, 4, 12; 14:1, 3, 10, 13; 15:3, 8, 15, 20, 24, 25, 28; 1Co 1:2, 8; 2:5^2; 3:10, 12; 4:9; 5:3, 5; 7:29; 8:5; 9:3, 12, 13; 10:6, 11; 11:2, 10, 23^2, 29; 12:22; 15:1, 3, 4; 16:2, 6, 8, 10, 11, 13, 22; 2Co 1:9^2, 10, 11, 16^2, 22; 2:6, 13, 17; 3:2, 3^2, 7; 4:2, 8, 18^2; 5:16, 20; 6:9; 7:5, 12; 8:3, 6, 17; 9:11; 10:4, 7; 11:12, 26; 12:1^2, 9; 13:2; Gal 2:4, 7; 3:10, 12^2, 13, 18^2; 4:11; 5:7, 15; 6:17; Eph 1:8, 10; 2:20; 3:15; 4:8, 17, 24; 5:6, 14, 18; 6:3, 6, 11, 13, 18^2; Php 1:6, 22, 26, 29^2; 2:8, 10, 16, 17, 27^3; 3:5, 12, 14, 15, 19; Col 1:7, 16, 20^2; 2:8^2, 22; 3:1, 2^2, 10, 14, 22; 1Th 2:4, 5; 4:12; 5:3^2, 8, 21; 2Th 1:10; 2:15; 3:8; 1Ti 1:14, 16, 19; 3:1, 16; 4:12, 14; 5:9, 11, 12, 22; 6:2; 2Ti 1:6, 17, 18; 2:7, 22; 4:8, 15; Tit 1:2; 3:6, 13; Phm 1:9; Heb 3:1, 6, 11; 4:3, 4; 5:7, 13; 6:1, 2, 7, 20; 7:11, 16^2; 8:4, 5, 6, 10; 9:6, 13; 10:16, 24, 26, 28; 11:12, 13, 21, 29; 12:2, 11, 25; 13:1; Jas 1:26; 2:3, 21; 3:5, 6^2; 4:3, 11, 13; 5:5, 17; 1Pe 1:13, 17; 2:12, 24; 3:12; 4:4, 14; 5:7; 2Pe 1:18; 2:1, 5, 21^2; 3:4, 17; 1Jn 2:12; 3:1, 6, 9, 17; 4:16, 17; 3Jn 1:6; Jude 1:6; Rev 1:9, 10, 11, 17; 2:17, 22, 24, 25; 3:10, 11, 12^2, 18, 21^2; 4:2, 4^2, 9, 10; 5:1^2, 3, 7, 10, 13^3; 6:2, 16^2; 7:1^3, 3, 10, 11, 15; 8:3, 5, 10^2; 9:4, 7; 10:2^2, 5^2, 8^2; 11:2, 9, 10, 11, 12, 16^2; 12:1, 3; 13:1^3, 10, 12, 14, 16^2; 14:1^2, 6, 9^2, 12, 13, 14^2, 15, 16, 19; 16:1, 2^2, 3, 4, 8, 10, 12, 14, 18, 21; 17:1, 3, 5, 9; 18:19^2, 24; 19:2, 4, 12^2, 14, 16^2, 19, 20, 21^2; 20:4^2, 8, 11; 21:5, 12, 13^4, 14, 23, 25; 22:2, 4.

OUR (1200)

Ge 1:26^2; 5:29; 19:9, 31, 32^3, 34^2; 23:6; 24:60; 29:26; 31:1^2, 14, 16^2, 32; 33:12; 34:9, 14, 15, 16, 17, 21, 22, 23, 31; 37:26, 27^3; 41:12; 42:9, 12, 13, 21, 32; 43:4, 7, 8, 18^2, 21, 22^2, 28; 44:8, 16, 25, 26^2, 31; 46:34^2; 47:3, 15, 18^6, 19^3, 25^2; Ex 1:10; 3:18; 5:3, 8; 8:10, 26, 27; 10:9^3, 25, 26^2; 12:27; 17:3, 9; 34:9^2; Lev 25:20; Nu 10:31; 11:6; 13:33; 14:3; 20:3, 4, 15^2, 16, 19; 21:2; 27:3, 4^2; 31:49; 32:5, 16^2, 17, 18, 19, 25, 26^2, 27; 36:2, 3, 4; Dt 1:6, 19, 20, 25, 28, 41; 2:1, 8, 29, 33, 36, 37; 3:3^2; 4:7; 5:2, 3, 24, 25, 27^2; 6:4, 20, 22, 23, 24, 25^2; 18:16; 21:7^2; 26:3, 7^3, 15; 29:15, 18, 29^2; 31:17; 32:3, 27, 31^2; Jos 2:11, 14, 19, 24; 5:13; 7:9; 9:11^2, 13, 19, 24; 17:4; 18:6; 21:2; 22:19, 23, 27, 28^2, 29; 24:17^4, 18, 24; Jdg 6:13; 7:18; 9:3, 8, 10, 12, 14; 10:10; 11:2, 6, 8, 10, 12, 19, 24; 13:23; 14:3; 16:23^3, 24^5; 18:5, 19; 19:18, 19; 20:23, 28; 21:7, 18; Ru 2:20^2; 4:3; 1Sa 2:2; 4:3; 5:7, 10, 11; 7:8; 8:20; 9:7, 12; 12:10, 19; 14:6, 10^2; 16:16; 17:9, 47; 20:29; 24:15; 25:14, 16, 17; 29:4; 2Sa 7:22; 10:12^2; 15:15; 18:12; 19:9, 41, 43; 22:32; 1Ki 1:2, 11, 43, 47; 8:21, 40, 53, 57^2, 58^2, 59, 61, 65; 12:10; 18:5; 20:31^2; 2Ki 2:19; 4:9; 18:22; 19:19; 22:13; 1Ch 12:17, 19; 13:2^2, 3; 15:13; 16:14, 35; 17:20; 19:13^2; 28:2, 8; 29:10, 13, 15^2, 16, 18; 2Ch 2:4, 5; 6:31; 10:10; 13:10, 11, 12; 14:7, 11^2; 19:7; 20:6, 7, 9, 12^2; 28:13^2; 29:6^2, 9^3; 32:8^2, 11; 34:21; Ezr 4:3; 5:12; 7:27; 8:17, 18, 21^3, 22, 23^2, 25, 30, 31, 33; 9:6^3, 7^5, 8^4, 9^3, 10, 13^4, 15; 10:2, 3^2, 14^3; Ne 4:4, 9, 11, 15, 20, 23; 5:2, 3^3, 4, 5^6, 8, 9^2; 6:1, 16^2; 8:10; 9:9, 16, 32^4, 34^4, 36, 37^3, 38^3; 10:29, 30^2, 32, 33, 34^3, 35, 36^5, 37^6, 38, 39; 13:2, 4, 18, 27; Job 8:9; 15:10; 22:20; 28:22; 31:15; 36:26; 37:5, 19^2, 23; Ps 8:1, 9; 12:4^3; 18:31; 20:5^2, 7; 22:4; 33:20^2, 21, 22; 35:21; 40:3; 44:1^2, 2^2, 5^2, 7^2, 8, 9, 10, 13, 18^2, 20^2, 24, 25; 46:1, 7, 11; 47:3, 4, 6; 48:1, 8, 14^2; 50:3; 59:11; 60:10, 12; 62:8; 65:1, 3, 5; 66:8, 9^2, 11, 12; 67:6; 68:19^2, 20; 77:13; 78:3, 5; 79:4, 9^2, 10, 12; 80:6^2; 81:1, 3; 84:9; 85:4, 9, 12; 89:17, 18^2; 90:1, 8^2, 9^2, 10, 12, 14, 17^3; 92:13; 94:23; 95:1, 6, 7; 98:3; 99:5, 8, 9^2; 103:10^2, 12; 105:7; 106:6, 7, 47; 108:11, 13; 113:5; 115:3; 116:5; 118:23; 122:2, 9; 123:2^2; 124:1, 2, 8; 126:2^2, 4; 135:2, 5; 136:23, 24; 137:2, 3^2; 141:7; 144:12^2, 13^3, 14^2; 147:1, 5, 7; Pr 1:13; Ecc 1:10; SS 1:16, 17^2; 2:9, 12, 15; 7:13; 8:8; Isa 1:10; 3:6; 4:1^3; 25:9; 26:8, 13; 28:15^2; 33:2^2, 20, 21, 22^3; 35:2; 36:7; 37:20; 38:20; 40:3, 8; 42:17; 47:4; 52:10; 53:1, 4^2, 5^2; 55:7; 56:12; 59:10, 12^4, 13^3; 61:2, 6; 63:16^3, 17, 18; 64:6^2, 7, 8, 9, 11^2; Jer 3:22, 23, 24^2, 25^6; 4:10; 5:19, 24; 6:24; 8:14; 9:18^2, 19^3, 21^2; 11:21; 14:7^2, 20^2, 22^2; 16:10, 19; 17:12; 18:12, 18; 20:10; 21:13; 23:6, 36; 26:16; 31:6; 33:16; 35:6, 8^3, 10; 37:3; 42:2, 6^2, 20; 43:2; 44:17^3, 19; 46:16^2; 50:28; 51:10, 34, 35^2, 51; La 3:40, 41^2, 46; 4:17^2, 18^4, 19, 20; 5:1, 2^2, 3, 4, 5, 7, 9^2, 10, 15^2, 16, 17^2, 21; Eze 11:15; 33:10, 21, 24; 36:2; 37:11^2; 40:1; Da 1:13; 9:6^3, 7, 8^3, 9, 10, 12, 13^2, 14, 15, 16^2, 17; Hos 6:1; 7:5; 8:2; 14:2^2, 3^2; Joel 1:16^2; Am 6:13; Mic 2:4; 4:5, 11; 5:5^2, 6^2; 7:17, 19^2, 20; Hab 3:2^2; Zec 1:6; 9:7; 13:9; Mal 2:10; Mt 3:9; 6:9, 11, 12^2; 8:17^2; 20:33; 21:42; 23:30; 25:8; 27:25; Mk 11:10; 12:11, 29; Lk 1:55, 71, 72, 73, 74, 75, 78, 79; 3:8; 7:5^2; 10:11; 11:3, 4; 13:26; 17:5, 10; 19:14; 22:49; 23:2, 41; 24:20, 22, 24, 32; Jn 3:11; 4:12, 20; 6:31; 7:35, 51; 8:39, 53; 9:20; 11:11, 48^2; 12:38; 14:23; Ac 1:17; 2:11, 39; 3:12, 13; 4:25; 5:30; 6:4; 7:2, 11, 12, 15, 17, 19^2, 38, 39, 44, 45; 10:28; 13:17, 31, 32; 15:10, 11, 24, 25, 26; 16:20; 17:20, 28; 19:27, 37; 20:21; 21:3, 5^2, 7, 21, 25, 28^2; 22:3, 14; 24:14; 26:5, 6, 7; 27:7, 10^2; 28:17^2; Ro 1:4, 7; 3:5; 4:1, 12, 17, 24, 25^2; 5:1, 3, 5, 11, 21; 6:6, 23; 7:5, 25; 8:16, 18, 23^2, 26, 27, 39; 9:10; 10:16; 13:11; 15:6, 30; 16:1, 9, 18, 20, 23; 1Co 1:1, 2, 3, 6, 7, 8, 9, 10, 30; 2:7; 4:12; 5:4^2, 7; 6:11; 9:1; 10:1, 6; 12:24; 15:3, 14, 31, 57; 16:12; 2Co 1:1, 2, 3, 4, 5^2, 7^3, 8, 9, 10, 11, 12^3, 18, 22; 3:2^2, 3, 5; 4:3, 6, 10^2, 11, 17, 18; 5:2, 4, 9, 13^2; 6:3, 11, 12; 7:3, 4, 13, 14; 8:9, 13, 17, 19, 22, 23, 24; 9:3; 10:11^2, 13, 14, 15^3; 12:18; 13:9; Gal 1:3, 4^2; 2:4, 16; 4:6, 26; 6:14, 18; Eph 1:2, 3, 14, 17; 2:3, 14; 3:11; 5:20; 6:12, 24; Php 1:2; 3:20, 21; 4:20; Col 1:1, 2, 3, 7^2; 2:13; 4:3, 8, 9, 14; 1Th 1:2, 3^2, 5; 2:1, 2, 4, 5, 8, 9, 17, 19^3, 20; 3:2, 5, 7, 9, 11^2, 13^2; 5:9, 23, 28; 2Th 1:1, 8, 10, 11, 12^2; 2:1^2, 14^2, 16^2; 3:7, 14, 18; 1Ti 1:1^2, 2, 12, 14; 2:3; 4:10; 6:1, 3, 14, 17; 2Ti 1:2, 8, 10; 4:15; Tit 1:3, 4^2; 2:10, 13; 3:4, 6, 14; Phm 1:1^2, 2^2, 3; Heb 1:1; 3:6; 4:15, 16; 6:20; 7:14, 26; 9:14; 10:22^2; 12:2^2, 9, 10^2, 29; 13:9, 20, 23; Jas 1:27; 2:1, 21; 3:9; 1Pe 1:3; 2:24; 2Pe 1:1, 2, 3, 8, 11, 14, 16; 2:20; 3:2, 4, 15^2, 18; 1Jn 1:1^2, 3, 4, 9^2, 10; 2:1, 2; 3:5, 14, 16^2, 19, 20^2, 21; 4:10; 5:4; 2Jn 1:12; 3Jn 1:12; Jude 1:4^2, 17, 21, 25^2; Rev 1:5; 4:11; 5:10; 6:10; 7:3, 10, 12; 11:15; 12:10^3; 19:1, 5, 6.

OURS (20)

Ge 26:20; 34:21, 23; Dt 21:20; Jos 9:12; 22:24, 25, 27; Ru 3:2; 2Ch 14:7; Eze 35:10; Mk 12:7; Lk 20:14; 1Co 1:2; 2Co 3:4; 7:5; 1Th 3:12; 2Pe 1:1; 1Jn 2:2; Rev 1:9.

OURSELVES (45)

Ge 11:4^2; 34:16; 43:7; 44:16; Nu 31:50; 32:17; Dt 2:35; 3:7; Jos 22:17; Jdg 19:19; 2Sa 19:42; 2Ki 7:9; Ezr 8:21; Job 34:4; Pr 7:18; Isa 7:6; 58:3; Jer 26:19; Da 3:16; Jn 4:42; Ac 21:1; Ro 8:23; 15:1; 1Co 11:31; 15:30; 2Co 1:4, 9, 12; 3:1, 5^2; 4:2, 5^2; 5:12; 6:4; 7:1; 10:12; 12:19; Gal 2:17; 1Th 3:1; 2Th 3:9; 2Pe 1:18; 1Jn 1:8.

OUT (2407)

Ge 2:9, 19, 22, 23; 3:22, 24; 4:8, 10, 16, 22; 6:14; 7:23; 8:7, 8, 9, 10, 12, 16, 17, 18, 19; 9:10, 18, 24; 10:5, 32; 11:31; 12:4, 5, 9; 13:11; 14:5, 8, 14, 17, 18; 15:7, 14; 18:12; 19:5, 8, 9, 10, 12, 14^2, 16, 17, 24, 29; 22:3, 10, 11; 23:16; 24:7, 10, 11, 13, 15, 22, 29, 30, 31, 43, 45, 53, 63; 25:25, 26; 27:3, 9, 34; 28:10, 14; 30:14, 16; 31:4, 33; 34:1, 6, 24, 28; 35:5, 14; 37:7, 28; 38:24, 25, 28^2, 29^2, 30; 39:12, 13, 15, 18; 40:14, 17; 41:2, 3, 13, 18, 46; 43:23, 30, 31; 44:15; 45:1, 25; 46:1; 47:10, 30; 48:14; 50:24; Ex 1:10; 2:10, 11, 13, 23; 3:7, 8, 10, 11, 12, 17, 20; 4:4^2, 6, 7; 5:8, 10; 6:1, 6, 7, 11, 13, 26, 27; 7:2, 4, 5^2, 15, 19; 8:5, 6, 12, 16, 17; 9:9, 10, 15, 19, 22, 23, 29^2, 33^2; 10:11, 12, 13, 21, 22, 28; 11:1, 10; 12:17, 22, 39, 42, 51; 13:3^3, 8, 9, 14^2, 16, 18; 14:8, 10, 11, 15, 16, 21, 26, 27; 15:12, 25; 16:1^2, 3, 4, 6, 27, 29, 32; 17:1, 3, 4, 6, 9, 14; 18:1, 7, 18; 19:2, 5, 17, 22, 24; 20:2^2; 21:27; 22:6, 23, 27; 23:15, 23, 28, 29, 30, 31; 24:13; 25:11, 18, 29, 31, 36; 27:8; 28:28, 35; 29:12, 46; 32:1, 4, 7, 8, 11, 12, 19, 23, 24, 25, 32, 33; 33:1, 2, 8; 34:1, 4, 11, 18, 24, 34^2; 36:1, 3; 37:2, 7, 16, 17, 22, 25; 38:7; 39:3, 21, 30; 40:4, 23, 36, 37; Lev 1:15; 2:9, 13; 4:7, 18, 25, 30, 34; 5:9; 6:12, 13; 8:15; 9:9, 23, 24; 10:2; 11:45; 13:12, 20, 25, 39, 42, 45, 56; 14:38, 40, 43, 45; 16:17, 18, 24; 17:13; 18:24, 25, 28^2; 19:31, 36; 20:22, 23; 22:33; 23:43; 24:8, 10^2; 25:38, 42, 55; 26:10, 13, 14, 15, 26, 33, 45; 27:33; Nu 1:1; 2:9, 16, 17^2, 24, 31, 34; 9:1, 8, 17, 18, 19, 20, 21^2, 22^2, 23; 10:2, 5, 6^2, 12, 13, 17, 21, 25, 28, 29, 33, 34, 35; 11:2, 20, 24, 26, 31, 32^2; 12:4^2, 13; 13:3; 14:25; 15:41; 16:13, 14, 22, 27, 35, 37, 39, 46; 17:9; 19:16; 20:5, 8^2, 10, 11, 16^2, 18, 20, 22; 21:5, 11, 13, 23, 28, 32, 33; 22:5, 6, 11, 19, 36; 23:22; 24:2, 6, 8, 17^2, 19; 26:4, 11; 27:17^2, 21; 28:7; 31:3, 28, 30, 47; 32:11, 21, 23, 39; 33:1, 3^2, 38, 52, 55; 35:4; Dt 1:19, 22, 27, 33, 40, 44; 2:1, 12, 21, 22, 23, 24, 32; 3:1, 16; 4:12, 15, 20^2, 33, 34, 36, 37, 38, 45, 46; 5:4, 6^2, 15, 22, 23, 26; 6:12^2, 19, 21, 23; 7:1, 6, 8, 17, 19, 22, 24; 8:4, 9, 14^2, 15; 9:3, 4^2, 5, 10, 12, 14, 17, 23, 26, 28, 29; 10:1, 3^2, 4; 11:23; 12:3, 16, 24, 29; 13:3, 5, 10^2; 14:2; 15:23; 16:1; 18:5, 12; 19:1; 20:1; 21:2; 22:25, 27; 23:4; 24:9, 11; 25:4, 6, 11, 17, 18, 19; 26:7, 8; 27:26; 28:6, 19, 32; 29:5, 7, 20, 21, 25; 31:1; 32:26, 39; 33:18, 21, 22, 27; Jos 2:2, 3^2, 6, 7^2, 10, 23; 3:1, 3, 10; 4:16, 17, 18, 20; 5:4, 5; 6:1, 22^2, 23^2; 7:2^2, 9, 23; 8:3^2, 5, 14, 18^2, 22, 26; 9:13, 17, 24; 10:22, 23; 11:4; 13:6, 10, 13; 14:11^2, 12; 15:7, 9, 14; 16:7; 17:13, 18; 18:4, 8, 12, 14, 15, 19, 20; 19:1, 13, 17, 24, 29, 32, 34, 40; 21:3, 4; 22:3; 23:5^2, 9, 13; 24:5, 6, 10, 12, 17, 18; Jdg 1:23, 24, 27, 28, 29, 30, 31, 33, 35; 2:1, 3, 12, 15, 16, 18, 21, 23; 3:9, 15, 22^2, 23; 4:18, 22; 5:4, 12, 28; 6:6, 8^2, 13, 14, 19, 20, 30, 38; 7:15, 21, 23, 24; 8:5, 22, 25; 9:8, 15, 20^2, 27, 29, 33, 34, 35^2, 38, 39, 41, 42, 43; 10:10, 14; 11:13, 16, 23, 31, 34, 40; 12:1, 2; 13:9; 14:9, 14^2; 15:4, 9, 18, 19; 16:20, 21, 25^2; 18:2, 11, 14, 17, 23; 19:22, 24, 27, 28, 30; 20:1, 10, 20, 21, 25, 31, 33, 37, 42; 21:17, 21; Ru 1:7, 13; 2:3^2, 16, 18; 3:15, 18; 1Sa 1:15, 16; 2:5, 28; 3:3, 12; 4:1; 5:10; 6:6; 7:3, 6, 8, 9, 11; 8:8, 18, 20; 9:10, 11; 10:2, 18, 19, 23; 11:2, 7; 12:6, 8, 10; 13:10, 14, 17, 23; 14:11, 26, 27, 34, 38; 15:6, 11^2, 13, 18; 17:4, 8, 20^2, 23, 25^2, 33, 49, 55, 56; 18:6, 27, 30; 19:3^2, 8^2; 20:11, 12, 17, 35, 37; 21:5; 23:15, 22, 23, 24; 24:2, 8^2, 14, 21; 25:15; 26:4, 5, 14, 20; 27:1; 28:12, 13, 17, 18; 30:21, 22; 2Sa 1:7; 2:13, 23, 26; 3:25; 4:5, 9; 5:18, 20^2, 22, 24; 6:1, 2, 6, 8, 20; 7:6, 23^2; 10:3, 7, 8; 11:1, 3, 13, 17, 22, 23; 12:11, 31; 13:9, 15, 17, 18; 14:7; 15:2, 5, 16, 17; 16:5^2, 7^2; 17:1, 19, 21^2, 22, 23; 18:2^2, 3, 4, 8, 12, 24, 25, 28; 19:7^2, 15, 19; 20:7^2, 8, 10; 21:10, 17; 22:7, 9, 13, 17, 20; 23:16; 24:12, 16, 20; 1Ki 1:29, 30; 2:30, 46; 3:7; 4:33; 6:1, 12, 27; 8:9, 16, 21, 22, 38, 51^2, 52, 53^2, 54; 9:9; 10:13; 11:12, 18, 29^2, 31, 32, 34; 12:18, 25, 28; 13:2, 3, 4^3, 5, 21, 28; 14:21, 24; 16:20; 17:20, 21; 19:11, 13, 21; 20:16, 17, 18^2, 19, 27, 33, 39; 21:10, 26; 22:22, 25, 32, 34; 2Ki 2:3, 12, 21, 23, 24; 3:6, 9; 4:1, 18, 21, 25, 34, 35, 37, 39, 40^2; 5:2, 11; 6:5, 7^2, 13, 15; 7:10, 12, 13, 14, 16; 9:11, 15, 17, 19, 21, 23, 30, 32, 35; 10:9, 12, 22, 25, 26; 11:12, 14, 15; 14:27; 15:16; 16:3, 6, 7, 13; 17:7, 8, 11, 36; 18:12, 18, 28, 31; 19:9, 14, 31^2, 35; 21:2, 7, 13^2, 15; 22:9; 23:29; 24:7; 25:7; 1Ch 4:10; 5:20; 7:11; 8:13; 9:28, 32; 11:18; 12:17; 13:9, 11; 14:8, 11^2, 15^2; 15:13; 16:35; 17:5, 21^2; 19:3, 7, 8, 9; 20:1, 3, 4; 21:10; 23:29, 32; 28:7; 2Ch 2:4; 5:10; 6:5, 12, 13, 29; 7:11, 22; 8:16; 10:18; 12:7, 13; 13:9, 11, 14; 14:9, 10; 15:2; 16:2, 14; 18:24, 31, 33; 19:2, 4; 20:7, 9, 11, 17, 20, 21; 21:15, 19; 22:7; 23:11, 14^2; 24:12; 26:11, 19, 20; 28:3, 9; 29:7, 16^2, 18; 30:12; 31:1, 5; 32:18, 20; 33:2, 7, 15; 34:14, 17, 21, 25; 35:16, 20, 24; Ezr 1:7, 8; 4:4; 6:8, 12, 13; 8:25, 26, 29, 30, 31, 33; 9:5; Ne 2:12, 13; 3:17; 4:5, 10, 19, 21; 5:13^3, 15; 6:8; 8:1, 15, 16; 9:7, 18, 21, 27, 28; 10:32, 33; 11:1; 12:27; 13:8, 14, 25; Est 2:11, 22; 3:9, 12, 15; 4:1, 5, 6, 17; 5:2, 9; 7:7; 8:9, 14; 9:1, 13, 28; Job 1:11, 12; 2:5, 7, 11; 3:24; 7:11; 8:8; 9:3, 4, 8; 10:1, 6, 10, 18; 11:13; 13:9, 16; 15:13; 16:7, 20; 17:13; 18:5, 6; 20:15, 25^2; 21:17; 23:5, 14; 24:12; 26:7, 10; 27:21, 23; 28:25; 29:6; 30:8, 20; 31:38; 33:21, 23; 35:9, 12; 36:26, 29; 37:9, 18, 22; 38:1, 13, 14, 32, 41; 39:29; 40:6; 41:18, 19; Ps 6:6; 7:15; 9:5; 10:15; 14:7; 16:4; 18:8, 12, 16, 19, 42; 19:4; 22:2, 9, 14^2; 27:3, 12; 30:1; 31:17; 34:6, 17; 37:7; 40:2^2; 41:6; 42:4; 44:2, 9, 20; 51:1, 9; 53:6; 55:17, 23; 57:2; 58:2, 6; 59:7; 60:6, 10; 62:8; 66:17; 68:7; 69:3, 16, 24, 28; 72:12; 75:8; 77:1^2, 2; 78:16, 20, 21, 52, 55; 79:3, 6; 80:8^2, 11; 81:5, 7, 10; 84:2; 88:1, 9; 89:26; 94:4; 102:T, 26; 104:2, 23; 105:37, 39, 41, 43; 106:29, 45; 107:6, 14, 23, 28^2, 41; 108:7, 11; 109:13, 14, 21; 114:1; 118:12; 119:45, 94, 139, 146, 155; 124:7; 126:6; 130:1; 135:7; 136:6, 11; 138:7; 139:3; 140:5; 142:2; 143:6, 11; 149:9; Pr 1:21, 23, 24; 2:3; 3:21; 4:21; 6:19; 7:6, 10, 15; 8:1, 4, 27, 29; 9:1, 3, 15; 10:9, 31; 12:23; 13:9, 16; 14:5; 16:4; 17:14; 18:15; 19:5, 9, 26; 20:5, 8, 20, 26, 27; 21:13; 22:10^2; 23:4; 24:20; 25:2, 4; 26:20; 30:17; 31:16, 18; Ecc 2:1; 7:25; 8:11, 17; 12:9; SS 1:3; 3:11; 7:13; 8:11; Isa 1:15, 16; 2:3; 3:7; 5:2; 7:3; 10:23, 30; 11:11; 13:3; 14:11, 19, 26, 27; 15:4^2, 5; 16:8, 10, 12; 17:10, 11; 19:20; 22:5, 12, 16; 23:11; 24:11, 18; 25:11^2; 26:14, 17, 21; 27:8; 28:20, 27; 29:4^2, 18, 21; 30:1, 14, 24; 31:3; 34:1, 3, 11; 36:3, 13, 16; 37:9, 14, 32^2, 36; 40:6, 22^2, 26; 42:2, 3, 5^3, 13, 14, 25; 43:8, 13, 17^2, 25; 44:3, 7, 13, 24^2, 26; 45:12; 46:6^2, 7; 47:13; 48:13, 14, 20, 21; 49:9; 50:6, 9; 51:4, 6, 13, 22; 52:11^2; 53:2, 12; 54:3; 55:11, 12; 57:4, 6, 13, 14; 58:2; 62:1; 65:2, 14^2, 20; 66:24; Jer 1:9, 14; 2:6; 3:8; 4:1, 4, 7^2, 31; 5:6; 6:1, 7^2, 11, 12, 25, 29; 7:18, 20, 22; 10:3, 12, 13, 18, 25; 11:4^2, 11, 12, 15; 12:5, 13; 14:16^2; 15:1; 16:13, 14, 15^2; 17:8, 19, 22; 18:23; 19:2, 13; 20:8, 18; 21:9, 12; 22:4, 20^2, 28; 23:3, 7, 8^2, 19, 39; 26:23; 27:2; 30:7, 10, 15, 23; 31:4, 6, 32, 37, 40; 32:4, 9, 10, 21, 29; 34:7, 13^2; 35:16; 36:30; 37:5, 7, 10; 38:8, 10, 13, 22, 23; 39:7, 14; 41:6, 10; 42:18^2; 44:6, 17, 18, 19^2, 25^2; 45:3; 46:3, 27; 47:2; 48:4, 12, 20, 31, 44, 45; 49:2^2, 3; 50:8, 25; 51:12, 15, 16, 25, 34, 39, 44, 45, 48; 52:11; La 1:17; 2:4, 8, 11, 18, 19^2; 3:8^2; 4:11; Eze 1:4, 11, 13, 22, 23; 2:9; 3:18, 22, 23, 25; 4:10, 11; 6:6, 11, 14; 7:8; 8:3; 9:1, 7, 8; 10:7^2; 11:7, 9, 13; 12:3, 4^2, 5, 6, 7^2; 13:2, 17; 14:9, 13, 19, 22; 15:7; 16:5, 27, 36; 17:6, 7^2; 20:6^2, 8, 9, 10, 13, 14, 21, 22, 28, 38, 41; 21:12, 19, 20, 31^2; 22:22, 31; 23:8, 43; 25:7, 13, 16, 17; 26:5; 27:26, 28, 33; 28:18; 29:4; 30:9^2, 15; 31:12; 32:7; 33:8, 27; 34:13; 35:3; 36:18, 24; 37:1, 21; 38:4, 8; 39:9, 17, 29; 42:15; 44:3, 8, 15, 19; 46:2, 8, 9^3, 10^2, 12^2, 18; 47:1, 2; Da 2:14, 34, 45; 3:26^2; 4:36; 5:7; 6:23; 7:3, 10; 8:9; 9:11, 15, 27; 11:4, 11, 20, 40, 44; Hos 1:11; 2:10, 15; 5:1, 10; 7:14; 8:2, 5; 9:4, 13, 15; 11:1, 9; 12:9; 13:4; Joel 1:14; 2:28, 29; 3:7, 18; Am 2:10; 3:1; 4:3^2; 5:3^2, 8; 6:10; 7:2, 5, 12; 9:6; Jnh 1:5, 7; 4:5; Mic 1:11; 2:1, 13; 3:4; 4:2, 10; 5:2; 6:4; 7:9, 15, 17; Na 1:6; Hab 1:2; 2:11; 3:13, 14; Zep 1:4, 11, 17; 2:13; 3:8; Hag 1:9; 2:5; Zec 1:16; 2:2; 4:7, 12; 5:3, 4; 6:1, 5, 7, 12; 12:1, 9, 10; 14:3, 8; Mal 3:10, 14; 4:2; Mt 2:6, 7, 15; 3:5, 9, 16; 5:13, 26, 29; 7:4, 5, 15, 22; 8:3, 16, 31, 32, 34; 9:17, 27, 31, 32, 33, 34, 38; 10:1, 5, 8, 16; 11:7, 8, 9, 16; 12:11, 13^2, 14, 19, 20, 24, 26, 27^2, 28, 34, 35^2, 43; 13:1, 3, 41^2, 52; 14:25, 26, 29, 30, 31; 15:11, 17, 18, 19, 22, 23; 17:18, 19, 27; 18:9, 28; 20:1, 3, 5, 6; 21:12, 17, 39; 22:10, 15; 23:24; 24:4, 17, 26^2, 32; 25:1, 6^2, 8, 25; 26:15, 28, 30, 51, 55, 69, 71; 27:18, 32, 46, 50, 53, 60; 28:14; Mk 1:5, 10, 12, 23, 25, 26, 34, 39, 41, 45; 2:12, 13; 3:5^2, 6, 11, 14, 15, 21, 22, 23; 4:1, 3, 22; 5:2, 5, 8, 10, 13, 14, 30, 40; 6:7, 12, 13, 24, 38, 48, 49, 54; 7:15, 19, 20, 21, 26; 8:15; 9:18, 25, 26, 28, 29, 38, 43, 47; 11:11, 13, 15, 19; 12:8, 38, 44^2; 13:5, 15, 28; 14:24, 26, 48, 68; 15:10, 18, 20, 34, 46; 16:8, 9, 17, 20; Lk 1:22, 62; 2:8; 3:7, 8; 4:29, 33, 35^2, 36, 41, 42; 5:3, 4, 13, 27, 37; 6:10, 12, 42^2, 45^3; 7:12, 13, 24, 25, 26, 32; 8:2, 3, 5, 8, 17, 22, 28, 29, 33, 35^2, 38, 46; 9:1, 2, 6, 38, 40, 49, 51; 10:2, 3, 35; 11:14, 15, 18, 19^2, 20, 24, 27; 12:15, 33, 59; 13:15, 28, 32; 14:5, 19, 21, 23, 35; 15:15, 18, 28; 16:17;

SHALL (467)

SHE (1011)

SO (3003)

For "SO" as a proper name see the Main Concordance.

THAT (5758)

THE (55728)

24, 28, 29, 30^2; **3:**1^2, 2, 3^3, 4, 5^4, 6, 7, 8, 9^2, 10^2, 11^2, 14^2, 17, 18, 20, 21; **4:**1, 2, 3^4, 4, 5, 7, 9, 10, 11, 12, 15^3, 18, 21^2, 22, 23^2; **Col 1:**1, 2, 3, 4^2, 5^4, 6^2, 8, 9^2, 10^2, 12^4, 13^3, 14, 15^3, 18^7, 20, 23^3, 24^2, 25^2, 26^2, 27^3; **2:**2^2, 3, 7, 8, 9^2, 10, 11^4, 12^2, 13, 14^2, 15^2, 17^2, 18^2, 19^2, 20, 23; **3:**1, 6, 7, 10^2, 13, 15, 16, 17^3, 18, 20, 22, 23, 24^2; **4:**3, 5^2, 7^2, 8, 10, 11^2, 12, 14, 15^2, 16^3, 17^2; **1Th 1:**1^4, 5, 6^4, 7, 8, 9, 10^2; **2:**2, 3, 4^2, 8, 9, 13^3, 14^2, 15^2, 16^3, 19^2; **3:**2, 5, 8, 9^2, 11, 12, 13; **4:**1, 2^2, 5, 6, 10, 12, 13, 15^3, 16^5, 17^4; **5:**2^3, 5^4, 8^2, 12, 13, 14^2, 19, 21, 23^2, 24, 26, 27^2, 28; **2Th 1:**1^3, 2^2, 3, 4, 5, 7, 8, 9^3, 10, 12^3; **2:**1, 2^2, 3^3, 6, 7^3, 8^4, 9^3, 10, 11, 12, 13^5, 14, 15; **3:**1^2, 3^2, 4^2, 5, 6^3, 8, 9, 12^2, 16^2, 17, 18; **1Ti 1:**1, 2^2, 5, 7, 8, 9^3, 10, 11^2, 14^2, 15^2, 16, 17^2, 18^2; **2:**4, 5, 6, 7^3, 14^2; **3:**2^2, 6^2, 7, 9^2, 11, 12, 15^4, 16^4; **4:**1^2, 3, 5, 6^4, 8^2, 10^2, 12, 13, 14; **5:**5, 6, 7, 8, 9, 10^2, 13, 14, 16^2, 17^3, 18^4, 20, 21^2, 22^2, 24^3, 25; **6:**1, 2, 3, 5, 7, 10^2, 12^4, 13^2, 14, 15^2, 19^2, 20, 21; **2Ti 1:**1^2, 2, 6^2, 8^2, 9, 10^2, 13, 14^3, 15, 16^2, 17, 18^2; **2:**1, 2^2, 5^2, 6^3, 7, 8, 9, 10^3, 15, 18^3, 19^3, 21^2, 22^2, 24, 25^2, 26^2; **3:**1, 3, 6, 7, 8^2, 9, 11^2, 15, 17; **4:**1^3, 2, 3, 4, 5^2, 6, 7^3, 8^3, 13^2, 14^2, 17^4, 18, 19, 21, 22; **Tit 1:**1^3, 2^2, 3^2, 4, 5, 6^2, 9, 10, 11, 13, 14^2, 15; **2:**2, 3^2, 4, 5, 6, 10, 11, 13^2, 15; **3:**1, 4, 5^2, 7, 9, 13, 15; **Phm 1:**2, 3, 5^2, 7^2, 9, 13, 15, 16, 20, 25^2; **Heb 1:**1^2, 2, 3^5, 4^2, 5, 6, 7, 8^2, 9, 10^5, 12, 13; **2:**2, 3, 4, 5, 6, 7, 9^2, 10, 11^2, 12^2, 13, 14^3, 17^2; **3:**1^2, 2, 3^2, 4, 5, 6, 7, 8^3, 12, 14^2, 15, 17; **4:**1, 2^2, 3^2, 4^2, 5, 6, 9, 12^3, 13, 14^3, 16; **5:**3^2, 5, 6, 7^2, 9, 10, 12, 13, 14; **6:**1^2, 2^3, 4^2, 5^4, 6, 7^2, 8, 10, 11, 16, 17^2, 18, 19^3, 20; **7:**1^2, 3, 4^2, 5^3, 6, 7^2, 8^3, 9^2, 10, 11^6, 12^2, 13, 16^3, 17, 18, 19, 21, 22, 26, 27^3, 28^4; **8:**1^4, 2^3, 4^2, 5^3, 6^3, 8^5, 9^3, 10^3, 11^3, 13; **9:**1, 2^4, 3^2, 4^6, 5^4, 6^2, 7^4, 8^4, 9^4, 10^2, 11^2, 12^2, 13^2, 14^3, 15^4, 16^3, 17, 18, 19^5, 20^2, 21^3, 22^2, 23^3, 24, 25^3, 26^5, 28; **10:**1^4, 2, 4, 5, 7, 8, 9^2, 10^2, 11, 12, 15, 16^2, 19^2, 20, 21, 23, 25^3, 26^2, 27, 28^2, 29^4, 30, 31^2, 32^2, 34, 36; **11:**2, 3, 7^2, 9^2, 10, 11, 12^4, 13, 15, 17, 19, 21, 22^2, 23, 24, 25^2, 26^2, 27, 28^5, 29^3, 30^2, 31^2, 32, 33, 34^4, 37, 38^2; **12:**1^2, 2^5, 4, 5, 6, 9, 11, 13, 14, 15, 16, 17, 20, 21, 22^3, 23^4, 24^3, 26^3, 27^2; **13:**4^3, 5, 6, 7^2, 8, 10, 11^5, 12^2, 13^2, 14, 15, 20^5; **Jas 1:**1^3, 3, 6^2, 7, 9, 10, 11^4, 12^3, 17^2, 18, 20, 21^2, 22, 23, 25^2, 27; **2:**3^3, 5^3, 6^3, 7^2, 8, 9, 10, 12, 17, 19, 21, 23, 25^3, 26^2; **3:**3^2, 4, 5^2, 6^5, 7, 8, 9, 10, 11, 13, 14, 15, 17; **4:**4^2, 5, 6^2, 7, 10, 11^2, 12, 15, 17; **5:**1, 3, 4^6, 5, 7^4, 8, 9^2, 10^4, 11^2, 14^4, 15^3, 16, 17, 18^2, 19, 20; **1Pe 1:**1, 2^4, 3^3, 5^3, 9^2, 10^3, 11^4, 12^3, 13, 14, 18, 19, 20^2, 21, 22^2, 23, 24^4, 25^3; **2:**3, 4, 6, 7^3, 8, 9, 10, 11, 12^2, 13^3, 15, 17^2, 19, 24, 25; **3:**1^3, 2, 3, 4, 5^3, 7^3, 12^5, 15^2, 18^4, 19, 20^2, 21^4; **4:**1, 2^2, 3, 4, 5^2, 6^4, 7, 11^4, 12, 13, 14^2, 17^3, 18^3; **5:**1^2, 3, 4^2, 5^3, 8, 9^3, 10, 11, 12^2; **2Pe 1:**1, 2, 4^3, 10, 11, 12, 13, 16, 17^3, 18, 19^4, 20, 21^2; **2:**1^2, 2, 5^2, 6^2, 7, 8, 9^3, 10^2, 11^2, 13, 14, 15^3, 16, 18, 20^4, 21^2, 22^2; **3:**2^4, 3, 4, 5^2, 6, 7^3, 8, 9, 10^5, 12^5, 13, 15, 16^2, 17, 18; **1Jn 1:**1^2, 2^3, 3, 5, 6^2, 7^3, 8; **2:**1^2, 2^3, 4^2, 7^2, 8^2, 9^2, 10, 11^3, 13^3, 14^3, 15^5, 16^6, 17^3, 18^3, 20^2, 21^2, 22^6, 23^4, 24^3, 27; **3:**1^4, 4, 8^6, 10^3, 11^2, 12, 13, 17, 19, 23, 24; **4:**1^2, 2^2, 3^3, 4^3, 5^4, 6^2, 9, 14^3, 15, 16, 17, 18; **5:**1^2, 2, 4^3, 5^2, 6^4, 8^4, 9, 10^2, 11, 12^2, 13^2, 14, 18^2, 19^3, 20^2; **2Jn 1:**1^4, 2, 3^2, 4^2, 5, 6, 7^4, 9^4, 13; **3Jn 1:**1^2, 3^2, 4, 5, 6, 7^3, 8, 9, 10^2, 12, 14^2; **Jude 1:**1, 3^3, 4, 5, 6^2, 7^2, 8, 9^4, 10, 11, 12^2, 13, 14^2, 15^4, 17, 18, 19^2, 20, 21, 23^2, 25; **Rev 1:**1, 2^2, 3^3, 4^3, 5^6, 7^3, 8^4, 9^4, 10^2, 11, 12, 13, 15, 16, 17^2, 18^2, 20^8; **2:**1^5, 5^2, 6^2, 7^5, 8^5, 9, 10^3, 11^3, 12^4, 13, 14^2, 15^2, 16, 17^3, 18^4, 20, 23, 24, 26^2, 28, 29^2; **3:**1^5, 2, 5, 6^2, 7^4, 9, 10^3, 12^5, 13^2, 14^6, 15, 18, 20^2, 21, 22^2; **4:**1, 2, 3^3, 4, 5^3, 6^3, 7^4, 8^2, 9^2, 10^3; **5:**1^2, 2^2, 3^2, 4, 5^5, 6^6, 7^3, 8^5, 9, 10, 11^4, 12, 13^4, 14^2; **6:**1^4, 3^3, 4, 5^3, 6^3, 7^4, 8^3, 9^5, 10^2, 11, 12^3, 13^2, 14, 15^8, 16^6, 17; **7:**1^6, 2^6, 3^5, 4^2, 5^3, 6^3, 7^3, 8^3, 9^2, 10^2, 11^5, 13, 14^3, 15^2, 16, 17^3; **8:**1, 2, 3^5, 4^5, 5^4, 6^2, 7^5, 8^3, 9^3, 10^4, 11^4, 12^6, 13^4; **9:**1^7, 2^5, 3^3, 4^3, 5^2, 7, 9^2, 11^2, 12, 13^3, 14^4, 15, 16^2, 17^4, 18, 19^2, 20^2; **10:**1, 2^2, 3^3, 4^2, 5^3, 6^3, 7^4, 8^6, 9^2, 10^2; **11:**1^3, 2^3, 4^4, 6^4, 7^2, 8^2, 10^3, 11, 13^4, 14^2, 15^4, 16, 17, 18^5, 19; **12:**1^2, 4^6, 5, 6^2, 7^2, 9^4, 10^5, 11^3, 12^3, 13^4, 14^5, 15^3, 16^4, 17^4; **13:**1^4, 2^3, 3^5, 4^4, 5, 7, 8^6, 10^4, 11, 12^4, 14^6, 15^3, 17^4, 18^2; **14:**1, 2^2, 3^6, 4^2, 6^2, 7^5, 8^3, 9^3, 10^5, 11^3, 12^2, 13^3, 14, 15^5, 16^3, 17, 18^5, 19^3, 20^4; **15:**1, 2^3, 3^5, 5^3, 6^3, 7^3, 8^5; **16:**1^4, 2^5, 3^3, 4^2, 5^3, 6, 7, 8^3, 9^2, 10^3, 11, 12^5, 13^6, 14^4, 16^2, 17^4, 18, 19^7, 20, 21^3; **17:**1^4, 2^5, 3^2, 4^2, 5^4, 6^4, 7^5, 8^8, 9^2, 10, 11^2, 12^2, 13, 14^2, 15^3, 16^3, 17, 18^4; **18:**1, 2, 3^6, 7, 8, 9^3, 11^2, 14, 15, 17^2, 18, 19, 20, 21^3, 22^2, 23^4, 24^3; **19:**1, 2^3, 3, 4^3, 5, 6, 7^2, 8^2, 9^4, 10^3, 13, 14, 15^4, 17^3, 18^2, 19^5, 20^7, 21^6; **20:**1^2, 2^2, 3^3, 4^3, 5^4, 6^2, 7, 8^5, 9^4, 10^4, 12^5, 13^3, 14^3, 15^2; **21:**1^2, 2^2, 3^2, 4, 5, 6^6, 8^8, 9^6, 10^2, 11, 12^4, 13^4, 14^5, 15^2, 16^3, 17, 18^2, 19^6, 20^8, 21^3, 22^3, 23^5, 24^3, 26^2, 27; **22:**1^5, 2^9, 3^3, 5^4, 6^6, 7^2, 8^3, 9^2, 10^3, 13^6, 14^4, 15^4, 16^4, 17^4, 18^3, 19^2, 21^2.

THEIR (3701)

Ge 1:11, 12^2, 21, 24, 25^3; **2:**1; **6:**12; **7:**3, 14; **8:**16; **9:**23^4; **10:**5^3, 20^2, 31^2, 32^2; **11:**7; **13:**6; **14:**8, 11, 24; **15:**13; **17:**8; **18:**16, 20, 26; **19:**33, 35, 36; **22:**17; **23:**13; **24:**32, 59, 60, 61; **25:**13, 16, 18; **26:**31; **31:**53; **32:**11, 15; **33:**2, 6, 13; **34:**13, 18, 20^2, 21, 23^3, 25, 27, 28, 29^2; **35:**4; **36:**7^2, 19, 30, 40, 43; **37:**2, 4, 12, 16, 21, 25^3, 32; **40:**1; **42:**6, 24, 25^2, 26^2, 28, 29, 35^2, 36; **43:**2, 11, 24^2, 25, 33; **44:**3^2, 13^2; **45:**21, 25, 27; **46:**5^3, 6, 17, 32; **47:**1, 12, 17^5, 20, 22; **48:**6; **49:**5, 6^3, 7^2, 19, 28; **50:**8^2, 15, 17; **Ex 1:**14^2, 21; **2:**11, 16, 17^2, 18, 23^3, 24; **3:**7^2; **4:**5, 31; **5:**4, 7, 21; **6:**9, 14, 16, 19, 26; **7:**11, 12, 22; **8:**7, 18, 26; **9:**20^2, 21, 34; **10:**7; **11:**2; **12:**4, 34^2, 51; **13:**17, 21; **14:**5^2, 22^2, 25, 26, 29^2, 31; **18:**19; **19:**8, 9, 10, 14, 21, 24; **22:**9, 23, 30; **23:**6, 24^3, 27, 32, 33; **24:**12; **25:**20; **27:**19; **28:**10, 38; **29:**10, 15, 19, 20^2, 21^2, 25, 28, 33, 45, 46^2; **30:**19, 21; **32:**3, 13, 25, 32, 34; **33:**6, 8; **34:**7, 13^3, 15^2, 16^2; **35:**18, 22; **36:**4, 36, 38^2; **37:**9; **38:**17, 19^2, 28; **40:**15^2, 31, 38; **Lev 4:**15; **6:**17; **7:**34, 36, 38; **8:**2, 14, 16, 18, 22, 24^3, 25, 28, 30^2; **10:**1, 5, 19^2; **11:**8^2, 11^2, 24, 25, 27^2, 28, 35; **15:**31; **16:**16^2, 21, 22, 27; **17:**7; **18:**3, 29; **20:**4, 5, 11^2, 12^2, 13^2, 16^2, 17, 18, 24, 27^2; **21:**5^3, 6^3, 7^2; **23:**4, 18; **24:**9, 14; **25:**3, 32, 33, 34^2, 45; **26:**4, 20, 36^2, 39^3, 40^4, 41^3, 43, 44^2, 45^3; **Nu 1:**2, 3, 16, 18^2, 20, 22, 24, 26, 28, 30, 32, 34, 36, 38, 40, 42, 45, 52, 53; **2:**3, 9, 10, 16, 18, 24, 25, 31, 32^2, 34; **3:**4, 15, 20, 26, 31, 36, 37, 39, 40, 45; **4:**2, 22, 27^2, 28, 29, 31, 32^3, 34, 38, 40, 42, 44, 46; **5:**3; **6:**15; **7:**3, 7, 8, 9, 10, 87; **8:**7^2, 10, 12, 15, 21, 22, 25, 26^2; **10:**14, 18, 22, 25; **11:**1, 12, 24, 33; **13:**4; **14:**1, 6, 9, 23, 35, 44; **15:**25; **16:**15, 26, 27^2, 32^2, 34, 38; **17:**2, 6^2, 10; **18:**12, 17^2, 18, 20, 21, 22, 24; **20:**8^2, 11, 21; **21:**2, 3, 24; **23:**21; **24:**7^4, 8^2; **25:**2, 18; **26:**12, 15, 20, 23, 26, 28, 35, 37, 38, 42, 44, 48, 57, 59; **27:**5, 7^2, 14, 19; **28:**31; **29:**6, 11, 18, 19, 21, 24, 27, 30, 33, 37; **31:**8, 10, 12, 29; **32:**15, 17, 29, 30, 36, 41; **33:**2^2, 4^2, 52^3; **34:**14, 15, 19; **35:**3^2, 7; **36:**3, 4^2, 6, 11^2, 12^2; **Dt 1:**8; **2:**5, 9, 12^2, 21, 22, 23, 28; **3:**7; **4:**7, 9, 10, 37, 38; **5:**29^2, 30; **6:**2; **7:**3^2, 5^4, 10^2, 16, 24^2, 25; **9:**5, 14, 27^2; **10:**9^2, 11^2, 15; **11:**6^2, 9; **12:**2, 3^5, 4, 12, 29, 30^2, 31^4; **13:**13; **14:**8^2, 27, 29; **18:**1, 2^2, 5, 8, 18; **19:**1; **20:**11, 18, 19; **21:**6; **24:**16^2; **29:**8, 17, 25, 28; **31:**3, 4, 7^2, 11, 13, 18, 20^2, 21, 28; **32:**5, 8, 16^2, 20, 21, 25, 26, 29, 30, 31, 32^3, 33, 35^3, 36, 37, 38^2, 49; **33:**29; **Jos 1:**6; **3:**15; **4:**8, 18^2, 21; **5:**1, 6, 7^2; **6:**8; **7:**6, 11, 12^2; **8:**2, 13, 19, 20, 33; **9:**5^2, 14, 17; **10:**5, 19, 20, 24^2, 40, 42; **11:**4, 6^2, 9^2, 12, 13, 16, 17, 20, 21, 23; **12:**6^2, 7^2; **13:**12, 14, 23, 28, 33; **14:**2, 3, 4, 12; **15:**2, 4, 12, 32, 36, 41, 44, 46, 51, 54, 57, 59, 60, 62; **16:**4, 5, 9; **17:**2, 4, 11; **18:**1, 2, 7^2, 8, 10, 11, 12, 24, 28; **19:**1, 6, 7, 9, 10, 15, 16, 18, 22, 23, 25, 30, 31, 33, 38, 39, 41, 47^2, 48; **20:**4; **21:**3, 8, 16, 18, 19, 22, 24, 25, 26, 27, 29, 31, 32, 33, 35, 37, 39, 41, 43, 44^3; **22:**6, 7, 9, 32; **23:**1, 2, 5, 7; **24:**8; **Jdg 1:**2, 3, 4, 7, 17, 27; **2:**2, 3, 10, 12, 14, 17^3, 18, 19^2, 20, 22; **3:**4, 6^4, 7, 18, 25; **4:**5; **5:**18, 20; **6:**3, 5^3, 9; **7:**2, 5, 6^3, 8, 12, 19^2, 20^2, 22; **8:**3, 12, 19, 21, 26, 33, 34^2; **9:**24^2, 26, 27, 35, 57; **10:**12; **12:**1, 2; **13:**20; **14:**19^3; **16:**18, 23, 24; **18:**1, 2, 7, 8, 12, 14, 21^3, 26, 27, 29; **19:**21; **20:**2, 13, 14, 15, 22, 33; **21:**2, 6, 22, 23, 24; **1Sa 1:**19; **2:**25; **4:**2; **6:**6, 7, 10, 13, 18; **7:**4; **8:**7; **9:**16; **10:**10, 12; **11:**6; **12:**9; **13:**2, 6^2, 20; **14:**20, 21, 30, 46, 47; **15:**20; **17:**1, 2, 17, 18, 21, 51, 52, 53; **18:**13, 16, 27; **19:**20; **21:**11, 13^2; **22:**2; **23:**5; **25:**10, 13; **28:**1; **29:**1, 2, 5; **30:**2, 3; **31:**7, 9^2, 12, 13; **2Sa 1:**11; **2:**25, 26, 27; **3:**18, 30; **4:**12; **5:**2^2, 21; **6:**5, 19; **7:**7, 10, 23, 24; **10:**3, 4, 8, 17, 18^3; **12:**30; **13:**29, 30, 31; **15:**30, 36; **16:**14; **18:**17, 28; **19:**6, 8; **20:**2, 3; **22:**41, 46; **23:**17, 19; **1Ki 1:**7, 41; **2:**4, 5, 15, 33; **4:**8, 28; **6:**27^2; **7:**9, 25, 43; **8:**7, 8, 11, 34, 35, 37, 44, 45^3, 47, 48^3, 49^3, 50; **9:**9^2, 21; **10:**5; **11:**2, 8; **12:**27^2; **13:**11, 12; **14:**15, 22; **15:**16, 32; **16:**2, 13, 26; **18:**28^2, 29, 37; **20:**1, 12, 16, 23, 24, 32^2; **22:**10^2; **2Ki 1:**14; **2:**1; **3:**27; **6:**20, 22, 23; **7:**7^3, 13, 14, 15; **8:**12^4; **9:**13; **10:**7, 32; **11:**12; **13:**5; **14:**6^2; **15:**16; **16:**15^2; **17:**7, 9^2, 14^2, 15, 16, 17, 19, 21, 23, 31, 32, 33, 34, 40, 41^3; **18:**12, 27^2, 37; **19:**17, 18, 26, 29; **21:**8, 14^2, 15; **22:**17; **23:**2, 9, 35; **25:**23^2, 24; **1Ch 1:**29; **2:**16; **3:**9, 19; **4:**3, 27, 31, 32, 33, 38^2, 39, 41^3; **5:**7^2, 9, 10, 13, 15, 20^2, 24^2, 25; **6:**19, 32, 33, 44, 48, 54^2, 59, 60, 64, 66, 69, 70, 71, 73, 75, 76, 77, 79, 81; **7:**2^2, 4, 5, 7, 9, 21, 22, 28, 29, 30, 32, 40; **8:**28, 32, 38; **9:**1, 2^2, 9^2, 17^2, 19, 22^2, 23, 25^3, 32, 34, 38, 44; **10:**7, 9^2, 10, 12^2; **11:**2^2, 14, 19^2, 21; **12:**3, 8, 19, 30, 32^2, 39, 40; **13:**2, 8; **14:**12; **15:**15, 16, 17, 18; **16:**21; **17:**6, 9, 22; **19:**4, 7, 9, 18^3; **20:**2; **21:**12; **23:**22, 24^2, 32^2; **24:**2, 3, 6, 19^2, 30, 31; **25:**3, 6, 7, 8; **26:**6, 8^2, 12^2, 13, 20, 31^2; **27:**1; **28:**15, 18; **29:**9, 18, 20, 21, 24; **2Ch 2:**11; **3:**13; **4:**4, 14, 20; **5:**8, 9, 11, 12, 13, 14; **6:**25, 26, 28, 34, 35^3, 37, 38^3, 39^3; **7:**3, 6^2, 10, 14^3, 22; **8:**8, 14; **9:**4^2; **11:**11, 13, 14, 16^2; **13:**12, 14, 15, 16, 18, 19; **14:**4; **15:**4, 12^2; **17:**14; **18:**9^2; **19:**4; **20:**13, 25, 27, 33^2; **21:**3; **22:**5; **24:**10, 18^2, 23, 24^2; **25:**4^3, 5, 15; **26:**11, 13, 19; **27:**2; **28:**6, 8, 15, 18; **29:**6^2, 15, 22^2, 23, 24, 26, 30, 34; **30:**7, 9, 16, 17, 22^2, 27; **31:**1^2, 2, 5, 6^2, 10, 15^2, 16^3, 17^3, 19; **32:**13, 17; **33:**17; **34:**5, 25, 30, 32, 33^2; **35:**2, 10^2, 15^2; **36:**15, 17; **Ezr 1:**6; **2:**59, 62, 65, 69, 70^2; **3:**1, 3, 8^2, 9, 10^2; **4:**5, 9, 17, 23; **5:**3, 5, 6, 8, 10^2; **6:**5, 6, 13, 18^2, 20, 21; **7:**16, 17; **8:**24; **9:**1, 2^2, 11^2, 12^2; **10:**3, 19^3; **Ne 3:**5^3, 18, 23; **4:**2, 3, 4^2, 5^2, 6, 13, 15, 17; **5:**1^2, 6, 11, 14, 15; **6:**6, 9, 16; **7:**3^2, 61, 64, 67, 73^2; **8:**6^2, 15, 16^2, 17; **9:**1, 2^3, 3^2, 4, 6, 9, 11, 15^2, 17^2, 19, 20^2, 21^2, 23^2, 24^2, 26, 27^2, 28, 29, 35^2, 38; **10:**10, 28^2, 29, 30, 39; **11:**1, 9, 12, 14, 19, 23, 25, 30; **12:**7, 9, 24, 40, 41, 45; **13:**10, 11, 13^2, 24, 25^3; **Est 1:**17, 20; **3:**13; **4:**8; **8:**9, 11^2, 13; **9:**2^2, 5, 10, 15, 16^2, 22^3, 24, 27, 28, 31^3; **Job 1:**4^2, 5; **2:**11, 12^2; **3:**15, 18; **4:**21; **5:**12, 13, 15; **6:**4, 17, 18; **8:**4, 8, 10; **9:**5, 26; **11:**9, 20; **12:**6^2, 18, 24; **14:**12; **15:**18, 35; **16:**10; **17:**2, 4, 9; **18:**4; **21:**8^3, 9, 10^2, 11^2, 13, 16^2, 29; **22:**6, 16^2, 18, 19, 20; **24:**5^2, 17, 18, 23; **26:**8; **27:**14, 15; **29:**8, 9^2, 10^2, 17, 22, 25; **30:**2^2, 4, 5, 9, 10, 12; **33:**15, 16; **34:**21, 24, 25, 26; **35:**13; **36:**6, 10, 11^2, 14, 15^2, 20, 28; **37:**8; **38:**15^2, 20^2, 32, 35, 40; **39:**3^2, 4; **40:**13, 20, 22; **42:**15^2, 16; **Ps 2:**2, 3^2; **4:**7; **5:**9^4, 10^3; **9:**5, 6, 15, 16; **10:**17; **11:**2^2, 6; **12:**2; **14:**1, 6; **16:**4^2; **17:**7, 10^2, 14^2; **18:**40, 45; **19:**3, 4^2; **20:**8; **21:**10^2, 12; **22:**4, 7, 13^2; **25:**22; **28:**3^2, 4^3, 9; **31:**18; **33:**6; **34:**5, 15, 17; **35:**6, 7, 8, 16, 17; **37:**7^2, 12, 13, 15^3, 18, 25, 26, 32, 33, 39; **38:**12; **39:**11^2; **40:**3, 15; **44:**1, 3^2, 12, 14; **46:**3; **49:**6^2, 10, 11^3, 13^2, 14^2; **53:**1; **55:**3, 9, 19, 23; **56:**1, 2; **58:**4, 6, 7, 10; **59:**7^2, 12^3; **62:**4^2; **64:**3^2, 5, 8^2; **65:**7; **68:**21, 23; **69:**23^2, 25^2; **70:**3; **72:**14; **73:**4, 6, 7^2, 8, 9^2, 10, 17; **74:**4, 6, 8; **76:**5; **78:**4, 5, 6, 7, 8, 12, 28^2, 30, 33^2, 35^2, 36^2, 37, 38, 44^2, 46^2, 47^2, 48^2, 53, 55^2, 57, 58^2, 63^2, 64^2; **79:**10; **81:**6^2, 12^2, 14^2, 15; **83:**2, 11^2, 16; **84:**5; **85:**2; **89:**17, 32^2; **90:**10, 16; **91:**12; **93:**3^2; **94:**23^2; **98:**8; **99:**8; **102:**17, 28; **103:**17; **104:**3, 11, 17, 21^2, 22, 27, 29; **105:**14, 16, 24, 29^2, 30^2, 31, 32^2, 33^2, 35^2, 36^2, 37; **106:**11, 14, 18, 20, 25, 27, 29, 35, 36, 37^2, 38^2, 39, 41, 42^2, 43, 44^2, 45; **107:**5, 6^2, 13^2, 14, 17^2, 19^2, 26^2, 27, 28^2, 30, 38^2, 39, 41^2, 42; **109:**2, 10, 13, 15, 25; **113:**8; **115:**2, 4, 7, 9, 10, 11; **119:**2, 70, 118; **123:**2; **124:**3, 6; **125:**3; **127:**5; **129:**3; **130:**8; **132:**12; **135:**6, 12, 17; **136:**21; **140:**2, 3^2, 5, 8^2, 9; **141:**4, 6, 10; **144:**12; **145:**15, 19; **146:**4^2; **147:**3, 11; **149:**2^2, 5, 6^2, 8^2; **Pr 1:**5, 15, 16, 18, 31^2; **2:**15; **8:**21; **9:**15; **10:**15; **11:**3, 5, 31; **12:**21; **13:**25; **14:**8, 14, 20, 24, 31; **17:**5, 6, 26; **18:**11; **20:**29; **22:**23; **23:**11^2; **24:**1, 2^2; **29:**16; **30:**11^2, 12^2, 25, 26, 29; **31:**5, 7^2; **Ecc 2:**3; **4:**1, 9; **8:**13; **9:**3, 6^3; **12:**4, 11; **SS 2:**13; **3:**3; **5:**7; **7:**12, 13; **Isa 1:**4; **2:**4^2, 7^4, 8^3, 20; **3:**4, 8, 9^2, 10, 11, 16^2, 17, 18; **5:**11, 12, 13^2, 14^2, 17, 21^2, 24^2, 28^4, 29^2; **6:**2^2, 4, 10^5; **8:**19, 21^2; **9:**3, 4^2, 11; **10:**2^2, 13^2, 17, 25, 27^2, 32; **11:**7; **13:**8, 10^2, 11, 16^4, 18; **14:**1, 2^3, 9, 21^2, 25; **15:**4^2, 5, 8^3; **16:**4, 8; **17:**7^2, 8^2, 9; **19:**3, 20, 22; **23:**13; **24:**6, 14; **25:**11^3; **26:**16, 19, 21; **27:**11^2; **28:**9; **29:**13^4, 15^2, 22, 23; **30:**4, 6^2; **31:**1^2, 3, 4^2, 8, 9^2; **33:**7, 9, 19; **34:**2, 3^3, 7, 17; **35:**10; **36:**12^2, 22; **37:**18, 19, 27, 30; **38:**19; **40:**6, 31; **41:**1, 17, 22, 29^2; **42:**4, 11, 15; **43:**9; **44:**9, 11, 18^2, 26; **45:**1, 12; **46:**1, 6, 7; **48:**19; **49:**22^2, 23^2, 26^2; **50:**2; **51:**7, 11, 14; **52:**8^2, 15; **53:**3, 11; **54:**3, 17; **55:**12; **56:**7, 11; **57:**8; **58:**1^2; **59:**5, 6^3, 7^3, 8, 18, 20, 21; **60:**8, 9, 10, 11; **61:**6, 7^3, 9^2; **63:**3, 6, 8, 9, 10; **65:**2, 4, 6, 7^2, 14, 21, 22, 23; **66:**3^3, 17, 18^2, 20, 24^2; **Jer 1:**15^2, 16^2; **2:**11, 13, 26^4, 27^2; **3:**16, 17, 21^2, 24^2; **4:**23; **5:**3, 4, 5, 6^3, 7, 16, 27, 28, 31; **6:**3^2, 10, 12^3, 15, 19, 23, 27; **7:**19, 24, 26, 28, 30, 31; **8:**1, 7, 10^2, 12, 13^2, 16, 19^2; **9:**3, 5, 6, 8, 14^2, 16; **10:**5, 7, 15, 21; **11:**8, 10^2, 14, 18, 22^2, 23; **12:**2^2, 14; **13:**10; **14:**3^3, 4, 6, 10^3, 12, 14, 16^3; **15:**7, 8^2, 9; **16:**3^2, 4, 15, 17^2, 18^4, 20; **17:**1^2, 2^2, 25^2; **18:**15, 16^2, 17^2, 20, 21^4, 22, 23^3; **19:**4, 5, 7^3, 9^2; **20:**4, 5, 11; **21:**7^2; **22:**4^2, 9, 13; **23:**3, 8, 10, 11, 12, 16, 17, 21, 22^2, 26, 27, 31, 32; **24:**6, 7^2, 10; **25:**12, 14^2, 36, 38; **26:**10; **27:**4; **29:**23; **30:**3, 8^2, 9^2, 10, 19, 20^2, 21^3; **31:**5, 13, 17, 24, 32, 33^3, 34^2; **32:**13, 18, 22, 30^2, 32^2, 33^2, 34, 35, 38, 39^2, 44; **33:**8, 12, 20, 26; **34:**10, 11, 20^3, 21^2; **35:**14, 16; **36:**3^2, 6, 7, 24, 31; **37:**10; **38:**4, 18, 23; **40:**7, 8, 9; **41:**5^2, 12, 17; **43:**1, 12^2; **44:**5, 15; **46:**5, 8, 21, 26, 27; **47:**3^3; **48:**34, 35; **49:**7, 11, 18, 20, 21^2, 29^4, 32^2, 35, 37^2; **50:**4, 5, 6^2, 7^3, 9^2, 10, 27, 33, 34^3, 40, 42, 45; **51:**5^2, 18, 28^2, 30^2, 55, 56; **La 1:**11, 22; **2:**9, 10^2, 12^3, 15^2, 16^2, 20; **3:**46, 60^2, 61^2, 63, 64, 65; **4:**2, 3^2, 7^3, 8^2, 10^3, 14, 20; **5:**7, 8, 12, 14; **Eze 1:**5, 7^2, 8^2, 9, 10, 11^2, 18, 23, 24^2, 25, 26; **2:**3, 6; **4:**4, 5, 17; **5:**10^2; **6:**5, 9^4, 13^4; **7:**13, 18^2, 19^5, 20^2, 24^2, 27^2; **8:**16^2, 17; **9:**10; **10:**10, 12^5, 16^2, 19, 21, 22; **11:**19, 20, 21^2, 22; **12:**16, 19^3; **13:**2, 3, 6^3, 17, 18^2, 22^2; **14:**3^2, 5, 10, 11^2, 13, 14, 16, 17, 18, 19, 20, 21, 22^2, 23^2; **16:**40, 45^2, 47^2; **18:**23; **19:**4, 7^2, 8^2; **20:**4, 8, 16^2, 18^3, 24^2, 26, 28^3, 30; **21:**15, 23, 28; **22:**10^2, 26, 27, 31; **23:**3^3, 8, 15^2, 17, 24, 30, 36, 37^3, 39^2, 42, 45, 47^3; **24:**25^5; **25:**4^2, 13, 15; **26:**16^3; **27:**9, 10, 11, 29, 30^2, 31, 35^2; **28:**7, 25, 26^2; **29:**7^3, 8, 14, 16; **30:**7, 11; **31:**4^2, 14; **32:**7, 10, 23, 24, 25^2, 26^3, 27^4, 29, 30^2; **33:**2^2, 11, 17, 31^2; **34:**10, 13, 14, 23, 24, 27^3, 30; **35:**5^2; **36:**5^2, 12^2, 17^4, 18, 19^2, 23, 37; **37:**10, 20, 21, 23^4, 25^3, 26, 27; **38:**4, 16; **39:**14, 22, 23^2, 24^2, 26^2, 27, 28^2; **42:**4; **43:**7^4, 8^3, 9^2, 10; **44:**10^2, 12^2, 13, 18^2, 19, 20^3, 28; **45:**4, 5, 8; **46:**16, 18^2; **47:**12^4; **48:**29; **Da 1:**16; **3:**21, 27^3, 28^2, 29; **6:**24^2; **7:**12; **8:**23; **11:**8^3, 15, 27, 32; **Hos 1:**7; **2:**5, 17; **3:**5^2; **4:**7, 8, 9^2, 12, 18^3, 19; **5:**4^3, 5, 6, 7^2, 15^2; **7:**2^2, 3^2, 6^2, 7^2, 14^2, 16^2; **8:**4^2, 13^2, 14^2; **9:**4, 6^2, 9^2, 13, 15^3, 16^2; **10:**2^4, 8, 10, 14; **11:**4, 6^3, 11; **12:**11; **13:**2, 16^4; **14:**4; **Joel 1:**3^2, 7^2; **2:**7, 17, 22^2; **3:**6, 13, 21; **Am 2:**4, 8, 14; **3:**10, 12^2; **5:**11; **6:**2; **7:**11, 17; **9:**4, 14^2, 15; **Ob 1:**12^2, 13^5, 14^3; **Jnh 1:**13; **3:**8^2, 10; **4:**11^2; **Mic 2:**1^2, 6, 9^2, 13^2; **3:**2, 3^2, 7; **4:**3^2, 5, 13^2; **5:**5; **6:**12, 16; **7:**4, 13, 16^4, 17; **Na 1:**10, 13; **2:**2, 5, 7, 11; **3:**12, 13; **Hab 1:**6, 7, 8^3, 9, 11; **2:**7, 15; **Zep 1:**9, 13^2, 17^2, 18^2; **2:**7^2, 8, 9, 10, 14, 15; **3:**6^3, 11, 13; **Hag 1:**10, 12^2, 14; **2:**22^2; **Zec 1:**21; **2:**9; **5:**9; **7:**2, 11^2, 12; **8:**8, 12; **9:**7^2, 16; **10:**6, 7^3, 9; **11:**3, 5^2, 6, 16; **12:**5^2, 12^3, 13^2, 14; **14:**12^6; **Mal 3:**5, 11; **4:**6^2; **Mt 1:**21; **2:**9, 11, 12; **3:**6; **4:**6, 8, 20, 21^2, 22, 23; **6:**2, 5, 7, 15, 16^2; **7:**6, 16, 20, 29; **8:**11, 22, 34; **9:**2, 4, 29, 30, 35; **10:**17, 21; **12:**9, 15, 21, 25; **13:**15^5, 43, 54, 58; **14:**14, 35; **15:**2, 8^2, 9, 26, 27; **16:**8; **17:**12, 25; **18:**10, 31; **20:**8, 25, 34^2; **21:**7, 8; **22:**7, 16, 18; **23:**5^2; **24:**45; **25:**1, 3, 4, 7, 10; **26:**43, 67; **27:**39; **28:**11; **Mk 1:**5, 18, 19, 20, 23, 39; **2:**5, 8; **3:**5; **5:**17; **6:**6, 52; **7:**3, 5, 6^2, 7, 27; **8:**17; **9:**48; **10:**32, 42; **11:**7, 8; **12:**15, 41, 44; **13:**12; **14:**40, 56, 59, 65; **15:**19, 29; **16:**2, 14^2, 18^2; **Lk 1:**16, 17, 20, 51, 52, 77; **2:**8, 22, 39, 44^2; **3:**15; **4:**6, 11, 15; **5:**2, 6, 7, 11, 15, 20, 30; **6:**1, 18, 23, 26; **8:**3, 12, 14; **9:**5, 47, 60; **10:**38; **11:**17, 48; **12:**36, 42; **13:**1, 29; **16:**4, 8; **18:**9; **19:**35, 36; **20:**23; **21:**1, 4^2; **23:**23, 24, 25, 48, 51; **24:**5^2, 11, 17, 31^2, 43, 45; **Jn 2:**11, 15; **3:**19; **4:**30, 38; **5:**28; **7:**31, 50; **8:**30; **10:**39; **11:**19, 45, 55; **12:**11, 37, 40^4, 42; **13:**12; **15:**22, 25; **17:**20; **19:**6; **20:**10; **Ac 1:**9^2, 19; **2:**41, 45, 46, 47; **4:**23^2, 24, 26, 29; **5:**14, 16, 38; **6:**1, 6; **7:**6, 12, 13, 16, 19, 34, 35, 39, 41, 54, 57^2, 58; **8:**10, 17; **9:**15, 24; **10:**9; **11:**23, 30; **12:**20, 25; **13:**3, 4, 5, 17, 18, 19^2, 22, 27, 33, 50, 51; **14:**2, 5, 14, 16, 17, 23; **15:**3, 9, 22, 26; **16:**19, 24, 33, 35; **17:**21; **18:**26; **19:**12, 18, 19; **21:**5, 21, 24^3; **22:**4, 5, 22, 23; **23:**21, 28, 29, 30, 31; **24:**1, 21; **25:**13, 16, 19; **26:**18, 20^2; **27:**19, 43; **28:**6, 27^5; **Ro 1:**18, 21^2, 24^2, 26, 27, 30; **2:**15^3; **3:**3, 8, 13^3, 14, 15, 16, 18; **8:**5^2; **10:**2, 3, 18^2; **11:**9, 10^2, 11, 12^3, 15^2, 24, 27, 30; **13:**6; **15:**27; **16:**4, 5, 18, 23; **1Co 1:**2; **3:**19; **8:**7, 12; **9:**13, 14; **10:**5; **14:**3, 35; **16:**19; **2Co 3:**14, 15; **6:**16; **8:**2^2, 3^2, 14; **9:**14^2; **11:**15^2; **12:**14^2; **13:**13; **Gal 2:**13; **Eph 1:**10; **2:**16; **4:**14, 17, 18^2, 29; **5:**24, 28^2; **6:**6^2, 9; **Php 3:**19^6; **Col 2:**23^3; **3:**22^2; **1Th 2:**16^2; **5:**13; **1Ti 1:**9, 19; **3:**11, 13; **4:**14; **5:**4^3, 11^2, 12, 14; **6:**1, 2, 17^2; **2Ti 2:**17, 26; **3:**2, 6, 9; **4:**3^2, 4; **Tit 1:**12, 15, 16; **2:**4, 5, 9; **3:**13; **Heb 2:**10, 14, 15^2; **3:**10, 19; **4:**6, 11; **6:**6; **7:**5^2, 27; **8:**9, 10^3, 12^2; **9:**6; **10:**2, 16^2, 17; **11:**14, 16, 20, 35, 39; **13:**3, 7^2, 17^2, 24; **Jas 1:**27; **5:**3; **1Pe 1:**24; **2:**23; **3:**1, 5^2, 12, 16; **4:**19; **2Pe 2:**2, 3^3, 9, 13^2, 21; **3:**3, 16; **1Jn 2:**19; **2Jn 1:**13; **3Jn 1:**6, 14; **Jude 1:**6^2, 8, 13, 16^2, 18; **Rev 3:**4; **4:**4, 10, 11; **6:**11, 17; **7:**9, 11, 14, 17^2; **9:**4, 7^2, 8^2, 9, 10, 16, 17^2, 18, 19^3, 20, 21^4; **11:**5^2, 7, 8^2, 9, 11, 12, 16^2; **12:**8, 11^2; **14:**1, 2, 5, 11, 13^2; **15:**6; **16:**10, 11^2; **17:**13, 17^2; **18:**11, 15, 17, 19; **19:**18, 19, 21; **20:**4^3; **21:**3, 4, 8, 24; **22:**4, 14.

THEIRS (21)

Ge 34:28; **Ex 29:**9; **Nu 23:**10; **33:**54; **1Sa 25:**7; **1Ki 22:**13; **2Ch 18:**12; **Ne 5:**5; **Isa 61:**7; **Jer 44:**28; **Eze 16:**52; **46:**17; **Jnh 2:**8; **Mt 5:**3, 10; **Ro 9:**4^2, 5; **1Co 7:**30; **Heb 1:**4; **8:**6.

THEM (5162)

Ge 1:14, 15, 17, 22, 26, 27, 28^2; **2:**19^2; **3:**7,

21; **5:**2^{3}; **6:**1, 2, 4, 7, 13^{2}, 19, 21; **7:**14, 15; **9:**1, 19; **11:**3, 6, 8, 9; **13:**6; **14:**10, 15^{3}, 24; **15:**5, 10, 11; **17:**23; **18:**2^{2}, 8^{2}, 16^{2}; **19:**1^{2}, 3, 5^{2}, 6, 8^{2}, 9, 12, 16^{2}, 17^{2}, 18; **20:**8, 14; **21:**14^{2}, 27; **22:**6, 8; **23:**8; **24:**53, 56; **25:**6, 26; **26:**4, 15, 18^{2}, 27, 30, 31; **27:**13, 14^{2}, 15; **29:**5, 6, 7, 9; **30:**28, 31, 32, 35^{2}, 37, 40, 42; **31:**5, 9, 34^{2}, 37, 46, 55; **32:**2, 4, 16, 23; **34:**8, 14, 21^{2}, 23, 25; **35:**4, 5^{2}; **36:**7^{2}; **37:**2, 4, 6, 13, 17^{2}, 18, 22, 25; **38:**18, 26, 28; **39:**14; **40:**3, 4^{2}, 6, 8^{2}, 11, 17, 22; **41:**3, 6, 8^{2}, 12, 13, 19, 21, 23, 30, 38; **42:**7^{2}, 9^{2}, 12, 14, 17, 18, 23, 24^{3}, 25^{2}, 27, 29, 36; **43:**2, 11^{2}, 16, 23, 24, 27, 34; **44:**4^{2}, 6^{2}, 11, 15, 28; **45:**15, 19, 21^{2}, 22, 24, 26, 27; **46:**6; **47:**2, 6^{3}, 11, 17^{2}, 20, 22; **48:**6, 9^{2}, 10^{2}, 12, 13^{2}, 20; **49:**7^{2}, 19, 28^{2}, 29; **50:**12, 19, 21^{2}; **Ex 1:**7, 10, 11^{2}, 13, 14, 16, 17, 18, 21; **2:**11, 17, 18, 25; **3:**7, 8^{2}, 9, 13^{2}, 16, 20; **4:**18, 20, 30, 31; **5:**5, 7, 8, 13, 20; **6:**1^{2}, 3, 4^{2}, 6, 13; **7:**6, 13; **8:**2, 14; **9:**2^{2}, 11, 17, 27; **10:**1, 2, 4, 19, 26, 27; **12:**5, 6^{2}, 21, 27, 36, 38, 42; **13:**17, 21^{3}; **14:**4, 5, 7, 9, 10, 17, 19^{2}, 23^{2}, 25, 27, 28; **15:**5, 7, 9^{3}, 10, 12, 13, 16, 17^{2}, 19, 21, 25^{2}; **16:**3, 4, 12, 15, 19, 20^{2}, 23; **18:**8, 9, 16, 20^{2}, 21, 22^{2}, 25; **19:**7, 10^{2}, 12, 14, 21, 22, 24, 25; **20:**5^{2}, 11; **21:**1; **22:**5, 11, 30^{2}; **23:**13, 23, 24^{2}, 29, 30, 31, 32, 33; **24:**14; **25:**3, 8^{2}, 10, 12, 13, 20, 26, 28^{2}, 37, 40; **26:**1, 6, 11, 19, 37; **27:**6; **28:**5, 9, 12, 20, 23, 25, 26, 27, 33, 40, 41^{2}, 43; **29:**1, 3^{2}, 4, 8, 9, 13^{2}, 17, 22, 24, 25^{2}, 29, 30, 33, 35, 46^{2}; **30:**5, 12^{3}, 29^{2}, 30; **31:**11; **32:**2^{2}, 3, 8, 10^{2}, 12^{3}, 13, 19, 21, 24, 25, 27, 34; **34:**1, 15, 31^{2}, 32, 33; **35:**1, 23, 29, 35^{2}; **36:**8, 13, 24, 36^{2}, 38; **37:**3, 4, 8, 9, 13, 28; **38:**6; **39:**6, 7, 18, 19, 20, 25, 43; **40:**11, 12, 14, 15; **Lev 1:**2, 12; **2:**12; **3:**3, 4, 9, 10, 11, 14, 15, 16; **4:**8, 9, 10, 20; **5:**8; **6:**10, 18; **7:**4, 5, 7, 34, 36; **8:**6, 10, 11, 13^{3}, 27, 28^{2}, 30; **9:**2, 7, 13, 14, 22; **10:**1, 2, 4, 5, 11, 14, 17; **11:**4, 11, 26, 31, 32, 33, 35, 43^{2}; **12:**7; **13:**39, 59; **14:**12, 23, 24, 51; **15:**2, 14, 15, 27, 29, 31^{2}; **16:**4, 7, 12, 16, 21, 23, 28; **17:**2, 5^{2}, 7, 8^{2}, 10; **18:**2, 5^{2}, 30; **19:**2, 10, 31, 37; **20:**6, 8, 12, 13, 18, 22, 23, 27; **21:**1, 8^{2}, 23; **22:**3, 9^{2}, 16^{3}, 18, 25, 31; **23:**2, 10, 22, 43; **24:**6, 12; **25:**2, 31, 43, 44, 46^{2}; **26:**36^{2}, 37, 41^{2}, 43^{2}, 44^{4}; **27:**2; **Nu 1:**19, 49; **2:**5, 12, 20, 27; **3:**6, 16; **4:**12^{2}, 19, 27, 37, 41, 45; **5:**3^{2}, 4, 12, 23; **6:**2, 7, 16, 20, 23, 27; **7:**5^{2}, 6, 10; **8:**6, 7^{3}, 8, 10, 13, 15, 16, 17, 19, 21^{3}; **9:**6, 8; **10:**2, 33^{2}, 34; **11:**1^{2}, 3, 4, 12^{2}, 16, 17, 21, 22^{2}, 24, 25, 26, 28, 29, 31, 32, 33; **12:**4, 5, 9^{2}; **13:**3^{2}, 17, 23^{2}, 26^{2}, 33; **14:**2, 9^{2}, 10, 11, 12^{2}, 13, 14^{2}, 16^{2}, 19, 20, 23, 28, 31, 45^{2}; **15:**2, 18, 23, 26, 38, 39; **16:**2, 3^{3}, 7, 9, 15^{2}, 19, 21, 26, 30^{2}, 31, 32, 33, 34, 38, 39, 45, 46, 47; **17:**2, 4, 6, 9; **18:**16, 20, 24, 26; **19:**6, 9, 10, 17, 21; **20:**6, 10, 12, 13, 20, 21^{2}, 25, 26, 28; **21:**1, 3^{2}, 6, 16, 25, 30^{2}, 33, 35; **22:**6^{2}, 7, 8, 11^{3}, 12, 18, 20; **23:**2, 9^{2}, 11, 13^{3}, 21^{2}, 22, 25^{2}, 27; **24:**8^{2}, 9, 10; **25:**2, 3, 4^{2}, 8, 11^{2}, 17; **26:**3, 10, 43, 53, 62, 64, 65; **27:**7^{2}, 17^{3}; **28:**2, 3; **30:**12^{3}, 14^{2}, 15^{2}; **31:**3, 6, 13, 15, 30, 47, 51; **32:**7, 8, 9, 13, 17, 19, 20, 28, 29^{2}, 33, 41; **33:**4, 51, 54, 56; **34:**2; **35:**2, 6, 10, 15; **Dt 1:**3, 8, 13, 15, 16, 25, 29, 39, 42; **2:**5, 6, 9, 11, 12^{3}, 14, 15^{2}, 19^{2}, 20, 21^{2}, 22^{2}, 23, 34, 36; **3:**3, 4, 6, 20, 22, 28; **4:**1, 5, 6, 7, 9^{3}, 10, 13, 19, 31, 37, 45; **5:**1^{2}, 9^{2}, 22^{2}, 29, 30, 31^{2}; **6:**2, 7^{2}, 8^{2}, 9; **7:**2^{5}, 3, 5, 12, 15, 16, 17, 18, 20, 21, 22, 23^{2}, 24, 25; **8:**19; **9:**2, 3^{4}, 4^{2}, 5, 10, 12, 14, 17^{2}, 28^{5}; **10:**2, 4, 9, 11, 15; **11:**4^{2}, 6^{2}, 9, 16, 18^{2}, 19^{2}, 20; **12:**14, 18, 21, 22, 29; **13:**2; **14:**19; **15:**20; **17:**3, 8, 9, 16; **18:**2, 4, 5, 18^{2}; **19:**1, 3, 8; **20:**1, 3, 17, 19^{3}, 20; **21:**5, 10, 18; **22:**19, 24^{2}; **23:**6, 8, 18; **24:**8; **25:**5, 11; **26:**2, 13, 16; **27:**2, 3, 4, 5, 7, 26; **28:**13, 14, 25^{2}, 26, 31, 32, 39^{2}, 41, 55, 57; **29:**1, 2, 7, 17, 25^{2}, 26^{2}, 28^{2}; **30:**1, 17; **31:**4, 5^{2}, 6, 7^{2}, 10, 11, 16, 17^{4}, 19^{2}, 20^{2}, 21^{4}, 23, 28; **32:**11^{2}, 19, 20, 21^{2}, 23^{2}, 24^{2}, 25, 26, 28, 30^{2}, 35, 38^{2}, 46, 47; **33:**2, 9, 17; **Jos 1:**2, 6, 15^{2}, 18; **2:**4, 5^{2}, 6^{2}, 9, 13, 15, 16, 21, 22, 23; **3:**6, 14; **4:**3^{3} 5, 7, 8^{4}, 11, 12, 22; **6:**1; **6:**5, 6, 8, 13, 18, 23; **7:**1, 2, 5^{2}, 11^{2}, 13, 21^{2}, 23^{2}, 25; **8:**3, 5, 6^{2}, 9, 10, 11, 12, 15, 16, 22^{3}, 24^{2}, 29, 33, 35; **9:**11^{2}, 15^{2}, 16, 18^{2}, 19^{2}, 20^{3}, 21^{3}, 26^{2}; **10:**1, 8^{3}, 9, 10^{4}, 11^{2}, 19^{3}, 20, 25, 26, 27^{2}, 39, 41; **11:**6^{2}, 7^{2}, 8^{3}, 9, 11, 12^{2}, 14, 17^{2}, 19, 20^{2}, 21; **12:**6; **13:**6, 8^{2}, 12, 14, 33; **14:**1, 12; **17:**4, 13, 18; **18:**4, 6, 7, 8, 10; **19:**49; **20:**4, 9; **21:**2, 10, 11, 17, 44^{3}; **22:**2, 6^{2}, 7^{2}, 12, 15, 33; **23:**1, 2, 5^{2}, 7^{3}, 12^{2}, 16; **24:**6, 7^{2}, 8^{2}, 11, 12, 13, 25; **Jdg 1:**3, 7, 22, 25, 28, 29, 30^{2}, 33, 34; **2:**3, 12^{2}, 14^{3}, 15^{3}, 16, 17, 18^{4}, 19, 21, 22, 23^{2}; **3:**8, 9^{2}, 15, 23, 25, 27; **4:**2; **5:**21; **6:**1, 8, 9, 19^{2}, 20, 35^{2}; **7:**1, 4^{2}, 16, 17, 24; **8:**2, 8, 12^{2}, 16, 20, 21, 23, 25, 34, 35; **9:**1, 7, 27, 36, 38, 43^{2}, 44, 49, 57; **10:**7^{2}, 8, 14, 16; **11:**7, 9, 11, 21, 25, 26, 32; **12:**3, 4; **13:**1; **14:**9^{2}, 12, 18, 19; **15:**3^{2}, 4, 7, 8^{2}, 11, 13, 16; **16:**3^{3}, 8, 12, 13, 25, 26, 29; **17:**4^{2}; **18:**2, 4, 6, 8, 9, 18, 21, 23, 27, 28; **19:**6, 8, 15, 23, 24^{3}, 25, 29; **20:**10, 13, 17, 20, 23, 25^{2}, 28, 31, 32^{2}, 39, 41^{2}, 42, 43^{2}, 44, 46; **21:**7, 12, 14, 18, 22^{4}, 23; **Ru 1:**6, 7, 9, 13, 19, 20; **2:**16; **1Sa 2:**8^{3}, 10, 23, 25; **3:**13; **4:**2; **5:**6^{2}, 8; **6:**6, 7, 10, 12, 15, 19^{2}; **7:**7, 10, 11; **8:**8, 9^{4}, 11, 14, 22^{2}; **9:**4^{2}, 11, 14, 20, 22; **10:**2, 4, 5, 6, 18, 25; **11:**7, 8, 11^{2}, 12; **12:**5, 8, 9^{2}; **13:**16, 22; **14:**8, 9, 10, 11, 12, 21, 32^{2}, 34^{3}, 36^{2}, 37, 47, 48; **15:**2, 3^{2}, 4, 6, 15, 18^{2}, 21, 24; **16:**5, 20; **17:**3, 18, 23, 36, 39^{3}, 40; **18:**16; **19:**8, 15; **20:**21, 40; **21:**2; **22:**4, 7, 18; **23:**18, 26; **24:**7; **25:**5, 7, 8, 14, 15, 16, 18, 20; **26:**12, 13; **28:**23; **30:**2^{2}, 8^{3}, 15, 17^{2}, 20, 21, 22; **31:**1, 7, 12, 13; **2Sa 1:**4, 10, 11; **2:**5, 7, 13, 14; **3:**22, 36; **4:**7, 12; **5:**3, 19, 20, 21, 23^{2}; **7:**10^{2}; **8:**1, 2^{3}, 5, 7; **10:**3, 4, 9, 10, 16, 19; **11:**23; **12:**11, 17, 31^{2}; **13:**30; **14:**6; **15:**35, 36^{2}; **17:**11, 15, 17, 18^{2}, 20; **18:**1, 14, 16; **20:**3^{3}, 8; **21:**2^{3}, 6, 9^{3}, 10, 12^{2}; **22:**15, 28, 38, 39, 42, 43^{2}; **23:**11, 19; **24:**1, 12, 24; **1Ki 1:**33; **2:**5, 7, 32^{2}; **3:**17; **5:**9^{4}, 12, 14; **6:**12, 15, 35^{2}; **7:**25, 46, 51; **8:**4, 14, 21, 34, 35, 36, 37, 44, 46^{3}, 48, 50, 52, 53; **9:**6, 7, 9^{2}, 12, 13, 25; **10:**17, 19, 28, 29; **11:**2^{2}, 18, 29; **12:**7^{2}, 9, 10, 16, 17; **13:**12; **14:**15, 27, 28, 31; **15:**18, 22, 24, 29; **16:**23; **18:**4^{2}, 10, 13, 22, 23^{2}, 26, 27, 28, 29, 33, 40^{3}; **19:**2, 21; **20:**7, 18^{2}, 19, 23, 24, 25, 27^{2}, 30^{2}; **21:**8^{2}, 10, 11; **22:**6, 10, 43, 50; **2Ki 1:**2, 3, 5, 7; **2:**6, 8, 11, 12, 16^{2}, 17, 18, 24^{2}; **3:**3, 9, 21, 24; **4:**33, 39^{2}, 44; **5:**12, 22, 23^{3}, 24; **6:**3, 4, 5, 11, 16, 18, 19^{2}, 21^{3}, 22^{2}, 23^{2}, 33; **7:**8^{2}, 10, 12, 13, 14, 15; **8:**24; **9:**11, 13, 17, 18, 19, 20; **10:**1, 6^{3}, 7^{2}, 8, 14^{3}, 17, 18, 22, 25^{2}; **11:**4^{4}, 5; **12:**7, 18; **13:**2, 3, 6, 7, 11, 18, 23^{4}; **14:**26, 27; **15:**7, 38; **16:**20; **17:**6, 7, 8, 11, 15^{4}, 18, 20^{3}, 21, 22, 23, 24, 25, 26^{2}, 28, 29, 32, 35^{4}; **18:**11, 12, 13, 18, 19, 23; **19:**3, 6, 11, 12, 18; **20:**13^{2}, 15; **21:**3, 8^{2}, 9, 14, 21; **22:**5, 6, 7, 15; **23:**4, 12^{2}, 16, 20; **24:**2, 3, 20; **25:**20^{2}, 21, 24; **1Ch 4:**41; **5:**11, 20^{2}, 25, 26; **6:**32, 54; **7:**3, 22; **8:**7; **9:**28^{2}; **10:**1, 7, 12; **11:**3, 21; **12:**17^{2}, 18^{2}, 21, 39; **13:**2; **14:**8, 10^{2}, 11, 12, 14^{2}; **15:**2, 12, 18; **16:**21, 31, 32, 38, 41; **17:**9^{2}; **18:**1, 5, 7; **19:**4^{2}, 5, 10, 16, 17^{2}; **20:**3; **21:**10; **22:**2, 4, 14, 18; **23:**22, 31; **24:**3, 5, 19; **25:**7; **26:**32; **29:**8; **2Ch 1:**16, 17; **2:**2, 16^{2}, 18^{2}; **3:**10, 16^{2}; **4:**4, 6, 7^{2}, 8, 17; **5:**1, 5; **6:**3, 25^{2}, 26, 27, 28, 34, 36^{3}; **7:**19, 20, 22^{3}; **8:**2; **9:**8^{2}, 11, 16, 18; **10:**7^{2}, 9, 10, 13, 16, 17; **11:**11, 12, 14, 23^{2}; **12:**5, 7^{2}, 10, 11; **13:**7, 10, 13, 16, 17; **14:**7, 9, 13, 14; **15:**4, 6, 9, 15^{2}; **16:**6, 8; **17:**8, 9; **18:**5, 9, 31; **19:**4, 6, 9, 10; **20:**10^{2}, 12, 16^{2}, 17, 23, 25, 27, 32; **21:**1, 3; **22:**8, 12; **23:**3, 6, 12, 14; **24:**5, 10, 13, 17, 19^{2}; **25:**5, 10, 12^{2}, 14^{3}, 20; **26:**9, 23; **27:**5; **28:**5, 9^{3}, 15^{2}, 21, 23^{2}, 24; **29:**3, 4, 8, 23, 32, 34; **30:**1, 7, 10, 12, 14, 16, 18, 24, 27; **31:**1, 2, 6, 19; **32:**1, 6^{2}, 18^{2}, 22, 26; **33:**3, 8, 11, 15; **34:**4^{2}, 6, 12^{2}, 16, 23; **35:**2, 11, 12, 13, 15; **36:**7, 15, 17^{2}; **Ezr 1:**6, 8^{2}; **2:**62, 63; **3:**3; **4:**4^{2}, 5, 20, 23; **5:**1, 2^{2}, 3, 9, 10, 12, 14, 15; **6:**9, 22^{2}; **7:**17, 25; **8:**1, 13, 14, 15, 17^{2}, 25, 26, 28, 29^{2}; **9:**2, 12; **10:**10, 16, 44; **Ne 1:**2, 9^{2}; **2:**9, 17, 18, 20; **3:**2, 7, 23^{2}, 27, 29, 30; **4:**4, 11^{2}, 12, 13, 14; **5:**7^{3}, 8, 11^{2}, 12, 15; **6:**3, 4, 17; **7:**3^{3}, 64, 65; **8:**5, 9, 12, 17; **9:**6, 10, 11, 12^{2}, 13^{2}, 14^{2}, 15^{4}, 17^{2}, 19^{2}, 20^{2}, 21, 22^{2}, 23, 24^{3}, 26^{2}, 27^{5}, 28^{3}, 29^{2}, 30^{3}, 31^{2}, 34, 35^{2}; **10:**31; **11:**21; **12:**9, 24, 32, 38, 43; **13:**2, 9, 10, 11^{3}, 15, 16, 17, 21, 25^{3}, 29, 30; **Est 2:**3^{2}; **3:**4, 8, 9; **4:**4; **5:**8, 11; **6:**8, 9; **8:**10, 11, 17; **9:**1^{2}, 2^{2}, 3, 5^{2}, 16, 21, 22, 23, 24, 26, 27, 28, 31; **Job 1:**4, 5^{2}, 6, 15, 17, 19; **2:**1; **5:**14, 15; **8:**4; **9:**5; **11:**20; **12:**15, 23^{2}, 24, 25; **15:**19; **17:**4; **20:**15, 19, 29; **21:**8, 9, 17, 26; **22:**6, 19, 29; **24:**17, 20^{2}, 23; **26:**5; **27:**15; **29:**24^{2}, 25; **30:**2, 9, 13; **31:**15, 27; **32:**15; **33:**16; **34:**25, 26^{2}; **36:**7^{2}, 9, 10^{2}, 13, 15; **37:**11, 12, 21; **38:**20; **39:**14, 15^{2}; **40:**13; **42:**9, 15; **Ps 2:**4, 5^{2}, 9^{2}; **5:**10^{2}, 11^{2}, 12; **7:**7; **9:**6, 20; **10:**9, 17; **11:**4; **12:**5^{2}; **17:**13^{2}; **18:**14, 37, 38, 41, 42^{2}; **19:**11^{2}; **21:**9^{3}, 12^{2}; **22:**4, 18; **24:**9; **25:**9, 14; **28:**4^{3}, 5^{2}, 9; **31:**12, 20^{2}; **33:**19^{2}; **34:**7, 16, 17^{2}, 19, 20; **35:**5, 6, 8^{2}, 10^{2}, 24, 25; **36:**8; **37:**10, 12, 33^{2}, 40^{4}; **38:**16; **40:**5; **41:**10; **43:**3^{2}; **44:**3^{2}; **45:**16; **48:**6, 7, 13; **49:**11^{2}; **53:**5^{2}; **54:**5; **55:**13^{2}, 19^{2}; **56:**7; **58:**7; **59:**8, 11^{3}, 12, 13^{2}; **62:**10; **64:**5, 7, 8^{3}; **68:**2, 22^{2}, 25^{2}, 27; **69:**22, 24^{2}, 27^{2}, 34; **72:**14; **73:**10, 18^{2}, 20; **74:**8, 11; **76:**11; **78:**4, 6, 11, 13, 14, 15, 21, 24, 25, 27, 28, 29, 31^{2}, 34, 38, 42, 45^{2}, 49, 50^{2}, 52, 53, 54, 55^{2}, 59, 66, 72^{2}; **80:**5^{2}; **81:**12; **82:**4; **83:**4, 8, 9, 13, 15^{2}, 18; **85:**8; **88:**8; **89:**9; **94:**23^{3}; **96:**12; **97:**10; **98:**9; **99:**3, 6, 7^{2}, 8; **102:**14, 26; **104:**8, 24, 27, 28; **105:**14, 17, 24, 27, 38, 40^{2}, 44; **106:**4, 8, 9, 10^{2}, 11, 15^{2}, 21, 23^{2}, 26^{2}, 27, 29, 32, 34, 36, 41^{2}, 42^{2}, 43, 46^{2}; **107:**6, 7, 8, 12, 13, 14, 15, 19, 20^{2}, 21, 22, 28, 30, 31, 32, 38, 40; **109:**15, 27; **111:**2, 6; **113:**8; **115:**8^{3}; **118:**10, 11, 12; **119:**33, 47, 52, 93, 129, 140, 152, 165, 167; **126:**2; **127:**5; **132:**12; **135:**18^{3}; **136:**11; **137:**9; **139:**16, 17, 18, 22^{2}; **140:**10; **144:**6; **145:**15, 19; **146:**6; **147:**4, 18; **148:**5, 6, 13; **149:**3, 9; **Pr 1:**10, 12, 15, 32^{2}; **3:**3^{2}, 21; **4:**5, 19, 21^{2}, 22; **5:**17; **6:**21^{2}; **7:**3^{2}; **8:**8, 9; **10:**16^{2}; **11:**3, 5, 6; **12:**6, 26; **14:**3; **15:**6; **17:**15; **19:**7; **20:**1, 5, 10, 12, 26; **21:**7; **22:**2, 5, 18^{2}, 23; **23:**21; **24:**22, 25; **28:**4, 13, 27; **31:**7, 21, 24, 29; **Ecc 1:**14; **2:**5, 14, 18; **3:**5, 18, 19; **4:**16; **5:**8, 11^{2}, 19; **6:**2^{2}; **7:**28; **8:**13; **9:**2, 5, 11, 12; **10:**9^{2}; **11:**8; **12:**1, 12; **SS 3:**4, 8; **4:**2, 4; **5:**3; **6:**6; **Isa 1:**2, 14, 23; **2:**9; **3:**4, 9^{2}, 10, 11, 12; **5:**25, 27; **8:**7, 14, 15; **9:**4, 10, 11, 13, 16; **10:**6, 19, 20, 26; **11:**6, 14; **13:**2^{2}, 8^{2}, 17; **14:**1^{2}, 2^{2}, 9, 20, 22; **16:**14; **17:**2, 11^{4}, 13; **18:**6; **19:**1, 4, 12, 14, 16, 17, 18, 20^{2}, 21, 22^{3}, 25; **23:**1; **25:**12^{2}; **26:**11^{2}, 14^{3}, 16; **27:**4^{2}, 5^{3}, 11^{3}; **28:**13; **29:**23; **30:**5, 8, 20, 22^{2}, 28, 30, 31, 32^{2}; **31:**8; **33:**21^{2}; **34:**2^{2}, 7, 15, 16, 17; **35:**10; **36:**1, 4, 8; **37:**3, 6, 11, 12, 19; **38:**16; **39:**2^{2}, 4; **40:**7, 11, 22, 24^{2}, 26^{2}; **41:**1, 2, 3, 4, 12, 15, 16^{3}, 17^{2}, 22, 28^{2}; **42:**5, 9, 10, 11, 12, 16^{3}, 22^{3}, 25^{3}; **43:**6^{2}, 9^{2}; **44:**9, 11, 26; **45:**21; **47:**6^{2}, 13, 14, 15; **48:**3^{2}, 5^{3}, 6^{2}, 7^{2}, 13, 21^{2}; **49:**10^{4}, 18^{2}; **50:**9; **51:**8^{2}, 11; **52:**4, 5; **56:**5^{2}, 7, 8; **57:**6, 13^{2}, 19; **58:**2; **59:**8^{2}, 21; **61:**3, 8^{2}, 9; **63:**3^{2}, 6, 9^{4}, 10, 11^{2}, 12, 13, 19; **64:**5; **65:**8, 9, 21, 22, 23; **66:**4^{2}, 19, 20, 21; **Jer 1:**8, 17^{3}; **2:**3, 25, 28, 34, 37; **4:**12, 29; **5:**3^{2}, 5, 6^{2}, 9, 10^{2}, 13^{2}, 16, 19, 29; **6:**9, 10, 15, 18, 21, 24, 30; **7:**16, 22^{2}, 23, 27^{2}, 28, 33; **8:**3, 4, 13^{2}; **9:**2, 7, 9, 13, 14, 16^{3}, 17, 18, 22; **10:**2, 5, 11, 14, 18; **11:**2, 3, 4, 5, 6, 7, 8^{2}, 10, 11^{2}, 12, 14, 20, 22, 23; **12:**2, 3^{2}, 6, 9, 14^{2}, 15^{2}; **13:**10, 12, 13, 14^{2}, 19; **14:**10^{2}, 12^{2}, 13, 14^{3}, 15, 16^{2}, 17; **15:**1^{2}, 2, 3, 4, 7, 8, 16, 17, 19; **16:**6, 7^{2}, 11^{2}, 15^{2}, 16^{2}, 18, 19, 21^{2}; **17:**18^{3}, 20; **18:**15^{2}, 17^{2}, 20, 21, 22, 23^{2}; **19:**7, 9^{2}, 11, 15; **20:**4^{3}, 12; **21:**3, 4, 7^{2}; **22:**7, 13; **23:**2^{2}, 3^{2}, 4^{2}, 8, 12, 15, 18, 21, 22, 32^{2}, 33; **24:**6^{6}, 7, 9^{2}, 10^{2}; **25:**6, 9^{3}, 10, 14, 16, 18, 26, 27, 28, 30^{2}; **26:**2, 3, 4, 19; **27:**4, 15, 17, 18, 22^{3}; **28:**14; **29:**8, 9, 17^{2}, 18^{3}, 19, 21^{2}, 22, 23; **30:**3, 8, 9, 19^{2}, 20, 21; **31:**5, 8^{3}, 9^{2}, 10, 11, 13, 23, 28^{2}, 32^{3}, 34; **32:**14, 18, 20, 22, 23^{4}, 33, 37^{4}, 39^{2}, 40^{3}, 41^{2}, 42^{2}; **33:**6, 7, 8, 13, 24, 26; **34:**10^{2}, 11, 13, 16, 22; **35:**2^{2}, 4, 5, 15, 16, 17^{3}; **36:**3^{2}, 4, 6, 13, 14, 15, 18, 23^{2}, 25, 26, 31^{2}, 32; **37:**5; **38:**4, 11, 19, 26, 27; **39:**4, 5, 10; **40:**9, 10, 11, 14; **41:**5, 6^{2}, 7^{2}, 8^{3}, 10, 18; **42:**9, 17^{2}; **43:**1, 9, 10^{2}; **44:**6, 27; **45:**5; **46:**15, 21^{2}, 26; **47:**2; **48:**9, 19, 33; **49:**20, 29, 32, 36, 37^{3}; **50:**6^{2}, 7^{2}, 21, 27^{3}, 33^{2}, 43, 45; **51:**17, 39^{2}, 40, 48; **52:**3, 26^{2}, 27; **La 1:**17, 22; **2:**21^{2}; **3:**20, 40, 63, 64, 65, 66^{2}; **4:**4, 15, 16^{2}; **Eze 1:**6, 8, 9, 10, 11, 12, 13, 15, 16, 17, 19, 20, 21; **2:**4, 5, 6^{2}, 7; **3:**4, 6, 9^{2}, 11^{2}, 13, 15, 17, 26, 27; **4:**9^{2}, 13; **5:**2, 3, 4^{2}, 13^{2}; **6:**2, 10, 12, 14; **7:**13^{2}, 19^{2}, 20, 22, 27^{2}; **8:**11^{2}, 13, 17, 18^{4}; **9:**2, 7, 10^{2}; **10:**2, 7, 10, 16, 17^{2}, 19^{2}; **11:**1, 4, 16^{3}, 19^{4}, 22^{2}; **12:**6^{2}, 7, 10, 11^{2}, 12, 14, 15^{2}, 16, 23^{2}, 28; **13:**6, 17, 20, 22; **14:**3, 4^{2}; **15:**7^{3}; **16:**17, 18^{2}, 19, 20, 21, 33, 36, 37^{2}, 50, 53, 54, 61; **17:**3, 9, 12^{2}; **18:**11, 14, 28; **19:**12; **20:**3, 4^{3}, 5^{3}, 6^{3}, 7, 8^{2}, 9, 10^{2}, 11^{4}, 12^{2}, 13^{4}, 14, 15^{3}, 17^{3}, 21^{4}, 22, 23^{3}, 25, 26^{2}, 27, 28^{2}, 29, 38, 40; **21:**6, 14, 23^{2}; **22:**18, 26, 28, 29, 30, 31^{2}; **23:**6, 13, 15, 16^{3}, 17^{2}, 22, 23^{2}, 24, 36, 37, 40, 43, 45, 46^{2}, 47^{2}; **24:**3, 6, 20, 27; **25:**2, 3, 17^{3}; **28:**25, 26; **29:**12, 14^{2}, 21; **30:**9, 23, 26; **32:**10^{2}, 19, 24, 25, 26, 31; **33:**2, 6, 7, 10, 11, 25, 27, 28, 31, 32^{2}, 33; **34:**2, 4, 6, 10^{3}, 11, 12^{2}, 13^{4}, 14, 15, 20, 21, 23^{3}, 24, 25, 26, 27^{2}, 28^{2}, 29, 30; **35:**10, 11^{2}; **36:**12, 18, 19^{2}, 20, 23, 37; **37:**2, 4, 8^{3}, 10, 12^{2}, 13, 17, 19^{2}, 21^{3}, 22^{2}, 23^{2}, 24, 26^{3}, 27, 28; **38:**4, 5, 7, 8, 11, 15, 17; **39:**9^{2}, 10^{2}, 12, 13^{2}, 14, 15, 18, 21, 23^{2}, 24^{2}, 26, 27^{3}, 28^{2}, 29; **40:**22, 26, 42; **41:**16; **42:**5, 9, 11; **43:**8^{2}, 9^{2}, 10, 11^{2}, 24^{3}; **44:**11, 12, 14, 18, 19, 23, 28, 29, 30; **46:**10, 18, 20; **47:**12, 14, 22; **48:**12, 21; **Da 1:**4, 5, 7, 14, 16, 18^{2}, 19, 20^{2}; **2:**3, 13, 18, 21, 34, 35, 38, 44; **3:**14, 19, 20, 27^{2}; **4:**7, 17^{2}, 25, 32; **5:**1, 2, 3, 21, 23; **6:**2^{2}, 24; **7:**8, 20, 21, 24; **8:**9, 10; **10:**7, 12, 21; **11:**7, 8, 18, 24, 34, 37, 38, 39, 40; **12:**6; **Hos 1:**6, 7, 10; **2:**5, 7^{3}, 12^{2}, 18; **4:**9^{2}, 12, 16, 19^{2}; **5:**2, 4, 5^{2}, 6, 7, 10, 14^{3}; **7:**2, 7^{2}, 12^{4}, 13^{3}, 15^{2}; **8:**5, 10, 12^{2}, 13; **9:**2, 4^{2}, 6^{2}, 9, 12^{3}, 14^{3}, 15^{3}, 17; **10:**5, 10^{3}; **11:**3^{2}, 4^{2}, 5, 7, 11; **12:**10^{2}; **13:**2, 6, 7, 8^{4}, 14^{2}; **14:**4^{2}, 9^{3}; **Joel 2:**3^{5}, 6, 10, 17, 19; **3:**2^{2}, 6, 7^{2}, 8, 12; **Am 1:**6; **2:**9; **4:**5, 9; **5:**8, 11, 22^{2}; **6:**10; **7:**8; **8:**2; **9:**1, 2^{2}, 3^{3}, 4^{2}, 6, 14, 15; **Ob 1:**11, 13; **Jnh 1:**10^{2}; **3:**5, 7, 8, 10; **Mic 2:**2^{2}, 12, 13^{2}; **3:**3, 4^{2}, 5, 6; **4:**4, 7, 12; **7:**4, 14, 15; **Na 2:**2; **3:**18; **Hab 1:**10, 12^{2}, 15^{3}; **2:**6, 8, 17; **3:**2^{2}; **Zep 1:**13, 18; **2:**7, 9, 11; **3:**8, 9, 13, 19; **Hag 1:**6; **2:**2; **Zec 1:**21; **2:**9^{2}; **6:**3; **7:**14^{2}; **8:**8^{2}; **9:**14, 15, 16; **10:**3, 5, 6^{4}, 8^{3}, 9, 10^{4}, 12; **11:**5^{3}, 6, 8, 12, 13; **12:**8^{2}; **13:**1, 9^{3}; **14:**18, 21; **Mal 1:**8, 13^{2}; **2:**2, 5, 13, 15, 17; **3:**3, 7, 17; **4:**1^{2}; **Mt 2:**4, 7, 8, 9; **3:**7; **4:**21, 24; **5:**2, 17^{2}; **6:**1, 8, 26, 32; **7:**6, 12, 16, 20, 23, 24, 26; **8:**4, 30, 32; **9:**15^{2}, 28, 30, 36; **10:**1, 18, 21, 26, 29; **11:**25; **12:**1, 4, 11, 16, 25, 27; **13:**3, 11, 13, 14, 15, 24, 28, 29, 30, 31, 33, 34, 39, 42, 50, 52, 57; **14:**6, 14, 16, 18, 19^{2}, 23, 25, 27; **15:**14, 16, 30^{2}, 32, 36^{2}; **16:**1, 4, 6, 12; **17:**1, 2, 3, 5, 7, 9, 13, 22, 27^{2}; **18:**2, 12, 17, 20; **19:**2, 4, 13^{3}, 14, 15, 26, 28; **20:**2^{2}, 4, 6, 7, 8, 10, 12, 13, 17, 22, 23, 25^{3}, 31^{2}, 32, 34; **21:**2^{3}, 3^{2}, 6, 7^{2}, 8, 13, 14, 17, 31, 36^{2}, 37, 42, 45; **22:**1, 3, 6^{2}, 20, 21, 28, 35, 41, 43; **23:**3, 4^{2}, 7, 30, 34; **24:**39, 45; **25:**2, 3, 14, 19; **26:**10, 19, 27, 31, 36, 38, 40, 43, 44, 45, 48, 70, 73, 74; **27:**10, 17, 26, 48, 56; **28:**9, 10, 13, 16, 18, 19, 20; **Mk 1:**20, 22, 31, 44; **2:**2, 3, 8, 12, 13, 17, 19^{2}, 20, 27; **3:**2, 4, 5, 12, 14^{2}, 17, 23^{2}, 28; **4:**2, 11, 13, 15, 21, 33, 34; **5:**10, 12, 13, 19, 39, 40, 43; **6:**4, 5, 7^{2}, 11, 13, 31, 33^{3}, 34^{2}, 37^{2}, 39, 41^{2}, 46, 48^{3}, 50, 51, 56; **7:**9, 36; **8:**3^{2}, 4, 6^{2}, 7^{2}, 9, 13, 14, 15, 17, 21, 27, 30, 31; **9:**1, 2^{2}, 3, 4, 7, 8, 9, 14^{2}, 16, 31, 33, 36^{2}; **10:**1, 6, 13^{2}, 14^{2}, 16^{2}, 27, 30, 32, 39, 42^{3}; **11:**2, 6^{2}, 17; **12:**1, 2, 4, 5, 12, 16, 17, 28^{2}; **13:**5, 9, 12, 20; **14:**7, 10, 13, 16, 23, 24, 27, 34, 37, 40, 41, 44, 60, 69, 70, 71; **15:**8, 12, 15, 40; **16:**12, 13, 14, 15, 18, 19, 20; **Lk 1:**6, 22^{2}; **2:**7, 9^{2}, 10, 15, 17, 18, 19, 34, 38, 46^{2}, 50, 51^{2}; **3:**13, 16, 18, 20; **4:**2, 21, 23, 26, 27, 35, 39, 40, 41^{2}, 42; **5:**7, 14, 25, 29, 31, 34, 35, 36; **6:**1, 3, 5, 9, 10, 13, 17, 19, 31, 32, 35^{2}, 39, 47, 49; **7:**6, 18, 19, 38^{3}, 42^{2}, 44; **8:**3, 31, 32^{3}, 37, 55, 56; **9:**1, 2, 3, 5, 10, 11^{2}, 13, 14, 16^{2}, 18, 21, 23, 34, 45, 46, 48, 54, 55; **10:**1, 2, 9, 21, 35; **11:**2, 5, 15, 17, 19, 31, 46, 47, 49; **12:**6, 15, 16, 24, 30, 37^{3}, 38, 42; **13:**4, 23; **14:**5, 7, 19, 23, 25; **15:**2, 3, 4, 12; **16:**15, 28, 29^{2}, 30; **17:**14, 15, 23, 27, 29, 31; **18:**1, 7, 15^{2}, 16, 29, 31, 34; **19:**11, 13, 27^{3}, 29, 32, 33, 46; **20:**15, 17, 19, 23, 25, 41; **21:**6, 8, 10, 13, 29; **22:**4, 6, 13, 15, 19, 23, 24^{2}, 25^{3}, 35, 36, 40, 41, 45, 46, 47, 50, 55, 58, 66; **23:**14, 20, 22, 28, 34; **24:**4, 5, 10, 11, 13, 15, 17, 18, 25, 27, 29, 30^{2}, 33, 35, 36^{2}, 38, 40, 41, 44, 46, 50^{2}, 51^{2}; **Jn 1:**38; **2:**7, 8, 19, 24; **3:**22; **4:**32, 40; **5:**17, 19, 21, 39; **6:**10, 13, 17, 20, 31, 32, 39, 53, 61, 64; **7:**6, 21, 45, 49; **8:**2, 7, 21, 27, 42; **10:**3, 4, 6, 8, 16, 20, 27, 28^{2}, 29^{2}, 32, 34, 35; **11:**11, 14, 19, 37, 44, 46^{2}, 49, 52^{2}; **12:**35, 36, 40, 47; **13:**1, 5, 12, 17, 22, 23; **14:**21; **15:**22, 24; **16:**19; **17:**6, 8^{2}, 9, 10, 11, 12^{3}, 13, 14^{2}, 15^{2}, 17, 18, 19, 20, 21, 22, 23^{2}, 26^{3}; **18:**4, 5, 7, 18, 29; **19:**5, 16, 23^{2}, 24, 40; **20:**17, 18, 19, 20, 22, 23, 25, 26^{2}; **21:**3, 5, 10, 12, 13, 20, 24, 25; **Ac 1:**3, 4^{2}, 7, 10; **2:**3, 4^{2}, 6, 8, 11, 13, 40^{2}; **3:**3, 5^{2}, 8, 11, 12; **4:**3, 7^{2}, 8, 14, 15, 18^{2}, 21^{2}, 23, 24, 33, 34^{2}; **5:**13, 15^{2}, 16, 18, 19, 22, 23, 26, 27, 33, 35, 38, 40^{4}; **6:**1, 3, 6; **7:**19, 24, 25, 26, 34, 36, 42, 44, 45^{2}, 60; **8:**3, 11, 14, 15, 16, 17, 18; **9:**2, 21, 27, 28, 39^{2}, 40, 41; **10:**8^{2}, 20^{2}, 23, 24, 28, 46, 48; **11:**3, 4, 12, 15, 17, 20^{2}, 21, 23, 28; **12:**1, 10, 17, 25; **13:**2, 3^{2}, 4, 5, 8, 13, 15, 17, 20, 21, 42, 43^{2}, 46, 50, 51; **14:**3, 5^{2}, 13, 15, 18, 22, 23^{2}, 27; **15:**2, 3, 4, 7, 8^{2}, 9, 12, 20^{2}, 22, 23, 25, 33, 37, 38^{2}; **16:**7, 10, 19, 20, 22, 23, 24, 25, 30, 33, 34^{2}, 37, 39^{3}, 40; **17:**2, 5, 6, 7, 9, 13, 16, 18, 26, 32, 34; **18:**2, 3, 6, 11, 16, 20; **19:**2, 6^{2}, 9^{2}, 12, 15, 16^{3}, 19, 25; **20:**1, 18, 30, 36, 38; **21:**1, 4, 7, 19, 20, 21, 25, 26^{2}, 40; **22:**2, 4, 5, 30; **23:**6, 8, 10^{2}, 21^{2}, 23, 31; **25:**3, 6, 11, 16; **26:**10, 11^{4}, 17, 18, 30; **27:**9, 21, 33, 35, 40, 42, 43; **28:**14, 17, 23^{2}, 27; **Ro 1:**19^{2}, 24, 26, 28, 32; **2:**3, 15; **4:**11; **6:**19; **9:**5, 25, 26, 33; **10:**2, 5, 14; **11:**8, 9, 14, 23, 27, 32; **15:**15, 27^{2}; **16:**4, 14, 15, 17; **1Co 2:**14; **6:**13, 15; **7:**8, 31; **10:**4, 5, 7, 8^{2}, 9, 10, 11; **11:**2; **12:**6, 11, 18^{2}; **14:**10; **15:**10, 29; **16:**3; **2Co 2:**13; **4:**17; **5:**15, 19; **6:**16^{2}, 17; **8:**22; **9:**2^{2}, 13; **11:**8; **Gal 2:**2, 5, 14; **3:**12; **4:**9, 15, 17; **Eph 2:**3, 16; **4:**18; **5:**7, 11; **6:**4, 6, 9; **Php 1:**28; **3:**8; **Col 1:**27; **2:**15^{2}; **3:**14, 19; **1Th 2:**16; **3:**3; **4:**17; **5:**3, 13; **2Th 2:**11; **1Ti 1:**18, 20; **3:**10^{2}; **4:**3, 15, 16; **5:**11, 16^{2}, 24^{2}; **6:**2^{4}, 18; **2Ti 2:**14^{2}, 17, 25^{2}, 26; **3:**5, 11; **4:**3, 16; **Tit 1:**13; **2:**7, 9^{2}, 10; **Heb 1:**12; **2:**11; **4:**2, 6, 8; **5:**1; **6:**10; **7:**23, 25; **8:**9^{3}, 10, 11; **9:**13, 15; **10:**8^{2}, 16^{2}; **11:**13^{2}, 16, 30, 38, 39; **12:**9, 19, 25; **13:**9, 17; **Jas 2:**25; **3:**3; **1Pe 1:**11, 12; **2:**8; **3:**1, 7; **4:**4; **2Pe 1:**4, 9, 12; **2:**1, 3, 4^{2}, 6^{2}, 8, 17, 19, 21^{2}, 22; **3:**1, 16; **1Jn 2:**19; **3:**24; **4:**4, 5; **3Jn 1:**6, 10; **Jude 1:**10, 11, 23; **Rev 2:**2, 16, 27^{2}; **3:**5, 9; **4:**4; **5:**10, 13; **6:**11; **7:**14, 15, 16, 17; **8:**2, 6, 12; **9:**5^{2}, 6, 11; **10:**6; **11:**5^{2}, 7^{2}, 9, 10, 11^{2}, 12; **12:**4, 10, 11; **13:**7, 14; **14:**9, 13, 19; **15:**1, 2; **16:**6, 14; **17:**14; **19:**15, 20, 21; **20:**6, 8, 9, 10, 11, 13; **21:**3^{2}, 14; **22:**5, 8^{2}, 18.

THEMSELVES (236)

Ge 3:7; **10:**1; **21:**29; **30:**40; **34:**22; **43:**15, 32^{2}; **44:**14; **50:**18; **Ex 12:**39; **18:**22, 26; **19:**22; **32:**8, 31; **34:**15, 16; **Lev 17:**7; **20:**5; **Nu 8:**7, 21, 26; **23:**9, 24; **Dt 9:**12; **31:**14, 16; **Jos 8:**15, 27; **11:**14; **24:**1; **Jdg 2:**17; **5:**2; **6:**2; **8:**27, 33; **9:**8, 51; **18:**30; **19:**22; **20:**22; **1Sa 2:**5; **3:**13; **14:**11; **21:**4; **2Sa 2:**25; **10:**8; **12:**19; **1Ki 14:**23; **18:**23, 28; **2Ki 3:**9; **11:**11; **12:**8; **17:**9, 15, 16, 17; **23:**3; **1Ch 5:**25; **15:**14; **19:**9; **21:**20; **2Ch 5:**11; **7:**14; **12:**6, 7^{2}; **21:**11, 13; **23:**7; **29:**15, 34; **30:**3, 11, 15, 17, 18, 24; **31:**4, 18; **34:**32; **35:**14^{2}; **Ezr 6:**20^{2}, 21; **9:**1, 2; **Ne 4:**16; **8:**16; **9:**2, 18; **10:**28, 29; **12:**29, 30; **13:**22; **Est 8:**11, 13; **9:**16, 27, 31; **Job 1:**6; **2:**1; **3:**14; **24:**7, 16; **Ps 22:**29;

THEN (2931)

THERE (1873)

THESE (1120)

THEY (6563)

5:14; 6:18, 20[3]; 7:6; 8:10[2], 12; 9:25, 26; 11:8[2]; 12:7[2], 15, 25; 14:21; 15:24, 35; 16:10; 17:12; 19:12, 15, 18, 23, 24; 21:8, 11, 12[2], 13, 14, 18, 26; 22:16, 17; 24:2[2], 3, 4, 6, 7[2], 8, 10[2], 11[2], 16[2], 17, 18, 21, 22[2], 24[4]; 29:22, 23, 24; 30:1, 3, 4, 5[2], 6, 7, 8, 10[2], 11, 12[2], 13[2], 14[2]; 31:13; 32:3, 4, 15, 16[2]; 33:15; 34:19, 20[2], 23, 25, 27, 28; 35:9; 36:9[2], 11[2], 12[2], 13, 14; 37:8, 12; 38:35, 40; 39:2[2], 3, 4, 13, 16; 40:12; 41:6, 17[2], 23, 25; 42:11; **Ps** 1:4; 2:3; 5:9, 10; 6:7, 10; 7:2; 9:3, 15[2], 20; 10:10[2]; 11:2; 14:1, 3, 5; 16:3; 17:10, 11[2], 12, 14; 18:7, 18, 37, 38[2], 41, 44[2], 45[2]; 19:2[2], 10[2], 13; 20:8; 21:11[2]; 22:4, 5[2], 7, 16, 18, 26, 31; 23:4; 25:3, 6, 19; 27:2; 28:4, 5; 31:13, 18; 32:6, 9; 33:15; 35:5, 7, 8[2], 11, 12, 13, 15[2], 16[2], 20, 21, 27; 36:8; 37:2[2], 7, 10, 19[2], 20, 26, 28, 40; 38:12; 40:5, 12; 41:7; 44:3; 45:15[2]; 48:4, 5[2]; 49:11, 14; 52:6; 53:1, 3, 5; 55:3, 10, 21; 56:1, 5[2], 6[3], 8; 57:6[3]; 58:3, 7, 8, 9, 10[2]; 59:3, 4, 6, 7[3], 12, 13, 14, 15; 62:4[4], 9[2]; 63:9[2], 10; 64:3, 4[2], 5[3], 6, 7, 9; 65:13; 66:4[2], 6; 68:3; 69:21, 23, 26, 28; 71:11; 72:17; 73:4, 5[2], 6, 8[2], 11, 12, 19; 74:4, 5, 6, 7[2], 8[2]; 76:5; 78:6, 7, 8, 10, 11, 17, 18[2], 19, 22, 25, 29[3], 30[2], 32[2], 34[2], 35, 36, 37, 39, 40, 41[2], 42, 44, 53, 56[2], 57, 58[2]; 79:1[2], 2, 3, 7, 12; 82:5[3]; 83:3[2], 4, 5[2], 17[2]; 84:4, 6[2], 7; 86:9; 87:7[2]; 88:17[2]; 89:16[2], 31, 51; 90:5, 10; 91:12; 92:7, 12, 13, 14[2]; 94:2, 4, 5[2], 6[2], 7, 11, 21; 95:9, 10[2], 11; 96:13; 99:6, 7; 101:3, 6; 102:26[3]; 104:7, 8[2], 9[2], 11, 12, 22[2], 28[2], 29[2], 30, 32; 105:12, 13, 18, 27, 28, 35, 38, 40, 44, 45; 106:3, 7[3], 12, 13, 14[2], 15, 16, 19, 20, 21, 24[2], 25, 28, 29, 32, 33, 34, 35, 36, 37, 38[2], 39[3], 43[2]; 107:4, 5, 6, 7, 11, 12, 13, 18, 19, 23, 24, 26, 27[2], 28, 30, 36[2], 37, 39; 109:2, 3[2], 4, 5, 10, 25[2], 28[3]; 111:2, 8; 115:5[2], 6[2], 7[3]; 118:11, 12[2]; 119:1, 2, 3[2], 24, 74, 87, 98, 111, 138, 150, 155, 158, 165; 120:7; 124:3; 127:5[2]; 129:1, 2[2], 6; 135:16[2], 17; 137:3, 7; 138:4, 5; 139:18, 20; 140:3, 5, 8, 10; 141:7, 9; 142:6; 144:5; 145:4, 5, 6, 7, 11; 146:4; 147:9, 20; 148:5; **Pr** 1:9, 11, 16, 18, 28[2], 29, 30, 31; 3:2, 22; 4:16[4], 17, 19, 22; 6:22[3]; 7:5; 8:9; 9:18; 15:22; 16:5, 13; 18:8, 11; 19:7; 21:7, 22; 22:22; 23:5[2], 35[2]; 24:22; 26:22; 30:15, 24, 25, 26, 27; 31:5; **Ecc** 1:7; 3:11, 12, 18[2]; 4:1[2], 9, 11; 5:1, 11; 8:10; 9:1, 3[2], 5[2], 6; 10:13; 11:3, 8; 12:3; **SS** 1:4; 3:3; 5:7[4]; 6:5; **Isa** 1:2, 4[2], 11, 14, 18[3], 23[2]; 2:4[2], 6[2], 8, 12, 20, 21; 3:9[3], 10, 11, 12; 5:11, 12[2], 24, 26, 29[3], 30; 6:2[3], 3, 10, 13; 7:1, 19, 22, 25; 8:12, 15[2], 20[2], 21[3], 22[2]; 9:3, 13, 20[2], 21; 10:28[3], 29, 32[2]; 11:9, 14[3], 16; 13:5, 8[2], 18[2]; 14:2, 7, 10[2], 16, 21; 15:3[2], 5[3], 7[2]; 16:7; 17:8[2], 9, 12[2], 13, 14; 18:6; 19:3, 14, 16, 20, 21[3], 22; 21:5[4], 15; 22:2, 3; 23:5, 13[2], 18; 24:5, 9, 11, 14[3], 22[2]; 25:9, 11; 26:10[2], 11, 14[2], 16[2]; 27:10[2], 11; 28:7[3], 12, 13; 29:23[3]; 30:4, 10; 31:8; 33:12; 34:17; 35:2, 9, 10; 36:19; 37:3, 19[2], 27, 38; 38:19; 39:3[2], 4[2], 7; 40:15[2], 17, 24[4], 31[3]; 41:5, 25, 27, 29; 42:9, 16, 22[2], 24[2], 25[2]; 43:2, 9, 14, 17, 21; 44:4, 9[2], 11, 18[4], 26; 45:14[3], 16, 24; 46:2[2], 6[2], 7[2]; 47:9, 14[2], 15; 48:3, 5, 7, 13, 21; 49:9, 10, 12, 21, 22, 23[2], 26; 50:9; 51:11, 14[2], 20[2]; 52:6, 8[2], 15[4]; 56:10[5], 11[4]; 57:2[2], 6[2], 12; 58:2[4], 3; 59:4[2], 5, 6[2], 7, 8[2], 18, 19; 60:7, 11, 21[2]; 61:3, 4[2], 7[2], 9; 62:4, 6, 12; 63:8, 10, 13, 14, 19; 65:7, 17, 21[2], 22, 23[3], 24[2], 25; 66:2, 3, 4[2], 5, 6, 17, 18, 19, 20[2], 24[2]; **Jer** 1:15, 19; 2:5[2], 6, 11, 13, 15[2], 24, 26, 27[4], 28, 30; 3:17[2], 18, 21; 4:2, 17, 22[5], 24, 30; 5:2[2], 3[3], 4[2], 5[2], 7, 8, 12[2], 13, 17[3], 22[3], 23, 24, 27, 28[2]; 6:3, 10[2], 14[2], 15[5], 19, 23[5], 28[3], 30; 7:17, 18, 19[2], 24[3], 26[2], 27[2], 30, 31, 32; 8:2[4], 4, 5[2], 6, 9[3], 11[2], 12[6], 16, 17, 19; 9:2, 3[4], 5[2], 6, 10, 13[2], 14[2], 16; 10:3, 4[2], 5[4], 8[2], 14, 15[2], 18, 21, 25[2]; 11:8[3], 10[2], 11[2], 12[2], 14, 18, 19; 12:2[2], 5, 6[3], 10, 13[2], 16[3]; 13:11, 12; 14:2, 3[3], 10[2], 12[2], 14, 15, 16[2], 18; 15:2, 7, 16, 20; 16:4[3], 6, 10, 11, 15, 16[2], 17, 18, 20, 21; 17:11, 13, 15, 23[2], 25; 18:12, 15[2], 18, 20, 22; 19:4[4], 5, 9, 11, 13, 15; 20:5, 11; 21:1, 6; 22:7, 9, 12, 18[2], 28; 23:3, 4, 8[2], 12[3], 13, 14[3], 16[2], 17[2], 21[2], 22[2], 25, 27[2], 32[2]; 24:2, 3, 7[2], 8[2], 10; 25:5, 14, 16[2], 18, 28, 33; 26:3[2], 10, 23; 27:10, 14, 15, 16, 18, 22[2]; 28:14; 29:5, 6, 9, 17, 19, 23[2], 28; 30:9, 14, 19[2]; 31:1, 9[3], 11, 12[4], 16, 32, 33, 34, 37; 32:14, 23[3], 29, 32[2], 33[2], 34, 35[2], 38, 39, 40; 33:5, 7, 8, 9, 11, 24; 34:5, 10[2], 11[2], 16, 18[2], 22; 35:6, 14[2], 15, 17[2]; 36:7, 15, 16[2], 17, 20[2], 24, 31; 37:5, 8, 9, 10, 15[2]; 38:6[2], 7, 9[2], 13, 18, 19, 20, 22, 25, 27; 39:4[2], 5, 14, 16; 40:8, 12[3]; 41:1, 7, 12[2], 13, 17, 18; 42:5; 43:3, 5, 6, 7; 44:2, 3[3], 5[2], 6, 10[2], 12[4], 14, 27; 46:5[3], 6, 15, 16[3], 17, 21[2], 22, 23[3]; 47:2[2]; 48:5[2], 12[2], 13, 32, 33, 36, 39; 49:9[3], 23[2]; 50:5[2], 6, 7, 9, 36[2], 37[2], 38, 42[5]; 51:2, 4, 7, 14, 17, 18[2], 24, 28, 30[2], 38, 39[2], 57; 52:4, 7[2], 17, 18; **La** 1:2, 6, 8, 11[2], 14[2], 19[2], 21[2]; 2:7, 8, 10, 12[2], 14[2], 15, 16, 20; 3:14, 23, 53, 63, 64; 4:8[2], 9, 14[2], 15[2], 19; **Eze** 1:8, 9[2], 12[2], 16, 17[2], 20, 21[2], 24[2], 25; 2:3, 5[3], 6[2], 7[2]; 3:6, 7, 8, 9, 11, 15, 25, 26, 27; 4:17; 5:13, 17; 6:9[3], 10, 11, 13[2], 14[2]; 7:14, 18, 19[2], 20, 21, 22, 25, 26, 27; 8:6, 9, 12, 16, 17[2], 18; 9:2, 6, 7, 8, 9, 10; 10:11[3], 17[2], 19[2], 20; 11:3, 15, 16, 18, 20[2], 21; 12:2[2], 3[3], 4[2], 5, 6, 7, 11, 15, 16[3], 19, 23; 13:6[2], 9[2], 10[2], 21; 14:10, 11[2], 14, 15, 16[2], 18[2], 20[2], 22; 15:3, 7, 8; 16:16, 37, 39[2], 40, 41, 47, 49, 50, 51, 52, 55; 17:23; 18:23; 19:4, 8, 9[2]; 20:1, 8[4], 9, 12, 13[2], 16, 20, 21[3], 24, 25, 26, 28[2], 38[2], 49; 21:7, 12; 22:7[2], 10, 18, 25, 26[3], 27, 28, 29, 31; 23:3, 4, 10, 17, 24[3], 25[3], 26, 29[2], 37[4], 38[2], 39[3], 40[2], 42, 44[2], 45, 47; 24:27; 25:3, 4[2], 11, 13, 14[2], 17; 26:4, 6, 10, 12[2], 16, 17; 27:5[2], 6[2], 10, 11[2], 12, 13, 15, 16, 17, 19, 21, 22, 24, 30[2], 31[2], 32[2]; 28:7, 8, 13, 22, 23, 24, 25[2], 26[3]; 29:7[2], 9, 13, 14, 16, 21; 30:6, 7, 8, 11, 19, 25, 26; 31:14; 32:3, 12, 15, 16[2], 20, 21[2], 24, 25[2], 26, 27, 29[2], 30[2]; 33:11, 29[2], 31[3], 32, 33; 34:5[3], 6, 12, 14[2], 22, 25, 27, 28[2], 29, 30[2]; 35:12, 15; 36:3, 5[2], 8, 11, 12, 17, 18[2], 19, 20[3], 21, 35, 38; 37:9, 10, 11, 17, 19, 21, 22, 23[2], 24[2], 25[2], 27; 38:8, 17, 23; 39:6, 9, 10[3], 14, 15, 16, 18, 23[2], 26[3], 28; 40:18, 24, 48; 41:19; 42:6, 11, 13, 14[5]; 43:7, 8[2], 10, 11[3], 26[2]; 44:11[2], 12[2], 13[2], 15, 16[2], 17[3], 18[2], 19[4], 20[2], 22[2], 23, 24[2], 29; 46:10[2]; 47:11, 12, 22; 48:14; **Da** 1:5[2], 15, 16, 19; 2:2, 7, 11, 38; 3:3, 7, 9, 12, 24, 27, 28; 4:7; 5:3, 4[2], 8, 15; 6:4[2], 12, 13, 16, 22, 24; 7:22; 8:25; 10:7; 11:6, 31, 33, 34[2], 35; **Hos** 1:10, 11; 2:4, 8, 21, 22, 23; 3:1, 5; 4:2, 7[2], 8, 10[3], 12[2], 13, 14[2], 18; 5:4, 6[2], 7[2], 15[3]; 6:7[2], 9; 7:1, 2[2], 3, 4, 6, 7, 12, 13[3], 14[2], 15, 16[3]; 8:4[3], 5, 6, 7, 9, 10[2], 12, 13[3]; 9:3, 4, 6, 9, 10[3], 12, 16[2], 17[2]; 10:2, 3, 4, 8; 11:2[3], 3, 5[2], 7, 10, 11; 12:8, 11; 13:2[3], 3, 6[4], 16[2]; **Joel** 1:18; 2:4[2], 5, 7[3], 8[2], 9[4], 17; 3:2, 3[3], 8, 19; **Am** 2:4[2], 6, 7, 8[2]; 3:3, 10; 6:2, 9; 7:2; 8:7, 12, 14[2]; 9:2[2], 3[2], 4, 12, 14[3]; **Ob** 1:5[3], 16[2], 18, 19; **Jnh** 1:5, 7, 8, 10[2], 11, 13, 14, 15, 16; 3:5, 10[2]; **Mic** 1:7, 16; 2:1, 2[2], 4, 13; 3:4[2], 5[2], 7, 11; 4:3[2], 11, 12[2]; 5:1, 4, 6; 7:3[2], 16, 17[3]; **Na** 1:9, 10[2], 12[2], 15; 2:3, 4[2], 5[2], 8, 11; 3:12, 13, 16[2], 17; **Hab** 1:7[2], 8, 9, 10[3], 11; 2:7, 15; **Zep** 1:13[2], 17[2]; 2:7[2], 10; 3:4, 7[2], 13[2], 16, 18, 19; **Hag** 1:14; 2:14[2]; **Zec** 1:4, 5, 6, 9, 10, 11, 15; 3:5; 4:10; 5:9[2], 10; 6:7[2]; 7:11[2], 12, 13[2], 14[2]; 8:8; 9:2, 15[3], 16, 17; 10:2[2], 5[2], 6, 8, 9[3], 11, 12; 11:6, 12, 13; 12:6, 10[3]; 13:2, 9[3]; 14:12, 13, 17, 18; **Mal** 1:4[2]; 2:15; 3:17; 4:3; **Mt** 1:18, 23; 2:5, 9[3], 10[2], 11[3], 12, 13, 18; 3:6; 4:6, 18[2], 20, 21, 22; 5:4, 5, 6, 7, 8, 9, 12, 15, 16; 6:2, 5[2], 7[2], 14, 16[3], 26[2], 28; 7:6, 15[2]; 8:28, 29, 32, 34[2]; 9:8[2], 11, 15, 17[2], 24, 28, 31, 32, 36; 10:17, 19; 11:16, 18, 19, 20, 21; 12:2, 10, 14, 22, 24, 27, 36, 41, 45; 13:6[2], 13[2], 15[3], 16[2], 41, 42, 48, 51, 54[2], 57; 14:5, 12, 15, 16, 17, 20, 26[2], 32, 34[2], 35; 15:2[2], 9, 12, 14, 31[2], 32[2], 34, 36, 37; 16:5, 7, 12, 14, 28; 17:6, 8[2], 9, 12[2], 14, 16, 22, 23; 18:7, 31; 19:3, 6, 7, 12, 25; 20:5, 7, 10, 11[2], 12, 18, 22, 23, 24, 30[2], 31, 33, 34; 21:1, 7, 15, 16, 20[2], 23, 25, 26, 27, 31, 35, 37, 38, 39, 41, 45, 46[2]; 22:3, 5, 10, 16[3], 19, 21, 22[3], 24, 30, 33, 42; 23:3[4], 4[2], 5[2], 6, 7, 25; 24:3, 30, 31, 39; 25:5, 9, 10, 11, 44, 46; 26:4, 5, 8[2], 15, 21, 22, 26, 30[2], 59, 60, 66, 67; 27:2, 4, 7, 9, 10, 13, 16, 18, 21, 22, 23, 28, 29[2], 30, 31[3], 32[3], 33, 34, 35[2], 36, 37, 42, 47, 53[2], 54, 55, 63, 66; 28:4, 9, 10, 12, 15, 17[2]; **Mk** 1:5, 16, 18, 20, 21, 27[2], 29[2], 30, 34, 37[2]; 2:4[2], 8, 12, 16, 19[2], 20, 23, 24; 3:2, 4, 6, 8, 11, 13, 14, 21[2], 30, 31, 32; 4:6[2], 7, 12[2], 15, 17[3], 33, 36, 41; 5:1, 15[3], 35, 36, 38, 40, 42; 6:2, 3, 12, 13, 30, 31, 32, 34, 35, 36, 37, 38[2], 40, 42, 49[3], 50, 51, 52, 53[2], 54, 55[2], 56[2]; 7:3, 4[4], 7, 27, 32, 36, 37; 8:1, 2, 3, 5, 6, 7, 11, 14, 16, 19, 20, 22, 24, 28; 9:1, 2, 6, 8[2], 9[2], 10, 11, 13[2], 14[2], 15, 18, 20, 30[2], 31, 32, 33, 34[2]; 10:4, 8, 10, 32, 33, 35, 37, 39, 40, 41, 46, 49; 11:1, 4[2], 6, 7, 8, 12, 18, 19, 20[2], 27, 28, 31, 32, 33; 12:3, 4, 5[3], 6, 8, 12[4], 13, 14[2], 16[2], 17, 19, 25[2], 38, 40, 44; 13:4; 14:2, 5, 11, 16, 18, 19[2], 22, 23, 26[2], 32, 40, 51, 53, 55[2], 64, 65; 15:1, 4, 13, 14, 17, 18, 19[2], 20[3], 21, 22, 23, 24[2], 25, 27, 31, 35; 16:1, 2, 3, 4[2], 5[3], 6, 8[2], 11[2], 12, 13, 14, 17[2], 18[4]; **Lk** 1:2, 7[2], 22, 58, 59[2], 61, 62; 2:6, 9, 16, 17[2], 20[2], 39, 42, 43, 44[2], 45[2], 46, 48, 50; 3:12; 4:11, 22, 28, 29, 32, 36, 38, 41, 42[2]; 5:6[2], 7[3], 9, 11, 19[2], 22, 26, 33, 35; 6:7, 8, 11[2], 22, 39; 7:4[2], 16[2], 20, 29[2], 30, 31, 32; 8:6, 10[2], 12, 13[4], 14[3], 19, 22, 23[2], 25[2], 26, 31, 33, 34, 35[3], 37, 40, 45, 53; 9:6, 10[3], 12, 13, 17, 19, 27, 31, 32[2], 34[2], 36[2], 37, 40, 43, 45[3], 54, 56, 57; 10:7, 13, 30; 11:19, 26, 32, 34, 46, 48, 49[2]; 12:1, 24[2], 27, 36, 53; 13:2, 4; 14:4, 6, 12, 14, 18; 15:24; 16:28, 29, 30, 31[2]; 17:1, 12, 14[2], 37; 18:1, 8, 15, 32, 34, 37, 43; 19:11, 15, 25, 33, 34, 35, 37, 40, 44[2], 48; 20:2, 5, 6, 7, 10, 11, 12, 13, 14[2], 15, 16, 19[2], 20[3], 25, 26[2], 28, 36[4], 41, 46, 47; 21:7[2], 12[2], 16, 24, 27, 30; 22:2, 5, 9, 13[2], 23, 35, 49, 54, 55, 64, 65, 67, 70, 71; 23:2, 5, 11, 12, 18, 21, 23, 25, 26[2], 30, 33[2], 34[3], 35, 36, 48, 56[2]; 24:1, 2, 3[2], 4, 8, 9[2], 11, 14, 15, 16, 17, 19, 20, 22, 23[2], 24, 28[2], 29, 31, 32, 33[2], 36, 37[2], 41, 42, 45, 52, 53; **Jn** 1:21, 22, 37, 38, 39; 2:3, 7, 8, 12, 22; 3:26; 4:23, 30, 35, 40, 42, 45[2], 52; 5:12, 23; 6:2, 9, 11, 12, 13, 14, 15, 17, 19[3], 21[2], 22, 24, 25[2], 28, 30, 34, 42, 45, 49, 63; 7:25, 26, 30, 31, 52; 8:3, 6, 7, 10, 19, 25, 27, 33, 39, 41, 59; 9:10, 11, 12, 13, 16, 17, 18, 19, 22, 24[2], 26, 28, 34[2], 35; 10:4, 5[3], 6, 10, 16, 27, 28, 39, 41; 11:8, 31, 34, 41, 42, 47, 53, 56[3], 57; 12:13, 16[2], 18, 21[2], 37, 39, 40, 42[2], 43; 14:24; 15:20[4], 21[2], 22[2], 24[3], 25; 16:2, 3[2], 18, 19; 17:3, 6[2], 7, 8[3], 9, 11[2], 13, 14, 16, 19, 21, 22, 23, 25; 18:3, 5, 6, 7, 12, 18, 21, 28, 30, 40; 19:2, 3, 6, 15, 18, 23, 24[2], 29, 31, 33[2], 37[2], 42; 20:2[2], 9, 13[3], 20, 23[2]; 21:3[3], 5, 6[2], 8, 9[2], 12, 15; **Ac** 1:6[2], 10, 11, 12, 13[3], 14, 19, 23, 24, 26; 2:1, 2, 3, 6, 7, 12, 13, 18, 37, 42, 45, 46[2]; 3:10[2]; 4:1, 2, 3[2], 7, 13[4], 14[2], 15, 16[2], 18, 21[2], 24[3], 28, 31[3], 32[2]; 5:9, 13, 18, 21[3], 22, 26[2], 27, 33[2], 40[2], 41, 42; 6:5, 6, 10, 11, 12[2], 13, 15; 7:6, 7[2], 9, 19, 25, 35, 39, 40, 41[2], 45, 52, 54[2], 57[2], 59; 8:4, 6, 11, 12[2], 14, 15[3], 16, 17, 25, 36[2], 39; 9:7, 8, 24, 26, 29, 30, 38; 10:9, 18, 39, 46, 47, 48[2]; 11:18[2], 22, 30; 12:10[3], 15[2], 16[2], 19, 20[3], 22, 25; 13:2, 3[2], 5[2], 6[3], 14[2], 27, 28[2], 29[2], 31, 45, 48, 50, 51; 14:1, 6, 7, 11, 12[2], 14, 18, 19, 21[2], 22, 23, 24, 25[2], 26[3], 27, 28; 15:3[2], 4[3], 11, 12, 13, 22, 23, 24, 30, 33, 35, 36, 39[2]; 16:3, 4[2], 7[2], 8, 19, 20, 23[2], 31, 32, 37[2], 38[2], 39, 40[3]; 17:1[2], 5[2], 6[2], 7, 8, 9, 10, 11, 13, 18, 19[2], 20, 26[2], 32; 18:3, 13, 17, 19, 20, 26; 19:2, 3, 5, 6, 9, 13, 16, 17, 19, 28[2], 32, 34[2], 37, 38; 20:18, 21, 37[2], 38[2]; 21:4, 6, 20[3], 21, 22, 24, 25, 27, 29, 30, 31, 32, 40; 22:2[2], 9, 18, 22, 23, 25; 23:9, 12, 14, 21[3], 27, 28, 32[2], 33; 24:1, 13[2], 14, 18, 19, 20; 25:3[2], 7, 14, 17, 18, 19; 26:5[2], 7, 10, 18, 20, 31[2]; 27:3, 13[4], 17[3], 18, 19, 27, 28[2], 29, 30, 36, 38[3], 39[4], 40[2]; 28:2, 4, 6, 10[2], 15, 17, 18, 21, 23, 25, 27[3], 28; **Ro** 1:21[2], 22[2], 25, 28, 29[3], 30[2], 31, 32[2]; 2:14[2], 15, 26[2]; 3:2, 12, 17; 4:7, 17; 9:7[2], 26, 32[2]; 10:1, 2, 3[2], 14[5], 15[2], 18[2]; 11:3[2], 8[2], 10, 11, 20, 23[2], 28[2], 31[2]; 15:27[3], 28; 16:4, 7[2], 18; **1Co** 2:8[2], 14[2]; 4:19; 7:9[2], 14, 29, 30[2], 36; 8:7[2]; 9:10, 25; 10:1, 2, 3, 4, 6, 33; 12:12, 19; 13:8[2]; 14:21, 23, 34, 35[2]; 15:11, 35; 16:4, 15, 17, 18; **2Co** 1:20; 4:4; 6:16; 8:3[2], 4, 5[2], 14, 23; 10:4, 12[2]; 11:12, 22[3], 23; 12:21; **Gal** 1:23, 24; 2:6, 7, 9[3], 10, 12, 14; 4:17; 5:12, 17; 6:12, 13[2]; **Eph** 4:18, 19; **Php** 1:17, 28; 3:21; 4:18; **Col** 2:2[3], 22, 23; 3:21; 4:9, 11; **1Th** 1:9[2]; 2:15, 16[2]; 5:3; **2Th** 1:9; 2:10[2], 11; 3:11[2], 12; **1Ti** 1:7[4]; 2:15; 3:9, 10; 4:3; 5:11, 12[2], 13[3]; 6:2[2], 19[2]; **2Ti** 2:10, 18[2], 23, 26; 3:6, 9; 4:3, 4; **Tit** 1:11[3], 13, 16[3]; 2:3, 4, 8, 10[2]; 3:13[2], 14; **Heb** 1:11[2], 12; 3:10, 11, 16[2], 18, 19; 4:2[2], 3, 5; 6:6[2]; 8:5, 9, 10, 11; 9:10, 13; 10:2; 11:13[5], 14, 15[3], 16, 23[2], 29, 35, 37[4], 38, 40; 12:10, 20, 25[2]; 13:17; **Jas** 2:6, 7; 3:4[2]; 4:1; **1Pe** 1:12[2]; 2:8[3], 12[2], 23; 3:1, 2, 5, 14; 4:4[2], 5, 6; **2Pe** 1:8, 21; 2:1, 3, 4, 11, 12[3], 13[4], 14[3], 15, 18[2], 19[2], 20[3]; 3:4, 5, 16; **1Jn** 2:19[4]; 4:1, 5; **3Jn** 1:5, 6, 7; **Jude** 1:4, 7, 10[2], 11[3], 12, 13, 15, 16[2], 18; **Rev** 2:9, 22; 3:4[2], 9; 4:4, 6, 8, 10, 11; 5:8, 9, 10, 11, 12; 6:8, 9, 10, 11[2], 16; 7:9, 10, 11, 13[2], 14[2], 15, 16[2]; 9:4, 5[2], 6, 7, 9, 10[2], 11, 19, 20, 21; 11:2, 3, 6[3], 7, 11, 12[2]; 12:8, 11[2]; 13:4; 14:3, 4[3], 5, 13, 20; 15:2, 6; 16:4, 6[2], 9[3], 11[2], 13, 14[2], 16, 21; 17:8, 10, 13, 14, 16[2]; 18:9, 10, 14, 15, 18[2], 19; 19:3, 4; 20:4[2], 6, 8, 9, 10, 12; 21:3; 22:4, 5[2], 14.

THIS (3712)

Ge 2:4, 23, 24; 3:13, 14; 5:1; 6:9, 15; 7:1; 8:12; 9:12, 17; 10:1; 11:6, 10, 27; 12:7, 12; 13:10; 14:1, 13; 15:1, 4, 7, 18; 16:13; 17:4, 10, 21; 18:4, 10, 12; 19:7, 9, 13, 14, 19, 21; 20:5, 6, 10, 11, 13, 16; 21:6, 26, 30; 22:14, 16; 24:5, 7, 8, 9, 13, 14, 43, 50, 58; 25:12, 19, 22, 26; 26:3, 7, 10, 11, 33; 27:46; 28:15, 16, 17[3], 20, 22; 29:25, 27, 33, 35; 30:6, 20, 31, 43; 31:1, 13, 40, 41, 48, 51[2], 52[4]; 32:2, 4, 5, 10, 32; 33:10; 34:4, 30; 35:12, 20; 36:1, 9, 24, 43; 37:2, 6, 9, 10, 21, 22[2], 32; 38:23, 28, 29; 39:9, 14, 17, 19; 40:12, 14, 18; 41:24, 36, 38, 39; 42:15[2], 18, 20, 21, 25, 28, 33; 43:6, 11, 29; 44:5[2], 13, 15, 29; 45:9, 17, 19, 21, 23; 48:4, 15, 18, 20; 49:28; 50:17, 24, 25; **Ex** 1:18, 22; 2:6, 9, 12, 15; 3:3, 6, 12[2], 14, 15, 21; 4:5, 17, 22; 5:1, 6, 10, 15, 22[2], 23; 6:9, 26; 7:17[2], 23; 8:1, 17, 19, 20, 22, 23, 24, 32; 9:1, 5, 13, 14, 16, 18, 27; 10:3, 6, 7, 17; 11:4; 12:2, 3, 11, 14, 17[2], 25, 26, 42; 13:3, 5[2], 8, 9, 10, 14, 15, 19; 14:4; 15:1; 16:3[2], 4, 16, 22, 23, 32; 17:6, 14; 18:11, 14, 23; 19:3; 20:22; 21:31; 22:9, 11; 23:15; 24:8; 25:9, 15, 30; 26:17, 37; 27:21; 28:32, 43; 29:1, 9, 22[2], 28, 38, 42; 30:9, 10, 13, 21, 31, 37; 31:13; 32:1, 5, 13, 23, 24, 27, 29; 33:1, 13; 34:9, 18; 35:4; 36:6, 22; 39:23; **Lev** 2:2; 3:14, 17; 4:20[2], 21, 26, 31, 35; 5:13, 18; 6:7, 9, 20; 7:12, 35, 36; 8:5; 9:6; 10:3, 9, 15, 19, 20; 12:8; 13:31; 14:8, 31, 36, 53; 15:3, 15, 30; 16:3, 16, 29, 30, 34; 17:2, 5, 7; 18:24; 19:25; 21:24; 22:24; 23:14[2], 18, 21, 27, 31, 41[2]; 24:3, 8; 25:13; 26:16, 18, 27, 44; **Nu** 1:54; 3:1; 4:4, 6, 19, 24, 28, 31, 33, 37, 41, 45; 5:4, 13, 19, 21, 22, 24, 29, 30; 6:13, 21, 23; 7:17, 23, 29, 35, 41, 47, 53, 59, 65, 71, 77, 83; 8:4, 7, 14, 24, 26; 9:3; 10:8, 13, 28; 11:6, 11, 15; 12:2, 7; 13:27; 14:2, 3, 14, 15, 27, 29, 32, 35[2], 39, 41; 15:11, 12, 13, 15, 21, 24; 16:4, 6, 21, 28, 31, 40, 45; 17:5, 10; 18:11[2], 23, 28, 32; 19:2, 10, 14, 21; 20:4, 5, 10, 12, 14; 21:2, 5, 17; 22:4, 10, 16, 30[2]; 23:5, 16; 24:14, 23; 25:7; 27:11, 12, 16; 28:2, 3, 6, 8, 10, 13, 14, 17, 24; 29:7; 30:1; 31:21, 29; 32:5, 8, 10, 15, 20, 22, 23, 32; 33:2; 34:6, 9, 12, 13; 35:5, 14; 36:5, 6; **Dt** 1:4, 5, 6, 8, 31, 32, 35; 2:3, 7, 22, 25; 3:14, 18, 26, 27, 28; 4:6[2], 8, 22, 26, 32, 39, 44, 48; 5:3, 25, 28; 6:25; 7:5; 8:11, 17; 9:4, 6, 7, 13, 27; 10:10; 11:5; 13:14; 15:2, 9, 10, 15; 17:4[2], 5, 18, 19; 18:3, 16[2]; 19:4, 7, 10, 20; 20:15; 21:7, 8, 20; 22:5, 14, 16, 19, 25, 26; 24:18, 22; 25:9; 26:9[2], 16, 17, 18; 27:3, 8, 26; 28:13, 58[3], 61; 29:4, 6, 7, 9, 12, 13, 14, 19[2], 20, 21, 24[3], 25, 27[2], 29; 30:10, 18, 19; 31:7, 9, 11, 12, 13, 19, 21, 22, 23, 24, 25, 26, 30; 32:6, 19, 27, 29, 34, 44, 46[2], 51; 33:1, 7; 34:4, 6; **Jos** 1:8, 13; 2:3, 9[2], 17, 18; 3:4, 10; 4:9, 24; 5:4, 9, 12; 6:3, 9, 14, 25, 26[2]; 7:5, 7, 9, 13, 20, 25, 26; 8:14, 19, 27, 28, 29; 9:12, 20, 24, 27; 10:2, 25, 27; 11:1, 6, 16; 12:2; 13:2, 6, 13, 15, 24, 29, 31, 32; 14:10, 12; 15:4, 20, 63; 16:5, 8, 10; 17:1, 2; 18:14, 19, 28; 19:8; 21:42; 22:3, 16, 17, 22[2], 28, 31, 34; 23:9, 13, 15; 24:2, 15, 27, 32; **Jdg** 1:21, 26, 32; 2:2[2], 20; 3:2, 12; 4:9, 14; 5:1, 3, 30; 6:8, 13, 20, 24, 26, 29, 39; 7:4[2], 14; 8:1, 3, 9; 9:3, 7, 24, 25, 29, 42, 46; 10:4; 11:15, 27, 37, 39; 13:20, 23; 14:4; 15:3, 6, 7, 18; 16:15; 17:5, 13; 18:3, 12[2]; 19:11, 23[2], 24; 20:3, 6, 9, 10, 12, 25; 21:3, 11, 18; **Ru** 1:14, 19; 2:10; 3:10; 4:6, 7, 12, 14, 18; **1Sa** 1:3, 7, 27; 2:14, 17, 20, 27; 4:6, 7, 14, 16; 5:5; 6:9, 10, 16, 18, 20; 8:6, 8, 11; 9:6, 13, 15, 16, 17, 24; 10:11, 18, 27; 11:7, 9, 13; 12:2, 5, 8, 16, 20; 14:29, 35, 45[2]; 15:2, 14[2]; 16:8, 9; 17:10, 17, 25, 26[3], 27, 32, 33, 36, 37, 46, 56; 18:5, 8; 19:6, 17, 24; 20:2, 3, 12, 19, 21, 31, 39; 21:11, 15[3]; 22:15; 23:17, 25, 28; 24:4, 10, 11, 16; 25:9, 10[2], 21, 27, 33; 27:11; 28:10, 18; 29:3, 5; 30:8, 15, 20, 25[2]; **2Sa** 1:17, 18; 2:5, 6, 26; 3:8[2], 28, 33, 38; 4:3, 8; 6:8, 22; 7:5, 6, 8, 17, 18, 19[2], 21, 27[2]; 10:5, 7, 17; 11:3, 6, 19, 21, 25[3]; 12:5, 7, 8, 11, 12, 14, 21, 31; 13:12, 17, 18, 20, 21, 28, 32; 14:13[2], 15, 19[2], 20, 33; 15:6, 8; 16:9, 10, 11, 17; 17:4, 6, 7; 18:10, 11, 14, 18; 19:7, 11, 21, 22, 36, 42; 20:21; 22:1; 23:17; 24:12, 23; **1Ki** 1:27, 49; 2:23, 30, 40; 3:6[2], 9, 10, 11, 17, 18, 19, 23; 5:2, 7, 10, 11; 6:12, 17; 7:8, 28, 31, 37; 8:18, 27, 28, 29[3], 30, 31, 33, 35, 38, 42, 43, 61; 9:3, 7, 8[3], 9, 13, 21; 11:11, 31, 33, 39; 12:2, 15, 19, 22, 24[2], 30, 32; 13:2, 3, 16, 21, 33, 34; 14:2, 6, 7, 10, 14, 15; 15:21; 17:14, 20, 21; 18:39; 19:2; 20:2, 5, 6, 7, 9, 12, 13[2], 14[2], 24, 28[2], 33, 39, 42; 21:7, 19[2], 29; 22:11, 20, 27[2], 32; **2Ki** 1:2, 4, 6, 7, 11[2], 13, 16[2]; 2:12, 19, 21[2], 22; 3:7, 16[2], 17[2], 18; 4:9, 13, 16, 43[2]; 5:6, 7, 8, 18[2], 20, 26; 6:11, 19[2], 28, 32, 33; 7:1[2], 2, 9[2], 18, 19; 8:5[2], 8, 9, 22; 9:1, 3, 6, 11, 12, 15, 18, 19, 25, 26, 36, 37; 10:2, 5, 6, 24, 27; 11:5; 12:17; 13:23; 14:7; 15:20; 16:6; 17:7, 12, 27, 34, 41; 18:12, 14, 16, 19[2], 22, 25[2], 29, 30, 31; 19:1, 3[2], 6, 9, 20, 21, 29[2], 31, 32[2], 33, 34; 20:1, 5, 6[2], 9, 17; 21:7, 12, 15; 22:13[2], 15, 16[2], 17, 18, 19, 20; 23:3, 21[2], 23, 24, 27; 24:20; 25:26; **1Ch** 4:14, 41, 43; 5:26; 11:11, 19; 13:4, 11; 16:7; 17:4, 5, 7, 15, 16, 17, 19; 19:8, 17; 20:3; 21:3, 7, 8, 10, 11, 17, 23; 22:8; 24:19; 25:1; 27:1, 6, 24; 28:7, 8, 19; 29:1, 3, 14, 16, 18; **2Ch** 1:10[2], 11; 2:3, 4; 6:8, 18, 20[3], 21, 22, 24, 26, 29, 32, 33, 34, 40; 7:12, 15, 16, 20, 21[3], 22; 8:8, 14; 10:2, 15, 19; 11:2, 4[2], 17; 12:5, 7; 14:11; 16:5, 10; 18:10, 19, 26[2], 31; 19:2, 10; 20:1, 7, 9, 12, 15[2], 17, 26[2]; 21:10, 12, 18; 23:4; 24:11, 20, 22; 25:15, 16, 17; 29:9, 25, 28; 30:9, 26; 31:1, 7, 10, 11, 20; 32:9, 10, 12, 15, 17, 20; 33:7; 34:21[2], 23, 24[2], 25, 26, 27, 28, 31, 32; 35:14, 18, 19, 20, 21, 25; 36:23; **Ezr** 1:2, 9; 2:69; 3:12; 4:11, 13, 14, 15[2], 16, 17, 19, 21, 22[2]; 5:3[2], 4, 6, 9[2], 11, 12, 13, 16, 17[2]; 6:2, 7[2], 8, 11[2], 12[2], 17; 7:6, 11, 17, 24, 27; 8:23, 35; 9:2, 3, 4, 10, 13, 15; 10:2, 4, 13[2], 14, 15; **Ne** 1:11[2]; 2:2, 10, 18, 19; 3:10; 4:9; 5:13[3], 16, 18; 6:2, 3, 7[2], 8, 13, 16[2]; 7:5; 8:9, 10, 11, 15, 17; 9:10, 18, 32, 38; 13:3, 4, 6, 14, 15, 17, 18[2], 21, 22, 27; **Est** 1:1, 18, 21; 2:4, 7, 13, 23; 3:2, 9; 4:11, 13, 14[2], 15, 16; 5:7, 13, 14; 6:3, 9, 11; 7:3[2], 6; 8:12; 9:1, 13, 14, 17, 26, 29; **Job** 1:1, 5, 20, 22; 2:10; 3:1; 5:27; 6:10; 7:15; 9:2; 10:13[2]; 11:2, 6; 12:9; 13:1, 16; 17:8; 21:2, 6; 22:21; 23:15; 24:25; 27:12[2];

THOSE (1368)

TO (20933)

UPON (351)

US (1431)

WAS (4158)

3:18, 20; 4:6; 2Pe 2:7, 8, 16, 21; 3:5, 6; 1Jn 1:1, 2; 3:8; 5:18; 3Jn 1:7; Jude 1:3^2, 4, 9; Rev 1:4, 8, 9, 10, 12, 13, 15, 16, 18; 2:13; 4:1, 2^2, 6, 7^3, 8^2; 5:4^2, 12; 6:2^2, 4^2, 5^2, 8^3, 11^2, 12, 14; 7:9; 8:1, 3, 7^3, 8, 12^2, 13; 9:1, 5, 8, 9, 16, 18, 19; 10:1^2, 2, 4, 11; 11:1^2, 8, 13, 17, 19^2; 12:2^2, 4^2, 5, 7, 8, 9^2, 14, 17; 13:3, 5, 7^2, 8, 14^2, 15; 14:1, 2, 5, 14^2, 15, 16^2; 15:5, 8; 16:8, 10, 12, 18, 21; 17:3, 4^2, 5, 6^2, 8^2, 11; 18:1, 18, 24; 19:4, 8, 11, 20; 20:10, 11^2, 12, 13, 15^2; 21:1, 5, 11, 16^2, 17^2, 18, 19, 21.

WE (1884)

Ge 3:2; 11:4; 13:8; 19:2, 5, 13, 34; 20:13; 22:5^2; 24:25, 50; 26:22, 28^2, 29; 29:5, 8^2, 27; 31:14, 49; 32:6; 34:14^2, 15, 16, 21, 30; 37:7, 26^2, 32; 38:23; 40:8; 41:12, 38; 42:2, 11, 21^3, 22, 30, 31^3, 32; 43:4, 5, 7^2, 8^2, 10^2, 18, 20, 21^3, 22^2; 44:8^3, 16^5, 20^2, 22, 24^2, 26^4; 47:4, 15, 18, 19^4, 25^2; 48:7; 50:15, 18; Ex 1:10; 5:16; 8:26^2, 27; 9:28; 10:9^2, 26^4; 12:33; 14:5^2, 12; 15:24; 16:3^3, 7, 8; 19:8; 20:19^2; 24:3, 7^2, 14; 32:1, 23; Lev 25:20^2; Nu 9:7^2; 10:29^2, 31, 32; 11:4, 5^2, 6^2, 18^2, 20; 12:11; 13:27, 28, 30^2, 31^2, 32^2, 33^3; 14:2, 4, 7, 9, 40^2; 16:12, 14; 17:12^3, 13; 20:3, 4, 10, 15, 16^2, 17^3, 18, 19^4; 21:2, 5, 7^2, 22^3, 30^2; 31:50; 32:5, 16, 17^2, 18, 19, 25, 32^2; Dt 1:19^2, 22^2, 28^3, 41^2; 2:1^2, 8^2, 13, 14^2, 27^2, 29, 33, 34^2, 35^2; 3:1, 3, 4^2, 6^2, 7, 8, 10, 12, 29; 4:7; 5:24^2, 25^3, 26, 27; 6:21, 24, 25; 7:17^2; 12:8, 30; 18:16, 21; 26:7; 29:7, 8, 16^2, 29; 30:12, 13; Jos 1:16^2, 17^2; 2:10, 11, 14^2, 18, 19, 20^2; 4:23; 5:1; 6:17; 7:7; 8:5, 6^2; 9:6, 7, 8, 9, 11, 12^2, 13, 19^2, 20^3, 22, 24^2, 25; 17:14; 22:17, 23, 24, 26, 27, 28^2, 31; 24:15, 17, 18, 21, 22, 24; Jdg 1:3, 24; 8:6, 15; 9:28^2, 38; 10:10, 15; 11:6, 8, 10, 24; 13:15^2, 17, 22^2; 14:15; 15:10, 13^2; 16:5^2; 18:9; 19:12^2, 18, 19^2, 22; 20:13, 23, 28, 32, 39; 21:7^2, 16, 18^2, 22^2; Ru 1:10; 4:11; 1Sa 5:8; 6:2^2, 4, 9; 7:6; 8:19, 20; 9:7^4; 10:14^2; 11:1, 3^2, 10, 12; 12:10^3, 12, 19^2; 14:8, 9^3, 10; 15:15; 16:11; 17:9; 20:42; 23:3^2, 20; 25:7, 8, 15, 16; 30:14^2, 22^2; 2Sa 5:1; 7:22; 11:23; 12:18^2; 13:25; 14:7^2, 14; 15:14^2; 16:20; 17:5, 6, 12^2, 13; 18:3; 19:10, 42^3, 43^3; 20:1, 19; 21:4^2, 5; 1Ki 3:18; 5:6; 8:47^3; 12:4, 9, 16; 17:12; 18:5^2; 20:23^2, 25^2, 31; 22:3, 7, 8, 15; 2Ki 2:16; 3:8, 11, 13; 4:13; 6:1, 15, 28, 29^2; 7:3, 4^6, 9^2, 10, 12^2; 10:4, 5^3, 13^2; 18:22, 26; 1Ch 11:1; 12:18^2; 13:3; 15:13; 16:35^2; 17:20; 29:13, 14^2, 15, 16; 2Ch 2:16; 6:37^2; 10:4, 9, 16; 13:10, 11; 14:7^2, 11^2; 18:3, 5, 6, 7, 14; 20:9, 12^2; 25:16; 28:13; 29:18, 19; 31:10; Ezr 4:2, 3, 14^2, 16; 5:8, 9, 10^2, 11^2; 8:15, 21, 22, 23, 31, 32^2, 33; 9:7, 9, 10^2, 14, 15^2; 10:2, 4, 12, 13^2; Ne 1:6, 7^2; 2:17^2, 20; 4:1, 4, 6, 9, 10, 11, 15^2, 19, 21; 5:2^2, 3, 4, 5^3, 8, 12^3, 16; 9:33, 36, 37, 38; 10:30, 31^2, 32, 34, 35, 36, 37^3, 39; 13:27; Est 5:5; 7:4; Job 2:10; 5:27; 8:9; 9:32; 15:9^2; 17:16; 18:2, 3; 19:28; 21:14, 15^2; 26:14; 32:13; 37:19^2; 38:35; Ps 12:4^2; 20:5, 7, 8, 9; 21:13; 33:20, 21, 22; 35:21, 25^2; 36:9; 44:1, 5^2, 8^2, 17, 20, 22^2, 25; 46:2; 48:8^2, 9; 55:14; 60:12; 64:6; 65:3, 4; 66:12; 74:8, 9; 75:1^2; 78:3, 4^2; 79:4, 8, 13^2; 80:3, 7, 18^2, 19; 81:5^2; 90:7, 9, 10^2, 12, 14, 15; 95:7; 100:3^2; 103:14^2; 106:6^2, 47; 108:13; 115:18; 118:26; 123:3, 4; 124:7^2; 126:1, 3; 129:8; 132:6^2; 137:1^2, 2, 4; Pr 1:13, 14; 24:12; SS 1:4^2, 11; 6:1, 13; 8:8^2, 9^2; Isa 1:9^2; 2:3; 4:1; 5:19^2; 8:18; 9:10^2; 10:29; 14:10; 16:6; 20:6^3; 22:13; 24:16; 25:9^2; 26:1, 8, 12, 13, 17, 18^5; 28:15^3; 30:16^2; 33:2; 36:7, 11; 38:20; 41:22, 23^2, 26^2; 42:24; 46:5; 51:23; 53:2, 3, 4, 5, 6; 58:3^2; 59:9^2, 10^3, 11^3, 12; 63:17, 19; 64:3, 5^2, 6, 8^2, 9^2, 11; 66:5; Jer 2:31^2; 3:22, 25^3; 4:13; 5:12; 6:16, 17, 24; 7:10; 8:8^2, 14^2, 15, 20; 9:19^2; 13:12; 14:7, 9, 19^2, 20^2; 15:2; 16:10^2; 18:12; 20:10; 26:19; 35:6, 8^2, 10, 11^3; 36:16; 38:25; 41:8; 42:2, 3^2, 5, 6^3, 13, 14^2, 20; 44:16, 17^6, 18^2, 19^2, 25^2; 48:14, 29; 50:7; 51:9, 51^2; La 2:16^3; 3:22, 42, 47; 4:17, 18, 20^2; 5:3, 4^2, 5, 6, 7, 9, 16, 21; Eze 11:3; 20:32; 21:10; 33:10^2, 24; 35:10; 37:11; Da 2:4, 7, 23, 36; 3:16, 17^2, 18^2, 24; 6:5; 9:5^3, 6, 7, 8^2, 9, 10, 11, 13, 14, 15^2, 18^2; Hos 6:2; 8:2; 10:3^3; 14:2, 3^2; Am 6:10, 13; 8:5^2; Ob 1:1; Jnh 1:6, 11; 3:9; Mic 2:4; 4:2, 5; 5:5; Hab 1:12; Zec 1:11; 8:23; Mal 1:4^2, 6, 7; 2:10^2, 17; 3:7, 8, 13, 14, 15; Mt 2:2; 3:9; 6:12, 31^3; 7:22; 9:14; 11:3, 17^2; 12:38; 14:17; 15:33; 16:7; 17:19, 27; 19:27; 20:18, 22, 33; 21:25, 26^2, 27; 22:16; 23:30^2; 25:37, 38, 39, 44; 26:65; 27:42, 63; 28:13, 14; Mk 2:12; 4:30^2, 38; 5:9; 6:37; 8:16; 9:28, 38^2; 10:28, 33, 35^2, 39; 11:31, 32, 33; 12:14, 15^2; 14:58, 63; 15:32; Lk 3:8, 10, 12, 14; 4:23; 5:26; 7:19, 20, 32^2; 9:12, 13^2, 49^2; 10:11; 11:4; 13:26; 15:32; 17:10^2; 18:28^2, 31; 19:14; 20:5, 6, 7, 21; 22:49, 71^2; 23:2, 41^2; 24:21; Jn 1:14, 16, 41, 45; 3:2, 11^4; 4:20, 22^2, 42^3; 6:5, 28, 30, 42, 68, 69; 7:27, 35; 8:33^2, 41^2, 48, 52; 9:4, 20^2, 21, 24, 28, 29^2, 31, 40; 10:33; 11:16, 47, 48; 12:21, 34; 14:5^2, 23; 16:18, 30; 17:11, 22; 18:30, 31; 19:7, 15; 20:2, 25; 21:24; Ac 2:11, 32, 37; 3:12, 15; 4:9, 12, 16^2, 17, 20^2; 5:23^3, 28, 29, 32; 6:3, 11, 14; 7:40; 10:22, 33, 39, 47; 11:12; 13:32, 46^2; 14:15^2, 22; 15:10, 11^2, 19, 20, 24, 25, 27^2, 36; 16:10, 11, 12^2, 13^3, 16^2, 28, 37; 17:19, 20, 28^2, 29^2, 32; 19:2, 25, 40^2; 20:6^2, 7, 8, 13^2, 14, 15^2, 35; 21:1^3, 2, 3^2, 4, 5^2, 6, 7^2, 8, 10, 12^2, 14, 15, 16, 17, 22, 23, 25; 23:9, 14^2, 15; 24:2, 3, 5, 6, 8; 26:14; 27:1, 2^2, 3, 4, 5^2, 7^2, 8, 12, 15, 16^2, 18, 20, 26, 27, 29; 28:1, 10^2, 11, 12, 13^2, 14^2, 15, 16, 21, 22^2; Ro 1:5; 2:2; 3:5, 8^2, 9^3, 19, 20, 28, 31^2; 4:1, 9; 5:1^2, 2^3, 3^2, 6, 8, 9^2, 10^3, 11^2; 6:1^2, 2^2, 4^2, 5^2, 6^2, 8^3, 9, 15^2; 7:4, 5^2, 6^2, 7, 14; 8:12, 15, 16, 17^4, 22, 23^2, 24, 25^3, 26^2, 28, 31, 36^2, 37; 9:14, 29^2, 30; 10:8; 12:5, 6; 13:11; 14:8^6, 10; 15:1, 4; 1Co 1:23; 2:6, 7, 12^2, 13, 16; 3:9; 4:8, 9, 10^3, 11^4, 12^5, 13^3; 6:3; 8:1^2, 4, 6^2, 8^3; 9:4, 5, 11^2, 12^3, 25; 10:8, 9, 16^2, 17^2, 22^2; 11:16, 31^2, 32^3; 12:13^2, 23^2; 13:9^2, 12^2; 14:26; 15:11, 15^2, 19^2, 30, 32, 49^2, 51^2, 52; 2Co 1:4^2, 6^3, 7, 8^4, 9^2, 10, 12^2, 13, 14, 24^2; 2:11, 15, 16, 17^2; 3:1^2, 5, 12^2, 13, 18; 4:1^2, 2^4, 5, 7, 8, 10, 11, 13, 14, 16^3, 18; 5:1^3, 2, 3^2, 4^3, 6^3, 7, 8, 9^2, 10, 11^3, 12, 13^2, 14, 16^3, 20^2, 21; 6:1, 3, 4, 9, 11, 12, 16; 7:1, 2^3, 3, 5^2, 13^2, 14; 8:1, 5, 6, 18, 19^2, 20^2, 21, 22; 9:4; 10:2, 3^2, 4, 5^2, 6, 7, 11^4, 12, 13, 14^3, 15, 16^2; 11:4, 6, 21; 12:18, 19^3; 13:4^2, 6, 7^3, 8, 9^2; Gal 1:8^2, 9; 2:4, 5, 9, 10, 15, 16^2, 17^2; 3:14, 23, 24, 25; 4:3^2, 5, 31; 5:5^2, 25; 6:9^2, 10; Eph 1:7, 11, 12; 2:3, 5, 10, 18; 3:12, 20; 4:13, 14, 15, 25; 5:30; 6:22; Php 3:3^2, 16, 17, 20; Col 1:3^2, 4, 9^2, 10, 14, 28^2; 4:3; 1Th 1:2, 3, 4, 5, 8; 2:2^2, 3^2, 4^2, 5^2, 6^2, 7, 8^2, 9^2, 10, 11, 13, 17^2, 18, 19; 3:1^2, 2, 3, 4^3, 6, 7, 8, 9^2, 10^2; 4:1^2, 2, 6, 9, 10, 11, 13, 14^2, 15^2, 17^2; 5:1, 5, 8, 10^2, 12, 14; 2Th 1:3, 4, 11, 12; 2:1, 13, 15; 3:2, 4^2, 6, 7^2, 8^3, 9^2, 10^2, 11, 12; 1Ti 1:8, 9; 2:2; 4:10^2; 6:7^2, 8^2; 2Ti 1:9; 2:11^2, 12^3, 13; Tit 2:13; 3:3^2, 5, 7; Phm 1:6; Heb 2:1^3, 3^2, 5, 8, 9; 3:1, 6^3, 14^3, 19; 4:2, 3, 13, 14^2, 15^3, 16; 5:11; 6:3, 9^2, 11, 12, 18, 19; 7:15, 19; 8:1^2; 9:5, 14; 10:10, 19, 21, 23, 24, 26^2, 30, 39; 11:1^2, 3; 12:1, 9^3, 10, 25^2, 28; 13:6, 10, 14^2, 18^2; Jas 1:18; 3:1, 2, 3^2, 9^2; 4:13, 15; 5:11; 1Pe 2:24; 2Pe 1:3, 16^3, 18^2, 19; 3:13; 1Jn 1:1^4, 2^2, 3^2, 4, 5, 6^2, 7^2, 8^2, 9, 10^3; 2:1, 3^3, 5^2, 18, 28; 3:1^2, 2^5, 10, 11, 14^3, 16^2, 19^3, 21, 22^2, 24^2; 4:6^2, 9, 10, 11, 12, 13^2, 14, 16, 17^2, 19; 5:2^2, 9, 14^2, 15^5, 18, 19^2, 20^3; 2Jn 1:5^2, 6; 3Jn 1:8^2, 12, 14; Jude 1:3; Rev 7:3; 11:17.

WERE (2530)

Ge 2:1, 4, 9^2, 25; 3:7^2, 11, 19; 4:8; 5:2; 6:1, 2, 4^2; 7:11, 16, 19, 23; 8:1; 9:18, 19^2, 23; 10:10, 21, 25, 29; 11:5; 12:6; 13:6^2, 7, 13^2; 14:7, 13; 17:26; 18:11; 19:11, 14; 20:8; 23:20; 24:32^2, 54; 25:3, 4^2, 16, 24; 26:27, 35; 27:1, 23; 28:8, 12; 29:2, 3; 30:35, 38, 39, 41, 42; 31:1, 4, 10; 32:7; 34:5, 7, 25; 35:1, 2, 16, 26^2; 36:5^2, 7^2, 12, 13, 15, 16^2, 17^2, 18, 19^2, 20^2, 21, 29, 30, 31, 40, 43; 37:7, 9, 11, 25^2; 38:12, 27; 39:20; 40:5, 6, 7, 10, 13, 16, 17^2; 41:4, 5, 50; 42:5, 13, 30, 32, 35^2; 43:7, 18^3, 25, 27, 34; 44:3; 45:3^2, 16, 24; 46:15^2, 18, 20, 22^2, 25, 26, 27, 31; 47:3, 14, 27, 28; 48:7, 10; 49:31^2, 32; 50:8, 23; Ex 1:7, 12, 15; 2:5, 11; 4:16^2; 5:14^2, 19^2; 6:14^3, 15^2, 16, 17, 18, 19^2, 21, 22, 24^2, 25, 27; 8:14, 18; 9:11, 26, 31, 32; 10:8, 11; 12:37; 14:8, 10^2, 11, 21, 27; 15:27; 16:17; 17:3, 11^2, 16; 22:21; 23:9; 27:8; 32:15, 16, 25, 29; 33:5; 34:1, 30; 35:22, 26, 29; 36:4, 6, 9, 15, 28, 29^2, 30; 37:13, 14, 15^2, 17, 19, 20, 22; 38:2, 14, 15, 16, 17^3, 19^2, 20, 21, 25, 27; 39:4, 13, 14; Lev 7:35^2, 36; 15:10; 18:27, 28, 30; 19:34; Nu 1:16^2, 18, 20^2, 22^2, 24^2, 26^2, 28^2, 30^2, 32^2, 34^2, 36^2, 38^2, 40^2, 42^2, 44, 45^2, 47; 2:33; 3:2, 3^2, 17, 18, 20, 21, 22, 23, 25, 27, 28, 29, 31, 32, 33, 34, 35, 36, 38^2; 4:36, 38, 40, 42, 44, 49; 7:2^2, 8, 9^2, 84, 87, 88; 9:6; 11:18, 22^2, 26^2, 29; 12:8; 13:3; 14:6, 37; 15:26, 32; 16:2, 27, 33, 35, 38; 19:18; 20:13; 21:32; 22:3, 22, 34, 40; 25:6; 26:4, 5, 7^2, 9^3, 12, 14^2, 15, 18^2, 19, 20, 21, 22^2, 23, 25^2, 26, 27^2, 28, 30, 33, 34^2, 35, 36, 37^3, 38, 40, 41^2, 42^2, 43^2, 44, 47^2, 48, 50^2, 57^2, 58, 62; 27:1, 14; 31:5, 8, 16^2, 26, 47, 48; 32:1, 38, 39; 33:4, 9, 40; 36:1; Dt 1:18, 26; 2:11, 21; 3:5^2; 4:35, 43, 46; 5:5, 15; 6:21; 7:7^2; 9:10, 15; 10:2, 19, 22; 11:2, 4; 12:15; 15:15, 22; 16:12; 24:18, 22; 25:18^2; 28:62, 67^2; 32:29; 34:7; Jos 4:7; 5:6, 7^2, 8^2; 6:9; 7:4; 8:16^2, 22, 24, 33^2; 9:4, 13, 16, 24; 10:1, 2^2, 11, 20, 26, 33; 11:2, 8, 22; 13:23, 28; 14:2, 12^2; 15:21, 46, 63; 16:9; 17:1, 3, 9, 12^2; 18:2, 20; 19:15^2, 16, 22, 23, 30, 31, 35, 38, 39, 48; 21:4^2, 5, 6, 10^2, 19, 20, 21, 26, 27, 33, 34, 40^2, 41; 22:30, 33; 24:32; Jdg 1:19, 21, 27, 35^2; 2:14, 15; 3:4, 8, 14; 4:17; 5:6, 13, 14, 15; 6:29; 7:19, 20, 23, 24; 8:10^2, 19, 26; 9:3, 27, 29; 10:17; 11:2; 12:2, 6; 14:4; 15:6; 16:2, 12, 17, 25, 27^2; 17:2, 4; 18:3, 7^2, 22, 26, 30; 19:11, 16, 22; 20:16^2, 31, 32^2, 36, 41; 21:9, 14^2, 23; Ru 1:2^2; 2:23; 1Sa 1:3, 13; 2:5^2, 12, 17, 22, 27; 3:1, 2; 4:4, 7, 10, 15, 19; 5:4, 12; 6:13; 7:7, 10, 13, 14; 8:10; 9:3, 4, 11, 14, 22, 27; 10:9, 14; 11:9, 11^2; 13:2^2, 4, 7, 11^2, 15, 16; 14:2, 11, 17^2, 21, 22, 24, 31, 41^2, 49, 51; 15:9, 17; 17:11, 21, 52; 18:6; 19:5; 20:20; 22:2^2, 11, 17; 23:24, 26^2; 24:3; 25:7^2, 15^2, 16^2, 20, 43; 26:7, 12, 16; 29:2, 4; 30:2, 6, 10, 16, 21, 26, 27; 2Sa 1:14, 23^4, 26; 2:3, 15, 17, 18, 30, 31; 3:2, 5, 34^2, 36; 4:2^2; 5:2, 13; 6:3, 5, 13; 7:19; 8:2, 17, 18; 9:12; 10:5, 8, 9, 14, 19^2; 11:7, 16; 12:1, 18, 19, 31; 13:23, 30; 14:27, 32; 15:4, 14, 22, 24^2, 30; 16:6; 17:17^2; 18:1, 7, 12; 19:6^2, 8, 9, 14, 17, 41, 43; 20:3, 8, 15, 25; 21:2^2, 9, 13, 22; 22:10, 16, 18, 38; 23:17, 22, 24, 39; 24:9; 1Ki 1:9, 41^2; 2:32; 3:2, 18; 4:2, 10, 13, 20^2, 21, 22; 5:12; 6:5, 7, 10, 25; 7:4, 5, 6, 9, 10, 11, 19, 20, 22, 24, 25, 28, 29^2, 31, 32^2, 33^2, 35, 37^2, 45, 47, 48; 8:5, 8; 9:20, 22, 23; 10:10, 19, 21^2, 28; 11:2, 29; 12:8, 17, 31; 13:8, 20; 14:24; 15:27; 16:21; 18:6, 10; 20:12, 16, 23, 27, 33; 22:10, 12, 43, 48; 2Ki 2:1, 11, 15; 4:6, 39; 6:20, 32; 7:3, 10; 9:25; 10:1, 4, 6^2, 17; 11:2, 9^2, 10, 14^2, 15; 12:3, 21; 13:21; 14:4; 15:4, 35; 17:9, 14, 23, 41^2; 19:12^2, 18, 35; 23:7, 11, 13, 16; 24:11, 14; 25:4, 5, 13, 15, 19, 25, 28; 1Ch 1:19, 23, 29, 31, 33, 43, 51, 54; 2:1, 3, 9, 16^2, 18, 23, 33, 50, 52; 3:1, 4, 5^2, 6, 9, 20; 4:2, 3, 4, 6, 12, 14, 18, 23, 31, 32, 33, 38, 41^2; 5:1, 10, 13, 14, 17, 18, 20, 23, 24^2, 25; 6:48, 49, 50, 54^3, 55, 56, 57, 60^3, 61, 62, 63, 66, 67; 7:3, 5^2, 8, 11^2, 12, 16, 17, 19, 21, 29, 33, 40; 8:3, 6^3, 8, 10, 13, 16, 18, 21, 25, 27, 28, 38^2, 40^2; 9:1, 2, 3, 9, 13^2, 18, 19, 22, 23, 24, 26^2, 28^3, 29, 32, 33^3, 34, 44^2; 11:2, 10, 19, 24, 26; 12:1^2, 2^3, 8^3, 14, 20, 21^2, 38^2, 40; 13:8; 15:19, 20, 21, 23, 24^2, 26^2, 27^3; 16:5, 6, 19, 38, 41, 42^2; 17:17^2; 18:16, 17; 19:5, 7, 9, 10, 11, 15, 19; 20:3, 4, 8; 21:5, 20, 29; 23:3, 9, 10, 11, 14, 17, 24^2, 27, 29, 30^2, 31^2; 24:1^2, 4^2, 5, 30, 31; 25:2, 5^2, 6^2; 26:6^2, 7, 8^2, 9, 11, 13, 14, 17, 18, 19^2, 20, 21^3, 22, 26^2, 28, 29, 30, 31, 32; 27:1, 2, 4, 5, 7, 8, 9, 10, 11, 12, 13, 14, 15, 22, 31; 29:15; 2Ch 1:16; 2:17^2; 3:15; 4:3, 4, 6, 16, 19, 21; 5:5, 6, 9, 11, 12^2; 6:38; 7:6^2; 8:7, 9, 10; 9:18, 20^2, 28; 10:8, 17; 11:10, 12; 13:14, 17, 18^2; 14:8, 13; 15:5, 13; 16:8; 17:8, 19; 18:9, 11; 20:22^2, 33, 36, 37^2; 21:2^2, 13; 22:11; 23:8^2, 9, 13^3, 14, 18; 24:13, 14^2, 26; 25:5, 10, 12; 28:12, 15^2, 23; 29:6, 23, 29, 31, 34, 35; 30:7, 8, 15, 17, 21; 31:1, 13, 16, 18, 19^2; 32:9^2, 13, 18, 31; 34:4^2, 9, 12^2, 13, 14, 33; 35:7, 11, 14, 15, 17, 18; 36:21; Ezr 1:11; 2:59, 62; 4:1, 20; 5:2, 5; 6:20; 8:3, 13, 16^2, 20, 33; 10:9, 16; Ne 2:10, 12; 3:7, 17, 18, 22; 4:1, 7^2, 15, 16, 17; 5:2, 3, 4, 8, 16, 18^2; 6:2, 9, 16, 17, 18; 7:1, 4, 61, 64, 68; 8:2, 4, 7, 9, 14; 9:3, 4, 12, 19, 25, 26, 27, 28, 30, 35; 10:1, 8; 11:1, 13, 14, 20, 21, 22, 23, 30; 12:1, 7, 8, 12, 22, 23, 24, 25, 27^2, 28, 44^2; 13:3, 13^2, 15, 16; Est 1:3, 5^2, 6, 14^2, 21; 2:8, 19, 23; 3:6, 12^2, 13; 4:12; 5:6; 6:14; 7:2; 8:9^2; 9:1, 2, 16, 26; Job 1:13, 14^2, 18; 3:12; 4:7; 5:8; 8:9; 9:15, 20^2, 33; 15:7; 16:4; 19:23^2, 24; 22:3^2, 8, 16; 29:5, 10; 30:5^2, 6, 8; 32:4, 11, 22; 34:14; 38:4, 6, 21; 39:16; 42:15; Ps 18:9, 15, 17, 37; 22:5^2; 31:12; 33:6; 35:13; 39:12; 40:5; 48:5; 50:12; 53:5; 55:12^2; 65:3; 77:16, 19; 78:8^2, 37^2, 39, 53, 57, 64; 80:10; 81:6; 87:5; 90:2; 99:6, 8; 105:12; 106:7, 43; 107:5, 23, 27, 29, 30, 39; 119:5; 126:1, 2; 133:3; 139:16, 18; 141:6; 148:5; Pr 3:20; 8:24^2, 25; Ecc 2:7; 4:8, 16^2; 7:10; SS 1:6; 6:11; 8:1, 7; Isa 6:2^2, 3; 7:2, 23; 9:1; 10:15; 12:1; 14:9^2; 22:2, 3^2; 26:17, 18; 27:4, 7, 13^2; 29:16; 37:12^2, 19, 36; 40:15; 41:22, 25^2; 43:9; 46:3; 48:4^2, 8; 49:19; 50:1; 51:1^2; 52:3, 14^2, 15; 54:1, 6; 57:10; 58:2; 59:10; 63:14; 64:5; Jer 1:5; 2:3, 36; 4:24^2, 25; 6:14; 7:13, 26; 8:11; 9:1; 11:18; 15:1, 16; 17:23; 19:15; 22:24; 24:1; 28:5; 33:7, 11; 34:1, 7^2; 36:12, 28, 32; 37:5, 10^2, 15; 40:1, 6, 7^2; 41:1, 2, 3^2, 7, 10^2, 11, 13^2, 16, 18; 42:2, 8; 44:12, 15^2, 17, 19, 20; 49:18; 50:24^2; 52:7, 8, 17, 19, 23, 25, 30, 32; La 1:7, 14; 2:4, 14^2; 3:52; 4:7, 10, 18, 19; Eze 1:1, 7^2, 11^2, 18^2, 23; 2:10; 3:15; 7:20; 8:1, 16^2; 9:6, 8; 10:3, 12^2, 15, 20^2; 11:1; 14:14, 16, 18, 20; 16:3, 4^3, 5^3, 7^2, 8, 13^2, 22, 27, 28^2, 29, 31, 49, 50, 52, 55^2; 19:7^2, 11; 20:16, 21, 25; 21:30; 23:2, 3, 4, 20, 42; 26:17; 27:7, 8^2, 9, 11, 15, 21; 28:12, 13^4, 14^2, 15^2, 16, 18; 29:7, 13; 31:13, 15, 16^2; 32:27, 31; 34:5^2, 6, 12; 36:17, 19, 35; 37:2; 38:8; 39:18, 23; 40:2, 7^2, 9, 10, 12, 16^2, 17, 18, 30, 38, 39^2, 40^2, 41^2, 42^2, 43^2, 44, 48^2, 49; 41:2, 3, 6^3, 7, 11, 13, 16, 18, 19, 20, 22, 25, 26; 42:4, 5, 6, 10, 11, 12; 46:22; 48:11; Da 1:5^2, 6, 16; 2:13, 29, 34, 35, 41, 42, 47; 3:13, 21, 27, 28; 4:12, 31, 36; 5:9, 15; 6:2, 4, 24; 7:2, 4, 8, 9^2, 10, 12; 8:3, 12; 10:3, 12; Hos 2:12; 6:7; 8:7; 10:14; 13:6^2; Am 4:11; Ob 1:11; Jnh 1:5; Mic 1:13^2; Na 3:9^2, 10^3; Hab 1:5; 3:8, 14; Zep 3:7, 19; Hag 2:15, 16^2; Zec 1:8, 18; 3:4; 5:9; 6:1, 7; 7:6^2, 7^2, 14; 8:9, 10; 11:11; Mt 1:17; 2:10, 16, 20; 3:4, 6; 4:18^2, 21, 24; 5:12; 7:28; 8:16^2, 27, 28; 9:8, 32, 36; 11:7, 21, 23; 12:1, 3, 23; 13:6, 54; 14:20^2, 26, 33, 36; 15:12, 31, 37^2; 17:9, 23; 18:31; 19:8, 12^2, 13, 25; 20:9, 10, 12, 24, 29, 30; 21:12, 15, 20, 46; 22:22, 25, 28, 33, 41; 23:37; 24:24, 38; 25:2^2, 10^2; 26:8, 21, 22, 26, 43, 59, 69; 27:32, 38, 44, 52, 54^2, 55, 56, 61; 28:3, 4, 11, 13, 15; Mk 1:5, 16, 22, 27; 2:6, 8, 15^2, 16, 18, 25; 3:2, 10, 20, 30; 4:1, 6, 36, 41; 5:13, 15, 20, 40, 42; 6:2, 8, 14, 31, 34, 42, 50, 51, 52, 56; 7:2, 35, 37; 8:8^2, 9, 25; 9:2, 4, 6, 9, 15, 30, 32, 33; 10:5, 10, 13, 24, 26, 32^3, 46; 11:12, 15; 12:12, 17, 20, 23, 41; 13:22; 14:1^2, 4, 11, 18, 19, 22, 40, 55, 67; 15:40^2, 41; 16:2, 5, 8, 10, 12, 14; Lk 1:2^2, 6, 7, 10, 21, 59, 65^2; 2:6, 8, 9, 18, 20, 38, 43^2, 48, 49; 3:15^2, 21; 4:20, 22, 25, 27, 28, 32, 36, 42; 5:2, 9, 10, 17, 22, 26, 29; 6:3, 7, 8, 11, 18; 7:16, 21, 39; 8:1, 3, 4, 19, 23, 35, 37, 40, 52, 56; 9:7, 14, 17^2, 18, 32, 33, 34, 43, 45, 57; 10:13, 38; 11:52; 12:1, 49; 13:1, 2, 4, 17^2, 34; 14:24, 25; 15:1, 16; 16:14, 16; 17:10, 14, 17, 27, 28; 18:9, 15; 19:11, 32, 33, 45, 47; 20:19, 26, 29, 33, 45; 21:5; 22:2^2, 5, 63; 23:10, 32; 24:4, 13, 14, 16, 28^2, 31, 32, 36, 37; Jn 1:3, 48; 3:2, 19, 23; 4:27; 6:11, 19, 21^2, 24, 61; 7:1, 11, 15, 39, 43; 8:6, 20, 39, 42; 9:10, 16, 22, 33, 34, 40, 41; 10:8, 19; 12:11, 20; 13:1; 14:2; 17:6; 18:3, 15, 30, 36; 19:11; 20:4, 19, 20, 25, 26^2; 21:2, 6, 8, 18, 25; Ac 1:10, 13^2; 2:1, 2, 4, 5, 37, 41^2, 43, 44, 47; 3:1, 10, 11; 4:1, 2^2, 6, 13^2, 21, 31^2, 32, 34; 5:13, 14, 16, 17^2, 24, 33, 36, 37; 6:1, 15; 7:9, 16, 26, 54, 59; 8:1, 7, 12; 9:17, 21, 26; 10:2, 9, 38, 45; 11:24, 26; 12:11, 12, 16; 13:1, 2, 42, 45, 48^2, 52; 14:4; 15:1, 2, 4, 22, 30, 31, 32, 33; 16:5, 15, 16^2, 23, 25^2, 26, 33, 38^2; 17:4, 5, 8, 11; 18:3, 8, 14; 19:5, 7, 12^2, 13, 14, 17, 28, 32^2; 20:8^2, 12, 13; 21:16, 18, 27, 30, 31, 37, 40; 22:20, 23, 24, 29; 23:4, 6, 9, 13, 27, 28; 24:9; 25:3, 14; 26:10; 27:1, 4, 15, 16, 27^2, 30, 36, 37, 44; 28:9, 10, 15, 24; Ro 1:21, 27; 2:26; 3:6; 4:17, 23; 5:6, 8, 10^2, 19; 6:3^2, 4, 17, 20^2; 7:5^2; 8:24; 9:3, 11, 32; 11:6, 7, 19, 20, 24^2, 30; 15:21, 26, 27; 16:7; 1Co 1:13, 15, 26^5; 2:4; 3:2; 4:18; 5:3; 6:11^4, 20; 7:7, 21^2, 23, 30^2; 10:1, 2, 5, 7, 9, 10, 11; 11:5; 12:2^2, 13^2, 17^2, 19; 16:15; 2Co 1:8; 3:14; 5:20; 7:5, 9^2, 13, 15; 8:3, 10; 9:2; 11:21; 12:12, 13; Gal 1:10, 17; 2:6, 14; 3:16, 23, 27; 4:3^2, 8, 14^2; 5:7, 13; Eph 1:11, 12, 13^2; 2:1, 3, 5, 12, 13, 17^2; 4:4^2, 21, 22, 30; 5:8; 6:7; Col 1:16^2, 21^2; 2:7, 11, 13, 17; 3:15; 1Th 2:6, 7, 8, 10, 17; 3:3, 4, 7; 2Th 3:7^2, 10; 1Ti 5:1; 6:12; Tit 3:3; Heb 2:15; 3:16^2, 19; 8:4; 9:2, 5, 9; 10:6, 8, 33^2; 11:2, 9, 13^2, 16, 23, 29, 31, 35, 36, 37^3, 39; 13:3^2; Jas 2:22; 5:6; 1Pe 1:12, 18; 2:8, 10, 21, 25; 3:5, 9, 20; 4:12; 2Pe 1:16, 18, 21; 2:1, 20; 1Jn 3:12^2; Rev 1:14^2, 15; 3:15; 4:4^3, 5, 6^2, 11; 5:8, 9; 6:8, 11^2; 7:4, 5, 9^2, 11; 8:2, 7, 9; 9:2, 3, 4, 5, 8, 15, 17, 19, 20; 10:1; 11:13^2, 15, 16, 18; 14:4, 20; 15:6, 8; 16:5, 9; 17:2; 18:23^2; 19:14, 20, 21; 20:3, 4, 5, 12^2, 13^2, 14; 21:12, 13, 14, 19, 21.

WHEN (2816)

Ge 2:4^2, 17; 3:5, 6; 4:12; 5:1, 2, 3, 6, 9, 12, 15, 18, 21, 25, 28; 6:1, 4; 7:6; 8:11; 9:21, 24; 11:10, 12, 14, 16, 18, 20, 22, 24, 31; 12:4, 12, 14, 15; 14:10, 14; 15:17; 16:4, 16; 17:1, 22, 24; 18:2, 16, 33; 19:1, 15, 16, 29, 33^2, 35^2; 20:8, 13; 21:4, 5, 15; 22:3, 9; 24:14, 22, 41, 42, 52, 54; 25:20, 24, 26, 29; 26:7, 8, 34; 27:1, 5, 27, 34, 40, 42, 45; 28:6, 11, 16; 29:3, 10, 23, 25, 31, 33, 34, 35; 30:1, 9, 16, 30, 38^2; 31:19, 25, 49; 32:2, 6, 10, 17, 19, 20, 25; 34:2, 5; 35:1, 7; 36:33, 34, 35, 36, 37, 38, 39; 37:4, 5, 7, 10, 14, 21, 23, 28, 29; 38:12, 13, 15, 27, 29; 39:3, 13, 15, 19; 40:6, 13, 14, 16; 41:1, 2, 14, 15, 18, 46, 55, 56; 42:1, 6, 21, 29, 35; 43:2, 16, 18, 26, 34; 44:4^2, 6, 14, 24, 30; 45:1, 4, 16, 27^2; 46:1, 28, 33; 47:15, 18, 24, 29, 30; 48:2, 8, 17; 49:15, 28, 33; 50:4, 10, 11, 15, 17; Ex 1:16; 2:2, 3, 10, 15, 18; 3:4, 12, 21; 4:6, 7, 14, 21, 31; 5:13, 19, 20; 6:28; 7:5, 7, 9; 8:15, 17, 18; 9:23, 29, 34; 11:1; 12:6, 13^2, 23, 25, 26, 27; 13:5, 8, 14, 15, 17; 14:5, 18, 31; 15:19, 23; 16:8, 14, 15, 18, 21, 32;

WHICH (707)

WHO (5081)

WHOM (394)

WHOSE (278)

23:7, 8[2]; **26:**3; **30:**7; **31:**9[2]; **33:**16; **36:**7; **45:**1; **57:**8, 15, 20; **58:**11; **65:**4; **Jer 5:**15[2]; **17:**5, 7; **32:**18; **37:**13; **44:**28; **46:**18; **48:**15; **51:**57; **La 3:**25; **Eze 3:**6; **11:**21; **17:**16[2]; **20:**9, 14, 22; **21:**25[2], 29[2]; **23:**20[2]; **24:**6; **26:**10; **32:**27; **38:**8; **40:**2, 3; **42:**2; **Da 12:**1; **Hos 7:**4; **Joel 3:**19; **Am 5:**27; **Mic 2:**7; **5:**2; **Hab 1:**11; **Zec 6:**12; **Mt 1:**3, 5[2], 6; **3:**11; **22:**20[2], 28, 42; **24:**46; **26:**3; **Mk 1:**7; **7:**25; **12:**16[2], 23; **Lk 3:**16; **6:**6; **12:**37, 38; **13:**1; **16:**1; **20:**24, 33; **Jn 1:**27; **4:**46; **6:**42; **11:**2; **18:**26; **Ac 10:**6; **13:**25; **14:**13; **16:**1[2]; **27:**23; **Ro 4:**7[2], 8; **14:**1, 2; **16:**23; **Php 3:**8; **4:**3; **1Ti 4:**2; **5:**17; **Tit 1:**6; **Heb 3:**17; **11:**10, 34; **12:**23; **1Jn 5:**16; **Jude 1:**4; **Rev 2:**18[2]; **9:**11; **13:**8, 12; **17:**8; **19:**11; **21:**27.

WILL (10192)

See also the selected listing for "WILL" in the Main Concordance.

Ge 1:29; **2:**17, 18, 24[2]; **3:**3, 4, 5[2], 14[2], 15[3], 16[4], 17, 18[2], 19[2]; **4:**7, 12[2], 14[3], 15; **5:**29; **6:**3[2], 7, 17, 18[2], 20; **7:**4[2]; **8:**21[2], 22; **9:**2, 3, 5[3], 11[2], 13, 15[2], 16, 25; **11:**6, 7; **12:**1, 2[4], 3[3], 7, 12[3], 13[2]; **13:**15, 16; **14:**23[2], 24; **15:**2, 3, 4[2], 8, 13[2], 14[2], 15, 16; **16:**10[2], 11, 12[3]; **17:**2[2], 4, 5[2], 6[3], 7, 8[2], 11, 14, 15, 16[5], 17[2], 19[3], 20[5], 21[2]; **18:**10[2], 12, 13, 14[2], 18[2], 19[2], 21[2], 23, 24, 25, 26, 28[2], 29, 30, 31, 32; **19:**2, 15, 17, 19, 20, 21[2]; **20:**4, 7[3], 11; **21:**6, 10, 12, 13, 18, 23; **22:**2, 5[2], 8, 14[2], 17[2], 18; **23:**6, 9, 13[2]; **24:**3, 4, 7[2], 8, 14, 33, 39, 40, 41[2], 42, 49, 58[2]; **25:**23[3]; **26:**3[4], 4[3], 22, 24[2], 29; **27:**33, 39, 40[3], 41, 46; **28:**13, 14[3], 15[3], 20[3], 21, 22[2]; **29:**8, 27, 32, 34, 35; **30:**13, 15, 20, 26, 28, 31[2], 32, 33[2]; **31:**3, 8[2], 52[2]; **32:**9, 11, 12[2], 20[2], 26, 28; **33:**13; **34:**11, 15, 16, 17, 22, 23, 30; **35:**3, 10[2], 11[2], 12; **37:**8, 10, 26, 35; **38:**16, 17, 23; **40:**13[2], 19[2]; **41:**16, 30[3], 31[2], 32, 36, 40, 44; **42:**15[2], 16, 18, 33, 34[2], 37, 38[2]; **43:**3, 4[2], 5[3], 8, 9[2], 14; **44:**9[2], 10[2], 17, 22, 23, 26, 29, 31[2], 32; **45:**6, 11[2], 18, 20, 28; **46:**3, 4[3], 31[2], 34; **47:**16, 19, 25, 29, 30; **48:**4[3], 5[2], 6[2], 19[4], 20, 21; **49:**1, 4, 7, 8[3], 10, 11[2], 12, 13[2], 15, 16, 17, 19[2], 20[2]; **50:**5, 21, 24, 25; **Ex 1:**10[2]; **2:**9; **3:**3, 12[3], 18, 19, 20[3], 21[2], 22[2]; **4:**9, 12[2], 14, 15[2], 16[2], 21[2], 23; **5:**2, 10, 11, 18; **6:**1[4], 6[3], 7[3], 8[2], 12; **7:**1, 3, 4[3], 5, 9, 17[3], 18[3], 19[2]; **8:**2, 3[2], 4, 8, 10, 11[2], 16, 21[2], 22[3], 23[2], 26, 28, 29[2]; **9:**3, 4[2], 5, 9[2], 14, 17, 18, 19[2], 22, 28, 29[3]; **10:**3, 4, 5[2], 6, 7, 8, 9, 12, 14, 21, 26, 28, 29; **11:**1[3], 4, 5, 6[2], 7[2], 8[2], 9; **12:**4, 12[2], 13[3], 23[3], 25, 33; **13:**9, 16, 19; **14:**3, 4[4], 13[3], 14, 17[3], 18; **15:**1, 2[2], 9[6], 13[2], 14[2], 15[3], 16[2], 17, 18, 26; **16:**4[3], 6, 7, 8, 12[3], 25, 26, 28; **17:**6[2], 9, 14, 16; **18:**15, 18, 19, 22[2], 23[2]; **19:**5, 6, 8, 9[2], 11, 22, 24; **20:**7, 19[2], 20, 24, 25; **21:**6, 13, 19, 28, 34, 36; **22:**11, 13, 15, 23, 24[3], 27[2]; **23:**7, 21, 22[2], 23[2], 25[2], 26[2], 27[2], 28, 29, 30, 31[3], 33[2]; **24:**3, 7[2], 12; **25:**8, 9, 16, 21, 22; **26:**13[2], 25, 33; **27:**7; **28:**28, 29, 30, 32, 35[2], 38[4], 43; **29:**21, 26, 29, 37[2], 42, 43[2], 44[2], 45, 46; **30:**6, 8, 12, 16, 20, 21, 25, 29[2], 36; **31:**13, 17; **32:**1, 5, 10, 13[3], 23, 30, 33, 34[2]; **33:**1, 2, 3, 5, 12, 14[2], 16[2], 17, 19[6], 22, 23[2]; **34:**1, 10[3], 11, 12, 15[2], 16, 24[2]; **40:**9, 10, 15[2]; **Lev 1:**3, 4; **3:**4, 10, 15; **4:**9, 20[2], 26[2], 31[2], 35[2]; **5:**1, 3, 4, 10, 13[3], 16[2], 17, 18[2]; **6:**7[2], 18, 27; **7:**18[3]; **8:**33, 35; **9:**4; **10:**3[2], 6[2], 7, 9, 15; **11:**24[2], 25, 26, 27, 28, 31, 32[3], 33, 39, 40[2]; **12:**2, 5, 7, 8[2]; **13:**6, 14, 17, 34, 58; **14:**8, 9, 20, 31, 36, 46, 53[2]; **15:**3[2], 4[2], 5, 6, 7, 8, 9, 10[2], 11, 13, 15, 16, 17, 18, 19[2], 20[2], 21, 22, 23, 24[2], 25, 26[2], 27[2], 28, 30, 31; **16:**2, 13[2], 16, 22, 30[2]; **17:**5, 10[2], 15[2], 16; **18:**5, 28; **19:**5, 7, 8, 17, 22, 24, 25, 29, 31; **20:**3[2], 5[2], 6[2], 9, 11, 12, 13, 14, 16, 17, 20[2], 21, 24[2], 27; **21:**15; **22:**2, 4, 6, 7, 20, 23, 25, 27, 29; **23:**11, 18, 30, 43; **24:**12, 15; **25:**6, 18, 19[2], 20, 21[2], 22[2], 28[2], 41, 45, 46; **26:**4[2], 5[3], 6[5], 7[2], 8[3], 9[2], 10[2], 11[2], 12[2], 14, 16[5], 17[4], 18[2], 19, 20[3], 21, 22[3], 24[2], 25[3], 26[4], 28[2], 29, 30[2], 31[2], 32[2], 33[4], 34[2], 35, 36[4], 37[2], 38[2], 39[2], 40, 42[2], 43[3], 44, 45; **27:**8, 12[2], 14[2], 15, 18[2], 19, 21[2], 23, 24, 32; **Nu 1:**53; **2:**5, 7, 9, 10, 12, 14, 16, 17[2], 18, 20, 22, 24, 25, 27, 29, 31; **4:**15, 20; **5:**3, 9, 10, 24, 27[3], 28[2], 31[2]; **6:**27[2]; **8:**14, 19; **9:**13; **10:**6, 9, 10, 29[2], 30, 32; **11:**17[4], 18[3], 19, 21, 23[2]; **14:**3, 8[2], 9, 11[2], 12[2], 13, 14, 15, 23[2], 24[2], 27, 28, 29, 30, 31, 32, 33, 34, 35[3], 40, 41, 42, 43[3]; **15:**10, 16, 25, 26, 28, 39[2], 40[2]; **16:**5[3], 7, 12, 14[2], 22, 26, 28, 30; **17:**5[2], 10[2], 12, 13; **18:**3, 5, 13, 20[2], 22[2], 23, 24, 27, 28, 30, 32[3]; **19:**7, 8, 10[2], 11, 12[2], 14, 15, 16, 19, 21; **20:**8[2], 12, 17[2], 18, 19[2], 24[2], 26[2]; **21:**2[2], 7, 16, 22[2]; **22:**6, 8, 11, 17, 19[2], 34; **23:**3[2], 13, 23, 27; **24:**7[4], 14, 17[3], 18[3], 19, 20, 22, 24[3]; **25:**13; **26:**55; **27:**13, 17[2], 20, 21[3]; **30:**4, 5[2], 7, 8, 9, 11, 12[2]; **31:**2, 23, 24; **32:**11, 15[2], 17, 18, 19, 20[2], 21, 22, 23[2], 25, 26, 27, 31, 32[2]; **33:**54, 55[3], 56; **34:**2[2], 3[2], 4, 5, 6[2], 8, 9, 11, 12[2]; **35:**2, 3, 4, 5, 6, 12, 13, 15; **36:**3[2], 4[2], 8; **Dt 1:**13, 17, 22, 30, 36[2], 38[2], 39[3], 41, 42[2]; **2:**4, 5, 9, 19, 25[3], 27[2]; **3:**21, 22, 28[3]; **4:**6[2], 22[2], 26[3], 27[3], 28, 29, 30, 31; **5:**11, 25[2], 27, 33; **6:**15[2], 25; **7:**4[3], 10[2], 12, 13[2], 14[2], 15[3], 16, 19, 20, 22[3], 23, 24[4], 25, 26; **8:**9[2], 14[2], 19, 20; **9:**3[3], 5, 14, 28; **10:**2, 10; **11:**14, 15[2], 16, 17[5], 23[2], 24[2], 25[2]; **12:**5, 10[3], 11, 14, 18, 25, 26, 28, 29, 30; **13:**11[2], 17[2]; **14:**23, 24, 25; **15:**4, 6[5], 9[2], 10, 11, 17, 18, 20; **16:**2, 6, 7, 11, 15[3], 16; **17:**8, 9, 10, 13[2], 17, 20; **18:**6, 12, 14, 15, 16, 18[3], 19; **19:**10[2], 20[2]; **20:**1, 8, 18[2]; **21:**8, 9, 18, 20, 21; **22:**9, 16; **23:**14, 21[2], 22; **24:**13[2], 15; **25:**1, 3, 6, 7, 9; **26:**2, 17[3], 19[2]; **28:**1, 2, 3, 4, 5, 6, 7[3], 8[2], 9, 10[2], 11, 12[3], 13[2], 15, 16, 17, 18, 19, 20, 21, 22[2], 23, 24[2], 25[3], 26[2], 27, 28, 29[3], 30[6], 31[6], 32[2], 33[2], 34, 35, 36[2], 37[2], 38[3], 39[3], 40[3], 41[3], 42, 43[2], 44[4], 45[2], 46, 48[2], 49[2], 51[2], 52[2], 53[2], 54, 55[3], 56, 57, 59, 60[2], 61, 62, 63[2], 64[2], 65[2], 66, 67[3], 68[3]; **29:**19[2], 20[4], 21, 22, 23[2], 24, 25; **30:**3, 4, 5[3], 6, 7, 8, 9[2], 12, 13, 16[2], 18[2], 20; **31:**3[4], 4, 5, 6, 8[2], 11, 14, 16[2], 17[5], 18, 20, 21[2], 23[2], 26, 27, 29[2]; **32:**1, 3, 7[2], 20[2], 21[2], 22, 23, 24[2], 25[3], 29, 35[2], 36, 37, 39, 41, 42, 43[2], 47, 50, 52[2]; **33:**17, 19[2], 21, 23, 25[2], 27, 28, 29[2]; **34:**4[2]; **Jos 1:**3, 4, 5[3], 6, 8, 9, 11, 16[2], 17, 18; **2:**12, 13[2], 14, 16, 17, 19[3], 20; **3:**4, 5, 7, 10[2], 11, 13; **6:**5[2], 18[2], 26[2]; **7:**3, 9[3], 12, 25; **8:**5[2], 6[2], 7, 18; **9:**20[3], 23; **10:**8, 25; **11:**6; **13:**6; **14:**9, 12; **15:**16; **17:**17, 18; **18:**3, 4[2], 6, 8; **22:**18, 27[2], 28; **23:**5[3], 13[2], 15, 16[2]; **24:**15[2], 18, 19, 20, 21, 24, 27[2]; **Jdg 1:**1, 3, 12, 24; **2:**1, 3[3], 21, 22[2]; **4:**7, 8, 9[3], 22; **5:**3[3]; **6:**16[2], 18, 36, 37[3]; **7:**4, 7, 11; **8:**7, 9, 23[3]; **10:**13, 18[2]; **11:**8, 9, 10, 24[2], 31[2], 37; **13:**5[2], 7[2], 16; **14:**12, 15; **15:**3, 13[2]; **16:**5; **17:**3, 13; **18:**5, 10, 25[2]; **19:**12, 24; **20:**8[2], 28; **21:**1, 17, 22; **Ru 1:**9, 10, 16[3], 17[2]; **2:**22; **3:**1, 2, 4, 5, 11, 13, 18; **4:**4[4], 10, 15; **1Sa 1:**11[3], 14, 22[2], 28; **2:**9[2], 10[4], 25[2], 30[2], 31[2], 32[3], 33[2], 34[2], 35[4], 36; **3:**11, 12, 14; **4:**8, 9; **5:**11; **6:**3[2], 5, 9, 20; **7:**3, 5; **8:**9[2], 11[4], 12, 13, 14, 15, 16, 17[2], 18[2], 20; **9:**5, 6, 8[2], 13[3], 16[2], 17, 19[2], 26; **10:**2[2], 3[3], 4[2], 5[3], 6[3], 8; **11:**1, 2, 3, 7, 9, 10, 12; **12:**3, 10, 15, 17[2], 19, 22, 23, 25; **13:**12, 14, 19; **14:**6, 8, 9, 10[2], 37, 40, 45; **15:**2, 26, 33; **16:**1, 2, 3, 11, 16[2]; **17:**9[2], 25[3], 26, 27, 32, 36, 37, 46[3], 47[2]; **18:**17[2], 21; **19:**3[2], 6; **20:**3, 10, 12[2], 18[2], 20, 21, 31; **22:**3, 7[2], 16, 23; **23:**11[3], 12[2], 17[3], 20, 23[2]; **24:**4, 10, 12, 13, 20[2], 21; **25:**8, 28, 29[2], 31; **26:**6, 10[4], 21, 25; **27:**1[3], 12; **28:**1, 2[2], 10, 19[3], 23; **29:**4; **30:**8[2], 15[2], 22, 24[2]; **31:**4; **2Sa 2:**6, 26; **3:**12, 13, 18; **5:**2[2], 6, 8[2], 19[2], 24; **6:**21, 22[3]; **7:**9, 10[3], 11[2], 12[3], 13[2], 14[3], 15, 16[2], 21, 26[3], 27, 29; **9:**7[3], 10, 11; **10:**2, 11, 12; **11:**11, 12, 15; **12:**10, 11[2], 12, 14, 23[2], 28[2]; **13:**13, 24; **14:**7, 8, 10, 11[2], 15[2], 16, 21; **15:**8, 14[2], 21, 25, 28, 33, 34[2]; **16:**3, 12, 18[2], 19, 21[2]; **17:**2, 3[2], 8, 9, 10, 12[3], 13[2], 16; **18:**2, 4, 22; **19:**7[2], 26[2], 33, 34, 36, 38[2]; **20:**6[2], 21; **21:**3, 6, 17[2]; **22:**50[2]; **23:**5; **24:**24; **1Ki 1:**5, 13, 14, 17, 20, 21, 24, 30[2], 51, 52[2]; **2:**4, 8, 9, 17, 18, 20, 26, 30, 32, 37[2], 38, 42[2], 44, 45[2]; **3:**12[4], 13[2], 14; **5:**5[2], 6[2], 8, 9[3]; **6:**12, 13[2]; **8:**19, 27, 29, 40, 42; **9:**3, 5, 7[3], 8[2], 9; **11:**2, 11, 12[2], 13[2], 32, 33, 34, 35, 36, 37[3], 38[3], 39; **12:**4, 7[2], 11[2], 14[2], 26, 27[2]; **13:**2[3], 3[2], 7, 22, 32; **14:**3[2], 5, 10[2], 11[2], 12, 13[2], 14[2], 15[3], 16; **15:**19; **16:**3, 4[2]; **17:**1, 4, 14[2]; **18:**1, 5, 12, 14, 15, 21, 23, 24, 37; **19:**17[2], 20; **20:**6, 9, 13[2], 14[4], 22, 23, 25, 28[2], 31, 34[2], 36, 39; **21:**2[2], 4, 6[2], 19, 21, 22, 23, 24[2], 29[2]; **22:**4, 6, 11, 12, 15, 20, 21, 22[2], 25, 30; **2Ki 1:**2, 4[2], 6[2], 16[2]; **2:**2, 4, 6, 10, 21; **3:**7[2], 17[3], 18, 19[2]; **4:**16, 30, 43; **5:**5, 8, 10[2], 16, 17[2], 20, 27; **6:**3, 8, 11, 19; **7:**1, 2[2], 4[2], 9, 12[3], 13[2], 18, 19[2]; **8:**1, 8, 9, 10[2], 12[2], 13; **9:**7, 8[2], 9, 10[2], 26, 36, 37[2]; **10:**5[2], 6, 10, 18, 19, 24, 30; **13:**17, 19; **15:**12; **16:**15; **17:**39; **18:**14, 23, 27, 30[2], 31, 32; **19:**4[2], 7[2], 10, 11, 28[2], 29[2], 30, 31[2], 32[2], 33[2], 34; **20:**1, 5[2], 6[3], 8[3], 9, 17[3], 18[3], 19; **21:**4, 7, 8[3], 12, 13[2], 14[2]; **22:**17[2], 20[3]; **23:**27[2]; **25:**24; **1Ch 4:**10; **10:**4; **11:**2[2], 5, 6; **12:**18, 19; **13:**2; **14:**10[2], 15; **16:**18[2], 33[2]; **17:**8, 9[3], 10[2], 11[2], 12[2], 13[3], 14[2], 19, 24[4], 25, 27; **19:**2, 12, 13; **21:**23[2], 24; **22:**5, 9[5], 10[4], 13, 19; **28:**6[2], 7, 9[2], 20, 21[2]; **2Ch 1:**12[3]; **2:**5, 8, 10, 12, 14, 16[2]; **6:**9, 18, 31; **7:**14[4], 15, 16, 18, 20[3], 21, 22; **10:**4, 7[2], 11[2], 14[2]; **12:**7[3], 8; **13:**12[2]; **15:**2[2], 7; **16:**3, 9; **18:**3[2], 5, 10, 11, 14, 19, 20, 21[2], 24, 29; **19:**10[2], 11[3]; **20:**9[3], 12, 16[2], 17[3], 20[2], 37; **21:**15; **24:**20; **25:**8; **26:**18; **28:**13, 23[2]; **29:**10; **30:**8, 9[3]; **32:**11, 15, 17; **33:**4, 7, 8[2]; **34:**25[2], 28[3]; **35:**21; **Ezr 4:**3, 13[2], 15, 16, 21; **6:**8; **7:**18; **10:**4, 11; **Ne 1:**8, 9; **2:**6[2], 7, 8[2], 17, 20[2]; **4:**2[3], 11[2], 12, 20; **5:**12[3]; **6:**7, 9[2], 11; **9:**29; **10:**31[3], 36, 37[2], 39; **13:**21; **Est 1:**17[2], 18[2], 20; **3:**9; **4:**13, 14[2], 16[2]; **5:**3, 6[2], 8[2]; **6:**13; **7:**2[2], 8; **9:**12[2]; **Job 1:**11, 21; **2:**4, 5; **4:**2; **5:**1[3], 19[2], 20, 21, 22, 23[2], 24[2], 25[2], 26; **6:**24; **7:**7, 8[3], 10[2], 11[3], 13[2], 19, 21[3]; **8:**2, 5, 6, 7[2], 10[2], 21, 22[2]; **9:**19, 27[2], 28; **10:**1, 2, 8, 9; **11:**3[2], 15[2], 16, 17[2], 18[2], 19[2], 20[3]; **12:**2, 7[2], 8; **13:**7[2], 8[2], 15[2], 16, 18, 19, 20, 22, 25[2]; **14:**3, 7[2], 9, 12, 14[2], 15[3], 16, 17[2]; **15:**17, 28, 29[3], 30[3], 31, 32[2], 33, 34[2]; **16:**3, 22; **17:**3, 4, 5, 9[2], 10, 16[2]; **18:**2; **19:**2, 22, 25, 26, 27, 28, 29[2]; **20:**7[2], 9[2], 11, 14[2], 15[2], 16[2], 17, 18, 20, 21, 22[2], 23, 25, 26, 27[2], 28; **21:**19; **22:**15, 21, 23, 25, 26[2], 27[3], 28[2], 29, 30[2]; **23:**10; **24:**15; **27:**4[2], 5[2], 6[2], 10[2], 11[2], 14, 15[2], 17[2], 19; **29:**18, 19[2], 20; **30:**23; **31:**6, 14[2]; **32:**10, 14, 17[2], 21[2]; **33:**28, 31, 33; **34:**17, 31, 32; **35:**2, 14; **36:**2, 3, 11, 12; **38:**3; **39:**9[2], 10, 11[2]; **40:**2, 5, 7, 14; **41:**3[2], 4, 6[2], 8, 12; **42:**4[2], 8[2]; **Ps 1:**5, 6; **2:**7, 8, 9[2]; **3:**2, 6; **4:**2[2], 3, 8; **5:**7[2]; **6:**10[2]; **7:**2, 12[2], 17[2]; **9:**1[2], 2[2], 8[2], 10, 18; **10:**6, 16; **11:**6[2], 7; **12:**4, 5[2], 7; **13:**1[2], 2, 3, 4[2], 6; **14:**4; **15:**5; **16:**4[2], 7, 8, 9, 10[2], 11; **17:**3[2], 6, 15[2]; **18:**49[2]; **19:**13; **20:**5[2]; **21:**7, 8[2], 9[3], 10, 12, 13; **22:**22[2], 25, 26[2], 27[2], 29[2], 30[2], 31; **23:**4, 6[2]; **24:**5; **25:**3[2], 12, 13[2], 15; **26:**12; **27:**2, 3[2], 5[2], 6[3], 8, 10, 13; **28:**1, 5, 7; **30:**1, 6, 9[2], 12; **31:**7; **32:**5, 6, 7, 8[2], 9; **34:**1[2], 2, 11, 20, 21[2], 22; **35:**9, 10, 17, 18[2], 28; **37:**2[2], 4, 5, 6, 9[2], 10[2], 11, 15[2], 17, 18, 19[2], 20[3], 22[2], 24, 26, 27, 28[3], 29, 33, 34[2], 38[2]; **38:**15; **39:**1[2], 6; **40:**3, 8; **41:**2[2], 3, 5, 8; **42:**5, 6, 11; **43:**4[2], 5; **44:**8; **45:**6[2], 12[2], 16[2], 17[2]; **46:**2, 5[2], 10[2]; **48:**14; **49:**3[2], 4[2], 11, 14[3], 15[2], 17[2], 19[2]; **50:**3, 7[2], 15[2], 21, 22; **51:**7[2], 13[2], 14, 15, 17, 19[2]; **52:**5[3], 6[2], 9[3]; **53:**4; **54:**6[2]; **55:**19, 22[2], 23[2]; **56:**3, 4, 9[2], 11, 12; **57:**1, 7, 8, 9[2]; **58:**5, 9, 10, 11; **59:**10[2], 11, 13, 16[2]; **60:**6, 9[2], 12[2]; **61:**8; **62:**2, 3, 6, 12; **63:**3, 4[2], 5[2], 9[2], 10, 11[3]; **64:**5, 7[2], 8[2], 9[2]; **65:**1, 2; **66:**13, 15[2]; **67:**6[2], 7[2]; **68:**16, 21, 22[2], 29, 31[2]; **69:**30, 31, 32, 35[2], 36[2]; **71:**6, 11, 14[2], 15, 16[2], 20[2], 21, 22[2], 23, 24; **72:**2, 3, 4[2], 5, 6, 7[2], 8, 9[2], 10[2], 11[2], 12, 13, 14, 17[2]; **73:**15, 20, 24, 27, 28; **74:**8, 9, 10[2]; **75:**9[2], 10[2]; **77:**7[2], 10, 11[2], 12; **78:**2[2], 4[2]; **79:**5[2], 13[2]; **80:**4, 18[2]; **81:**8, 10; **82:**2, 7[2]; **83:**16; **85:**5[2], 6, 8[2], 12[2]; **86:**7[2], 9[2], 11, 12[2]; **87:**4[2], 5[2], 6, 7; **89:**1[2], 2, 4, 21[2], 22[2], 23, 24[2], 25, 26, 27, 28[2], 29, 32, 33[2], 34, 35, 36, 37, 46[2]; **90:**13; **91:**1, 2, 3, 4[3], 5, 7, 8, 10[2], 11, 12[2], 13[2], 14[2], 15[4], 16; **92:**7, 9[2], 12[2], 13, 14[2]; **94:**3[2], 8, 14[2], 15[2], 16[2], 23[2]; **96:**10, 12, 13[2]; **98:**9; **101:**1[2], 2[3], 3[2], 4, 5[2], 6[2], 7[2], 8[2]; **102:**13, 15[2], 16, 17[2], 21, 26[4], 27, 28[2]; **103:**9[2], 21; **104:**9, 33[2]; **105:**11[2]; **108:**1, 2, 3[2], 7, 10[2], 13[2]; **109:**28[3], 29, 30[2]; **110:**2[2], 3[2], 4, 5, 6, 7[2]; **111:**1; **112:**2[2], 5, 6[2], 7, 8[2], 9, 10[3]; **115:**8[2], 12[3], 13; **116:**2, 13, 14, 17, 18; **118:**6, 7, 17[2], 19, 21, 28[2]; **119:**7, 8, 16, 17[2], 23, 27, 33, 34, 42, 44, 45, 46[2], 55, 60, 61, 78, 82, 84, 88, 93, 95, 106, 109, 116, 117[2], 145, 146; **120:**3, 4; **121:**3[2], 4, 6, 7[2], 8; **122:**8, 9; **125:**3, 5; **126:**5, 6; **127:**5; **128:**2[2], 3[2]; **130:**8; **132:**3, 4, 11[2], 12, 14, 15[2], 16[2], 17, 18[2]; **135:**14, 18[2]; **138:**1[2], 2[2], 8; **139:**10[2], 11, 12[2]; **140:**8, 13[2]; **141:**5, 6[2], 7; **142:**7; **143:**7, 10; **144:**9[2], 12[2], 13[2], 14[2]; **145:**1[2], 2, 4[2], 5[2], 6[2], 7, 10[2], 11, 20, 21; **146:**2[2]; **148:**6; **Pr 1:**9, 13, 14, 22[2], 26[2], 28[4], 31, 32[2], 33; **2:**5, 9, 10[2], 11[2], 12, 16, 20, 21[2], 22[2]; **3:**2, 4, 6, 8, 10[2], 18, 22, 23[2], 24[2], 26[2]; **4:**4, 6[2], 8[2], 9, 10, 12[2]; **5:**11, 12, 23; **6:**9[2], 11, 15[2], 22[3], 29, 33, 34, 35[2]; **7:**2, 5, 20, 23; **9:**6, 8[2], 9[2], 11[2], 12[2]; **10:**7[2], 9, 24[2], 30[2], 31; **11:**15, 21[2], 25[2], 28[2], 29[2]; **12:**11, 24; **13:**3, 13; **14:**7, 11[2], 14, 19, 26; **15:**10, 12, 27, 31; **16:**3, 5, 14; **17:**2[2], 5, 11, 13; **18:**21; **19:**5[2], 9[2], 16, 17, 19, 20, 24, 25[2], 27; **20:**13[2], 20, 21, 22; **21:**7, 13, 17[2], 25, 28[2]; **22:**6, 8, 9, 11, 13, 14, 15, 23[2], 27, 29[2]; **23:**5, 8[2], 9, 11, 13, 15, 16, 18, 33, 34, 35[2]; **24:**8, 12, 14, 18, 20, 22, 24, 25[2], 34; **25:**5, 8, 10, 16, 17, 22[2]; **26:**4, 5, 26, 27[2]; **27:**14, 18[2], 22, 26, 27; **28:**8, 10[2], 16, 17, 18, 19[2], 20[2], 21, 23, 25, 27; **29:**1, 14, 16, 17[2], 19, 21, 25; **30:**6, 10[2], 17[2]; **Ecc 1:**9[2], 11; **2:**1, 15, 16[2], 19[2]; **3:**14[2], 15[2], 17[2], 22; **4:**11; **6:**12; **7:**18, 26[2]; **8:**3, 5[2], 8, 12, 13[2], 15; **9:**5, 6, 12; **10:**10, 14; **11:**1, 3, 4[2], 6[2], 8, 9; **12:**1, 14; **SS 1:**4, 11; **3:**2[2]; **4:**6; **5:**8; **7:**8[2], 12; **8:**9[2]; **Isa 1:**15[2], 19, 20, 24, 25[2], 26[2], 27, 28[2], 29[2], 30, 31[2]; **2:**2[3], 3[3], 4[5], 9, 11[2], 12, 17[2], 18, 19, 20, 21; **3:**4[2], 5[2], 6, 7, 10[2], 11, 17[2], 18, 24, 25, 26[2]; **4:**1[2], 2[2], 3, 4[2], 5[2], 6; **5:**1, 5[5], 6[3], 9, 10, 13[3], 14, 15, 16[2], 17[2], 24, 30[3]; **6:**8, 13[2]; **7:**7[2], 8, 9, 12[2], 13, 14[4], 15, 16, 17[2], 18, 19, 20, 21, 22[2], 23, 24[2], 25[2]; **8:**2, 4, 7, 8, 10[2], 14[3], 15[3], 17[2], 21[3], 22[2]; **9:**1[2], 5[2], 6[2], 7[3], 8, 9, 10[2], 14, 17[2], 19[3], 20[3], 21[2]; **10:**3[3], 4, 12[2], 16[2], 17[2], 18, 19, 20[2], 21[2], 22, 23, 25[2], 26[2], 27[2], 29, 32[2], 33[3], 34[2]; **11:**1[2], 2, 3[2], 4[4], 5, 6[3], 7[3], 8, 9[2], 10[3], 11, 12[2], 13[3], 14[4], 15[3], 16; **12:**1[2], 2, 3, 4; **13:**6, 7[2], 8[4], 10[3], 11[3], 12, 13[2], 14[2], 15[2], 16[2], 17, 18[3], 19, 20[3], 21[4], 22[2]; **14:**1[4], 2[3], 4, 10[2], 13[3], 14[2], 20[2], 22[2], 23[2], 24[2], 25[3], 29[2], 30[4], 32; **15:**9; **16:**4[3], 5[2], 14[2]; **17:**1[2], 2[2], 3[2], 4[2], 5, 6, 7, 8[2], 9[2], 11; **18:**3[2], 4[2], 5, 6[2], 7[2]; **19:**2[2], 3[3], 4[2], 5[2], 6[3], 7[2], 8[2], 9[2], 10[2], 16[2], 17[2], 18[2], 19, 20[3], 21[4], 22[4], 23[3], 24, 25; **20:**4, 5, 6; **21:**2, 16, 17; **22:**14, 18[3], 19[2], 20, 21[2], 22, 23[2], 24, 25[4]; **23:**5, 12, 15[2], 16, 17[3], 18[3]; **24:**1, 2, 3, 13, 18[2], 21, 22[2], 23[2]; **25:**1, 2, 3[2], 6, 7, 8[3], 9, 10[2], 11[2], 12[2]; **26:**1, 3, 19[3], 21[2]; **27:**1[2], 6[2], 9[3], 12[2], 13[2]; **28:**2, 3, 4, 5, 6, 11, 13[2], 16, 17[3], 18[3], 19[3], 21[2], 22; **29:**2[3], 3[2], 4[4], 5, 6, 7, 8, 11, 12, 14[3], 15, 17, 18[2], 19[2], 20[3], 22[2], 23[3], 24[2]; **30:**3[2], 5, 13, 14[2], 16[4], 17[2], 19[3], 20[2], 21, 22[2], 23[3], 24, 25, 26[2], 29[2], 30[2], 31[2], 32; **31:**2, 3[3], 4, 5[4], 7, 8[4], 9[2]; **32:**1[2], 2, 3[2], 4[2], 5, 10[3], 14[2], 16, 17[2], 18, 20; **33:**1[2], 5, 6, 10[3], 12[2], 16[4], 17, 18, 19, 20[3], 21[4], 22, 23[2], 24[2]; **34:**2[2], 3[3], 4[2], 7[3], 9[2], 10[4], 11[3], 12[2], 13[2], 14[3], 15[3], 16[3], 17; **35:**1[2], 2[4], 4[3], 5, 6[2], 7[2], 8[5], 9[4], 10[5]; **36:**8, 12, 15[2], 16, 18; **37:**4[2], 7[2], 10, 11, 29[2], 30[2], 31, 32[2], 33[2], 34[2], 35; **38:**1, 5, 6[2], 7, 8, 11[2], 15, 20[2], 21, 22[2]; **39:**6[3], 7[3], 8; **40:**5[2], 18[2], 20[2], 25, 28, 31[4]; **41:**7, 10[2], 11[2], 12[2], 13, 14, 15[2], 16[4], 17[2], 18[2], 19[2], 23; **42:**1[2], 2, 3[3], 4[2], 6[3], 8, 13[4], 15[2], 16[5], 17, 23; **43:**2[4], 4, 5, 6, 10, 14, 28[2]; **44:**2, 3[2], 4, 5[4], 7, 11[2], 21, 26, 27, 28[2]; **45:**1, 2[3], 3, 5, 13[3], 14[4], 16[2], 17[2], 23[3], 24[2], 25[2]; **46:**4[4], 5[2], 10[2], 11[2], 13[2]; **47:**1, 3[3], 5, 7, 8, 9[2], 11[4], 12[2], 14; **48:**6[2], 11, 14[2], 15[2]; **49:**3, 6, 7[2], 8[4], 9, 10[3], 11[2], 12, 13, 15, 18[2], 19[2], 20, 21, 22[3], 23[5], 25[3], 26[3]; **50:**7[2], 8, 9[3], 11; **51:**3[4], 4[2], 5[2], 6[4], 8[3], 11[5], 14[3], 22, 23; **52:**1, 3, 6[2], 8, 10[2], 12[3], 13[2], 15[4]; **53:**10[4], 11[3], 12[2]; **54:**3[2], 4[3], 6, 7, 8, 10, 11, 12, 13[2], 14[5], 15[2], 17[2]; **55:**2, 3, 5[2], 7[2], 11[2], 12[3], 13[4]; **56:**1, 3, 5[3], 7[3], 8, 12; **57:**12[2], 13[3], 14, 16[2], 18[2], 19; **58:**8[4], 9[4], 10[2], 11[4], 12[3], 14[2]; **59:**2, 5, 8, 18[2], 19[3], 20, 21; **60:**3, 5[4], 6[2], 7[4], 10[3], 11[2], 12[3], 13[2], 14[3], 15, 16[2], 17[3], 18[2], 19[4], 20[4], 21[2], 22[2]; **61:**3, 4[2], 5[2], 6[4], 7[4], 8, 9[2], 11; **62:**1[2], 2[3], 3, 4[4], 5[2], 6, 8[2], 9[2], 12[2]; **63:**7, 8; **64:**12[2]; **65:**6[3], 7, 8[2], 9[4], 10, 12[2], 13[6], 14[2], 15[3], 16[3], 17[3], 18[2], 19[2], 20[3], 21[2], 22[3], 23[2], 24[2], 25[4]; **66:**1[2], 4[2], 5, 11[2], 12[2], 13[2], 14[4], 15, 16[2], 17, 18, 19[3], 20[2], 21, 22[2], 23, 24[4]; **Jer 1:**8, 14, 15[2], 16, 17, 19[3]; **2:**9, 19[2], 20, 24, 31, 35, 36, 37[2]; **3:**5[2], 12[2], 14, 15[2], 16[4], 17[3], 18[2], 22[2]; **4:**1, 2[2], 4, 7, 9[3], 10, 11, 14, 27[2], 28[3]; **5:**1, 5, 6[3], 12[3], 14, 17[3], 18, 19[2], 31; **6:**2, 3[2], 8, 10, 11, 12, 15[2], 16[2], 17, 18, 21[3], 26; **7:**3, 7, 9, 14, 15, 16, 20[2], 23[2], 27[2], 32[2], 33[2], 34[2]; **8:**1, 2[3], 3, 9[2], 10, 12[2], 13[5], 17[2]; **9:**7, 10, 11[2], 15, 16[2], 22, 25; **10:**4, 11, 15, 18[2], 22; **11:**4[2], 5, 11[2], 12[2], 14, 16[2], 21, 22[2], 23[2]; **12:**4[2], 5, 7[2], 10[2], 11[2], 12[3], 13[2], 14[2], 15[2], 16, 17; **13:**9, 10, 14[2], 16, 17[3], 18, 19[3], 21[2], 24, 26, 27; **14:**10, 12[3], 13[2], 15[2], 16[3]; **15:**3, 4, 5[3], 6, 7[2], 8[3], 9[4], 11[2], 13, 14[3], 18, 19[2], 20[3], 21; **16:**4[5], 6[3], 7[2], 9, 13[3], 14, 15[2], 16[4], 18, 19, 21[3]; **17:**3, 4[3], 6[3], 8, 11[2], 13[2], 14[2], 25[3], 26, 27[2]; **18:**2, 8, 10, 12[3], 16[3], 17[2], 18[2]; **19:**3, 6, 7[3], 8[3], 9[2], 11[2], 12[2], 13; **20:**4[4], 5[2], 6[2], 9, 10[2], 11[3]; **21:**2[2], 4, 5, 6[2], 7[3], 9[3], 10[2], 12, 14[3]; **22:**4, 5, 6, 7[2], 8[2], 9, 10, 11, 12[2], 14, 18[2], 19, 21, 22[3], 23, 25, 26[2], 27, 28, 30[3]; **23:**2, 3[3], 4[4], 5[2], 6[3], 7, 8[2], 12[4], 15, 17[2], 19, 20[2], 26, 27, 33, 34, 39, 40[2]; **24:**6[4], 7[4], 8, 9, 10; **25:**6, 9[3], 10, 11[2], 12[2], 13, 14[2], 16[2], 26, 27, 29[2], 30[3], 31[3], 33[3], 34, 35, 37, 38[2]; **26:**3[3], 6, 9[2], 13, 15, 18[2]; **27:**6[2], 7[2], 8[2], 9, 10[3], 11[2], 12, 13[2], 14, 15[2], 16, 17, 22[3]; **28:**2, 3, 4[2], 9, 11, 13, 14[3]; **29:**7, 10, 12[2], 13, 14[4], 17[2], 18[2], 21[2], 22, 28, 32[4]; **30:**3, 7[4], 8[3], 9[2], 10[3], 11[4], 16[4], 17, 18[3], 19[5], 20[3], 21[5], 22[2], 23, 24[2]; **31:**1[2], 2[2], 4[3], 5[2], 6, 8[3], 9[4], 10[2], 11, 12[4], 13[3], 14[2], 16[2], 17, 18, 22[3], 23, 24, 25, 27, 28, 29, 30[2], 31, 32, 33[4], 34[4], 36, 37, 38, 39, 40[2]; **32:**3, 4[3], 5[3], 14, 15, 24, 25, 28, 29[2], 36, 37[2], 38[2], 39[2], 40[4], 41[2], 42, 43, 44[3]; **33:**3, 5[3], 6[3], 7[2], 8[2], 9[3], 10, 11, 12, 13, 14, 15[3], 16[3], 17, 18, 21, 22, 26[3]; **34:**2, 3[3], 4, 5[2], 17, 18, 20[2], 21, 22[3]; **35:**7, 13, 15, 19; **36:**3[2], 7[2], 30[2], 31[2]; **37:**7, 8[2], 9[2], 17, 19, 20; **38:**2[4], 3[2], 9, 15, 16, 17[3], 18[4], 19, 20[3], 22[2], 23[4], 25; **39:**16, 17[2], 18[3]; **40:**4, 9, 10, 15; **42:**3, 4[3], 6[3], 10[2], 11, 12[2], 13, 14[2], 16[3], 17[3], 18[3], 20, 22; **43:**10[3], 11, 12[3], 13[2]; **44:**8, 12[5], 13, 14[2], 16, 17[3], 25, 26, 27, 28[3], 29[4]; **45:**4, 5[2]; **46:**8[2], 10[2], 12[4], 15[2], 16[3], 17, 18, 19, 21[2], 22[2], 23, 24, 26[2], 27[3], 28[3]; **47:**2[4], 3[2], 5[3]; **48:**1[3], 2[4], 4[2], 7[2], 8[3], 9[2], 12[3], 13, 15[2], 16, 18, 35, 41[2], 42, 44[3], 47; **49:**2[4], 3, 4, 5[3], 6, 8, 10[4], 11, 12, 13[2], 15, 16, 17[3], 18[2], 19[2], 20[2], 21[2], 22[2], 26[2], 27[2], 29[3], 32[4], 33[3], 35, 36[3], 37[3], 38, 39; **50:**2[3], 3[3], 4, 5[3], 9[4], 10[2], 12[3], 13[3], 18, 19[3], 20[4], 30[2], 32[4], 34, 36[2], 37[2], 38[2], 39[3], 40[2], 44[2], 45[2], 46[2]; **51:**1, 2[2], 4, 6, 8, 11, 12, 14[2], 18, 24, 25, 26[2], 29, 33, 36[2], 37, 39, 40, 41[2], 42[2], 43, 44[3], 47[4], 48[2], 52[2], 53, 55[4], 56[4], 57[2], 58, 62[3], 64[3]; **La 3:**24, 32, 49; **4:**21[2], 22[3]; **Eze 2:**1, 5; **3:**8, 9, 18[3], 19[2], 20[4], 21[2], 22, 25[2], 26[2], 27[3]; **4:**3[2], 5, 8, 13[2], 15, 16[2], 17[3]; **5:**2, 4, 8, 9[2], 10[4], 11[2], 12[3], 13[4], 14, 15, 16[4], 17[4]; **6:**3, 4[3], 5[2], 6[2], 7[2], 8[2], 9[2], 10, 11, 12[4], 13, 14[2]; **7:**3[2], 4[3], 8, 9[3], 11, 13[3], 14, 15[2], 16, 17[2], 18[3], 19[4], 20, 21[2], 22[3], 24[3], 25[2], 26[4], 27[6]; **8:**6[2], 13, 15, 18[3]; **9:**10[2]; **11:**3, 7, 8, 9, 10[3], 11[3], 12, 13, 17[2], 18, 19[2], 20[3], 21; **12:**3, 11[2], 12[3], 13[5], 14[2], 15, 16[2], 19[2], 20[3], 23[2], 24, 25[3], 28[2]; **13:**5, 9[4], 11[3], 12, 13[2], 14[5], 15[2], 18, 20[2], 21[3], 23[3]; **14:**4, 5, 7, 8[3], 9, 10[2], 11[4], 21, 22[4], 23[2]; **15:**6, 7[3], 8; **16:**37[3], 38[2], 39[3], 40[2], 41[3], 42[3], 43, 44, 53, 55[2], 58, 59, 60[2], 61[2], 62[2], 63; **17:**9[4], 10[2], 15[3], 17, 19, 20[3], 21[3], 22[2], 23[4], 24[2]; **18:**3, 4, 9, 13[4], 17[2], 18, 19, 20[5], 21[2], 22[2], 24[3], 26[2], 27, 28[2], 30[2], 31; **20:**3, 4[2], 11, 13, 20, 21, 30, 31, 32, 33, 34, 35[2], 36, 37[2], 38[4], 39, 40[3], 41[2], 42, 43[2], 44, 47[3], 48[2]; **21:**3, 4, 5[2], 7[3], 13, 17[2], 21[4], 22, 23[2], 24, 26[3], 27[3], 29, 30, 31[2], 32[3]; **22:**2[2], 4, 5, 13, 14[2], 15[2], 16, 19, 20, 21[3], 22[2], 31; **23:**22[2], 24[4], 25[6], 26, 27[2], 29[3], 31, 32[2], 33, 34[2], 36, 45, 47[2], 48, 49[2]; **24:**6, 9, 13, 14[4], 21, 22[2], 23[3], 24[3], 26, 27[5]; **25:**4[2], 5[2], 7[4], 9, 10[2], 11[2], 13[3], 14[3], 16, 17[2]; **26:**2, 3, 4[2], 5[2], 6[2], 8[2], 9, 10[3], 11[3], 12[2], 13[2], 14[3], 15, 16[2], 17, 20[3], 21[4]; **27:**26, 27, 28, 29[2], 30[2], 31[3], 32, 36; **28:**7, 8[2], 9[2], 10, 19, 22[2],

WITH (5912)

YOU (13727)

YOUR (6631)

134, 135^{3}, 136, 137, 139, 140^{2}, 141, 142^{2}, 143, 144, 145, 146, 147, 148, 149^{2}, 150, 151, 152, 153, 154, 155, 156^{2}, 157, 158, 159^{2}, 160^{2}, 161, 162, 163, 164, 165, 166^{2}, 167, 168^{2}, 169, 170, 171, 172^{2}, 173^{2}, 174^{2}, 175, 176^{2}; **121**:3, 5^{2}, 7, 8; **122**:2, 7^{2}, 9; **128**:2, 3^{4}, 5, 6; **130**:2, 7; **131**:3; **132**:8^{2}, 9^{2}, 10^{2}, 11^{2}, 12^{2}; **134**:2; **135**:9, 13^{2}; **137**:9; **138**:1, 2^{6}, 4, 7^{2}, 8^{2}; **139**:5, 7^{2}, 10^{2}, 14, 16^{2}, 17, 20^{2}; **140**:13; **142**:7^{2}; **143**:1, 2, 5^{2}, 7, 8, 10^{2}, 11^{2}, 12^{2}; **144**:5, 6, 7; **145**:1, 2, 4^{2}, 5^{2}, 6^{2}, 7^{2}, 10, 11^{2}, 12^{2}, 13^{2}, 16; **146**:3, 10; **147**:12, 13^{2}, 14; **Pr 1**:8^{2}, 9^{2}, 14, 22, 26; **2**:2^{2}, 10^{2}; **3**:1, 2, 3^{2}, 5^{2}, 6^{2}, 7, 8^{2}, 9^{2}, 10^{2}, 21, 22, 23^{2}, 24, 26^{2}, 27, 28, 29; **4**:4, 9, 10, 12, 13, 15, 21^{2}, 23, 24^{2}, 25^{2}, 26, 27; **5**:2, 9^{2}, 10^{2}, 11^{2}, 15^{2}, 16^{2}, 18^{2}; **6**:1, 2, 3^{3}, 4^{2}, 9, 20^{2}, 21^{2}, 25, 26; **7**:2, 3^{2}, 4, 25; **9**:6, 11^{2}, 12; **16**:3; **19**:18; **22**:17, 18^{2}, 19, 27, 28; **23**:2, 8, 9, 12^{2}, 15, 16, 17, 18, 19, 22^{2}, 25, 26^{2}, 33^{2}; **24**:10, 12, 13, 14^{2}, 17^{2}, 27^{3}, 28^{2}; **25**:7, 8, 9, 10, 17, 21; **27**:2^{2}, 10^{3}, 23^{2}, 27^{2}; **29**:17^{2}; **30**:32^{2}; **31**:3^{2}; **Ecc 5**:1, 2^{3}, 4, 6^{2}; **7**:9, 17, 21, 22; **9**:7^{2}, 8, 9^{4}, 10^{2}; **10**:4, 20^{3}; **11**:1, 6^{2}, 9^{4}, 10^{2}; **12**:1^{2}; **SS 1**:2, 3^{2}, 4, 7^{3}, 8, 10^{2}, 15; **2**:14^{4}; **4**:1^{3}, 2, 3^{4}, 4, 5, 9^{2}, 10^{3}, 11^{3}, 13; **5**:1, 9^{2}; **6**:1^{2}, 5^{2}, 6, 7^{2}; **7**:1^{2}, 2^{2}, 3, 4^{3}, 5^{2}, 6, 7^{2}, 8^{2}, 9; **8**:5, 6^{2}, 13; **Isa 1**:5^{2}, 6^{2}, 7^{3}, 11, 13^{2}, 14^{2}, 15^{2}, 16, 18, 22^{2}, 23, 25^{2}, 26^{2}; **2**:6; **3**:12, 14, 25^{2}; **4**:1; **6**:7^{3}; **7**:3, 5, 9, 11, 17^{2}, 20^{3}; **8**:8, 10^{2}; **10**:3, 22, 27^{2}; **12**:1; **14**:9, 11^{2}, 13, 16, 19, 20^{2}, 30^{2}; **16**:3, 9^{2}; **17**:10^{2}; **19**:12; **20**:2^{2}; **22**:2, 3, 7, 12, 14, 16^{2}, 18^{2}, 19^{2}, 21^{3}; **23**:7, 10, 12, 14; **25**:1, 12; **26**:8^{2}, 9, 11^{4}, 13, 17, 19^{2}, 20; **28**:17^{2}, 18^{2}, 22^{2}; **29**:1, 4^{3}, 5, 10^{2}; **30**:3, 15^{2}, 16, 20^{2}, 21, 22^{2}, 23, 29; **31**:7; **32**:11^{2}, 12, 20^{2}; **33**:3, 4, 6, 11, 17, 18, 20, 23; **35**:4; **36**:11, 12, 17; **37**:4^{2}, 6, 17, 23^{2}, 24, 29^{3}; **38**:1, 3, 5^{4}, 17^{2}, 18^{2}, 19; **39**:4, 6^{2}, 7^{2}; **40**:1, 9^{2}, 26; **41**:10, 12, 13^{2}, 14, 21^{2}, 22, 24; **42**:6, 20; **43**:3^{4}, 4, 5, 14^{2}, 15^{2}, 23, 24^{3}, 25^{2}, 26, 27^{2}, 28; **44**:3^{2}, 22^{2}, 23, 24, 27; **45**:9; **46**:3, 4; **47**:2^{3}, 3^{2}, 6, 8, 9^{2}, 10^{2}, 12^{2}, 13; **48**:4^{2}, 8, 17^{2}, 18^{2}, 19^{2}; **49**:16, 17, 18^{2}, 19^{2}, 20^{2}, 21, 22^{2}, 23^{3}, 25, 26^{3}; **50**:1^{4}, 11; **51**:2, 6, 7, 13, 15, 16, 20^{2}, 22^{3}, 23^{2}; **52**:1, 2^{2}, 7, 8, 12; **54**:2^{4}, 3, 4^{2}, 5^{3}, 6, 8, 11, 12^{3}, 13^{2}; **55**:2^{2}, 3, 5, 8^{2}, 9^{2}; **57**:4, 5, 6^{2}, 7^{2}, 8^{4}, 9^{2}, 10^{2}, 11, 12^{2}, 13; **58**:1, 3^{2}, 4^{2}, 7^{2}, 8^{4}, 10^{2}, 11^{2}, 12, 13^{2}, 14^{2}; **59**:2^{3}, 3^{4}, 12, 21^{3}; **60**:1, 3^{2}, 4^{3}, 5, 6, 9^{2}, 10, 11, 14^{2}, 16^{2}, 17^{2}, 18^{4}, 19^{4}, 20^{4}, 21; **61**:5^{2}; **62**:2^{2}, 3, 4^{3}, 5^{2}, 6, 8^{2}, 11; **63**:2, 14, 15^{4}, 16, 17^{3}, 18^{3}, 19; **64**:2^{2}, 5, 7^{2}, 8, 9, 10; **65**:7^{2}, 15; **66**:5^{2}, 9, 14, 20, 22; **Jer 1**:9; **2**:2, 5, 9, 16, 17, 19^{3}, 20^{2}, 22, 25^{2}, 30^{3}, 33, 34, 36, 37^{2}; **3**:2, 5, 13^{3}, 14, 16, 18; **4**:1, 3, 4, 7^{2}, 14, 18^{2}, 30^{3}; **5**:3, 7, 14, 17^{4}, 19^{2}, 25^{2}; **6**:8, 9, 16, 20^{2}; **7**:3^{2}, 5^{2}, 6, 7, 14, 15, 21^{2}, 22, 23, 25, 29; **9**:4^{2}, 20^{2}; **10**:6, 7, 17, 24, 25^{2}; **11**:4^{2}, 5, 7, 15^{2}, 20, 21; **12**:1, 6^{2}, 13; **13**:1, 4, 16^{2}, 17, 18^{3}, 20, 21, 22^{3}, 25, 26^{3}, 27^{3}; **14**:7, 9, 21^{3}; **15**:11, 13^{4}, 14, 15, 16^{2}, 17; **16**:9^{2}, 11, 12, 13; **17**:3^{4}, 4^{2}, 16, 22^{2}; **18**:11^{3}, 20, 23^{2}; **20**:4^{2}, 6^{2}, 12; **21**:4, 14^{2}; **22**:2^{2}, 7, 15, 17^{2}, 20^{2}, 21^{2}, 22^{3}, 25; **23**:39; **25**:5^{3}, 6, 7, 28, 34; **26**:11, 13^{3}, 14, 15; **27**:2, 4, 6, 9^{5}, 10, 12, 13; **28**:7; **29**:6^{2}, 13, 16, 21, 25; **30**:10, 12^{2}, 13^{2}, 14^{3}, 15^{3}, 16, 17, 22; **31**:4, 7^{2}, 16^{3}, 17^{2}, 21; **32**:7^{2}, 8, 17, 19^{3}, 21, 23; **34**:3, 5^{2}, 13, 14, 16, 17; **35**:6, 15^{3}, 18; **37**:18, 19; **38**:5, 12, 16, 17^{2}, 20, 22^{2}, 23; **39**:16, 18; **40**:2, 4, 10, 14, 15; **42**:2, 3, 4, 5, 9, 12, 13, 20, 21; **44**:3, 8, 9^{2}, 10, 21^{3}, 22^{2}, 25^{3}; **45**:5; **46**:3, 4^{3}, 12^{2}, 14, 15, 19, 27; **47**:6; **48**:6, 7, 18^{2}, 27^{2}, 28, 32^{2}, 46^{2}; **49**:4^{3}, 11^{2}, 16^{2}; **50**:12, 14, 31; **51**:6, 13, 24, 36, 45; **La 1**:10; **2**:13, 14^{3}, 15, 16, 17, 18^{2}, 19^{3}, 21; **3**:23, 55, 56, 65; **4**:22^{4}; **5**:19; **Eze 2**:1, 8; **3**:3, 9, 11, 24, 26^{2}, 27; **4**:3, 4^{2}, 6, 7, 8, 9, 15; **5**:1^{2}, 2, 3, 9, 10^{2}, 11, 12^{2}, 16; **6**:2, 3, 4^{4}, 5^{2}, 6^{3}, 7, 11^{2}; **7**:3^{2}, 4, 8^{2}, 9; **9**:8; **10**:2; **11**:5, 15^{3}; **12**:3, 4, 5, 6^{2}, 18^{2}, 25; **13**:4, 8, 17^{2}, 18, 20^{2}, 21^{3}, 22, 23; **14**:6^{2}; **16**:3^{3}, 4, 6^{2}, 7^{2}, 8, 11^{2}, 12^{3}, 13^{2}, 14^{3}, 15^{4}, 16^{2}, 18, 20^{2}, 22^{4}, 23, 25^{3}, 26^{2}, 27^{3}, 29, 31^{2}, 32, 33^{2}, 34^{2}, 36^{6}, 37^{2}, 39^{5}, 41^{3}, 43^{3}, 45^{4}, 46^{2}, 47, 48^{2}, 49, 51, 52^{5}, 53, 54, 55^{2}, 56^{2}, 57, 58^{2}, 60, 61^{2}, 63^{2}; **17**:5; **18**:25, 29, 30^{2}; **19**:2, 10^{2}; **20**:5, 7^{2}, 18, 19, 20, 27, 30, 31^{3}, 36, 39^{2}, 40^{3}, 42, 43, 44^{2}, 46, 47; **21**:2, 12, 14, 16, 24^{3}, 30, 32^{2}; **22**:4^{2}, 12, 13, 14^{2}, 15; **23**:21^{3}, 22, 25^{3}, 26^{2}, 29^{2}, 31^{2}, 32, 33, 34, 35^{2}, 40^{2}, 49^{2}; **24**:13^{2}, 14^{2}, 16, 17^{4}, 21^{2}, 22, 23^{5}, 27; **25**:2, 4^{2}, 6^{3}; **26**:8^{2}, 9^{2}, 10^{2}, 11^{3}, 12^{5}, 13^{2}, 15, 17^{2}, 18^{2}, 20; **27**:4^{3}, 5, 6^{2}, 7^{3}, 8^{3}, 9^{2}, 10^{2}, 11^{4}, 12^{2}, 13, 14, 15, 16^{2}, 17, 18, 19^{2}, 21, 22, 24, 25, 26, 27^{5}, 28, 33^{3}, 34^{2}; **28**:2, 4^{2}, 5^{4}, 7^{2}, 13, 15, 16, 17^{4}, 18^{2}, 21; **29**:2, 3, 4^{5}, 5, 8, 10, 21; **32**:2^{2}, 5^{2}, 6^{2}, 8, 9, 10, 12; **33**:2, 11, 12, 17, 25, 26, 30, 31, 32; **34**:18^{3}, 19, 21, 31; **35**:2, 4, 8^{4}, 9, 11; **36**:13, 14, 15, 22, 24, 25^{2}, 26, 28^{2}, 29, 31^{2}, 32^{2}, 33^{2}; **37**:12, 13, 14, 17, 18, 25; **38**:2, 4^{4}, 9, 10, 13, 15; **39**:3^{4}, 4, 20; **40**:4^{2}; **43**:27; **44**:6, 7, 8, 30^{3}; **45**:9; **47**:14^{2}; **Da 1**:10^{2}, 12, 13; **2**:4, 5, 28^{3}, 29, 30, 38, 47; **3**:12, 17, 18; **4**:19^{2}, 22^{2}, 26, 27^{3}, 31; **5**:11^{4}, 16, 17^{2}, 18, 23^{5}, 26, 28; **6**:16, 20; **7**:5; **9**:5, 6^{2}, 11, 13, 15, 16^{6}, 17^{3}, 18^{3}, 19^{4}, 24^{2}; **10**:12^{3}, 14, 17, 21; **11**:14; **12**:1^{2}, 9, 13^{2}; **Hos 1**:9; **2**:1^{2}, 2; **3**:1^{2}; **4**:4, 5, 6^{2}, 13^{2}, 14^{2}; **5**:13; **6**:4; **8**:1, 5; **9**:1, 5, 7^{2}, 10; **10**:12, 13^{2}, 14^{2}, 15; **12**:6^{2}, 9^{2}; **13**:4, 9, 10^{3}, 14^{2}; **14**:1^{3}, 8; **Joel 1**:2^{2}, 3^{2}, 5, 13, 14; **2**:12, 13^{3}, 14, 17^{2}, 23, 26, 27, 28^{3}; **3**:4, 5, 7, 8, 10^{2}, 11, 17; **Am 2**:11^{2}; **3**:2, 11^{2}; **4**:1, 4^{2}, 5, 9^{2}, 10^{4}, 12; **5**:12^{2}, 17, 21^{2}, 23^{2}, 26^{3}; **6**:2, 4, 5, 7; **7**:12^{2}, 17^{3}; **8**:10^{3}, 14; **9**:15; **Ob 1**:3^{2}, 4, 7^{3}, 9, 10, 12, 15^{2}; **Jnh 1**:6, 8; **2**:3, 4^{2}, 7; **Mic 1**:16; **2**:10; **4**:9, 10; **5**:1, 9^{3}, 10^{2}, 11^{2}, 12, 13^{3}, 14^{2}; **6**:1, 5, 8, 9, 10, 13, 14, 16; **7**:4, 5^{2}, 10, 11^{2}, 14^{3}; **Na 1**:13^{2}, 14^{3}, 15^{2}; **2**:1, 13^{3}; **3**:5^{4}, 12, 13^{3}, 14, 16, 17^{2}, 18^{3}, 19^{4}; **Hab 1**:5, 13; **2**:7, 10^{2}, 16^{2}, 17; **3**:2^{2}, 8^{3}, 9, 11^{2}, 13^{2}, 15; **Zep 1**:11; **3**:14, 15^{2}, 16, 17, 20^{2}; **Hag 1**:4, 5, 6, 7, 11; **2**:17; **Zec 1**:2, 4^{3}, 5, 6; **3**:4, 8; **6**:15; **7**:10; **8**:9, 13, 14, 16, 17; **9**:9, 11, 12, 13^{2}; **11**:1^{2}, 9; **13**:6; **14**:1; **Mal 1**:5, 6, 8, 9, 10, 13; **2**:2^{3}, 3^{3}, 8, 13^{2}, 14^{3}, 15^{2}, 16, 17; **3**:7, 11^{2}; **4**:3; **Mt 1**:20; **4**:6, 7, 10; **5**:12, 16^{3}, 20, 23^{2}, 24^{3}, 25, 29^{3}, 30^{3}, 33, 36, 37^{2}, 40^{2}, 43^{2}, 44, 45, 47, 48; **6**:1^{2}, 3^{2}, 4^{2}, 6^{3}, 8, 9, 10^{2}, 14, 15^{2}, 17^{2}, 18^{2}, 21^{2}, 22^{2}, 23^{2}, 25^{2}, 26, 32; **7**:3^{2}, 4^{3}, 5^{2}, 6, 11^{2}, 22^{2}; **9**:2, 4, 5, 6, 11, 14, 18, 22, 29; **10**:9, 12, 13^{2}, 14^{2}, 17, 20, 27, 29, 30; **11**:10, 26, 29; **12**:2, 13, 27^{2}, 37^{2}, 47; **13**:16^{2}, 27, 32; **15**:2, 3, 4, 6, 28; **16**:6, 11; **17**:16, 24, 27; **18**:8^{2}, 9, 14, 15^{2}, 33, 35^{2}; **19**:8^{2}, 19^{2}, 21; **20**:14, 21^{3}, 26, 27; **21**:5; **22**:17, 37^{4}, 39, 44^{2}; **23**:11, 23, 32, 34, 37, 38; **24**:3, 20, 42; **25**:8, 21, 23, 25, 34; **26**:18, 42, 52, 73; **27**:4, 24; **Mk 1**:2, 44; **2**:5, 9^{2}, 11; **3**:5, 32; **5**:9, 19, 23, 34^{2}, 35; **6**:8, 11, 18; **7**:5, 9, 10^{2}, 13, 29; **8**:17; **9**:18, 38, 43, 45, 47; **10**:5, 19, 37^{3}, 43, 49, 52; **11**:25^{2}; **12**:30^{5}, 31, 33^{4}, 36^{2}; **13**:9, 23; **Lk 1**:13^{2}, 36, 44, 61; **2**:29, 30, 32, 35, 48; **3**:14; **4**:8, 11, 12, 21, 23; **5**:14, 20, 22, 23, 24; **6**:10, 22, 23, 24, 27, 29^{2}, 35^{2}, 36, 38, 41^{2}, 42^{5}; **7**:27, 44, 48, 50; **8**:20, 25, 30, 48, 49; **9**:5, 40, 41, 49; **10**:6, 11, 17, 20, 21, 27^{6}; **11**:2^{2}, 11, 13^{2}, 19^{2}, 34^{5}, 36, 42, 47, 48; **12**:1, 7, 15, 20, 22^{2}, 29, 30, 32, 33, 34^{2}, 35, 58; **13**:12, 34, 35; **14**:9, 10^{2}, 12^{3}; **15**:19^{2}, 21, 27^{2}, 29, 30; **16**:2, 6, 7, 12, 15, 25^{2}; **17**:3, 19, 20; **18**:20, 42^{2}; **19**:5, 16, 18, 20, 22, 39, 42, 43, 44; **20**:43^{2}; **21**:13, 14, 15, 18, 28^{2}, 34; **22**:32^{2}, 36, 53; **23**:14^{2}, 28, 42, 46; **24**:38; **Jn 2**:17, 18; **4**:16, 18, 35, 50, 53; **5**:8, 10, 11, 20, 42, 45^{2}; **6**:26, 49, 58; **7**:3; **8**:11, 13^{2}, 17, 19, 21, 24^{2}, 38, 41, 42, 44^{2}, 52, 54, 56; **9**:10, 17, 19, 26, 41; **10**:34; **11**:15, 23; **12**:15, 28, 30, 36; **13**:14^{2}, 38; **14**:1, 27; **15**:11; **16**:7, 20, 22^{2}, 24, 26; **17**:1^{2}, 5, 6, 11, 14, 17; **18**:11, 31, 34, 35^{2}, 39; **19**:14, 15, 26, 27; **20**:17^{2}, 27^{2}; **21**:6, 18; **Ac 2**:17^{3}, 27, 28, 35^{2}, 38, 39; **3**:17, 19, 22^{2}, 25^{2}, 26; **4**:25, 27, 28, 29^{2}, 30^{2}; **5**:3, 4, 9, 28; **7**:3^{2}, 6, 32, 33, 37, 43, 51, 52; **8**:20, 21, 22; **9**:13, 14, 34; **10**:4, 31^{2}; **11**:14; **12**:8^{2}, 15; **13**:33, 35, 41; **14**:10, 17; **15**:23, 24; **16**:31; **17**:23, 28; **18**:6^{2}, 15; **20**:30, 31; **22**:13, 16, 18, 20; **23**:5, 21, 35^{2}; **24**:2, 22; **25**:5; **26**:16, 17, 24^{2}; **27**:22, 25; **28**:22, 25; **Ro 1**:8; **2**:5^{2}, 17; **4**:18; **6**:12, 13^{2}, 14, 19^{2}; **8**:10^{2}, 11, 36; **9**:7; **10**:6, 8^{2}, 9^{2}, 10^{2}; **11**:3^{2}, 28; **12**:1^{2}, 2, 11, 20; **13**:9, 11; **14**:10^{2}, 13^{2}, 15^{3}, 21; **15**:9, 24; **16**:17, 19, 20; **1Co 1**:5^{2}; **2**:5; **4**:6, 15; **5**:2, 6; **6**:8, 15, 19^{2}, 20; **7**:5, 14, 16^{2}, 21, 35; **8**:9, 11, 12; **11**:17; **14**:9, 16^{2}, 20, 23; **15**:1, 14, 17^{2}, 34^{2}, 55^{2}, 58; **16**:3, 13; **2Co 1**:6^{2}, 11, 24^{2}; **2**:8, 10; **4**:5, 15; **5**:11; **6**:13; **7**:2, 7^{3}, 9; **8**:6, 7, 8, 9, 11^{3}, 14, 24; **9**:2^{2}, 10^{2}, 11, 13^{2}; **10**:6, 15; **11**:3^{2}; **12**:14, 19; **13**:9; **Gal 3**:1, 3, 16; **4**:15^{2}, 16; **5**:13, 14; **6**:13, 18; **Eph 1**:13, 15^{2}, 18; **2**:1; **3**:13, 16, 17; **4**:22^{2}, 23, 26, 29; **5**:19, 22, 25; **6**:1, 2, 4, 5, 6, 9, 11, 13, 14, 15; **Php 1**:5, 9, 19, 25, 26; **2**:4, 5, 12, 17, 20, 25; **4**:5, 6, 7^{2}, 10, 15, 17, 19, 23; **Col 1**:4, 8, 21^{2}, 23; **2**:5, 12, 13^{2}; **3**:1, 2, 3, 4, 5, 8, 9, 15, 16, 18, 19, 20, 21, 22, 23; **4**:1, 6, 8; **1Th 1**:3^{3}, 5, 8; **2**:14; **3**:2, 5, 6, 7, 10, 12, 13; **4**:11^{3}, 12; **5**:23; **2Th 1**:3, 4, 11; **2**:17; **3**:5; **1Ti 4**:14, 15, 16^{2}; **5**:1, 23^{2}; **6**:12, 20; **2Ti 1**:4, 5^{3}; **2**:15; **4**:5^{2}, 9, 15, 21, 22; **Tit 2**:7; **3**:12; **Phm 1**:2, 5^{2}, 6, 7, 13, 14, 19, 21, 22, 25; **Heb 1**:5, 8^{2}, 9^{2}, 10, 12, 13^{2}; **2**:12^{2}; **3**:1, 8, 9, 15; **4**:7; **5**:5; **6**:9, 10, 11; **10**:7, 9, 32, 34, 35; **11**:18; **12**:4^{2}, 12, 13; **13**:5, 7, 17, 24; **Jas 1**:3; **2**:2, 8, 18; **3**:14; **4**:1, 3, 8^{2}, 9^{2}, 12, 14; **5**:2^{2}, 3^{2}, 4, 12^{2}, 16; **1Pe 1**:7, 9^{2}, 13^{2}, 17, 18, 20, 21, 22; **2**:2, 11, 12, 16, 18, 20, 25; **3**:1, 2, 3, 4, 7^{2}, 15, 16; **5**:2, 7, 8, 9; **2Pe 1**:5, 8, 10, 13, 19; **3**:2, 17^{2}; **1Jn 2**:12; **2Jn 1**:4, 10, 13; **3Jn 1**:2, 3, 6; **Jude 1**:12, 20; **Rev 1**:9; **2**:2^{3}, 4, 5, 6, 9^{2}, 13^{2}, 19^{3}, 23; **3**:1, 2, 8, 9, 11, 15, 18^{2}; **4**:11; **5**:9; **10**:9^{2}; **11**:17, 18^{4}; **14**:15, 18; **15**:3^{2}, 4^{2}; **16**:6, 7; **18**:10, 14, 23^{2}; **19**:10; **22**:9.

YOURS (86)

Ge 1:29; **20**:7; **31**:32; **45**:20; **48**:6; **Ex 11**:8; **Nu 18**:11, 13, 14, 15, 18^{2}; **Dt 9**:21; **11**:24; **20**:1; **Jos 17**:18; **Jdg 1**:3; **4**:9; **7**:18; **1Sa 2**:23; **25**:6; **2Sa 16**:4; **1Ki 1**:47^{2}; **3**:9, 22^{2}; **5**:6; **20**:4; **21**:19; **22**:23; **2Ki 2**:10; **18**:19; **1Ch 12**:18; **21**:24; **29**:11^{3}; **2Ch 1**:10; **2**:8; **18**:22; **20**:15; **21**:14; **Job 42**:2; **Ps 71**:16; **74**:16^{2}; **86**:8; **89**:11^{2}; **119**:94; **128**:2; **Pr 5**:17; **Isa 36**:4; **45**:14; **63**:19; **Jer 32**:20; **38**:22; **Da 2**:39; **Am 6**:2; **Mal 3**:12; **Mt 17**:27; **18**:32; **Mk 2**:18; **11**:24; **Lk 4**:7; **5**:33; **6**:20; **15**:30, 31, 32; **22**:42; **Jn 15**:20; **17**:6, 9, 10; **1Co 3**:21, 22; **10**:29; **16**:18; **2Co 6**:12; **Eph 6**:9; **2Th 1**:11; **1Pe 1**:2; **2Pe 1**:2; **Jude 1**:2.

YOURSELF (191)

Ge 6:14; **14**:21; **28**:2; **31**:32; **33**:9; **Ex 9**:17; **10**:3; **19**:23; **20**:4, 19; **34**:2; **Lev 9**:7; **18**:20, 23; **19**:18, 34; **25**:6; **Nu 5**:20; **Dt 5**:8; **8**:17; **9**:4; **23**:12, 13; **Jos 14**:12; **Jdg 8**:21; **19**:5, 6, 8, 9; **Ru 3**:3; **4**:6, 8; **1Sa 20**:8; **25**:26; **28**:2; **2Sa 16**:21; **17**:11; **20**:4; **22**:26^{2}, 27^{2}; **1Ki 1**:17; **2**:2, 5, 36; **3**:11; **11**:31; **14**:2, 9; **17**:13; **18**:1; **20**:40; **21**:20; **2Ki 5**:10; **22**:19; **1Ch 17**:21; **2Ch 21**:15; **25**:19; **34**:27^{2}; **Ne 9**:10; **Job 5**:27; **15**:8; **18**:4; **33**:5; **35**:8; **38**:3, 34; **40**:7, 8, 10^{2}; **Ps 10**:1; **18**:25^{2}, 26^{2}; **37**:4; **44**:23; **45**:3; **59**:5; **65**:6; **80**:15, 17; **89**:46; **119**:102; **Pr 6**:3^{2}, 5; **22**:25; **23**:4; **25**:6; **26**:4; **30**:32; **Ecc 7**:16, 22; **Isa 22**:16; **26**:15; **47**:8, 10; **51**:9; **52**:1, 2; **63**:14; **64**:12; **Jer 1**:17; **2**:22; **4**:30^{2}; **13**:22; **20**:4; **32**:8; **38**:18, 23; **45**:5; **La 2**:18; **3**:43, 44; **5**:21; **Eze 3**:19, 21, 24; **4**:4, 9; **16**:17, 24; **23**:30, 40; **28**:4; **33**:9; **Da 5**:17, 22, 23; **9**:15; **10**:12; **Hos 1**:2; **Am 7**:17; **Ob 1**:3; **Mal 2**:15, 16; **Mt 4**:6; **8**:4; **19**:19; **21**:21; **22**:39; **27**:40; **Mk 1**:44; **11**:23; **12**:31, 33; **14**:30; **15**:30; **Lk 4**:9, 23; **5**:14; **6**:42; **7**:6; **10**:27; **12**:20; **17**:8; **23**:37, 39; **Jn 1**:22; **7**:4; **14**:22; **21**:18; **Ac 5**:3; **16**:28; **21**:24; **23**:3; **24**:8; **25**:10; **26**:1; **Ro 2**:1, 5, 17, 21; **12**:3^{2}; **13**:9; **14**:22; **Gal 5**:14; **6**:1; **1Ti 4**:7, 13, 15, 16; **5**:22; **2Ti 2**:15; **Jas 2**:8.

YOURSELVES (213)

Ge 34:9; **35**:2; **45**:5, 12; **47**:24; **Ex 18**:18; **19**:4, 15; **20**:22, 23; **23**:9; **30**:37; **Lev 11**:24, 43^{2}, 44^{2}; **16**:29, 31; **17**:11; **18**:24, 30; **19**:4, 28; **20**:7, 25; **23**:27, 32; **26**:1; **Nu 11**:18; **15**:39; **16**:3, 21; **29**:7; **31**:18, 19; **32**:20; **Dt 4**:9, 15, 16, 23; **7**:17, 25; **9**:16; **10**:19; **14**:1; **18**:21; **19**:2, 7; **20**:14; **21**:9; **28**:68; **29**:16; **31**:14, 19; **Jos 2**:16; **3**:5; **7**:13, 14; **8**:2; **17**:15; **22**:16, 19; **23**:3, 12; **24**:15, 22; **Jdg 15**:12; **1Sa 2**:29; **7**:3^{2}; **8**:17; **10**:19; **16**:5; **2Ki 11**:8; **1Ch 15**:12; **2Ch 29**:5, 31; **35**:4, 6; **Ezr 10**:11; **Ne 13**:25; **Job 19**:5, 29; **27**:12; **42**:8; **Isa 1**:16; **26**:20; **29**:9; **43**:22; **48**:2; **50**:11; **58**:10; **62**:6; **Jer 2**:17, 28; **4**:4; **7**:21; **25**:7; **26**:15; **37**:9; **44**:7^{2}, 8^{2}; **47**:5; **49**:14; **Eze 18**:31; **20**:7, 18, 30, 31, 43^{2}; **24**:23; **34**:3; **36**:31; **47**:21, 22; **Hos 10**:12; **Am 3**:9; **5**:26; **Mic 1**:16; **2**:3; **6**:15; **Na 2**:1; **Hag 1**:4; **Zec 7**:6; **Mt 3**:9; **6**:19, 20; **16**:8; **23**:13, 31; **25**:9; **Mk 6**:31; **9**:50; **Lk 3**:8; **11**:46, 52; **12**:11, 33, 57; **13**:28; **16**:9, 15; **17**:3, 14; **21**:14, 30; **23**:28; **Jn 3**:28; **6**:43; **15**:8; **18**:31; **Ac 2**:22, 40; **4**:19; **5**:39; **13**:46; **18**:15; **20**:28, 34; **27**:21; **Ro 6**:11, 13, 16; **12**:10; **13**:14; **15**:5, 14; **1Co 3**:16, 18; **6**:8; **7**:5; **10**:15; **11**:13; **15**:58; **2Co 3**:2; **7**:11^{2}, 12; **9**:13; **13**:5^{2}; **Gal 3**:27; **5**:1, 2; **Eph 2**:8; **Php 1**:27; **2**:3; **Col 3**:8, 12; **4**:2; **1Th 4**:9; **2Th 3**:7; **Heb 10**:34; **13**:3; **Jas 1**:22; **2**:4; **4**:7, 10; **5**:5; **1Pe 1**:22; **2**:1, 13, 18; **4**:1; **5**:5, 6; **1Jn 5**:21; **Jude 1**:20, 21.

BIBLICAL–LANGUAGE INDEX–LEXICONS

FEATURES OF THE HEBREW TO ENGLISH AND ARAMAIC TO ENGLISH INDEX–LEXICONS

G/K NUMBER
Matches the number at the end of context lines; one- to four-digit numbers are Hebrew, five-digit numbers are Aramaic (see the introduction, pages xii, xv).

LEXICAL FORM and TRANSLITERATION
See the transliteration and pronunication table below.

FREQUENCY COUNT
Indicates the total number of occurrences of this Hebrew or Aramaic word in the biblical text (see the introduction, page xv).

10008 אֱדַיִן *’^{e}ḏayin* (57)

then (11)

NIV WORD and (FREQUENCY COUNT)
NIV words are listed according to their exact textual spelling and are organized according to frequency (see the introduction, page xv).

as soon as (1) +10168+10427

MULTIPLE WORDS / MULTIPLE NUMBERS
More than one NIV word and/or more than one G/K number indicate multiple-word translations (see the introduction, pages xii, xiii, xv).

that day^{s} (1)

SUPERSCRIPT “S”
Indicates “substitution” translation (see the introduction, pages xiii-xv).

untranslated (11)

UNTRANSLATED
Always the final entry, indicates the number of times the NIV did not translate the Hebrew or Aramaic word for stylistic reasons (see the introduction, pages xv, xvi).

Variant; not used

VARIANT; NOT USED
Notes words of variant spelling and variant readings in the G/K number list that were not used in translating the NIV (see the introduction, pages xv, xvi).

HEBREW AND ARAMAIC TRANSLITERATION AND PRONUNCIATION TABLE

Hebrew	*English*	*Sound*
א	’	[no sound]
בּ	*b*	*b*oy
ב	*ḇ*	*v*ote
גּ	*g*	*g*irl
ג	*g̱*	*g*irl
דּ	*d*	*d*og
ד	*ḏ*	*d*og
ה	*h*	*h*ot
ו	*w*	*v*ote
ז	*z*	*z*ip
ח	*ḥ*	Ba*ch*
ט	*ṭ*	*t*ip
י	*y*	*y*es
כּ	*k*	*k*it
כ ך	*ḵ*	Ba*ch*
ל	*l*	*l*et
מ ם	*m*	*m*other
נ ן	*n*	*n*ot
ס	*s*	*s*ip
ע	‘	[no sound]
פּ	*p*	*p*ot
פ ף	*p̱*	*ph*one
צ ץ	*ṣ*	si*ts*
ק	*q*	tor*q*ue
ר	*r*	*r*ot
שׂ	*ś*	*s*ip
שׁ	*š*	*sh*ip
תּ	*t*	*t*ip
ת	*ṯ*	*t*ip
ָ	*ā*	f*a*ther
ֵ	*ē*	th*ey*
ֹ	*ō*	ph*o*ne
וֹ	*ô*	ph*o*ne
וּ	*û*	t*u*ne
ַ	*a*	f*a*ther
ֶ	*e*	g*e*t
ִ	*i*	p*i*n, mach*i*ne
ָ	*o*	ph*o*ne
ֻ	*u*	s*u*re
ְ	^{e}	s*e*lect [if vocal]
ֲ	^{a}	b*a*ton
ֱ	^{e}	s*e*lect
ֳ	^{o}	m*o*tel

HEBREW TO ENGLISH INDEX–LEXICON OF THE OLD TESTAMENT

1 א '
Variant; not used

2 אָ־ *-ā'* (1)
untranslated (1)

3 אָב *'āḇ* (1209)
father (527)
fathers (264)
father's (121)
forefathers (80)
families (57) +1074
families (36)
family (25) +1074
family (14)
forefather (11)
ancestral (9)
them[S] (9) +2257
fathers' (5)
father's (4) +4200
parents (3) +562+2256
ancestor (2)
ancestors (2)
clans (2)
forefathers (2) +3
grandfather's (2)
he[S] (2) +3870
him[S] (2) +2257
parents (2)
clan (1) +1074+5476
clans (1) +1074
family possessions (1)
fatherless (1) +401
forefather's (1)
forefathers (1) +8037
grandfather (1)
group (1) +1074+2755
he[S] (1) +2023
he[S] (1) +3276
him[S] (1) +2023
him[S] (1) +3276
his[S] (1) +2023
his[S] (1) +2257
them[S] (1) +3870
them[S] (1) +4013
they[S] (1) +4013
untranslated (10)

4 אֵב *'ēḇ* (2)
growing (1)
new growth (1)

5 אֲבַגְתָא *'ăḇag̱tā'* (1)
Abagtha (1)

6 אָבַד *'āḇad* (185)
perish (43)
destroy (28)
destroyed (18)
lost (11)
perished (9)
destruction (5)
gone (5)
perishes (4)
perishing (4)
ruined (4)
annihilate (3)
come to nothing (3)
comes to nothing (2)
destroys (2)
lose (2)
wipe out (2)
annihilation (1)
banish (1)
be destroyed (1)
broken (1)
brought ruin (1)
certainly be destroyed (1) +6
come to ruin (1)
corrupts (1)
dead (1)
demolish (1)
destroy completely (1) +6
destroying (1)
die (1)
died (1)
dying (1)
elude (1)
expelled (1)
exterminate (1)
give up (1)
have no (1) +4946
have nowhere (1) +4946
kill (1)
loses (1) +8
not escape (1) +4960
perish (1) +6
ruin (1)
silence (1)
squanders (1)
surely be destroyed (1) +6
swept (1)
vanished (1)
wandering (1)
wiped out (1)
without (1)
untranslated (2)

7 אֹבֵד *'ōḇēḏ* (2)
ruin (2)

8 אֲבֵדָה *'ăḇēḏāh* (4)
lost property (2)
loses (1) +6
lost (1)

9 אֲבַדֹּה *'ăḇaddōh* (1)
destruction (1)

10 אֲבַדּוֹ *'ăḇaddô* (1)
untranslated (1)

11 אֲבַדּוֹן *'ăḇaddôn* (5)
destruction (5)

12 אַבְדָן *'aḇdān* (1)
destroying (1)

13 אָבְדָן *'āḇdān* (1)
destruction (1)

14 אָבָה *'āḇāh* (53)
would (13)
refused (11) +4202
willing (11)
unwilling (7) +4202
accept (2)
refuse (2) +4202
will (2)
agree to demands (1)
consent (1)
submit (1)
would have (1)
yield (1)

15 אֵבֶה *'ēḇeh* (1)
papyrus (1)

16 אֲבוֹי *'ăḇôy* (1)
sorrow (1)

17 אֵבוּס *'ēḇûs* (3)
manger (3)

18 אִבְחָה *'iḇḥāh* (1)
slaughter (1)

19 אֲבַטִּיחַ *'ăḇattiyaḥ* (1)
melons (1)

20 אָבִי1 *'āḇiy1* (1)
oh that (1)

21 אָבִי2 *'āḇiy2*
Variant; not used

22 אָבִי3 *'āḇiy3*
Variant; not used

23 אֲבִי *'ăḇiy* (1)
Abijah (1)

24 אֲבִיאֵל *'ăḇiy'ēl* (3)
Abiel (3)

25 אֲבִיאָסָף *'ăḇiy'āsāp̱* (1)
Abiasaph (1)

26 אָבִיב *'āḇiyḇ* (8)
Abib (5)

- headed (1)
- heads (1)
- that[S] (1)

27 אֲבִיבַעַל 'ᵃḇiyḇaʻal
- Variant; not used

28 אֲבִיגַיִל 'ᵃḇiyḡayil (19)
- Abigail (17)
- untranslated (2)

29 אֲבִידָן 'ᵃḇiyḏān (5)
- Abidan (5)

30 אֲבִידָע 'ᵃḇiyḏāʻ (2)
- Abida (2)

31 אֲבִיָּה 'ᵃḇiyyāh (28)
- Abijah (25)
- Abijah's (3)

32 אֲבִיָּהוּ 'ᵃḇiyyāhû (2)
- Abijah (2)

33 אֲבִיהוּא 'ᵃḇiyhû' (12)
- Abihu (12)

34 אֲבִיהוּד 'ᵃḇiyhûḏ (1)
- Abihud (1)

35 אֲבִיהַיִל 'ᵃḇiyhayil (2)
- Abihail (2)

36 אֶבְיוֹן 'eḇyôn (61)
- needy (46)
- poor (14)
- needy (1) +132

37 אֲבִיּוֹנָה 'ᵃḇiyyônāh (1)
- desire (1)

38 אֲבִיחַיִל 'ᵃḇiyhayil (4)
- Abihail (4)

39 אֲבִיטוּב 'ᵃḇiytûḇ (1)
- Abitub (1)

40 אֲבִיטַל 'ᵃḇiytāl (2)
- Abital (2)

41 אֲבִיָּם 'ᵃḇiyyām
- Variant; not used

42 אֲבִימָאֵל 'ᵃḇiymā'ēl (2)
- Abimael (2)

43 אֲבִימֶלֶךְ 'ᵃḇiymeleḵ (66)
- Abimelech (60)
- Abimelech's (2)
- he[S] (2)
- him[S] (1)
- his[S] (1)

44 אֲבִינָדָב 'ᵃḇiynāḏāḇ (12)
- Abinadab (9)
- Abinadab's (2)
- untranslated (1)

45 אֲבִינֹעַם 'ᵃḇiynōʻam (4)
- Abinoam (4)

46 אֲבִינֵר 'ᵃḇiynēr (1)
- Abner (1)

47 אֶבְיָסָף 'eḇyāsāp̄ (3)
- Ebiasaph (3)

48 אֲבִיעֶזֶר 'ᵃḇiyʻezer (7)
- Abiezer (6)
- Abiezrites (1)

49 אֲבִי עֶזְרִי 'ᵃḇiy ʻezriy (3)
- Abiezrites (2)
- Abiezrite (1)

50 אֲבִי־עַלְבוֹן 'ᵃḇiy-ʻalḇôn (1)
- Abi-Albon (1)

51 אָבִיר 'āḇiyr (6)
- mighty one (6)

52 אַבִּיר 'abbiyr (17)
- mighty (4)
- bulls (2)
- stallions (2)
- warriors (2)
- angels (1)
- great (1)
- head (1)
- steeds (1)
- strong (1)
- stubborn-hearted (1) +4213
- valiant men (1) +4213

53 אֲבִירָם 'ᵃḇiyrām (11)
- Abiram (11)

54 אֲבִישַׁג 'ᵃḇiyšaḡ (5)
- Abishag (5)

55 אֲבִישׁוּעַ 'ᵃḇiyšûaʻ (5)
- Abishua (5)

56 אֲבִישׁוּר 'ᵃḇiyšûr (2)
- Abishur (1)
- Abishur's (1)

57 אֲבִישַׁי 'ᵃḇiyšay (19)
- Abishai (19)

58 אֲבִישָׁלוֹם 'ᵃḇiyšālôm (2)
- Abishalom (2)

59 אֶבְיָתָר 'eḇyāṯār (30)
- Abiathar (28)
- he[S] (1)
- them[S] (1) +2256+7401

60 אָבַךְ 'āḇaḵ (1)
- rolls upward (1)

61 1אָבַל 'āḇal1 (32)
- mourn (11)
- mourned (9)
- mourns (4)
- mourning (2)
- grieve (1)
- grieving (1)
- in mourning (1)
- lament (1)
- made lament (1)
- pretend in mourning (1)

62 2אָבַל 'āḇal2 (7)
- parched (3)
- dries up (2)
- dried up (1)
- dry up (1)

63 1אָבֵל 'āḇēl1 (8)
- mourn (2)
- mourners (2)
- grief (1)
- grieve (1)
- mourning (1)
- weeping (1)

64 2אָבֵל 'āḇēl2 (1)
- Abel (1)

65 אֵבֶל 'ēḇel (24)
- mourning (15)
- mourn (2)
- ceremony of mourning (1)
- moan (1)
- mourn (1) +6913
- period of mourning (1)
- sorrow (1)
- time of mourning (1)
- weep (1)

66 אֲבָל 'ᵃḇāl (11)
- but (3)
- however (2)
- indeed (1)
- not at all (1)
- now (1)
- surely (1)
- well (1)
- yes but (1)

67 אֻבָל 'uḇāl (3)
- canal (3)

68 אָבֵל בֵּית מַעֲכָה 'āḇēl bêyṯ maʻᵃḵāh (4)
- Abel Beth Maacah (4)

69 אָבֵל הַשִּׁטִּים 'āḇēl haššittiym (1)
- Abel Shittim (1)

70 אָבֵל כְּרָמִים 'āḇēl kᵉrāmiym (1)
- Abel Keramim (1)

71 אָבֵל מְחוֹלָה 'āḇēl mᵉhôlāh (3)
- Abel Meholah (3)

72 אָבֵל מַיִם 'āḇēl mayim (1)
- Abel Maim (1)

73 אָבֵל מִצְרַיִם 'āḇēl misrayim (1)
- Abel Mizraim (1)

74 אֶבֶן 'eḇen (273)
- stone (93)
- stones (89)
- rock (8)
- rocks (7)
- stone (5) +928+2021+8083
- weights (5)
- gems (4)
- stoned (4) +8083
- hailstones (3) +453
- slingstones (3) +7845
- blocks (2)
- differing weights (2) +74+2256
- onyx (2) +8732
- ore (2)
- sapphire (2) +6209
- some[S] (2)
- stone (2) +928+2021+6232
- stoned (2) +928+2021+6232
- another[S] (1)
- capstone (1) +8036
- charm (1) +2834
- chrysolite (1) +9577
- cornerstone (1) +7157
- cover (1)
- fieldstones (1) +8969
- gem (1)
- hail (1) +1352
- hailstones (1)
- hailstones (1) +1352
- jewels (1)
- marble (1) +8880
- masons (1) +3093
- plumb line (1)
- plumb line (1) +974
- sling stones (1) +928+2021
- sparkling jewels (1) +734
- standard (1)
- stone (1) +8083
- stonecutters (1) +2935
- stoned (1) +928+2021+8083
- stoned to death (1) +8083
- stonemasons (1) +3093+7815
- stoning (1) +928+2021+8083
- them (1) +928+2021+4392
- them[S] (1)
- them[S] (1) +2021+9109
- these[S] (1) +2021
- two differing weights (1) +74+2256
- untranslated (4)

75 אֶבֶן הָעֵזֶר 'eḇen hāʻēzer (3)
- Ebenezer (3)

76 אֲבָנָה 'ᵃḇānāh (1)
- Abana (1)

77 אַבְנֵט 'aḇnēṭ (9)
- sash (6)
- sashes (3)

78 אָבְנַיִם 'oḇnayim (2)
- delivery stool (1)
- wheel (1)

79 אַבְנֵר 'aḇnēr (62)
- Abner (55)
- Abner's (3)
- him[S] (2)

he^{S} (1)
untranslated (1)

80 אָבַס *'āḇas* (2)
choice (1)
fattened (1)

81 אֲבַעְבֻּעֹת *'^{a}ḇa'bu'ōṯ* (2)
festering (2)

82 אֶבֶץ *'eḇeṣ* (1)
Ebez (1)

83 אִבְצָן *'iḇṣān* (2)
Ibzan (2)

84 אָבַק *'āḇaq* (2)
wrestled (2)

85 אָבָק *'āḇāq* (6)
dust (4)
fine dust (1)
powder (1)

86 אֲבָקָה *'^{a}ḇāqāh* (1)
spices (1)

87 אָבַר *'āḇar* (1)
take flight (1)

88 אֵבֶר *'ēḇer* (3)
wings (2)
feathers (1)

89 אֶבְרָה *'eḇrāh* (4)
feathers (2)
pinions (2)

90 אַבְרָהָם *'aḇrāhām* (175)
Abraham (153)
Abraham's (11)
he^{S} (6)
him^{S} (2)
his^{S} (1)
his^{S} (1) +4200
untranslated (1)

91 אַבְרֵךְ *'aḇrēḵ* (1)
make way (1)

92 אַבְרָם *'aḇrām* (61)
Abram (50)
Abram's (5)
him^{S} (3)
he^{S} (1)
his^{S} (1)
untranslated (1)

93 אַבְשַׁי *'aḇšay* (6)
Abishai (6)

94 אַבְשָׁלוֹם *'aḇšālôm* (109)
Absalom (88)
Absalom's (10)
he^{S} (6)
him^{S} (2)
Absalom's (1) +4200
untranslated (2)

95 אֹבֹת *'ōḇōṯ* (4)
Oboth (4)

96 אָגֵא *'āḡē'* (1)
Agee (1)

97 אֲגַג *'^{a}ḡaḡ* (8)
Agag (7)
untranslated (1)

98 אֲגָגִי *'^{a}ḡāḡiy* (5)
Agagite (5)

99 אֲגֻדָּה *'^{a}guddāh* (4)
bunch (1)
cords (1)
foundation (1)
group (1)

100 אֱגוֹז *'^{e}ḡôz* (1)
nut trees (1)

101 אָגוּר *'āḡûr* (1)
Agur (1)

102 אֲגוֹרָה *'^{a}ḡôrāh* (1)
piece (1)

103 אֵגֶל *'ēḡel* (1)
drops (1)

104 אֶגְלַיִם *'eglayim* (1)
Eglaim (1)

105 אָגַם *'āgam*
Variant; not used

106 1אֲגַם *'^{a}gam1* (9)
pools (3)
ponds (2)
marshes (1)
pool (1)
pool (1) +4784
swampland (1) +4784

107 2אֲגַם *'^{a}gam2*
Variant; not used

108 אָגֵם *'āḡēm* (1)
sick (1)

109 אַגְמוֹן *'agmôn* (5)
reed (3)
cord (1)
reeds (1)

110 אַגָּן *'aggān* (3)
bowls (2)
goblet (1)

111 אֲגַף *'^{a}ḡap̱* (7)
troops (7)

112 אָגַר *'āḡar* (3)
gather grapes (1)
gathers (1)
gathers crops (1)

113 אֲגַרְטָל *'^{a}gartāl* (2)
dishes (2)

114 אֶגְרֹף *'egrōp̱* (2)
fist (1)
fists (1)

115 אִגֶּרֶת *'iggereṯ* (10)
letters (6)
letter (4)

116 אֵד *'ēḏ* (2)
streams (2)

117 אָדַב *'āḏaḇ* (1)
grieve (1)

118 אַדְבְּאֵל *'aḏb^{e}'ēl* (2)
Adbeel (2)

119 אֲדַד *'^{a}ḏaḏ* (1)
Hadad (1)

120 אִדּוֹ *'iddô* (2)
Iddo (2)

121 אֱדוֹם *'^{e}ḏôm* (104)
Edom (79)
Edom (11) +824
Edomites (10)
Edom's (2)
Edomites (1) +1201
untranslated (1)

122 אֲדוֹמִי *'^{a}ḏômiy* (12)
Edomite (8)
Edomites (4)

123 אָדוֹן *'āḏôn* (332)
lord (142)
master (105)
master's (28)
Lord (17)
lords (5)
lord's (4) +4200
masters (4)
sir (3)
you^{S} (3) +3276
lord's (2)
sovereign (2)
fellow officers (1) +6269
gods (1)
he^{S} (1) +3276
her^{S} (1) +851+2257
him^{S} (1) +3276
husbands (1)
owner (1)
supervisors (1)
the Lord (1)
your^{S} (1) +3276
untranslated (7)

124 אַדּוֹן *'addôn* (1)
Addon (1)

125 אֲדוֹנִיָּה *'^{a}dôniyyāh*
Variant; not used

126 אֲדוֹרַיִם *'^{a}dôrayim* (1)
Adoraim (1)

127 אֲדוֹרָם *'^{a}ḏôrām*
Variant; not used

128 אֹדוֹת *'ōḏôṯ* (11)
because of (4) +6584
about (3) +6584
concerned (1)
for sake (1) +6584
untranslated (2)

129 אַדִּיר *'addiyr* (27)
nobles (7)
mighty (6)
leaders (3)
majestic (3)
mighty one (2)
glorious (1)
leader (1)
mightier (1)
picked troops (1)
splendid (1)
stately (1)

130 אֲדַלְיָא *'^{a}ḏalyā'* (1)
Adalia (1)

131 אָדַם *'āḏēm* (10)
dyed red (6)
red (3)
ruddy (1)

132 1אָדָם *'āḏām1* (549)
man (278)
men (82)
men (23) +1201
people (20)
human (13)
man's (13)
one (13)
man (10) +1201
mankind (10)
anyone (9)
mankind (6) +1201
person (5)
men's (3)
persons (3)
someone (3)
body (2)
everyone (2)
man's (2) +1201
man's (2) +4200
mortal men (2) +1201
all mankind (1) +1201
all men (1) +1201+2021
another^{S} (1) +2021
any (1)
anyone (1) +3972
charioteers (1) +8207
deserted (1) +401+4946
else^{S} (1)
every (1)
everyone (1) +2021+3972

everyone (1) +3972
giver[S] (1)
he[S] (1)
him[S] (1) +2021
his[S] (1)
his[S] (1) +2021
human (1) +1201
human being (1)
low (1) +1201
low among men (1) +1201
lowborn men (1) +1201
man-made (1) +3338+5126
men (1) +1201+2021
mortals (1)
natural (1) +2021+3869+3972
needy (1) +36
nobody (1) +4202
other[S] (1)
others[S] (1)
people (1) +1201
people (1) +5883
rabble (1) +8044
reflects the man (1) +2021+4200
scoundrel (1) +1175
slaves (1) +5883
son (1)
successor (1) +339+995+8611
they[S] (1) +2021
those[S] (1)
whoever (1) +2021+3972
untranslated (8)

133 2אָדָם *'ādām2*
Variant; not used

134 3אָדָם *'ādām3* (12)
Adam (11)
Adam's (1)

135 4אָדָם *'ādām4*
Variant; not used

136 5אָדָם *'ādām5* (2)
Adam (1)
untranslated (1)

137 אָדֹם *'ādōm* (9)
red (7)
ruddy (1)
untranslated (1)

138 אֹדֶם *'ōdem* (3)
ruby (3)

139 אֱדֹם *'ᵉdōm*
Variant; not used

140 אֲדַמְדָּם *'adamdām* (6)
reddish-white (4) +4237
reddish (2)

141 1אֲדָמָה *'adāmāh1* (226)
land (120)
ground (42)
earth (30)
soil (11)
dust (4)
lands (3)
clay (2)
country (2)
crops (2)
fields (2)
native land (2)
below (1) +2021+6584
crops (1) +2021+7262
farmer (1) +408+6268
her[S] (1) +3776
home (1)
homeland (1)

142 2אֲדָמָה *'adāmāh2* (1)
Adamah (1)

143 3אֲדָמָה *'adāmāh3*
Variant; not used

144 אַדְמָה *'admāh* (5)
Admah (5)

145 אַדְמוֹנִי *'admôniy* (3)
ruddy (2)
red (1)

146 אֲדָמִי הַנֶּקֶב *'adāmiy hanneqeb* (1)
Adami Nekeb (1)

147 אֲדֻמִּים *'adummiym* (2)
Adummim (2)

148 אַדְמָתָא *'admātā'* (1)
Admatha (1)

149 אֶדֶן *'eden* (58)
bases (41)
base (2)
footings (1)
those[S] (1)
untranslated (13)

150 אַדָּן *'addān* (1)
Addon (1)

151 אֲדֹנָי *'adōnāy* (442)
sovereign (291)
the Lord (91)
Lord (57)
the Lord's (3)

152 אֲדֹנִי בֶזֶק *'adōniy bezeq* (3)
Adoni-Bezek (3)

153 אֲדֹנִיָּה *'adōniyyāh* (7)
Adonijah (7)

154 אֲדֹנִיָּהוּ *'adōniyyāhû* (19)
Adonijah (17)
Adonijah's (1) +4200
untranslated (1)

155 אֲדֹנִי־צֶדֶק *'adōniy-sedeq* (2)
Adoni-Zedek (2)

156 אֲדֹנִיקָם *'adōniyqām* (3)
Adonikam (3)

157 אֲדֹנִירָם *'adōniyrām* (4)
Adoniram (4)

158 אָדַר *'ādar* (3)
majestic (2)
glorious (1)

159 אֶדֶר *'eder* (2)
handsome (1)
rich (1)

160 אֲדָר *'adār* (8)
Adar (8)

161 1אַדָּר *'addār1* (1)
Addar (1)

162 2אַדָּר *'addār2* (1)
Addar (1)

163 אֲדַרְכֹנִים *'adarkōniym* (2)
darics (2)

164 אֲדֹרָם *'adōrām*
Variant; not used

165 1אַדְרַמֶּלֶךְ *'adrammelek1* (1)
Adrammelech (1)

166 2אַדְרַמֶּלֶךְ *'adrammelek2* (2)
Adrammelech (2)

167 אֶדְרֶעִי *'edre'iy* (8)
Edrei (8)

168 אַדֶּרֶת *'adderet* (12)
cloak (5)
robe (2)
garment (1)
prophet's garment (1)
rich pastures (1)
royal robes (1)
splendid (1)

169 אָדַשׁ *'ādaš*
Variant; not used

170 אָהַב *'āhab* (217)
love (93)
loves (38)
loved (33)
lovers (12)
friends (8)
allies (4)
friend (4)
in love with (3)
fell in love with (2)
like (2)
liked (2)
adore (1)
attracted to (1)
both[S] (1) +2021+2021+2256+8533
chosen ally (1)
dearly (1)
desires (1)
likes (1)
on friendly terms (1)
resents (1) +4202
show love (1)
showed love (1)
value (1)
was loved (1)
were loved (1)
untranslated (2)

171 אֹהַב *'ōhab* (2)
love (1)
thing loved (1)

172 אַהַב *'ahab* (2)
lovers (1)
loving (1)

173 1אַהֲבָה *'ahᵃbāh1* (33)
love (26)
friendship (2)
loved (2)
lovingly (1)
that[S] (1)
untranslated (1)

174 2אַהֲבָה *'ahᵃbāh2*
Variant; not used

175 אֲהַבְהָבַי *'ahabhābay*
Variant; not used

176 אֹהַד *'ōhad* (2)
Ohad (2)

177 אֲהָהּ *'ahāh* (15)
Ah (9)
oh (3)
Alas (1)
not so (1)
what (1)

178 אַהֲוָא *'ahᵃwā'* (3)
Ahava (3)

179 אֵהוּד *'ēhûd* (9)
Ehud (8)
untranslated (1)

180 אֱהִי *'ᵉhiy* (3)
where (2)
where (1) +686

181 אֶהְיֶה *'ehyeh*
Variant; not used

182 1אָהַל *'āhal1* (3)
moved tents (1)
pitch tent (1)
pitched tents (1)

183 2אָהַל *'āhal2* (1)
bright (1)

184 אָהָל *'āhāl*
Variant; not used

185 1אֹהֶל *'ōhel1* (351)
tent (260)
tents (45)
home (10)

homes (9)
dwellings (3)
it[S] (3) +2021
house (2)
tabernacle (2)
another[S] (1)
broke camp (1) +4946+5825
camps (1)
house (1) +1074
household (1)
nomads (1) +928+8905
sanctuary (1)
tent site (1)
tent-dwelling (1) +928+2021
untranslated (8)

186 2אֹהֶל *'ōhel2* (1)
Ohel (1)

187 אֵהֶל *'ēhel*
Variant; not used

188 אָהֳלָה *'oh[o]lāh* (5)
Oholah (5)

189 אֲהָלוֹת *'[a]hālôt* (2)
aloes (2)

190 אָהֳלִיאָב *'oh[o]liy'āb* (5)
Oholiab (5)

191 אָהֳלִיבָה *'oh[o]liybāh* (6)
Oholibah (6)

192 אָהֳלִיבָמָה *'oh[o]liybāmāh* (8)
Oholibamah (8)

193 1אֲהָלִים *'[a]hāliym1* (2)
aloes (2)

194 2אֲהָלִים *'[a]hāliym2*
Variant; not used

195 אַהֲרֹן *'ah[a]rôn* (347)
Aaron (300)
Aaron's (31)
he[S] (5)
his[S] (3)
Aaron's (1) +4200
Aaronic (1) +1201
family of Aaron (1)
him[S] (1)
untranslated (4)

196 אוֹ *'ô* (320)
or (247)
whether or (13)
either or (4)
if (3)
when (3)
whether (3)
and (2)
also (1)
at all (1) +1524+7785
either (1)
if (1) +4537
nor (1)
or else (1)
or so (1)
over a year (1) +2296+2296+3427+9102
rather than (1)
which way (1) +3545+6584+6584+8520
untranslated (35)

197 אַו *'aw* (1)
crave (1)

198 אוּאֵל *'û'ēl* (1)
Uel (1)

199 1אוֹב *'ôb1* (1)
wineskins (1)

200 2אוֹב *'ôb2* (16)
mediums (9)
medium (2)
ghostlike (1) +3869
medium (1) +1266
medium (1) +8626
one[S] (1) +1266
spirit (1)

201 אוֹבִיל *'ôbiyl* (1)
Obil (1)

202 אוּד *'ûd* (3)
burning stick (2)
firewood (1)

203 1אָוָה *'āwāh1* (29)
crave (4)
desired (3)
desires (3)
craves (2)
longed for (2)
crave other food (1) +9294
craved other food (1)
craves for more (1) +9294
desire (1)
enthralled (1)
gave in to craving (1) +9294
like (1)
long for (1)
pleases (1)
set desire on (1)
want (1)
yearns for (1)
untranslated (3)

204 2אָוָה *'āwāh2* (1)
run a line (1)

205 אַוָּה *'awwāh* (7)
want (3)
craving (1) +5883
earnestness (1) +5883
please (1)
pleases (1)

206 אוּזַי *'ûzay* (1)
Uzai (1)

207 אוּזָל *'ûzāl* (3)
Uzal (3)

208 אוֹי *'ôy* (24)
woe (19)
Alas (2)
Ah (1)
alas (1)
in trouble (1)

209 אֱוִי *'[e]wiy* (2)
Evi (2)

210 אוֹיָה *'ôyāh* (1)
woe (1)

211 1אֱוִיל *'[e]wiyl1* (25)
fool (16)
fools (7)
fool's (1)
wicked fools (1)

212 2אֱוִיל *'[e]wiyl2*
Variant; not used

213 אֱוִיל מְרֹדַךְ *'[e]wiyl m[e]rōdak* (2)
Evil-Merodach (2)

214 1אוּל *'ûl1* (1)
bodies (1)

215 2אוּל *'ûl2* (1)
untranslated (1)

216 אֱוִלִי *'[e]wiliy* (1)
foolish (1)

217 1אוּלַי *'ûlay1* (2)
Ulai (2)

218 2אוּלַי *'ûlay2* (45)
perhaps (25)
what if (9)
it may be (3)
maybe (3)
but (1)
but perhaps (1)
if not (1)
may yet (1)
were it to (1)

219 1אוּלָם *'ûlām1* (19)
but (5) +2256
but (4)
nevertheless (2) +2256
though (2)
but if (1)
however (1) +2256
if (1)
otherwise (1)
yet (1)
untranslated (1)

220 2אוּלָם *'ûlām2* (4)
Ulam (4)

221 3אוּלָם *'ûlām3*
Variant; not used

222 אִוֶּלֶת *'iwwelet* (25)
folly (22)
foolish (2)
sinful folly (1)

223 אוֹמָר *'ômār* (3)
Omar (3)

224 אָוֶן *'āwen* (77)
evil (23)
evildoers (16) +7188
wicked (6)
sin (3)
wrong (3)
calamity (1)
deceit (1)
disaster (1)
distress (1)
evildoer (1) +7188
false (1)
hardship (1)
harm (1)
idol (1)
iniquity (1)
injustice (1)
malice (1)
malicious (1)
misfortune (1)
nothing (1)
on no account (1) +6584
punishment (1)
sins (1)
slander (1)
sorrow (1)
suffering (1)
trouble (1)
unjust (1)
villain (1) +408
wicked men (1) +7188
wickedness (1)

225 2אָוֶן *'āwen2* (2)
Aven (1)
Heliopolis (1)

226 1אוֹן *'ôn1* (12)
power (3)
manhood (2)
man (1)
sign of strength (1)
strength (1)
vigor (1)
weak (1) +401
wealth (1)
wealthy (1)

227 2אוֹן *'ôn2* (1)
on (1)

228 3אוֹן *'ôn3* (3)
on (3)

229 אוֹנוֹ *'ônô* (5)
Ono (5)

230 אוֹנִי *'ôniy* (1)
mourners (1)

231 אוֹנָם *'ônām* (4)
Onam (4)

232 אוֹנָן *'ônān* (8)
Onan (7)
untranslated (1)

233 אוּפָז *'ûp̱āz* (2)
finest gold (1) +4188
Uphaz (1)

234 1אוֹפִיר *'ôp̱iyr1* (13)
Ophir (11)
gold of Ophir (1)
there[s] (1)

235 2אוֹפִיר *'ôp̱iyr2*
Variant; not used

236 אוֹפַן *'ôp̱an* (35)
wheels (23)
wheel (8)
cartwheel (1) +6322
untranslated (3)

237 אוּץ *'ûs* (10)
delayed (1) +4202
eager (1)
haste (1)
hasty (1) +928+8079
in haste (1)
pressing (1)
run (1)
small (1)
try (1)
urged (1)

238 אוֹצָר *'ôsār* (79)
treasures (22)
treasuries (20)
storehouses (9)
treasury (7)
riches (2)
storehouse (2)
supplies (2)
treasure (2)
arsenal (1)
fortune (1)
put in charge of the storerooms (1) +732+6584
storehouse (1) +1074
storerooms (1)
storerooms (1) +4200+5969
stores (1)
treasury (1) +1074
vats (1)
vaults (1)
wealth (1)
untranslated (2)

239 1אוֹר *'ôr1* (45)
shine (8)
give light (6)
make shine (6)
light (4)
brightened (2)
gives light (2)
brightens (1)
dawned (1)
daybreak (1)
give light (1) +240
gives sight (1)
giving light (1)
keep burning (1)
leaves glistening (1)
light fires (1)
lights up (1)
lit up (1)
look with favor (1) +7156
made light shine (1)
make fires (1)
radiant (1)
resplendent with light (1)
shining ever brighter (1) +2143+2256

240 2אוֹר *'ôr2* (119)
light (83)
lightning (7)
daybreak (3) +1332+2021
daylight (3)
dawn (2) +1332+2021
shining (2)
sun (2)
brightens (1)
broad daylight (1) +3427
dawn (1)
daybreak (1)
daylight (1) +1332+2021
give light (1) +239
gleam (1)
glint (1)
lamp (1)
light of day (1)
lights (1)
new day (1)
shine (1) +2118
sunlight (1) +2780
sunrise (1)
sunshine (1)
untranslated (1)

241 1אוּר *'ûr1* (6)
fire (4)
east (1)
light (1)

242 2אוּר *'ûr2* (7)
Urim (7)

243 3אוּר *'ûr3* (4)
Ur (4)

244 4אוּר *'ûr4* (1)
Ur (1)

245 1אוֹרָה *'ôrāh1* (3)
light (1)
morning (1)
time of happiness (1)

246 2אוֹרָה *'ôrāh2* (1)
herbs (1)

247 אוּרִי *'ûriy* (7)
Uri (7)

248 אוּרִיאֵל *'ûriy'ēl* (4)
Uriel (4)

249 אוּרִיָּה *'ûriyyāh* (36)
Uriah (29)
him[s] (3)
Uriah's (2)
untranslated (2)

250 אוּרִיָּהוּ *'ûriyyāhû* (3)
Uriah (3)

251 אוּרִים *'ûriym*
Variant; not used

252 אוּת *'ûṯ* (4)
give consent (2)
agreed (1)
consent (1)

253 1אוֹת *'ôṯ1* (79)
sign (36)
miraculous signs (17)
signs (14)
miraculous sign (3)
symbols (2)
accounts (1)
banners (1)
example (1)
mark (1)
standards (1)
wonders (1)
untranslated (1)

254 2אוֹת *'ôṯ2*
Variant; not used

255 אָז *'āz* (141)
then (65)
at that time (11)
and (5)
long ago (5) +4946
ever since (2) +4946
now (2)
since (2) +4946
so (2)
time (2)
about this time (1)
after (1)
already (1)
already (1) +4946
and (1) +2256
distant past (1)
from (1) +4946
meanwhile (1)
now (1) +4946
of old (1)
old (1)
once (1)
past (1)
that will mean (1)
thus (1)
when (1) +4946
untranslated (29)

256 אֶזְבַּי *'ezbāy* (1)
Ezbai (1)

257 אֵזוֹב *'ēzôḇ* (10)
hyssop (10)

258 אֵזוֹר *'ēzôr* (14)
belt (9)
belt (1) +5516
belts (1) +2513
it[s] (1) +2021
loincloth (1)
sash (1)

259 אֲזַי *'ᵃzay* (3)
untranslated (3)

260 אַזְכָּרָה *'azkārāh* (7)
memorial portion (6)
memorial offering (1)

261 אָזַל *'āzal* (5)
gone (2)
disappears (1)
go about (1)
off goes (1)

262 אֶזֶל *'ezel* (1)
Ezel (1)

263 1אָזַן *'āzan1* (41)
listen (19)
hear (11)
pay attention (3)
give ear (2)
ear perceived (1)
give a hearing (1) +7754
listened (1)
paid attention (1)
pays attention (1)
turned a deaf ear (1) +4202

264 2אָזַן *'āzan2* (1)
pondered (1)

265 אֹזֶן *'ōzen* (188)
ears (58)
ear (25)
hearing (24)
to (19) +928
pay attention (7) +5742
give ear (6) +5742
heard (3) +928
before (2) +928
let know (2) +906+1655
listen (2) +5742
revealed (2) +1655
tells (2) +906+1655

they[S] (2)
bring to attention (1) +1655
confiding in (1) +906+1655
ear lobe (1)
hear (1) +5742
heard (1)
heard (1) +606+928
in person (1) +928
listen (1) +7992
listen carefully (1) +928+9048
listen closely (1) +928+9048
listen closely (1) +5742
listen well (1) +5742
listened (1) +928
listened attentively to (1) +448
listens (1) +9048
make sure hears (1) +928+8492
makes listen (1) +1655
news (1) +2245
paid any attention (1) +4200+5742+9048
paid attention (1) +5742
revealed (1) +906+1655
speaks (1) +1655
tell (1) +906+1655
tell (1) +928+1819
told (1) +928+1819
wearing (1) +928
whoever[S] (1)
untranslated (7)

266 **אָזֵן** *'āzēn* (1)
equipment (1)

267 **אֻזֵּן שֶׁאֱרָה** *'uzzēn še'ᵉrāh* (1)
Uzzen Sheerah (1)

268 **אַזְנוֹת תָּבוֹר** *'aznôt̲ tāb̲ôr* (1)
Aznoth Tabor (1)

269 1**אָזְנִי** *'āzniy1* (1)
Ozni (1)

270 2**אָזְנִי** *'āzniy2* (1)
Oznite (1)

271 **אֲזַנְיָה** *'ᵃzanyāh* (1)
Azaniah (1)

272 **אֲזִקִּים** *'ᵃziqqiym* (2)
chains (2)

273 **אָזַר** *'āzar* (17)
armed (4)
arms (2)
brace (2) +2743
prepare for battle (2)
armed yourself (1)
binds (1)
clothed (1)
get ready (1) +5516
provide (1)
strengthen (1)
untranslated (1)

274 **אֶזְרוֹעַ** *'ezrôa'* (2)
arm (1)
it[S] (1) +3276

275 **אֶזְרָח** *'ezrāh* (17)
native-born (12)
born (1)
citizens (1)
native soil (1)
native-born (1) +824
native-born (1) +824+2021

276 **אֶזְרָחִי** *'ezrāhiy* (3)
Ezrahite (3)

277 1**אָח** *'āh1* (2)
Alas (1)
oh (1)

278 2**אָח** *'āh2* (632)
brother (211)
brothers (201)
relatives (67)
fellow (19)
associates (17)
brother's (17)
other[S] (15)
countrymen (10)
another[S] (7)
fellow countrymen (5)
kinsmen (5)
relative (5)
family (3)
people (3)
brother Israelite (2)
countryman (2)
cousins (2)
friends (2)
he[S] (2) +3870
nephew (2) +1201
others[S] (2)
among yourselves (1) +408+448
anyone else[S] (1)
associate (1)
brother Israelites (1)
brotherhood (1)
brothers (1) +562
companions (1)
each (1) +408+2257
equally (1) +408+2257+3869
equally among them (1) +408+2257+3869
families (1)
fellow Jews (1)
fellow Levites (1)
him[S] (1) +3870
people from Benjamin (1) +2157
people from Judah (1) +2157
priests[S] (1) +2157
them[S] (1)
them[S] (1) +2257
two men (1) +408+2256+3481
uncle (1)
uncle's (1) +562
very own brother (1) +562+1201+3870
untranslated (10)

279 **אַח** *'ah* (3)
firepot (2)
untranslated (1)

280 **אֹחַ** *'ōah* (1)
jackals (1)

281 **אַחְאָב** *'ah'āb̲* (92)
Ahab (79)
Ahab's (7)
he[S] (3)
he[S] (1) +1201+6687
untranslated (2)

282 **אֶחָב** *'ehāb̲* (1)
Ahab (1)

283 **אַחְבָּן** *'ahbān* (1)
Ahban (1)

284 **אָחַד** *'āhad̲*
Variant; not used

285 **אֶחָד** *'ehād̲* (976)
one (466)
a (78)
each (58)
first (39)
same (32)
other[S] (27)
any (16)
single (13)
another[S] (12)
eleven (6) +6926
once (6)
the (6)
certain (5)
an (4)
eleventh (4) +6926
forty-one (4) +752+2256
man[S] (4)
only (4)
twenty-first (4) +2256+6929
twenty-one (4) +2256+6929
unit (4)
any (3) +3972
common (3)
eleven (3) +6925
next (3)
once (3) +7193
one and the same (3)
some (3)
thirty-one (3) +2256+8993
together (3) +285+448
41,500 (2) +547+752+2256+2256+2822+4395
621 (2) +2256+4395+6929+9252
agree (2) +2118+3869
alike (2)
all (2)
identical (2)
numbered (2) +3869
second (2)
the other[S] (2)
unique (2)
yearly (2) +928+9102
151,450 (1) +547+547+752+2256+2256 +2256+2256+2822+2822+4395+4395
61 (1) +2256+9252
61,000 (1) +547+2256+9252
721 (1) +2256+2256+4395+6929+8679
all (1) +928
all the same (1)
all together (1) +408+3869
alone (1) +928
annual (1) +928+2021+9102
another (1)
appointed (1)
back and forth (1) +285+2178+2178+2256
daily (1) +3427+4200
did the same[S] (1) +285+448+2489
each one (1)
equally (1) +3869
fellow[S] (1)
few (1)
for a while (1) +3427
forty-first (1) +752+2256
in unison (1) +3869
joined together (1) +3869+6641
none (1) +4202
once for all (1)
one time (1)
one way (1) +928
one-tenth (1) +6928
only a few (1)
over here (1) +4200+6298
over there (1) +4200+6298
same one (1)
shoulder to shoulder (1) +8900
singleness (1)
some other[S] (1)
someone (1)
someone (1) +2021+6639
suddenly (1) +928
third[S] (1)
thirty-first (1) +2256+8993
time and again (1) +2256+4202+4202+9109
together (1) +3869
undivided (1)
unheard-of (1)
unity (1)
whatever[S] (1)
wherever (1) +889+928+2021+5226
whose[S] (1) +2021+2021+9108
untranslated (81)

286 **אָחוּ** *'āhû* (3)
reeds (3)

287 **אֵחוּד** *'ēhûd̲* (1)
Ehud (1)

288 1**אַחֲוָה** *'ahᵃwāh1* (1)
brotherhood (1)

289 2**אַחֲוָה** *'ahᵃwāh2* (1)
what say (1)

290 אָחוּז *'āhûz*
Variant; not used

291 אֲחוֹחַ *'ahôah* (1)
Ahoah (1)

292 אֲחוֹחִי *'ahôhiy* (5)
Ahohite (4)
Ahohite (1) +1201

293 אֲחוּמַי *'ahûmay* (1)
Ahumai (1)

294 אָחוֹר *'āhôr* (41)
back (14)
backs (2)
backward (2)
behind (2)
hindquarters (2)
rear (2)
west (2)
away (1)
backsliding (1)
backward (1) +4200
behind (1) +4946
deserted (1) +6047
drawn back (1) +6047
future (1)
is driven back (1) +6047
made retreat (1) +8740
on both sides (1) +2256+7156
overthrows (1) +8740
retreating (1) +6047
time to come (1)
under control (1) +928
withdrawn (1) +8740

295 אָחוֹת *'āhôt* (119)
sister (88)
sisters (11)
other[S] (4)
sister's (4)
together (2) +448+851
another[S] (1)
untranslated (9)

296 1אָחַז *'āhaz1* (65)
seized (9)
grip (4)
seizes (3)
caught (2)
grips (2)
hold (2)
seize (2)
supports (2)
take (2)
took (2)
took hold (2)
accept possession (1)
acquire property (1)
acquired (1)
acquired property (1)
are caught (1)
are taken (1)
bar (1)
being taken (1)
catch (1)
clinging (1)
closely followed (1)
did so[S] (1)
embracing (1)
fastened (1)
grasp (1)
grasping (1)
grasps (1)
handle (1)
held (1)
hold fast (1)
hold out (1)
in (1)
inserted (1)
kept from closing (1) +9073
see (1)
share (1)
steady (1)
take hold (1)
take on (1)
wearing (1)
untranslated (3)

297 2אָחַז *'āhaz2* (3)
attached to (1)
covers (1)
was attached (1)

298 אָחָז *'āhāz* (42)
Ahaz (41)
untranslated (1)

299 אֲחֻזָּה *'ahuzzāh* (66)
property (28)
possession (14)
land (4) +824
possess (4)
family land (3) +8441
place (2)
site (2)
family property (1)
hold (1)
hold as a possession (1)
lands (1)
occupied (1)
property (1) +824
territory (1)
that[S] (1)
untranslated (1)

300 אַחְזַי *'ahzay* (1)
Ahzai (1)

301 אֲחַזְיָה *'ahazyāh* (7)
Ahaziah (7)

302 אֲחַזְיָהוּ *'ahazyāhû* (31)
Ahaziah (27)
Ahaziah's (4)

303 אֲחֻזָּם *'ahuzzām* (1)
Ahuzzam (1)

304 אֲחֻזַּת *'ahuzzat* (1)
Ahuzzath (1)

305 אֵחִי *'ēhiy* (1)
Ehi (1)

306 אֲחִי *'ahiy* (2)
Ahi (2)

307 אֲחִיאָם *'ahiy'ām* (2)
Ahiam (2)

308 אֲחִיָּה *'ahiyyāh* (18)
Ahijah (16)
Ahiah (1)
Ahijah's (1)

309 אֲחִיָּהוּ *'ahiyyāhû* (5)
Ahijah (5)

310 אֲחִיהוּד *'ahiyhûd* (1)
Ahihud (1)

311 אַחְיוֹ *'ahyô* (6)
Ahio (6)

312 אֲחִיחֻד *'ahiyhud* (1)
Ahihud (1)

313 אֲחִיטוּב *'ahiytûb* (15)
Ahitub (15)

314 אֲחִילוּד *'ahiylûd* (5)
Ahilud (5)

315 אֲחִימוֹת *'ahiymôt* (1)
Ahimoth (1)

316 אֲחִימֶלֶךְ *'ahiymelek* (18)
Ahimelech (18)

317 אֲחִימַן *'ahiyman* (4)
Ahiman (4)

318 אֲחִימַעַץ *'ahiyma'as* (15)
Ahimaaz (15)

319 אַחְיָן *'ahyān* (1)
Ahian (1)

320 אֲחִינָדָב *'ahiynādāb* (1)
Ahinadab (1)

321 אֲחִינֹעַם *'ahiynō'am* (7)
Ahinoam (7)

322 אֲחִיסָמָךְ *'ahiysāmāk* (3)
Ahisamach (3)

323 אֲחִיעֶזֶר *'ahiy'ezer* (6)
Ahiezer (6)

324 אֲחִיקָם *'ahiyqām* (20)
Ahikam (20)

325 אֲחִירָם *'ahiyrām* (1)
Ahiram (1)

326 אֲחִירָמִי *'ahiyrāmiy* (1)
Ahiramite (1)

327 אֲחִירַע *'ahiyra'* (5)
Ahira (5)

328 אֲחִישַׁחַר *'ahiyšahar* (1)
Ahishahar (1)

329 אֲחִישָׁר *'ahiyšār* (1)
Ahishar (1)

330 אֲחִיתֹפֶל *'ahiytōpel* (20)
Ahithophel (17)
Ahithophel's (3)

331 אַחְלָב *'ahlāb* (1)
Ahlab (1)

332 אַחֲלַי *'ahalay* (2)
if only (1)
oh that (1)

333 אַחְלָי *'ahlāy* (2)
Ahlai (2)

334 אַחְלָמָה *'ahlāmāh* (2)
amethyst (2)

335 אֲחַסְבַּי *'ahasbay* (1)
Ahasbai (1)

336 אָחַר *'āhar* (17)
delay (5)
delayed (2)
slow (2)
detain (1)
hold back (1)
late (1)
linger (1)
lost time (1)
remained (1)
stay up late (1)
took longer (1)

337 1אַחֵר *'ahēr1* (166)
other (83)
another (39)
others (12)
else (4)
next (4)
another (3) +6388
different (2)
more (2)
more (2) +6388
additional (1)
changed (1) +2200
new (1)
other gods (1)
second (1)
set farther back (1) +2021+2958
someone else (1)
someone else's (1)
strange (1)
sword[S] (1)
various (1)
what[S] (1)
untranslated (3)

338 2אַחֵר *'ahēr2* (1)
Aher (1)

339 אַחַר *'ahar* (716)
after (205)
behind (42)
followed (27) +2143
follow (20) +2143
next to (17)
with (16)
afterward (14) +4027
to (13)
follow (12)
from (12) +4946
followed (11)
following (11)
after that (10)
then (10)
behind (9) +4946
in the course of time (8) +4027
afterward (7)
back (6)
followed (6) +995
following (6) +2143
some time later (6) +465+1821+2021+2021
pursue (5)
pursuing (5)
since (5)
after (4) +4027
of (4)
west (4)
later (3)
later (3) +4027
now (3)
some time later (3) +4027
succeed (3)
after this (2)
against (2)
around (2)
away from (2) +4946
back (2) +4946
beyond (2)
chasing (2)
finished (2)
flee (2)
follow (2) +2118
followers (2)
follows (2) +995
in addition to (2)
join (2)
outlived (2) +799+3427
pursue (2) +8938
pursuing (2) +4946
rear (2)
tending (2)
then (2) +4027
after (1) +4946
after a while (1) +465+1821+2021+2021
after the time of (1)
afterward (1) +4026
again (1)
at (1)
back (1) +7155
backs (1)
butt (1)
calling to arms (1) +2410
chasing (1) +1944
departing from (1) +4946
descendants (1)
deserted (1) +4946+6590
devoted to (1) +2143
ends up (1)
ever (1)
far side (1)
follow (1) +995
follow (1) +1815
follow (1) +3655
follow (1) +4946+7756
follow (1) +6296
follow (1) +7756
followed (1) +2118
followed (1) +3655
followed (1) +7756
followed in (1) +995
followers (1) +889+2021+6639
followers (1) +2143
follows (1)
follows (1) +4027
for (1)
from then on (1) +4027+4946
future (1)
gave support (1) +6468
go over the branches a second time (1) +6994
go over the vines again (1) +6618
greedy (1) +2143
how long (1) +5503+6388
imitated (1)
in (1)
in hot pursuit (1)
in the course of time (1) +4027+4946
last of all (1)
later (1) +465+1821+2021+2021
later (1) +2296
later (1) +4027+4946
lead on (1) +3870
lead to do the same[S] (1) +466+2177+2388
leaves behind (1)
led (1) +2143
left (1) +4946
loyal to (1)
lust after (1) +2388
lusted after (1) +2388
next (1)
next after (1)
next in line (1)
over (1)
pursue (1) +2143
pursue (1) +3655
pursued (1) +2143
pursuing (1) +2143
pursuit (1)
right behind (1)
runs after for favors (1) +2388
shortly after (1)
since (1) +889
some time after (1)
some time later (1)
succeeded (1)
successive years (1) +9102+9102
successor (1)
successor (1) +132+995+8611
supported (1)
supported (1) +2118
then (1) +2256
those[S] (1) +889+2021+6639
toward (1)
under the command of (1)
when (1)
worshiping (1)
untranslated (83)

340 אחרון *'ah[a]rôn* (51)
last (11)
end (10)
next (4)
western (4)
future (2)
later (2)
rear (2)
second (2)
then (2) +928+2021
to come (2)
end (1) +928+2021+2118
follow (1)
he[S] (1) +408+2021+2021
later (1) +928+2021
present (1)
then (1)
this[S] (1)
time (1)
west (1)
yet to come (1)

341 אַחְרַח *'ahrah* (1)
Aharah (1)

342 אֲחַרְחֵל *'[a]harhēl* (1)
Aharhel (1)

343 אַחֲרַי *'ah[a]ray* (1)
in the end (1)

344 אַחֲרִית *'ah[a]riyṯ* (61)
end (20)
to come (8)
future (7)
last (4)
future hope (3)
left (3)
descendants (2)
at last (1)
end of life (1)
far side (1)
final destiny (1)
final outcome (1)
future (1) +3427
later (1)
later in time (1) +928
latter part (1)
latter part of life (1)
least (1)
outcome (1)
what happens (1)
what might happen (1)

345 אֲחֹרַנִּית *'[a]horanniyṯ* (7)
back (2)
backward (2)
go back (1) +8740
gone down (1) +3718
turned the other way (1)

346 אֲחַשְׁדַּרְפָּן *'[a]hašdarpān* (4)
satraps (4)

347 אֲחַשְׁוֵרוֹשׁ *'[a]hašwērôš* (31)
Xerxes (31)

348 אֲחַשְׁרֹשׁ *'[a]hašērōš* (1)
untranslated (1)

349 אֲחַשְׁתָּרִי *'[a]haštāriy*
Variant; not used

350 אֲחַשְׁתְּרָן *'[a]hašt[e]rān* (2)
for king (1)
royal (1)

351 1אַט *'at1* (5)
gently (2) +4200
gentle (1)
meekly (1)
slowly (1) +4200

352 2אַט *'at2*
Variant; not used

353 1אָטָד *'ātāḏ1* (4)
thornbush (3)
thorns (1)

354 2אָטָד *'ātāḏ2* (2)
Atad (2)

355 אֵטוּן *'ētûn* (1)
linen (1)

356 אִטִּים *'ittiym* (1)
spirits of the dead (1)

357 אָטַם *'ātam* (8)
narrow (4)
holds (1)
shuts (1)
stopped (1)
stops (1)

358 אָטַר *'ātar* (1)
close (1)

359 אָטֵר *'ātēr* (5)
Ater (5)

360 אִטֵּר *'ittēr* (2)
left-handed (2) +3338+3545

361 אִי *'ēy* (40)
where (16)
where (9) +2296
what (3) +2296
which (2) +2296
by what (1) +2296
no more (1)
what (1)
where (1) +5226
which way (1) +2006+2021+2296
which way (1) +2296
why (1) +2296+4200
untranslated (3)

362 1אִי *'iy1* (36)
islands (15)
coastlands (8)
coasts (5)
island (2)
coast (1)
distant shores (1)
distant shores (1) +3542
maritime (1)
shore (1)
shores (1)

363 2אִי *'iy2* (3)
hyenas (3)

364 3אִי *'iy3* (1)
not (1)

365 4אִי *'iy4* (2)
pity (1)
woe (1)

366 אָיַב *'āyaḇ* (1)
enemy (1)

367 אֹיֵב *'ōyēḇ* (284)
enemies (191)
enemy (70)
foes (12)
foe (3)
enemy's (1)
his own[s] (1) +2021
their[s] (1) +3870
whom[s] (1)
untranslated (4)

368 אֵיבָה *'ēyḇāh* (5)
hostility (4)
enmity (1)

369 אֵיד *'ēyḏ* (24)
disaster (16)
calamity (3)
destruction (2)
fall (1)
ruin (1)
siege ramps (1) +784

370 1אַיָּה *'ayyāh1* (4)
black kite (2)
falcon's (1)
vultures (1)

371 2אַיָּה *'ayyāh2* (6)
Aiah (4)
Aiah's (2)

372 אַיֵּה *'ayyēh* (44)
where (43)
untranslated (1)

373 אִיּוֹב *'iyyôḇ* (58)
Job (49)
Job's (5)
he[s] (3)
untranslated (1)

374 אִיזֶבֶל *'iyzeḇel* (22)
Jezebel (18)
Jezebel's (3)
she[s] (1)

375 אֵיךְ *'ēyḵ* (61)
how (47)
why (6)
what (4)
how gladly (1)
too (1)
what else (1)
untranslated (1)

376 אִיכָבוֹד *'iyḵāḇôḏ* (2)
Ichabod (1)
Ichabod's (1)

377 אֵיכָה *'ēyḵāh* (17)
how (12)
where (2)
but how (1)
see how (1)
what (1)

378 אֵיכֹה *'ēyḵōh* (1)
where (1)

379 אֵיכָכָה *'ēyḵāḵāh* (4)
how (2)
untranslated (2)

380 1אַיִל *'ayil1* (161)
ram (88)
rams (61)
its[s] (4) +2021
it[s] (2) +2021
leading men (2)
leaders (1)
ruler (1)
rulers (1)
untranslated (1)

381 2אַיִל *'ayil2* (5)
oaks (4)
sacred oaks (1)

382 3אַיִל *'ayil3* (30)
jambs (9)
projecting walls (9)
jambs (1) +4647
untranslated (11)

383 4אַיִל *'ayil4*
Variant; not used

384 אֱיָל *'ĕyāl* (1)
strength (1)

385 אַיָּל *'ayyāl* (12)
deer (9)
young stag (3) +6762

386 אֵיל פָּארָן *'ēyl pā'rān* (1)
El Paran (1)

387 אַיָּלָה *'ayyālāh* (10)
doe (5)
deer (3)
does (2)

388 אֵילוֹ *'iylô*
Variant; not used

389 אַיָּלוֹן *'ayyālôn* (10)
Aijalon (10)

390 1אֵילוֹן *'ēylôn1* (4)
Elon (4)

391 2אֵילוֹן *'ēylôn2* (1)
Elon (1)

392 אֵילוֹן בֵּית חָנָן *'ēylôn bēyṯ ḥānān* (1)
Elon Bethhanan (1)

393 אֵילוֹת *'ēylôṯ* (4)
Elath (3)
untranslated (1)

394 אֱיָלוּת *'ĕyālûṯ* (1)
strength (1)

395 אֵילָם *'ēylām* (64)
portico (44)
hall (3)
colonnade (1) +6647
porticoes (1)
temple porch (1)
untranslated (14)

396 אֵילִם *'ēylim* (6)
Elim (5)
where[s] (1) +928

397 אֵילַת *'ēylaṯ* (4)
Elath (4)

398 אָיֹם *'āyōm* (3)
majestic (2)
feared (1)

399 אֵימָה *'ēymāh* (17)
terror (7)
terrors (4)
fear (2)
dreadful (1)
fearsome (1)
great fear (1)
wrath (1)

400 אֵימִים *'ēymiym* (3)
Emites (3)

401 1אַיִן *'ayin1* (790)
no (209)
there is no (98)
not (93)
nothing (32)
there was no (29)
without (29)
is not (20)
none (10)
cannot (9)
without (9) +4946
gone (8)
there will be no (8)
be no more (7)
never (7)
lack (6)
there is none (6)
are no more (5)
beyond (5)
don't (5)
is no more (5)
neither (5)
be no (4)
is no (4)
is there no (4)
no (4) +4946
nor (4) +2256
there is not (4)
there was none (4)
there were no (4)
were not (4)
it is not (3)
nothing (3) +3972
there is no (3) +1172
was not (3)
is that not (2)
is there not (2)
isn't (2)
it's not (2)
lacks (2)
none (2) +408
nothing (2) +1821
nothing (2) +4399
senseless (2) +4213
there are no (2)
there is nothing (2)
there is nothing (2) +4399
there was not (2)
there was nothing (2)
there will be none (2)
was no more (2)
was there no (2)
waterless (2) +4784
without (2) +928
won't (2)
all alone (1) +9108
allowed (1) +646
am no more (1)

any[S] (1)
are not (1)
aren't (1)
bare (1) +928+4399
be nothing (1) +1194
before (1) +3954
boundless (1) +7897
cannot (1) +3946
countless (1) +5031
deserted (1) +132+4946
deserted (1) +3782
deserted (1) +3782+4946
disappeared (1)
endless (1) +7891
endless (1) +7897
fatherless (1) +3
free from (1)
gone from (1) +907
here are no (1)
in vain (1)
incomprehensible (1) +1069
incurable (1) +5340
innumerable (1) +5031
is never (1)
is nothing (1)
isn't there (1)
it was impossible (1)
it was not (1)
kept secret (1) +5583
lack (1) +928
lack (1) +4200
loses (1)
more (1) +4200
more than (1) +4200
naught (1)
nearly (1) +3869
neither (1) +4946
never (1) +4200+6409
none (1) +4946
none will be (1) +4946
nor (1) +677
nor (1) +1685+2256
nor (1) +2256+4946
nothing at all (1) +700+2256
nothing whatever (1) +1821+3972
or (1)
or (1) +561+2256
otherwise (1) +561
powerless (1) +445+3338+4200
powerless (1) +445+4200
powerless (1) +3946
regardless (1) +4200+9068
so[S] (1)
surely (1) +561
than (1)
there is neither (1)
there is no (1) +3972
there is no (1) +4946
there is nothing (1) +3972
there were no (1) +1172
there were not (1)
there will not be (1)
too (1)
unclean (1) +3196
uncovered (1) +1064
unless (1)
unsearchable (1) +2984
was no (1)
weak (1) +226
will not (1)
without (1) +4200
without (1) +6330
without any payment (1) +2855
without equal (1) +3202+4946
worthless (1) +2914
wouldn't (1)
untranslated (18)

402 2אַיִן *'ayin2* (17)
where (12)
where (5) +4946

403 אִין *'iyn* (1)
don't (1)

404 אִיעֶזֶר *'iy'ezer* (1)
Iezer (1)

405 אִיעֶזְרִי *'iy'ezriy* (1)
Iezerite (1)

406 אֵיפָה *'ēyp̱āh* (40)
ephah (29)
basket (4)
differing measures (1) +406+2256
measure (1)
measures (1)
measuring basket (1)
two differing measures (1) +406+2256

407 אֵיפֹה *'ēyp̱ōh* (10)
where (8)
what (1)
where from (1)

408 1אִישׁ *'iyš1* (2189)
man (612)
men (523)
each (160)
one (106)
husband (64)
man's (32)
anyone (29)
every (18)
everyone (18)
people (16)
Israelites (14) +3776
soldiers (12) +4878
someone (12)
any (11)
some[S] (10)
they[S] (9) +2021
person (8)
they[S] (7)
everyone (6) +3972
he[S] (6) +2021
Israelite (6) +1074+3776+4946
those[S] (6)
he[S] (5)
Israelite (5) +3776
none (5) +4202
swordsmen (5) +2995+8990
them[S] (5)
warrior (5) +4878
all (4)
army (4) +4878
husbands (4)
male (4)
those[S] (4) +2021
another[S] (3)
anyone (3) +2021+4769
foot soldiers (3) +8081
him[S] (3)
him[S] (3) +2021
they (3)
who (3)
anyone (2) +408
anyone (2) +3972
at war with (2) +4878
champion (2) +1227+2021
each (2) +408
father (2)
fellow (2)
Israelite (2) +1201+3776+4946
mankind (2)
merchants (2) +9365
mourners[S] (2)
neighbor[S] (2)
none (2) +401
servants (2)
their[S] (2)
them[S] (2) +2021
valiant fighter (2) +1201+2657
valiant fighters (2) +2657
warriors (2) +2657
whoever (2)
whoever (2) +889
whoever (2) +2021+4769
you[S] (2)
a[S] (1)
accuser (1) +8190
adulteress (1) +851
all together (1) +285+3869
allies (1) +1382
among yourselves (1) +278+448
another creature[S] (1)
any (1) +408
any (1) +3972
any man (1) +408
any man (1) +2021+4769
anyone (1) +2021
anyone (1) +2021+3972
anyone's (1)
archers (1) +928+2021+4619+8008
army (1)
Benjamin (1) +1201+3549
Benjamite (1) +1228
Benjamite (1) +3549
Benjamites (1) +1228+4946
blood relatives (1) +1460
Boaz[S] (1) +2021
brother (1)
captive (1)
census (1) +6296
champions (1) +2657
child (1)
close friend (1) +8934
counselor (1) +6783
counselors (1) +6783
cubs (1)
descendant (1) +2446+4946
deserve to (1)
deserved (1)
each (1) +278+2257
eloquent (1) +1821
enemies (1) +5194
Ephraimites (1) +713
equally (1) +278+2257+3869
equally among them (1) +278+2257+3869
everyone (1) +2021+3972
everyone's (1) +928
experienced fighter (1) +4878
experienced fighting men (1) +1475+2657+4878
famous (1) +9005
farmer (1) +141+6268
fellow townsmen (1) +6551
fellowman (1)
followers (1) +889+2143+6640
forces (1)
friend[S] (1)
friends (1) +8934
Gibeonites (1) +1500
Gileadites (1) +1680
give in marriage (1) +4200+5989
great soldiers (1) +4878
group (1)
guards (1) +5464
he[S] (1) +340+2021+2021
he[S] (1) +2021+2021+6640+8886
he[S] (1) +2021+5283
high (1) +1201
highborn (1) +1201
himself[S] (1) +2021
his[S] (1) +2021
hunter (1) +7473
husband's (1)
in the prime of life (1)
Israel (1) +3776
Israelite (1) +2021+3778
kings[S] (1)
leaders (1) +8031
liar (1) +3942
madman (1) +8713
man (1) +408+2256
man's body (1)

mankind (1) +1414
marries (1) +2118+2118+4200
marries (1) +2118+4200
marry (1) +2118+4200
members (1)
men (1) +1201
men's (1)
Moabites (1) +4566
mockers (1) +4371
more[S] (1)
neighbor's (1)
Ninevites (1) +5770
none[S] (1)
officials (1)
one and all (1)
one party[S] (1)
one[S] (1) +2424
opponent (1)
oppressor (1) +9412
ready for battle (1) +2021+4200+4878+7372
remain unmarried (1) +1194+2118+4200+4200+6328
sailors (1) +641
scoffers (1) +4371
scoundrel (1) +1175
scoundrel (1) +1175+2021
slanderers (1) +4383
slept with (1) +3359+4200+5435
soldier (1) +7372
soldiers (1) +1505+4878
soldiers (1) +7372
soldiers (1) +8081
some of them[S] (1)
son (1)
son (1) +2446
spies (1) +8078
steward[S] (1)
steward[S] (1) +889+1074+2021+6584
strongest defenders (1) +2657
talker (1) +8557
tall (1) +4500
tend livestock (1) +2118+5238
tended livestock (1) +2118+5238
the parties (1) +2084+2256+8276
their[S] (1) +2021
their[S] (1) +3373
them (1)
they[S] (1) +3315
they[S] (1) +7159
this[S] (1)
together (1) +907+2084+8276
townspeople (1) +6551
tribe of Benjamin (1) +3549
troublemaker (1) +1175
trusted friends (1) +8934
two men (1) +278+2256+3481
unmarried (1) +2118+4200+4202
untraveled (1) +1172+4946+6296
villain (1) +224
virgin (1) +3359+4202
voluntarily (1) +4213+6584+6590
well-known (1) +9005
who (1) +2021+6504
whoever (1) +889+3972
untranslated (243)

409 2אִישׁ *'iyš2*
Variant; not used

410 אִישׁ־בֹּשֶׁת *'iyš-bōšet* (11)
Ish-Bosheth (11)

411 אִישׁ־טוֹב *'iyš-tôb*
Variant; not used

412 אִישְׁהוֹד *'iyšhôd* (1)
Ishhod (1)

413 אִישׁוֹן *'iyšôn* (5)
apple (2)
apple (1) +1426
dark (1) +696
untranslated (1)

414 אִישַׁי *'iyšay* (1)
Jesse (1)

415 אִיתוֹן *'iytôn* (2)
entrance (1)
untranslated (1)

416 אִיתַי *'iytay* (1)
Ithai (1)

417 אִיתִיאֵל *'iytiy'ēl* (3)
Ithiel (3)

418 אִיתָמָר *'iytāmār* (21)
Ithamar (19)
Ithamar's (2)

419 1אֵיתָן *'ēytān1* (13)
rich (2)
constant (1)
enduring (1)
ever flowing (1)
everlasting (1)
flowing stream (1)
hard (1)
long established (1)
never-failing (1)
place (1)
secure (1)
steady (1)

420 2אֵיתָן *'ēytān2* (8)
Ethan (8)

421 אַךְ *'ak* (161)
but (31)
surely (21)
only (16)
however (8)
but only (5)
nevertheless (5)
yet (5)
alone (4)
just (4)
nothing but (4)
also (2)
and (2)
indeed (2)
so (2)
after (1)
although (1)
as long as (1)
as surely as (1)
be sure (1)
both (1)
but (1) +3954
but also (1)
but too (1)
complete (1)
completely (1)
except (1)
fully (1)
furthermore (1)
just after (1)
mere (1)
once more (1) +2021+7193
only (1) +8370
provided (1) +561
really (1)
scarcely (1)
surely (1) +6964
though (1)
very (1)
untranslated (26)

422 אַכַּד *'akkad* (1)
Akkad (1)

423 אַכְזָב *'akzāb* (2)
deceptive (2)

424 אַכְזִיב *'akziyb* (4)
Aczib (4)

425 אַכְזָר *'akzār* (4)
deadly (1)
fierce (1)
heartless (1)
ruthlessly (1) +4200

426 אַכְזָרִי *'akzāriy* (8)
cruel (7)
merciless (1)

427 אַכְזְרִיּוּת *'akz'riyyût* (1)
cruel (1)

428 אֲכִילָה *'ᵃkiylāh* (1)
food (1)

429 אָכִישׁ *'ākiyš* (21)
Achish (19)
untranslated (2)

430 אָכַל *'ākal* (820)
eat (359)
ate (70)
devour (44)
consume (31)
be eaten (25)
eats (25)
eaten (23)
devoured (22)
eating (22)
consumed (19)
devours (10)
consuming (9)
food (8)
consumes (6)
feed on (6)
be consumed (5)
enjoy (5)
ate up (4)
burns (4)
gave to eat (4)
eaten (3) +430
eater (3)
feast (3)
fed (3)
be devoured (2)
been destroyed (2)
destroy (2)
destroyed (2)
devouring (2)
eat up (2)
enjoys (2)
feasting (2)
feed (2)
give[S] (2)
had to eat (2)
make eat (2)
make eat food (2)
needed (2)
shared (2)
burn up (1)
burned (1)
burned up (1)
claimed (1)
crushed completely (1) +2256+4730
dine on (1)
dined (1)
dried up (1)
earn (1)
eat away (1)
eaten away (1)
eaten provisions (1) +430
eats away (1)
enjoyed (1)
feast on (1)
feasting (1) +2256+9272
feeding (1)
feeds on (1)
free to eat (1) +430
get food (1)
give to eat (1)
had food enough (1)
have food (1)
have plenty to eat (1) +430
have[S] (1)
is eaten (1)
is eaten (1) +430

kept (1)
lick up (1)
like (1)
live on (1)
meal (1) +4312
must eat (1) +430
needs (1)
pests (1)
prepare food to eat (1)
prepares (1)
provided for (1) +2118+2256+4200+4312
put an end (1)
ruins (1)
sap (1)
sat (1)
scarce (1) +928+5017
share in (1)
sharing (1) +4946
stay for a meal (1) +4312
stripped (1)
stripped clean (1)
supposed to dine (1) +3782+3782
taste (1)
took space (1)
use (1)
used up (1) +430
would[s] (1)
untranslated (16)

431 אֹכֶל *'oḵel* (39)
food (36)
it[s] (1)
mealtime (1) +2021+6961
prey (1)

432 אֻכָל *'uḵāl* (1)
Ucal (1)

433 אָכְלָה *'oḵlāh* (17)
food (11)
fuel (3)
eat (2)
devour (1)

434 1אָכֵן *'āḵēn1* (18)
surely (7)
but (4)
yet (2)
actually (1)
because surely (1)
how (1)
truly (1)
untranslated (1)

435 2אָכֵן *'āḵēn2*
Variant; not used

436 אָכַף *'āḵap̱* (1)
drives on (1)

437 אֶכֶף *'eḵep̱* (1)
hand (1)

438 אִכָּר *'ikkār* (7)
farmers (4)
farmer (1)
people (1)
work fields (1)

439 אַכְשָׁף *'aḵšāp̱* (3)
Acshaph (3)

440 1אַל *'al1* (730)
not (511)
don't (64)
no (52)
nor (14) +2256
never (11)
or (5)
nor (3)
without (3)
cannot (2)
from (2)
neither (2)
never (2) +4200+6409
nothing (2)
stop (2)
abstain from sexual relations (1) +448+851+5602
always (1) +2893
better than (1)
beware (1) +9068
forget (1) +2349
immortality (1) +4638
instead of (1)
neither (1) +2256
never (1) +6524
or (1) +2256
overlook (1) +7155
untranslated (44)

441 2אַל *'al2*
Variant; not used

442 1אֵל *'ēl1*
Variant; not used

443 2אֵל *'ēl2*
Variant; not used

444 3אֵל *'ēl3*
Variant; not used

445 4אֵל *'ēl4* (5)
power (3) +3338
powerless (1) +401+3338+4200
powerless (1) +401+4200

446 5אֵל *'ēl5* (237)
God (199)
god (19)
God's (5)
mighty (4)
gods (3)
mighty one (3)
great (1)
heavenly beings (1) +1201
his[s] (1)
mighty (1) +1201

447 6אֵל *'ēl6* (9)
these (7)
those (2)

448 אֶל *'el* (5516)
to (3052)
into (160)
against (128)
on (114)
in (102)
at (91)
for (74)
toward (57)
with (51)
enter (36) +995
before (30)
over (23)
upon (20)
concerning (17)
entered (17) +995
of (16)
about (16)
reached (13) +995
among (12)
by (12)
into (11) +9348
around (10)
lay with (7) +995
near (7)
because of (6)
sleep with (6) +995
enters (5) +995
slept with (5) +995
along (4)
arrived (4) +995
attack (4)
attack (4) +6590
in front of (4) +7156
lie with (4) +995
after (3)
as for (3)
at (3) +4578
attack (3) +995
decorated (3)
facedown (3) +7156
facing (3) +7156
from (3)
in front of (3) +4578
straight ahead (3) +6298+7156
together (3) +285+285
up to (3)
wherever (3) +889+3972
above (2)
above (2) +1068
all the way to (2)
along with (2)
approaches (2) +995
be buried (2) +665+7700
beside (2)
down to (2)
faced (2) +7156
facing each other (2) +4691+4691
fall in (2) +6015
hands together (2) +4090+4090
in addition to (2)
in front of (2)
include (2)
inside (2) +9348
into presence (2)
next to (2) +3338
next to (2) +6298
on (2) +4578
onto (2)
received (2) +995
together (2) +295+851
under (2)
abstain from sexual relations (1) +440+851+5602
abutted (1)
according to (1)
across (1)
adjoining (1) +7156
among (1) +9348
among yourselves (1) +278+408
and (1)
approached (1) +995
arrive (1) +995
as (1)
as far as (1)
as far as (1) +4578
at the sight of (1)
ate (1) +995+7931
attack (1) +7756
attacked (1) +7756
attacking (1) +6590
attentive to (1)
away (1) +2021+2025+2575
because (1)
befall (1) +628
before (1) +7156
belonged to (1)
belonged to (1) +2118
belongs to (1)
beside (1) +3338
bordering (1)
both and (1)
buried (1) +995+7700
call to mind (1) +4213+8740
care (1) +4213+8492
care about (1) +4213+8492
checked on (1) +8938
committed adultery with (1) +995
concerned about (1) +4213+8492
concerned for (1)
consult (1)
consult (1) +2143
counting on (1) +906+5883+5951
covered (1)
decorated with (1)
definitely (1) +3922
did the same[s] (1) +285+285+2489
done so[s] (1) +995+7931

during (1)
entered (1) +6073
entering (1) +995
entrusted to (1) +3338
every kind (1) +2385+2385+4946
faced (1)
faced forward (1) +4578+7156
filled with gladness (1) +1637+8524
find (1) +995
fit for (1)
fixed on (1)
follow (1) +3338
for the sake of (1)
from (1) +7156
go sleep with (1) +995
guest (1) +995+1074
have (1)
have on hand (1) +3338+9393
here (1)
impressed (1)
in accordance with (1)
in charge of (1)
in front of (1) +4578+7156
in the front line (1) +4578+7156
in vain (1) +2855
inherit (1) +2118
inquire of (1) +2011
inquire of (1) +7928
inquired of (1) +606
inside (1)
inside (1) +1074+2021
into (1) +7163
invade (1) +995
invaded (1) +995
invaded (1) +6590
invader (1) +995
join (1)
joining (1)
keep away (1) +3870+7928
lie with (1) +7928
listened attentively to (1) +265
look in the face (1) +5951+7156
lusted after (1) +6311
lying on (1)
lying with (1) +995
make turn (1) +5989
married (1) +995
meet (1)
meet (1) +7156
occupied (1) +6641
occupy (1) +995
on account of (1)
on the faces of (1)
on the side of (1)
onto (1) +9348
opposite (1)
opposite (1) +7156
out of (1)
overboard (1) +2021+3542
overruled (1) +2616
overtook (1) +995
participate in (1) +2118
reach (1) +995
reached (1) +6590
reaches (1) +995
reflected on (1) +4213+5989
rejoined (1) +2143
replace (1) +995+9393
right in (1)
see (1) +6524
showed concern for (1) +7155
sleeps with (1) +995
southern (1) +5582+6991
southward (1) +2021+3545
square (1) +752+8062+8063
square (1) +752+8063
stops to think (1) +4213+8740
surmounted by (1)
that (1)
their (1) +2157
thought (1) +606+3276
to (1) +4578
to (1) +9348
to within (1)
took (1) +995
touched (1) +995
toward (1) +2006
toward (1) +5790
toward (1) +7156
use (1) +2143
went in to spend the night with (1) +995
untranslated (1171)

449 אֵל אֱלֹהֵי יִשְׂרָאֵל *'ēl 'ᵉlōhēy yiśrā'ēl* (1)
El Elohe Israel (1)

450 אֵל בֵּית־אֵל *'ēl bēyṯ-'ēl* (1)
El Bethel (1)

451 אֵל בְּרִית *'ēl bᵉriyṯ* (1)
El-Berith (1)

452 אֵלָא *'ēlā'* (1)
Ela (1)

453 אֶלְגָּבִישׁ *'elgāḇiyš* (3)
hailstones (3) +74

454 אַלְגּוּמִּים *'algûmmiym* (3)
algumwood (2) +6770
algum (1)

455 אֶלְדָּד *'eldāḏ* (2)
Eldad (2)

456 אֶלְדָּעָה *'eldā'āh* (2)
Eldaah (2)

457 1אָלָה *'ālāh1* (8)
swears the oath (2)
take an oath (2)
bound under an oath (1)
cursing (1)
take oaths (1)
utter a curse (1)

458 2אָלָה *'ālāh2* (1)
mourn (1)

459 3אָלָה *'ālāh3*
Variant; not used

460 4אָלָה *'ālāh4* (34)
oath (10)
curses (8)
curse (7)
object of cursing (3)
required (2) +928+5957
accursed (1)
public charge (1)
put under oath (1) +9048
sworn agreement (1)

461 1אֵלָה *'ēlāh1* (13)
oak (6)
oak tree (3)
terebinth (2)
great tree (1)
tree (1)

462 2אֵלָה *'ēlāh2* (13)
Elah (12)
Elah's (1)

463 3אֵלָה *'ēlāh3* (3)
Elah (3)

464 אַלָּה *'allāh* (1)
oak (1)

465 אֵלֶּה *'ēlleh* (747)
these (481)
this (55)
those (15)
them (12)
they (12)
this^{S} (12) +1821+2021+2021
such (10)
others^{S} (7)
some time later (6) +339+1821+2021+2021
some (5)
following^{S} (4)
the (4)
here (3)
who (3)
altogether (2) +2256
men^{S} (2)
now (2) +928+2021+2021+3427
one group^{S} (2)
that (2)
us^{S} (2)
what^{S} (2) +1821+2021+2021
after a while (1) +339+1821+2021+2021
all this (1)
all^{S} (1)
animals^{S} (1)
as follows (1)
case^{S} (1)
each other (1)
everything (1) +1821+2021+2021+3972
gave the message (1) +1819+1821+2021+2021+3972
his^{S} (1)
impartially (1) +465+6640
later (1) +339+1821+2021+2021
next^{S} (1)
share their duties (1) +6640
she (1)
that happened (1) +1821+2021+2021
that^{S} (1) +1821+2021+2021
the craftsmen^{S} (1)
the first^{S} (1)
the men of the ambush^{S} (1)
the men^{S} (1)
the others^{S} (1)
the total^{S} (1)
their^{S} (1) +2021
things^{S} (1)
this is how (1) +928+3972
this is how (1) +1821+2021+2021+3869
this is why (1) +6584
two^{S} (1)
very (1)
what (1)
who^{S} (1)
whose^{S} (1) +1426+2257
your^{S} (1)
untranslated (69)

466 אֱלֹהִים *'ᵉlōhiym* (2602)
God (2242)
gods (205)
god (59)
God's (25)
he^{S} (7)
he^{S} (7) +3378+3870
judges (4)
him^{S} (3) +3378+3870
angels (2) +1201+2021
goddess (2)
he^{S} (2) +2021
his^{S} (2) +3378+3870
angels (1) +1201
divine (1)
God's (1) +4200
God's (1) +4946
God-fearing (1) +2021+3710
godly (1)
great (1)
he^{S} (1) +824+2021
he^{S} (1) +3378
he^{S} (1) +3378+5646
heavenly beings (1)
high (1)
him^{S} (1)
him^{S} (1) +2021
him^{S} (1) +3378+4013
his^{S} (1) +3276
I^{S} (1)
idols (1)
it^{S} (1) +778+2021

lead to do the same[s] (1) +339+2177+2388
majestic (1)
mighty (1)
sacred (1)
shrine (1) +1074
spirit (1)
them[s] (1) +1074+2021+3998
them[s] (1) +2157
there[s] (1) +928+1074
very (1) +4200
untranslated (13)

467 אִלּוּ *'illû* (2)
if (2)

468 אֱלוֹהַּ *'ᵉlôah* (58)
God (46)
god (7)
God's (4)
untranslated (1)

469 1אֱלוּל *'ᵉlûl1* (1)
Elul (1)

470 2אֱלוּל *'ᵉlûl2* (1)
untranslated (1)

471 1אֵלוֹן *'ēlôn1* (10)
great tree (4)
great trees (4)
large tree (1)
tree (1)

472 2אֵלוֹן *'ēlôn2* (2)
Elon (2)

473 1אַלּוֹן *'allôn1* (8)
oak (4)
oaks (4)

474 2אַלּוֹן *'allôn2* (1)
Allon (1)

475 אַלּוֹן בָּכוּת *'allôn bāḵûṯ* (1)
Allon Bacuth (1)

476 1אַלּוּף *'allûp̱1* (9)
close friends (2)
friend (2)
allies (1)
companion (1)
gentle (1)
oxen (1)
partner (1)

477 2אַלּוּף *'allûp̱2* (60)
chiefs (16)
leaders (3)
divisions (1)
untranslated (40)

478 אָלוּשׁ *'ālûš* (2)
Alush (2)

479 אֶלְזָבָד *'elzāḇāḏ* (2)
Elzabad (2)

480 אָלַח *'ālah* (3)
corrupt (3)

481 אֶלְחָנָן *'elhānān* (4)
Elhanan (4)

482 אֱלִיאָב *'ᵉliy'āḇ* (21)
Eliab (20)
he[s] (1)

483 אֱלִיאֵל *'ᵉliy'ēl* (10)
Eliel (10)

484 אֱלִיאָתָה *'ᵉliy'āṯāh* (1)
Eliathah (1)

485 אֱלִידָד *'ᵉliyḏāḏ* (1)
Elidad (1)

486 אֶלְיָדָע *'elyāḏā'* (4)
Eliada (4)

487 אַלְיָה *'alyāh* (5)
fat tail (5)

488 אֵלִיָּה *'ēliyyāh* (8)
Elijah (8)

489 אֵלִיָּהוּ *'ēliyyāhû* (63)
Elijah (60)
Elijah's (1)
him[s] (1)
untranslated (1)

490 אֱלִיהוּ *'ᵉliyhû* (4)
Elihu (4)

491 אֱלִיהוּא *'ᵉliyhû'* (7)
Elihu (6)
he[s] (1)

492 אֶלְיְהוֹעֵינַי *'elyᵉhô'ēynay* (2)
Eliehoenai (2)

493 אֶלְיוֹעֵינַי *'elyô'ēynay* (7)
Elioenai (7)

494 אֶלְיַחְבָּא *'elyahbā'* (2)
Eliahba (2)

495 אֱלִיחֹרֶף *'ᵉliyhōreṗ* (1)
Elihoreph (1)

496 אֱלִיל *'ᵉliyl* (20)
idols (15)
worthless (2)
idolatries (1)
images (1)
untranslated (1)

497 אֱלִימֶלֶךְ *'ᵉliymeleḵ* (6)
Elimelech (6)

498 אֶלְיָסָף *'elyāsāp̱* (6)
Eliasaph (6)

499 אֱלִיעֶזֶר *'ᵉliy'ezer* (14)
Eliezer (14)

500 אֱלִיעָם *'ᵉliy'ām* (2)
Eliam (2)

501 אֱלִיעֵנַי *'ᵉliy'ēnay* (1)
Elienai (1)

502 אֱלִיפַז *'ᵉliyp̱az* (15)
Eliphaz (14)
him[s] (1)

503 אֱלִיפַל *'ᵉliyp̱al* (1)
Eliphal (1)

504 אֱלִיפְלֵהוּ *'ᵉliyp̱ᵉlēhû* (2)
Eliphelehu (2)

505 אֱלִיפֶלֶט *'ᵉliyp̱elet* (8)
Eliphelet (8)

506 אֱלִיצוּר *'ᵉliysûr* (5)
Elizur (5)

507 אֱלִיצָפָן *'ᵉliysāp̄ān* (4)
Elizaphan (4)

508 אֱלִיקָא *'ᵉliyqā'* (1)
Elika (1)

509 אֶלְיָקִים *'elyāqiym* (12)
Eliakim (12)

510 אֱלִישֶׁבַע *'ᵉliyšeḇa'* (1)
Elisheba (1)

511 אֱלִישָׁה *'ᵉliyšāh* (3)
Elishah (3)

512 אֱלִישׁוּעַ *'ᵉliyšûa'* (3)
Elishua (3)

513 אֶלְיָשִׁיב *'elyāšiyḇ* (17)
Eliashib (15)
Eliashib's (1)
it[s] (1) +1074

514 אֱלִישָׁמָע *'ᵉliyšāmā'* (16)
Elishama (16)

515 אֱלִישָׁע *'ᵉliyšā'* (58)
Elisha (54)
Elisha's (3)
he[s] (1)

516 אֱלִישָׁפָט *'ᵉliyšāp̄āṯ* (1)
Elishaphat (1)

517 אֱלִיָּתָה *'ᵉliyyāṯāh* (1)
Eliathah (1)

518 אַלְלַי *'allay* (2)
what misery (1)
woe (1)

519 1אָלַם *'ālam1* (8)
silent (6)
be silenced (1)
speechless (1)

520 2אָלַם *'ālam2* (1)
binding (1)

521 אֵלֶם *'ēlem*
Variant; not used

522 אִלֵּם *'illēm* (6)
mute (4)
that cannot speak (1)
those who cannot speak (1)

523 אַלְמֻגִּים *'almuggiym* (3)
almugwood (3) +6770

524 אֲלֻמָּה *'ᵃlummāh* (5)
sheaves (2)
it[s] (1)
sheaf (1)
sheaves of grain (1)

525 אַלְמוֹדָד *'almôḏāḏ* (2)
Almodad (2)

526 אַלַּמֶּלֶךְ *'allammeleḵ* (1)
Allammelech (1)

527 1אַלְמָן *'almān1* (1)
forsaken (1)

528 2אַלְמָן *'almān2* (1)
strongholds (1)

529 אַלְמֹן *'almōn* (1)
widowhood (1)

530 אַלְמָנָה *'almānāh* (54)
widow (31)
widows (18)
widow's (4)
untranslated (1)

531 אַלְמָנוּת *'almānûṯ* (4)
widow's (2)
widowhood (1)
widows (1)

532 אַלְמֹנִי *'almōniy* (3)
certain (1) +7141
friend (1) +7141
such and such (1) +7141

533 אֵלֹנִי *'ēlōniy* (1)
Elonite (1)

534 אֶלְנַעַם *'elnā'am* (1)
Elnaam (1)

535 אֶלְנָתָן *'elnāṯān* (7)
Elnathan (7)

536 אֶלָּסָר *'ellāsār* (2)
Ellasar (2)

537 אֶלְעָד *'el'āḏ* (1)
Elead (1)

538 אֶלְעָדָה *'el'āḏāh* (1)
Eleadah (1)

539 אֶלְעוּזַי *'el'ûzay* (1)
Eluzai (1)

540 אֶלְעָזָר *'el'āzār* (72)
Eleazar (70)
Eleazar's (2)

541 אֶלְעָלֵא *'el'ālē'* (1)
Elealeh (1)

542 אֶלְעָלֵה *'el'ālēh* (4)
Elealeh (4)

543 אֶלְעָשָׂה *'el'āśāh* (6)
Eleasah (4)
Elasah (2)

544 1אָלַף *'ālap1* (4)
learn (1)
prompts (1)
teach (1)
teaches (1)

545 2אָלַף *'ālap2* (1)
increase by thousands (1)

546 1אֶלֶף *'elep1* (7)
herds (5)
oxen (2)

547 2אֶלֶף *'elep2* (495)
thousand (223)
thousands (31)
24,000 (14) +752+2256+6929
25,000 (14) +2256+2822+6929
10,000 (9) +6930
4,500 (8) +752+2256+2822+4395
1,000 (5)
1,254 (4) +752+2256+2822+4395
36,000 (3) +2256+8993+9252
40,500 (3) +752+2256+2822+4395
5,000 (3) +2822
53,400 (3) +752+2256+2256+2822+4395+8993
603,550 (3) +547+2256+2256+2256 +2822+2822+4395+4395+8993+9252
eleven hundred (3) +2256+4395
1,052 (2) +2256+2822+9109
1,247 (2) +752+2256+4395+8679
1,775 (2) +2256+2256+2256+2822+4395+8679+8679
16,000 (2) +6925+9252
18,000 (2) +6925+9046
200,000 (2) +4395
30,500 (2) +2256+2822+4395+8993
32,200 (2) +2256+2256+4395+8993+9109
35,400 (2) +752+2256+2256+2822+4395+8993
4,600 (2) +752+2256+4395+9252
41,500 (2) +285+752+2256+2256+2822+4395
45,650 (2) +752+2256+2256+2256 +2822+2822+4395+9252
46,500 (2) +752+2256+2256+2822+4395+9252
54,400 (2) +752+752+2256+2256+2822+4395
57,400 (2) +752+2256+2256+2822+4395+8679
59,300 (2) +2256+2256+2822+4395+8993+9596
6,720 (2) +2256+4395+6929+8679+9252
62,700 (2) +2256+2256+4395+8679+9109+9252
7,337 (2) +2256+4395+8679+8679+8993+8993
74,600 (2) +752+2256+2256+4395+8679+9252
fourteen hundred (2) +752+2256+4395
million (2) +547
seventeen hundred (2) +2256+4395+8679
units of a thousand (2)
1,017 (1) +2256+6925+8679
1,017 (1) +6925+8679
1,222 (1) +2256+4395+6929+9109
1,290 (1) +2256+4395+9596
1,335 (1) +2256+2822+4395+8993+8993
1,365 (1) +2256+2256+2256+2822+4395+8993+9252
1,760 (1) +2256+2256+4395+8679+9252
108,100 (1) +547+2256+2256+4395+4395+9046
120,000 (1) +2256+4395+6929
14,700 (1) +752+2256+4395+6925+8679
151,450 (1) +285+547+752+2256 +2256+2256+2256+2822+2822+4395+4395
153,600 (1) +547+2256+2256+2256 +2822+4395+4395+8993+9252
157,600 (1) +547+2256+2256+2256 +2822+4395+4395+8679+9252
16,750 (1) +2256+2822+4395+6925+8679+9252
17,200 (1) +2256+4395+6925+8679
180,000 (1) +2256+4395+9046
186,400 (1) +547+547+752+2256+2256 +2256+4395+4395+9046+9252
2,000 (1)
2,056 (1) +2256+2822+9252
2,067 (1) +2256+8679+9252
2,172 (1) +2256+2256+4395+8679+9109
2,172 (1) +2256+4395+8679+9109
2,200 (1) +2256+4395
2,300 (1) +2256+4395+8993
2,322 (1) +2256+4395+6929+8993+9109
2,400 (1) +752+2256+4395
2,600 (1) +2256+4395+9252
2,630 (1) +2256+2256+4395+8993+9252
2,750 (1) +2256+2822+4395+8679
2,812 (1) +2256+4395+6925+9046+9109
2,818 (1) +2256+4395+6925+9046+9046
20,000 (1) +6929
20,200 (1) +2256+4395+6929
20,800 (1) +2256+4395+6929+9046
22,000 (1) +2256+6929+9109
22,034 (1) +752+2256+2256+2256+6929+8993+9109
22,200 (1) +2256+2256+4395+6929+9109
22,273 (1) +2256+2256+2256 +4395+6929+8679+8993+9109
22,600 (1) +2256+2256+4395+6929+9109+9252
23,000 (1) +2256+6929+8993
25,100 (1) +2256+2256+2822+4395+6929
26,000 (1) +2256+6929+9252
28,600 (1) +2256+2256+4395+6929+9046+9252
280,000 (1) +2256+4395+9046
3,000 (1) +8993
3,023 (1) +2256+2256+6929+8993+8993
3,200 (1) +2256+4395+8993
3,600 (1) +2256+4395+8993+9252
3,630 (1) +2256+2256+4395+8993+8993+9252
3,700 (1) +2256+4395+8679+8993
3,930 (1) +2256+4395+8993+8993+9596
300,000 (1) +4395+8993
307,500 (1) +547+2256+2256+2822 +4395+4395+8679+8993
32,000 (1) +2256+8993+9109
32,500 (1) +2256+2256+2822+4395+8993+9109
337,500 (1) +547+547+2256+2256+2256 +2822+4395+4395+8679+8993+8993
337,500 (1) +547+547+2256+2256 +2822+4395+4395+8679+8993+8993
37,000 (1) +2256+8679+8993
40,000 (1) +752
42,360 (1) +752+2256+4395+8052+8993+9252
42,360 (1) +752+4395+8052+8993+9252
43,730 (1) +752+2256+2256+2256 +4395+8679+8993+8993
44,760 (1) +752+752+2256+2256 +2256+4395+8679+9252
45,400 (1) +752+752+2256+2256+2822+4395
45,600 (1) +752+2256+2256+2822+4395+9252
5,400 (1) +752+2256+2822+4395
50,000 (1) +2822
52,700 (1) +2256+2256+2822+4395+8679+9109
6,200 (1) +2256+4395+9252
6,800 (1) +2256+4395+9046+9252
60,500 (1) +2256+2822+4395+9252
601,730 (1) +547+2256+2256+4395 +4395+8679+8993+9252
61,000 (1) +285+2256+9252
61,000 (1) +2256+8052+9252
64,300 (1) +752+2256+2256+4395+8993+9252
64,400 (1) +752+752+2256+2256+4395+9252
675,000 (1) +547+547+2256+2256 +2822+4395+8679+9252
7,000 (1) +8679
7,100 (1) +2256+4395+8679
7,500 (1) +2256+2822+4395+8679
70,000 (1) +8679
72,000 (1) +2256+8679+9109
76,500 (1) +2256+2256+2822+4395+8679+9252
8,580 (1) +2256+2256+2822+4395+9046+9046
8,600 (1) +2256+4395+9046+9252
80,000 (1) +9046
87,000 (1) +2256+8679+9046
eighteen thousand (1) +2256+8052+9046
fifteen hundred feet (1) +564
five hundred yards (1) +564
thirty-six hundred (1) +2256+4395+8993+9252
thirty-three hundred (1) +2256+4395+8993+8993
three thousand feet (1) +564
twelve hundred (1) +2256+4395
twenty-seven hundred (1) +2256+4395+8679
twenty-six hundred (1) +2256+4395+9252
units of 1,000 (1)
vast (1) +547
untranslated (6)

548 3אֶלֶף *'elep3* (12)
clans (9)
clan (1)
unit (1)
units (1)

549 4אֶלֶף *'elep4*
Variant; not used

550 אֱלִיפֶלֶט *'elpelet* (1)
Elpelet (1)

551 אֶלְפַּעַל *'elpa'al* (3)
Elpaal (3)

552 אָלַץ *'ālas* (1)
prodded (1)

553 אֶלְצָפָן *'elsāpān* (2)
Elzaphan (2)

554 אַלְקוּם *'alqûm* (1)
army (1)

555 אֶלְקָנָה *'elqānāh* (21)
Elkanah (20)
untranslated (1)

556 אֶלְקֹשִׁי *'elqōšiy* (1)
Elkoshite (1)

557 אֶלְתּוֹלַד *'eltôlad* (2)
Eltolad (2)

558 אֶלְתְּקֵא *'elt'qē'* (1)
Eltekeh (1)

559 אֶלְתְּקֵה *'elt'qēh* (1)
Eltekeh (1)

560 אֶלְתְּקוֹן *'elt'qôn* (1)
Eltekon (1)

561 אִם *'im* (1070)
if (522)
but (39) +3954
or (39)
not (34)
when (27)
except (24) +3954

though (22)
whether (16)
surely (14) +4202
only (11) +3954
if (10) +3954
even if (9)
that (8)
no (7)
only (7)
but if (6)
since (6)
unless (6) +3954
although (5)
or (5) +2256
never (4)
unless (4) +4202
whenever (4)
yet if (4)
and (3)
however (3) +3954
neither (3)
only if (3)
until (3) +6330
but (2) +4202
but only (2) +3954
don't (2)
if (2) +3907
instead (2) +3954
nor (2)
other than (2) +3954
surely (2) +3954
than (2) +3954
that (2) +4202
though (2) +3954
till (2) +4202
until (2) +889+6330
whether (2) +4202
without (2) +3954
after (1) +3983
although (1) +3954
as (1)
as if (1)
as long as (1) +6388
because (1)
because (1) +3610+4202
but (1)
cannot (1)
certainly (1) +4202
even (1) +3954
even though (1)
except (1) +1194
however (1)
if even (1)
if indeed (1)
if only (1)
indeed (1) +3954
never (1) +2721
never (1) +4200+5905
never (1) +6330+6409
nor (1) +2256
not (1) +3954
not even (1)
not one (1)
nothing (1) +3972+4946
or (1) +401+2256
other than (1)
otherwise (1) +401
please (1)
provided (1) +421
rather (1)
rather (1) +3954
so (1) +3610+4202
suppose (1)
surely (1) +401
till (1) +6330
unless (1) +1194
unless (1) +3954+4200+7156
unless (1) +3954+4202
until (1) +3954
whether (1) +2022+4202
while (1)
why (1) +4027+4200+4537
won't until (1) +3954
yet (1) +3954
you (1) +3870
untranslated (145)

562 אֵם *'ēm* (220)
mother (134)
mother's (60)
mothers (8)
parents (3) +3+2256
birth (2) +1061
grandmother (2)
she[s] (2) +2257
birth (1) +5055
brothers (1) +278
fork (1)
grandmother's (1)
mothers' (1)
uncle's (1) +278
very own brother (1) +278+1201+3870
untranslated (2)

563 אָמָה *'āmāh* (56)
maidservant (16)
servant (14)
maidservants (9)
slave girls (4)
female (3)
servant's (2)
slave girl (2)
her[s] (1) +3870
me[s] (1) +3870
slave born in household (1) +1201
slave woman (1)
slave woman's (1)
slaves (1) +2256+6269

564 1אַמָּה *'ammāh1* (255)
cubits (163)
cubit (37)
about six hundred feet (2) +752+4395
long cubits (2)
seventy-five feet (2) +2822
18 inches (1)
45 feet (1) +8993
450 feet (1) +4395+8993
75 feet (1) +2822
doorposts (1)
fifteen feet (1) +928+2021+6924
fifteen hundred feet (1) +547
five hundred yards (1) +547
four and a half feet (1) +8993
more than thirteen feet (1) +9596
over nine feet (1) +2256+2455+9252
seven and a half feet (1) +928+2021+2822
six feet (1) +752
thirty feet (1) +928+2021+6929
three feet (1)
three thousand feet (1) +547
time (1)
twenty feet (1) +2822+6926
twenty-seven feet (1) +6926+9046
yards (1)
untranslated (29)

565 2אַמָּה *'ammāh2* (1)
Ammah (1)

566 3אַמָּה *'ammāh3*
Variant; not used

567 4אַמָּה *'ammāh4*
Variant; not used

568 אֵמָה *'ēmāh*
Variant; not used

569 אֻמָּה *'ummāh* (3)
tribal (2)
peoples (1)

570 1אָמוֹן *'āmôn1* (2)
craftsman (1)
craftsmen (1)

571 2אָמוֹן *'āmôn2* (17)
Amon (15)
Amon's (2)

572 3אָמוֹן *'āmôn3* (1)
Amon (1)

573 1אֵמוּן *'ēmûn1* (2)
faithful (2)

574 2אֵמוּן *'ēmûn2* (6)
faithful (2)
faith (1)
trustworthy (1)
truthful (1)
unfaithful (1) +4202

575 אֱמוּנָה *'ᵉmûnāh* (49)
faithfulness (20)
truth (6)
faithful (5)
faithfully (5) +928
entrusted with (2) +928
trustworthy (2)
truthful (2)
complete honesty (1)
faith (1)
integrity (1)
safe (1)
steady (1)
sure foundation (1)
trust (1)

576 אָמוֹץ *'āmôs* (13)
Amoz (13)

577 אָמִי *'āmiy* (1)
Ami (1)

578 אֲמִינוֹן *'ᵃmiynôn* (1)
Amnon (1)

579 אַמִּיץ *'ammiys* (6)
mighty (2)
bravest (1) +4213
strength (1)
strong (1)
vast (1)

580 אָמִיר *'āmiyr* (2)
branches (1)
undergrowth (1)

581 1אָמַל *'āmal1* (16)
languish (2)
wither (2)
fade (1)
fails (1)
faint (1)
languishes (1)
pine away (1)
pines away (1)
waste away (1)
wasted away (1)
wastes away (1)
weak-willed (1) +4226
withered (1)
withers (1)

582 2אָמַל *'āmal2*
Variant; not used

583 אֻמְלַל *'umlal* (1)
faint (1)

584 אֲמֵלָל *'ᵃmēlāl* (1)
feeble (1)

585 אֲמָם *'ᵃmām* (1)
Amam (1)

586 1אָמַן *'āman1* (97)
believe (20)
faithful (15)
trust (8)
believed (7)
trustworthy (4)
be established (2)

come true (2)
firm (2)
have faith (2)
places trust (2)
put trust (2)
be confirmed (1)
be trusted (1)
be upheld (1)
be verified (1)
believes (1)
certain (1)
confident (1)
despairs (1) +4202
endure (1)
enduring (1)
fails (1) +4202
firmly (1)
have assurance (1)
lasting (1)
lingering (1)
loyal (1)
never fail (1)
not fail (1)
prolonged (1)
reliable (1)
stand (1)
stand firm (1) +4394
stand firm in faith (1)
stand still (1)
sure (1)
trusted (1)
trusted advisers (1)
trusting (1)
trusts (1)
trustworthy (1) +8120
was attested (1)

587 2אָמַן *'āman2* (9)
nurse (2)
are carried (1)
brought up (1)
cared (1)
foster fathers (1)
guardians (1)
guardians of children (1)
nurtured (1)

588 אָמָּן *'āmmān* (1)
craftsman's (1)

589 אָמֵן *'āmēn* (30)
amen (26)
truth (2)
amen so be it (1) +589

590 אֹמֶן *'ōmen* (1)
perfect (1)

591 1אֲמָנָה *'ᵃmānāh1* (2)
binding agreement (1)
regulated (1)

592 2אֲמָנָה *'ᵃmānāh2* (2)
Amana (1)
untranslated (1)

593 1אָמְנָה *'omnāh1* (2)
really (1)
true (1)

594 2אָמְנָה *'omnāh2* (1)
bringing up (1)

595 אֹמְנָה *'ōmnāh* (1)
doorposts (1)

596 אַמְנוֹן *'amnôn* (27)
Amnon (25)
Amnon's (1)
him[s] (1)

597 אָמְנָם *'omnām* (9)
true (4)
indeed (2)
be assured (1)
doubtless (1)
unthinkable (1) +4202

598 אֻמְנָם *'umnām* (5)
really (3)
indeed (1)
really (1) +677

599 אָמֵץ *'āmēs* (41)
courageous (11)
strong (4)
strengthen (3)
managed (2)
raised up (2)
determined (1)
encourage (1)
established (1)
hardened (1)
hardhearted (1) +906+4222
increases (1)
let grow (1)
marshal (1)
muster (1)
obstinate (1)
opposed (1) +6584
reinforced (1)
steady (1)
strengthened (1)
stronger (1)
supported (1)
take heart (1) +4213
take heart (1) +4222
victorious (1)

600 אָמֹץ *'āmōs* (2)
powerful (2)

601 אֹמֶץ *'ōmes* (1)
grow stronger (1) +3578

602 אַמְצָה *'amsāh* (1)
strong (1)

603 אַמְצִי *'amsiy* (2)
Amzi (2)

604 אֲמַצְיָה *'ᵃmasyāh* (9)
Amaziah (9)

605 אֲמַצְיָהוּ *'ᵃmasyāhû* (31)
Amaziah (29)
Amaziah's (2)

606 1אָמַר *'āmar1* (5317)
said (1958)
says (610)
say (506)
asked (215)
replied (185)
answered (161)
saying (138)
tell (93)
told (84)
thought (47)
ask (45)
ordered (28)
message (18)
added (15)
spoke (14)
commanded (13)
answer (12)
speak (12)
promised (10)
declared (9)
shouted (9)
continued (8)
word (8)
thinking (7)
uttered (7) +2256+5951
called (6)
cried (6)
prayed (6)
think (6)
call (5)
exclaimed (5)
gave orders (5)
asking (4)
declare (4)
reply (4)
reported (4)
spoken (4)
tells (4)
asks (3)
be called (3)
be said (3)
called out (3)
cried out (3)
intend (3)
suggested (3)
announced (2)
be (2)
challenge (2)
claim (2)
claims (2)
command (2)
commands (2)
cry out (2)
demanded (2)
is said (2)
name (2)
order (2)
read (2)
replied (2) +8938
responded (2)
say (2) +606
set (2)
shout (2)
shouting (2)
talked (2)
telling (2)
thinks (2)
want (2)
add (1)
advised (1)
afraid[s] (1)
agreed (1)
assured (1)
be named (1)
be told (1)
been given (1)
boast (1)
boasted (1)
boasts (1)
brought up (1)
call out (1)
called back (1)
calling out (1)
came (1)
claimed (1)
commemorate (1)
complain (1)
confessed (1)
cries (1)
cry (1)
cry out (1) +4200+5951
declares (1) +606
demand (1)
demanding (1)
directed (1)
exclaim (1)
explain (1)
gave (1)
gave an order (1)
gave the order (1)
give (1)
goes (1)
greeted (1)
heard (1) +265+928
indicate (1)
indicated (1)
inquired of (1) +448
insisted (1)
instructed (1)
intended (1)
issued orders (1)
keep saying (1) +606
makes speech (1) +609

news (1)
objected (1)
offered (1)
plan (1)
plead (1)
proclaiming (1)
promised (1) +606
proposed (1)
protest (1)
provided (1)
question (1)
realize (1) +4200+4222
recite (1)
recite (1) +2256+6699
repeated (1)
replies (1)
report (1)
reporting (1)
respond (1)
say (1) +2256+6699
saying (1) +4200
search (1) +928
sent word (1)
shows (1)
snorts (1)
so sure (1) +606
speaks (1)
spoke up (1)
suggest (1)
swear (1)
talking (1)
tell (1) +1821
think (1) +928+4213
think (1) +928+4222
thinks (1) +928+4222
thought (1) +448+3276
told (1) +4200+8938
urged (1)
use (1)
used (1)
uttered (1)
wanted (1)
warned (1)
warning (1)
was said (1)
was told (1)
words (1)
untranslated (878)

607 2אָמַר *'āmar2* (2)
boast (1)
full of boasting (1)

608 אֹמֶר *'ōmer* (5)
speech (2)
promise (1)
what[s] (1)
word (1)

609 1אֵמֶר *'ēmer1* (48)
words (33)
arguments (2)
what say (2) +7023
words (2) +7023
answers (1)
appointed (1)
keeps saying (1) +8740
lies (1) +9214
makes speech (1) +606
pleading (1)
those[s] (1)
what said (1) +7023
what say (1)

610 2אֵמֶר *'ēmer2*
Variant; not used

611 1אִמֵּר *'immēr1* (1)
fawns (1)

612 2אִמֵּר *'immēr2* (8)
Immer (8)

613 3אִמֵּר *'immēr3* (2)
Immer (2)

614 אִמְרָה *'imrāh* (37)
word (13)
promise (11)
words (4)
promises (2)
speech (2)
command (1)
prayer (1)
what have to say (1)
what say (1)
untranslated (1)

615 אֶמְרָה *'emrāh*
Variant; not used

616 אֱמֹרִי *'^{e}mōriy* (87)
Amorites (76)
Amorite (10)
it[s] (1) +1473+2021

617 אִמְרִי *'imriy* (2)
Imri (2)

618 אֲמַרְיָה *'^{a}maryāh* (13)
Amariah (12)
Amariah's (1)

619 אֲמַרְיָהוּ *'^{a}maryāhû* (3)
Amariah (3)

620 אַמְרָפֶל *'amrāpel* (2)
Amraphel (2)

621 אֶמֶשׁ *'emeš* (5)
last night (3)
night (1)
yesterday (1)

622 אֱמֶת *'^{e}met* (127)
faithfulness (34)
truth (29)
true (20)
faithful (5)
sure (5)
faithfully (4)
faithfully (4) +928
security (3)
truthful (3)
honorably (2) +928
reliable (2)
right (2)
truly (2) +928
trustworthy (2)
assurance (1)
assuredly (1) +928
fairly (1)
fairness (1)
faithful (1) +928+2143
faithfully (1) +6913
integrity (1)
lasting (1)
really (1) +928
sound (1)

623 אַמְתַּחַת *'amtahat* (15)
sack (7)
sacks (7)
it[s] (1) +2257

624 אֲמִתַּי *'^{a}mitay* (2)
Amittai (2)

625 אָן *'ān* (42)
where (17) +2025
how long (12) +2025+6330
anywhere else (2) +625+2025+2025+2256
where (2)
which way (2) +2025
anywhere (1) +625+2025+2025+2256
how long (1) +6330
when (1) +2025+6330
wherever (1) +2025
untranslated (1)

626 אָנָּא *'ānnā'* (7)
O (5)
I ask (1)
oh (1)

627 1אָנָה *'ānāh1* (3)
groan (1)
lament (1)
mourning (1)

628 2אָנָה *'ānāh2* (4)
befall (1) +448
befalls (1) +4200
lets happen (1) +3338+4200
trying to pick a quarrel (1)

629 אָנָּה *'ānnāh* (6)
O (6)

630 אֲנוּ *'^{a}nû* (1)
untranslated (1)

631 אָנוּשׁ *'ānûš* (8)
incurable (3)
beyond cure (1)
despair (1)
grievous (1)
incurable wound (1)
no cure (1)

632 1אֱנוֹשׁ *'^{e}nôš1* (42)
man (20)
men (9)
mortal (4)
man's (2)
friends (1) +8934
he[s] (1)
his[s] (1)
mankind (1)
one (1)
ordinary (1)
very few (1) +4663

633 2אֱנוֹשׁ *'^{e}nôš2* (7)
Enosh (7)

634 אָנַח *'ānah* (13)
groan (7)
groaning (2)
grieve (1)
groaned (1)
groans (1)
moan (1)

635 אֲנָחָה *'^{a}nāhāh* (11)
groaning (6)
sighing (4)
groans (1)

636 אֲנַחְנוּ *'^{a}nahnû* (121)
we (103)
us (6)
we're (2)
our (1)
untranslated (9)

637 אֲנָחֲרָת *'^{a}nāh^{a}rat* (1)
Anaharath (1)

638 אֲנִי *'^{a}niy* (874)
I (790)
me (26)
myself (21)
we (6)
I'll (3)
my (2)
each of us (1) +2085+2256
I'm (1)
me alone (1) +3276
mine (1)
my life (1)
yes[s] (1)
untranslated (20)

639 אֳנִי *'^{o}niy* (7)
ships (3)
fleet (1)
fleet of trading ships (1) +9576
galley (1)
it[s] (1) +9576

640 אֲנִיָּה '^{a}niyyāh (2)
lament (1)
lamentation (1)

641 אֳנִיָּה '^{o}niyyāh (32)
ships (16)
ship (3)
boats (1)
cargo (1) +889+928+2021+3998
fleet of ships (1)
fleet of trading ships (1) +2143+4200+9576
fleet of trading ships (1) +2143+9576
fleet of trading ships (1) +9576
it^{s} (1) +9576
sail (1) +928+2021+2143
sailors (1) +408
these^{s} (1)
they^{s} (1)
trading ship (1) +9576
untranslated (1)

642 אֲנִיעָם '^{a}niy'ām (1)
Aniam (1)

643 אֲנָךְ '^{a}nāḵ (4)
plumb line (3)
true to plumb (1)

644 אָנֹכִי 'ānōḵiy (359)
I (326)
I'm (8)
me (5)
myself (5)
I'll (3)
it^{s} (1)
we (1)
untranslated (10)

645 אָנַן 'ānan (2)
complain (1)
complained (1)

646 אָנַס 'ānas (1)
allowed (1) +401

647 אָנַף 'ānap̱ (14)
angry (14)

648 אָנָף 'ānāp̱
Variant; not used

649 אֲנָפָה '^{a}nāp̱āh (2)
heron (2)

650 אָנַק 'ānaq (4)
groan (3)
lament (1)

651 1אֲנָקָה '^{a}nāqāh1 (4)
groans (2)
groaning (1)
wail (1)

652 2אֲנָקָה '^{a}nāqāh2 (1)
gecko (1)

653 אָנַשׁ 'ānaš (1)
ill (1)

654 אָסָא 'āsā' (58)
Asa (50)
Asa's (7)
untranslated (1)

655 אָסוּךְ 'āsûḵ (1)
little^{s} (1)

656 אָסוֹן 'āsôn (5)
harm (3)
serious injury (2)

657 אֵסוּר 'ēsûr (3)
bindings (1)
chains (1)
imprisoned (1) +1074+2021+5989

658 אָסִיף 'āsiyp̱ (3)
ingathering (2)
harvest (1)

659 אָסִיר 'āsiyr (14)
prisoners (8)
captives (2)
captive (1)
held (1)
untranslated (2)

660 1אַסִּיר 'assiyr1 (4)
captives (2)
captive (1)
prisoners (1)

661 2אַסִּיר 'assiyr2 (4)
Assir (4)

662 אָסָם 'āsām (2)
barns (2)

663 אַסְנָה 'asnāh (1)
Asnah (1)

664 אָסְנַת 'āsnaṯ (3)
Asenath (3)

665 אָסַף 'āsap̱ (199)
gathered (18)
gather (17)
assembled (14)
be gathered (9)
assemble (6)
harvest (5)
rear guard (5)
was gathered (5)
brought together (4)
called together (4) +2256+8938
gathered together (4)
take away (4)
are taken away (3)
collected (3)
cure (3)
gather together (3)
gathered up (3)
mustered (3)
accumulated (2)
be buried (2) +448+7700
gather in (2)
gather up (2)
gathers (2)
gathers up (2)
no longer shine (2) +5586
put (2)
withdraw (2)
admit (1)
are gathered (1)
assembling (1)
banded together (1) +2021+2653+4200
be brought back (1)
be collected (1)
be gathered (1) +665
be gathered up (1)
be herded together (1) +669
be recovered (1)
been brought (1)
been gathered (1)
bring (1)
bring back (1)
brought (1)
brought back (1)
called together (1)
came together (1)
cured (1)
do so more (1)
drew up (1)
dying (1)
gather around (1)
gathering (1)
get (1)
gone (1)
got together (1)
had brought (1)
harvested (1)
is gathered in (1)
is harvested (1)
join (1)
join forces (1)
joined forces (1)
joined forces (1) +3481
lose (1)
massing together (1)
muster (1)
rallied (1)
receive (1)
regrouped (1) +3480
remove (1)
return (1)
returned (1)
set aside (1)
steal away (1)
store away (1)
summon (1)
surely gather (1) +665
sweep away (1) +6066
take (1)
taken (1)
taken away (1)
together (1)
took (1)
took into service (1)
victims (1)
wane (1)
was^{s} (1)
were brought together (1)
were caught (1)
were gathered (1)
were mustered (1)
withdrawn (1)
withdraws (1)
withdrew (1)

666 אָסָף 'āsāp̱ (46)
Asaph (45)
Asaph's (1)

667 אָסֹף 'āsōp̱ (3)
storehouse (1)
storehouse (1) +1074
storerooms (1)

668 אֹסֶף 'ōsep̱ (3)
gathers (1)
harvest of fruit (1)
untranslated (1)

669 אֲסֵפָה '^{a}sēp̱āh (1)
be herded together (1) +665

670 אֲסֻפָּה '^{a}suppāh (1)
collected sayings (1) +1251

671 אֲסַפְסֻף '^{a}sap̱sup̱ (1)
rabble (1)

672 אַסְפָּתָא 'aspāṯā' (1)
Aspatha (1)

673 אָסַר 'āsar (73)
bound (9)
obligated (4)
obligates (4)
be tied (2)
hitch up (2)
prison (2) +1074
prisoners (2)
tie up (2)
tied (2)
ties (2)
are bound (1)
be kept in prison (1)
be tied up (1)
been captured (1)
bind (1)
binding (1)
captives (1)
fetters (1)
had made ready (1)
harness (1)
hitch (1)
hitched (1)
hitched up (1)
instruct (1)

is held captive (1)
join in (1)
made ready (1)
obligate (1)
obligation taken (1)
prison (1) +1074+2021
put (1)
put in bonds (1)
put in chains (1)
start (1)
stay (1)
take prisoner (1)
tether (1)
tethered (1)
tie up (1) +673
ties securely (1) +673
was confined (1)
went into (1)
were bound (1)
were confined (1)
were held (1)
were taken prisoner (1)
wore (1)
untranslated (3)

674 אִסָּר *'issār* (11)
pledge (6)
pledges (5)

675 אֵסַר־חַדֹּן *'ēsar-haddōn* (3)
Esarhaddon (3)

676 אֶסְתֵּר *'estēr* (55)
Esther (42)
Esther's (5)
she[s] (4)
her[s] (1)
who[s] (1)
untranslated (2)

677 1אַף *'ap1* (134)
and (8)
too (7)
and (6) +2256
even (6)
how much less (6) +3954
also (4)
how much more (4)
how much more (4) +3954
how much worse (3) +3954
no sooner (3) +1153
surely (3)
all (2)
and also (2)
how much more so (2) +3954
now (2)
then (2)
too (2) +2256
yes (2)
also (1) +2256
but also (1)
but even (1)
but now (1)
even (1) +2256
even (1) +2256+3954
how (1)
how much better (1) +3954
how much less (1) +3954+4202
how much more (1) +2256+3954
if (1)
in all this (1)
indeed (1)
indeed (1) +2256+3954
moreover (1)
no (1)
nor (1) +401
or (1)
really (1)
really (1) +598
really (1) +3954
rejoice greatly (1) +1635+1638
though (1)
till (1) +2256
together with (1) +2256
true (1)
very (1)
whether (1)
yet (1) +2256
untranslated (37)

678 2אַף *'ap2* (277)
anger (173)
wrath (15)
face (14)
nostrils (12)
angry (11) +3013
nose (10)
angry (4)
faces (4)
very angry (4) +3013
patient (3) +800
fury (2)
noses (2)
anger (1) +3013
angry (1) +3019
before (1) +928
before (1) +4200
breath (1)
brow (1)
double (1)
fell facedown (1) +2556+4200
furious (1) +3013+4394
gives patience (1) +799
great rage (1) +3034
hot-tempered (1)
life breath (1) +8120
long-suffering (1) +800
not angry (1) +8740
passion (1)
patience (1) +802
pride (1) +1470
quick-tempered (1) +7920
resentment (1)
snout (1)
which[s] (1) +2257
untranslated (1)

679 אָפַד *'āpad* (2)
fasten (1)
fastened (1)

680 1אֵפֹד *'ēpōd1* (49)
ephod (46)
it[s] (1) +2021
untranslated (2)

681 2אֵפֹד *'ēpōd2* (1)
Ephod (1)

682 אֲפֻדָּה *'ªpuddāh* (3)
skillfully woven (2)
covered (1)

683 אַפֶּדֶן *'appeden* (1)
royal (1)

684 אָפָה *'āpāh* (13)
bake (5)
baked (5)
bakes (1)
baking (1)
be baked (1)

685 אֹפֶה *'ōpeh* (11)
baker (8)
bakers (2)
baked goods (1) +4407+5126

686 אֵפוֹא *'ēpô'* (15)
then (7)
now (3)
so (2)
how (1) +928+4537
oh (1) +4769+5989
where (1) +180

687 אָפוּנָה *'āpûnāh*
Variant; not used

688 אֲפִיחַ *'ªpiyah* (1)
Aphiah (1)

689 אָפִיל *'āpiyl* (1)
ripen later (1)

690 1אַפַּיִם *'appayim1*
Variant; not used

691 2אַפַּיִם *'appayim2* (2)
Appaim (2)

692 1אָפִיק *'āpiyq1* (18)
ravines (8)
streams (4)
valleys (2)
channels (1)
rows (1)
streams (1) +5707
tubes (1)

693 2אָפִיק *'āpiyq2* (1)
mighty (1)

694 אֹפֶל *'ōpel* (9)
darkness (4)
thick darkness (2)
deepest night (1) +4017+6547
gloom (1)
shadows (1)

695 אָפֵל *'āpēl* (1)
pitch dark (1)

696 אֲפֵלָה *'ªpēlāh* (10)
gloom (2)
dark (1)
dark (1) +413
darkness (1)
deep darkness (1)
deep shadows (1)
night (1)
total darkness (1) +3125
utter darkness (1)

697 אֶפְלָל *'eplāl* (2)
Ephlal (2)

698 אֹפֶן *'ōpen* (1)
aptly (1) +6584

699 אָפֵס *'āpēs* (5)
come to an end (1)
gone (1)
used up (1)
vanish (1)
vanished (1)

700 אֶפֶס *'epes* (43)
ends (14)
no (5)
none (5)
without (3) +928
but (2) +3954
not (2)
only (2)
amount to nothing (1)
but (1)
however (1) +3954
lately (1) +928
nothing (1)
nothing at all (1) +401+2256
or (1) +2256
vanish away (1)
whether (1) +2256
yet (1) +3954

701 אֹפֶס *'ōpes* (1)
ankle-deep (1)

702 אֶפֶס דַּמִּים *'epes dammiym* (1)
Ephes Dammim (1)

703 אֶפַע *'epa'* (1)
worthless (1)

704 אֶפְעֶה *'ep'eh* (3)
adder (2)
adders (1)

705 אָפַף *'āpap* (5)
entangled (2)

engulfing (1)
surround (1)
swirled about (1)

706 אָפַק *'āp̱aq* (7)
are withheld (1)
control himself (1)
controlling himself (1)
felt compelled (1)
held myself back (1)
hold yourself back (1)
restrained himself (1)

707 אֲפֵק *'ap̱ēq* (9)
Aphek (9)

708 אֲפֵקָה *'ap̱ēqāh* (1)
Aphekah (1)

709 אֵפֶר *'ēp̱er* (22)
ashes (20)
dust (2)

710 אֲפֵר *'ap̱ēr* (2)
headband (2)

711 אֶפְרֹחַ *'ep̱rōah* (5)
young (2)
young ones (1)
untranslated (2)

712 אַפִּרְיוֹן *'appiryôn* (1)
carriage (1)

713 אֶפְרַיִם *'ep̱rayim* (180)
Ephraim (148)
Ephraim's (12)
Ephraim (6) +1201
Ephraimites (4) +1201
Ephraim (2) +824
Ephraimite (2) +1201
Ephraimites (2)
Ephraimite (1)
Ephraimites (1) +408
Ephraimites (1) +4946
untranslated (1)

714 1אֶפְרָת *'ep̱rāṯ1* (4)
Ephrath (4)

715 2אֶפְרָת *'ep̱rāṯ2* (1)
Ephrath (1)

716 1אֶפְרָתָה *'ep̱rāṯāh1* (3)
Ephrathah (3)

717 2אֶפְרָתָה *'ep̱rāṯāh2* (2)
Ephrathah (2)

718 אֶפְרָתִי *'ep̱rāṯiy* (5)
Ephraimite (3)
Ephrathite (1)
Ephrathites (1)

719 אֶצְבֹּן *'esbōn* (2)
Ezbon (2)

720 אֶצְבַּע *'esba'* (31)
finger (17)
fingers (11)
forefinger (2)
toes (1)

721 1אָצִיל *'āsiyl1* (1)
farthest corners (1)

722 2אָצִיל *'āsiyl2* (1)
leaders (1)

723 אַצִּיל *'assiyl* (3)
arms (1) +3338
long (1)
wrists (1) +3338

724 אָצַל *'āsal* (5)
denied (1)
reserved (1)
smaller (1)
take (1)
took (1)

725 אֵצֶל *'ēsel* (61)
beside (30)
near (6)
side (4)
at (2)
at side (2)
away (2) +4946
by (2)
next to (2)
with (2)
close to (1)
close to (1) +7940
go to bed with (1) +8886
neared (1) +2143
next to (1) +4946
to (1)
untranslated (3)

726 2אֵצֶל *'ēsel2*
Variant; not used

727 1אָצֵל *'āsēl1* (6)
Azel (6)

728 2אָצֵל *'āsēl2* (1)
Azel (1)

729 אֲצַלְיָהוּ *'asalyāhû* (2)
Azaliah (2)

730 אֹצֶם *'ōsem* (2)
Ozem (2)

731 אֶצְעָדָה *'es'āḏāh* (2)
armlets (1)
band (1)

732 אָצַר *'āsar* (5)
stored up (2)
be stored up (1)
hoard (1)
put in charge of the storerooms (1) +238+6584

733 אֵצֶר *'ēser* (5)
Ezer (5)

734 אֶקְדָּח *'eqdāh* (1)
sparkling jewels (1) +74

735 אַקּוֹ *'aqqô* (1)
wild goat (1)

736 אֲרָא *'arā'* (1)
Ara (1)

737 אֶרְאֵל *'er'ēl* (1)
brave men (1)

738 אֲרִאֵל *'ari'ēl* (2)
best men (2)

739 1אַרְאֵלִי *'ar'ēliy1* (2)
Areli (2)

740 2אַרְאֵלִי *'ar'ēliy2* (1)
Arelite (1)

741 אָרַב *'āraḇ* (41)
ambush (9)
lie in wait (8)
lies in wait (5)
in ambush (3)
set an ambush (3)
hidden (2)
lay in wait (2)
ambush set (1)
ambushes (1)
bandits (1)
hide (1)
lurked (1)
lurks (1)
lying in wait (1)
took up concealed positions (1)
untranslated (1)

742 אֲרָב *'arāḇ* (1)
Arab (1)

743 אֶרֶב *'ereḇ* (2)
cover (1)
wait (1)

744 אֹרֶב *'ōreḇ* (2)
intrigue (1)
trap (1)

745 אַרְבֵּאל *'arḇē'l*
Variant; not used

746 אַרְבֶּה *'arbeh* (24)
locusts (15)
locust (5)
great locusts (2)
great locust (1)
they[s] (1) +2021

747 אָרְבָּה *'ārbāh* (1)
cleverness (1)

748 אֲרֻבָּה *'arubbāh* (9)
floodgates (6)
nests (1)
window (1)
windows (1)

749 אֲרֻבּוֹת *'arubbôṯ* (1)
Arubboth (1)

750 אַרְבִּי *'arbiy* (1)
Arbite (1)

751 ארנבן *'rnḇn*
Variant; not used

752 1אַרְבַּע *'arba'1* (456)
four (172)
forty (78)
fourteenth (19) +6925
24,000 (14) +547+2256+6929
fourteen (12) +6925
twenty-fourth (9) +2256+6929
4,500 (8) +547+2256+2822+4395
fourteen (7) +6926
forty-two (5) +2256+9109
fourth (5)
twenty-four (5) +2256+6929
1,254 (4) +547+2256+2822+4395
all fours (4)
forty-one (4) +285+2256
fourteenth (4) +6926
40,500 (3) +547+2256+2822+4395
430 (3) +2256+4395+8993
53,400 (3) +547+2256+2256+2822+4395+8993
fortieth (3)
forty-five (3) +2256+2822
1,247 (2) +547+2256+4395+8679
345 (2) +2256+2822+4395+8993
35,400 (2) +547+2256+2256+2822+4395+8993
4,600 (2) +547+2256+4395+9252
403 (2) +2256+4395+8993
41,500 (2) +285+547+2256+2256+2822+4395
42 (2) +2256+9109
435 (2) +2256+2822+4395+8993
45,650 (2) +547+2256+2256+2256+2822+2822+4395+9252
46,500 (2) +547+2256+2256+2822+4395+9252
54,400 (2) +547+752+2256+2256+2822+4395
57,400 (2) +547+2256+2256+2822+4395+8679
74 (2) +2256+8679
74,600 (2) +547+2256+4395+8679+9252
about six hundred feet (2) +564+4395
forty-eight (2) +2256+9046
fourteen hundred (2) +547+2256+4395
14,700 (1) +547+2256+4395+6925+8679
148 (1) +2256+4395+9046
151,450 (1) +285+547+547+2256+2256+2256+2256+2822+2822+4395+4395
186,400 (1) +547+547+547+2256+2256+2256+4395+4395+9046+9252

2,400 (1) +547+2256+4395
22,034 (1) +547+2256+2256+2256+6929+8993+9109
242 (1) +2256+4395+9109
245 (1) +2256+2256+2822+4395
245 (1) +2256+2822+4395
284 (1) +2256+4395+9046
324 (1) +2256+4395+6929+8993
34 (1) +2256+8993
40 (1)
40,000 (1) +547
410 (1) +2256+4395+6927
42,360 (1) +547+2256+4395+8052+8993+9252
42,360 (1) +547+4395+8052+8993+9252
420 (1) +2256+4395+6929
43,730 (1) +547+2256+2256+2256+4395+8679+8993+8993
44,760 (1) +547+752+2256+2256+2256+4395+8679+9252
45,400 (1) +547+752+2256+2256+2822+4395
45,600 (1) +547+2256+2256+2822+4395+9252
454 (1) +752+2256+2822+4395
468 (1) +2256+4395+9046+9252
5,400 (1) +547+2256+2822+4395
64,300 (1) +547+2256+2256+4395+8993+9252
64,400 (1) +547+752+2256+2256+4395+9252
642 (1) +2256+2256+4395+9109+9252
642 (1) +2256+4395+9109+9252
648 (1) +2256+4395+9046+9252
743 (1) +2256+2256+4395+8679+8993
743 (1) +2256+4395+8679+8993
745 (1) +2256+2822+4395+8679
840 (1) +2256+4395+9046
845 (1) +2256+2822+4395+9046
945 (1) +2256+2256+2822+4395+9596
each^s (1)
forty-first (1) +285+2256
forty-nine (1) +2256+9596
forty-seven (1) +2256+8679
four-fifths (1) +3338
six feet (1) +564
square (1) +448+8062+8063
square (1) +448+8063
untranslated (8)

753 2אַרְבַּע *'arba'2*
Variant; not used

754 אַרְבָּעִים *'arbā'iym*
Variant; not used

755 אָרַג *'ārag* (14)
weaver's (4)
weaver (3)
weavers (2)
did weaving (1) +1428
spin (1)
weave (1)
wove (1)
woven (1) +5126

756 אֶרֶג *'ereg* (2)
loom (1)
weaver's shuttle (1)

757 אַרְגָּב *'argāb*
Variant; not used

758 1אַרְגֹּב *'argōb1* (4)
Argob (4)

759 2אַרְגֹּב *'argōb2* (1)
Argob (1)

760 אַרְגְּוָן *'argᵉwān* (1)
purple (1)

761 אַרְגַּז *'argaz* (3)
chest (3)

762 אֹרְגִים *'ōrgiym*
Variant; not used

763 אַרְגָּמָן *'argāmān* (38)
purple (36)
purple material (1)
tapestry (1)

764 אַרְדְּ *'ard* (3)
Ard (3)

765 אַרְדּוֹן *'ardôn* (1)
Ardon (1)

766 אַרְדִּי *'ardiy* (1)
Ardite (1)

767 אֲרִדַי *'ᵃriday* (1)
Aridai (1)

768 אָרָה *'ārāh* (2)
gathered (1)
pick (1)

769 אָרוֹד *'ᵃrôd*
Variant; not used

770 אַרְוָד *'arwād* (2)
Arvad (2)

771 1אֲרוֹדִי *'ᵃrôdiy1* (2)
Arodi (2)

772 2אֲרוֹדִי *'ᵃrôdiy2* (1)
Arodite (1)

773 אַרְוָדִי *'arwādiy* (2)
Arvadites (2)

774 אֻרְוָה *'urwāh* (4)
stalls (3)
pens (1)

775 אָרוּז *'ārûz* (1)
tightly knotted (1)

776 אֲרוּכָה *'ᵃrûkāh* (6)
health (2)
repairs (2)
healing (1)
healing for wound (1)

777 אֲרוּמָה *'ᵃrûmāh* (1)
Arumah (1)

778 אֲרוֹן *'ᵃrôn* (202)
ark (181)
chest (10)
it^s (4) +2021
it^s (2)
coffin (1)
it^s (1) +466+2021
it^s (1) +1382+2021
untranslated (2)

779 אֲרַוְנָה *'ᵃrawnāh* (11)
Araunah (8)
he^s (1)
untranslated (2)

780 אֶרֶז *'erez* (73)
cedar (53)
cedars (19)
them^s (1) +6770

781 אַרְזָה *'arzāh* (1)
beams of cedar (1)

782 1אָרַח *'ārah1* (7)
traveler (4)
going out (1)
keeps company (1) +2495+4200
travelers (1)

783 2אָרַח *'ārah2* (4)
Arah (4)

784 אֹרַח *'ōrah* (56)
path (17)
paths (11)
way (9)
ways (5)
course (4)
roads (2)
age of childbearing (1) +851+2021+3869
conduct (1)
destiny (1)
end (1)
journey (1)
path (1) +2006
siege ramps (1) +369
untranslated (1)

785 אֹרְחָה *'ōrhāh* (4)
caravans (3)
caravan (1)

786 אֲרֻחָה *'ᵃruhāh* (6)
allowance (2)
meal (1)
provisions (1)
untranslated (2)

787 אֲרִי *'ᵃriy* (34)
lion (17)
lions (12)
lions' (2)
fierce lion (1)
lion's (1)
young lion (1) +4097

788 אֻרִי *'uriy* (1)
Uri (1)

789 1אֲרִיאֵל *'ᵃriy'ēl1* (5)
altar hearth (2)
hearth (1)
untranslated (2)

790 2אֲרִיאֵל *'ᵃriy'ēl2* (4)
Ariel (4)

791 3אֲרִיאֵל *'ᵃriy'ēl3* (1)
Ariel (1)

792 אֲרִידָתָא *'ᵃriydātā'* (1)
Aridatha (1)

793 1אַרְיֵה *'aryēh1* (46)
lion (34)
lion's (4)
lions (4)
cubs (1) +1594
it^s (1) +1581+2021
untranslated (2)

794 2אַרְיֵה *'aryēh2* (1)
Arieh (1)

795 אֻרִיָּה *'uryāh*
Variant; not used

796 אַרְיוֹךְ *'aryôk* (2)
Arioch (2)

797 אֻרִים *'uriym*
Variant; not used

798 אֲרִיסַי *'ᵃriysay* (1)
Arisai (1)

799 אָרַךְ *'ārak* (35)
live long (8) +3427
long (4)
lengthen (2)
outlived (2) +339+3427
prolong (2)
been long (1)
delay (1)
endure (1)
enjoy a long life (1) +3427
enjoy long life (1) +3427
give long (1)
gives patience (1) +678
go by (1)
have long (1)
lives a long time (1)
living long (1)
made long (1)
maintains (1)
patient (1)
remained (1)

stayed (1) +8905
stick out (1)

800 אָרֵךְ *'ārēḵ* (15)
slow (9)
patient (3) +678
long (1)
long-suffering (1) +678
patience (1) +8120

801 אָרֹךְ *'ārōḵ* (3)
long time (2)
longer (1)

802 אֹרֶךְ *'ōreḵ* (94)
long (65)
length (12)
wide (2)
endless (1)
extended (1)
forever (1) +3427+4200
lengthwise (1)
longer (1)
many years (1) +3427
patience (1) +678
prolong (1)
so long (1) +3427
spreading (1)
square (1) +2256+8145
total wingspan (1) +4053
untranslated (3)

803 1אֶרֶךְ *'ereḵ1*
Variant; not used

804 2אֶרֶךְ *'ereḵ2* (1)
Erech (1)

805 אַרְכִּי *'arkiy* (6)
Arkite (5)
Arkites (1)

806 אֲרָם *'^{a}rām* (129)
Aram (69)
Arameans (42)
Aramean (7)
Aramean kingdom (2)
their^S (2)
them^S (2)
they^S (2)
it^S (1)
untranslated (2)

807 אֲרַם מַעֲכָה *'^{a}ram ma'^{a}ḵāh* (1)
Aram Maacah (1)

808 אֲרַם נַהֲרַיִם *'^{a}ram nah^{a}rayim* (5)
Aram Naharaim (5)

809 אֲרַם צוֹבָה *'^{a}ram ṣôḇāh* (1)
Aram Zobah (1)

810 אַרְמוֹן *'armôn* (33)
fortresses (19)
citadels (4)
citadel (3)
palaces (3)
fortress (1)
palace (1)
stronghold (1)
strongholds (1)

811 אֲרָמִי *'^{a}rāmiy* (5)
in Aramaic (5)

812 אֲרַמִּי *'^{a}rammiy* (13)
Aramean (8)
Arameans (4)
untranslated (1)

813 אַרְמֹנִי *'armōniy* (1)
Armoni (1)

814 אֲרָן *'^{a}rān* (2)
Aran (2)

815 1אֹרֶן *'ōren1* (1)
pine (1)

816 2אֹרֶן *'ōren2* (1)
Oren (1)

817 אַרְנֶבֶת *'arneḇeṯ* (2)
rabbit (2)

818 אַרְנוֹן *'arnôn* (25)
Arnon (24)
Arnon's (1)

819 אֲרַנְיָה *'^{a}ranyāh*
Variant; not used

820 אַרְנָן *'arnān* (1)
Arnan (1)

821 אָרְנָן *'ārnān* (12)
Araunah (9)
he^S (1)
him^S (1)
untranslated (1)

822 אַרְפָּד *'arpāḏ* (6)
Arpad (6)

823 אַרְפַּכְשַׁד *'arpaḵšaḏ* (9)
Arphaxad (9)

824 אֶרֶץ *'ereṣ* (2505)
land (1150)
earth (524)
Egypt (184) +5213
ground (160)
country (92)
countries (39)
lands (34)
Canaan (29) +4046
world (20)
region (18)
territory (17)
Edom (11) +121
Gilead (8) +1680
Israel (7) +3776
around^S (6)
it^S (6) +2021
Judah (6) +3373
wild (6)
area (5)
earth's (5)
fields (5)
Moab (5) +4566
countryside (4)
district (4)
Goshen (4) +1777
land (4) +299
neighboring (4)
soil (4)
territories (4)
dust (3)
floor (3)
its^S (3) +2021
Assyria (2) +855
cities (2) +9133
community (2)
empire (2)
Ephraim (2) +713
Judah^S (2) +2021
lower Egypt (2) +5213
Midian (2) +4518
Negev (2) +5582
Shinar (2) +9114
the other^S (2) +2021+7895
there^S (2) +2021
they^S (2) +2021+6639
upper Egypt (2) +7356
areas of land (1)
army (1)
Babylon (1) +951
Babylon (1) +4169
Babylonia (1) +9114
Bashan (1) +1421
battlefield (1)
Benjamin (1) +1228
clay (1)
community (1) +2021+6639
desert (1) +4497
districts (1)
down (1) +2025
fail (1) +2025+5877
field (1)
floor space (1)
foreign (1)
Galilee (1) +1665
he^S (1) +466+2021
here^S (1) +928+2021
here^S (1) +2021
homeland (1) +4580
homeland (1) +5226
in midair (1)
+1068+1068+2021+2021+2256+9028
it^S (1) +2021+2021+2296
land's (1) +928
little distance (1) +3896
Naphtali (1) +5889
nations (1)
nations (1) +1580
native land (1)
native-born (1) +275
native-born (1) +275+2021
native-born (1) +928+2021+3528
neighbors (1)
on foot (1) +2021+6584
other nationalities (1) +2021+6639
peoples (1)
Philistines (1) +7149
place (1)
plain (1) +6677
plateau (1) +4793
property (1) +299
shore (1)
soil (1) +6760
some distance (1) +2021+3896
some distance (1) +3896
suitable (1)
Tema (1) +9401
their^S (1) +2021+6639
them^S (1) +2021+6551
there (1) +928
there^S (1) +928+2021
there^S (1) +928+2257
there^S (1) +2025+4046
tracts of land (1)
Uz (1) +6420
vicinity (1)
where^S (1)
whole earth (1) +9315
whole world (1) +9315
untranslated (42)

825 אַרְצָא *'arṣā'* (1)
Arza (1)

826 אָרַר *'ārar* (63)
cursed (32)
curse (11)
be cursed (7)
brings a curse (5)
put a curse on (2)
under a curse (2)
curse (1) +4423
curse bitterly (1) +826
this^S (1)

827 אֲרָרַט *'^{a}rāraṭ* (4)
Ararat (4)

828 אֲרָרִי *'^{a}rāriy*
Variant; not used

829 אָרַשׂ *'āraś* (11)
pledged to be married (5)
betroth (3)
betrothed (2)
pledged (1)

830 אֲרֶשֶׁת *'^{a}rešeṯ* (1)
request (1)

831 אַרְתַּחְשַׁסְתְּא *'artaḥšast'* (10)
Artaxerxes (9)
untranslated (1)

832 אֲשַׂרְאֵל *'[a]śar'ēl* (1)
Asarel (1)

833 אֲשַׂרְאֵלָה *'[a]śar'ēlāh* (1)
Asarelah (1)

834 אַשְׂרְאֵלִי *'aśri'ēliy* (1)
Asrielite (1)

835 אַשְׂרִיאֵל *'aśriy'ēl* (3)
Asriel (3)

836 1אֵשׁ *'ēš1* (379)
fire (259)
burn down (9) +928+2021+8596
fiery (9)
set on fire (9) +928+2021+3675
burned (8) +928+2021+8596
lightning (7)
burning (6)
be burned up (4) +928+2021+8596
burn (4) +928+2021+8596
burned up (4) +928+2021+8596
set fire (4) +3675
set on fire (4) +928+2021+8596
burn up (3) +928+2021+8596
burned down (3) +928+2021+8596
burning (3) +2021+6584
flame (3)
coals (2)
fire (2) +4258
fires (2)
flaming (2)
it[s] (2) +2021
use for fuel (2) +1277
are burned up (1) +928+2021+8596+8596
be burned (1) +928+2021+8596
be burned down (1) +928+2021+8596
blazing (1)
burn (1) +4805
burn to death (1) +928+2021+8596
burned (1) +928+2021+8938
burned down (1) +2021+8596
burned to death (1) +928+2021+8596
charred (1) +928+1277+2021
firepot (1) +3963
flashes (1) +928
fuel for fire (1) +928+1896
fuel for flames (1) +928+1896
kindled (1) +7706
lightning (1) +4259
lit (1) +1277
on fire (1) +928+1277+2021
set ablaze (1) +928+2021+3675
set fire to (1) +928+2021+8596
set fire to (1) +928+2021+8938
set on fire (1) +3675
used for fuel (1) +1198+8596
untranslated (5)

837 2אֵשׁ *'ēš2*
Variant; not used

838 אִשׁ *'iš* (1)
one (1)

839 אַשְׁבֵּל *'ašbēl* (3)
Ashbel (3)

840 אַשְׁבֵּלִי *'ašbēliy* (1)
Ashbelite (1)

841 אֶשְׁבָּן *'ešbān* (2)
Eshban (2)

842 אַשְׁבֵּעַ *'ašbēa'*
Variant; not used

843 אֶשְׁבַּעַל *'ešba'al* (2)
Esh-Baal (2)

844 אֶשֶׁד *'āšēd̲* (7)
slopes (5)
mountain slopes (2)

845 אֶשֶׁד *'ešed̲*
Variant; not used

846 אַשְׁדּוֹד *'ašdôd̲* (17)
Ashdod (15)
untranslated (2)

847 אַשְׁדּוֹדִי *'ašdôd̲iy* (6)
people of Ashdod (2)
Ashdod (1)
from Ashdod (1)
men of Ashdod (1)
untranslated (1)

848 אַשְׁדּוֹדִית *'ašdôd̲iyt̲* (1)
language of Ashdod (1)

849 אַשְׁדּוֹת הַפִּסְגָּה *'ašdôt̲ happisgāh*
Variant; not used

850 אֶשְׁדָּת *'ešdāt̲* (1)
mountain slopes (1)

851 אִשָּׁה *'iššāh* (781)
wife (253)
woman (167)
women (103)
wives (91)
married (10) +4374
wife's (9)
each (7)
give in marriage (7) +4200+5989
her[s] (6) +2021
mother (6)
one (6)
she[s] (6) +2021
widow (6)
gave in marriage (5) +4200+5989
harem (5) +1074
marry (5) +2118+4200
married (4) +4200+4374
marry (4) +4200+4374
marry (4) +4374
woman's (4)
married (3) +2118+4200
adulteress (2) +2424
harem (2)
her[s] (2)
mate (2)
together (2) +295+448
abstain from sexual relations (1) +440+448+5602
adulteress (1) +408
age of childbearing (1) +784+2021+3869
be given in marriage (1) +4200+5989
become wife (1) +4200+4374
gave in marriage (1) +5989
girl (1) +3251
give in marriage (1) +2021+5989
her[s] (1) +123+2257
her[s] (1) +2257
married (1) +2118
married (1) +2257+4200+4200+4374
married (1) +5951
married to (1) +2118+4200
Naomi[s] (1) +2021
others[s] (1) +2021
period (1) +2006
queens[s] (1)
she[s] (1) +2257
stillborn child (1) +5878
them[s] (1)
they[s] (1) +1201+2021
they[s] (1) +2021
took in marriage (1) +4200+4374
was given in marriage (1) +4200+5989
widow (1) +4637
wife (1) +1249
women's (1)
untranslated (32)

852 אִשֶּׁה *'iššeh* (65)
offering made by fire (38)
offerings made by fire (19)
made by fire (2)
offering by fire (2)
sacrifice made by fire (2)
offering made by fire (1) +7933
offerings made with fire (1)

853 אֲשׁוּיָה *'[a]šûyāh*
Variant; not used

854 אֱשׁוּן *'[e]šûn* (1)
pitch darkness (1) +3125

855 אַשּׁוּר *'aššûr* (151)
Assyria (120)
Assyrian (9)
Asshur (7)
Assyrians (5)
Assyrians (5) +1201
Assyria (2) +824
Assyria's (1)
Shalmaneser[s] (1) +4889
untranslated (1)

856 אֲשׁוּרִי *'[a]šûriy* (1)
Ashuri (1)

857 אַשּׁוּרִם *'aššûrim* (1)
Asshurites (1)

858 אַשְׁחוּר *'ašḥûr* (2)
Ashhur (2)

859 אָשְׁיָה *'āšyāh* (2)
towers (1)
untranslated (1)

860 אֲשִׁימָא *'[a]šiymā'* (1)
Ashima (1)

861 אָשִׁישׁ *'āšiyš* (1)
men (1)

862 אֲשִׁישָׁה *'[a]šiyšāh* (4)
cake of raisins (2)
raisins (1)
sacred cakes (1)

863 אֶשֶׁךְ *'ešek̲* (1)
testicles (1)

864 1אֶשְׁכּוֹל *'eškôl1* (9)
cluster of grapes (3)
clusters (3)
cluster (2)
clusters of fruit (1)

865 2אֶשְׁכֹּל *'eškôl2* (4)
Eshcol (4)

866 3אֶשְׁכֹּל *'eškōl3* (2)
Eshcol (2)

867 אַשְׁכְּנַז *'ašk[e]naz* (3)
Ashkenaz (3)

868 אֶשְׁכָּר *'eškār* (2)
gifts (1)
paid (1) +8740

869 אֶשֶׁל *'ēšel* (3)
tamarisk tree (3)

870 אָשֵׁם *'āšam* (35)
guilty (15)
bear guilt (3)
condemned (2)
sin (2)
admit guilt (1)
declare guilty (1)
devastated (1)
guilty of wrongdoing (1) +870
held guilty (1)
innocent (1)
pay for it (1)
suffering (1)
unpunished (1) +4202
very guilty (1) +870
wronged (1)

871 אָשָׁם *'āšām* (47)
guilt offering (29)
guilt offerings (5)
penalty (4)
guilt (2)

wrong (2)
its[S] (1) +2021
making amends for sin (1)
restitution (1) +8740
sins (1)
untranslated (1)

872 אָשֵׁם *'āšēm* (2)
convict (1)
punished (1)

873 אַשְׁמָה *'ašmāh* (19)
guilt (13)
guilty (2)
guilt offering (1)
guilty of sins (1)
requiring payment (1)
shame (1)

874 אַשְׁמוּרָה *'ašmûrāh* (7)
watches of the night (3)
watch (2)
last watch of the night (1) +1332
last watch of the night (1) +1332+2021

875 אַשְׁמָן *'ašmān* (1)
strong (1)

876 אֶשְׁנָב *'ešnāḇ* (2)
lattice (2)

877 אַשְׁנָה *'ašnāh* (2)
Ashnah (2)

878 אֶשְׁעָן *'eš'ān* (1)
Eshan (1)

879 אַשָּׁף *'aššāp̱* (2)
enchanters (2)

880 אַשְׁפָּה *'ašpāh* (6)
quiver (5)
quivers (1)

881 אַשְׁפְּנַז *'ašpᵉnaz* (1)
Ashpenaz (1)

882 אֶשְׁפָּר *'ešpār* (2)
cake of dates (2)

883 אַשְׁפֹּת *'ašpōṯ* (7)
dung (4)
ash heap (2)
ash heaps (1)

884 אַשְׁקְלוֹן *'ašqᵉlôn* (12)
Ashkelon (12)

885 אֶשְׁקְלוֹנִי *'ešqᵉlôniy* (1)
Ashkelon (1)

886 1אָשַׁר *'āšar1* (6)
walk (2)
are guided (1)
guide (1)
guides (1)
keep right (1)

887 2אָשַׁר *'āšar2* (11)
call blessed (4)
be blessed (1)
bless (1)
call happy (1)
called blessed (1)
encourage (1)
spoke well of (1)
untranslated (1)

888 אָשֵׁר *'āšēr* (43)
Asher (37)
Asher (5) +1201
Asher's (1) +4946

889 אֲשֶׁר *'ᵃšer* (5501)
that (538)
who (527)
as (270) +3869
which (222)
what (178)
whom (120)
where (79)
just as (58) +3869
whose (42)
those (41)
when (41)
when (38) +3869
until (30) +6330
whatever (30) +3972
because (28)
for (28)
how (28)
just as (24) +3869+3972
because (21) +3610
as (18)
what (18) +3869
whatever (18)
just as (17) +3869+4027
after (14) +3869
because (14) +6584
if (13)
as (12) +3869+4027
like (12) +3869
so that (11)
the one[S] (10)
wherever (10) +928+3972
though (8)
administrator[S] (7) +6584
whatever (7) +3869
anyone (6)
because (6) +9393
he[S] (6)
so (6)
them[S] (6)
as (5) +3869+3972
because (5) +3869
since (5)
whatever (5) +3869+3972
him[S] (4)
of (4)
something (4)
the covenant[S] (4)
things (4)
whoever (4)
at (3)
because (3) +6813
before (3) +4202+6330
for (3) +3610
if (3) +3869
just as (3)
since (3) +3610
territory[S] (3)
the land[S] (3)
these (3)
this (3)
wherever (3) +448+3972
wherever (3) +928+2006+2021
wherever (3) +928+5226
although (2)
as much as (2) +3869
as soon as (2) +3869
because (2) +928
even as (2) +3869
even though (2)
exactly as (2) +3869+4027
for (2) +9393
here (2)
how much (2)
it[S] (2)
just the way (2) +3869
just what (2) +3869+4027
one[S] (2)
others[S] (2)
peoples[S] (2)
sometimes (2) +3780
such (2)
the creatures[S] (2)
the day[S] (2)
the man[S] (2)
the men[S] (2)
the name[S] (2)
the ones[S] (2)
the property[S] (2)
the steward[S] (2) +6584
the way[S] (2)
the ways[S] (2)
there (2)
they[S] (2)
until (2) +561+6330
what (2) +3869+4027
whatever (2) +3869+4027
where (2) +928
wherever (2)
wherever (2) +928+2021+3972+5226
whoever (2) +408
whoever (2) +4769
with (2)
abundantly (1) +3907+6330+6330
according to (1)
according to (1) +3869
although (1) +928+3972
any (1)
anything (1) +3972
as (1) +928
as (1) +928+3972
as easily as (1) +3869
as long as (1) +3869
as soon as (1)
as though (1) +3869
because (1) +3869+7023
because (1) +4946
because of (1) +3869
but (1)
by (1)
cargo (1) +641+928+2021+3998
closest friend (1) +3869+3870+5883+8276
covenant[S] (1)
creature[S] (1)
creatures[S] (1)
crowd (1) +3972+6641
disaster[S] (1)
do not know where am going (1) +2143+2143+6584
edict[S] (1)
else[S] (1)
everything else (1)
exactly as (1) +3869+3972
exactly like (1) +3869+3972+4027
except (1) +4202
finally (1) +6330
followers (1) +339+2021+6639
followers (1) +408+2143+6640
for (1) +928
for (1) +6584
from (1) +928
gods[S] (1)
governor[S] (1) +6584
have (1) +4200
houses[S] (1)
if only (1) +3869
in (1)
in accordance with (1) +3869
in accordance with (1) +3972
in proportion to (1) +3869+5002
in the end (1) +6330
including (1)
instead of (1) +9393
it (1)
just as (1) +3869+3972+4027
just as (1) +3972+4200
just what (1) +3869
keeper[S] (1) +6584
kind (1) +3869
lest (1) +4202
life (1) +2118+3427
like (1)
like (1) +3869+3972
like (1) +3869+4027
living thing[S] (1)
make countless (1) +4202+6218+8049
man[S] (1)
matter[S] (1)
men[S] (1)

mission (1) +1821+8938
more (1) +3869
moving from place to place (1) +928+2143+2143
my people[s] (1)
no sooner than (1) +3869
nothing (1) +3972+4202
now that (1) +3869
one (1)
or (1)
or (1) +4202
other[s] (1) +907
otherwise (1) +4202+5100
people[s] (1) +928+3972
place[s] (1)
possessions[s] (1)
predecessor (1) +2118+4200+7156
proper place (1) +2118+5226+9004
property[s] (1)
property[s] (1) +2118+4200
replies[s] (1)
responsible for (1) +928+4200
robe[s] (1)
same (1) +3869
same as (1)
share (1) +3869+4200
shared hardships (1) +928+6700+6700
she[s] (1)
since (1) +339
since (1) +928
since (1) +4946
since (1) +9393
so (1) +3869
so that (1) +3610
so with (1) +3869
some other place[s] (1)
some[s] (1)
someone (1)
son[s] (1)
steward[s] (1) +408+1074+2021+6584
steward[s] (1) +1074+6584
such as (1)
surviving (1) +3855+3856
than (1) +4946
that (1) +6330
the areas[s] (1)
the celebration[s] (1)
the cup[s] (1)
the girl[s] (1)
the gods[s] (1)
the person[s] (1)
the place[s] (1)
the places[s] (1)
the plans[s] (1)
the storehouses[s] (1) +928+2157+3972
the temple[s] (1)
the terms[s] (1)
the territory[s] (1)
the total[s] (1)
the vineyard[s] (1)
then (1)
then (1) +3869
this is how (1) +3869
those[s] (1) +339+2021+6639
till (1) +6330
town[s] (1)
under (1)
very things (1) +3869+4027
vows[s] (1)
what (1) +4017
whatever (1) +928+3972
whatever (1) +3869+3972+4027
when (1) +6584
whenever (1) +928+3972
whenever (1) +3869
wherever (1) +285+928+2021+5226
wherever (1) +928
wherever (1) +928+2021+5226
wherever (1) +2021+3972+5226+6584
wherever (1) +2025+9004
wherever (1) +3972+6584
wherever (1) +3972+9004
wherever (1) +4946
wherever[s] (1) +5226
while (1)
while (1) +3869
whoever (1) +408+3972
whose (1) +4200
yet (1)
yet (1) +1172+4946
you[s] (1)
untranslated (2620)

890 אֶשֶׁר *'ešer* (2)
blessed (1)
happy (1)

891 אֹשֶׁר *'ōšer* (1)
happy (1)

892 אָשֻׁר *'āšur* (9)
steps (4)
feet (2)
foothold (1)
place to stand (1)
tracked down (1)

893 1אַשֻּׁר *'aššur1*
Variant; not used

894 2אַשֻּׁר *'aššur2*
Variant; not used

895 אֲשֵׁרָה *'ᵃšērāh* (40)
Asherah poles (22)
Asherah pole (14)
Asherah (3)
Asherahs (1)

896 אָשֵׁרִי *'āšēriy* (1)
people of Asher (1)

897 אַשְׁרֵי *'ašrēy* (44)
blessed (37)
how happy (4)
blessings (1)
happy (1)
untranslated (1)

898 אֲשֻׁרִים *'ᵃšuriym*
Variant; not used

899 אָשַׁשׁ *'āšaš* (1)
fix in mind (1)

900 אֶשְׁתָּאוֹל *'eštā'ôl* (7)
Eshtaol (7)

901 אֶשְׁתָּאֻלִי *'eštā'uliy* (1)
Eshtaolites (1)

902 אֶשְׁתּוֹן *'eštôn* (2)
Eshton (2)

903 אֶשְׁתְּמֹה *'ešt^emōh* (1)
Eshtemoh (1)

904 אֶשְׁתְּמֹעַ *'ešt^emōa'* (5)
Eshtemoa (5)

905 אַתְּ *'at* (65)
you (50)
how did it go (1) +4769
untranslated (14)

906 1אֵת *'ēt1* (10942)
aloud (5) +5951+7754
entreat (3) +2704+7156
ordained (3) +3338+4848
sought the favor of (3) +2704+7156
take a census (3) +5951+8031
installed (2) +3338+4848
let know (2) +265+1655
openhanded (2) +3338+7337+7337
ordination (2) +3338+4848
tells (2) +265+1655
accepted (1) +5951+7156
began (1) +5951+7754
come into presence (1) +7156+8011
confiding in (1) +265+1655
consecrated (1) +3338+4848
count (1) +5951+8031
counted (1) +5951+8031
counting on (1) +448+5883+5951
did so[s] (1) +2021+6913+7175
did[s] (1) +3877+4213+4392
disheartened (1) +4222+5022
given word (1) +7023+7198
hardhearted (1) +599+4222
has sexual relations with (1) +1655+6872
have sexual relations (1) +6872+8011
helped (1) +2616+3338
helped find strength (1) +2616+3338
include in the census (1) +5951+8031
inquire of (1) +7023+8626
intercede with (1) +2704+7156
interceded with (1) +2704+7156
keep themselves alive (1) +4392+5883+8740
let go (1) +3338+5663
looked (1) +6524
offering body (1) +7316+8079
ordain (1) +3338+4848
out (1) +5951
relieve himself (1) +2257+6114+8079
relieving himself (1) +2257+6114+8079
revealed (1) +265+1655
saw (1) +5951+6524
seek favor (1) +2704+7156
sent on way (1) +8938
sought favor (1) +2704+7156
stared with a fixed gaze (1) +2256+6641+7156+8492
sulking (1) +6015+7156
sworn (1) +3338+5951
tell (1) +265+1655
tightfisted (1) +3338+7890
undergo circumcision (1) +1414+4576+6889
uttered a word (1) +3076+4383
wanted (1) +5883+8626
wanted to kill (1) +1335+5883
wept so loudly (1) +928+1140+5989+7754
worry (1) +4213+8492
untranslated (10870)

907 2אֵת *'ēt2* (935)
with (405)
from (93) +4946
against (34)
to (28)
among (14)
along with (13)
his (13) +2257
before (9) +7156
and (8)
have (8)
near (7)
of (7) +4946
for (5)
in (5)
slept with (5) +8886
by (4)
left (4) +2143+4946
through (4) +4946
upon (4)
doing (3) +4946
had (3) +5162
lies with (3) +8886
pronounced on (3) +1819
sleeps with (3) +8886
the LORD's (3) +3378+4946
allied with (2)
away from (2) +4946
before (2)
close to (2)
has (2)
have (2) +3780
help (2)
in front of (2) +7156
lay with (2) +8886
leave (2) +2143+4946
of (2)

within (2)
about (1)
accompanied (1) +2143
accompanied (1) +6590
accompanied by (1)
accompany (1) +3655
according to (1)
account for (1) +3108
adding to (1) +2256
all around (1)
alongside (1)
among (1) +4946
among (1) +8905
and (1) +2256
and together (1)
any of (1) +4946
as (1)
as well as (1)
ask (1) +8626
assist (1) +6641
away (1) +4946
because of (1)
both and (1)
bring (1) +995
by (1) +4946
by myself (1) +3276+4946
company (1) +2118
concern (1)
confide in (1) +4213
decreed (1)
determined (1) +4946
fighting with (1) +2118
following (1) +6639
for (1) +4946
forsaking (1) +4946
gain support (1) +2118+3338
given to (1)
gone from (1) +401
had (1)
help (1) +2118
helped (1)
helping (1)
in addition to (1)
in hand (1)
in possession (1)
in sight (1) +7156
in view (1) +7156
inquire of (1) +2011+4946
into (1)
know (1)
leaves (1) +2143+4946
left (1) +4946
lie with (1) +8886
lies with (1) +8886+8886
lost (1) +4946+5877
lying with (1) +8886
my (1) +3276
near (1) +2143
next to (1)
on (1)
on (1) +4946
on behalf of (1) +4946
on side (1)
oppose (1)
other[S] (1) +889
out of (1) +4946
over (1)
own (1)
past (1) +4946
representative (1) +4946
send (1) +995+4946
sent by (1) +4946
served (1) +6641+7156
shared with (1)
show (1)
sleeping with (1) +2446+8886+8887
sleeps with (1) +2446+8886+8887
some (1) +4946
supported (1) +2118+3338
through (1)
to (1) +7156
together (1)
together (1) +408+2084+8276
together with (1)
told (1) +4946+9048
toward (1)
under (1)
under (1) +7156
under care (1)
with (1) +7156
with the help of (1)
with the help of (1) +4946
within sight of (1) +7156
your (1) +3870
untranslated (130)

908 3אֵת *'ēṯ3* (5)
plowshares (3)
mattocks (2)

909 אֶתְבַּעַל *'eṯba'al* (1)
Ethbaal (1)

910 אָתָה *'āṯāh* (21)
come (7)
bring (2)
comes (2)
advance (1)
assembled (1)
be restored (1)
came (1)
come forward (1)
coming (1)
holds (1)
pass (1)
sweeps over (1)
things to come (1)

911 אַתָּה *'atāh* (745)
you (621)
yourself (17)
your (4)
you're (2)
your own (2)
it (1)
you alone (1) +911
you yourself (1)
you'll (1)
yours (1)
untranslated (93)

912 אָתוֹן *'āṯôn* (34)
donkey (13)
donkeys (12)
female donkeys (2)
her[S] (2) +2021
colt (1) +1201
donkey's (1)
female (1)
she[S] (1) +2021
them[S] (1) +2021

913 אַתּוּק *'atûq* (1)
untranslated (1)

914 אַתַּי *'atiy* (7)
untranslated (7)

915 אִתַּי *'itay* (8)
Ittai (7)
Ithai (1)

916 אַתִּיק *'atiyq* (5)
galleries (3)
gallery (2)

917 אַתֶּם *'atem* (283)
you (244)
yourselves (10)
your (3)
yours (2)
people[S] (1)
you and your men (1)
untranslated (22)

918 אֵתָם *'ēṯām* (4)
Etham (4)

919 אֶתְמוֹל *'eṯmôl* (8)
before (2) +8997
day (1) +3427
formerly (1) +4946+8997
in the past (1) +1685+1685+8997
lately (1)
long (1) +4946
previously (1) +3869+8997

920 אַתֵּן *'atēn* (4)
you (4)

921 אֶתְנָה *'eṯnāh* (1)
pay (1)

922 אֶתְנִי *'eṯniy* (1)
Ethni (1)

923 אֵתָנִים *'ēṯāniym* (1)
Ethanim (1)

924 אֶתְנַן *'eṯnan* (11)
earnings (2)
payment (2)
wages (2)
hire as a prostitute (1)
pay (1) +5989
temple gifts (1)
wages of a prostitute (1)
untranslated (1)

925 אֶתְנָן *'eṯnān* (1)
Ethnan (1)

926 אֲתָרִים *'ᵃṯāriym* (1)
Atharim (1)

927 ב *ḇ*
Variant; not used

928 בְּ־ *bᵉ-* (15567)
in (4676)
with (1047)
on (956)
at (580)
by (501)
when (497)
of (303)
to (281)
into (274)
against (260)
among (241)
through (183)
for (160)
among (111) +9348
from (98)
over (89)
as (80)
through (62) +3338
because of (59)
during (59)
among (52) +7931
according to (50)
while (48)
throughout (47) +3972
in (45) +9348
when (45) +3427
before (36) +3270
obey (36) +7754+9048
hand over (35) +3338+5989
upon (34)
under (33)
there[S] (28) +2023
after (27)
throughout (26)
along (25)
enter (25) +995
in (24) +7931
handed over (23) +3338+5989
follow (22) +2143
about (20)
whenever (20)
with (20) +3338
within (20)
within (20) +7931

to (19) +265
by (18) +3338
near (18)
obeyed (18) +7754+9048
with (17) +9348
because (16)
how (16) +4537
if (16)
has (15)
inquired of (15) +8626
inside (15) +9348
to (15) +3338
to (15) +7754
within (15) +9348
used (14)
have (12)
here (12) +2296
had (11)
when (11) +6961
with (11) +7931
around (10)
followed (10) +2143
seems (10) +6524
where (10)
wherever (10) +889+3972
wherever (10) +3972
burn down (9) +836+2021+8596
east (9) +6298
inside (9)
into (9) +9348
safely (9) +8934
set on fire (9) +836+2021+3675
without (9) +4202
and (8)
be handed over (8) +3338+5989
burned (8) +836+2021+8596
entered (8) +995
in spite of (8)
seemed (8) +6524
think (8) +6524
through (8) +9348
before (7)
outside (7) +2021+2575
pleased (7) +3512+6524
that (7)
toward (7)
along with (6) +9348
amid (6)
any (6)
before (6) +2021+8037
despite (6)
invade (6) +995
like (6)
secretly (6) +2021+6260
there[s] (6) +3731
this is how (6) +2296
unintentionally (6) +8705
use (6)
within (6) +6388
against (5) +7156
always (5) +3972+6961
at the cost of (5)
beyond (5) +6298
displeased (5) +6524+8317
faithfully (5) +575
has (5) +2118
on account of (5)
pleased with (5) +2834+5162+6524
pleases (5) +3202+6524
ruthlessly (5) +7266
stone (5) +74+2021+8083
using (5)
accidentally (4) +8705
accompanied by (4)
across (4) +6298
allotted (4) +1598+2021
be burned up (4) +836+2021+8596
beside (4)
burn (4) +836+2021+8596
burned up (4) +836+2021+8596
consult (4) +2011
every morning (4) +928+1332+1332+2021+2021
faithfully (4) +622
have (4) +3338
in exchange for (4)
inner room (4) +2540+2540
inquire of (4) +2011
invaded (4) +995
near (4) +7931
out of (4)
seem (4) +6524
set on fire (4) +836+2021+8596
there[s] (4) +1195+2021
there[s] (4) +2023+9348
there[s] (4) +2257
to (4) +6524
touch (4) +2118
unintentionally (4) +1172+1981
wearing (4)
whether (4)
with (4) +6524
as (3) +2006
at the risk of (3)
at the time of (3)
before (3) +4202
between (3) +9348
burn up (3) +836+2021+8596
burned down (3) +836+2021+8596
called out (3) +1524+7754+7924
cost (3)
daily (3) +3427+3427
each year (3) +9102+9102
early (3) +8040
every last male (3) +7815+8874
favorably disposed toward (3) +2834+6524
first (3) +2021+9378
follows (3) +2143
has (3) +3780
heard (3) +265
including (3)
king's (3) +4889
later (3)
like (3) +3202+6524
made (3)
male (3) +7815+8874
on high (3) +2021+5294
on the basis of (3)
saw (3) +6524
secret (3) +4537
share (3) +5951
some (3)
though (3)
through (3) +7931
throughout (3) +1473+3972
under (3) +3338
upon (3) +7931
whenever (3) +3972
wherever (3) +889+2006+2021
wherever (3) +889+5226
wild (3) +2021+8441
without (3) +700
all (2)
all day long (2) +2021+2021+2085+3427
allotted (2) +1598+2021+5989
alone (2) +1727+2257
along with (2)
anywhere (2) +3972+5226
as (2) +6961
as before (2) +3869+7193+7193
as long as (2)
as long as live (2) +6388
as soon as (2)
assassinate (2) +3338+8938
associate with (2) +995
at (2) +6961
because (2) +889
because of (2) +1673
before (2) +265
before (2) +3270+4202
bloodshed (2) +995+1947
boldly (2) +3338+8123
by (2) +6524
by means of (2)
by what means (2) +4537
certainly be handed over (2) +3338+5989+5989
chosen (2) +7924+9005
deceitfully (2) +5327
disobeyed (2) +4202+7754+9048
distressed (2) +6524+8317
do (2)
down (2)
each (2)
each day (2) +3427+3427
earlier (2) +2021+9378
entrusted with (2) +575
everywhere (2) +3972
exceedingly (2) +4394+4394
fill (2)
first (2) +2021+8037
fleet-footed (2) +7824+8079
following (2)
following (2) +8079
for each day (2) +1821+3427+3427
for nothing (2) +1896+8198
from (2) +9348
fully obey (2) +7754+9048+9048
greatly (2) +4394+4394
guilty (2) +3338
had (2) +3338
hand over (2) +3338+6037
handed over (2) +3338+6037
have respect for (2) +3700+6524
honorably (2) +622
in charge of (2)
in obedience to (2)
in return for (2)
inside (2) +1074+2021
intersecting (2) +9348
invades (2) +995
its (2) +2023
joyfully (2) +8525
just as (2)
led by (2) +8031
make a survey of (2) +2143
my (2) +3276+8079
near (2) +6298
now (2) +465+2021+2021+3427
on (2) +7931
on high (2) +7757
over (2) +8031
overwhelmed (2) +2118+4202+6388+8120
play (2) +3338+5594
playing the harp (2) +3338+5594
please (2) +3202+6524
please (2) +3837+6524
pleased (2) +3202+6524
pleased (2) +3837+6524
privately (2) +2021+6260
purchased (2) +4374+4697
quietly (2) +2021+4319
reached (2) +995
required (2) +460+5957
sees (2) +6524
sell (2) +4084+5989
sold for (2) +2118
stone (2) +74+2021+6232
stoned (2) +74+2021+6232
struck (2) +2118
supervising (2)
taking with (2) +3338
then (2) +340+2021
there[s] (2) +1074+2021
there[s] (2) +9076
thought (2) +6524
throughout (2) +6017
throughout (2) +9348
truly (2) +622
up to (2)
very (2) +4394+4394
what (2)
what (2) +4537

when (2) +2021+3427
where (2) +889
where[s] (2) +2023
wherever (2)
wherever (2) +889+2021+3972+5226
wherever goes (2) +928+995+2256+3655
while (2) +3427
wholeheartedly (2) +3972+4213
wholeheartedly (2) +3972+4222
wholeheartedly (2) +4222+8969
with help (2)
without (2) +401
withstand (2) +995
withstand (2) +6641+7156
wounds (2) +995
yearly (2) +285+9102
ability (1) +2683+4213
aboard (1)
above (1) +2021+5294
accuse (1) +1821+8492
across (1)
affected (1)
after (1) +1821
after (1) +1896+4946
after (1) +3427
after (1) +8079
after (1) +9005
again (1) +1685+2021+2021+2085+7193
against (1) +6330
alive (1) +5883
all (1) +285
all night long (1) +2021+4326
allotted (1) +1598+2021+2118
alone (1) +285
along (1) +6298
along (1) +9348
along with (1) +3338
along with (1) +7931
alongside (1)
aloud (1) +1524+7754
aloud (1) +7754
already (1) +2021+9378
although (1) +889+3972
angry (1) +3013+6524
annual (1) +285+2021+9102
annual (1) +2021+7193+9102
annually (1) +2256+3972+9102+9102
anywhere in (1) +1473+3972
appealed to (1) +3512+6524
appear (1) +2118+3869+6524
approve of (1) +3202+6524
archers (1) +408+2021+4619+8008
archers (1) +2021+4619+8008
are burned up (1) +836+2021+8596+8596
arrayed in (1)
as (1) +889
as (1) +889+3972
as directs (1)
as done before (1) +3869+7193+7193
as long as (1) +3427
as long as (1) +3972+6961
as long as (1) +6388
as one (1) +9348
as usually did (1) +3427+3427+3869
assaults (1) +8938
assemble (1) +2021+6590+7736
assisted (1) +2616+3338
assuredly (1) +622
at (1) +2006+2021
at (1) +6298
at (1) +7931
at (1) +9348
at once (1) +2021+2021+2085+3427
at once (1) +2021+2021+2085+6961
at once (1) +2021+3427
at other times (1) +7193+7193
at stake (1)
at the blast (1) +1896
at the time (1)
attached to (1)
attack (1) +3338+8938
attack (1) +3718
attack (1) +5877
attacked (1) +3338+8938
attacked (1) +5877
attacked (1) +6590
attacks (1) +3338+8938
bare (1) +401+4399
based on (1)
be a virgin (1) +1436
be burned (1) +836+2021+8596
be burned down (1) +836+2021+8596
be defeated (1) +3338+5989
be taken captive (1) +2021+4090+9530
bears (1)
because (1) +2256+3610+3610
because (1) +3610
because (1) +3610+3610
because of (1) +3338
been handed over (1) +3338+5989
before (1) +678
before (1) +2021+9378
beginning with (1)
behind (1)
belong to (1) +2118
belonged to (1) +8079
bent on (1) +6783
beset (1) +995
beside (1) +2668
beside (1) +3338
besiege (1) +995+2021+5189
besieged (1) +2837
between (1)
bind themselves with (1) +995
blind (1) +2021+5782+6427
boasted (1) +1540+7023
borrowed (1) +5957
bought (1) +2021+4084+7864
bring about (1) +2118
brings (1)
brought (1) +3338
brought with (1) +2118+3338
brutally (1) +7266
burn to death (1) +836+2021+8596
burned (1) +836+2021+8938
burned to death (1) +836+2021+8596
buy (1) +4084
by (1) +9348
by day (1) +3429
by means (1)
cargo (1) +641+889+2021+3998
carried (1) +3338+4374
carry off (1) +995+2021+8660
carrying (1)
cause (1) +3338
centrally located in (1) +9348
charred (1) +836+1277+2021
close to (1)
clung to (1)
come into (1) +5877
commit (1) +2143
committed (1) +2143
compels (1)
concealed in (1)
concerning (1)
consider (1) +4222
consider (1) +6524
considered (1) +6524
constantly (1) +3972+6961
consult (1) +1821+2011
containing (1)
contrary to (1) +3869+4202
counted off (1) +5031+6296
covered (1) +2118
covers (1) +995
cruelly (1) +2622
customary (1) +3869+7193+7193
daily (1) +1821+3427+3427
daily (1) +2257+3427+3427
day by day (1) +1821+2257+3427+3427
day by day (1) +1821+3427+3427
dealing with (1)
debtor (1) +5957
deceived (1) +5792+5793
deceptively (1) +6817
defiantly (1) +7418
delegation (1) +3338+6269
deliberately (1) +6893
delivered (1) +3338
despise (1) +1022+6524
despise (1) +6524+7837
despises (1) +1022+6524
despises (1) +6524+7837
despite (1) +4200+8611
diligently obey (1) +7754+9048+9048
disapprove (1) +6524+8317
disobedience (1) +4202+7754+9048
disobey (1) +1194+7754+9048
displease (1) +2834+4202+5162+6524
displease (1) +6524+8273
displeasing (1) +2834+4202+5162+6524
displeasing (1) +6524+8273
distributed among (1)
do that[s] (1) +2118+2257+3338
done by (1) +3338
doubly (1) +2021+9109
drew (1) +3338+4848
driving (1)
due annually (1) +1896+4946+9102+9102
during (1) +3427
each day's (1) +2257+3427+3427
each day's (1) +3427+3427
each morning (1) +928+1332+1332+2021+2021
eagerly (1) +3972+8356
east (1) +2025+4667+6298
east (1) +2025+4667+6298+9087
east (1) +4667+6298+9087
encounter (1) +995
end (1) +340+2021+2118
entered (1) +995+9348
entering (1) +995
entering (1) +995+7931
entering (1) +995+9348
enters (1) +995
entrusted to (1) +3338
even after (1)
even if (1)
evening (1) +928+2021+2021+6847+6847
every (1)
every day (1) +3427+3427
every evening (1) +928+2021+2021+6847+6847
every Sabbath (1) +8701+8701
everyone's (1) +408
everywhere (1) +3972+5226
fairly (1) +7406
faithful (1) +622+2143
far back in (1) +3752
far off (1) +8158
fault (1) +4200+8611
favorable toward (1) +2834+5162+6524
feeds (1) +5966+9094
few (1) +5031+5071
fiercely (1) +2021+6677
fifteen feet (1) +564+2021+6924
filled (1) +2118+3972
filled with (1) +7931
flashed back and forth (1) +4374+9348
flashes (1) +836
follow (1) +2143+8079
follow (1) +8079
followed (1)
followed (1) +6590+8079
for (1) +889
for (1) +1685+8611
for (1) +3338
for (1) +6524
for (1) +9348
forcefully (1) +3338
formerly (1) +2021+8037
fought in (1) +3655
free from (1) +4202

from (1) +889
from (1) +3338
from (1) +6524
from now (1) +6388
from the time (1)
fuel for fire (1) +836+1896
fuel for flames (1) +836+1896
fully determined (1) +4222+8969
galled (1) +6524+8317
gave in (1) +7754+9048
gave victory (1) +3338+5989
get (1)
give (1) +3338+5989
given by (1)
giving credit to (1) +9005
glad (1) +3512+6524
gladly (1) +3206+4222
go (1) +2006+2143
gone (1) +2118+4202
gone (1) +4202+6641
had (1) +2118
had (1) +7023
had (1) +7931
had chance (1) +2118+3338
hand over (1) +3338+4835
hand over (1) +3338+5162
hand over to (1) +3338+5989
handed (1) +3338+5989
handed over (1) +3338+5162
handed over (1) +3338+5796
handing over (1) +3338+5989
handing over (1) +3338+6037
harbor (1) +4328+7931
harbor in (1)
harnessed to (1)
harshly (1) +2622
has (1) +3338
hasty (1) +237+8079
have (1) +2118
have (1) +3338+5162
have (1) +3780
have (1) +5055
have (1) +7023
have a claim on (1)
heard (1) +265+606
here[S] (1) +824+2021
here[S] (1) +2021+2021+2296+5226
here[S] (1) +2021+4497
here[S] (1) +2023
here[S] (1) +5226
his (1) +2257
his[S] (1) +2021+4889
hold (1) +2118+3338
holding (1) +3338
holds (1) +2118+3338
how (1)
how (1) +686+4537
hurl insults (1) +7080+8557
if (1) +3427
imagine (1) +5381
imprisoned (1) +5464+5989
in (1) +1060
in (1) +4213
in (1) +4595
in accordance with (1)
in charge of (1) +3338
in each corner (1) +928+5243+5243
in equal amounts (1) +963+963
in keeping with (1)
in payment for (1)
in person (1) +265
in possession (1)
in regard to (1)
in response to (1)
in the name of (1)
in view of (1)
include (1) +9348
inquire of (1) +8626
inquires of (1) +1821+8626
inquiring of (1) +8626
inserted into (1)
inside (1) +5055
inside (1) +7931
insist on paying for (1) +4697+7864+7864
inspire (1) +4222+5989
intentionally (1) +7402
interwoven (1) +2021+8054
into (1) +7931
invade (1) +6296
invade (1) +6590
invaded (1) +6590
invoke (1) +7023+7924
involved in (1)
Israel's (1) +3776
Israelite (1) +1201+3776
Israelite (1) +3776
its[S] (1) +2021+6551
join (1) +2118
joined in (1) +9348
just before (1) +3270
keep (1) +2143
keeping watch (1) +6524+8011
kept (1) +2143
killing (1) +3338+8938
lack (1) +401
lack (1) +4202
laden with (1)
laid siege (1) +995+2021+5189
lamb (1) +2021+3897+8445
lamb (1) +2021+4166+8445
land's (1) +824
lately (1) +700
later (1) +340+2021
later in time (1) +344
lead life (1) +2143
leads (1) +2021+8037
leave (1)
led life (1) +2143
let get away (1) +2006+8938
let touch (1) +995
leveled completely (1) +2021+9164+9168
lie in state (1) +3883+8886
like (1) +9348
liked (1) +3837+6524
likes (1) +2021+3202+4200
listen carefully (1) +265+9048
listen carefully (1) +7754+9048
listen closely (1) +265+9048
listened (1) +265
live (1) +2021+2644
live (1) +2143
lived (1) +1074+2021
living in (1)
long ago (1) +2021+8037
look (1) +6524
look carefully (1) +6524+8011
looked (1) +2118+6524
lose heart (1) +1327+7931+8120
lost self-confidence (1) +4394+5877+6524
loudly (1) +1524+7754
made (1) +4374
made a fatal mistake (1) +5883+9494
made pay for (1) +8031+8740
made with (1)
make enter (1) +995
make fine speeches (1) +2488+4863
make full restitution (1) +8031+8740
make sure hears (1) +265+8492
makes (1)
mark (1)
measured out (1) +4500+9419
mention (1) +7023+9019
monthly (1) +2544+2544
mortal (1) +5883
mounted (1) +2021+6061
moving from place to place (1) +889+2143+2143
must sell (1) +2021+4084+4835+4835
my (1) +3276
nails down (1) +2616+5021
named (1) +7924+9005
native-born (1) +824+2021+3528
nomads (1) +185+8905
not please (1) +6524+8317
not want (1) +6524+8273
now (1)
obey (1) +2143
obey fully (1) +7754+9048+9048
obeying (1) +7754+9048
obeys (1) +7754+9048
of (1) +9348
off (1)
offer (1)
on (1) +9348
on board (1)
on board (1) +9348
on each side (1)
on fire (1) +836+1277+2021
on side (1)
on the condition that (1) +2296
on the tip of tongue (1) +2674+4383
once (1)
one (1)
one by one (1) +5031
one of[S] (1)
one way (1) +285
only (1) +1727+2257
only if (1)
oppose (1) +995
oppressed (1) +2021+6913+6945
out here (1) +2021+2575
outdoor (1) +2021+2575
over (1) +9348
overrun (1)
paid (1)
painted (1) +2021+7037+8531
parallel (1) +7156
part of (1)
pay with (1)
peaceably (1) +8934
peacefully (1) +8934
penned up (1) +1074+2021+3973
people[S] (1) +889+3972
pierce (1)
pierce (1) +995
pierced (1) +995
pierced (1) +5737
placed seal (1) +2597+3159
please (1) +2256+3202+3838+6524
please (1) +3838+6524
pleased (1) +3201+6524
pleased (1) +3838+6524
pleased with (1) +2834+5951+6524
pleased with (1) +3202+6524
pleased with (1) +3512+6524
pleased with (1) +3837+6524
pleases (1) +3512+6524
plot against (1) +3108+4222
prefer (1) +3202+6524
present in (1)
preserved (1) +2021+2645+8492
presumptuously (1) +2295
prevailed upon (1) +2616
privately (1) +2021+4319
privately (1) +2021+8952
proclaim (1) +7924
proclaimed (1) +7924
promised (1) +1819+7023
prone to (1)
protect (1) +3829+8883
pursues (1) +8740
put in jeopardy (1) +1414+5951+9094
put on (1) +5516+8492
puts up a bold front (1) +6451+7156
quickly (1) +4559
raiding (1) +995
rationed (1) +5374
rationed (1) +5486
reached (1) +2118
reached (1) +9048
reaches to (1)
ready for battle (1) +2021+4878+7372
really (1) +622

regarding (1)
regards (1) +5162+6524
regular flow (1) +1414+2307
regularly (1) +3427+3427+4200
repay (1) +8031+8740
responsible for (1) +889+4200
responsible for (1) +4200+8611
responsible for (1) +6015
result of (1)
ride (1) +2143
risked (1)
roars (1) +5989+7754
Sabbath after Sabbath (1)
+928+2021+2021+3427+3427+8701+8701
sacrificed (1) +5989+6296
sail (1) +641+2021+2143
sandaled (1) +2021+5837
satisfied (1) +3512+6524
satisfied (1) +8934
scarce (1) +430+5017
scorned the idea (1) +1022+6524
screamed (1) +1524+7754+7924
search (1) +606
seem (1) +2118+6524
seem (1) +4017+6524
seemed (1) +2118+6524
seize (1) +3338+8492
sell for (1) +2118
set ablaze (1) +836+2021+3675
set fire to (1) +836+2021+8596
set fire to (1) +836+2021+8938
set on (1)
set with (1)
seven and a half feet (1) +564+2021+2822
shamefully (1) +2365
shared hardships (1) +889+6700+6700
sharply (1) +2622
shoot (1) +2021+8008
shout (1) +7754+7924
shout aloud (1) +1744+7924
shouted (1) +7754+7924
shouted (1) +7754+8123+9558
since (1) +889
sing (1) +7023+8492
sing songs (1) +4200+7754+8123+9048
sins defiantly (1) +3338+6913+8123
sins unintentionally (1) +6913+8705
sleeping with (1) +5989+8888
sling stones (1) +74+2021
smoothly (1) +4797
so quickly (1) +7328
some of (1)
someone else[s] (1) +3338
soon (1) +7940
speak (1) +7023
spreads feathers to run (1)
+2021+5257+5294
stargazers (1) +2600+3919
stationed at (1)
stoned (1) +74+2021+8083
stoning (1) +74+2021+8083
strike (1) +2118
striking (1) +2118
suddenly (1) +285
suddenly (1) +7328+7353
suddenly (1) +7353
suffer (1)
suffered (1) +2118
surely hand over (1) +3338+5989+5989
surrender (1) +3338+6037
surrounded by (1) +9348
sweep away (1) +4053+7674
take great delight (1) +8464+8525
take hold of (1) +2118
take in (1)
taken (1) +3338
taken great pains (1) +6715
taken into account (1)
takes the stand (1) +7756
tell (1) +265+1819
tent-dwelling (1) +185+2021
that (1) +3907
the storehouses[s] (1) +889+2157+3972
their[s] (1) +2157+4090
them[s] (1) +74+2021+4392
then[s] (1) +2296
then[s] (1) +2021+2021+2085+3427
there[s] (1)
there[s] (1) +824
there[s] (1) +1195+2021
there[s] (1) +2021+2215
there[s] (1) +466+1074
there[s] (1) +824+2021
there[s] (1) +824+2257
there[s] (1) +951
there[s] (1) +1014+2021
there[s] (1) +1028
there[s] (1) +1074+2021+3752
there[s] (1) +1078
there[s] (1) +1618
there[s] (1) +2006+2021
there[s] (1) +2021+2215
there[s] (1) +2021+4722
there[s] (1) +2021+5207
there[s] (1) +2021+6551
there[s] (1) +2023+8148
there[s] (1) +2025+9463
there[s] (1) +2157
there[s] (1) +2257+7931
there[s] (1) +2257+9348
there[s] (1) +2972
there[s] (1) +4392+9348
there[s] (1) +5213
there[s] (1) +5707+7724
there[s] (1) +8931
think (1) +606+4213
think (1) +606+4222
thinks (1) +606+4222
thirty feet (1) +564+2021+6929
this (1) +3907
this is how (1) +465+3972
this is the way (1) +4392
thoughtlessly (1) +1051+4200+8557
thoughts (1) +5883+6783
through fault (1)
throughout (1) +7931
thunders (1) +5989+7754
till (1)
timely (1) +6961
to (1) +4200+6288
to (1) +4213
to avenge (1)
to each man (1) +9005
to get (1)
together with (1)
told (1) +265+1819
told (1) +7023+8492
took (1)
took with (1) +3338
tried (1) +4213+9365
troubled (1) +6524+8273
under control (1) +294
under cover (1) +9564
underfoot (1) +8079
unharmed (1) +8934
unintentionally (1) +4202+7402
unnoticed (1) +2021+4319
unscathed (1) +8934
upset (1) +6524+8317
urgently (1) +2622
use name as a curse (1) +8678
used (1) +3338
used for (1)
uses (1) +3338
value (1) +1540+6524
valued (1) +1540+6524
very old (1) +995+2021+2416+3427
vigorously (1) +6437
walk (1) +2006+2143
walking along (1) +2006+2021
wanted to do (1) +3202+6524
watch (1) +6524
waylaid (1) +2006+2021+8492
wearing (1) +265
went aboard (1) +3718
wept so loudly (1) +906+1140+5989+7754
were put in chains (1) +2414+8415
west (1) +6298
whatever (1) +889+3972
when (1) +8040
when began (1) +3427
whenever (1) +889+3972
whenever (1) +3427
whenever (1) +3972+6961
whenever (1) +6961
where[s] (1) +396
where[s] (1) +2021+5226
where[s] (1) +2177
where[s] (1) +2257
where[s] (1) +5226
where[s] (1) +6152+8234
wherever (1) +285+889+2021+5226
wherever (1) +889
wherever (1) +889+2021+5226
wherever (1) +2021+3972+5226
wholeheartedly (1) +4213+8969
why (1) +4537
willfully (1) +4222
wish (1) +3202+6524
wish (1) +3512+6524
wished (1) +3202+6524
with (1) +2118
with (1) +8079
with in hand (1)
within (1) +2668
within (1) +3752
within (1) +5055+9348
without (1) +1172
without meaning (1) +2021+2039
withstood (1) +6641+7156
won (1) +5951+6524
workmen (1) +2021+4856+6913
worn (1) +5432
worth (1)
your (1) +2257
your (1) +3870
untranslated (2479)

929 בִּאָה *bi'āh* (1)
entrance (1)

930 בָּאַר *bā'ar* (3)
clearly (1)
expound (1)
make plain (1)

931 1בְּאֵר *b^e'ēr1* (39)
well (30)
pit (2)
wells (2)
full of pits (1) +931
well (1) +4784
well's (1)
wells (1) +4784

932 2בְּאֵר *b^e'ēr2* (2)
Beer (2)

933 3בְּאֵר *b^e'ēr3*
Variant; not used

934 בֹּאר *bō'r*
Variant; not used

935 בְּאֵר אֵילִים *b^e'ēr 'ēyliym* (1)
Beer Elim (1)

936 בְּאֵר לַחַי רֹאִי *b^e'ēr lahay rō'iy* (3)
Beer Lahai Roi (3)

937 בְּאֵר שֶׁבַע *b^e'ēr šeba'* (34)
Beersheba (34)

938 בְּאֵרָא *b^e'ērā'* (1)
Beera (1)

939 בְּאֵרָה *b^e'ērāh* (1)
Beerah (1)

940 בְּאֵרוֹת b^{e}'ērôṯ (5)
Beeroth (5)

941 בְּאֵרִי b^{e}'ēriy (2)
Beeri (2)

942 בְּאֵרֹת בְּנֵי־יַעֲקָן b^{e}'ērōṯ b^{e}nēy-ya^{a}qān
Variant; not used

943 בְּאֵרֹתִי b^{e}'ērōṯiy (5)
Beerothite (4)
people of Beeroth (1)

944 בָּאַשׁ bā'aš (17)
stench (3)
stink (2)
bring shame (1)
give a bad smell (1) +5580
loathsome (1)
made stench (1) +8194
made yourself a stench (1)
making a stench (1)
reeked (1)
rot (1)
smell (1)
smelled bad (1)
so odious (1) +944

945 בְּאֹשׁ b^{e}'ōš (3)
stench (3)

946 בְּאֻשׁ b^{e}'uš (2)
bad (1)
bad fruit (1)

947 בָּאְשָׁה bā'^{e}šāh (1)
weeds (1)

948 בַּאֲשֶׁר ba'^{a}šer
Variant; not used

949 בָּבָה bāḇāh (1)
apple (1)

950 בֵּבַי bēḇay (6)
Bebai (6)

951 בָּבֶל bāḇel (262)
Babylon (242)
Babylon's (3)
Babylonians (2) +1201
Babel (1)
Babylon (1) +824
Babylonia (1)
Babylonian (1) +1201
he^{S} (1) +4889
him^{S} (1) +4889
his^{S} (1) +4889
there^{S} (1) +928
untranslated (7)

952 בַּג baḡ (1)
untranslated (1)

953 בָּגַד bāḡaḏ (49)
unfaithful (16)
betrayed (5)
broken faith (4)
treacherous (4)
betray (2)
betrays (2)
break faith (2)
faithless (2)
traitor (2)
acted treacherously (1)
betraying (1)
breaking faith (1)
faithless (1) +954
how treacherous (1) +953
traitors (1)
undependable (1)
utterly unfaithful (1) +953

954 1בֶּגֶד beḡeḏ1 (2)
faithless (1) +953
treachery (1)

955 2בֶּגֶד beḡeḏ2 (217)
clothes (79)
garments (48)
clothing (23)
robes (17)
garment (14)
cloak (8)
cloth (8)
tunic (2)
wardrobe (2)
articles of clothing (1)
blankets (1) +2927
cloaks (1)
clothed (1)
clothed (1) +4252
clothes (1) +6886
covers (1)
fold of cloak (1)
rags (1)
those^{S} (1)
untranslated (6)

956 בֹּגְדוֹת bōḡ^{e}ḏôṯ (1)
treacherous (1)

957 בָּגוֹד bāḡôḏ (2)
unfaithful (2)

958 בִּגְוַי biḡway (6)
Bigvai (6)

959 בִּגְלַל biḡlal
Variant; not used

960 בִּגְתָא biḡtā' (1)
Bigtha (1)

961 בִּגְתָן biḡṯān (1)
Bigthana (1)

962 בִּגְתָנָא biḡṯānā' (1)
Bigthana (1)

963 1בַּד baḏ1 (162)
alone (40) +4200
in addition to (18) +4200+4946
only (16) +4200
besides (9) +4200+4946
only one (8) +4200
by themselves (4) +4200+4392
apart (3) +4200
as well as (2) +4200+4946
in addition to (2) +4200
limbs (2)
not counting (2) +4200+4946
not including (2) +4200+4946
set (2)
all (1) +4200
all alone (1) +4200
all by myself (1) +3276+4200
along with (1) +4200+4946
also (1) +4200
anyone (1) +4200
besides (1) +4200
by himself (1) +2257+4200
by itself (1) +2257+4200
by itself (1) +4200
by myself (1) +3276+4200
even though (1) +4200
in addition (1) +4200
in addition (1) +4200+4946
in equal amounts (1) +928+963
into another set (1) +4200
into one set (1) +4200
more than (1) +4200+4946
myself (1) +3276
only (1) +2314+4200
only exception (1) +4200
only one (1) +2257+4200
other than (1) +1194+4200
other than (1) +4200+4946
parts (1)
separate (1) +3657+4200
separate (1) +4200
this one (1) +4200
untranslated (23)

964 2בַּד baḏ2 (41)
poles (31)
carrying poles (2)
their^{S} (2) +2021
bars of gates (1)
branches (1)
gates (1)
main branches (1) +4751
they^{S} (1) +2021
untranslated (1)

965 3בַּד baḏ3 (23)
linen (22)
undergarments (1) +4829

966 4בַּד baḏ4 (3)
boasts (2)
idle talk (1)

967 5בַּד baḏ5 (2)
false prophets (2)

968 בָּדָא bāḏā' (2)
choosing (1)
making up (1)

969 בָּדַד bāḏaḏ (3)
alone (1)
straggler (1)
wandering alone (1)

970 בָּדָד bāḏāḏ (11)
alone (6)
alone (1) +4200
apart (1) +4200
by itself (1) +4200
deserted (1)
desolate (1)

971 בְּדַד b^{e}ḏaḏ (2)
Bedad (2)

972 בְּדֵי b^{e}ḏēy
Variant; not used

973 בֵּדְיָה bēḏ^{e}yāh (1)
Bedeiah (1)

974 בְּדִיל b^{e}ḏiyl (5)
tin (4)
plumb line (1) +74

975 בָּדִיל bāḏiyl (1)
impurities (1)

976 בָּדַל bāḏal (42)
set apart (7)
separate (5)
separated (4)
distinguish (3)
separated themselves (3)
set aside (3)
separate yourselves (2)
severing completely (2)
be expelled (1)
defected (1)
dismissed (1)
employed (1)
excluded (1)
kept themselves separate (1)
make a distinction (1)
selected (1)
single out (1)
singled out (1)
surely exclude (1) +976
was set apart (1)

977 בָּדָל bāḏāl (1)
piece (1)

978 בְּדֹלַח b^{e}ḏōlah (2)
aromatic resin (1)
resin (1)

979 בְּדָן b^{e}ḏān (1)
Bedan (1)

980 בָּדַק bāḏaq (1)
repaired (1)

981 בֶּדֶק beḏeq (10)
damage (2)

repair (1) +2616
repairing (1)
seams (1)
shipwrights (1) +2616
untranslated (4)

982 בִּדְקַר *bidqar* (1)
Bidkar (1)

983 בֹּהוּ *bōhû* (3)
empty (2)
desolation (1)

984 בְּהוֹן *bᵉhôn* (2)
thumbs (2) +3338

985 בַּהַט *bahat* (1)
porphyry (1)

986 בָּהִיר *bāhiyr* (1)
bright (1)

987 בָּהַל *bāhal* (39)
terrified (10)
dismayed (3)
hurried (2)
make afraid (2)
terrifies (2)
alarm (1)
alarmed (1)
am bewildered (1)
dismayed (1) +4394
eager (1)
hurry (1)
immediately (1)
in a hurry (1)
in agony (1)
in anguish (1) +4394
quick (1)
quickly (1)
quickly gained (1)
raced (1)
sudden (1)
terrify (1)
terror (1)
terror seize (1)
tremble (1)
was shaken (1)

988 בֶּהָלָה *behālāh* (4)
terror (2)
misfortune (1)
sudden terror (1)

989 בְּהֵמָה *bᵉhēmāh* (190)
animals (63)
animal (44)
livestock (33)
cattle (17)
beasts (13)
beast (5)
herds (3)
another[s] (1)
beasts of burden (1) +2256+2651
brute beast (1)
kinds of cattle (1) +989+2256
livestock (1) +5238
mount (1)
mounts (1)
one[s] (1)
wild beasts (1)
untranslated (2)

990 בְּהֵמוֹת *bᵉhēmôt* (1)
behemoth (1)

991 בֹּהֶן *bōhen* (14)
big toe (5)
thumb (5)
big toes (2)
thumbs (2)

992 בֹּהַן *bōhan* (2)
Bohan (2)

993 בֹּהַק *bōhaq* (1)
harmless rash (1)

994 בַּהֶרֶת *baheret* (12)
spot (7)
bright spot (2)
spots (2)
untranslated (1)

995 בּוֹא *bô'* (2581)
come (374)
came (285)
bring (177)
went (174)
brought (165)
go (105)
coming (71)
comes (67)
arrived (48)
enter (36) +448
enter (31)
returned (29)
enter (25) +928
took (22)
bringing (19)
entered (19)
go in (19)
went in (18)
entered (17) +448
take (14)
bring in (13)
gone (13)
reached (13) +448
come in (12)
entering (12)
brought in (11)
came in (11)
reached (11) +6330
bring back (10)
went into (10)
brings (8)
entered (8) +928
enters (8)
brought back (7)
fulfilled (7)
lay with (7) +448
put (7)
set (7)
well advanced (7)
followed (6) +339
get (6)
go into (6)
invade (6) +928
reached (6)
sleep with (6) +448
sunset (6) +2021+9087
went back (6)
attack (5) +6584
enters (5) +448
goes (5)
happened (5)
slept with (5) +448
approached (4) +6330
arrived (4) +448
back (4)
came back (4)
carried off (4)
entrance (4)
flee (4)
flows (4)
going (4)
going on duty (4)
included (4)
invaded (4) +928
lie with (4) +448
overtake (4)
reached (4) +2025
return (4)
arriving (3)
attack (3) +448
attack (3) +4200
bring about (3)
bring into (3)
brought into (3)
comes true (3)
entered (3) +4200
get in (3)
give (3)
going in (3)
is brought (3)
marched (3)
overtakes (3)
returning (3)
sailed (3)
setting (3)
taken (3)
toward (3) +2025+3870
was brought (3)
advance (2)
approach (2)
approaches (2) +448
approaching (2)
arrival (2)
arrives (2)
associate with (2) +928
at hand (2)
attack (2)
attacked (2) +6584
be brought (2)
been brought into (2)
bloodshed (2) +928+1947
bow (2)
bring down (2)
bringing in (2)
brought to pass (2)
came home (2)
came to pass (2)
carried (2)
carry (2)
certainly come (2) +995
come into (2)
come true (2)
delivered (2)
enter (2) +6584
entering (2) +4200
follows (2) +339
get there (2)
go back (2)
go now (2) +2143
goes down (2)
goes in (2)
happens (2)
inserted (2)
invade (2)
invades (2) +928
kept (2)
led (2)
led in campaigns (2) +2256+3655+4200+7156
led on military campaigns (2) +2256+3655
left (2) +4946
march (2)
placed (2)
present (2)
presented (2)
put in (2)
reach (2) +6330
reached (2) +928
received (2) +448
set out (2)
sets (2)
sunset (2) +2021+6961+9087
were brought (2)
wherever goes (2) +928+928+2256+3655
withstand (2) +928
wounds (2) +928
accompanied (1) +8079
actually come (1) +995
admitted (1)
advanced (1)
advancing (1)
all the way to (1)
all the way to (1) +3870+6330
all the way to (1) +6330
appear (1)

appeared (1)
apply (1)
approached (1)
approached (1) +448
are[s] (1)
are brought (1)
arrive (1)
arrive (1) +448
arrive (1) +6330
arrived (1) +6330
arrives (1) +7024
assembled (1) +7736
associate (1)
at hand (1) +4200+7940
at hand (1) +7940
ate (1) +448+7931
attacking (1) +6584
attacks (1) +6584
awaits (1)
away (1)
be[s] (1)
be brought in (1)
be heard[s] (1)
be inserted (1)
be right there (1)
be taken (1)
became (1)
been brought (1)
been taken into (1)
begin (1)
beset (1) +928
besiege (1) +928+2021+5189
bind themselves with (1) +928
blessed (1) +1388
border (1)
bound (1)
break into (1)
bring (1) +907
bring home (1)
bring out (1)
bringing into (1)
broke (1)
brought about (1)
brought in as wives (1)
built up (1)
buried (1)
buried (1) +448+7700
by all means go (1) +2143
calling together (1) +2256+8938
came along (1)
came back (1) +2143+2256
came bringing (1)
came up (1)
came with (1)
carried away (1)
carried back (1)
carry back (1)
carry off (1)
carry off (1) +928+2021+8660
carry out duties (1) +2256+3655
caused to come (1)
check (1) +4200+7156
collapses (1) +8691
come back (1)
come home (1)
come on (1)
come to rest (1)
comes (1) +995
comes by (1)
comes in (1)
comes true (1) +995
committed adultery with (1) +448
confront (1)
consort (1)
covers (1) +928
crept (1)
crowded into (1)
deported (1) +1583
does[s] (1)
done so[s] (1) +448+7931
edge (1)
encounter (1) +928
encroach (1)
enter (1) +4200
entered (1) +928+9348
entered (1) +2025
entered (1) +6584
entered and went (1)
entering (1) +448
entering (1) +928
entering (1) +928+7931
entering (1) +928+9348
entering (1) +2025
entering (1) +6330
enters (1) +928
enters (1) +2025
enters (1) +4200
escort (1)
every spring (1) +9102
extending (1)
fallen (1)
find (1) +448
fled (1)
float (1)
flowing (1)
follow (1) +339
followed in (1) +339
fulfill (1)
future (1)
gain (1)
gave (1)
give in (1)
given (1)
go (1) +2143
go about business (1) +2256+3655
go at once (1) +2143+2256
go down (1)
go home (1)
go in (1) +2143+2256
go sleep with (1) +448
going down (1)
gone into (1)
granted (1)
guest (1) +448+1074
had (1)
had brought (1)
had brought in (1)
had[s] (1)
hand over (1)
happen (1)
harbor (1)
harvested (1)
has (1)
have (1)
here (1)
hid in (1)
imported (1)
in (1)
insert (1)
intermarry (1)
into (1)
invade (1) +448
invade (1) +2025+9004
invaded (1) +448
invaded (1) +6584
invader (1) +448
invading (1) +4200
invited (1)
is (1)
join (1) +6330
journeyed (1)
laid siege (1) +928+2021+5189
last (1)
lead (1)
lead (1) +2256+3655
lead (1) +2256+3655+4200+7156
led into (1)
ledges (1)
let touch (1) +928
lie with (1) +6584
listed (1)
lying with (1) +448
made attack (1)
make (1)
make enter (1) +928
make go down (1)
married (1) +448
migration (1)
moved (1)
moved into (1)
moved out (1)
moves (1)
moving (1)
occupy (1) +448
offer (1)
on (1)
on duty (1) +2256+3655
oppose (1) +928
out (1)
over (1)
overtook (1) +448
overwhelm (1) +6584
pass (1)
passed (1)
pierce (1) +928
pierced (1) +928
place (1)
placing (1)
poured (1)
produce (1)
provide (1)
pulled back (1)
put (1) +4200+7156
put (1) +4200+9202
putting (1)
raiding (1) +928
reach (1)
reach (1) +448
reached (1) +4200
reaches (1) +448
received (1)
received (1) +4200
reentered (1) +2256+8740
replace (1) +448+9393
report back (1)
reported (1)
resound (1)
rest (1)
return (1) +995
return (1) +2143
return (1) +6388
rose (1)
sank in (1)
send (1)
send (1) +907+4946
sent (1)
serve (1) +2256+3655
set foot (1)
share (1)
shave head in mourning (1) +7947
shed (1)
sleeps with (1) +448
stay (1) +4202
stayed away (1) +4202
stepped (1)
stole into (1) +1704+4200
successor (1) +132+339+8611
sunset (1) +2021+3064
swarm (1)
sweep on (1) +995
swept in (1)
take (1) +1198
take (1) +6584
take along (1)
take back (1)
take home (1)
take into (1)
take out (1)
take part (1)
taken place (1)
takes place (1)
taking (1)
time is ripe (1) +7891

to the vicinity of (1) +3870+6330
took (1) +448
took back (1)
took back (1) +2256+8938
took into (1)
touch (1)
touched (1) +448
toward (1) +3870
travel about (1) +2256+3655
traveled (1)
treads (1)
turn (1)
very old (1) +928+2021+2416+3427
visit (1)
was brought into (1)
was taken (1)
went in to spend the night with (1) +448
went inside (1)
went on (1)
went out (1)
went over (1)
were (1)
were taken (1)
what[s] (1) +2021
wielding (1) +2025+4200+5087
will[s] (1)
work (1)
untranslated (88)

996 1בּוּז *bûz1* (13)
despises (4)
despise (3)
scorns (2)
derides (1)
scorn (1)
utterly scorned (1) +996

997 2בּוּז *bûz2* (11)
contempt (9)
despised (1)
laughingstock (1)

998 3בּוּז *bûz3* (3)
Buz (3)

999 בּוּזָה *bûzāh* (1)
despised (1)

1000 1בּוּזִי *bûziy1* (2)
Buzite (2)

1001 2בּוּזִי *bûziy2* (1)
Buzi (1)

1002 בַּוַּי *bawway*
Variant; not used

1003 בּוּךְ *bûḵ* (3)
bewildered (1)
mill about (1)
wandering around in confusion (1)

1004 1בּוּל *bûl1* (1)
Bul (1)

1005 2בּוּל *bûl2* (1)
block (1)

1006 3בּוּל *bûl3* (1)
produce (1)

1007 בּוּנָה *bûnāh* (1)
Bunah (1)

1008 בּוּס *bûs* (12)
trample down (4)
kicking about (2)
loathes (1)
trample (1)
trampled (1)
trampled down (1)
trampled underfoot (1)
trampling (1)

1009 בּוּץ *bûṣ* (8)
fine linen (6)
linen (1)
white linen (1)

1010 בּוֹצֵץ *bôṣēṣ* (1)
Bozez (1)

1011 בּוּקָה *bûqāh* (1)
pillaged (1)

1012 בּוֹקֵר *bôqēr* (1)
shepherd (1)

1013 בּוּר *bûr* (1)
concluded (1)

1014 בּוֹר *bôr* (71)
pit (26)
cistern (19)
well (7)
cisterns (5)
dungeon (3)
dungeon (2) +1074
wells (2)
death (1)
hole (1)
one[s] (1)
quarry (1) +5217
slimy pit (1) +8622
there[s] (1) +928+2021
untranslated (1)

1015 בּוֹר הַסִּרָה *bôr hassirāh*
Variant; not used

1016 בּוֹר־עָשָׁן *bôr-ʿāšān* (1)
Bor Ashan (1)

1017 1בּוֹשׁ *bôš1* (120)
put to shame (41)
ashamed (24)
disgraced (8)
shame (6)
shamed (4)
disappointed (3)
disgrace (3)
disgraceful (3)
dismayed (3)
be disgraced (2)
despair (2)
have shame at all (2) +1017
bear shame (1)
bring shame (1)
brings shame (1)
disgraces (1)
distressed (1)
embarrassment (1)
felt ashamed (1)
felt shame (1)
frustrate (1)
humiliated (1)
infamy (1)
let be dashed (1)
let be put to shame (1)
shameful (1)
shamelessly (1) +4202
suffer shame (1)
utter shame (1) +1425
untranslated (1)

1018 2בּוֹשׁ *bôš2* (2)
so long (2)

1019 בּוּשָׁה *bûšāh* (4)
shame (4)

1020 בַּז *baz* (25)
plunder (15)
plundered (4)
loot (2) +1024
despoil (1) +4200+5989
looted (1)
plunder (1) +1024
taken captive (1)

1021 בָּזָא *bāzāʾ* (2)
divided (2)

1022 בָּזָה *bāzāh* (44)
despised (19)
despise (7)
contemptible (3)
was despised (3)
be despised (2)
despises (2)
contemptuous (1)
despise (1) +928+6524
despises (1) +928+6524
is despised (1)
ridiculed (1)
scorned the idea (1) +928+6524
show contempt (1)
shown contempt (1)

1023 בִּזָּה *bizzāh* (10)
plunder (7)
booty (1)
pillage (1)
plundered (1)

1024 בָּזַז *bāzaz* (43)
plunder (11)
carried off (4)
carry off (4)
plundered (3)
loot (2)
loot (2) +1020
looted (2)
took (2)
be plundered (1)
collect (1)
make spoil (1)
plunder (1) +1020
plunderers (1)
robbing (1)
snatch (1)
take (1)
taken plunder (1)
taking as plunder (1)
took as plunder (1)
totally plundered (1) +1024

1025 בִּזָּיוֹן *bizzāyôn* (1)
disrespect (1)

1026 בִּזְיוֹתְיָה *bizyôtyāh* (1)
Biziothiah (1)

1027 בָּזָק *bāzāq* (1)
flashes of lightning (1)

1028 בֶּזֶק *bezeq* (3)
Bezek (2)
there[s] (1) +928

1029 בָּזַר *bāzar* (2)
distribute (1)
scatter (1)

1030 בִּזְּתָא *bizzᵉtāʾ* (1)
Biztha (1)

1031 בָּחוֹן *bāḥôn* (1)
tester of metals (1)

1032 בַּחוּן *baḥûn* (1)
siege towers (1)

1033 1בָּחוּר *bāḥûr1* (50)
young men (34)
young man (6)
able (3)
men (3)
bridegrooms (1)
sons (1)
strong young men (1)
younger men (1)

1034 2בָּחוּר *bāḥûr2*
Variant; not used

1035 בְּחוּרוֹת *bᵉḥûrôṯ* (2)
youth (2)

1036 בְּחוּרִים *bᵉḥûriym* (1)
youth (1)

1037 1בַּחוּרִים *baḥûriym1*
Variant; not used

1038 2בַּחוּרִים *bahûriym2* (5)
Bahurim (5)

1039 בַּחִין *bahiyn* (1)
untranslated (1)

1040 בָּחִיר *bāhiyr* (13)
chosen (13)

1041 1בָּחַל *bāhal1* (1)
detested (1)

1042 2בָּחַל *bāhal2* (1)
untranslated (1)

1043 בָּחַן *bāhan* (29)
test (11)
be tested (3)
examine (3)
tested (3)
tests (2)
challenge (1)
examines (1)
probe (1)
searches (1)
testing (1)
tried (1)
untranslated (1)

1044 בַּחַן *bahan* (1)
watchtower (1)

1045 1בֹּחַן *bōhan1*
Variant; not used

1046 2בֹּחַן *bōhan2* (1)
tested (1)

1047 1בָּחַר *bāhar1* (166)
chosen (63)
choose (42)
chose (27)
chooses (7)
choice (4)
best (3)
prefer (3)
selected (2)
acceptable (1)
adopt (1)
choose (1) +7864
decide (1)
desirable (1)
desire (1)
discern (1)
find (1)
finest (1)
selects (1)
sided with (1) +4200
tested (1)
would rather be (1)
untranslated (2)

1048 2בָּחַר *bāhar2*
Variant; not used

1049 בַּחֲרוּמִי *bah^{a}rûmiy* (1)
Baharumite (1)

1050 בַּחֲרֻמִי *bahurimiy*
Variant; not used

1051 בָּטָא *bātā'* (4)
carelessly (1)
rash words came (1)
reckless words (1)
thoughtlessly (1) +928+4200+8557

1052 בָּטוּחַ *bātûah*
Variant; not used

1053 1בָּטַח *bātah1* (119)
trust (45)
trusts (15)
trusted (10)
depending (8)
depend (4)
feel secure (4)
put trust (4)
rely (3)
secure (3)
confident (2)
let persuade to trust (2)
on basing (2)
put confidence (2)
relied (2)
trusting (2)
unsuspecting (2)
basing confidence (1)
bold (1)
depended (1)
has full confidence (1) +4213
led to believe (1)
made trust (1)
persuaded to trust (1)
reckless (1)
safe (1)

1054 2בָּטַח *bātah2* (1)
stumble (1)

1055 1בֶּטַח *betah1* (42)
safety (24)
secure (4)
confidence (2)
safely (2) +4200
securely (2)
unsuspecting (2)
complacency (1)
feeling of security (1)
security (1)
trustfully (1) +4200
unsuspecting (1) +4200
without a care (1)

1056 2בֶּטַח *betah2*
Variant; not used

1057 בִּטְחָה *bithāh* (1)
trust (1)

1058 בַּטֻּחָה *battuhāh* (1)
secure (1)

1059 בִּטָּחוֹן *bittāhôn* (3)
confidence (2)
hope (1)

1060 בָּטַל *bātal* (1)
cease (1)

1061 1בֶּטֶן *beten1* (72)
womb (28)
belly (4)
birth (4)
abdomen (3)
stomach (3)
birth (2) +562
body (2)
heart (2)
inmost being (2) +2540
inmost parts (2) +2540
bodies (1)
born (1)
borne (1)
bowl-shaped part (1)
brothers (1) +1201
children (1) +2021+7262
children (1) +7262
conceived (1)
craving (1)
depths (1)
descendants (1) +7262
infants (1) +7262
inside (1)
offspring (1)
pregnancy (1)
still hunger (1) +4848
waist (1)
within (1)
untranslated (2)

1062 2בֶּטֶן *beten2* (1)
Beten (1)

1063 בָּטְנָה *botnāh* (1)
pistachio nuts (1)

1064 בְּטֹנִים *b^{e}tōniym* (1)
Betonim (1)

1065 בִּי *biy* (12)
O (4)
please (3)
but (2)
please (1) +5528
untranslated (2)

1066 בָּיַי *bāyay*
Variant; not used

1067 בִּין *biyn* (171)
understand (29)
discerning (16)
understanding (11)
consider (8)
understood (5)
give understanding (4)
have understanding (4)
instructed (4)
understands (4)
discern (3)
discernment (3)
gain (3)
perceive (3)
clever (2)
gain understanding (2)
gives thought (2)
gives understanding (2)
look (2)
ponder (2)
realized (2)
show regard (2)
skilled (2)
able (1)
acted wisely (1)
brilliant (1)
cared for (1)
checked (1)
comprehended (1)
consider carefully (1)
considers (1)
distinguish (1)
dwell on (1)
enlighten (1)
explain (1)
explaining (1)
feel (1)
find (1)
gave full attention (1)
give discernment (1)
give thought (1)
have concern (1) +1981
insight (1)
insights have (1)
instruct (1)
instructing (1)
intelligent (1)
know (1)
knows (1)
learned (1)
learning (1)
let understand (1)
look lustfully (1)
looked closely (1)
master (1)
note well (1) +1067
noticed (1)
observe (1)
pays heed (1)
prudent (1)
quick to understand (1) +4529
realize (1)
regard (1)
see (1)
sensible (1)
show (1)
show favor (1)
skillful (1)

take heed (1)
take note (1)
teacher (1)
tell the meaning (1)
think (1)
thinking (1)
understand clearly (1) +1069
well (1)
untranslated (2)

1068 בַּיִן *bayin* (410)
between (164)
among (31)
at twilight (11) +2021+6847
from (6)
at (3)
between (3) +4946
above (2) +448
as (2)
on forehead (2) +6524
on foreheads (2) +6524
or (2)
whether (2)
with (2)
above (1)
above (1) +6584
against (1)
alternated with (1)
among (1) +4946
attached to (1)
difference between (1)
distinction between (1)
every (1)
from (1) +4200
front of heads (1) +6524
have (1) +2118
in (1) +928
in midair (1) +824+1068+2021+2021+2256+9028
in the midst of (1)
midst (1)
of (1) +4946
on (1)
out (1) +4946
out of (1) +4946
relationships between (1)
separate (1) +5911
separated (1) +7233
slung on back (1) +4190
the difference between (1)
to (1)
together (1)
using (1)
witness (1) +9048
womb (1) +8079
untranslated (147)

1069 בִּינָה *biynāh* (38)
understanding (24)
insight (2)
wisdom (2)
discernment (1)
good sense (1)
great skill (1) +2682+3359
incomprehensible (1) +401
intelligence (1)
understand (1)
understand (1) +3359
understand clearly (1) +1067
understood (1) +3359
untranslated (1)

1070 בֵּיצָה *bēyṣāh* (6)
eggs (5)
untranslated (1)

1071 בִּיר *bayir*
Variant; not used

1072 בִּירָה *biyrāh* (18)
citadel (14)
forts (2)
palatial structure (2)

1073 בִּירָנִיָּה *biyrāniyyāh*
Variant; not used

1074 1בַּיִת *bayiṯ1* (2045)
house (770)
temple (436)
palace (120)
household (81)
houses (81)
home (71)
family (67)
families (57) +3
family (25) +3
people (21)
land (15)
palace (15) +4889
homes (10)
hold (8)
buildings (6)
households (6)
Israelite (6) +408+3776+4946
place (6)
prison (6) +2021+6045
estate (5)
harem (5) +851
inside (5) +4946
Israel (5) +3776
shrines (5)
behind (4) +4946
building (4)
families (4)
family line (4)
hall (4)
it[s] (4) +2021
Judah (4) +3373
prison (4) +2021+3975
room (4)
that[s] (4)
dynasty (3)
armory (2) +3998
center (2)
court (2)
division (2)
dungeon (2) +1014
inside (2) +928+2021
inside (2) +2025
its[s] (2) +2021
its[s] (2) +3378
palace grounds (2) +4889
prison (2) +673
prison (2) +2021+3989
prison (2) +3975
quarters (2)
residence (2)
sanctuary (2)
shelter (2)
storehouses (2) +5800
temple area (2)
temples (2)
there[s] (2) +928+2021
those[s] (2)
tribe (2)
tribes (2)
web (2)
apartment (1)
banquet hall (1) +3516
born in the same home (1) +4580
bottles (1)
camps (1) +5661
clan (1)
clan (1) +3+5476
clans (1) +3
descendants (1)
descendants (1) +5270
dungeon (1) +3975
dwellings (1)
full (1) +6017
group (1) +3+2755
guest (1) +448+995
guests (1) +1591
house (1) +185
house (1) +4632
imprisoned (1) +657+2021+5989
in (1) +2021+2025
inner (1)
inside (1)
inside (1) +448+2021
inside (1) +4200+4946
interior (1)
interior (1) +2025+4946
inward (1) +2025
Israelite (1) +3776
Israelites (1) +3776
it[s] (1) +513
it[s] (1) +1251
it[s] (1) +3378
kitchens (1) +1418
lived (1) +928+2021
living with (1)
lodge (1) +4472
main hall (1)
mansions (1)
mansions (1) +8041
palace (1) +4895
palaces (1)
pen up (1) +2025
penned up (1) +928+2021+3973
possessions (1)
prison (1)
prison (1) +673+2021
prison (1) +2021+4551
prison (1) +2021+7213
prison (1) +5464
prisons (1) +3975
realm (1)
sanctuary (1) +5219
shrine (1)
shrine (1) +466
slave by birth (1) +3535
stall (1)
steward[s] (1) +408+889+2021+6584
steward[s] (1) +889+6584
storehouse (1) +238
storehouse (1) +667
strong fortress (1) +5181
that[s] (1) +2021+2021+2296
them[s] (1) +466+2021+3998
them[s] (1) +2023
there[s] (1) +466+928
there[s] (1) +928+2021+3752
there[s] (1) +7281
there[s] (1) +8235
they[s] (1) +3441
tomb (1)
town (1)
treasury (1) +238
under (1) +4200
underneath (1) +4946
wall (1)
where[s] (1)
wine stewards (1) +8042
workers (1) +6275
untranslated (42)

1075 2בַּיִת *bayiṯ2* (3)
among (1)
between (1)
meet (1)

1076 3בַּיִת *bayiṯ3*
Variant; not used

1077 בֵּית אָוֶן *bēyṯ 'āwen* (7)
Beth Aven (7)

1078 בֵּית־אֵל *bēyṯ-'ēl* (71)
Bethel (70)
there[s] (1) +928

1079 בֵּית אַרְבֵּאל *bēyṯ 'arḇē'l* (1)
Beth Arbel (1)

1080 בֵּית אַשְׁבֵּעַ *bēyṯ 'ašbēa'* (1)
Beth Ashbea (1)

1081 בֵּית בַּעַל מְעוֹן *bēyṯ ba'al m''ôn* (1)
Beth Baal Meon (1)

1082 בֵּית בִּרְאִי *bēyt bir'iy* (1)
Beth Biri (1)

1083 בֵּית בָּרָה *bēyt bārāh* (2)
Beth Barah (2)

1084 בֵּית־גָּדֵר *bēyt-gādēr* (1)
Beth Gader (1)

1085 בֵּית גָּמוּל *bēyt gāmûl* (1)
Beth Gamul (1)

1086 בֵּית דִּבְלָתַיִם *bēyt diblātayim* (1)
Beth Diblathaim (1)

1087 בֵּית־דָּגוֹן *bēyt-dāgôn* (2)
Beth Dagon (2)

1088 בֵּית הָאֱלִי *bēyt hā'ᵉliy* (1)
of Bethel (1)

1089 בֵּית הָאֵצֶל *bēyt hā'ēṣel* (1)
Beth Ezel (1)

1090 בֵּית הַגִּלְגָּל *bēyt haggilgāl* (1)
Beth Gilgal (1)

1091 בֵּית הַגָּן *bēyt haggān* (1)
Beth Haggan (1)

1092 בֵּית הַמֶּרְחָק *bēyt hammerḥāq*
Variant; not used

1093 בֵּית הַיְשִׁימוֹת *bēyt hayᵉšiymôt* (4)
Beth Jeshimoth (4)

1094 בֵּית־הַכֶּרֶם *bēyt-hakkerem* (2)
Beth Hakkerem (2)

1095 בֵּית־הַלַּחְמִי *bēyt-hallaḥmiy* (4)
of Bethlehem (3)
the Bethlehemite (1)

1096 בֵּית־הַמַּרְכָּבוֹת *bēyt-hammarkābôt* (1)
Beth Marcaboth (1)

1097 בֵּית הָעֵמֶק *bēyt hā'ēmeq* (1)
Beth Emek (1)

1098 בֵּית הָעֲרָבָה *bēyt hā'ᵃrābāh* (4)
Beth Arabah (4)

1099 בֵּית הָרָם *bēyt hārām* (1)
Beth Haram (1)

1100 בֵּית הָרָן *bēyt hārān* (1)
Beth Haran (1)

1101 בֵּית הַשִּׁטָּה *bēyt haššiṭṭāh* (1)
Beth Shittah (1)

1102 בֵּית־חָגְלָה *bēyt-ḥoglāh* (3)
Beth Hoglah (3)

1103 בֵּית־חוֹרוֹן *bēyt-ḥôrôn* (14)
Beth Horon (14)

1104 בֵּית חָנָן *bēyt ḥānān*
Variant; not used

1105 בֵּית כָּר *bēyt kār* (1)
Beth Car (1)

1106 בֵּית לְבָאוֹת *bēyt lᵉbā'ôt* (1)
Beth Lebaoth (1)

1107 בֵּית לֶחֶם *bēyt leḥem* (41)
Bethlehem (40)
untranslated (1)

1108 בֵּית לְעַפְרָה *bēyt lᵉ'aprāh* (1)
Beth Ophrah (1)

1109 בֵּית מִלּוֹא *bēyt millô'* (4)
Beth Millo (4)

1110 בֵּית מְעוֹן *bēyt mᵉ'ôn* (1)
Beth Meon (1)

1111 בֵּית מַעֲכָה *bēyt ma'ᵃkāh*
Variant; not used

1112 בֵּית מַרְכָּבוֹת *bēyt markābôt* (1)
Beth Marcaboth (1)

1113 בֵּית נִמְרָה *bēyt nimrāh* (2)
Beth Nimrah (2)

1114 בֵּית עֶדֶן *bēyt 'eden* (1)
Beth Eden (1)

1115 בֵּית־עַזְמָוֶת *bēyt-'azmāwet* (1)
Beth Azmaveth (1)

1116 בֵּית־עֲנוֹת *bēyt-'ᵃnôt* (1)
Beth Anoth (1)

1117 בֵּית־עֲנָת *bēyt-'ᵃnāt* (3)
Beth Anath (3)

1118 בֵּית־עֵקֶד *bēyt-'ēqed* (2)
Beth Eked (2)

1119 בֵּית עַשְׁתָּרוֹת *bēyt 'aštārôt*
Variant; not used

1120 בֵּית פֶּלֶט *bēyt pelet* (2)
Beth Pelet (2)

1121 בֵּית פְּעוֹר *bēyt pᵉ'ôr* (4)
Beth Peor (4)

1122 בֵּית פַּצֵּץ *bēyt paṣṣēṣ* (1)
Beth Pazzez (1)

1123 בֵּית־צוּר *bēyt-ṣûr* (4)
Beth Zur (4)

1124 בֵּית־רְחוֹב *bēyt-rᵉḥôb* (2)
Beth Rehob (2)

1125 בֵּית רָפָא *bēyt rāpā'* (1)
Beth Rapha (1)

1126 בֵּית־שְׁאָן *bēyt-šᵉ'ān* (9)
Beth Shan (9)

1127 בֵּית שֶׁמֶשׁ *bēyt šemeš* (20)
Beth Shemesh (20)

1128 בֵּית־שִׁמְשִׁי *bēyt-šimšiy* (2)
of Beth Shemesh (2)

1129 בֵּית תּוֹגַרְמָה *bēyt tôgarmāh* (2)
Beth Togarmah (2)

1130 בֵּית־תַּפּוּחַ *bēyt-tappûah* (1)
Beth Tappuah (1)

1131 בִּיתָן *biytān* (3)
palace (3)

1132 1בָּכָא *bākā'1* (4)
balsam trees (4)

1133 2בָּכָא *bākā'2* (1)
Baca (1)

1134 בָּכָה *bākāh* (114)
wept (36)
weep (26)
weeping (16)
wailing (5)
mourned (3)
wept (3) +1140
mourn (2)
wailed (2)
bitterly weeps (1) +1134
cried (1)
crying (1)
grieved (1)
mourning (1)
sob (1)
sobbing (1)
tears (1)
weep (1) +1134
weep at all (1) +1134
weep bitterly (1) +1134
weeping (1) +1140
wept aloud (1)
wept bitterly (1) +1135+2221
wept much (1) +1134
wet with tears (1)

1135 בֶּכֶה *bekeh* (1)
wept bitterly (1) +1134+2221

1136 בִּכּוּרָה *bikkûrāh* (4)
early figs (1)
early fruit (1)
fig ripe (1)
ripen early (1)

1137 בִּכּוּרִים *bikkûriym* (17)
firstfruits (12)
first ripe (1)
first ripe fruit (1)
first ripe grain (1)
untranslated (2)

1138 בְּכוֹרַת *bᵉkôrat* (1)
Becorath (1)

1139 בָּכוּת *bākût*
Variant; not used

1140 בְּכִי *bᵉkiy* (29)
weeping (14)
weep (4)
wept (3) +1134
weeps (2)
tears (1)
weep (1) +5951
weeping (1) +1134
weeping bitterly (1) +1140
wept so loudly (1) +906+928+5989+7754

1141 בֹּכִים *bōkiym* (2)
Bokim (2)

1142 בְּכִירָה *bᵉkiyrāh* (6)
older (6)

1143 בְּכִית *bᵉkiyt* (1)
mourning (1)

1144 בָּכַר *bākar* (4)
bear (1)
bearing first child (1)
firstborn belongs to (1) +4200
give the rights of the firstborn (1)

1145 בֵּכֶר *bēker* (1)
young camels (1)

1146 בֶּכֶר *beker* (5)
Beker (5)

1147 בְּכֹר *bᵉkōr* (122)
firstborn (108)
oldest (3)
firstborn male (2)
first (1)
first male offspring (1)
first male offspring (1) +7081+8167
poorest of the poor (1) +1924
untranslated (5)

1148 בְּכֹרָה *bᵉkōrāh* (10)
birthright (6)
ages (1) +7584
firstborn (1)
rights as firstborn (1)
rights of the firstborn (1)

1149 בִּכְרָה *bikrāh* (1)
she-camel (1)

1150 בֹּכְרוּ *bōkrû* (2)
Bokeru (2)

1151 בַּכְרִי *bakriy* (1)
Bekerite (1)

1152 בִּכְרִי *bikriy* (8)
Bicri (8)

1153 1בַּל *bal1* (69)
not (34)
cannot (6)
no (5)
never (3)
no sooner (3) +677
never (2) +4200+5905
never (2) +4200+6409
nor (2) +2256
nothing (2)
blind (1) +8011
don't (1)
ignorant (1) +3359

immovable (1) +4572
in order that no (1)
never (1) +2256+6329+6409
untouched (1) +7212
without (1)
worthless (1) +3603
untranslated (1)

1154 2בַּל *bal2*
Variant; not used

1155 בֵּל *bēl* (3)
Bel (3)

1156 בַּלְאֲדָן *bal'ᵃdān* (2)
Baladan (2)

1157 בֵּלְאשַׁצַּר *bēl'šaṣṣar* (1)
Belshazzar's (1)

1158 בָּלַג *bālag* (4)
flashes (1)
have joy (1)
rejoice (1)
smile (1)

1159 בִּלְגָּה *bilgāh* (3)
Bilgah (2)
Bilgah's (1)

1160 בִּלְגַּי *bilgay* (1)
Bilgai (1)

1161 בִּלְדַּד *bildad* (5)
Bildad (5)

1162 1בָּלָה *bālāh1* (16)
wear out (6)
worn out (2)
decay (1)
did[s] (1)
long enjoy (1)
made grow old (1)
oppress (1)
wasted away (1)
wastes away (1)
untranslated (1)

1163 2בָּלָה *bālāh2* (1)
Balah (1)

1164 3בָּלַהּ *bālah3* (1)
untranslated (1)

1165 בָּלֶה *bāleh* (5)
old (2)
worn (1)
worn out (1)
worn-out (1)

1166 בַּלָּהָה *ballāhāh* (10)
terrors (6)
horrible end (3)
sudden terror (1)

1167 1בִּלְהָה *bilhāh1* (10)
Bilhah (9)
she[s] (1)

1168 2בִּלְהָה *bilhāh2* (1)
Bilhah (1)

1169 בִּלְהָן *bilhān* (4)
Bilhan (4)

1170 בְּלוֹי *bᵉlôy* (3)
old (2)
worn-out (1)

1171 בֵּלְטְשַׁאצַּר *bēlṭᵉša'ṣṣar* (2)
Belteshazzar (2)

1172 בְּלִי *bᵉliy* (58)
no (9)
not (7)
lack (6)
without (6)
unintentionally (4) +928+1981
there is no (3) +401
no (2) +4946
without (2) +4200
deserted (1) +3782+4946
destruction (1)
guiltless (1) +7322
lacking (1)
lacking (1) +4946
nameless (1) +9005
no longer (1)
no more (1)
nothing (1) +4537
relentless (1) +3104
there were no (1) +401
unnoticed (1) +4946+8492
untraveled (1) +408+4946+6296
without (1) +928
without (1) +3869
without (1) +4946
yet (1) +889+4946
untranslated (2)

1173 בְּלִיל *bᵉliyl* (3)
fodder (3)

1174 בְּלִימָה *bᵉliymāh*
Variant; not used

1175 בְּלִיַּעַל *bᵉliyya'al* (27)
wicked (6)
scoundrels (3) +1201
wicked (3) +1201
destruction (2)
vile (2)
corrupt (1)
evil men (1)
scoundrel (1) +132
scoundrel (1) +408
scoundrel (1) +408+2021
troublemaker (1) +408
troublemakers (1)
troublemakers (1) +1201
wickedness (1)
worthless (1)
untranslated (1)

1176 1בָּלַל *bālal1* (44)
mixed (38)
confuse (1)
confused (1)
fed (1)
mixes (1)
poured (1)
untranslated (1)

1177 2בָּלַל *bālal2*
Variant; not used

1178 בָּלַם *bālam* (1)
controlled (1)

1179 בָּלַס *bālas* (1)
took care of (1)

1180 1בָּלַע *bāla'1* (44)
swallowed up (9)
swallow up (7)
swallowed (7)
swallow (3)
be swallowed up (2)
destroy (2)
swallows (2)
consumed (1)
destroying (1)
devoured (1)
devours (1)
for an instant (1) +6330+8371
gulps down (1)
is swallowed up (1)
moment (1)
ruin (1)
torn (1)
uneaten (1) +4202
untranslated (1)

1181 2בָּלַע *bāla'2*
Variant; not used

1182 3בָּלַע *bāla'3* (6)
are led astray (1)
at wits' end (1) +2683+3972
befuddled (1)
bring to nothing (1)
confuse (1)
turn (1)

1183 1בֶּלַע *bela'1* (1)
what swallowed (1)

1184 2בֶּלַע *bela'2* (1)
harmful (1)

1185 3בֶּלַע *bela'3* (12)
Bela (12)

1186 4בֶּלַע *bela'4* (2)
Bela (2)

1187 בַּלְעֲדֵי *bal'ᵃdēy* (17)
apart from (3) +4946
besides (3) +4946
cannot (2)
other than (2) +4946
without (2) +4946
besides (1)
except (1) +4946
not (1) +4946
nothing (1)
without (1)

1188 בַּלְעִי *bal'iy* (1)
Belaite (1)

1189 1בִּלְעָם *bil'ām1* (60)
Balaam (53)
Balaam's (4)
he[s] (1)
him[s] (1)
the two of them[s] (1) +1192+2256

1190 2בִּלְעָם *bil'ām2* (1)
Bileam (1)

1191 בָּלַק *bālaq* (2)
devastate (1)
stripped (1)

1192 בָּלָק *bālāq* (43)
Balak (34)
Balak's (2)
the two of them[s] (1) +1189+2256
them[s] (1) +6269
untranslated (5)

1193 בִּלְשָׁן *bilšān* (2)
Bilshan (2)

1194 בִּלְתִּי *biltiy* (112)
not (37)
no (14)
keep from (5)
nothing (5)
neither (4)
without (3)
except (2)
fail (2)
never (2)
prevent (2) +5989
unless (2)
avoid (1)
be kept from (1) +1757+4200
be nothing (1) +401
besides (1)
but (1)
ceremonially unclean (1) +3196
didn't (1)
disobey (1) +928+7754+9048
except (1) +561
except for (1)
failing (1)
forbidden (1) +7422
free from (1)
from (1)
insatiable (1) +8425
instead of (1) +4200
no more (1)

not (1) +4946
only (1) +4202
other than (1) +963+4200
refusing (1)
remain unmarried (1) +408+2118+4200+4200+6328
stop (1)
unable (1)
unceasing (1) +6239
unless (1) +561
worthless (1) +3603
untranslated (7)

1195 1בָּמָה *bāmāh1* (105)
high places (62)
high place (20)
heights (9)
there[S] (4) +928+2021
mound (2)
shrines (1)
there (1) +928+2021
tops (1)
waves (1)
untranslated (4)

1196 2בָּמָה *bāmāh2* (1)
Bamah (1)

1197 בִּמְהָל *bimhāl* (1)
Bimhal (1)

1198 בְּמוֹ *bᵉmô* (12)
from (2)
in (2)
with (2)
take (1) +995
through (1)
used for fuel (1) +836+8596
untranslated (3)

1199 בָּמוֹת *bāmôṯ* (2)
Bamoth (2)

1200 בָּמוֹת בַּעַל *bāmôṯ ba'al* (2)
Bamoth Baal (2)

1201 1בֵּן *bēn1* (4932)
son (1847)
sons (814)
Israelites (483) +3776
descendants (229)
children (175)
old (153)
people (85)
Ammonites (79) +6648
young (54)
Israelite (50) +3776
men (35)
men (23) +132
Israel (21) +3776
Benjamites (17) +1228
Reubenites (17) +8017
Gadites (16) +1514
Levites (15) +4290
Benjamin (13) +1228
descendant (12)
son's (12)
them[S] (12) +3776
Judah (11) +3373
age (10)
foreigners (10) +5797
man (10) +132
Ammon (9) +6648
children's (9)
company (9)
Danites (9) +1968
Hittites (9) +3147
Merarites (9) +5356
they[S] (9) +3776
Ammonite (8) +6648
people (8) +6639
Gad (7) +1514
Kohathite (7) +7740
Merarite (7) +5356
countrymen (6) +6639
Ephraim (6) +713
exiles (6) +1583
Gershonites (6) +1767
grandson (6)
mankind (6) +132
Reuben (6) +8017
Asher (5) +888
Assyrians (5) +855
boy (5)
foreigner (5) +5797
line (5)
Manasseh (5) +4985
Naphtali (5) +5889
peoples (5)
Simeon (5) +9058
sons' (5)
their[S] (5) +2257
year-old (5) +9102
Zebulun (5) +2282
able men (4) +2657
age (4) +9102
Anakites (4) +6737
brave (4) +2657
Dan (4) +1968
descended (4)
Ephraimites (4) +713
grandchildren (4) +1201
grandsons (4)
Issachar (4) +3779
Kohathites (4) +7740
man (4)
Simeonites (4) +9058
child (3)
cousin (3) +1856
grandson (3) +1201
grandsons (3) +1201
Israelites' (3) +3776
Kohathites (3) +7741
Levites (3) +4291
one[S] (3)
princes (3)
princes (3) +4889
scoundrels (3) +1175
their[S] (3) +3870
whose[S] (3)
wicked (3) +1175
ages (2) +9102
angels (2) +466+2021
Babylonians (2) +951
born (2)
calf (2) +1330
calves (2)
common people (2) +6639
condemned to (2)
cubs (2)
Ephraimite (2) +713
father[S] (2)
fruitful vine (2) +7238
Gershonite (2) +1767
grandchildren (2)
him[S] (2) +3870
hostages (2) +9510
Israelite (2) +408+3776+4946
Israelites (2) +3776+4946
Joseph (2) +3441
lambs (2) +7366
lay people (2) +6639
man's (2) +132
Manassites (2) +4985
mortal men (2) +132
nephew (2) +278
overnight (2) +4326
they[S] (2) +5797
valiant fighter (2) +408+2657
young men (2)
Aaronic (1) +195
able (1) +2657
able-bodied (1) +2657
Ahohite (1) +292
all mankind (1) +132
all men (1) +132+2021
angels (1) +466
anointed (1) +2021+3658
army (1)
arrows (1) +8008
arrows[S] (1)
babies (1)
Babylonian (1) +951
Benjamin (1) +408+3549
birth (1)
bravely (1) +2657+4200
bravest soldier (1) +2657
brood (1)
brothers (1) +1061
bull (1) +1330
calves (1) +1330
children (1) +1887
children's (1) +4200
choice (1)
clans (1)
colt (1) +912
courageous (1) +2657
cousins on their father's side (1) +1856
Cushites (1) +3934
deserve to (1)
deserves (1)
deserves to (1)
destitute (1) +2710
disciple (1)
Edomites (1) +121
Egyptians (1) +5213
especially bred (1) +2021+8247
evildoers (1) +6594
families (1)
fertile (1) +9043
fighting (1) +2657
foal (1)
foreigner (1) +2021+5797
foreigners (1) +2021+5797
Gad (1) +1532
Gershonite (1) +1769
Gershonites (1) +1768
Gershonites (1) +1769
Gilead (1) +1680
goats (1) +6436
granddaughters (1) +1426
Greeks (1) +3436
Hacmonite (1) +2685
he[S] (1) +281+6687
heavenly beings (1) +446
high (1) +408
highborn (1) +408
him[S] (1) +2021+3778
him[S] (1) +2023
his people[S] (1) +3147
human (1) +132
Israelite (1) +928+3776
Israelite (1) +3776+4200
Israelite (1) +3776+4946
Israelites (1) +3776+6639
Jaakanites (1) +3622
Judah's (1) +3373
Kedar (1) +7723
Kohathite (1) +7741
Korahites (1) +7948
low (1) +132
low among men (1) +132
lowborn men (1) +132
Maacathite (1) +5084
members (1)
men (1) +132+2021
men (1) +408
mighty (1) +446
Moabites (1) +4566
murderer (1) +8357
must die (1) +4638
my[S] (1) +2257
native (1) +6639
nephews (1) +2157
noisy boasters (1) +8623
of Gilead (1) +1682

of Judah (1) +3373
one (1)
one who will inherit (1) +5479
opening of the womb (1) +5402
oppressed (1) +6715
people (1) +132
prince (1) +4889
proud (1) +8832
proud beasts (1) +8832
rebellious (1) +5308
Reuben (1) +8018
Reubenite (1) +8017
servant (1)
singers (1) +8876
slave born in household (1) +563
soldiers (1) +2657
some^{S} (1)
sparks (1) +8404
successors (1)
their^{S} (1)
their^{S} (1) +1769+2021
their^{S} (1) +6648
them^{S} (1) +3620
them^{S} (1) +4013
them^{S} (1) +6648
these men^{S} (1) +2021+5566
they^{S} (1) +851+2021
they^{S} (1) +1201+1514+2256+8017
they^{S} (1) +1228
they^{S} (1) +1968
they^{S} (1) +2257
they^{S} (1) +6648
tribe (1)
tribes (1)
troops (1) +1522
troublemakers (1) +1175
vassal (1)
very own brother (1) +278+562+3870
vultures (1) +5979
warriors (1) +2657
who^{S} (1) +3776
Zadokites (1) +7401
Zerahites (1) +2438
untranslated (237)

1202 2בֵּן *bēn2*
Variant; not used

1203 בֶּן־אֲבִינָדָב *ben-'*^{a}*biynāḏāḇ* (1)
Ben-Abinadab (1)

1204 בֶּן־אוֹנִי *ben-'ôniy* (1)
Ben-Oni (1)

1205 בֶּן־גֶּבֶר *ben-geḇer* (1)
Ben-Geber (1)

1206 בֶּן־דֶּקֶר *ben-deqer* (1)
Ben-Deker (1)

1207 בֶּן־הֲדַד *ben-h*^{a}*ḏaḏ* (25)
Ben-Hadad (24)
Ben-Hadad's (1)

1208 בֶּן־הִנֹּם *ben-hinnōm* (10)
Ben Hinnom (10)

1209 בֶּן־זוֹחֵת *ben-zôhēṯ* (1)
Ben-Zoheth (1)

1210 בֶּן־חוּר *ben-hûr* (1)
Ben-Hur (1)

1211 בֶּן־חַיִל *ben-hayil* (1)
Ben-Hail (1)

1212 בֶּן־חָנָן *ben-hānān* (1)
Ben-Hanan (1)

1213 בֶּן־חֶסֶד *ben-hesed* (1)
Ben-Hesed (1)

1214 בֶּן־עַמִּי *ben-'ammiy* (1)
Ben-Ammi (1)

1215 בָּנָה *bānāh* (377)
built (114)
build (96)
building (24)
rebuilt (23)
rebuild (14)
be rebuilt (12)
built up (12)
builders (9)
build up (7)
builds (6)
be built (4)
fortified (4)
rebuilding (3)
been built (2)
been rebuilt (2)
build a family (2)
erect (2)
is built (2)
made (2)
rebuilt (2) +2256+8740
set up (2)
using^{S} (2)
be established (1)
be restored (1)
besieged (1) +6584
builds up (1)
constructed (1)
construction (1)
craftsmen (1)
did work (1)
done this^{S} (1) +3378+4200+4640
erected (1)
establish (1)
form (1)
indeed built (1) +1215
lined (1)
make firm (1)
newly built (1)
partitioned off (1)
prosper (1)
rebuild (1) +2256+8740
repairing (1)
restored (1)
stands firm (1)
was built (1)
were used (1)
worked (1)
untranslated (5)

1216 בְּנֹב *b*^{e}*nōḇ*
Variant; not used

1217 בְּנוֹ *b*^{e}*nô* (2)
Beno (2)

1218 בִּנּוּי *binnûy* (8)
Binnui (8)

1219 בְּנוֹת *b*^{e}*nôṯ*
Variant; not used

1220 בָּנִי *bāniy* (13)
Bani (13)

1221 בֻּנִּי *bunniy* (3)
Bunni (3)

1222 בְּנֵי־בְרַק *b*^{e}*nēy-ḇ*^{e}*raq* (1)
Bene Berak (1)

1223 בְּנֵי יַעֲקָן *b*^{e}*nēy ya*^{a}*qān* (2)
Bene Jaakan (2)

1224 בִּנְיָה *binyāh* (1)
building (1)

1225 בְּנָיָה *b*^{e}*nāyāh* (11)
Benaiah (11)

1226 בְּנָיָהוּ *b*^{e}*nāyāhû* (31)
Benaiah (31)

1227 בֵּנַיִם *bēnayim* (2)
champion (2) +408+2021

1228 בִּנְיָמִין *binyāmiyn* (168)
Benjamin (111)
Benjamites (17) +1201
Benjamin (13) +1201
Benjamites (11)
Benjamite (4)
Benjamin's (2)
tribe of Benjamin (2)
Benjamin (1) +824
Benjamite (1) +408
Benjamite (1) +4946
Benjamites (1) +408+4946
Benjamites (1) +4946
they^{S} (1) +1201
untranslated (2)

1229 בֶּן־יְמִינִי *ben-y*^{e}*miyniy* (10)
Benjamite (7)
Benjamites (1)
men of Benjamin (1)
untranslated (1)

1230 בִּנְיָן *binyān* (7)
building (4)
outer wall (2)
wall (1)

1231 בְּנִינוּ *b*^{e}*niynû* (1)
Beninu (1)

1232 בִּנְעָא *bin'ā'* (2)
Binea (2)

1233 בְּסוֹדְיָה *b*^{e}*sôḏ*^{e}*yāh* (1)
Besodeiah (1)

1234 בֵּסַי *bēsay* (2)
Besai (2)

1235 בֹּסֶר *bōser* (5)
sour grapes (3)
grape (1)
unripe grapes (1)

1236 בַּעֲבוּר *ba*^{a}*ḇûr*
Variant; not used

1237 1בַּעַד *ba'aḏ1* (104)
for (48)
through (8)
behind (5)
from (4)
behind (3) +4946
in (3)
around (2)
on behalf of (2)
around (1) +4946+6017
barred in (1) +1378
by (1)
for (1) +3954
of (1)
on (1)
on behalf (1)
over (1)
seals off (1) +3159
untranslated (20)

1238 2בַּעַד *ba'aḏ2*
Variant; not used

1239 1בָּעָה *bā'āh1* (3)
ask (2)
pillaged (1)

1240 2בָּעָה *bā'āh2* (2)
bulging (1)
causes to boil (1)

1241 בְּעוּלָה *b*^{e}*'ûlāh* (1)
Beulah (1)

1242 בְּעוֹר *b*^{e}*'ôr* (10)
Beor (10)

1243 בִּעוּת *bi'ûṯ* (2)
terrors (2)

1244 1בֹּעַז *bō'az1* (22)
Boaz (22)

1245 2בֹּעַז *bō'az2* (2)
Boaz (2)

1246 בָּעַט *bā'aṭ* (2)
kicked (1)

scorn (1)

1247 בְּעִי *b^{e}ʻiy*
Variant; not used

1248 בְּעִיר *b^{e}ʻiyr* (7)
livestock (4)
animals (1)
cattle (1)
untranslated (1)

1249 1בָּעַל *bāʻal1* (15)
husband (4)
be married (1)
has a husband (1)
married (1)
married (1) +1251
marries (1)
marries (1) +2256+4374
marry (1)
marrying (1)
ruled (1)
ruled over (1)
wife (1) +851

1250 2בָּעַל *bāʻal2*
Variant; not used

1251 1בַּעַל *baʻal1* (164)
Baal (55)
Baals (18)
citizens (18)
owner (14)
husband (6)
Baal worship (3)
Baal's (3)
husbands (2)
two-horned (2) +2021+7967
with (2)
accuser (1) +5477
allied (1) +1382
archers (1) +2932
bird on the wing (1) +4053
birds (1) +4053
captain (1)
charmer (1) +4383
collected sayings (1) +670
creditor (1) +2257+3338+5408
dreamer (1) +2021+2706
filled with (1)
given to gluttony (1) +5883
has (1)
him[S] (1) +2023
hot-tempered (1) +2779
husband's (1)
involved in (1)
it[S] (1) +1074
man (1)
man's (1)
married (1) +1249
master (1)
men (1)
one who destroys (1) +5422
one who gives (1)
owned (1)
owner's (1)
people (1)
possessor (1)
practice (1)
related by marriage (1)
riders (1) +7304
rulers (1)
schemer (1) +4659
tenants (1)
they[S] (1) +3972+4463+8901
those who deserve (1)
those who get (1)
those who have (1)
under oath (1) +8652
who[S] (1) +8901

1252 2בַּעַל *baʻal2* (3)
Baal (3)

1253 בַּעַל בְּרִית *baʻal b^{e}riyṯ* (2)
Baal-Berith (2)

1254 בַּעַל גָּד *baʻal gāḏ* (3)
Baal Gad (3)

1255 בַּעַל הָמוֹן *baʻal hāmôn* (1)
Baal Hamon (1)

1256 בַּעַל זְבוּב *baʻal z^{e}ḇûḇ* (4)
Baal-Zebub (4)

1257 בַּעַל חָנָן *baʻal ḥānān* (5)
Baal-Hanan (5)

1258 בַּעַל חָצוֹר *baʻal ḥāṣôr* (1)
Baal Hazor (1)

1259 בַּעַל חֶרְמוֹן *baʻal ḥermôn* (2)
Baal Hermon (2)

1260 בַּעַל מְעוֹן *baʻal m^{e}ʻôn* (3)
Baal Meon (3)

1261 בַּעַל פְּעוֹר *baʻal p^{e}ʻôr* (2)
Baal Peor (2)

1262 בַּעַל־פְּרָצִים *baʻal-p^{e}rāṣiym* (4)
Baal Perazim (4)

1263 בַּעַל צְפֹן *baʻal ṣ^{e}pōn* (3)
Baal Zephon (3)

1264 בַּעַל שָׁלִשָׁה *baʻal šālišāh* (1)
Baal Shalishah (1)

1265 בַּעַל תָּמָר *baʻal tāmār* (1)
Baal Tamar (1)

1266 1בַּעֲלָה *ba^{a}ʻlāh1* (4)
medium (1) +200
mistress (1)
one[S] (1) +200
owned (1)

1267 2בַּעֲלָה *ba^{a}ʻlāh2* (6)
Baalah (6)

1268 בְּעָלוֹת *b^{e}ʻālôṯ* (1)
Bealoth (1)

1269 בְּעֶלְיָדָע *b^{e}ʻelyāḏāʻ* (1)
Beeliada (1)

1270 בְּעַלְיָה *b^{e}ʻalyāh* (1)
Bealiah (1)

1271 בַּעֲלִיס *ba^{a}ʻliys* (1)
Baalis (1)

1272 בַּעֲלַת *ba^{a}ʻlāṯ* (4)
Baalath (4)

1273 בַּעֲלַת בְּאֵר *ba^{a}ʻlaṯ b^{e}ʼēr* (1)
Baalath Beer (1)

1274 בְּעֹן *b^{e}ʻōn* (1)
Beon (1)

1275 בַּעֲנָא *ba^{a}ʻnāʼ* (3)
Baana (3)

1276 בַּעֲנָה *ba^{a}ʻnāh* (9)
Baanah (9)

1277 1בָּעַר *bāʻar1* (63)
burn (11)
burned (5)
burning (5)
blazed (4)
burn up (3)
fire (3)
light (3)
ablaze (2)
blazing (2)
burned up (2)
burns (2)
consume (2)
set ablaze (2)
use for fuel (2) +836
blazed forth (1)
blazes (1)
charred (1) +836+928+2021
consumed (1)
consumes (1)
fires (1)
flare up (1)
kindled (1)
lit (1) +836
on fire (1) +836+928+2021
raged (1)
sacrificed (1)
sets ablaze (1)
started (1)
use for fuel (1)

1278 2בָּעַר *bāʻar2* (24)
purge (12)
rid (3)
destroyed (2)
removed (2)
got rid of (1)
graze (1)
grazes (1)
laid waste (1)
ruined (1)

1279 3בָּעַר *bāʻar3* (7)
senseless (5)
brutal (1)
give senseless (1)

1280 בַּעַר *baʻar* (5)
senseless (3)
ignorant (1)
stupid (1)

1281 בַּעֲרָא *ba^{a}ʻrāʼ* (1)
Baara (1)

1282 בְּעֵרָה *b^{e}ʻērāh* (1)
fire (1)

1283 בַּעֲשֵׂיָה *ba^{a}ʻśēyāh* (1)
Baaseiah (1)

1284 בַּעְשָׁא *baʻšāʼ* (28)
Baasha (25)
Baasha's (2)
he[S] (1)

1285 בְּעֶשְׁתְּרָה *b^{e}ʻešt^{e}rāh* (1)
Be Eshtarah (1)

1286 בָּעַת *bāʻaṯ* (16)
overwhelmed (2)
terrified (2)
terrify (2)
afraid (1)
alarm (1)
fill with terror (1)
frighten (1)
frightening (1)
makes tremble (1)
overwhelm (1)
startle (1)
tormented (1)
tormenting (1)

1287 בְּעָתָה *b^{e}ʻāṯāh* (2)
terror (2)

1288 בֹּץ *bōṣ* (1)
mud (1)

1289 בִּצָּה *biṣṣāh* (4)
marsh (2)
swamps (1)
untranslated (1)

1290 בָּצוּר *bāṣûr* (26)
fortified (22)
walls (2)
unsearchable (1)
untranslated (1)

1291 בֵּצַי *bēṣay* (3)
Bezai (3)

1292 1בָּצִיר *bāṣiyr1* (7)
grape harvest (4)
full grape harvest (1)
grapes (1)

vineyard (1)

1293 2בָּצִיר *bāṣiyr2* (1)
dense (1)

1294 בָּצָל *bāṣāl* (1)
onions (1)

1295 בְּצַלְאֵל *bᵉṣal'ēl* (9)
Bezalel (9)

1296 בַּצְלוּת *baṣlûṯ* (2)
Bazluth (2)

1297 בַּצְלִית *baṣliyṯ*
Variant; not used

1298 בָּצַע *bāṣa'* (16)
cut off (3)
greedy (3)
breaking ranks (1)
bring down (1)
builds (1)
complete (1)
finished (1)
fulfilled (1)
go after ill-gotten gain (1) +1299
greedy (1) +1299
make unjust gain (1)
make unjust gain (1) +1299

1299 בֶּצַע *beṣa'* (23)
gain (9)
dishonest gain (3)
unjust gain (2)
cut off (1)
go after ill-gotten gain (1) +1298
greed (1)
greedy (1) +1298
ill-gotten gain (1)
ill-gotten gains (1)
make unjust gain (1) +1298
plunder (1)
selfish gain (1)

1300 בְּצַעֲנַנִּים *bᵉṣa'ᵃnanniym*
Variant; not used

1301 1בָּצֵק *bāṣēq1* (2)
swell (1)
swollen (1)

1302 2בָּצֵק *bāṣēq2* (5)
dough (5)

1303 בִּצְקָלוֹן *biṣqālôn*
Variant; not used

1304 בָּצְקַת *bāṣqaṯ* (2)
Bozkath (2)

1305 1בָּצַר *bāṣar1* (7)
grape pickers (2)
harvest (2)
gathered (1)
gathering grapes (1)
harvest grapes (1)

1306 2בָּצַר *bāṣar2* (1)
breaks (1)

1307 3בָּצַר *bāṣar3* (4)
be thwarted (1)
fortifies (1)
impossible (1)
strengthen (1)

1308 4בָּצַר *bāṣar4*
Variant; not used

1309 1בֶּצֶר *beṣer1* (2)
gold (1)
nuggets (1)

1310 2בֶּצֶר *beṣer2* (1)
Bezer (1)

1311 3בֶּצֶר *beṣer3* (4)
Bezer (4)

1312 1בָּצְרָה *boṣrāh1* (1)
pen (1)

1313 2בָּצְרָה *boṣrāh2* (8)
Bozrah (8)

1314 בַּצָּרָה *baṣṣārāh* (3)
trouble (2)
drought (1)

1315 בִּצָּרוֹן *biṣṣārôn* (1)
fortress (1)

1316 בַּצֹּרֶת *baṣṣōreṯ* (1)
drought (1)

1317 בַּקְבּוּק *baqbûq* (2)
Bakbuk (2)

1318 בַּקְבֻּק *baqbuq* (3)
jar (3)

1319 בַּקְבֻּקְיָה *baqbuqyāh* (3)
Bakbukiah (3)

1320 בַּקְבַּקַּר *baqbaqqar* (1)
Bakbakkar (1)

1321 בֻּקִּי *buqqiy* (5)
Bukki (5)

1322 בֻּקִּיָּהוּ *buqqiyyāhû* (2)
Bukkiah (2)

1323 בָּקִיעַ *bāqiya'* (2)
bits (1)
breaches in defenses (1)

1324 בָּקַע *bāqa'* (51)
divided (3)
ripped open (3)
split (3)
was broken through (3)
broke (2)
burst forth (2)
cracked (2)
divide (2)
hatch (2)
opened up (2)
split apart (2)
were divided (2)
be split (1)
been broken through (1)
break forth (1)
break through (1)
breaks up (1)
burst (1)
chopped up (1)
conquer (1)
cut (1)
gush forth (1)
invaded (1)
is hatched (1)
mauled (1)
ready to burst (1)
rip open (1)
shook (1)
splits (1)
taken by storm (1)
tear apart (1)
tore open (1)
tunnels (1) +3284
unleash (1)
were dashed to pieces (1)

1325 בֶּקַע *beqa'* (2)
beka (2)

1326 בִּקְעָה *biq'āh* (20)
plain (9)
valley (7)
valleys (4)

1327 1בָּקַק *bāqaq1* (8)
be completely laid waste (1) +1327
destroyers (1)
devastate (1)
laid waste (1)
lay waste (1)
lose heart (1) +928+7931+8120
ruin (1)

1328 2בָּקַק *bāqaq2* (1)
spreading (1)

1329 בָּקַר *bāqar* (7)
look after (2)
consider (1)
look (1)
pick out (1)
seek (1)
seeking guidance (1)

1330 בָּקָר *bāqār* (184)
cattle (40)
herds (32)
oxen (31)
bull (27) +7228
bulls (14)
herd (10)
bulls (5) +7228
bull (4)
ox (4)
animals (2)
calf (2) +1201
heifer (2) +6320
bull (1) +1201
calves (1) +1201
cattle (1) +5238
cow (1)
cows (1)
cows' (1)
herds (1) +5238
herds (1) +6373
oxgoad (1) +4913
plowing (1)
young cow (1) +6320

1331 1בֹּקֶר *bōqer1*
Variant; not used

1332 2בֹּקֶר *bōqer2* (212)
morning (179)
every morning (4)
+928+928+1332+2021+2021
dawn (3)
daybreak (3) +240+2021
dawn (2) +240+2021
morning's (2)
mornings (2)
break of day (1) +7155
daybreak (1) +2021+7155
daybreak (1) +7155
daylight (1) +240+2021
each morning (1)
+928+928+1332+2021+2021
each morning (1)
+1332+2021+2021+4200+4200
hold back overnight (1) +4328+6330
last watch of the night (1) +874
last watch of the night (1) +874+2021
morning light (1)
untranslated (4)

1333 בַּקָּרָה *baqqārāh* (1)
looks after (1)

1334 בִּקֹּרֶת *biqqōreṯ* (1)
due punishment (1)

1335 בָּקַשׁ *bāqaš* (225)
seek (58)
seeking (12)
look for (10)
looked for (10)
search for (10)
searched for (7)
looking for (6)
sought (5)
tried (5)
searched (4)
seeks (4)
find (3)
hold accountable (3) +3338+4946
search (3)

search out (3)
trying (3)
bent on (2)
call to account (2)
conspired (2)
demand (2)
in search of (2)
intend (2)
searching for (2)
seek out (2)
sought out (2)
take (2)
trying to take (2)
want (2)
about to (1)
ask for (1)
asked (1)
asked for (1)
asked for permission (1)
asking for (1)
be sought (1)
beg (1)
begging (1)
call to account (1) +3338+4946
carefully investigated (1) +2011+2256
demanded (1)
demanded payment (1)
finds (1)
gone in search of (1)
hold responsible (1) +3338+4946
inquiring of (1)
intended (1)
invites (1)
looking for a chance (1)
looks for (1)
looks to (1)
petitioned (1)
plans (1)
plead with (1)
pleaded (1)
pleaded with (1)
promote (1)
promotes (1)
pursue (1)
pursues (1)
pursuing (1)
questioned (1)
search be made for (1)
search made for (1)
searching (1)
seek an audience with (1) +7156
seek help (1)
seek to (1)
set out (1)
snare (1)
sought to (1)
straining (1)
tried to take (1)
try to find (1)
try to get (1)
trying to (1)
trying to get (1)
want to (1)
want to do (1)
wanted to (1)
wanted to kill (1) +906+5883
wanted to make (1) +4200
was investigated (1)
went in search of (1)

1336 בַּקָּשָׁה *baqqāšāh* (8)
request (7)
asked (1)

1337 1בַּר *bar1* (4)
son (4)

1338 2בַּר *bar2* (7)
pure (3)
bright (1)
empty (1)
favorite (1)
radiant (1)

1339 3בַּר *bar3* (13)
grain (11)
wheat (2)

1340 4בַּר *bar4* (1)
wilds (1)

1341 1בֹּר *bōr1* (5)
cleanness (5)

1342 2בֹּר *bōr2* (2)
thoroughly purge away (1) +2021+3869+7671
washing soda (1)

1343 1בָּרָא *bārā'1* (48)
created (21)
create (10)
were created (6)
creator (3)
are created (2)
creating (2)
brings about (1)
creates (1)
done (1)
not yet created (1)

1344 2בָּרָא *bārā'2* (1)
fattening (1)

1345 3בָּרָא *bārā'3* (5)
clear (1)
clear land (1)
cut down (1)
make (1)
untranslated (1)

1346 4בָּרָא *bārā'4*
Variant; not used

1347 בְּרֹאדַךְ־בַּלְאֲדָן *b^erō'd̠ak̠-bal'^ad̠ān*
Variant; not used

1348 בִּרְאִי *bir'iy*
Variant; not used

1349 בְּרָאיָה *b^erā'yāh* (1)
Beraiah (1)

1350 בַּרְבֻּר *barbur* (1)
fowl (1)

1351 בָּרַד *bārad̠* (1)
hail (1)

1352 בָּרָד *bārād̠* (29)
hail (21)
hail (1) +74
hailstones (1)
hailstones (1) +74
hailstorm (1)
hailstorm (1) +2443
it^s (1) +2021
storm (1)
untranslated (1)

1353 בָּרֹד *bārōd̠* (4)
dappled (2)
spotted (2)

1354 1בֶּרֶד *bered̠1* (1)
Bered (1)

1355 2בֶּרֶד *bered̠2* (1)
Bered (1)

1356 1בָּרָה *bārāh1* (6)
eat (3)
food (1)
give to eat (1)
urged to eat (1)

1357 2בָּרָה *bārāh2*
Variant; not used

1358 בָּרוּךְ *bārûk̠* (26)
Baruch (26)

1359 בָּרוּר *bārûr* (2)
purify (1) +2200
sincerely (1)

1360 בְּרוֹשׁ *b^erôš* (19)
pine (7)
pine trees (4)
pine tree (3)
pines (3)
pine (1) +6770
spears of pine (1)

1361 בְּרוֹת *b^erôt̠* (1)
firs (1)

1362 בָּרוּת *bārût̠* (1)
food (1)

1363 בֵּרוֹתָה *bērôt̠āh* (1)
Berothah (1)

1364 בִּרְזָוִת *birzāwit̠* (1)
untranslated (1)

1365 בִּרְזָיִת *birzāyit̠* (1)
Birzaith (1)

1366 בַּרְזֶל *barzel* (76)
iron (62)
iron-smelting (3)
ax (2)
iron tool (2)
blacksmith (1) +3093
head (1)
iron axhead (1)
iron chains (1)
irons (1)
tool of iron (1)
untranslated (1)

1367 בַּרְזִלַּי *barzillay* (12)
Barzillai (12)

1368 1בָּרַח *bārah1* (65)
fled (32)
flee (5)
fleeing (3)
running away (3)
come away (1)
drives out (1)
drove away (1)
drove out (1)
escaping (1)
extend (1)
extended (1)
flees (1)
flees headlong (1) +1368
fleeting (1)
fly away (1)
go back (1)
gone back (1)
leave at once (1)
make flee (1)
put to flight (1)
ran away (1)
ran off (1)
run away (1)
run off (1)
takes to flight (1)

1369 2בָּרַח *bārah2*
Variant; not used

1370 3בָּרַח *bārah3*
Variant; not used

1371 בָּרִחַ *bāriah* (4)
fugitives (2)
gliding (2)

1372 בַּרְחֻמִי *barhumiy* (1)
Barhumite (1)

1373 בֵּרִי *bēriy* (1)
Beri (1)

1374 בָּרִיא *bāriy'* (14)
fat (4)
healthy (3)
fat (2) +1414
choice (1)
choice sheep (1)

choicest (1)
nourished (1) +1414
stall-fed (1)

1375 בְּרִיאָה *b^e riy'āh* (1)
something totally new (1)

1376 בִּרְיָה *biryāh* (3)
food (3)

1377 בָּרִיחַ *bāriyah* (1)
Bariah (1)

1378 בְּרִיחַ *b^e riyah* (41)
bars (17)
crossbars (11)
crossbar (2)
bar (1)
barred gates (1)
barred in (1) +1237
bars of gates (1)
gate (1)
gate bars (1)
untranslated (5)

1379 בֵּרִים *bēriym* (1)
Berites (1)

1380 בְּרִיעָה *b^e riy'āh* (11)
Beriah (11)

1381 בְּרִיעִי *b^e riy'iy* (1)
Beriite (1)

1382 בְּרִית *b^e riyt* (284)
covenant (246)
treaty (26)
agreement (3)
compact (3)
agreements (1)
alliance (1)
allied (1) +1251
allies (1) +408
it^S (1) +778+2021
marriage covenant (1)

1383 בֹּרִית *bōriyt* (2)
soap (2)

1384 1בָּרַךְ *bārak1* (3)
had kneel down (1)
kneel (1)
knelt down (1) +1386+6584

1385 2בָּרַךְ *bārak2* (327)
blessed (86)
bless (79)
praise (63)
be blessed (23)
praised (8)
blesses (7)
give blessing (6)
congratulate (3)
curse (3)
cursed (3)
extol (3)
pronounce blessings (3)
blessing (2)
gave blessing (2)
be praised (1)
bless (1) +1385
bless abundant (1) +1385
bless at all (1) +1385
blessed (1) +1385
blessed again and again (1) +1385
blessings given (1)
commended (1)
counted blessed (1)
do so^S (1)
done nothing but bless (1) +1385
give greetings (1)
given (1)
giving blessing (1) +1388
greet (1)
greet (1) +7925
greeted (1)
greets (1)
invokes a blessing (1)
invokes a blessing on himself (1)
is blessed (1)
pronounce blessing (1)
pronounced (1)
richly bless (1) +1385
surely bless (1) +1385
thank (1)
worships (1)
untranslated (1)

1386 בֶּרֶךְ *berek* (26)
knees (15)
knee (3)
lap (2)
for (1) +6584
knee-deep (1)
kneel (1)
kneeling (1) +4156+6584
knelt down (1) +1384+6584
untranslated (1)

1387 בָּרַכְאֵל *barak'ēl* (2)
Barakel (2)

1388 1בְּרָכָה *b^e rākāh1* (68)
blessing (37)
blessings (14)
blessed (2)
blessed (2) +5989
gift (2)
peace (2)
present (2)
special favor (2)
bless (1) +5989
blessed (1) +995
generous (1)
giving blessing (1) +1385
good (1)

1389 2בְּרָכָה *b^e rākāh2* (1)
Beracah (1)

1390 3בְּרָכָה *b^e rākāh3* (2)
Beracah (2)

1391 בְּרֵכָה *b^e rēkāh* (18)
pool (13)
pools (2)
pool (1) +4784
reservoirs (1) +4784
untranslated (1)

1392 בֶּרֶכְיָה *berekyāh* (7)
Berekiah (7)

1393 בֶּרֶכְיָהוּ *berekyāhû* (4)
Berekiah (4)

1394 בְּרֹמִים *b^e rōmiym* (1)
multicolored (1)

1395 בַּרְנֵעַ *barnēa'*
Variant; not used

1396 בֶּרַע *bera'* (1)
Bera (1)

1397 בָּרַק *bāraq* (1)
send forth lightning (1) +1398

1398 1בָּרָק *bāraq1* (21)
lightning (11)
flash like lightning (3)
bolts of lightning (2)
flashing (1)
gleaming point (1)
glittering (1)
lightning bolts (1)
send forth lightning (1) +1397

1399 2בָּרָק *bāraq2* (14)
Barak (12)
Barak's (1)
he^S (1)

1400 בְּרַק *b^e raq*
Variant; not used

1401 בַּרְקוֹס *barqôs* (2)
Barkos (2)

1402 בַּרְקָן *barqōn* (2)
briers (2)

1403 בָּרֶקֶת *bāreqet* (2)
beryl (2)

1404 בָּרְקַת *borqat* (1)
beryl (1)

1405 1בָּרַר *bārar1* (15)
pure (3)
choice (2)
chosen (2)
show yourself pure (2)
be purified (1)
choose (1)
cleanse (1)
purge (1)
purified (1)
tests (1)

1406 2בָּרַר *bārar2* (2)
polished (1)
sharpen (1)

1407 בִּרְשַׁע *birša'* (1)
Birsha (1)

1408 בֵּרֹתַי *bērōtay* (1)
Berothai (1)

1409 בֵּרֹתִי *bērōtiy* (1)
Berothite (1)

1410 בְּשׂוֹר *b^e śôr* (3)
Besor (2)
untranslated (1)

1411 בֹּשֶׂם *bōśem* (30)
spices (21)
spice (3)
fragrance (2)
fragrant (2)
perfumes (1)
spice-laden (1)

1412 בָּשְׂמַת *bāś^e mat* (7)
Basemath (7)

1413 בָּשַׂר *bāśar* (24)
proclaim (4)
bring good tidings (2)
bringing good news (2)
brought the news (2)
proclaim the news (2)
take the news (2)
bring good news (1)
bring tidings (1)
bringing news (1)
brings good news (1)
do so^S (1)
hear good news (1)
messenger of good tidings (1)
preach good news (1)
proclaimed (1)
proclaiming (1)

1414 בָּשָׂר *bāśār* (270)
flesh (75)
meat (64)
body (21)
himself (10) +2257
mankind (10)
skin (8) +6425
creature (7)
bodies (5)
people (5)
life (4)
flesh and blood (3)
men (3)
creatures (2)
everyone (2) +3972
fat (2) +1374
gaunt (2) +1987
it^S (2)

kind (2)
living thing (2)
mortal man (2)
skin (2)
be circumcised (1) +4576+6889
blood relative (1) +8638
bodily (1) +4946
body (1) +6872
circumcised (1) +4576+6889
close relative (1) +8638
completely (1) +2256+4946+5883+6330
genitals (1)
lean (1) +8369
lustful (1) +1541
mankind (1) +408
meal (1)
mortal (1)
myself (1) +3276
nothing but skin (1) +2256+6425
nourished (1) +1374
one[s] (1) +3972
put in jeopardy (1) +928+5951+9094
regular flow (1) +928+2307
that[s] (1)
them (1) +4392
those[s] (1)
undergo circumcision (1) +906+4576+6889
was circumcised (1) +4576+6889
you (1) +3870
untranslated (12)

1415 בְּשׂרָה *bᵉśōrāh* (6)
news (3)
good news (2)
reward for news (1)

1416 בַּשֶּׁבֶת *baššebet*
Variant; not used

1417 בְּשַׁגַּם *bᵉšaggam*
Variant; not used

1418 בָּשַׁל *bāšal* (28)
cook (10)
cooked (5)
boiled (3)
boil (2)
baked (1)
burned to cook (1)
cooked (1) +1419
kitchens (1) +1074
ripe (1)
ripened (1)
roast (1)
roasted (1)

1419 בָּשֵׁל *bāšēl* (2)
boiled (1)
cooked (1) +1418

1420 בִּשְׁלָם *bišlām* (1)
Bishlam (1)

1421 1בָּשָׁן *bāšān1* (60)
Bashan (59)
Bashan (1) +824

1422 2בָּשָׁן *bāšān2*
Variant; not used

1423 בָּשְׁנָה *bošnāh* (1)
disgraced (1) +4374

1424 בָּשַׁס *bāšas* (1)
trample (1)

1425 בֹּשֶׁת *bōšet* (30)
shame (20)
disgraced (2)
disgrace (1) +7156
humiliation (1) +7156
shame (1) +6872
shameful god (1)
shameful gods (1)
shameful idol (1)
shaming (1)
utter shame (1) +1017

1426 1בַּת *bat1* (588)
daughter (245)
daughters (205)
women (15)
people (14) +6639
surrounding settlements (10)
settlements (9)
villages (7)
surrounding villages (6)
granddaughter (5)
woman (5)
owls (4) +3613
daughter's (3)
girl (3)
girls (2)
horned owl (2) +3613
maidens (2)
owl (2) +3613
year-old (2) +9102
young women (2)
adopted (1) +4200+4374
age (1) +9102
apple (1) +413
branches (1)
city (1)
cousin (1) +1856
descendant (1)
Egypt (1) +5213
eyes (1) +6524
granddaughters (1) +1201
inhabitants (1)
old (1)
outlying villages (1)
people (1)
princess (1) +4889
she[s] (1) +7281
sister (1)
songs (1) +8877
whose[s] (1) +465+2257
whose[s] (1) +7524
young (1)
untranslated (24)

1427 2בַּת *bat2* (14)
baths (8)
bath (6)

1428 3בַּת *bat3* (1)
did weaving (1) +755

1429 בָּתָה *bātāh* (1)
wasteland (1)

1430 בֹּתָה *bōtāh*
Variant; not used

1431 בַּתָּה *battāh* (1)
steep (1)

1432 1בְּתוּאֵל *bᵉtû'ēl1* (9)
Bethuel (9)

1433 2בְּתוּאֵל *bᵉtû'ēl2* (1)
Bethuel (1)

1434 בְּתוּל *bᵉtûl* (1)
Bethul (1)

1435 בְּתוּלָה *bᵉtûlāh* (51)
virgin (25)
maidens (7)
virgins (6)
young women (4)
maiden (3)
daughters (1)
girl (1)
girls (1) +5855
unmarried (1)
women (1)
young woman (1)

1436 בְּתוּלִים *bᵉtûliym* (9)
proof of virginity (3)
never marry (2)
be a virgin (1) +928
proof that a virgin (1)
to be a virgin (1)
virgin (1)

1437 בִּתְיָה *bityāh* (1)
Bithiah (1)

1438 בָּתַק *bātaq* (1)
hack to pieces (1)

1439 בָּתַר *bātar* (2)
cut (1)
cut in half (1)

1440 1בֶּתֶר *beter1* (3)
pieces (2)
halves (1)

1441 2בֶּתֶר *beter2* (1)
rugged (1)

1442 בַּת־רַבִּים *bat-rabbiym* (1)
Bath Rabbim (1)

1443 בִּתְרוֹן *bitrôn* (1)
Bithron (1)

1444 בַּת־שֶׁבַע *bat-šeba'* (12)
Bathsheba (12)

1445 בַּת־שׁוּעַ *bat-šûa'*
Variant; not used

1446 ג *g*
Variant; not used

1447 גֵּא *gē'* (1)
pride (1)

1448 גָּאָה *gā'āh* (6)
highly exalted (2) +1448
grow tall (1)
hold head high (1)
risen (1)

1449 גֵּאָה *gē'āh* (1)
pride (1)

1450 גֵּאֶה *gē'eh* (8)
proud (7)
pride (1)

1451 גְּאוּאֵל *gᵉ'û'ēl* (1)
Geuel (1)

1452 גַּאֲוָה *ga'ᵃwāh* (18)
pride (7)
arrogance (2)
majesty (2)
back (1)
conceit (1)
glorious (1)
proud (1)
proud (1) +6913
surging (1)
triumph (1)

1453 גְּאוּלִים *gᵉ'ûliym* (1)
redemption (1)

1454 גָּאוֹן *gā'ôn* (49)
pride (23)
majesty (6)
arrogance (5)
proud (5)
thickets (3)
splendor (2)
arrogant (1)
glory (1)
lush thicket (1)
majestic (1)
pomp (1)

1455 גֵּאוּת *gē'ût* (8)
majesty (2)
pride (2)
arrogance (1)
column (1)
glorious things (1)
surging (1)

1456 גַּאֲיוֹן *ga'ᵃyôn* (1)
arrogant (1)

1457 1גָּאַל *gā'al1* (103)
redeemed (18)
redeem (17)
redeemer (17)
avenger (13)
kinsman-redeemer (7)
be redeemed (3)
do it^{s} (2)
redeem (2) +1457
redeems (2)
relative (2)
rescue (2)
claim (1)
close relative (1)
defender (1)
delivered (1)
do so^{s} (1)
has the right to do it^{s} (1)
is redeemed (1)
kinsman-redeemers (1)
near of kin (1)
redeem himself (1)
redeemable (1)
redeems (1) +1457
untranslated (4)

1458 2גָּאַל *gā'al2* (11)
defiled (4)
defile himself (2)
unclean (2)
are defiled (1)
are stained (1)
stained (1)

1459 גֹּאַל *gō'al* (1)
defiled (1)

1460 גְּאֻלָּה *g^{e}'ullāh* (14)
redemption (4)
redeem (3)
right of redemption (2)
as nearest relative duty (1)
blood relatives (1) +408
it^{s} (1) +3276
redeemed (1)
right to redeem (1)

1461 1גַּב *gab̲1* (10)
rims (3)
mounds (2)
back (1)
backs (1)
eyebrows (1) +6524
mound (1)
strong (1)

1462 2גַּב *gab̲2* (2)
defenses (2)

1463 1גֵּב *gēb̲1* (3)
cisterns (1)
full of ditches (1) +1463

1464 2גֵּב *gēb̲2* (1)
beams (1)

1465 גֶּבֶא *geb̲e'* (2)
cistern (1)
marshes (1)

1466 גֵּבָה *gēb̲āh* (1)
locusts (1)

1467 גָּבַהּ *gāb̲ah* (33)
proud (5)
exalted (3)
haughty (3)
towered (3)
high (2)
higher (2)
soar (2)
arrogant (1)
build high (1)
builds high (1)
devoted (1)
exalts (1)
highest (1)
made higher (1)
make grow tall (1)
pride (1)
pride (1) +4213
taller (1)
tower proudly (1)
upward (1)

1468 גָּבֵהַּ *gāb̲ēah* (4)
haughty (1)
pride (1) +8120
proud (1)
towered (1)

1469 גָּבֹהַּ *gāb̲ōah* (38)
high (19)
tall (2)
arrogant (1)
exalted (1)
haughty (1)
height (1) +7757
heights (1)
lofty (1)
long (1)
longer (1)
official (1)
one^{s} (1)
others^{s} (1)
proud (1)
so proudly (1) +1469
taller (1)
towers (1)
untranslated (1)

1470 גֹּבַהּ *gōb̲ah* (18)
height (4)
high (3)
tall (2)
conceit (1)
haughty (1)
heights (1)
higher (1)
pride (1)
pride (1) +678
raised (1)
splendor (1)
untranslated (1)

1471 גַּבְהוּת *gab̲hûṯ* (2)
arrogance (1)
arrogant (1)

1472 גָּבוֹל *gāb̲ôl*
Variant; not used

1473 גְּבוּל *g^{e}b̲ûl* (249)
territory (58)
boundary (44)
border (36)
borders (10)
boundaries (10)
it^{s} (9) +2021
country (7)
land (7)
area (4)
boundary stone (4)
region (3)
rim (3)
throughout (3) +928+3972
coastline (2)
vicinity (2)
allotted portions (1)
allotted territory (1)
anywhere (1) +3972
anywhere in (1) +928+3972
areas (1)
bank (1)
borderland (1)
boundary stones (1)
coast (1)
districts (1)
domain (1)
Egypt (1) +5213
end (1) +7895
homeland (1)
it^{s} (1)
it^{s} (1) +616+2021
limits (1)
neighboring territory (1)
part (1)
parts (1)
places (1)
the borders (1)
wall (1)
walls (1)
untranslated (23)

1474 גְּבוּלָה *g^{e}b̲ûlāh* (2)
boundary stones (1)
field (1)

1475 גִּבּוֹר *gibbôr* (160)
warriors (27)
mighty (23)
mighty men (17)
fighting men (12) +2657
warrior (11)
brave warriors (6) +2657
mighty man (4)
strong (4)
heroes (3)
man (3)
special guard (3)
able men (2) +2657
best fighting men (2) +2657
fighting men (2)
hero (2)
mighty warrior (2)
mighty warriors (2)
powerful (2)
standing (2) +2657
valiant soldier (2) +2657
warrior's (2)
another^{s} (1)
blameless (1) +9459
brave fighting men (1) +2657
brave man (1) +2657
brave warrior (1) +2657
capable men (1) +2657
champion (1)
experienced fighting men (1) +408+2657+4878
fighter (1)
fighters (1)
good fighters (1)
leaders (1)
men (1)
mighty (1) +3946
mighty men (1) +2657
mighty warrior (1) +2657
military staff (1)
noblest (1) +4946
officers (1)
principal (1)
soldiers (1)
strong man (1)
troops (1) +2657
very capable men (1) +2657
warriors (1) +2657
untranslated (2)

1476 גְּבוּרָה *g^{e}b̲ûrāh* (62)
power (16)
strength (14)
might (11)
achievements (8)
mighty acts (4)
things^{s} (2)
acts of power (1)
mighty power (1)
mighty works (1)
source of strength (1)
victory (1)
warriors (1)
untranslated (1)

1477 גִּבֵּחַ *gibbēah* (1)
bald forehead (1)

1478 גַּבַּחַת *gabbahat* (4)
forehead (3)
other[S] (1)

1479 גֹּבַי *gōbay* (2)
locusts (1)
swarms of locusts (1)

1480 גַּבַּי *gabbay* (1)
Gabbai (1)

1481 גֵּבִים *gēbiym* (1)
Gebim (1)

1482 גְּבִינָה *g^ebiynāh* (1)
cheese (1)

1483 גָּבִיעַ *gābiya'* (14)
cups (6)
cup (4)
bowls (1)
one[S] (1)
untranslated (2)

1484 גְּבִיר *g^ebiyr* (2)
lord (2)

1485 גְּבִירָה *g^ebiyrāh* (13)
mistress (7)
queen mother (3)
position as queen mother (2)
queen (1)

1486 גָּבִישׁ *gābiyš* (1)
jasper (1)

1487 גָּבַל *gābal* (5)
borders (1)
formed the boundary (1)
put limits (1)
put limits around (1)
set up (1)

1488 גְּבַל *g^ebal* (1)
Gebal (1)

1489 גְּבָל *g^ebāl* (1)
Gebal (1)

1490 גִּבְלִי *gibliy* (2)
Gebalites (1)
men of Gebal (1)

1491 גַּבְלֻת *gablut* (2)
braided (2)

1492 גִּבֵּן *gibbēn* (1)
hunchbacked (1)

1493 גַּבְנֹן *gabnôn* (2)
rugged (2)

1494 גֶּבַע *geba'* (15)
Geba (15)

1495 גִּבְעָא *gib'ā'* (1)
Gibea (1)

1496 1גִּבְעָה *gib'āh1* (67)
hills (36)
hill (26)
heights (2)
hilltops (2)
untranslated (1)

1497 2גִּבְעָה *gib'āh2* (49)
Gibeah (48)
untranslated (1)

1498 גִּבְעוֹנִי *gib'ôniy* (8)
Gibeonites (6)
Gibeonite (1)
of Gibeon (1)

1499 גִּבְעֹל *gib'ōl* (1)
in bloom (1)

1500 גִּבְעוֹן *gib'ôn* (39)
Gibeon (38)
Gibeonites (1) +408

1501 גִּבְעַת *gib'at*
Variant; not used

1502 גִּבְעַת הָעֲרָלוֹת *gib'at hā'ᵃrālôt* (1)
Gibeath Haaraloth (1)

1503 גִּבְעָתִי *gib'ātiy* (1)
Gibeathite (1)

1504 גָּבַר *gābar* (25)
rose (3)
triumph (3)
great (2)
strengthen (2)
winning (2)
arrogantly (1)
confirm (1)
flooded (1)
greater (1)
increasing (1)
needed (1)
overpowered (1)
overwhelmed (1)
prevailed (1)
prevails (1)
stronger (1)
strongest (1)
vaunts himself (1)

1505 1גֶּבֶר *geber1* (66)
man (39)
men (7)
one (3)
man's (2)
any[S] (1)
blameless (1) +9459
boy (1)
each[S] (1)
families (1)
he[S] (1)
him[S] (1)
husband's (1)
men's (1)
mighty man (1)
ruler (1) +8031
soldiers (1) +408+4878
strong man (1)
whoever[S] (1)
untranslated (1)

1506 2גֶּבֶר *geber2* (1)
Geber (1)

1507 גִּבָּר *gibbār* (1)
Gibbar (1)

1508 גַּבְרִיאֵל *gabriy'ēl* (2)
Gabriel (2)

1509 גְּבֶרֶת *g^eberet* (2)
queen (2)

1510 גִּבְּתוֹן *gibb^etôn* (6)
Gibbethon (5)
it[S] (1)

1511 גָּג *gāg* (31)
roof (10)
roofs (7)
top (3)
roof of house (1)
top of the wall (1)
untranslated (1)

1512 1גַּד *gad1* (2)
coriander (2)

1513 2גַּד *gad2* (3)
fortune (1)
good fortune (1)
untranslated (1)

1514 גָּד *gād* (70)
Gad (43)
Gadites (16) +1201
Gad (7) +1201
Gad's (1)
they[S] (1) +1201+1201+2256+8017
untranslated (2)

1515 גִּדְגָּד *gidgād*
Variant; not used

1516 גֻּדְגֹּדָה *gudgōdāh* (2)
Gudgodah (1)
untranslated (1)

1517 1גָּדַד *gādad1* (5)
cut yourselves (2)
cut himself (1)
cut themselves (1)
slashed themselves (1)

1518 2גָּדַד *gādad2* (3)
band together (1)
marshal troops (1)
thronged (1)

1519 גָּדָה *gādāh*
Variant; not used

1520 גַּדָּה *gaddāh*
Variant; not used

1521 1גְּדוּד *g^edûd1* (1)
ridges (1)

1522 2גְּדוּד *g^edûd2* (33)
troops (5)
raiders (3)
raiding bands (3)
band of raiders (2)
bands (2)
forces (2)
raiding party (2)
troop (2)
band of rebels (1)
bandits (1)
divisions (1)
invaders (1)
marauders (1)
men ready for battle (1) +4878+7372
raid (1)
them[S] (1) +2021
troops (1) +1201
untranslated (3)

1523 גְּדוּדָה *g^edûdāh* (1)
slashed (1)

1524 גָּדוֹל *gādôl* (529)
great (244)
large (41)
high (23)
greatest (17)
loud (16)
greater (9)
mighty (9)
older (9)
heavy (8)
old (7)
vast (7)
very (6)
greatly (5)
terrible (5)
bitterly (4)
important (4)
much (4)
oldest (4)
powerful (4)
strong (4)
called out (3) +928+7754+7924
even more (3)
larger (3)
many (3)
aloud (2) +7754
awful (2)
became more and more powerful (2) +2143+2143+2256
deep (2)
fierce (2)
great (2) +4394
huge (2)
louder (2)

loudly (2)
more (2)
such (2)
wealthy (2)
wonders (2)
all (1)
aloud (1) +928+7754
at all (1) +196+7785
awful (1) +2098
became more and more powerful (1) +2143+2256
better (1)
big (1)
boastful (1) +1819
chief (1)
deeds (1)
destroyed (1) +4394+4804+5782
devastated (1) +4394+4804+5782
difficult (1)
far (1)
feat (1) +1821
fine (1) +2256+3202
great amount (1)
grievous (1)
hard (1)
harsh (1)
highly regarded (1) +4394
hot-tempered (1) +2779
huge (1) +4200+4394+6330
immense (1)
imposing (1) +4200+5260
intense (1) +4394
large (1) +4394
leaders (1)
leading (1)
loud (1) +4394+6330
loudly (1) +928+7754
main (1)
most important (1)
nobles (1)
noisy din (1) +7754
nothing (1) +1821+2256+4202+7785
older (1) +4946
power (1)
preeminent (1)
prominent (1)
rich (1)
screamed (1) +928+7754+7924
serious (1)
shout (1) +7754+7924
so much (1)
solemn (1)
strange (1)
stronger (1)
such (1) +2296
terrified (1) +3707+3711
thick (1)
top (1)
total (1) +4394
trembled violently (1) +3006+3010+4394+6330
utterly (1)
vast (1) +4394
vast (1) +4394+4394
violent (1)
well-to-do (1)
untranslated (2)

1525 גְּדוּלָּה *g^eḏûllāh* (13)
great (3)
greatness (3)
great thing (2)
great deeds (1)
honor (1)
majesty (1)
recognition (1)
untranslated (1)

1526 גִּדּוּף *giddûp̱* (2)
scorn (1)
taunts (1)

1527 גְּדוּפָה *g^eḏûp̱āh* (1)
taunt (1)

1528 גִּדּוּפָה *giddûp̱āh* (1)
insults (1)

1529 1גְּדוֹר *g^eḏôr1* (4)
Gedor (4)

1530 2גְּדוֹר *g^eḏôr2* (3)
Gedor (3)

1531 גְּדִי *g^eḏiy* (17)
young goat (7) +6436
young goat (5)
goat (1)
goatskins (1) +6425+6436
lambs (1)
young goats (1)
young goats (1) +6436

1532 1גָּדִי *gāḏiy1* (15)
Gadites (12)
Gad (1)
Gad (1) +1201
of Gad (1)

1533 2גָּדִי *gāḏiy2* (2)
Gadi (2)

1534 גַּדִּי *gaddiy* (1)
Gaddi (1)

1535 גַּדִּיאֵל *gaddiy'ēl* (1)
Gaddiel (1)

1536 גִּדְיָה *giḏyāh* (5)
banks (2)
at flood stage (1) +3972+4848+6584
at flood stage (1) +3972+6584
untranslated (1)

1537 גְּדִיָּה *g^eḏiyyāh* (1)
young goats (1)

1538 1גָּדִישׁ *gāḏiyš1* (3)
sheaves (1)
shocks (1)
shocks of grain (1)

1539 2גָּדִישׁ *gāḏiyš2* (1)
tomb (1)

1540 גָּדַל *gāḏal* (117)
great (17)
greater (8)
grown up (7)
exalted (6)
grew up (6)
exalt (5)
grew (5)
reared (4)
defied (2) +6584
gives great (2)
glorify (2)
honored (2)
make great (2)
wealthy (2)
boast (1)
boast so much (1) +3870+7023
boasted (1) +928+7023
boosting (1)
brought up (1)
developed (1)
displayed (1)
exalt himself (1)
great (1) +4394
great things done (1)
greatness (1)
grew older (1)
grow long (1)
grown (1)
grows up (1)
increased (1)
lifted up (1)
made great (1)
made grow (1)
made threats (1)
magnificent (1)
magnify (1)
make greater (1)
make grow (1)
make so much of (1)
mocking (1)
most (1)
nourished (1)
pile high (1)
powerful (1)
raised (1)
raising (1)
reached (1) +6330
rear (1)
rearing (1)
rich (1)
set up to be great (1)
show greatness (1)
superior (1)
trained (1)
triumphed (1)
undertook great (1)
value (1) +928+6524
valued (1) +928+6524
well-nurtured (1)
yielding (1)
untranslated (1)

1541 גָּדֵל *gāḏēl* (4)
lustful (1) +1414
more and more powerful (1) +2025+2143+2256+4200+5087+6330
stature (1)
wealth (1)

1542 גֹּדֶל *gōḏel* (13)
majesty (4)
greatness (3)
arrogance (1)
beauty (1)
great (1)
great power (1)
strength (1)
willful pride (1) +7262

1543 גִּדֵּל *giddēl* (4)
Giddel (4)

1544 גָּדִל *gāḏil* (2)
festooned (1)
tassels (1)

1545 גְּדַלְיָה *g^eḏalyāh* (6)
Gedaliah (6)

1546 גְּדַלְיָהוּ *g^eḏalyāhû* (26)
Gedaliah (25)
Gedaliah's (1)

1547 גִּדַּלְתִּי *giddaltiy* (2)
Giddalti (2)

1548 גָּדַע *gāḏaʻ* (23)
cut down (4)
cut off (3)
broke (2)
cut to pieces (2)
be cut off (1)
be felled (1)
be sheared off (1)
been cast down (1)
been felled (1)
broke down (1)
broken (1)
broken down (1)
cut short (1)
cut through (1)
cuts through (1)
is cut off (1)

1549 גִּדְעוֹן *giḏʻôn* (39)
Gideon (35)
he^s (3)
Gideon's (1)

1550 גִּדְעֹם *giḏʻōm* (1)
Gidom (1)

1551 גִּדְעֹנִי *gid'ōniy* (5)
Gideoni (5)

1552 גָּדַף *gādap* (7)
blasphemed (5)
blasphemes (1)
revile (1)

1553 גָּדַר *gādar* (10)
masons (2)
repair (2)
barred (1)
blocked (1)
build up (1)
repairer of walls (1)
wall in (1) +1555
walled (1)

1554 גֶּדֶר *geder* (1)
Geder (1)

1555 גָּדֵר *gādēr* (14)
wall (7)
walls (3)
fence (1)
wall in (1) +1553
wall of protection (1)
untranslated (1)

1556 1גְּדֵרָה *g^{e}dērāh1* (9)
pens (4)
walls (3)
pens (1) +7366
wall (1)

1557 2גְּדֵרָה *g^{e}dērāh2* (2)
Gederah (2)

1558 גְּדֵרוֹת *g^{e}dērôt* (2)
Gederoth (2)

1559 גְּדֵרִי *g^{e}dēriy* (1)
Gederite (1)

1560 גִּדֶרֶת *gideret*
Variant; not used

1561 גְּדֵרָתִי *g^{e}dērātiy* (1)
Gederathite (1)

1562 גְּדֵרֹתַיִם *g^{e}dērōtayim* (1)
Gederothaim (1)

1563 גֵּה *gēh*
Variant; not used

1564 גָּהָה *gāhāh* (1)
heal (1)

1565 גֵּהָה *gēhāh* (1)
medicine (1)

1566 גָּהַר *gāhar* (3)
stretched out (2)
bent down (1)

1567 גַּו *gaw* (3)
back (2)
backs (1)

1568 1גֵּו *gēw1* (7)
back (5)
backs (2)

1569 2גֵּו *gēw2* (1)
fellow men (1)

1570 1גּוֹב *gôb1* (2)
Gob (2)

1571 2גּוֹב *gôb2* (1)
swarms (1)

1572 גּוּב *gûb*
Variant; not used

1573 גּוֹג *gôg* (10)
Gog (10)

1574 גּוּד *gûd* (3)
attack (1)
attacked (1)
invading (1)

1575 1גֵּוָה *gēwāh1* (3)
pride (2)
lift up (1)

1576 2גֵּוָה *gēwāh2* (1)
back (1)

1577 גּוּז *gûz* (2)
drove in (1)
pass (1)

1578 גּוֹזָל *gôzāl* (2)
young (1)
young pigeon (1)

1579 גּוֹזָן *gôzān* (5)
Gozan (5)

1580 גּוֹי *gôy* (561)
nations (410)
nation (114)
people (8)
gentiles (5)
gentile (2)
peoples (2)
another^{s} (1)
countries (1)
each national group (1) +1580
foreign (1)
it^{s} (1) +2021
kind (1)
nations (1) +824
pagan nations (1)
they^{s} (1)
untranslated (10)

1581 גְּוִיָּה *g^{e}wiyyāh* (13)
bodies (4)
body (4)
carcass (1)
corpses (1)
dead (1)
it^{s} (1) +793+2021
untranslated (1)

1582 גּוֹיִם *gôyim* (3)
Goiim (2)
Goyim (1)

1583 גּוֹלָה *gôlāh* (41)
exile (16)
exiles (15)
exiles (6) +1201
captive (1)
deported (1) +995
those^{s} (1) +2021
took (1) +2143

1584 גּוֹלָן *gôlān* (6)
Golan (4)
untranslated (2)

1585 גּוּמָּץ *gûmmāṣ* (1)
pit (1)

1586 1גּוּנִי *gûniy1* (4)
Guni (4)

1587 2גּוּנִי *gûniy2* (1)
Gunite (1)

1588 גָּוַע *gāwa'* (24)
die (8)
died (4)
breathed his last (4)
perish (3)
perished (2)
breathes his last (1)
close to death (1)
fell dead (1)

1589 גּוּף *gûp* (1)
shut (1)

1590 גּוּפָה *gûpāh* (2)
bodies (1)
untranslated (1)

1591 1גּוּר *gûr1* (81)
living (24)
dwell (10)
live (7)
settle (6)
stay (4)
stayed (3)
aliens (2)
live for a while (2)
lived (2)
settled (2)
stay for a while (2)
staying (2)
strangers (2)
alien (1)
can^{s} (1)
for a while stayed (1)
gather together (1)
guests (1) +1074
linger (1)
live awhile (1)
lived as an alien (1)
lives (1)
living as an alien (1)
nomads (1)
settles (1)
untranslated (1)

1592 2גּוּר *gûr2* (6)
conspire (2)
attack (1) +1592
attacks (1)
stir up (1)

1593 3גּוּר *gûr3* (10)
afraid (3)
fear (2)
revere (2)
terrified (2)
dreaded (1)

1594 4גּוּר *gûr4* (7)
cubs (3)
cub (2)
cubs (1) +793
young (1)

1595 5גּוּר *gûr5* (1)
Gur (1)

1596 גֹּור *gôr* (2)
cubs (2)

1597 גּוּר־בַּעַל *gûr-bā'al* (1)
Gur Baal (1)

1598 גּוֹרָל *gôrāl* (77)
lot (37)
lots (17)
allotment (5)
allotted (4) +928+2021
allotted (3)
allotted (2) +928+2021+5989
allotted (2) +2118
allotted (1) +928+2021+2118
allotted inheritance (1)
drawing lots (1)
portions (1)
territory allotted (1)
untranslated (2)

1599 גּוּשׁ *gûš* (1)
scabs (1) +6760

1600 גֵּז *gēz* (4)
fleece (1)
harvested (1)
mown field (1)
wool from shearing (1)

1601 גִּזְבָּר *gizbār* (1)
treasurer (1)

1602 גָּזָה *gāzāh* (1)
brought forth (1)

1603 גִּזָּה *gizzāh* (7)
fleece (6)

untranslated (1)

1604 גִּזֹנִי *gizôniy* (1)
Gizonite (1)

1605 גָּזַז *gāzaz* (15)
shear (3)
shearers (3)
shearing (3)
be cut off (1)
cut off (1)
shave heads (1) +7942
shaved (1)
sheep-shearing time (1)
sheepshearers (1)

1606 גָּזֵז *gāzēz* (2)
Gazez (2)

1607 גָּזִית *gāziyṯ* (11)
dressed (3)
dressed stone (3)
cut (2)
blocks of stone (1)
dressed stones (1)
stone (1)

1608 גָּזַל *gāzal* (30)
rob (3)
snatched (3)
been robbed (2)
commit robbery (2) +1611
seized (2)
are robbed (1)
be forcibly taken (1)
caught (1)
commit robbery (1) +1610
commits robbery (1) +1611
exploit (1)
injured (1)
robbed (1)
robbed (1) +1609
robs (1)
seize (1)
snatch away (1)
steal (1)
stolen (1)
stolen (1) +1611
take by force (1)
tear (1)
withhold (1)

1609 גֵּזֶל *gēzel* (2)
denied (1)
robbed (1) +1608

1610 גָּזֵל *gāzēl* (4)
commit robbery (1) +1608
robbery (1)
stolen (1)
stolen goods (1)

1611 גְּזֵלָה *gᵉzēlāh* (6)
commit robbery (2) +1608
commits robbery (1) +1608
plunder (1)
stolen (1) +1608
what stolen (1)

1612 גָּזָם *gāzām* (3)
locust swarm (2)
locusts (1)

1613 גַּזָּם *gazzām* (2)
Gazzam (2)

1614 גֶּזַע *gezaʻ* (3)
stump (2)
take root (1) +9245

1615 1גָּזַר *gāzar1* (12)
are cut off (2)
be cut off (1)
cut (1)
cut down (1)
cut in two (1)
decide (1)
decreed (1)
divided (1)
excluded (1)
there are no (1)
was cut off (1)

1616 2גָּזַר *gāzar2* (1)
devour (1)

1617 1גֶּזֶר *gezer1* (2)
asunder (1)
pieces (1)

1618 2גֶּזֶר *gezer2* (15)
Gezer (14)
there[s] (1) +928

1619 גִּזְרָה *gizrāh* (8)
courtyard (7)
appearance (1)

1620 גְּזֵרָה *gᵉzērāh*
Variant; not used

1621 גִּזְרִי *gizriy* (1)
untranslated (1)

1622 גָּהָה *gāhāh*
Variant; not used

1623 גָּחוֹן *gāhôn* (2)
belly (2)

1624 גַּחַל *gahal* (16)
coals (6)
burning coals (5)
bolts (2)
embers (1)
hot coals (1)
untranslated (1)

1625 גַּחֶלֶת *gaheleṯ* (2)
burning coal (1)
coals (1)

1626 גַּחַם *gaham* (1)
Gaham (1)

1627 גַּחַר *gahar* (2)
Gahar (2)

1628 גַּיְא *gay'* (60)
valley (50)
valleys (7)
it[s] (1) +2215
untranslated (2)

1629 גֵּיא חֲרָשִׁים *gēy' ḥᵃrāšiym* (1)
Ge Harashim (1)

1630 גִּיד *giyḏ* (7)
sinews (3)
tendon (2) +5962
tendons (2)

1631 1גִּיחַ *giyah1* (6)
brought (1)
burst (1)
charged out (1)
in agony (1)
surge (1)
thrashing about (1)

1632 2גִּיחַ *giyah2* (1)
Giah (1)

1633 גִּיחוֹן *giyhôn* (6)
Gihon (6)

1634 גֵּיחֲזִי *gēyhᵃziy* (12)
Gehazi (12)

1635 1גִּיל *giyl1* (47)
rejoice (25)
glad (11)
rejoices (3)
great joy (1) +1635
joy (1)
joyful (1)
rejoice greatly (1) +677+1638
rejoiced (1)
untranslated (2)

1636 2גִּיל *giyl2* (1)
age (1)

1637 3גִּיל *giyl3* (8)
gladness (5)
delight (1)
filled with gladness (1) +448+8524
jubilant (1)

1638 גִּילָה *giylāh* (2)
delight (1)
rejoice greatly (1) +677+1635

1639 גִּילֹנִי *giylōniy* (2)
Gilonite (2)

1640 גִּינַת *giynaṯ* (2)
Ginath (2)

1641 גִּישׁ *giyš* (1)
untranslated (1)

1642 גֵּישָׁן *gēyšān* (1)
Geshan (1)

1643 1גַּל *gal1* (18)
heap (8)
heap of ruins (2)
pile (2)
piles of stone (2) +5898
heap of rubble (1)
pile of rocks (1)
piles of stones (1)
rubble (1)

1644 2גַּל *gal2* (16)
waves (13)
breakers (1)
fountain (1)
surging (1)

1645 גֵּל *gēl* (3)
dung (1)
excrement (1)
excrement (1) +7362

1646 גֹּל *gōl*
Variant; not used

1647 גַּלָּב *gallāḇ* (1)
barber's (1)

1648 גִּלְבֹּעַ *gilbōaʻ* (8)
Gilboa (8)

1649 1גַּלְגַּל *galgal1* (9)
wheels (3)
wagons (2)
chariot wheels (1)
wheel (1)
whirling wheels (1)
whirlwind (1)

1650 2גַּלְגַּל *galgal2* (2)
tumbleweed (2)

1651 1גִּלְגָּל *gilgāl1* (1)
wheels (1)

1652 2גִּלְגָּל *gilgāl2* (40)
Gilgal (39)
untranslated (1)

1653 גֻּלְגֹּלֶת *gulgōleṯ* (12)
one by one (4) +4200+4392
skull (2)
each (1) +5031
each one (1)
head (1)
individually (1) +4200
person (1)
total (1)

1654 גֶּלֶד *gēleḏ* (1)
skin (1)

1655 גָּלָה *gālāh* (188)
carried into exile (11)
have sexual relations with (11) +6872

deported (7)
be exposed (4)
dishonored (4) +6872
expose (4)
uncovered (4)
exposed (3)
go into exile (3)
have sexual relations (3) +6872
open (3)
opened (3)
revealed (3)
taken captive (3)
taken into exile (3)
be revealed (2)
been carried into exile (2)
been revealed (2)
betray (2)
betrays (2)
committed (2)
departed (2)
exile (2)
exiled (2)
have relations with (2) +6872
laid bare (2)
let know (2) +265+906
made known (2)
revealed (2) +265
revealed himself (2)
sent into exile (2)
surely go into exile (2) +1655
tells (2) +265+906
took captive (2)
took into exile (2)
uncover (2)
unsealed (2)
went into captivity (2)
went into exile (2)
airing (1)
banished (1)
bare (1)
be carried into exile (1)
be exiled (1)
be laid bare (1)
been shown (1)
been torn off (1)
being carried into exile (1)
bring to attention (1) +265
brought (1)
captive (1)
captivity (1)
carried away (1)
carried into exile (1) +1655
carried on openly (1)
carry away (1)
carry into exile (1)
carry off (1)
certainly go into exile (1) +1655
clearly reveal myself (1) +1655
confiding in (1) +265+906
disclose (1)
dishonor bed (1) +4053
dishonor bed (1) +6872
dishonor by having sexual relations with (1) +6872
dishonor by to have sexual relations (1) +6872
dishonors bed (1) +4053
disrobing (1)
driven out (1)
free (1)
go (1)
go into exile (1) +1655
gone into exile (1)
has sexual relations with (1) +906+6872
lay bare (1)
led captive (1)
let enjoy (1)
let see (1)
lift (1)
makes listen (1) +265
remove (1)
removed (1)
revealed (1) +265+906
revealing (1)
reveals (1)
send into exile (1)
set out (1)
showed themselves (1)
speak (1)
speaks (1) +265
strip (1) +6872
strip off (1)
stripped (1)
stripped away (1)
take off (1)
taken (1)
tell (1) +265+906
was given (1)
was uncovered (1)
were taken captive (1)
word come (1)
would^{s} (1) +1655
untranslated (2)

1656 גִּלֹה *gilōh* (2)
Giloh (2)

1657 גֻּלָּה *gullāh* (15)
bowl-shaped (6)
springs (4)
bowl (3)
untranslated (2)

1658 גִּלּוּלִים *gillûliym* (48)
idols (46)
idolatry (2)

1659 גְּלוֹם *g^{e}lôm* (1)
fabric (1)

1660 גָּלוֹן *gālôn*
Variant; not used

1661 גָּלוּת *gālûṯ* (15)
exiles (7)
exile (5)
captives (1)
communities (1)
communities of captives (1)

1662 גָּלַח *gālah* (23)
shave (5)
shave off (5)
shaved off (3)
cut hair (2)
shaved (2)
be shaved (1)
been shaved (1)
were shaved (1)
untranslated (3)

1663 גִּלָּיוֹן *gillāyôn* (2)
mirrors (1)
scroll (1)

1664 1גָּלִיל *gāliyl1* (4)
rings (1)
rods (1)
turned in sockets (1)
untranslated (1)

1665 2גָּלִיל *gāliyl2* (6)
Galilee (5)
Galilee (1) +824

1666 גְּלִילָה *g^{e}liylāh* (3)
regions (2)
region (1)

1667 גְּלִילוֹת *g^{e}liylôṯ* (3)
Geliloth (3)

1668 גַּלִּים *galliym* (2)
Gallim (2)

1669 גָּלְיָת *golyāṯ* (6)
Goliath (6)

1670 1גָּלַל *gālal1* (17)
roll (4)
rolled (3)
commit (2)
attack (1)
come rolling in (1)
lay wallowing (1)
roll on (1)
rolled away (1)
rolled up (1)
rolls (1)
trusts (1)

1671 2גָּלַל *gālal2*
Variant; not used

1672 1גָּלָל *gālāl1* (2)
dung (1)
filth (1)

1673 2גָּלָל *gālāl2* (10)
because of (7)
because of (2) +928
because (1)

1674 3גָּלָל *gālāl3* (3)
Galal (3)

1675 גִּלֲלַי *gil^{a}lay* (1)
Gilalai (1)

1676 גָּלַם *gālam* (1)
rolled up (1)

1677 גֹּלֶם *gōlem* (1)
unformed body (1)

1678 גַּלְמוּד *galmûḏ* (4)
barren (3)
Haggard (1)

1679 גָּלַע *gāla'* (3)
breaks out (1)
defies (1)
quick to quarrel (1)

1680 גִּלְעָד *gil'āḏ* (102)
Gilead (85)
Gilead (8) +824
Gileadites (3)
Gilead (1) +1201
Gilead's (1)
Gileadites (1) +408
them^{s} (1) +2418
there^{s} (1) +5206
untranslated (1)

1681 גַּלְעֵד *gal'ēḏ* (2)
Galeed (2)

1682 גִּלְעָדִי *gil'āḏiy* (11)
Gileadite (8)
of Gilead (2)
of Gilead (1) +1201

1683 גָּלַשׁ *gālaš* (2)
descending (2)

1684 גֻּלֹּת *gullōṯ*
Variant; not used

1685 גַּם *gam* (769)
also (106)
even (64)
too (62)
and (53) +2256
and (49)
also (26) +2256
even (15) +2256
both (13)
then (9)
moreover (8) +2256
but (6)
or (6)
yes (6)
either (5)
moreover (5)
now (5)
though (5)

as well (4)
neither (4) +4202
or (4) +2256
too (4) +2256
again (3)
as well as (3) +2256
indeed (3)
just as (3)
nor (3)
nor (3) +4202
now (3) +2256
then (3) +2256
and also (2)
another (2)
as for (2)
besides (2) +2256
but (2) +2256
but also (2)
even (2) +3954
in turn (2)
indeed (2) +2256
more (2)
neither (2)
no (2)
so (2) +2256
surely (2)
therefore (2) +2256
together with (2) +2256
yes (2) +2256
yet (2)
yet (2) +2256
after (1) +2256
again (1) +928+2021+2021+2085+7193
along with (1) +2256
although (1) +3954
and even (1)
and indeed (1)
and now (1)
as well as (1)
besides (1)
both and (1)
but even (1)
but even (1) +2256
certainly (1)
even if (1)
ever (1)
finally (1) +2256
for (1) +928+8611
for some time (1) +1685+8997+9453
furthermore (1)
furthermore (1) +2256
in spite of (1)
in the past (1) +919+1685+8997
including (1) +2256
instead (1) +2256
joined (1) +2256
kept provoking (1) +4087+4088
mere (1)
moreover (1) +3954
next (1)
no sooner than (1)
nor (1) +401+2256
nor (1) +2256
nor (1) +2256+4202
or (1) +3954
rather (1) +2256
since (1)
so (1)
still (1) +2256
than (1) +2256
that (1) +2256
therefore (1)
very well (1)
when (1)
whether (1)
with (1)
with (1) +2256
untranslated (200)

1686 גָּמָא *gāmā'* (2)
eats up (1)
give (1)

1687 גֹּמֶא *gōme'* (4)
papyrus (4)

1688 גֹּמֶד *gōmeḏ* (1)
about a foot and a half (1)

1689 גַּמָּדִים *gammāḏiym* (1)
men of Gammad (1)

1690 גָּמוּל *gāmûl* (1)
Gamul (1)

1691 גְּמוּל *g^emûl* (19)
what done (4)
what deserve (3)
retribution (2)
benefits (1)
deeds (1)
deserve (1)
deserves (1) +3338
due (1)
kindness (1)
something done (1)
what deserves (1)
what[s] (1)
work (1)

1692 גְּמוּלָה *g^emûlāh* (3)
retribution (1)
way[s] (1)
what done (1)

1693 גִּמְזוֹ *gimzô* (1)
Gimzo (1)

1694 גָּמַל *gāmal* (37)
weaned (7)
done (5)
dealt with (2)
repay (2)
treated (2)
was weaned (2)
been good (1)
benefits (1)
brings (1)
brought (1)
brought up (1)
committed (1)
did (1)
do good (1)
good (1)
goodness (1)
is weaned (1)
paying back (1)
produced (1)
repaying (1)
reward (1)
ripening (1)
young child (1)

1695 גָּמָל *gāmāl* (54)
camels (46)
camel (3)
camels' (2)
camel's (1)
camel-loads (1) +5362
untranslated (1)

1696 גְּמַלִּי *g^emalliy* (1)
Gemalli (1)

1697 גַּמְלִיאֵל *gamliy'ēl* (5)
Gamaliel (5)

1698 גָּמַר *gāmar* (5)
bring to an end (1)
failed (1)
fulfill (1)
fulfills (1)
no more (1)

1699 גֹּמֶר1 *gōmer1* (5)
Gomer (5)

1700 גֹּמֶר2 *gōmer2* (1)
Gomer (1)

1701 גְּמַרְיָה *g^emaryāh* (1)
Gemariah (1)

1702 גְּמַרְיָהוּ *g^emaryāhû* (4)
Gemariah (4)

1703 גַּן *gan* (41)
garden (39)
gardens (2)

1704 גָּנַב *gānaḇ* (40)
steal (9)
stolen (3)
steals (2)
stole (2)
stole away (2)
are stolen (1)
be considered stolen (1)
deceive (1)
deceived (1) +4213
deceived (1) +4222
kidnapping (1) +5883
kidnaps (1)
snatches away (1)
steal away (1)
steal in (1)
stealing (1)
stole into (1) +995+4200
swept away (1)
taken secretly (1)
thief (1)
was forcibly carried off (1) +1704
was secretly brought (1)
was stolen (1)
was stolen (1) +1704
untranslated (1)

1705 גַּנָּב *gannāḇ* (17)
thief (9)
thieves (7)
kidnapper (1)

1706 גְּנֵבָה *g^enēḇāh* (2)
stolen (1)
theft (1)

1707 גְּנֻבַת *g^enuḇaṯ* (2)
Genubath (2)

1708 גַּנָּה *gannāh* (16)
gardens (9)
garden (6)
grove (1)

1709 גֶּנֶז1 *genez1* (2)
treasury (2)

1710 גֶּנֶז2 *genez2* (1)
rugs (1)

1711 גַּנְזַךְ *ganzaḵ* (1)
storerooms (1)

1712 גַּנִּים *ganniym*
Variant; not used

1713 גָּנַן *gānan* (8)
defend (4)
shield (4)

1714 גִּנְּתוֹי *ginn^eṯôy*
Variant; not used

1715 גִּנְּתוֹן *ginn^eṯôn* (3)
Ginnethon (2)
Ginnethon's (1)

1716 גָּעָה *gā'āh* (2)
bellow (1)
lowing (1)

1717 גֹּעָה *gō'āh* (1)
Goah (1)

1718 גָּעַל *gā'al* (10)
abhor (4)
despised (2)
abhorred (1)
despise (1)
fail (1)
was defiled (1)

1719 גֹּעַל *gō'al* (1)
despised (1)

1720 גַּעַל *ga'al* (9)
Gaal (9)

1721 גָּעַר *gā'ar* (14)
rebuke (7)
rebuked (3)
rebukes (2)
prevent (1)
reprimanded (1)

1722 גְּעָרָה *g^e'ārāh* (15)
rebuke (12)
threat (3)

1723 גָּעַשׁ *gā'aš* (10)
trembled (4)
surging (2)
are shaken (1)
roll (1)
stagger (1)
untranslated (1)

1724 גַּעַשׁ *ga'aš* (4)
Gaash (4)

1725 גַּעְתָּם *ga'tām* (3)
Gatam (3)

1726 1גַּף *gap1* (1)
highest point (1) +5294

1727 2גַּף *gap2* (3)
alone (2) +928+2257
only (1) +928+2257

1728 גֶּפֶן *gepen* (55)
vine (36)
vines (16)
grapevine (2) +3516
grapevines (1)

1729 גֹּפֶר *gōper* (1)
cypress (1)

1730 גָּפְרִית *gopriyt* (7)
burning sulfur (4)
sulfur (3)

1731 גֵּר *gēr* (92)
alien (61)
aliens (26)
stranger (3)
alien's (1)
strangers (1)

1732 גִּר *gir* (1)
chalk (1)

1733 גֵּרָא *gērā'* (9)
Gera (9)

1734 גָּרָב *gārāb* (3)
festering (2)
festering sores (1)

1735 1גָּרֵב *gārēb1* (2)
Gareb (2)

1736 2גָּרֵב *gārēb2* (1)
Gareb (1)

1737 גַּרְגַּר *gargar* (1)
olives (1)

1738 גַּרְגְּרוֹת *garg^{e}rôt* (4)
neck (4)

1739 גִּרְגָּשִׁי *girgāšiy* (7)
Girgashites (7)

1740 גָּרַד *gārad* (1)
scraped himself (1)

1741 גָּרָה *gārāh* (15)
stirs up (3)
ask (2)
provoke to war (2)
carry the battle (1) +2256+8740
engage (1)
opposed (1)
prepare for war (1)
provoke (1)
resist (1)
wage war (1) +2021+4200+4878
untranslated (1)

1742 1גֵּרָה *gērāh1* (11)
cud (11)

1743 2גֵּרָה *gērāh2* (5)
gerahs (5)

1744 גָּרוֹן *gārôn* (9)
throat (3)
mouths (1)
neck (1)
necks (1)
shout aloud (1) +928+7924
throats (1)
untranslated (1)

1745 גֵּרוּת כִּמְהָם *gērût kimhām* (1)
Geruth Kimham (1)

1746 גָּרַז *gāraz* (1)
am cut off (1)

1747 גִּרְזִי *girziy* (1)
Girzites (1)

1748 גְּרִזִים *g^{e}riziym* (4)
Gerizim (4)

1749 גַּרְזֶן *garzen* (4)
ax (3)
chisel (1)

1750 1גָּרַם *gāram1* (1)
leave (1)

1751 2גָּרַם *gāram2* (2)
break in pieces (1)
dash (1)

1752 גֶּרֶם *gerem* (5)
bare (1)
bone (1)
bones (1)
limbs (1)
rawboned (1)

1753 גַּרְמִי *garmiy* (1)
Garmite (1)

1754 גָּרֹל *gārōl* (1)
untranslated (1)

1755 גֹּרֶן *gōren* (36)
threshing floor (32)
threshing floors (3)
threshing floor (1) +1841

1756 גָּרַס *garas* (2)
broken (1)
consumed (1)

1757 1גָּרַע *gāra'1* (21)
be reduced (2)
be taken (2)
cut off (2)
be kept from (1) +1194+4200
be taken away (1)
deprive (1)
disappear (1)
hinder (1)
limit (1)
omit (1)
reduce (1)
reduce the number (1)
reduced (1)
subtract (1)
take (1)
take away (1)
taken (1)
withdraw favor (1)

1758 2גָּרַע *gāra'2* (1)
draws up (1)

1759 גָּרַף *gārap* (1)
swept away (1)

1760 גָּרַר *gārar* (5)
catches (1)
chew (1)
drag away (1)
driving (1)
trimmed (1)

1761 גְּרָר *g^{e}rār* (10)
Gerar (10)

1762 גֶּרֶשׂ *gereś* (2)
crushed (1)
crushed grain (1)

1763 1גָּרַשׁ *gāraš1* (46)
drive out (8)
drive (7)
divorced (5)
drove out (5)
drove away (3)
driven (2)
driving out (2)
drove (2)
be driven (1)
been banished (1)
been driven out (1)
cast aside (1)
drive away (1)
drive out (1) +1763
driving (1)
emptied (1)
get rid of (1)
removed (1)
were banished (1)

1764 2גָּרַשׁ *gāraš2* (3)
be stirred up (1)
cast up (1)
tossing (1)

1765 גֶּרֶשׁ *gereš* (1)
yield (1)

1766 גְּרֻשָׁה *g^{e}rušāh* (1)
dispossessing (1)

1767 גֵּרְשׁוֹן *gēršôn* (17)
Gershon (9)
Gershonites (6) +1201
Gershonite (2) +1201

1768 גֵּרְשֹׁם *gēršōm* (14)
Gershom (7)
Gershon (6)
Gershonites (1) +1201

1769 גֵּרְשֻׁנִּי *gēršunniy* (13)
Gershonite (7)
Gershonites (3)
Gershonite (1) +1201
Gershonites (1) +1201
their[S] (1) +1201+2021

1770 גְּשׁוּר *g^{e}šûr* (9)
Geshur (8)
they[S] (1) +2256+5083

1771 גְּשׁוּרִי *g^{e}šûriy* (6)
Geshurites (3)
people of Geshur (3)

1772 גָּשַׁם *gāšam* (1)
bring rain (1)

1773 1גֶּשֶׁם *gešem1* (35)
rain (24)
showers (3)
rains (2)
rainy (2)
abundant showers (1)
downpour (1) +4764
shower (1)
winter rains (1)

1774 2גֶּשֶׁם *gešem2* (3)
Geshem (3)

1775 גֹּשֶׁם *gōšem* (1)
showers (1)

1776 גַּשְׁמוּ *gašmû* (1)
Geshem (1)

1777 גֹּשֶׁן *gōšen* (15)
Goshen (11)
Goshen (4) +824

1778 גִּשְׁפָּא *gišpā'* (1)
Gishpa (1)

1779 גָּשַׁשׁ *gāšaš* (2)
feeling way (1)
grope along (1)

1780 גַּת1 *gat1* (5)
winepress (4)
winepresses (1)

1781 גַּת2 *gat2* (34)
Gath (34)

1782 גַּת3 *gat3*
Variant; not used

1783 גַּת הַחֵפֶר *gat hahēper* (2)
Gath Hepher (2)

1784 גַּת־רִמּוֹן *gat-rimmôn* (4)
Gath Rimmon (4)

1785 גִּתִּי *gitiy* (10)
Gittite (8)
Gath (1)
Gittites (1)

1786 גִּתַּיִם *gitayim* (2)
Gittaim (2)

1787 גִּתִּית *gitiyt* (3)
gittith (3)

1788 גֶּתֶר *geter* (2)
Gether (2)

1789 ד *d*
Variant; not used

1790 דָּאַב *dā'ab* (3)
dim (1)
faint (1) +5883
sorrow (1)

1791 דְּאָבָה *d'ābāh* (1)
dismay (1)

1792 דְּאָבוֹן *d'ābôn* (1)
despairing (1)

1793 דָּאַג *dā'ag* (7)
afraid (1)
dread (1)
dreaded (1)
has worries (1)
troubled (1)
worried (1)
worrying (1)

1794 דָּאג *dā'g* (1)
fish (1)

1795 דֹּאֵג *dō'ēg* (8)
Doeg (6)
untranslated (2)

1796 דְּאָגָה *d'āgāh* (6)
anxiety (2)
fear (2)
anxious (1)
restless (1)

1797 דָּאָה1 *dā'āh1* (5)
soared (2)
swooping down (2)
swoop down (1)

1798 דָּאָה2 *dā'āh2* (1)
red kite (1)

1799 דֹּאר *dō'r* (1)
Dor (1)

1800 דֹּב *dōb* (12)
bear (10)
bears (2)

1801 דֹּבֶא *dōbe'* (1)
strength (1)

1802 דְּבָאָה *d'bā'āh*
Variant; not used

1803 דָּבַב *dābab* (1)
flowing gently (1)

1804 דִּבָּה *dibbāh* (9)
slander (3)
bad report (2)
report (2)
bad reputation (1)
whispering (1)

1805 דְּבוֹרָה1 *d'bôrāh1* (4)
bees (3)
swarm of bees (1)

1806 דְּבוֹרָה2 *d'bôrāh2* (10)
Deborah (10)

1807 דִּבְיֹנִים *dibyōniym* (1)
seed pods (1)

1808 דְּבִיר1 *d'biyr1* (15)
inner sanctuary (14)
most holy place (1) +7731

1809 דְּבִיר2 *d'biyr2* (1)
Debir (1)

1810 דְּבִיר3 *d'biyr3* (13)
Debir (11)
untranslated (2)

1811 דְּבֵלָה *d'bēlāh* (5)
poultice (2)
cake of pressed figs (1)
cakes of pressed figs (1)
fig cakes (1)

1812 דִּבְלָה *diblāh* (1)
Diblah (1)

1813 דִּבְלַיִם *diblayim* (1)
Diblaim (1)

1814 דִּבְלָתַיִם *diblātayim*
Variant; not used

1815 דָּבַק *dābaq* (54)
hold fast (7)
cling (5)
bound (2)
clung (2)
held fast (2)
keep (2)
make stick (2)
stay (2)
sticks (2)
ally (1)
almost upon (1)
are joined fast (1)
caught up (1)
clings (1)
defiled (1) +4583
drawn (1)
follow (1) +339
found (1)
froze (1)
joined (1)
laid low (1)
not escape (1)
overtake (1)
overtook (1)
plague (1)
pressed hard (1)
pressed hard after (1)
pressing (1)
reduced to (1)
stayed (1)
stayed close (1)
stick together (1)
sticking (1)
stuck (1)
tightly joined (1)
united (1)
untranslated (1)

1816 דָּבֵק *dābēq* (3)
held fast (1)
sticks closer (1)
touched (1)

1817 דֶּבֶק *debeq* (3)
sections (2)
welding (1)

1818 דָּבַר1 *dābar1* (5)
departure (1)
destroy (1)
destroyed (1)
subdued (1)
subdues (1)

1819 דָּבַר2 *dābar2* (1140)
said (197)
speak (170)
spoken (99)
spoke (85)
say (67)
promised (51)
tell (49)
speaking (38)
told (37)
speaks (18)
talked (17)
says (14)
talking (14)
talk (11)
saying (10)
gave (6)
pronounced (6)
reported (6)
declared (5)
decreed (5)
directed (5)
made (5)
proclaimed (5)
repeated (5)
replied (5)
say (5) +1821
warned (5)
asked (4)
given (4)
praying (4)
promise (4)
speak out (4)
words (4)
ask (3)
give (3)
instructed (3)
preached (3)
pronounce (3)
pronounced on (3) +907
spoke up (3)
telling (3)
threatened (3)
announce (2)
answered (2)
declare (2)
foretold (2)
full of (2)
give answer (2) +1821
give message (2)
liars (2) +9214
proclaim (2)
promises made (2)
propose (2)
sang (2)
speak up (2)
spreads (2)
tells (2)
threaten (2)
address (1)
announced (1)

are said (1)
argued (1)
asking (1)
asks (1)
boastful (1) +1524
break out (1)
commanded (1)
complain (1)
contend (1)
decree (1)
described (1)
dictate (1)
discussed (1)
encourage (1) +4213+6584
encouraged (1) +4222+6584
ever say (1) +1821
explained (1)
fluent (1) +4200+4554
fomenting (1)
gave the message (1) +465+1821+2021+2021+3972
give an answer (1)
give opinion (1)
gives (1)
giving (1)
imagine (1)
instructed (1) +7023
invite (1)
is spoken (1)
lie (1) +3942
lie (1) +9214
lied (1) +3942
lies (1) +8736
lying (1) +3942
lying (1) +9214
made request (1)
make (1)
make many promises (1) +1821
make promise (1) +1821
make request (1)
mention (1)
mentioned (1)
message (1)
message came (1)
named (1)
ordered (1)
persuade (1) +4213+6584
plea (1)
pleaded (1)
pleads (1)
predicted (1)
proclaiming (1)
proclaims (1)
promise (1) +1821
promised (1) +928+7023
promises (1)
promises (1) +1821
prophesied (1) +5553
rebukes (1)
recited (1)
reciting (1)
recommended (1)
request (1) +1821
requested (1)
ridicule (1)
said (1) +1821
said (1) +1821+2021
said a word (1)
shouted (1)
silent (1) +4202
slander (1)
speak well (1) +1819
speak with words (1)
speech (1) +4537
spoken (1) +1821
spoken (1) +7023
spoken kindly (1) +4213+6584
state (1)
suggested (1)
talking together (1)
taught (1)
tell (1) +265+928
thought (1)
told (1) +265+928
urging (1)
used to say (1) +1819
utter (1)
will^{s} (1) +1821
untranslated (26)

1820 3דָּבַר *dāḇar3*
Variant; not used

1821 דָּבָר *dāḇār* (1455)
word (339)
words (226)
events (51)
this^{s} (44) +2021+2021+2296
annals (37) +3427
things (33)
message (31)
what^{s} (31) +2021
thing (27)
matter (24)
what said (21)
nothing (19) +4202
promise (15)
anything (14)
say (13)
this^{s} (12) +465+2021+2021
command (11)
everything (11) +2021+3972
what^{s} (11)
said (10)
answer (9)
answer (8) +8740
report (8)
what say (8)
anything (7) +3972
records (7)
terms (7)
because of (6) +6584
case (6)
commandments (6)
it^{s} (6) +2021
reported (6) +8740
some time later (6) +339+465+2021+2021
asked (5)
cases (5)
everything (5) +3972
instructions (5)
promises (5)
say (5) +1819
this^{s} (5) +2021
account (4)
advice (4)
commanded (4)
it^{s} (4) +2021+2021+2296
plan (4)
promised (4)
sayings (4)
something (4)
told (4)
affairs (3)
annals (3)
answered (3) +8740
because (3) +6584
commands (3)
concerning (3) +6584
conversation (3)
instruction (3)
lies (3) +9214
questions (3)
request (3)
speak (3)
way (3)
what^{s} (3) +2021+2021+2296
about (2) +6584
achievements (2)
affair (2)
bidding (2)
charge (2)
conduct (2)
counsel (2)
decree (2)
deeds (2)
dispute (2)
doing (2)
empty words (2) +8557
for (2) +6584
for each day (2) +928+3427+3427
give answer (2) +1819
nothing (2) +401
nothing (2) +3972+4202
occasion (2)
order (2)
predicting (2)
regulations (2)
relationship (2)
required (2)
requirement (2)
requirements (2)
saying (2)
some (2)
speaks (2)
spoke (2)
story (2)
thoughts (2)
verdict (2) +5477
voice (2)
what asks (2)
what written (2)
what^{s} (2) +465+2021+2021
written (2)
accusations (1)
accuse (1) +928+8492
activity (1)
after (1) +928
after a while (1) +339+465+2021+2021
amount (1)
animal^{s} (1)
answer (1) +6699
answers (1) +8740
anything (1) +1821+2021+3972+4946
anything (1) +2021+3972
anything (1) +3972+4946
as a result of (1) +6584
ask (1) +2011
at all (1)
behavior (1)
business (1)
cases (1) +8191
cause (1)
charges (1)
claims (1)
compliments (1) +5833
concerned (1)
conferred (1)
conferred (1) +2118
consult (1) +928+2011
curses (1)
customary (1) +4027
daily (1) +928+3427+3427
danger (1)
day by day (1) +928+2257+3427+3427
day by day (1) +928+3427+3427
decided (1) +6641
decisions (1)
deed (1)
defiance (1)
demand (1)
details (1)
directed (1)
disease (1)
disputes (1)
done (1)
duties (1)
duty (1)
edict (1)
eloquent (1) +408
else (1)
enough (1)
ever say (1) +1819
everything (1) +465+2021+2021+3972

feat (1) +1524
flaw (1) +8273
fulfilled (1)
gave the message (1) +465+1819+2021+2021+3972
harm (1) +8273
how (1)
idea (1)
in behalf of (1) +6584
inquires of (1) +928+8626
instructed (1)
it[S] (1)
language (1)
later (1) +339+465+2021+2021
lesson (1)
lies (1) +3942
make many promises (1) +1819
make promise (1) +1819
matters (1)
mere talk (1) +8557
mission (1) +889+8938
need (1)
news (1)
nothing (1) +1524+2256+4202+7785
nothing whatever (1) +401+3972
offering (1)
one[S] (1)
ones[S] (1)
ordered (1)
plans (1)
plot (1)
prediction (1)
promise (1) +1819
promises (1) +1819
prophecy (1)
proposal (1)
proposed (1)
question (1)
record (1)
refrain (1)
reports (1)
request (1) +1819
requested (1)
responded (1)
revelation (1)
rule (1)
said (1) +1819
said (1) +1819+2021
says (1)
secret (1)
sins (1) +6411
situation (1)
slandered (1) +6613+8492
slanders (1) +6613+8492
something to say (1)
songs (1) +8877
speak up (1)
speaking (1)
speaking (1) +7754
speech (1)
speeches (1)
spoken (1)
spoken (1) +1819
such[S] (1)
suggested (1) +2021+2021+2296
suggestion (1)
tell (1) +606
text (1)
that happened (1) +465+2021+2021
that said (1)
that[S] (1) +465+2021+2021
the word (1)
them[S] (1) +2021+2021+2296
them[S] (1) +3870
theme (1)
they[S] (1) +3870
this (1) +2021+2021+2296
this is how (1) +465+2021+2021+3869
this[S] (1)
thought (1)
threatened (1)
threats (1)
through (1) +3869
times (1)
transfer of property (1) +3972+9455
trouble (1)
what foretold (1)
what happened (1)
what have to say (1)
what said (1) +7754
what says (1)
what spoke (1)
what[S] (1) +7754
whatever (1) +4537
whisper (1)
why (1)
will[S] (1) +1819
words (1) +7023
work (1)
year (1) +9102
untranslated (48)

1822 1דֶּבֶר *deber1* (49)
plague (43)
plagues (3)
pestilence (2)
diseases (1)

1823 2דֶּבֶר *deber2*
Variant; not used

1824 דֹּבֶר *dōber* (2)
pasture (2)

1825 דִּבֵּר *dibbēr* (1)
word (1)

1826 דִּבְרָה *dibrāh* (5)
as for (1) +6584
because (1) +6584
cause (1)
order (1)
therefore (1) +6584+8611

1827 דֹּבְרוֹת *dōbrôt* (1)
rafts (1)

1828 דִּבְרִי *dibriy* (1)
Dibri (1)

1829 דָּבְרַת *dāberat* (3)
Daberath (3)

1830 דַּבֶּרֶת *dabberet* (1)
instruction (1)

1831 דְּבַשׁ *debaš* (54)
honey (52)
honeycomb (1) +3626
honeycomb (1) +7430

1832 1דַּבֶּשֶׁת *dabbešet1* (1)
humps (1)

1833 2דַּבֶּשֶׁת *dabbešet2* (1)
Dabbesheth (1)

1834 דָּג *dāg* (18)
fish (17)
fishing (1)

1835 1דָּגָה *dāgāh1* (1)
increase (1)

1836 2דָּגָה *dāgāh2* (15)
fish (15)

1837 דָּגוֹן *dāgôn* (13)
Dagon (8)
Dagon's (2)
his[S] (1)
his body[S] (1)
untranslated (1)

1838 1דָּגַל *dāgal1* (1)
outstanding (1)

1839 2דָּגַל *dāgal2* (3)
in procession (1)
lift up banners (1)
troops with banners (1)

1840 דֶּגֶל *degel* (14)
standard (11)
standards (2)
banner (1)

1841 דָּגָן *dāgān* (40)
grain (38)
bread (1)
threshing floor (1) +1755

1842 דָּגַר *dāgar* (2)
care for young (1)
hatches eggs (1)

1843 דַּד *dad* (4)
bosom (2)
bosoms (1)
breasts (1)

1844 דָּדָה *dādāh* (2)
leading (1)
walk humbly (1)

1845 דֹּדָוָהוּ *dōdāwāhû* (1)
Dodavahu (1)

1846 דֹּדִי *dōdiy*
Variant; not used

1847 דְּדָן *dedān* (10)
Dedan (10)

1848 דְּדָנִי *dedāniy* (1)
Dedanites (1)

1849 דֹּדָנִים *dōdāniym*
Variant; not used

1850 דָּהַם *dāham* (1)
taken by surprise (1)

1851 דָּהַר *dāhar* (1)
galloping (1)

1852 דַּהֲרָה *daharāh* (2)
galloping (2)

1853 דּוּב *dûb* (1)
drain away (1)

1854 דַּוָּג *dawwāg* (2)
fishermen (1)
untranslated (1)

1855 דּוּגָה *dûgāh* (1)
fishhooks (1) +6106

1856 דּוֹד *dôd* (61)
lover (28)
uncle (11)
love (8)
cousin (3) +1201
beloved (2)
others[S] (2)
cousin (1)
cousin (1) +1426
cousins on their father's side (1) +1201
lover's (1) +4200
lovers (1)
relative (1)
untranslated (1)

1857 דּוּד *dûd* (8)
basket (3)
baskets (2)
caldrons (1)
kettle (1)
pot (1)

1858 דָּוִד *dāwid* (1075)
David (906)
David's (69)
he[S] (47)
him[S] (18)
David's (8) +4200
his[S] (4)
David's line (1)
you[S] (1)
untranslated (21)

1859 דּוּדָאִים *dûdā'iym* (6)
mandrakes (5)
mandrake plants (1)

1860 דּוֹדָה *dôdāh* (3)
aunt (2)
father's sister (1)

1861 דּוֹדוֹ *dôdô* (4)
Dodo (3)
untranslated (1)

1862 דּוֹדַי *dôday* (3)
Dodai (3)

1863 דּוּדַי *dûday*
Variant; not used

1864 דָּוָה *dāwāh* (1)
monthly period (1) +5614

1865 דָּוֶה *dāweh* (5)
faint (2)
menstrual cloth (1)
monthly period (1)
monthly period (1) +5614

1866 דּוּחַ *dûah* (3)
cleanse (1)
rinsed (1)
washed (1)

1867 דְּוַי *dᵉway* (2)
ill (1)
sickbed (1) +6911

1868 דַּוָּי *dawwāy* (3)
faint (2)
afflicted (1)

1869 דּוֹיֵג *dôyēg* (1)
untranslated (1)

1870 דּוּךְ *dûk* (1)
crushed (1)

1871 דּוּכִיפַת *dûkiypat* (2)
hoopoe (2)

1872 1דּוּמָה *dûmāh1* (2)
silence (1)
silence of death (1)

1873 2דּוּמָה *dûmāh2* (1)
Dumah (1)

1874 3דּוּמָה *dûmāh3* (3)
Dumah (3)

1875 דּוּמִיָּה *dûmiyyāh* (4)
awaits (1)
rest (1)
silent (1)
still (1)

1876 דּוּמָם *dûmām* (3)
lifeless (1)
quietly (1)
silence (1)

1877 דּוּמֶּשֶׂק *dûmmeśeq* (1)
Damascus (1)

1878 דּוֹן *dôn*
Variant; not used

1879 דּוּן *dûn*
Variant; not used

1880 דּוֹנַג *dônag* (4)
wax (4)

1881 דּוּץ *dûs* (1)
goes (1)

1882 דּוּק *dûq*
Variant; not used

1883 1דּוּר *dûr1* (1)
pile wood (1)

1884 2דּוּר *dûr2* (1)
dwell (1)

1885 3דּוּר *dûr3* (2)
all around (1) +2021+3869
ball (1)

1886 1דּוֹר *dôr1* (1)
house (1)

1887 2דּוֹר *dôr2* (151)
generation (44)
generations to come (37)
all generations (14) +1887+2256
generations (12)
descendants (6)
those[S] (4)
generations (3) +1887+2256
all generations (2) +1887
age-old (1) +1887+2256
all time (1) +1887+2256
always (1) +1887+2256+4200
another[S] (1)
children (1) +1201
company (1)
endless generations (1) +1887+2256
generations long past (1) +1887+2256+9102
generations to come (1) +1887+2256
many generations (1) +1887+2256
people (1)
people of time (1)
through all generations (1) +1887
to come (1) +1887+2256
untranslated (3)

1888 3דּוֹר *dôr3* (3)
Dor (3)

1889 דּוּשׁ *dûš* (16)
thresh (3)
threshed (2)
be trampled (1)
go on threshing (1) +1889
is threshed (1)
is trampled down (1)
tear (1)
threshing (1)
threshing grain (1)
threshing time (1)
trample (1)
treading out grain (1)

1890 דָּחָה *dāhāh* (7)
are brought down (1)
driving away (1)
pushed back (1) +1890
thrown down (1)
tottering (1)
trip (1)

1891 דָּחַח *dāhah*
Variant; not used

1892 דְּחִי *dᵉhiy* (2)
stumbling (2)

1893 דֹּחַן *dōhan* (1)
millet (1)

1894 דָּחַף *dāhap* (4)
spurred on (2)
eager (1)
rushed (1)

1895 דָּחַק *dāhaq* (2)
afflicted (1)
jostle (1)

1896 דַּי *day* (39)
whenever (5) +4946
enough (4)
from (3) +4946
as much as wanted (2)
as often as (2) +4946
for nothing (2) +928+8198
afford (1) +3338+5162
afford (1) +3338+5595
after (1) +928+4946
as far as possible (1) +3869
at the blast (1) +928
deserves (1) +3869
due annually (1) +928+4946+9102+9102
enough (1) +4200+4537
fuel for fire (1) +836+928
fuel for flames (1) +836+928
just enough (1)
means (1)
no end (1) +3869
often (1) +4946
plenty (1)
room enough (1)
sufficient (1)
sufficient means (1) +3869
swarms (1)
whatever (1)
whenever (1) +3954+4946

1897 דִּיבוֹן *diybôn* (9)
Dibon (9)

1898 דִּיבוֹן גָּד *diybôn gād* (2)
Dibon Gad (2)

1899 דִּיג *diyg* (1)
catch (1)

1900 דַּיָּג *dayyāg* (2)
fishermen (2)

1901 דַּיָּה *dayyāh* (2)
falcon (1)
falcons (1)

1902 דְּיוֹ *dᵉyô* (1)
ink (1)

1903 דִּי זָהָב *diy zāhāb* (1)
Dizahab (1)

1904 דִּימוֹן *diymôn* (2)
Dimon (1)
Dimon's (1)

1905 דִּימוֹנָה *diymônāh* (1)
Dimonah (1)

1906 1דִּין *diyn1* (24)
judge (8)
contend (2)
govern (2)
plead (2)
vindicate (2)
administer (1)
arguing with each other (1)
defend rights (1)
defended (1)
governs (1)
provide justice (1)
punish (1)
vindicated (1)

1907 2דִּין *diyn2* (19)
cause (3)
judgment (3)
justice (3)
rights (3)
case (2)
judge (1)
lawsuits (1) +1907+4200
quarrels (1)
untranslated (1)

1908 דַּיָּן *dayyān* (2)
defender (1)
judge (1)

1909 דִּינָה *diynāh* (8)
Dinah (7)
Dinah's (1)

1910 דִּיפַת *diypat*
Variant; not used

1911 דָּיֵק *dāyēq* (6)
siege works (6)

1912 דַּיִשׁ *dayiš* (1)
threshing (1)

1913 1דִּישׁוֹן *diyšôn1* (1)
ibex (1)

1914 2דִּישׁוֹן *diyšôn2* (8)
Dishon (7)
Dishan (1)

1915 דִּישָׁן *diyšān* (4)
Dishan (4)

1916 דַּךְ *dak̲* (4)
oppressed (3)
hurts (1)

1917 דָּכָא *dāk̲ā'* (18)
crush (7)
crushed (4)
broke (1)
contrite (1)
crushes (1)
crushing (1)
dejected (1)
humbled themselves (1)
was crushed (1)

1918 1דַּכָּא *dakkā'1* (3)
contrite (1)
crushed (1)
crushing (1)

1919 2דַּכָּא *dakkā'2* (1)
dust (1)

1920 דָּכָה *dāk̲āh* (6)
crushed (4)
contrite (1)
untranslated (1)

1921 דַּכָּה *dakkāh*
Variant; not used

1922 דֳּכִי *dᵒk̲iy* (1)
pounding waves (1)

1923 1דַּל *dal1* (1)
door (1)

1924 2דַּל *dal2* (48)
poor (36)
weak (4)
grew weaker and weaker (1) +2143+2256
haggard (1)
helpless (1)
humble (1)
needy (1)
poorest of the poor (1) +1147
scrawny (1)
weakest (1)

1925 דָּלַג *dālag̲* (5)
scale (2)
avoid stepping (1)
leap (1)
leaping (1)

1926 1דָּלָה *dālāh1* (5)
draw water (1)
draws out (1)
drew water (1) +1926
lifted out of the depths (1)

1927 2דָּלָה *dālāh2* (1)
hang limp (1)

1928 3דָּלָה *dālāh3*
Variant; not used

1929 1דַּלָּה *dallāh1* (2)
hair (1) +8031
loom (1)

1930 2דַּלָּה *dallāh2* (5)
poorest (5)

1931 דָּלַח *dālah* (3)
churning (1)
muddied (1)
stirred (1)

1932 דְּלִי *dᵉliy* (2)
bucket (1)
buckets (1)

1933 דְּלָיָה *dᵉlāyāh* (4)
Delaiah (4)

1934 דְּלָיָהוּ *dᵉlāyāhû* (3)
Delaiah (3)

1935 דְּלִילָה *dᵉliylāh* (6)
Delilah (6)

1936 דָּלִית *dāliyt̲* (8)
branches (6)
boughs (2)

1937 1דָּלַל *dālal1* (7)
in need (2)
dwindle (1)
fade (1)
impoverished (1)
in great need (1)
weak (1)

1938 2דָּלַל *dālal2* (1)
dangles (1)

1939 דִּלְעָן *dil'ān* (1)
Dilean (1)

1940 1דָּלַף *dālap̲1* (2)
leaks (1)
pour out tears (1)

1941 2דָּלַף *dālap̲2* (1)
weary (1)

1942 דֶּלֶף *delep̲* (2)
constant dripping (2) +3265

1943 דַּלְפוֹן *dalp̲ôn* (1)
Dalphon (1)

1944 דָּלַק *dālaq* (9)
chased (1)
chasing (1) +339
fervent (1)
flaming (1)
hunt down (1)
hunts down (1)
inflamed (1)
kindle (1)
set on fire (1)

1945 דַּלֶּקֶת *dalleqet̲* (1)
inflammation (1)

1946 דֶּלֶת *delet̲* (88)
doors (46)
door (21)
gates (10)
leaves (2)
columns (1)
gate (1)
it[s] (1) +2021
lid (1)
outside (1) +4946
untranslated (4)

1947 דָּם *dām* (359)
blood (282)
bloodshed (17)
bloodthirsty (6)
guilty of bloodshed (4)
it[s] (4) +2021
guilt of blood (3)
lifeblood (3) +5883
bleeding (2)
bloodguilt (2)
bloodshed (2) +928+995
bloodshed (2) +1947+4200
guilt of bloodshed (2)
guilt of shedding blood (2)
blood shed (1)
blood vengeance (1)
blood-stained (1)
bloodshed (1) +5477
bloodshed (1) +9161
bloodstains (1)
death (1)
destruction (1)
do anything that endangers life (1) +6584+6641
flow (1)
guilt of murder (1) +5883
guilty of blood (1)
guilty of murder (1)
innocent man (1) +5929
it[s] (1)
it[s] (1) +2023+4946
it[s] (1) +2257
killing (1)
massacre (1)
murder (1)
murdering (1)
other[s] (1)
person[s] (1)
shedding of blood (1)
untranslated (3)

1948 1דָּמָה *dāmāh1* (29)
compare (4)
compared (3)
is like (3)
be like (2)
am like (1)
are like (1)
been like (1)
equal (1)
intending (1)
intends (1)
like (1)
liken (1)
make myself like (1)
match (1)
meditate (1)
plan (1)
planned (1)
plotted (1)
think (1)
thought (1)
told parables (1)

1949 2דָּמָה *dāmāh2* (4)
be silenced (1)
ceasing (1)
silence (1)
unceasingly (1) +4202

1950 3דָּמָה *dāmāh3* (13)
ruined (3)
destroy (2)
perish (2)
are destroyed (1)
be completely destroyed (1) +1950
be wiped out (1)
disaster awaits (1)
float away (1)

1951 דֻּמָּה *dumāh* (1)
silenced (1)

1952 דְּמוּת *dᵉmût̲* (25)
likeness (5)
like (4)
looked like (4)
looked (3)
figure (2)
appearance (1)
figures (1)
form (1)
image (1)
like (1) +3869
sketch (1)
untranslated (1)

1953 דְּמִי *dᵉmiy* (1)
prime (1)

1954 דֳּמִי *dᵒmiy* (3)
rest (2)
silent (1)

1955 דִּמְיוֹן *dimyôn* (1)
like (1)

1956 דַּמִּים *dammiym*
Variant; not used

1957 1דָּמַם *dāmam1* (24)
silent (6)
be silenced (2)
be still (2)
ceasing (1)
find rest (1)
keeps quiet (1)
quieted (1)
quietly (1)
rest (1)
silence (1)
silenced (1)
stand still (1)
still (1)
stood still (1)
stops (1)
wait (1)
waiting in silence (1)

1958 2דָּמַם *dāmam2*
Variant; not used

1959 3דָּמַם *dāmam3* (5)
be destroyed (1)
be silenced (1)
doomed to perish (1)
perish (1)
will be laid waste (1)

1960 דְּמָמָה *d^{e}māmāh* (3)
hushed (1)
whisper (1)
whisper (1) +7754

1961 דֹּמֶן *dōmen* (6)
refuse (6)

1962 דִּמְנָה *dimnāh* (1)
Dimnah (1)

1963 דָּמַע *dāma‘* (2)
weep bitterly (1) +1963

1964 דֶּמַע *dema‘* (1)
vats (1)

1965 דִּמְעָה *dim‘āh* (23)
tears (21)
weeping (2)

1966 דַּמֶּשֶׂק *dammeśeq* (39)
Damascus (37)
untranslated (2)

1967 דְּמֶשֶׂק *d^{e}meśeq*
Variant; not used

1968 1דָּן *dān1* (50)
Dan (33)
Danites (9) +1201
Dan (4) +1201
Danite (1) +4200+4751
Danites (1)
they^{s} (1) +1201
untranslated (1)

1969 2דָּן *dān2* (20)
Dan (20)

1970 דָּן יַעַן *dān ya‘an* (1)
Dan Jaan (1)

1971 דָּנִאֵל *dāni’ēl* (3)
untranslated (3)

1972 דַּנָּה *dannāh* (1)
Dannah (1)

1973 דִּנְהָבָה *dinhāḇāh* (2)
Dinhabah (2)

1974 דָּנִי *dāniy* (5)
Danites (3)
Dan (1)
men of Dan (1)

1975 דָּנִיֵּאל *dāniyyē’l* (29)
Daniel (29)

1976 דֵּעַ *dēa‘* (5)
what know (3)
knowledge (2)

1977 דָּעָה *dā‘āh*
Variant; not used

1978 דֵּעָה *dē‘āh* (6)
knowledge (4)
knows (1)
teach (1) +3723

1979 דְּעוּאֵל *d^{e}‘û’ēl* (5)
Deuel (5)

1980 דָּעַךְ *dā‘aḵ* (9)
snuffed out (5)
died out (1)
extinguished (1)
goes out (1)
vanish (1)

1981 1דַּעַת *da‘aṯ1* (91)
knowledge (68)
know (5)
unintentionally (4) +928+1172
acknowledgment (2)
experienced (1) +2256+9312
has knowledge (1) +3359
have concern (1) +1067
have knowledge (1) +3359
it^{s} (1)
learning (1)
man of knowledge (1) +3359
notions (1)
understanding (1)
well informed (1) +3359
what know (1)
what teach (1)

1982 2דַּעַת *da‘aṯ2*
Variant; not used

1983 3דַּעַת *da‘aṯ3*
Variant; not used

1984 דֳּפִי *d^{o}piy* (1)
slander (1) +5989

1985 דָּפַק *dāp̱aq* (3)
driven hard (1)
knocking (1)
pounding (1)

1986 דָּפְקָה *dop̱qāh* (2)
Dophkah (2)

1987 דַּק *daq* (14)
thin (6)
fine (2)
gaunt (2) +1414
dwarfed (1)
finely ground (1)
gentle (1)
untranslated (1)

1988 דֹּק *dōq* (1)
canopy (1)

1989 דִּקְלָה *diqlāh* (2)
Diklah (2)

1990 דָּקַק *dāqaq* (13)
powder (3)
ground (2)
be ground (1)
break to pieces (1)
broke to pieces (1)
broke up (1)
crush (1)
fine (1)
grind (1)
pounded (1)

1991 דָּקַר *dāqar* (11)
run through (3)
be thrust through (1)
drove through (1)
fatally wounded (1)
pierced (1)
racked with hunger (1)
ran through (1)
stab (1)
wounded (1)

1992 דֶּקֶר *deqer*
Variant; not used

1993 דַּר *dar* (1)
mother-of-pearl (1)

1994 דֵּרָאוֹן *dērā’ôn* (2)
contempt (1)
loathsome (1)

1995 דָּרְבָן *dārḇān* (1)
goads (1)

1996 דָּרְבֹנָה *dārḇōnāh* (1)
goads (1)

1997 דַּרְדַּע *darda‘* (2)
Darda (2)

1998 דַּרְדַּר *dardar* (2)
thistles (2)

1999 דָּרוֹם *dārôm* (19)
south (17)
south wind (1)
southward (1)

2000 1דְּרוֹר *d^{e}rôr1* (2)
swallow (2)

2001 2דְּרוֹר *d^{e}rôr2* (1)
liquid (1)

2002 3דְּרוֹר *d^{e}rôr3* (7)
freedom (5)
freedom for slaves (1)
liberty (1)

2003 דָּרְיָוֶשׁ *dāryāweš* (10)
Darius (10)

2004 דַּרְיוֹשׁ *daryôš*
Variant; not used

2005 דָּרַךְ *dārak̠* (63)
bend (4)
trampled (4)
treads (4)
draw (3)
tread (3)
treading (3)
guide (2)
marches (2)
set (2)
strung (2)
trodden (2)
aim (1)
archer (1)
bent (1)
come (1)
cross over (1)
direct (1)
directs (1)
draw the bow (1)
drew (1)
enables to go (1)
go (1)
guides (1)
handle (1)
lead (1)
led (1)
make ready to shoot (1)
march on (1)
overran (1)
press (1)
set feet (1)
set foot on (1)
step (1)
string (1)
trample down (1)
treads out (1)
trod (1)

use (1)
walked (1)
walks (1)
with bows (1) +8008
untranslated (2)

2006 דֶּרֶךְ *derek* (713)
ways (180)
way (177)
road (61)
journey (30)
path (21)
conduct (18)
toward (15)
direction (9)
roads (9)
through (8)
route (7)
life (5)
what done (5)
pass by (4) +6296
paths (4)
side (4)
to (4)
as (3) +928
by (3)
highway (3)
mission (3)
on (3)
roadside (3)
wherever (3) +889+928+2021
works (3)
all do (2)
course (2)
distance (2)
does (2)
facing (2)
go to (2)
passageway (2)
street (2)
trackless (2) +4202
what[s] (2) +2021
action (1)
along (1)
at (1) +928+2021
behavior (1)
by way of (1)
course of life (1)
crossroads (1)
custom (1)
did (1)
dispersed (1) +2143+4200
distant (1) +2021+8049
do so[s] (1) +4946+8740
done (1)
everything do (1)
extending (1)
fate (1)
favors (1)
follow (1)
following (1)
go (1) +928+2143
god (1)
how behaved (1)
how live (1)
in the way should go (1) +6584+7023
justice (1)
leads (1)
leads to (1)
let get away (1) +928+8938
line (1)
long (1)
main road (1) +2006
man of integrity (1) +9448
march (1)
missions (1)
northward (1) +2021+7600
on way (1) +6913
path (1) +784
period (1) +851
place (1)
room (1)
routes (1)
running here and there (1) +8592
siege ramp (1)
skilled (1) +3512
streets (1)
strength (1)
teaching (1)
that[s] (1)
there[s] (1) +928+2021
things did (1)
toward (1) +448
toward (1) +6584
toward (1) +6584+7156
travel (1) +6296
traveled (1)
traveled (1) +2143
traveling (1)
upright (1) +3838
vigor (1)
walk (1)
walk (1) +928+2143
walked (1)
walking along (1) +928+2021
waylaid (1) +928+2021+8492
what did (1)
where[s] (1) +2021
which way (1) +361+2021+2296
untranslated (40)

2007 דַּרְכְּמוֹנִים *darkmôniym* (4)
drachmas (4)

2008 דַּרְמֶשֶׂק *darmeśeq* (6)
Damascus (6)

2009 דָּרַע *dāra'*
Variant; not used

2010 דַּרְקוֹן *darqôn* (2)
Darkon (2)

2011 דָּרַשׁ *dāraš* (164)
seek (34)
inquire of (19)
sought (11)
consult (5)
seeking (5)
consult (4) +928
inquire of (4) +928
call to account (3)
demand an accounting (3)
cares for (2)
consults (2)
hold accountable (2) +3338+4946
investigate (2)
let inquire of (2) +4200
look (2)
require (2)
search for (2)
searches (2)
seek help (2)
seek out (2)
seeks (2)
sought out (2)
study (2)
appeal (1)
are pondered (1)
ask (1)
ask (1) +1821
asked (1)
avenges (1)
call to account (1) +4946+6640
care about (1)
care for (1)
carefully investigated (1) +1335+2256
cares (1)
certainly demand (1) +2011
comes looking for (1)
consult (1) +928+1821
consulted (1)
find out (1)
follow (1)
give an accounting (1)
guidance (1)
inquire (1)
inquire of (1) +448
inquire of (1) +907+4946
inquire of (1) +4200
inquired about (1) +2011
inquired of (1)
inquiring (1)
let inquire of (1)
let inquire of at all (1) +2011+4200
look for (1)
look to (1)
make investigation (1)
probe (1)
rally (1)
required (1) +6584
revealed myself (1)
search was made (1)
searched (1)
searches for (1)
seek will (1)
selects (1)
sought after (1)
worked for (1)
would (1)
yield to the plea (1)
untranslated (1)

2012 דָּשָׁא *dāšā'* (2)
green (1)
produce (1)

2013 דֶּשֶׁא *deše'* (14)
grass (4)
green (4)
vegetation (3)
grass (1) +4604
new grass (1)
new growth (1)

2014 1דָּשֵׁן *dāšēn1* (11)
prosper (2)
remove ashes (2)
accept (1)
anoint (1)
are fully satisfied (1)
be soaked (1)
gives health (1)
is covered (1)
thrive (1)

2015 2דָּשֵׁן *dāšēn2* (2)
fresh (1)
rich (1)

2016 דֶּשֶׁן *dešen* (16)
ashes (7)
abundance (3)
ash (1)
choice food (1)
oil (1)
rich (1)
richest of fare (1)
richest of foods (1) +2256+2693

2017 דָּת *dāṯ* (22)
edict (8)
law (6)
laws (2)
command (1)
customs (1)
order (1)
orders (1)
prescribed (1)
untranslated (1)

2018 דָּתָן *dāṯān* (10)
Dathan (10)

2019 דֹּתָן *dōṯān* (3)
Dothan (3)

2020 ה *h*
Variant; not used

2021 הַ־ *ha-* (30369)
the (16201)

a (759)
who (468)
that (205)
his[s] (157)
this (150)
those (145)
today (137) +3427
their[s] (95)
an (78)
what (67)
your[s] (59)
these (54)
he[s] (44)
this[s] (44) +1821+2021+2296
each (40)
today (39) +2021+2296+3427
O (35)
my[s] (31)
what[s] (31) +1821
him[s] (29) +4889
they[s] (28) +6639
he[s] (26) +4889
one (26)
its[s] (25)
her[s] (22)
any (21)
always (18) +3427+3972
anyone (18)
they[s] (18)
which (18)
whoever (18)
now (17) +2021+2296+3427
other[s] (17)
he[s] (16) +3913
them[s] (16) +6639
now (14) +3427
our[s] (14)
you[s] (13)
this[s] (12) +465+1821+2021
at twilight (11) +1068+6847
everything (11) +1821+3972
whatever (11)
him[s] (10)
it[s] (10) +6551
tonight (10) +4326
burn down (9) +836+928+8596
it[s] (9) +1473
set on fire (9) +836+928+3675
some[s] (9)
they[s] (9) +408
burned (8) +836+928+8596
every (8)
everyone (7) +3972+5883
it[s] (7)
outside (7) +928+2575
before (6) +928+8037
he[s] (6) +408
her[s] (6) +851
his[s] (6) +4889
it[s] (6) +824
it[s] (6) +1821
prison (6) +1074+6045
secretly (6) +928+6260
she[s] (6) +851
some time later (6) +339+465+1821+2021
sunset (6) +995+9087
as long as (5) +3427+3972
it[s] (5) +4640
stone (5) +74+928+8083
this[s] (5) +1821
those[s] (5) +6639
allotted (4) +928+1598
be burned up (4) +836+928+8596
burn (4) +836+928+8596
burned up (4) +836+928+8596
day after day (4) +3427+3972
every morning (4) +928+928+1332+1332+2021
falsely (4) +4200+9214
first (4) +3427+3869
his own[s] (4)
in vain (4) +4200+8736
it[s] (4) +1074
it[s] (4) +1821+2021+2296
it[s] (4) +1947
it[s] (4) +3542
its[s] (4) +380
prison (4) +1074+3975
set on fire (4) +836+928+8596
them[s] (4) +7931
there[s] (4) +928+1195
those[s] (4) +408
Trans-Euphrates (4) +5643+6298
who[s] (4) +3913
anyone (3) +408+4769
burn up (3) +836+928+8596
burned down (3) +836+928+8596
burning (3) +836+6584
daybreak (3) +240+1332
east (3) +4667+9087
ever since (3) +2021+2296+3427+6330
first (3) +928+9378
forever (3) +3427+3972
he[s] (3) +7149
him[s] (3) +408
his own[s] (3) +4889
it[s] (3) +185
it[s] (3) +778
it[s] (3) +2215
it[s] (3) +5438
it[s] (3) +5596
it[s] (3) +5999
it[s] (3) +6219
its[s] (3) +824
its[s] (3) +4640
men[s] (3)
misuse (3) +4200+5951+8736
on high (3) +928+5294
she[s] (3) +5855
them (3) +6639
them[s] (3) +3913
them[s] (3) +7971
what[s] (3)
what[s] (3) +1821+2021+2296
what[s] (3) +5126
wherever (3) +889+928+2006
whose (3)
wild (3) +928+8441
all day long (2) +928+2021+2085+3427
allotted (2) +928+1598+5989
Amaziah[s] (2) +4889
angels (2) +466+1201
anyone (2) +3972+5883
anything (2)
anything (2) +3972+3998
certain (2)
champion (2) +408+1227
chief officer (2) +7372+8569
completely (2) +3972+4200
continual (2) +3427+3972
continually (2) +3427+3972
dawn (2) +240+1332
daybreak (2) +6590+8840
earlier (2) +928+9378
east (2) +2025+4667+9087
everyone (2) +3972+6639
first (2) +928+8037
forever (2) +6330+6409
he[s] (2) +466
he[s] (2) +2021+2085+5883
he[s] (2) +8357
her[s] (2) +912
her[s] (2) +5855
here[s] (2) +2021+2296+5226
him[s] (2) +5853
his own[s] (2) +3913
inside (2) +928+1074
it[s] (2) +380
it[s] (2) +836
it[s] (2) +4966
it[s] (2) +5577
it[s] (2) +7228
it[s] (2) +7339
it[s] (2) +8120
its[s] (2) +1074
its[s] (2) +2958
its[s] (2) +3284
its[s] (2) +7228
its[s] (2) +9133
Judah[s] (2) +824
misuses (2) +4200+5951+8736
never (2) +3427+3972+4202
now (2) +465+928+2021+3427
now (2) +3869+6961
one's (2)
one[s] (2) +6639
prison (2) +1074+3989
privately (2) +928+6260
quietly (2) +928+4319
someone (2)
someone[s] (2)
something[s] (2)
still (2) +2021+2296+3427+6330
stone (2) +74+928+6232
stoned (2) +74+928+6232
sunrise (2) +2436+9087
sunset (2) +995+6961+9087
the other[s] (2) +824+7895
their own[s] (2)
their[s] (2) +964
their[s] (2) +6639
them[s] (2)
them[s] (2) +408
them[s] (2) +3051
them[s] (2) +3338
them[s] (2) +3972+6639
them[s] (2) +4131
them[s] (2) +5853
them[s] (2) +8993
then (2) +340+928
there[s] (2) +824
there[s] (2) +928+1074
they[s] (2) +824+6639
they[s] (2) +3913
they[s] (2) +7366
this very (2)
those[s] (2) +5877
two-horned (2) +1251+7967
used to (2) +4200+8037
what[s] (2) +465+1821+2021
what[s] (2) +2006
when (2) +928+3427
where[s] (2) +5226
wherever (2) +889+928+3972+5226
whoever (2) +408+4769
whose[s] (2)
above (1) +928+5294
abroad (1) +2575+4200
accuses (1) +4200+5477+7756
after a while (1) +339+465+1821+2021
afternoon (1) +3427+5742
again (1) +928+1685+2021+2085+7193
age of childbearing (1) +784+851+3869
ago (1) +3427
Ai[s] (1) +6551
all around (1) +1885+3869
all men (1) +132+1201
all night long (1) +928+4326
all-night (1) +3972+4326
allotted (1) +928+1598+2118
already (1) +928+9378
annual (1) +285+928+9102
annual (1) +928+7193+9102
anointed (1) +1201+3658
another[s] (1)
another[s] (1) +132
another[s] (1) +2215+2296+4946
another[s] (1) +9019
any man (1) +408+4769
anyone (1) +408
anyone (1) +408+3972
anyone[s] (1) +4637
anything (1) +1821+1821+3972+4946

anything (1) +1821+3972
anything[S] (1)
archers (1) +408+928+4619+8008
archers (1) +928+4619+8008
are burned up (1) +836+928+8596+8596
around (1) +2575+4946
assemble (1) +928+6590+7736
at (1) +928+2006
at last (1) +7193
at once (1) +928+2021+2085+3427
at once (1) +928+2021+2085+6961
at once (1) +928+3427
at once (1) +3427
at this time (1) +3427
away (1) +448+2025+2575
awhile (1) +3427+3869
banded together (1) +665+2653+4200
be burned (1) +836+928+8596
be burned down (1) +836+928+8596
be taken captive (1) +928+4090+9530
before (1) +928+9378
below (1) +141+6584
below deck (1) +3752+6208
besiege (1) +928+995+5189
blind (1) +928+5782+6427
Boaz[S] (1) +408
both[S] (1) +170+2021+2256+8533
bought (1) +928+4084+7864
breeding (1) +3501+7366
brings to ruin (1) +4200+6156+8273
burn to death (1) +836+928+8596
burned (1) +836+928+8938
burned down (1) +836+8596
burned to death (1) +836+928+8596
callous (1) +2693+3869
captain (1) +2480+8042
cargo (1) +641+889+928+3998
carry off (1) +928+995+8660
charred (1) +836+928+1277
children (1) +1061+7262
commander in chief (1) +6584+7372
community (1) +824+6639
crops (1) +141+7262
daily (1) +3427+4200
David's[S] (1)
daybreak (1) +1332+7155
daylight (1) +240+1332
did so[S] (1) +906+6913+7175
distant (1) +2006+8049
doing this[S] (1) +3569+6894
doubly (1) +928+9109
dreamer (1) +1251+2706
each day (1) +2021+3427+3427+4200+4200
each day (1) +3427+4200
each morning (1) +928+928+1332+1332+2021
each morning (1) +1332+1332+2021+4200+4200
each[S] (1) +4090
end (1) +340+928+2118
enthrones (1) +3782+4058+4200
especially bred (1) +1201+8247
evening (1) +928+928+2021+6847+6847
evening (1) +6847+6961
ever (1) +3427+3972
every day (1) +3427+4200
every evening (1) +928+928+2021+6847+6847
everyone (1) +132+3972
everyone (1) +408+3972
everyone[S] (1)
everything (1) +465+1821+2021+3972
everything (1) +3972
everything (1) +3972+4856
everywhere (1) +3972+5226
fiercely (1) +928+6677
fifteen feet (1) +564+928+6924
fight (1) +3655+4200+4878
followers (1) +339+889+6639
for life (1) +3427+3972
foreigner (1) +1201+5797
foreigners (1) +1201+5797
forevermore (1) +6330+6409
formerly (1) +928+8037
from now on (1) +3427+3972
furthermore (1) +2256+9108
gave the message (1) +465+1819+1821+2021+3972
get out of here (1) +2025+2575+8938
give in marriage (1) +851+5989
God-fearing (1) +466+3710
hard (1) +3668+4200+4607
he himself[S] (1) +3913
he[S] (1) +340+408+2021
he[S] (1) +408+2021+6640+8886
he[S] (1) +408+5283
he[S] (1) +466+824
he[S] (1) +3381+3913
he[S] (1) +3758+5566
he[S] (1) +4855
he[S] (1) +5853
he[S] (1) +7595
her[S] (1) +6320
here[S] (1) +824
here[S] (1) +824+928
here[S] (1) +928+2021+2296+5226
here[S] (1) +928+4497
here[S] (1) +5226
him[S] (1) +132
him[S] (1) +466
him[S] (1) +1201+3778
him[S] (1) +3450
him[S] (1) +3759+5566
him[S] (1) +4889+6460
him[S] (1) +5782
him[S] (1) +5999
him[S] (1) +7127
him[S] (1) +7140
him[S] (1) +7149
him[S] (1) +8357
himself[S] (1) +408
his own[S] (1) +367
his own[S] (1) +2021+2418+5566
his[S] (1) +132
his[S] (1) +408
his[S] (1) +928+4889
his[S] (1) +4637
his[S] (1) +5566
immediately (1) +3427+3869
imprisoned (1) +657+1074+5989
in (1) +1074+2025
in broad daylight (1) +2021+2296+4200+6524+9087
in broad daylight (1) +5584+9087
in midair (1) +824+1068+1068+2021+2256+9028
infamous (1) +3238+9005
inside (1) +448+1074
interwoven (1) +928+8054
Israel's[S] (1)
Israelite (1) +408+3778
it[S] (1) +778
it[S] (1) +3136
it[S] (1) +4058
it[S] (1) +4114
it[S] (1) +4640
it's[S] (1) +3427
it[S] (1) +258
it[S] (1) +466+778
it[S] (1) +616+1473
it[S] (1) +680
it[S] (1) +778+1382
it[S] (1) +793+1581
it[S] (1) +824+2021+2296
it[S] (1) +1352
it[S] (1) +1580
it[S] (1) +1946
it[S] (1) +2021+2085+5226
it[S] (1) +2021+2296+6551
it[S] (1) +2021+2296+8878
it[S] (1) +2021+2645+7606
it[S] (1) +2162
it[S] (1) +2570
it[S] (1) +2633
it[S] (1) +2706
it[S] (1) +2851
it[S] (1) +3051
it[S] (1) +3855
it[S] (1) +4084
it[S] (1) +4223
it[S] (1) +4258
it[S] (1) +4722
it[S] (1) +4784
it[S] (1) +4889+9133
it[S] (1) +4963
it[S] (1) +5120
it[S] (1) +5261
it[S] (1) +6130
it[S] (1) +6174
it[S] (1) +6322
it[S] (1) +6592
it[S] (1) +6639
it[S] (1) +6727
it[S] (1) +6770
it[S] (1) +7498
it[S] (1) +7663
it[S] (1) +7815
it[S] (1) +8288
it[S] (1) +8367
it[S] (1) +8385
it[S] (1) +8407
it[S] (1) +8441
it[S] (1) +8538
it[S] (1) +8701
it[S] (1) +8947
it[S] (1) +9024
it[S] (1) +9043
it[S] (1) +9310
its[S] (1) +871
its[S] (1) +928+6551
its[S] (1) +2633
its[S] (1) +3720
its[S] (1) +4058+4200
its[S] (1) +6425
its[S] (1) +6592
its[S] (1) +7175
Jacob's[S] (1)
Jether[S] (1) +5853
just (1) +3427
just now (1) +3427
laid siege (1) +928+995+5189
lamb (1) +928+3897+8445
lamb (1) +928+4166+8445
last night (1) +4326
last watch of the night (1) +874+1332
lasting (1) +2021+2296+3427+6330
later (1) +339+465+1821+2021
later (1) +340+928
leads (1) +928+8037
leveled completely (1) +928+9164+9168
likes (1) +928+3202+4200
live (1) +928+2644
lived (1) +928+1074
long ago (1) +928+8037
long life (1) +2644+4200
man's[S] (1)
mealtime (1) +431+6961
men (1) +132+1201
midnight (1) +2942+4326
mounted (1) +928+6061
must sell (1) +928+4084+4835+4835
Naomi[S] (1) +851
native-born (1) +275+824
native-born (1) +824+928+3528
natural (1) +132+3869+3972
nightfall (1) +4326
noon (1) +3427+4734
northward (1) +2006+7600
nothing (1) +3972+4202
now (1) +7193
on each side (1) +2021+2296+2296+4946+4946+4946+4946+6298+6298
on fire (1) +836+928+1277

on foot (1) +824+6584
on high (1) +4200+5294
on high (1) +5294
on the west (1) +4427+9087
once again (1) +3869+8037
once more (1) +421+7193
one another (1) +6639
one^S (1) +4131
one^S (1) +5566
oppressed (1) +928+6913+6945
other nationalities (1) +824+6639
others^S (1)
others^S (1) +851
out here (1) +928+2575
outdoor (1) +928+2575
outer (1) +2575+4200
outside the family (1) +2025+2424+2575
overboard (1) +448+3542
painted (1) +928+7037+8531
penned up (1) +928+1074+3973
people^S (1)
perjurers (1) +4200+8678+9214
perjury (1) +4200+8678+9214
permanently (1) +4200+7552
places^S (1)
plotting (1) +3086+8288
preserved (1) +928+2645+8492
prison (1) +673+1074
prison (1) +1074+4551
prison (1) +1074+7213
privately (1) +928+4319
privately (1) +928+8952
put out (1) +2575+3655
ready for battle (1) +408+4200+4878+7372
ready for battle (1) +928+4878+7372
recently (1) +3427
reflects a face (1) +2021+4200+7156+7156
reflects the man (1) +132+4200
regular (1) +3427+3972
Sabbath after Sabbath (1)
+928+928+2021+3427+3427+8701+8701
safely (1) +4200+8934
said (1) +1819+1821
sail (1) +641+928+2143
sandaled (1) +928+5837
Saul's^S (1)
scoundrel (1) +408+1175
see (1) +4200+6524+8011
set ablaze (1) +836+928+3675
set farther back (1) +337+2958
set fire to (1) +836+928+8596
set fire to (1) +836+928+8938
seven and a half feet (1) +564+928+2822
seven-day periods (1) +3427+8679
she^S (1)
she^S (1) +912
she^S (1) +4893
shoot (1) +928+8008
similar (1) +3869+5260
sling stones (1) +74+928
sober (1) +3516+3655+4946
some distance (1) +824+3896
someone (1) +285+6639
someone^S (1) +5877
someone^S (1) +8011
southward (1) +448+3545
spreads feathers to run (1) +928+5257+5294
spring (1) +4784+6524
spring (1) +9102+9588
steward^S (1) +408+889+1074+6584
still (1) +2021+2296+3427+3869
stoned (1) +74+928+8083
stoning (1) +74+928+8083
such (1)
such^S (1) +6913
suggested (1) +1821+2021+2296
sunset (1) +995+3064
tent-dwelling (1) +185+928
that happened (1) +465+1821+2021
that^S (1) +465+1821+2021
that^S (1) +1074+2021+2296
the place^S (1)
their^S (1) +408
their^S (1) +465
their^S (1) +824+6639
their^S (1) +1201+1769
their^S (1) +2498+4200
their^S (1) +3913
their^S (1) +4131
them^S (1) +74+928+4392
them^S (1) +3192
them^S (1) +74+9109
them^S (1) +466+1074+3998
them^S (1) +824+6551
them^S (1) +912
them^S (1) +1522
them^S (1) +1821+2021+2296
them^S (1) +2021+2296+6639
them^S (1) +2143
them^S (1) +3192
them^S (1) +3192+9109
them^S (1) +4283
them^S (1) +4291
them^S (1) +5566
them^S (1) +5987
them^S (1) +6109
them^S (1) +6296
them^S (1) +6929+7983
them^S (1) +7194
them^S (1) +7700
them^S (1) +7736
them^S (1) +7983
them^S (1) +9149
then^S (1) +928+2021+2085+3427
then^S (1) +2021+2085+6961
there^S (1) +928+1195
there^S (1) +928+2215
there^S (1) +824+928
there^S (1) +928+1014
there^S (1) +928+1074+3752
there^S (1) +928+2006
there^S (1) +928+2215
there^S (1) +928+4722
there^S (1) +928+5207
there^S (1) +928+6551
there^S (1) +3720
there^S (1) +8441
there^S (1) +9399
these men^S (1) +1201+5566
these men^S (1) +4856+6913
these^S (1) +74
these^S (1) +2693
they^S (1) +132
they^S (1) +746
they^S (1) +851
they^S (1) +851+1201
they^S (1) +964
they^S (1) +2256+2657+3405+8569
they^S (1) +3374
they^S (1) +3452
they^S (1) +3972+6639
they^S (1) +4291
they^S (1) +4619
they^S (1) +4784
they^S (1) +4855
they^S (1) +5954
they^S (1) +6296
they^S (1) +7736
they^S (1) +8103
they^S (1) +8569
they^S (1) +9133
thirty feet (1) +564+928+6929
this (1) +1821+2021+2296
this is how (1) +465+1821+2021+3869
this kind of sore (1) +5596+5999
this^S (1) +2021+2296+5126
this^S (1) +9108
thoroughly purge away (1)
+1342+3869+7671
those^S (1) +339+889+6639
those^S (1) +1583
those^S (1) +2651
those^S (1) +7156
those^S (1) +7239
those^S (1) +8599
those^S (1) +8636
tomorrow^S (1)
two^S (1)
unnoticed (1) +928+4319
useless (1) +4200+9214
very old (1) +928+995+2416+3427
wage war (1) +1741+4200+4878
walking along (1) +928+2006
waylaid (1) +928+2006+8492
what^S (1) +995
what^S (1) +2021+2296+5184
what^S (1) +4856
whatever^S (1) +3655
where^S (1) +928+5226
where^S (1) +2006
where^S (1) +2021+2667+2958
wherever (1) +285+889+928+5226
wherever (1) +889+3972+5226+6584
wherever (1) +889+928+5226
wherever (1) +928+3972+5226
wherever (1) +3972+4946+5226
which way (1) +361+2006+2296
which^S (1) +7366
which^S (1) +8965
who (1) +408+6504
whoever (1) +132+3972
whoever^S (1)
whom (1)
whose^S (1) +285+2021+9108
without meaning (1) +928+2039
woman's monthly uncleanness (1)
+3240+5614
workmen (1) +928+4856+6913
year (1) +3427+4200
years (1) +6961+9102
yet (1) +2021+2085+3427+6330
yet (1) +2021+2156+3427+6330
yet (1) +3427
Ziklag^S (1) +6551
untranslated (10017)

2022 ־הַ h^a- (743)
whether (12)
if (11)
not (8)
when (4)
don't (3)
as you know (2) +4202
or (2)
rather (2)
aren't (1)
isn't (1)
not only (1)
only (1) +4202
so (1)
surely (1)
unless (1) +4202
what about (1) +4202
whether (1) +561+4202
untranslated (690)

2023 ָה - *ah* (3129)
her (1141)
it (539)
its (257)
the^S (95)
she (67)
their (67)
them (28)
there^S (28) +928
his (13)
the city^S (12)
the land^S (12)
whose (12)
herself (8)
herself (7) +5883
this (7)
which^S (7)
there^S (6) +6584

your (6)
a^S (5)
her (5) +4200
her own (5)
there^S (4) +928+9348
him (3)
one (3)
that city^S (3)
there^S (3)
this^S (3)
Hagar^S (2)
hers (2)
its (2) +928
its (2) +4200
its land^S (2)
its^S (2)
Jerusalem^S (2)
land^S (2)
she (2) +5883
that^S (2)
the town^S (2)
where^S (2) +928
which (2)
wisdom^S (2)
you (2)
all this^S (1)
an^S (1)
another^S (1)
city^S (1)
Dinah's^S (1)
Edom's^S (1)
Edom^S (1)
Egypt^S (1)
Hannah^S (1)
he^S (1) +3
here^S (1) +928
hers (1) +4200
herself (1) +4222
herself (1) +7931
him^S (1) +3
him^S (1) +1201
him^S (1) +1251
his former righteousness^S (1)
his nurse^S (1)
his^S (1) +3
in (1)
Israel's^S (1)
it^S (1) +1947+4946
its (1) +6584
its inhabitants^S (1)
its own (1)
its people^S (1)
Judah^S (1)
Moab^S (1)
my law^S (1)
Nineveh^S (1) +5226
piece^S (1)
that (1)
that day^S (1)
that place^S (1)
that time^S (1)
that's (1)
the (1)
the courtyard^S (1)
the daughter's^S (1)
the dove^S (1)
the earth^S (1)
the fire^S (1)
the first woman^S (1)
the girl^S (1)
the goat^S (1)
the kingdom^S (1)
the lampstand^S (1)
the pit^S (1)
the place^S (1)
the plot^S (1)
the spring^S (1)
the sword^S (1)
the temple^S (1)
their land^S (1)
their lands^S (1)
them^S (1) +1074
themselves (1)
there^S (1) +928+8148
there^S (1) +5226
these^S (1)
this city^S (1)
this land^S (1)
those (1)
tongue^S (1)
Tyre^S (1)
what happened^S (1)
whom (1)
word^S (1)
your own (1)
your wife^S (1)
yourself (1) +4222
Zion^S (1)
untranslated (687)

2024 הֹ - *ōh* (53)
his (9)
they (4)
them (3)
its (2)
it (1)
their (1)
those (1)
untranslated (32)

2025 2 הָ - *āh2* (1116)
to (292)
on (95)
at (58)
there (58) +9004
into (51)
in (37)
more (36) +5087
west (28) +3542
north (26) +7600
toward (25)
where (17) +625
where (16) +9004
east (13) +7708
how long (12) +625+6330
for (9)
northern (9) +7600
south (9) +5582
outside (8) +2575
east (7) +4667
east (7) +7711
upward (6) +4200+5087
out (5) +2575
south (5) +9402
above (4) +4200+4946+5087
reached (4) +995
the Jordan^S (4) +9004
above (3) +4200+5087
eastern (3) +7711
from (3)
in it^S (3) +9004
on (3) +5087
over (3) +4200+4946+5087
south (3) +5582+9402
southern (3) +5582
toward (3) +995+3870
westward (3) +3542
after (2)
anywhere else (2) +625+625+2025+2256
each year (2) +3427+3427+4946
east (2) +2021+4667+9087
eastern (2) +4667
head (2) +2256+4946+5087+8900
higher (2) +5087
highly (2) +4200+5087
in the presence of (2) +5584
inside (2)
inside (2) +1074
it^S (2) +9004
outside (2) +2575+4946
south (2) +2025+5582+9402
top (2) +4200+4946+5087
up (2) +4200+5087
very (2) +4200+5087
western (2) +3542
wherever (2) +9004
which way (2) +625
across (1)
advance (1) +7156
against (1)
along (1)
among (1)
annual (1) +3427+3427+4946
anywhere (1) +625+625+2025+2256
as far as (1)
at each successive level (1) +2025+4200+4200+5087+5087
away (1) +448+2021+2575
back^S (1) +9004
beyond (1) +5087
deep (1) +5087
depth (1) +4200+5087
down (1) +824
downstream (1) +4200+4946+5087
east (1) +928+4667+6298
east (1) +928+4667+6298+9087
east (1) +4667+6298
eastern (1) +7708
eastward (1) +2025+4667+7711
eastward (1) +4667
eastward (1) +7708
eastward (1) +7711
entered (1) +995
entering (1) +995
enters (1) +995
exceedingly (1) +4200+5087
extend eastward (1) +7708
extend out (1) +2575
extend westward (1) +3542
facing (1)
fail (1) +824+5877
get out of here (1) +2021+2575+8938
heights (1) +4200+5087
here (1) +2178
here^S (1) +5213
high above (1) +4200+4946+5087
higher than (1) +4200+5087+8049
in (1) +1074+2021
in ascending stages (1) +2025+4200+4200+5087+5087
inside^S (1) +9004
interior (1) +1074+4946
invade (1) +995+9004
inward (1) +1074
join (1)
magnificence (1) +5087
more (1) +4200+5087
more and more powerful (1) +1541+2143+2256+4200+5087+6330
northern (1) +4946+7600
older (1) +5087
on to (1)
onto (1)
outer (1) +4200+4946+5087
outside (1) +2667
outside (1) +7339
outside the family (1) +2021+2424+2575
over (1)
over and above (1) +4200+5087
overturned (1) +2200+4200+5087
pen up (1) +1074
project upward (1) +4200+5087
severe (1) +4200+5087
southeast (1) +2025+5582+7711
southeast (1) +5582+7711
the land^S (1) +9004
there^S (1) +824+4046
there^S (1) +928+9463
to (1) +9004
top (1) +4200+5087
top (1) +5087
top of (1) +4200+4946+5087
upstream (1) +4200+5087
upward (1) +4200+4946+5087

very (1) +4200+5087+6330
west (1) +5115
western[s] (1) +4667
when (1) +625+6330
where[s] (1) +7730
wherever (1) +625
wherever (1) +889+9004
wielding (1) +995+4200+5087
young and old (1) +2256+5087
untranslated (115)

2026 הֵא *hē'* (2)
here (1)
surely (1)

2027 הֶאָח *he'āh* (12)
Aha (11)
Ah (1)

2028 הָאֲחַשְׁתָּרִי *hā'ᵃhaštāriy* (1)
Haahashtari (1)

2029 הָאֱלִי *hā'ᵉliy*
Variant; not used

2030 הָאֶלֶף *hā'eleḇ* (1)
Haeleph (1)

2031 הָאַמָּה *hā'ammāh*
Variant; not used

2032 הָאֵצֶל *hā'ēṣel*
Variant; not used

2033 הָאַרְבַּע *hā'arba'*
Variant; not used

2034 הָאֲרָרִי *hā'rāriy*
Variant; not used

2035 1הַב *haḇ1* (33)
give (12)
ascribe (9)
come (5)
bring (2)
appoint (1)
choose (1)
do (1)
praise (1)
put (1)

2036 2הַב *haḇ2*
Variant; not used

2037 הַבְהַב *haḇhaḇ* (1)
given (1)

2038 הָבַל *hāḇal* (5)
worthless (2)
fill with false hopes (1)
meaningless talk (1) +2039
take pride (1)

2039 1הֶבֶל *heḇel1* (73)
meaningless (34)
worthless idols (9)
breath (5)
in vain (5)
worthless (4)
dishonest (1)
empty talk (1)
fleeting (1)
futile (1)
futility (1)
less meaning (1) +8049
meaningless talk (1) +2038
mere breath (1)
no meaning (1)
nonsense (1)
utterly meaningless (1) +2039
utterly useless (1) +2256+8198
vapor (1)
without meaning (1) +928+2021
worthless idols (1) +8736

2040 2הֶבֶל *heḇel2* (8)
Abel (8)

2041 הָבְנִים *hoḇniym* (2)
ebony (1)
untranslated (1)

2042 הָבַר *hāḇar* (2)
astrologers (1) +9028
untranslated (1)

2043 הֵגֵא *hēgē'* (1)
Hegai (1)

2044 הַגִּדְגָּד *haggidgāḏ*
Variant; not used

2045 הַגְּדוֹלִים *haggᵉḏôliym* (1)
Haggedolim (1)

2046 הַגּוֹיִם *haggôyim*
Variant; not used

2047 1הָגָה *hāgāh1* (25)
meditate (3)
plot (3)
growls (1)
lament (1)
meditates (1)
moan (1)
moan mournfully (1) +2047
moaned (1)
mutter (1)
mutters (1)
ponder (1)
speak (1)
speaks (1)
tell (1)
think (1)
utter (1)
utter a sound (1)
uttering (1)
utters (1)
weighs (1)

2048 2הָגָה *hāgāh2* (3)
remove (2)
drives out (1)

2049 הֶגֶה *hegeh* (3)
moan (1)
mourning (1)
rumbling (1)

2050 הָגוּת *hāgûṯ* (1)
utterance (1)

2051 הֵגַי *hēgay* (3)
Hegai (3)

2052 הָגִיג *hāgiyg* (2)
meditated (1)
sighing (1)

2053 הִגָּיוֹן *higgāyôn* (4)
Higgaion (1)
meditation (1)
melody (1)
mutter (1)

2054 הָגִין *hāgiyn* (1)
corresponding (1)

2055 הַגִּלְגָּל *haggilgal*
Variant; not used

2056 הַגָּן *haggān*
Variant; not used

2057 הָגָר *hāgār* (12)
Hagar (11)
she[s] (1)

2058 הַגְרִי *hagriy* (7)
Hagrites (4)
Hagri (2)
Hagrite (1)

2059 הֵד *hēḏ* (1)
joy (1)

2060 הֲדַד *hᵃdaḏ* (13)
Hadad (12)
untranslated (1)

2061 הֲדַדְעֶזֶר *hᵃdaḏ'ezer* (21)
Hadadezer (17)
Hadadezer's (2)
who[s] (2)

2062 הֲדַד־רִמּוֹן *hᵃdaḏ-rimmôn* (1)
Hadad Rimmon (1)

2063 הָדָה *hāḏāh* (1)
put (1)

2064 הֹדּוּ *hōddû* (2)
India (2)

2065 הֲדוּרִים *hᵃḏûriym* (1)
mountains (1)

2066 1הֲדוֹרָם *hᵃḏôrām1* (2)
Hadoram (2)

2067 2הֲדוֹרָם *hᵃḏôrām2* (2)
Adoniram (1)
Hadoram (1)

2068 הִדַּי *hidday* (1)
Hiddai (1)

2069 הֹדַיְוָהוּ *hōḏaywāhû* (1)
untranslated (1)

2070 הָדַךְ *hāḏak* (1)
crush (1)

2071 הֲדֹם *hᵃḏōm* (6)
footstool (5) +8079
footstool (1)

2072 הֲדַס *hᵃḏas* (6)
myrtle trees (3)
myrtle (2)
myrtles (1)

2073 הֲדַסָּה *hᵃḏassāh* (1)
Hadassah (1)

2074 הָדַף *hāḏaḇ* (11)
shoves (2)
depose (1)
drive out (1)
driven (1)
driven out (1)
push away (1)
push down (1)
shove (1)
thrusting out (1)
thwarts (1)

2075 הָדַר *hāḏar* (6)
are shown respect (1) +7156
exalt yourself (1)
favoritism (1) +7156
show favoritism (1)
show respect (1)
splendor (1)

2076 הֲדַר *hᵃḏar*
Variant; not used

2077 הָדָר *hāḏār* (30)
splendor (12)
majesty (10)
majestic (2)
blessing (1)
choice (1)
dignity (1)
glory (1)
honor (1)
nobles (1)

2078 הֶדֶר *heḏer* (1)
splendor (1)

2079 הֲדָרָה *hᵃḏārāh* (5)
splendor (4)
glory (1)

2080 הֲדַרְעֶזֶר *hᵃḏar'ezer*
Variant; not used

2081 הָהּ *hāh* (1)
Alas (1)

2082 הוֹ *hô* (2)
anguish (1) +2082

2083 הוּ *hû* (1)
it (1)

2084 ־הוּ *-hû* (1083)
him (484)
it (147)
his (137)
them (36)
he (20)
their (18)
its (13)
the[s] (10)
his own (6)
a[s] (4)
David[s] (4)
they (4)
which (4)
someone (3)
each (2)
Moses[s] (2)
Pekahiah[s] (2)
whose (2)
your (2)
Abram[s] (1)
Asahel's[s] (1)
Ben-Hadad[s] (1)
both of you (1) +2256+3870
Cyrus[s] (1)
God[s] (1)
idol[s] (1)
Joab[s] (1)
meal[s] (1)
my (1)
Nadab[s] (1)
one's (1)
that day[s] (1)
the altar[s] (1)
the child[s] (1)
the clouds[s] (1)
the idol[s] (1)
the inside[s] (1)
the lamb[s] (1)
the lion[s] (1)
the manna[s] (1)
the mountain[s] (1)
the parties (1) +408+2256+8276
the stand[s] (1)
the water[s] (1)
their own (1)
theirs (1)
this (1)
together (1) +408+907+8276
who (1)
whom (1)
you (1)
untranslated (146)

2085 הוּא *hû'* (1888)
he (438)
that (379)
it (191)
she (82)
this (54)
they (40)
that is (34)
who (32)
himself (22)
that same (19)
one (11)
same (10)
which (9)
him (7)
his (6)
those (6)
these (4)
Jotham[s] (3)
the man[s] (3)
this city[s] (3)
Abram[s] (2)
all day long (2) +928+2021+2021+3427
far and wide (2) +2134+2256+4946
he[s] (2) +2021+2021+5883
its (2)
only[s] (2)
that man[s] (2)
that very (2)
the animal[s] (2)
the LORD[s] (2)
them (2)
what (2)
you (2)
again (1) +928+1685+2021+2021+7193
any[s] (1)
anyone (1)
at once (1) +928+2021+2021+3427
at once (1) +928+2021+2021+6961
Baal[s] (1)
Balaam[s] (1)
Beerah[s] (1)
daughter[s] (1)
David[s] (1)
death[s] (1)
each of us (1) +638+2256
Elah[s] (1)
Elijah[s] (1)
Elisha[s] (1)
else (1)
fire[s] (1)
Gaal[s] (1)
Gehazi[s] (1)
Hannah[s] (1)
he alone (1)
he himself (1)
herself (1)
it[s] (1) +2021+2021+5226
joy[s] (1)
let it be (1) +4027
man[s] (1)
mine (1)
my vow[s] (1)
Naaman[s] (1)
Naomi[s] (1)
other[s] (1)
priests[s] (1)
regular[s] (1)
Ruth[s] (1)
she's (1)
Shem[s] (1)
something[s] (1)
such (1)
that part[s] (1)
that person[s] (1)
that slave[s] (1)
that son[s] (1)
that's (1)
the city[s] (1)
the father[s] (1)
the key[s] (1)
the Makirites[s] (1)
the person[s] (1)
the prophet[s] (1)
the slave[s] (1)
the woman[s] (1)
then[s] (1) +928+2021+2021+3427
then[s] (1) +2021+2021+6961
things[s] (1)
this man[s] (1)
this same (1)
very (1)
which[s] (1)
who[s] (1)
whoever (1)
whose (1)
yet (1) +2021+2021+3427+6330
untranslated (444)

2086 1הוֹד *hôd1* (24)
splendor (10)
majesty (3)
glory (2)
honor (2)
proud (2)
authority (1)
best strength (1)
face (1)
glorious (1)
majestic (1)

2087 2הוֹד *hôd2* (1)
Hod (1)

2088 הוֹדְוָה *hôdwāh* (2)
Hodaviah (2)

2089 הוֹדַוְיָה *hôdawyāh* (3)
Hodaviah (3)

2090 הוֹדַוְיָהוּ *hôdawyāhû* (1)
Hodaviah (1)

2091 הוֹדִיָּה *hôdiyyāh* (6)
Hodiah (5)
Hodiah's (1)

2092 1הָוָה *hāwāh1* (1)
fall (1)

2093 2הָוָה *hāwāh2* (5)
be (2)
become (1)
get (1)
lie (1)

2094 1הַוָּה *hawwāh1* (3)
craving (1)
desire (1)
evil desires (1)

2095 2הַוָּה *hawwāh2* (13)
destroying (2)
destruction (2)
ruin (2)
corrupt (1)
deadly (1)
destructive forces (1)
disaster (1)
malice (1)
malicious (1)
misery (1)

2096 הוֹה *hôāh* (3)
calamity (3)

2097 הוֹהָם *hôhām* (1)
Hoham (1)

2098 הוֹי *hôy* (51)
woe (36)
Alas (5)
come (4)
Ah (3)
oh (2)
awful (1) +1524

2099 הוֹלֵלוֹת *hôlēlôt* (4)
madness (4)

2100 הוֹלֵלוּת *hôlēlût* (1)
madness (1)

2101 הוּם *hûm* (4)
distraught (1)
shook (1)
stirred (1)
throng (1)

2102 הוֹמָם *hômām* (1)
Homam (1)

2103 הוּן *hûn* (1)
thinking it easy (1)

2104 הוֹן *hôn* (26)
wealth (15)
enough (2)
wealth of goods (2)
money (1)
pittance (1) +4202
possessions (1)
rich (1)
riches (1)
treasures (1)

valuable things (1) +3701

2105 הוֹר *hôr*
Variant; not used

2106 הוֹשָׁמָע *hôšāmā‘* (1)
Hoshama (1)

2107 הוֹשֵׁעַ *hôšēa‘* (16)
Hoshea (12)
Hosea (2)
him[S] (1)
Joshua (1)

2108 הוֹשַׁעְיָה *hôša‘yāh* (3)
Hoshaiah (3)

2109 הוּת *hûṯ* (1)
assault (1)

2110 הוֹתִיר *hôṯiyr* (2)
Hothir (2)

2111 הָזָה *hāzāh* (1)
dream (1)

2112 הַחִירוֹת *hahiyrôṯ*
Variant; not used

2113 הִי *hiy* (1)
woe (1)

2114 ־הִי *-hiy* (1)
his (1)

2115 הִיא *hiy'*
Variant; not used

2116 הֵידָד *hēyḏāḏ* (7)
shouts of joy (3)
shout (1)
shout in triumph (1) +6702
shouting (1)
shouts (1)

2117 הֻיְּדוֹת *huyyᵉḏôṯ* (1)
songs of thanksgiving (1)

2118 הָיָה *hāyāh* (3577)
be (715)
was (305)
came (165)
become (164)
were (159)
is (97)
been (77)
are (76)
became (59)
had (50) +4200
have (48) +4200
come (26)
happened (26)
will (19)
am (17)
had (16)
happen (16)
have (16)
remain (14)
lived (12) +3427
belong to (11) +4200
has (11)
hold (10)
becomes (9)
fall (9)
comes (8)
lived (8)
remained (8)
set (8)
go (7)
bring (6)
continue (6)
done (6)
fell (6)
has (6) +4200
lie (6)
made (6)
serve (6)
went (6)
belonged to (5) +4200
bring (5) +4200
consider (5) +4200
ended (5) +9362
fallen (5)
has (5) +928
left (5)
marry (5) +851+4200
stay (5)
stayed (5)
belongs to (4) +4200
endure (4)
included (4)
keep (4)
last (4)
leave (4)
numbered (4)
one day (4) +2256
rest (4)
spread (4)
took place (4)
touch (4) +928
appears (3)
coming (3)
end (3) +9362
ending (3) +9362
extend (3)
given (3)
keep (3) +4200
kept (3)
lay (3)
make (3)
married (3) +851+4200
may (3)
put (3)
stand (3)
taken (3)
use (3)
used (3)
wear (3) +6584
agree (2) +285+3869
allotted (2) +1598
applies (2)
arose (2)
bind (2) +3213+4200
brought (2)
come what may (2) +4537
connecting (2)
did (2)
do (2)
extended (2)
follow (2) +339
fulfilled (2)
get (2)
help (2) +6640
lies (2)
living (2)
lying (2)
occur (2)
overwhelmed (2) +928+4202+6388+8120
owned (2) +5238
preceded (2) +4200+7156
reached (2)
receive (2) +4200
regard as (2) +4200
rule (2) +6584
serve as (2)
served (2)
settled (2)
sold for (2) +928
spent (2)
struck (2) +928
take place (2)
turn to (2)
turned into (2) +4200
use (2) +4200
wear (2)
abound (1) +7172
acquired (1) +4200
act (1)
allotted (1) +928+1598+2021
amount to (1)
amounted to (1)
appear (1)
appear (1) +928+3869+6524
appeared (1)
apply (1)
aroused (1) +6584
arranged (1) +4595
attach (1)
be (1) +2118
be treated as (1)
become (1) +4200
becoming (1)
began (1)
beginning (1)
being (1)
belong (1)
belong to (1) +928
belonged to (1) +448
belonging to (1) +4200
belongs (1)
bring about (1) +928
brings (1)
broke out (1)
brought about (1) +4946
brought with (1) +928+3338
came (1) +2118
came into being (1)
came on (1)
came to (1)
came to be (1)
carried by (1) +6584
caught (1)
cause (1) +4946
certainly come true (1) +2118
come into being (1) +2118
comes of (1)
committed (1)
company (1) +907
compare with (1) +3869
complete (1) +4946+7891
condemn (1) +2631+4200
conferred (1) +1821
consist of (1)
continued (1) +2143
controlled (1) +4200
could not (1) +6584
count (1) +4200
covered (1) +928
decide (1) +6584+7023
decided (1) +4213+6640
designate (1)
do that[S] (1) +928+2257+3338
downcast (1) +4200
drove back (1) +6584
earlier (1)
end (1) +340+928+2021
ends (1)
endure (1) +4200
engaged in (1)
escapes (1) +7129
exhausted (1)
exists (1)
extending (1)
fared (1)
feared (1) +3007
fighting with (1) +907
filled (1) +928+3972
find (1)
follow (1)
followed (1) +339
formed (1)
fulfilled (1) +4027
future (1) +4537+8611
gain support (1) +907+3338
gained (1)
give (1)
give (1) +4200
give shelter (1) +6261
goes (1) +8079
gone (1)

gone (1) +928+4202
got (1) +4200
grew worse and worse (1) +2617+2716+4394
had (1) +928
had (1) +6584
had chance (1) +928+3338
had part in (1) +4946
had to (1) +6584
happening (1)
happens (1)
harbor (1) +4222+6640
harbored (1) +4200
has (1) +6640
have (1) +928
have (1) +1068
have (1) +6584
having (1) +4200
help (1) +907
help (1) +4200
hold (1) +928+3338
holds (1) +928+3338
in office (1)
inclined (1) +2296
include (1)
increase (1)
incurs (1)
inherit (1) +448
into marry (1) +4200
join (1) +928
joined (1)
lasted (1)
led the way (1) +3338+8037
left (1) +4200
lend (1)
let (1)
life (1) +889+3427
looked (1) +928+6524
made angry (1) +7911
made fall (1) +4200+4842
make sport of (1) +4200+5442
making (1)
married (1) +851
married to (1) +851+4200
marries (1) +408+2118+4200
marries (1) +408+4200
marries (1) +4200
marry (1) +408+4200
marry into (1) +4200
mattered (1)
mount (1) +4853
moved (1)
observe (1)
occurred (1)
once (1)
owes (1)
own (1) +4200
participate in (1) +448
passed (1)
predecessor (1) +889+4200+7156
prepare (1) +3922
produced (1)
proper place (1) +889+5226+9004
property[s] (1) +889+4200
prove to be (1)
proved to be (1)
provided for (1) +430+2256+4200+4312
raise (1)
raised (1)
reached (1) +928
reaching (1)
ready (1)
rebel (1) +5308
received (1)
received (1) +4200
regard (1) +4200+7156
remain unmarried (1) +408+1194+4200+4200+6328
remains (1)
required (1)
rested (1)
restored (1)
retains (1)
retains (1) +4200
ruled (1) +4889
run (1)
seem (1)
seem (1) +928+6524
seemed (1)
seemed (1) +928+6524
sell for (1) +928
serve (1) +4200
serve (1) +4200+7156
served (1) +4200+7156
served as (1)
serving (1)
share (1) +4200
shed (1)
shine (1) +240
show (1) +4200
shows to be (1) +4200
sprang up (1)
standing (1)
start (1)
started (1)
staying (1)
steals forth (1)
stretched (1)
strike (1)
strike (1) +928
striking (1) +928
suffer (1)
suffered (1) +928
suffered (1) +4200
supply (1) +4200
supported (1) +339
supported (1) +907+3338
surely become (1) +2118
surely take place (1)
surround (1) +4946+6017
take (1)
take (1) +4200
take care of (1) +4200+5466
take care of (1) +6125
take command (1) +4200+5464
take hold of (1) +928
take the place of (1) +9393
tasted (1)
taught (1) +3723
tend livestock (1) +408+5238
tended livestock (1) +408+5238
testify (1) +6332
took care of (1) +6125
touches (1) +6584
treated (1)
treated (1) +6640
treating (1)
turn against (1) +4200+8477
turned (1)
turned out (1)
unite (1) +3480+4200+4222
unmarried (1) +408+4200+4202
used to (1)
using (1)
want[s] (1)
was altogether (1) +2118
was committed (1)
wasn't (1) +4202
weighed (1)
went over (1) +6017
when (1) +4946
with (1) +928
work (1)
you (1)
untranslated (887)

2119 הַיָּה *hayyāh* (1)
untranslated (1)

2120 הֵיךְ *hēyk̲* (2)
how (2)

2121 הֵיכָל *hēyk̲āl* (80)
temple (54)
outer sanctuary (7)
palace (7)
main hall (6)
palaces (4)
sanctuary (1)
temples (1)

2122 הֵילֵל *hēylēl* (1)
morning star (1)

2123 הֵימָם *hēymām* (1)
Homam (1)

2124 הֵימָן *hēymān* (17)
Heman (16)
his[s] (1)

2125 הִין *hiyn* (22)
hin (22)

2126 הַיַּרְקוֹן *hayyarqôn*
Variant; not used

2127 הַיְשִׁימוֹת *hayšiymôt̲*
Variant; not used

2128 הָכַר *hāk̲ar*
Variant; not used

2129 הַכָּרָה *hakkārāh* (1)
look (1)

2130 הַכֶּרֶם *hakkerem*
Variant; not used

2131 הַל *hal*
Variant; not used

2132 הֲלֹא *hᵃlōʼ*
Variant; not used

2133 הָלָא *hālāʼ* (1)
driven away (1)

2134 הָלְאָה *hālʼāh* (16)
on (4)
beyond (2) +2256+4946
far and wide (2) +2085+2256+4946
beyond (1) +4200+4946
beyond (1) +4946
continuing (1)
forward (1)
on the other side of (1) +2256+4946+6298
outside (1) +4946
some distance away (1)
way (1)

2135 הַלּוֹחֵשׁ *hallôḥēš* (2)
Hallohesh (2)

2136 הִלּוּלִים *hillûliym* (2)
festival (1)
offering of praise (1)

2137 הַלָּז *hallāz* (7)
this (3)
that (2)
the (1)
there's (1)

2138 הַלָּזֶה *hallāzeh* (3)
that (2)
this (1)

2139 הַלֵּזוּ *hallēzû*
Variant; not used

2140 הַלַּחְמִי *hallaḥmiy*
Variant; not used

2141 הָלִיךְ *hāliyk̲* (1)
path (1)

2142 הֲלִיכָה *hᵃliyk̲āh* (7)
procession (2)
affairs (1)
traveling merchants (1)
way (1)
ways (1)
untranslated (1)

2143 הָלַךְ *hālak̲* (1556)
go (327)
went (171)
come (94)
walk (87)
walked (38)
left (32)
gone (29)
followed (27) +339
follow (22) +928
follow (20) +339
going (15)
moved (15)
set out (15)
led (14)
came (11)
went away (11)
followed (10) +928
take (10)
walking (10)
went out (9)
walks (8)
go about (7)
go back (7)
goes (7)
leave (7)
continue (6)
continued (6)
following (6) +339
live (6)
go out (5)
left (5) +4946
marched (5)
returned (5)
run (5)
traveled (5)
went off (5)
went on (5)
brought (4)
coming (4)
fled (4)
go (4) +2256+8740
go away (4)
go off (4)
lead (4)
leave (4) +4946
left (4) +907+4946
be (3)
did[s] (3)
follow (3)
followed (3)
follows (3) +928
go ahead (3)
going about (3)
grow (3)
on way (3)
ran (3)
taking (3)
wandered (3)
withdrew (3)
advanced (2)
away (2)
bandit (2)
be on way (2)
became more and more powerful (2)
+1524+2143+2256
been (2)
began (2)
carry (2)
departs (2)
disappears (2)
done[s] (2)
flow (2)
flowed (2)
get (2)
get out (2)
go (2) +2143
go now (2) +995
go way (2)
goes about (2)
going back (2)
going back and forth (2)
gossip (2) +8215
leader (2) +4200+7156
leads away (2)
leave (2) +907+4946
make a survey of (2) +928
march (2)
marched out (2)
marching (2)
minister (2)
move (2)
moved about (2)
remain (2)
return (2)
rode (2)
sent (2)
set sail (2)
spread (2)
stay (2)
took (2)
travel (2)
walk about (2)
way (2)
weak as (2)
went on way (2)
went over (2)
went up (2)
were on way (2)
about (1)
accompanied (1) +907
accompanied by (1) +6640
accompany (1) +4200+5584
advances (1)
all the way (1)
all this time (1)
associates (1)
attended by (1) +4200+8079
banish (1)
be on way (1) +2256+5825
became more and more powerful (1)
+1524+2256
blows (1)
by all means go (1) +995
came back (1) +995+2256
cause to walk (1)
climbed up (1)
closer and closer (1) +2256+7929
comes (1)
commit (1) +928
committed (1) +928
concern (1)
conduct (1)
consult (1) +448
continued (1) +2118
continued to grow (1)
course (1)
crawl (1)
depart (1)
departed (1)
deported (1)
devoted to (1)
devoted to (1) +339
disappeared (1) +4946+6524
dispersed (1) +2006+4200
do not know where am going (1)
+889+2143+6584
drive (1)
driven (1)
drove back (1)
enabled to walk (1)
entered (1) +6330
escape (1)
escorted (1)
exiled (1)
fade away (1)
faithful (1) +622+928
flashed back and forth (1)
flashed down (1)
fleeing (1)
fleet of trading ships (1) +641+4200+9576
fleet of trading ships (1) +641+9576
floated (1)
flowing (1)
flows (1)
flows away (1)
flying (1)
follow (1) +928+8079
follow along (1)
followers (1) +339
followers (1) +408+889+6640
freely strut (1)
get away (1)
get back (1)
get rid of (1)
go (1) +928+2006
go (1) +995
go aside (1)
go at once (1) +995+2256
go at once (1) +2143
go forward (1)
go in (1) +995+2256
go on (1)
go on way (1)
go over (1)
go to and fro (1)
go up (1)
goes down (1)
goes out (1) +2143
goes to and fro (1)
going around (1)
going off (1)
gone (1) +2143
gone away (1)
gone off (1) +2143
gone up (1)
greedy (1) +339
grew even wilder (1) +2256+6192
grew louder and louder (1)
+2256+2618+4394
grew stronger and stronger (1) +2256+2618
grew stronger and stronger (1) +2256+7997
grew weaker and weaker (1) +1924+2256
have go (1)
hurry (1) +4559
increased more and more (1)
+2143+2256+8041
invaded (1) +4200
join (1) +6584
join (1) +6640
journey (1)
journeyed (1)
keep (1) +928
keep on (1)
keeping all the way (1) +2143
kept (1)
kept (1) +928
kept coming (1) +2143
kept on (1)
kept on (1) +8743
lead (1) +4200+7156
lead life (1) +928
lead on (1) +2256+5627
leading (1)
leads (1)
leads a life (1)
leave (1) +4946+6640
leave (1) +4946+6643
leaves (1) +907+4946
leaving (1)
led (1) +339
led life (1) +928
left (1) +4946+6640
live (1) +928
lived (1)
made walk (1)
made way (1)
make flow (1)
man[s] (1)
marches (1)
melting away (1) +2256+4570
more and more powerful (1)
+1541+2025+2256+4200+5087+6330

moved back and forth (1)
moves (1)
moves about (1)
moves along (1)
moving (1)
moving about (1)
moving from place to place (1)
moving from place to place (1) +889+928+2143
near (1) +907
neared (1) +725
obey (1) +928
off (1)
passed away (1)
passing (1)
persisted (1)
proceed (1)
proceeded (1)
prowled (1)
prowling (1)
pursue (1) +339
pursued (1) +339
pursuing (1) +339
ran down (1)
receded steadily (1) +2256+8740+8740
rejoined (1) +448
resort to (1) +4200+7925
return (1) +995
return (1) +2256+7155
return (1) +8740
ride (1) +928
rides (1)
roam (1) +2256+3718
roamed (1)
rode off (1)
rougher and rougher (1) +2256+6192
roving (1)
runs along (1)
sail (1) +641+928+2021
sending (1)
sending on (1)
set off (1)
shining ever brighter (1) +239+2256
slanderer (1) +8215
stalks (1)
stream (1)
surely leave (1) +2143+4946+6584
sweep (1)
take back (1)
take part (1) +6640
take possession (1)
take turns (1) +3427
taken (1)
them[s] (1) +2021
took (1) +1583
took to (1)
travel along (1)
traveled (1) +2006
travelers (1) +5986
traveling (1)
tripping along with mincing steps (1) +2256+3262
trudge (1)
turned (1)
turning (1)
use (1) +448
very well go (1) +2143
walk (1) +928+2006
walk continually (1)
walked along (1)
walked along (1) +2143
walked around (1)
walked back and forth (1)
walked on (1)
walking along (1)
walking along (1) +2143
walking around (1)
walks around (1)
wanders (1)
ways (1)
went (1) +2143
went about (1)
went along (1) +2143
went around (1)
went back (1)
went down (1)
went forth (1)
went forward (1)
went home (1)
went in (1)
went out (1) +2143
will[s] (1)
with (1)
withdraw (1)
withdrew (1) +4946
untranslated (78)

2144 הֵלֶךְ *hēlek̲* (2)
oozing out (1)
traveler (1)

2145 1הָלַל *hālal1* (4)
radiance (1)
shone (1)
show (1)
throws out flashes (1)

2146 2הָלַל *hālal2* (146)
praise (89)
boast (11)
praised (7)
worthy of praise (6)
boasts (4)
glory (4)
give praise (3)
praises (3)
be praised (2)
praising (2)
bring praise (1)
cheering (1)
extol (1)
exult (1)
gave thanks (1)
giving praise (1)
had wedding songs (1)
is praised (1)
make boast (1)
renown (1)
sang (1)
sang praises (1)
sing praise (1)
sing praises (1)
that purpose[s] (1)

2147 3הָלַל *hālal3* (16)
arrogant (3)
go mad (2)
makes fools of (2)
acted like a madman (1)
boast (1)
drive furiously (1)
foolish (1)
gone mad (1)
mock (1)
rail (1)
storm (1)
turns into a fool (1)

2148 הִלֵּל *hillēl* (2)
Hillel (2)

2149 הַלְלוּיָה *halᵉlûyāh*
Variant; not used

2150 הָלַם *hālam* (8)
beat (1)
laid low (1)
smashed (1)
strike (1)
strikes (1)
struck (1)
thundered (1)
trampled down (1)

2151 הֲלֹם *hᵃlōm* (12)
here (4)
this far (2) +6330
in all directions (1)
now (1)
over here (1)
to (1)
untranslated (2)

2152 הֵלֶם *hēlem* (1)
Helem (1)

2153 הַלְמוּת *halmût̲* (1)
hammer (1)

2154 1הָם *hām1* (1)
Ham (1)

2155 2הָם *hām2* (1)
wealth (1)

2156 הֵם *hēm* (562)
they (321)
those (39)
them (14)
these (13)
that (10)
who (6)
it (5)
themselves (4)
things[s] (3)
men[s] (2)
such[s] (2)
the gatekeepers[s] (2)
this (2)
all[s] (1)
his net[s] (1)
Israelites[s] (1)
our own[s] (1)
people[s] (1)
the (1)
the Benjamites[s] (1)
the Israelites[s] (1)
the others[s] (1)
the people[s] (1)
the places[s] (1)
the priests[s] (1)
the spies[s] (1)
their idols[s] (1)
those same (1)
yet (1) +2021+2021+3427+6330
you (1)
untranslated (122)

2157 ־הֶם *-hem* (3048)
them (1103)
their (915)
they (116)
the[s] (54)
their (35) +4200
themselves (27)
their own (20)
those (18)
the people[s] (11)
it (9)
these (7)
whose (7)
men[s] (6)
who (6)
her (5)
his (5)
its (5)
their own (5) +4200
theirs (4)
which (4)
whom (4)
him (3)
Israel[s] (3)
Moses and Aaron[s] (3)
my people[s] (3)
the idols[s] (3)
the Israelites[s] (3)
theirs (3) +4200
a[s] (2)
each (2)
its own (2)

people^{s} (2)
the (2)
the Gibeonites^{s} (2)
the Hagrites^{s} (2)
the posts^{s} (2)
them^{s} (2) +4053
these^{s} (2)
you (2)
your (2)
both^{s} (1)
doing so^{s} (1)
each other^{s} (1) +9109
Elijah and Elisha^{s} (1) +9109
enemies^{s} (1)
his descendants^{s} (1)
his followers^{s} (1)
his precepts^{s} (1)
Israelites^{s} (1)
it^{s} (1)
itself (1)
lovers^{s} (1)
man's^{s} (1)
my accusers^{s} (1)
nephews (1) +1201
officials^{s} (1)
one kind after another (1) +4200+5476
one^{s} (1) +4200
others^{s} (1) +4946
people from Benjamin (1) +278
people from Judah (1) +278
priests^{s} (1) +278
related^{s} (1)
such things^{s} (1)
that (1)
the Ammonites^{s} (1)
the bodies^{s} (1)
the brothers^{s} (1)
the cherubim^{s} (1)
the Egyptians^{s} (1)
the envoys^{s} (1)
the gatekeepers^{s} (1)
the heavens^{s} (1)
the Hebronites^{s} (1)
the Kohathite^{s} (1)
the Levites^{s} (1)
the man and the woman^{s} (1)
the men^{s} (1)
the messengers^{s} (1)
the Philistines^{s} (1)
the pots^{s} (1)
the procession^{s} (1)
the sea^{s} (1)
the shepherds^{s} (1)
the spies^{s} (1)
the stands^{s} (1)
the storehouses^{s} (1) +889+928+3972
the storerooms^{s} (1)
the waters (1)
their (1) +448
their (1) +928+4090
their (1) +4946
their (1) +6584
their own (1) +7156
theirs (1) +4946
them^{s} (1) +466
them^{s} (1) +8533
themselves (1) +7156
there^{s} (1) +928
there^{s} (1) +6584
these days^{s} (1)
these men^{s} (1)
these things^{s} (1)
this threat^{s} (1)
thorns^{s} (1)
those Israelites^{s} (1)
us (1) +2256+3276
where^{s} (1) +6584
women^{s} (1)
your troops^{s} (1)
untranslated (567)

2158 הַמְּדָתָא *hamm^{e}dāṯā'* (5)
Hammedatha (5)

2159 הָמָה *hāmāh* (34)
roar (5)
disturbed (3)
laments (3)
loud (2)
rage (2)
roaring (2)
snarling (2)
astir (1)
brawler (1)
bustles about (1)
cry out (1)
groaned (1)
growl (1)
in uproar (1)
moaning (1)
noise (1) +7754
noisy (1)
pound (1)
pounds (1)
raging (1)
tumult (1)
yearns (1)

2160 הֵמָּה *hēmmāh*
Variant; not used

2161 ־הֵמָה *-hēmāh* (1)
the^{s} (1)

2162 הָמוֹן *hāmôn* (84)
hordes (18)
army (11)
crowd (7)
wealth (5)
many (4)
all (2) +3972
commotion (2)
masses (2)
multitudes (2)
noise (2)
noisy (2)
roar (2)
vast army (2)
abundance (1)
army (1) +2657
clamor (1)
confusion (1)
great amount (1)
heavy (1)
it^{s} (1) +2021
large (1)
multitude (1)
people (1)
populace (1)
raging (1)
roaring (1)
rumble (1)
tenderness (1) +5055
throng (1)
thunder (1)
troops (1)
tumult (1)
turmoil (1)
uproar (1) +7754
untranslated (2)

2163 הֲמוֹן גּוֹג *h^{a}môn gôg* (2)
Hamon Gog (2)

2164 הֲמוֹנָה *h^{a}mônāh* (1)
Hamonah (1)

2165 הַמַּחְלְקוֹת *hammaḥl^{e}qôṯ*
Variant; not used

2166 הֶמְיָה *hemyāh* (1)
noise (1)

2167 הֲמֻלָּה *h^{a}mullāh* (2)
storm (1)
tumult (1) +7754

2168 הַמֹּלֶכֶת *hammōleḵeṯ* (1)
Hammoleketh (1)

2169 1הָמַם *hāmam1* (17)
routed (3)
threw into confusion (2)
drives over (1)
eliminated (1)
resounds (1)
rout (1)
ruin (1)
threw into a panic (1)
throw into confusion (1)
throwing into confusion (1) +4539
thrown into confusion (1)
troubling (1)
untranslated (2)

2170 2הָמַם *hāmam2*
Variant; not used

2171 הָמַן *hāman* (1)
unruly (1)

2172 הָמָן *hāmān* (54)
Haman (43)
Haman's (5)
he^{s} (5)
untranslated (1)

2173 הֲמָסִים *h^{a}māsiym* (1)
twigs (1)

2174 הַמִּצְפֶּה *hammispeh*
Variant; not used

2175 הַמַּרְכָּבוֹת *hammarkāḇôṯ*
Variant; not used

2176 1הֵן *hēn1* (100)
if (15)
but (7)
surely (7)
see (6)
look (4)
now (4)
when (4)
since (2)
though (2)
yet (2)
agreed (1)
but if (1)
even (1)
for (1)
full well (1)
here (1)
oh (1)
only (1)
what if (1)
untranslated (38)

2177 ־הֶן *-hen* (183)&
their (77)
them (46)
they (8)
the^{s} (3)
it (2)
its (2)
their (2) +4200
their own (2)
both^{s} (1)
lead to do the same^{s} (1) +339+466+2388
the girls^{s} (1)
the rooms^{s} (1)
the woman and her sister^{s} (1)
theirs (1)
these^{s} (1)
things (1)
where^{s} (1) +928
which (1)
which^{s} (1)
untranslated (30)

2178 1הֵנָּה *hēnnāh1* (51)
here (25)
left^{s} (2)
now (2)
right^{s} (2)
back and forth (1) +285+285+2178+2256

here (1) +2025
here (1) +6330
in any direction (1) +2178+2256
nearby (1)
on this side (1)
opposite (1)
since (1) +6330
the present time (1)
then (1)
there (1)
this (1)
this day^{s} (1)
thus far (1) +6330
toward it (1)
yet (1) +6330
untranslated (2)

2179 2הֵנָּה *hēnnāh2* (47)
they (8)
these (5)
them (4)
things^{s} (2)
those (2)
both (1)
cows^{s} (1)
given even more (1) +2179+2256+3578+3869+3869
people^{s} (1)
plans^{s} (1)
such (1)
their (1) +4200
themselves (1)
what is the meaning (1) +4537
untranslated (16)

2180 הִנֵּה *hinnēh* (1061)
see (81)
look (61)
here (57)
there (57)
saw (43)
now (33)
if (28)
surely (24)
found (12)
yes (9)
how (6)
indeed (6)
listen (6)
suddenly (6)
but (5)
this (4)
beware (3)
even (3)
that (3)
already (2)
appeared (2)
as soon as (2)
discovered (2)
just (2)
just then (2) +2256
remember (2)
so (2)
suppose (2)
very well (2)
very well then (2)
what (2)
when (2)
after all (1)
all at once (1) +2296
be sure (1)
behold (1)
certainly (1)
come (1)
come then (1)
consider (1)
for (1)
heard (1)
here now (1)
it is still there (1)
just as (1)
meanwhile (1)
nevertheless (1)
not (1)
now then (1)
ready (1)
ready to do (1)
realized (1)
right now (1)
showed (1)
since (1)
soon (1)
suddenly appeared (1)
sure (1)
surely (1) +3954
then (1)
therefore (1)
think (1)
this is how (1)
this is why (1)
though (1)
too (1)
unless (1)
very well (1) +5528
well (1)
what can do (1)
untranslated (550)

2181 הֵנָה- *-h^{e}nāh* (3)&
its (1)
them (1)
they (1)

2182 הֲנָחָה *h^{a}nāḥāh* (1)
holiday (1)

2183 הִנֹּם *hinnōm* (3)
Hinnom (3)

2184 הֵנַע *hēna'* (3)
Hena (3)

2185 הֲנָפָה *h^{a}nāp̱āh*
Variant; not used

2186 הַנֶּקֶב *hanneqeḇ*
Variant; not used

2187 הַס *has* (7)
be silent (2)
be still (2)
hush (1)
quiet (1)
silence (1)

2188 הָסָה *hāsāh* (1)
silenced (1)

2189 הַסְּנָאָה *hass^{e}nā'āh* (1)
Hassenaah (1)

2190 הַסְּנֻאָה *hass^{e}nu'āh* (2)
Hassenuah (2)

2191 הַסֹּפֶרֶת *hassōp̱ereṯ* (1)
Hassophereth (1)

2192 הָעֲבָרִים *hā'^{a}ḇāriym*
Variant; not used

2193 הָעֵזֶר *hā'ēzer*
Variant; not used

2194 הָעַמֹּנִי *hā'ammōniy*
Variant; not used

2195 הָעֵמֶק *hā'ēmeq*
Variant; not used

2196 הָעֲרָבָה *hā'^{a}rāḇāh*
Variant; not used

2197 הָעֲרָלוֹת *hā'^{a}rālôṯ*
Variant; not used

2198 הֲפֻגָה *h^{a}p̱ugāh* (1)
relief (1)

2199 הַפּוּךְ *happûḵ*
Variant; not used

2200 הָפַךְ *hāp̱aḵ* (94)
turned (21)
turn (8)
overthrew (5)
changed (4)
overthrow (4)
be changed (2)
be turned (2)
turned back (2)
was changed (2)
wheel around (2) +3338
are (1)
be brought (1)
be overturned (1)
been turned over (1)
came tumbling (1)
change (1)
changed (1) +337
deceitful (1)
devastate (1)
distort (1)
disturbed (1)
flashing back and forth (1)
got down (1)
is transformed (1)
lays bare (1)
left (1)
overcome (1)
overthrown (1)
overthrows (1)
overturn (1)
overturned (1) +2025+4200+5087
overturns (1)
overwhelm (1)
purify (1) +1359
restore (1)
routed (1) +6902
swirl (1)
takes shape (1)
the tables were turned (1)
turn into (1)
turned about (1) +3338
turned and became (1)
turned around (1)
turned into (1)
turned over (1)
turning (1)
turns (1)
unreliable (1)
was overcome (1)
was overthrown (1)
was sapped (1)
was turned (1)

2201 הֵפֶךְ *hēpeḵ* (3)
opposite (1)
turn upside down (1)
very opposite (1)

2202 הֲפֵכָה *h^{a}pēḵāh* (1)
catastrophe (1)

2203 הֲפַכְפַּךְ *h^{a}p̱akp̱aḵ* (1)
devious (1)

2204 הַפִּצֵּץ *happiṣṣēṣ* (1)
Happizzez (1)

2205 הֻצַּב *huṣṣaḇ*
Variant; not used

2206 הַצֹּבֵבָה *haṣṣōḇēḇāh* (1)
Hazzobebah (1)

2207 הַצְּבָיִים *haṣṣ^{e}ḇāyiym*
Variant; not used

2208 הַצָּלָה *haṣṣālāh* (1)
deliverance (1)

2209 הַצְלֶלְפּוֹנִי *haṣṣ^{e}lelpôniy* (1)
Hazzelelponi (1)

2210 הֹצֶן *hōṣen* (1)
weapons (1)

2211 הַצֻּרִים *haṣṣuriym*
Variant; not used

2212 הַקּוֹץ *haqqôṣ* (5)
Hakkoz (5)

2213 הַקּוֹרֵא *haqqôrē'*
Variant; not used

2214 הַקָּטָן *haqqāṭān* (1)
Hakkatan (1)

2215 הַר *har* (560)
mountains (143)
mount (119)
mountain (114)
hill country (82)
hills (40)
hill (32)
mountain shrines (4)
mountaintops (4) +8031
it[s] (3) +2021
another[s] (1) +2021+2296+4946
hillside (1)
hillside (1) +7521
hilltop (1)
hilltop (1) +8031
hilltops (1) +8031
it[s] (1) +1628
mountain clefts (1)
mountain haunts (1)
mountain regions (1)
mountaintop (1) +8031
range (1)
there (1) +928+2021
there[s] (1) +928+2021
untranslated (5)

2216 הֹר *hōr* (12)
Hor (12)

2217 הָרָא *hārā'* (1)
Hara (1)

2218 הָרֹאֶה *hārō'eh* (1)
Haroeh (1)

2219 הַרְאֵל *har'ēl* (1)
altar hearth (1)

2220 הַרְבָּה *harbāh*
Variant; not used

2221 הַרְבֵּה *harbēh* (50)
much (10)
many (8)
great (4)
great quantity (4) +4394
more (3)
quantities (2)
abundance (1)
abundance (1) +4394
abundant supply (1)
all (1)
extensive (1)
full (1)
great (1) +4394
great numbers (1) +4394
greatly (1)
greatly (1) +4394
large (1)
large amount (1) +4394
large number (1)
overrighteous (1) +7404
overwicked (1) +8399
seldom (1) +4202
so much (1)
very (1) +4394
wept bitterly (1) +1134+1135

2222 הָרַג *hārag* (167)
killed (53)
kill (46)
slain (9)
put to death (7)
killing (6)
murdered (4)
slay (4)
kills (3)
put (3)
destroyed (2)
slaughter (2)
slayer (2)
be killed (1)
be ravaged (1)
been killed (1)
destroy (1)
destroying (1)
executed (1)
face death (1)
murder (1)
murderer (1)
murderers (1)
murdering (1)
murders (1)
must certainly put to death (1) +2222
put to death (1) +2222
put to death (1) +4638
ravage (1)
slaughter (1) +4200+5422
slaughter takes place (1) +2223
slaughtered (1)
slaughtering (1)
slew (1)
untranslated (3)

2223 הֶרֶג *hereg* (5)
slaughter (2)
killed (1)
killing (1)
slaughter takes place (1) +2222

2224 הֲרֵגָה *hᵃrēgāh* (5)
slaughter (5)

2225 הָרָה *hārāh* (45)
conceived (16)
pregnant (16)
conceive (7)
with child (2)
conceives (1)
gave birth (1)
is born (1)
untranslated (1)

2226 הָרֶה *hāreh* (12)
pregnant (7)
with child (2)
enlarged (1)
expectant mothers (1)
pregnant women (1)

2227 הָרוּם *hārûm* (1)
Harum (1)

2228 הֵרוֹן *hērôn* (1)
childbearing (1)

2229 הֲרוֹרִי *hᵃrôriy* (1)
Harorite (1)

2230 הָרִיָּה *hāriyyāh* (1)
pregnant women (1)

2231 הֵרָיוֹן *hērāyôn* (2)
conceive (1)
conception (1)

2232 הֲרִיסָה *hᵃriysāh* (1)
ruins (1)

2233 הֲרִיסוּת *hᵃriysûṯ* (1)
waste (1)

2234 הָרָם *hārām*
Variant; not used

2235 הֹרָם *hōrām* (1)
Horam (1)

2236 הַרְמוֹן *harmôn* (1)
Harmon (1)

2237 הָרָן *hārān* (7)
Haran (7)

2238 הָרַס *hāras* (43)
tear down (7)
overthrow (3)
tears down (3)
broken down (2)
destroyed (2)
force way through (2)
in ruins (2)
torn down (2)
are torn down (1)
be overturned (1)
been broken down (1)
being destroyed (1)
break (1)
break down (1)
demolish (1)
demolished (1)
destroy (1)
is destroyed (1)
laid waste (1) +2256+2990
left in ruins (1)
must demolish (1) +2238
ousted (1)
overthrew (1)
overthrown (1)
pull down (1)
threw down (1)
was destroyed (1)

2239 הֶרֶס *heres* (1)
destruction (1)

2240 הֲרָרִי *hᵃrāriy* (5)
Hararite (5)

2241 הַשַּׁחַר *haššahar*
Variant; not used

2242 הַשִּׁטָּה *haššiṭṭāh*
Variant; not used

2243 הַשִּׁטִּים *haššiṭṭiym*
Variant; not used

2244 הָשֵׁם *hāšēm* (1)
Hashem (1)

2245 הַשְׁמָעוּת *hašmā'ûṯ* (1)
news (1) +265

2246 הַתַּאֲוָה *hata'ᵃwāh*
Variant; not used

2247 הִתּוּךְ *hitûḵ* (1)
melted (1)

2248 הִתְחַבְּרוּת *hiṯhabbᵉrûṯ*
Variant; not used

2249 הִתְיַחֵשׂ *hityahēś*
Variant; not used

2250 הַתִּיכוֹן *hatiyḵôn*
Variant; not used

2251 הֲתָךְ *hᵃṯāḵ* (4)
Hathach (3)
him[s] (1)

2252 הָתַל *hāṯal* (1)
taunt (1)

2253 הֲתֻלִים *hᵃṯuliym* (1)
mockers (1)

2254 הָתַת *hāṯaṯ*
Variant; not used

2255 ו *w*
Variant; not used

2256 וְ- *wᵉ*- (50531)
and (19275)
but (1877)
then (1821)
so (1179)
or (931)
when (596)
with (333)
also (251)
now (246)
so that (236)

that (175)
yet (143)
while (113)
nor (109) +4202
and then (91)
as (89)
for (88)
after (77)
both and (76)
however (73)
together with (73)
nor (70)
and when (64)
as for (61)
if (60)
therefore (58)
and also (56)
even (56)
and (53) +1685
along with (48)
and so (44)
as well as (41)
because (41)
including (40)
though (39)
also (26) +1685
but when (25)
twenty-five (23) +2822+6929
even though (22)
again (20)
since (19)
instead (18)
in this way (17)
meanwhile (17)
until (17)
even (15) +1685
twenty-two (15) +6929+9109
24,000 (14) +547+752+6929
25,000 (14) +547+2822+6929
all generations (14) +1887+1887
at this (14)
nor (14) +440
or (14) +4202
thus (13)
both (12)
but as for (12)
although (11)
and now (11)
next (11)
250 (10) +2822+4395
and yet (10)
but also (10)
include (10)
on each side (10) +4946+4946+7024+7024
only (10)
till (10)
whether or (10)
nevertheless (9)
too (9)
twenty-fourth (9) +752+6929
4,500 (8) +547+752+2822+4395
and that (8)
moreover (8)
moreover (8) +1685
and as well (7)
and though (7)
and too (7)
either or (7)
finally (7)
twenty-third (7) +6929+8993
uttered (7) +606+5951
and (6) +677
besides (6)
but now (6)
but then (6)
on both sides[s] (6) +2296+2296+4946+4946
thirty-three (6) +8993+8993
thirty-two (6) +8993+9109
twenty-seventh (6) +6929+8679
twenty-three (6) +6929+8993
whenever (6)
120 (5) +4395+6929
but (5) +219
even if (5)
forty-two (5) +752+9109
indeed (5)
just as (5)
or (5) +561
sent for (5) +4200+7924+8938
to (5)
twenty-four (5) +752+6929
twenty-nine (5) +6929+9596
1,254 (4) +547+752+2822+4395
128 (4) +4395+6929+9046
afterward (4)
and after (4)
before (4)
called together (4) +665+8938
eighty-five (4) +2822+9046
forty-one (4) +285+752
go (4) +2143+8740
nor (4) +401
now that (4)
on (4)
on either side (4) +4946+4946+7024+7024
one day (4)
one day (4) +2118
or (4) +1685
so when (4)
that is (4)
that is why (4)
too (4) +1685
twenty-eight (4) +6929+9046
twenty-first (4) +285+6929
twenty-one (4) +285+6929
yes (4)
127 (3) +2256+4395+6929+8679
29 (3) +6929+9596
32 (3) +8993+9109
36,000 (3) +547+8993+9252
40,500 (3) +547+752+2822+4395
430 (3) +752+4395+8993
53,400 (3) +547+752+2256+2822+4395+8993
603,550 (3) +547+547+2256+2256+2822+2822+4395+4395+8993+9252
after that (3)
and afterward (3)
and even (3)
and since (3)
as soon as (3)
as well as (3) +1685
between (3) +4946+6330
each people (3) +6639+6639
each province (3) +4519+4519
eleven hundred (3) +547+4395
fifty-two (3) +2822+9109
find out (3) +3359+8011
forty-five (3) +752+2822
generations (3) +1887+1887
in (3)
neither (3) +4202
now (3) +1685
otherwise (3)
parents (3) +3+562
see (3) +3359+8011
sent for (3) +7924+8938
seventy-five (3) +2822+8679
seventy-seven (3) +8679+8679
so then (3)
then (3) +1685
then when (3)
thirty-five (3) +2822+8993
thirty-ninth (3) +8993+9596
thirty-one (3) +285+8993
thirty-seventh (3) +8679+8993
twenty-fifth (3) +2822+6929
1,052 (2) +547+2822+9109
1,247 (2) +547+752+4395+8679
1,775 (2) +547+2256+2256+2822+4395+8679+8679
112 (2) +4395+6925+9109
123 (2) +4395+6929+8993
130 (2) +4395+8993
137 (2) +2256+4395+8679+8993
150 (2) +2822+4395
220 (2) +4395+6929
223 (2) +4395+6929+8993
30,500 (2) +547+2822+4395+8993
32,200 (2) +547+2256+4395+8993+9109
320 (2) +4395+6929+8993
345 (2) +752+2822+4395+8993
35,400 (2) +547+752+2256+2822+4395+8993
372 (2) +4395+8679+8993+9109
390 (2) +4395+8993+9596
392 (2) +4395+8993+9109+9596
4,600 (2) +547+752+4395+9252
403 (2) +752+4395+8993
41,500 (2) +285+547+752+2256+2822+4395
42 (2) +752+9109
435 (2) +752+2822+4395+8993
45,650 (2) +547+752+2256+2256+2822+2822+4395+9252
46,500 (2) +547+752+2256+2822+4395+9252
52 (2) +2822+9109
54,400 (2) +547+752+752+2256+2822+4395
57,400 (2) +547+752+2256+2822+4395+8679
59,300 (2) +547+2256+2822+4395+8993+9596
6,720 (2) +547+4395+6929+8679+9252
62,700 (2) +547+2256+4395+8679+9109+9252
621 (2) +285+4395+6929+9252
65 (2) +2822+9252
652 (2) +2822+4395+9109+9252
666 (2) +4395+9252+9252+9252
7,337 (2) +547+4395+8679+8679+8993+8993
74 (2) +752+8679
74,600 (2) +547+752+2256+4395+8679+9252
760 (2) +4395+8679+9252
95 (2) +2822+9596
973 (2) +4395+8679+8993+9596
98 (2) +9046+9596
altogether (2) +465
and because (2)
and included (2)
and so that (2)
anywhere else (2) +625+625+2025+2025
as surely as (2)
at either end[s] (2) +2296+2296+4946+4946
at that time (2)
became more and more powerful (2) +1524+2143+2143
besides (2) +1685
beyond (2) +2134+4946
but (2) +1685
but even (2)
differing weights (2) +74+74
each dish (2) +4094+4094
each gate (2) +9133+9133
each lampstand (2) +4963+4963
even when (2)
far and wide (2) +2085+2134+4946
fifty-five (2) +2822+2822
followed by (2)
forty-eight (2) +752+9046
fourteen hundred (2) +547+752+4395
from (2)
fully accomplishes (2) +6913+7756
furthermore (2)
head (2) +2025+4946+5087+8900
here (2)
how (2)
imported (2) +3655+6590
in turn (2)
included (2)
indeed (2) +1685
just then (2) +2180

led in campaigns (2) +995+3655+4200+7156
led on military campaigns (2) +995+3655
neither (2)
nevertheless (2) +219
ninety-nine (2) +9596+9596
ninety-six (2) +9252+9596
nor (2) +1153
now when (2)
or (2) +3954
rather than (2) +4202
rebuilt (2) +1215+8740
send for (2) +4374+8938
seventeen hundred (2) +547+4395+8679
sixty-six (2) +9252+9252
sixty-two (2) +9109+9252
slaves (2) +6269+9148
so (2) +1685
still (2)
summoned (2) +7924+8938
them[s] (2) +2286+7518
therefore (2) +1685
thirty-eight (2) +8993+9046
thirty-eighth (2) +8993+9046
thirty-second (2) +8993+9109
thirty-seven (2) +8679+8993
together with (2) +1685
too (2) +677
treaty of friendship (?) +3208+8934
twenty-second (2) +6929+9109
twenty-seven (2) +6929+8679
us (2) +3276+3870
various kinds of service (2) +6275+6275
where (2)
wherever goes (2) +928+928+995+3655
with the help of (2)
yes (2) +1685
yet (2) +1685
1,017 (1) +547+6925+8679
1,222 (1) +547+4395+6929+9109
1,290 (1) +547+4395+9596
1,335 (1) +547+2822+4395+8993+8993
1,365 (1) +547+2256+2256 +2822+4395+8993+9252
1,760 (1) +547+2256+4395+8679+9252
105 (1) +2822+4395
108,100 (1) +547+547+2256+4395+4395+9046
110 (1) +4395+6927
119 (1) +4395+6926+9596
120,000 (1) +547+4395+6929
122 (1) +2256+4395+6929+9109
122 (1) +4395+6929+9109
133 (1) +2256+4395+8993+8993
138 (1) +4395+8993+9046
139 (1) +4395+8993+9596
14,700 (1) +547+752+4395+6925+8679
148 (1) +752+4395+9046
151,450 (1) +285+547+547+752+2256 +2256+2256+2822+2822+4395+4395
153,600 (1) +547+547+2256+2256 +2822+4395+4395+8993+9252
156 (1) +2822+4395+9252
157,600 (1) +547+547+2256+2256 +2822+4395+4395+8679+9252
16,750 (1) +547+2822+4395+6925+8679+9252
160 (1) +4395+9252
162 (1) +2256+4395+9109+9252
17,200 (1) +547+4395+6925+8679
172 (1) +4395+8679+9109
180 (1) +4395+9046
180,000 (1) +547+4395+9046
182 (1) +2256+4395+9046+9109
186,400 (1) +547+547+547+752+2256 +2256+4395+4395+9046+9252
187 (1) +2256+4395+8679+9046
188 (1) +4395+9046+9046
2,056 (1) +547+2822+9252
2,067 (1) +547+8679+9252
2,172 (1) +547+2256+4395+8679+9109
2,172 (1) +547+4395+8679+9109
2,200 (1) +547+4395
2,300 (1) +547+4395+8993
2,322 (1) +547+4395+6929+8993+9109
2,400 (1) +547+752+4395
2,600 (1) +547+4395+9252
2,630 (1) +547+2256+4395+8993+9252
2,750 (1) +547+2822+4395+8679
2,812 (1) +547+4395+6925+9046+9109
2,818 (1) +547+4395+6925+9046+9046
20,200 (1) +547+4395+6929
20,800 (1) +547+4395+6929+9046
205 (1) +2822+4395
207 (1) +4395+8679
209 (1) +4395+9596
212 (1) +4395+6925+9109
218 (1) +4395+6925+9046
22 (1) +6929+9109
22,000 (1) +547+6929+9109
22,034 (1) +547+752+2256+2256+6929+8993+9109
22,200 (1) +547+2256+4395+6929+9109
22,273 (1) +547+2256+2256+4395 +6929+8679+8993+9109
22,600 (1) +547+2256+4395+6929+9109+9252
23,000 (1) +547+6929+8993
232 (1) +4395+8993+9109
242 (1) +752+4395+9109
245 (1) +752+2256+2822+4395
245 (1) +752+2822+4395
25,100 (1) +547+2256+2822+4395+6929
26,000 (1) +547+6929+9252
273 (1) +2256+4395+8679+8993
28 (1) +6929+9046
28,600 (1) +547+2256+4395+6929+9046+9252
280,000 (1) +547+4395+9046
284 (1) +752+4395+9046
288 (1) +4395+9046+9046
3,023 (1) +547+2256+6929+8993+8993
3,200 (1) +547+4395+8993
3,600 (1) +547+4395+8993+9252
3,630 (1) +547+2256+4395+8993+8993+9252
3,700 (1) +547+4395+8679+8993
3,930 (1) +547+4395+8993+8993+9596
307,500 (1) +547+547+2256 +2822+4395+4395+8679+8993
318 (1) +4395+6925+8993+9046
32,000 (1) +547+8993+9109
32,500 (1) +547+2256+2822+4395+8993+9109
323 (1) +4395+6929+8993+8993
324 (1) +752+4395+6929+8993
328 (1) +4395+6929+8993+9046
337,500 (1) +547+547+547+2256+2256 +2822+4395+4395+8679+8993+8993
337,500 (1) +547+547+547+2256 +2822+4395+4395+8679+8993+8993
34 (1) +752+8993
35 (1) +2822+8993
350 (1) +2822+4395+8993
365 (1) +2256+2822+4395+8993+9252
37,000 (1) +547+8679+8993
410 (1) +752+4395+6927
42,360 (1) +547+752+4395+8052+8993+9252
420 (1) +752+4395+6929
43,730 (1) +547+752+2256+2256 +4395+8679+8993+8993
44,760 (1) +547+752+752 +2256+2256+4395+8679+9252
45,400 (1) +547+752+752+2256+2822+4395
45,600 (1) +547+752+2256+2822+4395+9252
454 (1) +752+752+2822+4395
468 (1) +752+4395+9046+9252
5,400 (1) +547+752+2822+4395
52,700 (1) +547+2256+2822+4395+8679+9109
530 (1) +2822+4395+8993
550 (1) +2822+2822+4395
56 (1) +2822+9252
595 (1) +2256+2822+2822+4395+9596
6,200 (1) +547+4395+9252
6,800 (1) +547+4395+9046+9252
60,500 (1) +547+2822+4395+9252
601,730 (1) +547+547+2256 +4395+4395+8679+8993+9252
61 (1) +285+9252
61,000 (1) +285+547+9252
61,000 (1) +547+8052+9252
62 (1) +9109+9252
623 (1) +4395+6929+8993+9252
628 (1) +4395+6929+9046+9252
64,300 (1) +547+752+2256+4395+8993+9252
64,400 (1) +547+752+752+2256+4395+9252
642 (1) +752+2256+4395+9109+9252
642 (1) +752+4395+9109+9252
648 (1) +752+4395+9046+9252
650 (1) +2822+4395+9252
655 (1) +2822+2822+4395+9252
666 (1) +2256+4395+9252+9252+9252
667 (1) +4395+8679+9252+9252
67 (1) +8679+9252
675 (1) +2822+4395+8679+9252
675,000 (1) +547+547+547 +2256+2822+4395+8679+9252
690 (1) +4395+9252+9596
7,100 (1) +547+4395+8679
7,500 (1) +547+2822+4395+8679
72 (1) +8679+9109
72,000 (1) +547+8679+9109
721 (1) +285+2256+4395+6929+8679
725 (1) +2822+4395+6929+8679
730 (1) +4395+8679+8993
736 (1) +4395+8679+8993+9252
743 (1) +752+2256+4395+8679+8993
743 (1) +752+4395+8679+8993
745 (1) +752+2822+4395+8679
76,500 (1) +547+2256+2822+4395+8679+9252
775 (1) +2822+4395+8679+8679
777 (1) +2256+4395+8679+8679+8679
782 (1) +2256+4395+8679+9046+9109
8,580 (1) +547+2256+2822+4395+9046+9046
8,600 (1) +547+4395+9046+9252
807 (1) +4395+8679+9046
815 (1) +2822+4395+6926+9046
822 (1) +4395+6929+9046+9109
830 (1) +4395+8993+9046
832 (1) +4395+8993+9046+9109
840 (1) +752+4395+9046
845 (1) +752+2822+4395+9046
87,000 (1) +547+8679+9046
895 (1) +2256+2822+4395+9046+9596
905 (1) +2822+4395+9596
910 (1) +4395+6924+9596
912 (1) +4395+6926+9109+9596
928 (1) +4395+6929+9046+9596
930 (1) +4395+8993+9596
945 (1) +752+2256+2822+4395+9596
950 (1) +2822+4395+9596
956 (1) +2256+2822+4395+9252+9596
962 (1) +2256+4395+9109+9252+9596
969 (1) +2256+4395+9252+9596+9596
accompanied by (1)
adding to (1) +907
after (1) +1685
after this (1)
again and again (1) +8899+8938
age-old (1) +1887+1887
all time (1) +1887+1887
along with (1) +1685
also (1) +677
also included (1)
alternate[s] (1) +2298+7194+8232
alternated[s] (1) +7194+8232
always (1) +1887+1887+4200
and (1) +255

and (1) +907
and (1) +6330
and again (1)
and alike (1)
and after (1)
and as (1)
and as for (1)
and either (1)
and even after (1)
and even though (1)
and likewise (1)
and still (1)
and that is why (1)
and what about (1)
and whenever (1)
and with (1)
annually (1) +928+3972+9102+9102
anywhere (1) +625+625+2025+2025
army (1) +6639+7736
as far as (1)
as surely as live (1) +2644+2644+5883
as well (1)
as well as (1) +3869
assassinated (1) +4637+5782
at that (1)
back and forth (1) +285+285+2178+2178
be on way (1) +2143+5825
bearing (1)
beasts of burden (1) +989+2651
became more and more powerful (1) +1524+2143
because (1) +928+3610+3610
because (1) +4202
been brought to attention (1) +5583+9048
bordering each side[s] (1) +2296+2296+4946+4946
both of you (1) +2084+3870
both[s] (1) +170+2021+2021+8533
bring (1) +3655+4374
but (1) +3463
but (1) +8370
but even (1) +1685
but too (1)
but while (1)
by the time (1)
by then (1)
calling together (1) +995+8938
came back (1) +995+2143
carefully investigated (1) +1335+2011
carry out duties (1) +995+3655
carry the battle (1) +1741+8740
cities (1) +6551+6551
closer and closer (1) +2143+7929
commander-in-chief (1) +8031+8569
completely (1) +1414+4946+5883+6330
cover up (1) +4059+8740
crushed completely (1) +430+4730
deception (1) +4213+4213
did so[s] (1) +2932+4374+8008
differing measures (1) +406+406
each of us (1) +638+2085
each table (1) +8947+8947
each town (1) +6551+6551
eighteen thousand (1) +547+8052+9046
eighty-six (1) +9046+9252
eighty-three (1) +8993+9046
endless generations (1) +1887+1887
enslaved (1) +3899+4200+4200+6269+9148
especially (1)
even (1) +677
even (1) +677+3954
even then (1)
even while (1)
every city (1) +6551+6551
every day (1) +3427+3427+3972
every family (1) +5476+5476
every province (1) +4519+4519
except for (1) +4202
executed (1) +4637+5782
exorbitant interest (1) +5968+9552
experienced (1) +1981+9312
feasting (1) +430+9272
fifteen (1) +2822+6927
fifty-second (1) +2822+9109
finally (1) +1685
fine (1) +1524+3202
for instance (1)
forty-first (1) +285+752
forty-nine (1) +752+9596
forty-seven (1) +752+8679
fully obeyed (1) +6913+9048
furthermore (1) +1685
furthermore (1) +2021+9108
furthermore (1) +6388
furthermore (1) +6964
generations long past (1) +1887+1887+9102
generations to come (1) +1887+1887
given even more (1) +2179+2179+3578+3869+3869
go about business (1) +995+3655
go at once (1) +995+2143
go in (1) +995+2143
grapes or raisins (1) +3313+4300+6694
great wrath (1) +2405+7912
grew even wilder (1) +2143+6192
grew louder and louder (1) +2143+2618+4394
grew stronger and stronger (1) +2143+2618
grew stronger and stronger (1) +2143+7997
grew weaker and weaker (1) +1924+2143
had brought (1) +4374+8938
had executed (1) +4637+5782
had removed (1) +4374+8938
harem (1) +8721+8721
have to do with (1) +4200+4200
here is what (1) +2296+2296+3869+3869
how much more (1) +677+3954
however (1) +219
if then (1)
in addition (1)
in addition to (1)
in any direction (1) +2178+2178
in any direction (1) +3907+3907
in midair (1) +824+1068+1068+2021+2021+9028
in order for (1)
including (1) +1685
including and (1)
increased more and more (1) +2143+2143+8041
indeed (1) +677+3954
instead (1) +1685
interest of any kind (1) +5968+9552
invite (1) +7924+8938
joined (1) +1685
just who (1) +4769+4769
kills (1) +4637+5782+5883
kinds of cattle (1) +989+989
laid waste (1) +2238+2990
later (1)
lead (1) +995+3655
lead (1) +995+3655+4200+7156
lead on (1) +2143+5627
likewise (1)
made good escape (1) +4880+5674
man (1) +408+408
many generations (1) +1887+1887
many years (1) +3427+9102
marauding (1) +6296+8740
marries (1) +1249+4374
meanwhile (1) +3907+3907+6330+6330
melting away (1) +2143+4570
more and more powerful (1) +1541+2025+2143+4200+5087+6330
movements (1) +4569+4604
much too numerous (1) +6786+8041
neither (1) +440
never (1) +1153+6329+6409
nine-and-a-half (1) +2942+9596
ninety-eight (1) +9046+9596
no more than (1)
nor (1) +401+1685
nor (1) +401+4946
nor (1) +561
nor (1) +1685
nor (1) +1685+4202
nothing (1) +1524+1821+4202+7785
nothing at all (1) +401+700
nothing but skin (1) +1414+6425
now (1) +6964
numbers increased greatly (1) +7238+8049
obey (1) +6913+9068
on both (1) +2296+2296+4946+4946
on both sides (1) +294+7156
on both sides[s] (1) +2296+2296+4946
on duty (1) +995+3655
on each side[s] (1) +2296+2296+4946+4946
on the other side of (1) +2134+4946+6298
once more (1)
one of the other peoples (1) +6639+6639
or (1) +401+561
or (1) +440
or (1) +700
or even (1)
otherwise (1) +4202
over nine feet (1) +564+2455+9252
pay close attention (1) +7992+9048
please (1) +928+3202+3838+6524
provided for (1) +430+2118+4200+4312
raised (1) +5951+5989
raped (1) +6700+8886
rapes (1) +2616+6640+8886
rapes (1) +6640+8886+9530
rather (1)
rather (1) +1685
realize (1) +3359+8011
realized (1) +3359+8011
reappears (1) +7255+8740
rebuild (1) +1215+8740
recaptured (1) +4374+8740
receded steadily (1) +2143+8740+8740
recite (1) +606+6699
reentered (1) +995+8740
reopened (1) +2916+8740
return (1) +2143+7155
richest of foods (1) +2016+2693
roam (1) +2143+3718
rougher and rougher (1) +2143+6192
ruined (1) +2472+2476
say (1) +606+6699
scream for help (1) +7754+7924+8123
screamed for help (1) +7754+7924+8123
sent for (1) +4374+8938
sent word (1) +5583+8938
sent word (1) +7924+8938
serve (1) +995+3655
seventeen (1) +6927+8679
shining ever brighter (1) +239+2143
shouted (1) +5951+7754+7924
similarly (1)
sixty-eight (1) +9046+9252
sixty-five (1) +2822+9252
slaves (1) +563+6269
square (1) +802+8145
square (1) +4946+4946+7024+7024
staggering burden (1) +4842+7050
stared with a fixed gaze (1) +906+6641+7156+8492
stayed night (1) +3782+4328
still (1) +1685
strip off clothes (1) +6910+7320
summon (1) +4374+8938
suppose (1)
surely (1)
than (1) +1685
than (1) +4202
that (1) +1685
the parties (1) +408+2084+8276
the two of them[s] (1) +1189+1192
them[s] (1) +59+7401
then (1) +339
then (1) +6964
they[s] (1) +1201+1201+1514+8017

they^S (1) +1770+5083
they^S (1) +2021+2657+3405+8569
thirty-fifth (1) +2822+8993
thirty-first (1) +285+8993
thirty-six (1) +8993+9252
thirty-six hundred (1) +547+4395+8993+9252
thirty-sixth (1) +8993+9252
thirty-three hundred (1) +547+4395+8993+8993
through (1)
tightly shut up (1) +6037+6037
till (1) +677
time and again (1) +285+4202+4202+9109
to come (1) +1887+1887
together with (1) +677
together with (1) +6330
took back (1) +995+8938
travel about (1) +995+3655
tripping along with mincing steps (1) +2143+3262
twelve hundred (1) +547+4395
twenty-seven hundred (1) +547+4395+8679
twenty-six (1) +6929+9252
twenty-six hundred (1) +547+4395+9252
twenty-sixth (1) +6929+9252
two differing measures (1) +406+406
two differing weights (1) +74+74
two men (1) +278+408+3481
two-and-a-half (1) +2942+9109
undivided loyalty (1) +4202+4213+4213
upon (1)
us (1) +2157+3276
us (1) +3276+4013
utterly useless (1) +2039+8198
various gates (1) +9133+9133
various peoples (1) +6639+6639
various provinces (1) +4519+4519
violated (1) +6700+8886
what (1) +2296+2296+3869+3869
what (1) +2296+2297+3869+3869
what about (1)
when also (1)
whether (1)
whether (1) +700
who (1)
whoever he may be (1) +6424+6699
whole assembly (1) +6337+7736
with (1) +1685
with both (1)
yet (1) +677
yet (1) +6964
yet also (1)
young and old (1) +2025+5087
untranslated (20271)

2257 ־וֹ -ô (12080)
his (4456)
him (2172)
he (548)
it (499)
its (373)
the^S (338)
their (286)
them (182)
his own (140)
his (81) +4200
whose (56)
himself (55)
a^S (40)
her (36)
they (31)
whom (26)
your (26)
himself (18) +5883
his (13) +907
one (13)
who (13)
David^S (11)
that^S (11)
the altar^S (11)
himself (10) +1414
himself (10) +4213
its own (10)
the king^S (10)
the king's^S (10)
their own (10)
each (9)
them^S (9) +3
you (9)
God^S (8)
his own (8) +4200
those^S (8)
he (7) +5883
God's^S (6)
man's^S (6)
the man^S (6)
the LORD^S (6)
the value^S (5)
their^S (5) +1201
this^S (5)
Aaron^S (4)
an^S (4)
David's^S (4)
Elijah^S (4)
Elisha^S (4)
Gideon^S (4)
its (4) +4200
Jacob^S (4)
Jehoram^S (4)
Jehu^S (4)
Moses^S (4)
she (4)
the gateway^S (4)
their (4) +4200
there^S (4) +928
which (4)
Abram^S (3)
any^S (3)
anyone (3)
Eliakim's^S (3)
Jehoiachin^S (3)
Joseph^S (3)
Moses'^{S} (3)
my (3)
same^S (3)
Saul's^S (3)
Solomon^S (3)
there^S (3)
these^S (3)
whose (3) +4200
Aaron's^S (2)
Abraham^S (2)
Ahab^S (2)
Ahaziah^S (2)
alone (2) +928+1727
Amnon^S (2)
Gehazi^S (2)
he (2) +3338
here^S (2)
him^S (2) +3
his (2) +6640
Hosea^S (2)
Isaac^S (2)
Israel's^S (2)
Jehoiachin's^S (2)
Jehoram's^S (2)
Jeremiah^S (2)
Joab^S (2)
Joash^S (2)
Job's^S (2)
Joseph's^S (2)
Josiah^S (2)
Josiah's^S (2)
man^S (2)
Nebuchadnezzar^S (2)
Noah^S (2)
own (2)
owner (2) +4200
Saul^S (2)
she^S (2) +562
Solomon's^S (2)
the area^S (2)
the ark^S (2)
the king of the south^S (2)
the lamps^S (2)
the LORD's^S (2)
the man himself^S (2)
the man's^S (2)
the neighbor^S (2)
the person^S (2)
the table^S (2)
their own (2) +4200
them^S (2) +6269
they^S (2) +6269
tribe^S (2)
your own (2)
Zedekiah's^S (2)
Abijah's^S (1)
Abishai^S (1)
Abraham's^S (1)
Absalom's^S (1)
Achan^S (1)
Adonijah^S (1)
Ahab's^S (1)
Ahaz^S (1)
Amasa^S (1)
Amon's^S (1)
animal^S (1)
another^S (1)
any such thing^S (1)
Baal's^S (1)
Baruch^S (1)
Benaiah^S (1)
both^S (1)
by himself (1) +963+4200
by itself (1) +963+4200
consecrate himself (1) +3338+4848
creditor (1) +1251+3338+5408
daily (1) +928+3427+3427
day by day (1) +928+1821+3427+3427
did this^S (1) +3338+5742
did^S (1) +3338+5989
do that^S (1) +928+2118+3338
each (1) +278+408
each day's (1) +928+3427+3427
Egypt^S (1)
Ehud^S (1)
Eleazar^S (1)
Elisha's^S (1)
enemy^S (1)
equally (1) +278+408+3869
equally among them (1) +278+408+3869
every (1)
every^S (1)
God's name^S (1)
Gog^S (1)
Hadad^S (1)
Haman^S (1)
Hanun^S (1)
he himself (1)
Heman's^S (1)
her husband^S (1)
her son^S (1)
her^S (1) +123+831
her^S (1) +851
herself (1)
him (1) +3338
him (1) +5883
him^S (1) +3162
him^S (1) +6660
himself (1) +4222
himself (1) +8031
himself (1) +8638
himself (1) +9005
his (1) +928
his (1) +6584
his body^S (1)
his descendants^S (1)
his father's^S (1)
his father^S (1)
his neighbor^S (1)
his own (1) +4213+4946

his own (1) +5883
his^{S} (1) +3
inner sanctuary^{S} (1)
Israel^{S} (1)
it^{S} (1)
it^{S} (1) +623
it^{S} (1) +1947
it^{S} (1) +2308
it^{S} (1) +2942
it^{S} (1) +3338
it^{S} (1) +8031
it^{S} (1) +9005
its own (1) +5883
itself (1)
Jacob's^{S} (1)
Jehoahaz^{S} (1)
Jehoiakim's^{S} (1)
Jehu's^{S} (1)
Jeriah^{S} (1)
Jesse^{S} (1)
Jethro^{S} (1)
Joab's^{S} (1)
Job^{S} (1)
Joshua^{S} (1)
Judah's^{S} (1)
Laban^{S} (1)
Lot's^{S} (1)
Manasseh^{S} (1)
married (1) +851+4200+4200+4374
my companion^{S} (1)
my^{S} (1) +1201
Naaman's^{S} (1)
Naboth's^{S} (1)
Neco^{S} (1)
not circumcised (1) +4200+6889
Obed-Edom^{S} (1)
of his own (1) +3655+3751
one's (1)
one^{S} (1)
only (1) +928+1727
only one (1) +963+4200
opposite^{S} (1)
others^{S} (1)
Othniel^{S} (1)
person^{S} (1)
Pharaoh's^{S} (1)
pillar^{S} (1)
Potiphar^{S} (1)
Rehoboam^{S} (1)
relieve himself (1) +906+6114+8079
relieving himself (1) +906+6114+8079
riches^{S} (1)
royal^{S} (1)
Sennacherib's^{S} (1)
servant^{S} (1)
Shalmaneser's^{S} (1) +4200
Shaul's^{S} (1)
she^{S} (1) +851
she^{S} (1) +3304
she^{S} (1) +7108
Sheba^{S} (1)
Sherebiah's^{S} (1)
Shimei^{S} (1)
soldier^{S} (1)
someone (1)
someone's (1)
something^{S} (1)
stolen goods (1) +4200+4202
such^{S} (1)
that man's line^{S} (1)
that month^{S} (1)
that nation^{S} (1)
that person^{S} (1)
the angel^{S} (1)
the animal^{S} (1)
the article^{S} (1)
the basket^{S} (1)
the bells^{S} (1)
the Benjamites^{S} (1)
the boy's^{S} (1)
the boy^{S} (1)
the bread^{S} (1)
the calf^{S} (1)
the captain^{S} (1)
the cloud^{S} (1)
the coming storm^{S} (1)
the contaminated part^{S} (1)
the country^{S} (1)
the defender^{S} (1)
the enemy's^{S} (1)
the ephod^{S} (1)
the gold^{S} (1)
the grapes^{S} (1)
the injured man^{S} (1)
the lambs^{S} (1)
the offender^{S} (1)
the one (1)
the other half of Manasseh^{S} (1)
the other man^{S} (1)
the people^{S} (1)
the person (1)
the Philistine's^{S} (1)
the pillar^{S} (1)
the platform^{S} (1)
the pot^{S} (1)
the priest^{S} (1)
the rim^{S} (1)
the robe^{S} (1)
the scroll^{S} (1)
the servant^{S} (1)
the shore^{S} (1)
the slave^{S} (1)
the snake^{S} (1)
the successor^{S} (1)
the tribe^{S} (1)
the value^{S} (1)
the wicked^{S} (1)
the wood^{S} (1)
their^{S} (1)
theirs (1) +4200
them^{S} (1) +278
them^{S} (1) +6639
them^{S} (1) +7366
themselves (1) +5883
there^{S} (1) +824+928
there^{S} (1) +928+7931
there^{S} (1) +928+9348
they (1) +5883
they^{S} (1)
they^{S} (1) +1201
this (1)
this altar^{S} (1)
this god's^{S} (1)
this matter^{S} (1)
this^{S} (1) +3769+4202
Uzziah^{S} (1)
walled (1) +2570+4200
where^{S} (1) +928
which^{S} (1) +678
which^{S} (1) +7366
who^{S} (1)
whose^{S} (1) +465+1426
your (1) +928
your brother's^{S} (1)
your father^{S} (1)
your side^{S} (1)
your tithe^{S} (1)
yourself (1)
yourself (1) +4213
yourself (1) +5883
Zechariah's^{S} (1)
Zechariah^{S} (1)
untranslated (2076)

2258 וְדָן *w^{e}ḏān*
Variant; not used

2259 וָהֵב *wāhēḇ* (1)
Waheb (1)

2260 וָו *wāw* (13)
hooks (13)

2261 וָזָר *wāzār* (1)
guilty (1)

2262 וַיְזָתָא *wayzāṯā'* (1)
Vaizatha (1)

2263 וָלָד *wālāḏ* (1)
children (1)

2264 וַנְיָה *wanyāh* (1)
Vaniah (1)

2265 וָפְסִי *wop̱siy* (1)
Vophsi (1)

2266 וַשְׁנִי *wašniy*
Variant; not used

2267 וַשְׁתִּי *waštiy* (10)
Vashti (10)

2268 ז *z*
Variant; not used

2269 1זְאֵב *z^{e}'ēḇ1* (7)
wolf (4)
wolves (3)

2270 2זְאֵב *z^{e}'ēḇ2* (6)
Zeeb (6)

2271 זֹאת *zō'ṯ*
Variant; not used

2272 זָבַד *zāḇaḏ* (1)
presented (1)

2273 זֵבֶד *zēḇeḏ* (1)
gift (1)

2274 זָבָד *zāḇāḏ* (8)
Zabad (8)

2275 זַבְדִּי *zaḇdiy* (3)
Zabdi (3)

2276 זַבְדִּיאֵל *zaḇdiy'ēl* (2)
Zabdiel (2)

2277 זְבַדְיָה *z^{e}ḇaḏyāh* (6)
Zebadiah (6)

2278 זְבַדְיָהוּ *z^{e}ḇaḏyāhû* (3)
Zebadiah (3)

2279 זְבוּב *z^{e}ḇûḇ* (2)
flies (2)

2280 זָבוּד *zāḇûḏ* (2)
Zabud (1)
untranslated (1)

2281 זְבוּדָּה *z^{e}ḇûddāh* (1)
untranslated (1)

2282 זְבוּלוּן *z^{e}ḇûlûn* (45)
Zebulun (40)
Zebulun (5) +1201

2283 זְבוּלֹנִי *z^{e}ḇûlōniy* (3)
Zebulun (1)
Zebulunite (1)
untranslated (1)

2284 זָבַח *zāḇaḥ* (134)
sacrifice (39)
sacrificed (18)
offer sacrifices (17)
offered (10)
offer (9)
offered sacrifices (8)
sacrificing (6)
sacrifices (4)
slaughter (3)
slaughtered (3)
made sacrifices (2) +2285
preparing (2)
sacrifice (2) +2285
butchered (1)
do^{S} (1)
making (1)
offer sacrifice (1)

offered a sacrifice (1)
offering (1)
offering sacrifices (1)
offers (1)
sacrifices offer (1)
untranslated (2)

2285 1זֶבַח *zebah1* (162)
sacrifices (57)
sacrifice (47)
offering (24)
offerings (15)
sacrificed (13)
made sacrifices (2) +2284
sacrifice (2) +2284
feasting (1)
it^s (1) +8968

2286 2זֶבַח *zebah2* (12)
Zebah (10)
them^s (2) +2256+7518

2287 זַבַּי *zabbay* (2)
Zabbai (2)

2288 זְבִידָה *zᵉbiydāh* (1)
Zebidah (1)

2289 זְבִינָא *zᵉbiynā'* (1)
Zebina (1)

2290 זָבַל *zābal* (1)
treat with honor (1)

2291 1זְבֻל *zᵉbul1* (6)
Zebul (6)

2292 2זְבֻל *zᵉbul2* (5)
magnificent (2)
heavens (1)
lofty throne (1)
princely mansions (1)

2293 זָג *zāg* (1)
skins (1)

2294 זֵד *zēd* (13)
arrogant (10)
haughty (1)
proud (1)
willful sins (1)

2295 זָדוֹן *zādôn* (11)
pride (4)
arrogant (2)
arrogance (1)
conceited (1)
contempt (1)
overweening pride (1) +6301
presumptuously (1) +928

2296 זֶה *zeh* (1778)
this (1082)
these (109)
that (49)
this^s (44) +1821+2021+2021
today (39) +2021+2021+3427
here (17)
now (17) +2021+2021+3427
one (17)
such (16)
it (13)
here (12) +928
he (9)
where (9) +361
another^s (7)
on both sides^s (6) +2256+2296+4946+4946
this is how (6) +928
this very (6)
other^s (5)
what (5)
it^s (4) +1821+2021+2021
side^s (4)
the (4)
the other^s (4)
ever since (3) +2021+2021+3427+6330
now (3)
really (3)
same (3)
so (3) +6584
such (3) +3869
that same (3)
thing^s (3)
those (3)
very (3)
what (3) +361
what^s (3) +1821+2021+2021
another messenger^s (2)
at either end^s (2) +2256+2296+4946+4946
here^s (2) +2021+2021+5226
how (2)
man^s (2)
she (2)
so (2) +3869
still (2) +2021+2021+3427+6330
them (2)
there (2)
therefore (2) +6584
this is how (2)
which (2)
which (2) +361
who (2)
all at once (1) +2180
an (1)
another messenger (1)
another^s (1) +2021+2215+4946
back^s (1)
bordering each side^s (1) +2256+2296+4946+4946
by what (1) +361
except for (1)
from (1) +4946
front^s (1)
he's (1)
her (1)
here is what (1) +2256+2296+3869+3869
here^s (1) +928+2021+2021+5226
how (1) +4537
in broad daylight (1) +2021+2021+4200+6524+9087
inclined (1) +2118
it^s (1) +824+2021+2021
it^s (1) +2021+2021+6551
it^s (1) +2021+2021+8878
its^s (1)
just (1) +6964
lasting (1) +2021+2021+3427+6330
later (1) +339
Leah^s (1)
long for^s (1)
neither (1) +4202
now (1) +3954
now (1) +6964
of what use (1) +4200+4537
on both (1) +2256+2296+4946+4946
on both sides^s (1) +2256+2296+4946
on each side (1) +2021+2021+2296+4946+4946+4946+4946+6298+6298
on each side^s (1) +2256+2296+4946+4946
on the condition that (1) +928
once (1)
one condition^s (1)
over a year (1) +196+2296+3427+9102
right where (1)
same amount^s (1)
so (1)
still (1) +2021+2021+3427+3869
such (1) +1524
such offerings^s (1)
such questions^s (1)
suggested (1) +1821+2021+2021
that's (1)
that^s (1) +1074+2021+2021
the condition^s (1)
the first one^s (1)
the younger one^s (1)
the^s (1)
them^s (1) +1821+2021+2021
them^s (1) +2021+2021+6639
then (1)
then (1) +928
this (1) +1821+2021+2021
this fellow's^s (1) +4200
this is what (1)
this^s (1) +2021+2021+5126
today (1) +3427
what (1) +2256+2296+3869+3869
what (1) +2256+2297+3869+3869
what (1) +4769
what do I care about (1) +3276+4200+4200+4537
what^s (1) +2021+2021+5184
which way (1) +361
which way (1) +361+2006+2021
whom (1)
why (1) +361+4200
why (1) +6584
woman (1)
you^s (1)
untranslated (145)

2297 זֹה *zōh* (11)
this (6)
one (1)
such (1) +3869
what (1) +2256+2296+3869+3869
untranslated (2)

2298 זָהָב *zāhāb* (388)
gold (365)
golden (9)
Gold (2)
pure gold (2) +2298
alternate^s (1) +2256+7194+8232
nuggets of gold (1)
untranslated (7)

2299 זָהַם *zāham* (1)
finds repulsive (1)

2300 זַהַם *zaham* (1)
Zaham (1)

2301 1זָהַר *zāhar1* (1)
shine (1)

2302 2זָהַר *zāhar2* (22)
warn (8)
take warning (3)
dissuade (2)
give warning (2)
be warned (1)
is warned (1)
taken warning (1)
teach (1)
took warning (1)
warned (1)
untranslated (1)

2303 זֹהַר *zōhar* (2)
bright (1)
brightness (1)

2304 זִו *ziw* (2)
Ziv (2)

2305 זוֹ *zô* (2)
for this (1)
untranslated (1)

2306 זוּ *zû* (15)
the (4)
as (1)
it (1)
such (1)
that (1)
things (1)
where (1)
who (1)
whose (1)
untranslated (3)

2307 זוּב *zûb* (42)
flowing (19)

discharge (9)
gushed out (3)
man[s] (3)
bodily discharge (1)
discharge (1) +2308
flow (1)
fruitful (1)
has a discharge (1) +2308
regular flow (1) +928+1414
running sore (1)
waste away (1)

2308 זוֹב *zôḇ* (13)
discharge (7)
discharge (1) +2307
discharge (1) +3240
has a discharge (1) +2307
it[s] (1) +2257
untranslated (2)

2309 זוּזִים *zûziym* (1)
Zuzites (1)

2310 זוּחַ *zûah*
Variant; not used

2311 זוֹחֵת *zōhēṯ* (1)
Zoheth (1)

2312 זָוִית *zāwiyṯ* (2)
corners (1)
pillars (1)

2313 זוּל *zûl* (1)
pour out (1)

2314 זוּלָה *zûlāh* (16)
but (6)
except (4)
besides (2)
apart from (1)
only (1)
only (1) +963+4200
only (1) +4202

2315 זוּן *zûn*
Variant; not used

2316 זוּעַ *zûa'* (3)
make tremble (1)
showed fear (1)
tremble (1)

2317 זְוָעָה *z'wā'āh* (6)
abhorrent (4)
object of dread (1)
terror (1)

2318 1זוּר *zûr1* (4)
broken (1)
cleansed (1)
crush (1)
squeezed (1)

2319 2זוּר *zûr2* (6)
turned (2)
deserted (1)
estranged (1)
go astray (1)
stranger (1)

2320 3זוּר *zûr3* (1)
offensive (1)

2321 זָזָא *zāzā'* (1)
Zaza (1)

2322 זָחַח *zāhah* (2)
swing out (2)

2323 1זָחַל *zāhal1* (2)
crawl (1)
glide (1)

2324 2זָחַל *zāhal2* (1)
fearful (1)

2325 זֹחֶלֶת *zōheleṯ* (1)
Zoheleth (1)

2326 זִיד *ziyḏ* (10)
arrogant (2)
arrogance (1)
arrogantly treated (1)
contemptuous (1)
cooking (1)
defied (1)
presumes (1)
schemes (1)
treated arrogantly (1)

2327 זֵידוֹן *zēyḏôn* (1)
raging (1)

2328 1זִיז *ziyz1* (2)
creatures (2)

2329 2זִיז *ziyz2* (1)
overflowing (1)

2330 זִיזָא *ziyzā'* (3)
Ziza (3)

2331 זִיזָה *ziyzāh* (1)
Ziza (1)

2332 זִינָא *ziynā'*
Variant; not used

2333 זִיעַ *ziya'* (1)
Zia (1)

2334 1זִיף *ziyp̱1* (8)
Ziph (7)
there[s] (1) +4497

2335 2זִיף *ziyp̱2* (2)
Ziph (2)

2336 זִיפָה *ziyp̱āh* (1)
Ziphah (1)

2337 זִיפִי *ziyp̱iy* (3)
Ziphites (3)

2338 זִיקוֹת *ziyqôṯ* (2)
flaming torches (1)
torches (1)

2339 זַיִת *zayiṯ* (38)
olive (9)
olive tree (8)
olive groves (7)
olives (7)
olive trees (4)
olive grove (1)
olive trees (1) +3658
olives from trees (1)

2340 זֵיתָן *zēyṯān* (1)
Zethan (1)

2341 זַךְ *zaḵ* (11)
pure (6)
clear (2)
flawless (1)
innocent (1)
upright (1)

2342 זָכָה *zāḵāh* (8)
kept pure (2)
pure (2)
acquit (1)
justified (1)
keep pure (1)
make yourselves clean (1)

2343 זְכוֹכִית *z'ḵôḵiyṯ* (1)
crystal (1)

2344 זְכוּר *z'ḵûr* (4)
men (4)

2345 זָכוּר *zāḵûr*
Variant; not used

2346 זַכּוּר *zakkûr* (10)
Zaccur (10)

2347 זַכַּי *zakkay* (3)
Zaccai (2)
untranslated (1)

2348 זָכַךְ *zāḵaḵ* (4)
pure (2)
brighter (1)
untranslated (1)

2349 1זָכַר *zāḵar1* (225)
remember (116)
remembered (23)
be remembered (15)
remembers (8)
invoke (4)
mention (4)
consider (2)
mentioned (2)
petition (2)
proclaim (2)
recalled (2)
remind (2)
tell (2)
are remembered (1)
be invoked (1)
brought to mind (1)
burns memorial (1)
call on (1)
carry on the memory (1)
cause to be honored (1)
commemorate (1)
disregarding (1) +4202
done this[s] (1)
draw attention to (1)
forget (1) +440
hold (1)
honor (1)
made mention of (1)
make petition (1)
mindful (1)
perpetuate memory (1) +9005
praise (1)
recalling (1)
record (1)
reflect on (1)
reflects on (1)
remember (1) +2349
remember well (1) +2349
reminded (1)
reminder (1)
review the past (1)
summons (1)
think about (1)
thought (1)
trust (1)
well remember (1) +2349
worthy of mention (1)
untranslated (4)

2350 2זָכָר *zāḵar2* (1)
males (1)

2351 זָכָר *zāḵār* (82)
male (37)
men (17)
males (11)
man (9)
son (3)
boy (1)
boys (1) +3251
not a virgin (1) +3359+5435
slept with (1) +3359+4200+5435
slept with (1) +3359+5435

2352 זֵכֶר *zēḵer* (23)
memory (11)
renown (3)
name (2)
remembered (2)
celebrate (1) +5580
fame (1)
name by which remembered (1)
name of renown (1)
remembers (1)

2353 1זֶכֶר *zeker1* (1)
Zeker (1)

2354 2זֶכֶר *zeker2*
Variant; not used

2355 זִכָּרוֹן *zikkārôn* (24)
memorial (9)
reminder (3)
remembered (2)
remembrance (2)
chronicles (1)
commemorate (1)
commemorated (1)
historic right (1)
maxims (1)
pagan symbols (1)
remind (1)
something remembered (1)

2356 זִכְרִי *zikriy* (12)
Zicri (12)

2357 זְכַרְיָה *zᵉkaryāh* (25)
Zechariah (24)
Zechariah's (1)

2358 זְכַרְיָהוּ *zᵉkaryāhû* (16)
Zechariah (16)

2359 זֻלּוּת *zullût* (1)
vile (1)

2360 זַלְזַל *zalzal* (1)
shoots (1)

2361 1זָלַל *zālal1* (7)
gluttons (2)
despise (1)
despised (1)
gorge (1)
profligate (1)
worthless (1)

2362 2זָלַל *zālal2* (2)
tremble (1)
trembled (1)

2363 זַלְעָפָה *zal'āpāh* (3)
feverish (1)
indignation (1)
scorching (1)

2364 זִלְפָּה *zilpāh* (7)
Zilpah (7)

2365 1זִמָּה *zimmāh1* (29)
lewdness (6)
wickedness (3)
consequences of lewdness (2)
lewd (2)
wicked schemes (2)
evil (1)
evil intent (1)
evil schemes (1)
lewd act (1)
lewd acts (1)
penalty for lewdness (1)
plans (1)
schemes (1)
shameful (1)
shameful crimes (1)
shamefully (1) +928
shameless (1)
wicked (1)
untranslated (1)

2366 2זִמָּה *zimmāh2* (3)
Zimmah (3)

2367 זְמוֹרָה *zᵉmôrāh* (5)
branch (3)
vines (2)

2368 זַמְזֻמִּים *zamzummiym* (1)
Zamzummites (1)

2369 1זָמִיר *zāmiyr1* (7)
singing (2)
songs (2)
music and song (1)
song (1)
theme of song (1)

2370 2זָמִיר *zāmiyr2*
Variant; not used

2371 זְמִירָה *zᵉmiyrāh* (1)
Zemirah (1)

2372 זָמַם *zāmam* (13)
determined (3)
plot (2)
carry out purpose (1)
considers (1)
decided (1)
intended (1)
plan (1)
planned (1)
planned evil (1)
resolved (1)

2373 זָמָם *zāmām* (1)
plans (1)

2374 זָמַן *zāman* (3)
set (2)
designated (1)

2375 זְמָן *zᵉmān* (4)
time (2)
designated times (1)
time appointed (1)

2376 1זָמַר *zāmar1* (45)
sing praise (18)
make music (10)
sing praises (8)
sing (7)
music (1)
praise (1)

2377 2זָמַר *zāmar2* (3)
prune (2)
pruned (1)

2378 זֶמֶר *zemer* (1)
mountain sheep (1)

2379 1זִמְרָה *zimrāh1* (7)
song (3)
music (2)
singing (2)

2380 2זִמְרָה *zimrāh2* (1)
best products (1)

2381 1זִמְרִי *zimriy1* (17)
Zimri (16)
Zimri's (1)

2382 2זִמְרִי *zimriy2* (1)
Zimri (1)

2383 זִמְרָן *zimrān* (2)
Zimran (2)

2384 זִמְרָת *zimrāt*
Variant; not used

2385 זַן *zan* (3)
every kind (1) +448+2385+4946
various (1)

2386 זָנַב *zānab* (2)
attack from the rear (1)
cut off (1)

2387 זָנָב *zānāb* (11)
tail (9)
stubs (1)
tails (1)

2388 1זָנָה *zānāh1* (62)
prostitute (12)
prostituted (5)
unfaithful (5)
engaged in prostitution (4)
turn to prostitution (3)
committed adultery (2)
lusted after (2) +339
prostitutes (2)
adulterous (1)
carried on prostitution (1)
caused to prostitute themselves (1)
commit adultery (1)
continue prostitution (1) +2388
did[s] (1)
engage in prostitution (1)
engaging in prostitution (1)
guilty of prostitution (1)
guilty of the vilest adultery (1) +2388
indulge in sexual immorality (1)
lead to do the same[s] (1) +339+466+2177
led to prostitute themselves (1)
lust after (1) +339
making a prostitute (1)
ply her trade (1)
promiscuous (1)
prostituting (1)
prostitution (1)
runs after for favors (1) +339
that[s] (1) +4392
turned to prostitution (1)
use as a prostitute (1) +9373
untranslated (2)

2389 2זָנָה *zānāh2*
Variant; not used

2390 זֹנָה *zōnāh* (33)
prostitute (20)
prostitutes (7)
harlot (2)
prostitution (2)
harlots (1)
prostitute's (1)

2391 1זָנוֹחַ *zānôah1* (4)
Zanoah (4)

2392 2זָנוֹחַ *zānôah2* (1)
Zanoah (1)

2393 זְנוּנִים *zᵉnûniym* (12)
prostitution (4)
adulterous (1)
adulterous look (1)
adultery (1)
idolatry (1)
unfaithfulness (1)
wanton lust (1)
untranslated (2)

2394 זְנוּת *zᵉnût* (9)
prostitution (7)
immorality (1)
unfaithfulness (1)

2395 1זָנַח *zānah1* (1)
stink (1)

2396 2זָנַח *zānah2* (19)
rejected (11)
reject (4)
cast off (1)
deprived (1)
removed (1)
throw out (1)

2397 זָנַק *zānaq* (1)
springing out (1)

2398 זָעָה *zā'āh*
Variant; not used

2399 זֵעָה *zē'āh* (1)
sweat (1)

2400 זַעֲוָה *zaᵃwāh* (7)
terror (1)
thing of horror (1)
untranslated (5)

2401 זַעֲוָן *zaᵃwān* (2)
Zaavan (2)

2402 זְעֵיר *zᵉ'ēyr*
Variant; not used

2403 זָעַךְ *zā'ak* (1)
are cut short (1)

2404 זָעַם *zā'am* (12)
denounce (3)
angry (2)
accursed (1)
denounced (1)
expresses wrath (1)
fury shown (1)
under the wrath (1)
under wrath (1)
vent fury (1)

2405 זַעַם *za'am* (22)
wrath (15)
indignation (3)
anger (1)
fierce (1)
great wrath (1) +2256+7912
insolent (1)

2406 1זָעַף *zā'ap̱1* (3)
angry (1)
rages (1)
raging (1)

2407 2זָעַף *zā'ap̱2* (2)
dejected (1)
looking worse (1)

2408 זַעַף *za'ap̱* (6)
rage (2)
raging (2)
enraged (1)
wrath (1)

2409 זָעֵף *zā'ēp̱* (2)
angry (2)

2410 זָעַק *zā'aq* (74)
cry out (18)
cried out (16)
cried (5)
cries out (4)
called (3)
cry (3)
crying out (2)
summon (2)
assembled (1)
call out (1)
called out to fight (1)
calling to arms (1) +339
cried for help (1)
cried out for help (1)
cry for help (1) +7754
cry out for help (1)
gathered together (1)
howl (1)
issued a proclamation (1)
make appeals (1)
sent up a cry (1)
summoned (1)
summoning (1)
wail (1)
wailing (1) +2411
weeping aloud (1)
were called (1)
were called together (1)
untranslated (1)

2411 זְעָקָה *z''āqāh* (18)
cry (7)
outcry (3)
cry out (1) +7754
cry out (1) +9048
crying (1)
lament (1) +6424
lamentation (1)
shouts (1)
wailing (1)
wailing (1) +2410

2412 זִפְרוֹן *ziprôn* (1)
Ziphron (1)

2413 זֶפֶת *zepeṯ* (3)
pitch (3)

2414 1זֵק *zēq1* (4)
chains (2)
fetters (1)
were put in chains (1) +928+8415

2415 2זֵק *zēq2* (1)
firebrands (1)

2416 1זָקֵן *zāqēn1* (26)
old (22)
aged (1) +4394
grew old (1)
grow old (1)
very old (1) +928+995+2021+3427

2417 זָקָן *zāqān* (19)
beard (11)
beards (5)
chin (2)
hair (1)

2418 2זָקֵן *zāqēn2* (180)
elders (122)
old (32)
aged (5)
dignitaries (2)
leaders (2)
leading (2)
chief (1)
elder (1)
elderly (1)
his own^{s} (1) +2021+2021+5566
of ripe old age (1)
older (1)
older (1) +3427+4200
them^{s} (1) +1680
veteran (1)
women^{s} (1)
untranslated (5)

2419 זֹקֶן *zōqen* (1)
old age (1)

2420 זִקְנָה *ziqnāh* (6)
old age (3)
old (2)
grew old (1)

2421 זְקֻנִים *z'quniym* (4)
old age (4)

2422 זָקַף *zāqap̱* (2)
lifts up (2)

2423 זָקַק *zāqaq* (7)
refined (3)
distill (1)
finest (1)
purified (1)
refine (1)

2424 זָר *zār* (70)
foreigners (14)
foreign (8)
strangers (7)
another (4)
anyone else (4)
adulteress (3)
else (3)
stranger (3)
unauthorized (3)
adulteress (2) +851
alien (2)
aliens (2)
anyone other than a priest (2)
strange (2)
distant sources (1)
enemies (1)
foreigners' (1)
illegitimate (1)
imported (1)
one^{s} (1)
one^{s} (1) +408
other (1)
outside a priest's family (1)
outside the family (1) +2021+2025+2575
unauthorized person (1)

2425 זֵר *zēr* (10)
molding (10)

2426 זָרָא *zārā'* (1)
loathe (1)

2427 זָרַב *zāraḇ* (1)
dry (1)

2428 זְרֻבָּבֶל *z'rubbāḇel* (21)
Zerubbabel (21)

2429 זֶרֶד *zereḏ* (4)
Zered (3)
untranslated (1)

2430 1זָרָה *zārāh1* (38)
scatter (18)
scattered (5)
winnow (4)
spread (3)
winnows out (2)
are scattered (1)
is scattered (1)
spread out (1)
throw away (1)
were scattered (1)
winnowing (1)

2431 2זָרָה *zārāh2* (1)
discern (1)

2432 זְרוֹעַ *z'rôa'* (90)
arm (53)
arms (15)
strength (6)
power (4)
shoulder (2)
allies (1)
arm of power (1)
armed forces (1)
army (1)
forces (1)
power (1) +3946
powerful (1)
shoulders (1)
strengthened (1) +2616
strong arms (1) +3338

2433 זֵרוּעַ *zērûa'* (2)
seeds (1)
seeds (1) +2446

2434 זַרְזִיף *zarziyp̱*
Variant; not used

2435 זַרְזִיר *zarziyr* (1)
strutting rooster (1) +5516

2436 זָרַח *zārah* (18)
rises (5)
rise (2)
rose (2)
sunrise (2) +2021+9087
appears (1)
broke out (1)
dawned (1)
dawns (1)
shine (1)
shining (1)
sunrise (1) +9087

2437 1זֶרַח *zerah1* (1)
dawn (1)

2438 2זֶרַח *zerah2* (21)
Zerah (20)
Zerahites (1) +1201

2439 זַרְחִי *zarhiy* (6)
Zerahite (4)
Zerahites (2)

2440 זְרַחְיָה *z'rahyāh* (5)
Zerahiah (5)

2441 1זָרַם *zāram1* (1)
sweep away (1)

2442 2זָרַם *zāram2* (1)
poured down (1)

2443 זֶרֶם *zerem* (9)
storm (4)
driving rain (1) +4784
hailstorm (1) +1352
rains (1)
thunderstorm (1)
torrents (1)

2444 זִרְמָה *zirmāh* (2)
emission (1)
that[s] (1)

2445 זָרַע *zāra'* (56)
sow (16)
plant (9)
planted (4)
sown (4)
planted crops (2)
seed-bearing (2) +2446
sower (2)
sows (2)
be able to have children (1) +2446
be planted (1)
bearing (1)
have descendants (1)
is shed (1)
plant (1) +2446
plant seed (1)
plant with seed (1)
planting (1)
pregnant (1)
scatter (1)
scattered (1)
seed (1) +2446
sowed (1)
sowing seed (1)

2446 זֶרַע *zera'* (230)
descendants (82)
offspring (35)
seed (25)
children (20)
family (5)
grain (5)
semen (5)
line (4)
people (4)
descent (3)
blood (2)
descendant (2)
descended (2)
family line (2)
posterity (2)
seed-bearing (2) +2445
be able to have children (1) +2445
brood (1)
child (1)
crops (1)
descendant (1) +408+4946
fertile (1)
have sexual relations (1) +4200+5989+8888
Jews[s] (1)
origin (1)
plant (1)
plant (1) +2445
planter (1) +5432
planting (1)
produce (1) +3655+9311
race (1)
righteous (1) +7404
seed (1) +2445
seed to sow (1) +5433
seeds (1) +2433
seedtime (1)
sleeping with (1) +907+8886+8887
sleeps with (1) +907+8886+8887
son (1) +408
sons (1)
stock (1)
their[s] (1) +3870
them[s] (1) +3870
various kinds (1)
untranslated (2)

2447 זֵרֹעִים *zērō'iym* (1)
vegetables (1)

2448 זֵרְעֹנִים *zēr'ōniym* (1)
vegetables (1)

2449 זָרַף *zārap̱* (1)
watering (1)

2450 1זָרַק *zāraq1* (35)
sprinkled (15)
sprinkle (11)
been sprinkled (2)
scatter (2)
scattered (1)
sprinkles (1)
sprinkling (1)
toss (1)
tossed (1)

2451 2זָרַק *zāraq2*
Variant; not used

2452 1זָרַר *zārar1*
Variant; not used

2453 2זָרַר *zārar2* (1)
sneezed (1)

2454 זֶרֶשׁ *zereš* (4)
Zeresh (4)

2455 זֶרֶת *zereṯ* (7)
span (5)
breadth of hand (1)
over nine feet (1) +564+2256+9252

2456 זַתּוּא *zatû'* (4)
Zattu (4)

2457 זֵתָם *zēṯām* (2)
Zetham (2)

2458 זֵתָר *zēṯar* (1)
Zethar (1)

2459 ח *ḥ*
Variant; not used

2460 חֹב *ḥōḇ* (1)
heart (1)

2461 חָבָא *ḥāḇā'* (36)
hid (7)
hidden (7)
hiding (5)
hide (3)
hid themselves (2)
be protected (1)
become hard (1)
force into hiding (1)
hidden away (1)
hidden himself (1)
hide themselves (1)
hide yourselves (1)
hushed (1)
secretly (1)
stay there (1)
stepped aside (1)
uses[s] (1)

2462 חָבַב *ḥāḇaḇ* (1)
love (1)

2463 חֹבָב *ḥōḇāḇ* (2)
Hobab (2)

2464 חָבָה *ḥāḇāh* (2)
conceal himself (1)
hide (1)

2465 חֻבָּה *ḥubbāh* (1)
Hubbah (1)

2466 חָבוֹר *ḥāḇôr* (3)
Habor (3)

2467 חַבּוּרָה *ḥabbûrāh* (7)
bruise (2)
wounds (2)
Blows (1)
injuring (1)
welts (1)

2468 חָבַט *ḥāḇaṭ* (5)
beat (1)
is beaten out (1)
thresh (1)
threshed (1)
threshing (1)

2469 חֲבַיָּה *ḥᵃḇayyāh* (2)
Hobaiah (2)

2470 חֶבְיוֹן *ḥeḇyôn* (1)
hidden (1)

2471 1חָבַל *ḥāḇal1* (12)
hold in pledge (2)
demanded security (1)
require a pledge for a loan (1) +2478
seized for a debt (1)
take as a pledge (1)
take as a pledge (1) +2471
take as security for a debt (1)
take in pledge (1)
taken in pledge (1)
taking as security (1)

2472 2חָבַל *ḥāḇal2* (12)
destroy (3)
acted very wickedly (1) +2472
be broken (1)
is broken (1)
offend (1)
pay for it (1)
ruin (1)
ruined (1) +2256+2476
work havoc (1)

2473 3חָבַל *ḥāḇal3* (3)
conceived (1)
in labor (1)
pregnant (1)

2474 1חֶבֶל *ḥeḇel1* (2)
procession (2)

2475 2חֶבֶל *ḥeḇel2* (49)
cords (11)
ropes (9)
region (4)
portion (3)
land (2)
rope (2)
share (2)
allotted (1)
boundary lines (1)
by (1)
cord (1)
district (1)
fate (1)
it[s] (1)
lands (1)
length (1)
length of cord (1)
lengths (1)
line (1)
measured (1)
noose (1)
portions (1)
rigging (1)

2476 3חֶבֶל *ḥeḇel3* (1)
ruined (1) +2256+2472

2477 חֵבֶל *ḥēḇel* (8)
pain (3)
pains (2)
anguish (1)
labor pains (1)
pangs (1)

2478 חֲבֹל *ḥᵃḇōl* (3)
require a pledge for a loan (1) +2471

what took in pledge (1)
what took in pledge for a loan (1)

2479 חִבֵּל *ḥibbēl* (1)
rigging (1)

2480 חֹבֵל *ḥōḇēl* (5)
seamen (3)
captain (1) +2021+8042
seamen (1) +3542

2481 חֲבֹלָה *ḥᵃḇōlāh* (1)
what took in pledge (1)

2482 חֹבְלִים *ḥōḇliym* (2)
union (2)

2483 חֲבַצֶּלֶת *ḥᵃḇasseleṯ* (2)
crocus (1)
rose (1)

2484 חֲבַצִּנְיָה *ḥᵃḇassinyāh* (1)
Habazziniah (1)

2485 חָבַק *ḥāḇaq* (13)
embrace (3)
embraced (3)
embraces (2)
folds (1)
hold in arms (1)
hug (1)
lie (1)
untranslated (1)

2486 חִבֻּק *ḥibbuq* (2)
folding (2)

2487 חֲבַקּוּק *ḥᵃḇaqqûq* (2)
Habakkuk (2)

2488 1חָבַר *ḥāḇar1* (1)
make fine speeches (1) +928+4863

2489 2חָבַר *ḥāḇar2* (28)
attached (2)
be fastened (2)
fasten (2)
fasten together (2)
joined (2)
made an alliance (2)
agreed (1)
allied with (1)
allies (1)
among (1)
casts spells (1) +2490
coming to an agreement (1)
did the same[s] (1) +285+285+448
do the same[s] (1)
enchanter (1) +2490
is closely compacted (1)
join (1)
join together (1)
joined forces (1)
joined to (1)
touched (1)
touching (1)

2490 1חֶבֶר *ḥeḇer1* (7)
bands (1)
casts spells (1) +2489
enchanter (1) +2489
magic spells (1)
share (1)
share with (1)
spells (1)

2491 2חֶבֶר *ḥeḇer2* (11)
Heber (10)
Heber's (1)

2492 חָבֵר *ḥāḇēr* (15)
associated with (3)
companions (2)
friend (2)
friends (2)
kind (1)
partner (1)
united (1)
untranslated (3)

2493 חַבָּר *ḥabbār* (1)
traders (1)

2494 חֲבַרְבֻּרוֹת *ḥᵃḇarburôṯ* (1)
spots (1)

2495 חֶבְרָה *ḥeḇrāh* (1)
keeps company (1) +782+4200

2496 1חֶבְרוֹן *ḥeḇrôn1* (63)
Hebron (62)
untranslated (1)

2497 2חֶבְרוֹן *ḥeḇrôn2* (10)
Hebron (10)

2498 חֶבְרוֹנִי *ḥeḇrôniy* (6)
Hebronites (4)
Hebronite (1)
their[s] (1) +2021+4200

2499 חֶבְרִי *ḥeḇriy* (1)
Heberite (1)

2500 חֲבֶרֶת *ḥᵃḇereṯ* (1)
partner (1)

2501 חֹבֶרֶת *ḥōḇereṯ* (4)
set (4)

2502 חָבַשׁ *ḥāḇaš* (32)
saddled (9)
bind up (3)
binds up (3)
put (2)
saddle (2)
bandaged (1)
been bound up (1)
bound up (1)
did so[s] (1)
dressed (1)
fastened (1)
govern (1)
have saddled (1)
remedy (1)
shroud (1)
twisted (1)
wrapped around (1)
untranslated (1)

2503 חֲבִתִּים *ḥᵃḇitiym* (1)
offering bread (1)

2504 חַג *ḥag* (62)
feast (33)
festival (19)
festivals (4)
religious feasts (2)
festal procession (1)
festival offerings (1)
festival sacrifices (1)
yearly festivals (1)

2505 חָגָּא *ḥāggā'* (1)
terror (1)

2506 1חָגָב *ḥāgāḇ1* (5)
grasshopper (2)
grasshoppers (2)
locusts (1)

2507 2חָגָב *ḥāgāḇ2* (1)
Hagab (1)

2508 חֲגָבָא *ḥᵃgāḇā'*
Variant; not used

2509 חֲגָבָה *ḥᵃgāḇāh* (2)
Hagaba (1)
Hagabah (1)

2510 חָגַג *ḥāgag* (16)
celebrate (9)
celebrate a festival (1)
celebrate the feast (1)
festive (1)
hold a festival (1)
reeled (1)
reveling (1)
untranslated (1)

2511 חָגוּ *ḥāgû* (3)
clefts (3)

2512 חֲגוֹר *ḥᵃgôr* (3)
belt (2)
sashes (1)

2513 חָגוֹר *ḥāgôr* (1)
belts (1) +258

2514 חֲגוֹרָה *ḥᵃgôrāh* (5)
bear arms (1) +2520
belt (1)
coverings (1)
sash (1)
warrior's belt (1)

2515 חַגִּי *ḥaggiy* (3)
Haggi (2)
Haggite (1)

2516 חַגַּי *ḥaggay* (9)
Haggai (9)

2517 חַגִּיָּה *ḥaggiyyāh* (1)
Haggiah (1)

2518 חַגִּית *ḥaggiyṯ* (5)
Haggith (5)

2519 חָגְלָה *ḥoglāh* (4)
Hoglah (4)

2520 חָגַר *ḥāgar* (43)
put on (13)
wearing (4)
armed (3) +3998
tied around (3)
tuck cloak into belt (2) +5516
wear (2)
bear arms (1) +2514
belt (1)
cloak tucked into belt (1) +5516
clothed (1)
fastened on (1)
gird (1)
in (1)
put sackcloth around (1)
puts on armor (1)
restrained (1)
sets about work (1) +5516
strapped (1)
tie (1)
tie around (1)
tied (1)
was armed (1)

2521 1חַד *ḥaḏ1* (4)
sharp (3)
sharpened (1)

2522 2חַד *ḥaḏ2* (1)
each (1)

2523 חָדַד *ḥāḏaḏ* (5)
sharpened (2)
fiercer (1)
is sharpened (1)
slash (1)

2524 חֲדַד *ḥᵃḏaḏ* (2)
Hadad (2)

2525 1חָדָה *ḥāḏāh1* (2)
delighted (1)
made glad (1)

2526 2חָדָה *ḥāḏāh2* (1)
be included (1)

2527 3חָדָה *ḥāḏāh3* (2)
sharpens (2)

2528 חַדָּה *ḥaddāh*
Variant; not used

2529 חַדּוּד *ḥaddûḏ* (1)
jagged (1)

2530 חֶדְוָה *hedwāh* (2)
joy (2)

2531 חָדִיד *hādiyd* (3)
Hadid (3)

2532 1חָדַל *hādal1* (59)
stopped (10)
stop (8)
refrain (5)
fail (4)
ceased (3)
give up (3)
let alone (3)
not (2)
abandoned (1)
absent (1)
always be (1) +4202
cease (1)
do not (1)
don't (1)
failing (1)
fails (1)
gone away (1)
keep (1)
leave alone (1) +4946
no enough (1)
no more (1)
over (1)
past (1)
refrain from (1)
refuse (1)
show restraint (1)
silent (1)
stop trusting in (1) +4946
untranslated (1)

2533 2חָדַל *hādal2*
Variant; not used

2534 חָדֵל *hādēl* (3)
fleeting (1)
refuse (1)
rejected (1)

2535 חֶדֶל *hedel* (1)
this world (1)

2536 חַדְלָי *hadlāy* (1)
Hadlai (1)

2537 חֵדֶק *hēdeq* (2)
brier (1)
thorns (1)

2538 חִדֶּקֶל *hiddeqel* (2)
Tigris (2)

2539 חָדַר *hādar* (1)
closing in from every side (1)

2540 חֶדֶר *heder* (35)
room (6)
bedroom (4) +5435
inner room (4) +928+2540
rooms (3)
bedroom (2)
bedroom (2) +4753
chambers (2)
inmost being (2) +1061
inmost parts (2) +1061
bedrooms (1)
chamber (1)
constellations (1)
homes (1)
inner room (1)
private room (1)
shrine (1)

2541 חַדְרָךְ *hadrāk* (1)
Hadrach (1)

2542 חָדַשׁ *hādaš* (10)
renew (4)
restore (2)
bring new (1)
is renewed (1)
reaffirm (1)
repaired (1)

2543 חָדָשׁ *hādāš* (53)
new (50)
fresh (1)
recently (1)
recently (1) +4946+7940

2544 1חֹדֶשׁ *hōdeš1* (283)
month (193)
months (30)
new Moon (7)
new Moons (7)
new Moon festivals (4)
new Moon festival (3)
another[s] (1)
mating time (1)
monthly (1)
monthly (1) +928+2544
new moon (1)
new Moon festivals (1) +8031
whole month (1) +3427
untranslated (31)

2545 2חֹדֶשׁ *hōdeš2* (1)
Hodesh (1)

2546 חֲדָשָׁה *hădāšāh* (1)
Hadashah (1)

2547 חָדְשִׁי *hodšiy*
Variant; not used

2548 חֲדָתָּה *hădatāh*
Variant; not used

2549 חוּב *hûb* (1)
because of (1)

2550 חוֹב *hôb* (1)
loan (1)

2551 חוֹבָה *hôbāh* (1)
Hobah (1)

2552 1חוּג *hûg1* (1)
marks out (1)

2553 2חוּג *hûg2* (3)
circle (1)
horizon (1)
vaulted (1)

2554 חוּד *hûd* (4)
tell (2)
given (1)
set forth (1)

2555 1חָוָה *hāwāh1* (6)
tell (3)
display (1)
explain (1)
show (1)

2556 2חָוָה *hāwāh2* (173)
worship (39)
bow down (33)
bowed down (30)
worshiped (23)
pay honor (7)
worshiping (7)
bowed (6)
bowing down (5)
bowed in worship (2)
prostrated himself (2)
worships (2)
bow (1)
bow down to worship (1)
bowed low (1)
bows down (1)
fell facedown (1) +678+4200
fell prostrate (1)
honor (1)
humbly bow (1)
kneeling (1)
knelt (1)
paid homage (1)
paid honor (1)
reverence (1)
worshiped leaned (1)
untranslated (3)

2557 1חַוָּה *hawwāh1* (3)
settlements (3)

2558 2חַוָּה *hawwāh2* (2)
eve (2)

2559 חוֹזָי *hôzāy*
Variant; not used

2560 1חוֹחַ *hôah1* (12)
thistle (4)
hook (2)
thorns (2)
brambles (1)
briers (1)
thickets (1)
thornbush (1)

2561 2חוֹחַ *hôah2*
Variant; not used

2562 חוּט *hût* (7)
circumference (1) +6015
cord (1)
cord (1) +9535
line (1)
ribbon (1)
thread (1)
threads (1)

2563 חִוִּי *hiwwiy* (25)
Hivites (23)
Hivite (2)

2564 חֲוִילָה *hăwiylāh* (7)
Havilah (7)

2565 1חוּל *hûl1* (10)
swirling down (2)
dancing (1)
fall (1)
flash (1)
join (1)
turned (1)
wait (1)
wait patiently (1)
untranslated (1)

2566 2חוּל *hûl2* (2)
Hul (2)

2567 1חוֹל *hôl1* (23)
sand (21)
grains of sand (2)

2568 2חוֹל *hôl2*
Variant; not used

2569 חוּם *hûm* (4)
dark-colored (4)

2570 חוֹמָה *hômāh* (133)
wall (81)
walls (43)
city wall (2)
walled (2)
it[s] (1) +2021
walled (1) +2257+4200
untranslated (3)

2571 חוּס *hûs* (24)
look with pity (6) +6524
show pity (4) +6524
concerned (2)
looked with pity (2) +6524
show mercy (2)
have pity (1)
look with compassion (1) +6524
mercy (1)
mind (1)
showing pity (1) +6524
spare (1)
spared (1)
take pity (1)

2572 חוֹף *ḥôp̱* (7)
coast (4) +3542
coast (1)
haven (1)
seashore (1) +3542

2573 חוּפָם *ḥûp̱ām* (1)
Hupham (1)

2574 חוּפָמִי *ḥûp̱āmiy* (1)
Huphamite (1)

2575 חוּץ *ḥûṣ* (164)
outside (49) +4946
streets (38)
street (13)
outside (8)
outside (8) +2025
outside (7) +928+2021
out (5) +2025
out (4) +4946
outer (3)
fields (2)
outside (2) +2025+4946
abroad (1) +2021+4200
area (1) +4946
around (1) +2021+4946
away (1) +448+2021+2025
countryside (1)
elsewhere (1)
extend out (1) +2025
get out of here (1) +2021+2025+8938
land (1)
market areas (1)
out (1)
out here (1) +928+2021
outdoor (1) +928+2021
outer (1) +2021+4200
outside the family (1) +2021+2025+2424
put out (1) +2021+3655
relieve yourself (1) +3782
without (1) +4946
untranslated (7)

2576 חוֹק *ḥôq*
Variant; not used

2577 חוּקֹק *ḥûqōq* (1)
Hukok (1)

2578 1חָוַר *ḥāwar1* (1)
grow pale (1)

2579 2חָוַר *ḥāwar2*
Variant; not used

2580 1חוּר *ḥûr1* (2)
white (2)

2581 2חוּר *ḥûr2* (15)
Hur (15)

2582 חוֹרוֹן *ḥôrôn*
Variant; not used

2583 חוֹרָי *ḥôrāy* (1)
fine linen (1)

2584 חוּרַי *ḥûray* (1)
Hurai (1)

2585 חוּרִי *ḥûriy* (1)
Huri (1)

2586 חוּרָם *ḥûrām* (11)
Hiram (6)
Huram (2)
he^s (1)
Hiram's (1)
untranslated (1)

2587 חוּרָם אָבִי *ḥûrām 'āḇiy* (2)
Huram-Abi (2)

2588 חַוְרָן *ḥawrān* (2)
Hauran (2)

2589 חוֹרֹנַיִם *ḥôrōnayim* (5)
Horonaim (5)

2590 1חוּשׁ *ḥûš1* (18)
come quickly (7)
hasten (2)
do swiftly (1)
go quickly (1)
hurried (1)
hurry (1)
ready (1)
rushes (1)
sudden (1)
swooping (1)
untranslated (1)

2591 2חוּשׁ *ḥûš2* (3)
dismayed (1)
find enjoyment (1)
greatly disturbed (1)

2592 חוּשָׁה *ḥûšāh* (1)
Hushah (1)

2593 חוּשַׁי *ḥûšay* (14)
Hushai (12)
untranslated (2)

2594 חוּשִׁים *ḥûšiym* (2)
Hushim (2)

2595 חוּשָׁם *ḥûšām* (4)
Husham (4)

2596 חַוֹּת יָאִיר *hawwōṯ yā'iyr* (4)
Havvoth Jair (4)

2597 1חוֹתָם *ḥôṯām1* (14)
seal (10)
signet ring (2)
placed seal (1) +928+3159
sealed together (1) +6037

2598 2חוֹתָם *ḥôṯām2* (2)
Hotham (2)

2599 חֲזָאֵל *ḥ^{a}zā'ēl* (23)
Hazael (21)
he^s (1)
his^s (1)

2600 חָזָה *ḥāzāh* (54)
see (13)
saw (5)
seen (5)
visions (5)
gaze (3)
look (3)
see visions (3)
sees (3)
are^s (1)
gave (1)
give visions (1)
gloat (1)
looked (1)
looks (1)
observed (1)
observes (1)
prophesy (1)
received (1)
saw visions (1) +2606
select (1)
stargazers (1) +928+3919
vision saw (1)

2601 חָזֶה *ḥāzeh* (13)
breast (11)
breasts (2)

2602 1חֹזֶה *ḥōzeh1* (17)
seer (11)
seers (5)
prophets (1)

2603 2חֹזֶה *ḥōzeh2* (1)
agreement (1)

2604 חֲזָהאֵל *ḥ^{a}zāh'ēl*
Variant; not used

2605 חֲזוֹ *ḥ^{a}zô* (1)
Hazo (1)

2606 חָזוֹן *ḥāzôn* (35)
vision (22)
visions (8)
revelation (4)
saw visions (1) +2600

2607 חָזוּת *ḥāzûṯ* (5)
prominent (2)
vision (2)
agreement (1)

2608 חֲזוֹת *ḥ^{a}zôṯ* (1)
visions (1)

2609 חֲזִיאֵל *ḥ^{a}ziy'ēl* (1)
Haziel (1)

2610 חֲזָיָה *ḥ^{a}zāyāh* (1)
Hazaiah (1)

2611 חֶזְיוֹן *ḥezyôn* (1)
Hezion (1)

2612 חִזָּיוֹן *ḥizzāyôn* (9)
vision (5)
visions (2)
dreams (1)
revelation (1)

2613 חֲזִיז *ḥ^{a}ziyz* (3)
thunderstorm (2) +7754
storm clouds (1)

2614 חֲזִיר *ḥ^{a}ziyr* (7)
pig (2)
pig's (2)
pigs (2)
boars (1)

2615 חֵזִיר *ḥēziyr* (2)
Hezir (2)

2616 חָזַק *ḥāzaq* (290)
strong (41)
repaired (18)
made repairs (14)
strengthen (12)
repair (10)
took hold (7)
hardened (6)
severe (5)
strengthened (5)
stronger (5)
encourage (4)
firmly (4)
hard (4)
repairs made (4)
take hold (4)
took (4)
gripped (3)
harden (3)
hold fast (3)
powerful (3)
seizes (3)
armed (2)
embraced (2)
encouraged (2)
encouraged (2) +3338
established himself firmly (2)
fasten (2)
fight bravely (2)
grabbed (2)
held (2)
help (2)
holds fast (2)
seize (2)
take (2)
took courage (2)
urged (2)
assisted (1) +928+3338
assisted (1) +3338
be sure (1)
began (1) +3338
brace yourselves (1) +5516
captured (1)
carried out repairs (1)

caught (1)
caught hold (1)
caulk (1)
cling (1)
clings (1)
come (1)
conquered (1) +6584
courage (1)
courageously (1)
devote (1)
devoted (1)
do best (1)
embrace (1)
encourages (1)
equipped (1)
fortified (1)
found strength (1)
gave power (1)
gave strength (1)
gave strong support (1) +6640
give strength (1)
given strength (1)
gone[s] (1)
grasped (1)
grasping (1)
grew in strength (1)
grips (1)
harsh (1)
have strength (1)
heavier (1)
held secure (1)
help (1) +3338
helped (1)
helped (1) +906+3338
helped find strength (1) +906+3338
hold back (1)
hold on (1)
holding (1)
holding on (1)
join (1) +6584
kept (1)
lay hold (1)
leans (1)
made harder (1)
made strong (1)
maintain (1)
maintains (1)
marshaled strength (1)
nails down (1) +928+5021
overpowered (1)
overruled (1) +448
overruled (1) +6584
preserve (1)
press (1)
prevailed upon (1) +928
proved stronger (1)
rallied strength (1)
rapes (1) +2256+6640+8886
recovery (1)
reinforce (1)
reinforced (1)
repair (1) +981
repairing (1)
resist (1)
restored (1)
restoring (1)
seized (1)
shipwrights (1) +981
showed strength (1)
stay (1)
strengthen position (1)
strengthened (1) +2432
strengthened himself (1)
strengthening his own position (1)
strengthens (1)
strong (1) +3338
support (1)
supported (1)
supports (1) +6640
take courage (1)
take firm hold (1)
take up (1)
takes hold (1)
triumphed (1)
unswerving (1)
victorious (1)
was strengthened (1)
worked hard (1)
untranslated (3)

2617 חָזָק *ḥāzāq* (57)
mighty (23)
strong (12)
powerful (6)
hardened (2) +5195
power (2)
stronger (2)
bitter (1)
fiercest (1)
good (1)
grew worse and worse (1) +2118+2716+4394
hard (1)
harder (1)
loud (1)
severe (1)
stubborn (1) +4213
unyielding (1) +7156

2618 חָזֵק *ḥāzēq* (2)
grew louder and louder (1) +2143+2256+4394
grew stronger and stronger (1) +2143+2256

2619 חֵזֶק *ḥēzeq* (1)
strength (1)

2620 חֹזֶק *ḥōzeq* (5)
mighty (3)
power (1)
strength (1)

2621 חֶזְקָה *ḥezqāh* (4)
became powerful (1)
become strong (1)
gained power (1)
strong (1)

2622 חָזְקָה *ḥāzqāh* (5)
cruelly (1) +928
force (1)
harshly (1) +928
sharply (1) +928
urgently (1) +928

2623 חִזְקִי *ḥizqiy* (1)
Hizki (1)

2624 חִזְקִיָּה *ḥizqiyyāh* (13)
Hezekiah (9)
he[s] (1)
Hezekiah's (1)
Hezekiah's (1) +4200
Hizkiah (1)

2625 חִזְקִיָּהוּ *ḥizqiyyāhû* (74)
Hezekiah (66)
Hezekiah's (5)
he[s] (2)
Hezekiah's (1) +4200

2626 חָח *ḥāḥ* (8)
hooks (4)
hook (2)
brooches (1)
untranslated (1)

2627 חָטָא *ḥāṭā'* (239)
sinned (68)
committed (23)
sin (23)
caused to commit (20)
sins (19)
purify (9)
sinning (6)
sinner (5)
caused to sin (4)
wronged (4)
purify himself (3)
bear the blame (2)
do wrong (2)
done wrong (2)
led into sin (2)
purified (2)
sinful (2)
wrongs (2)
a sin committed (1) +2631
be purified (1)
bore the loss (1)
bring sin (1)
cause to sin (1)
cleanse (1)
commit (1)
commit a sin (1)
commits sin (1)
committed (1) +2628
committed a sin (1) +2631
crime committed (1)
failed to do (1)
fails to find (1)
fails to reach (1)
fault (1)
find missing (1)
forfeiting (1)
forfeits (1)
lead into sin (1)
make out to be guilty (1)
make sin (1)
miss (1)
miss the way (1)
offended (1)
offered for a sin offering (1)
offers (1)
presented for a sin offering (1)
purified themselves (1)
purify yourselves (1)
purifying (1)
retreat (1)
sin offerings (1)
sinned greatly (1) +2628
sinner's (1)
wicked (1)
untranslated (5)

2628 חֵטְא *ḥēṭ'* (34)
sins (8)
sin (5)
guilty of sin (3)
consequences of sin (2)
guilty (2)
held responsible (2) +5951
sinful (2)
become guilty (1) +5951+6584
committed (1) +2627
consequences of sins (1)
errors (1)
guilt (1)
guilty (1) +5951
punished for sins (1)
shortcomings (1)
sinned greatly (1) +2627
untranslated (1)

2629 חַטָּא *ḥaṭṭā'* (19)
sinners (13)
criminals (1)
sinful (1)
sinned (1)
sinner (1)
sinning (1)
wicked people (1)

2630 חֶטְאָה *ḥeṭ'āh* (1)
sinning (1)

2631 חֲטָאָה *ḥᵃṭā'āh* (8)
sin (2)
a sin committed (1) +2627
committed a sin (1) +2627
condemn (1) +2118+4200

guilt (1)
sin offerings (1)
sins (1)

2632 חַטָּאָה *ḥaṭṭā'āh*
Variant; not used

2633 חַטָּאת *ḥaṭṭā'ṯ* (298)
sin offering (105)
sin (85)
sins (74)
sin offerings (8)
punishment (3)
cleansing (1)
iniquities (1)
it[s] (1) +2021
its[s] (1) +2021
offense (1)
purification from sin (1)
purification offering (1)
sinful thing (1)
sinner (1)
sinning (1)
that[s] (1)
wickedness (1)
wronged (1)
wrongs (1)
wrongs (1) +6913
untranslated (8)

2634 חָטַב *ḥāṭaḇ* (9)
woodcutters (3) +6770
cut (2)
carved (1)
chop (1)
cut down (1)
woodsmen (1)

2635 חֲטֻבוֹת *ḥ^eṭuḇôṯ* (1)
colored (1)

2636 חִטָּה *ḥiṭṭāh* (30)
wheat (30)

2637 חַטּוּשׁ *ḥaṭṭûš* (5)
Hattush (5)

2638 חֲטִיטָא *ḥ^eṭiyṭā'* (2)
Hatita (2)

2639 חַטִּיל *ḥaṭṭiyl* (2)
Hattil (2)

2640 חֲטִיפָא *ḥ^eṭiypā'* (2)
Hatipha (2)

2641 חָטַם *ḥāṭam* (1)
hold back (1)

2642 חָטַף *ḥāṭap̱* (3)
catch (1)
catches (1)
seize (1)

2643 חֹטֶר *ḥōṭer* (2)
rod (1)
shoot (1)

2644 1חַי *ḥay1* (238)
life (108)
as surely as lives (46)
as surely as live (23)
live (12)
lived (9)
as live (6)
lives (6)
as lives (3)
living (3)
as surely as live (2) +5883
lifetime (2)
as surely as live (1) +2256+2644+5883
creature (1)
life will not be worth living (1) +4200+4537
life-giving (1)
lifetime (1) +3427
live (1) +928+2021
long life (1) +2021+4200
nourish (1)
old (1) +3427+9102
untranslated (8)

2645 2חַי *ḥay2* (146)
living (62)
alive (34)
live (15)
fresh (8)
raw (5)
lives (3)
life (2)
lifetime (2)
next year (2)
next year (2) +6961
as surely as live (1)
flowing (1)
green (1)
it[s] (1) +2021+2021+7606
lived (1)
living creatures (1)
living thing (1)
others[s] (1)
preserved (1) +928+2021+8492
raw (1) +4695
vigorous (1)

2646 3חַי *ḥay3* (1)
family (1)

2647 חִיאֵל *ḥiy'ēl* (1)
Hiel (1)

2648 חִידָה *ḥiyḏāh* (17)
riddle (8)
hard questions (2)
riddles (2)
allegory (1)
answer (1)
hidden things (1)
intrigue (1)
scorn (1)

2649 חָיָה *ḥāyāh* (275)
live (90)
lived (43)
preserve life (12)
spared (10)
long live (9)
surely live (9) +2649
keep alive (7)
let live (7)
recover (6)
revive (5)
save life (5)
kept alive (3)
leave alive (3)
preserve (3)
restored to life (3)
allowed to live (2)
bring back to life (2)
came to life (2)
certainly recover (2) +2649
come to life (2)
preserves life (2)
revived (2)
save (2)
save lives (2)
spare (2)
survive (2)
survived (2)
allow to live (1)
bring to life (1)
brought back to life (1)
choose life (1)
die (1) +4202
flourish (1)
give life (1)
gives life (1)
healed (1)
live again (1)
live on (1)
lives (1)
makes alive (1)
preserved life (1)
protect lives (1)
raised (1)
recovered (1)
recovery (1) +2716+4946
renew (1)
restore life (1)
restored (1)
saved lives (1)
saving (1)
spare life (1)
spare lives (1)
spared lives (1)
sparing (1)
stay alive (1)
will[s] (1)
untranslated (5)

2650 חָיֶה *ḥāyeh* (1)
vigorous (1)

2651 1חַיָּה *ḥayyāh1* (103)
animals (25)
beasts (25)
living creatures (13)
living (8)
animal (7)
wild animals (6)
beast (4)
creatures (3)
living creature (2)
wild beasts (2)
animal (1) +7473
beasts of burden (1) +989+2256
creature (1)
livestock (1)
living things (1)
ones[s] (1)
those[s] (1) +2021
wild animal (1)

2652 2חַיָּה *ḥayyāh2* (13)
life (3)
hunger (1)
live (1)
lives (1)
me (1) +3276
renewal (1)
them (1) +4392
very being (1)
untranslated (3)

2653 3חַיָּה *ḥayyāh3* (3)
band (1)
banded together (1) +665+2021+4200
people (1)

2654 חַיּוּת *ḥayyûṯ* (1)
living (1)

2655 1חִיל *ḥiyl1* (47)
in anguish (4)
in labor (4)
tremble (4)
gave birth (2)
shakes (2)
was given birth (2)
wounded (2)
writhe (2)
writhe in pain (2)
writhed (2)
writhes (2)
at birth (1)
be born (1)
bears (1)
brings (1)
brought forth (1)
brought to birth (1)
felt pain (1)
goes into labor (1)
in deep anguish (1)
in distress (1)
suffers torment (1)
trembles (1)
twists (1)

were brought forth (1)
writhe in agony (1) +2655
writhe in agony (1) +4394
writhed in pain (1)
untranslated (1)

2656 2חִיל *ḥiyl2* (2)
endure (1)
prosperous (1)

2657 חַיִל *ḥayil* (246)
army (77)
wealth (25)
fighting men (12) +1475
strength (11)
brave warriors (6) +1475
riches (5)
able men (4) +1201
brave (4) +1201
force (4)
troops (4)
valiant (4)
capable (3)
forces (3)
noble character (3)
soldiers (3)
strong (3)
able men (2) +1475
able-bodied (2)
best fighting men (2) +1475
caravan (2)
might (2)
mighty things (2)
power (2)
standing (2)
standing (2) +1475
valiant fighter (2) +408+1201
valiant fighters (2) +408
valiant soldier (2) +1475
victory (2)
warriors (2) +408
worthy (2)
able (1)
able (1) +1201
able-bodied (1) +1201
armed force (1)
armed forces (1) +7372
armies (1)
army (1) +2162
army (1) +7372
battle (1)
brave (1)
brave fighting men (1) +1475
brave man (1) +1475
brave warrior (1) +1475
bravely (1) +1201+4200
bravest soldier (1) +1201
capable men (1) +1475
champions (1) +408
company (1)
courageous (1) +1201
experienced fighting men (1) +408+1475+4878
fighting (1)
fighting (1) +1201
goods (1)
mighty (1)
mighty men (1) +1475
mighty warrior (1) +1475
military (1)
military leaders (1)
noble (1)
one^s (1)
profit (1)
skills (1)
soldiers (1) +1201
special ability (1)
strongest defenders (1) +408
they^s (1) +2021+2256+3405+8569
troops (1) +1475
valiantly (1)
very capable men (1) +1475
warriors (1) +1201
warriors (1) +1475
wealthy (1)
untranslated (3)

2658 חֵיל *ḥēyl* (7)
ramparts (3)
defense (1)
outer fortifications (1)
wall (1)
walls (1)

2659 3חִיל *ḥiyl3* (6)
pain (5)
anguish (1)

2660 חִילָה *ḥiylāh* (1)
pain (1)

2661 חִילֵז *ḥiylēz*
Variant; not used

2662 חֵילֵךְ *ḥēylēḵ* (1)
Helech (1)

2663 חֵילָם *ḥēylām* (2)
Helam (2)

2664 חִילֵן *ḥiylēn* (1)
Hilen (1)

2665 חִין *ḥiyn* (1)
graceful (1)

2666 חַיִץ *ḥayiṣ* (1)
flimsy wall (1)

2667 חִיצוֹן *ḥiyṣôn* (25)
outer (20)
away from (1)
both outer (1)
outside (1)
outside (1) +2025
where^s (1) +2021+2021+2958

2668 חֵיק *ḥēyq* (39)
arms (6)
cloak (5)
lap (4)
laps (4)
gutter (3)
breast (2)
heart (2)
loves (2)
beside (1) +928
bosom (1)
embrace (1)
floor (1)
garment (1)
love (1)
returned unanswered (1) +8740
secret (1)
within (1) +928
untranslated (2)

2669 חִירָה *ḥiyrāh* (2)
Hirah (2)

2670 חִירוֹם *ḥiyrôm* (3)
Hiram (2)
he^s (1)

2671 חִירָם *ḥiyrām* (22)
Hiram (15)
Huram (3)
he^s (1)
Hiram's (1)
untranslated (2)

2672 חִירֹת *ḥiyrōṯ*
Variant; not used

2673 חִישׁ *ḥiyš* (1)
quickly (1)

2674 חֵךְ *ḥēḵ* (18)
mouth (6)
roof of mouth (3)
taste (3)
tongue (2)
lips (1)
on the tip of tongue (1) +928+4383
roof of mouths (1)
speech (1)

2675 חָכָה *ḥāḵāh* (14)
wait (7)
delay (1)
lie in ambush (1)
long for (1)
longs (1)
wait in hope (1)
waited (1)
waits for (1)

2676 חַכָּה *ḥakkāh* (3)
hooks (2)
fishhook (1)

2677 חֲכִילָה *ḥᵃḵiylāh* (3)
Hakilah (3)

2678 חֲכַלְיָה *ḥᵃḵalyāh* (2)
Hacaliah (2)

2679 חַכְלִילִי *ḥaḵliyliy* (1)
darker (1)

2680 חַכְלִלוּת *ḥaḵlilûṯ* (1)
bloodshot (1)

2681 חָכַם *ḥāḵam* (28)
wise (13)
skillful (2)
wisdom (2)
wiser (2)
deal shrewdly (1)
extremely wise (1) +2682
make wiser (1)
makes wiser (1)
making wise (1)
overwise (1) +3463
skill (1)
teach wisdom (1)
untranslated (1)

2682 חָכָם *ḥāḵām* (138)
wise (105)
skilled (7)
skilled (6) +4213
wisdom (4)
craftsmen (2)
skilled craftsmen (2)
wiser (2)
advisers (1)
craftsmen (1) +4213
extremely wise (1) +2681
great skill (1) +1069+3359
shrewd (1)
skillful (1)
those^s (1)
unwise (1) +4202
wise (1) +4213
wisest (1)

2683 חָכְמָה *ḥoḵmāh* (149)
wisdom (131)
skill (7)
learning (2)
skilled (2)
ability (1) +928+4213
at wits' end (1) +1182+3972
skill (1) +4213
that^s (1)
wisdom (1) +8120
wise (1)
wise advice (1)

2684 חָכְמוֹת *ḥoḵmôṯ* (4)
wisdom (4)

2685 חַכְמֹנִי *ḥaḵmōniy* (2)
Hacmoni (1)
Hacmonite (1) +1201

2686 חָכַר *ḥāḵar* (1)
attack (1)

2687 חֹל *ḥōl* (7)
common (4)
common use (1)
not holy (1)
ordinary (1)

2688 חָלָא *ḥālā'* (1)
afflicted with a disease (1)

2689 1חֶלְאָה *ḥel'āh1* (5)
deposit (3)
encrusted (1)
untranslated (1)

2690 2חֶלְאָה *ḥel'āh2* (2)
Helah (2)

2691 חֶלְאָם *ḥēlā'm*
Variant; not used

2692 חָלָב *ḥālāḇ* (44)
milk (41)
cheeses (1) +3043
suckling (1)
well nourished (1) +4848

2693 1חֵלֶב *ḥēleḇ1* (92)
fat (64)
fat portions (7)
finest (5)
best (3)
callous hearts (2)
callous (1) +2021+3869
curds (1)
fattened (1)
flesh (1)
richest of foods (1) +2016+2256
these^{s} (1) +2021
untranslated (5)

2694 2חֵלֶב *ḥēleḇ2*
Variant; not used

2695 חֶלְבָּה *ḥelbāh* (1)
Helbah (1)

2696 חֶלְבּוֹן *ḥelbôn* (1)
Helbon (1)

2697 חֶלְבְּנָה *ḥelb'nāh* (1)
galbanum (1)

2698 חֶלֶד *ḥeleḏ* (5)
world (2)
fleeting life (1)
life (1)
span of years (1)

2699 חֵלֶד *ḥēleḏ* (2)
Heled (2)

2700 חֹלֶד *ḥōleḏ* (1)
weasel (1)

2701 חֻלְדָּה *ḥuldāh* (2)
Huldah (2)

2702 חֶלְדַּי *ḥelday* (3)
Heldai (3)

2703 1חָלָה *ḥālāh1* (56)
ill (13)
weak (8)
illness (4)
diseased (3)
faint (3)
wounded (3)
been wounded (2)
grievous (2)
afflicted (1)
beyond healing (1)
cause to suffer (1)
concerned (1)
crushing (1) +4394
fatal (1)
grieve (1)
hurt (1)
incurable (1)
inflamed (1) +2779
injured (1)
lay ill (1)
makes sick (1)
pretend to be ill (1)
pretended to be ill (1)
sick (1)
suffering (1)
wear themselves out (1)

2704 2חָלָה *ḥālāh2* (17)
entreat (3) +906+7156
sought the favor of (3) +906+7156
appeal (1)
court favor (1) +7156
curry favor with (1) +7156
implore (1) +7156
intercede with (1) +906+7156
interceded with (1) +906+7156
seek favor (1) +906+7156
seek favor (1) +7156
sought (1)
sought favor (1) +906+7156
sought favor (1) +7156

2705 חַלָּה *ḥallāh* (14)
cakes (6)
cake (3)
loaf (2)
cake (1) +4312
loaves of bread (1)
untranslated (1)

2706 חֲלוֹם *ḥ^{a}lôm* (65)
dream (28)
dreams (14)
had a dream (6) +2731
dream had (2) +2731
dreamer (2) +2731
had dream (2) +2731
had dreams (2) +2731
dreamed (1)
dreamer (1) +1251+2021
dreaming (1)
dreams (1) +2731
dreams encourage to have (1) +2731
foretells by dreams (1) +2731
interpreters of dreams (1)
it^{s} (1) +2021
untranslated (1)

2707 חַלּוֹן *ḥallôn* (32)
window (13)
windows (10)
openings (7)
parapet openings (1)
untranslated (1)

2708 חֹלוֹן *ḥōlôn* (3)
Holon (3)

2709 חַלּוֹנִי *ḥallônāy*
Variant; not used

2710 חֲלוֹף *ḥ^{a}lôp̱* (1)
destitute (1) +1201

2711 חֲלוּשָׁה *ḥ^{a}lûšāh* (1)
defeat (1)

2712 חֲלַח *ḥ^{a}lah* (3)
Halah (3)

2713 חַלְחוּל *ḥalḥûl* (1)
Halhul (1)

2714 חַלְחָלָה *ḥalḥālāh* (4)
anguish (2)
pain (1)
tremble (1)

2715 חָלַט *ḥālaṭ* (1)
pick up (1)

2716 חֳלִי *ḥ^{o}liy* (24)
disease (5)
illness (5)
sickness (4)
affliction (1)
evil (1)
grew worse and worse (1) +2118+2617+4394
ill (1)
illnesses (1)
infirmities (1)
injured (1)
injury (1)
recovery (1) +2649+4946
suffering (1)

2717 1חֲלִי *ḥ^{a}liy1* (2)
jewels (1)
ornament (1)

2718 2חֲלִי *ḥ^{a}liy2* (1)
Hali (1)

2719 חֶלְיָה *ḥelyāh* (1)
jewelry (1)

2720 1חָלִיל *ḥāliyl1* (6)
flutes (4)
flute (2)

2721 2חָלִיל *ḥāliyl2* (21)
far be it (12)
forbid (4)
never (3)
never (1) +561
of course not (1)

2722 חֲלִיפָה *ḥ^{a}liyp̱āh* (12)
sets (6)
change (1)
clothes (1)
new (1)
renewal (1)
shifts (1)
wave upon wave (1)

2723 חֲלִיצָה *ḥ^{a}liyṣāh* (2)
belongings (1)
weapons (1)

2724 חֵלְכָה *ḥēl'ḵāh* (3)
victims (2)
victim (1)

2725 1חָלַל *ḥālal1* (135)
began (25)
desecrated (11)
profane (11)
begin (8)
desecrate (7)
profaned (7)
begun (6)
defile (5)
defiled (5)
desecrating (5)
enjoy (4)
started (4)
beginning (3)
being profaned (3)
first time (2)
grew (2)
violate (2)
am profaned (1)
be defamed (1)
be desecrated (1)
becoming (1)
been defiled (1)
been profaned (1)
break (1)
bring low (1)
defiles herself (1)
degrade (1)
desecrates (1)
disgrace (1)
disgraces (1)
dishonor (1)
drove in disgrace (1)
launch (1)
let be profaned (1)
proceeded (1)
treating with contempt (1)

undertook (1)
violates (1)
was desecrated (1)
untranslated (3)

2726 2חָלַל *ḥālal2* (8)
killed (1)
pierce (1)
pierced (1)
pierced through (1)
slay (1)
was pierced (1)
wounded (1)
wounds (1)

2727 3חָלַל *ḥālal3* (2)
make music (1)
playing (1)

2728 1חָלָל *ḥālāl1* (92)
slain (38)
killed (21)
dead (6)
wounded (5)
casualties (4)
body (3)
victims (3)
slaughter (2)
bodies (1)
dead bodies (1)
die (1)
fall in battle (1) +5877
flattering (1)
hurt (1)
mortally wounded man (1)
people (1)
slain in battle (1)
violent (1)

2729 2חָלָל *ḥālāl2* (3)
defiled (2)
profane (1)

2730 1חָלַם *ḥālam1* (2)
grow strong (1)
restored to health (1)

2731 2חָלַם *ḥālam2* (27)
had a dream (6) +2706
had a dream (5)
dream had (2) +2706
dreamer (2) +2706
dreams (2)
had dream (2) +2706
had dreams (2) +2706
dream (1)
dreamed (1)
dreams (1) +2706
dreams encourage to have (1) +2706
foretells by dreams (1) +2706
untranslated (1)

2732 חֵלֶם *ḥēlem*
Variant; not used

2733 חַלָּמוּת *hallāmût* (1)
egg (1)

2734 חַלָּמִישׁ *hallāmiyš* (5)
flint (1)
flinty (1)
flinty rock (1)
hard (1)
hard rock (1)

2735 חֵלֹן *ḥēlōn* (5)
Helon (5)

2736 1חָלַף *ḥālap1* (26)
changed (3)
new (3)
change (2)
changing (1)
comes along (1)
disappear (1)
discarded (1)
exchange (1)
glided past (1)
go (1)
goes by (1)
let renew (1)
over (1)
renew (1)
replace (1)
skim past (1)
sprout (1)
sweep on (1)
sweep past (1)
sweeping (1)
violated (1)

2737 2חָלַף *ḥālap2* (2)
pierced (1)
pierces (1)

2738 1חֵלֶף *ḥēlep1* (1)
Heleph (1)

2739 2חֵלֶף *ḥēlep2* (2)
for (1)
in return for (1)

2740 1חָלַץ *ḥālas1* (23)
deliver (4)
rescued (3)
be delivered (2)
delivers (2)
torn out (2)
delivered (1)
escape (1)
is rescued (1)
offer (1)
rescue (1)
robbed (1)
take off (1)
unsandaled (1) +5837
withdrawn (1)
untranslated (1)

2741 2חָלַץ *ḥālas2* (21)
armed (12)
armed guard (2)
arm (1)
arm ourselves (1)
arm yourselves (1)
armed for battle (1)
army (1)
soldiers (1)
strengthen (1)

2742 חֶלֶץ *ḥeles* (5)
Helez (5)

2743 חֲלָצַיִם *hᵃlāsayim* (11)
brace (2) +273
flesh and blood (2) +3655+4946
waist (2)
body (1)
heart (1)
stomach (1)
waists (1)
untranslated (1)

2744 1חָלָק *halaq1* (9)
flatters (2)
seductive (2)
deceitful (1)
flattering (1)
smooth (1)
smooths (1)
speak deceit (1)

2745 2חָלַק *ḥālaq2* (56)
divide (9)
divided (6)
dividing (3)
share (3)
be divided (2)
distribute (2)
gave (2)
parcel out (2)
accomplice (1) +6640
allots (1)
allotting (1)
apportioned (1)
assigns (1)
be allotted (1)
be distributed (1)
be divided up (1)
distributed (1)
distributes (1)
distributing supplies (1)
divide up (1)
divided up (1)
divides (1)
get share of property (1)
give a portion (1)
give a share (1)
given (1)
is dispersed (1)
is distributed (1)
made assignments (1)
received (1)
scatter (1)
scattered (1)
separated into divisions (1)
took some of the things (1)
were split (1)

2746 3חָלַק *ḥālaq3*
Variant; not used

2747 1חָלָק *ḥālāq1* (9)
flattering (3)
smooth (2)
flattery (1)
pleasant (1)
slippery (1)
smoother (1)

2748 2חָלָק *ḥālāq2* (2)
Halak (2)

2749 1חֵלֶק *ḥēleq1* (1)
smooth (1)

2750 2חֵלֶק *ḥēleq2* (66)
share (16)
portion (14)
lot (6)
allotment (4)
portions (4)
parts (3)
reward (3)
fate (2)
plot of ground (2)
benefits (1)
fields (1)
have say (1) +6699
inheritance (1)
land (1)
lives (1)
owns (1)
part (1)
plot (1)
possession (1)
that[s] (1)
untranslated (1)

2751 3חֵלֶק *ḥēleq3* (2)
Helek (2)

2752 חַלֻּק *halluq* (1)
smooth (1)

2753 1חֶלְקָה *ḥelqāh1* (2)
smooth (2)

2754 2חֶלְקָה *ḥelqāh2* (23)
field (10)
field (4) +8441
plot (2)
plot of ground (2)
portion (2)
another[s] (1)
piece (1)
tract (1)

2755 חֲלֻקָּה *hᵃluqqāh* (1)
group (1) +3+1074

2756 חֲלַקָּה *ḥ^{a}laqqāh*
Variant; not used

2757 חֶלְקִי *ḥelqiy* (1)
Helekite (1)

2758 חֶלְקָי *ḥelqāy* (1)
Helkai (1)

2759 חִלְקִיָּה *ḥilqiyyāh* (15)
Hilkiah (13)
he^{S} (1)
Hilkiah's (1)

2760 חִלְקִיָּהוּ *ḥilqiyyāhû* (19)
Hilkiah (18)
he^{S} (1)

2761 חֲלַקְלַק *ḥ^{a}laqlaq* (4)
slippery (2)
intrigue (1)
not sincere (1)

2762 חֶלְקַת *ḥelqaṯ* (2)
Helkath (2)

2763 חֶלְקַת הַצֻּרִים *ḥelqaṯ hassuriym* (1)
Helkath Hazzurim (1)

2764 1חָלַשׁ *ḥālaš1* (1)
laid low (1)

2765 2חָלַשׁ *ḥālaš2* (2)
laid low (1)
overcame (1)

2766 חַלָּשׁ *ḥallāš* (1)
weakling (1)

2767 1חָם *ḥām1* (4)
father-in-law (4)

2768 2חָם *ḥām2* (2)
swelter (1)
warm (1)

2769 3חָם *ḥām3* (16)
Ham (15)
Hamites (1)

2770 חֹם *ḥōm* (9)
heat (8)
hot (1)

2771 חֵמָא *ḥēmā'*
Variant; not used

2772 חֶמְאָה *ḥem'āh* (10)
curds (6)
cream (2)
butter (1)
curdled milk (1)

2773 חָמַד *ḥāmaḏ* (21)
covet (6)
desire (2)
treasure (2)
choice (1)
chooses (1)
coveted (1)
delight (1)
delight in (1)
delighted (1)
desirable (1)
lust after (1)
pleasing (1)
precious (1)
wealth (1)

2774 חֶמֶד *ḥemeḏ* (6)
handsome (3)
fruitful (1)
lush (1)
pleasant (1)

2775 חֶמְדָּה *ḥemdāh* (16)
pleasant (3)
desired (2)
fine (2)
treasures (2) +3998
desirable (1)
desire (1)
regret (1)
stately (1)
valuable (1)
valuables (1)
value (1)

2776 חֲמֻדוֹת *ḥ^{a}muḏôṯ* (9)
highly esteemed (3)
best (1)
choice (1)
costly gifts (1)
precious (1)
riches (1)
value (1)

2777 חֶמְדָּן *ḥemdān* (2)
Hemdan (2)

2778 חֵמָה *ḥēmāh* (1)
careful (1)

2779 חֵמָה *ḥēmāh* (123)
wrath (75)
anger (12)
fury (8)
rage (5)
venom (4)
angry (2)
burning (2)
fierce (2)
furious (2)
poison (2)
easily angered (1)
enraged (1) +4848
hot (1)
hot-tempered (1)
hot-tempered (1) +1251
hot-tempered (1) +1524
indignation (1)
inflamed (1) +2703
stinging (1)

2780 חַמָּה *ḥammāh* (6)
sun (4)
heat (1)
sunlight (1) +240

2781 חַמּוּאֵל *ḥammû'ēl* (1)
Hammuel (1)

2782 חֲמוּטַל *ḥ^{a}mûtal* (3)
Hamutal (3)

2783 חָמוּל *ḥāmûl* (3)
Hamul (3)

2784 חָמוּלִי *ḥāmûliy* (1)
Hamulite (1)

2785 חַמּוֹן *ḥammôn* (2)
Hammon (2)

2786 חָמוּץ *ḥāmûṣ*
Variant; not used

2787 חָמוֹץ *ḥāmôṣ* (1)
oppressed (1)

2788 חַמּוּק *ḥammûq* (1)
graceful (1)

2789 1חֲמוֹר *ḥ^{a}môr1* (98)
donkey (47)
donkeys (45)
donkey's (3)
donkeys (1) +2789
male donkeys (1)

2790 2חֲמוֹר *ḥ^{a}môr2*
Variant; not used

2791 3חֲמוֹר *ḥ^{a}môr3* (13)
Hamor (12)
his^{S} (1)

2792 חָמוֹת *ḥāmôṯ* (11)
mother-in-law (11)

2793 חֹמֶט *ḥōmeṭ* (1)
skink (1)

2794 חֻמְטָה *ḥumṭāh* (1)
Humtah (1)

2795 חֲמִיטַל *ḥ^{a}miytal* (2)
untranslated (2)

2796 חָמִיץ *ḥāmiyṣ* (1)
mash (1)

2797 חֲמִישִׁי *ḥ^{a}miyšiy* (45)
fifth (43)
five-sided (1)
one fifth (1)

2798 חָמַל *ḥāmal* (41)
spare (12)
pity (6)
spared (4)
had pity (2)
have pity (2)
mercy (2)
allow pity (1)
bear (1)
compassion (1)
concern (1)
felt sorry (1)
had compassion (1)
had concern (1)
in compassion spares (1)
mercilessly (1) +4202
refrained (1)
show mercy (1)
take pity (1)
unrelenting (1) +4202

2799 חֶמְלָה *ḥemlāh* (2)
merciful (1)
mercy (1)

2800 חֻמְלָה *ḥumlāh*
Variant; not used

2801 חָמַם *ḥāmam* (23)
warm (8)
hot (6)
warms (2)
aroused (1)
burn with lust (1)
heat (1)
in a rage (1) +4222
lets warm (1)
warming (1)
untranslated (1)

2802 חַמָּן *ḥammān* (8)
incense altars (8)

2803 1חָמַס *ḥāmas1* (8)
do violence (2)
harms (1)
laid waste (1)
mistreated (1)
stripped (1)
violence (1)
wrong (1)

2804 2חָמַס *ḥāmas2*
Variant; not used

2805 חָמָס *ḥāmās* (60)
violence (43)
violent (5)
destroyed (2)
malicious (2)
crime (1)
fiercely (1)
plunder (1)
ruthless (1)
terror (1)
violent (1) +4848
wrong (1)
wronged (1)

2806 1חָמֵץ *ḥāmēṣ1* (4)
rises (1)
was grieved (1)

yeast (1)
yeast added (1)

2807 2חָמֵץ *ḥāmēs2* (1)
cruel (1)

2808 3חָמֵץ *ḥāmēs3* (1)
stained crimson (1)

2809 4חָמֵץ *ḥāmēs4* (11)
yeast (3)
anything containing yeast (2)
anything with yeast in it (1)
bread made with yeast (1)
containing yeast (1)
leavened bread (1)
made with yeast (1)
with yeast in it (1)

2810 חֹמֶץ *hōmes* (6)
vinegar (4)
wine vinegar (1)
untranslated (1)

2811 חָמַק *hāmaq* (2)
left (1)
wander (1)

2812 1חָמַר *hāmar1* (2)
foam (1)
foaming (1)

2813 2חָמַר *ḥamar2* (4)
in torment (2)
red (1)
untranslated (1)

2814 3חָמַר *hāmar3* (1)
coated (1)

2815 חֶמֶר *hemer* (1)
foaming (1)

2816 1חֹמֶר *hōmer1* (1)
churning (1)

2817 2חֹמֶר *hōmer2* (17)
clay (11)
mortar (4)
mud (2)

2818 3חֹמֶר *hōmer3* (13)
homer (10)
heaps (1) +2818
homers (1)

2819 חֵמָר *hēmār* (3)
tar (3)

2820 חַמְרָן *hamrān*
Variant; not used

2821 חָמַשׁ *hāmaš* (5)
armed (1)
armed for battle (1)
fully armed (1)
outposts (1) +7895
take a fifth (1)

2822 חָמֵשׁ *hameš* (504)
five (164)
fifty (77)
twenty-five (23) +2256+6929
fifteenth (15) +6925
25,000 (14) +547+2256+6929
250 (10) +2256+4395
4,500 (8) +547+752+2256+4395
fifteen (8) +6926
fifteen (6) +6925
500 (5) +4395
captain (5) +8569
fifth (5)
1,254 (4) +547+752+2256+4395
eighty-five (4) +2256+9046
fifties (4)
40,500 (3) +547+752+2256+4395
5,000 (3) +547
50 (3)
53,400 (3) +547+752+2256+2256+4395+8993
603,550 (3) +547+547+2256+2256+2256+2822+4395+4395+8993+9252
fiftieth (3)
fifty-two (3) +2256+9109
forty-five (3) +752+2256
seventy-five (3) +2256+8679
thirty-five (3) +2256+8993
twenty-fifth (3) +2256+6929
1,052 (2) +547+2256+9109
1,775 (2) +547+2256+2256+2256+4395+8679+8679
150 (2) +2256+4395
30,500 (2) +547+2256+4395+8993
345 (2) +752+2256+4395+8993
35,400 (2) +547+752+2256+2256+4395+8993
41,500 (2) +285+547+752+2256+2256+4395
435 (2) +752+2256+4395+8993
45,650 (2) +547+752+2256+2256+2256+2822+4395+9252
46,500 (2) +547+752+2256+2256+4395+9252
52 (2) +2256+9109
54,400 (2) +547+752+752+2256+2256+4395
57,400 (2) +547+752+2256+2256+4395+8679
59,300 (2)+547+2256+2256+4395+8993+9596
65 (2) +2256+9252
652 (2) +2256+4395+9109+9252
95 (2) +2256+9596
fifteenth (2) +6926
fifty-five (2) +2256+2822
men[S] (2)
seventy-five feet (2) +564
1,335 (1) +547+2256+4395+8993+8993
1,365 (1) +547+2256+2256+2256+4395+8993+9252
105 (1) +2256+4395
151,450 (1) +285+547+547+752+2256+2256+2256+2256+2822+4395+4395
153,600 (1) +547+547+2256+2256+2256+4395+4395+8993+9252
156 (1) +2256+4395+9252
157,600 (1) +547+547+2256+2256+2256+4395+4395+8679+9252
16,750 (1)+547+2256+4395+6925+8679+9252
2,056 (1) +547+2256+9252
2,750 (1) +547+2256+4395+8679
205 (1) +2256+4395
245 (1) +752+2256+2256+4395
245 (1) +752+2256+4395
25,100 (1) +547+2256+2256+4395+6929
307,500 (1) +547+547+2256+2256+4395+4395+8679+8993
32,500 (1)+547+2256+2256+4395+8993+9109
337,500 (1) +547+547+547+2256+2256+2256+4395+4395+8679+8993+8993
337,500 (1) +547+547+547+2256+2256+4395+4395+8679+8993+8993
35 (1) +2256+8993
350 (1) +2256+4395+8993
365 (1) +2256+2256+4395+8993+9252
45,400 (1) +547+752+752+2256+2256+4395
45,600 (1) +547+752+2256+2256+4395+9252
454 (1) +752+752+2256+4395
5,400 (1) +547+752+2256+4395
50,000 (1) +547
52,700 (1) +547+2256+2256+4395+8679+9109
530 (1) +2256+4395+8993
550 (1) +2256+2822+4395
56 (1) +2256+9252
595 (1) +2256+2256+2822+4395+9596
60,500 (1) +547+2256+4395+9252
650 (1) +2256+4395+9252
655 (1) +2256+2822+4395+9252
675 (1) +2256+4395+8679+9252
675,000 (1) +547+547+547+2256+2256+4395+8679+9252
7,500 (1) +547+2256+4395+8679
725 (1) +2256+4395+6929+8679
745 (1) +752+2256+4395+8679
75 feet (1) +564
76,500 (1) +547+2256+2256+4395+8679+9252
775 (1) +2256+4395+8679+8679
8,580 (1) +547+2256+2256+4395+9046+9046
815 (1) +2256+4395+6926+9046
845 (1) +752+2256+4395+9046
895 (1) +2256+2256+4395+9046+9596
905 (1) +2256+4395+9596
945 (1) +752+2256+2256+4395+9596
950 (1) +2256+4395+9596
956 (1) +2256+2256+4395+9252+9596
captains (1) +8569
fifteen (1) +2256+6927
fifty-second (1) +2256+9109
seven and a half feet (1) +564+928+2021
sixty-five (1) +2256+9252
thirty-fifth (1) +2256+8993
twenty feet (1) +564+6926
untranslated (13)

2823 1חֹמֶשׁ *hōmeš1* (1)
fifth (1)

2824 2חֹמֶשׁ *hōmeš2* (4)
stomach (3)
belly (1)

2825 חֲמִשִּׁים *hamiššiym*
Variant; not used

2826 חֲמֻשִׁים *hamušiym*
Variant; not used

2827 חֵמֶת *hēmeṯ* (4)
skin (3)
wineskin (1)

2828 חֲמָת *hamāṯ* (24)
Hamath (24)

2829 1חַמַּת *hammaṯ1* (1)
Hammath (1)

2830 2חַמַּת *hammaṯ2* (1)
Hammath (1)

2831 חַמֹּת דֹּאר *hammōṯ dō'r* (1)
Hammoth Dor (1)

2832 חֲמַת צוֹבָה *hamāṯ sôbāh* (1)
Hamath Zobah (1)

2833 חֲמָתִי *hamāṯiy* (2)
Hamathites (2)

2834 1חֵן *hēn1* (69)
favor (41)
grace (5)
pleased with (5) +928+5162+6524
favorably disposed toward (3) +928+6524
bless (2)
gracious (2)
alluring (1) +3202
charm (1)
charm (1) +74
displease (1) +928+4202+5162+6524
displeasing (1) +928+4202+5162+6524
esteemed (1)
favorable toward (1) +928+5162+6524
graceful (1)
kindhearted (1)
ornament to grace (1)
pleased with (1) +928+5951+6524

2835 2חֵן *hēn2* (1)
Hen (1)

2836 חֵנָדָד *hēnāḏāḏ* (4)
Henadad (4)

2837 1חָנָה *hānāh1* (143)
camped (77)
encamped (12)
camp (11)
encamp (9)
set up camp (4)
took up positions (3)

besiege (2) +6584
made camp (2)
pitched camp (2)
set up tents (2)
attacked (1)
besieged (1) +928
besieged (1) +6584
camping (1)
defend (1)
encamps (1)
laid siege to (1) +6584
living (1)
nearly over (1)
remain in camp (1)
remained in camp (1)
set up (1)
settle (1)
settled (1)
stay (1)
untranslated (4)

2838 2חָנָה *ḥānāh2*
Variant; not used

2839 חַנָּה *hannāh* (13)
Hannah (12)
her^s (1)

2840 1חֲנוֹךְ *ḥ^{a}nôḵ1* (16)
Enoch (10)
Hanoch (6)

2841 2חֲנוֹךְ *ḥ^{a}nôḵ2*
Variant; not used

2842 חָנוּן *ḥānûn* (11)
Hanun (11)

2843 חַנּוּן *hannûn* (13)
gracious (12)
compassionate (1)

2844 חָנוּת *ḥānûṯ* (1)
vaulted cell (1)

2845 1חָנַט *ḥānaṭ1* (1)
forms (1)

2846 2חָנַט *ḥānaṭ2* (3)
embalmed (2)
embalm (1)

2847 חֲנֻטִים *ḥ^{a}nuṭiym* (1)
embalming (1)

2848 חַנִּיאֵל *hanniy'ēl* (2)
Hanniel (2)

2849 חָנִיךְ *ḥāniyḵ* (1)
trained men (1)

2850 חֲנִינָה *ḥ^{a}niynāh* (1)
favor (1)

2851 חֲנִית *ḥ^{a}niyṯ* (49)
spear (38)
spears (8)
it^s (1) +2021
its^s (1)
untranslated (1)

2852 חָנַךְ *ḥānaḵ* (5)
dedicated (3)
dedicate (1)
train (1)

2853 חֲנֻכָּה *ḥ^{a}nukkāh* (8)
dedication (6)
offerings for dedication (2)

2854 חֲנֹכִי *ḥ^{a}nōḵiy* (1)
Hanochite (1)

2855 חִנָּם *ḥinnām* (32)
without cause (7)
for nothing (5)
for no reason (4)
needless (2)
useless (2)
without reason (2)
at no cost (1)
cost nothing (1)
costs nothing (1)
harmless soul (1) +5929
in vain (1) +448
innocent (1)
undeserved (1)
without any payment (1) +401
without any reason (1)
without paying anything (1)

2856 חֲנַמְאֵל *ḥ^{a}nam'ēl* (4)
Hanamel (4)

2857 חֲנָמַל *ḥ^{a}nāmal* (1)
sleet (1)

2858 1חָנַן *ḥānan1* (78)
have mercy (14)
gracious (13)
merciful (8)
kind (4)
plead (3)
begged (2)
generous (2)
have pity (2)
making supplication (2)
pleaded (2)
show mercy (2)
beg (1)
beg for mercy (1)
begged for favor (1)
charming (1)
cried for mercy (1)
do a kindness (1)
favor (1)
generously (1)
gets mercy (1)
grace is shown (1)
gracious (1) +2858
graciously given (1)
lift up for mercy (1)
made^s (1)
moves to pity (1)
pity (1)
plead for mercy (1)
prayed (1)
show favor (1)
shows favor (1)
shows mercy (1)
take pity (1)
untranslated (1)

2859 2חָנַן *ḥānan2* (1)
loathsome (1)

2860 חָנָן *ḥānān* (12)
Hanan (12)

2861 חֲנַנְאֵל *ḥ^{a}nan'ēl* (4)
Hananel (4)

2862 חֲנָנִי *ḥ^{a}nāniy* (11)
Hanani (11)

2863 חֲנַנְיָה *ḥ^{a}nanyāh* (25)
Hananiah (24)
he^s (1)

2864 חֲנַנְיָהוּ *ḥ^{a}nanyāhû* (3)
Hananiah (3)

2865 חָנֵס *ḥānēs* (1)
Hanes (1)

2866 1חָנֵף *ḥānēp̱1* (11)
defiled (4)
completely defiled (1) +2866
corrupt (1)
desecrated (1)
godless (1)
pollute (1)
pollutes (1)

2867 2חָנֵף *ḥānēp̱2*
Variant; not used

2868 3חָנֵף *ḥānēp̱3* (13)
godless (10)
ungodly (3)

2869 חֹנֶף *ḥōnep̱* (1)
ungodliness (1)

2870 חֲנֻפָּה *ḥ^{a}nuppāh* (1)
ungodliness (1)

2871 חָנַק *ḥānaq* (2)
hanged himself (1)
strangled (1)

2872 חַנָּתֹן *hannāṯôn* (1)
Hannathon (1)

2873 1חָסַד *ḥāsaḏ1* (1)
shame (1)

2874 2חָסַד *ḥāsaḏ2* (2)
show yourself faithful (2)

2875 1חֶסֶד *ḥeseḏ1* (3)
disgrace (3)

2876 2חֶסֶד *ḥeseḏ2* (248)
love (129)
kindness (41)
unfailing love (32)
great love (6)
mercy (6)
loving (5)
kindnesses (3)
unfailing kindness (3)
acts of devotion (2)
devotion (2)
favor (2)
approval (1)
devout (1)
faithful (1)
faithfully (1)
glory (1)
good favor (1)
grace (1)
kind (1)
kindly (1)
loving-kindness (1)
loyal (1)
merciful (1)
well (1)
untranslated (4)

2877 3חֶסֶד *ḥeseḏ3*
Variant; not used

2878 חֲסַדְיָה *ḥ^{a}saḏyāh* (1)
Hasadiah (1)

2879 חָסָה *ḥāsāh* (37)
take refuge (23)
find refuge (3)
takes refuge (3)
taken refuge (2)
trust (2)
have a refuge (1)
makes refuge (1)
refuge (1)
took refuge (1)

2880 1חֹסָה *ḥōsāh1* (4)
Hosah (4)

2881 2חֹסָה *ḥōsāh2* (1)
Hosah (1)

2882 חָסוּת *ḥāsûṯ* (1)
untranslated (1)

2883 חָסִיד *ḥāsiyḏ* (35)
saints (15)
faithful (6)
godly (4)
loving (2)
consecrated (1)
devoted (1)
favored (1)
holy (1)
merciful (1)
ungodly (1) +4202

untranslated (2)

2884 חֲסִידָה *ḥ^{a}siyḏāh* (6)
stork (6)

2885 חָסִיל *ḥāsiyl* (6)
grasshoppers (2)
locusts (2)
grasshopper (1)
young locusts (1)

2886 חֲסִין *ḥ^{a}siyn* (1)
mighty (1)

2887 חָסַל *ḥāsal* (1)
devour (1)

2888 חָסַם *ḥāsam* (2)
block the way (1)
muzzle (1)

2889 חָסַן *ḥāsan* (1)
hoarded (1)

2890 חֹסֶן *ḥōsen* (5)
rich store (1)
riches (1)
treasure (1)
treasures (1)
wealth (1)

2891 חָסֹן *ḥāsōn* (2)
mighty (1)
strong (1)

2892 חַסְפַּס *ḥaspas* (1)
flakes (1)

2893 1חָסֵר *ḥāsēr1* (23)
lack (3)
lacks (3)
lacked (2)
run dry (2)
always (1) +440
depriving (1)
goes hungry (1)
gone down (1)
had nothing (1) +3972
have too little (1)
in want (1)
made lower (1)
needs (1) +4728
number is less than (1)
recede (1)
scarce (1)
withholds (1)

2894 2חָסֵר *ḥāsēr2* (17)
lacks (9)
lack (3)
lacked (2)
have no (1)
lacking (1)
short (1)

2895 חֶסֶר *ḥeser* (2)
poverty (1)
want (1)

2896 חֹסֶר *ḥōser* (3)
lack (1)
poverty (1)
untranslated (1)

2897 חַסְרָה *ḥasrāh* (1)
Hasrah (1)

2898 חֶסְרוֹן *ḥesrôn* (1)
lacking (1)

2899 1חַף *ḥap̱1* (1)
clean (1)

2900 2חַף *ḥap̱2*
Variant; not used

2901 חָפָא *ḥāp̱āʼ* (1)
secretly did (1)

2902 חָפָה *ḥāp̱āh* (12)
covered (4)
overlaid (3)
cover (2)
are sheathed (1)
paneled (1)
was covered (1)

2903 1חֻפָּה *ḥuppāh1* (3)
canopy (1)
chamber (1)
pavilion (1)

2904 2חֻפָּה *ḥuppāh2* (1)
Huppah (1)

2905 חָפַז *ḥāp̱az* (10)
alarm (1)
alarmed (1)
dismay (1)
fled (1)
headlong flight (1)
hurried (1)
hurrying (1)
terrified (1)
took to flight (1)
untranslated (1)

2906 חִפָּזוֹן *ḥippāzôn* (3)
haste (3)

2907 חֻפִּים *ḥuppiym* (3)
Huppites (2)
Huppim (1)

2908 חֹפֶן *ḥōp̱en* (6)
handfuls (2) +4850
hands (2)
hollow of hands (1)
two handfuls (1) +4850

2909 חָפְנִי *ḥop̱niy* (5)
Hophni (5)

2910 חָפַף *ḥāp̱ap̱* (1)
shields (1)

2911 1חָפֵץ *ḥāp̱ēs1* (74)
pleased (9)
desire (7)
delights (6)
delighted (5)
pleases (5)
want (5)
delight (4)
desires (3)
delight in (2)
displeases (2) +4202
eager (2)
take pleasure (2)
will (2)
delights in (1)
desired (1) +3139
favors (1)
find delight (1)
find pleasure (1)
finds delight (1)
finds pleasure (1)
fond (1)
found pleasure (1)
have delight (1)
have desire (1)
have pleasure (1)
meant (1)
pleasure (1)
rather (1)
take any pleasure in (1) +2911
take delight (1)
willing (1)
wished (1)

2912 2חָפֵץ *ḥāp̱as2* (1)
sways (1)

2913 3חָפֵץ *ḥāp̱ēs3* (12)
desire (3)
delight (2)
delight in (1)
delights in (1)
loves (1)
prefer (1)
takes pleasure in (1)
wanted (1)
willing (1)

2914 חֵפֶץ *ḥēp̱es* (38)
please (5)
delight (3)
desire (3)
desired (3)
pleasure (3)
wants (3)
activity (2)
wanted (2)
care (1)
delightful (1)
desires (1)
eager (1)
just right (1)
matter (1)
pleased (1)
precious (1)
purpose (1)
such things^{s} (1)
want (1)
will (1)
wish (1)
worthless (1) +401

2915 חֶפְצִי־בָהּ *ḥep̱siy-ḇāh* (2)
Hephzibah (2)

2916 1חָפַר *ḥāp̱ar1* (22)
dug (10)
spy out (3)
dig a hole (1)
digs (1)
dug up (1)
look about (1)
paws (1)
reopened (1) +2256+8740
scoops out (1)
search for (1)
seeks out (1)

2917 2חָפֵר *ḥāp̱ar2* (17)
confusion (4)
disgrace (3)
disgraced (3)
humiliated (2)
abashed (1)
ashamed (1)
covered with shame (1)
disappointed (1)
dismay (1)

2918 1חֵפֶר *ḥēp̱er1* (7)
Hepher (7)

2919 2חֵפֶר *ḥēp̱er2* (2)
Hepher (2)

2920 חֶפְרִי *ḥep̱riy* (1)
Hepherite (1)

2921 חֲפָרַיִם *ḥ^{a}p̱ārayim* (1)
Hapharaim (1)

2922 חָפְרַע *ḥop̱raʻ* (1)
Hophra (1)

2923 חֲפַרְפָּרָה *ḥ^{a}p̱arpārāh* (1)
rodents (1)

2924 חָפַשׂ *ḥāp̱aś* (24)
disguised himself (5)
search (3)
in disguise (2)
searches (2)
be ransacked (1)
becomes like (1)
devised (1)
examine (1)
go into hiding (1)
hunt down (1)
inquired (1)

look around (1)
plot (1)
search for (1)
searched (1)
track down (1)

2925 חֵפֶשׂ *ḥēp̱eś* (1)
plan (1)

2926 חָפַשׁ *ḥāp̱aš* (1)
been freed (1)

2927 חֹפֶשׁ *ḥōp̱eš* (1)
blankets (1) +955

2928 חֻפְשָׁה *ḥup̱šāh* (1)
freedom (1)

2929 חָפְשׁוּת *ḥop̱šûṯ* (1)
untranslated (1)

2930 חָפְשִׁי *ḥop̱šiy* (17)
free (9)
free (2) +8938
exempt from taxes (1) +6913
freed (1)
freed (1) +8938
set apart (1)
set free (1) +8938
untranslated (1)

2931 חָפְשִׁית *ḥop̱šiyṯ* (2)
separate (2)

2932 חֵץ *ḥēṣ* (55)
arrows (38)
arrow (12)
archers (1) +1251
did so^{s} (1) +2256+4374+8008
untranslated (3)

2933 1חָצַב *ḥāṣēḇ1* (16)
dug (3)
cut out (2)
dig (2)
cut in pieces (1)
cut to pieces (1)
engraved (1)
hewing (1)
hewn out (1)
prepare (1)
swings (1)
were cut (1)
untranslated (1)

2934 2חָצַב *ḥāṣaḇ2* (1)
strikes (1)

2935 חֹצֵב *ḥōṣēḇ* (8)
stonecutters (5)
masons (2)
stonecutters (1) +74

2936 חָצָה *ḥāṣāh* (15)
divided (5)
be divided (1)
divide (1)
divide equally (1)
divide up (1)
dividing (1)
live out half (1)
parceled out (1)
rising up (1)
set apart (1)
untranslated (1)

2937 1חָצוֹר *ḥāṣôr1* (18)
Hazor (18)

2938 2חָצוֹר *ḥāṣôr2*
Variant; not used

2939 חָצוֹר חֲדַתָּה *ḥāṣôr ḥᵃḏatāh* (1)
Hazor Hadattah (1)

2940 חֲצוֹת *ḥᵃṣôṯ* (3)
midnight (2) +4326
middle (1)

2941 חֻצוֹת *ḥuṣôṯ*
Variant; not used

2942 חֲצִי *ḥᵃṣiy* (125)
half (79)
half-tribe (18) +8657
middle (6)
half-tribe (5) +4751
half-district (4) +7135
halfway (2)
two (2)
half-tribe (1)
it^{s} (1) +2257
midnight (1) +2021+4326
midst (1)
nine-and-a-half (1) +2256+9596
two-and-a-half (1) +2256+9109
untranslated (3)

2943 1חֵצִי *ḥēṣiy1* (5)
arrow (5)

2944 2חֵצִי *ḥēṣiy2*
Variant; not used

2945 1חָצִיר *ḥāṣiyr1* (20)
grass (19)
hay (1)

2946 2חָצִיר *ḥāṣiyr2* (1)
leeks (1)

2947 3חָצִיר *ḥāṣiyr3*
Variant; not used

2948 4חָצִיר *ḥāṣiyr4* (1)
home (1)

2949 חֵצֶן *ḥēṣen*
Variant; not used

2950 חֹצֶן *ḥōṣen* (3)
arms (2)
folds of robe (1)

2951 1חָצַץ *ḥāṣaṣ1* (2)
come to an end (1)
in ranks (1)

2952 2חָצַץ *ḥāṣaṣ2* (1)
singers (1)

2953 חָצָץ *ḥāṣāṣ* (2)
gravel (2)

2954 חַצְצוֹן תָּמָר *ḥaṣṣôn tāmār* (2)
Hazazon Tamar (2)

2955 חִצְצֵר *ḥaṣṣar* (12)
blew (1)
blew trumpets (1)
blow (1)
played (1)
sounding (1)
trumpeters (1)
untranslated (6)

2956 חֲצֹצְרָה *ḥᵃṣōṣᵉrāh* (29)
trumpets (25)
trumpeters (3)
horn (1)

2957 חָצַר *ḥāṣar*
Variant; not used

2958 חָצֵר *ḥāṣēr* (191)
courtyard (59)
court (48)
villages (45)
courts (21)
courtyards (4)
its^{s} (2) +2021
settlements (2)
enclosed (1)
set farther back (1) +337+2021
surrounding villages (1)
where^{s} (1) +2021+2021+2667
untranslated (6)

2959 2חָצֵר *ḥāṣēr2*
Variant; not used

2960 חֲצַר־אַדָּר *ḥᵃṣar-'addār* (1)
Hazar Addar (1)

2961 חֲצַר גַּדָּה *ḥᵃṣar gaddāh* (1)
Hazar Gaddah (1)

2962 חָצֵר הַתִּיכוֹן *ḥāṣēr hatiyḵôn* (1)
Hazer Hatticon (1)

2963 חֲצַר סוּסָה *ḥᵃṣar sûsāh* (1)
Hazar Susah (1)

2964 חֲצַר סוּסִים *ḥᵃṣar sûsiym* (1)
Hazar Susim (1)

2965 חֲצַר עֵינוֹן *ḥᵃṣar ʿēynôn* (1)
Hazar Enan (1)

2966 חֲצַר עֵינָן *ḥᵃṣar ʿēynān* (3)
Hazar Enan (3)

2967 חֲצַר שׁוּעָל *ḥᵃṣar šûʿāl* (4)
Hazar Shual (4)

2968 חֶצְרוֹ *ḥeṣrô* (2)
Hezro (2)

2969 1חֶצְרוֹן *ḥeṣrôn1* (16)
Hezron (16)

2970 2חֶצְרוֹן *ḥeṣrôn2* (1)
Hezron (1)

2971 חֶצְרוֹנִי *ḥeṣrôniy* (2)
Hezronite (2)

2972 חֲצֵרוֹת *ḥᵃṣērôṯ* (6)
Hazeroth (5)
there^{s} (1) +928

2973 חֲצֵרִים *ḥᵃṣēriym*
Variant; not used

2974 חֶצְרַי *ḥeṣray* (1)
untranslated (1)

2975 חֲצַרְמָוֶת *ḥᵃṣarmāweṯ* (2)
Hazarmaveth (2)

2976 חֹק *ḥōq* (129)
decrees (75)
share (11)
decree (8)
statutes (4)
limits (2)
ordinance (2)
allotment (1)
appointed time (1)
barrier (1)
boundaries (1)
boundary (1)
conditions (1)
custom (1)
daily bread (1)
daily bread (1) +4312
horizon (1)
law (1)
laws (1)
limit (1)
make laws (1) +2980
portions (1)
precepts (1)
prescribed portion (1)
quota (1)
regular allotment (1)
regular share (1)
regulations (1)
statute (1)
territory (1)
time (1)
tradition (1)
untranslated (2)

2977 חָקָה *ḥāqāh* (4)
portrayed (2)
carvings (1)
putting marks (1)

2978 חֻקָּה *ḥuqqāh* (104)
decrees (52)

ordinance (23)
regulations (7)
statutes (5)
customs (3)
practices (3)
requirement (3)
rules (3)
fixed laws (1)
laws (1)
regular (1)
requirements (1)
share (1)

2979 חֲקוּפָא *ḥ^{a}qûp̱ā'* (2)
Hakupha (2)

2980 חָקַק *ḥāqaq* (19)
marked out (2)
scepter (2)
captains (1)
chiseling (1)
decrees (1)
draw (1)
engraved (1)
inscribe (1)
lawgiver (1)
leader's (1)
make laws (1)
make laws (1) +2976
portrayed (1)
princes (1)
ruler's staff (1)
scepters (1)
were written (1)

2981 חֵקֶק *ḥēqeq*
Variant; not used

2982 חֻקֹּק *ḥuqqōq* (1)
Hukkok (1)

2983 חָקַר *ḥāqar* (27)
explore (4)
search (3)
examined (2)
was determined (2)
be searched out (1)
dense (1) +4202
discovered (1)
probe (1)
questions (1)
sample (1)
search out (1)
searched (1)
searched out (1)
searches for (1)
searching for (1)
sees through (1)
sound out (1)
test (1)
tested (1)
took up (1)

2984 חֵקֶר *ḥēqer* (13)
fathom (2)
fathomed (2)
searching (2)
finding out (1)
inquiry (1)
mysteries (1)
recesses (1)
seek (1)
unsearchable (1) +401
what learned (1)

2985 1חֹר *ḥōr1* (13)
nobles (12)
noble (1)

2986 2חֹר *ḥōr2* (7)
hole (2)
holes (2)
lairs (1)
latch-opening (1)
sockets (1)

2987 חֻר *ḥur* (2)
hole (1)
pits (1)

2988 חֹר הַגִּדְגָּד *hōr haggidg̱āḏ* (2)
Hor Haggidgad (2)

2989 חֲרָאִים *ḥ^{a}rā'iym* (3)
filth (2)
untranslated (1)

2990 1חָרֵב *ḥārēḇ1* (37)
laid waste (6)
dried up (5)
dry up (5)
desolate (3)
ruined (3)
been dried (2)
dry (2)
parched (2)
devastated (1)
horror (1)
laid waste (1) +2238+2256
lay waste (1)
left deserted (1)
lies in ruins (1)
makes run dry (1)
utterly ruined (1) +2990

2991 2חָרֵב *ḥārēḇ2* (4)
kill (2)
must have fought (1) +2991

2992 3חָרֵב *ḥārēḇ3* (10)
in ruins (3)
dry (2)
ruin (2)
desolate (1)
desolate waste (1)
ruined (1)

2993 4חָרֵב *ḥārēḇ4*
Variant; not used

2994 5חָרֵב *ḥārēḇ5*
Variant; not used

2995 חֶרֶב *ḥereḇ* (412)
sword (362)
swords (31)
swordsmen (5) +408+8990
dagger (3)
knives (2)
war (2)
killed (1) +4200+5782+7023
tool (1)
weapons (1)
untranslated (4)

2996 1חֹרֶב *ḥōreḇ1* (13)
heat (6)
drought (3)
dry (3)
fever (1)

2997 2חֹרֶב *ḥōreḇ2* (4)
object of horror (1)
rubble (1)
ruined (1)
waste (1)

2998 חֹרֵב *ḥōrēḇ* (17)
Horeb (17)

2999 חָרְבָּה *ḥorbāh* (43)
ruins (21)
ruin (7)
desolate (5)
in ruins (3)
deserts (1)
desolation (1)
places lying in ruins (1)
ruined (1)
ruined homes (1)
waste (1)
wasteland (1)

3000 חֲרָבָה *ḥārāḇāh* (8)
dry ground (4)
dry land (3)
dry up (1) +5989

3001 חֲרָבוֹן *ḥ^{a}rāḇôn* (1)
heat (1)

3002 חַרְבוֹנָא *harḇônā'* (1)
Harbona (1)

3003 חַרְבוֹנָה *harḇônāh* (1)
Harbona (1)

3004 חָרַג *ḥārag̱* (2)
come trembling (2)

3005 חַרְגֹּל *hargōl* (1)
cricket (1)

3006 חָרַד *ḥāraḏ* (39)
make afraid (9)
tremble (5)
trembled (4)
come trembling (2)
frighten away (2)
trembling (2)
alarm (1)
fear (1)
frighten (1)
gone to trouble (1) +3010
pounds (1)
quaking with fear (1)
routing (1)
shudder (1)
startled (1)
strike with terror (1)
terrify (1)
terror filled (1) +4394
trembled violently (1) +1524+3010+4394+6330
trembles (1)
untranslated (1)

3007 חָרֵד *ḥārēḏ* (6)
trembles (2)
fear (1)
feared (1) +2118
tremble (1)
trembled (1)

3008 1חֲרֹד *ḥ^{a}rōḏ1* (1)
Harod (1)

3009 2חֲרֹד *ḥ^{a}rōḏ2*
Variant; not used

3010 1חֲרָדָה *ḥ^{a}rāḏāh1* (9)
fear (2)
panic (2)
terror (2)
gone to trouble (1) +3006
horror (1)
trembled violently (1) +1524+3006+4394+6330

3011 2חֲרָדָה *ḥ^{a}rāḏāh2* (2)
Haradah (2)

3012 חֲרֹדִי *ḥ^{a}rōḏiy* (2)
Harodite (2)

3013 1חָרָה *ḥārāh1* (92)
angry (22)
burned (18)
angry (11) +678
burn (6)
aroused (4)
burns (4)
fret (4)
very angry (4) +678
burned (2) +4394
anger (1) +678
angry (1) +928+6524
burning (1)
compete (1)
flared (1)
flared up (1)
furious (1) +678+4394

furious (1) +4394
fury (1) +4394
have more and more (1)
loses temper (1) +3013
rage (1)
raged (1)
troubled (1)
zealously (1)
untranslated (1)

3014 2חָרָה *ḥārāh2*
Variant; not used

3015 חַרְהֲיָה *ḥarhªyāh* (1)
Harhaiah (1)

3016 חֲרוּזִים *ḥªrûziym* (1)
strings of jewels (1)

3017 חָרוּל *ḥārûl* (3)
weeds (2)
undergrowth (1)

3018 חֲרוּמַף *ḥªrûmap̱* (1)
Harumaph (1)

3019 חָרוֹן *ḥārôn* (40)
fierce (28)
wrath (5)
burning (2)
angry (1) +678
burning anger (1)
dry (1)
heat (1)
hot (1)

3020 חֲרוּפִי *ḥªrûp̱iy* (1)
Haruphite (1)

3021 1חָרוּץ *ḥārûṣ1* (6)
gold (5)
untranslated (1)

3022 2חָרוּץ *ḥārûṣ2* (1)
trench (1)

3023 3חָרוּץ *ḥārûṣ3* (4)
sharp (1)
sledge (1)
sledges (1)
threshing sledge (1)

3024 4חָרוּץ *ḥārûṣ4* (1)
maimed (1)

3025 5חָרוּץ *ḥārûṣ5* (2)
decision (2)

3026 6חָרוּץ *ḥārûṣ6* (5)
diligent (5)

3027 7חָרוּץ *ḥārûṣ7* (1)
Haruz (1)

3028 חַרְחוּר *ḥarḥûr* (2)
Harhur (2)

3029 חַרְחֲיָה *ḥarḥªyāh*
Variant; not used

3030 חַרְחַס *ḥarḥas* (1)
Harhas (1)

3031 חַרְחֻר *ḥarḥur* (1)
scorching heat (1)

3032 חֶרֶט *ḥereṭ* (2)
pen (1)
tool (1)

3033 חַרְטֹם *ḥarṭōm* (11)
magicians (10)
them[s] (1)

3034 חֳרִי *ḥªriy* (6)
fierce (3)
burning (1)
great rage (1) +678
hot (1)

3035 1חֹרִי *ḥōriy1* (1)
bread (1)

3036 2חֹרִי *ḥōriy2* (3)
Hori (3)

3037 3חֹרִי *ḥōriy3* (7)
Horite (4)
Horites (3)

3038 חָרִיט *ḥāriyṭ* (2)
bags (1)
purses (1)

3039 חִרְיוֹנִים *ḥiryyôniym*
Variant; not used

3040 חָרִיף *ḥāriyp̱* (2)
Hariph (2)

3041 חֲרִיפוֹת *ḥªriyp̱ôṯ*
Variant; not used

3042 חֲרִיפִי *ḥªriyp̱iy* (1)
untranslated (1)

3043 1חָרִיץ *ḥāriyṣ1* (1)
cheeses (1) +2692

3044 2חָרִיץ *ḥāriyṣ2* (2)
picks (2)

3045 חָרִישׁ *ḥāriyš* (3)
ground (1)
plowing (1)
plowing season (1)

3046 חֲרִישִׁי *ḥªriyšiy* (1)
scorching (1)

3047 חָרַךְ *ḥārak̠* (1)
roast (1)

3048 חֲרַכִּים *ḥªrakkiym* (1)
lattice (1)

3049 1חָרַם *ḥāram1* (50)
totally destroyed (13)
completely destroyed (6)
completely destroy (4)
totally destroy (3)
destroy completely (2)
destroyed (2)
destroying completely (2)
annihilate (1)
be destroyed (1)
bring about destruction (1)
Completely destroy (1)
Completely destroy (1) +3049
destroy (1)
destroy totally (1)
destroying (1)
devote (1)
devoted and destroyed (1)
devoted to destruction (1) +3051
devotes (1)
exterminate (1)
forfeit (1)
kill (1)
must destroy totally (1) +3049

3050 2חָרַם *ḥāram2* (1)
disfigured (1)

3051 1חֵרֶם *ḥērem1* (29)
devoted things (6)
devoted (4)
destruction (3)
set apart for destruction (2)
them[s] (2) +2021
condemned things (1)
curse (1)
destroyed (1)
determined should die (1)
devoted to destruction (1)
devoted to destruction (1) +3049
devoted to God (1)
devoted to the LORD (1)
it[s] (1) +2021
that which is devoted (1)
totally destroyed (1)
untranslated (1)

3052 2חֵרֶם *ḥērem2* (9)
net (5)
fishnets (2)
nets (1)
trap (1)

3053 חָרִם *ḥārim* (11)
Harim (10)
Harim's (1)

3054 חֳרֵם *ḥªrēm* (1)
Horem (1)

3055 חָרְמָה *ḥormāh* (9)
Hormah (9)

3056 חֶרְמוֹן *ḥermôn* (14)
Hermon (13)
heights of Hermon (1)

3057 חֶרְמֹנִים *ḥermōniym*
Variant; not used

3058 חֶרְמֵשׁ *ḥermēš* (3)
sickle (2)
sickles (1)

3059 1חָרָן *ḥārān1* (10)
Haran (10)

3060 2חָרָן *ḥārān2* (2)
Haran (2)

3061 חֹרֹנִי *ḥōrōniy* (3)
Horonite (3)

3062 חַרְנֶפֶר *ḥarnep̱er* (1)
Harnepher (1)

3063 1חֶרֶס *ḥeres1* (1)
itch (1)

3064 2חֶרֶס *ḥeres2* (2)
sun (1)
sunset (1) +995+2021

3065 3חֶרֶס *ḥeres3* (2)
Heres (2)

3066 חַרְסָה *ḥarsāh*
Variant; not used

3067 חַרְסוּת *ḥarsûṯ* (1)
untranslated (1)

3068 חַרְסִית *ḥarsiyṯ* (1)
Potsherd (1)

3069 1חָרַף *ḥārap̱1* (1)
all winter (1)

3070 2חָרַף *ḥārap̱2* (39)
taunted (4)
defied (3)
defy (3)
insult (3)
insulted (3)
insulting (3)
mocked (3)
heaped insults on (2)
reproach (2)
ridicule (2)
shows contempt (2)
taunt (2)
discredit (1)
hurled (1)
mock (1)
rebuking (1)
risked (1) +4200+4637
taunts (1)
treats with contempt (1)

3071 3חָרַף *ḥārap̱3*
Variant; not used

3072 4חָרַף *ḥārap̱4* (1)
promised (1)

3073 חָרֵף *ḥārēp̱* (1)
Hareph (1)

3074 חֹרֶף *ḥōrep̱* (7)
winter (5)

prime (1)
season (1)

3075 חֶרְפָּה *herpāh* (73)
disgrace (17)
reproach (16)
scorn (10)
insults (5)
object of scorn (5)
shame (4)
contempt (3)
scorned (3)
insolence (2)
humiliation (1)
insult (1)
insulted (1)
mock (1)
mocked (1)
objects of reproach (1)
offensive (1)
slur (1)

3076 1חָרַץ *hāraṣ1* (10)
been decreed (2)
decreed (2)
bark (1) +4383
been determined (1)
determined (1)
is decreed (1)
pronounced (1)
uttered a word (1) +906+4383

3077 2חָרַץ *hāraṣ2* (1)
move quickly (1)

3078 חַרְצֹב *harṣōḇ* (2)
chains (1)
struggles (1)

3079 חַרְצָן *harṣān* (1)
seeds (1)

3080 חָרַק *hāraq* (5)
gnash (3)
gnashed (1)
gnashes (1)

3081 1חָרַר *hārar1* (9)
be charred (1)
burn (1)
burned up (1)
burns (1)
chars (1)
glows (1)
is charred (1)
kindling (1)
parched (1)

3082 2חָרַר *hārar2*
Variant; not used

3083 חֲרֵרִים *h^{a}rēriym* (1)
parched places (1)

3084 חֶרֶשׂ *hereś* (17)
clay (9)
potsherd (2)
potsherds (2)
earthenware (1)
fragment (1)
piece of broken pottery (1)
pieces (1)

3085 חֲרֶשֶׁת *h^{a}rešeṯ*
Variant; not used

3086 1חָרַשׁ *hāraš1* (27)
plow (6)
plot (3)
be plowed (2)
plowed (2)
plowing (2)
craftsman (1)
devises (1)
farmer (1)
inscribed (1)
plan (1)
planted (1)
plots (1)
plotting (1) +2021+8288
plowman (1)
plowmen (1)
plows (1)
tools (1)

3087 2חָרֵשׁ *hārēš2* (47)
silent (15)
quiet (8)
says nothing (3)
deaf (2)
altogether silent (1) +3087
fail to speak (1)
holds tongue (1)
keeps silent (1)
kept quiet (1)
made no move (1)
reduce to silence (1)
remain silent (1) +3087
said no more (1)
say nothing (1)
saying nothing (1)
says nothing (1) +3087
still (1)
stop (1)
turn a deaf ear (1)
without saying a word (1)

3088 1חֶרֶשׁ *hereš1*
Variant; not used

3089 2חֶרֶשׁ *hereš2* (1)
secretly (1)

3090 3חֶרֶשׁ *hereš3* (1)
Heresh (1)

3091 1חֹרֶשׁ *hōreš1* (3)
forest (1)
thickets (1)
wooded areas (1)

3092 2חֹרֶשׁ *hōreš2* (4)
Horesh (4)

3093 חָרָשׁ *hārāš* (38)
craftsmen (11)
craftsman (8)
carpenters (4)
carpenters (3) +6770
blacksmith (2)
blacksmith (1) +1366
carpenter (1) +6770
craftsman's (1)
cutter (1)
makers (1)
masons (1) +74
skilled (1)
stonemasons (1) +74+7815
stonemasons (1) +7815
workers (1)

3094 חֵרֵשׁ *hērēš* (9)
deaf (8)
untranslated (1)

3095 חַרְשָׁא *haršā'* (2)
Harsha (2)

3096 חֲרָשִׁים *h^{a}rāšiym*
Variant; not used

3097 חֲרֶשֶׁת *h^{a}rešeṯ*
Variant; not used

3098 1חֲרֹשֶׁת *h^{a}rōšeṯ1* (4)
cut (2)
work (2)

3099 חֲרֹשֶׁת הַגּוֹיִם *h^{a}rōšeṯ haggôyim* (3)
Harosheth Haggoyim (3)

3100 חָרַת *hāraṯ* (1)
engraved (1)

3101 חֶרֶת *hereṯ* (1)
Hereth (1)

3102 חֲשׂוּפָא *h^{a}śûpā'* (2)
Hasupha (2)

3103 חֲשׂוּפַי *h^{a}śûpay*
Variant; not used

3104 חָשַׂךְ *hāśak* (27)
hold back (3)
withheld (3)
kept (2)
bring relief (1)
halted (1)
hesitate (1)
holds (1)
is relieved (1)
is spared (1)
keep (1)
keep silent (1) +7023
preserve (1)
punished less (1) +4200+4752
relentless (1) +1172
reserve (1)
restrain (1)
spare (1)
spares (1)
sparing (1)
too easy on (1)
uses with restraint (1)
withholds (1)

3105 חָשִׂף *hāśip* (1)
small flocks (1)

3106 1חָשַׂף *hāśap1* (11)
bared (2)
draw (1)
lay bare (1)
lift up (1)
pull up (1)
scooping (1)
strip bare (1)
stripped off bark (1) +3106
strips bare (1)

3107 2חָשַׂף *hāśap2*
Variant; not used

3108 חָשַׁב *hāšaḇ* (112)
think (6)
devised (5)
plot (5)
plan (4)
plots (4)
are regarded (3)
count (3)
devise (3)
plotting (3)
thought (3)
was considered (3)
are considered (2)
be considered (2)
be reckoned (2)
considered (2)
determine (2)
devises (2)
intended (2)
make (2)
planning (2)
purposed (2) +4742
seem (2)
seems (2)
were considered (2)
account (1)
account for (1) +907
am counted (1)
be credited (1)
be taken (1)
care for (1)
compute (1)
consider (1)
consider themselves (1)
considers (1)
counted (1)
counts (1)

credited (1)
determine the value (1)
determined (1)
devise plans (1)
devising (1)
esteemed (1)
execute (1)
has in mind (1) +4222
hold (1)
honored (1)
imagine (1)
improvise (1)
is considered (1)
is thought (1)
make plans (1) +4742
mean (1)
planned (1)
plans (1)
plans have (1) +4742
plot against (1) +928+4222
plotted (1)
plotted (1) +4742
regard (1)
regarded (1)
require an accounting (1)
respected (1)
scheming (1)
threatened (1)
treats (1)
tried (1)
was credited (1)
were thought (1)

3109 חֵשֶׁב *ḥēšeḇ* (8)
waistband (7)
skillfully woven waistband (1)

3110 חֹשֵׁב *ḥōšēḇ* (12)
skilled craftsman (8)
designer (1)
designers (1)
designers (1) +4742
skillful men (1)

3111 חַשְׁבַּדָּנָה *ḥašbaddānāh* (1)
Hashbaddanah (1)

3112 חֲשֻׁבָה *ḥ^ašuḇāh* (1)
Hashubah (1)

3113 1חֶשְׁבּוֹן *ḥešbôn1* (3)
scheme of things (2)
planning (1)

3114 2חֶשְׁבּוֹן *ḥešbôn2* (38)
Heshbon (38)

3115 חִשָּׁבוֹן *ḥiššāḇôn* (2)
machines (1)
schemes (1)

3116 חֲשַׁבְיָה *ḥ^ašaḇyāh* (12)
Hashabiah (12)

3117 חֲשַׁבְיָהוּ *ḥ^ašaḇyāhû* (3)
Hashabiah (3)

3118 חֲשַׁבְנָה *ḥ^ašaḇnāh* (1)
Hashabnah (1)

3119 חֲשַׁבְנְיָה *ḥ^ašaḇn^eyāh* (2)
Hashabneiah (2)

3120 חָשָׁה *ḥāšāh* (16)
silent (8)
not speak (2)
aren't do something (1)
calmed (1)
doing nothing (1)
hushed (1)
keeping it to ourselves (1)
not saying (1)

3121 חַשּׁוּב *ḥaššûḇ* (5)
Hasshub (5)

3122 חָשׁוּק *ḥāšûq* (8)
bands (8)

3123 חֻשִׁים *ḥušiym* (1)
Hushim (1)

3124 חָשַׁךְ *ḥāšaḵ* (17)
dark (5)
darkened (3)
darkens (2)
dim (2)
black (1)
blacker (1)
brings darkness (1)
darken (1)
made dark (1)

3125 חֹשֶׁךְ *ḥōšeḵ* (80)
darkness (70)
dark (4)
black (1)
dark place (1)
dusk (1)
gloom (1)
pitch darkness (1) +854
total darkness (1) +696

3126 חָשֹׁךְ *ḥāšōḵ* (1)
obscure (1)

3127 חֲשֵׁכָה *ḥăš^eḵāh* (1)
darkness (1)

3128 חֲשֵׁכָה *ḥ^ašēḵāh* (7)
darkness (4)
dark (3)

3129 חָשַׁל *ḥāšal* (1)
lagging (1)

3130 חֻשָׁם *ḥāšum* (5)
Hashum (5)

3131 חֻשִׁם *ḥušim* (1)
Hushites (1)

3132 חֶשְׁמוֹן *ḥešmôn* (1)
Heshmon (1)

3133 חַשְׁמַל *ḥašmal* (3)
glowing metal (3)

3134 חַשְׁמַן *ḥašman* (1)
envoys (1)

3135 חַשְׁמֹנָה *ḥašmōnāh* (2)
Hashmonah (2)

3136 חֹשֶׁן *ḥōšen* (25)
breastpiece (23)
it (1) +2021
untranslated (1)

3137 1חָשַׁק *ḥāšaq1* (8)
desired (2) +3139
set affection (2)
attracted (1)
in love kept (1)
loves (1)
set (1)

3138 2חָשַׁק *ḥāšaq2* (3)
bands (2)
make bands (1)

3139 חֵשֶׁק *ḥēšeq* (4)
desired (2) +3137
desired (1) +2911
longed for (1)

3140 חִשֻּׁק *ḥiššuq* (1)
spokes (1)

3141 חִשֻּׁר *ḥiššur* (1)
hubs (1)

3142 חַשְׁרָה *ḥašrāh*
Variant; not used

3143 חֲשַׁשׁ *ḥ^ašaš* (2)
chaff (1)
dry grass (1)

3144 חֻשָׁתִי *ḥušātiy* (5)
Hushathite (5)

3145 1חַת *ḥat1* (2)
dread (1)
fear (1)

3146 2חַת *ḥat2* (2)
broken (1)
terrified (1)

3147 חֵת *ḥēṯ* (14)
Hittites (9) +1201
Hittite (2)
Hittites (2)
his people[s] (1) +1201

3148 חָטָא *ḥāṭā'*
Variant; not used

3149 חָתָה *ḥāṯāh* (4)
heap (1)
scoop (1)
snatch up (1)
taking (1)

3150 חִתָּה *ḥitāh* (1)
terror (1)

3151 חִתּוּל *ḥitûl* (1)
splint (1)

3152 חַתְחַת *ḥathaṯ* (1)
dangers (1)

3153 חִתִּי *ḥitiy* (48)
Hittites (25)
Hittite (23)

3154 חִתִּית *ḥitiyṯ* (9)
terror (8)
untranslated (1)

3155 חָתַךְ *ḥāṯaḵ* (1)
are decreed (1)

3156 חָתַל *ḥāṯal* (2)
wrapped in cloths (1) +3156

3157 חֲתֻלָּה *ḥ^ṯullāh* (1)
wrapped (1)

3158 חֶתְלוֹן *ḥeṯlôn* (2)
Hethlon (2)

3159 חָתַם *ḥāṯam* (26)
sealed (12)
seal (2)
seal up (2)
affixing seals (1)
be sealed up (1)
blocked (1)
enclosed (1)
model (1)
placed seal (1) +928+2597
seals off (1) +1237
shut in (1)
stops (1)
untranslated (1)

3160 חֹתֶמֶת *ḥōṯemeṯ* (1)
seal (1)

3161 חָתַן *ḥāṯan* (11)
son-in-law (5)
intermarry (4)
allied himself by marriage (1)
made an alliance (1)

3162 חֹתֵן *ḥōṯēn* (21)
father-in-law (19)
brother-in-law (1)
him[s] (1) +2257

3163 חָתָן *ḥāṯān* (20)
bridegroom (10)
son-in-law (6)
sons-in-law (3)
related by marriage (1)

3164 חֲתֻנָּה *ḥ^ṯunnāh* (1)
wedding (1)

3165 חֹתֶנֶת *ḥōṯeneṯ* (1)
mother-in-law (1)

3166 חָתַף *ḥāṯap̱* (1)
snatches away (1)

3167 חֶתֶף *ḥeṯep̱* (1)
bandit (1)

3168 חָתַר *ḥāṯar* (8)
dug (3)
dig (2)
break into (1)
dig down (1)
row (1)

3169 חָתַת *ḥāṯaṯ* (54)
discouraged (10)
terrified (9)
dismayed (7)
shattered (7)
filled with terror (3)
terrify (3)
afraid (2)
be shattered (2)
shatter (2)
broken (1)
cracked (1)
dreaded (1)
fail (1)
frighten (1)
frightened (1)
panic (1)
stood in awe (1)
terror (1)

3170 1חֲתַת *ḥᵃṯaṯ1* (1)
something dreadful (1)

3171 2חֲתַת *ḥᵃṯaṯ2* (1)
Hathath (1)

3172 ט *ṭ*
Variant; not used

3173 טֵאטֵא *ṭēʾṭēʾ* (1)
sweep (1)

3174 טָבְאַל *ṭāḇᵉʾal* (1)
Tabeel (1)

3175 טָבְאֵל *ṭāḇᵉʾēl* (1)
Tabeel (1)

3176 טָבַב *ṭāḇaḇ*
Variant; not used

3177 טִבָּה *ṭibbāh*
Variant; not used

3178 טְבוּלִים *ṭᵉḇûliym* (1)
turbans (1)

3179 טַבּוּר *ṭabbûr* (2)
center (2)

3180 טָבַח *ṭāḇaḥ* (11)
slaughter (3)
slaughtered (3)
be slaughtered (1)
prepared (1)
slaughter (1) +3181
slaughters (1)
slay (1)

3181 1טֶבַח *ṭeḇaḥ1* (12)
slaughter (9)
animal (1)
meat (1)
slaughter (1) +3180

3182 2טֶבַח *ṭeḇaḥ2* (1)
Tebah (1)

3183 3טֶבַח *ṭeḇaḥ3* (1)
Tebah (1)

3184 טַבָּח *ṭabbāḥ* (32)
guard (13)
imperial guard (12)
cook (2)
untranslated (5)

3185 טַבָּחָה *ṭabbāḥāh* (1)
cooks (1)

3186 טִבְחָה *ṭiḇḥāh* (3)
butchered (1)
meat (1)
slaughtered (1)

3187 טִבְחַת *ṭiḇḥaṯ* (1)
Tebah (1)

3188 טָבַל *ṭāḇal* (16)
dip (8)
dipped (4)
bathe (1)
plunge (1)
soaked (1)
touched (1)

3189 טְבַלְיָהוּ *ṭᵉḇalyāhû* (1)
Tabaliah (1)

3190 טָבַע *ṭāḇaʿ* (10)
sink (2)
sunk (2)
are drowned (1)
fallen (1)
sank (1)
sank down (1)
were set (1)
were settled in place (1)

3191 טַבָּעוֹת *ṭabbāʿôṯ* (2)
Tabbaoth (2)

3192 טַבַּעַת *ṭabbaʿaṯ* (50)
rings (34)
ring (5)
signet ring (5)
signet rings (2)
them (1) +2021
them[s] (1) +2021
them[s] (1) +2021+9109
untranslated (1)

3193 טַבְרִמֹּן *ṭaḇrimmōn* (1)
Tabrimmon (1)

3194 טֵבֵת *ṭēḇēṯ* (1)
Tebeth (1)

3195 טַבָּת *ṭabbāṯ* (1)
Tabbath (1)

3196 טָהוֹר *ṭāhôr* (95)
pure (42)
clean (32)
ceremonially clean (13)
unclean (3) +4202
ceremonially unclean (1) +1194
flawless (1)
free from impurity (1)
unclean (1) +401
untranslated (1)

3197 טָהֵר *ṭāhēr* (93)
clean (23)
be cleansed (12)
cleanse (12)
pronounce clean (9)
cleansed (8)
purify (7)
purified (4)
ceremonially clean (3)
purify themselves (3)
purified themselves (2)
make ceremonially clean (1)
pronounces clean (1)
pronouncing clean (1)
pure (1)
purge (1)
purged (1)
purified themselves ceremonially (1)
purifier (1)
purify yourselves (1)
unclean (1) +4202

3198 טֹהַר *ṭōhar* (4)
purification (2)
clean (1)
clear (1)

3199 טְהָר *ṭᵉhār* (1)
splendor (1)

3200 טָהֳרָה *ṭohᵒrāh* (13)
cleansing (3)
ceremonial cleansing (2)
pronounced clean (2)
purification (2)
purified (2)
clean (1)
cleansed (1)

3201 1טוֹב *ṭôḇ1* (29)
pleases (7)
in high spirits (5) +4213
did well (2)
feel better (2)
beautiful (1)
better (1) +3201
doing good (1)
done well (1)
favorably disposed (1)
go well (1)
make prosper (1)
pleased (1) +928+6524
pleasing (1)
prosper (1)
well off (1)
untranslated (1)

3202 2טוֹב *ṭôḇ2* (489)
good (241)
better (64)
best (17)
well (10)
fine (9)
prosperity (9)
right (7)
better off (6)
gracious (6)
pleases (6)
beautiful (5) +5260
pleases (5) +928+6524
favorable (4)
goodness (4)
precious (4)
choice (3)
kind (3)
like (3) +928+6524
beautiful (2)
favorably (2)
glad (2)
happy (2)
please (2)
please (2) +928+6524
pleased (2) +928+6524
pleasing (2)
prospers (2) +5162
rich (2)
satisfaction (2)
success (2)
very well (2)
alluring (1) +2834
approve of (1) +928+6524
attractive (1)
benefited (1)
better (1) +4946
bounty (1)
celebrating (1) +3427
celebration (1)
cheerful (1)
delightful (1)
favor (1)
festive (1)
fine (1) +1524+2256
finest (1)
flourishing (1)
generous man (1) +6524
graciously (1)
handsome (1)

handsome (1) +5260
handsome (1) +9307
happiness (1)
healthier (1)
help (1)
impressive (1)
intelligent (1) +8507
joyful (1)
likes (1) +928+2021+4200
lovely (1)
mean more (1)
noble (1)
pleasant (1)
please (1) +928+2256+3838+6524
pleased with (1) +928+6524
prefer (1) +928+6524
profitable (1)
profitable (1) +6087
prosper (1)
prosper (1) +5162
prospered (1)
prosperous (1)
relief (1)
sinful (1) +4202
sound (1)
the other[S] (1)
valid (1)
wanted to do (1) +928+6524
wealth (1)
well off (1)
well-being (1)
wicked (1) +4202
wish (1) +928+6524
wished (1) +928+6524
without equal (1) +401+4946
worthwhile (1)
wrong (1) +4202
untranslated (2)

3203 3טוֹב *tôḇ3* (1)
sweet (1)

3204 4טֹב *tôḇ4* (4)
Tob (4)

3205 5טוֹב *tôḇ5*
Variant; not used

3206 טוּב *tûḇ* (32)
good things (7)
goodness (6)
best (3)
prosperity (3)
bounty (2)
good (2)
attractive (1)
best things (1)
blessings (1)
fair (1)
finest wares (1)
gladly (1) +928+4222
joy (1)
prosper (1)
rich produce (1)

3207 טוֹב אֲדוֹנִיָּה *tôḇ ʾᵃdôniyyāh* (1)
Tob-Adonijah (1)

3208 טוֹבָה *tôḇāh* (67)
good (22)
prosperity (9)
good things (7)
favor (3)
well (3)
bounty (2)
good thing (2)
kindly (2)
treaty of friendship (2) +2256+8934
enjoyment (1)
fair (1)
good deeds (1)
good do (1) +3512
good work (1)
goodness (1)
goods (1)
gracious (1)
in behalf (1) +6584
joy (1)
prosperous (1)
satisfaction (1)
unharmed (1)
welfare (1)
well-being (1)

3209 טוֹבִיָּה *tôḇiyyāh* (17)
Tobiah (14)
Tobijah (2)
Tobiah's (1)

3210 טוֹבִיָּהוּ *tôḇiyyāhû* (1)
Tobijah (1)

3211 טָוָה *tāwāh* (2)
spun (2)

3212 טוּחַ *tûah* (11)
covered (3)
cover (2)
been plastered (1)
overlaying (1)
plaster (1)
plastered (1)
whitewash (1) +9521
whitewashed (1)

3213 טוֹטָפֹת *tôtāpōṯ* (3)
bind (2) +2118+4200
symbol (1)

3214 טוּל *tûl* (14)
hurl (2)
hurled (2)
threw (2)
throw (2)
be hurled out (1)
fall (1)
hurl away (1) +3232
is cast (1)
overpowering (1)
sent (1)

3215 טוּר *tûr* (26)
row (9)
rows (9)
course (2)
courses (2)
ledge of stone (1)
sets (1)
untranslated (2)

3216 טוּשׂ *tûś* (1)
swooping down (1)

3217 טָחָה *tāhāh* (1)
bowshot (1) +8008

3218 טְחוֹן *tᵉhôn* (1)
millstones (1)

3219 טֻחוֹת *tuhôṯ* (2)
heart (1)
inner parts (1)

3220 טָחַח *tāhah* (1)
plastered over (1)

3221 טָחַן *tāhan* (7)
grinding (2)
ground (2)
grind (1)
grind grain (1)
ground to powder (1) +3512

3222 טַחֲנָה *tahᵃnāh* (1)
grinding (1)

3223 טֹחֲנָה *tōhᵃnāh* (1)
grinders (1)

3224 טְחֹרִים *tᵉhōriym* (8)
tumors (2)
untranslated (6)

3225 טִיחַ *tiyah* (1)
whitewash (1)

3226 טִיט *tiyt* (13)
mud (7)
clay (2)
mire (2)
dirt (1)
muddy (1)

3227 טִירָה *tiyrāh* (7)
camps (3)
ledge (1)
locations (1)
place (1)
towers (1)

3228 טַל *tal* (31)
dew (31)

3229 טָלָא *tālāʾ* (8)
spotted (6)
gaudy (1)
patched (1)

3230 טְלָאִים *tᵉlāʾiym* (1)
Telaim (1)

3231 טָלֶה *tāleh* (3)
lamb (2)
lambs (1)

3232 טַלְטֵלָה *taltēlāh* (1)
hurl away (1) +3214

3233 טָלַל *tālal* (1)
roofing over (1)

3234 1טֶלֶם *telem1* (1)
Telem (1)

3235 2טֶלֶם *telem2* (1)
Telem (1)

3236 טַלְמוֹן *talmôn* (5)
Talmon (5)

3237 1טָמֵא *tāmēʾ1* (163)
unclean (62)
defiled (28)
defile (12)
pronounce unclean (8)
defile yourselves (6)
defiles (5)
defiled herself (4)
ceremonially unclean (3)
defiling (3)
desecrated (3)
make himself unclean (3)
defile themselves (2)
defiled yourself (2)
impure (2)
make himself ceremonially unclean (2)
make yourselves unclean (2)
be made unclean (1)
became defiled (1)
been defiled (1)
corrupt (1)
defile himself (1)
defiled yourselves (1)
defiles herself (1)
desecrate (1)
impurity (1)
let become defiled (1)
make unclean (1)
pronounce ceremonially unclean (1)
pronounce unclean (1) +3237
pronounced unclean (1)
remains unclean (1) +3238

3238 2טָמֵא *tāmēʾ2* (87)
unclean (64)
ceremonially unclean (12)
defiled (7)
impure (1)
infamous (1) +2021+9005
pagan (1)
remains unclean (1) +3237

3239 טֻמְאָה *tom'āh*
Variant; not used

3240 טֻמְאָה *ṭum'āh* (36)
uncleanness (16)
unclean (6)
impurity (4)
impurities (2)
ceremonially unclean (1)
discharge (1) +2308
filthiness (1)
impure (1)
things that make unclean (1)
unclean practices (1)
woman's monthly uncleanness (1) +2021+5614
untranslated (1)

3241 טָמָה *ṭāmāh* (1)
considered stupid (1)

3242 טָמַם *ṭāmam*
Variant; not used

3243 טָמַן *ṭāman* (31)
hidden (10)
hid (6)
hide (3)
buried (2)
buries (2)
bury (2)
hiding (2)
grave (1)
lies in wait (1)
set (1)
treasures hidden (1) +8561

3244 טֶנֶא *ṭene'* (4)
basket (4)

3245 טָנַף *ṭānap̱* (1)
soil (1)

3246 טָעָה *ṭā'āh* (1)
lead astray (1)

3247 טָעַם *ṭā'am* (11)
taste (4)
tasted (2)
tastes (2)
merely tasted (1) +3247
sees (1)

3248 טַעַם *ṭa'am* (13)
pretended to be insane (2) +9101
tasted (2)
decree (1)
discernment (1)
discreetly (1)
discretion (1)
flavor (1)
good judgment (1)
judgment (1)
tastes (1)
untranslated (1)

3249 1טָעַן *ṭā'an1* (1)
pierced (1)

3250 2טָעַן *ṭā'an2* (1)
load (1)

3251 1טַף *ṭap̱1* (42)
children (27)
women and children (6)
little ones (4)
little children (2)
boys (1) +2351
families (1)
girl (1) +851

3252 2טַף *ṭap̱2*
Variant; not used

3253 1טָפַח *ṭāp̱aḥ1* (1)
spread out (1)

3254 2טָפַח *ṭāp̱aḥ2* (1)
cared for (1)

3255 טֶפַח *ṭep̱aḥ* (2)
handbreadth (2)

3256 טֹפַח *ṭōp̱aḥ* (5)
handbreadth (5)

3257 1טְפָחָה *ṭap̱hāh1* (1)
handbreadth (1)

3258 2טְפָחָה *ṭap̱hāh2* (1)
eaves (1)

3259 טִפֻּחִים *ṭippuḥiym* (1)
cared for (1)

3260 טָפַל *ṭāp̱al* (3)
cover (1)
smear (1)
smeared (1)

3261 טִפְסָר *ṭip̱sār* (2)
commander (1)
officials (1)

3262 טָפַף *ṭāp̱ap̱* (1)
tripping along with mincing steps (1) +2143+2256

3263 טָפַשׁ *ṭāp̱aš* (1)
unfeeling (1)

3264 טָפַת *ṭāp̱aṯ* (1)
Taphath (1)

3265 טָרַד *ṭāraḏ* (2)
constant dripping (2) +1942

3266 טְרוֹם *ṭ'rôm* (1)
untranslated (1)

3267 טָרַח *ṭārah* (1)
loads (1)

3268 טֹרַח *ṭōraḥ* (2)
burden (1)
problems (1)

3269 טָרִי *ṭāriy* (2)
fresh (1)
open (1)

3270 טֶרֶם *ṭerem* (56)
before (36) +928
before (9)
not yet (4)
before (2) +928+4202
before (1) +4946
just before (1) +928
no yet (1)
no yet (1) +3972
still not (1)

3271 טָרַף *ṭārap̱* (25)
tear to pieces (4)
tear (3)
tearing (3)
been torn to pieces (1) +3271
give (1)
killed (1)
mangles (1)
prey (1)
raged (1)
ravenous (1)
surely been torn to pieces (1) +3271
tearing prey (1)
tears (1)
torn to pieces (1)
was torn to pieces by a wild animal (1) +3271

3272 טֶרֶף *ṭerep̱* (22)
prey (13)
food (4)
victims (2)
game (1)
kill (1)
torn (1)

3273 טָרָף *ṭārāp̱* (2)
freshly plucked (1)
new (1)

3274 טְרֵפָה *ṭ'rēp̱āh* (9)
torn by wild animals (5)
animal torn by beasts (1)
animals torn by wild beasts (1)
prey (1)
remains (1)

3275 י *y*
Variant; not used

3276 ־ִי *-iy* (6489)
my (3486)
me (1800)
I (381)
my (77) +4200
the[s] (52)
my own (43)
me (35) +5883
mine (33) +4200
I (29) +5883
myself (27)
our (25)
us (18)
mine (16)
a[s] (9)
myself (9) +5883
I'm (4)
my (4) +5883
my own (4) +4200
her (3)
his (3)
me (3) +7156
myself (3) +4213
we (3)
you[s] (3) +123
here[s] (2)
him (2)
I've (2)
me (2) +3883
my (2) +928+8079
this[s] (2)
us (2) +2256+3870
you (2)
all by myself (1) +963+4200
an[s] (1)
by myself (1) +907+4946
by myself (1) +963+4200
he[s] (1) +3
he[s] (1) +123
her (1) +4200
her own (1)
here[s] (1) +6584
here[s] (1) +6640
him[s] (1) +3
him[s] (1) +123
his[s] (1) +466
I (1) +4213
I (1) +5055
I (1) +7023
I (1) +8120
it[s] (1) +274
it[s] (1) +1460
it[s] (1) +4213
it[s] (1) +7754
its (1)
me (1) +2652
me (1) +8120
me alone (1) +638
mine (1) +4200+8611
mine (1) +6643
mine (1) +9393
my (1) +907
my (1) +928
my (1) +4200+7156
my (1) +6640
my (1) +7156
my life (1)
my life's (1)
my own (1) +4200+8611
myself (1) +963
myself (1) +1414

myself (1) +3338
our own (1)
ours (1) +4200
their[s] (1) +3776+6639
them[s] (1) +6639
they[s] (1) +7366
thought (1) +448+606
us (1) +2157+2256
us (1) +2256+4013
what do I care about (1) +2296+4200+4200+4537
your (1)
your[s] (1) +123
untranslated (353)

3277 יָאַב *yā'aḇ* (1)
longing for (1)

3278 יָאָה *yā'āh* (1)
due (1)

3279 יַאֲזַנְיָה *ya'ᵃzanyāh* (2)
Jaazaniah (2)

3280 יַאֲזַנְיָהוּ *ya'ᵃzanyāhû* (2)
Jaazaniah (2)

3281 יָאִיר *yā'iyr* (8)
Jair (8)

3282 1יָאַל *yā'al1* (4)
become fools (2)
foolish (1)
foolishly (1)

3283 2יָאַל *yā'al2* (19)
determined (3)
pleased (3)
agreed (2)
bold (2)
be so kind as (1)
began (1)
by all means (1)
content (1)
intent on (1)
please (1) +5528
tried (1)
willing (1)
untranslated (1)

3284 יְאֹר *y'ōr* (65)
Nile (31)
river (13)
streams (10)
canals (2)
its[s] (2) +2021
riverbank (1) +8557
rivers (1)
streams of the Nile (1)
tunnels (1) +1324
untranslated (3)

3285 יָאִרִי *yā'iriy* (1)
Jairite (1)

3286 יָאַשׁ *yā'aš* (6)
despair (1)
despairing (1)
give up (1)
hopeless (1)
no use (1)
use (1)

3287 יֹאשִׁיָּה *yō'šiyyāh* (1)
Josiah (1)

3288 יֹאשִׁיָּהוּ *yō'šiyyāhû* (52)
Josiah (47)
Josiah's (3)
him[s] (1)
untranslated (1)

3289 יאתון *yi'tôn*
Variant; not used

3290 יְאָתְרַי *y'āṯray* (1)
Jeatherai (1)

3291 יָבַב *yāḇaḇ* (1)
cried out (1)

3292 יְבוּל *yᵉḇûl* (12)
crops (7)
harvest (2)
grapes (1)
harvests (1)
produce (1)

3293 יְבוּס *yᵉḇûs* (4)
Jebus (3)
untranslated (1)

3294 יְבוּסִי *yᵉḇûsiy* (41)
Jebusites (32)
Jebusite (9)

3295 יִבְחָר *yiḇḥār* (3)
Ibhar (3)

3296 יָבִין *yāḇiyn* (8)
Jabin (6)
him[s] (1) +4046+4889
Jabin's (1)

3297 יָבַל *yāḇal* (18)
bring (5)
are led in (1)
be brought (1)
be carried (1)
be led forth (1)
been carried (1)
bring back (1)
is carried (1)
is delivered (1)
is led (1)
led (1)
sends (1)
taken (1)
was led (1)

3298 1יָבָל *yāḇāl1* (2)
flow (1)
flowing streams (1) +4784

3299 2יָבָל *yāḇāl2* (1)
Jabal (1)

3300 יִבְלְעָם *yiḇlᵉ'ām* (3)
Ibleam (3)

3301 יַבֶּלֶת *yabbeleṯ* (1)
anything with warts (1)

3302 יָבַם *yāḇam* (3)
fulfill the duty of a brother-in-law (2)
fulfill duty as a brother-in-law (1)

3303 יָבָם *yāḇām* (2)
husband's brother (2)

3304 יְבָמָה *yᵉḇāmāh* (5)
brother's widow (1)
brother's wife (1)
her[s] (1) +3871
she[s] (1) +2257
sister-in-law (1)

3305 יַבְנְאֵל *yaḇn'ēl* (2)
Jabneel (2)

3306 יַבְנֵה *yaḇnēh* (1)
Jabneh (1)

3307 יִבְנְיָה *yiḇnᵉyāh* (1)
Ibneiah (1)

3308 יִבְנִיָּה *yiḇniyyāh* (1)
Ibnijah (1)

3309 יַבֹּק *yabbōq* (7)
Jabbok (7)

3310 יְבֶרֶכְיָהוּ *yᵉḇerekyāhû* (1)
Jeberekiah (1)

3311 יִבְשָׂם *yiḇśām* (1)
Ibsam (1)

3312 1יָבֵשׁ *yāḇēš1* (63)
dried up (15)
withered (8)
dry up (7)
wither (6)
dry (5)
withers (5)
dries up (2)
wither away (2)
completely dry (1)
completely withered (1) +3312
drought (1)
fail (1)
made shrivel (1)
make dry (1)
overthrow (1)
parched (1)
shriveled up (1)
wither completely (1) +3312
withered away (1)

3313 2יָבֵשׁ *yāḇēš2* (10)
dry (8)
grapes or raisins (1) +2256+4300+6694
lost (1)

3314 3יָבֵשׁ *yāḇēš3* (3)
Jabesh (3)

3315 4יָבֵשׁ *yāḇēš4* (9)
Jabesh (8)
they[s] (1) +408

3316 יָבֵשׁ גִּלְעָד *yāḇēš gil'āḏ* (12)
Jabesh Gilead (12)

3317 יַבָּשָׁה *yabbāšāh* (14)
dry ground (10)
dry land (2)
land (2)

3318 יַבֶּשֶׁת *yabbešeṯ* (2)
dry land (1)
ground (1)

3319 יִגְאָל *yig'āl* (3)
Igal (3)

3320 יָגַב *yāḡaḇ* (2)
fields (2)

3321 יָגֵב *yāḡēḇ* (1)
fields (1)

3322 יָגְבְּהָה *yogbᵉhāh* (2)
Jogbehah (2)

3323 יִגְדַּלְיָהוּ *yiḡdalyāhû* (1)
Igdaliah (1)

3324 1יָגָה *yāḡāh1* (7)
brings grief (1)
brought (1)
brought grief (1)
grief (1)
grieve (1)
torment (1)
tormentors (1)

3325 2יָגָה *yāḡāh2* (1)
been removed (1)

3326 יָגוֹן *yāḡôn* (14)
sorrow (13)
anguish (1)

3327 יָגוּר *yāḡûr* (1)
Jagur (1)

3328 יָגוֹר *yāḡôr* (2)
fear (2)

3329 יָגִיעַ *yāḡiya'* (1)
weary (1) +3946

3330 יְגִיעַ *yᵉḡiya'* (16)
labor (4)
fruits of labor (2)
products (2)
fruit of labor (1) +4090
heavy work (1)
possessions (1)
produce (1)

toil (1)
wealth (1)
work (1)
worked (1)

3331 יְגִיעָה *yᵉgiyʻāh* (1)
wearies (1)

3332 יָגְלִי *yog̱liy* (1)
Jogli (1)

3333 יָגַע *yāg̱aʻ* (26)
wearied (6)
weary (5)
labored (3)
worn out (3)
toil (2)
exhaust (1)
labor (1)
struggle (1)
tired (1)
toiled (1)
wear out (1)
wearies (1)

3334 יָגָע *yāg̱āʻ* (1)
what toiled for (1)

3335 יָגֵעַ *yāg̱ēaʻ* (3)
wearisome (1)
weary (1)
worn out (1)

3336 יָגֹר *yāg̱ōr* (5)
dread (2)
dreaded (2)
feared (1)

3337 יְגַר שָׂהֲדוּתָא *yᵉg̱ar śāhᵃdûṯāʼ* (1)
Jegar Sahadutha (1)

3338 יָד *yāḏ* (1627)
hand (538)
hands (349)
through (62) +928
hand over (35) +928+5989
power (34)
from (33) +4946
handed over (23) +928+5989
with (20) +928
by (18) +928
to (15) +928
care (14)
to (12) +6584
be handed over (8) +928+5989
afford (7) +5952
arm (7)
next to (7) +6584
arms (6)
command (6)
control (5)
direction (5)
next section (5) +6584
side (5)
supervision (5)
against (4) +4946+9393
finger (4)
have (4) +928
possession (4)
spacious (4) +8146
clutches (3)
fist (3)
hands (3) +4090
hold accountable (3) +1335+4946
next (3) +6584
ordained (3) +906+4848
power (3) +445
special gifts (3) +9556
strength (3)
under (3) +928
along (2) +6584
armrests (2)
as much as pleases (2) +5522
assassinate (2) +928+8938
authority (2)
axles (2)
bank (2)
be sure of this (2) +3338+4200
boldly (2) +928+8123
by (2) +6584
certainly be handed over (2) +928+5989+5989
encouraged (2) +2616
grasp (2)
guilty (2) +928
had (2) +928
hand over (2) +928+6037
handed (2)
handed over (2) +928+6037
he (2) +2257
hold accountable (2) +2011+4946
installed (2) +906+4848
left-handed (2) +360+3545
liberality (2)
monument (2)
next to (2) +448
openhanded (2) +906+7337+7337
ordain (2) +4848
ordination (2) +906+4848
paw (2)
place (2)
play (2) +928+5594
playing the harp (2) +928+5594
projection (2)
projections (2)
prospers (2) +5952
rebelled (2) +8123
seized (2) +8492
supports (2)
taking with (2) +928
them[s] (2) +2021
thumbs (2) +984
times (2)
wheel around (2) +2200
wrist (2)
you (2) +3870
abandon (1) +4946+8332
accompanied by (1) +6584
actions (1)
adjoining (1) +6584
adjoining section (1) +6584
afford (1) +1896+5162
afford (1) +1896+5595
against (1) +4946
agent (1) +4200
along (1)
along (1) +4200
along with (1) +928
arms (1) +723
as a direct result (1) +9393
as prescribed by (1) +6584
assistant (1) +6584
assisted (1) +928+2616
assisted (1) +2616
assisted (1) +6584
attack (1) +928+8938
attack (1) +6584+6590
attacked (1) +928+8938
attacks (1) +928+8938
be defeated (1) +928+5989
because of (1) +928
beckon (1) +5677
beckon (1) +5951
been handed over (1) +928+5989
began (1) +2616
beside (1) +448
beside (1) +928
beside (1) +4200
beside (1) +6584
body (1)
border (1)
borders (1)
bounty (1)
bracelets (1) +6584+7543
broad (1) +8146
brought (1) +928
brought with (1) +928+2118
call to account (1) +1335+4946
carried (1) +928+4374
cause (1) +928
commanded (1)
companies (1)
consecrate himself (1) +2257+4848
consecrate himself (1) +4848
consecrated (1) +906+4848
creditor (1) +1251+2257+5408
custody (1)
customers (1) +6086
customers (1) +6088
debts (1) +5391
dedicate (1) +4848
dedicated (1) +4848
delegation (1) +928+6269
delivered (1) +928
deserves (1) +1691
did this[s] (1) +2257+5742
did[s] (1) +2257+5989
discourage (1) +8332
discouraging (1) +8332
do (1) +5126
do that[s] (1) +928+2118+2257
don't say a word (1) +6584+7023+8492
done by (1) +928
drew (1) +928+4848
entrusted to (1) +448
entrusted to (1) +928
fists (1)
follow (1) +448
for (1) +928
for (1) +6584
force (1)
forcefully (1) +928
four-fifths (1) +752
from (1) +928
gain support (1) +907+2118
gave victory (1) +928+5989
give (1) +928+5989
give up (1) +8332
given over (1) +5599+6584
had chance (1) +928+2118
hand over (1) +928+4835
hand over (1) +928+5162
hand over to (1) +928+5989
handed (1) +928+5989
handed (1) +4946
handed over (1) +928+5162
handed over (1) +928+5796
handing over (1) +928+5989
handing over (1) +928+6037
handiwork (1) +5126
has (1) +928
have (1) +928+5162
have (1) +3780+9393
have on hand (1) +448+9393
have on hand (1) +3780+9393
help (1) +2616
help (1) +4200
help (1) +6640
help (1) +6640+8883
helped (1) +906+2616
helped find strength (1) +906+2616
him (1) +2257
hold (1)
hold (1) +928+2118
hold responsible (1) +1335+4946
holding (1) +928
holds (1) +928+2118
in charge of (1) +928
it[s] (1) +2257
it[s] (1) +3870
killing (1) +928+8938
labor (1)
large (1) +8146
leadership (1)
led the way (1) +2118+8037
let go (1) +906+5663
lets happen (1) +628+4200

little by little (1) +6584
lost courage (1) +8332
made subject to (1) +4044+9393
man-made (1) +132+5126
marched past (1) +6296+6584
memorial (1)
myself (1) +3276
nakedness (1)
near (1) +6584
nearby (1) +6584
of (1) +4946
ordain (1) +906+4848
ordained (1) +4848
ordered (1)
overpowered (1) +6451+6584
pledged (1) +5989
plenty of room (1) +8146
portion (1)
powerless (1) +401+445+4200
put in charge (1) +6584+6641
put up security (1) +4200+9546
reached out (1) +8938
reaches out (1) +8938
reaching (1) +8938
remaining (1)
reward earned (1) +7262
rich (1) +5952
ruled (1) +4939
seize (1) +928+8492
set apart (1) +4848
set free (1) +4946+8938
shapes (1) +5126
shares (1)
shed by (1) +4946
shores (1)
sided with (1) +6640
signpost (1)
sins defiantly (1) +928+6913+8123
snare (1)
someone else[s] (1) +928
stroke (1)
strong (1) +2616
strong arms (1) +2432
submit (1) +5989
submit (1) +8132
submitted (1) +5989
supported (1) +907+2118
surely hand over (1) +928+5989+5989
surrender (1) +928+6037
surrenders (1) +5989
swore (1) +5951
sworn (1) +906+5951
take charge of (1) +9393
taken (1) +928
things did (1) +5126
those[s] (1)
tightfisted (1) +906+7890
to (1) +9393
took with (1) +928
turned about (1) +2200
unable to support (1) +4572
under (1) +4946
under care (1)
used (1) +928
uses (1) +928
vicinity (1)
wants to give (1) +5952
war clubs (1) +5234
waves (1)
weak (1) +8333
with (1) +4200
with (1) +6584
wrists (1)
wrists (1) +723
untranslated (72)

3339 יִדְאֲלָה *yidʾᵃlāh* (1)
Idalah (1)

3340 יִדְבָּשׁ *yidbāš* (1)
Idbash (1)

3341 יָדַד *yādad* (3)
cast (3)

3342 יְדִדוּת *yᵉdidût* (1)
love (1)

3343 1יָדָה *yādāh1* (3)
shoot (1)
threw (1)
throw down (1)

3344 2יָדָה *yādāh2* (111)
praise (44)
give thanks (35)
confess (10)
thanksgiving (3)
confessed (2)
confessing (2)
extol (2)
admit (1)
brings praise (1)
confesses (1)
confession (1)
gave thanks (1)
led in thanksgiving (1) +9378
praised (1)
praises (1)
praising (1)
psalm of thanks (1)
thank (1)
thanking (1)
thanks (1)

3345 יַדּוֹ *yaddaw* (1)
untranslated (1)

3346 יִדּוֹ *yiddô* (1)
Iddo (1)

3347 יָדוֹן *yādôn* (1)
Jadon (1)

3348 יַדּוּעַ *yaddûaʿ* (3)
Jaddua (3)

3349 יְדוּתוּן *yᵉdûtûn* (16)
Jeduthun (15)
his[s] (1)

3350 יַדַּי *yadday* (1)
Jaddai (1)

3351 יָדִיד *yādiyd* (8)
love (3)
beloved (2)
loved one (1)
lovely (1)
loves (1)

3352 יְדִידָה *yᵉdiydāh* (1)
Jedidah (1)

3353 יְדִידוֹת *yᵉdiydôt* (1)
wedding (1)

3354 יְדִידְיָהּ *yᵉdiydyāh* (1)
Jedidiah (1)

3355 יְדָיָה *yᵉdāyāh* (2)
Jedaiah (2)

3356 יְדִיעֲאֵל *yᵉdiyʿᵃʾēl* (6)
Jediael (6)

3357 יְדִיתוּן *yᵉdiytûn* (4)
Jeduthun (1)
untranslated (3)

3358 יִדְלָף *yidlāp* (1)
Jidlaph (1)

3359 יָדַע *yādaʿ* (949)
know (422)
knows (43)
knew (39)
known (23)
acknowledge (21)
understand (15)
teach (13)
realize (12)
make known (11)
tell (11)
made known (10)
learned (9)
aware (8)
find out (8)
know how (8)
show (7)
know about (6)
knowing (6)
learn (6)
be sure (5) +3359
knew about (5)
knowledge (5)
realized (5)
be known (4)
experienced (4)
knows how (4)
lay with (4)
see (4)
understanding (4)
acknowledged (3)
answer (3)
be sure (3)
confront (3)
consider (3)
find out (3) +2256+8011
is known (3)
know (3) +3359
make myself known (3)
observe (3)
see (3) +2256+8011
skilled (3)
unknown (3) +4202
cares for (2)
chosen (2)
concern (2)
concerned about (2)
found out (2)
friends (2)
gain (2)
have (2)
have sex with (2)
ignorant (2) +4202
is made aware (2)
learns (2)
let know (2)
recognized (2)
respected (2)
revealed myself (2)
take notice (2)
unaware (2) +4202
understood (2)
able (1)
acknowledges (1)
acquaintances (1)
agreed (1)
apply (1)
approval (1)
are known (1)
assured (1)
assured (1) +3359
attaining (1)
be found out (1)
be made known (1)
be recognized (1)
be remembered (1)
be sure know (1) +3359
become aware (1)
become known (1)
been discovered (1)
been known (1)
behaved (1)
by surprise (1) +4202
can (1)
can read (1) +6219
cannot read (1) +4202+6219
care about (1)
care for (1)
cared for (1)
close friend (1)

close friends (1)
closest friend (1)
closest friends (1)
come to (1)
comprehend (1)
decide (1)
display (1)
displayed (1)
endowed with (1)
enjoy (1)
experts (1)
familiar with (1)
feel (1)
find (1)
foresee (1)
great skill (1) +1069+2682
had experience (1)
had intimate relations with (1)
had regard for (1)
had the least inkling (1) +3359
has knowledge (1) +1981
have concern for (1)
have knowledge (1) +1981
have to do with (1)
ignorant (1) +1153
inform (1)
instructed (1)
is respected (1)
know all about (1)
know for certain (1) +3359
know how to read (1) +6219
know what it is like (1)
know what means (1)
knowing about (1)
knowing how (1)
knows very well (1) +3359
lain with (1)
leading (1)
learn the difference between (1)
learned about (1)
learning (1)
lets be known (1)
letting know (1)
made himself known (1)
make himself known (1)
make predictions (1)
makes known (1)
man of knowledge (1) +1981
mourners (1) +5631
must understand (1) +3359
not a virgin (1) +2351+5435
note (1)
notice (1)
noticed (1)
perceive (1)
perceiving (1)
proclaim (1)
raped (1)
realize (1) +2256+8011
realized (1) +2256+8011
realizing (1)
recognizes (1)
remember (1)
reveal myself (1)
revealed (1)
show how to distinguish (1)
showed (1)
shown (1)
shown himself (1)
shows (1)
skillful (1)
sleep with (1)
slept with (1)
slept with (1) +408+4200+5435
slept with (1) +2351+4200+5435
slept with (1) +2351+5435
slept with (1) +5435
stranger (1) +4202
strangers (1) +4202
suffer (1)
taught a lesson (1)
teaching (1)
tell the difference (1)
think (1)
think it over (1)
think over (1)
told (1)
trained (1)
understand (1) +1069
understands (1)
understood (1) +1069
unfamiliar (1) +4202
virgin (1) +408+4202
want to do with (1)
was discovered (1)
was known (1)
watched over (1)
watches over (1)
well informed (1) +1981
were seen (1)
untranslated (14)

3360 יָדָע *yāḏā'* (2)
Jada (2)

3361 יְדַעְיָה *y^{e}ḏa'yāh* (11)
Jedaiah (9)
Jedaiah's (2)

3362 יִדְּעֹנִי *yidd^e'ōniy* (11)
spiritists (9)
spiritist (2)

3363 יָהּ *yāh* (49)
the LORD (44)
LORD (4)
he^s (1)

3364 יָהַב *yāhaḇ*
Variant; not used

3365 יְהָב *y^{e}hāḇ* (1)
cares (1)

3366 יָהַד *yāhaḏ* (1)
became Jews (1)

3367 יָהְדַּי *yāhdāy* (1)
Jahdai (1)

3368 יְהֻדִיָּה *y^{e}huḏiyyāh*
Variant; not used

3369 יֵהוּא *yēhû'* (58)
Jehu (52)
he^s (4)
Jehu's (2)

3370 יְהוֹאָחָז *y^{e}hô'āḥāz* (20)
Jehoahaz (18)
Ahaziah (2)

3371 יְהוֹאָשׁ *y^{e}hô'āš* (17)
Jehoash (9)
Joash (8)

3372 יְהוּד *y^{e}hûḏ* (1)
Jehud (1)

3373 יְהוּדָה *y^{e}hûḏāh* (819)
Judah (772)
Judah (11) +1201
Judah's (11)
Judah (6) +824
Judah (4) +1074
Jews (3)
Judean (2)
Judah's (1) +1201
of Judah (1) +1201
their^s (1) +408
they^s (1)
Yaudi (1)
untranslated (5)

3374 1יְהוּדִי *y^{e}hûḏiy1* (82)
Jews (57)
Jew (10)
Jewish (4)
men of Judah (3)
Judean (1)
they^s (1) +2021
untranslated (6)

3375 2יְהוּדִי *y^{e}hûḏiy2* (4)
Jehudi (4)

3376 1יְהוּדִית *y^{e}hûḏiyṯ1* (6)
in Hebrew (5)
language of Judah (1)

3377 2יְהוּדִית *y^{e}hûḏiyṯ2* (1)
Judith (1)

3378 יהוה *yhwh* (6829)&
the LORD (6030)
LORD (399)
the LORD's (243)
he^s (35)
the LORD's (27) +4200
him^s (16)
his^s (13)
he^s (7) +466+3870
him^s (3) +466+3870
its^s (3) +1074
the LORD's (3) +907+4946
his^s (2) +466+3870
me^s (2)
done this^s (1) +1215+4200+4640
he^s (1) +466
he^s (1) +466+5646
he^s (1) +4855
him^s (1) +466+4013
the angel (1) +4855
the LORD's (1) +4946+6640
the LORD himself (1) +7156
untranslated (38)

3379 יְהוֹזָבָד *y^{e}hôzāḇāḏ* (4)
Jehozabad (4)

3380 יְהוֹחָנָן *y^{e}hôḥānān* (9)
Jehohanan (9)

3381 יְהוֹיָדָע *y^{e}hôyāḏā'* (51)
Jehoiada (50)
he^s (1) +2021+3913

3382 יְהוֹיָכִין *y^{e}hôyāḵiyn* (10)
Jehoiachin (10)

3383 יְהוֹיָקִים *y^{e}hôyāqiym* (36)
Jehoiakim (34)
Jehoiakim's (2)

3384 יְהוֹיָרִיב *y^{e}hôyāriyḇ* (2)
Jehoiarib (2)

3385 יְהוּכַל *y^{e}hûḵal* (1)
Jehucal (1)

3386 יְהוֹנָדָב *y^{e}hônāḏāḇ* (8)
Jonadab (5)
Jehonadab (3)

3387 יְהוֹנָתָן *y^{e}hônāṯān* (82)
Jonathan (68)
he^s (3)
Jonathan's (3)
Jehonathan (2)
me^s (1)
untranslated (5)

3388 יְהוֹסֵף *y^{e}hôsēp̱* (1)
Joseph (1)

3389 יְהוֹעַדָּה *y^{e}hô'addāh* (2)
Jehoaddah (2)

3390 יְהוֹעַדִּין *y^{e}hô'addiyn* (1)
Jehoaddin (1)

3391 יְהוֹעַדָּן *y^{e}hô'addān* (2)
Jehoaddin (1)
untranslated (1)

3392 יְהוֹצָדָק *y^{e}hôṣāḏāq* (8)
Jehozadak (8)

3393 יְהוֹרָם *y^{e}hôrām* (29)
Jehoram (16)

Joram (13)

3394 יְהוֹשֶׁבַע *yehôšeba'* (1)
Jehosheba (1)

3395 יְהוֹשַׁבְעַת *yehôšaḇ'aṯ* (2)
Jehosheba (2)

3396 יְהוֹשָׁמָע *yehôšāmā'*
Variant; not used

3397 יְהוֹשֻׁעַ *yehôšua'* (218)
Joshua (203)
he[S] (8)
him[S] (2)
untranslated (5)

3398 1יְהוֹשָׁפָט *yehôšāp̱āṭ1* (82)
Jehoshaphat (79)
Jehoshaphat's (2)
untranslated (1)

3399 2יְהוֹשָׁפָט *yehôšāp̱āṭ2* (2)
Jehoshaphat (2)

3400 יָהִיר *yāhiyr* (2)
arrogant (2)

3401 יְהַלֶּלְאֵל *yehallel'ēl* (2)
Jehallelel (2)

3402 יָהֲלֹם *yāhalōm* (3)
emerald (3)

3403 יַהַץ *yahaṣ* (7)
Jahaz (7)

3404 יַהְצָה *yahṣāh* (2)
Jahzah (2)

3405 יוֹאָב *yô'āḇ* (145)
Joab (132)
Joab's (8)
he[S] (2)
they[S] (1) +2021+2256+2657+8569
who[S] (1)
untranslated (1)

3406 יוֹאָח *yô'āh* (11)
Joah (11)

3407 יוֹאָחָז *yô'āhāz* (4)
Jehoahaz (3)
Joahaz (1)

3408 יוֹאֵל *yô'ēl* (20)
Joel (20)

3409 יוֹאָשׁ *yô'āš* (47)
Joash (30)
Jehoash (16)
him[S] (1)

3410 יוֹב *yôḇ*
Variant; not used

3411 1יוֹבָב *yôḇāḇ1* (2)
Jobab (2)

3412 2יוֹבָב *yôḇāḇ2* (7)
Jobab (7)

3413 יוֹבֵל *yôḇēl* (27)
jubilee (20)
trumpets (3) +8795
ram's horn (1)
rams' horns (1)
trumpets (1) +7967
year of jubilee (1)

3414 1יוּבַל *yûḇal1* (1)
stream (1)

3415 2יוּבָל *yûḇal2* (1)
Jubal (1)

3416 יוֹזָבָד *yôzāḇāḏ* (11)
Jozabad (11)

3417 יוֹזָכָר *yôzāḵār*
Variant; not used

3418 יוֹחָא *yôḥā'* (2)
Joha (2)

3419 יוֹחָנָן *yôḥānān* (24)
Johanan (24)

3420 יוּטָּה *yûṭṭāh* (3)
Juttah (3)

3421 יוֹיָדָע *yôyāḏā'* (5)
Joiada (5)

3422 יוֹיָכִין *yôyāḵiyn* (1)
Jehoiachin (1)

3423 יוֹיָקִים *yôyāqiym* (4)
Joiakim (4)

3424 יוֹיָרִיב *yôyāriyḇ* (5)
Joiarib (4)
Joiarib's (1)

3425 יוֹכֶבֶד *yôḵeḇeḏ* (2)
Jochebed (2)

3426 יוּכַל *yûḵal* (1)
Jehucal (1)

3427 1יוֹם *yôm1* (2298)
day (950)
days (474)
today (137) +2021
time (122)
when (45) +928
today (39) +2021+2021+2296
annals (37) +1821
years (21)
always (18) +2021+3972
life (17)
now (17) +2021+2021+2296
reign (17)
now (14) +2021
lived (12) +2118
times (10)
as long as (9) +3972
lifetime (9)
period (9)
live long (8) +799
years (8) +9102
year (7)
reigns (6)
as long as (5) +2021+3972
day after day (4) +2021+3972
first (4) +2021+3869
three-day (4) +8993
annual (3)
as long as lived (3) +3972
daily (3) +928+3427
day's (3)
ever since (3) +2021+2021+2296+6330
forever (3) +2021+3972
some time (3)
those[S] (3)
all day long (2) +928+2021+2021+2085
always (2) +3972
as long as lives (2) +3972
continual (2) +2021+3972
continually (2) +2021+3972
daily (2) +3427
date (2)
daytime (2)
during (2)
each day (2) +928+3427
each year (2) +2025+3427+4946
for each day (2) +928+1821+3427
live (2)
never (2) +2021+3972+4202
now (2) +465+928+2021+2021
outlived (2) +339+799
rest (2) +3972
some time later (2) +4946
still (2) +2021+2021+2296+6330
weeks (2) +8651
when (2) +928+2021
while (2) +928
whole (2)
after (1) +928
afternoon (1) +2021+5742
age (1)
age (1) +8044
ago (1) +2021
allotted time (1)
annual (1) +2025+3427+4946
as long as (1) +928
as long as endure (1) +3869
as long as live (1) +3972
as long as live (1) +3972+4200+6409
as long as live (1) +4946
as usually did (1) +928+3427+3869
at once (1) +928+2021
at once (1) +928+2021+2021+2085
at once (1) +2021
at this time (1) +2021
awhile (1) +2021+3869
based on the rate paid (1) +3869
birthday (1) +3528
broad daylight (1) +240
celebrating (1) +3202
daily (1) +285+4200
daily (1) +928+1821+3427
daily (1) +928+2257+3427
daily (1) +2021+4200
day (1) +919
day after day (1)
day by day (1) +928+1821+2257+3427
day by day (1) +928+1821+3427
daylight (1)
days as (1)
days of life (1)
distant future (1) +8041
during (1) +928
during that time (1)
each day (1) +2021+2021+3427+4200+4200
each day (1) +2021+4200
each day's (1) +928+2257+3427
each day's (1) +928+3427
each day's (1) +3427
each[S] (1)
endures (1)
enjoy a long life (1) +799
enjoy long life (1) +799
enjoyed long life (1) +8428
ever (1) +2021+3972
ever (1) +3972
ever (1) +4946
ever since (1) +4946
every day (1)
every day (1) +928+3427
every day (1) +2021+4200
every day (1) +2256+3427+3972
fate (1)
first (1) +3869
for a while (1) +285
for life (1) +2021+3972
forever (1) +802+4200
from now on (1) +2021+3972
full (1)
full moon (1) +4057
full years (1) +9102
future (1) +344
future (1) +4737
how long must wait (1) +3869+4537
if (1) +928
immediately (1) +2021+3869
in lifetime (1) +3972
in little more than (1) +6584
in the course of time (1) +3427+4200+4946
in trouble (1) +7997
it's (1) +2021
it[S] (1)
just (1) +2021
just now (1) +2021
lasting (1) +2021+2021+2296+6330
later on (1) +4946
length of days (1) +9102
life (1) +889+2118
life span (1) +5031
lifetime (1) +2644
light (1)

lingering (1) +3427+6584
lived (1)
lives (1) +9102
long ago (1) +4946+7710
many years (1) +802
many years (1) +2256+9102
never (1) +4202+4946
night (1)
noon (1) +2021+4734
old (1) +2644+9102
old (1) +4946+7710
older (1) +2418+4200
older (1) +3888
one month (1) +3732
other days (1) +3427
over a year (1) +196+2296+2296+9102
past (1) +8037
recently (1) +2021
regular (1) +2021+3972
regularly (1) +928+3427+4200
Sabbath after Sabbath (1)
+928+928+2021+2021+3427+8701+8701
season (1)
select a day (1) +3427+4200+4946
set time (1) +4595
seven-day (1) +8679
seven-day periods (1) +2021+8679
since (1) +4200+4946
so long (1) +802
span of life (1)
still (1) +2021+2021+2296+3869
sun (1)
take turns (1) +2143
that day (1) +3427
then[s] (1) +928+2021+2021+2085
this[s] (1)
today (1)
today (1) +2296
tomorrow (1) +4737
two[s] (1)
used to be (1) +6409
very old (1) +928+995+2021+2416
when (1)
when (1) +4946
when began (1) +928
whenever (1) +928
while (1) +3972
while continues (1) +3972
whole month (1) +2544
year (1) +2021+4200
yet (1) +2021
yet (1) +2021+2021+2085+6330
yet (1) +2021+2021+2156+6330
younger (1) +4200+7582
untranslated (65)

3428 2יוֹם *yôm2*
Variant; not used

3429 יוֹמָם *yômām* (51)
day (23)
by day (19)
in the daytime (2)
by day (1) +928
constant (1)
day after day (1) +9458
during the day (1)
during the daytime (1)
every day (1)
in daytime (1)

3430 יָוָן *yāwān* (11)
Greece (6)
Javan (4)
Greeks (1)

3431 יָוֵן *yāwēn* (2)
mire (1)
miry (1)

3432 יוֹנָדָב *yônādāb* (7)
Jonadab (7)

3433 1יוֹנָה *yônāh1* (32)
dove (14)
doves (8)
pigeons (8)
pigeon (2)

3434 2יוֹנָה *yônāh2* (19)
Jonah (18)
Jonah's (1)

3435 3יוֹנָה *yônāh3*
Variant; not used

3436 יְוָנִי *y[e]wāniy* (1)
Greeks (1) +1201

3437 יוֹנֵק *yônēq* (12)
infants (6)
infant (2)
infant's (1)
nursed (1)
nursing (1)
tender shoot (1)

3438 יוֹנֶקֶת *yôneqet* (6)
shoots (4)
new shoots (1)
young shoots (1)

3439 יוֹנַת אֵלֶם רְחֹקִים *yônat 'ēlem r[e]hōqiym*
Variant; not used

3440 יוֹנָתָן *yônātān* (42)
Jonathan (42)

3441 יוֹסֵף *yôsēp* (213)
Joseph (180)
Joseph's (19)
he[s] (5)
him[s] (4)
Joseph (2) +1201
his[s] (1)
they[s] (1) +1074
untranslated (1)

3442 יוֹסִפְיָה *yôsipyāh* (1)
Josiphiah (1)

3443 יוֹעֵאלָה *yô'ē'lāh* (1)
Joelah (1)

3444 יוֹעֵד *yô'ēd* (1)
Joed (1)

3445 יוֹעֶזֶר *yô'ezer* (1)
Joezer (1)

3446 יוֹעֵץ *yô'ēṣ* (21)
counselor (7)
advisers (6)
counselors (5)
adviser (1)
encouraged (1)
one to give counsel (1)

3447 יוֹעָשׁ *yô'āš* (2)
Joash (2)

3448 יוֹצֵאת *yôṣē't* (1)
going into captivity (1)

3449 יוֹצָדָק *yôṣādāq* (4)
Jozadak (4)

3450 יוֹצֵר *yôṣēr* (20)
potter (11)
potter's (4)
him[s] (1) +2021
potters (1)
pottery (1)
pottery (1) +3998
pottery (1) +5574

3451 יוֹקִים *yôqiym* (1)
Jokim (1)

3452 1יוֹרֶה *yôreh1* (2)
archers (1)
they[s] (1) +2021

3453 2יוֹרֶה *yôreh2* (3)
autumn (2)
untranslated (1)

3454 יוֹרָה *yôrāh* (1)
Jorah (1)

3455 יוֹרַי *yôray* (1)
Jorai (1)

3456 יוֹרָם *yôrām* (20)
Joram (14)
Jehoram (4)
him[s] (1)
Jehoram's (1)

3457 יוּשַׁב חֶסֶד *yûšab hesed* (1)
Jushab-Hesed (1)

3458 יוֹשִׁבְיָה *yôšibyāh* (1)
Joshibiah (1)

3459 יוֹשָׁה *yôšāh* (1)
Joshah (1)

3460 יוֹשַׁוְיָה *yôšawyāh* (1)
Joshaviah (1)

3461 יוֹשָׁפָט *yôšāpāt* (2)
Joshaphat (2)

3462 יוֹתָם *yôtām* (24)
Jotham (22)
Jotham's (2)

3463 יוֹתֵר *yôtēr* (10)
advantage (1)
anything in addition (1)
benefits (1)
but (1) +2256
gain (1)
not only (1)
overwise (1) +2681
profit (1)
rest (1)
than (1) +4946

3464 יְזוּאֵל *y[e]zû'ēl* (1)
untranslated (1)

3465 יְזִיאֵל *y[e]ziy'ēl* (1)
Jeziel (1)

3466 יִזִּיָּה *yizziyyāh* (1)
Izziah (1)

3467 יָזִיז *yāziyz* (1)
Jaziz (1)

3468 יִזְלִיאָה *yizliy'āh* (1)
Izliah (1)

3469 יָזַן *yāzan* (1)
lusty (1)

3470 יְזַנְיָה *y[e]zanyāh* (1)
Jezaniah (1)

3471 יְזַנְיָהוּ *y[e]zanyāhû* (1)
Jaazaniah (1)

3472 יֶזַע *yeza'* (1)
perspire (1)

3473 יִזְרָח *yizrāh* (1)
Izrahite (1)

3474 יִזְרַחְיָה *yizrahyāh* (3)
Izrahiah (2)
Jezrahiah (1)

3475 1יִזְרְעֶאל *yizr[e]'e'l1* (2)
Jezreel (2)

3476 2יִזְרְעֶאל *yizr[e]'e'l2* (34)
Jezreel (34)

3477 יִזְרְעֵאלִי *yizr[e]'ē'liy* (13)
Jezreelite (7)
of Jezreel (5)
untranslated (1)

3478 יְחֻבָּה *y[e]hubbāh* (1)
untranslated (1)

3479 יַחַד *yāhad* (3)
join (2)

give undivided (1)

3480 יַחַד *yaḥaḏ* (46)
together (14)
all (8)
alike (3)
completely (2)
each other (2)
alone (1)
along with (1)
also (1)
both (1)
by no means (1) +4202
in force (1)
now (1)
regrouped (1) +665
side by side (1)
together in unity (1)
unite (1) +2118+4200+4222
with (1)
untranslated (5)

3481 יַחְדָּו *yaḥdāw* (96)
together (57)
all (7)
both (4)
alike (3)
as well (2)
fitted (2) +9447
together with (2)
alone (1)
altogether (1)
assemble (1) +5602
assemble (1) +7695
be reunited (1) +7695
came together (1) +7695
each other (1)
even (1)
joined forces (1) +665
people^{s} (1)
two men (1) +278+408+2256
with (1)
with one accord (1)
untranslated (6)

3482 יַחְדּוֹ *yaḥdô* (1)
Jahdo (1)

3483 יַחְדַּי *yaḥdōy*
Variant; not used

3484 יַחְדִּיאֵל *yaḥdiy'ēl* (1)
Jahdiel (1)

3485 יֶחְדְּיָהוּ *yeḥ^{e}dyāhû* (2)
Jehdeiah (2)

3486 יְחוּאֵל *y^{e}ḥû'ēl* (1)
untranslated (1)

3487 יַחֲזִיאֵל *yaḥ^{a}ziy'ēl* (6)
Jahaziel (6)

3488 יַחְזְיָה *yaḥz^{e}yāh* (1)
Jahzeiah (1)

3489 יְחֶזְקֵאל *y^{e}ḥezqē'l* (3)
Ezekiel (2)
Jehezkel (1)

3490 יְחִזְקִיָּה *y^{e}ḥizqiyyāh* (3)
Hezekiah (3)

3491 יְחִזְקִיָּהוּ *y^{e}ḥizqiyyāhû* (41)
Hezekiah (37)
Hezekiah's (2)
he^{s} (1)
Jehizkiah (1)

3492 יַחְזֵרָה *yaḥzērāh* (1)
Jahzerah (1)

3493 יְחִיאֵל *y^{e}ḥiy'ēl* (14)
Jehiel (14)

3494 יְחִיאֵלִי *y^{e}ḥiy'ēliy* (2)
Jehieli (2)

3495 יָחִיד *yāḥiyḏ* (12)
only son (5)
only child (3)
lonely (2)
precious life (2)

3496 יְחִיָּה *y^{e}ḥiyyāh* (1)
Jehiah (1)

3497 יָחִיל *yāḥiyl* (1)
wait (1)

3498 יָחַל *yāḥal* (45)
put hope (14)
hope (7)
wait (7)
waited (6)
expect (1)
expectantly (1)
given hope (1)
hope unfulfilled (1)
linger (1)
looked (1)
looking (1)
wait for (1)
wait in hope (1)
untranslated (2)

3499 יַחְלְאֵל *yaḥl^{e}'ēl* (2)
Jahleel (2)

3500 יַחְלְאֵלִי *yaḥl^{e}'ēliy* (1)
Jahleelite (1)

3501 יָחַם *yāḥam* (6)
in heat (2)
breeding (1) +2021+7366
conceived (1)
mate (1)
mated (1)

3502 יַחְמוּר *yaḥmûr* (2)
roe deer (1)
roebucks (1)

3503 יַחְמַי *yaḥmay* (1)
Jahmai (1)

3504 יָחֵף *yāḥēp̱* (5)
barefoot (4)
bare (1)

3505 יַחְצְאֵל *yaḥs^{e}'ēl* (2)
Jahzeel (1)
Jahziel (1)

3506 יַחְצְאֵלִי *yaḥs^{e}'ēliy* (1)
Jahzeelite (1)

3507 יַחֲצִיאֵל *yaḥ^{a}siy'ēl* (1)
Jahziel (1)

3508 יָחַר *yāḥar* (1)
untranslated (1)

3509 יָחַשׂ *yāḥaś* (20)
family (2)
listed (2)
listed in genealogy (2)
be listed in the genealogical record (1)
deal with genealogies (1)
enrolled in the genealogical records (1)
genealogical record listed (1)
kept a genealogical record (1)
listed in genealogical records (1)
names in the genealogical records (1)
registered (1)
registration by families (1)
was listed in the genealogies (1)
were entered in the genealogical records (1)
were recorded in the genealogies (1)
were registered (1)
were registered by genealogy (1)

3510 יַחַשׂ *yaḥaś* (1)
genealogical (1)

3511 יַחַת *yaḥaṯ* (8)
Jahath (7)
Jehath (1)

3512 יָטַב *yāṭaḇ* (115)
go well (14)
do good (10)
good (10)
pleased (7) +928+6524
reform (4)
make prosper (3)
well (3)
do what is right (2)
enjoy (2)
thoroughly (2)
treated well (2)
adorned (1)
appealed to (1) +928+6524
arranged (1)
best (1)
better (1)
brought success (1)
cheer up (1) +4213
commends (1)
correctly (1)
delighted (1)
do right (1)
do^{s} (1)
doing good (1)
enjoying (1)
found favor (1)
give joy (1)
gives (1)
glad (1) +928+6524
glad (1) +4213
goes well (1)
good do (1) +3208
good done (1)
greater (1)
ground to powder (1) +3221
have a right (1)
have any right (1)
in good spirits (1) +4213
inclined (1)
kind (1)
make famous (1)
make more prosperous (1)
makes cheerful (1)
please (1)
pleased (1)
pleased with (1) +928+6524
pleases (1) +928+6524
prosper (1)
really change (1) +3512
satisfied (1) +928+6524
share (1)
show kindness (1)
skilled (1)
skilled (1) +2006
skillfully (1)
stately (1)
stately bearing (1)
surely make prosper (1) +3512
tends (1)
thorough (1)
to pieces (1)
treat well (1)
very (1)
well provided for (1)
wish (1) +928+6524

3513 יָטְבָה *yoṭ^{e}ḇāh* (1)
Jotbah (1)

3514 יָטְבָתָה *yoṭ^{e}ḇāṯāh* (3)
Jotbathah (3)

3515 יְטוּר *y^{e}ṭûr* (3)
Jetur (3)

3516 יַיִן *yayin* (141)
wine (132)
grapevine (2) +1728
wineskins (2) +5532
banquet (1) +5492
banquet hall (1) +1074
old wine (1)
sober (1) +2021+3655+4946

wine offerings (1)

3517 יַךְ *yak̲*
Variant; not used

3518 יְכוֹנְיָה *yᵉk̲ônyāh*
Variant; not used

3519 יָכַח *yāk̲ah* (59)
rebuke (14)
punish (3)
rebuked (3)
rebukes (3)
chosen (2)
judge (2)
settle disputes (2)
accuse (1)
accuses (1)
arbitrate (1)
are vindicated (1)
argue (1)
argue case (1)
arguments (1)
be chastened (1)
complained (1)
convict (1)
correct (1)
correction (1)
corrects (1)
decide (1)
defend (1)
defender (1)
disciplines (1)
give decisions (1)
lodging a charge (1)
pleads (1)
present case (1)
prove (1)
proved wrong (1)
reason together (1)
rebuke frankly (1) +3519
reproves (1)
surely rebuke (1) +3519
use[S] (1)

3520 1יָכִין *yāk̲iyn1* (6)
Jakin (6)

3521 2יָכִין *yāk̲iyn2* (2)
Jakin (2)

3522 יָכִינִי *yāk̲iyniy* (1)
Jakinite (1)

3523 יָכֹל *yāk̲ōl* (194)
cannot (45) +4202
could (38)
able (23)
can (22)
can't (7) +4202
overcome (5)
must (4)
overpower (3)
prevail (3)
succeed (3)
allowed (2)
bear (2)
can do (2)
overcame (2)
allowed to (1)
attain (1)
avail (1)
can (1) +3523
can certainly do (1) +3523
cannot bear (1) +4202
cannot stand (1) +4202
could do (1)
could risk (1)
dare (1)
dares (1)
endure (1)
ever able (1) +3523
failed (1) +4202
gained the victory (1)
have time (1) +4538
incapable (1) +4202
powerless (1) +4202
prevailed (1)
surely triumph (1) +3523
too heavy a burden to carry (1) +4202+5951
troubled (1) +4202+9200
unable (1) +4202
will (1)
won (1)
untranslated (4)

3524 יְכָלְיָה *yᵉk̲olyāh* (2)
Jecoliah (1)
untranslated (1)

3525 יְכָלְיָהוּ *yᵉk̲olyāhû* (1)
Jecoliah (1)

3526 יְכָנְיָה *yᵉk̲onyāh* (7)
Jehoiachin (6)
untranslated (1)

3527 יְכָנְיָהוּ *yᵉk̲onyāhû* (1)
Jehoiachin (1)

3528 יָלַד *yālad̲* (495)
father (147)
bore (49)
gave birth (46)
had (31)
born (24)
were born (20)
give birth (16)
borne (13)
in labor (12)
gives birth (8)
have (7)
midwives (7)
was born (7)
is born (5)
be born (4)
bear children (4)
has (4)
mother (4)
bear (3)
bears (3)
given birth (3)
having children (3)
baby (2)
been born (2)
birth (2)
borne children (2)
childless (2) +4202
descendants (2)
had a baby (2)
had a son (2)
had children (2)
have children (2)
in childbirth (2)
midwife (2)
was descended (2)
arrives (1)
be brought forth (1)
bear a child (1)
bearing children (1)
begotten (1)
birthday (1) +3427
bore a child (1)
bore young (1)
bring forth (1)
bring to delivery (1)
child was born (1)
childbirth (1)
children (1)
children born (1)
daughter (1)
descendant (1)
fathered (1)
fathers (1)
forefather (1)
gave life (1)
give delivery (1)
giving birth (1)
had sons (1)
has son (1)
have a child (1)
have a son (1)
help in childbirth (1)
indicated ancestry (1)
lay (1)
making bud (1)
men[S] (1)
native-born (1) +824+928+2021
near the time of delivery (1)
newborn (1)
placed at birth (1)
remained childless (1) +4202
son be born (1)
women[S] (1)
yet unborn (1)
untranslated (10)

3529 יֶלֶד *yeled̲* (90)
child (21)
children (20)
young men (11)
boy (8)
boys (5)
baby (4)
boy's (3)
young (3)
sons (2)
youth (2)
babies (1)
baby's (1)
brood (1)
gives birth prematurely (1) +3655
little ones (1)
pagans (1) +5799
son (1)
young man (1)
youths (1)
untranslated (2)

3530 יַלְדָּה *yaldāh* (3)
girls (2)
girl (1)

3531 יַלְדוּת *yaldût* (3)
youth (2)
young (1)

3532 יָלַה *yālah* (1)
wasted away (1)

3533 יִלּוֹד *yillôd̲* (5)
born (4)
children born (1)

3534 יָלוֹן *yālôn* (1)
Jalon (1)

3535 יָלִיד *yāliyd̲* (13)
descendants (6)
born (3)
those born (3)
slave by birth (1) +1074

3536 יָלַל *yālal* (30)
wail (26)
turn to wailing (1)
wails (1)
weep (1)
untranslated (1)

3537 יְלֵל *yᵉlēl* (1)
howling (1)

3538 יְלָלָה *yᵉlālāh* (5)
wailing (3)
lamentation (1)
wail (1)

3539 יַלֶּפֶת *yallep̱et̲* (2)
running sores (2)

3540 יֶלֶק *yeleq* (9)
grasshoppers (3)
locusts (2)
young locusts (2)
swarm of locusts (1)

young locust (1)

3541 יַלְקוּט *yalqût* (1)
pouch (1)

3542 יָם *yām* (395)
sea (262)
west (37)
west (28) +2025
seas (21)
seashore (5)
seashore (5) +8557
western (5)
coast (4) +2572
it[s] (4) +2021
high seas (3) +4213
westward (3) +2025
coast (2)
river (2)
western (2) +2025
coast (1) +8557
distant shores (1) +362
extend westward (1) +2025
lake (1)
overboard (1) +448+2021
seafarers (1) +6296
seamen (1) +2480
seashore (1) +2572
shore (1) +8557
south (1)
waters (1)
untranslated (1)

3543 יְמוּאֵל *y‘mû’ēl* (2)
Jemuel (2)

3544 יְמִימָה *y‘miymāh* (1)
Jemimah (1)

3545 1יָמִין *yāmiyn1* (140)
right (118)
south (12)
left-handed (2) +360+3338
south (2) +4946
hand (1)
southward (1) +448+2021
which way (1) +196+6584+6584+8520
untranslated (3)

3546 2יָמִין *yāmiyn2* (6)
Jamin (6)

3547 יָמִינִי *yāmiyniy* (1)
Jaminite (1)

3548 יְמָנִי *y‘māyniy* (2)
untranslated (2)

3549 יְמִינִי *y‘miyniy* (4)
Benjamin (1)
Benjamin (1) +408+1201
Benjamite (1) +408
tribe of Benjamin (1) +408

3550 יִמְלָא *yimlā’* (2)
Imlah (2)

3551 יִמְלָה *yimlāh* (2)
Imlah (2)

3552 יַמְלֵךְ *yamlēk* (1)
Jamlech (1)

3553 יֵמִם *yēmim* (1)
hot springs (1)

3554 יָמַן *yāman* (5)
turn to the right (2)
go to the right (1)
right-handed (1)
to the right (1)

3555 יִמְנָה *yimnāh* (5)
Imnah (4)
Imnite (1)

3556 יְמָנִי *y‘māniy* (33)
right (24)
south (9)

3557 יִמְנָע *yimnā‘* (1)
Imna (1)

3558 יָמַר *yāmar* (1)
changed (1)

3559 יִמְרָה *yimrāh* (1)
Imrah (1)

3560 יָמַשׁ *yāmaš* (1)
untranslated (1)

3561 יָנָה *yānāh* (19)
oppress (5)
oppressor (3)
mistreat (2)
oppressors (2)
take advantage of (2)
crush (1)
do wrong (1)
driving (1)
mistreated (1)
oppresses (1)

3562 יָנוֹחַ *yānôah* (3)
Janoah (3)

3563 יָנוֹחָה *yānôhāh*
Variant; not used

3564 יָנוּם *yānûm* (1)
untranslated (1)

3565 יָנִים *yāniym* (1)
Janim (1)

3566 יְנִיקָה *y‘niyqāh* (1)
shoot (1)

3567 יָנַק *yānaq* (16)
nurse (7)
nursed (4)
drink (1)
feast on (1)
female (1)
nourished (1)
suck (1)

3568 יַנְשׁוּף *yanšûp* (3)
great owl (3)

3569 1יָסַד *yāsad1* (41)
laid the foundations (5)
the foundation was laid (4)
established (3)
laid the foundation (3)
founded (2)
ordained (2)
set (2)
the foundation laid (2)
assigned (1)
assigned to positions (1)
begun (1)
doing this[s] (1) +2021+6894
foundations (1)
foundations be laid (1)
instructed (1)
laid foundations (1)
lay (1)
lay foundations (1)
lays the foundation (1)
made a place (1)
provide a foundation (1)
sets (1)
sure (1)
the foundation been laid (1)
the foundations were laid (1)
was founded (1)

3570 2יָסַד *yāsad2* (2)
conspire (1)
gather (1)

3571 יְסֻד *y‘sud*
Variant; not used

3572 יְסוֹד *y‘sôd* (20)
base (9)
foundations (6)
foundation (2)
foot (1)
restoration (1)
stand firm (1)

3573 יְסוּדָה *y‘sûdāh* (1)
foundation (1)

3574 יִסּוֹר *yissôr* (1)
correct (1)

3575 יָסַךְ *yāsak*
Variant; not used

3576 יִסְכָּה *yiskāh* (1)
Iscah (1)

3577 יִסְמַכְיָהוּ *yismakyāhû* (1)
Ismakiah (1)

3578 יָסַף *yāsap* (217)
again (26)
again (22) +6388
add (21)
severely (12)
more (9)
longer (8)
more (7) +6388
added (6)
longer (5) +6388
once more (5)
anymore (4) +6388
continued (4)
make even heavier (4)
anymore (3)
do again (3)
multiply (3)
adding (2)
adds (2)
all the more (2) +6388
enlarged (2)
far exceeded (2)
increased (2)
never (2) +4202
once again (2)
once again (2) +6388
once more (2) +6388
promote (2)
adds length (1)
another (1)
another (1) +6388
any longer (1)
any longer (1) +6388
back (1) +6388
be added (1)
bring (1)
bring more and more (1)
brings (1)
by far (1)
carried still further (1)
continued (1) +6388
destroy (1)
do again (1) +6388
else (1)
ever (1)
farther (1)
gains (1)
gave (1)
given even more (1) +2179+2179+2256+3869+3869
grow stronger (1) +601
had reaffirm (1)
heap (1)
heaping (1)
increase (1)
increase (1) +6584
join (1)
later (1)
make again (1) +6388
make increase (1)
making more (1)
more (1) +8041
more and more (1)
more and more (1) +3972+6584

more besides (1)
multiplies (1)
over (1)
persist (1)
prolong (1)
reach out[s] (1)
still another (1) +6388
still more (1)
stirring up more (1)
stop (1) +4202
stopped (1) +4202+6388
were added (1) +6388
untranslated (6)

3579 1יָסַר *yāsar1* (42)
discipline (10)
punish (5)
scourged (4)
disciplines (3)
instructs (2)
scourge (2)
take warning (2)
accept correction (1)
be corrected (1)
be warned (1)
been disciplined (1)
catch (1)
chastened severely (1) +3579
correct (1)
corrects (1)
disciplined (1)
instructed (1)
taught (1)
trained (1)
warning (1)

3580 2יָסַר *yāsar2*
Variant; not used

3581 יָסֹר *yāsōr*
Variant; not used

3582 יָע *yā‘* (9)
shovels (9)

3583 1יַעְבֵּץ *ya‘bēs1* (1)
Jabez (1)

3584 2יַעְבֵּץ *ya‘bēs2* (3)
Jabez (3)

3585 יָעַד *yā‘aḏ* (28)
meet (8)
banded together (3)
assemble (2)
challenge (2)
gathered (2)
joined forces (2)
appointed (1)
met by agreement (1)
ordered (1)
placed (1)
selected (1)
selects (1)
set (1)
summon (1)
turned (1)

3586 יַעְדָּה *ya‘dāh* (2)
Jadah (2)

3587 יֶעְדוֹ *ye‘dô* (1)
Iddo (1)

3588 יֶעְדִּי *ye‘diy* (1)
untranslated (1)

3589 יָעָה *yā‘āh* (1)
sweep away (1)

3590 יְעוּאֵל *yᵉ‘û’ēl* (6)
Jeuel (2)
untranslated (4)

3591 יְעוּץ *yᵉ‘ûs* (1)
Jeuz (1)

3592 יָעוּר *yā‘ûr* (1)
untranslated (1)

3593 יְעוּשׁ *yᵉ‘ûš* (9)
Jeush (9)

3594 יָעַז *yā‘az* (1)
arrogant (1)

3595 יַעֲזִיאֵל *ya‘ᵃziy’ēl* (1)
Jaaziel (1)

3596 יַעֲזִיָּהוּ *ya‘ᵃziyyāhû* (2)
Jaaziah (2)

3597 יַעְזֵיר *ya‘zēyr* (13)
Jazer (13)

3598 יָעַט *yā‘at* (1)
arrayed (1)

3599 יְעִיאֵל *yᵉ‘iy’ēl* (13)
Jeiel (13)

3600 יָעִיר *yā‘iyr* (1)
Jair (1)

3601 יְעִישׁ *yᵉ‘iyš* (3)
untranslated (3)

3602 יַעְכָּן *ya‘kān* (1)
Jacan (1)

3603 יָעַל *yā‘al* (23)
gain (3)
of value (2)
succeed (2)
worthless idols (2) +4202
advantage (1)
benefit (1)
benefit in the least (1) +3603
best (1)
did good (1)
do good (1)
have value (1)
profit (1)
unprofitable (1) +4202
useless (1) +4202
worthless (1) +1153
worthless (1) +1194
worthless (1) +4202

3604 1יָעֵל *yā‘ēl1* (3)
wild goats (2)
goats (1)

3605 2יָעֵל *yā‘ēl2* (6)
Jael (6)

3606 יַעֲלָא *ya‘ᵃlā’* (1)
Jaala (1)

3607 1יַעֲלָה *ya‘ᵃlāh1* (1)
deer (1)

3608 2יַעֲלָה *ya‘ᵃlāh2* (1)
Jaala (1)

3609 יַעְלָם *ya‘lām* (4)
Jalam (4)

3610 1יַעַן *ya‘an1* (99)
because (34)
because (21) +889
because (3) +3954
because of (3)
for (3) +889
since (3) +889
for (2)
because (1) +561+4202
because (1) +928
because (1) +928+2256+3610
because (1) +928+3610
but since (1)
in (1)
since (1)
since (1) +3954
so (1) +561+4202
so that (1) +889
therefore (1) +4027+4200
while (1)
why (1) +4537
untranslated (15)

3611 2יַעַן *ya‘an2*
Variant; not used

3612 יָעֵן *yā‘ēn* (1)
ostriches (1)

3613 יַעֲנָה *ya‘ᵃnāh* (8)
owls (4) +1426
horned owl (2) +1426
owl (2) +1426

3614 יַעְנַי *ya‘nay* (1)
Janai (1)

3615 1יָעֵף *yā‘ēp̱1* (8)
faint (2)
tired (2)
exhaust (1)
fall (1)
labor (1)
tire (1)

3616 2יָעֵף *yā‘ēp̱2* (1)
swift flight (1) +3618

3617 3יָעֵף *yā‘ēp̱3* (3)
weary (2)
exhausted (1)

3618 יְעָף *yᵉ‘āp̱* (1)
swift flight (1) +3616

3619 יָעַץ *yā‘as* (59)
consulted (5)
advice gave (3) +6783
advise (3)
advised (3)
planned (3)
advice (2)
advice given (2) +6783
counsels (2)
determined (2)
planned (2) +6783
plot (2)
plotted (2)
purposed (2)
advice offered (1)
advise (1) +6783
agreed (1)
confer (1)
conferred (1)
conferring (1)
conspire (1)
consult (1)
consulted advisers (1)
consulting (1)
counsel (1)
counseled (1)
decided (1)
give advice (1)
give counsel (1)
giving advice (1) +6783
intend (1)
makes plans (1)
makes up (1)
planning (1) +6783
plotted (1) +6783
promote (1)
seeking advice (1)
take advice (1)
take counsel (1)
warn (1)

3620 יַעֲקֹב *ya‘ᵃqōḇ* (349)
Jacob (316)
Jacob's (17)
he[s] (7)
him[s] (5)
his[s] (2)
Jacob's (1) +4200
them[s] (1) +1201

3621 יַעֲקֹבָה *ya‘ᵃqōḇāh* (1)
Jaakobah (1)

3622 יַעֲקָן *ya'ᵃqān* (1)
Jaakanites (1) +1201

3623 1יַעַר *ya'ar1* (57)
forest (38)
forests (7)
thickets (3)
woods (3)
finest of forests (2) +4149
thicket (2)
forested (1)
groves (1)

3624 2יַעַר *ya'ar2* (1)
honeycomb (1)

3625 3יַעַר *ya'ar3* (1)
Jaar (1)

3626 1יַעֲרָה *ya'ᵃrāh1* (1)
honeycomb (1) +1831

3627 2יַעֲרָה *ya'ᵃrāh2*
Variant; not used

3628 יַעְרָה *ya'rāh*
Variant; not used

3629 יַעֲרֵי אֹרְגִים *ya'ᵃrēy 'ōrᵉgiym* (1)
Jaare-Oregim (1)

3630 יְעָרִים *yᵉ'āriym* (1)
Jearim (1)

3631 יַעֲרֶשְׁיָה *ya'ᵃrešyāh* (1)
Jaareshiah (1)

3632 יַעֲשׂוּ *ya'ᵃśû* (1)
Jaasu (1)

3633 יַעֲשַׂי *ya'ᵃśāy* (1)
untranslated (1)

3634 יַעֲשִׂיאֵל *ya'ᵃśiy'ēl* (2)
Jaasiel (2)

3635 יִפְדְיָה *yipdᵉyāh* (1)
Iphdeiah (1)

3636 יָפָה *yāpāh* (8)
beautiful (3)
adorn (1)
adorn yourself (1)
delightful (1)
majestic (1)
most excellent (1)

3637 יָפֶה *yāpeh* (42)
beautiful (23)
beautiful (3) +5260
lovely (3)
beautiful (2) +9307
handsome (2) +5260
sleek (2) +5260
fair (1)
fine (1)
handsome (1)
handsome appearance (1)
proper (1)
sleek (1) +9307
well-built (1) +9307

3638 יְפֵה־פִיָּה *yᵉpēh-piyyāh*
Variant; not used

3639 יָפוֹ *yāpô* (4)
Joppa (4)

3640 יָפַח *yāpah* (1)
gasping for breath (1)

3641 יָפֵחַ *yāpēah* (1)
breathing out (1)

3642 יְפִי *yᵉpiy* (19)
beauty (18)
beautiful (1)

3643 1יָפִיעַ *yāpiya'1* (1)
Japhia (1)

3644 2יָפִיעַ *yāpiya'2* (4)
Japhia (4)

3645 יְפֵיפִיָּה *yᵉpēypiyyāh* (1)
beautiful (1)

3646 יַפְלֵט *yaplēt* (3)
Japhlet (2)
Japhlet's (1)

3647 יַפְלֵטִי *yaplētiy* (1)
Japhletites (1)

3648 יְפֻנֶּה *yᵉpunneh* (16)
Jephunneh (16)

3649 יָפַע *yāpa'* (8)
shine forth (2)
light (1)
makes flash (1)
shine (1)
shines forth (1)
shone forth (1)
smile (1)

3650 יִפְעָה *yip'āh* (2)
shining splendor (1)
splendor (1)

3651 יֶפֶת *yepet* (11)
Japheth (11)

3652 1יִפְתָּח *yiptāh1* (1)
Iphtah (1)

3653 2יִפְתָּח *yiptāh2* (29)
Jephthah (22)
him[s] (2)
he[s] (1)
his[s] (1)
Jephthah's (1)
untranslated (2)

3654 יִפְתַּח־אֵל *yiptah-'ēl* (2)
Iphtah El (2)

3655 יָצָא *yāṣā'* (1076)
brought out (100)
came out (84)
went out (82)
go out (57)
go (40)
come out (39)
left (38)
bring out (35)
leave (24)
come (21)
went (20)
serve (14)
marched out (12)
gone out (11)
out (11)
set out (10)
bring (8)
brought (8)
coming out (8)
came (7)
comes (7)
get out (7)
going out (7)
spread (7)
goes out (6)
take (6)
comes out (5)
extending (5)
took (5)
bring forth (4)
bringing out (4)
brings out (4)
coming (4)
escape (4)
go free (4)
gone (4)
leaving (4)
march out (4)
produces (4)
released (4)
removed (4)
returned (4)
spreading (4)
surrender (4)
took out (4)
came forward (3)
fell (3)
free (3)
going (3)
had brought (3)
lead out (3)
led out (3)
marching out (3)
projecting (3)
send out (3)
sent (3)
went on (3)
withdrew (3)
be brought out (2)
began (2)
break out (2)
bringing (2)
brings (2)
burst out (2)
come forth (2)
come up (2)
continued (2)
depart (2)
departed (2)
departure (2)
did[s] (2)
drive out (2)
experienced soldiers (2) +7372
exported (2)
flesh and blood (2) +2743+4946
flow out (2)
flows (2)
forth (2)
given (2)
goes (2)
going off duty (2)
gone from (2)
has (2)
imported (2) +2256+6590
is (2)
led (2)
led in campaigns (2) +995+2256+4200+7156
led on military campaigns (2) +995+2256
marches out (2)
move out (2)
produce (2)
promised (2) +4946+7023
ready for military service (2) +7372
ready to go out (2) +7372
remove (2)
said (2) +4946+7023
sank (2)
stepped forward (2)
take out (2)
taken (2)
taken out (2)
took from (2)
utter (2)
wherever goes (2) +928+928+995+2256
your own flesh and blood (2) +3870+4946
accompany (1) +907
advance (1)
advanced (1)
advancing (1)
announced (1)
appearing (1)
arise (1)
arisen (1)
arises (1)
avoid (1)
away (1)
become known (1)
been brought out (1)
born (1) +4946+8167
breaks out (1)
breathed her last (1) +5883

bring (1) +2256+4374
bringing forth (1)
budded (1) +7258
burst forth (1)
call out (1)
came out (1) +3655
carried away (1)
carried out (1)
carry (1)
carry out (1)
carry out duties (1) +995+2256
charges (1)
cleared (1)
collapse (1)
coming forth (1)
continue (1)
crawling out (1)
crossed (1)
dart (1)
departs (1)
descendants (1) +3751+5883
descended (1)
direct descendants (1) +3751
do[s] (1)
draw (1)
drawn (1)
drew out (1)
empties (1)
empty (1)
encamped (1) +4722
end (1)
escaped (1)
escapes (1)
ever goes outside (1) +3655
exacted (1)
extend (1)
extended (1)
falls (1)
fight (1) +2021+4200+4878
flash (1)
flashed (1)
flashed out (1)
flowed (1)
flowing (1)
flying (1)
follow (1)
follow (1) +339
followed (1)
followed (1) +339
followed (1) +6640
forges (1)
fought in (1) +928
fought in (1) +4200
found (1)
freed (1)
gives (1)
gives birth prematurely (1) +3529
gives vent to (1)
go about (1)
go about business (1) +995+2256
go into (1)
go off (1)
go off duty (1)
go off to war (1)
go up (1)
goes over (1)
grows out (1)
gushed out (1) +8041
had difficulty taking possession of (1) +4946
have leave (1)
headed (1)
imported (1)
issue (1)
joined (1)
lay (1)
lead (1) +995+2256
lead (1) +995+2256+4200+7156
leads forth (1)
leaves (1)
led out (1) +4200+7156
left (1) +3655
made come out (1)
make shine (1)
make spew out (1) +4946+7023
makes come up (1)
march on (1)
marched into (1)
met expenses (1)
of (1) +4946
of his own (1) +2257+3751
on duty (1) +995+2256
on the way (1)
on way (1)
out came (1)
out comes (1)
out goes (1)
paid (1)
passing (1)
pierced (1)
pour out (1)
pours (1)
prevails (1)
produce (1) +2446+9311
produced (1)
promote (1)
pursue (1) +339
put away (1)
put out (1) +2021+2575
reached (1)
release (1)
risen (1)
rises (1)
rising (1)
rode out (1)
rush (1)
rushed out (1)
say (1) +4946+7023
send away (1)
sent out (1)
serve (1) +995+2256
serve in (1)
set free (1)
sets free (1)
shines out (1)
slip out (1)
sober (1) +2021+3516+4946
sow (1)
speak (1)
spoke (1)
spreads (1)
spring (1)
spring up (1)
springs up (1)
starting (1)
stepped out (1)
stretch (1)
surely come out (1) +3655
surely march out (1) +3655
surrender (1) +3655
surrendered (1)
take back (1)
telling (1)
took part in (1) +4200
travel about (1) +995+2256
turned out (1)
undertook (1)
unsheathed (1) +4946+9509
uttered (1) +4946
venture out (1)
vindicated (1) +7407
was brought out (1)
went away (1)
went outside (1)
were (1)
whatever[s] (1) +2021
untranslated (18)

3656 יָצַב *yāṣab* (49)
stood (6)
stand (5)
confront (3)
stand up (3)
took stand (3)
present themselves (2)
present yourselves (2)
presented themselves (2)
serve (2)
stay (2)
take positions (2)
commits himself (1)
kept distance (1) +4946+5584
place (1)
present himself (1)
sided (1)
stand firm (1)
stand out (1)
stand still (1)
standing (1)
station myself (1)
take a stand (1)
take place (1)
take stand (1)
take up positions (1)
took places (1)
wait (1)
withstand (1) +6640

3657 יָצַג *yāṣag* (17)
set (4)
made (2)
placed (2)
leave (1)
leave behind (1)
maintain (1)
make bare (1)
place (1)
presented (1)
separate (1) +963+4200
touch (1)
untranslated (1)

3658 1יִצְהָר *yiṣhār1* (23)
oil (20)
anointed (1) +1201+2021
olive oil (1)
olive trees (1) +2339

3659 2יִצְהָר *yiṣhār2* (9)
Izhar (9)

3660 יִצְהָרִי *yiṣhāriy* (4)
Izharites (4)

3661 1יָצוּעַ *yāṣûa‘1* (5)
bed (2)
bed (1) +6911
couch (1)
marriage bed (1)

3662 2יָצוּעַ *yāṣûa‘2* (3)
untranslated (3)

3663 יִצְחָק *yiṣḥāq* (110)
Isaac (102)
Isaac's (3)
he[s] (2)
his[s] (1)
who[s] (1)
untranslated (1)

3664 יִצְחָר *yiṣḥār* (1)
untranslated (1)

3665 יָצִיא *yāṣiy'* (2)
sons (1) +5055
untranslated (1)

3666 יָצִיעַ *yāṣiya‘* (3)
floor (1)
side rooms (1)
structure (1)

3667 יָצַע *yāṣa‘* (4)
are spread out (1)
lay (1)
lying (1)
make bed (1)

3668 יָצַק *yāṣaq* (52)
pour (11)

cast (10)
poured (6)
poured out (4)
firm (2)
hard (2)
pouring (2)
were cast (2)
been anointed (1)
beset (1)
frozen (1)
hard (1) +2021+4200+4607
is smelted (1)
pour out (1)
ran (1)
serve (1)
served (1)
set down (1)
spread out (1)
washed away (1)
untranslated (1)

3669 **יְצֻקָה** *ye suqāh* (1)
one piece with (1)

3670 **יָצַר** *yāsar* (43)
formed (15)
maker (4)
planned (4)
forms (3)
made (2)
preparing (2)
shapes (2)
brings on (1)
creator (1)
fashioned (1)
forged (1)
form (1)
make (1)
makes (1)
man (1)
ordained (1)
was formed (1)
untranslated (1)

3671 **1יֵצֶר** *yēser1* (9)
inclination (2)
creation (1)
desire (1) +4742
disposed (1)
formed (1)
mind (1)
motive (1)
pot (1)

3672 **2יֵצֶר** *yēser2* (3)
Jezer (3)

3673 **יִצְרִי** *yisriy* (2)
Izri (1)
Jezerite (1)

3674 **יְצֻרִים** *ye suriym* (1)
frame (1)

3675 **יָצַת** *yāsat* (28)
set on fire (9) +836+928+2021
set fire (4) +836
kindle (3)
been burned (2)
are burned (1)
burn (1)
burns (1)
kindled (1)
set ablaze (1) +836+928+2021
set on fire (1)
set on fire (1) +836
sets ablaze (1)
untranslated (2)

3676 **יֶקֶב** *yeqeb* (16)
winepress (7)
vats (3)
winepresses (3)
presses (2)
wine vat (1)

3677 **יְקַבְצְאֵל** *ye qabs^e 'ēl* (1)
Jekabzeel (1)

3678 **יָקַד** *yāqad* (8)
be kept burning (3)
burn (2)
burning (1)
burns (1)
kindled (1)

3679 **יְקֹד** *ye qōd* (2)
blazing (1)
fire (1)

3680 **יָקְדְעָם** *yoqd^e 'ām* (1)
Jokdeam (1)

3681 **יָקֶה** *yāqeh* (1)
Jakeh (1)

3682 **יְקָהָה** *ye qāhāh* (2)
obedience (2)

3683 **יָקוּד** *yāqûd* (1)
hearth (1)

3684 **יָקוֹט** *yāqôt* (1)
fragile (1)

3685 **יְקוּם** *ye qûm* (3)
living thing (2)
living creature (1)

3686 **יָקוֹשׁ** *yāqôš*
Variant; not used

3687 **יָקוּשׁ** *yāqûš* (4)
fowler (1)
fowler's (1)
men who snare birds (1)
snares (1) +7062

3688 **יְקוּתִיאֵל** *ye qûtiy'ēl* (1)
Jekuthiel (1)

3689 **יָקַח** *yāqah* (1)
insolent (1)

3690 **יָקְטָן** *yoqtān* (6)
Joktan (6)

3691 **יָקִים** *yāqiym* (2)
Jakim (2)

3692 **יַקִּיר** *yaqqiyr* (1)
dear (1)

3693 **יְקַמְיָה** *ye qamyāh* (3)
Jekamiah (3)

3694 **יְקַמְעָם** *ye qam'ām* (2)
Jekameam (2)

3695 **יָקְמְעָם** *yāqm'ām* (2)
Jokmeam (2)

3696 **יָקְנְעָם** *yoqn^e 'ām* (4)
Jokneam (4)

3697 **יָקַע** *yāqa'* (8)
killed and exposed (2)
turned away in disgust (2)
been killed and exposed (1)
kill and expose (1)
turn away (1)
wrenched (1)

3698 **יְקִפָּאוֹן** *ye qippā'ôn*
Variant; not used

3699 **יָקַץ** *yāqas* (11)
awoke (6)
woke up (3)
awakened (1)
wake up (1)

3700 **יָקַר** *yāqar* (11)
precious (4)
have respect for (2) +928+6524
costly (1)
make scarcer (1)
priced (1)
seldom (1)
well known (1) +4394

3701 **יָקָר** *yāqār* (35)
precious (18)
high-grade (2)
rare (2)
beauty (1)
fine (1)
good quality (1)
honored (1)
outweighs (1) +4946
priceless (1)
prizes (1)
quality (1)
splendor (1)
valuable things (1) +2104
very (1)
worthy (1)
untranslated (1)

3702 **יְקָר** *ye qār* (17)
honor (7)
riches (2)
honor (1) +6913
precious things (1)
price (1)
rare (1)
respect (1) +5989
splendor (1)
treasures (1)
valuables (1)

3703 **יִקְרָה** *yiqrāh*
Variant; not used

3704 **יָקֹשׁ** *yāqaš* (9)
are ensnared (1)
are trapped (1)
be ensnared (1)
be snared (1)
been trapped (1)
fowler's (1)
laid (1)
set a trap (1)
snared (1)

3705 **יָקְשָׁן** *yoqšān* (4)
Jokshan (4)

3706 **יָקְתְאֵל** *yoqt^e 'ēl* (2)
Joktheel (2)

3707 **1יָרֵא** *yārē'1* (332)
afraid (118)
fear (91)
awesome (24)
feared (12)
revere (11)
worship (10)
be feared (4)
dreadful (4)
revered (4)
terrified (4) +4394
awesome wonders (3)
fears (3)
intimidate (3)
stand in awe (3)
alarmed (2)
frightened (2)
have fear (2)
have reverence (2)
revering (2)
worshiped (2)
are feared (1)
awesome deeds (1)
awesome works (1)
believer (1)
despair (1)
dreaded (1)
dreadful (1) +4394
feared (1) +3711
fearfully (1)
fearing (1)
filled with fear (1) +4394
frighten (1)

held in awe (1)
is feared (1)
made afraid (1)
not daring (1)
overawed (1)
respect (1)
respects (1)
reverent (1)
shown reverence (1)
stood in awe (1) +4394
terrified (1) +1524+3711
terrified (1) +4394+4394
terrify (1)
terror (1)

3708 2יָרֵא *yārē'2*
Variant; not used

3709 3יָרֵא *yārē'3*
Variant; not used

3710 4יָרֵא *yārē'4* (52)
fear (32)
fears (7)
afraid (4)
feared (3)
worshiped (2)
God-fearing (1) +466+2021
revere (1)
worship (1)
worshiping (1)

3711 יִרְאָה *yir'āh* (45)
fear (34)
piety (3)
reverence (2)
awesome (1)
feared (1)
feared (1) +3707
fears (1)
revere (1)
terrified (1) +1524+3707

3712 יִרְאוֹן *yir'ôn* (1)
iron (1)

3713 יִרְאִיָּיה *yir'iyyāyh* (2)
Irijah (2)

3714 יָרֵב *yārēḇ* (2)
great (2)

3715 יְרֻבַּעַל *y[e]rubba'al* (14)
Jerub-Baal (11)
Jerub-Baal's (3)

3716 יָרָבְעָם *yārāḇ[e]'ām* (104)
Jeroboam (94)
Jeroboam's (6)
he[s] (4)

3717 יְרֻבֶּשֶׁת *y[e]rubbešeṯ* (1)
Jerub-Besheth (1)

3718 יָרַד *yāraḏ* (384)
went down (63)
go down (61)
come down (28)
came down (24)
bring down (19)
down (13)
brought down (8)
gone down (8)
go (7)
take down (7)
coming down (6)
fall (6)
going down (5)
took down (4)
come (3)
comes down (3)
descend (3)
descended (3)
gone (3)
leave (3) +4946
let down (3)
lowered (3)
overflow (3)
be brought down (2)
continued down (2)
descending (2)
falling (2)
fell (2)
flowing (2)
goes down (2)
lead down (2)
pull down (2)
went (2)
abandon (1) +4946
abandoned (1)
are brought down (1)
attack (1)
attack (1) +928
been brought down (1)
been taken down (1)
bowed (1)
brings down (1)
brought (1)
came (1)
came down (1) +3718
came out (1)
carried down (1)
climbed down (1)
consign (1)
continued (1)
cut down (1)
descends (1)
do so[s] (1)
fail (1)
fall down (1)
fallen (1)
falls (1)
flattens (1)
flow (1)
flow from (1)
flowed down (1)
flowing down (1)
goes down (1) +4200+4752
gone down (1) +345
got off (1) +4946+6584
haul down (1)
leading down (1)
leave (1) +4946+9348
led down (1)
let flow (1)
let go down (1)
letting run down (1)
made flow down (1)
march down (1)
moved down (1)
overflowing (1)
poured (1)
prostrate (1)
pulls down (1)
puts (1)
ran down (1)
removed (1)
road down (1)
roam (1) +2143+2256
running down (1)
sank (1)
sank down (1)
send down (1)
sends (1)
sent down (1)
settled (1)
sink (1)
so[s] (1)
step down (1)
stepped down (1)
subdue (1)
subdued (1)
take (1)
take off (1) +4946+6584
taken (1)
toward evening (1) +4394
was taken down (1)
went aboard (1) +928
went out (1)
will[s] (1)
untranslated (5)

3719 יֶרֶד *yereḏ* (7)
Jared (6)
Jered (1)

3720 יַרְדֵּן *yardēn* (183)
Jordan (172)
Jordan's (3)
river (2)
its[s] (1) +2021
there[s] (1) +2021
untranslated (4)

3721 1יָרָה *yārāh1* (27)
shoot (10)
shot (3)
cast (1)
fallen (1)
hurled (1)
laid (1)
motions (1)
overthrown (1)
set up (1)
shoot arrows (1)
shooting (1)
shot arrows (1)
shot with arrows (1) +3721
throws (1)
untranslated (1)

3722 2יָרָה *yārāh2* (3)
be refreshed (1)
showers (1)
water (1)

3723 3יָרָה *yārāh3* (45)
teach (25)
instruct (3)
teaches (3)
taught (2)
determine (1)
direct (1)
display (1)
get directions (1)
give guidance (1)
guide (1)
instructed (1)
instruction (1)
instructs (1)
showed (1)
taught (1) +2118
teach (1) +1978

3724 יָרַהּ *yārah* (1)
afraid (1)

3725 יְרוּאֵל *y[e]rû'ēl* (1)
Jeruel (1)

3726 יָרוֹחַ *yārôah* (1)
Jaroah (1)

3727 יָרוּם *yārûm*
Variant; not used

3728 יָרוֹק *yārôq* (1)
green thing (1)

3729 יְרוּשָׁא *y[e]rûšā'* (1)
Jerusha (1)

3730 יְרוּשָׁה *y[e]rûšāh* (1)
Jerusha (1)

3731 יְרוּשָׁלַםִ *y[e]rûšālami* (643)
Jerusalem (631)
there[s] (6) +928
Jerusalem's (3)
the city[s] (1)
untranslated (2)

3732 1יֶרַח *yerah1* (12)
month (5)
months (5)

moon (1)
one month (1) +3427

3733 2יֶרַח *yeraḥ2* (2)
Jerah (2)

3734 יָרֵחַ *yārēaḥ* (27)
moon (27)

3735 יְרִחוֹ *y^{e}riḥô* (57)
Jericho (56)
there[s] (1)

3736 יְרֹחָם *y^{e}rōḥām* (10)
Jeroham (10)

3737 יְרַחְמְאֵל *y^{e}raḥm^{e}'ēl* (8)
Jerahmeel (8)

3738 יְרַחְמְאֵלִי *y^{e}raḥm^{e}'ēliy* (2)
Jerahmeel (1)
Jerahmeelites (1)

3739 יַרְחָע *yarḥā'* (2)
Jarha (2)

3740 יָרַט *yāraṭ* (2)
reckless (1)
thrown (1)

3741 יְרִיאֵל *y^{e}riy'ēl* (1)
Jeriel (1)

3742 1יָרִיב *yāriyḇ1* (3)
contend (2)
accusers (1)

3743 2יָרִיב *yāriyḇ2* (3)
Jarib (3)

3744 יְרִיבַי *y^{e}riyḇay* (1)
Jeribai (1)

3745 יְרִיָּה *y^{e}riyyāh* (1)
Jeriah (1)

3746 יְרִיָּהוּ *y^{e}riyyāhû* (2)
Jeriah (2)

3747 יְרִיחֹה *y^{e}riyḥōh*
Variant; not used

3748 יְרִימוֹת *y^{e}riymôṯ* (7)
Jerimoth (7)

3749 יְרִיעָה *y^{e}riy'āh* (54)
curtains (18)
curtain (14)
other[s] (4)
tent (3)
shelter (2)
dwellings (1)
shelters (1)
tent curtains (1)
untranslated (10)

3750 יְרִיעוֹת *y^{e}riy'ôṯ* (1)
Jerioth (1)

3751 יָרֵךְ *yārēḵ* (34)
side (9)
thigh (9)
hip (5)
base (3)
breast (2)
attacked viciously (1) +5782+6584+8797
descendants (1) +3655+5883
direct descendants (1) +3655
leg (1)
legs (1)
of his own (1) +2257+3655

3752 יְרֵכָה *y^{e}rēḵāh* (30)
far end (6)
ends (4)
utmost heights (4)
far (3)
depths (2)
remote area (2)
below deck (1) +2021+6208
border (1)
end (1)
far back in (1) +928
rear (1)
there[s] (1) +928+1074+2021
within (1) +928
untranslated (2)

3753 יָרַם *yāram*
Variant; not used

3754 יַרְמוּת *yarmûṯ* (7)
Jarmuth (7)

3755 יְרָמוֹת *y^{e}rāmôṯ*
Variant; not used

3756 יְרֵמוֹת *y^{e}rēmôṯ* (7)
Jeremoth (5)
Jerimoth (2)

3757 יְרֵמַי *y^{e}rēmay* (1)
Jeremai (1)

3758 יִרְמְיָה *yirm^{e}yāh* (18)
Jeremiah (16)
he[s] (1) +2021+5566
Jeremiah's (1)

3759 יִרְמְיָהוּ *yirm^{e}yāhû* (129)
Jeremiah (123)
he[s] (2)
him[s] (2)
him[s] (1) +2021+5566
Jeremiah's (1)

3760 יָרַע *yāra'* (1)
faint (1)

3761 יִרְפְּאֵל *yirp^{e}'ēl* (1)
Irpeel (1)

3762 יָרַק *yāraq* (3)
spit (1)
spit (1) +3762

3763 יָרָק *yārāq* (3)
vegetable (2)
vegetables (1)

3764 יֶרֶק *yereq* (8)
green (4)
tender shoots (2)
grass (1)
plants (1)

3765 יַרְקוֹן *yarqôn*
Variant; not used

3766 יֵרָקוֹן *yērāqôn* (6)
mildew (5)
deathly pale (1)

3767 יָרְקְעָם *yorq^{o}'ām* (1)
Jorkeam (1)

3768 יְרַקְרַק *y^{e}raqraq* (3)
greenish (2)
shining (1)

3769 1יָרַשׁ *yāraš1* (232)
possess (48)
take possession (31)
drive out (24)
driven out (11)
inherit (11)
drove out (9)
took possession (9)
take over (6)
took over (6)
dispossess (5)
taken over (5)
heir (4)
occupy (4)
taken possession (4)
dislodge (3)
destroy (2)
possessed (2)
take (2)
become poor (1)
belonged (1)
capturing (1)
certainly drive out (1) +3769
conquer (1)
conqueror (1)
destitute (1)
displaces (1)
dispossessing (1)
drive from (1)
drive out completely (1) +3769
drove (1)
drove out completely (1) +3769
fell heir (1)
gain possession (1)
gave as an inheritance (1)
give (1)
given (1)
gives (1)
grow poor (1)
heirs (1)
inheritance (1)
inherited (1)
inherits (1)
leave as an inheritance (1)
make inherit (1)
make vomit up (1)
new owners (1)
occupied (1)
own (1)
poor (1)
prosperous (1) +6807
push out (1)
rob (1)
seize (1)
seized property (1)
sends poverty (1)
share in the inheritance (1)
take away possessions (1)
this[s] (1) +2257+4202
won (1)
untranslated (2)

3770 2יָרַשׁ *yāraš2*
Variant; not used

3771 יְרֵשָׁה *y^{e}rēšāh* (2)
conquered (2)

3772 יְרֻשָּׁה *y^{e}ruššāh* (14)
possession (7)
own (2)
heirs (1)
heritage (1)
inheritance (1)
part (1)
possess (1)

3773 יִשְׂחָק *yiśḥāq* (2)
Isaac (2)

3774 יְשִׂימִאֵל *y^{e}śiymi'ēl* (1)
Jesimiel (1)

3775 יָשַׂם *yāśam*
Variant; not used

3776 יִשְׂרָאֵל *yiśrā'ēl* (2506)
Israel (1712)
Israelites (483) +1201
Israelites (72)
Israelite (50) +1201
Israel's (35)
Israel (21) +1201
Israelite (16)
Israelites (14) +408
them[s] (12) +1201
they[s] (9) +1201
Israel (7) +824
them[s] (7)
Israelite (6) +408+1074+4946
Israel (5) +1074
Israelite (5) +408
Israel's (3) +4200
Israelites' (3) +1201
Israelite (2) +408+1201+4946
Israelites (2) +1201+4946

their[s] (2)
them[s] (2) +3972+7736
her[s] (1)
her[s] (1) +141
Israel (1) +408
Israel (1) +6639
Israel's (1) +928
Israelite (1) +928
Israelite (1) +928+1201
Israelite (1) +1074
Israelite (1) +1201+4200
Israelite (1) +1201+4946
Israelite (1) +4946
Israelites (1) +1074
Israelites (1) +1201+6639
Israelites (1) +4946
the whole land[s] (1)
their[s] (1) +3276+6639
their[s] (1) +6584
them[s] (1) +3972
they[s] (1) +3972
who[s] (1) +1201
untranslated (18)

3777 יְשַׂרְאֵלָה *y'śar'ēlāh* (1)
Jesarelah (1)

3778 יִשְׂרְאֵלִי *yiśr'ēliy* (5)
Israelite (3)
him[s] (1) +1201+2021
Israelite (1) +408+2021

3779 יִשָּׂשכָר *yiśśāśk̲ār* (43)
Issachar (38)
Issachar (4) +1201
untranslated (1)

3780 יֵשׁ *yēš* (138)
there is (27)
have (12) +4200
is (11)
is there (8)
be (5)
are (4)
have (4)
will (4)
am (3)
has (3) +928
there are (3)
there was (3)
has (2)
have (2) +907
owned (2) +4200
sometimes (2) +889
are there (1)
continue (1)
do (1)
had (1)
had (1) +4200
have (1) +928
have (1) +3338+9393
have on hand (1) +3338+9393
it is (1)
lies (1)
owns (1) +4200
so[s] (1)
there were (1)
there will be (1)
this is (1)
wealth (1)
were (1)
yes (1)
untranslated (25)

3781 יִשְׁאָל *yiš'āl*
Variant; not used

3782 יָשַׁב *yāšab̲* (1093)
live (141)
lived (91)
people (73)
live in (68)
sit (59)
settled (43)
stay (40)
living (39)
sitting (39)
living in (33)
stayed (32)
sat (31)
inhabitants (30)
sat down (22)
remained (18)
dwell (13)
inhabited (13)
lived in (12)
settle (12)
enthroned (11)
sits (11)
dwelling (10)
lives (10)
remain (9)
seated (9)
dwell in (8)
occupied (8)
reigned (8)
staying (8)
wait (6)
married (5)
settle down (5)
sit enthroned (5)
men (4)
sits enthroned (4)
be (3)
inhabitant (3)
left (3)
lived at (3)
sit down (3)
at rest (2)
be inhabited (2)
dwells (2)
dwelt (2)
everyone (2) +3972
king (2)
lies (2)
make dwell (2)
marrying (2)
occupy (2)
reign (2)
resettle (2)
resettled (2)
residents (2)
ruling (2)
seat (2)
seats (2)
situated (2)
stand (2)
stays (2)
took seat (2)
took up residence (2)
were (2)
avoid (1) +4946
brought to live (1)
citizens (1)
continually (1)
crouching (1)
deserted (1) +401
deserted (1) +401+4946
deserted (1) +1172+4946
deserted (1) +4202
did so[s] (1)
dwellers (1)
dwellings (1)
endures (1)
enthrones (1) +2021+4058+4200
give (1)
go (1)
had live (1)
have a home (1)
held court (1)
hide in (1)
hold out (1)
intact (1)
kings (1)
lay in wait (1)
let live (1)
lie (1)
live securely (1)
living at (1)
lounging (1)
made dwell (1)
make live (1)
makes dwell (1)
meet (1)
meeting (1)
mounted like jewels (1) +4859+6584
occupants (1)
peopled (1)
reigns (1)
relieve yourself (1) +2575
remains (1)
rest (1)
rested (1)
restore (1)
rule (1)
sat up (1)
sat waiting (1)
securely (1)
set up (1)
sets (1)
settle in (1)
settle on (1)
settles (1)
sit as judge (1)
spent (1)
stay (1) +3782
stay in (1)
stay up (1)
stayed at home (1)
stayed night (1) +2256+4328
stopping (1)
succeeded (1)
successor (1)
supposed to dine (1) +430+3782
taken seat (1)
takes (1) +6584
takes seat (1)
throne (1)
thrones (1)
took place (1)
took places (1)
took seats (1)
was (1)
withdrew (1)
untranslated (27)

3783 יֹשֵׁב בַּשֶּׁבֶת *yōšēb̲ baššeb̲et̲* (1)
Josheb-Basshebeth (1)

3784 יֶשֶׁבְאָב *yešeb̲'āb̲* (1)
Jeshebeab (1)

3785 יִשְׁבּוֹ בְּנֹב *yišbô b'nōb̲* (1)
untranslated (1)

3786 יִשְׁבָּח *yišbāh* (1)
Ishbah (1)

3787 יִשְׁבִּי בְּנֹב *yišbiy b'nōb̲* (1)
Ishbi-Benob (1)

3788 יָשֻׁבִי לֶחֶם *yāšub̲iy lehem* (1)
Jashubi Lehem (1)

3789 יִשְׁבַּעַל *yišba'al*
Variant; not used

3790 יָשָׁבְעָם *yāšāb̲'ām* (3)
Jashobeam (3)

3791 יִשְׁבָּק *yišbāq* (2)
Ishbak (2)

3792 יָשְׁבְּקָשָׁה *yošb'qāšāh* (2)
Joshbekashah (2)

3793 1יָשׁוּב *yāšûb̲1* (4)
Jashub (4)

3794 2יָשׁוּב *yāšûb̲2*
Variant; not used

3795 יָשׁוּבִי *yāšûbiy* (1)
Jashubite (1)

3796 יִשְׁוָה *yišwāh* (2)
Ishvah (2)

3797 יְשׁוֹחָיָה *yᵉšôhāyāh* (1)
Jeshohaiah (1)

3798 1יִשְׁוִי *yišwiy1* (4)
Ishvi (4)

3799 2יִשְׁוִי *yišwiy2* (1)
Ishvite (1)

3800 1יֵשׁוּעַ *yēšûaʿ1* (28)
Jeshua (27)
Joshua (1)

3801 2יֵשׁוּעַ *yēšûaʿ2* (1)
Jeshua (1)

3802 יְשׁוּעָה *yᵉšûʿāh* (78)
salvation (47)
deliverance (9)
savior (6)
victories (5)
save (2)
victorious (2)
deliver (1)
deliverer (1)
rescue (1)
safety (1)
saves (1)
saving (1)
victory (1)

3803 יֶשַׁח *yešah* (1)
empty (1)

3804 יָשַׁט *yāšaṭ* (3)
extend (1)
extended (1)
held out (1)

3805 יִשַׁי *yišay* (41)
Jesse (34)
Jesse's (5)
him[s] (1)
untranslated (1)

3806 יָשִׁיב *yāšiyb* (1)
untranslated (1)

3807 יִשִּׁיָּה *yiššiyyāh* (6)
Isshiah (5)
Ishijah (1)

3808 יִשִּׁיָּהוּ *yiššiyyāhû* (1)
Isshiah (1)

3809 יְשִׁימָה *yᵉšiymāh*
Variant; not used

3810 יְשִׁימוֹן *yᵉšiymôn* (13)
wasteland (7)
Jeshimon (4)
waste (1)
wastelands (1)

3811 יְשִׁימוֹת *yᵉšiymôṯ*
Variant; not used

3812 יַשִּׁימָוֶת *yaššiymāweṯ* (1)
untranslated (1)

3813 יָשִׁישׁ *yāšiyš* (4)
aged (2)
old (1)
old men (1)

3814 יְשִׁישַׁי *yᵉšiyšay* (1)
Jeshishai (1)

3815 יָשַׁם *yāšam*
Variant; not used

3816 יִשְׁמָא *yišmāʾ* (1)
Ishma (1)

3817 יִשְׁמָעֵאל *yišmāʿēʾl* (48)
Ishmael (47)
he[s] (1)

3818 יִשְׁמְעֵאלִי *yišmᵉʿēʾliy* (8)
Ishmaelites (6)
Ishmaelite (2)

3819 יִשְׁמַעְיָה *yišmaʿyāh* (1)
Ishmaiah (1)

3820 יִשְׁמַעְיָהוּ *yišmaʿyāhû* (1)
Ishmaiah (1)

3821 יִשְׁמְרַי *yišmᵉray* (1)
Ishmerai (1)

3822 1יָשֵׁן *yāšēn1* (18)
sleep (8)
fell asleep (2)
sleep (2) +9104
sleeping (2)
asleep (1)
put to sleep (1)
sleeps (1)
smolders (1)

3823 2יָשֵׁן *yāšēn2* (3)
chronic (1)
last year's harvest (1) +3824
lived a long time (1)

3824 יָשָׁן *yāšān* (6)
old (3)
it[s] (2)
last year's harvest (1) +3823

3825 3יָשֵׁן *yāšēn3* (7)
asleep (2)
sleep (2)
sleeping (2)
slept (1)

3826 4יָשֵׁן *yāšēn4* (1)
Jashen (1)

3827 יְשָׁנָה *yᵉšānāh* (3)
Jeshanah (3)

3828 יָשַׁע *yāšaʿ* (184)
save (86)
saved (22)
be saved (11)
saves (10)
rescue (8)
help (7)
deliver (5)
gave victory (4)
rescued (3)
worked salvation (3)
am saved (2)
avenging (2)
bring victory (2)
give victory (2)
are saved (1)
avenged (1)
be delivered (1)
brought about victory (1) +9591
came to rescue (1)
deliverance (1)
get help for (1)
having salvation (1)
help at all (1) +3828
is saved (1)
kept safe (1)
preserve (1)
salvation (1)
saving (1)
spare (1)
untranslated (1)

3829 יֵשַׁע *yēšaʿ* (36)
salvation (15)
savior (13)
safety (2)
victory (2)
deliver (1)
protect (1) +928+8883
save (1)
saving (1)

3830 יֹשַׁע *yōšaʿ*
Variant; not used

3831 יִשְׁעִי *yišʿiy* (5)
Ishi (4)
who[s] (1)

3832 יְשַׁעְיָה *yᵉšaʿyāh* (4)
Jeshaiah (4)

3833 יְשַׁעְיָהוּ *yᵉšaʿyāhû* (35)
Isaiah (30)
Jeshaiah (3)
untranslated (2)

3834 יִשְׁפָּה *yišpāh* (1)
Ishpah (1)

3835 יָשְׁפֵה *yāšpēh* (3)
jasper (3)

3836 יִשְׁפָּן *yišpān* (1)
Ishpan (1)

3837 יָשַׁר *yāšar* (27)
make straight (4)
right (3)
please (2) +928+6524
pleased (2) +928+6524
best (1)
channeled (1)
consider right (1)
fix directly (1)
go straight (1)
good (1)
hammered evenly (1)
keeps straight (1)
level (1)
liked (1) +928+6524
makes straight (1)
pleased with (1) +928+6524
upright (1)
went straight (1)
untranslated (2)

3838 1יָשָׁר *yāšār1* (117)
upright (48)
right (44)
fit (3)
just (2)
straight (2)
alliance (1)
conscientious (1) +4222
faultless (1)
in accord with (1) +4222
innocent (1)
level (1)
please (1) +928+2256+3202+6524
please (1) +928+6524
pleased (1) +928+6524
reliable (1)
right and true (1)
righteous (1)
safe (1)
stretched out (1)
truth (1)
upright (1) +2006
uprightness (1)
worthy (1)

3839 2יָשָׁר *yāšār2* (2)
Jashar (2)

3840 יֵשֶׁר *yēšer* (1)
Jesher (1)

3841 יֹשֶׁר *yōšer* (14)
upright (4)
honest (2)
straight (2)
uprightness (2)
integrity (1)
integrity (1) +4222
right (1)
unduly (1) +4946

3842 יִשְׁרָה *yišrāh* (1)
upright (1)

3843 יְשֻׁרוּן *yᵉšurûn* (4)
Jeshurun (4)

3844 יָשֵׁשׁ *yāšēš* (1)
aged (1)

3845 יָתֵד *yāṯēḏ* (25)
tent pegs (7)
peg (4)
pin (3)
tent peg (3)
stakes (2)
those[S] (2)
firm place (1)
pegs (1)
something to dig with (1)
untranslated (1)

3846 יָתוֹם *yāṯôm* (42)
fatherless (36)
orphans (2)
fatherless child (1)
fatherless children (1)
orphan (1)
orphan's (1)

3847 יְתוּר *yᵉṯûr*
Variant; not used

3848 יַתִּיר *yaṯiyr* (4)
Jattir (4)

3849 יִתְלָה *yiṯlāh* (1)
Ithlah (1)

3850 יִתְמָה *yiṯmāh* (1)
Ithmah (1)

3851 1יָתָן *yāṯān1*
Variant; not used

3852 2יָתָן *yāṯān2*
Variant; not used

3853 יַתְנִיאֵל *yaṯniy'ēl* (1)
Jathniel (1)

3854 יִתְנָן *yiṯnān* (1)
Ithnan (1)

3855 יָתַר *yāṯar* (105)
left (24)
rest (20)
remaining (7)
left over (6)
remain (5)
be left (3)
leave (3)
spare (3)
had left over (2)
remains (2)
some (2)
allow to remain (1)
are left (1)
be left alive (1)
been left alive (1)
escaped (1)
excel (1)
grant abundant (1)
had some left over (1)
have left over (1)
holding out (1)
it[S] (1) +2021
keep (1)
kept (1)
leaving (1)
more (1)
most (1)
preserve (1)
remained (1)
sparing (1)
still (1)
stopped (1) +4202
survived (1)
surviving (1) +889+3856
survivors (1)
was detained (1)
was left (1)
untranslated (2)

3856 1יֶתֶר *yeṯer1* (95)
other (45)
rest (21)
left (5)
survivors (3)
excelling (2)
last (2)
remaining (2)
wealth (2)
arrogant (1)
even far (1) +4394
full (1)
leave (1)
little left (1) +7129+8636
others (1)
power (1)
remnant (1)
surviving (1)
surviving (1) +889+3855
untranslated (3)

3857 2יֶתֶר *yeṯer2* (7)
thongs (3)
bow (1)
cords of tent (1)
strings (1)
untranslated (1)

3858 3יֶתֶר *yeṯer3* (9)
Jether (8)
Jethro (1)

3859 יִתְרָא *yiṯrā'* (1)
Jether (1)

3860 יִתְרָה *yiṯrāh* (2)
wealth (2)

3861 יִתְרוֹ *yiṯrô* (9)
Jethro (8)
he[S] (1)

3862 יִתְרוֹן *yiṯrôn* (10)
gain (3)
better (2)
advantage (1)
gained (1)
increase (1)
profit (1)
success (1)

3863 יִתְרִי *yiṯriy* (5)
Ithrite (4)
Ithrites (1)

3864 יִתְרָן *yiṯrān* (3)
Ithran (3)

3865 יִתְרְעָם *yiṯrᵉʿām* (2)
Ithream (2)

3866 יֹתֶרֶת *yōṯereṯ* (11)
covering (11)

3867 יְתֵת *yᵉṯēṯ* (2)
Jetheth (2)

3868 כ *k*
Variant; not used

3869 כְּ־ *kᵉ-* (2914)
like (899)
as (425)
as (270) +889
when (112)
according to (86)
just as (58) +889
about (41)
when (38) +889
in (30)
in accordance with (30)
as soon as (24)
just as (24) +889+3972
what (21)
for (20)
what (18) +889
just as (17) +889+4027
just as (16)
same (16)
such (15)
after (14) +889
at (13)
after (12)
as (12) +889+4027
like (12) +889
to (12)
as if (11)
same as (11)
while (9)
as though (8)
by (8)
such as (8)
with (8)
whatever (7) +889
because (6)
like (6) +5126
similar (6)
as (5) +889+3972
because (5) +889
following (5)
whatever (5) +889+3972
alike (4)
first (4) +2021+3427
in keeping with (4)
unlike (4) +4202
whenever (4)
as common as (3)
how (3) +4537
if (3) +889
into (3)
like (3) +5260
so (3)
soon (3) +5071
such (3) +2296
whatever (3)
according to (2) +6584
agree (2) +285+2118
almost (2) +5071
as before (2) +928+7193+7193
as much as (2) +889
as soon as (2) +889
at once (2) +8092
because of (2)
but (2)
compared to (2)
conformed to (2) +6913
equal (2)
even as (2) +889
exactly as (2) +889+4027
follow (2) +6913
followed (2)
had (2)
how many (2) +4537+6330
how often (2) +4537
imitate (2) +6913
in the order of (2)
in way (2)
indeed (2)
just the way (2) +889
just what (2) +889+4027
now (2) +2021+6961
numbered (2) +285
out of (2)
so (2) +2296
way (2)
what (2) +889+4027
what deserve (2) +5126
whatever (2) +889+4027
whatever (2) +3972
according to (1) +889
according to (1) +7023
according to the rules (1)
accordingly (1) +7023

adhere to (1) +6913
after (1) +9005
against (1) +4202
age of childbearing (1) +784+851+2021
all (1)
all around (1) +1885+2021
all together (1) +285+408
among (1)
and (1)
appear (1) +928+2118+6524
appropriate (1)
as (1) +4027
as (1) +6961
as (1) +8611
as deserve (1)
as done before (1) +928+7193+7193
as easily as (1) +889
as far as (1)
as far as possible (1) +1896
as for (1)
as good as (1)
as in the case of (1)
as in times past (1) +3972
as is the case (1)
as long as (1) +889
as long as endure (1) +3427
as many (1)
as many as (1)
as measureless as (1)
as much as (1)
as much as (1) +7023
as soon as (1) +4027
as surely as (1)
as though (1) +889
as usual (1) +8997+9453
as usually (1)
as usually did (1) +928+3427+3427
as well as (1)
as well as (1) +2256
as with (1)
at (1) +6590
awhile (1) +2021+3427
based on the rate paid (1) +3427
because (1) +889+7023
because of (1) +889
both alike (1)
both and (1)
by the time (1)
callous (1) +2021+2693
closest friend (1) +889+3870+5883+8276
compare with (1)
compare with (1) +2118
contrary to (1) +928+4202
contrary to (1) +4202
customary (1) +928+7193+7193
deserves (1) +1896
desire (1)
equal to (1)
equally (1)
equally (1) +278+408+2257
equally (1) +285
equally among them (1) +278+408+2257
even (1)
even for (1)
exactly as (1) +889+3972
exactly like (1) +889+3972+4027
exactly like (1) +4027
fared like (1)
few (1) +5071
first (1) +3427
follow (1)
followed the example (1) +6913+6913
from (1)
fulfill (1) +4027+6913+7023
ghostlike (1) +200
given even more (1) +2179+2179+2256+3578+3869
heart and soul (1) +4222
here is what (1) +2256+2296+2296+3869
how (1)
how long (1) +4537
how long must wait (1) +3427+4537
how many (1) +4537
how many more (1) +4537
how quickly (1) +5071
if (1)
if only (1) +889
immediately (1) +2021+3427
in a moment (1) +5071
in accordance with (1) +889
in accordance with (1) +4027
in proportion to (1)
in proportion to (1) +889+5002
in proportion to (1) +7023
in the way (1)
in unison (1) +285
joined together (1) +285+6641
just as (1) +889+3972+4027
just as (1) +3972
just as (1) +4027
just like (1)
just like (1) +4027
just like (1) +7023
just what (1) +889
kind (1)
kind (1) +889
large enough (1)
like (1) +889+3972
like (1) +889+4027
like (1) +1952
like (1) +5477
like (1) +6524
like (1) +6886
might well have (1) +5071
mistake for (1) +8011
more (1)
more (1) +889
natural (1) +132+2021+3972
nearly (1) +401
no end (1) +1896
no sooner than (1)
no sooner than (1) +889
not[s] (1)
nothing but (1)
nothing more than (1)
now that (1) +889
obeyed (1) +7756
of (1)
of little value (1) +5071
once again (1) +2021+8037
one for each (1) +5031
only (1)
or (1)
outcome different (1) +4202
persisted in (1) +6913
prescribed (1) +5477
previously (1) +919+8997
quotas (1) +5477
remains (1)
same (1) +889
scarcely (1) +5071
share (1) +889+4200
similar (1) +2021+5260
so (1) +889
so (1) +6584
so many (1) +4537
so that (1) +7023
so with (1)
so with (1) +889
some (1)
some (1) +5071
soon (1) +5071+7775
sort (1)
spokesman (1) +7023
standing (1)
still (1) +2021+2021+2296+3427
such (1) +2297
suddenly (1) +8092
sufficient means (1) +1896
suitable (1) +5584
suitable for (1) +5584
than (1)
the same as (1)
then (1) +889
this is how (1) +465+1821+2021+2021
this is how (1) +889
thoroughly purge away (1) +1342+2021+7671
though (1)
through (1) +1821
together (1) +285
too (1)
treated as (1)
usual (1)
very things (1) +889+4027
what (1) +2256+2296+2296+3869
what (1) +2256+2296+2297+3869
what deserve (1)
what deserve for (1)
what deserves (1)
whatever (1) +889+3972+4027
whenever (1) +889
whether (1)
while (1) +889
without (1) +1172
yet (1)
untranslated (264)

3870 ךָ *-kā* (7096)
your (3454)
you (2610)
the[s] (85)
your own (65)
yourself (43)
your (28) +4200
yours (24) +4200
you (21) +5883
yours (19)
him (10)
a[s] (8)
your (8) +4200
he[s] (7) +466+3378
yourselves (7)
his (6)
your (5)
its (4)
my (4)
your own (4) +4200
yourself (4) +4222
yourself (4) +5883
him[s] (3) +466+3378
their[s] (3) +1201
toward (3) +995+2025
what are you doing (3) +4200+4537
an[s] (2)
he[s] (2) +3
he[s] (2) +278
him[s] (2) +1201
his[s] (2) +466+3378
their (2)
this[s] (2)
us (2) +2256+3276
you (2) +3338
your own flesh and blood (2) +3655+4946
your very own (2) +4200
yourself (2) +4213
yourselves (2) +4222
yourselves (2) +5883
all the way to (1) +995+6330
any[s] (1)
boast so much (1) +1540+7023
both of you (1) +2084+2256
closest friend (1) +889+3869+5883+8276
each other[s] (1)
he[s] (1) +6269
her (1)
her[s] (1) +563
here[s] (1) +6584
him[s] (1) +278
him[s] (1) +6269
his[s] (1) +8276
I[s] (1) +6269
Israelite[s] (1)

it[S] (1) +3338
its[S] (1)
keep away (1) +448+7928
lead on (1) +339
me (1)
me[S] (1) +563
me[S] (1) +6269
one[S] (1)
their[S] (1) +367
their[S] (1) +2446
them[S] (1) +3
them[S] (1) +1821
them[S] (1) +2446
them[S] (1) +4621
they[S] (1) +1821
to the vicinity of (1) +995+6330
toward (1) +995
very own brother (1) +278+562+1201
what right have you (1) +4200+4537
whose (1)
you (1) +561
you (1) +1414
you (1) +4213
you (1) +8120
you yourself (1) +7156
you[S] (1)
your (1) +907
your (1) +928
your own self (1)
untranslated (592)

3871 ךָ *-k* (1287)
your (615)
you (484)
the[S] (13)
your (10) +4200
you (4) +5883
you (3)
her (2)
their (2)
whose (2)
you (2) +7156
your own (2)
yours (2)
yourself (2)
yourselves (2)
her[S] (1) +3304
these[S] (1)
this city[S] (1)
what is the matter (1) +4200+4537
whom (1)
your (1) +4946
your (1) +6584
yours (1) +4200
yourself (1) +4213
yourself (1) +4222
untranslated (132)

3872 כָּאַב *kā'aḇ* (8)
in pain (2)
ache (1)
brought grief (1)
feels pain (1)
ruin (1)
sharp (1)
wounds (1)

3873 כְּאֵב *kᵉ'ēḇ* (6)
pain (3)
anguish (2)
suffering (1)

3874 כָּאָה *kā'āh* (3)
brokenhearted (1) +4222
disheartened (1) +4213
lose heart (1)

3875 כָּאֶה *kā'eh* (1)
untranslated (1)

3876 כַּאֲשֶׁר *ka'ᵃšer*
Variant; not used

3877 1כָּבֵד *kāḇēḏ1* (115)
honor (19)
heavy (8)
honored (6)
hardened (4)
honors (4)
be honored (3)
gain glory (3)
honorable (3)
glorify (2)
glorious (2)
highly respected (2)
honoring (2)
made heavy (2)
multiply (2)
nobles (2)
put heavy (2)
renowned (2)
was held in honor (2)
abounding (1)
am glorified (1)
am honored (1)
be held in honor (1)
bring glory (1)
bring honor (1)
burden (1)
did[S] (1) +906+4213+4392
distinguished (1)
distinguished himself (1)
dull (1)
failing (1)
fierce (1)
gain glory for myself (1)
gained glory for yourself (1)
give glory (1)
glorified (1)
glory (1)
grew fierce (1)
grievous (1)
harden (1)
harder (1)
heavy (1) +3878
heavy (1) +4394
held in honor (1)
increased (1)
is honored (1)
laid heavy (1)
make dull (1)
makes wealthy (1)
outweigh (1) +4946
placed a heavy burden (1)
pretend to be somebody (1)
proud (1)
reward (1)
reward handsomely (1) +3877
reward handsomely (1) +3877+4394
stopped up (1) +4946+9048
unyielding (1)
was honored (1)
wealthy (1)
weighed down (1)
untranslated (1)

3878 2כָּבֵד *kāḇēḏ2* (40)
heavy (8)
great (4)
large (4)
severe (4)
difficult (2)
worst (2) +4394
bitterly (1) +4394
dense (1)
great numbers (1) +4394
heavier (1)
heavy (1) +3877
large (1) +4394
loaded (1)
severe (1) +4394
slow (1)
solemn (1)
strong (1)
terrible (1) +4394
thick (1)
tired (1)
unyielding (1)
untranslated (1)

3879 3כָּבֵד *kāḇēḏ3* (14)
liver (13)
heart (1)

3880 כֹּבֶד *kōḇeḏ* (4)
dense (1)
heat (1)
heavy (1)
piles (1)

3881 כְּבֵדֻת *kᵉḇēḏuṯ* (1)
difficulty (1)

3882 כָּבָה *kāḇāh* (24)
quenched (7)
quench (4)
go out (3)
put out (2)
snuff out (2)
extinguished (1)
goes out (1)
gone out (1)
quench fire (1)
snuffed out (1)
unquenchable (1) +4202

3883 1כָּבוֹד *kāḇôḏ1* (200)
glory (120)
honor (33)
glorious (10)
splendor (6)
pomp (3)
wealth (3)
dignity (2)
honored (2)
me (2) +3276
riches (2)
soul (2)
vast (2)
abundance (1)
gloriously (1)
heart (1)
honor (1) +5989
honorable (1)
honored (1) +6913
honoring (1)
lie in state (1) +928+8886
men of rank (1)
respect (1)
rewarded (1)
splendid (1)
tongue (1)

3884 2כָּבוֹד *kāḇôḏ2* (2)
elegant (1)
glorious (1)

3885 כְּבוּדָּה *kᵉḇûddāh* (1)
possessions (1)

3886 כָּבוּל *kāḇûl* (2)
Cabul (2)

3887 כַּבּוֹן *kabbôn* (1)
Cabbon (1)

3888 כַּבִּיר *kabbiyr* (10)
mighty (4)
blustering (1)
feeble (1) +4202
flooding downpour (1) +8851
fortune (1)
great (1)
older (1) +3427

3889 כָּבִיר *kāḇiyr* (2)
goats' hair (2) +6436

3890 כֶּבֶל *keḇel* (2)
shackles (2)

3891 כָּבַס *kāḇas* (51)
wash (36)
washed (5)
washerman's (3)

be washed (2)
been washed (2)
launderer's (1)
wash away (1)
untranslated (1)

3892 כָּבַר *kābar* (2)
abundance (1)
multiplies (1)

3893 1כְּבָר *kᵉbār1* (9)
already (5)
before (1)
long since (1)
now (1)
untranslated (1)

3894 2כְּבָר *kᵉbār2* (8)
Kebar (8)

3895 1כְּבָרָה *kᵉbārāh1* (1)
sieve (1)

3896 2כְּבָרָה *kᵉbārāh2* (3)
little distance (1) +824
some distance (1) +824
some distance (1) +824+2021

3897 כֶּבֶשׂ *kebeś* (107)
male lambs (35)
lambs (25)
lamb (19)
male lamb (15)
sheep (3)
lamb (1) +928+2021+8445
sheep (1) +7366
untranslated (8)

3898 כִּבְשָׂה *kibśāh* (8)
ewe lamb (4)
ewe lambs (2)
lamb (1)
lambs (1)

3899 כָּבַשׁ *kābaš* (15)
is subdued (2)
been enslaved (1)
enslaved (1) +2256+4200+4200+6269+9148
forced (1)
is subject (1)
make men slaves (1) +6269
molest (1)
overcome (1)
subdue (1)
subdued (1)
subject (1)
tread underfoot (1)
was brought under control (1)
untranslated (1)

3900 כֶּבֶשׁ *kebeš* (1)
footstool (1)

3901 כִּבְשָׁן *kibšān* (4)
furnace (4)

3902 כַּד *kad* (18)
jar (12)
jars (3)
large jars (1)
pitcher (1)
untranslated (1)

3903 כַּדּוּר *kaddûr*
Variant; not used

3904 כְּדֵי *kᵉdēy*
Variant; not used

3905 כַּדְכֹּד *kadkōd* (2)
rubies (2)

3906 כְּדָרְלָעֹמֶר *kᵉdārlā'ōmer* (5)
Kedorlaomer (5)

3907 כֹּה *kōh* (577)
this is what (471)
this (16)
ever so (12)
here (4)
so (3)
if (2) +561
this is how (2)
abundantly (1) +889+6330+6330
in any direction (1) +2256+3907
like this (1)
meanwhile (1) +2256+3907+6330+6330
now (1)
over there (1)
same (1)
such (1)
that (1)
that (1) +928
that is what (1)
there (1)
this (1) +928
this way (1)
what (1)
what happened (1)
untranslated (49)

3908 1כָּהָה *kāhāh1* (12)
faded (5)
weak (2)
faint (1)
falter (1)
grown dim (1)
totally blinded (1) +3908

3909 2כָּהָה *kāhāh2* (1)
restrain (1)

3910 כֵּהֶה *kēheh* (4)
despair (1)
dull (1)
smoldering (1)
weak (1)

3911 כֵּהָה *kēhāh* (1)
heal (1)

3912 כָּהַן *kāhan* (23)
serve as priests (12)
priest (2)
priests (2)
serve as priest (2)
served as priests (2)
high priest (1)
served as priest (1)
serving as priests (1)

3913 כֹּהֵן *kōhēn* (750)
priest (390)
priests (300)
he[s] (16) +2021
priest's (5)
who[s] (4) +2021
them[s] (3) +2021
his own[s] (2) +2021
priestly (2)
they[s] (2) +2021
he himself[s] (1) +2021
he[s] (1) +2021+3381
idolatrous priests (1)
priesthood (1)
Priests (1)
royal advisers (1)
their[s] (1) +2021
untranslated (19)

3914 כְּהֻנָּה *kᵉhunnāh* (14)
priesthood (9)
priestly office (2)
priests (2)
priestly service (1)

3915 כּוּב *kûb*
Variant; not used

3916 כּוֹבַע *kôba'* (6)
helmets (4)
helmet (2)

3917 כָּוָה *kāwāh* (2)
be burned (1)
being scorched (1)

3918 כְּוִיָּה *kᵉwiyyāh* (2)
burn (2)

3919 כּוֹכָב *kôkāb* (37)
stars (33)
star (2)
stargazers (1) +928+2600
starry (1)

3920 כּוּל *kûl* (37)
contain (3)
endure (3)
held (3)
hold (3)
provide (3)
provided (3)
feed (2)
supplied (2)
supplied provisions (2)
sustain (2)
bear (1)
conducts (1)
given provisions (1)
hold in (1)
holding (1)
holding in (1)
holds (1)
provide supplies (1)
supply with food (1)
sustained (1)
sustains (1)

3921 כּוּמָז *kûmāz* (2)
necklaces (1)
ornaments (1)

3922 1כּוּן *kûn1* (219)
established (23)
prepared (14)
establish (10)
prepare (10)
be established (9)
provided (9)
steadfast (6)
ready (5)
founded (4)
get ready (4)
made preparations (4)
formed (3)
is firmly established (3)
provide (3)
right (3)
set (3)
set in place (3)
been proved (2)
direct (2)
establishes (2)
firm (2)
is established (2)
loyal (2)
turn (2)
was carried out (2)
was established (2)
about to (1)
aim (1)
appear (1) +4604
appointed (1)
are prepared (1)
be restored (1)
be secure (1)
be set (1)
be trusted (1)
been firmly decided (1)
been made ready (1)
bent on (1)
brought about (1)
build (1)
built (1)
commit (1)
confirmed (1)
could (1)
definite information (1)

definitely (1) +448
determines (1)
devote (1)
devoted (1)
done[s] (1)
encourage (1) +4213
endure (1)
erected (1)
establishing (1)
fashions (1)
find out (1)
finish (1)
form (1)
full (1)
gave a firm (1)
have ready (1)
is (1)
is made ready (1)
keep loyal (1)
lays up (1)
made plans (1)
made ready (1)
make (1)
make preparation (1)
make preparations (1)
make secure (1)
makes firm (1)
makes secure (1)
on the alert (1)
ordained (1)
piles (1)
prepare (1) +2118
preparing (1)
provides (1)
put in place (1)
refreshed (1)
secure (1)
set in order (1)
set on (1)
set up (1)
sets (1)
spread (1)
stand (1)
steadfastly (1)
stood (1)
stood (1) +5163+8079
store up (1)
stores (1)
string (1)
succeed (1)
supplied provisions (1)
supplies (1)
supply (1)
support (1)
sustain (1)
took (1)
was arranged (1)
was firmly established (1)
was reestablished (1)
were attached (1)
were formed (1)
were prepared (1)
untranslated (4)

3923 כּוּן2 *kûn2* (1)
Cun (1)

3924 כַּוָּן *kawwān* (2)
cakes (1)
cakes of bread (1)

3925 כּוֹנַנְיָהוּ *kônanyāhû* (3)
untranslated (3)

3926 כּוֹס1 *kôs1* (31)
cup (26)
goblet (2) +7694
cups (1)
give a drink (1) +9197
lot (1) +4987

3927 כּוֹס2 *kôs2* (3)
little owl (2)
owl (1)

3928 כּוּר1 *kûr1*
Variant; not used

3929 כּוּר2 *kûr2* (9)
furnace (9)

3930 כּוֹר עָשָׁן *kôr ʿāšān*
Variant; not used

3931 כּוֹרֶשׁ *kôreš* (15)
Cyrus (15)

3932 כּוּשׁ1 *kûš1* (29)
Cush (26)
Cushite (3)

3933 כּוּשׁ2 *kûš2* (1)
Cush (1)

3934 כּוּשִׁי1 *kûšiy1* (25)
Cushite (14)
Cushites (7)
Cushites (1) +1201
Ethiopian (1)
Nubians (1)
untranslated (1)

3935 כּוּשִׁי2 *kûšiy2* (2)
Cushi (2)

3936 כּוּשָׁן *kûšān* (1)
Cushan (1)

3937 כּוּשַׁן רִשְׁעָתַיִם *kûšan riš'āṯayim* (4)
Cushan-Rishathaim (2)
him[s] (1)
whom[s] (1)

3938 כּוֹשָׁרָה *kôšārāh* (1)
singing (1)

3939 כּוּת *kûṯ* (1)
Cuthah (1)

3940 כּוּתָה *kûṯāh* (1)
Cuthah (1)

3941 כָּזַב *kāzaḇ* (16)
lie (3)
false (2)
lying (2)
prove false (2)
considered a liar (1)
deceive (1)
fail (1)
liar (1) +8120
liars (1)
mislead (1)
prove a liar (1)

3942 כָּזָב *kāzāḇ* (31)
lies (11)
lying (5)
lie (4)
false gods (3)
false (2)
deceptive (1)
liar (1) +408
lie (1) +1819
lied (1) +1819
lies (1) +1821
lying (1) +1819

3943 כֹּזֵבָא *kōzēḇā'* (1)
Cozeba (1)

3944 כָּזְבִּי *kāzbiy* (2)
Cozbi (2)

3945 כְּזִיב *kᵉziyḇ* (1)
Kezib (1)

3946 כֹּחַ1 *kōah1* (126)
strength (56)
power (31)
might (4)
powerful (4)
ability (2)
able (2) +6806
helpless (2) +4202+6806
powerless (2) +4202
wealth (2)
cannot (1) +401
crops (1)
firm (1)
great (1)
helpless (1) +4946
mighty (1)
mighty (1) +1475
power (1) +2432
powerless (1) +401
qualified (1)
resources (1)
shout (1)
strengthened (1)
very strong (1) +6793
vigorous (1)
weakness (1) +4202
weary (1) +3329
yield (1)
untranslated (3)

3947 כֹּחַ2 *kōah2* (1)
monitor lizard (1)

3948 כָּחַד *kāhaḏ* (32)
hide (8)
hidden (3)
conceal (2)
hiding (2)
annihilated (1)
are destroyed (1)
denied (1)
destroy (1)
got rid of (1)
hides (1)
keep (1)
keep back (1)
led to downfall (1)
lost (1)
perish (1)
perishing (1)
ruined (1)
was hidden (1)
were destroyed (1)
wipe out (1)
wiped (1)

3949 כָּחַל *kāhal* (1)
painted (1)

3950 כָּחַשׁ *kāhaš* (22)
cringe (3)
lied (3)
lying (2)
come cringing (1)
cower (1)
deceive (1)
deceiving (1)
disown (1)
disowns (1)
fail (1)
fails (1)
lie (1)
lies (1)
thin (1)
treachery (1)
unfaithful (1)
untrue (1)

3951 כַּחַשׁ *kahaš* (6)
lies (4)
deception (1)
gauntness (1)

3952 כֶּחָשׁ *kehāš* (1)
deceitful (1)

3953 כִּי1 *kiy1* (1)
branding (1)

3954 כִּי2 *kiy2* (4486)
for (1059)
that (564)
because (531)

when (221)
if (149)
but (108)
though (54)
since (46)
surely (43)
but (39) +561
how (39)
except (24) +561
and (20)
yet (19)
even (14)
so (14)
although (12)
only (12)
only (11) +561
if (10) +561
as (8)
now (8)
why (8)
because of (6)
by (6)
even though (6)
how much less (6) +677
unless (6) +561
because (5) +6584
indeed (5)
whenever (5)
yes (5)
after (4)
how much more (4) +677
however (4)
if not (4) +4295
then (4)
because (3) +3610
even if (3)
how much worse (3) +677
however (3) +561
if not (3)
instead (3)
just (3)
now that (3)
or (3)
therefore (3)
until (3) +6330
while (3)
after all (2)
as for (2)
because (2) +4027+6584
because (2) +6813
but (2) +700
but only (2)
but only (2) +561
certainly (2)
even (2) +1685
for (2) +4027+6584
how much more so (2) +677
in fact (2)
instead (2) +561
nevertheless (2)
no (2)
or (2) +2256
other than (2) +561
out of (2)
perhaps (2)
so that (2)
still (2)
suppose (2)
surely (2) +561
than (2) +561
though (2) +561
too (2)
what (2)
whether (2)
without (2) +561
all (1)
although (1) +561
although (1) +1685
as well (1)
at (1)
at all (1)
at least (1)
because (1) +4200+4537
because (1) +9393
because of (1) +4946+7156
because that will mean (1)
before (1) +401
but (1) +421
clearly (1) +8011
despite (1)
even (1) +561
even (1) +677+2256
even when (1)
ever (1)
for (1) +1237
for otherwise (1)
for surely (1)
greater (1)
how much better (1) +677
how much less (1) +677+4202
how much more (1) +677+2256
how well (1)
however (1) +700
if anything but (1)
if so (1) +6964
in doing this (1)
in order to (1)
indeed (1) +561
indeed (1) +677+2256
is that why (1)
it was the custom of (1)
just because (1)
moreover (1)
moreover (1) +1685
not (1) +561
not only (1)
now (1) +2296
on the contrary (1)
once (1)
or (1) +1685
other than (1)
rather (1)
rather (1) +561
rather (1) +4202
really (1)
really (1) +677
rightly (1)
since (1) +3610
since (1) +4027+6584
since (1) +9393
so (1) +4394
surely (1) +2180
surely (1) +6964
that if (1)
that really (1)
this (1)
till (1) +6330
truly (1)
unless (1) +561+4200+7156
unless (1) +561+4202
until (1) +561
very well then (1)
well (1)
what more (1) +4537
when (1) +4200+7023
whenever (1) +1896+4946
where (1)
with (1)
won't until (1) +561
yes (1) +4202
yet (1) +561
yet (1) +700
untranslated (1232)

3955 כִּי־אִם *kiy-'im*
Variant; not used

3956 כִּי עַל כֵּן *kiy 'al kēn*
Variant; not used

3957 כִּיד *kiyd̲* (1)
destruction (1)

3958 כִּידוֹד *kiyd̲ôd̲* (1)
sparks (1)

3959 כִּידוֹן *kiyd̲ôn* (9)
javelin (5)
lance (2)
spear (1)
spears (1)

3960 כִּידוֹר *kiyd̲ôr* (1)
attack (1)

3961 כִּידֹן *kiyd̲ōn* (1)
Kidon (1)

3962 כִּיּוֹן *kiyyûn* (1)
pedestal (1)

3963 כִּיּוֹר *kiyyôr* (23)
basin (12)
basins (6)
firepot (1) +836
pan (1)
platform (1)
untranslated (2)

3964 כִּילַי *kiylay* (2)
scoundrel (1)
scoundrel's (1)

3965 כֵּילַפּוֹת *kēylappôt̲* (1)
hatchets (1)

3966 כִּימָה *kiymāh* (3)
Pleiades (3)

3967 כִּיס *kiys* (6)
bag (3)
bags (1)
purse (1)
untranslated (1)

3968 כִּיר *kiyr* (1)
cooking pot (1)

3969 כִּישׁוֹר *kiyšôr* (1)
distaff (1)

3970 כָּכָה *kāk̲āh* (37)
so (5)
this (4)
this is how (4)
this is what (4)
in this way (3)
in the same way (2)
such a thing (2)
as (1)
because of (1) +6584
in this manner (1)
like this (1)
such (1)
such and such (1)
that (1)
thus (1)
true (1)
untranslated (4)

3971 כִּכָּר *kikkār* (68)
talents (38)
plain (10)
talent (9)
bread (2) +4312
loaf (2)
cover (1)
crust (1)
loaf (1) +4312
loaves (1)
region (1)
surrounding region (1)
whole region (1)

3972 כֹּל *kōl* (5417)
all (3246)
every (311)
whole (265)
everything (189)
any (155)
entire (82)
everyone (49)

throughout (47) +928
anyone (38)
anything (37)
no (31) +4202
whatever (30) +889
each (26)
just as (24) +889+3869
whoever (22)
always (18) +2021+3427
whatever (17)
a (16)
altogether (14)
none (14) +4202
throughout (14)
one (13)
rest (13)
everything (11) +1821+2021
nothing (11) +4202
total (11)
wherever (10) +889+928
wherever (10) +928
as long as (9) +3427
other[s] (9)
those[s] (9)
anything (7) +1821
anywhere (7)
everyone (7) +2021+5883
full (7)
everyone (6) +408
always (5) +928+6961
as (5) +889+3869
as long as (5) +2021+3427
completely (5)
everything (5) +1821
whatever (5) +889+3869
both (4)
day after day (4) +2021+3427
everything (4) +5126
in all (4)
much (4)
some (4) +4946
any (3) +285
as long as lived (3) +3427
at all (3)
everything (3) +4213
everywhere (3)
forever (3) +2021+3427
fully (3)
nothing (3) +401
throughout (3) +928+1473
throughout (3) +4200
whenever (3) +928
wherever (3) +448+889
all (2) +2162
always (2) +3427
an (3)
anyone (2) +408
anyone (2) +2021+5883
anyone (2) +5883
anything (2) +2021+3998
anything (2) +4399
anywhere (2) +928+5226
as long as (2) +6388
as long as lives (2) +3427
completely (2) +2021+4200
continual (2) +2021+3427
continually (2) +2021+3427
during (2)
even (2)
ever (2)
everyone (2) +1414
everyone (2) +2021+6639
everyone (2) +3782
everyone (2) +5883
everything (2) +3998
everywhere (2) +928
everywhere (2) +5226
great (2)
great (2) +8044
in full force (2)
it[s] (2)
never (2) +2021+3427+4202
no (2) +4202+4946
nothing (2) +1821+4202
rest (2) +3427
something (2)
them[s] (2) +2021+6639
them[s] (2) +3776+7736
this[s] (2)
together (2)
totaled (2)
various (2)
what[s] (2)
whatever (2) +3869
wherever (2) +889+928+2021+5226
wholeheartedly (2) +928+4213
wholeheartedly (2) +928+4222
your[s] (2)
abundant (1)
all kinds (1) +4946
all over (1)
all-night (1) +2021+4326
although (1) +889+928
always (1)
among (1) +4200
annually (1) +928+2256+9102+9102
any (1) +408
anyone (1) +132
anyone (1) +408+2021
anything (1) +889
anything (1) +1821+1821+2021+4946
anything (1) +1821+2021
anything (1) +1821+4946
anything (1) +3998
anywhere (1) +1473
anywhere in (1) +928+1473
around (1)
as (1)
as (1) +889+928
as (1) +6645+8611
as in times past (1) +3869
as long as (1)
as long as (1) +928+6961
as long as live (1) +3427
as long as live (1) +3427+4200+6409
at flood stage (1) +1536+4848+6584
at flood stage (1) +1536+6584
at random (1)
at wits' end (1) +1182+2683
body (1)
constantly (1) +928+6961
covered with (1)
crowd (1) +889+6641
depth (1)
detailed (1)
details (1)
dire (1)
eagerly (1) +928+8356
ever (1) +2021+3427
ever (1) +3427
everlasting (1) +6409
every day (1) +2256+3427+3427
every way (1)
everyone (1) +132
everyone (1) +132+2021
everyone (1) +408+2021
everyone else (1) +7736
everyone's (1)
everything (1) +465+1821+2021+2021
everything (1) +2021
everything (1) +2021+4856
everything (1) +5626
everything (1) +8214
everywhere (1) +928+5226
everywhere (1) +2021+5226
exactly as (1) +889+3869
exactly like (1) +889+3869+4027
farthest recesses (1) +9417
filled (1) +928+2118
for life (1) +2021+3427
four[s] (1)
from now on (1) +2021+3427
full force (1)
gave the message (1) +465+1819+1821+2021+2021
had nothing (1) +2893
in accordance with (1) +889
in lifetime (1) +3427
just as (1) +889+3869+4027
just as (1) +889+4200
just as (1) +3869
like (1) +889+3869
long (1)
men[s] (1)
more (1)
more and more (1) +3578+6584
natural (1) +132+2021+3869
no yet (1) +3270
none (1) +4202+4946
none (1) +4202+5883
nothing (1) +561+4946
nothing (1) +889+4202
nothing (1) +2021+4202
nothing but (1)
nothing whatever (1) +401+1821
numbered (1)
one[s] (1) +1414
only (1)
open (1)
people[s] (1) +889+928
prosperity (1) +8044
regular (1) +2021+3427
rest[s] (1)
shrub (1) +8489
so far as (1) +4200
solid (1)
something (1) +3998
sound (1)
still (1) +6388
such (1)
such (1) +4946
that[s] (1)
the storehouses[s] (1) +889+928+2157
them[s] (1) +3776
them[s] (1) +6551
there is no (1) +401
there is nothing (1) +401
these things[s] (1)
these[s] (1)
they[s] (1) +1251+4463+8901
they[s] (1) +2021+6639
they[s] (1) +3776
things (1) +3998
this is how (1) +465+928
throng (1)
through (1)
throughout (1) +4946
throughout (1) +6584+7156
total (1) +4200+5031
total (1) +7212
transfer of property (1) +1821+9455
utter (1)
vast (1)
we (1) +5646
whatever (1) +889+3869+4027
whatever (1) +889+928
whenever (1)
whenever (1) +889+928
whenever (1) +928+6961
whenever (1) +4200
wherever (1) +889+2021+5226+6584
wherever (1) +889+6584
wherever (1) +889+9004
wherever (1) +928+2021+5226
wherever (1) +2021+4946+5226
while (1) +3427
while continues (1) +3427
who[s] (1)
whoever (1) +132+2021
whoever (1) +408+889
untranslated (310)

3973 1כָּלָא *kālā' 1* (17)
were restrained (2)

am confined (1)
confined (1)
contain (1)
hold back (1)
imprisoned (1)
keeping (1)
kept (1)
penned up (1) +928+1074+2021
refuse (1)
seal (1)
stop (1)
stopped falling (1)
withheld (1)
withhold (1)
untranslated (1)

3974 2כָּלָא *kālā'2* (1)
finish (1)

3975 כֶּלֶא *kele'* (10)
prison (4) +1074+2021
prison (2)
prison (2) +1074
dungeon (1) +1074
prisons (1) +1074

3976 כִּלְאָב *kil'āḇ* (1)
Kileab (1)

3977 כִּלְאַיִם *kil'ayim* (4)
two kinds (3)
different kinds (1)

3978 כֶּלֶב *keleḇ* (32)
dogs (19)
dog (10)
dog's (2)
male prostitute (1)

3979 כָּלֵב *kālēḇ* (35)
Caleb (29)
Caleb's (6)

3980 כָּלֵב אֶפְרָתָה *kālēḇ 'eprāṯāh* (1)
Caleb Ephrathah (1)

3981 כָּלִבּוֹ *kālibbiw*
Variant; not used

3982 כָּלִבִּי *kālibbiy* (2)
Calebite (1)
untranslated (1)

3983 1כָּלָה *kālāh1* (206)
finished (55)
destroyed (14)
destroy (11)
fail (9)
spend (8)
completed (6)
finish (6)
perish (6)
end (4)
put an end (4)
consume (3)
ended (3)
gone (3)
spent (3)
vanish (3)
cease (2)
come to an end (2)
complete (2)
completely (2)
consumed (2)
determined (2)
fails (2)
finishing (2)
fulfill (2)
used up (2)
very (2)
after (1)
after (1) +561
all (1)
bent on (1)
blind (1)
came to an end (1)
completely (1) +6330
completely destroyed (1) +6330
completion (1)
concludes (1)
crushed (1)
decided (1)
destroy completely (1)
destroys (1)
disappear (1)
done (1)
eliminate (1)
ending (1)
failed (1)
faints (1)
faints with longing (1)
finally (1)
full (1)
given full vent (1)
grow weary (1)
hanging (1)
intended (1)
longed (1)
made an end (1)
make an end (1)
meet (1)
overcome (1)
ravage (1)
settled (1)
stopped (1)
strip bare (1)
vanishes (1)
wastes away (1)
wear out (1)
were completed (1)
wipe (1)
wiped (1)
wiped out (1)
yearns (1)
untranslated (2)

3984 2כָּלָה *kālāh2*
Variant; not used

3985 כָּלֶה *kāleh*
Variant; not used

3986 3כָּלָה *kālāh3* (21)
end (6)
completely destroy (5) +6913
destroy completely (3) +6913
destruction (2)
bad (1)
completely (1)
destructive (1)
power to destroy (1)
totally (1)

3987 כַּלָּה *kallāh* (34)
bride (15)
daughter-in-law (14)
daughters-in-law (5)

3988 כְּלֻהַי *kᵉluhiy* (1)
Keluhi (1)

3989 כְּלוּא *kᵉlû'* (2)
prison (2) +1074+2021

3990 1כְּלוּב *kᵉlûḇ1* (3)
basket (2)
cages (1)

3991 2כְּלוּב *kᵉlûḇ2* (2)
Kelub (2)

3992 כְּלוּבָי *kᵉlûḇāy* (1)
Caleb (1)

3993 כְּלוּהוּ *kᵉlûhû* (1)
untranslated (1)

3994 כְּלוּלֹת *kᵉlûlōṯ* (1)
bride (1)

3995 1כֶּלַח *kelah1* (2)
full vigor (1)
vigor (1)

3996 2כֶּלַח *kelah2* (2)
Calah (2)

3997 כָּל־חֹזֶה *kol-ḥōzeh* (2)
Col-Hozeh (2)

3998 כְּלִי *kᵉliy* (325)
articles (67)
furnishings (21)
armor-bearer (18) +5951
weapons (14)
utensils (13)
instruments (11)
jar (9)
pot (9)
article (8)
equipment (8)
accessories (7)
jars (7)
weapon (7)
things (6)
armor (5)
jewelry (5)
belongings (4)
goods (4)
objects (4)
supplies (4)
armed (3) +2520
object (3)
vessels (3)
anything (2)
anything (2) +2021+3972
armor-bearers (2) +5951
armory (2) +1074
bag (2)
bags (2)
everything (2) +3972
goblets (2) +5482
household articles (2)
jewels (2)
one[s] (2)
packed (2)
pottery (2)
treasures (2) +2775
another[s] (1)
anything (1) +3972
baggage (1)
basket (1)
boats (1)
cargo (1) +641+889+928+2021
clothing (1)
container (1)
dishes (1)
goblets (1)
instruments (1) +8877
it[s] (1)
jewel (1)
kinds (1)
material (1)
methods (1)
other[s] (1)
possessions (1)
pots (1)
pottery (1) +3450
sacks (1)
something (1) +3972
specific things (1) +5466
storage jar (1)
storage jars (1)
them[s] (1) +466+1074+2021
thing (1)
things (1) +3972
tool (1)
weapon (1) +4878
weapon (1) +4878+7372
weapon (1) +5424
weapons (1) +4878
yokes (1)
untranslated (23)

3999 כְּלִיא *kᵉliy'* (2)
untranslated (2)

4000 כִּלְיָה *kilyāh* (31)
kidneys (18)
heart (4)
mind (3)
inmost being (2)
hearts (1)
kernels (1)
minds (1)
spirit (1)

4001 כִּלָּיוֹן *killāyôn* (2)
destruction (1)
weary with longing (1)

4002 כִּלְיוֹן *kilyôn* (3)
Kilion (3)

4003 כָּלִיל *kāliyl* (15)
perfect (3)
whole (3)
completely (2)
entirely (2)
perfection (1)
solid (1)
totally (1)
whole burnt offering (1)
whole burnt offerings (1)

4004 כַּלְכֹּל *kalkōl* (2)
Calcol (2)

4005 כָּלַל *kālal* (2)
brought to perfection (2)

4006 כְּלָל *k^{e}lāl* (1)
Kelal (1)

4007 כָּלַם *kālam* (38)
ashamed (6)
disgraced (6)
humiliated (3)
blush (2)
disgrace (2)
mistreat (2)
be disgraced (1)
be put to shame (1)
been in disgrace (1)
blush with shame (1)
despairing (1)
disgraces (1)
embarrass (1)
fear disgrace (1)
humbled (1)
in disgrace (1)
lacked (1)
put to shame (1)
puts to shame (1)
rebuke (1)
reproached (1)
shameful treatment (1)
were shocked (1)

4008 כִּלְמַד *kilmad* (1)
Kilmad (1)

4009 כְּלִמָּה *k^{e}limmāh* (30)
disgrace (12)
shame (9)
scorn (3)
dishonor (1)
dishonors (1)
humiliation (1)
mocking (1)
shamed (1)
taunts (1)

4010 כְּלִמּוּת *k^{e}limmût* (1)
shame (1)

4011 כַּלְנֵה *kalnēh* (2)
Calneh (2)

4012 כַּלְנוֹ *kalnô* (1)
Calno (1)

4013 ־כֶם *-kem* (2658)
you (1268)
your (940)
the[s] (52)
your (48) +4200
yourselves (36)
your own (18)
yourselves (12) +5883
their (4)
yours (4) +4200
your own (3) +4200
yours (3)
them[s] (2) +7700
you (2) +5883
yourselves (2) +7156
a[s] (1)
an[s] (1)
every[s] (1)
him[s] (1) +466+3378
see for yourselves (1) +6524+8011
the (1)
the people[s] (1)
their (1) +4200
them (1)
them[s] (1) +3
them[s] (1) +1201
they (1)
they[s] (1) +3
think (1) +4200+8492
us (1) +2256+3276
what do you mean (1) +4200+4537
you (1) +6795
you (1) +7156
you're (1)
your (1) +4946
your (1) +6584
yourselves (1) +4222
yourselves (1) +7418
untranslated (241)

4014 כָּמַהּ *kāmah* (1)
longs for (1)

4015 כַּמָּה *kammāh*
Variant; not used

4016 כִּמְהָם *kimhām* (3)
Kimham (3)

4017 כְּמוֹ *k^{e}mô* (141)
like (80)
as (25)
according to (2)
with (2)
all (1)
as though (1)
as well as (1)
but (1)
deepest night (1) +694+6547
equal (1)
equal to (1)
even so (1)
for (1)
in a moment (1) +8092
kind (1)
or (1)
same (1)
seem (1) +928+6524
such (1) +4027
such as (1)
thus (1)
what (1) +889
whether (1)
worse (1) +4202
worth (1)
untranslated (11)

4018 כִּמְוֹהָם *kimwhām* (1)
untranslated (1)

4019 כְּמוֹשׁ *k^{e}môš* (9)
Chemosh (8)
untranslated (1)

4020 כְּמִישׁ *k^{e}miyš*
Variant; not used

4021 כַּמֹּן *kammōn* (3)
cummin (3)

4022 כָּמַס *kāmas* (1)
kept in reserve (1)

4023 כָּמַר *kāmar* (4)
aroused (1)
deeply moved (1) +8171
filled with (1)
hot (1)

4024 כֹּמֶר *kōmer* (3)
idolatrous priests (1)
pagan (1)
pagan priests (1)

4025 כַּמְרִיר *kamriyr* (1)
blackness (1)

4026 1כֵּן *kēn1* (20)
right (7)
honest (5)
afterward (1) +339
agreed (1)
aright (1)
correctly (1)
order (1)
truly (1)
unjustly (1) +4202
yes (1)

4027 2כֵּן *kēn2* (752)
therefore (146) +4200
so (88)
therefore (52) +6584
that is why (34) +6584
this (32)
so (25) +6584
same (23)
that (20)
just as (17) +889+3869
afterward (14) +339
as (12) +889+3869
so (10) +4200
in the course of time (8) +339
such (7)
as (6)
because (5) +6584
but (5) +4200
this is why (5) +6584
after (4) +339
true (4)
what (4)
in this way (3)
it[s] (3)
later (3) +339
some time later (3) +339
that is what (3)
then (3) +4200
this is what (3)
and (2)
because (2) +3954+6584
exactly (2)
exactly as (2) +889+3869
for (2) +3954+6584
for (2) +4200
in way (2)
just what (2) +889+3869
like (2)
like that (2)
like this (2)
more (2)
no (2) +4202
no wonder (2) +6584
so that (2) +6584
surely (2) +4200
that is how (2)
that is the way (2)
then (2) +339
this is how (2)
very well (2) +4200
what (2) +889+3869
whatever (2) +889+3869
accordingly (1)
alike (1)
also (1)

also sweet[s] (1)
and (1) +4200
and (1) +6584
and so (1) +6584
as (1) +3869
as soon as (1) +3869
as well (1)
because (1) +4200
because of (1) +6584
because of this (1) +4200
because of this (1) +6584
custom (1) +6913
customary (1) +1821
empty (1) +4202
enough (1)
exactly like (1) +889+3869+3972
exactly like (1) +3869
follow (1) +6913
follow lead (1) +6913
followed (1) +6913
follows (1) +339
for (1)
from then on (1) +339+4946
fulfill (1) +3869+6913+7023
fulfilled (1) +2118
further (1)
futile (1) +4202
greatly (1)
happening[s] (1)
how (1) +6584
however (1) +4200
in accordance with (1) +3869
in the course of time (1) +339+4946
in the same order (1)
in the same way (1)
it must be (1)
just as (1)
just as (1) +889+3869+3972
just as (1) +3869
just for that (1) +4200
just like (1) +3869
later (1) +339+4946
let it be (1) +2085
like (1) +889+3869
nevertheless (1) +4200
not (1)
nothing (1) +4202
particularly (1) +4200
similar (1)
since (1) +3954+6584
since (1) +6584
so much (1)
so then (1) +4200
still (1) +4200
such (1) +4017
that (1) +6584
that was how (1)
that's why (1) +6584
then (1)
then (1) +6584
therefore (1) +3610+4200
this reason (1)
this was the kind (1)
this was what (1)
this way (1)
thus (1)
too (1)
tried (1) +6913
unlike (1) +4202+6913
very things (1) +889+3869
very well (1)
whatever (1) +889+3869+3972
why (1) +561+4200+4537
yes (1)
yet (1)
yet (1) +4200
untranslated (85)

4028 3כֵּן *kēn3*
Variant; not used

4029 4כֵּן *kēn4* (10)
stand (8)
basework (1) +5126
mast (1) +9568

4030 5כֵּן *kēn5* (6)
position (2)
instead of (1) +6584
place (1)
succeeded (1) +6584+6641
successor (1) +6584+6641

4031 6כֵּן *kēn6* (5)
gnats (4)
flies (1)

4032 ־ךְ *-ḵen* (19)
your (13)
you (5)
your own (1)

4033 כָּנָה *kānāh* (4)
bestow a title of honor (1)
flatter (1)
flattery (1)
take (1)

4034 כַּנֵּה *kannēh* (1)
Canneh (1)

4035 כַּנָּה *kannāh* (1)
root (1)

4036 כִּנּוֹר *kinnôr* (42)
harp (21)
harps (19)
lutes (1)
lyre (1)

4037 כָּנְיָהוּ *konyāhû* (3)
Jehoiachin (3)

4038 כִּנָּם *kinnām* (2)
gnats (2)

4039 כְּנָנִי *k[e]nāniy* (1)
Kenani (1)

4040 כְּנַנְיָה *k[e]nanyāh* (1)
Kenaniah (1)

4041 כְּנַנְיָהוּ *k[e]nanyāhû* (2)
Kenaniah (2)

4042 כָּנַנְיָהוּ *kānanyāhû* (3)
Conaniah (3)

4043 כָּנַס *kānas* (11)
gather (3)
gathers (2)
amassed (1)
assemble (1)
bring (1)
gather together (1)
storing up wealth (1)
wrap around (1)

4044 כָּנַע *kāna'* (36)
humbled himself (5)
subdued (5)
humbled themselves (4)
humbled yourself (3)
subdue (3)
humble himself (2)
subjected (2)
were subdued (2)
are humbled (1)
humble (1)
humble themselves (1)
humbled (1)
made subject to (1) +3338+9393
repented (1)
silence (1)
was subdued (1)
were subjugated (1)
untranslated (1)

4045 כִּנְעָה *kin'āh* (1)
belongings (1)

4046 1כְּנַעַן *k[e]na'an1* (89)
Canaan (51)
Canaan (29) +824
Canaanite (5)
him[s] (1) +3296+4889
Phoenicia (1)
there[s] (1) +824+2025
untranslated (1)

4047 2כְּנַעַן *k[e]na'an2* (4)
merchants (2)
merchant (1)
merchants (1) +6639

4048 כִּנְעָן *kin'ān* (1)
traders (1)

4049 כְּנַעֲנָה *k[e]na[a]nāh* (5)
Kenaanah (5)

4050 1כְּנַעֲנִי *k[e]na[a]niy1* (71)
Canaanites (56)
Canaanite (13)
Canaan (1)
in Canaan (1)

4051 2כְּנַעֲנִי *k[e]na[a]niy2* (2)
merchants (2)

4052 כָּנַף *kānap̱* (1)
hidden (1)

4053 כָּנָף *kānāp̱* (111)
wings (56)
wing (14)
corner (3)
corners (3)
corner of garment (2)
ends (2)
flying (2)
fold (2)
them[s] (2) +2157
bird (1) +7606
bird on the wing (1) +1251
birds (1) +1251
birds (1) +7606
clothes (1)
dishonor bed (1) +1655
dishonors bed (1) +1655
each[s] (1)
edges (1)
folds of garment (1)
hem (1)
hem of robe (1)
kind[s] (1)
kinds[s] (1)
other[s] (1)
piece (1)
quarters (1)
sweep away (1) +928+7674
those[s] (1)
total wingspan (1) +802
winged (1)
untranslated (4)

4054 כִּנְּרוֹת *kinrôṯ* (3)
Kinnereth (3)

4055 כִּנֶּרֶת *kinnereṯ* (4)
Kinnereth (4)

4056 כְּנָת *k[e]nāṯ* (2)
associates (1)
untranslated (1)

4057 כֶּסֶא *kese'* (3)
full moon (1)
full moon (1) +3427
moon full (1)

4058 כִּסֵּא *kissē'* (135)
throne (110)
thrones (8)
chair (4)
seat (3)
seat of honor (3)
those[s] (2)
authority (1)
enthrones (1) +2021+3782+4200

it[s] (1) +2021
its[s] (1) +2021+4200
untranslated (1)

4059 כָּסָה *kāsāh* (153)
covered (37)
cover (26)
covers (15)
covering (7)
decorating (4)
be covered (3)
cover (3) +4832
cover up (3)
hide (3)
put on (3)
wearing (3)
were covered (3)
around (2)
clothed (2)
conceal (2)
concealed (2)
conceals (2)
keeps (2)
overwhelms (2)
provides (2)
put over (2)
are covered (1)
bathing (1)
blindfolds (1) +7156
buried (1)
closed (1)
clothe (1)
cover themselves (1)
cover up (1) +2256+8740
covered herself (1)
covered up (1)
covers over (1)
decorate (1)
engulfed (1)
fills (1)
flood (1)
is shrouded (1)
keep (1)
overlooks (1)
overwhelm (1)
overwhelmed (1)
shield (1)
was covered (1)
wear (1)
untranslated (2)

4060 כֶּסֶה *kēseh*
Variant; not used

4061 כִּסֵּה *kissēh*
Variant; not used

4062 כָּסוּי *kāsûy* (2)
cover (1) +5989
covering (1)

4063 כְּסוּלּוֹת *k[e]sûlôṯ* (1)
Kesulloth (1)

4064 כְּסוּת *k[e]sûṯ* (9)
covering (2)
cloak (1)
clothing (1)
cover (1)
cover the offense (1) +6524
garment (1)
uncovered (1) +401
untranslated (1)

4065 כָּסַח *kāsah* (2)
cut (1)
is cut down (1)

4066 כֵּסְיָה *kēsyāh*
Variant; not used

4067 1כְּסִיל *k[e]siyl1* (70)
fool (36)
fools (21)
foolish (9)
fool's (4)

4068 2כְּסִיל *k[e]siyl2* (4)
Orion (3)
constellations (1)

4069 3כְּסִיל *k[e]siyl3* (1)
Kesil (1)

4070 כְּסִילוּת *k[e]siylûṯ* (1)
folly (1)

4071 כָּסַל *kāsal* (1)
foolish (1)

4072 1כֶּסֶל *kesel1* (7)
loins (5)
back (1)
waist (1)

4073 2כֶּסֶל *kesel2* (6)
trust (3)
confidence (1)
stupidity (1)
trusts in (1)

4074 כִּסְלָה *kislāh* (2)
confidence (1)
folly (1)

4075 כִּסְלֵו *kislēw* (3)
Kislev (2)
untranslated (1)

4076 כְּסָלוֹן *k[e]sālôn* (1)
Kesalon (1)

4077 כִּסְלוֹן *kislôn* (1)
Kislon (1)

4078 כַּסְלֻחִים *kasluḥiym* (2)
Casluhites (2)

4079 כִּסְלֹת תָּבוֹר *kislōṯ tāḇôr* (1)
Kisloth Tabor (1)

4080 כָּסַם *kāsam* (2)
keep hair trimmed (1) +4080

4081 כֻּסֶּמֶת *kussemeṯ* (3)
spelt (3)

4082 כָּסַס *kāsas* (1)
determine amount needed (1)

4083 כָּסַף *kāsaḇ* (6)
hungry (1)
long for (1)
longed (1) +4083
shameful (1) +4202
yearns (1)

4084 כֶּסֶף *keseḇ* (401)
silver (303)
money (61)
price (7)
bought (2) +5239
sell (2) +928+5989
shekels (2)
silver (2) +4084
value (2) +6886
bought (1) +928+2021+7864
buy (1) +928
it[s] (1) +2021
must sell (1) +928+2021+4835+4835
pay (1) +5989
pay (1) +8740
pay (1) +9202
payment (1)
property (1)
value (1)
what paid (1)
untranslated (8)

4085 כָּסִפְיָא *kāsiḇyā'* (2)
Casiphia (2)

4086 כֶּסֶת *keseṯ* (2)
magic charms (2)

4087 כָּעַס *kā'as* (54)
provoked to anger (19)
provoke to anger (7)
provoking to anger (6)
provoked (4)
angered (3)
angry (2)
provoke (2)
provoked to anger (2) +4088
incensed (1)
kept provoking (1) +1685+4088
make angry (1)
provoke to anger (1) +4088
provoking (1)
thrown insults (1)
trouble (1)
vexed (1)
untranslated (1)

4088 כַּעַס *ka'as* (22)
grief (4)
sorrow (4)
provoked to anger (2) +4087
anger (1)
angered (1)
annoyance (1)
anxiety (1)
displeasure (1)
frustration (1)
ill-tempered (1)
kept provoking (1) +1685+4087
provocation (1)
provoke to anger (1) +4087
provoked to anger (1)
taunt (1)

4089 כַּעַשׂ *ka'aś* (4)
anger (1)
anguish (1)
grief (1)
resentment (1)

4090 כַּף *kaḇ* (193)
hands (76)
hand (32)
dish (12)
dishes (12)
palm (6)
soles (6)
feet (5) +8079
foot (4) +8079
sole (4)
hands (3) +3338
socket (3)
grasp (2)
handful (2) +4850
hands together (2) +448+4090
palm of hand (2)
arms (1)
be taken captive (1) +928+2021+9530
clutches (1)
each[s] (1) +2021
earnings (1) +7262
fingers (1)
from (1) +4946
fruit of labor (1) +3330
handles (1)
palms of hands (1)
paws (1)
pocket (1)
their[s] (1) +928+2157
those[s] (1) +8079
took a handful (1) +4848
untranslated (6)

4091 כֵּף *kēḇ* (2)
rocks (2)

4092 כָּפָה *kāḇāh* (1)
soothes (1)

4093 כִּפָּה *kippāh* (4)
palm branch (2)
branches (1)
fronds (1)

4094 1כְּפוֹר *k[e]ḇôr1* (8)
bowls (3)

each dish (2) +2256+4094
untranslated (2)

4095 2כְּפוֹר *kᵉp̱ôr2* (3)
frost (3)

4096 כָּפִיס *kāp̱iys* (1)
beams (1)

4097 כְּפִיר *kᵉp̱iyr* (30)
lion (7)
lions (7)
great lion (4)
young lions (4)
strong lion (3)
great lions (1)
he[S] (1)
young (1)
young lion (1)
young lion (1) +787

4098 כְּפִירָה *kᵉp̱iyrāh* (4)
Kephirah (4)

4099 כְּפִירִים *kᵉp̱iyriym* (2)
villages (2)

4100 כָּפַל *kāp̱al* (5)
folded double (2)
fold double (1)
strike twice (1)
untranslated (1)

4101 כֶּפֶל *kep̱el* (3)
bridle (1) +8270
double (1)
two sides (1)

4102 כָּפַן *kāp̱an* (1)
sent out (1)

4103 כָּפָן *kāp̱ān* (2)
famine (1)
hunger (1)

4104 כָּפַף *kāp̱ap̱* (5)
are bowed down (2)
bow down (1)
bowed down in distress (1)
bowing (1)

4105 1כָּפַר *kāp̱ar1* (101)
make atonement (58)
making atonement (6)
atonement made (5)
made atonement (4)
atone (3)
be atoned for (3)
forgave (2)
forgive (2)
makes atonement (2)
accept atonement (1)
appease (1)
atoned for (1)
atonement (1)
atonement be made (1)
atonement made (1) +4113
atonement was made (1)
be annulled (1)
be atoned (1)
is atoned for (1)
make amends (1)
pacify (1) +7156
pardon (1)
ward off with a ransom (1)
untranslated (2)

4106 2כָּפָר *kāp̱ar2* (1)
coat (1)

4107 כָּפָר *kāp̱ār* (2)
villages (2)

4108 1כֹּפֶר *kōp̱er1* (1)
villages (1)

4109 2כֹּפֶר *kōp̱er2* (1)
pitch (1)

4110 3כֹּפֶר *kōp̱er3* (2)
henna (1)
henna blossoms (1)

4111 4כֹּפֶר *kōp̱er4* (13)
ransom (8)
bribe (2)
bribes (1)
compensation (1)
payment (1)

4112 כְּפַר הָעַמֹּנִי *kᵉp̱ar hāʿammōniy* (1)
Kephar Ammoni (1)

4113 כִּפֻּרִים *kippuriym* (8)
atonement (6)
atonement made (1) +4105
atoning (1)

4114 כַּפֹּרֶת *kappōreṯ* (27)
atonement cover (15)
cover (10)
atonement (1)
it (1) +2021

4115 כָּפַשׁ *kāp̱aš* (1)
trampled (1)

4116 1כַּפְתּוֹר *kap̱tôr1* (3)
Caphtor (3)

4117 2כַּפְתּוֹר *kap̱tôr2* (18)
buds (8)
bud (6)
columns (1)
tops of the pillars (1)
untranslated (2)

4118 כַּפְתֹּרִי *kap̱tōriy* (3)
Caphtorites (3)

4119 1כַּר *kar1* (12)
lambs (8)
battering rams (3)
choice lambs (1) +4946+7366

4120 2כַּר *kar2* (3)
meadows (2)
fields (1)

4121 3כַּר *kar3* (1)
saddle (1)

4122 כָּר *kār*
Variant; not used

4123 כֹּר *kōr* (7)
cors (6)
cor (1)

4124 כִּרְבֵּל *kirbēl* (1)
was clothed (1)

4125 1כָּרָה *kārāh1* (15)
dug (5)
digs (3)
pierced (2)
cut out (1)
dig (1)
is dug (1)
plots (1)
sank (1)

4126 2כָּרָה *kārāh2* (4)
barter (1)
barter away (1)
bought (1)
untranslated (1)

4127 3כָּרָה *kārāh3* (1)
prepared a feast (1) +4130

4128 4כָּרָה *kārāh4*
Variant; not used

4129 5כָּרָה *kārāh5*
Variant; not used

4130 כֵּרָה *kērāh* (1)
prepared a feast (1) +4127

4131 1כְּרוּב *kᵉrûḇ1* (91)
cherubim (66)
cherub (15)
them[S] (2) +2021
one[S] (1) +2021
their[S] (1) +2021
untranslated (6)

4132 2כְּרוּב *kᵉrûḇ2* (2)
Kerub (2)

4133 כָּרִי *kāriy* (3)
Carites (2)
untranslated (1)

4134 כְּרִית *kᵉriyṯ* (2)
Kerith (2)

4135 כְּרִיתוּת *kᵉriyṯûṯ* (4)
divorce (4)

4136 כַּרְכֹּב *karkōḇ* (2)
ledge (2)

4137 כַּרְכֹּם *karkōm* (1)
saffron (1)

4138 כַּרְכְּמִישׁ *karkᵉmiyš* (3)
Carchemish (3)

4139 כַּרְכַּס *karkas* (1)
Carcas (1)

4140 כִּרְכָּרָה *kirkārāh* (1)
camels (1)

4141 כָּרַם *kāram*
Variant; not used

4142 1כֶּרֶם *kerem1* (93)
vineyards (49)
vineyard (41)
grapes (1)
vintage (1)
untranslated (1)

4143 2כֶּרֶם *kerem2*
Variant; not used

4144 כֹּרֵם *kōrēm* (5)
work vineyards (2)
vine growers (1)
vineyards (1)
working fields and vineyards (1)

4145 1כַּרְמִי *karmiy1* (8)
Carmi (8)

4146 2כַּרְמִי *karmiy2* (1)
Carmite (1)

4147 כַּרְמִיל *karmiyl* (3)
crimson (3)

4148 כְּרָמִים *kᵉrāmiym*
Variant; not used

4149 1כַּרְמֶל *karmel1* (15)
fertile field (5)
finest of forests (2) +3623
orchards (2)
fertile (1)
fertile fields (1)
fertile lands (1)
fertile pasturelands (1)
fruitful land (1)
untranslated (1)

4150 2כַּרְמֶל *karmel2* (7)
Carmel (7)

4151 3כַּרְמֶל *karmel3* (15)
Carmel (15)

4152 4כַּרְמֶל *karmel4* (3)
new grain (2)
heads of new grain (1)

4153 כַּרְמְלִי *karmᵉliy* (7)
of Carmel (5)
Carmelite (2)

4154 כְּרָן *kᵉrān* (2)
Keran (2)

4155 כִּרְסֵם *kirsēm* (1)
ravage (1)

4156 כָּרַע *kāra'* (36)
sank (3)
bow (2)
bow down (2)
fell (2)
kneel down (2)
knelt down (2)
made bow (2)
bend down (1)
bowed down (1)
bows down (1)
bring down (1)
brought to knees (1)
cringe (1)
crouch (1)
crouch down (1)
crouches (1)
cutting down (1)
down (1)
faltering (1)
got down (1)
kneel (1)
kneeling (1) +1386+6584
knelt (1)
made miserable (1) +4156
sleep with (1) +6584
slumped down (1)
went into labor (1)

4157 כֶּרַע *kera'* (9)
legs (8)
leg bones (1)

4158 כַּרְפַּס *karpas* (1)
hangings of linen (1)

4159 כָּרַר *kārar* (2)
danced (1)
dancing (1)

4160 כָּרֵשׂ *kārēś* (1)
stomach (1)

4161 כַּרְשְׁנָא *karšᵉnā'* (1)
Carshena (1)

4162 כָּרַת *kāraṯ* (289)
cut off (56)
made (45)
be cut off (37)
make (27)
cut down (20)
destroy (14)
cut (8)
fail to have (8) +4200
kill (6)
be destroyed (4)
destroyed (4)
making (4)
be cut down (3)
made a covenant (3)
be ruined (2)
covenanted (2)
put an end (2)
renewed (2)
was cut off (2)
are cut off (1)
banish (1)
be broken (1)
be consumed (1)
be cut out (1)
be rid of (1)
be struck down (1)
be taken (1)
be without (1) +4946
been broken off (1)
been cut off (1)
been snatched (1)
cease (1)
chop down (1)
conquered (1)
cut up (1)
cutting (1)
cutting (1) +9163
cutting off (1)
destruction (1)
disappear (1)
entered (1)
fell (1)
felling (1)
form (1)
is cut down (1)
killing (1)
killing off (1)
leave no (1)
made a pact (1)
make a treaty (1)
makes (1)
makes a covenant (1)
must surely be cut off (1) +4162
take away (1)
vanished (1)
were cut off (1)
wipe out (1)
untranslated (1)

4163 כְּרֹת *kᵉrōṯ*
Variant; not used

4164 כְּרֻתוֹת *kᵉruṯôṯ* (3)
trimmed beams (3)

4165 כְּרֵתִי *kᵉrēṯiy* (11)
Kerethites (10)
Kerethite (1)

4166 כֶּשֶׂב *keśeḇ* (13)
lamb (5)
sheep (4)
lamb (1) +928+2021+8445
lambs (1)
sheep (1) +8445
young of the flock (1)

4167 כִּשְׂבָּה *kiśbāh* (1)
lamb (1)

4168 כֶּשֶׂד *keśeḏ* (1)
Kesed (1)

4169 כַּשְׂדִּים *kaśdiym* (82)
Babylonians (49)
Babylonian (12)
Chaldeans (8)
Babylonia (5)
astrologers (2)
Chaldea (2)
Babylon (1) +824
Babylonians' (1)
untranslated (2)

4170 כָּשָׂה *kāśāh* (1)
sleek (1)

4171 כָּשַׁח *kāšah*
Variant; not used

4172 כַּשִּׁיל *kaššiyl* (1)
axes (1)

4173 כָּשַׁל *kāšal* (65)
stumble (23)
fall (5)
stumbled (4)
stumbles (3)
be brought down (2)
downfall (2)
give way (2)
overthrow (2)
are brought down (1)
bring to ruin (1)
cause to fall (1)
caused to stumble (1)
fails (1)
faltered (1)
feeblest (1)
giving out (1)
made stumble (1)
make fall (1)
overthrown (1)
sapped (1)
stagger (1)
staggers (1)
stumble and fall (1) +4173
stumbling (1)
weak (1)
without success (1)
untranslated (3)

4174 כִּשָּׁלוֹן *kiššālôn* (1)
fall (1)

4175 כָּשַׁף *kāšap̱* (6)
sorcerers (3)
engages in witchcraft (1)
sorceress (1)
witchcraft (1)

4176 כֶּשֶׁף *kešep̱* (6)
sorceries (3)
witchcraft (3)

4177 כַּשָּׁף *kaššāp̱* (1)
sorcerers (1)

4178 כָּשֵׁר *kāšēr* (3)
bring (1)
succeed (1)
thinks right (1)

4179 כִּשְׁרוֹן *kišrôn* (3)
achievement (1) +5126
benefit (1)
skill (1)

4180 כָּתַב *kāṯaḇ* (225)
written (107)
write (25)
wrote (23)
recorded (9)
write down (6)
wrote down (5)
be written (3)
inscribed (3)
signed (3)
were recorded (3)
be listed (2)
engraved (2)
was recorded (2)
were written (2)
write a description (2)
writes (2)
wrote out (2)
been recorded (1)
copied (1) +5467
decree be issued (1)
issue decrees (1) +4180
listed (1)
lodged (1)
map out (1)
order be written (1)
put in writing (1)
putting in writing (1)
record (1)
record (1) +9005
register (1)
was written (1)
was written down (1)
were listed (1)
words (1)
writing (1)
written descriptions (1)
wrote description (1)
untranslated (3)

4181 כְּתָב *kᵉṯāḇ* (17)
script (5)
records (3)
text (3)
book (1)
directions written (1)
document (1)
letter (1)
prescribed (1)
writing (1)

4182 כְּתֹבֶת *k^{e}ṯōḇeṯ* (1)
marks (1)

4183 כִּתִּיִּים *kitiyyim* (10)
Kittim (4)
Cyprus (3)
western coastlands (1)
untranslated (2)

4184 כָּתִית *kāṯiyṯ* (5)
pressed (2)
pressed olives (2)
pressed olive (1)

4185 כֹּתֶל *kōṯel* (1)
wall (1)

4186 כִּתְלִישׁ *kiṯliyš* (1)
Kitlish (1)

4187 כָּתַם *kāṯam* (1)
stain (1)

4188 כֶּתֶם *keṯem* (9)
gold (5)
fine gold (1)
finest gold (1) +233
pure gold (1)
purest gold (1) +7058

4189 כֻּתֹּנֶת *kutōneṯ* (29)
robe (13)
tunics (6)
tunic (5)
garments (4)
garment (1)

4190 כָּתֵף *kāṯēp̱* (68)
side (18)
shoulders (10)
shoulder pieces (8)
slope (8)
shoulder (5)
backs (3)
projecting walls (2)
slopes (2)
arm (1)
flank (1)
handles (1)
one[s] (1)
sides (1)
sidewalls (1)
slung on back (1) +1068
supports (1) +7193
wall (1)
untranslated (3)

4191 כְּתֹף *k^{e}ṯōp̱*
Variant; not used

4192 1כָּתַר *kāṯar1* (1)
bear (1)

4193 2כָּתַר *kāṯar2* (4)
encircle (1)
gather about (1)
hem in (1)
surrounded (1)

4194 3כָּתַר *kāṯar3* (1)
crowned (1)

4195 כֶּתֶר *keṯer* (3)
crown (2)
crest (1)

4196 כֹּתֶרֶת *kōṯereṯ* (24)
capitals (11)
capital (5)
circular frame (1)
untranslated (7)

4197 כָּתַשׁ *kāṯaš* (1)
grind (1)

4198 כָּתַת *kāṯaṯ* (16)
beat (3)
crushed (3)
are broken to pieces (1)
are defeated (1)
battered to pieces (1) +8625
be broken to pieces (1)
beat down (1)
broke into pieces (1)
crush (1)
oppress (1)
shattered (1)
was crushed (1)

4199 ל *l*
Variant; not used

4200 1לְ־ *l^e-* (20495)
to (4730)
for (1684)
of (756)
before (542) +7156
in (365)
with (219)
as (210)
by (209)
why (165) +4537
from (157)
therefore (146) +4027
forever (137) +6409
on (137)
into (110)
at (102)
have (94)
against (91)
had (90)
his (81) +2257
through (79)
my (77) +3276
that (74)
before (71)
in front of (66) +7156
according to (61)
so that (60)
had (50) +2118
has (50)
to (50) +7156
have (48) +2118
your (48) +4013
ahead (45) +7156
about (42)
alone (40) +963
over (40)
your (36) +3870
their (35) +2157
mine (33) +3276
belongs to (28)
so (26)
the LORD's (26) +3378
belong to (25)
to (25) +7023
upon (25)
when (25)
before (24) +4946+7156
yours (24) +3870
belonging to (23)
our (22) +5646
by (21) +7156
in order to (21)
among (20)
like (19)
presence (19) +7156
and (18)
every (18)
forever (18) +5905
in addition to (18) +963+4946
toward (17)
belonged to (16)
concerning (16)
only (16) +963
against (13) +7156
before (13) +5584
as for (12)
forever (12) +6329
have (12) +3780
after (11)
belong to (11) +2118
from (11) +4946+7156
for (10) +7156
so (10) +4027
under (10)
your (10) +3871
besides (9) +963+4946
to (9) +7754
David's (8) +1858
fail to have (8) +4162
from (8) +7156
his own (8) +2257
never (8) +4202+6409
only one (8) +963
formerly (7) +7156
give in marriage (7) +851+5989
meet (7) +7156
on behalf (7)
Solomon's (7) +8976
with (7) +7156
because of (6)
has (6) +2118
near (6)
near (6) +7156
serve (6) +6641+7156
their (6) +4564
upward (6) +2025+5087
before (5) +6524
belonged to (5) +2118
bring (5) +2118
but (5) +4027
close to (5) +6645
consider (5) +2118
destined for (5)
ever (5) +6409
for sake (5)
gave in marriage (5) +851+5989
have to do with (5)
her (5) +2023
marry (5) +851+2118
on side (5)
sent for (5) +2256+7924+8938
their own (5) +2157
used to (5) +7156
what (5) +4537
while (5)
with (5) +7023
above (4) +2025+4946+5087
always (4) +5905
belongs to (4) +2118
by themselves (4) +963+4392
concerns (4)
escape with (4) +8965
falsely (4) +2021+9214
father's (4) +3
given to (4)
great (4) +8044
greet (4) +8626+8934
greeted (4) +8626+8934
in honor (4)
in vain (4) +2021+8736
in vain (4) +8198
its (4) +2257
king's (4) +4889
lord's (4) +123
married (4) +851+4374
marry (4) +851+4374
my own (4) +3276
one by one (4) +1653+4392
owned (4)
owns (4)
plentiful (4) +8044
received (4)
Saul's (4) +8620
their (4) +2257
throughout (4)
till (4)
to belong (4)
within (4)
your own (4) +3870
yours (4) +4013

above (3) +2025+5087
along (3)
apart (3) +963
as if (3)
as soon as (3)
attack (3) +995
awaits (3)
become (3)
below (3) +4752
between (3)
by (3) +7023
down (3) +4752
entered (3) +995
eternal (3) +6409
face (3) +7156
faced (3)
get (3)
great amount (3) +8044
greatly (3) +8044
in abundance (3) +8044
in behalf of (3)
Israel's (3) +3776
keep (3) +2118
large numbers (3) +8044
leading (3) +7156
leads to (3)
married (3) +851+2118
mean by (3)
misuse (3) +2021+5951+8736
never (3) +4202+5905
opposite (3) +7156
over (3) +2025+4946+5087
related to (3)
sight (3) +7156
theirs (3) +2157
then (3) +4027
throughout (3) +3972
to belonged (3)
until (3)
watch (3) +6524
watched (3) +6524
what are you doing (3) +3870+4537
whose (3) +2257
whose (3) +4769
without (3) +4202
your own (3) +4013
a matter of (2)
accompanies (2) +7156
according to (2) +7023
across (2)
after (2) +7891
along with (2) +6645
always (2) +6409
any (2)
applies to (2)
as (2) +6645
as long as (2) +7156
as much as (2) +7023
as well as (2) +963+4946
assigned to (2)
at (2) +7156
at random (2) +9448
at table[s] (2) +7156
at the point of (2)
be sure of this (2) +3338+3338
Belonging to (2)
bent on (2)
beside (2) +6645
beside (2) +7156
bind (2) +2118+3213
bloodshed (2) +1947+1947
bottom (2) +4752+4946
brings (2)
cause (2)
clan by clan (2) +5476
completely (2) +2021+3972
covered with (2) +7156
do for (2)
during (2)
each (2)
entered service (2) +6641+7156
entering (2) +995
eternal (2) +6329
ever (2) +6329
extensive (2) +8044
for (2) +4027
forever (2) +6330+6409
from (2) +4974
gently (2) +351
give (2)
given (2)
have in common (2)
highly (2) +2025+5087
his (2) +4564
his[s] (2) +8976
holding (2)
in (2) +5584
in (2) +6961
in accordance with (2)
in addition to (2) +963
in behalf (2)
in connection with (2)
in front of (2) +5584
in order that (2)
in presence (2) +5584+6524
in such a way that (2)
in way (2) +7156
inside (2) +7156
its (2) +2023
just as (2) +6645
large quantities (2) +8044
leader (2) +2143+7156
led in campaigns (2) +995+2256+3655+7156
let inquire of (2) +2011
liable to (2)
long ago (2) +4946+8158
man's (2) +132
many (2) +8044
mean to (2)
misuses (2) +2021+5951+8736
much (2) +8044
never (2) +440+6409
never (2) +1153+5905
never (2) +1153+6409
never again (2) +4202+6409
not counting (2) +963+4946
not including (2) +963+4946
of (2) +4946+7156
of (2) +7156
on account of (2)
on behalf of (2)
opposite (2) +5584
ours (2) +5646
own (2)
owned (2) +3780
owner (2) +2257
parallel to (2) +6645
Pharaoh's (2) +7281
plenty (2) +8044
preceded (2) +2118+7156
preceded (2) +7156
receive (2) +2118
regard (2) +5584+8492
regard as (2) +2118
representing (2)
resist (2) +6641+7156
safely (2) +1055
see (2) +7156
seems to (2) +7156
served (2) +6641+7156
serving (2) +6641+7156
some (2)
surely (2) +4027
their (2) +2177
their own (2) +2257
to (2) +6524
to belongs (2)
top (2) +2025+4946+5087
turned into (2) +2118
under (2) +7156
up (2) +2025+5087
use (2) +2118
used to (2) +2021+8037
very (2) +2025+5087
very well (2) +4027
watching (2) +6524
when (2) +6961
when (2) +7023
without (2) +1172
withstand (2) +6641+7156
won (2) +5951+7156
your very own (2) +3870
Aaron's (1) +195
above (1)
above (1) +4946+4946+5087+6645
abroad (1) +2021+2575
Absalom's (1) +94
abundant (1) +8044
accompanied (1)
accompany (1) +2143+5584
accused of (1)
accuses (1) +2021+5477+7756
acquired (1) +2118
adjoining (1) +6645
Adonijah's (1) +154
adopted (1) +1426+4374
adorned (1) +7596+9514
affects (1)
again (1) +6409
agent (1) +3338
agreed with (1) +7754+9048
ahead (1)
ahead (1) +4946+7156
alike (1) +6645
all (1) +963
all alone (1) +963
all by myself (1) +963+3276
allotted (1)
allowed (1)
alone (1) +970
along (1) +3338
along with (1)
along with (1) +963+4946
alongside (1) +6645
alongside of (1) +6645
also (1) +963
always (1) +1887+1887+2256
always (1) +6329
among (1) +3972
and (1) +4027
anyone (1) +963
apart (1) +970
around (1)
as (1) +6961
as a result (1)
as in (1)
as long as live (1) +3427+3972+6409
as well as (1) +6645
asked how they were (1) +8626+8934
assaults (1) +5596+5596
assigned (1)
assistant (1) +6641+7156
at (1) +6645
at (1) +7023
at advance (1) +7156
at each successive level (1) +2025+2025+4200+5087+5087
at hand (1) +995+7940
at sanctuary[s] (1) +7156
at the head of (1) +7156
attack (1)
attack (1) +6913
attains (1)
attend (1) +6641+7156
attend (1) +7156
attended by (1) +2143+8079
attending (1) +7156
attention (1) +7156
avoid (1) +4202+6843
awaits (1) +7156
backward (1) +294
bake thoroughly (1) +8596+8599
banded together (1) +665+2021+2653

be given in marriage (1) +851+5989
be kept from (1) +1194+1757
became (1)
because (1)
because (1) +3954+4537
because (1) +4027
because of this (1) +4027
become (1) +2118
become wife (1) +851+4374
befalls (1) +628
before (1) +678
before (1) +5584+6524
before eyes (1) +7156
before time (1) +4946+7156
beforehand (1) +4946+7156
belonging to (1) +2118
beside (1) +3338
besides (1)
besides (1) +963
beyond (1) +2134+4946
bodyguard (1) +8031+9068
bordering (1) +6645
borne by (1)
bravely (1) +1201+2657
bring (1)
bringing (1)
brings to ruin (1) +2021+6156+8273
brought (1)
but (1)
but why (1) +4537
by (1) +4946
by (1) +6524
by himself (1) +963+2257
by itself (1) +963
by itself (1) +963+2257
by itself (1) +970
by myself (1) +963+3276
call in honor of (1) +7727
check (1) +995+7156
children's (1) +1201
choose (1)
come across (1) +7156+7925
committed (1)
condemn (1) +2118+2631
consult (1) +7156
contains (1)
continually (1) +6329
continually (1) +8092
controlled (1)
controlled (1) +2118
corresponding to (1)
count (1) +2118
covered (1) +8492
crown (1)
crowns (1) +8031
cry out (1) +606+5951
daily (1) +285+3427
daily (1) +2021+3427
Danite (1) +1968+4751
depth (1) +2025+5087
despite (1) +928+8611
despoil (1) +1020+5989
directed to (1)
directly in front of (1) +5790
directly opposite (1) +5790+7156
dispersed (1) +2006+2143
done this[s] (1) +1215+3378+4640
doomed to (1)
downcast (1) +2118
downstream (1) +2025+4946+5087
droves (1) +8044
each day (1) +2021+2021+3427+3427+4200
each day (1) +2021+3427
each morning (1) +1332+1332+2021+2021+4200
each[s] (1) +5031
endless (1) +5905
endure (1) +2118
enough (1) +1896+4537
enslaved (1) +2256+3899+4200+6269+9148
enter (1) +995
enter service (1) +6641+7156
entered the service (1) +6641+7156
enters (1) +995
enthrones (1) +2021+3782+4058
even though (1) +963
ever (1) +7156
ever again (1) +5905+5905
ever since (1) +4946
everlasting (1) +5905
everlasting (1) +6409
every day (1) +2021+3427
exceedingly (1) +2025+5087
extends to (1) +4946
faced (1) +7156
far and wide (1) +4946+6330+8158
far away (1) +4946+6330+8158
fault (1) +928+8611
fell facedown (1) +678+2556
fight (1) +2021+3655+4878
find (1)
finds (1)
firstborn belongs to (1) +1144
fit for (1)
fleet of trading ships (1) +641+2143+9576
fluent (1) +1819+4554
for life (1) +6409
for relief from (1) +4946+7156
for the sake of (1)
for the use of (1)
forced to (1)
forever (1) +802+3427
forward (1) +7156
fought in (1) +3655
found (1) +7156+8011
from (1) +1068
from (1) +4946
from among (1)
from place to place (1) +5023
gain (1)
gave permission (1)
girl's (1) +5855
give (1) +2118
give (1) +7156
give in marriage (1) +408+5989
given over to (1)
God's (1) +466
goes down (1) +3718+4752
going (1)
got (1) +2118
great number (1) +8044
great numbers (1) +8044
great quantities (1) +4394+8044
had (1) +3780
had (1) +5162
had been (1) +7156
harbored (1) +2118
hard (1) +2021+3668+4607
has (1) +5162
has to do with (1)
have (1) +889
have (1) +5989
have part (1)
have regard for (1) +5564
have right (1)
have sexual relations (1) +2446+5989+8888
have the right (1)
have to do with (1) +2256+4200
having (1)
having (1) +2118
hear (1) +5877+7156
heights (1) +2025+5087
help (1)
help (1) +2118
help (1) +3338
help (1) +6913
her (1) +3276
here (1) +7156
hers (1) +2023
Hezekiah's (1) +2624
Hezekiah's (1) +2625
high above (1) +2025+4946+5087
higher than (1) +2025+5087+8049
his[s] (1) +90
his[s] (1) +4889+5213
his[s] (1) +5557
his[s] (1) +8620
hold (1)
how was (1) +8934
how was going (1) +8934
how were (1) +8934
however (1) +4027
huge (1) +1524+4394+6330
hunt down (1) +4511+7421
imposing (1) +1524+5260
in (1) +7156
in accordance with (1) +7023
in addition (1) +963
in addition (1) +963+4946
in ascending stages (1) +2025+2025+4200+5087+5087
in broad daylight (1) +2021+2021+2296+6524+9087
in charge of (1)
in debt (1) +5957
in earlier times (1) +7156
in eyes (1) +7156
in front of (1) +6524
in fulfillment of (1)
in large numbers (1) +8044
in opposition to (1)
in path (1) +7156
in possession (1)
in preparation for (1)
in service (1) +7156
in the course of time (1) +3427+3427+4946
in the eyes of (1) +7156
in the face of (1) +5584
in the sight of (1)
in this way (1)
inclines to (1)
individually (1) +1653
inner (1) +7156
inner (1) +7163
inquire of (1) +2011
inside (1) +1074+4946
inside (1) +7163
instead of (1)
instead of (1) +1194
instead of (1) +7156
intimate with (1)
into (1) +7163
into another set (1) +963
into marry (1) +2118
into one set (1) +963
invaded (1) +2143
invading (1) +995
involved in (1)
Israelite (1) +1201+3776
it means (1)
its[s] (1) +2021+4058
Jacob's (1) +3620
jointed (1) +4946+5087+8079
just as (1) +889+3972
just for that (1) +4027
keep (1)
keeps company (1) +782+2495
kept (1)
killed (1) +2995+5782+7023
Korah's (1) +7946
lack (1) +401
large amount (1) +8044
larger (1) +8044
lasting (1) +6409
later (1)
later (1) +7891
lawsuits (1) +1907+1907
lead (1) +995+2256+3655+7156
lead (1) +2143+7156
lead (1) +7156
lead across (1) +6296+7156
lead to (1)
leading into (1)

leading into (1) +7023
leading to (1)
learned (1) +5583
leaves (1)
led (1) +7156
led out (1) +3655+7156
led to (1)
left (1) +2118
length (1) +6645
let inquire of at all (1) +2011+2011
lets happen (1) +628+3338
life will not be worth living (1) +2644+4537
like (1) +6645
likes (1) +928+2021+3202
long (1) +6409
long ago (1) +6409
long life (1) +2021+2644
lover's (1) +1856
made fall (1) +2118+4842
make serve (1) +8492
make sport of (1) +2118+5442
married (1) +851+2257+4200+4374
married to (1) +851+2118
marries (1) +408+2118
marries (1) +408+2118+2118
marries (1) +2118
marry (1) +408+2118
marry into (1) +2118
match for (1)
mighty (1) +8044
mine (1) +3276+8611
more (1) +401
more (1) +2025+5087
more (1) +8044
more and more powerful (1)
+1541+2025+2143+2256+5087+6330
more for (1)
more quickly than (1) +7156
more readily than (1) +7156
more than (1) +401
more than (1) +963+4946
Moses' (1) +5407
my (1) +3276+7156
my own (1) +3276+8611
Nebuchadnezzar's (1) +5557
never (1) +401+6409
never (1) +561+5905
never (1) +4202+7156
nevertheless (1) +4027
next to (1)
next to (1) +5584
next to (1) +6298
not circumcised (1) +2257+6889
numerous (1) +8044
obey (1)
obey (1) +7754+9048
of (1) +4946+8611
of what use (1) +2296+4537
of what use (1) +4537
offered a kiss of homage (1) +5975+7023
older (1) +2418+3427
on behalf of (1) +5466
on behalf of (1) +5790
on high (1) +2021+5294
once for all (1) +5905
one kind after another (1) +2157+5476
one[S] (1) +2157
only (1) +963+2314
only exception (1) +963
only one (1) +963+2257
open (1) +7156
opposite (1) +6645
other than (1) +963+1194
other than (1) +963+4946
ours (1) +3276
ours (1) +5646+7156
out (1)
out of way (1) +4946+7156
outer (1) +2021+2575
outer (1) +2025+4946+5087
over (1) +4946+6584
over (1) +7156
over and above (1) +2025+5087
over here (1) +285+6298
over there (1) +285+6298
overlooking (1) +7156
overtake (1)
overtakes (1)
overturned (1) +2025+2200+5087
own (1) +2118
owning (1)
owns (1) +3780
paid any attention (1) +265+5742+9048
particularly (1) +4027
pay (1)
people's (1) +6639
per (1)
perjurers (1) +2021+8678+9214
perjury (1) +2021+8678+9214
permanently (1) +2021+7552
permanently (1) +7552
piece by piece (1) +5984
plentifully (1) +7859
powerless (1) +401+445
powerless (1) +401+445+3338
preceding (1) +7156
predecessor (1) +889+2118+7156
present (1) +5877+7156
present (1) +7156
previous (1) +7156
project upward (1) +2025+5087
property[S] (1) +889+2118
provide with (1)
provided for (1) +430+2118+2256+4312
provides for (1)
punished less (1) +3104+4752
put (1) +995+7156
put (1) +995+9202
put up security (1) +3338+9546
quantities (1) +8044
quarrel between (1)
quite innocently (1) +9448
reached (1) +995
ready for (1)
ready for battle (1) +408+2021+4878+7372
realize (1) +606+4222
receive (1)
received (1) +995
received (1) +2118
receives (1) +5989
reduced to servitude (1) +6268+6269
referring to (1)
reflects a face (1) +2021+2021+7156+7156
reflects the man (1) +132+2021
regard (1) +2118+7156
regarded (1)
regarded in the sight of (1) +7156
regardless (1) +401+9068
regards (1) +5162+7156
regularly (1) +928+3427+3427
relating to (1)
relation to (1)
remain unmarried (1)
+408+1194+2118+4200+6328
renowned (1) +9005
represent (1)
represented (1)
resisted (1) +5584+6641
resort to (1) +2143+7925
responding to (1) +6645
responsible for (1)
responsible for (1) +889+928
responsible for (1) +928+8611
responsible for (1) +5584
rests with (1)
retains (1) +2118
reward (1)
right before (1)
right before (1) +5584
right for (1)
risked (1) +3070+4637
ruined (1) +7914
ruthlessly (1) +425
safely (1) +2021+8934
safely (1) +8934
same as (1)
saying (1) +606
see (1) +2021+6524+8011
see (1) +6524
see to it (1) +6524
seeks (1)
select a day (1) +3427+3427+4946
self-control (1) +5110+8120
sent for (1) +7924+8938
separate (1) +963
separate (1) +963+3657
servants' (1) +6269
serve (1) +2118
serve (1) +2118+7156
serve (1) +7156
served (1) +2118+7156
service of (1)
setting the time (1) +5503
severe (1) +2025+5087
Shalmaneser's[S] (1) +2257
share (1) +889+3869
share (1) +2118
Shimei's (1) +9059
show (1) +2118
show (1) +7156
shows to be (1) +2118
sided with (1) +1047
since (1) +3427+4946
sing songs (1) +928+7754+8123+9048
slaughter (1) +2222+5422
slept with (1) +408+3359+5435
slept with (1) +2351+3359+5435
slow down (1) +6806+8206
slowly (1) +351
so as (1)
so as to (1)
so far as (1) +3972
so many (1) +8044
so then (1) +4027
Solomon's (1) +8611+8976
some years later (1) +7891+9102
started (1) +6991
stationed at (1)
still (1) +4027
stole into (1) +995+1704
stolen goods (1) +2257+4202
storerooms (1) +238+5969
straight ahead (1) +5790
straight to (1)
struck (1)
subject to (1)
succeed against (1) +5584
such as (1)
suffered (1) +2118
summoned (1) +7924+8938
supply (1) +2118
take (1) +2118
take care of (1) +2118+5466
take command (1) +2118+5464
take for (1) +5989+7156
taken (1)
taken from (1) +4946+7156
testify (1) +6332+6699
than (1)
that[S] (1) +8079
the LORD's (1) +3378
their (1) +2179
their (1) +4013
their[S] (1) +2021+2498
theirs (1) +2257
therefore (1) +3610+4027
think (1) +4013+8492
this fellow's[S] (1) +2296
this one (1) +963
thoughtlessly (1) +928+1051+8557
thus (1)
to (1) +928+6288
to (1) +4946

to (1) +6584+7156
to fulfill (1)
to honor (1)
to the point of (1)
to the very end (1) +6409+6813
to turned (1)
together with (1)
told (1) +606+8938
took in marriage (1) +851+4374
took part in (1) +3655
top (1) +2025+5087
top of (1) +2025+4946+5087
tore apart (1) +7973+7974+9109
total (1)
total (1) +3972+5031
treated the same as (1) +6645
troubles (1)
trustfully (1) +1055
tuned to (1)
turn against (1) +2118+8477
turn into (1)
under (1) +1074
under blessing (1) +7156
under direction (1) +7156
under supervision (1) +7156
unintentionally (1) +8705
unite (1) +2118+3480+4222
unless (1) +561+3954+7156
unmarried (1) +408+2118+4202
unsuspecting (1) +1055
unto (1)
upstream (1) +2025+5087
upward (1) +2025+4946+5087
used as (1)
used by (1)
used for (1)
used in (1)
useless (1) +2021+9214
uses (1)
valued at (1)
very (1) +466
very (1) +2025+5087+6330
wage war (1) +1741+2021+4878
walled (1) +2257+2570
want (1)
wanted to make (1) +1335
was given in marriage (1) +851+5989
watched (1) +7156
wear (1)
were fettered (1) +5602+5733
what do I care about (1) +2296+3276+4200+4537
what do you mean (1) +4013+4537
what is doing (1) +4537
what is the matter (1) +3871+4537
what right have you (1) +3870+4537
when (1) +3954+7023
whenever (1) +3972
whenever (1) +7023
where[S] (1) +4564
where[S] (1) +7156
wherever (1)
wherever (1) +8079
whether (1)
while (1) +6961
whose (1) +889
why (1) +361+2296
why (1) +561+4027+4537
why (1) +4537+8611
wielding (1) +995+2025+5087
wish well (1) +8934
with (1) +3338
with (1) +6645
without (1) +401
worship (1) +7156
year (1) +2021+3427
yet (1) +4027
younger (1) +3427+7582
yours (1) +3871
Zedekiah's (1) +7409
untranslated (7405)

4201 לְ־2 *lᵉ-2*
Variant; not used

4202 לֹא *lō'* (5189)
not (2963)
no (613)
never (155)
nor (109) +2256
cannot (101)
nothing (68)
without (67)
cannot (45) +3523
neither (42)
don't (33)
no (31) +3972
didn't (30)
none (29)
nothing (19) +1821
isn't (14)
none (14) +3972
or (14)
or (14) +2256
surely (14) +561
won't (13)
before (12)
haven't (11)
nor (11)
nothing (11) +3972
refused (11) +14
without (9) +928
failed (8)
never (8) +4200+6409
can't (7) +3523
nothing (7) +4399
refused (7)
unwilling (7) +14
aren't (5)
forbidden (5) +6913
hasn't (5)
never (5) +6388
none (5) +408
refuse (5)
little (4)
neither (4) +1685
unjust (4) +9419
unless (4) +561
unlike (4) +3869
wouldn't (4)
before (3) +889+6330
before (3) +928
beyond (3)
fail (3)
fails (3)
injustice (3) +5477
instead of (3)
more than (3)
neither (3) +2256
never (3) +4200+5905
nor (3) +1685
unclean (3) +3196
unknown (3) +3359
without (3) +4200
as you know (2) +2022
before (2) +928+3270
but (2) +561
can't (2)
childless (2) +3528
disobeyed (2) +928+7754+9048
disobeyed (2) +9048
displeases (2) +2911
doesn't (2)
forbidden (2) +7422
free from (2)
from (2)
hardly (2)
helpless (2) +3946+6806
ignorant (2) +3359
lack (2)
never (2) +2021+3427+3972
never (2) +3578
never (2) +6330+6409
never again (2) +4200+6409
no (2) +3972+4946
no (2) +4027
nothing (2) +1821+3972
overwhelmed (2) +928+2118+6388+8120
powerless (2) +3946
rather than (2)
rather than (2) +2256
refuse (2) +14
shouldn't (2)
that (2) +561
till (2) +561
trackless (2) +2006
unable (2)
unaware (2) +3359
useless (2) +7503
whether (2) +561
worthless idols (2) +3603
against (1) +3869
agreed (1)
always be (1) +2532
anything[S] (1)
as[S] (1)
avoid (1) +4200+6843
barely (1)
because (1) +561+3610
because (1) +2256
before (1) +6330
before (1) +6388
before elapsed (1) +4848
better than (1)
bottled-up (1) +7337
but (1)
by no means (1) +3480
by surprise (1) +3359
can hardly breathe (1) +5972+8636
cannot bear (1) +3523
cannot read (1) +3359+6219
cannot stand (1) +3523
certainly (1) +561
cloudless (1) +6265
contrary (1)
contrary to (1)
contrary to (1) +928+3869
contrary to (1) +3869
couldn't (1)
delayed (1) +237
dense (1) +2983
denying (1)
deserted (1) +3782
despairs (1) +586
die (1) +2649
disobedience (1) +928+7754+9048
disobey (1) +9048
disorder (1) +6043
displease (1) +928+2834+5162+6524
displeasing (1) +928+2834+5162+6524
disregarding (1) +2349
either (1)
else (1)
empty (1) +4027
ever (1)
except (1) +889
except for (1) +2256
fail (1) +8505
failed (1) +3523
failed (1) +6388+7756
fails (1) +586
feeble (1) +3888
feeble (1) +6437
free from (1) +928
free of (1)
futile (1) +4027
gives way (1) +6641
go unanswered (1) +6699
gone (1) +928+2118
gone (1) +928+6641
hidden (1) +8011
how much less (1) +677+3954
if (1)
ignored (1) +4213+8492

in vain (1)
incapable (1) +3523
keeps (1) +4614
lack (1) +928
lest (1) +889
little value (1) +4399
make countless (1) +889+6218+8049
many (1) +5071
measureless (1) +4499
mercilessly (1) +2798
neglected (1) +5757
neither (1) +2296
never (1) +3427+4946
never (1) +4200+7156
never (1) +5905+6330
never (1) +6409
never (1) +8041
never (1) +9458
nobody (1) +132
none (1) +285
none (1) +3972+4946
none (1) +3972+5883
none (1) +4399
nor (1) +1685+2256
nothing (1) +889+3972
nothing (1) +1524+1821+2256+7785
nothing (1) +2021+3972
nothing (1) +4027
nothing (1) +4312
nothing (1) +5126
Nowhere (1)
nowhere (1)
of no account (1)
only (1) +1194
only (1) +2022
only (1) +2314
only (1) +8370
only[s] (1)
or (1) +889
other than (1)
otherwise (1) +889+5100
otherwise (1) +2256
outcome different (1) +3869
past (1)
pittance (1) +2104
powerless (1)
powerless (1) +3523
precious (1) +5877
rather (1) +3954
refused (1) +9048
remained childless (1) +3528
resents (1) +170
scarcely (1)
seldom (1) +2221
shameful (1) +4083
shamelessly (1) +1017
silent (1) +1819
since (1)
sinful (1) +3202
so (1) +561+3610
stay (1) +995
stayed away (1) +995
still to come (1) +6913
stolen goods (1) +2257+4200
stop (1)
stop (1) +3578
stopped (1) +3578+6388
stopped (1) +3855
stops (1)
stranger (1) +3359
strangers (1) +3359
surely (1)
than (1) +2256
this[s] (1) +2257+3769
till (1)
time and again (1) +285+2256+4202+9109
too (1)
too heavy a burden to carry (1) +3523+5951
troubled (1) +3523+9200
turned a deaf ear (1) +263
unable (1) +3523
unafraid (1) +7064
unceasingly (1) +1949
unchanged (1) +4614
unclean (1) +3197
uncut (1) +7786
undivided loyalty (1) +2256+4213+4213
uneaten (1) +1180
unfaithful (1) +574
unfamiliar (1) +3359
unfanned (1) +5870
ungodly (1) +2883
unintentionally (1) +928+7402
unjust (1) +5477
unjustly (1) +4026
unless (1)
unless (1) +561+3954
unless (1) +2022
unlike (1)
unlike (1) +4027+6913
unmarried (1) +408+2118+4200
unprofitable (1) +3603
unpunished (1) +870
unquenchable (1) +3882
unrelenting (1) +2798
unrighteousness (1) +7406
unruly (1) +4340
unsharpened (1) +7837
unsuccessful (1) +7503
unsuited (1) +5534
unthinkable (1) +597
untiring (1) +7028
unwise (1) +2682
useless (1)
useless (1) +3603
useless (1) +6122
virgin (1) +408+3359
wasn't (1) +2118
weakness (1) +3946
what about (1) +2022
whether (1) +561+2022
who[s] (1)
wicked (1) +3202
withheld[s] (1) +4763
withhold (1)
worse (1) +4017
worthless (1) +3603
wrong (1) +3202
yes (1) +3954
untranslated (329)

4203 לֹא דְבָר *lō' d̲āb̲ār* (2)
Lo Debar (2)

4204 לֹא עַמִּי *lō' 'ammiy* (1)
Lo-Ammi (1)

4205 לֹא רֻחָמָה *lō' ruḥāmāh* (2)
Lo-Ruhamah (2)

4206 לָאָה *lā'āh* (19)
weary (3)
worn out (3)
try patience (2)
burdened (1)
can no longer (1)
cannot (1)
could not (1)
discouraged (1)
frustrated (1)
impatient (1)
lazy (1)
not be able (1)
wears herself out (1)
weary themselves (1)

4207 לֵאָה *lē'āh* (34)
Leah (28)
Leah's (5)
untranslated (1)

4208 לָאז *lā'z*
Variant; not used

4209 לָאַט *lā'aṭ*
Variant; not used

4210 לָאֵל *lā'ēl* (1)
Lael (1)

4211 לְאֹם *l^e'ōm* (35)
peoples (18)
nations (8)
people (4)
nation (1)
nations' (1)
other[s] (1)
others[s] (1)
subjects (1)

4212 לְאֻמִּים *l^e'ummiym* (1)
Leummites (1)

4213 לֵב *lēb̲* (600)
heart (310)
hearts (74)
mind (21)
judgment (11)
himself (10) +2257
attention (7)
minds (7)
skilled (6) +2682
in high spirits (5) +3201
understanding (5)
brokenhearted (3) +8689
everything (3) +3972
high seas (3) +3542
myself (3) +3276
tenderly (3) +6584
arrogant (2) +5951
conscience-stricken (2) +5782
considered (2) +8492
courage (2)
imagination (2)
senseless (2) +401
thoughts (2)
wholehearted devotion (2) +8969
wholeheartedly (2) +928+3972
will (2)
willing (2) +5618
willing (2) +5951
wise (2)
yourself (2) +3870
ability (1)
ability (1) +928+2683
accord (1)
again give allegiance (1) +8740
am forgotten (1) +4946+8894
anxious striving (1) +8301
attitude (1)
bravest (1) +579
call to mind (1) +448+8740
care (1) +448+8492
care about (1) +448+8492
careful attention (1)
cares (1) +6584+8492
cheer up (1) +3512
chest (1)
concerned about (1) +448+8492
confide in (1) +907
conscience (1)
consider (1) +6584+8492
consider (1) +8492
consider well (1) +8883
craftsmen (1) +2682
dared (1) +4848
deceived (1) +1704
deception (1) +2256+4213
decided (1) +2118+6640
desire (1)
did[s] (1) +906+3877+4392
discourage (1) +5648
discouraged (1) +5648
disheartened (1) +3874
encourage (1) +1819+6584
encourage (1) +3922
encouragingly (1) +6584
enraged (1) +6192

faithless (1) +6047
glad (1) +3512
has full confidence (1) +1053
head (1)
heartache (1) +6780
his own (1) +2257+4946
I (1) +3276
idea (1) +4946
ignored (1) +4202+8492
in (1) +928
in good spirits (1) +3512
inclined (1) +5742
intent (1)
intention (1) +8492
it^s (1) +3276
kindly (1)
led astray (1) +5742
merrymakers (1) +8524
obstinate (1) +7997
opinions (1)
persist in own way (1) +9244
persuade (1) +1819+6584
pride (1) +1467
proud (1) +8123
purpose (1)
reason (1)
reflected on (1) +448+5989
refreshed (1) +6184
resolved (1) +6584+8492
rip open (1) +6033+7973
sense (1)
skill (1) +2683
spirit (1)
spoken kindly (1) +1819+6584
stops to think (1) +448+8740
stubborn (1) +2617
stubborn-hearted (1) +52
stunned (1) +7028
take heart (1) +599
take note (1) +8883
them (1) +4392
themselves (1) +4392
think (1) +606+928
think (1) +5989
think about (1) +6584+6590
to (1) +928
tried (1) +928+9365
undivided loyalty (1) +2256+4202+4213
valiant men (1) +52
very (1)
voluntarily (1) +408+6584+6590
wholeheartedly (1) +928+8969
willful (1)
willing (1) +5605
willingly (1) +4946
wisdom (1)
wise (1) +2682
worry (1) +906+8492
you (1) +3870
yourself (1) +2257
yourself (1) +3871
untranslated (3)

4214 לֵב קָמָי *lēḇ qāmāy* (1)
Leb Kamai (1)

4215 לָבֹא *lāḇō'*
Variant; not used

4216 לְבֶא *leḇe'* (1)
lions (1)

4217 לְבֹא חֲמָת *l^{e}ḇō' ḥ^{a}māṯ* (12)
Lebo Hamath (12)

4218 לִבְאָה *liḇ'āh* (1)
mate (1)

4219 לְבָאוֹת *l^{e}ḇā'ôṯ* (1)
Lebaoth (1)

4220 1לָבַב *lāḇaḇ1* (3)
stolen heart (2)
become wise (1)

4221 2לָבַב *lāḇaḇ2* (2)
made bread (1)
make special bread (1) +4223

4222 לֵבָב *lēḇāḇ* (252)
heart (120)
hearts (46)
mind (10)
give careful thought (5) +8492
yourself (4) +3870
conscience (3)
heart's (2)
minds (2)
understanding (2)
wholehearted devotion (2) +8969
wholeheartedly (2) +928+3972
wholeheartedly (2) +928+8969
yourselves (2) +3870
breasts (1)
brokenhearted (1) +3874
conscientious (1) +3838
consider (1) +928
consider better (1) +8123
convictions (1) +6640
courage (1)
deceived (1) +1704
disheartened (1) +906+5022
downhearted (1) +8317
encouraged (1) +1819+6584
enticed (1) +7331
fainthearted (1) +8205
fainthearted (1) +8216
filled with pride (1) +8123
fully determined (1) +928+8969
gladly (1) +928+3206
harbor (1) +2118+6640
hardhearted (1) +599+906
has in mind (1) +3108
heart and soul (1) +3869
herself (1) +2023
himself (1) +2257
in a rage (1) +2801
in accord with (1) +3838
indecisive (1) +8205
inspire (1) +928+5989
integrity (1) +3841
intend (1) +6640
intent (1)
plot against (1) +928+3108
profound (1)
proud (1) +8123
purpose (1)
realize (1) +606+4200
take heart (1) +599
themselves (1) +4392
think (1) +606+928
think (1) +5989
think (1) +6584+6590
thinks (1) +606+928
unite (1) +2118+3480+4200
willfully (1) +928
yourself (1) +2023
yourself (1) +3871
yourselves (1) +4013
untranslated (4)

4223 לְבִבָה *l^{e}ḇiḇāh* (3)
bread (1)
it^s (1) +2021
make special bread (1) +4221

4224 לְבַד *l^{e}ḇad*
Variant; not used

4225 לַבָּה *labbāh* (1)
flames (1)

4226 לִבָּה *libbāh* (1)
weak-willed (1) +581

4227 1לְבוֹנָה *l^{e}ḇônāh1*
Variant; not used

4228 2לְבוֹנָה *l^{e}ḇônāh2* (1)
Lebonah (1)

4229 לָבוּשׁ *lāḇûš* (15)
clothed (7)
in (3)
armed (1)
covered (1)
dress (1)
dressed (1)
wore (1)

4230 לְבוּשׁ *l^{e}ḇûš* (31)
clothing (5)
garments (5)
garment (4)
robe (4)
clothed (3)
clothes (2)
coat (1)
dressed (1)
gown (1)
military tunic (1) +4496
put on (1)
put on (1) +5989
robed (1)
robes (1)

4231 לָבַט *lāḇaṭ* (3)
comes to ruin (2)
come to ruin (1)

4232 לְבִי *l^{e}ḇiy*
Variant; not used

4233 לָבִיא *lāḇiy'* (11)
lioness (7)
lion (3)
lions (1)

4234 לְבִיָּא *l^{e}ḇiyyā'* (1)
lioness (1)

4235 1לָבַן *lāḇan1* (5)
made spotless (2)
leaving white (1)
white (1)
whiter (1)

4236 2לָבַן *lāḇan2* (3)
bricks (1)
make bricks (1) +4246
making bricks (1) +4246

4237 1לָבָן *lāḇān1* (29)
white (24)
reddish-white (4) +140
whiter (1)

4238 2לָבָן *lāḇān2* (54)
Laban (45)
Laban's (5)
he^s (2)
him^s (1)
untranslated (1)

4239 3לָבָן *lāḇān3* (1)
Laban (1)

4240 לָבֵן *lāḇēn*
Variant; not used

4241 לְבָנָהא *l^{e}ḇānāh'*
Variant; not used

4242 לִבְנֶה *liḇneh* (2)
poplar (2)

4243 לִבְנָה *liḇnāh* (18)
Libnah (17)
it^s (1)

4244 1לְבָנָה *l^{e}ḇānāh1* (3)
moon (3)

4245 2לְבָנָה *l^{e}ḇānāh2* (2)
Lebana (1)
Lebanah (1)

4246 לְבֵנָה *l^{e}ḇēnāh* (12)
bricks (5)
brick (2)
altars of brick (1)

clay tablet (1)
make bricks (1) +4236
making bricks (1) +4236
pavement (1)

4247 לְבֹנָה *l^eḇōnāh* (21)
incense (20)
frankincense (1)

4248 לְבָנוֹן *l^eḇānôn* (71)
Lebanon (68)
cedar of Lebanon (2)
there[s] (1)

4249 לִבְנִי 1 *liḇniy1* (5)
Libni (5)

4250 לִבְנִי 2 *liḇniy2* (2)
Libnite (1)
Libnites (1)

4251 לִבְנָת *liḇnāṯ*
Variant; not used

4252 לָבַשׁ *lāḇaš* (98)
put on (23)
clothed (15)
clothe (10)
wear (9)
dress (5)
came upon (3)
dressed (3)
dressed in (3)
robed (3)
covered (2)
wore (2)
clad (1)
clothed (1) +955
clothes (1)
dress in (1)
provide (1)
provided with clothes (1)
put clothes on (1)
put on (1) +9432
put on as clothing (1)
put on clothes (1)
put on robes (1)
puts on (1)
putting on (1)
robe (1)
vestments (1)
wear clothes (1)
worn (1)
untranslated (3)

4253 לֹג *lōg̱* (5)
log (5)

4254 לֹד *lōḏ* (4)
Lod (4)

4255 לִדְבִר *liḏḇir*
Variant; not used

4256 לֵדָה *lēḏāh* (4)
deliver (2)
birth (1)
in labor (1)

4257 לֹה *lōh* (1)
untranslated (1)

4258 לַהַב *lahaḇ* (12)
flames (3)
fire (2) +836
flame (2)
flashing (2)
aflame (1)
blade (1)
it[s] (1) +2021

4259 לֶהָבָה *lehāḇāh* (19)
flame (6)
flames (3)
flaming (3)
blaze (2)
blazing (1)
burned (1)
flashes (1)
lightning (1) +836
point (1)

4260 לְהָבִים *l^ehāḇiym* (2)
Lehabites (2)

4261 לַהַג *lahag̱* (1)
study (1)

4262 לָהַד *lāhaḏ* (1)
Lahad (1)

4263 לָהַהּ *lāhah* (1)
madman (1)

4264 לָהָה *lāhāh*
Variant; not used

4265 לָהַט 1 *lāhaṭ1* (10)
sets ablaze (2)
blazes (1)
burned up (1)
consumed (1)
consumes (1)
flames (1)
in flames (1)
set afire (1)
set on fire (1)

4266 לָהַט 2 *lāhaṭ2* (1)
ravenous beasts (1)

4267 לַהַט *lahaṭ* (1)
flaming (1)

4268 לְהָטִים *l^ehāṭiym* (1)
secret arts (1)

4269 לָהַם *lāham* (2)
choice morsels (2)

4270 לָהֵן *lahēn*
Variant; not used

4271 לִהְלֵהַּ *lihlēah*
Variant; not used

4272 לַהֲקָה *lah^aqāh* (1)
group (1)

4273 לוּ *lû* (25)
if (12)
if only (8)
let (1)
oh (1)
what if (1)
will (1)
untranslated (1)

4274 לוֹ דְבָר *lô ḏ^eḇār* (2)
Lo Debar (2)

4275 לוּב *lûḇ* (6)
Libyans (4)
Libya (2)

4276 לוּד *lûḏ* (9)
Lud (2)
Ludites (2)
Lydia (2)
Lydians (1)
men of Lydia (1)
untranslated (1)

4277 לָוָה 1 *lāwāh1* (12)
join (5)
bind themselves (2)
accompany (1)
attached (1)
be joined (1)
bound himself (1)
joined (1)

4278 לָוָה 2 *lāwāh2* (14)
lend (4)
borrow (3)
borrower (2)
lender (2)
lend freely (1)
lends (1)
lends freely (1)

4279 לוּז 1 *lûz1* (6)
devious (2)
let out (2)
deceit (1)
perverse (1)

4280 לוּז 2 *lûz2* (1)
almond (1)

4281 לוּז 3 *lûz3* (8)
Luz (7)
untranslated (1)

4282 לוּזָה *lûzāh*
Variant; not used

4283 לוּחַ *lûaḥ* (43)
tablets (33)
tablet (3)
boards (2)
panels (1)
surfaces (1)
them[s] (1) +2021
they[s] (1)
timbers (1)

4284 לוּחִית *lûḥiyṯ* (2)
Luhith (2)

4285 לוֹחֵשׁ *lôḥēš*
Variant; not used

4286 לוּט *lûṭ* (4)
covered (1)
enfolds (1)
pulled over (1)
wrapped (1)

4287 לוֹט 1 *lôṭ1* (1)
shroud (1)

4288 לוֹט 2 *lôṭ2* (33)
Lot (30)
he[s] (1)
Lot's (1)
untranslated (1)

4289 לוֹטָן *lôṭān* (7)
Lotan (5)
Lotan's (2)

4290 לֵוִי 1 *lēwiy1* (62)
Levi (42)
Levites (15) +1201
Levite (2)
Levites (2)
Levites (1) +4751

4291 לֵוִי 2 *lēwiy2* (288)
Levites (245)
Levite (26)
Levi (5)
Levites (3) +1201
Levitical (2)
them[s] (2) +2021
Levites (1) +5476
they[s] (1) +2021
untranslated (3)

4292 לִוְיָה *liwyāh* (2)
garland (2)

4293 לִוְיָתָן *liwyāṯān* (6)
Leviathan (4)
leviathan (2)

4294 לוּל *lûl* (1)
stairway (1)

4295 לוּלֵא *lûlē'* (14)
if not (5)
if not (4) +3954
unless (2)
but (1)
not (1)
still (1)

4296 לוּן *lûn* (19)
grumbled (7)

grumble (3)
constant grumbling (1) +9442
grumbling (1)
grumbling (1) +9442
howl (1)
made grumble (1)
untranslated (4)

4297 לוּשׁ *lûš* (6)
knead (2)
kneaded (2)
kneading (1)
untranslated (1)

4298 לָוִשׁ *lāwiš* (1)
untranslated (1)

4299 לָזוּת *lāzûṯ* (1)
corrupt talk (1)

4300 לַח *lah* (6)
fresh (2)
green (2)
fresh-cut (1)
grapes or raisins (1) +2256+3313+6694

4301 לֵחַ *lēah* (1)
strength (1)

4302 1לְחוּם *lᵉhûm1* (1)
entrails (1)

4303 2לְחוּם *lᵉhûm2* (1)
blows (1)

4304 לֻחוֹת *luhôṯ* (1)
untranslated (1)

4305 1לְחִי *lᵉhiy1* (20)
cheeks (4)
jawbone (4)
cheek (3)
jaws (3)
face (2)
jaw (2)
jowls (1)
neck (1)

4306 2לְחִי *lᵉhiy2* (4)
Lehi (4)

4307 לַחַי רֹאִי *lahay rōʾiy*
Variant; not used

4308 לָחַךְ *lāhak̲* (6)
lick (3)
lick up (1)
licked up (1)
licks up (1)

4309 1לָחַם *lāham1* (171)
fight (70)
fought (30)
attacked (15)
fighting (11)
attack (7)
attacking (5)
battle (5)
make war (5)
fights (4)
war (3)
made war (2)
at war (1)
engage in battle (1)
fight (1) +4309
fight battle (1)
military (1)
military exploits (1)
overpower (1)
overpower (1) +6584
pressed attack (1)
stormed (1)
waging war (1)
wars (1)
untranslated (1)

4310 2לָחַם *lāham2* (6)
eat (4)
consuming (1)
dine (1)

4311 לָחֵם *lāhem* (1)
war (1)

4312 לֶחֶם *lehem* (299)
food (124)
bread (116)
loaves of bread (6)
something[S] (3)
bread (2) +3971
meal (2)
provisions (2)
something to eat (2) +7326
baked (1)
cake (1) +2705
crops (1)
daily bread (1) +2976
eat (1)
feast (1)
feed (1)
food (1) +7326
fruit (1)
loaf (1) +3971
loaves (1)
meal (1) +430
nothing (1) +4202
overfed (1) +8430
provided for (1) +430+2118+2256+4200
stay for a meal (1) +430
swallow up (1)
untranslated (25)

4313 לַחְמִי *lahmiy* (1)
Lahmi (1)

4314 לַחְמָס *lahmās* (1)
Lahmas (1)

4315 לָחַץ *lāhas* (19)
oppressed (6)
oppress (4)
oppressors (2)
confined (1)
crushing (1)
hold shut (1)
oppressing (1)
press (1)
pressed close (1)
severely oppressing (1) +4316

4316 לַחַץ *lahas* (12)
affliction (2)
nothing but (2)
oppressed (2)
oppression (2)
severely oppressing (1) +4315
way[S] (1)
untranslated (2)

4317 לָחַשׁ *lāhaš* (3)
charmer (1)
whisper (1)
whispering among themselves (1)

4318 לַחַשׁ *lahaš* (5)
charmed (2)
barely whisper a prayer (1) +7440
charms (1)
enchanter (1)

4319 לָט *lāt* (7)
secret arts (3)
quietly (2) +928+2021
privately (1) +928+2021
unnoticed (1) +928+2021

4320 לֹט *lōt* (2)
myrrh (2)

4321 לְטָאָה *lᵉtāʾāh* (1)
wall lizard (1)

4322 לְטוּשִׁים *lᵉtûšiym* (1)
Letushites (1)

4323 לָטַשׁ *lātaš* (5)
sharpened (2)
fastens piercing (1)
forged (1)
sharpen (1)

4324 לֹיָה *lōyāh* (3)
wreaths (3)

4325 לַיִל *layil* (8)
night (6)
untranslated (2)

4326 לַיְלָה *laylāh* (227)
night (189)
nights (14)
tonight (10) +2021
midnight (2) +2940
overnight (2) +1201
all night long (1) +928+2021
all-night (1) +2021+3972
dark (1)
last night (1) +2021
midnight (1) +2021+2942
nightfall (1)
nightfall (1) +2021
nighttime (1)
nocturnal (1)
untranslated (1)

4327 לִילִית *liyliyṯ* (1)
night creatures (1)

4328 לִין *liyn* (69)
spend the night (17)
spent the night (6)
stay (6)
remain (4)
spent (3)
dwell (2)
spend (2)
stay at night (2)
at home (1)
camp (1)
camped (1)
endure (1)
for the night (1)
harbor (1) +928+7931
hold back overnight (1) +1332+6330
kept (1)
leave overnight (1)
left (1)
lie all night (1)
remains (1)
resides (1)
rest (1)
resting (1)
rests (1)
roost (1)
sleeping (1)
spend days (1)
spend nights (1)
spent the nights (1)
stay night (1)
stay tonight (1)
stayed night (1) +2256+3782
stays at night (1)
stays only a night (1) +5742
stopped for the night (1)

4329 לִיץ *liys* (6)
mock (2)
mocks (2)
mocker (1)
mocking (1)

4330 1לַיִשׁ *layiš1* (3)
lion (2)
lionesses (1)

4331 2לַיִשׁ *layiš2* (2)
Laish (2)

4332 3לַיִשׁ *layiš3* (4)
Laish (4)

4333 לַיְשָׁה *layšāh* (1)
Laishah (1)

4334 לָכַד *lāḵaḏ* (121)
captured (33)
took (17)
capture (9)
be captured (6)
was taken (6)
be caught (4)
take (4)
takes (4)
caught (3)
taken (3)
was chosen (3)
captures (2)
ensnare (2)
was captured (2)
are caught (1)
are trapped (1)
assumed (1)
be taken captive (1)
catch (1)
catch (1) +4334
catches (1)
cling together (1)
conquered (1)
ensnared (1)
entangle (1)
frozen (1)
held fast (1)
is captured (1)
is caught (1)
seize (1)
taking possession (1)
took prisoner (1)
trapped (1)
was caught (1)
were caught (1)
were taken (1)

4335 לֶכֶד *leḵeḏ* (1)
snared (1)

4336 לֵכָה *lēḵāh* (1)
Lecah (1)

4337 לָכִישׁ *lāḵiyš* (24)
Lachish (24)

4338 לָכֵן *lāḵēn*
Variant; not used

4339 לֻלָאוֹת *lulā'ôṯ* (13)
loops (11)
untranslated (2)

4340 לָמַד *lāmaḏ* (87)
teach (30)
learn (15)
taught (14)
learned (3)
teaches (3)
trains (3)
teaching (2)
train (2)
trained (2)
accept (1)
adopted (1)
cultivated (1)
experienced (1)
imparted (1)
instructors (1)
learn well (1) +4340
teachers (1)
unruly (1) +4202
were trained (1)
untranslated (2)

4341 לִמֻּד *limmuḏ* (6)
accustomed to (2)
disciples (1)
instructed (1)
one taught (1)
taught (1)

4342 לָמָּה *lāmmāh*
Variant; not used

4343 לָמוֹ *lāmô*
Variant; not used

4344 לְמוֹ *lᵉmô* (4)
for (1)
in (1)
over (1)
untranslated (1)

4345 לְמוּאֵל *lᵉmû'ēl* (2)
Lemuel (2)

4346 לְמוֹאֵל *lᵉmô'l*
Variant; not used

4347 לֶמֶךְ *lemeḵ* (11)
Lamech (11)

4348 לְמַעַן *lᵉma'an*
Variant; not used

4349 לֵן *lēn*
Variant; not used

4350 לֹעַ *lōa'* (1)
throat (1)

4351 לָעַב *lā'aḇ* (1)
mocked (1)

4352 לָעַג *lā'aḡ* (21)
mock (6)
mocks (6)
ridiculed (3)
maliciously mocked (1) +4352
mocked (1)
scoff (1)
scoffs (1)
strange (1)

4353 לַעַג *la'aḡ* (7)
scorn (3)
derision (1)
foreign (1)
ridicule (1)
ridiculed (1)

4354 לָעֵג *lā'ēḡ*
Variant; not used

4355 לַעְדָּה *la'dāh* (1)
Laadah (1)

4356 לַעְדָּן *la'dān* (7)
Ladan (7)

4357 לָעַז *lā'az* (1)
foreign tongue (1)

4358 לָעַט *lā'aṭ* (1)
let have (1)

4359 לָעִיר *lā'iyr*
Variant; not used

4360 לַעֲנָה *la'ᵃnāh* (8)
bitter (3)
gall (3)
bitterness (2)

4361 לְעַנּוֹת *lᵉ'annôṯ* (1)
leannoth (1)

4362 1לָעַע *lā'a'1* (2)
impetuous (1)
rashly (1)

4363 2לָעַע *lā'a'2* (1)
drink (1)

4364 לְעַפְרָה *lᵉ'aprāh*
Variant; not used

4365 לַפִּיד *lappiyḏ* (13)
torches (5)
torch (4)
firebrands (1)
flaming torches (1)
lightning (1)
untranslated (1)

4366 לַפִּידוֹת *lappiyḏôṯ* (1)
Lappidoth (1)

4367 לִפְנֵי *lip̄nēy*
Variant; not used

4368 לִפְנָי *lip̄nāy*
Variant; not used

4369 לָפַת *lāp̄aṯ* (3)
reached toward (1)
turn aside (1)
turned (1)

4370 לֵץ *lēṣ* (16)
mocker (11)
mockers (4)
proud mockers (1)

4371 לָצוֹן *lāṣôn* (3)
mockers (1) +408
mockery (1)
scoffers (1) +408

4372 לָצַץ *lāṣaṣ* (1)
mockers (1)

4373 לַקּוּם *laqqûm* (1)
Lakkum (1)

4374 לָקַח *lāqaḥ* (966)
take (238)
took (238)
get (46)
taken (32)
accept (23)
bring (20)
brought (20)
married (16)
taking (14)
take away (12)
receive (11)
received (11)
married (10) +851
took away (10)
marry (8)
accepted (7)
choose (7)
accepts (6)
carried off (6)
got (6)
selected (6)
takes (6)
capture (5)
captured (5)
marries (5)
bring back (4)
married (4) +851+4200
marry (4) +851
marry (4) +851+4200
put (4)
seize (4)
seized (4)
taken away (4)
was taken (4)
be taken (3)
been captured (3)
carried (3)
carried away (3)
collected (3)
respond to (3)
select (3)
took hold (3)
use (3)
am taken (2)
carry away (2)
collect (2)
found (2)
is taken (2)
keep (2)
kill (2) +5883
led away (2)
picked up (2)
purchased (2) +928+4697
send for (2) +2256+8938
takes away (2)
took as prisoners (2)
was taken away (2)

were taken (2)
accepting (1)
acquiring (1)
adopted (1) +1426+4200
appoint (1)
are gathered (1)
are taken (1)
arrest (1)
be brought (1)
be taken away (1)
become wife (1) +851+4200
been taken (1)
been taken away (1)
being led away (1)
blow away (1)
bring (1) +2256+3655
buy (1)
buys (1)
captivate (1)
carried (1) +928+3338
catch (1)
caught (1)
choose as wives (1)
chose (1)
come back (1)
did[s] (1)
did so[s] (1)
did so[s] (1) +2256+2932+8008
disgraced (1) +1423
drew (1)
find (1)
flashed back and forth (1) +928+9348
flashing (1)
force to give (1)
get back (1)
gets (1)
given (1)
grabbed (1)
had brought (1)
had brought (1) +2256+8938
had removed (1) +2256+8938
have (1)
have come (1)
invites (1)
kept (1)
learn (1)
learned (1)
loaded (1)
made (1) +928
make (1)
married (1) +851+2257+4200+4200
marries (1) +1249+2256
need (1)
open to (1)
pledged to marry (1)
prefer (1)
prepare (1)
recaptured (1) +2256+8740
receives (1)
removed (1)
responded to (1)
retake (1)
sampled (1)
sent for (1)
sent for (1) +2256+8938
share (1)
snatched (1)
strip of (1)
stripped (1)
suffer (1)
summon (1) +2256+8938
take up (1)
takes life (1)
taking hold (1)
took down (1)
took in marriage (1) +851+4200
took out (1)
took over (1)
took prisoner (1)
use as (1)
wag (1)
want (1)
was captured (1)
wins (1)
untranslated (22)

4375 לֶקַח *leqaḥ* (9)
instruction (3)
learning (3)
beliefs (1)
persuasive words (1)
teaching (1)

4376 לִקְחִי *liqḥiy* (1)
Likhi (1)

4377 לָקַט *lāqaṭ* (37)
gather (11)
gathered (8)
glean (6)
pick up (3)
be gathered up (1)
collected (1)
gather up (1)
gathering (1)
gathers (1)
gleaned (1)
gleans (1)
picked up (1)
picked up scraps (1)

4378 לֶקֶט *leqeṭ* (2)
gleanings (2)

4379 לָקַק *lāqaq* (7)
lapped (2)
licked up (2)
lap (1)
lick up (1)
untranslated (1)

4380 לָקַשׁ *lāqaš* (1)
glean (1)

4381 לֶקֶשׁ *leqeš* (2)
second crop (1)
untranslated (1)

4382 לָשָׁד *lāšāḏ* (2)
something made (1)
strength (1)

4383 לָשׁוֹן *lāšôn* (117)
tongue (62)
tongues (23)
language (11)
bay (3)
languages (3)
wedge (2)
words (2)
bark (1) +3076
charmer (1) +1251
deceit (1) +9567
fangs (1)
gulf (1)
lips (1)
object of malicious talk (1) +6584+6590+8557
on the tip of tongue (1) +928+2674
slanderers (1) +408
speech (1)
uttered a word (1) +906+3076

4384 לִשְׁכָּה *liškāh* (47)
rooms (21)
room (13)
storerooms (5)
side rooms (2)
chambers (1)
hall (1)
priests' rooms (1) +7731
that[s] (1)
untranslated (2)

4385 1לֶשֶׁם *lešem1* (2)
jacinth (2)

4386 2לֶשֶׁם *lešem2* (2)
Leshem (2)

4387 לָשַׁן *lāšan* (3)
slander (1)
slanders (1)
untranslated (1)

4388 לֶשַׁע *leša'* (1)
Lasha (1)

4389 לַשָּׁרוֹן *laššārôn* (1)
Lasharon (1)

4390 לֵתֶךְ *lēṯeḵ* (1)
lethek (1)

4391 מ *m*
Variant; not used

4392 ָם - *ām* (3952)
them (1550)
their (1012)
they (251)
the[s] (124)
their own (43)
it (31)
whose (15)
a[s] (14)
these (12)
those (12)
you (11)
its (10)
which[s] (10)
the people[s] (9)
themselves (9) +5883
his (7)
Israel[s] (6)
men[s] (6)
themselves (6)
who (6)
the Israelites[s] (5)
them (5) +5883
by themselves (4) +963+4200
he (4)
one by one (4) +1653+4200
the creatures[s] (4)
they (4) +5883
this (4)
us (4)
all[s] (3)
each (3)
her (3)
him (3)
our (3)
she (3)
that[s] (3)
the cherubim[s] (3)
the Levites[s] (3)
the men[s] (3)
the rest[s] (3)
your (3)
courts[s] (2)
gods[s] (2)
Judah[s] (2)
my people[s] (2)
our fathers[s] (2)
that (2)
the enemies[s] (2)
the shields[s] (2)
the wicked[s] (2)
these articles[s] (2)
whom (2)
almost to a man (1) +6330+9462
an[s] (1)
anyone (1)
Babylon[s] (1)
battle[s] (1)
did[s] (1) +906+3877+4213
each[s] (1)
Egypt[s] (1)
else's (1)
extremes[s] (1)
him (1)
his enemies[s] (1)
his offerings[s] (1)

his own (1)
his sons[s] (1)
its people[s] (1)
keep themselves alive (1) +906+5883+8740
man's[s] (1)
man[s] (1)
men (1)
Moses and Aaron[s] (1)
one's own (1)
priests[s] (1)
prophets[s] (1)
that person[s] (1)
that[s] (1) +2388
the Arameans[s] (1)
the army[s] (1)
the Canaanites[s] (1)
the case[s] (1)
the censers[s] (1)
the days[s] (1)
the enemies[s] (1)
the flock[s] (1) +5883
the forces[s] (1)
the Gibeonites[s] (1)
the goats[s] (1)
the gods[s] (1)
the hair[s] (1)
the Horites[s] (1)
the kings[s] (1)
the Midianite[s] (1)
the Midianites[s] (1)
the nations[s] (1)
the nobles and officials[s] (1)
the others[s] (1)
the people (1)
the priests[s] (1)
the procession[s] (1)
the ropes[s] (1)
the servants[s] (1)
the stones[s] (1)
the things[s] (1)
the water[s] (1)
their enemies[s] (1)
their gods[s] (1)
their leaders[s] (1)
their sons[s] (1)
their temples[s] (1)
theirs (1)
them (1) +74+928+2021
them (1) +1414
them (1) +2652
them (1) +4213
themselves (1) +4213
themselves (1) +4222
there[s] (1) +928+9348
these offerings[s] (1)
they (1) +9307
this is the way (1) +928
those nations[s] (1)
your brothers[s] (1)
your lovers[s] (1)
your sons[s] (1)
untranslated (637)

4393 מַאֲבוּס *ma'abûs* (1)
granaries (1)

4394 מְאֹד *m^e'ōd* (296)
very (71)
greatly (22)
great (18)
so (7)
large (6)
most (6)
very (6) +6330
great quantity (4) +2221
terrified (4) +3707
very much (4)
beyond measure (3) +6330
how (3)
all (2)
burned (2) +3013
closely (2)
deep (2)
desperate (2)
exceedingly (2) +928+4394
exceedingly (2) +4394
fully (2)
great (2) +1524
greatly (2) +928+4394
large (2) +8041
much (2)
overweening (2)
strength (2)
thoroughly (2)
utterly (2)
utterly (2) +6330
very (2) +928+4394
worst (2) +3878
abundance (1) +2221
abundantly (1)
accumulate large amounts (1) +8049
aged (1) +2416
almost (1)
at a distance (1) +8158
badly (1)
behaved in the vilest manner (1) +9493
beyond number (1) +8041
bitterly (1)
bitterly (1) +3878
boundless (1) +8146
come quickly (1) +4554
coming quickly (1) +4554
completely (1)
critically (1)
crushing (1) +2703
destroyed (1) +1524+4804+5782
devastated (1) +1524+4804+5782
devout (1)
dismayed (1) +987
dreadful (1) +3707
enough (1)
even far (1) +3856
even more (1)
ever-present (1) +5162
exceedingly (1)
exhausted (1) +6545
far (1)
filled with fear (1) +3707
firmly (1)
full well (1)
furious (1) +678+3013
furious (1) +3013
furious (1) +7911
fury (1) +3013
great (1) +1540
great (1) +2221
great numbers (1) +2221
great numbers (1) +3878
great quantities (1) +4200+8044
greatly (1) +2221
greatly (1) +4394
grew louder and louder (1) +2143+2256+2618
grew worse and worse (1) +2118+2617+2716
heavy (1) +3877
highly (1)
highly regarded (1) +1524
huge (1)
huge (1) +1524+4200+6330
in anguish (1) +987
intense (1) +1524
kept bringing pressure (1) +7210
large (1) +1524
large (1) +3878
large amount (1) +2221
least (1)
long way (1) +8158
lost self-confidence (1) +928+5877+6524
loud (1) +1524+6330
make as great as you like (1) +8049
many (1) +8041
more (1)
more than (1)
much (1) +6330
quickly (1)
reward handsomely (1) +3877+3877
severe (1) +3878
severe (1) +8041
so (1) +3954
so (1) +4394
so highly (1)
so much (1)
stand firm (1) +586
stood in awe (1) +3707
strongly (1)
tempest rages (1) +8548
terrible (1) +3878
terrified (1) +3707+4394
terror filled (1) +3006
too (1)
total (1) +1524
toward evening (1) +3718
trembled violently (1) +1524+3006+3010+6330
utter (1)
vast (1) +1524
vast (1) +1524+4394
very (1) +2221
very (1) +6786
violently (1)
well known (1) +3700
without restraint (1) +6330
writhe in agony (1) +2655
untranslated (3)

4395 1מֵאָה *mē'āh1* (581)
hundred (233)
hundreds (18)
250 (10) +2256+2822
100 (8)
4,500 (8) +547+752+2256+2822
units of a hundred (6)
120 (5) +2256+6929
200 (5)
500 (5) +2822
1,254 (4) +547+752+2256+2822
128 (4) +2256+6929+9046
127 (3) +2256+2256+6929+8679
40,500 (3) +547+752+2256+2822
430 (3) +752+2256+8993
53,400 (3) +547+752+2256+2256+2822+8993
603,550 (3) +547+547+2256+2256+2256+2822+2822+4395+8993+9252
eleven hundred (3) +547+2256
1,247 (2) +547+752+2256+8679
1,775 (2) +547+2256+2256+2256+2822+8679+8679
112 (2) +2256+6925+9109
123 (2) +2256+6929+8993
130 (2) +2256+8993
137 (2) +2256+2256+8679+8993
150 (2) +2256+2822
200,000 (2) +547
220 (2) +2256+6929
223 (2) +2256+6929+8993
30,500 (2) +547+2256+2822+8993
300 (2) +8993
32,200 (2) +547+2256+2256+8993+9109
320 (2) +2256+6929+8993
345 (2) +752+2256+2822+8993
35,400 (2) +547+752+2256+2256+2822+8993
372 (2) +2256+8679+8993+9109
390 (2) +2256+8993+9596
392 (2) +2256+8993+9109+9596
4,600 (2) +547+752+2256+9252
403 (2) +752+2256+8993
41,500 (2) +285+547+752+2256+2256+2822
435 (2) +752+2256+2822+8993
45,650 (2) +547+752+2256+2256+2256+2822+2822+9252
46,500 (2) +547+752+2256+2256+2822+9252

54,400 (2) +547+752+752+2256+2256+2822
57,400 (2) +547+752+2256+2256+2822+8679
59,300 (2) +547+2256+2256+2822+8993+9596
6,720 (2) +547+2256+6929+8679+9252
62,700 (2) +547+2256+2256+8679+9109+9252
621 (2) +285+2256+6929+9252
652 (2) +2256+2822+9109+9252
666 (2) +2256+9252+9252+9252
7,337 (2) +547+2256+8679+8679+8993+8993
74,600 (2) +547+752+2256+2256+8679+9252
760 (2) +2256+8679+9252
800 (2) +9046
973 (2) +2256+8679+8993+9596
about six hundred feet (2) +564+752
fourteen hundred (2) +547+752+2256
hundredth (2)
seventeen hundred (2) +547+2256+8679
units of hundreds (2)
1,222 (1) +547+2256+6929+9109
1,290 (1) +547+2256+9596
1,335 (1) +547+2256+2822+8993+8993
1,365 (1) +547+2256+2256+2256+2822+8993+9252
1,760 (1) +547+2256+2256+8679+9252
105 (1) +2256+2822
108,100 (1) +547+547+2256+2256+4395+9046
110 (1) +2256+6927
112 (1) +6925+9109
119 (1) +2256+6926+9596
120,000 (1) +547+2256+6929
122 (1) +2256+2256+6929+9109
122 (1) +2256+6929+9109
133 (1) +2256+2256+8993+8993
138 (1) +2256+8993+9046
139 (1) +2256+8993+9596
14,700 (1) +547+752+2256+6925+8679
148 (1) +752+2256+9046
151,450 (1) +285+547+547+752+2256+2256+2256+2256+2822+2822+4395
153,600 (1) +547+547+2256+2256+2256+2822+4395+8993+9252
156 (1) +2256+2822+9252
157,600 (1) +547+547+2256+2256+2256+2822+4395+8679+9252
16,750 (1) +547+2256+2822+6925+8679+9252
160 (1) +2256+9252
162 (1) +2256+2256+9109+9252
17,200 (1) +547+2256+6925+8679
172 (1) +2256+8679+9109
180 (1) +2256+9046
180,000 (1) +547+2256+9046
182 (1) +2256+2256+9046+9109
186,400 (1) +547+547+547+752+2256+2256+2256+4395+9046+9252
187 (1) +2256+2256+8679+9046
188 (1) +2256+9046+9046
2,172 (1) +547+2256+2256+8679+9109
2,172 (1) +547+2256+8679+9109
2,200 (1) +547+2256
2,300 (1) +547+2256+8993
2,322 (1) +547+2256+6929+8993+9109
2,400 (1) +547+752+2256
2,600 (1) +547+2256+9252
2,630 (1) +547+2256+2256+8993+9252
2,750 (1) +547+2256+2822+8679
2,812 (1) +547+2256+6925+9046+9109
2,818 (1) +547+2256+6925+9046+9046
20,200 (1) +547+2256+6929
20,800 (1) +547+2256+6929+9046
205 (1) +2256+2822
207 (1) +2256+8679
209 (1) +2256+9596
212 (1) +2256+6925+9109
218 (1) +2256+6925+9046
22,200 (1) +547+2256+2256+6929+9109
22,273 (1) +547+2256+2256+2256+6929+8679+8993+9109
22,600 (1) +547+2256+2256+6929+9109+9252
232 (1) +2256+8993+9109
242 (1) +752+2256+9109
245 (1) +752+2256+2256+2822
245 (1) +752+2256+2822
25,100 (1) +547+2256+2256+2822+6929
273 (1) +2256+2256+8679+8993
28,600 (1) +547+2256+2256+6929+9046+9252
280,000 (1) +547+2256+9046
284 (1) +752+2256+9046
288 (1) +2256+9046+9046
3,200 (1) +547+2256+8993
3,600 (1) +547+2256+8993+9252
3,630 (1) +547+2256+2256+8993+8993+9252
3,700 (1) +547+2256+8679+8993
3,930 (1) +547+2256+8993+8993+9596
300,000 (1) +547+8993
307,500 (1) +547+547+2256+2256+2822+4395+8679+8993
318 (1) +2256+6925+8993+9046
32,500 (1) +547+2256+2256+2822+8993+9109
323 (1) +2256+6929+8993+8993
324 (1) +752+2256+6929+8993
328 (1) +2256+6929+8993+9046
337,500 (1) +547+547+547+2256+2256+2256+2822+4395+8679+8993+8993
337,500 (1) +547+547+547+2256+2256+2822+4395+8679+8993+8993
350 (1) +2256+2822+8993
365 (1) +2256+2256+2822+8993+9252
410 (1) +752+2256+6927
42,360 (1) +547+752+2256+8052+8993+9252
42,360 (1) +547+752+8052+8993+9252
420 (1) +752+2256+6929
43,730 (1) +547+752+2256+2256+2256+8679+8993+8993
44,760 (1) +547+752+752+2256+2256+2256+8679+9252
45,400 (1) +547+752+752+2256+2256+2822
45,600 (1) +547+752+2256+2256+2822+9252
450 feet (1) +564+8993
454 (1) +752+752+2256+2822
468 (1) +752+2256+9046+9252
5,400 (1) +547+752+2256+2822
52,700 (1) +547+2256+2256+2822+8679+9109
530 (1) +2256+2822+8993
550 (1) +2256+2822+2822
595 (1) +2256+2256+2822+2822+9596
6,200 (1) +547+2256+9252
6,800 (1) +547+2256+9046+9252
60,500 (1) +547+2256+2822+9252
601,730 (1) +547+547+2256+2256+4395+8679+8993+9252
623 (1) +2256+6929+8993+9252
628 (1) +2256+6929+9046+9252
64,300 (1) +547+752+2256+2256+8993+9252
64,400 (1) +547+752+752+2256+2256+9252
642 (1) +752+2256+2256+9109+9252
642 (1) +752+2256+9109+9252
648 (1) +752+2256+9046+9252
650 (1) +2256+2822+9252
655 (1) +2256+2822+2822+9252
666 (1) +2256+2256+9252+9252+9252
667 (1) +2256+8679+9252+9252
675 (1) +2256+2822+8679+9252
675,000 (1) +547+547+547+2256+2256+2822+8679+9252
690 (1) +2256+9252+9596
7,100 (1) +547+2256+8679
7,500 (1) +547+2256+2822+8679
721 (1) +285+2256+2256+6929+8679
725 (1) +2256+2822+6929+8679
730 (1) +2256+8679+8993
736 (1) +2256+8679+8993+9252
743 (1) +752+2256+2256+8679+8993
743 (1) +752+2256+8679+8993
745 (1) +752+2256+2822+8679
76,500 (1) +547+2256+2256+2822+8679+9252
775 (1) +2256+2822+8679+8679
777 (1) +2256+2256+8679+8679+8679
782 (1) +2256+2256+8679+9046+9109
8,580 (1) +547+2256+2256+2822+9046+9046
8,600 (1) +547+2256+9046+9252
807 (1) +2256+8679+9046
815 (1) +2256+2822+6926+9046
822 (1) +2256+6929+9046+9109
830 (1) +2256+8993+9046
832 (1) +2256+8993+9046+9109
840 (1) +752+2256+9046
845 (1) +752+2256+2822+9046
895 (1) +2256+2256+2822+9046+9596
905 (1) +2256+2822+9596
910 (1) +2256+6924+9596
912 (1) +2256+6926+9109+9596
928 (1) +2256+6929+9046+9596
930 (1) +2256+8993+9596
945 (1) +752+2256+2256+2822+9596
950 (1) +2256+2822+9596
956 (1) +2256+2256+2822+9252+9596
962 (1) +2256+2256+9109+9252+9596
969 (1) +2256+2256+9252+9596+9596
hundredfold (1) +9134
thirty-six hundred (1) +547+2256+8993+9252
thirty-three hundred (1) +547+2256+8993+8993
twelve hundred (1) +547+2256
twenty-seven hundred (1) +547+2256+8679
twenty-six hundred (1) +547+2256+9252
two hundred (1)
untranslated (7)

4396 2מֵאָה *mēʼāh2* (2)
hundred (2)

4397 מַאֲוַיִּים *maʼawiyyiym* (1)
desires (1)

4398 מְאוּם *meʼûm* (1)
untranslated (1)

4399 מְאוּמָה *meʼûmāh* (32)
anything (10)
nothing (7) +4202
anything (2) +3972
nothing (2) +401
there is nothing (2) +401
all (1)
any kind (1)
bare (1) +401+928
fault (1)
little value (1)
little value (1) +4202
none (1) +4202
something (1)
untranslated (1)

4400 מָאוֹס *māʼôs* (1)
refuse (1)

4401 מָאוֹר *māʼôr* (19)
light (13)
lights (4)
cheerful (1)
moon (1)

4402 מְאוּרָה *meʼûrāh* (1)
nest (1)

4403 מֵאָז *mēʼāz*
Variant; not used

4404 מֹאזְנַיִם *mōʼznayim* (15)
scales (12)

balance (2)
set of scales (1) +5486

4405 מְאָיוֹת m^{e}'āyôṯ
Variant; not used

4406 מֵאַיִן mē'ayin
Variant; not used

4407 מַאֲכָל ma'^{a}ḵāl (30)
food (21)
fruit (4)
baked goods (1) +685+5126
devoured (1)
meal (1)
something to eat (1)
supplies (1)

4408 מַאֲכֶלֶת ma'^{a}ḵeleṯ (4)
knife (3)
knives (1)

4409 מַאֲכֹלֶת ma'^{a}ḵōleṯ (2)
fuel (2)

4410 מַאֲמָץ ma'^{a}māṣ (1)
efforts (1)

4411 מַאֲמָר ma'^{a}mār (3)
command (1)
decree (1)
instructions (1)

4412 מָאַן mā'an (46)
refused (22)
refuse (15)
refuses (2)
refusing (2)
absolutely refuses (1) +4412
incurable (1) +8324
rejected (1)
resist (1)

4413 מָאֵן mā'ēn
Variant; not used

4414 מֵאֵן mē'ēn
Variant; not used

4415 1מָאַס mā'as1 (74)
rejected (34)
reject (12)
despise (8)
despised (3)
despises (3)
be rejected (1)
denied (1)
disdained (1)
refuse (1)
rejected completely (1) +4415
rejects (1)
ridiculed (1)
scorn (1)
spurn (1)
spurned (1)
utterly rejected (1) +4415
vile (1)

4416 2מָאַס mā'as2 (2)
festering (1)
vanish (1)

4417 מְאַסֵּף m^{e}'assēp̱
Variant; not used

4418 מַאֲפֶה ma'^{a}p̱eh (1)
baked (1)

4419 מַאֲפֵל ma'^{a}p̱ēl (1)
darkness (1)

4420 מַאְפֵּלְיָה ma'pēlyāh (1)
great darkness (1)

4421 מָאַר mā'ar (4)
destructive (3)
painful (1)

4422 מַאֲרָב ma'^{a}rāḇ (5)
ambush (1)
hiding place (1)
place of ambush (1)
troops (1)
wait (1)

4423 מְאֵרָה m^{e}'ērāh (5)
curse (2)
curses (2)
curse (1) +826

4424 מֵאֲשֶׁר mē'^{a}šer
Variant; not used

4425 מֵאֵת mē'ēṯ
Variant; not used

4426 מִבְדָּלוֹת miḇdālôṯ (1)
set aside (1)

4427 מָבוֹא māḇô' (24)
entrance (7)
enter (2)
place where sets (2)
setting (2)
west (2) +9087
do[s] (1)
entrances (1) +7339
entryway (1)
gateway (1)
go down (1)
how to get into (1)
on the west (1) +2021+9087
outskirts (1)
untranslated (1)

4428 מְבוּכָה m^{e}ḇûḵāh (2)
confusion (1)
terror (1)

4429 מַבּוּל mabbûl (14)
flood (11)
floodwaters (3) +4784

4430 מְבוֹנִים m^{e}ḇôniym
Variant; not used

4431 מְבוּסָה m^{e}ḇûsāh (3)
aggressive (2)
trampling (1)

4432 מַבּוּעַ mabbûa' (3)
bubbling springs (1) +4784
spring (1)
springs (1)

4433 מְבוּקָה m^{e}ḇûqāh (1)
plundered (1)

4434 מְבוּשִׁים m^{e}ḇûšiym (1)
private parts (1)

4435 מִבְחוֹר miḇḥôr (2)
choicest (1)
major (1)

4436 1מִבְחָר miḇḥār1 (12)
choicest (4)
best (3)
choice possessions (1)
elite (1)
fine (1)
finest (1)
pick (1)

4437 2מִבְחָר miḇḥār2 (1)
Mibhar (1)

4438 מַבָּט mabbāṭ (3)
hope (1)
relied on (1)
trusted in (1)

4439 מִבְטָא miḇṭā' (2)
rash promise (2)

4440 מִבְטָח miḇṭāḥ (15)
trust (4)
confidence (2)
secure (2)
security (2)
hope (1)
reliance (1)
source of confidence (1)
trusted (1)
what relies on (1)

4441 מַבָּךְ mabbāḵ (1)
sources (1)

4442 מַבֵּל mabbēl (1)
fire (1)

4443 מַבְלִיגִית maḇliygiyṯ (1)
comforter (1)

4444 מְבֻלָּקָה m^{e}ḇulāqāh
Variant; not used

4445 מִבְנֶה miḇneh (1)
buildings (1)

4446 מְבֻנַּי m^{e}ḇunnay (1)
Mebunnai (1)

4447 מַבְנִית maḇniyṯ
Variant; not used

4448 1מִבְצָר miḇṣār1 (36)
fortified (21)
strongholds (5)
fortresses (3)
fortified cities (2)
defenses (1)
fortified city (1)
fortified places (1)
fortress (1)
mightiest fortresses (1) +5057

4449 2מִבְצָר miḇṣār2 (2)
Mibzar (2)

4450 3מִבְצָר miḇṣār3 (1)
ore (1)

4451 מִבְרָח miḇrāḥ (2)
fleeing (1)
untranslated (1)

4452 מִבְשָׂם miḇśām (3)
Mibsam (3)

4453 מְבַשְּׁלוֹת m^{e}ḇašš^{e}lôṯ (1)
places for fire (1)

4454 מָג māg (2)
official (2)

4455 מַגְבִּישׁ magbiyš (1)
Magbish (1)

4456 מִגְבָּלוֹת migbālôṯ (1)
braided (1)

4457 מִגְבָּעָה migbā'āh (4)
headbands (3)
headbands (1) +6996

4458 מֶגֶד meg̱eḏ (12)
best (2)
choice (2)
valuable gifts (2)
articles of value (1)
costly gifts (1)
delicacy (1)
finest (1)
fruitfulness (1)
precious (1)

4459 מְגִדּוֹ m^{e}giddô (11)
Megiddo (11)

4460 מִגְדּוֹל migdôl (1)
untranslated (1)

4461 מְגִדּוֹן m^{e}giddôn (1)
Megiddo (1)

4462 מַגְדִּיאֵל magdiy'ēl (2)
Magdiel (2)

4463 1מִגְדָּל migdāl1 (48)
tower (28)
towers (13)

watchtower (2)
watchtower (2) +5915
high platform (1)
they[s] (1) +1251+3972+8901
watchtowers (1)

4464 2מִגְדָּל *mig̱dāl2*
Variant; not used

4465 מִגְדֹּל *mig̱dōl* (6)
Migdol (6)

4466 מִגְדַּל־אֵל *mig̱dal-'ēl* (1)
Migdal El (1)

4467 מִגְדַּל־גָּד *mig̱dal-gaḏ* (1)
Migdal Gad (1)

4468 מִגְדַּל־עֵדֶר *mig̱dal-'ēḏer* (1)
Migdal Eder (1)

4469 מִגְדָּנוֹת *mig̱dānôṯ*
Variant; not used

4470 מָגוֹג *māg̱ôg* (4)
Magog (4)

4471 1מָגוֹר *māg̱ôr1* (8)
terror (7)
terrors (1)

4472 2מָגוֹר *māg̱ôr2* (11)
pilgrimage (2)
alien (1)
live as an alien (1)
lived (1)
living (1)
lodge (1) +1074
lodging (1)
stayed (1)
staying (1)
where lived (1)

4473 3מָגוֹר *māg̱ôr3*
Variant; not used

4474 מָגוֹר מִסָּבִיב *māg̱ôr missāḇiyḇ* (1)
Magor-Missabib (1)

4475 מְגוֹרָה *m^{e}g̱ôrāh* (3)
dread (1)
dreads (1)
fears (1)

4476 מְגוּרָה *m^{e}g̱ûrāh* (1)
barn (1)

4477 מַגְזֵרָה *mag̱zērāh* (1)
axes (1)

4478 מַגָּל *maggāl* (2)
sickle (2)

4479 מְגִלָּה *m^{e}g̱illāh* (21)
scroll (17)
scroll (4) +6219

4480 מְגַמָּה *m^{e}g̱ammāh* (1)
hordes (1)

4481 מָגַן *māg̱an* (3)
delivered (1)
hand over (1)
present (1)

4482 1מָגֵן *māg̱ēn1* (63)
shield (34)
shields (17)
small shields (6)
armed (2)
kings (1)
large[s] [shields] (1)
rulers (1)
shields small (1)

4483 2מָגֵן *māg̱ēn2*
Variant; not used

4484 מֶגֶן *meg̱en*
Variant; not used

4485 מְגִנָּה *m^{e}g̱innāh* (1)
veil (1)

4486 מִגְעֶרֶת *mig̱'ereṯ* (1)
rebuke (1)

4487 מַגֵּפָה *maggēp̱āh* (26)
plague (19)
blow (2)
casualties (1)
losses (1)
plagues (1)
slaughter (1)
untranslated (1)

4488 מַגְפִּיעָשׁ *mag̱piy'āš* (1)
Magpiash (1)

4489 מָגַר *māg̱ar* (2)
cast (1)
thrown (1)

4490 מְגֵרָה *m^{e}g̱ērāh* (4)
saws (2)
axes (1)
saw (1)

4491 מִגְרוֹן *mig̱rôn* (2)
Migron (2)

4492 מִגְרָעוֹת *mig̱rā'ôṯ* (1)
offset ledges (1)

4493 מֶגְרָפָה *meg̱rāp̱āh* (1)
clods (1)

4494 מִגְרָשׁ *mig̱rāš* (119)
pasturelands (41)
pastureland (5)
farm (1)
open land (1)
pastureland (1) +8441
shorelands (1)
untranslated (69)

4495 מִגְרְשׁוֹת *mig̱r^{e}šôṯ*
Variant; not used

4496 מַד *maḏ* (11)
tunic (3)
clothes (2)
clothing (1)
decreed (1)
garment (1)
military tunic (1) +4230
robes (1)
saddle blankets (1)

4497 1מִדְבָּר *miḏbār1* (270)
desert (256)
open (3)
wasteland (2)
wilderness (2)
barren wilderness (1)
desert (1) +824
deserts (1)
here[s] (1) +928+2021
open country (1)
there[s] (1)
there[s] (1) +2334

4498 2מִדְבָּר *miḏbār2* (1)
mouth (1)

4499 מָדַד *māḏaḏ* (51)
measured (30)
measured off (5)
measure off (3)
be measured (2)
measure (2)
consider (1)
drags on (1)
measure distance (1)
measure the full payment (1)
measureless (1) +4202
poured into measures (1)
stretched himself out (1)
untranslated (2)

4500 1מִדָּה *middāh1* (55)
measurements (12)
size (10)
measuring (9)
section (7)
huge (2)
at regular intervals (1)
district (1)
great (1)
great size (1)
length (1)
long (1)
measure (1)
measured out (1) +928+9419
measures (1)
number (1)
standard (1)
tall (1)
tall (1) +408
untranslated (2)

4501 2מִדָּה *middāh2* (1)
tax (1)

4502 מַדְהֵבָה *maḏhēḇāh* (1)
fury (1)

4503 מָדוּ *māḏû* (2)
garments (2)

4504 2מַדְוֶה *maḏweh2* (2)
diseases (2)

4505 מַדּוּחִים *maddûḥiym* (1)
misleading (1)

4506 1מָדוֹן *māḏôn1* (29)
dissension (7)
quarrelsome (6)
disputes (2)
quarrel (2)
strife (2)
conflict (1)
contends (1)
source of contention (1)
untranslated (7)

4507 2מָדוֹן *māḏôn2* (2)
Madon (2)

4508 מַדּוּעַ *maddûa'* (72)
why (70)
what (1)
what's the meaning of (1)

4509 מְדוּרָה *m^{e}ḏûrāh* (2)
fire pit (1)
wood (1)

4510 מִדְחֶה *miḏheh* (1)
ruin (1)

4511 מַדְחֵפָה *maḏhēp̱āh* (1)
hunt down (1) +4200+7421

4512 מָדַי *māḏay* (16)
Media (7)
Medes (5)
Madai (2)
Mede (1)
Median (1)

4513 מָדִי *māḏiy* (1)
Mede (1)

4514 מַדַּי *madday*
Variant; not used

4515 מָדִין *māḏiyn* (1)
untranslated (1)

4516 מִדִּין *middiyn* (1)
Middin (1)

4517 1מִדְיָן *miḏyān1*
Variant; not used

4518 2מִדְיָן *miḏyān2* (59)
Midian (32)
Midianites (12)
Midianite (8)
Midian (2) +824

Midian's (2)
them[s] (1)
untranslated (2)

4519 מְדִינָה *m^e^diynāh* (51)
provinces (20)
province (10)
provincial (5)
each province (3) +2256+4519
district (1)
every province (1) +2256+4519
parts (1)
regions (1)
various provinces (1) +2256+4519
untranslated (5)

4520 מִדְיָנִי *midyāniy* (8)
Midianite (5)
Midianites (3)

4521 מְדֹכָה *m^e^dōkāh* (1)
mortar (1)

4522 מַדְמֵן *madmēn* (1)
Madmen (1)

4523 1מַדְמֵנָה *madmēnāh1* (1)
manure (1)

4524 2מַדְמֵנָה *madmēnāh2* (1)
Madmenah (1)

4525 1מַדְמַנָּה *madmannāh1* (1)
Madmannah (1)

4526 2מַדְמַנָּה *madmannāh2* (1)
Madmannah (1)

4527 1מְדָן *m^e^dān1* (2)
Medan (2)

4528 2מְדָן *m^e^dān2*
Variant; not used

4529 מַדָּע *maddā'* (6)
knowledge (4)
quick to understand (1) +1067
thoughts (1)

4530 מֹדָע *mōdā'* (2)
kinsman (1)
relative (1)

4531 מֹדַעַת *mōda'at* (1)
kinsman (1)

4532 מַדְקֵרָה *madqērāh* (1)
pierce (1)

4533 מַדְרֵגָה *madrēgāh* (2)
cliffs (1)
mountainside (1)

4534 מִדְרָךְ *midrāk* (1)
put on (1)

4535 מִדְרָשׁ *midrāš* (2)
annotations (2)

4536 מְדֻשָׁה *m^e^dušāh* (1)
crushed (1)

4537 מָה *māh* (755)
what (343)
why (165) +4200
how (69)
why (33)
how (16) +928
why (13) +6584
whatever (7)
what (5) +4200
how long (4) +6330
what mean (4)
who (4)
how (3) +3869
O (3)
secret (3) +928
what are you doing (3) +3870+4200
what's the matter (3)
by what means (2) +928
come what may (2) +2118
how many (2) +3869+6330
how often (2) +3869
not (2)
what (2) +928
anything (1)
because (1) +3954+4200
but why (1) +4200
enough (1) +1896+4200
ever so (1)
future (1) +2118+8611
how (1) +686+928
how (1) +2296
how find things (1)
how long (1) +3869
how long must wait (1) +3427+3869
how many (1) +3869
how many more (1) +3869
how much (1)
if (1) +196
life will not be worth living (1) +2644+4200
not[s] (1)
nothing (1) +1172
of what use (1) +2296+4200
of what use (1) +4200
so many (1) +3869
speech (1) +1819
that (1)
this is how (1)
what (1) +6584
what about (1)
what do I care about (1) +2296+3276+4200+4200
what do you mean (1) +4013+4200
what is doing (1) +4200
what is the matter (1) +3871+4200
what is the meaning (1)
what is the meaning (1) +2179
what is the meaning of (1)
what is troubling (1)
what is wrong (1)
what kind (1)
what like (1)
what more (1) +3954
what right have you (1) +3870+4200
what's (1)
whatever (1) +1821
when (1) +6330
where (1)
whether (1)
which (1)
why (1) +561+4027+4200
why (1) +928
why (1) +3610
why (1) +4200+8611
why (1) +9393
untranslated (15)

4538 מָהַהּ *māhah* (8)
wait (2)
delay (1)
delayed (1)
have time (1) +3523
hesitated (1)
linger (1)
waited (1)

4539 מְהוּמָה *m^e^hûmāh* (12)
panic (4)
turmoil (3)
confusion (2)
throwing into confusion (1) +2169
tumult (1)
unrest (1)

4540 מְהוּמָן *m^e^hûmān* (1)
Mehuman (1)

4541 מְהֵיטַבְאֵל *m^e^hēytab'ēl* (3)
Mehetabel (3)

4542 מָהִיר *māhiyr* (4)
skilled (1)
skillful (1)
speeds (1)
well versed (1)

4543 מָהַל *māhal* (1)
diluted (1)

4544 מַהֲלָךְ *mah^a^lāk* (5)
journey (1)
passageway (1)
place (1)
visit (1)
untranslated (1)

4545 מַהֲלָל *mah^a^lāl* (1)
praise (1)

4546 מַהֲלַלְאֵל *mah^a^lal'ēl* (7)
Mahalalel (7)

4547 מַהֲלֻמוֹת *mah^a^lumôt* (2)
beating (1)
beatings (1)

4548 מָהֵם *māhēm*
Variant; not used

4549 מַהֲמֹרוֹת *mah^a^mōrôt* (1)
miry pits (1)

4550 מַהְפֵּכָה *mahpēkāh* (6)
overthrown (3)
overthrew (2)
destruction (1)

4551 מַהְפֶּכֶת *mahpeket* (4)
stocks (3)
prison (1) +1074+2021

4552 מְחוֹלָה *m^e^hôlāh*
Variant; not used

4553 מְחֻקְצָעוֹת *m^e^huqṣā'ôt*
Variant; not used

4554 1מָהַר *māhar1* (82)
quickly (26)
hurried (9)
quick (6)
at once (4)
hurry (4)
bring at once (3)
soon (3)
swift (3)
immediately (2)
act at once (1)
all at once (1)
are swept away (1)
come quickly (1)
come quickly (1) +4394
coming quickly (1) +4394
darting (1)
dash (1)
do now (1)
early (1)
fearful (1)
fluent (1) +1819+4200
go at once (1)
hasten (1)
hastily (1)
hasty (1)
impetuous (1)
lost no time (1)
move quickly (1)
rash (1)
run after (1)
sudden (1)

4555 2מָהַר *māhar2* (2)
must pay bride-price (1) +4555

4556 1מַהֵר *mahēr1*
Variant; not used

4557 2מַהֵר *mahēr2*
Variant; not used

4558 מֹהַר *mōhar* (3)
bride-price (1)
price for bride (1)
price for the bride (1)

4559 מְהֵרָה *m^ehērāh* (20)
quickly (7)
at once (2)
soon (2)
hurriedly (1)
hurry (1)
hurry (1) +2143
immediately (1)
quickly (1) +928
speedily (1)
swiftly (1)
swiftly (1) +6330
very soon (1)

4560 מַהֲרַי *mah^aray* (3)
Maharai (3)

4561 מַהֵר שָׁלָל חָשׁ בַּז *mahēr šālāl hāš baz* (2)
Maher-Shalal-Hash-Baz (2)

4562 מַהֲתַלָּה *mah^atallāh* (1)
illusions (1)

4563 מוֹ *mô*
Variant; not used

4564 מוֹ־ *-mô* (119)
them (47)
their (23)
their (6) +4200
themselves (5)
him (3)
they (3)
us (3)
his (2) +4200
it (2)
the[S] (2)
each other[S] (1)
he (1)
his (1)
his people[S] (1)
its (1)
my enemies[S] (1)
Shem[S] (1)
those (1)
water[S] (1)
where[S] (1) +4200
who (1)
untranslated (12)

4565 מוֹאָב1 *mô'āḇ1* (2)
Moab (2)

4566 מוֹאָב2 *mô'āḇ2* (179)
Moab (136)
Moabites (12)
Moab (7) +8441
Moab's (7)
Moabite (7)
Moab (5) +824
its[S] (1)
Moabites (1) +408
Moabites (1) +1201
there[S] (1) +8441
they[S] (1)

4567 מוֹאָבִי *mô'āḇiy* (16)
Moabitess (6)
Moabite (5)
Moabites (4)
Moab (1)

4568 מוֹאל *mô'l*
Variant; not used

4569 מוֹבָא *môḇā'* (3)
entrances (1)
movements (1) +2256+4604
untranslated (1)

4570 מוּג *mûg* (17)
melt away (3)
melting in fear (2)
melts (2)
collapses (1)
disheartened (1)
flow (1)
made waste away (1)
melt (1)
melted away (1)
melting away (1) +2143+2256
quake (1)
soften (1)
toss about (1)

4571 מוֹד *môḏ* (1)
shook (1)

4572 מוֹט1 *môṭ1* (41)
be shaken (8)
fall (5)
be moved (4)
removed (2)
slip (2)
slipping (2)
topple (2)
are shaken (1)
be uprooted (1)
be uprooted (1) +9247
bring down (1)
gives way (1)
immovable (1) +1153
is thoroughly shaken (1) +4572
let fall (1)
quaking (1)
shake (1)
slipped (1)
slips (1)
staggering (1)
unable to support (1) +3338
untranslated (1)

4573 מוֹט2 *môṭ2* (4)
carrying frame (2)
pole (1)
yoke (1)

4574 מוֹטָה *môṭāh* (12)
yoke (8)
bars (2)
crossbars (1)
poles (1)

4575 מוּךְ *mûḵ* (5)
poor (4)
poor to pay (1)

4576 מוּל1 *mûl1* (31)
circumcised (7)
be circumcised (4)
been circumcised (2)
was circumcised (2)
are[S] (1)
be circumcised (1) +1414+6889
been circumcised (1) +6889
circumcise (1)
circumcise (1) +6889
circumcise yourselves (1)
circumcised (1) +1414+6889
circumcising (1)
did so[S] (1)
had[S] (1)
must be circumcised (1) +4576
undergo circumcision (1) +906+1414+6889
was circumcised (1) +1414+6889
were circumcised (1)
untranslated (1)

4577 מוּל2 *mûl2* (3)
cut off (3)

4578 מוּל3 *mûl3* (35)
at (3) +448
in front of (3) +448
corner (2)
in front of (2) +4946
near (2)
on (2) +448
on (2) +4946
opposite (2)
toward (2)
as far as (1) +448
before (1)
border (1)
faced forward (1) +448+7156
facing (1)
from (1) +4946
in front of (1) +448+7156
in the front line (1) +448+7156
in the front part (1)
in the vicinity of (1)
next to (1) +4946
off (1) +4946
opposite direction (1)
to (1)
to (1) +448

4579 מוֹלָדָה *môlāḏāh* (4)
Moladah (4)

4580 מוֹלֶדֶת *môleḏeṯ* (22)
native (4)
relatives (3)
birth (2)
family (2)
family background (2)
people (2)
born (1)
born in the same home (1) +1074
children (1)
homeland (1) +824
natives (1)
untranslated (2)

4581 מוּלָה *mûlāh* (1)
circumcision (1)

4582 מוֹלִיד *môliyḏ* (1)
Molid (1)

4583 מוּם *mûm* (21)
defect (8)
blemish (3)
flaw (2)
shame (2)
abuse (1)
defects (1)
defiled (1) +1815
injured (1) +5989
injures (1) +5989
physical defect (1)

4584 מְוּמְכָן *m^ewmuḵān* (1)
untranslated (1)

4585 מוּסָב *mûsāḇ*
Variant; not used

4586 מוּסָד *mûsāḏ* (2)
foundation (1)
foundation laid (1)

4587 מוֹסָד *môsāḏ* (8)
foundations (8)

4588 מוּסָדָה *mûsāḏāh* (2)
foundation (1)
untranslated (1)

4589 מוֹסָדָה *môsāḏāh* (5)
foundations (3)
foundation (1)
founded (1)

4590 מוּסָךְ *mûsāḵ* (1)
canopy (1)

4591 מוֹסֵר *môsēr* (5)
chains (3)
noose (1) +6577
shackles (1)

4592 מוּסָר *mûsār* (50)
discipline (21)
instruction (10)
correction (6)
disciplined (2)
lesson (2)
punishment (2)

punished (1)
punishing (1)
rebuke (1)
taught (1)
teaches (1)
warning (1)
warnings (1)

4593 1מוֹסֵרָה *môsērāh1* (8)
bonds (3)
chains (2)
ropes (1)
shackles (1)
yoke of straps (1)

4594 2מוֹסֵרָה *môsērāh2* (1)
Moserah (1)

4595 מוֹעֵד *mô'ēḏ* (223)
meeting (147)
appointed feasts (24)
appointed time (15)
time (7)
appointed (2)
festivals (2)
seasons (2)
anniversary (1)
appointed feast (1)
appointed seasons (1)
appointed times (1)
army (1)
arranged (1) +2118
assembly (1)
assigned portion (1)
certain place (1)
council (1)
designated (1)
feast (1)
feasts (1)
festival offerings (1)
in (1) +928
occasion (1)
opportunity (1)
place of meeting (1)
place where met (1)
place where worshiped (1)
ready (1)
set time (1) +3427
time set (1)
times (1)

4596 מוֹעָד *mô'āḏ* (1)
ranks (1)

4597 מוּעָדָה *mû'āḏāh* (1)
designated (1)

4598 מוֹעַדְיָה *mô'aḏyāh* (1)
Moadiah's (1)

4599 מוּעָף *mû'āp̱* (1)
gloom (1)

4600 מוֹעֵצָה *mô'ēṣāh* (7)
counsel (1)
devices (1)
inclinations (1)
intrigues (1)
plans (1)
schemes (1)
traditions (1)

4601 מוּעָקָה *mû'āqāh* (1)
burdens (1)

4602 מוֹפַעַת *môp̱a'aṯ* (1)
untranslated (1)

4603 מוֹפֵת *môp̱ēṯ* (36)
wonders (17)
sign (7)
wonder (3)
miracles (2)
miraculous sign (2)
portent (2)
miracle (1)
symbolic of things to come (1)
symbols (1)

4604 1מוֹצָא *môṣā'1* (27)
exits (3)
flowing springs (2) +4784
imported (2)
spring (2) +4784
stages (2)
appear (1) +3922
came from (1)
east (1)
go (1)
grass (1) +2013
issuing (1)
mine (1)
movements (1) +2256+4569
outlet (1)
rises (1)
springs (1) +4784
utter (1)
what passes (1)
what uttered (1)
where dawns (1)
word that comes from (1)

4605 2מוֹצָא *môṣā'2* (5)
Moza (5)

4606 מוֹצָאָה *môṣā'āh* (2)
origins (1)
untranslated (1)

4607 1מוּצָק *mûṣāq1* (7)
cast metal (3)
cast (1)
cast bronze (1)
cast in molds (1)
hard (1) +2021+3668+4200

4608 2מוּצָק *mûṣāq2* (2)
distress (1)
restriction (1)

4609 מוּצָקָה *mûṣāqāh* (2)
channels (1)
one piece with (1)

4610 מוּק *mûq* (1)
scoff (1)

4611 מוֹקֵד *môqēḏ* (2)
burning (1)
glowing embers (1)

4612 מוֹקְדָה *môq'ḏāh* (1)
hearth (1)

4613 מוֹקֵשׁ *môqēš* (27)
snare (12)
snares (6)
trap (3)
traps (3)
ensnared (1)
snared (1)
trapped (1)

4614 1מור *mûr1* (14)
exchanged (3)
divided up (1)
exchange (1)
give way (1)
keeps (1) +4202
make a substitution (1) +4614
make substitution (1)
substitute (1)
substitute (1) +4614
unchanged (1) +4202

4615 2מור *mûr2*
Variant; not used

4616 מוֹרָא *môrā'* (12)
fear (4)
terror (3)
awesome (1)
awesome deeds (1)
feared (1)
respect (1)
reverence (1)

4617 מוֹרַג *môraḡ* (3)
threshing sledges (2)
threshing sledge (1)

4618 מוֹרָד *môrāḏ* (5)
road down (2)
hammered (1)
slope (1)
slopes (1)

4619 1מוֹרֶה *môreh1* (5)
archers (1)
archers (1) +408+928+2021+8008
archers (1) +928+2021+8008
they[s] (1) +2021
untranslated (1)

4620 2מוֹרֶה *môreh2* (3)
autumn rains (2)
autumn (1)

4621 3מוֹרֶה *môreh3* (4)
teachers (2)
teacher (1)
them[s] (1) +3870

4622 4מוֹרֶה *môreh4* (3)
Moreh (3)

4623 1מוֹרָה *môrāh1* (3)
razor (3)

4624 2מוֹרָה *môrāh2*
Variant; not used

4625 1מוֹרָשׁ *môrāš1* (2)
inheritance (1)
place (1)

4626 2מוֹרָשׁ *môrāš2* (1)
desires (1)

4627 מוֹרָשָׁה *môrāšāh* (9)
possession (9)

4628 מוֹרֶשֶׁת גַּת *môrešeṯ gaṯ* (1)
Moresheth Gath (1)

4629 מוֹרַשְׁתִּי *môraštiy* (2)
of Moresheth (2)

4630 1מושׁ *mûš1* (3)
feel (2)
touch (1)

4631 2מושׁ *mûš2* (21)
leave (3)
depart (2)
shaken (2)
departed (1)
fails (1)
give way (1)
go away (1)
left place (1)
move (1)
moved (1)
moving (1)
remove (1)
save (1)
takes (1)
vanish (1)
without (1)
untranslated (1)

4632 מוֹשָׁב *môšāḇ* (43)
live (12)
settlements (5)
seat (3)
dwelling (2)
seating (2)
where settle (3)
council (1)
dwelling place (1)
dwellings (1)
home (1)
house (1) +1074
houses (1)

length of time (1)
members (1)
place (1)
places where lived (1)
region where lived (1)
settled (1)
situated (1)
stood (1)
throne (1)
untranslated (1)

4633 1מוּשִׁי *mûšiy1* (8)
Mushi (8)

4634 2מוּשִׁי *mûšiy2* (2)
Mushite (1)
Mushites (1)

4635 מוֹשִׁיעַ *môšiya'* (21)
savior (11)
deliverer (3)
rescue (3)
deliverers (2)
rescues (1)
save (1)

4636 מוֹשָׁעָה *môšā'āh* (1)
saves (1)

4637 מוּת *mûṯ* (809)
die (200)
died (162)
dead (103)
put to death (43)
kill (36)
killed (31)
death (30)
be put to death (26)
dies (25)
must be put to death (19) +4637
surely die (7) +4637
assassinated (5)
die (5) +4637
dying (5)
kill (4) +4637
must die (4) +4637
shall be put to death (4) +4637
slay (4)
surely be put to death (4) +4637
certainly die (3) +4637
putting to death (3)
be murdered (2)
brings death (2)
causing to die (2)
destroy (2)
died a natural death (2)
killing (2)
kills (2)
perish (2)
put[s] (2)
slain (2)
anyone[s] (1) +2021
as good as dead (1)
assassinated (1) +2256+5782
assassination (1)
be killed (1)
body (1)
bring about death (1)
certainly be put to death (1) +4637
die out (1)
doomed to die (1) +4637
end (1)
executed (1) +2256+5782
failed (1)
fell dead (1)
go down (1)
had executed (1) +2256+5782
his[s] (1) +2021
in fact die (1) +4637
is put to death (1)
killed (1) +5782
killing off (1)
kills (1) +2256+5782+5883
lifeless (1)
lives (1)
lose life (1)
make die (1)
man[s] (1)
messengers of death (1)
mortal (1)
murder (1)
must be put to death (1)
put death (1)
put to death (1) +4637
ready to die (1)
risked (1) +3070+4200
slays (1)
someone[s] (1)
stillborn infant (1)
struck down and died (1)
was killed (1)
was put to death (1)
were put to death (1)
widow (1) +851
untranslated (10)

4638 מָוֶת *māweṯ* (151)
death (109)
die (11)
died (11)
dies (5)
deadly (3)
dead (2)
capital offense (1) +5477
deadly plague (1)
death's (1)
dying (1)
immortality (1) +440
kill (1)
must die (1) +1201
plague (1)
put to death (1) +2222
untranslated (1)

4639 מוֹתָר *môṯār* (3)
profit (2)
advantage (1)

4640 מִזְבֵּחַ *mizbēah* (403)
altar (337)
altars (50)
it[s] (5) +2021
its[s] (4) +2021
done this[s] (1) +1215+3378+4200
untranslated (6)

4641 מֶזֶג *mezeḡ* (1)
blended wine (1)

4642 מָזֶה *māzeh* (1)
wasting (1)

4643 מַזֶּה *mazzeh*
Variant; not used

4644 מִזֶּה *mizzeh*
Variant; not used

4645 מִזָּה *mizzāh* (3)
Mizzah (3)

4646 מָזוּ *māzû* (1)
barns (1)

4647 מְזוּזָה *m^{e}zûzāh* (19)
doorposts (4)
doorframe (3)
doorframes (3)
doorpost (2)
doorway (1) +7339
doorways (1) +7339
gatepost (1) +9133
gateposts (1) +9133
jambs (1)
jambs (1) +382
posts (1)

4648 מָזוֹן *māzôn* (2)
provisions (2)

4649 1מָזוֹר *māzôr1* (3)
sores (2)
sore (1)

4650 2מָזוֹר *māzôr2* (1)
trap (1)

4651 1מֵזַח *mēzah1* (1)
harbor (1)

4652 2מֵזַח *mēzah2* (1)
belt (1)

4653 מָזִיחַ *māziyah* (1)
disarms (1) +8332

4654 מַזְכִּיר *mazkiyr* (9)
recorder (9)

4655 מַזָּל *mazzāl* (1)
constellations (1)

4656 מִזְלָג *mizlāḡ*
Variant; not used

4657 מַזְלֵג *mazlēḡ* (7)
meat forks (4)
fork (2)
forks (1)

4658 מִזְלָגָה *mizlāḡāh*
Variant; not used

4659 מְזִמָּה *m^{e}zimmāh* (19)
discretion (4)
crafty (2)
purposes (2)
schemes (2)
wicked schemes (2)
discernment (1)
evil intent (1)
evil schemes (1)
plan (1)
purpose (1)
schemer (1) +1251
thoughts (1)

4660 מִזְמוֹר *mizmôr* (57)
psalm (57)

4661 מַזְמֵרָה *mazmērāh* (4)
pruning hooks (3)
pruning knives (1)

4662 מְזַמֶּרֶת *m^{e}zammereṯ* (5)
wick trimmers (5)

4663 מִזְעָר *miz'ār* (4)
in a very short time (1) +5071+6388
very few (1) +632
very few (1) +5071
very soon (1) +5071+6388

4664 מָזָר *māzar*
Variant; not used

4665 מִזְרֶה *mizreh* (2)
shovel (1)
winnowing fork (1)

4666 מַזָּרוֹת *mazzārôṯ* (1)
constellations (1)

4667 מִזְרָח *mizrāh* (74)
east (34)
east (7) +2025
rising (6)
sunrise (5)
east (3) +2021+9087
sunrise (3) +9087
east (2) +2021+2025+9087
east (2) +9087
eastern (2) +2025
east (1) +928+2025+6298
east (1) +928+2025+6298+9087
east (1) +928+6298+9087
east (1) +2025+6298
eastern (1)
eastern (1) +9087
eastward (1) +2025
eastward (1) +2025+2025+7711
western[s] (1) +2025

untranslated (1)

4668 מְזָרִים *m^ezāriym* (1)
driving winds (1)

4669 מִזְרָע *mizrā'* (1)
sown field (1)

4670 מִזְרָק *mizrāq* (32)
sprinkling bowls (15)
sprinkling bowl (13)
bowl used for sprinkling (1)
bowlful (1)
bowls (1)
sacred bowls (1)

4671 מֵחַ *mēaḥ* (2)
fat animals (1)
rich (1)

4672 מֹחַ *mōaḥ* (1)
marrow (1)

4673 1מָחָא *māḥā'1* (3)
clap (2)
clapped (1)

4674 2מָחָא *māḥā'2*
Variant; not used

4675 מַחֲבֵא *maḥ^abē'* (1)
shelter (1)

4676 מַחֲבֹא *maḥ^abō'* (1)
hiding places (1)

4677 מְחַבְּרוֹת *m^eḥabb^erôt* (2)
fittings (1)
joists (1)

4678 מַחְבֶּרֶת *maḥberet* (8)
set (6)
seam (2)

4679 מַחֲבַת *maḥ^abat* (5)
griddle (3)
baking (1)
pan (1)

4680 מַחֲגֹרֶת *maḥ^agōret* (1)
sackcloth (1) +8566

4681 1מָחָה *māḥāh1* (34)
blot out (11)
be blotted out (3)
blotted out (2)
wipe (2)
wiped out (2)
wipes (2)
be wiped away (1)
be wiped out (1)
blots out (1)
completely blot out (1) +4681
ruin (1)
swept away (1)
wash off (1)
wipe away (1)
wipe out (1)
wiped (1)
wiping (1)

4682 2מָחָה *māḥāh2* (1)
continue (1)

4683 3מָחָה *māḥāh3* (1)
meats (1)

4684 מְחוּגָה *m^eḥûgāh* (1)
compasses (1)

4685 מָחוֹז *māḥôz* (1)
haven (1)

4686 מְחוּיָאֵל *m^eḥûyā'ēl* (2)
Mehujael (2)

4687 מַחֲוִים *maḥ^awiym* (1)
Mahavite (1)

4688 1מָחוֹל *māḥôl1* (6)
dancing (4)
dance (2)

4689 2מָחוֹל *māḥôl2* (1)
Mahol (1)

4690 מַחֲזֶה *maḥ^azeh* (4)
vision (3)
visions (1)

4691 מֶחֱזָה *meḥ^ezāh* (3)
facing each other (2) +448+4691

4692 מַחֲזִיאוֹת *maḥ^aziy'ôt* (2)
Mahazioth (2)

4693 מְחִי *m^eḥiy* (1)
blows (1)

4694 מְחִידָא *m^eḥiydā'* (2)
Mehida (2)

4695 מִחְיָה *miḥyāh* (8)
food (1)
living thing (1)
new life (1)
raw (1) +2645
raw flesh (1)
recover (1)
relief (1)
save lives (1)

4696 מְחִיָּיאֵל *m^eḥiyyāy'ēl*
Variant; not used

4697 1מְחִיר *m^eḥiyr1* (15)
price (6)
purchased (2) +928+4374
charge (1)
cost (1)
insist on paying for (1) +928+7864+7864
money (1)
sale (1)
worth (1)
untranslated (1)

4698 2מְחִיר *m^eḥiyr2* (1)
Mehir (1)

4699 מַחֲלֵב *maḥ^alēb*
Variant; not used

4700 מַחֲלֶה *maḥ^aleh* (2)
disease (1)
sickness (1)

4701 מַחֲלָה *maḥ^alāh* (4)
disease (2)
diseases (1)
sickness (1)

4702 מַחְלָה *maḥlāh* (5)
Mahlah (5)

4703 מְחֹלָה *m^eḥōlāh* (8)
dancing (5)
dances (2)
dance (1)

4704 מְחִלָּה *m^eḥillāh* (1)
holes (1)

4705 מַחְלוֹן *maḥlôn* (4)
Mahlon (3)
Mahlon's (1)

4706 1מַחְלִי *maḥliy1* (12)
Mahli (12)

4707 2מַחְלִי *maḥliy2* (2)
Mahlite (1)
Mahlites (1)

4708 מַחֲלֻיִים *maḥ^aluyiym* (2)
wounded (1)
untranslated (1)

4709 מַחֲלָף *maḥ^alāp* (1)
pans (1)

4710 מַחְלָפָה *maḥ^alāpāh* (3)
braids (3)

4711 מַחֲלָצוֹת *maḥ^alāṣôt* (2)
fine robes (1)
rich garments (1)

4712 מַחְלְקוֹת *maḥl^eqôt*
Variant; not used

4713 מַחֲלֹקֶת *maḥ^alōqet* (42)
divisions (19)
division (17)
tribal divisions (2)
army divisions (1)
groups (1)
portions (1)
untranslated (1)

4714 1מָחֲלַת *māḥ^alat1* (2)
mahalath (2)

4715 2מָחֲלַת *māḥ^alat2* (2)
Mahalath (2)

4716 מְחֹלָתִי *m^eḥōlātiy* (2)
Meholathite (1)
of Meholah (1)

4717 מַחְמָאֹת *maḥmā'ōt* (1)
butter (1)

4718 מַחְמָד *maḥmād* (13)
treasures (4)
delight (3)
cherished (1)
lovely (1)
pleasing (1)
treasured (1)
value (1)
value (1) +6524

4719 מַחְמֹד *maḥmōd* (2)
treasures (1)
untranslated (1)

4720 מַחְמָל *maḥmāl* (1)
object (1)

4721 מַחְמֶצֶת *maḥmeṣet* (2)
anything with yeast in it (1)
made with yeast (1)

4722 מַחֲנֶה *maḥ^aneh* (214)
camp (144)
army (23)
camps (8)
forces (5)
troops (3)
armies (2)
dwelling (2)
fighting (2)
group (2)
groups (2)
lines (2)
attendants (1)
band (1)
company (1)
droves (1)
encamped (1) +3655
force (1)
it[S] (1) +2021
it[S] (1) +5213
Midianites[S] (1)
there[S] (1) +928+2021
tribes (1)
units (1)
unwalled (1)
untranslated (6)

4723 מַחֲנֵה־דָן *maḥ^anēh-dān* (2)
Mahaneh Dan (2)

4724 מַחֲנַיִם *maḥ^anayim* (14)
Mahanaim (14)

4725 מַחֲנָק *maḥ^anāq* (1)
strangling (1)

4726 מַחְסֶה *maḥseh* (20)
refuge (18)
shelter (2)

4727 מַחְסוֹם *maḥsôm* (1)
muzzle (1)

4728 מַחְסוֹר *mahsôr* (13)
poverty (4)
lack (2)
need (2)
scarcity (2)
lacks (1)
needs (1) +2893
poor (1)

4729 מַחְסֵיָה *mahsēyāh* (2)
Mahseiah (2)

4730 מָחַץ *māhas* (13)
crush (3)
crushed (2)
crushed completely (1) +430+2256
crushing (1)
cut to pieces (1)
injures (1)
pierce (1)
shattered (1)
smite (1)
wounded (1)

4731 מַחַץ *mahas* (1)
wounds (1)

4732 מַחְצֵב *mahsēb* (3)
dressed (3)

4733 מֶחֱצָה *meh^esāh* (2)
half (2)

4734 מַחֲצִית *mah^asiyt* (16)
half (13)
half as much (1)
half share (1)
noon (1) +2021+3427

4735 מָחַק *māhaq* (1)
crushed (1)

4736 מֶחְקָר *mehqār* (1)
depths (1)

4737 מָחָר *māhār* (52)
tomorrow (43)
in the future (4)
days to come (1)
ever (1)
future (1) +3427
some day (1)
tomorrow (1) +3427

4738 מַחֲרָאָה *mah^arā'āh* (1)
latrine (1)

4739 מַחֲרֵשָׁה *mah^arēšāh* (2)
plowshares (2)

4740 מָחֳרָת *moh^orāt* (32)
next day (22)
day after (6)
next (3)
following (1)

4741 מַחְשֹׂף *mahśōp* (1)
exposing (1)

4742 מַחֲשָׁבָה *mah^ašābāh* (56)
thoughts (14)
plans (9)
plan (3)
plots (3)
purposes (3)
artistic designs (2)
imaginations (2)
purposed (2) +3108
scheme (2)
schemes (2)
artistic craftsmanship (1)
design (1)
designed (1)
designers (1) +3110
desire (1) +3671
devised (1)
make plans (1) +3108
overthrow (1)
plans have (1) +3108
plotted (1) +3108
plotting (1)
things planned (1)
ways (1)
what thinking (1)

4743 מַחְשָׁךְ *mahšāk* (7)
darkness (5)
dark places (1)
darkest (1)

4744 מַחַת *mahat* (3)
Mahath (3)

4745 מְחִתָּה *m^ehittāh* (11)
ruin (4)
terror (3)
object of horror (1)
ruined (1)
ruins (1)
undoing (1)

4746 מַחְתָּה *mahtāh* (22)
censers (11)
censer (4)
firepans (3)
trays (3)
it[s] (1)

4747 מַחְתֶּרֶת *mahteret* (2)
breaking in (2)

4748 מַטְאֲטֵא *mat'^atē'* (1)
broom (1)

4749 מַטְבֵּחַ *matbēah* (1)
place to slaughter (1)

4750 מָטֶה *māteh*
Variant; not used

4751 מַטֶּה *matteh* (253)
tribe (124)
staff (37)
tribes (21)
tribal (8)
rod (6)
half-tribe (5) +2942
staffs (5)
supply (4)
club (3)
branches (2)
scepter (2)
arrows (1)
bar (1)
branch (1)
Danite (1) +1968+4200
family (1)
Levites (1) +4290
main branches (1) +964
one[s] (1)
spear (1)
supplies (1)
them[s] (1)
untranslated (25)

4752 מַטָּה *mattāh* (19)
below (3) +4200
bottom (3)
down (3) +4200
bottom (2) +4200+4946
lower (2)
goes down (1) +3718+4200
going down to (1)
less (1)
punished less (1) +3104+4200
untranslated (2)

4753 מִטָּה *mittāh* (28)
bed (17)
couch (4)
bedroom (2) +2540
beds (2)
bier (1)
carriage (1)
couches (1)

4754 מֻטֶּה *mutteh* (1)
injustice (1)

4755 מֻטָּה *muttāh*
Variant; not used

4756 מִטְהָר *mithār*
Variant; not used

4757 מַטְוֶה *matweh* (1)
what spun (1)

4758 מָטִיל *mātiyl* (1)
rods (1)

4759 מַטְמוֹן *matmôn* (5)
hidden treasure (2)
hidden (1)
riches (1)
treasure (1)

4760 מַטָּע *mattā'* (7)
planted (2)
planting (2)
base (1)
land for crops (1)
untranslated (1)

4761 מַטְעָם *mat'ām* (8)
tasty food (6)
delicacies (2)

4762 מִטְפַּחַת *mitpahat* (2)
cloaks (1)
shawl (1)

4763 מָטַר *mātar* (18)
rained down (3)
had rain (2)
rain down (2)
sent rain (2)
had[s] (1)
pour down (1)
rain (1)
rain (1) +4764
rained (1)
send (1)
send rain (1)
water (1)
withheld[s] (1) +4202

4764 מָטָר *mātār* (38)
rain (34)
showers (2)
downpour (1) +1773
rain (1) +4763

4765 מַטְרֵד *matrēd* (2)
Matred (2)

4766 מַטָּרָה *mattārāh* (16)
guard (13)
target (3)

4767 מַטְרִי *matriy* (1)
Matri's (1)

4768 מַי *may*
Variant; not used

4769 מִי *miy* (424)
who (285)
whom (34)
what (17)
which (11)
whose (11)
if only (10) +5989
oh (8) +5989
anyone (7)
whoever (6)
anyone (3) +408+2021
if only (3)
whose (3) +4200
how (2)
one (2)
someone (2)
whoever (2) +408+2021
whoever (2) +889
any man (1) +408+2021

how did it go (1) +905
how I long for (1) +5761+5989
I wish (1) +5989
just who (1) +2256+4769
oh (1) +686+5989
oh how I wish (1) +5989
others[S] (1)
what (1) +2296
untranslated (6)

4770 מֵי הַיַּרְקוֹן *mēy hayyarqôn* (1)
Me Jarkon (1)

4771 מֵי זָהָב *mēy zāhāḇ* (2)
Me-Zahab (2)

4772 מֵידְבָא *mēyḏᵉḇā'* (5)
Medeba (5)

4773 מֵידָד *mēyḏāḏ* (2)
Medad (2)

4774 מֵיטָב *mēyṭāḇ* (6)
best (5)
untranslated (1)

4775 מִיכָא *miyḵā'* (4)
Mica (4)

4776 מִיכָאֵל *miyḵā'ēl* (13)
Michael (13)

4777 מִיכָה *miyḵāh* (33)
Micah (24)
Micah's (6)
his[S] (1)
Mica (1)
Micaiah (1)

4778 מִיכָהוּ *miyḵāhû* (1)
untranslated (1)

4779 מִיכָיָה *miyḵāyāh* (4)
Micaiah (3)
untranslated (1)

4780 מִיכָיָהוּ *miyḵāyāhû* (1)
Micaiah (1)

4781 מִיכָיְהוּ *miyḵāyᵉhû* (21)
Micaiah (19)
Micah (1)
Micah's (1)

4782 מִיכָל *miyḵāl* (1)
brook (1) +4784

4783 מִיכַל *miyḵal* (17)
Michal (17)

4784 מַיִם *mayim* (581)
water (359)
waters (140)
flood (3)
floodwaters (3) +4429
rain (3)
springs (3) +5078
tears (3)
flowing springs (2) +4604
river (2)
sea (2)
spring (2)
spring (2) +4604
spring (2) +6524
springs (2) +6524
that[S] (2)
waterless (2) +401
well-watered (2) +9272
brook (1) +4782
bubbling springs (1) +4432
dam (1)
driving rain (1) +2443
floodwaters (1) +8041
floodwaters (1) +8673
flow (1)
flowing streams (1) +3298
it[S] (1) +2021
melted (1)
pool (1)
pool (1) +106
pool (1) +1391
reservoirs (1) +1391
reservoirs (1) +5224
seas (1)
spring (1) +2021+6524
spring of water (1)
springs (1) +4604
stream (1)
swampland (1) +106
they[S] (1) +2021
water supply (1)
water's (1)
watercourse (1) +7104
watering (1)
waves (1)
well (1) +931
wells (1) +931
untranslated (18)

4785 מִיָּמִין *miyyāmiyn* (4)
Mijamin (4)

4786 מִין *miyn* (31)
kind (18)
kinds (9)
various kinds (1)
untranslated (3)

4787 מֵינֶקֶת *mēyneqeṯ* (6)
nurse (4)
nursing mothers (1)
untranslated (1)

4788 מֵיסָךְ *mēysāḵ* (1)
untranslated (1)

4789 מֵיפַעַת *mēyp̄a'aṯ* (4)
Mephaath (4)

4790 מִיץ *miys* (3)
churning (1)
stirring up (1)
twisting (1)

4791 מֵישָׁא *mēyšā'* (1)
Mesha (1)

4792 מִישָׁאֵל *miyšā'ēl* (7)
Mishael (7)

4793 מִישׁוֹר *miyšôr* (23)
plateau (9)
justice (2)
level (2)
level ground (2)
plains (2)
justly (1)
plain (1)
plateau (1) +824
smooth (1)
straight (1)
uprightness (1)

4794 מֵישַׁךְ *mēyšaḵ* (1)
Meshach (1)

4795 מֵישַׁע *mēyša'* (1)
Mesha (1)

4796 מֵישָׁע *mēyšā'* (1)
Mesha (1)

4797 מֵישָׁרִים *mēyšāriym* (19)
right (6)
equity (3)
fair (2)
uprightly (2)
alliance (1)
integrity (1)
justice (1)
level (1)
smoothly (1) +928
straight (1)

4798 מֵיתָר *mēyṯār* (9)
ropes (7)
cords (1)
drawn bow (1)

4799 מַכְאֹב *maḵ'ōḇ* (16)
pain (7)
suffering (4)
sorrows (2)
grief (1)
pains (1)
woes (1)

4800 מַכְבֵּנָה *maḵḇēnāh* (1)
Macbenah (1)

4801 מַכְבַּנַּי *maḵḇannay* (1)
Macbannai (1)

4802 מַכְבֵּר *maḵḇēr* (1)
thick cloth (1)

4803 מִכְבָּר *miḵḇār* (6)
grating (6)

4804 מַכָּה *makkāh* (48)
wounds (9)
wound (4)
losses (3)
struck down (3)
blow (2)
injury (2)
plagues (2)
slaughter (2)
afflictions (1)
attack (1)
beatings (1)
blows (1)
calamities (1)
casualties (1)
destroyed (1) +1524+4394+5782
devastated (1) +1524+4394+5782
disaster (1)
disasters (1)
flogged (1) +5782
force (1)
ground (1)
inflicted (1)
plague (1)
slaughtered (1)
sores (1)
struck down (1) +5782
victory (1)
untranslated (2)

4805 מִכְוָה *miḵwāh* (5)
burn (4)
burn (1) +836

4806 מָכוֹן *māḵôn* (17)
place (11)
foundation (2)
dwelling place (1)
foundations (1)
site (1)
untranslated (1)

4807 מְכוֹנָה *mᵉḵônāh* (25)
movable stands (7)
stand (6)
stands (6)
foundation (1)
place (1)
untranslated (4)

4808 מְכוּרָה *mᵉḵûrāh* (3)
ancestry (3)

4809 מָכִי *māḵiy* (1)
Maki (1)

4810 מָכִיר *māḵiyr* (22)
Makir (20)
Makir's (1)
Makirites (1)

4811 מָכִירִי *māḵiyriy* (1)
Makirite (1)

4812 מָכַךְ *māḵaḵ* (3)
are brought low (1)

sag (1)
wasted away (1)

4813 מִכְלָא *miḵlā'* (3)
pens (2)
pen (1)

4814 מִכְלוֹל *miḵlôl* (2)
full (1)
fully (1)

4815 מַכְלוּל *maḵlûl* (1)
beautiful garments (1)

4816 מִכְלוֹת *miḵlôṯ* (1)
solid (1)

4817 מִכְלָל *miḵlāl* (1)
perfect (1)

4818 מַכֹּלֶת *makkōleṯ* (1)
food (1)

4819 מִכְמָן *miḵmān* (1)
treasures (1)

4820 מִכְמָס *miḵmās* (2)
Micmash (2)

4821 מִכְמָר *miḵmār* (2)
net (1)
nets (1)

4822 מַכְמֹר *maḵmōr*
Variant; not used

4823 מִכְמֶרֶת *miḵmereṯ* (3)
dragnet (2)
nets (1)

4824 מִכְמֹרֶת *miḵmōreṯ*
Variant; not used

4825 מִכְמָשׂ *miḵmāś* (9)
Micmash (9)

4826 מִכְמְתָת *miḵmᵉṯāṯ* (2)
Micmethath (2)

4827 מַכְנַדְבַי *maḵnaḏbay* (1)
Macnadebai (1)

4828 מְכֹנָה *mᵉḵōnāh* (1)
Meconah (1)

4829 מִכְנָס *miḵnās* (5)
undergarments (4)
undergarments (1) +965

4830 מֶכֶס *meḵes* (6)
tribute (6)

4831 מִכְסָה *miḵsāh* (2)
number (1)
value (1) +6886

4832 מִכְסֶה *miḵseh* (16)
covering (12)
cover (3) +4059
coverings (1)

4833 מְכַסֶּה *mᵉḵasseh* (4)
awnings (1)
clothes (1)
cover (1)
layer of fat (1)

4834 מַכְפֵּלָה *maḵpēlāh* (6)
Machpelah (6)

4835 מָכַר *māḵar* (80)
sold (19)
sell (17)
selling (7)
sells (7)
be sold (5)
sold himself (4)
seller (3)
sells himself (3)
been sold (2)
were sold (2)
be sold back (1)
enslaved (1)
hand over (1) +928+3338
must be sold (1) +4929
must sell (1) +928+2021+4084+4835
offer yourselves for sale (1)
sell land (1) +4928
sellers (1)
sold themselves (1)
sold yourself (1)

4836 מֶכֶר *meḵer* (3)
merchandise (1)
pay (1) +5989
worth (1)

4837 מַכָּר *makkār* (2)
treasurers (2)

4838 מִכְרֶה *miḵreh* (1)
pits (1)

4839 מְכֵרָה *mᵉḵērāh* (1)
swords (1)

4840 מִכְרִי *miḵriy* (1)
Micri (1)

4841 מְכֵרָתִי *mᵉḵērāṯiy* (1)
Mekerathite (1)

4842 מִכְשׁוֹל *miḵšôl* (14)
stumbling block (4)
obstacles (2)
downfall (1)
fallen (1)
made fall (1) +2118+4200
make stumble (1)
makes fall (1)
staggering burden (1) +2256+7050
stumble (1)
stumbling blocks (1)

4843 מַכְשֵׁלָה *maḵšēlāh* (2)
heap of ruins (1)
heaps of rubble (1)

4844 מִכְתָּב *miḵtāḇ* (9)
writing (5)
inscription (1) +7334
letter (1)
written (1)
untranslated (1)

4845 מְכִתָּה *mᵉḵittāh* (1)
pieces (1)

4846 מִכְתָּם *miḵtām* (6)
miktam (6)

4847 מַכְתֵּשׁ *maḵtēš* (3)
hollow place (1)
market district (1)
mortar (1)

4848 1מָלֵא *mālē'1* (253)
filled (46)
fill (38)
full (35)
be filled (10)
over (8)
wholeheartedly (7)
completed (5)
covered (5)
fulfilled (5)
was filled (4)
filling (3)
fills (3)
ordained (3) +906+3338
satisfy (3)
set (3)
installed (2) +906+3338
laden with (2)
ordain (2) +3338
ordination (2) +906+3338
passed (2)
aloud (1)
are filled (1)
at flood stage (1) +1536+3972+6584
bathed in (1)
be paid in full (1)
bear (1)
before elapsed (1) +4202
came (1)
come (1)
come to an end (1)
confirm (1)
consecrate himself (1) +2257+3338
consecrate himself (1) +3338
consecrated (1) +906+3338
cover (1)
cover (1) +7156
crowded (1)
dared (1) +4213
dedicate (1) +3338
dedicated (1) +3338
did completely (1)
drenched (1)
drew (1) +928+3338
enraged (1) +2779
enriched (1)
finish (1)
finished (1)
fulfilling (1)
fulfillment (1)
give full (1)
given (1)
gorge (1)
grant (1)
have fill (1)
heaping up (1)
highly (1)
is satisfied (1)
last (1)
live out (1)
make succeed (1)
making full (1)
midst (1)
mount (1) +4853
mounted (1)
numbered (1)
ordain (1) +906+3338
ordained (1) +3338
overflowing (1)
presented the full number (1)
prosper (1)
provide (1)
racked with (1)
set apart (1) +3338
shown (1)
still hunger (1) +1061
take up (1)
taking full (1)
took a handful (1) +4090
unite (1)
uses (1)
violent (1) +2805
well nourished (1) +2692
were filled (1)
untranslated (2)

4849 2מָלֵא *mālē'2* (60)
filled (31)
full (21)
abundance (1)
loaded (1)
loud (1)
mother's^{s} (1)
strewn with (1)
strong (1)
weighed down (1)
untranslated (1)

4850 מְלֹא *mᵉlō'* (38)
everything in (8)
all that is in (5)
filled (3)
full (3)
handful (2) +4090
handfuls (2) +2908
take a handful (2) +7858+7859
all that in (1)

all who are in (1)
all who were in (1)
bowlful (1) +6210
cover (1)
fullness (1)
group (1)
length (1)
take (1)
third[s] (1)
two handfuls (1) +2908
whole band (1)
untranslated (1)

4851 1מִלֹּא *millō'*
Variant; not used

4852 מְלֵאָה *m^{e}lē'āh* (3)
crops (1)
granaries (1)
juice (1)

4853 מִלֻּאָה *millu'āh* (4)
mount (1) +2118
mount (1) +4848
mounted (1)
settings (1)

4854 מִלֻּאִים *millu'iym* (14)
ordination (7)
mounted (2)
ordination offering (2)
ordination offerings (1)
ordination ram (1)
settings (1)

4855 מַלְאָךְ *mal'āḵ* (213)
angel (98)
messengers (60)
messenger (23)
angels (9)
men (8)
envoys (6)
delegation (1)
he[s] (1) +2021
he[s] (1) +3378
men[s] (1)
official (1)
spies (1)
the angel (1) +3378
they[s] (1) +2021
untranslated (1)

4856 מְלָאכָה *m^{e}lā'ḵāh* (167)
work (87)
regular work (12) +6275
workers (7) +6913
anything (3)
duties (3)
task (3)
workmen (3) +6913
business (2)
crafts (2)
project (2)
property (2)
service (2)
use (2) +6913
administrators (1) +6913
anything useful (1)
assist (1)
been used (1) +6913
building (1)
craftsmanship (1)
deeds (1)
details (1)
do (1)
done (1)
droves (1)
everything (1) +2021+3972
kinds (1)
made (1)
master craftsmen (1) +6913
matter (1)
merchants (1) +6913
part (1)
performed (1)
projects (1)
purpose (1)
responsible (1)
responsible (1) +6275
settings (1) +9513
something useful (1)
supplies (1)
these men[s] (1) +2021+6913
what[s] (1) +2021
work (1) +6913
worked (1)
working (1) +6913
workmen (1)
workmen (1) +928+2021+6913
untranslated (4)

4857 מַלְאֲכוּת *mal'ăḵûṯ* (1)
message (1)

4858 מַלְאָכִי *mal'āḵiy* (1)
Malachi (1)

4859 מִלֵּאת *millē'ṯ* (1)
mounted like jewels (1) +3782+6584

4860 מַלְבּוּשׁ *malbûš* (8)
robes (4)
clothes (3)
clothing (1)

4861 מַלְבֵּן *malbēn* (3)
brick pavement (1)
brickmaking (1)
brickwork (1)

4862 מָלָה *mālāh*
Variant; not used

4863 מִלָּה *millāh* (38)
words (24)
speaking (2)
speeches (2)
word (2)
anything to say (1)
byword (1)
make fine speeches (1) +928+2488
reply (1) +8740
said (1)
say (1)
what say (1)
what[s] (1)

4864 מִלּוֹא *millô'* (6)
supporting terraces (6)

4865 מַלּוּחַ *mallûah* (1)
salt herbs (1)

4866 מַלּוּךְ *mallûḵ* (6)
Malluch (6)

4867 מְלוּכָה *m^{e}lûḵāh* (25)
kingdom (11)
royal (7)
kingship (3)
dominion (1)
king (1)
queen (1)
rule (1)

4868 מַלּוּכִי *mallûḵiy* (1)
Malluch's (1)

4869 מָלוֹן *mālôn* (8)
lodging place (2)
camp (1)
camp overnight (1)
parts (1)
place (1)
place where they stopped for the night (1)
place where we stopped for the night (1)

4870 מְלוּנָה *m^{e}lûnāh* (2)
hut (2)

4871 מַלּוֹתִי *mallôṯiy* (2)
Mallothi (2)

4872 1מָלַח *mālah1* (1)
vanish (1)

4873 2מָלַח *mālah2* (4)
be salted (1)
season (1)
were rubbed with salt (1) +4873

4874 1מֶלַח *melah1* (2)
clothes (2)

4875 2מֶלַח *melah2* (30)
salt (29)
untranslated (1)

4876 מַלָּח *mallāh* (4)
mariners (2)
sailors (2)

4877 מְלֵחָה *m^{e}lēhāh* (3)
salt (1)
salt flats (1)
salt waste (1)

4878 מִלְחָמָה *milhāmāh* (319)
battle (135)
war (74)
fighting (16)
fight (14)
soldiers (12) +408
wars (6)
warrior (5) +408
army (4) +408
army (4) +6639
battles (4)
military (3)
warfare (3)
at war with (2) +408
battle formation (2)
battle lines (2)
fighting (2) +6913
military age (2)
armed (1)
at war (1)
at war (1) +6913
attack (1)
attacked (1)
battle (1) +7372
experienced fighter (1) +408
experienced fighting men (1) +408+1475+2657
fight (1) +2021+3655+4200
force (1) +6639
great soldiers (1) +408
men ready for battle (1) +1522+7372
ready for battle (1) +408+2021+4200+7372
ready for battle (1) +928+2021+7372
soldiers (1) +408+1505
soldiers (1) +9530
struggle (1)
that[s] (1)
time of war (1)
wage war (1) +1741+2021+4200
war cry (1)
weapon (1) +3998
weapon (1) +3998+7372
weapons (1) +3998
well-trained (1) +6913
went to war (1) +6913
untranslated (3)

4879 מֶלֶט *melet* (1)
clay (1)

4880 1מָלַט *mālat1* (95)
escaped (20)
escape (17)
save (7)
flee (5)
rescued (4)
run (4)
be delivered (3)
rescue (3)
saved (3)
deliver (2)

delivers (2)
go free (2)
got away (2)
let get away (2)
be saved (1)
escape (1) +4880
escape (1) +7127
escaping (1)
get away (1)
is kept safe (1)
lay eggs (1)
made escape (1)
made good escape (1) +2256+5674
release (1)
retrieved (1)
save (1) +4880
shoot out (1)
slip out (1)
slipped away (1)
spared (1)
were saved (1)

4881 2מָלַט *mālaṭ2*
Variant; not used

4882 מְלַטְיָה *mᵉlaṭyāh* (1)
Melatiah (1)

4883 מְלִיכוּ *mᵉliyḵû* (1)
untranslated (1)

4884 מְלִילָה *mᵉliylāh* (1)
kernels (1)

4885 מֵלִיץ *mēliyṣ* (5)
envoys (1)
intercessor (1)
interpreter (1)
mediator (1)
spokesmen (1)

4886 מְלִיצָה *mᵉliyṣāh* (2)
parables (1)
ridicule (1)

4887 1מָלַךְ *mālaḵ1* (350)
king (151)
reigned (70)
reign (37)
made king (24)
reigns (9)
ruled (9)
make king (7)
rule (5)
proclaimed king (3)
set up king (2) +4889
acknowledged as king (1)
appoint as king (1)
came to power (1)
confirmed as king (1)
crown (1)
extend (1)
give king (1) +4889
intend to reign (1) +4887
king (1) +4889
kingship (1)
made king (1) +4889
made queen (1)
make king (1) +4889
put on throne (1)
queen (1)
reigned (1) +4889
ruled over (1)
ruling (1)
set a king (1) +4889
set up kings (1)
surely be king (1) +4887
took control (1)
was made ruler (1)
untranslated (8)

4888 2מָלַךְ *mālaḵ2* (1)
pondered (1)

4889 1מֶלֶךְ *meleḵ1* (2527)
king (1840)
kings (271)
king's (172)
royal (65)
him^s (29) +2021
he^s (26) +2021
palace (15) +1074
his^s (6) +2021
king's (4) +4200
his own^s (3) +2021
king's (3) +928
princes (3) +1201
reign (3)
Amaziah^s (2) +2021
palace grounds (2) +1074
ruled (2)
set up king (2) +4887
give king (1) +4887
he^s (1) +951
him^s (1) +951
him^s (1) +2021+6460
him^s (1) +3296+4046
his^s (1) +928+2021
his^s (1) +951
his^s (1) +4200+5213
it^s (1) +2021+9133
king (1) +4887
kingdom (1)
kingdoms (1)
kings' (1)
made king (1) +4887
majesty (1)
make king (1) +4887
prince (1) +1201
princess (1) +1426
reigned (1) +4887
rule over (1)
ruled (1) +2118
rulers (1)
set a king (1) +4887
Shalmaneser^s (1) +855
untranslated (55)

4890 2מֶלֶךְ *meleḵ2* (2)
Melech (2)

4891 מֹלֶךְ *mōleḵ* (9)
Molech (9)

4892 מַלְכֹּדֶת *malkōḏeṯ* (1)
trap (1)

4893 מַלְכָּה *malkāh* (35)
queen (30)
queen's (2)
queens (2)
she^s (1) +2021

4894 מִלְכָּה *milkāh* (11)
Milcah (11)

4895 מַלְכוּת *malkûṯ* (90)
kingdom (35)
reign (19)
royal (16)
realm (5)
empire (2)
kingdoms (2)
royal position (2)
became king (1)
king (1)
kingship (1)
palace (1) +1074
position as king (1)
royalty (1)
rule (1)
untranslated (2)

4896 מַלְכִּיאֵל *malkiy'ēl* (3)
Malkiel (3)

4897 מַלְכִּיאֵלִי *malkiy'ēliy* (1)
Malkielite (1)

4898 מַלְכִּיָּה *malkiyyāh* (15)
Malkijah (15)

4899 מַלְכִּיָּהוּ *malkiyyāhû* (1)
Malkijah (1)

4900 מַלְכִּי־צֶדֶק *malkiy-ṣeḏeq* (2)
Melchizedek (2)

4901 מַלְכִּירָם *malkiyrām* (1)
Malkiram (1)

4902 מַלְכִּי־שׁוּעַ *malkiy-šûa‘* (5)
Malki-Shua (5)

4903 מַלְכָּם *malkām* (4)
Molech (3)
Malcam (1)

4904 מִלְכֹּם *milkōm* (3)
Molech (3)

4905 מַלְכֵּן *malkēn* (1)
untranslated (1)

4906 מְלֶכֶת *mᵉleḵeṯ* (5)
queen (5)

4907 מֹלֶכֶת *mōleḵeṯ*
Variant; not used

4908 1מָלַל *mālal1* (5)
wither (2)
be blunted (1)
dry (1)
withers away (1)

4909 2מָלַל *mālal2* (2)
are cut off (1)
circumcise (1)

4910 3מָלַל *mālal3* (4)
proclaim (1)
said (1)
say (1)
speak (1)

4911 4מָלַל *mālal4* (1)
signals (1)

4912 מִלְלַי *milᵉlay* (1)
Milalai (1)

4913 מַלְמָד *malmāḏ* (1)
oxgoad (1) +1330

4914 מָלַץ *mālaṣ* (1)
sweet (1)

4915 מֶלְצַר *melṣar* (2)
guard (2)

4916 מָלַק *mālaq* (2)
wring (1)
wring off (1)

4917 מַלְקוֹחַ *malqôaḥ* (7)
spoils (4)
plunder (2)
all^s (1)

4918 מַלְקוֹחַיִם *malqôḥayim* (1)
roof of mouth (1)

4919 מַלְקוֹשׁ *malqôš* (8)
spring rains (4)
rain in spring (1)
spring (1)
spring rain (1)
springtime (1) +6961

4920 מֶלְקָחַיִם *melqāḥayim* (6)
tongs (3)
wick trimmers (3)

4921 מֶלְתָּחָה *meltāḥāh* (1)
wardrobe (1)

4922 מַלְתָּעוֹת *maltā‘ôṯ* (1)
fangs (1)

4923 מַמְּגוּרָה *mammᵉgûrāh* (1)
granaries (1)

4924 מֵמַד *mēmāḏ* (1)
dimensions (1)

4925 מְמוּכָן *mᵉmûḵān* (3)
Memucan (3)

4926 מָמוֹת *māmôṯ* (2)
deadly (1)
death (1)

4927 מַמְזֵר *mamzēr* (2)
foreigners (1)
one born of a forbidden marriage (1)

4928 מִמְכָּר *mimkār* (10)
sold (2)
what sold (2)
goods (1)
land sold (1)
money from sale (1)
release (1)
sale (1)
sell land (1) +4835

4929 מִמְכֶּרֶת *mimkereṯ* (1)
must be sold (1) +4835

4930 מַמְלָכָה *mamlāḵāh* (117)
kingdom (58)
kingdoms (45)
royal (7)
kings (2)
kingship (2)
reign (2)
royal power (1)

4931 מַמְלָכוּת *mamlāḵûṯ* (9)
kingdom (4)
realm (3)
reign (1)
royal (1)

4932 מִמְסָךְ *mimsāḵ* (2)
bowls of mixed wine (2)

4933 מֶמֶר *memer* (1)
bitterness (1)

4934 1מַמְרֵא *mamrē'1* (8)
Mamre (8)

4935 2מַמְרֵא *mamrē'2* (2)
Mamre (2)

4936 מַמְּרֹרִים *mammᵉrōriym* (1)
misery (1)

4937 מִמְשַׁח *mimšaḥ* (1)
anointed (1)

4938 מִמְשָׁל *mimšāl* (3)
power (2)
leaders (1)

4939 מֶמְשָׁלָה *memšālāh* (17)
dominion (4)
govern (4)
kingdom (3)
ruled (2)
authority (1)
forces (1)
rule (1)
ruled (1) +3338

4940 מִמְשָׁק *mimšāq* (1)
place (1)

4941 מַמְתַקִּים *mamṯaqiym* (2)
sweet (1)
sweetness (1)

4942 1מָן *mān1* (13)
manna (13)

4943 2מָן *mān2* (1)
what (1)

4944 1מֵן *mēn1* (2)
music of strings (1)
strings (1)

4945 2מֵן *mēn2* (1)
share (1)

4946 מִן *min* (7531)
from (2540)
of (592)
than (182)
out of (179)
from (155) +6584
some (123)
in (116)
on (98)
at (94)
from (93) +907
more than (93)
before (82) +7156
because of (54) +7156
too (54)
by (50)
outside (49) +2575
from (45) +7156
with (44)
because of (43)
any (40)
for (39)
to (37)
from (33) +3338
one (32)
from (25) +6640
before (24) +4200+7156
among (23)
since (21)
above (19) +5087
in addition to (18) +963+4200
below (17) +9393
of (17) +7156
because (16)
from (16) +7931
from (16) +9348
on every side (16) +6017
not (15)
as (14)
above (13) +6584
out of (13) +9348
through (13)
without (13)
from (12) +339
no (12)
above (11)
after (11)
from (11) +4200+7156
from among (11)
part (11)
away from (10)
away from (10) +6584
on each side (10) +2256+4946+7024+7024
rather than (10)
against (9)
behind (9) +339
besides (9) +963+4200
of one piece with (9)
on (9) +6584
so (9)
when (9)
without (9) +401
because (8) +7156
off (8) +6584
around (7) +6017
better than (7)
by (7) +7156
north (7) +7600
of (7) +907
under (7) +9393
whether (7)
Israelite (6) +408+1074+3776
on both sides[s] (6) +2256+2296+2296+4946
over (6)
before (5)
far away (5) +8158
from (5) +5584
greater than (5)
inside (5) +1074
left (5) +2143
long ago (5) +255
off (5)
toward (5)
whenever (5) +1896
where (5) +402
above (4) +2025+4200+5087
against (4) +3338+9393
among (4) +7931
at (4) +7156
behind (4) +1074
beneath (4) +9393
beyond (4)
both (4)
far from (4)
later (4) +7891
leave (4) +2143
left (4) +907+2143
malice aforethought (4) +8533+8997+9453
most (4)
no (4) +401
of (4) +6640
of (4) +9348
on either side (4) +2256+4946+7024+7024
out (4) +2575
out of (4) +6584
some (4) +3972
south (4) +5582
that (4)
through (4) +907
until (4)
within (4)
across (3) +6298
after (3) +7891
against (3) +6584
against (3) +7156
ancient (3) +6409
apart from (3) +1187
away (3)
away from (3) +6640
back (3) +9004
behind (3) +1237
belong to (3)
besides (3) +1187
between (3) +1068
between (3) +2256+6330
doing (3) +907
east (3) +7710
either (3)
escape (3) +7156
ever since (3)
from (3) +1896
higher than (3) +6584
hold accountable (3) +1335+3338
into (3)
leave (3) +3718
left (3) +7756
northern (3) +7600
out (3) +9004
over (3) +2025+4200+5087
so that (3)
the LORD's (3) +907+3378
unaware of (3) +6623
under (3)
about (2)
along (2)
as often as (2) +1896
as well as (2) +963+4200
at either end[s] (2) +2256+2296+2296+4946
at set times (2) +6330+6961+6961
away (2) +725
away (2) +9004
away from (2) +339
away from (2) +907
back (2) +339
before (2) +6584
beside (2) +7396
between (2)
beyond (2) +2134+2256
beyond (2) +6298
bottom (2) +4200+4752
by (2) +6640
cannot (2)

caused by (2)
dictated (2) +7023
distant (2) +5305
distant (2) +8158
each year (2) +2025+3427+3427
east (2) +6298
even more than (2)
ever (2) +6409
ever since (2) +255
excluded from (2)
extend from (2)
extended from (2)
extending from (2)
far and wide (2) +2085+2134+2256
far from (2) +5584
flesh and blood (2) +2743+3655
from (2) +6584+7156
from (2) +9393
from every side (2) +6017
from out of (2) +9348
future (2) +8158
got off (2) +6584+7563
had the habit (2) +8997+9453
head (2) +2025+2256+5087+8900
hold accountable (2) +2011+3338
in front of (2) +4578
in regard to (2)
instead of (2)
Israelite (2) +408+1201+3776
Israelites (2) +1201+3776
just above (2) +5087
leave (2) +907+2143
leave alone (2) +6073
left (2) +995
left of (2)
less than (2)
like (2)
long ago (2) +4200+8158
long ago (2) +6409
long ago (2) +7710
long ago (2) +8158
made of (2)
mine (2) +5761
nearby (2) +5584
never (2)
no (2) +1172
no (2) +3972+4202
north (2) +8520
not counting (2) +963+4200
not including (2) +963+4200
nothing but (2)
of (2) +4200+7156
of one piece (2)
on (2) +4578
only (2)
other than (2) +1187
out (2)
out from (2)
outside (2) +2025+2575
over (2) +5087
over (2) +6584
promised (2) +3655+7023
pursuing (2) +339
said (2) +3655+7023
separated from (2) +6584
since (2) +255
so many (2) +8044
so not (2)
so that not (2)
some (2) +7921
some of (2)
some time later (2) +3427
south (2) +3545
speak (2) +7023
to (2) +6640
top (2) +2025+4200+5087
turning from (2)
upon (2)
where (2) +9004
without (2) +1187
your own flesh and blood (2) +3655+3870
abandon (1) +3338+8332
abandon (1) +3718
about to (1) +6964+7940
above (1) +4200+4946+5087+6645
above (1) +5087+6584
according to (1)
across from (1) +6298
across the way (1) +5584
after (1) +339
after (1) +928+1896
after (1) +7895
after (1) +7921
against (1) +3338
ahead (1) +4200+7156
all around (1) +6017
all kinds (1) +3972
all life (1) +6388
all sorts (1) +7896
all the way from (1)
allots (1)
along (1) +6298
along with (1) +963+4200
alongside (1) +6298
aloof (1) +5584
already (1) +255
always (1) +6388
am forgotten (1) +4213+8894
among (1) +907
among (1) +1068
annual (1) +2025+3427+3427
another[s] (1) +2021+2215+2296
any (1) +6388
any of (1) +907
anything (1) +1821+1821+2021+3972
anything (1) +1821+3972
area (1) +2575
around (1) +1237+6017
around (1) +2021+2575
as long as (1)
as long as live (1) +3427
as much as (1) +8049
Asher's (1) +888
avert (1) +6296+6584
avoid (1)
avoid (1) +3782
away (1) +907
away (1) +6584
away (1) +6640
away from (1) +5584
away from (1) +7156
be without (1) +4162
because (1) +889
because of (1) +3954+7156
because of (1) +5584
because of (1) +6584
because of (1) +9004
before (1) +3270
before (1) +6640
before (1) +8997+9453
before time (1) +4200+7156
beforehand (1) +4200+7156
behind (1) +294
belonging to (1)
belongs to (1)
Benjamite (1) +1228
Benjamites (1) +408+1228
Benjamites (1) +1228
beside (1) +6584
better (1) +3202
beyond (1) +2134
beyond (1) +2134+4200
bodily (1) +1414
bordering each side[s] (1) +2256+2296+2296+4946
born (1) +3655+8167
branch of (1) +9348
brief (1) +7940
broke camp (1) +185+5825
broke off (1) +8740
brought about (1) +2118
by (1) +907
by (1) +4200
by (1) +6298
by (1) +6584
by (1) +7023
by (1) +9348
by myself (1) +907+3276
by not (1)
call to account (1) +1335+3338
call to account (1) +2011+6640
cause (1) +2118
causes (1)
certain (1)
choice lambs (1) +4119+7366
citizens of[s] (1)
complete (1) +2118+7891
completely (1) +1414+2256+5883+6330
concerning (1)
confront (1)
confronting (1) +7156
consent (1)
constant (1) +5584
deaf (1) +9048
defense against (1) +7156
departing from (1) +339
deprived of (1)
descendant (1) +408+2446
deserted (1) +132+401
deserted (1) +339+6590
deserted (1) +401+3782
deserted (1) +1172+3782
determined (1) +907
dictate (1) +7023
dictated (1) +7023+7924
dictating (1) +7023
dictation (1) +7023
directed by (1)
directly from (1)
disappeared (1) +2143+6524
do away with (1) +6073+9348
do so[s] (1) +2006+8740
down (1)
down (1) +8031
downstream (1) +2025+4200+5087
driven from (1)
due annually (1) +928+1896+9102+9102
during (1)
eastward (1) +7710
eluded (1) +6015+7156
entire (1) +7895
enveloped (1) +6017
Ephraimites (1) +713
escaped from (1)
even beyond (1) +6584
ever (1) +3427
ever since (1) +3427
ever since (1) +4200
every (1) +7891
every kind (1) +448+2385+2385
excelled (1)
except (1) +1187
except for (1)
extends to (1) +4200
face (1) +7156
faced (1)
facing (1)
facing (1) +5584
fail (1) +6073
failed (1) +6980
failed to keep (1) +6073
far and wide (1) +4200+6330+8158
far away (1) +4200+6330+8158
far away (1) +5305
few (1)
follow (1) +339+7756
for (1) +907
for (1) +6584
for (1) +7156
for fear of (1)
for fear of (1) +7156
for lack of (1)
for relief from (1) +4200+7156

for sake (1) +7156
former (1) +7710
formerly (1) +919+8997
forsaking (1) +907
free from (1)
from (1) +255
from (1) +2296
from (1) +4090
from (1) +4200
from (1) +4578
from (1) +5584+6524
from (1) +6017
from (1) +6298
from (1) +6524
from (1) +6640+7156
from (1) +7891
from inside (1)
from then on (1) +339+4027
frontal (1) +5584
gaunt (1) +9043
give up (1) +8740
God's (1) +466
gone from (1) +9348
got off (1) +3718+6584
had difficulty taking possession of (1) +3655
had part in (1) +2118
handed (1) +3338
have no (1) +6
have no (1) +6259+6524
have nowhere (1) +6
helpless (1) +3946
high above (1) +2025+4200+5087
higher (1) +5087
higher (1) +6584
his (1) +5647
his own (1) +2257+4213
hold responsible (1) +1335+3338
idea (1) +4213
in (1) +6584
in (1) +7931
in (1) +9348
in addition (1) +963+4200
in deference to (1) +7156
in front of (1) +7156
in presence (1)
in the course of time (1) +339+4027
in the course of time (1) +3427+3427+4200
including (1)
inquire of (1) +907+2011
inside (1) +1074+4200
inside (1) +7163
interior (1) +1074+2025
Israelite (1) +1201+3776
Israelite (1) +3776
Israelites (1) +3776
it[S] (1) +1947+2023
its[S] (1) +5288
jointed (1) +4200+5087+8079
just (1) +6964
keep from (1)
kept distance (1) +3656+5584
kept from (1)
Lacking (1) +1172
larger share of (1)
later (1)
later (1) +339+4027
later on (1) +3427
leave (1)
leave (1) +2143+6640
leave (1) +2143+6643
leave (1) +3718+9348
leave (1) +6015
leave (1) +6590
leave (1) +7756
leave (1) +9004
leave alone (1) +2532
leave alone (1) +6641
leaves (1) +907+2143
leaving (1) +5825
leaving (1) +6296
left (1)
left (1) +339
left (1) +907
left (1) +2143+6640
left (1) +5825
left (1) +6590
left (1) +7756+9348
lived (1)
long (1) +919
long (1) +6409
long (1) +8158
long ago (1) +3427+7710
lost (1)
lost (1) +907+5877
lost (1) +5877
lower (1) +9393
made from (1)
made up of (1)
make room for (1) +7156
make spew out (1) +3655+7023
meet (1) +7156
member (1)
more (1)
more than (1) +963+4200
most of (1)
much more than (1)
near (1)
near (1) +7396
nearby (1) +7940
neither (1) +401
never (1) +3427+4202
next to (1) +725
next to (1) +4578
next to (1) +7396
no longer be (1) +6073
no more (1)
noblest (1) +1475
none (1) +401
none (1) +3972+4202
none will be (1) +401
nor (1) +401+2256
northern (1) +2025+7600
not (1) +1187
not (1) +1194
not harm (1) +5927
nothing (1) +561+3972
now (1) +255
obscure (1) +6680+9048
of (1) +1068
of (1) +3338
of (1) +3655
of (1) +4200+8611
of (1) +6584
of (1) +7895
of all (1) +9348
off (1) +4578
often (1) +1896
old (1) +3427+7710
older (1) +1524
on (1) +907
on behalf of (1) +907
on both (1) +2256+2296+2296+4946
on both sides[S] (1) +2256+2296+2296
on each side (1) +2021+2021+2296+2296+4946+4946+4946+4946+6298+6298
on each side[S] (1) +2256+2296+2296+4946
on high (1) +5087
on high (1) +5294
on terms (1) +6640
on the basis of (1)
on the other side of (1) +2134+2256+6298
on this side of (1) +6298
once (1)
opposing (1)
opposite (1) +5584
or (1)
other than (1) +963+4200
others[S] (1) +2157
out (1) +1068
out (1) +7156
out of (1) +907
out of (1) +1068
out of (1) +5584
out of (1) +7156
out of (1) +7931
out of way (1) +4200+7156
outer (1) +2025+4200+5087
outnumber (1) +8045
outnumber (1) +8049
outside (1) +1946
outside (1) +2134
outweigh (1) +3877
outweighs (1) +3701
over (1) +4200+6584
pad (1) +9393
past (1) +907
past (1) +6584
peels (1) +6584
permission (1)
poured out (1) +9161
presence (1) +6584
prevent from (1)
projecting from (1)
protection from (1) +7156
received from (1)
recently (1) +2543+7940
recovery (1) +2649+2716
reject (1) +6584+7156+8938
reject (1) +6584+7156+8959
representative (1) +907
represented (1)
rest of (1)
resting on (1) +9393
rid (1) +6584+8959
risked (1) +5584+8959
say (1) +3655+7023
select a day (1) +3427+3427+4200
send (1) +907+995
sent by (1) +907
set free (1) +3338+8938
sharing (1) +430
shed by (1) +3338
side (1) +6298
sides (1) +6017+6298
since (1) +889
since (1) +3427+4200
so cannot (1)
so that no (1)
sober (1) +2021+3516+3655
some (1) +907
some distance away (1) +8158
some distance away (1) +8178
some distance from (1) +7156
southern (1) +5582
southernmost (1) +7895
southward (1) +9402
spared from (1) +7156
spoke the word (1) +7023
square (1) +2256+4946+7024+7024
started (1)
starting out from (1)
stop trusting in (1) +2532
stopped (1)
stopped (1) +6590
stopped up (1) +3877+9048
such (1) +3972
surely leave (1) +2143+2143+6584
surpasses (1)
surround (1) +2118+6017
take off (1) +3718+6584
taken (1)
taken from (1) +4200+7156
than (1) +889
than (1) +3463
than deserved (1)
the LORD's (1) +3378+6640
their (1) +2157
theirs (1) +2157
there (1) +9004
there is no (1) +401
those[S] (1)
throughout (1) +3972
till no more (1)

tilting away from (1) +7156
to (1) +4200
to (1) +6584
to (1) +7156
to (1) +9393
to nothing (1) +8024
told (1) +907+9048
top of (1) +2025+4200+5087
unaware (1) +6524+6623
under (1) +3338
under (1) +7156
underneath (1) +1074
underneath (1) +9393
unduly (1) +3841
unnoticed (1) +1172+8492
unsheathed (1) +3655+9509
untraveled (1) +408+1172+6296
upward (1) +2025+4200+5087
used (1)
uttered (1) +3655
utterly (1)
was spent for making (1) +6913
west (1) +6298
when (1) +255
when (1) +2118
when (1) +3427
whenever (1) +1896+3954
wherever (1) +889
wherever (1) +2021+3972+5226
while (1)
will (1)
willingly (1) +4213
with (1) +7396
with the help of (1) +907
withdrew (1) +2143
without (1) +1172
without (1) +2575
without being aware (1) +6524
without equal (1) +401+3202
worked (1)
worse than (1)
yet (1) +889+1172
your (1) +3871
your (1) +4013
untranslated (1167)

4947 מַנְגִּינָה *mangiynāh* (1)
mock in songs (1)

4948 1מָנָה *mānāh1* (28)
counted (4)
provided (4)
assigned (3)
count (3)
be counted (2)
number (2)
take a census (2)
appoint (1)
appointed (1)
counts (1)
destine (1)
determines (1)
raise (1)
was numbered (1)
were assigned (1)

4949 מָנֶה *māneh* (5)
minas (4)
mina (1)

4950 2מָנָה *mānāh2* (12)
share (3)
piece of meat (1)
portion (1)
portions (1)
portions of food (1)
portions of meat (1)
presents (1)
presents of food (1)
some[s] (1)
special food (1)

4951 מֹנֶה *mōneh* (2)
times (2)

4952 מִנְהָג *minhāḡ* (2)
driving (1)
that[s] (1)

4953 מִנְהָרָה *minhārāh* (1)
shelters (1)

4954 מָנוֹד *mānôḏ* (1)
shake (1)

4955 1מָנוֹחַ *mānôaḥ1* (7)
resting place (2)
came to rest (1)
home (1)
place to set (1)
places of rest (1)
rest (1)

4956 2מָנוֹחַ *mānôaḥ2* (18)
Manoah (15)
he[s] (1)
untranslated (2)

4957 מְנוּחָה *m^{e}nûḥāh* (21)
rest (6)
resting place (6)
place of rest (2)
easily (1)
peace and rest (1)
place to rest (1)
places of rest (1)
quiet (1)
resting (1)
staff (1)

4958 מָנוֹל *mānôl*
Variant; not used

4959 מָנוֹן *mānôn* (1)
grief (1)

4960 מָנוֹס *mānôs* (8)
refuge (4)
escape (1)
flee (1)
flee in haste (1) +5674
not escape (1) +6

4961 מְנוּסָה *m^{e}nûsāh* (2)
fleeing (1)
flight (1)

4962 מָנוֹר *mānôr* (4)
rod (4)

4963 מְנוֹרָה *m^{e}nôrāh* (41)
lampstand (26)
lampstands (5)
each lampstand (2) +2256+4963
each lampstand (1) +4963
it[s] (1) +2021
lamp (1)
untranslated (3)

4964 מִנְּזָר *minn^{e}zār* (1)
guards (1)

4965 מֻנָּח *munnāḥ* (3)
open area (3)

4966 מִנְחָה *minḥāh* (211)
grain offering (92)
grain offerings (42)
offering (18)
tribute (13)
gift (11)
offerings (9)
gifts (8)
sacrifice (5)
grain (2)
it[s] (2) +2021
offering of grain (2)
sacrifices (2)
evening sacrifice (1) +6590
sacrifice (1) +6590
untranslated (3)

4967 מְנֻחוֹת *m^{e}nuḥôṯ*
Variant; not used

4968 מְנַחֵם *m^{e}naḥēm* (8)
Menahem (7)
Menahem's (1)

4969 1מָנַחַת *mānaḥaṯ1* (2)
Manahath (2)

4970 2מָנַחַת *mānaḥaṯ2* (1)
Manahath (1)

4971 מָנַחְתִּי *mānaḥtiy* (2)
Manahathites (2)

4972 מְנִי *m^{e}niy* (1)
destiny (1)

4973 1מִנִּי *minniy1* (1)
Minni (1)

4974 2מִנִּי *minniy2* (34)
from (12)
than (3)
with (3)
by (2)
from (2) +4200
out of (2)
since (2)
before (1)
ever since (1)
of (1)
untranslated (5)

4975 מִנְיָמִין *minyāmiyn* (3)
Miniamin (2)
Miniamin's (1)

4976 1מִנִּית *minniyṯ1* (2)
Minnith (2)

4977 2מִנִּית *minniyṯ2*
Variant; not used

4978 מִנְלֶה *minleh* (1)
possessions (1)

4979 מָנַע *māna'* (29)
kept (4)
withheld (4)
withhold (4)
keep (2)
keeps (2)
refuse (2)
are denied (1)
been withheld (1)
denied (1)
deprived (1)
do not run (1)
held back (1)
hoards (1)
keep back (1)
not set (1)
refused (1)
restrain (1)

4980 מַנְעוּל *man'ûl* (6)
bolts (5)
lock (1)

4981 מִנְעָל *min'āl* (1)
bolts of gates (1)

4982 מַנְעַמִּים *man'ammiym* (1)
delicacies (1)

4983 מְנַעַנְעִים *m^{e}na'an'iym* (1)
sistrums (1)

4984 מְנַקִּית *m^{e}naqiyṯ* (4)
bowls (3)
bowls used for drink offerings (1)

4985 מְנַשֶּׁה *m^{e}naššeh* (145)
Manasseh (130)
Manasseh's (6)
Manasseh (5) +1201
Manassites (2) +1201
tribe of Manasseh (1)
untranslated (1)

4986 מְנַשִּׁי *m^{e}naššiy* (4)
Manasseh (3)

Manassites (1)

4987 מְנָת *m^{e}nāṯ* (9)
portions (3)
portion (2)
assigned (1)
contributed (1)
food (1)
lot (1) +3926

4988 מָס *mās* (1)
despairing man (1)

4989 מַס *mas* (23)
forced labor (14)
slave (2)
forced laborers (1)
labor force (1)
laborers (1)
slave labor (1)
slave labor force (1)
tribute (1)
untranslated (1)

4990 מֵסַב *mēsaḇ* (4)
around (2)
surround (1)
table (1)

4991 מְסִבָּה *m^{e}sibbāh* (1)
around (1)

4992 מִסָּבִיב *missāḇiyḇ*
Variant; not used

4993 1מַסְגֵּר *masgēr1* (3)
prison (3)

4994 2מַסְגֵּר *masgēr2* (4)
artisans (4)

4995 מִסְגֶּרֶת *misgereṯ* (18)
rim (6)
panels (5)
side panels (2)
strongholds (2)
dens (1)
untranslated (2)

4996 מַסָּד *massaḏ* (1)
foundation (1)

4997 מִסְדְּרוֹן *misd^{e}rôn* (1)
porch (1)

4998 מָסָה *māsāh* (4)
consume (1)
drench (1)
made melt with fear (1)
melts (1)

4999 1מַסָּה *massāh1* (3)
trials (2)
testings (1)

5000 2מַסָּה *massāh2* (1)
despair (1)

5001 3מַסָּה *massāh3* (5)
Massah (5)

5002 מִסָּה *missāh* (1)
in proportion to (1) +889+3869

5003 מַסְוֶה *masweh* (3)
veil (3)

5004 מְסוּכָה *m^{e}sûḵāh* (1)
thorn hedge (1)

5005 מַסָּח *massāh* (1)
take turns (1)

5006 מִסְחָר *mishar* (1)
revenues (1)

5007 מָסַךְ *māsaḵ* (5)
mixed (2)
mingle (1)
mixing (1)
poured (1)

5008 מֶסֶךְ *meseḵ* (1)
mixed with spices (1)

5009 מָסָךְ *māsāḵ* (25)
curtain (17)
shielding (3)
covering (2)
curtains (1)
defenses (1)
shields (1)

5010 מְסֻכָּה *m^{e}suḵāh* (1)
adorned (1)

5011 1מַסֵּכָה *massēḵāh1* (26)
cast idol (5)
idol cast (3)
images (3)
cast (2)
cast idols (2)
idol (2)
image (2)
cast images (1)
cast metal (1)
forming an alliance (1) +5818
idol cast from metal (1)
idols (1)
idols cast (1)
idols made of metal (1)

5012 2מַסֵּכָה *massēḵāh2* (2)
blanket (1)
sheet (1)

5013 3מַסֵּכָה *massēḵāh3*
Variant; not used

5014 מִסְכֵּן *miskēn* (4)
poor (4)

5015 מְסֻכָּן *m^{e}sukkān*
Variant; not used

5016 מִסְכְּנוֹת *misk^{e}nôṯ* (7)
store (6)
buildings to store (1)

5017 מִסְכֵּנֻת *miskēnuṯ* (1)
scarce (1) +430+928

5018 מַסֶּכֶת *masseḵeṯ* (3)
fabric (3)

5019 מְסִלָּה *m^{e}sillāh* (27)
road (10)
highway (6)
roads (3)
highways (2)
courses (1)
main road (1)
pilgrimage (1)
steps (1)
straight ahead (1)
ways (1)

5020 מַסְלוּל *maslûl* (1)
highway (1)

5021 מַסְמֵר *masmēr* (4)
nails (3)
nails down (1) +928+2616

5022 מָסַס *māsas* (21)
melt (6)
melted (3)
melted away (2)
be soaked (1)
disheartened (1) +906+4222
dropped (1)
made lose (1)
melt with fear (1) +5022
melts (1)
waste away (1)
wastes away (1)
weak (1)

5023 מַסַּע *massa‘* (12)
journey (2)
travels (2)
from place to place (1) +4200
having set out (1)
order of march (1)
setting out (1)
stages in journey (1)
traveled from place to place (1)
traveling from place to place (1)
way (1)

5024 1מַסָּע *massā‘1* (1)
quarry (1)

5025 2מַסָּע *massā‘2* (1)
dart (1)

5026 מִסְעָד *mis‘āḏ* (1)
supports (1)

5027 מִסְפֵּד *mispēḏ* (16)
wailing (5)
mourning (4)
wail (2)
weeping (2)
howl (1) +6913
lamented (1) +6199
mourns (1)

5028 מִסְפּוֹא *mispô’* (5)
fodder (4)
feed (1)

5029 מִסְפָּחָה *mispāhāh* (2)
veils (2)

5030 מִסְפַּחַת *mispahaṯ* (3)
rash (3)

5031 1מִסְפָּר *mispār1* (133)
number (47)
listed (15)
counted (8)
few (7)
list (6)
as many as (3)
how many (2)
number (2) +5152
numbered (2)
numbers (2)
account (1)
all (1)
allotted (1)
any (1)
bowmen (1) +8008
census (1)
count (1)
counted off (1) +928+6296
countless (1) +401
during (1)
each (1) +1653
each[s] (1) +4200
few (1) +928+5071
in all (1)
innumerable (1) +401
inventory (1)
length (1)
life span (1) +3427
limit (1)
listing (1)
many (1)
measure (1)
one by one (1) +928
one for each (1) +3869
only a few (1)
only a few (1) +5493
so many (1) +8041
total (1) +3972+4200
very few (1) +5493
untranslated (10)

5032 2מִסְפָּר *mispār2* (1)
Mispar (1)

5033 מִסְפֶּרֶת *mispereṯ* (1)
Mispereth (1)

5034 מָסַר *māsar* (2)
supplied (1)

the means of (1)

5035 מֹסֵרוֹת *mōsērôṯ* (2)
Moseroth (2)

5036 מֹסָרָם *mōsārām*
Variant; not used

5037 מָסֹרֶת *māsōreṯ* (1)
bond (1)

5038 מִסַּת *missaṯ*
Variant; not used

5039 מִסְתּוֹר *mistôr* (1)
hiding place (1)

5040 מַסְתֵּר *mastēr* (1)
hide (1)

5041 מִסְתָּר *mistār* (10)
ambush (2)
hiding (2)
secret places (2)
cover (1)
hiding places (1)
secret (1)
untranslated (1)

5042 מַעֲבָד *maᵃḇāḏ* (1)
deeds (1)

5043 מַעֲבֶה *maᵃḇeh* (1)
molds (1)

5044 מַעֲבָר *maᵃḇār* (3)
ford (1)
pass (1)
stroke (1)

5045 מַעְבָּרָה *ma'bārāh* (8)
fords (5)
pass (2)
river crossings (1)

5046 1מַעְגָּל *ma'gāl1* (3)
camp (3)

5047 2מַעְגָּל *ma'gāl2* (13)
paths (8)
path (2)
carts (1)
way (1)
ways (1)

5048 מָעַד *mā'aḏ* (8)
turn (2)
bent (1)
lame (1)
slip (1)
slipping (1)
wavering (1)
wrenched (1)

5049 מַעֲדַי *maᵃḏay* (1)
Maadai (1)

5050 מַעַדְיָה *ma'aḏyāh* (1)
Moadiah (1)

5051 מַעֲדַנּוֹת *maᵃḏannôṯ* (2)
beautiful (1)
confidently (1)

5052 מַעֲדַנִּים *maᵃḏanniym* (3)
delicacies (2)
delight (1)

5053 מַעְדֵּר *ma'dēr* (1)
hoe (1)

5054 מָעָה *mā'āh* (1)
numberless grains (1)

5055 מֵעֶה *mē'eh* (33)
body (4)
bowels (4)
heart (4)
anguish (2)
inside (2)
stomach (2)
within (2)
birth (1) +562
children (1) +7368
flesh (1)
have (1) +928
I (1) +3276
inside (1) +928
intestines (1)
line (1)
sons (1) +3665
stomachs (1)
tenderness (1) +2162
within (1) +928+9348
womb (1)

5056 מָעוֹג *mā'ôg̱* (1)
bread (1)

5057 מָעוֹז *mā'ôz* (35)
fortress (8)
refuge (8)
stronghold (7)
fortresses (2)
helmet (2) +8031
protection (2)
height (1)
mightiest fortresses (1) +4448
protect (1)
strength (1)
strong (1)
untranslated (1)

5058 מָעוֹזֶן *mā'ôzen* (1)
fortresses (1)

5059 מָעוֹךְ *mā'ôḵ* (1)
Maoch (1)

5060 1מָעוֹן *mā'ôn1*
Variant; not used

5061 2מָעוֹן *mā'ôn2* (18)
dwelling (7)
dwelling place (4)
haunt (4)
den (1)
refuge (1)
where live (1)

5062 3מָעוֹן *mā'ôn3* (3)
Maon (2)
Maonites (1)

5063 4מָעוֹן *mā'ôn4* (6)
Maon (6)

5064 מְעוּנִים *mᵉ'ûniym* (5)
Meunites (3)
Meunim (2)

5065 מְעוֹנֹתַי *mᵉ'ônōṯay* (2)
Meonothai (2)

5066 מָעוּף *mā'ûp̱* (1)
gloom (1)

5067 מָעוֹר *mā'ôr* (1)
naked bodies (1)

5068 מַעַזְיָה *ma'azyāh* (1)
Maaziah (1)

5069 מַעַזְיָהוּ *ma'azyāhû* (1)
Maaziah (1)

5070 מָעַט *mā'aṭ* (22)
few (4)
decrease (2)
smaller (2)
decreased (1)
dwindles away (1)
gathered little (1)
give less (1)
just a few (1)
let diminish (1)
little (1)
make few in number (1)
make weak (1)
no less than (1)
numbers decreased (1)
reduce to nothing (1)
small (1)
trifling (1)

5071 מְעַט *mᵉ'aṭ* (101)
little (33)
few (12)
not enough (5)
only a few (5)
little while (3)
smaller (3)
soon (3) +3869
almost (2) +3869
isn't enough (2)
short distance (2)
soon (2) +6388
almost (1) +6388
brief (1)
brink (1)
few (1) +928+5031
few (1) +3869
few in number (1) +5493
fewest (1)
how quickly (1) +3869
in a moment (1) +3869
in a very short time (1) +4663+6388
little more (1)
little while (1) +6388
little while (1) +8092
many (1) +4202
might well have (1) +3869
moment's (1)
of little value (1) +3869
only a little (1)
scarcely (1) +3869
short (1)
some (1)
some (1) +3869
soon (1) +3869+7775
too few (1)
too little (1)
very few (1) +4663
very soon (1) +4663+6388
wasn't enough (1)
waste away (1)

5072 מְעֻטָּה *mᵉ'uṭṭāh*
Variant; not used

5073 מַעֲטֶה *maᵃṭeh* (1)
garment (1)

5074 מַעֲטֶפֶת *maᵃṭep̱eṯ* (1)
capes (1)

5075 מְעִי *mᵉ'iy* (1)
heap (1)

5076 מָעַי *mā'ay* (1)
Maai (1)

5077 מְעִיל *mᵉ'iyl* (28)
robe (20)
cloak (4)
robes (2)
garment (1)
untranslated (1)

5078 מַעְיָן *ma'yān* (23)
springs (10)
spring (5)
springs (3) +4784
fountain (2)
fountains (1)
well (1)
wells (1)

5079 מְעִינִים *mᵉ'iyniym* (2)
untranslated (2)

5080 מָעַךְ *mā'aḵ* (4)
bruised (1)
fondled (1)
stuck (1)
were fondled (1)

5081 1מַעֲכָה *maᵃḵāh1* (3)
Maacah (3)

5082 2מַעֲכָה *maʿᵃkāh2* (19)
Maacah (19)

5083 מַעֲכַת *maʿᵃkāt* (1)
they[s] (1) +1770+2256

5084 מַעֲכָתִי *maʿᵃkātiy* (8)
Maacah (3)
Maacathite (3)
Maacathite (1) +1201
Maacathites (1)

5085 מָעַל *māʿal* (36)
unfaithful (13)
unfaithful (7) +5086
acted unfaithfully (2) +5086
acted unfaithfully (1)
betray (1)
break faith (1) +5086
broke faith (1)
commits a violation (1) +5086
forsaking (1) +5086
more and more unfaithful (1) +5086+8049
most unfaithful (1) +5086
treachery (1) +5086
unfaithfulness (1) +5086
unfaithfulness guilty of (1) +5086
unfaithfulness showed (1) +5086
violating the ban (1)
untranslated (1)

5086 1מַעַל *maʿal1* (29)
unfaithful (7) +5085
unfaithfulness (6)
acted unfaithfully (2) +5085
break faith (1) +5085
commits a violation (1) +5085
disobedience (1)
falsehood (1)
forsaking (1) +5085
matter (1)
more and more unfaithful (1) +5085+8049
most unfaithful (1) +5085
treachery (1) +5085
turning away (1)
unfaithfulness (1) +5085
unfaithfulness guilty of (1) +5085
unfaithfulness showed (1) +5085
untranslated (1)

5087 2מַעַל *maʿal2* (140)
more (36) +2025
above (19) +4946
upward (6) +2025+4200
above (4) +2025+4200+4946
above (3) +2025+4200
on (3) +2025
over (3) +2025+4200+4946
head (2) +2025+2256+4946+8900
higher (2) +2025
highly (2) +2025+4200
just above (2) +4946
over (2) +4946
top (2) +2025+4200+4946
up (2) +2025+4200
very (2) +2025+4200
above (1) +4200+4946+4946+6645
above (1) +4946+6584
at each successive level (1) +2025+2025+4200+4200+5087
beyond (1) +2025
deep (1) +2025
depth (1) +2025+4200
downstream (1) +2025+4200+4946
exceedingly (1) +2025+4200
heights (1) +2025+4200
high above (1) +2025+4200+4946
higher (1) +4946
higher than (1) +2025+4200+8049
in ascending stages (1) +2025+2025+4200+4200+5087
jointed (1) +4200+4946+8079
magnificence (1) +2025
more (1) +2025+4200
more and more powerful (1) +1541+2025+2143+2256+4200+6330
older (1) +2025
on high (1) +4946
outer (1) +2025+4200+4946
over and above (1) +2025+4200
overturned (1) +2025+2200+4200
project upward (1) +2025+4200
severe (1) +2025+4200
top (1)
top (1) +2025
top (1) +2025+4200
top of (1) +2025+4200+4946
upstream (1) +2025+4200
upward (1) +2025+4200+4946
very (1) +2025+4200+6330
wielding (1) +995+2025+4200
young and old (1) +2025+2256
untranslated (15)

5088 מֵעַל *mēʿal*
Variant; not used

5089 מֹעַל *mōʿal* (1)
lifted (1)

5090 מַעֲלֶה *maʿᵃleh* (16)
pass (7)
hill (2)
way (2)
ascent (1)
going up (1)
mount (1)
stairs (1)
way up (1)

5091 1מַעֲלָה *maʿᵃlāh1* (1)
what is going through (1)

5092 2מַעֲלָה *maʿᵃlāh2* (48)
steps (22)
ascents (15)
stairway (2)
flight of stairs (1)
journey (1)
lofty palace (1)
most exalted (1) +9366
untranslated (5)

5093 מַעְלָה *maʿlah*
Variant; not used

5094 מַעֲלִיל *maʿᵃliyl* (1)
untranslated (1)

5095 מַעֲלָל *maʿᵃlāl* (42)
deeds (16)
actions (8)
done (6)
practices (3)
dealings (1)
do (1)
evil practices (1)
sins (1)
ways (1)
what doing (1)
wicked deeds (1)
work (1)
untranslated (1)

5096 מַעֲמָד *maʿᵃmād* (5)
attending (2)
duty (1)
places (1)
position (1)

5097 מָעֳמָד *moʿᵒmād* (1)
foothold (1)

5098 מַעֲמָסָה *maʿᵃmāsāh* (1)
immovable (1)

5099 מַעֲמַקִּים *maʿᵃmaqqiym* (5)
depths (3)
deep (2)

5100 מַעַן *maʿan* (271)
so that (78)
to (36)
that (24)
for sake (22)
for the sake of (22)
because of (17)
so (17)
then (10)
and (7)
in order to (6)
for (5)
therefore (4)
bent on (1)
for then (1)
in behalf of (1)
in this way (1)
otherwise (1) +889+4202
that is why (1)
this (1)
thus (1)
till (1)
untranslated (14)

5101 1מַעֲנֶה *maʿᵃneh1* (7)
answer (2)
giving an apt reply (1) +7023
reply (1)
respond (1)
say (1)
way to refute (1)

5102 2מַעֲנֶה *maʿᵃneh2* (1)
ends (1)

5103 מַעֲנָה *maʿᵃnāh* (2)
acre (1) +7538
furrows (1)

5104 מְעוֹנָה *meʿōnāh* (9)
dens (5)
refuge (2)
den (1)
dwelling place (1)

5105 מַעֲנִית *maʿᵃniyt* (1)
untranslated (1)

5106 מַעַץ *maʿas* (1)
Maaz (1)

5107 מַעֲצֵבָה *maʿᵃsēbāh* (1)
torment (1)

5108 מַעֲצָד *maʿᵃsād* (2)
chisel (1)
tool (1)

5109 מַעְצוֹר *maʿsôr* (1)
hinder (1)

5110 מַעְצָר *maʿsār* (1)
self-control (1) +4200+8120

5111 מַעֲקֶה *maʿᵃqeh* (1)
parapet (1)

5112 מַעֲקַשִּׁים *maʿᵃqaššiym* (1)
rough places (1)

5113 מַעַר *maʿar* (2)
available space (1)
nakedness (1)

5114 1מַעֲרָב *maʿᵃrāb1* (9)
wares (8)
merchants (1) +6842

5115 2מַעֲרָב *maʿᵃrāb2* (15)
west (12)
place of setting (1)
west (1) +2025
untranslated (1)

5116 מַעֲרֶה *maʿᵃreh*
Variant; not used

5117 1מְעָרָה *meʿārāh1* (40)
cave (30)
caves (6)
den (1)
untranslated (3)

5118 2מְעָרָה *mᵉʿārāh2* (1)
wasteland (1)

5119 מַעֲרָךְ *maʿᵃrāḵ* (1)
plans (1)

5120 מַעֲרָכָה *maʿᵃrāḵāh* (19)
armies (3)
battle line (3)
ranks (3)
lines (2)
battle lines (1)
battle positions (1)
battlefield (1) +8441
facing each other (1) +7925
forces (1)
it[s] (1) +2021
proper kind (1)
row (1)

5121 מַעֲרֶכֶת *maʿᵃreḵeṯ* (10)
set out on the table (3)
consecrated bread (2)
row (2)
rows (1)
set out (1)
setting out the consecrated bread (1)

5122 מַעֲרֹם *maʿᵃrōm* (1)
naked (1)

5123 מַעֲרָץ *maʿᵃrāṣ*
Variant; not used

5124 מַעֲרָצָה *maʿᵃrāṣāh* (1)
great power (1)

5125 מַעֲרָת *maʿᵃrāṯ* (1)
Maarath (1)

5126 מַעֲשֶׂה *maʿᵃśeh* (236)
work (60)
works (17)
made (14)
what done (11)
what made (10)
deeds (8)
things (7)
like (6) +3869
everything (4) +3972
worked (4)
do (3)
like (3)
practices (3)
what[s] (3) +2021
crops (2)
deed (2)
done (2)
done (2) +6913
fashioned (2)
labor (2)
network (2) +8407
objects (2)
occupation (2)
products (2)
shape (2)
what deserve (2) +3869
what did (2)
working (2)
accomplished (1)
achievement (1) +4179
acting (1)
actions (1)
acts (1)
baked goods (1) +685+4407
baking (1)
basework (1) +4029
construction (1)
crafted (1)
creature made (1)
crime (1) +8288
crop (1)
customs (1)
design (1)
do (1) +3338
does (1)
duties (1)
formed (1)
fruit (1)
handiwork (1) +3338
how made (1)
idols made (1)
interwoven chains (1) +9249
is done (1) +6913
making (1)
man-made (1) +132+3338
network (1) +8422+8422
nothing (1) +4202
performance (1)
perfumes (1) +5351
projects (1)
property (1)
sculptured (1) +7589
shapes (1) +3338
structure (1)
that does (1)
that done (1)
that made (1)
things did (1)
things did (1) +3338
this[s] (1) +2021+2021+2296
trouble (1)
undertook (1)
verses (1)
way (1)
well-dressed hair (1) +5250
what do (1)
what make (1)
whatever do (1)
work (1) +6913
woven (1) +755
wrongdoing (1)
untranslated (2)

5127 מַעְשַׂי *maʿśay* (1)
Maasai (1)

5128 מַעֲשֵׂיָה *maʿᵃśēyāh* (16)
Maaseiah (16)

5129 מַעֲשֵׂיָהוּ *maʿᵃśēyāhû* (7)
Maaseiah (7)

5130 מַעֲשֵׂר *maʿᵃśēr* (32)
tithe (13)
tithes (13)
tenth (5)
setting aside a tenth (1) +6923

5131 מַעֲשַׁקּוֹת *maʿᵃšaqqôṯ* (2)
extortion (1)
tyrannical (1) +8041

5132 מֹף *mōp̱* (1)
Memphis (1)

5133 מִפְגָּע *mip̱gāʿ* (1)
target (1)

5134 מַפָּח *mappāḥ* (1)
gasp (1)

5135 מַפֻּחַ *mappuaḥ* (1)
bellows (1)

5136 מְפִיבֹשֶׁת *mᵉp̱iyḇōšeṯ* (15)
Mephibosheth (15)

5137 מֻפִּים *muppiym* (1)
Muppim (1)

5138 מֵפִיץ *mēp̱iyṣ* (1)
club (1)

5139 מַפָּל *mappāl* (2)
folds (1)
sweepings (1)

5140 מִפְלָאוֹת *mip̱lāʾôṯ* (1)
wonders (1)

5141 מִפְלַגָּה *mip̱laggāh* (1)
subdivisions (1)

5142 מַפָּלָה *mappālāh* (1)
ruins (1)

5143 מַפֵּלָה *mappēlāh* (2)
ruin (2)

5144 מִפְלָט *mip̱lāṭ* (1)
place of shelter (1)

5145 מִפְלֶצֶת *mip̱leṣeṯ* (4)
pole[s] (2)
repulsive (2)

5146 מִפְלָשׂ *mip̱lāś* (1)
hang poised (1)

5147 מַפֶּלֶת *mappeleṯ* (8)
fall (3)
downfall (2)
carcass (1)
fallen (1)
shipwreck (1)

5148 מִפְעָל *mip̱ʿāl* (1)
deeds (1)

5149 מִפְעָלָה *mip̱ʿālāh* (2)
what done (1)
works (1)

5150 מַפָּץ *mappāṣ* (1)
deadly (1)

5151 מַפֵּץ *mappēṣ* (1)
war club (1)

5152 מִפְקָד *mip̱qāḏ* (5)
number (2) +5031
appointment (1)
designated part (1)
inspection (1)

5153 מִפְרָץ *mip̱rāṣ* (1)
coves (1)

5154 מַפְרֶקֶת *map̱reqeṯ* (1)
neck (1)

5155 מִפְרָשׂ *mip̱rāś* (2)
sail (1)
spreads out (1)

5156 מִפְשָׂעָה *mip̱śāʿāh* (1)
buttocks (1)

5157 מִפְתָּח *mip̱tāḥ* (1)
open (1)

5158 מַפְתֵּחַ *map̱tēaḥ* (3)
key (2)
key for opening (1)

5159 מִפְתָּן *mip̱tān* (8)
threshold (8)

5160 מֵץ *mēṣ* (1)
oppressor (1)

5161 מֹץ *mōṣ* (8)
chaff (8)

5162 מָצָא *māṣāʾ* (456)
found (108)
find (85)
be found (25)
finds (16)
was found (12)
is found (11)
were (9)
been found (8)
were found (8)
come upon (7)
meet (7)
discovered (6)
finding (6)
is caught (6)
met (6)
pleased with (5) +928+2834+6524
present (5)
are (3)
came upon (3)

discover (3)
had (3) +907
handed (3)
came (2)
comprehend (2)
fathom (2)
happened (2)
have enough (2)
is (2)
lived (2)
overtook (2)
prospers (2) +3202
reach (2)
still (2)
survives (2)
was (2)
acquire (1)
acquired (1)
acquires (1)
afford (1) +1896+3338
are found (1)
be room enough (1)
be seen (1)
become (1)
been brought (1)
before (1)
bring a reward (1)
brings (1)
brings upon (1)
came across (1)
captured (1)
catch (1)
caught up (1)
comes (1)
detect (1)
discover meaning (1)
displease (1) +928+2834+4202+6524
displeasing (1) +928+2834+4202+6524
do (1)
doing (1)
enough (1)
ever-present (1) +4394
fall on (1)
favorable toward (1) +928+2834+6524
find out (1)
following (1)
found courage (1)
found out (1)
found to be true (1)
gain (1)
gained (1)
get (1)
had (1)
had (1) +4200
hand over (1) +928+3338
handed over (1) +928+3338
happened to (1)
has (1) +4200
have (1)
have (1) +928+3338
here (1)
hit (1)
is attained (1)
is captured (1)
is found (1) +5162
lay hold (1)
lay on (1)
lies (1)
lift (1)
looking for (1)
lot (1)
overcome (1)
overtake (1)
possess (1)
probe (1)
prosper (1) +3202
reaches (1)
reaped (1)
regards (1) +928+6524
regards (1) +4200+7156
search (1)
seize (1)
seized (1)
solved (1)
spreads (1)
still out (1)
took (1)
uncovered (1)
was caught (1)
were caught (1)
win (1)
untranslated (9)

5163 מַצָּב *maṣṣāḇ* (10)
outpost (4)
detachment (1)
garrison (1)
office (1)
outposts (1)
stood (1) +3922+8079
stood (1) +8079

5164 מֻצָּב *muṣṣāḇ* (2)
pillar (1)
towers (1)

5165 מַצָּבָה *maṣṣāḇāh* (1)
outpost (1)

5166 מִצָּבָה *miṣṣāḇāh*
Variant; not used

5167 מַצֵּבָה *maṣṣēḇāh* (34)
sacred stones (14)
pillar (10)
sacred stone (5)
monument (1)
pillars (1)
sacred pillars (1)
stone pillars (1)
untranslated (1)

5168 מְצֹבָיָה *m^{e}ṣōḇāyāh* (1)
Mezobaite (1)

5169 מַצֶּבֶת1 *maṣṣeḇeṯ1* (2)
stump (1)
stumps (1)

5170 מַצֶּבֶת2 *maṣṣeḇeṯ2* (2)
pillar (2)

5171 מְצָד *m^{e}ṣāḏ* (11)
strongholds (7)
fortress (2)
stronghold (2)

5172 מָצָה *māṣāh* (7)
be drained out (2)
drain dry (1)
drained to dregs (1) +9272
drink down (1)
drink up (1)
wrung out (1)

5173 מֹצָה *mōṣāh* (1)
Mozah (1)

5174 מַצָּה1 *maṣṣāh1* (53)
bread made without yeast (14)
unleavened bread (20)
without yeast (5)
bread without yeast (3)
bread (2)
made without yeast (2)
feast of unleavened bread (1)
prepared without yeast (1)
unleavened (1)
untranslated (4)

5175 מַצָּה2 *maṣṣāh2* (3)
quarrel (1)
quarrels (1)
strife (1)

5176 מֻצְהָב *muṣhāḇ*
Variant; not used

5177 מִצְהָלוֹת *miṣhālôṯ* (2)
lustful neighings (1)
neighing (1) +7754

5178 מָצוֹד1 *māṣôḏ1* (2)
net (1)
snare (1)

5179 מָצוֹד2 *māṣôḏ2* (1)
plunder (1)

5180 מְצוּדָה1 *m^{e}ṣûḏāh1* (3)
snare (2)
prey (1)

5181 מְצוּדָה2 *m^{e}ṣûḏāh2* (18)
fortress (9)
stronghold (7)
prison (1)
strong fortress (1) +1074

5182 מְצוֹדָה1 *m^{e}ṣôḏāh1* (1)
net (1)

5183 מְצוֹדָה2 *m^{e}ṣôḏāh2* (2)
fortress (1)
prison (1)

5184 מִצְוָה *miṣwāh* (184)
commands (138)
command (11)
commanded (4)
ordered (4)
commandments (3)
prescribed (3)
admonition (2)
commanded (2) +7422
instructions (2)
law (2)
commandment (1)
gave (1)
laws (1)
order (1)
orders (1)
rules (1)
terms (1)
way prescribed (1)
what ordered (1)
what^{s} (1) +2021+2021+2296
untranslated (3)

5185 מְצוֹלָה *m^{e}ṣôlāh* (12)
depths (9)
deep (2)
ravine (1)

5186 מָצוֹק *māṣôq* (6)
distress (3)
suffering (2)
stress (1)

5187 מָצוּק *māṣûq* (2)
foundations (1)
stood (1)

5188 מְצוּקָה *m^{e}ṣûqāh* (7)
distress (4)
anguish (3)

5189 מָצוֹר1 *māṣôr1* (22)
siege (15)
besieged (2)
besiege (1) +928+995+2021
laid siege (1) +928+995+2021
ramparts (1)
siege works (1)
siegeworks (1)

5190 מָצוֹר2 *māṣôr2* (4)
fortified (2)
defense (1)
stronghold (1)

5191 מָצוֹר3 *māṣôr3* (5)
Egypt (5)

5192 מָצוֹר4 *māṣôr4*
Variant; not used

5193 מְצוּרָה *m^{e}ṣûrāh* (8)
fortified (5)

defenses (1)
fortress (1)
siege works (1)

5194 מַצּוּת *maṣṣûṯ* (1)
enemies (1) +408

5195 מֵצַח *mēṣaḥ* (13)
forehead (8)
hardened (2) +2617
brazen look (1)
foreheads (1)
untranslated (1)

5196 מִצְחָה *miṣḥāh* (1)
greaves (1)

5197 מְצִלָּה *m^{e}ṣillāh* (1)
bells (1)

5198 מְצֻלָה *m^{e}ṣulāh*
Variant; not used

5199 מְצִלְתַּיִם *m^{e}ṣiltayim* (13)
cymbals (13)

5200 מִצְנֶפֶת *miṣnepeṯ* (12)
turban (11)
untranslated (1)

5201 מַצָּע *maṣṣā'* (1)
bed (1)

5202 מִצְעָד *miṣ'āḏ* (3)
steps (2)
submission (1)

5203 1מִצְעָר *miṣ'ār1* (5)
small (2)
humble (1)
little while (1)
only a few (1)

5204 2מִצְעָר *miṣ'ār2* (1)
Mizar (1)

5205 1מִצְפֶּה *miṣpeh1* (2)
place that overlooks (1)
watchtower (1)

5206 2מִצְפֶּה *miṣpeh2* (5)
Mizpah (4)
there^{s} (1) +1680

5207 מִצְפָּה *miṣpāh* (41)
Mizpah (39)
there^{s} (1) +928+2021
untranslated (1)

5208 מַצְפּוֹן *maṣpôn* (1)
hidden treasures (1)

5209 מָצַץ *māṣaṣ* (1)
drink deeply (1)

5210 מֵצַר *mēṣar* (3)
anguish (2)
distress (1)

5211 מַצָּרָה *maṣṣārāh*
Variant; not used

5212 מִצְרִי *miṣriy* (24)
Egyptian (21)
Egyptian's (2)
Egyptians (1)

5213 מִצְרַיִם *miṣrayim* (687)
Egypt (374)
Egypt (184) +824
Egyptians (82)
Egyptian (10)
Egypt's (5)
Mizraim (4)
lower Egypt (2) +824
them^{s} (2)
country (1)
Egypt (1) +1426
Egypt (1) +1473
Egyptians (1) +1201
here^{s} (1) +2025
his^{s} (1) +4200+4889
it^{s} (1) +4722
lower Egypt (1)
the Egyptians (1)
there^{s} (1)
there^{s} (1) +928
they^{s} (1)
who^{s} (1)
untranslated (11)

5214 מַצְרֵף *maṣrēp̱* (2)
crucible (2)

5215 מַק *maq* (2)
decay (1)
stench (1)

5216 1מַקֶּבֶת *maqqeḇeṯ1* (4)
hammer (3)
hammers (1)

5217 2מַקֶּבֶת *maqqeḇeṯ2* (1)
quarry (1) +1014

5218 מַקֵּדָה *maqqēḏāh* (9)
Makkedah (9)

5219 מִקְדָּשׁ *miqdāš* (75)
sanctuary (61)
sanctuaries (4)
holy place (2)
holiest (1)
holy places (1)
holy things (1)
it^{s} (1)
most holy place (1) +7731
sanctuary (1) +1074
shrine (1)
temple (1)

5220 מַקְהֵל *maqhēl* (2)
great assembly (1)
great congregation (1)

5221 מַקְהֵלוֹת *maqhēlôṯ* (2)
Makheloth (2)

5222 מִקְוֵא *miqwē'*
Variant; not used

5223 1מִקְוֶה *miqweh1* (5)
hope (5)

5224 2מִקְוֶה *miqweh2* (3)
collecting (1)
gathered (1)
reservoirs (1) +4784

5225 מִקְוָה *miqwāh* (1)
reservoir (1)

5226 מָקוֹם *māqôm* (401)
place (268)
home (14)
places (12)
land (5)
room (5)
site (4)
spot (4)
where^{s} (4)
dwelling place (3)
wherever (3) +889+928
anywhere (2) +928+3972
dwell (2)
everywhere (2) +3972
here^{s} (2) +2021+2021+2296
seat (2) +8699
sites (2)
space (2)
there^{s} (2)
where^{s} (2) +2021
wherever (2) +889+928+2021+3972
area (1)
base (1)
channels (1)
commands (1)
countries (1)
direction (1)
dwelling (1)
everywhere (1) +928+3972
everywhere (1) +2021+3972
haunt (1)
here^{s} (1) +928
here^{s} (1) +928+2021+2021+2296
here^{s} (1) +2021
homeland (1)
homeland (1) +824
homes (1)
it^{s} (1)
it^{s} (1) +2021+2021+2085
Nineveh^{s} (1) +2023
points (1)
position (1)
positions (1)
post (1)
proper place (1) +889+2118+9004
regions (1)
reside (1)
rest (1)
sanctuary (1) +7731
seated (1) +5989
somewhere (1)
suitable (1)
there^{s} (1) +2023
town (1)
town records (1) +9133
way (1)
where (1) +361
where dwells (1)
where lived (1)
where^{s} (1) +928
where^{s} (1) +928+2021
wherever (1) +285+889+928+2021
wherever (1) +889+2021+3972+6584
wherever (1) +889+928+2021
wherever (1) +928+2021+3972
wherever (1) +2021+3972+4946
wherever^{s} (1) +889
untranslated (13)

5227 מָקוֹר *māqôr* (18)
fountain (9)
spring (3)
assembly (1)
flow (1)
it^{s} (1)
source of (1)
springs (1)
well (1)

5228 מִקָּח *miqqāḥ* (1)
bribery (1) +8816

5229 מַקָּחוֹת *maqqāḥôṯ* (1)
merchandise (1)

5230 מִקְטָר *miqṭār* (1)
burning (1)

5231 מֻקְטָר *muqṭār* (1)
incense (1)

5232 מְקַטֶּרֶת *m^{e}qaṭṭereṯ* (1)
incense altars (1)

5233 מִקְטֶרֶת *miqṭereṯ* (2)
censer (2)

5234 מַקֵּל *maqqēl* (18)
staff (7)
branches (6)
branch (1)
staffs (1)
stick of wood (1)
sticks (1)
war clubs (1) +3338

5235 מִקְלוֹת *miqlôṯ* (4)
Mikloth (4)

5236 מִקְלָט *miqlāṭ* (20)
refuge (17)
place of refuge (1)
protection (1)

untranslated (1)

5237 מִקְלַעַת *miqla'aṯ* (4)
carved (2) +7844
carved (1)
engraving (1)

5238 מִקְנֶה *miqneh* (76)
livestock (45)
cattle (4)
flocks (4)
herdsmen (2) +8286
owned (2) +2118
acquired (1)
animal (1)
animals (1)
bought (1)
cattle (1) +1330
droves of livestock (1)
flocks (1) +7366
flocks and herds (1)
herds (1)
herds (1) +1330
herds and flocks (1)
herds of livestock (1)
herdsmen (1)
livestock (1) +989
sheep and goats (1) +7366
tend livestock (1) +408+2118
tended livestock (1) +408+2118
that[s] (1)
untranslated (1)

5239 מִקְנָה *miqnāh* (15)
bought (4)
purchase (3)
bought (2) +4084
price (2)
paid (1)
property (1)
untranslated (2)

5240 מִקְנֵיָהוּ *miqnēyāhû* (2)
Mikneiah (2)

5241 מִקְסָם *miqsām* (2)
divinations (2)

5242 מָקַץ *māqaṣ* (1)
Makaz (1)

5243 מִקְצוֹעַ *miqṣôa'* (12)
corners (5)
angle (4)
angle of the wall (1)
in each corner (1) +928+928+5243

5244 מַקְצֻעָה *maqṣu'āh* (1)
chisels (1)

5245 מָקַק *māqaq* (10)
waste away (4)
rot (3)
be dissolved (1)
fester (1)
wasting away (1)

5246 מִקְרָא *miqrā'* (23)
assembly (15)
assemblies (3)
another[s] (1) +7731
assemble (1)
calling together (1)
convocations (1) +7924
read (1)

5247 מִקְרֶה *miqreh* (10)
fate (4)
destiny (2)
as it turned out (1) +7936
by chance (1)
something happened (1)
that[s] (1)

5248 מְקָרֶה *m^eqāreh* (1)
rafters (1)

5249 מְקֵרָה *m^eqērāh* (2)
house (1)
summer palace (1)

5250 מִקְשֶׁה *miqšeh* (1)
well-dressed hair (1) +5126

5251 1מִקְשָׁה *miqšāh1* (9)
hammered (5)
hammered out (2)
hammer out (1) +6913
untranslated (1)

5252 2מִקְשָׁה *miqšāh2* (2)
field of melons (1)
melon patch (1)

5253 1מַר *mar1* (41)
bitter (18)
bitterness (7)
bitterly (4)
anguish (3)
bitter suffering (2)
bitter anguish (1)
deadly (1)
discontented (1) +5883
fierce (1) +5883
hot-tempered (1) +5883
in anguish (1) +5883
ruthless (1)

5254 2מַר *mar2* (1)
drop (1)

5255 מֹר *mōr* (12)
myrrh (12)

5256 1מָרָא *mārā'1*
Variant; not used

5257 2מָרָא *mārā'2* (1)
spreads feathers to run (1) +928+2021+5294

5258 3מָרָא *mārā'3*
Variant; not used

5259 4מָרָא *mārā'4* (1)
Mara (1)

5260 מַרְאֶה *mar'eh* (103)
appearance (14)
looked (10)
vision (10)
appears (5)
beautiful (5) +3202
appear (3)
appeared (3)
beautiful (3) +3637
like (3) +3869
that[s] (3)
face (2)
handsome (2) +3637
sight (2)
sleek (2) +3637
ugly (2) +8273
what sees (2)
clearly (1)
eye (1)
features (1)
handsome (1) +3202
huge (1)
imposing (1) +1524+4200
look (1)
look at (1)
looked (1) +8011
pattern (1)
saw (1) +6524
see (1)
see (1) +6524
seem (1)
sights (1)
sights (1) +6524
similar (1) +2021+3869
what[s] (1)
untranslated (14)

5261 1מַרְאָה *mar'āh1* (11)
vision (5)
visions (5)
it[s] (1) +2021

5262 2מַרְאָה *mar'āh2* (1)
mirrors (1)

5263 מֻרְאָה *mur'āh* (1)
crop (1)

5264 מְראוֹן *m^er'ôn*
Variant; not used

5265 מְרַאֲשׁוֹת *m^era'^{a}šôṯ* (13)
near head (4)
head (2)
under head (2)
by head (1)
heads (1)
untranslated (3)

5266 מֵרַב *mēraḇ* (4)
Merab (4)

5267 מַרְבַד *marḇaḏ* (2)
covered (1) +8048
coverings bed (1)

5268 מִרְבָּה *mirbāh* (1)
so much (1)

5269 מַרְבֶּה *marbeh* (3)
abundance (1)
increase (1)
untranslated (1)

5270 מַרְבִּית *marbiyṯ* (5)
most (2)
descendants (1) +1074
greatness (1)
profit (1)

5271 מַרְבֵּץ *marbēṣ* (2)
lair (1)
resting place (1)

5272 מַרְבֵּק *marbēq* (4)
fattened (3)
stall (1)

5273 מַרְגּוֹעַ *margôa'* (1)
rest (1)

5274 מַרְגְּלוֹת *marg^{e}lôṯ* (6)
feet (4)
legs (1)
untranslated (1)

5275 מַרְגֵּמָה *margēmāh* (1)
sling (1)

5276 מַרְגֵּעָה *margē'āh* (1)
place of repose (1)

5277 מָרַד *māraḏ* (25)
rebelled (12)
rebel (7)
revolt (2)
rebelling (1)
rebellion (1)
rebellious (1)
untranslated (1)

5278 1מֶרֶד *mereḏ1* (1)
rebellion (1)

5279 2מֶרֶד *mereḏ2* (2)
Mered (2)

5280 מַרְדּוּת *mardûṯ* (1)
rebellious (1)

5281 מְרֹדָךְ *m^erōḏāḵ* (1)
Marduk (1)

5282 מְרֹדַךְ־בַּלְאֲדָן *m^erōḏaḵ-bal'^{a}ḏān* (2)
Merodach-Baladan (2)

5283 מָרְדֳּכַי *morḏ^{o}kay* (60)
Mordecai (49)
Mordecai's (5)
he[s] (3)
him[s] (2)

he[s] (1) +408+2021

5284 מִרְדָּף *murdāp̱* (1)
aggression (1)

5285 מָרָה *mārāh*
Variant; not used

5286 1מָרָה *mārāh1* (44)
rebelled (20)
rebellious (9)
rebel (3)
defied (2)
rebels (2)
defying (1)
disobedient (1)
disobeyed (1)
hostility (1)
most rebellious (1) +5286
rebelling (1)
rebellion (1)

5287 2מָרָה *mārāh2*
Variant; not used

5288 3מָרָה *mārāh3* (5)
Marah (4)
its[s] (1) +4946

5289 מֹרָה *mōrāh* (2)
bitterness (1)
source of grief (1) +8120

5290 מַרְהֵבָה *marhēḇāh*
Variant; not used

5291 מָרוּד *mārûḏ* (3)
wandering (2)
wanderer (1)

5292 מֵרוֹז *mērôz* (1)
Meroz (1)

5293 מָרוֹחַ *mārôah* (1)
damaged (1)

5294 מָרוֹם *mārôm* (54)
on high (10)
heights (9)
heavens (4)
exalted (3)
high (3)
on high (3) +928+2021
pride (3)
above (1) +928+2021
arrogance (1)
exalted (1) +6639
haughty (1)
heaven (1)
height (1)
heights (1) +8031
heights above (1)
heights of heaven (1)
high positions (1)
highest point (1)
highest point (1) +1726
lofty (1)
on heights (1)
on high (1) +2021
on high (1) +2021+4200
on high (1) +4946
skies (1)
spreads feathers to run (1) +928+2021+5257

5295 מֵרוֹם *mērôm* (2)
Merom (2)

5296 מֵרוֹץ *mērôṣ* (1)
race (1)

5297 1מְרוּצָה *m[e]rûṣāh1* (5)
course (2)
runs (1)
untranslated (2)

5298 2מְרוּצָה *m[e]rûṣāh2* (1)
extortion (1)

5299 מְרוּקִים *m[e]rûqiym* (1)
beauty treatments (1)

5300 מָרוֹת *mārôṯ* (1)
Maroth (1)

5301 מַרְזֵחַ *marzēaḥ* (2)
feasting (1)
funeral meal (1)

5302 מָרַח *māraḥ* (1)
apply (1)

5303 מֶרְחָב *merḥāḇ* (6)
spacious place (3)
meadow (1)
setting free (1)
whole (1)

5304 מֶרְחָבְיָה *merḥāḇyāh*
Variant; not used

5305 מֶרְחָק *merḥāq* (18)
afar (4)
distant (4)
distant (2) +4946
far away (2)
distant lands (1)
far away (1) +4946
far-off (1)
faraway (1)
some distance away (1)
stretches afar (1)

5306 מַרְחֶשֶׁת *marḥešeṯ* (2)
pan (2)

5307 מָרַט *māraṭ* (14)
polished (5)
lost hair (2) +8031
smooth-skinned (2)
burnished (1)
made raw (1)
pulled (1)
pulled out beard (1)
pulled out hair (1)

5308 מְרִי *m[e]riy* (23)
rebellious (17)
rebellion (3)
bitter (1)
rebel (1) +2118
rebellious (1) +1201

5309 מְרִיא *m[e]riy'* (8)
fattened calves (3)
fattened animals (2)
choice (1)
fattened calf (1)
yearling (1)

5310 מֵרִיב *mēriyḇ*
Variant; not used

5311 מְרִיב בַּעַל *m[e]riyḇ ba'al* (3)
Merib-Baal (2)
who[s] (1)

5312 1מְרִיבָה *m[e]riyḇāh1* (2)
quarreling (1)
rebelled (1)

5313 2מְרִיבָה *m[e]riyḇāh2* (7)
Meribah (7)

5314 מְרִי־בַעַל *m[e]riy-ḇa'al* (1)
who[s] (1)

5315 מְרִיבַת קָדֵשׁ *m[e]riyḇaṯ qāḏēš* (4)
Meribah Kadesh (4)

5316 מְרָיָה *m[e]rāyāh* (1)
Meraiah (1)

5317 מֹרִיָּה *mōriyyāh* (2)
Moriah (2)

5318 מְרָיוֹת *m[e]rāyôṯ* (6)
Meraioth (6)

5319 מִרְיָם *miryām* (15)
Miriam (13)
her[s] (1)
she[s] (1)

5320 מְרִירוּת *m[e]riyrûṯ* (1)
bitter grief (1)

5321 מְרִירִי *m[e]riyriy* (1)
deadly (1)

5322 מֹרֶךְ *mōreḵ* (1)
fearful (1)

5323 מֶרְכָּב *merkāḇ* (3)
chariot (1)
seat (1)
sits (1)

5324 מֶרְכָּבָה *merkāḇāh* (44)
chariots (21)
chariot (20)
untranslated (3)

5325 מַרְכָּבוֹת *markāḇôṯ*
Variant; not used

5326 מַרְכֹּלֶת *markōleṯ* (1)
marketplace (1)

5327 1מִרְמָה *mirmāh1* (39)
deceit (12)
deceitful (9)
dishonest (4)
lies (4)
deception (3)
false (3)
deceitfully (2) +928
deceitfully (1)
treachery (1)

5328 2מִרְמָה *mirmāh2* (1)
Mirmah (1)

5329 מְרֵמוֹת *m[e]rēmôṯ* (7)
Meremoth (6)
Meremoth's (1)

5330 מִרְמָס *mirmās* (7)
trampled underfoot (2)
beaten down (1)
trample down (1) +8492
trampled (1)
what trampled (1) +8079
where run (1)

5331 מֵרֹנֹתִי *mērōnōṯiy* (2)
Meronothite (1)
of Meronoth (1)

5332 מֶרֶס *meres* (1)
Meres (1)

5333 מַרְסְנָא *mars[e]nā'* (1)
Marsena (1)

5334 מֵרַע *mēra'* (1)
evil (1)

5335 1מֵרֵעַ *mērēa'1* (8)
friend (3)
friends (3)
companions (1)
personal adviser (1)

5336 2מֵרֵעַ *mērēa'2*
Variant; not used

5337 מִרְעֶה *mir'eh* (13)
pasture (12)
place where fed (1)

5338 מַרְעִית *mar'iyṯ* (10)
pasture (8)
fed (1)
flock (1)

5339 מַרְעֲלָה *mar'[a]lāh* (1)
Maralah (1)

5340 1מַרְפֵּא *marpē'1* (14)
healing (8)
remedy (3)
healed (1)
health (1)
incurable (1) +401

5341 2מַרְפֵּא *marpē'2* (2)
at peace (1)
calmness (1)

5342 מַרְפֵּה *marpēh*
Variant; not used

5343 מִרְפָּשׂ *mirpāś* (1)
what muddied (1)

5344 מָרַץ *māraṣ* (4)
ails (1)
beyond all remedy (1)
bitter (1)
painful (1)

5345 מַרְצֵעַ *marṣēa'* (2)
awl (2)

5346 מַרְצֶפֶת *marṣepeṯ* (1)
base (1)

5347 מָרַק *māraq* (4)
be scoured (1)
cleanse away (1)
polish (1)
polished (1)

5348 מָרָק *mārāq* (3)
broth (3)

5349 מֶרְקָח *merqāh* (1)
perfume (1)

5350 מֶרְקָחָה *merqāhāh* (2)
pot of ointment (1)
spices (1)

5351 מִרְקַחַת *mirqahaṯ* (3)
fragrant (1)
perfumes (1) +5126
took care of mixing (1) +8379

5352 מָרַר *mārar* (14)
bitter (2)
made bitter (2)
bitterly (1)
bitterness attacked (1)
furiously (1)
grieve bitterly (1)
grieves (1)
in bitter distress (1)
made taste bitterness (1)
rage (1)
rebel (1)
suffered (1)

5353 מָרֹר *mārōr* (5)
bitter herbs (3)
bitter things (1)
bitterness (1)

5354 מְרֵרָה *m'rērāh* (1)
gall (1)

5355 מְרֹרָה *m'rōrāh* (2)
liver (1)
venom (1)

5356 1מְרָרִי *m'rāriy1* (39)
Merari (21)
Merarites (9) +1201
Merarite (7) +1201
Merarite (2)

5357 2מְרָרִי *m'rāriy2* (1)
Merarite (1)

5358 1מָרֵשָׁה *mārēšāh1* (6)
Mareshah (6)

5359 2מָרֵשָׁה *mārēšāh2* (2)
Mareshah (2)

5360 מִרְשַׁעַת *mirša'aṯ* (1)
wicked (1)

5361 מְרָתַיִם *m'rāṯayim* (1)
Merathaim (1)

5362 1מַשָּׂא *maśśā'1* (36)
burden (8)
load (7)
carry (5)
burdens (2)
carrying (2)
singing (2)
what to carry (2)
camel-loads (1) +1695
carried about (1)
desire (1)
loads (1)
oppression (1)
take away (1) +5911
that[s] (1)
tribute (1)

5363 2מַשָּׂא *maśśā'2* (30)
oracle (27)
oracles (1)
prophecies (1)
prophecy (1)

5364 3מַשָּׂא *maśśā'3* (2)
Massa (2)

5365 מַשֹּׂא *maśśō'* (1)
partiality (1) +7156

5366 מַשָּׂאָה *maśśā'āh* (1)
clouds of smoke (1)

5367 מַשְׂאוֹת *maś'ôṯ*
Variant; not used

5368 מַשְׂאֵת *maś'ēṯ* (15)
gifts (2)
tax (2)
burden (1)
cloud (1)
gift (1)
lifting up (1)
portion (1)
portions (1)
present (1)
signal (1)
smoke (1)
untranslated (2)

5369 1מִשְׂגָּב *miśgāḇ1* (17)
fortress (9)
stronghold (5)
refuge (2)
high (1)

5370 2מִשְׂגָּב *miśgāḇ2*
Variant; not used

5371 מַשֶּׂגֶת *maśśeḡeṯ*
Variant; not used

5372 מְשׂוּכָה *m'śûkkāh* (1)
hedge (1)

5373 מַשּׂוֹר *maśśôr* (1)
saw (1)

5374 מְשׂוּרָה *m'śûrāh* (4)
measure out (1)
measurements of quantity (1)
quantity (1)
rationed (1) +928

5375 1מָשׂוֹשׂ *māśôś1* (16)
joy (6)
delight (2)
gaiety (2)
rejoices (2)
celebrations (1)
joyful (1)
merriment (1)
rejoice greatly (1) +8464

5376 2מָשׂוֹשׂ *māśôś2* (1)
withers away (1)

5377 מִשְׂחָק *miśhāq* (1)
scoff (1)

5378 מַשְׂטֵמָה *maśṭēmāh* (2)
hostility (2)

5379 מְשֻׂכָה *m'śuḵāh* (1)
blocked (1)

5380 מַשְׂכִּיל *maśkiyl* (14)
maskil (13)
psalm of praise (1)

5381 מַשְׂכִּית *maśkiyṯ* (6)
carved (1)
carved images (1)
evil conceits (1)
idol (1)
imagine (1) +928
settings (1)

5382 מַשְׂכֹּרֶת *maśkōreṯ* (4)
wages (3)
rewarded (1)

5383 מַשְׂמֵרָה *maśmērāh* (1)
nails (1)

5384 מִשְׂפָּח *miśpāh* (1)
bloodshed (1)

5385 מִשְׂרָה *miśrāh* (2)
government (2)

5386 מִשְׂרָפוֹת *miśrāp̄ôṯ* (2)
burned (1)
funeral fire (1)

5387 מִשְׂרְפוֹת מַיִם *miśr'p̄ôṯ mayim* (2)
Misrephoth Maim (2)

5388 מַשְׂרֵקָה *maśrēqāh* (2)
Masrekah (2)

5389 מַשְׂרֵת *maśrēṯ* (1)
pan (1)

5390 מַשׁ *maš*
Variant; not used

5391 מַשָּׁא *maššā'* (4)
debts (1)
debts (1) +3338
exacting of usury (1)
usury (1)

5392 מֵשָׁא *mēšā'* (1)
Mesha (1)

5393 מַשְׁאָב *maš'āḇ* (1)
watering places (1)

5394 מַשָּׁאָה *maššā'āh* (1)
make a loan (1) +5957

5395 מַשֻּׁאָה *maššu'āh*
Variant; not used

5396 מַשָּׁאוֹן *maššā'ôn* (1)
deception (1)

5397 מַשֻּׁאוֹת *maššu'ôṯ* (2)
ruin (1)
ruins (1)

5398 מִשְׁאָל *miš'āl* (2)
Mishal (2)

5399 מִשְׁאָלָה *miš'ālāh* (2)
desires (1)
requests (1)

5400 מִשְׁאֶרֶת *miš'ereṯ* (4)
kneading trough (2)
kneading troughs (2)

5401 מִשְׁבְּצוֹת *mišb'ṣôṯ* (9)
filigree (3)
settings (3)
filigree settings (2)
interwoven (1)

5402 מַשְׁבֵּר *mašbēr* (3)
point of birth (2)
opening of the womb (1) +1201

5403 מִשְׁבָּר *mišbār* (5)
waves (3)

breakers (2)

5404 מִשְׁבַּת *mišbāṯ* (1)
destruction (1)

5405 מִשְׁגֶּה *mišgeh* (1)
mistake (1)

5406 מָשָׁה *māšāh* (3)
drew out (2)
drew (1)

5407 מֹשֶׁה *mōšeh* (767)
Moses (709)
he^{S} (19)
him^{S} (17)
Moses' (13)
his^{S} (3)
Moses' (1) +4200
untranslated (5)

5408 מַשֶּׁה *maššeh* (1)
creditor (1) +1251+2257+3338

5409 מְשׁוֹאָה *m^{e}šô'āh* (3)
ruin (1)
wasteland (1)
wastelands (1)

5410 מַשּׁוּאָה *maššû'āh*
Variant; not used

5411 מְשׁוֹבָב *m^{e}šôḇāḇ* (1)
Meshobab (1)

5412 מְשׁוּבָה *m^{e}šûḇāh* (14)
backsliding (4)
faithless (4)
waywardness (2)
backslidings (1)
turn away (1)
turn from (1)
untranslated (1)

5413 מְשׁוּגָה *m^{e}šûgāh* (1)
error (1)

5414 מָשׁוֹט *māšôṭ* (1)
oars (1)

5415 מִשּׁוֹט *miššôṭ* (1)
oars (1)

5416 מְשִׁסָּה *m^{e}šiwssāh* (1)
untranslated (1)

5417 מָשַׁח *māšaḥ* (71)
anointed (33)
anoint (24)
spread (4)
anointing (3)
was anointed (2)
been anointed (1)
decorates (1)
oil (1)
rubbed (1)
use (1)

5418 1מִשְׁחָה *mišḥāh1* (21)
anointing (21)

5419 2מִשְׁחָה *mišḥāh2* (2)
portion (1)
untranslated (1)

5420 1מָשְׁחָה *mošḥāh1* (1)
anointing (1)

5421 2מָשְׁחָה *mošḥāh2* (1)
portion (1)

5422 מַשְׁחִית *mašḥiyṯ* (16)
destroyer (4)
destructive (2)
corruption (1)
deathly pale (1)
destroy (1)
destroyers (1)
destroys (1)
destruction (1)
one who destroys (1) +1251
slaughter (1) +2222+4200
traps (1)
undoing (1)

5423 מִשְׁחָר *mišḥār* (1)
dawn (1)

5424 מַשְׁחֵת *mašḥēṯ* (1)
weapon (1) +3998

5425 מִשְׁחַת *mišḥaṯ* (1)
disfigured (1)

5426 מָשְׁחָת *mošḥāṯ* (1)
deformed (1)

5427 מִשְׁטוֹחַ *mišṭôaḥ* (3)
place to spread (2)
places for spreading (1)

5428 מִשְׁטָר *mišṭār* (1)
dominion (1)

5429 מֶשִׁי *mešiy* (2)
costly fabric (1)
costly garments (1)

5430 מְשֵׁיזַבְאֵל *m^{e}šēyzaḇ'ēl* (3)
Meshezabel (3)

5431 מָשִׁיחַ *māšiyaḥ* (38)
anointed (38)

5432 מָשַׁךְ *māšaḵ* (36)
drew (2)
tall (2)
archers (1) +8008
be delayed (1)
be prolonged (1)
bear (1)
cheering (1)
continue (1)
deferred (1)
delay (1)
drag away (1)
dragged off (1)
drags away (1)
drags off (1)
draw along (1)
drawn (1)
extend (1)
follow (1)
go at once (1)
joins (1)
lead the way (1)
led (1)
lure (1)
patient (1)
planter (1) +2446
prolong (1)
pull in (1)
pulled (1)
pulled up (1)
sound long (1)
sounds a long blast (1)
spread out (1)
take away (1)
worn (1) +928

5433 1מֶשֶׁךְ *mešeḵ1* (2)
price (1)
seed to sow (1) +2446

5434 2מֶשֶׁךְ *mešeḵ2* (10)
Meshech (10)

5435 מִשְׁכָּב *miškāḇ* (46)
bed (23)
beds (6)
bedroom (4) +2540
lies with (2)
bedding (1)
bier (1)
couch (1)
lie in death (1)
mat (1)
not a virgin (1) +2351+3359
slept with (1) +408+3359+4200
slept with (1) +2351+3359
slept with (1) +2351+3359+4200
slept with (1) +3359
taking rest (1) +8886

5436 מֹשְׁכוֹת *mōš^{e}ḵôṯ* (1)
cords (1)

5437 מְשַׁכֶּלֶת *m^{e}šakkeleṯ*
Variant; not used

5438 מִשְׁכָּן *miškān* (139)
tabernacle (102)
dwelling place (8)
tents (5)
dwellings (4)
dwelling (3)
it^{S} (3) +2021
dwelling places (2)
where dwells (2)
habitat (1)
homes (1)
houses (1)
lived (1)
place where dwell (1)
resting place (1)
tent (1)
untranslated (3)

5439 1מָשַׁל *māšal1* (17)
be like (2)
is like (2)
quote (2)
tell (2)
become like (1)
byword (1)
liken (1)
poets (1)
quote proverb (1)
quotes proverbs (1)
quoting (1)
reduced to (1)
telling (1)

5440 2מָשַׁל *māšal2* (81)
rule (28)
ruler (16)
rules (7)
ruled (6)
rulers (4)
ruler's (3)
govern (2)
ruling (2)
actually rule (1) +5440
controls (1)
dominion (1)
exercised (1)
gain control (1)
has right (1)
in charge (1)
made ruler (1)
make rulers (1)
master (1)
untranslated (2)

5441 3מָשַׁל *māšal3*
Variant; not used

5442 1מָשָׁל *māšāl1* (40)
oracle (7)
proverb (7)
proverbs (7)
byword (6)
discourse (2)
parable (2)
parables (2)
saying (2)
make sport of (1) +2118+4200
object of scorn (1)
ridicule (1) +5951
taunt (1)
taunt (1) +5951

5443 2מָשָׁל *māšāl2* (1)
Mashal (1)

5444 1מֹשֶׁל *mōšel1* (1)
equal (1)

5445 2מֹשֶׁל *mōšel2* (2)
power (1)
rule (1)

5446 מְשֹׁל *mᵉšōl*
Variant; not used

5447 מִשְׁלוֹחַ *mišlôah* (3)
giving (2)
lay (1)

5448 מִשְׁלָח *mišlāh* (7)
put to (6)
places where turned loose (1)

5449 מִשְׁלַחַת *mišlahat* (2)
band (1)
discharged (1)

5450 מְשֻׁלָּם *mᵉšullām* (25)
Meshullam (25)

5451 מְשִׁלֵּמוֹת *mᵉšillēmôt* (2)
Meshillemoth (2)

5452 מְשֶׁלֶמְיָה *mᵉšelemyāh* (1)
Meshelemiah (1)

5453 מְשֶׁלֶמְיָהוּ *mᵉšelemyāhû* (3)
Meshelemiah (3)

5454 מְשִׁלֵּמִית *mᵉšillēmiyt* (1)
Meshillemith (1)

5455 מְשֻׁלֶּמֶת *mᵉšullemet* (1)
Meshullemeth (1)

5456 מִשְׁלֹשׁ *mišlōš*
Variant; not used

5457 מְשַׁמָּה *mᵉšammāh* (7)
waste (4)
dried up (2)
object of horror (1)

5458 מִשְׁמָן *mišmān* (5)
fat (2)
richest (1)
sturdiest (1)
sturdy (1)

5459 מִשְׁמַנָּה *mišmannāh* (1)
Mishmannah (1)

5460 מַשְׁמַנִּים *mašmanniym* (1)
choice food (1)

5461 1מִשְׁמָע *mišmā'1* (1)
what hears (1)

5462 2מִשְׁמָע *mišmā'2* (4)
Mishma (4)

5463 מִשְׁמַעַת *mišma'at* (4)
bodyguard (3)
subject to (1)

5464 1מִשְׁמָר *mišmār1* (22)
custody (6)
guard (4)
else[s] (1)
guarded (1) +9068
guards (1)
guards (1) +408
imprisoned (1) +928+5989
other[s] (1)
posts (1)
prison (1) +1074
section (1)
services (1)
take command (1) +2118+4200
under guard (1) +6584

5465 2מִשְׁמָר *mišmār2*
Variant; not used

5466 מִשְׁמֶרֶת *mišmeret* (78)
duties (10)
requirements (7)
care (5)
responsibilities (4)
kept (3)
responsible (3)
service (3)
duty (2)
guarding (2) +9068
have charge of (2) +9068
keep (2)
order (2)
responsible for care (2)
what requires (2)
assigned (1)
guard (1)
guard (1) +9068
guarding (1)
guards (1)
in charge (1)
lead (1)
loyal (1) +9068
mission (1)
obligations (1)
on behalf of (1) +4200
positions (1)
post (1)
responsibility (1)
responsible (1) +9068
safe (1)
services (1)
serving (1)
specific things (1) +3998
take care of (1)
take care of (1) +2118+4200
under guard (1)
use (1)
watch (1)
untranslated (5)

5467 מִשְׁנֶה *mišneh* (34)
second (8)
next in rank (5)
double (4)
twice as much (4)
second District (3)
double portion (2)
copied (1) +4180
copy (1)
matching (1)
new quarter (1)
other (1)
second in rank (1)
second-in-command (1)
twice (1)

5468 מְשִׁסָּה *mᵉšissāh* (6)
plundered (3)
loot (2)
victim (1)

5469 מִשְׁעוֹל *miš'ôl* (1)
narrow path (1)

5470 מִשְׁעִי *miš'iy* (1)
make clean (1)

5471 מִשְׁעָם *miš'ām* (1)
Misham (1)

5472 מִשְׁעָן *miš'ān* (4)
supplies (2)
support (2)

5473 מַשְׁעֵן *maš'ēn* (1)
supply (1)

5474 מַשְׁעֵנָה *maš'ēnāh* (1)
support (1)

5475 מִשְׁעֶנֶת *miš'enet* (11)
staff (9)
cane (1)
staffs (1)

5476 מִשְׁפָּחָה *mišpāhāh* (304)
clan (131)
clans (124)
peoples (8)
families (7)
family (7)
clan by clan (2) +4200
people (2)
clan (1) +3+1074
each clan (1) +5476
every family (1) +2256+5476
kinds (1)
kingdoms (1)
Levites (1) +4291
nation (1)
one kind after another (1) +2157+4200
untranslated (13)

5477 מִשְׁפָּט *mišpāt* (424)
justice (94)
laws (83)
just (28)
judgment (24)
right (13)
cause (11)
judgments (11)
regulations (11)
specified (8)
ordinances (7)
punishment (6)
law (5)
sentence (5)
case (4)
prescribed (4)
rights (4)
standards (4)
decision (3)
injustice (3) +4202
ordinance (3)
prescribed way (3)
requirements (3)
what requires (3)
commands (2)
court (2)
custom (2)
decisions (2)
judge (2)
judging (2)
justly (2)
legal (2)
practice (2)
practices (2)
proper procedure (2)
sentenced (2)
specifications (2)
trial (2)
verdict (2) +1821
what do[s] (2)
accuser (1) +1251
accuses (1) +2021+4200+7756
always do (1)
bloodshed (1) +1947
capital offense (1) +4638
charges (1)
customs (1)
decided (1)
defense (1)
deserve (1)
deserving (1)
dimensions (1)
disputes decided (1)
do (1)
due (1)
honest (1)
honestly (1)
inquiring (1)
judge (1) +9149
judges (1) +6913
justice of cause (1)
kind (1)
lawsuits (1)
like (1) +3869
making decisions (1)
manner (1)
means of making decisions (1)

place of judgment (1)
plan (1)
precepts (1)
prescribed (1) +3869
proper place (1)
punish (1) +6913
quotas (1) +3869
regulation (1)
regulations prescribed (1)
render judgment (1) +9149
right way (1)
rightfully (1)
rule (1)
share (1)
standards measuring (1)
statutes (1)
unjust (1) +4202
verdict (1)
vindication (1)
way prescribed (1)
untranslated (5)

5478 מִשְׁפְּתַיִם *mišpᵉṯayim* (2)
campfires (1)
two saddlebags (1)

5479 מֶשֶׁק *mešeq* (1)
one who will inherit (1) +1201

5480 מַשָּׁק *maššāq* (1)
swarm (1)

5481 מְשֻׁקָּד *mᵉšuqqāḏ* (6)
shaped like almond flowers (4)
untranslated (2)

5482 1מַשְׁקֶה *mašqeh1* (19)
cupbearer (10)
cupbearers (2)
goblets (2) +3998
liquid (1)
position (1)
water (1)
well watered (1)
well-watered (1)

5483 2מַשְׁקֶה *mašqeh2*
Variant; not used

5484 מִשְׁקוֹל *mišqôl* (1)
weigh out (1)

5485 מַשְׁקוֹף *mašqôp̄* (3)
top (2)
tops (1)

5486 מִשְׁקָל *mišqāl* (49)
weight (20)
weighing (16)
weighed (6)
exact weight (1)
force (1)
paid (1) +5989
rationed (1) +928
set of scales (1) +4404
weighed out (1)
untranslated (1)

5487 מִשְׁקֶלֶת *mišqeleṯ* (2)
plumb line (2)

5488 מִשְׁקָע *mišqā'* (1)
clear (1)

5489 מִשְׁרָה *mišrāh* (1)
juice (1)

5490 מִשְׁרָעִי *mišrā'iy* (1)
Mishraites (1)

5491 מָשַׁשׁ *māšaš* (9)
grope (2)
searched through (2)
felt (1)
grope about (1)
touched (1)
touches (1)
untranslated (1)

5492 מִשְׁתֶּה *mišteh* (46)
banquet (12)
feast (12)
feasting (8)
drink (3)
drinking (2)
banquet (1) +3516
banquets (1)
dinner (1)
feasts (1)
meal (1)
table (1)
that[s] (1)
untranslated (2)

5493 1מַת *mōṯ1* (20)
men (11)
few (3)
few in number (1) +5071
friends (1)
little (1)
only a few (1) +5031
people (1)
very few (1) +5031

5494 2מֹת *mōṯ2*
Variant; not used

5495 מַתְבֵּן *maṯbēn* (1)
straw (1)

5496 מֶתֶג *meṯeḡ* (4)
bit (3)
halter (1)

5497 מֶתֶג הָאַמָּה *meṯeḡ hā'ammāh* (1)
Metheg Ammah (1)

5498 מָתוֹק *māṯôq* (12)
sweet (10)
sweeter (2)

5499 מְתוּשָׁאֵל *mᵉṯûšā'ēl* (2)
Methushael (2)

5500 מְתוּשֶׁלַח *mᵉṯûšelah* (6)
Methuselah (6)

5501 מָתַח *māṯah* (1)
spreads out (1)

5502 מִתְחָה *miṯhāh*
Variant; not used

5503 מָתַי *māṯay* (43)
how long (27) +6330
when (11)
how long (2)
for how long (1) +6330
how long (1) +339+6388
setting the time (1) +4200

5504 מַתְכֹּנֶת *maṯkōneṯ* (5)
formula (2)
number (1)
original design (1)
standard measure (1)

5505 מַתְלָאָה *matlā'āh*
Variant; not used

5506 מְתַלְּעוֹת *mᵉṯallᵉ'ôṯ* (3)
fangs (2)
jaws (1)

5507 מְתֹם *mᵉṯōm* (4)
health (2)
all (1)
soundness (1)

5508 1מַתָּן *matān1* (5)
gift (3)
gifts (2)

5509 2מַתָּן *matān2* (3)
Mattan (3)

5510 1מַתָּנָה *matānāh1* (17)
gifts (9)
gift (5)
bribe (1)
bribes (1)
given (1)

5511 2מַתָּנָה *matānāh2* (2)
Mattanah (2)

5512 מִתְנִי *miṯniy* (1)
Mithnite (1)

5513 מַתְּנַי *matnay* (3)
Mattenai (3)

5514 מַתַּנְיָה *matanyāh* (13)
Mattaniah (13)

5515 מַתַּנְיָהוּ *matanyāhû* (3)
Mattaniah (3)

5516 מָתְנַיִם *māṯnayim* (47)
waist (16)
side (4)
waists (4)
backs (3)
body (2)
loins (2)
there[s] (2)
tuck cloak into belt (2) +2520
armor (1)
belt (1) +258
bodies (1)
brace yourselves (1) +2616
cloak tucked into belt (1) +2520
get ready (1) +273
heart (1)
make wear (1) +6584+6590
put on (1) +928+8492
sets about work (1) +2520
strutting rooster (1) +2435
tucking cloak into belt (1) +9113

5517 מָתַק *māṯaq* (6)
sweet (4)
enjoyed sweet (1)
feasts on (1)

5518 מָתֵק *māṯēq* (2)
pleasant (1)
pleasantness (1)

5519 מֹתֶק *mōṯeq* (1)
sweet (1)

5520 מִתְקָה *miṯqāh* (2)
Mithcah (2)

5521 מִתְרְדָת *miṯrᵉḏāṯ* (2)
Mithredath (2)

5522 מַתָּת *mataṯ* (6)
gift (3)
as much as pleases (2) +3338
gifts he does not give (1) +9214

5523 מַתַּתָּה *matatāh* (1)
Mattattah (1)

5524 מַתִּתְיָה *matityāh* (4)
Mattithiah (4)

5525 מַתִּתְיָהוּ *matityāhû* (4)
Mattithiah (4)

5526 נ *n*
Variant; not used

5527 ־ָן *- ān* (36)
their (9)
they (5)
them (4)
each (2)
the creatures[s] (1)
the rooms[s] (1)
the[s] (1)
you (1)
untranslated (12)

5528 1נָא *nā'1* (405)
please (59)
now (22)

I beg you (5)
then (4)
come now (3) +6964
I would like (2)
all right (1)
but (1)
I pray (1)
if you will (1)
O (1)
please (1) +1065
please (1) +3283
quick (1)
right now (1)
so (1)
therefore (1)
very well (1) +2180
we pray (1)
untranslated (297)

5529 2נָא *nā'2* (1)
raw (1)

5530 נֹא *nō'* (4)
Thebes (4)

5531 נֹא אָמוֹן *nō' 'āmôn* (1)
Thebes (1)

5532 נֹאד *nōḏ* (7)
skin (2)
wineskins (2) +3516
jars (1)
scroll (1)
wineskin (1)

5533 נָאָה *nā'āh* (3)
beautiful (2)
adorns (1)

5534 נָאוֶה *nā'weh* (10)
fitting (4)
lovely (4)
beautiful (1)
unsuited (1) +4202

5535 נָאַם *nā'am* (1)
declare (1)

5536 נְאֻם *nᵉ'um* (376)
declares (363)
oracle (9)
says (3)
declared (1)

5537 נָאַף *nā'ap̱* (31)
commit adultery (7)
adulterers (6)
committed adultery (5)
adulteress (3)
adulterer (2)
adulterous (2)
adultery (2)
commits adultery (2)
adulteries (1)
untranslated (1)

5538 נַאֲפוּפִים *na'ᵃp̱ûp̱iym* (1)
unfaithfulness (1)

5539 נִאֻפִים *ni'up̱iym* (2)
adulteries (1)
adultery (1)

5540 נָאַץ *nā'as* (24)
spurned (5)
despise (4)
revile (2)
treated with contempt (2)
despised (1)
is blasphemed (1)
made show utter contempt (1) +5540
rejected (1)
rejecting (1)
reviled (1)
reviles (1)
spurns (1)
treat with contempt (1)
treating with contempt (1)

5541 נְאָצָה *nᵉ'āṣāh* (2)
disgrace (2)

5542 נֶאָצָה *ne'āṣāh* (3)
blasphemies (2)
contemptible things (1)

5543 נָאַק *nā'aq* (2)
groan (1) +5544
groans (1)

5544 נְאָקָה *nᵉ'āqāh* (4)
groaning (2)
groan (1) +5543
groaned (1)

5545 נָאַר *nā'ar* (2)
abandoned (1)
renounced (1)

5546 נֹב *nōḇ* (6)
Nob (6)

5547 נָבָא *nāḇā'* (115)
prophesy (47)
prophesying (28)
prophesied (26)
prophesies (8)
acts like a prophet (1)
frantic prophesying (1)
poses as a prophet (1)
prophetic (1)
untranslated (2)

5548 נָבַב *nāḇaḇ*
Variant; not used

5549 1נְבוֹ *nᵉḇô1* (11)
Nebo (11)

5550 2נְבוֹ *nᵉḇô2* (1)
Nebo (1)

5551 3נְבוֹ *nᵉḇô3* (1)
Nebo (1)

5552 נְבוּ שַׂר־סְכִים *nᵉḇû śar-sᵉḵiym* (1)
Nebo-Sarsekim (1)

5553 נְבוּאָה *nᵉḇû'āh* (3)
prophecy (2)
prophesied (1) +1819

5554 נָבוּב *nāḇûḇ* (4)
hollow (3)
witless (1)

5555 נְבוּזַרְאֲדָן *nᵉḇûzar'ᵃḏān* (15)
Nebuzaradan (15)

5556 נְבוּכַדְנֶאצַּר *nᵉḇûkaḏne'ssar* (28)
Nebuchadnezzar (26)
his^{s} (1)
untranslated (1)

5557 נְבוּכַדְרֶאצַּר *nᵉḇûkaḏre'ssar* (34)
Nebuchadnezzar (31)
his^{s} (1) +4200
Nebuchadnezzar's (1) +4200
untranslated (1)

5558 נְבוּשַׁזְבָּן *nᵉḇûšazbān* (1)
Nebushazban (1)

5559 נָבוֹת *nāḇôṯ* (22)
Naboth (17)
Naboth's (4)
he^{s} (1)

5560 נָבַח *nāḇah* (1)
bark (1)

5561 1נֹבַח *nōḇah1* (1)
Nobah (1)

5562 2נֹבַח *nōḇah2* (2)
Nobah (2)

5563 נִבְחַז *niḇhaz* (1)
Nibhaz (1)

5564 נָבַט *nāḇat* (70)
look (20)
looked (7)
consider (6)
see (3)
tolerate (3)
gaze (2)
have regard for (2)
look down (2)
look up (2)
looks (2)
seen (2)
detect (1)
esteem (1)
have regard for (1) +4200
let look (1)
look around (1)
look on (1)
look with favor (1) +7156
looked around (1)
looked over (1)
looks down (1)
observe (1)
sees (1)
stare (1)
viewed (1)
views (1)
watch (1)
watches over (1)
watching (1)
untranslated (1)

5565 נְבָט *nᵉḇāt* (25)
Nebat (25)

5566 נָבִיא *nāḇiy'* (316)
prophet (152)
prophets (150)
he^{s} (1) +2021+3758
him^{s} (1) +2021+3759
his own^{s} (1) +2021+2021+2418
his^{s} (1) +2021
one^{s} (1) +2021
prophecy (1)
prophesy (1)
prophet's (1)
them^{s} (1) +2021
these men^{s} (1) +1201+2021
those who prophesy (1)
untranslated (3)

5567 נְבִיאָה *nᵉḇiy'āh* (6)
prophetess (6)

5568 נְבָיוֹת *nᵉḇāyôṯ* (5)
Nebaioth (5)

5569 נֵבֶךְ *nēḇeḵ* (1)
springs (1)

5570 1נָבֵל *nāḇēl1* (20)
fading (3)
fall (3)
wither (3)
lose heart (2)
withers (2)
crumbles (1)
die away (1)
only wear out (1) +5570
shrivel up (1)
shriveled (1)
withered (1)

5571 2נָבַל *nāḇal2* (5)
dishonor (1)
dishonors (1)
played the fool (1)
rejected (1)
treat with contempt (1)

5572 1נָבָל *nāḇāl1* (19)
fool (9)
foolish (4)
fools (2)
base (1)
lawless (1)
no understanding (1)

wicked fools (1)

5573 2נָבָל *nāḇāl2* (21)
Nabal (18)
Nabal's (2)
he[S] (1)

5574 1נֵבֶל *nēḇel1* (11)
skin (3)
wineskin (2)
jars (1)
jugs (1)
pots (1)
pottery (1) +3450
skins (1)
water jars (1)

5575 2נֵבֶל *nēḇel2* (27)
lyres (15)
lyre (7)
harps (4)
harp (1)

5576 נְבָלָה *nᵉḇālāh* (13)
disgraceful thing (4)
folly (3)
disgraceful (2)
vileness (2)
outrageous things (1)
wicked thing (1)

5577 נְבֵלָה *nᵉḇēlāh* (48)
body (13)
carcasses (13)
carcass (5)
dead bodies (5)
anything found dead (3)
it[S] (2) +2021
already dead (1)
animal found dead (1)
bodies (1)
found dead (1)
lifeless forms (1)
untranslated (2)

5578 נַבְלוּת *naḇlûṯ* (1)
lewdness (1)

5579 נְבַלַּט *nᵉḇallāṭ* (1)
Neballat (1)

5580 נָבַע *nāḇaʿ* (11)
gushes (2)
bubbling (1)
celebrate (1) +2352
give a bad smell (1) +944
overflow (1)
pour forth (1)
pour out (1)
poured out (1)
spew (1)
utter (1)

5581 נִבְשָׁן *niḇšān* (1)
Nibshan (1)

5582 נֶגֶב *negeḇ* (111)
south (38)
Negev (36)
south (9) +2025
southern (6)
south (4) +4946
south (3) +2025+9402
southern (3) +2025
Negev (2) +824
south (2) +2025+2025+9402
south (2) +9402
southeast (1) +2025+2025+7711
southeast (1) +2025+7711
southern (1) +448+6991
southern (1) +4946
southland (1)
southland (1) +8441

5583 נָגַד *nāḡaḏ* (372)
tell (93)
told (87)
was told (23)
reported (15)
declare (14)
proclaim (11)
announce (8)
explain (6)
report (5)
answered (4)
give (4)
inform (4)
revealed (4)
said (4)
declared (3)
explained (3)
foretold (3)
show (3)
brought report (2)
denounces (2)
foretell (2)
heard (2)
informed (2)
messenger (2)
speak (2)
telling (2)
tells (2)
warned (2)
admit (1)
announces (1)
announcing (1)
assured (1) +5583
be sure to tell (1) +5583
been brought to attention (1) +2256+9048
been shown (1)
been told (1)
been told about (1) +5583
confess (1)
confront (1)
declares (1)
declaring (1)
describe (1)
disclose (1)
do so[S] (1)
explaining (1)
expose (1)
exposed (1)
give an answer (1)
give answer (1) +5583
kept secret (1) +401
learn (1)
learned (1) +4200
let know (1)
made clear (1)
make known (1)
message (1)
messenger[S] (1)
must report (1) +5583
parade (1)
proclaiming (1)
report came back (1)
reveals (1)
sent word (1) +2256+8938
showed (1)
shown (1)
speak up (1)
spoke (1)
tell answer (1)
tell the news (1)
testify (1)
testimony (1)
told answer (1)
utter (1)
was reported (1)
were clearly told (1) +5583
word came (1)
untranslated (4)

5584 נֶגֶד *negeḏ* (151)
before (29)
opposite (15)
before (13) +4200
in the presence of (7)
in front of (6)
from (5) +4946
facing (3)
in (3)
near (3)
presence (3)
before (2) +7156
by (2)
distance (2)
far from (2) +4946
in (2) +4200
in front of (2) +4200
in presence (2) +4200+6524
in the presence of (2) +2025
in the sight of (2)
nearby (2) +4946
opposite (2) +4200
regard (2) +4200+8492
straight in (2)
accompany (1) +2143+4200
across the way (1) +4946
against (1)
aloof (1) +4946
away from (1) +4946
because of (1) +4946
before (1) +4200+6524
bent on (1) +7156
beyond (1)
constant (1) +4946
defend (1) +6641
directly (1)
facing (1) +4946
from (1) +4946+6524
frontal (1) +4946
in broad daylight (1) +2021+9087
in sight (1)
in the face of (1) +4200
kept distance (1) +3656+4946
known to (1)
next to (1) +4200
opposite (1) +4946
out of (1) +4946
resisted (1) +4200+6641
responsible for (1) +4200
right before (1) +4200
risked (1) +4946+8959
some distance (1)
straight (1)
straight through (1)
succeed against (1) +4200
suitable (1) +3869
suitable for (1) +3869
to (1)
with (1)
untranslated (3)

5585 נָגַהּ *nāḡah* (6)
turns into light (2)
burning (1)
dawned (1)
give (1)
shine (1)

5586 1נֹגַהּ *nōḡah1* (19)
brightness (5)
brilliant light (2)
dawn (2)
no longer shine (2) +665
radiance (2)
bright (1)
flashing (1)
glow (1)
light (1)
ray of brightness (1)
splendor (1)

5587 2נֹגַהּ *nōḡah2* (2)
Nogah (2)

5588 נְגֹהָה *nᵉḡōhāh* (1)
brightness (1)

5589 נְגוֹ *nᵉḡô*
Variant; not used

5590 נָגַח *nāgaḥ* (11)
gore (3)
gores (3)
butting (1)
charged (1)
engage in battle (1)
push back (1)
untranslated (1)

5591 נַגָּח *naggāḥ* (2)
goring (2)

5592 נָגִיד *nāgiyḏ* (44)
leader (13)
ruler (12)
prince (3)
in charge (2)
officers (2)
official in charge (2)
administrators (1)
chief (1)
commanders (1)
leaders (1)
nobles (1)
officer (1)
officer in charge (1)
rulers (1)
supervisor (1)
worthy things (1)

5593 נְגִינָה *n^egiynāh* (14)
stringed instruments (9)
mock in song (2)
music (1)
song (1)
songs (1)

5594 נָגַן *nāgan* (15)
harpist (2)
play (2)
play (2) +928+3338
play the harp (2)
playing the harp (2) +928+3338
musicians (1)
playing (1)
plays (1)
plays an instrument (1)
sing (1)

5595 נָגַע *nāga'* (150)
touches (43)
touched (24)
touch (17)
came (6)
come (4)
reached (4)
arrived (3)
reaches (3)
struck (3)
afflicted (2)
get (2)
reach (2)
reaching (2)
strike (2)
strikes (2)
add (1)
afford (1) +1896+3338
approach (1)
are plagued (1)
attack (1)
befall (1)
bother (1)
bring down (1)
brought down (1)
casts down (1)
draws near (1)
drew near (1)
extend (1)
follows (1)
happened (1)
inflicted (1)
is[s] (1)
laid (1)
let themselves be driven back (1)
level (1)
molest (1)
molests (1)
near (1)
pierces (1)
plagued (1)
put (1)
seize (1)
stricken (1)
touching (1)
went (1)
untranslated (1)

5596 נֶגַע *nega'* (78)
mildew (15)
infectious (11)
sore (11)
contamination (3)
disaster (3)
infected person (3)
it[s] (3) +2021
affected article (2)
afflictions (2)
contaminated (2)
diseases (2)
article[s] (1)
assault (1)
assaults (1) +4200+5596
Blows (1)
contaminated article (1)
flogging (1)
floggings (1)
infected person (1) +5999
infection (1)
person[s] (1)
plague (1)
scourge (1)
sores (1)
spreading mildew (1) +7669
stricken (1)
this kind of sore (1) +2021+5999
wounds (1)
untranslated (3)

5597 נָגַף *nāgap̱* (49)
be defeated (5)
strike (5)
been defeated (4)
strike down (3)
struck down (3)
were defeated (3)
afflicted (2)
been routed (2)
struck (2)
stumble (2)
was defeated (2)
was routed (2)
bring defeat upon (1)
defeated (1)
defeating (1)
defeating (1) +5597
hit (1)
inflicts (1)
injures (1)
plague (1)
routed (1)
strike with a plague (1)
struck with a plague (1)
were beaten (1)
were routed (1)

5598 נֶגֶף *negep̱* (7)
plague (6)
causes to stumble (1)

5599 נָגַר *nāgar* (10)
rushing (2)
delivered over (1)
flow (1)
given over (1) +3338+6584
hand over (1)
pour (1)
pours out (1)
spilled (1)
stretched out (1)

5600 נִגֶּרֶת *niggereṯ*
Variant; not used

5601 נָגַשׂ *nāgaś* (23)
slave drivers (5)
oppressor (3)
require payment (2)
ruler (2)
driver's (1)
exacted (1)
exploit (1)
hard pressed (1)
in distress (1)
oppress (1)
oppress each other (1)
oppressors (1)
slave driver's (1)
tax collector (1)
was oppressed (1)

5602 נָגַשׁ *nāgaš* (125)
approached (12)
bring (11)
come near (11)
brought (7)
came (7)
approach (6)
went up (5)
come (4)
take (4)
went (3)
advanced (2)
brought close (2)
came up (2)
close (2)
come close (2)
come forward (2)
come here (2)
get so close (2)
go (2)
go up (2)
presented (2)
abstain from sexual relations (1) +440+448+851
assemble (1) +3481
be brought (1)
be overtaken (1)
bring in (1)
bring near (1)
brings (1)
came forward (1)
came near (1)
came over (1)
confront (1)
done so[s] (1)
draw near (1)
drew near (1)
get out (1)
give more space (1)
go near (1)
march out (1)
moved forward (1)
offered (1)
overtake (1)
place (1)
present (1)
sacrifice (1)
set (1)
set forth (1)
step forward (1)
stepped forward (1)
took (1)
touch (1)
went close (1)
went over (1)
were fettered (1) +4200+5733

5603 נֵד *nēḏ* (4)
heap (2)
wall (2)

5604 נָדָא *nādā'* (1)
untranslated (1)

5605 נָדַב *nādab* (17)
brought as freewill offerings (1) +5607
freewill offerings (1)
gave freewill offerings (1)
gave willingly (1)
give generously (1)
given freely (1)
given willingly (1)
prompts to give (1)
volunteered (1)
volunteered himself for service (1)
willing (1)
willing (1) +4213
willing (1) +8120
willing response (1)
willing volunteers (1)
willingly given (1)
willingly offer themselves (1)

5606 נָדָב *nādāb* (20)
Nadab (19)
Nadab's (1)

5607 נְדָבָה *n^edābāh* (26)
freewill offerings (10)
freewill offering (7)
freely (2)
willing (2)
abundant (1)
brought as freewill offerings (1) +5605
freewill (1)
voluntarily (1)
untranslated (1)

5608 נְדַבְיָה *n^edabyāh* (1)
Nedabiah (1)

5609 נִדְגָּלוֹת *nidgālôt*
Variant; not used

5610 נָדַד *nādad* (28)
flee (5)
fled (3)
banished (2)
fugitives (2)
strays (2)
be cast aside (1)
could not (1)
flapped (1)
flee in haste (1) +5610
flown away (1)
fluttering (1)
fly away (1)
in flight (1)
nothing (1)
refugees (1)
strayed (1)
wanderers (1)
wanders about (1)

5611 נְדֻדִים *n^edudiym* (1)
toss (1) +8425

5612 נָדָה *nādāh* (2)
exclude (1)
put off (1)

5613 נֵדֶה *nēdeh* (1)
fee (1)

5614 נִדָּה *niddāh* (29)
period (7)
cleansing (6)
monthly period (3)
unclean thing (3)
act of impurity (1)
corruption (1)
defilement (1)
impurity (1)
impurity of monthly period (1)
monthly flow (1)
monthly period (1) +1864
monthly period (1) +1865
polluted (1)
woman's monthly uncleanness (1) +2021+3240

5615 1נָדַח *nādah1* (55)
banish (6)
banished (6)
exiles (5)
been scattered (3)
drive (2)
fugitives (2)
led astray (2)
strays (2)
are drawn away (1)
be driven away (1)
be enticed (1)
be thrust (1)
been banished (1)
been driven (1)
chased away (1)
disperses (1)
drive out (1)
driven (1)
driven away (1)
enticed (1)
estranged (1)
exiled (1)
hunted (1)
outcast (1)
pushing (1)
scatter (1)
scattered (1)
seduced (1)
spewed out (1)
straying (1)
topple (1)
turn (1)
turn away (1)
were exiled (1)
untranslated (1)

5616 2נָדַח *nādah2* (3)
bring (1)
putting (1)
swings (1)

5617 נֹדִי *nōdiy*
Variant; not used

5618 נָדִיב *nādiyb* (27)
nobles (8)
princes (5)
willing (3)
noble (2)
ruler (2)
willing (2) +4213
great man's (1)
nobleman (1)
officials (1)
prince's (1)
royal (1)

5619 נְדִיבָה *n^ediybāh* (3)
noble (2)
dignity (1)

5620 1נָדָן *nādān1* (1)
sheath (1)

5621 2נָדָן *nādān2* (1)
gifts (1)

5622 נָדַף *nādap* (9)
windblown (3)
blow away (2)
blows away (1)
fleeting (1)
is blown away (1)
refute (1)

5623 נָדַר *nādar* (31)
made a vow (4) +5624
vowed (3) +5624
made vow (2) +5624
make a vow (2) +5624
makes a vow (2) +5624
vow (2)
vow made (2) +5624
made a vow (1)
made vow (1)
made vows (1) +5624
make a special vow (1) +7098
make a vow (1)
make vows (1)
make vows (1) +5624
makes a vow (1)
making a vow (1)
making vow (1)
vowed (1)
vows (1)
vows made (1) +5624
vows to give (1)

5624 נֶדֶר *nēder* (60)
vows (21)
vow (13)
made a vow (4) +5623
vowed (3)
vowed (3) +5623
made vow (2) +5623
make a vow (2) +5623
makes a vow (2) +5623
vow made (2) +5623
fulfill a special vow (1) +7098
made vows (1) +5623
make vows (1) +5623
makes a special vow (1) +7098
special vow (1) +7098
special vows (1) +7098
vows made (1) +5623
what promised (1)

5625 נֹהַּ *nōah* (1)
value (1)

5626 ־נָה *-nāh* (214)
it (84)
her (22)
them (9)
its (6)
which[s] (5)
they (4)
she (3)
that (3)
the lampstand[s] (3)
him (2)
the[s] (2)
this (2)
everything (1) +3972
himself (1)
incense[s] (1)
one (1)
so[s] (1)
the animal[s] (1)
the city[s] (1)
the flock[s] (1)
the food[s] (1)
the land[s] (1)
their (1)
themselves (1)
which (1)
widow[s] (1)
untranslated (55)

5627 1נָהַג *nāhag1* (30)
carried off (3)
guiding (3)
lead (3)
led (3)
drive (2)
guide (2)
drive away (1)
driven away (1)
drives (1)
driving (1)
drove (1)
drove ahead (1)
guided (1)
lead away (1)

lead on (1) +2143+2256
led forth (1)
led in triumphal procession (1)
led out (1)
made blow (1)
take (1)

5628 2נָהַג *nāhag2* (1)
moan (1)

5629 1נָהָה *nāhāh1* (3)
mourned (1)
taunt (1)
wail (1)

5630 2נָהָה *nāhāh2*
Variant; not used

5631 נְהִי *n[e]hiy* (7)
wail (2)
mourners (1) +3359
mournful song (1)
mourning (1)
wail (1) +5951
wailing (1)

5632 נִהְיָה *nihyāh*
Variant; not used

5633 נָהַל *nāhal* (10)
guide (3)
brought (1)
gently leads (1)
lead (1)
leads (1)
move along (1)
put (1)
took care of (1)

5634 נַהֲלָל *nah[a]lāl* (2)
Nahalal (2)

5635 1נַהֲלֹל *nah[a]lōl1* (1)
water holes (1)

5636 2נַהֲלֹל *nah[a]lōl2* (1)
Nahalol (1)

5637 נָהַם *nāham* (5)
groan (2)
growl (1)
roar (1)
roaring (1)

5638 נַהַם *naham* (2)
roar (2)

5639 נְהָמָה *n[e]hāmāh* (2)
anguish (1)
roaring (1)

5640 נָהַק *nāhaq* (2)
bray (1)
brayed (1)

5641 1נָהַר *nāhar1* (3)
stream (3)

5642 2נָהַר *nāhar2* (3)
radiant (2)
rejoice (1)

5643 נָהָר *nāhār* (119)
river (58)
rivers (23)
streams (12)
Trans-Euphrates (4) +2021+6298
canal (3)
seas (3)
Euphrates[S] (2)
flood (2)
riverbed (2)
waters (2)
canals (1)
currents (1)
rivers (1) +5707
untranslated (5)

5644 נְהָרָה *n[e]hārāh* (1)
light (1)

5645 נַהֲרַיִם *nah[a]rayim*
Variant; not used

5646 1נוּ־ *-nû1* (1656)
us (701)
our (670)
we (94)
our (22) +4200
our own (12)
ourselves (10)
ours (7)
the[S] (6)
it (5)
we (5) +5883
ourselves (3) +5883
us (3) +5883
me (2)
ours (2) +4200
a[S] (1)
each other (1) +9109
he[S] (1) +466+3378
here[S] (1)
one (1)
ours (1) +4200+7156
that (1)
us (1) +6524
us deserve (1)
we (1) +3972
we're (1)
what[S] (1)
you (1)
untranslated (101)

5647 2נוּ־ *-nû2* (511)
him (174)
it (85)
them (48)
he (24)
his (10)
my wrath[S] (8)
they (8)
animal[S] (2)
its (2)
the altar[S] (2)
the ephod[S] (2)
the servant[S] (2)
themselves (2)
whom (2)
Abimelech[S] (1)
Absalom[S] (1)
all he has[S] (1)
all[S] (1)
another[S] (1)
any[S] (1)
drink[S] (1)
Edom[S] (1)
hers (1)
his (1) +4946
his own (1)
Jeremiah[S] (1)
Judah[S] (1)
man[S] (1)
manna[S] (1)
one (1)
the blood[S] (1)
the man[S] (1)
the meat[S] (1)
the oil[S] (1)
the roof[S] (1)
the sacred portion[S] (1)
the wicked[S] (1)
their (1)
their own (1)
there[S] (1)
these tithes[S] (1)
this bread[S] (1)
those[S] (1)
what (1)
who (1)
untranslated (109)

5648 נוא *nû'* (9)
forbids (2)
discourage (1) +4213
discouraged (1) +4213
forbid (1)
forbidden (1)
refuse (1)
thwarts (1)
untranslated (1)

5649 נוּב *nûḇ* (4)
bear fruit (1)
brings forth (1)
increase (1)
make thrive (1)

5650 נֹוב *nôḇ* (1)
untranslated (1)

5651 נוֹבַי *nôḇāy* (1)
untranslated (1)

5652 נוּג *nûḡ* (1)
sorrows (1)

5653 נוּד *nûḏ* (26)
flee (3)
mourn (3)
wanderer (2)
away (1)
comfort (1)
comforted (1)
drive away (1)
fluttering (1)
go astray (1)
make wander (1)
moaning (1)
mourn loss (1)
shake (1)
shake head in scorn (1)
shake heads in scorn (1)
show sympathy (1)
swaying (1)
sways (1)
sympathize (1)
sympathy (1)
untranslated (1)

5654 1נוֹד *nôḏ1* (1)
lament (1)

5655 2נוֹד *nôḏ2* (1)
Nod (1)

5656 נוֹדָב *nôḏāḇ* (1)
Nodab (1)

5657 1נָוָה *nāwāh1* (1)
at rest (1)

5658 2נָוָה *nāwāh2* (1)
praise (1)

5659 1נָוֶה *nāweh1* (32)
pasture (9)
dwelling (3)
house (3)
grazing land (2)
homeland (2)
pastureland (2)
abode (1)
dwelling place (1)
dwelling places (1)
haunt (1)
haunts (1)
home (1)
land (1)
pastures (1)
pleasant place (1)
property (1)
settlement (1)

5660 2נָוֶה *nāweh2*
Variant; not used

5661 3נָוָה *nāwāh3* (15)
pastures (7)
camps (1) +1074
dwell (1)
dwellings (1)

grasslands (1)
haunts (1)
meadows (1)
pasturelands (1)
place (1)

5662 נָוֹת *nāwôṯ* (1)
untranslated (1)

5663 1נוּחַ *nûah1* (143)
leave (11)
given rest (8)
put (8)
rest (7)
left (6)
kept (5)
rested (5)
set (5)
at rest (4)
give rest (4)
leave alone (4)
place (4)
placed (4)
find rest (3)
gave rest (3)
gives rest (3)
settle (3)
subside (3)
allowed (2)
came to rest (2)
granted rest (2)
laid (2)
put down (2)
set up (2)
allied (1)
allowed to remain (1)
be set (1)
brought (1)
cast (1)
comes to rest (1)
deposited (1)
forsake (1)
get relief (1)
give peace (1)
gives relief (1)
giving rest (1)
got relief (1)
have rest (1)
lay (1)
lay to rest (1)
lays (1)
left unweighed (1)
let be idle (1)
let go (1) +906+3338
let remain (1)
lowered (1)
permits (1)
remain (1)
reposes (1)
resides (1)
resting (1)
safely (1)
save (1)
saved (1)
set down (1)
settled (1)
settled down (1)
store (1)
store up (1)
subsided (1)
throw (1)
tolerate (1)
touch (1)
wait patiently (1)
waited (1)

5664 2נוּחַ *nûah2*
Variant; not used

5665 נוֹחַ *nôah* (1)
resting place (1)

5666 נוֹחָה *nôhāh* (1)
Nohah (1)

5667 נוּט *nûṭ* (1)
shake (1)

5668 נָוִית *nāwiyṯ* (5)
untranslated (5)

5669 נָזֶל *nāzel*
Variant; not used

5670 נוּם *nûm* (6)
slumber (3)
sleep (2)
slumbers (1)

5671 נוּמָה *nûmāh* (1)
drowsiness (1)

5672 1נוּן *nûn1* (2)
continue (1)
untranslated (1)

5673 2נוּן *nûn2* (30)
Nun (30)

5674 נוּס *nûs* (160)
fled (63)
flee (38)
flees (7)
ran (7)
fleeing (6)
run (5)
escape (3)
flee away (3)
escaped (2)
fugitives (2)
draining away (1)
drives along (1)
fled back (1)
fled up (1)
flee in haste (1) +4960
flight (1)
forced to flee (1) +5674
fugitive (1)
get away (1)
get away (1) +5674
gone (1)
hurried to bring (1)
keep (1)
leave (1)
made good escape (1) +2256+4880
on the run (1)
put to flight (1)
retreat (1)
routed (1)
running away (1)
turned and ran (1)
untranslated (1)

5675 נוּעַ *nûa'* (42)
shake (5)
hold sway (3)
shaken (3)
make wander about (2)
restless (2)
stagger (2)
staggered (2)
tosses (2)
wander about (2)
crooked (1)
disturb (1)
grope (1)
is shaken (1)
made wander (1)
moving (1)
reels (1) +5675
set trembling (1)
shaking (1)
shook (1)
sways (1)
tremble (1)
trembled (1)
wander (1)
wandering (1)
untranslated (3)

5676 נוֹעַדְיָה *nô'aḏyāh* (2)
Noadiah (2)

5677 1נוּף *nûp̱1* (35)
wave (12)
waved (4)
presented (3)
present (2)
use (2)
beckon (1) +3338
put (1)
raise (1)
raised (1)
raises (1)
shake (1)
shakes (1)
sweep (1)
used (1)
uses (1)
was waved (1) +9485
wield (1)

5678 2נוּף *nûp̱2* (2)
gave (1)
perfumed (1)

5679 נוֹף *nôp̱* (1)
loftiness (1)

5680 נוּץ *nûs* (1)
flee (1)

5681 נוֹצָה *nôsāh* (3)
plumage (2)
feathers (1)

5682 נוּק *nûq*
Variant; not used

5683 נוּשׁ *nûš* (1)
helpless (1)

5684 1נָזָה *nāzāh1* (24)
sprinkle (17)
spattered (2)
sprinkled (2)
is spattered (1)
sprinkles (1)
untranslated (1)

5685 2נָזָה *nāzāh2*
Variant; not used

5686 נָזִיד *nāziyḏ* (6)
stew (6)

5687 נָזִיר *nāziyr* (16)
Nazirite (8)
Nazirites (2)
prince (2)
untended vines (2)
princes (1)
separation (1)

5688 נָזַל *nāzal* (11)
flow (3)
descend (1)
made flow (1)
pour down moisture (1)
quaked (1)
shower down (1)
spread abroad (1)
streaming down (1)
streams (1)

5689 נֹזֵל *nōzēl* (5)
streams (3)
running water (1)
surging (1)

5690 נֶזֶם *nezem* (17)
ring (5)
earrings (4)
rings (4)
earring (2)
nose ring (2)

5691 נֵזֶק *nēzeq* (1)
disturbing (1)

5692 1נָזַר *nāzar1* (5)
consecrated themselves (1)
fast (1)
keep separate (1)
separates himself (1)
treat with respect (1)

5693 2נָזַר *nāzar2* (5)
separation (2)
abstain (1)
dedicate (1)
Nazirite (1)

5694 נֵזֶר *nēzer* (25)
crown (7)
separation (6)
dedicated (3)
diadem (3)
Nazirite (2)
dedication (1)
hair (1)
symbol of separation (1)
untranslated (1)

5695 נֹחַ *nōah* (47)
Noah (40)
Noah's (3)
he^{s} (2)
his^{s} (2)

5696 נַחְבִּי *nahbiy* (1)
Nahbi (1)

5697 1נָחָה *nāḥāh1* (35)
lead (11)
guide (9)
led (6)
guided (4)
guides (2)
disperses (1)
lead out (1)
ushers (1)

5698 2נָחָה *nāḥāh2*
Variant; not used

5699 נַחוּם *nahûm* (1)
Nahum (1)

5700 נְחוּם *n*^{e}*hûm* (1)
Nehum (1)

5701 נָחוֹר *nāḥôr* (18)
Nahor (16)
Nahor's (2)

5702 נָחוּשׁ *nāḥûš* (1)
bronze (1)

5703 נְחוּשָׁה *n*^{e}*ḥûšāh* (10)
bronze (8)
bronze-tipped (1)
copper (1)

5704 נְחִילוֹת *n*^{e}*ḥiylôṯ* (1)
flutes (1)

5705 נָחִיר *nāḥiyr* (1)
nostrils (1)

5706 נָחַל *nāhal* (59)
inherit (6)
assign as an inheritance (2)
distribute (2)
gave inheritance (2)
giving as an inheritance (2)
inheritance (2)
lead to inherit (2)
receive inheritance (2)
received (2)
received inheritance (2)
allotted (1)
assign inheritance (1)
assigned (1)
been allotted (1)
bestowing (1)
cause to inherit (1)
divide (1)
divide as inheritance (1)
divide for an inheritance (1)
dividing (1)
gave (1)
get inheritance (1)
give as an inheritance (1)
give inheritance (1)
has inherit (1)
have inheritance (1)
have inheritance (1) +5709
help assign (1)
heritage (1)
inherit land (1)
inheritance given (1)
inherits (1)
leaves an inheritance (1)
pass on as an inheritance (1)
possess (1)
possessed (1)
reassign (1)
receive (1)
receive inheritance (1) +5709
received as an inheritance (1)
take as inheritance (1)
take possession (1)
will (1)
wills (1)
untranslated (1)

5707 1נַחַל *nahal1* (139)
valley (34)
gorge (19)
river (17)
streams (12)
ravine (11)
ravines (9)
stream (8)
wadi (7)
brook (5)
torrent (3)
torrents (2)
valleys (2)
course (1)
intermittent streams (1)
poplars (1) +6857
rivers (1)
rivers (1) +5643
shaft (1)
stream beds (1)
streams (1) +692
there^{s} (1) +928+7724
untranslated (1)

5708 2נַחַל *nahal2*
Variant; not used

5709 1נַחֲלָה *nah*^{a}*lāh1* (222)
inheritance (185)
heritage (5)
inherit (3)
part (3)
property (3)
inheritances (2)
one^{s} (2)
territory (2)
that^{s} (2)
ancestral property (1)
estate (1)
have inheritance (1) +5706
inherited (1)
it^{s} (1)
land (1)
land inherited (1)
land inherits (1)
lands (1)
place (1)
receive inheritance (1) +5706
territories (1)
territory inherit (1)
untranslated (2)

5710 2נַחֲלָה *nah*^{a}*lāh2* (1)
disease (1)

5711 3נַחֲלָה *nah*^{a}*lāh3* (2)
wadi (2)

5712 נַחֲלִיאֵל *nah*^{a}*liy'ēl* (2)
Nahaliel (2)

5713 נֶחֱלָמִי *neh*^{e}*lāmiy* (3)
Nehelamite (3)

5714 נָחַם *nāham* (108)
comfort (23)
comforted (5)
express sympathy (5)
relent (5)
be comforted (4)
change mind (4)
comforts (4)
was grieved (4)
console (3)
grieved (3)
have compassion (3)
relented (3)
am grieved (2)
be consoled (2)
comforter (2)
comforters (2)
compassion (2)
consoled (2)
give comfort (2)
relents (2)
be avenged (1)
change minds (1)
consoling himself (1)
find comfort (1)
get relief (1)
given comfort (1)
giving comfort (1)
had compassion (1)
have pity (1)
look with compassion (1)
pity (1)
reassured (1)
reconsider (1)
recovered from grief (1)
relent and do not bring (1)
relent and not bring (1)
relent so that not bring (1)
relented and did not (1)
repent (1)
repented (1)
repents (1)
show compassion (1)
showed pity (1)
was comforted (1)
was consoled (1)
were consoled (1)

5715 נַחַם *naham* (1)
Naham (1)

5716 נֹחַם *nōham* (1)
compassion (1)

5717 נֶחָמָה *nehāmāh* (2)
comfort (1)
consolation (1)

5718 נְחֶמְיָה *n*^{e}*hemyāh* (8)
Nehemiah (8)

5719 נִחֻמִים *nihumiym* (3)
comfort (1)
comforting (1)
compassion (1)

5720 נַחֲמָנִי *nah*^{a}*māniy* (1)
Nahamani (1)

5721 נַחְנוּ *nahnû* (6)
we (5)
untranslated (1)

5722 נָחַץ *nāhas* (1)
urgent (1)

5723 נָחַר *nāhar* (2)
angry (1)

blow fiercely (1)

5724 נַחַר *naḥar* (1)
snorting (1)

5725 נַחֲרָה *naḥᵉrāh* (1)
snorting (1)

5726 נַחְרַי *naḥray* (2)
Naharai (2)

5727 נָחַשׁ *nāḥaš* (11)
divination (2)
find things out by divination (1) +5727
interprets omens (1)
learned by divination (1)
practice divination (1)
sorcery (1)
took as a good sign (1)
uses for divination (1) +5727

5728 נַחַשׁ *naḥaš* (2)
sorcery (2)

5729 1נָחָשׁ *nāḥāš1* (31)
snake (14)
serpent (11)
snakes (3)
serpent's (2)
venomous snakes (1)

5730 2נָחָשׁ *nāḥāš2*
Variant; not used

5731 3נָחָשׁ *nāḥāš3* (9)
Nahash (8)
him[s] (1)

5732 נַחְשׁוֹן *naḥšôn* (10)
Nahshon (10)

5733 1נְחֹשֶׁת *nᵉḥōšeṯ1* (140)
bronze (128)
bronze shackles (5)
copper (4)
chains (1)
wealth (1)
were fettered (1) +4200+5602

5734 2נְחֹשֶׁת *nᵉḥōšeṯ2*
Variant; not used

5735 נְחֻשְׁתָּא *nᵉḥuštā'* (1)
Nehushta (1)

5736 נְחֻשְׁתָּן *nᵉḥuštān* (1)
Nehushtan (1)

5737 נָחַת *nāḥaṯ* (10)
bend (2)
bring down (1)
come (1)
come down (1)
descend (1)
go down (1)
impresses (1)
level (1)
pierced (1) +928

5738 1נַחַת *naḥaṯ1* (1)
coming down (1)

5739 2נַחַת *naḥaṯ2* (6)
rest (2)
comfort (1)
peace (1)
quiet (1)
tranquillity (1)

5740 3נַחַת *naḥaṯ3* (5)
Nahath (5)

5741 נָחֵת *nāḥēṯ* (1)
going down (1)

5742 נָטָה *nāṭāh* (217)
stretch out (22)
stretched out (20)
outstretched (18)
turn (12)
pitched (10)
pay attention (7) +265
turned (7)
give ear (6) +265
stretches out (5)
upraised (5)
deprive (4)
deny (3)
pervert (3)
spread out (3)
took aside (3)
turn aside (3)
turned away (3)
deprive of justice (2)
evening (2)
extended (2)
held out (2)
listen (2) +265
parted (2)
pitch (2)
spread (2)
swerve (2)
afternoon (1) +2021+3427
applying (1)
be stretched out (1)
bend (1)
bent down (1)
brandishes (1)
conspired (1)
did this[s] (1) +2257+3338
directs (1)
extend (1)
get back on (1)
get off (1)
giving (1)
go ahead (1)
go forward (1)
grow long (1)
hear (1) +265
hold out (1)
inclined (1) +4213
kept away (1)
lay (1)
lead (1)
leaning (1)
led astray (1)
led astray (1) +4213
let be drawn (1)
let down (1)
lie down (1)
listen closely (1) +265
listen well (1) +265
measures (1)
misleads (1)
outspread (1)
paid any attention (1) +265+4200+9048
paid attention (1) +265
part (1)
perverted (1)
plot (1)
pushed (1)
raised (1)
set (1)
shakes (1)
showed (1)
shown (1)
siding (1)
slipped (1)
spreads out (1)
stay (1)
stays only a night (1) +4328
strayed (1)
stretch wide (1)
stretched (1)
throw (1)
thrust (1)
turn away (1)
turned aside (1)
turning (1)
turning aside (1)
went over (1)
withholds (1)
won over (1)
yield (1)
untranslated (3)

5743 נְטוֹפָתִי *nᵉṭôp̱āṯiy* (11)
Netophathite (8)
Netophathites (3)

5744 נָטִיל *nāṭiyl* (1)
who trade with (1)

5745 נָטִיעַ *nāṭiya'* (1)
plants (1)

5746 נְטִישׁוֹת *nᵉṭiyšôṯ* (3)
branches (2)
spreading branches (1)

5747 נָטַל *nāṭal* (4)
giving (1)
laid (1)
lifted up (1)
weighs (1)

5748 נֵטֶל *nēṭel* (1)
burden (1)

5749 נָטַע *nāṭa'* (59)
plant (28)
planted (19)
are planted (1)
farmers (1)
firmly embedded (1)
implanted (1)
pitch (1)
plants (1)
replanted (1)
set in place (1)
set out (1)
set up (1)
untranslated (2)

5750 נֶטַע *neṭa'* (4)
garden (1)
plant (1)
plants (1)
set out (1)

5751 נְטָעִים *nᵉṭā'iym* (1)
Netaim (1)

5752 נָטַף *nāṭap̱* (18)
drip (3)
prophesy (3)
preach (2)
dripped (1)
dripping (1)
drop (1)
fell gently (1)
poured (1)
poured down (1)
poured down rain (1)
preaching (1)
prophet (1)
prophets say (1)

5753 נָטָף *nāṭāp̱* (1)
gum resin (1)

5754 נֶטֶף *neṭep̱* (1)
drops (1)

5755 נְטִפָה *nᵉṭip̱āh* (2)
earrings (1)
pendants (1)

5756 נְטֹפָה *nᵉṭōp̱āh* (2)
Netophah (2)

5757 1נָטַר *nāṭar1* (9)
angry (2)
bear a grudge against (1)
harbor anger (1)
maintains wrath (1)
neglected (1) +4202
take care of (1)
tenants (1)
tend (1)

5758 2נָטַר *nāṭar2*
Variant; not used

5759 נָטַשׁ *nāṭaš* (40)
abandoned (5)
forsake (5)
left (4)
leave (3)
reject (3)
spread out (3)
abandon (1)
be abandoned (1)
brought down (1)
cast out (1)
deserted (1)
drawn (1)
drop (1)
forgo (1)
hangs loose (1)
let (1)
rejected (1)
scattered (1)
spread (1)
spreading out (1)
stopped thinking (1)
throw (1)
unused (1)

5760 נִי *niy* (1)
wail (1)

5761 ־נִי *-niy* (1315)
me (1011)
I (204)
my (28)
us (12)
myself (3)
him (2)
mine (2) +4946
we (2)
how I long for (1) +4769+5989
I'll (1)
untranslated (49)

5762 נִיב *niyḇ* (2)
it[s] (1)
praise (1)

5763 נֵיבָי *neyḇāy* (1)
Nebai (1)

5764 נִיד *niyḏ* (1)
comfort (1)

5765 נִידָה *niyḏāh* (1)
unclean (1)

5766 נָיוֹת *nāyôṯ* (6)
Naioth (6)

5767 נִיחֹחַ *niyhōah* (43)
pleasing (39)
fragrant incense (4) +8194

5768 1נִין *niyn1*
Variant; not used

5769 2נִין *niyn2* (3)
offspring (2)
children (1)

5770 נִינְוֵה *niynᵉwēh* (17)
Nineveh (16)
Ninevites (1) +408

5771 נִיס *niys* (1)
untranslated (1)

5772 נִיסָן *niysān* (2)
Nisan (2)

5773 נִיצוֹץ *niyṣôṣ* (1)
spark (1)

5774 1נִיר *niyr1* (2)
break up (2)

5775 2נִיר *niyr2* (5)
lamp (5)

5776 3נִיר *niyr3* (3)
unplowed ground (2)
field (1)

5777 1נָכָא *nāḵā'1* (1)
were driven out (1)

5778 2נָכָא *nāḵā'2* (1)
grieve (1)

5779 נָכֵא *nāḵē'* (3)
crushed (2)
crushes (1)

5780 נְכֹאת *nᵉḵō'ṯ* (2)
spices (2)

5781 נֶכֶד *neḵeḏ* (3)
descendants (3)

5782 נָכָה *nāḵāh* (501)
struck down (57)
killed (39)
struck (34)
defeated (32)
strike (28)
put (24)
attacked (21)
kill (15)
attack (13)
beat (10)
kills (10)
strike down (9)
inflicted (7)
conquered (5)
cut down (5)
destroy (5)
afflict (4)
afflicted (4)
attacks (4)
fought (4)
hits (4)
murdered (4)
slain (4)
subdued (4)
take (4)
assassinated (3)
defeat (3)
hit (3)
killing (3)
pin (3)
punished (3)
put to death (3)
slaughtered (3)
stabbed (3)
strikes (3)
beat down (2)
beaten (2)
broke through (2)
conscience-stricken (2) +4213
defeating (2)
destroyed (2)
flog (2)
had beaten (2)
inflict (2)
kill (2) +5883
overpowered (2)
punish (2)
slapped (2)
slaughtering (2)
strike together (2)
striking (2)
striking down (2)
takes life (2) +5883
victory (2)
were destroyed (2)
wounded (2)
annihilate (1)
assailant (1)
assassinated (1) +2256+4637
assassins (1)
attacked viciously (1) +3751+6584+8797
be beaten (1)
be struck down (1)
beating (1)
beats (1)
being beaten (1)
blazed (1)
blighted (1)
blind (1) +928+2021+6427
break up (1)
chewed (1)
clapped (1)
conquers (1)
dealt (1)
destroyed (1) +1524+4394+4804
devastated (1) +1524+4394+4804
drove (1)
executed (1)
executed (1) +2256+4637
fall (1)
fallen (1)
fell upon (1)
flogged (1) +4804
give lashes (1)
had executed (1) +2256+4637
had struck down (1)
harm (1)
have flogged (1)
him[s] (1) +2021
hitting (1)
indeed defeated (1) +5782
inflicted casualties (1)
injured (1)
is blighted (1)
is struck (1)
killed (1) +2995+4200+7023
killed (1) +4637
killed (1) +8357
killed off (1)
kills (1) +2256+4637+5883
lashes (1)
must certainly put (1) +5782
overthrow (1)
person[s] (1)
plunge (1)
plunged (1)
putting to death (1)
putting to rout (1)
routed (1)
sacked (1)
send down (1)
shot (1)
slay (1)
smash (1)
smitten (1)
strikes down (1)
strikes the blow (1)
struck (1) +5782
struck down (1) +4804
struck the blow (1)
tear down (1)
thrust (1)
was killed (1)
was put to death (1)
were afflicted (1)
were beaten (1)
wound (1)
wounds was given (1)
untranslated (4)

5783 נָכֶה *nāḵeh* (3)
contrite (1)
crippled (1)
lame (1)

5784 נֵכֶה *nēḵeh* (1)
attackers (1)

5785 נְכֹה *nᵉḵōh* (4)
Neco (3)
untranslated (1)

5786 נְכוֹ *nᵉḵô* (4)
Neco (4)

5787 1נָכוֹן *nāḵôn1* (1)
fate (1)

5788 2נָכוֹן *nāḵôn2*
Variant; not used

5789 3נָכוֹן *nāḵôn3* (1)
Nacon (1)

5790 נֹכַח *nōḵah* (25)
opposite (5)
before (3)
facing (3)
faces (2)
approval (1)
directly in front of (1) +4200
directly opposite (1) +4200+7156
in front of (1)
in full view (1) +6524
in the presence of (1) +7156
on behalf of (1) +4200
open before (1) +7156
straight ahead (1) +4200
toward (1) +448
toward (1) +6330
vicinity (1)

5791 נָכֹחַ *nāḵōah* (8)
right (3)
honest (1)
honesty (1)
proper (1)
uprightly (1)
uprightness (1)

5792 נָכַל *nāḵal* (4)
cheat (1)
conspire (1)
deceived (1) +928+5793
plotted (1)

5793 נֵכֶל *nēḵel* (1)
deceived (1) +928+5792

5794 נְכָסִים *n^{e}ḵāsiym* (5)
possessions (2)
riches (2)
wealth (1)

5795 1נָכַר *nāḵar1* (45)
recognized (9)
recognize (5)
acknowledge (4)
show partiality (4) +7156
know (2)
are recognized (1)
concerned (1)
disguises himself (1)
distinguish (1)
examine to see (1)
favor (1)
is known (1)
know how (1)
make friends with (1)
misunderstand (1)
notice (1)
paid regard (1)
realized (1)
regard (1)
remembers (1)
see (1)
takes note of (1)
tell (1)
took note (1)
took notice (1)
untranslated (1)

5796 2נָכַר *nāḵar2* (5)
handed over (1) +928+3338
made foreign (1)
pretend to be someone else (1)
pretended to be a stranger (1)
pretense (1)

5797 נֵכָר *nēḵār* (36)
foreign (16)
foreigners (10) +1201
foreigner (5) +1201
they^{s} (2) +1201
alien (1)
foreigner (1) +1201+2021
foreigners (1) +1201+2021

5798 נֶכֶר *nēḵer* (2)
disaster (1)
misfortune (1)

5799 נָכְרִי *noḵriy* (46)
foreign (14)
foreigner (10)
wayward (6)
alien (4)
foreigners (4)
another (1)
another man's (1)
foreigners (1) +6639
pagans (1) +3529
someone else (1)
stranger (1)
wild (1)
untranslated (1)

5800 נְכֹת *n^{e}ḵōṯ* (3)
storehouses (2) +1074
untranslated (1)

5801 נָלָה *nālāh* (1)
stop (1)

5802 נִמְבְזָה *n^{e}miḇzāh*
Variant; not used

5803 נְמוּאֵל *n^{e}mû'ēl* (3)
Nemuel (3)

5804 נְמוּאֵלִי *n^{e}mû'ēliy* (1)
Nemuelite (1)

5805 נְמָלָה *n^{e}mālāh* (2)
ant (1)
ants (1)

5806 נָמֵס *nāmēs*
Variant; not used

5807 נָמֵר *nāmēr* (6)
leopard (4)
leopards (2)

5808 נִמְרֹד *nimrōḏ* (4)
Nimrod (4)

5809 נִמְרָה *nimrāh* (1)
Nimrah (1)

5810 נִמְרִים *nimriym* (2)
Nimrim (2)

5811 נִמְשִׁי *nimšiy* (5)
Nimshi (5)

5812 נֵס *nēs* (21)
banner (14)
battle standard (2)
pole (2)
sail (1)
signal (1)
warning sign (1)

5813 נְסִבָּה *n^{e}sibbāh* (1)
turn of events (1)

5814 נָסָה *nāsāh* (36)
test (14)
tested (8)
put to the test (6)
used to (2)
did^{s} (1)
testing (1)
tried (1)
try (1)
venture (1)
ventures (1)

5815 נָסַח *nāsah* (4)
be uprooted (1)
tear (1)
tears down (1)
torn (1)

5816 1נְסִיךְ *nāsiyḵ1* (2)
drink offerings (1)
metal images (1)

5817 2נְסִיךְ *nāsiyḵ2* (4)
princes (3)
leaders (1)

5818 1נָסַךְ *nāsaḵ1* (23)
poured out (7)
pour out (6)
pouring out (3)
casts (2)
brought (1)
forming an alliance (1) +5011
pour (1)
pouring out of drink offerings (1)
pouring out of offerings (1)

5819 2נָסַךְ *nāsaḵ2* (1)
covers (1)

5820 3נָסַךְ *nāsaḵ3* (2)
installed (1)
was appointed (1)

5821 1נֶסֶךְ *neseḵ1* (60)
drink offerings (32)
drink offering (27)
libations (1)

5822 2נֶסֶךְ *neseḵ2* (4)
images (3)
metal god (1)

5823 1נסס *nāsas1* (1)
sick (1)

5824 2נָסַס *nāsas2* (2)
be unfurled (1)
sparkle (1)

5825 נָסַע *nāsa'* (146)
set out (49)
left (43)
moved on (6)
traveled (5)
went (5)
move (3)
broke camp (2)
brought out (2)
move on (2)
moved (2)
pulled up (2)
withdrew (2)
advance (1)
are pulled up (1)
be on way (1) +2143+2256
been pulled down (1)
broke camp (1) +185+4946
journeyed (1)
leaving (1) +4946
led (1)
left (1) +4946
let loose (1)
marching (1)
move about (1)
move out (1)
out (1)
put to one side (1)
quarries (1)
removed from quarry (1)
setting out (1)
tore loose (1)
uproots (1)
wander (1)
went out (1)
untranslated (1)

5826 נָסַק *nāsaq*
Variant; not used

5827 נִסְרֹךְ *nisrōḵ* (2)
Nisroch (2)

5828 נֵעָה *nē'āh* (1)
Neah (1)

5829 נֹעָה *nō'āh* (4)
Noah (4)

5830 נְעוּרִים *n*^{e}*'ûriym* (46)
youth (37)
young (5)
childhood (3)
boyhood (1)

5831 נְעוּרוֹת *n*^{e}*'ûrôṯ* (1)
youth (1)

5832 נְעִיאֵל *n*^{e}*'iy'ēl* (1)
Neiel (1)

5833 נָעִים1 *nā'iym1* (11)
pleasant (4)
beautiful (1)
charming (1)
compliments (1) +1821
contentment (1)
gracious (1)
pleasing (1)
pleasures (1)

5834 נָעִים2 *nā'iym2* (2)
melodious (1)
singer (1)

5835 נָעַל1 *nā'al1* (6)
locked (2)
bolt (1)
bolted (1)
locked up (1)
sealed (1)

5836 נָעַל2 *nā'al2* (2)
put sandals on (1)
sandals (1)

5837 נַעַל *na'al* (22)
sandals (14)
sandal (6)
sandaled (1) +928+2021
unsandaled (1) +2740

5838 נָעֵם *nā'ēm* (8)
pleasant (2)
dear (1)
delicious (1)
go well (1)
more favored (1)
pleasing (1)
well (1)

5839 נַעַם *na'am* (1)
Naam (1)

5840 נֹעַם *nō'am* (7)
favor (3)
pleasant (2)
beauty (1)
pleasing (1)

5841 נַעֲמָה1 *na*^{a}*'māh1* (4)
Naamah (4)

5842 נַעֲמָה2 *na*^{a}*'māh2* (1)
Naamah (1)

5843 נָעֳמִי *nā*^{o}*'miy* (21)
Naomi (19)
Naomi's (1)
she[S] (1)

5844 נַעֲמִי *na*^{a}*'miy* (1)
Naamite (1)

5845 נַעֲמָן *na*^{a}*'mān* (16)
Naaman (14)
Naaman's (2)

5846 נַעֲמָנִים *na*^{a}*'māniym* (1)
finest (1)

5847 נַעֲמָתִי *na*^{a}*'māṯiy* (4)
Naamathite (4)

5848 נַעֲצוּץ *na*^{a}*'ṣûṣ* (2)
thornbush (1)
thornbushes (1)

5849 נָעַר1 *nā'ar1* (1)
growl (1)

5850 נָעַר2 *nā'ar2* (11)
swept (2)
am shaken off (1)
drop leaves (1)
keeps (1)
shake (1)
shake myself free (1)
shake off (1)
shake out (1)
shaken out (1)
shook out (1)

5851 נָעַר3 *nā'ar3*
Variant; not used

5852 נַעַר1 *na'ar1*
Variant; not used

5853 נַעַר2 *na'ar2* (253)
boy (48)
servant (29)
young (25)
young man (23)
men (21)
servants (14)
child (13)
young men (11)
boy's (4)
boys (4)
young officers (4)
children (3)
youth (3)
foreman (2) +5893
him[S] (2) +2021
steward (2)
them[S] (2) +2021
underlings (2)
aide (1)
assistants (1)
attendants (1)
attendants (1) +9250
boy (1) +7783
child's (1)
he[S] (1)
he[S] (1) +2021
helper (1)
Jether[S] (1) +2021
man (1)
men's (1)
personal attendants (1) +9250
personal servant (1) +9250
servant's (1)
sons (1)
workers (1)
youths (1)
youths (1) +7783
untranslated (22)

5854 נֹעַר *nō'ar* (4)
youth (3)
child's (1)

5855 נַעֲרָה1 *na*^{a}*'rāh1* (63)
girl (19)
girl's (10)
maids (7)
servant girls (5)
girls (4)
she[S] (3) +2021
young (3)
her[S] (2) +2021
young woman (2)
attendants (1)
girl's (1) +4200
girls (1) +1435
she[S] (1)
untranslated (4)

5856 נַעֲרָה2 *na*^{a}*'rāh2* (3)
Naarah (3)

5857 נַעֲרָה3 *na*^{a}*'rāh3* (1)
Naarah (1)

5858 נַעֲרַי *na*^{a}*'ray* (1)
Naarai (1)

5859 נְעַרְיָה *n*^{e}*'aryāh* (3)
Neariah (3)

5860 נַעֲרָן *na*^{a}*'rān* (1)
Naaran (1)

5861 נְעֹרֶת *n*^{e}*'ōreṯ* (2)
piece of string (1) +7348
tinder (1)

5862 נֹף *nōp̱* (7)
Memphis (7)

5863 נֶפֶג *nep̱eg̱* (4)
Nepheg (4)

5864 נָפָה1 *nāp̱āh1* (1)
sieve (1)

5865 נָפָה2 *nāp̱āh2*
Variant; not used

5866 נְפוּסִים *n*^{e}*p̱ûsiym* (1)
Nephussim (1)

5867 נְפוּשְׁסִים *n*^{e}*p̱ûš*^{e}*siym* (1)
Nephussim (1)

5868 נָפוֹת *nāp̱ôṯ* (1)
Naphoth (1)

5869 נָפוֹת דֹּאר *nāp̱ôṯ dō'r* (3)
Naphoth Dor (3)

5870 נָפַח *nāp̱ah* (11)
boiling (2)
blast (1)
blew away (1)
blow (1)
breathe last (1) +5883
breathed (1)
broken (1)
fans (1)
sniff contemptuously (1)
unfanned (1) +4202

5871 נֹפַח *nōp̱ah* (1)
Nophah (1)

5872 נְפִילִים *n*^{e}*p̱iyliym* (3)
Nephilim (3)

5873 נְפִיסִים *n*^{e}*p̱iysiym* (1)
untranslated (1)

5874 נָפִישׁ *nāp̱iyš* (3)
Naphish (3)

5875 נְפִישְׁסִים *n*^{e}*p̱iyš*^{e}*siym* (1)
untranslated (1)

5876 נֹפֶךְ *nōp̱eḵ* (4)
turquoise (4)

5877 נָפַל *nāp̱al* (435)
fall (102)
fell (67)
fallen (40)
falls (23)
cast (13)
allotted (4)
collapsed (4)
down (4)
downfall (4)
failed (4)
gone over (4)
make fall (4)
allot (3)
bring down (3)
came (3)
cut down (3)
fall down (3)
falling (3)
fell down (3)
put (3)
bring (2)
brought down (2)
defected (2)

deserting (2)
downcast (2)
falls prostrate (2)
fell prostrate (2)
going to death (2)
got down (2)
have cut down (2)
inferior (2)
lay (2)
lie fallen (2)
lying (2)
seized (2) +6584
surrender (2)
those[S] (2) +2021
threw (2)
threw arms around (2) +6584+7418
threw down (2)
waste away (2)
afraid (1) +6584+7065
allocate (1)
allots (1)
assail (1) +6584
attack (1) +928
attacked (1)
attacked (1) +928
become (1)
bowed down (1) +6584+7156
bowed down to the ground (1) +6584+7156
brings on (1)
cast down (1)
casting (1)
cause to fall (1)
caused to fall (1)
collapse (1)
collapses (1)
come into (1) +928
come over (1)
confined (1)
consisted of (1)
cracked (1) +7288
crumble (1)
cutting down (1)
defeated (1)
deserts (1)
died (1)
do not count (1)
down came (1)
dropped out (1)
drops (1)
erodes (1)
fail (1) +824+2025
fall in battle (1) +2728
fall limp (1)
fallen down (1)
falls down (1)
fell dead (1)
frown (1) +7156
give birth (1)
give up (1)
given birth (1)
gone down (1)
happens (1)
have fall (1)
hear (1) +4200+7156
hurtling down (1)
killed (1)
knocks out (1)
lay prostrate (1)
left (1)
let fall (1)
lie (1)
lived in hostility toward (1) +6584+7156
lose (1)
lost (1) +907+4946
lost (1) +4946
lost self-confidence (1) +928+4394+6524
made come down (1)
make (1)
make drop (1)
make lie down (1)
making (1)
neglect (1)
overpower (1)
overwhelmed (1) +6584
perish (1)
pleading (1) +9382
plunge (1)
precious (1) +4202
present (1) +4200+7156
reach (1)
settled (1)
settles (1)
sink (1)
slaughter (1)
slay (1)
someone[S] (1) +2021
stilled (1)
strewn (1)
stumble (1)
such force[S] (1)
surely come to ruin (1) +5877
surrenders (1)
those[S] (1)
threw arms around (1) +6584
throw (1)
throw in (1)
throwing himself down (1)
thrown (1)
tumbles (1)
wastes away (1)
were[S] (1)
untranslated (2)

5878 נֵפֶל *nēp̱el* (3)
stillborn child (2)
stillborn child (1) +851

5879 1נָפַץ *nāp̱as1* (17)
shatter (9)
smash (2)
broke (1)
broken (1)
crushed to pieces (1)
dash to pieces (1)
dashes (1)
separate (1)

5880 2נָפַץ *nāp̱as2* (3)
scatter (1)
scattered (1)
scattering (1)

5881 נֶפֶץ *nep̱es* (1)
cloudburst (1)

5882 נָפַשׁ *nāp̱aš* (3)
be refreshed (1)
refreshed himself (1)
rested (1)

5883 נֶפֶשׁ *nep̱eš* (757)
life (129)
soul (105)
lives (36)
me (35) +3276
I (29) +3276
person (22)
you (21) +3870
himself (18) +2257
heart (16)
yourselves (12) +4013
people (11)
myself (9) +3276
themselves (9) +4392
anyone (7)
everyone (7) +2021+3972
he (7) +2257
herself (7) +2023
appetite (6)
creatures (6)
spirit (5)
them (5) +4392
we (5) +5646
body (4)
creature (4)
dead body (4)
death (4)
man (4)
my (4) +3276
one (4)
souls (4)
they (4) +4392
you (4) +3871
yourself (4) +3870
breath (3)
dead (3)
desire (3)
hearts (3)
lifeblood (3) +1947
needs (3)
ourselves (3) +5646
persons (3)
someone (3)
those[S] (3)
us (3) +5646
anyone (2) +2021+3972
anyone (2) +3972
as surely as live (2) +2644
desires (2)
everyone (2) +3972
he[S] (2) +2021+2021+2085
hunger (2)
hungry (2) +8281
kill (2) +4374
kill (2) +5782
long (2) +5951
members (2)
mind (2)
neck (2)
she (2) +2023
takes life (2) +5782
thing (2)
you (2) +4013
yourselves (2) +3870
affection (1)
alive (1) +928
all (1)
another[S] (1)
appetites (1)
as surely as live (1) +2256+2644+2644
be a willing party (1) +5951
being (1)
breathe last (1) +5870
breathed her last (1) +3655
closest friend (1) +889+3869+3870+8276
completely (1) +1414+2256+4946+6330
corpse (1)
cost (1)
counting on (1) +448+906+5951
courage (1)
craved (1)
craving (1)
craving (1) +205
descendants (1) +3655+3751
die (1)
discontented (1) +5253
dying (1)
earnest (1)
earnestness (1) +205
enemies (1) +8533
faint (1) +1790
feel (1)
fierce (1) +5253
given to gluttony (1) +1251
greed (1)
greedy man (1) +8146
guilt of murder (1) +1947
he[S] (1)
heart's (1)
hearts' (1)
herself (1)
him (1) +2257
him[S] (1)
his own (1) +2257
hot-tempered (1) +5253
how it feels (1)

hunger (1) +8199
impatient (1) +7918
in all[s] (1)
in anguish (1) +5253
its own (1) +2257
just what wanted (1)
keep themselves alive (1) +906+4392+8740
keep themselves alive (1) +8740
kidnapping (1) +1704
kill (1)
kills (1) +2256+4637+5782
livelihood (1)
living soul (1)
made a fatal mistake (1) +928+9494
member (1)
minds (1)
mortal (1) +928
murders (1) +8357
none (1) +3972+4202
people (1) +132
perfume (1)
personal vows (1) +6886
pleased (1)
plunder (1) +7693
relish (1) +5951
slave (1)
slaves (1) +132
stouthearted (1) +6437
that[s] (1)
the flock[s] (1) +4392
themselves (1) +2257
these[s] (1)
they (1) +2257
thirst (1)
thirsty (1) +8799
thoughts (1) +928+6783
threatened (1) +6330
throats (1)
wait to kill (1) +9068
wanted (1) +906+8626
wanted to kill (1) +906+1335
weary (1) +6546
willing (1)
wished (1)
wishes (1)
yourself (1) +2257
zeal (1)
untranslated (46)

5884 נֶפֶת *nepeṯ*
Variant; not used

5885 נֹפֶת *nōp̱eṯ* (5)
honey (3)
honey from the comb (1)
sweetness as the honeycomb (1)

5886 נֶפְתּוֹחַ *nep̱tôaḥ* (2)
Nephtoah (2)

5887 נַפְתּוּלִים *nap̱tûliym* (1)
had a struggle (1) +7349

5888 נַפְתֻּחִים *nap̱tuḥiym* (2)
Naphtuhites (2)

5889 נַפְתָּלִי *nap̱tāliy* (51)
Naphtali (44)
Naphtali (5) +1201
Naphtali (1) +824
untranslated (1)

5890 1נֵץ *nēṣ1* (2)
blossomed (1) +6590
flowers (1)

5891 2נֵץ *nēṣ2* (3)
hawk (3)

5892 נָצָא *nāṣā'*
Variant; not used

5893 1נָצַב *nāṣaḇ1* (74)
standing (14)
set up (9)
set (5)
stood (5)
stand (3)
district officers (2)
foreman (2) +5853
officials (2)
attendants (1)
attending (1)
decreed (1)
deputy (1)
district governors (1)
erected as a monument (1)
establish (1)
foremen (1) +8569
healthy (1)
is (1)
keeps intact (1)
leader (1)
life (1)
made (1)
made stand firm (1)
piled up (1)
present yourself (1)
presides (1)
ready (1)
repointing (1)
resting (1)
stands firm (1)
stay (1)
stood by (1)
stood firm (1)
stood upright (1)
takes place (1)
takes stand (1)
wait (1)
waiting (1)
untranslated (2)

5894 2נָצַב *nāṣaḇ2*
Variant; not used

5895 1נִצָּב *niṣṣāḇ1*
Variant; not used

5896 2נִצָּב *niṣṣāḇ2* (1)
handle (1)

5897 1נָצָה *nāṣāh1* (8)
fighting (3)
rebelled (2)
fight broke out (1)
fought (1)
got into a fight (1)

5898 2נָצָה *nāṣāh2* (8)
lie in ruins (2)
piles of stone (2) +1643
desolate (1)
laid waste (1)
laid waste (1) +5898

5899 3נָצָה *nāṣāh3*
Variant; not used

5900 נִצָּה *niṣṣāh* (2)
blossoms (1)
flower (1)

5901 1נֹצָה *nōṣāh1* (1)
contents (1)

5902 2נֹצָה *nōṣāh2*
Variant; not used

5903 נְצוּרִים *nᵉṣûriym*
Variant; not used

5904 נָצַח *nāṣaḥ* (65)
director of music (56)
foremen (2)
supervise (2)
direct (1)
directing (1)
does always (1)
supervised (1)
supervising (1)

5905 1נֵצַח *nēṣaḥ1* (43)
forever (18) +4200
always (4) +4200
never (3) +4200+4202
never (2) +1153+4200
endless (1) +4200
eternal (1)
ever again (1) +4200+5905
everlasting (1)
everlasting (1) +4200
flamed unchecked (1) +9068
forever (1)
glory (1)
majesty (1)
never (1) +561+4200
never (1) +4202+6330
once for all (1) +4200
splendor (1)
unending (1)
utmost (1)

5906 2נֵצַח *nēṣaḥ2* (2)
blood (2)

5907 1נְצִיב *nᵉṣiyḇ1* (12)
garrisons (4)
outpost (3)
garrison (1)
governor (1)
pillar (1)
untranslated (2)

5908 2נְצִיב *nᵉṣiyḇ2* (1)
Nezib (1)

5909 נְצִיחַ *nᵉṣiyaḥ* (2)
Neziah (2)

5910 נָצִיר *nāṣiyr* (1)
untranslated (1)

5911 נָצַל *nāṣal* (212)
rescue (42)
deliver (40)
save (32)
delivered (17)
rescued (12)
delivers (6)
saved (6)
be saved (3)
snatched (3)
be delivered (2)
defended (2)
escape (2)
free yourself (2)
protect (2)
recovered (2)
rescues (2)
saves (2)
surely deliver (2) +5911
be rescued (1)
come to rescue (1)
defender (1)
deliverance (1)
delivering (1)
ease (1)
escapes (1)
ever delivered (1) +5911
free (1)
plunder (1)
plundered (1)
protected (1)
rescued at all (1) +5911
rescuing (1)
retake (1)
safe (1)
separate (1) +1068
snatch (1)
spared (1)
stripped off (1)
succeed in the rescue (1) +5911
take (1)
take away (1) +5362
take back (1)
taken away (1)

taken refuge (1)
took away (1)
was spared (1)
untranslated (1)

5912 נִצָּנִים *nissāniym*
Variant; not used

5913 1נָצַץ *nāsas1* (1)
gleamed (1)

5914 2נָצַץ *nāsas2* (3)
in bloom (2)
blossoms (1)

5915 נָצַר *nāsar* (61)
keep (15)
protect (8)
guards (5)
guard (4)
obey (4)
guarded (2)
preserve (2)
watch over (2)
watchtower (2) +4463
crafty (1)
guard well (1)
hidden (1)
is spared (1)
keep safe (1)
keep watch over (1)
keeping secret vigil (1)
keeps (1)
kept (1)
maintaining (1)
observe (1)
preserves (1)
tends (1)
watcher (1)
watchman (1)
watchmen (1)
untranslated (1)

5916 נֵצֶר *nēser* (4)
branch (2)
family line (1) +9247
shoot (1)

5917 נִצְּרָה *nissᵉrāh* (1)
watch (1)

5918 1נָקַב *nāqab1* (16)
designated (3)
pierce (2)
pierces (2)
been given (1)
bestow (1)
bored (1)
holes (1)
name (1)
notable (1)
pierced (1)
were designated (1)
were registered (1)

5919 2נָקַב *nāqab2* (3)
blasphemes (2)
blasphemed (1)

5920 1נֶקֶב *neqeb1* (1)
mountings (1)

5921 2נֶקֶב *neqeb2*
Variant; not used

5922 נְקֵבָה *nᵉqēbāh* (22)
female (16)
woman (3)
daughter (1)
girl (1)
women (1)

5923 נָקֹד *nāqōd* (9)
speckled (9)

5924 נֹקֵד *nōqēd* (2)
raised sheep (1)
shepherds (1)

5925 נְקֻדָּה *nᵉquddāh* (1)
studded (1)

5926 נִקֻּדִים *niqqudiym* (3)
moldy (2)
cakes (1)

5927 נָקָה *nāqāh* (41)
go unpunished (9)
innocent (3)
leave the guilty unpunished (3) +5927
be banished (2)
be released (2)
hold guiltless (2)
let go entirely unpunished (2) +5927
be cleared of guilt (1)
consider innocent (1)
destitute (1)
forgive (1)
go unpunished (1) +5927
guiltless (1)
have a right to get even (1)
hold innocent (1)
indeed go unpunished (1) +5927
let go unpunished (1)
not be held responsible (1)
not harm (1) +4946
pardon (1)
pardoned (1)

5928 נְקוֹדָא *nᵉqôdā'* (4)
Nekoda (4)

5929 נָקִי *nāqiy* (43)
innocent (30)
released (2)
clean (1)
exempt (1)
free (1)
free from blame (1)
free from obligation (1)
harmless soul (1) +2855
innocent man (1) +1947
not binding (1)
not held responsible (1)
not responsible (1)
without guilt (1)

5930 נָקִיא *nāqiy'*
Variant; not used

5931 נִקָּיוֹן *niqqāyôn* (5)
innocence (2)
clean (1)
empty stomachs (1) +9094
purity (1)

5932 נָקִיק *nāqiyq* (3)
crevices (2)
crevice (1)

5933 נָקַם *nāqam* (35)
avenge (6)
takes vengeance (2)
took revenge (2) +5934
avenge (1) +5934
avenge (1) +5935
avenge myself (1)
avenge themselves (1)
avenge wrongs (1)
avenged (1)
avenged myself (1)
avenger (1)
avenging (1)
be punished (1)
bent on revenge (1)
doing so (1)
get revenge (1)
get revenge (1) +5934
is avenged (1)
must be punished (1) +5933
punished (1)
seek revenge (1)
suffer vengeance (1)
take revenge (1)
take revenge (1) +5934
take vengeance (1)
take vengeance (1) +5935
vengeance (1)

5934 נָקָם *nāqām* (17)
vengeance (7)
take vengeance (2) +8740
took revenge (2) +5933
avenge (1)
avenge (1) +5933
avenged (1)
get revenge (1) +5933
revenge (1)
take revenge (1) +5933

5935 נְקָמָה *nᵉqāmāh* (27)
vengeance (17)
avenges (2)
avenges (2) +5989
avenge (1)
avenge (1) +5933
avenged (1) +5989
avenged (1) +6913
revenge (1)
take vengeance (1) +5933

5936 נָקַע *nāqa'* (3)
turned away in disgust (2)
turned away (1)

5937 1נָקַף *nāqap1* (2)
cut down (1)
destroyed (1)

5938 2נָקַף *nāqap2* (17)
surrounded (2)
circling (1)
cut hair (1)
cycle go on (1)
drawn (1)
echoes along (1)
encircled (1)
engulfed (1)
go around (1)
march around (1) +6015
run course (1)
station themselves (1)
station yourselves (1)
surround (1)
untranslated (2)

5939 נֹקֶף *nōqep* (2)
beaten (2)

5940 נִקְפָּה *niqpāh* (1)
rope (1)

5941 נָקַר *nāqar* (6)
gouge out (2)
gouged out (1)
pecked out (1)
pierces (1)
were hewn (1)

5942 נְקָרָה *nᵉqārāh* (2)
caverns (1)
cleft (1)

5943 נָקַשׁ *nāqaš* (4)
be ensnared (1)
seize (1)
set a trap (1)
set traps (1)

5944 1נֵר *nēr1* (44)
lamps (23)
lamp (16)
lights (2)
them[s] (1)
untranslated (2)

5945 2נֵר *nēr2* (17)
Ner (17)

5946 נֵרְגַל *nērgal* (1)
Nergal (1)

5947 נֵרְגַל שַׂר־אֶצֶר *nērgal śar-'eser* (3)
Nergal-Sharezer (3)

5948 נֵרְדְּ *nērd* (3)
nard (2)
perfume (1)

5949 נֵרִיָּה *nēriyyāh* (7)
Neriah (7)

5950 נֵרִיָּהוּ *nēriyyāhû* (3)
Neriah (3)

5951 נָשָׂא *nāśā'* (656)
carry (36)
bear (35)
lift up (32)
carried (26)
carrying (26)
up (26)
armor-bearer (18) +3998
lifted up (16)
take up (14)
took (12)
forgive (10)
raise (10)
brought (8)
held responsible (7) +6411
lifted (7)
take (7)
uttered (7) +606+2256
bring (6)
carried off (6)
took up (6)
aloud (5) +906+7754
bearing (5)
carries (5)
lift (5)
look (5) +6524
swore with uplifted (5)
take away (5)
accept (4) +7156
aloud (4) +7754
carry off (4)
endure (4)
exalted (4)
get (4)
loaded (4)
lofty (4)
pick up (4)
picks up (4)
rose (4)
show partiality (4) +7156
spread (4)
suffer (4)
be carried off (3)
bore (3)
forgiving (3)
looked (3) +6524
married (3)
misuse (3) +2021+4200+8736
offer (3)
picked up (3)
put (3)
share (3) +928
sworn with uplifted (3)
take a census (3) +906+8031
armor-bearers (2) +3998
arrogant (2) +4213
be lifted up (2)
be raised (2)
bearer (2)
brought back (2)
carried away (2)
forgave (2)
held responsible (2) +2628
long (2) +5883
misuses (2) +2021+4200+8736
pay (2)
pray (2) +9525
receive (2)
released (2) +8031
rise (2)
rise up (2)
shows partiality (2) +7156
spare (2)
suffered (2)
support (2)
take a census (2) +8031
taken (2)
wear (2)
willing (2) +4213
with uplifted swore (2)
won (2) +4200+7156
abounds (1)
accept (1)
accepted (1) +906+7156
are forgiven (1)
armed (1)
at all forgive (1) +5951
be a willing party (1) +5883
be carried (1)
be exalted (1)
be forgiven (1)
be raised up (1)
be taken away (1)
bear up (1)
bear with (1)
beckon (1) +3338
become guilty (1) +2628+6584
been exalted (1)
began (1) +906+7754
begin (1)
borne fruit (1)
bring upon (1)
carried (1) +6673
carriers (1) +6025
carries off (1)
carry about (1)
carry away (1)
carry back (1)
casts (1)
caught up (1)
chose (1)
clothed with (1)
containing (1)
continued on journey (1) +8079
count (1) +906+8031
counted (1) +906+8031
counting on (1) +448+906+5883
cry out (1) +606+4200
disdainful (1)
ease (1)
elevated (1)
elevating (1)
equipped (1)
exalt itself (1)
exalted yourself (1)
gather (1)
gave assistance (1)
grant (1) +7156
granted request (1) +7156
guilty (1)
guilty (1) +2628
had (1)
handle (1)
have respect for (1)
helped (1)
high (1)
highly regarded (1) +7156
honored (1) +7156
include in the census (1) +906+8031
incur (1)
is carried off (1)
is exalted (1)
let shine (1)
lifts up (1)
loaded up (1)
look in the face (1) +448+7156
look with longing (1) +6524
looked about (1) +6524
looks (1) +6524
loudly (1) +7754
made (1)
make (1)
man of rank (1) +7156
married (1) +851
mount up (1)
mourn (1) +7806
moved (1)
must be carried (1) +5951
out (1)
out (1) +906
pardon (1)
pardoned (1)
pardons (1)
partial (1) +7156
placed (1)
pleased with (1) +928+2834+6524
prepare (1)
produce (1)
prominent (1) +7156
provide (1)
pull up (1)
put himself forward (1)
put in jeopardy (1) +928+1414+9094
raised (1)
raised (1) +2256+5989
raising (1)
rear (1)
rebel (1)
receive (1) +7156
relish (1) +5883
respect (1) +7156
responsible for (1)
ridicule (1) +5442
rise again (1)
rises high (1)
rouse themselves (1)
saw (1) +906+6524
served (1)
set yourselves (1)
share (1)
share in (1) +6584
shouted (1) +2256+7754+7924
showed partiality (1) +7156
shown honor (1) +7156
shown partiality (1) +7156
sing (1)
snatch up (1)
suffer for (1)
suffering for (1)
supplied (1)
swear with uplifted (1)
sweep away (1)
sweeps away (1)
swore (1) +3338
sworn (1) +906+3338
take in marriage (1)
taken anything (1) +5951
taken as wives (1)
taken up (1)
takes (1)
takes up (1)
taunt (1) +5442
toil (1)
too heavy a burden to carry (1) +3523+4202
took away (1)
took notice (1) +6524
transport (1)
trembles (1)
turn (1)
uplifted (1)
wail (1) +5631
was highly regarded (1)
was raised (1)
wearing (1)
weep (1) +1140
won (1) +928+6524
wore (1)
untranslated (11)

5952 נָשַׂג *nāśag* (50)
overtake (14)
afford (7) +3338
overtook (6)
catch up (2)

continue until (2)
overtaken (2)
prospers (2) +3338
accompany (1)
attain (1)
catch (1)
caught up (1)
certainly overtake (1) +5952
equal (1)
move (1)
overtaking (1)
put (1)
reach (1)
reaches (1)
rich (1) +3338
wants to give (1) +3338
untranslated (1)

5953 נְשׂוּאָה *n^eśû'āh* (1)
images that are carried about (1)

5954 1נָשִׂיא *nāśiy'1* (131)
leader (43)
leaders (29)
prince (29)
princes (10)
chiefs (3)
ruler (3)
rulers (2)
chief (1)
chief leader (1) +5954
himself[S] (1)
leaders' (1)
they[S] (1) +2021
untranslated (6)

5955 2נָשִׂיא *nāśiy'2* (4)
clouds (4)

5956 נָשַׂק *nāśaq* (3)
broke out (1)
burn up (1)
kindles a fire (1)

5957 1נָשָׁא *nāšā'1* (18)
creditor (3)
required (2) +460+928
borrowed (1) +928
creditors (1)
debtor (1) +928
exacting (1)
in debt (1) +4200
lending (1)
lent (1)
loan made (1)
make a loan (1) +5394
making loan (1)
moneylender (1)
subject to tribute (1)
usury charging (1)

5958 2נָשָׁא *nāšā'2* (15)
deceive (4)
let deceive (4)
deceived (3)
are deceived (1)
completely deceived (1) +5958
take by surprise (1)

5959 נָשַׁב *nāšab̲* (3)
blows (1)
drove away (1)
stirs up (1)

5960 1נָשָׁה *nāšāh1* (9)
forget (3)
forgotten (2)
made forget (1)
not endow (1)
surely forget (1) +5960

5961 2נָשָׁה *nāšāh2*
Variant; not used

5962 נָשֶׁה *nāšeh* (2)
tendon (2) +1630

5963 נְשִׁי *n^ešiy* (2)
debts (1)
untranslated (1)

5964 נְשִׁיָּה *n^ešiyyāh* (1)
oblivion (1)

5965 נְשִׁיקָה *n^ešiyqāh* (2)
kisses (2)

5966 1נָשַׁךְ *nāšak̲1* (11)
bite (3)
bites (3)
bitten (2)
bit (1)
feeds (1) +928+9094
is bitten (1)

5967 2נָשַׁךְ *nāšak̲2* (5)
charge interest (1)
charge interest (1) +5968
debtors (1)
earn interest (1)
untranslated (1)

5968 נֶשֶׁךְ *nešek̲* (12)
usury (5)
interest (2)
charge interest (1) +5967
exorbitant interest (1) +2256+9552
interest of any kind (1) +2256+9552
untranslated (2)

5969 נִשְׁכָּה *niškāh* (3)
living quarters (1)
room (1)
storerooms (1) +238+4200

5970 נָשַׁל *nāšal* (7)
take off (2)
drive out (1)
drives out (1)
driving out (1)
drop off (1)
fly off (1)

5971 נָשַׁם *nāšam* (1)
gasp (1)

5972 נְשָׁמָה *n^ešāmāh* (24)
breath (11)
breathed (4)
blast (2)
spirit (2)
breath (1) +8120
breathes (1)
breathing (1)
can hardly breathe (1) +4202+8636
life (1)

5973 נָשַׁף *nāšap̲* (2)
blew (1)
blows (1)

5974 נֶשֶׁף *nešep̲* (12)
dusk (4)
twilight (3)
dawn (2)
darkening (1)
morning (1)
night (1)

5975 1נָשַׁק *nāšaq1* (30)
kissed (17)
kiss (9)
kiss good-by (2)
kissed good-by (1)
offered a kiss of homage (1) +4200+7023

5976 2נָשַׁק *nāšaq2* (5)
armed (2)
armed (1) +8227
brushing (1)
submit (1)

5977 1נֶשֶׁק *nešeq1* (10)
weapons (6)
armory (1)
battle (1)
fray (1)
weapon (1)

5978 2נֶשֶׁק *nešeq2*
Variant; not used

5979 נֶשֶׁר *nešer* (26)
eagle (15)
eagles (5)
eagle's (2)
vulture (2)
eagles' (1)
vultures (1) +1201

5980 נָשַׁת *nāšat̲* (4)
cease (1)
dry up (1)
exhausted (1)
parched (1)

5981 נִשְׁתְּוָן *ništ^ewān*
Variant; not used

5982 נְתוּנִים *n^et̲ûniym*
Variant; not used

5983 נָתַח *nāt̲ah* (9)
cut (4)
cut into pieces (4)
cut up (1)

5984 נֵתַח *nēt̲ah* (13)
pieces (8)
piece (2)
parts (1)
piece by piece (1) +4200
pieces of meat (1)

5985 נָתִיב *nāt̲iyb̲* (5)
path (3)
hidden path (1)
wake (1)

5986 נְתִיבָה *n^et̲iyb̲āh* (21)
paths (11)
path (3)
way (2)
bypaths (1)
road (1)
roads (1)
streets (1)
travelers (1) +2143

5987 נָתִין *nāt̲iyn* (17)
temple servants (15)
them[S] (1) +2021
untranslated (1)

5988 נָתַךְ *nāt̲ak̲* (21)
poured out (7)
be melted (3)
melt (2)
paid out (2)
pour out (2)
poured down (2)
be poured out (1)
been poured out (1)
is poured out (1)

5989 נָתַן *nāt̲an* (2016)
give (344)
gave (231)
put (169)
given (147)
giving (58)
make (55)
gives (45)
made (37)
set (36)
hand over (35) +928+3338
handed over (23) +928+3338
placed (23)
let (19)
be given (18)
grant (14)
pay (14)
place (14)

yield (13)
bring (12)
delivered (12)
granted (11)
appointed (10)
if only (10) +4769
send (9)
spread (9)
assigned (8)
be handed over (8) +928+3338
entrusted (8)
hand over (8)
oh (8) +4769
deliver (7)
exchanged (7)
give in marriage (7) +851+4200
give over (7)
sent (7)
lay (6)
offered (6)
repay (6)
sell (6)
allow (5)
attach (5)
gave in marriage (5) +851+4200
get (5)
give in marriage (5)
give up (5)
paid (5)
set up (5)
show (5)
take (5)
allowed (4)
been given (4)
bring down (4)
fasten (4)
fastened (4)
gave over (4)
laid (4)
makes (4)
offer (4)
provide (4)
provided (4)
provides (4)
setting (4)
thunders (4) +7754
was given (4)
applied (3)
attached (3)
bringing down (3)
brought (3)
cause (3)
caused (3)
deal (3)
do (3)
establish (3)
give back (3)
given over (3)
paying (3)
produce (3)
resounded (3)
stationed (3)
surrender (3)
treat (3)
turn (3)
turned (3)
was issued (3)
allotted (2) +928+1598+2021
appoint (2)
are (2)
are given (2)
attaching (2)
avenges (2) +5935
be given wholly (2) +5989
be issued (2)
been put (2)
bestows (2)
blessed (2) +1388
causes (2)
certainly be handed over (2) +928+3338+5989
contributed (2)
dedicated (2)
deliver over (2)
delivered over (2)
delivers (2)
direct (2)
distributing (2)
do so[s] (2)
entrust (2)
established (2)
gifts (2)
handed over (2)
hang (2)
is given (2)
kept (2)
left (2)
lend (2)
lends (2)
lifting (2)
made turn (2)
maintain (2)
making (2)
permit (2)
presented (2)
prevent (2) +1194
proclaim (2)
providing (2)
puts (2)
putting (2)
raised (2)
received (2)
reported (2)
reward (2)
sell (2) +928+4084
thrown (2)
thunder (2) +7754
turn into (2)
turn over (2)
wrap (2)
yields (2)
abandoned (1)
allotted (1)
allow to possess (1)
allowing (1)
allows (1)
announced (1)
announces (1)
appoints (1)
are laid (1)
are put (1)
arranged (1)
ascribe (1)
avenged (1) +5935
barter (1)
be (1)
be bought (1)
be defeated (1) +928+3338
be given in marriage (1) +851+4200
be handed over (1)
be injured (1)
be left (1)
be supplied (1)
bears (1)
became (1)
been allotted (1)
been committed (1)
been handed over (1) +928+3338
been published (1)
been subjected (1)
bestow (1)
bestowed (1)
bless (1) +1388
bow (1)
bowed (1)
breeds (1)
bringing (1)
brings (1)
bury (1)
buy (1)
called together (1)
came (1)
carry out (1)
cast (1)
charge (1)
charging (1)
choose (1)
committed (1)
confirm (1)
consign (1)
costs (1)
cover (1) +4062
credited (1)
cry aloud (1) +7754
cut (1) +8582
deliver (1) +5989
demand (1)
designate (1)
designated (1)
despoil (1) +1020+4200
destined (1)
devote (1)
devoted (1)
did[s] (1) +2257+3338
dispenses (1)
display (1)
distribute (1)
distributed (1)
does (1)
drop (1)
dry up (1) +3000
enabled (1)
endow (1)
exchange (1)
falls (1)
filled (1)
flourishes (1)
from (1)
gave in marriage (1)
gave in marriage (1) +851
gave in pledge (1)
gave up (1)
gave victory (1) +928+3338
give (1) +928+3338
give (1) +5989
give away (1)
give generously (1) +5989
give in marriage (1) +408+4200
give in marriage (1) +851+2021
give permission (1)
given in pledge (1)
given up (1)
gives gifts (1)
gives over (1)
glad to give (1) +5989
granted requests (1)
granting (1)
grants (1)
growl (1) +7754
growled (1) +7754
hand over to (1) +928+3338
handed (1) +928+3338
handing over (1) +928+3338
hands over (1)
has sexual relations (1) +8888
have (1)
have (1) +4200
have sexual relations (1) +2446+4200+8888
have sexual relations (1) +8888
healing (1) +8337
hold (1)
hold accountable (1) +6584
honor (1) +3883
how I long for (1) +4769+5761
I wish (1) +4769
imparts (1)
imposed (1)
imprisoned (1) +657+1074+2021
imprisoned (1) +928+5464
inflict (1)
injured (1) +4583
injures (1) +4583
inserted (1)

inspire (1) +928+4222
instruct (1)
is drawn (1)
is thrown (1)
issued (1)
join (1)
keep (1)
leave (1)
let be heard (1)
let have (1)
let out (1)
lifts (1)
made face (1) +7156
made ready (1)
make restitution (1)
make turn (1) +448
marry (1)
must certainly give (1) +5989
oh (1) +686+4769
oh how I wish (1) +4769
open (1) +7341
ordained (1)
paid (1) +5486
pay (1) +924
pay (1) +4084
pay (1) +4836
pay (1) +8510
perform (1)
permitted to do (1)
pile (1)
piled (1)
pitch (1)
plant (1)
pledged (1) +3338
pour (1)
pour out (1)
produces (1)
producing (1)
prove to be (1)
pulled (1)
push (1)
put in place (1)
put on (1) +4230
put out (1)
put up (1)
raise (1)
raised (1) +2256+5951
raises (1)
raising (1)
receive (1)
receives (1) +4200
recite (1)
reduced (1)
reflected on (1) +448+4213
replaced (1) +9393
resolved (1) +7156
resound (1)
respect (1) +3702
reward (1) +7190
rewarded (1) +8510
rises (1)
roared (1) +7754
roars (1) +928+7754
sacrificed (1) +928+6296
seated (1) +5226
send down (1)
send out (1)
share (1)
shares (1)
sing (1) +7754
slander (1) +1984
sleeping with (1) +928+8888
sparkles (1) +6524
spend (1)
spreads (1)
stained (1)
store (1)
stored (1)
strike (1)
subjected (1)
submit (1) +3338
submitted (1) +3338
suffer (1) +6584
supplied (1)
supplies (1)
supply (1)
surely hand over (1) +928+3338+5989
surrenders (1) +3338
take for (1) +4200+7156
think (1) +4213
think (1) +4222
thunders (1) +928+7754
tie (1) +6584
tie up (1)
traded (1)
treated (1)
turned (1) +7156
turned into (1)
turned over (1)
turns (1)
use (1)
was entrusted (1)
was given in marriage (1) +851+4200
was left hanging (1)
wept so loudly (1) +906+928+1140+7754
were assigned (1)
were given (1)
were given over (1)
wins (1)
untranslated (34)

5990 נָתָן *nāṯān* (42)
Nathan (42)

5991 נְתַנְאֵל *n^eṯan'ēl* (14)
Nethanel (14)

5992 נְתַנְיָה *n^eṯanyāh* (15)
Nethaniah (15)

5993 נְתַנְיָהוּ *n^eṯanyāhû* (5)
Nethaniah (5)

5994 נְתַן־מֶלֶךְ *n^eṯan-meleḵ* (1)
Nathan-Melech (1)

5995 נָתַס *nāṯas* (1)
break up (1)

5996 נָתַע *nāṯa'* (1)
are broken (1)

5997 נָתַץ *nāṯaṣ* (42)
broke down (6)
tore down (6)
break down (4)
demolished (4)
tear down (3)
torn down (3)
demolish (2)
destroyed (2)
pulled down (2)
be broken up (1)
been torn down (1)
breaks down (1)
bring down to ruin (1)
broken down (1)
destroy (1)
lay in ruins (1)
shattered (1)
tear out (1)
tears down (1)

5998 נָתַק *nāṯaq* (27)
break (2)
broken (2)
snapped (2)
are purged out (1)
are shattered (1)
are snapped (1)
broke away (1)
drag off (1)
draw away (1)
is broken (1)
is torn (1)
lured away (1)
pull off (1)
set (1)
snaps (1)
tear (1)
tear away (1)
tear off (1)
tore off (1)
torn (1)
torn off (1)
uprooted (1) +9247
were drawn away (1)
were lured away (1)

5999 נֶתֶק *neṯeq* (14)
itch (7)
it[s] (3) +2021
diseased area (1)
him[s] (1) +2021
infected person (1) +5596
this kind of sore (1) +2021+5596

6000 1נָתַר *nāṯar1* (1)
let loose (1)

6001 2נָתַר *nāṯar2* (3)
hopping (1)
leaps (1)
made tremble (1)

6002 3נָתַר *nāṯar3* (3)
released (1)
sets free (1)
untie (1)

6003 נֶתֶר *neṯer* (2)
soda (2)

6004 נָתַשׁ *nāṯaš* (20)
uproot (11)
be uprooted (3)
uprooted (3)
completely uproot (1) +6004
was uprooted (1)

6005 ס *s*
Variant; not used

6006 סְאָה *s^e'āh* (9)
seahs (6)
seah (3)

6007 סְאוֹן *s^e'ôn* (1)
boot (1)

6008 סָאַן *sā'an* (1)
warrior's (1)

6009 סַאסְּאָה *sa'ss^e'āh* (1)
warfare (1)

6010 1סָבָא *sāḇā'1* (6)
drink fill (1)
drink too much (1)
drunk (1)
drunkard (1)
drunkards (1)
untranslated (1)

6011 סֹבֶא *sōḇe'* (3)
choice wine (1)
drinks (1)
wine (1)

6012 2סָבָא *sāḇā'2*
Variant; not used

6013 סְבָא *s^eḇā'* (4)
Seba (4)

6014 סְבָאִי *s^eḇā'iy* (2)
Sabeans (2)

6015 סָבַב *sāḇaḇ* (163)
surrounded (15)
turned (12)
surround (10)
turn (8)
changed (4)
go about (3)

moved (3)
prowl about (3)
turning (3)
circle around (2)
coiled around (2)
curved (2)
fall in (2) +448
led around (2)
made rounds (2)
made way around (2)
march around (2)
marched around (2)
measure around (2) +6017
pass (2)
round (2)
settings (2)
turn about (2)
turned around (2)
turned away (2)
turns (2)
went around (2)
winds through (2)
all around (1)
around (1)
be turned over (1)
become (1)
began (1)
bring back (1)
bring over (1)
brought around (1)
carried around (1)
change (1)
changing (1)
circled (1)
circuit (1)
circumference (1) +2562
coming around (1)
cross (1)
curved around (1)
dragged (1)
eluded (1) +4946+7156
encircled (1) +6017
encircled (1) +6017+6017
encircling (1)
engulf (1)
gather around (1)
gathered around (1)
go (1)
go around (1)
hinged (1)
is rolled (1)
leave (1) +4946
march around (1) +5938
on every side (1)
once again (1)
put around (1)
responsible for (1) +928
returned home (1)
roundabout (1)
sent around (1)
shielded (1)
sit down (1)
skirted (1)
stand aside (1)
stepped aside (1)
sulking (1) +906+7156
surrounding (1)
surrounds (1)
swarmed around (1)
swirled about (1)
swung open (1)
took away (1)
turn against (1)
turn away (1) +7156
turn over (1)
turned (1) +7156
turned over (1)
waged against from all sides (1)
walk about (1)
walk through (1)
went (1)
went throughout (1)
were changed (1)
were mounted (1)
untranslated (2)

6016 סִבָּה *sibbāh* (1)
turn of events (1)

6017 סָבִיב *sābiyb̲* (319)
around (108)
surrounding (27)
all around (23)
all around (17) +6017
on every side (16) +4946
on all sides (13)
on every side (9)
around (7) +4946
all (5)
neighbors (5)
surround (5)
every side (4)
surrounded (4)
around (3) +6017
about (2)
circular in shape (2) +6318
from every side (2) +4946
measure around (2) +6015
neighboring (2)
surrounds (2)
throughout (2) +928
all around (1) +4946
all over (1) +6017+6584
along (1)
area around (1)
around (1) +1237+4946
back and forth (1) +6017
circular band (1) +6318
completely (1)
completely surrounding (1) +6017
course (1)
covered with (1) +6017+8470
encircled (1) +6015
encircled (1) +6015+6017
encircling (1)
enveloped (1) +4946
escorted by (1)
everything around (1)
everywhere (1)
from (1) +4946
full (1) +1074
in (1)
on (1)
outside walls (1)
overrun (1)
ringed about (1)
round about (1)
sides (1) +4946+6298
stationed around (1)
surround (1) +2118+4946
surrounding (1) +6017
turn (1)
went over (1) +2118
untranslated (19)

6018 סָבַךְ *sāb̲ak̲* (2)
entangled (1)
entwines (1)

6019 סְבָךְ *sᵉb̲ak̲* (3)
thickets (2)
thicket (1)

6020 סְבֹךְ *sᵉb̲ōk̲* (2)
lair (1)
thicket (1)

6021 סִבְּכַי *sibbᵉkay* (4)
Sibbecai (4)

6022 סָבַל *sāb̲al* (9)
bear (2)
sustain (2)
burden (1)
carried (1)
carry (1)
drags himself along (1)
draw heavy loads (1)

6023 סֵבֶל *sēb̲el* (3)
burden (1)
labor force (1)
materials (1)

6024 סֹבֶל *sōb̲el* (3)
burden (2)
burdens (1)

6025 סַבָּל *sabbāl* (5)
carriers (2)
laborers (2)
carriers (1) +5951

6026 סִבְלוֹת *sib̲lôt̲* (6)
yoke (2)
forced labor (1)
hard labor (1)
work (1)
working (1)

6027 סִבֹּלֶת *sibbōlet̲* (1)
Sibboleth (1)

6028 סִבְרַיִם *sib̲rayim* (1)
Sibraim (1)

6029 סַבְתָּא *sab̲tā'* (1)
Sabta (1)

6030 סַבְתָּה *sab̲tāh* (1)
Sabtah (1)

6031 סַבְתְּכָא *sab̲tᵉkā'* (2)
Sabteca (2)

6032 סָגַד *sāgad̲* (5)
bow down (2)
bows down (2)
untranslated (1)

6033 סְגוֹר *sᵉgôr* (1)
rip open (1) +4213+7973

6034 סָגוּר *sāgûr* (9)
pure (8)
finest gold (1)

6035 סְגֻלָּה *sᵉgullāh* (8)
treasured possession (6)
personal treasures (1)
treasure (1)

6036 סֶגֶן *segen* (17)
officials (12)
commanders (3)
officers (1)
rulers (1)

6037 סָגַר *sāgar* (82)
shut (21)
put in isolation (5)
be shut (4)
gave over (3)
be shut up (2)
close (2)
close up (2)
closed (2)
closed up (2)
delivered (2)
hand over (2)
hand over (2) +928+3338
handed over (2) +928+3338
isolate (2)
keep in isolation (2)
sold (2)
surrender (2)
are closed (1)
closed in (1)
confine (1)
confined (1)
confines in prison (1)
deliver up (1)
delivered up (1)

filled in (1)
given up (1)
handing over (1) +928+3338
hemmed in (1)
imprisoned himself (1)
imprisons (1)
is barred (1)
locked (1)
sealed together (1) +2597
shut yourself (1)
shuts (1)
surrender (1) +928+3338
tightly shut up (1) +2256+6037
turned over (1)
will[s] (1)

6038 סָגָר *sāgār* (1)
javelin (1)

6039 סַגְרִיר *sagriyr* (1)
rainy (1)

6040 סַד *saḏ* (2)
shackles (2)

6041 סָדִין *sāḏiyn* (4)
linen garments (4)

6042 סְדֹם *sᵉḏōm* (39)
Sodom (38)
the city[s] (1)

6043 סֵדֶר *sēḏer* (1)
disorder (1) +4202

6044 סַהַר *sahar* (1)
rounded (1)

6045 סֹהַר *sōhar* (8)
prison (6) +1074+2021
untranslated (2)

6046 סוֹא *sô'* (1)
So (1)

6047 סוּג1 *sûg1* (24)
be turned (5)
move (4)
deserted (1) +294
disloyal (1)
drawn back (1) +294
faithless (1) +4213
is driven back (1) +294
moves (1)
overtake (1)
retreating (1) +294
store up (1)
turn (1)
turn away (1)
turn back (1)
turned (1)
turned away (1)
turning (1)

6048 סוּג2 *sûg̱2* (1)
encircled (1)

6049 סוּג3 *sûg̱3* (1)
untranslated (1)

6050 סוּגַר *sûg̱ar* (1)
cage (1)

6051 סוֹד *sôḏ* (21)
council (7)
confidence (4)
company (1)
confides (1)
conspiracy (1)
conspire (1)
counsel (1)
fellowship (1)
gathered (1)
intimate (1)
intimate friendship (1)
plan (1)

6052 סוֹדִי *sôḏiy* (1)
Sodi (1)

6053 סוּחַ *sûaḥ* (1)
Suah (1)

6054 סוּחָה *sûḥāh* (1)
refuse (1)

6055 סוֹטַי *sôṭay* (2)
Sotai (2)

6056 סוּךְ1 *sûḵ1* (2)
spurred on (1)
stir up (1)

6057 סוּךְ2 *sûḵ2* (10)
use (3)
healing balm (1)
perfume (1)
pour (1)
put on (1)
put on lotions (1)
used lotions at all (1) +6057

6058 סוּךְ3 *sûḵ3*
Variant; not used

6059 סְוֵנֵה *sᵉwēnēh* (3)
Aswan (3)

6060 סְוֵנִים *sᵉwēniym*
Variant; not used

6061 סוּס1 *sûs1* (138)
horses (87)
horse (30)
horseman (3) +8206
horseback (2)
horses' (2)
mounted (2) +8206
war-horses (2)
horse's (1)
horsemen (1) +8206
mounted (1) +928+2021
stallions (1)
them[s] (1)
work horses (1)
untranslated (4)

6062 סוּס2 *sûs2* (1)
untranslated (1)

6063 סוּסָה *sûsāh* (1)
mare (1)

6064 סוּסִי *sûsiy* (1)
Susi (1)

6065 סוּסִים *sûsiym*
Variant; not used

6066 סוּף1 *sûp̱1* (6)
sweep away (2)
demolished (1)
die out (1)
meet end (1)
sweep away (1) +665

6067 סוֹף *sôp̱* (5)
end (2)
conclusion (1)
destiny (1)
rear (1)

6068 סוּף2 *sûp̱2* (28)
red (24)
reeds (2)
rushes (1)
seaweed (1)

6069 סוּף3 *sûp̱3* (1)
Suph (1)

6070 סוּפָה1 *sûp̱āh1* (15)
whirlwind (6)
gale (2)
storm (2)
tempest (2)
stormy (1)
whirlwinds (1)
windstorm (1)

6071 סוּפָה2 *sûp̱āh2* (1)
Suphah (1)

6072 סוֹפֶרֶת *sôp̱ereṯ* (1)
Sophereth (1)

6073 סוּר1 *sûr1* (301)
removed (31)
remove (28)
turn away (22)
turn (10)
turned away (10)
away (7)
take away (7)
cut off (6)
leave (6)
turn aside (6)
take (5)
turned (5)
depart (4)
got rid of (4)
left (4)
shuns (4)
stop (4)
took off (4)
turned aside (4)
get rid of (3)
keep (3)
lifted (3)
taken away (3)
turning (3)
turning aside (3)
avoids (2)
cease (2)
come (2)
come in (2)
deny (2)
departed (2)
deposed (2)
go (2)
gone (2)
is removed (2)
leave alone (2) +4946
put away (2)
rejected (2)
rid (2)
shun (2)
stopped (2)
stray (2)
take off (2)
throw away (2)
took (2)
took away (2)
turned in (2)
abolish (1)
banish (1)
been removed (1)
broke away (1)
carry away (1)
circumcise (1) +6889
clear (1)
cleared away (1)
come over (1)
denied (1)
denies (1)
deprives (1)
dethroned (1)
deviate (1)
did away with (1)
do away with (1) +4946+9348
dragged (1)
end (1)
entered (1) +448
escape (1)
expelled (1)
fail (1) +4946
failed to keep (1) +4946
far (1)
give up (1)
give up pursuit (1)
go away (1)
go over (1)

gone over (1)
hardened rebels (1) +6253
instead of (1)
is abolished (1)
keep free (1)
lay aside (1)
led astray (1)
left undone (1)
made come off (1)
make leave (1)
move (1)
move back (1)
moved away (1)
no longer be (1) +4946
pass away (1)
past (1)
put aside (1)
put out (1)
removal (1)
removes (1)
return (1)
sent away (1)
set aside (1)
shows no (1)
shunned (1)
silences (1)
slip (1)
snatch away (1)
stay (1)
strip off (1)
take back (1)
taken (1)
turns (1)
turns away (1)
vanish (1)
ward off (1)
went over (1)
went up (1)
untranslated (2)

6074 2סוּר *sûr2* (1)
corrupt (1)

6075 3סוּר *sûr3* (1)
Sur (1)

6076 סוֹרִי *sôriy*
Variant; not used

6077 1סוּת *sûṯ1* (18)
incited (4)
urged (3)
entices (2)
misleading (2)
drew away (1)
inciting (1)
let mislead (1)
mislead (1)
misled (1)
urged on (1)
wooing (1)

6078 2סוּת *sûṯ2* (2)
robes (1)
untranslated (1)

6079 סָחַב *sāḥaḇ* (5)
dragged away (3)
drag away (1)
drag down (1)

6080 סְחָבָה *sᵉḥāḇāh* (3)
rags (2)
untranslated (1)

6081 סָחָה *sāḥāh* (1)
scrape away (1)

6082 סְחִי *sᵉḥiy* (1)
scum (1)

6083 סְחִיפָה *sᵉḥiyp̄āh*
Variant; not used

6084 סָחִישׁ *sāḥiyš* (1)
what springs from (1)

6085 סָחַף *sāḥap̄* (2)
be laid low (1)
driving (1)

6086 סָחַר *sāḥar* (21)
merchants (8)
did business with (4)
trade (3)
customers (1) +3338
gone (1)
merchant (1)
pounds (1)
traders (1)
trafficked (1)

6087 סַחַר *saḥar* (7)
marketplace (1)
merchandise (1)
profit (1)
profitable (1) +3202
profits (1)
trading (1)
untranslated (1)

6088 סְחֹרָה *sᵉḥōrāh* (1)
customers (1) +3338

6089 סֹחֵרָה *sōḥērāh* (1)
rampart (1)

6090 סֹחֶרֶת *sōḥereṯ* (1)
costly stones (1)

6091 סֵט *sēṭ* (1)
faithless (1)

6092 סִיג *siyg̱* (7)
dross (7)

6093 סִיד *siyḏ*
Variant; not used

6094 סִיוָן *siywān* (1)
Sivan (1)

6095 סִיחוֹן *siyḥôn* (37)
Sihon (34)
he[s] (2)
Sihon's (1)

6096 1סִין *siyn1* (2)
Pelusium (2)

6097 2סִין *siyn2* (4)
sin (4)

6098 סִינִי *siyniy* (2)
Sinites (2)

6099 סִינַי *siynay* (35)
Sinai (35)

6100 סִינִים *siyniym*
Variant; not used

6101 סִיס *siys* (2)
swift (2)

6102 סִיסְרָא *siysᵉrā'* (21)
Sisera (20)
Sisera's (1)

6103 סִיעָא *siy'ā'* (1)
Sia (1)

6104 סִיעֲהָא *siy'ᵃhā'* (1)
Siaha (1)

6105 סִיר *siyr* (29)
pot (11)
pots (11)
cooking pot (2)
washbasin (2) +8176
caldron (1)
cooking pots (1)
pan (1)

6106 סִירָה *siyrāh* (5)
thorns (3)
fishhooks (1) +1855
thornbushes (1)

6107 סַךְ *sāḵ* (1)
multitude (1)

6108 סֹךְ *sōḵ* (4)
cover (1)
dwelling (1)
lair (1)
tent (1)

6109 סֻכָּה *sukkāh* (32)
tabernacles (9)
booths (7)
shelter (3)
tents (3)
canopy (2)
dwelling (1)
hut (1)
pavilion (1)
shelters (1)
shrine (1)
tent (1)
them[s] (1) +2021
thicket (1)

6110 סִכּוּת *sikkûṯ*
Variant; not used

6111 סֻכּוֹת *sukkôṯ* (18)
Succoth (18)

6112 סֻכּוֹת בְּנוֹת *sukkôṯ bᵉnôṯ* (1)
Succoth Benoth (1)

6113 סֻכִּיִּים *sukkiyyiym* (1)
Sukkites (1)

6114 1סָכַךְ *sāḵaḵ1* (18)
covered (2)
guardian (2)
overshadowing (2)
conceal (1)
cover (1)
hedged in (1)
overshadowed (1)
relieve himself (1) +906+2257+8079
relieving himself (1) +906+2257+8079
shelter (1)
shield (1)
shielded (1)
shields (1)
shut up (1)
spread protection (1)

6115 2סָכַךְ *sāḵaḵ2* (2)
knit together (2)

6116 סֹכֵךְ *sōḵēḵ* (1)
protective shield (1)

6117 סְכָכָה *sᵉḵāḵāh* (1)
Secacah (1)

6118 סָכַל *sāḵal* (8)
done a foolish thing (3)
acted foolishly (1)
acted like a fool (1)
foolish (1)
turn into foolishness (1)
turns into nonsense (1)

6119 סָכָל *sāḵāl* (8)
fool (4)
foolish (1)
senseless (1)
stupid (1)
untranslated (1)

6120 סֶכֶל *seḵel* (1)
fools (1)

6121 סִכְלוּת *siḵlûṯ* (6)
folly (6)

6122 1סָכַן *sāḵan1* (9)
be of benefit (1)
been in the habit of (1) +6122
benefit (1)
familiar with (1)
profit (1)

profits (1)
submit (1)
useless (1) +4202

6123 2סָכַן *sāḵan2* (1)
too poor (1)

6124 3סָכַן *sāḵan3* (1)
be endangered (1)

6125 סֹכֵן *sōḵēn* (3)
steward (1)
take care of (1) +2118
took care of (1) +2118

6126 1סָכַר *sāḵar1* (2)
be silenced (1)
been closed (1)

6127 2סָכַר *sāḵar2* (1)
hand over (1)

6128 3סָכַר *sāḵar3* (1)
hired (1)

6129 סָכַת *sāḵat* (1)
silent (1)

6130 סַל *sal* (15)
basket (12)
baskets (2)
it[s] (1) +2021

6131 סָלָא *sālā'* (1)
worth their weight (1)

6132 סַלֻּא *sallu'* (2)
Sallu (2)

6133 סִלָּא *sillā'* (1)
Silla (1)

6134 סָלַד *sālaḏ* (1)
joy (1)

6135 סֶלֶד *seleḏ* (2)
Seled (2)

6136 1סָלָה *sālāh1* (2)
reject (1)
rejected (1)

6137 2סָלָה *sālāh2* (2)
be bought (2)

6138 סֶלָה *selāh* (74)
Selah (74)

6139 סַלּוּ *sallû* (2)
Sallu (1)
Sallu's (1)

6140 סָלוּא *sālû'* (1)
Salu (1)

6141 סִלּוֹן *sillôn* (2)
briers (1)
thorns (1)

6142 סָלַח *sālah* (47)
forgive (26)
be forgiven (13)
release (3)
forgiven (2)
forgives (1)
pardon (1)
untranslated (1)

6143 סַלָּח *sallāh* (1)
forgiving (1)

6144 סַלַּי *sallay* (1)
Sallai (1)

6145 סְלִיחָה *s[e]liyhāh* (3)
forgiving (2)
forgiveness (1)

6146 סַלְכָה *salḵāh* (4)
Salecah (4)

6147 1סָלַל *sālal1* (2)
esteem (1)
set yourself (1)

6148 2סָלַל *sālal2* (10)
build up (4)
build (2)
built up (1)
extol (1)
is a highway (1)
pile up (1)

6149 סֹלְלָה *sōl[e]lāh* (11)
siege ramps (4)
ramp (3)
siege ramp (3)
ramps (1)

6150 סֻלָּם *sullām* (1)
stairway (1)

6151 סַלְסִלָּה *salsillāh* (1)
branches (1)

6152 1סֶלַע *sela'1* (58)
rock (30)
rocks (9)
crags (4)
cliff (2)
cliffs (2)
mountain (2)
cliff (1) +9094
rocky (1)
rocky crag (1)
rocky crags (1)
stone (1)
stronghold (1)
where[s] (1) +928+8234
untranslated (2)

6153 2סֶלַע *sela'2* (4)
Sela (4)

6154 סֶלַע הַמַּחְלְקוֹת *sela' hammahl[e]qôṯ* (1)
Sela Hammahlekoth (1)

6155 סָלְעָם *sāl[e]'ām* (1)
katydid (1)

6156 סָלַף *sālap̄* (7)
overthrows (2)
twists (2)
brings to ruin (1) +2021+4200+8273
frustrates (1)
ruins (1)

6157 סֶלֶף *selep̄* (2)
deceitful (1)
duplicity (1)

6158 סָלַק *sālaq* (1)
go up (1)

6159 סֹלֶת *sōleṯ* (53)
fine flour (46)
flour (6)
fine (1)

6160 סַם *sam* (16)
fragrant (14)
fragrant spices (1)
untranslated (1)

6161 סַמְגַּר *samgar* (1)
Samgar (1)

6162 סַמְגַּר־נְבוֹ *samgar-n[e]ḇô*
Variant; not used

6163 סְמָדַר *s[e]māḏar* (3)
blossoming (1)
blossoms (1)
in bloom (1)

6164 סָמַךְ *sāmaḵ* (48)
lay (17)
laid (6)
sustained (3)
upholds (3)
leans (2)
steadfast (2)
sustain (2)
sustains (2)
allies (1)
bracing (1)
gained confidence (1)
gave support (1)
laid siege (1)
lies heavily (1)
relied (1)
rely (1)
rested (1)
secure (1)
strengthen (1)

6165 סְמַכְיָהוּ *s[e]makyāhû* (1)
Semakiah (1)

6166 סֶמֶל *semel* (5)
idol (2)
image (2)
shape (1)

6167 סָמַם *sāmam*
Variant; not used

6168 סָמַן *sāman* (1)
plot (1)

6169 סָמַר *sāmar* (2)
stood on end (1)
trembles (1)

6170 סָמָר *sāmār* (1)
swarm (1)

6171 סְנָאָה *s[e]nā'āh* (2)
Senaah (2)

6172 סַנְבַלַּט *sanḇallat* (10)
Sanballat (10)

6173 סַנָּה *sannāh*
Variant; not used

6174 סְנֶה *s[e]neh* (6)
bush (5)
it[s] (1) +2021

6175 סֶנֶּה *senneh* (1)
Seneh (1)

6176 סְנוּאָה *s[e]nû'āh*
Variant; not used

6177 סַנְוֵרִים *sanwēriym* (3)
blindness (3)

6178 סַנְחֵרִיב *sanhēriyḇ* (13)
Sennacherib (13)

6179 סַנְסַנָּה *sansannāh* (1)
Sansannah (1)

6180 סַנְסִנָּה *sansinnāh* (1)
fruit (1)

6181 סְנַפִּיר *s[e]nappiyr* (5)
fins (5)

6182 סָס *sās* (1)
worm (1)

6183 סִסְמַי *sismay* (2)
Sismai (2)

6184 סָעַד *sā'aḏ* (12)
refresh (2)
sustains (2)
grant support (1)
have something to eat (1)
made secure (1)
refreshed (1) +4213
supported (1)
sustain (1)
uphold (1)
upholding (1)

6185 סָעָה *sā'āh* (1)
tempest (1) +8120

6186 1סָעִיף *sā'iyp̄1* (4)
cave (2)
overhanging (2)

6187 2סָעִיף *sā'iyp̄2* (2)
boughs (1)

branches (1)

6188 סָעַף *sā'ap̱* (1)
lop off (1)

6189 סֵעֵף *sē'ēp̱* (1)
double-minded (1)

6190 סְעַפָּה *s^{e}'appāh* (2)
boughs (2)

6191 סְעִפִּים *s^{e}'ippiym* (1)
opinions (1)

6192 סָעַר *sā'ar* (7)
enraged (1) +4213
grew even wilder (1) +2143+2256
lashed by storms (1)
rougher and rougher (1) +2143+2256
scattered with a whirlwind (1)
stormed out (1)
swirling (1)

6193 סַעַר *sa'ar* (8)
storm (4)
tempest (1)
violent winds (1)
whirlwind (1)
wind (1)

6194 סְעָרָה *s^{e}'arah* (18)
storm (5)
whirlwind (3)
gale (1)
storms (1)
stormy (1)
tempest (1)
tempest (1) +8120
violent wind (1) +8120
violent winds (1) +8120
windstorm (1) +8120
untranslated (2)

6195 1סַף *sap̱1* (7)
basins (3)
basin (1)
bowls (1)
cup (1)
untranslated (1)

6196 2סַף *sap̱2*
Variant; not used

6197 3סַף *sap̱3* (25)
threshold (7)
doorkeepers (5) +9068
thresholds (5)
doorway (2)
doorframes (1)
doorkeeper (1) +9068
doors (1)
doorways (1)
entrance (1)
untranslated (1)

6198 4סַף *sap̱4* (1)
Saph (1)

6199 סָפַד *sāp̱aḏ* (30)
mourn (12)
mourned (8)
lament (3)
be mourned (2)
beat (1)
lamented (1) +5027
mourners (1)
walk in mourning (1)
weep (1)

6200 סָפָה *sāp̱āh* (16)
be swept away (4)
sweep away (2)
are caught (1)
be destroyed (1)
being swept away (1)
bring disaster (1)
perish (1)
perished (1)
sweeps away (1)
swept away (1)
take (1)
take off (1)

6201 סָפוֹן *sāp̱ôn*
Variant; not used

6202 1סָפַח *sāp̱ah1* (4)
appoint (1)
huddled (1)
share (1)
unite (1)

6203 2סָפַח *sāp̱ah2* (1)
pouring (1)

6204 סַפַּחַת *sappahat̠* (2)
rash (2)

6205 סִפַּי *sippay* (1)
Sippai (1)

6206 1סָפִיחַ *sāp̱iyah1* (4)
what grows by itself (2)
what grows of itself (2)

6207 2סָפִיחַ *sāp̱iyah2* (1)
torrents (1)

6208 סְפִינָה *s^{e}p̱iynāh* (1)
below deck (1) +2021+3752

6209 סַפִּיר *sappiyr* (11)
sapphires (5)
sapphire (4)
sapphire (2) +74

6210 סֵפֶל *sēp̱el* (2)
bowl (1)
bowlful (1) +4850

6211 סָפַן *sāp̱an* (6)
covered (1)
paneled (1)
panels (1)
roofing (1)
was kept (1)
was roofed (1)

6212 סִפֻּן *sippun* (2)
ceiling (2)

6213 סַפְסִיג *sap̱siyg̱* (1)
glaze (1)

6214 סָפַף *sāp̱ap̱* (1)
doorkeeper (1)

6215 1סָפַק *sāp̱aq1* (6)
beat (2)
clap (1)
punishes (1)
scornfully claps hands (1)
struck together (1)

6216 2סָפַק *sāp̱aq2* (1)
wallow (1)

6217 סֶפֶק *sep̱eq* (1)
riches (1)

6218 סָפַר *sāp̱ar* (105)
tell (18)
told (17)
count (12)
count off (6)
declare (6)
proclaim (4)
counted (3)
telling (3)
be recorded (2)
be told (2)
recount (2)
talk (2)
were told (2)
acknowledge (1)
appraised (1)
be counted (1)
boasted (1)
census taken (1) +6222
conscripted (1)
counted out (1)
declared (1)
gave account (1)
inform (1)
is declared (1)
keeping records (1)
make countless (1) +889+4202+8049
proclaimed (1)
recite (1)
record (1)
recounted (1)
repeated (1)
speak (1)
state (1)
took a census (1)
utter (1)
wait (1)
were counted (1)
write (1)
untranslated (1)

6219 1סֵפֶר *sēp̱er1* (188)
book (104)
scroll (23)
letter (12)
letters (10)
deed (6)
certificate (4)
dispatches (4)
scroll (4) +4479
it^{S} (3) +2021
literature (2)
written (2)
books (1)
can read (1) +3359
cannot read (1) +3359+4202
deeds (1)
documents (1)
indictment (1)
know how to read (1) +3359
record (1)
records (1)
scriptures (1)
them^{S} (1)
untranslated (3)

6220 2סֵפֶר *sēp̱er2*
Variant; not used

6221 סֹפֵר *sōp̱ēr* (56)
secretary (28)
scribe (11)
secretaries (4)
scribes (2)
teacher (2)
writing (2)
chief officer (1)
commander's (1)
man learned (1)
officer in charge (1)
scribe's (1)
secretary's (1)
writer (1)

6222 1סְפָר *s^{e}p̱ār1* (1)
census taken (1) +6218

6223 2סְפָר *s^{e}p̱ār2* (1)
Sephar (1)

6224 סְפָרַד *s^{e}p̱āraḏ* (1)
Sepharad (1)

6225 סִפְרָה *sip̱rāh* (1)
record (1)

6226 סְפַרְוַיִם *s^{e}p̱arwayim* (7)
Sepharvaim (6)
untranslated (1)

6227 סְפַרְוִים *s^{e}p̱arwiym* (1)
Sepharvites (1)

6228 סְפֹרוֹת *s^{e}p̱ōrôt̠* (1)
measure (1)

6229 סֹפְרִים *sōp̄ᵉriym*
Variant; not used

6230 סֹפֶרֶת *sōp̄eret̲*
Variant; not used

6231 סֶפֶת *sep̄et̲*
Variant; not used

6232 סָקַל *sāqal* (22)
stone (5)
be stoned (2)
been stoned (2)
stone (2) +74+928+2021
stoned (2) +74+928+2021
cleared of stones (1)
must be stoned to death (1) +6232
pelted (1)
remove (1)
stoning (1)
surely be stoned (1) +6232
throwing (1)

6233 סַר *sār* (1)
captain (1)

6234 סַר *sar* (3)
sullen (3)

6235 סָרָב *sārāb̲* (1)
briers (1)

6236 סַרְגּוֹן *sargôn* (1)
Sargon (1)

6237 סֶרֶד *sered̲* (2)
Sered (2)

6238 סַרְדִּי *sardiy* (1)
Seredite (1)

6239 1סָרָה *sārāh1* (1)
unceasing (1) +1194

6240 2סָרָה *sārāh2* (7)
rebellion (4)
crime (1)
revolt (1)
revolted against (1)

6241 סִרָה *sirāh* (1)
Sirah (1)

6242 סָרוּחַ *sārûah* (3)
flowing (1)
lounge (1)
lounging (1)

6243 1סָרַח *sārah1* (3)
hang (1)
hang down (1)
spreading (1)

6244 2סָרַח *sārah2* (1)
decayed (1)

6245 סֶרַח *serah* (1)
length (1)

6246 סִרְיוֹן *siryôn* (2)
armor (2)

6247 סָרִיס *sāriys* (45)
eunuchs (10)
official (9)
officials (9)
officer (5)
court officials (4)
eunuch (4)
officers (2)
attendants (1)
palace officials (1)

6248 1סֶרֶן *seren1* (1)
axles (1)

6249 2סֶרֶן *seren2* (21)
rulers (21)

6250 סַרְעַפָּה *sar'appāh* (1)
boughs (1)

6251 סָרַף *sārap̲* (1)
burn (1)

6252 סִרְפָּד *sirpād̲* (1)
briers (1)

6253 1סָרַר *sārar1* (17)
stubborn (6)
rebellious (4)
obstinate (2)
stubbornly (2)
defiant (1)
hardened rebels (1) +6073
rebels (1)

6254 2סָרַר *sārar2* (1)
in charge (1)

6255 סְתָו *sᵉtāw* (1)
winter (1)

6256 סְתוּר *sᵉtûr* (1)
Sethur (1)

6257 סְתָיו *sᵉtāyw* (1)
untranslated (1)

6258 סָתַם *sātam* (12)
stopped up (3)
blocked (2)
being closed (1)
blocking off (1)
close up (1)
closed up (1)
inmost place (1)
seal up (1)
stop up (1)

6259 סָתַר *sātar* (83)
hide (35)
hidden (10)
hid (9)
hiding (4)
conceal (2)
concealed (2)
is hidden (2)
secret (2)
are hidden (1)
away (1)
be sheltered (1)
certainly hide (1) +6259
covers (1)
go into hiding (1)
have no (1) +4946+6524
hide yourself (1)
hides (1)
hides himself (1)
hiding place (1)
take refuge (1)
takes refuge (1)
undetected (1)
vanish (1)
untranslated (1)

6260 סֵתֶר *sēter* (35)
secret (8)
secretly (6) +928+2021
shelter (5)
hiding place (2)
privately (2) +928+2021
refuge (2)
concealed (1)
covering (1)
hidden (1)
hiding (1)
hiding places (1)
ravine (1)
secret place (1)
sly (1)
thundercloud (1) +8308
veil (1)

6261 סִתְרָה *sitrāh* (1)
give shelter (1) +2118

6262 סִתְרִי *sitriy* (1)
Sithri (1)

6263 ע '
Variant; not used

6264 1עָב *'āb1* (3)
overhang (1)
overhanging roof (1)
overhangs (1)

6265 2עָב *'āb2* (30)
clouds (19)
cloud (7)
clouds of the sky (2) +8836
cloudless (1) +4202
thick clouds (1)

6266 3עָב *'āb3* (1)
thickets (1)

6267 עַב *'ab̲*
Variant; not used

6268 עָבַד *'ābad̲* (290)
serve (88)
worship (37)
served (28)
worshiped (13)
do (11)
work (10)
serving (8)
subject to (8)
ministers (6)
enslave (3)
enslaved (3)
labor (3)
subject (3)
work for (3)
worked (3)
worked for (3)
worshiping (3)
burdened (2)
farm (2)
hold in bondage (2)
serves (2)
till (2)
used (2)
work (2) +6275
workers (2)
works (2)
be cultivated (1)
be plowed (1)
been plowed (1)
been worked (1)
been[s] (1)
bondage (1) +6275
cultivate (1)
do work (1)
do[s] (1)
doing (1)
done (1)
drove (1)
efforts (1)
enslaving (1)
farmer (1) +141+408
fulfilling by doing (1)
keep working (1)
laborer (1)
led (1)
make slaves (1)
make work (1)
making work (1)
observe (1)
perform (1)
profits (1)
put to work (1)
reduced to servitude (1) +4200+6269
servant (1)
serve as slaves (1)
services (1)
slave (1)
subjects (1)
subjugate (1)
submit (1)
to subject (1)
worship (1) +6275

untranslated (3)

6269 עֶבֶד1 *'eḇeḏ1* (806)
servant (325)
servants (156)
officials (77)
men (48)
slaves (30)
officers (16)
menservants (15)
slave (15)
attendants (14)
slavery (14)
manservant (8)
male slaves (7)
servant's (7)
subject (7)
official (4)
subjects (3)
attendant (2)
in bondage (2)
male slave (2)
officer (2)
retinue (2)
serve (2)
slaves (2) +2256+9148
them^{S} (2) +2257
they^{S} (2) +2257
vassal (2)
vassals (2)
as a slave (1) +6275
court (1)
delegation (1) +928+3338
enslaved (1) +2256+3899+4200+4200+9148
envoys (1)
fellow officers (1) +123
government officials (1)
he^{S} (1) +3870
him^{S} (1) +3870
I^{S} (1) +3870
in service (1)
lowest of slaves (1) +6269
make men slaves (1) +3899
me^{S} (1) +3870
messengers (1)
reduced to servitude (1) +4200+6268
servants men (1)
servants the (1)
servants' (1)
servants' (1) +4200
served (1)
service (1)
slaves (1) +563+2256
slaves male (1)
subordinates (1)
them^{S} (1) +1192
they^{S} (1) +8620
worship (1)
untranslated (9)

6270 עֶבֶד2 *'eḇeḏ2* (6)
Ebed (6)

6271 עֲבַד *ᵃḇaḏ* (1)
what do (1)

6272 עַבְדָּא *'aḇdā'* (2)
Abda (2)

6273 עֹבֵד־אֱדוֹם *'ōḇēḏ-'ᵉdôm* (20)
Obed-Edom (18)
him^{S} (1)
his^{S} (1)

6274 עַבְדְּאֵל *'aḇdᵉ'ēl* (1)
Abdeel (1)

6275 עֲבֹדָה *ᵃḇōḏāh* (144)
work (39)
service (24)
regular work (12) +4856
labor (7)
duties (5)
serving (5)
use (5)
ceremony (3)
ministering (3)
campaign (2)
constructing (2)
job (2)
ministry (2)
slavery (2)
task (2)
various kinds of service (2) +2256+6275
work (2) +6268
as a slave (1) +6269
assist (1)
bondage (1)
bondage (1) +6268
by (1)
craft (1)
cultivate (1)
demands (1)
doing (1)
doing work (1)
effect (1)
farmed (1)
posts (1)
regular service (1) +7372
required (1)
responsible (1)
responsible (1) +4856
served (1)
slaves (1)
tasks (1)
workers (1) +1074
worship (1) +6268
untranslated (2)

6276 עֲבֻדָּה *ᵃḇuddāh* (2)
servants (2)

6277 עַבְדּוֹן1 *'aḇdôn1* (6)
Abdon (6)

6278 עַבְדּוֹן2 *'aḇdôn2* (3)
Abdon (3)

6279 עַבְדִּי *'aḇdiy* (3)
Abdi (3)

6280 עַבְדִּיאֵל *'aḇdiy'ēl* (1)
Abdiel (1)

6281 עֹבַדְיָה *'ōḇaḏyāh* (11)
Obadiah (11)

6282 עֹבַדְיָהוּ *'ōḇaḏyāhû* (9)
Obadiah (9)

6283 עֶבֶד־מֶלֶךְ *'eḇeḏ-meleḵ* (6)
Ebed-Melech (6)

6284 עֲבֵד נְגוֹ *ᵃḇēḏ nᵉgô* (1)
Abednego (1)

6285 עַבְדֻת *'aḇduṯ* (3)
bondage (2)
slavery (1)

6286 עָבָה *'āḇāh* (3)
thicker (2)
heavy (1)

6287 עֲבוֹט *ᵃḇôṭ* (4)
pledge (2)
offering as a pledge (1)
untranslated (1)

6288 עֲבוּר1 *ᵃḇûr1* (49)
for the sake of (11)
because of (6)
so that (5)
for sake (4)
to (4)
because (3)
for (2)
in order to (2)
on account of (2)
so (2)
that (2)
for this purpose (1)
then (1)
to (1) +928+4200
while (1)
untranslated (2)

6289 עֲבוּר2 *ᵃḇûr2* (2)
food (1)
produce (1)

6290 עָבוֹת1 *'āḇôṯ1* (4)
leafy (3)
shade (1)

6291 עָבוֹת2 *'āḇôṯ2* (5)
thick foliage (4)
boughs (1)

6292 עָבַט1 *'āḇaṭ1* (5)
borrow (1)
freely lend (1) +6292
get (1)
lend (1)

6293 עָבַט2 *'āḇaṭ2* (1)
swerving (1)

6294 עַבְטִיט *'aḇṭiyṭ* (1)
extortion (1)

6295 עֳבִי *ᵒḇiy* (6)
thick (2)
thickness (2)
dense (1)
molds (1)

6296 עָבַר1 *'āḇar1* (551)
crossed (31)
pass (30)
cross (28)
cross over (23)
passed (21)
crossed over (17)
go (17)
crossing (12)
went (10)
passed by (9)
pass by (8)
pass through (8)
went on (8)
go over (7)
sacrificed (6)
violated (6)
come (5)
go on (5)
moved on (5)
swept (5)
pass by (4) +2006
sacrifice (4)
take away (4)
advanced (3)
came along (3)
come over (3)
continued (3)
going (3)
led (3)
over (3)
pass away (3)
passed through (3)
spread (3)
traveled (3)
bring across (2)
broken (2)
came by (2)
comes (2)
disobey (2)
get through (2)
go beyond (2)
go on way (2)
go past (2)
going down (2)
gone (2)
gone by (2)
had pass (2)
journey (2)
led through (2)
make (2)

marched (2)
pass on (2)
passed along (2)
passer-by (2)
passes (2)
passing by (2)
passing through (2)
past (2)
put (2)
send (2)
spare (2)
sweep through (2)
sweeps by (2)
swept by (2)
taken away (2)
travel (2)
travelers (2)
travels (2)
turn over (2)
walked (2)
according to the weight current (1)
advance (1)
avert (1) +4946+6584
be over (1)
been (1)
beyond (1)
blown (1)
blows (1)
breed (1)
bring across (1) +6296
brought (1)
brought over (1)
came to the other side (1)
carried over (1)
carry over (1)
cast off (1)
cause to pass (1)
cease (1)
census (1) +408
coming (1)
coming over (1)
continue on (1)
continued along (1)
continued on (1)
counted off (1) +928+5031
cover (1)
cover (1) +6584
cross over without fail (1) +6296
crosses over (1)
crossing over (1)
did so[s] (1)
disobeyed (1)
disobeying (1)
disregarded (1)
driven (1)
enter (1)
exceed (1)
expelled (1)
explored (1) +9365
extended (1)
fail (1)
fall (1)
felt (1)
fleeting (1)
flowing (1)
follow (1) +339
forded (1)
forgive (1)
forgives (1)
forth (1)
give over (1)
go away (1)
goes (1)
goes across (1)
goes through (1)
going over (1)
gone on (1)
had pass by (1)
have no limit (1)
have shave (1) +9509
have sounded (1)
invade (1)
invade (1) +928
irresistible (1)
issued (1)
jealous (1) +6584+7863+8120
kept on going (1)
know no limits (1)
laid (1)
lead across (1) +4200+7156
leaving (1) +4946
led around (1)
let pass (1)
made work (1)
make cross (1)
marauding (1) +2256+8740
march on (1)
marched on (1)
marched past (1) +3338+6584
marching (1)
missed (1)
moved on ahead (1)
moved on beyond (1)
moves on (1)
on the way (1)
on way (1)
outran (1)
over going (1)
overcome (1)
overflow (1)
overlook (1)
overrun (1)
overstep (1)
overwhelmed (1) +8031
overwhelming (1)
pass into other hands (1)
passed away (1)
passes by (1)
passing (1)
perish (1)
perishing (1)
provide safe-conduct (1)
put a yoke (1)
put an end (1)
ran (1)
ran past (1)
reclaimed (1)
remove (1)
removed (1)
repealed (1)
roam (1)
sacrificed (1) +928+5989
sacrifices (1)
sail (1)
seafarers (1) +3542
send out (1)
sent (1)
sent across (1)
sent over (1)
sent throughout (1)
set free (1)
shave (1)
sin (1)
sound (1)
spreading among (1)
surrounded (1)
sweep (1)
sweeps on (1)
swept away (1)
swim (1)
take note as pass (1)
take over (1)
taken from (1)
taken over (1)
them[s] (1) +2021
they[s] (1) +2021
through (1)
took (1)
took off (1)
transfer (1)
transgressed (1)
travel (1) +2006
traveled along (1)
traveling through (1)
turn away (1)
turned aside (1)
untraveled (1) +408+1172+4946
used (1)
vanishes (1)
violate (1)
violation (1)
wade through (1)
walk on (1)
walk over (1)
walked over (1)
went as far as (1)
went away (1)
went forward (1)
went over (1)
went up (1)
untranslated (11)

6297 2עָבַר *'āḇar2* (8)
very angry (4)
angers (1)
angry (1)
hotheaded (1)
meddles (1)

6298 1עֵבֶר *'ēḇer1* (92)
east (9) +928
side (9)
other side (6)
beyond (5) +928
across (4) +928
beyond (4)
Trans-Euphrates (4) +2021+5643
across (3) +4946
straight ahead (3) +448+7156
beyond (2) +4946
east (2) +4946
near (2) +928
next to (2) +448
across from (1) +4946
along (1)
along (1) +928
along (1) +4946
alongside (1) +4946
at (1) +928
by (1) +4946
east (1)
east (1) +928+2025+4667
east (1) +928+2025+4667+9087
east (1) +928+4667+9087
east (1) +2025+4667
east side (1)
from (1) +4946
goes on (1)
land beyond (1)
next to (1) +4200
on each side (1) +2021+2021+2296+2296+4946+4946+4946+4946+6298
on the other side of (1) +2134+2256+4946
on this side of (1) +4946
over here (1) +285+4200
over there (1) +285+4200
side (1) +4946
sides (1)
sides (1) +4946+6017
space (1)
this side (1)
west (1)
west (1) +928
west (1) +4946
untranslated (6)

6299 2עֵבֶר *'ēḇer2* (15)
Eber (15)

6300 עָבָר *'āḇār*
Variant; not used

6301 עֶבְרָה *'eḇrāh* (34)
wrath (21)
anger (4)

fury (4)
insolence (2)
rage (2)
overweening pride (1) +2295

6302 עֲבָרָה *ʿᵃḇārāh* (3)
fords (2)
ford (1)

6303 עִבְרִי1 *ʿiḇriy1* (34)
Hebrew (16)
Hebrews (16)
woman[S] (1)
untranslated (1)

6304 עִבְרִי2 *ʿiḇriy2* (1)
Ibri (1)

6305 עֲבָרִים *ʿᵃḇāriym* (5)
Abarim (5)

6306 עֶבְרֹן *ʿeḇrōn*
Variant; not used

6307 עַבְרֹנָה *ʿaḇrōnāh* (2)
Abronah (2)

6308 עָבַשׁ *ʿāḇaš* (1)
shriveled (1)

6309 עָבַת *ʿāḇaṯ* (1)
conspire (1)

6310 עֲבֹת *ʿᵃḇōṯ* (19)
ropes (7)
chains (4)
rope (3)
chains (1) +9249
cords (1)
fetters (1)
harness (1)
ties (1)

6311 עָגַב *ʿāg̱aḇ* (8)
lusted after (3) +6584
lovers (1)
lusted (1)
lusted after (1)
lusted after (1) +448
untranslated (1)

6312 עֲגָבָה *ʿᵃg̱āḇāh* (2)
love (1)
lust (1)

6313 עֲגָבִים *ʿᵃg̱āḇiym* (1)
devotion (1)

6314 עֻגָה *ʿug̱āh* (7)
cake of bread (2)
cakes (2)
bread (1)
cake (1)
flat cake (1)

6315 עָגוּר *ʿāg̱ûr* (2)
thrush (2)

6316 עָגִיל *ʿāg̱iyl* (2)
earrings (2)

6317 עֲגִילָה *ʿᵃg̱iylāh* (1)
shields (1)

6318 עָגֹל *ʿāg̱ōl* (6)
circular in shape (2) +6017
round (2)
circular band (1) +6017
rounded (1)

6319 עֵגֶל *ʿēg̱el* (36)
calf (19)
calves (10)
shape of a calf (3)
calf-idol (2)
calf-idols (1)
shape of calves (1)

6320 עֶגְלָה1 *ʿeg̱lāh1* (11)
heifer (6)
heifer (2) +1330
heifer's (1)
her[S] (1) +2021
young cow (1) +1330

6321 עֶגְלָה2 *ʿeg̱lāh2* (2)
Eglah (2)

6322 עֲגָלָה *ʿᵃg̱ālāh* (24)
cart (13)
carts (8)
cartwheel (1) +236
it[S] (1) +2021
threshing cart (1)

6323 עֶגְלוֹן1 *ʿeg̱lôn1* (5)
Eglon (4)
who[S] (1)

6324 עֶגְלוֹן2 *ʿeg̱lôn2* (8)
Eglon (8)

6325 עֶגְלַיִם *ʿeg̱layim*
Variant; not used

6326 עֶגְלַת שְׁלִשִׁיָּה *ʿeg̱laṯ šᵉlišiyyāh* (2)
Eglath Shelishiyah (2)

6327 עָגַם *ʿāg̱am* (1)
grieved (1)

6328 עָגַן *ʿāg̱an* (1)
remain unmarried (1) +408+1194+2118+4200+4200

6329 עַד1 *ʿaḏ1* (48)
ever (16)
forever (12) +4200
forever (3) +6330
ancient (2)
eternal (2) +4200
ever (2) +4200
ever and ever (2)
everlasting (2)
always (1) +4200
continually (1) +4200
eternal (1)
ever (1) +6330
forever (1)
never (1) +1153+2256+6409
of old (1)

6330 עַד2 *ʿaḏ2* (1261)
to (322)
until (224)
till (94)
as far as (70)
forever (44) +6409
until (30) +889
how long (27) +5503
up to (21)
and (13)
all the way to (12)
how long (12) +625+2025
reached (11) +995
before (9)
at (8)
or (8)
as (7)
by (7)
for (6)
until (6) +8611
very (6) +4394
ever (5) +6409
forevermore (5) +6409
while (5)
after (4)
approached (4) +995
even (4)
from (4)
how long (4) +4537
still (4)
always (3) +6409
among (3)
and alike (3)
before (3) +889+4202
between (3) +2256+4946
beyond measure (3) +4394
but (3)
ever since (3) +2021+2021+2296+3427
forever (3) +6329
out to (3)
reaches to (3)
through (3)
until (3) +561
until (3) +3954
when (3)
as far away as (2)
at set times (2) +4946+6961+6961
come to (2)
down to (2)
enough (2)
everlasting (2) +6409
forever (2) +2021+6409
forever (2) +4200+6409
from beginning to (2)
how many (2) +3869+4537
in (2)
in the end (2)
lasts (2)
more (2) +6409
never (2) +4202+6409
of (2)
reach (2) +995
still (2) +2021+2021+2296+3427
this far (2) +2151
till (2) +8611
until (2) +561+889
up (2)
utterly (2) +4394
with (2)
abundantly (1) +889+3907+6330
against (1) +928
all the way to (1) +995
all the way to (1) +995+3870
all the way up (1)
almost to a man (1) +4392+9462
and (1) +2256
arrive (1) +995
arrived (1) +995
as long as (1)
at the point of (1)
before (1) +4202
by then (1)
completely (1) +1414+2256+4946+5883
completely (1) +3983
completely destroyed (1) +3983
down to (1) +9462
end (1)
endless (1) +6409
ends (1)
entered (1) +2143
entering (1) +995
even as far as (1)
even enough (1)
ever (1) +6329
extends to (1)
far and wide (1) +4200+4946+8158
far and wide (1) +8158
far away (1) +4200+4946+8158
finally (1) +889
for an instant (1) +1180+8371
for how long (1) +5503
forevermore (1) +2021+6409
founded on (1)
here (1) +2178
hold back overnight (1) +1332+4328
how long (1) +625
huge (1) +1524+4200+4394
in the end (1) +889
including (1)
into (1)
join (1) +995
lasted so long (1)
lasting (1) +2021+2021+2296+3427
lasting (1) +6409
led to (1)

loud (1) +1524+4394
meanwhile (1) +2256+3907+3907+6330
more and more powerful (1) +1541+2025+2143+2256+4200+5087
much (1) +4394
near (1)
never (1) +561+6409
never (1) +4202+5905
on (1) +6964
only (1)
over (1)
prior (1)
reach to (1)
reached (1) +1540
reached height (1) +8003
reaching to (1)
reduces to (1)
since (1)
since (1) +2178
so much (1)
so much that (1)
still in force (1)
swiftly (1) +4559
that (1) +889
this far (1) +7024
though (1)
threatened (1) +5883
thus far (1) +2178
till (1) +561
till (1) +889
till (1) +3954
till (1) +6961
to the point of (1)
to the vicinity of (1) +995+3870
together with (1) +2256
toward (1)
toward (1) +5790
trembled violently (1) +1524+3006+3010+4394
until the end of (1)
until the time for (1)
very (1) +2025+4200+5087
waited (1)
when (1) +625+2025
when (1) +4537
when (1) +8611
while (1) +8611
while still (1)
without (1) +401
without restraint (1) +4394
yet (1)
yet (1) +2021+2021+2085+3427
yet (1) +2021+2021+2156+3427
yet (1) +2178
yet (1) +6964
untranslated (91)

6331 3עַד *'ad3* (1)
prey (1)

6332 עֵד *'ēd* (73)
witness (38)
witnesses (18)
testify (3)
testimony (3)
call in as witnesses (1) +6386
evidence (1)
had witnessed (1) +6386
have the transaction witnessed (1) +6386
testify (1) +2118
testify (1) +4200+6699
those who speak up for (1)
witnessed (1) +6386
untranslated (3)

6333 עִדֹּא *'iddō'* (1)
Iddo (1)

6334 1עָדָה *'ādāh1* (2)
prowls (1)
takes away (1)

6335 2עָדָה *'ādāh2* (8)
adorned (2)
adorn (1)
adorns (1)
decked (1)
put on (1)
put on jewelry (1) +6344
take up (1)

6336 3עָדָה *'ādāh3* (8)
Adah (8)

6337 1עֵדָה *'ēdāh1* (148)
community (69)
assembly (50)
followers (10)
people (4)
band (2)
company (2)
assembled (1)
community's (1)
flocking together (1)
herd (1)
household (1)
swarm (1)
whole assembly (1) +2256+7736
untranslated (4)

6338 2עֵדָה *'ēdāh2* (5)
witness (4)
witnesses (1)

6339 3עֵדָה *'ēdāh3*
Variant; not used

6340 עִדָּה *'iddāh* (1)
filthy (1)

6341 עִדּוֹ *'iddô* (4)
Iddo (4)

6342 עִדּוֹא *'iddô'* (3)
Iddo (2)
Iddo's (1)

6343 עֵדוּת *'ēdût* (83)
testimony (37)
statutes (29)
stipulations (4)
copy of covenant (2)
covenant (2)
regulations (2)
requirements (2)
statute (2)
demands (1)
warnings gave (1) +6386
warnings given (1) +6386

6344 עֲדִי *'ᵃdiy* (14)
ornaments (5)
jewelry (2)
beautiful jewelry (1) +7382
bridle (1) +8270
desires (1)
jewels (1)
most beautiful of jewels (1) +6344
put on jewelry (1) +6335

6345 עֲדָיָא *'ᵃdāyā'* (1)
untranslated (1)

6346 עֲדִיאֵל *'ᵃdiy'ēl* (3)
Adiel (3)

6347 עֲדָיָה *'ᵃdāyāh* (8)
Adaiah (8)

6348 עֲדָיָהוּ *'ᵃdāyāhû* (1)
Adaiah (1)

6349 1עָדִין *'ādiyn1* (1)
wanton (1)

6350 2עָדִין *'ādiyn2* (4)
Adin (4)

6351 עֲדִינָא *'ᵃdiynā'* (1)
Adina (1)

6352 עֲדִינוֹ *'ᵃdiynô*
Variant; not used

6353 עֲדִיתַיִם *'ᵃdiytayim* (1)
Adithaim (1)

6354 עַדְלַי *'adlay* (1)
Adlai (1)

6355 עֲדֻלָּם *'ᵃdullām* (8)
Adullam (8)

6356 עֲדֻלָּמִי *'ᵃdullāmiy* (3)
Adullamite (2)
of Adullam (1)

6357 עָדַן *'ādan* (1)
reveled (1)

6358 1עֵדֶן *'ēden1* (3)
delicacies (1)
delights (1)
finery (1)

6359 2עֵדֶן *'ēden2* (14)
Eden (14)

6360 3עֵדֶן *'ēden3* (2)
Eden (2)

6361 עֶדֶן *'eden* (3)
Eden (3)

6362 עֲדֶן *'ᵃden* (1)
yet (1)

6363 עַדְנָא *'adnā'* (2)
Adna (2)

6364 עֲדֶנָה *'ᵃdenāh* (1)
still (1)

6365 עַדְנָה *'adnāh* (1)
Adnah (1)

6366 עֶדְנָה *'ednāh* (1)
pleasure (1)

6367 עַדְנַח *'adnah* (1)
Adnah (1)

6368 עַדְעָדָה *'ad'ādāh* (1)
Adadah (1)

6369 עָדַף *'ādap* (9)
additional (2)
left (2)
balance (1)
exceed number (1)
exceeded number (1)
have too much (1)
left over (1)

6370 1עָדַר *'ādar1* (2)
help (1)
volunteered to serve (1)

6371 2עָדַר *'ādar2* (2)
cultivated (2)

6372 3עָדַר *'ādar3* (7)
missing (3)
fail (1)
left (1)
nowhere to be found (1)
saw to it that was lacking (1)

6373 1עֵדֶר *'ēder1* (39)
flock (15)
flocks (15)
herds (3)
each herd (1) +6373
flocks and herds (1)
herds (1) +1330
sheep (1)
untranslated (1)

6374 2עֵדֶר *'ēder2* (2)
Eder (2)

6375 3עֵדֶר *'ēder3* (1)
Eder (1)

6376 עֶדֶר *'eder* (1)
Eder (1)

6377 עַדְרִיאֵל *'aḏriy'ēl* (2)
Adriel (2)

6378 עֲדָשִׁים *'aḏāšiym* (4)
lentils (3)
lentil (1)

6379 עַוָּא *'awwā'* (1)
Avva (1)

6380 עוּב *'ûḇ* (1)
covered with the cloud (1)

6381 עוֹבֵד *'ôḇēḏ* (10)
Obed (10)

6382 עוֹבָל *'ôḇāl* (2)
Obal (2)

6383 עוּג *'ûḡ* (1)
bake (1)

6384 עוֹג *'ôḡ* (22)
Og (20)
Og's (2)

6385 עוּגָב *'ûḡāḇ* (4)
flute (4)

6386 1עוּד *'ûḏ1* (44)
warned (5)
warn (4)
testify (3)
admonished (2)
call as witnesses (2)
sustains (2)
acting as witness (1)
been warned (1)
bind (1)
brought charges against (1)
call in as witnesses (1) +6332
call to testify (1)
commended (1)
gave charge (1)
give warning (1)
had witnessed (1) +6332
have testify (1)
have the transaction witnessed (1) +6332
say (1)
solemnly declared (1)
stand firm (1)
testified (1)
warn solemnly (1) +6386
warned (1) +6386
warned solemnly (1) +6386
warnings gave (1) +6343
warnings given (1) +6343
witnessed (1) +6332
untranslated (1)

6387 2עוּד *'ûḏ2*
Variant; not used

6388 עוֹד *'ôḏ* (491)
longer (74)
again (72)
still (54)
more (35)
again (22) +3578
while still (16)
other (11)
another (9)
anymore (8)
continued (8)
more (7) +3578
yet (7)
further (6)
within (6) +928
longer (5) +3578
never (5) +4202
also (4)
anymore (4) +3578
besides (4)
once again (4)
another (3) +337
any longer (3)
any more (3)
else (3)
all the more (2) +3578
as long as (2) +3972
as long as live (2) +928
even (2)
ever (2)
left (2)
more (2) +337
once again (2) +3578
once more (2) +3578
overwhelmed (2) +928+2118+4202+8120
remain (2)
remained (2)
remains (2)
soon (2) +5071
still another (2)
while (2)
added (1)
all life (1) +4946
almost (1) +5071
always (1) +4946
another (1) +3578
any (1) +4946
any longer (1) +3578
as long as (1)
as long as (1) +561
as long as (1) +928
awaits (1)
back (1)
back (1) +3578
before (1) +4202
but also (1)
continue (1)
continued (1) +3578
do again (1) +3578
even as (1)
even more (1)
ever again (1)
failed (1) +4202+7756
for (1)
from now (1) +928
from now on (1)
furthermore (1) +2256
how long (1) +339+5503
in (1)
in a very short time (1) +4663+5071
kept on (1)
left now (1)
little while (1) +5071
long time (1)
make again (1) +3578
moreover (1)
next (1)
not enough (1) +7781
now (1)
on (1)
once more (1)
only (1)
others (1)
reappears (1) +8011
reconsider (1) +8740
regain (1) +6806
return (1) +995
since then (1)
something else (1)
stands (1)
still (1) +3972
still (1) +8636
still another (1) +3578
stopped (1) +3578+4202
time (1)
very soon (1) +4663+5071
were added (1) +3578
yet to come (1)
untranslated (29)

6389 עוֹדֵד *'ôḏēḏ* (3)
Oded (3)

6390 1עָוָה *'āwāh1* (17)
done wrong (6)
perverted (2)
am staggered (1)
bowed down (1)
did wrong (1)
does wrong (1)
made crooked (1)
perverse (1)
ruin (1)
sinning (1)
warped (1)

6391 2עָוָה *'āwāh2*
Variant; not used

6392 1עַוָּה *'awwāh1* (3)
ruin (3)

6393 2עַוָּה *'awwāh2*
Variant; not used

6394 עִוָּה *'iwwāh* (3)
Ivvah (3)

6395 עוּז *'ûz* (6)
flee for safety (2)
bring to a place of shelter (1)
look for help (1)
strong (1)
take cover (1)

6396 1עֲוִיל *'awiyl1* (2)
children (1)
little boys (1)

6397 2עֲוִיל *'awiyl2* (1)
evil men (1)

6398 1עַוִּים *'awwiym1* (3)
Avvites (3)

6399 2עַוִּים *'awwiym2* (1)
Avvim (1)

6400 עֲוִית *'awiyṯ* (2)
Avith (2)

6401 1עָוַל *'āwal1* (2)
doing evil (1)
evil (1)

6402 2עוּל *'ûl2* (5)
calved (1)
have young (1)
nursing young (1)
sheep (1)
such[s] (1)

6403 3עוּל *'ûl3* (3)
infant (2)
baby at breast (1)

6404 עָוֶל *'āwel* (22)
evil (5)
sin (4)
dishonest (3)
wrong (3)
dishonestly (1)
doing wrong (1)
fault (1)
guilt (1)
pervert (1) +6913
unjust (1)
ways (1)

6405 עַוָּל *'awwāl* (5)
wicked (2)
evil man (1)
unjust (1)
unrighteous (1)

6406 עַוְלָה *'awlāh* (32)
wicked (7)
wickedness (7)
evil (5)
wrong (5)
injustice (3)
crime (1)
false (1)
iniquity (1)
unjust (1)

wickedly (1)

6407 עוֹלֵל *'ôlēl* (11)
children (7)
infant (1)
infants (1)
little children (1)
little ones (1)

6408 עוֹלָל *'ôlāl* (9)
children (7)
infants (2)

6409 עוֹלָם *'ôlām* (440)
forever (137) +4200
everlasting (56)
forever (44) +6330
lasting (26)
forever (21)
ancient (13)
ever (9)
regular (9)
never (8) +4200+4202
of old (7)
eternal (5)
ever (5) +4200
ever (5) +6330
for ever (5)
forevermore (5) +6330
long ago (4)
always (3)
always (3) +6330
ancient (3) +4946
eternal (3) +4200
old (3)
age-old (2)
always (2) +4200
ancient times (2)
eternity (2)
ever (2) +4946
everlasting (2) +6330
for life (2)
forever (2) +2021+6330
forever (2) +4200+6330
long (2)
long ago (2) +4946
more (2) +6330
never (2) +440+4200
never (2) +1153+4200
never (2) +4202+6330
never again (2) +4200+4202
permanent (2)
again (1) +4200
ages (1)
all eternity (1)
all time (1)
any time (1)
as long as live (1) +3427+3972+4200
continue (1)
continued (1)
early times (1)
endless (1) +6330
everlasting (1) +3972
everlasting (1) +4200
for life (1) +4200
forevermore (1) +2021+6330
gone by (1)
lasting (1) +4200
lasting (1) +6330
lasting (1) +9458
life (1)
long (1) +4200
long (1) +4946
long ago (1) +4200
long time (1)
never (1) +401+4200
never (1) +561+6330
never (1) +1153+2256+6329
never (1) +4202
to come (1)
to the very end (1) +4200+6813
used to be (1) +3427
untranslated (2)

6410 עוּן *'ûn*
Variant; not used

6411 עָוֹן *'āwōn* (234)
sin (59)
sins (49)
guilt (35)
wickedness (13)
iniquity (12)
iniquities (10)
punishment (9)
held responsible (7) +5951
crime (4)
guilty (4)
wicked (4)
consequences of sin (3)
responsibility for offenses (3)
blame (2)
offense (2)
sinful (2)
wrong (2)
affliction (1)
crimes (1)
evil deeds (1)
faults (1)
offenses (1)
punished (1)
punished (1) +7936
punishment for sins (1)
sins (1) +1821
wrongdoing (1)
wrongdoings (1)
wrongs (1)
untranslated (2)

6412 עוֹנָה *'ônāh*
Variant; not used

6413 עִוְעִים *'iw'iym* (1)
dizziness (1)

6414 עוּף1 *'ûp̱1* (26)
fly away (4)
darting (3)
flew (3)
fly (3)
flying (3)
flies (2)
cast (1)
flies away (1)
fly along (1)
fly off (1)
hovering overhead (1)
swoop down (1)
untranslated (2)

6415 עוּף2 *'ûp̱2*
Variant; not used

6416 עוֹף *'ôp̱* (71)
birds (54)
bird (12)
flying (2)
winged (2)
winged creature (1)

6417 עוֹפַי *'ôp̱ay* (1)
untranslated (1)

6418 עוּץ1 *'ûs1* (2)
consider (1)
devise (1)

6419 עוּץ2 *'ûs2* (5)
Uz (5)

6420 עוּץ3 *'ûs3* (3)
Uz (2)
Uz (1) +824

6421 עוּק *'ûq* (2)
crush (1)
crushes (1)

6422 עָוַר1 *'āwar1* (5)
put out (3)
blinds (2)

6423 עוּר2 *'ûr2* (1)
uncovered (1) +6880

6424 עוּר3 *'ûr3* (82)
awake (16)
stir up (8)
awaken (6)
rouse (6)
stirred up (6)
wake up (5)
raised (4)
arouse (3)
moved (3)
arise (2)
aroused (2)
be roused (2)
stirs up (2)
wakens (2)
being stirred up (1)
gloated (1)
is wakened (1)
lament (1) +2411
lash (1)
raise up (1)
rising (1)
roused (1)
roused himself (1)
rouses (1)
stir (1)
strives (1)
thrive (1)
wakened (1)
whoever he may be (1) +2256+6699

6425 עוֹר *'ôr* (99)
skin (39)
leather (14)
hides (13)
hide (8)
skin (8) +1414
skins (6)
face (3) +7156
body (1)
flesh (1)
goatskins (1) +1531+6436
its[s] (1) +2021
nothing but skin (1) +1414+2256
untranslated (3)

6426 עִוֵּר *'iwwēr* (26)
blind (26)

6427 עִוָּרוֹן *'iwwārôn* (2)
blind (1) +928+2021+5782
blindness (1)

6428 עַוֶּרֶת *'awweret̠* (1)
blind (1)

6429 עוּשׁ *'ûš* (1)
quickly (1)

6430 עָוַת *'āwat̠* (11)
pervert (3)
cheating (1)
deprive (1)
frustrates (1)
is twisted (1)
made crooked (1)
stoop (1)
wronged (1)
wronging (1)

6431 עוּת *'ût̠* (1)
sustains (1)

6432 עַוָּתָה *'awwāt̠āh* (1)
wrong done (1)

6433 עוּתַי *'ût̠ay* (2)
Uthai (2)

6434 עַז *'az* (23)
strong (5)
mighty (4)
fierce (3)
powerful (3)

fierce-looking (1) +7156
fortified (1)
great (1)
harshly (1)
stern-faced (1) +7156
strength (1)
stronger (1)
stronghold (1)

6435 עָז *'āz* (1)
power (1)

6436 עֵז *'ēz* (74)
male goat (24) +8538
goats (11)
goat (8)
goat hair (7)
young goat (7) +1531
goat (2) +7618
goat (2) +8538
goat (2) +8544
goats' hair (2) +3889
male goats (2) +8538
goat (1) +8445
goats (1) +1201
goats' (1)
goatskins (1) +1531+6425
male goats (1) +7618
young goat (1)
young goats (1) +1531

6437 עֹז *'ōz* (94)
strength (38)
strong (12)
power (11)
mighty (8)
might (6)
fortified (3)
stronghold (3)
praise (2)
feeble (1) +4202
firm (1)
fortress (1)
great (1)
great power (1)
hard (1)
stouthearted (1) +5883
strongholds (1)
stubborn (1)
vigorously (1) +928
untranslated (1)

6438 עֻזָּא *'uzzā'* (11)
Uzzah (6)
Uzza (5)

6439 עֲזָאזֵל *'azā'zēl* (4)
scapegoat (4)

6440 1עָזַב *'āzab1* (212)
forsake (37)
forsaken (34)
leave (28)
left (19)
abandoned (18)
deserted (11)
forsook (8)
abandon (6)
forsaking (5)
free (5)
rejected (4)
neglect (3)
desert (2)
deserts (2)
fails (2)
leaves (2)
rejecting (2)
be abandoned (1)
be laid waste (1)
be left (1)
been abandoned (1)
change (1)
commits (1)
disregarded (1)
forfeit (1)
forsakes (1)
gave up (1)
give free rein (1)
give up (1)
go (1)
ignores (1)
is forsaken (1)
is neglected (1)
lays (1)
left behind (1)
left destitute (1)
renounces (1)
stop (1)
stopped showing (1)
turn from (1)
vanish (1)

6441 2עָזַב *'āzab2* (4)
be sure help (1) +6441
restore wall (1)
restored (1)

6442 עִזְבוֹנִים *'izbôniym* (7)
merchandise (7)

6443 עַזְבּוּק *'azbûq* (1)
Azbuk (1)

6444 עַזְגָּד *'azgād* (4)
Azgad (4)

6445 עַזָּה *'azzāh* (20)
Gaza (20)

6446 עֻזָּה *'uzzāh* (3)
Uzzah (3)

6447 1עֲזוּבָה *'azûbāh1*
Variant; not used

6448 2עֲזוּבָה *'azûbāh2* (4)
Azubah (4)

6449 עֱזוּז *'ezûz* (3)
power (2)
violence (1)

6450 עִזּוּז *'izzûz* (2)
reinforcements (1)
strong (1)

6451 עָזַז *'āzaz* (10)
brazen (1)
fixed securely (1)
makes powerful (1)
oppressive (1)
overpowered (1) +3338+6584
puts up a bold front (1) +928+7156
show strength (1)
strong (1)
triumph (1)
triumphant (1)

6452 עָזָז *'āzāz* (1)
Azaz (1)

6453 עֲזַזְיָהוּ *'azazyāhû* (3)
Azaziah (3)

6454 עֻזִּי *'uzziy* (11)
Uzzi (11)

6455 עֻזִּיָּא *'uzziyyā'* (1)
Uzzia (1)

6456 עֲזִיאֵל *'aziy'ēl* (1)
Aziel (1)

6457 עֻזִּיאֵל *'uzziy'ēl* (16)
Uzziel (16)

6458 עָזִּיאֵלִי *'āzziy'ēliy* (2)
Uzzielites (2)

6459 עֻזִּיָּה *'uzziyyāh* (8)
Uzziah (8)

6460 עֻזִּיָּהוּ *'uzziyyāhû* (19)
Uzziah (17)
him[s] (1) +2021+4889
Uzziah's (1)

6461 עֲזִיזָא *'aziyzā'* (1)
Aziza (1)

6462 1עַזְמָוֶת *'azmāwet1* (6)
Azmaveth (6)

6463 2עַזְמָוֶת *'azmāwet2* (2)
Azmaveth (2)

6464 עַזָּן *'azzān* (1)
Azzan (1)

6465 עָזְנִיָּה *'ozniyyāh* (2)
black vulture (2)

6466 עָזַק *'āzaq* (1)
dug up (1)

6467 עֲזֵקָה *'azēqāh* (7)
Azekah (7)

6468 עָזַר *'āzar* (82)
help (42)
helped (12)
helps (6)
helper (2)
added (1)
allied with (1)
allies (1)
am helped (1)
assist (1)
came to rescue (1)
cohorts (1)
gave support (1) +339
give support (1)
helpers (1)
helping (1)
is helped (1)
protect (1)
receive help (1) +6469
support (1)
supported (1)
sustain (1)
was helped (1)
were helped (1)
untranslated (1)

6469 1עֵזֶר *'ēzer1* (22)
help (13)
helper (5)
receive help (1) +6468
staff (1)
strength (1)
untranslated (1)

6470 2עֵזֶר *'ēzer2* (4)
Ezer (4)

6471 1עֶזֶר *'ezer1*
Variant; not used

6472 2עֶזֶר *'ezer2* (1)
Ezer (1)

6473 עַזֻּר *'azzur* (3)
Azzur (3)

6474 עֶזְרָא *'ezrā'* (22)
Ezra (21)
Ezra's (1)

6475 עֲזַרְאֵל *'azar'ēl* (6)
Azarel (6)

6476 1עֶזְרָה *'ezrāh1* (26)
help (19)
aid (3)
allies (1)
helper (1)
influence (1)
support (1)

6477 2עֶזְרָה *'ezrāh2* (1)
Ezrah (1)

6478 עֲזָרָה *'azārāh* (9)
ledge (6)
court (2)

outer court (1)

6479 עֶזְרִי *‘ezriy* (1)
Ezri (1)

6480 עַזְרִיאֵל *‘azriy’ēl* (3)
Azriel (3)

6481 עֲזַרְיָה *‘ᵃzaryāh* (32)
Azariah (31)
Azariah’s (1)

6482 עֲזַרְיָהוּ *‘ᵃzaryāhû* (16)
Azariah (14)
Azariah’s (1)
Azariahu (1)

6483 עַזְרִיקָם *‘azriyqām* (6)
Azrikam (6)

6484 עַזָּתִי *‘azzāṯiy* (2)
Gaza (1)
people of Gaza (1)

6485 עֵט *‘ēṭ* (4)
pen (2)
tool (2)

6486 1עָטָה *‘āṭāh1* (15)
cover (5)
wrapped (2)
covered (1)
covered with a mantle (1)
veiled (1)
wearing (1)
wrap around himself (1)
wrapped himself (1)
wraps around him (1)
wraps himself (1)

6487 2עָטָה *‘āṭāh2* (3)
is grasped (1)
take firm hold (1) +6487

6488 עָטוּף *‘āṭûp̱* (2)
faint (1)
weak (1)

6489 עֲטִין *‘ᵃṭiyn* (1)
body (1)

6490 עֲטִישָׁה *‘ᵃṭiyšāh* (1)
snorting (1)

6491 עֲטַלֵּף *‘ᵃṭallēp̱* (3)
bat (2)
bats (1)

6492 עָטָם *‘āṭām*
Variant; not used

6493 1עָטַף *‘āṭap̱1* (3)
clothe (1) +8884
mantled (1)
turns (1)

6494 2עָטַף *‘āṭap̱2* (11)
faint (8)
ebbed away (1)
ebbing away (1)
weak (1)

6495 3עָטַף *‘āṭap̱3*
Variant; not used

6496 1עָטַר *‘āṭar1* (2)
closing in (1)
surround (1)

6497 2עָטַר *‘āṭar2* (5)
crowned (2)
bestower of crowns (1)
crown (1)
crowns (1)

6498 1עֲטָרָה *‘ᵃṭārāh1* (23)
crown (18)
wreath (3)
crowns (2)

6499 2עֲטָרָה *‘ᵃṭārāh2* (1)
Atarah (1)

6500 עֲטָרוֹת *‘ᵃṭārôṯ* (4)
Ataroth (4)

6501 עַטְרוֹת אַדָּר *‘aṭrôṯ ’addār* (2)
Ataroth Addar (2)

6502 עַטְרוֹת בֵּית יוֹאָב *‘aṭrôṯ bêyṯ yô’āḇ* (1)
Atroth Beth Joab (1)

6503 עַטְרוֹת שׁוֹפָן *‘aṭrôṯ šôp̱ān* (1)
Atroth Shophan (1)

6504 עַי *‘ay* (38)
Ai (36)
city[s] (1)
who (1) +408+2021

6505 עִי *‘iy* (5)
heap of rubble (3)
broken man (1)
rubble (1)

6506 1עֵיבָל *‘ēyḇāl1* (4)
Ebal (4)

6507 2עֵיבָל *‘ēyḇāl2* (3)
Ebal (3)

6508 3עֵיבָל *‘ēyḇāl3*
Variant; not used

6509 עַיָּה *‘ayyāh* (2)
Aija (1)
Ayyah (1)

6510 עִיּוֹן *‘iyyôn* (3)
Ijon (3)

6511 עֲיוֹת *‘ᵃyôṯ* (1)
untranslated (1)

6512 1עִיט *‘iyṭ1* (1)
hurled insults (1)

6513 2עִיט *‘iyṭ2* (2)
pounce (1)
pounced (1)

6514 עַיִט *‘ayiṭ* (8)
bird of prey (3)
birds of prey (3)
birds (1)
carrion birds (1) +7606

6515 עֵיטָם *‘ēyṭām* (5)
Etam (5)

6516 עִיֵּי הָעֲבָרִים *‘iyyēy hā‘ᵃḇāriym* (2)
Iye Abarim (2)

6517 עִיִּים *‘iyyiym* (2)
Iim (1)
Iyim (1)

6518 עֵילוֹם *‘ēylôm*
Variant; not used

6519 עִילַי *‘iylay* (1)
Ilai (1)

6520 1עֵילָם *‘ēylām1* (16)
Elam (15)
Elam’s (1)

6521 2עֵילָם *‘ēylām2* (13)
Elam (12)
untranslated (1)

6522 עֲיָם *‘ᵃyām* (1)
scorching (1)

6523 עָיַן *‘āyan* (2)
kept jealous eye on (1)
untranslated (1)

6524 1עַיִן *‘ayin1* (896)
eyes (437)
sight (63)
eye (36)
looked (25)
presence (14)
seems (10) +928
spring (10)
seemed (8) +928
think (8) +928
pleased (7) +928+3512
face (6)
look (6)
look with pity (6) +2571
before (5) +4200
displeased (5) +928+8317
look (5) +5951
pleased with (5) +928+2834+5162
pleases (5) +928+3202
seem (4) +928
show pity (4) +2571
to (4) +928
with (4) +928
favorably disposed toward (3) +928+2834
fountain (3)
like (3) +928+3202
looked (3) +5951
saw (3) +928
watch (3) +4200
watched (3) +4200
watching (3)
appearance (2)
by (2) +928
distressed (2) +928+8317
full view (2)
have respect for (2) +928+3700
in presence (2) +4200+5584
look after (2) +6584+8492
looked with pity (2) +2571
on forehead (2) +1068
on foreheads (2) +1068
please (2) +928+3202
please (2) +928+3837
pleased (2) +928+3202
pleased (2) +928+3837
sees (2) +928
sparkled (2)
spring (2) +4784
springs (2) +4784
thought (2) +928
to (2) +4200
watching (2) +4200
angry (1) +928+3013
appealed to (1) +928+3512
appear (1) +928+2118+3869
approve of (1) +928+3202
before (1) +4200+5584
begrudge (1) +8317
by (1) +4200
consider (1) +928
considered (1) +928
cover the offense (1) +4064
despise (1) +928+1022
despise (1) +928+7837
despises (1) +928+1022
despises (1) +928+7837
disappeared (1) +2143+4946
disapprove (1) +928+8317
displease (1) +928+2834+4202+5162
displease (1) +928+8273
displeasing (1) +928+2834+4202+5162
displeasing (1) +928+8273
downcast (1) +8814
eyebrows (1) +1461
eyes (1) +1426
eyesight (1)
favorable toward (1) +928+2834+5162
for (1) +928
fountains (1)
from (1) +928
from (1) +4946
from (1) +4946+5584
front of heads (1) +1068
galled (1) +928+8317
generous man (1) +3202
glad (1) +928+3512
glance (1)
gleam (1)
have no (1) +4946+6259

have no compassion (1) +8317
in broad daylight (1) +2021+2021+2296+4200+9087
in front of (1) +4200
in full view (1) +5790
judgment (1)
keeping watch (1) +928+8011
like (1) +3869
liked (1) +928+3837
look (1) +928
look carefully (1) +928+8011
look with compassion (1) +2571
look with longing (1) +5951
looked (1) +906
looked (1) +928+2118
looked about (1) +5951
looks (1) +5951
lost self-confidence (1) +928+4394+5877
never (1) +440
not please (1) +928+8317
not want (1) +928+8273
outward appearance (1)
please (1) +928+2256+3202+3838
please (1) +928+3838
pleased (1) +928+3201
pleased (1) +928+3838
pleased with (1) +928+2834+5951
pleased with (1) +928+3202
pleased with (1) +928+3512
pleased with (1) +928+3837
pleases (1) +928+3512
pools (1)
prefer (1) +928+3202
regards (1) +928+5162
satisfied (1) +928+3512
saw (1) +906+5951
saw (1) +5260
scorned the idea (1) +928+1022
see (1) +448
see (1) +2021+4200+8011
see (1) +4200
see (1) +5260
see (1) +8011
see (1) +8492
see for yourselves (1) +4013+8011
see to it (1) +4200
seem (1) +928+2118
seem (1) +928+4017
seemed (1) +928+2118
show (1)
show ill will (1) +8317
showing pity (1) +2571
sights (1) +5260
sparkles (1) +5989
sparkling (1)
spring (1) +2021+4784
springs (1)
stay awake (1) +7219
stingy (1) +8273
stingy man (1) +8273
those[s] (1)
took notice (1) +5951
troubled (1) +928+8273
unaware (1) +4946+6623
upset (1) +928+8317
us (1) +5646
value (1) +928+1540
value (1) +4718
valued (1) +928+1540
wanted to do (1) +928+3202
watch (1)
watch (1) +928
watches (1)
well (1)
what see (1)
winks maliciously (1) +7975
wish (1) +928+3202
wish (1) +928+3512
wished (1) +928+3202
without being aware (1) +4946
won (1) +928+5951
untranslated (36)

6525 עַיִן2 *'ayin2*
Variant; not used

6526 עַיִן3 *'ayin3* (5)
Ain (5)

6527 עֵין גֶּדִי *'ēyn gediy* (6)
En Gedi (6)

6528 עֵין גַּנִּים *'ēyn ganniym* (3)
En Gannim (3)

6529 עֵין־דּאֹר *'ēyn-dō'r* (3)
Endor (3)

6530 עֵין הַקּוֹרֵא *'ēyn haqqôrē'* (1)
En Hakkore (1)

6531 עֵין הַתַּנִּין *'ēyn hatanniyn*
Variant; not used

6532 עֵין חַדָּה *'ēyn ḥaddāh* (1)
En Haddah (1)

6533 עֵין חָצוֹר *'ēyn ḥāṣôr* (1)
En Hazor (1)

6534 עֵין חֲרֹד *'ēyn ḥ[a]rōd*
Variant; not used

6535 עֵין מִשְׁפָּט *'ēyn mišpāṭ* (1)
En Mishpat (1)

6536 עֵין עֶגְלַיִם *'ēyn 'eglayim* (1)
En Eglaim (1)

6537 עֵין רֹגֵל *'ēyn rōgēl* (4)
En Rogel (4)

6538 עֵין רִמּוֹן *'ēyn rimmôn* (1)
En Rimmon (1)

6539 עֵין שֶׁמֶשׁ *'ēyn šemeš* (2)
En Shemesh (2)

6540 עֵין תַּפּוּחַ *'ēyn tappûaḥ* (1)
En Tappuah (1)

6541 עֵינוֹן *'ēynôn*
Variant; not used

6542 עֵינַיִם *'ēynayim* (2)
Enaim (2)

6543 עֵינָם *'ēynām* (1)
Enam (1)

6544 עֵינָן *'ēynān* (5)
Enan (5)

6545 עִיף *'iyp* (5)
exhausted (2)
exhausted (1) +4394
faint (1)
fainting (1)

6546 עָיֵף *'āyēp* (18)
weary (6)
exhausted (3)
famished (2)
tired (2)
faint (1)
parched (1)
thirsty (1)
weary (1) +5883
worn out (1)

6547 עֵיפָה1 *'ēypāh1* (2)
darkness (1)
deepest night (1) +694+4017

6548 עֵיפָה2 *'ēypāh2* (1)
ephah (1)

6549 עֵיפָה3 *'ēypāh3* (4)
ephah (4)

6550 עֵיפַי *'ēypay* (1)
Ephai (1)

6551 עִיר1 *'iyr1* (1092)
city (512)
towns (262)
cities (126)
town (100)
it[s] (10) +2021
villages (8)
hometown (3)
Ai[s] (1) +2021
another[s] (1)
citadel (1)
cities (1) +2256+6551
each town (1) +2256+6551
each towns (1) +6551
every city (1) +2256+6551
fellow townsmen (1) +408
inner shrine (1)
it[s] (1) +2021+2021+2296
its[s] (1)
its[s] (1) +928+2021
places (1)
them[s] (1)
them[s] (1) +824+2021
them[s] (1) +3972
there[s] (1) +928+2021
townspeople (1) +408
villages (1) +7252
which[s] (1)
Ziklag[s] (1) +2021
untranslated (46)

6552 עִיר2 *'iyr2* (2)
anguish (1)
wrath (1)

6553 עִיר3 *'iyr3* (1)
Ir (1)

6554 עִיר4 *'iyr4* (2)
donkey (1)
untranslated (1)

6555 עַיִר *'ayir* (7)
donkeys (3)
colt (2)
donkeys' (1)
male donkeys (1)

6556 עִיר הַהֶרֶס *'iyr haheres*
Variant; not used

6557 עִיר הַחֶרֶס *'iyr haḥeres*
Variant; not used

6558 עִיר הַמֶּלַח *'iyr hammelaḥ*
Variant; not used

6559 עִיר הַתְּמָרִים *'iyr hatt[e]māriym*
Variant; not used

6560 עִיר נָחָשׁ *'iyr nāḥāš* (1)
Ir Nahash (1)

6561 עִיר שֶׁמֶשׁ *'iyr šemeš* (1)
Ir Shemesh (1)

6562 עִירָא *'iyrā'* (6)
Ira (6)

6563 עִירָד *'iyrād* (2)
Irad (2)

6564 עִירוּ *'iyrû* (1)
Iru (1)

6565 עִירִי *'iyriy* (1)
Iri (1)

6566 עִירָם *'iyrām* (2)
Iram (2)

6567 עֵירֹם *'ēyrōm* (10)
naked (9)
nakedness (1)

6568 עַיִשׁ *'ayiš* (1)
bear (1)

6569 עַיַּת *'ayyat* (1)
Aiath (1)

6570 עַכְבּוֹר *'akbôr* (7)
Acbor (7)

6571 עַכָּבִישׁ *ʿakkāḇiyš* (2)
spider's (2)

6572 עַכְבָּר *ʿaḵbār* (6)
rats (5)
rat (1)

6573 עַכּוֹ *ʿakkô* (1)
Acco (1)

6574 עָכוֹר *ʿāḵôr* (5)
Achor (5)

6575 עָכָן *ʿāḵān* (6)
Achan (6)

6576 עָכַס *ʿāḵas* (1)
ornaments jingling (1)

6577 עֶכֶס *ʿeḵes* (2)
bangles (1)
noose (1) +4591

6578 עַכְסָה *ʿaḵsāh* (5)
Acsah (5)

6579 עָכַר *ʿāḵar* (14)
brings trouble (4)
brought trouble (3)
bring trouble (2)
made trouble (2)
increased (1)
troubler (1)
wretched (1)

6580 עָכָר *ʿāḵār* (1)
Achar (1)

6581 עָכְרָן *ʿoḵrān* (5)
Ocran (5)

6582 עַכְשׁוּב *ʿaḵšûḇ* (1)
vipers (1)

6583 עַל 1 *ʿal1* (4)
Most High (4)

6584 עַל 2 *ʿal2* (5780)
on (1149)
against (400)
over (376)
to (319)
for (250)
in (248)
upon (166)
from (155) +4946
at (128)
by (92)
with (79)
of (61)
because of (57)
about (53)
therefore (52) +4027
above (45)
in charge of (43)
that is why (34) +4027
concerning (31)
along (29)
because (29)
around (27)
near (26)
beside (25)
so (25) +4027
into (24)
according to (18)
from (18)
facedown (15) +7156
under (15)
because (14) +889
above (13) +4946
on (13) +7156
why (13) +4537
to (12) +3338
attack (10)
away from (10) +4946
bears (10) +7924
border (10)
over (10) +7156
within (10)
on (9) +4946
toward (9)
after (8)
along with (8)
as (8)
before (8)
near (8) +7156
off (8) +4946
on top of (8)
together with (8)
administrator[s] (7) +889
next to (7) +3338
wearing (7)
attacked (6) +6590
because of (6) +1821
in (6) +7156
in front of (6) +7156
next to (6)
there[s] (6) +2023
among (5)
attack (5) +995
attack (5) +6590
because (5) +3954
because (5) +4027
before (5) +7156
east (5) +7156
for sake (5)
had charge of (5)
next section (5) +3338
this is why (5) +4027
across (4)
bear (4) +7924
because of (4) +128
connected to (4)
enter (4) +6590
have (4)
in accordance with (4)
in addition to (4)
in command (4) +7372
out of (4) +4946
than (4)
upon (4) +7156
about (3) +128
according to (3) +7023
against (3) +4946
attacking (3) +7756
because (3) +1821
burning (3) +836+2021
concerning (3) +1821
covered with (3)
faces (3) +7156
facing (3) +7156
had to (3)
higher than (3) +4946
in opposition to (3)
in spite of (3)
invaded (3) +6590
lusted after (3) +6311
next (3) +3338
on account of (3)
oppose (3)
past (3)
responsible for (3)
rested on (3)
so (3) +2296
tenderly (3) +4213
throughout (3)
top (3)
toward (3) +7156
up to (3)
wear (3) +2118
when (3)
about (2) +1821
according to (2) +3869
across (2) +7156
across from (2) +7156
along (2) +3338
and (2)
as for (2)
as though (2)
as well as (2)
attached to (2)
attacked (2) +995
await (2)
because (2) +3954+4027
before (2) +4946
besides (2)
besiege (2) +2837
by (2) +3338
cover (2)
crown (2)
decorated with (2)
defied (2) +1540
enter (2) +995
fighting (2)
for (2) +1821
for (2) +3954+4027
from (2) +4946+7156
from (2) +7156
got off (2) +4946+7563
in behalf (2)
in front of (2)
inner (2)
look after (2) +6524+8492
lying on (2) +7156
mating with (2) +6590
more than (2)
no wonder (2) +4027
on behalf (2)
onto (2)
outside (2)
over (2) +4946
prostrate (2) +7156
protect (2) +6641
responsibility for (2)
rests on (2)
rule (2) +2118
rule over (2)
seized (2) +5877
separated from (2) +4946
set on (2)
so that (2) +4027
the steward[s] (2) +889
therefore (2) +2296
though (2)
threw arms around (2) +5877+7418
to (2) +7931
too (2)
wore (2)
above (1) +1068
above (1) +4946+5087
above (1) +7156
accompanied by (1) +3338
accuse (1) +7212
add (1)
adjoining (1) +3338
adjoining section (1) +3338
adorned (1) +6590
afraid (1) +5877+7065
against (1) +7156
against side (1)
ahead (1) +7156
all over (1) +6017+6017
all the way to (1)
although (1)
and (1) +4027
and alike (1)
and so (1) +4027
anoint (1)
apart from (1)
aptly (1) +698
aroused (1) +2118
as a result of (1) +1821
as far as (1)
as for (1) +1826
as part of (1)
as prescribed by (1) +3338
assail (1) +5877
assaults (1) +7756
assistant (1) +3338
assisted (1) +3338

assume the responsibility for carrying out (1) +6641
at (1) +6813
at (1) +7156
at flood stage (1) +1536+3972
at flood stage (1) +1536+3972+4848
at heels (1) +7418
at side (1)
attack (1) +3338+6590
attacked (1) +7756
attacked viciously (1) +3751+5782+8797
attacking (1)
attacking (1) +995
attacks (1) +995
attacks (1) +7756
attendants (1) +6641
avert (1) +4946+6296
away (1) +4946
because (1) +1826
because of (1) +3970
because of (1) +4027
because of (1) +4946
because of (1) +6813
because of this (1) +4027
become guilty (1) +2628+5951
been under (1) +6590
below (1) +141+2021
beside (1) +3338
beside (1) +4946
beside (1) +7156
besieged (1) +1215
besieged (1) +2837
better than (1)
between (1)
beyond (1)
binding on (1)
blessed (1)
bordering (1)
borne on (1) +7156
bowed down (1) +5877+7156
bowed down to the ground (1) +5877+7156
bracelets (1) +3338+7543
by (1) +4946
by (1) +7023
care for (1)
cares (1) +4213+8492
carried by (1) +2118
carry on (1) +7756
charged against (1)
commander in chief (1) +2021+7372
confronted (1) +6641
confronted (1) +7756
conquered (1) +2616
consider (1) +4213+8492
contribute (1)
corresponding to (1) +7156
could not (1) +2118
cover (1) +6296
credited to (1)
crossing (1) +7156
crowns (1)
deal with (1)
decide (1) +2118+7023
demanded (1) +7023
depend on (1)
directed to (1)
do anything that endangers life (1) +1947+6641
do not know where am going (1) +889+2143+2143
don't say a word (1) +3338+7023+8492
drove back (1) +2118
during (1)
east (1) +7156+7710
embraced (1) +7418
encircle (1) +7443
encourage (1) +1819+4213
encouraged (1) +1819+4222
encouragingly (1) +4213
entered (1) +995
even beyond (1) +4946
expressed (1) +7023
extend toward (1)
extended (1) +7156
falsely (1) +9214
feed on (1)
fight (1)
follows (1) +7925
for (1) +889
for (1) +1386
for (1) +3338
for (1) +4946
for sake (1) +128
gave a high rank in (1) +8492
given over (1) +3338+5599
got off (1) +3718+4946
governor[S] (1) +889
had (1)
had (1) +2118
had to (1) +2118
hanging on (1)
has (1)
have (1) +2118
help (1)
here[S] (1) +3276
here[S] (1) +3870
higher (1) +4946
highest (1) +8031
his (1) +2257
hold accountable (1) +5989
how (1)
how (1) +4027
in (1) +4946
in accordance with (1) +7023
in behalf (1) +3208
in behalf of (1)
in behalf of (1) +1821
in charge (1) +6641
in control (1)
in hands (1)
in hostility toward (1) +7156
in little more than (1) +3427
in preference to (1) +7156
in presence (1)
in presence of (1)
in store for (1)
in the light of (1)
in the presence of (1)
in the way should go (1) +2006+7023
including (1)
increase (1) +3578
instead of (1) +4030
invade (1) +6590
invaded (1) +995
its (1) +2023
jealous (1) +6296+7863+8120
join (1) +2143
join (1) +2616
keeper[S] (1) +889
kneeling (1) +1386+4156
knelt down (1) +1384+1386
laid siege to (1) +2837
leader (1)
leads to (1)
lie with (1) +995
lingering (1) +3427+3427
little by little (1) +3338
lived in hostility toward (1) +5877+7156
load (1)
loaded with (1)
longed for (1)
make wear (1) +5516+6590
manned (1)
marched past (1) +3338+6296
more and more (1) +3578+3972
mounted like jewels (1) +3782+4859
near (1) +3338
nearby (1)
nearby (1) +3338
nearest (1) +7156
object of malicious talk (1) +4383+6590+8557
obligates (1)
of (1) +4946
on (1) +7023
on behalf of (1)
on foot (1) +824+2021
on no account (1) +224
on side (1)
opposed (1) +599
opposed (1) +6641
over (1) +4200+4946
over higher (1)
overflow (1) +6590
overpower (1) +4309
overpowered (1) +3338+6451
overruled (1) +2616
overwhelm (1) +995
overwhelmed (1) +5877
part (1)
part of (1)
past (1) +4946
peels (1) +4946
persuade (1) +1819+4213
placed on (1)
presence (1) +4946
protects (1) +6641
put in charge (1) +3338+6641
put in charge of the storerooms (1) +238+732
reaches to (1)
reason (1)
received gladly (1) +8523
reclining (1)
regarding (1)
reign over (1)
reject (1) +4946+7156+8938
reject (1) +4946+7156+8959
repay (1) +8031+8740
required (1) +2011
required of (1)
resolved (1) +4213+8492
responsible (1)
rest on (1)
rid (1) +4946+8959
ring (1)
ruled over (1)
serve (1) +6641
set against (1)
share in (1) +5951
shave (1) +7947
simply (1) +7023
since (1)
since (1) +3954+4027
since (1) +4027
sleep with (1) +4156
so (1) +3869
spoken kindly (1) +1819+4213
stand up (1) +6641+6642
steward[S] (1) +408+889+1074+2021
steward[S] (1) +889+1074
strike (1)
succeeded (1) +4030+6641
successor (1) +4030+6641
suffer (1) +5989
supervised (1)
supporting (1)
surely leave (1) +2143+2143+4946
take (1) +995
take care of (1)
take off (1) +3718+4946
takes (1) +3782
that (1) +4027
that's why (1) +4027
the duty of (1)
their (1) +2157
their[S] (1) +3776
then (1) +4027
there[S] (1) +2157
therefore (1) +1826+8611
think (1) +4222+6590
think about (1) +4213+6590
this is why (1) +465

threw arms around (1) +5877
throughout (1) +3972+7156
tie (1) +5989
to (1) +4200+7156
to (1) +4946
to reach (1)
took up (1) +6641
touches (1) +2118
toward (1) +2006
toward (1) +2006+7156
under guard (1) +5464
upside down (1) +7156
used (1)
used for (1)
using (1)
voluntarily (1) +408+4213+6590
watch over (1) +8492
wear (1) +6590
wearing around (1)
weigh down (1)
what (1) +4537
when (1) +889
where[s] (1) +2157
where[s] (1) +6642
wherever (1) +889+2021+3972+5226
wherever (1) +889+3972
which way (1) +196+3545+6584+8520
while still alive (1) +7156
why (1) +2296
will (1) +7023
with (1) +3338
with (1) +7156
worn (1)
yet (1)
your (1) +3871
your (1) +4013
untranslated (913)

6585 עֹל *'ōl* (40)
yoke (36)
it[s] (3)
yoked (1) +6590

6586 עַל־כֵּן *'al-kēn*
Variant; not used

6587 עֻלָּא *'ullā'* (1)
Ulla (1)

6588 עַלְבּוֹן *'albôn*
Variant; not used

6589 עִלֵּג *'illēg* (1)
stammering (1)

6590 עָלָה *'ālāh* (901)
went up (111)
go up (76)
brought up (46)
came up (31)
go (24)
bring up (23)
come up (23)
offered (14)
come (13)
sacrificed (13)
offer (12)
up (12)
attack (11)
sacrifice (11)
gone up (10)
bring (9)
coming up (9)
lifted (9)
rise (8)
rises (8)
went (8)
climbed (7)
attacked (6) +6584
led up (6)
marched up (6)
set up (6)
ascended (5)
attack (5) +6584
attacked (5)
came (5)
chews (5)
marched (5)
presented (5)
rising (5)
sacrificing (5)
take up (5)
ascend (4)
attack (4) +448
brought (4)
chew (4)
climb up (4)
conscripted (4)
enter (4) +6584
goes up (4)
going up (4)
grow (4)
return (4)
rose (4)
send up (4)
took (4)
climbed up (3)
grew up (3)
growing (3)
invaded (3) +6584
lying on (3)
makes rise (3)
march (3)
offered sacrifices (3)
offerings (3)
present (3)
returned (3)
used (3)
withdraw (3)
withdrew (3)
advance (2)
advances (2)
aroused (2)
assemble (2)
attacking (2)
carried (2)
carried up (2)
carry up (2)
climb (2)
climbs (2)
daybreak (2) +2021+8840
get (2)
go back (2)
go on up (2)
go straight up (2)
gone (2)
got on (2)
imported (2) +2256+3655
invaded (2)
is (2)
lift (2)
made (2)
mating with (2) +6584
offered up (2)
offering (2)
raged (2)
reached (2)
reaches (2)
sets up (2)
soar (2)
spring up (2)
sprinkled (2)
take (2)
taken (2)
withdrawn (2)
accompanied (1) +907
adorned (1) +6584
advanced (1)
appeared (1)
approach (1)
are exalted (1)
are recorded (1)
ascending (1)
ascent (1)
assemble (1) +928+2021+7736
at (1) +3869
attack (1) +3338+6584
attacked (1) +928
attacking (1) +448
attacks (1)
back (1)
been under (1) +6584
billowed up (1)
blazed up (1)
blossomed (1) +5890
blow away (1)
blowing in (1)
bring back (1)
bringing up (1)
brought along (1)
brought back (1)
building (1)
burning (1)
carried away (1)
casting up (1)
charge (1)
charged (1)
charging (1)
chosen (1)
climbed in (1)
climbing up (1)
come back (1)
comes (1)
comes out (1)
coming (1)
coming out (1)
consider (1)
continued (1)
continued up (1)
decorated (1)
deserted (1) +339+4946
drag away (1)
entered (1)
evening sacrifice (1) +4966
exalted (1)
falls (1)
filled (1)
first light of dawn (1) +8840
flare up (1)
flared (1)
flourishing (1)
flowed over (1)
followed (1) +928+8079
gathered (1)
get up (1)
goes (1)
going (1)
gone ahead (1)
grow up (1)
had come up (1)
had go up (1)
haul up (1)
have (1)
headed (1)
helped up (1)
invade (1) +928
invade (1) +6584
invaded (1) +448
invaded (1) +928
is on way (1)
kept burning (1)
lead (1)
leading to (1)
leave (1) +4946
left (1) +4946
lights (1)
made come up (1)
made grow up (1)
make come (1)
make come up (1)
make offerings (1)
make wear (1) +5516+6584
makes offering (1)
making (1)
mount (1)
mounted up (1)

move away (1)
moved away (1)
moved up (1)
object of malicious talk (1) +4383+6584+8557
offer up (1)
offers (1)
on (1)
on way (1)
on way up (1)
overflow (1) +6584
overgrown (1)
overrun (1)
paid (1)
passed (1)
presented offerings (1)
progressed (1)
pull out (1)
pulls up (1)
put on (1)
raises up (1)
ran (1)
ran up (1)
reached (1) +448
restore (1)
retreated (1)
sacrifice (1) +4966
sacrifice (1) +6592
scale (1)
send (1)
serve (1)
should go up (1) +6590
sprinkle (1)
stepped out (1)
steps (1)
stir up (1)
stirs up (1)
stopped (1) +4946
surely bring back (1) +6590
surpass (1)
swarm (1)
take away (1)
taken up (1)
think (1) +4222+6584
think about (1) +4213+6584
took up (1)
upper (1)
voluntarily (1) +408+4213+6584
walking (1)
wear (1)
wear (1) +6584
weighed (1)
went back (1)
went off (1)
went over (1)
worked (1)
yoked (1) +6585
untranslated (22)

6591 עָלֶה *'āleh* (18)
leaves (7)
leaf (5)
branches (1)
green leaf (1)
untranslated (4)

6592 1עֹלָה *'ōlāh1* (288)
burnt offering (159)
burnt offerings (109)
offering (7)
sacrifice (2)
burnt (1)
it[s] (1) +2021
its[s] (1) +2021
offerings (1)
sacrifice (1) +6590
sacrifices (1)
them[s] (1)
untranslated (4)

6593 2עֹלָה *'ōlāh2*
Variant; not used

6594 1עַלְוָה *'alwāh1* (1)
evildoers (1) +1201

6595 2עַלְוָה *'alwāh2* (2)
Alvah (2)

6596 עֲלוּמִים *'alûmiym* (5)
youth (3)
youthful vigor (1)
untranslated (1)

6597 עַלְוָן *'alwān* (2)
Alvan (2)

6598 עֲלוּקָה *'alûqāh* (1)
leech (1)

6599 עָלוֹת *'ālôt* (1)
Aloth (1)

6600 עָלַז *'ālaz* (17)
rejoice (7)
jubilant (2)
triumph (2)
glad (1)
leaps for joy (1)
made merry (1)
reveling (1)
shout with laughter (1)
untranslated (1)

6601 עָלֵז *'ālēz* (1)
revelers (1)

6602 עֲלָטָה *'alātāh* (4)
dusk (3)
darkness (1)

6603 1עֵלִי *'ēliy1* (33)
Eli (27)
Eli's (4)
who[s] (1)
untranslated (1)

6604 2עֵלִי *'ēliy2* (1)
Most High (1)

6605 עֱלִי *'eliy* (1)
pestle (1)

6606 עִלִּי *'illiy* (2)
upper (2)

6607 עַלְיָה *'alyāh* (1)
untranslated (1)

6608 עֲלִיָּה *'aliyyāh* (19)
upper room (6)
room (4)
room above (2)
upper chambers (2)
upper parts (2)
upper rooms (2)
room over (1)

6609 1עֶלְיוֹן *'elyôn1* (22)
upper (15)
high (2)
imposing (2)
top (2)
most exalted (1)

6610 2עֶלְיוֹן *'elyôn2* (31)
Most High (31)

6611 עַלִּיז *'alliyz* (7)
revelry (3)
rejoice (2)
carefree (1)
revelers (1)

6612 עֲלִיל *'aliyl* (1)
furnace (1)

6613 עֲלִילָה *'aliylāh* (24)
actions (6)
what done (5)
deeds (4)
did (1)
do (1)
done (1)
mighty deeds (1)
misdeeds (1)
practices (1)
slandered (1) +1821+8492
slanders (1) +1821+8492
works (1)

6614 עֲלִילִיָּה *'aliyliyyāh* (1)
deeds (1)

6615 עַלְיָן *'alyān*
Variant; not used

6616 עָלִיץ *'āliys*
Variant; not used

6617 עֲלִיצֻת *'aliysut* (1)
gloating (1)

6618 1עָלַל *'ālal1* (18)
abuse (2)
abused (1)
brings grief (1)
cut down (1)
deal (1)
dealt (1)
dealt harshly (1)
glean thoroughly (1) +6618
go over a second time (1)
go over the vines again (1) +339
made a fool (1)
mistreat (1)
take part in (1)
treated (1)
treated harshly (1)
was inflicted (1)

6619 2עָלַל *'ālal2* (1)
buried (1)

6620 3עָלַל *'ālal3* (1)
youths (1)

6621 4עָלַל *'ālal4*
Variant; not used

6622 עֹלֵלוֹת *'ōlēlôt* (6)
few grapes (2)
gleanings (2)
gleaning (1)
gleanings of grapes (1)

6623 עָלַם *'ālam* (29)
hidden (4)
ignore (4)
unaware of (3) +4946
hard (2)
hide (2)
bring (1)
close (1)
close (1) +6623
closes (1)
hiding (1)
hypocrites (1)
make shut (1)
obscures (1)
secret (1)
shut (1)
swollen (1)
turn away (1)
unaware (1) +4946+6524

6624 עֶלֶם *'elem* (2)
boy (1)
young man (1)

6625 עַלְמָה *'almāh* (7)
maiden (2)
maidens (2)
girl (1)
virgin (1)
virgins (1)

6626 עַלְמוֹן *'almôn* (1)
Almon (1)

6627 עַלְמוֹן דִּבְלָתַיִם *'almôn diblātayim* (2)
Almon Diblathaim (2)

6628 עֲלָמוֹת *ʿălāmôṯ* (2)
alamoth (2)

6629 עַל־מוּת *ʿal-mûṯ*
Variant; not used

6630 עֲלֶמֶת1 *ʿālemeṯ1* (1)
Alemeth (1)

6631 עֲלֶמֶת2 *ʿālemeṯ2* (3)
Alemeth (3)

6632 עָלַס *ʿālas* (3)
enjoy (1)
enjoy ourselves (1)
flap joyfully (1)

6633 עָלַע *ʿālaʿ* (1)
feast on (1)

6634 עָלַף *ʿālap̱* (6)
faint (2)
decorated (1)
disguise herself (1)
fainted (1)
withered away (1)

6635 עֻלְפֶּה *ʿulpeh*
Variant; not used

6636 עָלַץ *ʿālaṣ* (8)
rejoice (3)
rejoices (2)
triumph (2)
jubilant (1)

6637 עֹלָתָה *ʿōlāṯāh* (2)
injustice (1)
untranslated (1)

6638 עַם1 *ʿam1* (32)
people (32)

6639 עַם2 *ʿam2* (1836)
people (1261)
peoples (100)
nations (90)
men (72)
army (48)
troops (31)
they[s] (28) +2021
them[s] (16) +2021
people (14) +1426
soldiers (10)
nation (9)
people (8) +1201
people's (7)
countrymen (6) +1201
fighting men (6)
those[s] (5) +2021
army (4) +4878
Israelites[s] (4)
nationality (4)
others[s] (4)
each people (3) +2256+6639
them (3) +2021
common people (2) +1201
creatures (2)
everyone (2) +2021+3972
humble (2) +6714
lay people (2) +1201
lives (2)
one[s] (2) +2021
their[s] (2) +2021
them[s] (2) +2021+3972
they[s] (2) +824+2021
those[s] (2)
anyone else[s] (1)
army (1) +2256+7736
common people (1)
community (1) +824+2021
everyone (1)
exalted (1) +5294
fellow townsmen (1) +9133
followers (1) +339+889+2021
following (1) +907
force (1) +4878
force of men (1)
forces (1)
foreigners (1) +5799
guests (1)
Israel (1) +3776
Israelites (1) +1201+3776
it[s] (1) +2021
leaders (1) +8031
man (1)
merchants (1) +4047
multitude (1)
nationalities (1)
native (1) +1201
one another (1) +2021
one of the other peoples (1) +2256+6639
other nationalities (1) +824+2021
people's (1) +4200
person (1)
population (1)
soldier (1)
soldiers (1) +7372
someone (1) +285+2021
their[s] (1) +824+2021
their[s] (1) +3276+3776
them[s] (1) +2021+2021+2296
them[s] (1) +2257
them[s] (1) +3276
they[s] (1)
they[s] (1) +2021+3972
those[s] (1) +339+889+2021
various peoples (1) +2256+6639
untranslated (37)

6640 עִם *ʿim* (1049)
with (527)
to (63)
against (42)
and (25)
from (25) +4946
among (24)
in (15)
for (13)
near (12)
along with (11)
toward (10)
together with (8)
at (7)
before (7)
like (7)
on (5)
sleeps with (5) +8886
join (4)
lie with (4) +8886
of (4) +4946
away from (3) +4946
beside (3)
by (3)
have (3)
help (3)
slept with (3) +8886
accompanied by (2)
accompany (2)
also (2)
around (2)
as well as (2)
by (2) +4946
come to bed with (2) +8886
has sexual relations with (2) +8886
help (2) +2118
his (2) +2257
in company with (2)
into (2)
lay with (2) +8886
sleep with (2) +8886
to (2) +4946
to belong (2)
accompanied by (1) +2143
accomplice (1) +2745
allies[s] (1) +8611
allots to (1)
and alike (1)
and all (1)
as long as (1)
aside (1)
attitude (1)
away (1) +4946
because of (1)
bed with (1) +8886
before (1) +4946
belong to (1)
besides (1)
both and (1)
call to account (1) +2011+4946
concerning (1)
convictions (1) +4222
decided (1) +2118+4213
demand (1)
desire (1)
despite (1)
done this[s] (1) +8886
dwell with (1)
endued with (1)
even as (1)
followed (1)
followed (1) +3655
followers (1) +408+889+2143
from (1)
from (1) +4946+7156
gave strong support (1) +2616
give (1)
harbor (1) +2118+4222
has (1)
has (1) +2118
he[s] (1) +408+2021+2021+8886
help (1) +3338
help (1) +3338+8883
here (1)
here[s] (1) +3276
impartially (1) +465+465
in mind (1)
in spite of (1)
in store (1)
in the care of (1)
in the presence of (1)
intend (1) +4222
join (1) +2143
leave (1) +2143+4946
left (1) +2143+4946
lies with (1) +8886
manned by (1)
my (1) +3276
of (1)
on terms (1) +4946
present (1)
rapes (1) +2256+2616+8886
rapes (1) +2256+8886+9530
share their duties (1) +465
sided with (1) +3338
sleeping with (1) +8886
support (1)
supports (1) +2616
take part (1) +2143
the LORD's (1) +3378+4946
took care of (1)
treated (1) +2118
treated (1) +6913
when (1)
where (1)
with help (1)
with the help of (1)
withstand (1) +3656
untranslated (106)

6641 עָמַד *ʿāmaḏ* (525)
stood (82)
stand (64)
standing (53)
stopped (19)
appointed (10)
stationed (8)
stands (7)
stay (7)
stop (7)
assigned (6)

present (6)
serve (6) +4200+7156
stood still (6)
endure (5)
stand up (5)
stood up (5)
arise (4)
endures (4)
have stand (4)
ministering (4)
put in place (4)
set (4)
stayed (4)
had stand (3)
presented (3)
raised (3)
remain (3)
remains (3)
serve (3)
set in place (3)
stand firm (3)
appear (2)
appoint (2)
came to a halt (2)
confirmed (2)
delay (2)
enables to stand (2)
entered service (2) +4200+7156
last (2)
minister (2)
perform (2)
propped up (2)
protect (2) +6584
remained (2)
resist (2) +4200+7156
rise (2)
rose up (2)
served (2)
served (2) +4200+7156
serving (2) +4200+7156
set up (2)
stand ground (2)
stayed behind (2)
take stand (2)
took places (2)
took stand (2)
unchanged (2)
unchanged (2) +9393
upright (2)
wait (2)
withstand (2) +928+7156
withstand (2) +4200+7156
act (1)
appeared (1)
appointing (1)
as did[S] (1)
assist (1) +907
assistant (1) +4200+7156
assume the responsibility for carrying out (1) +6584
attend (1) +4200+7156
attendants (1) +6584
avoid (1)
be (1)
be presented (1)
broke out (1)
built (1)
calm (1)
can[S] (1)
claim (1)
come (1)
come forward (1)
confronted (1) +6584
crowd (1) +889+3972
decided (1) +1821
defend (1) +5584
do anything that endangers life (1) +1947+6584
emerge (1)
enduring (1)
enter service (1) +4200+7156
entered the service (1) +4200+7156
establish (1)
face (1)
fulfillment (1)
gets up (1)
gives stability (1)
gives way (1) +4202
gone (1) +928+4202
had pledge (1)
had serve (1)
halt (1)
halted (1)
held (1)
in charge (1) +6584
installed (1)
joined together (1) +285+3869
keep on (1)
leave alone (1) +4946
linger (1)
live (1)
made stand (1)
making strong (1)
muster (1)
occupied (1) +448
on duty (1)
opposed (1) +6584
performed (1)
persists (1)
pillar (1)
pledged (1)
position (1)
post (1)
posted (1)
posting (1)
protects (1) +6584
put in charge (1) +3338+6584
putting in place (1)
raise (1)
raised up (1)
reach (1)
rebuilding (1)
rebuilt (1)
rely (1)
repair (1)
replaced (1) +9393
represent (1)
resist (1)
resisted (1) +4200+5584
rise up (1)
rises (1)
serve (1) +6584
served (1) +907+7156
sets up (1)
stand the strain (1)
stand up (1) +6584+6642
standing trial (1)
stands firm (1)
stared with a fixed gaze (1) +906+2256+7156+8492
staying (1)
stays (1)
stirred up (1)
stood by (1)
stood firm (1)
stood in places (1)
stood waiting (1)
succeed (1)
succeeded (1) +4030+6584
successor (1) +4030+6584
successor (1) +9393
surviving (1)
to feet (1)
tolerated (1)
took (1)
took up (1) +6584
uphold (1)
was (1)
were (1)
withstood (1) +928+7156
worked (1)
untranslated (9)

6642 עֹמֶד *'ômed* (8)
feet (1)
place where standing (1)
places (1)
positions (1)
posts (1)
stand up (1) +6584+6641
standing (1)
where[S] (1) +6584

6643 עִמָּד *'immād* (45)
with (16)
to (6)
against (2)
in (2)
besides (1)
for (1)
leave (1) +2143+4946
mine (1) +3276
oppose (1)
oppose (1) +8189
surround (1)
toward (1)
untranslated (11)

6644 עֶמְדָּה *'emdāh* (1)
protection (1)

6645 1עֻמָּה *'ummāh1* (32)
close to (5) +4200
along with (2) +4200
as (2) +4200
beside (2) +4200
just as (2) +4200
parallel to (2) +4200
above (1) +4200+4946+4946+5087
adjoining (1) +4200
alike (1) +4200
alongside (1) +4200
alongside of (1) +4200
as (1) +3972+8611
as well as (1) +4200
at (1) +4200
bordering (1) +4200
length (1) +4200
like (1) +4200
opposite (1) +4200
responding to (1) +4200
treated the same as (1) +4200
with (1) +4200
untranslated (2)

6646 2עֻמָּה *'ummāh2* (1)
Ummah (1)

6647 עַמּוּד *'ammûd* (112)
pillars (38)
posts (36)
pillar (25)
columns (2)
colonnade (1) +395
column (1)
one[S] (1)
untranslated (8)

6648 עַמּוֹן *'ammôn* (106)
Ammonites (79) +1201
Ammon (9) +1201
Ammonite (8) +1201
Ammon (5)
Ammonites (1)
their[S] (1) +1201
them[S] (1) +1201
they[S] (1) +1201
untranslated (1)

6649 עַמּוֹנִי *'ammôniy* (21)
Ammonite (13)
Ammonites (6)
Ammon (1)
untranslated (1)

6650 עָמוֹס *'āmôs* (7)
Amos (7)

6651 עָמוֹק *'āmôq* (2)
Amok (1)
Amok's (1)

6652 עַמִּי *'ammiy*
Variant; not used

6653 עַמִּיאֵל *'ammiy'ēl* (6)
Ammiel (6)

6654 עַמִּיהוּד *'ammiyhûḏ* (10)
Ammihud (10)

6655 עַמִּיזָבָד *'ammiyzāḇāḏ* (1)
Ammizabad (1)

6656 עַמִּיחוּר *'ammiyḥûr* (1)
untranslated (1)

6657 עַמִּינָדָב *'ammiynāḏāḇ* (13)
Amminadab (13)

6658 עָמִיר *'āmiyr* (4)
sheaves (2)
cut grain (1)
grain (1)

6659 עַמִּישַׁדָּי *'ammiyšaddāy* (5)
Ammishaddai (5)

6660 עָמִית *'āmiyṯ* (12)
neighbor (4)
another[s] (1)
close (1)
countryman (1)
countrymen (1)
him[s] (1)
him[s] (1) +2257
neighbor's (1)
other[s] (1)

6661 עָמַל *'āmal* (11)
labor (3)
toils (2)
efforts (1)
poured effort (1)
tend (1)
toiled (1)
worked (1)
works (1)

6662 1עָמָל *'āmāl1* (55)
trouble (15)
work (8)
labor (5)
misery (5)
toil (5)
oppressive (2)
toilsome (2)
wrong (2)
abuse (1)
bitter labor (1)
burdens (1)
distress (1)
efforts (1)
making trouble (1)
miserable (1)
suffering (1)
things[s] (1)
what toiled for (1)
what[s] (1)

6663 2עָמָל *'āmāl2* (1)
Amal (1)

6664 1עָמֵל *'āmēl1* (4)
misery (2)
laborer's (1)
workman's (1)

6665 2עָמֵל *'āmēl2* (5)
labors (1)
toil (1)
toiled for (1)
toiling (1)
toilsome (1)

6666 עַמְלֵץ *'amlēṣ*
Variant; not used

6667 עֲמָלֵק *'ᵃmālēq* (39)
Amalekites (25)
Amalek (12)
Amalekite (1)
their[s] (1)

6668 עֲמָלֵקִי *'ᵃmālēqiy* (12)
Amalekites (9)
Amalekite (3)

6669 1עָמַם *'āmam1* (1)
rival (1)

6670 2עָמַם *'āmam2* (2)
hidden (1)
lost luster (1)

6671 עַמֹּנָה *'ammōnāh* (1)
untranslated (1)

6672 עִמָּנוּ אֵל *'immānû 'ēl* (2)
Immanuel (2)

6673 עָמַס *'āmas* (9)
laid (2)
bears burdens (1)
burdensome (1)
carried (1) +5951
loaded (1)
loading (1)
move (1)
upheld (1)

6674 עֲמַסְיָה *'ᵃmasyāh* (1)
Amasiah (1)

6675 עַמְעָד *'am'āḏ* (1)
Amad (1)

6676 עָמַק *'āmaq* (9)
deep (3)
deepest (1)
go to great depths (1)
greatly (1)
made deep (1)
profound (1)
sunk deep (1)

6677 עֵמֶק *'ēmeq* (68)
valley (52)
valleys (11)
plain (2)
fiercely (1) +928+2021
plain (1) +824
plains (1)

6678 עָמֹק *'āmōq* (17)
deep (13)
cunning (1)
deeper (1)
most profound (1) +6678

6679 עֹמֶק *'ōmeq* (2)
deep (1)
depths (1)

6680 עָמֵק *'āmēq* (3)
obscure (2)
obscure (1) +4946+9048

6681 עֵמֶק קְצִיץ *'ēmeq q'ṣiyṣ* (1)
Emek Keziz (1)

6682 1עָמַר *'āmar1* (1)
gathers (1)

6683 2עָמַר *'āmar2* (2)
treat as a slave (1)
treats as a slave (1)

6684 1עֹמֶר *'ōmer1* (8)
sheaf (4)
sheaves (3)
sheaf of grain (1)

6685 2עֹמֶר *'ōmer2* (6)
omer (5)
omers (1)

6686 עֲמֹרָה *'ᵃmōrāh* (19)
Gomorrah (19)

6687 עָמְרִי *'omriy* (18)
Omri (15)
Omri's (2)
he[s] (1) +281+1201

6688 עַמְרָם *'amrām* (14)
Amram (13)
Amram's (1)

6689 עַמְרָמִי *'amrāmiy* (2)
Amramites (2)

6690 עֲמָשָׂא *'ᵃmāśā'* (16)
Amasa (15)
whose[s] (1)

6691 עֲמָשַׂי *'ᵃmāśay* (5)
Amasai (5)

6692 עֲמַשְׁסַי *'ᵃmašsay* (1)
Amashsai (1)

6693 עֲנָב *'ᵃnāḇ* (2)
Anab (2)

6694 עֵנָב *'ēnāḇ* (19)
grapes (12)
good grapes (2)
grape (2)
grapes or raisins (1) +2256+3313+4300
raisin (1)
untranslated (1)

6695 עָנַג *'ānag* (10)
delight (2)
find delight (2)
delicate (1)
delight yourself (1)
enjoy (1)
find joy (1)
mocking (1)
sensitive (1)

6696 עֹנֶג *'ōneg* (2)
delight (1)
luxurious (1)

6697 עָנֹג *'ānōg* (3)
sensitive (2)
delicate (1)

6698 עָנַד *'ānaḏ* (2)
fasten (1)
put on (1)

6699 1עָנָה *'ānāh1* (314)
answered (74)
answer (73)
replied (41)
said (29)
answers (9)
asked (7)
respond (7)
responded (6)
testify (5)
reply (4)
testifies (4)
spoke (3)
answering (2)
declare (2)
give (2)
help (2)
said in reply (2)
spoke up (2)
accept (1)
accuse (1)
answer (1) +1821
answer given (1)
arguing (1)
be answered (1)
come to relief (1)
dispute (1)
echo (1)
explained (1)
gave ruling (1)
get response (1)
give answer (1)

give testimony (1)
gives (1)
gives back answer (1)
giving testimony (1)
go unanswered (1) +4202
had[s] (1)
have answer (1)
have say (1) +2750
recite (1) +606+2256
reported (1)
said a word (1)
save (1)
say (1)
say (1) +606+2256
says (1)
shout (1)
shouted (1)
tell (1)
testified (1)
testify (1) +4200+6332
testimony (1)
told (1)
whoever he may be (1) +2256+6424
untranslated (4)

6700 2עָנָה *'ānāh2* (81)
afflicted (12)
deny (6)
oppress (5)
humble (4)
oppressed (4)
humbled (3)
subdue (3)
afflict (2)
humble yourself (2)
mistreated (2)
raped (2)
violated (2)
be afflicted (1)
bring affliction (1)
broke (1)
bruised (1)
deny himself (1)
disgraced (1)
dishonored (1)
disturbed (1)
do[s] (1) +6700
force (1)
hardships endured (1)
humble ourselves (1)
made suffer (1)
mistreat (1)
oppressors (1)
overwhelmed (1)
punish (1)
raped (1) +2256+8886
ravished (1)
shared hardships (1) +889+928+6700
stilled (1)
stoop down (1)
subdued (1)
submit (1)
suffered (1)
suffered affliction (1)
take advantage of (1)
use (1)
violate women (1)
violated (1) +2256+8886
violates (1)
untranslated (1)

6701 3עָנָה *'ānāh3* (3)
burden (2) +6721
keeps occupied (1)

6702 4עָנָה *'ānāh4* (15)
sing (6)
sang (4)
sound (2) +7754
howl (1)
shout in triumph (1) +2116
singing (1)

6703 עֹנָה *'ōnāh* (1)
marital rights (1)

6704 עֲנָה *'ᵃnāh* (12)
Anah (12)

6705 עָנָו *'ānāw* (25)
humble (7)
afflicted (4)
poor (4)
oppressed (2)
afflicted (1) +6714
helpless (1)
meek (1)
needy (1)
them[s] (1)
untranslated (3)

6706 עֻנּוֹ *'unnô* (1)
untranslated (1)

6707 עָנוּב *'ānûḇ* (1)
Anub (1)

6708 עֲנָוָה *'ᵃnāwāh* (6)
humility (5)
stoop down (1)

6709 עַנְוָה *'anwāh*
Variant; not used

6710 עֲנוֹק *'ᵃnôq* (1)
Anak (1)

6711 עֲנוּשִׁים *'ᵃnûšiym* (1)
fines (1)

6712 עֲנוֹת *'ᵃnôṯ*
Variant; not used

6713 עֱנוּת *'ᵉnûṯ* (1)
suffering (1)

6714 עָנִי *'āniy* (79)
poor (40)
afflicted (14)
oppressed (4)
needy (3)
helpless (2)
humble (2) +6639
weak (2)
afflicted (1) +6705
distress (1)
gentle (1)
humble (1)
meek (1)
suffer (1)
wretched (1)
untranslated (5)

6715 עֳנִי *'ᵒniy* (37)
affliction (14)
suffering (9)
misery (8)
distress (1)
grief (1)
hardship (1)
oppressed (1) +1201
persecute (1)
taken great pains (1) +928

6716 עֻנִּי *'unniy* (3)
Unni (3)

6717 עֲנָיָה *'ᵃnāyāh* (2)
Anaiah (2)

6718 עָנָיו *'ānāyw*
Variant; not used

6719 עָנִים *'āniym* (1)
Anim (1)

6720 עֵנִים *'ēniym* (1)
untranslated (1)

6721 עִנְיָן *'inyān* (8)
burden (2) +6701
business (1)
cares (1)
labor (1)
misfortune (1) +8273
task (1)
work (1)

6722 עָנֵם *'ānēm* (1)
Anem (1)

6723 עֲנָמִים *'ᵃnāmiym* (2)
Anamites (2)

6724 עֲנַמֶּלֶךְ *'ᵃnammeleḵ* (1)
Anammelech (1)

6725 1עָנַן *'ānan1* (1)
bring clouds (1) +6727

6726 2עָנַן *'ānan2* (10)
practiced sorcery (2)
sorcery (2)
cast spells (1)
mediums (1)
practice divination (1)
practice sorcery (1)
soothsayers' (1)
sorceress (1)

6727 1עָנָן *'ānān1* (87)
cloud (63)
clouds (17)
mist (2)
bring clouds (1) +6725
it[s] (1) +2021
morning mist (1)
smoke (1)
them[s] (1)

6728 2עָנָן *'ānān2* (1)
Anan (1)

6729 עֲנָנָה *'ᵃnānāh* (1)
cloud (1)

6730 עֲנָנִי *'ᵃnāniy* (1)
Anani (1)

6731 1עֲנָנְיָה *'ᵃnānᵉyāh1* (1)
Ananiah (1)

6732 2עֲנָנְיָה *'ᵃnānᵉyāh2* (1)
Ananiah (1)

6733 עָנָף *'ānāp̱* (7)
branches (6)
branch (1)

6734 עָנֵף *'ānēp̱* (1)
full of branches (1)

6735 עָנַק *'ānaq* (3)
necklace (1)
supply liberally (1) +6735

6736 1עֲנָק *'ᵃnāq1* (3)
chain (1)
chains (1)
jewel (1)

6737 2עֲנָק *'ᵃnāq2* (17)
Anakites (7)
Anak (6)
Anakites (4) +1201

6738 1עָנֵר *'ānēr1* (2)
Aner (2)

6739 2עָנֵר *'ānēr2* (1)
Aner (1)

6740 עָנַשׁ *'ānaš* (8)
suffer (2)
fine (1)
imposed a levy (1)
must be fined (1) +6740
punish (1)
punished (1)

6741 עֹנֶשׁ *'ōneš* (2)
levy (1)
penalty (1)

6742 עֲנָת *'ᵃnāṯ* (2)
Anath (2)

6743 1עֲנָתוֹת *ʿ[a]nāṯôṯ1* (13)
Anathoth (13)

6744 2עֲנָתוֹת *ʿ[a]nāṯôṯ2* (2)
Anathoth (2)

6745 עַנְּתֹתִי *ʿann[e]ṯōṯiy* (5)
from Anathoth (3)
Anathothite (2)

6746 עַנְתֹתִיָּה *ʿanṯōṯiyyāh* (1)
Anthothijah (1)

6747 עָסִיס *ʿāsiys* (5)
new wine (3)
nectar (1)
wine (1)

6748 עָסַס *ʿāsas* (1)
trample down (1)

6749 עָעַר *ʿāʿar*
Variant; not used

6750 עֳפָאִים *ʿ[o]p̱āʾyim*
Variant; not used

6751 עֳפִי *ʿ[o]p̱iy* (1)
branches (1)

6752 1עָפַל *ʿāp̱al1* (1)
puffed up (1)

6753 2עָפַל *ʿāp̱al2* (1)
presumption (1)

6754 1עֹפֶל *ʿōp̱el1* (6)
tumors (6)

6755 2עֹפֶל *ʿōp̱el2* (8)
hill of Ophel (4)
citadel (1)
hill (1)
Ophel (1)
stronghold (1)

6756 עָפְנִי *ʿop̱niy* (1)
Ophni (1)

6757 עַפְעַפַּיִם *ʿap̱ʿappayim* (10)
eyelids (3)
eyes (3)
first rays (1)
gaze (1)
glances (1)
rays (1)

6758 עָפַף *ʿāp̱ap̱* (1)
brandish (1)

6759 עָפַר *ʿāp̱ar* (1)
showering (1)

6760 עָפָר *ʿāp̱ār* (110)
dust (81)
earth (5)
rubble (5)
soil (4)
ground (3)
ashes (2)
powder (2)
clay (1)
dirt (1)
earthen ramps (1)
material (1)
plaster (1)
sand (1)
scabs (1) +1599
soil (1) +824

6761 עֵפֶר *ʿēp̱er* (4)
Epher (4)

6762 עֹפֶר *ʿōp̱er* (5)
young stag (3) +385
fawns (2)

6763 1עָפְרָה *ʿop̱rāh1* (1)
Ophrah (1)

6764 2עָפְרָה *ʿop̱rāh2* (7)
Ophrah (7)

6765 עַפְרָה *ʿap̱rāh*
Variant; not used

6766 1עֶפְרוֹן *ʿep̱rôn1* (12)
Ephron (8)
Ephron's (2)
he[s] (1)
him[s] (1)

6767 2עֶפְרוֹן *ʿep̱rôn2* (2)
Ephron (2)

6768 עֶפְרַיִן *ʿep̱rayin* (1)
untranslated (1)

6769 עֹפֶרֶת *ʿōp̱ereṯ* (9)
lead (9)

6770 עֵץ *ʿēṣ* (329)
wood (100)
trees (69)
tree (61)
timber (12)
wooden (10)
gallows (9)
logs (9)
stick (7)
shaft (4)
almugwood (3) +523
carpenters (3) +3093
stick of wood (3)
sticks (3)
woodcutters (3) +2634
algumwood (2) +454
timbers (2)
beams (1)
branches (1) +8457
carpenter (1) +3093
carpenters (1)
firewood (1)
it[s] (1) +2021
loads of wood (1)
lumber (1)
olive (1) +9043
paneling (1) +7596
piece of wood (1)
pine (1) +1360
plant life (1)
stalks (1)
that[s] (1)
them[s] (1) +780
wooden idol (1)
woodpile (1)
woodwork (1)
untranslated (10)

6771 1עָצַב *ʿāṣaḇ1* (2)
like image (1)
shaped (1)

6772 2עָצַב *ʿāṣaḇ2* (14)
distressed (2)
grieve (2)
grieved (2)
be grieved (1)
be injured (1)
filled with grief (1)
grieving (1)
interfered with (1)
twist (1)
was filled with pain (1)
was grieved (1)

6773 עָצָב *ʿāṣāḇ* (17)
idols (13)
images (4)

6774 עַצָּב *ʿaṣṣāḇ* (1)
workers (1)

6775 1עֶצֶב *ʿeṣeḇ1* (1)
pot (1)

6776 2עֶצֶב *ʿeṣeḇ2* (6)
hard work (1)
harsh (1)
pain (1)
toil (1)
toiling (1)
trouble (1)

6777 1עֹצֶב *ʿōṣeḇ1* (1)
idols (1)

6778 2עֹצֶב *ʿōṣeḇ2* (4)
pain (2)
offensive (1)
suffering (1)

6779 עִצָּבוֹן *ʿiṣṣāḇôn* (3)
painful toil (2)
pains (1)

6780 עַצֶּבֶת *ʿaṣṣeḇeṯ* (5)
grief (1)
heartache (1) +4213
sorrows (1)
sufferings (1)
wounds (1)

6781 עָצָה *ʿāṣāh* (1)
winks (1)

6782 עָצֶה *ʿāṣeh* (1)
backbone (1)

6783 1עֵצָה *ʿēṣāh1* (88)
counsel (23)
advice (15)
plans (9)
plan (4)
advice gave (3) +3619
purpose (3)
schemes (3)
strategy (3)
advice given (2) +3619
planned (2) +3619
purposes (2)
advise (1) +3619
bent on (1) +928
consultation (1)
counselor (1) +408
counselors (1) +408
decision (1)
giving advice (1) +3619
harmony (1) +8934
planned (1)
planning (1) +3619
plot (1)
plots (1)
plotted (1) +3619
predictions (1)
sense (1)
that[s] (1)
thoughts (1) +928+5883
verdict (1)
untranslated (1)

6784 2עֵצָה *ʿēṣāh2*
Variant; not used

6785 3עֵצָה *ʿēṣāh3* (2)
trees (1)
wooden idols (1)

6786 עָצוּם *ʿāṣûm* (31)
mighty (8)
powerful (7)
stronger (6)
strong (4)
great (1)
much too numerous (1) +2256+8041
power (1)
strength (1)
throngs (1)
very (1) +4394

6787 עֶצְיוֹן גֶּבֶר *ʿeṣyôn geḇer* (7)
Ezion Geber (7)

6788 עָצַל *ʿāṣal* (1)
hesitate (1)

6789 עָצֵל *ʿāṣēl* (14)
sluggard (13)

sluggard's (1)

6790 עַצְלָה *'aslāh* (1)
laziness (1)

6791 עַצְלוּת *'aslût* (1)
idleness (1)

6792 עֲצַלְתַּיִם *'ᵃsaltayim* (1)
lazy (1)

6793 1עָצַם *'āsam1* (18)
many (6)
numerous (3)
crush bones (1)
height of power (1)
made numerous (1)
more (1)
power (1)
powerful (1)
strength (1)
vast (1)
very strong (1) +3946

6794 2עָצַם *'āsam2* (2)
sealed (1)
shuts (1)

6795 1עֶצֶם *'esem1* (126)
bones (80)
very (11)
blood (6)
bone (6)
body (3)
same (3)
bodies (2)
being (1)
frame (1)
itself (1)
limb (1)
those[s] (1)
vigor (1)
you (1) +4013
untranslated (8)

6796 2עֶצֶם *'esem2* (3)
Ezem (3)

6797 1עֹצֶם *'ōsem1* (3)
strength (2)
might (1)

6798 2עֹצֶם *'ōsem2* (1)
frame (1)

6799 עַצְמָה *'asmāh*
Variant; not used

6800 עָצְמָה *'osmāh* (2)
potent (1)
power (1)

6801 עַצְמוֹן *'asmôn* (3)
Azmon (2)
where[s] (1)

6802 עֲצֻמוֹת *'ᵃsumôt* (1)
arguments (1)

6803 עֵצֶן *'ēsen*
Variant; not used

6804 עֶצְנִי *'esniy* (1)
untranslated (1)

6805 עָצַץ *'āsas*
Variant; not used

6806 עָצַר *'āsar* (46)
slave (5)
shut up (4)
able (2) +3946
be stopped (2)
helpless (2) +3946+4202
retain (2)
stopped (2)
was stopped (2)
able (1)
been kept (1)
close up (1)
closed up (1) +6806
confined (1)
detain (1)
detained (1)
govern (1)
holds back (1)
keep (1)
kept (1)
prevail (1)
refrained (1)
regain (1) +6388
restricted (1)
seized (1)
shut (1)
slow down (1) +4200+8206
stay (1)
stops (1)
was banished (1)
was checked (1)
was confined (1)
was shut in (1)

6807 עֶצֶר *'eser* (1)
prosperous (1) +3769

6808 עֹצֶר *'ōser* (3)
oppression (2)
barren (1)

6809 עֲצָרָה *'ᵃsārāh* (11)
assembly (5)
assemblies (2)
sacred assembly (2)
closing assembly (1)
crowd (1)

6810 עָקַב *'āqab* (5)
deceived (1)
deceiver (1) +6810
grasped heel (1)
holds back (1)

6811 1עָקֵב *'āqēb1* (13)
heel (4)
heels (2)
ambush (1)
body (1)
footprints (1)
hoofs (1)
step (1)
steps (1)
tracks (1)

6812 2עָקֵב *'āqēb2* (1)
deceivers (1)

6813 עֵקֶב *'ēqeb* (15)
because (3) +889
because (2) +3954
for (2)
at (1) +6584
because (1)
because of (1) +6584
bring (1)
if (1)
reward (1)
to the end (1)
to the very end (1) +4200+6409

6814 1עָקֹב *'āqōb1* (1)
footprints (1)

6815 2עָקֹב *'āqōb2* (2)
deceitful (1)
rough ground (1)

6816 עֹקֶב *'ōqeb*
Variant; not used

6817 עָקְבָה *'āqbāh* (1)
deceptively (1) +928

6818 עָקַד *'āqad* (1)
bound (1)

6819 עָקֹד *'āqōd* (7)
streaked (7)

6820 עֵקֶד *'ēqed*
Variant; not used

6821 עָקָה *'āqāh* (1)
stares (1)

6822 עַקּוּב *'aqqûb* (8)
Akkub (8)

6823 עָקַל *'āqal* (1)
perverted (1)

6824 עֲקַלְקַל *'ᵃqalqāl* (2)
crooked ways (1)
winding (1)

6825 עֲקַלָּתוֹן *'ᵃqallātôn* (1)
coiling (1)

6826 עֲקָן *'ᵃqān* (2)
Akan (2)

6827 1עָקַר *'āqar1* (2)
uproot (1)
uprooted (1)

6828 2עָקַר *'āqar2* (5)
hamstrung (4)
hamstring (1)

6829 עָקָר *'āqār* (12)
barren (8)
sterile (2)
childless (1)
without young (1)

6830 1עֵקֶר *'ēqer1* (1)
member (1)

6831 2עֵקֶר *'ēqer2* (1)
Eker (1)

6832 עַקְרָב *'aqrāb* (9)
scorpions (6)
scorpion (3)

6833 עֶקְרוֹן *'eqrôn* (22)
Ekron (22)

6834 עֶקְרוֹנִי *'eqrôniy* (2)
Ekron (1)
people of Ekron (1)

6835 עָקַשׁ *'āqaš* (5)
distort (1)
perverse (1)
pronounce guilty (1)
takes crooked (1)
turned crooked (1)

6836 1עִקֵּשׁ *'iqqēš1* (11)
perverse (6)
crooked (3)
warped (1)
wicked (1)

6837 2עִקֵּשׁ *'iqqēš2* (3)
Ikkesh (3)

6838 עִקְּשׁוּת *'iqqᵉšût* (2)
corrupt (1)
perversity (1)

6839 1עָר *'ār1* (2)
adversaries (1)
enemy (1)

6840 2עָר *'ār2* (6)
Ar (6)

6841 עֵר *'ēr* (10)
Er (9)
untranslated (1)

6842 1עָרַב *'ārab1* (17)
puts up security (4)
make a bargain (2)
come to aid (1)
devote (1)
ensure (1)
guarantee safety (1)
guaranteed safety (1)

merchants (1) +5114
mortgaging (1)
pledge (1)
put up security (1)
puts up security (1) +6859
trade (1)

6843 2עָרַב *ʿāraḇ2* (5)
mingled (2)
avoid (1) +4200+4202
join (1)
share (1)

6844 3עָרַב *ʿāraḇ3* (8)
please (2)
sweet (2)
acceptable (1)
found pleasure (1)
pleasant (1)
pleasing (1)

6845 4עָרַב *ʿāraḇ4* (3)
evening (2)
turns to gloom (1)

6846 1עֶרֶב *ʿereḇ1*
Variant; not used

6847 2עֶרֶב *ʿereḇ2* (134)
evening (110)
at twilight (11) +1068+2021
dusk (2)
evenings (2)
night (2)
evening (1) +928+928+2021+2021+6847
evening (1) +2021+6961
every evening (1) +928+928+2021+2021+6847
fading (1)
untranslated (1)

6848 3עֶרֶב *ʿereḇ3*
Variant; not used

6849 1עֵרֶב *ʿēreḇ1* (9)
knitted material (9)

6850 2עֵרֶב *ʿēreḇ2* (5)
foreign people (2)
foreigners (1)
of foreign descent (1)
other people (1)

6851 1עֲרַב *ʿᵃraḇ1* (7)
Arabia (6)
Arabian (1)

6852 2עֲרַב *ʿᵃraḇ2*
Variant; not used

6853 עָרֵב *ʿārēḇ* (2)
sweet (1)
tastes sweet (1)

6854 1עֹרֵב *ʿōrēḇ1* (10)
raven (6)
ravens (4)

6855 2עֹרֵב *ʿōrēḇ2* (7)
Oreb (7)

6856 עָרֹב *ʿārōḇ* (9)
swarms of flies (5)
flies (4)

6857 1עֲרָבָה *ʿᵃrāḇāh1* (5)
poplars (3)
poplar trees (1)
poplars (1) +5707

6858 2עֲרָבָה *ʿᵃrāḇāh2* (58)
Arabah (28)
plains (17)
desert (4)
wasteland (3)
wastelands (2)
wilderness (2)
deserts (1)
untranslated (1)

6859 עֲרֻבָּה *ʿᵃrubbāh* (2)
assurance (1)
puts up security (1) +6842

6860 עֵרָבוֹן *ʿērāḇôn* (3)
pledge (3)

6861 עַרְבִי *ʿarḇiy* (8)
Arabs (5)
Arab (2)
untranslated (1)

6862 עֲרָבִי *ʿᵃrāḇiy* (2)
Arab (1)
nomad (1)

6863 עַרְבָתִי *ʿarḇātiy* (2)
Arbathite (2)

6864 עָרַג *ʿārag̱* (3)
pants (2)
pant (1)

6865 1עֲרָד *ʿᵃrāḏ1* (1)
Arad (1)

6866 2עֲרָד *ʿᵃrāḏ2* (4)
Arad (4)

6867 1עָרָה *ʿārāh1* (14)
exposed (2)
tear down (2)
dishonor (1)
emptied (1)
empty (1)
give over to death (1)
is poured (1)
make bald (1)
poured out (1)
stripped (1)
stripped naked (1)
uncovers (1)

6868 2עָרָה *ʿārāh2* (1)
plants (1)

6869 3עָרָה *ʿārāh3* (1)
Arah (1)

6870 עֲרוּגָה *ʿᵃrûg̱āh* (4)
beds (2)
plot (2)

6871 עָרוֹד *ʿārôḏ* (1)
his[s] (1)

6872 עֶרְוָה *ʿerwāh* (54)
have sexual relations with (11) +1655
nakedness (11)
dishonored (4) +1655
dishonor (3)
have sexual relations (3) +1655
have relations with (2) +1655
indecent (2)
shame (2)
unprotected (2)
body (1) +1414
dishonor bed (1) +1655
dishonor by having sexual relations with (1) +1655
dishonor by to have sexual relations (1) +1655
has sexual relations with (1) +906+1655
have sexual relations (1) +906+8011
naked (1)
shame (1) +1425
strip (1) +1655
untranslated (5)

6873 עָרוֹם *ʿārôm* (16)
naked (12)
stripped (3)
that way[s] (1)

6874 עָרוּם *ʿārûm* (11)
prudent (8)
crafty (3)

6875 1עֲרוֹעֵר *ʿᵃrôʿēr1*
Variant; not used

6876 2עֲרוֹעֵר *ʿᵃrôʿēr2* (16)
Aroer (16)

6877 עָרוּץ *ʿārûṣ* (1)
dry (1)

6878 1עֵרִי *ʿēriy1* (2)
Eri (2)

6879 2עֵרִי *ʿēriy2* (1)
Erite (1)

6880 עֶרְיָה *ʿeryāh* (6)
bare (4)
nakedness (1)
uncovered (1) +6423

6881 עֲרִיסָה *ʿᵃriysāh* (4)
ground meal (4)

6882 עֲרִיפִים *ʿᵃriyp̱iym* (1)
clouds (1)

6883 עָרִיץ *ʿāriyṣ* (21)
ruthless (17)
fierce (2)
cruel (1)
warrior (1)

6884 עֲרִירִי *ʿᵃriyriy* (4)
childless (4)

6885 עָרַךְ *ʿāraḵ* (75)
took up positions (5)
arrange (4)
deployed (4)
prepared (4)
arranged (3)
compare (3)
prepare (3)
spread (3)
drew up (2)
drew up line (2)
formed battle lines (2)
judge quality (2)
marshaled (2)
set (2)
set out (2)
take up positions (2)
accuse (1)
been prepared (1)
compare with (1)
deployed forces (1)
draw up case (1)
drawing up (1)
drawn up (1)
drew up lines (1)
formation (1)
formed lines (1)
handle (1)
in formation (1)
keep (1)
laid out (1)
lay (1)
lay out (1)
line up (1)
ready (1)
recount (1)
set out (1) +6886
set up (1)
set value (1)
state (1)
stationed (1)
sustain (1)
taxed (1)
tend (1)
tended (1)
value sets (1)
untranslated (1)

6886 עֵרֶךְ *ʿēreḵ* (33)
value (11)
proper value (3)
set value (3)
value (2) +4084
assessments (1)

clothes (1) +955
equivalent values (1)
form (1)
like (1) +3869
personal vows (1) +5883
price set (1)
set out (1) +6885
specified amount (1)
that[s] (1)
value (1) +4831
what belongs (1)
worth (1)
untranslated (1)

6887 עָרַל *'āral* (2)
be exposed (1)
regard as forbidden (1) +6889

6888 עָרֵל *'ārēl* (35)
uncircumcised (29)
faltering (2)
closed (1)
forbidden (1)
untranslated (2)

6889 עָרְלָה *'orlāh* (15)
foreskins (3)
be circumcised (1) +1414+4576
been circumcised (1) +4576
circumcise (1) +4576
circumcise (1) +6073
circumcised (1) +1414+4576
flesh (1)
foreskin (1)
not circumcised (1) +2257+4200
regard as forbidden (1) +6887
undergo circumcision (1) +906+1414+4576
was circumcised (1) +1414+4576
untranslated (1)

6890 1עָרַם *'āram1* (1)
piled up (1)

6891 2עָרַם *'āram2* (6)
craftiness (1)
cunning (1)
learn prudence (1)
shows prudence (1)
very crafty (1) +6891

6892 עֹרֶם *'ōrem*
Variant; not used

6893 עָרְמָה *'ormāh* (5)
prudence (3)
deliberately (1) +928
ruse (1)

6894 עֲרֵמָה *'ᵃrēmāh* (11)
heaps (3)
doing this[s] (1) +2021+3569
grain (1)
grain pile (1)
heap (1)
heaps of grain (1)
in heaps (1) +6894
mound (1)

6895 עַרְמוֹן *'ermôn* (2)
plane trees (2)

6896 עֵרָן *'ērān* (1)
Eran (1)

6897 עֵרָנִי *'ērāniy* (1)
Eranite (1)

6898 עַרְעוֹר *'ar'ôr*
Variant; not used

6899 עַרְעָר *'ar'ār* (3)
bush (2)
destitute (1)

6900 עַרְעָרָה *'ar'ārāh*
Variant; not used

6901 עֲרֹעֵרִי *'ᵃrō'ēriy* (1)
Aroerite (1)

6902 עֹרֶף *'ōreḇ* (33)
stiff-necked (11) +7996
backs (7)
stiff-necked (7) +7997
neck (4)
back (2)
routed (1) +2200
untranslated (1)

6903 1עָרַף *'ārap1* (2)
drop (1)
fall (1)

6904 2עָרַף *'ārap2* (6)
break neck (3)
breaks neck (1)
demolish (1)
neck was broken (1)

6905 עָרְפָּה *'ārpāh* (2)
Orpah (2)

6906 עֲרָפֶל *'ᵃrāpel* (15)
thick darkness (4)
blackness (2)
dark cloud (2)
dark clouds (2)
darkness (2)
deep darkness (2)
deep gloom (1)

6907 עָרַץ *'āras* (15)
terrified (4)
dread (2)
shake (2)
cause terror (1)
feared (1)
give way to panic (1)
is feared (1)
stand in awe (1)
terrify (1)
torment (1)

6908 עָרַק *'āraq* (2)
gnawing pains (1)
roamed (1)

6909 עַרְקִי *'arqiy* (2)
Arkites (2)

6910 עָרַר *'ārar* (4)
be leveled (1) +6910
strip off clothes (1) +2256+7320
stripped bare (1)

6911 עֶרֶשׂ *'ereś* (10)
bed (4)
couches (2)
bed (1) +3661
couch (1)
sickbed (1) +1867
untranslated (1)

6912 עֵשֶׂב *'ēśeḇ* (33)
grass (11)
plants (8)
growing (4)
plant (4)
vegetation (2)
green thing (1)
pasture (1)
tender plants (1)
untranslated (1)

6913 1עָשָׂה *'āśāh1* (2637)
do (405)
did (286)
made (270)
done (263)
make (161)
doing (61)
does (55)
follow (39)
prepare (30)
celebrate (25)
deal (24)
built (22)
obey (22)
maker (21)
show (21)
carry out (20)
be done (18)
act (17)
sacrifice (16)
committed (14)
inflict (14)
provide (14)
celebrated (13)
prepared (13)
keep (11)
acted (10)
bring (10)
been done (9)
gave (9)
observe (9)
performed (9)
shown (9)
accomplish (8)
makes (8)
offer (8)
treated (8)
work (8)
brought (7)
making (7)
present (7)
treat (7)
workers (7) +4856
bear (6)
build (6)
perform (6)
worked (6)
commits (5)
completely destroy (5) +3986
deal with (5)
forbidden (5) +4202
is done (5)
obeys (5)
produce (5)
showed (5)
uphold (5)
acquired (4)
appointed (4)
be made (4)
carried out (4)
exploits (4)
give (4)
grant (4)
observed (4)
provided (4)
put (4)
use (4)
used (4)
working (4)
yield (4)
achieve (3)
acting (3)
be granted (3)
brought about (3)
caused (3)
conduct (3)
destroy completely (3) +3986
do work (3)
engage (3)
gain (3)
gained (3)
held (3)
instituted (3)
offered (3)
performs (3)
practice (3)
produced (3)
sends (3)
showing (3)
shows (3)
supervise (3)
used to make (3)
waged (3)

were carved (3)
workmen (3) +4856
works (3)
achieved (2)
acts (2)
are done (2)
bake (2)
be fulfilled (2)
be prepared (2)
been made (2)
been observed (2)
behaved (2)
busy (2)
carrying out (2)
carved (2)
conformed to (2) +3869
consulted (2)
deal (2) +6913
deals (2)
dealt (2)
done (2) +5126
dug (2)
establishes (2)
fight (2)
fighting (2) +4878
follow (2) +3869
formed (2)
fought (2)
fulfill (2)
fully accomplishes (2) +2256+7756
get (2)
happen (2)
happens (2)
harm (2) +8273
harm (2) +8288
imitate (2) +3869
inflicted (2)
introduced (2)
kept (2)
maintain (2)
obeyed (2)
open (2)
ordained (2)
practices (2)
put into practice (2)
responsible (2)
serve (2)
set up (2)
shaping (2)
undertaken (2)
use (2) +4856
was celebrated (2)
worship (2)
yielded (2)
accomplished (1)
accomplishing (1)
add (1)
adhere to (1) +3869
administer (1)
administrators (1) +4856
am (1)
amassed (1)
answer (1)
applies (1)
apply (1)
are (1)
artificial (1)
assign (1)
assigned (1)
at war (1) +4878
at work (1)
attack (1) +4200
attend to (1)
avenged (1) +5935
be (1)
be carried out (1)
be completed (1)
be paid back (1)
be presented (1)
be used (1)
bearing (1)
became famous (1) +9005
been (1)
been committed (1)
been constructed (1)
been followed (1)
been used (1) +4856
began (1)
behave (1)
behaves (1)
bring up (1)
bulges with flesh (1) +7089
cancel debts (1) +9024
careful to carry out (1) +6913
carried on (1)
carried through (1)
carrying on (1)
carves (1)
cast (1)
celebrating (1)
celebration (1)
certainly carry out (1) +6913
certainly do (1) +6913
certainly make (1) +6913
comes (1)
commit (1)
committing (1)
construct (1)
constructed (1)
continue (1)
continued (1)
cooked (1)
copied (1)
created (1)
creature (1)
crop (1)
custom (1)
custom (1) +4027
customary (1)
deeds (1)
defends (1)
defiled[S] (1)
deserve (1)
did so[S] (1) +906+2021+7175
diligent (1)
displayed (1)
do (1) +6913
do great things (1) +6913
do something (1)
dressed (1)
earners (1)
earns (1)
engaged in (1)
erected (1)
establish (1)
established (1)
evildoer (1) +8288
evildoer (1) +8402
evildoers (1) +8402
executed (1)
exempt from taxes (1) +2930
exercises (1)
express (1)
faithfully (1) +622
fashion (1)
fashioned (1)
finished (1)
fit for (1)
follow (1) +4027
follow lead (1) +4027
followed (1) +4027
followed the example (1) +3869+6913
founded (1)
fulfill (1) +3869+4027+7023
fulfilled (1)
fulfills (1)
fully obeyed (1) +2256+9048
gains (1)
get ready (1)
give over (1)
given (1)
goes on (1)
going (1)
got ready (1)
granted (1)
grow (1)
hammer (1) +8393
hammer out (1) +5251
handle (1)
handled (1)
have (1)
have[S] (1)
help (1)
help (1) +4200
holding (1)
honor (1) +3702
honored (1) +3883
howl (1) +5027
in charge (1)
is built (1)
is carried out (1)
is done (1) +5126
is made (1)
judge[S] (1)
judges (1) +5477
keeping (1)
keeps (1)
make provision (1)
make up (1)
manage (1)
marks off (1)
master craftsmen (1) +4856
may do (1)
measured (1)
meet (1)
merchants (1) +4856
molded (1)
mount (1)
mounted (1)
mourn (1) +65
move (1)
obey (1) +2256+9068
observance (1)
occurs (1)
officiate (1)
on way (1) +2006
oppressed (1) +928+2021+6945
Pack (1)
pack (1)
passes through (1)
persist (1)
persisted in (1) +3869
pervert (1) +6404
piled (1)
presents (1)
proclaimed (1)
proud (1) +1452
provides (1)
providing (1)
punish (1) +5477
put forth (1)
put in jeopardy (1) +9214
ready (1)
received (1)
reduces (1)
render (1)
rescued (1) +9591
resist (1)
resorted (1)
rich (1)
roughs out (1)
sacrificed (1)
secures (1)
serve (1) +7372
set (1)
shapes (1)
sins defiantly (1) +928+3338+8123
sins unintentionally (1) +928+8705
still to come (1) +4202
stir up (1)
such[S] (1) +2021
surely show (1) +6913
surely sprout (1) +6913

take (1)
take action (1)
take part (1) +7928
take place (1)
taken care of (1)
taking place (1)
these men[s] (1) +2021+4856
trained (1)
treated (1) +6640
tried (1) +4027
trim (1)
trimmed (1)
turns to (1)
unlike (1) +4027+4202
upheld (1)
upholds (1)
use to make (1)
useful (1)
wage (1)
waging (1)
was happening (1)
was made (1)
was spent for making (1) +4946
well-trained (1) +4878
went about (1)
went on (1)
went to war (1) +4878
were made (1)
were practiced (1)
were prepared (1)
were[s] (1)
won (1)
work (1) +4856
work (1) +5126
worker (1)
workers (1)
working (1) +4856
workmen (1) +928+2021+4856
works out (1)
wrongdoing (1) +8400
wrongs (1) +2633
untranslated (97)

6914 2**עָשָׂה** *'āśāh2* (3)
caressed (3)

6915 **עֲשָׂהאֵל** *'aśāh'ēl* (18)
Asahel (17)
he[s] (1)

6916 **עֵשָׂו** *'ēśāw* (97)
Esau (79)
Esau's (14)
he[s] (3)
untranslated (1)

6917 **עָשׂוֹר** *'āśôr* (16)
tenth (12)
ten-stringed (3)
ten (1)

6918 **עֲשִׂיאֵל** *'aśiy'ēl* (1)
Asiel (1)

6919 **עֲשָׂיָה** *'aśāyāh* (8)
Asaiah (8)

6920 **עֲשִׂירִי** *'aśiyriy* (29)
tenth (29)

6921 **עָשַׂק** *'āśaq* (1)
disputed (1)

6922 **עֵשֶׂק** *'ēśeq* (1)
Esek (1)

6923 **עָשַׂר** *'āśar* (9)
take a tenth (2)
be sure to set aside a tenth (1) +6923
collect tithes (1)
give a tenth (1) +6923
receive tithes (1)
setting aside a tenth (1) +5130

6924 **עֶשֶׂר** *'eśer* (59)
ten (57)
910 (1) +2256+4395+9596
fifteen feet (1) +564+928+2021

6925 **עָשָׂר** *'āśār* (205)
twelve (51) +9109
12 (24) +9109
fourteenth (19) +752
fifteenth (15) +2822
twelfth (15) +9109
fourteen (12) +752
eleventh (8) +6954
thirteenth (8) +8993
fifteen (6) +2822
eighteen (4) +9046
seventeenth (4) +8679
sixteen (4) +9252
eleven (3) +285
sixteenth (3) +9252
112 (2) +2256+4395+9109
16,000 (2) +547+9252
18 (2) +9046
18,000 (2) +547+9046
eighteenth (2) +9046
nineteenth (2) +9596
thirteen (2) +8993
1,017 (1) +547+2256+8679
1,017 (1) +547+8679
112 (1) +4395+9109
13 (1) +8993
14,700 (1) +547+752+2256+4395+8679
16,750 (1) +547+2256+2822+4395+8679+9252
17,200 (1) +547+2256+4395+8679
2,812 (1) +547+2256+4395+9046+9109
2,818 (1) +547+2256+4395+9046+9046
212 (1) +2256+4395+9109
218 (1) +2256+4395+9046
318 (1) +2256+4395+8993+9046
eleven (1) +6954
nineteen (1) +9596
untranslated (1)

6926 **עֶשְׂרֵה** *'eśrēh* (136)
twelve (30) +9109
sixteen (14) +9252
thirteen (10) +8993
eighteenth (9) +9046
fifteen (8) +2822
eighteen (7) +9046
fourteen (7) +752
twelfth (7) +9109
eleven (6) +285
eleventh (5) +6954
seventeen (5) +8679
eleven (4) +6954
eleventh (4) +285
fourteenth (4) +752
thirteenth (3) +8993
fifteenth (2) +2822
nineteenth (2) +9596
seventeenth (2) +8679
119 (1) +2256+4395+9596
815 (1) +2256+2822+4395+9046
912 (1) +2256+4395+9109+9596
hundred and twenty thousand (1) +8052+9109
nineteen (1) +9596
twenty feet (1) +564+2822
twenty-seven feet (1) +564+9046

6927 **עֲשָׂרָה** *'aśārāh* (65)
ten (59)
110 (1) +2256+4395
410 (1) +752+2256+4395
fifteen (1) +2256+2822
seventeen (1) +2256+8679
untranslated (2)

6928 **עִשָּׂרוֹן** *'iśśārôn* (33)
two-tenths (11) +9109
three-tenths (8) +8993
one-tenth (4)
tenth (4)
one-tenth (1) +285
untranslated (5)

6929 **עֶשְׂרִים** *'eśriym* (316)
twenty (119)
twenty-five (23) +2256+2822
twenty-two (15) +2256+9109
24,000 (14) +547+752+2256
25,000 (14) +547+2256+2822
twentieth (9)
twenty-fourth (9) +752+2256
twenty-third (7) +2256+8993
twenty-seventh (6) +2256+8679
twenty-three (6) +2256+8993
120 (5) +2256+4395
twenty-four (5) +752+2256
twenty-nine (5) +2256+9596
128 (4) +2256+4395+9046
twenty-eight (4) +2256+9046
twenty-first (4) +285+2256
twenty-one (4) +285+2256
127 (3) +2256+2256+4395+8679
29 (3) +2256+9596
twenty-fifth (3) +2256+2822
123 (2) +2256+4395+8993
20 (2)
220 (2) +2256+4395
223 (2) +2256+4395+8993
320 (2) +2256+4395+8993
6,720 (2) +547+2256+4395+8679+9252
621 (2) +285+2256+4395+9252
twenty-second (2) +2256+9109
twenty-seven (2) +2256+8679
1,222 (1) +547+2256+4395+9109
120,000 (1) +547+2256+4395
122 (1) +2256+2256+4395+9109
122 (1) +2256+4395+9109
2,322 (1) +547+2256+4395+8993+9109
20,000 (1) +547
20,200 (1) +547+2256+4395
20,800 (1) +547+2256+4395+9046
22 (1) +2256+9109
22,000 (1) +547+2256+9109
22,034 (1) +547+752+2256+2256+2256+8993+9109
22,200 (1) +547+2256+2256+4395+9109
22,273 (1) +547+2256+2256+2256+4395+8679+8993+9109
22,600 (1) +547+2256+2256+4395+9109+9252
23,000 (1) +547+2256+8993
25,100 (1) +547+2256+2256+2822+4395
26,000 (1) +547+2256+9252
28 (1) +2256+9046
28,600 (1) +547+2256+2256+4395+9046+9252
3,023 (1) +547+2256+2256+8993+8993
323 (1) +2256+4395+8993+8993
324 (1) +752+2256+4395+8993
328 (1) +2256+4395+8993+9046
420 (1) +752+2256+4395
623 (1) +2256+4395+8993+9252
628 (1) +2256+4395+9046+9252
721 (1) +285+2256+2256+4395+8679
725 (1) +2256+2822+4395+8679
822 (1) +2256+4395+9046+9109
928 (1) +2256+4395+9046+9596
them[s] (1) +2021+7983
thirty feet (1) +564+928+2021
twenty-six (1) +2256+9252
twenty-sixth (1) +2256+9252
untranslated (2)

6930 **עֲשֶׂרֶת** *'aśereṯ* (52)
ten (39)
10,000 (9) +547
tens (3)
ten-acre (1) +7538

6931 1**עָשׁ** *'āš1* (7)
moth (4)
moths (2)
moth's cocoon (1)

6932 2עָשׁ *'āš2*
Variant; not used

6933 3עָשׁ *'āš3* (1)
bear (1)

6934 עָשׁוֹק *'āšôq* (1)
oppressor (1)

6935 עֲשׁוּקִים *ᵃšûqiym* (3)
oppression (3)

6936 עָשׁוֹת *'āšôṯ* (1)
wrought (1)

6937 עַשְׁוָת *'ašwāṯ* (1)
Ashvath (1)

6938 עָשִׁיר *'āšiyr* (23)
rich (21)
wealth (1)
wealthy (1)

6939 עָשַׁן *'āšan* (6)
smoke (2)
anger smolder (1)
burn (1)
covered with smoke (1)
smolder (1)

6940 1עָשָׁן *'āšān1* (25)
smoke (23)
cloud of smoke (1)
smoking (1)

6941 2עָשָׁן *'āšān2* (4)
Ashan (4)

6942 עָשֵׁן *'āšēn* (2)
in smoke (1)
smoldering (1)

6943 עָשַׁק *'āšaq* (37)
oppress (7)
oppressed (7)
defraud (4)
oppresses (3)
cheated (2)
oppressor (2)
oppressors (2)
cheats (1)
crushed (1)
mistreat (1)
oppression (1)
practice extortion (1) +6945
practiced extortion (1) +6945
rages (1)
take advantage (1)
taken by extortion (1) +6945
tormented (1)

6944 עֵשֶׁק *'ēšeq* (1)
Eshek (1)

6945 עֹשֶׁק *'ōšeq* (15)
oppression (6)
extortion (3)
oppressed (1)
oppressed (1) +928+2021+6913
practice extortion (1) +6943
practiced extortion (1) +6943
taken by extortion (1) +6943
tyranny (1)

6946 עָשְׁקָה *'ošqāh* (1)
troubled (1)

6947 עָשַׁר *'āšar* (17)
rich (7)
bring wealth (1)
brings wealth (1)
enrich (1)
enriched (1)
get rich (1)
give wealth (1) +6948
made rich (1)
pretends to be rich (1)
richer (1) +6948
wealth (1)

6948 עֹשֶׁר *'ōšer* (37)
wealth (21)
riches (14)
give wealth (1) +6947
richer (1) +6947

6949 עָשַׁשׁ *'āšaš* (3)
weak (3)

6950 1עָשַׁת *'āšat1* (1)
sleek (1)

6951 2עָשַׁת *'āšat2* (1)
take notice (1)

6952 עֶשֶׁת *'ešeṯ* (1)
polished (1)

6953 עַשְׁתּוּת *'aštûṯ* (1)
have (1)

6954 עַשְׁתֵּי *'aštēy* (18)
eleventh (8) +6925
eleventh (5) +6926
eleven (4) +6926
eleven (1) +6925

6955 עֶשְׁתֹּנֹת *'eštōneṯ* (1)
plans (1)

6956 עַשְׁתֹּרֶת *'aštōreṯ* (9)
Ashtoreths (6)
Ashtoreth (3)

6957 עַשְׁתְּרֹת *'ašteret* (4)
lambs (4)

6958 עַשְׁתָּרֹת *'aštārōṯ* (6)
Ashtaroth (6)

6959 עַשְׁתְּרֹת קַרְנַיִם *'ašt'rōṯ qarnayim* (1)
Ashteroth Karnaim (1)

6960 עַשְׁתְּרָתִי *ᵃšt'rāṯiy* (1)
Ashterathite (1)

6961 עֵת *'ēṯ* (297)
time (179)
times (26)
season (12)
when (11) +928
always (5) +928+3972
when (3)
as (2) +928
at (2) +928
at set times (2) +4946+6330+6961
days (2)
in (2) +4200
next year (2) +2645
now (2)
now (2) +2021+3869
proper time (2)
sunset (2) +995+2021+9087
when (2) +4200
appointed time (1)
as (1) +3869
as (1) +4200
as long as (1) +928+3972
at once (1) +928+2021+2021+2085
circumstances (1)
constantly (1) +928+3972
doom (1)
due time (1)
end (1)
evening (1) +2021+6847
future (1)
hour (1)
mealtime (1) +431+2021
occasion (1)
old (1)
past (1) +8037
punishment (1)
ripens (1)
seasons (1)
spring (1) +9102+9588
springtime (1) +4919
then[S] (1) +2021+2021+2085
till (1) +6330
time after time (1) +8041
timely (1) +928
whenever (1) +928
whenever (1) +928+3972
while (1) +4200
years (1) +2021+9102
untranslated (8)

6962 עֵת קָצִין *'ēṯ qāsiyn* (1)
Eth Kazin (1)

6963 עָתַד *'āṯaḏ* (2)
crumbling (1)
get ready (1)

6964 עַתָּה *'atāh* (434)
now (317)
then (10)
come now (3) +5528
therefore (3)
already (2)
but (2)
longer (2)
soon (2)
when (2)
about to (1) +4946+7940
although (1)
always (1)
further (1)
furthermore (1)
furthermore (1) +2256
going to (1)
if so (1) +3954
just (1) +2296
just (1) +4946
now (1) +2256
now (1) +2296
now then (1)
on (1) +6330
right now (1)
so (1)
surely (1) +421
surely (1) +3954
that day (1)
that time on (1)
then (1) +2256
this (1)
this day (1)
this time on (1)
yet (1) +2256
yet (1) +6330
untranslated (65)

6965 עָתוּד *'āṯûḏ* (2)
treasures (1)
untranslated (1)

6966 עַתּוּד *'atûḏ* (29)
male goats (15)
goats (12)
leaders (2)

6967 עִתִּי *'itiy* (1)
appointed for the task (1)

6968 עַתַּי *'atay* (4)
Attai (4)

6969 עָתִיד *'āṯiyḏ* (6)
ready (3)
doom (1)
poised (1)
untranslated (1)

6970 עֲתָיָה *ᵃṯāyāh* (1)
Athaiah (1)

6971 עָתִיק *'āṯiyq* (1)
fine (1)

6972 עַתִּיק *'atiyq* (2)
from ancient times (1)
taken (1)

6973 עֲתָךְ *ᵃṯāḵ* (1)
Athach (1)

6974 עַתְלַי *'atlāy* (1)
Athlai (1)

6975 עֲתַלְיָה *ᵃtalyāh* (7)
Athaliah (7)

6976 עֲתַלְיָהוּ *ᵃtalyāhû* (10)
Athaliah (10)

6977 עָתַם *'ātam* (1)
be scorched (1)

6978 עָתְנִי *'otniy* (1)
Othni (1)

6979 עָתְנִיאֵל *'otniy'ēl* (7)
Othniel (7)

6980 עָתַק *'ātaq* (9)
moved (2)
copied (1)
fail (1)
failed (1) +4946
growing old (1)
moved on (1)
moves (1)
went on (1)

6981 עָתָק *'ātāq* (4)
arrogance (1)
arrogant (1)
arrogantly (1)
outstretched (1)

6982 עָתֵק *'ātēq* (1)
enduring (1)

6983 1עָתַר *'ātar1* (20)
pray (7)
answered prayer (4)
prayed (4)
was moved by entreaty (2)
answered prayers (1)
prays (1)
respond to pleas (1)

6984 2עָתַר *'ātar2* (2)
multiplies (1)
without restraint (1)

6985 1עָתָר *'ātār1* (1)
worshipers (1)

6986 2עָתָר *'ātar2* (1)
fragrant (1)

6987 עֶתֶר *'eter* (2)
Ether (2)

6988 עֲתֶרֶת *ᵃteret* (1)
abundant (1)

6989 פ *p*
Variant; not used

6990 פָּאָה *pā'āh* (1)
scatter (1)

6991 1פֵּאָה *pē'āh1* (85)
side (33)
boundary (4)
edges (4)
end (4)
corners (2)
distant places (2) +7899
foreheads (2)
border (1)
edge (1)
front (1)
places (1)
sides (1)
southern (1) +448+5582
started (1) +4200
untranslated (27)

6992 2פֵּאָה *pē'āh2* (1)
remotest frontiers (1)

6993 3פֵּאָה *pē'āh3*
Variant; not used

6994 1פָּאַר *pā'ar1* (1)
go over the branches a second time (1)
+339

6995 2פָּאַר *pā'ar2* (13)
display splendor (3)
adorn (2)
endowed with splendor (2)
boast (1)
bring honor (1)
crowns (1)
displays glory (1)
leave the honor (1)
raise itself (1)

6996 פְּאֵר *pᵉ'ēr* (7)
turbans (2)
adorns head (1)
crown of beauty (1)
headbands (1) +4457
headdresses (1)
turban (1)

6997 פֹּארָה *pō'rāh* (7)
branches (5)
leafy boughs (1)
untranslated (1)

6998 פֻּארָה *pu'rāh* (1)
boughs (1)

6999 פָּארוּר *pā'rûr* (2)
grows pale (1) +7695
turns pale (1) +7695

7000 פָּארָן *pā'rān* (10)
Paran (10)

7001 פַּג *pag* (1)
early fruit (1)

7002 פִּגּוּל *piggûl* (4)
impure (2)
unclean (1)
unclean meat (1)

7003 פָּגַע *pāga'* (46)
touched (6)
strike down (4)
struck down (4)
meet (2)
meets (2)
plead (2)
strike (2)
attack (1)
attacked (1)
bordered (1)
come across (1)
come to the help of (1)
do^{s} (1)
extended (1)
find (1)
found (1)
harmed (1)
intercede (1)
intervene (1)
kill (1)
laid (1)
made intercession (1)
make plead (1)
met (1)
praying (1)
reached (1)
spare (1)
strike mark (1)
urge (1)
urged (1)
untranslated (1)

7004 פֶּגַע *pega'* (2)
chance (1)
disaster (1) +8273

7005 פַּגְעִיאֵל *pag'iy'ēl* (5)
Pagiel (5)

7006 פָּגַר *pāgar* (2)
exhausted (2)

7007 פֶּגֶר *peger* (21)
bodies (7)
dead bodies (7)
carcasses (2)
lifeless idols (2)
corpse (1)
dead (1)
lifeless forms (1)

7008 פָּגַשׁ *pāgaš* (14)
met (6)
have in common (2)
meet (2)
attack (1)
comes (1)
meet together (1)
meets (1)

7009 פָּדָה *pādāh* (60)
redeem (22)
redeemed (15)
ransom (4)
delivered (2)
ransomed (2)
be ransomed (1)
be redeemed (1)
been ransomed (1) +7009
buy back (1)
let be redeemed (1)
must redeem (1) +7009
ransoms (1)
redeem (1) +7009
redeems (1)
redemption (1)
rescued (1)
untranslated (1)

7010 פְּדַהְאֵל *pᵉdah'ēl* (1)
Pedahel (1)

7011 פְּדָהצוּר *pᵉdāhṣûr* (5)
Pedahzur (5)

7012 פְּדוּיִם *pᵉdûyim* (3)
redemption (2)
redeem (1)

7013 פָּדוֹן *pādôn* (2)
Padon (2)

7014 פְּדוּת *pᵉdût* (3)
redemption (2)
ransom (1)

7015 פְּדָיָה *pᵉdāyāh* (7)
Pedaiah (7)

7016 פְּדָיָהוּ *pᵉdāyāhû* (1)
Pedaiah (1)

7017 פִּדְיוֹם *pidyôm* (1)
redemption (1)

7018 פִּדְיוֹן *pidyôn* (2)
ransom (1)
redeem (1)

7019 פַּדָּן *paddān* (1)
Paddan (1)

7020 פַּדַּן אֲרָם *paddan ᵃrām* (10)
Paddan Aram (10)

7021 פָּדַע *pāda'* (1)
spare (1)

7022 פֶּדֶר *peder* (3)
fat (3)

7023 פֶּה *peh* (498)
mouth (199)
mouths (40)
command (39)
to (25) +4200
lips (13)
opening (8)
face (7)
with (5) +4200
word (5)
commanded (4)
end (4)

speech (4)
spoken (4)
testimony (4)
according to (3) +6584
by (3) +4200
number (3)
according to (2) +4200
as much as (2) +4200
commands (2)
dictated (2) +4946
man (2)
other[S] (2)
promised (2) +3655+4946
pronounced (2)
required (2)
said (2)
said (2) +3655+4946
speak (2)
speak (2) +4946
speak up (2) +7337
what say (2) +609
when (2) +4200
words (2) +609
according to (1) +3869
accordingly (1) +3869
amount (1)
as much as (1) +3869
at (1) +4200
beak (1)
because (1) +889+3869
big talk (1)
boast so much (1) +1540+3870
boasted (1) +928+1540
by (1) +4946
by (1) +6584
collar (1)
collar (1) +9389
consulting (1) +8626
decide (1) +2118+6584
demanded (1) +6584
dictate (1) +4946
dictated (1)
dictated (1) +4946+7924
dictating (1) +4946
dictation (1) +4946
direction (1)
don't say a word (1) +3338+6584+8492
double-edged (1)
double-edged (1) +9109
drank in (1) +7196
expressed (1) +6584
fruit (1)
fulfill (1) +3869+4027+6913
gape (1) +8143
give command (1) +7337
given word (1) +906+7198
giving an apt reply (1) +5101
had (1) +928
have (1) +928
hunger (1)
I (1) +3276
in accordance with (1) +4200
in accordance with (1) +6584
in proportion to (1) +3869
in the way should go (1) +2006+6584
inquire of (1) +906+8626
instructed (1) +1819
invoke (1) +928+7924
jaws (1)
just like (1) +3869
keep silent (1) +3104
killed (1) +2995+4200+5782
leading into (1) +4200
made a vow (1) +7198
make spew out (1) +3655+4946
mention (1) +928+9019
neck (1)
offered a kiss of homage (1) +4200+5975
on (1) +6584
orders (1)
portion (1)
promised (1) +928+1819
requires (1)
say (1)
say (1) +3655+4946
say (1) +7337
sayings (1)
share (1)
simply (1) +6584
sing (1) +928+8492
sneer (1) +8143
so that (1) +3869
speak (1) +928
speaks (1) +7337
spoke the word (1) +4946
spoken (1) +1819
spokesman (1) +3869
talk (1)
taste (1)
told (1) +928+8492
two-thirds (1) +9109
what said (1) +609
when (1) +3954+4200
whenever (1) +4200
will (1) +6584
words (1) +1821
words (1) +7339
untranslated (10)

7024 פֹּה *pōh* (70)
here (43)
on each side (10) +2256+4946+4946+7024
on either side (4) +2256+4946+4946+7024
other[S] (2)
side (2)
arrives (1) +995
square (1) +2256+4946+4946+7024
this far (1) +6330
untranslated (3)

7025 פּוּאָה *pû'āh* (3)
Puah (3)

7026 פֻּוָּאָה *puww'āh* (1)
Puah (1)

7027 פּוּאִי *pû'iy* (1)
Puite (1)

7028 פּוּג *pûg* (4)
feeble (1)
paralyzed (1)
stunned (1) +4213
untiring (1) +4202

7029 פּוּגָה *pûgāh* (1)
relief (1)

7030 פֻּוָּה *puwwāh*
Variant; not used

7031 1פּוּחַ *pûah1* (3)
breaks (2)
blow (1)

7032 2פּוּחַ *pûah2* (12)
pours out (4)
breathe (1)
breathe out (1)
gives (1)
malign (1)
sneers (1)
speaks (1)
stir up (1)
witness (1)

7033 פּוּט *pût* (7)
Put (7)

7034 פּוּטִיאֵל *pûtiy'ēl* (1)
Putiel (1)

7035 פּוֹטִיפַר *pôtiypar* (2)
Potiphar (2)

7036 פּוֹטִי פֶרַע *pôtiy pera'* (3)
Potiphera (3)

7037 פּוּךְ *pûk* (4)
turquoise (2)
paint (1)
painted (1) +928+2021+8531

7038 פּוֹל *pôl* (2)
beans (2)

7039 1פּוּל *pûl1*
Variant; not used

7040 2פּוּל *pûl2* (3)
Pul (2)
him[S] (1)

7041 פּוּן *pûn* (1)
in despair (1)

7042 פּוֹנֶה *pôneh*
Variant; not used

7043 פּוּנִי *pûniy*
Variant; not used

7044 פּוּנֹן *pûnōn* (2)
Punon (2)

7045 פּוּעָה *pû'āh* (1)
Puah (1)

7046 פּוּץ *pûs* (67)
scattered (21)
scatter (11)
disperse (7)
were scattered (5)
been scattered (4)
dispersed (2)
overflow (2)
attacker (1)
be scattered (1)
blow away (1)
broken (1)
dog (1)
driven (1)
go out (1)
is scattered (1)
scattering (1)
scatters (1)
separated (1)
sow (1)
spread out (1)
unleash (1)
untranslated (1)

7047 2פּוּץ *pûs2*
Variant; not used

7048 1פּוּק *pûq1* (2)
stumble (1)
totter (1)

7049 2פּוּק *pûq2* (7)
receives (2)
gains (1)
let succeed (1)
obtains (1)
provision (1)
spend (1)

7050 פּוּקָה *pûqāh* (1)
staggering burden (1) +2256+4842

7051 1פּוּר *pûr1*
Variant; not used

7052 2פּוּר *pûr2* (8)
Purim (5)
pur (3)

7053 פּוּרָה *pûrāh* (2)
measures (1)
winepress (1)

7054 פּוֹרָתָא *pôrātā'* (1)
Poratha (1)

7055 1פּוּשׁ *pûš1* (4)
frolic (1)
gallops headlong (1)
leap (1)
untranslated (1)

7056 2פּוּשׁ *pûš2* (1)
scattered (1)

7057 פּוּתִי *pûṯiy* (1)
Puthites (1)

7058 פַּז *paz* (9)
pure gold (5)
gold (2)
fine gold (1)
purest gold (1) +4188

7059 1פָּזַז *pāzaz1* (1)
fine (1)

7060 2פָּזַז *pāzaz2* (2)
leaping (1)
limber (1)

7061 פָּזַר *pāzar* (10)
scattered (5)
been scattered (1)
dispersed (1)
gives freely (1)
scattered abroad (1)
scatters (1)

7062 1פַּח *paḥ1* (24)
snare (14)
snares (5)
trap (4)
snares (1) +3687

7063 2פַּח *paḥ2* (2)
sheets (1)
thin sheets (1)

7064 פָּחַד *pāḥaḏ* (25)
afraid (3)
fear (2)
overwhelmed with dread (2) +7065
terrified (2)
brought down to terror (1)
come trembling (1)
feared (1)
fears (1)
fill (1)
filled with dread (1)
in awe (1)
live in terror (1)
looked in fear (1)
made shake (1)
showed fear (1)
throb (1)
tremble (1)
trembles (1)
turn in fear (1)
unafraid (1) +4202

7065 1פַּחַד *paḥaḏ1* (49)
fear (14)
terror (13)
dread (8)
calamity (2)
overwhelmed with dread (2) +7064
afraid (1) +5877+6584
awe (1)
cares (1)
disaster (1)
dreaded (1)
peril (1)
terrifying (1)
terrors (1)
threat (1)
what[s] (1)

7066 2פַּחַד *paḥaḏ2* (2)
thighs (1)
untranslated (1)

7067 פַּחְדָּה *paḥdāh* (1)
awe (1)

7068 פֶּחָה *peḥāh* (28)
governors (15)
governor (10)
officer (2)
officers (1)

7069 פָּחַז *pāḥaz* (2)
adventurers (1)
arrogant (1)

7070 פַּחַז *paḥaz* (1)
turbulent (1)

7071 פַּחֲזוּת *paḥᵃzûṯ* (1)
reckless (1)

7072 פָּחַח *pāḥaḥ* (1)
trapped (1)

7073 פֶּחָם *peḥām* (4)
coals (3)
charcoal (1)

7074 פַּחַת *paḥaṯ* (10)
pit (7)
cave (2)
pitfalls (1)

7075 פַּחַת מוֹאָב *paḥaṯ mô'āḇ* (6)
Pahath-Moab (6)

7076 פְּחֶתֶת *pᵉḥeṯeṯ* (1)
mildew (1)

7077 פִּטְדָה *piṭdāh* (4)
topaz (4)

7078 פְּטִירִים *pᵉṭiyriym* (1)
untranslated (1)

7079 פַּטִּישׁ *paṭṭiyš* (3)
hammer (3)

7080 פָּטַר *pāṭar* (9)
open (4)
breaching (1)
eluded (1)
hurl insults (1) +928+8557
released (1)
were exempt from duties (1)

7081 פֶּטֶר *peṭer* (11)
first offspring (5)
firstborn (3)
first male offspring (1) +1147+8167
firstborn (1) +8167
firstborn (1) +8715

7082 פִּטְרָה *piṭrāh* (1)
firstborn (1)

7083 פִּי־בֶסֶת *piy-ḇeseṯ* (1)
Bubastis (1)

7084 פִּי הַחִירוֹת *piy haḥiyrôṯ* (4)
Pi Hahiroth (4)

7085 פִּיד *piyḏ* (4)
misfortune (2)
calamities (1)
distress (1)

7086 פִּיחַ *piyaḥ* (2)
soot (2)

7087 פִּיכֹל *piyḵōl* (3)
Phicol (3)

7088 פִּים *piym* (1)
two thirds of a shekel (1)

7089 פִּימָה *piymāh* (1)
bulges with flesh (1) +6913

7090 פִּינְחָס *piynḥās* (25)
Phinehas (25)

7091 פִּינֹן *piynōn* (2)
Pinon (2)

7092 פִּיפִיּוֹת *piypiyyôṯ* (2)
double-edged (1)
many teeth (1)

7093 פִּישׁוֹן *piyšôn* (1)
Pishon (1)

7094 פִּיתוֹן *piyṯôn* (2)
Pithon (2)

7095 פַּךְ *paḵ* (3)
flask (3)

7096 פָּכָה *pāḵāh* (1)
flowing (1)

7097 פֹּכֶרֶת הַצְּבָיִים *pōḵereṯ hassᵉḇāyiym* (2)
Pokereth-Hazzebaim (2)

7098 פָּלָא *pālā'* (73)
wonders (17)
wonderful (15)
marvelous (10)
miracles (5)
amazing (3)
hard (3)
difficult (2)
am wonderfully made (1)
are wonderful (1)
astound (1)
astounding (1)
display awesome power (1)
fulfill a special vow (1) +5624
greatly (1)
impossible (1)
magnificent (1)
make a special vow (1) +5623
makes a special vow (1) +5624
send fearful (1)
show wonder (1)
showed wonderful (1)
special vow (1) +5624
special vows (1) +5624
unheard-of (1)
wonder (1)

7099 פֶּלֶא *pele'* (13)
wonders (4)
miracles (3)
wonderful (2)
astonishing things (1)
astounding (1)
marvelous things (1)
wonder (1)

7100 פִּלְאִי *pil'iy* (3)
beyond understanding (1)
wonderful (1)
untranslated (1)

7101 פַּלֻּאִי *pallu'iy* (1)
Palluite (1)

7102 פְּלָאיָה *pᵉlā'yāh* (2)
Pelaiah (2)

7103 פָּלַג *pālag* (4)
was divided (2)
confound (1)
cuts (1)

7104 1פֶּלֶג *peleḡ1* (10)
streams (9)
watercourse (1) +4784

7105 2פֶּלֶג *peleḡ2* (7)
Peleg (7)

7106 פְּלַגָּה *pᵉlaggāh* (3)
districts (2)
streams (1)

7107 פְּלֻגָּה *pᵉluggāh* (1)
subdivision (1)

7108 פִּלֶגֶשׁ *pileḡeš* (37)
concubine (21)
concubines (14)
lovers (1)
she[s] (1) +2257

7109 פִּלְדָּשׁ *pildāš* (1)
Pildash (1)

7110 פְּלָדֹת *pᵉlāḏōṯ* (1)
metal (1)

7111 פָּלָה *pālāh* (5)
deal differently (1)

distinguish (1)
make a distinction (1)
makes a distinction (1)
set apart (1)

7112 **פַּלּוּא** *pallû'* (5)
Pallu (5)

7113 **פְּלוֹנִי** *p^{e}lôniy* (3)
Pelonite (3)

7114 **פָּלַח** *pālah* (5)
pierces (2)
bring forth (1)
cut up (1)
plows (1)

7115 **פֶּלַח** *pelah* (6)
millstone (3)
halves (2)
part (1)

7116 **פִּלְחָא** *pilhā'* (1)
Pilha (1)

7117 **פָּלַט** *pālat* (26)
deliverer (5)
rescue (5)
delivered (4)
deliver (3)
delivers (2)
save (2)
calve (1)
carry off (1)
let escape (1)
saves (1)
survive (1)

7118 **פֶּלֶט** *pelet* (2)
Pelet (2)

7119 **פַּלֵּט** *pallēt* (1)
deliverance (1)

7120 **1פַּלְטִי** *paltiy1* (2)
Palti (1)
Paltiel (1)

7121 **2פַּלְטִי** *paltiy2* (1)
Paltite (1)

7122 **פִּלְטָי** *piltāy* (1)
Piltai (1)

7123 **פַּלְטִיאֵל** *paltiy'ēl* (2)
Paltiel (2)

7124 **פְּלַטְיָה** *p^{e}latyāh* (3)
Pelatiah (3)

7125 **פְּלַטְיָהוּ** *p^{e}latyāhû* (2)
Pelatiah (2)

7126 **פְּלָיָה** *p^{e}lāyāh* (1)
Pelaiah (1)

7127 **פָּלִיט** *pāliyt* (18)
escape (6)
escaped (2)
fugitives (2)
anyone[s] (1)
escape (1) +4880
fugitive (1)
him[s] (1) +2021
man who escaped (1)
man[s] (1)
renegades (1)
survivor (1)

7128 **פָּלֵיט** *pālēyt* (4)
escaped (1)
fugitives (1)
refugees (1)
survive (1)

7129 **פְּלֵיטָה** *p^{e}lēytāh* (30)
remnant (6)
deliverance (4)
escape (4)
survivors (4)
escaped (3)
fugitives (3)
band of survivors (2)
escapes (1) +2118
little left (1) +3856+8636
place to escape (1)
survivor (1)

7130 **פָּלִיל** *pāliyl* (2)
concede (1)
court (1)

7131 **פְּלִילָה** *p^{e}liylāh* (1)
decision (1)

7132 **פְּלִילִי** *p^{e}liyliy* (2)
to be judged (2)

7133 **פְּלִילִיָּה** *p^{e}liyliyyāh* (1)
rendering decisions (1)

7134 **1פֶּלֶךְ** *peleḵ1* (2)
crutch (1)
spindle (1)

7135 **2פֶּלֶךְ** *peleḵ2* (8)
district (4)
half-district (4) +2942

7136 **1פָּלַל** *pālal1* (4)
expected (1)
furnished justification (1)
intervened (1)
mediate (1)

7137 **2פָּלַל** *pālal2* (80)
pray (30)
prayed (28)
praying (10)
prays (5)
intercede (2)
prayer (2)
offer prayer (1) +9525
plead (1)
untranslated (1)

7138 **פָּלָל** *pālāl* (1)
Palal (1)

7139 **פְּלַלְיָה** *p^{e}lalyāh* (1)
Pelaliah (1)

7140 **פַּלְמֹנִי** *palmōniy* (1)
him[s] (1) +2021

7141 **פְּלֹנִי** *p^{e}lōniy* (3)
certain (1) +532
friend (1) +532
such and such (1) +532

7142 **1פָּלַס** *pālas1* (4)
make level (1)
make smooth (1)
mete out (1)
prepared (1)

7143 **2פָּלַס** *pālas2* (2)
examines (1)
gives thought (1)

7144 **פֶּלֶס** *peles* (2)
balances (1)
scales (1)

7145 **פָּלַץ** *pālas* (1)
makes tremble (1)

7146 **פַּלָּצוּת** *pallāsûṯ* (4)
fear (1)
horror (1)
terror (1)
trembling (1)

7147 **פָּלַשׁ** *pālaš* (5)
roll (4)
untranslated (1)

7148 **פְּלֶשֶׁת** *p^{e}lešeṯ* (9)
Philistia (7)
Philistines (2)

7149 **פְּלִשְׁתִּי** *p^{e}lištiy* (289)
Philistines (200)
Philistine (62)
they[s] (8)
Philistine's (4)
he[s] (3) +2021
them[s] (3)
him[s] (1) +2021
his[s] (1)
Philistia (1)
Philistines (1) +824
their[s] (1)
untranslated (4)

7150 **פֶּלֶת** *peleṯ* (2)
Peleth (2)

7151 **פְּלֻת** *p^{e}luṯ* (1)
distinction (1)

7152 **פְּלֵתִי** *p^{e}lēṯiy* (7)
Pelethites (7)

7153 **פֶּן** *pen* (133)
or (49)
not (16)
otherwise (9)
lest (8)
so that not (6)
if (4)
might (4)
no (3)
and (2)
because (2)
for (2)
so not (2)
that no (2)
that not (2)
can't (1)
for if (1)
in order that not (1)
may (1)
not be allowed (1)
or else (1)
perhaps (1)
so cannot (1)
so that no (1)
that (1)
too (1)
won't (1)
would (1)
untranslated (9)

7154 **פַּנַּג** *pannag* (1)
confections (1)

7155 **פָּנָה** *pānāh* (134)
turned (27)
turn (18)
facing (14)
looked (4)
prepare (4)
look (3)
return (3)
turning (3)
turns (3)
faces (2)
give attention (2)
left (2)
look with favor (2)
turned back (2)
turns away (2)
accept (1)
approaches (1)
back (1)
back (1) +339
break camp (1)
break of day (1) +1332
cleared ground (1)
daybreak (1) +1332
daybreak (1) +1332+2021
emptied (1)
expected (1)
face (1)

faced (1)
fading (1)
fled (1)
glancing (1)
go (1)
goes (1)
looked around (1)
looking (1)
looking back (1)
notice (1)
overlook (1) +440
pass away (1)
pays attention (1)
prepared (1)
respond (1)
return (1) +2143+2256
showed concern for (1) +448
surveyed (1)
tied (1)
turn around (1)
turn back (1)
turn to help (1)
turned (1) +8900
turned around (1)
turned away (1)
turns back (1)
untranslated (5)

7156 פָּנֶה *pāneh* (2127)
before (542) +4200
face (211)
presence (108)
before (82) +4946
in front of (66) +4200
because of (54) +4946
to (50) +4200
ahead (45) +4200
from (45) +4946
faces (35)
front (25)
before (24) +4200+4946
by (21) +4200
before (19)
presence (19) +4200
of (17) +4946
sight (17)
facedown (15) +6584
against (13) +4200
on (13) +6584
from (11) +4200+4946
for (10) +4200
over (10) +6584
surface (10)
before (9) +907
facing (9)
because (8) +4946
from (8) +4200
near (8) +6584
open (8)
by (7) +4946
formerly (7) +4200
meet (7) +4200
with (7) +4200
in (6) +6584
in front of (6) +6584
near (6) +4200
serve (6) +4200+6641
against (5) +928
before (5) +6584
east (5) +6584
used to (5) +4200
accept (4) +5951
at (4) +4946
determined (4) +8492
in front of (4) +448
show partiality (4) +5795
show partiality (4) +5951
upon (4) +6584
against (3) +4946
east (3)
entreat (3) +906+2704
escape (3) +4946
face (3) +4200
face (3) +6425
facedown (3) +448
faces (3) +6584
facing (3) +448
facing (3) +6584
leading (3) +4200
me (3) +3276
opposite (3) +4200
sight (3) +4200
sought the favor of (3) +906+2704
straight ahead (3) +448+6298
toward (3) +6584
accompanies (2) +4200
across (2) +6584
across from (2) +6584
advisers (2) +8011
as long as (2) +4200
at (2) +4200
at table[s] (2) +4200
attitude (2)
audience (2)
before (2) +5584
beside (2) +4200
covered with (2) +4200
entered service (2) +4200+6641
face to face (2)
faced (2)
faced (2) +448
faced each other (2) +8011
floor (2)
from (2) +4946+6584
from (2) +6584
in front of (2)
in front of (2) +907
in way (2) +4200
inside (2) +4200
leader (2) +2143+4200
led in campaigns (2) +995+2256+3655+4200
looking (2)
lying on (2) +6584
of (2) +4200
of (2) +4200+4946
preceded (2) +2118+4200
preceded (2) +4200
prostrate (2) +6584
reject (2) +8740
repulse (2) +8740
resist (2) +4200+6641
see (2) +4200
seems to (2) +4200
served (2) +4200+6641
serving (2) +4200+6641
shows partiality (2) +5951
top (2)
under (2) +4200
withstand (2) +928+6641
withstand (2) +4200+6641
won (2) +4200+5951
you (2) +3871
yourselves (2) +4013
above (1) +6584
accepted (1) +906+5951
adjoining (1) +448
advance (1) +2025
against (1) +6584
ahead (1) +4200+4946
ahead (1) +6584
all (1)
appear before (1) +8011
appearance (1)
appearing (1)
approach (1)
are shown respect (1) +2075
assistant (1) +4200+6641
at (1) +6584
at advance (1) +4200
at sanctuary[s] (1) +4200
at the head of (1) +4200
attend (1) +4200
attend (1) +4200+6641
attending (1) +4200
attention (1)
attention (1) +4200
awaits (1) +4200
away from (1) +4946
because of (1) +3954+4946
before (1) +448
before eyes (1) +4200
before time (1) +4200+4946
beforehand (1) +4200+4946
beginning (1)
bent on (1) +5584
beside (1) +6584
blade (1)
blindfolds (1) +4059
border (1)
borne on (1) +6584
bowed down (1) +5877+6584
bowed down to the ground (1) +5877+6584
check (1) +995+4200
come across (1) +4200+7925
come into presence (1) +906+8011
condition (1)
confronting (1) +4946
consult (1) +4200
corresponding to (1) +6584
countenance (1)
court favor (1) +2704
cover (1) +4848
crossing (1) +6584
curry favor with (1) +2704
defense against (1) +4946
determine (1) +8492
determined (1) +8492+8492
directly opposite (1) +4200+5790
disgrace (1) +1425
earlier times (1)
east (1) +6584+7710
edge (1)
eluded (1) +4946+6015
end (1)
enter service (1) +4200+6641
entered the service (1) +4200+6641
ever (1) +4200
expression (1)
extended (1) +6584
face (1) +4946
faced (1) +4200
faced forward (1) +448+4578
favoritism (1) +2075
field (1)
fierce-looking (1) +6434
for (1)
for (1) +4946
for fear of (1) +4946
for relief from (1) +4200+4946
for sake (1) +4946
forward (1) +4200
found (1) +4200+8011
from (1) +448
from (1) +4946+6640
front columns (1)
frown (1) +5877
give (1) +4200
grant (1) +5951
granted request (1) +5951
ground (1)
had been (1) +4200
had special access to (1) +8011
head (1)
headed for (1) +8492
hear (1) +4200+5877
here (1) +4200
highly regarded (1) +5951
honored (1) +5951
humiliation (1) +1425
implore (1) +2704
in (1)
in (1) +4200
in deference to (1) +4946

in earlier times (1) +4200
in eyes (1) +4200
in front (1)
in front of (1) +448+4578
in front of (1) +4946
in hostility toward (1) +6584
in path (1) +4200
in preference to (1) +6584
in service (1) +4200
in sight (1) +907
in the eyes of (1) +4200
in the front line (1) +448+4578
in the presence of (1) +5790
in view (1) +907
inner (1) +4200
instead of (1) +4200
intended (1)
intercede with (1) +906+2704
interceded with (1) +906+2704
lead (1)
lead (1) +995+2256+3655+4200
lead (1) +2143+4200
lead (1) +4200
lead across (1) +4200+6296
led (1) +4200
led out (1) +3655+4200
lifetime (1)
lived in hostility toward (1) +5877+6584
look in the face (1) +448+5951
look with favor (1) +239
look with favor (1) +5564
looked (1)
looked (1) +8492
looks (1)
made face (1) +5989
make room for (1) +4946
man of rank (1) +5951
meet (1) +448
meet (1) +4946
meet with (1) +8011
more quickly than (1) +4200
more readily than (1) +4200
mouth (1)
my (1) +3276
my (1) +3276+4200
nearest (1) +6584
never (1) +4200+4202
obstinate (1) +7997
on both sides (1) +294+2256
open (1) +4200
open before (1) +5790
opening (1)
opposite (1) +448
ours (1) +4200+5646
out (1) +4946
out of (1) +4946
out of way (1) +4200+4946
outer (1)
over (1) +4200
overlooking (1) +4200
pacify (1) +4105
parallel (1) +928
partial (1) +5951
partiality (1) +5365
preceding (1) +4200
predecessor (1) +889+2118+4200
present (1)
present (1) +4200
present (1) +4200+5877
previous (1) +4200
prominent (1) +5951
protection from (1) +4946
put (1) +995+4200
puts up a bold front (1) +928+6451
receive (1) +5951
reflects a face (1) +2021+2021+4200+7156
regard (1) +2118+4200
regarded in the sight of (1) +4200
regards (1) +4200+5162
region (1)
reject (1) +4946+6584+8938
reject (1) +4946+6584+8959
renounce (1) +8740
resist (1)
resolved (1) +5989
respect (1) +5951
scalp (1)
see (1) +8011
seek an audience with (1) +1335
seek favor (1) +906+2704
seek favor (1) +2704
seen for myself (1) +8011
serve (1) +2118+4200
serve (1) +4200
served (1) +907+6641
served (1) +2118+4200
show (1) +4200
showed partiality (1) +5951
shown honor (1) +5951
shown partiality (1) +5951
some distance from (1) +4946
sought favor (1) +906+2704
sought favor (1) +2704
spared from (1) +4946
stared with a fixed gaze (1) +906+2256+6641+8492
stern-faced (1) +6434
sulking (1) +906+6015
table^{S} (1)
take for (1) +4200+5989
taken from (1) +4200+4946
that^{S} (1)
the LORD himself (1) +3378
their own (1) +2157
themselves (1) +2157
those^{S} (1) +2021
throughout (1) +3972+6584
tilting away from (1) +4946
to (1) +907
to (1) +4200+6584
to (1) +4946
toward (1)
toward (1) +448
toward (1) +2006+6584
turn away (1) +6015
turned (1) +5989
turned (1) +6015
turned (1) +8492
under (1) +907
under (1) +4946
under blessing (1) +4200
under direction (1) +4200
under supervision (1) +4200
unless (1) +561+3954+4200
unyielding (1) +2617
upside down (1) +6584
watched (1) +4200
way (1)
where^{S} (1) +4200
while still alive (1) +6584
with (1) +907
with (1) +6584
within sight of (1) +907
withstood (1) +928+6641
worship (1) +4200
you (1) +4013
you yourself (1) +3870
untranslated (121)

7157 פִּנָּה *pinnāh* (31)
corner (15)
corners (5)
cornerstone (3)
leaders (2)
capstone (1) +8031
corner defenses (1)
cornerstone (1) +74
cornerstones (1)
street corner (1)
strongholds (1)

7158 1פְּנוּאֵל *p^{e}nû'ēl1* (2)
Penuel (2)

7159 2פְּנוּאֵל *p^{e}nû'ēl2* (6)
Peniel (5)
they^{S} (1) +408

7160 1פְּנִיאֵל *p^{e}niy'ēl1* (1)
untranslated (1)

7161 2פְּנִיאֵל *p^{e}niy'ēl2* (1)
Peniel (1)

7162 פְּנִיִּים *p^{e}niyyyim*
Variant; not used

7163 פְּנִימָה *p^{e}niymāh* (13)
inside (2)
within (2)
in (1)
inner (1) +4200
inner sanctuary (1)
inside (1) +4200
inside (1) +4946
into (1) +448
into (1) +4200
inward (1)
untranslated (1)

7164 פְּנִימִי *p^{e}niymiy* (31)
inner (25)
inner sanctuary (2)
innermost (2)
far end (1)
inside (1)

7165 פְּנִינִים *p^{e}niyniym* (7)
rubies (6)
untranslated (1)

7166 פְּנִנָּה *p^{e}ninnāh* (3)
Peninnah (3)

7167 פָּנַק *pānaq* (1)
pampers (1)

7168 פַּס *pas* (5)
richly ornamented (3)
ornamented (2)

7169 פַּס דַּמִּים *pas dammiym* (1)
Pas Dammim (1)

7170 פָּסַג *pāsag* (1)
view (1)

7171 פִּסְגָּה *pisgāh* (8)
Pisgah (8)

7172 פִּסָּה *pissāh* (1)
abound (1) +2118

7173 1פָּסַח *pāsah1* (4)
pass over (3)
passed over (1)

7174 2פָּסַח *pāsah2* (3)
became crippled (1)
danced (1)
waver (1)

7175 פֶּסַח *pesah* (49)
Passover (36)
Passover lamb (4)
Passover lambs (3)
Passover offerings (3)
did so^{S} (1) +906+2021+6913
its^{S} (1) +2021
Passover animals (1)

7176 פָּסֵחַ *pāsēah* (4)
Paseah (4)

7177 פִּסֵּחַ *pissēah* (14)
lame (11)
crippled (3)

7178 פָּסִיל *pāsiyl* (23)
idols (16)
images (5)
carved idols (1)
carved images (1)

7179 פָּסַךְ *pāsak* (1)
Pasach (1)

7180 פָּסַל *pāsal* (6)
chisel out (2)
chiseled out (2)
carved (1)
cut (1)

7181 פֶּסֶל *pesel* (31)
idol (11)
idols (7)
carved image (5)
image (4)
carved (2)
carved images (1)
images (1)

7182 פָּסַס *pāsas* (1)
vanished (1)

7183 פִּסְפָּה *pispāh* (1)
Pispah (1)

7184 פָּעָה *pā'āh* (1)
cry out (1)

7185 פָּעוּ *pā'û* (2)
Pau (2)

7186 פְּעוֹר *p^e'ôr* (9)
Peor (9)

7187 פָּעִי *pā'iy*
Variant; not used

7188 פָּעַל *pā'al* (57)
evildoers (16) +224
do (12)
done (9)
does (2)
made (2)
act (1)
affect (1)
bestow (1)
bring (1)
devise (1)
did (1)
evildoer (1) +224
fashions (1)
forges (1)
maker (1)
makes ready (1)
plot (1)
practice (1)
wicked men (1) +224
works (1)
works out (1)

7189 פֹּעַל *pō'al* (37)
deeds (8)
work (7)
works (5)
what done (4)
conduct (2)
labor (2)
performed exploits (2)
acts (1)
did (1)
made (1)
something (1)
wages (1)
what did (1)
what[S] (1)

7190 פְּעֻלָּה *p^e'ullāh* (14)
wages (3)
deeds (2)
recompense (2)
reward (2)
work (2)
payment (1)
reward (1) +5989
works (1)

7191 פְּעֻלְּתַי *p^e'ull^etay* (1)
Peullethai (1)

7192 פָּעַם *pā'am* (5)
troubled (3)
stir (1)
troubles (1)

7193 פַּעַם *pa'am* (117)
times (44)
time (14)
feet (10)
twice (5)
now (3)
once (3) +285
once more (3)
as before (2) +928+3869+7193
encounter (2)
footsteps (2)
one more (2)
steps (2)
again (1) +928+1685+2021+2021+2085
annual (1) +928+2021+9102
anvil (1)
as done before (1) +928+3869+7193
at last (1) +2021
at other times (1) +928+7193
campaign (1)
clatter (1)
customary (1) +928+3869+7193
forms (1)
level (1)
moment (1)
now (1) +2021
once (1)
once more (1) +421+2021
other[S] (1)
sets (1)
supports (1) +4190
thrust (1)
twice over (1)
untranslated (1)

7194 פַּעֲמוֹן *pa'^amôn* (7)
bells (4)
alternate[S] (1) +2256+2298+8232
alternated[S] (1) +2256+8232
them[S] (1) +2021

7195 פַּעְנֵחַ *pa'nēaḥ*
Variant; not used

7196 פָּעַר *pā'ar* (4)
open (2)
drank in (1) +7023
opens (1)

7197 פַּעֲרַי *pa'^aray* (1)
Paarai (1)

7198 פָּצָה *pāṣāh* (15)
opened (3)
deliver (2)
open wide (2)
opens (2)
delivers (1)
given word (1) +906+7023
made a vow (1) +7023
open (1)
opened wide (1)
promised (1)

7199 1פָּצַח *pāṣaḥ1*
Variant; not used

7200 2פָּצַח *pāṣaḥ2* (9)
burst (6)
break (1)
break in pieces (1)
untranslated (1)

7201 פְּצִירָה *p^eṣiyrāh* (1)
sharpening (1)

7202 פָּצַל *pāṣal* (2)
peeled (1)
peeling (1)

7203 פְּצָלוֹת *p^eṣālôṯ* (1)
stripes (1)

7204 פָּצַם *pāṣam* (1)
torn open (1)

7205 פָּצַע *pāṣa'* (3)
been emasculated (1)
bruised (1)
wounded (1)

7206 פֶּצַע *peṣa'* (8)
wounds (4)
wound (2)
bruises (1)
wounding (1)

7207 פָּצַץ *pāṣaṣ* (3)
breaks in pieces (1)
crumbled (1)
crushed (1)

7208 פַּצֵּץ *paṣṣēṣ*
Variant; not used

7209 פִּצֵּץ *piṣṣēṣ*
Variant; not used

7210 פָּצַר *pāṣar* (7)
insisted (2)
arrogance (1)
kept bringing pressure (1) +4394
persisted (1)
persuaded (1)
urged (1)

7211 פִּק *piq* (1)
give way (1)

7212 פָּקַד *pāqaḏ* (301)
punish (45)
counted (23)
number (19)
numbered (13)
numbers (12)
appoint (11)
were counted (11)
appointed (9)
assigned (9)
count (8)
mustered (8)
care for (6)
missing (6)
put in charge (6)
appointed as governor (5)
punished (5)
come (3)
empty (3)
punishes (3)
surely come to aid (3) +7212
assign (2)
be punished (2)
deal (2)
enroll (2)
examine (2)
gracious (2)
mobilized (2)
officers (2)
punishing (2)
supervisors (2)
total (2)
were appointed (2)
accuse (1) +6584
assembled (1)
be called to arms (1)
be missed (1)
be missing (1)
be robbed (1)
bestow punishment (1)
bestowed care on (1)
bring (1)
bring punishment (1)
called to account (1)
came (1)
come to aid (1)
come to the aid of (1)
commit (1)
concerned about (1)
counted (1) +7212
destroy (1)
did[S] (1)

experience (1)
fails to come (1)
harm (1)
in charge (1)
in charge of (1)
lack (1)
listed (1)
longed for (1)
missed (1)
misses at all (1) +7212
missing (1) +7212
muster forces (1)
mustering (1)
numbering (1)
placed (1)
post (1)
posted (1)
prescribed (1)
punishments come (1)
put (1)
put away (1)
see (1)
send (1)
sets (1)
store (1)
summoned (1)
take care of (1)
take stock of (1)
total (1) +3972
untouched (1) +1153
visit (1)
was counted (1)
was entrusted (1) +7214
watch over (1)
watched over and seen (1) +7212
were counted in the census (1)
were found missing (1)
were recorded (1)
were registered (1)
untranslated (6)

7213 פְּקֻדָּה *p^{e}quddāh* (32)
punished (4)
punishment (3)
appointed (2)
appointed order (2)
guards (2)
judgment (2)
assignment (1)
charge (1)
enrollment (1)
governor (1)
having charge (1)
in charge (1)
mustered (1)
officials (1)
oversight (1)
place of leadership (1)
prison (1) +1074+2021
providence (1)
reckoning (1)
responsible (1)
stored up (1)
visits (1)
what usually happens (1)

7214 פִּקָּדוֹן *piqqāḏôn* (3)
held in reserve (1)
something entrusted (1)
was entrusted (1) +7212

7215 פְּקִדֻת *p^{e}qiḏuṯ* (1)
guard (1)

7216 פְּקוֹד *p^{e}qôḏ* (2)
Pekod (2)

7217 פְּקוּדִים *p^{e}qûḏiym* (1)
amounts (1)

7218 פִּקּוּדִים *piqqûḏiym* (24)
precepts (24)

7219 פָּקַח *pāqah* (20)
open (7)
opened (4)
be opened (2)
fix (1)
gives sight (1)
keep watchful (1)
opens (1)
stay awake (1) +6524
were opened (1)
untranslated (1)

7220 פֶּקַח *peqah* (11)
Pekah (10)
Pekah's (1)

7221 פִּקֵּחַ *piqqēah* (2)
see (1)
sight (1)

7222 פְּקַחְיָה *p^{e}qahyāh* (3)
Pekahiah (2)
Pekahiah's (1)

7223 פְּקַח־קוֹחַ *p^{e}qah-qôah* (1)
release from darkness (1)

7224 פָּקִיד *pāqiyḏ* (13)
chief officer (3)
in charge (3)
commissioners (2)
officer (2)
deputy (1)
direction (1)
supervisors (1)

7225 פְּקָעִים *p^{e}qā'iym* (3)
gourds (3)

7226 פַּקֻּעֹת *paqqu'ōṯ* (1)
gourds (1)

7227 פֶּקֶר *peqer*
Variant; not used

7228 פַּר *par* (132)
bull (47)
bulls (30)
bull (27) +1330
bull's (9)
bulls (5) +1330
young bulls (3)
it^s (2) +2021
its^s (2) +2021
bull calves (1)
its^s (1)
one^s (1)
oxen (1)
untranslated (3)

7229 פָּרָא *pārā'* (1)
thrives (1)

7230 פֶּרֶא *pere'* (9)
wild donkey (4)
wild donkeys (3)
donkeys (1)
wild donkey's (1)

7231 פִּרְאָם *pir'ām* (1)
Piram (1)

7232 פַּרְבָּר *parbār* (2)
court (2)

7233 פָּרַד *pāraḏ* (26)
separates (3)
spread out (3)
are scattered (1)
be parted (1)
be scattered (1)
be separated (1)
consort (1)
deserts (1)
divided (1)
keeps apart (1)
left (1)
out of joint (1)
part company (1)
parted (1)
parted company (1)
scattered (1)
separated (1)
separated (1) +1068
set apart by themselves (1)
unfriendly (1)
was separated (1)
were parted (1)

7234 פֶּרֶד *pereḏ* (14)
mules (10)
mule (4)

7235 פִּרְדָּה *pirdāh* (3)
mule (3)

7236 פַּרְדֵּס *pardēs* (3)
forest (1)
orchard (1)
parks (1)

7237 פְּרֻדֹת *p^{e}ruḏōṯ* (1)
seeds (1)

7238 1פָּרָה *pārāh1* (29)
fruitful (14)
make fruitful (5)
fruitful vine (2) +1201
made fruitful (2)
bear fruit (1)
flourish (1)
increased (1)
numbers increased greatly (1) +2256+8049
produces (1)
spring up (1)

7239 2פָּרָה *pārāh2* (26)
cows (18)
heifer (6)
cow (1)
those^s (1) +2021

7240 3פָּרָה *pārāh3* (1)
Parah (1)

7241 פֶּרֶה *pereh* (1)
wild donkey (1)

7242 פֻּרָה *purāh* (2)
Purah (2)

7243 פְּרוּדָא *p^{e}rûḏā'* (1)
Peruda (1)

7244 פְּרוֹזִים *p^{e}rôziym* (1)
untranslated (1)

7245 פָּרוּחַ *pārûah* (1)
Paruah (1)

7246 פַּרְוַיִם *parwayim* (1)
Parvaim (1)

7247 פַּרְוָר *parwār* (1)
court (1)

7248 פָּרוּר *pārûr* (3)
pot (3)

7249 פֵּרוֹת *pērôṯ*
Variant; not used

7250 פָּרָז *pārāz* (2)
warriors (1)
untranslated (1)

7251 פְּרָזוֹן *p^{e}rāzôn* (2)
village life (1)
warriors (1)

7252 פְּרָזוֹת *p^{e}rāzôṯ* (2)
city without walls (1)
villages (1) +6551

7253 פְּרָזִי *p^{e}rāziy* (4)
country (1)
rural (1)
unwalled (1)
unwalled villages (1)

7254 פְּרִזִּי *p^{e}rizziy* (23)
Perizzites (23)

7255 1פָּרַח *pāraḥ1* (34)
flourish (5)
blossom (4)
broken out (3)
budded (3)
bud (2)
spring up (2)
blossomed (1)
break out (1)
breaking out (1)
breaks out all over (1) +7255
bring to bud (1)
broke out (1)
burst into bloom (1) +7255
make flourish (1)
reappears (1) +2256+8740
spreading (1)
sprout (1)
sprouted (1)
thrive (1)

7256 2פָּרַח *pāraḥ2* (2)
birds (2)

7257 3פָּרַח *pāraḥ3*
Variant; not used

7258 פֶּרַח *peraḥ* (17)
blossoms (8)
blossom (3)
floral work (2)
budded (1) +3655
flowers (1)
untranslated (2)

7259 פִּרְחַח *pirḥaḥ* (1)
tribe (1)

7260 פָּרַט *pāraṭ* (1)
strum away (1)

7261 פֶּרֶט *pereṭ* (1)
grapes that have fallen (1)

7262 פְּרִי *pᵉriy* (120)
fruit (80)
crops (7)
produce (4)
young (4)
fruits (3)
deserve (2)
firstfruits (2) +8040
fruitful (2)
children (1) +1061
children (1) +1061+2021
crops (1) +141+2021
descendants (1)
descendants (1) +1061
earnings (1) +4090
fruitage (1)
fruitfulness (1)
infants (1) +1061
offspring (1)
result (1)
reward earned (1) +3338
rewarded (1)
what deserve (1)
willful pride (1) +1542
untranslated (1)

7263 פְּרִידָא *pᵉriydā'* (1)
Perida (1)

7264 1פָּרִיץ *pāriys1* (1)
ferocious (1)

7265 2פָּרִיץ *pāriys2* (5)
violent (3)
robbers (2)

7266 פֶּרֶךְ *perek* (6)
ruthlessly (5) +928
brutally (1) +928

7267 פָּרֹכֶת *pārōket* (25)
curtain (25)

7268 פָּרַם *pāram* (3)
tear (2)
torn (1)

7269 פַּרְמַשְׁתָּא *parmaštā'* (1)
Parmashta (1)

7270 פַּרְנָךְ *parnāk* (1)
Parnach (1)

7271 1פָּרַס *pāras1* (14)
split (11)
hoofs (1)
offer food (1)
share (1)

7272 פֶּרֶס *peres* (2)
vulture (2)

7273 2פָּרַס *pāras2* (28)
Persia (26)
Persian (2)

7274 פַּרְסָה *parsāh* (21)
hoof (12)
hoofs (6)
untranslated (3)

7275 פָּרְסִי *pārsiy* (1)
Persian (1)

7276 1פָּרַע *pāra'1* (1)
take the lead (1)

7277 2פָּרַע *pāra'2* (15)
unkempt (3)
ignores (2)
avoid (1)
cast off restraint (1)
get out of control (1)
hold back (1)
ignore (1)
ignored (1)
loosen (1)
promoted wickedness (1)
running wild (1)
taking away (1)

7278 1פֶּרַע *pera'1* (2)
leaders (1)
princes (1)

7279 2פֶּרַע *pera'2* (2)
hair (1) +8552
hair long (1)

7280 3פֶּרַע *pera'3*
Variant; not used

7281 פַּרְעֹה *par'ōh* (274)
Pharaoh (206)
Pharaoh's (51)
his[s] (5)
he[s] (4)
him[s] (2)
Pharaoh's (2) +4200
royal (1)
she[s] (1) +1426
there[s] (1) +1074
untranslated (1)

7282 1פַּרְעֹשׁ *par'ōš1* (2)
flea (2)

7283 2פַּרְעֹשׁ *par'ōš2* (6)
Parosh (6)

7284 פִּרְעָתוֹן *pir'āṯôn* (1)
Pirathon (1)

7285 פִּרְעָתוֹנִי *pir'āṯôniy* (5)
Pirathonite (3)
from Pirathon (1)
untranslated (1)

7286 פַּרְפַּר *parpar* (1)
Pharpar (1)

7287 פָּרַץ *pāras* (50)
broken out (4)
broke down (3)
broken down (3)
urged (3)
break down (2)
break out (2)
increased (2)
spread (2)
spread out (2)
again and again bursts (1) +7288+7288
are broken down (1)
break (1)
break all bounds (1)
breaking away (1)
breaks open (1)
breaks through (1)
brim over (1)
broke out (1)
broke out in anger (1)
broken (1)
broken into (1)
broken out (1) +7288
broken through (1)
burst forth (1)
cuts (1)
destroy (1)
dispersing (1)
far and wide (1)
gaps (1)
increase (1)
many (1)
prosperous (1)
tear down (1)
urging (1)
went out (1)
untranslated (1)

7288 1פֶּרֶץ *peres1* (19)
gap (3)
breach (2)
break out (2)
wrath (2)
again and again bursts (1) +7287+7288
breaching of walls (1)
breaks (1)
breaks in the wall (1)
broken (1)
broken out (1) +7287
broken places (1)
cracked (1) +5877
gap in the wall (1)

7289 2פֶּרֶץ *peres2* (15)
Perez (15)

7290 פֶּרֶץ עֻזָּא *peres 'uzzā'* (2)
Perez Uzzah (2)

7291 פַּרְצִי *parsiy* (1)
Perezite (1)

7292 פְּרָצִים *pᵉrāsiym* (1)
Perazim (1)

7293 פָּרַק *pāraq* (10)
take off (2)
free (1)
freed (1)
rip to pieces (1)
tearing off (1)
throw off (1)
took off (1)
tore apart (1)
was stripped (1)

7294 פֶּרֶק *pereq* (2)
crossroads (1)
plunder (1)

7295 פָּרָק *pārāq* (1)
untranslated (1)

7296 1פָּרַר *pārar1* (48)
break (8)
broken (6)
breaking (5)
broke (4)
foils (2)
frustrate (2)

nullifies (2) +7296
be broken (1)
be thwarted (1)
discredit (1)
fail (1)
frustrated (1)
frustrating (1)
no longer stirred (1)
nullified (1)
nullifies (1)
nullify (1)
put away (1)
revoking (1)
take (1)
thwart (1)
thwarts (1)
undermine (1)
violate (1)
was revoked (1)

7297 2פָּרַר *pārar2* (4)
is split asunder (1) +7297
shattered (1)
split open (1)

7298 פָּרַשׂ *pāraś* (68)
spread (21)
spread out (19)
spreading (4)
scattered (3)
spreading out (2)
throw (2)
be scattered (1)
cast (1)
chop up (1)
display (1)
exposes (1)
extended (1)
gives (1)
held out (1)
laid (1)
opens (1)
scatters (1)
spreads (1)
spreads out (1)
stretch out (1)
stretches out (1)
stretching out (1)
unrolled (1)

7299 פַּרְשֵׁז *parśēz* (1)
spreading (1)

7300 1פָּרַשׁ *pāraš1* (3)
clear (1)
made clear (1)
making clear (1)

7301 2פָּרַשׁ *pāraš2* (1)
poisons (1)

7302 1פֶּרֶשׁ *pereš1* (7)
offal (6)
untranslated (1)

7303 2פֶּרֶשׁ *pereš2* (1)
Peresh (1)

7304 1פָּרָשׁ *pārāš1* (18)
horses (14)
war horses (2)
riders (1) +1251
steeds (1)

7305 2פָּרָשׁ *pārāš2* (38)
horsemen (27)
charioteers (6)
cavalry (5)

7306 פַּרְשֶׁגֶן *paršegen* (1)
copy (1)

7307 פַּרְשְׁדֹן *parš^{e}ḏōn* (1)
back (1)

7308 פָּרָשָׁה *pārāšāh* (2)
exact amount (1)
full account (1)

7309 פַּרְשַׁנְדָּתָא *paršandāṯā'* (1)
Parshandatha (1)

7310 פְּרָת *p^{e}rāṯ* (19)
Euphrates (15)
Perath (4)

7311 פֹּרָת *pōrāṯ*
Variant; not used

7312 פַּרְתְּמִים *partmiym* (3)
most noble (1)
nobility (1)
princes (1)

7313 פָּשָׂה *pāśāh* (20)
spread (14)
spread (2) +7313
spreading (2) +7313

7314 פָּשַׂע *pāśa'* (1)
march (1)

7315 פֶּשַׂע *peśa'* (1)
step (1)

7316 פָּשַׂק *pāśaq* (2)
offering body (1) +906+8079
speaks rashly (1) +8557

7317 פַּשׁ *paš* (1)
wickedness (1)

7318 פָּשַׁח *pāšah* (1)
mangled (1)

7319 פַּשְׁחוּר *pašḥûr* (14)
Pashhur (13)
he^{S} (1)

7320 פָּשַׁט *pāšat* (43)
raided (7)
strip (7)
stripped (4)
take off (4)
skin (2)
stripped off (2)
took off (2)
advance (1)
go raiding (1)
made a dash (1)
raiding (1)
remove (1)
removed (1)
rob (1)
rushed (1)
rushed forward (1)
skinned (1)
strip off (1)
strip off clothes (1) +2256+6910
strip the dead (1)
swept down (1)
taken off (1)

7321 פָּשַׁע *pāša'* (41)
rebelled (13)
in rebellion (4)
rebels (3)
transgressors (3)
committed (2)
rebel (2)
rebellion (2)
revolted (2)
sin (2)
sinned (2)
do wrong (1)
in revolt (1)
offended (1)
rebellious (1)
sinners (1)
wrongs (1)

7322 פֶּשַׁע *peša'* (93)
sins (20)
offenses (14)
rebellion (13)
transgressions (11)
transgression (8)
sin (7)
offense (5)
rebellious (3)
crime (1)
disobeys (1)
guilt of rebellion (1)
guiltless (1) +1172
illegal possession (1)
penalty of sin (1)
rebels (1)
sinful (1)
sinfulness (1)
sinned (1)
wrong (1)
wrongs (1)

7323 פֵּשֶׁר *pēšer* (1)
explanation (1)

7324 פֵּשֶׁת *pēšeṯ* (16)
linen (12)
flax (4)

7325 פִּשְׁתָּה *pištāh* (4)
flax (2)
wick (2)

7326 פַּת *paṯ* (14)
piece (2)
something to eat (2) +4312
bread (1)
crumble (1) +7359
crust (1)
food (1)
food (1) +4312
it^{S} (1)
little (1)
pebbles (1)
pieces (1)
some (1)

7327 פֹּת *pōṯ* (2)
scalps (1)
sockets (1)

7328 פִּתְאֹם *piṯ'ōm* (25)
suddenly (13)
sudden (4)
in an instant (2)
all at once (1)
at once (1)
by surprise (1)
so quickly (1) +928
suddenly (1) +928+7353
unexpectedly (1)

7329 פַּת־בַּג *paṯ-baḡ* (6)
food (4)
choice food (1)
provisions (1)

7330 פִּתְגָם *piṯgām* (2)
edict (1)
sentence (1)

7331 1פָּתָה *pāṯāh1* (27)
entice (5)
deceive (2)
enticed (2)
enticing (2)
allure (1)
be deceived (1)
be persuaded (1)
been enticed (1)
coax (1)
deceived (1)
easily deceived (1)
enticed (1) +4222
entices (1)
flatter (1)
is enticed (1)
lure (1)
seduces (1)
simple (1)

talks too much (1) +8557
was deceived (1)

7332 2פָּתָה *pāṯāh2* (1)
extend the territory (1)

7333 פְּתוּאֵל *p^{e}ṯû'ēl* (1)
Pethuel (1)

7334 פִּתּוּחַ *pitûah* (11)
engraved (2)
art of engraving (1) +7338
carved paneling (1)
engrave (1) +7338
engraved (1) +7338
engraves (1)
experienced in engraving (1) +7338
inscription (1)
inscription (1) +4844
untranslated (1)

7335 פְּתוֹר *p^{e}ṯôr* (2)
Pethor (2)

7336 פְּתוֹת *p^{e}ṯôṯ* (1)
scraps (1)

7337 1פָּתַח *pāṯah1* (136)
open (44)
opened (33)
be opened (4)
loose (2)
openhanded (2) +906+3338+7337
speak up (2) +7023
takes off (2)
were opened (2)
are opened (1)
be poured out (1)
be released (1)
be set free (1)
bottled-up (1) +4202
break open (1)
breaking up (1)
draw (1)
drawn (1)
expose (1)
expound (1)
free yourself (1)
freed (1)
freeing (1)
give command (1) +7023
go (1)
loosened (1)
make flow (1)
market (1)
open wide (1)
opened up (1)
opens (1)
reach (1)
release (1)
removed (1)
say (1) +7023
set free (1)
speaks (1) +7023
strip (1)
take off (1)
throw open (1)
thrown open (1)
uncovers (1)
unloaded (1)
unlocked (1)
unsealed (1)
unstopped (1)
unstrung (1)
untied (1)
was opened (1)
wide open (1) +7337
untranslated (2)

7338 2פָּתַח *pāṯah2* (9)
engrave (3)
art of engraving (1) +7334
carved (1)
engrave (1) +7334
engraved (1)
engraved (1) +7334
experienced in engraving (1) +7334

7339 פֶּתַח *peṯah* (163)
entrance (110)
door (15)
doorway (9)
doors (5)
entrances (3)
doorways (2)
gate (2)
gates (2)
it[s] (2) +2021
doorway (1) +4647
doorways (1) +4647
entrance (1) +9133
entrances (1) +4427
gateways (1) +9133
mouth (1)
one[s] (1)
outside (1)
outside (1) +2025
parapet opening (1)
words (1) +7023
untranslated (2)

7340 פֵּתַח *pēṯah* (1)
unfolding (1)

7341 פִּתָּחוֹן *pitāhôn* (2)
open (1)
open (1) +5989

7342 פְּתַחְיָה *p^{e}ṯahyāh* (4)
Pethahiah (4)

7343 1פֶּתִי *petiy1* (16)
simple (15)
simplehearted (1)

7344 2פֶּתִי *petiy2* (3)
simple ways (2)
ignorance (1)

7345 פְּתִיגִיל *p^{e}ṯiygiyl* (1)
fine clothing (1)

7346 פְּתַיּוּת *p^{e}ṯayyûṯ* (1)
undisciplined (1)

7347 פְּתִיחָה *p^{e}ṯiyhāh* (2)
drawn sword (1)
drawn swords (1)

7348 פָּתִיל *pāṯiyl* (11)
cord (8)
fastened (1)
piece of string (1) +5861
strands (1)

7349 פָּתַל *pāṯal* (5)
show yourself shrewd (2)
crooked (1)
had a struggle (1) +5887
wily (1)

7350 פְּתַלְתֹּל *p^{e}ṯaltōl* (1)
crooked (1)

7351 פִּתֹם *pitōm* (1)
Pithom (1)

7352 פֶּתֶן *peṯen* (6)
cobra (3)
serpents (2)
cobras (1)

7353 פֶּתַע *peṯa'* (7)
suddenly (3)
instant (2)
suddenly (1) +928
suddenly (1) +928+7328

7354 פָּתַר *pāṯar* (9)
interpret (4)
interpreted (2)
given interpretation (1)
giving interpretation (1)
said in interpretation (1)

7355 פִּתְרוֹן *pitārôn* (5)
meaning (2)
means (2)
interpretations (1)

7356 פַּתְרוֹס *paṯrôs* (5)
Upper Egypt (2)
Upper Egypt (2) +824
Upper [Egypt] (1)

7357 פַּתְרֻסִים *paṯrusiym* (2)
Pathrusites (2)

7358 פַּתְשֶׁגֶן *paṯšegen* (3)
copy (3)

7359 פָּתַת *pāṯaṯ* (1)
crumble (1) +7326

7360 צ *s*
Variant; not used

7361 צֵא *sē'*
Variant; not used

7362 צֵאָה *sē'āh* (2)
excrement (1)
excrement (1) +1645

7363 צֹאָה *sō'āh* (5)
filth (3)
untranslated (2)

7364 צֹאִי *sō'iy* (2)
filthy (2)

7365 צֶאֱלִים *se'^{e}liym* (2)
lotus plants (1)
lotuses (1)

7366 צֹאן *sō'n* (275)
sheep (97)
flocks (69)
flock (66)
sheep and goats (11)
animals (6)
shepherds (3) +8286
lambs (2) +1201
they[s] (2) +2021
animal from flock (1)
breeding (1) +2021+3501
choice lambs (1) +4119+4946
ewes (1)
flocks (1) +5238
goats (1)
pens (1) +1556
rest[s] (1)
sheep (1) +3897
sheep and goats (1) +5238
sheep goats or (1)
sheep or goats (1)
them[s] (1) +2257
they[s] (1) +3276
which[s] (1) +2021
which[s] (1) +2257
untranslated (3)

7367 צַאֲנָן *sa'^{a}nān* (1)
Zaanan (1)

7368 צֶאֱצָאִים *se'^{e}sā'iym* (11)
offspring (4)
descendants (3)
all that comes out (1)
children (1) +5055
crops (1)
that comes out (1)

7369 1צָב *sāḇ1* (2)
covered (1)
wagons (1)

7370 2צָב *sāḇ2* (1)
great lizard (1)

7371 1צָבָא *sāḇā'1* (14)
conscripting (2)
fight (2)
fought (2)

attack (1)
do battle (1)
fighting (1)
serve (1) +7372
served (1)
served (1) +7371
take part (1) +7372

7372 2צָבָא *sāḇā'2* (487)
Almighty (285)
army (59)
divisions (21)
division (20)
battle (12)
host (8)
hosts (8)
armies (6)
war (6)
forces (5)
in command (4) +6584
serve (4)
starry host (4)
stars (4)
hard service (3)
chief officer (2) +2021+8569
experienced soldiers (2) +3655
heavenly hosts (2)
ready for military service (2) +3655
ready to go out (2) +3655
troops (2)
armed forces (1) +2657
army (1) +2657
array (1)
battle (1) +4878
commander in chief (1) +2021+6584
commanders (1) +8569
company (1)
men ready for battle (1) +1522+4878
multitudes (1)
powers (1)
ready for battle (1) +408+2021+4200+4878
ready for battle (1) +928+2021+4878
regular service (1) +6275
serve (1) +6913
serve (1) +7371
soldier (1) +408
soldiers (1)
soldiers (1) +408
soldiers (1) +6639
starry hosts (1)
take part (1) +7371
vast array (1)
weapon (1) +3998+4878
untranslated (3)

7373 3צְבָא *sāḇā'3* (1)
gazelles (1)

7374 צְבָאָה *sᵉḇā'āh* (2)
gazelles (2)

7375 צְבֹאִים *sᵉḇō'iym* (5)
Zeboiim (5)

7376 צֹבֵבָה *sōḇēḇāh*
Variant; not used

7377 צָבָה *sāḇāh* (2)
swell (1)
swells (1)

7378 צֹבֶה *sōḇeh*
Variant; not used

7379 צָבֶה *sāḇeh* (1)
swell (1)

7380 צָבוּעַ *sāḇûa'* (1)
speckled (1)

7381 צָבַט *sāḇaṭ* (1)
offered (1)

7382 1צְבִי *sᵉḇiy1* (18)
beautiful (6)
glory (4)
beauty (2)
most beautiful (2)
beautiful jewelry (1) +6344
jewel (1)
most beautiful (1) +7382

7383 2צְבִי *sᵉḇiy2* (11)
gazelle (10)
gazelles (1)

7384 צִבְיָא *siḇyā'* (1)
Zibia (1)

7385 צִבְיָה *siḇyāh* (2)
Zibiah (2)

7386 צְבִיָּה *sᵉḇiyyāh* (2)
gazelle (2)

7387 צְבֹיִים *sᵉḇōyiym* (3)
untranslated (3)

7388 צָבַע *sāḇa'*
Variant; not used

7389 צֶבַע *seḇa'* (3)
colorful garments (2)
garments (1)

7390 צִבְעוֹן *siḇ'ôn* (8)
Zibeon (8)

7391 צְבֹעִים *sᵉḇō'iym* (2)
Zeboim (2)

7392 צָבַר *sāḇar* (7)
build (1)
heaped up (1)
heaps up (1)
heaps up wealth (1)
piled (1)
store up (1)
stored up (1)

7393 צִבֻּר *sibbur* (1)
piles (1)

7394 צִבָּרוֹן *sibbārôn*
Variant; not used

7395 צֶבֶת *sebeṯ* (1)
bundles (1)

7396 1צַד *sad1* (34)
side (14)
sides (5)
arm (2)
beside (2) +4946
opposite sides (2) +7521
backs (1)
flank (1)
near (1) +4946
next to (1) +4946
other^s (1)
vicinity (1)
with (1) +4946
untranslated (2)

7397 2צַד *sad2*
Variant; not used

7398 צְדָד *sāḏāḏ* (2)
Zedad (2)

7399 1צָדָה *sāḏāh1* (2)
do intentionally (1)
hunting down (1)

7400 2צָדָה *sāḏāh2* (1)
are destroyed (1)

7401 צָדוֹק *sāḏôq* (53)
Zadok (51)
them^s (1) +59+2256
Zadokites (1) +1201

7402 צְדִיָּה *sᵉḏiyyāh* (2)
intentionally (1) +928
unintentionally (1) +928+4202

7403 צִדִּים *siddiym* (1)
Ziddim (1)

7404 צַדִּיק *saddiyq* (206)
righteous (178)
innocent (13)
just (3)
right (2)
righteous one (2)
upright (2)
honest (1)
in the right (1)
overrighteous (1) +2221
righteous (1) +2446
righteousness (1)
untranslated (1)

7405 צָדַק *sāḏaq* (40)
righteous (11)
innocent (3)
acquit (2)
acquitting (2)
declare not guilty (2)
justify (2)
vindicated (2)
admit in the right (1)
appear righteous (1)
be reconsecrated (1)
cleared (1)
innocence (1)
justifying (1)
lead to righteousness (1)
made appear righteous (1)
made seem righteous (1)
maintain rights (1)
prove innocence (1)
prove right (1)
proved right (1)
right (1)
see that gets justice (1)
vindicates (1)

7406 צֶדֶק *seḏeq* (118)
righteousness (58)
righteous (16)
honest (8)
right (7)
justice (5)
accurate (3)
fairly (3)
just (3)
righteously (2)
truth (2)
cleared (1)
fairly (1) +928
integrity (1)
justly (1)
rightful (1)
rights (1)
true (1)
unrighteousness (1) +4202
vindication (1)
untranslated (2)

7407 צְדָקָה *sᵉḏāqāh* (159)
righteousness (98)
right (20)
righteous (9)
righteous acts (7)
righteous things (4)
innocence (2)
justice (2)
prosperity (2)
vindication (2)
claim (1)
honesty (1)
integrity (1)
just (1)
righteous act (1)
righteous deeds (1)
righteous state (1)
righteous will (1)
righteously (1)
salvation (1)
vindicated (1) +3655
untranslated (2)

7408 צִדְקִיָּה *sidqiyyāh* (7)
Zedekiah (7)

7409 צִדְקִיָּהוּ *sidqiyyāhû* (57)
Zedekiah (53)
Zedekiah's (2)
his[s] (1)
Zedekiah's (1) +4200

7410 צָהַב *sāhab* (1)
polished (1)

7411 צָהֹב *sāhōb* (3)
yellow (3)

7412 1צָהַל *sāhal1* (9)
acclaim (1)
cry out (1) +7754
held a celebration (1)
neigh (1)
neighing (1)
shout (1)
shout aloud (1)
shout for joy (1)
untranslated (1)

7413 2צָהַל *sāhal2* (1)
make shine (1)

7414 צָהַר *sāhar* (1)
crush olives (1)

7415 צֹהַר *sōhar* (1)
roof (1)

7416 צָהֳרַיִם *soh^orayim* (23)
noon (11)
midday (7)
noonday (3)
high noon (1)
noonday sun (1)

7417 צַו *saw* (1)
idols (1)

7418 צַוָּאר *sawwā'r* (42)
neck (25)
necks (7)
threw arms around (2) +5877+6584
at heels (1) +6584
defiantly (1) +928
embraced (1) +6584
head (1)
shoulders (1)
yourselves (1) +4013
untranslated (2)

7419 צוֹבָא *sôbā'* (2)
Zobah (2)

7420 צוֹבָה *sôbāh* (10)
Zobah (10)

7421 צוּד *sûd* (17)
ensnare (4)
hunt (3)
hunts (2)
hunt down (1)
hunt down (1) +4200+4511
hunted (1)
hunted (1) +7421
preys upon (1)
stalk (1)
stalked (1)

7422 צָוָה *sāwāh* (504)
commanded (210)
command (45)
gave (25)
ordered (22)
commands (13)
giving (13)
gave orders (10)
give (10)
instructed (9)
appointed (8)
do (8)
told (8)
gave order (7)
directed (6)
gave command (5)
order (5)
tell (5)
been commanded (4)
give command (4)
given (4)
orders (4)
charged (3)
commission (3)
decreed (3)
gave instructions (3)
give orders (3)
instructions (3)
laid down (3)
put in order (3)
was commanded (3)
commanded (2) +5184
forbidden (2) +4202
given order (2)
given orders (2)
giving orders (2)
ordained (2)
send (2)
appoint (1)
are directed (1)
bestows (1)
commander (1)
commanding (1)
commissioned (1)
decree (1)
decrees (1)
determined (1)
direct (1)
directs (1)
dispatch (1)
forbidden (1)
forbidden (1) +1194
gave a charge (1)
gave an order (1)
gave commands (1)
gave the order (1)
give a message (1)
give commands (1)
give the order (1)
given a command (1)
given an order (1)
given the command (1)
giving instructions (1)
issue an order (1)
left instructions (1)
marshaled (1)
prescribed (1)
put in charge (1)
puts in command (1)
say (1)
sent (1)
sent word (1)
summon (1)
urge (1)
untranslated (2)

7423 צָוַח *sāwah* (1)
shout (1)

7424 צְוָחָה *s^ewāhāh* (4)
cries (1)
cry (1)
cry of distress (1)
cry out (1)

7425 צוּלָה *sûlāh* (1)
watery deep (1)

7426 צוּם *sûm* (21)
fasted (12)
fast (5)
fasted (1) +7426
fasted (1) +7427
fasting (1)

7427 צוֹם *sôm* (26)
fasting (10)
fast (9)
day of fasting (1)
fasted (1) +7426
fasts (1)
time of fasting (1)
untranslated (3)

7428 צוּעָר *sû'ār* (5)
Zuar (5)

7429 1צוּף *sûp1* (3)
closed (1)
made float (1)
overwhelmed (1)

7430 2צוּף *sûp2* (2)
comb (1)
honeycomb (1) +1831

7431 3צוּף *sûp3* (3)
Zuph (3)

7432 צוֹפַח *sôpah* (2)
Zophah (2)

7433 צוֹפַי *sôpay* (1)
Zophai (1)

7434 צוּפִי *sûpiy* (1)
Zuphite (1)

7435 צוֹפִים *sôpiym*
Variant; not used

7436 צוֹפַר *sôpar* (4)
Zophar (4)

7437 1צוּץ *sûs1* (8)
flourish (2)
blossomed (1) +7488
bud (1)
budded (1)
flourishes (1)
resplendent (1)
springs up (1)

7438 2צוּץ *sûs2* (1)
peering (1)

7439 צוּק *sûq* (11)
inflict (3)
besiege (2)
oppressor (2)
compels (1)
imposed (1)
nagging (1)
press (1)

7440 2צוּק *sûq2* (1)
barely whisper a prayer (1) +4318

7441 צוֹק *sôq* (1)
trouble (1)

7442 צוּקָה *sûqāh* (3)
distress (1)
fearful (1)
trouble (1)

7443 1צוּר *sûr1* (35)
besieging (7)
besieged (6)
laid siege (5)
besiege (3)
lay siege (3)
besieges (1)
encircle (1) +6584
enclose (1)
hem in (1)
put into bags (1)
siege (1)
stirring up (1)
take (1)
tied up (1)
tuck away (1)
under siege (1)

7444 2צוּר *sûr2* (4)
harass (2)
attack (1)

oppose (1)

7445 3צוּר *ṣûr3* (2)
cast (1)
fashioning (1)

7446 4צוּר *ṣûr4* (74)
rock (60)
rocks (8)
rocky (3)
crag (1)
crags (1)
strength (1)

7447 5צוּר *ṣûr5*
Variant; not used

7448 6צוּר *ṣûr6* (5)
Zur (5)

7449 7צוּר *ṣûr7*
Variant; not used

7450 צוֹר *ṣôr* (42)
Tyre (42)

7451 צוּרָה *ṣûrāh* (6)
design (3)
forms (1)
untranslated (2)

7452 צוּרִיאֵל *ṣûriy'ēl* (1)
Zuriel (1)

7453 צוּרִישַׁדָּי *ṣûriyšadday* (5)
Zurishaddai (5)

7454 צַוְּרֹנִים *ṣaww[e]rōniym* (1)
necklace (1)

7455 צוּת *ṣûṯ* (1)
set on fire (1)

7456 צַח *ṣaḥ* (4)
clear (1)
radiant (1)
scorching (1)
shimmering (1)

7457 צִחֶה *ṣiḥeh* (1)
parched (1)

7458 צָחַח *ṣāḥaḥ* (1)
whiter (1)

7459 צְחִחִי *ṣ[e]ḥiḥiy* (1)
untranslated (1)

7460 צָחִיחַ *ṣāḥiyaḥ* (5)
bare (4)
exposed places (1)

7461 צְחִיחָה *ṣ[e]ḥiyḥāh* (1)
sun-scorched land (1)

7462 צַחֲנָה *ṣaḥ[a]nāh* (1)
smell (1)

7463 צַחְצָחוֹת *ṣaḥṣāḥôṯ* (1)
sun-scorched land (1)

7464 צָחַק *ṣāḥaq* (13)
laugh (4)
laughed (2)
make sport (2)
caressing (1)
indulge in revelry (1)
joking (1)
mocking (1)
performed (1)

7465 צְחֹק *ṣ[e]ḥōq* (2)
laughter (1)
scorn (1)

7466 צַחַר *ṣāḥar* (1)
Zahar (1)

7467 צָחֹר *ṣāḥōr* (1)
white (1)

7468 צֹחַר *ṣōḥar* (5)
Zohar (5)

7469 1צִי *ṣiy1* (4)
ships (3)
ship (1)

7470 2צִי *ṣiy2* (6)
desert creatures (4)
creatures of the desert (1)
desert tribes (1)

7471 צִיבָא *ṣiyḇā'* (16)
Ziba (15)
Ziba's (1)

7472 צִיד *ṣiyḏ* (1)
packed (1)

7473 1צַיִד *ṣayiḏ1* (14)
game (7)
hunter (2)
wild game (2)
animal (1) +2651
hunter (1) +408
hunting (1)

7474 2צַיִד *ṣayiḏ2* (5)
food (2)
provisions (2)
food supply (1)

7475 צַיָּד *ṣayyāḏ* (1)
hunters (1)

7476 צֵידָה *ṣēyḏāh* (10)
provisions (6)
food (2)
supplies (1)
untranslated (1)

7477 צִידוֹן *ṣiyḏôn* (20)
Sidon (20)

7478 צִידוֹן רַבָּה *ṣiyḏôn rabbāh* (2)
Greater Sidon (2)

7479 צִידֹנִי *ṣiyḏōniy* (16)
Sidonians (15)
people of Sidon (1)

7480 צִיָּה *ṣiyyāh* (16)
dry (5)
parched (4)
desert (2)
drought (2)
parched land (2)
dry land (1)

7481 צָיוֹן *ṣāyôn* (2)
desert (2)

7482 צִיּוֹן *ṣiyyôn* (154)
Zion (152)
Zion's (2)

7483 צִיּוּן *ṣiyyûn* (3)
marker (1)
road signs (1)
tombstone (1)

7484 צִיחָא *ṣiyḥā'* (3)
Ziha (3)

7485 צִינֹק *ṣiynōq* (1)
neck-irons (1)

7486 צִיעֹר *ṣiy'ōr* (1)
Zior (1)

7487 צִיף *ṣiyp̱* (1)
untranslated (1)

7488 1צִיץ *ṣiyṣ1* (14)
flowers (7)
flower (3)
plate (3)
blossomed (1) +7437

7489 2צִיץ *ṣiyṣ2* (1)
Ziz (1)

7490 3צִיץ *ṣiyṣ3* (1)
salt (1)

7491 צִיצָה *ṣiyṣāh* (1)
flower (1)

7492 צִיצִת *ṣiyṣiṯ* (4)
tassels (2)
hair (1)
tassel (1)

7493 1צִיר *ṣiyr1* (1)
delegation (1)

7494 2צִיר *ṣiyr2* (1)
hinges (1)

7495 3צִיר *ṣiyr3* (6)
envoy (3)
ambassadors (1)
envoys (1)
messenger (1)

7496 4צִיר *ṣiyr4* (5)
anguish (1)
labor pains (1)
pain (1)
pangs (1)
those[s] (1)

7497 5צִיר *ṣiyr5* (2)
idols (1)
untranslated (1)

7498 צֵל *ṣēl* (53)
shadow (27)
shade (16)
shadows (4)
protection (2)
shelter (2)
evening shadows (1)
it[s] (1) +2021

7499 צָלָה *ṣālāh* (3)
roast (1)
roasted (1)
roasts (1)

7500 צִלָּה *ṣillāh* (3)
Zillah (3)

7501 צְלוּל *ṣ[e]lûl* (1)
round loaf (1)

7502 1צָלַח *ṣālaḥ1* (10)
came in power (6)
came forcefully (1)
come in power (1)
rushed (1)
sweep through (1)

7503 2צָלַח *ṣālaḥ2* (55)
prosper (7)
succeed (7)
prospered (5)
victorious (4)
gave success (3)
successful (3)
give success (2)
grant success (2)
have success (2)
thrive (2)
useless (2) +4202
achieve purpose (1)
avail (1)
granted success (1)
helped (1)
made successful (1)
make success (1)
prevail (1)
prosperous (1)
prospers (1)
rose (1)
succeeded (1)
succeeded in carrying out (1)
unsuccessful (1) +4202
useful (1)
victoriously (1)
win (1)

7504 צְלֹחִית *ṣ[e]lōḥiyṯ* (1)
bowl (1)

7505 צַלַּחַת *sallahaṯ* (4)
dish (3)
pans (1)

7506 צְלַחַת *sēlahaṯ*
Variant; not used

7507 צָלִי *sāliy* (3)
meat (1)
roast (1)
roasted (1)

7508 צְלִיל *s^{e}liyl* (1)
untranslated (1)

7509 1צָלַל *sālal1* (4)
tingle (2)
make tingle (1)
quivered (1)

7510 2צָלַל *sālal2* (1)
sank (1)

7511 3צָלַל *ṣālal3* (2)
evening shadows fell (1)
overshadowing (1)

7512 1צֶלֶם *selem1* (15)
idols (6)
image (5)
models (2)
figures (1)
untranslated (1)

7513 2צֶלֶם *selem2* (2)
fantasies (1)
phantom (1)

7514 1צַלְמוֹן *salmôn1* (1)
Zalmon (1)

7515 2צַלְמוֹן *salmôn2* (2)
Zalmon (2)

7516 צַלְמָוֶת *salmāweṯ* (18)
deep shadow (4)
shadow of death (3)
darkness (2)
deep darkness (2)
deep shadows (2)
deepest gloom (2)
blackest (1)
blackness (1)
thick darkness (1)

7517 צַלְמֹנָה *salmōnāh* (2)
Zalmonah (2)

7518 צַלְמֻנָּע *salmunnā'* (12)
Zalmunna (10)
them[S] (2) +2256+2286

7519 צָלַע *sāla'* (4)
lame (3)
limping (1)

7520 צֶלַע *sela'* (4)
fall (1)
falls (1)
slip (1)
stumbled (1)

7521 1צֵלָע *sēlā'1* (41)
side (10)
side rooms (9)
sides (4)
boards (2)
opposite sides (2) +7396
another[S] (1)
beams (1)
floor (1)
hillside (1) +2215
leaves (1)
one[S] (1)
planks (1)
rib (1)
ribs (1)
side room (1)
untranslated (4)

7522 2צֵלָע *sēlā'2* (12)
Zela (1)
Zelah (1)

7523 צָלָף *sālāp̱* (1)
Zalaph (1)

7524 צְלָפְחָד *s^{e}lāp̱^{e}hāḏ* (11)
Zelophehad (5)
Zelophehad's (4)
who[S] (1)
whose[S] (1) +1426

7525 צֶלְצַח *selsah* (1)
Zelzah (1)

7526 צְלָצַל *s^{e}lāsal* (1)
swarms of locusts (1)

7527 1צִלְצָל *ṣilṣāl1* (1)
whirring (1)

7528 2צִלְצָל *silsāl2* (1)
spears (1)

7529 צֶלְצְלִים *selseliym* (3)
cymbals (3)

7530 צֶלֶק *seleq* (2)
Zelek (2)

7531 צִלְּתַי *sill^{e}ṯay* (2)
Zillethai (2)

7532 1צָמֵא *sāmē'1* (11)
thirsty (6)
thirst (2)
thirsts (2)
suffer thirst (1)

7533 צָמָא *sāmā'* (17)
thirst (15)
parched ground (1)
thirsty (1)

7534 2צָמֵא *sāmē'2* (9)
thirsty (8)
dry (1)

7535 צִמְאָה *sim'āh* (1)
dry (1)

7536 צִמָּאוֹן *simmā'ôn* (3)
thirsty ground (2)
thirsty (1)

7537 צָמַד *sāmaḏ* (5)
joined in worshiping (2)
harness (1)
strapped (1)
yoked themselves (1)

7538 צֶמֶד *semeḏ* (15)
yoke (3)
pair (2)
two (2)
acre (1) +5103
oxen (1)
string (1)
team (1)
teams (1)
ten-acre (1) +6930
together (1)
yoke of oxen (1)

7539 צַמָּה *sammāh* (4)
veil (4)

7540 צִמּוּקִים *simmûqiym* (4)
cakes of raisins (3)
raisin cakes (1)

7541 צָמַח *sāmah* (33)
grow (3)
grown (3)
sprouted (3)
make grow (2)
make sprout (2)
makes grow (2)
appear (1)
branch out (1)
bring to fruition (1)
causes to grow (1)
flourish (1)
flourishing (1)
grew (1)
growing (1)
made grow (1)
make spring up (1)
produce (1)
spring into being (1)
spring up (1)
springs forth (1)
springs up (1)
sprout (1)
sprouting (1)
sprung up (1)

7542 צֶמַח *semah* (12)
branch (5)
crops (1)
grew (1)
growth (1)
head (1)
plant (1)
sprout (1)
vegetation (1)

7543 1צָמִיד *sāmiyḏ1* (6)
bracelets (5)
bracelets (1) +3338+6584

7544 2צָמִיד *sāmiyḏ2* (1)
lid (1)

7545 צַמִּים *sammiym* (1)
snare (1)

7546 צָמַק *sāmaq* (1)
dry (1)

7547 צֶמֶר *semer* (16)
wool (13)
woolen (2)
woolen garment (1)

7548 צְמָרִי *s^{e}māriy* (2)
Zemarites (2)

7549 צְמָרַיִם *s^{e}mārayim* (2)
Zemaraim (2)

7550 צַמֶּרֶת *sammereṯ* (5)
top (3)
shoot (1)
tops (1)

7551 צָמַת *sāmaṯ* (15)
destroy (4)
destroyed (3)
put to silence (2)
cease to flow (1)
end (1)
seek to destroy (1)
silence (1)
silenced (1)
wears out (1)

7552 צְמִתֻת *s^{e}miṯuṯ* (2)
permanently (1) +2021+4200
permanently (1) +4200

7553 צֵן *sēn* (3)
thorns (2)
hooks (1)

7554 צִן *sin* (10)
Zin (10)

7555 צֹנֶא *sōnā'*
Variant; not used

7556 צֹנֶה *sōneh* (1)
flocks (1)

7557 1צִנָּה *sinnāh1* (1)
coolness (1)

7558 2צִנָּה *sinnāh2* (20)
shield (9)
large[S] [shields] (4)

large shields (3)
shields (3)
buckler (1)

7559 3צִנָּה *sinnāh3*
Variant; not used

7560 צָנוּעַ *sānûa'* (1)
humility (1)

7561 צָנוּף *sānûp̱*
Variant; not used

7562 צִנּוֹר *ṣinnôr* (2)
water shaft (1)
waterfalls (1)

7563 צָנַח *sānah* (3)
got off (2) +4946+6584
untranslated (1)

7564 צְנִינִים *sᵉniyniym* (2)
thorns (2)

7565 צָנִיף *sāniyp̱* (5)
turban (3)
diadem (1)
untranslated (1)

7566 צְנִיפָה *sᵉniyp̱āh* (1)
tiaras (1)

7567 צָנַם *sānam*
Variant; not used

7568 צָנֻם *sānum* (1)
withered (1)

7569 צְנָן *sᵉnān* (1)
Zenan (1)

7570 צָנַע *sāna'* (1)
humbly (1)

7571 צָנַף *sānap̱* (3)
put on (1)
roll up tightly (1) +7571+7572

7572 צְנֵפָה *sᵉnēp̱āh* (1)
roll up tightly (1) +7571+7571

7573 צִנְצֶנֶת *sinseneṯ* (1)
jar (1)

7574 צַנְתָּרוֹת *santārôṯ* (1)
pipes (1)

7575 צָעַד *sā'ad̠* (8)
marched (2)
climb (1)
marched off (1)
strode through (1)
taken steps (1) +7576
walk (1)
walking along (1)

7576 צַעַד *sa'ad̠* (14)
step (5)
steps (5)
path (2)
stride (1)
taken steps (1) +7575

7577 1צְעָדָה *sᵉ'ād̠āh1* (2)
marching (2)

7578 2צְעָדָה *sᵉ'ād̠āh2* (1)
ankle chains (1)

7579 צָעָה *sā'āh* (5)
cowering prisoners (1)
lay down (1)
pour (1)
pour out (1)
striding forward (1)

7580 צָעוֹר *sā'ôr* (2)
untranslated (2)

7581 צָעִיף *sā'iyp̱* (3)
veil (3)

7582 1צָעִיר *sā'iyr1* (23)
younger (7)
young (3)
youngest (3)
least (2)
little (2)
small (2)
lowly (1)
servants (1)
smallest (1)
younger (1) +3427+4200

7583 2צָעִיר *sā'iyr2* (1)
Zair (1)

7584 צְעִירָה *sᵉ'iyrāh* (1)
ages (1) +1148

7585 צָעַן *sā'an* (1)
moved (1)

7586 צֹעַן *sō'an* (7)
Zoan (7)

7587 צְעַנִּים *sᵉ'anniym* (1)
untranslated (1)

7588 צַעֲנַנִּים *sa'ᵃnanniym* (2)
Zaanannim (2)

7589 צַעֲצֻעִים *sa'ᵃsu'iym* (1)
sculptured (1) +5126

7590 צָעַק *sā'aq* (55)
cried out (16)
cry out (9)
cried for help (3)
cries out (3)
beg (2)
called out (2)
cried (2)
crying out (2)
were called out (2)
appealed (1)
burst out (1)
cried out for help (1) +7754
cry (1)
cry aloud (1)
cry out (1) +7590
scream for help (1)
screamed (1)
shout (1)
summoned (1)
was called up (1)
were called to arms (1)
were summoned (1)

7591 צְעָקָה *sᵉ'āqāh* (21)
cry (9)
outcry (3)
cries (2)
cry (2) +7754
wailing (2)
cries of distress (1)
crying out (1)
outcry (1) +7754

7592 צָעַר *sā'ar* (3)
brought low (1)
disdained (1)
little ones (1)

7593 צֹעַר *sō'ar* (10)
Zoar (10)

7594 צָפַד *sāp̱ad̠* (1)
shriveled (1)

7595 1צָפָה *sāp̱āh1* (38)
watchman (11)
lookout (4)
watchmen (4)
watch (3)
he^{s} (1) +2021
keep watch (1)
keeping watch (1)
lie in wait (1)
look (1)
looking (1)
lookouts (1)
marked (1)
standing watch (1)
wait in expectation (1)
watch in hope (1)
watched (1)
watches over (1)
watching (1)
untranslated (2)

7596 2צָפָה *sāp̱āh2* (47)
overlaid (27)
overlay (11)
covered (4)
adorned (1) +4200+9514
coating (1)
paneling (1) +6770
spread (1)
untranslated (1)

7597 3צָפָה *sāp̱āh3* (1)
flowing (1)

7598 צְפוֹ *sᵉp̱ô* (3)
Zepho (3)

7599 צִפּוּי *sippûy* (5)
overlaid (3)
overlay (2)

7600 1צָפוֹן *sāp̱ôn1* (151)
north (97)
north (26) +2025
northern (9) +2025
north (7) +4946
northern (4)
northern (3) +4946
north wind (1)
northern (1) +2025+4946
northward (1) +2006+2021
sacred mountain (1)
untranslated (1)

7601 2צָפוֹן *sāp̱ôn2* (3)
Zaphon (3)

7602 צְפוֹן *sᵉp̱ôn* (2)
Zephon (2)

7603 1צְפוֹנִי *sᵉp̱ôniy1* (1)
northern (1)

7604 2צְפוֹנִי *sᵉp̱ôniy2* (1)
Zephonite (1)

7605 צָפוּעַ *sāp̱ûa'* (1)
untranslated (1)

7606 1צִפּוֹר *sippôr1* (40)
bird (18)
birds (12)
bird's (2)
sparrow (2)
bird (1) +4053
birds (1) +4053
carrion birds (1) +6514
it^{s} (1) +2021+2021+2645
poultry (1)
untranslated (1)

7607 2צִפּוֹר *sippôr2* (7)
Zippor (7)

7608 צַפַּחַת *sappahaṯ* (7)
jug (6)
jar (1)

7609 צְפִי *sᵉp̱iy*
Variant; not used

7610 צְפִיָּה *sippiyyāh* (1)
towers (1)

7611 צִפְיוֹן *sip̱yôn*
Variant; not used

7612 צִפְיוֹנִי *sip̱yôniy*
Variant; not used

7613 צַפִּיחִת *sappiyhiṯ* (1)
wafers (1)

7614 צֹפִים *sōpiym* (1)
Zophim (1)

7615 צָפִין *sāpiyn* (1)
untranslated (1)

7616 צָפִיעַ *sāpiya'* (1)
manure (1)

7617 צְפִיעָה *s^epiy'āh* (1)
offshoots (1)

7618 צָפִיר *sāpiyr* (6)
goat (2) +6436
goat (1)
male goats (1)
male goats (1) +6436
untranslated (1)

7619 צְפִירָה *s^epiyrāh* (3)
doom (2)
crown (1)

7620 צָפִית *sāpiyt* (1)
rugs (1)

7621 צָפַן *sāpan* (34)
store up (3)
stored up (3)
cherish (2)
hidden (2)
hide (2)
keep safe (2)
restraining (2)
waylay (2)
closed (1)
concealed (1)
hid (1)
holds in store (1)
is concealed (1)
is stored up (1)
kept on record (1)
lurk (1)
secret (1)
set (1)
stores up (1)
treasured (1)
treasured place (1)
treasures (1)
untranslated (2)

7622 צְפַנְיָה *s^epanyāh* (8)
Zephaniah (8)

7623 צְפַנְיָהוּ *s^epanyāhû* (2)
Zephaniah (2)

7624 צָפְנַת פַּעְנֵחַ *sāp^enat pa'nēah* (1)
Zaphenath-Paneah (1)

7625 צֶפַע *sepa'* (1)
viper (1)

7626 צִפְעֹנִי *sip'ōniy* (4)
vipers (2)
viper (1)
viper's (1)

7627 צָפַף *sāpap* (4)
whisper (2)
chirp (1)
cried (1)

7628 צַפְצָפָה *sapsāpāh* (1)
willow (1)

7629 צָפַר *sāpar* (1)
leave (1)

7630 צְפַרְדֵּעַ *s^epardēa'* (13)
frogs (13)

7631 צִפֹּרָה *sippōrāh* (3)
Zipporah (3)

7632 צִפֹּרֶן *sippōren* (2)
nails (1)
point (1)

7633 צֶפֶת *sepet* (1)
capital (1)

7634 צְפַת *s^epat* (1)
Zephath (1)

7635 צְפָתָה *s^epatāh* (1)
Zephathah (1)

7636 צָקוּן *sāqûn*
Variant; not used

7637 צִקְלַג *siqlag* (15)
Ziklag (14)
it[s] (1)

7638 צִקְלוֹן *siqqālôn* (1)
untranslated (1)

7639 צַר 1 *sar1* (47)
distress (20)
trouble (11)
narrow (3)
small (3)
distressed (2)
adversity (1)
anguish (1)
anguished (1)
critical (1)
grieve (1)
misery (1)
pent-up (1)
tightly (1)

7640 צַר 2 *sar2* (68)
enemies (28)
foes (19)
enemy (11)
foe (3)
adversaries (2)
adversary (2)
hostile (1)
opponent (1)
oppressor (1)

7641 צַר 3 *sar3* (1)
flint (1)

7642 צַר 4 *sar4*
Variant; not used

7643 צֵר *sēr* (1)
Zer (1)

7644 צֹר 1 *sōr1* (5)
flint (3)
edge (1)
flint knife (1)

7645 צֹר 2 *sōr2*
Variant; not used

7646 צָרַב *sārab* (1)
be scorched (1)

7647 צָרָב *sārāb* (1)
scorching (1)

7648 צָרֶבֶת *sārebet* (2)
scar (2)

7649 צְרֵדָה *s^erēdāh* (1)
Zeredah (1)

7650 צָרָה 1 *sārāh1* (70)
trouble (24)
distress (22)
troubles (8)
anguish (4)
calamity (2)
difficulties (2)
adversity (1)
calamities (1)
distressed (1)
distresses (1)
groan (1)
hardship (1)
hostility (1)
oppressed (1)

7651 צָרָה 2 *sārāh2* (1)
rival (1)

7652 צִרָה *sirāh*
Variant; not used

7653 צְרוּיָה *s^erûyāh* (26)
Zeruiah (25)
Zeruiah's (1)

7654 צְרוּעָה *s^erû'āh* (1)
Zeruah (1)

7655 צְרוֹר 1 *s^erôr1* (7)
purse (2)
bag (1)
bundle (1)
pouch (1)
pouches (1)
sachet (1)

7656 צְרוֹר 2 *s^erôr2* (2)
pebble (1)
piece (1)

7657 צְרוֹר 3 *s^erôr3* (1)
Zeror (1)

7658 צָרַח *sārah* (2)
raise the battle cry (1)
shouting (1)

7659 צֶרַח *serah*
Variant; not used

7660 צֹרִי *sōriy* (5)
from Tyre (1)
men from Tyre (1)
of Tyre (1)
Tyre (1)
Tyrians (1)

7661 צֳרִי *s^oriy* (6)
balm (6)

7662 צְרִי *s^eriy* (1)
Zeri (1)

7663 צְרִיחַ *s^eriyah* (4)
stronghold (2)
it[s] (1) +2021
pits (1)

7664 צֹרֶךְ *sōrek* (1)
need (1)

7665 צָרַע *sāra'* (20)
had leprosy (6)
leprosy (4)
leprous (4)
diseased (2)
disease (1)
has an infectious skin disease (1)
infectious skin disease (1)
person[s] (1)

7666 צָרְעָה *sor'āh* (10)
Zorah (10)

7667 צִרְעָה *sir'āh* (3)
hornet (3)

7668 צָרְעִי *sor'iy* (1)
Zorites (1)

7669 צָרַעַת *sāra'at* (35)
skin disease (10)
infectious disease (7)
mildew (6)
leprosy (5)
disease (2)
infectious skin diseases and mildew (1)
it[s] (1)
leprous (1)
spreading mildew (1)
spreading mildew (1) +5596

7670 צָרְעָתִי *sor'ātiy* (2)
Zorathites (2)

7671 צָרַף *sārap* (34)
goldsmith (6)
refined (5)
flawless (3)

goldsmiths (2)
refine (2)
silversmith (2)
been tested (1)
examine (1)
fashions (1)
proved true (1)
refiner (1)
refiner's (1)
refining goes on (1) +7671
sift (1)
test (1)
thoroughly purge away (1) +1342+2021+3869
untranslated (3)

7672 צֹרְפִי *ṣōrpiy* (1)
goldsmiths (1)

7673 צָרְפַת *ṣārᵉpat* (3)
Zarephath (3)

7674 1צָרַר *ṣārar1* (30)
distress (3)
bring distress (2)
in distress (2)
in labor (2)
besiege (1)
bind up (1)
bound securely (1)
distressed (1)
frustrated (1)
gave trouble (1)
hampered (1)
kept in confinement (1)
lay siege (1)
mended (1)
oppress (1)
oppressed (1)
small (1)
stored up (1)
sweep away (1) +928+4053
trouble (1)
tying (1)
weakened (1)
wrapped (1)
wrapped up (1)
wraps up (1)

7675 2צָרַר *ṣārar2* (26)
enemies (7)
enemy (4)
foes (4)
oppressed (2)
adversaries (1)
foe (1)
give trouble (1)
hostile (1)
oppose (1)
oppressing (1)
rival wife (1)
treat as enemies (1)
treated as enemies (1)

7676 3צָרַר *ṣārar3*
Variant; not used

7677 4צָרַר *ṣārar4*
Variant; not used

7678 צְרֵרָה *ṣᵉrērāh* (1)
Zererah (1)

7679 צֶרֶת *ṣereṯ* (1)
Zereth (1)

7680 צֶרֶת הַשַּׁחַר *ṣereṯ haššaḥar* (1)
Zereth Shahar (1)

7681 צָרְתָן *ṣārᵉtān* (4)
Zarethan (4)

7682 ק *q*
Variant; not used

7683 קֵא *qē'* (1)
vomit (1)

7684 קָאַת *qā'aṯ* (5)
desert owl (4)
owl (1)

7685 קַב *qaḇ* (1)
cab (1)

7686 קָבַב *qāḇaḇ* (14)
curse (8)
cursed (2)
put a curse on (2)
curse at all (1) +7686

7687 קֵבָה *qēḇāh* (2)
body (1)
inner parts (1)

7688 קֻבָּה *qubbāh* (1)
tent (1)

7689 קִבּוּץ *qibbûṣ* (1)
collection (1)

7690 קְבוּרָה *qᵉḇûrāh* (14)
tomb (5)
grave (4)
burial (2)
buried (1)
have burial (1) +7699
proper burial (1)

7691 קָבַל *qāḇal* (14)
accept (3)
took (3)
opposite (2)
received (2)
agreed (1)
take choice (1)
untranslated (2)

7692 קְבֹל *qᵉḇōl* (2)
battering rams (1)
in front of (1)

7693 קָבַע *qāḇa'* (6)
rob (3)
plunder (1)
plunder (1) +5883
robbing (1)

7694 קֻבַּעַת *qubba'aṯ* (2)
goblet (2) +3926

7695 קָבַץ *qāḇaṣ* (127)
gather (38)
gathered (15)
assembled (12)
assemble (10)
gathers (5)
called together (4)
brought together (3)
gather together (3)
bring (2)
came together (2)
collect (2)
come together (2)
were assembled (2)
amasses (1)
assemble (1) +3481
assemble yourselves (1)
be gathered (1)
be reunited (1) +3481
bring back (1)
bring together (1)
came together (1) +3481
collected (1)
come and join (1)
gather in (1)
gathered together (1)
grows pale (1) +6999
join (1)
joined forces (1)
mobilized (1)
mustered (1)
picked up (1)
rallied (1)
shepherd (1)
stored up (1)
surely bring together (1) +7695
takes captive (1)
turns pale (1) +6999
were brought (1)
were gathered (1)

7696 קַבְצְאֵל *qaḇṣᵉ'ēl* (3)
Kabzeel (3)

7697 קְבֻצָה *qᵉḇuṣāh* (1)
gather (1)

7698 קִבְצַיִם *qiḇṣayim* (1)
Kibzaim (1)

7699 קָבַר *qāḇar* (133)
buried (54)
was buried (31)
bury (30)
burying (7)
be buried (4)
be sure to bury (1) +7699
gravediggers (1)
have burial (1) +7690
is buried (1)
untranslated (2)

7700 קֶבֶר *qeḇer* (68)
grave (18)
tomb (16)
graves (10)
tombs (9)
burial (5)
be buried (2) +448+665
buried (2)
them^S (2) +4013
burial place (1)
burial site (1)
buried (1) +448+995
them^S (1) +2021

7701 קִבְרוֹת הַתַּאֲוָה *qiḇrôṯ hata'ᵃwāh* (5)
Kibroth Hattaavah (5)

7702 קָדַד *qāḏaḏ* (15)
bowed down (7)
bowed low (5)
bowed (2)
bowed heads (1)

7703 קִדָּה *qiddāh* (2)
cassia (2)

7704 קְדוּמִים *qᵉḏûmiym* (1)
age-old (1)

7705 קָדוֹשׁ *qāḏôš* (116)
holy (62)
holy one (43)
consecrated (4)
sacred (4)
saints (2)
untranslated (1)

7706 קָדַח *qāḏaḥ* (5)
kindle (1)
kindled (1)
kindled (1) +836
light (1)
sets ablaze (1)

7707 קַדַּחַת *qaddaḥaṯ* (2)
fever (2)

7708 קָדִים *qāḏiym* (67)
east (38)
east (13) +2025
east wind (7)
eastward (2)
desert wind (1)
east winds (1)
eastern (1) +2025
eastward (1) +2025
extend eastward (1) +2025
hot east wind (1)
untranslated (1)

7709 קָדַם *qāḏam* (26)
come before (4)
confronted (4)
come to meet (2)
confront (2)
bring (1)
come (1)
comes before (1)
go (1)
go before (1)
has a claim against (1)
in front (1)
meet (1)
met (1)
quick (1)
receive (1)
rise (1)
stay open (1)
welcomed (1)

7710 קֶדֶם *qeḏem* (61)
east (17)
of old (8)
eastern (7)
long ago (5)
ancient (3)
east (3) +4946
before (2)
gone by (2)
long ago (2) +4946
ancient times (1)
before began (1)
days of old (1)
east (1) +6584+7156
eastward (1) +4946
eternal (1)
everlasting (1)
forever (1)
former (1) +4946
long ago (1) +3427+4946
old (1) +3427+4946
past (1)

7711 קֵדֶם *qēḏem* (26)
east (10)
east (7) +2025
eastern (3) +2025
eastward (1) +2025
eastward (1) +2025+2025+4667
southeast (1) +2025+2025+5582
southeast (1) +2025+5582
untranslated (2)

7712 קַדְמָה *qaḏmāh* (6)
before (3)
old (1)
past (1)
untranslated (1)

7713 קִדְמָה *qiḏmāh* (4)
east (4)

7714 1קֵדְמָה *qēḏmāh1*
Variant; not used

7715 2קֵדְמָה *qēḏmāh2* (2)
Kedemah (2)

7716 קַדְמוֹן *qaḏmôn* (1)
eastern (1)

7717 קְדֵמוֹת *qᵉḏēmôṯ* (4)
Kedemoth (4)

7718 קַדְמִיאֵל *qaḏmiyʾēl* (8)
Kadmiel (8)

7719 1קַדְמֹנִי *qaḏmōniy1* (10)
eastern (3)
east (2)
former (2)
old (1)
past (1)
untranslated (1)

7720 2קַדְמֹנִי *qaḏmōniy2* (1)
Kadmonites (1)

7721 קָדְקֹד *qoḏqōḏ* (12)
top of head (3)
brow (2)
head (2)
skulls (2)
crown of head (1)
crowns (1)
heads (1)

7722 קָדַר *qāḏar* (17)
darkened (3)
mourning (3)
darken (2)
mourn (2)
black (1)
blackened (1)
clothed with gloom (1)
dark (1)
go dark (1)
grief (1)
wail (1)

7723 קֵדָר *qēḏār* (12)
Kedar (10)
Kedar (1) +1201
Kedar's (1)

7724 קִדְרוֹן *qiḏrôn* (11)
Kidron (10)
there[S] (1) +928+5707

7725 קַדְרוּת *qaḏrûṯ* (1)
darkness (1)

7726 קְדֹרַנִּית *qᵉḏōranniyṯ* (1)
mourners (1)

7727 קָדַשׁ *qāḏaš* (171)
consecrate (30)
consecrated (22)
dedicated (10)
consecrate yourselves (9)
consecrated themselves (7)
dedicates (7)
holy (7)
keep holy (7)
makes holy (7)
show myself holy (7)
set apart (6)
prepare (5)
consecration (3)
made holy (3)
been consecrated (2)
declare holy (2)
dedicate (2)
honor as holy (2)
keeping holy (2)
make holy (2)
regard as holy (2)
sacred (2)
set aside (2)
acknowledge holiness (1)
be acknowledged as holy (1)
be consecrated (1)
call in honor of (1) +4200
celebrate holy (1)
consecrate themselves (1)
consecrating (1)
consecrating themselves (1)
consecrating themselves (1) +7731
defiled (1)
done[S] (1)
have purified (1)
holiness (1)
purified herself (1)
send (1)
set apart as holy (1)
show himself holy (1)
show holiness (1)
showed himself holy (1)
solemnly consecrate (1) +7727
uphold holiness (1)
untranslated (1)

7728 1קָדֵשׁ *qāḏēš1* (11)
shrine prostitutes (5)
shrine prostitute (4)
prostitutes of the shrines (1)
untranslated (1)

7729 2קָדֵשׁ *qāḏēš2* (14)
Kadesh (14)

7730 קֶדֶשׁ *qeḏeš* (12)
Kedesh (11)
where[S] (1) +2025

7731 קֹדֶשׁ *qōḏeš* (433)
holy (136)
sanctuary (72)
sacred (65)
most holy (23) +7731
holy place (14)
most holy place (11) +7731
holy things (10)
holiness (9)
most holy place (8)
sacred offerings (8)
consecrated (7)
holy offerings (5)
most holy offerings (5) +7731
most holy things (3) +7731
sacred offering (3)
dedicated (2)
dedicated things (2)
holy furnishings (2)
sacred gifts (2)
sacred objects (2)
something holy (2)
things dedicated (2)
another[S] (1) +5246
consecrated gifts (1) +7731
consecrated things (1)
consecrating themselves (1) +7727
dedicate (1)
dedicated gifts (1)
gifts dedicated (1)
holy one (1)
holy ones (1)
holy precincts (1)
it[S] (1)
most holy place (1) +1808
most holy place (1) +5219
most sacred (1) +7731
most sacred food (1) +7731
offering (1)
offerings (1)
priests' rooms (1) +4384
sacred portion (1)
sacred things (1)
sanctuary (1) +5226
sanctuary area (1)
set apart (1)
temple (1)
things[S] (1)
what holy (1)
untranslated (7)

7732 קָדֵשׁ בַּרְנֵעַ *qāḏēš barnēaʿ* (10)
Kadesh Barnea (10)

7733 קָהָה *qāhāh* (4)
set on edge (3)
dull (1)

7734 קְהָיוֹן *qēhāyôn*
Variant; not used

7735 קָהַל *qāhal* (39)
gathered (9)
assembled (8)
assemble (5)
came together (3)
gather (2)
gathered together (2)
mustered (2)
summoned (2)
called together (1)
came as a group (1)
convenes a court (1)

crowded (1)
gather together (1)
summoned to assemble (1)

7736 קָהָל *qāhāl* (123)
assembly (72)
community (13)
company (5)
horde (4)
crowd (3)
mob (3)
throng (3)
army (2)
gathered (2)
hordes (2)
alliance (1)
army (1) +2256+6639
assemble (1) +928+2021+6590
assembled (1) +995
congregation (1)
everyone else (1) +3972
people (1)
them[s] (1) +3776+3972
them[s] (1) +2021
them[s] (1) +3776+3972
they[s] (1) +2021
whole assembly (1) +2256+6337
untranslated (2)

7737 קְהִלָּה *qᵉhillāh* (2)
assembly (1)
meeting (1)

7738 קֹהֶלֶת *qōheleṯ* (7)
teacher (7)

7739 קְהֵלָתָה *qᵉhēlāṯāh* (2)
Kehelathah (2)

7740 קְהָת *qᵉhāṯ* (32)
Kohath (18)
Kohathite (7) +1201
Kohathites (4) +1201
Kohath's (2)
untranslated (1)

7741 קְהָתִי *qᵉhāṯiy* (15)
Kohathite (7)
Kohathites (3)
Kohathites (3) +1201
Kohath (1)
Kohathite (1) +1201

7742 1קָו *qāw1* (20)
rule (8)
measuring line (7)
line (4)
measure (1)

7743 2קָו *qāw2* (3)
strange speech (2) +7743

7744 3קָו *qāw3*
Variant; not used

7745 קְוֵא *qᵉwēʾ* (2)
Kue (2)

7746 קוֹבַע *qôḇaʿ* (2)
helmet (1)
helmets (1)

7747 1קָוָה *qāwāh1* (47)
hope in (7)
wait (7)
look (5)
looked for (4)
hope (3)
hoped (2)
trusted (2)
wait for (2)
eager (1)
expect (1)
hope for (1)
hoped for (1)
in hope (1)
long for (1)
look for (1)
look in hope (1)
put trust (1)
waited for (1)
waited patiently for (1) +7747
waiting (1)
waiting eagerly (1)
waits (1)

7748 2קָוָה *qāwāh2* (2)
be gathered (1)
gather (1)

7749 קָוֶה *qāweh* (3)
untranslated (3)

7750 קְוֵה *qᵉwēh* (2)
Kue (2)

7751 קוֹחַ *qôah*
Variant; not used

7752 קוּט *qûṭ* (7)
loathe (4)
abhor (1)
angry (1)
loathing (1)

7753 קוֹט *qôṭ*
Variant; not used

7754 קוֹל *qôl* (506)
voice (101)
sound (62)
obey (36) +928+9048
obeyed (18) +928+9048
voices (17)
to (15) +928
listen (12)
thunder (12)
noise (11)
to (9) +4200
cry (8)
cry for mercy (6) +9384
sounds (6)
aloud (5) +906+5951
proclamation (5)
roar (5)
aloud (4) +5951
thunders (4) +5989
blast (3)
called out (3) +928+1524+7924
cries (3)
plea (3)
word (3)
aloud (2)
aloud (2) +1524
crackling (2)
cry (2) +7591
crying (2)
disobeyed (2) +928+4202+9048
fully obey (2) +928+9048+9048
hear (2)
heard (2)
heard (2) +9048
lowing (2)
response (2)
shout (2)
shouts of joy (2) +8262
sound (2) +6702
sounding (2)
speech (2)
thunder (2) +5989
thunderstorm (2) +2613
what say (2)
what says (2)
words (2)
acclamation (1)
agreed with (1) +4200+9048
aloud (1) +928
aloud (1) +928+1524
argue (1) +9048
began (1) +906+5951
blast (1) +8795
bleating (1)
calling (1) +7924
calls (1)
clamor (1)
clatter (1) +8323
command (1)
cooing (1)
crack (1)
cried out (1)
cried out for help (1) +7590
cry aloud (1) +5989
cry for help (1) +2410
cry for help (1) +8776
cry out (1) +2411
cry out (1) +7412
diligently obey (1) +928+9048+9048
disobedience (1) +928+4202+9048
disobey (1) +928+1194+9048
gave in (1) +928+9048
give a hearing (1) +263
growl (1)
growl (1) +5989
growled (1) +5989
hears (1) +9048
hears (1) +9048+9048
hiss (1)
it[s] (1) +3276
listen (1) +9048
listen carefully (1) +928+9048
loud (1)
loudly (1) +928+1524
loudly (1) +5951
music (1)
neighing (1) +5177
news (1)
noise (1) +2159
noisy din (1) +1524
obey (1) +4200+9048
obey fully (1) +928+9048+9048
obeying (1) +928+9048
obeys (1) +928+9048
outcry (1) +7591
rebuke (1)
resound (1)
roared (1) +5989
roaring (1) +8614
roars (1) +928+5989
say (1)
scream for help (1) +2256+7924+8123
screamed (1) +928+1524+7924
screamed for help (1) +2256+7924+8123
shout (1) +928+7924
shout (1) +1524+7924
shout (1) +8123
shouted (1) +928+7924
shouted (1) +928+8123+9558
shouted (1) +2256+5951+7924
shouting (1) +9558
shouts (1)
sing (1) +5989
sing songs (1) +928+4200+8123+9048
song (1)
sound (1) +8123
speaking (1) +1821
taunts (1)
thunders (1) +928+5989
tumult (1) +2167
tune (1)
uproar (1) +2162
uproar (1) +9558
very (1)
war cry (1)
weeping (1)
wept so loudly (1) +906+928+1140+5989
what have to say (1)
what said (1)
what said (1) +1821
what saying (1)
what[s] (1)
what[s] (1) +1821
whisper (1) +1960
untranslated (23)

7755 קוֹלָיָה *qôlāyāh* (2)
Kolaiah (2)

7756 קוּם *qûm* (630)
got up (50)
rise (28)
rise up (28)
get up (24)
arise (22)
set up (17)
rose (16)
stand (16)
establish (13)
raise up (11)
set out (11)
fulfill (10)
come (9)
go (9)
raised up (9)
at once (8)
established (8)
stood up (8)
restore (7)
rose up (7)
stand up (7)
foes (5)
stood (5)
arose (4)
confirm (4)
erected (4)
keep (4)
prepared (4)
adversaries (3)
attacking (3) +6584
carried out (3)
confirms (3)
endure (3)
enemies (3)
fulfilled (3)
help up (3)
kept (3)
left (3) +4946
now (3)
proceeded (3)
rises (3)
rises up (3)
set (3)
standing (3)
up (3)
begin (2)
build (2)
came (2)
confirmed (2)
decreed (2)
deeded (2)
fully accomplishes (2) +2256+6913
get ready (2)
gets up (2)
got ready (2)
grows up (2)
hurry (2)
maintain (2)
place (2)
raise (2)
raises (2)
raising up (2)
rise to power (2)
risen up (2)
rouse (2)
stands (2)
start (2)
stepped forward (2)
succeeded (2) +9393
supported (2)
survive (2)
went (2)
accomplish (1)
accuses (1) +2021+4200+5477
all right do it[s] (1)
appear (1)
appears (1)
appointed (1)
arise and come (1)
assaults (1) +6584
attack (1)
attack (1) +448
attacked (1) +448
attacked (1) +6584
attacks (1)
attacks (1) +6584
be (1)
become (1)
been kept (1)
began (1)
belong (1)
binding (1)
break out (1)
brighter (1)
bring (1)
came out (1)
came to power (1)
carries out (1)
carry on (1)
carry on (1) +6584
carry out (1)
changed (1) +7756
come forward (1)
come on (1)
come out (1)
confirming (1)
confronted (1) +6584
confronts (1)
convict (1)
crept up (1)
do[s] (1)
done (1)
erect (1)
establish the custom (1)
exalted (1)
failed (1) +4202+6388
final (1)
follow (1) +339
follow (1) +339+4946
followed (1) +339
gave (1)
get away (1)
get it to its feet (1) +7756
go up (1)
gone (1)
grew up (1)
grown (1)
has effect (1)
have (1)
heaped up (1)
hold (1)
hurried (1)
in turn (1)
incited (1)
keep (1) +7756
leave (1) +4946
left (1)
left (1) +4946+9348
lift up (1)
made (1)
make good (1)
makes rise (1)
moved (1)
moved out (1)
obeyed (1) +3869
opposed (1)
opposite (1)
piled up (1)
prevails (1)
produce (1)
provide (1)
raised (1)
rebelled (1)
remain (1)
remains (1)
revolted (1)
risen (1)
send (1)
set to work (1)
setting up (1)
sit up (1)
soon (1)
started (1)
station (1)
stilled (1)
stir up (1)
stood ground (1)
strengthen (1)
succeed (1)
surely stand (1) +7756
surged forward (1)
take place (1)
takes the stand (1) +928
turned (1)
undertakes (1)
uphold (1)
was set up (1)
went out (1)
went to work (1)
withdrew (1)
withstand (1)
untranslated (64)

7757 קוֹמָה *qômāh* (46)
high (28)
height (2)
on high (2) +928
tallest (2)
deep (1)
diameter (1)
height (1) +1469
higher (1)
length (1)
lengths (1)
lofty trees (1) +8123
low (1) +9166
on high (1)
stature (1)
untranslated (2)

7758 קוֹמְמִיּוּת *qôm*e*miyyûṯ* (1)
with heads held high (1)

7759 קוֹנֵן *qônēn*
Variant; not used

7760 קוֹעַ *qôa'* (1)
Koa (1)

7761 קוֹף *qôp̱* (2)
apes (2)

7762 קוּץ1 *qûs1* (8)
dread (2)
abhorred (1)
detest (1)
disgusted (1)
filled with dread (1)
hostile (1)
resent (1)

7763 קוּץ2 *qûs2* (1)
tear apart (1)

7764 קוֹץ1 *qôs1* (12)
thorns (10)
thornbushes (2)

7765 קוֹץ2 *qôs2*
Variant; not used

7766 קוֹץ3 *qôs3* (1)
Koz (1)

7767 קְוֻצּוֹת *q*e*wussôṯ* (2)
hair (2)

7768 קַוְקָו *qawqāw*
Variant; not used

7769 קוּר1 *qûr1* (2)
dug wells (2)

7770 קוּר2 *qûr2* (2)
cobwebs (1)
web (1)

7771 קוֹרָה *qôrāh* (5)
beams (1)
ceiling beams (1)
pole (1)
roof (1)
tree (1)

7772 קוּשׁ *qûš* (1)
ensnare (1)

7773 קוּשָׁיָהוּ *qûšāyāhû* (1)
Kushaiah (1)

7774 קָה *qāh*
Variant; not used

7775 קָט *qāṭ* (1)
soon (1) +3869+5071

7776 קֶטֶב *qeteḇ* (4)
plague (2)
destruction (1)
destructive (1)

7777 קְטוֹרָה *qᵉṭôrāh* (1)
incense (1)

7778 קְטוּרָה *qᵉṭûrāh* (4)
Keturah (4)

7779 קָטַל *qāṭal* (3)
slay (2)
kills (1)

7780 קֶטֶל *qeṭel* (1)
slaughter (1)

7781 1קָטֹן *qāṭōn1* (4)
not enough (1)
not enough (1) +6388
skimping (1)
unworthy (1)

7782 קֹטֶן *qōṭen* (2)
little finger (2)

7783 1קָטָן *qāṭān1* (47)
small (12)
least (9)
younger (8)
young (5)
youngest (4)
little (2)
boy (1) +5853
lesser (1)
light (1)
low (1)
smaller (1)
smallest (1)
youths (1) +5853

7784 2קָטָן *qāṭān2*
Variant; not used

7785 2קָטֹן *qāṭōn2* (54)
small (14)
youngest (14)
least (7)
young (7)
little (3)
younger (3)
simple (2)
at all (1) +196+1524
brief (1)
lesser (1)
nothing (1) +1524+1821+2256+4202

7786 קָטַף *qāṭap̱* (5)
break off (1)
broke off (1)
gathered (1)
pick (1)
uncut (1) +4202

7787 1קָטַר *qāṭar1* (115)
burn (35)
burn incense (18)
burned incense (14)
burned (12)
burning incense (11)
burned sacrifices (4)
burn sacrifices (3)
make offerings (2)
be burned (1)
burn offerings (1)
burned up (1) +7787
burning (1)
burns incense (1)
make offering (1)
offer (1)
offer sacrifices (1)
offered up (1)
perfumed (1)
present (1)
presented offerings (1)
presenting (1)
untranslated (2)

7788 2קָטַר *qāṭar2* (1)
enclosed (1)

7789 קִטֵּר *qiṭṭēr* (1)
incense (1)

7790 קִטְרוֹן *qiṭrôn* (1)
Kitron (1)

7791 קְטֻרוֹת *qᵉṭurôṯ*
Variant; not used

7792 קְטֹרֶת *qᵉṭōreṯ* (60)
incense (59)
offering (1)

7793 קַטָּת *qaṭṭāṯ* (1)
Kattath (1)

7794 1קִיא *qiy'1* (9)
vomit (2)
vomit out (2)
vomited out (2)
spit out (1)
vomit up (1)
vomited (1)

7795 2קִיא *qiy'2* (3)
vomit (3)

7796 קָיָה *qāyāh*
Variant; not used

7797 קַיִת *qayiṯ*
Variant; not used

7798 קִיטוֹר *qiyṭôr* (4)
smoke (2)
clouds (1)
dense smoke (1)

7799 קִים *qiym* (1)
foes (1)

7800 קִימָה *qiymāh* (1)
standing (1)

7801 קִין *qiyn* (8)
chant (3)
composed laments (1)
sang lament (1)
take up a lament (1)
took up lament (1) +7806
wailing (1)

7802 1קַיִן *qayin1* (1)
spearhead (1)

7803 2קַיִן *qayin2* (16)
Cain (16)

7804 3קַיִן *qayin3* (2)
Kenites (2)

7805 4קַיִן *qayin4* (1)
Kain (1)

7806 1קִינָה *qiynāh1* (18)
lament (13)
laments (2)
mourn (1) +5951
took up lament (1) +7801
weeping (1)

7807 2קִינָה *qiynāh2* (1)
Kinah (1)

7808 קֵינִי *qēyniy* (12)
Kenites (7)
Kenite (5)

7809 קֵינָן *qēynān* (6)
Kenan (6)

7810 קִיץ *qiys* (23)
awake (7)
wake up (4)
awakens (2)
rouse (2)
all summer (1)
awakened (1)
awakes (1)
awoke (1)
come to life (1)
rise (1)
roused (1)
wake (1)

7811 קַיִץ *qayis* (20)
summer (10)
summer fruit (3)
ripe fruit (2)
ripened fruit (2)
cakes of figs (1)
fruit (1)
harvest (1)

7812 קִיצוֹן *qiysôn* (4)
end (4)

7813 קִיקָיוֹן *qiyqāyôn* (5)
vine (5)

7814 קִיקָלוֹן *qiyqālôn* (1)
disgrace (1)

7815 1קִיר *qiyr1* (74)
wall (38)
walls (16)
every last male (3) +928+8874
male (3) +928+8874
sides (3)
side (2)
agony (1)
ceiling (1)
city (1)
it[s] (1) +2021
roof (1)
stonemasons (1) +74+3093
stonemasons (1) +3093
untranslated (2)

7816 2קִיר *qiyr2* (1)
Kir (1)

7817 3קִיר *qiyr3* (4)
Kir (4)

7818 קִיר־חֶרֶשׂ *qiyr-hereś* (3)
Kir Hareseth (3)

7819 קִיר חֲרֶשֶׂת *qiyr hᵃrešeṯ* (2)
Kir Hareseth (2)

7820 קֵירֹס *qēyrōs* (2)
Keros (2)

7821 קִישׁ *qiyš* (21)
Kish (21)

7822 קִישׁוֹן *qiyšôn* (6)
Kishon (6)

7823 קִישִׁי *qiyšiy* (1)
Kishi (1)

7824 קַל *qal* (13)
swift (7)
fleet-footed (2) +928+8079
foam (1)
speedily (1)
swifter (1)
swiftly (1)

7825 1קֹל *qōl1* (1)
little (1)

7826 2קֹל *qōl2*
Variant; not used

7827 קָלָה *qālah* (1)
untranslated (1)

7828 1קָלָה *qālāh1* (4)
burned (1)
roasted (1)
roasted grain (1)
searing pain (1)

7829 2קָלָה *qālāh2* (7)
base (1)
be a nobody (1)
be degraded (1)
be despised (1)
dishonors (1)
little known (1)
small (1)

7830 קָלוֹן *qālôn* (17)
shame (9)
disgrace (3)
insult (2)
disgraceful (1)
insults (1)
shameful ways (1)

7831 קַלַּחַת *qallahaṯ* (2)
caldron (1)
pot (1)

7832 קָלַט *qālat* (1)
stunted (1)

7833 קָלִי *qāliy* (6)
roasted grain (4)
roasted (1)
untranslated (1)

7834 קַלָּי *qallāy* (1)
Kallai (1)

7835 קֵלָיָה *qēlāyāh* (1)
Kelaiah (1)

7836 קְלִיטָא *qᵉliytā'* (3)
Kelita (3)

7837 קָלַל *qālal* (81)
curse (12)
cursed (8)
curses (7)
lighten (5)
swifter (5)
cursing (3)
make lighter (3)
blasphemer (2)
not serious (2)
receded (2)
be considered accursed (1)
become undignified (1)
blaspheme (1)
call a curse down (1)
called curses down (1)
called down a curse (1)
called down curses (1) +7839
cast lots (1)
comes easily (1)
considered trivial (1)
despise (1) +928+6524
despises (1) +928+6524
disdained (1)
easy (1)
humble (1)
humbled (1)
is cursed (1)
lift (1)
made contemptible (1)
pronounce a curse on (1)
put a curse on (1)
revile (1)
simple (1)
small (1)
swaying (1)
swift (1)
treat with contempt (1)
treated with contempt (1)
trivial (1)
unsharpened (1) +4202
unworthy (1)
vile (1)

7838 קָלָל *qālāl* (2)
burnished (2)

7839 קְלָלָה *qᵉlālāh* (33)
curse (12)
curses (7)
cursing (5)
object of cursing (4)
condemnation (2)
accursed (1)
called down curses (1) +7837
pronounce curses (1)

7840 קָלַס *qālas* (4)
deride (1)
jeered (1)
mock (1)
scorned (1)

7841 קֶלֶס *qeles* (3)
derision (2)
reproach (1)

7842 קַלָּסָה *qallāsāh* (1)
laughingstock (1)

7843 1קָלַע *qāla'1* (4)
hurl away (1)
hurl out (1)
sling (1)
slung (1)

7844 2קָלַע *qāla'2* (3)
carved (2) +5237
carved (1)

7845 1קֶלַע *qela'1* (6)
sling (3)
slingstones (3) +74

7846 2קֶלַע *qela'2* (15)
curtains (15)

7847 קַלָּע *qallā'* (1)
men armed with slings (1)

7848 קְלֹקֵל *qᵉlōqēl* (1)
miserable (1)

7849 קִלְּשׁוֹן *qillᵉšôn* (1)
forks (1)

7850 קָמָה *qāmāh* (8)
standing grain (6)
grainfield (1)
stalk (1)

7851 קְמוּאֵל *qᵉmû'ēl* (3)
Kemuel (3)

7852 קָמוֹן *qāmôn* (1)
Kamon (1)

7853 קִמּוֹשׂ *qimmôś* (3)
briers (1)
nettles (1)
thorns (1)

7854 קֶמַח *qemah* (14)
flour (13)
meal (1)

7855 קָמַט *qāmat* (2)
bound (1)
were carried off (1)

7856 קָמַי *qāmāy*
Variant; not used

7857 קָמַל *qāmal* (2)
wither (1)
withers (1)

7858 קָמַץ *qāmas* (3)
take a handful (2) +4850+7859
take a handful (1)

7859 קֹמֶץ *qōmes* (4)
take a handful (2) +4850+7858
handful (1)
plentifully (1) +4200

7860 קֵן *qēn* (13)
nest (11)
house (1)
rooms (1)

7861 קָנָא *qānā'* (33)
jealous (5)
envy (4)
envious (3)
suspects (3)
envied (2)
jealous (2) +7863
made jealous (2)
very zealous (2) +7861
zealous (2)
aroused jealousy (1)
jealousy (1)
make envious (1)
provokes to jealousy (1)
stirred up jealous anger (1)
zeal (1)
zealous (1) +7863

7862 קַנָּא *qannā'* (6)
jealous (6)

7863 קִנְאָה *qin'āh* (43)
jealousy (15)
zeal (15)
jealous anger (4)
envy (3)
jealous (2) +7861
jealous (1)
jealous (1) +6296+6584+8120
zealous (1) +7861
untranslated (1)

7864 1קָנָה *qānāh1* (78)
buy (20)
bought (19)
get (7)
buyer (6)
acquire (2)
be bought (2)
purchase (2)
purchased (2)
acquired (1)
acquires (1)
bought (1) +928+2021+4084
bought back (1)
buyers (1)
buying (1)
buys (1) +7871
choose (1) +1047
gains (1)
gets (1)
insist on paying (1) +7864
insist on paying for (1) +928+4697+7864
master (1)
reclaim (1)
taken (1)
untranslated (1)

7865 2קָנָה *qānāh2* (6)
creator (3)
brought forth (2)
created (1)

7866 קָנֶה *qāneh* (58)
rod (12)
branches (10)
reed (5)
branch (4)
reeds (4)
calamus (3)

shaft (2)
stalk (2)
cane (1)
fragrant calamus (1)
joint (1)
measuring rod (1)
scales (1)
untranslated (11)

7867 3קָנָה *qānāh3* (3)
Kanah (3)

7868 קַנּוֹא *qannô'* (2)
jealous (2)

7869 קְנַז *qᵉnaz* (11)
Kenaz (11)

7870 קְנִזִּי *qᵉnizziy* (4)
Kenizzite (3)
Kenizzites (1)

7871 קִנְיָן *qinyān* (11)
goods (3)
buys (1) +7864
creatures (1)
have (1)
herds (1)
livelihood (1)
possessed (1)
property (1)
untranslated (1)

7872 קִנָּמוֹן *qinnāmôn* (3)
cinnamon (3)

7873 קָנַן *qānan* (6)
make nests (1)
makes nest (1)
nest (1)
nested (1)
nestled (1)
untranslated (1)

7874 קֶנֶץ *qenes* (1)
end (1) +8492

7875 קְנָת *qᵉnāṯ* (2)
Kenath (2)

7876 קָסַם *qāsam* (22)
diviners (6)
divination (2)
divinations (2)
consult (1)
omen (1)
practice divination (1) +7877
practiced divination (1)
practiced divination (1) +7877
practices divination (1) +7877
seek an omen (1) +7877
soothsayer (1)
tell fortunes (1)
utter divinations (1)
untranslated (2)

7877 קֶסֶם *qesem* (11)
divination (2)
divinations (2)
fee for divination (1)
lot (1)
oracle (1)
practice divination (1) +7876
practiced divination (1) +7876
practices divination (1) +7876
seek an omen (1) +7876

7878 קָסַס *qāsas* (1)
stripped (1)

7879 קֶסֶת *qeseṯ* (3)
kit (2)
writing kit (1)

7880 קָעָה *qā'āh*
Variant; not used

7881 קְעִילָה *qᵉ'iylāh* (18)
Keilah (18)

7882 קַעֲקַע *qa'ᵃqa'* (1)
tattoo (1)

7883 קְעָרָה *qᵉ'ārāh* (17)
plate (13)
plates (4)

7884 קָפָא *qāp̄ā'* (4)
complacent (1)
congealed (1)
curdle (1)
untranslated (1)

7885 קִפָּאוֹן *qippā'ôn* (1)
frost (1)

7886 קָפַד *qāp̄aḏ* (1)
rolled up (1)

7887 קִפֹּד *qippōḏ* (3)
screech owl (2)
owls (1)

7888 קְפָדָה *qᵉp̄āḏāh* (1)
terror (1)

7889 קִפּוֹז *qippôz* (1)
owl (1)

7890 קָפַץ *qāp̄as* (7)
shut (2)
bounding (1)
gathered up (1)
shuts (1)
tightfisted (1) +906+3338
withheld (1)

7891 קֵץ *qēs* (67)
end (40)
later (4) +4946
after (3) +4946
climax (3)
after (2) +4200
remotest (2)
afar (1)
complete (1) +2118+4946
course (1)
endless (1) +401
every (1) +4946
from (1) +4946
fulfilled (1)
later (1) +4200
limit (1)
passed (1)
prospects (1)
some years later (1) +4200+9102
time is ripe (1) +995

7892 קָצַב *qāsaḇ* (2)
cut (1)
sheep just shorn (1)

7893 קֶצֶב *qeseḇ* (3)
shape (2)
roots (1)

7894 1קָצָה *qāṣāh1* (4)
cutting off (1)
reduce size (1)
scraped (1)
scraped off (1)

7895 קָצֶה *qāseh* (93)
end (28)
ends (16)
edge (11)
border (3)
mouth (3)
other[s] (4)
outskirts (3)
foot (2)
frontier (2)
part (2)
the other[s] (2) +824+2021
after (1) +4946
distant (1)
end (1) +1473
entire (1) +4946
every part (1)
extreme (1)
far end (1)
farthest (1)
most distant land (1)
of (1) +4946
other[s] (1) +9028
outposts (1) +2821
southernmost (1) +4946
tip (1)
untranslated (3)

7896 2קָצָה *qāṣāh2* (35)
ends (11)
corners (9)
end (4)
all sorts (2)
tip (2)
all (1)
all sorts (1) +4946
other[s] (1)
outer fringe (1)
quarters (1)
ruin (1)
untranslated (1)

7897 קֵצֶה *qēseh* (5)
end (2)
boundless (1) +401
endless (1) +401
number (1)

7898 קָצוּ *qāsû* (3)
ends (2)
borders (1)

7899 קָצוּץ *qāsûs* (3)
distant places (2) +6991
distant (1)

7900 קָצוּר *qāsûr* (1)
narrower (1)

7901 קְצוֹת *qᵉsôṯ*
Variant; not used

7902 קֶצַח *qesah* (3)
caraway (3)

7903 קָצִין *qāsiyn* (12)
commander (4)
rulers (3)
leader (2)
commanders (1)
leaders (1)
ruler (1)

7904 1קְצִיעָה *qᵉsiy'āh1* (1)
cassia (1)

7905 2קְצִיעָה *qᵉsiy'āh2* (1)
Keziah (1)

7906 קְצִיץ *qᵉsiys*
Variant; not used

7907 1קָצִיר *qāsiyr1* (49)
harvest (37)
harvests (3)
harvest time (2)
harvesting (2) +7917
harvesting grain (1)
reap (1) +7917
reaper (1)
reaping (1)
untranslated (1)

7908 2קָצִיר *qāsiyr2* (5)
branches (2)
boughs (1)
shoots (1)
twigs (1)

7909 1קָצַע *qāsa'1* (1)
have scraped (1)

7910 2קָצַע *qāsa'2* (3)
corners (3)

7911 קָצַף *qāsap̱* (34)
angry (23)
angered (2)
enraged (2)
anger (1)
angry (1) +7912
aroused wrath (1)
furious (1) +4394
made angry (1) +2118
provoked to anger (1)
very angry (1) +7912

7912 1קֶצֶף *qesep̱1* (28)
wrath (13)
anger (7)
angry (3)
angry (1) +7911
discord (1)
fury (1)
great wrath (1) +2256+2405
very angry (1) +7911

7913 2קֶצֶף *qesep̱2* (1)
twig (1)

7914 קְצָפָה *qᵉsāp̱āh* (1)
ruined (1) +4200

7915 1קָצַץ *qāsas1* (11)
cut off (4)
took away (3)
cut (1)
cut free (1)
shatters (1)
stripped off (1)

7916 2קָצַץ *qāsas2*
Variant; not used

7917 1קָצַר *qāsar1* (36)
reap (15)
harvesters (5)
reaper (3)
harvesting (2) +7907
gather (1)
harvest (1)
harvesting (1)
harvests (1)
reap (1) +7907
reaped (1)
reapers (1)
reaps (1)
untranslated (3)

7918 2קָצַר *qāsar2* (14)
cut short (3)
short (2)
angry (1)
bear no longer (1)
grew weary (1)
impatient (1)
impatient (1) +5883
short (1) +7918
tired (1)
too short (1)

7919 קֹצֶר *qōser* (1)
discouragement (1) +8120

7920 קָצֵר *qāsēr* (5)
drained (2)
few (1)
quick-tempered (1) +678
quick-tempered (1) +8120

7921 קְצָת *qᵉsāṯ* (9)
end (2)
some (2) +4946
after (1) +4946
corners (1)
far away (1)
untranslated (2)

7922 קַר *qar* (3)
cold (1)
cool (1)
even-tempered (1) +8120

7923 קֹר *qōr* (1)
cold (1)

7924 1קָרָא *qārā'1* (737)
called (139)
call (81)
named (55) +9005
summoned (45)
read (33)
called (27) +9005
proclaim (23)
summon (18)
calls (15)
be called (14)
invited (12)
proclaimed (12)
called out (11)
calling (11)
bears (10) +6584
cried out (9)
call out (7)
cry out (7)
gave (7)
invite (7)
call (6) +9005
cry (6)
shouted (6)
is called (5)
sent for (5) +2256+4200+8938
bear (4) +6584
call upon (4)
called together (4)
name (4) +9005
proclaiming (4)
summons (4)
are called (3)
call on (3)
called out (3) +928+1524+7754
cried (3)
guests (3)
named (3)
sent for (3) +2256+8938
was called (3)
announced (2)
asks (2)
be called (2) +9005
be reckoned (2)
call in (2)
chosen (2) +928+9005
declared (2)
famous (2) +9005
gave name (2)
given (2)
read aloud (2)
say (2)
summoned (2) +2256+8938
were summoned (2)
announce (1)
appeal (1)
be known as (1)
be known as (1) +9005
be mentioned (1)
be named (1) +9005
been called (1)
been invited as guests (1)
been named (1) +9005
being called (1)
being summoned (1)
bleat (1)
blurts out (1)
brag (1)
bring out (1)
call back (1)
call for help (1)
call yourselves (1)
called down (1)
called in (1)
calling (1) +7754
calling (1) +9005
calling down (1)
calling for help (1)
calling forth (1)
calling out (1)
calls in (1)
claims (1)
convocations (1) +5246
cries out (1)
decreed (1)
dictated (1) +4946+7023
did^{s} (1)
exclaim (1)
foretold (1)
get (1)
give (1)
got (1)
grasping (1)
herald (1)
invitation (1)
invite (1) +2256+8938
invites (1)
invoke (1) +928+7023
is called (1) +9005
is called together (1)
known as (1)
make an offer (1)
make proclamation (1)
men of high rank (1)
name (1)
named (1) +928+9005
offer (1)
pray (1)
prayed (1)
preach (1)
proclaim (1) +928
proclaimed (1) +928
pronounced (1)
raised a cry (1)
reading (1)
scream for help (1) +2256+7754+8123
screamed (1) +928+1524+7754
screamed for help (1) +2256+7754+8123
sent for (1) +4200+8938
sent word (1) +2256+8938
shout (1)
shout (1) +928+7754
shout (1) +1524+7754
shout aloud (1) +928+1744
shouted (1) +928+7754
shouted (1) +2256+5951+7754
shouted the news (1)
summoned (1) +4200+8938
voices (1)
was called (1) +9005
was read aloud (1)
were appointed (1)
were called (1)
were counted (1)
were invited (1)
word (1)
untranslated (8)

7925 2קָרָא *qārā'2* (138)
meet (78)
against (13)
met (5)
happened (4)
toward (3)
attack (2)
came toward (2)
come upon (2)
follows (2)
meet in battle (2)
oppose (2)
breaks out (1)
brought upon (1)
come (1)
come across (1) +4200+7156
comes (1)
facing each other (1) +5120
fall upon (1)
fight (1)
follows (1) +6584
greet (1) +1385
happen (1)

happened to be (1) +7936
help (1)
into (1)
opposite (1)
out came to meet (1)
resort to (1) +2143+4200
seized (1)
wage (1)
welcomed (1)
went to meet (1)
untranslated (2)

7926 1קֹרֵא *qōrē'1* (2)
partridge (2)

7927 2קֹרֵא *qōrē'2* (3)
Kore (3)

7928 קָרַב *qārab̲* (280)
bring (36)
present (36)
offer (22)
brought (15)
come near (11)
approached (9)
come (9)
presented (9)
brings (7)
go near (7)
offers (7)
approach (6)
came (6)
near (6)
offered (5)
went (5)
brought forward (4)
brought near (3)
came near (3)
come forward (3)
drew near (3)
had come forward (3)
about (2)
acceptable (2)
advance (2)
bring near (2)
came forward (2)
come here (2)
join (2)
made an offering (2)
offering (2)
sacrificed (2)
add (1)
appear (1)
approaches (1)
approaching (1)
bring forward (1)
bring here (1)
bringing (1)
bringing near (1)
brought offering (1)
brought to a close (1)
came together (1)
cause to come near (1)
closer (1)
come closer (1)
comes (1)
comes near (1)
draw near (1)
draws near (1)
encroach (1)
go (1)
gone near (1)
have brought (1)
have come near (1)
inquire of (1) +448
joined (1)
keep away (1) +448+3870
lie with (1) +448
made (1)
made offerings (1)
make (1)
march up (1)
meet (1)
offer sacrifices (1)
offer up (1)
present yourselves (1)
presenting (1)
presents (1)
reach (1)
reached (1)
soon (1)
stood (1)
take part (1) +6913
went near (1)
untranslated (2)

7929 קָרֵב *qārēb̲* (12)
draw near (2)
approached (1)
approaches (1)
came (1)
closer (1)
closer and closer (1) +2143+2256
comes near (1)
even comes near (1) +7929
goes near (1)
going (1)

7930 קְרָב *qᵉrāb̲* (9)
war (5)
battle (4)

7931 קֶרֶב *qereb̲* (225)
among (52) +928
in (24) +928
within (20) +928
among (18)
from (16) +4946
inner parts (16)
with (11) +928
midst (6)
heart (5)
among (4) +4946
near (4) +928
them[s] (4) +2021
through (3) +928
upon (3) +928
inmost being (2)
on (2) +928
to (2) +6584
along with (1) +928
at (1) +928
ate (1) +448+995
body (1)
done so[s] (1) +448+995
entering (1) +928+995
filled with (1) +928
folds (1)
had (1) +928
harbor (1) +928+4328
hearts (1)
herself (1) +2023
in (1) +4946
inside (1) +928
into (1) +928
lose heart (1) +928+1327+8120
middle (1)
mind (1)
minds (1)
out of (1) +4946
presence (1)
ranks (1)
stomach (1)
there[s] (1) +928+2257
thick (1)
throughout (1) +928
untranslated (7)

7932 קִרְבָה *qirb̲āh* (2)
come near (1)
near (1)

7933 קָרְבָּן *qorbān* (80)
offering (58)
offerings (7)
gifts (2)
offers (2)
gift (1)
offered (1)
offering made by fire (1) +852
sacrifice (1)
untranslated (7)

7934 קֻרְבָּן *qurbān* (2)
contribution (1)
contributions (1)

7935 קַרְדֹּם *qardōm* (5)
axes (4)
ax (1)

7936 1קָרָה *qārāh1* (27)
met (4)
happen (3)
happened (3)
laid beams (2)
as it turned out (1) +5247
beams (1)
come (1)
come true (1)
comes (1)
gave success (1)
give success (1)
happened to be (1) +7925
lays beams (1)
make beams (1)
meet (1)
overtake (1)
overtakes (1)
punished (1) +6411
select (1)

7937 קָרֶה *qāreh* (1)
emission (1)

7938 2קָרָה *qārāh2* (6)
cold (5)
icy blast (1)

7939 3קָרָה *qārāh3*
Variant; not used

7940 קָרוֹב *qārôb̲* (77)
near (38)
nearest (5)
neighbors (3)
approach (2)
close (2)
warriors (2)
about to (1) +4946+6964
always (1)
at hand (1) +995
at hand (1) +995+4200
brief (1) +4946
close at hand (1)
close relative (1)
close relative (1) +8638
close to (1) +725
close to heart (1)
closely associated (1)
closely related (1)
closest (1)
come near (1)
dependent (1)
fellowman (1)
invites (1)
kinsmen (1)
nearby (1)
nearby (1) +4946
nearer (1)
neighbor (1)
recently (1) +2543+4946
shorter (1)
soon (1) +928

7941 קָרוּת *qārût̲*
Variant; not used

7942 קָרַח *qāraḥ* (6)
must shave (1) +7947
shave head (1)
shave heads (1) +1605
shave heads (1) +7947

was rubbed bare (1)
untranslated (1)

7943 קֶרַח *qerah* (7)
ice (4)
cold (1)
frost (1)
hail (1)

7944 קֵרֵחַ *qērēah* (3)
baldhead (2)
bald (1)

7945 קָרֵחַ *qārēah* (14)
Kareah (14)

7946 קֹרַח *qōrah* (37)
Korah (34)
Korah's (2)
Korah's (1) +4200

7947 קָרְחָה *qorhāh* (11)
shaved (3)
baldness (1)
make bald (1) +8143
must shave (1) +7942
shave (1) +6584
shave (1) +8492
shave head in mourning (1) +995
shave heads (1) +7942
tear out hair (1)

7948 קָרְחִי *qorhiy* (8)
Korahite (3)
Korahites (3)
Korah (1)
Korahites (1) +1201

7949 קָרַחַת *qārahaṯ* (4)
head (2)
bald head (1)
side[s] (1)

7950 קְרִי *qᵉriy* (7)
hostile (6)
hostility (1)

7951 קָרִיא *qāriy'* (3)
appointed (1)
officials (1)
untranslated (1)

7952 קְרִיאָה *qᵉriy'āh* (1)
message (1)

7953 קִרְיָה *qiryāh* (29)
city (20)
town (5)
cities (3)
one[s] (1)

7954 קְרִיּוֹת *qᵉriyyôṯ* (3)
Kerioth (3)

7955 קְרִיּוֹת חֶצְרוֹן *qᵉriyyôṯ hesrôn* (1)
Kerioth Hezron (1)

7956 קִרְיַת *qiryaṯ* (1)
Kiriath (1)

7957 קִרְיַת אַרְבַּע *qiryaṯ 'arba'* (7)
Kiriath Arba (7)

7958 קִרְיַת־בַּעַל *qiryaṯ-ba'al* (2)
Kiriath Baal (2)

7959 קִרְיַת הָאַרְבַּע *qiryaṯ hā'arba'* (2)
Kiriath Arba (2)

7960 קִרְיַת חֻצוֹת *qiryaṯ husôṯ* (1)
Kiriath Huzoth (1)

7961 קִרְיַת יְעָרִים *qiryaṯ yᵉ'āriym* (19)
Kiriath Jearim (19)

7962 קִרְיַת־סַנָּה *qiryaṯ-sannāh* (1)
Kiriath Sannah (1)

7963 קִרְיַת־סֵפֶר *qiryaṯ-sēp̱er* (4)
Kiriath Sepher (4)

7964 קִרְיָתַיִם *qiryāṯayim* (7)
Kiriathaim (6)
untranslated (1)

7965 קָרַם *qāram* (2)
cover (1)
covered (1)

7966 קָרַן *qāran* (4)
radiant (3)
horns (1)

7967 קֶרֶן *qeren* (75)
horns (44)
horn (23)
two-horned (2) +1251+2021
brow (1)
hillside (1)
him[s] (1)
rays (1)
trumpets (1) +3413
tusks (1)

7968 קֶרֶן הַפּוּךְ *qeren happûḵ* (1)
Keren-Happuch (1)

7969 קַרְנַיִם *qarnayim* (1)
Karnaim (1)

7970 קָרַס *qāras* (2)
stoop (1)
stoops low (1)

7971 קֶרֶס *qeres* (10)
clasps (7)
them[s] (3) +2021

7972 קַרְסֹל *qarsōl* (2)
ankles (2)

7973 קָרַע *qāra'* (63)
tore (26)
torn (12)
tear (10)
rend (2)
tore away (2)
be split apart (1)
cut off (1)
makes large (1)
most certainly tear away (1) +7973
rip open (1) +4213+6033
shade (1)
slandered (1)
tear off (1)
tore apart (1) +4200+7974+9109
was split apart (1)

7974 קְרָעִים *qᵉrā'iym* (4)
pieces (2)
rags (1)
tore apart (1) +4200+7973+9109

7975 קָרַץ *qāras* (5)
been taken (1)
maliciously wink (1)
purses (1)
winks (1)
winks maliciously (1) +6524

7976 קֶרֶץ *qeres* (1)
gadfly (1)

7977 קַרְקַע1 *qarqa'1* (7)
floor (5)
bottom (1)
floors (1)

7978 קַרְקַע2 *qarqa'2* (1)
Karka (1)

7979 קַרְקַר *qarqar*
Variant; not used

7980 קַרְקֹר *qarqōr* (1)
Karkor (1)

7981 קָרַר1 *qārar1* (2)
pours out (2)

7982 קָרַר2 *qārar2* (1)
battering down (1)

7983 קֶרֶשׁ *qereš* (51)
frames (27)
frame (8)
those[s] (2)
deck (1)
them[s] (1) +2021
them[s] (1) +2021+6929
untranslated (11)

7984 קֶרֶת *qereṯ* (5)
city (5)

7985 קַרְתָּה *qartāh* (2)
Kartah (2)

7986 קַרְתָּן *qartān* (1)
Kartan (1)

7987 קַשְׂוָה *qaśwāh* (4)
pitchers (3)
jars (1)

7988 קְשִׂיטָה *qᵉśiytāh* (3)
pieces of silver (2)
piece of silver (1)

7989 קַשְׂקֶשֶׂת *qaśqeśeṯ* (8)
scales (7)
coat of scale armor (1) +9234

7990 קַשׁ *qaš* (16)
stubble (7)
chaff (6)
straw (2)
piece of straw (1)

7991 קִשֻּׁאָה *qiššu'āh* (1)
cucumbers (1)

7992 קָשַׁב *qāšaḇ* (46)
listen (14)
pay attention (12)
hear (4)
listened (3)
listens (2)
paid attention (2)
alert (1) +7993
attendance (1)
attentively (1)
gave heed (1)
heard (1)
heed (1)
listen (1) +265
pay close attention (1) +2256+9048
turning (1)

7993 קֶשֶׁב *qešeḇ* (4)
alert (1)
alert (1) +7992
paid attention (1)
response (1)

7994 קַשָּׁב *qaššāḇ* (2)
attentive (2)

7995 קַשֻּׁב *qaššuḇ* (3)
attentive (3)

7996 קָשָׁה *qāšāh* (29)
stiff-necked (11) +6902
harden (2)
put heavy (2)
cruel (1)
difficult (1)
distressed (1)
great difficulty (1)
hard (1)
hardens (1)
hardship (1)
harshly (1)
having great difficulty (1)
heavy (1)
made stubborn (1)
resisted (1)
stubbornly refused (1)
treats harshly (1)

7997 קָשֶׁה *qāšeh* (36)
stiff-necked (7) +6902
harshly (5)

cruel (3)
fierce (3)
hard (2)
harsh (2)
stubborn (2)
bad news (1)
deeply troubled (1) +8120
desperate times (1)
difficult (1)
dire (1)
grew stronger and stronger (1) +2143+2256
in trouble (1) +3427
obstinate (1) +4213
obstinate (1) +7156
strong (1)
surly (1)
unyielding (1)

7998 קָשָׁה *qāšah* (1)
harden (1)

7999 קֹשְׁט *qōšṭ* (1)
true (1)

8000 קֹשֶׁט *qōšeṭ* (1)
bow (1)

8001 קְשִׁי *qᵉšiy* (1)
stubbornness (1)

8002 קִשְׁיוֹן *qišyôn* (2)
Kishion (2)

8003 קָשַׁר *qāšar* (44)
conspired (10)
plotted (7)
bind (4)
conspired (4) +8004
tie (3)
tied (3)
became one with (1)
carried out (1)
closely bound up (1)
conspiracy led (1) +8004
conspirators (1)
hold (1)
is bound up (1)
put on (1)
put on a leash (1)
raising a conspiracy (1)
reached height (1) +6330
strong (1)
stronger (1)

8004 קֶשֶׁר *qešer* (16)
conspiracy (5)
conspired (4) +8003
treason (4)
conspiracy led (1) +8003
rebellion (1)
traitor (1)

8005 קִשֻּׁרִים *qiššuriym* (2)
sashes (1)
wedding ornaments (1)

8006 1קָשַׁשׁ *qāšaš1* (8)
gathering (4)
gather (2)
gather together (2)

8007 2קָשַׁשׁ *qāšaš2*
Variant; not used

8008 קֶשֶׁת *qešeṯ* (76)
bow (45)
bows (14)
rainbow (4)
archer (1) +9530
archers (1) +408+928+2021+4619
archers (1) +928+2021+4619
archers (1) +5432
archers (1) +8227
arrow (1)
arrows (1)
arrows (1) +1201
bowmen (1) +5031
bowshot (1) +3217
did so[s] (1) +2256+2932+4374
shoot (1) +928+2021
with bows (1) +2005

8009 קַשָּׁת *qaššāṯ* (1)
archer (1) +8050

8010 ר *r*
Variant; not used

8011 1רָאָה *rā'āh1* (1303)
see (342)
saw (305)
seen (102)
look (52)
looked (37)
appeared (33)
sees (27)
examine (25)
show (23)
appear (20)
showed (17)
shown (12)
consider (10)
be seen (9)
realized (9)
find out (8)
seeing (8)
appears (7)
watching (7)
examines (6)
enjoy (5)
looks (5)
watch (5)
find (4)
have regard for (4)
learned (4)
noticed (4)
watched (4)
been seen (3)
find out (3) +2256+3359
observe (3)
remember (3)
see (3) +2256+3359
advisers (2) +7156
be shown (2)
decide (2)
face (2)
faced each other (2) +7156
had[s] (2)
here (2)
inspect (2)
knows (2)
let see (2)
look after (2)
look around (2)
look down on (2)
look for (2)
look over (2)
looking (2)
meet (2)
notice (2)
observed (2)
present himself (2)
provide (2)
revealed (2)
view (2)
were exposed (2)
Ah (1)
allowed to see (1)
appear before (1) +7156
appearing (1)
are given (1)
attract (1)
be found (1)
be provided (1)
bear in mind (1)
beheld (1)
being seen (1)
blind (1) +1153
catch glimpse (1)
caught sight of (1)
cherished (1)
choose (1)
chose (1)
chosen (1)
clearly (1) +3954
come into presence (1) +906+7156
come into view (1)
compare (1)
consider carefully (1)
considers (1)
conspicuous (1)
contemplating (1)
display (1)
displayed (1)
ever seeing (1) +8011
experienced (1)
faced (1)
found (1)
found (1) +4200+7156
gaze (1)
gazing (1)
glimpse (1)
gloat (1)
had a vision (1)
had special access to (1) +7156
have sexual relations (1) +906+6872
hidden (1) +4202
indeed seen (1) +8011
inspected (1)
keeping watch (1) +928+6524
knew (1)
knowing (1)
let gloat (1)
listen (1)
listen carefully (1)
look carefully (1) +928+6524
looked (1) +5260
looked things over (1)
looking at each other (1)
lookout (1)
looks down on (1)
made see (1)
make look (1)
make see (1)
meet with (1) +7156
met (1)
mistake for (1) +3869
only look (1) +8011
paid attention (1)
please (1)
present (1)
present myself (1)
present yourself (1)
probe (1)
realize (1)
realize (1) +2256+3359
realized (1) +2256+3359
realizing (1)
reappears (1) +6388
reason (1)
recognize (1)
regard (1)
regarded (1)
respect (1)
revealing (1)
reveals (1)
saw clearly (1) +8011
see (1) +2021+4200+6524
see (1) +6524
see (1) +7156
see for yourselves (1) +4013+6524
see visions (1)
seems (1)
seen for myself (1) +7156
selected (1)
show himself (1)
showing (1)
sight (1)
someone[s] (1) +2021

stare (1)
suffered (1)
took note (1)
turn (1)
uncovered (1)
understand (1)
very well (1)
viewed (1)
visible (1)
visit (1)
was seen (1)
were shown (1)
untranslated (37)

8012 2רָאָה *rā'āh2* (1)
red kite (1)

8013 רָאֶה *rā'eh*
Variant; not used

8014 1רֹאֶה *rō'eh1* (12)
seer (10)
seer's (1)
seers (1)

8015 2רֹאֶה *rō'eh2* (1)
seeing visions (1)

8016 3רֹאֶה *rō'eh3*
Variant; not used

8017 רְאוּבֵן *r^e'ûḇēn* (72)
Reuben (45)
Reubenites (17) +1201
Reuben (6) +1201
Reubenite (1) +1201
they[s] (1) +1201+1201+1514+2256
untranslated (2)

8018 רְאוּבֵנִי *r^e'ûḇēniy* (18)
Reubenites (13)
Reuben (2)
men of Reuben (1)
Reuben (1) +1201
Reubenite (1)

8019 רַאֲוָה *ra'^{a}wāh* (1)
spectacle (1)

8020 רְאוּמָה *r^e'ûmāh* (1)
Reumah (1)

8021 רְאוּת *r^e'ûṯ* (1)
feast on (1)

8022 רֹאִי *rō'iy*
Variant; not used

8023 רְאִי *r^e'iy* (1)
mirror (1)

8024 רֳאִי *r^o'iy* (4)
features (1)
sees (1)
spectacle (1)
to nothing (1) +4946

8025 רְאָיָה *r^e'āyāh* (4)
Reaiah (4)

8026 רְאִית *r^e'iyṯ* (1)
untranslated (1)

8027 רָאַם *rā'am* (1)
raised up (1)

8028 רְאֵם *r^e'ēm* (9)
wild ox (6)
wild oxen (2)
him[s] (1)

8029 1רָאמוֹת *rā'môṯ1* (2)
coral (2)

8030 2רָאמוֹת *rā'môṯ2* (5)
Ramoth (5)

8031 1רֹאשׁ *rō'š1* (603)
head (217)
heads (124)
top (45)
chief (33)
leaders (19)
first (16)
tops (10)
beginning (8)
hair (8)
chiefs (6)
companies (6)
leader (6)
mountaintops (4) +2215
summit (3)
take a census (3) +906+5951
topmost (3)
ends (2)
finest (2)
helmet (2) +5057
high (2)
leading (2)
led by (2) +928
lost hair (2) +5307
over (2) +928
prominent place (2)
released (2) +5951
take a census (2) +5951
all (1)
any (1)
authority (1)
begin (1)
bodyguard (1) +4200+9068
branches off (1)
capstone (1) +7157
choicest gifts (1)
command (1)
commander-in-chief (1) +2256+8569
commanders (1)
company (1)
count (1) +906+5951
counted (1) +906+5951
crest (1)
crowns (1) +4200
detachments (1)
director (1)
directors (1)
divisions (1)
down (1) +4946
each (1)
fine (1)
foremost (1)
full (1)
hair (1) +1929
headwaters (1)
heights (1) +5294
highest (1)
highest (1) +6584
hilltop (1) +2215
hilltops (1) +2215
himself (1) +2257
include in the census (1) +906+5951
it[s] (1) +2257
it[s] (1) +8552
junction (1)
leaders (1) +408
leaders (1) +6639
leading men (1)
made pay for (1) +928+8740
make full restitution (1) +928+8740
masters (1)
men (1)
mountaintop (1) +2215
new Moon festivals (1) +2544
oldest (1)
outstanding (1)
overwhelmed (1) +6296
peaks (1)
raiding parties (1)
reaches (1)
repay (1) +928+8740
repay (1) +6584+8740
ruler (1) +1505
rulers (1)
special (1)
sum (1)
tip (1)
untranslated (11)

8032 2רֹאשׁ *rō'š2* (12)
poison (5)
poisoned (3)
bitterness (2)
gall (1)
poisonous weeds (1)

8033 3רֹאשׁ *rō'š3* (1)
Rosh (1)

8034 4רֹאשׁ *rō'š4*
Variant; not used

8035 רִאשָׁה *ri'šāh* (1)
before (1)

8036 רֹאשָׁה *rō'šah* (1)
capstone (1) +74

8037 רִאשׁוֹן *ri'šôn* (182)
first (100)
former (19)
beginning (13)
before (6) +928+2021
earlier (6)
before (4)
first (2) +928+2021
old (2)
used to (2) +2021+4200
ancestors (1)
chief (1)
chief officials (1)
days of old (1)
early (1)
fathers (1)
forefathers (1) +3
formerly (1) +928+2021
front (1)
highest (1)
lead (1)
leads (1) +928+2021
led the way (1) +2118+3338
long (1)
long ago (1) +928+2021
of old (1)
older (1)
once again (1) +2021+3869
one in the lead (1)
past (1)
past (1) +3427
past (1) +6961
predecessors (1)
previous (1)
used to (1)
untranslated (3)

8038 רִאשֹׁנִי *ri'šôniy* (1)
first (1)

8039 רַאֲשׁוֹת *ra'^{a}šôṯ*
Variant; not used

8040 רֵאשִׁית *rē'šîṯ* (51)
first (13)
firstfruits (8)
beginning (7)
best (6)
early (3) +928
firstfruits (2) +7262
beginnings (1)
choice (1)
choice parts (1)
early (1)
finest (1)
firstfruits of harvest (1)
foremost (1)
leaders (1)
mainstay (1)
starting (1)
supreme (1)
when (1) +928

8041 1רַב *rab̲1* (425)
many (162)
great (73)
long (18)
numerous (14)
abundant (12)
mighty (10)
much (10)
abounding (8)
large (8)
enough (6)
larger (6)
vast (6)
full (4)
more (4)
greatly (3)
number (3)
plenty (3)
crowd (2)
deep (2)
fully (2)
gone too far (2)
great deal (2)
heavy (2)
large (2) +4394
large amount (2)
long enough (2)
rushing (2)
so great (2)
so many (2)
weighs heavily (2)
abundantly (1)
all abound (1)
beyond number (1) +4394
chief (1)
convinced (1)
distant (1)
distant future (1) +3427
floodwaters (1) +4784
gone far enough (1)
great quantities (1)
greater (1)
greater power (1)
gushed out (1) +3655
high (1)
huge (1)
increased more and more (1) +2143+2143+2256
increasing (1)
larger number (1)
mansions (1) +1074
many (1) +4394
more (1) +3578
most (1)
much too numerous (1) +2256+6786
multitude (1)
multitudes (1)
never (1) +4202
numbers (1)
old (1)
older (1)
powerful (1)
quantities (1)
quantity (1)
rich (1)
richly (1)
severe (1) +4394
severely (1)
so (1)
so many (1) +5031
so much (1)
stronger (1)
surging (1)
time after time (1) +6961
too long (1)
tyrannical (1) +5131
utterly (1)
very (1)
what (1)
whole (1)
wide (1)

8042 2רַב *rab̲2* (33)
commander (23)
chief (3)
high (2)
officers (2)
captain (1) +2021+2480
wine stewards (1) +1074
untranslated (1)

8043 3רַב *rab̲3* (3)
archers (2)
archer (1)

8044 רֹב *rōb̲* (152)
many (31)
great (24)
numerous (6)
all (5)
great (4) +4200
much (4)
plentiful (4) +4200
abundant (3)
great amount (3) +4200
greatly (3) +4200
in abundance (3) +4200
large numbers (3) +4200
abundance (2)
extensive (2) +4200
great (2) +3972
great numbers (2)
greatness (2)
large (2)
large quantities (2) +4200
many (2) +4200
much (2) +4200
plenty (2) +4200
so many (2) +4946
abound (1)
abundant (1) +4200
advanced (1)
age (1) +3427
droves (1) +4200
great number (1)
great number (1) +4200
great numbers (1) +4200
great quantities (1) +4200+4394
harsh (1)
in abundance (1)
in large numbers (1) +4200
increased (1)
large amount (1) +4200
larger (1) +4200
load (1)
long (1)
mighty (1) +4200
more (1) +4200
multitude (1)
numerous (1) +4200
prosperity (1) +3972
quantities (1) +4200
rabble (1) +132
size (1)
so many (1)
so many (1) +4200
surpassing (1)
thick (1)
widespread (1)
untranslated (7)

8045 1רָבַב *rāb̲ab̲1* (20)
many (7)
great (3)
numerous (3)
increased (2)
abound (1)
do[s] (1)
increase in number (1)
outnumber (1) +4946
tens of thousands (1)

8046 2רָבַב *rāb̲ab̲2* (1)
shot (1)

8047 רְבָבָה *rᵉb̲āb̲āh* (18)
ten thousand (6)
tens of thousands (5)
countless (1)
grow (1)
myriads (1)
ten thousands (1)
thousands (1)
untranslated (2)

8048 רָבַד *rāb̲ad̲* (1)
covered (1) +5267

8049 1רָבָה *rāb̲āh1* (179)
increase (14)
many (10)
increase in number (9)
increased (9)
increase numbers (8)
numerous (8)
multiplied (5)
make numerous (4)
multiply (4)
thrive (4)
great (3)
greater (3)
greatly (3)
increases (3)
much (3)
multiplies (3)
gave many (2)
give larger (2)
had many (2)
increase the number (2)
increasing (2)
keep (2)
long (2)
make great (2)
more (2)
reared (2)
take many (2)
abundant (1)
accumulate large amounts (1) +4394
acquire great numbers (1)
add to numbers (1)
adding (1)
as much as (1) +4946
before[s] (1)
built many (1)
built more (1)
distant (1) +2006+2021
done more (1)
enlarge (1)
enlarged (1)
freely (1)
gaining (1)
gathered much (1)
generously gave (1)
get more (1)
give more (1)
greatly increase (1) +8049
grew up (1)
grow large (1)
have many (1)
heap (1)
higher than (1) +2025+4200+5087
increased in number (1)
increased number (1)
increased numbers (1)
kept on (1)
lavished (1)
less meaning (1) +2039
made many (1)
made numerous (1)
make as great as you like (1) +4394
make countless (1) +889+4202+6218
make many (1)
make numerous (1) +8049
make plentiful (1)
makes grow (1)
many times (1)
more and more (1)

more and more unfaithful (1) +5085+5086
multiply the number (1)
numbers increased (1)
numbers increased greatly (1) +2256+7238
offer many (1)
outnumber (1) +4946
piles up (1)
repeatedly (1)
so does[s] (1)
so increase (1) +8049
time after time (1)
too much (1)
use an abundance (1)
whole (1)
yet more (1)
untranslated (5)

8050 2רָבָה *rāḇāh2* (1)
archer (1) +8009

8051 רַבָּה *rabbāh* (15)
Rabbah (15)

8052 רִבּוֹא *ribbô'* (11)
20,000 (2) +9109
42,360 (1) +547+752+2256+4395+8993+9252
42,360 (1) +547+752+4395+8993+9252
61,000 (1) +547+2256+9252
eighteen thousand (1) +547+2256+9046
hundred and twenty thousand (1) +6926+9109
many thousands (1)
ten thousand (1)
tens of thousands (1)
untranslated (1)

8053 רְבִיבִים *r'ḇiyḇiym* (6)
showers (5)
abundant rain (1)

8054 רָבִיד *rāḇiyḏ* (3)
chain (1)
interwoven (1) +928+2021
necklace (1)

8055 רְבִיעִי *r'ḇiy'iy* (57)
fourth (44)
quarter (9)
fourth generation (2)
four-sided (1)
square (1)

8056 רַבִּית *rabbiyṯ* (1)
Rabbith (1)

8057 רָבַךְ *rāḇaḵ* (3)
mixing (1)
well-kneaded (1)
well-mixed (1)

8058 רִבְלָה *riḇlāh* (11)
Riblah (11)

8059 רַב מָג *raḇ māḡ*
Variant; not used

8060 רַב־סָרִיס *raḇ-sāriys*
Variant; not used

8061 1רָבַע *rāḇa'1* (4)
have sexual relations with (2)
lying down (1)
mate (1)

8062 2רָבַע *rāḇa'2* (12)
square (9)
rectangular (2)
square (1) +448+752+8063

8063 1רֶבַע *reḇa'1* (7)
directions (2)
quarter (2)
sides (1)
square (1) +448+752
square (1) +448+752+8062

8064 2רֶבַע *reḇa'2* (2)
Reba (2)

8065 1רֹבַע *rōḇa'1* (2)
fourth part (1)
quarter (1)

8066 2רֹבַע *rōḇa'2*
Variant; not used

8067 רִבֵּעַ *ribbēa'* (4)
fourth generation (4)

8068 רְבֻעַת *r'ḇu'aṯ*
Variant; not used

8069 רָבַץ *rāḇas* (30)
lie down (11)
lay down (2)
lie (2)
lying (2)
rest (2)
build (1)
crouching (1)
fall (1)
fallen down (1)
have lie down (1)
lies (1)
lies down (1)
lying down (1)
makes lie down (1)
rest flocks (1)
sitting (1)

8070 רֵבֶץ *rēḇes* (4)
resting place (2)
dwelling place (1)
where lay (1)

8071 רִבְקָה *riḇqāh* (30)
Rebekah (29)
Rebekah's (1)

8072 רַב־שָׁקֵה *raḇ-šāqēh* (16)
field commander (12)
commander (4)

8073 רֶגֶב *regeḇ* (2)
clods of earth (1)
soil (1)

8074 רָגַז *rāḡaz* (41)
tremble (7)
rage (4)
shook (4)
disturbed (3)
shakes (2)
trembled (2)
all astir (1)
anger (1)
come trembling (1)
convulsed (1)
enraged (1)
in anguish (1)
made tremble (1)
make tremble (1)
pounded (1)
provoke (1)
quake (1)
quarrel (1)
rages (1)
rouse (1)
shake (1)
shaken (1)
shudder (1)
trembles (1)
unrest (1)

8075 רֹגֶז *rōgez* (7)
turmoil (3)
excitement (1)
roar (1)
trouble (1)
wrath (1)

8076 רַגָּז *raggāz* (1)
anxious (1)

8077 רָגְזָה *rogzāh* (1)
shudder (1)

8078 רָגַל *rāḡal* (26)
spies (8)
spied out (4)
spy out (4)
spying (2)
explore (1)
explored (1)
scouts (1)
secret messengers (1)
slander (1)
slandered (1)
spies (1) +408
taught to walk (1)

8079 רֶגֶל *regel* (252)
feet (131)
foot (43)
legs (6)
feet (5) +4090
footstool (5) +2071
foot (4) +4090
times (4)
steps (3)
big toes (2)
fleet-footed (2) +928+7824
following (2) +928
footsteps (2)
my (2) +928+3276
accompanied (1) +995
after (1) +928
ankles (1)
attended by (1) +2143+4200
belonged to (1) +928
continued on journey (1) +5951
follow (1) +928
follow (1) +928+2143
followed (1) +928+6590
goes (1) +2118
hasty (1) +237+928
jointed (1) +4200+4946+5087
letting range free (1) +8938
offering body (1) +906+7316
pace (1)
relieve himself (1) +906+2257+6114
relieving himself (1) +906+2257+6114
service (1)
step (1)
stood (1) +3922+5163
stood (1) +5163
that[s] (1) +4200
those[s] (1) +4090
underfoot (1) +928
underfoot (1) +9393
what trampled (1) +5330
wherever (1) +4200
with (1) +928
womb (1) +1068
untranslated (12)

8080 רֹגֵל *rōḡēl*
Variant; not used

8081 רַגְלִי *ragliy* (12)
foot soldiers (6)
foot soldiers (3) +408
on foot (2)
soldiers (1) +408

8082 רֹגְלִים *rōḡ'liym* (2)
Rogelim (2)

8083 רָגַם *rāḡam* (16)
stone (5) +74+928+2021
stoned (4) +74
must stone (1) +8083
stone (1)
stone (1) +74
stoned (1) +74+928+2021
stoned to death (1) +74
stoning (1) +74+928+2021

8084 רֶגֶם *regem* (1)
Regem (1)

8085 רֶגֶם מֶלֶךְ *regem meleḵ* (1)
Regem-Melech (1)

8086 רִגְמָה *rigmāh* (1)
great throng (1)

8087 רָגַן *rāgan* (7)
gossip (4)
grumbled (2)
complain (1)

8088 1רָגַע *rāga'1* (7)
become (1)
churned up (1)
churns up (1)
in an instant (1)
instant (1)
moment (1)
stirs up (1)

8089 2רָגַע *rāga'2* (5)
bring rest (1)
cease (1)
find repose (1)
give rest (1)
repose (1)

8090 3רָגַע *rāga'3* (1)
broken (1)

8091 רָגֵעַ *rāgēa'* (1)
live quietly (1)

8092 רֶגַע *rega'* (22)
moment (9)
at once (2) +3869
in a moment (2)
at another time (1)
at any time (1)
continually (1) +4200
in a moment (1) +4017
in an instant (1)
little while (1) +5071
peace (1)
sudden (1)
suddenly (1) +3869

8093 רָגַשׁ *rāgaš* (1)
conspire (1)

8094 רֶגֶשׁ *regeš* (1)
throng (1)

8095 רִגְשָׁה *rigšāh* (1)
noisy crowd (1)

8096 רָדַד *rād̲ad̲* (2)
beaten (1)
subdues (1)

8097 1רָדָה *rād̲āh1* (23)
rule (11)
ruled (3)
officials (2)
directed (1)
leading (1)
rule over (1)
ruler (1)
subdued (1)
subdues (1)
trample the grapes (1)

8098 2רָדָה *rād̲āh2* (2)
scooped out (1)
taken (1)

8099 רַדַּי *radday* (1)
Raddai (1)

8100 רְדִיד *r^{e}d̲iyd̲* (2)
cloak (1)
shawls (1)

8101 רָדַם *rād̲am* (7)
fell into a deep sleep (2)
in a deep sleep (1)
lay fast asleep (1)
lie still (1)
sleep (1)
sleeps (1)

8102 רֹדָן *rōd̲ān* (3)
Rodanim (2)
Rhodes (1)

8103 רָדַף *rād̲ap̲* (144)
pursue (33)
pursued (27)
pursuing (11)
pursues (9)
chased (8)
pursuers (7)
chase (6)
persecute (5)
persecutors (4)
follow (3)
pursuit (3)
went in pursuit (3)
chases (2)
go (2)
in pursuit (2)
came by in pursuit (1)
devise (1)
driven (1)
driven away (1)
hound (1)
hounded (1)
hunts (1)
hurried (1)
past (1)
plague (1)
press on (1)
pursuer (1)
put to flight (1)
routs (1)
run after (1)
set out in pursuit (1)
they[s] (1) +2021
untranslated (2)

8104 רָהַב *rāhab̲* (4)
made bold (1)
overwhelm (1)
press plea (1)
rise up (1)

8105 רַהַב *rahab̲* (6)
Rahab (6)

8106 רֹהַב *rōhab̲*
Variant; not used

8107 רָהָב *rāhāb̲* (1)
proud (1)

8108 רָהְגָּה *rāhgāh* (1)
Rohgah (1)

8109 רָהָה *rāhāh*
Variant; not used

8110 1רַהַט *rahat1* (3)
troughs (2)
troughs (1) +9216

8111 2רַהַט *rahat2* (1)
tresses (1)

8112 רָהִיט *rāhiyt* (1)
rafters (1)

8113 רוּד *rûd̲* (4)
restless (1)
roam (1)
trouble (1)
unruly (1)

8114 רוֹדָנִים *rôd̲āniym*
Variant; not used

8115 רָוָה *rāwāh* (14)
drench (2)
satisfy (2)
drenched (1)
drink deep (1)
drunk its fill (1)
feast (1)
lavished on (1)
quenched its thirst (1)
refresh (1)
refreshes (1)
sated (1)
watering (1)

8116 רָוֶה *rāweh* (4)
well-watered (2)
drowned (1)
watered land (1)

8117 רוֹהֲגָה *rôh^{a}gāh* (1)
untranslated (1)

8118 רָוַח *rāwah* (3)
find relief (1)
relief come (1)
spacious (1)

8119 רֶוַח *rewah* (2)
relief (1)
space (1)

8120 רוּחַ *rûah* (379)
spirit (176)
wind (79)
breath (31)
winds (13)
mind (5)
heart (4)
side (4)
spirits (4)
blast (3)
sides (3)
anger (2)
courage (2)
feelings (2)
it[s] (2) +2021
overwhelmed (2) +928+2118+4202+6388
air (1)
breath (1) +5972
breeze (1)
breezes (1)
cool (1)
deep sleep (1) +9554
deeply troubled (1) +7997
discouragement (1) +7919
empty (1)
even-tempered (1) +7922
hostility (1)
I (1) +3276
inspired (1)
inspires (1)
jealous (1) +6296+6584+7863
liar (1) +3941
life (1)
life breath (1) +678
long-winded (1)
lose heart (1) +928+1327+7931
me (1) +3276
motives (1)
pant (1) +8634
patience (1) +800
pride (1) +1468
quick-tempered (1) +7920
rage (1)
resentment (1)
revived (1) +8740
self-control (1) +4200+5110
source of grief (1) +5289
strength (1)
temper (1)
tempest (1) +6185
tempest (1) +6194
trustworthy (1) +586
violent wind (1) +6194
violent winds (1) +6194
whirlwind (1)
willing (1) +5605
windstorm (1) +6194
wisdom (1) +2683
you (1) +3870
untranslated (4)

8121 רְוָחָה *r^{e}wāhāh* (2)
relief (2)

8122 רְוָיָה *r^{e}wāyāh* (2)
overflows (1)

place of abundance (1)

8123 1רוּם *rûm1* (194)
exalted (20)
exalt (16)
present (10)
high (9)
lift up (7)
raised (6)
haughty (5)
lifted high (5)
raise (5)
remove (5)
provided (4)
tall (4)
exalts (3)
lift (3)
raised up (3)
be exalted (2)
boldly (2) +928+3338
brought up (2)
lifted (2)
lifted up (2)
lifts (2)
lofty (2)
offer (2)
presenting (2)
proud (2)
rebelled (2) +3338
rose (2)
take (2)
as a special gift set aside (1)
be lifted up (1)
brandish (1)
build on high (1)
consider better (1) +4222
contributed (1)
displays (1)
donated (1)
exalt himself (1)
exult (1)
filled with pride (1) +4222
greater (1)
heights (1)
held up (1)
higher (1)
highest (1)
holds up (1)
honored (1)
is removed (1)
let triumph (1)
lift out (1)
lifts up (1)
lofty trees (1) +7757
loud (1)
made grow tall (1)
picked up (1)
present (1) +9556
present a portion (1)
presented (1)
proud (1) +4213
proud (1) +4222
raised and taken an oath (1)
rebuild (1)
rise (1)
rise up (1)
rises (1)
scream for help (1) +2256+7754+7924
screamed for help (1) +2256+7754+7924
set apart (1)
set high (1)
set up (1)
shout (1) +7754
shouted (1) +928+7754+9558
sing songs (1) +928+4200+7754+9048
sins defiantly (1) +928+3338+6913
sound (1) +7754
stop (1)
take out (1)
take up (1)
taller (1)
took away (1)
took up (1)
towering (1)
triumph (1)
triumphed (1)
turn (1)
upraised (1)
very top (1)
was presented (1) +9556
untranslated (4)

8124 2רוּם *rûm2* (6)
haughty (2)
pride (2)
haughtiness (1)
high (1)

8125 רוֹם *rôm* (1)
high (1)

8126 רוּמָה *rûmāh* (1)
Rumah (1)

8127 רוֹמָה *rômāh* (1)
proudly (1)

8128 רוֹמָם *rômām* (2)
praise (2)

8129 רוֹמֵמֻת *rômēmuṯ* (1)
rise up (1)

8130 רוּן *rûn* (1)
wakes from stupor (1)

8131 רוּעַ *rûaʿ* (45)
shout (8)
shout aloud (4)
shout for joy (4)
shouted (3)
gave a shout (2) +9558
shout in triumph (2)
shouting (2)
cry aloud (1) +8275
cry out (1)
crying out (1)
extol (1)
give a shout (1) +9558
give a war cry (1)
made noise (1) +9558
raise the battle cry (1)
raise the war cry (1)
raised a shout (1) +9558
raised the battle cry (1)
shout with joy (1)
shouted for joy (1)
shouts (1)
signal (1)
sound (1)
sound a blast (1)
sound alarm (1)
sound of battle cry (1)
triumph (1)

8132 רוּץ *rûṣ* (103)
run (20)
ran (19)
guards (10)
couriers (6)
running (5)
hurried (4)
guard (3)
hurry (3)
rush (3)
advance (2)
chase (2)
guardroom (2) +9288
another[s] (1)
attack (1)
busy (1)
charge (1)
charged (1)
charging (1)
courier (1)
dart about (1)
gallop along (1)
go (1)
go quickly (1)
hasten (1)
quickly brought (1)
raced (1)
ran off (1)
runner (1)
runs (1)
rushed forward (1)
rushes (1)
served quickly (1)
submit (1) +3338
untranslated (3)

8133 רוּשׁ *rûš* (23)
poor (19)
oppressed (1)
poverty (1)
pretends to be poor (1)
weak (1)

8134 רוּת *rûṯ* (12)
Ruth (12)

8135 רָזָה *rāzāh* (2)
destroys (1)
waste away (1)

8136 רָזֶה *rāzeh* (2)
lean (1)
poor (1)

8137 1רָזוֹן *rāzôn1* (3)
wasting disease (2)
short (1)

8138 2רָזוֹן *rāzôn2* (1)
prince (1)

8139 רְזוֹן *rᵉzôn* (1)
Rezon (1)

8140 רָזִי *rāziy* (2)
waste away (2)

8141 רָזַם *rāzam* (1)
flash (1)

8142 רָזַן *rāzan* (6)
rulers (5)
princes (1)

8143 רָחַב *rāhaḇ* (25)
enlarges (3)
broaden (2)
enlarge (2)
boasts (1)
broad (1)
enlarged (1)
extend (1)
gape (1) +7023
give relief (1)
given room (1)
greedy (1)
make bald (1) +7947
multiplied (1)
open wide (1)
opened wide (1)
opens the way (1)
set free (1)
sneer (1) +7023
swell with joy (1)
wide (1)
wider (1)

8144 רַחַב *rahaḇ* (2)
spacious place (1)
vast expanses (1)

8145 רֹחַב *rōhaḇ* (103)
wide (69)
width (11)
breadth (3)
thick (3)
deep (2)
distance (2)
broad (1)
from front to back (1)
length (1)

projected (1)
span (1)
square (1) +802+2256
widened (1)
untranslated (6)

8146 1רָחָב *rāḥāḇ1* (21)
spacious (4) +3338
broad (2)
proud (2)
spacious (2)
boundless (1) +4394
broad (1) +3338
freedom (1)
gaping (1)
greedy man (1) +5883
large (1)
large (1) +3338
plenty of room (1) +3338
spread out (1)
thick (1)
wider (1)

8147 2רָחָב *rāḥāḇ2* (5)
Rahab (5)

8148 1רְחֹב *r[e]ḥōḇ1* (43)
streets (15)
square (10)
public square (6)
public squares (5)
squares (4)
one[S] (1)
open square (1)
there[S] (1) +928+2023

8149 2רְחֹב *r[e]ḥōḇ2* (7)
Rehob (7)

8150 3רְחֹב *r[e]ḥōḇ3* (3)
Rehob (3)

8151 רְחֹבוֹת *r[e]ḥōḇôṯ* (3)
Rehoboth (3)

8152 רְחַבְיָה *r[e]ḥaḇyāh* (2)
Rehabiah (2)

8153 רְחַבְיָהוּ *r[e]ḥaḇyāhû* (3)
Rehabiah (2)
his[S] (1)

8154 רְחַבְעָם *r[e]ḥaḇʿām* (50)
Rehoboam (43)
he[S] (3)
Rehoboam's (3)
untranslated (1)

8155 רְחֹבֹת עִיר *r[e]ḥōḇōṯ ʿiyr* (1)
Rehoboth Ir (1)

8156 רְחוּם *r[e]ḥûm* (4)
Rehum (4)

8157 רַחוּם *raḥûm* (13)
compassionate (10)
merciful (3)

8158 רָחוֹק *rāḥôq* (85)
far (12)
distant (11)
afar (10)
distance (10)
far away (9)
far away (5) +4946
distant (2) +4946
distant place (2)
future (2) +4946
long ago (2) +4200+4946
long ago (2) +4946
long way (2)
at a distance (1) +4394
away (1)
beyond (1)
beyond reach (1)
far and wide (1) +4200+4946+6330
far and wide (1) +6330
far away (1) +4200+4946+6330
far off (1)
far off (1) +928
far-off (1)
farthest (1)
long (1) +4946
long way (1) +4394
past (1)
some distance away (1) +4946
widely (1)

8159 רָחִיט *rāḥiyṭ* (1)
untranslated (1)

8160 רֵחַיִם *rēḥayim* (5)
millstones (2)
hand mill (1)
handmill (1)
pair of millstones (1)

8161 1רָחֵל *rāḥēl1* (4)
sheep (3)
ewes (1)

8162 2רָחֵל *rāḥēl2* (47)
Rachel (40)
Rachel's (5)
her[S] (1)
she[S] (1)

8163 רָחַם *rāḥam* (47)
have compassion (15)
compassion (4)
has compassion (4)
show love (4)
mercy (3)
show compassion (3)
have mercy (2)
loved (2)
show mercy (2)
find compassion (1)
finds mercy (1)
full of compassion (1)
had compassion (1)
have great compassion (1) +8163
love (1)
pity (1)

8164 רָחָם *rāḥām* (1)
osprey (1)

8165 1רַחַם *raḥam1* (1)
Raham (1)

8166 2רַחַם *raḥam2*
Variant; not used

8167 רֶחֶם *reḥem* (31)
womb (20)
birth (4)
born (1) +3655+4946
first male offspring (1) +1147+7081
firstborn (1) +7081
girl (1)
mothers (1)
woman (1)
wombs (1)

8168 רָחָמָה *rāḥāmāh* (1)
osprey (1)

8169 רַחֲמָה *raḥ[a]māh* (1)
two[S] (1)

8170 רֻחָמָה *ruḥāmāh*
Variant; not used

8171 רַחֲמִים *raḥ[a]miym* (40)
compassion (18)
mercy (11)
compassions (1)
deeply moved (1) +4023
favor (1)
great mercy (1)
kindest acts (1)
merciful (1)
pitied (1)
pity (1)
sympathy (1)
untranslated (2)

8172 רַחֲמָנִי *raḥ[a]māniy* (1)
compassionate (1)

8173 1רָחַף *rāḥap̄1* (3)
hovering (1)
hovers (1)
tremble (1)

8174 2רָחַף *rāḥap̄2*
Variant; not used

8175 רָחַץ *rāḥaṣ* (73)
bathe (25)
wash (23)
washed (10)
bathed (4)
washing (4)
are cleansed (1)
bathing (1)
drenched (1)
plunge (1)
wash away (1)
washed myself (1)
were washed (1)

8176 רַחַץ *raḥaṣ* (2)
washbasin (2) +6105

8177 רַחְצָה *raḥṣāh* (2)
washing (2)

8178 רָחַק *rāḥaq* (58)
far (12)
far away (7)
drive far (3)
keep far (3)
put away (2)
remove far (2)
sent far away (2)
stand aloof (2)
taken (2)
alienated (1)
avoid (1)
away (1)
distance away (1)
extended (1)
extending (1)
far off (1)
far removed (1)
go far (1)
gone some distance (1)
have nothing to do (1)
is severed (1)
keep distance (1)
must very far (1) +8178
no near (1)
refrain (1)
send far (1)
some distance away (1) +4946
stays far (1)
strayed far (1)
went far (1)
withdraw far (1)

8179 רָחֵק *rāḥēq* (1)
far (1)

8180 רָחַשׁ *rāḥaš* (1)
stirred (1)

8181 רַחַת *raḥaṯ* (1)
fork (1)

8182 רָטַב *rāṭaḇ* (1)
drenched (1)

8183 רָטֹב *rāṭōḇ* (1)
well-watered plant (1)

8184 רָטָה *rāṭāh*
Variant; not used

8185 רֶטֶט *reṭeṭ* (1)
panic (1)

8186 רֻטֲפַשׁ *ruṭ[a]p̄aš* (1)
is renewed (1)

8187 רָטַשׁ *rātaš* (6)
be dashed to pieces (1)
be dashed to the ground (1)
dash to the ground (1)
strike down (1)
were dashed to pieces (1)
were dashed to the ground (1)

8188 רִי *riy* (1)
moisture (1)

8189 1רִיב *riyḇ1* (71)
quarreled (7)
bring charges (6)
contend (4)
defend (4)
accuse (3)
rebuked (3)
complain (2)
quarrel (2)
rebuke (2)
take up (2)
accused (1)
argue (1)
argue the case (1)
bring a case (1)
bring a charge (1)
charges (1)
contended (1)
contends (1)
criticized (1)
defender (1)
defends (1)
defends cause (1)
dispute (1)
fights (1)
in court (1)
judgment (1)
oppose (1)
oppose (1) +6643
plead (1)
plead case (1)
plead cause (1)
plead the case (1)
pleads (1)
quarrel (1) +8189
quarrels (1)
took to task (1)
took up (1)
upheld (1)
uphold (1)
uphold cause (1)
vigorously defend (1) +8189
untranslated (3)

8190 2רִיב *riyḇ2* (60)
case (11)
cause (9)
strife (7)
dispute (4)
attacks (2)
charge (2)
complaint (2)
disputes (2)
lawsuit (2)
quarrel (2)
quarreling (2)
accusation (1)
accuser (1) +408
accusing (1)
cases of dispute (1)
charges (1)
contend (1)
court (1)
distress (1)
grievance (1)
justice (1)
lawsuits (1)
oppose (1)
strives (1)
struggle (1)
taunts (1)

8191 רִיבָה *riyḇāh* (2)
cases (1) +1821
plea (1)

8192 רִיבַי *riyḇay* (2)
Ribai (2)

8193 רִיחַ *riyah* (11)
smell (2)
accept (1)
catches the scent (1)
caught the smell (1) +8194
comes close (1)
delight (1)
enjoy fragrance (1)
smelled (1)
stand (1)
take delight (1)

8194 רֵיחַ *rēyah* (58)
aroma (40)
fragrance (8)
fragrant incense (4) +5767
smell (2)
caught the smell (1) +8193
made stench (1) +944
scent (1)
that[s] (1)

8195 רִיפוֹת *riyp̱ôṯ* (2)
grain (2)

8196 רִיפַת *riyp̱aṯ* (2)
Riphath (2)

8197 1רִיק *riyq1* (19)
draw (3)
drawn (3)
emptying (2)
pour out (2)
poured out (2)
brandish (1)
called out (1)
draw out (1)
empty (1)
leaves empty (1)
pour (1)
poured (1)

8198 2רִיק *riyq2* (12)
in vain (4) +4200
for nothing (2) +928+1896
in vain (2)
delusions (1)
empty (1)
no purpose (1)
utterly useless (1) +2039+2256

8199 רֵיק *rēyq* (14)
empty (4)
fantasies (2)
worthless (2)
adventurers (1)
emptied (1)
hunger (1) +5883
idle (1)
reckless (1)
vulgar (1)

8200 רֵיקָם *rēyqām* (16)
empty-handed (9)
empty (3)
unfilled (1)
unsatisfied (1)
without cause (1)
without excuse (1)

8201 1רִיר *riyr1* (1)
flowing (1)

8202 2רִיר *riyr2* (2)
saliva (1)
white (1)

8203 רֵישׁ *rēyš* (7)
poverty (7)

8204 רֹךְ *rōḵ* (1)
gentle (1)

8205 רַךְ *raḵ* (18)
gentle (5)
tender (5)
inexperienced (2)
responsive (2)
weak (2)
fainthearted (1) +4222
indecisive (1) +4222

8206 רָכַב *rāḵaḇ* (78)
riding (10)
mounted (6)
rider (6)
put (4)
rode (4)
horseman (3) +6061
ride (3)
riders (3)
rides (3)
drive (2)
mounted (2) +6061
ridden (2)
ride on (2)
rode off (2)
set (2)
came riding (1)
cause to ride (1)
driver (1)
drivers (1)
got into chariot (1)
got on (1)
had ride (1)
had ride along (1)
horsemen (1) +6061
in a chariot (1)
lead (1)
led on horseback (1)
let ride (1)
made ride (1)
mount (1)
moved (1)
ride forth (1)
ride off (1)
rides on (1)
riding in chariots (1)
slow down (1) +4200+6806
take (1)
taken (1)
took by chariot (1)

8207 רֶכֶב *reḵeḇ* (121)
chariots (78)
chariot (26)
charioteers (3)
riders (3)
chariot horses (2)
upper (2)
charioteers (1) +132
chariots and charioteers (1)
upper one (1)
untranslated (4)

8208 רַכָּב *rakkāḇ* (3)
chariot driver (2)
horseman (1)

8209 רֵכָב *rēḵāḇ* (13)
Recab (13)

8210 רִכְבָה *riḵḇāh* (1)
saddle (1)

8211 רֵכָבִי *rēḵāḇiy* (4)
Recabite (2)
Recabites (2)

8212 רֵכָה *rēḵāh* (1)
Recah (1)

8213 רְכוּב *rᵉḵûḇ* (1)
chariot (1)

8214 רְכוּשׁ *rᵉḵûš* (28)
possessions (11)

goods (7)
property (3)
wealth (2)
equipment (1)
equipped (1)
everything (1) +3972
flocks (1)
riches (1)

8215 רָכִיל *rāḵiyl* (6)
gossip (2) +2143
slander (1)
slanderer (1) +2143
slanderous (1)
spreading slander (1)

8216 רָכַךְ *rāḵaḵ* (6)
lose (2)
fainthearted (1) +4222
made faint (1)
soothed (1)
soothing (1)

8217 רָכַל *rāḵal* (17)
merchants (6)
traded (6)
merchant (2)
traders (2)
traded with (1)

8218 רָכָל *rāḵāl* (1)
Racal (1)

8219 רְכֻלָּה *rᵉḵullāh* (4)
trade (2)
merchandise (1)
trading (1)

8220 רָכַס *rāḵas* (2)
tied (2)

8221 רֶכֶס *reḵes* (1)
rugged places (1)

8222 רֹכֶס *rōḵes* (1)
intrigues (1)

8223 רָכַשׁ *rāḵaš* (5)
accumulated (2)
acquired (2)
untranslated (1)

8224 רֶכֶשׁ *reḵeš* (4)
chariot horses (1)
fast horses (1)
horses (1)
team (1)

8225 1רָם *rām1*
Variant; not used

8226 2רָם *rām2* (7)
ram (7)

8227 1רָמָה *rāmāh1* (4)
hurled (2)
archers (1) +8008
armed (1) +5976

8228 2רָמָה *rāmāh2* (8)
betrayed (2)
deceive (2)
deceived (2)
betray (1)
deceives (1)

8229 3רָמָה *rāmāh3* (5)
lofty shrines (3)
hill (1)
lofty shrine (1)

8230 4רָמָה *rāmāh4* (36)
Ramah (33)
Ramoth (2)
untranslated (1)

8231 רִמָּה *rimmāh* (7)
maggots (2)
worm (2)
worms (2)
maggot (1)

8232 1רִמּוֹן *rimmôn1* (32)
pomegranates (24)
pomegranate (4)
alternate[S] (1) +2256+2298+7194
alternated[S] (1) +2256+7194
pomegranate tree (1)
untranslated (1)

8233 2רִמּוֹן *rimmôn2* (3)
Rimmon (3)

8234 3רִמּוֹן *rimmôn3* (9)
Rimmon (8)
where[S] (1) +928+6152

8235 4רִמּוֹן *rimmôn4* (3)
Rimmon (2)
there[S] (1) +1074

8236 רִמּוֹן פֶּרֶץ *rimmôn peres* (2)
Rimmon Perez (2)

8237 רִמּוֹנוֹ *rimmônô* (1)
Rimmono (1)

8238 רָמוֹת *rāmôṯ* (1)
untranslated (1)

8239 רָמוּת *rāmûṯ* (1)
remains (1)

8240 רָמוֹת גִּלְעָד *rāmôṯ gil'āḏ* (20)
Ramoth Gilead (20)

8241 רָמוֹת־נֶגֶב *rāmôṯ-negeḇ* (1)
Ramoth Negev (1)

8242 רֹמַח *rōmah* (15)
spears (10)
spear (5)

8243 רַמְיָה *ramyāh* (1)
Ramiah (1)

8244 1רְמִיָּה *rᵉmiyyāh1* (7)
faulty (2)
lazy (2)
lax (1)
laziness (1)
shiftless (1)

8245 2רְמִיָּה *rᵉmiyyāh2* (8)
deceit (4)
deceitful (2)
deceitfully (2)

8246 רַמִּים *rammiym*
Variant; not used

8247 רַמָּכָה *rammāḵāh* (1)
especially bred (1) +1201+2021

8248 רְמַלְיָהוּ *rᵉmalyāhû* (13)
Remaliah (11)
Remaliah's (2)

8249 1רָמַם *rāmam1* (1)
full (1)

8250 2רָמַם *rāmam2* (5)
rose (2)
exalted (1)
get away (1)
rose upward (1)

8251 רוֹמַמְתִּי עֶזֶר *rōmamtiy 'ezer* (2)
Romamti-Ezer (2)

8252 רָמַס *rāmas* (19)
trample (4)
trampled (4)
trampled underfoot (3)
aggressor (1)
be trampled (1)
mauls (1)
trample down (1)
trampling (1)
tread (1)
treading (1)
trod down (1)

8253 רָמַשׂ *rāmaś* (17)
moves (5)
move (4)
moves along (2)
creature that moves (1)
creatures that move (1)
moved (1)
moves about (1)
moving (1)
prowl (1)

8254 רֶמֶשׂ *remeś* (17)
creatures that move (5)
creature (2)
creatures (2)
crawling things (1)
creature that moves (1)
creatures that move along the ground (1)
moves (1)
reptiles (1)
sea creatures (1)
small creatures (1)
teeming creatures (1)

8255 רֶמֶת *remeṯ* (1)
Remeth (1)

8256 רָמַת הַמִּצְפֶּה *rāmaṯ hammispeh* (1)
Ramath Mizpah (1)

8257 רָמַת לְחִי *rāmaṯ lᵉhiy* (1)
Ramath Lehi (1)

8258 רָמָתִי *rāmāṯiy* (1)
Ramathite (1)

8259 רָמָתַיִם *rāmāṯayim* (1)
Ramathaim (1)

8260 רֹן *rōn* (1)
songs (1)

8261 רָנָה *rānāh* (1)
rattles (1)

8262 1רִנָּה *rinnāh1* (33)
cry (10)
singing (4)
song (4)
songs of joy (4)
shouts of joy (3)
plea (2)
shouts of joy (2) +7754
joy (1)
pride (1)
rejoicing (1)
sing (1)

8263 2רִנָּה *rinnāh2* (1)
Rinnah (1)

8264 רָנַן *rānan* (53)
sing for joy (15)
shout for joy (11)
sing (9)
cry out (2)
rejoice (2)
call forth songs of joy (1)
calls aloud (1)
cries aloud (1)
ever sing for joy (1) +8264
joyfully sing (1)
jubilant song (1)
made sing (1)
sang (1)
shout (1)
shouted for joy (1)
sing joyfully (1)
sings (1)
songs of joy (1)

8265 רְנָנָה *rᵉnānāh* (4)
joyful songs (1)
mirth (1)
shout of joy (1)
singing (1)

8266 רְנָנִים *rᵉnāniym* (1)
ostrich (1)

8267 רִסָּה *rissāh* (2)
Rissah (2)

8268 1רָסִיס *rāsiys1* (1)
dampness (1)

8269 2רָסִיס *rāsiys2* (1)
pieces (1)

8270 1רֶסֶן *resen1* (4)
bit (1)
bridle (1) +4101
bridle (1) +6344
restraint (1)

8271 2רֶסֶן *resen2* (1)
Resen (1)

8272 רָסַס *rāsas* (1)
moisten (1)

8273 רַע *ra‘* (351)
evil (190)
wicked (24)
bad (23)
wrong (10)
harm (8)
trouble (8)
disaster (5)
wild (4)
poor (3)
ugly (3)
deadly (2)
ferocious (2)
grievous (2)
harm (2) +6913
heavy (2)
malice (2)
no good (2)
painful (2)
ruin (2)
sad (2)
sin (2)
terrible (2)
ugly (2) +5260
bitter (1)
brings to ruin (1) +2021+4200+6156
crimes (1)
cruel (1)
destroying (1)
destruction (1)
difficult (1)
disaster (1) +7004
displease (1) +928+6524
displeasing (1) +928+6524
distressing (1)
dreadful (1)
flaw (1) +1821
great (1)
hardships (1)
harm (1) +1821
harmful (1)
horrible (1)
hurt (1)
immoral (1)
impure (1)
look sad (1)
mean (1)
miserable (1)
misery (1)
misfortune (1) +6721
not want (1) +928+6524
not[S] (1)
one way[S] (1)
savage (1)
serious (1)
severe (1)
stern (1)
stingy (1) +6524
stingy man (1) +6524
surely suffer (1) +8317
troubled (1) +928+6524
ugly (1) +9307
undesirable (1)
unfavorable (1)
unjust (1)
vile (1)
violence (1)
worse (1)
worst (1)
wretched (1)
untranslated (1)

8274 2רַע *ra‘2*
Variant; not used

8275 1רֵעַ *rēa‘1* (3)
cry aloud (1) +8131
shouting (1)
thunder (1)

8276 2רֵעַ *rēa‘2* (188)
neighbor (52)
other[S] (29)
friend (26)
neighbor's (18)
friends (15)
another[S] (12)
neighbors (7)
companions (3)
countrymen (3)
another man's (2)
companion (2)
fellow Israelite (2)
another's[S] (1)
associates (1)
closest friend (1) +889+3869+3870+5883
each other[S] (1)
fellow (1)
friendship (1)
his[S] (1) +3870
husband (1)
lovers (1)
neighbors' (1)
one who is close (1)
opponent (1)
opponent's (1)
the parties (1) +408+2084+2256
together (1) +408+907+2084
untranslated (2)

8277 3רֵעַ *rēa‘3* (2)
thoughts (2)

8278 רֹעַ *rōa‘* (19)
evil (9)
bad (4)
wicked (2)
sad (1)
sadness (1)
sinful (1)
ugly (1)

8279 1רָעֵב *rā‘ēḇ1* (13)
hungry (6)
causing to hunger (1)
famished (1)
feel the famine (1)
goes hungry (1)
hunger (1)
let go hungry (1)
starving (1)

8280 רָעָב *rā‘āḇ* (101)
famine (91)
hunger (6)
starvation (2)
starve (2)

8281 2רָעֵב *rā‘ēḇ2* (20)
hungry (17)
hungry (2) +5883
starving (1)

8282 רְעָבוֹן *r‘āḇôn* (3)
starving (2)
famine (1)

8283 רָעַד *rā‘aḏ* (3)
greatly distressed (1)
trembles (1)
trembling (1)

8284 רַעַד *ra‘aḏ* (2)
trembling (2)

8285 רְעָדָה *r‘āḏāh* (4)
trembling (4)

8286 1רָעָה *rā‘āh1* (172)
shepherd (42)
shepherds (37)
tend (8)
feed (7)
graze (7)
tending (6)
pasture (5)
feed on (4)
feeds on (3)
grazing (3)
herdsmen (3)
shepherds (3) +7366
take care of (3)
browse (2)
browses (2)
eat (2)
find pasture (2)
grazed (2)
herdsmen (2) +5238
pastured (2)
rule (2)
shepherd's (2)
cared for (1)
devour (1)
drive away (1)
enjoy pasture (1)
graze flock (1)
grazing flocks (1)
grazing the flocks (1)
herding (1)
keeping (1)
kept (1)
lead (1)
leaders (1)
nourish (1)
prey on (1)
shaved (1)
shepherd flock (1)
shepherded (1)
shepherdess (1)
tends (1)
untranslated (4)

8287 2רָעָה *rā‘āh2* (5)
companion (3)
attended at wedding (1)
make friends (1)

8288 3רָעָה *rā‘āh3* (318)
disaster (79)
evil (48)
wickedness (32)
harm (26)
calamity (18)
trouble (17)
ruin (8)
wrong (8)
wicked (6)
calamities (4)
disasters (4)
troubles (4)
wrongdoing (4)
bad (3)
distress (3)
misfortune (3)
badly (2)
crimes (2)
danger (2)
destruction (2)
evil deeds (2)
evil thing (2)
harm (2) +6913
misery (2)
another[S] (1)

awful crime (1)
awful thing (1)
crime (1) +5126
cruelty (1)
deeds of evildoers (1)
defeat (1)
discomfort (1)
displeased (1) +8317
downfall (1)
evil intent (1)
evildoer (1) +6913
fate (1)
fault (1)
harming (1)
it[s] (1) +2021
malice (1)
offense (1)
peril (1)
plotting (1) +2021+3086
punishment (1)
sin (1)
sins (1)
something desperate (1)
very disturbed (1) +8317
wicked thing (1)
wickedness is great (1) +8288
worst (1)
wrongs (1)
untranslated (5)

8289 4רָעָה *rā‘āh4*
Variant; not used

8290 5רָעָה *rā‘āh5*
Variant; not used

8291 רֵעֶה *rē‘eh* (4)
friend (2)
personal adviser (1)
untranslated (1)

8292 רֵעָה *rē‘āh* (4)
companions (1)
friends (1)
girls (1)
untranslated (1)

8293 רְעוּ *r^e‘û* (5)
Reu (5)

8294 רְעוּאֵל *r^e‘û’ēl* (10)
Reuel (10)

8295 1רְעוּת *r^e‘ûṯ1* (6)
mate (2)
another's[s] (1)
another[s] (1)
someone else (1)
untranslated (1)

8296 2רְעוּת *r^e‘ûṯ2* (7)
chasing after (7)

8297 רְעִי *r^e‘iy* (1)
pasture-fed (1)

8298 רֵעִי *rē‘iy* (1)
Rei (1)

8299 רַעְיָה *ra‘yāh* (9)
darling (9)

8300 רֵעְיָה *rē‘yāh*
Variant; not used

8301 רַעְיוֹן *ra‘yôn* (3)
chasing after (2)
anxious striving (1) +4213

8302 רָעַל *rā‘al* (1)
brandished (1)

8303 רַעַל *ra‘al* (1)
reeling (1)

8304 רְעָלָה *r^e‘ālāh* (1)
veils (1)

8305 רְעֵלָיָה *r^e‘ēlāyāh* (1)
Reelaiah (1)

8306 1רָעַם *rā‘am1* (11)
resound (3)
thundered (3)
thunders (3)
thunder (2)

8307 2רָעַם *rā‘am2* (2)
distorted with fear (1)
irritate (1)

8308 רַעַם *ra‘am* (6)
thunder (4)
shout (1)
thundercloud (1) +6260

8309 רַעְמָא *ra‘mā’* (2)
Raamah (2)

8310 1רַעְמָה *ra‘māh1* (1)
flowing mane (1)

8311 2רַעְמָה *ra‘māh2* (3)
Raamah (3)

8312 3רַעְמָה *ra‘māh3*
Variant; not used

8313 רַעַמְיָה *ra‘amyāh* (1)
Raamiah (1)

8314 רַעְמְסֵס *ra‘m^{e}sēs* (5)
Rameses (5)

8315 רָעַן *rā‘an* (1)
flourish (1)

8316 רַעֲנָן *ra‘^{a}nān* (19)
spreading (11)
green (3)
fine (1)
flourishing (1)
green tree (1)
thriving (1)
verdant (1)

8317 1רָעַע *rā‘a‘1* (95)
evil (10)
wicked (10)
harm (6)
displeased (5) +928+6524
evildoers (5)
bring disaster (4)
bad (3)
brought trouble (3)
do harm (3)
distressed (2) +928+6524
doing evil (2)
mistreated (2)
acted wickedly (1)
begrudge (1) +6524
bring trouble (1)
brought misfortune (1)
brought to grief (1)
brought tragedy (1)
crushed (1)
destruction brought (1)
did evil (1)
disapprove (1) +928+6524
displeased (1)
displeased (1) +8288
do evil (1)
do wicked thing (1)
doing wrong (1)
done evil (1)
done wrong (1) +8317
downhearted (1) +4222
galled (1) +928+6524
grudging (1)
harming (1)
have no compassion (1) +6524
hurts (1)
leads to evil (1)
look sad (1)
not please (1) +928+6524
persist in doing evil (1) +8317
show ill will (1) +6524
sinned (1)
suffers harm (1)
surely suffer (1) +8273
treat worse (1)
trouble came (1)
upset (1) +928+6524
very disturbed (1) +8288
vile (1)
wickedly (1)
wronged (1)

8318 2רָעַע *rā‘a‘2* (6)
break (1)
broken (1)
come to ruin (1)
is broken up (1) +8318
shatters (1)

8319 רָעַף *rā‘ap̱* (5)
overflow (2)
let drop (1)
rain down (1)
showers fall (1)

8320 רָעַץ *rā‘aṣ* (2)
shattered (2)

8321 1רָעַשׁ *rā‘aš1* (30)
shake (6)
tremble (6)
trembles (4)
quake (3)
quaked (3)
made tremble (2)
shook (2)
make leap (1)
quaking (1)
shaken (1)
sway (1)

8322 2רָעַשׁ *rā‘aš2*
Variant; not used

8323 רַעַשׁ *ra‘aš* (17)
earthquake (7)
rumbling (2)
battle (1)
clatter (1) +7754
commotion (1)
frenzied (1)
noise (1)
rattling (1)
rattling sound (1)
tremble (1)

8324 1רָפָא *rāp̱ā’1* (69)
heal (21)
healed (10)
heals (5)
be healed (4)
physicians (4)
recover (3)
be cured (2)
cure (2)
dress (2)
fresh (2)
are healed (1)
be repaired (1)
been healed (1)
gone (1)
incurable (1) +4412
makes fresh (1)
mend (1)
physician (1)
repaired (1)
see that is completely healed (1) +8324
wholesome (1)
untranslated (2)

8325 2רָפָא *rāp̱ā’2* (3)
Rapha (3)

8326 רִפְאוּת *rip̱’ûṯ* (1)
health (1)

8327 1רְפָאִים *r^{e}p̱ā’iym1* (8)
dead (5)

departed spirits (1)
spirits of the dead (1)
spirits of the departed (1)

8328 2רְפָאִים *rᵉpā'iym2* (11)
Rephaites (10)
who[s] (1)

8329 3רְפָאִים *rᵉpā'iym3* (8)
Rephaim (8)

8330 רְפָאֵל *rᵉpā'ēl* (1)
Rephael (1)

8331 רָפַד *rāp̱aḏ* (3)
leaving a trail (1)
refresh (1)
spread out (1)

8332 1רָפָה *rāp̱āh1* (46)
leave (4)
go limp (3)
hang limp (3)
lazy (3)
let alone (3)
let go (3)
abandon (2)
give (2)
lowered (2)
withdraw (2)
abandon (1) +3338+4946
almost (1)
disarms (1) +4653
discourage (1) +3338
discouraging (1) +3338
fail (1)
falter (1)
feeble (1)
give up (1) +3338
leave alone (1)
lost courage (1) +3338
refrain (1)
sinks down (1)
slack (1)
still (1)
stop (1)
subsided (1)
wait (1)
weak (1)

8333 רָפֶה *rāp̱eh* (4)
feeble (2)
weak (1)
weak (1) +3338

8334 2רָפָה *rāp̱āh2* (1)
Raphah (1)

8335 3רָפָה *rāp̱āh3* (4)
Rapha (4)

8336 רָפוּא *rāp̱û'* (1)
Raphu (1)

8337 רְפוּאָה *rᵉp̱û'āh* (3)
healing (1) +5989
remedies (1)
remedy (1)

8338 רֶפַח *rep̱ah* (1)
Rephah (1)

8339 רְפִידָה *rᵉp̱iyḏāh* (1)
base (1)

8340 רְפִידִים *rᵉp̱iyḏiym* (5)
Rephidim (5)

8341 רְפָיָה *rᵉp̱āyāh* (5)
Rephaiah (5)

8342 רִפָּיוֹן *rippāyôn* (1)
hang limp (1)

8343 רַפְסֹדוֹת *rap̱sōḏôṯ* (1)
rafts (1)

8344 רָפַף *rāp̱ap̱* (1)
quake (1)

8345 רָפַק *rāp̱aq* (1)
leaning (1)

8346 רָפַשׂ *rāp̱aś* (5)
humble yourself (1)
humbled (1)
muddied (1)
muddy (1)
muddying (1)

8347 רֶפֶשׁ *rep̱eš* (1)
mire (1)

8348 רֶפֶת *rep̱eṯ* (1)
stalls (1)

8349 רַץ *raṣ* (1)
bars (1)

8350 רָץ *rāṣ*
Variant; not used

8351 1רָצָא *rāṣā'1* (1)
sped forth (1)

8352 2רָצָא *rāṣā'2*
Variant; not used

8353 רָצַד *rāṣaḏ* (1)
gaze in envy (1)

8354 1רָצָה *rāṣāh1* (52)
accept (10)
be accepted (5)
pleased with (4)
enjoy (3)
pleased (3)
delights in (2)
please (2)
approve (1)
be acceptable (1)
dear to (1)
delight (1)
devotion (1)
enjoyed (1)
favored (1)
favors (1)
finds favor with (1)
held in high esteem (1)
in delight (1)
join (1)
loved (1)
pleasing (1)
put in (1)
received favorably (1)
regain favor (1)
show favor (1)
showed favor (1)
take delight in (1)
take pleasure (1)
take pleasure in (1)
takes delight (1)

8355 2רָצָה *rāṣāh2* (4)
pay for (2)
been paid for (1)
make amends (1)

8356 רָצוֹן *rāṣôn* (56)
favor (15)
accepted (7)
acceptable (5)
pleased (4)
pleases (4)
will (4)
delights (3)
desires (2)
goodwill (2)
pleasure (2)
delight (1)
eagerly (1) +928+3972
favored (1)
fitting (1)
good pleasure (1)
please (1)
pleasing (1)
wished (1)

8357 רָצַח *rāṣah* (47)
murderer (12)
accused of murder (7)
murder (6)
accused (3)
he[s] (2) +2021
killed (2)
murdered (2)
anyone[s] (1)
be murdered (1)
him[s] (1) +2021
kill (1)
killed (1) +5782
killed a person (1)
kills a man (1)
kills another (1)
murderer (1) +1201
murderers (1)
murders (1) +5883
put to death (1)
throw down (1)

8358 רֶצַח *reṣah* (2)
mortal agony (1)
slaughter (1)

8359 רִצְיָא *riṣyā'* (1)
Rizia (1)

8360 רְצִין *rᵉṣiyn* (11)
Rezin (10)
Rezin's (1)

8361 רָצַע *rāṣa'* (1)
pierce (1)

8362 רָצַף *rāṣap̱* (1)
inlaid (1)

8363 1רֶצֶף *reṣep̱1* (1)
baked over hot coals (1)

8364 2רֶצֶף *reṣep̱2* (2)
Rezeph (2)

8365 1רִצְפָּה *riṣpāh1* (1)
live coal (1)

8366 2רִצְפָּה *riṣpāh2* (4)
Rizpah (4)

8367 רִצְפָּה *riṣp̱āh* (7)
pavement (5)
it[s] (1) +2021
mosaic pavement (1)

8368 רָצַץ *rāṣaṣ* (20)
oppressed (4)
splintered (3)
broken (2)
crushed (2)
bruised (1)
brutally oppressed (1)
cracked (1)
cruel (1)
crush (1)
discouraged (1)
jostled each other (1)
smashed to pieces (1)
trampled (1)

8369 1רַק *raq1* (3)
lean (2)
lean (1) +1414

8370 2רַק *raq2* (109)
only (30)
but (22)
however (13)
except (5)
nevertheless (4)
surely (3)
yet (3)
always (2)
except that (2)
although (1)
and (1)
as for (1)

be sure (1)
but (1) +2256
but also (1)
but only (1)
moreover (1)
nothing but (1)
only (1) +421
only (1) +4202
really (1)
sheer (1)
untranslated (12)

8371 רֹק *rōq* (3)
for an instant (1) +1180+6330
spit (1)
spitting (1)

8372 רָקַב *rāqab̲* (2)
rot (2)

8373 רָקָב *rāqāb̲* (5)
decay (2)
rot (1)
rots (1)
something rotten (1)

8374 רֹקֶב *rōqeb̲*
Variant; not used

8375 רִקָּבוֹן *riqqāb̲ôn* (1)
rotten (1)

8376 רָקַד *rāqad̲* (9)
skipped (2)
dance (1)
dance about (1)
dancing (1)
jolting (1)
leap (1)
leap about (1)
makes skip (1)

8377 רַקָּה *raqqāh* (5)
temple (3)
temples (2)

8378 רַקּוֹן *raqqôn* (1)
Rakkon (1)

8379 רָקַח *rāqaḥ* (8)
perfumer (3)
blended (1)
makes perfume (1)
mixing in (1)
perfume (1) +9043
took care of mixing (1) +5351

8380 רֶקַח *reqaḥ* (1)
spiced (1)

8381 רֹקַח *rōqaḥ* (2)
blend (1)
fragrant blend (1)

8382 רַקָּח *raqqāḥ* (1)
perfume-makers (1)

8383 רִקֻּחַ *riqquaḥ* (1)
perfumes (1)

8384 רַקָּחָה *raqqāḥāh* (1)
perfumers (1)

8385 רָקִיעַ *rāqiya'* (17)
expanse (13)
heavens (2)
it^{s} (1) +2021
skies (1)

8386 רָקִיק *rāqiyq* (8)
wafers (5)
wafer (3)

8387 רָקַם *rāqam* (9)
embroiderer (7)
embroiderers (1)
was woven together (1)

8388 רָקֶם *rāqem* (1)
Rakem (1)

8389 1רֶקֶם *reqem1* (1)
Rekem (1)

8390 2רֶקֶם *reqem2* (4)
Rekem (4)

8391 רִקְמָה *riqmāh* (12)
embroidered (4)
embroidered work (2)
embroidered cloth (1)
embroidered dress (1)
embroidered garments (1)
highly embroidered (1)
varied colors (1)
various colors (1)

8392 רָקַע *rāqa'* (11)
spread out (3)
hammered out (2)
hammered (1)
overlays (1)
spreading out (1)
stamp (1)
stamped (1)
trampled (1)

8393 רִקֻּעַ *riqqua'* (1)
hammer (1) +6913

8394 רָקַק *rāqaq* (1)
spits (1)

8395 רַקַּת *raqqat̲* (1)
Rakkath (1)

8396 רֹשׁ *rōš*
Variant; not used

8397 רִשְׁיוֹן *rišyôn* (1)
authorized (1)

8398 רָשַׁם *rāšam* (1)
written (1)

8399 רָשַׁע *rāša'* (35)
condemn (7)
acted wickedly (3)
condemning (3)
guilty (3)
condemns (2)
done evil (2)
wicked (2)
condemned (1)
declare guilty (1)
did wrong (1)
do wrong (1)
doing wrong (1)
done wrong (1)
guilty of wickedness (1)
inflicted punishment (1)
let be condemned (1)
overwicked (1) +2221
refute (1)
violated (1)
untranslated (1)

8400 רֶשַׁע *reša'* (30)
wickedness (16)
wicked (5)
evil (2)
ill-gotten (2)
dishonest (1)
evil deeds (1)
injustice (1)
it^{s} (1)
wrongdoing (1) +6913

8401 רָשָׁע *rāšā'* (264)
wicked (237)
guilty (9)
evil (3)
wickedness (3)
he^{s} (2)
him^{s} (2)
deserves (1)
evildoers (1)
in the wrong (1)
one in the wrong (1)
outlaw (1)
they^{s} (1)
ungodly (1)
untranslated (1)

8402 רִשְׁעָה *riš'āh* (15)
wickedness (11)
crime (1)
evildoer (1) +6913
evildoers (1) +6913
wicked (1)

8403 רִשְׁעָתַיִם *riš'āt̲ayim*
Variant; not used

8404 1רֶשֶׁף *rešep̲1* (7)
pestilence (2)
blazing (1)
bolts of lightning (1)
burns (1)
flashing (1)
sparks (1) +1201

8405 2רֶשֶׁף *rešep̲2* (1)
Resheph (1)

8406 רָשַׁשׁ *rāšaš* (2)
been crushed (1)
destroy (1)

8407 רֶשֶׁת *rešet̲* (22)
net (16)
network (2) +5126
it^{s} (1) +2021
network (1)
snare (1)
trap (1)

8408 רַתּוֹק *ratôq* (2)
chains (1)
untranslated (1)

8409 רָתַח *rāt̲aḥ* (3)
bring to a boil (1) +8410
churning (1)
makes churn (1)

8410 רֶתַח *ret̲aḥ* (1)
bring to a boil (1) +8409

8411 רַתִּיקָה *ratiyqāh* (1)
chains (1)

8412 רָתַם *rāt̲am* (1)
harness (1)

8413 רֹתֶם *rōt̲em* (4)
broom tree (3)
tree (1)

8414 רִתְמָה *rit̲māh* (2)
Rithmah (2)

8415 רָתַק *rāt̲aq* (2)
were put in chains (1) +928+2414
untranslated (1)

8416 רְתֻקוֹת *r^{e}t̲uqôt̲* (1)
chains (1)

8417 רְתֵת *r^{e}t̲ēt̲* (1)
trembled (1)

8418 שׂ *ś*
Variant; not used

8419 שְׂאֹר *ś^{e}'ōr* (5)
yeast (5)

8420 1שְׂאֵת *ś^{e}'ēt̲1* (7)
honor (2)
splendor (2)
accepted (1)
lofty place (1)
rises up (1)

8421 2שְׂאֵת *ś^{e}'ēt̲2* (7)
swelling (6)
swollen (1)

8422 שְׂבָכָה *ś^{e}b̲āk̲āh* (17)
network (12)

lattice (1)
mesh (1)
network (1) +5126+8422
untranslated (1)

8423 שְׂבָם *ś^{e}ḇām* (1)
Sebam (1)

8424 שִׂבְמָה *śiḇmāh* (5)
Sibmah (5)

8425 שָׂבַע *śāḇaʿ* (100)
satisfied (30)
filled (9)
satisfy (9)
full (6)
get enough (3)
have enough (3)
satisfies (3)
endured (2)
fill (2)
had enough (2)
has enough (2)
have abundant (2)
too much (2)
all want (1)
all wanted (1)
content (1)
eat fill (1)
eaten enough (1)
eats fill (1)
enjoy (1)
enjoy plenty (1)
feast on (1)
fully repaid (1)
gorge (1)
had fill (1)
had plenty (1)
have fill (1)
have more than enough (1)
have plenty (1)
have to spare (1)
have too much (1)
insatiable (1) +1194
overwhelm (1)
satisfy fully (1)
supplied all needs (1)
toss (1) +5611
well watered (1)
untranslated (1)

8426 שָׂבָע *śāḇāʿ* (8)
abundance (7)
overflowing (1)

8427 שֹׂבַע *śōḇaʿ* (7)
all want (2)
fill (2)
all could eat (1)
all wanted (1)
content (1)

8428 שָׂבֵעַ *śāḇēaʿ* (10)
full (7)
abounding (1)
content (1)
enjoyed long life (1) +3427

8429 שָׂבְעָה *śoḇʿāh* (4)
abundant (1)
enough (1)
glutted (1)
satisfy (1)

8430 שִׂבְעָה *śiḇʿāh* (1)
overfed (1) +4312

8431 1שָׂבַר *śāḇar1* (2)
examining (2)

8432 2שָׂבַר *śāḇar2* (6)
look (2)
wait (2)
hope (1)
hoped (1)

8433 שֵׂבֶר *śēḇer* (2)
hope (1)
hopes (1)

8434 שְׂגָא *śāgāʾ* (2)
extol (1)
makes great (1)

8435 שָׂגַב *śāgaḇ* (20)
protect (4)
be exalted (2)
exalted (2)
is exalted (2)
lifted (2)
lofty (2)
high (1)
is kept safe (1)
safe (1)
strengthened (1)
strong (1)
unscalable (1)

8436 שָׂגָה *śāgāh* (4)
grow (1)
increase (1)
prosperous (1)
thrive (1)

8437 שְׂגוּב *ś^{e}gûḇ* (3)
Segub (3)

8438 שַׂגִּיא *śaggiyʾ* (2)
exalted (1)
great (1)

8439 שְׂגִיב *ś^{e}giyḇ* (1)
untranslated (1)

8440 שָׂדַד *śāḏaḏ* (3)
break up the ground (1)
harrowing (1)
till (1)

8441 שָׂדֶה *śāḏeh* (322)
field (128)
fields (76)
wild (24)
country (17)
land (11)
open country (8)
Moab (7) +4566
field (4) +2754
ground (4)
open (4)
territory (4)
family land (3) +299
region (3)
wild (3) +928+2021
area (2)
countryside (2)
mainland (2)
open field (2)
soil (2)
battlefield (1) +5120
it^{S} (1) +2021
lands (1)
outlying districts (1)
pastureland (1) +4494
place (1)
southland (1) +5582
there^{S} (1) +2021
there^{S} (1) +4566
untranslated (7)

8442 שָׂדַי *śāḏay* (13)
field (9)
fields (2)
slopes (1)
wild (1)

8443 שִׂדִּים *śiddiym* (3)
Siddim (3)

8444 שְׂדֵרָה *ś^{e}ḏērāh* (4)
ranks (3)
planks (1)

8445 שֶׂה *śeh* (47)
sheep (26)
lamb (11)
another^{S} (2)
flock (2)
animals (1)
goat (1) +6436
lamb (1) +928+2021+3897
lamb (1) +928+2021+4166
one^{S} (1)
sheep (1) +4166

8446 שָׂהֵד *śāhēḏ* (1)
advocate (1)

8447 שָׂהֲדוּתָא *śāh^{a}ḏûṯāʾ*
Variant; not used

8448 שַׂהֲרֹנִים *śah^{a}rōniym* (3)
ornaments (2)
crescent necklaces (1)

8449 שׂוֹבֶךְ *śôḇeḵ* (1)
thick branches (1)

8450 1שׂוּג *śûg1*
Variant; not used

8451 2שׂוּג *śûg2* (1)
make grow (1)

8452 שׂוּחַ *śûah* (1)
meditate (1)

8453 שַׂוְחָט *śawhāt*
Variant; not used

8454 שׂוּט *śûṭ* (1)
turn aside (1)

8455 שׂוּךְ *śûḵ* (2)
block (1)
put a hedge (1)

8456 שׂוֹךְ *śôḵ* (1)
branches (1)

8457 שׂוֹכָה *śôḵāh* (1)
branches (1) +6770

8458 שׂוֹכֹה *śôḵōh* (5)
Socoh (5)

8459 שׂוֹכוֹ *śôḵô* (3)
Soco (3)

8460 שׂוּכָתִי *śûḵāṯiy* (1)
Sucathites (1)

8461 שׂוּמָה *śûmāh* (1)
intention (1)

8462 שׂוּר *śûr*
Variant; not used

8463 שׂוֹרָה *śôrāh* (1)
place (1)

8464 שׂוּשׂ *śûś* (27)
rejoice (11)
delight (2)
glad (2)
rejoicing (2)
delight greatly (1) +8464
delighted (1)
gladly (1)
happy (1)
please (1)
pleased (1)
rejoice greatly (1) +5375
take delight (1)
take great delight (1) +928+8525

8465 שֵׂחַ *śēah* (1)
thoughts (1)

8466 שָׂחָה *śāhāh* (3)
flood (1)
swim (1)
swimmer (1)

8467 שָׂחוּ *śāhû* (1)
deep enough to swim in (1)

8468 שְׂחוֹק *ś^{e}hôq* (15)
laughter (7)

laughingstock (3)
object of ridicule (3)
pleasure (1)
ridiculed (1)

8469 שָׂחַט *śāḥaṭ* (1)
squeezed (1)

8470 שָׂחִיף *śāḥiyp̱* (1)
covered with (1) +6017+6017

8471 שָׂחַק *śāḥaq* (36)
laugh (7)
laughs (6)
celebrating (3)
rejoicing (3)
celebrate (1)
danced (1)
entertain (1)
fight hand to hand (1)
frolic (1)
joking (1)
joyful (1)
laughed (1)
make a pet (1)
mock (1)
perform (1)
play (1)
playing (1)
revelers (1)
scoffs (1)
scorned (1)
smiled (1)

8472 שְׂחֹת *śuḥōṯ*
Variant; not used

8473 שֵׂט *śēṭ* (1)
rebels (1)

8474 שָׂטָה *śāṭāh* (6)
goes astray (2)
gone astray (2)
turn (2)

8475 שָׂטַם *śāṭam* (6)
assails (1)
attack (1)
held a grudge against (1)
holds a grudge against (1)
hostility (1)
revile (1)

8476 שָׂטַן *śāṭan* (6)
accusers (3)
accuse (2)
slander (1)

8477 שָׂטָן *śāṭān* (27)
Satan (18)
adversary (4)
oppose (2)
accuser (1)
adversaries (1)
turn against (1) +2118+4200

8478 1שִׂטְנָה *śiṭnāh1* (1)
accusation (1)

8479 2שִׂטְנָה *śiṭnāh2* (1)
Sitnah (1)

8480 שִׂיא *śiy'* (1)
pride (1)

8481 שִׂיאוֹן *śiy'ôn* (1)
Siyon (1)

8482 שִׂיב *śiyḇ* (2)
gray (1)
gray-haired (1)

8483 שֵׂיב *śēyḇ* (1)
age (1)

8484 שֵׂיבָה *śēyḇāh* (19)
old age (6)
gray head (5)
gray hair (2)
aged (1)
gray (1)
gray hairs (1)
gray-haired (1)
hair gray (1)
white hair (1)

8485 שִׂיג *śiyg̱* (1)
busy (1)

8486 1שִׂיד *śiyḏ1* (2)
coat (2)

8487 2שִׂיד *śiyḏ2* (4)
lime (2)
plaster (2)

8488 1שִׂיחַ *śiyaḥ1* (21)
meditate (7)
consider (3)
speak (3)
mused (2)
tell (2)
complain (1)
deep in thought (1)
in distress (1)
mock (1)

8489 2שִׂיחַ *śiyaḥ2* (4)
bushes (2)
brush (1)
shrub (1) +3972

8490 3שִׂיחַ *śiyaḥ3* (13)
complaint (7)
anguish (1)
complaints (1)
lament (1)
meditation (1)
sort of things he says (1)
thoughts (1)

8491 שִׂיחָה *śiyḥāh* (3)
meditate (2)
devotion (1)

8492 שִׂים *śiym* (587)
put (106)
set (50)
make (48)
made (35)
placed (16)
set up (13)
give (11)
laid (11)
appointed (8)
lay (8)
makes (7)
place (7)
turn (7)
established (5)
gave (5)
give careful thought (5) +4222
puts (5)
bring (4)
determined (4) +7156
put in place (4)
put up (4)
putting (4)
took (4)
turned (4)
appoint (3)
brought (3)
fasten (3)
named (3) +9005
performed (3)
provide (3)
take (3)
assign (2)
attached (2)
charges (2)
considered (2) +4213
consigning to labor (2)
fastened (2)
fix (2)
given (2)
giving (2)
leaving (2)
look after (2) +6524+6584
mark out (2)
pay (2)
planted (2)
posted (2)
prepare (2)
prepares (2)
reduce (2)
reduced (2)
regard (2) +4200+5584
seized (2) +3338
served (2)
sets (2)
turn into (2)
accuse (1) +928+1821
added (1)
applied (1)
attach (1)
avenged (1)
be sure to appoint (1) +8492
become (1)
care (1) +448+4213
care about (1) +448+4213
cares (1) +4213+6584
caused to turn (1)
charge (1)
clap (1)
concerned about (1) +448+4213
consider (1)
consider (1) +4213
consider (1) +4213+6584
controls (1)
covered (1) +4200
depends on (1)
designate (1)
destroy (1) +9039
determine (1) +7156
determined (1) +7156+8492
did[s] (1)
displayed (1)
does (1)
don't say a word (1) +3338+6584+7023
drew up (1)
end (1) +7874
erected (1)
establish (1)
establishes (1)
exacted (1)
examine (1)
fastens (1)
float (1)
formed (1)
gave a high rank in (1) +6584
grants (1)
had (1)
had brought (1)
had take up positions (1)
harbor (1)
headed for (1) +7156
hung (1)
ignored (1) +4202+4213
imposed (1)
increased (1)
inflict (1)
intention (1) +4213
keep (1)
keeps (1)
lay up (1)
left (1)
lifted (1)
light (1)
list (1)
loaded (1)
looked (1) +7156
make serve (1) +4200
make sure hears (1) +265+928
making (1)
marked off (1)

offers (1)
piled (1)
pitched (1)
plant (1)
pondered (1)
ponders (1)
poured (1)
prepared (1)
presented (1)
preserve (1)
preserved (1) +928+2021+2645
press charges (1)
pressed (1)
provided (1)
put in charge (1)
put on (1) +928+5516
repay (1)
replace (1) +9393
replaced (1)
require (1)
resolved (1) +4213+6584
see (1) +6524
seize (1) +928+3338
separated (1)
serve (1)
set in place (1)
sets up (1)
setting (1)
shave (1) +7947
shedding (1)
showed (1)
shrouded (1)
sing (1) +928+7023
slandered (1) +1821+6613
slanders (1) +1821+6613
spread (1)
stared with a fixed gaze (1) +906+2256+6641+7156
stationed (1)
stirs up (1)
strap (1)
take up positions (1)
think (1) +4013+4200
throw (1)
thrown (1)
told (1) +928+7023
trample down (1) +5330
treat (1)
turned (1) +7156
turned into (1)
unnoticed (1) +1172+4946
use (1)
used (1)
was placed (1)
was set (1)
watch over (1) +6584
waylaid (1) +928+2006+2021
worry (1) +906+4213
untranslated (20)

8493 שֵׂךְ *śēk̲* (1)
barbs (1)

8494 שֹׂךְ *śōk̲* (1)
dwelling (1)

8495 שָׂכָה *śāk̲āh*
Variant; not used

8496 שֻׂכָּה *śukkāh* (1)
harpoons (1)

8497 שֶׂכוּ *śek̲û* (1)
Secu (1)

8498 שֶׂכְוִי *śek̲wiy* (1)
mind (1)

8499 שְׂכִיָה *śāk̲ᵉyāh* (1)
Sakia (1)

8500 שְׂכִיָּה *śᵉk̲iyyāh* (1)
vessel (1)

8501 שַׂכִּין *śakkiyn* (1)
knife (1)

8502 שָׂכִיר *śāk̲iyr* (18)
hired man (5)
hired worker (4)
hired (3)
servant bound by contract (2)
hired hand (1)
laborers (1)
man hired (1)
mercenaries (1)

8503 שָׂכַךְ1 *śāk̲ak̲1* (2)
cover (1)
hide (1)

8504 שָׂכַךְ2 *śāk̲ak̲2*
Variant; not used

8505 שָׂכַל1 *śāk̲al1* (61)
wise (13)
understand (6)
successful (4)
prosper (3)
prudent (3)
understanding (3)
instruct (2)
act wisely (1)
careful (1)
fail (1) +4202
gaining wisdom (1)
gave thought (1)
gave understanding (1)
give attention (1)
give insight (1)
gives heed (1)
giving attention (1)
guides (1)
had great success (1)
had regard for (1)
has regard for (1)
have insight (1)
insight (1)
instructed (1)
met with success (1)
ponder (1)
showed understanding (1) +8507
showing aptitude (1)
skilled (1)
succeeds (1)
successfully (1)
takes note (1)
understands (1)
wisely (1)

8506 שָׂכַל2 *śāk̲al2* (1)
crossing (1)

8507 שֶׂכֶל *śek̲el* (16)
understanding (4)
wisdom (3)
capable (1)
discretion (1)
intelligence (1)
intelligent (1) +3202
meaning (1)
name (1)
showed understanding (1) +8505
wise (1)
untranslated (1)

8508 שִׂכְלוּת *śiklût̲* (1)
folly (1)

8509 שָׂכַר *śāk̲ar* (20)
hired (9)
hire (3)
been hired (1)
earn wages (1) +8509
hire themselves out (1)
hired (1) +8509
hires (1)
untranslated (1)

8510 שָׂכָר1 *śāk̲ār1* (28)
wages (10)
reward (6)
pay (2)
rewarded (2)
fare (1)
money paid for hire (1)
paid (1) +9202
pay (1) +5989
return (1)
rewarded (1) +5989
worth (1)
untranslated (1)

8511 שָׂכָר2 *śāk̲ār2* (2)
Sacar (2)

8512 שֶׂכֶר *śek̲er* (2)
reward (1)
wage (1)

8513 שְׂלָו *śᵉlāw* (4)
quail (4)

8514 שַׂלְמָא *śalmā'* (2)
Salma (2)

8515 שַׂלְמָה1 *śalmāh1* (16)
clothes (5)
cloak (4)
garment (2)
robes (2)
clothing (1)
garments (1)
robe (1)

8516 שַׂלְמָה2 *śalmāh2*
Variant; not used

8517 שַׂלְמוֹן *śalmôn* (4)
Salmon (4)

8518 שַׂלְמַי *śalmay*
Variant; not used

8519 שָׂלַק *śālaq*
Variant; not used

8520 שְׂמֹאל *śᵉmō'l* (54)
left (45)
north (6)
north (2) +4946
which way (1) +196+3545+6584+6584

8521 שִׂמְאֵל *śim'ēl* (5)
to the left (3)
go to the left (1)
left-handed (1)

8522 שְׂמָאלִי *śᵉmā'liy* (9)
north (4)
left (3)
untranslated (2)

8523 שָׂמַח *śāmah* (157)
rejoice (42)
glad (30)
rejoiced (11)
gloat (5)
rejoices (5)
brings joy (4)
bring joy (3)
delight (3)
happy (3)
joy (3)
make glad (3)
rejoicing (3)
enjoy (2)
gladly (2)
joyful (2)
let gloat (2)
pleased (2)
be[s] (1)
bring happiness (1)
cheers (1)
cheers up (1)
delights (1)
elated (1)
exult (1)
filled with joy (1)
give joy (1)

given cause to rejoice (1)
given joy (1) +8525
giving joy (1)
gladdens (1)
gladness (1)
glee (1)
gloats (1)
happy (1) +8525
held a celebration (1)
joyous (1)
made rejoice (1)
made very glad (1) +8523
make merry (1)
makes glad (1)
makes merry (1)
received gladly (1) +6584
rejoiced (1) +8525
share joy (1) +8525
shines brightly (1)
take pleasure (1)
untranslated (2)

8524 שָׂמֵחַ *śāmēah* (20)
happy (5)
joyful (2)
rejoicing (2)
cheerful (1)
cheering (1)
delight (1)
delight in (1)
filled with gladness (1) +448+1637
filled with joy (1)
gloat (1)
joy (1)
merrymakers (1) +4213
rejoice (1)
rejoicing (1) +8525

8525 שִׂמְחָה *śimhāh* (94)
joy (46)
gladness (10)
rejoicing (6)
pleasure (5)
rejoice (3)
joyful (2)
joyfully (2)
joyfully (2) +928
rejoiced (2)
celebrate (1)
delight (1)
delights (1)
enjoyment (1)
given joy (1) +8523
glad occasions (1)
glee (1)
happiness (1)
happy (1) +8523
joyful songs (1)
pleased (1)
rejoiced (1) +8523
rejoicing (1) +8524
revelry (1)
share joy (1) +8523
take great delight (1) +928+8464

8526 שְׂמִיכָה *śᵉmiyk̲āh* (1)
covering (1)

8527 שָׂמַךְ *śāmak̲*
Variant; not used

8528 שַׂמְלָה *śamlāh* (4)
Samlah (4)

8529 שִׂמְלָה *śimlāh* (31)
clothes (12)
clothing (7)
cloak (4)
garment (3)
cloth (2)
best clothes (1)
untranslated (2)

8530 שַׂמְלַי *śamlay*
Variant; not used

8531 שָׂמַם *śāmam* (1)
painted (1) +928+2021+7037

8532 שְׂמָמִית *śᵉmāmiyt̲* (1)
lizard (1)

8533 שָׂנֵא *śānē'* (148)
hate (59)
hated (16)
hates (14)
foes (11)
enemies (9)
malice aforethought (4) +4946+8997+9453
adversaries (3)
dislikes (3)
enemy (3)
foe (2)
unloved (2)
abhor (1)
am not loved (1)
are shunned (1)
both[s] (1) +170+2021+2021+2256
detest (1)
enemies (1) +5883
enemy's (1)
hate (1) +8534
have hatred (1) +8534
hostile (1)
is hated (1)
malicious (1)
not love (1)
not loved (1)
not[s] (1)
refuses (1)
shunned (1)
them[s] (1) +2157
thoroughly hated (1) +8533
untranslated (2)

8534 שִׂנְאָה *śin'āh* (17)
hatred (8)
hate (2)
hate (1) +8533
hated (1)
hates (1)
have hatred (1) +8533
malice (1)
malice aforethought (1)
untranslated (1)

8535 שָׂנִיא *śāniy'* (1)
not love (1)

8536 שְׂנִיר *śᵉniyr* (4)
Senir (4)

8537 1שָׂעִיר *śā'iyr1* (3)
hairy (2)
shaggy (1)

8538 2שָׂעִיר *śā'iyr2* (54)
male goat (24) +6436
goat (10)
male goat (7)
goat's (3)
goats (3)
goat (2) +6436
male goats (2) +6436
wild goats (2)
it[s] (1) +2021

8539 3שָׂעִיר *śā'iyr3* (2)
goat idols (2)

8540 4שָׂעִיר *śā'iyr4* (1)
showers (1)

8541 1שֵׂעִיר *śē'iyr1* (35)
Seir (35)

8542 2שֵׂעִיר *śē'iyr2* (1)
Seir (1)

8543 3שֵׂעִיר *śē'iyr3* (3)
Seir (3)

8544 1שְׂעִירָה *śᵉ'iyrāh1* (2)
goat (2) +6436

8545 2שְׂעִירָה *śᵉ'iyrāh2* (1)
Seirah (1)

8546 שְׂעִפִּים *śᵉ'ippiym* (2)
disquieting (1)
troubled thoughts (1)

8547 1שָׂעַר *śā'ar1* (3)
shudder (3)

8548 2שָׂעַר *śā'ar2* (4)
storm out (1)
sweeps out (1)
swept away (1)
tempest rages (1) +4394

8549 3שָׂעַר *śā'ar3* (1)
fear (1)

8550 1שַׂעַר *śa'ar1* (3)
horror (3)

8551 2שַׂעַר *śa'ar2* (1)
wind (1)

8552 שֵׂעָר *śē'ār* (28)
hair (23)
hairy (2)
garment of hair (1)
hair (1) +7279
it[s] (1) +8031

8553 שַׂעֲרָה *śa'ᵃrāh* (7)
hair (3)
hair of head (2)
hairs (2)

8554 שְׂעָרָה *śᵉ'ārāh* (2)
storm (2)

8555 שְׂעֹרָה *śᵉ'ōrāh* (34)
barley (33)
untranslated (1)

8556 שְׂעֹרִים *śᵉ'ōriym* (1)
Seorim (1)

8557 שָׂפָה *śāp̲āh* (178)
lips (97)
rim (14)
edge (10)
bank (7)
language (6)
seashore (5) +3542
speech (5)
chattering (2)
empty words (2) +1821
mouth (2)
talk (2)
tongue (2)
band (1)
banks (1)
border (1)
coast (1) +3542
hurl insults (1) +928+7080
mere talk (1) +1821
object of malicious talk (1) +4383+6584+6590
riverbank (1) +3284
shore (1)
shore (1) +3542
speaks rashly (1) +7316
talker (1) +408
talks too much (1) +7331
thoughtlessly (1) +928+1051+4200
what said (1)
whisper (1)
words (1)
untranslated (7)

8558 שָׂפַח *śāp̲ah* (1)
bring sores on (1)

8559 שָׂפָם *śāp̲ām* (5)
lower part of face (3)
faces (1)
mustache (1)

8560 שִׂפְמוֹת *śip̲môt̲* (1)
Siphmoth (1)

8561 שָׂפַן *śāp̱an* (1)
treasures hidden (1) +3243

8562 1שָׂפַק *śāp̱aq1* (2)
claps in derision (1)
clasp hands (1)

8563 2שָׂפַק *śāp̱aq2* (1)
enough (1)

8564 שֶׂפֶק *śep̱eq*
Variant; not used

8565 שֵׂפֶק *śēp̱eq* (1)
plenty (1)

8566 שַׂק *śaq* (48)
sackcloth (42)
sack (3)
sacks (2)
sackcloth (1) +4680

8567 שָׂקַד *śāqaḏ* (1)
been bound (1)

8568 שָׂקַר *śāqar* (1)
flirting (1)

8569 שַׂר *śar* (421)
officials (78)
commanders (74)
princes (41)
commander (36)
officers (31)
leaders (29)
nobles (18)
chief (17)
ruler (14)
prince (10)
leader (8)
captain (7)
rulers (7)
captain (5) +2822
leading (3)
officials in charge (3)
warden (3)
chief officer (2) +2021+7372
command (2)
governor (2)
in charge (2)
captains (1) +2822
chief men (1)
chief officials (1)
commander-in-chief (1) +2256+8031
commanders (1) +7372
dignitaries (1)
foremen (1) +5893
head (1)
heads (1)
masters (1)
mighty (1)
officer (1)
they[s] (1) +2021
they[s] (1) +2021+2256+2657+3405
untranslated (15)

8570 שַׂרְאֶצֶר *śar'eṣer* (3)
Sharezer (3)

8571 שָׂרַג *śārag̱* (2)
close-knit (1)
woven together (1)

8572 שָׂרַד *śāraḏ* (1)
left (1)

8573 שְׂרָד *śᵉrāḏ* (4)
woven (4)

8574 שֶׂרֶד *śereḏ* (1)
marker (1)

8575 1שָׂרָה *śārāh1* (3)
struggled (3)

8576 2שָׂרָה *śārāh2* (5)
ladies (1)
of royal birth (1)
queen (1)
queens (1)
women of nobility (1)

8577 3שָׂרָה *śārāh3* (38)
Sarah (35)
Sarah's (1)
she[s] (1)
untranslated (1)

8578 שְׂרוּג *śᵉrûg̱* (5)
Serug (5)

8579 שְׂרוֹךְ *śᵉrôḵ* (2)
thong (2)

8580 שֶׂרַח *śeraḥ* (3)
Serah (3)

8581 שָׂרַט *śāraṭ* (3)
cut (1) +8583
injure themselves (1) +8581

8582 שֶׂרֶט *śereṭ* (1)
cut (1) +5989

8583 שָׂרֶטֶת *śāreṭeṯ* (1)
cut (1) +8581

8584 שָׂרַי *śāray* (17)
Sarai (15)
she[s] (1)
untranslated (1)

8585 שָׂרִיג *śāriyg̱* (3)
branches (3)

8586 1שָׂרִיד *śāriyḏ1* (29)
survivors (17)
survive (4)
left (2)
survivor (2)
few (1)
men who were left (1)
survived (1)
untranslated (1)

8587 2שָׂרִיד *śāriyḏ2* (2)
Sarid (2)

8588 שְׂרָיָה *śᵉrāyāh* (19)
Seraiah (17)
Seraiah's (1)
untranslated (1)

8589 שְׂרָיָהוּ *śᵉrāyāhû* (1)
Seraiah (1)

8590 שִׂרְיוֹן *śiryôn* (2)
Sirion (2)

8591 שָׂרִיק *śāriyq* (1)
combed (1)

8592 שָׂרַךְ *śāraḵ* (1)
running here and there (1) +2006

8593 שַׂר־סְכִים *śar-sᵉkiym*
Variant; not used

8594 שָׂרַע *śāra'* (3)
deformed (2)
stretch out (1)

8595 שַׂרְעַפִּים *śar'appiym* (2)
anxiety (1)
anxious thoughts (1)

8596 שָׂרַף *śārap̱* (117)
burned (27)
burn (13)
burn down (9) +836+928+2021
burned (8) +836+928+2021
be burned up (4) +836+928+2021
burn (4) +836+928+2021
burned up (4) +836+928+2021
burns (4)
set on fire (4) +836+928+2021
burn up (3) +836+928+2021
burned down (3) +836+928+2021
set fire to (3)
be burned (2)
been burned up (2)
burn up (2)
are burned up (1) +836+928+2021+8596
bake thoroughly (1) +4200+8599
be burned (1) +836+928+2021
be burned down (1) +836+928+2021
be destroyed (1)
being burned (1)
burn as sacrifices (1)
burn down (1)
burn to death (1) +836+928+2021
burned as sacrifices (1)
burned down (1) +836+2021
burned to death (1)
burned to death (1) +836+928+2021
burned up (1)
destroy (1)
destroyed (1)
destroyed by fire (1)
is burned (1)
made (1)
make a fire (1)
set fire to (1) +836+928+2021
used for fuel (1) +836+1198
untranslated (2)

8597 1שָׂרָף *śārāp̱1* (7)
seraphs (2)
venomous (2)
snake (1)
snakes (1)
venomous serpent (1)

8598 2שָׂרָף *śārāp̱2* (1)
Saraph (1)

8599 שְׂרֵפָה *śᵉrēp̱āh* (13)
fire (3)
burned (2)
burning (2)
bake thoroughly (1) +4200+8596
burned-out (1)
burning waste (1)
smoldering remains (1)
those[s] (1) +2021
untranslated (1)

8600 שָׂרַק *śāraq*
Variant; not used

8601 1שָׂרֹק *śārōq1* (1)
brown (1)

8602 2שָׂרֹק *śārōq2* (1)
choicest vines (1)

8603 1שֹׂרֵק *śōrēq1* (2)
choice vine (1)
choicest vines (1)

8604 2שֹׂרֵק *śōrēq2* (1)
Sorek (1)

8605 שְׂרֵקָה *śᵉrēqāh* (1)
choicest branch (1)

8606 שָׂרַר *śārar* (7)
choose princes (1)
govern (1)
governed (1)
lord it (1) +8606
rule (1)
ruler (1)

8607 שָׂשׂוֹן *śāśôn* (22)
joy (14)
gladness (6)
joyful (1)
rejoicing (1)

8608 שָׂתַם *śāṯam* (1)
shuts out (1)

8609 שָׂתַר *śāṯar* (1)
outbreak (1)

8610 שׂ *ś*
Variant; not used

8611 שֶׁ־ *ša-* (142)
that (15)
who (15)
which (7)
until (6) +6330
the one^{s} (4)
whose (4)
because (3)
whom (3)
he^{s} (2)
till (2) +6330
allies^{s} (1) +6640
as (1) +3869
as (1) +3972+6645
body^{s} (1)
despite (1) +928+4200
fault (1) +928+4200
for (1) +928+1685
future (1) +2118+4537
how (1)
it^{s} (1)
mine (1) +3276+4200
my own (1) +3276+4200
of (1) +4200+4946
responsible for (1) +928+4200
since (1)
so that (1)
Solomon's (1) +4200+8976
successor (1) +132+339+995
than (1)
the produce^{s} (1)
therefore (1) +1826+6584
when (1) +6330
where (1)
while (1) +6330
why (1) +4200+4537
wisdom^{s} (1)
untranslated (55)

8612 שָׁאַב *šā'aḇ* (19)
draw water (5)
draw (4)
drew (4)
carriers (3)
carry (1)
drew water (1)
filled (1)

8613 שָׁאַג *šā'ag* (21)
roar (7)
roaring (4)
roared (3)
roars (2)
comes roar (1)
groan (1)
roar mightily (1) +8613
untranslated (1)

8614 שְׁאָגָה *š'āḡāh* (7)
roar (3)
groaning (2)
groans (1)
roaring (1) +7754

8615 1שָׁאָה *šā'āh1* (4)
turned into (2)
lie ruined (1)
ruined (1)

8616 2שָׁאָה *šā'āh2* (2)
roar (2)

8617 3שָׁאָה *šā'āh3* (1)
watched closely (1)

8618 שַׁאֲוָה *ša'ᵃwāh* (1)
untranslated (1)

8619 שְׁאוֹל *š'ôl* (66)
grave (55)
death (6)
depths (2)
depths of the grave (2)
realm of death (1)

8620 שָׁאוּל *šā'ûl* (406)
Saul (327)
Saul's (34)
he^{s} (12)
Shaul (9)
him^{s} (6)
Saul's (4) +4200
his^{s} (3)
his^{s} (1) +4200
they^{s} (1) +6269
untranslated (9)

8621 שָׁאוּלִי *šā'ûliy* (1)
Shaulite (1)

8622 1שָׁאוֹן *šā'ôn1* (1)
slimy pit (1) +1014

8623 2שָׁאוֹן *šā'ôn2* (17)
uproar (5)
roaring (3)
roar (2)
brawlers (1)
great tumult (1)
loud noise (1)
noise (1)
noisy boasters (1) +1201
roar of battle (1)
tumult (1)

8624 שְׁאָט *š'āt* (3)
malice (3)

8625 שְׁאִיָּה *š'iyyāh* (1)
battered to pieces (1) +4198

8626 שָׁאַל *šā'al* (174)
ask (39)
asked (36)
inquired of (15) +928
question (6)
asks (4)
greet (4) +4200+8934
greeted (4) +4200+8934
request (4)
consult (3)
questioned (3)
asking (2)
have request to make (2) +8629
ask (1) +907
asked how they were (1) +4200+8934
be given over (1)
beg (1)
beggars (1)
borrows (1)
consulted (1)
consulting (1) +7023
demand (1)
demanding (1)
demands (1)
desired (1)
earnestly asked for permission (1) +8626
earnestly asked permission (1) +8626
find out (1)
gave (1)
gave what asked for (1)
get answer (1) +8626
give (1)
have request (1) +8629
inquire (1)
inquire of (1) +906+7023
inquire of (1) +928
inquires of (1) +928+1821
inquiring of (1) +928
investigate (1)
invoking (1)
looks (1)
make^{s} (1)
medium (1) +200
obtain decisions (1)
pray (1)
prayed (1)
questioned closely (1) +8626
require (1)
said (1)
tell (1)
took (1)
wanted (1) +906+5883
was borrowed (1)
wish (1)
untranslated (7)

8627 שְׁאָל *š'āl* (1)
Sheal (1)

8628 שְׁאָלָה *š'ālāh*
Variant; not used

8629 שְׁאֵלָה *š'ēlāh* (13)
petition (6)
have request to make (2) +8626
have request (1) +8626
prayed for (1)
request (1)
what asked for (1)
what^{s} (1)

8630 שְׁאַלְתִּיאֵל *š'altiy'ēl* (6)
Shealtiel (6)

8631 שָׁאַן *šā'an* (5)
security (2)
at ease (1)
at rest (1)
enjoy ease (1)

8632 שְׁאָן *š'ān*
Variant; not used

8633 שַׁאֲנָן *ša'ᵃnān* (10)
complacent (3)
insolence (2)
at ease (1)
feel secure (1)
peaceful (1)
proud (1)
undisturbed (1)

8634 1שָׁאַף *šā'ap̱1* (11)
pant (3)
hotly pursue (2)
hurries back (1)
long for (1)
longing for (1)
pant (1) +8120
pursue (1)
sniffing (1)

8635 2שָׁאַף *šā'ap̱2* (3)
trample (2)
hounded (1)

8636 שָׁאַר *šā'ar* (133)
left (52)
remained (10)
remain (9)
leave (7)
left behind (6)
leaving (5)
rest (5)
survived (5)
survive (3)
survivors (3)
have left (2)
leave alive (2)
spare (2)
been kept (1)
can hardly breathe (1) +4202+5972
left alone (1)
left survivor (1)
little left (1) +3856+7129
remains (1)
remnant (1)
remnant spare (1)
reserve (1)
sparing (1)
still (1)
still (1) +6388
survives (1)
those^{s} (1) +2021
untranslated (8)

8637 שְׁאָר *še'ār* (25)
rest (10)
remnant (9)
survivors (3)
other (1)
remainder (1)
remaining (1)

8638 שְׁאֵר *še'ēr* (18)
flesh (5)
close relative (3)
meat (2)
blood relative (1) +1414
body (1)
close relative (1) +1414
close relative (1) +7940
close relatives (1)
food (1)
himself (1) +2257
relative (1)

8639 שְׁאָר יָשׁוּב *še'ār yāšûḇ* (1)
Shear-Jashub (1)

8640 שַׁאֲרָה *ša'arāh*
Variant; not used

8641 שֶׁאֱרָה *še'erāh* (1)
Sheerah (1)

8642 שְׁאֵרִית *še'ēriyṯ* (66)
remnant (44)
rest (7)
survivors (7)
remain (2)
remaining (2)
descendant (1)
last (1)
left (1)
other (1)

8643 שֵׁאת *šē'ṯ* (1)
ruin (1)

8644 שְׁבָא *šeḇā'* (23)
Sheba (22)
Sabeans (1)

8645 שְׁבָאִים *šeḇā'iym* (1)
Sabeans (1)

8646 שְׁבָבִים *šeḇāḇiym* (1)
broken in pieces (1)

8647 שָׁבָה *šāḇāh* (46)
captors (4)
carried off (4)
taken captive (4)
captured (3)
took captive (3)
are held captive (2)
captives (2)
conquerors (2)
take captive (2)
takes captive (2) +8647
be taken captive (1)
been captured (1)
been carried captive (1)
been taken captive (1)
captured (1) +8660
carried away (1)
held captive (1)
is taken away (1)
led in train (1)
made captives of (1)
make captives (1)
seized (1)
take captives (1) +8660
taken (1)
taken as prisoners (1) +8664
takes captive (1)
took as prisoners (1) +8664

8648 שְׁבוֹ *šeḇô* (2)
agate (2)

8649 שְׁבוּאֵל *šeḇû'ēl* (3)
Shubael (3)

8650 שְׁבוּל *šeḇûl*
Variant; not used

8651 שָׁבוּעַ *šāḇûa'* (20)
weeks (7)
sevens (4)
seven (3)
weeks (2) +3427
bridal week (1)
feast of weeks (1)
week (1)
untranslated (1)

8652 שְׁבוּעָה *šeḇû'āh* (29)
oath (17)
swear (2)
curse (1)
denounce (1)
oath swore (1)
put oath (1) +8678
sworn (1)
sworn allegiance (1) +8678
sworn judgments (1)
takes an oath (1) +8678
them^{s} (1)
under oath (1) +1251

8653 שָׁבוּר *šāḇûr* (1)
injured (1)

8654 שְׁבוּת *šeḇûṯ* (29)
fortunes (14)
captivity (7)
exiled (1)
made prosperous again (1) +8740
untranslated (6)

8655 שָׁבַח1 *šāḇaḥ1* (9)
commend (2)
extol (2)
glory (2)
declared (1)
glorify (1)
receive praise (1)

8656 שָׁבַח2 *šāḇaḥ2* (3)
keeps (1)
still (1)
stilled (1)

8657 שֵׁבֶט *šēḇeṭ* (190)
tribes (74)
tribe (44)
rod (23)
half-tribe (18) +2942
scepter (15)
tribal (3)
club (2)
staff (2)
chief men (1)
javelins (1)
peoples (1)
punish (1)
rulers (1)
shepherd's rod (1)
stick (1)
untranslated (2)

8658 שְׁבָט *šeḇāṭ* (1)
Shebat (1)

8659 שָׁבִי *šāḇiy*
Variant; not used

8660 שְׁבִי *šeḇiy* (48)
captivity (17)
exile (13)
captives (8)
captured (4)
prisoners (2)
captured (1) +8647
carry off (1) +928+995+2021
prisoner (1)
take captives (1) +8647

8661 שֹׁבִי *šōḇiy* (1)
Shobi (1)

8662 שֹׁבָי *šōḇay* (2)
Shobai (2)

8663 שָׁבִיב *šāḇiyḇ* (1)
flame (1)

8664 שִׁבְיָה *šiḇyāh* (9)
prisoners (3)
captives (2)
captivity (2)
taken as prisoners (1) +8647
took as prisoners (1) +8647

8665 שְׁבִיָּה *šeḇiyyāh* (1)
captive (1)

8666 שְׁבִיל *šeḇiyl* (3)
paths (1)
way (1)
untranslated (1)

8667 שָׁבִיס *šāḇiys* (1)
headbands (1)

8668 שְׁבִיעִי *šeḇiy'iy* (97)
seventh (97)

8669 שְׁבִית *šeḇiyṯ* (14)
fortunes (4)
captives (1)
untranslated (9)

8670 שֹׁבֶל *šōḇel* (1)
skirts (1)

8671 שַׁבְּלוּל *šabbelûl* (1)
slug (1)

8672 שִׁבֹּלֶת1 *šibbōleṯ1* (16)
heads of grain (8)
heads (3)
grain (2)
branches (1)
leftover grain (1)
Shibboleth (1)

8673 שִׁבֹּלֶת2 *šibbōleṯ2* (3)
floods (1)
floodwaters (1) +4784
flowing (1)

8674 שֶׁבְנָא *šeḇnā'* (7)
Shebna (7)

8675 שֶׁבְנָה *šeḇnāh* (2)
Shebna (2)

8676 שְׁבַנְיָה *šeḇanyāh* (5)
Shebaniah (5)

8677 שְׁבַנְיָהוּ *šeḇanyāhû* (1)
Shebaniah (1)

8678 שָׁבַע *šāḇa'* (186)
swore (35)
swear (29)
promised on oath (21)
sworn (21)
took an oath (7)
swore an oath (6)
charge (5)
made swear (4)
take oaths (4)
made swear an oath (3)
made take an oath (3)
make swear (3)
oath (3)
put under oath (3)
taken an oath (3)
solemnly swore (2)
swears (2)
swore oath (2)
takes an oath (2)
bound under a strict oath (1) +8678
bound with the oath (1)
confirmed by oath (1)
declared on oath (1)
gave oath (1)
gave solemn oath (1)

given oath (1)
made swear an oath (1) +8678
perjurers (1) +2021+4200+9214
perjury (1) +2021+4200+9214
pledged on oath (1)
pronounced solemn oath (1)
put oath (1) +8652
ratified by oath (1)
solemnly promised (1)
swear allegiance (1)
swearing (1)
swears falsely (1)
sworn allegiance (1) +8652
sworn an oath (1)
taken oath (1)
takes an oath (1) +8652
took oath (1)
took the oath (1)
use name as a curse (1) +928
want to swear (1)

8679 1שֶׁבַע *šeḇa‘1* (487)
seven (286)
seventy (57)
seventh (9)
twenty-seventh (6) +2256+6929
70 (5)
seventeen (5) +6926
seventeenth (4) +6925
127 (3) +2256+2256+4395+6929
seventy-five (3) +2256+2822
seventy-seven (3) +2256+8679
thirty-seventh (3) +2256+8993
1,247 (2) +547+752+2256+4395
1,775 (2) +547+2256+2256 +2256+2822+4395+8679
137 (2) +2256+2256+4395+8993
372 (2) +2256+4395+8993+9109
57,400 (2) +547+752+2256+2256+2822+4395
6,720 (2) +547+2256+4395+6929+9252
62,700 (2) +547+2256+2256+4395+9109+9252
7,337 (2) +547+2256+4395+8679+8993+8993
74 (2) +752+2256
74,600 (2) +547+752+2256+2256+4395+9252
760 (2) +2256+4395+9252
973 (2) +2256+4395+8993+9596
seven (2) +8679
seventeen hundred (2) +547+2256+4395
seventeenth (2) +6926
thirty-seven (2) +2256+8993
twenty-seven (2) +2256+6929
1,017 (1) +547+2256+6925
1,017 (1) +547+6925
1,760 (1) +547+2256+2256+4395+9252
14,700 (1) +547+752+2256+4395+6925
157,600 (1) +547+547+2256+2256 +2256+2822+4395+4395+9252
16,750 (1) +547+2256+2822+4395+6925+9252
17,200 (1) +547+2256+4395+6925
172 (1) +2256+4395+9109
187 (1) +2256+2256+4395+9046
2,067 (1) +547+2256+9252
2,172 (1) +547+2256+2256+4395+9109
2,172 (1) +547+2256+4395+9109
2,750 (1) +547+2256+2822+4395
207 (1) +2256+4395
22,273 (1) +547+2256+2256+2256 +4395+6929+8993+9109
273 (1) +2256+2256+4395+8993
3,700 (1) +547+2256+4395+8993
307,500 (1) +547+547+2256+2256 +2822+4395+4395+8993
337,500 (1) +547+547+547+2256+2256 +2256+2822+4395+4395+8993+8993
337,500 (1) +547+547+547+2256+2256 +2822+4395+4395+8993+8993
37,000 (1) +547+2256+8993
43,730 (1) +547+752+2256+2256 +2256+4395+8993+8993
44,760 (1) +547+752+752+2256 +2256+2256+4395+9252
52,700 (1) +547+2256+2256+2822+4395+9109
601,730 (1) +547+547+2256+2256 +4395+4395+8993+9252
667 (1) +2256+4395+9252+9252
67 (1) +2256+9252
675 (1) +2256+2822+4395+9252
675,000 (1) +547+547+547+2256 +2256+2822+4395+9252
7,000 (1) +547
7,100 (1) +547+2256+4395
7,500 (1) +547+2256+2822+4395
70,000 (1) +547
72 (1) +2256+9109
72,000 (1) +547+2256+9109
721 (1) +285+2256+2256+4395+6929
725 (1) +2256+2822+4395+6929
730 (1) +2256+4395+8993
736 (1) +2256+4395+8993+9252
743 (1) +752+2256+2256+4395+8993
743 (1) +752+2256+4395+8993
745 (1) +752+2256+2822+4395
76,500 (1) +547+2256+2256+2822+4395+9252
775 (1) +2256+2822+4395+8679
777 (1) +2256+2256+4395+8679+8679
782 (1) +2256+2256+4395+9046+9109
807 (1) +2256+4395+9046
87,000 (1) +547+2256+9046
forty-seven (1) +752+2256
many (1)
seven-day (1) +3427
seven-day periods (1) +2021+3427
sevenfold (1)
seventeen (1) +2256+6927
twenty-seven hundred (1) +547+2256+4395
untranslated (7)

8680 2שֶׁבַע *šeḇa‘2* (9)
Sheba (9)

8681 3שֶׁבַע *šeḇa‘3* (1)
Sheba (1)

8682 4שֶׁבַע *šeḇa‘4*
Variant; not used

8683 שִׁבְעָה *šiḇ‘āh* (1)
Shibah (1)

8684 שִׁבְעִים *šiḇ‘iym*
Variant; not used

8685 שִׁבְעָנָה *šiḇ‘ānāh* (1)
seven (1)

8686 שִׁבְעָתַיִם *šiḇ‘āṯayim*
Variant; not used

8687 שָׁבַץ *šāḇas* (2)
filigree settings (1)
weave (1)

8688 שָׁבָץ *šāḇās* (1)
throes of death (1)

8689 1שָׁבַר *šāḇar1* (147)
break (19)
broken (16)
smashed (10)
be broken (9)
broke (9)
be destroyed (5)
break down (4)
cut off (4)
shattered (4)
smash (4)
brokenhearted (3) +4213
injured (3)
is broken (3)
are broken (2)
are crushed (2)
breaking to pieces (2)
breaks (2)
broke up (2)
crush (2)
destroy (2)
destroyed (2)
is injured (2)
mauled (2)
was broken off (2)
were wrecked (2)
abolish (1)
are broken off (1)
are shattered (1)
be broken off (1)
be broken up (1)
be injured (1)
be smashed (1)
been broken (1)
been grieved (1)
break to pieces (1)
break to pieces (1) +8689
break up (1)
breaks down (1)
breaks in pieces (1)
bring to the moment of birth (1)
broke off (1)
broken off (1)
crushed (1)
demolish (1)
desolate (1)
fixed (1)
is shattered (1)
quench (1)
shattering (1)
stripped (1)
suffered (1)
was broken (1)
were crushed (1)
untranslated (1)

8690 2שָׁבַר *šāḇar2* (21)
buy (11)
sell (3)
buy grain (2)
sold grain (2)
buying (1)
pay for (1)
selling (1)

8691 1שֶׁבֶר *šeḇer1* (44)
destruction (14)
wound (7)
destroyed (3)
disaster (2)
fracture (2)
break in pieces (1)
broken (1)
brokenness (1)
bruises (1)
collapses (1) +995
crash (1)
crippled (1)
crushed (1)
crushes (1)
downfall (1)
fractures (1)
injury (1)
ruin (1)
thrashing (1)
untranslated (2)

8692 2שֶׁבֶר *šeḇer2* (9)
grain (9)

8693 3שֶׁבֶר *šeḇer3* (1)
Sheber (1)

8694 שֵׁבֶר *šēḇer* (1)
interpretation (1)

8695 שִׁבָּרוֹן *šibbārôn* (2)
broken (1)
destruction (1)

8696 שְׁבָרִים *šᵉḇāriym* (1)
stone quarries (1)

8697 שָׁבַת *šāḇaṯ* (72)
put an end (14)
rested (4)
stopped (4)
come to an end (3)
remove (3)
rest (3)
stop (3)
bring an end (2)
cease (2)
ended (2)
gone (2)
put a stop (2)
abandoned (1)
abstained from work (1)
blot out (1)
bring to an end (1)
cause to stop (1)
cut off (1)
did away with (1)
disappear (1)
discard (1)
do away with (1)
do not work (1)
have rest (1)
have[s] (1)
leave (1)
left without (1)
makes cease (1)
must observe a sabbath (1) +8701
need not (1)
no (1)
observe sabbath (1) +8701
removed (1)
revert (1)
rid (1)
ruined (1)
settles (1)
silence (1)
stilled (1)
stopping (1)

8698 2שָׁבַת *šāḇaṯ2*
Variant; not used

8699 1שֶׁבֶת *šeḇeṯ1* (6)
seat (2) +5226
home (1)
lie (1)
reign (1)
site (1)

8700 2שֶׁבֶת *šeḇeṯ2* (2)
Do-Nothing (1)
loss of time (1)

8701 שַׁבָּת *šabbāṯ* (111)
sabbath (66)
sabbaths (30)
another[s] (1)
every sabbath (1) +928+8701
every sabbath (1) +8701
it[s] (1) +2021
must observe a sabbath (1) +8697
observe sabbath (1) +8697
sabbath after sabbath (1)
+928+928+2021+2021+3427+3427+8701
sabbath days (1)
sabbath rests (1)
weeks (1)
untranslated (2)

8702 שַׁבָּתוֹן *šabbāṯôn* (11)
rest (7)
day of rest (4)

8703 שַׁבְּתַי *šabbᵉṯay* (3)
Shabbethai (3)

8704 שָׁגַג *šāgag* (4)
deceived (1)
erred (1)
went astray (1)
wrong committed unintentionally (1) +8705

8705 שְׁגָגָה *šᵉgāgāh* (19)
unintentionally (6) +928
accidentally (4) +928
mistake (2)
error (1)
not intentional (1)
sins unintentionally (1) +928+6913
unintentional wrong (1)
unintentionally (1) +4200
wrong (1)
wrong committed unintentionally (1) +8704

8706 שָׁגָה *šāgāh* (21)
stagger (3)
stray (3)
captivated (2)
led astray (2)
sins unintentionally (2)
deceiver (1)
erred (1)
gone astray (1)
leads (1)
leads astray (1)
let stray (1)
unintentionally (1)
wandered (1)
wrong (1)

8707 שָׁגֵה *šāgēh* (1)
Shagee (1)

8708 שָׁגַח *šāgah* (3)
gazing (1)
stare (1)
watches (1)

8709 שְׁגִיאָה *šᵉgiy'āh* (1)
errors (1)

8710 שִׁגָּיוֹן *šiggāyôn* (2)
shiggaion (1)
shigionoth (1)

8711 שָׁגַל *šāgal* (4)
been ravished (1)
raped (1)
ravish (1)
ravished (1)

8712 שֵׁגָל *šēgal* (2)
queen (1)
royal bride (1)

8713 שָׁגַע *šāga'* (7)
carry on (1)
drive mad (1)
insane (1)
madman (1)
madman (1) +408
madmen (1)
maniac (1)

8714 שִׁגָּעוֹן *šiggā'ôn* (3)
madness (2)
madman (1)

8715 שֶׁגֶר *šeger* (5)
calves (4)
firstborn (1) +7081

8716 שַׁד *šaḏ* (21)
breasts (17)
breast (4)

8717 שֵׁד *šēḏ* (2)
demons (2)

8718 1שֹׁד *šōḏ1* (3)
breasts (2)
breast (1)

8719 2שֹׁד *šōḏ2* (25)
destruction (13)
ruin (4)
violence (3)
oppression (2)
havoc (1)
loot (1)
untranslated (1)

8720 שָׁדַד *šāḏaḏ* (59)
destroyer (7)
destroyed (6)
destroy (5)
ruined (4)
destroyers (3)
is destroyed (3)
are destroyed (2)
be destroyed (2)
destroying (2)
destroys (2)
devastated (2)
marauders (2)
are ruined (1)
assail (1)
be devastated (1)
be ruined (1)
been destroyed (1)
dead (1)
doomed to destruction (1)
in ruins (1)
lies in ruins (1)
looter (1)
perish (1)
raid (1)
ravage (1)
robbers (1)
robs (1)
shatter (1)
takes loot (1)
utterly ruined (1) +8720

8721 שִׁדָּה *šiddāh* (2)
harem (1) +2256+8721

8722 שָׁדוּד *šāḏûḏ*
Variant; not used

8723 שַׁדּוּן *šaddûn* (1)
judgment (1)

8724 שַׁדַּי *šadday* (48)
Almighty (48)

8725 שְׁדֵיאוּר *šᵉḏēy'ûr* (5)
Shedeur (5)

8726 שַׁדִּין *šaddiyn* (1)
untranslated (1)

8727 שְׁדֵמָה *šᵉḏēmāh* (5)
fields (4)
terraces (1)

8728 שָׁדַף *šāḏap̱* (3)
scorched (3)

8729 שְׁדֵפָה *šᵉḏēp̱āh* (2)
scorched (2)

8730 שִׁדָּפוֹן *šiddāp̱ôn* (5)
blight (5)

8731 שַׁדְרַךְ *šadraḵ* (1)
Shadrach (1)

8732 1שֹׁהַם *šōham1* (11)
onyx (9)
onyx (2) +74

8733 2שֹׁהַם *šōham2* (1)
Shoham (1)

8734 שָׁו *šāw*
Variant; not used

8735 שׁוּא *šû'*
Variant; not used

8736 שָׁוְא *šāw'* (54)
false (15)
in vain (4) +2021+4200
worthless (4)
in vain (3)
lies (3)
misuse (3) +2021+4200+5951
deceitful (2)
falsehood (2)

futility (2)
misuses (2) +2021+4200+5951
deceit (1)
destruction (1)
empty plea (1)
falsely (1)
futile (1)
idol (1)
idols (1)
lies (1) +1819
meaningless (1)
nothing (1)
worthless idols (1)
worthless idols (1) +2039
worthless things (1)
untranslated (1)

8737 **שְׁוָא** *šᵉwā'* (2)
Sheva (2)

8738 **שׁוֹא** *šô'* (1)
ravages (1)

8739 **שׁוֹאָה** *šô'āh* (12)
ruin (3)
desolate (2)
storm (2)
catastrophe (1)
destroyed (1)
disaster (1)
ruins (1)
trouble (1)

8740 **1שׁוּב** *šûb1* (1069)
return (157)
returned (99)
turn (50)
bring back (39)
go back (37)
again (34)
restore (34)
turn back (34)
come back (23)
brought back (21)
went back (21)
back (20)
turned (16)
turn away (15)
restored (14)
turned away (13)
put back (10)
repent (10)
turned back (10)
give back (9)
send back (9)
answer (8) +1821
repay (8)
came back (7)
take back (7)
turns (7)
turns away (7)
recovered (6)
reported (6) +1821
returns (6)
answer (5)
bring (5)
change (5)
go (5)
took back (5)
go (4) +2143+2256
pay back (4)
refuse (4)
relent (4)
rewarded (4)
take (4)
withdrew (4)
answered (3) +1821
bringing back (3)
make return (3)
regain (3)
restores (3)
returning (3)
started back (3)
stop (3)
stopped (3)
turned around (3)
again and again (2)
be sure to take back (2) +8740
bring down (2)
brought (2)
come (2)
coming back (2)
ever return (2) +8740
give (2)
keep (2)
left (2)
once more (2)
oppose (2)
pay (2)
rebuilt (2) +1215+2256
reject (2) +7156
repaid (2)
repented (2)
reply (2)
repulse (2) +7156
restrain (2)
retreat (2)
revert (2)
revoked (2)
rewards (2)
sent (2)
sent back (2)
take vengeance (2) +5934
turn around (2)
turn away (2) +8740
turning (2)
withdraw (2)
withholds (2)
again (1) +9108
again be used (1)
again give allegiance (1) +4213
another (1)
answer give (1)
answered (1)
answers (1) +1821
arrived (1)
back again (1)
be brought back (1)
been returned (1)
break (1)
bring in (1)
broke off (1) +4946
brought down (1)
by all means send (1) +8740
call to mind (1) +448+4213
came again (1)
carry the battle (1) +1741+2256
caused to roam (1)
changed (1)
changed mind (1)
changed minds (1)
continually (1)
cover up (1) +2256+4059
depart (1)
departs (1)
did^{s} (1)
do so^{s} (1) +2006+4946
dole out (1)
draw back (1)
drew back (1)
drives (1)
dwell (1)
escaping (1)
flow back (1)
flowed back (1)
forced to restore (1)
gave (1)
get back (1)
give up (1) +4946
gives back (1)
go back (1) +345
go on (1)
going back (1)
hold back (1)
keep themselves alive (1) +906+4392+5883
keep themselves alive (1) +5883
keeps saying (1) +609
left behind (1)
lose (1)
made go back (1)
made pay for (1) +928+8031
made prosperous again (1) +8654
made retreat (1) +294
make full restitution (1) +928+8031
make go (1)
make right (1)
marauding (1) +2256+6296
mislead (1)
no longer (1)
not angry (1) +678
overruling (1)
overthrows (1) +294
paid (1)
paid (1) +868
paid back (1)
pass again (1)
passed (1)
pay (1) +4084
pays back (1)
pays back (1) +8740
penitent (1)
prompt to answer (1)
pull back (1)
pursues (1) +928
raised (1)
ran (1)
reappears (1) +2256+7255
rebuild (1) +1215+2256
recaptured (1) +2256+4374
receded steadily (1) +2143+2256+8740
recoil (1)
recoils (1)
reconsider (1) +6388
recover (1)
reentered (1) +995+2256
refreshes (1)
refund (1)
renew (1)
renounce (1) +7156
reopened (1) +2256+2916
repay (1) +928+8031
repay (1) +6584+8031
repaying (1)
repents (1)
reply (1) +4863
rescue (1)
respond (1)
responded (1)
rest (1)
restitution (1) +871
restitution made (1)
restore again (1)
restorer (1)
restrained (1)
retire (1)
retreats (1)
return (1) +2143
return (1) +8740
returned unanswered (1) +2668
reverse (1)
reversed (1)
revived (1) +8120
reviving (1)
revoke (1)
roll back (1)
say (1)
send (1)
sending back (1)
shy away (1)
something else (1)
stops to think (1) +448+4213
strayed (1)
subsides (1)
supply (1)
surely return (1) +8740

take away (1)
take back (1) +8740
taken back (1)
takes back (1) +8740
try again (1)
turn again (1)
turned again (1)
turned to go (1)
turning away (1)
vent (1)
ward off (1)
were brought back (1)
withdrawn (1) +294
withheld (1)
withhold (1)
untranslated (33)

8741 2שׁוּב *šûḇ2*
Variant; not used

8742 שׁוּבָאֵל *šûḇā'ēl* (3)
Shubael (3)

8743 1שׁוֹבָב *šôḇāḇ1* (3)
faithless (2)
kept on (1) +2143

8744 2שׁוֹבָב *šôḇāḇ2* (4)
Shobab (4)

8745 שׁוֹבֵב *šôḇēḇ* (3)
unfaithful (2)
traitors (1)

8746 שׁוּבָה *šûḇāh* (1)
repentance (1)

8747 שׁוֹבָךְ *šôḇaḵ* (2)
Shobach (2)

8748 שׁוֹבָל *šôḇāl* (9)
Shobal (9)

8749 שׁוֹבֵק *šôḇēq* (1)
Shobek (1)

8750 1שָׁוָה *šāwāh1* (14)
compare (2)
be like (1)
count equal (1)
equal (1)
get what deserved (1)
gives satisfaction (1)
in best interest (1)
is like (1)
justify (1)
leveled (1)
liken (1)
stilled (1)
waited patiently (1)

8751 2שָׁוָה *šāwāh2* (7)
bestowed (2)
makes (2)
brought forth (1)
set (1)
set heart (1)

8752 שָׁוֶה *šāweh*
Variant; not used

8753 שָׁוֵה *šāwēh* (1)
Shaveh (1)

8754 שָׁוֵה קִרְיָתַיִם *šāwēh qiryāṯayim* (1)
Shaveh Kiriathaim (1)

8755 1שׁוּחַ *šûah1* (1)
leads down (1)

8756 2שׁוּחַ *šûah2* (2)
Shuah (2)

8757 1שׁוּחָה *šûḥāh1* (5)
pit (4)
rifts (1)

8758 2שׁוּחָה *šûḥāh2* (1)
Shuhah's (1)

8759 שַׁוְחָט *šawḥāṭ*
Variant; not used

8760 שׁוּחִי *šûḥiy* (5)
Shuhite (5)

8761 שׁוּחָם *šûḥām* (1)
Shuham (1)

8762 שׁוּחָמִי *šûḥāmiy* (2)
Shuhamite (2)

8763 1שׁוּט *šûṭ1* (13)
oarsmen (2)
range (2)
roaming (2)
go (1)
go here and there (1)
go up and down (1)
gone (1)
rush here and there (1)
wander (1)
went around (1)

8764 2שׁוּט *šûṭ2* (3)
despise (1)
malicious (1)
maligned (1)

8765 1שׁוֹט *šôṭ1* (12)
whips (5)
scourge (3)
whip (2)
lash (1)
untranslated (1)

8766 2שׁוֹט *šôṭ2*
Variant; not used

8767 שׁוּל *šûl* (11)
hem (5)
skirts (4)
train of robe (1)
untranslated (1)

8768 שׁוֹלָל *šôlāl* (4)
stripped (2)
barefoot (1)
untranslated (1)

8769 שׁוּלַמִּית *šûlammiyṯ* (2)
Shulammite (2)

8770 שׁוּמִים *šûmiym* (1)
garlic (1)

8771 1שׁוּנִי *šûniy1* (2)
Shuni (2)

8772 2שׁוּנִי *šûniy2* (1)
Shunite (1)

8773 שׁוּנֵם *šûnēm* (3)
Shunem (3)

8774 שׁוּנַמִּי *šûnammiy* (8)
Shunammite (8)

8775 שָׁוַע *šāwa'* (22)
cry for help (7)
cried for help (4)
call for help (3)
called for help (3)
cry out (3)
cry out for help (1)
plead for relief (1)

8776 שֶׁוַע *šewa'* (1)
cry for help (1) +7754

8777 1שׁוֹעַ *šôa'1* (2)
highly respected (1)
rich (1)

8778 2שׁוֹעַ *šôa'2* (1)
Shoa (1)

8779 3שׁוֹעַ *šôa'3* (1)
crying out (1)

8780 1שׁוּעַ *šûa'1* (1)
cries for help (1)

8781 2שׁוּעַ *šûa'2* (3)
Shua (3)

8782 3שׁוּעַ *šûa'3* (1)
wealth (1)

8783 שׁוּעָא *šû'ā'* (1)
Shua (1)

8784 שַׁוְעָה *šaw'āh* (11)
cry (7)
cry for help (3)
outcry (1)

8785 1שׁוּעָל *šû'āl1* (7)
foxes (3)
jackals (3)
fox (1)

8786 2שׁוּעָל *šû'āl2* (1)
Shual (1)

8787 3שׁוּעָל *šû'āl3* (1)
Shual (1)

8788 שׁוֹעֵר *šô'ēr* (37)
gatekeepers (29)
doorkeepers (4)
gatekeeper (2)
keep watch (1)
keeper of gate (1)

8789 1שׁוּף *šûp̱1* (2)
crush (2)

8790 2שׁוּף *šûp̱2* (1)
strike (1)

8791 שׁוֹפָךְ *šôp̱aḵ* (2)
Shophach (2)

8792 שׁוּפָם *šûp̱ām* (1)
Shupham (1)

8793 שׁוּפָמִי *šûp̱āmiy* (1)
Shuphamite (1)

8794 שׁוֹפָן *šôp̱ān*
Variant; not used

8795 שׁוֹפָר *šôp̱ār* (72)
trumpet (44)
trumpets (18)
trumpets (3) +3413
ram's horn (2)
blast (1) +7754
horns (1)
rams' horns (1)
trumpet (1) +9558
untranslated (1)

8796 1שׁוּק *šûq1* (3)
overflow (2)
water (1)

8797 שׁוֹק *šôq* (19)
thigh (12)
legs (5)
attacked viciously (1) +3751+5782+6584
leg (1)

8798 2שׁוּק *šûq2* (4)
street (2)
streets (2)

8799 שׁוֹקֵק *šôqēq* (2)
thirsty (1) +5883
unquenched (1)

8800 1שׁוּר *šûr1* (14)
see (5)
behold (1)
care for (1)
gaze (1)
lie in wait (1)
look (1)
lurk (1)
pays attention (1)
perceive (1)
view (1)

8801 2שׁוּר *šûr2* (4)
carriers (1)
comes (1)

descend (1)
went (1)

8802 שׁוֹר *šôr* (79)
ox (38)
bull (16)
cattle (13)
animal (2)
bulls (2)
calf (2)
herd (2)
oxen (2)
cow (1)
one[S] (1)

8803 3שׁוּר *šûr3* (3)
wall (3)

8804 4שׁוּר *šûr4* (6)
Shur (6)

8805 שׁוּרָה *šûrāh* (1)
terraces (1)

8806 שׁוֹרֵר *šôrēr* (6)
slander (2)
adversaries (1)
enemies (1)
oppressors (1)
slanderers (1)

8807 שַׁוְשָׁא *šawšā'* (1)
Shavsha (1)

8808 1שׁוּשַׁן *šûšan1* (17)
lilies (11)
lily (6)

8809 2שׁוּשַׁן *šûšan2* (21)
Susa (21)

8810 שׁוּשַׁק *šûšaq* (1)
untranslated (1)

8811 שׁוּתֶלַח *šûṯelah* (4)
Shuthelah (4)

8812 שָׁזַף *šāzap̱* (3)
darkened (1)
saw (1)
seen (1)

8813 שָׁזַר *šāzar* (21)
finely twisted (21)

8814 שַׁח *šah* (1)
downcast (1) +6524

8815 שָׁחַד *šāhaḏ* (2)
bribing (1)
pay a ransom (1)

8816 שֹׁחַד *šōhaḏ* (23)
bribe (12)
bribes (6)
gift (2)
bribery (1) +5228
reward (1)
those who love bribes (1)

8817 שָׁחָה *šāhāh* (2)
fall prostrate (1)
weighs down (1)

8818 שְׁחוֹר *š^{e}hôr* (1)
soot (1)

8819 שְׁחוּת *š^{e}hûṯ* (1)
trap (1)

8820 שָׁחַח *šāhah* (19)
brought low (3)
be brought low (2)
bow down (1)
bowed head (1)
bowing (1)
bring down (1)
collapse (1)
collapsed (1)
cowered (1)
crouch (1)
downcast (1)
faint (1)
humbled (1)
humbles (1)
mumble (1)
untranslated (1)

8821 1שָׁחַט *šāhaṭ1* (81)
slaughtered (35)
slaughter (23)
killed (5)
sacrifices (2)
be slaughtered (1)
butchered (1)
dead (1)
deadly (1)
kill (1)
killing (1)
offer (1)
sacrifice (1)
sacrificed (1)
sacrifices slaughtered (1)
slaughtering (1)
slay (1)
was killed (1)
were slaughtered (1)
untranslated (2)

8822 2שָׁחַט *šāhaṭ2* (5)
hammered (5)

8823 שַׁחֲטָה *šah^{a}ṭāh* (1)
slaughter (1)

8824 שְׁחִיטָה *š^{e}hiyṭāh* (1)
kill (1)

8825 שְׁחִין *š^{e}hiyn* (13)
boil (6)
boils (5)
sores (1)
untranslated (1)

8826 שָׁחִיס *šāhiys* (1)
what springs from (1)

8827 שְׁחִית *š^{e}hiyṯ* (2)
grave (1)
traps (1)

8828 שַׁחַל *šahal* (7)
lion (6)
untranslated (1)

8829 שְׁחֵלֶת *š^{e}hēleṯ* (1)
onycha (1)

8830 שַׁחַף *šahap̱* (2)
gull (2)

8831 שַׁחֶפֶת *šahepeṯ* (2)
wasting disease (1)
wasting diseases (1)

8832 שַׁחַץ *šahas* (2)
proud (1) +1201
proud beasts (1) +1201

8833 שַׁחֲצוּמָה *šah^{a}ṣûmāh* (1)
Shahazumah (1)

8834 שַׁחֲצִימָה *šah^{a}ṣiymāh* (1)
untranslated (1)

8835 שָׁחַק *šāhaq* (4)
beat fine (2)
grind (1)
wears away (1)

8836 שַׁחַק *šahaq* (21)
clouds (8)
skies (8)
clouds of the sky (2) +6265
dust (1)
skies above (1)
sky (1)

8837 1שָׁחַר *šāhar1* (1)
grows black (1)

8838 2שָׁחַר *šāhar2* (13)
earnestly seek (2)
careful (1)
conjure away (1)
eagerly (1)
foraging (1)
longs for (1)
look (1)
look for (1)
looked for (1)
search for (1)
seek (1)
seeks (1)

8839 שָׁחֹר *šāhōr* (6)
black (5)
dark (1)

8840 שַׁחַר *šahar* (24)
dawn (14)
daybreak (2)
daybreak (2) +2021+6590
day dawns (1)
first light of dawn (1) +6590
light of dawn (1)
morning (1)
sun rises (1)
untranslated (1)

8841 שַׁחֲרוּת *šah^{a}rûṯ* (1)
vigor (1)

8842 שְׁחַרְחֹר *š^{e}harhōr* (1)
dark (1)

8843 שְׁחַרְיָה *š^{e}haryāh* (1)
Shehariah (1)

8844 שַׁחֲרַיִם *šah^{a}rayim* (1)
Shaharaim (1)

8845 שָׁחַת *šāhaṯ* (146)
destroy (60)
destroyed (11)
corrupt (10)
destroying (5)
cut down (3)
destroys (3)
ruin (3)
ruined (3)
act corruptly (2)
corrupted (2)
depraved (2)
destruction (2)
devastate (2)
raiding parties (2)
ravage (2)
acted corruptly (1)
afflicting (1)
allowed to fall into ruin (1)
battering (1)
blemished (1)
cause devastation (1)
cause of destruction (1)
clip off (1)
corrupt practices (1)
corruption (1)
devastated (1)
devouring (1)
doing so[S] (1)
downfall (1)
endanger (1)
given to corruption (1)
killed (1)
laid waste (1)
overthrow (1)
polluted (1)
ravaging (1)
ravening (1)
spilled (1)
steal (1)
stifling (1)
struck down (1)
sure to become utterly corrupt (1) +8845
tear down (1)

violated (1)
was marred (1)
was ruined (1)
wasted (1)
untranslated (1)

8846 שַׁחַת *šaḥaṯ* (23)
pit (17)
corruption (2)
decay (2)
dungeon (1)
slime pit (1)

8847 שִׁטָּה *šiṭṭāh* (29)
acacia (25)
acacia wood (3)
acacias (1)

8848 שָׁטַח *šāṭaḥ* (6)
enlarges (1)
exposed (1)
scattered (1)
spread out (1)
spread out (1) +8848

8849 שֹׁטֵט *šōṭēṭ* (1)
whips (1)

8850 שִׁטִּים *šiṭṭiym* (4)
Shittim (4)

8851 שָׁטַף *šāṭap̱* (31)
overwhelming (3)
torrents (3)
engulf (2)
flood (2)
overflow (2)
wash away (2)
washed (2)
be rinsed (1)
be swept away (1)
charging (1)
engulfed (1)
flooding (1)
flooding downpour (1) +3888
flowed (1)
flowed abundantly (1)
overflowing (1)
rinsed (1)
rinsing (1)
rushing (1)
sweep over (1)
swept away (1)
swirling over (1)

8852 שֶׁטֶף *šeṭep̱* (6)
flood (2)
overwhelming (2)
rise (1)
torrents of rain (1)

8853 שֹׁטֵר *šāṭar* (25)
officials (10)
officers (6)
foremen (5)
officer (1)
overseer (1)
scribes (1)
serve as officials (1)

8854 שֹׁטֵר *šōṭēr*
Variant; not used

8855 שִׁטְרַי *šiṭray* (1)
Shitrai (1)

8856 שַׁי *šay* (3)
gifts (3)

8857 שְׁיָא *š'yā'* (1)
untranslated (1)

8858 שִׁיאֹן *šiy'ōn* (1)
Shion (1)

8859 1שִׁיבָה *šiyḇāh1* (1)
stay (1)

8860 2שִׁיבָה *šiyḇāh2* (1)
captives (1)

8861 שָׁיָה *šāyāh* (1)
deserted (1)

8862 שִׁיזָא *šiyzā'* (1)
Shiza (1)

8863 שִׂיחַ *šiyaḥ* (5)
downcast (4)
down (1)

8864 שִׁיחָה *šiyḥāh* (3)
pit (1)
pitfalls (1)
untranslated (1)

8865 שִׁיחוֹר *šiyḥôr* (4)
Shihor (4)

8866 שִׁיחוֹר לִבְנָת *šiyḥôr liḇnāṯ* (1)
Shihor Libnath (1)

8867 שִׁיט *šiyṭ*
Variant; not used

8868 שַׁיִט *šayiṭ* (1)
oars (1)

8869 שִׁילֹה *šiylōh*
Variant; not used

8870 שִׁילוֹ *šiylô* (3)
Shiloh (3)

8871 שֵׁילָל *šēylāl*
Variant; not used

8872 שִׁילֹנִי *šiylōniy* (6)
Shilonite (4)
of Shiloh (1)
Shilonites (1)

8873 שִׁימוֹן *šiymôn* (1)
Shimon (1)

8874 שִׁין *šiyn* (6)
every last male (3) +928+7815
male (3) +928+7815

8875 שַׁיִן *šayin* (2)
urine (2)

8876 1שִׁיר *šiyr1* (87)
sing (33)
singers (27)
musicians (6)
sang (5)
women[s] (5)
choirs (2)
be sung (1)
echo (1)
musician (1)
praised in song (1)
sang song (1)
singers (1) +1201
singing (1)
sings (1)
untranslated (1)

8877 2שִׁיר *šiyr2* (79)
song (47)
songs (11)
musical (6)
music (5)
singing (4)
instruments (1) +3998
sing (1)
singers (1)
songs (1) +1426
songs (1) +1821
untranslated (1)

8878 שִׁירָה *šiyrāh* (13)
song (11)
it[s] (1) +2021+2021+2296
songs (1)

8879 שְׁיָרָה *š'yārāh*
Variant; not used

8880 שַׁיִשׁ *šayiš* (1)
marble (1) +74

8881 שִׁישָׁא *šiyšā'* (1)
Shisha (1)

8882 שִׁישַׁק *šiyšaq* (7)
Shishak (7)

8883 1שִׁית *šiyṯ1* (86)
make (9)
put (9)
set (7)
made (6)
laid (3)
bring (2)
give (2)
granted (2)
is demanded (2)
lay (2)
place (2)
take (2)
turn (2)
alert (1)
applied (1)
apply (1)
appointed (1)
assign (1)
change (1)
close (1)
consider well (1) +4213
demands (1)
drawn up (1)
endowed (1)
establish (1)
gave a place (1)
halt (1)
harbors (1)
have (1)
help (1) +3338+6640
hold (1)
make turn (1)
makes (1)
pay (1)
perform (1)
placed (1)
placing (1)
posted (1) +8883
protect (1) +928+3829
set out (1)
strike (1)
take note (1) +4213
treat (1)
turned (1)
wrestle (1)
untranslated (3)

8884 2שִׁית *šiyṯ2* (2)
clothe (1) +6493
dressed (1)

8885 שַׁיִת *šayiṯ* (7)
thorns (7)

8886 שָׁכַב *šākaḇ* (211)
rested (36)
lie down (20)
lie (18)
lay down (13)
lying (10)
lay (8)
rest (8)
lies (7)
sleep (5)
sleeps with (5) +6640
slept with (5) +907
lie with (4) +6640
lying down (4)
lies down (3)
lies with (3) +907
sleeps with (3) +907
slept with (3) +6640
be laid (2)
come to bed with (2) +6640
has sexual relations with (2) +6640
laid (2)
lay with (2) +907

lay with (2) +6640
put (2)
sleep with (2) +6640
slept (2)
bed with (1) +6640
done this[s] (1) +6640
go (1)
go to bed with (1) +725
go to sleep (1)
gone to bed (1)
he[s] (1) +408+2021+2021+6640
laid low (1)
laid to rest (1)
lain down (1)
lay down to sleep (1)
lie around (1)
lie in state (1) +928+3883
lie with (1) +907
lies with (1) +907+8886
lies with (1) +6640
lying with (1) +907
made lie down (1)
raped (1) +2256+6700
rapes (1) +2256+2616+6640
rapes (1) +2256+6640+9530
resting (1)
sleeping (1)
sleeping with (1) +907+2446+8887
sleeping with (1) +6640
sleeps (1)
sleeps with (1) +907+2446+8887
stayed (1)
take rest (1)
taking rest (1) +5435
tip over (1)
violated (1) +2256+6700
untranslated (5)

8887 שִׁכְבָה *šik̲bāh* (9)
emission (4)
layer (1)
sleeping with (1) +907+2446+8886
sleeps with (1) +907+2446+8886
untranslated (2)

8888 שְׁכֹבֶת *š*^{e}*k̲ōbet̲* (4)
has sexual relations (1) +5989
have sexual relations (1) +2446+4200+5989
have sexual relations (1) +5989
sleeping with (1) +928+5989

8889 שָׁכָה *šāk̲āh* (1)
well-fed (1)

8890 שְׁכוֹל *š*^{e}*k̲ôl* (3)
loss of children (2)
forlorn (1)

8891 שַׁכּוּל *šakkûl* (6)
alone (2)
robbed of cubs (2)
childless (1)
robbed (1)

8892 שְׁכוּלָה *š*^{e}*k̲ûlāh* (1)
bereaved (1)

8893 שִׁכּוֹר *šikkôr* (13)
drunkards (4)
drunk (2)
drunkard (2)
getting drunk (2) +9272
drunkard's (1)
drunken (1)
drunken men (1)

8894 שָׁכַח *šāk̲aḥ* (101)
forget (42)
forgotten (22)
forgot (11)
be forgotten (9)
ignore (4)
forgets (2)
ignored (2)
am forgotten (1) +4213+4946
ever forget (1) +8894
is forgotten (1)
made forget (1)
make forget (1)
neglect (1)
overlook (1)
unmindful (1)

8895 שָׁכֵחַ *šāk̲ēaḥ* (2)
forget (2)

8896 שָׁכַךְ *šāk̲ak̲* (5)
subsided (2)
receded (1)
rid (1)
untranslated (1)

8897 שָׁכֹל *šāk̲al* (23)
miscarry (3)
bereaved (2)
deprive of children (2)
leave childless (2)
make childless (2)
bereave (1)
bereaves (1)
bring bereavement (1)
cast fruit (1)
childless (1)
deprived of children (1)
lose (1)
made childless (1)
make unproductive (1)
miscarried (1)
rob of children (1)
unproductive (1)

8898 שִׁכֻּלִים *šikkuliym* (1)
bereavement (1)

8899 שָׁכַם *šāk̲am* (66)
early (18)
again and again (11)
got up early (5)
get up early (4)
got up (4)
early got up (3)
early in the morning (3)
rose (3)
rose early (3)
early the next morning (2)
again and again (1) +2256+8938
eager (1)
early arose (1)
early morning get up (1)
go early (1)
laid (1)
morning (1)
rise early (1)
untranslated (2)

8900 1שְׁכֶם *š*^{e}*k̲em1* (22)
shoulders (9)
shoulder (7)
head (2) +2025+2256+4946+5087
backs (1)
ridge of land (1)
shoulder to shoulder (1) +285
turned (1) +7155

8901 2שְׁכֶם *š*^{e}*k̲em2* (48)
Shechem (43)
there[s] (2)
its[s] (1)
they[s] (1) +1251+3972+4463
who[s] (1) +1251

8902 3שְׁכֶם *š*^{e}*k̲em3* (15)
Shechem (12)
Shechem's (3)

8903 שֶׁכֶם *šek̲em* (3)
Shechem (3)

8904 שִׁכְמִי *šik̲miy* (1)
Shechemite (1)

8905 שָׁכַן *šāk̲an* (131)
live (26)
dwell (21)
dwelling (8)
live in (6)
settled (5)
dwell in (4)
dwells (4)
nest (3)
stayed (3)
dwelt (2)
dwelt in (2)
have a home (2) +9393
let live (2)
lived in (2)
lives (2)
living (2)
remain (2)
rest (2)
set up (2)
settle (2)
abode (1)
allow to dwell (1)
among (1) +907
at rest (1)
came to rest (1)
camp (1)
come to dwell (1)
dwells in (1)
encamped (1)
find shelter (1)
inhabit (1)
inhabited (1)
let settle (1)
lie (1)
lie down to rest (1)
lived (1)
lives in (1)
made a dwelling (1)
make home (1)
make sleep (1)
nomads (1) +185+928
placed (1)
resides (1)
rests (1)
settled in (1)
stands (1)
stay (1)
stayed (1) +799
untranslated (1)

8906 שֶׁכֶן *šek̲en*
Variant; not used

8907 שָׁכֵן *šāk̲ēn* (21)
neighbors (11)
neighbor (3)
neighboring (2)
living (1)
neighboring peoples (1)
one living in (1)
people who live in (1)
untranslated (1)

8908 שְׁכַנְיָה *š*^{e}*k̲anyāh* (9)
Shecaniah (8)
Shecaniah's (1)

8909 שְׁכַנְיָהוּ *š*^{e}*k̲anyāhû* (2)
Shecaniah (2)

8910 שָׁכַר *šāk̲ar* (18)
drunk (6)
make drunk (4)
made drunk (3)
drank freely (1)
drink fill (1)
get drunk (1)
have fill (1)
keep on getting drunk (1)

8911 שֵׁכָר *šēk̲ār* (23)
beer (11)
fermented drink (9)
drinks (2)
drunkards (1) +9272

8912 שָׁכֻר *šāk̠ur* (1)
made drunk (1)

8913 1שִׁכָּרוֹן *šikkārôn1* (3)
drunkenness (2)
drunk (1)

8914 2שִׁכָּרוֹן *šikkārôn2* (1)
Shikkeron (1)

8915 שַׁל *šal* (1)
irreverent act (1)

8916 שַׁלְאֲנָן *šal'^{a}nan* (1)
secure (1)

8917 שָׁלָב *šālab̠* (2)
set parallel (2)

8918 שָׁלָב *šālāb̠* (3)
uprights (3)

8919 שָׁלַג *šālag̠* (1)
snow fallen (1)

8920 1שֶׁלֶג *šeleg̠1* (19)
snow (16)
snowy (2)
snows (1)

8921 2שֶׁלֶג *šeleg̠2* (1)
soap (1)

8922 1שָׁלָה *šālāh1* (7)
at ease (1)
have peace (1)
live at ease (1)
negligent (1)
raise hopes (1)
secure (1)
undisturbed (1)

8923 2שָׁלָה *šālāh2* (1)
takes away (1)

8924 1שֵׁלָה *šēlāh1* (1)
what^{s} (1)

8925 2שֵׁלָה *šēlāh2* (8)
Shelah (8)

8926 שִׁלֹה *šilōh* (22)
Shiloh (22)

8927 שַׁלְהֶבֶת *šalheb̠et̠* (2)
flame (2)

8928 שַׁלְהֶבֶתְיָה *šalheb̠etyāh* (1)
mighty flame (1)

8929 שָׁלֵו *šālēw* (8)
at ease (2)
carefree (2)
prosperous (1)
quiet (1)
respite (1)
well (1)

8930 שָׁלוּ *šālû* (1)
felt secure (1)

8931 שִׁלוֹ *šilô* (7)
Shiloh (6)
there^{s} (1) +928

8932 שַׁלְוָה *šalwāh* (8)
feel secure (3)
complacency (1)
felt secure (1)
peace and quiet (1)
security (1)
unconcerned (1) +9200

8933 שִׁלּוּחִים *šillûḥiym* (3)
parting gifts (1)
sent away (1)
wedding gift (1)

8934 שָׁלוֹם *šālôm* (236)
peace (113)
all right (9)
safe (9)
safely (9) +928
come in peace (5)
prosperity (5)
greet (4) +4200+8626
greeted (4) +4200+8626
well (4)
how are (3)
success (3)
cordially (2)
good health (2)
in peace (2)
peaceful (2)
peacefully (2)
prosper (2)
treaty of friendship (2) +2256+3208
triumph (2)
all is well (1)
asked how they were (1) +4200+8626
benefit (1)
blessing (1)
close friend (1) +408
completely (1)
contentment (1)
desires (1)
friendly relations (1)
friends (1)
friends (1) +408
friends (1) +632
good (1)
goodwill (1)
greet (1)
grow well (1)
harmony (1) +6783
how is (1)
how was (1)
how was (1) +4200
how was going (1) +4200
how were (1) +4200
kind (1)
order (1)
peace and prosperity (1)
peaceably (1)
peaceably (1) +928
peaceful relations (1)
peacefully (1) +928
peacetime (1)
perfect peace (1) +8934
prospers (1)
safely (1) +2021+4200
safely (1) +4200
satisfied (1) +928
secure (1)
sound (1)
soundness (1)
trusted friends (1) +408
unharmed (1)
unharmed (1) +928
unscathed (1)
unscathed (1) +928
welcome (1)
welfare (1)
well-being (1)
wish well (1) +4200
yes^{s} (1)
untranslated (3)

8935 שַׁלּוּם *šallûm* (26)
Shallum (25)
Shallum's (1)

8936 שִׁלּוּם *šillûm* (4)
retribution (2)
bribes (1)
reckoning (1)

8937 שַׁלּוּן *šallûn* (1)
Shallun (1)

8938 שָׁלַח *šālaḥ* (847)
sent (310)
send (113)
let go (55)
sent away (22)
sending (20)
sent out (17)
lay (11)
sent word (11)
reached out (10)
sends (10)
send away (9)
stretched out (7)
send on way (5)
sent for (5) +2256+4200+7924
sent on way (5)
set free (5)
called together (4) +665+2256
lift (4)
release (4)
send word (4)
sent off (4)
set (4)
stretch out (4)
divorce (3)
reach out (3)
sent back (3)
sent for (3)
sent for (3) +2256+7924
shoot (3)
stirs up (3)
assassinate (2) +928+3338
been sent (2)
dismissed (2)
divorced (2)
drive out (2)
extend (2)
free (2)
free (2) +2930
gave orders (2)
gave over (2)
pursue (2) +339
raise (2)
reached (2)
reached down (2)
replied (2) +606
send back (2)
send for (2) +2256+4374
send forth (2)
send out (2)
sent message (2)
shot (2)
summoned (2) +2256+7924
thrust (2)
unleashed (2)
was sent (2)
abandoned (1)
again and again (1) +2256+8899
appealed (1)
assaults (1) +928
assigned (1)
attack (1) +928+3338
attacked (1) +928+3338
attacks (1) +928+3338
banished (1)
be sent (1)
be sure to let go (1) +8938
being sent (1)
brought (1)
burned (1) +836+928+2021
calling together (1) +995+2256
cast (1)
checked on (1) +448
come back (1)
delivered (1)
demanded (1)
directed (1)
dispatched (1)
divorces (1)
do let go (1) +8938
does^{s} (1)
ended (1)
exile (1)
extends (1)
force (1)
freed (1) +2930

gave (1)
gave away in marriage (1)
get out of here (1) +2021+2025+2575
give an order (1)
had brought (1) +2256+4374
had removed (1) +2256+4374
holds (1)
invite (1) +2256+7924
killing (1) +928+3338
laid (1)
lay snares (1)
lays (1)
leave (1)
left to himself (1)
let down (1)
let get away (1)
let get away (1) +928+2006
let grow (1)
let loose (1)
lets loose (1)
lets stray (1)
letting go (1)
letting range free (1) +8079
lowered (1)
made flourish (1)
makes pour (1)
mission (1) +889+1821
ordered (1)
pointing (1)
provided (1)
pushed (1)
put (1)
put out (1)
putting (1)
reach down (1)
reached out (1) +3338
reaches out (1) +3338
reaching (1) +3338
reject (1) +4946+6584+7156
released (1)
releases (1)
remove (1)
return (1)
rushing (1)
see on way (1)
seize (1)
send a message (1)
send for (1)
send urgent (1) +8938
sending away (1)
sends out (1)
sent a message (1)
sent for (1) +2256+4374
sent for (1) +4200+7924
sent for help (1)
sent forth (1)
sent messengers (1)
sent on way (1) +906
sent word (1) +2256+5583
sent word (1) +2256+7924
set fire to (1) +836+928+2021
set free (1) +2930
set free (1) +3338+4946
shooting (1)
spared (1)
specify (1)
spreading (1)
summon (1)
summon (1) +2256+4374
summoned (1)
summoned (1) +4200+7924
swing (1)
throw off (1)
told (1) +606+4200
took back (1) +995+2256
turned (1)
unleash (1)
use (1)
use to do (1)
vent (1)
was sent away (1)
were sent (1)
were sent on way (1)
untranslated (17)

8939 שֶׁלַח1 *šelah1* (7)
weapon (3)
sword (2)
defenses (1)
weapons (1)

8940 שֶׁלַח2 *šelah2* (1)
Siloam (1)

8941 שֶׁלַח3 *šelah3* (9)
Shelah (9)

8942 שִׁלֹחַ *šilōah* (1)
Shiloah (1)

8943 שְׁלֻחוֹת *šᵉluhôṯ* (1)
shoots (1)

8944 שִׁלְחִי *šilhiy* (2)
Shilhi (2)

8945 שְׁלָחִים *šᵉlāhiym* (1)
plants (1)

8946 שִׁלְחִים *šilhiym* (1)
Shilhim (1)

8947 שֻׁלְחָן *šulhān* (71)
table (52)
tables (12)
each table (1) +2256+8947
it[s] (1) +2021
untranslated (4)

8948 שָׁלַט *šālat* (8)
enable (1)
enables (1)
got the upper hand (1)
have control (1)
let rule (1)
lorded it over (1)
lords it over (1)
overpower (1)

8949 שֶׁלֶט *šelet* (7)
shields (6)
small shields (1)

8950 שִׁלְטוֹן *šiltôn* (2)
power (1)
supreme (1)

8951 שַׁלֶּטֶת *šalleteṯ* (1)
brazen (1)

8952 שְׁלִי *šᵉliy* (1)
privately (1) +928+2021

8953 שִׁלְיָה *šilyāh* (1)
afterbirth (1)

8954 שַׁלִּיט *šalliyt* (4)
governor (1)
power (1)
ruler (1)
rulers (1)

8955 שָׁלִישׁ1 *šāliyš1* (2)
basket (1)
bowlful (1)

8956 שָׁלִישׁ2 *šāliyš2* (1)
lutes (1)

8957 שָׁלִישׁ3 *šāliyš3* (16)
officers (5)
officer (3)
captains (2)
chariot officers (2)
chariot officer (1)
chief officers (1)
untranslated (2)

8958 שְׁלִישִׁי *šᵉliyšiy* (105)
third (93)
three (7)
day after (1)
day after tomorrow (1)
one-third (1)
that[s] (1)
upper (1)

8959 שָׁלַךְ *šālaḵ* (125)
threw (26)
throw (14)
cast (8)
thrust (7)
thrown (6)
put (5)
throw away (3)
throw down (3)
thrown down (3)
get rid of (2)
hurled (2)
hurled down (2)
threw down (2)
thrown away (2)
thrown out (2)
throws (2)
toss (2)
are cast (1)
banish (1)
be thrown (1)
be thrown out (1)
cast away (1)
cast out (1)
did[s] (1)
divide (1)
dropped (1)
dropping (1)
flung (1)
hurl (1)
hurls (1)
hurls down (1)
in ruins (1)
knocked (1)
pelt (1)
pushed back (1)
pushed down (1)
reject (1) +4946+6584+7156
rid (1) +4946+6584
risked (1) +4946+5584
scatter (1)
scattered (1)
set down (1)
shedding (1)
snatched (1)
sprinkle (1)
threw away (1)
threw out (1)
throw off (1)
thrown aside (1)
was brought low (1)
were thrown out (1)

8960 שָׁלָךְ *šālāḵ* (2)
cormorant (2)

8961 שַׁלֶּכֶת1 *šalleḵeṯ1* (1)
cut down (1)

8962 שַׁלֶּכֶת2 *šalleḵeṯ2* (1)
Shalleketh (1)

8963 שָׁלַל1 *šālal1* (2)
pull out (1) +8963

8964 שָׁלַל2 *šālal2* (14)
plunder (4)
plundered (4)
plunder (2) +8965
seize (2)
becomes prey (1)
loot (1) +8965

8965 שָׁלָל *šālāl* (74)
plunder (49)
escape with (4) +4200
spoils (4)
loot (3)
plunder (2) +8964

booty (1)
goods (1)
loot (1) +8964
plundered (1)
prey (1)
property (1)
share of plunder (1)
spoil (1)
value (1)
which^{s} (1) +2021
untranslated (2)

8966 1שָׁלֵם *šālēm1* (117)
repay (18)
fulfill (12)
pay (9)
make restitution (6)
pay back (6)
reward (6)
at peace (4)
finished (3)
made peace (3)
repays (3)
made a treaty of peace (2)
made an end (2)
must make restitution (2) +8966
repaying (2)
restore (2)
accomplish (1)
be fulfilled (1)
be repaid (1)
bring punishment (1)
carries out (1)
committed (1)
completed (1)
end (1)
fulfilled (1)
fulfilled obligations (1)
fulfilling (1)
fulfills (1)
is rewarded (1)
keep (1)
make good (1)
make pay (1)
make peace (1)
makes live at peace (1)
must certainly make restitution (1) +8966
must pay (1) +8966
offer (1)
paid back (1)
pay back in full (1)
pay for the loss (1)
pays back (1)
peaceful (1)
present (1)
receive due (1)
repaid (1)
repay in full (1) +8966
restitution (1)
returns (1)
unscathed (1)

8967 שְׁלָם *š^{e}lām*
Variant; not used

8968 שֶׁלֶם *šelem* (87)
fellowship (34)
fellowship offerings (32)
fellowship offering (20)
it^{s} (1) +2285

8969 2שָׁלֵם *šālēm2* (27)
fully committed (4)
accurate (2)
fully devoted (2)
whole (2)
wholehearted devotion (2) +4213
wholehearted devotion (2) +4222
wholeheartedly (2) +928+4222
allies (1)
dressed (1)
fieldstones (1) +74
friendly (1)
full measure (1)
fully determined (1) +928+4222
richly (1)
safely (1)
uncut (1)
wholeheartedly (1) +928+4213
untranslated (1)

8970 3שָׁלֵם *šālēm3* (2)
Salem (2)

8971 4שָׁלֵם *šālēm4*
Variant; not used

8972 1שִׁלֵּם *šillēm1*
Variant; not used

8973 2שִׁלֵּם *šillēm2* (3)
Shillem (3)

8974 שִׁלֻּמָה *šillumāh* (1)
punishment (1)

8975 שַׁלָּמָה *šallāmāh*
Variant; not used

8976 שְׁלֹמֹה *š^{e}lōmōh* (293)
Solomon (235)
Solomon's (26)
he^{s} (12)
Solomon's (7) +4200
him^{s} (6)
his^{s} (2)
his^{s} (2) +4200
Solomon's (1) +4200+8611
untranslated (2)

8977 שְׁלֹמוֹת *š^{e}lōmôṯ* (4)
Shelomoth (3)
untranslated (1)

8978 שַׁלְמַי *šalmay* (2)
Shalmai (2)

8979 שְׁלֹמִי *š^{e}lōmiy* (1)
Shelomi (1)

8980 שִׁלֵּמִי *šillēmiy* (1)
Shillemite (1)

8981 שְׁלֻמִיאֵל *š^{e}lumiy'ēl* (5)
Shelumiel (5)

8982 שֶׁלֶמְיָה *šelemyāh* (5)
Shelemiah (5)

8983 שֶׁלֶמְיָהוּ *šelemyāhû* (5)
Shelemiah (5)

8984 1שְׁלֹמִית *š^{e}lōmiyṯ1* (7)
Shelomith (6)
untranslated (1)

8985 2שְׁלֹמִית *š^{e}lōmiyṯ2* (2)
Shelomith (2)

8986 שַׁלְמַן *šalman* (1)
Shalman (1)

8987 שַׁלְמַנְאֶסֶר *šalman'eser* (2)
Shalmaneser (2)

8988 שַׁלְמֹנִים *šalmōniym* (1)
gifts (1)

8989 שֵׁלָנִי *šēlāniy* (2)
of Shelah (1)
Shelanite (1)

8990 שָׁלַף *šālap̱* (25)
swordsmen (5) +408+2995
draw (4)
drawn (4)
armed (3)
handle (2)
drew (1)
grow (1)
pull out (1)
pulls (1)
removed (1)
took off (1)
untranslated (1)

8991 שֶׁלֶף *šelep̱* (2)
Sheleph (2)

8992 שָׁלַשׁ *šālaš* (10)
did the third time (1)
divide into three (1)
do a third time (1)
day after tomorrow (1)
third (1)
three (1)
three years old (1)
three-year-old (1)
untranslated (2)

8993 שָׁלֹשׁ *šālōš* (601)
three (282)
thirty (83)
third (12)
thirteen (10) +6926
thirteenth (8) +6925
three-tenths (8) +6928
twenty-third (7) +2256+6929
thirty-three (6) +2256+8993
thirty-two (6) +2256+9109
twenty-three (6) +2256+6929
30 (5)
three-day (4) +3427
32 (3) +2256+9109
36,000 (3) +547+2256+9252
430 (3) +752+2256+4395
53,400 (3) +547+752+2256+2256+2822+4395
603,550 (3) +547+547+2256+2256+2256+2822+2822+4395+4395+9252
thirteenth (3) +6926
thirty-five (3) +2256+2822
thirty-ninth (3) +2256+9596
thirty-one (3) +285+2256
thirty-seventh (3) +2256+8679
123 (2) +2256+4395+6929
130 (2) +2256+4395
137 (2) +2256+2256+4395+8679
223 (2) +2256+4395+6929
30,500 (2) +547+2256+2822+4395
300 (2) +4395
32,200 (2) +547+2256+2256+4395+9109
320 (2) +2256+4395+6929
345 (2) +752+2256+2822+4395
35,400 (2) +547+752+2256+2256+2822+4395
372 (2) +2256+4395+8679+9109
390 (2) +2256+4395+9596
392 (2) +2256+4395+9109+9596
403 (2) +752+2256+4395
435 (2) +752+2256+2822+4395
59,300 (2) +547+2256+2256+2822+4395+9596
7,337 (2) +547+2256+4395+8679+8679+8993
973 (2) +2256+4395+8679+9596
them^{s} (2) +2021
thirteen (2) +6925
thirty-eight (2) +2256+9046
thirty-eighth (2) +2256+9046
thirty-second (2) +2256+9109
thirty-seven (2) +2256+8679
1,335 (1) +547+2256+2822+4395+8993
1,365 (1) +547+2256+2256+2256+2822+4395+9252
13 (1) +6925
133 (1) +2256+2256+4395+8993
138 (1) +2256+4395+9046
139 (1) +2256+4395+9596
153,600 (1) +547+547+2256+2256+2256+2822+4395+4395+9252
2,300 (1) +547+2256+4395
2,322 (1) +547+2256+4395+6929+9109
2,630 (1) +547+2256+2256+4395+9252
22,034 (1) +547+752+2256+2256+2256+6929+9109
22,273 (1) +547+2256+2256+2256+4395+6929+8679+9109

23,000 (1) +547+2256+6929
232 (1) +2256+4395+9109
273 (1) +2256+2256+4395+8679
3,000 (1) +547
3,023 (1) +547+2256+2256+6929+8993
3,200 (1) +547+2256+4395
3,600 (1) +547+2256+4395+9252
3,630 (1) +547+2256+2256+4395+8993+9252
3,700 (1) +547+2256+4395+8679
3,930 (1) +547+2256+4395+8993+9596
300,000 (1) +547+4395
307,500 (1) +547+547+2256+2256+2822+4395+4395+8679
318 (1) +2256+4395+6925+9046
32,000 (1) +547+2256+9109
32,500 (1) +547+2256+2256+2822+4395+9109
323 (1) +2256+4395+6929+8993
324 (1) +752+2256+4395+6929
328 (1) +2256+4395+6929+9046
337,500 (1) +547+547+547+2256+2256+2256+2822+4395+4395+8679+8993
337,500 (1) +547+547+547+2256+2256+2822+4395+4395+8679+8993
34 (1) +752+2256
35 (1) +2256+2822
350 (1) +2256+2822+4395
365 (1) +2256+2256+2822+4395+9252
37,000 (1) +547+2256+8679
42,360 (1) +547+752+2256+4395+8052+9252
42,360 (1) +547+752+4395+8052+9252
43,730 (1) +547+752+2256+2256+2256+4395+8679+8993
45 feet (1) +564
450 feet (1) +564+4395
530 (1) +2256+2822+4395
601,730 (1) +547+547+2256+2256+4395+4395+8679+9252
623 (1) +2256+4395+6929+9252
64,300 (1) +547+752+2256+2256+4395+9252
730 (1) +2256+4395+8679
736 (1) +2256+4395+8679+9252
743 (1) +752+2256+2256+4395+8679
743 (1) +752+2256+4395+8679
830 (1) +2256+4395+9046
832 (1) +2256+4395+9046+9109
930 (1) +2256+4395+9596
eighty-three (1) +2256+9046
four and a half feet (1) +564
people[s] (1) +9109
thirtieth (1)
thirty-fifth (1) +2256+2822
thirty-first (1) +285+2256
thirty-six (1) +2256+9252
thirty-six hundred (1) +547+2256+4395+9252
thirty-sixth (1) +2256+9252
thirty-three hundred (1) +547+2256+4395+8993
this time[s] (1) +9102
three-pronged (1) +9094
untranslated (9)

8994 שֶׁלֶשׁ *šēleš* (1)
Shelesh (1)

8995 שָׁלִשָׁה *šālišāh* (1)
Shalisha (1)

8996 שִׁלְשָׁה *šilšāh* (1)
Shilshah (1)

8997 שִׁלְשׁוֹם *šilšôm* (25)
before (6) +9453
malice aforethought (4) +4946+8533+9453
before (2) +919
had the habit (2) +4946+9453
as usual (1) +3869+9453
before (1) +4946+9453
for some time (1) +1685+1685+9453
formerly (1) +919+4946
had been (1) +9453
in the past (1) +919+1685+1685
in the past (1) +9453
past (1) +9453
previously (1) +919+3869
untranslated (2)

8998 שָׁלִשִׁי *šālišiy* (2)
three (2)

8999 שְׁלִשִׁיָּה *šᵉlišiyyāh*
Variant; not used

9000 שִׁלֵּשִׁים *šillēšiym* (5)
third (4)
third generation (1)

9001 שְׁלֹשִׁים *šᵉlōšiym*
Variant; not used

9002 שִׁלְתָּה *šiltāh*
Variant; not used

9003 שַׁלְתִּיאֵל *šaltiy'ēl* (3)
Shealtiel (3)

9004 שָׁם *šām* (836)
there (400)
where (101)
there (58) +2025
which[s] (18)
it[s] (17)
where (16) +2025
here (9)
in which[s] (5)
in it[s] (4)
the Jordan[s] (4) +2025
back (3) +4946
in it[s] (3) +2025
out (3) +4946
away (2) +4946
behind (2)
in (2)
in Zion[s] (2)
it[s] (2) +2025
that place[s] (2)
them[s] (2)
where (2) +4946
wherever (2) +2025
whom[s] (2)
among which[s] (1)
at Pas Dammim[s] (1)
back (1)
back[s] (1) +2025
because of (1) +4946
beside (1)
Gath[s] (1)
Hebron[s] (1)
in such places[s] (1)
in that place[s] (1)
in them[s] (1)
inside[s] (1) +2025
into it[s] (1)
invade (1) +995+2025
leave (1) +4946
nearby (1)
place (1)
proper place (1) +889+2118+5226
right there (1)
Samaria[s] (1)
see (1)
that land[s] (1)
the chest[s] (1)
the city[s] (1)
the land[s] (1) +2025
the north[s] (1)
them (1)
there (1) +4946
to (1) +2025
what[s] (1)
when (1)
wherever (1)
wherever (1) +889+2025
wherever (1) +889+3972
untranslated (141)

9005 1שֵׁם *šēm1* (864)
name (563)
names (62)
named (55) +7924
named (44)
called (27) +7924
called (10)
fame (10)
name's (7)
call (6) +7924
renown (6)
famous (5)
name (4) +7924
honor (3)
named (3) +8492
be called (2) +7924
chosen (2) +928+7924
famous (2) +7924
after (1) +928
after (1) +3869
be known as (1) +7924
be named (1) +7924
became famous (1) +6913
been named (1) +7924
byword (1)
calling (1) +7924
famous (1) +408
giving credit to (1) +928
himself (1) +2257
infamous (1) +2021+3238
is called (1) +7924
it[s] (1) +2257
memorable (1)
named (1) +928+7924
nameless (1) +1172
perpetuate memory (1) +2349
record (1) +4180
renowned (1) +4200
that[s] (1)
to each man (1) +928
was called (1) +7924
well-known (1) +408
word (1)
untranslated (28)

9006 2שֵׁם *šēm2* (17)
Shem (17)

9007 שַׁמָּא *šammā'* (2)
Shamma (1)
Shammah (1)

9008 שֶׁמְאֵבֶר *šem'ēḇer* (1)
Shemeber (1)

9009 שִׁמְאָה *šim'āh* (1)
Shimeah (1)

9010 שִׁמְאָם *šim'ām* (1)
Shimeam (1)

9011 שַׁמְגַּר *šamgar* (2)
Shamgar (2)

9012 שָׁמַד *šāmaḏ* (90)
destroy (31)
destroyed (24)
be destroyed (6)
are destroyed (5)
destruction (3)
demolish (2)
wipe out (2)
annihilate (1)
annihilation (1)
be overthrown (1)
been decimated (1)
been destroyed (1)
brought to ruin (1)
certainly be destroyed (1) +9012
completely destroyed (1)
crushed (1)
cut off (1)
exterminating (1)

get rid of (1)
perished (1)
shatter (1)
totally destroy (1) +9012

9013 שֶׁמֶד *šemed* (1)
Shemed (1)

9014 1שַׁמָּה *šammāh1* (40)
desolate (7)
waste (7)
horror (6)
object of horror (5)
ruin (4)
laid waste (3)
desolation (1)
desolations (1)
destroyed (1)
devastate (1)
horrible (1)
in ruins (1)
thing of horror (1)
wasteland (1)

9015 2שַׁמָּה *šammāh2* (7)
Shammah (7)

9016 שַׁמְהוּת *šamhût* (1)
Shamhuth (1)

9017 שְׁמוּאֵל *šᵉmû'ēl* (141)
Samuel (127)
he[S] (5)
Samuel's (4)
him[S] (2)
Shemuel (1)
untranslated (2)

9018 שַׁמּוּעַ *šammûa'* (5)
Shammua (5)

9019 שְׁמוּעָה *šᵉmû'āh* (27)
news (8)
report (7)
message (5)
rumor (3)
another[S] (1) +2021
mention (1) +928+7023
reports (1)
rumors (1)

9020 שָׁמוּר *šāmûr* (1)
untranslated (1)

9021 שַׁמּוֹת *šammôt* (1)
Shammoth (1)

9022 שָׁמַח *šāmah*
Variant; not used

9023 שָׁמַט *šāmat* (10)
stumbled (2)
be thrown down (1)
cancel (1)
cancel debt (1)
lie unplowed (1)
lose (1)
threw down (1)
throw down (1)
untranslated (1)

9024 שְׁמִטָּה *šᵉmiṭṭāh* (5)
canceling debts (2)
cancel debts (1) +6913
it[S] (1) +2021
time for canceling debts (1)

9025 שַׁמַּי *šammay* (6)
Shammai (5)
Shammai's (1)

9026 שְׁמִידָע *šᵉmiydā'* (3)
Shemida (3)

9027 שְׁמִידָעִי *šᵉmiydā'iy* (1)
Shemidaite (1)

9028 שָׁמַיִם *šāmayim* (416)
heaven (154)
heavens (141)
sky (46)
air (40)
starry (9)
highest heavens (6) +9028
skies (6)
heavenly (2)
astrologers (1) +2042
heaven's (1)
highest heaven (1) +9028
horizon (1)
in midair (1) +824+1068+1068+2021+2021+2256
other[S] (1) +7895
skies above (1) +9028
untranslated (2)

9029 שְׁמִינִי *šᵉmiyniy* (28)
eighth (27)
following[S] (1)

9030 שְׁמִינִית *šᵉmiyniyt* (3)
sheminith (3)

9031 1שָׁמִיר *šāmiyr1* (8)
briers (8)

9032 2שָׁמִיר *šāmiyr2* (3)
as hard as flint (1)
flint (1)
hardest stone (1)

9033 3שָׁמִיר *šāmiyr3* (1)
Shamir (1)

9034 4שָׁמִיר *šāmiyr4* (3)
Shamir (3)

9035 שְׁמִירָמוֹת *šᵉmiyrāmôt* (5)
Shemiramoth (4)
untranslated (1)

9036 שַׁמְלַי *šamlay* (1)
untranslated (1)

9037 1שָׁמֵם *šāmēm1* (94)
appalled (19)
desolate (15)
causes desolation (4)
deserted (4)
devastated (4)
lay waste (4)
lies desolate (4)
completely destroy (2)
demolished (2)
destitute (2)
destroyed (2)
horrified (2)
ruin (2)
was laid waste (2)
are appalled (1)
are demolished (1)
astonished (1)
be demolished (1)
be destroyed (1)
be laid waste (1)
brought devastation (1)
cause to be appalled (1)
desolation (1)
desolations (1)
destroy yourself (1)
dismayed (1)
fill with horror (1)
him[S] (1)
in ruins (1)
laid waste (1)
made desolate (1)
overwhelmed (1)
ravaged (1)
ruined (1)
strip (1)
stripped (1)
was left so desolate (1)
were terrified (1)
without help (1)
untranslated (1)

9038 2שָׁמֵם *šāmēm2* (2)
desolate (2)

9039 שְׁמָמָה *šᵉmāmāh* (56)
desolate (30)
waste (5)
desolation (3)
ruins (3)
wasteland (3)
desolate place (2)
laid waste (2)
barren (1)
demolished (1)
desolate waste (1)
despair (1)
destroy (1) +8492
ravaged (1)
ruined (1)
utterly desolate (1)

9040 שִׁמָּמָה *šimmāh* (1)
desolate (1)

9041 שִׁמָּמוֹן *šimmāmôn* (2)
despair (2)

9042 1שָׁמֵן *šāmēn1* (5)
fat (1)
filled with food (1)
grew fat (1)
make calloused (1)
well-nourished (1)

9043 שֶׁמֶן *šemen* (193)
oil (155)
olive oil (13)
olive (4)
perfume (3)
fertile (2)
best (1)
cosmetic lotions (1)
fat (1)
fertile (1) +1201
fine perfume (1)
gaunt (1) +4946
it[S] (1) +2021
lotions (1)
oils (1)
ointments (1)
olive (1) +6770
perfume (1) +8379
perfumes (1)
rich food (1)
wild olive (1)
untranslated (1)

9044 שָׁמָן *šāmān* (2)
richness (2)

9045 2שָׁמֵן *šāmēn2* (10)
fertile (3)
rich (3)
luxury (1)
plentiful (1)
sleek (1)
vigorous (1)

9046 שְׁמֹנֶה *šᵉmōneh* (147)
eight (29)
eighty (16)
eighteenth (9) +6926
eighteen (7) +6926
128 (4) +2256+4395+6929
eighteen (4) +6925
eighty-five (4) +2256+2822
twenty-eight (4) +2256+6929
eighth (3)
18 (2) +6925
18,000 (2) +547+6925
80 (2)
800 (2) +4395
98 (2) +2256+9596
eighteenth (2) +6925
forty-eight (2) +752+2256
thirty-eight (2) +2256+8993

thirty-eighth (2) +2256+8993
108,100 (1) +547+547+2256+2256+4395+4395
138 (1) +2256+4395+8993
148 (1) +752+2256+4395
180 (1) +2256+4395
180,000 (1) +547+2256+4395
182 (1) +2256+2256+4395+9109
186,400 (1) +547+547+547+752+2256+2256+2256+4395+4395+9252
187 (1) +2256+2256+4395+8679
188 (1) +2256+4395+9046
2,812 (1) +547+2256+4395+6925+9109
2,818 (1) +547+2256+4395+6925+9046
20,800 (1) +547+2256+4395+6929
218 (1) +2256+4395+6925
28 (1) +2256+6929
28,600 (1) +547+2256+2256+4395+6929+9252
280,000 (1) +547+2256+4395
284 (1) +752+2256+4395
288 (1) +2256+4395+9046
318 (1) +2256+4395+6925+8993
328 (1) +2256+4395+6929+8993
468 (1) +752+2256+4395+9252
6,800 (1) +547+2256+4395+9252
628 (1) +2256+4395+6929+9252
648 (1) +752+2256+4395+9252
782 (1) +2256+2256+4395+8679+9109
8,580 (1) +547+2256+2256+2822+4395+9046
8,600 (1) +547+2256+4395+9252
80,000 (1) +547
807 (1) +2256+4395+8679
815 (1) +2256+2822+4395+6926
822 (1) +2256+4395+6929+9109
830 (1) +2256+4395+8993
832 (1) +2256+4395+8993+9109
840 (1) +752+2256+4395
845 (1) +752+2256+2822+4395
87,000 (1) +547+2256+8679
895 (1) +2256+2256+2822+4395+9596
928 (1) +2256+4395+6929+9596
eighteen thousand (1) +547+2256+8052
eightieth (1)
eighty-six (1) +2256+9252
eighty-three (1) +2256+8993
ninety-eight (1) +2256+9596
sixty-eight (1) +2256+9252
twenty-seven feet (1) +564+6926

9047 **שְׁמֹנִים** *šᵉmōniym*
Variant; not used

9048 **שָׁמַע** *šāma'* (1161)
heard (293)
hear (238)
listen (225)
listened (40)
obey (36) +928+7754
hears (27)
obey (19)
obeyed (18) +928+7754
proclaim (15)
obeyed (13)
agreed (9)
be heard (9)
hearing (8)
listening (8)
understand (8)
is heard (6)
listen carefully (4) +9048
listens (4)
paid attention (4)
was heard (4)
do (3)
heed (3)
let hear (3)
pay attention (3)
proclaimed (3)
resound (3)
sound (3)
agree (2)
are heard (2)
declare (2)
discerning (2)
disobeyed (2) +928+4202+7754
disobeyed (2) +4202
foretold (2)
fully obey (2) +928+7754+9048
give (2)
heard (2) +7754
mark my words (2)
obedient (2)
obeying (2)
proclaiming (2)
raise (2)
received a report (2)
sang (2)
summon (2)
administering (1)
agreed with (1) +4200+7754
announce (1)
announced (1)
are heeded (1)
argue (1) +7754
be heeded (1)
been brought to attention (1) +2256+5583
been heard (1)
been heard of (1)
been proclaimed (1)
been^{s} (1)
boast (1)
bring word (1)
called up (1)
careful to obey (1) +9048
cause to hear (1)
caused to hear (1)
certainly hear (1) +9048
complied (1)
comply (1)
cry out (1)
cry out (1) +2411
deaf (1) +4946
did (1)
diligently obey (1) +928+7754+9048
disobedience (1) +928+4202+7754
disobey (1) +928+1194+7754
disobey (1) +4202
ever hearing (1) +9048
expect to be heard (1)
faithfully obey (1) +9048
find out (1)
fully obeyed (1) +2256+6913
gave in (1) +928+7754
get back to (1)
have^{s} (1)
heard (1) +9051
heard definitely (1) +9048
hears (1) +7754
hears (1) +7754+9048
hears (1) +9048
heeds (1)
is proclaimed (1)
is reported (1)
issued an order (1)
learn (1)
let be heard (1)
listen (1) +7754
listen carefully (1) +265+928
listen carefully (1) +928+7754
listen closely (1) +265+928
listen in (1)
listened to (1)
listens (1) +265
made hear (1)
made known (1)
made proclamation (1)
make hear (1)
make heard (1)
obedience (1)
obey (1) +4200+7754
obey fully (1) +928+7754+9048
obeying (1) +928+7754
obeys (1)
obeys (1) +928+7754
obscure (1) +4946+6680
overheard (1)
paid any attention (1) +265+4200+5742
pay close attention (1) +2256+7992
playing (1)
plots (1)
proclaims (1)
pronounced (1)
put under oath (1) +460
reached (1)
reached (1) +928
received (1)
received message (1)
refused (1) +4202
resounds (1)
sing songs (1) +928+4200+7754+8123
sound be heard (1)
sounding (1)
stopped up (1) +3877+4946
summoned (1)
surely heard (1) +9048
tell (1)
told (1)
told (1) +907+4946
was overheard (1)
were heard (1)
witness (1) +1068
word came (1)
untranslated (10)

9049 1**שֶׁמַע** *šema'1* (1)
clash (1)

9050 2**שֶׁמַע** *šema'2* (5)
Shema (5)

9051 **שֵׁמַע** *šēma'* (17)
fame (4)
report (3)
reports (3)
hear (2)
news (2)
heard (1) +9048
rumor (1)
word (1)

9052 **שָׁמָע** *šāmā'* (1)
Shama (1)

9053 **שֹׁמַע** *šōma'* (4)
reports (2)
fame (1)
reputation (1)

9054 **שְׁמַע** *šᵉma'* (1)
Shema (1)

9055 **שִׁמְעָא** *šim'ā'* (5)
Shimea (4)
Shammua (1)

9056 **שִׁמְעָה** *šim'āh* (3)
Shimeah (3)

9057 **שְׁמָעָה** *šᵉmā'āh* (1)
Shemaah (1)

9058 **שִׁמְעוֹן** *šim'ôn* (44)
Simeon (30)
Simeon (5) +1201
Simeonites (4) +1201
Simeonites (3)
Shimeon (1)
untranslated (1)

9059 1**שִׁמְעִי** *šim'iy1* (45)
Shimei (42)
he^{s} (1)
Shimei's (1) +4200
untranslated (1)

9060 2**שִׁמְעִי** *šim'iy2* (2)
Shimei (1)
Shimeites (1)

9061 שְׁמַעְיָה *šᵉmaʿyāh* (34)
Shemaiah (32)
his[S] (1)
Shemaiah's (1)

9062 שְׁמַעְיָהוּ *šᵉmaʿyāhû* (7)
Shemaiah (7)

9063 שִׁמְעֹנִי *šimʿōniy* (4)
Simeon (2)
Simeonite (1)
Simeonites (1)

9064 שִׁמְעָת *šimʿāt̠* (2)
Shimeath (2)

9065 שִׁמְעָתִי *šimʿātiy* (1)
Shimeathites (1)

9066 שֵׁמֶץ *šēmes* (2)
faint (1)
whisper (1)

9067 שִׁמְצָה *šimsāh* (1)
laughingstock (1)

9068 שָׁמַר *šāmar* (469)
keep (83)
careful (46)
obey (21)
observe (20)
kept (19)
carefully (16)
guard (16)
keeps (10)
watch (9)
watchmen (8)
keeping (7)
guards (6)
watches over (6)
doorkeepers (5) +6197
in charge (5)
keeper (5)
maintain (5)
obeyed (5)
protect (5)
take care of (5)
watch over (5)
celebrate (4)
responsible (4)
be sure (3)
care (3)
do (3)
guarded (3)
guarding (3)
heeds (3)
observed (3)
on guard (3)
protects (3)
watched over (3)
watchman (3)
be careful (2)
beware (2)
carried out (2)
carrying out (2)
cling (2)
faithful (2)
follow (2)
followed (2)
guard yourself (2)
guarding (2) +5466
have charge of (2) +5466
keep safe (2)
kept myself (2)
make sure (2)
obeys (2)
perform (2)
protected (2)
safekeeping (2)
see (2)
serve (2)
waiting (2)
watches (2)
watching (2)
watching over (2)
assures (1)
be protected (1)
be sure to keep (1) +9068
beware (1) +440
bodyguard (1) +4200+8031
cared for (1)
careful (1) +9068
careful to do (1)
carefully observe (1) +9068
cherishes (1)
consider (1)
continue (1)
continued (1)
defending (1)
did[S] (1)
done (1)
doorkeeper (1) +6197
eyed (1)
faithfully carried out (1)
flamed unchecked (1) +5905
give (1)
guard (1) +5466
guarded (1) +5464
had charge of (1)
have charge of (1)
heed (1)
hoarded (1)
keep away (1)
keep close watch on (1)
keep penned up (1)
keep track of (1)
keepers (1)
keeps close watch (1)
kept a record (1)
kept in mind (1)
kept penned up (1)
kept themselves (1)
kept watch (1)
living (1)
looks after (1)
loyal (1) +5466
must (1)
obey (1) +2256+6913
obeying (1)
observing (1)
on duty (1)
on duty at (1)
paid attention (1)
pay attention (1)
performed (1)
performing (1)
preserve (1)
preserved (1)
put (1)
regardless (1) +401+4200
remains (1)
responsible (1) +5466
responsible for (1)
secured (1)
see to it (1)
shepherd (1)
spare (1)
spies (1)
take care (1)
tended sheep (1)
under siege (1)
wait to kill (1) +5883
was set aside (1)
watch carefully (1)
untranslated (1)

9069 1שֶׁמֶר *šemer1* (5)
dregs (3)
aged wine (1)
wines (1)

9070 2שֶׁמֶר *šemer2* (3)
Shemer (3)

9071 שֹׁמֵר *šōmēr* (3)
Shomer (3)

9072 שָׁמְרָה *šāmrāh* (1)
guard (1)

9073 שְׁמֻרָה *šᵉmurāh* (1)
kept from closing (1) +296

9074 1שִׁמְרוֹן *šimrôn1* (2)
Shimron (2)

9075 2שִׁמְרוֹן *šimrôn2* (3)
Shimron (3)

9076 שֹׁמְרוֹן *šōmrôn* (109)
Samaria (105)
the city[S] (2)
there[S] (2) +928

9077 שִׁמְרוֹן מְראוֹן *šimrôn mᵉrʾôn* (1)
Shimron Meron (1)

9078 שִׁמְרִי *šimriy* (4)
Shimri (4)

9079 שְׁמַרְיָה *šᵉmaryāh* (3)
Shemariah (3)

9080 שְׁמַרְיָהוּ *šᵉmaryāhû* (1)
Shemariah (1)

9081 שִׁמֻּרִים *šimmuriym* (2)
vigil (2)

9082 שְׁמִרִימוֹת *šᵉmiriymôt̠*
Variant; not used

9083 שִׁמְרִית *šimriyt̠* (1)
Shimrith (1)

9084 שִׁמְרֹנִי *šimrōniy* (1)
Shimronite (1)

9085 שֹׁמְרֹנִי *šōmrōniy* (1)
people of Samaria (1)

9086 שִׁמְרָת *šimrāt̠* (1)
Shimrath (1)

9087 שֶׁמֶשׁ *šemeš* (135)
sun (102)
sunset (6) +995+2021
east (3) +2021+4667
sunrise (3) +4667
east (2) +2021+2025+4667
east (2) +4667
sunrise (2) +2021+2436
sunset (2) +995+2021+6961
west (2) +4427
battlements (1)
broad daylight (1)
east (1) +928+2025+4667+6298
east (1) +928+4667+6298
eastern (1) +4667
in broad daylight (1) +2021+2021+2296+4200+6524
in broad daylight (1) +2021+5584
on the west (1) +2021+4427
sunlight (1)
sunrise (1) +2436
sunshine (1)

9088 שִׁמְשׁוֹן *šimšôn* (38)
Samson (33)
Samson's (3)
he[S] (2)

9089 שִׁמְשַׁי *šimšay*
Variant; not used

9090 שִׁמְשִׁי *šimšiy*
Variant; not used

9091 שַׁמְשְׁרַי *šamšᵉray* (1)
Shamsherai (1)

9092 שֻׁמָתִי *šumātiy* (1)
Shumathites (1)

9093 שַׁן *šan*
Variant; not used

9094 1שֵׁן *šēn1* (56)
teeth (26)
ivory (10)
tooth (9)
cliff (1)

cliff (1) +6152
crag (1)
empty stomachs (1) +5931
fangs (1)
feeds (1) +928+5966
put in jeopardy (1) +928+1414+5951
three-pronged (1) +8993
untranslated (3)

9095 2שֵׁן *šēn2* (1)
Shen (1)

9096 שָׁנָא *šānā'* (1)
dull (1)

9097 שֵׁנָא *šēnā'* (1)
sleep (1)

9098 שִׁנְאָב *šin'āb* (1)
Shinab (1)

9099 שִׁנְאָן *šin'ān* (1)
thousands (1)

9100 שֶׁנְאַצַּר *šen'assar* (1)
Shenazzar (1)

9101 1שָׁנָה *šānāh1* (24)
change (2)
different (2)
do again (2)
pretended to be insane (2) +3248
put aside (2)
repeats (2)
again (1)
alter (1)
changes (1)
changing (1)
deprive (1)
did again (1)
disguise yourself (1)
more (1)
moved (1)
rebellious (1)
strike twice (1)
was given (1)

9102 2שָׁנָה *šānāh2* (878)
years (409)
year (303)
years (8) +3427
year-old (5) +1201
age (4) +1201
each year (3) +928+9102
spring (3) +9588
ages (2) +1201
them[s] (2)
year-old (2) +1426
yearly (2) +285+928
age (1) +1426
ages (1)
annual (1) +285+928+2021
annual (1) +928+2021+7193
annually (1) +928+2256+3972+9102
day (1)
due annually (1) +928+1896+4946+9102
each year (1) +9102
every spring (1) +995
full years (1) +3427
generations long past (1) +1887+1887+2256
it[s] (1)
its[s] (1)
length of days (1) +3427
lives (1) +3427
many years (1) +2256+3427
old (1) +2644+3427
over a year (1) +196+2296+2296+3427
some years later (1) +4200+7891
spring (1) +2021+9588
spring (1) +6961+9588
successive years (1) +339+9102
this time[s] (1) +8993
time (1)
year (1) +1821
year's (1)
years (1) +2021+6961
untranslated (103)

9103 3שָׁנָה *šānāh3*
Variant; not used

9104 שֵׁנָה *šēnāh* (23)
sleep (19)
sleep (2) +3822
sleep of death (1)
slumber (1)

9105 שֶׁנְהַבִּים *šenhabbiym* (2)
ivory (2)

9106 1שָׁנִי *šāniy1* (42)
scarlet yarn (31) +9357
scarlet (7)
scarlet thread (2)
scarlet (1) +9357
scarlet wool (1) +9357

9107 2שָׁנִי *šāniy2*
Variant; not used

9108 שֵׁנִי *šēniy* (157)
second (75)
other (33)
another (12)
second time (10)
again (5)
after (1)
again (1) +8740
all alone (1) +401
another part (1)
each (1)
following (1)
furthermore (1) +2021+2256
middle (1)
next (1)
one (1)
second in command (1)
this time (1)
this[s] (1) +2021
whose[s] (1) +285+2021+2021
untranslated (8)

9109 שְׁנַיִם *šᵉnayim* (772)
two (374)
both (52)
twelve (51) +6925
twelve (30) +6926
12 (24) +6925
each (16)
twelfth (15) +6925
twenty-two (15) +2256+6929
second (12)
two-tenths (11) +6928
pair (9)
double (8)
twelfth (7) +6926
thirty-two (6) +2256+8993
forty-two (5) +752+2256
32 (3) +2256+8993
fifty-two (3) +2256+2822
together (3)
1,052 (2) +547+2256+2822
112 (2) +2256+4395+6925
20,000 (2) +8052
32,200 (2) +547+2256+2256+4395+8993
372 (2) +2256+4395+8679+8993
392 (2) +2256+4395+8993+9596
42 (2) +752+2256
52 (2) +2256+2822
62,700 (2) +547+2256+2256+4395+8679+9252
652 (2) +2256+2822+4395+9252
other (2)
pairs (2) +9109
sides (2)
sixty-two (2) +2256+9252
thirty-second (2) +2256+8993
twenty-second (2) +2256+6929
twice (2)
1,222 (1) +547+2256+4395+6929
112 (1) +4395+6925
122 (1) +2256+2256+4395+6929
122 (1) +2256+4395+6929
162 (1) +2256+2256+4395+9252
172 (1) +2256+4395+8679
182 (1) +2256+2256+4395+9046
2,172 (1) +547+2256+2256+4395+8679
2,172 (1) +547+2256+4395+8679
2,322 (1) +547+2256+4395+6929+8993
2,812 (1) +547+2256+4395+6925+9046
212 (1) +2256+4395+6925
22 (1) +2256+6929
22,000 (1) +547+2256+6929
22,034 (1) +547+752+2256+2256+2256+6929+8993
22,200 (1) +547+2256+2256+4395+6929
22,273 (1) +547+2256+2256+2256+4395+6929+8679+8993
22,600 (1) +547+2256+2256+4395+6929+9252
232 (1) +2256+4395+8993
242 (1) +752+2256+4395
32,000 (1) +547+2256+8993
32,500 (1) +547+2256+2256+2822+4395+8993
52,700 (1) +547+2256+2256+2822+4395+8679
62 (1) +2256+9252
642 (1) +752+2256+2256+4395+9252
642 (1) +752+2256+4395+9252
72 (1) +2256+8679
72,000 (1) +547+2256+8679
782 (1) +2256+2256+4395+8679+9046
822 (1) +2256+4395+6929+9046
832 (1) +2256+4395+8993+9046
912 (1) +2256+4395+6926+9596
962 (1) +2256+2256+4395+9252+9596
another (1)
both sides (1)
double-edged (1) +7023
doubly (1) +928+2021
each other (1) +5646
each other[s] (1) +2157
each[s] (1)
Elijah and Elisha[s] (1) +2157
few (1)
fifty-second (1) +2256+2822
hundred and twenty thousand (1) +6926+8052
inner and outer[s] (1)
people[s] (1) +8993
some[s] (1)
them[s] (1) +74+2021
them[s] (1) +2021+3192
time and again (1) +285+2256+4202+4202
tore apart (1) +4200+7973+7974
two at a time (1) +9109
two-and-a-half (1) +2256+2942
two-thirds (1) +7023
untranslated (38)

9110 שְׁנִינָה *šᵉniynāh* (4)
object of ridicule (3)
ridicule (1)

9111 1שָׁנַן *šānan1* (8)
sharp (4)
sharpen (2)
embittered (1)
make sharp (1)

9112 2שָׁנַן *šānan2* (1)
impress (1)

9113 שָׁנַס *šānas* (1)
tucking cloak into belt (1) +5516

9114 שִׁנְעָר *šin'ār* (8)
Babylonia (3)
Shinar (2)
Shinar (2) +824
Babylonia (1) +824

9115 שָׁסָה *šāsāh* (11)
plundered (4)

raiders (2)
loot (1)
looted (1)
looting (1)
pillage (1)
plunderers (1)

9116 שָׁסַס *šāsas* (6)
plundered (3)
be looted (1)
plunder (1)
ransacked (1)

9117 שָׁסַע *šāsa'* (9)
completely divided (3) +9118
completely divided (1)
divided (1) +9118
rebuked (1)
tear open (1)
tore apart (1)
torn (1)

9118 שֶׁסַע *šesa'* (4)
completely divided (3) +9117
divided (1) +9117

9119 שָׁסַף *šāsap̄* (1)
put to death (1)

9120 שָׁעָה *šā'āh* (11)
look (6)
have regard (1)
look with favor (1)
looked with favor (1)
pay attention (1)
turn away (1)

9121 שַׁעֲטָה *šᵉ'āṭāh* (1)
galloping (1)

9122 שַׁעַטְנֵז *ša'aṭnēz* (2)
woven (1)
woven material (1)

9123 שֹׁעַל *šō'al* (3)
handful (1)
handfuls (1)
hollow of hand (1)

9124 שַׁעַלְבִים *ša'albiym* (2)
Shaalbim (2)

9125 שַׁעֲלַבִּין *ša'ᵃlabbiyn* (1)
Shaalabbin (1)

9126 שַׁעַלְבֹנִי *ša'albōniy* (2)
Shaalbonite (2)

9127 שַׁעֲלִים *ša'ᵃliym* (1)
Shaalim (1)

9128 שָׁעַן *šā'an* (22)
rely (5)
lean (3)
leaning (3)
relied (3)
leaned (2)
rest (2)
depended (1)
leans (1)
lie (1)
untranslated (1)

9129 שָׁעַע1 *šā'a'1* (4)
blind yourselves (1)
close (1)
closed (1)
sightless (1)

9130 שָׁעַע2 *šā'a'2* (6)
delight (3)
brought joy (1)
dandled (1)
play (1)

9131 שַׁעַף *ša'ap̄* (2)
Shaaph (2)

9132 שַׁעַר *šā'ar* (1)
thinking (1)

9133 שַׁעַר1 *ša'ar1* (374)
gate (177)
gates (75)
gateway (29)
towns (18)
city gate (11)
entrance (10)
cities (6)
court (5)
city gates (4)
courts (4)
gateways (4)
town (3)
cities (2) +824
each gate (2) +2256+9133
its[S] (2) +2021
town gate (2)
assembly at the gate (1)
end[S] (1)
entrance (1) +7339
fellow townsmen (1) +6639
gatepost (1) +4647
gateposts (1) +4647
gateways (1) +7339
it[S] (1) +2021+4889
opposite[S] (1)
other[S] (1)
they[S] (1) +2021
town records (1) +5226
various gates (1) +2256+9133
untranslated (5)

9134 שַׁעַר2 *ša'ar2* (1)
hundredfold (1) +4395

9135 שֹׁעָר *šō'ār* (1)
poor (1)

9136 שַׁעֲרוּר *ša'ᵃrûr* (2)
shocking thing (1)
something horrible (1)

9137 שַׁעֲרוּרִי *ša'ᵃrûriy* (3)
horrible thing (2)
untranslated (1)

9138 שְׁעַרְיָה *šᵉ'aryāh* (2)
Sheariah (2)

9139 שַׁעֲרַיִם *ša'ᵃrayim* (3)
Shaaraim (3)

9140 שַׁעַשְׁגַז *ša'ašgaz* (1)
Shaashgaz (1)

9141 שַׁעֲשׁוּעִים *ša'ᵃšû'iym* (9)
delight (7)
delighting (1)
filled with delight (1)

9142 שָׁפָה *šāp̄āh* (2)
bare (1)
stick out (1)

9143 שְׁפוֹ *šᵉp̄ô* (2)
Shepho (2)

9144 שְׁפוֹט *šᵉp̄ôṭ* (2)
judgment (1)
punishment (1)

9145 שְׁפוּפָם *šᵉp̄ûp̄ām*
Variant; not used

9146 שְׁפוּפָן *šᵉp̄ûp̄ān* (1)
Shephuphan (1)

9147 שְׁפוֹת *šᵉp̄ôṯ* (1)
cheese (1)

9148 שִׁפְחָה *šip̄ḥāh* (63)
servant (19)
maidservant (12)
maidservants (11)
female (7)
servant girl (3)
maid (2)
slave girl (2)
slaves (2) +2256+6269
women (2)
enslaved (1) +2256+3899+4200+4200+6269
servant girls (1)
serve (1)

9149 שָׁפַט *šāp̄aṭ* (204)
judge (69)
judges (26)
led (12)
rulers (8)
execute judgment (6)
govern (5)
decide (4)
judged (4)
judging (4)
vindicate (4)
defend (3)
lead (3)
leaders (3)
defend the cause (2)
delivered (2)
governed (2)
rule (2)
ruler (2)
sentence (2)
administer (1)
argue (1)
be judged (1)
bring judgment (1)
bring justice (1)
bring to judgment (1)
brought to trial (1)
condemn (1)
confront with evidence (1)
decide dispute (1)
decided (1)
defend cause (1)
defending (1)
enter into judgment (1)
executing judgment (1)
given[S] (1)
gives judgment (1)
goes to court (1)
is tried (1)
judge (1) +5477
judge in office (1)
judges decide (1)
judges in office (1)
leader (1)
leading (1)
pass judgment (1)
play the judge (1) +9149
pleads case (1)
punish (1)
render judgment (1) +5477
ruled (1)
serve as judge (1)
serve as judges (1)
served (1)
served as judges (1)
them[S] (1) +2021
uphold (1)
untranslated (3)

9150 שֶׁפֶט *šep̄eṭ* (16)
punishment (9)
judgment (3)
acts of judgment (2)
judgments (1)
Penalties (1)

9151 שָׁפָט *šāp̄āṭ* (8)
Shaphat (8)

9152 שְׁפַטְיָה *šᵉp̄aṭyāh* (10)
Shephatiah (10)

9153 שְׁפַטְיָהוּ *šᵉp̄aṭyāhû* (3)
Shephatiah (3)

9154 שִׁפְטָן *šip̄ṭān* (1)
Shiphtan (1)

9155 שְׁפִי1 *šᵉp̄iy1* (10)
barren heights (7)

barren height (1)
barren hill (1)
untranslated (1)

9156 2שְׁפִי *šᵉp̱iy2*
Variant; not used

9157 1שֻׁפִּים *šuppiym1* (1)
Shuppim (1)

9158 2שֻׁפִּים *šuppiym2* (2)
Shuppites (2)

9159 שְׁפִיפֹן *šᵉp̱iyp̱ōn* (1)
viper (1)

9160 שָׁפִיר *šāp̱iyr* (1)
Shaphir (1)

9161 שָׁפַךְ *šāp̱aḵ* (117)
pour out (33)
shed (25)
poured out (11)
build (6)
shedding (4)
outpoured (3)
pours out (3)
be poured out (2)
be shed (2)
built (2)
pour (2)
pours (2)
sheds (2)
am poured out (1)
be poured (1)
been shed (1)
bloodshed (1) +1947
build up (1)
drain out (1)
dumped (1)
ebb away (1)
ebbs away (1)
flowed (1)
lavished (1)
lost (1)
outpouring (1)
poured out (1) +4946
pouring out (1)
scattered (1)
spilled out (1)
spills (1)
untranslated (2)

9162 שֶׁפֶךְ *šep̱eḵ* (2)
heap (1)
where thrown (1)

9163 שָׁפְכָה *šop̱kāh* (1)
cutting (1) +4162

9164 1שָׁפֵל *šāp̱ēl1* (30)
humbled (6)
brought low (4)
bring low (3)
bring down (2)
brings down (1)
brings low (1)
casts (1)
come down (1)
descended (1)
fades (1)
humble (1)
humbles (1)
humiliate (1)
lay low (1)
lays low (1)
leveled completely (1) +928+2021+9168
levels (1)
low (1)
stoops down (1)

9165 שֵׁפֶל *šēp̱el* (2)
low (1)
low estate (1)

9166 שָׁפָל *šāp̱āl* (18)
lowly (8)
deep (3)
humiliated (2)
low (2)
deeper (1)
low (1) +7757
lowliest (1)

9167 2שָׁפֵל *šāp̱ēl2*
Variant; not used

9168 שִׁפְלָה *šip̱lāh* (1)
leveled completely (1) +928+2021+9164

9169 שְׁפֵלָה *šᵉp̱ēlāh* (20)
western foothills (13)
foothills (7)

9170 שִׁפְלוּת *šip̱lûṯ* (1)
idle (1)

9171 שָׁפָם *šāp̱ām* (1)
Shapham (1)

9172 שְׁפָם *šᵉp̱ām* (2)
Shepham (2)

9173 שֻׁפָּם *šuppim*
Variant; not used

9174 שִׁפְמוֹת *šip̱ᵃmôṯ*
Variant; not used

9175 שִׁפְמִי *šip̱miy* (1)
Shiphmite (1)

9176 1שָׁפָן *šāp̱ān1* (4)
coney (2)
coneys (2)

9177 2שָׁפָן *šāp̱ān2* (30)
Shaphan (30)

9178 שָׁפַע *šāp̱aʿ*
Variant; not used

9179 שֶׁפַע *šep̱aʿ* (1)
abundance (1)

9180 שִׁפְעָה *šip̱ʿāh* (6)
flood (2)
troops (2)
herds (1)
many (1)

9181 שִׁפְעִי *šip̱ʿiy* (1)
Shiphi (1)

9182 שָׁפַר *šāp̱ar* (1)
delightful (1)

9183 1שֶׁפֶר *šep̱er1* (1)
beautiful (1)

9184 2שֶׁפֶר *šep̱er2* (2)
Shepher (2)

9185 1שִׁפְרָה *šip̱rāh1* (1)
fair (1)

9186 2שִׁפְרָה *šip̱rāh2* (1)
Shiphrah (1)

9187 שַׁפְרוּר *šap̱rûr* (1)
untranslated (1)

9188 שַׁפְרִיר *šap̱riyr* (1)
royal canopy (1)

9189 שָׁפַת *šāp̱aṯ* (5)
put on (3)
establish (1)
lay (1)

9190 1שְׁפַתַּיִם *šᵉp̱atayim1* (1)
campfires (1)

9191 2שְׁפַתַּיִם *šᵉp̱atayim2* (1)
double-pronged hooks (1)

9192 שֶׁצֶף *šesep̱* (1)
surge (1)

9193 1שָׁקַד *šāqaḏ1* (12)
watching (3)
did not hesitate (1)
guard (1)
have an eye for (1)
lie awake (1)
lie in wait (1)
stand guard (1)
watch (1)
watch kept (1)
watched (1)

9194 2שָׁקַד *šāqaḏ2*
Variant; not used

9195 3שָׁקַד *šāqaḏ3*
Variant; not used

9196 שָׁקֵד *šāqēḏ* (4)
almond tree (2)
almonds (2)

9197 שָׁקָה *šāqāh* (62)
water (10)
watered (6)
drink (5)
made drink (4)
gave a drink (3)
give to drink (3)
gave (2)
get a drink (2)
get to drink (2)
give drink (2)
got to drink (2)
have drink (2)
drench (1)
gave water (1)
give (1)
give a drink (1)
give a drink (1) +3926
give water (1)
given (1)
given a drink (1)
given to drink (1)
gives drink (1)
irrigated (1)
let drink (1)
made to drink (1)
make drink (1)
rich (1)
watering (1)
waters (1)
wine served (1)
untranslated (1)

9198 שִׁקּוּי *šiqqûy* (3)
drink (2)
nourishment (1)

9199 שִׁקּוּץ *šiqqûṣ* (28)
vile images (9)
abomination (3)
detestable god (3)
detestable idols (3)
abominable idols (1)
abominations (1)
detestable acts (1)
detestable images (1)
detestable things (1)
filth (1)
forbidden food (1)
vile (1)
vile god (1)
vile goddess (1)

9200 שָׁקַט *šāqaṭ* (42)
at peace (5)
quiet (5)
rest (4)
had peace (3)
peaceful (3)
quietness (3)
calm (2)
had rest (2)
have peace (2)
in peace (2)
calms (1)
enjoyed peace (1)

grant relief (1)
left (1)
lies hushed (1)
silent (1)
still (1)
troubled (1) +3523+4202
unconcerned (1) +8932
unsuspecting (1)
untranslated (1)

9201 שֶׁקֶט *šeqeṭ* (1)
quiet (1)

9202 שָׁקַל *šāqal* (23)
weighed out (7)
pay (2)
weigh (2)
weigh out (2)
be weighed (1)
be weighed (1) +9202
paid (1) +8510
pay (1) +4084
put (1) +995+4200
spend (1)
took revenue (1)
weighed (1)
untranslated (1)

9203 שֶׁקֶל *šeqel* (88)
shekels (45)
shekel (39)
price (1)
weighs (1)
which[s] (1)
untranslated (1)

9204 שִׁקְמָה *šiqmāh* (7)
sycamore-fig trees (5)
fig trees (1)
sycamore-figs (1)

9205 שָׁקַע *šāqaʿ* (6)
sink (2)
died down (1)
let settle (1)
sinks (1)
tie down (1)

9206 שְׁקַעֲרוּרָה *šᵉqaʿᵃrūrāh* (1)
depressions (1)

9207 שָׁקַף *šāqap̱* (22)
looked down (6)
looks down (4)
looked out (2)
overlooking (2)
watched (2)
appears (1)
look down (1)
looked (1)
looms (1)
overlooks (1)
peered (1)

9208 שֶׁקֶף *šāqeḇ* (1)
frames (1)

9209 שְׁקֻפִים *šᵉquḇlym* (2)
clerestory (1)
windows placed high (1)

9210 שָׁקַץ *šāqas* (7)
defile (2)
detest (2)
disdained (1)
utterly abhor (1) +9210

9211 שֶׁקֶץ *šeqes* (11)
detestable (7)
detest (3)
abominable things (1)

9212 שָׁקַק *šāqaq* (4)
charging (1)
pounce (1)
rush (1)
rushing back and forth (1)

9213 שָׁקַר *šāqar* (6)
false (2)
betray (1)
deal falsely (1)
deceive (1)
lie (1)

9214 שֶׁקֶר *šeqer* (113)
lies (21)
lying (16)
false (14)
deceptive (4)
falsely (4) +2021+4200
lie (4)
without cause (4)
deceit (3)
deceitful (3)
falsehood (3)
falsely (3)
fraud (3)
lies (3) +1821
not true (3)
false gods (2)
liar (2)
liars (2) +1819
wrong (2)
deceiver (1)
deception (1)
disillusionment (1)
falsely (1) +6584
gifts he does not give (1) +5522
in vain (1)
liars (1)
lie (1) +1819
lies (1) +609
lying (1) +1819
perjurers (1) +2021+4200+8678
perjury (1) +2021+4200+8678
pretense (1)
put in jeopardy (1) +6913
useless (1) +2021+4200
vain hope (1)
without reason (1)

9215 שַׁקָּר *šaqqār*
Variant; not used

9216 שֹׁקֶת *šōqeṯ* (2)
trough (1)
troughs (1) +8110

9217 1שֵׁר *šēr1* (1)
bracelets (1)

9218 2שֵׁר *šēr2*
Variant; not used

9219 שֹׁר *šōr* (3)
body (1)
cord (1)
navel (1)

9220 שָׁרָב *šārāḇ* (2)
burning sand (1)
desert heat (1)

9221 שֵׁרֵבְיָה *šērēḇyāh* (8)
Sherebiah (8)

9222 שַׁרְבִיט *šarḇiyt* (4)
scepter (4)

9223 1שָׁרָה *šārāh1* (2)
deliver (1)
unleashes (1)

9224 2שָׁרָה *šārāh2* (1)
vineyards (1)

9225 שֵׁרָה *šērāh*
Variant; not used

9226 שָׁרוּחֶן *šārûhen* (1)
Sharuhen (1)

9227 שָׁרוֹן *šārôn* (6)
Sharon (6)

9228 שָׁרוֹנִי *šārôniy* (1)
Sharonite (1)

9229 שְׁרוּקָה *šᵉrûqāh* (1)
untranslated (1)

9230 שֵׁרוּת *šērûṯ*
Variant; not used

9231 שִׁרְטַי *širtay* (1)
untranslated (1)

9232 שָׁרַי *šāray* (1)
Sharai (1)

9233 שִׁרְיָה *širyāh* (1)
javelin (1)

9234 שִׁרְיוֹן *širyôn* (8)
armor (3)
breastplate (1)
coat of armor (1)
coat of scale armor (1) +7989
coats of armor (1)
untranslated (1)

9235 שָׁרִיר *šāriyr* (1)
muscles (1)

9236 שְׁרֵמוֹת *šᵉrēmôṯ* (1)
untranslated (1)

9237 שָׁרַץ *šāras* (14)
moves about (3)
multiply (2)
move about (1)
multiplied (1)
swarm (1)
swarms (1)
teem (1)
teem (1) +9238
teemed (1)
teems (1)
untranslated (1)

9238 שֶׁרֶץ *šeres* (15)
creatures (4)
creature (3)
animals (1)
crawling thing (1)
creatures that move along the ground (1)
insects (1)
insects that swarm (1)
move along (1)
swarming things (1)
teem (1) +9237

9239 שָׁרַק *šāraq* (12)
scoff (7)
hiss (1)
hisses (1)
signal (1)
whistle (1)
whistles (1)

9240 שְׁרֵקָה *šᵉrēqāh* (7)
scorn (5)
derision (1)
object of scorn (1)

9241 שְׁרִקָה *šᵉriqāh* (2)
object of scorn (1)
whistling (1)

9242 שָׁרַר *šārar*
Variant; not used

9243 שָׁרָר *šārār* (1)
Sharar (1)

9244 שְׁרִרוּת *šᵉrirûṯ* (10)
stubbornness (7)
stubborn (2)
persist in own way (1) +4213

9245 שָׁרַשׁ *šāraš* (8)
be uprooted (1)
take root (1)
take root (1) +1614
taken root (1)
taking root (1)

took root (1) +9247
uproot (1)
uprooted (1)

9246 שֶׁרֶשׁ *šereš* (1)
Sheresh (1)

9247 שֹׁרֶשׁ *šōreš* (33)
roots (15)
root (12)
be uprooted (1) +4572
depths (1)
family line (1) +5916
soles (1)
took root (1) +9245
uprooted (1) +5998

9248 שַׁרְשָׁה *šaršāh*
Variant; not used

9249 שַׁרְשְׁרָה *šarš^{e}rāh* (8)
chains (5)
chain (1)
chains (1) +6310
interwoven chains (1) +5126

9250 שָׁרַת *šārat̲* (100)
minister (29)
ministering (14)
serve (8)
service (6)
aide (4)
assist (4)
servants (4)
served (4)
ministered (3)
servant (3)
attendant (2)
attending (2)
ministers (2)
attendants (1)
attendants (1) +5853
attended (1)
ministering (1) +9251
officials (1)
on duty (1)
personal attendants (1) +5853
personal servant (1) +5853
serving (1)
supply (1)
take care of (1)
waited on (1)
untranslated (3)

9251 שָׁרֵת *šārēt̲* (1)
ministering (1) +9250

9252 1שֵׁשׁ *šēš1* (271)
six (116)
sixty (23)
sixteen (14) +6926
sixteen (4) +6925
36,000 (3) +547+2256+8993
603,550 (3) +547+547+2256+2256+2256+2822+2822+4395+4395+8993
sixteenth (3) +6925
16,000 (2) +547+6925
4,600 (2) +547+752+2256+4395
45,650 (2) +547+752+2256+2256+2256+2822+2822+4395
46,500 (2) +547+752+2256+2256+2822+4395
6,720 (2) +547+2256+4395+6929+8679
62,700 (2) +547+2256+2256+4395+8679+9109
621 (2) +285+2256+4395+6929
65 (2) +2256+2822
652 (2) +2256+2822+4395+9109
666 (2) +2256+4395+9252+9252
74,600 (2) +547+752+2256+2256+4395+8679
760 (2) +2256+4395+8679
ninety-six (2) +2256+9596
sixty-six (2) +2256+9252
sixty-two (2) +2256+9109
1,365 (1) +547+2256+2256+2256+2822+4395+8993
1,760 (1) +547+2256+2256+4395+8679
153,600 (1) +547+547+2256+2256+2256+2822+4395+4395+8993
156 (1) +2256+2822+4395
157,600 (1) +547+547+2256+2256+2256+2822+4395+4395+8679
16,750 (1) +547+2256+2822+4395+6925+8679
160 (1) +2256+4395
162 (1) +2256+2256+4395+9109
186,400 (1) +547+547+547+752+2256+2256+2256+4395+4395+9046
2,056 (1) +547+2256+2822
2,067 (1) +547+2256+8679
2,600 (1) +547+2256+4395
2,630 (1) +547+2256+2256+4395+8993
22,600 (1) +547+2256+2256+4395+6929+9109
26,000 (1) +547+2256+6929
28,600 (1) +547+2256+2256+4395+6929+9046
3,600 (1) +547+2256+4395+8993
3,630 (1) +547+2256+2256+4395+8993+8993
365 (1) +2256+2256+2822+4395+8993
42,360 (1) +547+752+2256+4395+8052+8993
42,360 (1) +547+752+4395+8052+8993
44,760 (1) +547+752+752+2256+2256+2256+4395+8679
45,600 (1) +547+752+2256+2256+2822+4395
468 (1) +752+2256+4395+9046
56 (1) +2256+2822
6,200 (1) +547+2256+4395
6,800 (1) +547+2256+4395+9046
60 (1)
60,500 (1) +547+2256+2822+4395
601,730 (1) +547+547+2256+2256+4395+4395+8679+8993
61 (1) +285+2256
61,000 (1) +285+547+2256
61,000 (1) +547+2256+8052
62 (1) +2256+9109
623 (1) +2256+4395+6929+8993
628 (1) +2256+4395+6929+9046
64,300 (1) +547+752+2256+2256+4395+8993
64,400 (1) +547+752+752+2256+2256+4395
642 (1) +752+2256+2256+4395+9109
642 (1) +752+2256+4395+9109
648 (1) +752+2256+4395+9046
650 (1) +2256+2822+4395
655 (1) +2256+2822+2822+4395
666 (1) +2256+2256+4395+9252+9252
667 (1) +2256+4395+8679+9252
67 (1) +2256+8679
675 (1) +2256+2822+4395+8679
675,000 (1) +547+547+547+2256+2256+2822+4395+8679
690 (1) +2256+4395+9596
736 (1) +2256+4395+8679+8993
76,500 (1) +547+2256+2256+2822+4395+8679
8,600 (1) +547+2256+4395+9046
956 (1) +2256+2256+2822+4395+9596
962 (1) +2256+2256+4395+9109+9596
969 (1) +2256+2256+4395+9596+9596
eighty-six (1) +2256+9046
over nine feet (1) +564+2256+2455
sixth (1)
sixty-eight (1) +2256+9046
sixty-five (1) +2256+2822
thirty-six (1) +2256+8993
thirty-six hundred (1) +547+2256+4395+8993
thirty-sixth (1) +2256+8993
twenty-six (1) +2256+6929
twenty-six hundred (1) +547+2256+4395
twenty-sixth (1) +2256+6929
untranslated (3)

9253 2שֵׁשׁ *šēš2* (3)
marble (3)

9254 3שֵׁשׁ *šēš3* (39)
linen (21)
fine linen (17)
untranslated (1)

9255 שָׁשָׁא *šāšā'* (1)
drag along (1)

9256 שֵׁשְׁבַּצַּר *šēšbassar* (2)
Sheshbazzar (2)

9257 שָׁשָׁה *šāšāh* (1)
sixth (1)

9258 שָׁשַׁי *šāšay* (1)
Shashai (1)

9259 שֵׁשַׁי *šēšay* (3)
Sheshai (3)

9260 שֵׁשִׁי *šēšiy*
Variant; not used

9261 שִׁשִּׁי *šiššiy* (28)
sixth (28)

9262 שִׁשִּׁים *šiššiym*
Variant; not used

9263 שֵׁשַׁךְ *šēšak̲* (2)
Sheshach (2)

9264 שֵׁשָׁן *šēšān* (5)
Sheshan (4)
he^s (1)

9265 שָׁשַׁק *šāšaq* (2)
Shashak (2)

9266 שָׁשַׁר *šāšar* (2)
red (2)

9267 שֵׁת *šāt̲*
Variant; not used

9268 1שֵׁת *šēt̲1* (3)
buttocks (2)
foundations (1)

9269 2שֵׁת *šēt̲2* (9)
Seth (8)
Sheth (1)

9270 3שֵׁת *šēt̲3*
Variant; not used

9271 1שָׁתָה *šāt̲āh1* (1)
workers in cloth (1)

9272 2שָׁתָה *šāt̲āh2* (215)
drink (127)
drank (28)
drinking (23)
drinks (8)
drunk (6)
must drink (3) +9272
drinkers (2)
getting drunk (2) +8893
well-watered (2) +4784
be drunk (1)
dine (1)
drained to dregs (1) +5172
drinks in (1)
drinks up (1)
drunkards (1) +8911
feasted (1)
feasting (1) +430+2256
get a drink (1)
have a drink (1)
refresh (1)
untranslated (2)

9273 שָׁתוֹת *šāt̲ôt̲*
Variant; not used

9274 1שְׁתִי š^{e}ṯiy1 (9)
woven (9)

9275 2שְׁתִי š^{e}ṯiy2 (1)
drunkenness (1)

9276 שְׁתִיָּה š^{e}ṯiyyāh (1)
drink in own way (1)

9277 שָׁתִיל šāṯiyl (1)
shoots (1)

9278 שָׁתַל šāṯal (10)
planted (5)
plant (2)
been planted (1)
is planted (1)
is transplanted (1)

9279 שֻׁתַלְחִי šuṯalḥiy (1)
Shuthelahite (1)

9280 שָׁתַם šāṯam (2)
sees clearly (2)

9281 שְׁתֻם š^{e}ṯum
Variant; not used

9282 שָׁתַן šāṯan
Variant; not used

9283 שָׁתַע šāṯa' (2)
dismayed (2)

9284 שָׁתַק šāṯaq (4)
calm (2)
calm down (1)
dies down (1)

9285 שֵׁתָר šēṯār (1)
Shethar (1)

9286 שָׁתַת šāṯaṯ (2)
destined (1)
lay claim (1)

9287 ת ṯ
Variant; not used

9288 תָּא tā' (17)
alcoves (8)
alcove (2)
guardroom (2) +8132
alcoves for the guards (1)
untranslated (4)

9289 1תָּאַב tā'aḇ1 (2)
long for (2)

9290 2תָּאַב tā'aḇ2 (1)
abhor (1)

9291 תַּאֲבָה ta'^{a}ḇāh (1)
longing (1)

9292 תָּאָה ta'āh (2)
run a line (1)
untranslated (1)

9293 תְּאוֹ t^{e}'ô (2)
antelope (2)

9294 1תַּאֲוָה ta'^{a}wāh1 (21)
desire (5)
longing (2)
longings (2)
bounty (1)
choicest (1)
crave other food (1) +203
craved (1)
craves for more (1) +203
craving (1)
cravings (1)
desires (1)
gave in to craving (1) +203
pleasing (1)
selfish ends (1)
what craved (1)

9295 2תַּאֲוָה ta'^{a}wāh2
Variant; not used

9296 תְּאוֹמִים t^{e}'ômiym
Variant; not used

9297 תַּאֲלָה ta'^{a}lāh (1)
curse (1)

9298 תָּאַם tā'am (2)
has twin (2)

9299 תַּאֲנָה ta'^{a}nāh (1)
in heat (1)

9300 תְּאֵנָה t^{e}'ēnāh (39)
fig tree (15)
figs (13)
fig trees (6)
fig (2)
ones^{s} (1)
those^{s} (1)
tree (1)

9301 תֹּאֲנָה tō'^{a}nāh (1)
occasion (1)

9302 תַּאֲנִיָּה ta'^{a}niyyāh (2)
mourn (1)
mourning (1)

9303 תְּאֻנִים t^{e}'uniym (1)
efforts (1)

9304 תַּאֲנַת שִׁלֹה ta'^{a}naṯ šilōh (1)
Taanath Shiloh (1)

9305 1תָּאַר tā'ar1 (6)
turned (3)
curved (1)
headed (1)
went down (1)

9306 2תָּאַר tā'ar2 (2)
makes an outline (1)
marks (1)

9307 תֹּאַר tō'ar (15)
form (4)
beautiful (2) +3637
bearing (1)
beauty (1)
fine-looking (1)
handsome (1) +3202
look like (1)
sleek (1) +3637
they (1) +4392
ugly (1) +8273
well-built (1) +3637

9308 תַּרְאֲעָ ta'rēa' (1)
Tarea (1)

9309 תְּאַשּׁוּר t^{e}'aššûr (3)
cypress (2)
cypress wood (1)

9310 תֵּבָה tēḇāh (28)
ark (25)
basket (2)
it^{s} (1) +2021

9311 תְּבוּאָה t^{e}ḇû'āh (43)
harvest (11)
crops (6)
income (4)
produce (4)
brings forth (1)
comes (1)
crop (1)
crop comes in (1)
enough (1)
fruit (1)
gain (1)
harvesting crops (1)
produce (1) +2446+3655
produced (1)
produces (1)
product (1)
revenue (1)
what is taken (1)
yield (1)
yields returns (1)
untranslated (2)

9312 תְּבוּנָה t^{e}ḇûnāh (42)
understanding (28)
ability (3)
insight (2)
cleverly fashioned (1)
detect (1)
discernment (1)
experienced (1) +1981+2256
judgment (1)
reasoning (1)
skillful (1)
wisdom (1)
words of insight (1)

9313 תְּבוּסָה t^{e}ḇûsāh (1)
downfall (1)

9314 תָּבוֹר tāḇôr (10)
Tabor (10)

9315 תֵּבֵל tēḇēl (36)
world (30)
earth (3)
whole earth (1) +824
whole world (1) +824
world's (1)

9316 תֶּבֶל teḇel (2)
perversion (2)

9317 תֻּבַל tuḇal (8)
Tubal (8)

9318 תַּבְלִית taḇliyṯ (1)
destruction (1)

9319 תְּבַלֻּל t^{e}ḇallul (1)
defect (1)

9320 תֶּבֶן teḇen (17)
straw (17)

9321 תִּבְנִי tiḇniy (3)
Tibni (3)

9322 תַּבְנִית taḇniyṯ (20)
plans (3)
looked like (2)
pattern (2)
plan (2)
adorn (1)
form (1)
formed (1)
image (1)
kinds (1)
replica (1)
untranslated (5)

9323 תַּבְעֵרָה taḇ'ērāh (2)
Taberah (2)

9324 תֵּבֵץ tēḇēṣ (3)
Thebez (2)
it^{s} (1)

9325 תִּגְלַת פִּלְאֶסֶר tiglaṯ pil'eser (3)
Tiglath Pileser (3)

9326 תַּגְמוּל tagmûl (1)
goodness (1)

9327 תִּגְרָה tigrāh (1)
blow (1)

9328 תֹּגַרְמָה tōgarmāh (2)
Togarmah (2)

9329 תִּדְהָר tiḏhār (2)
fir (2)

9330 תַּדְמֹר taḏmōr (2)
Tadmor (2)

9331 תִּדְעָל tiḏ'āl (2)
Tidal (2)

9332 תֹּהוּ tōhû (20)
nothing (3)
empty (2)

formless (2)
waste (2)
barren (1)
chaos (1)
confusion (1)
empty space (1)
false (1)
in vain (1)
ruined (1)
useless (1)
useless idols (1)
wasteland (1)
worthless (1)

9333 תְּהוֹם *tᵉhôm* (36)
deep (19)
depths (6)
deep waters (3)
deep springs (2)
ocean depths (2)
deeps (1)
oceans (1)
seas (1)
springs (1)

9334 תָּהֳלָה *tohᵒlāh* (1)
error (1)

9335 תְּהִלָּה *tᵉhillāh* (58)
praise (46)
praised (2)
praises (2)
boast (1)
glory (1)
hymn of praise (1)
praiseworthy deeds (1)
psalm of praise (1)
renown (1)
theme of praise (1)
untranslated (1)

9336 תַּהֲלוּכָה *tahᵃlûk̲āh*
Variant; not used

9337 תַּהְפֻּכוֹת *tahpuk̲ôt̲* (10)
perverse (6)
confusing things (1)
deceit (1)
perverseness (1)
perversity (1)

9338 תָּו *tāw* (3)
mark (1)
put a mark (1) +9344
sign (1)

9339 תּוֹאֲמִים *tôʼᵃmiym* (6)
twin (3)
double (2)
twins (1)

9340 תּוּבַל קַיִן *tûb̲al qayin* (2)
Tubal-Cain (1)
Tubal-Cain's (1)

9341 תּוּבְנָה *tûb̲ᵉnāh* (1)
untranslated (1)

9342 תּוּגָה *tûg̲āh* (4)
grief (3)
sorrow (1)

9343 תּוֹדָה *tôd̲āh* (32)
thanksgiving (9)
thank offerings (8)
thank (4)
praise (2)
songs of thanksgiving (2)
choir (1)
choirs that gave thanks (1)
choirs to give thanks (1)
confession (1)
expression of thankfulness (1)
giving thanks (1)
thank offering (1)

9344 1תָּוָה *tāwāh1* (3)
making marks (1)
put a mark (1) +9338
untranslated (1)

9345 2תָּוָה *tāwāh2* (1)
vexed (1)

9346 תּוֹחַ *tôah* (1)
Toah (1)

9347 תּוֹחֶלֶת *tôhelet̲* (5)
hope (2)
expected (1)
hoped (1)
prospect (1)

9348 תָּוֶךְ *tāwek̲* (420)
among (111) +928
in (45) +928
middle (27)
with (17) +928
from (16) +4946
inside (15) +928
within (15) +928
midst (13)
out of (13) +4946
among (12)
center (11)
into (11) +448
into (9) +928
through (8) +928
along with (6) +928
within (5)
of (4) +4946
there[s] (4) +928+2023
between (3) +928
from (2) +928
from out of (2) +4946
heart (2)
inside (2) +448
intersecting (2) +928
presence (2)
throughout (2) +928
along (1) +928
among (1) +448
as one (1) +928
at (1) +928
branch of (1) +4946
by (1) +928
by (1) +4946
central (1)
centrally located in (1) +928
do away with (1) +4946+6073
entered (1) +928+995
entering (1) +928+995
flashed back and forth (1) +928+4374
for (1) +928
gone from (1) +4946
in (1) +4946
include (1) +928
inner part (1)
interior (1)
joined in (1) +928
leave (1) +3718+4946
left (1) +4946+7756
like (1) +928
of (1) +928
of all (1) +4946
on (1) +928
on board (1) +928
onto (1) +448
over (1) +928
ranks (1)
surrounded by (1) +928
there[s] (1) +928+2257
there[s] (1) +928+4392
to (1) +448
two (1)
within (1) +928+5055
untranslated (25)

9349 תּוֹכֵחָה *tôk̲ēhāh* (4)
rebuke (2)
punishment (1)
reckoning (1)

9350 תּוֹכַחַת *tôk̲ahat̲* (24)
correction (8)
rebuke (8)
argument (1)
arguments (1)
complaint (1)
corrections (1)
punish (1)
punished (1)
rebukes (1)
reply (1)

9351 תּוֹלָד *tôlād̲* (1)
Tolad (1)

9352 תּוֹלְדוֹת *tôlēd̲ôt̲* (39)
records (14)
account (10)
listed genealogy (3)
genealogical records (2)
genealogy (2)
account of line (1)
account of the family (1)
birth (1)
descendants (1)
family line (1)
genealogical record (1)
lines of descent (1)
order of birth (1)

9353 תּוֹלוֹן *tôlôn* (1)
untranslated (1)

9354 תּוֹלָל *tôlāl* (1)
tormentors (1)

9355 1תּוֹלָע *tôlāʻ1* (2)
crimson (1)
purple (1)

9356 2תּוֹלָע *tôlāʻ2* (6)
Tola (6)

9357 תּוֹלֵעָה *tôlēʻāh* (41)
scarlet yarn (31) +9106
worm (5)
worms (2)
maggots (1)
scarlet (1) +9106
scarlet wool (1) +9106

9358 תּוֹלָעִי *tôlāʻiy* (1)
Tolaite (1)

9359 תּוֹעֵבָה *tôʻēb̲āh* (118)
detestable practices (30)
detestable (19)
detestable things (18)
detests (13)
detestable thing (7)
detest (6)
detestable idols (6)
detestable ways (3)
things detestable (3)
loathsome (2)
things[s] (2)
abhors (1)
abominations (1)
detestable god (1)
detestable offense (1)
detestable sins (1)
repulsive (1)
thing detestable (1)
what detestable (1)
untranslated (1)

9360 תּוֹעָה *tôʻāh* (2)
error (1)
trouble (1)

9361 תּוֹעָפוֹת *tôʻāp̲ôt̲* (4)
strength (2)
choicest (1)
peaks (1)

9362 תּוֹצָאוֹת *tôṣāʼôt̲* (25)
ended (5) +2118

out (5)
end (3) +2118
ending (3) +2118
escape (1)
exits (1)
extended (1)
farthest limits (1)
wellspring (1)
untranslated (4)

9363 תָּוְקְהַת *tāwqᵉhaṯ* (1)
untranslated (1)

9364 תּוֹקְעִים *tôqᵉʻiym* (1)
strike hands in pledge (1)

9365 תּוּר *tûr* (24)
explore (6)
explored (5)
merchants (2) +408
cautious (1)
explored (1) +6296
exploring (1)
find (1)
going (1)
investigate (1)
ranges (1)
search out (1)
searched out (1)
sent to spy out (1)
tried (1) +928+4213

9366 תּוֹר1 *tôr1* (5)
earrings (2)
turn (2)
most exalted (1) +5092

9367 תּוֹר2 *tôr2* (14)
doves (9)
dove (5)

9368 תּוֹרָה *tôrāh* (223)
law (168)
laws (16)
regulations (15)
teaching (8)
instruction (5)
instructions (2)
matters of law (1)
teaching of law (1)
teaching of the law (1)
teachings (1)
usual way of dealing (1)
untranslated (4)

9369 תּוֹשָׁב *tôšāḇ* (13)
temporary resident (5)
stranger (2)
guest (1)
living (1)
people living (1)
strangers (1)
temporary residents (1)
tenants (1)

9370 תּוּשִׁיָּה *tûšiyyāh* (11)
sound judgment (3)
success (2)
victory (2)
wisdom (2)
insight (1)
true wisdom (1)

9371 תּוֹתָח *tôṯāḥ* (1)
club (1)

9372 תָּזַז *tāzaz* (1)
cut down (1)

9373 תַּזְנוּת *taznûṯ* (22)
prostitution (8)
promiscuity (5)
lust (2)
favors (1)
illicit favors (1)
promiscuous (1)
prostitute (1)
use as a prostitute (1) +2388
untranslated (2)

9374 תַּחְבֻּלוֹת *taḥbulôṯ* (7)
guidance (4)
advice (1)
direction (1)
untranslated (1)

9375 תֹּחוּ *tōḥû* (1)
Tohu (1)

9376 תַּחְכְּמֹנִי *taḥkᵉmōniy* (1)
Tahkemonite (1)

9377 תַּחֲלֻאִים *taḥᵃlu'iym* (5)
diseases (3)
pain (1)
ravages (1)

9378 תְּחִלָּה *tᵉḥillāh* (23)
beginning (7)
first (3) +928+2021
began (2)
earlier (2) +928+2021
first (2)
first time (2)
already (1) +928+2021
before (1) +928+2021
led in thanksgiving (1) +3344
untranslated (2)

9379 תַּחְמָס *taḥmās* (2)
screech owl (2)

9380 תַּחַן *taḥan* (2)
Tahan (2)

9381 תַּחֲנָה *taḥᵃnāh* (1)
set up camp (1)

9382 תְּחִנָּה1 *tᵉḥinnāh1* (25)
plea (10)
petition (4)
plea for mercy (2)
supplication (2)
cry for mercy (1)
gracious (1)
mercy (1)
pleading (1) +5877
pleas (1)
request (1)
supplications (1)

9383 תְּחִנָּה2 *tᵉḥinnāh2* (1)
Tehinnah (1)

9384 תַּחֲנוּן *taḥᵃnûn* (18)
cry for mercy (6) +7754
cry for mercy (2)
pray (2)
begging for mercy (1)
mercy (1)
petition (1)
petitions (1)
pleading (1)
requests (1)
supplication (1)
supplications (1)

9385 תַּחֲנִי *taḥᵃniy* (1)
Tahanite (1)

9386 תַּחֲנֹתִי *taḥᵃnōṯiy*
Variant; not used

9387 תַּחְפַּנְחֵס *taḥpanḥēs* (8)
Tahpanhes (7)
untranslated (1)

9388 תַּחְפְּנֵיס *taḥpᵉnēys* (3)
Tahpenes (3)

9389 תַּחְרָא *taḥrā'* (2)
collar (1)
collar (1) +7023

9390 תַּחְרֵעַ *taḥrēaʻ* (1)
Tahrea (1)

9391 תַּחַשׁ1 *taḥaš1* (14)
sea cows (12)
hides of sea cows (1)
leather (1)

9392 תַּחַשׁ2 *taḥaš2* (1)
Tahash (1)

9393 תַּחַת1 *taḥaṯ1* (511)
under (150)
succeeded (65)
for (34)
in place of (24)
in place (23)
instead of (18)
below (17) +4946
beneath (15)
below (10)
under (7) +4946
because (6) +889
succeed (5)
against (4) +3338+4946
beneath (4) +4946
instead (4)
where (4)
with (4)
at feet (3)
in (3)
in return for (3)
place (3)
replace (3)
while married to (3)
among (2)
at the foot of (2)
for (2) +889
from (2) +4946
have a home (2) +8905
in exchange for (2)
on (2)
succeeded (2) +7756
to (2)
to compensate for (2)
unchanged (2) +6641
underneath (2)
although (1)
amid (1)
as a direct result (1) +3338
at foot of (1)
at the spot (1)
because (1) +3954
by (1)
from (1)
have (1) +3338+3780
have on hand (1) +448+3338
have on hand (1) +3338+3780
homes (1)
in exchange (1)
in position (1)
in stead (1)
in the place of (1)
instead of (1) +889
land[s] (1)
legs (1)
lower (1) +4946
made subject to (1) +3338+4044
mine (1) +3276
on behalf (1)
on the spot (1)
pad (1) +4946
position (1)
replace (1) +448+995
replace (1) +8492
replaced (1) +5989
replaced (1) +6641
resting on (1) +4946
riding (1)
since (1) +889
since (1) +3954
submission (1)
succeeds (1)
successor (1) +6641
supported (1)

take charge of (1) +3338
take the place of (1)
take the place of (1) +2118
to (1) +3338
to (1) +4946
underfoot (1) +8079
underneath (1) +4946
undersides (1)
when (1)
where stand (1)
why (1) +4537
untranslated (26)

9394 2תַּחַת *taḥaṯ2* (4)
Tahath (4)

9395 3תַּחַת *taḥaṯ3* (2)
Tahath (2)

9396 תַּחְתּוֹן *taḥtôn* (14)
lower (11)
lowest (3)

9397 תַּחְתִּי *taḥtiy* (19)
below (7)
depths (4)
lower (4)
lowest (2)
beneath (1)
foot (1)

9398 תַּחְתִּים חָדְשִׁי *taḥtiym ḥoḏšiy* (1)
Tahtim Hodshi (1)

9399 תִּיכוֹן *tiykôn* (10)
middle (7)
center (2)
there[s] (1) +2021

9400 תִּילוֹן *tiylôn* (1)
Tilon (1)

9401 תֵּימָא *tēymā'* (5)
Tema (4)
Tema (1) +824

9402 1תֵּימָן *tēymān1* (23)
south (8)
south (5) +2025
south (3) +2025+5582
south (2) +2025+2025+5582
south (2) +5582
south wind (2)
southward (1) +4946

9403 2תֵּימָן *tēymān2* (11)
Teman (11)

9404 תֵּימָנִי *tēymāniy* (8)
Temanite (6)
Temanites (2)

9405 תֵּימְנִי *tēymᵉniy* (1)
Temeni (1)

9406 תִּימָרָה *tiymārāh* (2)
billows (1)
column (1)

9407 תִּיצִי *tiysiy* (1)
Tizite (1)

9408 תִּירוֹשׁ *tiyrôš* (38)
new wine (34)
grapes (1)
juice (1)
new (1)
wine (1)

9409 תִּירְיָא *tiyryā'* (1)
Tiria (1)

9410 תִּירָס *tiyrās* (2)
Tiras (2)

9411 תַּיִשׁ *tayiš* (4)
male goats (2)
goats (1)
he-goat (1)

9412 תֹּךְ *tōḵ* (4)
threats (2)
oppression (1)
oppressor (1) +408

9413 תָּכָה *tāḵāh* (1)
bow down (1)

9414 תְּכוּנָה *tᵉkûnāh* (3)
arrangement (1)
dwelling (1)
supply (1)

9415 תֻּכִּיִּים *tukkiyyiym* (2)
baboons (2)

9416 תִּכְלָה *tiḵlāh* (1)
perfection (1)

9417 תַּכְלִית *taḵliyṯ* (5)
boundary (1)
end (1)
farthest recesses (1) +3972
limits (1)
nothing but (1)

9418 תְּכֵלֶת *tᵉḵēleṯ* (49)
blue (42)
blue yarn (3)
blue cloth (2)
blue material (2)

9419 תָּכַן *tāḵan* (18)
just (5)
unjust (4) +4202
weighs (2)
amount been determined (1)
are weighed (1)
hold firm (1)
marked off (1)
measured out (1) +928+4500
understood (1)
weighed (1)

9420 1תֹּכֶן *tōḵen1* (2)
full quota (1)
size (1)

9421 2תֹּכֶן *tōḵen2* (1)
token (1)

9422 תָּכְנִית *toḵniyṯ* (2)
perfection (1)
plan (1)

9423 תַּכְרִיךְ *taḵriyḵ* (1)
robe (1)

9424 תֵּל *tēl* (5)
heap of ruins (1)
mound (1)
mounds (1)
ruin (1)
ruins (1)

9425 תֵּל אָבִיב *tēl 'āḇiyḇ* (1)
Tel Abib (1)

9426 תֵּל חַרְשָׁא *tēl ḥaršā'* (2)
Tel Harsha (2)

9427 תֵּל מֶלַח *tēl melaḥ* (2)
Tel Melah (2)

9428 תָּלָא *tālā'* (3)
determined (1)
hung (1)
suspense (1)

9429 תַּלְאֻבוֹת *tal'uḇôṯ* (1)
burning heat (1)

9430 תְּלָאָה *tᵉlā'āh* (5)
hardship (2)
hardships (2)
burden (1)

9431 תְּלַאשָּׂר *tᵉla'śśār* (2)
Tel Assar (2)

9432 תִּלְבֹּשֶׁת *tilbōšeṯ* (1)
put on (1) +4252

9433 תִּלְגַת פִּלְנְאֶסֶר *tillᵉgaṯ pilnᵉ'eser* (3)
Tiglath-Pileser (3)

9434 תָּלָה *tālāh* (28)
hanged (8)
hung (7)
hang (5)
hanging (3)
been hung up (1)
is hung (1)
suspends (1)
were hanged (1)
untranslated (1)

9435 תָּלוּל *tālûl* (1)
lofty (1)

9436 תֶּלַח *telaḥ* (1)
Telah (1)

9437 תְּלִי *tᵉliy* (1)
quiver (1)

9438 תָּלַל *tālal* (9)
deceive (2)
made a fool of (2)
act deceitfully (1)
cheated (1)
deceives (1)
deluded (1)
making a fool of (1)

9439 תֶּלֶם *telem* (5)
furrows (2)
plowed (2)
furrow (1)

9440 תַּלְמַי *talmay* (6)
Talmai (6)

9441 תַּלְמִיד *talmiyḏ* (1)
student (1)

9442 תְּלֻנּוֹת *tᵉlunnôṯ* (8)
grumbling (5)
complaints (1)
constant grumbling (1) +4296
grumbling (1) +4296

9443 תָּלַע *tāla'* (1)
clad in scarlet (1)

9444 תַּלְפִּיּוֹת *talpiyyôṯ* (1)
elegance (1)

9445 תְּלַשָּׂר *tᵉlaśśār*
Variant; not used

9446 תַּלְתַּל *taltāl* (1)
wavy (1)

9447 תָּם *tām* (16)
blameless (8)
fitted (2) +3481
flawless (1)
innocent (1)
integrity (1)
perfect (1)
quiet (1)
strong (1)

9448 תֹּם *tōm* (25)
blameless (8)
integrity (6)
at random (2) +4200
clear (2)
full (2)
full measure (1)
last (1)
man of integrity (1) +2006
quite innocently (1) +4200
righteous (1)

9449 תָּמַהּ *tāmah* (10)
aghast (1)
amazed (1)
appalled (1)
astounded (1)
look aghast (1)

looked in astonishment (1)
stunned (1)
surprised (1)
utterly amazed (1) +9449

9450 תֻּמָּה *tummāh* (5)
integrity (4)
blameless (1)

9451 תִּמָּהוֹן *timmāhôn* (2)
confusion (1)
panic (1)

9452 תַּמּוּז *tammûz* (1)
Tammuz (1)

9453 תְּמוֹל *t'môl* (23)
before (6) +8997
malice aforethought (4) +4946+8533+8997
yesterday (4)
had the habit (2) +4946+8997
as usual (1) +3869+8997
before (1) +4946+8997
for some time (1) +1685+1685+8997
had been (1) +8997
in the past (1) +8997
past (1) +8997
untranslated (1)

9454 תְּמוּנָה *t'mûnāh* (10)
form (7)
image (1)
kind (1)
likeness (1)

9455 תְּמוּרָה *t'mûrāh* (6)
substitute (2)
had for (1)
return (1)
trading (1)
transfer of property (1) +1821+3972

9456 תְּמוּתָה *t'mûṯāh* (2)
death (1)
die (1)

9457 תֶּמַח *temah* (2)
Temah (2)

9458 תָּמִיד *tāmiyḏ* (104)
always (23)
regular (23)
continually (12)
regularly (12)
ever (8)
daily sacrifice (5)
forever (3)
constantly (2)
at all times (1)
constant (1)
continual (1)
continued (1)
continuing (1)
continuously (1)
daily (1)
day after day (1) +3429
endless (1)
keep on (1)
kept (1)
lasting (1) +6409
long (1)
never (1) +4202
often (1)
untranslated (1)

9459 תָּמִים *tāmiym* (91)
without defect (47)
blameless (19)
perfect (8)
full (3)
good faith (2)
whole (2)
all (1)
blameless (1) +1475
blameless (1) +1505
entire (1)
right answer (1)
truth (1)
untranslated (4)

9460 תֻּמִּים *tummiym* (5)
Thummim (5)

9461 תָּמַךְ *tāmaḵ* (21)
uphold (3)
gains (2)
holds (2)
lay hold (2)
accepting (1)
gain (1)
grasps (1)
held (1)
held up (1)
hold fast (1)
lead straight (1)
made secure (1)
support (1)
taken hold (1)
took hold (1)
upholds (1)

9462 תָּמַם *tāmam* (63)
gone (5)
completely (4)
end (4)
perish (3)
all (2)
blameless (2)
completed (2)
finished (2)
over (2)
put an end (2)
show yourself blameless (2)
vanish (2)
all gone (1)
almost to a man (1) +4392+6330
burn away (1)
burned (1)
burned away (1)
consumed (1)
cook well (1)
destroy (1)
destroyed (1)
die (1)
died (1)
done (1)
doomed (1)
down to (1) +6330
ended (1)
fail (1)
have get ready (1)
last (1)
meet end (1)
overtaken (1)
perfect (1)
perished (1)
perishing (1)
settled (1)
spent (1)
stop (1)
untranslated (5)

9463 תִּמְנָה *timnāh* (12)
Timnah (11)
there[s] (1) +928+2025

9464 תִּמְנִי *timniy* (1)
Timnite's (1)

9465 תִּמְנַע *timna'* (6)
Timna (6)

9466 תִּמְנַת־חֶרֶס *timnaṯ-heres* (1)
Timnath Heres (1)

9467 תִּמְנַת־סֶרַח *timnaṯ-serah* (2)
Timnath Serah (2)

9468 תֶּמֶס *temes* (1)
melting away (1)

9469 1תָּמָר *tāmār1* (12)
palms (5)
palm (3)
palm tree (2)
palm trees (2)

9470 2תָּמָר *tāmār2* (22)
Tamar (22)

9471 3תָּמָר *tāmār3* (4)
Tamar (3)
untranslated (1)

9472 1תֹּמֶר *tōmer1* (1)
palm (1)

9473 2תֹּמֶר *tōmer2* (1)
scarecrow (1)

9474 תִּמֹרָה *timōrāh* (20)
palm trees (14)
palm tree (2)
palm tree decorations (2)
palm tree designs (1)
untranslated (1)

9475 תַּמְרוּק *tamrûq* (3)
beauty treatments (2)
cosmetics (1)

9476 1תַּמְרוּרִים *tamrûriym1* (3)
bitter (1)
bitterly (1)
great (1)

9477 2תַּמְרוּרִים *tamrûriym2* (1)
guideposts (1)

9478 תַּן *tan* (15)
jackals (13)
jackal (1)
untranslated (1)

9479 1תָּנָה *tānāh1* (2)
sold (2)

9480 2תָּנָה *tānāh2* (1)
commemorate (1)

9481 תְּנוּאָה *t'nû'āh* (2)
against (1)
fault (1)

9482 תְּנוּבָה *t'nûḇāh* (5)
fruit (3)
crops (1)
food (1)

9483 תְּנוּךְ *t'nûḵ* (8)
lobe (5)
lobes (2)
untranslated (1)

9484 תְּנוּמָה *t'nûmāh* (5)
slumber (5)

9485 תְּנוּפָה *t'nûpāh* (30)
wave offering (21)
waved (5)
blows (1)
uplifted (1)
was waved (1) +5677
wave offerings (1)

9486 תַּנּוּר *tannûr* (15)
oven (8)
furnace (3)
ovens (3)
firepot (1)

9487 תַּנְחוּמוֹת *tanhûmôṯ* (2)
consolation (1)
consolations (1)

9488 תַּנְחוּמִים *tanhûmiym* (3)
comforting (1)
consolation (1)
console (1)

9489 תַּנְחֻמֶת *tanhumeṯ* (2)
Tanhumeth (2)

9490 תַּנִּין *tanniyn* (15)
monster (5)

snake (3)
serpent (2)
creatures of the sea (1)
great sea creatures (1)
jackal (1)
monster of the deep (1)
serpents (1)

9491 1תִּנְשֶׁמֶת *tinšemeṯ1* (1)
chameleon (1)

9492 2תִּנְשֶׁמֶת *tinšemeṯ2* (2)
white owl (2)

9493 תָּעַב *tā'aḇ* (22)
vile (4)
abhor (3)
detest (3)
abhorred (2)
despise (2)
abhors (1)
behaved in the vilest manner (1) +4394
degraded (1)
detest (1) +9493
loathed (1)
rejected (1)
repulsive (1)

9494 תָּעָה *tā'āh* (51)
led astray (6)
leads astray (4)
go astray (3)
lead astray (3)
wandered (3)
went astray (3)
reel (2)
stray (2)
strayed (2)
wayward (2)
deceive himself (1)
did[s] (1)
error (1)
falters (1)
go about (1)
gone astray (1)
had wander (1)
made a fatal mistake (1) +928+5883
made wander (1)
make stagger (1)
make wander (1)
makes stagger (1)
mislead (1)
sends wandering (1)
spread (1)
staggers around (1)
strays (1)
wander about (1)
wandering around (1)
wandering off (1)
untranslated (1)

9495 תֹּעוּ *tō'û* (2)
Tou (2)

9496 תְּעוּדָה *t^{e}'ûḏāh* (3)
testimony (2)
method of legalizing transactions (1)

9497 תֹּעִי *tō'iy* (3)
Tou (2)
he[s] (1)

9498 1תְּעָלָה *t^{e}'ālāh1* (9)
aqueduct (3)
trench (3)
channel (1)
channels (1)
tunnel (1)

9499 2תְּעָלָה *t^{e}'ālāh2* (2)
healing (2)

9500 תַּעֲלוּלִים *ta^{a}lûliym* (2)
harsh treatment (1)
mere children (1)

9501 תַּעֲלֻם *ta^{a}lum*
Variant; not used

9502 תַּעֲלֻמָה *ta^{a}lumāh* (3)
secrets (2)
hidden things (1)

9503 תַּעֲנוּג *ta^{a}nûḡ* (5)
delight (1)
delights (1)
delights of the heart (1)
live in luxury (1)
pleasant (1)

9504 תַּעֲנִית *ta^{a}niyṯ* (1)
self-abasement (1)

9505 תַּעְנַךְ *ta^{a}naḵ* (7)
Taanach (7)

9506 תָּעַע *tā'a'* (2)
scoffed (1)
tricking (1)

9507 תְּעֻפָה *t^{e}'upāh* (1)
darkness (1)

9508 תַּעֲצֻמוֹת *ta^{a}sumôṯ* (1)
strength (1)

9509 תַּעַר *ta'ar* (13)
scabbard (5)
razor (4)
have shave (1) +6296
knife (1)
sheath (1)
unsheathed (1) +3655+4946

9510 תַּעֲרוּבוֹת *ta^{a}rûḇôṯ* (2)
hostages (2) +1201

9511 תַּעְתֻּעִים *ta'tu'iym* (2)
mockery (2)

9512 1תֹּף *tōp̱1* (16)
tambourines (9)
tambourine (4)
music of tambourines (2)
music of tambourine (1)

9513 2תֹּף *tōp̱2* (1)
settings (1) +4856

9514 תִּפְאֶרֶת *tip̱'ereṯ* (51)
glorious (11)
glory (11)
splendor (9)
honor (7)
fine (3)
beautiful (2)
boasted (2)
adorned (1) +4200+7596
elation (1)
finery (1)
look (1)
pride (1)
untranslated (1)

9515 1תַּפּוּחַ *tappûah1* (6)
apple tree (3)
apples (3)

9516 2תַּפּוּחַ *tappûah2* (1)
Tappuah (1)

9517 3תַּפּוּחַ *tappûah3* (5)
Tappuah (5)

9518 תְּפוּצָה *t^{e}p̱ûṣāh* (1)
shattered (1)

9519 תֻּפִינִים *tupiyniym* (1)
broken (1)

9520 תָּפַל *tāp̱al*
Variant; not used

9521 1תָּפֵל *tāp̱ēl1* (5)
whitewash (4)
whitewash (1) +3212

9522 2תָּפֵל *tāp̱ēl2* (2)
tasteless (1)
worthless (1)

9523 תֹּפֶל *tōp̱el* (1)
Tophel (1)

9524 תִּפְלָה *tip̱lāh* (3)
wrongdoing (2)
repulsive thing (1)

9525 תְּפִלָּה *t^{e}p̱illāh* (77)
prayer (60)
prayers (10)
petition (2)
pray (2) +5951
offer prayer (1) +7137
plea (1)
pray (1)

9526 תִּפְלֶצֶת *tip̱leseṯ* (1)
terror (1)

9527 תִּפְסַח *tip̱sah* (2)
Tiphsah (2)

9528 תָּפַף *tāp̱ap̱* (2)
beat (1)
playing tambourines (1)

9529 תָּפַר *tāp̱ar* (4)
mend (1)
sew (1)
sewed (1)
sewed together (1)

9530 תָּפַשׂ *tāp̱aś* (65)
captured (8)
seize (4)
seized (4)
take (4)
took (4)
capture (3)
arrested (2)
be caught (2)
caught (2)
grasped (2)
taken (2)
was trapped (2)
archer (1) +8008
are caught (1)
be captured (1)
be taken captive (1) +928+2021+4090
been caught in the act (1)
brandishing (1)
capturing (1)
carry (1)
covered (1)
deal with (1)
dishonor (1)
handle (1)
hold (1)
occupy (1)
play (1)
rapes (1) +2256+6640+8886
reaper (1)
recapture (1)
soldiers (1) +4878
surely be captured (1) +9530
take captive (1)
take hold (1)
taken over (1)
took hold (1)
untranslated (1)

9531 1תֹּפֶת *tōp̱eṯ1* (1)
spit (1)

9532 2תֹּפֶת *tōp̱eṯ2* (9)
Topheth (9)

9533 תָּפְתֶּה *top̱teh* (1)
Topheth (1)

9534 תָּקְהַת *toqhaṯ* (1)
Tokhath (1)

9535 1תִּקְוָה *tiqwāh1* (2)
cord (1)
cord (1) +2562

9536 2תִּקְוָה *tiqwāh2* (32)
hope (30)
expectation (1)
hopes (1)

9537 3תִּקְוָה *tiqwāh3* (2)
Tikvah (2)

9538 תְּקוּמָה *t^{e}qûmāh* (1)
able to stand (1)

9539 תְּקוֹמֵם *t^{e}qômēm*
Variant; not used

9540 תָּקוֹעַ *tāqôa'* (1)
trumpet (1)

9541 תְּקוֹעַ *t^{e}qôa'* (7)
Tekoa (7)

9542 תְּקוֹעִי *t^{e}qô'iy* (7)
from Tekoa (4)
men of Tekoa (2)
Tekoite (1)

9543 תְּקוּפָה *t^{e}qûp̱āh* (4)
turn (2)
circuit (1)
course (1)

9544 תַּקִּיף *taqqiyp̱* (2)
stronger (1)
untranslated (1)

9545 תָּקַן *tāqan* (3)
set in order (1)
straighten (1)
straightened (1)

9546 תָּקַע *tāqa'* (70)
blow (10)
sounded (10)
blew (7)
sound (7)
blowing (5)
sounding (3)
plunged (2)
sounds (2)
strikes in pledge (2)
blow trumpets (1)
blows (1)
camped (1)
carried (1)
clap (1)
claps (1)
drive (1)
driven (1)
drove (1)
fastened (1)
had blown (1)
hung up (1)
pitch (1)
pitched (1)
put up security (1) +3338+4200
signal (1)
sounded blast (1)
struck in pledge (1)
tighten (1)
tightened (1)
untranslated (2)

9547 תֵּקַע *tēqa'* (1)
sounding (1)

9548 תָּקַף *tāqap̱* (3)
overpower (1)
overpowered (1)
overwhelm (1)

9549 תֹּקֶף *tōqep̱* (3)
authority (1)
might (1)
power (1)

9550 תַּרְאֲלָה *tar'^{a}lāh* (1)
Taralah (1)

9551 תַּרְבּוּת *tarbûṯ* (1)
brood (1)

9552 תַּרְבִּית *tarbiyṯ* (7)
excessive interest (4)
exorbitant interest (1) +2256+5968
interest of any kind (1) +2256+5968
untranslated (1)

9553 תִּרְגֵּם *tirgēm* (1)
language (1)

9554 תַּרְדֵּמָה *tardēmāh* (7)
deep sleep (6)
deep sleep (1) +8120

9555 תִּרְהָקָה *tirhāqāh* (2)
Tirhakah (2)

9556 תְּרוּמָה *t^{e}rûmāh* (76)
offering (19)
portion (12)
contributions (8)
offerings (7)
presented (4)
contribution (3)
special gifts (3) +3338
part (2)
set aside (2)
special gift (2)
bribes (1)
district (1)
gift (1)
portion as a special gift (1)
present (1) +8123
present an offering (1)
special gifts (1)
special portion (1)
was presented (1) +8123
untranslated (5)

9557 תְּרוּמִיָּה *t^{e}rûmiyyāh* (1)
special gift (1)

9558 תְּרוּעָה *t^{e}rû'āh* (36)
battle cry (5)
shouts (3)
shouts of joy (3)
blast (2)
cry (2)
gave a shout (2) +8131
war cries (2)
acclaim (1)
give a shout (1) +8131
made noise (1) +8131
raised a shout (1) +8131
resounding (1)
shout (1)
shout for joy (1)
shouted (1) +928+7754+8123
shouting (1)
shouting (1) +7754
shouts for joy (1)
signaling (1)
sound the trumpets (1)
trumpet (1) +8795
trumpet blast (1)
trumpet blasts (1)
uproar (1) +7754

9559 תְּרוּפָה *t^{e}rûp̱āh* (1)
healing (1)

9560 תִּרְזָה *tirzāh* (1)
cypress (1)

9561 תֶּרַח *terah* (11)
Terah (10)
he^s (1)

9562 תָּרַח *tārah* (2)
Terah (2)

9563 תִּרְחֲנָה *tirh^{a}nāh* (1)
Tirhanah (1)

9564 תָּרְמָה *tormāh* (1)
under cover (1) +928

9565 תַּרְמוּק *tarmûq* (1)
Variant; not used

9566 תַּרְמוּת *tarmûṯ* (1)
untranslated (1)

9567 תַּרְמִית *tarmiyṯ* (5)
delusions (2)
deceit (1)
deceit (1) +4383
deceitfulness (1)

9568 תֹּרֶן *tōren* (3)
flagstaff (1)
mast (1)
mast (1) +4029

9569 תַּרְעִית *tar'iyṯ*
Variant; not used

9570 תַּרְעֵלָה *tar'ēlāh* (3)
makes stagger (2)
made stagger (1)

9571 תִּרְעָתִים *tir'āṯiym* (1)
Tirathites (1)

9572 תְּרָפִים *t^{e}rāp̱iym* (15)
household gods (8)
idol (3)
idols (3)
idolatry (1)

9573 1תִּרְצָה *tirṣāh1* (5)
Tirzah (5)

9574 2תִּרְצָה *tirṣāh2* (13)
Tirzah (13)

9575 תֶּרֶשׁ *tereš* (2)
Teresh (2)

9576 1תַּרְשִׁישׁ *taršiyš1* (25)
Tarshish (16)
fleet of trading ships (1) +639
fleet of trading ships (1) +641
fleet of trading ships (1) +641+2143
fleet of trading ships (1) +641+2143+4200
it^s (1) +639
it^s (1) +641
that port^s (1)
trade (1)
trading ship (1) +641

9577 2תַּרְשִׁישׁ *taršiyš2* (7)
chrysolite (6)
chrysolite (1) +74

9578 3תַּרְשִׁישׁ *taršiyš3* (3)
Tarshish (3)

9579 תִּרְשָׁתָא *tiršāṯā'* (5)
governor (5)

9580 תַּרְתָּן *tartān* (2)
supreme commander (2)

9581 תַּרְתָּק *tartāq* (1)
Tartak (1)

9582 תְּשׂוּמָה *t^{e}śûmāh* (1)
left (1)

9583 תְּשֻׁאָה *t^{e}šu'āh* (5)
commotion (1)
shout (1)
shouts (1)
storm (1)
thunders (1)

9584 תִּשְׁבֶּה *ṯišbeh*
Variant; not used

9585 תִּשְׁבִּי *tišbiy* (6)
Tishbite (6)

9586 תִּשְׁבֵּי *tišbēy* (1)
Tishbe (1)

9587 תַּשְׁבֵּץ *tašbēṣ* (1)
woven (1)

9588 תְּשׁוּבָה *t^{e}šûḇāh* (8)
spring (3) +9102
answering (1)

answers (1)
spring (1) +2021+9102
spring (1) +6961+9102
went back (1)

9589 תְּשֻׁוָּה *tᵉšuwwāh* (1)
untranslated (1)

9590 תַּשְׁוִית *taświyṯ*
Variant; not used

9591 תְּשׁוּעָה *tᵉšûʿāh* (34)
salvation (12)
victory (12)
help (2)
brought about victory (1) +3828
deliverance (1)
delivered (1)
rescue (1)
rescued (1) +6913
save (1)
saves (1)
savior (1)

9592 תְּשׁוּקָה *tᵉšûqāh* (3)
desire (2)
desires (1)

9593 תְּשׁוּרָה *tᵉšûrāh* (1)
gift (1)

9594 תֻּשִׁיָּה *tušiyyāh*
Variant; not used

9595 תְּשִׁיעִי *tᵉšiyʿiy* (18)
ninth (18)

9596 תֵּשַׁע *tēšaʿ* (77)
nine (12)
ninth (5)
twenty-nine (5) +2256+6929
29 (3) +2256+6929
thirty-ninth (3) +2256+8993
390 (2) +2256+4395+8993
392 (2) +2256+4395+8993+9109
59,300 (2) +547+2256+2256+2822+4395+8993
95 (2) +2256+2822
973 (2) +2256+4395+8679+8993
98 (2) +2256+9046
nineteenth (2) +6925
nineteenth (2) +6926
ninety (2)
ninety-nine (2) +2256+9596
ninety-six (2) +2256+9252
1,290 (1) +547+2256+4395
119 (1) +2256+4395+6926
139 (1) +2256+4395+8993
209 (1) +2256+4395
3,930 (1) +547+2256+4395+8993+8993
595 (1) +2256+2256+2822+2822+4395
690 (1) +2256+4395+9252
895 (1) +2256+2256+2822+4395+9046
90 (1)
905 (1) +2256+2822+4395
910 (1) +2256+4395+6924
912 (1) +2256+4395+6926+9109
928 (1) +2256+4395+6929+9046
930 (1) +2256+4395+8993
945 (1) +752+2256+2256+2822+4395
950 (1) +2256+2822+4395
956 (1) +2256+2256+2822+4395+9252
962 (1) +2256+2256+4395+9109+9252
969 (1) +2256+2256+4395+9252+9596
forty-nine (1) +752+2256
more than thirteen feet (1) +564
nine-and-a-half (1) +2256+2942
nineteen (1) +6925
nineteen (1) +6926
ninety-eight (1) +2256+9046

9597 תִּשְׁעִים *tišʿiym*
Variant; not used

ARAMAIC TO ENGLISH INDEX-LEXICON OF THE OLD TESTAMENT

10001 א '
Variant; not used

10002 ־ָא *-ā'* (831)
the (412)
O (26)
a (15)
this (7)
his^{S} (4)
these (4)
he^{S} (3) +10421
him^{S} (3) +10421
that (3)
an (2)
continually (2) +10089+10753
ever (2) +10550
he^{S} (2) +10421+10453
his^{S} (2) +10421
immediately (2) +10734
my^{S} (2)
as soon as (1) +10089+10168+10530
as soon as (1) +10168+10232+10341
certainly (1) +10327
cordial greetings (1) +10002+10353+10720
ever (1) +10527+10550
forever (1) +10378+10550
forever (1) +10509+10527
forever (1) +10527+10550
forever (1) +10550
it^{S} (1)
it^{S} (1) +10418
it^{S} (1) +10424
it^{S} (1) +10614
its^{S} (1)
never end (1) +10509+10527
order (1) +10302+10682
she^{S} (1) +10423
sundown (1) +10436+10728
them^{S} (1) +10038
they^{S} (1) +10353+10553
this^{S} (1) +10418
Trans-Euphrates (1) +10468+10526
what^{S} (1) +10418
when (1) +10089+10530
who^{S} (1) +10131
untranslated (314)

10003 אַב *'aḇ* (9)
father (6)
fathers (2)
predecessors (1)

10004 אֵב *'ēḇ* (3)
fruit (3)

10005 אֲבַד *'^{a}ḇaḏ* (7)
execute (2)
completely destroyed (1) +10221+10722
destroyed (1)
executed (1)
execution (1)
perish (1)

10006 אֶבֶן *'eḇen* (8)
rock (3)
stone (3)
large stones (2) +10146

10007 אִגְּרָה *'igg^{e}rāh* (3)
letter (3)

10008 אֱדַיִן *'^{e}ḏayin* (57)
then (13) +10089
then (11)
so (8) +10089
so (3)
when (2) +10089
also (1) +10358
and (1) +10221
as soon as (1) +10168+10427
at this (1)
finally (1)
now (1)
that day^{S} (1)
therefore (1) +10089
thus (1) +10089
untranslated (11)

10009 אֲדָר *'^{a}ḏār* (1)
Adar (1)

10010 אִדַּר *'iddar* (1)
threshing floor (1)

10011 אֲדַרְגָּזַר *'^{a}ḏargāzar* (2)
advisers (2)

10012 אַדְרַזְדָּא *'aḏrazdā'* (1)
with diligence (1)

10013 אֶדְרָע *'eḏrā'* (1)
force (1)

10014 אַזְדָּא *'azdā'* (2)
firmly (2)

10015 אֲזָה *'^{a}zāh* (3)
heated (1)
hot (1)
hotter (1)

10016 אֲזַל *'^{a}zal* (7)
returned (2)
went (2)
go (1)
untranslated (2)

10017 אַח *'ah* (2)
brother Jews (1)
untranslated (1)

10018 אַחֲוָיָה *'ah^{a}wāyāh*
Variant; not used

10019 אֲחִידָה *'^{a}hiyḏāh* (1)
riddles (1)

10020 אַחְמְתָא *'ahm^{e}ṯā'* (1)
Ecbatana (1)

10021 אַחַר *'ahar* (3)
after (1)
in the future (1) +10180
to come (1) +10180+10201

10022 אַחֲרִי *'ah^{a}riy* (1)
to come (1)

10023 אָחֳרִי *'oh^{o}riy* (6)
another (3)
a^{S} (1)
one (1)
other (1)

10024 אָחֳרֵין *'oh^{o}rēyn* (1)
finally (1) +10221+10527

10025 אָחֳרָן *'oh^{o}rān* (5)
another (2)
one (1)
other (1)
someone else (1)

10026 אֲחַשְׁדַּרְפַּן *'^{a}hašdarpan* (9)
satraps (9)

10027 אִילָן *'iylān* (6)
tree (6)

10028 אֵימְתָן *'ēym^{e}ṯān* (1)
frightening (1)

10029 אִיתַי *'iyṯay* (19)
there is (3)
are (2)
do (1)
have (1) +10089
in fact (1)
there are (1)
unharmed (1) +10244+10379
will be left with (1) +10378
untranslated (8)

10030 אֲכַל *'^{a}ḵal* (7)
devoured (2)
ate (1)
denounced (1) +10642
devour (1)
eat (1)
falsely accused (1) +10642

10031 אַל *'al* (4)
don't (2)

not (2)

10032 אֵל *'ēl* (1)
these (1)

10033 אֱלָהּ *'ᵉlāh* (96)
God (73)
gods (15)
god (6)
untranslated (2)

10034 אֵלֶּה *'ēlleh* (2)
untranslated (2)

10035 אֲלוּ *'ᵃlû* (5)
there (4)
untranslated (1)

10036 אִלֵּין *'illēyn* (5)
the others[S] (1)
those (1)
untranslated (3)

10037 אִלֵּךְ *'illēḵ* (14)
these (8)
untranslated (6)

10038 אֲלַף *'ᵃlap̱* (5)
thousands (2)
them[S] (1) +10002
thousand (1)
untranslated (1)

10039 אַמָּה *'ammāh* (4)
ninety feet (3) +10749
nine feet (1) +10747

10040 אֻמָּה *'ummāh* (8)
nations (6)
nation (1)
people (1)

10041 אֲמַן *'ᵃman* (3)
trustworthy (2)
trusted (1)

10042 אֲמַר *'ᵃmar* (71)
said (6)
tell (6)
told (5)
asked (3)
command (3)
commanded (2)
gave orders (2)
interpret (2) +10600
ordered (2)
say (2)
decreed (1)
gave explanation (1)
gave the order (1)
saying (1)
spoke (1)
summoned (1) +10085+10378
untranslated (32)

10043 אִמַּר *'immar* (3)
male lambs (3)

10044 אֲנָה *'ᵃnāh* (16)
I (15)
me (1)

10045 אִנּוּן *'innûn* (4)
those (1)
untranslated (3)

10046 אֱנוֹשׁ *'ᵉnôš* (2)
untranslated (2)

10047 אֲנַחְנָא *'ᵃnaḥnā'* (4)
we (4)

10048 אֲנַס *'ᵃnas* (1)
difficult (1)

10049 אֲנַף *'ᵃnap̱* (2)
attitude (1) +10614
prostrate (1) +10542

10050 אֱנָשׁ *'ᵉnāš* (25)
man (8)
men (6)
people (3)
anyone (2) +10353
everyone (1) +10353
human (1)
mankind (1) +10120
people (1) +10120
people (1) +10240
whoever (1) +10168+10353

10051 אַנְתְּ *'ant* (14)
untranslated (14)

10052 אַנְתָּה *'antāh* (15)
you (13)
untranslated (2)

10053 אַנְתּוּן *'antûn* (1)
you (1)

10054 אֱסוּר *'ᵉsûr* (3)
bound (2)
imprisonment (1)

10055 אָסְנַפַּר *'āsᵉnapar* (1)
Ashurbanipal (1)

10056 אָסְפַּרְנָא *'āsᵉparnā'* (7)
with diligence (3)
be sure (1)
diligence (1)
fully (1)
surely (1)

10057 אֱסָר *'ᵉsār* (7)
decree (7)

10058 אָע *'āʿ* (5)
timbers (2)
wood (2)
beam (1)

10059 אַף *'ap̱* (4)
also (2) +10221
even (1) +10221
nor (1) +10221+10379

10060 אֲפָרְסָי *'ᵃp̱ārᵉsāy* (1)
Persia (1)

10061 אֲפַרְסְכָי *'ᵃp̱arsᵉḵāy* (2)
officials (2)

10062 אֲפַרְסַתְכָי *'ᵃp̱arsaṯᵉḵāy* (1)
officials (1)

10063 אַפְּתֹם *'appᵉṯōm* (1)
revenues (1)

10064 אֶצְבַּע *'esbaʿ* (3)
fingers (1)
toes (1)
toes (1) +10655

10065 אַרְבַּע *'arbaʿ* (8)
four (8)

10066 אַרְגְּוָן *'argᵉwān* (3)
purple (3)

10067 אֲרוּ *'ᵃrû* (5)
there (5)

10068 אֳרַח *'ᵒrah* (2)
ways (2)

10069 אַרְיֵה *'aryēh* (10)
lions' (5)
lions (4)
lion (1)

10070 אַרְיוֹךְ *'aryôḵ* (5)
Arioch (4)
untranslated (1)

10071 אֲרִיךְ *'ᵃriyḵ* (1)
proper (1)

10072 אַרְכֻבָּה *'arḵubbāh* (1)
knees (1)

10073 אַרְכָה *'arḵāh* (2)
continue (1)
live (1) +10089+10261

10074 אַרְכְּוָי *'arkᵉwāy* (2)
Erech (1)
untranslated (1)

10075 אֲרַע *'ᵃraʿ* (21)
earth (14)
ground (3)
land (2)
inferior (1)
world (1)

10076 אַרְעִי *'arʿiy* (1)
floor (1)

10077 אֲרַק *'ᵃraq* (1)
earth (1)

10078 אַרְתַּחְשַׁשְׂתְּא *'artaḥšaśt'* (7)
Artaxerxes (6)
untranslated (1)

10079 אֹשׁ *'ōš* (3)
foundations (3)

10080 אֶשָּׁא *'eššā'* (1)
fire (1)

10081 אָשַׁף *'āšap̱* (6)
enchanters (4)
enchanter (2)

10082 אֻשַּׁרְנָא *'uššarnā'* (2)
structure (2)

10083 אֶשְׁתַּדּוּר *'eštadûr* (2)
rebellion (1)
sedition (1)

10084 אָת *'āṯ* (3)
signs (2)
miraculous signs (1)

10085 אֲתָה *'ᵃṯāh* (16)
brought (3)
brought in (2)
came (2)
come (2)
bring in (1)
coming (1)
gone (1)
summoned (1) +10042+10378
was brought (1)
went (1)
were brought (1)

10086 אַתּוּן *'atûn* (10)
furnace (10)

10087 אֲתַר *'ᵃṯar* (5)
site (2)
place (1)
places (1)
trace (1)

10088 ב *ḇ*
Variant; not used

10089 בְּ־ *bᵉ-* (227)
in (79)
then (13) +10008
with (11)
on (9)
at (8)
so (8) +10008
over (7)
by (6)
of (6)
from (4)
have (3)
continually (2) +10002+10753
throughout (2) +10353
to (2)
under (2)
underfoot (2) +10655
when (2) +10008
about (1)
among (1)

as soon as (1) +10002+10168+10530
be handed over (1) +10311+10314
because (1)
daily (1) +10317+10317
Daniel's (1) +10181
during (1)
had (1)
handed over (1) +10311+10314
have (1) +10029
his (1) +10192
immediately (1) +10096
in (1) +10135
in (1) +10135+10464
live (1) +10073+10261
loudly (1) +10264
on (1) +10135
place[S] (1) +10135+10193
place[S] (1) +10193
possess (1) +10311
something to do with (1)
therefore (1) +10008
thus (1) +10008
wearing (1)
when (1) +10002+10530
wherever (1) +10168+10353
while (1)
with regard to (1)
untranslated (32)

10090 בְּאִישׁ *bi'yš* (1)
wicked (1)

10091 בְּאֵשׁ *b^e'ēš* (1)
distressed (1)

10092 בָּאתַר *bā'ṯar* (3)
after (3)

10093 בָּבֶל *bāḇel* (25)
Babylon (24)
its[S] (1)

10094 בָּבְלִי *bāḇ^{e}liy* (1)
Babylon (1)

10095 בְּדַר *b^{e}ḏar* (1)
scatter (1)

10096 בְּהִילוּ *b^{e}hiylû* (1)
immediately (1) +10089

10097 בְּהַל *b^{e}hal* (11)
terrified (3)
alarm (1)
alarmed (1)
amazement (1) +10755
at once (1)
disturbed (1)
frightened (1)
hurried (1)
troubled (1)

10098 בְּטֵל *b^{e}ṭal* (6)
stop (2)
came to a standstill (1)
stop work (1)
stopped (1)
untranslated (1)

10099 בֵּין *bēyn* (3)
among (1)
between (1)
untranslated (1)

10100 בִּינָה *biynāh* (1)
discerning (1) +10313

10101 בִּירָה *biyrāh* (1)
citadel (1)

10102 בִּית *biyṯ* (1)
spent the night (1)

10103 בַּיִת *bayiṯ* (44)
house (17)
temple (16)
home (2)
houses (2)
archives (1) +10148
archives (1) +10515
hall (1)
residence (1)
treasury (1)
treasury (1) +10148
untranslated (1)

10104 בָּל *bāl* (1)
determined (1) +10682

10105 בֵּלְאשַׁצַּר *bēl'šassar* (2)
Belshazzar (2)

10106 בְּלָה *b^{e}lāh* (1)
oppress (1)

10107 בְּלוֹ *b^{e}lô* (3)
tribute (3)

10108 בֵּלְטְשַׁאצַּר *bēlṭ^{e}ša'ṣṣar* (8)
Belteshazzar (8)

10109 בֵּלְשַׁאצַּר *bēlša'ṣṣar* (5)
Belshazzar (4)
Belshazzar's (1)

10110 בֵּן *bēn*
Variant; not used

10111 בְּנָה *b^{e}nāh* (22)
rebuild (7)
built (3)
be rebuilt (2)
building (2)
is built (2)
rebuilding (2)
build (1)
constructing (1)
construction (1)
under construction (1)

10112 בִּנְיָן *binyān* (1)
building (1)

10113 בְּנַס *b^{e}nas* (1)
angry (1)

10114 בְּעָה *b^e'āh* (12)
asked (2)
prays (2) +10115
asked for (1)
look for (1)
plead (1)
praying (1)
prays (1)
request (1)
sought out (1)
tried (1)

10115 בָּעוּ *bā'û* (2)
prays (2) +10114

10116 בְּעֵל *b^e'ēl* (3)
commanding officer (3) +10302

10117 בִּקְעָה *biq'āh* (1)
plain (1)

10118 בְּקַר *b^{e}qar* (5)
a search made (2)
a search be made (1)
inquire (1)
searched (1)

10119 1בַּר *bar1* (8)
field (5)
wild (3)

10120 2בַּר *bar2* (19)
son (5)
exiles (4) +10145
descendant (2)
sons (2)
age (1) +10732
children (1)
mankind (1) +10050
people (1)
people (1) +10050
young (1)

10121 1בְּרַךְ *b^{e}raḵ1* (1)
got down (1)

10122 2בְּרַךְ *b^{e}raḵ2* (4)
praise (2)
praised (2)

10123 בְּרֵךְ *b^{e}rēḵ* (1)
knees (1)

10124 בְּרַם *b^{e}ram* (5)
but (3)
however (1)
nevertheless (1)

10125 בְּשַׂר *b^{e}śar* (3)
creature (1)
flesh (1)
men (1)

10126 בַּת *baṯ* (2)
baths (2)

10127 ג *g*
Variant; not used

10128 גַּב *gaḇ* (2)
back (1)
untranslated (1)

10129 גֹּב *gōḇ* (10)
den (10)

10130 גְּבוּרָה *g^{e}ḇûrāh* (2)
power (2)

10131 גְּבַר *g^{e}ḇar* (21)
men (12)
some[S] (3)
man (2)
soldiers (1)
who[S] (1) +10002
untranslated (2)

10132 גִּבַּר *gibbar* (1)
strongest soldiers (1) +10264

10133 גְּדָבַר *g^{e}ḏāḇar* (2)
treasurers (2)

10134 גְּדַד *g^{e}ḏaḏ* (2)
cut down (2)

10135 גַּו *gaw* (13)
into (6) +10378
in (1) +10089
in (1) +10089+10464
middle (1)
of (1) +10427
on (1) +10089
place[S] (1) +10089+10193
untranslated (1)

10136 9גֵּוָה *gēwāh* (1)
pride (1)

10137 גּוּחַ *gûaḥ* (1)
churning up (1)

10138 גּוֹן *gôn*
Variant; not used

10139 גִּזְבַּר *gizbar* (1)
treasurers (1)

10140 גְּזַר *g^{e}zar* (6)
diviners (3)
cut out (1)
diviner (1)
was cut out (1)

10141 גְּזֵרָה *g^{e}zērāh* (3)
announced (1)
decree (1)
solitary (1)

10142 גִּיר *giyr* (1)
plaster (1)

10143 גַּלְגַּל *galgal* (1)
wheels (1)

10144 גְּלָה *g^{e}lāh* (9)
deported (2)

revealer (2)
reveals (2)
been revealed (1)
reveal (1)
was revealed (1)

10145 גָּלוּ *gālû* (4)
exiles (4) +10120

10146 גְּלָל *g^e^lāl* (2)
large stones (2) +10006

10147 גְּמַר *g^e^mar* (1)
greetings (1)

10148 גְּנַז *g^e^naz* (3)
archives (1) +10103
treasury (1)
treasury (1) +10103

10149 גַּף *gap̱* (3)
wings (3)

10150 גְּרַם *g^e^ram* (1)
bones (1)

10151 גְּשֵׁם *g^e^šēm* (6)
body (3)
bodies (1)
lives (1)
untranslated (1)

10152 ד *d*
Variant; not used

10153 דְּ־ *d^e^-*
Variant; not used

10154 דָּא *dā'* (6)
this (2)
each (1)
others[S] (1)
together (1) +10154+10378

10155 דֹּב *dōḇ* (1)
bear (1)

10156 דְּבַח *d^e^ḇah1* (1)
present (1)

10157 דְּבַח *d^e^ḇah2* (1)
sacrifices (1)

10158 דְּבַק *d^e^ḇaq* (1)
united (1) +10180+10180+10554

10159 דִּבְרָה *diḇrāh* (2)
so that (1) +10168+10527
so that (1) +10168+10542

10160 דְּהַב *d^e^haḇ* (23)
gold (23)

10161 דְּהוּא *d^e^hû'*
Variant; not used

10162 דֶּהָיֵא *dehāyē'*
Variant; not used

10163 דּוּר *dûr* (13)
live (2)
peoples (2)
lived (1)
shelter (1)
untranslated (7)

10164 דּוּרָא *dûrā'* (1)
Dura (1)

10165 דּוּשׁ *dûš* (1)
trampling down (1)

10166 דַּחֲוָה *dah^a^wāh* (1)
entertainment (1)

10167 דְּחַל *d^e^hal* (6)
terrifying (2)
awesome (1)
feared (1)
made afraid (1)
reverence (1)

10168 דִּי *diy* (348)
of (46)
that (46)
who (18)
which (9)
until (8) +10527
whom (8)
so that (6)
those (5)
anyone (4) +10426
from (4)
because (3)
because (3) +10353+10619
for (3) +10353+10619
in (3)
when (3) +10341
with (3)
but (2)
for (2)
just as (2)
what (2)
whatever (2) +10353
whoever (2) +10426
any more than (1) +10195+10341
as (1)
as (1) +10527
as soon as (1) +10002+10089+10530
as soon as (1) +10002+10232+10341
as soon as (1) +10008+10427
because (1) +10427
because of (1) +10378+10619
by (1) +10353+10619
during (1)
even as (1) +10353+10619
hoping (1) +10527
if (1)
just as (1) +10353+10619
one (1)
over (1)
since (1) +10353+10619
so that (1) +10159+10527
so that (1) +10159+10542
surely (1) +10427+10643
this is the meaning (1) +10353+10619
though (1) +10353+10619
whatever (1) +10408
when (1) +10427
wherever (1) +10089+10353
while (1) +10527
whoever (1) +10050+10353
whoever (1) +10353
whose (1)
untranslated (135)

10169 1דִּין *diyn1* (2)
administer justice (1)
untranslated (1)

10170 2דִּין *diyn2* (5)
court (2)
judgment (1)
just (1)
punished (1) +10191+10522

10171 2דַּיָּן *dayyān* (2)
judges (2)

10172 דִּינָיֵא *diynāyē'*
Variant; not used

10173 דֵּךְ *dēḵ* (13)
this (12)
untranslated (1)

10174 דִּכֵּן *dikkēn* (3)
that (1)
this (1)
untranslated (1)

10175 דְּכַר *d^e^ḵar* (3)
rams (3)

10176 דִּכְרוֹן *diḵrôn* (1)
memorandum (1)

10177 דָּכְרָן *doḵrān* (2)
archives (1) +10515
records (1) +10515

10178 דְּלַק *d^e^laq* (1)
all ablaze (1) +10471

10179 דְּמָה *d^e^māh* (2)
like (1)
looked like (1)

10180 דְּנָה *d^e^nāh* (58)
this (30)
that (2)
ago (1) +10427+10622
as follows (1) +10341
before (1) +10427+10622
in the future (1) +10021
so (1) +10353+10619
such (1) +10341
that is why (1) +10542
the (1)
then (1) +10353+10619
therefore (1) +10353+10619
these (1)
this (1) +10341
this made (1) +10353+10619
to come (1) +10021+10201
united (1) +10158+10180+10554
untranslated (10)

10181 דָּנִיֵּאל *dāniyyē'l* (52)
Daniel (46)
Daniel's (1)
Daniel's (1) +10089
he[S] (1)
him[S] (1)
untranslated (2)

10182 דְּקַק *d^e^qaq* (10)
crushed (3)
crush (2)
breaks (1)
broke to pieces (1)
broken to pieces (1)
crushing (1)
smashed (1)

10183 דָּר *dār* (4)
generation (4)

10184 דָּרְיָוֶשׁ *dār^e^yāweš* (15)
Darius (15)

10185 דְּרָע *d^e^rā'* (1)
arms (1)

10186 דָּת *dāṯ* (14)
law (7)
laws (4)
decree (2)
penalty (1)

10187 דֶּתֶא *deṯe'* (2)
grass (2)

10188 דְּתָבַר *d^e^ṯāḇar* (2)
judges (2)

10189 ה *h*
Variant; not used

10190 הֲ־ *h^a^-* (7)
is it true (1) +10609
untranslated (6)

10191 ־ָה *-āh* (63)
the (15)
Trans-Euphrates (12) +10468+10526
its[S] (2)
immediately (1) +10734
it[S] (1) +10424
punished (1) +10170+10522
suddenly (1) +10734
that (1)
that province[S] (1) +10468+10526
this (1)
your[S] (1)
untranslated (26)

10192 ־ֵהּ *-ēh* (159)
his (47)

him (24)
it (16)
its (10)
he (7)
the[S] (5)
their (3)
a[S] (1)
his (1) +10089
his (1) +10378
his own (1)
man[S] (1)
same[S] (1)
untranslated (41)

10193 הָ־ *-ah* (52)
it (15)
its (7)
them (5)
place[S] (1) +10089
place[S] (1) +10089+10135
the[S] (1)
which (1)
untranslated (21)

10194 הָא *hā'* (1)
look (1)

10195 הֵא *hē'* (1)
any more than (1) +10168+10341

10196 הַדָּבַר *haddāḇar* (4)
advisers (4)

10197 הַדָּם *haddām* (2)
pieces (2)

10198 הֲדַר1 *h^adar1* (3)
glorified (1)
glorify (1)
honor (1)

10199 הֲדַר2 *h^adar2* (3)
honor (1)
majesty (1)
splendor (1)

10200 הוּא *hû'* (16)
he (5)
it (1)
that (1)
that tree[S] (1)
untranslated (8)

10201 הֲוָה *h^wāh* (71)
be (11)
was (7)
became (2)
happen (2)
were (2)
appear (1)
continued (1)
had (1) +10542
have (1)
keep (1)
kept (1)
must (1)
remain (1)
stay (1)
take place (1)
to come (1) +10021+10180
untranslated (36)

10202 הוּךְ *hûḵ*
Variant; not used

10203 הוֹן־ *-hôn* (61)
their (17)
them (17)
the[S] (3)
their own (1)
they (1)
untranslated (22)

10204 הִי־ *-hiy* (76)
his (26)
its (14)
him (11)
he (5)
it (4)
one (1)
the[S] (1)
untranslated (14)

10205 הִיא *hiy'* (8)
it (1)
itself (1)
there (1)
this (1)
untranslated (4)

10206 הֵיכַל *hēyḵal* (13)
temple (8)
palace (5)

10207 הֲלַךְ *h^alaḵ* (7)
go (3)
walk (1)
walking (1)
walking around (1)
untranslated (1)

10208 הֲלָךְ *h^lāḵ* (3)
duty (3)

10209 הֹם־ *-hōm* (12)
their (5)
them (4)
untranslated (3)

10210 הִמּוֹ *himmô* (12)
them (6)
they (1)
untranslated (5)

10211 המונך *hmwnḵ* (3)
untranslated (3)

10212 הַמְיָנֵךְ *hamyānaḵ* (3)
chain (3)

10213 הֵן *hēn* (16)
if (11)
even if (1)
then (1)
untranslated (3)

10214 הֵן־ *-hēn* (8)
the others[S] (1)
them (1)
untranslated (6)

10215 הַנְזָקָה *hanzāqāh*
Variant; not used

10216 הַצְדָּא *hasdā'*
Variant; not used

10217 הַרְהֹר *harhōr* (1)
images (1)

10218 הִתְבְּהָלָה *hiṯb^ehālāh*
Variant; not used

10219 הִתְנַדָּבוּ *hiṯnaddāḇû*
Variant; not used

10220 וּ *w*
Variant; not used

10221 וְ־ *w^e-* (751)
and (400)
or (20)
but (19)
then (9)
now (5)
so (5)
so that (5)
moreover (3)
nor (3) +10379
that (3)
together with (3)
with (3)
also (2)
also (2) +10059
120 (1) +10395+10574
and (1) +10008
and now (1)
and that (1)
and when (1)
as (1)
as for (1)
at this (1)
completely destroyed (1) +10005+10722
even (1) +10059
finally (1)
finally (1) +10024+10527
furthermore (1)
including (1)
instead (1)
next (1)
nor (1)
nor (1) +10059+10379
period of time (1) +10232+10530
set to work (1) +10624+10742
sixty-two (1) +10749+10775
therefore (1)
till (1)
until (1)
when (1)
while (1)
yes (1)
yet (1)
untranslated (241)

10222 ז *z*
Variant; not used

10223 זְבַן *z^eḇan* (1)
gain (1)

10224 זְהִיר *z^ehiyr* (1)
careful (1)

10225 זוּד *zûḏ* (1)
pride (1)

10226 זוּן *zûn* (1)
was fed (1)

10227 זוּעַ *zû'a* (4)
dreaded (1)
fear (1)
untranslated (2)

10228 זִיו *ziyw* (6)
face pale (3)
dazzling (1)
look so pale (1) +10731
splendor (1)

10229 זָכוּ *zāḵû* (1)
innocent (1)

10230 זְכַרְיָה *z^eḵaryāh* (2)
Zechariah (2)

10231 זְמַן1 *z^eman1* (2)
conspired (1)
untranslated (1)

10232 זְמַן2 *z^eman2* (11)
time (5)
times (2)
as soon as (1) +10002+10168+10341
period of time (1) +10221+10530
seasons (1)
set times (1)

10233 זְמָר *z^emār* (4)
music (4)

10234 זַמָּר *zammār* (1)
singers (1)

10235 זַן *zan* (4)
kinds (4)

10236 זְעֵיר *z^e'ēyr* (6)
little (5)
little longer (1)

10237 זְעִק *z^e'iq* (1)
called (1)

10238 זְקַף *z^eqaḇ* (1)
be lifted up (1)

10239 זְרֻבָּבֶל *zᵉrubbāḇel* (1)
Zerubbabel (1)

10240 זְרַע *zᵉraʿ* (1)
people (1) +10050

10241 ח *h*
Variant; not used

10242 חֲבוּלָה *ḥᵃḇûlāh* (1)
wrong (1)

10243 חֲבַל *ḥᵃḇal* (6)
be destroyed (3)
destroy (2)
hurt (1)

10244 חֲבָל *ḥᵃḇāl* (3)
threat (1)
unharmed (1) +10029+10379
wound (1)

10245 חֲבַר *ḥᵃḇar* (3)
friends (3)

10246 חַבְרָה *haḇrāh* (1)
others (1)

10247 חַגַּי *haggay* (2)
Haggai (2)

10248 חַד *haḏ* (15)
a (5)
one (5)
first (3)
same (1)
times (1)

10249 חֲדֵה *ḥᵃḏēh* (1)
chest (1)

10250 חֶדְוָה *hedwāh* (1)
joy (1)

10251 חֲדַת *ḥᵃḏaṯ*
Variant; not used

10252 חֲוָה *ḥᵃwāh* (15)
interpret (5) +10600
tell (4)
explain (2)
doˢ (1)
explain (1) +10600
reveal (1)
tells (1)

10253 חוּט *hûṭ* (1)
repairing (1)

10254 חִוָּר *hiwwār* (1)
white (1)

10255 חֲזָה *ḥᵃzāh* (31)
looked (8)
saw (7)
hadˢ (3)
see (3)
watched (3)
looking (1)
realize (1)
usual (1)
vision (1)
watch (1)
watching (1)
untranslated (1)

10256 חֱזוּ *ḥᵉzû* (12)
visions (6)
vision (4)
dream (1) +10267
looked (1)

10257 חֲזוֹת *ḥᵃzôṯ* (2)
visible (2)

10258 חַטָּאָה *hattāʾāh* (3)
sin (1)
wickedness (1)
untranslated (1)

10259 חֲטָי *ḥᵃṭāy* (2)
sins (1)
untranslated (1)

10260 חַטָּיָא *hattāyāʾ* (1)
sin offering (1)

10261 חַי *hay* (7)
living (4)
live (1) +10073+10089
lives (1)
well-being (1)

10262 חֲיָה *ḥᵃyāh* (6)
live (5)
spared (1)

10263 חֵיוָה *hēywāh* (20)
beasts (7)
beast (6)
animals (5)
animal (2)

10264 חַיִל *hayil* (7)
army (1)
compelled (1)
loud (1)
loudly (1) +10089
powers (1)
strongest soldiers (1) +10132
untranslated (1)

10265 חַכִּים *hakkiym* (14)
wise (14)

10266 חָכְמָה *hoḵmāh* (8)
wisdom (7)
thatˢ (1)

10267 חֵלֶם *hēlem* (22)
dream (20)
dream (1) +10256
dreams (1)

10268 חֲלַף *ḥᵃlap̄* (4)
pass by (4)

10269 חֲלָק *ḥᵃlāq* (3)
live (2)
nothing (1) +10379

10270 חֲמָה *ḥᵃmāh* (2)
furious (1)
furious (1) +10416

10271 חֲמַר *ḥᵃmar* (6)
wine (6)

10272 חִנְטָה *hinṭāh* (2)
wheat (2)

10273 חֲנֻכָּה *ḥᵃnukkāh* (4)
dedication (4)

10274 חֲנַן *ḥᵃnan* (2)
asking for help (1)
kind (1)

10275 חֲנַנְיָה *ḥᵃnanyāh* (1)
Hananiah (1)

10276 חַסִּיר *hassiyr* (1)
wanting (1)

10277 חֲסַן *ḥᵃsan* (2)
possess (1)
possessed (1)

10278 חֱסֵן *ḥᵉsēn* (2)
mighty (1)
power (1)

10279 חֲסַף *ḥᵃsap̄* (9)
clay (5)
baked clay (2)
baked clay (1) +10298
clay (1) +10298

10280 חֲצַף *ḥᵃṣap̄* (2)
harsh (1)
urgent (1)

10281 חֲרַב *ḥᵃraḇ* (1)
was destroyed (1)

10282 חַרְטֹם *harṭōm* (5)
magicians (3)
magician (2)

10283 חֲרַךְ *ḥᵃraḵ* (1)
was singed (1)

10284 חֲרַץ *ḥᵃraṣ* (1)
legs (1) +10626

10285 חֲשַׁב *ḥᵃšaḇ* (1)
are regarded (1)

10286 חֲשׁוֹךְ *ḥᵃšôḵ* (1)
darkness (1)

10287 חֲשַׁח *ḥᵃšah* (1)
need (1)

10288 חַשְׁחָה *hašhāh* (1)
needed (1)

10289 חַשְׁחוּ *hašhû* (1)
needed (1)

10290 חֲשַׁל *ḥᵃšal* (1)
smashes (1)

10291 חֲתַם *ḥᵃṯam* (1)
sealed (1)

10292 ט *ṭ*
Variant; not used

10293 טְאֵב *ṭᵉʾēḇ* (1)
overjoyed (1) +10678

10294 טָב *ṭāḇ* (2)
pleases (1)
pure (1)

10295 טַבָּח *ṭabbāh* (1)
guard (1)

10296 טוּר *ṭûr* (2)
mountain (2)

10297 טְוָת *ṭᵉwāṯ* (1)
without eating (1)

10298 טִין *ṭiyn* (2)
baked clay (1) +10279
clay (1) +10279

10299 טַל *ṭal* (5)
dew (5)

10300 טְלַל *ṭᵉlal* (1)
found shelter (1)

10301 1טְעֵם *ṭᵉʿēm1* (3)
eat (2)
ate (1)

10302 2טְעֵם *ṭᵉʿēm2* (30)
decree (5)
decree (4) +10682
commanding officer (3) +10116
order (3)
attention (2)
authorized (2) +10682
accountable (1)
command (1)
commanded (1) +10682
decreed (1) +10682
decrees (1)
drinking (1)
order (1) +10002+10682
order (1) +10682
prescribed (1) +10427
report (1)
tact (1)

10303 טְפַר *ṭᵉp̄ar* (2)
claws (1)
nails (1)

10304 טְרַד *ṭᵉraḏ* (4)
driven away (2)
was driven away (2)

10305 טַרְפְּלָי *ṭarpᵉlāy* (1)
men from Tripolis (1)

10306 י *y*
Variant; not used

10307 ־ִי *-iy* (72)
my (33)
I (14)
me (12)
my (1) +10621
myself (1) +10380
untranslated (11)

10308 יְבַל *yebal* (3)
brought (2)
take (1)

10309 יַבֶּשָׁה *yabbešāh* (1)
earth (1)

10310 יְגַר *yegar*
Variant; not used

10311 יַד *yad* (17)
hand (7)
hands (3)
hand (2) +10589
be handed over (1) +10089+10314
direction (1)
handed over (1) +10089+10314
possess (1) +10089
power (1)

10312 יְדָה *yedāh* (2)
giving thanks (1)
thank (1)

10313 יְדַע *yeda'* (47)
know (11)
tell (8)
acknowledge (3)
interpret (3) +10600
explained (2)
inform (2)
made known (2)
shown (2)
understand (2)
acknowledged (1)
certain (1) +10327+10427
discerning (1) +10100
gave (1)
information (1)
knew (1)
knows (1)
learned (1)
remember (1)
showed (1)
teach (1)
untranslated (1)

10314 יְהַב *yehab* (28)
given (4)
gave (3)
was given (3)
be given (1)
be handed over (1)
be handed over (1) +10089+10311
be paid (1)
entrusted (1)
give (1)
give up (1)
gives (1)
handed over (1) +10089+10311
laid (1)
lavished (1)
made (1)
paid (1)
placed (1)
pronounced (1)
thrown (1)
were allowed (1)
were paid (1)

10315 יְהוּד *yehûd* (7)
Judah (6)
untranslated (1)

10316 יְהוּדָי *yehûdāy* (10)
Jews (9)
Jewish (1)

10317 יוֹם *yôm* (16)
days (6)
day (3)
time (3)
daily (1) +10089+10317
long history (1) +10427+10550
times (1)

10318 יוֹצָדָק *yôṣādāq* (1)
Jozadak (1)

10319 יְחַט *yeḥaṭ*
Variant; not used

10320 יְטַב *yeṭab* (1)
seems best (1)

10321 יְכִל *yekil* (14)
able (5)
can (5)
defeating (1)
unable (1) +10379
untranslated (2)

10322 יַם *yam* (2)
sea (2)

10323 יְסַף *yesap* (1)
became even greater (1) +10339+10650

10324 יְעַט *ye'aṭ* (1)
agreed (1)

10325 יָעֵט *yā'ēṭ* (2)
advisers (2)

10326 יְצַב *yeṣab* (1)
know the true meaning (1)

10327 יַצִּיב *yaṣṣiyb* (5)
certain (1) +10313+10427
certainly (1) +10002
stands (1)
true (1)
true meaning (1)

10328 יְקַד *yeqad* (8)
blazing (8) +10471

10329 יְקֵדָה *yeqēdāh* (1)
blazing (1)

10330 יַקִּיר *yaqqiyr* (2)
honorable (1)
too difficult (1)

10331 יְקָר *yeqār* (7)
glory (6)
honor (1)

10332 יְרוּשְׁלֶם *yerûšelem* (26)
Jerusalem (26)

10333 יְרַח *yeraḥ* (2)
month (1)
months (1)

10334 יַרְכָה *yarkāh* (1)
thighs (1)

10335 יִשְׂרָאֵל *yiśrā'ēl* (8)
Israel (7)
Israelites (1) +10553

10336 יֵשׁוּעַ *yēšûa'* (1)
Jeshua (1)

10337 יָת *yāt* (1)
untranslated (1)

10338 יְתִב *yetib* (5)
living (1)
seated (1)
settled (1)
sit (1)
took seat (1)

10339 יַתִּיר *yatiyr* (8)
became even greater (1) +10323+10650
exceptional (1)
keen (1)
most (1)
outstanding (1)
so (1)
very (1)
untranslated (1)

10340 כ *k*
Variant; not used

10341 כְּ־ *ke-* (41)
like (14)
as (6)
in accordance with (4)
when (3) +10168
at (2)
how (2) +10408
according to (1)
after (1)
any more than (1) +10168+10195
as follows (1) +10180
as soon as (1) +10002+10168+10232
for (1)
in way (1)
such (1) +10180
this (1) +10180
when (1)

10342 ־ָךְ *-k* (118)
your (46)
you (40)
there[s] (1) +10444
yours (1)
yourself (1)
yourself (1) +10381
untranslated (28)

10343 כְּדַב *kedab* (1)
misleading (1)

10344 כִּדְבָּה *kidbāh*
Variant; not used

10345 כָּה *kāh* (1)
this (1) +10527

10346 כְּהַל *kehal* (4)
could (2)
able (1)
can (1)

10347 כָּהֵן *kāhēn* (8)
priests (6)
priest (2)

10348 כַּוָּה *kawwāh* (1)
windows (1)

10349 ־כוֹן *-kôn* (10)
you (8)
your (2)

10350 כּוֹרֶשׁ *kôreš* (8)
Cyrus (7)
untranslated (1)

10351 כִּיל *kiyl*
Variant; not used

10352 כַּכַּר *kakkar* (1)
talents (1)

10353 כֹּל *kōl* (105)
all (36)
any (9)
whole (7)
no (4) +10379
because (3) +10168+10619
for (3) +10168+10619
anyone (2) +10050
every (2)
everything (2)
throughout (2) +10089
whatever (2) +10168
a[s] (1)
anyone (1)
by (1) +10168+10619
cordial greetings (1) +10002+10002+10720
do so[s] (1) +10544+10708

entire (1)
even as (1) +10168+10619
everyone (1) +10050
just as (1) +10168+10619
none (1) +10379
other[S] (1)
since (1) +10168+10619
so (1) +10180+10619
then (1) +10180+10619
therefore (1) +10180+10619
they[S] (1) +10002+10553
this is the meaning (1) +10168+10619
this made (1) +10180+10619
though (1) +10168+10619
wherever (1) +10089+10168
whoever (1) +10050+10168
whoever (1) +10168
untranslated (11)

10354 כְּלַל *kᵉlal* (8)
are restored (2)
finished (2)
restore (2)
restoring (1)
untranslated (1)

10355 ־כֹם *-kōm* (5)
you (3)
your (2)

10356 כְּמָה *kᵉmāh*
Variant; not used

10357 כֵּן *kēn* (8)
this (2)
untranslated (6)

10358 כְּנֵמָא *kᵉnēmā'* (5)
also (1) +10008
as follows (1)
this (1)
untranslated (2)

10359 כְּנַשׁ *kᵉnaš* (3)
assembled (1)
crowded around (1)
summoned (1) +10378+10714

10360 כְּנָת *kᵉnāt* (7)
associates (6)
fellow (1)

10361 כַּסְדָּי *kasdāy*
Variant; not used

10362 כְּסַף *kᵉsap̱* (13)
silver (12)
money (1)

10363 כְּעַן *kᵉ'an* (13)
now (6)
furthermore (1)
now then (1)
the present (1)
untranslated (4)

10364 כְּעֶנֶת *kᵉ'enet̲* (3)
now (1)
untranslated (2)

10365 כְּעֶת *kᵉ'et̲* (1)
untranslated (1)

10366 כְּפַת *kᵉp̱at̲* (4)
firmly tied (1)
tie up (1)
tied up (1)
were bound (1)

10367 כֹּר *kōr* (1)
cors (1)

10368 כַּרְבְּלָה *karbᵉlāh* (1)
turbans (1)

10369 כְּרָה *kᵉrāh* (1)
troubled (1)

10370 כָּרוֹז *kārôz* (1)
herald (1)

10371 כְּרַז *kᵉraz* (1)
proclaimed (1)

10372 כָּרְסֵא *korsē'* (3)
throne (2)
thrones (1)

10373 כַּשְׂדָּי *kaśdāy* (15)
astrologers (6)
astrologer (1)
Babylonians (1)
Chaldean (1)
untranslated (6)

10374 כְּתַב *kᵉt̲ab̲* (8)
wrote (4)
read (1)
was written (1)
write down (1)
wrote down (1)

10375 כְּתָב *kᵉt̲āb̲* (12)
writing (5)
inscription (2)
put in writing (2) +10673
decree (1)
limit (1)
what written (1)

10376 כְּתַל *kᵉt̲al* (2)
wall (1)
walls (1)

10377 ל *l*
Variant; not used

10378 לְ־ *lᵉ-* (364)
to (102)
for (22)
of (11)
into (7)
forever (6) +10550
had (6)
into (6) +10135
in (3)
against (2)
as (2)
before (2) +10619
on (2)
why (2) +10408
against (1) +10608
applied to (1)
at (1)
because of (1) +10168+10619
by (1)
extends to (1)
forever (1) +10002+10550
his (1) +10192
in favor of (1)
later (1) +10636
near (1) +10619
never (1) +10379+10550
so that (1)
summoned (1) +10042+10085
summoned (1) +10359+10714
together (1) +10154+10154
toward (1)
what (1) +10408
will be left with (1) +10029
with (1)
with (1) +10619
untranslated (170)

10379 לָא *lā'* (82)
not (38)
no (10)
cannot (4)
no (4) +10353
without (4)
nor (3) +10221
never (2)
before (1)
neither (1)
never (1) +10378+10550
none (1) +10353
nor (1) +10059+10221
nothing (1)
nothing (1) +10269
rather than (1)
unable (1) +10321
unharmed (1) +10029+10244
weren't (1)
untranslated (6)

10380 לֵב *lēb̲* (1)
myself (1) +10307

10381 לְבַב *lᵉb̲ab̲* (7)
mind (3)
heart (2)
mind (1) +10669
yourself (1) +10342

10382 לְבוּשׁ *lᵉb̲ûš* (2)
clothes (1)
clothing (1)

10383 לְבַשׁ *lᵉb̲aš* (3)
clothed (3)

10384 לָהּ *lāh*
Variant; not used

10385 לָהֵן1 *lāhēn1* (3)
so (1)
so then (1)
therefore (1)

10386 לָהֵן2 *lāhēn2* (7)
except (4)
but (2)
unless (1)

10387 לֵוָי *lēwāy* (4)
Levites (4)

10388 לְוָת *lᵉwāt̲* (1)
from (1) +10427

10389 לְחֶם *lᵉhem* (1)
banquet (1)

10390 לְחֵנָה *lᵉhēnāh* (3)
concubines (3)

10391 לֵילֵי *lēylēy* (5)
night (5)

10392 לִשָּׁן *liššān* (7)
men of every language (6)
language (1)

10393 מ *m*
Variant; not used

10394 מָא *mā'*
Variant; not used

10395 מְאָה *mᵉ'āh* (8)
hundred (7)
120 (1) +10221+10574

10396 מֹאזְנֵא *mō'zᵉnē'* (1)
scales (1)

10397 מֵאמַר *mē'mar* (2)
declare (1)
requested (1)

10398 מָאן *mā'n* (7)
articles (4)
goblets (3)

10399 מְגִלָּה *mᵉgillāh* (1)
scroll (1)

10400 מְגַר *mᵉgar* (1)
overthrow (1)

10401 מַדְבַּח *madbah* (1)
altar (1)

10402 מִדָּה *middāh* (4)
taxes (3)
revenues (1)

10403 מְדוֹר *mᵉdôr* (3)
live (2)

lived (1)

10404 מָדַי *māḏay* (7)
Medes (4)
Mede (1)
Media (1)
untranslated (1)

10405 מָדָיָא *māḏāyā'*
Variant; not used

10406 מְדִינָה *mᵉdiynāh* (11)
province (7)
provincial (2)
district (1)
provinces (1)

10407 מְדָר *mᵉḏār* (1)
live (1)

10408 מָה *māh* (14)
what (5)
how (2) +10341
why (2) +10378
things (1)
what (1) +10378
whatever (1)
whatever (1) +10168
why (1) +10542

10409 מוֹת *môṯ* (1)
death (1)

10410 מָזוֹן *māzôn* (2)
food (2)

10411 מְחָא *mᵉḥā'* (4)
struck (2)
hold back (1)
impaled (1)

10412 מַחְלְקָה *mahlᵉqāh* (1)
groups (1)

10413 מְטָא *mᵉṭā'* (8)
approached (1)
came (1)
happened (1)
issued (1)
reached (1)
reaches (1)
touched (1)
touching (1)

10414 מִישָׁאֵל *miyšā'ēl* (1)
Mishael (1)

10415 מֵישַׁךְ *mēyšaḵ* (14)
Meshach (13)
untranslated (1)

10416 מְלָא *mᵉlā'* (2)
filled (1)
furious (1) +10270

10417 מַלְאַךְ *mal'aḵ* (2)
angel (2)

10418 מִלָּה *millāh* (24)
matter (4)
words (3)
command (2)
decided (2)
things (2)
decree (1)
dream[S] (1)
it[S] (1) +10002
speak (1) +10425
substance (1) +10646
thing (1)
this[S] (1) +10002
voices (1)
what asks (1)
what said (1)
what[S] (1) +10002

10419 1מְלַח *mᵉlah1* (1)
under obligation (1) +10420

10420 2מְלַח *mᵉlah2* (3)
salt (2)
under obligation (1) +10419

10421 מֶלֶךְ *meleḵ* (180)
king (137)
kings (11)
royal (9)
king's (6)
he[S] (3) +10002
him[S] (3) +10002
he[S] (2) +10002+10453
his[S] (2) +10002
kingdoms (1)
royal interests (1)
them[S] (1)
untranslated (4)

10422 מְלַךְ *mᵉlaḵ* (1)
advice (1)

10423 מַלְכָּה *malkāh* (2)
queen (1)
she[S] (1) +10002

10424 מַלְכוּ *malkû* (57)
kingdom (30)
kingdoms (7)
reign (5)
royal (4)
sovereignty (2)
dominion (1)
government affairs (1)
it[S] (1) +10002
it[S] (1) +10191
realm (1)
royal authority (1)
sovereign power (1)
throne (1)
untranslated (1)

10425 מְלַל *mᵉlal* (5)
spoke (2)
answered (1)
speak (1) +10418
speaking (1)

10426 מַן *man* (10)
anyone (4) +10168
what (2)
who (2)
whoever (2) +10168

10427 מִן *min* (125)
from (41)
of (8)
partly (7)
to (5)
with (3)
because of (2)
before (2) +10621
from (2) +10621
one (2)
out of (2)
according to (1)
ago (1) +10180+10622
among (1)
as soon as (1) +10008+10168
because (1) +10168
before (1) +10180+10622
by (1)
by (1) +10621
certain (1) +10313+10327
for (1)
from (1) +10388
greater than (1)
in (1) +10608
issue (1) +10621
long history (1) +10317+10550
more than (1)
of (1) +10135
on (1)
over (1) +10543
partly (1) +10636
prescribed (1) +10302
some (1)
surely (1) +10168+10643
when (1) +10168
untranslated (27)

10428 מְנֵא *mᵉnē'* (3)
mene (3)

10429 מִנְדָּה *mindāh*
Variant; not used

10430 מַנְדַּע *manda'* (4)
knowledge (2)
sanity (2)

10431 מְנָה *mᵉnāh* (5)
appointed (2)
appoint (1)
numbered (1)
set (1)

10432 מִנְחָה *minhāh* (2)
grain offerings (1)
offering (1)

10433 מִנְיָן *minyān* (1)
each (1)

10434 מַעֲבָד *ma'ᵃḇāḏ* (1)
does (1)

10435 מְעֵה *mᵉ'ēh* (1)
belly (1)

10436 מֶעָל *me'āl* (1)
sundown (1) +10002+10728

10437 מָרֵא *mārē'* (6)
Lord (2)
lord (2)
untranslated (2)

10438 מְרַד *mᵉraḏ* (1)
rebellion (1)

10439 מָרָד *mārāḏ* (2)
rebellious (2)

10440 מְרַט *mᵉrat* (1)
were torn off (1)

10441 מֹשֶׁה *mōšeh* (1)
Moses (1)

10442 מְשַׁח *mᵉšah1* (2)
oil (1)
olive oil (1)

10443 מְשַׁח *mᵉšah2*
Variant; not used

10444 מִשְׁכַּב *miškaḇ* (6)
bed (5)
there[S] (1) +10342

10445 מִשְׁכַּן *miškan* (1)
dwelling (1)

10446 מַשְׁרוֹקִי *mašrôqiy* (4)
flute (4)

10447 מִשְׁתֵּא *mištē'* (1)
banquet (1)

10448 מַתְּנָה *matᵉnāh* (3)
gifts (3)

10449 נ *n*
Variant; not used

10450 ־נָא *-nā'* (11)
us (7)
our (1)
the[S] (1)
we (1)
untranslated (1)

10451 נְבָא *nᵉḇā'* (1)
prophesied (1)

10452 נְבוּאָה *nᵉḇû'āh* (1)
preaching (1)

10453 נְבוּכַדְנֶצַּר *nᵉḇûḵadneṣṣar* (31)
Nebuchadnezzar (28)

he[S] (2) +10002+10421
untranslated (1)

10454 נְבִזְבָּה *neḇizbāh* (2)
rewards (2)

10455 נְבִיא *neḇiy'* (8)
prophet (3)
prophets (1)
untranslated (4)

10456 נֶבְרְשָׁה *neḇreššāh* (1)
lampstand (1)

10457 נְגַד *neg̱aḏ* (1)
flowing (1)

10458 נֶגֶד *neg̱eḏ* (1)
toward (1)

10459 נְגַהּ *negah* (1)
first light (1)

10460 נְגוֹ *negô*
Variant; not used

10461 נְדַב *neḏaḇ* (4)
freely given (1)
freewill offerings (1)
wish (1)
untranslated (1)

10462 נִדְבָּךְ *niḏbāḵ* (2)
courses (1)
untranslated (1)

10463 נְדַד *neḏaḏ* (1)
could not (1)

10464 נִדְנֶה *niḏneh* (1)
in (1) +10089+10135

10465 נְהוֹר *nehôr* (1)
untranslated (1)

10466 נְהִיר *nehiyr* (1)
light (1)

10467 נַהִירוּ *nahiyrû* (2)
insight (2)

10468 נְהַר *nehar* (15)
Trans-Euphrates (12) +10191+10526
river (1)
that province[S] (1) +10191+10526
Trans-Euphrates (1) +10002+10526

10469 נוּד *nûḏ* (1)
flee (1)

10470 נְוָלוּ *newālû* (3)
piles of rubble (2)
pile of rubble (1)

10471 נוּר *nûr* (17)
blazing (8) +10328
fire (8)
all ablaze (1) +10178

10472 נְזַק *nezaq* (4)
detriment (1)
suffer (1)
suffer loss (1)
troublesome (1)

10473 נְחָשׁ *nehāš* (9)
bronze (9)

10474 נְחַת *nehaṯ* (6)
coming down (2)
deposit (1)
deposited (1)
stored (1)
was deposed (1)

10475 נְטַל *netal* (2)
raised (1)
was lifted (1)

10476 נְטַר *netar* (1)
kept (1)

10477 ־נִי *-niy* (18)
me (17)
untranslated (1)

10478 נִיחוֹחַ *niyhôha* (2)
incense (1)
pleasing (1)

10479 נְכַס *neḵas* (2)
property (1)
treasury (1)

10480 נְמַר *nemar* (1)
leopard (1)

10481 נְסַח *nesah* (1)
be pulled (1)

10482 1נְסַךְ *nesaḵ1* (1)
presented (1)

10483 2נְסַךְ *nesaḵ2* (1)
drink offerings (1)

10484 נְפַל *nep̱al* (12)
fall down (5)
fell (3)
came (1)
fell down (1)
have occasion (1)
untranslated (1)

10485 נְפַק *nep̱aq* (12)
taken (3)
appeared (1)
came out (1)
come out (1)
coming out (1)
gone out (1)
issued (1)
removed (1)
took (1)
untranslated (1)

10486 נִפְקָה *nip̱qāh* (2)
costs (1)
expenses (1)

10487 נִצְבָּה *nisbāh* (1)
strength (1)

10488 נְצַח *nesah* (1)
distinguished himself (1)

10489 נְצַל *nesal* (3)
save (2)
saves (1)

10490 נְקֵא *neqē'* (1)
white (1)

10491 נְקַשׁ *neqaš* (1)
knocked (1)

10492 נְשָׂא *neśā'* (3)
revolt (1)
swept away (1)
take (1)

10493 נְשִׁין *nešiyn* (1)
wives (1)

10494 נִשְׁמָה *nišmāh* (1)
life (1)

10495 נְשַׁר *nešar* (2)
eagle (2)

10496 נִשְׁתְּוָן *ništewān* (5)
letter (4)
written reply (1)

10497 נְתִין *neṯiyn* (1)
temple servants (1)

10498 נְתַן *neṯan* (7)
gives (3)
paid (1)
provide (1)
supply (1)
untranslated (1)

10499 נְתַר *neṯar* (1)
strip off (1)

10500 ס *s*
Variant; not used

10501 סַבְּכָא *sabbeḵā'*
Variant; not used

10502 סְבַל *seḇal* (1)
be laid (1)

10503 סְבַר *seḇar* (1)
try (1)

10504 סְגִד *seg̱iḏ* (12)
worship (10)
paid honor (1)
worshiped (1)

10505 סְגַן *seg̱an* (5)
prefects (4)
in charge (1) +10647

10506 סְגַר *seg̱ar* (1)
shut (1)

10507 סוּמְפֹּנְיָה *sûmpōnyāh* (4)
pipes (3)
untranslated (1)

10508 סוּף *sûp̱* (2)
bring to an end (1)
fulfilled (1)

10509 סוֹף *sôp̱* (5)
distant parts (1)
end (1)
ends (1)
forever (1) +10002+10527
never end (1) +10002+10527

10510 סוּפֹּנְיָא *sûpōnyā'*
Variant; not used

10511 סְטַר *setar*
Variant; not used

10512 סִיפֹּנְיָא *siypōnyā'*
Variant; not used

10513 סְלִק *selaq* (8)
came up (4)
lift out (1)
took up (1)
turned (1)
was lifted (1)

10514 סְעַד *se'aḏ* (1)
helping (1)

10515 סְפַר *sep̱ar* (5)
archives (1) +10103
archives (1) +10177
book (1)
books (1)
records (1) +10177

10516 סָפַר *sāp̱ar* (6)
secretary (4)
teacher (2)

10517 סַרְבָּל *sarbāl* (2)
robes (2)

10518 סָרַךְ *sāraḵ* (5)
administrators (5)

10519 1סְתַר *seṯar1* (1)
hidden (1)

10520 2סְתַר *seṯar2* (1)
destroyed (1)

10521 ע *'*
Variant; not used

10522 עֲבַד *'aḇaḏ* (28)
done (3)
do (2)
made (2)
be carried out (1)
be cut into (1)
be done (1)
be made (1)

being carried on (1)
carried out (1)
celebrated (1)
cut into (1)
does (1)
gave (1)
make (1)
neglect (1) +10712
obey (1)
performed (1)
performs (1)
provide (1)
punished (1) +10170+10191
waging (1)
untranslated (3)

10523 עֲבֵד *ᵃḇēḏ* (9)
servants (6)
servant (1)
untranslated (2)

10524 עֲבֵד נְגוֹ *ᵃḇēḏ nᵉgô* (14)
Abednego (13)
untranslated (1)

10525 עֲבִידָה *ᵃḇiyḏāh* (6)
work (3)
administrators (1)
affairs (1)
service (1)

10526 עֲבַר *ᵃḇar* (14)
Trans-Euphrates (12) +10191+10468
that province[S] (1) +10191+10468
Trans-Euphrates (1) +10002+10468

10527 עַד *ʿad* (35)
until (8) +10168
until (4)
for (3)
during (2)
as (1) +10168
ever (1) +10002+10550
finally (1) +10024+10221
forever (1) +10002+10509
forever (1) +10002+10550
hoping (1) +10168
never end (1) +10002+10509
on (1)
so that (1) +10159+10168
this (1) +10345
to (1)
up to (1)
while (1) +10168
untranslated (5)

10528 עֲדָה *ᵃdāh* (9)
repealed (2)
stripped (2)
deposes (1)
pass away (1)
taken (1)
taken away (1)
was (1)

10529 עִדּוֹא *ʿiddôʾ* (2)
Iddo (2)

10530 עִדָּן *ʿiddān* (13)
times (6)
time (3)
as soon as (1) +10002+10089+10168
period of time (1) +10221+10232
situation (1)
when (1) +10002+10089

10531 עוֹד *ʿôḏ* (1)
still (1)

10532 עֲוָיָה *ᵃwāyāh* (1)
wickedness (1)

10533 עוֹף *ʿôp̄* (2)
bird (1)
birds (1)

10534 עוּר *ʿûr* (1)
chaff (1)

10535 עֵז *ʿēz* (1)
male goats (1) +10615

10536 עִזְקָה *ʿizqāh* (2)
rings (1)
signet ring (1)

10537 עֶזְרָא *ʿezrāʾ* (3)
Ezra (3)

10538 עֲזַרְיָה *ᵃzaryāh* (1)
Azariah (1)

10539 עֵטָה *ʿēṭāh* (1)
wisdom (1)

10540 עַיִן *ʿayin* (5)
eyes (4)
eye (1)

10541 עִיר *ʿiyr* (3)
messenger (2)
messengers (1)

10542 עַל *ʿal* (114)
to (16)
on (13)
over (8)
for (7)
against (6)
about (4)
in (4)
around (3)
lying in (3)
of (3)
among (1)
concerning (1)
had (1) +10201
lying (1)
lying on (1)
prostrate (1) +10049
rule (1)
so that (1) +10159+10168
than (1)
that is why (1) +10180
toward (1)
why (1) +10408
untranslated (35)

10543 עֵלָּא *ʿēllāʾ* (1)
over (1) +10427

10544 עִלָּה *ʿillāh* (3)
basis for charges (1)
do so[S] (1) +10353+10708
grounds for charges (1)

10545 עֲלָוָה *ᵃlāwāh* (1)
burnt offerings (1)

10546 עִלָּי *ʿillāy* (20)
most High (10)
untranslated (10)

10547 עִלִּי *ʿilliy* (1)
upstairs room (1)

10548 עֶלְיוֹן *ʿelyôn* (4)
most High (3)
his[S] (1)

10549 עֲלַל *ᵃlal* (17)
brought (3)
came (2)
went (2)
came in (1)
came into (1)
take (1)
took (1)
was brought (1)
went in (1)
were brought (1)
untranslated (3)

10550 עָלַם *ʿālam* (20)
forever (6) +10378
eternal (2)
ever (2) +10002
everlasting (2)
ancient (1)
ever (1)
ever (1) +10002+10527
forever (1) +10002
forever (1) +10002+10378
forever (1) +10002+10527
long history (1) +10317+10427
never (1) +10378+10379

10551 עֵלְמָי *ʿēlmāy* (1)
Elamites (1)

10552 עֲלַע *ᵃlaʿ* (1)
ribs (1)

10553 עַם *ʿam* (15)
people (7)
peoples (6)
Israelites (1) +10335
they[S] (1) +10002+10353

10554 עִם *ʿim* (22)
with (10)
for (2)
to (2)
against (1)
among (1)
as well as (1)
at (1)
like (1)
of (1)
united (1) +10158+10180+10180
untranslated (1)

10555 עַמִּיק *ʿammiyq* (1)
deep (1)

10556 עֲמַר *ᵃmar* (1)
wool (1)

10557 עַן *ʿan*
Variant; not used

10558 עֲנָה *ᵃnāh* (30)
said (13)
answered (5)
replied (5)
asked (3)
ordered (1)
shouted (1)
untranslated (2)

10559 עֲנֵה *ᵃnēh* (1)
oppressed (1)

10560 עֲנָן *ᵃnān* (1)
clouds (1)

10561 עֲנַף *ᵃnap̄* (4)
branches (4)

10562 עֲנָשׁ *ᵃnāš* (1)
confiscation (1)

10563 עֶנֶת *ʿeneṯ*
Variant; not used

10564 עֳפִי *ᵒpiy* (3)
leaves (3)

10565 עֲצִיב *ᵃṣiyḇ* (1)
anguished (1)

10566 עֲקַר *ᵃqar* (2)
were uprooted (1)
untranslated (1)

10567 עִקַּר *ʿiqqar* (3)
stump (3)

10568 עָר *ʿār* (2)
adversaries (1)
untranslated (1)

10569 עֲרַב *ᵃraḇ* (4)
mixed (2)
mixes (1)
mixture (1)

10570 עֲרָד *ᵃrāḏ* (1)
wild donkeys (1)

10571 ערוה *ʿarwāh* (1)
dishonored (1)

10572 עשב *ʿᵃśab* (5)
grass (4)
plants (1)

10573 עשר *ʿᵃśar* (6)
ten (4)
twelve (2) +10775

10574 עשרין *ʿeśriyn* (1)
120 (1) +10221+10395

10575 עשת *ʿᵃšat* (1)
planned (1)

10576 עת *ʿet*
Variant; not used

10577 עתיד *ʿᵃtiyd* (1)
ready (1)

10578 עתיק *ʿatiyq* (3)
ancient (3)

10579 פ *p*
Variant; not used

10580 פחה *pehāh* (10)
governor (6)
governors (4)

10581 פחר *pehār* (1)
untranslated (1)

10582 פטיש *pattiyš* (2)
trousers (1)
untranslated (1)

10583 פלג1 *pᵉlag1* (1)
divided (1)

10584 פלג2 *pᵉlag2* (1)
half (1)

10585 פלגה *pᵉluggāh* (1)
divisions (1)

10586 פלח *pᵉlah* (10)
serve (7)
workers (1)
worship (1)
worshiped (1)

10587 פלחן *polhān* (1)
worship (1)

10588 פם *pum* (6)
mouth (4)
lips (1)
mouths (1)

10589 פס *pas* (2)
hand (2) +10311

10590 פסנתרין *pᵉsantēriyn* (4)
harp (4)

10591 פרזל *parzel* (20)
iron (20)

10592 פרס *pᵉras* (1)
is divided (1)

10593 פרס *pᵉrēs* (2)
parsin (1)
Peres (1)

10594 פרס *pāras* (6)
Persians (4)
Persia (2)

10595 פרסי *parsāy* (2)
Persian (1)
untranslated (1)

10596 פרק *pᵉraq* (1)
renounce (1)

10597 פרש *pᵉraš* (1)
translated (1)

10598 פרשגן *paršegen* (3)
copy (3)

10599 פשר1 *pᵉšar1* (2)
give interpretations (1) +10600
interpret (1)

10600 פשר2 *pᵉšar2* (32)
means (7)
interpret (5) +10252
interpretation (4)
interpret (3)
interpret (3) +10313
interpret (2) +10042
meaning (2)
explain (1)
explain (1) +10252
give interpretations (1) +10599
mean (1)
meant (1)
untranslated (1)

10601 פתגם *pitgām* (6)
answer (1)
decision (1)
defend (1) +10754
edict (1)
reply (1)
report (1)

10602 פתח *pᵉtah* (2)
opened (1)
were opened (1)

10603 פתי *pᵉtāy* (2)
wide (2)

10604 צ *s*
Variant; not used

10605 צבה *sᵉbāh* (10)
wanted to (4)
wishes (4)
pleases (1)
wanted (1)

10606 צבו *sᵉbû* (1)
situation (1)

10607 צבע *sᵉbaʿ* (5)
be drenched (2)
was drenched (2)
drenched (1)

10608 צד *sad* (2)
against (1) +10378
in (1) +10427

10609 צדא *sᵉdāʾ* (1)
is it true (1) +10190

10610 צדקה *sidqāh* (1)
right (1)

10611 צואר *sawwaʾr* (3)
neck (3)

10612 צלה *sᵉlāh* (2)
pray (1)
prayed (1)

10613 צלח *sᵉlah* (4)
making rapid progress (1)
promoted (1)
prosper (1)
prospered (1)

10614 צלם *sᵉlēm* (17)
image (10)
statue (5)
attitude (1) +10049
it[s] (1) +10002

10615 צפיר *sᵉpiyr* (1)
male goats (1) +10535

10616 צפר *sippar* (4)
birds (3)
bird (1)

10617 ק *q*
Variant; not used

10618 קבל *qᵉbal* (3)
receive (2)
took over (1)

10619 קבל *qᵒbēl* (29)
because (3) +10168+10353
for (3) +10168+10353
before (2) +10378
because of (1) +10168+10378
by (1) +10168+10353
even as (1) +10168+10353
just as (1) +10168+10353
near (1) +10378
since (1) +10168+10353
so (1) +10180+10353
then (1) +10180+10353
therefore (1) +10180+10353
this is the meaning (1) +10168+10353
this made (1) +10180+10353
though (1) +10168+10353
with (1) +10378
untranslated (8)

10620 קדיש *qaddiyš* (13)
holy (7)
saints (5)
they[s] (1)

10621 קדם *qᵒdām* (46)
to (11)
before (7)
before (2) +10427
from (2) +10427
by (1) +10427
former (1)
in presence (1)
in sight (1)
into presence (1)
issue (1) +10427
my (1) +10307
presence (1)
untranslated (16)

10622 קדמה *qadmāh* (2)
ago (1) +10180+10427
before (1) +10180+10427

10623 קדמי *qadmāy* (3)
first (2)
earlier (1)

10624 קום *qûm* (36)
set up (9)
stood (4)
issue (2)
rise (2)
sets (2)
appoint (1)
appointed (1)
arise (1)
come (1)
endure (1)
get up (1)
got up (1)
installed (1)
issues (1)
leaped to feet (1)
set (1)
set to work (1) +10221+10742
sets up (1)
standing (1)
was raised up (1)
untranslated (2)

10625 קטל *qᵉtal* (7)
put to death (4)
was slain (2)
killed (1)

10626 קטר *qᵉtar* (3)
difficult problems (2)
legs (1) +10284

10627 קיט *qayit* (1)
summer (1)

10628 קים *qᵉyām* (2)
edict (2)

10629 קַיָּם *qayyām* (2)
endures (1)
restored (1)

10630 קִיתְרֹס *qiyṯrōs* (4)
zither (4)

10631 קָל *qāl* (7)
sound (4)
voice (2)
untranslated (1)

10632 קְנָה *q^{e}nāh* (1)
buy (1)

10633 1קְצַף *q^{e}sap̱1* (1)
furious (1)

10634 2קְצַף *q^{e}sap̱2* (1)
wrath (1)

10635 קְצַץ *q^{e}sas* (1)
trim off (1)

10636 קְצָת *q^{e}sāṯ* (3)
end (1)
later (1) +10378
partly (1) +10427

10637 קְרָא *q^{e}rāʾ* (11)
read (4)
been read (1)
call (1)
called (1)
called out (1)
proclaimed (1)
reads (1)
was read (1)

10638 קְרֵב *q^{e}rēḇ* (9)
approached (2)
came forward (1)
came near (1)
led (1)
offer sacrifices (1)
offered (1)
sacrifice (1)
went (1)

10639 קְרָב *q^{e}rāḇ* (1)
war (1)

10640 קִרְיָה *qiryāh* (9)
city (9)

10641 קֶרֶן *qeren* (14)
horn (9)
horns (5)

10642 קְרַץ *q^{e}ras* (2)
denounced (1) +10030
falsely accused (1) +10030

10643 קְשֹׁט *q^{e}šōṭ* (2)
right (1)
surely (1) +10168+10427

10644 קַתְרוֹס *qaṯrôs* (4)
untranslated (4)

10645 ר *r*
Variant; not used

10646 רֵאשׁ *rēʾš* (14)
head (4)
mind (4)
heads (2)
saw (2)
leaders (1)
substance (1) +10418

10647 רַב *raḇ* (23)
great (11)
boastfully (2)
chief (2)
boastful (1)
commander (1)
enormous (1)
huge (1)
imposing (1)
in charge (1) +10505
large (1)
many (1) +10678

10648 רְבָה *r^{e}ḇāh* (6)
grew large (2)
great (1)
grew (1)
grown (1)
placed in a high position (1)

10649 רִבּוֹ *ribbô* (3)
ten thousand (2)
untranslated (1)

10650 רְבוּ *r^{e}ḇû* (5)
greatness (3)
became even greater (1) +10323+10339
high position (1)

10651 רְבִיעָי *r^{e}ḇiyʿāy* (10)
fourth (6)
untranslated (4)

10652 רַבְרְבָנִין *raḇr^{e}ḇāniyn* (9)
nobles (8)
untranslated (1)

10653 1רְגַז *r^{e}gaz1* (1)
angered (1)

10654 2רְגַז *r^{e}gaz2* (1)
rage (1)

10655 רְגַל *r^{e}gal* (8)
feet (4)
underfoot (2) +10089
toes (1) +10064
untranslated (1)

10656 רְגַשׁ *r^{e}gaš* (3)
went as a group (3)

10657 רֵו *rēw* (2)
appearance (1)
looks (1)

10658 רוּחַ *rûha* (11)
spirit (6)
mind (1)
qualities (1)
wind (1)
winds (1)
untranslated (1)

10659 1רוּם *rûm1* (4)
arrogant (1)
exalt (1)
promoted (1)
set up (1)

10660 2רוּם *rûm2* (5)
high (2)
top (2)
height (1)

10661 רָז *rāz* (9)
mystery (6)
mysteries (3)

10662 רְחוּם *r^{e}hûm* (4)
Rehum (4)

10663 רַחִיק *rahiyq* (1)
away (1)

10664 רַחֲמִין *rah^{a}miyn* (1)
mercy (1)

10665 רְחַץ *r^{e}has* (1)
trusted (1)

10666 רֵיחַ *rêyha* (1)
smell (1)

10667 רְמָה *r^{e}māh* (12)
be thrown (5)
threw (2)
thrown (2)
impose (1)
throw (1)
were set in place (1)

10668 רְעוּ *r^{e}ʿû* (2)
decision (1)
will (1)

10669 רַעְיוֹן *raʿyôn* (6)
thoughts (2)
mind (1)
mind (1) +10381
untranslated (2)

10670 רַעֲנַן *raʿ^{a}nan* (1)
prosperous (1)

10671 רְעַע *r^{e}ʿaʿ* (2)
break (1)
breaks to pieces (1)

10672 רְפַס *r^{e}p̱as* (2)
trampled (2)

10673 רְשַׁם *r^{e}šam* (7)
put in writing (2) +10375
been published (1)
publish (1)
put in writing (1)
was written (1)
wrote (1)

10674 שׂ *ś*
Variant; not used

10675 שָׂב *śāḇ* (5)
elders (5)

10676 שַׂבְּכָא *śabb^{e}ḵāʾ* (4)
lyre (4)

10677 שְׂגָא *ś^{e}gāʾ* (3)
greatly (2)
grow (1)

10678 שַׂגִּיא *śaggiyʾ* (13)
abundant (2)
deeply (1)
enormous (1)
even more (1)
fill (1)
great (1)
greatly (1)
large (1)
many (1)
many (1) +10647
overjoyed (1) +10293
so (1)

10679 שָׂהֲדוּ *śāh^{a}ḏû*
Variant; not used

10680 שְׂטַר *ś^{e}ṭar* (1)
sides (1)

10681 שִׂיב *śiyḇ*
Variant; not used

10682 שִׂים *śiym* (26)
issued (5)
decree (4) +10302
issue (3)
authorized (2) +10302
appointed (1)
called (1) +10721
commanded (1) +10302
decreed (1) +10302
determined (1) +10104
order (1) +10002+10302
order (1) +10302
pay (1)
pays (1)
placed (1)
placing (1)
turned into (1)

10683 שְׂכַל *ś^{e}ḵal* (1)
thinking (1)

10684 שָׂכְלְתָנוּ *śāḵl^{e}ṯānû* (3)
intelligence (2)
understanding (1)

10685 שִׁלָּה *šillāh* (1)
untranslated (1)

10686 שְׂנָא *š^{e}nāʾ* (2)
enemies (1)
untranslated (1)

10687 שְׂעַר *š^{e}ʿar* (3)
hair (3)

10688 שׂ *š*
Variant; not used

10689 שְׁאֵל *š^{e}ʾēl* (6)
asked (3)
ask (1)
asks (1)
questioned (1)

10690 שְׁאֵלָה *š^{e}ʾēlāh* (1)
verdict (1)

10691 שְׁאַלְתִּיאֵל *š^{e}ʾaltiyʾēl* (1)
Shealtiel (1)

10692 שְׁאָר *š^{e}ʾār* (12)
rest (5)
elsewhere (2)
left (2)
other (2)
anything else (1)

10693 שְׁבַח *š^{e}ḇah* (5)
praise (2)
praised (2)
honored (1)

10694 שְׁבַט *š^{e}ḇat* (1)
tribes (1)

10695 שְׁבִיב *š^{e}ḇiyḇ* (2)
flames (1)
flaming (1)

10696 שְׁבַע *š^{e}ḇaʿ* (6)
seven (6)

10697 שְׁבַק *š^{e}ḇaq* (5)
leave (2)
be left (1)
not interfere (1)
remain (1)

10698 שְׁבַשׁ *š^{e}ḇaš* (1)
baffled (1)

10699 שֵׁגַל *šēḡal* (3)
wives (3)

10700 שְׁדַר *š^{e}ḏar* (1)
made every effort (1)

10701 שַׁדְרַךְ *šaḏraḵ* (14)
Shadrach (13)
untranslated (1)

10702 שְׁוָה *š^{e}wāh* (3)
be turned into (1)
given (1)
untranslated (1)

10703 שׁוּר *šûr* (4)
walls (3)
untranslated (1)

10704 שׁוּשַׁנְכָי *šûšanḵāy* (1)
of Susa (1)

10705 שְׁחַת *š^{e}haṯ* (3)
corrupt (1)
corruption (1)
wicked (1)

10706 שֵׁיזִב *šēyziḇ* (9)
rescue (5)
rescued (2)
rescues (1)
save (1)

10707 שֵׁיצִיא *šēysiyʾ* (1)
completed (1)

10708 שְׁכַח *š^{e}ḵah* (18)
was found (5)
find (4)
found (4)
do so^s (1) +10353+10544
leaving (1)
obtain (1)
untranslated (2)

10709 שְׁכַן *š^{e}ḵan* (2)
caused to dwell (1)
nesting places (1)

10710 שְׁלֵה *š^{e}lēh* (1)
contented (1)

10711 שָׁלֻה *šāluh*
Variant; not used

10712 שָׁלוּ *šālû* (4)
anything (1)
fail (1)
neglect (1) +10522
negligent (1)

10713 שְׁלֵוָה *š^{e}lēwāh* (1)
prosperity (1)

10714 שְׁלַח *š^{e}lah* (14)
sent (9)
are sent (1)
lifts (1)
send (1)
sending message (1)
summoned (1) +10359+10378

10715 שְׁלֵט *š^{e}lēt* (7)
made ruler (2)
ruler (2)
harmed (1)
overpowered (1)
rule (1)

10716 שִׁלְטֹן *šiltōn* (2)
officials (2)

10717 שָׁלְטָן *šol^{e}tān* (14)
dominion (7)
authority (2)
power (2)
authority to rule (1)
part (1)
rulers (1)

10718 שַׁלִּיט *šalliyt* (10)
sovereign (4)
authority (1)
mighty (1)
officer (1)
ruler (1)
rules (1)
ruling (1)

10719 שְׁלִם *š^{e}lim* (3)
brought to an end (1)
deliver (1)
finished (1)

10720 שְׁלָם *š^{e}lām* (4)
prosper (2)
cordial greetings (1) +10002+10002+10353
greetings (1)

10721 שֻׁם *šum* (12)
name (4)
called (3)
names (3)
called (1) +10682
named (1)

10722 שְׁמַד *š^{e}maḏ* (1)
completely destroyed (1) +10005+10221

10723 שְׁמַיִן *š^{e}mayin* (38)
heaven (29)
air (3)
heavens (3)
sky (3)

10724 שְׁמַם *š^{e}mam* (1)
greatly perplexed (1)

10725 שְׁמַע *š^{e}maʿ* (9)
heard (4)
hear (3)
hears (1)
obey (1)

10726 שָׁמְרַיִן *šomrayin* (2)
Samaria (2)

10727 שְׁמַשׁ *š^{e}maš1* (1)
attended (1)

10728 שְׁמַשׁ *š^{e}maš2* (1)
sundown (1) +10002+10436

10729 שִׁמְשַׁי *šimšay* (4)
Shimshai (4)

10730 שֵׁן *šēn* (5)
teeth (3)
untranslated (2)

10731 1שְׁנָה *š^{e}nāh1* (22)
different (5)
changed (4)
change (3)
changes (2)
turned (2)
altered (1)
defied (1)
grew (1)
look so pale (1) +10228
scorched (1)
untranslated (1)

10732 2שְׁנָה *š^{e}nāh2* (7)
year (5)
age (1) +10120
years (1)

10733 3שְׁנָה *š^{e}nāh* (1)
sleep (1)

10734 שָׁעָה *šāʿāh* (5)
immediately (2) +10002
immediately (1) +10191
suddenly (1) +10191
time (1)

10735 שְׁפַט *š^{e}p̱at* (1)
magistrates (1)

10736 שַׁפִּיר *šappiyr* (2)
beautiful (2)

10737 1שְׁפַל *š^{e}p̱al1* (4)
humbled (2)
humble (1)
subdue (1)

10738 2שְׁפַל *š^{e}p̱al2* (1)
lowliest (1)

10739 שְׁפַר *š^{e}p̱ar* (3)
pleased (2)
pleasure (1)

10740 שְׁפַרְפָּר *š^{e}p̱arpār* (1)
dawn (1)

10741 שָׁק *šāq* (1)
legs (1)

10742 שְׁרָה *š^{e}rāh* (6)
solve (2)
dwells (1)
gave way (1)
set to work (1) +10221+10624
unbound (1)

10743 שְׁרֹשׁ *š^{e}rōš* (3)
roots (3)

10744 שְׁרֹשׁוּ *š^{e}rōšû* (1)
banishment (1)

10745 שְׁרֹשִׁי *š^{e}rōšiy* (1)
untranslated (1)

10746 שֵׁשְׁבַּצַּר *šēšbassar* (2)
Sheshbazzar (2)

10747 שֵׁת *šēṯ* (2)
nine feet (1) +10039
sixth (1)

10748 שְׁתָה *š^eṯāh* (5)
drank (4)
drink (1)

10749 שִׁתִּין *šittiyn* (4)
ninety feet (3) +10039
sixty-two (1) +10221+10775

10750 שְׁתַר בּוֹזְנַי *š^eṯar bôz^enay* (4)
Shethar-Bozenai (4)

10751 ת *ṯ*
Variant; not used

10752 תְּבַר *t^eḇar* (1)
brittle (1)

10753 תְּדִיר *t^eḏiyr* (2)
continually (2) +10002+10089

10754 תּוּב *tûḇ* (8)
restored (2)
returned (2)
defend (1) +10601
gave (1)
received (1)
spoke (1)

10755 תְּוַהּ *t^ewah* (1)
amazement (1) +10097

10756 תּוֹר *tôr* (7)
cattle (4)
bulls (3)

10757 תְּחוֹת *t^eḥôṯ* (5)
under (4)
untranslated (1)

10758 תְּלַג *t^elag̱* (1)
snow (1)

10759 תְּלִיתָי *t^eliyṯāy* (2)
third (1)
untranslated (1)

10760 תְּלָת *t^elāṯ* (11)
three (10)
third (1)

10761 תַּלְתָּא *taltā'* (3)
third highest (3)

10762 תְּלָתִין *t^elāṯiyn* (2)
thirty (2)

10763 תְּמַהּ *t^emah* (3)
wonders (3)

10764 תַּמָּה *tammāh* (4)
there (2)
untranslated (2)

10765 תִּנְיָן *tinyān* (1)
second (1)

10766 תִּנְיָנוּת *tinyānûṯ* (1)
once more (1)

10767 תִּפְתָּי *tiptāy* (2)
magistrates (2)

10768 תַּקִּיף *taqqiyp̱* (5)
powerful (2)
strong (2)
mighty (1)

10769 תְּקַל *t^eqal* (1)
been weighed (1)

10770 תְּקֵל *t^eqēl* (2)
tekel (2)

10771 תְּקַן *t^eqan* (1)
was restored (1)

10772 תְּקִף *t^eqip̱* (5)
strong (3)
enforce (1)
hardened (1)

10773 תְּקֹף *t^eqōp̱* (1)
might (1)

10774 תְּקָף *t^eqāp̱* (1)
power (1)

10775 תְּרֵין *t^erēyn* (4)
twelve (2) +10573
second (1)
sixty-two (1) +10221+10749

10776 תְּרַע *t^era'* (2)
court (1)
opening (1)

10777 תָּרָע *tārā'* (1)
gatekeepers (1)

10778 תַּרְתֵּין *tartēyn*
Variant; not used

10779 תַּתְּנַי *tat^enay* (4)
Tattenai (4)

FEATURES OF THE GREEK TO ENGLISH INDEX–LEXICON

G/K NUMBER
Matches the number at the end of context lines (see the introduction, pages xii, xv).

LEXICAL FORM and TRANSLITERATION
See the transliteration and pronunication table below.

FREQUENCY COUNT
Indicates the total number of occurrences of this Greek word in the biblical text (see the introduction, page xv).

257 ἄλλος *allos* (155)

another (42) ← **NIV WORD and (FREQUENCY COUNT)** NIV words are listed according to their exact textual spelling and are organized according to frequency (see the introduction, page xv).

one another (1) *+257+4639* ← **MULTIPLE WORDS / MULTIPLE NUMBERS** More than one NIV word and/or more than one G/K number indicate multiple-word translations (see the introduction, pages xii, xiii, xv).

gospel[S] (1) ← **SUPERSCRIPT "S"** Indicates "substitution" translation (see the introduction, pages xiii-xv).

untranslated (5) ← **UNTRANSLATED** Always the final entry, indicates the number of times the NIV did not translate the Greek word for stylistic reasons (see the introduction, pages xv, xvi).

Variant; not used ← **VARIANT; NOT USED** Notes words of variant spelling and variant readings in the G/K number list that were not used in translating the NIV (see the introduction, pages xv, xvi).

GREEK TRANSLITERATION AND PRONUNCIATION TABLE

Greek	*English*	*Sound*
Α, α	*A, a*	f*a*ther
Β, β	*B, b*	*b*oy
Γ, γ	*G, g*	*g*irl
Δ, δ	*D, d*	*d*og
Ε, ε	*E, e*	g*e*t
Ζ, ζ	*Z, z*	a*dz*e
Η, η	*Ē, ē*	th*ey*
Θ, θ	*Th, th*	*th*ey
Ι, ι	*I, i*	p*i*n, mach*i*ne
Κ, κ	*K, k*	*k*it
Λ, λ	*L, l*	*l*et
Μ, μ	*M, m*	*m*other
Ν, ν	*N, n*	*n*ot
Ξ, ξ	*X, x*	fo*x*
Ο, ο	*O, o*	h*o*t
Π, π	*P, p*	*p*ot
Ρ, ρ	*R, r*	*r*ot
Σ, σ, ς	*S, s, s*	*s*ip
Τ, τ	*T, t*	*t*ip
Υ, υ	*Y, y*	p*u*t
Φ, φ	*Ph, ph*	*ph*one
Χ, χ	*Ch, ch*	Ba*ch*
Ψ, ψ	*Ps, ps*	li*ps*
Ω, ω	*Ō, ō*	ph*o*ne
γγ	*ng*	thi*ng*
γκ	*nk*	thi*nk*
γξ	*nx*	thi*nks*
γχ	*nch*	thi*nk*
εὐ	*eu*	*you*
ηὐ	*ēu*	s*ay you*
οὐ	*ou*	thr*ou*gh
υἱ	*hui*	*hwee*
ʽ	*h*	*h*ot
ῥ	*rh*	myr*rh*
ᾳ	*ā*	f*a*ther
ῃ	*ē*	th*ey*
ῳ	*ō*	ph*o*ne

GREEK TO ENGLISH INDEX–LEXICON OF THE NEW TESTAMENT

1 α *a*
Variant; not used

2 Ἀαρών *Aarōn* (5)
Aaron (4)
Aaron's (1)

3 Ἀβαδδών *Abaddōn* (1)
Abaddon (1)

4 ἀβαρής *abarēs* (1)
burden (1)

5 ἀββά *abba* (3)
Abba (3)

6 Ἅβελ *Habel* (4)
Abel (4)

7 Ἀβιά *Abia* (3)
Abijah (3)

8 Ἀβιαθάρ *Abiathar* (1)
Abiathar (1)

9 Ἀβιληνή *Abilēnē* (1)
Abilene (1)

10 Ἀβιούδ *Abioud* (2)
Abiud (2)

11 Ἀβραάμ *Abraam* (73)
Abraham (64)
Abraham's (9)

12 ἄβυσσος *abyssos* (9)
Abyss (8)
deep (1)

13 Ἅγαβος *Hagabos* (2)
Agabus (2)

14 ἀγαθοεργέω *agathoergeō* (2)
do good (1)
shown kindness (1)

15 ἀγαθοεργός *agathoergos*
Variant; not used

16 ἀγαθοποιέω *agathopoieō* (9)
do good (3)
doing good (3)
are good (1)
do what is right (1)
does what is good (1)

17 ἀγαθοποιΐα *agathopoiia* (1)
do good (1)

18 ἀγαθοποιός *agathopoios* (1)
who do right (1)

19 ἀγαθός *agathos* (102)
good (89)
kind (2)
right (2)
better (1)
clear (1)
favor (1)
generous (1)
goods (1)
helpful (1)
pleasant (1)
useful (1)
untranslated (1)

20 ἀγαθωσύνη *agathōsynē* (4)
goodness (3)
good (1)

21 ἀγαλλίασις *agalliasis* (5)
joy (2)
delight (1)
glad (1)
great joy (1)

22 ἀγαλλιάω *agalliaō* (11)
rejoices (2)
be glad (1)
enjoy (1)
filled with joy (1)
filled with joy (1) *+5915*
full of joy (1)
glad (1)
greatly rejoice (1)
overjoyed (1) *+5897*
rejoiced (1)

23 ἄγαμος *agamos* (4)
unmarried (4)

24 ἀγανακτέω *aganakteō* (7)
indignant (6)
saying indignantly (1)

25 ἀγανάκτησις *aganaktēsis* (1)
indignation (1)

26 ἀγαπάω *agapaō* (143)
love (74)
loved (40)
loves (22)
love (2) *+27*
truly love (2)
longed for (1)
loving (1)
showed love (1)

27 ἀγάπη *agapē* (116)
love (109)
love (2) *+26*
love (2) *+2400*
it[s] (1) *+3836*
love feasts (1)
loves (1)

28 ἀγαπητός *agapētos* (61)
dear friends (22)
dear (13)
love (11)
dear friend (9)
loved (3)
dearly loved (1)
friends (1)
so dear (1)

29 Ἁγάρ *Hagar* (2)
Hagar (2)

30 ἀγγαρεύω *angareuō* (3)
forced (2)
forces (1)

31 ἀγγεῖον *angeion* (1)
jars (1)

32 ἀγγελία *angelia* (2)
message (2)

33 ἀγγέλλω *angellō* (1)
with the news (1)

34 ἄγγελος *angelos* (176)
angel (86)
angels (81)
messenger (4)
angel's (2)
messengers (2)
spies (1)

35 ἄγγος *angos* (1)
baskets (1)

36 ἀγέλη *agelē* (7)
herd (7)

37 ἀγενεαλόγητος *agenealogētos* (1)
without genealogy (1)

38 ἀγενής *agenēs* (1)
lowly (1)

39 ἁγιάζω *hagiazō* (28)
sanctified (7)
sanctify (4)
made holy (3)
hallowed (2)
make holy (2)
makes sacred (2)
sanctified (2) *+1639*
set apart (2)
consecrated (1)
holy (1)
made holy (1) *+1639*
makes holy (1)

40 ἁγιασμός *hagiasmos* (10)
holiness (4)

holy (2)
sanctifying (2)
be sanctified (1)
holy life (1)

41 ἅγιος *hagios* (234)
holy (161)
saints (45)
God's people (9)
sacred (4)
holy people (3)
sanctuary (3)
believers (1)
consecrated (1) *+2813*
devoted (1)
God's holy people (1)
holy one (1)
holy ones (1)
holy place (1)
most holy place (1) *+41*

42 ἁγιότης *hagiotēs* (1)
holiness (1)

43 ἁγιωσύνη *hagiōsynē* (3)
holiness (2)
holy (1) *+1877*

44 ἀγκάλη *ankalē* (1)
arms (1)

45 ἄγκιστρον *ankistron* (1)
line (1)

46 ἄγκυρα *ankyra* (4)
anchors (3)
anchor (1)

47 ἄγναφος *agnaphos* (2)
unshrunk (2)

48 ἁγνεία *hagneia* (2)
purity (2)

49 ἁγνίζω *hagnizō* (7)
purified (2)
ceremonial cleansing (1)
ceremonially clean (1)
purification rites (1)
purifies (1)
purify (1)

50 ἁγνισμός *hagnismos* (1)
purification (1)

51 ἀγνοέω *agnoeō* (22)
ignorant (5)
not understand (3)
unknown (3)
not know (2)
unaware (2)
don't know (1)
ignorance (1)
ignored (1)
ignores (1)
not realizing (1)
not recognize (1)
uninformed (1)

52 ἀγνόημα *agnoēma* (1)
sins committed in ignorance (1)

53 ἄγνοια *agnoia* (4)
ignorance (4)

54 ἁγνός *hagnos* (8)
pure (6)
innocent (1)
purity (1)

55 ἁγνότης *hagnotēs* (2)
pure (1)
purity (1)

56 ἁγνῶς *hagnōs* (1)
sincerely (1)

57 ἀγνωσία *agnōsia* (2)
are ignorant (1) *+2400*
ignorant (1)

58 ἄγνωστος *agnōstos* (1)
unknown (1)

59 ἀγορά *agora* (11)
marketplaces (6)
marketplace (5)

60 ἀγοράζω *agorazō* (30)
buy (13)
bought (9)
purchased (2)
selling (2)
buying (1)
buys (1)
redeemed (1)
spend (1)

61 ἀγοραῖος *agoraios* (2)
courts are open (1) *+72*
marketplace (1)

62 ἄγρα *agra* (2)
catch (2)

63 ἀγράμματος *agrammatos* (1)
unschooled (1)

64 ἀγραυλέω *agrauleō* (1)
living out (1)

65 ἀγρεύω *agreuō* (1)
catch (1)

66 ἀγριέλαιος *agrielaios* (2)
olive tree that is wild (1)
wild olive shoot (1)

67 ἄγριος *agrios* (3)
wild (3)

68 Ἀγρίππας *Agrippas* (11)
Agrippa (11)

69 ἀγρός *agros* (36)
field (22)
countryside (5)
fields (5)
country (3)
it[s] (1) *+3836*

70 ἀγρυπνέω *agrypneō* (4)
alert (1)
keep watch (1)
on guard (1)
on the watch (1)

71 ἀγρυπνία *agrypnia* (2)
have gone without sleep (1) *+1877*
sleepless nights (1)

72 ἄγω *agō* (69)
brought (25)
bring (10)
led (8)
go (6)
took (3)
bringing (2)
listen (2)
take (2)
brought to trial (1)
courts are open (1) *+61*
for (1)
influenced (1)
leads (1)
leave (1) *+1949*
led away (1)
swayed (1)
taken (1)
took (1) *+4161*
untranslated (1)

73 ἀγωγή *agōgē* (1)
way of life (1)

74 ἀγών *agōn* (6)
fight (2)
opposition (1)
race (1)
struggle (1)
struggling (1)

75 ἀγωνία *agōnia* (1)
anguish (1)

76 ἀγωνίζομαι *agōnizomai* (8)
fight (2)
competes in the games (1)
fought (1)
make every effort (1)
strive (1)
struggling (1)
wrestling (1)

77 Ἀδάμ *Adam* (9)
Adam (9)

78 ἀδάπανος *adapanos* (1)
free of charge (1)

79 Ἀδδί *Addi* (1)
Addi (1)

80 ἀδελφή *adelphē* (25)
sister (15)
sisters (8)
believing wife (1) *+1222*
woman (1)

81 ἀδελφός *adelphos* (342)
brothers (204)
brother (104)
brothers (12) *+467*
brother's (8)
believers (3)
him[s] (2) *+899+3836*
man (2)
own people (2)
another[s] (1)
believing man (1)
fellow (1)
him[s] (1) *+1609+3836*
people (1)

82 ἀδελφότης *adelphotēs* (2)
brotherhood of believers (1)
brothers (1)

83 ἄδηλος *adēlos* (2)
not clear (1)
unmarked (1)

84 ἀδηλότης *adēlotēs* (1)
uncertain (1)

85 ἀδήλως *adēlōs* (1)
aimlessly (1)

86 ἀδημονέω *adēmoneō* (3)
troubled (2)
distressed (1)

87 ᾅδης *hadēs* (10)
Hades (5)
depths (2)
grave (2)
hell (1)

88 ἀδιάκριτος *adiakritos* (1)
impartial (1)

89 ἀδιάλειπτος *adialeiptos* (2)
constantly (1)
unceasing (1)

90 ἀδιαλείπτως *adialeiptōs* (4)
continually (3)
constantly (1)

91 ἀδιαφθορία *adiaphthoria*
Variant; not used

92 ἀδικέω *adikeō* (28)
harm (5)
done wrong (3)
do wrong (2)
does wrong (2)
hurt (2)
wronged (2)
damage (1)

did wrong (1)
do harm (1)
guilty (1)
harm done (1)
inflict injury (1)
injured (1)
mistreated (1)
mistreating (1)
torment (1)
unfair (1)
wrong (1)

93 ἀδίκημα *adikēma* (3)
crime (1)
crimes (1)
misdemeanor (1)

94 ἀδικία *adikia* (25)
wickedness (9)
evil (4)
unjust (2)
unrighteousness (2)
dishonest (1)
evildoers (1) *+2239*
harm (1)
nothing false (1) *+4024*
sin (1)
worldly (1)
wrong (1)
wrongdoing (1)

95 ἀδικοκρίτης *adikokritēs*
Variant; not used

96 ἄδικος *adikos* (13)
unjust (3)
unrighteous (3)
dishonest (2)
wicked (2)
evildoers (1)
ungodly (1)
worldly (1)

97 ἀδίκως *adikōs*
Variant; not used

98 Ἀδμίν *Admin*
Variant; not used

99 ἀδόκιμος *adokimos* (8)
depraved (1)
disqualified (1)
fail the test (1) *+1639*
failed the test (1) *+1639*
rejected (1)
to have failed (1) *+1639*
unfit (1)
worthless (1)

100 ἄδολος *adolos* (1)
pure (1)

101 Ἀδραμυττηνός *Adramyttēnos* (1)
from Adramyttium (1)

102 Ἀδρίας *Adrias* (1)
Adriatic sea (1)

103 ἀδρότης *hadrotēs* (1)
liberal (1)

104 ἀδυνατέω *adynateō* (2)
impossible (2)

105 ἀδύνατος *adynatos* (10)
impossible (7)
crippled (1)
powerless (1)
weak (1)

106 ᾄδω *adō* (5)
sang (3)
sing (2)

107 ἀεί *aei* (7)
always (7)

108 ἀετός *aetos* (5)
eagle (3)
vultures (2)

109 ἄζυμος *azymos* (9)
feast of unleavened Bread (4)
unleavened Bread (2)
bread without yeast (1)
feast of unleavened Bread (1) *+2465*
without yeast (1)

110 Ἀζώρ *Azōr* (2)
Azor (2)

111 Ἄζωτος *Azōtos* (1)
Azotus (1)

112 ἀηδία *aēdia*
Variant; not used

113 ἀήρ *aēr* (7)
air (6)
sky (1)

114 ἀθανασία *athanasia* (3)
immortality (2)
immortal (1)

115 ἀθάνατος *athanatos*
Variant; not used

116 ἀθέμιτος *athemitos* (2)
against law (1)
detestable (1)

117 ἄθεος *atheos* (1)
without God (1)

118 ἄθεσμος *athesmos* (2)
lawless (2)

119 ἀθετέω *atheteō* (16)
rejects (6)
reject (2)
rejected (2)
set aside (2)
broken (1)
frustrate (1)
refuse (1)
setting aside (1)

120 ἀθέτησις *athetēsis* (2)
do away (1)
set aside (1)

121 Ἀθῆναι *Athēnai* (4)
Athens (4)

122 Ἀθηναῖος *Athēnaios* (2)
Athenians (1)
Athens (1)

123 ἀθλέω *athleō* (2)
competes (1)
competes as an athlete (1)

124 ἄθλησις *athlēsis* (1)
contest (1)

125 ἀθροίζω *athroizō* (1)
assembled together (1)

126 ἀθυμέω *athymeō* (1)
become discouraged (1)

127 ἀθῷος *athōos* (2)
innocent (2)

128 αἴγειος *aigeios* (1)
goatskins (1) *+1293*

129 αἰγιαλός *aigialos* (6)
shore (3)
beach (2)
sandy beach (1)

130 Αἰγύπτιος *Aigyptios* (5)
Egyptian (3)
Egyptians (2)

131 Αἴγυπτος *Aigyptos* (25)
Egypt (20)
Egypt (5) *+1178*

132 ἀΐδιος *aidios* (2)
eternal (1)
everlasting (1)

133 αἰδώς *aidōs* (1)
decency (1)

134 Αἰθίοψ *Aithiops* (2)
Ethiopian (1) *+467*
Ethiopians (1)

135 αἷμα *haima* (97)
blood (87)
man (2) *+2779+4922*
subject to bleeding (2) *+1877+4868*
bleeding (1) *+3836+4868*
bleeding (1) *+3836+4380*
blood money (1) *+5507*
blood red (1) *+6055*
natural descent (1)
shedding blood (1)

136 αἱματεκχυσία *haimatekchysia* (1)
shedding of blood (1)

137 αἱμορροέω *haimorroeō* (1)
subject to bleeding (1)

138 Αἰνέας *Aineas* (2)
Aeneas (2)

139 αἴνεσις *ainesis* (1)
praise (1)

140 αἰνέω *aineō* (8)
praising (5)
praise (3)

141 αἴνιγμα *ainigma* (1)
poor (1) *+1877*

142 αἶνος *ainos* (2)
praise (1)
praised (1) *+1443*

143 Αἰνών *Ainōn* (1)
Aenon (1)

144 αἴξ *aix*
Variant; not used

145 αἱρέομαι *haireomai* (3)
chose (2)
choose (1)

146 αἵρεσις *hairesis* (9)
sect (4)
party (2)
differences (1)
factions (1)
heresies (1)

147 αἱρετίζω *hairetizō* (1)
chosen (1)

148 αἱρετικός *hairetikos* (1)
divisive (1)

149 αἴρω *airō* (101)
take (15)
picked up (9)
take away (7)
pick up (6)
taken (6)
get (5)
took (5)
taken away (4)
takes away (4)
took away (4)
carry (3)
take up (3)
takes (3)
away with (2)
go (2)
lift up (2)
pull away (2)
raised (2)
called out in a loud voice (1) *+5889*
carried (1)
cuts off (1)
deprived (1)

get out (1)
get rid of (1)
hoisted aboard (1)
keep in suspense (1) *+3836+6034*
looked (1) *+3836+4057*
put (1)
removed (1)
rid (1)
take out (1)
taken down (1)
taking out (1)
weighed anchor (1)
untranslated (1)

150 αἰσθάνομαι *aisthanomai* (1)
grasp (1)

151 αἴσθησις *aisthēsis* (1)
insight (1)

152 αἰσθητήριον *aisthētērion* (1)
themselves (1)

153 αἰσχροκερδής *aischrokerdēs* (2)
pursuing dishonest gain (2)

154 αἰσχροκερδῶς *aischrokerdōs* (1)
greedy for money (1)

155 αἰσχρολογία *aischrologia* (1)
filthy language (1)

156 αἰσχρός *aischros* (4)
disgrace (1)
disgraceful (1)
dishonest (1)
shameful (1)

157 αἰσχρότης *aischrotēs* (1)
obscenity (1)

158 αἰσχύνη *aischynē* (6)
shame (3)
shameful (2)
humiliated (1) *+3552*

159 αἰσχύνομαι *aischynomai* (5)
ashamed (4)
unashamed (1) *+3590*

160 αἰτέω *aiteō* (70)
ask (23)
asked for (9)
ask for (8)
asked (8)
asks (6)
asks for (4)
asking (3)
asked (1) *+161*
asked favor (1)
beg (1) *+1797+3836*
called for (1)
demand (1)
demanded (1)
pray (1)
request (1)
urgently requested (1) *+4151*

161 αἴτημα *aitēma* (3)
asked (1) *+160*
demand (1)
requests (1)

162 αἰτία *aitia* (20)
basis for a charge (3)
reason (3)
why (3) *+1328+4005*
charge (1)
charge (1) *+5770*
charge against (1)
charges (1)
guilty of crime (1)
proper ground (1)
situation (1)
so (1) *+1328+4005*
that is why (1) *+1328+4005*
therefore (1) *+1328+4005*
untranslated (1)

163 αἰτίαμα *aitiama*
Variant; not used

164 αἰτιάομαι *aitiaomai*
Variant; not used

165 αἴτιος *aitios* (5)
basis (1)
basis for a charge (1)
grounds for the death penalty (1) *+2505*
reason (1)
source (1)

166 αἰτίωμα *aitiōma* (1)
charges (1)

167 αἰφνίδιος *aiphnidios* (2)
suddenly (1)
unexpectedly (1)

168 αἰχμαλωσία *aichmalōsia* (3)
captivity (2)
led captives in his train (1) *+169*

169 αἰχμαλωτεύω *aichmalōteuō* (1)
led captives in his train (1) *+168*

170 αἰχμαλωτίζω *aichmalōtizō* (4)
gain control over (1)
making a prisoner (1)
take captive (1)
taken as prisoners (1)

171 αἰχμάλωτος *aichmalōtos* (1)
prisoners (1)

172 αἰών *aiōn* (122)
ever (44)
forever (23) *+1650+3836*
age (20)
ages (7)
never (4) *+1650+3590+3836+4024*
world (4)
eternal (2)
never (2) *+1650+3836+4024*
universe (2)
again (1) *+1650+3836*
ages past (1)
ever (1) *+1650+3836*
ever (1) *+1666+3836*
forever (1) *+1650*
forever (1) *+1650+2465*
forevermore (1) *+1650+3836+4246*
life (1)
long ago (1)
long ago (1) *+608*
never again (1) *+1650+3590+3836+4024*
time (1)
ways (1)
untranslated (1)

173 αἰώνιος *aiōnios* (71)
eternal (63)
beginning of time (2) *+5989*
everlasting (2)
ages (1)
forever (1)
never (1) *+1650+3590+3836+4024*
untranslated (1)

174 ἀκαθαρσία *akatharsia* (10)
impurity (6)
impure (1)
sexual impurity (1)
to be impure (1) *+2093*
unclean (1)

175 ἀκαθάρτης *akathartēs*
Variant; not used

176 ἀκάθαρτος *akathartos* (31)
evil (23)
unclean (6)
filth (1)
impure (1)

177 ἀκαιρέομαι *akaireomai* (1)
had no opportunity (1)

178 ἀκαίρως *akairōs* (1)
out of season (1)

179 ἄκακος *akakos* (2)
blameless (1)
naive (1)

180 ἄκανθα *akantha* (14)
thorns (9)
thornbushes (2)
which[S] (2) *+3836*
untranslated (1)

181 ἀκάνθινος *akanthinos* (2)
of thorns (2)

182 ἄκαρπος *akarpos* (7)
unfruitful (3)
unproductive (2)
fruitless (1)
without fruit (1)

183 ἀκατάγνωστος *akatagnōstos* (1)
cannot be condemned (1)

184 ἀκατακάλυπτος *akatakalyptos* (2)
uncovered (2)

185 ἀκατάκριτος *akatakritos* (2)
hasn't been found guilty (1)
without a trial (1)

186 ἀκατάλυτος *akatalytos* (1)
indestructible (1)

187 ἀκατάπαστος *akatapastos*
Variant; not used

188 ἀκατάπαυστος *akatapaustos* (1)
never stop (1)

189 ἀκαταστασία *akatastasia* (5)
disorder (3)
revolutions (1)
riots (1)

190 ἀκατάστατος *akatastatos* (2)
restless (1)
unstable (1)

191 ἀκατάσχετος *akataschetos*
Variant; not used

192 Ἀκελδαμάχ *Hakeldamach* (1)
Akeldama (1)

193 ἀκέραιος *akeraios* (3)
innocent (2)
pure (1)

194 ἀκηδεμονέω *akēdemoneō*
Variant; not used

195 ἀκλινής *aklinēs* (1)
unswervingly (1)

196 ἀκμάζω *akmazō* (1)
ripe (1)

197 ἀκμήν *akmēn* (1)
still (1)

198 ἀκοή *akoē* (24)
message (4)
ears (3)
heard (3)
ever hearing (2) *+201*
news (2)
rumors (2)
what heard (2)
ear (1)
hearing (1)
learn (1)
reports (1)
sense of hearing (1)
what ears want to hear (1)

199 ἀκολουθέω *akoloutheō* (90)
followed (41)
follow (32)
following (6)
accompanied (2)

behind (1)
come (1)
follow (1) +3958
followed out (1) +2002
following behind (1)
follows (1)
is one of us (1) +1609+3552
went with (1)
untranslated (1)

200 ἀκουστός *akoustos*
Variant; not used

201 ἀκούω *akouō* (428)
heard (199)
hear (99)
listen (40)
hears (18)
hearing (14)
heard about (10)
listens (9)
listening (8)
listened (5)
heard of (3)
ever hearing (2) +198
understand (2)
accept (1)
aware of (1)
ever hearing (1) +201
hear (1) +1639+4047
hear (1) +4015
heard (1) +1639
hearers (1)
it[S] (1) +608+794+4005
learned (1)
obey (1)
reached (1) +1650
reported (1)
say (1) +1609+1666
told (1)
understands (1)
whispered[S] (1)
untranslated (2)

202 ἀκρασία *akrasia* (2)
lack of self-control (1)
self-indulgence (1)

203 ἀκρατής *akratēs* (1)
without self-control (1)

204 ἄκρατος *akratos* (1)
full strength (1)

205 ἀκρίβεια *akribeia* (1)
thoroughly (1) +2848

206 ἀκριβέστατος *akribestatos*
Variant; not used

207 ἀκριβής *akribēs* (1)
strictest (1)

208 ἀκριβόω *akriboō* (2)
found out exact (1)
learned (1)

209 ἀκριβῶς *akribōs* (9)
accurate (2)
accurately (1)
careful (1)
carefully (1)
more adequately (1)
very careful (1)
very well (1)
well (1)

210 ἀκρίς *akris* (4)
locusts (4)

211 ἀκροατήριον *akroatērion* (1)
audience room (1)

212 ἀκροατής *akroatēs* (4)
hear (1)
heard (1) +1181
listen (1)
listens (1) +1639

213 ἀκροβυστία *akrobystia* (20)
uncircumcised (5)
not circumcised (4)
uncircumcision (4)
before circumcised (1) +1877
gentiles (1)
they (1) +899+3836
uncircumcised (1) +1877
uncircumcised (1) +2400
untranslated (2)

214 ἀκρογωνιαῖος *akrogōniaios* (2)
chief cornerstone (1) +1639
cornerstone (1)

215 ἀκροθίνιον *akrothinion* (1)
plunder (1)

216 ἄκρον *akron* (6)
ends (2)
end (1)
other[S] (1)
tip (1)
top (1)

217 Ἀκύλας *Akylas* (6)
Aquila (6)

218 ἀκυρόω *akyroō* (3)
nullify (2)
set aside (1)

219 ἀκωλύτως *akōlytōs* (1)
without hindrance (1)

220 ἄκων *akōn* (1)
not voluntarily (1)

221 ἅλα *hala*
Variant; not used

222 ἀλάβαστρον *alabastron*
Variant; not used

223 ἀλάβαστρος *alabastros* (4)
alabaster jar (3)
jar (1)

224 ἀλαζονεία *alazoneia* (2)
boasting (1)
brag (1) +1877+3836

225 ἀλαζών *alazōn* (2)
boastful (2)

226 ἀλαλάζω *alalazō* (2)
clanging (1)
wailing (1)

227 ἀλάλητος *alalētos* (1)
words cannot express (1)

228 ἄλαλος *alalos* (3)
mute (2)
robbed him of speech (1)

229 ἅλας *halas* (8)
salt (6)
it[S] (2) +3836

230 ἀλείφω *aleiphō* (9)
poured on (4)
anoint (2)
anointed (1)
put oil on (1)
put on (1)

231 ἀλεκτοροφωνία *alektorophōnia* (1)
when the rooster crows (1)

232 ἀλέκτωρ *alektōr* (11)
rooster (11)

233 Ἀλεξανδρεύς *Alexandreus* (2)
Alexandria (1)
of Alexandria (1)

234 Ἀλεξανδρῖνος *Alexandrinos* (2)
Alexandrian (2)

235 Ἀλέξανδρος *Alexandros* (6)
Alexander (5)
he[S] (1) +3836

236 ἄλευρον *aleuron* (2)
flour (1)
large amount of flour (1) +4929+5552

237 ἀλήθεια *alētheia* (109)
truth (93)
true (5)
assure (1) +2093+3306
certainly (1) +2093
deny truth (1) +2848+6017
how true (1) +2093
right (1) +2093
true (1) +1877
truly (1) +1877
truthful (1)
truthfully (1)
truthfulness (1)
untranslated (1)

238 ἀληθεύω *alētheuō* (2)
speaking truth (1)
telling truth (1)

239 ἀληθής *alēthēs* (26)
true (9)
valid (5)
real (3)
truth (3)
integrity (2)
genuine (1)
really (1)
reliable (1)
truthful (1)

240 ἀληθινός *alēthinos* (28)
true (26)
right (1)
sincere (1)

241 ἀλήθω *alēthō* (2)
grinding (1)
grinding grain (1)

242 ἀληθῶς *alēthōs* (18)
surely (6)
really (3)
the truth (3)
truly (2)
actually (1)
true (1)
with certainty (1)
without a doubt (1)

243 ἁλιεύς *halieus* (5)
fishermen (3)
fishers (2)

244 ἁλιεύω *halieuō* (1)
fish (1)

245 ἁλίζω *halizō* (2)
made salty (1)
salted (1)

246 ἀλίσγημα *alisgēma* (1)
polluted (1)

247 ἀλλά *alla* (638)
but (414)
instead (20)
yet (16)
no (14)
rather (11)
on the contrary (10)
only (7)
and (6)
in fact (5)
indeed (5)
but rather (4)
nevertheless (4)
but only (3)
however (3)
now (3)
if not (2)
so (2)

again (1)
although (1)
and what is more (1) +1145+2779+4047+4246+5250
but (1) +2445
but instead (1)
certainly (1)
even (1)
even though (1)
except (1)
except that (1)
for (1)
if (1)
in addition (1) +2779
indeed (1) +2779
instead (1) +3437
instead of (1)
just (1)
on contrary (1) +1883
on the contrary (1) +3437+4498
surely (1) +1145
then (1)
though (1)
to some extent (1) +608+3538
what (1)
what is more (1) +1254+2779+3667+4024
what is more (1) +3529
yes (1)
untranslated (82)

248 ἀλλάσσω *allassō* (6)
changed (3)
change (2)
exchanged (1)

249 ἀλλαχόθεν *allachothen* (1)
other way (1)

250 ἀλλαχοῦ *allachou* (1)
somewhere else (1)

251 ἀλληγορέω *allēgoreō* (1)
taken figuratively (1)

252 ἀλληλουϊά *hallēlouia* (4)
Hallelujah (4)

253 ἀλλήλων *allēlōn* (100)
one another (46)
each other (32)
themselves (3)
each other's (2)
together (2) +4639
yourselves (2)
all the others (1)
mutual (1)
one another's (1)
one body (1)
others (1)
parted company (1) +608+714
talked the matter over (1) +1368+4639
them (1)
untranslated (5)

254 ἀλλογενής *allogenēs* (1)
foreigner (1)

255 ἀλλοιόω *alloioō*
Variant; not used

256 ἅλλομαι *hallomai* (3)
jumped up (1)
jumping (1)
welling up (1)

257 ἄλλος *allos* (155)
another (42)
other (34)
others (33)
someone else (6)
else (5)
some (5)
more (4)
still another (2)
still others (2)
that one (2)
another (1) +5516
another's (1)
anyone else (1)
anything (1)
gospel[s] (1)
one (1)
one (1) +1651+4024
one another (1) +257+4639
other (1) +1254
other than (1)
others (1) +1254
some (1) +1254
some more (1)
someone (1)
untranslated (5)

258 ἀλλοτριεπίσκοπος *allotriepiskopos* (1)
meddler (1)

259 ἀλλότριος *allotrios* (14)
others (4)
someone else's (3)
stranger (2)
another (1)
foreign (1)
not his own (1)
not their own (1)
stranger's (1)

260 ἀλλόφυλος *allophylos* (1)
gentile (1)

261 ἄλλως *allōs* (1)
not (1)

262 ἀλοάω *aloaō* (3)
treading out the grain (2)
thresher (1)

263 ἄλογος *alogos* (3)
brute (1)
unreasonable (1)
unreasoning (1)

264 ἀλόη *aloē* (1)
aloes (1)

265 ἅλς *hals*
Variant; not used

266 ἁλυκός *halykos* (1)
salt spring (1)

267 ἄλυπος *alypos* (1)
less anxiety (1)

268 ἅλυσις *halysis* (11)
chains (6)
chain (3)
chained hand (1) +1297
chained hand (1) +1313

269 ἀλυσιτελής *alysitelēs* (1)
no advantage (1)

270 ἄλφα *alpha* (3)
Alpha (3)

271 Ἁλφαῖος *Halphaios* (5)
Alphaeus (5)

272 ἅλων *halōn* (2)
threshing floor (2)

273 ἀλώπηξ *alōpēx* (3)
foxes (2)
fox (1)

274 ἅλωσις *halōsis* (1)
caught (1)

275 ἅμα *hama* (10)
together (3)
at the same time (2)
and (1)
besides (1)
early in the morning (1) +4745
one thing more (1)
with (1)

276 ἀμαθής *amathēs* (1)
ignorant (1)

277 ἀμαράντινος *amarantinos* (1)
never fade away (1)

278 ἀμάραντος *amarantos* (1)
fade (1)

279 ἁμαρτάνω *hamartanō* (43)
sin (14)
sinned (12)
sinning (7)
sins (5)
commit a sin (1) +281
doing wrong (1)
done wrong (1)
leave your life of sin (1) +3600
sinful (1)

280 ἁμάρτημα *hamartēma* (4)
sins (3)
sin (1)

281 ἁμαρτία *hamartia* (173)
sins (74)
sin (73)
be guilty of sin (3) +2400
sin (2) +4472
sin offering (2)
sin offerings (2) +4309
sinful (2)
sinning (2)
commit a sin (1) +279
guilt (1)
guilty of sin (1) +2400
promotes sin (1) +1356
sin (1) +2237
sin's (1)
sinned (1) +1639+4472
sins (1) +1639
sins (1) +3836+4472
sins (1) +4472
what is sinful (1)
what sin was (1)
without sin (1) +4024

282 ἀμάρτυρος *amartyros* (1)
without testimony (1)

283 ἁμαρτωλός *hamartōlos* (47)
sinners (29)
sinner (9)
sinful (6)
sinful life (1)
sinner (1) +467
sinner (1) +476

284 Ἀμασίας *Amasias*
Variant; not used

285 ἄμαχος *amachos* (2)
not quarrelsome (1)
peaceable (1)

286 ἀμάω *amaō* (1)
mowed (1)

287 ἀμέθυστος *amethystos* (1)
amethyst (1)

288 ἀμελέω *ameleō* (4)
ignore (1)
neglect (1)
paid no attention (1)
turned away (1)

289 ἄμεμπτος *amemptos* (5)
blameless (2)
blamelessly (1)
faultless (1) +1181
nothing wrong with (1)

290 ἀμέμπτως *amemptōs* (2)
blameless (2)

291 ἀμέριμνος *amerimnos* (2)
free from concern (1)
out of trouble (1)

292 ἀμετάθετος *ametathetos* (2)
unchangeable (1)
unchanging (1)

293 ἀμετακίνητος *ametakinētos* (1)
nothing move (1)

294 ἀμεταμέλητος *ametamelētos* (2)
irrevocable (1)
no regret (1)

295 ἀμετανόητος *ametanoētos* (1)
unrepentant (1)

296 ἄμετρος *ametros* (2)
beyond limits (2) *+1650+3836*

297 ἀμήν *amēn* (123)
the truth (74)
amen (30)
untranslated (18)

298 ἀμήτωρ *amētōr* (1)
mother (1)

299 ἀμίαντος *amiantos* (4)
pure (2)
faultless (1)
spoil (1)

300 Ἀμιναδάβ *Aminadab* (3)
Amminadab (3)

301 ἄμμον *ammon*
Variant; not used

302 ἄμμος *ammos* (5)
sand (4)
shore (1)

303 ἀμνός *amnos* (4)
lamb (4)

304 ἀμοιβή *amoibē* (1)
repaying (1) *+625*

305 ἄμορφος *amorphos*
Variant; not used

306 ἄμπελος *ampelos* (9)
vine (7)
grapes (1)
grapevine (1)

307 ἀμπελουργός *ampelourgos* (1)
took care of the vineyard (1)

308 ἀμπελών *ampelōn* (23)
vineyard (23)

309 Ἀμπλιᾶτος *Ampliatos* (1)
Ampliatus (1)

310 ἀμύνομαι *amynomai* (1)
went to defense (1)

311 ἀμφιβάλλω *amphiballō* (1)
casting a net (1)

312 ἀμφίβληστρον *amphiblēstron* (1)
net (1)

313 ἀμφιέζω *amphiezō* (1)
clothes (1)

314 ἀμφιέννυμι *amphiennymi* (3)
dressed (2)
clothes (1)

315 Ἀμφίπολις *Amphipolis* (1)
Amphipolis (1)

316 ἄμφοδον *amphodon* (1)
street (1)

317 ἀμφότεροι *amphoteroi* (14)
both (11)
all (1)
them all (1) *+3836*
two (1)

318 ἀμώμητος *amōmētos* (1)
blameless (1)

319 ἄμωμον *amōmon* (1)
spice (1)

320 ἄμωμος *amōmos* (8)
blameless (3)
without blemish (2)
without fault (2)
unblemished (1)

321 Ἀμών *Amōn* (2)
Amon (2)

322 Ἀμώς *Amōs* (1)
Amos (1)

323 ἄν *an* (166)
would (39)
whoever (19) *+4005*
if (17)
until (13) *+2401*
anyone (7)
before (4) *+2401*
whom (4) *+4005*
anyone who (3) *+4005*
whatever (2) *+4005*
whatever (2) *+4005+5516*
when (2) *+6055*
wherever (2) *+3963*
whoever (2) *+4015*
all who (1) *+4012*
all whom (1) *+4012*
any (1)
any (1) *+4005+5516*
as (1) *+2776*
as soon as (1) *+6055*
before (1) *+2445+4570*
could (1)
everyone (1) *+4246*
everything (1) *+4012+4246*
except (1) *+1623+3614*
had (1) *+2400*
if any (1) *+4005*
might (1)
once (1) *+608+4005*
pray (1) *+2377*
so that (1) *+3968*
somehow or other (1) *+6055*
survive (1) *+5392*
the one (1) *+4005*
till (1) *+2401*
until (1) *+948+4005*
what (1) *+5516*
what going on (1) *+4047+5515*
whatever (1) *+1650+4005*
whatever (1) *+4012*
whatever (1) *+5516*
when (1)
when (1) *+2471*
when (1) *+4005*
when (1) *+1650+4005*
which (1) *+5515*
whoever (1) *+3836*
untranslated (17)

324 ἀνά *ana* (13)
each (2)
among (1) *+3545*
at (1)
between (1) *+3545*
each (1) *+1651+1667*
each one (1) *+3836*
extra (1) *+1545*
from (1)
into (1) *+3545*
one at a time (1) *+3538*
two by two (1) *+1545+1545*
untranslated (1)

325 ἀναβαθμός *anabathmos* (2)
steps (2)

326 ἀναβαίνω *anabainō* (82)
went up (23)
going up (7)
come up (5)
go up (4)
went (4)
ascend (3)
ascended (3)
came up (3)
climbed (3)
coming (2)
coming up (2)
grew up (2)
ascending (1)
climbed aboard (1)
climbs in (1)
comes up (1)
conceived (1)
decided (1) *+2093+2840+3836*
go (1)
goes up (1)
gone (1)
grows (1)
left (1)
marched (1)
reached (1)
returned (1)
returning (1)
rise (1)
rises (1)
rose (1)
went upstairs (1)
were up (1) *+1639*
untranslated (1)

327 ἀναβάλλω *anaballō* (1)
adjourned the proceedings (1)

328 ἀναβιβάζω *anabibazō* (1)
pulled up (1)

329 ἀναβλέπω *anablepō* (24)
looked up (5)
received sight (5)
receive sight (4)
looking up (3)
see (3)
see again (2)
able to see (1)
restore sight (1)

330 ἀνάβλεψις *anablepsis* (1)
recovery of sight (1)

331 ἀναβοάω *anaboaō* (1)
cried out (1)

332 ἀναβολή *anabolē* (1)
delay (1) *+4472*

333 ἀνάγαιον *anagaion* (2)
upper room (2)

334 ἀναγγέλλω *anangellō* (14)
told (4)
reported (2)
declare (1)
explain (1)
make known (1)
making known (1)
openly confessed (1) *+2018*
preach (1)
proclaim (1)
tell (1)

335 ἀναγεννάω *anagennaō* (2)
born again (1)
given new birth (1)

336 ἀναγινώσκω *anaginōskō* (32)
read (24)
reading (5)
reader (2)
reads (1)

337 ἀναγκάζω *anankazō* (9)
compelled (2)
force (2)
made (2)
compel (1)
drove to it (1)
make (1)

338 ἀναγκαῖος *anankaios* (8)
necessary (2)
close (1)
daily necessities (1) *+5970*
had (1) *+1639*
indispensable (1)
more necessary (1)
necessary for (1)

339 ἀναγκαστῶς *anankastōs* (1)
must (1)

340 ἀνάγκη *anankē* (17)
necessary (3)
compulsion (2)
distress (2)
hardships (2)
must (2)
compelled (1) *+2130*
crisis (1)
forced (1) *+2848*
had (1)
must (1) *+2400*
need (1) *+2400*

341 ἀναγνωρίζω *anagnōrizō* (1)
told (1)

342 ἀνάγνωσις *anagnōsis* (3)
public reading (1)
read (1)
reading (1)

343 ἀνάγω *anagō* (23)
put out to sea (5)
sail (4)
brought (2)
sailed (2)
set sail (2)
bring out (1)
bring up (1)
brought back (1)
led (1)
led up (1)
set out (1)
taken upstairs (1)
took (1)

344 ἀναδείκνυμι *anadeiknymi* (2)
appointed (1)
show (1)

345 ἀνάδειξις *anadeixis* (1)
appeared publicly (1)

346 ἀναδέχομαι *anadechomai* (2)
received (1)
welcomed (1)

347 ἀναδίδωμι *anadidōmi* (1)
delivered (1)

348 ἀναζάω *anazaō* (3)
alive again (2)
sprang to life (1)

349 ἀναζητέω *anazēteō* (3)
look for (2)
looking for (1)

350 ἀναζώννυμι *anazōnnymi* (1)
prepare for action (1) *+3836+4019*

351 ἀναζωπυρέω *anazōpyreō* (1)
fan into flame (1)

352 ἀναθάλλω *anathallō* (1)
renewed (1)

353 ἀνάθεμα *anathema* (6)
cursed (2)
eternally condemned (2)
curse (1)
taken a solemn oath (1) *+354*

354 ἀναθεματίζω *anathematizō* (4)
bound with an oath (1)
call down curses (1)
taken a solemn oath (1) *+353*
taken an oath (1)

355 ἀναθεωρέω *anatheōreō* (2)
consider (1)
looked carefully at (1)

356 ἀνάθημα *anathēma* (1)
gifts dedicated to God (1)

357 ἀναίδεια *anaideia* (1)
boldness (1)

358 ἀναίρεσις *anairesis* (1)
death (1)

359 ἀναιρέω *anaireō* (24)
kill (9)
killed (4)
put to death (4)
executed (2)
get rid of (1)
killing (1)
overthrow (1)
sets aside (1)
took (1)

360 ἀναίτιος *anaitios* (2)
innocent (2)

361 ἀνακαθίζω *anakathizō* (2)
sat up (2)

362 ἀνακαινίζω *anakainizō* (1)
brought back (1)

363 ἀνακαινόω *anakainoō* (2)
renewed (2)

364 ἀνακαίνωσις *anakainōsis* (2)
renewal (1)
renewing (1)

365 ἀνακαλύπτω *anakalyptō* (2)
removed (1)
unveiled (1)

366 ἀνακάμπτω *anakamptō* (4)
return (2)
come back (1)
go back (1)

367 ἀνάκειμαι *anakeimai* (14)
reclining at the table (4)
at the table (2)
guests (2)
at the meal (1) *+3836*
dinner guests (1)
eating (1)
having dinner (1)
reclining (1)
seated (1)

368 ἀνακεφαλαιόω *anakephalaioō* (2)
bring together under one head (1)
summed up (1)

369 ἀνακλίνω *anaklinō* (6)
take places at the feast (2)
have recline at the table (1)
have sit down (1)
placed (1)
sit down (1)

370 ἀνακόπτω *anakoptō*
Variant; not used

371 ἀνακράζω *anakrazō* (5)
cried out (5)

372 ἀνακραυγάζω *anakraugazō*
Variant; not used

373 ἀνακρίνω *anakrinō* (16)
examined (3)
judged (2)
raising questions (2)
called to account (1)
cross-examined (1)
discerned (1)
examining (1)
judge (1)
judges (1)
judgment (1)
makes judgments about (1)
sit in judgment on (1)

374 ἀνάκρισις *anakrisis* (1)
investigation (1)

375 ἀνακυλίω *anakyliō*
Variant; not used

376 ἀνακύπτω *anakyptō* (4)
straightened up (2)
stand up (1)
straighten up (1)

377 ἀναλαμβάνω *analambanō* (13)
taken up (4)
get (1)
lifted up (1)
put on (1)
take aboard (1)
take up (1)
taken (1)
taken back (1)
took (1)
took aboard (1)

378 ἀνάλημψις *analēmpsis* (1)
taken up (1)

379 ἀναλίσκω *analiskō*
Variant; not used

380 ἀνάλλομαι *anallomai*
Variant; not used

381 ἀναλογία *analogia* (1)
proportion (1)

382 ἀναλογίζομαι *analogizomai* (1)
consider (1)

383 ἄναλος *analos* (1)
saltiness (1)

384 ἀναλόω *analoō* (2)
destroy (1)
destroyed (1)

385 ἀνάλυσις *analysis* (1)
departure (1)

386 ἀναλύω *analyō* (2)
depart (1)
to return (1) *+4536*

387 ἀναμάρτητος *anamartētos* (1)
without sin (1)

388 ἀναμένω *anamenō* (1)
wait for (1)

389 ἀναμιμνήσκω *anamimnēskō* (6)
remembered (2)
remember (1)
remembers (1)
remind (1)
remind of (1)

390 ἀνάμνησις *anamnēsis* (4)
remembrance (3)
reminder (1)

391 ἀνανεόομαι *ananeoomai* (1)
made new (1)

392 ἀνανήφω *ananēphō* (1)
come to senses (1)

393 Ἁνανίας *Hananias* (11)
Ananias (11)

394 ἀναντίρρητος *anantirrētos* (1)
undeniable (1)

395 ἀναντιρρήτως *anantirrētōs* (1)
without raising any objection (1)

396 ἀνάξιος *anaxios* (1)
not competent (1)

397 ἀναξίως *anaxiōs* (1)
unworthy manner (1)

398 ἀνάπαυσις *anapausis* (5)
rest (4)
stop (1) *+2400*

399 ἀναπαύω *anapauō* (12)
refreshed (3)
resting (2)
get rest (1)
give rest (1)
refresh (1)
rest (1)
rests (1)
take life easy (1)
wait (1)

400 ἀναπείθω *anapeithō* (1)
persuading (1)

401 ἀνάπειρος *anapeiros* (2)
crippled (2)

402 ἀναπέμπω *anapempō* (5)
sent back (2)
send (1)
sending back (1)
sent (1)

403 ἀναπηδάω *anapēdaō* (1)
jumped to his feet (1)

404 ἀναπίπτω *anapiptō* (12)
sit down (3)
reclined at the table (2)
sat down (2)
leaned back (1)
leaning back (1)
returned to place (1) *+4099*
sit down to eat (1)
take (1) *+1650*

405 ἀναπληρόω *anaplēroō* (6)
finds himself (1)
fulfill (1)
fulfilled (1)
heap up to the limit (1)
make up for (1)
supplied (1)

406 ἀναπολόγητος *anapologētos* (2)
no excuse (1)
without excuse (1)

407 ἀναπράσσω *anaprassō*
Variant; not used

408 ἀναπτύσσω *anaptyssō* (1)
unrolling (1)

409 ἀνάπτω *anaptō* (2)
kindled (1)
set on fire (1)

410 ἀναρίθμητος *anarithmētos* (1)
countless (1)

411 ἀνασείω *anaseiō* (2)
stirred up (1)
stirs up (1)

412 ἀνασκευάζω *anaskeuazō* (1)
troubling (1)

413 ἀνασπάω *anaspaō* (2)
pull out (1)
pulled up (1)

414 ἀνάστασις *anastasis* (42)
resurrection (37)
rise (3)
raised to life again (1)
rising (1)

415 ἀναστατόω *anastatoō* (3)
agitators (1)
caused trouble (1)
revolt (1)

416 ἀνασταυρόω *anastauroō* (1)
crucifying all over again (1)

417 ἀναστενάζω *anastenazō* (1)
sighed deeply (1) *+3836+4460*

418 ἀναστρέφω *anastrephō* (10)
live (3)
conduct (1)
conducted ourselves (1)
lived (1)
overturned (1)
return (1)
treated (1)
went back (1)

419 ἀναστροφή *anastrophē* (13)
way of life (4)
lives (3)
behavior (2)
life (2)
do (1)
live (1)

420 ἀνασῴζω *anasōzō*
Variant; not used

421 ἀνατάσσομαι *anatassomai* (1)
draw up (1)

422 ἀνατέλλω *anatellō* (9)
came up (2)
rises (2)
causes to rise (1)
dawned (1)
descended (1)
just after sunrise (1) *+2463+3836*
rising (1)

423 ἀνατίθημι *anatithēmi* (2)
discussed (1)
set before (1)

424 ἀνατολή *anatolē* (10)
east (7)
east (2) *+2463*
rising sun (1)

425 ἀνατολικός *anatolikos*
Variant; not used

426 ἀνατρέπω *anatrepō* (2)
destroy (1)
ruining (1)

427 ἀνατρέφω *anatrephō* (3)
brought up (2)
cared for (1)

428 ἀναφαίνω *anaphainō* (2)
appear (1)
sighting (1)

429 ἀναφέρω *anapherō* (10)
offer (2)
offered (2)
bore (1)
led (1)
led up (1)
offering (1)
take away (1)
taken up (1)

430 ἀναφωνέω *anaphōneō* (1)
exclaimed (1)

431 ἀνάχυσις *anachysis* (1)
flood (1)

432 ἀναχωρέω *anachōreō* (14)
withdrew (5)
left (3)
returned (2)
drew (1)
go away (1)
gone (1)
withdrew (1) *+1696*

433 ἀνάψυξις *anapsyxis* (1)
refreshing (1)

434 ἀναψύχω *anapsychō* (1)
refreshed (1)

435 ἀνδραποδιστής *andrapodistēs* (1)
slave traders (1)

436 Ἀνδρέας *Andreas* (13)
Andrew (13)

437 ἀνδρίζομαι *andrizomai* (1)
men of courage (1)

438 Ἀνδρόνικος *Andronikos* (1)
Andronicus (1)

439 ἀνδροφόνος *androphonos* (1)
murderers (1)

440 ἀνεγκλησία *anenklēsia*
Variant; not used

441 ἀνέγκλητος *anenklētos* (5)
blameless (3)
free from accusation (1)
nothing against them (1)

442 ἀνεκδιήγητος *anekdiēgētos* (1)
indescribable (1)

443 ἀνεκλάλητος *aneklalētos* (1)
inexpressible (1)

444 ἀνέκλειπτος *anekleiptos* (1)
not be exhausted (1)

445 ἀνεκτός *anektos* (5)
more bearable (5)

446 ἀνελεήμων *aneleēmōn* (1)
ruthless (1)

447 ἀνέλεος *aneleos* (1)
without mercy (1)

448 ἀνεμίζω *anemizō* (1)
blown by the wind (1)

449 ἄνεμος *anemos* (31)
wind (19)
winds (10)
squall (2) *+3278*

450 ἀνένδεκτος *anendektos* (1)
bound to come (1) *+2262+3590*

451 ἀνεξεραύνητος *anexeraunētos* (1)
unsearchable (1)

452 ἀνεξίκακος *anexikakos* (1)
not resentful (1)

453 ἀνεξιχνίαστος *anexichniastos* (2)
beyond tracing out (1)
unsearchable (1)

454 ἀνεπαίσχυντος *anepaischyntos* (1)
does not need to be ashamed (1)

455 ἀνεπίλημπτος *anepilēmptos* (3)
above reproach (1)
blame (1)
no open to blame (1)

456 ἀνέρχομαι *anerchomai* (3)
went up (2)
go up (1)

457 ἄνεσις *anesis* (5)
freedom (1)
peace (1)
relief (1)
relieved (1)
rest (1)

458 ἀνετάζω *anetazō* (2)
question (1)
questioned (1)

459 ἄνευ *aneu* (3)
without (2)
apart from (1)

460 ἀνεύθετος *aneuthetos* (1)
unsuitable (1)

461 ἀνευρίσκω *aneuriskō* (2)
finding (1)

found (1)

462 ἀνέχομαι *anechomai* (15)
put up with (8)
bear with (2)
bearing with (1)
doing that^{s} (1)
endure (1)
enduring (1)
listen (1)

463 ἀνεψιός *anepsios* (1)
cousin (1)

464 ἄνηθον *anēthon* (1)
dill (1)

465 ἀνήκω *anēkō* (3)
fitting (1)
out of place (1) *+4024*
what you ought to do (1) *+3836*

466 ἀνήμερος *anēmeros* (1)
brutal (1)

467 ἀνήρ *anēr* (217)
men (64)
man (63)
husband (37)
brothers (12) *+81*
husbands (12)
husband's (2)
Jew (2) *+2681*
man's (2)
characters (1)
divorced (1) *+608+668*
Ethiopian (1) *+134*
faithful to her husband (1) *+1222+1651*
he^{s} (1) *+3836*
him^{s} (1) *+3836*
Jews (1) *+2681*
marriage (1)
mature (1) *+5455*
murderer (1) *+5838*
owner of (1) *+4005*
prophet (1) *+4737*
sinner (1) *+283*
terrorists (1) *+3836+4974*
you (1)
untranslated (8)

468 ἀνθίστημι *anthistēmi* (14)
opposed (4)
resist (4)
do so^{s} (1)
oppose (1)
rebelling against (1)
resists (1)
stand up against (1)
stand your ground (1)

469 ἀνθομολογέομαι *anthomologeomai* (1)
gave thanks (1)

470 ἄνθος *anthos* (4)
flowers (2)
blossom (1)
flower (1)

471 ἀνθρακιά *anthrakia* (2)
fire (1)
fire of burning coals (1)

472 ἄνθραξ *anthrax* (1)
coals (1)

473 ἀνθρωπάρεσκος *anthrōpareskos* (2)
win favor (2)

474 ἀνθρώπινος *anthrōpinos* (7)
human (3)
among men (1)
common to man (1)
I put this in human terms (1) *+3306*
man (1)

475 ἀνθρωποκτόνος *anthrōpoktonos* (3)
murderer (3)

476 ἄνθρωπος *anthrōpos* (550)
man (277)
men (136)
people (18)
man's (12)
human (9)
everyone (6) *+4246*
men's (5)
him^{s} (4) *+3836*
self (4)
child (3)
fellow (3)
mankind (3)
being (2)
everybody (2) *+4246*
everyone (2)
king (2) *+995*
landowner (2) *+3867*
men (2) *+3836+3836+5626*
others (2)
pay attention who they are (2) *+1063+4725*
person (2)
they^{s} (2) *+3836*
you^{s} (2)
all (1) *+4246*
all the world (1) *+1639+4005+5515*
anyone^{s} (1) *+3836*
cripple (1) *+822*
enemy (1) *+2398*
friend (1)
from everyday life (1) *+2848*
from human point of view (1) *+2848*
he^{s} (1) *+1697+3836*
he^{s} (1) *+3836*
him^{s} (1) *+1877+3836+4047*
human (1) *+2848*
human being (1)
human reasons (1)
husband (1)
Jew (1) *+2681*
judge by external appearance (1) *+3284+4725*
merchant (1) *+1867*
no one (1) *+4029*
one^{s} (1)
outwardly (1) *+2032+3836*
owner of a house (1) *+3867*
Roman citizen (1) *+4871*
Roman citizens (1) *+4871*
self (1) *+2840+3836*
sinner (1) *+283*
someone^{s} (1)
something man made up (1) *+2848*
suppose one (1) *+5515*
them^{s} (1)
them^{s} (1) *+3836*
those^{s} (1)
who^{s} (1) *+3836*
untranslated (15)

477 ἀνθυπατεύω *anthypateuō*
Variant; not used

478 ἀνθύπατος *anthypatos* (5)
proconsul (4)
proconsuls (1)

479 ἀνίημι *aniēmi* (4)
came loose (1)
leave (1)
not (1)
untied (1)

480 ἀνίλεως *anileōs*
Variant; not used

481 ἄνιπτος *aniptos* (2)
unwashed (2)

482 ἀνίστημι *anistēmi* (107)
got up (15)
get up (13)
stood up (13)
rise (9)
raise up (5)
rose (5)
rise again (4)
stand up (3)
appeared (2)
arise (2)
come back to life (2)
appears (1)
became ruler (1)
came forward (1)
come (1)
got ready (1)
have children (1) *+5065*
helped to her feet (1)
left (1)
left (1) *+608*
opposes (1) *+2093*
opposition arose (1)
raised (1)
raised again (1)
raised from the dead (1)
raised to life (1)
raised up (1)
raising (1)
raising up (1)
risen (1)
rises (1)
rising (1)
rose again (1)
send (1)
set out (1)
stand up (1) *+3981*
standing up (1)
started out (1) *+2002*
stood (1)
untranslated (6)

483 Ἄννα *Hanna* (2)
Anna (1)
Annas (1)

484 Ἄννας *Hannas* (3)
Annas (3)

485 ἀνόητος *anoētos* (6)
foolish (5)
how foolish you are (1) *+6043*

486 ἄνοια *anoia* (2)
folly (1)
furious (1) *+4398*

487 ἀνοίγω *anoigō* (77)
opened (38)
open (21)
opening (3)
opens (3)
standing open (2)
began to speak (1) *+3306+3836+5125*
broke open (1)
flew open (1)
lay open (1)
restored (1)
speak (1) *+3836+5125*
spoken freely (1) *+3836+5125*
untranslated (3)

488 ἀνοικοδομέω *anoikodomeō* (2)
rebuild (2)

489 ἄνοιξις *anoixis* (1)
open (1)

490 ἀνομία *anomia* (15)
wickedness (5)
lawlessness (3)
breaks law (1) *+4472*
ever-increasing wickedness (1) *+490+1650+3836*
evil (1)
evildoers (1) *+2237+3836*
lawless acts (1)
transgressions (1)

491 ἄνομος *anomos* (9)
not having the law (3)

lawless (2)
free from law (1)
lawbreakers (1)
transgressors (1)
wicked (1)

492 ἀνόμως *anomōs* (2)
apart from the law (2)

493 ἀνόνητος *anonētos*
Variant; not used

494 ἀνορθόω *anorthoō* (3)
restore (1)
straightened up (1)
strengthen (1)

495 ἀνόσιος *anosios* (2)
unholy (2)

496 ἀνοχή *anochē* (2)
forbearance (1)
tolerance (1)

497 ἀνταγωνίζομαι *antagōnizomai* (1)
struggle (1)

498 ἀντάλλαγμα *antallagma* (2)
in exchange for (2)

499 ἀνταναπληρόω *antanaplēroō* (1)
fill up (1)

500 ἀνταποδίδωμι *antapodidōmi* (7)
repay (4)
in return (1)
pay back (1)
repaid (1)

501 ἀνταπόδομα *antapodoma* (2)
repaid (1)
retribution (1)

502 ἀνταπόδοσις *antapodosis* (1)
reward (1)

503 ἀνταποκρίνομαι *antapokrinomai* (2)
say (1)
talk back (1)

504 ἀντέχω *antechō* (4)
devoted to (2)
help (1)
hold firmly to (1)

505 ἀντί *anti* (22)
for (9)
because (4) *+4005*
instead (2)
with (2)
after (1)
as (1)
for this reason (1) *+4047*
in place (1)
untranslated (1)

506 ἀντιβάλλω *antiballō* (1)
discussing (1)

507 ἀντιδιατίθημι *antidiatithēmi* (1)
oppose (1)

508 ἀντίδικος *antidikos* (5)
adversary (2)
adversary who is taking to court (1)
enemy (1)
he[s] (1) *+3836*

509 ἀντίθεσις *antithesis* (1)
opposing ideas (1)

510 ἀντικαθίστημι *antikathistēmi* (1)
resisted (1)

511 ἀντικαλέω *antikaleō* (1)
invite back (1)

512 ἀντίκειμαι *antikeimai* (8)
oppose (3)
adversaries (1)
contrary (1)
enemy (1)
in conflict (1)
opponents (1)

513 ἄντικρυς *antikrys* (1)
off (1)

514 ἀντιλαμβάνω *antilambanō* (3)
benefit (1)
help (1)
helped (1)

515 ἀντιλέγω *antilegō* (11)
say (2)
contradict (1)
objected (1)
obstinate (1)
oppose (1)
opposes (1)
spoken against (1)
talk back (1)
talked against (1)
talking against (1)

516 ἀντίλημψις *antilēmpsis* (1)
those able to help (1)

517 ἀντιλογία *antilogia* (4)
argument (1)
doubt (1)
opposition (1)
rebellion (1)

518 ἀντιλοιδορέω *antiloidoreō* (1)
retaliate (1)

519 ἀντίλυτρον *antilytron* (1)
ransom (1)

520 ἀντιμετρέω *antimetreō* (1)
measured (1)

521 ἀντιμισθία *antimisthia* (2)
exchange (1)
penalty (1)

522 Ἀντιόχεια *Antiocheia* (18)
Antioch (18)

523 Ἀντιοχεύς *Antiocheus* (1)
from Antioch (1)

524 ἀντιπαρέρχομαι *antiparerchomai* (2)
passed by on the other side (2)

525 Ἀντιπᾶς *Antipas* (1)
Antipas (1)

526 Ἀντιπατρίς *Antipatris* (1)
Antipatris (1)

527 ἀντιπέρα *antipera* (1)
across (1)

528 ἀντιπίπτω *antipiptō* (1)
resist (1)

529 ἀντιστρατεύομαι *antistrateuomai* (1)
waging war against (1)

530 ἀντιτάσσω *antitassō* (5)
opposes (2)
opposed (1)
opposing (1)
rebels against (1)

531 ἀντίτυπος *antitypos* (2)
copy (1)
symbolizes (1)

532 ἀντίχριστος *antichristos* (5)
antichrist (4)
antichrists (1)

533 ἀντλέω *antleō* (4)
draw (1)
draw out (1)
draw water (1)
drawn (1)

534 ἄντλημα *antlēma* (1)
to draw with (1)

535 ἀντοφθαλμέω *antophthalmeō* (1)
head into (1)

536 ἄνυδρος *anydros* (4)
arid (2)
without rain (1)
without water (1)

537 ἀνυπόκριτος *anypokritos* (6)
sincere (6)

538 ἀνυπότακτος *anypotaktos* (4)
disobedient (1)
not subject (1)
rebellious (1)
rebels (1)

539 ἄνω *anō* (9)
above (5)
up (2)
heavenward (1)
the brim (1)

540 ἄνωθεν *anōthen* (13)
from above (3)
top (3)
again (2)
from (2)
all over again (1) *+4099*
for a long time (1)
from the beginning (1)

541 ἀνωτερικός *anōterikos* (1)
interior (1) *+3538*

542 ἀνώτερος *anōteros* (2)
first (1)
up (1)

543 ἀνωφελής *anōphelēs* (2)
unprofitable (1)
useless (1)

544 ἀξίνη *axinē* (2)
ax (2)

545 ἄξιος *axios* (41)
worthy (17)
deserves (5)
deserving (4)
deserve (3) *+1639*
deserve (2)
in keeping with (2)
worth (2)
advisable (1) *+1639*
deserved (1)
deserves (1) *+1639*
rightly so (1) *+1639*
untranslated (2)

546 ἀξιόω *axioō* (7)
consider worthy (1)
count worthy (1)
deserves (1)
found worthy of (1)
think it wise (1)
want (1)
worthy (1)

547 ἀξίως *axiōs* (6)
worthy (3)
in a manner worthy (2)
in a way worthy (1)

548 ἀόρατος *aoratos* (5)
invisible (5)

549 Ἀουλία *Aoulia*
Variant; not used

550 ἀπαγγέλλω *apangellō* (45)
told (13)
reported (12)
tell (6)
report (4)
proclaim (3)
confirm (1)
declare (1)
exclaimed (1)
exclaiming (1)

preached (1)
said (1)
tell about (1)

551 ἀπάγχω *apanchō* (1)
hanged (1)

552 ἀπάγω *apagō* (15)
led away (4)
leads (2)
took (2)
brought (1)
executed (1)
lead away (1)
lead out (1)
led (1)
led astray (1)
take (1)

553 ἀπαίδευτος *apaideutos* (1)
stupid (1)

554 ἀπαίρω *apairō* (3)
taken from (3)

555 ἀπαιτέω *apaiteō* (2)
demand back (1)
demanded from (1)

556 ἀπαλγέω *apalgeō* (1)
lost all sensitivity (1)

557 ἀπαλλάσσω *apallassō* (3)
cured (1)
free (1)
reconciled to (1)

558 ἀπαλλοτριόω *apallotrioō* (3)
alienated from (1)
excluded (1)
separated (1)

559 ἁπαλός *hapalos* (2)
tender (2)

560 ἀπαντάω *apantaō* (2)
meet (1)
met (1)

561 ἀπάντησις *apantēsis* (3)
meet (3)

562 ἅπαξ *hapax* (14)
once (7)
once for all (4)
again (2)
already (1)

563 ἀπαράβατος *aparabatos* (1)
permanent (1)

564 ἀπαρασκεύαστος *aparaskeuastos* (1)
unprepared (1)

565 ἀπαρνέομαι *aparneomai* (10)
disown (7)
deny (3)

566 ἀπαρτί *aparti*
Variant; not used

567 ἀπάρτι *aparti*
Variant; not used

568 ἀπαρτισμός *apartismos* (1)
complete (1)

569 ἀπαρχή *aparchē* (8)
firstfruits (6)
first (1)
first convert (1)

570 ἅπας *hapas* (34)
all (18)
everything (7)
whole (3)
everyone (2)
everybody (1)
none (1) *+4024*
unlimited (1)
untranslated (1)

571 ἀπασπάζομαι *apaspazomai* (1)
saying good-by to (1)

572 ἀπατάω *apataō* (3)
deceive (1)
deceived (1)
deceives (1)

573 ἀπάτη *apatē* (7)
deceitfulness (3)
deceitful (1)
deceives (1)
deceptive (1)
pleasures (1)

574 ἀπάτωρ *apatōr* (1)
without father (1)

575 ἀπαύγασμα *apaugasma* (1)
radiance (1)

576 ἀπαφρίζω *apaphrizō*
Variant; not used

577 ἀπείθεια *apeitheia* (6)
disobedience (4)
disobedient (2)

578 ἀπειθέω *apeitheō* (14)
disobedient (4)
disobeyed (2)
refused to believe (2)
disobey (1)
do not believe (1)
not obey (1)
reject (1)
rejects (1)
unbelievers (1)

579 ἀπειθής *apeithēs* (6)
disobedient (5)
disobey (1)

580 ἀπειλέω *apeileō* (2)
made threats (1)
warn (1)

581 ἀπειλή *apeilē* (3)
threats (2)
threaten (1)

582 ἄπειμι1 *apeimi1* (7)
absent (3)
absent from (1)
away (1)
in absence (1)
not present (1)

583 ἄπειμι2 *apeimi2* (1)
went (1)

584 ἀπεῖπον *apeipon* (1)
renounced (1)

585 ἀπείραστος *apeirastos* (1)
cannot tempted (1)

586 ἄπειρος *apeiros* (1)
not acquainted with (1)

587 ἀπεκδέχομαι *apekdechomai* (8)
eagerly await (1)
eagerly await for (1)
eagerly wait for (1)
wait for (1)
wait eagerly for (1)
waited (1)
waiting for (1)
waits (1)

588 ἀπεκδύομαι *apekdyomai* (2)
disarmed (1)
taken off (1)

589 ἀπέκδυσις *apekdysis* (1)
putting off (1)

590 ἀπελαύνω *apelaunō* (1)
had ejected from (1)

591 ἀπελεγμός *apelegmos* (1)
lose good name (1) *+1650+2262*

592 ἀπελεύθερος *apeleutheros* (1)
freedman (1)

593 Ἀπελλῆς *Apellēs* (1)
Apelles (1)

594 ἀπελπίζω *apelpizō* (1)
expecting to get back (1)

595 ἀπέναντι *apenanti* (5)
before (1)
defying (1) *+4556*
in front of (1)
opposite (1)
you can see (1) *+5148*

596 ἀπέραντος *aperantos* (1)
endless (1)

597 ἀπερισπάστως *aperispastōs* (1)
undivided (1)

598 ἀπερίτμητος *aperitmētos* (1)
uncircumcised (1)

599 ἀπέρχομαι *aperchomai* (118)
went (25)
go (21)
went away (18)
left (6)
went off (5)
went back (4)
go away (3)
gone (3)
leave (3)
crossed (2)
passed away (2)
returned (2)
went out (2)
came (1)
cross (1)
drew (1)
followed (1) *+3958*
go on (1)
go over (1)
go running off after (1) *+1503+3593*
goes away (1)
going away (1)
gone away (1)
gone from (1)
hurried away from (1) *+5444*
left from (1)
on their way (1)
passed (1)
past (1)
perversion (1) *+2283+3958+4922*
spread (1)
turned back (1) *+1650+3836+3958*
went up (1)
withdraw (1)
withdrew (1)

600 ἀπέχω *apechō* (19)
abstain from (4)
received in full (3)
are from (2)
avoid (2)
was from (2)
about from (1)
enough (1)
have back (1)
received (1)
received payment (1)
was (1)

601 ἀπιστέω *apisteō* (8)
not believe (6)
faithless (1)
not have faith (1)

602 ἀπιστία *apistia* (11)
unbelief (6)
lack of faith (4)
unbelieving (1)

603 ἄπιστος *apistos* (23)
unbelievers (7)
unbelieving (6)
unbeliever (5)
not a believer (2)
doubting (1) *+1181*
incredible (1)
not believe (1)

604 ἁπλόος *haploos* (2)
good (2)

605 ἁπλότης *haplotēs* (8)
generosity (2)
sincerity (2)
generous (1)
generously (1) *+1877*
holiness (1)
sincere devotion (1)

606 ἁπλοῦς *haplous*
Variant; not used

607 ἁπλῶς *haplōs* (1)
generously (1)

608 ἀπό *apo* (647)
from (335)
of (36)
by (23)
on (12)
in (11)
since (11)
for (10)
against (9)
at (7)
with (7)
away (4)
because of (4)
far off (3) *+3427*
because (2)
ever since (2) *+4005*
in part (2) *+3538*
out of (2)
since (2) *+4005*
some (2)
after (1)
again (1) *+785*
again (1) *+3814+3836*
ago (1) *+4005*
alike (1) *+1651*
as (1)
at the hands of (1)
before (1)
before (1) *+4725*
belonged to (1)
beyond (1)
both (1)
cut off from (1)
deserting (1) *+3572*
divorced (1) *+467+668*
down from (1)
elude (1) *+5771*
far away (1) *+3427*
for a distance of (1)
from among (1)
from the time (1) *+4005*
given (1) *+2400*
in the future (1) *+785*
it's (1) *+201+794+4005*
leaving (1) *+4513*
left (1)
left (1) *+482*
long ago (1) *+172*
now (1) *+785*
now (1) *+3814+3836*
now (1) *+4005*
on some points (1) *+3538*
once (1) *+323+4005*
out (1)
part (1)
parted company (1) *+253+714*
some of (1)
some time ago (1) *+792+2465*
sound asleep (1) *+2965+3836+5678*
that had touched (1) *+3836+5999*
to (1)
to some extent (1) *+247+3538*
unmarried (1) *+1222+3395*
who belonged to (1)
with ever-increasing glory (1) *+1518+1518+1650*
untranslated (118)

609 ἀποβαίνω *apobainō* (4)
happened (1)
landed (1) *+1178+1650+3836*
left (1)
result (1)

610 ἀποβάλλω *apoballō* (2)
throw away (1)
throwing aside (1)

611 ἀποβλέπω *apoblepō* (1)
looking ahead (1)

612 ἀπόβλητος *apoblētos* (1)
rejected (1)

613 ἀποβολή *apobolē* (2)
lost (1)
rejection (1)

614 ἀπογίνομαι *apoginomai* (1)
die (1)

615 ἀπογραφή *apographē* (2)
census (2)

616 ἀπογράφω *apographō* (4)
register (2)
census be taken of (1)
written (1)

617 ἀποδείκνυμι *apodeiknymi* (4)
accredited (1)
proclaiming (1)
prove (1)
put on display (1)

618 ἀπόδειξις *apodeixis* (1)
demonstration (1)

619 ἀποδεκατεύω *apodekateuō*
Variant; not used

620 ἀποδεκατόω *apodekatoo* (4)
give a tenth of (2)
collect a tenth from (1) *+2400*
give God a tenth of (1)

621 ἀπόδεκτος *apodektos* (2)
pleases (1)
pleasing (1)

622 ἀποδέχομαι *apodechomai* (7)
welcomed (3)
accepted (1)
acknowledge (1)
received (1)
welcome (1)

623 ἀποδημέω *apodēmeō* (6)
went away on a journey (2)
going on a journey (1)
set off (1)
went away (1)
went on journey (1)

624 ἀπόδημος *apodēmos* (1)
going away (1)

625 ἀποδίδωμι *apodidōmi* (48)
give (9)
pay back (6)
reward (4)
pay (3)
repay (3)
gave back (2)
given (2)
paid (2)
sold (2)
account (1) *+3364*
award (1)
fulfill (1)
give account for (1)
give back (1)
give share of (1)
got (1)
keep (1)
pays back (1)
produces (1)
reimburse (1)
repay the debt (1)
repaying (1) *+304*
to testify to (1) *+3457*
yielding (1)

626 ἀποδιορίζω *apodiorizō* (1)
divide (1)

627 ἀποδοκιμάζω *apodokimazō* (9)
rejected (9)

628 ἀποδοχή *apodochē* (2)
acceptance (2)

629 ἀπόθεσις *apothesis* (2)
put aside (1) *+1639*
removal from (1)

630 ἀποθήκη *apothēkē* (6)
barn (4)
barns (2)

631 ἀποθησαυρίζω *apothēsaurizō* (1)
lay up treasure (1)

632 ἀποθλίβω *apothlibō* (1)
pressing (1)

633 ἀποθνῄσκω *apothnēskō* (112)
died (49)
die (33)
dies (11)
dead (9)
dying (5)
death (2)
put to death (1) *+1877+5840*
who die (1)
untranslated (1)

634 ἀποκαθιστάνω *apokathistanō*
Variant; not used

635 ἀποκαθίστημι *apokathistēmi* (8)
completely restored (3)
restored (2)
restore (2)
restores (1)

636 ἀποκαλύπτω *apokalyptō* (26)
revealed (19)
reveal (3)
disclosed (2)
a revelation comes (1)
make clear (1)

637 ἀποκάλυψις *apokalypsis* (18)
revelation (9)
revealed (7)
revelations (2)

638 ἀποκαραδοκία *apokaradokia* (2)
eager expectation for (1)
eagerly expect (1)

639 ἀποκαταλλάσσω *apokatallassō* (3)
reconcile (2)
reconciled (1)

640 ἀποκατάστασις *apokatastasis* (1)
restore (1)

641 ἀπόκειμαι *apokeimai* (4)
destined (1)
in store (1)
laid away (1)
stored up (1)

642 ἀποκεφαλίζω *apokephalizō* (4)
beheaded (4)

643 ἀποκλείω *apokleiō* (1)
closes (1)

644 ἀποκόπτω *apokoptō* (6)
cut off (3)
cut (1)
cutting off (1)
emasculate (1)

645 ἀπόκριμα *apokrima* (1)
sentence (1)

646 ἀποκρίνομαι *apokrinomai* (231)
answered (80)
replied (59)
asked (17)
said (11)
answer (9)
gave answer (4)
declared (3)
spoke up (3)
going to answer (2)
made reply (2)
reply (2)
say (2)
answers (1)
demanded (1)
given answer (1)
in reply (1)
insisted (1)
replied (1) *+3306+4022*
replied (1) *+5774*
responded (1)
retorted (1)
say in reply (1)
spoke (1)
tell (1)
told (1)
untranslated (24)

647 ἀπόκρισις *apokrisis* (4)
answer (3)
answers (1)

648 ἀποκρύπτω *apokryptō* (4)
hidden (2)
hidden from (1)
kept hidden for (1)

649 ἀπόκρυφος *apokryphos* (3)
concealed (2)
hidden (1)

650 ἀποκτείνω *apokteinō* (74)
kill (34)
killed (26)
put to death (4)
kills (2)
take life (2)
die (1)
died (1)
execute (1)
killing (1)
strike dead (1)
untranslated (1)

651 ἀποκτέννω *apoktennō*
Variant; not used

652 ἀποκυέω *apokyeō* (2)
give birth (1)
gives birth to (1)

653 ἀποκυλίω *apokyliō* (4)
rolled away (2)
roll away (1)
rolled back (1)

654 ἀπολαλέω *apolaleō*
Variant; not used

655 ἀπολαμβάνω *apolambanō* (10)
receive (2)
received (2)
getting (1)
has back (1)
receive from (1)
repaid (1)
rewarded (1) *+3635*
took away from (1)

656 ἀπόλαυσις *apolausis* (2)
enjoyment (1)
pleasures (1)

657 ἀπολείπω *apoleipō* (7)
left (4)
remains (2)
abandoned (1)

658 ἀπολείχω *apoleichō*
Variant; not used

659 ἀπολιμπάνω *apolimpanō*
Variant; not used

660 ἀπόλλυμι *apollymi* (90)
lose (14)
lost (12)
destroyed (9)
perish (9)
destroy (8)
kill (7)
loses (7)
killed (4)
perishing (4)
drown (3)
ruined (3)
die (2)
bring to end (1)
executed (1)
kill (1) *+3836*
perishes (1)
spoils (1)
starving to death (1) *+3350*
vanished (1)
wasted (1)

661 Ἀπολλύων *Apollyōn* (1)
Apollyon (1)

662 Ἀπολλωνία *Apollōnia* (1)
Apollonia (1)

663 Ἀπολλῶς *Apollōs* (10)
Apollos (10)

664 ἀπολογέομαι *apologeomai* (10)
defend yourselves (2)
defense (2)
make defense (2)
defending (1)
defending ourselves (1)
made defense (1)
make a defense (1) *+2527*

665 ἀπολογία *apologia* (8)
defense (4)
answer (1)
defend (1)
defending (1)
eagerness clear (1)

666 ἀπολούω *apolouō* (2)
wash away (1)
washed (1)

667 ἀπολύτρωσις *apolytrōsis* (10)
redemption (8)
ransom (1)
released (1)

668 ἀπολύω *apolyō* (66)
release (15)
send away (7)
divorces (6)
let go (6)
dismissed (5)
released (5)
divorce (4)
sent away (4)
sent off (3)
set free (3)
dismiss (1)
divorced (1)
divorced (1) *+467+608*
forgive (1)
forgiven (1)
free (1)
leave (1)
send (1)

669 ἀπομάσσω *apomassō* (1)
wipe off against (1)

670 ἀπομένω *apomenō*
Variant; not used

671 ἀπονέμω *aponemō* (1)
treat (1)

672 ἀπονίπτω *aponiptō* (1)
washed (1)

673 ἀποπέμπω *apopempō*
Variant; not used

674 ἀποπίπτω *apopiptō* (1)
fell (1)

675 ἀποπλανάω *apoplanaō* (2)
deceive (1)
wandered from (1)

676 ἀποπλέω *apopleō* (4)
sailed (2)
sail (1)
set sail (1)

677 ἀποπλύνω *apoplynō*
Variant; not used

678 ἀποπνίγω *apopnigō* (2)
choked (1)
drowned (1)

679 ἀπορέω *aporeō* (6)
at a loss (2)
perplexed (2)
puzzled (1)
wondering (1)

680 ἀπορία *aporia* (1)
perplexity (1)

681 ἀπορίπτω *aporiptō* (1)
jump overboard (1)

682 ἀπορφανίζω *aporphanizō* (1)
torn away from (1)

683 ἀποσκευάζω *aposkeuazō*
Variant; not used

684 ἀποσκίασμα *aposkiasma* (1)
shifting (1)

685 ἀποσπάω *apospaō* (4)
draw away (1)
drew out (1)
torn away (1)
withdrew (1)

686 ἀποστασία *apostasia* (2)
rebellion (1)
to turn away from (1)

687 ἀποστάσιον *apostasion* (3)
divorce (2)
certificate of divorce (1)

688 ἀποστάτης *apostatēs*
Variant; not used

689 ἀποστεγάζω *apostegazō* (1)
made an opening in (1)

690 ἀποστέλλω *apostellō* (132)
sent (93)
send (15)
sending (5)
sent out (4)
send back (2)
send out (2)
sending out (2)
gave orders (1)
given orders (1)

ordered (1)
puts (1)
release (1) *+912+1877*
sent away (1)
sent for (1) *+3559*
sent message (1)
sent word (1)

691 ἀποστερέω *apostereō* (6)
cheat (1)
cheated (1)
defraud (1)
deprive (1)
failed to pay (1)
robbed (1)

692 ἀποστολή *apostolē* (4)
apostleship (2)
apostolic (1)
ministry of an apostle (1)

693 ἀπόστολος *apostolos* (80)
apostles (51)
apostle (19)
apostles' (5)
messenger (2)
super-apostles (2) *+5663*
representatives (1)

694 ἀποστοματίζω *apostomatizō* (1)
besiege with questions (1) *+4309+4498*

695 ἀποστρέφω *apostrephō* (9)
turn away from (4)
deserted (1)
put back (1)
turning from (1)
who inciting to rebellion (1)
who reject (1)

696 ἀποστυγέω *apostygeō* (1)
hate (1)

697 ἀποσυνάγωγος *aposynagōgos* (3)
put out of the synagogue (2)
put out of the synagogue (1) *+4472*

698 ἀποτάσσω *apotassō* (6)
left (2)
give up (1)
leaving (1)
said good-by (1)
say good-by (1)

699 ἀποτελέω *apoteleō* (2)
full-grown (1)
heal people (1) *+2617*

700 ἀποτίθημι *apotithēmi* (9)
put off (2)
rid of (2)
get rid of (1)
laid (1)
put (1)
put aside (1)
throw off (1)

701 ἀποτινάσσω *apotinassō* (2)
shake off (1)
shook off (1)

702 ἀποτίνω *apotinō* (1)
pay back (1)

703 ἀποτολμάω *apotolmaō* (1)
boldly (1)

704 ἀποτομία *apotomia* (2)
sternness (2)

705 ἀποτόμως *apotomōs* (2)
harsh (1)
sharply (1)

706 ἀποτρέπω *apotrepō* (1)
have nothing to do with (1)

707 ἀπουσία *apousia* (1)
absence (1)

708 ἀποφέρω *apopherō* (6)
carried away (2)
carried (1)
led away (1)
taken (1)
untranslated (1)

709 ἀποφεύγω *apopheugō* (3)
escape (1)
escaped (1)
escaping from (1)

710 ἀποφθέγγομαι *apophthengomai* (3)
addressed (1)
saying (1)
untranslated (1)

711 ἀποφορτίζομαι *apophortizomai* (1)
unload (1)

712 ἀπόχρησις *apochrēsis* (1)
use (1)

713 ἀποχωρέω *apochōreō* (3)
away from (1)
leaves (1)
left (1)

714 ἀποχωρίζω *apochōrizō* (2)
parted company (1) *+253+608*
receded (1)

715 ἀποψύχω *apopsychō* (1)
faint (1)

716 Ἄππιος *Appios* (1)
Appius (1)

717 ἀπρόσιτος *aprositos* (1)
unapproachable (1)

718 ἀπρόσκοπος *aproskopos* (3)
blameless (1)
clear (1)
not cause to stumble (1)

719 ἀπροσωπολήμπτως *aprosōpolēmptōs* (1)
impartially (1)

720 ἄπταιστος *aptaistos* (1)
falling (1)

721 ἅπτω *haptō* (39)
touched (20)
touch (10)
lights (2)
built (1)
handle (1)
harm (1)
hold on to (1)
light (1)
marry (1) *+1222*
touching (1)

722 Ἀπφία *Apphia* (1)
Apphia (1)

723 ἀπωθέω *apōtheō* (6)
reject (3)
rejected (2)
pushed aside (1)

724 ἀπώλεια *apōleia* (18)
destruction (10)
doomed to destruction (2)
destroyed (1)
destroyed (1) *+1650*
destructive (1)
perish (1) *+1639+1650*
waste (1)
waste (1) *+1181*

725 ἀρά *ara* (1)
cursing (1)

726 ἄρα *ara* (49)
then (12)
so (8)
therefore (5) *+4036*
consequently (2) *+4036*
therefore (2)
as to (1)
consequently (1)
if in fact (1) *+1642*
in that case (1)
in that case (1) *+2075*
otherwise (1) *+2075*
perhaps (1) *+1145+1623*
perhaps (1) *+1623*
so then (1)
then (1) *+1145*
thus (1) *+1145*
untranslated (9)

727 ἆρα *ara* (3)
does that mean that (1)
untranslated (2)

728 Ἀραβία *Arabia* (2)
Arabia (2)

729 Ἄραβοι *Araboi*
Variant; not used

730 Ἀράμ *Aram* (3)
ram (3)

731 ἄραφος *araphos* (1)
seamless (1)

732 Ἄραψ *Araps* (1)
Arabs (1)

733 ἀργέω *argeō* (1)
untranslated (1)

734 ἀργός *argos* (8)
doing nothing (2)
careless (1)
idle (1)
idlers (1)
ineffective (1)
lazy (1)
useless (1)

735 ἀργύρεος *argyreos* (3)
silver (3)

736 ἀργύριον *argyrion* (20)
money (12)
silver (3)
silver coins (3)
coins (1)
drachmas (1)

737 ἀργυροκόπος *argyrokopos* (1)
silversmith (1)

738 ἄργυρος *argyros* (5)
silver (5)

739 ἀργυροῦς *argyrous*
Variant; not used

740 Ἄρειος πάγος *Areios pagos* (2)
meeting of the Areopagus (2)

741 Ἀρεοπαγίτης *Areopagitēs* (1)
member of the Areopagus (1)

742 ἀρεσκεία *areskeia* (1)
please (1)

743 ἀρέσκω *areskō* (17)
please (10)
pleased (3)
trying to please (2)
displease (1) *+3590*
try to please (1)

744 ἀρεστός *arestos* (4)
pleases (2)
pleased (1) *+1639*
right (1)

745 Ἀρέτας *Haretas* (1)
Aretas (1)

746 ἀρετή *aretē* (5)
goodness (3)
excellent (1)

praises (1)

747 Ἀρηί *Arēi*
Variant; not used

748 ἀρήν *arēn* (1)
lambs (1)

749 ἀριθμέω *arithmeō* (3)
numbered (2)
count (1)

750 ἀριθμός *arithmos* (18)
number (12)
in number (1) *+3836+4005*
numbering (1) *+1639*
numbers (1)
untranslated (3)

751 Ἁριμαθαία *Harimathaia* (4)
Arimathea (4)

752 Ἀρίσταρχος *Aristarchos* (5)
Aristarchus (5)

753 ἀριστάω *aristaō* (3)
breakfast (1)
eat (1)
eating (1)

754 ἀριστερός *aristeros* (4)
left (3)
left hand (1)

755 Ἀριστόβουλος *Aristoboulos* (1)
Aristobulus (1)

756 ἄριστον *ariston* (4)
dinner (1)
feast (1)
luncheon (1)
meal (1)

757 ἀρκετός *arketos* (3)
enough (3)

758 ἀρκέω *arkeō* (8)
content (3)
enough (3)
satisfied (1)
sufficient (1)

759 ἄρκος *arkos* (1)
bear (1)

760 ἄρκτος *arktos*
Variant; not used

761 ἅρμα *harma* (4)
chariot (3)
chariots (1)

762 Ἁρμαγεδών *Harmagedōn* (1)
Armageddon (1)

763 Ἀρμίν *Armin*
Variant; not used

764 ἁρμόζω *harmozō* (1)
promised (1)

765 ἁρμός *harmos* (1)
joints (1)

766 ἀρνέομαι *arneomai* (34)
denied (10)
disown (5)
deny (4)
denies (3)
disowned (3)
denying (2)
disowns (2)
fail (1)
refused (1)
rejected (1)
renounce (1)
say no to (1)

767 Ἀρνί *Arni*
Variant; not used

768 ἀρνίον *arnion* (30)
lamb (28)
lamb's (1)
lambs (1)

769 ἀροτριάω *arotriaō* (3)
plowing (1)
plowman (1)
plows (1)

770 ἄροτρον *arotron* (1)
plow (1)

771 ἁρπαγή *harpagē* (3)
greed (2)
confiscation (1)

772 ἁρπαγμός *harpagmos* (1)
something to be grasped (1)

773 ἁρπάζω *harpazō* (14)
caught up (3)
snatch (3)
attacks (1)
carry off (1)
force (1)
lay hold of (1)
snatched up (1)
snatches away (1)
suddenly took away (1)
take by force (1)

774 ἅρπαξ *harpax* (5)
swindlers (2)
ferocious (1)
robbers (1)
swindler (1)

775 ἀρραβών *arrabōn* (3)
deposit guaranteeing (2)
deposit (1)

776 ἄρρην *arrēn*
Variant; not used

777 ἄρρητος *arrētos* (1)
inexpressible (1)

778 ἀρρωστέω *arrōsteō*
Variant; not used

779 ἄρρωστος *arrōstos* (5)
sick (5)

780 ἀρσενοκοίτης *arsenokoitēs* (2)
homosexual offenders (1)
perverts (1)

781 ἄρσην *arsēn* (9)
male (6)
men (3)

782 Ἀρτεμᾶς *Artemas* (1)
Artemas (1)

783 Ἄρτεμις *Artemis* (5)
Artemis (5)

784 ἀρτέμων *artemōn* (1)
foresail (1)

785 ἄρτι *arti* (36)
now (20)
now on (3)
still (3) *+2401*
again (1) *+608*
at last (1)
at once (1)
in the future (1) *+608*
just (1)
just now (1)
now (1) *+608*
this moment (1)
this very (1)
this very day (1)

786 ἀρτιγέννητος *artigennētos* (1)
newborn (1)

787 ἄρτιος *artios* (1)
thoroughly (1)

788 ἄρτος *artos* (95)
bread (63)
loaves (18)
food (4)
loaf (3)
loaves of bread (3)
consecrated bread (1) *+4606*
untranslated (3)

789 ἀρτύω *artyō* (3)
made salty (1)
make salty (1)
seasoned (1)

790 Ἀρφαξάδ *Arphaxad* (1)
Arphaxad (1)

791 ἀρχάγγελος *archangelos* (2)
archangel (2)

792 ἀρχαῖος *archaios* (11)
ancient (3)
long ago (2)
people long ago (2)
earliest (1)
early (1)
old (1)
some time ago (1) *+608+2465*

793 Ἀρχέλαος *Archelaos* (1)
Archelaus (1)

794 ἀρχή *archē* (56)
beginning (31)
first (5)
rulers (5)
corners (2)
power (2)
all along (1) *+3836*
demons (1)
dominion (1)
early (1)
elementary (1)
elementary truths (1) *+3836+5122*
it^{s} (1) *+201+608+4005*
positions of authority (1)
powers (1)
rule (1)
ruler (1)

795 ἀρχηγός *archēgos* (4)
author (3)
prince (1)

796 ἀρχιερατικός *archieratikos* (1)
high priest's (1)

797 ἀρχιερεύς *archiereus* (122)
chief priests (64)
high priest (51)
high priest's (3)
high priests (2)
chief priest (1)
high priesthood (1)

798 ἀρχιληστής *archilēstēs*
Variant; not used

799 ἀρχιποίμην *archipoimēn* (1)
chief shepherd (1)

800 Ἄρχιππος *Archippos* (2)
Archippus (2)

801 ἀρχισυνάγωγος *archisynagōgos* (9)
synagogue ruler (7)
synagogue rulers (2)

802 ἀρχιτέκτων *architektōn* (1)
builder (1)

803 ἀρχιτελώνης *architelōnēs* (1)
chief tax collector (1)

804 ἀρχιτρίκλινος *architriklinos* (3)
master of the banquet (2)
he^{s} (1) *+3836*

805 ἀρχοστασία *archostasia*
Variant; not used

806 ἄρχω *archō* (86)
began (52)
beginning (7)
begin (3)
begins (2)
became (1)
first (1)
late in afternoon (1) *+2465+3111*
rule over (1)
rulers (1)
started (1)
went on (1)
untranslated (15)

807 ἄρχων *archōn* (37)
rulers (12)
ruler (9)
prince (7)
leaders (3)
authorities (2)
magistrate (1)
prominent (1)
ruler's (1)
ruling (1)

808 ἄρωμα *arōma* (4)
spices (4)

809 Ἀσά *Asa* (2)
Asa (2)

810 ἀσάλευτος *asaleutos* (2)
cannot be shaken (1)
would not move (1) *+3531*

811 Ἀσάφ *Asaph*
Variant; not used

812 ἄσβεστος *asbestos* (3)
unquenchable (2)
never goes out (1)

813 ἀσέβεια *asebeia* (6)
ungodly (3)
godlessness (2)
ungodliness (1)

814 ἀσεβέω *asebeō* (1)
done in ungodly way (1)

815 ἀσεβής *asebēs* (10)
ungodly (8)
godless (1)
wicked (1)

816 ἀσέλγεια *aselgeia* (10)
debauchery (4)
filthy (1)
lewdness (1)
license for immorality (1)
lustful desires (1) *+2123*
sensuality (1)
shameful (1)

817 ἄσημος *asēmos* (1)
ordinary (1)

818 Ἀσήρ *Asēr* (2)
Asher (2)

819 ἀσθένεια *astheneia* (24)
weakness (8)
weaknesses (4)
weak (2)
crippled (1) *+2400*
diseases (1)
illness (1) *+3836+4922*
illnesses (1)
infirmities (1)
infirmity (1)
invalid (1)
sick (1) *+2400*
sickness (1)
sicknesses (1)

820 ἀσθενέω *astheneō* (34)
sick (12)
weak (11)
ill (2)
lay sick (2)
disabled (1)
feel weak (1)
invalid (1)
powerless (1)
sickness (1) *+3798*
weakened (1)
weakening (1)

821 ἀσθένημα *asthenēma* (1)
failings (1)

822 ἀσθενής *asthenēs* (25)
weak (14)
sick (6)
weaker (2)
cripple (1) *+476*
unimpressive (1)
weakness (1)

823 Ἀσία *Asia* (18)
province of Asia (15)
Asia (3)

824 Ἀσιανός *Asianos* (1)
from the province of Asia (1)

825 Ἀσιάρχης *Asiarchēs* (1)
officials of the province (1)

826 ἀσιτία *asitia* (1)
without food (1)

827 ἄσιτος *asitos* (1)
without food (1)

828 ἀσκέω *askeō* (1)
strive (1)

829 ἀσκός *askos* (12)
wineskins (9)
skins (3)

830 ἀσμένως *asmenōs* (1)
warmly (1)

831 ἄσοφος *asophos* (1)
unwise (1)

832 ἀσπάζομαι *aspazomai* (59)
greet (30)
send greetings (11)
sends greetings (6)
greeted (4)
call out to (1)
give greeting (1)
give greetings to (1)
greets (1)
pay respects to (1)
said good-by (1)
sends greetings to (1)
welcomed (1)

833 ἀσπασμός *aspasmos* (10)
greeting (6)
greeted (3)
greetings (1)

834 ἄσπιλος *aspilos* (4)
defect (1)
from being polluted (1)
spotless (1)
without spot (1)

835 ἀσπίς *aspis* (1)
vipers (1)

836 ἄσπονδος *aspondos* (1)
unforgiving (1)

837 ἀσσάριον *assarion* (2)
pennies (1)
penny (1)

838 Ἀσσάρων *Assarōn*
Variant; not used

839 ἆσσον *asson* (1)
along the shore (1)

840 Ἆσσος *Assos* (2)
Assos (2)

841 ἀστατέω *astateō* (1)
homeless (1)

842 ἀστεῖος *asteios* (2)
no ordinary (2)

843 ἀστήρ *astēr* (27)
stars (16)
star (11)

844 ἀστήρικτος *astēriktos* (2)
unstable (1)
unstable (1) *+6034*

845 ἄστοργος *astorgos* (2)
heartless (1)
without love (1)

846 ἀστοχέω *astocheō* (3)
turned (1)
wandered (1)
wandered away (1)

847 ἀστραπή *astrapē* (9)
flashes of lightning (4)
lightning (4)
light (1)

848 ἀστράπτω *astraptō* (2)
that gleamed like lightning (1)
which flashes (1)

849 ἄστρον *astron* (1)
star (1)

850 Ἀσύγκριτος *Asynkritos* (1)
Asyncritus (1)

851 ἀσύμφωνος *asymphōnos* (1)
disagreed (1) *+1639*

852 ἀσύνετος *asynetos* (5)
dull (2)
foolish (1)
no understanding (1)
senseless (1)

853 ἀσύνθετος *asynthetos* (1)
faithless (1)

854 ἀσφάλεια *asphaleia* (3)
certainty (1)
safety (1)
securely (1) *+1877+4246*

855 ἀσφαλής *asphalēs* (5)
definite (1)
exactly (1)
firm (1)
get at truth (1) *+1182*
safeguard (1)

856 ἀσφαλίζω *asphalizō* (4)
made secure (2)
fastened (1)
make secure (1)

857 ἀσφαλῶς *asphalōs* (3)
assured (1) *+1182*
carefully (1)
under guard (1)

858 ἀσχημονέω *aschēmoneō* (2)
acting improperly (1)
rude (1)

859 ἀσχημοσύνη *aschēmosynē* (2)
indecent acts (1)
shamefully (1)

860 ἀσχήμων *aschēmōn* (1)
unpresentable (1)

861 ἀσωτία *asōtia* (3)
debauchery (1)
dissipation (1)
wild (1)

862 ἀσώτως *asōtōs* (1)
wild (1)

863 ἀτακτέω *atakteō* (1)
idle (1)

864 ἄτακτος *ataktos* (1)
idle (1)

865 ἀτάκτως *ataktōs* (2)
idle (1)
idle (1) *+4344*

866 ἄτεκνος *ateknos* (2)
childless (1)
no children (1)

867 ἀτενίζω *atenizō* (14)
looked straight (2)
fastened (1)
gazing (1)
look steadily (1)
looked (1)
looked (1) *+2917*
looked closely at (1)
looked directly at (1)
looked intently (1)
looked straight at (1)
looking intently (1)
stare at (1)
stared at (1)

868 ἄτερ *ater* (2)
when no was present (1)
without (1)

869 ἀτιμάζω *atimazō* (6)
dishonor (2)
degrading of (1)
insulted (1)
suffering disgrace (1)
treated shamefully (1)

870 ἀτιμάω *atimaō* (1)
treated shamefully (1)

871 ἀτιμία *atimia* (7)
dishonor (2)
common (1)
disgrace (1)
ignoble (1)
shameful (1)
to my shame (1) *+2848*

872 ἄτιμος *atimos* (4)
without honor (2)
dishonored (1)
less honorable (1)

873 ἀτιμόω *atimoō*
Variant; not used

874 ἀτμίς *atmis* (2)
billows (1)
mist (1)

875 ἄτομος *atomos* (1)
flash (1)

876 ἄτοπος *atopos* (4)
wrong (2)
unusual (1)
wicked (1)

877 Ἀττάλεια *Attaleia* (1)
Attalia (1)

878 αὐγάζω *augazō* (1)
see (1)

879 αὐγή *augē* (1)
daylight (1)

880 Αὔγουστος *Augoustos* (1)
Augustus (1)

881 αὐθάδης *authadēs* (2)
arrogant (1)
overbearing (1)

882 αὐθαίρετος *authairetos* (2)
entirely on their own (1)
on own initiative (1)

883 αὐθεντέω *authenteō* (1)
have authority over (1)

884 αὐλέω *auleō* (3)
played the flute (2)
played (1)

885 αὐλή *aulē* (12)
courtyard (6)
palace (2)
court (1)
house (1)
pen (1)
sheep pen (1)

886 αὐλητής *aulētēs* (2)
flute players (2)

887 αὐλίζομαι *aulizomai* (2)
spend the night (1)
spent the night (1)

888 αὐλός *aulos* (1)
flute (1)

889 αὐξάνω *auxanō* (23)
grew (4)
grow (4)
grow up (2)
growing (2)
grows (2)
become greater (1)
enlarge (1)
greatly increased (1) *+2779+4437*
increase (1)
made grow (1)
makes grow (1)
rises (1)
spread (1)
spread widely (1)

890 αὔξησις *auxēsis* (2)
grow (1)
grows (1) *+4472*

891 αὔξω *auxō*
Variant; not used

892 αὔριον *aurion* (14)
tomorrow (8)
next day (3)
tomorrow (3) *+3836*

893 αὐστηρός *austēros* (2)
hard (2)

894 αὐτάρκεια *autarkeia* (2)
contentment (1)
need (1)

895 αὐτάρκης *autarkēs* (1)
content (1)

896 αὐτοκατάκριτος *autokatakritos* (1)
self-condemned (1)

897 αὐτόματος *automatos* (2)
all by itself (1)
by itself (1)

898 αὐτόπτης *autoptēs* (1)
eyewitnesses (1)

899 αὐτός *autos* (5593)
him (1382)
his (899)
them (807)
their (275)
he (219)
her (198)
it (185)
Jesus[S] (141)
they (124)
its (49)
himself (37)
same (37)
Paul[S] (19)
the people[S] (17)
Jesus's[S] (15)
the man[S] (15)
she (14)
his own (12)
God's[S] (11)
the man's[S] (10)
Christ[S] (9)
these (9)
yourselves (9)
myself (8)
that (8)
those (8)
you (8)
his disciples[S] (7)
themselves (7)
John[S] (6)
the city[S] (5)
the disciples[S] (5)
the Jews[S] (5)
whose (5)
God[S] (4)
itself (4)
ourselves (4)
the apostles[S] (4)
the beast[S] (4)
the boy[S] (4)
their own (4)
very (4)
which (4)
whom (4)
Abraham[S] (3)
he himself (3)
I (3)
Jesus and his disciples[S] (3)
John's[S] (3)
Moses[S] (3)
others (3)
own (3)
Peter and John[S] (3)
Peter[S] (3)
Saul[S] (3)
Stephen[S] (3)
that (3) *+3836*
the crowd[S] (3)
the plants[S] (3)
theirs (3)
them (3) *+4639*
them[S] (3) *+3412+3836*
there (3) *+1877*
this (3)
together (3) *+2093+3836*
we (3)
who (3)
here (2)
herself (2)
him[S] (2) *+81+3836*
his master[S] (2)
home (2) *+1650+3875*
home (2) *+3836+3875*
Joseph[S] (2)
Lazarus[S] (2)
love[S] (2)
named (2) *+3950*
Paul and Barnabas[S] (2)
Paul and Silas[S] (2)
Peter's[S] (2)
that is how (2) *+2848+3836*
that very (2)
the body[S] (2)
the child[S] (2)
the children[S] (2)
the Lord[S] (2)
the men[S] (2)
the servant[S] (2)
the vineyard[S] (2)
the women[S] (2)
the young man[S] (2)
there (2)
they themselves (2)
to himself (2) *+1877+2840+3836*
your (2)
yourself (2)

a fig tree[S] (1)
a man's[S] (1)
agree (1) *+3306+3836*
alive (1) *+1877*
along (1) *+5250*
Ananias[S] (1)
Apollos[S] (1)
as I did (1) *+4047*
as usual (1) *+2848+3836*
at once (1) *+3836+6052*
at their hands (1) *+5679*
Barnabas and Saul[S] (1)
before their very eyes (1) *+1063*
being like-minded (1) *+3836+5858*
believers[S] (1) *+1666*
both of you (1) *+2779+5148*
boy's[S] (1)
by himself (1) *+3668*
child's[S] (1)
Christ's[S] (1)
come together (1) *+1639+2093+3836*
comes together (1) *+2093+3836+5302*
death[S] (1)
Elizabeth[S] (1)
Elymas[S] (1)
equal (1) *+3836*
faith[S] (1)
Festus[S] (1)
for the express purpose (1) *+1650+4047*
for this very reason (1) *+4047*
governing[S] (1) *+4047*
had[S] (1)
he (1) *+1328+3836+5931*
he (1) *+5679*
he and his disciples (1)
he's (1)
he's (1) *+1639+6034*
he[S] (1) *+899+1877+3836+4460*
here (1) *+1877*
him (1) *+4639*
him (1) *+5679*
himself (1) *+2840*
himself[S] (1) *+3836+3950*
his fellow (1) *+3836+5250*
his own (1)
his parents[S] (1)
home (1) *+1650+3836+3875*
I (1) *+1609*
I myself (1)
immediately (1) *+1877+3836+6052*
in his sight (1) *+1967*
in one place (1) *+2093+3836*
in same way (1)
Isaac[S] (1)
Israel[S] (1)
its (1) *+1877*
its own (1)
its[S] (1) *+3836+4725*
Jairus[S] (1)
James[S] (1)
Jesus (1) *+2652*
Jesus' body[S] (1)
Jews'[S] (1)
John's (1) *+2722*
just as though (1) *+1651+2779+3836*
just like this (1) *+2848+3836*
Levi's[S] (1)
Levi[S] (1)
lies[S] (1)
live in harmony (1) *+3836+5858*
Lydda[S] (1)
Mary[S] (1)
men's[S] (1)
men[S] (1)
money[S] (1)
nearby (1) *+3836*
of the scrolls[S] (1)
of them (1) *+5201*
one (1) *+3836*
one another (1)
Paul's[S] (1)
perfectly united (1) *+2936+3836*
Pilate[S] (1)
pointing (1) *+1753+3836+5931*
put on board (1) *+1650+1837*
rider (1) *+2093+2764*
riders (1) *+2093+2764*
same things (1)
same way (1)
Saul's[S] (1)
serpent's (1) *+4058*
she (1) *+5679*
Simeon[S] (1)
spirit of unity (1) *+3836+5858*
such (1)
such beings (1)
surrounding (1) *+4309*
than they (1)
that country[S] (1)
that God[S] (1)
that one sheep[S] (1)
that rest[S] (1)
that same (1)
the ark[S] (1)
the beggar[S] (1)
the blessing[S] (1)
the commander's[S] (1)
the commander[S] (1)
the commandment[S] (1)
the council[S] (1)
the cross[S] (1)
the firstborn[S] (1)
the flock[S] (1)
the gentiles[S] (1)
the gospel[S] (1)
the island[S] (1)
the Israelites[S] (1)
the kings[S] (1)
the land[S] (1)
the messengers[S] (1)
the money[S] (1)
the net[S] (1)
the officers[S] (1)
the one[S] (1)
the other[S] (1)
the others (1)
the perfume[S] (1)
the pigs[S] (1)
the prophets[S] (1)
the same (1)
the servants[S] (1)
the slave girl[S] (1)
the son[S] (1)
the spirit[S] (1)
the star[S] (1)
the sun[S] (1)
the tongue[S] (1)
the tree[S] (1)
the two of you (1) *+2779+5148*
the two[S] (1)
the very one (1)
the very thing (1) *+4047*
the widow[S] (1)
the wine[S] (1)
their (1) *+3836*
their homes[S] (1)
their own number (1)
them out (1)
them[S] (1) *+3836+4546*
them[S] (1) *+3836+5284*
themselves (1) *+2840+3836*
themselves (1) *+3836+6034*
these men[S] (1)
they (1) *+213+3836*
they (1) *+1328*
they (1) *+3836+4057*
they (1) *+4123*
they (1) *+4639*
they (1) *+5679*
they[S] (1) *+899+2779+3412+3836*
they[S] (1) *+1204+3836*
they[S] (1) *+3412+3836*
they[S] (1) *+3836+6001*
this is why (1) *+1328*
this man[S] (1)
this perfume[S] (1)
this[S] (1) *+3836+4246*
Timothy[S] (1)
to their number (1) *+2093+3836*
told him (1) *+1181+4639*
Trembling (1) *+2400+5571*
two Israelites[S] (1)
what we are writing[S] (1) *+3836*
who are there (1) *+1877*
who belonged to their sect (1)
whole (1)
whose (1) *+4005*
widow (1) *+1222*
with a great crash (1) *+1639+3489+3836+4774*
with them (1) *+1328+5931*
you yourself (1)
you yourselves (1)
your slaves[S] (1)
Zechariah's[S] (1)
untranslated (675)

900 αὐτόφωρος *autophōros* (1)
caught in the act (1) *+2093+2898*

901 αὐτόχειρ *autocheir* (1)
with own hands (1)

902 αὐχέω *aucheō* (1)
makes boasts (1)

903 αὐχμηρός *auchmēros* (1)
dark (1)

904 ἀφαιρέω *aphaireō* (10)
cutting off (3)
take away (2)
take away from (1)
taken away (1)
taken away from (1)
takes away from (1)
taking away (1)

905 ἀφανής *aphanēs* (1)
hidden from (1)

906 ἀφανίζω *aphanizō* (5)
destroy (2)
disfigure (1)
perish (1)
vanishes (1)

907 ἀφανισμός *aphanismos* (1)
disappear (1)

908 ἄφαντος *aphantos* (1)
disappeared (1) *+1181*

909 ἀφεδρών *aphedrōn* (2)
untranslated (2)

910 ἀφειδία *apheidia* (1)
harsh treatment (1)

911 ἀφελότης *aphelotēs* (1)
sincere (1)

912 ἄφεσις *aphesis* (17)
forgiveness (13)
forgiven (1)
forgiven (1) *+2400*
freedom (1)
release (1) *+690+1877*

913 ἁφή *haphē* (2)
ligament (1)
ligaments (1)

914 ἀφθαρσία *aphtharsia* (7)
imperishable (3)
immortality (2)
imperishable (1) *+1877*
undying (1)

915 ἄφθαρτος *aphthartos* (7)
immortal (2)

imperishable (2)
can never perish (1)
last forever (1)
unfading (1)

916 ἀφθονία *aphthonia*
Variant; not used

917 ἀφθορία *aphthoria* (1)
integrity (1)

918 ἀφίημι *aphiēmi* (145)
left (37)
forgive (22)
forgiven (22)
let (19)
leave (8)
leave alone (5)
leaving (4)
deserted (3)
divorce (3)
canceled (2)
let go (2)
abandoned (1)
abandons (1)
allow (1)
consented (1)
forgives (1)
forsaken (1)
gave up (1)
have neglected (1)
leaves (1)
leaving behind (1)
let be (1)
let go of (1)
let go on (1)
neglecting (1)
refuse (1) *+4024*
tolerate (1)
untranslated (2)

919 ἀφικνέομαι *aphikneomai* (1)
heard about (1)

920 ἀφιλάγαθος *aphilagathos* (1)
not lovers of good (1)

921 ἀφιλάργυρος *aphilargyros* (2)
free from the love of money (1)
not a lover of money (1)

922 ἄφιξις *aphixis* (1)
leave (1)

923 ἀφίστημι *aphistēmi* (12)
left (3)
abandon (1)
away from (1)
fall away (1)
leave alone (1)
led in revolt (1)
take away from (1)
turn away from (1)
turns away from (1)
withdrew (1)

924 ἄφνω *aphnō* (3)
suddenly (3)

925 ἀφόβως *aphobōs* (4)
fearlessly (1)
nothing to fear (1)
without fear (1)
without the slightest qualm (1)

926 ἀφομοιόω *aphomoioō* (1)
like (1)

927 ἀφοράω *aphoraō* (2)
fix eyes (1)
see (1)

928 ἀφορίζω *aphorizō* (10)
separate (4)
set apart (3)
exclude (1)
separates (1)
took (1)

929 ἀφορμή *aphormē* (7)
opportunity (5)
ground (1)
indulge (1)

930 ἀφρίζω *aphrizō* (2)
foaming at the mouth (1)
foams at the mouth (1)

931 ἀφρός *aphros* (1)
foams at the mouth (1)

932 ἀφροσύνη *aphrosynē* (4)
as a fool (1) *+1877*
folly (1)
fool (1)
foolishness (1)

933 ἄφρων *aphrōn* (11)
fool (5)
foolish (5)
fools (1)

934 ἀφυπνόω *aphypnoō* (1)
fell asleep (1)

935 ἀφυστερέω *aphystereō*
Variant; not used

936 ἄφωνος *aphōnos* (4)
mute (1)
silent (1)
without meaning (1)
without speech (1)

937 Ἀχάζ *Achaz* (2)
Ahaz (2)

938 Ἀχαΐα *Achaia* (10)
Achaia (10)

939 Ἀχαϊκός *Achaikos* (1)
Achaicus (1)

940 ἀχάριστος *acharistos* (2)
ungrateful (2)

941 Ἀχάς *Achas*
Variant; not used

942 ἀχειροποίητος *acheiropoiētos* (3)
not built by human hands (1)
not done by the hands of men (1)
not made by man (1)

943 Ἀχίμ *Achim* (2)
Akim (2)

944 ἀχλύς *achlys* (1)
mist (1)

945 ἀχρεῖος *achreios* (2)
unworthy (1)
worthless (1)

946 ἀχρειόω *achreioō* (1)
become worthless (1)

947 ἄχρηστος *achrēstos* (1)
useless (1)

948 ἄχρι *achri* (48)
until (16)
to (10)
until (5) *+4005*
as far as (2)
up to (2)
as high as (1)
as long as (1) *+4005*
before (1)
even to (1)
even to the point of (1)
for (1)
just before (1) *+4005*
later (1)
right up to (1)
so much as (1)
then (1) *+4005*
to where (1)
until (1) *+323+4005*

949 ἄχυρον *achyron* (2)
chaff (2)

950 ἀψευδής *apseudēs* (1)
not lie (1)

951 ἀψίνθιον *apsinthion*
Variant; not used

952 ἄψινθος *apsinthos* (2)
bitter (1)
wormwood (1)

953 ἄψυχος *apsychos* (1)
lifeless (1)

954 β *b*
Variant; not used

955 Βάαλ *Baal* (1)
Baal (1)

956 Βαβυλών *Babylōn* (12)
Babylon (11)
untranslated (1)

957 βαθμός *bathmos* (1)
standing (1)

958 βάθος *bathos* (8)
deep (3)
depth (2)
extreme (1) *+2848*
shallow (1) *+2400+3590*
shallow (1) *+3590*

959 βαθύνω *bathynō* (1)
down deep (1)

960 βαθύς *bathys* (4)
deep (3)
very early in the morning (1) *+3986*

961 βάϊον *baion* (1)
branches (1)

962 Βαλαάμ *Balaam* (3)
Balaam (2)
Balaam's (1)

963 Βαλάκ *Balak* (1)
Balak (1)

964 βαλλάντιον *ballantion* (4)
purse (3)
purses (1)

965 βάλλω *ballō* (122)
thrown (26)
put (18)
throw (16)
threw (6)
hurled (4)
bring (3)
cast (3)
casting (3)
lying (3)
hurled down (2)
pour (2)
poured (2)
pours (2)
putting (2)
spewed (2)
swung (2)
toss (2)
did[s] (1)
drives (1)
drop (1)
entice (1) *+1967+4998*
fertilize (1) *+3162*
flinging (1)
flung (1)
gave (1)
gave (1) *+1650*
help (1)
impose (1)
jumped (1) *+1571*
laid (1)
lay (1)

let down (1)
lies (1)
planted (1)
prompted (1) *+1650+2840+3836*
scatters (1)
stone (1) *+2093*
swept (1)
thrown down (1)
untranslated (2)

966 βαπτίζω *baptizō* (77)
baptized (47)
baptize (12)
baptizing (8)
Baptist (2)
wash (2)
baptism (1)
baptism receive (1)
baptism undergo (1) *+967*
baptized (1) *+967*
baptized (1) *+3836*
baptized (1) *+5639*

967 βάπτισμα *baptisma* (20)
baptism (17)
baptism undergo (1) *+966*
baptized (1) *+966*
baptizing (1)

968 βαπτισμός *baptismos* (3)
baptisms (1)
ceremonial washings (1)
washing (1)

969 βαπτιστής *baptistēs* (12)
Baptist (12)

970 βάπτω *baptō* (4)
dipped (2)
dip (1)
dipping (1)

971 βαρ *bar*
Variant; not used

972 Βαραββᾶς *Barabbas* (11)
Barabbas (11)

973 Βαράκ *Barak* (1)
Barak (1)

974 Βαραχίας *Barachias* (1)
Berekiah (1)

975 βάρβαρος *barbaros* (6)
foreigner (2)
islanders (2)
barbarian (1)
non-Greeks (1)

976 βαρέω *bareō* (6)
burdened (2)
heavy (1)
under pressure (1)
very sleepy (1) *+5678*
weighed down (1)

977 βαρέως *bareōs* (2)
hardly (2)

978 Βαρθολομαῖος *Bartholomaios* (4)
Bartholomew (4)

979 Βαριησοῦς *Bariēsous* (1)
Bar-Jesus (1)

980 Βαριωνᾶ *Bariōna* (1)
son of Jonah (1)

981 Βαριωνᾶς *Bariōnas*
Variant; not used

982 Βαρναβᾶς *Barnabas* (28)
Barnabas (28)

983 βάρος *baros* (6)
burden (3)
burdens (1)
that far outweighs them all (1)
+1650+2848+5651+5651
to burden (1) *+2202*

984 Βαρσαββᾶς *Barsabbas* (2)
Barsabbas (2)

985 Βαρτιμαῖος *Bartimaios* (1)
Bartimaeus (1)

986 βαρύνω *barynō*
Variant; not used

987 βαρύς *barys* (6)
burdensome (1)
heavy (1)
important matters (1)
savage (1)
serious (1)
weighty (1)

988 βαρύτιμος *barytimos* (1)
very expensive (1)

989 βασανίζω *basanizō* (12)
tormented (4)
torture (4)
buffeted (1)
pain (1)
straining (1)
suffering (1)

990 βασανισμός *basanismos* (6)
torment (3)
agony (1)
sting (1)
torture (1)

991 βασανιστής *basanistēs* (1)
jailers to be tortured (1)

992 βάσανος *basanos* (3)
torment (2)
severe pain (1)

993 βασιλεία *basileia* (162)
kingdom (154)
kingdoms (3)
it[s] (1) *+1847+3836+3836*
king (1)
made king (1) *+3284+3836*
rule (1)
rules (1) *+2400*

994 βασίλειος *basileios* (2)
palaces (1)
royal (1)

995 βασιλεύς *basileus* (115)
king (82)
kings (27)
king (2) *+476*
king's (2)
he[s] (1) *+3836*
kings' (1)

996 βασιλεύω *basileuō* (21)
reign (10)
reigned (4)
kings (3)
king (2)
reigning (1)
reigns (1)

997 βασιλικός *basilikos* (5)
royal (2)
royal official (2)
king's (1)

998 βασιλίσκος *basiliskos*
Variant; not used

999 βασίλισσα *basilissa* (4)
queen (4)

1000 βάσις *basis* (1)
feet (1)

1001 βασκαίνω *baskainō* (1)
bewitched (1)

1002 βαστάζω *bastazō* (27)
carry (5)
carrying (4)
bear (3)
carried (3)
bear with (1)
borne (1)
carried away (1)
endured hardships (1)
gave birth (1)
help himself to (1)
pay (1)
picked up (1)
rides (1)
support (1)
take (1)
tolerate (1)

1003 βάτος1 *batos1* (5)
bush (4)
briers (1)

1004 βάτος2 *batos2* (1)
eight hundred gallons (1) *+1669*

1005 βάτραχος *batrachos* (1)
frogs (1)

1006 βατταλογέω *battalogeō* (1)
babbling (1)

1007 βδέλυγμα *bdelygma* (6)
abomination (2)
abominable (1)
abominations (1)
detestable (1)
what is shameful (1)

1008 βδελυκτός *bdelyktos* (1)
detestable (1)

1009 βδελύσσομαι *bdelyssomai* (2)
abhor (1)
vile (1)

1010 βέβαιος *bebaios* (8)
binding (1)
certain (1)
firm (1)
firmly (1)
guaranteed (1)
in force (1)
secure (1)
sure (1)

1011 βεβαιόω *bebaioō* (8)
confirmed (3)
strengthened (2)
confirm (1)
keep strong (1)
makes stand firm (1)

1012 βεβαίωσις *bebaiōsis* (2)
confirming (1)
confirms (1) *+1650*

1013 βέβηλος *bebēlos* (5)
godless (4)
irreligious (1)

1014 βεβηλόω *bebēloō* (2)
desecrate (2)

1015 Βεελζεβούλ *Beelzeboul* (7)
Beelzebub (7)

1016 Βελιάρ *Beliar* (1)
Belial (1)

1017 βελόνη *belonē* (1)
needle (1)

1018 βέλος *belos* (1)
arrows (1)

1019 βελτίων *beltiōn* (1)
very well (1)

1020 Βενιαμείν *Beniamein*
Variant; not used

1021 Βενιαμίν *Beniamin* (4)
Benjamin (4)

1022 Βερνίκη *Bernikē* (3)
Bernice (3)

1023 Βέροια *Beroia* (2)
Berea (2)

1024 Βεροιαῖος *Beroiaios* (1)
from Berea (1)

1025 Βέρος *Beros*
Variant; not used

1026 Βεωορσόρ *Beōorsor*
Variant; not used

1027 Βεώρ *Beōr* (1)
Beor (1)

1028 Βηθαβαρά *Bēthabara*
Variant; not used

1029 Βηθανία *Bēthania* (12)
Bethany (12)

1030 Βηθαραβά *Bētharaba*
Variant; not used

1031 Βηθεσδά *Bēthesda* (1)
Bethesda (1)

1032 Βηθζαθά *Bēthzatha*
Variant; not used

1033 Βηθλέεμ *Bēthleem* (8)
Bethlehem (8)

1034 Βηθσαϊδά *Bēthsaida* (7)
Bethsaida (7)

1035 Βηθσαϊδάν *Bēthsaidan*
Variant; not used

1036 Βηθφαγή *Bēthphagē* (3)
Bethphage (3)

1037 βῆμα *bēma* (12)
court (4)
judge's seat (2)
judgment seat (2)
convened the court (1) *+2093+2767+3836*
court (1) *+2093*
foot of ground (1) *+4546*
throne (1)

1038 Βηρεύς *Bēreus*
Variant; not used

1039 βήρυλλος *bēryllos* (1)
beryl (1)

1040 βία *bia* (3)
pounding (1)
use force (1) *+3552*
violence (1)

1041 βιάζω *biazō* (2)
forcefully advancing (1)
forcing way (1)

1042 βίαιος *biaios* (1)
violent (1)

1043 βιαστής *biastēs* (1)
forceful (1)

1044 βιβλαρίδιον *biblaridion* (3)
little scroll (3)

1045 βιβλιδάριον *biblidarion*
Variant; not used

1046 βιβλίον *biblion* (34)
book (13)
scroll (13)
books (3)
certificate (2)
it[s] (2) *+3836*
scrolls (1)

1047 βίβλος *biblos* (10)
book (8)
record (1)
scrolls (1)

1048 βιβρώσκω *bibrōskō* (1)
eaten (1)

1049 Βιθυνία *Bithynia* (2)
Bithynia (2)

1050 βίος *bios* (10)
property (2)
to live on (2)
civilian affairs (1) *+4548*
life (1)
life's (1)
lives (1)
possessions (1)
what he has and does (1)

1051 βιόω *bioō* (1)
live (1)

1052 βίωσις *biōsis* (1)
way lived (1)

1053 βιωτικός *biōtikos* (3)
life (1)
of this life (1)
such matters[s] (1)

1054 βλαβερός *blaberos* (1)
harmful (1)

1055 βλάπτω *blaptō* (2)
hurt (1)
injuring (1)

1056 βλαστάνω *blastanō* (4)
budded (1)
produced (1)
sprouted (1)
sprouts (1)

1057 βλαστάω *blastaō*
Variant; not used

1058 Βλάστος *Blastos* (1)
Blastus (1)

1059 βλασφημέω *blasphēmeō* (34)
slander (4)
blaspheme (3)
cursed (3)
hurled insults at (3)
blasphemed (2)
blasphemes (2)
blaspheming (2)
abusive (1)
abusively (1)
blasphemies (1) *+1060*
blasphemy (1)
bring into disrepute (1)
denounced (1)
heap abuse on (1)
insulting (1)
malign (1)
slandered (1)
slandering (1)
slanderously reported (1)
speak abusively against (1)
spoken blasphemy (1)
spoken of as evil (1)

1060 βλασφημία *blasphēmia* (18)
blasphemy (5)
slander (5)
blasphemous (2)
blaspheme (1)
blasphemies (1)
blasphemies (1) *+1059*
blasphemy against (1)
malicious talk (1)
slanderous (1)

1061 βλάσφημος *blasphēmos* (4)
abusive (1)
blasphemer (1)
blasphemy (1)
slanderous (1)

1062 βλέμμα *blemma* (1)
saw (1)

1063 βλέπω *blepō* (129)
see (49)
saw (8)
seen (6)
watch out (6)
see to it (5)
seeing (5)
sees (5)
ever seeing (3) *+1063*
look (3)
blind (2) *+3590*
careful (2)
consider carefully (2)
look at (2)
pay attention who they are (2) *+476+4725*
unseen (2) *+3590*
alert (1)
be (1)
be unable to see (1) *+3590*
before their very eyes (1) *+899*
careful that (1)
consider (1)
do[s] (1)
exposed (1)
facing (1)
gaze on (1)
has[s] (1)
have[s] (1)
looked at (1)
looking on (1)
looks (1)
looks at (1)
on guard (1)
on your guard (1)
saw that (1)
sight (1)
stared (1)
take care (1)
think (1)
watch out (1) *+4932*
watch out for (1)
untranslated (2)

1064 βλητέος *blēteos* (1)
must be poured (1)

1065 Βοανηργές *Boanērges* (1)
Boanerges (1)

1066 βοάω *boaō* (12)
calling (4)
called out (2)
shouting (2)
cried out (1)
cry aloud (1)
cry out (1)
shrieks (1) *+3489+5889*

1067 Βόες *Boes* (2)
Boaz (2)

1068 βοή *boē* (1)
cries (1)

1069 βοήθεια *boētheia* (2)
help (1)
ropes (1)

1070 βοηθέω *boētheō* (8)
help (6)
helped (2)

1071 βοηθός *boēthos* (1)
helper (1)

1072 βόθρος *bothros*
Variant; not used

1073 βόθυνος *bothynos* (3)
pit (3)

1074 βολή *bolē* (1)
throw (1)

1075 βολίζω *bolizō* (2)
took soundings (2)

1076 βολίς *bolis*
Variant; not used

1077 Βοόζ *Booz*
Variant; not used

1078 Βόος *Boos* (1)
Boaz (1)

1079 βόρβορος *borboros* (1)
mud (1)

1080 βορρᾶς *borras* (2)
north (2)

1081 βόσκω *boskō* (9)
feed (3)
feeding (3)
tending (3)

1082 Βοσόρ *Bosor*
Variant; not used

1083 βοτάνη *botanē* (1)
crop (1)

1084 βότρυς *botrys* (1)
clusters of grapes (1)

1085 βουλευτής *bouleutēs* (2)
member of the council (2)

1086 βουλεύω *bouleuō* (6)
consider (1)
decided (1)
made plans (1)
make plans (1)
plotted (1)
untranslated (1)

1087 βουλή *boulē* (12)
purpose (6)
will (2)
decided that (1) *+5502*
decision (1)
motives (1)
planned (1) *+1181*

1088 βούλημα *boulēma* (3)
choose (1)
plan (1)
will (1)

1089 βούλομαι *boulomai* (37)
want (9)
wanted (9)
chooses (3)
planned (2)
wanting (2)
willing (2)
chose (1)
counsel (1)
determined (1)
determines (1)
had in mind (1)
intended (1)
like (1)
liked (1)
wants (1)
will (1)

1090 βουνός *bounos* (2)
hill (1)
hills (1)

1091 βοῦς *bous* (8)
ox (4)
cattle (2)
oxen (2)

1092 βραβεῖον *brabeion* (2)
prize (2)

1093 βραβεύω *brabeuō* (1)
rule (1)

1094 βραδύνω *bradynō* (2)
delayed (1)
slow (1)

1095 βραδυπλοέω *bradyploeō* (1)
made slow headway (1)

1096 βραδύς *bradys* (3)
slow (2)
how slow (1)

1097 βραδύτης *bradytēs* (1)
slowness (1)

1098 βραχίων *brachiōn* (3)
arm (2)
power (1)

1099 βραχύς *brachys* (7)
little (3)
for a little while (1)
short (1)
short (1) *+1328*
untranslated (1)

1100 βρέφος *brephos* (8)
baby (4)
babies (2)
infancy (1)
newborn babies (1)

1101 βρέχω *brechō* (7)
rain (3)
wet (2)
rained (1)
sends rain (1)

1102 βριμάομαι *brimaomai*
Variant; not used

1103 βροντή *brontē* (12)
peals of thunder (4)
thunder (3)
thunders (3)
peal of thunder (1)
thundered (1)

1104 βροχή *brochē* (2)
rain (2)

1105 βρόχος *brochos* (1)
restrict (1) *+2095*

1106 βρυγμός *brygmos* (7)
gnashing (7)

1107 βρύχω *brychō* (1)
gnashed (1)

1108 βρύω *bryō* (1)
flow (1)

1109 βρῶμα *brōma* (17)
food (10)
foods (3)
what eat (2)
eating (1)
solid food (1)

1110 βρώσιμος *brōsimos* (1)
to eat (1)

1111 βρῶσις *brōsis* (11)
food (6)
rust (2)
eat (1)
eating (1)
meal (1)

1112 βυθίζω *bythizō* (2)
plunge (1)
sink (1)

1113 βυθός *bythos* (1)
open sea (1)

1114 βυρσεύς *byrseus* (3)
tanner (3)

1115 βύσσινος *byssinos* (5)
fine linen (5)

1116 βύσσος *byssos* (1)
fine linen (1)

1117 βωμός *bōmos* (1)
altar (1)

1118 γ *g*
Variant; not used

1119 Γαββαθᾶ *Gabbatha* (1)
Gabbatha (1)

1120 Γαβριήλ *Gabriēl* (2)
Gabriel (2)

1121 γάγγραινα *gangraina* (1)
gangrene (1)

1122 Γάδ *Gad* (1)
Gad (1)

1123 Γαδαρηνός *Gadarēnos* (1)
Gadarenes (1)

1124 Γάζα1 *Gaza1* (1)
Gaza (1)

1125 γάζα2 *gaza2* (1)
treasury (1)

1126 γαζοφυλάκιον *gazophylakion* (5)
place where the offerings were put (2)
temple treasury (2)
treasury (1)

1127 Γάϊος *Gaios* (5)
Gaius (5)

1128 γάλα *gala* (5)
milk (5)

1129 Γαλάτης *Galatēs* (1)
Galatians (1)

1130 Γαλατία *Galatia* (4)
Galatia (3)
Galatian (1)

1131 Γαλατικός *Galatikos* (2)
Galatia (1)
of Galatia (1)

1132 γαλήνη *galēnē* (3)
calm (3)

1133 Γαλιλαία *Galilaia* (62)
Galilee (62)

1134 Γαλιλαῖος *Galilaios* (10)
Galileans (5)
Galilean (4)
Galilee (1)

1135 Γαλλία *Gallia*
Variant; not used

1136 Γαλλίων *Galliōn* (3)
Gallio (3)

1137 Γαμαλιήλ *Gamaliēl* (2)
Gamaliel (2)

1138 γαμέω *gameō* (28)
marry (12)
marries (7)
married (5)
marrying (2)
get married (1)
got married (1) *+1222*

1139 γαμίζω *gamizō* (7)
given in marriage (4)
giving in marriage (1)
marries (1)
marry (1)

1140 γαμίσκω *gamiskō* (1)
given in marriage (1)

1141 γάμος *gamos* (16)
wedding (6)
wedding banquet (5)
banquet (2)
marriage (1)
wedding feast (1)
wedding hall (1)

1142 γάρ *gar* (1040)
for (502)

because (85)
but (10)
and (9)
now (7)
indeed (6)
in fact (4)
since (4)
after all (3)
why (3)
as (2)
in fact (2) *+2779*
so (2)
yes (2)
as for (1)
as it is (1) *+2779*
because of (1)
even though (1) *+1569*
even though (1) *+3525*
for (1) *+3590*
for example (1)
for to be sure (1)
how (1) *+3590*
if (1)
in (1)
likewise (1) *+2779*
moreover (1)
no (1)
rather (1)
suppose (1) *+1569*
surely (1)
the fact is (1)
the reason (1) *+1650+4047*
though (1)
what does it matter (1) *+5515*
yet (1)
you see (1)
untranslated (376)

1143 γαστήρ *gastēr* (9)
pregnant women (3) *+1877+2400*
with child (2) *+1877+2400*
gluttons (1)
pregnant (1) *+1877+2400*
pregnant woman (1) *+1877+2400*
with child (1) *+1877+5197*

1144 Γαύδη *Gaudē*
Variant; not used

1145 γέ *ge* (24)
do[s] (3) *+3590*
does[s] (2) *+3590*
really (2)
surely (2) *+1623*
yet (2)
and what is more (1) *+247+2779+4047+4246+5250*
perhaps (1) *+726+1623*
surely (1) *+247*
then (1)
then (1) *+726*
though (1) *+2779*
thus (1) *+726*
untranslated (6)

1146 Γεδεών *Gedeōn* (1)
Gideon (1)

1147 γέεννα *geenna* (12)
hell (12)

1148 Γεθσημανῆ *Gethsēmanē*
Variant; not used

1149 Γεθσημανί *Gethsēmani* (2)
Gethsemane (2)

1150 γείτων *geitōn* (4)
neighbors (4)

1151 γελάω *gelaō* (2)
laugh (2)

1152 γέλως *gelōs* (1)
laughter (1)

1153 γεμίζω *gemizō* (9)
filled (5)
fill (2)
full (1)
swamped (1)

1154 γέμω *gemō* (11)
full (5)
covered with (3)
filled (2)
full of (1)

1155 γενεά *genea* (43)
generation (29)
generations (5)
descendants (1)
it[s] (1) *+3836+4047*
kind (1)
past (1) *+4233*
times (1)
untranslated (4)

1156 γενεαλογέω *genealogeō* (1)
trace descent (1)

1157 γενεαλογία *genealogia* (2)
genealogies (2)

1158 γενέθλια *genethlia*
Variant; not used

1159 γενέθλιος *genethlios*
Variant; not used

1160 γενέσια *genesia* (2)
birthday (2)

1161 γένεσις *genesis* (5)
birth (2)
genealogy (1)
life (1)
untranslated (1)

1162 γενετή *genetē* (1)
birth (1)

1163 γένημα *genēma* (4)
fruit (3)
harvest (1)

1164 γεννάω *gennaō* (97)
father (40)
born (37)
become father (3)
gives birth to (2)
bear (1)
bears children (1)
became (1)
became father (1)
became the father of (1)
birth (1)
bore (1)
came descendants (1)
child (1)
conceived (1)
gave birth to (1)
had (1)
illegitimate children (1) *+1666+4518*
native (1) *+1877+4005*
produce (1)

1165 γέννημα *gennēma* (4)
brood (4)

1166 Γεννησαρέτ *Gennēsaret* (3)
Gennesaret (3)

1167 γέννησις *gennēsis*
Variant; not used

1168 γεννητός *gennētos* (2)
born (2)

1169 γένος *genos* (20)
kinds (3)
offspring (3)
people (3)
family (2)
native (2)
born (1)
children (1) *+5626*
countrymen (1)
Jews (1) *+1609+1877+3836*
kind (1)
sorts (1)
untranslated (1)

1170 Γερασηνός *Gerasēnos* (3)
Gerasenes (3)

1171 Γεργεσηνός *Gergesēnos*
Variant; not used

1172 γερουσία *gerousia* (1)
assembly of elders (1)

1173 γέρων *gerōn* (1)
old (1)

1174 γεύομαι *geuomai* (15)
taste (6)
tasted (4)
eat (2)
ate (1)
get a taste (1)
tasting (1)

1175 γεωργέω *geōrgeō* (1)
farmed (1)

1176 γεώργιον *geōrgion* (1)
field (1)

1177 γεωργός *geōrgos* (19)
tenants (12)
farmers (3)
farmer (2)
gardener (1)
them[s] (1) *+3836*

1178 γῆ *gē* (250)
earth (151)
land (31)
ground (20)
soil (13)
Egypt (5) *+131*
shore (5)
earthly (3)
country (2)
landed (2) *+2093+2262+3836*
region (2)
Sodom (2) *+5047*
world (2)
ashore (1) *+1650+3836*
ashore (1) *+2093*
Canaan (1) *+5913*
countryside (1)
earth's (1)
its[s] (1) *+3836*
landed (1) *+609+1650+3836*
Midian (1) *+3409*
them[s] (1) *+2093+2997+3836+3836*
world's (1)
untranslated (2)

1179 γῆρας *gēras* (1)
old age (1)

1180 γηράσκω *gēraskō* (2)
aging (1)
old (1)

1181 γίνομαι *ginomai* (668)
was (54)
be (49)
become (46)
came (41)
happened (28)
became (26)
were (20)
done (13)
happen (13)
is (13)
been (11)
made (11)
performed (8)
take place (8)

come (6)
are (5)
do (5)
took place (5)
be done (4)
become (4) *+1650*
by no means (4) *+3590*
get (4)
making (4)
not at all (4) *+3590*
appeared (3)
approached (3)
became (3) *+1650*
becomes (3)
being (3)
broke out (3)
comes (3)
happening (3)
happens (3)
absolutely not (2) *+3590*
arrived (2)
becoming (2)
born (2)
brought (2)
came up (2)
certainly not (2) *+3590*
had (2)
lived (2)
marries (2)
occurred (2)
once (2) *+1254*
perform (2)
promised (2) *+2039*
reached (2) *+2093*
seized (2) *+2093*
share (2) *+5171*
stood (2)
surpassed (2) *+1869*
taken place (2)
turned (2)
turned into (2)
went (2)
accomplished (1)
agreed (1) *+3924*
am (1)
and (1) *+2779*
approaching (1) *+1584*
arose (1)
arose (1) *+1254*
arriving (1)
at daybreak (1) *+2002+2465*
at hour (1) *+6052*
bear (1)
became (1) *+1639*
become of (1)
been (1) *+1639*
been (1) *+1650*
been turned into (1)
belong (1)
betrayed (1) *+4595*
brought about (1)
came about (1)
changed (1) *+2283*
come of (1)
come true (1)
complained (1) *+1198*
dawn (1) *+2465+3516*
daybreak (1) *+2465*
decided (1) *+1191*
developed (1)
did (1)
died (1) *+2505*
died (1) *+3738*
disappeared (1) *+908*
do (1) *+4475*
does (1)
does[S] (1) *+4048*
doing (1)
doubting (1) *+603*
early in the morning (1) *+4746*
entered (1) *+1656*
experienced (1)
faultless (1) *+289*
fell (1)
fell headlong (1) *+4568*
fell into trance (1) *+1749+2093*
finds (1) *+2351*
finished (1)
follow example (1) *+3629*
fright (1) *+1873*
gain freedom (1) *+1801*
given (1)
go (1)
grant (1)
granted (1)
grew (1)
grown up (1) *+3489*
happened (1) *+1639*
has (1)
have (1)
heard (1) *+212*
heard about (1) *+1196*
heard sound (1) *+5889*
held accountable (1) *+5688*
imitate (1) *+3629*
in fear (1) *+1873*
in the morning (1) *+2465*
introduced (1)
join with others following example (1) *+5213*
learned about (1) *+5745*
look somber (1) *+5034*
looked so much like (1) *+6059*
loses (1)
make (1)
man-made (1) *+1328+5931*
may never (1) *+3590*
moths have eaten (1) *+4963*
neared (1) *+1581*
need (1) *+2400+5970*
never (1) *+3590*
now (1) *+2779*
obey (1) *+5675*
on (1)
once (1) *+2779*
one day (1) *+1254*
one day (1) *+2779*
owns (1)
participate in (1) *+3128*
planned (1) *+1087*
plunged into (1)
praying (1) *+4666*
proved (1)
proved to be (1)
rang out (1)
reach (1) *+1650*
reached (1)
reaching (1) *+2093*
receive (1)
result (1)
result in (1) *+1666*
revealed (1) *+1871*
rewards (1) *+3633*
served (1)
set (1)
shared in (1) *+3581*
shouted (1) *+3189*
show (1) *+5745*
so (1) *+1254*
spending time (1) *+5990*
spent (1)
split (1)
spoken (1)
stand firm (1) *+1612*
starting (1)
suffered (1)
suffering (1)
supply (1)
take charge of (1) *+2062*
taken (1)
that are (1)
that evening (1) *+4070*
the next morning (1) *+2465*
the time came when (1) *+1254*
thinking (1) *+3836+5856*
to marry[S] (1) *+4048*
told him (1) *+899+4639*
trembled with fear (1) *+1958*
trembling (1) *+1958*
turn (1)
turned (1) *+1650*
turned out (1)
undergoes (1) *+3581*
unequaled (1) *+3888+4024*
unequaled (1) *+3888+4024+5525*
used (1)
visit (1)
wake up (1) *+1213*
was born (1)
was filled with (1)
was going on (1)
waste (1) *+724*
went on (1)
wept (1) *+2653+3088*
woke up (1) *+2031*
work together (1) *+5301*
untranslated (66)

1182 γινώσκω *ginōskō* (222)
know (91)
understand (17)
known (15)
knows (12)
knew (11)
learned (6)
find out (5)
aware (4)
knowing (4)
recognize (4)
recognized (4)
found out (3)
aware of (2)
know that (2)
knowledge (2)
made known (2)
understood (2)
acknowledge (1)
assured (1) *+857*
concluded (1)
discover (1)
do so[S] (1)
evidence (1)
evident (1)
felt (1)
find out about (1)
get at truth (1) *+855*
had (1)
keep in mind (1)
knew about (1)
know about (1)
know how (1)
knows about (1)
knows thoughts (1)
learn (1)
learned about (1)
mark (1)
not clear (1) *+4024*
realize (1)
realized (1)
receive news (1)
regarded (1)
remember (1)
saw (1)
see if (1)
speak (1)
sure (1)
sure (1) *+3857*
sure of (1)
unaware (1) *+4024*
union with (1)
untranslated (2)

1183 γλεῦκος *gleukos* (1)
wine (1)

1184 γλυκύς *glykys* (4)
fresh (1)
fresh water (1)
sweet (1)
tasted sweet (1) *+1639*

1185 γλῶσσα *glōssa* (50)
tongue (21)
tongues (19)
language (5)
languages (2)
speaking in tongues (2)
untranslated (1)

1186 γλωσσόκομον *glōssokomon* (2)
keeper of money bag (1) *+2400*
money (1)

1187 γναφεύς *gnapheus* (1)
untranslated (1)

1188 γνήσιος *gnēsios* (4)
true (2)
loyal (1)
sincerity (1)

1189 γνησίως *gnēsiōs* (1)
genuine (1)

1190 γνόφος *gnophos* (1)
darkness (1)

1191 γνώμη *gnōmē* (9)
judgment (2)
purpose (2)
advice (1)
agreeing (1) *+1651+4472*
consent (1)
decided (1) *+1181*
thought (1)

1192 γνωρίζω *gnōrizō* (25)
made known (5)
make known (5)
tell (4)
known (3)
know (2)
told about (2)
know about (1)
present (1)
remind of (1)
spread (1)

1193 γνώριμος *gnōrimos*
Variant; not used

1194 γνῶσις *gnōsis* (29)
knowledge (25)
considerate (1) *+2848*
knowing (1)
knows (1)
understanding (1)

1195 γνώστης *gnōstēs* (1)
well acquainted with (1)

1196 γνωστός *gnōstos* (15)
known (6)
know (3) *+1639*
explain (1) *+1639*
friends (1)
heard about (1) *+1181*
knew (1)
know (1)
outstanding (1)

1197 γογγύζω *gongyzō* (8)
grumble (3)
grumbling (2)
complained (1)
did[s] (1)
whispering (1)

1198 γογγυσμός *gongysmos* (4)
complained (1) *+1181*
complaining (1)
grumbling (1)
whispering (1)

1199 γογγυστής *gongystēs* (1)
grumblers (1)

1200 γόης *goēs* (1)
impostors (1)

1201 Γολγοθᾶ *Golgotha* (3)
Golgotha (3)

1202 Γόμορρα *Gomorra* (4)
Gomorrah (4)

1203 γόμος *gomos* (3)
cargoes (2)
cargo (1)

1204 γονεύς *goneus* (20)
parents (19)
they[s] (1) *+899+3836*

1205 γόνυ *gony* (12)
knees (5)
knee (3)
kneel (1) *+2828+3836*
knelt (1) *+3836+5502*
knelt down (1) *+3836+5502*
knelt down (1) *+5502*

1206 γονυπετέω *gonypeteō* (4)
fell on knees before (1)
knelt (1)
knelt before (1)
on knees (1)

1207 γράμμα *gramma* (14)
letters (3)
bill (2)
letter (2)
written (2)
get learning (1) *+3857*
learning (1)
scriptures (1)
written code (1)
wrote (1)

1208 γραμματεύς *grammateus* (63)
teachers of the law (57)
teacher of the law (2)
clerk (1)
scholar (1)
teachers (1)
untranslated (1)

1209 γραπτός *graptos* (1)
written (1)

1210 γραφή *graphē* (50)
scripture (30)
scriptures (18)
writings (2)

1211 γράφω *graphō* (191)
written (105)
write (40)
wrote (15)
writing (11)
described (2)
make it (2)
recorded (2)
write down (2)
written down (2)
wrote down (2)
describes (1)
do so[s] (1)
had a notice prepared (1) *+5518*
read (1) *+1639*
sent the letter (1)
with writing (1)
write an account (1)
wrote about (1)

1212 γραώδης *graōdēs* (1)
old wives' tales (1)

1213 γρηγορέω *grēgoreō* (22)
keep watch (8)
watch (3)
alert (2)
on guard (2)
awake (1)
kept watch (1)
stays awake (1)
wake up (1)
wake up (1) *+1181*
watchful (1)
watching (1)

1214 γυμνάζω *gymnazō* (4)
trained (2)
experts (1) *+2840*
train (1)

1215 γυμνασία *gymnasia* (1)
training (1)

1216 γυμνητεύω *gymnēteuō*
Variant; not used

1217 γυμνιτεύω *gymniteuō* (1)
in rags (1)

1218 γυμνός *gymnos* (16)
naked (7)
needed clothes (2)
needing clothes (2)
taken it off (1)
uncovered (1)
wearing nothing (1) *+2093+4314*
without clothes (1)
untranslated (1)

1219 γυμνότης *gymnotēs* (2)
nakedness (2)

1220 γυναικάριον *gynaikarion* (1)
weak-willed women (1)

1221 γυναικεῖος *gynaikeios* (1)
wives (1)

1222 γυνή *gynē* (215)
woman (90)
wife (58)
women (30)
wives (12)
dear woman (2)
widow (2)
wife's (2)
believing wife (1) *+80*
bride (1)
faithful to her husband (1) *+467+1651*
got married (1) *+1138*
leaves wife (1) *+2400*
married (1) *+1313*
married (1) *+3284*
married a woman (1) *+3284*
married to (1)
marry (1) *+721*
mother (1)
she[s] (1)
she[s] (1) *+3836*
unmarried (1) *+608+3395*
widow (1) *+899*
widow (1) *+5939*
woman's (1)
women's (1)
untranslated (1)

1223 Γώγ *Gōg* (1)
Gog (1)

1224 γωνία *gōnia* (9)
capstone (5) *+3051*
corners (3)
corner (1)

1225 δ *d*
Variant; not used

1226 Δαβίδ *Dabid*
Variant; not used

1227 δαιμονίζομαι *daimonizomai* (13)
demon-possessed (10)
possessed by a demon (1)
possessed by demons (1)

suffering from demon-possession (1)

1228 δαιμόνιον *daimonion* (63)
demons (42)
demon (15)
demon-possessed (5) *+2400*
gods (1)

1229 δαιμονιώδης *daimoniōdēs* (1)
of the devil (1)

1230 δαίμων *daimōn* (1)
demons (1)

1231 δάκνω *daknō* (1)
biting (1)

1232 δάκρυον *dakryon* (10)
tears (8)
tear (2)

1233 δακρύω *dakryō* (1)
wept (1)

1234 δακτύλιος *daktylios* (1)
ring (1)

1235 δάκτυλος *daktylos* (8)
finger (6)
fingers (1)
lift a finger (1)

1236 Δαλμανουθά *Dalmanoutha* (1)
Dalmanutha (1)

1237 Δαλματία *Dalmatia* (1)
Dalmatia (1)

1238 δαμάζω *damazō* (4)
tamed (2)
subdue (1)
tame (1)

1239 δάμαλις *damalis* (1)
heifer (1)

1240 Δάμαρις *Damaris* (1)
Damaris (1)

1241 Δαμασκηνός *Damaskēnos* (1)
the Damascenes (1)

1242 Δαμασκός *Damaskos* (15)
Damascus (15)

1243 Δάν *Dan*
Variant; not used

1244 δανείζω *daneizō*
Variant; not used

1245 δάνειον *daneion* (1)
debt (1)

1246 δανειστής *daneistēs*
Variant; not used

1247 δανίζω *danizō* (4)
lend (3)
borrow (1)

1248 Δανιήλ *Daniēl* (1)
Daniel (1)

1249 δάνιον *danion*
Variant; not used

1250 δανιστής *danistēs* (1)
moneylender (1)

1251 δαπανάω *dapanaō* (5)
spend (2)
spent (2)
pay expenses (1)

1252 δαπάνη *dapanē* (1)
cost (1)

1253 Δαυίδ *Dauid* (59)
David (57)
David's (2)

1254 δέ *de* (2787)
but (669)
and (257)
then (89)
now (82)
he (70) *+3836*
they (49) *+3836*
so (37)
Jesus[s] (25) *+3836*
however (23)
yet (17)
when (9)
she (8) *+3836*
while (7)
instead (6)
meanwhile (5)
another (4) *+4005*
even (4)
the man[s] (4) *+3836*
also (3)
and yet (3)
at this (3)
others (3) *+3836*
another (2)
as (2)
as it is (2) *+3814*
for (2)
if he does (2) *+1623+3590*
moreover (2)
nevertheless (2)
once (2) *+1181*
or (2)
others (2) *+4005*
rather (2)
some (2)
still (2)
that (2)
the disciples[s] (2) *+3836*
the men[s] (2) *+3836*
those (2) *+3836*
though (2)
where (2)
after this (1)
again (1)
and now (1)
and some (2) *+4005*
another (1) *+3836*
another man (1) *+4005*
arose (1) *+1181*
as for (1)
as it is (1) *+4022*
at other times (1) *+4047*
at this point (1) *+4047*
because (1)
but (1) *+1883+3836*
but (1) *+4022*
but as far as (1)
but in the other case (1) *+1695*
by (1)
by now (1)
Cornelius[s] (1) *+3836*
finally (1)
former (1)
if (1)
in addition (1)
in addition (1) *+2093*
in fact (1) *+2779*
indeed (1) *+2779*
instead (1) *+3814*
Jesus' followers[s] (1) *+3836*
just (1)
just as (1)
Mary[s] (1) *+3836*
nor anyone (1) *+4029*
not until (1) *+2453*
now that (1)
on (1)
once (1)
one day (1) *+1181*
or (1) *+4005*
or at least (1) *+1623+3590*
other (1) *+257*
others (1) *+257*
otherwise (1) *+1623+3590*
Pilate[s] (1) *+3836*
rather (1) *+3437*
remember this (1) *+4047*
similarly (1)
simply (1)
so (1) *+1181*
so he (1) *+3836*
so they (1) *+3836*
some (1) *+257*
still another (1)
still others (1) *+3836*
the expert in the law[s] (1) *+3836*
the father[s] (1) *+3836*
the man's[s] (1) *+3836*
the manager[s] (1) *+3836*
the other (1) *+4005*
the people[s] (1) *+3836*
the rioters[s] (1) *+3836*
the time came when (1) *+1181*
those who (1) *+3836*
to the other (1) *+4005*
what is more (1) *+247+2779+3667+4024*
when (1) *+1623*
when (1) *+6055*
which (1)
yes (1)
untranslated (1303)

1255 δέησις *deēsis* (18)
prayers (6)
prayer (4)
pray (2) *+4472*
praying (2)
requests (2)
petition (1)
pray for help (1)

1256 δεῖ *dei* (101)
must (57)
ought (13)
should (9)
had (8)
have (3)
belong (1)
due (1)
for work (1) *+1877+2237+4005*
had (1) *+1639*
necessary (1)
ought to (1)
should be (1)
shouldn't (1) *+4024*
have (1)
untranslated (2)

1257 δεῖγμα *deigma* (1)
example (1)

1258 δειγματίζω *deigmatizō* (2)
expose to public disgrace (1)
made spectacle (1)

1259 δείκνυμι *deiknymi* (33)
show (20)
showed (6)
shown (3)
bring about (1)
explain (1)
showing (1)
shows (1)

1260 δεικνύω *deiknyō*
Variant; not used

1261 δειλία *deilia* (1)
timidity (1)

1262 δειλιάω *deiliaō* (1)
afraid (1)

1263 δειλινός *deilinos*
Variant; not used

1264 δειλός *deilos* (3)
afraid (1)
cowardly (1)
so afraid (1)

1265 δεῖνα *deina* (1)
certain (1)

1266 δεινός *deinos*
Variant; not used

1267 δεινῶς *deinōs* (2)
fiercely (1)
terrible (1)

1268 δειπνέω *deipneō* (4)
supper (2)
eat (1)
my supper (1) *+5515*

1269 δειπνοκλήτορ *deipnoklētor*
Variant; not used

1270 δεῖπνον *deipnon* (16)
banquet (4)
supper (4)
banquets (3)
dinner (2)
evening meal (1)
meal (1)
untranslated (1)

1271 δεῖπνος *deipnos*
Variant; not used

1272 δεισιδαιμονία *deisidaimonia* (1)
religion (1)

1273 δεισιδαίμων *deisidaimōn* (1)
very religious (1)

1274 δέκα *deka* (25)
ten (24)
eighteen (1) *+2779+3893*

1275 δεκαδύο *dekadyo*
Variant; not used

1276 δεκαέξ *dekaex*
Variant; not used

1277 δεκαοκτώ *dekaoktō* (2)
eighteen (2)

1278 δεκαπέντε *dekapente* (3)
fifteen (1)
ninety feet deep (1) *+3976*
two miles (1) *+5084*

1279 Δεκάπολις *Dekapolis* (3)
Decapolis (3)

1280 δεκατέσσαρες *dekatessares* (5)
fourteen (5)

1281 δέκατος *dekatos* (7)
tenth (7)

1282 δεκατόω *dekatoō* (2)
collected a tenth (1)
paid the tenth (1)

1283 δεκτός *dektos* (5)
favor (2)
acceptable (1)
accepted (1)
accepts (1) *+1639*

1284 δελεάζω *deleazō* (3)
entice (1)
enticed (1)
seduce (1)

1285 δένδρον *dendron* (25)
tree (17)
trees (8)

1286 δεξιοβόλος *dexiobolos*
Variant; not used

1287 δεξιολάβος *dexiolabos* (1)
spearmen (1)

1288 δεξιός *dexios* (54)
right hand (31)
right (21)
right side (2)

1289 δέομαι *deomai* (22)
pray (5)
beg (4)
begged (3)
ask (2)
please (2) *+5148*
prayed (2)
implore (1)
plead (1)
pleaded with (1)
prayed to (1)

1290 δέος *deos* (1)
awe (1)

1291 Δερβαῖος *Derbaios* (1)
from Derbe (1)

1292 Δέρβη *Derbē* (3)
Derbe (3)

1293 δέρμα *derma* (1)
goatskins (1) *+128*

1294 δερμάτινος *dermatinos* (2)
leather (2)

1295 δέρρις *derris*
Variant; not used

1296 δέρω *derō* (15)
beat (7)
beaten with blows (2)
beating (2)
flogged (2)
slaps (1)
strike (1)

1297 δεσμεύω *desmeuō* (3)
arresting (1)
chained hand (1) *+268*
tie up (1)

1298 δεσμέω *desmeō*
Variant; not used

1299 δέσμη *desmē* (1)
bundles (1)

1300 δέσμιος *desmios* (16)
prisoner (11)
in prison (2)
prisoners (2)
arrested (1)

1301 δεσμός *desmos* (18)
chains (11)
chained (2)
imprisonment (2)
bound (1)
prison (1)
untranslated (1)

1302 δεσμοφύλαξ *desmophylax* (3)
jailer (3)

1303 δεσμωτήριον *desmōtērion* (4)
jail (2)
prison (2)

1304 δεσμώτης *desmōtēs* (2)
prisoners (2)

1305 δεσπότης *despotēs* (10)
masters (4)
sovereign Lord (4)
master (1)
sovereign (1)

1306 δεῦρο *deuro* (9)
come (7)
go (1)
now (1)

1307 δεῦτε *deute* (12)
come (12)

1308 δευτεραῖος *deuteraios* (1)
on the following day (1)

1309 δεύτερον *deuteron* (6)
second time (2)
again (1)
again (1) *+4099*
later (1)
second (1)

1310 δευτερόπρωτος *deuteroprōtos*
Variant; not used

1311 δεύτερος *deuteros* (37)
second (27)
second time (4) *+1666*
second time (2) *+1666+4099*
another (1)
inner (1)
second (1) *+4099*
twice (1)

1312 δέχομαι *dechomai* (56)
welcomes (9)
welcome (7)
welcomed (7)
receive (6)
receives (6)
received (5)
accept (3)
accepted (3)
take (3)
obtained (1)
receiving (1)
refused (1) *+4024*
taking (1)
took (1)
welcomed (1) *+1645+3552*
untranslated (1)

1313 δέω *deō* (43)
bound (16)
tied (5)
bind (4)
prisoners (3)
in prison (2)
tie (2)
ties up (2)
wrapped (2)
arrest (1)
chained (1)
chained hand (1) *+268*
compelled (1)
in chains (1)
married (1) *+1222*
put in chains (1)

1314 δή *dē* (5)
therefore (1)
untranslated (4)

1315 δηλαυγῶς *dēlaugōs*
Variant; not used

1316 δῆλος *dēlos* (3)
clear (1)
clearly (1)
gives away (1) *+4472*

1317 δηλόω *dēloō* (7)
bring to light (1)
indicate (1)
informed (1)
made clear (1)
pointing (1)
showing (1)
told of (1)

1318 Δημᾶς *Dēmas* (3)
Demas (3)

1319 δημηγορέω *dēmēgoreō* (1)
delivered a public address (1)

1320 Δημήτριος *Dēmētrios* (3)
Demetrius (3)

1321 δημιουργός *dēmiourgos* (1)
builder (1)

1322 δῆμος *dēmos* (4)
crowd (2)

people (1)
they^{s} (1) *+3836*

1323 δημόσιος *dēmosios* (4)
public (2)
publicly (2)

1324 δηνάριον *dēnarion* (16)
denarius (7)
a day's wages (2)
denarii (2)
eight months of a man's wages (1) *+1357*
eight months' wages (1) *+1357*
silver coins (1)
the money worth a year's wages (1) *+5559*
untranslated (1)

1325 δήποτε *dēpote*
Variant; not used

1326 δηποτοῦν *dēpotoun*
Variant; not used

1327 δήπου *dēpou* (1)
surely (1)

1328 διά *dia* (666)
through (180)
by (80)
because of (65)
for (30)
because (23)
therefore (23) *+4047*
why (23) *+5515*
with (15)
in (13)
because (10) *+3836*
for this reason (9) *+4047*
for sake (8)
for the sake of (8)
from (7)
that is why (5) *+4047*
the reason (5) *+4047*
at (4)
out of (4)
so (4) *+4047*
this is why (4) *+4047*
always (3) *+4246*
because (3) *+4047*
during (3)
for benefit (3)
how is it that (3) *+5515*
on (3)
on account of (3)
the result of (3)
afforded by (2)
continually (2) *+4246*
regularly (2) *+4246*
since (2)
so then (2) *+4047*
that was why (2) *+4047*
why (2) *+162+4005*
who (2) *+4005*
after (1)
as the result of (1)
briefly (1) *+3900*
bring about (1)
by all this (1) *+4047*
by means of (1)
by the authority of (1)
causes (1)
compared to (1)
days (1) *+2465*
due to (1)
enabling (1) *+1443+3836+5931*
for (1) *+3836*
for sakes (1)
for that very reason (1) *+4047*
for the benefit of (1)
for this very reason (1) *+4047*
forever (1) *+4246*
go through (1)
he (1) *+899+3836+5931*
in answer to (1)
in keeping with (1)
in the presence of (1)
in view of (1)
man-made (1) *+1181+5931*
night (1) *+3816+4246*
of (1)
on account (1)
on the basis of (1)
on the evidence of (1)
over a period (1)
patiently (1) *+5705*
reaching more and more (1) *+3836+4429+4498*
short (1) *+1099*
since (1) *+3836*
so (1) *+162+4005*
so (1) *+4005*
terrified (1) *+5832*
that is why (1) *+162+4005*
therefore (1) *+162+4005*
they (1) *+899*
this is why (1) *+899*
to bottom (1) *+3910*
traveled about the country (1) *+1451+4246*
under (1)
use (1)
using (1) *+5931*
visit on the way (1)
when (1)
why (1) *+4005*
with (1) *+899+5931*
with the help of (1)
untranslated (54)

1329 διαβαίνω *diabainō* (3)
come over (1)
go (1)
passed through (1)

1330 διαβάλλω *diaballō* (1)
accused (1)

1331 διαβεβαιόομαι *diabebaioomai* (2)
confidently affirm (1)
stress (1)

1332 διαβλέπω *diablepō* (3)
see clearly (2)
eyes opened (1)

1333 διάβολος *diabolos* (38)
devil (31)
devil's (3)
he^{s} (1) *+3836*
malicious talkers (1)
slanderers (1)
slanderous (1)

1334 διαγγέλλω *diangellō* (3)
give notice of (1)
proclaim (1)
proclaimed (1)

1335 διαγίνομαι *diaginomai* (3)
later (1)
lost (1)
was over (1)

1336 διαγινώσκω *diaginōskō* (2)
decide (1)
information (1)

1337 διαγνωρίζω *diagnōrizō*
Variant; not used

1338 διάγνωσις *diagnōsis* (1)
decision (1)

1339 διαγογγύζω *diagongyzō* (2)
mutter (1)
muttered (1)

1340 διαγρηγορέω *diagrēgoreō* (1)
fully awake (1)

1341 διάγω *diagō* (2)
live (1)
lived (1)

1342 διαδέχομαι *diadechomai* (1)
received (1)

1343 διάδημα *diadēma* (3)
crowns (3)

1344 διαδίδωμι *diadidōmi* (3)
distributed (1)
divides up (1)
give (1)

1345 διάδοχος *diadochos* (1)
succeeded (1) *+3284*

1346 διαζώννυμι *diazōnnymi* (3)
wrapped around (2)
wrapped around waist (1)

1347 διαθήκη *diathēkē* (33)
covenant (25)
covenants (3)
covenant make (2) *+1416*
will (2)
covenant made (1) *+1416*

1348 διαίρεσις *diairesis* (3)
different (3)

1349 διαιρέω *diaireō* (2)
divided between (1)
gives (1)

1350 διακαθαίρω *diakathairō* (1)
clear (1)

1351 διακαθαρίζω *diakatharizō* (1)
clear (1)

1352 διακατελέγχομαι *diakatelenchomai* (1)
refuted (1)

1353 διακελεύω *diakeleuō*
Variant; not used

1354 διακονέω *diakoneō* (37)
serves (6)
wait on (6)
served (4)
serve (3)
administer (2)
attended (2)
help (2)
helped (2)
care for (1)
cared for needs (1)
do the work (1)
helpers (1)
helping (1)
helping to support (1)
in the service of (1)
ministry (1)
serve as deacons (1)
serving (1)

1355 διακονία *diakonia* (34)
ministry (14)
service (9)
serve (3)
distribution (1)
help (1)
mission (1)
preparations to be made (1)
service that perform (1) *+3311+3836+4047*
serving (1)
task (1)
work (1)

1356 διάκονος *diakonos* (29)
servant (13)
servants (7)
minister (3)
deacons (2)
attendants (1)
deacon (1)
ministers (1)
promotes sin (1) *+281*

1357 διακόσιοι *diakosioi* (8)
1,260 (2) *+2008+5943*

two hundred (2)
276 (1) *+1573+1971*
eight months of a man's wages (1) *+1324*
eight months' wages (1) *+1324*
hundred yards (1) *+4388*

1358 διακούω *diakouō* (1)
hear case (1)

1359 διακρίνω *diakrinō* (19)
doubt (4)
doubts (2)
criticized (1)
discriminated (1)
disputing (1) *+1363*
hesitate (1)
hesitation (1)
interpret (1)
judge a dispute (1)
judged (1)
made distinction (1)
makes different (1)
recognizing (1)
waver (1)
weigh carefully (1)

1360 διάκρισις *diakrisis* (3)
distinguish from (1)
distinguishing between (1)
passing judgment (1)

1361 διακωλύω *diakōlyō* (1)
deter (1)

1362 διαλαλέω *dialaleō* (2)
discuss (1)
talking about (1)

1363 διαλέγομαι *dialegomai* (13)
reasoned (4)
arguing (2)
addresses (1)
argued about (1)
discoursed (1)
discussions (1)
disputing (1) *+1359*
spoke to (1)
talked (1)

1364 διαλείπω *dialeipō* (1)
stopped (1)

1365 διάλεκτος *dialektos* (6)
in Aramaic (3) *+1579*
language (3)

1366 διαλιμπάνω *dialimpanō*
Variant; not used

1367 διαλλάσσομαι *diallassomai* (1)
reconciled (1)

1368 διαλογίζομαι *dialogizomai* (16)
thinking (5)
discussed (4)
arguing about (1)
talked the matter over (1) *+253+4639*
talking (1)
talking about (1)
thought (1)
wondered (1)
wondering (1)

1369 διαλογισμός *dialogismos* (14)
thoughts (6)
thinking (3)
arguing (1)
argument (1)
disputable (1)
disputing (1)
doubts (1)

1370 διαλύω *dialyō* (1)
dispersed (1)

1371 διαμαρτύρομαι *diamartyromai* (15)
testified (3)
declared (2)
warn (2)
warned (2)
charge (1)
give charge (1)
testify (1)
testifying (1)
testifying to (1)
warns (1)

1372 διαμάχομαι *diamachomai* (1)
argued vigorously (1)

1373 διαμένω *diamenō* (5)
remain (2)
goes on (1)
remained (1)
stood (1)

1374 διαμερίζω *diamerizō* (11)
divided (4)
divided up (2)
divide (1)
divided among (1)
dividing up (1)
gave (1)
separated (1)

1375 διαμερισμός *diamerismos* (1)
division (1)

1376 διανέμω *dianemō* (1)
spreading (1)

1377 διανεύω *dianeuō* (1)
making signs (1) *+1639*

1378 διανόημα *dianoēma* (1)
thoughts (1)

1379 διάνοια *dianoia* (12)
minds (4)
mind (3)
thoughts (2)
understanding (2)
thinking (1)

1380 διανοίγω *dianoigō* (8)
opened (5)
explaining (1)
firstborn (1) *+3616*
open (1)

1381 διανυκτερεύω *dianyktereuō* (1)
spent the night (1) *+1639*

1382 διανύω *dianyō* (1)
continued (1)

1383 διαπαντός *diapantos*
Variant; not used

1384 διαπαρατριβή *diaparatribē* (1)
constant friction between (1)

1385 διαπεράω *diaperaō* (6)
crossed over (4)
cross over (1)
crossing over (1)

1386 διαπλέω *diapleō* (1)
sailed across (1)

1387 διαπονέομαι *diaponeomai* (2)
greatly disturbed (1)
troubled (1)

1388 διαπορεύομαι *diaporeuomai* (5)
going by (1)
going through (1)
passing through (1)
traveled (1)
went through (1)

1389 διαπορέω *diaporeō* (4)
perplexed (2)
puzzled (1)
wondering about (1)

1390 διαπραγματεύομαι *diapragmateuomai* (1)
gained (1)

1391 διαπρίω *diapriō* (2)
furious (2)

1392 διαρήγνυμι *diarēgnymi*
Variant; not used

1393 διαρήσσω *diarēssō*
Variant; not used

1394 διαρθρόω *diarthroō*
Variant; not used

1395 διαρπάζω *diarpazō* (3)
rob (2)
carry off (1)

1396 διαρρήγνυμι *diarrēgnymi* (5)
tore (3)
break (1)
broken (1)

1397 διασαφέω *diasapheō* (2)
explain (1)
told (1)

1398 διασείω *diaseiō* (1)
extort money (1)

1399 διασκορπίζω *diaskorpizō* (9)
scattered (5)
scattered seed (2)
squandered (1)
wasting (1)

1400 διασπάω *diaspaō* (2)
tore apart (1)
torn to pieces (1)

1401 διασπείρω *diaspeirō* (3)
scattered (3)

1402 διασπορά *diaspora* (3)
people live scattered among (1) *+3836*
scattered (1)
scattered throughout (1)

1403 διαστέλλω *diastellō* (7)
commanded (2)
gave orders (2)
authorization (1)
did so[s] (1)
warned (1)

1404 διάστημα *diastēma* (1)
later (1)

1405 διαστολή *diastolē* (3)
difference (2)
distinction (1)

1406 διαστρέφω *diastrephō* (7)
perverse (2)
depraved (1)
distort the truth (1) *+3281*
perverting (1)
subverting (1)
turn (1)

1407 διασῴζω *diasōzō* (8)
safely (2)
escaped (1)
heal (1)
healed (1)
in safety (1)
saved through (1)
spare (1)

1408 διαταγή *diatagē* (1)
put into effect (1)

1409 διάταγμα *diatagma* (1)
edict (1)

1410 διαταράσσω *diatarassō* (1)
greatly troubled (1)

1411 διατάσσω *diatassō* (17)
directed (2)
ordered (2)
told (2)
told to do (2)

commanded (1)
give directions (1)
instituted (1)
instructing (1)
made arrangement (1)
orders (1)
put into effect (1)
required (1)
the rule lay down (1)

1412 διατελέω *diateleō* (1)
last (1)

1413 διατηρέω *diatēreō* (2)
avoid (1)
treasured (1)

1414 διατί *diati*
Variant; not used

1415 διατίθεμαι *diatithemai*
Variant; not used

1416 διατίθημι *diatithēmi* (7)
covenant make (2) *+1347*
made (2)
confer (1)
conferred (1)
covenant made (1) *+1347*

1417 διατρίβω *diatribō* (9)
stayed (3)
spending (2)
remained (1)
spent (1)
spent some time (1)
stayed a while (1)

1418 διατροφή *diatrophē* (1)
food (1)

1419 διαυγάζω *diaugazō* (1)
dawns (1)

1420 διαυγής *diaugēs* (1)
transparent (1)

1421 διαφανής *diaphanēs*
Variant; not used

1422 διαφέρω *diapherō* (13)
valuable (2)
worth more than (2)
carry (1)
different from (1)
differs (1)
driven (1)
makes difference (1)
more valuable than (1)
spread (1)
superior (1)
what is best (1) *+3836*

1423 διαφεύγω *diapheugō* (1)
escaping (1)

1424 διαφημίζω *diaphēmizō* (3)
spread the news about (1)
spreading (1)
widely circulated (1)

1425 διαφθείρω *diaphtheirō* (6)
corrupt (1)
destroy (1)
destroyed (1)
destroying (1)
destroys (1)
wasting away (1)

1426 διαφθορά *diaphthora* (6)
decay (4)
body decayed (1) *+3972*
decay (1) *+1650+5715*

1427 διάφορος *diaphoros* (4)
superior (2)
different (1)
various (1)

1428 διαφυλάσσω *diaphylassō* (1)
guard carefully (1) *+3836*

1429 διαχειρίζω *diacheirizō* (2)
kill (1)
killed (1)

1430 διαχλευάζω *diachleuazō* (1)
made fun of (1)

1431 διαχωρίζω *diachōrizō* (1)
leaving (1)

1432 διγαμία *digamia*
Variant; not used

1433 δίγαμος *digamos*
Variant; not used

1434 διδακτικός *didaktikos* (2)
able to teach (2)

1435 διδακτός *didaktos* (3)
taught (3)

1436 διδασκαλία *didaskalia* (21)
teaching (10)
doctrine (5)
teach (2)
teachings (2) *+1438*
teachings (1)
things taught (1)

1437 διδάσκαλος *didaskalos* (59)
teacher (50)
teachers (8)
master (1)

1438 διδάσκω *didaskō* (97)
teach (35)
teaching (31)
taught (20)
teaches (4)
taught (2) *+1639*
teachings (2) *+1436*
instructed (1)
lecture (1)
teachings (1)

1439 διδαχή *didachē* (30)
teaching (23)
instruction (3)
taught (2)
careful instruction (1)
teachings (1)

1440 δίδραχμον *didrachmon* (2)
two-drachma (1)
untranslated (1)

1441 Δίδυμος *Didymos* (3)
Didymus (3)

1442 διδῶ *didō*
Variant; not used

1443 δίδωμι *didōmi* (416)
give (116)
given (107)
gave (74)
gives (13)
put (9)
pay (5)
grant (4)
granted (4)
offered (4)
giving (3)
let (3)
make (3)
offer (3)
arranged (2)
commanded (2) *+1953*
enable (2)
gave up (2)
give to the poor (2) *+1797*
perform (2)
placed (2)
produced (2)
show (2)
struck in the face (2) *+4825*
appointed (1)
assigned (1)
bear (1)
benefit (1) *+5921*
bring (1)
buy (1)
cast (1)
caused (1)
distributed (1)
does (1)
enabled (1)
enabled (1) *+1639*
enabling (1) *+1328+3836+5931*
entrusted (1)
gifts (1)
give (1) *+3836*
glorified (1) *+1518*
glorify (1) *+1518*
hinder (1) *+1600*
is (1)
is[s] (1)
lavished (1)
leave (1)
pass on (1)
payment (1)
plot (1) *+5206*
poured (1)
praised (1) *+142*
presented (1)
punish (1) *+1689*
puts (1)
receive (1)
repay (1)
rescue (1) *+5401*
rewarding (1) *+3635+3836*
set (1)
sound (1)
speak (1)
strengthen (1) *+3194*
take back (1)
took (1)
try hard (1) *+2238*
venture (1)
untranslated (5)

1444 διεγείρω *diegeirō* (6)
got up (2)
grew rough (1)
refresh (1)
stimulate to (1)
woke (1)

1445 διενθυμέομαι *dienthymeomai* (1)
thinking (1)

1446 διεξέρχομαι *diexerchomai*
Variant; not used

1447 διέξοδος *diexodos* (1)
corners (1)

1448 διερμηνεία *diermēneia*
Variant; not used

1449 διερμηνευτής *diermēneutēs* (1)
interpreter (1)

1450 διερμηνεύω *diermēneuō* (6)
interpret (3)
explained what said (1)
interprets (1)
translated (1)

1451 διέρχομαι *dierchomai* (42)
go through (4)
traveled through (3)
go (2)
go over (2)
goes through (2)
going through (2)
passing through (2)
traveled throughout (2)
went (2)
came (1)
come (1)

coming (1)
gone about (1)
gone through (1)
passed (1)
passed through (1)
pierce (1)
spread (1)
took the road through (1)
traveled (1)
traveled about (1)
traveled about the country (1) *+1328+4246*
traveled along (1)
visit on way (1)
walked around (1)
walked right through (1)
was coming (1) *+3516*
went around (1)
went on (1) *+4134*
went through (1)

1452 διερωτάω *dierōtaō* (1)
found out (1)

1453 διετής *dietēs* (1)
two years old (1)

1454 διετία *dietia* (2)
two years (2)

1455 διηγέομαι *diēgeomai* (8)
tell (3)
told (2)
described (1)
reported (1)
speak of (1)

1456 διήγησις *diēgēsis* (1)
account (1)

1457 διηνεκής *diēnekēs* (4)
forever (2) *+1650+3836*
endlessly (1) *+1650+3836*
for all time (1) *+1650+3836*

1458 διθάλασσος *dithalassos* (1)
sandbar (1) *+5536*

1459 διϊκνέομαι *diikneomai* (1)
penetrates (1)

1460 διΐστημι *diistēmi* (3)
later (1)
left (1)
untranslated (1)

1461 διϊστορέω *diistoreō*
Variant; not used

1462 διϊσχυρίζομαι *diischyrizomai* (2)
asserted (1)
insisting that (1)

1463 δικάζω *dikazō*
Variant; not used

1464 δικαιοκρισία *dikaiokrisia* (1)
righteous judgment (1)

1465 δίκαιος *dikaios* (79)
righteous (53)
right (11)
just (8)
upright (3)
innocent (2)
honest (1)
righteousness (1)

1466 δικαιοσύνη *dikaiosynē* (91)
righteousness (74)
justice (5)
what is right (5)
right (2)
acts of righteousness (1)
are justified (1) *+1650*
it[s] (1)
righteous (1) *+1877*
righteous life (1)

1467 δικαιόω *dikaioō* (39)
justified (19)
justify (4)
justifies (3)
proved right (3)
considered righteous (2)
declared righteous (2)
acknowledged that right (1)
acquitted (1)
freed (1)
justified before God (1)
make innocent (1)
vindicated (1)

1468 δικαίωμα *dikaiōma* (10)
regulations (3)
righteous (2)
act of righteousness (1)
justification (1)
requirements (1)
righteous decree (1)
righteous requirements (1)

1469 δικαίως *dikaiōs* (5)
justly (2)
as ought (1)
righteous (1)
upright (1)

1470 δικαίωσις *dikaiōsis* (2)
justification (2)

1471 δικαστής *dikastēs* (2)
judge (2)

1472 δίκη *dikē* (3)
justice (1)
punished (1) *+5514*
punishment (1)

1473 δίκτυον *diktyon* (12)
nets (8)
net (4)

1474 δίλογος *dilogos* (1)
sincere (1) *+3590*

1475 διό *dio* (53)
therefore (27)
so (12)
that is why (5)
this is why (4)
for this reason (1)
now (1)
so then (1)
untranslated (2)

1476 διοδεύω *diodeuō* (2)
passed through (1)
traveled about (1)

1477 Διονύσιος *Dionysios* (1)
Dionysius (1)

1478 διόπερ *dioper* (2)
therefore (2)

1479 διοπετής *diopetēs* (1)
image which fell from heaven (1)

1480 διόρθωμα *diorthōma* (1)
reforms (1)

1481 διόρθωσις *diorthōsis* (1)
the new order (1)

1482 διορύσσω *dioryssō* (4)
break in (2)
broken into (2)

1483 Διόσκουροι *Dioskouroi* (1)
twin gods Castor and Pollux (1)

1484 διότι *dioti* (23)
because (10)
for (6)
therefore (2)
since (1)
so (1)
untranslated (3)

1485 Διοτρέφης *Diotrephēs* (1)
Diotrephes (1)

1486 διπλόος *diploos* (4)
double (2)
pay back double (1) *+1488*
twice as much (1)

1487 διπλοῦς *diplous*
Variant; not used

1488 διπλόω *diploō* (1)
pay back double (1) *+1486*

1489 δίς *dis* (6)
twice (4)
again (2)

1490 δισμυριάς *dismyrias* (1)
two hundred million (1) *+3689*

1491 διστάζω *distazō* (2)
doubt (1)
doubted (1)

1492 δίστομος *distomos* (3)
double-edged (3)

1493 δισχίλιοι *dischilioi* (1)
two thousand (1)

1494 διϋλίζω *diylizō* (1)
strain out (1)

1495 διχάζω *dichazō* (1)
turn (1)

1496 διχοστασία *dichostasia* (2)
dissensions (1)
divisions (1)

1497 διχοτομέω *dichotomeō* (2)
cut to pieces (2)

1498 διψάω *dipsaō* (16)
thirsty (13)
thirst (2)
thirst for (1)

1499 δίψος *dipsos* (1)
thirst (1)

1500 δίψυχος *dipsychos* (2)
double-minded (2)

1501 διωγμός *diōgmos* (10)
persecution (5)
persecutions (5)

1502 διώκτης *diōktēs* (1)
persecutor (1)

1503 διώκω *diōkō* (45)
persecuted (15)
persecute (11)
pursue (5)
persecuting (4)
make every effort (2)
press on (2)
pursued (2)
follow (1)
go running off after (1) *+599+3593*
practice (1)
try (1)

1504 δόγμα *dogma* (5)
regulations (2)
decree (1)
decrees (1)
untranslated (1)

1505 δογματίζω *dogmatizō* (1)
submit to rules (1)

1506 δοκέω *dokeō* (62)
think (20)
thought (7)
thinks (6)
seems (3)
thinking (3)
expect (2)
seem (2)

seemed good (2)
think that (2)
considered (1)
considers himself (1) *+1639*
convinced (1)
decided (1)
found (1)
men[s] (1)
opinion (1)
regarded (1)
reputed (1)
seemed (1)
seemed to be leaders (1)
supposing (1)
take for (1) *+1639*
wants (1)
untranslated (1)

1507 δοκιμάζω *dokimazō* (22)
test (6)
approve (2)
approved (1)
approves (1)
be tested (1)
discern (1)
examine (1)
find out (1)
how interpret (1)
interpret (1)
proved (1)
refined (1)
test and approve (1)
tests (1)
think it worthwhile (1)
try out (1)

1508 δοκιμασία *dokimasia* (1)
tried (1)

1509 δοκιμή *dokimē* (7)
character (2)
proved (2)
proof (1)
severe trial (1) *+2568*
would stand the test (1)

1510 δοκίμιον *dokimion* (2)
proved genuine (1)
testing (1)

1511 δόκιμος *dokimos* (7)
approved (3)
approval (1)
stood the test (1)
test (1)
tested and approved (1)

1512 δοκός *dokos* (6)
plank (6)

1513 δόλιος *dolios* (1)
deceitful (1)

1514 δολιόω *dolioō* (1)
practice deceit (1)

1515 δόλος *dolos* (11)
deceit (5)
deceitful (1)
false (1)
sly (1) *+1877*
sly way (1)
trick (1)
trickery (1)

1516 δολόω *doloō* (1)
distort (1)

1517 δόμα *doma* (4)
gifts (3)
gift (1)

1518 δόξα *doxa* (165)
glory (112)
glorious (15)
praise (9)
splendor (9)
honor (5)
celestial beings (2)
brilliance (1)
glories (1)
glorified (1) *+1443*
glorify (1) *+1443*
glorious (1) *+1877*
glorious presence (1)
glorious splendor (1)
honored (1)
majesty (1)
shone with glory (1) *+2400*
with ever-increasing glory (1) *+608+1518+1650*
untranslated (2)

1519 δοξάζω *doxazō* (61)
glorify (12)
glorified (11)
praised (11)
honored (4)
praising (4)
bring glory to (3)
praise (3)
glorious (2)
glory (2)
brought glory (1)
gave praise to (1)
glorifies (1)
glorifying (1)
glory come to (1)
glory gave (1)
honor (1)
make much of (1)
take glory (1)

1520 Δορκάς *Dorkas* (2)
Dorcas (2)

1521 δόσις *dosis* (2)
giving (1)
untranslated (1)

1522 δότης *dotēs* (1)
giver (1)

1523 Δουβέριος *Douberios*
Variant; not used

1524 δουλαγωγέω *doulagōgeō* (1)
make slave (1)

1525 δουλεία *douleia* (5)
slavery (2)
bondage (1)
makes a slave (1)
slaves (1)

1526 δουλεύω *douleuō* (25)
serve (10)
serving (3)
slaves (3)
enslaved (2)
served (2)
in slavery (1)
serve as slaves (1)
serves (1)
slave (1)
slaving (1)

1527 δούλη *doulē* (3)
servant (2)
untranslated (1)

1528 δοῦλος1 *doulos1* (124)
servant (54)
servants (38)
slave (18)
slaves (11)
servant's (2)
slavery (1)

1529 δοῦλος2 *doulos2* (2)
in slavery (2)

1530 δουλόω *douloō* (8)
become slaves (2)
addicted (1)
be enslaved (1)
bound (1)
in slavery (1)
make a slave (1)
slave (1)

1531 δοχή *dochē* (2)
banquet (2)

1532 δράκων *drakōn* (13)
dragon (13)

1533 δράσσομαι *drassomai* (1)
catches (1)

1534 δραχμή *drachmē* (3)
coin (1)
silver coins (1)
untranslated (1)

1535 δρέπανον *drepanon* (8)
sickle (8)

1536 δρόμος *dromos* (3)
race (2)
work (1)

1537 Δρούσιλλα *Drousilla* (1)
Drusilla (1)

1538 δύναμαι *dynamai* (210)
can (85)
cannot (40) *+4024*
could (35)
able (24)
can't (5) *+4024*
cannot (3) *+3590*
couldn't (2) *+4024*
ready (2)
and cannot (1) *+4028*
can do (1)
cannot (1) *+4046*
cannot do (1) *+4024*
cannot do (1) *+4028*
competent (1)
enables (1)
may (1)
possible (1)
right (1)
unable (1) *+3590*
unable (1) *+4024*
untranslated (2)

1539 δύναμις *dynamis* (119)
power (73)
miracles (16)
ability (3)
miraculous powers (3)
powerful (3)
powers (3)
mighty (2)
as much as were able (1) *+2848*
bodies (1)
brilliance (1)
enabled (1)
excessive (1)
fury (1)
grasp the meaning (1) *+3836+3857*
heavenly bodies (1) *+3836+4041*
mighty one (1)
miracle (1)
miraculous powers (1) *+1920*
so powerfully (1) *+1877*
strength (1)
work miracles (1)
workers of miracles (1)
untranslated (1)

1540 δυναμόω *dynamoō* (2)
strengthened (1)
turned to strength (1)

1541 δυνάστης *dynastēs* (3)
important official (1)
ruler (1)
rulers (1)

1542 δυνατέω *dynateō* (3)
able (2)
powerful (1)

1543 δυνατός *dynatos* (32)
possible (10)
able (4)
strong (3)
could (2)
power (2)
powerful (2)
can (1) *+1639*
could have done so (1)
had power (1) *+1639*
impossible (1) *+4024*
influential (1)
leaders (1)
mighty (1)
possible (1) *+1639*
thorough (1)

1544 δύνω *dynō* (2)
setting (1)
sunset (1) *+2463*

1545 δύο *dyo* (134)
two (122)
extra (2)
seventy-two (2) *+1573*
42 (1) *+5477*
both[s] (1) *+3836*
extra (1) *+324*
forty-two (1) *+5477*
twenty to thirty gallons (1) *+2445+3583+5552*
two by two (1) *+1545*
two by two (1) *+324+1545*

1546 δυσβάστακτος *dysbastaktos* (1)
hardly carry (1)

1547 δυσεντερία *dysenteria*
Variant; not used

1548 δυσεντέριον *dysenterion* (1)
dysentery (1)

1549 δυσερμήνευτος *dysermēneutos* (1)
hard to explain (1)

1550 δύσις *dysis*
Variant; not used

1551 δύσκολος *dyskolos* (1)
hard (1)

1552 δυσκόλως *dyskolōs* (3)
hard (3)

1553 δυσμή *dysmē* (5)
west (5)

1554 δυσνόητος *dysnoētos* (1)
hard to understand (1)

1555 δυσφημέω *dysphēmeō* (1)
slandered (1)

1556 δυσφημία *dysphēmia* (1)
bad report (1)

1557 δώδεκα *dōdeka* (75)
twelve (61)
12,000 (13) *+5942*
untranslated (1)

1558 δωδέκατος *dōdekatos* (1)
twelfth (1)

1559 δωδεκάφυλον *dōdekaphylon* (1)
twelve tribes (1)

1560 δῶμα *dōma* (7)
roof (4)
roofs (2)
roof of house (1)

1561 δωρεά *dōrea* (11)
gift (10)
it[s] (1) *+3836*

1562 δωρεάν *dōrean* (9)
freely (3)
for nothing (1)
free gift (1)
free of charge (1)
without cost (1)
without paying for it (1)
without reason (1)

1563 δωρέομαι *dōreomai* (3)
given (2)
gave (1)

1564 δώρημα *dōrēma* (2)
gift (2)

1565 δῶρον *dōron* (19)
gift (8)
gifts (8)
gift devoted to God (1)
help (1)
offerings (1)

1566 δωροφορία *dōrophoria*
Variant; not used

1567 ε *e*
Variant; not used

1568 ἔα *ea* (1)
Ha (1)

1569 ἐάν *ean* (351)
if (205)
unless (31) *+3590*
whatever (11) *+4005*
whoever (6) *+4005*
when (5)
wherever (5) *+3963*
anyone (3)
suppose (3)
though (3)
what (3) *+4005*
whatever (3) *+5516*
anything (2) *+4005*
whatever (2) *+4012*
whenever (2) *+3963*
whenever (2) *+4006*
whoever (2) *+5516*
all who (1) *+4012*
anyone (1) *+4005*
anyone (1) *+4012*
anyone (1) *+4246+6034*
anyone (1) *+5516*
anyone who (1) *+4005*
anyone who (1) *+5516*
anything (1) *+4005+4246+4547*
anything (1) *+5516*
as for (1)
at least (1) *+2779*
but (1) *+3590*
even (1) *+2779*
even if (1)
even though (1) *+1142*
everyone (1)
everything (1) *+4012+4246*
fail (1) *+3590*
in keeping with income (1) *+2338+4005+5516*
just (1) *+2779*
like (1) *+6055*
man (1)
on (1)
only (1) *+3590*
provided that (1)
since (1)
suppose (1) *+1142*
suppose a (1) *+5515*
those whom (1) *+4005*
until (1) *+3590+4754*
what (1) *+4012*
whatever (1)
whatever (1) *+4005+5516*
whenever (1)
whenever (1) *+2471*
wherever (1) *+4023*
whether (1)
who (1) *+5516*
whoever (1) *+4015*
whom (1) *+4005*
without (1) *+3590*
would (1)
untranslated (21)

1570 ἐάνπερ *eanper* (3)
if (2)
untranslated (1)

1571 ἑαυτοῦ *heautou* (267)
himself (77)
themselves (29)
his own (16)
ourselves (15)
his (14)
itself (12)
their (11)
their own (9)
them (6)
each other (4)
one another (4)
he (3)
herself (3)
yourselves (3)
her (2)
they (2)
appeared (1) *+5746*
bringing (1) *+2400+3552*
claimed to be (1) *+4472*
claims to be (1) *+4472*
her own (1)
him (1)
his heart (1)
his self (1)
his senses (1)
inwardly (1) *+1877*
it (1)
jumped (1) *+965*
myself (1)
oneself (1)
others (1)
our (1)
our hearts (1)
own (1)
proper (1)
renounced marriage (1) *+2335+2336*
self-seeking (1) *+2426+3836*
their hearts (1)
to himself (1) *+1877*
we (1)
your hearts (1)
yours (1)
yourself (1)
untranslated (30)

1572 ἐάω *eaō* (11)
let (6)
allow (2)
allowed (1)
left (1)
no more (1)

1573 ἑβδομήκοντα *hebdomēkonta* (5)
seventy-two (2) *+1545*
276 (1) *+1357+1971*
seventy (1)
seventy-five (1) *+4297*

1574 ἑβδομηκοντάκις *hebdomēkontakis* (1)
seventy-seven times (1) *+2231*

1575 ἕβδομος *hebdomos* (9)
seventh (9)

1576 Ἔβερ *Eber* (1)
Eber (1)

1577 Ἑβραϊκός *Hebraikos*
Variant; not used

1578 Ἑβραῖος *Hebraios* (4)
Hebrews (2)

Hebraic Jews (1)
Hebrew (1)

1579 Ἑβραΐς *Hebrais* (3)
in Aramaic (3) *+1365*

1580 Ἑβραϊστί *Hebraisti* (7)
in Aramaic (5)
in Hebrew (2)

1581 ἐγγίζω *engizō* (42)
near (13)
approached (9)
approaching (3)
came near (2)
came up (2)
come near (2)
comes (2)
almost (1)
almost here (1)
comes near (1)
draw near (1)
drawing near (1)
drew near (1)
gathering around (1)
gets here (1)
neared (1) *+1181*

1582 ἐγγράφω *engraphō* (3)
written (1)
written in (1)
written on (1)

1583 ἔγγυος *engyos* (1)
guarantee (1)

1584 ἐγγύς *engys* (31)
near (22)
almost time (2)
approaching (1) *+1181*
from (1)
in danger of (1)
nearby (1)
nearer (1)
Sabbath day's walk from (1)
+2400+3847+4879
soon (1)

1585 ἐγγύτερον *engyteron*
Variant; not used

1586 ἐγείρω *egeirō* (143)
raised (45)
get up (15)
got up (11)
risen (10)
rise (8)
raised to life (7)
raised from the dead (6)
raise (5)
appear (3)
raise up (3)
raises (3)
woke up (3)
gets up (2)
helped up (2)
wake up (2)
woke (2)
appeared (1)
come (1)
come now (1)
go (1)
lift out (1)
lifted (1)
made (1)
made get up (1)
on your feet (1)
raise again (1)
raised again (1)
raised up (1)
rise again (1)
rising (1)
stand up (1)
stir up (1)

1587 ἔγερσις *egersis* (1)
resurrection (1)

1588 ἐγκάθετος *enkathetos* (1)
spies (1)

1589 ἐγκαίνια *enkainia* (1)
feast of Dedication (1)

1590 ἐγκαινίζω *enkainizō* (2)
opened (1)
put into effect (1)

1591 ἐγκακέω *enkakeō* (6)
lose heart (2)
become weary (1)
discouraged (1)
give up (1)
tire of (1)

1592 ἐγκαλέω *enkaleō* (7)
accusing (2)
accusation (1)
accusations (1)
being charged with (1)
bring any charge (1)
press charges (1)

1593 ἐγκαταλείπω *enkataleipō* (10)
abandoned (2)
deserted (2)
forsaken (2)
abandon (1)
forsake (1)
give up (1)
left (1)

1594 ἐγκατοικέω *enkatoikeō* (1)
living among (1)

1595 ἐγκαυχάομαι *enkauchaomai* (1)
boast (1)

1596 ἐγκεντρίζω *enkentrizō* (6)
grafted in (2)
graft in (1)
grafted (1)
grafted in among (1)
grafted into (1)

1597 ἐγκλείω *enkleiō*
Variant; not used

1598 ἔγκλημα *enklēma* (2)
charge (1)
charges (1)

1599 ἐγκομβόομαι *enkomboomai* (1)
clothe with (1)

1600 ἐγκοπή *enkopē* (1)
hinder (1) *+1443*

1601 ἐγκόπτω *enkoptō* (5)
cut in on (1)
hinder (1)
hindered from (1)
stopped (1)
weary (1)

1602 ἐγκράτεια *enkrateia* (4)
self-control (4)

1603 ἐγκρατεύομαι *enkrateuomai* (2)
control themselves (1)
goes into training (1)

1604 ἐγκρατής *enkratēs* (1)
disciplined (1)

1605 ἐγκρίνω *enkrinō* (1)
classify (1)

1606 ἐγκρύπτω *enkryptō* (2)
mixed (2)

1607 ἔγκυος *enkyos* (1)
expecting a child (1)

1608 ἐγχρίω *enchriō* (1)
put on (1)

1609 ἐγώ *egō* (2670)
me (748)
I (500)
my (481)
us (362)
our (289)
we (176)
mine (11)
I myself (7)
ours (6)
my own (5)
I (2) *+1877*
our own (2)
your (2)
as for me (1)
as surely as I live (1) *+2409*
equal with us (1) *+2777+2779*
for myself (1)
here (1) *+1877*
him[s] (1) *+81+3836*
I (1) *+899*
I (1) *+3836+6034*
I (1) *+6034*
I'm (1) *+1639*
intelligible (1) *+3808+3836*
is one of us (1) *+199+3552*
it[s] (1) *+3836+5013*
Jews (1) *+1169+1877+3836*
me (1) *+3836+3950*
me (1) *+3836+6034*
me (1) *+6034*
me say (1) *+4123*
myself (1) *+6034*
of mine (1) *+1650*
our companions (1) *+3836+5250*
ourselves (1)
say (1) *+201+1666*
them[s] (1) *+3836+4252*
this[s] (1) *+3364+3836+4047*
we'll (1)
what business is it of mine (1) *+5515*
with us (1)
yes (1) *+2627*
untranslated (50)

1610 ἐδαφίζω *edaphizō* (1)
dash to the ground (1)

1611 ἔδαφος *edaphos* (1)
ground (1)

1612 ἑδραῖος *hedraios* (3)
firm (1)
settled the matter (1) *+2705*
stand firm (1) *+1181*

1613 ἑδραίωμα *hedraiōma* (1)
foundation (1)

1614 Ἑζεκίας *Hezekias* (2)
Hezekiah (2)

1615 ἐθελοθρησκία *ethelothrēskia* (1)
self-imposed worship (1)

1616 ἐθίζω *ethizō* (1)
custom (1)

1617 ἐθνάρχης *ethnarchēs* (1)
governor (1)

1618 ἐθνικός *ethnikos* (4)
pagans (3)
pagan (1)

1619 ἐθνικῶς *ethnikōs* (1)
like a gentile (1)

1620 ἔθνος *ethnos* (162)
gentiles (81)
nations (37)
nation (23)
pagans (6)
people (6)
Nation (3)
gentile (2)
country (1)
gentile (1) *+1666*

heathen (1)
pagan (1)

1621 ἔθος *ethos* (12)
customs (6)
custom (4)
as usual (1) *+2848+3836*
in the habit of (1)

1622 ἔθω *ethō*
Variant; not used

1623 εἰ *ei* (502)
if (313)
except (36) *+3590*
but (10) *+3590*
only (10) *+3590*
since (10)
that (6)
though (6)
whether (6)
only (5) *+3590+4024*
though (4) *+2779*
never (3)
but only (2) *+3590*
if he does (2) *+1254+3590*
surely (2) *+1145*
unless (2) *+1760+3590*
unless (2) *+3590*
unless (2) *+3614*
whatever (2) *+5516*
but (1) *+2779*
even though (1)
evidently (1) *+3590*
except (1) *+323+3614*
except for (1) *+3590*
hoping (1) *+4803*
if (1) *+3525*
in the hope that (1)
nevertheless (1) *+3590*
no (1)
now that (1)
only (1)
only (1) *+3590+3668*
only to (1) *+3590+4029*
or at least (1) *+1254+3590*
otherwise (1) *+1254+3590*
otherwise (1) *+1760+3590*
perhaps (1) *+726*
perhaps (1) *+726+1145*
perhaps (1) *+5593*
somehow (1) *+4803*
surely (1) *+3605*
that (1) *+4803*
to see if (1)
undoubtedly (1) *+5593*
unless (1) *+4024*
until (1) *+3590+4020*
what (1) *+5516*
what if (1)
when (1)
when (1) *+1254*
whether or not (1)
untranslated (47)

1624 εἰδέα *eidea* (1)
appearance (1)

1625 εἶδον *eidon*
Variant; not used

1626 εἶδος *eidos* (5)
form (2)
appearance (1)
kind (1)
sight (1)

1627 εἰδωλεῖον *eidōleion* (1)
idol's temple (1)

1628 εἰδωλόθυτος *eidōlothytos* (9)
food sacrificed to idols (5)
sacrificed to idols (2)
sacrifice offered to an idol (1)
such food (1)

1629 εἰδωλολάτρης *eidōlolatrēs* (7)
idolaters (5)
idolater (2)

1630 εἰδωλολατρία *eidōlolatria* (4)
idolatry (4)

1631 εἴδωλον *eidōlon* (11)
idols (8)
idol (2)
it[s] (1) *+3836*

1632 εἰκῇ *eikē* (6)
for nothing (2)
idle notions (1)
nothing (1)
vain (1)
wasted (1)

1633 εἴκοσι *eikosi* (11)
twenty-four (6) *+5475*
twenty (2)
a hundred and twenty feet deep (1) *+3976*
three or three and a half miles (1) *+2445+4297+5084+5558*
twenty-three (1) *+5552*

1634 εἴκω *eikō* (1)
give in (1) *+3836+5717*

1635 εἰκών *eikōn* (23)
image (13)
likeness (4)
portrait (2)
images (1)
it[s] (1) *+2563+3836+3836*
portrait (1) *+2400*
realities (1)

1636 εἰλικρίνεια *eilikrineia* (3)
sincerity (3)

1637 εἰλικρινής *eilikrinēs* (2)
pure (1)
wholesome (1)

1638 εἰ μήν *ei mēn*
Variant; not used

1639 εἰμί *eimi* (2462)
is (705)
are (369)
was (302)
be (263)
am (130)
were (128)
been (36)
come (14)
have (14)
had (12)
means (9)
comes (8)
happen (7)
be (6) *+1650*
lived (6)
do (5)
isn't (5) *+4024*
mean (5)
means (5) *+3493*
stands for (5)
become (4) *+1650*
belong to (4) *+1666*
belonged to (4) *+1666*
has (4)
live (4)
stay (4)
stayed (4)
as (3)
become (3)
being (3)
belong (3)
belongs to (3) *+1666*
calls for (3)
deserve (3) *+545*
hate (3) *+3631*
it's (3)
know (3) *+1196*
remain (3)
will (3)
with (3)
aren't (2) *+4024*
aren't (2) *+4049*
began (2)
belongs to (2)
cannot (2) *+4024*
cease to be (2) *+4024*
companions (2) *+3552+3836*
companions (2) *+3836+5250*
controlled (2)
deserve (2) *+2653*
did (2)
follow (2)
form (2)
go (2)
had (2) *+2400*
leads to (2)
mean (2) *+2527*
meant (2)
pleases (2) *+2298*
sanctified (2) *+39*
saved (2) *+5392*
taught (2) *+1438*
to (2)
would (2)
accepts (1) *+1283*
advisable (1) *+545*
after he was circumcised (1) *+1877+4364*
all the world (1) *+476+4005+5515*
am present (1)
are (1) *+1650*
at work (1)
be diligent (1)
be that as it may (1)
bears (1) *+4472*
became (1) *+1181*
because are (1)
been (1) *+1181*
before this been (1) *+4732*
believer (1) *+4412*
belong to Lord (1) *+3261*
belong to (1)
belonged to (1)
belonging to Simon (1) *+4981*
belongs (1)
belongs to Christ (1) *+5986*
betray (1) *+3836+4140*
binds together (1) *+5278*
boast (1) *+3017*
break (1) *+4127*
bring (1) *+1650*
came about (1)
can (1) *+1543*
care very little (1) *+1650+1788*
catch (1) *+2436*
chief cornerstone (1) *+214*
come together (1) *+899+2093+3836*
come together (1) *+5251*
come upon (1) *+2158*
considers himself (1) *+1506*
consist (1)
continued (1)
cured (1) *+2543*
cut (1) *+3300*
deserves (1) *+545*
devoted to (1) *+4674*
disagreed (1) *+851*
does belong to (1)
done (1)
done (1) *+2237*
done (1) *+4472*
done (1) *+4556*
enabled (1) *+1443*
end (1) *+4639*
enjoy long life (1) *+3432*
enter (1) *+1656*
envious (1) *+3836+4057+4505*
equality (1) *+2698+3836*

exist (1)
existed (1)
exists (1)
explain (1) *+1196*
fail the test (1) *+99*
failed the test (1) *+99*
fall (1) *+4406*
find (1)
find (1) *+2351*
forgive (1) *+2664*
gathered (1)
gathered (1) *+2190*
get (1)
given fullness (1) *+4444*
gives life (1) *+2443*
had (1) *+338*
had (1) *+1256*
had (1) *+1877*
had authority (1) *+1877+2026*
had power (1) *+1543*
had taken part in a rebellion (1) *+3334*
had too much (1) *+3551*
happened (1)
happened (1) *+1181*
have (1) *+2400*
have all you want (1) *+3170*
have an obligation (1) *+4050*
have being (1)
have hope (1) *+1827*
have such a place (1)
he's (1)
he's (1) *+899+6034*
hear (1) *+201+4047*
heard (1) *+201*
hold terror (1) *+5832*
how far will they go (1) *+4047+5515*
I'm (1) *+1609*
in charge of (1) *+2093*
in other words (1) *+4047*
including (1) *+4005*
involves (1)
is (1) *+3493*
is now (1)
isn't (1) *+4049*
keep (1)
kept on (1)
know (1) *+5745*
last (1)
lasts (1)
leaders (1) *+4755*
let be (1)
listens (1) *+212*
lived (1) *+1695*
longs for (1) *+2160*
looks like (1)
looks like (1) *+3927*
made (1)
made holy (1) *+39*
make complete (1) *+4444*
making a complaint about[s] (1)
making signs (1) *+1377*
marveled (1) *+2513*
may (1)
meaning (1)
means (1) *+3306*
means (1) *+4005*
meet (1)
numbering (1) *+750*
of you (1) *+1877+3836+5148*
on (1)
on the evening (1) *+4070*
one (1)
one of (1) *+1666*
only (1) *+3666*
owe (1) *+4050*
owed money to (1) *+5971*
owns (1) *+2625*
owns (1) *+3261*
participate (1) *+3128*
perish (1) *+724+1650*
place (1)
please (1) *+2298*
pleased (1) *+744*
possible (1) *+1543*
previously seen (1) *+4632*
put aside (1) *+629*
put trust (1) *+4275*
read (1) *+1211*
read (1) *+2108*
receive (1)
rely (1) *+4275*
rely on (1) *+1666*
represent (1)
resembled (1) *+3927*
rest (1)
rightly so (1) *+545*
riot (1) *+2573*
Romans (1) *+4871*
sat (1) *+5153*
say (1)
settle matters (1) *+2333*
share (1) *+3128*
share with (1) *+5171*
show favoritism (1) *+4720*
show favoritism (1) *+4721*
sided with (1) *+5250*
sinned (1) *+281+4472*
sins (1) *+281*
spent the night (1) *+1381*
spread (1)
standing (1)
standing (1) *+2705*
stood (1) *+2392*
stood (1) *+2705*
stood (1) *+3023*
stood opposed (1) *+5641*
sums up (1)
take (1) *+2400*
take for (1) *+1506*
taken part (1) *+3128*
takes captive (1) *+5194*
tasted sweet (1) *+1184*
testify (1) *+3457*
testify (1) *+3459*
though (1)
to have failed (1) *+99*
treat (1)
valued highly (1) *+1952*
want (1)
was present (1)
went (1)
were (1) *+4537*
were present (1)
were up (1) *+326*
what shall we do (1) *+4036+5515*
while (1) *+1877+3836*
with a great crash (1) *+899+3489+3836+4774*
withdrew (1) *+5723*
wore clothing (1) *+1907*
work with (1) *+5301*
untranslated (120)

1640 εἶμι *eimi*
Variant; not used

1641 εἵνεκεν *heineken* (2)
because (1) *+4005*
untranslated (1)

1642 εἴπερ *eiper* (6)
if (2)
if in fact (1) *+726*
if indeed (1)
since (1)
untranslated (1)

1643 εἴπως *eipōs*
Variant; not used

1644 εἰρηνεύω *eirēneuō* (4)
live in peace (2)
be at peace (1)
live at peace (1)

1645 εἰρήνη *eirēnē* (92)
peace (82)
peace be with (4)
go I wish you well (1) *+1877+5632*
peacemakers (1) *+4472*
reconcile (1) *+1650+5261*
safe (1) *+1877*
the blessing of peace (1)
welcomed (1) *+1312+3552*

1646 εἰρηνικός *eirēnikos* (2)
peace (1)
peace-loving (1)

1647 εἰρηνοποιέω *eirēnopoieō* (1)
making peace (1)

1648 εἰρηνοποιός *eirēnopoios* (1)
peacemakers (1)

1649 εἴρω *eirō*
Variant; not used

1650 εἰς *eis* (1762)
to (467)
into (249)
in (165)
for (143)
on (48)
at (37)
as (26)
forever (23) *+172+3836*
against (17)
to (15) *+3836*
so that (14) *+3836*
among (12)
so that (11)
that (7) *+3836*
be (6) *+1639*
of (6)
with (6)
about (5)
before (5)
until (5)
back (4) *+3836+3958*
become (5) *+1181*
become (4) *+1639*
entered (4) *+2262*
for purpose (4)
leads to (4)
never (4) *+172+3590+3836+4024*
toward (4)
why (4) *+5515*
and so (3) *+3836*
brought (3)
in order that (3) *+3836*
leading to (3)
reached (3) *+2262*
where (3) *+4005*
among (2) *+3545+3836*
became (2) *+1181*
beyond limits (2) *+296+3836*
down upon (2)
forever (2) *+1457+3836*
home (2) *+899+3875*
never (2) *+172+3836+4024*
on to (2)
over (2)
that (2)
through (2)
throughout (2) *+3910*
to bring (2)
to do (2)
whatever (2) *+323+4005*
aboard (1)
across (1) *+3836+4305*
again (1) *+172+3836*
all over (1) *+3910*
and thus (1) *+3836*
are (1) *+1639*
are justified (1) *+1466*
are saved (1) *+5401*
arrived (1) *+2262*

as a result (1) *+3836*
as far as (1)
ashore (1) *+1178+3836*
at all (1) *+3836+4117*
attaining to (1)
away[s] (1) *+2557+3836*
be saved (1) *+5401*
become (1)
been (1) *+1181*
before (1) *+3545+3836*
before them (1) *+3545*
belonging (1) *+4348*
bring (1) *+1639*
brings into (1) *+1652*
burial (1) *+3645+5502*
by (1)
by itself (1) *+1651+3023+5536+6006*
care very little (1) *+1639+1788*
completely (1) *+3836+4117*
condemned (1) *+2262+3213*
confirms (1) *+1012*
decay (1) *+1426+5715*
destroyed (1) *+724*
discredited (1) *+3357+4029*
doing (1)
endlessly (1) *+1457+3836*
enter (1) *+4513*
Ephesus (1)
eventually (1) *+5465*
ever (1) *+172+3836*
ever-increasing wickedness (1) *+490+490+3836*
faith from first to last (1) *+4411+4411*
far off (1) *+3426*
for (1) *+3836*
for all time (1) *+1457+3836*
for the express purpose (1) *+899+4047*
for this reason (1) *+4047*
forever (1) *+172*
forever (1) *+172+2465*
forevermore (1) *+172+3836+4246*
from (1)
full of (1)
gave (1) *+965*
greatly (1) *+4353*
grew (1) *+2262+3836*
hand over to (1) *+4140+5931*
has enough (1) *+2400*
home (1) *+899+3836+3875*
home (1) *+3836+3875*
home (1) *+3836+3875+5148*
in agreement (1) *+1651+3836*
in dealing with (1)
in order that (1)
in order to (1)
in regard to (1)
indoors (1) *+3836+3864*
indoors (1) *+3875*
intended to bring (1)
it[s] (1) *+3795*
landed (1) *+609+1178+3836*
led to (1)
listen carefully (1) *+3836+4044+5148+5148+5502*
lose good name (1) *+591+2262*
make one (1) *+1651*
never (1) *+173+3590+3836+4024*
never again (1) *+172+3590+3836+4024*
next (1) *+3516+3836*
of mine (1) *+1609*
onto (1)
perish (1) *+724+1639*
prompted (1) *+965+2840+3836*
put on board (1) *+899+1837*
reach (1) *+1181*
reached (1) *+201*
reaching (1) *+2262*
reconcile (1) *+1645+5261*
regarding (1)
result (1) *+3836*
result in (1)
return (1) *+2262+3836+4099*
return (1) *+5715*
right into (1) *+2276+2401*
saved (1) *+4348+6034*
so (1) *+3836*
so as (1) *+3836*
so as to (1)
so then (1) *+3836*
spur on (1) *+4237*
take (1) *+404*
take (1) *+2884*
testifying (1) *+3457*
that far outweighs them all (1) *+983+2848+5651+5651*
that is why (1) *+4047*
the full extent of (1) *+5465*
the reason (1) *+1142+4047*
the reason (1) *+4047*
then will be able (1) *+3836*
there[s] (1) *+2038+3836*
this is the reason (1) *+4047*
this very reason (1) *+4047*
throughout (1)
throughout (1) *+4246*
till (1)
to (1) *+4047*
to be (1)
to cause (1)
to serve (1)
to this end (1) *+4005*
treat (1) *+4472*
turned (1) *+1181*
turned around (1) *+3836+3958+5138*
turned back (1) *+599+3836+3958*
under (1)
under power (1) *+5931*
unto (1)
up (1)
visit in advance (1) *+4601*
visited (1) *+2262*
what (1) *+5515*
where (1)
where (1) *+5536*
where[s] (1) *+3836+5596*
will turn out (1)
with (1) *+3836*
with ever-increasing glory (1) *+608+1518+1518*
without (1) *+3590*
untranslated (279)

1651 εἷς *heis* (343)
one (241)
a (16)
first (8)
a single (7)
the other[s] (6)
each (5) *+1667*
man (4)
alone (3)
an (3)
one (3) *+5516*
a unit (1)
agreeing (1) *+1191+4472*
alike (1) *+608*
among (1) *+1666*
another (1)
any (1)
by itself (1) *+1650+3023+5536+6006*
detail (1) *+1667*
each (1)
each (1) *+324+1667*
each (1) *+1651+2848*
each other (1) *+1651+3836*
everyone (1) *+1667*
faithful to her husband (1) *+467+1222*
first day (1)
in agreement (1) *+1650+3836*
in turn (1) *+2848*
in unison (1)
just as though (1) *+899+2779+3836*
make one (1) *+1650*
nothing (1) *+4028*
once (1)
one (1) *+257+4024*
one (1) *+1666*
one (1) *+3836*
one after the other (1) *+1667*
one at a time (1) *+1651+2848*
only (1) *+4028*
some (1) *+3538+3836*
someone (1)
the next day (1) *+2465+3552*
the one (1)
the only (1)
the same (1)
unity (1)
untranslated (12)

1652 εἰσάγω *eisagō* (11)
brought in (2)
brought into (2)
bring in (1)
brings into (1) *+1650*
brought (1)
led into (1)
take into (1)
taken into (1)
took into (1)

1653 εἰσακούω *eisakouō* (5)
heard (4)
listen (1)

1654 εἰσδέχομαι *eisdechomai* (1)
receive (1)

1655 εἴσειμι *eiseimi* (4)
enter (1)
entered into (1)
went (1)
went to (1)

1656 εἰσέρχομαι *eiserchomai* (195)
enter (54)
entered (34)
went into (16)
go into (7)
went in (7)
come in (6)
enters (6)
go in (6)
come (5)
came in (4)
went inside (4)
went to (4)
comes in (3)
fall into (3)
went (3)
arrived in (2)
came into (2)
entering (2)
gone (2)
arrived (1)
came (1)
came to (1)
come at (1)
come in among (1)
come to (1)
comes into (1)
enter (1) *+1639*
enter into (1)
entered (1) *+1181*
entered into (1)
get in (1)
go (1)
goes into (1)
going into (1)
gone into (1)
got to (1)
hurried (1) *+3552+5082*
reached (1)
reaped the benefits of (1)
started (1)

went into (1) *+4513*
untranslated (3)

1657 εἰσκαλέομαι *eiskaleomai* (1)
invited (1)

1658 εἴσοδος *eisodos* (5)
coming (1)
enter (1)
reception (1)
visit (1)
welcome into (1)

1659 εἰσπηδάω *eispēdaō* (1)
rushed in (1)

1660 εἰσπορεύομαι *eisporeuomai* (17)
enter (3)
enters (3)
come in (2)
going into (2)
came (1)
go into (1)
going (1)
moved about freely (1) *+1744+2779*
went in (1)
went into (1)
went to (1)

1661 εἰστρέχω *eistrechō* (1)
ran (1)

1662 εἰσφέρω *eispherō* (8)
lead into (2)
bringing to (1)
brought (1)
brought into (1)
carries (1)
do this[s] (1)
take into (1)

1663 εἶτα *eita* (15)
then (10)
after that (1)
and (1)
moreover (1)
once more (1) *+4099*
when (1)

1664 εἴτε *eite* (65)
or (28)
whether (18)
if (11)
where (3)
as for (1)
as for (1) *+5642*
such as (1)
untranslated (2)

1665 εἴωθα *eiōtha* (4)
custom (4)

1666 ἐκ *ek* (917)
from (314)
of (207)
by (53)
out of (45)
at (20)
with (19)
in (17)
on (13)
out (7)
for (6)
some of (6)
from among (5)
belong to (5)
belong to (4) *+1639*
belonged to (4) *+1639*
second time (4) *+1311*
through (4)
among (3)
because of (3)
belongs to (3) *+1639*
circumcised (3) *+4364*
since (3)
whose mother was (3)
because (2)
belonged to (2)
depends on (2)
have faith (2) *+4411*
over (2)
part of (2)
second time (2) *+1311+4099*
under (2)
according to means (1) *+2400+3836*
after (1)
among (1) *+1651*
as (1)
away from (1)
based on (1)
believe (1) *+4411*
believers[s] (1) *+899*
between (1)
completely (1) *+3336+4356*
descendant (1) *+2588+3836*
descendant (1) *+3875*
descended from (1)
descended from (1) *+5065*
ever (1) *+172+3836*
followed (1)
free and belong to no man (1) *+1801+4246*
from then on (1) *+4047*
gentile (1) *+1620*
heavenly (1) *+4041*
his native language (1) *+2625+3836*
illegitimate children (1) *+1164+4518*
imperfect (1) *+3538*
in answer to (1)
in front of (1) *+1885*
it depends on you (1) *+3836+5148*
Jews (1) *+4364*
lose (1) *+3496*
might say (1) *+3836+5125*
on account of (1)
one (1) *+1651*
one of (1)
one of (1) *+1639*
oppose (1) *+1885*
physically (1) *+5882*
reluctantly (1) *+3383*
rely on (1) *+1639*
result in (1) *+1181*
say (1) *+201+1609*
they the kind (1) *+4047*
third time (1) *+5569*
this is how (1) *+4047*
to (1)
wholeheartedly (1) *+2840*
whose mother (1)
without (1) *+4024*
untranslated (104)

1667 ἕκαστος *hekastos* (82)
each (54)
each (5) *+1651*
every (3)
everyone (3)
a man[s] (2)
anyone (1)
daily (1) *+2465+2848*
detail (1) *+1651*
each (1) *+324+1651*
each of (1)
each one (1)
every one (1)
everyone (1) *+1651*
everyone (1) *+4246*
him (1)
his (1)
one (1)
one after the other (1) *+1651*
yourself (1)
untranslated (1)

1668 ἑκάστοτε *hekastote* (1)
always (1)

1669 ἑκατόν *hekaton* (17)
hundred (8)
144,000 (3) *+5475+5477+5942*
144 (1) *+5475+5477*
153 (1) *+4299+5552*
eight hundred gallons (1) *+1004*
hundreds (1)
seventy-five pounds (1) *+3354*
thousand bushels (1) *+3174*

1670 ἑκατονταετής *hekatontaetēs* (1)
hundred years old (1)

1671 ἑκατονταπλασίων *hekatontaplasiōn* (3)
hundred times (3)

1672 ἑκατοντάρχης *hekatontarchēs* (20)
centurion (16)
centurions (2)
centurion's (1)
officers (1)

1673 ἑκατόνταρχος *hekatontarchos*
Variant; not used

1674 ἐκβαίνω *ekbainō* (1)
left (1)

1675 ἐκβάλλω *ekballō* (81)
drive out (20)
driving out (8)
drove out (5)
drives out (3)
take out (3)
threw (3)
thrown (3)
brings (2)
driven (2)
get rid of (2)
remove from (2)
send out (2)
threw out (2)
brings out (1)
brought out (1)
dragged (1)
drive (1)
driven out (1)
drove from (1)
exclude (1)
expelled (1)
leads (1)
out (1)
pluck out (1)
put out (1)
put outside (1)
puts out (1)
reject (1)
sent (1)
sent away (1)
sent off (1)
sent out (1)
take out of (1)
throw (1)
throw outside (1)
throwing (1)
took out (1)

1676 ἔκβασις *ekbasis* (2)
outcome (1)
way out (1)

1677 ἐκβλαστάνω *ekblastanō*
Variant; not used

1678 ἐκβολή *ekbolē* (1)
throw the cargo overboard (1)

1679 ἐκγαμίζω *ekgamizō*
Variant; not used

1680 ἐκγαμίσκω *ekgamiskō*
Variant; not used

1681 ἔκγονος *ekgonos* (1)
grandchildren (1)

1682 ἐκδαπανάω *ekdapanaō* (1)
everything I have expend (1)

1683 ἐκδέχομαι *ekdechomai* (6)

expecting (1)
looking forward to (1)
wait for (1)
waiting for (1)
waits (1)
waits for (1)

1684 ἔκδηλος *ekdēlos* (1)
clear (1)

1685 ἐκδημέω *ekdēmeō* (3)
away from (2)
away (1)

1686 ἐκδίδωμι *ekdidōmi* (4)
rented (3)
rent (1)

1687 ἐκδιηγέομαι *ekdiēgeomai* (2)
told (1)
told how (1)

1688 ἐκδικέω *ekdikeō* (6)
avenge (1)
avenged (1)
justice (1)
punish (1)
see that gets justice (1)
take revenge (1) *+4932*

1689 ἐκδίκησις *ekdikēsis* (9)
avenge (2)
justice (2)
avenged (1) *+4472*
punish (1)
punish (1) *+1443*
punishment (1)
readiness to see justice done (1)

1690 ἔκδικος *ekdikos* (2)
agent to bring punishment (1)
punish (1)

1691 ἐκδιώκω *ekdiōkō* (1)
drove out (1)

1692 ἔκδοτος *ekdotos* (1)
handed over (1)

1693 ἐκδοχή *ekdochē* (1)
expectation (1)

1694 ἐκδύω *ekdyō* (5)
took off (2)
stripped (1)
stripped of clothes (1)
unclothed (1)

1695 ἐκεῖ *ekei* (106)
there (72)
where (13)
here (2)
nearby (2)
at Berea[S] (1)
at his house (1)
but in the other case (1) *+1254*
in (1)
in that place (1)
lived (1) *+1639*
stayed (1) *+3531*
to the grove[S] (1)
untranslated (9)

1696 ἐκεῖθεν *ekeithen* (37)
from there (12)
that place (3)
there (3)
from that place (2)
from (1)
left (1) *+2002*
left that place (1)
left there (1) *+3553*
on (1)
on each side (1) *+1949+2779*
that (1)
that town[S] (1)
the synagogue[S] (1)
then (1)
where (1)
withdrew (1) *+432*
untranslated (5)

1697 ἐκεῖνος *ekeinos* (264)
that (99)
he (29)
those (28)
they (15)
this (9)
them (7)
him (6)
his (3)
she (3)
the (3)
these (3)
he himself (2)
that same (2)
that very (2)
the former[S] (2)
the man[S] (2)
the one (2)
their (2)
who (2)
he[S] (1) *+476+3836*
himself (1)
his disciples[S] (1)
it (1)
Jesus Christ[S] (1)
Jesus[S] (1)
John[S] (1)
Judas[S] (1)
Mary[S] (1)
next (1)
others (1)
Priscilla and Aquila[S] (1)
same (1)
that was the time (1) *+1877+2465+3836*
the disciples[S] (1)
the father[S] (1)
the other (1)
your brother[S] (1)
untranslated (25)

1698 ἐκεῖσε *ekeise* (2)
there (1)
where (1)

1699 ἐκζητέω *ekzēteō* (7)
earnestly seek (1)
held responsible (1)
held responsible for (1)
searched intently and with the greatest care (1) *+2001+2779*
seek (1)
seeks (1)
sought (1)

1700 ἐκζήτησις *ekzētēsis* (1)
controversies (1)

1701 ἐκθαμβέω *ekthambeō* (4)
alarmed (2)
deeply distressed (1)
overwhelmed with wonder (1)

1702 ἔκθαμβος *ekthambos* (1)
astonished (1)

1703 ἐκθαυμάζω *ekthaumazō* (1)
amazed (1)

1704 ἔκθετος *ekthetos* (1)
throw out (1)

1705 ἐκκαθαίρω *ekkathairō* (2)
cleanses (1)
get rid of (1)

1706 ἐκκαίω *ekkaiō* (1)
inflamed (1)

1707 ἐκκακέω *ekkakeō*
Variant; not used

1708 ἐκκεντέω *ekkenteō* (2)
pierced (2)

1709 ἐκκλάω *ekklaō* (3)
broken off (3)

1710 ἐκκλείω *ekkleiō* (2)
alienate (1)
excluded (1)

1711 ἐκκλησία *ekklēsia* (114)
church (74)
churches (34)
assembly (4)
congregation (1)
congregations (1)

1712 ἐκκλίνω *ekklinō* (3)
away (1)
turn (1)
turned away (1)

1713 ἐκκολυμβάω *ekkolymbaō* (1)
swimming away (1)

1714 ἐκκομίζω *ekkomizō* (1)
carried out (1)

1715 ἐκκοπή *ekkopē*
Variant; not used

1716 ἐκκόπτω *ekkoptō* (10)
cut down (5)
cut off (3)
cut from under (1)
cut out (1)

1717 ἐκκρεμάννυμι *ekkremannymi* (1)
hung on (1)

1718 ἐκλαλέω *eklaleō* (1)
tell (1)

1719 ἐκλάμπω *eklampō* (1)
shine (1)

1720 ἐκλανθάνομαι *eklanthanomai* (1)
forgotten (1)

1721 ἐκλέγομαι *eklegomai* (22)
chosen (9)
chose (8)
choose (3)
made a choice (1)
picked (1)

1722 ἐκλείπω *ekleipō* (4)
end (1)
fail (1)
gone (1)
stopped shining (1)

1723 ἐκλεκτός *eklektos* (22)
chosen (12)
elect (10)

1724 ἐκλογή *eklogē* (7)
chosen (3)
election (3)
elect (1)

1725 ἐκλύω *eklyō* (5)
collapse (2)
give up (1)
lose (1)
lose heart (1)

1726 ἐκμάσσω *ekmassō* (5)
wiped (4)
drying (1)

1727 ἐκμυκτηρίζω *ekmyktērizō* (2)
sneered at (1)
sneering at (1)

1728 ἐκνεύω *ekneuō* (1)
slipped away (1)

1729 ἐκνήφω *eknēphō* (1)
come back to senses (1)

1730 ἑκούσιος *hekousios* (1)
spontaneous (1) *+2848*

1731 ἑκουσίως *hekousiōs* (2)

deliberately (1)
willing (1)

1732 ἔκπαλαι *ekpalai* (2)
long (1)
long ago (1)

1733 ἐκπειράζω *ekpeirazō* (4)
put to the test (2)
test (2)

1734 ἐκπέμπω *ekpempō* (2)
sent away (1)
sent on way (1)

1735 ἐκπερισσῶς *ekperissōs* (1)
emphatically (1)

1736 ἐκπετάννυμι *ekpetannymi* (1)
held out (1)

1737 ἐκπηδάω *ekpēdaō* (1)
rushed out (1)

1738 ἐκπίπτω *ekpiptō* (10)
run aground (2)
dashed (1)
failed (1)
fall (1)
fall away (1)
fall from (1)
fallen away from (1)
falls (1)
fell off (1)

1739 ἐκπλέω *ekpleō* (3)
sailed (3)

1740 ἐκπληρόω *ekplēroō* (1)
fulfilled (1)

1741 ἐκπλήρωσις *ekplērōsis* (1)
end (1)

1742 ἐκπλήσσω *ekplēssō* (13)
amazed (9)
astonished (3)
overwhelmed with amazement (1) *+5669*

1743 ἐκπνέω *ekpneō* (3)
breathed his last (2)
died (1)

1744 ἐκπορεύομαι *ekporeuomai* (33)
come out (3)
comes out (3)
leaving (3)
out came (2)
went out (2)
came from (1)
came out (1)
come (1)
comes (1)
comes from (1)
coming out (1)
flowing from (1)
from came (1)
go out (1)
goes out (1)
going (1)
leave (1)
left (1)
moved about freely (1) *+1660+2779*
out come (1)
out comes (1)
out of (1)
spread (1)
started (1)
went (1)

1745 ἐκπορνεύω *ekporneuō* (1)
gave up to sexual immorality (1)

1746 ἐκπτύω *ekptyō* (1)
scorn (1)

1747 ἐκπυρόω *ekpyroō*
Variant; not used

1748 ἐκριζόω *ekrizoō* (4)
uprooted (2)
pulled up by the roots (1)
root up (1)

1749 ἔκστασις *ekstasis* (7)
trance (2)
amazed (1) *+3284*
amazement (1)
astonished (1) *+2014*
bewildered (1)
fell into trance (1) *+1181+2093*

1750 ἐκστρέφω *ekstrephō* (1)
warped (1)

1751 ἐκσῴζω *eksōzō*
Variant; not used

1752 ἐκταράσσω *ektarassō* (1)
throwing into an uproar (1)

1753 ἐκτείνω *ekteinō* (16)
stretch out (5)
reached out (4)
stretched out (2)
lay (1)
lower (1)
motioned with (1)
pointing (1) *+899+3836+5931*
reached for (1) *+3836+5931*

1754 ἐκτελέω *ekteleō* (2)
finish (2)

1755 ἐκτένεια *ekteneia* (1)
earnestly (1) *+1877*

1756 ἐκτενής *ektenēs* (1)
deeply (1)

1757 ἐκτενῶς *ektenōs* (3)
earnestly (2)
deeply (1)

1758 ἐκτίθημι *ektithēmi* (4)
explained (3)
placed outside (1)

1759 ἐκτινάσσω *ektinassō* (4)
shake off (2)
shook from (1)
shook out (1)

1760 ἐκτός *ektos* (8)
outside (2)
unless (2) *+1623+3590*
beyond (1)
not include (1)
otherwise (1) *+1623+3590*
out of (1)

1761 ἕκτος *hektos* (14)
sixth (13)
noon (1) *+6052*

1762 ἐκτρέπω *ektrepō* (5)
disabled (1)
turn aside (1)
turn away from (1)
turned away (1)
wandered away from (1)

1763 ἐκτρέφω *ektrephō* (2)
bring up (1)
feeds (1)

1764 ἔκτρομος *ektromos*
Variant; not used

1765 ἔκτρωμα *ektrōma* (1)
abnormally born (1)

1766 ἐκφέρω *ekpherō* (8)
carried out (2)
bring (1)
brought (1)
carry out (1)
led (1)
produces (1)
take out of (1)

1767 ἐκφεύγω *ekpheugō* (8)
escape (5)
escaped (1)
ran out (1)
slipped through (1)

1768 ἐκφοβέω *ekphobeō* (1)
frighten (1)

1769 ἔκφοβος *ekphobos* (2)
so frightened (1)
with fear (1)

1770 ἐκφύω *ekphyō* (2)
come out (2)

1771 ἐκφωνέω *ekphōneō*
Variant; not used

1772 ἐκχέω *ekcheō* (27)
poured out (14)
shed (5)
pour out (3)
run out (2)
rushed (1)
scattered (1)
spilled out (1)

1773 ἐκχύννομαι *ekchynnomai*
Variant; not used

1774 ἐκχωρέω *ekchōreō* (1)
get out (1)

1775 ἐκψύχω *ekpsychō* (3)
died (3)

1776 ἑκών *hekōn* (2)
by its own choice (1)
voluntarily (1)

1777 ἐλαία *elaia* (15)
olives (10)
mount of olives (2)
olive (1)
olive tree (1)
olive trees (1)

1778 ἔλαιον *elaion* (11)
oil (9)
olive oil (2)

1779 ἐλαιών *elaiōn* (1)
mount of olives (1)

1780 Ἐλαμίτης *Elamitēs* (1)
Elamites (1)

1781 ἐλάσσων *elassōn* (4)
cheaper (1)
lesser (1)
younger (1)
untranslated (1)

1782 ἐλαττονέω *elattoneō* (1)
have too little (1)

1783 ἐλαττόω *elattoō* (3)
made lower (2)
less (1)

1784 ἐλάττων *elattōn*
Variant; not used

1785 ἐλαύνω *elaunō* (5)
driven (3)
oars (1)
rowed (1)

1786 ἐλαφρία *elaphria* (1)
lightly (1)

1787 ἐλαφρός *elaphros* (2)
light (2)

1788 ἐλάχιστος *elachistos* (14)
least (7)
very little (3)
very small (2)
care very little (1) *+1639+1650*
trivial (1)

1789 Ἐλεάζαρ *Eleazar* (2)
Eleazar (2)

1790 ἐλεάω *eleaō*
Variant; not used

1791 ἐλεγμός *elegmos* (1)
rebuking (1)

1792 ἔλεγξις *elenxis* (1)
rebuked (1) *+2400*

1793 ἔλεγχος *elenchos* (1)
certain (1)

1794 ἐλέγχω *elenchō* (17)
rebuke (3)
exposed (2)
rebuked (2)
convict (1)
convict of guilt (1)
convicted (1)
convinced that is a sinner (1)
correct (1)
expose (1)
prove guilty (1)
rebukes (1)
refute (1)
show fault (1)

1795 ἐλεεινός *eleeinos* (2)
pitied more than (1)
pitiful (1)

1796 ἐλεέω *eleeō* (32)
have mercy on (11)
mercy (4)
had mercy on (3)
received mercy (3)
shown mercy (3)
have pity (2)
be merciful to (1)
had^{s} (1)
has mercy on (1)
receive mercy (1)
showing mercy (1)
to show mercy (1)

1797 ἐλεημοσύνη *eleēmosynē* (13)
gifts to the poor (2)
give to the needy (2) *+4472*
give to the poor (2) *+1443*
beg (1) *+160+3836*
begging (1) *+3836+4639*
gave to in need (1) *+4472*
gifts for the poor (1)
giving (1)
helping the poor (1) *+4472*
money (1) *+3284*

1798 ἐλεήμων *eleēmōn* (2)
merciful (2)

1799 ἔλεος *eleos* (27)
mercy (24)
merciful (2)
tender mercy (1) *+5073*

1800 ἐλευθερία *eleutheria* (11)
freedom (10)
be free (1)

1801 ἐλεύθερος *eleutheros* (23)
free (18)
exempt (1)
free and belong to no man (1) *+1666+4246*
gain freedom (1) *+1181*
released (1)
set free (1)

1802 ἐλευθερόω *eleutheroō* (7)
set free (5)
liberated (1)
sets free (1)

1803 ἔλευσις *eleusis* (1)
coming (1)

1804 ἐλεφάντινος *elephantinos* (1)
ivory (1)

1805 Ἐλιακείμ *Eliakeim*
Variant; not used

1806 Ἐλιακίμ *Eliakim* (3)
Eliakim (3)

1807 ἕλιγμα *heligma*
Variant; not used

1808 Ἐλιέζερ *Eliezer* (1)
Eliezer (1)

1809 Ἐλιούδ *Elioud* (2)
Eliud (2)

1810 Ἐλισάβετ *Elisabet* (9)
Elizabeth (9)

1811 Ἐλισαῖος *Elisaios* (1)
Elisha (1)

1812 Ἐλισσαῖος *Elissaios*
Variant; not used

1813 ἑλίσσω *helissō* (2)
roll up (1)
rolling up (1)

1814 ἕλκος *helkos* (3)
sores (3)

1815 ἑλκόω *helkoō* (1)
covered with sores (1)

1816 ἑλκύω *helkyō* (8)
dragged (3)
dragging (1)
draw (1)
draws (1)
drew (1)
haul in (1)

1817 Ἑλλάς *Hellas* (1)
Greece (1)

1818 Ἕλλην *Hellēn* (25)
Greeks (14)
Greek (5)
gentile (4)
gentiles (2)

1819 Ἑλληνικός *Hellēnikos* (1)
Greek (1)

1820 Ἑλληνίς *Hellēnis* (2)
Greek (2)

1821 Ἑλληνιστής *Hellēnistēs* (3)
Grecian Jews (2)
Greeks (1)

1822 Ἑλληνιστί *Hellēnisti* (2)
Greek (2)

1823 ἐλλογάω *ellogaō* (1)
charge (1)

1824 ἐλλογέω *ellogeō* (1)
taken into account (1)

1825 Ἐλμαδάμ *Elmadam* (1)
Elmadam (1)

1826 Ἐλμωδάμ *Elmōdam*
Variant; not used

1827 ἐλπίζω *elpizō* (31)
hope (11)
put hope (4)
hope for (2)
hoped (2)
hoping (2)
set hope (2)
expect (1)
expected (1)
have hope (1) *+1639*
hopes (1)
hopes are set (1)
hopes for (1)
puts hope (1)
trust (1)

1828 ἐλπίς *elpis* (53)
hope (51)
all hope (1)
untranslated (1)

1829 Ἐλύμας *Elymas* (1)
Elymas (1)

1830 ἐλωΐ *elōi* (4)
Eloi (4)

1831 ἐμαυτοῦ *emautou* (37)
myself (17)
my own (7)
me (4)
my (3)
I (2)
my own accord (2)
my (1) *+3836+4309*
untranslated (1)

1832 ἐμβαίνω *embainō* (16)
got (10)
get (2)
got into (2)
getting (1)
stepped (1)

1833 ἐμβάλλω *emballō* (1)
throw (1)

1834 ἐμβαπτίζω *embaptizō*
Variant; not used

1835 ἐμβάπτω *embaptō* (2)
dipped (1)
dips (1)

1836 ἐμβατεύω *embateuō* (1)
goes into great detail about (1)

1837 ἐμβιβάζω *embibazō* (1)
put on board (1) *+899+1650*

1838 ἐμβλέπω *emblepō* (12)
looked at (4)
saw (2)
blinded (1) *+4024*
look at (1)
looked closely at (1)
looked directly at (1)
looked straight at (1)
looking (1)

1839 ἐμβριμάομαι *embrimaomai* (5)
deeply moved (2)
rebuked harshly (1)
strong warning (1)
warned sternly (1)

1840 ἐμέω *emeō* (1)
spit (1)

1841 ἐμμαίνομαι *emmainomai* (1)
obsession (1) *+4360*

1842 Ἐμμανουήλ *Emmanouēl* (1)
Immanuel (1)

1843 Ἐμμαοῦς *Emmaous* (1)
Emmaus (1)

1844 ἐμμένω *emmenō* (4)
continue (1)
remain faithful to (1)
remain true to (1)
stayed in (1)

1845 ἐμμέσῳ *emmesō*
Variant; not used

1846 Ἑμμώρ *Hemmōr* (1)
Hamor (1)

1847 ἐμός *emos* (73)
my (43)
my own (9)
mine (5)
I (4)
me (4)
for me (3)

I have (2) *+3836*
it[s] (1) *+993+3836+3836*
it[s] (1) *+3836*
myself (1)

1848 ἐμπαιγμονή *empaigmonē* (1)
scoffing (1)

1849 ἐμπαιγμός *empaigmos* (1)
jeers (1)

1850 ἐμπαίζω *empaizō* (13)
mocked (8)
mock (2)
mocking (1)
outwitted (1)
ridicule (1)

1851 ἐμπαίκτης *empaiktēs* (2)
scoffers (2)

1852 ἐμπέμπω *empempō*
Variant; not used

1853 ἐμπεριπατέω *emperipateō* (1)
walk among (1)

1854 ἐμπιμπλάω *empimplaō*
Variant; not used

1855 ἐμπίμπλημι *empimplēmi* (5)
enjoyed company (1)
filled (1)
had enough (1)
provides with plenty (1)
well fed (1)

1856 ἐμπίμπρημι *empimprēmi* (1)
burned (1)

1857 ἐμπιπλάω *empiplaō*
Variant; not used

1858 ἐμπίπλημι *empiplēmi*
Variant; not used

1859 ἐμπίπρημι *empiprēmi*
Variant; not used

1860 ἐμπίπτω *empiptō* (7)
fall (5)
falls (1)
fell (1)

1861 ἐμπλέκω *emplekō* (2)
entangled in (1)
involved in (1)

1862 ἐμπλοκή *emplokē* (1)
braided (1)

1863 ἐμπνέω *empneō* (1)
breathing out (1)

1864 ἐμπορεύομαι *emporeuomai* (2)
carry on business (1)
exploit (1)

1865 ἐμπορία *emporia* (1)
business (1)

1866 ἐμπόριον *emporion* (1)
market (1) *+3875*

1867 ἔμπορος *emporos* (5)
merchants (4)
merchant (1) *+476*

1868 ἐμπρήθω *emprēthō*
Variant; not used

1869 ἔμπροσθεν *emprosthen* (47)
before (19)
in front of (7)
ahead (4)
at (2)
in presence (2)
in the presence (3)
surpassed (2) *+1181*
in faces (1)
in front (1)
in full view of (1)
on ahead (1)
to (1)
your (1) *+5148*
untranslated (2)

1870 ἐμπτύω *emptyō* (6)
spit on (3)
spit (2)
spit at (1)

1871 ἐμφανής *emphanēs* (2)
revealed (1) *+1181*
seen (1)

1872 ἐμφανίζω *emphanizō* (10)
show (3)
brought charges (2)
appear (1)
appeared (1)
appeared and presented the charges (1)
petition (1)
reported (1)

1873 ἔμφοβος *emphobos* (5)
afraid (1)
fright (1) *+1181*
frightened (1)
in fear (1) *+1181*
terrified (1)

1874 ἐμφυσάω *emphysaō* (1)
breathed on (1)

1875 ἔμφυτος *emphytos* (1)
planted in (1)

1876 ἐμφωνέω *emphōneō*
Variant; not used

1877 ἐν *en* (2749)
in (1415)
with (152)
by (140)
at (134)
on (92)
among (87)
to (37)
through (34)
when (24)
of (23)
as (17)
for (17)
among (14) *+3545*
during (10)
into (10)
about (8)
when (8) *+3836*
within (8)
because of (6)
this is how (6) *+4047*
throughout (6) *+3910*
when (6) *+4005*
on account of (5)
soon (5) *+5443*
under (5)
against (4)
from (4)
how (4) *+5515*
out of (4)
where (4) *+4005*
while (4)
according to (3)
everywhere (3) *+4246+5536*
pregnant women (3) *+1143+2400*
there (3) *+899*
while (3) *+3836*
while (3) *+4005*
along (2)
as (2) *+3836*
here (2) *+4047*
how (2)
I (2) *+1609*
in (2) *+3545*
over (2)
subject to bleeding (2) *+135+4868*
throughout (2)
to himself (2) *+899+2840+3836*
while in (2)
with child (2) *+1143+2400*
a public figure (1) *+4244*
across (1)
after he was circumcised (1) *+1639+4364*
after this (1) *+2759+3836*
alive (1) *+899*
always (1) *+2789+4246*
as a fool (1) *+932*
as a man (1) *+4922*
as has just been said (1) *+3306+3836*
as of first importance (1) *+4755*
at the time of (1)
because (1) *+4005*
before (1)
before (1) *+3545*
before (1) *+3545+3836*
before circumcised (1) *+213*
before the group (1) *+3545*
believe (1) *+4409*
belong to (1)
besides (1)
both of them (1) *+4005*
brag (1) *+224+3836*
briefly (1) *+3900*
by (1) *+5931*
by the power of (1)
caused by (1)
cheerfully (1) *+2660*
clearly (1) *+4244*
complete (1) *+4246*
conceived (1) *+3120+3836+5197*
confident (1) *+5712*
contained (1) *+2400*
contained (1) *+5639*
diligently (1) *+5082*
does[s] (1) *+3531+5148*
done by (1)
down (1)
earnestly (1) *+1755*
elsewhere (1) *+2283*
enemies (1) *+2397*
figuratively (1) *+4231*
figuratively speaking (1) *+4130*
for (1) *+3545+3836*
for work (1) *+1256+2237+4005*
from among (1)
generously (1) *+605*
gently (1) *+4460+4559*
gently (1) *+4559*
glorious (1) *+1518*
go I wish you well (1) *+1645+5632*
had (1) *+1639*
had authority (1) *+1639+2026*
have gone without sleep (1) *+71*
he[s] (1) *+899+899+3836+4460*
heavenly things (1) *+3836+4041*
here (1) *+899*
here (1) *+1609*
him[s] (1) *+476+3836+4047*
holy (1) *+43*
humbly (1) *+4559*
immediately (1) *+899+3836+6052*
immediately (1) *+5443*
imperishable (1) *+914*
in accordance with (1)
in presence (1)
in spite of (1)
in the cause of (1)
inside (1)
inwardly (1) *+1571*
inwardly (1) *+3220+3836*
its (1) *+899*
Jews (1) *+1169+1609+3836*
legalistic (1) *+3795*
made think (1) *+2840+3836+5502*
make up mind (1) *+2840+3836+5502*
meanwhile (1) *+3568+3836*
met personally (1) *+3836+3972+4725+4922*

native (1) *+1164+4005*
near (1)
next (1)
observing (1) *+4513*
of you (1) *+1639+3836+5148*
old (1) *+2465+4581*
on board (1) *+3836+4450*
on journey (1) *+4513*
one Sabbath (1) *+3836+4879*
one Sabbath (1) *+4879*
outward (1) *+3836+5745*
outwardly (1) *+3836+5745*
outwardly (1) *+4922*
painful (1) *+3383*
perfectly (1) *+4246*
perishable (1) *+5785*
poor (1) *+141*
preaching (1) *+3364*
pregnant (1) *+1143+2400*
pregnant woman (1) *+1143+2400*
put to death (1) *+633+5840*
quick (1) *+5443*
quickly (1) *+5443*
relationship to (1)
release (1) *+690+912*
returned (1) *+2059+3836*
righteous (1) *+1466*
safe (1) *+1645*
secret (1) *+3696*
securely (1) *+854+4246*
short time (1) *+3900*
show favoritism (1) *+4721*
sleeping (1) *+2761*
sly (1) *+1515*
so powerfully (1) *+1539*
soon afterward (1) *+2009+3836*
staying away from (1) *+4024+4344*
that was the time (1) *+1697+2465+3836*
there (1) *+3545*
there (1) *+3836+5536*
there[s] (1) *+2639+3836*
there[s] (1) *+3836+4047+4484*
Thessalonians (1) *+2553*
this kind of[s] (1) *+4231*
this makes (1) *+4047*
thus (1) *+4047*
to himself (1) *+1571*
today (1) *+2465+3836+4958*
true (1) *+237*
truly (1) *+237*
uncircumcised (1) *+213*
united with (1)
unseen (1) *+3220+3836*
unseen (1) *+3224+3836*
until (1) *+4005*
use deception (1) *+4111+4344*
wear (1)
what (1) *+5515*
when (1) *+2465*
where (1) *+4005+5536*
while (1) *+1639+3836*
who are there (1) *+899*
with (1) *+3545*
with child (1) *+1143+5197*
with regard to (1) *+3538*
with the help of (1)
within (1) *+3517+3836*
wondered about (1) *+2840+3836+5502*
you have (1) *+5148*
your (1) *+5148*
untranslated (267)

1878 ἐναγκαλίζομαι *enankalizomai* (2)
taking in his arms (1)
took in arms (1)

1879 ἐνάλιος *enalios* (1)
creatures of sea (1)

1880 ἐνάλλομαι *enallomai*
Variant; not used

1881 ἐνανθρωπέω *enanthrōpeō*
Variant; not used

1882 ἔναντι *enanti* (2)
before (2)

1883 ἐναντίον *enantion* (9)
before (2)
against (1)
but (1) *+1254+3836*
in public (1) *+3295+3836*
in the sight (1)
instead (1) *+3437+3836*
on contrary (1) *+247*
untranslated (1)

1884 ἐναντιόομαι *enantioomai*
Variant; not used

1885 ἐναντίος *enantios* (7)
against (3)
hostile (1)
in front of (1) *+1666*
oppose (1)
oppose (1) *+1666*

1886 ἐναργής *enargēs*
Variant; not used

1887 ἐνάρχομαι *enarchomai* (2)
began (1)
beginning (1)

1888 ἔνατος *enatos* (10)
ninth (7)
three in the afternoon (2)
three in the afternoon (1)
+2465+3836+6052

1889 ἐναφίημι *enaphiēmi*
Variant; not used

1890 ἐνδεής *endeēs* (1)
needy (1)

1891 ἔνδειγμα *endeigma* (1)
evidence (1)

1892 ἐνδείκνυμι *endeiknymi* (11)
show (5)
display (2)
show that (2)
did (1)
shown (1)

1893 ἔνδειξις *endeixis* (4)
demonstrate (2)
proof (1)
sign (1)

1894 ἕνδεκα *hendeka* (6)
eleven (6)

1895 ἐνδέκατος *hendekatos* (3)
eleventh (3)

1896 ἐνδέχομαι *endechomai* (1)
can (1)

1897 ἐνδημέω *endēmeō* (3)
at home (3)

1898 ἐνδιδύσκω *endidyskō* (2)
dressed in (1)
put on (1)

1899 ἔνδικος *endikos* (2)
deserved (1)
just (1)

1900 ἐνδόμησις *endomēsis*
Variant; not used

1901 ἐνδοξάζομαι *endoxazomai* (2)
glorified (2)

1902 ἔνδοξος *endoxos* (4)
expensive (1)
honored (1)
radiant (1)
wonderful (1)

1903 ἔνδυμα *endyma* (8)
clothes (7)
clothing (1)

1904 ἐνδυναμόω *endynamoō* (7)
strong (2)
gave strength (1)
given strength (1)
gives strength (1)
powerful (1)
strengthened (1)

1905 ἐνδύνω *endynō* (1)
worm way (1)

1906 ἔνδυσις *endysis* (1)
untranslated (1)

1907 ἐνδύω *endyō* (28)
put on (7)
clothe with (3)
clothed with (3)
dressed in (3)
wear (2)
wearing (2)
clothed (1)
in place (1)
putting on (1)
wore clothing (1) *+1639*
worn (1)
untranslated (3)

1908 ἐνδώμησις *endōmēsis* (1)
untranslated (1)

1909 ἐνέδρα *enedra* (2)
ambush (1)
plot (1)

1910 ἐνεδρεύω *enedreuō* (2)
waiting (1)
waiting in ambush for (1)

1911 ἔνεδρον *enedron*
Variant; not used

1912 ἐνειλέω *eneileō* (1)
wrapped in (1)

1913 ἔνειμι *eneimi* (7)
is (3)
change (1) *+4164*
inside (1)
untranslated (2)

1914 ἕνεκα *heneka*
Variant; not used

1915 ἕνεκεν *heneken* (24)
for (4)
because (4)
for reason (2)
for the sake of (2)
on account (4)
sake (2)
for sake (1)
of (1)
that (1)
why (1)
why (1) *+5515*
untranslated (1)

1916 ἐνενήκοντα *enenēkonta* (4)
ninety-nine (4) *+1933*

1917 ἐνεός *eneos* (1)
speechless (1)

1918 ἐνέργεια *energeia* (8)
power (2)
work (2)
working (2)
energy (1)
powerful (1)

1919 ἐνεργέω *energeō* (21)
at work in (8)
works in (2)
act (1)
at work (1)
at work within (1)

effective (1)
exerted in (1)
expressing (1)
produces in (1)
work (1)
work among (1)
works (1)
works out (1)

1920 ἐνέργημα *energēma* (2)
miraculous powers (1) *+1539*
working (1)

1921 ἐνεργής *energēs* (3)
active (2)
effective work (1)

1922 ἐνευλογέω *eneulogeō* (2)
blessed (1)
blessed through (1)

1923 ἐνέχω *enechō* (3)
burdened (1)
nursed a grudge against (1)
oppose (1)

1924 ἐνθάδε *enthade* (8)
here (6)
back (1)
there (1)

1925 ἔνθεν *enthen* (2)
from here (2)

1926 ἐνθυμέομαι *enthymeomai* (2)
considered (1)
entertain thoughts (1)

1927 ἐνθύμησις *enthymēsis* (4)
thoughts (3)
design (1)

1928 ἔνι *eni*
Variant; not used

1929 ἐνιαυτός *eniautos* (14)
year (10)
years (2)
annual (1) *+2848*
year after year (1) *+2848*

1930 ἐνίοτε *eniote*
Variant; not used

1931 ἐνίστημι *enistēmi* (7)
present (3)
the present (2)
be (1)
come (1)

1932 ἐνισχύω *enischyō* (2)
regained strength (1)
strengthened (1)

1933 ἐννέα *ennea* (5)
ninety-nine (4) *+1916*
nine (1)

1934 ἐννεύς *enneos*
Variant; not used

1935 ἐννεύω *enneuō* (1)
made signs (1)

1936 ἔννοια *ennoia* (2)
attitude (1)
attitudes (1)

1937 ἔννομος *ennomos* (2)
legal (1)
under law (1)

1938 ἐννόμως *ennomōs*
Variant; not used

1939 ἔννυχος *ennychos* (1)
while it was still dark (1)

1940 ἐνοικέω *enoikeō* (5)
lives in (2)
dwell in (1)
live with (1)
lived in (1)

1941 ἐνορκίζω *enorkizō* (1)
charge before (1)

1942 ἑνότης *henotēs* (2)
unity (2)

1943 ἐνοχλέω *enochleō* (2)
cause trouble (1)
troubled (1)

1944 ἔνοχος *enochos* (10)
guilty (2)
subject (2)
worthy (2)
answerable (1)
guilty of sinning against (1)
held (1)
in danger (1)

1945 ἔνταλμα *entalma* (3)
rules (2)
commands (1)

1946 ἐνταφιάζω *entaphiazō* (2)
burial (1)
prepare for burial (1)

1947 ἐνταφιασμός *entaphiasmos* (2)
burial (2)

1948 ἐντέλλω *entellō* (15)
command (6)
commanded (4)
commanded to keep (1)
gave instructions (1)
giving instructions (1)
instructed (1)
tells (1)

1949 ἐντεῦθεν *enteuthen* (9)
from (1)
from another place (1)
from here (1)
here (1)
leave (1) *+72*
of here (1)
on each side (1) *+1696+2779*
one on each side (1) *+1949+2779*
this place (1)

1950 ἔντευξις *enteuxis* (2)
intercession (1)
prayer (1)

1951 ἐντίθημι *entithēmi*
Variant; not used

1952 ἔντιμος *entimos* (5)
precious (2)
honor (1) *+2400*
person more distinguished than (1)
valued highly (1) *+1639*

1953 ἐντολή *entolē* (67)
command (17)
commands (15)
commandment (13)
commandments (10)
commanded (2) *+1443*
orders (2)
commanded (1) *+3284*
instructions (1)
law (1)
one's (1)
regulation (1)
requires (1)
with instructions (1) *+3284*
untranslated (1)

1954 ἐντόπιος *entopios* (1)
people there (1)

1955 ἐντός *entos* (2)
inside (1)
within (1)

1956 ἐντρέπω *entrepō* (9)
respect (3)
ashamed (1)
care about (1)
cared about (1)
feel ashamed (1)
respected (1)
shame (1)

1957 ἐντρέφω *entrephō* (1)
brought up (1)

1958 ἔντρομος *entromos* (3)
trembled with fear (1) *+1181*
trembling (1)
trembling (1) *+1181*

1959 ἐντροπή *entropē* (2)
shame (2)

1960 ἐντρυφάω *entryphaō* (1)
reveling (1)

1961 ἐντυγχάνω *entynchanō* (5)
appealed (1)
intercede (1)
intercedes (1)
interceding (1)
petitioned (1)

1962 ἐντυλίσσω *entylissō* (3)
wrapped (2)
folded up (1)

1963 ἐντυπόω *entypoō* (1)
engraved (1)

1964 ἐνυβρίζω *enybrizō* (1)
insulted (1)

1965 ἐνυπνιάζομαι *enypniazomai* (2)
dream (1)
dreamers (1)

1966 ἐνύπνιον *enypnion* (1)
dreams (1)

1967 ἐνώπιον *enōpion* (94)
before (37)
in the presence (9)
in the sight (5)
in front of (4)
in the eyes (4)
to (4)
against (2)
in presence (2)
in sight (2)
on behalf (2)
publicly (2) *+4246*
sight (2)
at (1)
by (1)
entice (1) *+965+4998*
in full view of (1)
in his sight (1) *+899*
on behalf of (1)
publicly (1) *+3836+4436*
with (1)
untranslated (11)

1968 Ἐνώς *Enōs* (1)
Enosh (1)

1969 ἐνωτίζομαι *enōtizomai* (1)
listen carefully (1)

1970 Ἑνώχ *Henōch* (3)
Enoch (3)

1971 ἕξ *hex* (13)
six (7)
half (2) *+3604*
276 (1) *+1357+1573*
666 (1) *+1980+2008*
a half (1) *+3604*
forty-six (1) *+2779+5477*

1972 ἐξαγγέλλω *exangellō* (1)
declare (1)

1973 ἐξαγοράζω *exagorazō* (4)
make the most of opportunity (1) *+2789+3836*
making the most of (1)
redeem (1)
redeemed from (1)

1974 ἐξάγω *exagō* (12)
led out (6)
brought out (2)
escort out (1)
escorted (1)
lead out (1)
leads out (1)

1975 ἐξαιρέω *exaireō* (8)
rescued (3)
gouge out (2)
rescue (2)
set free (1)

1976 ἐξαίρω *exairō* (1)
expel (1)

1977 ἐξαιτέω *exaiteō* (1)
asked (1)

1978 ἐξαίφνης *exaiphnēs* (5)
suddenly (5)

1979 ἐξακολουθέω *exakoloutheō* (3)
follow (3)

1980 ἑξακόσιοι *hexakosioi* (2)
1,600 (1) *+5943*
666 (1) *+1971+2008*

1981 ἐξαλείφω *exaleiphō* (5)
blot out from (1)
canceled (1)
wipe away from (1)
wipe from (1)
wiped out (1)

1982 ἐξάλλομαι *exallomai* (1)
jumped (1)

1983 ἐξανάστασις *exanastasis* (1)
resurrection (1)

1984 ἐξανατέλλω *exanatellō* (2)
sprang up (2)

1985 ἐξανίστημι *exanistēmi* (3)
have children (2) *+5065*
stood up (1)

1986 ἐξανοίγω *exanoigō*
Variant; not used

1987 ἐξαπατάω *exapataō* (6)
deceive (3)
deceived (3)

1988 ἐξάπινα *exapina* (1)
suddenly (1)

1989 ἐξαπορέω *exaporeō* (2)
despaired (1)
in despair (1)

1990 ἐξαποστέλλω *exapostellō* (12)
sent (7)
sent away (3)
send (1)
sent off (1)

1991 ἐξαρτάω *exartaō*
Variant; not used

1992 ἐξαρτίζω *exartizō* (2)
equipped (1)
up (1)

1993 ἐξαστράπτω *exastraptō* (1)
flash of lightning (1)

1994 ἐξαυτῆς *exautēs* (6)
at once (2)
immediately (1)
right now (1)
right then (1)
untranslated (1)

1995 ἐξεγείρω *exegeirō* (2)
raise (1)
raised up (1)

1996 ἔξειμι1 *exeimi1* (4)
get (1)
leave (1)
leaving (1)
left (1)

1997 ἔξειμι2 *exeimi2*
Variant; not used

1998 ἐξελέγχω *exelenchō*
Variant; not used

1999 ἐξέλκω *exelkō* (1)
dragged away (1)

2000 ἐξέραμα *exerama* (1)
vomit (1)

2001 ἐξεραυνάω *exeraunaō* (1)
searched intently and with the greatest care (1) *+1699+2779*

2002 ἐξέρχομαι *exerchomai* (217)
went out (37)
left (21)
came out (19)
come out (14)
go out (11)
leave (11)
came (8)
gone out (7)
went (6)
spread (5)
come (4)
go (4)
set out (4)
gone (3)
leaving (3)
out came (3)
came out of (2)
comes out (2)
coming (2)
get out (2)
go away (2)
going out (2)
got out (2)
landed (2)
leave (2) *+2032*
out of come (2)
went on (2)
went out from (2)
went out of (2)
at daybreak (1) *+1181+2465*
bringing (1)
came from (1)
come from (1)
come out of (1) *+4047*
comes (1)
coming from (1)
descended from (1) *+4019*
driven out (1)
escaped (1)
flowed out (1)
followed out (1) *+199*
issued (1)
known (1)
led out (1)
left (1) *+1696*
left (1) *+3854*
originate (1)
out (1)
out come (1)
rode out (1)
slipping away from (1)
started (1)
started out (1) *+482*
stepped (1)
take (1)
walked out (1)
went out (1) *+2032*
went out (1) *+4513*
went through (1)
untranslated (1)

2003 ἔξεστι *exesti* (31)
lawful (10)
permissible (4)
unlawful (4) *+4024*
right (3)
can (1)
have right (1)
have the right (1)
lawful for (1)
lawful for (1) *+4024*
legal (1)
may (1)
permitted (1)
the law (1)
the law forbids (1) *+4024*

2004 ἐξετάζω *exetazō* (3)
ask (1)
make a search (1)
search for (1)

2005 ἐξέφνης *exephnēs*
Variant; not used

2006 ἐξέχω *exechō*
Variant; not used

2007 ἐξηγέομαι *exēgeomai* (6)
told (2)
described (1)
made known (1)
reported (1)
telling about (1)

2008 ἑξήκοντα *hexēkonta* (9)
sixty (5)
1,260 (2) *+1357+5943*
666 (1) *+1971+1980*
seven miles (1) *+5084*

2009 ἑξῆς *hexēs* (5)
next (4)
soon afterward (1) *+1877+3836*

2010 ἐξηχέω *exēcheō* (1)
rang out (1)

2011 ἕξις *hexis* (1)
use (1)

2012 ἐξιστάνω *existanō*
Variant; not used

2013 ἐξιστάω *existaō*
Variant; not used

2014 ἐξίστημι *existēmi* (17)
amazed (7)
astonished (6)
out of mind (2)
astonished (1) *+1749*
utterly amazed (1) *+2513*

2015 ἐξισχύω *exischyō* (1)
power (1)

2016 ἔξοδος *exodos* (3)
departure (2)
exodus from Egypt (1)

2017 ἐξολεθρεύω *exolethreuō* (1)
completely cut off from (1)

2018 ἐξομολογέω *exomologeō* (10)
confess (3)
praise (3)
confessing (2)
consented (1)
openly confessed (1) *+334*

2019 ἐξορκίζω *exorkizō* (1)
charge under oath (1)

2020 ἐξορκιστής *exorkistēs* (1)
driving out evil spirits (1)

2021 ἐξορύσσω *exoryssō* (2)
digging through (1)
torn out (1)

2022 ἐξουδενέω *exoudeneō* (1)
rejected (1)

2023 ἐξουδενόω *exoudenoō*
Variant; not used

2024 ἐξουθενέω *exoutheneō* (11)
look down on (2)
treat with contempt (2)
amounts to nothing (1)
despised (1)
looked down on (1)
of little account (1)
refuse to accept (1)
rejected (1)
ridiculed (1)

2025 ἐξουθενόω *exouthenoō*
Variant; not used

2026 ἐξουσία *exousia* (102)
authority (53)
power (11)
right (9)
authorities (8)
authority over (2)
charge (2)
control (2)
ability (1)
disposal (1)
dominion (1)
exercise of freedom (1)
had authority (1) *+1639+1877*
in charge (1)
jurisdiction (1)
kingdom (1)
must (1) *+2400*
on authority (1) *+3284*
reigns (1)
rights (1)
with authority (1) *+2400*
untranslated (2)

2027 ἐξουσιάζω *exousiazō* (4)
belong to (2)
exercise authority over (1)
mastered (1)

2028 ἐξουσιαστικός *exousiastikos*
Variant; not used

2029 ἐξοχή *exochē* (1)
leading (1)

2030 ἐξυπνίζω *exypnizō* (1)
wake up (1)

2031 ἔξυπνος *exypnos* (1)
woke up (1) *+1181*

2032 ἔξω *exō* (62)
outside (25)
out (17)
away (3)
from (2)
leave (2) *+2002*
out of (2)
outsiders (2) *+3836*
foreign (1)
outwardly (1) *+476+3836*
went out (1) *+2002*
untranslated (6)

2033 ἔξωθεν *exōthen* (13)
outside (6)
on the outside (2)
from outward (1)
from the outside (1)
outer (1)
outsiders (1)
untranslated (1)

2034 ἐξωθέω *exōtheō* (2)
drove out (1)
run aground (1)

2035 ἐξώτερος *exōteros* (3)
outside (2)
untranslated (1)

2036 ἔοικα *eoika* (2)
like (2)

2037 ἑορτάζω *heortazō* (1)
keep the Festival (1)

2038 ἑορτή *heortē* (25)
feast (22)
Passover feast (1)
religious festival (1)
there[s] (1) *+1650+3836*

2039 ἐπαγγελία *epangelia* (52)
promise (23)
promised (9)
promises (9)
promised (2) *+1181*
what was promised (2) *+3836*
consent (1)
has promised (1)
promised (1) *+2040*
was promised (1)
what had been promised (1) *+3836*
what has been promised (1) *+3836*
what was promised (1)

2040 ἐπαγγέλλομαι *epangellomai* (15)
promised (8)
made promise (2)
promise (2)
profess (1)
professed (1)
promised (1) *+2039*

2041 ἐπάγγελμα *epangelma* (2)
promise (1)
promises (1)

2042 ἐπάγω *epagō* (3)
bringing on (1)
brought on (1)
make guilty of (1) *+2093*

2043 ἐπαγωνίζομαι *epagōnizomai* (1)
contend (1)

2044 ἐπαθροίζω *epathroizō* (1)
increased (1)

2045 Ἐπαίνετος *Epainetos* (1)
Epenetus (1)

2046 ἐπαινέω *epaineō* (6)
praise (2)
commended (1)
have praise (1)
sing praises to (1)
untranslated (1)

2047 ἔπαινος *epainos* (11)
praise (7)
commend (1)
commend (1) *+2400*
praised (1)
praiseworthy (1)

2048 ἐπαίρω *epairō* (19)
looked up (3) *+3836+4057*
lift up (2)
lifted up (2)
raised (2)
called out (1) *+5889*
hoisted (1)
look up (1) *+3836+4057*
looked (1) *+3836+4057*
looking (1) *+3836+4057*
open eyes (1) *+4057*
pushes forward (1)
sets up (1)
shouted (1) *+3836+5889*
taken up (1)

2049 ἐπαισχύνομαι *epaischynomai* (11)
ashamed of (7)
ashamed (4)

2050 ἐπαιτέω *epaiteō* (2)
beg (1)
begging (1)

2051 ἐπακολουθέω *epakoloutheō* (4)
accompanied (1)
devoting (1)
follow (1)
trail behind (1)

2052 ἐπακούω *epakouō* (1)
heard (1)

2053 ἐπακροάομαι *epakroaomai* (1)
listening (1)

2054 ἐπάν *epan* (3)
when (2)
as soon as (1)

2055 ἐπάναγκες *epanankes* (1)
requirements (1)

2056 ἐπανάγω *epanagō* (3)
put out (2)
on way back (1)

2057 ἐπαναμιμνήσκω *epanamimnēskō* (1)
remind again (1)

2058 ἐπαναπαύομαι *epanapauomai* (2)
rely on (1)
rest on (1)

2059 ἐπανέρχομαι *epanerchomai* (2)
return (1)
returned (1) *+1877+3836*

2060 ἐπανίστημι *epanistēmi* (2)
rebel against (2)

2061 ἐπανόρθωσις *epanorthōsis* (1)
correcting (1)

2062 ἐπάνω *epanō* (19)
on (7)
over (4)
above (3)
more than (2)
of (1)
take charge of (1) *+1181*
untranslated (1)

2063 ἐπάρατος *eparatos* (1)
curse on (1)

2064 ἐπαρκέω *eparkeō* (3)
help (2)
helping (1)

2065 ἐπαρχεία *eparcheia* (2)
province (2)

2066 ἐπάρχειος *eparcheios*
Variant; not used

2067 ἐπαρχικός *eparchikos*
Variant; not used

2068 ἔπαυλις *epaulis* (1)
place (1)

2069 ἐπαύριον *epaurion* (17)
next day (15)
following day (2)

2070 ἐπαυτοφώρῳ *epautophōrō*
Variant; not used

2071 Ἐπαφρᾶς *Epaphras* (3)
Epaphras (3)

2072 ἐπαφρίζω *epaphrizō* (1)
foaming up (1)

2073 Ἐπαφρόδιτος *Epaphroditos* (2)
Epaphroditus (2)

2074 ἐπεγείρω *epegeirō* (2)
stirred up (1)
stirred up against (1)

2075 ἐπεί *epei* (26)
since (9)
because (4)
if it could (1)
if it were (1)
if that were so (1)
in that case (1) *+726*
now if (1)
otherwise (1)
otherwise (1) *+726*
so (1)
then (1)
untranslated (4)

2076 ἐπειδή *epeidē* (10)
since (4)
because (2)
for (1)
when (1)
untranslated (2)

2077 ἐπειδήπερ *epeidēper* (1)
untranslated (1)

2078 ἐπεῖδον *epeidon* (2)
consider (1)
shown favor (1)

2079 ἔπειμι *epeimi* (5)
next day (3)
following (1)
next (1)

2080 ἐπείπερ *epeiper*
Variant; not used

2081 ἐπεισαγωγή *epeisagōgē* (1)
introduced (1)

2082 ἐπεισέρχομαι *epeiserchomai* (1)
come upon (1)

2083 ἔπειτα *epeita* (16)
then (10)
after that (2)
later (2)
also (1)
and after (1)

2084 ἐπέκεινα *epekeina* (1)
beyond (1)

2085 ἐπεκτείνομαι *epekteinomai* (1)
straining toward (1)

2086 ἐπενδύομαι *ependyomai* (2)
clothed (2)

2087 ἐπενδύτης *ependytēs* (1)
outer garment (1)

2088 ἐπέρχομαι *eperchomai* (9)
happen to (2)
attacks (1)
came (1)
come upon (1)
comes on (1)
coming (1)
coming on (1)
coming upon (1)

2089 ἐπερωτάω *eperōtaō* (56)
asked (35)
ask (5)
question (4)
ask questions (2)
asking (2)
questioned (2)
ask about (1)
ask for (1)
asked about (1)
asking questions (1)
demanded (1)
plied (1)

2090 ἐπερώτημα *eperōtēma* (1)
pledge (1)

2091 ἐπέχω *epechō* (5)
attention (1)
hold out (1)
noticed (1)
stayed a little longer (1) *+5989*
watch closely (1)

2092 ἐπηρεάζω *epēreazō* (2)
mistreat (1)
speak maliciously against (1)

2093 ἐπί *epi* (888)
on (260)
in (73)
to (71)
at (39)
over (38)
against (34)
for (33)
of (21)
before (15)
upon (14)
by (12)
with (9)
about (8)
because of (5)
around (3)
from (3)
together (3) *+899+3836*
above (2)
after (2)
among (2)
as long as (2) *+4012+5989*
because (2)
because (2) *+4005*
during (2)
generously (2) *+2330*
in accordance with (2)
in the account (2)
into (2)
landed (2) *+1178+2262+3836*
reached (2) *+1181*
reached (2) *+2262*
right at (2)
seized (2) *+1181*
seized (2) *+2095+3836+5931*
toward (2)
whatever (2) *+4012*
when (2)
a long time (1) *+4498*
across (1)
along (1)
any further (1) *+4498*
arrest (1) *+2095+3836+5931*
arrested (1) *+2095+3836+5931*
as long as (1) *+4012*
ashore (1) *+1178*
assure (1) *+237+3306*
at the time (1)
bedridden (1) *+2879+3187*
beside (1)
between (1)
caught in the act (1) *+900+2898*
certainly (1) *+237*
come together (1) *+899+1639+3836*
comes together (1) *+899+3836+5302*
convened the court (1) *+1037+2767+3836*
court (1) *+1037*
covers (1) *+3023*
decided (1) *+326+2840+3836*
died (1) *+3738*
drive out (1)
embraced (1) *+2158+3836+5549*
facedown (1) *+4725*
fell into trance (1) *+1181+1749*
from bad to worse (1) *+3836+5937*
get very far (1) *+4498+4621*
holding in (1)
how true (1) *+237*
in addition (1) *+1254*
in charge of (1) *+1639*
in connection with (1)
in front of (1)
in one place (1) *+899+3836*
in the days of (1)
in the time of (1)
inasmuch as (1) *+3525+4012+4036*
just then (1) *+4047*
make guilty of (1) *+2042*
more and more (1) *+4498*
near (1)
on and on (1) *+4498*
on the basis of (1)
only as long as (1) *+4012+5989*
opposes (1) *+482*
reached (1)
reaching (1) *+1181*
resting on (1)
rider (1) *+899+2764*
riders (1) *+899+2764*
riders (1) *+2764+3836*
right (1) *+237*
spend time (1) *+3531+5989*
stone (1) *+965*
struck (1) *+2262*
that is why (1) *+4047*
them[S] (1) *+1178+2997+3836+3836*
threw himself (1) *+4406+4725*
threw his arms around (1) *+2158+3836+5549*
throughout (1) *+4246*
to be impure (1) *+174*
to face (1)
to overcome (1)
to their number (1) *+899+3836*
to where (1)
trusted personal servant (1) *+3131+3836*
under (1)
up to (1)
wearing nothing (1) *+1218+4314*
what (1) *+4005*
where (1) *+4005*
while (1) *+4012*
you (1) *+5148*
untranslated (133)

2094 ἐπιβαίνω *epibainō* (6)
arriving in (1)
boarded (1)
came (1)
go on (1)
riding (1)
went on board (1)

2095 ἐπιβάλλω *epiballō* (18)
laid on (2)
seized (2) *+2093+3836+5931*
seized (2) *+3836+5931*
sews on (2)
arrest (1) *+2093+3836+5931*
arrested (1) *+2093+3836+5931*
arrested (1) *+3836+5931*
broke (1)
broke down (1)
lay on (1)
puts to (1)
restrict (1) *+1105*
share (1) *+3538*
threw over (1)

2096 ἐπιβαρέω *epibareō* (3)
be a burden to (2)
put it too severely (1)

2097 ἐπιβιβάζω *epibibazō* (3)
put on (2)
taken (1)

2098 ἐπιβλέπω *epiblepō* (3)
look at (1)
mindful of (1)
show special attention to (1)

2099 ἐπίβλημα *epiblēma* (4)
patch (4)

2100 ἐπιβοάω *epiboaō*
Variant; not used

2101 ἐπιβουλή *epiboulē* (4)
plot (2)
plan (1)
plots (1)

2102 ἐπιγαμβρεύω *epigambreuō* (1)
marry (1)

2103 ἐπίγειος *epigeios* (7)
earthly (4)
earthly things (2)
on earth (1)

2104 ἐπιγίνομαι *epiginomai* (1)
came up (1)

2105 ἐπιγινώσκω *epiginōskō* (44)
recognized (6)
know (5)
recognize (4)
known (3)
learned (3)
realized (3)
knew (2)
knows (2)
understood (2)
acknowledge (1)
come to understand (1)
find out (1)
found out (1)
fully known (1)
know fully (1)
learn the truth (1)
realize (1)
realized that (1)
recognition (1)
recognizing (1)
took note (1)
understand (1)
verify (1)

2106 ἐπίγνωσις *epignōsis* (20)
knowledge (14)
acknowledge (1) *+2262*
conscious (1)
full understanding (1)
know (1)
know better (1)
knowing (1)

2107 ἐπιγραφή *epigraphē* (5)
inscription (3)
written notice (2)

2108 ἐπιγράφω *epigraphō* (5)
write on (2)
read (1) *+1639*
this inscription (1) *+4005*
written (1)

2109 ἐπιδείκνυμι *epideiknymi* (7)
show (3)
call attention to (1)
make clear (1)
proving (1)
showing (1)

2110 ἐπιδέχομαι *epidechomai* (2)
have (1)
welcome (1)

2111 ἐπιδημέω *epidēmeō* (2)
lived there (1)
visitors from (1)

2112 ἐπιδιατάσσομαι *epidiatassomai* (1)
add to (1)

2113 ἐπιδίδωμι *epididōmi* (9)
give (5)
delivered (1)
gave (1)
gave way (1)
handed (1)

2114 ἐπιδιορθόω *epidiorthoō* (1)
straighten out (1)

2115 ἐπιδύω *epidyō* (1)
go down (1)

2116 ἐπιείκεια *epieikeia* (1)
kind (1)

2117 ἐπιεικής *epieikēs* (6)
considerate (3)
gentleness (2)
gentle (1)

2118 ἐπιζητέω *epizēteō* (13)
looking for (5)
a thorough search made for (1)
asks for (1)
looks for (1)
run after (1)
runs after (1)
sought so earnestly (1)
want to bring up (1)
wanted (1)

2119 ἐπιθανάτιος *epithanatios* (1)
condemned to die (1)

2120 ἐπίθεσις *epithesis* (4)
laying on (3)
laid on (1)

2121 ἐπιθυμέω *epithymeō* (16)
long (3)
covet (2)
desires (2)
longed (2)
want (2)
coveted (1)
did[s] (1)
eagerly desired (1) *+2123*
longing (1)
lustfully (1) *+3836+4639*

2122 ἐπιθυμητής *epithymetēs* (1)
setting hearts on (1)

2123 ἐπιθυμία *epithymia* (38)
desires (11)
evil desires (8)
desire (3)
cravings (2)
lust (2)
passions (2)
covetous desire (1)
desire (1) *+2400*
eagerly desired (1) *+2121*
evil desire (1)
longed for (1)
longing (1)
lustful desires (1) *+816*
passionate (1)
sinful desires (1)
what coveting was (1)

2124 ἐπιθύω *epithyō*
Variant; not used

2125 ἐπικαθίζω *epikathizō* (1)
sat (1)

2126 ἐπικαλέω *epikaleō* (29)
called (8)
call on (7)
appeal to (2)
calls on (2)
appealed (1)
appealed to (1)
bear (1)
belong (1)
call (1)
calling on (1)
known as (1)
made appeal (1)
made appeal to (1)
prayed (1)

2127 ἐπικάλυμμα *epikalymma* (1)
cover-up (1) *+2400*

2128 ἐπικαλύπτω *epikalyptō* (1)
covered (1)

2129 ἐπικατάρατος *epikataratos* (2)
cursed (2)

2130 ἐπίκειμαι *epikeimai* (7)
applying (1)
compelled (1) *+340*
continued raging (1) *+3900+4024*
crowding around (1)
insistently (1)
laid across (1)
on (1)

2131 ἐπικέλλω *epikellō* (1)
ran aground (1)

2132 ἐπικερδαίνω *epikerdainō*
Variant; not used

2133 ἐπικεφάλαιον *epikephalaion*
Variant; not used

2134 Ἐπικούρειος *Epikoureios* (1)
Epicurean (1)

2135 ἐπικουρία *epikouria* (1)
help (1)

2136 ἐπικράζω *epikrazō*
Variant; not used

2137 ἐπικρίνω *epikrinō* (1)
decided (1)

2138 ἐπιλαμβάνομαι *epilambanomai* (19)
took (6)
seized (2)
take hold (2)
arrested (1)
catch (1)
caught (1)
helps (1)
seizing (1)
taking hold of (1)
trap in (1)
turned on (1)
untranslated (1)

2139 ἐπιλάμπω *epilampō*
Variant; not used

2140 ἐπιλανθάνομαι *epilanthanomai* (8)
forget (3)
forgotten (2)
forgets (1)
forgetting (1)
forgot (1)

2141 ἐπιλέγω *epilegō* (2)
called (1)
chose (1)

2142 ἐπιλείπω *epileipō* (1)
not have (1)

2143 ἐπιλείχω *epileichō* (1)
licked (1)

2144 ἐπιλησμονή *epilēsmonē* (1)
forgetting (1)

2145 ἐπίλοιπος *epiloipos* (1)
rest (1)

2146 ἐπίλυσις *epilysis* (1)
interpretation (1)

2147 ἐπιλύω *epilyō* (2)
explained (1)
must be settled (1)

2148 ἐπιμαρτυρέω *epimartyreō* (1)
testifying that (1)

2149 ἐπιμέλεια *epimeleia* (1)
for needs (1)

2150 ἐπιμελέομαι *epimeleomai* (3)
look after (1)
take care of (1)
took care of (1)

2151 ἐπιμελῶς *epimelōs* (1)
carefully (1)

2152 ἐπιμένω *epimenō* (16)
stayed (3)
continue in (2)
kept on (2)
been there (1)
go on (1)
persevere in (1)
persist in (1)
remain (1)
spend (1)
spend time (1) *+5989*
stay (1)
stay on (1)

2153 ἐπινεύω *epineuō* (1)
declined (1) *+4024*

2154 ἐπίνοια *epinoia* (1)
thought (1)

2155 ἐπιορκέω *epiorkeō* (1)
break oath (1)

2156 ἐπίορκος *epiorkos* (1)
perjurers (1)

2157 ἐπιούσιος *epiousios* (2)
daily (2)

2158 ἐπιπίπτω *epipiptō* (11)
came on (2)
come upon (1) *+1639*
embraced (1) *+2093+3836+5549*
fallen on (1)
gripped with fear (1) *+5832*
pushing forward (1)
seized with fear (1) *+5832*
struck (1)
threw himself on (1)
threw his arms around (1) *+2093+3836+5549*

2159 ἐπιπλήσσω *epiplēssō* (1)
rebuke harshly (1)

2160 ἐπιποθέω *epipotheō* (9)
long (3)
crave (1)
hearts go out to (1)
intensely (1)
long for (1)
longing (1)
longs for (1) *+1639*

2161 ἐπιπόθησις *epipothēsis* (2)
longing (2)

2162 ἐπιπόθητος *epipothētos* (1)
long for (1)

2163 ἐπιποθία *epipothia* (1)
longing (1)

2164 ἐπιπορεύομαι *epiporeuomai* (1)
coming (1)

2165 ἐπιράπτω *epiraptō* (1)
sews (1)

2166 ἐπιρίπτω *epiriptō* (2)
cast on (1)
threw on (1)

2167 ἐπισείω *episeiō*
Variant; not used

2168 ἐπίσημος *episēmos* (2)
notorious (1)
outstanding (1)

2169 ἐπισιτισμός *episitismos* (1)
food (1)

2170 ἐπισκέπτομαι *episkeptomai* (11)
look after (2)
visit (2)
care for (1)
choose (1)
come (1)
come to (1)
come to help (1)
looked after (1)
showed concern (1)

2171 ἐπισκευάζομαι *episkeuazomai* (1)
got ready (1)

2172 ἐπισκηνόω *episkēnoō* (1)
rest on (1)

2173 ἐπισκιάζω *episkiazō* (5)
enveloped (3)
fall on (1)
overshadow (1)

2174 ἐπισκοπέω *episkopeō* (2)
see to it (1)
serving as overseers (1)

2175 ἐπισκοπή *episkopē* (4)
coming (1)
overseer (1)
place of leadership (1)
visits (1)

2176 ἐπίσκοπος *episkopos* (5)
overseer (3)
overseers (2)

2177 ἐπισπάομαι *epispaomai* (1)
become uncircumcised (1)

2178 ἐπισπείρω *epispeirō* (1)
sowed (1)

2179 ἐπίσταμαι *epistamai* (14)
know (6)
understand (2)
familiar (1)
knew (1)
know about (1)
know that (1)
understands (1)
well aware (1)

2180 ἐπίστασις *epistasis* (2)
pressure (1)
stirring up (1) *+4472*

2181 ἐπιστάτης *epistatēs* (7)
master (7)

2182 ἐπιστέλλω *epistellō* (3)
written (2)
write (1)

2183 ἐπιστήμη *epistēmē*
Variant; not used

2184 ἐπιστήμων *epistēmōn* (1)
understanding (1)

2185 ἐπιστηρίζω *epistērizō* (4)
strengthening (3)
strengthen (1)

2186 ἐπιστολή *epistolē* (24)
letter (15)
letters (9)

2187 ἐπιστομίζω *epistomizō* (1)
silenced (1)

2188 ἐπιστρέφω *epistrephō* (36)
turn (4)
turn to (4)
turned (4)
go (3)
turned around (3)
return (2)
returned (2)
turned to (2)
turning to (2)
turns (2)
bring back (1)
bring back to (1)
comes back (1)
go back (1)
returned to (1)
returns to (1)
turned back (1)
turning (1)

2189 ἐπιστροφή *epistrophē* (1)
had been converted (1) *+3836*

2190 ἐπισυνάγω *episynagō* (8)
gather (3)
gather together (2)
gathered (1)
gathered (1) *+1639*
gathers (1)

2191 ἐπισυναγωγή *episynagōgē* (2)
gathered to (1)
meeting together (1)

2192 ἐπισυντρέχω *episyntrechō* (1)
running (1)

2193 ἐπισυρράπτω *episyrraptō*
Variant; not used

2194 ἐπισύστασις *episystasis*
Variant; not used

2195 ἐπισφαλής *episphalēs* (1)
dangerous (1)

2196 ἐπισχύω *epischyō* (1)
insisted (1)

2197 ἐπισωρεύω *episōreuō* (1)
gather around (1)

2198 ἐπιταγή *epitagē* (7)
command (5)
authority (1)
commanding (1) *+2848+3306*

2199 ἐπιτάσσω *epitassō* (10)
gives orders (2)
order (2)
ordered (2)
command (1)
commands (1)
directed (1)
orders (1)

2200 ἐπιτελέω *epiteleō* (10)
attain goal (1)
bring to completion (1)
build (1)
carry it on to completion (1)
carry on (1)
completed (1)
completion (1)
finish (1)
perfecting (1)
undergoing (1)

2201 ἐπιτήδειος *epitēdeios* (1)
needs (1)

2202 ἐπιτίθημι *epitithēmi* (39)
put on (10)
placed on (6)
gave (2)
laying on (2)
place (2)
place on (2)
add to (1)
adds to (1)
attack (1)
beat (1) *+4435*
flogged (1) *+4435*
furnished with (1)
laid on (1)
lay on (1)
on lay (1)
placed (1)
placing on (1)
puts on (1)
putting on (1)
set on (1)
to burden (1) *+983*

2203 ἐπιτιμάω *epitimaō* (30)
rebuked (17)
rebuke (6)
warned (2)
gave orders (1)
said sternly (1)
sternly (1)
strictly warned (1) *+4133*
warning (1)

2204 ἐπιτιμία *epitimia* (1)
punishment (1)

2205 ἐπιτρέπω *epitrepō* (18)
let (5)
allowed (3)
gave permission (2)
permission (2)
permitted (2)
permit (1)
permits (1)
permitting (1)
received permission (1)

2206 ἐπιτροπεύω *epitropeuō*
Variant; not used

2207 ἐπιτροπή *epitropē* (1)
commission (1)

2208 ἐπίτροπος *epitropos* (3)
foreman (1)
guardians (1)
manager (1)

2209 ἐπιτυγχάνω *epitynchanō* (5)
gained (1)
have (1)
obtain (1)
received (1)
untranslated (1)

2210 ἐπιφαίνω *epiphainō* (4)
appeared (3)
shine on (1)

2211 ἐπιφάνεια *epiphaneia* (6)
appearing (5)
splendor (1)

2212 ἐπιφανής *epiphanēs* (1)
glorious (1)

2213 ἐπιφαύσκω *epiphauskō* (1)
shine on (1)

2214 ἐπιφέρω *epipherō* (2)
bring against (1)
bringing (1)

2215 ἐπιφωνέω *epiphōneō* (4)
shouted (2)
shouting (1)
shouting at (1)

2216 ἐπιφώσκω *epiphōskō* (2)
about to begin (1)
dawn (1)

2217 ἐπιχειρέω *epicheireō* (3)
tried (2)
undertaken (1)

2218 ἐπιχείρησις *epicheirēsis*
Variant; not used

2219 ἐπιχέω *epicheō* (1)
pouring on (1)

2220 ἐπιχορηγέω *epichorēgeō* (5)
add (1)
give (1)
receive (1)
supplies (1)
supported (1)

2221 ἐπιχορηγία *epichorēgia* (2)
help given (1)
supporting (1)

2222 ἐπιχρίω *epichriō* (2)
put on (2)

2223 ἐπιψαύω *epipsauō*
Variant; not used

2224 ἐποικοδομέω *epoikodomeō* (7)
build up (1)
building on (1)
builds (1)
builds on (1)
built (1)
built on (1)
built up (1)

2225 ἐποκέλλω *epokellō*
Variant; not used

2226 ἐπονομάζω *eponomazō* (1)
call (1)

2227 ἐποπτεύω *epopteuō* (2)
see (2)

2228 ἐπόπτης *epoptēs* (1)
eyewitnesses (1)

2229 ἔπος *epos* (1)
one might even say (1) *+3306+6055*

2230 ἐπουράνιος *epouranios* (19)
heavenly (8)
heavenly realms (5)
heaven (4)
heavenly things (1)
in heaven (1)

2231 ἑπτά *hepta* (88)
seven (85)
seventh (1)
seventy-seven times (1) *+1574*
week (1) *+2465*

2232 ἑπτάκις *heptakis* (4)
seven times (4)

2233 ἑπτακισχίλιοι *heptakischilioi* (1)
seven thousand (1)

2234 ἑπταπλασίων *heptaplasiōn*
Variant; not used

2235 Ἔραστος *Erastos* (3)
Erastus (3)

2236 ἐραυνάω *eraunaō* (6)
searches (3)
diligently study (1)
look into (1)
trying to find out (1)

2237 ἐργάζομαι *ergazomai* (41)
work (7)
do (5)
worked (3)
does (2)
doing (2)
done (2)
administered (1)
at work (1)
bring about (1)
brings (1)
busy (1)
carrying on (1)
done (1) *+1639*
earn (1)
earn living (1)
evildoers (1) *+490+3836*
for work (1) *+1256+1877+4005*
let do (1)
put to work (1)
sin (1) *+281*
work for a living (1)
work for (1)
work hard (1) *+3159*
worked for (1)
working (1)
works (1)

2238 ἐργασία *ergasia* (6)
business (2)
indulge (1)
making money (1)
money (1)
try hard (1) *+1443*

2239 ἐργάτης *ergatēs* (16)
workers (5)
worker (3)
workmen (3)
do (1)
evildoers (1) *+94*
men to work (1)
them[s] (1) *+3836*
workman (1)

2240 ἔργον *ergon* (169)
work (35)
deeds (29)
done (9)
works (9)
doing (8)
observing (8)
actions (7)
do (6)
miracles (6)
things (5)
acts (4)
deed (3)
action (2)
task (2)
thing (2)
what he did (2)
act (1)
actions deserve (1) *+2848*
activity (1)
behavior (1)
did (1)
did (1) *+3836*
does (1)
had done (1)
it[s] (1)
it[s] (1) *+3836+5516*
labor (1)
made (1)
miracle (1)
observe (1)
practices (1)
requirements (1)
something (1)
these[s] (1) *+2819*
ways (1)
what he does (1)
what she did (1)
what[s] (1) *+3836*
what[s] (1) *+3836+5516*
will (1)
untranslated (8)

2241 ἐρεθίζω *erethizō* (2)
embitter (1)
stirred to action (1)

2242 ἐρείδω *ereidō* (1)
stuck fast (1)

2243 ἐρεύγομαι *ereugomai* (1)
utter (1)

2244 ἐρημία *erēmia* (4)
remote place (2)
country (1)
deserts (1)

2245 ἔρημος *erēmos* (49)
desert (32)
solitary (4)
desolate (3)
remote (3)
desert region (1)
deserted (1)
lonely (1)
lonely places (1)
open country (1)
quiet (1)

solitary places (1)

2246 ἐρημόω *erēmoō* (5)
brought to ruin (2)
ruined (2)
ruin (1)

2247 ἐρήμωσις *erēmōsis* (3)
desolation (3)

2248 ἐρίζω *erizō* (1)
quarrel (1)

2249 ἐριθεία *eritheia* (7)
selfish ambition (5)
factions (1)
self-seeking (1)

2250 ἔριον *erion* (2)
wool (2)

2251 ἔρις *eris* (9)
quarreling (2)
strife (2)
arguments (1)
discord (1)
dissension (1)
quarrels (1)
rivalry (1)

2252 ἐρίφιον *eriphion* (1)
goats (1)

2253 ἔριφος *eriphos* (2)
goats (1)
young goat (1)

2254 Ἑρμᾶς *Hermas* (1)
Hermas (1)

2255 ἑρμηνεία *hermēneia* (2)
interpretation (2)

2256 ἑρμηνευτής *hermēneutēs*
Variant; not used

2257 ἑρμηνεύω *hermēneuō* (3)
means (2)
translated (1)

2258 Ἑρμῆς *Hermēs* (2)
Hermes (2)

2259 Ἑρμογένης *Hermogenēs* (1)
Hermogenes (1)

2260 ἑρπετόν *herpeton* (4)
reptiles (4)

2261 ἐρυθρός *erythros* (2)
red (2)

2262 ἔρχομαι *erchomai* (632)
come (195)
came (130)
comes (58)
coming (57)
went (47)
arrived (13)
go (10)
returned (6)
return (5)
entered (4) *+1650*
arrives (3)
came back (3)
come back (3)
going (3)
gone (3)
reached (3)
reached (3) *+1650*
traveled (3)
visit (3)
went back (3)
went out (3)
joined (2) *+4639*
landed (2) *+1178+2093+3836*
on way (2)
reached (2) *+2093*
returns (2)
rose (2)
accompanied by (1) *+2779*
acknowledge (1) *+2106*
approaching (1) *+4639*
arrival (1)
arrived (1) *+1650*
been (1)
bound to come (1) *+450+3590*
bring (1)
brought (1)
brought out (1)
comes home (1)
coming (1) *+3836*
coming back (1)
coming of (1)
condemned (1) *+1650+3213*
entered (1)
fall (1)
falling (1)
follow (1) *+3958*
followed (1)
gathered (1)
get here (1)
get in (1)
goes (1)
going to happen (1)
going to rain (1) *+3915*
grew (1) *+1650+3836*
has served (1)
here (1)
hurried off (1) *+5067*
join (1) *+4639*
landed (1)
lighting (1)
lose good name (1) *+591+1650*
made their way (1)
make visit (1)
next (1)
occurs (1)
on his way (1)
on their way (1)
passed by (1)
reaching (1) *+1650*
rest (1)
result (1)
return (1) *+1650+3836+4099*
returning (1)
see (1) *+4639*
set off (1)
struck (1) *+2093*
to come (1) *+3516*
visited (1) *+1650*
visited (1) *+4639*
went on (1)
untranslated (9)

2263 ἐρωτάω *erōtaō* (63)
asked (19)
ask (18)
urged (3)
asks (2)
begged (2)
invited (2)
please (2) *+5148*
pray (2)
prayer is (2)
questioned (2)
ask questions (1)
asked for (1)
asking (1)
beg (1)
praying (1)
question (1)
questioning (1)
request (1)
requesting (1)

2264 ἐσθής *esthēs* (8)
clothes (5)
dressed (1)
robe (1)
robes (1)

2265 ἔσθησις *esthēsis*
Variant; not used

2266 ἐσθίω *esthiō* (158)
eat (92)
ate (19)
eating (19)
eats (10)
eaten (4)
do[s] (2)
food (2)
abstains (1) *+3590*
consume (1)
does so[s] (1) *+4024*
drink (1)
eating of (1)
get food (1)
have a feast (1)
have dinner (1)
untranslated (2)

2267 ἔσθω *esthō*
Variant; not used

2268 Ἑσλί *Hesli* (1)
Esli (1)

2269 ἔσοπτρον *esoptron* (2)
mirror (1)
reflection mirror (1)

2270 ἑσπέρα *hespera* (3)
evening (3)

2271 ἑσπερινός *hesperinos*
Variant; not used

2272 Ἑσρώμ *Hesrōm* (3)
Hezron (3)

2273 ἑσσόομαι *hessoomai* (1)
inferior (1)

2274 ἔσχατος *eschatos* (52)
last (42)
end (2)
ends (2)
final (2)
last of all (1)
least important (1)
lowest (1)
now (1)

2275 ἐσχάτως *eschatōs* (1)
dying (1)

2276 ἔσω *esō* (9)
inner (2)
inside (2)
in (1)
into (1)
inwardly (1) *+3836*
right into (1) *+1650+2401*
untranslated (1)

2277 ἔσωθεν *esōthen* (12)
inside (4)
on the inside (2)
from inside (1)
from within (1)
inwardly (1)
on both sides (1) *+2779+3957*
under (1)
within (1)

2278 ἐσώτερος *esōteros* (2)
inner (2)

2279 ἑταῖρος *hetairos* (3)
friend (3)

2280 ἑτερόγλωσσος *heteroglōssos* (1)
strange tongues (1)

2281 ἑτεροδιδασκαλέω *heterodidaskaleō* (2)
teach false doctrines (1)
teaches false doctrines (1)

2282 ἑτεροζυγέω *heterozygeō* (1)
yoked together (1)

2283 ἕτερος *heteros* (98)
another (29)
other (29)
others (13)
different (4)
else (4)
some (3)
different from (2)
another (1) *+3836*
changed (1) *+1181*
day after (1)
elsewhere (1) *+1877*
foreigners (1)
his fellowman[s] (1) *+3836*
next (1)
perversion (1) *+599+3958+4922*
somebody else (1)
someone else (1)
still others (1)
untranslated (3)

2284 ἑτέρως *heterōs* (1)
differently (1)

2285 ἔτι *eti* (93)
still (31)
more (9)
again (7)
longer (7)
continue (5)
any more (4)
even (3)
any longer (2)
anymore (1)
as (1)
as long as still (1)
before long (1) *+3625*
besides (1)
just as (1) *+2317*
left (1)
longer (1) *+5989*
never again (1) *+4024*
never again (1) *+4028*
now (1)
on (1)
only (1)
other (1)
still (1) *+3814*
very while (1) *+4012+4012*
while still (1)
yes (1) *+5445*
untranslated (7)

2286 ἑτοιμάζω *hetoimazō* (40)
prepared (19)
prepare (10)
make preparations (5)
get ready (3)
kept ready (1)
made ready (1)
make ready (1)

2287 Ἕτοιμας *Hetoimas*
Variant; not used

2288 ἑτοιμασία *hetoimasia* (1)
readiness (1)

2289 ἕτοιμος *hetoimos* (17)
ready (14)
prepared (1)
right (1)
work already done (1)

2290 ἑτοίμως *hetoimōs* (3)
ready (2)
ready (1) *+2400*

2291 ἔτος *etos* (49)
years (40)
year (3)
years old (3)
eighty-four (1) *+3837+5475*
untranslated (2)

2292 εὖ *eu* (5)
well (2)
well done (2)
help (1) *+4472*

2293 Εὕα *Heua* (2)
eve (2)

2294 εὐαγγελίζω *euangelizō* (54)
preach the gospel (7)
preached (7)
preaching the gospel (5)
preached the good news (3)
preach (2)
preach the good news (2)
preached the gospel (2)
proclaiming the good news (2)
the good news preached (2)
the gospel preached (2)
announced (1)
bring good news (1)
bring news (1)
bringing good news (1)
brought good news about (1)
gospel preached (1) *+2295*
gospel to proclaim (1) *+2295*
had the gospel preached (1)
preach a gospel (1)
preach good news (1)
preaching (1)
preaching a gospel (1)
preaching the good news (1)
preaching gospel (1) *+2295*
tell good news (1)
tell the good news (1)
telling the good news (1)
telling the good news about (1)
the good news is preached (1)
told the good news about (1)

2295 εὐαγγέλιον *euangelion* (76)
gospel (60)
good news (6)
preaching gospel (2)
gospel preached (1) *+2294*
gospel to proclaim (1) *+2294*
it[s] (1) *+3836*
preach gospel (1)
preaching (1)
preaching gospel (1) *+2294*
proclaiming gospel (1)
spreading gospel (1)

2296 εὐαγγελιστής *euangelistēs* (3)
evangelist (2)
evangelists (1)

2297 εὐαρεστέω *euaresteō* (3)
pleased (2)
please (1)

2298 εὐάρεστος *euarestos* (9)
pleasing (5)
pleases (2) *+1639*
please (1)
please (1) *+1639*

2299 εὐαρέστως *euarestōs* (1)
acceptably (1)

2300 Εὔβουλος *Euboulos* (1)
Eubulus (1)

2301 εὖγε *euge* (1)
well done (1)

2302 εὐγενής *eugenēs* (3)
noble birth (1)
of more noble character than (1)
of noble birth (1)

2303 εὐγλωττία *euglōttia*
Variant; not used

2304 εὐδία *eudia* (1)
fair weather (1)

2305 εὐδοκέω *eudokeō* (21)
pleased (8)
well pleased (5)
delight (2)
delighted (2)
pleased with (1)
prefer (1) *+3437*
thought it best (1)
with pleased (1)

2306 εὐδοκία *eudokia* (9)
good pleasure (3)
desire (1)
good purpose (1)
goodwill (1)
on whom favor rests (1)
pleasure (1)
purpose (1)

2307 εὐεργεσία *euergesia* (2)
act of kindness shown to (1)
service (1)

2308 εὐεργετέω *euergeteō* (1)
doing good (1)

2309 εὐεργέτης *euergetēs* (1)
benefactors (1)

2310 εὔθετος *euthetos* (3)
fit (1)
fit for service (1)
useful (1)

2311 εὐθέως *eutheōs* (36)
immediately (19)
at once (8)
as soon as (1)
at that moment (1)
at this (1)
now (1)
quickly (1)
right away (1)
soon (1)
suddenly (1)
untranslated (1)

2312 εὐθυδρομέω *euthydromeō* (2)
sailed straight (2)

2313 εὐθυμέω *euthymeō* (3)
keep up courage (2)
happy (1)

2314 εὔθυμος *euthymos* (1)
encouraged (1)

2315 εὐθύμως *euthymōs* (1)
gladly (1)

2316 εὐθύνω *euthynō* (2)
go (1)
make straight (1)

2317 εὐθύς1 *euthys1* (51)
immediately (13)
at once (8)
as soon as (6)
quickly (4)
as soon as (2) *+4020*
at once (1) *+4020*
at this (1)
just as (1)
just as (1) *+2285*
just then (1)
right away (1)
shortly (1)
sudden (1)
the moment (1)
then (1)
very early in the morning (1) *+4745*
when (1)
without delay (1)
untranslated (5)

2318 εὐθύς2 *euthys2* (8)
straight (6)
right (2)

2319 εὐθύτης *euthytēs* (1)
righteousness (1)

2320 εὐκαιρέω *eukaireō* (3)
has the opportunity (1)
have a chance (1)
spent time (1)

2321 εὐκαιρία *eukairia* (2)
opportunity (2)

2322 εὔκαιρος *eukairos* (2)
opportune (1)
time of need (1)

2323 εὐκαίρως *eukairōs* (2)
in season (1)
opportunity (1)

2324 εὔκοπος *eukopos* (7)
easier (7)

2325 εὐλάβεια *eulabeia* (2)
reverence (1)
reverent (1)

2326 εὐλαβέομαι *eulabeomai* (1)
holy fear (1)

2327 εὐλαβής *eulabēs* (4)
devout (2)
God-fearing (1)
godly (1)

2328 εὐλογέω *eulogeō* (40)
blessed (19)
gave thanks (6)
bless (5)
praising (3)
blessing (2)
bless (1) *+2328*
gave thanks for (1)
give thanks (1)
praise (1)
praised (1)

2329 εὐλογητός *eulogētos* (8)
praise (4)
praised (3)
blessed (1)

2330 εὐλογία *eulogia* (16)
blessing (6)
praise (4)
generous gift (2)
generously (2) *+2093*
flattery (1)
thanksgiving (1)

2331 εὐμετάδοτος *eumetadotos* (1)
generous (1)

2332 Εὐνίκη *Eunikē* (1)
Eunice (1)

2333 εὐνοέω *eunoeō* (1)
settle matters (1) *+1639*

2334 εὔνοια *eunoia* (1)
wholeheartedly (1) *+3552*

2335 εὐνουχίζω *eunouchizō* (2)
made that way[s] (1) *+2336*
renounced marriage (1) *+1571+2336*

2336 εὐνοῦχος *eunouchos* (8)
eunuch (5)
eunuchs (1)
made that way[s] (1) *+2335*
renounced marriage (1) *+1571+2335*

2337 Εὐοδία *Euodia* (1)
Euodia (1)

2338 εὐοδόω *euodoō* (4)
go well (1)
in keeping with income (1) *+1569+4005+5516*
is getting along well (1)
way opened for (1)

2339 εὐπάρεδρος *euparedros* (1)
devotion (1)

2340 εὐπειθής *eupeithēs* (1)
submissive (1)

2341 εὐπερίσπαστος *euperispastos*
Variant; not used

2342 εὐπερίστατος *euperistatos* (1)
easily entangles (1)

2343 εὐποιΐα *eupoiia* (1)
do good (1)

2344 εὐπορέω *euporeō* (1)
ability (1)

2345 εὐπορία *euporia* (1)
good income (1)

2346 εὐπρέπεια *euprepeia* (1)
beauty (1)

2347 εὐπρόσδεκτος *euprosdektos* (5)
acceptable (4)
favor (1)

2348 εὐπρόσεδρος *euprosedros*
Variant; not used

2349 εὐπροσωπέω *euprosōpeō* (1)
make a good impression (1)

2350 εὐρακύλων *eurakylōn* (1)
the northeaster (1)

2351 εὑρίσκω *heuriskō* (176)
found (83)
find (53)
finds (13)
met (3)
finding (2)
appeared (1)
bring about (1)
considered (1)
decide (1)
discovered (1)
enjoyed (1)
evident (1)
find (1) *+1639*
find out (1)
finds (1) *+1181*
found that (1)
laid bare (1)
obtained (1)
prove (1)
provide (1)
recovered (1)
result (1)
were looking for (1) *+2671*
when found (1)
untranslated (3)

2352 εὐροκλύδων *euroklydōn*
Variant; not used

2353 εὐρύχωρος *eurychōros* (1)
broad (1)

2354 εὐσέβεια *eusebeia* (15)
godliness (12)
godly (3)

2355 εὐσεβέω *eusebeō* (2)
put religion into practice by caring for (1)
worship (1)

2356 εὐσεβής *eusebēs* (3)
devout (2)
godly (1)

2357 εὐσεβῶς *eusebōs* (2)
godly (1)
godly life (1)

2358 εὔσημος *eusēmos* (1)
intelligible (1)

2359 εὔσπλαγχνος *eusplanchnos* (2)
compassionate (2)

2360 εὐσχημονέω *euschēmoneō*
Variant; not used

2361 εὐσχημόνως *euschēmonōs* (3)
decently (1)
fitting (1)
win the respect (1)

2362 εὐσχημοσύνη *euschēmosynē* (1)
modesty (1)

2363 εὐσχήμων *euschēmōn* (5)
prominent (2)
high standing (1)
presentable (1)
right (1)

2364 εὐτόνως *eutonōs* (2)
vehemently (1)
vigorously (1)

2365 εὐτραπελία *eutrapelia* (1)
coarse joking (1)

2366 Εὔτυχος *Eutychos* (1)
Eutychus (1)

2367 εὐφημία *euphēmia* (1)
good report (1)

2368 εὔφημος *euphēmos* (1)
admirable (1)

2369 εὐφορέω *euphoreō* (1)
produced a good crop (1)

2370 εὐφραίνω *euphrainō* (14)
celebrate (5)
rejoice (3)
glad (2)
held a celebration (1)
lived (1)
make glad (1)
merry (1)

2371 Εὐφράτης *Euphratēs* (2)
Euphrates (2)

2372 εὐφροσύνη *euphrosynē* (2)
fills with joy (1)
joy (1)

2373 εὐχαριστέω *eucharisteō* (38)
thank (13)
gave thanks (7)
giving thanks (5)
given thanks (4)
give thanks (2)
gives thanks (2)
thanked (2)
give thanks for (1)
grateful (1)
thankful (1)

2374 εὐχαριστία *eucharistia* (15)
thanksgiving (8)
thanks (2)
expressions of thanks (1)
gratitude (1)
thank (1)
thankful (1)
thankfulness (1)

2375 εὐχάριστος *eucharistos* (1)
thankful (1)

2376 εὐχή *euchē* (3)
vow (2)
prayer (1)

2377 εὔχομαι *euchomai* (7)
pray (3)
pray (1) *+323*
prayed for (1)
prayer for (1)
wish (1)

2378 εὔχρηστος *euchrēstos* (3)
useful (2)
helpful (1)

2379 εὐψυχέω *eupsycheō* (1)
cheered (1)

2380 εὐωδία *euōdia* (3)
fragrant (2) *+4011*
aroma (1)

2381 εὐώνυμος *euōnymos* (9)
left (8)
south of (1)

2382 εὐωχία *euōchia*
Variant; not used

2383 ἐφάλλομαι *ephallomai* (1)
jumped on (1)

2384 ἐφάπαξ *ephapax* (5)
once for all (4)
at the same time (1)

2385 Ἐφεσῖνος *Ephesinos*
Variant; not used

2386 Ἐφέσιος *Ephesios* (5)
Ephesians (2)
of Ephesus (2)
Ephesian (1)

2387 Ἔφεσος *Ephesos* (16)
Ephesus (15)
he (1)

2388 ἐφευρετής *epheuretēs* (1)
invent (1)

2389 ἐφημερία *ephēmeria* (2)
division (1)
priestly division (1)

2390 ἐφήμερος *ephēmeros* (1)
daily (1)

2391 ἐφικνέομαι *ephikneomai* (2)
come (1)
reaches (1)

2392 ἐφίστημι *ephistēmi* (21)
appeared (2)
came (2)
came up (2)
stood beside (2)
bent (1)
close (1)
come (1)
come on (1)
coming up (1)
it was (1)
prepared (1)
rushed to (1)
stood (1) *+1639*
stood near (1)
stopped (1)
stopped at (1)
untranslated (1)

2393 ἐφοράω *ephoraō*
Variant; not used

2394 Ἐφραίμ *Ephraim* (1)
Ephraim (1)

2395 ἐφφαθά *ephphatha* (1)
Ephphatha (1)

2396 ἐχθές *echthes* (3)
yesterday (3)

2397 ἔχθρα *echthra* (6)
hatred (2)
hostility (2)
enemies (1) *+1877*
hostile (1)

2398 ἐχθρός *echthros* (32)
enemies (21)
enemy (10)
enemy (1) *+476*

2399 ἔχιδνα *echidna* (5)
vipers (4)
viper (1)

2400 ἔχω *echō* (708)
have (209)
has (91)
had (72)
need (25) *+5970*
with (21)
having (11)
is (7)
sick (7) *+2809*
are (6)
held (6)
was (6)
demon-possessed (5) *+1228*
get (5)
needs (5) *+5970*
possessed by (5)
without (5) *+3590*
hold (4)
take (4)
am (3)
be (3)
be guilty of sin (3) *+281*
hold to (3)
holding (3)
holds (3)
keep (3)
pregnant women (3) *+1143+1877*
thank (3) *+5921*
able (2)
belongs to (2)
excuse (2) *+4148*
felt (2)
had (2) *+1639*
have (2) *+3836*
love (2) *+27*
married to (2)
needed (2) *+5970*
possess (2)
reap (2)
rich (2) *+3836+5975*
were (2)
who had (2)
with child (2) *+1143+1877*
accompanied by (1)
according to means (1) *+1666+3836*
accusers (1) *+2991*
approach (1) *+4643*
are ignorant (1) *+57*
as follows (1) *+3836+4047+5596*
be bold (1) *+4244+4498*
be dependent on (1) *+5970*
be encouraged (1) *+4155*
been (1)
believe (1) *+4411*
believers (1) *+3836+4411*
belongs to you (1) *+5050*
benefit (1) *+5921*
bring (1)
bringing (1) *+1571+3552*
can (1)
can[s] (1)
cannot (1) *+4024*
collect a tenth from (1) *+620*
come (1)
commend (1) *+2047*
confident (1) *+4244*
consider (1)
considered (1) *+6055*
contained (1) *+1877*
could (1)
cover-up (1) *+2127*
covered (1) *+2848*
crippled (1) *+819*
demon-possessed (1) *+3836+3836+4460+4505*
desire (1) *+2123*
distressed (1) *+3383*
doing (1)
dwell (1) *+3531*
end (1) *+5465*
enjoy (1)
enjoyed (1)
enjoying favor (1) *+5921*
eyes (1) *+4057*
face (1)
filled with (1)
finish (1) *+5455*
following (1)
for now (1) *+3814+3836*
forgiven (1) *+912*
gave (1)
gave (1) *+4639*
give (1)
given (1) *+608*
glory in (1) *+3018*
glory over (1) *+3018*
got (1)
guilty of sin (1) *+281*
had (1) *+323*
had charge of (1)
harbor (1)
hard (1) *+4498*
hardened (1) *+4800*
has enough (1) *+1650*
has given (1)
has hold (1)
have (1) *+1639*
have kept (1)
have made (1)
haven't (1) *+3590*
holding on to (1)
honor (1) *+1952*
in leaf (1) *+5877*
in need (1) *+5970*
is ours (1)
is time of grief (1) *+3383*
is under (1)
it was so (1) *+4048*
keep hold of (1)
keeper of money bag (1) *+1186*
keeping (1)
leaves wife (1) *+1222*
live (1)
lived (1) *+2998+3836*
living (1) *+3836+6034*
made (1)
made up of (1)
maintained (1)
must (1) *+340*
must (1) *+2026*
nearby (1)
need (1) *+340*
need (1) *+1181+5970*
next (1)
next day (1)
obey (1) *+5717*
one who had (1)
persevered (1) *+5702*
portrait (1) *+1635*
preached (1) *+3062*
pregnant (1) *+1143+1877*
pregnant woman (1) *+1143+1877*
reaching (1)
ready (1) *+2290*
rebuked (1) *+1792*
remember (1) *+3644*
retain (1)
rules (1) *+993*
Sabbath day's walk from (1) *+1584+3847+4879*
sealed with (1) *+5382*
shallow (1) *+958+3590*
shone with glory (1) *+1518*
short (1) *+3900*
sick (1) *+819*
since going through (1)
spare (1) *+3590*
spread (1) *+3786*
stop (1) *+398*
suffer persecution (1) *+2568*
surrounded by (1)
take (1) *+1639*
taken (1)

thankful (1) *+5921*
that accompany (1)
their breastplates were (1) *+2606*
their hair (1) *+2582*
there is a judge (1) *+3212+3836*
treated with (1)
trembling (1) *+899+5571*
uncircumcised (1) *+213*
want (1)
was sick (1) *+2809*
was with (1)
were ill (1) *+2809*
which had (1)
who are (1)
who have (1)
who need (1) *+5970*
whose (1) *+4005*
whose[S] (1)
with (1) *+4005*
with authority (1) *+2026*
wounded (1) *+3836+4435*
untranslated (18)

2401 ἕως *heōs* (146)
to (31)
until (31)
until (13) *+323*
until (13) *+4005*
before (4) *+323*
how long (4) *+4536*
till (4)
how (3)
still (3) *+785*
until (3) *+4015*
up to (3)
while (3)
even (2)
for (2)
to the point (2)
while (2) *+4005*
and (1)
as far as (1)
as long as (1)
before (1)
before (1) *+4005*
fully (1) *+5465*
going on to (1)
of this (1) *+4047*
right into (1) *+1650+2276*
right on down to (1)
right up to (1)
till (1) *+323*
to where (1)
when (1) *+4005*
while (1) *+4015*
untranslated (8)

2402 ϛ *[stigma]*
Variant; not used

2403 ζ *z*
Variant; not used

2404 Ζαβουλών *Zaboulōn* (3)
Zebulun (3)

2405 Ζακχαῖος *Zakchaios* (3)
Zacchaeus (3)

2406 Ζάρα *Zara* (1)
Zerah (1)

2407 ζαφθάνι *zaphthani*
Variant; not used

2408 Ζαχαρίας *Zacharias* (11)
Zechariah (10)
Zechariah's (1)

2409 ζάω *zaō* (139)
live (50)
living (42)
alive (18)
lives (15)
lived (4)
came to life (2)
as surely as I live (1) *+1609*
belonged (1)
brought to life (1)
come to life (1)
life (1)
live on (1)
receive living (1)
returned to life (1)

2410 ζβέννυμι *zbennymi*
Variant; not used

2411 Ζεβεδαῖος *Zebedaios* (12)
Zebedee (10)
Zebedee's (2)

2412 ζεστός *zestos* (3)
hot (2)
the other[S] (1)

2413 ζεύγνυμι *zeugnymi*
Variant; not used

2414 ζεῦγος *zeugos* (2)
pair (1)
yoke (1)

2415 ζευκτηρία *zeuktēria* (1)
ropes (1)

2416 Ζεύς *Zeus* (2)
Zeus (2)

2417 ζέω *zeō* (2)
fervor (1)
with great fervor (1) *+3836+4460*

2418 ζηλεύω *zēleuō* (1)
earnest (1)

2419 ζῆλος *zēlos* (16)
jealousy (7)
envy (2)
zeal (2)
ardent concern (1)
concern (1)
enthusiasm (1)
raging (1)
zealous (1)

2420 ζηλόω *zēloō* (11)
eagerly desire (2)
zealous (2)
covet (1)
eager (1)
envy (1)
jealous (1)
jealous for (1)
jealous of (1)
zealous for (1)

2421 ζηλωτής *zēlōtēs* (8)
eager (3)
Zealot (2)
zealous (2)
zealous for (1)

2422 ζημία *zēmia* (4)
loss (4)

2423 ζημιόω *zēmioō* (6)
forfeit (2)
forfeits (1)
harmed (1)
lost (1)
suffer loss (1)

2424 Ζηνᾶς *Zēnas* (1)
Zenas (1)

2425 Ζήνων *Zēnōn*
Variant; not used

2426 ζητέω *zēteō* (117)
looking for (18)
seek (14)
look for (10)
tried (9)
trying (6)
seeking (5)
want (5)
seeks (4)
looked for a way (3)
watched for (3)
ask for (2)
in search of (2)
searching for (2)
try (2)
wanting (2)
asked for (1)
asking (1)
asking for (1)
asks for (1)
attempt (1)
demanded (1)
demanding (1)
determined (1)
gain (1)
got ready (1)
looks out for (1)
make effort to obtain (1)
ready (1)
required (1)
search (1)
search for (1)
searched for (1)
self-seeking (1) *+1571+3836*
set heart on (1)
set hearts on (1)
sought (1)
sought for (1)
tries (1)
trying to kill (1) *+3836+6034*
trying to take (1)
waiting (1)
wanted (1)
wants (1)
watching for (1)
works for (1)

2427 ζήτημα *zētēma* (5)
questions (2)
controversies (1)
points of dispute (1)
question (1)

2428 ζήτησις *zētēsis* (7)
controversies (2)
argument (1)
arguments (1)
debate (1)
discussion (1)
investigate (1)

2429 ζιζάνιον *zizanion* (8)
weeds (8)

2430 Ζμύρνα *Zmyrna*
Variant; not used

2431 Ζοροβαβέλ *Zorobabel* (3)
Zerubbabel (3)

2432 ζόφος *zophos* (5)
blackest (2)
darkness (1)
gloom (1)
gloomy (1)

2433 ζυγός *zygos* (6)
yoke (5)
pair of scales (1)

2434 ζύμη *zymē* (13)
yeast (12)
that[S] (1) *+3836*

2435 ζυμόω *zymoō* (4)
worked through the dough (2)
works through (2)

2436 ζωγρέω *zōgreō* (2)
catch (1) *+1639*
taken captive (1)

2437 ζωή *zōē* (135)
life (128)

living (2)
alive (1)
brings life (1)
lifetime (1)
live (1)
untranslated (1)

2438 ζώνη *zōnē* (8)
belt (4)
belts (2)
sash (1)
sashes (1)

2439 ζώννυμι *zōnnymi* (3)
dress (1)
dressed (1)
put on clothes (1)

2440 ζωννύω *zōnnyō*
Variant; not used

2441 ζῳογονέω *zōogoneō* (3)
die (1) *+3590*
gives life to (1)
preserve (1)

2442 ζῷον *zōon* (23)
living creatures (13)
living creature (4)
animals (2)
beasts (1)
untranslated (3)

2443 ζῳοποιέω *zōopoieō* (11)
gives life (4)
made alive (2)
come to life (1)
give life (1)
gives life (1) *+1639*
impart life (1)
life-giving (1)

2444 η *ē*
Variant; not used

2445 ἤ *ē* (341)
or (244)
than (31)
and (9)
before (3) *+4570*
either (2)
instead of (2) *+3437*
before (1) *+323+4570*
but (1)
but (1) *+247*
more than (1)
nor (1)
only (1) *+4024+4498*
some (1)
than (1) *+3437*
three or three and a half miles (1) *+1633+4297+5084+5558*
twenty to thirty gallons (1) *+1545+3583+5552*
unless (1)
whether (1)
untranslated (38)

2446 ἦ *ē*
Variant; not used

2447 ἦ μήν *ē mēn*
Variant; not used

2448 ἡγεμονεύω *hēgemoneuō* (2)
governor (2)

2449 ἡγεμονία *hēgemonia* (1)
reign (1)

2450 ἡγεμών *hēgemōn* (20)
governor (13)
governors (4)
governor's (2)
rulers (1)

2451 ἡγέομαι *hēgeomai* (28)
consider (8)
leaders (4)
considered (2)
ruler (2)
think (2)
bear in mind (1)
chief (1)
hold (1)
idea (1)
regard (1)
regarded (1)
rules (1)
thought (1)
understand (1)
who treated (1)

2452 ἡδέως *hēdeōs* (5)
gladly (2)
liked (1)
very gladly (1)
with delight (1)

2453 ἤδη *ēdē* (61)
already (33)
now (5)
by now (2)
by this time (2)
as good as dead (1) *+3739*
as soon as (1) *+4020*
at last (1) *+4537*
even now (1)
nearly (1)
not until (1) *+1254*
now at last (1) *+4537*
still (1)
untranslated (11)

2454 ἡδονή *hēdonē* (5)
pleasures (3)
desires (1)
pleasure (1)

2455 ἡδύοσμον *hēdyosmon* (2)
mint (1)
spices mint (1)

2456 ἦθος *ēthos* (1)
character (1)

2457 ἥκω *hēkō* (25)
come (18)
has come (2)
have come (2)
arrived (1)
here (1)
overtake (1)

2458 ἠλί1 *ēli1*
Variant; not used

2459 Ἠλί2 *Ēli2* (1)
Heli (1)

2460 Ἠλίας *Ēlias* (29)
Elijah (28)
Elijah's (1)

2461 ἡλικία *hēlikia* (8)
life (2)
of age (2)
age (1)
short (1) *+3625+3836*
stature (1)
untranslated (1)

2462 ἡλίκος *hēlikos* (3)
how much (1)
small (1)
what a great (1)

2463 ἥλιος *hēlios* (32)
sun (28)
east (2) *+424*
just after sunrise (1) *+422+3836*
sunset (1) *+1544*

2464 ἧλος *hēlos* (2)
nail (1)
nails (1)

2465 ἡμέρα *hēmera* (389)
day (180)
days (114)
time (32)
daily (5) *+2848*
daylight (4)
day after day (2) *+2848*
every day (2) *+2848*
some time ago (2) *+3836+4047+4574*
this[s] (2) *+3836+4047*
very day (2) *+4958*
years (2)
a week later (1) *+3552+3893*
always (1) *+3836+4246*
another[s] (1)
at daybreak (1) *+1181+2002*
broad daylight (1)
court (1)
daily (1) *+1667+2848*
dawn (1) *+1181+3516*
day after day (1) *+4246*
day by day (1) *+2848+4246*
daybreak (1) *+1181*
days (1) *+1328*
daytime (1)
during (1)
each day (1) *+3836*
feast of unleavened Bread (1) *+109*
forever (1) *+172+1650*
in the morning (1) *+1181*
late in afternoon (1) *+806+3111*
long (1) *+4498*
morning (1)
nine in the morning (1) *+3836+5569+6052*
noon (1) *+3545*
old (1) *+1877+4581*
Sabbath (1) *+3836+4879*
some time ago (1) *+608+792*
that was the time (1) *+1697+1877+3836*
the next day (1) *+1651+3552*
the next morning (1) *+1181*
them[s] (1) *+3836*
this day (1) *+3836+4958*
three in the afternoon (1) *+1888+3836+6052*
today (1) *+1877+3836+4958*
week (1) *+2231*
when (1) *+1877*
while (1)
untranslated (6)

2466 ἡμέτερος *hēmeteros* (7)
our (4)
our own (1)
ours (1)
us (1)

2467 ἡμιθανής *hēmithanēs* (1)
half dead (1)

2468 ἥμισυς *hēmisys* (5)
half (5)

2469 ἡμιώριον *hemiōrion* (1)
half an hour (1)

2470 ἡμίωρος *hēmiōros*
Variant; not used

2471 ἡνίκα *hēnika* (2)
when (1) *+323*
whenever (1) *+1569*

2472 ἤπερ *ēper* (1)
than (1)

2473 ἤπιος *ēpios* (2)
gentle (1)
kind (1)

2474 Ἤρ *Ēr* (1)
Er (1)

2475 ἤρεμος *ēremos* (1)
peaceful (1)

2476 Ἡρῴδης *Hērōdēs* (43)
Herod (38)
Herod's (5)

2477 Ἡρῳδιανοί *Hērōdianoi* (3)
Herodians (3)

2478 Ἡρῳδιάς *Hērōdias* (6)
Herodias (6)

2479 Ἡρῳδίων *Hērōdiōn* (1)
Herodion (1)

2480 Ἠσαΐας *Ēsaias* (22)
Isaiah (22)

2481 Ἠσαῦ *Ēsau* (3)
Esau (3)

2482 ἥσσων *hēssōn* (2)
harm (1)
less (1)

2483 ἡσυχάζω *hēsychazō* (5)
gave up (1)
lead a quiet life (1)
no objections (1)
rested (1)
silent (1)

2484 ἡσυχία *hēsychia* (4)
quiet (1)
quietness (1)
settle down (1) *+3552*
silent (1)

2485 ἡσύχιος *hēsychios* (2)
quiet (2)

2486 ἤτοι *ētoi* (1)
whether (1)

2487 ἡττάομαι *hēttaomai* (2)
mastered (1)
overcome (1)

2488 ἥττημα *hēttēma* (2)
defeated (1)
loss (1)

2489 ἥττων *hēttōn*
Variant; not used

2490 ἠχέω *ēcheō* (1)
resounding (1)

2491 ἦχος1 *ēchos1* (3)
blast (1)
news (1)
sound (1)

2492 ἦχος2 *ēchos2* (1)
roaring (1)

2493 ἠχώ *ēchō*
Variant; not used

2494 θ *th*
Variant; not used

2495 θά *tha*
Variant; not used

2496 θάβιτα *thabita*
Variant; not used

2497 Θαδδαῖος *Thaddaios* (2)
Thaddaeus (2)

2498 θάλασσα *thalassa* (91)
sea (56)
lake (23)
waves (4)
water (2)
coast (1)
seashore (1)
seashore (1) *+3836+5927*
water's edge (1)
waters (1)
untranslated (1)

2499 θάλπω *thalpō* (2)
cares for (1)
caring for (1)

2500 Θαμάρ *Thamar* (1)
Tamar (1)

2501 θαμβέω *thambeō* (3)
amazed (2)
astonished (1)

2502 θάμβος *thambos* (3)
amazed (1)
astonished (1) *+4321*
wonder (1)

2503 θανάσιμος *thanasimos* (1)
deadly poison (1) *+5516*

2504 θανατηφόρος *thanatēphoros* (1)
deadly (1)

2505 θάνατος *thanatos* (120)
death (104)
fatal (3)
died (2)
put to death (2) *+5462*
deadly (1)
death sentence (1)
die (1) *+3972*
died (1) *+1181*
exposed to death (1)
grounds for the death penalty (1) *+165*
plague (1)
untranslated (2)

2506 θανατόω *thanatoō* (11)
put to death (8)
died (1)
face death (1)
killed (1)

2507 θάπτω *thaptō* (11)
buried (7)
bury (4)

2508 Θάρα *Thara* (1)
Terah (1)

2509 θαρρέω *tharreō* (6)
bold (2)
confident (2)
confidence (1)
with confidence (1)

2510 θαρσέω *tharseō* (7)
take courage (3)
take heart (3)
cheer up (1)

2511 θάρσος *tharsos* (1)
was encouraged (1) *+3284*

2512 θαῦμα *thauma* (2)
astonished (1) *+2513*
wonder (1)

2513 θαυμάζω *thaumazō* (43)
amazed (11)
astonished (8)
surprised (5)
amazement (4)
amazed at (3)
astonished (1) *+2512*
astonishment (1)
flatter (1) *+4725*
marveled (1) *+1639*
marveled at (1)
marveling (1)
surprise (1)
utterly amazed (1) *+2014*
was amazed (1)
wonder (1)
wondering (1)
wondering why (1)

2514 θαυμάσιος *thaumasios* (1)
wonderful (1)

2515 θαυμαστός *thaumastos* (6)
marvelous (4)
remarkable (1)
wonderful (1)

2516 θεά *thea* (1)
goddess (1)

2517 θεάομαι *theaomai* (22)
seen (8)
saw (7)
see (4)
look at (1)
looked at (1)
visit (1)

2518 θεατρίζω *theatrizō* (1)
publicly exposed (1)

2519 θέατρον *theatron* (3)
theater (2)
spectacle (1)

2520 θεῖον *theion* (7)
sulfur (7)

2521 θεῖος *theios* (3)
divine (2)
divine being (1)

2522 θειότης *theiotēs* (1)
divine nature (1)

2523 θειώδης *theiōdēs* (1)
yellow as sulfur (1)

2524 Θέκλα *Thekla*
Variant; not used

2525 θέλημα *thelēma* (62)
will (53)
decision (1)
desires (1)
please (1)
unwilling (1) *+4024*
want (1)
wanted (1)
wants (1)
willing (1)
untranslated (1)

2526 θέλησις *thelēsis* (1)
will (1)

2527 θέλω *thelō* (207)
want (74)
wants (19)
wanted (17)
willing (15)
desire (7)
like (7)
will (7)
would (7)
refused (6) *+4024*
wish (6)
wanting (3)
chosen (2)
longed (2)
mean (2) *+1639*
trying (2)
wished (2)
wishes (2)
choose (1)
chooses (1)
choosing (1)
chose (1)
decided (1)
deliberately (1)
delights (1)
determined (1)
have desire (1)
make a defense (1) *+664*
pleased (1)
pleases (1)
prefer (1)
purposely (1)
refuse (1) *+4024*
refusing (1) *+4024*
request (1)

tries (1)
unwilling (1) *+4024*
want to (1)
wants to (1)
was (1)
willingness (1)
wish that (1)
wishing (1)
would rather (1)
untranslated (1)

2528 θεμέλιον *themelion* (1)
foundations (1)

2529 θεμέλιος *themelios* (15)
foundation (12)
foundations (3)

2530 θεμελιόω *themelioō* (5)
established (2)
foundation (1)
laid the foundations of (1)
steadfast (1)

2531 θεοδίδακτος *theodidaktos* (1)
taught by God (1)

2532 θεολόγος *theologos*
Variant; not used

2533 θεομαχέω *theomacheō*
Variant; not used

2534 θεομάχος *theomachos* (1)
fighting against God (1)

2535 θεόπνευστος *theopneustos* (1)
God-breathed (1)

2536 θεός *theos* (1316)
God (1149)
God's (123)
gods (8)
him[s] (7) *+3836*
god (5)
he[s] (5) *+3836*
his[s] (4) *+3836*
divine (2)
God-fearing (2) *+3836+5828*
godly (2) *+2848*
God fearing gentiles (1) *+3836+5828*
goddess (1)
godly (1)
in God's sight (1) *+3836+4123*
in God's sight (1) *+4123*
of God (1)
untranslated (3)

2537 θεοσέβεια *theosebeia* (1)
worship God (1)

2538 θεοσεβής *theosebēs* (1)
godly man (1)

2539 θεοστυγής *theostygēs* (1)
God-haters (1)

2540 θεότης *theotēs* (1)
Deity (1)

2541 Θεόφιλος *Theophilos* (2)
Theophilus (2)

2542 θεραπεία *therapeia* (3)
healing (2)
servants (1)

2543 θεραπεύω *therapeuō* (43)
healed (22)
heal (12)
cured (3)
healing (3)
cure (1)
cured (1) *+1639*
served (1)

2544 θεράπων *therapōn* (1)
servant (1)

2545 θερίζω *therizō* (21)
reap (10)
reaper (2)
reaps (2)
harvest (1)
harvested (1)
harvesters (1)
harvesting (1)
reap a harvest (1)
reap harvest (1)
reaping (1)

2546 θερισμός *therismos* (13)
harvest (10)
harvest field (2)
that[s] (1) *+3836*

2547 θεριστής *theristēs* (2)
harvesters (2)

2548 θερμαίνω *thermainō* (6)
warming (3)
keep warm (1)
warm (1)
warmed (1)

2549 θέρμη *thermē* (1)
heat (1)

2550 θέρος *theros* (3)
summer (3)

2551 Θεσσαλία *Thessalia*
Variant; not used

2552 Θεσσαλονικεύς *Thessalonikeus* (4)
from Thessalonica (2)
Thessalonians (2)

2553 Θεσσαλονίκη *Thessalonikē* (5)
Thessalonica (4)
Thessalonians (1) *+1877*

2554 Θευδᾶς *Theudas* (1)
Theudas (1)

2555 θεωρέω *theōreō* (58)
see (22)
saw (18)
sees (5)
watching (3)
can see (1)
look at (1)
looked on (1)
looks (1)
looks at (1)
see here (1) *+4047*
seeing (1)
seen (1)
think (1)
watched (1)

2556 θεωρία *theōria* (1)
sight (1)

2557 θήκη *thēkē* (1)
away[s] (1) *+1650+3836*

2558 θηλάζω *thēlazō* (5)
nursing mothers (3)
infants (1)
nursed (1)

2559 θῆλυς *thēlys* (5)
female (3)
women (2)

2560 θήρα *thēra* (1)
trap (1)

2561 θηρεύω *thēreuō* (1)
catch (1)

2562 θηριομαχέω *thēriomacheō* (1)
fought wild beasts (1)

2563 θηρίον *thērion* (45)
beast (35)
snake (2)
wild beasts (2)
animal (1)
animals (1)
brutes (1)
it[s] (1) *+1635+3836+3836*
wild animals (1)
untranslated (1)

2564 θησαυρίζω *thēsaurizō* (8)
store up (2)
hoarded wealth (1)
reserved (1)
save up (1)
stores up (1)
storing up (1)
sum of money (1)

2565 θησαυρός *thēsauros* (18)
treasure (8)
treasures (5)
stored up (4)
storeroom (1)

2566 θιγγάνω *thinganō* (3)
touch (2)
touches (1)

2567 θλίβω *thlibō* (10)
persecuted (2)
crowding (1)
distressed (1)
harassed (1)
hard pressed (1)
narrow (1)
those in trouble (1)
trouble (1)
troubled (1)

2568 θλῖψις *thlipsis* (45)
trouble (8)
troubles (7)
distress (6)
suffering (4)
hardships (3)
persecution (3)
afflictions (2)
sufferings (2)
trials (2)
affliction (1)
anguish (1)
hard pressed (1)
persecuted (1)
severe trial (1) *+1509*
suffer (1)
suffer persecution (1) *+2400*
tribulation (1)

2569 θνήσκω *thnēskō* (9)
dead (9)

2570 θνητός *thnētos* (6)
mortal (6)

2571 θορυβάζω *thorybazō* (1)
upset (1)

2572 θορυβέω *thorybeō* (4)
alarmed (1)
commotion (1)
noisy (1)
riot (1)

2573 θόρυβος *thorybos* (7)
uproar (3)
commotion (1)
disturbance (1)
riot (1)
riot (1) *+1639*

2574 θραυματίζω *thraumatizō*
Variant; not used

2575 θραύω *thrauō* (1)
oppressed (1)

2576 θρέμμα *thremma* (1)
flocks and herds (1)

2577 θρηνέω *thrēneō* (4)
sang a dirge (2)

mourn (1)
wailed for (1)

2578 θρῆνος *thrēnos*
Variant; not used

2579 θρησκεία *thrēskeia* (4)
religion (3)
worship (1)

2580 θρῆσκος *thrēskos* (1)
religious (1)

2581 θριαμβεύω *thriambeuō* (2)
leads in triumphal procession (1)
triumphing over (1)

2582 θρίξ *thrix* (15)
hair (11)
hairs (2)
their hair (1) *+2400*
untranslated (1)

2583 θροέω *throeō* (3)
alarmed (3)

2584 θρόμβος *thrombos* (1)
drops (1)

2585 θρόνος *thronos* (62)
throne (52)
thrones (7)
it[s] (1) *+3836*
them[s] (1) *+3836*
untranslated (1)

2586 θρύπτω *thryptō*
Variant; not used

2587 Θυάτειρα *Thyateira* (4)
Thyatira (4)

2588 θυγάτηρ *thygatēr* (28)
daughter (23)
daughters (4)
descendant (1) *+1666+3836*

2589 θυγάτριον *thygatrion* (2)
little daughter (2)

2590 θύελλα *thyella* (1)
storm (1)

2591 θύϊνος *thyinos* (1)
citron (1)

2592 θυμίαμα *thymiama* (6)
incense (5)
burning of incense (1)

2593 θυμιατήριον *thymiatērion* (1)
altar of incense (1)

2594 θυμιάω *thymiaō* (1)
burn incense (1)

2595 θυμομαχέω *thymomacheō* (1)
quarreling (1)

2596 θυμός *thymos* (18)
wrath (4)
fury (3)
anger (2)
maddening (2)
rage (2)
fits of rage (1)
furious (1) *+4398*
furious (1) *+4441*
fury (1) *+3489*
outbursts of anger (1)

2597 θυμόω *thymoō* (1)
furious (1) *+3336*

2598 θύρα *thyra* (39)
door (21)
doors (6)
gate (5)
entrance (4)
doorway (1)
gates (1)
outer entrance (1) *+4784*

2599 θυρεός *thyreos* (1)
shield (1)

2600 θυρίς *thyris* (2)
window (2)

2601 θυρωρός *thyrōros* (4)
door (1)
girl on duty (1)
one at the door (1)
watchman (1)

2602 θυσία *thysia* (28)
sacrifices (16)
sacrifice (11)
offering (1)

2603 θυσιαστήριον *thysiastērion* (23)
altar (22)
altars (1)

2604 θύω *thyō* (14)
kill (5)
sacrificed (2)
butchered (1)
killed (1)
offer sacrifices (1)
sacrifice (1)
sacrifices offered (1)
sacrificing (1)
untranslated (1)

2605 Θωμᾶς *Thōmas* (11)
Thomas (11)

2606 θώραξ *thōrax* (5)
breastplate (2)
breastplates (2)
their breastplates were (1) *+2400*

2607 ι *i*
Variant; not used

2608 Ἰάϊρος *Iairos* (2)
Jairus (2)

2609 Ἰακώβ *Iakōb* (27)
Jacob (26)
Jacob's (1)

2610 Ἰάκωβος *Iakōbos* (42)
James (41)
his[s] (1) *+3836*

2611 ἴαμα *iama* (3)
healing (3)

2612 Ἰαμβρῆς *Iambrēs* (1)
Jambres (1)

2613 Ἰανναί *Iannai* (1)
Jannai (1)

2614 Ἰάννης *Iannēs* (1)
Jannes (1)

2615 ἰάομαι *iaomai* (26)
healed (15)
heal (6)
healing (2)
freed (1)
heals (1)
you may be healed (1)

2616 Ἰάρετ *Iaret* (1)
Jared (1)

2617 ἴασις *iasis* (3)
heal (1)
heal people (1) *+699*
healed (1)

2618 ἴασπις *iaspis* (4)
jasper (3)
jasper (1) *+3345*

2619 Ἰάσων *Iasōn* (5)
Jason (4)
Jason's (1)

2620 ἰατρός *iatros* (6)
doctor (4)
doctors (1)
physician (1)

2621 Ἰαχίν *Iachin*
Variant; not used

2622 ιβ' *ib*
Variant; not used

2623 ἴδε *ide*
Variant; not used

2624 ἰδέα *idea*
Variant; not used

2625 ἴδιος *idios* (112)
his own (37)
their own (11)
his (10)
privately (6) *+2848*
aside (3) *+2848*
its own (3)
own (3)
their (3)
themselves (3)
your (3)
himself (2)
our own (2)
your own (2)
all had (1) *+3836*
alone (1)
alone (1) *+2848*
belongs (1)
friends (1)
her (1)
her own (1)
him (1)
his home (1) *+3836*
his native language (1) *+1666+3836*
his own home (1) *+3836*
his relatives (1)
home (1) *+3836*
its (1)
its proper (1)
owns (1) *+1639*
private (1)
proper (1)
whose (1)
your own (1) *+3836*
yourselves (1)
untranslated (3)

2626 ἰδιώτης *idiōtēs* (5)
not trained (1)
ordinary (1)
some who do not understand (1)
someone who does not understand (1)
those who do not understand (1)

2627 ἰδού *idou* (200)
look (14)
here (11)
see (10)
now (9)
there before (9)
behold (4)
suddenly (4)
here is (2)
I tell you (2)
there (2)
as can see (1)
as know (1)
but (1)
consider (1)
here's (1)
I assure you (1)
indeed (1) *+2779*
just then (1)
just then (1) *+2779*
listen (1)
on one occasion (1) *+2779*
see how (1)
so (1)
suddenly (1) *+2779*
surely (1)

without warning (1)
yes (1) *+1609*
yet (1)
untranslated (115)

2628 Ἰδουμαία *Idoumaia* (1)
Idumea (1)

2629 ἱδρώς *hidrōs* (1)
sweat (1)

2630 Ἰεζάβελ *Iezabel* (1)
Jezebel (1)

2631 Ἱεράπολις *Hierapolis* (1)
Hierapolis (1)

2632 ἱερατεία *hierateia* (2)
priesthood (1)
priests (1)

2633 ἱεράτευμα *hierateuma* (2)
priesthood (2)

2634 ἱερατεύω *hierateuō* (1)
serving as priest (1)

2635 Ἰερεμίας *Ieremias* (3)
Jeremiah (3)

2636 ἱερεύς *hiereus* (31)
priest (16)
priests (15)

2637 Ἰεριχώ *Ierichō* (7)
Jericho (6)
untranslated (1)

2638 ἱερόθυτος *hierothytos* (1)
offered in sacrifice (1)

2639 ἱερόν *hieron* (71)
temple (32)
temple courts (23)
temple area (10)
its[S] (1) *+3836*
temple grounds (1)
temple guard (1)
there[S] (1) *+1877+3836*
untranslated (2)

2640 ἱεροπρεπής *hieroprepēs* (1)
reverent (1)

2641 ἱερός *hieros* (2)
holy (1)
temple (1)

2642 Ἱεροσόλυμα *Hierosolyma*
Variant; not used

2643 Ἱεροσολυμίτης *Hierosolymitēs* (2)
people of Jerusalem (2)

2644 ἱεροσυλέω *hierosyleō* (1)
rob temples (1)

2645 ἱερόσυλος *hierosylos* (1)
robbed temples (1)

2646 ἱερουργέω *hierourgeō* (1)
priestly duty (1)

2647 Ἰερουσαλήμ *Ierousalēm* (139)
Jerusalem (136)
city of Jerusalem (2)
untranslated (1)

2648 ἱερωσύνη *hierōsynē* (3)
priesthood (3)

2649 Ἰεσσαί *Iessai* (5)
Jesse (5)

2650 Ἰεφθάε *Iephthae* (1)
Jephthah (1)

2651 Ἰεχονίας *Iechonias* (2)
Jeconiah (2)

2652 Ἰησοῦς *Iēsous* (916)
Jesus (882)
Jesus' (14)
he[S] (7) *+3836*
him[S] (6) *+3836*
Joshua (3)
he[S] (1)
his[S] (1) *+3836*
Jesus (1) *+899*
untranslated (1)

2653 ἱκανός *hikanos* (39)
many (5)
long (4)
large (3)
deserve (2) *+1639*
number (2)
some (2)
worthy (2)
bright (1)
competent (1)
considerable (1)
deserve (1)
enough (1)
equal (1)
fit (1)
great (1)
great number (1)
large number (1)
large numbers (1)
large sum (1)
much (1)
post bond (1)
qualified (1)
satisfy (1) *+4472*
sufficient (1)
wept (1) *+1181+3088*
untranslated (1)

2654 ἱκανότης *hikanotēs* (1)
competence (1)

2655 ἱκανόω *hikanoō* (2)
made competent (1)
qualified (1)

2656 ἱκετηρία *hiketēria* (1)
petitions (1)

2657 ἰκμάς *ikmas* (1)
moisture (1)

2658 Ἰκόνιον *Ikonion* (6)
Iconium (6)

2659 ἱλαρός *hilaros* (1)
cheerful (1)

2660 ἱλαρότης *hilarotēs* (1)
cheerfully (1) *+1877*

2661 ἱλάσκομαι *hilaskomai* (2)
make atonement for (1)
mercy on (1)

2662 ἱλασμός *hilasmos* (2)
atoning sacrifice (2)

2663 ἱλαστήριον *hilastērion* (2)
atonement cover (1)
sacrifice of atonement (1)

2664 ἵλεως *hileōs* (2)
forgive (1) *+1639*
never (1)

2665 Ἰλλυρικόν *Illyrikon* (1)
Illyricum (1)

2666 ἱμάς *himas* (4)
thongs (3)
flog (1)

2667 ἱματίζω *himatizō* (2)
dressed (2)

2668 ἱμάτιον *himation* (61)
clothes (23)
cloak (13)
cloaks (7)
garment (6)
robe (4)
garments (2)
clothing (1)
dressed (1) *+4314*
one[S] (1)
outer clothing (1)
stripped (1) *+3836+4351*
untranslated (1)

2669 ἱματισμός *himatismos* (5)
clothes (3)
clothing (2)

2670 ἱμείρομαι *himeiromai*
Variant; not used

2671 ἵνα *hina* (663)
so that (195)
to (165)
that (117)
in order that (16)
so (12)
for (11)
in order to (10)
or (7) *+3590*
to let (6)
want (5)
then (4)
so as to (3)
and (2)
let (2)
meant to be (2)
reason to (2)
therefore (2)
when (2)
aim is to (1)
as (1)
as to (1)
at (1)
because (1)
before (1) *+3590*
bent on (1)
by (1)
expecting to (1)
for fear that (1) *+3590*
for if (1) *+3607*
from (1) *+3590*
hoped (1)
if (1)
in the hope that (1)
intent that (1)
is to (1)
it was intended that (1)
lest (1) *+3590*
only (1)
purpose that (1)
purpose to (1)
rather than (1) *+3590*
this happened that (1)
to keep from (1) *+3590*
wants (1)
were looking for (1) *+2351*
which (1)
untranslated (72)

2672 ἱνατί *hinati* (6)
why (6)

2673 Ἰόππη *Ioppē* (10)
Joppa (10)

2674 Ἰορδάνης *Iordanēs* (15)
Jordan (15)

2675 ἰός *ios* (3)
poison (2)
corrosion (1)

2676 Ἰουδά *Iouda*
Variant; not used

2677 Ἰουδαία *Ioudaia* (44)
Judea (43)
Judean (1)

2678 ἰουδαΐζω *ioudaizō* (1)
follow Jewish customs (1)

2679 Ἰουδαϊκός *Ioudaikos* (1)
Jewish (1)

2680 Ἰουδαϊκῶς *Ioudaikōs* (1)
like a Jew (1)

2681 Ἰουδαῖος *Ioudaios* (194)
Jews (149)
Jew (18)
Jewish (18)
Jew (2) *+467*
Jewess (2)
Judean (2)
Jew (1) *+476*
Jewish community (1) *+4436*
Jews (1) *+467*

2682 Ἰουδαϊσμός *Ioudaismos* (2)
Judaism (2)

2683 Ἰούδας *Ioudas* (44)
Judas (32)
Judah (10)
Jude (1)
Judea (1)

2684 Ἰουλία *Ioulia* (1)
Julia (1)

2685 Ἰούλιος *Ioulios* (2)
Julius (2)

2686 Ἰουνία *Iounia*
Variant; not used

2687 Ἰουνιᾶς *Iounias* (1)
Junias (1)

2688 Ἰοῦστος *Ioustos* (3)
Justus (3)

2689 ἱππεύς *hippeus* (2)
cavalry (1)
horsemen (1)

2690 ἱππικός *hippikos* (1)
mounted (1)

2691 ἵππος *hippos* (17)
horses (9)
horse (7)
horses' (1)

2692 ἶρις *iris* (2)
rainbow (2)

2693 Ἰσαάκ *Isaak* (20)
Isaac (20)

2694 ἰσάγγελος *isangelos* (1)
like angels (1)

2695 Ἰσαχάρ *Isachar*
Variant; not used

2696 Ἰσκαριώθ *Iskariōth*
Variant; not used

2697 Ἰσκαριώτης *Iskariōtēs* (11)
Iscariot (11)

2698 ἴσος *isos* (8)
agree (2)
equal (2)
as (1)
equality (1) *+1639+3836*
in full (1) *+3836*
same (1)

2699 ἰσότης *isotēs* (3)
equality (2)
fair (1)

2700 ἰσότιμος *isotimos* (1)
as precious as (1)

2701 ἰσόψυχος *isopsychos* (1)
like (1)

2702 Ἰσραήλ *Israēl* (68)
Israel (53)
Israelites (6) *+5626*
Israel (3) *+3875*
Israel (3) *+5626*
Israel's (1)
Israelites (1) *+3836+5626*
people Israel (1) *+5626*

2703 Ἰσραηλίτης *Israēlitēs* (9)
of Israel (6)
Israelite (2)
Israelites (1)

2704 Ἰσσαχάρ *Issachar* (1)
Issachar (1)

2705 ἵστημι *histēmi* (163)
standing (40)
stand (33)
stood (29)
stand firm (8)
stood up (5)
stopped (5)
stands (3)
appear (2)
establish (2)
established (2)
got up (2)
standing firm (2)
there (2)
brought (1)
counted out (1)
feet (1)
had to wait (1)
hold (1)
holding (1)
is (1)
made stand (1)
make stand (1)
on trial (1) *+3212*
present (1)
presented (1)
produced (1)
proposed (1)
put (1)
set (1)
settled the matter (1) *+1612*
stand fast (1)
standing (1) *+1639*
stands firm (1)
stayed (1)
stood (1) *+1639*
stop (1)
take stand (1)
taken stand (1)
uphold (1)
waits (1)
was there (1)

2706 ἱστίον *histion*
Variant; not used

2707 ἱστορέω *historeō* (1)
get acquainted with (1)

2708 ἰσχυρός *ischyros* (28)
strong (8)
mighty (7)
loud (2)
more powerful than (2)
stronger (2)
forceful (1)
greatly (1)
more powerful (1)
power (1)
powerful (1)
severe (1)
stronger than (1)

2709 ἰσχύς *ischys* (10)
strength (6)
mighty (2)
power (1)
stronger (1)

2710 ἰσχύω *ischyō* (28)
could (8)
able (5)
strong (3)
healthy (2)
can do (1)
gave beating (1)
good (1)
grew (1)
had (1)
powerful (1)
takes effect (1)
unable (1) *+4024*
unable (1) *+4033*
value (1)

2711 ἴσως *isōs* (1)
perhaps (1)

2712 Ἰταλία *Italia* (4)
Italy (4)

2713 Ἰταλικός *Italikos* (1)
Italian (1)

2714 Ἰτουραῖος *Itouraios* (1)
Iturea (1)

2715 ἰχθύδιον *ichthydion* (2)
small fish (2)

2716 ἰχθύς *ichthys* (20)
fish (19)
untranslated (1)

2717 ἴχνος *ichnos* (3)
follow the same course (1)
footsteps (1)
steps (1)

2718 Ἰωαθάμ *Iōatham* (2)
Jotham (2)

2719 Ἰωακίμ *Iōakim*
Variant; not used

2720 Ἰωανάν *Iōanan* (1)
Joanan (1)

2721 Ἰωάννα *Iōanna* (2)
Joanna (2)

2722 Ἰωάννης *Iōannēs* (135)
John (119)
John's (14)
John's (1) *+899*
untranslated (1)

2723 Ἰωάς *Iōas*
Variant; not used

2724 Ἰώβ *Iōb* (1)
Job's (1)

2725 Ἰωβήδ *Iōbēd* (3)
Obed (3)

2726 Ἰωδά *Iōda* (1)
Joda (1)

2727 Ἰωήλ *Iōēl* (1)
Joel (1)

2728 Ἰωνάθας *Iōnathas*
Variant; not used

2729 Ἰωνάμ *Iōnam* (1)
Jonam (1)

2730 Ἰωνάν *Iōnan*
Variant; not used

2731 Ἰωνᾶς *Iōnas* (9)
Jonah (9)

2732 Ἰωράμ *Iōram* (2)
Jehoram (2)

2733 Ἰωρίμ *Iōrim* (1)
Jorim (1)

2734 Ἰωσαφάτ *Iōsaphat* (2)
Jehoshaphat (2)

2735 Ἰωσή *Iōsē*
Variant; not used

2736 Ἰωσῆς *Iōsēs* (4)
Joses (3)

Joseph (1)

2737 Ἰωσήφ *Iōsēph* (34)
Joseph (31)
Joseph's (3)

2738 Ἰωσήχ *Iōsēch* (1)
Josech (1)

2739 Ἰωσίας *Iōsias* (2)
Josiah (2)

2740 ἰῶτα *iōta* (1)
the smallest letter (1)

2741 κ *k*
Variant; not used

2742 κάβος *kabos*
Variant; not used

2743 κἀγώ *kagō*
Variant; not used

2744 κάδος *kados*
Variant; not used

2745 καθά *katha* (1)
as (1)

2746 καθαίρεσις *kathairesis* (3)
demolish (1)
pulling down (1)
tearing down (1)

2747 καθαιρέω *kathaireō* (9)
took down (3)
brought down (1)
demolish (1)
overthrew (1)
robbed (1)
take down (1)
tear down (1)

2748 καθαίρω *kathairō* (1)
prunes (1)

2749 καθάπερ *kathaper* (13)
just as (5)
like (2)
as (1)
for (1)
matched (1) *+2779+4048*
the same thing (1) *+2779*
untranslated (2)

2750 καθάπτω *kathaptō* (1)
fastened (1)

2751 καθαρίζω *katharizō* (31)
clean (7)
cleansed (5)
cured (4)
make clean (3)
purify (3)
cleanse (2)
made clean (2)
purified (2)
cleansing (1)
purifies (1)
wash (1)

2752 καθαρισμός *katharismos* (7)
ceremonial washing (2)
cleansing (2)
purification (2)
cleansed (1)

2753 κάθαρμα *katharma*
Variant; not used

2754 καθαρός *katharos* (26)
clean (11)
pure (11)
clear (3)
innocent (1)

2755 καθαρότης *katharotēs* (1)
clean (1)

2756 καθέδρα *kathedra* (3)
benches (2)
seat (1)

2757 καθέζομαι *kathezomai* (7)
seated (2)
sitting (2)
sat (1)
sat down (1)
stayed (1)

2758 καθεῖς *katheis*
Variant; not used

2759 καθεξῆς *kathexēs* (5)
after this (1) *+1877+3836*
as it had happened (1)
from place to place (1)
on (1) *+2779+3836*
orderly (1)

2760 καθερίζω *katherizō*
Variant; not used

2761 καθεύδω *katheudō* (22)
sleeping (10)
asleep (6)
sleep (2)
fell asleep (1)
sleeper (1)
sleeping (1) *+1877*
sleeps (1)

2762 καθηγητής *kathēgētēs* (2)
teacher (2)

2763 καθήκω *kathēkō* (2)
fit (1)
ought to be done (1)

2764 κάθημαι *kathēmai* (91)
sitting (28)
seated (12)
sit (12)
sits (10)
sat (8)
rider (4) *+3836*
sat down (4)
live (2)
living (2)
rider (2)
sitting down (2)
rider (1) *+899+2093*
riders (1) *+899+2093*
riders (1) *+2093+3836*
seat (1)
untranslated (1)

2765 καθημέραν *kathēmeran*
Variant; not used

2766 καθημερινός *kathēmerinos* (1)
daily (1)

2767 καθίζω *kathizō* (46)
sat down (15)
sit (10)
sat (4)
sit down (3)
ridden (2)
seated (2)
appoint as judges (1)
came to rest (1)
convened (1)
convened the court (1) *+1037+2093+3836*
place (1)
sets up (1)
sits (1)
sitting down (1)
stay (1)
stayed (1)

2768 καθίημι *kathiēmi* (4)
let down (2)
lowered (1)
lowered (1) *+5899*

2769 καθιστάνω *kathistanō*
Variant; not used

2770 καθίστημι *kathistēmi* (21)
made (5)
put in charge (5)
appointed (3)
appoint (1)
appoints (1)
becomes (1)
escorted (1)
keep (1)
puts in charge (1)
turn over to (1)
untranslated (1)

2771 καθό *katho*
Variant; not used

2772 καθολικός *katholikos*
Variant; not used

2773 καθόλου *katholou* (1)
at all (1)

2774 καθοπλίζω *kathoplizō* (1)
fully armed (1)

2775 καθοράω *kathoraō* (1)
clearly seen (1)

2776 καθότι *kathoti* (6)
because (3)
as (1)
as (1) *+323*
for (1)

2777 καθώς *kathōs* (182)
as (82)
just as (47)
even as (5)
like (3)
since (3)
because (2)
for (2)
in accordance with (2)
what (2)
according to (1)
and (1)
any more than (1) *+4024*
as much as (1)
as well as (1)
but (1) *+4024*
equal with us (1) *+1609+2779*
how (1)
just (1)
just as (1) *+2779*
just as (1) *+4048*
just what (1)
that (1)
that way (1)
the same (1) *+3931*
this agrees with (1)
this is why (1)
which agrees with (1)
untranslated (16)

2778 καθώσπερ *kathōsper* (1)
just as (1)

2779 καί *kai* (9139)
and (4847)
also (244)
then (230)
but (173)
even (104)
so (93)
or (58)
too (36)
yet (36)
and then (23)
with (23)
now (15)
when (15)
both (14)
and so (12)
and also (10)
as (10)
and yet (9)

as well (8)
still (7)
where (7)
while (7)
as well as (6)
in fact (6)
so that (6)
there (6)
and even (5)
nor (5)
what do want with (5) *+5515*
including (4)
though (4)
though (4) *+1623*
whether (4)
again (3)
along with (3)
and too (3)
even though (3)
if (3)
in turn (3)
nor (3) *+4024*
afterward (2)
because (2)
but even (2)
he (2)
in fact (2) *+1142*
in the same way (2) *+4048*
later (2)
man (2) *+135+4922*
meanwhile (2)
rather than (2) *+4024*
therefore (2)
thus (2)
until (2)
with that (2)
430 (1) *+5484+5558*
450 (1) *+4299+5484*
accompanied by (1) *+2262*
and (1) *+1181*
and (1) *+5538*
and alike (1) *+5445*
and as (1) *+4099*
and as well (1)
and both (1)
and even more (1) *+4707+5148*
and indeed (1)
and others (1)
and still (1)
and though (1)
and up (1)
and what is more (1) *+247+1145+4047+4246+5250*
as for (1)
as it is (1) *+1142*
at (1)
at least (1) *+1569*
at that (1)
at this (1)
both (1) *+4047*
both of you (1) *+899+5148*
but (1) *+1623*
but also (1)
but still (1)
by (1)
eighteen (1) *+1274+3893*
equal with us (1) *+1609+2777*
even (1) *+1569*
for (1)
forty-six (1) *+1971+5477*
fully convinced (1) *+3857+4275*
furthermore (1)
greatly increased (1) *+889+4437*
if so (1)
in addition (1) *+247*
in fact (1) *+1254*
in this same way (1) *+4048*
indeed (1)
indeed (1) *+247*
indeed (1) *+1254*
indeed (1) *+2627*
instead of (1) *+4049*
it is the same (1) *+4048*
it is with (1)
just (1) *+1569*
just as (1) *+2777*
just as though (1) *+899+1651+3836*
just then (1) *+2627*
likewise (1) *+1142*
likewise (1) *+4048*
matched (1) *+2749+4048*
more than that (1)
moved about freely (1) *+1660+1744*
neither (1) *+4024*
nor (1) *+3590*
now (1) *+1181*
on (1) *+2759+3836*
on both sides (1) *+2277+3957*
on each side (1) *+1696+1949*
on one occasion (1)
on one occasion (1) *+2627*
once (1)
once (1) *+1181*
once more (1) *+4099*
one day (1) *+1181*
one on each side (1) *+1949+1949*
or (1) *+4024*
or even (1)
rather than (1) *+3590*
same as (1) *+4005*
searched intently and with the greatest care (1) *+1699+2001*
so it is with (1) *+4048*
so too (1)
some (1)
soon (1)
suddenly (1) *+2627*
than that (1) *+3590*
the same as (1) *+6055*
the same thing (1) *+2749*
the same way (1) *+6055*
the two of you (1) *+899+5148*
their (1)
then (1) *+4099*
they[s] (1) *+899+899+3412+3836*
thirty-eight (1) *+3893+5558*
though (1) *+1145*
to this (1)
together with (1)
what is more (1) *+247+1254+3667+4024*
why do involve (1) *+5515*
without (1) *+3590*
without (1) *+4024*
yet even (1)
untranslated (2958)

2780 Καϊάφας *Kaiaphas* (9)
Caiaphas (9)

2781 καίγε *kaige*
Variant; not used

2782 Κάϊν *Kain* (3)
Cain (3)

2783 Καϊνάμ *Kainam* (2)
Cainan (1)
Kenan (1)

2784 Καϊνάν *Kainan*
Variant; not used

2785 καινός *kainos* (42)
new (39)
anew (2)
latest (1)

2786 καινότης *kainotēs* (2)
new (1)
new way (1)

2787 καινοφωνία *kainophōnia*
Variant; not used

2788 καίπερ *kaiper* (5)
even though (2)
though (2)
although (1)

2789 καιρός *kairos* (85)
time (50)
times (8)
opportunity (3)
age (2)
dates (2)
right time (2)
the proper time (2)
a while (1)
always (1) *+1877+4246*
appointed season (1)
at just the right time (1) *+2848*
due time (1)
find convenient (1) *+3561*
in seasons (1)
make the most of opportunity (1) *+1973+3836*
occasions (1)
opportune time (1)
present (1) *+3814+3836*
present time (1)
proper time (1)
season (1)
seasons (1)
untranslated (1)

2790 Καῖσαρ *Kaisar* (29)
Caesar (20)
Caesar's (9)

2791 Καισάρεια *Kaisareia* (17)
Caesarea (17)

2792 καίτοι *kaitoi* (2)
and yet (1)
yet (1)

2793 καίτοιγε *kaitoige* (1)
although in fact (1)

2794 καίω *kaiō* (12)
burning (5)
blazing (2)
burned (2)
all ablaze (1) *+4786*
flames (1)
light (1)

2795 κἀκεῖ *kakei*
Variant; not used

2796 κἀκεῖθεν *kakeithen*
Variant; not used

2797 κἀκεῖνος *kakeinos*
Variant; not used

2798 κακία *kakia* (11)
malice (5)
evil (3)
depravity (1)
trouble (1)
wickedness (1)

2799 κακοήθεια *kakoētheia* (1)
malice (1)

2800 κακολογέω *kakologeō* (4)
curses (2)
maligned (1)
say bad about (1)

2801 κακοπάθεια *kakopatheia* (1)
suffering (1)

2802 κακοπαθέω *kakopatheō* (3)
endure hardship (1)
suffering (1)
trouble (1)

2803 κακοποιέω *kakopoieō* (4)
do evil (2)
does what is evil (1)
doing evil (1)

2804 κακοποιός *kakopoios* (3)
criminal (1)

doing wrong (1)
do wrong (1)

2805 κακός *kakos* (50)
evil (25)
wrong (8)
crime (3)
harm (3)
bad (2)
wicked (2)
criminal (1) *+4472*
harm (1) *+4556*
ill effects (1)
ugly (1)
wretches (1)
wrongdoer (1) *+4556*
wrongs (1)

2806 κακοῦργος *kakourgos* (4)
criminals (3)
criminal (1)

2807 κακουχέω *kakoucheō* (2)
mistreated (2)

2808 κακόω *kakoō* (6)
harm (2)
mistreated (1)
oppressed (1)
persecute (1)
poisoned (1)

2809 κακῶς *kakōs* (16)
sick (7) *+2400*
wrong (2)
diseases (1) *+3798*
evil (1)
greatly (1)
terribly (1)
was sick (1) *+2400*
were ill (1) *+2400*
wretched (1)

2810 κάκωσις *kakōsis* (1)
oppression (1)

2811 καλάμη *kalamē* (1)
straw (1)

2812 κάλαμος *kalamos* (12)
reed (4)
staff (3)
rod (2)
stick (2)
pen (1)

2813 καλέω *kaleō* (148)
called (85)
call (12)
invited (11)
calls (8)
give (3)
host (2)
invite (2)
invites (2)
known as (2)
reckoned (2)
call (1) *+3836+3950*
calling received (1) *+3104*
consecrated (1) *+41*
gave (1)
given (1)
guests (1)
has (1)
host who invited (1)
name (1)
name (1) *+3836+3950*
named (1)
named (1) *+3950*
said to be (1)
tell (1)
was known as (1)
untranslated (4)

2814 καλλιέλαιος *kallielaios* (1)
cultivated olive tree (1)

2815 καλοδιδάσκαλος *kalodidaskalos* (1)
teach what is good (1)

2816 Καλοὶ λιμένες *Kaloi limenes* (1)
fair Havens (1)

2817 καλοκαγαθία *kalokagathia*
Variant; not used

2818 καλοποιέω *kalopoieō* (1)
doing what is right (1)

2819 καλός *kalos* (100)
good (65)
better (9)
right (5)
beautiful (3)
noble (3)
excellent (2)
fine (2)
best (1)
choice (1)
clear (1)
faithfully (1) *+6055*
firm (1)
goodness (1)
great (1)
it[s] (1) *+3836*
these[s] (1) *+2240*
untranslated (2)

2820 κάλυμμα *kalymma* (4)
veil (4)

2821 καλύπτω *kalyptō* (8)
veiled (2)
concealed (1)
cover (1)
cover over (1)
covers over (1)
hides (1)
swept over (1)

2822 καλῶς *kalōs* (37)
well (12)
good (8)
right (6)
the truth (2)
easily (1)
fine way (1)
good (1) *+4472*
granted (1)
honorably (1)
rightly (1)
the right thing (1)
very well (1)
well said (1)

2823 κάμηλος *kamēlos* (6)
camel (4)
camel's (2)

2824 κάμιλος *kamilos*
Variant; not used

2825 κάμινος *kaminos* (4)
furnace (4)

2826 καμμύω *kammyō* (2)
closed (2)

2827 κάμνω *kamnō* (2)
grow weary (1)
sick (1)

2828 κάμπτω *kamptō* (4)
bow (1)
bowed (1)
kneel (1) *+1205+3836*
should bow (1)

2829 κἄν *kan*
Variant; not used

2830 Κανά *Kana* (4)
Cana (4)

2831 Καναναῖος *Kananaios* (2)
Zealot (2)

2832 Κανανίτης *Kananitēs*
Variant; not used

2833 Κανδάκη *Kandakē* (1)
Candace (1)

2834 κανών *kanōn* (4)
area of activity (1)
field (1) *+3586+3836*
rule (1)
territory (1)

2835 Καπερναούμ *Kapernaoum*
Variant; not used

2836 καπηλεύω *kapēleuō* (1)
peddle for profit (1)

2837 καπνός *kapnos* (13)
smoke (13)

2838 Καππαδοκία *Kappadokia* (2)
Cappadocia (2)

2839 καραδοκία *karadokia*
Variant; not used

2840 καρδία *kardia* (157)
hearts (69)
heart (60)
mind (3)
minds (2)
to himself (2) *+899+1877+3836*
decided (1) *+326+2093+3836*
experts (1) *+1214*
heart's (1)
himself (1) *+899*
inmost (1)
made think (1) *+1877+3836+5502*
make up mind (1) *+1877+3836+5502*
prompted (1) *+965+1650+3836*
self (1) *+476+3836*
stand firm (1) *+3836+5114*
themselves (1) *+899+3836*
thought (1)
wholeheartedly (1) *+1666*
wondered about (1) *+1877+3836+5502*
untranslated (7)

2841 καρδιογνώστης *kardiognōstēs* (2)
know heart (1)
knows heart (1)

2842 Κάρπος *Karpos* (1)
Carpus (1)

2843 καρπός *karpos* (66)
fruit (41)
crop (6)
harvest (4)
crops (3)
benefit (2)
grain (2)
child bear (1) *+3120+3836*
descendants (1) *+3836+4019*
fruitful (1)
fruitful (1) *+5770*
grapes (1)
heads (1)
seeds (1)
untranslated (1)

2844 καρποφορέω *karpophoreō* (8)
bearing fruit (2)
produce a crop (2)
bear fruit (1)
bore fruit (1)
produces a crop (1)
produces grain (1)

2845 καρποφόρος *karpophoros* (1)
crops (1)

2846 καρτερέω *kartereō* (1)
persevered (1)

2847 κάρφος *karphos* (6)
speck (4)
speck of sawdust (2)

2848 κατά *kata* (477)
against (47)
according to (46)
in (40)
by (34)
as (17)
every (10)
about (6)
for (6)
in accordance with (6)
privately (6) *+2625*
to (6)
at (5)
because of (5)
daily (5) *+2465*
like (5)
on (4)
over (4)
with (4)
along (3)
aside (3) *+2625*
based on (3)
down (3)
in every (3)
in keeping with (3)
in various (3)
just as (3)
of (3)
through (3)
as for (2)
case (2) *+3836*
contrary to (2)
day after day (2) *+2465*
earthly (2) *+4922*
every (2) *+4246*
every day (2) *+2465*
from house to house (2) *+3875*
from one to another (2)
godly (2) *+2536*
in obedience to (2)
in the ordinary way (2) *+4922*
is concerned (2)
just as (2) *+4012*
natural (2) *+5882*
off (2)
on the basis of (2)
out of (2)
required (2)
that is how (2) *+899+3836*
throughout (2)
throughout (2) *+3910*
your own (2) *+5148*
a follower of (1)
actions deserve (1) *+2240*
after (1)
agrees with (1)
all over (1) *+3910*
alone (1) *+2625*
alone (1) *+3668*
among (1)
annual (1) *+1929*
anywhere else in (1)
as does (1)
as intended (1)
as much as were able (1) *+1539*
as on (1)
as to (1)
as usual (1) *+899+3836*
as usual (1) *+1621+3836*
as was (1)
at just the right time (1) *+2789*
before (1)
before (1) *+4725*
by means of (1)
by standards (1)
by the standards of (1)
carrying out (1)
commanding (1) *+2198+3306*
conforms to (1)
considerate (1) *+1194*
covered (1) *+2400*
daily (1) *+1667+2465*
day by day (1) *+2465+4246*
deny truth (1) *+237+6017*
depends on (1)
down from (1)
during (1)
each (1)
each (1) *+1651+1651*
everyone (1) *+4246*
extreme (1) *+958*
faced (1) *+4725*
followed (1)
forced (1) *+340*
found in (1)
from a worldly point of view (1) *+4922*
from after town (1)
from everyday life (1) *+476*
from house to house (1) *+3836+3875*
from human point of view (1) *+476*
from one synagogue to another (1) *+4246+5252*
from village to village (1) *+3267+3836*
great (1) *+5651*
happened (1) *+5175*
how (1) *+3836*
how (1) *+5515*
human (1) *+476*
in any way (1) *+3594+5573*
in conformity with (1)
in each (1)
in regard to (1)
in response to (1)
in the way does (1)
in their homes (1) *+3875*
in this way[S] (1) *+4922*
in turn (1) *+1651*
in whole (1)
indicating that (1) *+4005*
intensely (1) *+5651*
just as (1) *+4005+4048+5573*
just as (1) *+4005+5573*
just like this (1) *+899+3836*
leads to (1)
member (1) *+3517+3836*
most excellent (1) *+5651*
near (1)
observer of law (1) *+3795*
one at a time (1) *+1651+1651*
opposed to (1)
opposite (1)
orderly way (1) *+5423*
out of favoritism (1) *+4680*
over against (1)
prescribed by (1)
reasonable (1) *+3364*
required by (1)
requires (1)
something man made up (1) *+476*
spontaneous (1) *+1730*
surface (1) *+4725*
that (1) *+4005*
that far outweighs them all (1) *+983+1650+5651+5651*
that meets in (1)
this is (1) *+3836*
thoroughly (1) *+205*
to my shame (1) *+871*
to suit (1)
toward (1)
what has happened to (1) *+3836*
when (1)
when face to face (1) *+4725*
where (1)
with regard to (1)
year after year (1) *+1929*
your (1) *+5148*
untranslated (42)

2849 καταβαίνω *katabainō* (81)
come down (14)
went down (13)
came down (12)
coming down (9)
go down (6)
descended (3)
descending (3)
comes down (2)
down (2)
goes down (2)
going down (2)
arrived (1)
came (1)
come (1)
comes (1)
descend (1)
falling (1)
fell (1)
go downstairs (1)
gone down (1)
got down (1)
on the way (1)
went (1)
untranslated (1)

2850 καταβάλλω *kataballō* (2)
laying (1)
struck down (1)

2851 καταβαρέω *katabareō* (1)
burden to (1)

2852 καταβαρύνω *katabarynō* (1)
heavy (1)

2853 κατάβασις *katabasis* (1)
place where the road goes down (1)

2854 καταβιβάζω *katabibazō*
Variant; not used

2855 καταβοάω *kataboaō*
Variant; not used

2856 καταβολή *katabolē* (11)
creation (9)
become a father (1) *+3284+5065*
beginning (1)

2857 καταβραβεύω *katabrabeuō* (1)
disqualify for the prize (1)

2858 καταγγελεύς *katangeleus* (1)
advocating (1)

2859 καταγγέλλω *katangellō* (18)
proclaim (4)
proclaimed (3)
preach (2)
preached (2)
proclaiming (2)
advocating (1)
foretold (1)
preaching (1)
reported (1)
telling (1)

2860 καταγελάω *katagelaō* (3)
laughed at (3)

2861 καταγινώσκω *kataginōskō* (3)
condemn (2)
clearly in the wrong (1)

2862 κατάγνυμι *katagnymi* (4)
break (2)
broke (1)
broken (1)

2863 καταγράφω *katagraphō* (1)
write (1)

2864 κατάγω *katagō* (9)
bring (2)
brought (2)
bring down (1)
landed (1)
pulled up (1)
put in (1)
took down (1)

2865 καταγωνίζομαι *katagōnizomai* (1)
conquered (1)

2866 καταδέω *katadeō* (1)
bandaged (1)

2867 κατάδηλος *katadēlos* (1)
clear (1)

2868 καταδικάζω *katadikazō* (5)
condemned (4)
condemn (1)

2869 καταδίκη *katadikē* (1)
be condemned (1)

2870 καταδιώκω *katadiōkō* (1)
to look for (1)

2871 καταδουλόω *katadouloō* (2)
enslaves (1)
make slaves (1)

2872 καταδυναστεύω *katadynasteuō* (2)
exploiting (1)
under the power (1)

2873 κατάθεμα *katathema* (1)
curse (1)

2874 καταθεματίζω *katathematizō* (1)
call down curses (1)

2875 καταισχύνω *kataischynō* (13)
put to shame (3)
dishonors (2)
shame (2)
ashamed (1)
ashamed of (1)
disappoint (1)
embarrassed (1)
humiliate (1)
humiliated (1)

2876 κατακαίω *katakaiō* (12)
burned (4)
burned up (4)
burn (1)
burn up (1)
burning up (1)
consumed (1)

2877 κατακαλύπτω *katakalyptō* (3)
cover (3)

2878 κατακαυχάομαι *katakauchaomai* (4)
boast (1)
boast over (1)
triumphs over (1)
untranslated (1)

2879 κατάκειμαι *katakeimai* (12)
eating (3)
lying (2)
bedridden (1) *+2093+3187*
dinner (1)
in bed (1)
lie (1)
lying on (1)
reclining at the table (1)
sick in bed (1)

2880 κατακλάω *kataklaō* (2)
broke (2)

2881 κατακλείω *katakleiō* (2)
locked (1)
put (1)

2882 κατακληροδοτέω *kataklērodoteō*
Variant; not used

2883 κατακληρονομέω *kataklēronomeō* (1)
gave to as inheritance (1)

2884 κατακλίνω *kataklinō* (5)
at the table (1)
reclined at the table (1)
sat down (1)
sit down (1)
take (1) *+1650*

2885 κατακλύζω *kataklyzō* (1)
deluged (1) *+5623*

2886 κατακλυσμός *kataklysmos* (4)
flood (4)

2887 κατακολουθέω *katakoloutheō* (2)
followed (2)

2888 κατακόπτω *katakoptō* (1)
cut (1)

2889 κατακρημνίζω *katakrēmnizō* (1)
throw down the cliff (1)

2890 κατάκριμα *katakrima* (3)
condemnation (3)

2891 κατακρίνω *katakrinō* (18)
condemned (9)
condemn (7)
condemning (1)
condemns (1)

2892 κατάκρισις *katakrisis* (2)
condemn (1)
condemns (1)

2893 κατακύπτω *katakyptō* (1)
stooped down (1)

2894 κατακυριεύω *katakyrieuō* (4)
lord it over (2)
lording it over (1)
overpowered (1)

2895 καταλαλέω *katalaleō* (5)
slander (2)
speaks against (2)
accuse (1)

2896 καταλαλιά *katalalia* (2)
slander (2)

2897 κατάλαλος *katalalos* (1)
slanderers (1)

2898 καταλαμβάνω *katalambanō* (15)
caught (1)
caught in the act (1) *+900+2093*
found (1)
get the prize (1)
grasp (1)
obtained (1)
overtakes (1)
realize (1)
realized (1)
seizes (1)
surprise (1)
take hold (1)
taken hold of (1)
took hold of (1)
understood (1)

2899 καταλέγω *katalegō* (1)
put on the list (1)

2900 κατάλειμμα *kataleimma*
Variant; not used

2901 καταλείπω *kataleipō* (24)
left (11)
leave (4)
leaving (3)
leaves (1)
leaving behind (1)
neglect (1)
passing (1)
reserved (1)
stands (1)

2902 καταλιθάζω *katalithazō* (1)
stone (1)

2903 καταλλαγή *katallagē* (4)
reconciliation (4)

2904 καταλλάσσω *katallassō* (6)
reconciled (5)
reconciling (1)

2905 κατάλοιπος *kataloipos* (1)
remnant (1)

2906 κατάλυμα *katalyma* (3)
guest room (2)
inn (1)

2907 καταλύω *katalyō* (17)
destroy (6)
thrown down (3)
abolish (2)
destroyed (2)
fail (1)
guest (1)
lodging (1)
stop (1)

2908 καταμανθάνω *katamanthanō* (1)
see (1)

2909 καταμαρτυρέω *katamartyreō* (3)
testimony bringing against (3)

2910 καταμένω *katamenō* (1)
staying (1)

2911 καταμόνας *katamonas*
Variant; not used

2912 κατανάθεμα *katanathema*
Variant; not used

2913 καταναθεματίζω *katanathematizō*
Variant; not used

2914 καταναλίσκω *katanaliskō* (1)
consuming (1)

2915 καταναρκάω *katanarkaō* (3)
burden (2)
burden to (1)

2916 κατανεύω *kataneuō* (1)
signaled (1)

2917 κατανοέω *katanoeō* (14)
consider (3)
pay attention to (2)
faced the fact (1)
fix thoughts on (1)
look (1)
look more closely (1)
looked (1) *+867*
looking at (1)
looks at (1)
saw (1)
saw through (1)

2918 καταντάω *katantaō* (13)
arrived (4)
reach (2)
attain (1)
came (1)
came to (1)
come (1)
landed (1)
reached (1)
see fulfilled (1)

2919 κατάνυξις *katanyxis* (1)
stupor (1)

2920 κατανύσσομαι *katanyssomai* (1)
cut to (1)

2921 καταξιόω *kataxioō* (3)
counted worthy (2)
considered worthy of (1)

2922 καταπατέω *katapateō* (5)
trample (1)
trampled (1)
trampled on (1)
trampled under foot (1)
trampling on (1)

2923 κατάπαυσις *katapausis* (9)
rest (8)
resting (1)

2924 καταπαύω *katapauō* (4)
given rest (1)
keeping (1)
rested (1)
rests (1)

2925 καταπέτασμα *katapetasma* (6)
curtain (6)

2926 καταπίμπρημι *katapimprēmi*
Variant; not used

2927 καταπίνω *katapinō* (7)
swallowed up (2)
devour (1)
drowned (1)
overwhelmed (1)
swallow (1)
swallowing (1)

2928 καταπίπτω *katapiptō* (3)
fell (2)
fall (1)

2929 καταπλέω *katapleō* (1)
sailed (1)

2930 καταπονέω *kataponeō* (2)
distressed (1)
him[S] (1) *+3836*

2931 καταποντίζω *katapontizō* (2)
drowned (1)
sink (1)

2932 κατάρα *katara* (6)
curse (3)
accursed (1)
being cursed (1)
cursing (1)

2933 καταράομαι *kataraomai* (5)
curse (3)
cursed (2)

2934 καταργέω *katargeō* (27)
destroy (3)
destroyed (3)
nullify (3)
fading away (2)
released (2)
abolished (1)
abolishing (1)
alienated (1)
cease (1)
coming to nothing (1)
disappears (1)
do away with (1)
done away with (1)
fading (1)
pass away (1)
put behind (1)
taken away (1)
use up (1)
worthless (1)

2935 καταριθμέω *katarithmeō* (1)
number (1)

2936 καταρτίζω *katartizō* (13)
prepared (2)
preparing (2)
restore (2)
aim for perfection (1)
equip (1)
formed (1)
fully trained (1)
ordained (1)
perfectly united (1) *+899+3836*
supply (1)

2937 κατάρτισις *katartisis* (1)
perfection (1)

2938 καταρτισμός *katartismos* (1)
prepare (1)

2939 κατασείω *kataseiō* (4)
motioned (3)
motioned (1) *+3836+5931*

2940 κατασκάπτω *kataskaptō* (2)
ruins (1)
torn down (1)

2941 κατασκευάζω *kataskeuazō* (11)
built (3)
prepare (3)
builder of (2)
arranged (1)
prepared (1)
set up (1)

2942 κατασκηνόω *kataskēnoō* (4)
perch (2)
live (1)
perched (1)

2943 κατασκήνωσις *kataskēnōsis* (2)
nests (2)

2944 κατασκιάζω *kataskiazō* (1)
overshadowing (1)

2945 κατασκοπέω *kataskopeō* (1)
spy on (1)

2946 κατάσκοπος *kataskopos* (1)
spies (1)

2947 κατασοφίζομαι *katasophizomai* (1)
dealt treacherously with (1)

2948 καταστέλλω *katastellō* (2)
quiet (1)
quieted (1)

2949 κατάστημα *katastēma* (1)
way live (1)

2950 καταστολή *katastolē* (1)
modestly (1) *+3177*

2951 καταστρέφω *katastrephō* (2)
overturned (2)

2952 καταστρηνιάω *katastrēniaō* (1)
sensual desires overcome their dedication to (1)

2953 καταστροφή *katastrophē* (1)
ruins (1)

2954 καταστρώννυμι *katastrōnnymi* (1)
scattered (1)

2955 κατασύρω *katasyrō* (1)
drag off (1)

2956 κατασφάζω *katasphazō* (1)
kill (1)

2957 κατασφάττω *katasphattō*
Variant; not used

2958 κατασφραγίζω *katasphragizō* (1)
sealed (1)

2959 κατάσχεσις *kataschesis* (2)
possess (1)
took (1)

2960 κατατίθημι *katatithēmi* (2)
do (1)
grant (1)

2961 κατατομή *katatomē* (1)
mutilators (1)

2962 κατατοξεύω *katatoxeuō*
Variant; not used

2963 κατατρέχω *katatrechō* (1)
ran down (1)

2964 καταυγάζω *kataugazō*
Variant; not used

2965 καταφέρω *katapherō* (4)
bringing against (1)
cast against (1)
sinking (1)
sound asleep (1) *+608+3836+5678*

2966 καταφεύγω *katapheugō* (2)
fled (2)

2967 καταφθείρω *kataphtheirō* (1)
depraved (1)

2968 καταφιλέω *kataphileō* (6)
kissed (5)
kissing (1)

2969 καταφρονέω *kataphroneō* (9)
despise (4)
look down on (2)
scorning (1)
show contempt for (1)
show less respect (1)

2970 καταφρονητής *kataphronētēs* (1)
scoffers (1)

2971 καταφωνέω *kataphōneō*
Variant; not used

2972 καταχέω *katacheō* (2)
poured (1)
poured on (1)

2973 καταχθόνιος *katachthonios* (1)
under the earth (1)

2974 καταχράομαι *katachraomai* (2)
engrossed in (1)
make use of (1)

2975 καταψηφίζομαι *katapsēphizomai*
Variant; not used

2976 καταψύχω *katapsychō* (1)
cool (1)

2977 κατείδωλος *kateidōlos* (1)
full of idols (1)

2978 κατέναντι *katenanti* (8)
ahead (3)
in the sight (2)
opposite (2)
before (1)

2979 κατενώπιον *katenōpion* (3)
in sight (2)
before (1)

2980 κατεξουσιάζω *katexousiazō* (2)
exercise authority over (2)

2981 κατεργάζομαι *katergazomai* (22)
do (3)
produced (3)
brings (2)
done (2)
accomplished (1)
achieving (1)
carry out (1)
committed (1)
develops (1)
did (1)
does (1)
doing (1)
made (1)
produces (1)
result in (1)
work out (1)

2982 κατέρχομαι *katerchomai* (16)
came down (4)
went down (4)
landed (3)
went (2)
arrived (1)
came (1)
come down (1)

2983 κατεσθίω *katesthiō* (14)
ate up (3)
devour (3)
ate (1)
consume (1)
devoured (1)
devouring (1)

devours (1)
eat (1)
exploits (1)
squandered (1)

2984 κατέσθω *katesthō*
Variant; not used

2985 κατευθύνω *kateuthynō* (3)
clear (1)
direct (1)
guide (1)

2986 κατευλογέω *kateulogeō* (1)
blessed (1)

2987 κατεφίσταμαι *katephistamai* (1)
made a attack on (1)

2988 κατέχω *katechō* (17)
hold on to (2)
keep (2)
bound (1)
hold (1)
hold firmly (1)
hold to (1)
holding back (1)
holding to (1)
holds back (1)
made (1)
possessing (1)
retain (1)
suppress (1)
take (1)
theirs to keep (1)

2989 κατηγορέω *katēgoreō* (23)
accuse (5)
accusing (3)
accused (2)
accused of (1)
accuser (1)
accuses (1)
accusing of (1)
bring charges (1)
charge to bring against (1)
charges (1)
charges bringing against (1)
charges brought against (1)
charges making against (1)
he[s] (1) *+3836*
presented case (1)
press charges against (1)

2990 κατηγορία *katēgoria* (3)
accusation (1)
charge (1)
charges (1)

2991 κατήγορος *katēgoros* (4)
accusers (3)
accusers (1) *+2400*

2992 κατήγωρ *katēgōr* (1)
accuser (1)

2993 κατήφεια *katēpheia* (1)
gloom (1)

2994 κατηχέω *katēcheō* (8)
informed (1)
instruct (1)
instructed (1)
instructed in (1)
instructor (1)
receives instruction in (1)
reports (1)
taught (1)

2995 κατιόω *katioō* (1)
corroded (1)

2996 κατισχύω *katischyō* (3)
be able (1)
overcome (1)
prevailed (1)

2997 κατοικέω *katoikeō* (44)
inhabitants (7)
live (7)
living (5)
lived (4)
dwell (3)
in (2)
lived in (2)
lives (2)
living in (2)
dwells in (1)
home (1)
inhabit (1)
inhabitants of (1)
live in (1)
residents of (1)
settled (1)
staying (1)
them[s] (1) *+1178+2093+3836+3836*
untranslated (1)

2998 κατοίκησις *katoikēsis* (1)
lived (1) *+2400+3836*

2999 κατοικητήριον *katoikētērion* (2)
dwelling (1)
home (1)

3000 κατοικία *katoikia* (1)
live (1)

3001 κατοικίζω *katoikizō* (1)
live (1)

3002 κατοπτρίζω *katoptrizō* (1)
reflect (1)

3003 κατόρθωμα *katorthōma*
Variant; not used

3004 κάτω *katō* (9)
below (3)
down (3)
bottom (2)
to the ground (1)

3005 κατώτερος *katōteros* (1)
lower (1)

3006 κατωτέρω *katōterō* (1)
under (1)

3007 Καῦδα *Kauda* (1)
Cauda (1)

3008 καυμα *kauma* (2)
heat (1)
scorching heat (1)

3009 καυματίζω *kaumatizō* (4)
scorched (2)
scorch (1)
seared (1)

3010 καυματόω *kaumatoō*
Variant; not used

3011 καῦσις *kausis* (1)
burned (1)

3012 καυσόω *kausoō* (2)
fire (1)
heat (1)

3013 καυστηριάζω *kaustēriazō* (1)
seared as with a hot iron (1)

3014 καύσων *kausōn* (3)
heat of the day (1)
hot (1)
scorching heat (1)

3015 καυτηριάζω *kautēriazō*
Variant; not used

3016 καυχάομαι *kauchaomai* (36)
boast (16)
boasting (4)
rejoice (3)
boast about (2)
boasts (2)
take pride (2)
boast of (1)
boasted (1)
boasting about (1)
boasting of (1)
brag (1)
brag about (1)
glory (1)

3017 καύχημα *kauchēma* (11)
boast (4)
boasting (2)
pride (2)
boast (1) *+1639*
joy (1)
something to boast about (1)

3018 καύχησις *kauchēsis* (11)
boasting (4)
pride (2)
boast (1)
boasting about (1)
glory (1)
glory in (1) *+2400*
glory over (1) *+2400*

3019 Καφαρναούμ *Kapharnaoum* (16)
Capernaum (16)

3020 Κεγχρεαί *Kenchreai* (2)
Cenchrea (2)

3021 κέδρος *kedros*
Variant; not used

3022 Κεδρών *Kedrōn* (1)
Kidron (1)

3023 κεῖμαι *keimai* (24)
lying (4)
destined (2)
is (2)
laid (2)
there (2)
been (1)
by itself (1) *+1650+1651+5536+6006*
covers (1) *+2093*
laid out (1)
laid up (1)
lay (1)
made (1)
put here (1)
stood (1) *+1639*
under the control (1)
was (1)
untranslated (1)

3024 κειρία *keiria* (1)
strips of linen (1)

3025 κείρω *keirō* (4)
cut off (2)
hair cut (1)
shearer (1)

3026 κέλευσμα *keleusma* (1)
loud command (1)

3027 κελεύω *keleuō* (25)
ordered (18)
gave orders (2)
command (1)
commanding (1)
directed (1)
give order (1)
tell (1)

3028 κενεμβατεύω *kenembateuō*
Variant; not used

3029 κενοδοξία *kenodoxia* (1)
vain conceit (1)

3030 κενόδοξος *kenodoxos* (1)
conceited (1)

3031 κενός *kenos* (18)
empty-handed (3)
empty (2)
in vain (2)

useless (2)
vain (2)
failure (1)
foolish (1)
hollow (1)
nothing (1)
so[s] (1)
without effect (1)
untranslated (1)

3032 κενοφωνία *kenophōnia* (2)
chatter (2)

3033 κενόω *kenoō* (5)
deprive (1)
emptied (1)
made nothing (1)
no value (1)
prove hollow (1)

3034 κέντρον *kentron* (4)
sting (2)
goads (1)
stings (1)

3035 κεντυρίων *kentyriōn* (3)
centurion (3)

3036 κενῶς *kenōs* (1)
without reason (1)

3037 κεραία *keraia* (2)
least stroke of a pen (2)

3038 κεραμεύς *kerameus* (3)
potter's (2)
potter (1)

3039 κεραμικός *keramikos* (1)
pottery (1) *+5007*

3040 κεράμιον *keramion* (2)
jar (2)

3041 κέραμος *keramos* (1)
tiles (1)

3042 κεράννυμι *kerannymi* (3)
mix (1)
poured (1)
untranslated (1)

3043 κέρας *keras* (11)
horns (10)
horn (1)

3044 κεράτιον *keration* (1)
pods (1)

3045 κερδαίνω *kerdainō* (17)
win (5)
gained (4)
gain (3)
won over (2)
gains (1)
make money (1)
spared (1)

3046 κέρδος *kerdos* (3)
gain (2)
profit (1)

3047 κέρμα *kerma* (1)
coins (1)

3048 κερματιστής *kermatistēs* (1)
exchanging money (1)

3049 κεφάλαιον *kephalaion* (2)
price (1)
the point is this (1)

3050 κεφαλαιόω *kephalaioō*
Variant; not used

3051 κεφαλή *kephalē* (75)
head (50)
heads (18)
capstone (5) *+1224*
hair (1)
untranslated (1)

3052 κεφαλιόω *kephalioō* (1)
struck on the head (1)

3053 κεφαλίς *kephalis* (1)
untranslated (1)

3054 κηδεύω *kēdeuō*
Variant; not used

3055 κημόω *kēmoō* (1)
muzzle (1)

3056 κῆνσος *kēnsos* (4)
taxes (3)
tax (1)

3057 κῆπος *kēpos* (5)
garden (3)
grove (2)

3058 κηπουρός *kēpouros* (1)
gardener (1)

3059 κηρίον *kērion*
Variant; not used

3060 κήρυγμα *kērygma* (8)
preaching (5)
message (1)
proclamation (1)
what was preached (1)

3061 κῆρυξ *kēryx* (3)
herald (2)
preacher (1)

3062 κηρύσσω *kēryssō* (61)
preach (16)
preached (16)
preaching (10)
proclaim (3)
proclaimed (3)
proclaiming (3)
preaches (2)
message (1)
preach (1) *+3306*
preached (1) *+2400*
talk (1)
talking about (1)
tell (1)
told (1)
untranslated (1)

3063 κῆτος *kētos* (1)
huge fish (1)

3064 Κηφᾶς *Kēphas* (9)
Peter (5)
Cephas (4)

3065 κιβώριον *kibōrion*
Variant; not used

3066 κιβωτός *kibōtos* (6)
ark (6)

3067 κιθάρα *kithara* (4)
harp (2)
harps (2)

3068 κιθαρίζω *kitharizō* (2)
playing (1)
untranslated (1)

3069 κιθαρῳδός *kitharōdos* (2)
harpists (2)

3070 Κιλικία *Kilikia* (8)
Cilicia (7)
provinces of Cilicia (1)

3071 Κίλιξ *Kilix*
Variant; not used

3072 κινάμωμον *kinamōmon*
Variant; not used

3073 κινδυνεύω *kindyneuō* (4)
danger (2)
danger that (1)
endanger (1)

3074 κίνδυνος *kindynos* (9)
danger (9)

3075 κινέω *kineō* (8)
move (2)
shaking (2)
aroused (1)
remove (1)
removed (1)
stirring up (1)

3076 κίνησις *kinēsis*
Variant; not used

3077 κιννάμωμον *kinnamōmon* (1)
cinnamon (1)

3078 Κίς *Kis* (1)
Kish (1)

3079 κίχρημι *kichrēmi* (1)
lend (1)

3080 κλάδος *klados* (11)
branches (9)
twigs (2)

3081 κλαίω *klaiō* (40)
weep (10)
crying (5)
weeping (5)
wept (5)
mourn (4)
wailing (3)
cry (2)
wail (1)
weeping (1) *+4472*
weeping for (1)
wept and wept (1) *+4498*
with tears (1)
untranslated (1)

3082 κλάσις *klasis* (2)
breaking (1)
broke (1)

3083 κλάσμα *klasma* (9)
broken pieces (5)
pieces (4)

3084 Κλαῦδα *Klauda*
Variant; not used

3085 Κλαύδη *Klaudē*
Variant; not used

3086 Κλαυδία *Klaudia* (1)
Claudia (1)

3087 Κλαύδιος *Klaudios* (3)
Claudius (3)

3088 κλαυθμός *klauthmos* (9)
weeping (7)
weeping (1) *+3836*
wept (1) *+1181+2653*

3089 κλάω *klaō* (14)
broke (12)
break (2)

3090 κλείς *kleis* (6)
key (4)
keys (2)

3091 κλείω *kleiō* (16)
shut (8)
locked (5)
close (1)
has no pity (1) *+3836+5073*
shuts (1)

3092 κλέμμα *klemma* (1)
thefts (1)

3093 Κλεοπᾶς *Kleopas* (1)
Cleopas (1)

3094 κλέος *kleos* (1)
credit (1)

3095 κλέπτης *kleptēs* (16)
thief (12)

thieves (4)

3096 κλέπτω *kleptō* (13)
steal (10)
stealing (2)
stole (1)

3097 κλῆμα *klēma* (4)
branch (3)
branches (1)

3098 Κλήμης *Klēmēs* (1)
Clement (1)

3099 κληρονομέω *klēronomeō* (18)
inherit (15)
inherited (1)
share in the inheritance (1)
take inheritance (1)

3100 κληρονομία *klēronomia* (14)
inheritance (14)

3101 κληρονόμος *klēronomos* (15)
heir (8)
heirs (6)
inherit (1)

3102 κλῆρος *klēros* (11)
lots (5)
inheritance (1)
lot (1)
place (1)
share (1)
shared (1) *+3275+3836*
untranslated (1)

3103 κληρόω *klēroō* (1)
chosen (1)

3104 κλῆσις *klēsis* (11)
called (4)
calling (3)
call (1)
calling received (1) *+2813*
life (1)
situation (1)

3105 κλητός *klētos* (10)
called (9)
invited (1)

3106 κλίβανος *klibanos* (2)
fire (2)

3107 κλίμα *klima* (3)
regions (2)
untranslated (1)

3108 κλινάριον *klinarion* (1)
beds (1)

3109 κλίνη *klinē* (8)
bed (4)
mat (3)
bed of suffering (1)

3110 κλινίδιον *klinidion* (2)
mat (2)

3111 κλίνω *klinō* (7)
lay (2)
almost over (1)
bowed (1)
bowed down (1)
late in afternoon (1) *+806+2465*
routed (1)

3112 κλισία *klisia* (1)
groups (1)

3113 κλοπή *klopē* (2)
theft (2)

3114 κλύδων *klydōn* (2)
raging (1)
wave (1)

3115 κλυδωνίζομαι *klydōnizomai* (1)
tossed back and forth by the waves (1)

3116 Κλωπᾶς *Klōpas* (1)
Clopas (1)

3117 κνήθω *knēthō* (1)
itching (1)

3118 Κνίδος *Knidos* (1)
Cnidus (1)

3119 κοδράντης *kodrantēs* (2)
a fraction of a penny (1)
penny (1)

3120 κοιλία *koilia* (23)
stomach (8)
birth (4) *+3613*
womb (3)
appetites (1)
belly (1)
child bear (1) *+2843+3836*
conceived (1) *+1877+3836+5197*
mother (1)
within (1)
wombs (1)
untranslated (1)

3121 κοιμάω *koimaō* (18)
fallen asleep (7)
asleep (2)
died (2)
fell asleep (2)
dies (1)
fall asleep (1)
sleep (1)
sleeping (1)
sleeps (1)

3122 κοίμησις *koimēsis* (1)
natural sleep (1) *+3836+3836+5678*

3123 κοινός *koinos* (16)
unclean (5)
impure (4)
call impure (2)
common (1)
in common (1)
share (1)
shared (1)
unholy (1)

3124 κοινόω *koinoō* (12)
make unclean (7)
makes unclean (2)
ceremonially unclean (1)
defiled (1)
what makes unclean (1)

3125 κοινωνέω *koinōneō* (8)
share (2)
have (1)
participate (1)
share with (1)
shared (1)
shared in (1)
shares in (1)

3126 κοινωνία *koinōnia* (19)
fellowship (10)
sharing (3)
participation (2)
contribution (1)
fellowship of sharing (1)
partnership (1)
share (1)

3127 κοινωνικός *koinōnikos* (1)
share (1)

3128 κοινωνός *koinōnos* (10)
partner (2)
participants (1)
participate (1) *+1639*
participate in (1) *+1181*
partners (1)
share (1)
share (1) *+1639*
side by side (1)
taken part (1) *+1639*

3129 κοινῶς *koinōs*
Variant; not used

3130 κοίτη *koitē* (4)
bed (1)
marriage bed (1)
sexual immorality (1)
untranslated (1)

3131 κοιτών *koitōn* (1)
trusted personal servant (1) *+2093+3836*

3132 κόκκινος *kokkinos* (6)
scarlet (6)

3133 κόκκος *kokkos* (7)
seed (6)
kernel (1)

3134 κολάζω *kolazō* (2)
punish (1)
punishment (1)

3135 κολακεία *kolakeia* (1)
flattery (1)

3136 κόλασις *kolasis* (2)
punishment (2)

3137 Κολασσαεύς *Kolassaeus*
Variant; not used

3138 Κολασσαί *Kolassai*
Variant; not used

3139 κολαφίζω *kolaphizō* (5)
struck with fists (2)
brutally treated (1)
receive a beating (1)
torment (1)

3140 κολλάω *kollaō* (12)
join (2)
unites (2)
associate with (1)
became followers of (1)
cling (1)
hired out to (1)
piled up (1)
stay near (1)
sticks (1)
united to (1)

3141 κολλούριον *kollourion* (1)
salve (1)

3142 κολλυβιστής *kollybistēs* (3)
money changers (3)

3143 κολοβόω *koloboō* (4)
cut short (2)
shortened (2)

3144 Κολοσσαεύς *Kolossaeus*
Variant; not used

3145 Κολοσσαί *Kolossai* (1)
Colosse (1)

3146 κόλπος *kolpos* (6)
side (3)
bay (1)
lap (1)
untranslated (1)

3147 κολυμβάω *kolymbaō* (1)
swim (1)

3148 κολυμβήθρα *kolymbēthra* (3)
pool (3)

3149 κολωνία *kolōnia* (1)
Roman colony (1)

3150 κομάω *komaō* (2)
has long hair (2)

3151 κόμη *komē* (1)
long hair (1)

3152 κομίζω *komizō* (10)
receive (3)
brought (1)

receive back (1)
received (1)
received back (1)
receiving (1)
repaid (1)
reward (1)

3153 κομψότερον *kompsoteron* (1)
better (1)

3154 κονιάω *koniaō* (2)
whitewashed (2)

3155 κονιορτός *koniortos* (5)
dust (5)

3156 κοπάζω *kopazō* (3)
died down (3)

3157 κοπετός *kopetos* (1)
mourned deeply (1) *+3489+4472*

3158 κοπή *kopē* (1)
defeat (1)

3159 κοπιάω *kopiaō* (23)
labor (5)
hard work (2)
work (2)
work hard (2)
worked (2)
worked hard (2)
efforts (1)
grown weary (1)
hardworking (1)
labors (1)
tired (1)
weary (1)
work hard (1) *+2237*
worked for (1)

3160 κόπος *kopos* (18)
labor (5)
bothering (3) *+4218*
hard work (2)
bother (1) *+4218*
efforts (1)
labored (1)
laboring (1)
toil (1)
trouble (1)
work (1)
worked (1)

3161 κοπρία *kopria* (1)
manure pile (1)

3162 κόπριον *koprion* (1)
fertilize (1) *+965*

3163 κόπρος *kopros*
Variant; not used

3164 κόπτω *koptō* (8)
mourn (4)
cut (2)
mourned (1)
mourning (1)

3165 κόραξ *korax* (1)
ravens (1)

3166 κοράσιον *korasion* (8)
girl (6)
little girl (1)
she[s] (1) *+3836*

3167 κορβᾶν *korban* (1)
Corban (1)

3168 κορβανᾶς *korbanas* (1)
treasury (1)

3169 Κόρε *Kore* (1)
Korah's (1)

3170 κορέννυμι *korennymi* (2)
eaten as much as wanted (1)
have all you want (1) *+1639*

3171 Κορίνθιος *Korinthios* (2)
Corinthians (2)

3172 Κόρινθος *Korinthos* (6)
Corinth (6)

3173 Κορνήλιος *Kornēlios* (8)
Cornelius (8)

3174 κόρος *koros* (1)
thousand bushels (1) *+1669*

3175 κοσμέω *kosmeō* (10)
put in order (2)
adorned (1)
beautifully dressed (1)
decorate (1)
decorated (1)
dress (1)
make attractive (1)
make beautiful (1)
trimmed (1)

3176 κοσμικός *kosmikos* (2)
earthly (1)
worldly (1)

3177 κόσμιος *kosmios* (2)
modestly (1) *+2950*
respectable (1)

3178 κοσμίως *kosmiōs*
Variant; not used

3179 κοσμοκράτωρ *kosmokratōr* (1)
powers of world (1)

3180 κόσμος *kosmos* (186)
world (173)
it[s] (3) *+3836*
universe (2)
adornment (1)
earth (1)
it[s] (1)
material (1)
people (1)
world's (1)
worldly (1) *+3836*
untranslated (1)

3181 Κούαρτος *Kouartos* (1)
Quartus (1)

3182 κοῦμ *koum* (1)
koum (1)

3183 κοῦμι *koumi*
Variant; not used

3184 κουστωδία *koustōdia* (3)
guard (2)
guards (1)

3185 κουφίζω *kouphizō* (1)
lightened (1)

3186 κόφινος *kophinos* (6)
basketfuls (2)
basketfuls (2) *+4441*
basketfuls (1) *+4445*
baskets (1)

3187 κράβαττος *krabattos* (11)
mat (8)
mats (2)
bedridden (1) *+2093+2879*

3188 κράββατος *krabbatos*
Variant; not used

3189 κράζω *krazō* (56)
shouted (13)
cried out (7)
shouting (7)
called out (3)
cry out (3)
cries out (2)
cry (2)
crying out (2)
a loud voice (1)
called (1)
calling out (1)
calls out (1)
cried (1)
cried out (1) *+3306*
cried out (1) *+3489+5889*
crying out (1) *+3306*
exclaim (1)
exclaimed (1)
gave a shout (1) *+5889*
screams (1)
shout (1)
shouted (1) *+1181*
shouted all the more (1) *+3437+4498*
shrieked (1)
yelling (1)

3190 κραιπάλη *kraipalē* (1)
dissipation (1)

3191 κρανίον *kranion* (4)
skull (4)

3192 κράσπεδον *kraspedon* (5)
edge (4)
tassels (1)

3193 κραταιός *krataios* (1)
mighty (1)

3194 κραταιόω *krataioō* (4)
strong (2)
became strong (1)
strengthen (1) *+1443*

3195 κρατέω *krateō* (47)
arrest (8)
arrested (5)
took (5)
seized (4)
hold to (3)
hold on to (2)
clasped (1)
grabbed (1)
held on to (1)
hold firmly to (1)
hold on (1)
holding back (1)
holding on to (1)
holding to (1)
holds (1)
kept (1)
kept from (1)
lost connection with (1) *+4024*
not forgive (1)
not forgiven (1)
observe (1)
obtained (1)
remain true to (1)
take charge of (1)
take hold (1)
take hold of (1)

3196 κράτιστος *kratistos* (4)
most excellent (3)
excellency (1)

3197 κράτος *kratos* (12)
power (8)
might (2)
mighty deeds (1)
strength (1)

3198 κραυγάζω *kraugazō* (9)
shouting (4)
shouted (3)
called (1)
cry out (1)

3199 κραυγή *kraugē* (6)
brawling (1)
cries (1)
cry (1)
crying (1)
uproar (1)
voice (1)

3200 κρέας *kreas* (2)
meat (2)

3201 κρείσσων *kreissōn*
Variant; not used

3202 κρείττων *kreittōn* (19)
better (14)
superior to (2)
better (1) *+3437*
good (1)
greater (1)

3203 κρεμάννυμι *kremannymi* (7)
hanging (3)
hung (3)
hang (1)

3204 κρημνός *krēmnos* (3)
steep bank (3)

3205 Κρής *Krēs* (2)
Cretans (2)

3206 Κρήσκης *Krēskēs* (1)
Crescens (1)

3207 Κρήτη *Krētē* (5)
Crete (5)

3208 κριθή *krithē* (1)
barley (1)

3209 κρίθινος *krithinos* (2)
barley (1)
small barley (1)

3210 κρίμα *krima* (27)
judgment (12)
condemnation (3)
be punished (2) *+3284*
be judged (1) *+3284*
judge (1)
judgments (1)
lawsuits (1)
penalty (1)
punishment (1)
sentence (1)
sentenced (1)
the same way[S] (1)
way treated[S] (1)

3211 κρίνον *krinon* (2)
lilies (2)

3212 κρίνω *krinō* (114)
judge (37)
judged (14)
judges (7)
condemn (6)
condemned (6)
decided (4)
judging (4)
consider (3)
pass judgment on (3)
considers (2)
stand trial (2)
come under judgment (1)
condemning (1)
convinced (1)
decided that (1)
decision that (1)
decisions (1)
goes to law (1)
judgment (1)
judgment that (1)
made up (1)
made up mind (1)
make judgment (1) *+3213*
make up mind (1)
on trial (1)
on trial (1) *+2705*
pass judgment (1)
passed judgment on (1)
passing judgment on (1)
punish (1)
resolved (1)
stand on trial (1)
sue (1)
take judgment (1)
there is a judge (1) *+2400+3836*
tried (1)
until judge (1) *+4024*

3213 κρίσις *krisis* (47)
judgment (28)
justice (5)
condemned (2)
judge (2) *+4472*
judgments (2)
accusation (1)
accusations (1)
be condemned (1) *+4406+5679*
condemned (1) *+1650+2262*
decisions (1)
doom (1)
make judgment (1) *+3212*
verdict (1)

3214 Κρίσπος *Krispos* (2)
Crispus (2)

3215 κριτήριον *kritērion* (3)
court (1)
disputes (1)
judge cases (1)

3216 κριτής *kritēs* (19)
judge (14)
judges (4)
sitting in judgment (1)

3217 κριτικός *kritikos* (1)
judges (1)

3218 κρούω *krouō* (9)
knock (3)
knocks (3)
knocking (2)
knocked at (1)

3219 κρύπτη *kryptē* (1)
place hidden (1)

3220 κρυπτός *kryptos* (17)
secret (7)
hidden (4)
secrets (2)
inner (1)
inwardly (1) *+1877+3836*
is hidden (1)
unseen (1) *+1877+3836*

3221 κρύπτω *kryptō* (18)
hidden (9)
hid (7)
hide (1)
secretly (1)

3222 κρυσταλλίζω *krystallizō* (1)
clear as crystal (1)

3223 κρύσταλλος *krystallos* (2)
crystal (2)

3224 κρυφαῖος *kryphaios* (2)
secret (1)
unseen (1) *+1877+3836*

3225 κρυφῇ *kryphē* (1)
secret (1)

3226 κρύφιος *kryphios*
Variant; not used

3227 κτάομαι *ktaomai* (7)
bought (1)
buy (1)
control (1)
gain (1)
get (1)
pay for (1)
take along (1)

3228 κτῆμα *ktēma* (4)
wealth (2)
piece of property (1)
possessions (1)

3229 κτῆνος *ktēnos* (4)
animals (1)
cattle (1)
donkey (1)
mounts (1)

3230 κτήτωρ *ktētōr* (1)
owned (1) *+5639*

3231 κτίζω *ktizō* (15)
created (11)
creator (3)
create (1)

3232 κτίσις *ktisis* (19)
creation (15)
authority (1)
created things (1)
creature (1)
world (1)

3233 κτίσμα *ktisma* (4)
created (2)
creature (1)
creatures (1)

3234 κτίστης *ktistēs* (1)
creator (1)

3235 κυβεία *kybeia* (1)
cunning (1)

3236 κυβέρνησις *kybernēsis* (1)
those with gifts of administration (1)

3237 κυβερνήτης *kybernētēs* (2)
pilot (1)
sea captain (1)

3238 κυκλεύω *kykleuō* (1)
surrounded (1)

3239 κυκλόθεν *kyklothen* (3)
all around (1)
encircled (1)
surrounding (1)

3240 κυκλόω *kykloō* (4)
gathered around (2)
marched around (1)
surrounded (1)

3241 κύκλῳ *kyklō* (8)
around (3)
surrounding (2)
encircled (1)
from village to village (1) *+3267*
in a circle (1)

3242 κύλισμα *kylisma*
Variant; not used

3243 κυλισμός *kylismos* (1)
wallowing (1)

3244 κυλίω *kyliō* (1)
rolled around (1)

3245 κυλλός *kyllos* (4)
crippled (2)
maimed (2)

3246 κῦμα *kyma* (5)
waves (4)
surf (1)

3247 κύμβαλον *kymbalon* (1)
cymbal (1)

3248 κύμινον *kyminon* (1)
cummin (1)

3249 κυνάριον *kynarion* (4)
dogs (4)

3250 Κύπριος *Kyprios* (3)
from Cyprus (3)

3251 Κύπρος *Kypros* (5)
Cyprus (5)

3252 κύπτω *kyptō* (2)
bent (1)
stoop down (1)

3253 Κυρεῖνος *Kyreinos*
Variant; not used

3254 Κυρηναῖος *Kyrēnaios* (6)
from Cyrene (3)
of Cyrene (2)
Cyrene (1)

3255 Κυρήνη *Kyrēnē* (1)
Cyrene (1)

3256 Κυρήνιος *Kyrēnios* (1)
Quirinius (1)

3257 κυρία *kyria* (2)
dear lady (1)
lady (1)

3258 κυριακός *kyriakos* (2)
Lord's (2)

3259 κυριεύω *kyrieuō* (7)
lord it over (2)
authority over (1)
has mastery over (1)
Lord (1)
lords (1)
master (1)

3260 Κυρίνιος *Kyrinios*
Variant; not used

3261 κύριος *kyrios* (720)
Lord (600)
master (35)
Lord's (32)
sir (23)
master's (6)
masters (6)
owner (6)
lords (3)
owners (3)
belong to Lord (1) *+1639*
he^{s} (1) *+3836*
his majesty (1)
masters' (1)
owns (1) *+1639*
sirs (1)

3262 κυριότης *kyriotēs* (4)
authority (2)
dominion (1)
powers (1)

3263 κυρόω *kyroō* (2)
duly established (1)
reaffirm (1)

3264 κύων *kyōn* (5)
dogs (4)
dog (1)

3265 κῶλον *kōlon* (1)
bodies (1)

3266 κωλύω *kōlyō* (23)
hinder (3)
stop (3)
forbid (2)
keep from (2)
kept from (2)
prevented from (2)
hindered (1)
oppose (1)
opposes (1)
permit (1) *+3594*
restrained (1)
shouldn't (1)
stop from taking (1)
stops (1)
told to stop (1)

3267 κώμη *kōmē* (27)
village (16)
villages (8)
from village to village (1) *+2848+3836*
from village to village (1) *+3241*
town (1)

3268 κωμόπολις *kōmopolis* (1)
villages (1)

3269 κῶμος *kōmos* (3)
orgies (3)

3270 κώνωψ *kōnōps* (1)
gnat (1)

3271 Κῶς *Kōs* (1)
Cos (1)

3272 Κωσάμ *Kōsam* (1)
Cosam (1)

3273 κωφός *kōphos* (14)
deaf (5)
mute (4)
man who had been mute (2)
could not talk (1)
he^{s} (1) *+3836*
unable to speak (1)

3274 λ *l*
Variant; not used

3275 λαγχάνω *lanchanō* (4)
chosen by lot (1)
decide by lot (1)
received (1)
shared (1) *+3102+3836*

3276 Λάζαρος *Lazaros* (15)
Lazarus (15)

3277 λάθρα *lathra* (4)
quietly (2)
aside (1)
secretly (1)

3278 λαῖλαψ *lailaps* (3)
squall (2) *+449*
storm (1)

3279 λακάω *lakaō* (1)
burst (1)

3280 λακτίζω *laktizō* (1)
kick (1)

3281 λαλέω *laleō* (296)
speak (62)
speaking (38)
spoke (33)
said (25)
speaks (18)
spoken (17)
say (16)
told (16)
saying (6)
talk (6)
tell (5)
talked (4)
talking (4)
telling (3)
preached (2)
proclaimed (2)
says (2)
teach (2)
address (1)
announced (1)
boast (1) *+5665*
bring (1)
bring a message (1) *+4839*
claiming (1)
declaring (1)
distort the truth (1) *+1406*
he^{s} (1) *+3836*
help speaking about (1) *+3590*
insisted (1)
lies (1) *+3836+6022*
may declare (1)
message (1)
preaching (1)
presenting (1)
proclaim (1)
promised (1)
said (1) *+3306*
say about (1)
speak about (1)
speaker (1)
speech (1)
spoke about (1)
talking about (1)
tells (1)
use language (1)
utter (1)
utters (1)
whispered (1)
untranslated (5)

3282 λαλιά *lalia* (3)
accent (1)
language (1)
said (1)

3283 λαμά *lama*
Variant; not used

3284 λαμβάνω *lambanō* (257)
receive (38)
took (38)
received (37)
take (24)
accept (9)
taking (9)
receives (7)
accepts (5)
taken (4)
bring (3)
collect (3)
receiving (3)
seized (3)
accepted (2)
be punished (2) *+3210*
caught (2)
gathered (2)
get (2)
married (2)
marry (2)
seizing (2)
take up (2)
amazed (1) *+1749*
appointed (1)
be edified (1) *+3868*
be judged (1) *+3210*
be rewarded (1) *+3635*
become (1)
become a father (1) *+2856+5065*
circumcised (1) *+4362*
circumcised (1) *+4364*
collected (1)
collectors of tax (1)
collects (1)
commanded (1) *+1953*
decided to (1) *+5206*
devised a plan (1) *+5206*
draw (1)
draws (1)
faced (1) *+4278*
filled with awe (1) *+5832*
forgotten that (1) *+3330*
gets (1)
given (1)
got (1)
guiding (1)
had (1)
have (1)
judge by external appearance (1) *+476+4725*
laid plans (1) *+5206*
made (1)
made king (1) *+993+3836*
married (1) *+1222*
married a woman (1) *+1222*
money (1) *+1797*
obtained (1)
on authority (1) *+2026*

picked up (1)
plotted (1) *+5206*
put on (1)
reminded (1) *+5704*
repayment (1)
seizes (1)
selected (1)
show partiality (1) *+4725*
succeeded (1) *+1345*
take over (1)
takes (1)
takes advantage of (1)
to the decision (1) *+5206*
took up (1)
tried to do (1) *+4278*
was encouraged (1) *+2511*
with instructions (1) *+1953*
untranslated (4)

3285 Λάμεχ *Lamech* (1)
Lamech (1)

3286 λαμπάς *lampas* (9)
lamps (7)
lanterns (1)
torch (1)

3287 λαμπρός *lampros* (9)
bright (2)
fine (2)
shining (2)
clear (1)
elegant (1)
splendor (1)

3288 λαμπρότης *lamprotēs* (1)
brighter than (1) *+5642*

3289 λαμπρῶς *lamprōs* (1)
in luxury (1)

3290 λάμπω *lampō* (7)
shine (2)
shone (2)
gives light (1)
lights up (1)
made shine (1)

3291 λανθάνω *lanthanō* (6)
forget (2)
escaped notice (1)
go unnoticed (1)
keep secret (1)
without knowing (1)

3292 λαξευτός *laxeutos* (1)
cut in the rock (1)

3293 Λαοδίκεια *Laodikeia* (6)
Laodicea (6)

3294 Λαοδικεύς *Laodikeus* (1)
Laodiceans (1)

3295 λαός *laos* (142)
people (127)
peoples (4)
people's (3)
crowd (2)
assembled worshipers (1) *+3836+4436*
crowd (1) *+3836+4436*
in public (1) *+1883+3836*
public (1)
them[S] (1) *+3836*
those[S] (1) *+3836*

3296 λάρυγξ *larynx* (1)
throats (1)

3297 Λασαία *Lasaia* (1)
Lasea (1)

3298 Λασέα *Lasea*
Variant; not used

3299 λάσκω *laskō*
Variant; not used

3300 λατομέω *latomeō* (2)
cut (1) *+1639*
cut out (1)

3301 λατρεία *latreia* (5)
act of worship (1)
ministry (1)
service (1)
temple worship (1)
worship (1)

3302 λατρεύω *latreuō* (21)
serve (10)
worship (5)
minister (1)
serve at a sanctuary (1)
served (1)
worshiped (1)
worshiper (1)
worshipers (1)

3303 λάχανον *lachanon* (4)
garden plants (2)
garden herbs (1)
vegetables (1)

3304 Λεββαῖος *Lebbaios*
Variant; not used

3305 λεγιών *legiōn* (4)
legion (3)
legions (1)

3306 λέγω *legō* (2355)
said (784)
tell (216)
say (186)
asked (153)
replied (92)
told (92)
says (83)
saying (77)
answered (52)
called (31)
spoken (16)
ask (15)
speak (12)
spoke (10)
telling (10)
call (9)
claim (9)
declared (8)
talking (7)
talking about (7)
speaking (6)
words of (5)
claiming (4)
claims (4)
continued (4)
declares (4)
exclaimed (4)
asking (3)
asks (3)
calls (3)
claimed (3)
demanded (3)
is (3)
mean (3)
mention (3)
ordered (3)
speaks (3)
spoken of (3)
tells (3)
added (2)
answer (2)
calling (2)
challenged (2)
known as (2)
means (2)
meant (2)
meant (2) *+4309*
name (2)
objected (2)
protested (2)
replied (2) *+899*
say about (2)
shouted (2)
shouting (2)
speak of (2)
stated (2)
told (2) *+4192*
words (2)
accuse (1)
addressed (1)
addressed (1) *+4639*
adds (1)
admit (1)
advise (1)
agree (1) *+899+3836*
announced (1)
are words of (1)
as has just been said (1) *+1877+3836*
asks for (1)
assure (1) *+237+2093*
at this (1) *+4047*
began to speak (1) *+487+3836+5125*
begged (1)
begged (1) *+4151*
boasted (1)
boasts (1)
by (1) *+4005*
by saying (1) *+4005*
call out (1)
called out (1)
called out (1) *+3489+5889*
charged (1)
claimed (1)
commanded (1)
commanding (1) *+2198+2848*
cried (1)
cried out (1)
cried out (1) *+3189*
cry (1)
cry out (1)
crying out (1) *+3189*
directed (1)
discuss (1)
explain (1)
grant (1)
I put this in human terms (1) *+474*
inquired (1)
insisted (1)
made statement (1) *+4839*
means (1) *+1639*
named (1)
not saying a word (1) *+4029*
one might even say (1) *+2229+6055*
order (1)
pleading (1)
prayed (1)
praying (1)
preach (1)
preach (1) *+3062*
present (1)
promised (1)
prophesied (1) *+4736*
question (1)
quote (1)
referring (1)
remarking (1)
repeat (1) *+4099*
replied (1) *+646+4022*
reply (1)
respond (1)
said (1) *+3281*
sang (1)
sent for (1) *+5888*
shouting at the top of voice (1) *+3489+5889*
singing (1)
so-called (1)
so-called (1) *+6055*
speak about (1)
speaks of (1)
spoke about (1)
spoke up (1)

spoken (1) *+3306*
state (1)
take an example (1)
talk (1)
telling about (1)
testified (1)
thought (1)
turned (1)
urged (1)
used (1)
using argument (1)
warned (1)
welcome (1) *+5897*
welcomes (1) *+5897*
went on (1)
what[S] (1) *+3836*
with that (1) *+4047*
with the news (1)
with the plea (1)
with the words (1)
with this (1) *+4047*
word (1)
untranslated (286)

3307 λεῖμμα *leimma* (1)
remnant (1)

3308 λεῖος *leios* (1)
smooth (1)

3309 λείπω *leipō* (6)
have everything need (1) *+3594*
lack (1)
lacking (1)
lacks (1)
left (1)
untranslated (1)

3310 λειτουργέω *leitourgeō* (3)
performs religious duties (1)
share (1)
worshiping (1)

3311 λειτουργία *leitourgia* (6)
service (2)
ceremonies (1)
help (1)
ministry (1)
service that perform (1) *+1355+3836+4047*

3312 λειτουργικός *leitourgikos* (1)
ministering (1)

3313 λειτουργός *leitourgos* (5)
servants (2)
minister (1)
serves (1)
take care (1)

3314 λείχω *leichō*
Variant; not used

3315 Λέκτρα *Lektra*
Variant; not used

3316 λεμά *lema* (2)
lama (2)

3317 λέντιον *lention* (2)
towel (2)

3318 λεπίς *lepis* (1)
scales (1)

3319 λέπρα *lepra* (4)
leprosy (4)

3320 λεπρός *lepros* (9)
have leprosy (3)
leper (2)
man with leprosy (2)
had leprosy (1)
with leprosy (1)

3321 λεπτός *leptos* (3)
small copper coins (2)
penny (1)

3322 Λευί *Leui* (8)
Levi (8)

3323 Λευίς *Leuis*
Variant; not used

3324 Λευίτης *Leuitēs* (3)
Levite (2)
Levites (1)

3325 Λευιτικός *Leuitikos* (1)
Levitical (1)

3326 λευκαίνω *leukainō* (2)
bleach (1)
made white (1)

3327 λευκοβύσσινος *leukobyssinos*
Variant; not used

3328 λευκός *leukos* (25)
white (22)
bright (1)
ripe (1)
white (1) *+3336*

3329 λέων *leōn* (9)
lion (5)
lions (2)
lion's (1)
lions' (1)

3330 λήθη *lēthē* (1)
forgotten that (1) *+3284*

3331 λῆμψις *lēmpsis* (1)
receiving (1)

3332 ληνός *lēnos* (5)
winepress (3)
press (1)
winepress (1) *+3836+3885*

3333 λῆρος *lēros* (1)
nonsense (1)

3334 λῃστής *lēstēs* (15)
robbers (9)
leading a rebellion (3)
bandits (1)
had taken part in a rebellion (1) *+1639*
robber (1)

3335 λῆψις *lēpsis*
Variant; not used

3336 λίαν *lian* (12)
great (3)
very (3)
completely (1) *+1666+4356*
furious (1) *+2597*
greatly (1)
strongly (1)
violent (1) *+5901*
white (1) *+3328*

3337 λίβανος *libanos* (2)
frankincense (1)
incense (1)

3338 λιβανωτός *libanōtos* (2)
censer (2)

3339 Λιβερτῖνος *Libertinos* (1)
freedmen (1)

3340 Λιβύη *Libyē* (1)
Libya (1)

3341 Λιβυστῖνος *Libystinos*
Variant; not used

3342 λιθάζω *lithazō* (9)
stone (5)
stoned (3)
stoning (1)

3343 λίθινος *lithinos* (3)
stone (2)
of stone (1)

3344 λιθοβολέω *lithoboleō* (7)
stone (4)
stoned (2)
stoning (1)

3345 λίθος *lithos* (59)
stone (35)
stones (14)
another[S] (4)
boulder (1)
jasper (1) *+2618*
jewel (1)
millstone (1) *+3683*
stone's (1)
untranslated (1)

3346 λιθόστρωτος *lithostrōtos* (1)
stone Pavement (1)

3347 λικμάω *likmaō* (2)
crushed (2)

3348 λιμήν *limēn* (2)
harbor (2)

3349 λίμνη *limnē* (11)
lake (10)
water's (1)

3350 λιμός *limos* (12)
famine (7)
famines (3)
hunger (1)
starving to death (1) *+660*

3351 λίνον *linon* (2)
linen (1)
wick (1)

3352 Λίνος *Linos* (1)
Linus (1)

3353 λιπαρός *liparos* (1)
riches (1)

3354 λίτρα *litra* (2)
about a pint (1)
seventy-five pounds (1) *+1669*

3355 λίψ *lips* (1)
southwest (1)

3356 λογεία *logeia* (2)
collection (1)
collections (1)

3357 λογίζομαι *logizomai* (40)
credited (10)
consider (3)
think (3)
count (2)
realize (2)
reasoned (2)
regard (2)
regarded (2)
claim (1)
considered (1)
counting (1)
credit (1)
credits (1)
discredited (1) *+1650+4029*
expect (1)
held (1)
maintain (1)
numbered (1)
record of (1)
regards (1)
think about (1)
think that (1)

3358 λογικός *logikos* (2)
spiritual (2)

3359 λόγιον *logion* (3)
words (3)

3360 λόγιος *logios* (1)
learned (1)

3361 λογισμός *logismos* (2)
arguments (1)
thoughts (1)

3362 λογομαχέω *logomacheō* (1)
quarreling about words (1)

3363 λογομαχία *logomachia* (1)
quarrels about words (1)

3364 λόγος *logos* (331)
word (126)
words (53)
message (29)
saying (10)
teaching (9)
account (6)
speech (5)
this[S] (5) *+3836*
news (4)
question (4)
said (3)
command (2)
instruction (2)
matter (2)
report (2)
speaker (2)
speaking (2)
talk (2)
talking (2)
thing (2)
this[S] (2) *+3836+4047*
account (1) *+625*
accounts (1)
am about to tell (1) *+3836+4047*
appearance (1)
book (1)
conversation (1)
eloquence (1)
further word spoken (1) *+4707*
grievance (1)
heard (1)
it[S] (1) *+3836*
maliciously (1) *+4505*
ministry (1)
nothing (1) *+4029*
preaching (1) *+1877*
preaching (1) *+3836*
proposal (1)
questions (1)
reason (1)
reasonable (1) *+2848*
reply (1)
rule (1)
rumor (1)
say (1)
sentence (1)
settled accounts (1) *+5256*
something he said (1)
speak (1)
stated (1)
statement (1)
stories (1)
story (1)
teachings (1)
things (1)
this[S] (1) *+1609+3836+4047*
took at word (1) *+4409*
truths (1)
what said (1)
what says (1)
what[S] (1) *+3836*
why (1) *+5515*
word of mouth (1)
untranslated (15)

3365 λόγχη *lonchē* (1)
spear (1)

3366 λοιδορέω *loidoreō* (4)
hurled insults at (2)
cursed (1)
insult (1)

3367 λοιδορία *loidoria* (3)
insult (2)
slander (1)

3368 λοίδορος *loidoros* (2)
slanderer (1)
slanderers (1)

3369 λοιμός *loimos* (2)
pestilences (1)
troublemaker (1)

3370 λοιπός *loipos* (55)
rest (15)
other (9)
others (9)
finally (5) *+3836*
else (3)
finally (3)
now (2)
still (2) *+3836*
beyond that (1)
everybody else (1)
from now on (1) *+3836*
further (1)
remains (1)
since that time (1) *+3836*
survivors (1)

3371 Λουκᾶς *Loukas* (3)
Luke (3)

3372 Λούκιος *Loukios* (2)
Lucius (2)

3373 λουτρόν *loutron* (2)
washing (2)

3374 λούω *louō* (5)
washed (4)
had a bath (1)

3375 Λύδδα *Lydda* (3)
Lydda (3)

3376 Λυδία *Lydia* (2)
Lydia (1)
Lydia's (1)

3377 Λυκαονία *Lykaonia* (1)
Lycaonian (1)

3378 Λυκαονιστί *Lykaonisti* (1)
the Lycaonian language (1)

3379 Λυκία *Lykia* (1)
Lycia (1)

3380 λύκος *lykos* (6)
wolves (4)
wolf (2)

3381 λυμαίνω *lymainō* (1)
began destroy (1)

3382 λυπέω *lypeō* (26)
grieve (5)
distressed (3)
sad (3)
sorrowful (3)
grieved (2)
hurt (2)
sorrow (2)
caused grief (1)
caused sorrow (1)
filled with grief (1) *+5379*
made sorry (1)
saddened (1)
suffer grief (1)

3383 λύπη *lypē* (16)
sorrow (7)
grief (2)
pain (2)
distressed (1) *+2400*
is time of grief (1) *+2400*
painful (1)
painful (1) *+1877*
reluctantly (1) *+1666*

3384 Λυσανίας *Lysanias* (1)
Lysanias (1)

3385 Λυσίας *Lysias* (2)
Lysias (2)

3386 λύσις *lysis* (1)
divorce (1)

3387 λυσιτελέω *lysiteleō* (1)
better (1)

3388 Λύστρα *Lystra* (6)
Lystra (6)

3389 λύτρον *lytron* (2)
ransom (2)

3390 λυτρόω *lytroō* (3)
redeem (2)
redeemed (1)

3391 λύτρωσις *lytrōsis* (3)
redemption (2)
redeemed (1) *+4472*

3392 λυτρωτής *lytrōtēs* (1)
deliverer (1)

3393 λυχνία *lychnia* (12)
lampstands (6)
stand (4)
lampstand (2)

3394 λύχνος *lychnos* (14)
lamp (12)
lamps (1)
light (1)

3395 λύω *lyō* (42)
untie (8)
untying (4)
destroyed (3)
released (3)
broken (2)
destroy (2)
loose (2)
loosed (2)
set free (2)
take off (2)
break (1)
breaking (1)
breaks (1)
broken to pieces (1)
destruction (1)
dismissed (1)
freed (1)
freeing (1)
loosened (1)
release (1)
unmarried (1) *+608+1222*
untied (1)

3396 Λωΐς *Lōis* (1)
Lois (1)

3397 Λώτ *Lōt* (4)
Lot (3)
Lot's (1)

3398 μ *m*
Variant; not used

3399 Μάαθ *Maath* (1)
Maath (1)

3400 Μαγαδάν *Magadan* (1)
Magadan (1)

3401 Μαγδαλά *Magdala*
Variant; not used

3402 Μαγδαληνή *Magdalēnē* (12)
Magdalene (12)

3403 Μαγεδών *Magedōn*
Variant; not used

3404 μαγεία *mageia* (1)
magic (1)

3405 μαγεύω *mageuō* (1)
practiced sorcery (1)

3406 μαγία *magia*
Variant; not used

3407 μάγος *magos* (6)
Magi (4)
sorcerer (2)

3408 Μαγώγ *Magōg* (1)
Magog (1)

3409 Μαδιάμ *Madiam* (1)
Midian (1) *+1178*

3410 μαζός *mazos*
Variant; not used

3411 μαθητεύω *mathēteuō* (4)
become a disciple (1)
instructed (1)
make disciples (1)
won disciples (1)

3412 μαθητής *mathētēs* (261)
disciples (222)
disciple (24)
student (3)
them[s] (3) *+899+3836*
they[s] (2) *+3836*
all disciples (1) *+3836+4436*
disciples' (1)
followers (1)
them[s] (1) *+3836*
they[s] (1) *+899+3836*
they[s] (1) *+899+899+2779+3836*
untranslated (1)

3413 μαθήτρια *mathētria* (1)
disciple (1)

3414 Μαθθαῖος *Maththaios* (5)
Matthew (5)

3415 Μαθθάτ *Maththat* (2)
Matthat (2)

3416 Μαθθίας *Maththias* (2)
Matthias (2)

3417 Μαθουσαλά *Mathousala* (1)
Methuselah (1)

3418 Μαϊνάν *Mainan*
Variant; not used

3419 μαίνομαι *mainomai* (5)
out of mind (3)
insane (1)
raving mad (1)

3420 μακαρίζω *makarizō* (2)
call blessed (1)
consider blessed (1)

3421 μακάριος *makarios* (50)
blessed (44)
good (4)
fortunate (1)
happier (1)

3422 μακαρισμός *makarismos* (3)
blessedness (2)
joy (1)

3423 Μακεδονία *Makedonia* (22)
Macedonia (21)
Macedonian (1)

3424 Μακεδών *Makedōn* (5)
Macedonians (2)
from Macedonia (1)
Macedonian (1)
of Macedonia (1)

3425 μάκελλον *makellon* (1)
meat market (1)

3426 μακράν *makran* (10)
far (4)
far away (3)
far off (1) *+1650*
long way off (1)
some distance (1)

3427 μακρόθεν *makrothen* (14)
distance (6)
far off (3) *+608*
at a distance (2)
a distance (1)
far away (1) *+608*
long distance (1)

3428 μακροθυμέω *makrothymeō* (10)
patient (8)
putting off (1)
waiting patiently (1)

3429 μακροθυμία *makrothymia* (14)
patience (11)
great patience (1) *+4246*
patient (1)
patiently (1)

3430 μακροθύμως *makrothymōs* (1)
patiently (1)

3431 μακρός *makros* (4)
distant (2)
lengthy (2)

3432 μακροχρόνιος *makrochronios* (1)
enjoy long life (1) *+1639*

3433 μαλακία *malakia* (3)
sickness (3)

3434 μαλακός *malakos* (4)
fine clothes (2)
fine (1)
male prostitutes (1)

3435 Μαλελεήλ *Maleleēl* (1)
Mahalalel (1)

3436 μάλιστα *malista* (12)
especially (9)
especially so (1)
most (1)
very (1)

3437 μᾶλλον *mallon* (81)
more (22)
rather (15)
all the more (4)
instead (3)
especially (2)
instead of (2) *+2445*
more than (2)
all the harder (1)
all the more (1) *+4498*
all the more (1) *+5537*
better (1) *+3202*
do so (1) *+5968*
do so more and more (1) *+4355*
do this more and more (1) *+4355*
greater (1)
greater than ever (1)
happier (1) *+5897*
how greater (1)
instead (1) *+247*
instead (1) *+1883+3836*
instead of (1)
less (1)
more (1) *+4358*
more and more (1)
more than that (1)
much (1)
on the contrary (1) *+247+4498*
prefer (1) *+2305*
rather (1) *+1254*
really (1)
shouted all the more (1) *+3189+4498*
than (1) *+2445*
then (1)
very (1)
untranslated (4)

3438 Μάλχος *Malchos* (1)
Malchus (1)

3439 μάμμη *mammē* (1)
grandmother (1)

3440 μαμωνᾶς *mamōnas* (4)
money (2)
wealth (2)

3441 Μαναήν *Manaēn* (1)
Manaen (1)

3442 Μανασσῆς *Manassēs* (3)
Manasseh (3)

3443 μανθάνω *manthanō* (25)
learn (10)
learned (8)
get into the habit of being (1)
inquire about (1)
instructed (1)
know (1)
learning (1)
learns (1)
studied (1)

3444 μανία *mania* (1)
insane (1)

3445 μάννα *manna* (5)
manna (5)

3446 μαντεύομαι *manteuomai* (1)
fortune-telling (1)

3447 μαραίνω *marainō* (1)
fade away (1)

3448 μαράνα θά *marana tha* (1)
come Lord (1)

3449 μαργαρίτης *margaritēs* (9)
pearls (7)
pearl (1)
untranslated (1)

3450 Μάρθα *Martha* (13)
Martha (13)

3451 Μαρία *Maria* (54)
Mary (51)
Mary's (2)
she[s] (1) *+3836*

3452 Μαριάμ *Mariam*
Variant; not used

3453 Μᾶρκος *Markos* (8)
mark (8)

3454 μάρμαρος *marmaros* (1)
marble (1)

3455 μαρτυρέω *martyreō* (77)
testify (21)
testifies (6)
testified (5)
commended (4)
testifies to (3)
declared (2)
given[s] (2)
respected (2)
spoke well of (2)
testified about (2)
testify about (2)
testify to (2)
testimony (2)
witness (2)
appearing witness (1)
confirmed (1)
gave testimony (1)
give testimony (1)
given testimony (1)
known (1)
pointed out (1)
showed (1)
speak (1)
speak well of (1)
spoke well (1)
spread the word (1)
tell about (1)
testifying (1)
testimony (1) *+3456+4005*
told about (1)
vouch (1)
warn (1)
well known (1)

well spoken of (1)

3456 μαρτυρία *martyria* (37)
testimony (31)
certified (1) *+3836+5381*
evidence (1)
reputation (1)
statements (1)
testimony (1) *+3455+4005*
witness (1)

3457 μαρτύριον *martyrion* (20)
testimony (12)
witnesses (3)
testifies (1)
testify (1)
testify (1) *+1639*
testify to (1) *+625*
testifying (1) *+1650*

3458 μαρτύρομαι *martyromai* (4)
declare (2)
insist on it (1)
urging (1)

3459 μάρτυς *martys* (35)
witnesses (20)
witness (10)
bore testimony (1)
martyr (1)
testify (1)
testify (1) *+1639*
testimony (1)

3460 μασάομαι *masaomai* (1)
gnawed (1)

3461 μασθός *masthos*
Variant; not used

3462 μασσάομαι *massaomai*
Variant; not used

3463 μαστιγόω *mastigoō* (7)
flog (4)
flogged (2)
punishes (1)

3464 μαστίζω *mastizō* (1)
flog (1)

3465 μάστιξ *mastix* (6)
suffering (2)
diseases (1)
flogged (1)
flogging (1)
sicknesses (1)

3466 μαστός *mastos* (3)
breasts (1)
chest (1)
untranslated (1)

3467 ματαιολογία *mataiologia* (1)
meaningless talk (1)

3468 ματαιολόγος *mataiologos* (1)
mere talkers (1)

3469 μάταιος *mataios* (6)
futile (2)
worthless (2)
empty (1)
useless (1)

3470 ματαιότης *mataiotēs* (3)
empty (1)
frustration (1)
futility (1)

3471 ματαιόω *mataioō* (1)
futile (1)

3472 μάτην *matēn* (2)
in vain (2)

3473 Ματθαῖος *Matthaios*
Variant; not used

3474 Ματθάν *Matthan* (2)
Matthan (2)

3475 Ματθάτ *Matthat*
Variant; not used

3476 Ματθίας *Matthias*
Variant; not used

3477 Ματταθά *Mattatha* (1)
Mattatha (1)

3478 Ματταθίας *Mattathias* (2)
Mattathias (1)
of Mattathias (1)

3479 μάχαιρα *machaira* (29)
sword (20)
swords (7)
edge sword (1) *+5125*
sword (1) *+5125*

3480 μάχη *machē* (4)
quarrels (3)
conflicts (1)

3481 μάχομαι *machomai* (4)
quarrel (2)
argue sharply (1)
fighting (1)

3482 μεγαλαυχέω *megalaucheō*
Variant; not used

3483 μεγαλεῖος *megaleios* (1)
wonders (1)

3484 μεγαλειότης *megaleiotēs* (3)
divine majesty (1)
greatness (1)
majesty (1)

3485 μεγαλοπρεπής *megaloprepēs* (1)
majestic (1)

3486 μεγαλύνω *megalynō* (8)
exalted (1)
expand (1)
glorifies (1)
held in high honor (1)
highly regarded (1)
long (1)
praising (1)
shown great (1)

3487 μεγάλως *megalōs* (1)
greatly (1)

3488 μεγαλωσύνη *megalōsynē* (3)
majesty (3)

3489 μέγας *megas* (194)
great (89)
loud (31)
large (10)
greatest (5)
severe (4)
completely (3)
big (2)
furious (2)
high (2)
high officials (2)
huge (2)
much (2)
strong (2)
terrified (2) *+5828+5832*
violent (2)
at the top of (1)
at the top of voice (1) *+5889*
at the top of voices (1) *+5889*
called out (1) *+3306+5889*
complete (1)
cried out (1) *+3189+5889*
enormous (1)
fear (1) *+5832*
filled with joy (1) *+5915*
fury (1) *+2596*
gigantic (1)
greatly (1)
grown up (1) *+1181*
intense (1)
intensely (1)
long (1)
mourned deeply (1) *+3157+4472*
overjoyed (1) *+5379+5897+5915*
profound (1)
proud (1)
richly (1)
roar (1) *+5889*
shouted (1) *+3836+5774+5889*
shouted (1) *+5888+5889*
shouting at the top of voice (1) *+3306+5889*
shriek (1) *+5888+5889*
shrieks (1) *+1066+5889*
special (1)
surprising (1)
terrible (1)
terror (1) *+5832*
tremendous (1) *+5496*
very (1)
with a great crash (1) *+899+1639+3836+4774*

3490 μέγεθος *megethos* (1)
great (1)

3491 μεγιστάν *megistan* (3)
great (1)
high officials (1)
princes (1)

3492 μέγιστος *megistos* (1)
very great (1)

3493 μεθερμηνεύω *methermēneuō* (8)
means (5) *+1639*
means (2)
is (1) *+1639*

3494 μέθη *methē* (3)
drunkenness (3)

3495 μεθιστάνω *methistano*
Variant; not used

3496 μεθίστημι *methistēmi* (5)
brought (1)
led astray (1)
lose (1) *+1666*
move (1)
removing (1)

3497 μεθοδεία *methodeia* (2)
schemes (1)
scheming (1)

3498 μεθόριον *methorion*
Variant; not used

3499 μεθύσκω *methyskō* (5)
get drunk (3)
had too much to drink (1)
intoxicated (1)

3500 μέθυσος *methysos* (2)
drunkard (1)
drunkards (1)

3501 μεθύω *methyō* (5)
drunk (2)
drunkards (1)
get drunk (1)
gets drunk (1)

3502 μείγνυμι *meignymi* (4)
mixed (4)

3503 μειγνύω *meignyō*
Variant; not used

3504 μειζότερος *meizoteros* (1)
greater than (1)

3505 μείζων *meizōn* (47)
greater than (18)
greater (10)
greatest (8)
more (3)
largest (2)

all the louder (1)
bigger (1)
greater than (1) *+3836*
older (1)
one greater than (1)
weightier than (1)

3506 μέλας *melas* (6)
black (3)
ink (3)

3507 Μελεά *Melea* (1)
Melea (1)

3508 μέλει *melei* (10)
care (2)
cares (2)
swayed (2)
cared (1)
concerned (1)
showed concern (1)
trouble (1)

3509 μελετάω *meletaō* (2)
give yourself wholly to (1)
plot (1)

3510 μέλι *meli* (4)
honey (4)

3511 μελισσεῖον *melisseion*
Variant; not used

3512 μελισσῖον *melission*
Variant; not used

3513 μελίσσιος *melissios*
Variant; not used

3514 Μελίτη *Melitē* (1)
Malta (1)

3515 Μελιτήνη *Melitēnē*
Variant; not used

3516 μέλλω *mellō* (109)
about to (21)
going to (18)
will (17)
would (8)
to come (7)
coming (4)
later (4)
intend (3)
intended (2)
the future (2)
to be (2)
wanting (2)
about (1)
as (1)
close (1)
come (1)
dawn (1) *+1181+2465*
future (1)
going (1)
going to happen to (1)
nearly (1)
never (1) *+3600*
next (1) *+1650+3836*
should (1)
that are coming (1)
to (1)
to come (1) *+2262*
waiting for (1)
was (1)
was coming (1) *+1451*
untranslated (1)

3517 μέλος *melos* (34)
members (7)
part (6)
parts (6)
parts of body (3)
part of body (2)
bodies (1)
each one[s] (1)
member (1) *+2848+3836*
members of body (1)
nature (1)
part of the body (1)
parts of the body (1)
them[s] (1) *+3836+5148*
unite (1) *+4472*
within (1) *+1877+3836*

3518 Μελχί *Melchi* (2)
Melki (2)

3519 Μελχισέδεκ *Melchisedek* (8)
Melchizedek (8)

3520 μέλω *melō*
Variant; not used

3521 μεμβράνα *membrana* (1)
parchments (1)

3522 μέμφομαι *memphomai* (2)
blame (1)
found fault with (1)

3523 μεμψίμοιρος *mempsimoiros* (1)
faultfinders (1)

3524 μέμψις *mempsis*
Variant; not used

3525 μέν *men* (178)
some (6) *+4005*
some (5) *+3836*
indeed (2)
one (2) *+4005*
some (2)
though (2)
as far as (1)
certainly (1)
even though (1) *+1142*
he (1) *+3836*
his son[s] (1) *+3836*
however (1) *+4036*
if (1) *+1623*
in the one case (1) *+6045*
inasmuch as (1) *+2093+4012+4036*
latter (1)
now (1)
one (1) *+3836*
others (1) *+3836*
our fathers[s] (1) *+3836*
Paul[s] (1) *+3836*
Peter and John[s] (1) *+3836*
sometimes (1) *+4047*
the apostles[s] (1) *+3836*
the men[s] (1) *+3836*
then (1)
they (1) *+3836*
those who (1) *+4005*
to be sure (1)
to the one (1) *+4005*
untranslated (135)

3526 Μενάμ *Menam*
Variant; not used

3527 Μεννά *Menna* (1)
Menna (1)

3528 μενοῦν *menoun* (1)
rather (1)

3529 μενοῦνγε *menounge* (3)
but (1)
of course (1)
what is more (1) *+247*

3530 μέντοι *mentoi* (8)
but (4)
nevertheless (1)
really (1)
very (1)
yet (1)

3531 μένω *menō* (118)
remain (24)
stay (14)
lives (12)
remains (11)
stayed (11)
continue (4)
live (4)
endures (2)
enduring (2)
living (2)
remained (2)
staying (2)
be (1)
belong (1)
belongs (1)
continues (1)
does[s] (1) *+1877+5148*
dwell (1) *+2400*
facing (1)
hold (1)
keep on (1)
last (1)
lasting (1)
lasts (1)
left (1)
lived (1)
permanent place (1)
spend time (1) *+2093+5989*
spent (1)
stand (1)
stands (1)
stayed (1) *+1695*
stays (1)
still (1)
survives (1)
waited for (1)
would not move (1) *+810*
untranslated (3)

3532 μερίζω *merizō* (14)
divided (9)
assigned (2)
divide (1)
gave (1)
given (1)

3533 μέριμνα *merimna* (6)
worries (3)
anxieties (1)
anxiety (1)
concern (1)

3534 μεριμνάω *merimnaō* (19)
worry about (5)
concerned about (4)
worry (4)
worrying (2)
anxious about (1)
have concern (1)
takes interest (1)
worried (1)

3535 μερίς *meris* (5)
district (1)
in common (1)
part (1)
share (1)
what[s] (1)

3536 μερισμός *merismos* (2)
dividing (1)
gifts distributed (1)

3537 μεριστής *meristēs* (1)
arbiter (1)

3538 μέρος *meros* (42)
part (8)
place (3)
region (3)
in part (2) *+608*
parts (2)
area (1)
comparison with (1)
detail (1)
district (1)
dividing into shares (1) *+4472*
extent (1)

imperfect (1) *+1666*
interior (1) *+541*
matter (1)
on some points (1) *+608*
one at a time (1) *+324*
one[S] (1)
piece (1)
regions (1)
share (1)
share (1) *+2095*
side (1)
some (1) *+1651+3836*
to some extent (1) *+247+608*
trade (1)
while (1)
with regard to (1) *+1877*
untranslated (2)

3539 μεσάζω *mesazō*
Variant; not used

3540 μεσημβρία *mesēmbria* (2)
noon (1)
south (1)

3541 μεσιτεύω *mesiteuō* (1)
confirmed (1)

3542 μεσίτης *mesitēs* (6)
mediator (5)
mediator between (1)

3543 μεσονύκτιον *mesonyktion* (4)
midnight (3)
at midnight (1)

3544 Μεσοποταμία *Mesopotamia* (2)
Mesopotamia (2)

3545 μέσος *mesos* (58)
among (14) *+1877*
middle (5)
center (3)
among (2) *+1650+3836*
front of everyone (2) *+3836*
in (2) *+1877*
among (1)
among (1) *+324*
before (1) *+1650+3836*
before (1) *+1877*
before (1) *+1877+3836*
before the group (1) *+1877*
before them (1) *+1650*
between (1)
between (1) *+324*
fellowship (1)
for (1) *+1877+3836*
from (1)
in (1)
in two (1)
into (1) *+324*
midnight (1) *+3816*
midnight (1) *+3816+3836*
noon (1) *+2465*
open (1)
presence (1)
there (1) *+1877*
way (1)
with (1)
with (1) *+1877*
untranslated (6)

3546 μεσότοιχον *mesotoichon* (1)
dividing wall (1)

3547 μεσουράνημα *mesouranēma* (3)
midair (3)

3548 μεσόω *mesoō* (1)
halfway through (1)

3549 Μεσσίας *Messias* (2)
Messiah (2)

3550 μεστός *mestos* (9)
full (6)
full of (1)
soaked (1)
untranslated (1)

3551 μεστόω *mestoō* (1)
had too much (1) *+1639*

3552 μετά *meta* (468)
with (263)
after (66)
to (11)
along with (9)
against (8)
later (7)
among (6)
later (6) *+4047*
companions (5) *+3836*
between (3)
in (3)
after (2) *+3836*
afterward (2) *+4047*
away (2)
by (2)
companions (2) *+1639+3836*
joyfully (2) *+5915*
on (2)
through (2)
when (2)
a week later (1) *+2465+3893*
afraid (1) *+5832*
afterward (1)
along (1)
and (1)
and to (1)
before very long (1) *+4024+4498*
behind (1)
boldly (1) *+4244*
bringing (1) *+1571+2400*
close (1)
companions (1)
confidently (1) *+4244*
disastrous (1) *+5615*
finally (1) *+4047*
first (1) *+3836*
followed (1) *+4344*
following (1)
humiliated (1) *+158*
hurried (1) *+1656+5082*
hurried (1) *+4513+5082*
in presence (1) *+3836+4725*
involved in (1)
is one of us (1) *+199+1609*
separate from (1) *+4024*
settle down (1) *+2484*
some time after (1)
some time later (1) *+4047*
that would follow (1) *+4047*
the next day (1) *+1651+2465*
together with (1)
under (1)
urgently (1) *+4155+4498*
use force (1) *+1040*
welcomed (1) *+1312+1645*
when (1) *+3836*
when later (1)
wholeheartedly (1) *+2334*
yet (1) *+4047*
untranslated (24)

3553 μεταβαίνω *metabainō* (12)
leave (3)
move (2)
crossed over (1)
going on (1)
left (1)
left there (1) *+1696*
move around (1)
passed (1)
went on (1)

3554 μεταβάλλω *metaballō* (1)
changed minds (1)

3555 μετάγω *metagō* (2)
steered (1)
turn (1)

3556 μεταδίδωμι *metadidōmi* (5)
share with (2)
contributing (1)
impart (1)
share (1)

3557 μετάθεσις *metathesis* (3)
change (1)
removing (1)
taken (1)

3558 μεταίρω *metairō* (2)
left (1)
moved on (1)

3559 μετακαλέω *metakaleō* (4)
for (1)
send for (1)
sent for (1) *+690*
untranslated (1)

3560 μετακινέω *metakineō* (1)
moved (1)

3561 μεταλαμβάνω *metalambanō* (7)
eat (1) *+5575*
find convenient (1) *+2789*
receive a share (1)
receives (1)
share in (1)
take (1)
together (1)

3562 μετάλημψις *metalēmpsis* (1)
be received with (1)

3563 μεταλλάσσω *metallassō* (2)
exchanged (2)

3564 μεταμέλομαι *metamelomai* (6)
regret (2)
change mind (1)
changed mind (1)
repent (1)
seized with remorse (1)

3565 μεταμορφόω *metamorphoō* (4)
transfigured (2)
transformed (1)
transformed into (1)

3566 μετανοέω *metanoeō* (34)
repent (23)
repented (5)
refused to repent (2) *+4024*
who repents (2)
repents (1)
untranslated (1)

3567 μετάνοια *metanoia* (22)
repentance (19)
change of mind (1)
repent (1)
turn in repentance (1)

3568 μεταξύ *metaxy* (9)
between (6)
meanwhile (1) *+1877+3836*
next (1)
untranslated (1)

3569 μεταπέμπω *metapempō* (9)
sent for (5)
bring back (1)
come (1)
for (1)
have transferred (1)

3570 μεταστρέφω *metastrephō* (2)
pervert (1)
turned (1)

3571 μετασχηματίζω *metaschēmatizō* (5)
applied (1)
masquerade (1)
masquerades (1)
masquerading (1)

transform (1)

3572 μετατίθημι *metatithēmi* (6)
change (2)
brought back (1)
deserting (1) *+608*
taken away (1)
taken from (1)

3573 μετατρέπω *metatrepō* (1)
change (1)

3574 μεταφυτεύω *metaphyteuō*
Variant; not used

3575 μετέπειτα *metepeita* (1)
afterward (1)

3576 μετέχω *metechō* (8)
belonged to (1)
have (1)
have a part (1)
lives on (1)
partake (1)
shared in (1)
sharing in (1)
take part (1)

3577 μετεωρίζομαι *meteōrizomai* (1)
worry about (1)

3578 μετοικεσία *metoikesia* (4)
exile (4)

3579 μετοικίζω *metoikizō* (2)
send into exile (1)
sent (1)

3580 μετοχή *metochē* (1)
in common (1)

3581 μέτοχος *metochos* (6)
companions (1)
partners (1)
share in (1)
shared in (1) *+1181*
undergoes (1) *+1181*
who share in (1)

3582 μετρέω *metreō* (11)
measure (4)
measured (4)
use[s] (3)

3583 μετρητής *metrētēs* (1)
twenty to thirty gallons (1) *+1545+2445+5552*

3584 μετριοπαθέω *metriopatheō* (1)
deal gently (1)

3585 μετρίως *metriōs* (1)
greatly (1) *+4024*

3586 μέτρον *metron* (14)
measure (7)
apportioned (1)
field (1)
field (1) *+2834+3836*
limit (1)
measurement (1)
measuring (1)
untranslated (1)

3587 μέτωπον *metōpon* (8)
foreheads (5)
forehead (3)

3588 μέχρι *mechri* (17)
until (5)
to (4)
until (2) *+4005*
all the way to (1)
at (1)
even to the point of (1)
till (1)
to the point of (1)
untranslated (1)

3589 μέχρις *mechris*
Variant; not used

3590 μή *mē* (1039)
not (524)
no (58)
except (36) *+1623*
never (34) *+4024*
not (31) *+4024*
unless (31) *+1569*
don't (24)
but (10) *+1623*
only (10) *+1623*
without (8)
certainly not (7) *+4024*
or (7) *+2671*
nothing (6)
stop (6)
never (5)
only (5) *+1623+4024*
without (5) *+2400*
by no means (4) *+1181*
from (4)
neither (4)
never (4) *+172+1650+3836+4024*
not at all (4) *+1181*
or (4)
avoid (3)
cannot (3)
cannot (3) *+1538*
do[s] (3) *+1145*
don't (3) *+4024*
none (3)
that (3)
won't (3)
absolutely not (2) *+1181*
against (2)
blind (2) *+1063*
but only (2) *+1623*
certainly not (2) *+1181*
does[s] (2) *+1145*
doesn't (2)
fearing that (2) *+5828*
how (2)
if he does (2) *+1254+1623*
keep from (2)
no (2) *+4024*
not are you (2)
not at all (2) *+4024*
not only (2)
nothing (2) *+5516*
that (2) *+4803*
unless (2) *+1623*
unless (2) *+1623+1760*
unseen (2) *+1063*
abstains (1) *+2266*
at once (1) *+3890*
be unable to see (1) *+1063*
before (1) *+2671*
bound to come (1) *+450+2262*
but (1) *+1569*
cover (1) *+5746*
didn't (1)
die (1) *+2441*
displease (1) *+743*
ever (1)
ever no (1) *+4024*
evidently (1) *+1623*
except (1)
except for (1) *+1623*
fail (1) *+1569*
fail (1) *+4049*
for (1) *+1142*
for (1) *+4803*
for fear that (1) *+2671*
for fear that (1) *+4803*
free from fear of (1) *+5828*
from (1) *+2671*
haven't (1) *+2400*
help speaking about (1) *+3281*
how (1) *+1142*
how dare you (1)
if (1)
isn't at all (1) *+4024*
kept from (1)
lest (1) *+2671*
may never (1) *+1181*
may this never (1)
never (1) *+173+1650+3836+4024*
never (1) *+1181*
never (1) *+4024+4033*
never (1) *+4024+4537*
never (1) *+4024+4799*
never again (1) *+172+1650+3836+4024*
never again (1) *+4024*
nevertheless (1) *+1623*
no longer (1) *+4024*
nobody (1) *+5516*
none (1) *+5516*
nor (1) *+2779*
not (1) *+4029*
not anything (1) *+3594*
not one (1) *+4024*
nothing (1) *+4024+4029*
nothing (1) *+5515*
nothing ever (1)
only (1) *+1569*
only (1) *+1623+3668*
only to (1) *+1623+4029*
or at least (1) *+1254+1623*
otherwise (1) *+1254+1623*
otherwise (1) *+1623+1760*
prevent (1)
prevent from blowing (1) *+4463*
rather than (1) *+2671*
rather than (1) *+2779*
refused to worship (1) *+4686*
shallow (1) *+958*
shallow (1) *+958+2400*
shouldn't (1)
sincere (1) *+1474*
spare (1) *+2400*
than that (1) *+2779*
to keep from (1) *+2671*
to keep from (1) *+3836+4639*
to prevent (1)
together (1) *+6006*
unable (1) *+1538*
unashamed (1) *+159*
until (1) *+1569+4754*
until (1) *+1623+4020*
without (1) *+1569*
without (1) *+1650*
without (1) *+2779*
without light (1) *+5743*
untranslated (64)

3591 μήγε *mēge* (1)
not (1)

3592 μηδαμῶς *mēdamōs* (2)
surely not (2)

3593 μηδέ *mēde* (57)
or (25)
not (11)
and not (5)
nor (5)
not even (4)
and (1)
and don't (1)
don't (1)
go running off after (1) *+599+1503*
or anything (1) *+3836*
untranslated (2)

3594 μηδείς *mēdeis* (90)
not anyone (13)
nothing (11)
no (10)
no one (9)
not (8)
don't anyone (5)
not anything (5)
don't (3)
without (3)

anyone (2)
not any (2)
any (1)
any way (1)
anyone's (1)
don't anything (1)
don't this (1)
have everything need (1) *+3309*
haven't anything (1)
in any way (1) *+2848+5573*
nobody (1)
not any way (1)
not anybody (1)
not anything (1) *+3590*
not in the least (1)
permit (1) *+3266*
without anything (1)
untranslated (4)

3595 μηδέποτε *mēdepote* (1)
never (1)

3596 μηδέπω *mēdepō* (1)
not yet (1)

3597 Μῆδος *Mēdos* (1)
Medes (1)

3598 μηθαμῶς *mēthamōs*
Variant; not used

3599 μηθείς *mētheis*
Variant; not used

3600 μηκέτι *mēketi* (22)
no longer (9)
stop (3)
again (1)
any longer (1)
don't any more (1)
leave your life of sin (1) *+279*
never (1)
never (1) *+3516*
never again (1)
no (1)
no more (1)
not (1)

3601 μῆκος *mēkos* (3)
long (3)

3602 μηκύνω *mēkynō* (1)
grows (1)

3603 μηλωτή *mēlōtē* (1)
sheepskins (1)

3604 μήν1 *mēn1* (18)
months (11)
month (4)
half (2) *+1971*
a half (1) *+1971*

3605 μήν2 *mēn2* (1)
surely (1) *+1623*

3606 μηνύω *mēnyō* (4)
informed (1)
report (1)
showed (1)
told (1)

3607 μήποτε *mēpote* (25)
or (5)
otherwise (4)
so that not (3)
if you do (2)
that none (2) *+5516*
because (1)
for (1)
for if (1) *+2671*
if (1)
in the hope that (1)
never (1)
no (1)
only (1)
untranslated (1)

3608 μήπου *mēpou*
Variant; not used

3609 μήπω *mēpō* (2)
not yet (1)
yet before (1)

3610 μήπως *mēpōs*
Variant; not used

3611 μηρός *mēros* (1)
thigh (1)

3612 μήτε *mēte* (34)
or (13)
no (5)
nor (4)
not (4)
neither (3)
either (1)
without (1)
untranslated (3)

3613 μήτηρ *mētēr* (83)
mother (73)
birth (4) *+3120*
mother's (3)
mothers (2)
untranslated (1)

3614 μήτι *mēti* (17)
not (2)
surely not (2)
unless (2) *+1623*
except (1) *+323+1623*
untranslated (10)

3615 μήτιγε *mētige* (1)
how much more (1)

3616 μήτρα *mētra* (2)
firstborn (1) *+1380*
womb (1)

3617 μητραλῴας *mētralōas*
Variant; not used

3618 μητρολῴας *mētrolōas* (1)
mothers (1)

3619 μητρόπολις *mētropolis*
Variant; not used

3620 μιαίνω *miainō* (5)
corrupted (2)
ceremonial uncleanness (1)
defile (1)
pollute (1)

3621 μίασμα *miasma* (1)
corruption (1)

3622 μιασμός *miasmos* (1)
corrupt (1)

3623 μίγμα *migma* (1)
mixture (1)

3624 μίγνυμι *mignymi*
Variant; not used

3625 μικρός *mikros* (46)
little (20)
a little while (7)
small (7)
least (4)
short (2)
smallest (2)
before long (1) *+2285*
low (1)
short (1) *+2461+3836*
younger (1)

3626 Μίλητος *Milētos* (3)
Miletus (3)

3627 μίλιον *milion* (1)
mile (1)

3628 μιμέομαι *mimeomai* (4)
imitate (2)
follow (1)
follow example (1)

3629 μιμητής *mimētēs* (6)
imitators (3)
follow example (1) *+1181*
imitate (1)
imitate (1) *+1181*

3630 μιμνῄσκομαι *mimnēskomai* (23)
remember (10)
remembered (6)
remembering (2)
are mindful (1)
realize (1)
recall (1)
recalled (1)
recalling (1)

3631 μισέω *miseō* (40)
hate (13)
hates (12)
hated (9)
hate (3) *+1639*
hating (2)
detestable (1)

3632 μισθαποδοσία *misthapodosia* (3)
punishment (1)
reward (1)
rewarded (1)

3633 μισθαποδότης *misthapodotēs* (1)
rewards (1) *+1181*

3634 μίσθιος *misthios* (2)
hired men (2)

3635 μισθός *misthos* (29)
reward (17)
wages (7)
be rewarded (1) *+3284*
paid (1)
profit (1)
rewarded (1) *+655*
rewarding (1) *+1443+3836*

3636 μισθόω *misthoō* (2)
hire (1)
hired (1)

3637 μίσθωμα *misthōma* (1)
rented house (1)

3638 μισθωτός *misthōtos* (3)
hired hand (2)
hired men (1)

3639 Μιτυλήνη *Mitylēnē* (1)
Mitylene (1)

3640 Μιχαήλ *Michaēl* (2)
Michael (2)

3641 μνᾶ *mna* (9)
mina (4)
minas (2)
more[s] (1)
untranslated (2)

3642 μνάομαι *mnaomai*
Variant; not used

3643 Μνάσων *Mnasōn* (1)
Mnason (1)

3644 μνεία *mneia* (7)
remember (2) *+4472*
memories (1)
mentioning (1) *+4472*
remember (1)
remember (1) *+2400*
remembering (1) *+4472*

3645 μνῆμα *mnēma* (8)
tomb (4)
tombs (3)
burial (1) *+1650+5502*

3646 μνημεῖον *mnēmeion* (40)
tomb (31)

tombs (5)
graves (3)
untranslated (1)

3647 μνήμη *mnēmē* (1)
remember (1) *+4472*

3648 μνημονεύω *mnēmoneuō* (21)
remember (16)
forgets (1) *+4033*
remembered (1)
remembering (1)
spoke (1)
thinking (1)

3649 μνημόσυνον *mnēmosynon* (3)
memory (2)
memorial offering (1)

3650 μνηστεύω *mnēsteuō* (3)
pledged to be married (3)

3651 μογγιλάλος *mongilalos*
Variant; not used

3652 μογιλάλος *mogilalos* (1)
could hardly talk (1)

3653 μόγις *mogis* (1)
scarcely ever (1)

3654 μόδιος *modios* (3)
bowl (3)

3655 μοιχαλίς *moichalis* (7)
adulterous (4)
adulteress (2)
adultery (1)

3656 μοιχάω *moichaō* (4)
commits adultery (4)

3657 μοιχεία *moicheia* (3)
adultery (3)

3658 μοιχεύω *moicheuō* (15)
commit adultery (10)
commits adultery (2)
adultery (1)
become an adulteress (1)
committed adultery with (1)

3659 μοιχός *moichos* (3)
adulterers (2)
adulterer (1)

3660 μόλις *molis* (6)
difficulty (2)
hard (1)
hardly (1)
very rarely (1)
with difficulty (1)

3661 Μολόχ *Moloch* (1)
Molech (1)

3662 μολύνω *molynō* (3)
defile (1)
defiled (1)
soiled (1)

3663 μολυσμός *molysmos* (1)
that contaminates (1)

3664 μομφή *momphē* (1)
grievances (1)

3665 μονή *monē* (2)
home (1)
rooms (1)

3666 μονογενής *monogenēs* (9)
one and only (5)
only (2)
one and only son (1)
only (1) *+1639*

3667 μόνον *monon* (40)
only (24)
alone (3)
but (3)
just (3)
all alone (1)
all they asked was (1)
merely (1)
what is more (1) *+247+1254+2779+4024*
untranslated (3)

3668 μόνος *monos* (74)
only (38)
alone (12)
just (4)
simply (2)
all (1)
alone (1) *+2848*
by himself (1) *+899*
by myself (1)
by ourselves (1)
by themselves (1)
even (1)
just one (1) *+4047*
only (1) *+1623+3590*
only a single (1)
private (1)
whatever happens (1)
untranslated (6)

3669 μονόφθαλμος *monophthalmos* (2)
one eye (2)

3670 μονόω *monoō* (1)
left all alone (1)

3671 μορφή *morphē* (3)
nature (2)
form (1)

3672 μορφόω *morphoō* (1)
formed (1)

3673 μόρφωσις *morphōsis* (2)
embodiment (1)
form (1)

3674 μοσχοποιέω *moschopoieō* (1)
made in the form of a calf (1)

3675 μόσχος *moschos* (6)
calf (3)
calves (2)
ox (1)

3676 μουσικός *mousikos* (1)
musicians (1)

3677 μόχθος *mochthos* (3)
hardship (1)
toiled (1)
toiling (1)

3678 μυελός *myelos* (1)
marrow (1)

3679 μυέω *myeō* (1)
learned the secret (1)

3680 μῦθος *mythos* (5)
myths (4)
stories (1)

3681 μυκάομαι *mykaomai* (1)
roar (1)

3682 μυκτηρίζω *myktērizō* (1)
mocked (1)

3683 μυλικός *mylikos* (1)
millstone (1) *+3345*

3684 μύλινος *mylinos* (1)
millstone (1)

3685 μύλος *mylos* (4)
millstone (2)
hand mill (1)
large millstone (1) *+3948*

3686 μυλών *mylōn*
Variant; not used

3687 μυλωνικός *mylōnikos*
Variant; not used

3688 Μύρα *Myra* (1)
Myra (1)

3689 μυριάς *myrias* (8)
ten thousand (2)
thousands upon thousands (2)
fifty thousand (1) *+4297*
many thousands (1)
thousands (1)
two hundred million (1) *+1490*

3690 μυρίζω *myrizō* (1)
poured perfume on to prepare (1)

3691 μύριοι *myrioi* (1)
ten thousand (1)

3692 μυρίος *myrios* (2)
ten thousand (2)

3693 μύρον *myron* (15)
perfume (12)
it[S] (1) *+3836*
myrrh (1)
perfumes (1)

3694 Μύρρα *Myrra*
Variant; not used

3695 Μυσία *Mysia* (2)
Mysia (2)

3696 μυστήριον *mystērion* (27)
mystery (18)
secret (3)
mysteries (2)
secrets (2)
deep truths (1)
secret (1) *+1877*

3697 μυωπάζω *myōpazō* (1)
nearsighted (1)

3698 μώλωψ *mōlōps* (1)
wounds (1)

3699 μωμάομαι *mōmaomai* (2)
criticism (1)
discredited (1)

3700 μῶμος *mōmos* (1)
blemishes (1)

3701 μωραίνω *mōrainō* (4)
fools (1)
loses (1)
loses its saltiness (1)
made foolish (1)

3702 μωρία *mōria* (5)
foolishness (5)

3703 μωρολογία *mōrologia* (1)
foolish talk (1)

3704 μωρός *mōros* (12)
foolish (7)
fool (2)
fools (2)
foolishness (1)

3705 Μωσεύς *Mōseus*
Variant; not used

3706 Μωσῆς *Mōsēs*
Variant; not used

3707 Μωϋσῆς *Mōysēs* (80)
Moses (77)
Moses' (2)
he[S] (1) *+3836*

3708 ν *n*
Variant; not used

3709 Ναασσών *Naassōn* (3)
Nahshon (3)

3710 Ναγγαί *Nangai* (1)
Naggai (1)

3711 Ναζαρά *Nazara*
Variant; not used

3712 Ναζαράθ *Nazarath*
Variant; not used

3713 Ναζαράτ *Nazarat*
Variant; not used

3714 Ναζαρέθ *Nazareth* (12)
Nazareth (12)

3715 Ναζαρέτ *Nazaret*
Variant; not used

3716 Ναζαρηνός *Nazarēnos* (6)
of Nazareth (4)
Nazarene (2)

3717 Ναζωραῖος *Nazōraios* (13)
of Nazareth (11)
Nazarene (2)

3718 Ναθάμ *Natham* (1)
Nathan (1)

3719 Ναθάν *Nathan*
Variant; not used

3720 Ναθαναήλ *Nathanaēl* (6)
Nathanael (6)

3721 ναί *nai* (34)
yes (32)
so (1)
untranslated (1)

3722 Ναιμάν *Naiman* (1)
Naaman (1)

3723 Ναΐν *Nain* (1)
Nain (1)

3724 ναός *naos* (45)
temple (42)
shrines (1)
temples (1)
untranslated (1)

3725 Ναούμ *Naoum* (1)
Nahum (1)

3726 νάρδος *nardos* (2)
nard (2)

3727 Νάρκισσος *Narkissos* (1)
Narcissus (1)

3728 ναυαγέω *nauageō* (2)
shipwrecked (2)

3729 ναύκληρος *nauklēros* (1)
owner of the ship (1)

3730 ναῦς *naus* (1)
ship (1)

3731 ναύτης *nautēs* (3)
sailors (3)

3732 Ναχώρ *Nachōr* (1)
Nahor (1)

3733 νεανίας *neanias* (3)
young man (3)

3734 νεανίσκος *neaniskos* (11)
young man (7)
young men (4)

3735 Νεά πολις *Nea polis* (1)
Neapolis (1)

3736 Νεάπολις *Neapolis*
Variant; not used

3737 Νεεμάν *Neeman*
Variant; not used

3738 νεκρός *nekros* (129)
dead (123)
death (3)
corpse (1)
died (1) *+1181*
died (1) *+2093*

3739 νεκρόω *nekroō* (3)
as good as dead (1) *+2453*
dead (1)
put to death (1)

3740 νέκρωσις *nekrōsis* (2)
dead (1)
death (1)

3741 νεομηνία *neomēnia* (1)
new Moon celebration (1)

3742 νέος *neos* (23)
new (11)
younger (8)
young (3)
youngest (1)

3743 νεοσσός *neossos*
Variant; not used

3744 νεότης *neotēs* (4)
boy (2)
child (1)
young (1)

3745 νεόφυτος *neophytos* (1)
recent convert (1)

3746 Νέρων *Nerōn*
Variant; not used

3747 Νεύης *Neuēs*
Variant; not used

3748 νεύω *neuō* (2)
motioned (2)

3749 νεφέλη *nephelē* (25)
cloud (18)
clouds (7)

3750 Νεφθαλίμ *Nephthalim* (3)
Naphtali (3)

3751 νέφος *nephos* (1)
cloud (1)

3752 νεφρός *nephros* (1)
minds (1)

3753 νεωκόρος *neōkoros* (1)
guardian of the temple (1)

3754 νεωτερικός *neōterikos* (1)
of youth (1)

3755 νή *nē* (1)
I mean that just as surely (1)

3756 νήθω *nēthō* (2)
spin (2)

3757 νηπιάζω *nēpiazō* (1)
infants (1)

3758 νήπιος *nēpios* (14)
child (5)
infants (3)
children (2)
little children (2)
childish (1) *+3836*
infant (1)

3759 Νηρεύς *Nēreus* (1)
Nereus (1)

3760 Νηρί *Nēri* (1)
Neri (1)

3761 νησίον *nēsion* (1)
small island (1)

3762 νῆσος *nēsos* (9)
island (9)

3763 νηστεία *nēsteia* (5)
fasting (2)
fast (1)
gone without food (1)
hunger (1)

3764 νηστεύω *nēsteuō* (20)
fast (11)
fasting (6)
fasted (1)
untranslated (2)

3765 νῆστις *nēstis* (2)
hungry (2)

3766 νηφαλέος *nēphaleos*
Variant; not used

3767 νηφάλιος *nēphalios* (3)
temperate (3)

3768 νήφω *nēphō* (6)
self-controlled (5)
keep head (1)

3769 Νίγερ *Niger* (1)
Niger (1)

3770 Νικάνωρ *Nikanōr* (1)
Nicanor (1)

3771 νικάω *nikaō* (28)
overcomes (10)
overcome (8)
overcame (2)
conquer (1)
conqueror (1)
conquest (1)
overpower (1)
overpowers (1)
prevail (1)
triumphed (1)
victorious (1)

3772 νίκη *nikē* (1)
victory (1)

3773 Νικόδημος *Nikodēmos* (5)
Nicodemus (5)

3774 Νικολαΐτης *Nikolaitēs* (2)
Nicolaitans (2)

3775 Νικόλαος *Nikolaos* (1)
Nicolas (1)

3776 Νικόπολις *Nikopolis* (1)
Nicopolis (1)

3777 νῖκος *nikos* (4)
victory (4)

3778 Νινευή *Nineuē*
Variant; not used

3779 Νινευΐ *Nineui*
Variant; not used

3780 Νινευίτης *Nineuitēs* (3)
Nineveh (2)
Ninevites (1)

3781 νιπτήρ *nipter* (1)
basin (1)

3782 νίπτω *niptō* (17)
wash (10)
washed (4)
washing (3)

3783 νοέω *noeō* (14)
understand (7)
see (3)
imagine (1)
know (1)
reflect on (1)
understood (1)

3784 νόημα *noēma* (6)
minds (4)
schemes (1)
thought (1)

3785 νόθος *nothos* (1)
illegitimate children (1)

3786 νομή *nomē* (2)
pasture (1)
spread (1) *+2400*

3787 νομίζω *nomizō* (15)
thought (3)
expected (2)
think (2)
think that (2)
thinking (2)
assumed (1)

suppose (1)
thinks (1)
thought that (1)

3788 νομικός *nomikos* (9)
experts in the law (5)
expert in the law (2)
about law (1)
lawyer (1)

3789 νομίμως *nomimōs* (2)
according to the rules (1)
properly (1)

3790 νόμισμα *nomisma* (1)
coin (1)

3791 νομοδιδάσκαλος *nomodidaskalos* (3)
teachers of the law (2)
teacher of the law (1)

3792 νομοθεσία *nomothesia* (1)
receiving of the law (1)

3793 νομοθετέω *nomotheteō* (2)
founded (1)
law was given (1)

3794 νομοθέτης *nomothetēs* (1)
lawgiver (1)

3795 νόμος *nomos* (194)
law (181)
it[s] (2)
lawbreaker (2) *+4127*
laws (2)
it[s] (1) *+1650*
law's (1)
legalistic (1) *+1877*
observer of law (1) *+2848*
principle (1)
regulation (1)
that[s] (1)

3796 νοσέω *noseō* (1)
unhealthy (1)

3797 νόσημα *nosēma*
Variant; not used

3798 νόσος *nosos* (11)
diseases (5)
disease (3)
diseases (1) *+2809*
illnesses (1)
sickness (1) *+820*

3799 νοσσιά *nossia* (1)
chicks (1)

3800 νοσσίον *nossion* (1)
chicks (1)

3801 νοσσός *nossos* (1)
young (1)

3802 νοσφίζω *nosphizō* (3)
kept (1)
kept back (1)
steal (1)

3803 νότος *notos* (7)
south (5)
south wind (2)

3804 νουθεσία *nouthesia* (3)
instruction (1)
warn (1)
warnings (1)

3805 νουθετέω *noutheteō* (8)
warn (3)
admonish (2)
admonishing (1)
instruct (1)
warning (1)

3806 νουμηνία *noumēnia*
Variant; not used

3807 νουνεχῶς *nounechōs* (1)
wisely (1)

3808 νοῦς *nous* (24)
mind (15)
minds (4)
insight (1)
intelligible (1) *+1609+3836*
thinking (1)
understanding (1)
untranslated (1)

3809 Νύμφαν *Nymphan* (1)
Nympha (1)

3810 Νυμφᾶς *Nymphas*
Variant; not used

3811 νύμφη *nymphē* (8)
bride (5)
daughter-in-law (3)

3812 νυμφίος *nymphios* (16)
bridegroom (11)
he[s] (3) *+3836*
bridegroom's (1)
him[s] (1)

3813 νυμφών *nymphōn* (3)
bridegroom (3)

3814 νῦν *nyn* (147)
now (110)
present (9)
now on (4) *+3836*
now (3) *+3836*
as it is (2)
as it is (2) *+1254*
now on (2)
a short while ago (1)
again (1) *+608+3836*
at present (1)
for now (1) *+2400+3836*
in present (1)
instead (1) *+1254*
just (1)
now (1) *+608+3836*
now then (1)
present (1) *+2789+3836*
present time (1)
still (1) *+2285*
untranslated (3)

3815 νυνί *nyni* (20)
now (16)
as it is (1)
in fact (1)
indeed (1)
untranslated (1)

3816 νύξ *nyx* (61)
night (51)
nights (3)
each evening (1) *+3836*
last night (1) *+3836+4047*
midnight (1) *+3545*
midnight (1) *+3545+3836*
night (1) *+1328+4246*
tonight (1)
tonight (1) *+3836+4047*

3817 νύσσω *nyssō* (1)
pierced (1)

3818 νυστάζω *nystazō* (2)
became drowsy (1)
sleeping (1)

3819 νυχθήμερον *nychthēmeron* (1)
a night and a day (1)

3820 Νῶε *Nōe* (8)
noah (8)

3821 νωθρός *nōthros* (2)
lazy (1)
slow (1)

3822 νῶτος *nōtos* (1)
backs (1)

3823 ξ *x*
Variant; not used

3824 ξαίνω *xainō*
Variant; not used

3825 ξενία *xenia* (2)
guest room (1)
place where staying (1)

3826 ξενίζω *xenizō* (10)
entertained (2)
staying (2)
a guest (1)
be guests (1)
stay (1)
strange (1)
surprised (1)
think it strange (1)

3827 ξενοδοχέω *xenodocheō* (1)
showing hospitality (1)

3828 ξένος *xenos* (14)
foreigners (4)
stranger (4)
strange (2)
aliens (1)
foreign (1)
hospitality (1)
strangers (1)

3829 ξέστης *xestēs* (1)
pitchers (1)

3830 ξηραίνω *xērainō* (15)
withered (6)
withers (3)
becomes rigid (1)
dried up (1)
ripe (1)
shriveled (1)
stopped (1)
wither (1)

3831 ξηρός *xēros* (8)
shriveled (4)
dry (2)
land (1)
paralyzed (1)

3832 ξύλινος *xylinos* (2)
of wood (1)
wood (1)

3833 ξύλον *xylon* (20)
tree (11)
clubs (5)
wood (3)
stocks (1)

3834 ξυράω *xyraō* (3)
shaved (2)
shaved off (1)

3835 ο *o*
Variant; not used

3836 ὁ *ho* (19856)
the (7395)
who (381)
those who (271)
his (199)
a (164)
what (160)
the who (153)
that (143)
he who (108)
their (92)
your (77)
this (76)
the son (74)
him who (73)
he (70) *+1254*
those (70)
our (52)
they (49) *+1254*
my (41)
he (35)
whoever (35)

which (28)
anyone who (27)
her (26)
Jesus[s] (25) *+1254*
forever (23) *+172+1650*
they (22)
its (21)
an (15)
to (15) *+1650*
so that (14) *+1650*
you who (14)
one (12)
one who (12)
whom (12)
because (10) *+1328*
these (10)
things (10)
all things (9) *+4246*
son (9)
everything (8) *+4246*
she (8) *+1254*
the that (8)
when (8) *+1877*
he[s] (7) *+2652*
him[s] (7) *+2536*
O (7)
that (7) *+1650*
him[s] (6) *+2652*
so that (6)
companions (5) *+3552*
finally (5) *+3370*
he[s] (5) *+2536*
some (5)
some (5) *+3525*
this[s] (5) *+3364*
we (5)
back (4) *+1650+3958*
him[s] (4) *+476*
his[s] (4) *+2536*
Jesus[s] (4)
never (4) *+172+1650+3590+4024*
now on (4) *+3814*
rider (4) *+2764*
someone (4)
the man[s] (4) *+1254*
whose (4)
you (4)
a man[s] (3)
and so (3) *+1650*
anyone (3)
God[s] (3)
he[s] (3) *+3812*
in order that (3) *+1650*
it (3)
it[s] (3) *+3180*
looked up (3) *+2048+4057*
mother (3)
now (3) *+3814*
others (3)
others (3) *+1254*
people who (3)
that (3) *+899*
that which (3)
the man[s] (3)
them[s] (3) *+899+3412*
to (3)
together (3) *+899+2093*
while (3) *+1877*
affairs (2)
after (2) *+3552*
among (2) *+1650+3545*
anything (2)
as (2) *+1877*
associates (2) *+5250*
beyond limits (2) *+296+1650*
case (2) *+2848*
companions (2) *+1639+3552*
companions (2) *+1639+5250*
companions (2) *+5250*
each (2)
forever (2) *+1457+1650*
front of everyone (2) *+3545*
God-fearing (2) *+2536+5828*
have (2) *+2400*
him[s] (2) *+81+899*
home (2) *+899+3875*
household (2)
I have (2) *+1847*
in (2)
interests (2)
it[s] (2) *+1046*
it[s] (2) *+4450*
landed (2) *+1178+2093+2262*
men (2) *+476+3836+5626*
never (2) *+172+1650+4024*
outsiders (2) *+2032*
people (2)
possessions (2) *+5639*
rich (2) *+2400+5975*
seized (2) *+2093+2095+5931*
seized (2) *+2095+5931*
she who (2)
some time ago (2) *+2465+4047+4574*
still (2) *+3370*
such (2)
that is how (2) *+899+2848*
the disciples[s] (2) *+1254*
the men[s] (2) *+1254*
the one (2)
the son[s] (2)
them (2)
they[s] (2) *+476*
they[s] (2) *+3412*
this[s] (2) *+2465+4047*
this[s] (2) *+3364+4047*
those (2) *+1254*
those that (2)
those who are[s] (2) *+5626*
those whose (2)
to himself (2) *+899+1877+2840*
tomorrow (2) *+892*
what is (2)
what was promised (2) *+2039*
which[s] (2) *+180*
whoever (2) *+4246*
you (2) *+4725+5148*
according to means (1) *+1666+2400*
across (1) *+1650+4305*
after this (1) *+1877+2759*
again (1) *+172+1650*
again (1) *+608+3814*
agree (1) *+899+3306*
all (1)
all along (1) *+794*
all disciples (1) *+3412+4436*
all had (1) *+2625*
all who (1)
altogether (1) *+4246*
always (1) *+2465+4246*
am about to tell (1) *+3364+4047*
and thus (1) *+1650*
another (1) *+1254*
another (1) *+2283*
any (1)
any way (1) *+5515*
anyone[s] (1)
anyone[s] (1) *+476*
arrest (1) *+2093+2095+5931*
arrested (1) *+2093+2095+5931*
arrested (1) *+2095+5931*
arrived (1) *+4242*
as a result (1) *+1650*
as follows (1) *+2400+4047+5596*
as has just been said (1) *+1877+3306*
as to (1)
as usual (1) *+899+2848*
as usual (1) *+1621+2848*
ashore (1) *+1178+1650*
assembled worshipers (1) *+3295+4436*
at all (1) *+1650+4117*
at once (1) *+899+6052*
at the meal (1) *+367*
away[s] (1) *+1650+2557*
baptized (1) *+966*
be proud (1) *+5734+5858*
before (1) *+1650+3545*
before (1) *+1877+3545*
beg (1) *+160+1797*
began to speak (1) *+487+3306+5125*
begging (1) *+1797+4639*
being like-minded (1) *+899+5858*
believers (1) *+2400+4411*
believers (1) *+4411*
besides everything else (1) *+4211+6006*
betray (1) *+1639+4140*
bleeding (1) *+135+4380*
blemish[s] (1) *+5525*
blindfolded (1) *+4328+4725*
both[s] (1) *+1545*
brag (1) *+224+1877*
but (1) *+1254+1883*
call (1) *+2813+3950*
called (1) *+3950+4005*
certified (1) *+3456+5381*
child bear (1) *+2843+3120*
childish (1) *+3758*
circumstances (1)
come together (1) *+899+1639+2093*
comes together (1) *+899+2093+5302*
coming (1) *+2262*
companions (1) *+4309*
completely (1) *+1650+4117*
conceived (1) *+1877+3120+5197*
convened the court (1) *+1037+2093+2767*
Cornelius[s] (1) *+1254*
crowd (1) *+3295+4436*
decided (1) *+326+2093+2840*
demon-possessed (1) *+2400+3836+4460+4505*
descendant (1) *+1666+2588*
descendants (1) *+2843+4019*
did (1) *+2240*
dressed ready for service (1) *+4019+4322*
each day (1) *+2465*
each evening (1) *+3816*
each one (1) *+324*
each other (1) *+1651+1651*
elementary truths (1) *+794+5122*
embraced (1) *+2093+2158+5549*
enabling (1) *+1328+1443+5931*
endlessly (1) *+1457+1650*
envious (1) *+1639+4057+4505*
equal (1) *+899*
equality (1) *+1639+2698*
ever (1) *+172+1650*
ever (1) *+172+1666*
ever-increasing wickedness (1) *+490+490+1650*
everyone (1) *+4246*
everyone who (1)
evildoers (1) *+490+2237*
extraordinary (1) *+4024+5593*
family (1)
family (1) *+3875*
family (1) *+4123*
field (1) *+2834+3586*
finally (1) *+5465*
first (1) *+3552*
footstool (1) *+4546+5711*
for (1) *+1328*
for (1) *+1650*
for (1) *+1877+3545*
for (1) *+4639*
for all time (1) *+1457+1650*
for now (1) *+2400+3814*
forevermore (1) *+172+1650+4246*
from bad to worse (1) *+2093+5937*
from house to house (1) *+2848+3875*
from house to house (1) *+3864*
from now on (1) *+3370*
from town to town (1) *+4484*
from village to village (1) *+2848+3267*
give (1) *+1443*

give in (1) +1634+5717
God who[S] (1)
God's[S] (1)
God-fearing gentiles (1) +2536+5828
gods[S] (1)
grasp the meaning (1) +1539+3857
greater than (1) +3505
grew (1) +1650+2262
guard carefully (1) +1428
had been converted (1) +2189
had[S] (1) +4123
has (1) +5639
has no pity (1) +3091+5073
he (1) +899+1328+5931
he (1) +3525
he that (1)
he[S] (1) +235
he[S] (1) +467
he[S] (1) +476
he[S] (1) +476+1697
he[S] (1) +508
he[S] (1) +804
he[S] (1) +899+899+1877+4460
he[S] (1) +995
he[S] (1) +1333
he[S] (1) +2989
he[S] (1) +3261
he[S] (1) +3273
he[S] (1) +3281
he[S] (1) +3707
healed (1) +5392
heavenly bodies (1) +1539+4041
heavenly things (1) +1877+4041
her own (1)
her who (1)
her[S] (1) +4086
highly valued (1) +5734
him (1)
him whose (1)
him[S] (1) +81+1609
him[S] (1) +467
him[S] (1) +476+1877+4047
him[S] (1) +2930
him[S] (1) +4263
him[S] (1) +4737
him[S] (1) +5108
him[S] (1) +5986
himself[S] (1) +899+3950
his fellow (1) +899+5250
his fellowman[S] (1) +2283
his home (1) +2625
his native language (1) +1666+2625
his own (1)
his own home (1) +2625
his son[S] (1)
his son[S] (1) +3525
his[S] (1) +2610
his[S] (1) +2652
his[S] (1) +4511
home (1) +899+1650+3875
home (1) +1650+3875
home (1) +1650+3875+5148
home (1) +2625
house (1)
how (1) +2848
how (1) +4309
human standards (1) +4922
I (1) +1609+6034
illness (1) +819+4922
immediately (1) +899+1877+6052
in agreement (1) +1650+1651
in full (1) +2698
in God's sight (1) +2536+4123
in number (1) +750+4005
in one place (1) +899+2093
in order to (1)
in person (1) +3836+4242+5393
in presence (1) +3552+4725
in public (1) +1883+3295
indoors (1) +1650+3864
instead (1) +1883+3437
intelligible (1) +1609+3808
inwardly (1) +1877+3220
inwardly (1) +2276
Israelites (1) +2702+5626
it depends on you (1) +1666+5148
it that (1)
it[S] (1) +27
it[S] (1) +69
it[S] (1) +229
it[S] (1) +993+1847+3836
it[S] (1) +1155+4047
it[S] (1) +1561
it[S] (1) +1609+5013
it[S] (1) +1631
it[S] (1) +1635+2563+3836
it[S] (1) +1847
it[S] (1) +2240+5516
it[S] (1) +2295
it[S] (1) +2585
it[S] (1) +2819
it[S] (1) +3364
it[S] (1) +3693
it[S] (1) +3954
it[S] (1) +4047+4839
it[S] (1) +4384
it[S] (1) +4784
it[S] (1) +5853
it[S] (1) +5890
it[S] (1) +6029
it[S] (1) +6052
its[S] (1) +899+4725
its[S] (1) +1178
its[S] (1) +2639
its[S] (1) +4922
its[S] (1) +5393
Jesus' followers[S] (1) +1254
Jesus'[S] (1)
Jews (1) +1169+1609+1877
just after sunrise (1) +422+2463
just as though (1) +899+1651+2779
just like this (1) +899+2848
keep in suspense (1) +149+6034
kill (1) +660
kneel (1) +1205+2828
knelt (1) +1205+5502
knelt down (1) +1205+5502
landed (1) +609+1178+1650
last night (1) +3816+4047
lies (1) +3281+6022
listen carefully (1) +1650+4044+5148+5148+5502
live in harmony (1) +899+5858
lived (1) +2400+2998
living (1) +2400+6034
look up (1) +2048+4057
looked (1) +149+4057
looked (1) +2048+4057
looking (1) +2048+4057
lustfully (1) +2121+4639
made king (1) +993+3284
made think (1) +1877+2840+5502
make the most of opportunity (1) +1973+2789
make up mind (1) +1877+2840+5502
man whose[S] (1)
man's[S] (1)
Mary[S] (1) +1254
matters (1)
me (1) +1609+3950
me (1) +1609+6034
meanwhile (1) +1877+3568
member (1) +2848+3517
men who[S] (1)
men[S] (1)
met personally (1) +1877+3972+4725+4922
midnight (1) +3545+3816
might say (1) +1666+5125
money (1)
most (1) +4498
motioned (1) +2939+5931
my (1) +1831+4309
name (1) +2813+3950
natural sleep (1) +3122+3836+5678
nearby (1) +899
nearby (1) +4309+5536
never (1) +173+1650+3590+4024
never again (1) +172+1650+3590+4024
next (1) +1650+3516
nine in the morning (1) +2465+5569+6052
now (1) +608+3814
of you (1) +1639+1877+5148
on (1) +2759+2779
on board (1) +1877+4450
one (1) +899
one (1) +1651
one (1) +3525
one Sabbath (1) +1877+4879
or anything (1) +3593
others (1) +3525
our companions (1) +1609+5250
our fathers[S] (1) +3525
outward (1) +1877+5745
outwardly (1) +476+2032
outwardly (1) +1877+5745
own (1)
Paul[S] (1) +3525
people (1) +5626
people live scattered among (1) +1402
perfectly united (1) +899+2936
person who (1)
Peter and John[S] (1) +3525
Peter[S] (1)
Pilate[S] (1) +1254
pointing (1) +899+1753+5931
possess (1) +5639
possessions (1)
preaching (1) +3364
prepare for action (1) +350+4019
present (1) +2789+3814
prompted (1) +965+1650+2840
property (1) +5639
publicly (1) +1967+4436
reached for (1) +1753+5931
reaching more and more (1) +1328+4429+4498
resolutely (1) +4725+5114
result (1) +1650
return (1) +1650+2262+4099
returned (1) +1877+2059
rewarding (1) +1443+3635
riders (1) +2093+2764
Sabbath (1) +2465+4879
seashore (1) +2498+5927
seed (1) +5078
self (1) +476+2840
self-seeking (1) +1571+2426
service that perform (1) +1355+3311+4047
shared (1) +3102+3275
she[S] (1) +1222
she[S] (1) +3166
she[S] (1) +3451
short (1) +2461+3625
shouted (1) +2048+5889
shouted (1) +3489+5774+5889
sighed deeply (1) +417+4460
since (1) +1328
since that time (1) +3370
sins (1) +281+4472
so (1)
so (1) +1650
so as (1) +1650
so he (1) +1254
so that (1) +4639
so then (1) +1650
so they (1) +1254
some (1) +1651+3538
some way (1) +4802
some who (1)
something (1)
soon afterward (1) +1877+2009
sound asleep (1) +608+2965+5678
speak (1) +487+5125

spirit of unity (1) *+899+5858*
spoken freely (1) *+487+5125*
stand firm (1) *+2840+5114*
still others (1) *+1254*
stripped (1) *+2668+4351*
such a (1)
such things[S] (1) *+4998*
terms (1)
terrorists (1) *+467+4974*
that had touched (1) *+608+5999*
that is (1)
that same (1)
that was the time (1) *+1697+1877+2465*
that[S] (1) *+2434*
that[S] (1) *+2546*
the affairs (1)
the affairs[S] (1)
the apostles[S] (1) *+3525*
the expert in the law[S] (1) *+1254*
the father[S] (1) *+1254*
the interests (1)
the man (1)
the man's[S] (1) *+1254*
the manager[S] (1) *+1254*
the men[S] (1) *+3525*
the parts[S] (1) *+4047+5393*
the people (1)
the people[S] (1) *+1254*
the rioters[S] (1) *+1254*
the soldiers[S] (1)
the things (1)
the whom (1)
the wife (1)
their (1) *+899*
them[S] (1) *+476*
them[S] (1) *+899+4546*
them[S] (1) *+899+5284*
them[S] (1) *+1177*
them[S] (1) *+1178+2093+2997+3836*
them[S] (1) *+1609+4252*
them[S] (1) *+2239*
them[S] (1) *+2465*
them[S] (1) *+2585*
them[S] (1) *+3295*
them[S] (1) *+3412*
them[S] (1) *+3517+5148*
them[S] (1) *+3836+4556+5525*
them[S] (1) *+4063*
themselves (1) *+899+2840*
themselves (1) *+899+6034*
then will be able (1) *+1650*
there (1) *+1877+5536*
there is a judge (1) *+2400+3212*
there[S] (1) *+1650+2038*
there[S] (1) *+1877+2639*
there[S] (1) *+1877+4047+4484*
they (1) *+213+899*
they (1) *+899+4057*
they (1) *+3525*
they who (1)
they[S] (1) *+899+1204*
they[S] (1) *+899+3412*
they[S] (1) *+899+6001*
they[S] (1) *+899+899+2779+3412*
they[S] (1) *+1322*
they[S] (1) *+4998*
they[S] (1) *+5861*
things that (1)
thinking (1) *+1181+5856*
this day (1) *+2465+4958*
this is (1) *+2848*
this man[S] (1)
this or that (1) *+3840*
this way (1)
this[S] (1) *+899+4246*
this[S] (1) *+1609+3364+4047*
this[S] (1) *+4047+4839*
those who (1) *+1254*
those who marry[S] (1) *+5525*
those who who who (1)
those[S] (1) *+3295*

three in the afternoon (1) *+1888+2465+6052*
threw his arms around (1) *+2093+2158+5549*
to keep from (1) *+3590+4639*
to show that (1) *+4639*
to their number (1) *+899+2093*
today (1) *+1877+2465+4958*
tonight (1) *+3816+4047*
trusted personal servant (1) *+2093+3131*
trying to kill (1) *+2426+6034*
turned around (1) *+1650+3958+5138*
turned back (1) *+599+1650+3958*
under (1) *+4123+4546*
unnatural ones (1) *+4123+5882*
unseen (1) *+1877+3220*
unseen (1) *+1877+3224*
us who (1)
we who (1)
weapons fight with (1) *+3960+5127*
weeping (1) *+3088*
what had been promised (1) *+2039*
what had happened to (1)
what has been promised (1) *+2039*
what has happened to (1) *+2848*
what we are writing[S] (1) *+899*
what will happen (1) *+4471*
what you ought to do (1) *+465*
what[S] (1) *+2240*
what[S] (1) *+2240+5516*
what[S] (1) *+3306*
what[S] (1) *+3364*
whatever (1) *+4246*
whatever give (1)
when (1) *+3552*
when are tempted (1) *+4280+5250*
where[S] (1) *+1650+5596*
while (1) *+1639+1877*
who[S] (1) *+476*
whoever (1) *+323*
wife (1)
winepress (1) *+3332+3885*
with (1) *+1650*
with a great crash (1) *+899+1639+3489+4774*
with great fervor (1) *+2417+4460*
within (1) *+1877+3517*
wondered about (1) *+1877+2840+5502*
worldly (1) *+3180*
wounded (1) *+2400+4435*
you (1) *+3950+5148*
you (1) *+4364+5148*
you have (1) *+5050*
your family (1) *+5050*
your own (1)
your own (1) *+2625*
yours (1) *+5050*
untranslated (9007)

3837 ὀγδοήκοντα *ogdoēkonta* (2)
eight hundred (1)
eighty-four (1) *+2291+5475*

3838 ὄγδοος *ogdoos* (5)
eighth (3)
eight (1)
untranslated (1)

3839 ὄγκος *onkos* (1)
hinders (1)

3840 ὅδε *hode* (10)
these (7)
she (1)
this or that (1) *+3836*
untranslated (1)

3841 ὁδεύω *hodeuō* (1)
traveled (1)

3842 ὁδηγέω *hodēgeō* (5)
lead (2)
explains to (1)
guide (1)
leads (1)

3843 ὁδηγός *hodēgos* (5)
guides (3)
guide (2)

3844 ὁδοιπορέω *hodoiporeō* (1)
on their journey (1)

3845 ὁδοιπορία *hodoiporia* (2)
journey (1)
on the move (1)

3846 ὁδοποιέω *hodopoieō*
Variant; not used

3847 ὁδός *hodos* (100)
way (50)
road (17)
path (7)
ways (5)
journey (4)
roadside (3)
paths (2)
direction (1)
on a journey (1)
roads (1)
route (1)
Sabbath day's walk from (1) *+1584+2400+4879*
street (1)
streets (1)
walked along (1) *+4472*
way of life (1)
untranslated (3)

3848 ὀδούς *odous* (12)
teeth (10)
tooth (2)

3849 ὀδυνάω *odynaō* (4)
in agony (2)
anxiously (1)
grieved (1)

3850 ὀδύνη *odynē* (2)
anguish (1)
griefs (1)

3851 ὀδυρμός *odyrmos* (2)
deep sorrow (1)
mourning (1)

3852 Ὀζίας *Ozias* (2)
Uzziah (2)

3853 ὄζω *ozō* (1)
a bad odor (1)

3854 ὅθεν *hothen* (15)
where (3)
therefore (2)
and so (1)
for this reason (1)
from death[S] (1)
from there (1)
left (1) *+2002*
so then (1)
that (1)
this is how (1)
this is why (1)
untranslated (1)

3855 ὀθόνη *othonē* (2)
sheet (2)

3856 ὀθόνιον *othonion* (5)
strips of linen (4)
linen (1)

3857 οἶδα *oida* (319)
know (225)
knew (19)
knows (13)
knowing (12)
realize (8)
known (7)
understand (5)

idea (2)
acquainted with (1)
aware (1)
be sure (1) *+1182*
can see (1)
fathom (1)
fully convinced (1) *+2779+4275*
get learning (1) *+1207*
grasp the meaning (1) *+1539+3836*
had idea (1)
in mind (1)
knew about (1)
knew who was (1)
knows how (1)
knows thoughts (1)
learn (1)
recognize (1)
regard (1)
remember (1)
respect (1)
sure (1)
take note of (1)
tell (1)
though know (1)
understanding (1)
who knows (1)
untranslated (3)

3858 οἰκεῖος *oikeios* (3)
belong to family (1)
immediate family (1)
members of household (1)

3859 οἰκετεία *oiketeia* (1)
servants in household (1)

3860 οἰκέτης *oiketēs* (4)
servant (2)
servants (1)
slaves (1)

3861 οἰκέω *oikeō* (9)
lives (3)
living (3)
live (2)
lives in (1)

3862 οἴκημα *oikēma* (1)
cell (1)

3863 οἰκητήριον *oikētērion* (2)
dwelling (1)
home (1)

3864 οἰκία *oikia* (93)
house (66)
home (11)
household (4)
houses (4)
homes (3)
family (1)
from house to house (1) *+3836*
indoors (1) *+1650+3836*
live in (1)
untranslated (1)

3865 οἰκιακός *oikiakos* (2)
members of household (2)

3866 οἰκοδεσποτέω *oikodespoteō* (1)
manage homes (1)

3867 οἰκοδεσπότης *oikodespotēs* (12)
owner of the house (5)
landowner (2) *+476*
head of the house (1)
landowner (1)
owner (1)
owner of a house (1) *+476*
owner's (1)

3868 οἰκοδομέω *oikodomeō* (40)
build (12)
built (10)
builders (4)
building (3)
build up (2)
edifies (2)
be edified (1) *+3284*
builds up (1)
constructive (1)
emboldened (1)
rebuild (1)
rebuild (1) *+4099*
strengthened (1)

3869 οἰκοδομή *oikodomē* (18)
building (3)
building up (3)
buildings (3)
strengthening (3)
build up (2)
builds up (1)
built up (1)
edification (1)
be edified (1) *+3284*

3870 οἰκοδομία *oikodomia*
Variant; not used

3871 οἰκοδόμος *oikodomos* (1)
builders (1)

3872 οἰκονομέω *oikonomeō* (1)
be manager (1)

3873 οἰκονομία *oikonomia* (9)
administration (2)
job (2)
commission (1)
management (1)
put into effect (1)
trust (1)
work (1)

3874 οἰκονόμος *oikonomos* (10)
manager (4)
administering (1)
director of public works (1)
entrusted with work (1)
have been given a trust (1)
those entrusted with (1)
trustees (1)

3875 οἶκος *oikos* (114)
house (59)
home (14)
household (8)
family (7)
Israel (3) *+2702*
from house to house (2) *+2848*
home (2) *+899+1650*
home (2) *+899+3836*
descendant (1) *+1666*
family (1) *+3836*
from house to house (1) *+2848+3836*
home (1) *+899+1650+3836*
home (1) *+1650+3836*
home (1) *+1650+3836+5148*
home (1) *+5148*
households (1)
houses (1)
in their homes (1) *+2848*
indoors (1) *+1650*
itself[s] (1)
market (1) *+1866*
members of household (1)
palace (1)
palaces (1)
sanctuary (1)

3876 οἰκουμένη *oikoumenē* (15)
world (13)
Roman world (2)

3877 οἰκουργός *oikourgos* (1)
busy at home (1)

3878 οἰκουρός *oikouros*
Variant; not used

3879 οἰκτείρω *oikteirō*
Variant; not used

3880 οἰκτιρμός *oiktirmos* (5)
compassion (3)
mercy (2)

3881 οἰκτίρμων *oiktirmōn* (3)
merciful (2)
mercy (1)

3882 οἰκτίρω *oiktirō* (2)
compassion (2)

3883 οἶμαι *oimai*
Variant; not used

3884 οἰνοπότης *oinopotēs* (2)
drunkard (2)

3885 οἶνος *oinos* (34)
wine (32)
winepress (1) *+3332+3836*
untranslated (1)

3886 οἰνοφλυγία *oinophlygia* (1)
drunkenness (1)

3887 οἴομαι *oiomai* (3)
suppose (1)
supposing (1)
think (1)

3888 οἷος *hoios* (14)
as (5)
how (1)
like (1)
the (1)
unequaled (1) *+1181+4024*
unequaled (1) *+1181+4024+5525*
what (1)
what kinds of (1)
untranslated (2)

3889 οἱοσδηποτοῦν *hoiosdēpotoun*
Variant; not used

3890 ὀκνέω *okneō* (1)
at once (1) *+3590*

3891 ὀκνηρός *oknēros* (3)
lacking (1)
lazy (1)
trouble (1)

3892 ὀκταήμερος *oktaēmeros* (1)
eighth day (1)

3893 ὀκτώ *oktō* (8)
eight (4)
a week later (1) *+2465+3552*
eighteen (1) *+1274+2779*
eighth (1)
thirty-eight (1) *+2779+5558*

3894 ὀλεθρευτής *olethreutēs*
Variant; not used

3895 ὀλεθρεύω *olethreuō*
Variant; not used

3896 ὀλέθριος *olethrios*
Variant; not used

3897 ὄλεθρος *olethros* (4)
destruction (2)
destroyed (1)
ruin (1)

3898 ὀλιγοπιστία *oligopistia* (1)
little faith (1)

3899 ὀλιγόπιστος *oligopistos* (5)
of little faith (5)

3900 ὀλίγος *oligos* (40)
few (15)
little (8)
little while (3)
some (2)
a little (1)
a long time (1) *+4024+5989*
a short time (1)
briefly (1) *+1328*

briefly (1) *+1877*
continued raging (1) *+2130+4024*
great disturbance (1) *+4024+5431*
many (1) *+4024*
sharp (1) *+4024*
short (1) *+2400*
short time (1) *+1877*
small (1)

3901 ὀλιγόψυχος *oligopsychos* (1)
timid (1)

3902 ὀλιγωρέω *oligōreō* (1)
make light of (1)

3903 ὀλίγως *oligōs* (1)
just (1)

3904 ὀλοθρευτής *olothreutēs* (1)
destroying (1)

3905 ὀλοθρεύω *olothreuō* (1)
destroyer (1)

3906 ὁλοκαύτωμα *holokautōma* (3)
burnt offerings (3)

3907 ὁλοκληρία *holoklēria* (1)
complete healing (1)

3908 ὁλόκληρος *holoklēros* (2)
complete (1)
whole (1)

3909 ὀλολύζω *ololyzō* (1)
wail (1)

3910 ὅλος *holos* (108)
whole (52)
all (34)
throughout (6) *+1877*
entire (2)
throughout (2) *+1650*
throughout (2) *+2848*
all (1) *+4012*
all long (1)
all over (1)
all over (1) *+1650*
all over (1) *+2848*
completely (1)
steeped (1)
throughout (1)
to bottom (1) *+1328*
whole (1) *+4116*

3911 ὁλοτελής *holotelēs* (1)
through and through (1)

3912 Ὀλυμπᾶς *Olympas* (1)
Olympas (1)

3913 ὄλυνθος *olynthos* (1)
late (1)

3914 ὅλως *holōs* (4)
at all (2)
actually (1)
completely (1)

3915 ὄμβρος *ombros* (1)
going to rain (1) *+2262*

3916 ὁμείρομαι *homeiromai* (1)
loved (1)

3917 ὁμιλέω *homileō* (4)
talked (2)
talking (2)

3918 ὁμιλία *homilia* (1)
company (1)

3919 ὅμιλος *homilos*
Variant; not used

3920 ὁμίχλη *homichlē* (1)
mists (1)

3921 ὄμμα *omma* (2)
eyes (2)

3922 ὄμνυμι *omnymi*
Variant; not used

3923 ὀμνύω *omnyō* (26)
swears (10)
swore (5)
swear (4)
declared on oath (2)
swear by (2)
promised (1)
promised with an oath (1)
sworn (1)

3924 ὁμοθυμαδόν *homothymadon* (11)
together (4)
all (2)
agreed (1) *+1181*
as one man (1)
heart (1)
joined together (1)
united (1)

3925 ὁμοιάζω *homoiazō*
Variant; not used

3926 ὁμοιοπαθής *homoiopathēs* (2)
human like (1)
just like (1)

3927 ὅμοιος *homoios* (45)
like (36)
as (2)
like (1) *+4047*
looked like (1) *+3930*
looks like (1) *+1639*
of (1)
resembled (1) *+1639*
resembling (1) *+3970*
similar (1)

3928 ὁμοιότης *homoiotēs* (2)
like (1)
untranslated (1)

3929 ὁμοιόω *homoioō* (15)
like (8)
compare (4)
form (1)
made like (1)
say is like (1)

3930 ὁμοίωμα *homoiōma* (6)
likeness (2)
as (1)
like (1)
look like (1)
looked like (1) *+3927*

3931 ὁμοίως *homoiōs* (31)
in the same way (10)
likewise (3)
the same (3)
also (2)
like (1)
same (1)
similarly (1)
so (1)
so do (1)
the same (1) *+2777*
the same thing (1)
too (1)
untranslated (5)

3932 ὁμοίωσις *homoiōsis* (1)
likeness (1)

3933 ὁμολογέω *homologeō* (26)
acknowledge (6)
confess (6)
acknowledges (4)
acknowledged that (1)
acknowledges that (1)
admit (1)
admitted (1)
claim (1)
confessed (1)
made confession (1) *+3934*
promised (1)
tell plainly (1)
untranslated (1)

3934 ὁμολογία *homologia* (6)
profess (2)
confess (1)
confession (1)
made confession (1)
made confession (1) *+3933*

3935 ὁμολογουμένως *homologoumenōs* (1)
beyond all question (1)

3936 ὁμόσε *homose*
Variant; not used

3937 ὁμότεχνος *homotechnos* (1)
as (1)

3938 ὁμοῦ *homou* (4)
together (3)
untranslated (1)

3939 ὁμόφρων *homophrōn* (1)
live in harmony with (1)

3940 ὅμως *homōs* (3)
at the same time (1)
even in the case of (1)
just as (1)

3941 ὄναρ *onar* (6)
dream (6)

3942 ὀνάριον *onarion* (1)
young donkey (1)

3943 ὀνειδίζω *oneidizō* (9)
insult (3)
heaped insults on (2)
denounce (1)
finding fault (1)
insulted (1)
rebuked (1)

3944 ὀνειδισμός *oneidismos* (5)
disgrace (3)
insult (1)
insults (1)

3945 ὄνειδος *oneidos* (1)
disgrace (1)

3946 Ὀνήσιμος *Onēsimos* (2)
Onesimus (2)

3947 Ὀνησίφορος *Onēsiphoros* (2)
Onesiphorus (2)

3948 ὀνικός *onikos* (2)
large (1)
large millstone (1) *+3685*

3949 ὀνίνημι *oninēmi* (1)
benefit (1)

3950 ὄνομα *onoma* (231)
name (156)
named (31)
names (9)
named (2) *+899*
call (1) *+2813+3836*
called (1)
called (1) *+3836+4005*
called (1) *+4005*
himself[s] (1) *+899+3836*
invoke the name (1) *+3951*
me (1) *+1609+3836*
name (1) *+2813+3836*
name's (1)
named (1) *+2813*
people (1)
reputation (1)
title (1)
title given (1) *+3951*
you (1) *+3836+5148*
untranslated (18)

3951 ὀνομάζω *onomazō* (10)
a hint of (1)
confesses (1)

derives name (1)
designated (1)
designating (1)
invoke the name (1) *+3950*
known (1)
named (1)
title given (1) *+3950*
calls (1)

3952 ὄνος *onos* (5)
donkey (4)
donkey's (1)

3953 ὄντως *ontōs* (10)
really (5)
certainly (1)
indeed (1)
it is true (1)
surely (1)
truly (1)

3954 ὄξος *oxos* (6)
wine vinegar (4)
it[s] (1) *+3836*
untranslated (1)

3955 ὀξύς *oxys* (8)
sharp (7)
swift (1)

3956 ὀπή *opē* (2)
holes (1)
spring (1)

3957 ὄπισθεν *opisthen* (7)
behind (4)
after (1)
in back (1)
on both sides (1) *+2277+2779*

3958 ὀπίσω *opisō* (36)
after (11)
behind (5)
back (4) *+1650+3836*
follow (3)
follow (2) *+4513*
back (1)
follow (1) *+199*
follow (1) *+2262*
followed (1)
followed (1) *+599*
from (1)
overtake (1)
perversion (1) *+599+2283+4922*
turned around (1) *+1650+3836+5138*
turned back (1) *+599+1650+3836*
untranslated (1)

3959 ὁπλίζω *hoplizō* (1)
arm (1)

3960 ὅπλον *hoplon* (6)
instruments (2)
weapons (2)
armor (1)
weapons fight with (1) *+3836+5127*

3961 ὁποῖος *hopoios* (5)
the quality (1)
what (1)
what (1) *+5525*
what kind of (1)
whatever (1)

3962 ὁπότε *hopote*
Variant; not used

3963 ὅπου *hopou* (82)
where (58)
wherever (5) *+1569*
wherever (3)
here (2)
whenever (2) *+1569*
wherever (2) *+323*
above (1)
in the case of (1)
on the other side[s] (1)
since (1)
the place where (1)
together (1)
yet even (1)
untranslated (3)

3964 ὀπτάνομαι *optanomai* (1)
appeared (1)

3965 ὀπτασία *optasia* (4)
vision (3)
visions (1)

3966 ὀπτός *optos* (1)
broiled (1)

3967 ὀπώρα *opōra* (1)
fruit (1)

3968 ὅπως *hopōs* (53)
so that (16)
to (15)
that (10)
so (3)
how (2)
in order to (1)
so that (1) *+323*
then (1)
untranslated (4)

3969 ὅραμα *horama* (12)
vision (8)
had a vision (1) *+3972*
sight (1)
vision (1) *+3972*
seen (1)

3970 ὅρασις *horasis* (4)
appearance (1)
resembling (1) *+3927*
vision (1)
visions (1)

3971 ὁρατός *horatos* (1)
visible (1)

3972 ὁράω *horaō* (481)
saw (182)
see (122)
seen (62)
appeared (17)
look (14)
looked (9)
seeing (7)
here (4)
realized (4)
perceiving (3)
see that (3)
watched (3)
careful (2)
do it[s] (2)
here is (2)
look at (2)
looked at (2)
noticed (2)
noticing (2)
see to it (2)
sees (2)
appear (1)
body decayed (1) *+1426*
came upon (1)
consider (1)
consider (1) *+4309*
die (1) *+2505*
experience (1)
find (1)
found (1)
had a vision (1) *+3969*
indeed seen (1) *+3972*
listen (1)
make sure that (1)
mark my words (1)
met personally (1) *+1877+3836+4725+4922*
met with (1)
mourn (1) *+4292*
saw that (1)
seen of (1)
settle the matter (1)
show (1)
surely (1)
that's your responsibility (1) *+5148*
the sight of (1)
vision (1) *+3969*
visit (1)
watch out (1)
watching (1)
well (1)
your responsibility (1) *+5148*
untranslated (3)

3973 ὀργή *orgē* (36)
wrath (27)
anger (7)
angry (1)
punishment (1)

3974 ὀργίζω *orgizō* (8)
angry (4)
anger (2)
enraged (2)

3975 ὀργίλος *orgilos* (1)
quick-tempered (1)

3976 ὀργυιά *orgyia* (2)
a hundred and twenty feet deep (1) *+1633*
ninety feet deep (1) *+1278*

3977 ὀρέγω *oregō* (3)
eager for (1)
longing for (1)
sets heart on being (1)

3978 ὀρεινός *oreinos* (2)
hill country (2)

3979 ὄρεξις *orexis* (1)
lust (1)

3980 ὀρθοποδέω *orthopodeō* (1)
acting in line (1)

3981 ὀρθός *orthos* (2)
level (1)
stand up (1) *+482*

3982 ὀρθοτομέω *orthotomeō* (1)
correctly handles (1)

3983 ὀρθρίζω *orthrizō* (1)
came early in the morning (1)

3984 ὀρθρινός *orthrinos* (1)
early morning (1)

3985 ὄρθριος *orthrios*
Variant; not used

3986 ὄρθρος *orthros* (3)
dawn (1)
daybreak (1)
very early in the morning (1) *+960*

3987 ὀρθῶς *orthōs* (4)
correctly (2)
plainly (1)
what is right (1)

3988 ὁρίζω *horizō* (8)
appointed (2)
set (2)
decided (1)
declared (1)
decreed (1)
determined (1)

3989 ὄρινξ *orinx*
Variant; not used

3990 ὅριον *horion* (12)
region (6)
vicinity (5)
area (1)

3991 ὁρκίζω *horkizō* (2)
command to come out (1)
swear (1)

3992 ὅρκος *horkos* (10)
oath (6)
oaths (3)
untranslated (1)

3993 ὁρκωμοσία *horkōmosia* (4)
oath (4)

3994 ὁρμάω *hormaō* (5)
rushed (5)

3995 ὁρμή *hormē* (2)
pilot (1)
plot afoot (1)

3996 ὅρμημα *hormēma* (1)
violence (1)

3997 ὄρνεον *orneon* (3)
birds (2)
bird (1)

3998 ὄρνις *ornis* (2)
hen (2)

3999 ὁροθεσία *horothesia* (1)
exact places (1)

4000 ὅρος *horos*
Variant; not used

4001 ὄρος *oros* (65)
mountain (22)
mount (15)
mountains (9)
mountainside (8)
hill (5)
hills (3)
hillside (2)
place (1)

4002 ὀρύσσω *oryssō* (3)
dug (2)
dug a hole (1)

4003 ὀρφανός *orphanos* (2)
orphans (2)

4004 ὀρχέομαι *orcheomai* (4)
dance (2)
danced (2)

4005 ὅς *hos* (1409)
what (137)
who (123)
whom (113)
which (112)
that (82)
him (58)
he (43)
them (23)
whose (21)
whoever (19) *+323*
anyone (17)
one (16)
these (14)
this (14)
they (13)
until (13) *+2401*
it (12)
whatever (11) *+1569*
the (10)
the one (9)
those (8)
their (7)
whatever (7)
when (7)
his (6)
some (6) *+3525*
when (6) *+1877*
whoever (6) *+1569*
those who (5)
until (5) *+948*
whoever (5)
another (4) *+1254*
because (4) *+505*
where (4) *+1877*
whom (4) *+323*
anyone who (3) *+323*
as (3) *+5573*
her (3)
the life[S] (3)
this gospel[S] (3)
what (3) *+1569*
where (3) *+1650*
while (3) *+1877*
and some (2) *+1254*
anything (2) *+1569*
as (2)
because (2) *+2093*
ever since (2) *+608*
its (2)
one (2) *+3525*
others (2) *+1254*
since (2) *+608*
that which (2)
the man[S] (2)
the men[S] (2)
the one whom (2)
theirs (2)
things (2)
until (2) *+3588*
whatever (2) *+323+1650*
whatever (2) *+323+5516*
when (2) *+323*
while (2) *+2401*
who (2) *+1328*
why (2) *+162+1328*
a man[S] (1)
about (1) *+4309*
Abraham[S] (1)
ago (1) *+608*
all the world (1) *+476+1639+5515*
also (1)
another (1)
another man (1) *+1254*
any (1) *+323+5516*
anyone (1) *+1569*
anyone who (1)
anyone who (1) *+1569*
anything (1) *+1569+4246+4547*
anything that (1)
as long as (1) *+948*
be (1)
because (1) *+1641*
because (1) *+1877*
before (1) *+2401*
both of them (1) *+1877*
by (1) *+3306*
by saying (1) *+3306*
called (1) *+3836+3950*
called (1) *+3950*
children[S] (1)
Christ[S] (1)
discipline[S] (1)
duty (1) *+4053+4472*
faith[S] (1)
for work (1) *+1256+1877+2237*
from the time (1) *+608*
God[S] (1)
he who (1)
him (1) *+4123*
his faith[S] (1)
holiness[S] (1)
I (1)
if any (1) *+323*
in keeping with income (1) *+1569+2338+5516*
in number (1) *+750+3836*
in that case (1) *+4309*
in the same way (1) *+5573*
in these (1)
including (1) *+1639*
indicating that (1) *+2848*
it[S] (1) *+201+608+794*
just as (1) *+2848+4048+5573*
just as (1) *+2848+5573*
just as (1) *+5573*
just before (1) *+948*
matters (1)
means (1) *+1639*
native (1) *+1164+1877*
now (1) *+608*
of them (1)
on (1)
once (1) *+323+608*
one of these journeys[S] (1)
or (1) *+1254*
others (1)
owner of (1) *+467*
Paul[S] (1)
peace[S] (1)
same as (1) *+2779*
she (1)
so (1)
so (1) *+162+1328*
so (1) *+1328*
someone (1)
something (1)
such a man (1)
such a man's[S] (1)
testimony (1) *+3455+3456*
that (1) *+2848*
that day[S] (1)
that is why (1) *+162+1328*
that tribe[S] (1)
the authority[S] (1)
the death[S] (1)
the fact[S] (1)
the glory[S] (1)
the gospel[S] (1)
the Jesus[S] (1)
the lawless one[S] (1)
the man whose (1)
the matters (1)
the name[S] (1)
the one (1) *+323*
the other (1) *+1254*
the promise[S] (1)
the situation (1)
the son[S] (1)
the tabernacle[S] (1)
the whom (1)
then (1) *+948*
there (1)
therefore (1) *+162+1328*
therefore (1) *+5920*
these men[S] (1)
these waters[S] (1)
this ark[3] (1)
this hope[S] (1)
this inscription (1) *+2108*
this man[S] (1)
those for whom (1)
those who (1) *+3525*
those whom (1)
those whom (1) *+1569*
to the one (1) *+3525*
to the other (1) *+1254*
to this end (1) *+1650*
until (1) *+323+948*
until (1) *+1877*
what (1) *+2093*
what (1) *+5515*
what (1) *+5516*
whatever (1) *+323*
whatever (1) *+1569+5516*
when (1) *+1650+2401*
where (1) *+1877+5536*
where (1) *+2093*
where (1) *+4123*
whom (1) *+1569*
whose (1) *+899*
whose (1) *+2400*
with (1) *+2400*
you (1)
your (1)
untranslated (269)

4006 ὁσάκις *hosakis* (3)
whenever (2) *+1569*

as often as (1)

4007 ὅσγε *hosge*
Variant; not used

4008 ὅσιος *hosios* (8)
holy (7)
holy blessings promised (1)

4009 ὁσιότης *hosiotēs* (2)
holiness (2)

4010 ὁσίως *hosiōs* (1)
holy (1)

4011 ὀσμή *osmē* (6)
fragrance (3)
fragrant (2) *+2380*
smell (1)

4012 ὅσος *hosos* (109)
all who (11)
whatever (8)
what (6)
everything (5)
how much (5)
as (4)
everything (4) *+4246*
that (4)
who (4)
all (3)
all (3) *+4246*
those who (3)
all that (2)
as long as (2) *+2093+5989*
as much as (2)
how many (2)
just as (2) *+2848*
whatever (2) *+1569*
whatever (2) *+2093*
whatever (2) *+4246*
all (1) *+3910*
all of (1)
all who (1) *+323*
all who (1) *+1569*
all whom (1) *+323*
anyone (1) *+1569*
as as (1)
as long as (1) *+2093*
as many as (1)
ever (1)
everything (1) *+323+4246*
everything (1) *+1569+4246*
everything that (1)
inasmuch as (1) *+2093+3525+4036*
more (1)
only as long as (1) *+2093+5989*
other (1)
people (1)
so long as (1) *+5989*
those (1)
those whom (1)
very while (1) *+2285+4012*
what (1) *+1569*
whatever (1) *+323*
while (1) *+2093*
who ever (1)
untranslated (7)

4013 ὅσπερ *hosper*
Variant; not used

4014 ὀστέον *osteon* (4)
bones (4)

4015 ὅστις *hostis* (144)
who (33)
they (23)
which (15)
whoever (6)
that (5)
this (5)
it (4)
them (3)
these (3)
until (3) *+2401*
others (2)
she (2)
some (2)
someone (2)
whoever (2) *+323*
you (2)
a (1)
another who (1)
anyone who (1)
Barabbas[S] (1)
he (1)
hear (1) *+201*
her (1)
such regulations[S] (1)
that temple[S] (1)
the cavalry[S] (1)
the one (1)
the people[S] (1)
those (1)
those who (1)
we (1)
whatever (1)
while (1) *+2401*
whoever (1) *+1569*
whoever (1) *+4246*
you who (1)
your generosity[S] (1)
untranslated (11)

4016 ὀστοῦν *ostoun*
Variant; not used

4017 ὀστράκινος *ostrakinos* (2)
clay (2)

4018 ὄσφρησις *osphrēsis* (1)
sense of smell (1)

4019 ὀσφῦς *osphys* (8)
waist (2)
belt (1)
body (1)
descendants (1) *+2843+3836*
descended from (1) *+2002*
dressed ready for service (1) *+3836+4322*
prepare for action (1) *+350+3836*

4020 ὅταν *hotan* (123)
when (95)
whenever (5)
after (4)
as soon as (2)
as soon as (2) *+2317*
while (2)
any time (1)
as soon as (1) *+2453*
at once (1) *+2317*
before (1)
once (1)
the moment (1)
until (1) *+1623+3590*
untranslated (6)

4021 ὅτε *hote* (102)
when (83)
after (6)
as (4)
once (2)
while (2)
after (1) *+5538*
as soon as (1)
before (1)
untranslated (2)

4022 ὅτι *hoti* (1298)
that (492)
because (205)
for (145)
how (6)
since (5)
this (3)
as (2)
by (2)
of (2)
about (1)
although (1)
as it is (1) *+1254*
but (1) *+1254*
here (1)
how (1) *+5515*
if (1)
in this (1)
is that why (1)
replied (1) *+646+3306*
the fact that (1)
this message (1)
though (1)
though actually (1)
to be (1)
what (1)
which (1)
why (1)
why (1) *+5515*
untranslated (417)

4023 οὗ *hou* (24)
where (19)
one in which (1)
the place where (1)
there (1)
to which (1)
wherever (1) *+1569*

4024 οὐ *ou* (1621)
not (1032)
no (142)
don't (55)
cannot (40) *+1538*
never (34) *+3590*
not (31) *+3590*
never (15)
nothing (15)
didn't (8)
certainly not (7) *+3590*
cannot (6)
refused (6) *+2527*
can't (5) *+1538*
doesn't (5)
isn't (5) *+1639*
neither (5)
nothing (5) *+4029*
only (5) *+1623+3590*
aren't (4)
haven't (4)
never (4) *+172+1650+3590+3836*
no one (4) *+4246*
unlawful (4) *+2003*
without (4)
don't (3) *+3590*
fail (3)
no (3) *+4246*
no more (3)
no one (3) *+4029*
none (3)
none[S] (3) *+4956*
nor (3)
nor (3) *+2779*
aren't (2) *+1639*
cannot (2) *+1639*
cease to be (2) *+1639*
couldn't (2) *+1538*
few (2) *+4498*
never (2) *+172+1650+3836*
no (2) *+3590*
no (2) *+4029*
no at all (2)
not at all (2) *+3590*
nothing (2) *+5515*
nothing (2) *+5516*
rather than (2) *+2779*
refused to repent (2) *+3566*
a long time (1) *+3900+5989*
against (1)
any more than (1) *+2777*
before very long (1) *+3552+4498*
blinded (1) *+1838*
but (1) *+2777*

cannot (1) *+2400*
cannot do (1) *+1538*
continued raging (1) *+2130+3900*
declined (1) *+2153*
does so[s] (1) *+2266*
ever no (1) *+3590*
extraordinary (1) *+3836+5593*
from (1)
getting nowhere (1) *+4029+6067*
great disturbance (1) *+3900+5431*
greatly (1) *+3585*
impossible (1) *+1543*
is it possible that (1)
isn't (1)
isn't at all (1) *+3590*
lack (1)
lawful for (1) *+2003*
lost connection with (1) *+3195*
many (1) *+3900*
neither (1) *+2779*
never (1) *+173+1650+3590+3836*
never (1) *+3590+4033*
never (1) *+3590+4537*
never (1) *+3590+4799*
never (1) *+4537*
never again (1) *+172+1650+3590+3836*
never again (1) *+2285*
never again (1) *+3590*
no longer (1) *+3590*
no place (1) *+4544*
nobody (1)
nobody (1) *+5516*
none (1) *+570*
none (1) *+4029*
none (1) *+4246*
not clear (1) *+1182*
not even (1) *+4028*
not one (1) *+3590*
nothing (1) *+3590+4029*
nothing (1) *+4246*
nothing (1) *+4246+4839*
nothing at all (1) *+4029*
nothing false (1) *+94*
one (1) *+257+1651*
only (1) *+2445+4498*
or (1) *+2779*
out of place (1) *+465*
refuse (1)
refuse (1) *+918*
refuse (1) *+2527*
refused (1) *+1312*
refused (1) *+4657*
refusing (1) *+2527*
separate from (1) *+3552*
sharp (1) *+3900*
shouldn't (1)
shouldn't (1) *+1256*
staying away from (1) *+1877+4344*
the law forbids (1) *+2003*
unable (1) *+1538*
unable (1) *+2710*
unaware (1) *+1182*
unequaled (1) *+1181+3888*
unequaled (1) *+1181+3888+5525*
unless (1) *+1623*
unlike (1) *+6055*
until judge (1) *+3212*
unusual (1) *+5593*
unwilling (1) *+2525*
unwilling (1) *+2527*
wasn't (1)
what is more (1) *+247+1254+2779+3667*
without (1) *+1666*
without (1) *+2779*
without sin (1) *+281*
yet (1) *+4037*
untranslated (39)

4025 οὐά *oua* (1)
so (1)

4026 οὐαί *ouai* (46)
woe (42)
how dreadful (3)
woes (1)

4027 οὐδαμῶς *oudamōs* (1)
by no means (1)

4028 οὐδέ *oude* (143)
or (35)
nor (28)
not (18)
not even (15)
neither (8)
no (7)
and (5)
and no (3)
don't (2)
even not (2)
not either (2)
and cannot (1) *+1538*
and not (1)
and nothing (1)
and nothing (1) *+5516*
but not (1)
cannot do (1) *+1538*
haven't (1)
never (1)
never again (1) *+2285*
no (1) *+4246*
not even (1) *+4024*
nothing (1) *+1651*
only (1) *+1651*
untranslated (5)

4029 οὐδείς *oudeis* (234)
no one (89)
nothing (37)
no (21)
anyone (7)
none (7)
not any (6)
not one (6)
nothing (5) *+4024*
any (3)
anything (3)
no one (3) *+4024*
not anything (3)
no (2) *+4024*
no one who (2)
not (2)
not anyone (2)
at all (1)
conscience is clear (1) *+5323*
discredited (1) *+1650+3357*
getting nowhere (1) *+4024+6067*
haven't anything (1)
men (1)
men[s] (1)
never (1)
no anything (1)
no at all (1)
no one (1) *+476*
no truth (1)
no way (1)
no whatever (1)
nobody (1)
none (1) *+4024*
nor anyone (1) *+1254*
not (1) *+3590*
not a thing (1)
not anyone's (1)
not in the least (1)
not saying a word (1) *+3306*
nothing (1) *+3364*
nothing (1) *+3590+4024*
nothing at all (1) *+4024*
one (1)
only to (1) *+1623+3590*
was getting nowhere (1) *+6067*
without (1)
untranslated (7)

4030 οὐδέποτε *oudepote* (16)
never (13)
nothing ever (2)
no one ever (1)

4031 οὐδέπω *oudepō* (4)
not yet (2)
ever (1)
still not (1)

4032 οὐθείς *outheis*
Variant; not used

4033 οὐκέτι *ouketi* (47)
no longer (27)
any more (3)
again (2)
no more (2)
cannot again (1)
ever again (1)
forgets (1) *+3648*
from then on (1)
never (1) *+3590+4024*
never again (1)
no (1)
no any more (1)
not (1)
not anymore (1)
not longer (1)
still no (1)
unable (1) *+2710*

4034 οὐκοῦν *oukoun* (1)
then (1)

4035 Οὐλαμμαούς *Oulammaous*
Variant; not used

4036 οὖν *oun* (497)
then (110)
therefore (71)
so (62)
now (12)
but (5)
therefore (5) *+726*
at this (4)
and (3)
finally (3)
when (3)
consequently (2) *+726*
meanwhile (2)
now then (2)
so then (2)
thus (2)
after all (1)
again (1)
as (1)
at that point (1)
because of (1)
conclude then (1)
finally (1) *+5538*
however (1) *+3525*
inasmuch as (1) *+2093+3525+4012*
still (1)
that (1)
this made (1)
too (1)
well then (1)
what (1) *+5515*
what shall we do (1) *+1639+5515*
yet (1)
untranslated (192)

4037 οὔπω *oupō* (27)
not yet (16)
still not (3)
still to come (2)
before (1)
ever (1)
still no (1)
up to that time not (1)
yet (1) *+4024*
yet not (1)

4038 οὐρά *oura* (5)
tails (4)
tail (1)

4039 οὐράνιος *ouranios* (8)
heavenly (7)
in heaven (1)

4040 οὐρανόθεν *ouranothen* (2)
from heaven (2)

4041 οὐρανός *ouranos* (274)
heaven (220)
sky (21)
heavens (15)
air (9)
heavenly (3)
skies (2)
heavenly (1) *+1666*
heavenly bodies (1) *+1539+3836*
heavenly things (1) *+1877+3836*
untranslated (1)

4042 Οὐρβανός *Ourbanos* (1)
Urbanus (1)

4043 Οὐρίας *Ourias* (1)
Uriah's (1)

4044 οὖς *ous* (36)
ears (21)
ear (13)
hearing (1)
listen carefully (1)
+1650+3836+5148+5148+5502

4045 οὐσία *ousia* (2)
estate (1)
wealth (1)

4046 οὔτε *oute* (87)
nor (30)
neither (19)
or (14)
not (7)
and (1)
and no (1)
and none (1) *+5516*
cannot (1) *+1538*
don't (1)
either (1)
never (1) *+4537*
never (1) *+4799*
no (1)
not any (1)
nothing (1)
nothing (1) *+5516*
or even (1)
refuses to (1)
untranslated (3)

4047 οὗτος *houtos* (1382)
this (620)
these (207)
he (41)
that (39)
him (25)
therefore (23) *+1328*
they (21)
such (15)
them (15)
it (12)
for this reason (9) *+1328*
she (9)
those (7)
later (6) *+3552*
this is how (6) *+1877*
that is why (5) *+1328*
the reason (5) *+1328*
what (5)
who (5)
Jesus[s] (4)
so (4) *+1328*
this is why (4) *+1328*
this very (4)
because (3) *+1328*
the latter[s] (3)
afterward (2) *+3552*
for that reason (2) *+4123*
for this reason (2) *+5920*
here (2) *+1877*
his (2)
so (2)
so then (2) *+1328*
some time ago (2) *+2465+3836+4574*
that was why (2) *+1328*
this one (2)
this[s] (2) *+2465+3836*
this[s] (2) *+3364+3836*
above all (1) *+4754*
am about to tell (1) *+3364+3836*
and what is more (1)
+247+1145+2779+4246+5250
Andrew[s] (1)
any such person (1)
appointed (1)
as (1)
as follows (1) *+2400+3836+5596*
as I did (1) *+899*
at other times (1) *+1254*
at this (1) *+3306*
at this point (1) *+1254*
both (1) *+2779*
by all this (1) *+1328*
come out of (1) *+2002*
everything (1)
finally (1) *+3552*
first of all (1) *+4754*
following (1)
for that very reason (1) *+1328*
for the express purpose (1) *+899+1650*
for this reason (1) *+505*
for this reason (1) *+1650*
for this very reason (1) *+899*
for this very reason (1) *+1328*
from then on (1) *+1666*
governing[s] (1) *+899*
happening[s] (1)
he's (1)
hear (1) *+201+1639*
here (1)
him[s] (1) *+476+1877+3836*
his master[s] (1)
how far will they go (1) *+1639+5515*
in other words (1) *+1639*
in the following (1)
it[s] (1) *+1155+3836*
it[s] (1) *+3836+4839*
John's disciples[s] (1)
Judas[s] (1)
just one (1) *+3668*
just then (1) *+2093*
last night (1) *+3816+3836*
like (1) *+3927*
men[s] (1)
of this (1) *+2401*
others (1)
pray[s] (1) *+4472*
present (1)
remember this (1) *+1254*
see here (1) *+2555*
service that perform (1) *+1355+3311+3836*
so doing[s] (1)
some (1)
some time later (1) *+3552*
sometimes (1) *+3525*
such sins[s] (1)
that is why (1) *+1650*
that is why (1) *+2093*
that would follow (1) *+3552*
the Bereans[s] (1)
the parts[s] (1) *+3836+5393*
the passage above (1)
the reason (1) *+1142+1650*
the reason (1) *+1650*
the reason (1) *+5920*
the same (1)
the very thing (1) *+899*
the women[s] (1)
their (1)
their work[s] (1)
there[s] (1) *+1877+3836+4484*
they the kind (1) *+1666*
this is how (1) *+1666*
this is the reason (1) *+1650*
this makes (1) *+1877*
this same (1)
this very reason (1) *+1650*
this way (1)
this[s] (1) *+1609+3364+3836*
this[s] (1) *+3836+4839*
thus (1) *+1877*
to (1) *+1650*
tonight (1) *+3816+3836*
what going on (1) *+323+5515*
what I meant (1) *+4309*
what Paul said[s] (1)
which (1)
who are here (1)
with that (1) *+3306*
with this (1) *+3306*
yet (1) *+3552*
untranslated (169)

4048 οὕτως *houtōs* (208)
so (63)
in the same way (11)
in this way (8)
like this (8)
this (8)
this is how (8)
this is what (6)
that is how (5)
like (3)
then (3)
true (3)
in the same way (2) *+2779*
in these words (2)
like that (2)
likewise (2)
that (2)
that way (2)
this way (2)
according to (1)
and (1)
as (1)
as is[s] (1)
as it has (1)
as you are (1)
at that (1)
by this kind (1)
does[s] (1) *+1181*
exactly (1)
how (1)
in such a way (1)
in this same way (1) *+2779*
in way (1)
it is the same (1) *+2779*
it was so (1) *+2400*
just as (1) *+2777*
just as (1) *+2848+4005+5573*
just as if (1)
likewise (1) *+2779*
matched (1) *+2749+2779*
so it is with (1) *+2779*
so much (1)
so then (1)
such things (1)
that is why (1)
the same (1)
the way (1)
this is (1)
this is the way (1)
this the way (1)
to (1)
to marry[s] (1) *+1181*
with such (1)
untranslated (34)

4049 οὐχί *ouchi* (54)
not (37)
no (7)

didn't (3)
aren't (2) *+1639*
fail (1) *+3590*
instead of (1) *+2779*
isn't (1) *+1639*
shouldn't (1)
won't (1)

4050 ὀφειλέτης *opheiletēs* (7)
obligated (2)
debtors (1)
guilty (1)
have an obligation (1) *+1639*
owe (1) *+1639*
owed (1)

4051 ὀφειλή *opheilē* (3)
debt (1)
duty (1)
owe (1)

4052 ὀφείλημα *opheilēma* (2)
debts (1)
obligation (1)

4053 ὀφείλω *opheilō* (35)
ought (13)
owe (4)
owed (3)
bound by his oath (2)
must (2)
should (2)
debt (1)
debt remain outstanding (1)
duty (1) *+4005+4472*
had (1)
has to (1)
have (1)
owes (1)
should have (1)
sins (1)

4054 ὄφελον *ophelon* (4)
I wish (2)
how I wish that (1)
I hope (1)

4055 ὄφελος *ophelos* (3)
good (2)
gained (1)

4056 ὀφθαλμοδουλία *ophthalmodoulia* (2)
eye is on (2)

4057 ὀφθαλμός *ophthalmos* (100)
eyes (59)
eye (25)
looked up (3) *+2048+3836*
sight (3)
envious (1) *+1639+3836+4505*
envy (1) *+4505*
eyes (1) *+2400*
look up (1) *+2048+3836*
looked (1) *+149+3836*
looked (1) *+2048+3836*
looking (1) *+2048+3836*
open eyes (1) *+2048*
they (1) *+899+3836*
untranslated (1)

4058 ὄφις *ophis* (14)
snakes (6)
serpent (3)
snake (3)
serpent's (1)
serpent's (1) *+899*

4059 ὀφρῦς *ophrys* (1)
brow (1)

4060 ὀχετός *ochetos*
Variant; not used

4061 ὀχλέω *ochleō* (1)
tormented (1)

4062 ὀχλοποιέω *ochlopoieō* (1)
formed a mob (1)

4063 ὄχλος *ochlos* (174)
crowd (106)
people (30)
crowds (25)
multitude (3)
mob (2)
crowd of people (1)
crowds of people (1)
group (1)
many people (1)
multitudes (1)
number (1)
numbers of people (1)
them[s] (1) *+3836*

4064 Ὀχοζίας *Ochozias*
Variant; not used

4065 ὀχύρωμα *ochyrōma* (1)
strongholds (1)

4066 ὀψάριον *opsarion* (5)
fish (4)
small fish (1)

4067 ὀψέ *opse* (3)
after the Sabbath (1) *+4879*
evening (1)
in the evening (1)

4068 ὀψία *opsia*
Variant; not used

4069 ὄψιμος *opsimos* (1)
spring (1)

4070 ὄψιος *opsios* (15)
evening (12)
late (1)
on the evening (1) *+1639*
that evening (1) *+1181*

4071 ὄψις *opsis* (3)
face (2)
appearances (1)

4072 ὀψώνιον *opsōnion* (4)
expense (1)
pay (1)
support (1)
wages (1)

4073 π *p*
Variant; not used

4074 παγιδεύω *pagideuō* (1)
trap (1)

4075 παγίς *pagis* (5)
trap (4)
snare (1)

4076 πάγος *pagos*
Variant; not used

4077 πάθημα *pathēma* (16)
sufferings (10)
passions (2)
suffering (2)
suffered (1)
what was suffered (1)

4078 παθητός *pathētos* (1)
suffer (1)

4079 πάθος *pathos* (3)
lust (2)
lusts (1)

4080 παιδαγωγός *paidagōgos* (3)
guardians (1)
put in charge to lead (1)
supervision (1)

4081 παιδάριον *paidarion* (1)
boy (1)

4082 παιδεία *paideia* (6)
discipline (3)
training (2)
disciplined (1)

4083 παιδευτής *paideutēs* (2)
disciplined (1)
instructor (1)

4084 παιδεύω *paideuō* (13)
disciplined (3)
beaten (1)
discipline (1)
disciplines (1)
educated (1)
instruct (1)
punish (1)
punished (1)
taught (1)
teaches (1)
trained (1)

4085 παιδιόθεν *paidiothen* (1)
childhood (1)

4086 παιδίον *paidion* (52)
child (21)
children (7)
little child (7)
little children (7)
child's (2)
dear children (2)
baby (1)
boy's (1)
children's (1)
friends (1)
her[s] (1) *+3836*
children (1)

4087 παιδίσκη *paidiskē* (13)
servant girl (4)
slave woman (4)
girl (1)
maidservants (1)
servant girls (1)
slave girl (1)
slave woman's (1)

4088 παιδόθεν *paidothen*
Variant; not used

4089 παίζω *paizō* (1)
indulge in pagan revelry (1)

4090 παῖς *pais* (24)
servant (12)
boy (4)
attendants (1)
boys (1)
child (1)
child's (1)
children (1)
menservants (1)
servants (1)
young man (1)

4091 παίω *paiō* (5)
hit (2)
struck (2)
strikes (1)

4092 Πακατιανός *Pakatianos*
Variant; not used

4093 πάλαι *palai* (7)
long ago (3)
all along (1)
already (1)
in the past (1)
past (1)

4094 παλαιός *palaios* (19)
old (19)

4095 παλαιότης *palaiotēs* (1)
old way (1)

4096 παλαιόω *palaioō* (4)
wear out (2)
made obsolete (1)
obsolete (1)

4097 πάλη *palē* (1)
struggle (1)

4098 παλιγγενεσία *palingenesia* (2)
rebirth (1)
renewal (1)

4099 πάλιν *palin* (141)
again (84)
back (9)
once more (7)
then after (3)
another (2)
second time (2) *+1311+1666*
then (2)
yet (2)
again (1) *+1309*
all over again (1) *+540*
also (1)
and as (1) *+2779*
another time (1)
elsewhere (1)
later (1)
now (1)
once again (1)
once more (1) *+1663*
once more (1) *+2779*
rebuild (1) *+3868*
repeat (1) *+3306*
return (1) *+1650+2262+3836*
returned to place (1) *+404*
second (1) *+1311*
then (1) *+2779*
untranslated (13)

4100 παλινγενεσία *palingenesia*
Variant; not used

4101 παμπληθεί *pamplēthei* (1)
with one voice (1)

4102 πάμπολυς *pampolys*
Variant; not used

4103 Παμφυλία *Pamphylia* (5)
Pamphylia (5)

4104 πανδοκεῖον *pandokeion*
Variant; not used

4105 πανδοκεύς *pandokeus*
Variant; not used

4106 πανδοχεῖον *pandocheion* (1)
inn (1)

4107 πανδοχεύς *pandocheus* (1)
innkeeper (1)

4108 πανήγυρις *panēgyris* (1)
joyful assembly (1)

4109 πανοικεί *panoikei* (1)
whole family (1)

4110 πανοπλία *panoplia* (3)
full armor (2)
armor (1)

4111 πανουργία *panourgia* (5)
craftiness (2)
cunning (1)
duplicity (1)
use deception (1) *+1877+4344*

4112 πανοῦργος *panourgos* (1)
crafty (1)

4113 πανπληθεί *panplēthei*
Variant; not used

4114 πανταχῇ *pantachē* (1)
everywhere (1)

4115 πανταχόθεν *pantachothen*
Variant; not used

4116 πανταχοῦ *pantachou* (7)
everywhere (6)
whole (1) *+3910*

4117 παντελής *pantelēs* (2)
at all (1) *+1650+3836*
completely (1) *+1650+3836*

4118 πάντῃ *pantē* (1)
every (1)

4119 πάντοθεν *pantothen* (3)
from everywhere (1)
gold-covered (1) *+4328+5992*
on every side (1)

4120 παντοκράτωρ *pantokratōr* (10)
Almighty (10)

4121 πάντοτε *pantote* (41)
always (35)
at all times (2)
any (1)
constantly (1)
forever (1)
from now on (1)

4122 πάντως *pantōs* (8)
at all (2)
surely (2)
by all possible means (1)
certainly (1)
must (1)
quite (1)

4123 παρά *para* (194)
from (47)
with (26)
by (11)
at (9)
than (9)
along (7)
beside (4)
contrary to (3)
to (3)
among (2)
before (2)
for that reason (2) *+4047*
more than (2)
of (2)
other than (2)
rather than (2)
above (1)
against (1)
any more (1) *+4498*
beyond (1)
conceited (1) *+4932+5861*
family (1) *+3836*
had[s] (1) *+3836*
him (1) *+4005*
in (1)
in God's sight (1) *+2536*
in God's sight (1) *+2536+3836*
in presence (1)
in the presence (1)
me say (1) *+1609*
minus (1)
near (1)
on (1)
out (1)
past (1)
presence (1)
they (1) *+899*
under (1) *+3836+4546*
unnatural ones (1) *+3836+5882*
where (1) *+4005*
you have (1) *+5148*
untranslated (36)

4124 παραβαίνω *parabainō* (3)
break (2)
left (1)

4125 παραβάλλω *paraballō* (1)
crossed over (1)

4126 παράβασις *parabasis* (7)
breaking (1)
breaking a command (1)
sinner (1)
sins (1)
transgression (1)
transgressions (1)
violation (1)

4127 παραβάτης *parabatēs* (5)
lawbreaker (2) *+3795*
break (1) *+1639*
lawbreaker (1)
lawbreakers (1)

4128 παραβιάζομαι *parabiazomai* (2)
persuaded (1)
urged strongly (1)

4129 παραβολεύομαι *paraboleuomai* (1)
risking (1)

4130 παραβολή *parabolē* (50)
parable (30)
parables (15)
lesson (2)
figuratively speaking (1) *+1877*
illustration (1)
proverb (1)

4131 παραβουλεύομαι *parabouleuomai*
Variant; not used

4132 παραγγελία *parangelia* (5)
command (1)
gave strict orders (1) *+4133*
instruction (1)
instructions (1)
orders (1)

4133 παραγγέλλω *parangellō* (31)
command (7)
commanded (4)
ordered (4)
told (3)
instructions (2)
cautioned (1)
charge (1)
commands (1)
directives (1)
gave command (1)
gave rule (1)
gave strict orders (1) *+4132*
give instructions (1)
give this command (1)
required (1)
strictly warned (1) *+2203*

4134 παραγίνομαι *paraginomai* (37)
came (14)
arrived (4)
arriving (4)
appeared (3)
come (3)
arrive (1)
came back (1)
came to support (1)
come from (1)
coming (1)
get here (1)
present (1)
went on (1) *+1451*
untranslated (1)

4135 παράγω *paragō* (10)
went on (2)
going by (1)
pass away (1)
passing (1)
passing away (1)
passing by (1)
walked along (1)
walked beside (1)
went along (1)

4136 παραδειγματίζω *paradeigmatizō* (1)
subjecting to public disgrace (1)

4137 παράδεισος *paradeisos* (3)
paradise (3)

4138 παραδέχομαι *paradechomai* (6)
accept (3)
accepts (1)

entertain (1)
welcomed (1)

4139 παραδιατριβή *paradiatribē*
Variant; not used

4140 παραδίδωμι *paradidōmi* (119)
handed over (19)
betray (16)
betrayed (14)
hand over (9)
entrusted (6)
betrayer (4)
gave over (4)
passed on (4)
betrays (3)
committed (3)
gave up (3)
handed down (3)
arrest (2)
delivered (2)
gave (2)
given over (2)
put in prison (2)
turn over (2)
arrested (1)
betray (1) *+1639+3836*
betraying (1)
commended (1)
deliver (1)
delivered over (1)
given (1)
hand over to (1) *+1650+5931*
handing over (1)
hands over (1)
put (1)
putting into (1)
ripe (1)
risked (1)
surrender (1)
surrendered (1)
throwing (1)
traitor (1)
turned over (1)

4141 παράδοξος *paradoxos* (1)
remarkable (1)

4142 παράδοσις *paradosis* (13)
tradition (7)
traditions (3)
passed on (1)
teaching (1)
teachings (1)

4143 παραζηλόω *parazēloō* (4)
make envious (2)
arouse jealousy (1)
arouse to envy (1)

4144 παραθαλάσσιος *parathalassios* (1)
by the lake (1)

4145 παραθεωρέω *paratheōreō* (1)
overlooked (1)

4146 παραθήκη *parathēkē* (3)
deposit entrusted to (1)
have entrusted to (1)
what has been entrusted to care (1)

4147 παραινέω *paraineō* (2)
urge (1)
warned (1)

4148 παραιτέομαι *paraiteomai* (12)
excuse (2) *+2400*
nothing to do with (2)
refuse (2)
begged (1)
don't have anything to do with (1)
make excuses (1)
not put on such a list (1)
refused (1)
requested (1)

4149 παρακαθέζομαι *parakathezomai* (1)
sat (1)

4150 παρακαθίζω *parakathizō*
Variant; not used

4151 παρακαλέω *parakaleō* (109)
urge (20)
encourage (13)
begged (12)
pleaded with (7)
comforted (6)
encouraged (6)
urged (6)
encouraging (5)
appeal to (4)
invited (4)
plead with (3)
begging (2)
comfort (2)
comforts (2)
answer kindly (1)
appeal (1)
appease (1)
asked (1)
asking for help (1)
begged (1) *+3306*
call on (1)
exhort (1)
exhorted (1)
given (1)
listen to appeal (1)
making appeal (1)
pleading with (1)
received (1)
request that (1)
speaking encouragement to (1)
urgently requested (1) *+160*

4152 παρακαλύπτω *parakalyptō* (1)
hidden (1)

4153 παρακαταθήκη *parakatathēkē*
Variant; not used

4154 παράκειμαι *parakeimai* (2)
have (1)
right there (1)

4155 παράκλησις *paraklēsis* (29)
encouragement (10)
comfort (8)
appeal (2)
be encouraged (1) *+2400*
consolation (1)
encourage (1)
encouraged (1)
encouraging message (1)
exhortation (1)
greatly encouraged (1) *+4444*
preaching (1)
urgently (1) *+3552+4498*

4156 παράκλητος *paraklētos* (5)
counselor (4)
one who speaks in defense (1)

4157 παρακοή *parakoē* (3)
disobedience (2)
act of disobedience (1)

4158 παρακολουθέω *parakoloutheō* (4)
accompany (1)
followed (1)
investigated (1)
know all about (1)

4159 παρακούω *parakouō* (3)
refuses to listen (2)
ignoring (1)

4160 παρακύπτω *parakyptō* (5)
bending over (1)
bent over (1)
bent over to look (1)
look (1)
looks intently (1)

4161 παραλαμβάνω *paralambanō* (49)
took (15)
received (7)
take (6)
taken (4)
receive (2)
takes (2)
took along (2)
took aside (2)
took with (2)
accepted (1)
instructed (1)
received from (1)
receiving (1)
took (1) *+72*
took charge of (1)
traditions (1)

4162 παραλέγομαι *paralegomai* (2)
moved along (1)
sailed (1)

4163 παράλιος *paralios* (1)
coast (1)

4164 παραλλαγή *parallagē* (1)
change (1) *+1913*

4165 παραλογίζομαι *paralogizomai* (2)
deceive (2)

4166 παραλυτικός *paralytikos* (10)
paralytic (7)
paralyzed (3)

4167 παράλυτος *paralytos*
Variant; not used

4168 παραλύω *paralyō* (5)
paralytic (2)
paralytics (1)
paralyzed (1)
weak (1)

4169 παραμένω *paramenō* (4)
continue with (1)
continues (1)
continuing (1)
stay awhile (1)

4170 παραμυθέομαι *paramytheomai* (4)
comforting (2)
comfort (1)
encourage (1)

4171 παραμυθία *paramythia* (1)
comfort (1)

4172 παραμύθιον *paramythion* (1)
comfort (1)

4173 παράνοια *paranoia*
Variant; not used

4174 παρανομέω *paranomeō* (1)
violate the law (1)

4175 παρανομία *paranomia* (1)
wrongdoing (1)

4176 παραπικραίνω *parapikrainō* (1)
rebelled (1)

4177 παραπικρασμός *parapikrasmos* (2)
rebellion (2)

4178 παραπίπτω *parapiptō* (1)
fall away (1)

4179 παραπλέω *parapleō* (1)
sail past (1)

4180 παραπλήσιος *paraplēsios* (1)
almost (1)

4181 παραπλησίως *paraplēsiōs* (1)
too (1)

4182 παραπορεύομαι *paraporeuomai* (5)
passed by (2)
going (1)
passed (1)
went along (1)

4183 παράπτωμα *paraptōma* (20)
sins (8)
trespass (5)
transgression (2)
transgressions (2)
sin (1)
sin against (1)
trespasses (1)

4184 παραρρέω *pararreō* (1)
drift away (1)

4185 παράσημος *parasēmos* (1)
figurehead (1)

4186 παρασκευάζω *paraskeuazō* (4)
ready (2)
get ready (1)
prepared (1)

4187 παρασκευή *paraskeuē* (6)
day of preparation (3)
preparation day (2)
preparation (1)

4188 παραστάτις *parastatis*
Variant; not used

4189 παρατείνω *parateinō* (1)
kept on (1)

4190 παρατηρέω *paratēreō* (6)
watched closely (2)
carefully watched (1)
keeping a close watch (1)
kept close watch on (1)
observing (1)

4191 παρατήρησις *paratērēsis* (1)
careful observation (1)

4192 παρατίθημι *paratithēmi* (19)
set before (5)
commit (3)
told (2) *+3306*
committed (1)
did so[s] (1)
distribute (1)
entrust (1)
entrusted with (1)
give (1)
proving (1)
put before (1)
set a meal before (1) *+5544*

4193 παρατυγχάνω *paratynchanō* (1)
happened to be there (1)

4194 παραυτίκα *parautika* (1)
momentary (1)

4195 παραφέρω *parapherō* (4)
take (2)
blown along (1)
carried away (1)

4196 παραφρονέω *paraphroneō* (1)
out of mind (1)

4197 παραφρονία *paraphronia* (1)
madness (1)

4198 παραφροσύνη *paraphrosynē*
Variant; not used

4199 παραχειμάζω *paracheimazō* (4)
winter (2)
spend the winter (1)
wintered (1)

4200 παραχειμασία *paracheimasia* (1)
winter in (1)

4201 παραχράομαι *parachraomai*
Variant; not used

4202 παραχρῆμα *parachrēma* (18)
immediately (9)
at once (4)
instantly (2)
at that moment (1)
just (1)
so quickly (1)

4203 πάρδαλις *pardalis* (1)
leopard (1)

4204 παρεδρεύω *paredreuō* (1)
serve at (1)

4205 πάρειμι *pareimi* (25)
come (7)
have (2)
am (1)
am with (1)
are here (1)
are present (1)
be (1)
came for (1)
here (1)
is here (1)
leaving undone (1)
now have (1)
present (1)
sought an audience (1)
time (1)
was (1)
was with (1)
were present (1)

4206 παρεισάγω *pareisagō* (1)
secretly introduce (1)

4207 παρείσακτος *pareisaktos* (1)
infiltrated ranks (1) *+4209*

4208 παρεισδύω *pareisdyō* (1)
secretly slipped in (1)

4209 παρεισέρχομαι *pareiserchomai* (2)
added (1)
infiltrated ranks (1) *+4207*

4210 παρεισφέρω *pareispherō* (1)
make (1)

4211 παρεκτός *parektos* (3)
except for (2)
besides everything else (1) *+3836+6006*

4212 παρεμβάλλω *paremballō* (1)
build (1)

4213 παρεμβολή *parembolē* (10)
barracks (6)
camp (3)
armies (1)

4214 παρενοχλέω *parenochleō* (1)
make it difficult for (1)

4215 παρεπίδημος *parepidēmos* (3)
strangers (3)

4216 παρέρχομαι *parerchomai* (29)
pass away (10)
disappear (4)
pass (2)
after (1)
be taken (1)
be taken away (1)
come (1)
come along (1)
disobeyed (1)
getting (1)
gone (1)
neglect (1)
pass by (1)
passed by (1)
passing by (1)
past (1)

4217 πάρεσις *paresis* (1)
left unpunished (1)

4218 παρέχω *parechō* (16)
bothering (3) *+3160*
became (1)
bother (1) *+3160*
brought in (1)
cause (1)
do (1)
earned (1)
given proof (1) *+4411*
promote (1)
provide with (1)
provides with (1)
set (1)
showed (1)
turn (1)

4219 παρηγορία *parēgoria* (1)
comfort (1)

4220 παρθενία *parthenia* (1)
untranslated (1)

4221 παρθένος *parthenos* (15)
virgin (8)
virgins (3)
pure (1)
unmarried (1)
virgin's (1)
untranslated (1)

4222 Πάρθοι *Parthoi* (1)
Parthians (1)

4223 παρίημι *pariēmi* (1)
feeble (1)

4224 παριστάνω *paristanō*
Variant; not used

4225 παρίστημι *paristēmi* (41)
present (7)
offer (6)
standing near (5)
stood beside (2)
bring near (1)
come (1)
give (1)
handed over (1)
nearby (1)
presented (1)
prove (1)
provide (1)
put at disposal (1)
showed (1)
stand (1)
stand before (1)
stand trial before (1)
standing around (1)
standing by (1)
standing nearby (1)
stands (1)
stood around (1)
stood at side (1)
stood there (1)
take stand (1)

4226 Παρμενᾶς *Parmenas* (1)
Parmenas (1)

4227 πάροδος *parodos* (1)
passing (1)

4228 παροικέω *paroikeō* (2)
made home (1)
visitor to (1)

4229 παροικία *paroikia* (2)
stay (1)
strangers (1)

4230 πάροικος *paroikos* (4)
aliens (2)
settled as foreigner (1)
strangers (1)

4231 παροιμία *paroimia* (5)
figuratively (1) *+1877*
figure of speech (1)
figures of speech (1)
proverbs (1)
this kind of[s] (1) *+1877*

4232 πάροινος *paroinos* (2)

4233 παροίχομαι *paroichomai* (1)
past (1) *+1155*

4234 παρομοιάζω *paromoiazō* (1)
like (1)

4235 παρόμοιος *paromoios* (1)
like (1)

4236 παροξύνω *paroxynō* (2)
easily angered (1)
greatly distressed (1)

4237 παροξυσμός *paroxysmos* (2)
sharp disagreement (1)
spur on (1) *+1650*

4238 παροράω *paroraō*
Variant; not used

4239 παροργίζω *parorgizō* (2)
exasperate (1)
make angry (1)

4240 παροργισμός *parorgismos* (1)
angry (1)

4241 παροτρύνω *parotrynō* (1)
incited (1)

4242 παρουσία *parousia* (24)
coming (17)
comes (3)
arrived (1) *+3836*
being (1)
in person (1) *+3836+3836+5393*
presence (1)

4243 παροψίς *paropsis* (2)
dish (2)

4244 παρρησία *parrēsia* (31)
confidence (7)
plainly (4)
courage (3)
publicly (3)
a public figure (1) *+1877*
assurance (1)
be bold (1) *+2400+4498*
bold (1) *+5968*
boldly (1)
boldly (1) *+3552*
boldness (1)
clearly (1) *+1877*
confident (1) *+2400*
confidently (1) *+3552*
fearlessly (1)
freedom (1)
openly (1)
public (1)

4245 παρρησιάζομαι *parrēsiazomai* (9)
speaking boldly (2)
boldly (1)
dared (1)
fearlessly (1)
freely (1)
preached fearlessly (1)
speak boldly (1)
spoke boldly (1)

4246 πᾶς *pas* (1240)
all (666)
every (127)
everything (108)
everyone (92)
whole (24)
any (17)
anyone (15)
all things (9) *+3836*
everything (8) *+3836*
full (8)
everyone (6) *+476*
always (5)
anything (4)
everybody (4)
everything (4) *+4012*
great (4)
no one (4) *+4024*
one (4) *+4922*
all (3) *+4012*
always (3) *+1328*
everywhere (3) *+1877+5536*
no (3) *+4024*
all over (2)
continually (2) *+1328*
entire (2)
every (2) *+2848*
everybody (2) *+476*
everyone (2) *+6034*
everyone's (2)
publicly (2) *+1967*
regularly (2) *+1328*
very (2)
whatever (2)
whatever (2) *+4012*
whoever (2) *+3836*
absolute (1)
all (1) *+476*
altogether (1) *+3836*
always (1) *+1877+2789*
always (1) *+2465+3836*
and what is more (1)
+247+1145+2779+4047+5250
any and every (1)
anyone (1) *+1569+6034*
anything (1) *+1569+4005+4547*
complete (1)
complete (1) *+1877*
complete (1) *+4444*
completely (1)
day after day (1) *+2465*
day by day (1) *+2465+2848*
depth (1)
everybody's (1)
everyone (1) *+323*
everyone (1) *+1667*
everyone (1) *+2848*
everyone (1) *+3836*
everything (1) *+323+4012*
everything (1) *+1569+4012*
everywhere (1) *+5536*
finally (1) *+5731*
forever (1) *+1328*
forevermore (1) *+172+1650+3836*
free and belong to no man (1) *+1666+1801*
from one synagogue to another (1)
+2848+5252
fully (1)
great endurance (1) *+5705*
great humility (1) *+5425*
great patience (1) *+3429*
in all (1)
in everything (1)
night (1) *+1328+3816*
no (1) *+4028*
none (1)
none (1) *+4024*
nothing (1) *+4024*
nothing (1) *+4024+4839*
one (1)
perfectly (1) *+1877*
profound (1)
proper (1)
pure (1)
securely (1) *+854+1877*
strict (1)
sufficient (1)
the whole (1)
the world[s] (1)
this[s] (1) *+899+3836*
throughout (1) *+1650*
throughout (1) *+2093*
traveled about the country (1) *+1328+1451*
whatever (1) *+3836*
whoever (1) *+4015*
whole universe (1)
whole world (1)
without (1) *+6006*
untranslated (33)

4247 πάσχα *pascha* (29)
Passover (26)
Passover lamb (3)

4248 πάσχω *paschō* (41)
suffer (21)
suffered (14)
suffering (5)
suffers (1)

4249 Πάταρα *Patara* (1)
Patara (1)

4250 πατάσσω *patassō* (10)
strike (4)
struck (3)
killing (1)
strike down (1)
struck down (1)

4251 πατέω *pateō* (5)
trample (1)
trample on (1)
trampled (1)
trampled on (1)
treads (1)

4252 πατήρ *patēr* (413)
father (335)
fathers (35)
father's (21)
forefathers (13)
patriarchs (4)
ancestor (2)
father who (1)
parents (1)
them[s] (1) *+1609+3836*

4253 Πάτμος *Patmos* (1)
Patmos (1)

4254 πατραλῴας *patralōas*
Variant; not used

4255 πατριά *patria* (3)
family (1)
line (1)
peoples (1)

4256 πατριάρχης *patriarchēs* (4)
patriarch (2)
patriarchs (2)

4257 πατρικός *patrikos* (1)
fathers (1)

4258 πατρίς *patris* (8)
hometown (6)
country (1)
country of their own (1)

4259 Πατροβᾶς *Patrobas* (1)
Patrobas (1)

4260 πατρολῴας *patrolōas* (1)
kill their fathers (1)

4261 πατροπαράδοτος *patroparadotos* (1)
handed down from forefathers (1)

4262 πατρῷος *patrōos* (3)
fathers (2)
ancestors (1)

4263 Παῦλος *Paulos* (158)
Paul (150)
Paul's (6)
him[s] (1) *+3836*
Paulus (1)

4264 παύω *pauō* (15)
stopped (6)
finished (2)
done with (1)
ended (1)
keep (1)
stilled (1)

stop (1)
stops (1)
subsided (1)

4265 Πάφος *Paphos* (2)
Paphos (2)

4266 παχύνω *pachynō* (2)
calloused (2)

4267 πέδη *pedē* (3)
foot (2)
irons on feet (1)

4268 πεδινός *pedinos* (1)
level (1)

4269 πεζεύω *pezeuō* (1)
on foot (1)

4270 πεζῇ *pezē* (2)
on foot (2)

4271 πεζός *pezos*
Variant; not used

4272 πειθαρχέω *peitharcheō* (4)
obey (2)
obedient (1)
taken advice (1)

4273 πειθός *peithos* (1)
persuasive (1)

4274 πειθώ *peithō*
Variant; not used

4275 πείθω *peithō* (52)
convinced (7)
confident (5)
persuaded (5)
confidence (2)
confident of (2)
followers (2)
persuade (2)
put confidence (2)
convince (1)
convinced of (1)
convinced that (1)
dissuaded (1)
encouraged (1)
follow (1)
fully convinced (1) *+2779+3857*
give in (1)
listening to (1)
make obey (1)
obey (1)
obeying (1)
persuasively (1)
put trust (1) *+1639*
rely (1) *+1639*
satisfy (1)
secured the support (1)
set at rest (1)
sure (1)
trusted (1)
trusts (1)
trying to persuade (1)
trying to win the approval of (1)
urged (1)
won over (1)

4276 Πειλᾶτος *Peilatos*
Variant; not used

4277 πεινάω *peinaō* (23)
hungry (17)
go hungry (3)
hunger (3)

4278 πεῖρα *peira* (2)
faced (1) *+3284*
tried to do (1) *+3284*

4279 πειράζω *peirazō* (39)
tempted (11)
tested (8)
test (7)
tried (3)
tempt (2)
tempter (2)
trying to trap (2)
did[s] (1)
examine (1)
tempting (1)
trap (1)

4280 πειρασμός *peirasmos* (20)
temptation (8)
trial (4)
trials (4)
testing (2)
tempting (1)
when are tempted (1) *+3836+5250*

4281 πειράω *peiraō* (1)
tried (1)

4282 πεισμονή *peismonē* (1)
persuasion (1)

4283 πέλαγος *pelagos* (2)
depths (1)
open sea (1)

4284 πελεκίζω *pelekizō* (1)
beheaded (1)

4285 πεμπταῖος *pemptaios*
Variant; not used

4286 πέμπτος *pemptos* (4)
fifth (4)

4287 πέμπω *pempō* (79)
sent (44)
send (20)
sending (7)
sent (2) *+4707*
take (2)
provide (1)
send for (1)
sends (1)
untranslated (1)

4288 πένης *penēs* (1)
poor (1)

4289 πενθερά *penthera* (6)
mother-in-law (6)

4290 πενθερός *pentheros* (1)
father-in-law (1)

4291 πενθέω *pentheō* (10)
mourn (6)
mourning (2)
filled with grief (1)
grieved over (1)

4292 πένθος *penthos* (5)
mourning (3)
grief (1)
mourn (1) *+3972*

4293 πενιχρός *penichros* (1)
poor (1)

4294 πεντάκις *pentakis* (1)
five times (1)

4295 πεντακισχίλιοι *pentakischilioi* (6)
five thousand (6)

4296 πεντακόσιοι *pentakosioi* (2)
five hundred (2)

4297 πέντε *pente* (38)
five (35)
fifty thousand (1) *+3689*
seventy-five (1) *+1573*
three or three and a half miles (1) *+1633+2445+5084+5558*

4298 πεντεκαιδέκατος *pentekaidekatos* (1)
fifteenth (1)

4299 πεντήκοντα *pentēkonta* (7)
fifty (3)
153 (1) *+1669+5552*
450 (1) *+2779+5484*
fifties (1)
four hundred (1)

4300 πεντηκοστή *pentēkostē* (3)
Pentecost (3)

4301 πεποίθησις *pepoithēsis* (6)
confidence (4)
confident of (1)
untranslated (1)

4302 περ *per*
Variant; not used

4303 Πέραια *Peraia*
Variant; not used

4304 περαιτέρω *peraiterō* (1)
further (1)

4305 πέραν *peran* (22)
other side (7)
across (5)
on the other side (3)
across (1) *+1650+3836*
along (1)
crossed (1)
on the opposite shore (1)
regions across (1)
to the far shore (1)
to other side (1)

4306 πέρας *peras* (4)
ends (3)
end (1)

4307 Πέργαμος *Pergamos* (2)
Pergamum (2)

4308 Πέργη *Pergē* (3)
Perga (3)

4309 περί *peri* (332)
about (132)
for (52)
of (17)
around (11)
concerning (11)
in regard to (5)
on (5)
because (4)
in (4)
by (3)
to (3)
with (3)
against (2)
as (2)
from (2)
meant (2) *+3306*
on behalf (2)
sin offerings (2) *+281*
about (1) *+4005*
about (1) *+6059*
as for (1)
as to (1)
at (1)
besiege with questions (1) *+694+4498*
companions (1) *+3836*
concerned (1)
consider (1) *+3972*
go with (1)
how (1) *+3836*
in case (1)
in favor (1)
in that case (1) *+4005*
interest in (1)
my (1) *+1831+3836*
nearby (1) *+3836+5536*
over (1)
over the matter of (1)
regarding (1)
see about (1)
surrounding (1) *+899*
to do with (1)
to help (1)

what I meant (1) *+4047*
untranslated (45)

4310 περιάγω *periagō* (6)
groped about (1)
take along (1)
travel over (1)
went (1)
went around (1)
went through (1)

4311 περιαιρέω *periaireō* (5)
cutting loose (1)
gave up (1)
set sail (1)
take away (1)
taken away (1)

4312 περιάπτω *periaptō* (1)
kindled (1)

4313 περιαστράπτω *periastraptō* (2)
flashed around (2)

4314 περιβάλλω *periballō* (23)
dressed in (4)
wear (3)
clothed (2)
clothed in (2)
dressed (2)
clothe (2)
dressed (2) *+2668*
dressing in (1)
in (1)
robed in (1)
wearing (1)
wearing nothing (1) *+1218+2093*
wrap around (1)

4315 περιβλέπω *periblepō* (7)
looked around at (3)
looked around (2)
looked at (1)
looking around (1)

4316 περιβόλαιον *peribolaion* (2)
covering (1)
robe (1)

4317 περιδέω *perideō* (1)
around (1)

4318 περιεργάζομαι *periergazomai* (1)
busybodies (1)

4319 περίεργος *periergos* (2)
busybodies (1)
sorcery (1)

4320 περιέρχομαι *perierchomai* (3)
going about (1)
went about (1)
went around (1)

4321 περιέχω *periechō* (2)
astonished (1) *+2502*
says (1)

4322 περιζώννυμι *perizōnnymi* (6)
buckled around waist (1)
dress to serve (1)
dressed ready for service (1) *+3836+4019*
get ready (1)
wore (1)
untranslated (1)

4323 περιζωννύω *perizōnnyō*
Variant; not used

4324 περίθεσις *perithesis* (1)
wearing (1)

4325 περιΐστημι *periistēmi* (4)
avoid (2)
standing here (1)
stood around (1)

4326 περικάθαρμα *perikatharma* (1)
scum (1)

4327 περικαθίζω *perikathizō*
Variant; not used

4328 περικαλύπτω *perikalyptō* (3)
blindfolded (1)
blindfolded (1) *+3836+4725*
gold-covered (1) *+4119+5992*

4329 περίκειμαι *perikeimai* (5)
tied around (2)
bound (1)
subject to (1)
surrounded (1)

4330 περικεφαλαία *perikephalaia* (2)
helmet (2)

4331 περικρατής *perikratēs* (1)
secure (1)

4332 περικρύβω *perikrybō* (1)
in seclusion (1)

4333 περικυκλόω *perikykloō* (1)
encircle (1)

4334 περιλάμπω *perilampō* (2)
blazing around (1)
shone around (1)

4335 περιλείπομαι *perileipomai* (2)
left (2)

4336 περιλείχω *perileichō*
Variant; not used

4337 περίλυπος *perilypos* (4)
overwhelmed with sorrow (2)
greatly distressed (1)
very sad (1)

4338 περιμένω *perimenō* (1)
wait for (1)

4339 πέριξ *perix* (1)
around (1)

4340 περιοικέω *perioikeō* (1)
neighbors (1)

4341 περίοικος *perioikos* (1)
neighbors (1)

4342 περιούσιος *periousios* (1)
his very own (1)

4343 περιοχή *periochē* (1)
passage (1)

4344 περιπατέω *peripateō* (95)
walk (25)
live (17)
walking (14)
walked (4)
walks (4)
live a life (3)
act (2)
acting (2)
walk around (2)
behave (1)
daily life (1)
did[s] (1)
do (1)
eat (1)
followed (1) *+3552*
go (1)
idle (1) *+865*
live lives (1)
living (1)
moved about (1)
passing by (1)
prowls around (1)
retain the place in life (1)
staying away from (1) *+1877+4024*
use deception (1) *+1877+4111*
walk along (1)
walking around (1)
walks around (1)
went (1)
went around (1)
untranslated (1)

4345 περιπείρω *peripeirō* (1)
pierced (1)

4346 περιπίπτω *peripiptō* (3)
face (1)
fell into the hands of (1)
struck (1)

4347 περιποιέω *peripoieō* (3)
bought (1)
gain (1)
keep (1)

4348 περιποίησις *peripoiēsis* (5)
belonging (1) *+1650*
possession (1)
receive (1)
saved (1) *+1650+6034*
share (1)

4349 περιραίνω *perirainō*
Variant; not used

4350 περιραντίζω *perirantizō*
Variant; not used

4351 περιρήγνυμι *perirēgnymi* (1)
stripped (1) *+2668+3836*

4352 περισπάω *perispaō* (1)
distracted (1)

4353 περισσεία *perisseia* (4)
abundant provision (1)
greatly (1) *+1650*
overflowing (1)
prevalent (1)

4354 περίσσευμα *perisseuma* (5)
overflow (2)
plenty (2)
left over (1)

4355 περισσεύω *perisseuō* (39)
left over (5)
overflow (5)
excel (3)
abound (2)
have an abundance (2)
overflowing (2)
wealth (2)
abundance (1)
better (1)
do so more and more (1) *+3437*
do this more and more (1) *+3437*
enhances (1)
flow over (1)
give fully (1)
grew (1)
have to spare (1)
is (1)
lavished (1)
living in plenty (1)
make abound (1)
more (1)
overflows (1)
plenty (1)
surpasses (1) *+4498*
welled up (1)

4356 περισσός *perissos* (6)
advantage (1)
beyond (1)
completely (1) *+1666+3336*
more (1)
no need (1)
to the full (1)

4357 περισσότερον *perissoteron*
Variant; not used

4358 περισσότερος *perissoteros* (16)
more (2)
more than (2)
most severely (2)
special (2)

excessive (1)
freely (1)
greater (1)
harder than (1)
more (1) *+3437*
more important than (1)
much more (1)
very (1)

4359 περισσοτέρως *perissoterōs* (12)
more (2)
delighted (1) *+5897*
depth (1)
especially (1)
every (1)
extremely (1)
greater (1)
more careful (1)
more frequently (1)
much harder (1)
particularly (1)

4360 περισσῶς *perissōs* (4)
all the louder (2)
even more (1)
obsession (1) *+1841*

4361 περιστερά *peristera* (10)
doves (5)
dove (4)
pigeons (1)

4362 περιτέμνω *peritemnō* (17)
circumcised (12)
circumcise (4)
circumcised (1) *+3284*

4363 περιτίθημι *peritithēmi* (8)
put on (4)
put around (2)
set on (1)
treat with (1)

4364 περιτομή *peritomē* (36)
circumcision (18)
circumcised (6)
Jews (4)
circumcised (3) *+1666*
after he was circumcised (1) *+1639+1877*
circumcised (1) *+3284*
Jews (1) *+1666*
you (1) *+3836+5148*
untranslated (1)

4365 περιτρέπω *peritrepō* (1)
driving (1)

4366 περιτρέχω *peritrechō* (1)
ran throughout (1)

4367 περιφέρω *peripherō* (3)
blown here and there (1)
carried (1)
carry around (1)

4368 περιφρονέω *periphroneō* (1)
despise (1)

4369 περίχωρος *perichōros* (9)
region (3)
surrounding country (3)
country around (1)
countryside (1)
surrounding (1)

4370 περίψημα *peripsēma* (1)
refuse (1)

4371 περπερεύομαι *perpereuomai* (1)
boast (1)

4372 Περσίς *Persis* (1)
Persis (1)

4373 πέρυσι *perysi* (2)
last year (2)

4374 πετεινόν *peteinon* (14)
birds (14)

4375 πέτομαι *petomai* (5)
flying (4)
fly (1)

4376 πέτρα *petra* (15)
rock (12)
rocks (3)

4377 Πέτρος *Petros* (155)
Peter (150)
Peter's (5)

4378 πετρώδης *petrōdēs* (4)
rocky places (4)

4379 πήγανον *pēganon* (1)
rue (1)

4380 πηγή *pēgē* (11)
springs (5)
spring (2)
well (2)
bleeding (1) *+135+3836*
untranslated (1)

4381 πήγνυμι *pēgnymi* (1)
set up (1)

4382 πηδάλιον *pēdalion* (2)
rudder (1)
rudders (1)

4383 πηλίκος *pēlikos* (2)
how great (1)
what large (1)

4384 πηλός *pēlos* (6)
mud (4)
it[s] (1) *+3836*
untranslated (1)

4385 πήρα *pēra* (6)
bag (6)

4386 πηρόω *pēroō*
Variant; not used

4387 πήρωσις *pērōsis*
Variant; not used

4388 πῆχυς *pēchys* (4)
hour (2)
cubits (1)
hundred yards (1) *+1357*

4389 πιάζω *piazō* (12)
arrest (3)
seize (3)
caught (2)
arresting (1)
captured (1)
seized (1)
taking (1)

4390 πιέζω *piezō* (1)
pressed down (1)

4391 πιθανολογία *pithanologia* (1)
fine-sounding arguments (1)

4392 πιθός *pithos*
Variant; not used

4393 πικραίνω *pikrainō* (4)
be harsh (1)
bitter (1)
turn sour (1)
turned sour (1)

4394 πικρία *pikria* (4)
bitterness (2)
bitter (1)
bitterness (1) *+5958*

4395 πικρός *pikros* (2)
bitter (1)
salt water (1)

4396 πικρῶς *pikrōs* (2)
bitterly (2)

4397 Πιλᾶτος *Pilatos* (55)
Pilate (54)
Pilate's (1)

4398 πίμπλημι *pimplēmi* (24)
filled (15)
completed (2)
came (1)
fulfillment (1)
furious (1) *+486*
furious (1) *+2596*
time (1)
uproar (1) *+5180*
untranslated (1)

4399 πίμπρημι *pimprēmi* (1)
swell up (1)

4400 πινακίδιον *pinakidion* (1)
writing tablet (1)

4401 πινακίς *pinakis*
Variant; not used

4402 πίναξ *pinax* (5)
platter (4)
dish (1)

4403 πίνω *pinō* (72)
drink (46)
drinking (10)
drinks (8)
drank (5)
drink from (1)
drinks in (1)
take (1)

4404 πιότης *piotēs* (1)
nourishing (1)

4405 πιπράσκω *pipraskō* (9)
sold (7)
sales (1)
selling (1)

4406 πίπτω *piptō* (90)
fell (38)
fall (13)
fallen (8)
falls (8)
fell down (7)
collapsed (2)
fall down (2)
be condemned (1) *+3213+5679*
beat (1)
bow down (1)
bowed down (1)
came (1)
died (1)
drop out (1)
fails (1)
fall (1) *+1639*
fell to the ground (1)
threw himself (1) *+2093+4725*
untranslated (1)

4407 Πισιδία *Pisidia* (1)
Pisidia (1)

4408 Πισίδιος *Pisidios* (1)
Pisidian (1)

4409 πιστεύω *pisteuō* (241)
believe (114)
believed (57)
believes (23)
believers (7)
put faith (5)
trusts (5)
trust (4)
entrusted with (3)
faith (3)
believing (2)
entrusted (2)
put trust (2)
became believers (1)
believe (1) *+1877*
believe in (1)
believed in (1)

believed on (1)
come to believe (1)
committed (1)
did[s] (1)
do[s] (1)
entrust (1)
putting faith (1)
rely on (1)
took at word (1) *+3364*
trusted (1)

4410 πιστικός *pistikos* (2)
pure (2)

4411 πίστις *pistis* (242)
faith (221)
believe (4)
faithfulness (4)
have faith (2) *+1666*
belief (1)
believe (1) *+1666*
believe (1) *+2400*
believers (1) *+2400+3836*
believers (1) *+3836*
believing (1)
faith from first to last (1) *+1650+4411*
faithful (1)
given proof (1) *+4218*
pledge (1)
trusted (1)

4412 πιστός *pistos* (67)
faithful (36)
trustworthy (13)
believe (5)
believer (3)
believers (3)
can be trusted (2)
believer (1) *+1639*
believing (1)
faith (1)
reliable (1)
sure (1)

4413 πιστόω *pistoō* (1)
convinced (1)

4414 πλανάω *planaō* (39)
deceived (8)
deceive (6)
deceives (3)
going astray (3)
deceiving (2)
in error (2)
lead astray (2)
wandered off (2)
be deceived (1)
deluded (1)
leads astray (1)
led astray (1)
misleads (1)
misled (1)
mistaken (1)
wander (1)
wander off (1)
wandered (1)
wanders away (1)

4415 πλάνη *planē* (10)
error (3)
deceitful (1)
deception (1)
delusion (1)
falsehood (1)
perversion (1)

4416 πλάνης *planēs*
Variant; not used

4417 πλανήτης *planētēs* (1)
wandering (1)

4418 πλάνος *planos* (5)
deceiver (2)
deceivers (1)
deceiving (1)
impostors (1)

4419 πλάξ *plax* (3)
tablets (2)
stone tablets (1)

4420 πλάσμα *plasma* (1)
is formed (1)

4421 πλάσσω *plassō* (2)
formed (2)

4422 πλαστός *plastos* (1)
made up (1)

4423 πλατεῖα *plateia* (9)
streets (5)
great street (2)
street (2)

4424 πλάτος *platos* (4)
wide (3)
breadth (1)

4425 πλατύνω *platynō* (3)
make wide (1)
open wide (1)
opened wide (1)

4426 πλατύς *platys* (1)
wide (1)

4427 πλέγμα *plegma* (1)
braided hair (1)

4428 πλέκω *plekō* (3)
twisted together (3)

4429 πλεονάζω *pleonazō* (9)
increase (2)
increasing (2)
credited (1)
have too much (1)
increased (1)
make increase (1)
reaching more and more (1) *+1328+3836+4498*

4430 πλεονεκτέω *pleonekteō* (5)
exploit (2)
exploited (1)
outwit (1)
take advantage of (1)

4431 πλεονέκτης *pleonektēs* (4)
greedy (3)
greedy person (1)

4432 πλεονεξία *pleonexia* (10)
greed (8)
lust (1)
one grudgingly given (1)

4433 πλευρά *pleura* (5)
side (5)

4434 πλέω *pleō* (6)
sail (2)
sailed (2)
sailing (1)
travel by ship (1)

4435 πληγή *plēgē* (22)
plagues (10)
plague (3)
wound (2)
beat (1) *+2202*
beatings (1)
flogged (1)
flogged (1) *+2202*
punishment (1)
wounded (1) *+2400+3836*
wounds (1)

4436 πλῆθος *plēthos* (31)
number (6)
assembly (3)
crowd (3)
people (3)
all (2)
multitude (2)
assembled worshipers (1) *+3295+3836*
church (1)
crowd (1) *+3295+3836*
crowds (1)
great company (1)
great number (1)
group (1)
Jewish community (1) *+2681*
large number (1)
numerous (1)
pile (1)
publicly (1) *+1967+3836*

4437 πληθύνω *plēthynō* (11)
abundance (3)
increase (2)
give many descendants (1) *+4437*
greatly increased (1) *+889+2779*
grew in numbers (1)
increased (1)
increasing (1)
spread (1)

4438 πλήκτης *plēktēs* (2)
violent (2)

4439 πλήμμυρα *plēmmyra* (1)
flood (1)

4440 πλήν *plēn* (31)
but (14)
however (4)
only (4)
yet (4)
beyond (1)
except (1)
important thing (1)
in any case (1)
untranslated (1)

4441 πλήρης *plērēs* (16)
full (9)
basketfuls (2) *+3186*
always (1)
basketfuls (1) *+5083*
covered (1)
fully (1)
furious (1) *+2596*

4442 πληροφορέω *plērophoreō* (6)
discharge all (1)
fulfilled (1)
fully (1)
fully assured (1)
fully convinced (1)
fully persuaded (1)

4443 πληροφορία *plērophoria* (4)
complete (1)
conviction (1)
full assurance (1)
sure (1)

4444 πληρόω *plēroō* (86)
fulfilled (21)
fulfill (11)
filled (10)
complete (7)
fill (3)
come (2)
completed (2)
filled with (2)
finished (2)
full (2)
after had passed (1)
amply supplied (1)
bring to fulfillment (1)
come true (1)
complete (1) *+4246*
completing (1)
fill up (1)
fill with (1)
filled in (1)
fills (1)

finds fulfillment (1)
fully (1)
fully met (1)
given fullness (1) *+1639*
gone by (1)
greatly encouraged (1) *+4155*
happened (1)
make complete (1)
make complete (1) *+1639*
meet (1)
passed (1)
present in its fullness (1)
summed up (1)
untranslated (1)

4445 πλήρωμα *plērōma* (17)
fullness (7)
fulfillment (2)
basketfuls (1) *+3186*
basketfuls (1) *+5083*
everything (1)
full measure (1)
full number (1)
fully (1)
untranslated (2)

4446 πλησίον *plēsion* (17)
neighbor (15)
near (1)
other (1)

4447 πλησμονή *plēsmonē* (1)
indulgence (1)

4448 πλήσσω *plēssō* (1)
struck (1)

4449 πλοιάριον *ploiarion* (5)
boat (2)
boats (2)
small boat (1)

4450 πλοῖον *ploion* (68)
boat (39)
ship (17)
boats (5)
ships (3)
it[s] (2) *+3836*
on board (1) *+1877+3836*
ship's (1)

4451 πλοκή *plokē*
Variant; not used

4452 πλόος *ploos* (3)
voyage (2)
sailing (1)

4453 πλοῦς *plous*
Variant; not used

4454 πλούσιος *plousios* (28)
rich (26)
wealth (1)
wealthy (1)

4455 πλουσίως *plousiōs* (4)
richly (2)
generously (1)
rich (1)

4456 πλουτέω *plouteō* (12)
rich (7)
acquired wealth (1)
gained wealth (1)
get rich (1)
grew rich (1)
richly (1)

4457 πλουτίζω *ploutizō* (3)
enriched (1)
made rich (1)
making rich (1)

4458 πλοῦτος *ploutos* (22)
riches (14)
wealth (6)
rich (1)
value (1)

4459 πλύνω *plynō* (3)
wash (1)
washed (1)
washing (1)

4460 πνεῦμα *pneuma* (379)
spirit (325)
spirits (32)
breath (3)
ghost (2)
spirit's (2)
spiritual (2)
attitude (1)
demon-possessed (1) *+2400+3836+3836+4505*
gently (1) *+1877+4559*
he[s] (1) *+899+899+1877+3836*
heart (1)
mind (1)
prophecy (1)
sighed deeply (1) *+417+3836*
spirit which predicted the future (1) *+4780*
wind (1)
winds (1)
with great fervor (1) *+2417+3836*
untranslated (1)

4461 πνευματικός *pneumatikos* (26)
spiritual (25)
spiritually (1)

4462 πνευματικῶς *pneumatikōs* (2)
figuratively (1)
spiritually (1)

4463 πνέω *pneō* (7)
blew (2)
blowing (1)
blows (1)
prevent from blowing (1) *+3590*
wind (1)
wind blows (1)

4464 πνίγω *pnigō* (3)
choke (1)
choked (1)
drowned (1)

4465 πνικτός *pniktos* (3)
meat of strangled animals (3)

4466 πνοή *pnoē* (2)
breath (1)
wind (1)

4467 ποδαπός *podapos*
Variant; not used

4468 ποδήρης *podērēs* (1)
a robe reaching down to feet (1)

4469 ποδονιπτήρ *podoniptēr*
Variant; not used

4470 πόθεν *pothen* (29)
where from (16)
where (7)
from which (1)
how (1)
how can (1)
what causes (1)
why (1)
untranslated (1)

4471 ποία *poia*
Variant; not used

4472 ποιέω *poieō* (568)
do (157)
doing (43)
did (38)
done (37)
made (35)
make (26)
does (24)
performed (7)
produce (6)
bear (5)
committed (5)
give (4)
making (4)
treated (4)
appointed (3)
bears (3)
do with (3)
put into practice (3)
put up (3)
was (3)
acted (2)
be (2)
bring (2)
carry out (2)
cause (2)
formed (2)
give to the needy (2) *+1797*
given (2)
judge (2) *+3213*
kept (2)
makes (2)
perform (2)
performing (2)
practice (2)
practiced (2)
practices (2)
pray (2) *+1255*
preparing (2)
provide (2)
puts into practice (2)
remember (2) *+3644*
sin (2) *+281*
sins (2) *+281+3836*
spending (2)
tell (2) *+5745*
treat (2)
work (2)
accomplish (1)
accomplished (1)
accomplishing (1)
act (1)
acts (1)
agreeing (1) *+1191+1651*
are (1)
attack (1) *+4483*
avenged (1) *+1689*
bearing (1)
bears (1) *+1639*
been (1)
began (1)
breaks law (1) *+490*
bring about (1)
business (1) *+5515*
carrying out (1)
causes (1)
causing (1)
celebrate (1)
claim (1) *+4932*
claimed to be (1) *+1571*
claims to be (1) *+1571*
commits (1)
consider (1)
created things (1)
criminal (1) *+2805*
delay (1) *+332*
dividing into shares (1) *+3538*
done (1) *+1639*
duty (1) *+4005+4053*
earned (1)
exercise (1)
exercised (1)
following (1)
forced (1)
forcing (1)
gain (1)
gaining (1)
gave (1)
gave to in need (1) *+1797*
get (1)

gives away (1) *+1316*
good (1) *+2822*
grows (1) *+890*
had (1)
have (1)
have do (1)
he sacrificed[S] (1)
healing (1) *+5618*
held (1)
help (1) *+2292*
helping the poor (1) *+1797*
involved in (1)
keep (1)
keeps (1)
kept up (1)
live by (1)
lives by (1)
made out to be (1)
make out to be (1)
mentioning (1) *+3644*
mourned deeply (1) *+3157+3489*
obey (1)
peacemakers (1) *+1645*
pray[S] (1) *+4047*
prepared (1)
provided (1)
put (1)
put out of the synagogue (1) *+697*
reached (1)
redeemed (1) *+3391*
remember (1) *+3647*
remembering (1) *+3644*
satisfy (1) *+2653*
see (1)
set up (1)
show (1)
sinned (1) *+281+1639*
spend (1)
spent (1)
stayed (1)
stirring up (1) *+2180*
sweep away with the torrent (1) *+4533*
think about (1) *+4630*
those who do (1)
treat (1) *+1650*
turn into (1)
turned into (1)
unite (1) *+3517*
walked along (1) *+3847*
weeping (1) *+3081*
who do you think you are (1) *+4932+5515*
win (1)
worked (1)
wrote (1)
yielded (1)
yielding (1)
untranslated (3)

4473 ποίημα *poiēma* (2)
made (1)
workmanship (1)

4474 ποίησις *poiēsis* (1)
does (1)

4475 ποιητής *poiētēs* (6)
do (1)
do (1) *+1181*
doing (1)
keeping (1)
obey (1)
poets (1)

4476 ποικίλος *poikilos* (10)
all kinds of (4)
various (4)
many kinds (1)
various kinds (1)

4477 ποιμαίνω *poimainō* (11)
rule (3)
be shepherds of (2)
be shepherd (1)
be shepherd of (1)
looking after sheep (1)
shepherds (1)
take care of (1)
tends (1)

4478 ποιμήν *poimēn* (18)
shepherd (13)
shepherds (4)
pastors (1)

4479 ποίμνη *poimnē* (5)
flock (3)
flocks (1)
untranslated (1)

4480 ποίμνιον *poimnion* (5)
flock (5)

4481 ποῖος *poios* (33)
what (20)
which (4)
kind of (3)
what kind of (2)
a way (1)
how is it (1)
the (1)
what will happen (1) *+3836*

4482 πολεμέω *polemeō* (7)
fight (2)
fought (2)
make war (2)
makes war (1)

4483 πόλεμος *polemos* (18)
battle (6)
wars (5)
war (4)
attack (1) *+4472*
fights (1)
go war (1) *+5202*

4484 πόλις *polis* (162)
city (86)
town (51)
towns (12)
cities (8)
city's (1)
from town to town (1) *+3836*
there[S] (1) *+1877+3836+4047*
village (1)
untranslated (1)

4485 πολιτάρχης *politarchēs* (2)
city officials (2)

4486 πολιτεία *politeia* (2)
citizenship (2)

4487 πολίτευμα *politeuma* (1)
citizenship (1)

4488 πολιτεύομαι *politeuomai* (2)
conduct yourselves (1)
fulfilled duty (1)

4489 πολίτης *politēs* (4)
citizen (2)
neighbor (1)
subjects (1)

4490 πολλάκις *pollakis* (18)
often (10)
again and again (3)
many times (2)
constantly (1)
many a time (1)
untranslated (1)

4491 πολλαπλασίων *pollaplasiōn* (1)
many times as much (1)

4492 πολυεύσπλαγχνος *polyeusplanchnos*
Variant; not used

4493 πολύλαλος *polylalos*
Variant; not used

4494 πολυλογία *polylogia* (1)
many words (1)

4495 πολυμερῶς *polymerōs* (1)
at many times (1)

4496 πολυπλήθεια *polyplētheia*
Variant; not used

4497 πολυποίκιλος *polypoikilos* (1)
manifold (1)

4498 πολύς *polys* (413)
many (193)
great (35)
much (31)
large (30)
more (16)
most (8)
greater (6)
how much (4)
more than (3)
rushing (3)
very (3)
a great deal of (2)
all (2)
few (2) *+4024*
long (2)
majority (2)
number (2)
plentiful (2)
plenty (2)
strict (2)
a great deal (1)
a long time (1) *+2093*
again and again (1)
all silent (1) *+4968*
all the more (1) *+3437*
any further (1) *+2093*
any more (1) *+4123*
badly (1)
be bold (1) *+2400+4244*
before very long (1) *+3552+4024*
besiege with questions (1) *+694+4309*
better (1)
big (1)
bigger (1)
by far (1)
considerable (1)
deep (1)
earnestly (1)
even more so[S] (1) *+5080*
freely (1)
further (1)
generously (1)
get very far (1) *+2093+4621*
great deal (1)
greatly (1)
hard (1) *+2400*
high (1)
intense (1)
larger (1)
late in the day (1) *+6052*
long (1) *+2465*
long period (1)
long time (1)
loudly (1)
more and more (1) *+2093*
most (1) *+3836*
often (1)
on and on (1) *+2093*
on the contrary (1) *+247+3437*
only (1) *+2445+4024*
over (1)
plenty of (1)
reaching more and more (1) *+1328+3836+4429*
several (1)
severe (1)
severely (1)
shouted all the more (1) *+3189+3437*
so many (1)
strong (1)
strongly (1)
surpasses (1) *+4355*
urgently (1) *+3552+4155*

very hard (1)
very late (1) *+6052*
violent (1)
violently (1)
warmly (1)
wept and wept (1) *+3081*
widespread (1)
untranslated (4)

4499 πολύσπλαγχνος *polysplanchnos* (1)
full of compassion (1)

4500 πολυτελής *polytelēs* (3)
expensive (1)
great worth (1)
very expensive (1)

4501 πολύτιμος *polytimos* (3)
expensive (1)
great value (1)
greater worth (1)

4502 πολυτρόπως *polytropōs* (1)
in various ways (1)

4503 πόμα *poma* (2)
drink (2)

4504 πονηρία *ponēria* (7)
evil (3)
wickedness (2)
malice (1)
wicked ways (1)

4505 πονηρός *ponēros* (78)
evil (47)
wicked (11)
bad (7)
more wicked than (2)
crimes (1)
demon-possessed (1) *+2400+3836+3836+4460*
envious (1) *+1639+3836+4057*
envy (1) *+4057*
evil one (1)
evils (1)
guilty conscience (1) *+5287*
maliciously (1) *+3364*
painful (1)
serious (1)
sinful (1)

4506 πόνος *ponos* (4)
agony (1)
pain (1)
pains (1)
working (1)

4507 Ποντικός *Pontikos* (1)
of Pontus (1)

4508 Πόντιος *Pontios* (3)
Pontius (3)

4509 Πόντος *pontos* (2)
Pontus (2)

4510 Πόντος *Pontos*
Variant; not used

4511 Πόπλιος *Poplios* (2)
his[s] (1) *+3836*
Publius (1)

4512 πορεία *poreia* (2)
goes about his business (1)
way (1)

4513 πορεύομαι *poreuomai* (153)
go (61)
went (22)
going (13)
goes (7)
on way (4)
follow (2)
follow (2) *+3958*
gone (2)
left (2)
living (2)
went on way (2)
went out (2)
about (1)
accompany (1) *+5250*
came (1)
companions (1) *+5250*
continued on way (1)
depart (1)
departed (1)
enter (1) *+1650*
following (1)
go back (1)
go on way (1)
heading (1)
hurried (1) *+3552+5082*
leave (1)
leaving (1)
leaving (1) *+608*
observing (1) *+1877*
on journey (1) *+1877*
set out (1)
started out (1)
taken (1)
traveled (1)
walking (1)
walking away (1)
way (1)
went along (1)
went into (1) *+1656*
went out (1) *+2002*
untranslated (4)

4514 πορθέω *portheō* (3)
destroy (1)
raised havoc (1)
tried destroy (1)

4515 πορία *poria*
Variant; not used

4516 πορισμός *porismos* (2)
gain (1)
means to financial gain (1)

4517 Πόρκιος *Porkios* (1)
Porcius (1)

4518 πορνεία *porneia* (25)
sexual immorality (13)
adulteries (5)
immorality (2)
marital unfaithfulness (2)
illegitimate children (1) *+1164+1666*
sexual sin (1)
untranslated (1)

4519 πορνεύω *porneuō* (8)
committed adultery (3)
commit sexual immorality (1)
committing sexual immorality (1)
did[s] (1)
sexual immorality (1)
sins sexually (1)

4520 πόρνη *pornē* (12)
prostitute (8)
prostitutes (4)

4521 πόρνος *pornos* (10)
sexually immoral (7)
immoral (2)
adulterers (1)

4522 πόρρω *porrō* (4)
far (2)
farther (1)
long way off (1)

4523 πόρρωθεν *porrōthen* (2)
at a distance (1)
from a distance (1)

4524 πορρωτέρω *porrōterō*
Variant; not used

4525 πορφύρα *porphyra* (4)
purple (2)
purple robe (2)

4526 πορφύρεος *porphyreos* (4)
purple (4)

4527 πορφυρόπωλις *porphyropōlis* (1)
dealer in purple cloth (1)

4528 πορφυροῦς *porphyrous*
Variant; not used

4529 ποσάκις *posakis* (3)
how often (2)
how many times (1)

4530 πόσις *posis* (3)
drink (2)
drinking (1)

4531 πόσος *posos* (27)
how much (11)
how many (10)
how (1)
how great (1)
how much more (1)
what (1)
untranslated (2)

4532 ποταμός *potamos* (17)
river (9)
rivers (3)
streams (3)
torrent (2)

4533 ποταμοφόρητος *potamophorētos* (1)
sweep away with the torrent (1) *+4472*

4534 ποταπός *potapos* (7)
what kind of (4)
how great (1)
what magnificent (1)
what massive (1)

4535 ποταπῶς *potapōs*
Variant; not used

4536 πότε *pote* (19)
when (11)
how long (4) *+2401*
long (3)
to return (1) *+386*

4537 ποτέ *pote* (29)
once (6)
at one time (3)
ever (3)
formerly (3)
used to (2)
ago (1)
at last (1) *+2453*
had been (1)
never (1) *+3590+4024*
never (1) *+4024*
never (1) *+4046*
now at last (1) *+2453*
of the past (1)
previous (1)
were (1) *+1639*
when (1)
untranslated (1)

4538 πότερον *poteron* (1)
whether (1)

4539 ποτήριον *potērion* (31)
cup (29)
cups (1)
gives a cup (1) *+4540*

4540 ποτίζω *potizō* (16)
gave to drink (2)
give to drink (2)
offered to drink (2)
waters (2)
drunk (1)
gave (1)
give water (1)
given to drink (1)
gives a cup (1) *+4539*

gives water to (1)
made drink (1)
watered (1)

4541 Ποτίολοι *Potioloi* (1)
Puteoli (1)

4542 πότος *potos* (1)
carousing (1)

4543 πού *pou* (4)
a place where (1)
about (1)
somewhere (1)
untranslated (1)

4544 ποῦ *pou* (48)
where (43)
place (2)
what (2)
no place (1) *+4024*

4545 Πούδης *Poudēs* (1)
Pudens (1)

4546 πούς *pous* (93)
feet (76)
foot (8)
foot of ground (1) *+1037*
footstool (1) *+3836+5711*
legs (1)
them[S] (1) *+899+3836*
under (1) *+3836+4123*
untranslated (4)

4547 πρᾶγμα *pragma* (11)
matter (2)
anything (1) *+1569+4005+4246*
dispute (1)
practice (1)
thing (1)
things (1)
things that (1)
what (1)
untranslated (2)

4548 πραγματεία *pragmateia* (1)
civilian affairs (1) *+1050*

4549 πραγματεύομαι *pragmateuomai* (1)
put to work (1)

4550 πραιτώριον *praitōrion* (8)
palace (4)
Praetorium (2)
palace guard (1)
palace of the governor (1)

4551 πράκτωρ *praktōr* (2)
officer (2)

4552 πρᾶξις *praxis* (6)
action (1)
deeds (1)
function (1)
has done (1)
misdeeds (1)
practices (1)

4553 πρᾶος *praos*
Variant; not used

4554 πραότης *praotēs*
Variant; not used

4555 πρασιά *prasia* (1)
groups (1) *+4555*

4556 πράσσω *prassō* (39)
do (9)
done (6)
doing (4)
acted (1)
collect (1)
collected (1)
deeds (1)
defying (1) *+595*
did (1)
does (1)
done (1) *+1639*
harm (1) *+2805*
indulged (1)
live (1)
mind business (1)
observe (1)
practice (1)
practiced (1)
preach[S] (1)
put into practice (1)
them[S] (1) *+3836+3836+5525*
wrongdoer (1) *+2805*
untranslated (1)

4557 πραϋπαθία *praupathia* (1)
gentleness (1)

4558 πραΰς *praus* (4)
gentle (3)
meek (1)

4559 πραΰτης *prautēs* (11)
gentleness (3)
gentle (2)
gently (1) *+1877*
gently (1) *+1877+4460*
humbly (1) *+1877*
humility (1)
meekness (1)
true humility (1)

4560 πρέπω *prepō* (7)
proper (2)
appropriate (1)
fitting (1)
in accord (1)
meets need (1)
untranslated (1)

4561 πρεσβεία *presbeia* (2)
delegation (2)

4562 πρεσβευτής *presbeutēs*
Variant; not used

4563 πρεσβεύω *presbeuō* (2)
ambassador (1)
ambassadors (1)

4564 πρεσβυτέριον *presbyterion* (3)
body of elders (1)
council (1)
council of elders (1)

4565 πρεσβύτερος *presbyteros* (66)
elders (56)
elder (3)
older (3)
ancients (1)
old (1)
older man (1)
those who are older (1)

4566 πρεσβύτης *presbytēs* (3)
old man (2)
older (1)

4567 πρεσβῦτις *presbytis* (1)
older (1)

4568 πρηνής *prēnēs* (1)
fell headlong (1) *+1181*

4569 πρίζω *prizō* (1)
sawed in two (1)

4570 πρίν *prin* (13)
before (9)
before (3) *+2445*
before (1) *+323+2445*

4571 Πρίσκα *Priska* (6)
Priscilla (6)

4572 Πρίσκιλλα *Priskilla*
Variant; not used

4573 πρίω *priō*
Variant; not used

4574 πρό *pro* (47)
before (30)
ahead (4) *+4725*
at (3)
above (2)
some time ago (2) *+2465+3836+4047*
ago (1)
ahead (1)
before (1) *+4725*
just outside (1)
on ahead (1) *+4725*
untranslated (1)

4575 προάγω *proagō* (20)
go ahead of (2)
go on ahead of (2)
going ahead of (2)
went ahead of (2)
bring (1)
bring out (1)
brought (1)
brought before (1)
entering ahead of (1)
former (1)
leading (1)
led the way (1)
once made (1)
reaching ahead of (1)
runs ahead (1)
went ahead (1)

4576 προαιρέω *proaireō* (1)
decided (1)

4577 προαιτιάομαι *proaitiaomai* (1)
already made the charge (1)

4578 προακούω *proakouō* (1)
already heard about (1)

4579 προαμαρτάνω *proamartanō* (2)
sinned earlier (2)

4580 προαύλιον *proaulion* (1)
entryway (1)

4581 προβαίνω *probainō* (5)
well along (2)
going on (1)
gone farther (1)
old (1) *+1877+2465*

4582 προβάλλω *proballō* (2)
pushed to the front (1)
sprout leaves (1)

4583 προβατικός *probatikos* (1)
sheep Gate (1)

4584 προβάτιον *probation*
Variant; not used

4585 πρόβατον *probaton* (39)
sheep (38)
sheep's (1)

4586 προβιβάζω *probibazō* (1)
prompted (1)

4587 προβλέπω *problepō* (1)
planned (1)

4588 προγίνομαι *proginomai* (1)
committed beforehand (1)

4589 προγινώσκω *proginōskō* (5)
foreknew (2)
already know (1)
chosen before (1)
known (1)

4590 πρόγνωσις *prognōsis* (2)
foreknowledge (2)

4591 πρόγονος *progonos* (2)
my forefathers (1)
parents and grandparents (1)

4592 προγράφω *prographō* (4)
already written (1)

portrayed (1)
was written about (1)
written in the past (1)

4593 πρόδηλος *prodēlos* (3)
obvious (2)
clear (1)

4594 προδίδωμι *prodidōmi* (1)
given (1)

4595 προδότης *prodotēs* (3)
betrayed (1) *+1181*
traitor (1)
treacherous (1)

4596 πρόδρομος *prodromos* (1)
went before (1)

4597 προεῖπον *proeipon*
Variant; not used

4598 προελπίζω *proelpizō* (1)
first to hope (1)

4599 προενάρχομαι *proenarchomai* (2)
earlier made a beginning (1)
the first (1)

4600 προεπαγγέλλω *proepangellō* (2)
promised (1)
promised beforehand (1)

4601 προέρχομαι *proerchomai* (9)
going farther (2)
went on ahead (2)
go on (1)
got there ahead of (1)
leading (1)
visit in advance (1) *+1650*
walked (1)

4602 προετοιμάζω *proetoimazō* (2)
prepared in advance (2)

4603 προευαγγελίζομαι *proeuangelizomai* (1)
announced the gospel in advance (1)

4604 προέχω *proechō* (1)
better (1)

4605 προηγέομαι *proēgeomai* (1)
above (1)

4606 πρόθεσις *prothesis* (12)
purpose (5)
consecrated (3)
consecrated bread (1) *+788*
plan (1)
true (1)
wanted (1)

4607 προθεσμία *prothesmia* (1)
time set (1)

4608 προθυμία *prothymia* (5)
eagerness (3)
eager (1)
willingness (1)

4609 πρόθυμος *prothymos* (3)
willing (2)
eager (1)

4610 προθύμως *prothymōs* (1)
eager (1)

4611 πρόϊμος *proimos* (1)
autumn rains (1)

4612 προϊνός *proinos*
Variant; not used

4613 προΐστημι *proistēmi* (8)
manage (2)
devote (1)
devote to (1)
direct (1)
leadership (1)
manage and see that (1)
over (1)

4614 προκαλέω *prokaleō* (1)
provoking (1)

4615 προκαταγγέλλω *prokatangellō* (2)
foretold (1)
predicted (1)

4616 προκαταρτίζω *prokatartizō* (1)
finish the arrangements for (1)

4617 προκατέχω *prokatechō*
Variant; not used

4618 πρόκειμαι *prokeimai* (5)
marked out (1)
offered (1)
serve as (1)
set before (1)
there (1)

4619 προκηρύσσω *prokēryssō* (1)
preached (1)

4620 προκοπή *prokopē* (3)
progress (2)
advance (1)

4621 προκόπτω *prokoptō* (6)
advancing (1)
get very far (1) *+2093+4498*
go (1)
grew (1)
indulge (1)
nearly over (1)

4622 πρόκριμα *prokrima* (1)
partiality (1)

4623 προκυρόω *prokyroō* (1)
previously established (1)

4624 προλαμβάνω *prolambanō* (3)
beforehand (1)
caught (1)
goes ahead (1)

4625 προλέγω *prolegō* (15)
said before (2)
told ahead of time (2)
already gave warning (1)
already said (1)
already told (1)
did before[s] (1)
foretold (1)
repeat (1)
said previously (1)
spoke long ago (1)
spoken in the past (1)
telling (1)
warn (1)

4626 προμαρτύρομαι *promartyromai* (1)
predicted (1)

4627 προμελετάω *promeletaō* (1)
worry beforehand (1)

4628 προμεριμνάω *promerimnaō* (1)
worry beforehand about (1)

4629 προνοέω *pronoeō* (3)
careful (1)
provide for (1)
taking pains (1)

4630 πρόνοια *pronoia* (2)
foresight (1)
think about (1) *+4472*

4631 πρόοιδα *prooida*
Variant; not used

4632 προοράω *prooraō* (4)
foresaw (1)
previously seen (1) *+1639*
saw (1)
seeing what was ahead (1)

4633 προορίζω *proorizō* (6)
predestined (4)
decided beforehand (1)
destined (1)

4634 προπάσχω *propaschō* (1)
previously suffered (1)

4635 προπάτωρ *propatōr* (1)
forefather (1)

4636 προπέμπω *propempō* (9)
accompanied (2)
send on way (2)
assist on journey (1)
help on journey (1)
help on way (1)
send on their way (1)
sent on way (1)

4637 προπετής *propetēs* (2)
rash (2)

4638 προπορεύομαι *proporeuomai* (2)
go before (1)
go on (1)

4639 πρός *pros* (698)
to (379)
with (47)
for (24)
at (21)
against (17)
toward (8)
before (7)
in (7)
among (6)
around (6)
of (4)
in order to (3)
lead to (3)
them (3) *+899*
about (2)
as (2)
because (2)
into (2)
joined (2) *+2262*
so that (2)
addressed (1) *+3306*
approaching (1) *+2262*
begging (1) *+1797+3836*
beside (1)
comparing with (1)
concerning (1)
end (1) *+1639*
for (1) *+3836*
for a little while (1) *+6052*
gave (1) *+2400*
him (1) *+899*
in approaching (1)
in restraining (1)
in to (1)
join (1) *+2262*
leads to (1)
lustfully (1) *+2121+3836*
nearly (1)
on (1)
one another (1) *+257+257*
outside (1)
see (1) *+2262*
so as to (1)
so that (1) *+3836*
talked the matter over (1) *+253+1368*
they (1) *+899*
to keep from (1) *+3590+3836*
to see (1)
to show that (1) *+3836*
together (1) *+253*
told him (1) *+899+1181*
up to (1)
vicinity of (1)
visited (1) *+2262*
untranslated (117)

4640 προσάββατον *prosabbaton* (1)
day before the Sabbath (1)

4641 προσαγορεύω *prosagoreuō* (1)
designated to be (1)

4642 προσάγω *prosagō* (4)
bring (2)
approaching (1)
brought before (1)

4643 προσαγωγή *prosagōgē* (3)
access (2)
approach (1) *+2400*

4644 προσαιτέω *prosaiteō* (2)
beg (1)
begging (1)

4645 προσαίτης *prosaitēs* (1)
begging (1)

4646 προσαναβαίνω *prosanabainō* (1)
move (1)

4647 προσαναλαμβάνω *prosanalambanō*
Variant; not used

4648 προσαναλίσκω *prosanaliskō*
Variant; not used

4649 προσαναλόω *prosanaloō*
Variant; not used

4650 προσαναπληρόω *prosanaplēroō* (2)
supplied (1)
supplying (1)

4651 προσανατίθημι *prosanatithēmi* (1)
consult (1)

4652 προσανέχω *prosanechō*
Variant; not used

4653 προσαπειλέω *prosapeileō* (1)
further threats (1)

4654 προσαχέω *prosacheō*
Variant; not used

4655 προσδαπανάω *prosdapanaō* (1)
extra expense (1)

4656 προσδέομαι *prosdeomai* (1)
needed (1)

4657 προσδέχομαι *prosdechomai* (14)
waiting for (5)
wait for (2)
accepted (1)
looking forward to (1)
receive (1)
refused (1) *+4024*
welcome (1)
welcomes (1)
untranslated (1)

4658 προσδίδωμι *prosdidōmi*
Variant; not used

4659 προσδοκάω *prosdokaō* (16)
expect (5)
expecting (3)
looking forward to (2)
expected (1)
look forward to (1)
suspense (1)
waiting (1)
waiting expectantly (1)
waiting for (1)

4660 προσδοκία *prosdokia* (2)
anticipating (1)
apprehensive (1)

4661 προσεάω *proseaō* (1)
allow to hold course (1)

4662 προσεγγίζω *prosengizō*
Variant; not used

4663 προσεδρεύω *prosedreuō*
Variant; not used

4664 προσεργάζομαι *prosergazomai* (1)
earned more (1)

4665 προσέρχομαι *proserchomai* (86)
came to (34)
came (10)
went to (8)
come to (4)
going to (4)
came up (3)
went (3)
came forward (2)
came up to (2)
draw near (2)
agree to (1)
approach (1)
approached (1)
came before (1)
comes (1)
coming (1)
go to (1)
stepped forward (1)
visit (1)
went over (1)
went up (1)
went up to (1)
untranslated (2)

4666 προσευχή *proseuchē* (36)
prayer (16)
prayers (12)
place of prayer (2)
praying (2)
ask God (1)
pray (1)
prayed earnestly (1) *+4667*
praying (1) *+1181*

4667 προσεύχομαι *proseuchomai* (85)
pray (42)
prayed (17)
praying (12)
prayer (5)
prays (3)
make prayers (2)
pray for (2)
prayed earnestly (1) *+4666*
praying to (1)

4668 προσέχω *prosechō* (24)
on guard (4)
careful (2)
devote (2)
pay attention (2)
attention (1)
beware (1)
consider carefully (1)
follow (1)
followed (1)
guard (1)
indulging (1)
keep watch over (1)
paid close attention to (1)
pay attention to (1)
respond to (1)
served at (1)
watch (1)
watch out (1)

4669 προσηλόω *prosēloō* (1)
nailing (1)

4670 προσήλυτος *prosēlytos* (4)
converts to Judaism (2)
convert (1)
convert to Judaism (1)

4671 πρόσθεσις *prosthesis*
Variant; not used

4672 πρόσκαιρος *proskairos* (4)
only a short time (2)
a short time (1)
temporary (1)

4673 προσκαλέω *proskaleō* (29)
called (8)
called to (7)
called in (3)
call (2)
called together (2)
calling to (2)
sent for (2)
calling (1)
gathered together (1)
summoning (1)

4674 προσκαρτερέω *proskartereō* (10)
attendants (1)
continued (1)
devote (1)
devoted to (1) *+1639*
faithful (1)
followed everywhere (1)
give attention (1)
give full time (1)
joined constantly (1)
ready (1)

4675 προσκαρτέρησις *proskarterēsis* (1)
keep on (1)

4676 προσκεφάλαιον *proskephalaion* (1)
cushion (1)

4677 προσκληρόω *prosklēroō* (1)
joined (1)

4678 πρόσκλησις *prosklēsis*
Variant; not used

4679 προσκλίνω *prosklinō* (1)
rallied (1)

4680 πρόσκλισις *prosklisis* (1)
out of favoritism (1) *+2848*

4681 προσκολλάω *proskollaō* (2)
united to (2)

4682 πρόσκομμα *proskomma* (6)
causes men to stumble (2)
stumbling block (2)
stumble (1)
stumbling (1)

4683 προσκοπή *proskopē* (1)
stumbling block (1)

4684 προσκόπτω *proskoptō* (8)
strike (2)
stumble (2)
beat against (1)
cause fall (1)
stumbled over (1)
stumbles (1)

4685 προσκυλίω *proskyliō* (2)
rolled (1)
rolled in front of (1)

4686 προσκυνέω *proskyneō* (60)
worship (28)
worshiped (17)
knelt before (3)
worshipers (3)
fall down (1)
fell on knees in front of (1)
kneeling down (1)
on knees before (1)
paid homage (1)
refused to worship (1) *+3590*
reverence (1)
worshiping (1)
worships (1)

4687 προσκυνητής *proskynētēs* (1)
worshipers (1)

4688 προσλαλέω *proslaleō* (2)
talk with (1)
talked with (1)

4689 προσλαμβάνω *proslambanō* (12)
accept (2)
accepted (2)
took aside (2)
ate (1)
eaten (1)

invited to home (1)
rounded up (1)
welcome (1)
welcomed (1)

4690 προσλέγω *proslegō*
Variant; not used

4691 πρόσλημψις *proslēmpsis* (1)
acceptance (1)

4692 πρόσληψις *proslēpsis*
Variant; not used

4693 προσμένω *prosmenō* (7)
with (2)
continue in (1)
continues (1)
remain (1)
stay (1)
stayed (1)

4694 προσορμίζω *prosormizō* (1)
anchored (1)

4695 προσοφείλω *prosopheilō* (1)
owe (1)

4696 προσοχθίζω *prosochthizō* (2)
angry (2)

4697 προσπαίω *prospaiō*
Variant; not used

4698 πρόσπεινος *prospeinos* (1)
hungry (1)

4699 προσπήγνυμι *prospēgnymi* (1)
nailing to cross (1)

4700 προσπίπτω *prospiptō* (8)
fell at feet (3)
beat against (1)
fell (1)
fell at (1)
fell before (1)
fell down before (1)

4701 προσποιέω *prospoieō* (1)
acted as if (1)

4702 προσπορεύομαι *prosporeuomai* (1)
came to (1)

4703 προσρήγνυμι *prosrēgnymi* (2)
struck (2)

4704 προσρήσσω *prosrēssō*
Variant; not used

4705 προστάσσω *prostassō* (7)
commanded (5)
ordered (1)
set (1)

4706 προστάτις *prostatis* (1)
help (1)

4707 προστίθημι *prostithēmi* (19)
added (5)
add (2)
given (2)
sent (2) *+4287*
added to (1)
and even more (1) *+2779+5148*
brought (1)
buried (1)
further word spoken (1) *+3364*
increase (1)
proceeded (1)
went on (1)

4708 προστρέχω *prostrechō* (4)
ran up to (2)
outran (1) *+5441*
ran (1)

4709 προσφάγιον *prosphagion* (1)
fish (1)

4710 πρόσφατος *prosphatos* (1)
new (1)

4711 προσφάτως *prosphatōs* (1)
recently (1)

4712 προσφέρω *prospherō* (47)
brought (12)
offered (8)
offer (7)
offer sacrifices (3)
bringing (2)
offering (2)
bring (1)
get (1)
lifted (1)
made[s] (1)
offered as a sacrifice (1)
offered up (1)
offering made (1) *+4714*
offers (1)
presented with (1)
repeated[s] (1)
sacrifice (1)
sacrificed (1)
treating (1)

4713 προσφιλής *prosphilēs* (1)
lovely (1)

4714 προσφορά *prosphora* (9)
offering (3)
sacrifice (3)
offerings (2)
offering made (1) *+4712*

4715 προσφωνέω *prosphōneō* (7)
calling out (2)
appealed (1)
called forward (1)
called to (1)
said (1)
speak (1)

4716 προσχαίρω *proschairō*
Variant; not used

4717 πρόσχυσις *proschysis* (1)
sprinkling (1)

4718 προσψαύω *prospsauō* (1)
lift (1)

4719 προσωπολημπτέω *prosōpolēmpteō* (1)
show favoritism (1)

4720 προσωπολήμπτης *prosōpolēmptēs* (1)
show favoritism (1) *+1639*

4721 προσωπολημψία *prosōpolēmpsia* (4)
favoritism (2)
show favoritism (1) *+1639*
show favoritism (1) *+1877*

4722 προσωποληπτέω *prosōpolēpteō*
Variant; not used

4723 προσωπολήπτης *prosōpolēptēs*
Variant; not used

4724 προσωποληψία *prosōpolēpsia*
Variant; not used

4725 πρόσωπον *prosōpon* (76)
face (24)
faces (7)
ahead (4) *+4574*
presence (3)
appearance (2)
pay attention who they are (2) *+476+1063*
sight (2)
you (2) *+3836+5148*
before (1) *+608*
before (1) *+2848*
before (1) *+4574*
blindfolded (1) *+3836+4328*
can see it[s] (1) *+1711*
faced (1) *+2848*
facedown (1) *+2093*
flatter (1) *+2513*
in person (1)
in presence (1) *+3552+3836*
its[s] (1) *+899+3836*
judge by external appearance (1) *+476+3284*
met personally (1) *+1877+3836+3972+4922*
on ahead (1) *+4574*
personally (1)
resolutely (1) *+3836+5114*
seen (1)
show partiality (1) *+3284*
surface (1) *+2848*
threw himself (1) *+2093+4406*
when face to face (1) *+2848*
untranslated (9)

4726 προτάσσω *protassō*
Variant; not used

4727 προτείνω *proteinō* (1)
stretched out (1)

4728 πρότερος *proteros* (11)
first (3)
earlier (2)
formerly (2)
before (1)
former (1)
once (1)
when (1)

4729 προτίθημι *protithēmi* (3)
planned (1)
presented (1)
purposed (1)

4730 προτρέπω *protrepō* (1)
encouraged (1)

4731 προτρέχω *protrechō* (1)
ran (1)

4732 προϋπάρχω *prouparchō* (2)
before this been (1) *+1639*
for some time (1)

4733 πρόφασις *prophasis* (6)
show (2)
excuse (1)
false motives (1)
pretending (1)
put on a mask to cover up (1)

4734 προφέρω *propherō* (2)
brings (2)

4735 προφητεία *prophēteia* (19)
prophecy (12)
prophecies (3)
prophesying (2)
gift of prophecy (1)
prophetic message (1)

4736 προφητεύω *prophēteuō* (28)
prophesy (12)
prophesied (7)
prophesies (5)
prophecy (1)
prophesied (1) *+3306*
prophesying (1)
spoke (1)

4737 προφήτης *prophētēs* (144)
prophets (80)
prophet (60)
prophet's (2)
him[s] (1) *+3836*
prophet (1) *+467*

4738 προφητικός *prophētikos* (2)
of prophets (1)
prophetic (1)

4739 προφῆτις *prophētis* (2)
prophetess (2)

4740 προφθάνω *prophthanō* (1)
first (1)

4741 προχειρίζω *procheirizō* (3)
appoint (1)

appointed (1)
chosen (1)

4742 προχειροτονέω *procheirotoneō* (1)
already chosen (1)

4743 Πρόχορος *Prochoros* (1)
Procorus (1)

4744 πρύμνα *prymna* (3)
stern (3)

4745 πρωΐ *prōi* (12)
early (3)
early in the morning (2)
in the morning (2)
at dawn (1)
early in the morning (1) *+275*
early morning (1)
morning (1)
very early in the morning (1) *+2317*

4746 πρωΐα *prōia* (2)
early in the morning (1)
early in the morning (1) *+1181*

4747 πρώϊμος *prōimos*
Variant; not used

4748 πρωϊνός *prōinos* (2)
morning (2)

4749 πρῷρα *prōra* (2)
bow (2)

4750 πρωτεύω *prōteuō* (1)
supremacy (1)

4751 πρωτοκαθεδρία *prōtokathedria* (4)
most important seats (4)

4752 πρωτοκλισία *prōtoklisia* (5)
place of honor (2)
places of honor (2)
places of honor at the table (1)

4753 πρωτόμαρτυς *prōtomartys*
Variant; not used

4754 πρῶτον *prōton* (58)
first (45)
first of all (4)
above all (1) *+4047*
after (1)
at first (1)
begins (1)
earlier (1)
first of all (1) *+4047*
in early days (1)
in the first place (1)
until (1) *+1569+3590*

4755 πρῶτος *prōtos* (97)
first (77)
leading (3)
before (2)
leaders (2)
most important (2)
worst (2)
as of first importance (1) *+1877*
beginning (1)
best (1)
chief official (1)
former (1)
leaders (1) *+1639*
old (1)
outer (1)
prominent (1)

4756 πρωτοστάτης *prōtostatēs* (1)
ringleader (1)

4757 πρωτοτόκια *prōtotokia* (1)
inheritance rights as the oldest son (1)

4758 πρωτότοκος *prōtotokos* (8)
firstborn (8)

4759 πρώτως *prōtōs* (1)
first (1)

4760 πταίω *ptaiō* (5)
at fault (1)
fall (1)
stumble (1)
stumble in (1)
stumbles (1)

4761 πτέρνα *pterna* (1)
heel (1)

4762 πτερύγιον *pterygion* (2)
highest point (2)

4763 πτέρυξ *pteryx* (5)
wings (5)

4764 πτηνός *ptēnos* (1)
birds (1)

4765 πτοέω *ptoeō* (2)
frightened (1)
startled (1)

4766 πτόησις *ptoēsis* (1)
give way (1)

4767 Πτολεμαΐς *Ptolemais* (1)
Ptolemais (1)

4768 πτύον *ptyon* (2)
winnowing fork (2)

4769 πτύρω *ptyrō* (1)
frightened (1)

4770 πτύσμα *ptysma* (1)
saliva (1)

4771 πτύσσω *ptyssō* (1)
rolled up (1)

4772 πτύω *ptyō* (3)
spit (3)

4773 πτῶμα *ptōma* (7)
body (3)
bodies (2)
carcass (1)
untranslated (1)

4774 πτῶσις *ptōsis* (2)
falling (1)
with a great crash (1)
+899+1639+3489+3836

4775 πτωχεία *ptōcheia* (3)
poverty (3)

4776 πτωχεύω *ptōcheuō* (1)
poor (1)

4777 πτωχός *ptōchos* (34)
poor (31)
beggar (2)
miserable (1)

4778 πυγμή *pygmē* (1)
ceremonial (1)

4779 Πύθιος *Pythios*
Variant; not used

4780 πύθων *pythōn* (1)
spirit which predicted the future (1) *+4460*

4781 πυκνός *pyknos* (3)
frequent (1)
frequently (1)
often (1)

4782 πυκτεύω *pykteuō* (1)
fight (1)

4783 πύλη *pylē* (10)
gate (6)
city gate (2)
city gates (1)
gates (1)

4784 πυλών *pylōn* (18)
gates (8)
gate (3)
door (1)
gateway (1)
it[s] (1) *+3836*
outer entrance (1) *+2598*
untranslated (3)

4785 πυνθάνομαι *pynthanomai* (12)
asked (5)
ask (2)
asking (1)
information (1)
inquired (1)
learning (1)
question (1)

4786 πῦρ *pyr* (71)
fire (57)
fiery (5)
burning (4)
flames (2)
all ablaze (1) *+2794*
spark (1)
untranslated (1)

4787 πυρά *pyra* (2)
fire (2)

4788 πύργος *pyrgos* (4)
tower (2)
watchtower (2)

4789 πυρέσσω *pyressō* (2)
with a fever (2)

4790 πυρετός *pyretos* (6)
fever (6)

4791 πύρινος *pyrinos* (1)
fiery red (1)

4792 πυρόω *pyroō* (6)
burn with passion (1)
fire (1)
flaming (1)
glowing (1)
inwardly burn (1)
refined (1)

4793 πυρράζω *pyrrazō* (2)
red (2)

4794 πυρρός *pyrros* (2)
fiery red (1)
red (1)

4795 Πύρρος *Pyrros* (1)
Pyrrhus (1)

4796 πύρωσις *pyrōsis* (3)
burning (2)
painful (1)

4797 πωλέω *pōleō* (22)
sold (8)
sell (7)
selling (5)
buying (2)

4798 πῶλος *pōlos* (12)
colt (12)

4799 πώποτε *pōpote* (6)
ever (3)
never (1)
never (1) *+3590+4024*
never (1) *+4046*

4800 πωρόω *pōroō* (5)
hardened (2)
deadened (1)
hardened (1) *+2400*
made dull (1)

4801 πώρωσις *pōrōsis* (3)
hardening (2)
stubborn (1)

4802 πῶς *pōs* (102)
how (77)
how is it (8)
how can (5)

what (3)
even (1)
some way (1)
some way (1) *+3836*
under what circumstances (1)
way (1)
why (1)
untranslated (3)

4803 πώς *pōs* (14)
so that (2)
somehow (2)
that (2) *+3590*
for (1) *+3590*
for fear that (1) *+3590*
hoping (1) *+1623*
in some way (1)
somehow (1) *+1623*
that (1)
that (1) *+1623*
untranslated (1)

4804 ρ *r*
Variant; not used

4805 Ῥαάβ *Rhaab* (2)
Rahab (2)

4806 ῥαββί *rhabbi* (15)
Rabbi (15)

4807 ῥαββονί *rhabboni*
Variant; not used

4808 ῥαββουνί *rhabbouni* (2)
Rabbi (1)
Rabboni (1)

4809 ῥαββωνί *rhabbōni*
Variant; not used

4810 ῥαβδίζω *rhabdizō* (2)
beaten (1)
beaten with rods (1)

4811 ῥάβδος *rhabdos* (12)
staff (5)
scepter (4)
measuring rod (1)
whip (1)
untranslated (1)

4812 ῥαβδοῦχος *rhabdouchos* (2)
officers (2)

4813 ῥαβιθά *rhabitha*
Variant; not used

4814 Ῥαγαύ *Rhagau* (1)
Reu (1)

4815 ῥᾳδιούργημα *rhadiourgēma* (1)
crime (1)

4816 ῥᾳδιουργία *rhadiourgia* (1)
trickery (1)

4817 ῥαίνω *rhainō*
Variant; not used

4818 Ῥαιφάν *Rhaiphan* (1)
Rephan (1)

4819 ῥακά *rhaka* (1)
Raca (1)

4820 ῥάκος *rhakos* (2)
cloth (2)

4821 Ῥαμά *Rhama* (1)
Ramah (1)

4822 ῥαντίζω *rhantizō* (4)
sprinkled (2)
sprinkled on (1)
sprinkled to cleanse (1)

4823 ῥαντισμός *rhantismos* (2)
sprinkled (1)
sprinkling (1)

4824 ῥαπίζω *rhapizō* (2)
slapped (1)
strikes (1)

4825 ῥάπισμα *rhapisma* (3)
struck in the face (2) *+1443*
beat (1)

4826 ῥάσσω *rhassō*
Variant; not used

4827 ῥαφίς *rhaphis* (2)
needle (2)

4828 ῥαχά *rhacha*
Variant; not used

4829 Ῥαχάβ *Rhachab* (1)
Rahab (1)

4830 Ῥαχήλ *Rhachēl* (1)
Rachel (1)

4831 Ῥεβέκκα *Rhebekka* (1)
Rebekah's (1)

4832 ῥέδη *rhedē* (1)
carriages (1)

4833 Ῥεμφάν *Rhemphan*
Variant; not used

4834 Ῥεφάν *Rhephan*
Variant; not used

4835 ῥέω *rheō* (1)
flow (1)

4836 Ῥήγιον *Rhēgion* (1)
Rhegium (1)

4837 ῥῆγμα *rhēgma* (1)
destruction (1)

4838 ῥήγνυμι *rhēgnymi* (7)
burst (3)
break forth (1)
tear to pieces (1)
threw to the ground (1)
throws to the ground (1)

4839 ῥῆμα *rhēma* (68)
word (16)
words (16)
things (6)
say (4)
matter (2)
bring a message (1) *+3281*
charge (1)
command (1)
it[S] (1) *+3836+4047*
made statement (1) *+3306*
meaning (1)
meant (1)
message (1)
nothing (1) *+4024+4246*
promised (1)
said (1)
saying (1)
sayings (1)
says (1)
thing (1)
this[S] (1) *+3836+4047*
what said (1)
untranslated (7)

4840 Ῥησά *Rhēsa* (1)
Rhesa (1)

4841 ῥήσσω *rhēssō*
Variant; not used

4842 ῥήτωρ *rhētōr* (1)
lawyer (1)

4843 ῥητῶς *rhētōs* (1)
clearly (1)

4844 ῥίζα *rhiza* (17)
root (16)
roots (1)

4845 ῥιζόω *rhizoō* (2)
rooted (2)

4846 ῥιπή *rhipē* (1)
twinkling (1)

4847 ῥιπίζω *rhipizō* (1)
tossed (1)

4848 ῥιπτέω *rhipteō*
Variant; not used

4849 ῥίπτω *rhiptō* (8)
dropped (1)
helpless (1)
laid (1)
threw (1)
threw down (1)
threw overboard (1)
throwing off (1)
thrown (1)

4850 Ῥοβοάμ *Rhoboam* (2)
Rehoboam (2)

4851 Ῥόδη *Rhodē* (1)
Rhoda (1)

4852 Ῥόδος *Rhodos* (1)
Rhodes (1)

4853 ῥοιζηδόν *rhoizēdon* (1)
with a roar (1)

4854 Ῥομφά *Rhompha*
Variant; not used

4855 ῥομφαία *rhomphaia* (7)
sword (7)

4856 ῥοπή *rhopē*
Variant; not used

4857 Ῥουβήν *Rhoubēn* (1)
Reuben (1)

4858 Ῥούθ *Rhouth* (1)
Ruth (1)

4859 Ῥοῦφος *Rhouphos* (2)
Rufus (2)

4860 ῥύμη *rhymē* (4)
street (2)
alleys (1)
streets (1)

4861 ῥύομαι *rhyomai* (17)
rescue (5)
rescued (4)
deliver (3)
delivered (3)
deliverer (1)
rescues (1)

4862 ῥυπαίνω *rhypainō* (1)
vile (1)

4863 ῥυπαρεύω *rhypareuō*
Variant; not used

4864 ῥυπαρία *rhyparia* (1)
moral filth (1)

4865 ῥυπαρός *rhyparos* (2)
shabby (1)
vile (1)

4866 ῥύπος *rhypos* (1)
dirt (1)

4867 ῥυπόω *rhypoō*
Variant; not used

4868 ῥύσις *rhysis* (3)
subject to bleeding (2) *+135+1877*
bleeding (1) *+135+3836+3836*

4869 ῥυτίς *rhytis* (1)
wrinkle (1)

4870 Ῥωμαϊκός *Rhōmaikos*
Variant; not used

4871 Ῥωμαῖος *Rhōmaios* (12)
Roman citizen (4)

Romans (2)
Roman (1)
Roman citizen (1) *+476*
Roman citizens (1)
Roman citizens (1) *+476*
Romans (1) *+1639*
Rome (1)

4872 Ῥωμαϊστί *Rhōmaisti* (1)
Latin (1)

4873 Ῥώμη *Rhōmē* (8)
Rome (8)

4874 ῥώννυμι *rhōnnymi* (1)
farewell (1)

4875 σ *s*
Variant; not used

4876 σαβαχθάνι *sabachthani* (2)
sabachthani (2)

4877 Σαβαώθ *Sabaōth* (2)
Almighty (2)

4878 σαββατισμός *sabbatismos* (1)
Sabbath-rest (1)

4879 σάββατον *sabbaton* (68)
Sabbath (51)
week (8)
after the Sabbath (1) *+4067*
day of the week (1)
one Sabbath (1) *+1877*
one Sabbath (1) *+1877+3836*
Sabbath (1) *+2465+3836*
Sabbath day (1)
Sabbath day's walk from (1) *+1584+2400+3847*
Sabbath days (1)
untranslated (1)

4880 σαγήνη *sagēnē* (1)
net (1)

4881 Σαδδουκαῖος *Saddoukaios* (14)
Sadducees (14)

4882 Σαδώκ *Sadōk* (2)
Zadok (2)

4883 σαίνω *sainō* (1)
unsettled (1)

4884 σάκκος *sakkos* (4)
sackcloth (4)

4885 Σαλά *Sala* (2)
Salmon (1)
Shelah (1)

4886 Σαλαθιήλ *Salathiēl* (3)
Shealtiel (3)

4887 Σαλαμίς *Salamis* (1)
Salamis (1)

4888 σαλεύω *saleuō* (15)
shaken (8)
swayed (2)
agitating (1)
shake (1)
shaken together (1)
shook (1)
unsettled (1)

4889 Σαλήμ *Salēm* (2)
Salem (2)

4890 Σαλίμ *Salim* (1)
Salim (1)

4891 Σαλμών *Salmōn* (2)
Salmon (2)

4892 Σαλμώνη *Salmōnē* (1)
Salmone (1)

4893 σάλος *salos* (1)
tossing (1)

4894 σάλπιγξ *salpinx* (11)
trumpet (7)
trumpet call (2)
trumpets (2)

4895 σαλπίζω *salpizō* (12)
sounded trumpet (7)
announce with trumpets (1)
sound (1)
sound trumpet (1)
sounded (1)
trumpet sound (1)

4896 σαλπιστής *salpistēs* (1)
trumpeters (1)

4897 Σαλώμη *Salōmē* (2)
Salome (2)

4898 Σαλωμών *Salōmōn*
Variant; not used

4899 Σαμάρεια *Samareia* (11)
Samaria (10)
Samaritan (1)

4900 Σαμαρία *Samaria*
Variant; not used

4901 Σαμαρίτης *Samaritēs* (9)
Samaritan (5)
Samaritans (4)

4902 Σαμαρῖτις *Samaritis* (2)
Samaritan (2)

4903 Σαμοθράκη *Samothrakē* (1)
Samothrace (1)

4904 Σάμος *Samos* (1)
Samos (1)

4905 Σαμουήλ *Samouēl* (3)
Samuel (3)

4906 Σαμφουρειν *Samphourein*
Variant; not used

4907 Σαμψών *Sampsōn* (1)
Samson (1)

4908 σανδάλιον *sandalion* (2)
sandals (1)
sandals (1) *+5686*

4909 σανίς *sanis* (1)
planks (1)

4910 Σαούλ *Saoul* (7)
Saul (7)

4911 σαπρός *sapros* (8)
bad (7)
unwholesome (1)

4912 Σάπφιρα *Sapphira* (1)
Sapphira (1)

4913 σάπφιρος *sapphiros* (1)
sapphire (1)

4914 σαργάνη *sarganē* (1)
basket (1)

4915 Σάρδεις *Sardeis* (3)
Sardis (3)

4916 σάρδινος *sardinos*
Variant; not used

4917 σάρδιον *sardion* (2)
carnelian (2)

4918 σαρδόνυξ *sardonyx* (1)
sardonyx (1)

4919 Σάρεπτα *Sarepta* (1)
Zarephath (1)

4920 σαρκικός *sarkikos* (7)
worldly (3)
material (2)
of the world (1)
sinful (1)

4921 σάρκινος *sarkinos* (4)
ancestry (1)
of human (1)
unspiritual (1)
worldly (1)

4922 σάρξ *sarx* (147)
flesh (33)
sinful nature (23)
body (20)
one (4) *+4246*
human (3)
people (3)
sinful man (3)
earthly (2) *+2848*
in the ordinary way (2) *+2848*
man (2) *+135+2779*
nature (2)
physical (2)
the world (2)
as a man (1) *+1877*
birth (1)
bodies (1)
corrupted flesh (1)
earthly (1)
external (1)
from a worldly point of view (1) *+2848*
human ancestry (1)
human effort (1)
human nature (1)
human standards (1) *+3836*
illness (1) *+819+3836*
in this way[s] (1) *+2848*
it[s] (1)
its[s] (1) *+3836*
life (1)
life on earth (1)
man (1)
mankind (1)
men (1)
met personally (1) *+1877+3836+3972+4725*
natural (1)
natural selves (1)
outwardly (1)
outwardly (1) *+1877*
perversion (1) *+599+2283+3958*
sensual (1)
sinful (1)
sinful human nature (1)
this world (1)
unspiritual (1)
world (1)
worldly manner (1)
untranslated (13)

4923 Σαρούχ *Sarouch*
Variant; not used

4924 σαρόω *saroō* (3)
swept clean (2)
sweep (1)

4925 Σάρρα *Sarra* (4)
Sarah (3)
Sarah's (1)

4926 Σαρών *Sarōn* (1)
Sharon (1)

4927 Σατάν *Satan*
Variant, not used

4928 Σατανᾶς *Satanas* (36)
Satan (35)
Satan's (1)

4929 σάτον *saton* (2)
amount (1)
large amount of flour (1) *+236+5552*

4930 Σαῦλος *Saulos* (17)
Saul (17)

4931 σβέννυμι *sbennymi* (6)
quenched (2)
extinguish (1)
going out (1)
put out (1)

snuff out (1)

4932 σεαυτοῦ *seautou* (96)
yourself (32)
yourselves (27)
you (9)
your own (4)
each other (3)
one another (3)
your (3)
claim (1) *+4472*
conceited (1) *+4123+5861*
take care of mat (1) *+5143*
take revenge (1) *+1688*
watch out (1) *+1063*
who do you think you are (1) *+4472+5515*
your life (1)
your very self (1)
untranslated (7)

4933 σεβάζομαι *sebazomai* (1)
worshiped (1)

4934 σέβασμα *sebasma* (2)
objects of worship (1)
worshiped (1)

4935 σεβαστός *sebastos* (3)
Emperor (1)
Emperor's (1)
imperial (1)

4936 σέβω *sebō* (10)
worship (3)
God-fearing (2)
worshiper of (2)
devout (1)
God-fearing Greeks (1)
worshiped (1)

4937 σειρά *seira*
Variant; not used

4938 σειρός *seiros*
Variant; not used

4939 σεισμός *seismos* (14)
earthquake (9)
earthquakes (3)
quake (1)
storm (1)

4940 σείω *seiō* (5)
shook (2)
shake (1)
shaken (1)
stirred (1)

4941 Σεκοῦνδος *Sekoundos* (1)
Secundus (1)

4942 Σελεύκεια *Seleukeia* (1)
Seleucia (1)

4943 σελήνη *selēnē* (9)
moon (9)

4944 σεληνιάζομαι *selēniazomai* (2)
seizures (2)

4945 Σεμεΐ *Semei*
Variant; not used

4946 Σεμεΐν *Semein* (1)
Semein (1)

4947 σεμίδαλις *semidalis* (1)
fine flour (1)

4948 σεμνός *semnos* (4)
worthy of respect (3)
noble (1)

4949 σεμνότης *semnotēs* (3)
holiness (1)
respect (1)
seriousness (1)

4950 Σέργιος *Sergios* (1)
Sergius (1)

4951 Σερούκ *Serouk*
Variant; not used

4952 Σερούχ *Serouch* (1)
Serug (1)

4953 Σήθ *Sēth* (1)
Seth (1)

4954 Σήμ *Sēm* (1)
Shem (1)

4955 σημαίνω *sēmainō* (6)
indicate (1)
indicating (1)
made known (1)
predicted (1)
show (1)
specifying (1)

4956 σημεῖον *sēmeion* (77)
miraculous signs (23)
sign (18)
signs (15)
miraculous sign (11)
none[s] (3) *+4024*
miracle (2)
mark (1)
miraculously (1)
signal (1)
the distinguishing mark (1)
wondrous sign (1)

4957 σημειόω *sēmeioō* (1)
take special note (1)

4958 σήμερον *sēmeron* (41)
today (32)
day (2)
very day (2) *+2465*
days (1)
this day (1)
this day (1) *+2465+3836*
today (1) *+1877+2465+3836*
today's (1)

4959 σημικίνθιον *sēmikinthion*
Variant; not used

4960 σήπω *sēpō* (1)
rotted (1)

4961 σηρικός *sērikos*
Variant; not used

4962 σής *sēs* (3)
moth (3)

4963 σητόβρωτος *sētobrōtos* (1)
moths have eaten (1) *+1181*

4964 σθενόω *sthenoō* (1)
firm (1)

4965 σιαγών *siagōn* (2)
cheek (2)

4966 σιαίνομαι *siainomai*
Variant; not used

4967 σιγάω *sigaō* (10)
quiet (3)
silent (3)
finished (1)
hidden (1)
kept this to themselves (1)
stop (1)

4968 σιγή *sigē* (2)
all silent (1) *+4498*
silence (1)

4969 σιδήρεος *sidēreos* (5)
iron (4)
of iron (1)

4970 σίδηρος *sidēros* (1)
iron (1)

4971 σιδηροῦς *sidērous*
Variant; not used

4972 Σιδών *Sidōn* (10)
Sidon (10)

4973 Σιδώνιος *Sidōnios* (1)
Sidon (1)

4974 σικάριος *sikarios* (1)
terrorists (1) *+467+3836*

4975 σίκερα *sikera* (1)
fermented drink (1)

4976 Σίλας *Silas* (12)
Silas (12)

4977 Σιλουανός *Silouanos* (4)
Silas (4)

4978 Σιλωάμ *Silōam* (3)
Siloam (3)

4979 Σιμαίας *Simaias*
Variant; not used

4980 σιμικίνθιον *simikinthion* (1)
aprons (1)

4981 Σίμων *Simōn* (75)
Simon (69)
Simon's (4)
belonging to Simon (1) *+1639*
his[s] (1)

4982 Σινά *Sina* (4)
Sinai (4)

4983 σίναπι *sinapi* (5)
mustard (5)

4984 σινδών *sindōn* (6)
linen cloth (3)
garment (1)
linen (1)
linen garment (1)

4985 σινιάζω *siniazō* (1)
sift (1)

4986 σιρικός *sirikos* (1)
silk (1)

4987 σιρός *siros* (1)
dungeons (1)

4988 σιτευτός *siteutos* (3)
fattened (3)

4989 σιτίον *sition* (1)
grain (1)

4990 σιτιστός *sitistos* (1)
fattened cattle (1)

4991 σιτομέτριον *sitometrion* (1)
food allowance (1)

4992 σῖτος *sitos* (14)
wheat (11)
grain (2)
kernel (1)

4993 Σιχάρ *Sichar*
Variant; not used

4994 Σιών *Siōn* (7)
Zion (7)

4995 σιωπάω *siōpaō* (10)
quiet (5)
silent (5)

4996 σιωπῇ *siōpē*
Variant; not used

4997 σκανδαλίζω *skandalizō* (29)
causes to sin (8)
fall away (7)
offend (2)
took offense (2)
cause to fall (1)
cause to sin (1)
causes fall into sin (1)
causes sin (1)
falls away (1)

go astray (1)
led into sin (1)
offended (1)
turn away (1)
untranslated (1)

4998 σκάνδαλον *skandalon* (15)
stumbling block (3)
makes fall (2)
cause people to sin (1)
causes sin (1)
entice (1) *+965+1967*
obstacle (1)
obstacles (1)
offense (1)
stumble (1)
such things[S] (1) *+3836*
they[S] (1) *+3836*
things that cause to sin (1)

4999 σκάπτω *skaptō* (3)
dig (2)
dug (1)

5000 Σκαριώθ *Skariōth*
Variant; not used

5001 Σκαριώτης *Skariōtēs*
Variant; not used

5002 σκάφη *skaphē* (3)
lifeboat (3)

5003 σκέλος *skelos* (3)
legs (3)

5004 σκέπασμα *skepasma* (1)
clothing (1)

5005 Σκευᾶς *Skeuas* (1)
Sceva (1)

5006 σκευή *skeuē* (1)
tackle (1)

5007 σκεῦος *skeuos* (23)
instrument (2)
jar (2)
objects (2)
possessions (2)
articles (1)
body (1)
goods (1)
jars (1)
kind (1)
merchandise (1)
partner (1)
pottery (1)
pottery (1) *+3039*
sea anchor (1)
sheet (1)
untranslated (4)

5008 σκηνή *skēnē* (21)
tabernacle (9)
shelters (3)
room (2)
tent (2)
dwelling (1)
dwelling place (1)
dwellings (1)
shrine (1)
tents (1)

5009 σκηνοπηγία *skēnopēgia* (1)
tabernacles (1)

5010 σκηνοποιός *skēnopoios* (1)
tentmaker (1)

5011 σκῆνος *skēnos* (1)
tent (1)

5012 σκηνόω *skēnoō* (5)
live (2)
dwell (1)
made his dwelling (1)
spread tent (1)

5013 σκήνωμα *skēnōma* (3)
dwelling place (1)
it[S] (1) *+1609+3836*
tent (1)

5014 σκιά *skia* (7)
shadow (6)
shade (1)

5015 σκιρτάω *skirtaō* (3)
leaped (2)
leap for joy (1)

5016 σκληροκαρδία *sklērokardia* (3)
hearts hard (2)
stubborn refusal (1)

5017 σκληρός *sklēros* (5)
hard (3)
harsh (1)
strong (1)

5018 σκληρότης *sklērotēs* (1)
stubbornness (1)

5019 σκληροτράχηλος *sklērotrachēlos* (1)
stiff-necked (1)

5020 σκληρύνω *sklērynō* (6)
harden (3)
hardened (1)
hardens (1)
obstinate (1)

5021 σκολιός *skolios* (4)
crooked (2)
corrupt (1)
harsh (1)

5022 σκόλοψ *skolops* (1)
thorn (1)

5023 σκοπέω *skopeō* (6)
fix eyes on (1)
look to (1)
see to it (1)
take note of (1)
watch (1)
watch out for (1)

5024 σκοπός *skopos* (1)
goal (1)

5025 σκορπίζω *skorpizō* (5)
scatters (3)
scattered (1)
scattered abroad (1)

5026 σκορπίος *skorpios* (5)
scorpions (3)
scorpion (2)

5027 σκοτεινός *skoteinos* (3)
full of darkness (2)
dark (1)

5028 σκοτία *skotia* (16)
darkness (11)
dark (5)

5029 σκοτίζομαι *skotizomai* (6)
darkened (5)
turned dark (1)

5030 σκότος *skotos* (31)
darkness (29)
dark (2)

5031 σκοτόω *skotoō* (2)
darkened (1)
darkness (1)

5032 σκύβαλον *skybalon* (1)
rubbish (1)

5033 Σκύθης *Skythēs* (1)
Scythian (1)

5034 σκυθρωπός *skythrōpos* (2)
downcast (1)
look somber (1) *+1181*

5035 σκύλλω *skyllō* (4)
bother (2)
harassed (1)
trouble (1)

5036 σκῦλον *skylon* (1)
spoils (1)

5037 σκωληκόβρωτος *skōlēkobrōtos* (1)
eaten by worms (1)

5038 σκώληξ *skōlēx* (1)
worm (1)

5039 σμαράγδινος *smaragdinos* (1)
emerald (1)

5040 σμάραγδος *smaragdos* (1)
emerald (1)

5041 σμῆγμα *smēgma*
Variant; not used

5042 σμίγμα *smigma*
Variant; not used

5043 σμύρνα1 *smyrna1* (2)
myrrh (2)

5044 Σμύρνα2 *Smyrna2* (2)
Smyrna (2)

5045 Σμυρναῖος *Smyrnaios*
Variant; not used

5046 σμυρνίζω *smyrnizō* (1)
mixed with myrrh (1)

5047 Σόδομα *Sodoma* (9)
Sodom (7)
Sodom (2) *+1178*

5048 Σολομών *Solomōn* (12)
Solomon (7)
Solomon's (5)

5049 σορός *soros* (1)
coffin (1)

5050 σός *sos* (26)
your (12)
yours (5)
belongs to you (1)
belongs to you (1) *+2400*
you (1)
you have (1) *+3836*
your family (1) *+3836*
your own (1)
yours (1) *+3836*
untranslated (2)

5051 σουδάριον *soudarion* (4)
burial cloth (1)
cloth (1)
handkerchiefs (1)
piece of cloth (1)

5052 Σουσάννα *Sousanna* (1)
Susanna (1)

5053 σοφία *sophia* (51)
wisdom (48)
wise (2)
superior wisdom (1) *+5667*

5054 σοφίζω *sophizō* (2)
cleverly invented (1)
make wise (1)

5055 σοφός *sophos* (20)
wise (18)
expert (1)
wiser (1)

5056 Σπανία *Spania* (2)
Spain (2)

5057 σπαράσσω *sparassō* (3)
convulsed (1)
shook violently (1)
throws into convulsions (1)

5058 σπαργανόω *sparganoō* (2)
wrapped in cloths (2)

5059 σπαταλάω *spatalaō* (2)
lives for pleasure (1)
self-indulgence (1)

5060 σπάω *spaō* (2)
drew (2)

5061 σπεῖρα *speira* (7)
company of soldiers (2)
detachment of soldiers (2)
regiment (2)
Roman troops (1)

5062 σπείρω *speirō* (52)
sow (9)
sown (9)
sows (8)
farmer (4)
seed sown (4)
received seed that fell (3)
sower (3)
plant (2)
planted (2)
scattering the seed (2)
sow seed (2)
sowed (2)
scattering seed (1)
sown seed (1)

5063 σπεκουλάτωρ *spekoulatōr* (1)
executioner (1)

5064 σπένδω *spendō* (2)
poured out like a drink offering (2)

5065 σπέρμα *sperma* (43)
seed (11)
descendants (10)
offspring (8)
children (3)
descendant (2)
have children (2) *+1985*
seeds (2)
become a father (1) *+2856+3284*
child (1)
descended from (1) *+1666*
family (1)
have children (1) *+482*

5066 σπερμολόγος *spermologos* (1)
babbler (1)

5067 σπεύδω *speudō* (6)
at once (1)
hurried off (1) *+2262*
immediately (1)
in a hurry (1)
quick (1)
speed (1)

5068 σπήλαιον *spēlaion* (6)
den (3)
caves (2)
cave (1)

5069 σπιλάς *spilas* (1)
blemishes (1)

5070 σπίλος *spilos* (2)
blots (1)
stain (1)

5071 σπιλόω *spiloō* (2)
corrupts (1)
stained (1)

5072 σπλαγχνίζομαι *splanchnizomai* (12)
had compassion (4)
have compassion (2)
took pity (2)
filled with compassion (1)
filled with compassion for (1)
heart went out (1)
take pity (1)

5073 σπλάγχνον *splanchnon* (11)
affection (3)
dearly (1)
has no pity (1) *+3091+3836*
heart (1)
hearts (1)
intestines (1)
tender mercy (1) *+1799*
tenderness (1)
very heart (1)

5074 σπόγγος *spongos* (3)
sponge (3)

5075 σποδός *spodos* (3)
ashes (3)

5076 σπορά *spora* (1)
seed (1)

5077 σπόριμος *sporimos* (3)
grainfields (3)

5078 σπόρος *sporos* (6)
seed (5)
seed (1) *+3836*

5079 σπουδάζω *spoudazō* (11)
do best (4)
make every effort (4)
eager (2)
made effort (1)

5080 σπουδαῖος *spoudaios* (3)
enthusiasm (1)
even more so[s] (1) *+4498*
zealous (1)

5081 σπουδαίως *spoudaiōs* (4)
all the more eager (1)
earnestly (1)
everything you can (1)
hard (1)

5082 σπουδή *spoudē* (12)
earnestness (3)
concern (1)
devoted (1)
diligence (1)
diligently (1) *+1877*
eager (1)
effort (1)
hurried (1) *+1656+3552*
hurried (1) *+3552+4513*
zeal (1)

5083 σπυρίς *spyris* (5)
basketfuls (2)
basket (1)
basketfuls (1) *+4441*
basketfuls (1) *+4445*

5084 στάδιον *stadion* (7)
stadia (2)
distance (1)
race (1)
seven miles (1) *+2008*
three or three and a half miles (1) *+1633+2445+4297+5558*
two miles (1) *+1278*

5085 στάμνος *stamnos* (1)
jar (1)

5086 στασιαστής *stasiastēs* (1)
insurrectionists (1)

5087 στάσις *stasis* (9)
dispute (3)
insurrection (2)
rioting (1)
riots (1)
standing (1)
uprising (1)

5088 στατήρ *statēr* (1)
four-drachma coin (1)

5089 σταυρός *stauros* (27)
cross (26)
crosses (1)

5090 σταυρόω *stauroō* (46)
crucified (31)
crucify (15)

5091 σταφυλή *staphylē* (3)
grapes (3)

5092 στάχυς1 *stachys1* (5)
heads of grain (3)
head (2)

5093 Στάχυς2 *Stachys2* (1)
Stachys (1)

5094 στέγη *stegē* (3)
roof (3)

5095 στέγω *stegō* (4)
stand (2)
protects (1)
put up with (1)

5096 στεῖρα *steira* (5)
barren (3)
barren woman (1)
barren women (1)

5097 στέλλω *stellō* (2)
avoid (1)
keep away (1)

5098 στέμμα *stemma* (1)
wreaths (1)

5099 στεναγμός *stenagmos* (2)
groaning (1)
groans (1)

5100 στενάζω *stenazō* (6)
groan (3)
burden (1)
grumble (1)
with a deep sigh (1)

5101 στενός *stenos* (3)
narrow (2)
small (1)

5102 στενοχωρέω *stenochōreō* (3)
withholding (2)
crushed (1)

5103 στενοχωρία *stenochōria* (4)
difficulties (1)
distress (1)
distresses (1)
hardship (1)

5104 στερεός *stereos* (4)
solid (3)
standing firm (1)

5105 στερεόω *stereoō* (3)
strong (2)
strengthened (1)

5106 στερέωμα *stereōma* (1)
firm (1)

5107 Στεφανᾶς *Stephanas* (3)
Stephanas (3)

5108 Στέφανος1 *Stephanos1* (7)
Stephen (6)
him[s] (1) *+3836*

5109 στέφανος2 *stephanos2* (18)
crown (15)
crowns (3)

5110 στεφανόω *stephanoō* (3)
crowned (2)
receive the victor's crown (1)

5111 στῆθος *stēthos* (5)
breast (1)
breasts (1)
chests (1)
untranslated (2)

5112 στήκω *stēkō*
Variant; not used

5113 στηριγμός *stērigmos* (1)
secure position (1)

5114 στηρίζω *stērizō* (13)
strengthen (6)
make strong (2)
establish (1)
firmly established (1)
fixed (1)
resolutely (1) *+3836+4725*
stand firm (1) *+2840+3836*

5115 στιβάς *stibas* (1)
branches (1)

5116 στίγμα *stigma* (1)
marks (1)

5117 στιγμή *stigmē* (1)
instant (1) *+5989*

5118 στίλβω *stilbō* (1)
dazzling (1)

5119 στοά *stoa* (4)
Colonnade (3)
covered colonnades (1)

5120 στοιβάς *stoibas*
Variant; not used

5121 Στοϊκός *Stoikos* (1)
stoic (1)

5122 στοιχεῖον *stoicheion* (7)
basic principles (3)
elements (2)
elementary truths (1) *+794+3836*
principles (1)

5123 στοιχέω *stoicheō* (5)
follow (1)
keep in step (1)
live up (1)
living (1)
walk (1)

5124 στολή *stolē* (9)
robes (4)
robe (3)
flowing robes (2)

5125 στόμα *stoma* (78)
mouth (42)
mouths (9)
lips (6)
face (4)
testimony (2)
words (2)
began to speak (1) *+487+3306+3836*
edge sword (1) *+3479*
might say (1) *+1666+3836*
speak (1) *+487+3836*
spoken freely (1) *+487+3836*
sword (1) *+3479*
that[S] (1)
untranslated (6)

5126 στόμαχος *stomachos* (1)
stomach (1)

5127 στρατεία *strateia* (2)
fight (1)
weapons fight with (1) *+3836+3960*

5128 στράτευμα *strateuma* (8)
troops (3)
armies (2)
army (2)
soldiers (1)

5129 στρατεύομαι *strateuomai* (7)
battle (1)
fight (1)
serves as a soldier (1)
serving as a soldier (1)
soldiers (1)
wage war (1)
war (1)

5130 στρατηγός *stratēgos* (10)
magistrates (5)
captain (3)
officers of guard (1)
officers of the temple guard (1)

5131 στρατιά *stratia* (2)
bodies (1)
host (1)

5132 στρατιώτης *stratiōtēs* (26)
soldiers (22)
soldier (3)
them[S] (1)

5133 στρατολογέω *stratologeō* (1)
commanding officer (1)

5134 στρατοπεδάρχης *stratopedarchēs*
Variant; not used

5135 στρατοπέδαρχος *stratopedarchos*
Variant; not used

5136 στρατόπεδον *stratopedon* (1)
armies (1)

5137 στρεβλόω *strebloo* (1)
distort (1)

5138 στρέφω *strephō* (21)
turned (7)
turn (5)
turning (2)
change (1)
returned (1)
turned around (1) *+1650+3836+3958*
turned away (1)
turned back (1)
turned toward (1)
turning around (1)

5139 στρηνιάω *strēniaō* (2)
luxury (1)
shared luxury (1)

5140 στρῆνος *strēnos* (1)
luxuries (1)

5141 στρουθίον *strouthion* (4)
sparrows (4)

5142 στρώννυμι *strōnnymi*
Variant; not used

5143 στρωννύω *strōnnyō* (6)
spread (3)
furnished (2)
take care of mat (1) *+4932*

5144 στυγητός *stygētos* (1)
hated (1)

5145 στυγνάζω *stygnazō* (2)
face fell (1)
overcast (1)

5146 στῦλος *stylos* (4)
pillar (2)
pillars (2)

5147 Στωϊκός *Stōikos*
Variant; not used

5148 σύ *sy* (2898)
you (1991)
your (700)
yours (15)
yourselves (11)
your own (8)
please (2) *+1289*
please (2) *+2263*
you (2) *+3836+4725*
you (2) *+6034*
you yourselves (2)
your own (2) *+2848*
and even more (1) *+2779+4707*
both of you (1) *+899+2779*
does[S] (1) *+1877+3531*
home (1) *+1650+3836+3875*
home (1) *+3875*
it depends on you (1) *+1666+3836*
listen carefully (1) *+1650+3836+4044+5148+5502*
of you (1) *+1639+1877+3836*
that's your responsibility (1) *+3972*
the two of you (1) *+899+2779*
them[S] (1) *+3517+3836*
us (1)
you (1) *+2093*
you (1) *+3836+3950*
you (1) *+3836+4364*
you can see (1) *+595*
you have (1) *+1877*
you have (1) *+4123*
you yourself (1)
you're (1)
your (1) *+1869*
your (1) *+1877*
your (1) *+2848*
your responsibility (1) *+3972*
yourself (1)
yourselves (1) *+6034*
untranslated (135)

5149 συγγένεια *syngeneia* (3)
family (1)
people (1)
relatives (1)

5150 συγγενής *syngenēs* (11)
relatives (8)
relative (2)
race (1)

5151 συγγενίς *syngenis* (1)
relative (1)

5152 συγγνώμη *syngnōmē* (1)
concession (1)

5153 συγκάθημαι *synkathēmai* (2)
sat (1) *+1639*
sitting with (1)

5154 συγκαθίζω *synkathizō* (2)
sat down together (1)
seated with (1)

5155 συγκακοπαθέω *synkakopatheō* (2)
endure with (1)
join in suffering (1)

5156 συγκακουχέομαι *synkakoucheomai* (1)
mistreated along with (1)

5157 συγκαλέω *synkaleō* (8)
called together (6)
calls together (2)

5158 συγκαλύπτω *synkalyptō* (1)
concealed (1)

5159 συγκάμπτω *synkamptō* (1)
bent (1)

5160 συγκαταβαίνω *synkatabainō* (1)
come with (1)

5161 συγκατάθεσις *synkatathesis* (1)
agreement (1)

5162 συγκατανεύω *synkataneuō*
Variant; not used

5163 συγκατατίθημι *synkatatithēmi* (1)
consented (1)

5164 συγκαταψηφίζομαι *synkatapsēphizomai* (1)
added (1)

5165 σύγκειμαι *synkeimai*
Variant; not used

5166 συγκεράννυμι *synkerannymi* (2)
combine with (1)
combined (1)

5167 συγκινέω *synkineō* (1)
stirred up (1)

5168 συγκλείω *synkleiō* (4)
bound over (1)

caught (1)
locked up (1)
prisoner (1)

5169 συγκληρονόμος *synklēronomos* (4)
heirs with (2)
co-heirs with (1)
heirs together with (1)

5170 συγκοινωνέω *synkoinōneō* (3)
share (2)
to do with (1)

5171 συγκοινωνός *synkoinōnos* (4)
share (2) *+1181*
companion (1)
share with (1) *+1639*

5172 συγκομίζω *synkomizō* (1)
buried (1)

5173 συγκρίνω *synkrinō* (3)
compare (2)
expressing (1)

5174 συγκύπτω *synkyptō* (1)
bent over (1)

5175 συγκυρία *synkyria* (1)
happened (1) *+2848*

5176 συγχαίρω *synchairō* (7)
rejoice with (4)
rejoices with (2)
shared joy (1)

5177 συγχέω *syncheō* (5)
baffled (1)
bewilderment (1)
confusion (1)
in an uproar (1)
stirred up (1)

5178 συγχράομαι *synchraomai* (1)
associate with (1)

5179 συγχύνω *synchynō*
Variant; not used

5180 σύγχυσις *synchysis* (1)
uproar (1) *+4398*

5181 συγχωρέω *synchōreō*
Variant; not used

5182 συζάω *syzaō* (3)
live with (2)
live (1)

5183 συζεύγνυμι *syzeugnymi* (2)
joined together (2)

5184 συζητέω *syzēteō* (10)
question (2)
argue with (1)
arguing (1)
arguing about (1)
asked (1)
debated (1)
debating (1)
discussed (1)
discussing (1)

5185 συζήτησις *syzētēsis*
Variant; not used

5186 συζητητής *syzētētēs* (1)
philosopher (1)

5187 σύζυγος *syzygos* (1)
yokefellow (1)

5188 συζωοποιέω *syzōopoieō* (2)
made alive with (2)

5189 συκάμινος *sykaminos* (1)
mulberry tree (1)

5190 συκῆ *sykē* (16)
fig tree (14)
figs (1)
tree (1)

5191 συκομορέα *sykomorea* (1)
sycamore-fig tree (1)

5192 σῦκον *sykon* (4)
figs (4)

5193 συκοφαντέω *sykophanteō* (2)
accuse falsely (1)
cheated out of (1)

5194 συλαγωγέω *sylagōgeō* (1)
takes captive (1) *+1639*

5195 συλάω *sylaō* (1)
robbed (1)

5196 συλλαλέω *syllaleō* (6)
talking with (3)
conferred with (1)
discussed with (1)
said (1)

5197 συλλαμβάνω *syllambanō* (16)
arrested (2)
capture (2)
help (2)
seized (2)
conceived (1)
conceived (1) *+1877+3120+3836*
have (1)
pregnant (1)
seize (1)
seizing (1)
taken (1)
with child (1) *+1143+1877*

5198 συλλέγω *syllegō* (8)
pick (2)
collect (1)
collected (1)
pull up (1)
pulled up (1)
pulling (1)
weed (1)

5199 συλλογίζομαι *syllogizomai* (1)
discussed (1)

5200 συλλυπέω *syllypeō* (1)
deeply distressed (1)

5201 συμβαίνω *symbainō* (8)
happened (3)
had to be (1)
happen (1)
happening (1)
of them (1) *+899*
untranslated (1)

5202 συμβάλλω *symballō* (6)
a help (1)
conferred (1)
dispute with (1)
go war (1) *+4483*
met (1)
pondered (1)

5203 συμβασιλεύω *symbasileuō* (2)
kings with (1)
reign with (1)

5204 συμβιβάζω *symbibazō* (7)
held together (2)
concluding (1)
instruct (1)
instructions to (1)
proving (1)
united (1)

5205 συμβουλεύω *symbouleuō* (4)
advised (1)
conspired (1)
counsel (1)
plotted (1)

5206 συμβούλιον *symboulion* (8)
council (1)
decided to (1) *+3284*
decision (1)
devised a plan (1) *+3284*
laid plans (1) *+3284*
plot (1) *+1443*
plotted (1) *+3284*
to the decision (1) *+3284*

5207 σύμβουλος *symboulos* (1)
counselor (1)

5208 Συμεών *Symeōn* (7)
Simeon (5)
Simon (2)

5209 συμμαθητής *symmathētēs* (1)
rest of the disciples (1)

5210 συμμαρτυρέω *symmartyreō* (3)
bearing witness (1)
confirms (1)
testifies with (1)

5211 συμμερίζομαι *symmerizomai* (1)
share (1)

5212 συμμέτοχος *symmetochos* (2)
partners with (1)
sharers together in (1)

5213 συμμιμητής *symmimētēs* (1)
join with others following example (1) *+1181*

5214 συμμορφίζω *symmorphizō* (1)
becoming like (1)

5215 σύμμορφος *symmorphos* (2)
conformed (1)
like (1)

5216 συμμορφόω *symmorphoō*
Variant; not used

5217 συμπαθέω *sympatheō* (2)
sympathize with (1)
sympathized with (1)

5218 συμπαθής *sympathēs* (1)
sympathetic (1)

5219 συμπαραγίνομαι *symparaginomai* (1)
gathered (1)

5220 συμπαρακαλέω *symparakaleō* (1)
mutually encouraged (1)

5221 συμπαραλαμβάνω *symparalambanō* (4)
take (1)
take with (1)
taking with (1)
took along (1)

5222 συμπαραμένω *symparamenō*
Variant; not used

5223 συμπάρειμι *sympareimi* (1)
present with (1)

5224 συμπάσχω *sympaschō* (2)
share in sufferings (1)
suffers with (1)

5225 συμπέμπω *sympempō* (2)
sending (1)
sending with (1)

5226 συμπεριέχω *symperiechō*
Variant; not used

5227 συμπεριλαμβάνω *symperilambanō* (1)
put arms around (1)

5228 συμπίνω *sympinō* (1)
drank (1)

5229 συμπίπτω *sympiptō* (1)
collapsed (1)

5230 συμπληρόω *symplēroō* (3)
approached (1)
came (1)
swamped (1)

5231 συμπνίγω *sympnigō* (5)
choke (2)

choked (2)
crushed (1)

5232 συμπολίτης *sympolitēs* (1)
fellow citizens with (1)

5233 συμπορεύομαι *symporeuomai* (4)
came (1)
traveling with (1)
walked along with (1)
went along with (1)

5234 συμποσία *symposia*
Variant; not used

5235 συμπόσιον *symposion* (1)
groups (1) *+5235*

5236 συμπρεσβύτερος *sympresbyteros* (1)
fellow elder (1)

5237 συμφέρω *sympherō* (15)
better (5)
good (3)
beneficial (1)
best (1)
brought together (1)
for good (1)
gained (1)
helpful (1)
is beneficial (1)

5238 σύμφημι *symphēmi* (1)
agree (1)

5239 σύμφορος *symphoros* (2)
good (2)

5240 συμφορτίζω *symphortizō*
Variant; not used

5241 συμφυλέτης *symphyletēs* (1)
countrymen (1)

5242 σύμφυτος *symphytos* (1)
united (1)

5243 συμφύω *symphyō* (1)
grew up with (1)

5244 συμφωνέω *symphōneō* (6)
agree (3)
agreed (1)
in agreement with (1)
match (1)

5245 συμφώνησις *symphōnēsis* (1)
harmony (1)

5246 συμφωνία *symphōnia* (1)
music (1)

5247 σύμφωνος *symphonos* (1)
mutual consent (1)

5248 συμψηφίζω *sympsēphizō* (1)
calculated (1)

5249 σύμψυχος *sympsychos* (1)
spirit (1)

5250 σύν *syn* (128)
with (75)
and (11)
together with (7)
along with (6)
associates (2) *+3836*
companions (2) *+1639+3836*
companions (2) *+3836*
accompanied (1) *+5302*
accompanied by (1)
accompany (1) *+4513*
along (1) *+899*
and what is more (1)
+247+1145+2779+4047+4246
as (1)
attendant of (1)
companions (1) *+4513*
his fellow (1) *+899+3836*
join in (1)
on (1)
our companions (1) *+1609+3836*
sided with (1) *+1639*
through (1)
when are tempted (1) *+3836+4280*
untranslated (8)

5251 συνάγω *synagō* (59)
gathered (12)
gather (10)
gathered together (5)
met (5)
assembled (3)
gathering (2)
got together (2)
invite in (2)
meeting (2)
met together (2)
store (2)
bring together (1)
called meeting (1)
called together (1)
came together (1)
caught (1)
come together (1) *+1639*
gather together (1)
harvests (1)
invited in (1)
picked up (1)
store away (1)
went (1)

5252 συναγωγή *synagōgē* (57)
synagogue (30)
synagogues (23)
congregation (1)
from one synagogue to another (1)
+2848+4246
meeting (1)
untranslated (1)

5253 συναγωνίζομαι *synagonizomai* (1)
join in struggle (1)

5254 συναθλέω *synathleō* (2)
contended at side (1)
contending as (1)

5255 συναθροίζω *synathroizō* (2)
called together (1)
gathered (1)

5256 συναίρω *synairō* (3)
settle (1)
settled accounts (1) *+3364*
settlement (1)

5257 συναιχμάλωτος *synaichmalōtos* (3)
fellow prisoner (2)
in prison with (1)

5258 συνακολουθέω *synakoloutheō* (3)
follow (1)
followed (1)
following (1)

5259 συναλίζω *synalizō* (1)
eating (1)

5260 συναλίσκομαι *synaliskomai*
Variant; not used

5261 συναλλάσσω *synallassō* (1)
reconcile (1) *+1645+1650*

5262 συναναβαίνω *synanabainō* (2)
come up with (1)
traveled with (1)

5263 συνανάκειμαι *synanakeimai* (7)
dinner guests (2)
at the table with (1)
ate with (1)
eating with (1)
fellow guests (1)
guests (1)

5264 συναναμείγνυμι *synanameignymi* (3)
associate with (3)

5265 συναναπαύομαι *synanapauomai* (1)
together refreshed (1)

5266 συναναστρέφομαι *synanastrephomai*
Variant; not used

5267 συναντάω *synantaō* (6)
met (4)
happen (1)
meet (1)

5268 συνάντησις *synantēsis*
Variant; not used

5269 συναντιλαμβάνομαι *synantilambanomai* (2)
help (1)
helps (1)

5270 συναπάγω *synapagō* (3)
carried away (1)
led astray (1)
willing to associate (1)

5271 συναποθνῄσκω *synapothnēskō* (3)
die with (2)
died with (1)

5272 συναπόλλυμι *synapollymi* (1)
killed with (1)

5273 συναποστέλλω *synapostellō* (1)
sent with (1)

5274 συναρμολογέω *synarmologeō* (2)
joined (1)
joined together (1)

5275 συναρπάζω *synarpazō* (4)
seized (3)
caught (1)

5276 συναυλίζομαι *synaulizomai*
Variant; not used

5277 συναυξάνω *synauxanō* (1)
grow together (1)

5278 σύνδεσμος *syndesmos* (4)
binds together (1) *+1639*
bond (1)
captive (1)
sinews (1)

5279 συνδέω *syndeō* (1)
fellow prisoners (1)

5280 συνδοξάζω *syndoxazō* (1)
share in glory (1)

5281 σύνδουλος *syndoulos* (10)
fellow servant (4)
fellow servants (3)
fellow servant with with (2)
servants (1)

5282 συνδρομή *syndromē* (1)
running (1)

5283 συνεγείρω *synegeirō* (3)
raised (1)
raised up with (1)
raised with (1)

5284 συνέδριον *synedrion* (22)
Sanhedrin (19)
councils (1)
local councils (1)
them[s] (1) *+899+3836*

5285 συνέδριος *synedrios*
Variant; not used

5286 σύνεδρος *synedros*
Variant; not used

5287 συνείδησις *syneidēsis* (30)
conscience (23)
consciences (4)
conscious (1)
felt guilty (1)
guilty conscience (1) *+4505*

5288 συνείδω *syneidō*
Variant; not used

5289 σύνειμι1 *syneimi1* (2)
companions (1)
were with (1)

5290 σύνειμι2 *syneimi2* (1)
gathering (1)

5291 συνεισέρχομαι *syneiserchomai* (2)
entered (1)
went with into (1)

5292 συνέκδημος *synekdēmos* (2)
accompany (1)
traveling companions (1)

5293 συνεκλεκτός *syneklektos* (1)
chosen together with (1)

5294 συνεκπορεύομαι *synekporeuomai*
Variant; not used

5295 συνελαύνω *synelaunō*
Variant; not used

5296 συνεπιμαρτυρέω *synepimartyreō* (1)
also testified (1)

5297 συνεπίσκοπος *synepiskopos*
Variant; not used

5298 συνεπιτίθημι *synepitithēmi* (1)
joined in the accusation (1)

5299 συνέπομαι *synepomai* (1)
accompanied by (1)

5300 συνεργέω *synergeō* (5)
fellow workers (1)
joins in the work (1)
worked with (1)
working together (1)
works (1)

5301 συνεργός *synergos* (13)
fellow worker (6)
fellow workers (5)
work together (1) *+1181*
work with (1) *+1639*

5302 συνέρχομαι *synerchomai* (30)
come together (5)
came together (3)
gathered (3)
come with (2)
accompanied (1) *+5250*
assemble (1)
assembled (1)
came (1)
came with (1)
come along with (1)
comes together (1) *+899+2093+3836*
continued with (1)
gathering (1)
going with (1)
meet together (1)
meetings (1)
met together (1)
there (1)
went along (1)
went with (1)
with (1)

5303 συνεσθίω *synesthiō* (5)
ate with (2)
eat (1)
eats with (1)
with eat (1)

5304 σύνεσις *synesis* (7)
understanding (4)
insight (2)
intelligence (1)

5305 συνετός *synetos* (4)
intelligent (2)
learned (2)

5306 συνευδοκέω *syneudokeō* (6)
approve of (2)
giving approval (2)
willing (2)

5307 συνευωχέομαι *syneuōcheomai* (2)
eating with (1)
feast with (1)

5308 συνεφίστημι *synephistēmi* (1)
joined in the attack (1)

5309 συνέχω *synechō* (12)
suffering (2)
compels (1)
covered (1)
crowding against (1)
devoted (1)
distressed (1)
guarding (1)
hem in (1)
overcome (1)
suffering from (1)
torn (1)

5310 συνήδομαι *synēdomai* (1)
delight (1)

5311 συνήθεια *synētheia* (3)
accustomed to (1)
custom (1)
practice (1)

5312 συνηλικιώτης *synēlikiōtēs* (1)
of own age (1)

5313 συνθάπτω *synthaptō* (2)
buried with (2)

5314 συνθλάω *synthlaō* (2)
broken to pieces (2)

5315 συνθλίβω *synthlibō* (2)
crowding against (1)
pressed around (1)

5316 συνθρύπτω *synthryptō* (1)
breaking (1)

5317 συνίημι *syniēmi* (26)
understand (14)
understood (4)
understanding (3)
understands (2)
did[S] (1)
realize (1)
wise (1)

5318 συνιστάω *synistaō*
Variant; not used

5319 συνίστημι *synistēmi* (17)
commend (6)
commends (2)
brings out more clearly (1)
commended (1)
demonstrates (1)
formed (1)
hold together (1)
prove that (1)
proved (1)
short (1)
standing with (1)

5320 συνίω *syniō*
Variant; not used

5321 συνοδεύω *synodeuō* (1)
traveling with (1)

5322 συνοδία *synodia* (1)
company (1)

5323 σύνοιδα *synoida* (2)
conscience is clear (1) *+4029*
full knowledge (1)

5324 συνοικέω *synoikeō* (1)
live with (1)

5325 συνοικοδομέω *synoikodomeō* (1)
built together (1)

5326 συνομιλέω *synomileō* (1)
talking with (1)

5327 συνομορέω *synomoreō* (1)
next door (1)

5328 συνοράω *synoraō* (2)
dawned on (1)
found out about (1)

5329 συνορία *synoria*
Variant; not used

5330 συνοχή *synochē* (2)
anguish (2)

5331 συνταράσσω *syntarassō*
Variant; not used

5332 συντάσσω *syntassō* (3)
commanded (1)
directed (1)
instructed (1)

5333 συντέλεια *synteleia* (6)
end (5)
very end (1)

5334 συντελέω *synteleō* (6)
end (1)
finality (1)
finished (1)
fulfilled (1)
make (1)
over (1)

5335 συντέμνω *syntemnō* (1)
speed (1)

5336 συντεχνίτης *syntechnitēs*
Variant; not used

5337 συντηρέω *syntēreō* (3)
preserved (1)
protected (1)
treasured up (1)

5338 συντίθημι *syntithēmi* (3)
agreed (2)
decided (1)

5339 συντόμως *syntomōs* (1)
briefly (1)

5340 συντρέχω *syntrechō* (3)
came running (1)
plunge with (1)
ran (1)

5341 συντρίβω *syntribō* (7)
broke (2)
broken (1)
bruised (1)
crush (1)
dash to pieces (1)
destroying (1)

5342 σύντριμμα *syntrimma* (1)
ruin (1)

5343 σύντροφος *syntrophos* (1)
brought up with (1)

5344 συντυγχάνω *syntynchanō* (1)
get near (1)

5345 Συντύχη *Syntychē* (1)
Syntyche (1)

5346 συντυχία *syntychia*
Variant; not used

5347 συνυποκρίνομαι *synypokrinomai* (1)
joined in hypocrisy (1)

5348 συνυπουργέω *synypourgeō* (1)
help (1)

5349 συνωδίνω *synōdinō* (1)
in the pains of childbirth (1)

5350 συνωμοσία *synōmosia* (1)
plot (1)

5351 Σύρα *Syra*
Variant; not used

5352 Συράκουσαι *Syrakousai* (1)
Syracuse (1)

5353 Συρία *Syria* (8)
Syria (8)

5354 Σύρος *Syros* (1)
Syrian (1)

5355 Συροφοινίκισσα *Syrophoinikissa* (1)
Syrian Phoenicia (1)

5356 Συροφοίνισσα *Syrophoinissa*
Variant; not used

5357 συρρήγνυμι *syrrēgnymi*
Variant; not used

5358 Σύρτις *Syrtis* (1)
sandbars of Syrtis (1)

5359 σύρω *syrō* (5)
dragged (2)
dragged off (1)
swept (1)
towing (1)

5360 συσπαράσσω *sysparassō* (2)
in a convulsion (1)
threw into a convulsion (1)

5361 σύσσημον *syssēmon* (1)
signal (1)

5362 σύσσωμος *syssōmos* (1)
members together of one body (1)

5363 συστασιαστής *systasiastēs*
Variant; not used

5364 συστατικός *systatikos* (1)
recommendation (1)

5365 συσταυρόω *systauroō* (5)
crucified with (5)

5366 συστέλλω *systellō* (1)
wrapped up (1)

5367 συστενάζω *systenazō* (1)
groaning (1)

5368 συστοιχέω *systoicheō* (1)
corresponds (1)

5369 συστρατιώτης *systratiōtēs* (2)
fellow soldier (2)

5370 συστρέφω *systrephō* (2)
came together (1)
gathered (1)

5371 συστροφή *systrophē* (2)
commotion (1)
conspiracy (1)

5372 συσχηματίζω *syschēmatizō* (2)
conform (1)
conform to the pattern of (1)

5373 Συχάρ *Sychar* (1)
Sychar (1)

5374 Συχέμ *Sychem* (2)
Shechem (2)

5375 σφαγή *sphagē* (3)
slaughter (2)
slaughtered (1)

5376 σφάγιον *sphagion* (1)
offerings (1)

5377 σφάζω *sphazō* (10)
slain (5)
had wound (1)
killed (1)
murder (1)
murdered (1)
slay (1)

5378 σφάλλω *sphallō*
Variant; not used

5379 σφόδρα *sphodra* (11)
greatly (2)
terrified (2) *+5828*
very (2)
filled with grief (1) *+3382*
great (1)
overjoyed (1) *+3489+5897+5915*
rapidly (1)
so (1)

5380 σφοδρῶς *sphodrōs* (1)
such violent (1)

5381 σφραγίζω *sphragizō* (15)
sealed (4)
seal up (2)
certified (1) *+3456+3836*
made sure that (1)
marked with a seal (1)
on placed seal (1)
put a seal (1)
putting a seal on (1)
set seal of ownership on (1)
untranslated (2)

5382 σφραγίς *sphragis* (16)
seal (10)
seals (5)
sealed with (1) *+2400*

5383 σφυδρόν *sphydron* (1)
ankles (1)

5384 σφυρόν *sphyron*
Variant; not used

5385 σχεδόν *schedon* (3)
almost (1)
nearly (1)
practically (1)

5386 σχῆμα *schēma* (2)
form (1)
in appearance (1)

5387 σχίζω *schizō* (11)
torn (5)
divided (2)
split (1)
tear (1)
tears (1)
torn open (1)

5388 σχίσμα *schisma* (8)
divided (3)
divisions (2)
tear (2)
division (1)

5389 σχοινίον *schoinion* (2)
cords (1)
ropes (1)

5390 σχολάζω *scholazō* (2)
devote (1)
unoccupied (1)

5391 σχολή *scholē* (1)
lecture hall (1)

5392 σῴζω *sōzō* (106)
saved (45)
save (37)
healed (12)
saved (2) *+1639*
bring safely (1)
cured (1)
delivered (1)
get better (1)
healed (1) *+3836*
made well (1)
make well (1)
saves (1)
survive (1)
survive (1) *+323*

5393 σῶμα *sōma* (142)
body (115)
bodies (14)
dead (1)
dead body (1)
in person (1) *+3836+3836+4242*
its[s] (1) *+3836*
person (1)
physical (1)
physically (1)
reality (1)
the parts[s] (1) *+3836+4047*
untranslated (4)

5394 σωματικός *sōmatikos* (2)
bodily (1)
physical (1)

5395 σωματικῶς *sōmatikōs* (1)
in bodily form (1)

5396 Σώπατρος *Sōpatros* (1)
Sopater (1)

5397 σωρεύω *sōreuō* (2)
heap (1)
loaded down (1)

5398 Σωσθένης *Sōsthenēs* (2)
Sosthenes (2)

5399 Σωσίπατρος *Sōsipatros* (1)
Sosipater (1)

5400 σωτήρ *sōtēr* (24)
savior (24)

5401 σωτηρία *sōtēria* (45)
salvation (36)
be saved (2)
are saved (1) *+1650*
be saved (1) *+1650*
deliverance (1)
rescue (1) *+1443*
save (1)
saved (1)
survive (1)

5402 σωτήριον *sōtērion*
Variant; not used

5403 σωτήριος *sōtērios* (5)
salvation (5)

5404 σωφρονέω *sōphroneō* (6)
in right mind (3)
clear minded (1)
self-controlled (1)
sober judgment (1)

5405 σωφρονίζω *sōphronizō* (1)
train (1)

5406 σωφρονισμός *sōphronismos* (1)
self-discipline (1)

5407 σωφρόνως *sōphronōs* (1)
self-controlled (1)

5408 σωφροσύνη *sōphrosynē* (3)
propriety (2)
reasonable (1)

5409 σώφρων *sōphrōn* (4)
self-controlled (3)
who is self-controlled (1)

5410 τ *t*
Variant; not used

5411 ταβέρναι *tabernai*
Variant; not used

5412 Ταβιθά *Tabitha* (2)
Tabitha (2)

5413 τάγμα *tagma* (1)
turn (1)

5414 τακτός *taktos* (1)
appointed (1)

5415 ταλαιπωρέω *talaipōreō* (1)
grieve (1)

5416 ταλαιπωρία *talaipōria* (2)
misery (2)

5417 ταλαίπωρος *talaipōros* (2)
wretched (2)

5418 ταλαντιαῖος *talantiaios* (1)
hundred pounds (1)

5419 τάλαντον *talanton* (14)
talents (7)
talent (3)
talents of money (1)
untranslated (3)

5420 ταλιθά *talitha* (1)
Talitha (1)

5421 ταμεῖον *tameion* (4)
inner rooms (2)
room (1)
storeroom (1)

5422 τανῦν *tanyn*
Variant; not used

5423 τάξις *taxis* (9)
order (6)
orderly (1)
orderly way (1) *+2848*
untranslated (1)

5424 ταπεινός *tapeinos* (8)
humble (4)
downcast (1)
in humble circumstances (1)
of low position (1)
timid (1)

5425 ταπεινοφροσύνη *tapeinophrosynē* (7)
humility (5)
great humility (1) *+4246*
humble (1)

5426 ταπεινόφρων *tapeinophrōn* (1)
humble (1)

5427 ταπεινόω *tapeinoō* (14)
humbled (4)
humbles (4)
humble (3)
lower (1)
made low (1)
need (1)

5428 ταπείνωσις *tapeinōsis* (4)
humble state (1)
humiliation (1)
low position (1)
lowly (1)

5429 ταράσσω *tarassō* (17)
troubled (6)
disturbed (2)
terrified (2)
throwing into confusion (2)
frightened (1)
startled (1)
stirred (1)
stirring up (1)
thrown into turmoil (1)

5430 ταραχή *tarachē*
Variant; not used

5431 τάραχος *tarachos* (2)
commotion (1)
great disturbance (1) *+3900+4024*

5432 Ταρσεύς *Tarseus* (2)
from Tarsus (1)
man from Tarsus (1)

5433 Ταρσός *Tarsos* (3)
Tarsus (3)

5434 ταρταρόω *tartaroō* (1)
sent to hell (1)

5435 τάσσω *tassō* (8)
appointed (2)
arranged (1)
assigned (1)
devoted (1)
established (1)
told (1)
untranslated (1)

5436 ταῦρος *tauros* (4)
bulls (3)
oxen (1)

5437 ταὐτά *tauta*
Variant; not used

5438 ταφή *taphē* (1)
burial place (1)

5439 τάφος *taphos* (7)
tomb (4)
tombs (2)
graves (1)

5440 τάχα *tacha* (2)
perhaps (1)
possibly (1)

5441 ταχέως *tacheōs* (15)
quickly (6)
soon (5)
easily (1)
hasty (1)
outran (1) *+4708*
very soon (1)

5442 ταχινός *tachinos* (2)
soon (1)
swift (1)

5443 τάχος *tachos* (8)
soon (5) *+1877*
immediately (1) *+1877*
quick (1) *+1877*
quickly (1) *+1877*

5444 ταχύς *tachys* (13)
soon (6)
quickly (3)
quick (2)
hurried away from (1) *+599*
in the next moment (1)

5445 τέ *te* (215)
and (42)
both (13)
but (4)
then (4)
so (3)
and also (2)
even (2)
and alike (1) *+2779*
as (1)
between (1)
or (1)
that is (1)
whether (1)
yes (1) *+2285*
untranslated (138)

5446 τεῖχος *teichos* (9)
wall (6)
walls (3)

5447 τεκμήριον *tekmērion* (1)
convincing proofs (1)

5448 τεκνίον *teknion* (8)
dear children (7)
children (1)

5449 τεκνογονέω *teknogoneō* (1)
have children (1)

5450 τεκνογονία *teknogonia* (1)
childbearing (1)

5451 τέκνον *teknon* (99)
children (73)
son (14)
child (5)
children's (2)
brood (1)
daughters (1)
dear children (1)
objects (1)
sons (1)

5452 τεκνοτροφέω *teknotropheō* (1)
bringing up children (1)

5453 τεκνόω *teknoō*
Variant; not used

5454 τέκτων *tektōn* (2)
carpenter (1)
carpenter's (1)

5455 τέλειος *teleios* (19)
perfect (10)
mature (5)
adults (1)
finish (1) *+2400*
mature (1) *+467*
perfection (1)

5456 τελειότης *teleiotēs* (2)
maturity (1)
perfect (1)

5457 τελειόω *teleioō* (22)
made perfect (8)
made complete (4)
finish (3)
make perfect (2)
clear (1)
complete (1)
completing (1)
over (1)
reach goal (1)

5458 τελείως *teleiōs* (1)
fully (1)

5459 τελείωσις *teleiōsis* (2)
accomplished (1)
perfection (1)

5460 τελειωτής *teleiōtēs* (1)
perfecter (1)

5461 τελεσφορέω *telesphoreō* (1)
mature (1)

5462 τελευτάω *teleutaō* (11)
died (5)
die (2)
put to death (2) *+2505*
dead (1)
end was near (1)

5463 τελευτή *teleutē* (1)
death (1)

5464 τελέω *teleō* (29)
finished (8)
completed (4)
fulfilled (4)
ended (2)
pay (2)
accomplished (1)
carried out (1)
done (1)
finish (1)
gratify (1)
keep (1)
made perfect (1)
obeys (1)
over (1)

5465 τέλος *telos* (40)
end (20)
fulfillment (2)
goal (2)
outcome (2)
result (2)
revenue (2)
destiny (1)
duty (1)

end (1) *+2400*
eventually (1) *+1650*
finally (1)
finally (1) *+3836*
fully (1) *+2401*
last (1)
the full extent of (1) *+1650*
untranslated (1)

5466 τελωνεῖον *telōneion*
Variant; not used

5467 τελώνης *telōnēs* (21)
tax collectors (15)
tax collector (6)

5468 τελώνιον *telōnion* (3)
tax collector's booth (2)
tax booth (1)

5469 τέρας *teras* (16)
wonders (13)
miracles (3)

5470 Τέρτιος *Tertios* (1)
Tertius (1)

5471 Τέρτουλλος *Tertoullos*
Variant; not used

5472 Τέρτυλλος *Tertyllos* (2)
Tertullus (2)

5473 τεσσαράκοντα *tessarakonta*
Variant; not used

5474 τεσσαρακονταετής *tessarakontaetēs*
Variant; not used

5475 τέσσαρες *tessares* (40)
four (29)
twenty-four (6) *+1633*
144,000 (3) *+1669+5477+5942*
144 (1) *+1669+5477*
eighty-four (1) *+2291+3837*

5476 τεσσαρεσκαιδέκατος *tessareskaidekatos* (2)
fourteen (1)
fourteenth (1)

5477 τεσσεράκοντα *tesserakonta* (22)
forty (15)
144,000 (3) *+1669+5475+5942*
144 (1) *+1669+5475*
42 (1) *+1545*
forty-six (1) *+1971+2779*
forty-two (1) *+1545*

5478 τεσσερακονταετής *tesserakontaetēs* (2)
forty years (2)

5479 τεταρταῖος *tetartaios* (1)
four days (1)

5480 τέταρτος *tetartos* (10)
fourth (9)
four (1)

5481 τετράγωνος *tetragōnos* (1)
square (1)

5482 τετράδιον *tetradion* (1)
four squads (1)

5483 τετρακισχίλιοι *tetrakischilioi* (5)
four thousand (5)

5484 τετρακόσιοι *tetrakosioi* (4)
four hundred (2)
430 (1) *+2779+5558*
450 (1) *+2779+4299*

5485 τετράμηνος *tetramēnos* (1)
four months (1)

5486 τετραπλόος *tetraploos* (1)
four times (1)

5487 τετραπλοῦς *tetraplous*
Variant; not used

5488 τετράπους *tetrapous* (3)
four-footed animals (2)
animals (1)

5489 τετραρχέω *tetrarcheō* (3)
tetrarch (3)

5490 τετράρχης *tetrarchēs* (4)
tetrarch (4)

5491 τεφρόω *tephroō* (1)
burning to ashes (1)

5492 τέχνη *technē* (3)
skill (1)
trade (1)
untranslated (1)

5493 τεχνίτης *technitēs* (4)
craftsmen (2)
architect (1)
workman (1)

5494 τήκομαι *tēkomai* (1)
melt (1)

5495 τηλαυγῶς *tēlaugōs* (1)
clearly (1)

5496 τηλικοῦτος *tēlikoutos* (4)
so large (1)
such (1)
such great (1)
tremendous (1) *+3489*

5497 τηνικαῦτα *tēnikauta*
Variant; not used

5498 τηρέω *tēreō* (71)
obey (16)
keep (10)
kept (10)
keeps (5)
held (3)
obeyed (3)
obeys (2)
protect (2)
reserved (2)
do (1)
do so[s] (1)
does (1)
guard (1)
guarding (1)
guards (1)
held over (1)
hold (1)
keep under guard (1)
keeps safe (1)
kept watch over (1)
not marry (1)
observe (1)
protected (1)
save (1)
saved (1)
stood (1)
take to heart (1)

5499 τήρησις *tērēsis* (3)
jail (2)
keeping (1)

5500 Τιβεριάς *Tiberias* (3)
Tiberias (3)

5501 Τιβέριος *Tiberios* (1)
Tiberius (1)

5502 τίθημι *tithēmi* (100)
put (21)
laid (10)
lay down (8)
placed (7)
appointed (5)
made (5)
lay (4)
make (3)
puts (3)
assign (2)
put in (2)
appoint (1)
appointing (1)
arranged (1)
brings out (1)
burial (1) *+1650+3645*
committed (1)
decided (1)
decided that (1) *+1087*
destined (1)
falling on (1)
fastened (1)
fell on (1)
got down (1)
knelt (1) *+1205+3836*
knelt down (1) *+1205*
knelt down (1) *+1205+3836*
laid down (1)
laid in (1)
lays (1)
lays down (1)
listen carefully (1) *+1650+3836+4044+5148+5148*
made think (1) *+1877+2840+3836*
make up mind (1) *+1877+2840+3836*
offer (1)
planted (1)
set (1)
set aside (1)
took off (1)
use (1)
wondered about (1) *+1877+2840+3836*

5503 τίκτω *tiktō* (18)
gave birth to (3)
give birth to (3)
born (2)
baby to be born (1)
bears children (1)
born to (1)
give birth (1)
give birth (1) *+6048*
given birth to (1)
gives birth to (1)
giving birth to a child (1)
have baby (1)
produces (1)

5504 τίλλω *tillō* (3)
pick (3)

5505 Τιμαῖος *Timaios* (1)
Timaeus (1)

5506 τιμάω *timaō* (21)
honor (16)
give recognition to (1)
honored (1) *+5507*
price set on (1) *+5507*
show proper respect to (1)
untranslated (1)

5507 τιμή *timē* (42)
honor (23)
money (3)
noble purposes (2)
price (2)
respect (2)
value (2)
blood money (1) *+135*
honorable (1)
honored (1) *+5506*
noble (1)
precious (1)
price set on (1) *+5506*
special treatment (1)
sum (1)

5508 τίμιος *timios* (13)
precious (6)
costly (2)
honored (2)
valuable (1)
very precious (1)
worth (1)

5509 τιμιότης *timiotēs* (1)
wealth (1)

5510 Τιμόθεος *Timotheos* (24)
Timothy (24)

5511 Τίμων *Timōn* (1)
Timon (1)

5512 τιμωρέω *timōreō* (2)
punished (2)

5513 τιμωρία *timōria* (1)
punished (1)

5514 τίνω *tinō* (1)
punished (1) *+1472*

5515 τίς *tis* (553)
what (220)
who (122)
why (73)
why (23) *+1328*
which (20)
whom (9)
whose (7)
how (6)
what do want with (5) *+2779*
how (4) *+1877*
why (4) *+1650*
how is it that (3) *+1328*
suppose one (3)
any (2)
nothing (2) *+4024*
one (2)
something (2)
was there ever (2)
all the world (1) *+476+1639+4005*
any way (1) *+3836*
anyone's (1)
business (1) *+4472*
each (1)
how (1) *+2848*
how (1) *+4022*
how far will they go (1) *+1639+4047*
my supper (1) *+1268*
nothing (1) *+3590*
suppose a (1)
suppose a (1) *+1569*
suppose one (1) *+476*
those (1)
what (1) *+1650*
what (1) *+1877*
what (1) *+4005*
what (1) *+4036*
what business is it of mine (1) *+1609*
what does it matter (1) *+1142*
what going on (1) *+323+4047*
what shall we do (1) *+1639+4036*
what the meaning of (1)
what's (1)
where (1)
which (1) *+323*
who do you think you are (1) *+4472+4932*
why (1) *+1915*
why (1) *+3364*
why (1) *+4022*
why (1) *+5920*
why do involve (1) *+2779*
untranslated (12)

5516 τὶς *tis* (534)
some (106)
a (85)
anyone (75)
one (35)
anything (31)
any (25)
someone (22)
something (18)
a certain (8)
he (7)
anybody (5)
an (4)
anyone who (4)
certain (4)
one (3) *+1651*
others (3)
several (3)
whatever (3) *+1569*
any one (2)
nothing (2) *+3590*
nothing (2) *+4024*
that none (2) *+3607*
the (2)
whatever (2) *+323+4005*
whatever (2) *+1623*
who (2)
whoever (2) *+1569*
a few (1)
a kind of (1)
and none (1) *+4046*
and nothing (1) *+4028*
another (1) *+257*
any (1) *+323+4005*
any other (1)
anyone (1) *+1569*
anyone who (1) *+1569*
anyone's (1)
anything (1) *+1569*
deadly poison (1) *+2503*
he who (1)
ideas[S] (1)
important (1)
in keeping with income (1) *+1569+2338+4005*
it[S] (1) *+2240+3836*
man's[S] (1)
members[S] (1)
named (1)
nobody (1) *+3590*
nobody (1) *+4024*
none (1) *+3590*
nothing (1) *+4046*
person who (1)
persons (1)
pieces (1)
some point (1)
somebody (1)
somewhat (1)
them (1)
thing (1)
what (1)
what (1) *+323*
what (1) *+1623*
what (1) *+4005*
what[S] (1) *+2240+3836*
whatever (1)
whatever (1) *+323*
whatever (1) *+1569+4005*
who (1) *+1569*
untranslated (34)

5517 Τίτιος *Titios* (1)
Titius (1)

5518 τίτλος *titlos* (2)
had a notice prepared (1) *+1211*
sign (1)

5519 Τίτος *Titos* (13)
Titus (13)

5520 τοί *toi*
Variant; not used

5521 τοιγαροῦν *toigaroun* (2)
therefore (2)

5522 τοίγε *toige*
Variant; not used

5523 τοίνυν *toinyn* (3)
then (2)
therefore (1)

5524 τοιόσδε *toiosde* (1)
untranslated (1)

5525 τοιοῦτος *toioutos* (57)
such (22)
such as these (4)
him (3)
like this (2)
so (2)
such a man (2)
this (2)
blemish[S] (1) *+3836*
he (1)
man like that (1)
men like him (1)
of a kind (1)
related trades[S] (1)
similar (1)
such a (1)
that (1)
them[S] (1) *+3836+3836+4556*
these (1)
they are the kind (1)
those who marry[S] (1) *+3836*
unequaled (1) *+1181+3888+4024*
what (1) *+3961*
untranslated (5)

5526 τοῖχος *toichos* (1)
wall (1)

5527 τόκος *tokos* (2)
interest (2)

5528 τολμάω *tolmaō* (16)
dare (6)
dared (5)
boldly (1)
courageously (1)
dares (1)
venture (1)
untranslated (1)

5529 τολμηρός *tolmēros* (1)
quite boldly (1)

5530 τολμηρότερον *tolmēroteron*
Variant; not used

5531 τολμηροτέρως *tolmēroterōs*
Variant; not used

5532 τολμητής *tolmētēs* (1)
bold (1)

5533 τομός *tomos* (1)
sharper (1)

5534 τόξον *toxon* (1)
bow (1)

5535 τοπάζιον *topazion* (1)
topaz (1)

5536 τόπος *topos* (94)
place (63)
places (6)
everywhere (3) *+1877+4246*
room (3)
area (2)
among (1)
by itself (1) *+1650+1651+3023+6006*
everywhere (1) *+4246*
foothold (1)
nearby (1) *+3836+4309*
opportunity (1)
rocks (1) *+5550*
sandbar (1) *+1458*
seat (1)
spot (1)
there (1) *+1877+3836*
where (1) *+1650*
where (1) *+1877+4005*
untranslated (4)

5537 τοσοῦτος *tosoutos* (20)
such great (4)
as much (2)
so many (2)
such (2)
this (2)
all (1)

all the more (1) *+3437*
all these (1)
enough (1)
long (1)
so much (1)
that (1)
these (1)

5538 τότε *tote* (160)
then (105)
at that time (11)
so (4)
that time (2)
that time on (2)
when (2)
after (1) *+4021*
and (1)
and (1) *+2779*
as soon as (1)
at that (1)
finally (1)
finally (1) *+4036*
formerly (1)
of that time (1)
once (1)
then on (1)
untranslated (23)

5539 τοὐναντίον *tounantion*
Variant; not used

5540 τοὔνομα *tounoma*
Variant; not used

5541 τοὔπισω *toupisō*
Variant; not used

5542 τουτέστιν *toutestin*
Variant; not used

5543 τράγος *tragos* (3)
goats (3)

5544 τράπεζα *trapeza* (15)
table (9)
tables (4)
deposit (1)
set a meal before (1) *+4192*

5545 τραπεζίτης *trapezitēs* (1)
bankers (1)

5546 τραῦμα *trauma* (1)
wounds (1)

5547 τραυματίζω *traumatizō* (2)
bleeding (1)
wounded (1)

5548 τραχηλίζω *trachēlizō* (1)
laid bare (1)

5549 τράχηλος *trachēlos* (7)
neck (3)
embraced (1) *+2093+2158+3836*
necks (1)
risked lives (1) *+5719*
threw his arms around (1) *+2093+2158+3836*

5550 τραχύς *trachys* (2)
rocks (1) *+5536*
rough (1)

5551 Τραχωνῖτις *Trachōnitis* (1)
Traconitis (1)

5552 τρεῖς *treis* (68)
three (63)
153 (1) *+1669+4299*
large (1)
large amount of flour (1) *+236+4929*
twenty to thirty gallons (1) *+1545+2445+3583*
twenty-three (1) *+1633*

5553 Τρεῖς ταβέρναι *Treis tabernai* (1)
three Taverns (1)

5554 τρέμω *tremō* (3)
trembling (2)
afraid (1)

5555 τρέφω *trephō* (9)
feeds (2)
taken care of (2)
brought up (1)
fattened (1)
feed (1)
food supply (1)
nursed (1)

5556 τρέχω *trechō* (20)
ran (6)
run (5)
running (3)
effort (1)
run race (1)
runners (1)
running a race (1)
rushing (1)
spread rapidly (1)

5557 τρῆμα *trēma* (1)
eye (1)

5558 τριάκοντα *triakonta* (11)
thirty (8)
430 (1) *+2779+5484*
thirty-eight (1) *+2779+3893*
three or three and a half miles (1) *+1633+2445+4297+5084*

5559 τριακόσιοι *triakosioi* (2)
the money worth a year's wages (1) *+1324*
untranslated (1)

5560 τρίβολος *tribolos* (2)
thistles (2)

5561 τρίβος *tribos* (3)
paths (3)

5562 τριετία *trietia* (1)
three years (1)

5563 τρίζω *trizō* (1)
gnashes (1)

5564 τρίμηνος *trimēnos* (1)
three months (1)

5565 τρίς *tris* (12)
three times (12)

5566 τρίστεγον *tristegon* (1)
third story (1)

5567 τρισχίλιοι *trischilioi* (1)
three thousand (1)

5568 τρίτον *triton* (8)
third time (6)
third (2)

5569 τρίτος *tritos* (48)
third (45)
nine (1) *+6052*
nine in the morning (1) *+2465+3836+6052*
third time (1) *+1666*

5570 τρίχινος *trichinos* (1)
made of hair (1)

5571 τρόμος *tromos* (5)
trembling (3)
fear (1)
Trembling (1) *+899+2400*

5572 τροπή *tropē* (1)
shadows (1)

5573 τρόπος *tropos* (13)
way (4)
as (3) *+4005*
in any way (1) *+2848+3594*
in the same way (1) *+4005*
just as (1) *+2848+4005*
just as (1) *+2848+4005+4048*
just as (1) *+4005*
lives (1)

5574 τροποφορέω *tropophoreō* (1)
endured (1)

5575 τροφή *trophē* (16)
food (12)
ate (1)
eat (1) *+3561*
keep (1)
untranslated (1)

5576 Τρόφιμος *Trophimos* (3)
Trophimus (3)

5577 τροφός *trophos* (1)
mother (1)

5578 τροφοφορέω *trophophoreō*
Variant; not used

5579 τροχιά *trochia* (1)
paths (1)

5580 τροχός *trochos* (1)
course (1)

5581 τρύβλιον *tryblion* (2)
bowl (2)

5582 τρυγάω *trygaō* (3)
gather (1)
gathered (1)
untranslated (1)

5583 τρυγών *trygōn* (1)
doves (1)

5584 τρυμαλιά *trymalia* (1)
eye (1)

5585 τρύπημα *trypēma* (1)
eye (1)

5586 Τρύφαινα *Tryphaina* (1)
Tryphena (1)

5587 τρυφάω *tryphaō* (1)
lived in luxury (1)

5588 τρυφή *tryphē* (2)
carouse (1)
luxury (1)

5589 Τρυφῶσα *Tryphōsa* (1)
Tryphosa (1)

5590 Τρῳάς *Trōas* (6)
Troas (6)

5591 Τρωγύλλιον *Trōgyllion*
Variant; not used

5592 τρώγω *trōgō* (6)
eats (2)
feeds on (2)
eating (1)
shares (1)

5593 τυγχάνω *tynchanō* (12)
enjoyed (1)
extraordinary (1) *+3836+4024*
gain (1)
had (1)
obtain (1)
perhaps (1)
perhaps (1) *+1623*
provide (1)
received (1)
taking part (1)
undoubtedly (1) *+1623*
unusual (1) *+4024*

5594 τυμπανίζω *tympanizō* (1)
tortured (1)

5595 τυπικῶς *typikōs* (1)
examples (1)

5596 τύπος *typos* (15)
pattern (4)
example (2)
examples (2)
model (2)

as follows (1) *+2400+3836+4047*
form (1)
idols (1)
marks (1)
where[s] (1) *+1650+3836*

5597 τύπτω *typtō* (13)
beat (5)
strike (2)
struck on (2)
beating (1)
strikes (1)
struck (1)
wound (1)

5598 Τύραννος1 *Tyrannos1* (1)
Tyrannus (1)

5599 τύραννος2 *tyrannos2*
Variant; not used

5600 τυρβάζω *tyrbazō*
Variant; not used

5601 Τύριος *Tyrios* (1)
people of Tyre (1)

5602 Τύρος *Tyros* (11)
Tyre (11)

5603 τυφλός *typhlos* (49)
blind (49)

5604 τυφλόω *typhloō* (3)
blinded (3)

5605 τυφόομαι *typhoomai* (3)
conceited (2)
become conceited (1)

5606 τύφω *typhō* (1)
smoldering (1)

5607 τυφωνικός *typhōnikos* (1)
of hurricane force (1)

5608 Τυχικός *Tychikos* (5)
Tychicus (5)

5609 υ *y*
Variant; not used

5610 ὑακίνθινος *hyakinthinos* (1)
dark blue (1)

5611 ὑάκινθος *hyakinthos* (1)
jacinth (1)

5612 ὑάλινος *hyalinos* (3)
of glass (2)
untranslated (1)

5613 ὕαλος *hyalos* (2)
glass (2)

5614 ὑβρίζω *hybrizō* (5)
insult (2)
insulted (1)
mistreat (1)
mistreated (1)

5615 ὕβρις *hybris* (3)
damage (1)
disastrous (1) *+3552*
insults (1)

5616 ὑβριστής *hybristēs* (2)
insolent (1)
violent man (1)

5617 ὑγιαίνω *hygiainō* (12)
sound (8)
enjoy good health (1)
healthy (1)
safe and sound (1)
well (1)

5618 ὑγιής *hygiēs* (11)
well (4)
cured (1)
freed (1)
healed (1)
healing (1) *+4472*
made well (1)
sound (1)
soundness (1)

5619 ὑγρός *hygros* (1)
green (1)

5620 ὑδρία *hydria* (3)
jars (1)
water jar (1)
water jars (1)

5621 ὑδροποτέω *hydropoteō* (1)
drinking only water (1)

5622 ὑδρωπικός *hydrōpikos* (1)
suffering from dropsy (1)

5623 ὕδωρ *hydōr* (76)
water (65)
waters (10)
deluged (1) *+2885*

5624 ὑετός *hyetos* (5)
rain (3)
it[s] (1)
raining (1)

5625 υἱοθεσία *huiothesia* (5)
adoption as sons (2)
adopted as sons (1)
full rights of sons (1)
sonship (1)

5626 υἱός *huios* (376)
son (299)
sons (36)
Israelites (6) *+2702*
people (6)
children (3)
guests (3)
Israel (3) *+2702*
child (2)
descendants (2)
man (2)
men (2) *+476+3836+3836*
those who are[s] (2) *+3836*
children (1) *+1169*
foal (1)
followers (1)
heirs (1)
Israelites (1) *+2702+3836*
one[s] (1)
people (1) *+3836*
people Israel (1) *+2702*
subjects (1)
whose[s] (1)

5627 ὕλη *hylē* (1)
forest (1)

5628 Ὑμέναιος *Hymenaios* (2)
Hymenaeus (2)

5629 ὑμέτερος *hymeteros* (11)
you (5)
your (2)
your own (2)
yours (2)

5630 ὑμνέω *hymneō* (4)
sung a hymn (2)
sing praises (1)
singing hymns (1)

5631 ὕμνος *hymnos* (2)
hymns (2)

5632 ὑπάγω *hypagō* (79)
go (44)
going (18)
get (2)
going away (2)
went (2)
away (1)
go I wish you well (1) *+1645+1877*
goes (1)
going back (1)
going out (1)
going over (1)
heading (1)
leave (1)
leaving (1)
on way (1)
returning (1)

5633 ὑπακοή *hypakoē* (15)
obedience (8)
obedient (3)
obey (3)
obeying (1)

5634 ὑπακούω *hypakouō* (21)
obey (14)
obeyed (4)
accepted (1)
answer (1)
obedient (1)

5635 ὕπανδρος *hypandros* (1)
married (1)

5636 ὑπαντάω *hypantaō* (10)
met (6)
went out to meet (2)
meet (1)
oppose (1)

5637 ὑπάντησις *hypantēsis* (3)
meet (3)

5638 ὕπαρξις *hyparxis* (2)
goods (1)
possessions (1)

5639 ὑπάρχω *hyparchō* (60)
was (9)
are (8)
is (7)
possessions (7)
be (3)
possessions (2) *+3836*
baptized (1) *+966*
being (1)
contained (1) *+1877*
gone (1)
has (1) *+3836*
have (1)
indulge (1)
loved money (1) *+5795*
means (1)
owned (1)
owned (1) *+3230*
possess (1)
possess (1) *+3836*
property (1)
property (1) *+3836*
that am (1)
was that belonged (1)
wasn't (1)
untranslated (6)

5640 ὑπείκω *hypeikō* (1)
submit (1)

5641 ὑπεναντίος *hypenantios* (2)
enemies (1)
stood opposed (1) *+1639*

5642 ὑπέρ *hyper* (150)
for (92)
about (7)
in (6)
more than (5)
above (4)
beyond (4)
for the sake of (4)
on behalf (4)
concerning (2)
for sake (2)
on behalf of (2)
over (2)
to (2)

according to (1)
as for (1) *+1664*
because of (1)
better than (1)
brighter than (1) *+3288*
Christ's (1) *+5986*
more (1)
shrewd (1) *+5861*
take place (1)
than (1)
to help (1)
untranslated (3)

5643 ὑπεραίρομαι *hyperairomai* (3)
conceited (1)
exalt himself (1)
untranslated (1)

5644 ὑπέρακμος *hyperakmos* (1)
getting along in years (1)

5645 ὑπεράνω *hyperanō* (3)
above (1)
far above (1)
higher (1)

5646 ὑπερασπίζω *hyperaspizō*
Variant; not used

5647 ὑπεραυξάνω *hyperauxanō* (1)
growing more and more (1)

5648 ὑπερβαίνω *hyperbainō* (1)
wrong (1)

5649 ὑπερβαλλόντως *hyperballontōs* (1)
more severely (1)

5650 ὑπερβάλλω *hyperballō* (5)
surpassing (2)
incomparable (1)
incomparably (1)
surpasses (1)

5651 ὑπερβολή *hyperbolē* (7)
all-surpassing (1)
great (1) *+2848*
intensely (1) *+2848*
most excellent (1) *+2848*
surpassingly great (1)
that far outweighs them all (1) *+983+1650+2848+5651*
utterly (1)

5652 ὑπερεγώ *hyperegō*
Variant; not used

5653 ὑπερείδω *hypereidō*
Variant; not used

5654 ὑπερέκεινα *hyperekeina* (1)
beyond (1)

5655 ὑπερεκπερισσοῦ *hyperekperissou* (3)
highest regard (1)
immeasurably (1)
most earnestly (1)

5656 ὑπερεκπερισσῶς *hyperekperissos*
Variant; not used

5657 ὑπερεκτείνω *hyperekteinō* (1)
going too far (1)

5658 ὑπερεκχύννω *hyperekchynnō* (1)
running over (1)

5659 ὑπερεντυγχάνω *hyperentynchanō* (1)
intercedes for (1)

5660 ὑπερέχω *hyperechō* (5)
better than (1)
governing (1)
supreme authority (1)
surpassing greatness (1)
transcends (1)

5661 ὑπερηφανία *hyperēphania* (1)
arrogance (1)

5662 ὑπερήφανος *hyperēphanos* (5)
proud (4)
arrogant (1)

5663 ὑπερλίαν *hyperlian* (2)
super-apostles (2) *+693*

5664 ὑπερνικάω *hypernikaō* (1)
more than conquerors (1)

5665 ὑπέρογκος *hyperonkos* (2)
boast (1) *+3281*
boastful (1)

5666 ὑπεροράω *hyperoraō* (1)
overlooked (1)

5667 ὑπεροχή *hyperochē* (2)
authority (1)
superior wisdom (1) *+5053*

5668 ὑπερπερισσεύω *hyperperisseuō* (2)
increased all the more (1)
knows no bounds (1)

5669 ὑπερπερισσῶς *hyperperissōs* (1)
overwhelmed with amazement (1) *+1742*

5670 ὑπερπλεονάζω *hyperpleonazō* (1)
poured out abundantly (1)

5671 ὑπερυψόω *hyperypsoō* (1)
exalted to the highest place (1)

5672 ὑπερφρονέω *hyperphroneō* (1)
think highly (1)

5673 ὑπερῷον *hyperōon* (4)
upstairs room (3)
room (1)

5674 ὑπέχω *hypechō* (1)
suffer (1)

5675 ὑπήκοος *hypēkoos* (3)
obedient (2)
obey (1) *+1181*

5676 ὑπηρετέω *hypēreteō* (3)
served (1)
supplied (1)
take care of needs (1)

5677 ὑπηρέτης *hypēretēs* (20)
officials (5)
guards (4)
servants (3)
officers (2)
temple guards (2)
attendant (1)
helper (1)
officer (1)
servant (1)

5678 ὕπνος *hypnos* (6)
natural sleep (1) *+3122+3836+3836*
sleep (1)
slumber (1)
sound asleep (1) *+608+2965+3836*
very sleepy (1) *+976*
untranslated (1)

5679 ὑπό *hypo* (220)
by (96)
under (37)
from (7)
of (3)
in (2)
subject to (2)
at (1)
at their hands (1) *+899*
be condemned (1) *+3213+4406*
established (1)
for (1)
he (1) *+899*
him (1) *+899*
on (1)
reached by (1)
result of (1)
she (1) *+899*
they (1) *+899*
untranslated (61)

5680 ὑποβάλλω *hypoballō* (1)
secretly persuaded (1)

5681 ὑπογραμμός *hypogrammos* (1)
example (1)

5682 ὑπόδειγμα *hypodeigma* (6)
example (4)
copies (1)
copy (1)

5683 ὑποδείκνυμι *hypodeiknymi* (6)
show (3)
warned (2)
showed (1)

5684 ὑποδεικνύω *hypodeiknyō*
Variant; not used

5685 ὑποδέχομαι *hypodechomai* (4)
gave lodging to (1)
opened home to (1)
welcomed (1)
welcomed into house (1)

5686 ὑποδέω *hypodeō* (3)
fitted (1)
sandals (1) *+4908*
wear (1)

5687 ὑπόδημα *hypodēma* (10)
sandals (10)

5688 ὑπόδικος *hypodikos* (1)
held accountable (1) *+1181*

5689 ὑποζύγιον *hypozygion* (2)
donkey (1)
donkey beast (1)

5690 ὑποζώννυμι *hypozōnnymi* (1)
passed under to hold together (1)

5691 ὑποκάτω *hypokatō* (11)
under (9)
untranslated (2)

5692 ὑπόκειμαι *hypokeimai*
Variant; not used

5693 ὑποκρίνομαι *hypokrinomai* (1)
pretended (1)

5694 ὑπόκρισις *hypokrisis* (6)
hypocrisy (5)
hypocritical (1)

5695 ὑποκριτής *hypokritēs* (17)
hypocrites (14)
hypocrite (2)
Hypocrites (1)

5696 ὑπολαμβάνω *hypolambanō* (5)
suppose (2)
hid (1)
reply (1)
show hospitality to (1)

5697 ὑπολαμπάς *hypolampas*
Variant; not used

5698 ὑπόλειμμα *hypoleimma* (1)
remnant (1)

5699 ὑπολείπω *hypoleipō* (1)
left (1)

5700 ὑπολήνιον *hypolēnion* (1)
pit for the winepress (1)

5701 ὑπολιμπάνω *hypolimpanō* (1)
leaving (1)

5702 ὑπομένω *hypomenō* (18)
endure (5)
stands firm (3)
endured (2)
perseveres (2)
patient (1)
persevered (1)
persevered (1) *+2400*
stayed (1)

stayed behind (1)
stood ground (1)

5703 ὑπομιμνήσκω *hypomimnēskō* (7)
remind (3)
call attention to (1)
remembered (1)
remind of (1)
reminding of (1)

5704 ὑπόμνησις *hypomnēsis* (3)
memory (1)
reminded (1) *+3284*
reminders (1)

5705 ὑπομονή *hypomonē* (31)
perseverance (13)
endurance (7)
patient endurance (4)
great endurance (1) *+4246*
patiently (1) *+1328*
persevering (1)
persistence (1)
standing firm (1)
to endure patiently (1)
to persevere (1)

5706 ὑπονοέω *hyponoeō* (3)
expected (1)
sensed (1)
think (1)

5707 ὑπόνοια *hyponoia* (1)
suspicions (1)

5708 ὑποπιάζω *hypopiazō*
Variant; not used

5709 ὑποπλέω *hypopleō* (2)
passed to the lee of (1)
sailed to the lee of (1)

5710 ὑποπνέω *hypopneō* (1)
gentle blow (1)

5711 ὑποπόδιον *hypopodion* (7)
footstool (5)
feet (1)
footstool (1) *+3836+4546*

5712 ὑπόστασις *hypostasis* (5)
being (1)
confidence (1)
confident (1) *+1877*
self-confident (1)
sure (1)

5713 ὑποστέλλω *hypostellō* (4)
hesitated (2)
draw back (1)
shrinks back (1)

5714 ὑποστολή *hypostolē* (1)
shrink back (1)

5715 ὑποστρέφω *hypostrephō* (35)
returned (18)
return (4)
came back (2)
returning (2)
decay (1) *+1426+1650*
go back (1)
home (1)
left (1)
on way home (1)
return (1) *+1650*
turn their backs (1)
went away (1)
went back (1)

5716 ὑποστρωννύω *hypostrōnnyō* (1)
spread (1)

5717 ὑποταγή *hypotagē* (4)
give in (1) *+1634+3836*
obedience (1)
obey (1) *+2400*
submission (1)

5718 ὑποτάσσω *hypotassō* (38)
submit (13)
put under (5)
subject (5)
subjected (3)
submissive (3)
in submission (2)
bring under control (1)
done[s] (1)
obedient (1)
placed under (1)
putting under (1)
subject to the control (1)
submits (1)

5719 ὑποτίθημι *hypotithēmi* (2)
point out (1)
risked lives (1) *+5549*

5720 ὑποτρέχω *hypotrechō* (1)
passed to the lee of (1)

5721 ὑποτύπωσις *hypotypōsis* (2)
example (1)
pattern (1)

5722 ὑποφέρω *hypopherō* (3)
bears up under (1)
endured (1)
stand up under (1)

5723 ὑποχωρέω *hypochōreō* (2)
withdrew (1)
withdrew (1) *+1639*

5724 ὑπωπιάζω *hypōpiazō* (2)
beat (1)
wear out (1)

5725 ὗς *hys* (1)
sow (1)

5726 ὑσσός *hyssos*
Variant; not used

5727 ὕσσωπος *hyssōpos* (2)
branches of hyssop (1)
hyssop plant (1)

5728 ὑστερέω *hystereō* (16)
lack (4)
inferior to (2)
destitute (1)
fall short (1)
fallen short (1)
gone (1)
in want (1)
lacked (1)
misses (1)
need (1)
needed (1)
worse (1)

5729 ὑστέρημα *hysterēma* (9)
lacking (2)
need (2)
could not give (1)
needed (1)
needs (1)
poverty (1)
what is lacking (1)

5730 ὑστέρησις *hysterēsis* (2)
need (1)
poverty (1)

5731 ὕστερος *hysteros* (13)
later (5)
finally (2)
finally (1) *+4246*
last of all (1)
later on (1)
then (1)
untranslated (2)

5732 ὑφαίνω *hyphainō*
Variant; not used

5733 ὑφαντός *hyphantos* (1)
woven (1)

5734 ὑψηλός *hypsēlos* (12)
high (6)
arrogant (1) *+5858*
be proud (1) *+3836+5858*
exalted above (1)
heaven (1)
highly valued (1) *+3836*
mighty (1)

5735 ὑψηλοφρονέω *hypsēlophroneō* (1)
be arrogant (1)

5736 ὕψιστος *hypsistos* (13)
most High (9)
highest (4)

5737 ὕψος *hypsos* (6)
high (3)
heaven (1)
high position (1)
on high (1)

5738 ὑψόω *hypsoō* (20)
lifted up (8)
exalted (5)
exalts (3)
lift up (2)
elevate (1)
made prosper (1)

5739 ὕψωμα *hypsōma* (2)
height (1)
pretension (1)

5740 φ *ph*
Variant; not used

5741 φάγος *phagos* (2)
glutton (2)

5742 φαιλόνης *phailonēs* (1)
cloak (1)

5743 φαίνω *phainō* (31)
appeared (7)
shine (3)
shining (3)
visible (2)
appear (1)
appear as (1)
appears (1)
be seen (1)
become (1)
gave light (1)
look (1)
obvious (1)
recognized (1)
see (1)
seemed (1)
seen (1)
shines (1)
show (1)
think (1)
without light (1) *+3590*

5744 Φάλεκ *Phalek* (1)
Peleg (1)

5745 φανερός *phaneros* (18)
open (2)
tell (2) *+4472*
clear (1)
disclosed (1)
know (1) *+1639*
knows (1)
laid bare (1)
learned about (1) *+1181*
obvious (1)
outward (1) *+1877+3836*
outwardly (1) *+1877+3836*
plain (1)
see (1)
show (1) *+1181*
shown (1)
well known (1)

5746 φανερόω *phaneroō* (49)
appeared (9)
revealed (9)
appears (4)
disclosed (3)
appear (2)
made known (2)
plain (2)
show (2)
showed (2)
appeared (1) +*1571*
brought to light (1)
cover (1) +*3590*
displayed (1)
expose (1)
made clear (1)
made plain (1)
makes visible (1)
proclaim clearly (1)
see (1)
seen plainly (1)
spreads (1)
visible (1)
untranslated (1)

5747 φανερῶς *phanerōs* (3)
distinctly (1)
openly (1)
publicly (1)

5748 φανέρωσις *phanerōsis* (2)
manifestation (1)
setting forth plainly (1)

5749 φανός *phanos* (1)
torches (1)

5750 Φανουήλ *Phanouēl* (1)
Phanuel (1)

5751 φαντάζω *phantazō* (1)
sight (1)

5752 φαντασία *phantasia* (1)
pomp (1)

5753 φάντασμα *phantasma* (2)
ghost (2)

5754 φάραγξ *pharanx* (1)
valley (1)

5755 Φαραώ *Pharaō* (5)
Pharaoh (3)
Pharaoh's (2)

5756 Φαρές *Phares* (3)
Perez (3)

5757 Φαρισαῖος *Pharisaios* (98)
Pharisees (84)
Pharisee (12)
Pharisee's (2)

5758 φαρμακεία *pharmakeia* (2)
magic spell (1)
witchcraft (1)

5759 φαρμακεύς *pharmakeus*
Variant; not used

5760 φάρμακον *pharmakon* (1)
magic arts (1)

5761 φάρμακος *pharmakos* (2)
practice magic arts (1)
those who practice magic arts (1)

5762 φάσις *phasis* (1)
news (1)

5763 φάσκω *phaskō* (3)
claimed (2)
asserting that (1)

5764 φάτνη *phatnē* (4)
manger (3)
stall (1)

5765 φαῦλος *phaulos* (6)
bad (3)
evil (3)

5766 φέγγος *phengos* (2)
light (2)

5767 φείδομαι *pheidomai* (10)
spare (9)
refrain (1)

5768 φειδομένως *pheidomenōs* (2)
sparingly (2)

5769 φελόνης *phelonēs*
Variant; not used

5770 φέρω *pherō* (66)
brought (17)
bring (12)
bear (6)
bringing (3)
came (2)
carried (2)
bearing (1)
bears (1)
blowing (1)
bore (1)
carry (1)
carrying (1)
charge (1) +*162*
did so[s] (1)
driven along (1)
fruitful (1) +*2843*
given (1)
go on (1)
lead (1)
leading (1)
let driven along (1)
multiplying (1)
origin (1)
produces (1)
prove (1)
put (1)
reach out (1)
sustaining (1)
take (1)
took (1)

5771 φεύγω *pheugō* (29)
flee (9)
fled (7)
escape (3)
ran off (3)
flee from (2)
elude (1) +*608*
escaped (1)
fled away (1)
run away (1)
runs away (1)

5772 Φῆλιξ *Phēlix* (9)
Felix (9)

5773 φήμη *phēmē* (2)
news (2)

5774 φημί *phēmi* (66)
said (25)
replied (17)
answered (7)
asked (3)
declared (2)
mean (2)
say (2)
claim (1)
declare (1)
replied (1) +*646*
shouted (1) +*3489+3836+5889*
untranslated (4)

5775 φημίζω *phēmizō*
Variant; not used

5776 Φῆστος *Phēstos* (13)
Festus (13)

5777 φθάνω *phthanō* (7)
come (3)
attained (2)
get (1)
precede (1)

5778 φθαρτός *phthartos* (6)
perishable (4)
mortal (1)
not last (1)

5779 φθέγγομαι *phthengomai* (3)
mouth words (1)
speak (1)
spoke (1)

5780 φθείρω *phtheirō* (9)
corrupted (3)
destroy (2)
corrupts (1)
destroys (1)
led astray (1)
perish (1) +*5785*

5781 φθινοπωρινός *phthinopōrinos* (1)
autumn (1)

5782 φθόγγος *phthongos* (2)
notes (1)
voice (1)

5783 φθονέω *phthoneō* (1)
envying (1)

5784 φθόνος *phthonos* (9)
envy (8)
envies (1)

5785 φθορά *phthora* (9)
corruption (1)
decay (1)
depravity (1)
destroyed (1)
destruction (1)
perish (1)
perish (1) +*5780*
perishable (1)
perishable (1) +*1877*

5786 φιάλη *phialē* (12)
bowl (7)
bowls (5)

5787 φιλάγαθος *philagathos* (1)
one who loves what is good (1)

5788 Φιλαδέλφεια *Philadelpheia* (2)
Philadelphia (2)

5789 φιλαδελφία *philadelphia* (6)
brotherly kindness (2)
brotherly love (2)
love for brothers (1)
loving each other as brothers (1)

5790 φιλάδελφος *philadelphos* (1)
love as brothers (1)

5791 φίλανδρος *philandros* (1)
love their husbands (1)

5792 φιλανθρωπία *philanthrōpia* (2)
kindness (1)
love (1)

5793 φιλανθρώπως *philanthrōpōs* (1)
in kindness (1) +*5968*

5794 φιλαργυρία *philargyria* (1)
love of money (1)

5795 φιλάργυρος *philargyros* (2)
loved money (1) +*5639*
lovers of money (1)

5796 φίλαυτος *philautos* (1)
lovers of themselves (1)

5797 φιλέω *phileō* (25)
love (13)
loves (6)
kiss (3)
loved (3)

5798 φιλήδονος *philēdonos* (1)
lovers of pleasure (1)

5799 φίλημα *philēma* (7)
kiss (7)

5800 Φιλήμων *Philēmōn* (1)
Philemon (1)

5801 Φίλητος *Philētos* (1)
Philetus (1)

5802 φιλία *philia* (1)
friendship (1)

5803 Φιλιππήσιος *Philippēsios* (1)
Philippians (1)

5804 Φίλιπποι *Philippoi* (4)
Philippi (4)

5805 Φίλιππος *Philippos* (36)
Philip (32)
Philip's (2)
Philippi (2)

5806 φιλόθεος *philotheos* (1)
lovers of God (1)

5807 Φιλόλογος *Philologos* (1)
Philologus (1)

5808 φιλονεικία *philoneikia* (1)
dispute (1)

5809 φιλόνεικος *philoneikos* (1)
contentious (1)

5810 φιλοξενία *philoxenia* (2)
entertain strangers (1)
hospitality (1)

5811 φιλόξενος *philoxenos* (3)
hospitable (2)
hospitality (1)

5812 φιλοπρωτεύω *philoprōteuō* (1)
loves to be first (1)

5813 φίλος *philos* (29)
friends (17)
friend (12)

5814 φιλοσοφία *philosophia* (1)
philosophy (1)

5815 φιλόσοφος *philosophos* (1)
philosophers (1)

5816 φιλόστοργος *philostorgos* (1)
devoted (1)

5817 φιλότεκνος *philoteknos* (1)
children (1)

5818 φιλοτιμέομαι *philotimeomai* (3)
ambition (1)
make it ambition (1)
make it goal (1)

5819 φιλοφρόνως *philophronōs* (1)
hospitably (1)

5820 φιλόφρων *philophrōn*
Variant; not used

5821 φιμόω *phimoō* (7)
quiet (2)
muzzle (1)
silence talk (1)
silenced (1)
speechless (1)
still (1)

5822 φλαγελλόω *phlagelloō*
Variant; not used

5823 Φλέγων *Phlegōn* (1)
Phlegon (1)

5824 φλογίζω *phlogizō* (2)
set on fire (1)
sets on fire (1)

5825 φλόξ *phlox* (7)
blazing (4)
flames (2)
fire (1)

5826 φλυαρέω *phlyareō* (1)
gossiping about (1)

5827 φλύαρος *phlyaros* (1)
gossips (1)

5828 φοβέομαι *phobeomai* (95)
afraid (41)
fear (14)
afraid of (12)
feared (4)
alarmed (2)
fearing that (2) *+3590*
God-fearing (2) *+2536+3836*
terrified (2) *+3489+5832*
terrified (2) *+5379*
be careful (1)
fear for (1)
fearing (1)
fears (1)
filled with awe (1)
free from fear of (1) *+3590*
God-fearing gentiles (1) *+2536+3836*
in fear (1)
respect (1)
reverence (1)
reverence for (1)
terrified (1)
who feared (1)
worship (1)

5829 φοβερός *phoberos* (3)
dreadful (1)
fearful (1)
terrifying (1)

5830 φοβέω *phobeō*
Variant; not used

5831 φόβητρον *phobētron* (1)
fearful events (1)

5832 φόβος *phobos* (47)
fear (18)
respect (5)
awe (3)
reverence (3)
terrified (2) *+3489+5828*
afraid (1)
afraid (1) *+3552*
alarm (1)
fear (1) *+3489*
feared (1)
fears (1)
filled with awe (1) *+3284*
gripped with fear (1) *+2158*
hold terror (1) *+1639*
reverent fear (1)
seized with fear (1) *+2158*
terrified (1)
terrified (1) *+1328*
terror (1)
terror (1) *+3489*
warning (1)

5833 Φοίβη *Phoibē* (1)
Phoebe (1)

5834 Φοινίκη *Phoinikē* (3)
Phoenicia (3)

5835 Φοινίκισσα *Phoinikissa*
Variant; not used

5836 φοῖνιξ1 *phoinix1* (2)
palm (1)
palm branches (1)

5837 Φοῖνιξ2 *Phoinix2* (1)
Phoenix (1)

5838 φονεύς *phoneus* (7)
murderers (3)
murderer (2)
murdered (1)
murderer (1) *+467*

5839 φονεύω *phoneuō* (12)
murder (6)
murdered (3)
commit murder (1)
kill (1)
murders (1)

5840 φόνος *phonos* (9)
murder (6)
murderous (1)
murders (1)
put to death (1) *+633+1877*

5841 φορέω *phoreō* (6)
bear (2)
wearing (2)
borne (1)
wear (1)

5842 φόρον *phoron* (1)
Forum (1)

5843 φόρος *phoros* (5)
taxes (5)

5844 φορτίζω *phortizō* (2)
burdened (1)
load down (1)

5845 φορτίον *phortion* (6)
burden (1)
burdens (1)
cargo (1)
help (1)
load (1)
loads (1)

5846 φόρτος *phortos*
Variant; not used

5847 Φορτουνᾶτος *Phortounatos* (1)
Fortunatus (1)

5848 φραγέλλιον *phragellion* (1)
whip (1)

5849 φραγελλόω *phragelloō* (2)
had flogged (2)

5850 φραγμός *phragmos* (4)
wall (2)
barrier (1)
country lanes (1)

5851 φράζω *phrazō* (1)
explain (1)

5852 φράσσω *phrassō* (3)
shut (1)
silenced (1)
stop (1)

5853 φρέαρ *phrear* (7)
well (3)
Abyss (1)
it[s] (1) *+3836*
shaft (1)
untranslated (1)

5854 φρεναπατάω *phrenapataō* (1)
deceives (1)

5855 φρεναπάτης *phrenapatēs* (1)
deceivers (1)

5856 φρήν *phrēn* (2)
thinking (1)
thinking (1) *+1181+3836*

5857 φρίσσω *phrissō* (1)
shudder (1)

5858 φρονέω *phroneō* (26)
have in mind (2)
mind (2)
agree with (1)
arrogant (1) *+5734*
attitude (1)

be proud (1) *+3836+5734*
being like-minded (1) *+899+3836*
concern (1)
concerned (1)
does so[s] (1)
feel (1)
live in harmony (1) *+899+3836*
minds set on (1)
on think (1)
purpose (1)
regards (1)
set minds on (1)
spirit of unity (1) *+899+3836*
take such a view of things (1)
take view (1)
think (1)
thought (1)
views are (1)
untranslated (1)

5859 φρόνημα *phronēma* (4)
mind (4)

5860 φρόνησις *phronēsis* (2)
understanding (1)
wisdom (1)

5861 φρόνιμος *phronimos* (14)
wise (8)
conceited (1)
conceited (1) *+4123+4932*
sensible (1)
shrewd (1)
shrewd (1) *+5642*
they[s] (1) *+3836*

5862 φρονίμως *phronimōs* (1)
shrewdly (1)

5863 φροντίζω *phrontizō* (1)
careful (1)

5864 φρουρέω *phroureō* (4)
guard (1)
guarded (1)
held prisoners (1)
shielded (1)

5865 φρυάσσω *phryassō* (1)
rage (1)

5866 φρύγανον *phryganon* (1)
brushwood (1)

5867 Φρυγία *Phrygia* (3)
Phrygia (3)

5868 φυγαδεύω *phygadeuō*
Variant; not used

5869 Φύγελος *Phygelos* (1)
Phygelus (1)

5870 φυγή *phygē* (1)
flight (1)

5871 φυλακή *phylakē* (46)
prison (31)
jail (3)
haunt (2)
watch (2)
cell (1)
guard (1)
guards (1)
imprisonments (1)
keeping watch (1) *+5875*
prisons (1)
time of night (1)
watch of the night (1)

5872 φυλακίζω *phylakizō* (1)
imprison (1)

5873 φυλακτήριον *phylaktērion* (1)
phylacteries (1)

5874 φύλαξ *phylax* (3)
guards (2)
sentries (1)

5875 φυλάσσω *phylassō* (31)
keep (5)
guard (4)
kept (3)
obey (3)
kept under guard (2)
on guard (2)
abstain from (1)
guarded (1)
guarding (1)
guards (1)
in obedience to (1)
keep from (1)
keeping watch (1) *+5871*
kept safe (1)
obeyed (1)
on guard against (1)
protect (1)
protected (1)

5876 φυλή *phylē* (31)
tribe (24)
tribes (5)
nations (1)
peoples (1)

5877 φύλλον *phyllon* (6)
leaves (5)
in leaf (1) *+2400*

5878 φύραμα *phyrama* (5)
batch (2)
batch of dough (2)
lump of clay (1)

5879 φυσικός *physikos* (3)
natural (2)
creatures of instinct (1)

5880 φυσικῶς *physikōs* (1)
instinct (1)

5881 φυσιόω *physioō* (7)
arrogant (2)
proud (2)
puffs up (2)
take pride (1)

5882 φύσις *physis* (14)
nature (7)
natural (2) *+2848*
birth (1)
kinds (1)
physically (1) *+1666*
unnatural ones (1) *+3836+4123*
untranslated (1)

5883 φυσίωσις *physiōsis* (1)
arrogance (1)

5884 φυτεία *phyteia* (1)
plant (1)

5885 φυτεύω *phyteuō* (11)
planted (7)
plants (3)
planting (1)

5886 φύω *phyō* (3)
came up (2)
grows (1)

5887 φωλεός *phōleos* (2)
holes (2)

5888 φωνέω *phōneō* (42)
called (9)
crows (7)
call (3)
called out (3)
calling (3)
crowed (3)
called to (2)
summoned (2)
asking for (1)
called in (1)
calls (1)
crow (1)
invite (1)
said (1)
sent for (1)
sent for (1) *+3306*
shouted (1) *+3489+5889*
shriek (1) *+3489+5889*

5889 φωνή *phōnē* (139)
voice (85)
sound (8)
voices (5)
rumblings (4)
roar (2)
shouts (2)
words (2)
at the top of voice (1) *+3489*
at the top of voices (1) *+3489*
blasts (1)
call (1)
called out (1) *+2048*
called out (1) *+3306+3489*
called out in a loud voice (1) *+149*
cried out (1) *+3189+3489*
cry (1)
gave a shout (1) *+3189*
heard sound (1) *+1181*
languages (1)
music (1)
peals (1)
roar (1) *+3489*
shouted (1) *+2048+3836*
shouted (1) *+3489+3836+5774*
shouted (1) *+3489+5888*
shouting at the top of voice (1) *+3306+3489*
shriek (1) *+3489+5888*
shrieks (1) *+1066+3489*
someone is saying (1)
sounded (1)
sounds (1)
thundering (1)
tone (1)
untranslated (5)

5890 φῶς *phōs* (73)
light (66)
daylight (2)
lights (2)
fire (1)
firelight (1)
it[s] (1) *+3836*

5891 φωστήρ *phōstēr* (2)
brilliance (1)
stars (1)

5892 φωσφόρος *phōsphoros* (1)
morning star (1)

5893 φωτεινός *phōteinos* (5)
full of light (3)
bright (1)
lighted (1)

5894 φωτίζω *phōtizō* (11)
enlightened (2)
bring to light (1)
brought to light (1)
give light (1)
gives light (1)
gives light to (1)
illuminated (1)
make plain to (1)
received light (1)
shines on (1)

5895 φωτισμός *phōtismos* (2)
light (2)

5896 χ *ch*
Variant; not used

5897 χαίρω *chairō* (74)
rejoice (17)
glad (13)
greetings (6)

delighted (3)
hail (3)
joy (3)
rejoicing (3)
delight (2)
happy (2)
joyful (2)
joyfully (2)
be glad (1)
delighted (1) *+4359*
full of joy (1)
full of joy (1) *+5915*
gladly (1)
gloat (1)
good-by (1)
happier (1) *+3437*
joy have (1) *+5915*
make rejoice (1)
overjoyed (1)
overjoyed (1) *+22*
overjoyed (1) *+3489+5379+5915*
pleased (1)
rejoices (1)
welcome (1) *+3306*
welcomes (1) *+3306*
untranslated (1)

5898 χάλαζα *chalaza* (4)
hail (2)
hailstones (1)
hailstorm (1)

5899 χαλάω *chalaō* (7)
let down (3)
lowered (3)
lowered (1) *+2768*

5900 Χαλδαῖος *Chaldaios* (1)
Chaldeans (1)

5901 χαλεπός *chalepos* (2)
terrible (1)
violent (1) *+3336*

5902 χαλιναγωγέω *chalinagōgeō* (2)
keep a tight rein on (1)
keep in check (1)

5903 χαλινός *chalinos* (2)
bits (1)
bridles (1)

5904 χαλινόω *chalinoō*
Variant; not used

5905 χάλκεος *chalkeos* (1)
bronze (1)

5906 χαλκεύς *chalkeus* (1)
metalworker (1)

5907 χαλκηδών *chalkēdōn* (1)
chalcedony (1)

5908 χαλκίον *chalkion* (1)
kettles (1)

5909 χαλκολίβανον *chalkolibanon* (2)
bronze (1)
burnished bronze (1)

5910 χαλκός *chalkos* (5)
money (2)
bronze (1)
copper (1)
gong (1)

5911 χαλκοῦς *chalkous*
Variant; not used

5912 χαμαί *chamai* (2)
on the ground (1)
to the ground (1)

5913 Χανάαν *Chanaan* (2)
Canaan (1)
Canaan (1) *+1178*

5914 Χαναναῖος *Chananaios* (1)
Canaanite (1)

5915 χαρά *chara* (59)
joy (44)
happiness (2)
joyfully (2) *+3552*
rejoicing (2)
filled with joy (1) *+22*
filled with joy (1) *+3489*
full of joy (1) *+5897*
glad (1)
happy (1)
joy have (1) *+5897*
overjoyed (1)
overjoyed (1) *+3489+5379+5897*
pleasant (1)

5916 χάραγμα *charagma* (8)
mark (7)
image (1)

5917 χαρακτήρ *charaktēr* (1)
exact representation (1)

5918 χάραξ *charax* (1)
embankment (1)

5919 χαρίζομαι *charizomai* (23)
forgive (5)
forgave (3)
canceled (2)
gave (2)
hand over (2)
forgiven (1)
forgiving (1)
freely given (1)
graciously give (1)
graciously given (1)
granted (1)
in grace gave (1)
released (1)
restored (1)

5920 χάριν *charin* (9)
for (2)
for this reason (2) *+4047*
because of (1)
for the sake of (1)
the reason (1) *+4047*
therefore (1) *+4005*
why (1) *+5515*

5921 χάρις *charis* (155)
grace (119)
favor (6)
thanks (5)
credit (3)
thank (3) *+2400*
commendable (2)
gift (2)
act of grace (1)
another[s] (1)
benefit (1) *+1443*
benefit (1) *+2400*
blessing (1)
enjoying favor (1) *+2400*
goodwill (1)
gracious (1)
gracious gift (1)
gratitude (1)
offering (1)
privilege (1)
thank (1)
thankful (1) *+2400*
thankfulness (1)

5922 χάρισμα *charisma* (17)
gift (8)
gifts (7)
gracious favor granted (1)
spiritual gift (1)

5923 χαριτόω *charitoō* (2)
freely given (1)
highly favored (1)

5924 Χαρράν *Charran* (2)
Haran (2)

5925 χάρτης *chartēs* (1)
paper (1)

5926 χάσμα *chasma* (1)
chasm (1)

5927 χεῖλος *cheilos* (7)
lips (6)
seashore (1) *+2498+3836*

5928 χειμάζω *cheimazō* (1)
took a battering from the storm (1)

5929 χείμαρρος *cheimarros* (1)
valley (1)

5930 χειμών *cheimōn* (6)
winter (4)
storm (1)
stormy (1)

5931 χείρ *cheir* (177)
hand (75)
hands (70)
seized (2) *+2093+2095+3836*
seized (2) *+2095+3836*
arms (1)
arrest (1) *+2093+2095+3836*
arrested (1) *+2093+2095+3836*
arrested (1) *+2095+3836*
by (1) *+1877*
clutches (1)
enabling (1) *+1328+1443+3836*
finger (1)
grasp (1)
hand over to (1) *+1650+4140*
he (1) *+899+1328+3836*
help (1)
man-made (1) *+1181+1328*
motioned (1) *+2939+3836*
pointing (1) *+899+1753+3836*
power (1)
reached for (1) *+1753+3836*
through (1) *+5250*
under power (1) *+1650*
using (1) *+1328*
with (1) *+1328*
wrists (1)
untranslated (6)

5932 χειραγωγέω *cheiragōgeō* (2)
by the hand (1)
led by the hand (1)

5933 χειραγωγός *cheiragōgos* (1)
someone to lead by the hand (1)

5934 χειρόγραφον *cheirographon* (1)
written code (1)

5935 χειροποίητος *cheiropoiētos* (6)
man-made (3)
built by hands (1)
done by the hands (1)
made by men (1)

5936 χειροτονέω *cheirotoneō* (2)
appointed (1)
chosen (1)

5937 χείρων *cheirōn* (11)
worse (4)
worse than (4)
from bad to worse (1) *+2093+3836*
more severely (1)
worse off than (1)

5938 Χερούβ *Cheroub* (1)
cherubim (1)

5939 χήρα *chēra* (26)
widow (12)
widows (10)
widows' (2)
widow (1) *+1222*
untranslated (1)

5940 χθές *chthes*
Variant; not used

5941 χιλίαρχος *chiliarchos* (21)
commander (17)
generals (2)
high ranking officers (1)
military commanders (1)

5942 χιλιάς *chilias* (23)
12,000 (13) *+1557*
thousand (5)
144,000 (3) *+1669+5475+5477*
thousands (2)

5943 χίλιοι *chilioi* (11)
thousand (8)
1,260 (2) *+1357+2008*
1,600 (1) *+1980*

5944 Χίος *Chios* (1)
Kios (1)

5945 χιτών *chitōn* (11)
tunic (5)
clothes (1)
clothing (1)
garment (1)
robes (1)
tunics (1)
undergarment (1)

5946 χιών *chiōn* (2)
snow (2)

5947 χις' *chis'*
Variant; not used

5948 χλαμύς *chlamys* (2)
robe (2)

5949 χλευάζω *chleuazō* (1)
sneered (1)

5950 χλιαρός *chliaros* (1)
lukewarm (1)

5951 Χλόη *Chloē* (1)
Chloe's (1)

5952 χλωρός *chlōros* (4)
green (2)
pale (1)
plant (1)

5953 χξς' *chxs'*
Variant; not used

5954 χοϊκός *choikos* (4)
earthly (2)
dust (1)
earth (1)

5955 χοῖνιξ *choinix* (2)
quart (1)
quarts (1)

5956 χοῖρος *choiros* (12)
pigs (12)

5957 χολάω *cholaō* (1)
angry (1)

5958 χολή *cholē* (2)
bitterness (1) *+4394*
gall (1)

5959 χόος *choos*
Variant; not used

5960 Χοραζίν *Chorazin* (2)
Korazin (2)

5961 χορηγέω *chorēgeō* (2)
provides (1)
supply (1)

5962 χορός *choros* (1)
dancing (1)

5963 χορτάζω *chortazō* (15)
satisfied (6)
feed (2)
well fed (2)
eat (1)
eat all they want (1)
fill (1)
filled (1)
gorged (1)

5964 χόρτασμα *chortasma* (1)
food (1)

5965 χόρτος *chortos* (15)
grass (9)
field (1)
hay (1)
plant (1)
stalk (1)
wheat (1)
wild (1)

5966 Χουζᾶς *Chouzas* (1)
Cuza (1)

5967 χοῦς *chous* (2)
dust (2)

5968 χράομαι *chraomai* (11)
use (4)
bold (1) *+4244*
do (1)
do so (1) *+3437*
in kindness (1) *+5793*
used (1)
uses (1)
untranslated (1)

5969 χράω *chraō*
Variant; not used

5970 χρεία *chreia* (49)
need (26) *+2400*
need (5)
needs (5) *+2400*
needs (4)
needed (2)
needed (2) *+2400*
be dependent on (1) *+2400*
daily necessities (1) *+338*
need (1) *+1181+2400*
responsibility (1)
who need (1) *+2400*

5971 χρεοφειλέτης *chreopheiletēs* (2)
debtors (1)
owed money to (1) *+1639*

5972 χρεωφειλέτης *chreōpheiletēs*
Variant; not used

5973 χρή *chrē* (1)
should (1)

5974 χρῄζω *chrēzō* (5)
need (4)
needs (1)

5975 χρῆμα *chrēma* (6)
money (3)
rich (2) *+2400+3836*
bribe (1)

5976 χρηματίζω *chrēmatizō* (9)
warned (5)
called (2)
revealed (1)
told (1)

5977 χρηματισμός *chrēmatismos* (1)
God's (1)

5978 χρήσιμος *chrēsimos* (1)
value (1)

5979 χρῆσις *chrēsis* (2)
relations (2)

5980 χρηστεύομαι *chrēsteuomai* (1)
kind (1)

5981 χρηστολογία *chrēstologia* (1)
smooth talk (1)

5982 χρηστός *chrēstos* (7)
good (2)
kind (2)
better (1)
easy (1)
kindness (1)

5983 χρηστότης *chrēstotēs* (10)
kindness (9)
good (1)

5984 χρῖσμα *chrisma* (3)
anointing (3)

5985 Χριστιανός *Christianos* (3)
Christian (2)
Christians (1)

5986 Χριστός *Christos* (528)
Christ (515)
Christ's (9)
anointed one (1)
belongs to Christ (1) *+1639*
Christ's (1) *+5642*
him[S] (1) *+3836*

5987 χρίω *chriō* (5)
anointed (4)
anointing (1)

5988 χρονίζω *chronizō* (5)
a long time in coming (1)
delay (1)
stayed so long (1)
staying away a long time (1)
taking a long time (1)

5989 χρόνος *chronos* (54)
time (27)
times (5)
as long as (2) *+2093+4012*
beginning of time (2) *+173*
long (2)
a long time (1) *+3900+4024*
delay (1)
instant (1) *+5117*
life (1)
lives (1)
longer (1) *+2285*
old (1)
only as long as (1) *+2093+4012*
past (1)
so long as (1) *+4012*
some time (1)
spend time (1) *+2093+3531*
spend time (1) *+2152*
stayed a little longer (1) *+2091*
while (1)
untranslated (1)

5990 χρονοτριβέω *chronotribeō* (1)
spending time (1) *+1181*

5991 χρύσεος *chryseos* (18)
golden (12)
of gold (5)
gold (1)

5992 χρυσίον *chrysion* (12)
gold (10)
gold jewelry (1)
gold-covered (1) *+4119+4328*

5993 χρυσοδακτύλιος *chrysodaktylios* (1)
wearing a gold ring (1)

5994 χρυσόλιθος *chrysolithos* (1)
chrysolite (1)

5995 χρυσόπρασος *chrysoprasos* (1)
chrysoprase (1)

5996 χρυσός *chrysos* (10)
gold (10)

5997 χρυσοῦς *chrysous*
Variant; not used

5998 χρυσόω *chrysoō* (2)
glittering (2)

5999 χρώς *chrōs* (1)
that had touched (1) *+608+3836*

6000 χωλός *chōlos* (14)
lame (10)
crippled (3)
cripples (1)

6001 χώρα *chōra* (28)
country (8)
region (8)
fields (3)
land (2)
area (1)
countryside (1)
ground (1)
they[s] (1) *+899+3836*
untranslated (3)

6002 Χοραζίν *Chōrazin*
Variant; not used

6003 χωρέω *chōreō* (10)
accept (3)
room for (2)
come (1)
goes (1)
holding (1)
make room for (1)
room (1)

6004 χωρίζω *chōrizō* (13)
separate (5)
leave (2)
do so[s] (1)
does[s] (1)
leaves (1)
left (1)
separated from (1)
set apart (1)

6005 χωρίον *chōrion* (10)
field (3)
land (2)
place (2)
estate (1)
lands (1)
plot of ground (1)

6006 χωρίς *chōris* (41)
without (23)
apart from (7)
besides (2)
not (2)
besides everything else (1) *+3836+4211*
by itself (1) *+1650+1651+3023+5536*
independent of (1)
separate from (1)
together (1) *+3590*
without (1) *+4246*
untranslated (1)

6007 χωρισμός *chōrismos*
Variant; not used

6008 χῶρος *chōros* (1)
northwest (1)

6009 ψ *ps*
Variant; not used

6010 ψάλλω *psallō* (5)
sing (2)
make music (1)
sing hymns (1)
sing songs of praise (1)

6011 ψαλμός *psalmos* (7)
Psalms (3)
psalms (2)
hymn (1)
Psalm (1)

6012 ψευδάδελφος *pseudadelphos* (2)
false brothers (2)

6013 ψευδαπόστολος *pseudapostolos* (1)
false apostles (1)

6014 ψευδής *pseudēs* (3)
false (2)
liars (1)

6015 ψευδοδιδάσκαλος *pseudodidaskalos* (1)
false teachers (1)

6016 ψευδολόγος *pseudologos* (1)
liars (1)

6017 ψεύδομαι *pseudomai* (12)
lie (4)
lying (3)
deny truth (1) *+237+2848*
falsely (1)
liars (1)
lied (1)
lied to (1)

6018 ψευδομαρτυρέω *pseudomartyreō* (5)
give false testimony (3)
gave false testimony (1)
testified falsely (1)

6019 ψευδομαρτυρία *pseudomartyria* (3)
false evidence (1)
false testimony (1)
false witnesses (1)

6020 ψευδόμαρτυς *pseudomartys* (1)
false witnesses (1)

6021 ψευδοπροφήτης *pseudoprophētēs* (11)
false prophets (7)
false prophet (4)

6022 ψεῦδος *pseudos* (10)
lie (4)
counterfeit (2)
falsehood (2)
deceitful (1)
lies (1) *+3281+3836*

6023 ψευδόχριστος *pseudochristos* (2)
false Christs (2)

6024 ψευδώνυμος *pseudōnymos* (1)
falsely called (1)

6025 ψεῦσμα *pseusma* (1)
falsehood (1)

6026 ψεύστης *pseustēs* (10)
liar (8)
liars (2)

6027 ψηλαφάω *psēlaphaō* (4)
touched (2)
reach out for (1)
touch (1)

6028 ψηφίζω *psēphizō* (2)
calculate (1)
estimate (1)

6029 ψῆφος *psēphos* (3)
it[s] (1) *+3836*
stone (1)
vote (1)

6030 ψιθυρισμός *psithyrismos* (1)
gossip (1)

6031 ψιθυριστής *psithyristēs* (1)
gossips (1)

6032 ψίξ *psix*
Variant; not used

6033 ψιχίον *psichion* (2)
crumbs (2)

6034 ψυχή *psychē* (102)
life (32)
soul (19)
souls (6)
lives (5)
heart (4)
everyone (2) *+4246*
minds (2)
you (2) *+5148*
all (1)
anyone (1) *+1569+4246*
being (1)
he's (1) *+899+1639*
I (1) *+1609*
I (1) *+1609+3836*
keep in suspense (1) *+149+3836*
living (1) *+2400+3836*
man (1)
me (1) *+1609*
me (1) *+1609+3836*
mind (1)
myself (1) *+1609*
people (1)
saved (1) *+1650+4348*
themselves (1) *+899+3836*
thing (1)
trying to kill (1) *+2426+3836*
unstable (1) *+844*
us[s] (1)
you[s] (1)
yourselves (1) *+5148*
untranslated (8)

6035 ψυχικός *psychikos* (6)
natural (3)
follow mere natural instincts (1)
unspiritual (1)
without the spirit (1)

6036 ψῦχος *psychos* (3)
cold (3)

6037 ψυχρός *psychros* (4)
cold (3)
one[s] (1)

6038 ψύχω *psychō* (1)
grow cold (1)

6039 ψωμίζω *psōmizō* (2)
feed (1)
give to the poor (1)

6040 ψωμίον *psōmion* (4)
bread (2)
piece of bread (2)

6041 ψώχω *psōchō* (1)
rub (1)

6042 Ὦ1 *Ō1* (3)
Omega (3)

6043 ὦ2 *ō2* (17)
O (4)
you (3)
how foolish you are (1) *+485*
oh (1)
untranslated (8)

6044 Ὠβήδ *Ōbēd*
Variant; not used

6045 ὧδε *hōde* (61)
here (50)
this (4)
here's (1)
in the one case (1) *+3525*
there (1)
this calls for (1)
untranslated (3)

6046 ᾠδή *ōdē* (7)
song (5)
songs (2)

6047 ὠδίν *ōdin* (4)
birth pains (2)
agony (1)
labor pains (1)

6048 ὠδίνω *ōdinō* (3)
give birth (1) *+5503*
have labor pains (1)
in the pains of childbirth (1)

6049 ὦμος *ōmos* (2)
shoulders (2)

6050 ὠνέομαι *ōneomai* (1)
bought (1)

6051 ᾠόν *ōon* (1)
egg (1)

6052 ὥρα *hōra* (106)
hour (52)
time (31)
moment (6)
hours (3)
at hour (1) +*1181*
at once (1) +*899+3836*
for a little while (1) +*4639*
immediately (1) +*899+1877+3836*
it[s] (1) +*3836*
late (1)
late in the day (1) +*4498*
little while (1)
nine (1) +*5569*
nine in the morning (1) +*2465+3836+5569*
noon (1) +*1761*
short (1)
three in the afternoon (1) +*1888+2465+3836*
very late (1) +*4498*

6053 ὡραῖος *hōraios* (4)
beautiful (4)

6054 ὠρύομαι *ōryomai* (1)
roaring (1)

6055 ὡς *hōs* (502)
as (152)
like (124)
when (33)
about (18)
just as (17)
as if (16)
how (11)
as though (5)
that (5)
while (5)
after (4)
and (3)
so (3)
like that of (2)
meaning (2)
of (2)
on (2)
on the pretext of (2)
regarded as (2)
resembled (2)
when (2) +*323*
according to (1)
and to which (1)
are (1)
as soon as (1)
as soon as (1) +*323*
at (1)
blood red (1) +*135*
considered (1) +*2400*
faithfully (1) +*2819*
for (1)
hardship like (1)
if only (1)
in accordance with (1)
is (1)
just (1)
just like (1)
like (1) +*1569*
looked like (1)
one might even say (1) +*2229+3306*
seem (1)
seemed (1)
since (1)
so-called (1) +*3306*
somehow or other (1) +*323*
something (1)
supposed (1)
that is (1)
the same as (1) +*2779*
the same way (1) +*2779*
the size of (1)
to (1)
unlike (1) +*4024*
what (1)
what sounded like (1)
when (1) +*1254*
untranslated (55)

6056 ὡσάν *hōsan*
Variant; not used

6057 ὡσαννά *hōsanna* (6)
Hosanna (6)

6058 ὡσαύτως *hōsautōs* (17)
in the same way (6)
likewise (2)
the same (2)
the same thing (2)
also (1)
similarly (1)
so also (1)
the same way (1)
too (1)

6059 ὡσεί *hōsei* (21)
about (10)
like (6)
about (1) +*4309*
as (1)
looked so much like (1) +*1181*
numbering about (1)
what seemed to be (1)

6060 Ὡσηέ *Hōsēe* (1)
Hosea (1)

6061 ὥσπερ *hōsper* (36)
as (15)
just as (10)
like (6)
as indeed (1)
the way (1)
unlike (1)
what (1)
untranslated (1)

6062 ὡσπερεί *hōsperei* (1)
as (1)

6063 ὥστε *hōste* (83)
so that (20)
so (19)
therefore (13)
that (9)
to (4)
as a result (3)
so then (3)
and (1)
consequently (1)
in order to (1)
now (1)
such that (1)
then (1)
untranslated (6)

6064 ὠτάριον *ōtarion* (2)
ear (2)

6065 ὠτίον *ōtion* (3)
ear (3)

6066 ὠφέλεια *ōpheleia* (2)
advantage (1)
value (1)

6067 ὠφελέω *opheleō* (15)
value (4)
good (2)
counts for (1)
devoted (1)
gain (1)
getting better (1)
getting nowhere (1) +*4024+4029*
good for (1)
good to (1)
help received (1)
was getting nowhere (1) +*4029*

6068 ὠφέλιμος *ōphelimos* (4)
value (2)
profitable (1)
useful (1)

FEATURES OF THE INDEX OF STRONG → GOODRICK/KOHLENBERGER NUMBERS

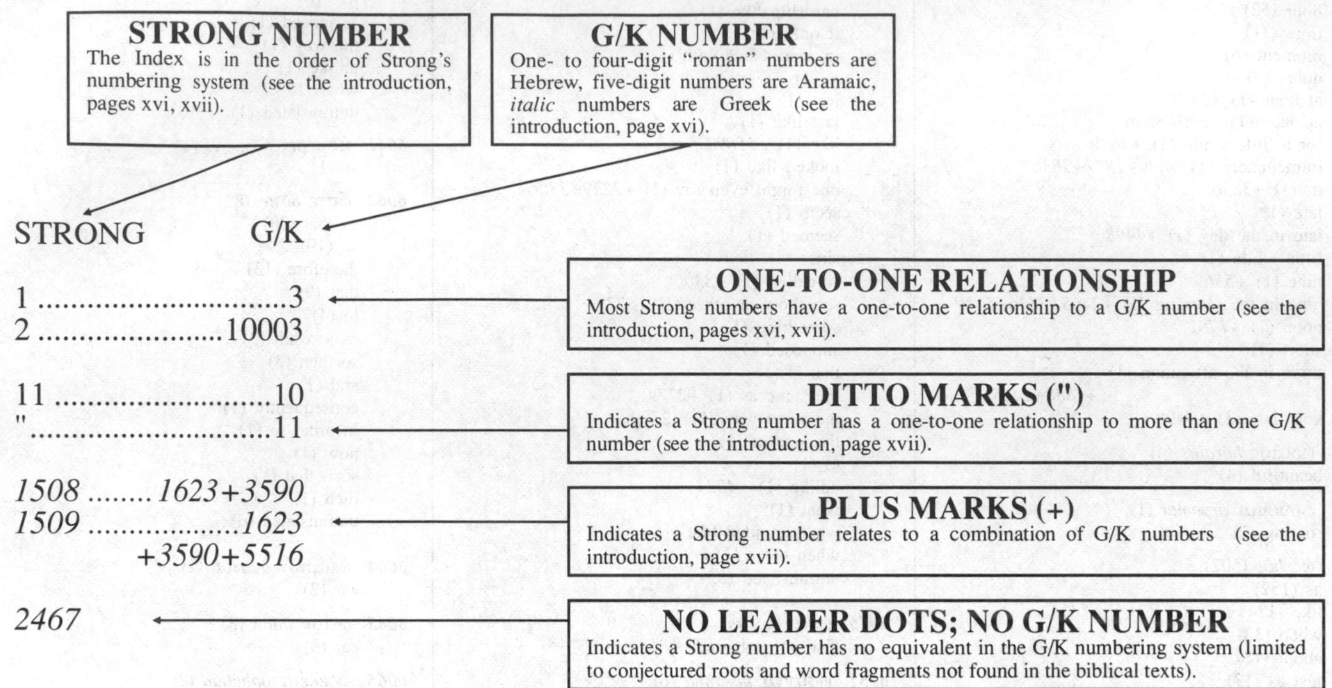

STRONG NUMBER
The Index is in the order of Strong's numbering system (see the introduction, pages xvi, xvii).
G/K NUMBER
One- to four-digit "roman" numbers are Hebrew, five-digit numbers are Aramaic, *italic* numbers are Greek (see the introduction, page xvi).
STRONG G/K
1 3
2 10003
ONE-TO-ONE RELATIONSHIP
Most Strong numbers have a one-to-one relationship to a G/K number (see the introduction, pages xvi, xvii).
11 10
" 11
DITTO MARKS (")
Indicates a Strong number has a one-to-one relationship to more than one G/K number (see the introduction, page xvii).
1508 .... 1623+3590
1509 1623
+3590+5516
PLUS MARKS (+)
Indicates a Strong number relates to a combination of G/K numbers (see the introduction, page xvii).
2467
NO LEADER DOTS; NO G/K NUMBER
Indicates a Strong number has no equivalent in the G/K numbering system (limited to conjectured roots and word fragments not found in the biblical texts).

FEATURES OF THE INDEX OF GOODRICK/ KOHLENBERGER → STRONG NUMBERS

G/K NUMBER
One- to four-digit "roman" numbers are Hebrew, five-digit numbers are Aramaic, *italic* numbers are Greek (see the introduction, page xvi).

STRONG NUMBER
"Roman" numbers are Hebrew or Aramaic; *italic* numbers are Greek (see the introduction, page xvii).

G/K STRONG

3 1
4 3

ONE-TO-ONE RELATIONSHIP
Most G/K numbers have a one-to-one relationship to a Strong number (see the introduction, page xvii).

10513 5559
" 5267

DITTO MARKS (")
Indicates a G/K number has a one-to-one relationship to more than one Strong number (see the introduction, page xvii).

1276 .... 1176+1803
1277 1176
+2532+3638

PLUS MARKS (+)
Indicates a G/K number relates to a combination of Strong numbers (see the introduction, pages xiii-xv).

1432
1433

NO LEADER DOTS; NO STRONG NUMBER
Indicates a G/K number has no equivalent in the Strong numbering system (see the introduction, page xvii).

NUMBERING SYSTEM INDEXES

INDEX OF STRONG → GOODRICK/KOHLENBERGER NUMBERS

HEBREW / ARAMAIC OLD TESTAMENT

STRONG	G/K
1	3
2	10003
3	4
4	10004
5	5
6	6
7	10005
8	7
9	8
10	9
11	10
"	11
12	12
13	13
14	14
15	20
"	1066
16	15
17	16
18	17
19	18
20	19
21	23
22	24
23	25
24	26
25	3+1500
26	28
27	29
28	30
29	31
"	32
30	33
31	34
32	35
"	38
33	49
34	36
35	37
36	39
37	40
38	41
39	42
40	43
41	44
42	45
43	47
44	48
45	50
"	6588
46	51
47	52
48	53
49	54
50	55
51	56
52	57
"	93
53	58
"	94
54	59
55	60
56	61
"	62
57	63
58	64
59	63

STRONG	G/K
"	64
60	65
61	66
62	68
63	69
"	2243
64	70
65	71
"	4552
66	72
67	73
68	74
69	10006
70	78
71	76
72	75
"	2193
73	77
74	46
"	79
75	80
76	81
77	82
78	83
79	84
80	85
81	86
82	87
83	88
84	89
85	90
86	91
87	92
88	95
89	96
90	97
91	98
92	99
93	100
94	101
95	102
96	103
97	104
98	106
"	107
99	108
100	109
101	110
102	111
103	112
104	10007
105	113
106	114
107	115
108	116
109	117
110	118
111	119
112	120
113	123
114	124
115	126
116	10008
117	129
118	130
119	131
120	132
"	133
"	135
121	134
"	136
122	137
123	121

STRONG	G/K
"	139
124	138
125	140
126	144
127	141
"	143
128	142
129+5346	146
130	122
131	147
132	145
133	148
134	149
135	150
136	151
137	152
138	125
"	153
"	154
139	155
140	156
141	157
142	158
143	160
144	10009
145	159
146	161
"	162
147	10010
148	10011
149	10012
150	163
151	127
"	164
152	165
"	166
153	10013
154	167
155	168
156	169
157	170
158	172
159	171
160	173
"	174
161	176
162	177
163	178
164	179
165	180
166	183
167	182
168	185
169	186
170	188
171	190
172	191
173	192
174	184
"	189
"	193
175	195
176	196
"	197
177	198
178	199
"	200
179	201
180	67
181	202
182	128
183	203
184	204

STRONG	G/K
185	205
186	206
187	207
188	208
189	209
190	210
191	211
192	213
193	212
"	214
"	215
194	218
195	217
196	216
197	221
198	220
199	219
200	222
201	223
202	226
203	227
204	228
205	224
"	230
206	225
207	229
208	231
209	232
210	233
211	234
"	235
212	236
213	237
214	238
215	239
216	240
217	241
218	243
"	244
219	245
"	246
220	774
221	247
"	788
222	248
223	249
"	250
224	242
"	251
"	797
225	252
226	253
227	255
228	10015
229	256
230	10014
231	257
232	258
233	259
234	260
235	261
236	10016
237	262
238	263
239	264
240	266
241	265
242	267
243	268
244	269
"	270
245	271
246	272

STRONG	G/K
247	273
248	274
249	275
250	276
251	278
252	10017
253	277
254	279
255	280
256	281
"	282
257	283
258	284
259	285
260	286
261	287
262	289
263	10018
264	288
265	291
266	292
267	293
268	294
269	295
270	290
"	296
"	297
271	298
272	299
273	300
274	301
"	302
275	303
276	304
277	306
278	305
279	307
280	10019
281	308
"	309
282	310
283	311
284	312
285	313
286	314
287	315
288	316
289	317
290	318
291	319
292	320
293	321
294	322
295	323
296	324
297	325
298	326
299	327
300	328
301	329
302	330
303	331
304	333
305	332
306	334
307	10020
308	335
309	336
310	339
"	343
311	10021
312	337
313	338

STRONG	G/K
314	340
315	341
316	342
317	10023
318	10024
319	344
320	10022
321	10025
322	345
323	346
324	10026
325	347
"	348
326	349
"	2028
327	350
328	351
"	356
329	353
"	354
330	355
331	357
332	358
333	359
334	360
335	361
336	364
337	365
"	388
338	363
339	362
340	366
341	367
342	368
343	369
344	370
345	371
346	372
347	373
348	374
349	375
"	377
"	379
350	376
351	378
352	380
"	381
"	382
"	383
"	442
"	443
"	444
"	444
353	384
354	385
355	387
356	390
"	391
"	472
357	389
358	392
"	1104
359	393
"	397
360	394
361	395
362	396
363	10027
364	386
365	387
366	398
367	399
"	568

STRONG	G/K
368	400
369	401
"	4406
370	402
371	403
372	404
373	405
374	406
375	407
376	408
"	409
377	899
378	410
379	412
380	413
"	854
381	408+2657
382	411
383	10029
384	417
385	418
386	419
387	420
388	923
389	421
390	422
391	423
392	424
393	425
394	426
395	427
396	428
397	429
398	430
399	10030
400	431
401	432
402	433
403	434
"	435
404	436
405	437
406	438
407	439
408	440
409	10031
410	445
"	446
411	447
412	10032
413	448
414	452
415	449
416	450
417	453
418	454
419	455
"	485
420	456
421	458
422	457
423	460
424	461
425	462
"	463
426	10033
427	464
428	187
"	459
"	465
429	10034
430	466
431	10035

STRONG	G/K
432	467
433	468
434	470
435	469
436	471
437	473
438	474
439	475
"	1139
440	533
441	476
"	477
442	478
443	479
444	480
445	481
446	482
447	483
448	484
"	517
449	485
450	486
451	487
452	488
"	489
453	490
"	491
454	492
"	493
455	494
456	495
457	496
458	497
459	10036
460	498
461	499
462	501
463	500
464	502
465	503
466	504
467	505
"	550
468	506
469	507
"	553
470	508
471	509
472	510
473	511
474	512
475	513
476	514
477	515
478	516
479	10037
480	518
481	519
"	520
482	521
483	522
484	523
485	524
486	525
487	526
488	527
"	528
489	529
490	530
491	531
492	532
493	534
494	535

STRONG	G/K
495	536
496	537
497	538
498	539
499	540
500	541
"	542
501	543
502	544
503	545
504	546
505	547
"	548
506	10038
507	549
"	2030
508	551
509	552
510	554
511	555
512	556
513	557
514	558
"	559
515	560
516	8845
517	562
518	561
519	563
520	564
"	567
521	10039
522	565
523	569
524	10040
525	570
526	571
527	572
528	572
529	573
"	574
530	575
531	576
532	577
533	579
534	580
535	581
"	582
536	583
537	584
538	585
539	586
"	587
540	10041
541	587
542	588
543	589
544	590
545	594
546	593
547	595
548	591
549	592
550	578
"	596
551	597
552	598
553	599
554	600
555	601
556	602
557	603
558	604
"	605
559	606
"	607
560	10042
561	609
"	610
"	611
562	608
563	10043
564	612
"	613
565	614
"	615
566	617
567	616
568	618
"	619
569	620
570	621
571	622
572	623
573	624
574	10028
575	625
576	10044
577	626
"	629
578	627
579	628
580	630
581	10045
582	632

STRONG	G/K
"	10046
583	633
584	634
585	635
586	10047
587	636
588	637
589	638
590	639
591	641
592	640
593	642
594	643
595	644
596	645
597	646
598	10048
599	647
600	10049
601	649
602	650
603	651
604	652
605	631
"	653
606	10050
607	10051
"	10052
608	10053
609	654
610	655
611	656
612	657
613	10054
614	658
615	659
616	660
617	661
618	662
619	663
620	10055
621	664
622	665
"	4417
623	666
624	667
625	668
626	669
627	670
628	671
629	10056
630	672
631	673
632	674
633	10057
634	675
635	676
636	10058
637	677
638	10059
639	678
"	690
640	679
641	681
642	682
643	683
644	684
"	685
645	686
646	680
647	688
648	689
649	691
650	692
"	693
651	695
652	694
653	696
654	697
655	698
656	699
657	700
"	701
658	702
"	1956
659	703
660	704
661	705
662	706
663	707
664	708
665	709
666	710
667	711
668	712
669	713
670	10060
671	10061
"	10062
672	714
"	715
"	716
"	717
673	718
674	10063

STRONG	G/K
675	719
676	720
677	10064
678	721
"	722
679	723
680	724
681	725
682	727
"	728
683	729
684	730
685	731
686	732
687	733
688	734
689	735
690	736
691	737
692	739
"	740
693	741
694	742
695	743
696	744
697	746
698	747
699	748
700	749
701	750
702	752
703	10065
704	753
705	754
706	752
707	755
708	756
709	758
"	759
710	760
711	10066
712	761
713	763
714	764
715	765
716	766
717	768
718	10067
719	770
720	769
721	773
722	771
"	772
723	774
"	795
724	776
725	777
726	145
727	778
728	779
"	819
729	775
730	780
731	781
732	782
733	783
734	784
735	10068
736	785
737	786
738	787
"	10069
739	738
740	790
"	791
741	789
742	767
743	792
744	793
745	794
746	796
"	10070
747	798
748	799
"	837
749	10071
750	800
"	803
751	804
752	801
753	802
754	10073
755	10072
756	10074
757	805
758	806
759	810
760	809
761	812
"	8246
762	811
763	808
"	5645
764	813
765	814

STRONG	G/K
766	815
767	816
768	817
769	818
770	820
771	821
772	10075
773	10076
774	822
775	823
776	824
777	825
778	10077
779	826
780	827
781	829
782	830
783	831
"	10078
784	836
785	10080
786	838
787	10079
788	839
789	840
790	841
791	842
792	843
793	845
794	844
795	846
796	847
797	848
798	849
799	850
800	836
801	852
802	851
803	853
"	859
804	855
805	856
"	857
806	858
807	860
808	861
809	862
810	863
811	864
812	865
"	866
813	867
814	868
815	869
816	870
817	871
818	872
819	873
820	875
821	874
822	876
823	877
824	878
825	879
826	10081
827	880
828	881
829	882
830	883
831	884
832	885
833	886
"	887
834	889
"	948
"	3876
"	4424
835	890
"	897
836	888
837	891
838	892
"	893
"	894
839	9309
840	832
841	833
842	895
843	896
"	898
844	835
845	834
846	10082
847	900
848	901
849	10083
850	902
851	903
"	904
852	10084
853	254
"	906
854	907
"	4425
855	908

STRONG	G/K
856	909
857	910
858	10085
859	905
"	911
"	914
"	917
"	920
860	912
861	10086
862	913
"	916
863	416
"	915
864	918
865	919
866	921
867	922
868	925
869	924
870	10087
"	10092
871	926
872	929
873	10090
874	930
875	931
876	932
877	934
878	938
879	935
880	939
881	940
882	941
883	936
"	4307
"	8022
884	933
"	937
"	8682
885	942
886	943
887	944
888	10091
889	945
890	947
891	946
892	949
893	950
894	951
895	10093
896	10094
897	952
898	953
899	954
"	955
900	956
901	957
902	958
903	960
904	961
"	962
905	963
"	964
"	4224
906	965
907	966
"	967
908	968
909	969
910	970
911	971
912	973
913	974
"	975
914	976
915	977
916	978
917	979
918	980
919	981
920	982
921	10095
922	983
923	985
924	10096
925	986
926	987
927	10218
"	10097
928	988
929	989
930	990
931	984
"	991
932	992
933	993
934	994
935	995
"	4215
936	996
937	997
938	998
939	999
940	1000

STRONG	G/K
941	1001
942	1002
943	1003
944	1005
"	1006
945	1004
946	1007
947	1008
948	1009
949	1010
950	1011
951	1012
952	1013
953	1014
"	1071
954	1017
"	1018
955	1019
956	10102
957	1020
958	1021
959	1022
"	5802
960	1022
961	1023
962	1024
963	1025
964	1026
965	1027
966	1028
967	1029
968	1030
969	1031
970	1033
"	1037
971	1032
"	1039
972	1040
973	1041
"	1042
974	1043
975	1044
976	1046
977	1034
"	1047
"	1048
978	1049
979	1035
980	1036
"	1038
981	1051
982	1052
"	1053
"	1054
983	1055
984	1056
985	1057
986	1059
987	1058
988	1060
989	10098
990	1061
991	1062
992	1063
993	1064
994	1065
995	1067
996	1068
"	1075
997	10099
998	1069
999	10100
1000	1070
1001	10101
1002	1072
1003	1073
1004	1074
"	1428
1005	10103
1006	1076
1007	1077
1008	1078
1009	745
"	1079
1010	1081
"	1110
1011	1082
"	1348
1012	1083
1013	1084
1014	1085
1015	1086
"	1814
1016	1087
1017	1088
"	2029
1018	726
"	1089
"	2032
1019	1090
1020	1093
"	2127
"	3811
1021	1094
"	2130

STRONG	G/K
1022	1095
"	2140
1023	1092
1024	1096
"	1112
"	2175
1025	1097
"	2195
1026	1098
"	2196
1027	1099
"	2234
1028	1100
1029	1101
"	2242
1030	1128
"	9090
1031	1102
1032	1103
"	2582
1033	1105
"	4122
1034	1106
1035	1107
1036	1108
"	4364
"	6765
1037	1109
1038	1111
1039	1113
1040	1114
1041	1115
1042	1116
"	6712
1043	1117
1044	1118
"	6820
1045	1119
1046	1120
1047	1121
1048	1122
"	7208
1049	1123
"	7449
1050	1124
1051	1125
1052	1126
"	8632
"	9093
1053	1127
1054	1130
1055	1131
1056	1133
1057	1132
1058	1134
1059	1135
1060	1147
1061	1137
1062	1148
1063	1136
1064	1138
1065	1140
1066	1141
1067	1142
1068	1143
1069	1144
1070	1145
1071	1146
1072	1149
1073	1136
1074	1150
1075	1152
1076	1151
1077	1153
"	1154
1078	1155
1079	10104
1080	10106
1081	1156
1082	1158
1083	1159
1084	1160
1085	1161
1086	1162
1087	1165
1088	1163
1089	1164
1090	1167
"	1168
1091	1166
1092	1169
1093	10107
1094	1170
1095	1171
1096	10108
1097	1172
"	4442
1098	1173
1099	1174
1100	1175
1101	1176
"	1177
1102	1178
1103	1179
1104	1180

STRONG	G/K
"	1181
"	1182
1105	1183
"	1184
1106	1185
"	1186
1107	1187
1108	1188
1109	1189
"	1190
1110	1191
"	4444
1111	1192
1112	1157
1113	10105
"	10109
1114	1193
1115	1194
1116	1195
1117	1196
1118	1197
1119	1198
1120	1199
"	1200
1121	1201
"	1217
"	4240
1122	1202
1123	10110
1124	10111
1125	1203
1126	1204
1127	1205
1128	1206
1129	1215
1130	1207
1131	1218
1132	1209
1133	1210
1134	1211
1135	1212
1136	1213
1137	1220
1138	1221
1139	1222
"	1400
1140	1224
1141	1225
"	1226
1142	1223
1143	1227
1144	1228
1145	1229
1146	1230
1147	10112
1148	1231
1149	10113
1150	1232
1151	1214
1152	1233
1153	1234
1154	1235
1155	1235
1156	10114
1157	1237
"	1238
1158	1239
"	1240
1159	10115
1160	1242
1161	1243
1162	1244
"	1245
1163	1246
1164	1247
1165	1248
1166	1241
"	1249
1167	1250
"	1251
1168	1252
1169	10116
1170	1253
1171	1254
1172	1266
1173	1267
1174	1255
1175	1268
"	6599
1176	1256
1177	1257
1178	1258
1179	1259
1180	1266
1181	1252+1195
1182	1269
1183	1270
1184	1270
1185	1271
1186	1260
1187	1261
1188	1262
1189	1263
1190	1264
1191	1272

STRONG	G/K
1192	1273
1193	1265
1194	1274
1195	1275
1196	1276
1197	1277
"	1278
"	1279
1198	1280
1199	1281
1200	1282
1201	1284
1202	1283
1203	1285
1204	1286
1205	1287
1206	1288
1207	1289
1208	1290
1209	1291
1210	1292
"	1293
1211	1294
1212	1295
1213	1296
"	1297
1214	1298
1215	1299
1216	1301
1217	1302
1218	1304
1219	1305
"	1306
"	1307
1220	1309
1221	1310
"	1311
1222	1309
1223	1312
1224	1313
"	7652
1225	1315
"	7394
1226	1314
"	1316
1227	1317
1228	1318
1229	1319
1230	1320
1231	1321
1232	1322
1233	1323
1234	1324
1235	1325
1236	10117
1237	1326
1238	1327
"	1328
1239	1329
1240	10118
1241	1330
1242	1331
"	1332
1243	1333
1244	1334
1245	1335
1246	1336
1247	10120
1248	1337
1249	1338
1250	1339
"	1340
1251	10119
1252	1341
1253	1342
1254	1343
"	1344
"	1345
1255	1347
1256	1349
1257	1350
1258	1351
1259	1352
1260	1354
"	1355
1261	1353
1262	1346
"	1356
"	1357
1263	1358
1264	1394
1265	1360
1266	1361
1267	1362
1268	1363
"	1408
1269	1364
"	1365
1270	1366
1271	1367
1272	1368
"	1369
"	1370
1273	1372
1274	1356
"	1357
1275	1373
1276	1379
1277	1374
1278	1375
1279	1376
1280	1378
1281	1371
1282	1377
1283	1380
1284	1381
1285	1382
1286	451
1287	1383
1288	1384
"	1385
1289	10121
"	10122
1290	1386
1291	10123
1292	1387
1293	1388
1294	1389
"	1390
1295	1391
1296	1392
"	1393
1297	10124
1298	1396
1299	1397
1300	1398
1301	1399
1302	1401
1303	1402
1304	1403
"	1404
1305	1359
"	1405
"	1406
1306	1407
1307	1409
1308	1410
1309	1415
1310	1418
1311	1419
1312	1420
1313	1411
1314	1411
1315	1412
1316	1421
"	1422
1317	1423
1318	1424
1319	1413
1320	1414
1321	10125
1322	1425
1323	1426
1324	1427
1325	10126
1326	1429
1327	1431
1328	1432
"	1433
1329	1434
1330	1435
1331	1436
1332	1437
1333	1438
1334	1439
1335	1440
1336	1441
1337	1442
1338	1443
1339	1444
1340	1445
1341	1447
1342	1448
1343	1450
1344	1449
1345	1451
1346	1452
1347	1454
1348	1455
1349	1456
1350	1453
"	1457
1351	1458
1352	1459
1353	1460
1354	1461
"	1462
1355	10128
1356	1463
"	1464
1357	1466
1358	10129
1359	1570
1360	1465
1361	1467
1362	1468
1363	1470
1364	1469
1365	1471
1366	1473
1367	1474
1368	1475
1369	1476
1370	10130
1371	1477
1372	1478
1373	1480
1374	1481
1375	1483
1376	1484
1377	1485
1378	1486
1379	1487
1380	1488
1381	1489
1382	1490
1383	1491
1384	1492
1385	1482
1386	1493
1387	1494
1388	1495
1389	1496
1390	1497
1391	1500
1392	1499
1393	1498
1394	1501
"	1502
1395	1503
1396	1504
1397	1505
1398	1506
1399	1504
1400	10131
1401	10132
1402	1507
1403	1508
1404	1509
1405	1510
1406	1511
1407	1512
1408	1513
1409	1513
1410	1514
1411	10133
1412	1516
1413	1517
"	1518
1414	10134
1415	1519
1416	1522
1417	1521
1418	1523
1419	1472
"	1524
"	2045
1420	1525
1421	1526
"	1528
1422	1527
1423	1531
1424	1533
1425	1532
1426	1534
1427	1535
1428	1536
1429	1537
1430	1538
"	1539
1431	1540
1432	1541
1433	1542
1434	1544
1435	1543
1436	1545
"	1546
1437	1547
1438	1548
1439	1549
1440	1550
1441	1551
1442	1552
1443	1553
1444	1555
1445	1554
1446	1529
"	1530
1447	1555
1448	1556
"	1560
1449	1557
1450	1558
1451	1559
1452	1561
1453	1562
1454	1563
1455	1564
1456	1565
1457	1566
1458	1567
1459	10135
1460	1568
"	1569
1461	1572
1462	1479
"	1571
1463	1573
1464	1574
1465	1576
1466	1576
1467	1575
"	10136
1468	1577
1469	1578
1470	1579
1471	1580
"	1582
1472	1581
1473	1583
1474	1584
1475	1585
1476	1586
1477	1587
1478	1588
1479	1589
1480	1590
1481	1591
"	1592
"	1593
1482	1594
1483	1595
1484	1596
1485	1597
1486	1598
1487	1599
"	1641
1488	1600
1489	1601
1490	10139
1491	1602
1492	1603
1493	1604
1494	1605
1495	1606
1496	1607
1497	1608
1498	1610
1499	1609
1500	1611
1501	1612
1502	1613
1503	1614
1504	1615
"	1616
1505	10140
1506	1617
1507	1618
1508	1619
1509	1620
1510	10141
1511	1621
"	1747
1512	1623
1513	1624
"	1625
1514	1626
1515	1627
1516	1628
1517	1630
1518	1622
"	1631
1519	10137
1520	1632
1521	1633
1522	1634
1523	1635
1524	1636
"	1637
1525	1638
1526	1639
1527	1640
1528	10142
1529	1642
1530	1643
"	1644
1531	1646
1532	1647
1533	1648
1534	1649
"	1650
1535	10143
1536	1651
1537	1652
"	2055
1538	1653
1539	1654
1540	1655
1541	10144
1542	1656
1543	1657
"	1684
1544	1658
1545	1659
1546	1661
1547	10145
1548	1662
1549	1663
1550	1664
1551	1665
1552	1666
1553	1667
1554	1668
1555	1669
1556	1670
"	1671
1557	1672
1558	1673
1559	959
"	1674
1560	10146
1561	1645
1562	1675
1563	1676
1564	1677
1565	1678
1566	1679
1567	1681
1568	1680
1569	1682
1570	1683
1571	1685
1572	1686
1573	1687
1574	1688
1575	1689
1576	1691
1577	1690
1578	1692
1579	1693
1580	1694
1581	1695
1582	1696
1583	1697
1584	1698
1585	10147
1586	1699
"	1700
1587	1701
"	1702
1588	1703
"	2056
1589	1704
1590	1705
1591	1706
1592	1707
1593	1708
1594	1708
1595	1709
"	1710
1596	10148
1597	1711
1598	1713
1599	1714
"	1715
1600	1716
1601	1717
1602	1718
1603	1720
1604	1719
1605	1721
1606	1722
1607	1723
1608	1724
1609	1725
1610	1726
"	1727
1611	10149
1612	1728
1613	1729
1614	1730
1615	1732
1616	1731
1617	1733
1618	1734
1619	1735
"	1736
1620	1737
1621	1738
1622	1739
1623	1740
1624	1741
1625	1742
1626	1743
1627	1744
1629	1746
1630	1748
1631	1749
1632	1754
1633	1750
"	1751
1634	1752
1635	10150
1636	1753
1637	1755
1638	1756
1639	1757
"	1758
1640	1759
1641	1760
1642	1761
1643	1762
1644	1763
"	1764
1645	1765
1646	1766
1647	1768
1648	1767
1649	1769
1650	1770
1651	1771
1652	1772
1653	1773
1654	1774
"	1776
1655	10151
1656	1775
1657	1777
1658	1778
1659	1779
1660	1780
1661	1781
1662	1783
1663	1785
1664	1786
1665	1787
1666	1788
1667	1784
1668	10154
1669	1790
1670	1791
1671	1792
1672	1793
1673	1795
"	1869
1674	1796
1675	1797
1676	1798
1677	1800
1678	10155
1679	1801
1680	1803
1681	1804
1682	1805
1683	1806
1684	10156
1685	10157
1686	1807
1687	1808
1688	1809
"	1810
"	4255
1689	1812
1690	1811
1691	1813
1692	1815
1693	10158
1694	1817
1695	1816
1696	1818
"	1819
"	1820
1697	1821
1698	1822
"	1823
1699	1824
1699'	1825
1700	1826
1701	10159
1702	1827
1703	1830
1704	1828
1705	1829
1706	1831
1707	1832
1708	1833
1709	1794
"	1834
1710	1836
1711	1835
1712	1837
1713	1838
"	1839
"	5609
1714	1840
1715	1841
1716	1842
1717	1843
1718	1844
1719	1847
"	1848
1720	1848
1721	1849
"	8102
"	8114
1722	10160
1723	10161
"	10162
1724	1850
1725	1851
1726	1852
1727	1853
1728	1854
1729	1855
1730	1856
1731	1857
1732	1858
1733	1860
1734	1846
"	1861
1735	1845
1736	1859
"	1863
1737	1862
1738	1864
1739	1865
1740	1866
1741	1867
1742	1868
1743	1870
1744	1871
1745	1872
1746	1873
"	1874
1747	1875
1748	1876
1749	1880
1750	1881
1751	1882
1752	1883
"	1884
1753	10163
1754	1885
"	3903
1755	1886
"	1887
1756	1799
"	1888
1757	10164
1758	1889
1759	10165
1760	1890
"	1891
1761	10166
1762	1892
1763	10167
1764	1893
1765	1894
1766	1895
1767	972
"	1896
"	3904
"	4514
1768	10168
1769	1897
1770	1899
1771	1900
1772	1901
1773	1902
1774	1903
1775	1904
1776	1905
1777	1878
"	1879
"	1906
1778	10169
1779	1907
"	8723
"	8726
1780	10170
1781	1908
1782	10171
1783	1909
1784	10172
1785	1911
1786	1912
1787	1914
1788	1913
1789	1915
1790	1916
1791	10173
1792	1917
1793	1918
"	1919
1794	1920
1795	1921
1796	1922
1797	10174
1798	10175
1799	10176
"	10177
1800	1924
1801	1925
1802	1926
"	1927
1803	1929
"	1930
1804	1931
1805	1932
1806	1933
"	1934
1807	1935
1808	1936
1809	1937
"	1938
1810	1939
1811	1940
"	1941
1812	1942
1813	1943
1814	1944
1815	10178
1816	1945
1817	1923
"	1928
"	1946
1818	1947
1819	1948
1820	1949
"	1950
1821	10179
1822	1951
1823	1952
1824	1953
"	1954
1825	1955
1826	1957
"	1958
"	1959
1827	1960
1828	1961
1829	1962
1830	1963
1831	1964
1832	1965
1833	1967
1834	1877
"	1966
"	2008
1835	1968
"	1969
1836	10180
1837	1972
1838	1973
1839	1974
1840	1971
"	1975
1841	10181
1842	1970
1843	1976
1844	1978
1845	1979
1846	1980
1847	1981
"	1982
"	1983
1848	1984
1849	1985
1850	1986
1851	1987
1852	1988
1853	1989
1854	1990
1855	10182
1856	1991
1857	1992
1858	1993
1859	10183
1860	1994
1861	1995
"	1996
1862	1997
1863	1998
1864	1999
1865	2001
"	2002
1866	2000
1867	2003
1868	10184
1869	2005
1870	2006
1871	2007
1872	10185
1873	2009
1874	2010
1875	2004
"	2011
1876	2012
1877	2013
1878	2014
1879	2015
1880	2016
1881	2017
1882	10186
1883	10187
1884	10188
1885	2018
1886	2019
1887	2026
1888	10194
"	10195
1889	2027
1890	2037
1891	2038
1892	2039
1893	2040
1894	2041
1895	2042
1896	2043
"	2051
1897	2047
1898	2048
1899	2049
1900	2050
1901	2052
1902	2053
1903	2054
1904	2057
1905	2058
1906	2059

STRONG	G/K
1907	10196
1908	2060
1909	2061
1910	2062
1911	2063
1912	2064
1913	2066
"	2067
1914	2068
1915	2070
1916	2071
1917	10197
1918	2072
1919	2073
1920	2074
1921	2065
"	2075
1922	10198
1923	10199
1924	2076
1925	2078
1926	2077
1927	2079
1928	2080
1929	2081
1930	2082
1931	2085
"	2115
1932	10200
"	10205
1933	2092
"	2093
1934	10201
1935	2086
1936	2087
1937	2088
1938	2089
1939	2069
"	2090
1940	2091
1941	2091
1942	2094
"	2095
1943	2096
1944	2097
1945	2098
1946	10202
1947	2099
1948	2100
1949	2101
1950	2102
1951	2103
1952	2104
1953	2106
1954	2107
1955	2108
1956	2110
1957	2111
1958	2113
1959	2116
1960	2117
1961	181
"	2118
1962	2119
1963	2120
1964	2121
1965	10206
1966	2122
1967	2123
1968	2124
1969	2125
1970	2128
"	2686
1971	2129
1972	2133
1973	2131
"	2134
1974	2136
1975	2137
"	4208
1976	2138
1977	2139
1978	2141
1979	2142
1980	2143
1981	10207
1982	2144
1983	10208
1984	2145
"	2146
"	2147
1985	2148
1986	2150
1987	2152
1988	2151
1989	2153
1990	2154
1991	2155
1992	2156
"	2160
"	2161
1993	2159
1994	10210
1995	2162
"	2171

STRONG	G/K
1996	2163
1997	2164
1998	2166
1999	2167
2000	2169
"	2170
2001	2172
2002	10211
"	10212
2003	2173
2004	2177
2005	2176
2006	10213
2007	2179
2008	2178
2009	2180
2010	2182
2011	1208
"	2183
2012	2184
2013	2187
"	2188
2014	2198
2015	2200
2016	2201
2017	2201
2018	2202
2019	2203
2020	2208
2021	2210
2022	2215
2023	2216
2024	2217
2025	2219
2026	2222
2027	2223
2028	2224
2029	2105
"	2225
2030	2226
"	2230
2031	10217
2032	2228
"	2231
2033	2229
2034	2232
2035	2233
2036	2235
2037	2227
2038	2236
2039	2237
2040	2238
2041	2239
2042	2215
2043	828
"	2034
"	2240
2044	2244
2045	2245
2046	2247
2047	2251
2048	2252
"	9438
2049	2253
2050	2109
"	2254
2051	2258
2052	2259
2053	2260
2054	2261
2055	2262
2056	2263
2057	2264
2058	2265
2059	2266
2060	2267
2061	2269
2062	2270
2063	2271
2064	2272
2065	2273
2066	2274
2067	2275
2068	2276
2069	2277
"	2278
2070	2279
2071	2280
2072	2281
2073	2291
"	2292
2074	2282
2075	2283
2076	2284
2077	2285
2078	2286
2079	2287
2080	2288
2081	2289
2082	2290
2083	2291
2084	10223
2085	2293
2086	2294
2087	2295

STRONG	G/K
2088	2296
2089	8445
2090	2297
2091	2298
2092	2299
2093	2300
2094	2301
"	2302
2095	10224
2096	2303
2097	2305
2098	2306
2099	2304
2100	2307
2101	2308
2102	2326
2103	10225
2104	2309
2105	2311
2106	2312
2107	2313
2108	2314
2109	2315
"	3469
2110	10226
2111	2316
"	2398
2112	10227
2113	2317
2114	2319
"	2320
2115	2318
2116	2318
2117	2321
2118	2310
"	2322
2119	2323
"	2324
2120	2325
2121	2327
2122	10228
2123	2328
"	2329
2124	2330
2125	2331
2126	2332
2127	2333
2128	2334
"	2335
2129	2336
2130	2337
2131	2338
"	2414
"	2415
2132	2339
2133	2340
2134	2341
2135	2342
2136	10229
2137	2343
2138	2344
"	2345
2139	2346
2140	2347
2141	2348
2142	2349
"	2350
"	4654
2143	2352
"	2354
2144	2353
2145	2351
2146	2355
2147	2356
2148	2357
"	2358
"	10230
2149	2359
2150	2360
2151	2361
"	2362
2152	2363
2153	2364
2154	2365
2155	2366
2156	2367
2157	2368
2158	2369
2159	2370
2160	2371
2161	2372
2162	2373
2163	2374
2164	10231
2165	2375
2166	10232
2167	2376
2168	2377
2169	2378
2170	10233
2171	10234
2172	2379
2173	2380
2174	2381
"	2382

STRONG	G/K
2175	2383
2176	2384
2177	2385
2178	10235
2179	2386
2180	2387
2181	2388
"	2389
"	2390
2182	2391
"	2392
2183	2393
2184	2394
2185	2390
2186	2395
"	2396
2187	2397
2188	2399
2189	2400
2190	2401
2191	2402
2192	10236
2193	2403
2194	2404
2195	2405
2196	2406
"	2407
2197	2408
2198	2409
2199	2410
2200	10237
2201	2411
2202	2412
2203	2413
2204	2416
2205	2418
2206	2417
2207	2419
2208	2421
2209	2420
2210	2422
2211	10238
2212	2423
2213	2425
2214	2424
"	2426
2215	2427
2216	2428
2217	10239
2218	2429
2219	2430
"	2431
"	4664
"	4668
2220	2432
2221	2433
2222	2434
"	2449
2223	2435
2224	2436
2225	2437
2226	2438
2227	2439
2228	2440
2229	2441
"	2442
2230	2443
2231	2444
2232	2445
2233	2446
2234	10240
2235	2447
"	2448
2236	2450
"	2451
2237	2452
"	2453
2238	2454
2239	2455
2240	2456
2241	2457
2242	2458
2243	2460
2244	2461
2245	2462
2246	2463
2247	2464
2248	10242
2249	2466
2250	2467
2251	2468
2252	2469
2253	2470
2254	2471
"	2472
"	2473
2255	10243
2256	2474
"	2475
"	2476
"	2477
"	2482
2257	10244
2258	2478
"	2481

STRONG	G/K
2259	2480
2260	2479
2261	2483
2262	2484
2263	2485
2264	2486
2265	2487
2266	2248
"	2488
"	2489
2267	2490
2268	2491
2269	10245
2270	2492
2271	2493
2272	2494
2273	10246
2274	2495
2275	2496
"	2497
"	6306
2276	2498
2277	2499
2278	2500
2279	2501
2280	2502
2281	2503
2282	2504
2283	2505
2284	2506
2285	2507
2286	2508
"	2509
2287	2510
2288	2511
2289	2513
2290	2512
"	2514
2291	2515
2292	2516
"	10247
2293	2517
2294	2518
2295	2519
2296	2520
2297	2522
2298	10248
2299	2521
2300	2523
"	2527
2301	2524
2302	2525
"	2526
2303	2529
2304	2530
2305	10250
2306	10249
2307	2531
2308	2532
"	2533
2309	2535
2310	2534
2311	2536
2312	2537
2313	2538
2314	2539
2315	2540
2316	2540
2317	2541
2318	2542
2319	2543
2320	2544
2321	2545
2322	2546
2323	10251
2324	10252
2325	2549
2326	2550
2327	2551
2328	2552
2329	2553
2330	2554
2331	2555
"	2556
2332	2558
2333	2557
2334	2596
2335	2559
2336	2560
2337	2561
2338	10253
2339	2562
2340	2563
2341	2564
2342	2565
"	2655
"	2656
2343	2566
2344	2567
"	2568
2345	2569
2346	2570
2347	2571
2348	2572
2349	2573

STRONG	G/K
2350	2574
2351	2575
2352	2987
2353	2580
2354	2581
2355	2583
2356	2986
2357	2578
2358	10254
2359	2585
2360	2584
2361	2586
"	2587
2362	2588
2363	2590
"	2591
2364	2592
2365	2593
2366	2594
"	3123
"	3131
2367	2595
2368	2597
2369	2598
2370	10255
2371	2599
"	2604
2372	2600
2373	2601
2374	2602
"	2603
2375	2605
2376	10256
2377	2606
2378	2608
2379	10257
2380	2607
2381	2609
2382	2610
2383	2611
2384	2612
2385	2613
2386	2614
2387	2615
2388	2616
2389	2617
2390	2618
2391	2619
2392	2620
2393	2621
2394	2622
2395	2623
2396	2624
"	2625
2397	2626
2398	2627
"	2630
"	3148
2399	2628
2400	2629
2401	2631
2402	10258
2403	2632
"	2633
2404	2634
2405	2635
2406	2636
2407	2637
2408	10259
2409	10260
2410	2638
2411	2639
2412	2640
2413	2641
2414	2642
2415	2643
2416	2644
"	2645
"	2646
"	2651
"	2652
"	2653
2417	10261
2418	10262
2419	2647
2420	2648
2421	2649
2422	2650
2423	10263
2424	2654
2425	2649
2426	2658
2427	2659
"	2660
2428	2657
"	2662
2429	10264
2430	2658
2431	2663
"	2691
2432	2661
"	2664
2433	2665
2434	2666
2435	2667

STRONG	G/K
2436	2576
"	2668
2437	2669
2438	2670
"	2671
2439	2590
2440	2673
2441	2674
2442	2675
2443	2676
2444	2677
2445	10265
2446	2678
2447	2679
2448	2680
2449	2681
2450	2682
2451	2683
2452	10266
2453	2685
2454	2684
2455	2687
2456	2688
2457	2689
2458	2690
2459	2693
2460	2694
2461	2692
2462	2695
2463	2696
2464	2697
2465	2698
2466	2699
2467	2700
2468	2701
2469	2702
2470	2703
"	2704
2471	2705
2472	2706
2473	2708
2474	2707
"	2709
2475	2710
2476	2711
2477	2712
2478	2713
2479	2714
2480	2715
2481	2717
2482	2718
2483	2716
2484	2719
2485	2720
2486	2721
2487	2722
2488	2723
2489	2724
"	3875
2490	2725
"	2726
"	2727
2491	2728
"	2729
2492	2730
"	2731
2493	10267
2494	2732
2495	2733
2496	2734
2497	2735
2498	2736
"	2737
2499	10268
2500	2739
2501	2738
2502	2740
"	2741
2503	2742
2504	2743
2505	2744
"	2745
"	2746
2506	2749
"	2750
2507	2751
2508	10269
2509	2747
2510	2748
2511	2747
2512	2752
2513	2753
"	2754
2514	2756
2515	2755
2516	2757
2517	2758
2518	2759
"	2760
2519	2761
2520	2762
2521	2211
"	2763
2522	2764
"	2765

STRONG	G/K
2523	2766
2524	2767
2525	2768
2526	2769
2527	2770
2528	10270
2529	2772
2530	2773
"	2776
2531	2774
2532	2775
2533	2777
2534	2771
"	2778
"	2779
2535	2780
2536	2781
2537	2782
"	2795
2538	2783
2539	2784
2540	2785
2541	2787
2542	2788
2543	2789
"	2790
2544	2791
2545	2792
2546	2793
2547	2794
2548	2796
2549	2797
2550	2798
"	2800
2551	2799
2552	2801
2553	2802
2554	2803
"	2804
2555	2805
2556	2786
"	2806
"	2807
"	2808
2557	2809
"	4721
2558	2810
2559	2811
2560	2812
"	2813
"	2814
2561	2815
2562	10271
2563	2816
"	2817
"	2818
2564	2819
2565	2798
2566	2820
2567	2821
2568	2822
2569	2823
2570	2824
2571	2821
2572	2825
"	2826
2573	2827
2574	2828
"	4217
2575	2829
"	2830
2576	2831
2577	2833
2578	2832
2579	2828+8041
2580	2834
2581	2835
2582	2836
2583	2837
2584	2839
2585	2840
"	2841
2586	2842
2587	2843
2588	2844
2589	2838
2590	2845
"	2846
"	2847
2591	10272
2592	2848
2593	2849
2594	2850
2595	2851
2596	2852
2597	10273
2598	2853
2599	2854
2600	2855
2601	2856
2602	2857
2603	2858
"	2859
2604	10274
2605	2860

STRONG	G/K
2606	2861
2607	2862
2608	2863
"	2864
"	10275
2609	2865
2610	2866
2611	2867
"	2868
2612	2869
2613	2870
2614	2871
2615	2872
2616	2873
"	2874
2617	2875
"	2876
2618	2877
2619	2878
2620	2879
2621	2880
"	2881
2622	2882
2623	2883
2624	2884
2625	2885
2626	2886
2627	10276
2628	2887
2629	2888
2630	2889
2631	10277
2632	10278
2633	2890
2634	2891
2635	10279
2636	2892
2637	2893
2638	2894
2639	2895
2640	2896
2641	2897
2642	2898
2643	2899
2644	2901
2645	2902
2646	2903
2647	2904
2648	2905
2649	2906
2650	2907
2651	2908
2652	2909
2653	2910
2654	2911
"	2912
2655	2913
2656	2914
2657	2915
2658	2916
2659	2917
2660	2918
"	2919
2661	7249
2662	2920
2663	2921
2664	2924
2665	2925
2666	2926
2667	2927
2668	2928
2669	2929
"	2931
2670	2930
2671	2932
2672	2933
"	2934
"	2935
2673	2936
2674	2937
"	2938
2675	2548
"	2939
2676	2940
2677	2942
"	2944
2678	2943
2679	4971
2680	4971
2681	2948
2682	2945
"	2946
"	2947
2683	2949
2684	2950
2685	10280
2686	2951
"	2952
2687	2953
2688	2954
2689	2956
2690	2955
"	2957
2691	2958
"	2973

STRONG	G/K
2692	2960
2693	1520
"	2961
2694	2250
"	2959
"	2962
2695	2968
"	2974
2696	2969
"	2970
2697	2971
2698	2972
2699	2958
2700	2975
2701	2963
2702	2964
"	6065
2703	2965
"	6541
2704	2966
2705	2967
2706	2976
2707	2977
2708	2978
2709	2979
2710	2980
2711	2981
2712	2577
"	2982
2713	2983
2714	2984
2715	2985
2716	2989
2717	2990
"	2991
2718	10281
2719	2995
2720	2992
2721	2996
"	2997
2722	2998
2723	2999
2724	3000
2725	3001
2726	3002
"	3003
2727	3004
2728	3005
2729	3006
2730	3007
2731	3010
2732	3011
2733	3009
"	3012
2734	3013
2735	1515
"	2044
"	2988
2736	3015
"	3029
2737	3016
2738	3017
2739	3018
2740	3019
2741	3020
"	3042
2742	3021
"	3022
"	3023
"	3025
"	3026
2743	3027
2744	3028
2745	3030
2746	3031
2747	3032
2748	3033
2749	10282
2750	3034
2751	3035
2752	3036
2753	3037
2754	3038
2755	3039
2756	3040
2757	3043
"	3044
2758	3045
2759	3046
2760	3047
2761	10283
2762	3048
2763	3049
"	3050
2764	3051
"	3052
2765	3054
2766	3053
2767	3055
2768	3056
2769	3057
2770	3058
2771	3059
"	3060
2772	3061

STRONG	G/K
2773	2589
2774	3062
2775	3063
"	3064
"	3066
2776	3065
2777	3067
"	3068
2778	3069
"	3070
"	3071
"	3072
2779	3074
2780	3073
2781	3075
2782	3024
"	3076
"	3077
2783	10284
2784	3078
2785	3079
2786	3080
2787	2579
"	3014
"	3081
"	3082
2788	3083
2789	3084
2790	3086
"	3087
2791	3089
2792	3090
2793	3091
"	3092
2794	3086
2795	3094
2796	3088
"	3093
2797	3095
2798	1629
"	3096
2799	3098
2800+1471	2046
2800+1471	3099
2801	3100
2802	3101
2803	3108
"	3110
2804	10285
2805	3109
2806	3111
2807	3112
2808	3113
2809	3114
2810	3115
2811	3116
"	3117
2812	3118
2813	3119
2814	3120
2815	3121
2816	10286
2817	3102
2818	10287
"	10288
2819	10289
2820	3104
2821	3124
"	3127
2822	3125
2823	3126
2824	3128
2825	3128
2826	3129
2827	10290
2828	3130
2829	3132
2830	3133
2831	3134
2832	3135
2833	3136
2834	3103
"	3106
"	3107
2835	3105
2836	3137
"	3138
2837	3139
2838	3122
2839	3140
2840	3141
2841	3142
2842	3143
2843	3144
2844	3145
"	3146
2845	3147
2846	3149
2847	3150
2848	3151
2849	3152
2850	3153
2851	3154
2852	3155
2853	3156

STRONG	G/K
2854	3157
2855	3158
2856	3159
2857	10291
2858	3160
2859	3161
"	3162
"	3165
2860	3163
2861	3164
2862	3166
2863	3167
2864	3168
2865	3169
2866	3170
2867	3171
2868	10293
2869	10294
2870	3174
"	3175
2871	3178
2872	3179
2873	3180
2874	3181
"	3183
2875	3182
2876	3184
2877	10295
2878	3186
2879	3185
2880	3187
2881	3188
2882	3189
2883	3190
2884	3191
2885	3192
2886	3193
2887	3194
2888	3195
2889	3196
2890	3196
2891	3197
2892	3198
"	3199
"	4756
2893	3200
2894	3173
2895	3512
2896	3176
"	3177
"	3201
"	3202
"	3205
"	3208
2897	3203
"	3204
2898	3206
2899	3207
2900	3209
"	3210
2901	3211
"	3684
2902	3212
"	3220
2903	3213
2904	3214
2905	3215
2906	10296
2907	3216
2908	10297
2909	3217
2910	3219
2911	3218
2912	3221
"	3223
2913	3222
2914	3224
2915	3225
2916	3226
2917	10298
2918	3227
2919	3228
2920	10299
2921	3229
2922	3231
2923	3230
2924	3231
2925	3232
2926	3233
2927	10300
2928	3234
"	3235
2929	3236
2930	3237
"	3239
2931	3238
2932	3240
2933	3241
"	3242
2934	3243
2935	3244
2936	3245
2937	3246
2938	3247
2939	10301

STRONG	G/K
2940	3248
2941	10301
2942	10302
2943	3250
2944	3249
2945	3251
"	3252
2946	3253
"	3254
2947	3255
"	3257
"	3258
2948	3256
2949	3259
2950	3260
2951	3261
2952	3262
2953	10303
2954	3263
2955	3264
2956	3265
2957	10304
2958	3266
2959	3267
2960	3268
2961	3269
2962	3270
2963	3271
2964	3272
2965	3273
2966	3274
2967	10305
2968	3277
2969	3278
2970	3279
"	3280
2971	3281
2972	3285
2973	3282
2974	3283
2975	3284
2976	3286
2977	3287
"	3288
2978	415
"	3289
2979	3290
2980	3291
2981	3292
2982	3293
2983	3294
2984	3295
2985	3296
2986	3297
2987	10308
2988	3298
2989	3299
2990	3301
2991	3300
2992	3302
2993	3303
2994	3304
2995	3305
2996	3306
2997	3307
2998	3308
2999	3309
3000	3310
3001	3312
3002	3313
3003	3314
"	3315
"	3316
3004	3317
3005	3311
3006	3318
3007	10309
3008	3319
3009	3320
3010	3321
3011	3322
3012	3323
3013	3324
"	5652
3014	3325
3015	3326
3016	3328
3017	3327
3018	3330
3019	3329
3020	3332
3021	3333
3022	3334
3023	3335
3024	3331
3025	3336
3026	3337
"	8447
"	10310
"	10679
3027	3338
3028	10311
3029	10312
3030	3339
3031	3340

STRONG	G/K
3032	3341
3033	3342
3034	3343
"	3344
3035	3345
"	3346
"	3350
3036	3347
3037	3348
3038	3349
"	3353
"	3357
3039	3351
3040	3352
3041	3354
3042	3355
3043	3356
3044	3358
3045	1977
"	3359
3046	10313
3047	3360
3048	3361
3049	3362
3050	3363
3051	2035
"	3364
3052	10314
3053	3365
3054	3366
3055	3372
3056	3367
3057	3368
3058	3369
3059	3370
3060	3371
3061	10315
3062	10316
3063	3373
3064	3374
3065	3375
3066	3376
3067	3376
"	3377
3068	3378
3069	3378
3070	3378+8011
3071	3378+5812
3072	3378+7404
3073	3378+8934
3074	3378+9004
3075	3379
3076	3380
3077	3381
3078	3382
3079	3383
"	3451
3080	3384
3081	3385
3082	3386
3083	3387
3084	3388
3085	3389
3086	3390
"	3391
3087	3392
3088	3393
"	3454
3089	3394
3090	3395
3091	3397
3092	3398
"	3399
3093	3400
3094	3401
3095	3402
3096	3403
"	3404
3097	3405
3098	3406
3099	3407
3100	3408
3101	3409
3102	3410
3103	3411
"	3412
3104	3413
3105	3414
3106	3415
3107	3416
3108	3417
3109	3418
3110	3419
3111	3421
3112	3422
3113	3423
3114	3424
3115	3425
3116	3426
3117	3427
"	3428
3118	10317
3119	3429
3120	3430
3121	3431

STRONG	G/K
3122	3432
3123	3433
3124	3434
3125	3436
3126	3437
3127	3438
3128	3439
3129	3440
3130	3441
3131	3442
3132	3443
3133	3444
3134	3445
3135	3447
3136	3449
"	10318
3137	3451
3138	3453
3139	3454
3140	3455
3141	3456
3142	3457
3143	3458
3144	3459
3145	3460
3146	3461
3147	3462
3148	3463
3149	3464
"	3465
3150	3466
3151	3467
3152	3468
3153	3470
"	3471
3154	3472
3155	3473
3156	3474
3157	3475
"	3476
3158	3477
3159	3477
3160	2465
"	3478
3161	3479
3162	3480
"	3481
3163	3482
3164	3484
3165	3485
3166	3487
3167	3488
3168	3489
3169	3490
"	3491
3170	3492
3171	3486
"	3493
3172	3494
3173	3495
3174	3496
3175	3497
3176	3498
3177	3499
3178	3500
3179	3501
3180	3502
3181	3503
3182	3504
3183	3505
3184	3506
3185	3507
3186	3508
3187	3509
3188	2249
"	3510
3189	3511
3190	3512
3191	10320
3192	3513
3193	3514
3194	3420
3195	3515
3196	3516
3197	3517
3198	3519
3199	3520
"	3521
3200	3522
3201	3523
3202	10321
3203	3524
"	3525
3204	3518
"	3526
"	3527
3205	3528
"	4256
3206	3529
3207	3530
3208	3531
3209	3533
3210	3534
3211	3535
3212	2143

STRONG	G/K
3213	3536
3214	3537
3215	3538
3216	4363
3217	3539
3218	3540
3219	3541
3220	3542
3221	10322
3222	3553
3223	3543
3224	3544
3225	3545
3226	3546
3227	3549
3228	3547
3229	3550
"	3551
3230	3552
3231	3554
3232	3555
3233	3548
"	3556
3234	3557
3235	3558
3236	3559
3237	3560
3238	3435
"	3561
3239	3562
"	3563
3240	4965
3241	3564
"	3565
3242	3566
3243	3567
"	4787
"	5682
3244	3568
3245	3569
"	3570
3246	3571
3247	3572
3248	3573
3249	6073
3250	3574
3251	3575
3252	3576
3253	3577
3254	3578
"	6231
3255	10323
3256	3579
"	3580
"	3581
3257	3582
3258	3583
"	3584
3259	3585
3260	3587
"	3588
3261	3589
3262	3590
3263	3591
3264	3623
3265	3592
"	3600
3266	3593
3267	3594
3268	3595
3269	3596
3270	3597
3271	3598
3272	10324
"	10325
3273	3599
3274	3601
3275	3602
3276	3603
3277	3604
3278	3605
3279	3606
"	3608
3280	3607
3281	3609
3282	3610
3283	3612
"	6720
3284	3613
3285	3614
3286	3615
3287	3617
3288	3616
"	3618
3289	3446
"	3619
"	6805
3290	3620
3291	3621
3292	3622
3293	3623
"	3624
"	3625
3294	3586
"	3628

STRONG	G/K
3295	3626
"	3627
3296	762
"	3629
3297	3630
3298	3631
3299	3632
"	3633
3300	3634
3301	3635
3302	3636
3303	3637
3304	3638
"	3645
3305	3639
3306	3640
3307	3641
3308	3642
3309	3643
"	3644
3310	3646
3311	3647
3312	3648
3313	3649
3314	3650
3315	3651
3316	3652
"	3653
3317	3654
3318	3448
"	3655
"	7361
3319	10707
3320	3656
"	7388
3321	10326
3322	3657
3323	3658
3324	3659
3325	3660
3326	3661
"	3662
"	3666
3327	3663
3328	3664
3329	3665
3330	10327
3331	3667
3332	3668
3333	3669
3334	7674
3335	3450
"	3670
3336	3671
3337	3672
3338	3674
3339	3673
3340	3672
3341	3675
3342	3676
3343	3677
3344	3678
"	3683
3345	10328
3346	10329
3347	3680
3348	3681
3349	3682
3350	3679
3351	3685
3352	3686
3353	3687
3354	3688
3355	3690
3356	3691
3357	3692
3358	10330
3359	3693
3360	3694
3361	3695
3362	3696
3363	3697
3364	3699
3365	3700
3366	3702
3367	10331
3368	3698
"	3701
"	3703
"	7941
3369	3704
3370	3705
3371	3706
3372	3707
"	3708
3373	3710
3374	3711
3375	3712
3376	3713
3377	3714
3378	3715
3379	3716
3380	3717
3381	3718
3382	3719
3383	3720
3384	3452
"	3709
"	3721
"	3722
"	3723
3385	3725
3386	3726
3387	3728
3388	3729
"	3730
3389	3731
3390	10332
3391	3732
3392	3733
3393	10333
3394	3734
3395	3736
3396	3737
3397	3738
3398	3739
3399	3740
"	8184
3400	3741
3401	3742
3402	3743
3403	3744
3404	3745
"	3746
3405	3735
"	3747
3406	3748
"	3755
"	3756
3407	3749
3408	3750
3409	3751
3410	10334
3411	3752
3412	3754
3413	3757
3414	3758
"	3759
3415	3760
3416	3761
3417	3762
3418	3764
3419	3763
3420	3766
3421	3767
3422	3768
3423	3769
3424	3771
3425	3772
3426	3780
3427	3782
"	3794
3428	3784
3429	3783
3430	3785
"	3787
3431	3786
3432	3795
3433	3788
3434	3790
3435	3791
3436	3792
3437	3793
"	3806
3438	3796
3439	3797
3440	3798
3441	3799
3442	3800
"	3801
3443	10336
3444	3802
3445	3803
3446	3773
3447	3804
3448	414
"	3805
3449	3807
"	3808
3450	3774
3451	3809
"	3812
3452	3810
3453	3813
3454	3814
3455	3775
3456	3815
3457	3816
3458	3817
3459	3818
3460	3819
"	3820
3461	3821
3462	3822
"	3823
3463	3825
3464	3826
3465	3824
3466	3827
3467	3828
"	3830
"	4635
3468	3829
3469	3831
3470	3832
"	3833
3471	3835
3472	3834
3473	3836
3474	3837
"	9223
3475	3840
3476	3841
3477	3838
"	3839
3478	3776
3479	10335
3480	3777
3481	3778
3482	3778
3483	3842
3484	3843
3485	3779
3486	3844
3487	10337
3488	10338
3489	3845
3490	3846
3491	3847
3492	3848
3493	10339
3494	3849
3495	3850
3496	3853
3497	3854
3498	3855
3499	3856
"	3857
3500	3858
3501	3859
3502	3860
3503	3861
3504	3862
3505	3863
3506	3864
3507	3865
3508	3866
3509	3867
3510	3872
3511	3873
3512	3874
3513	3877
3514	3880
3515	3878
3516	3879
3517	3881
3518	3882
3519	3883
3520	3884
"	3885
3521	3886
3522	3887
3523	3889
3524	3888
3525	3890
3526	3891
3527	3892
3528	3893
3529	3894
3530	3896
3531	3895
3532	3897
3533	3899
3534	3900
3535	3898
3536	3901
3537	3902
3538	10343
3539	3905
3540	3906
3541	3907
3542	10345
3543	3908
"	3909
3544	3910
3545	3911
3546	10346
3547	3912
3548	3913
3549	10347
3550	3914
3551	10348
3552	3915
3553	3916
3554	3917
3555	3918
3556	3919
3557	3920
3558	3921
3559	3922
"	5787
"	5788
3560	3923
3561	3924
3562	3925
3563	3926
"	3927
3564	3929
3565	3930
3566	3931
3567	10350
3568	3932
"	3933
3569	3934
3570	3935
3571	3934
3572	3936
3573	3937
"	8403
3574	3938
3575	3939
"	3940
3576	3941
3577	3942
3578	3943
3579	3944
3580	3945
3581	3946
"	3947
3582	3948
3583	3949
3584	3950
3585	3951
3586	3952
3587	3953
3588	3954
3589	3957
3590	3958
3591	3959
3592	3961
3593	3960
3594	3962
3595	3963
3596	3964
3597	3965
3598	3966
3599	3967
3600	3968
3601	3969
3602	3970
3603	3971
3604	10352
3605	3972
3606	10353
3607	3973
"	3974
"	3984
3608	3975
3609	3976
3610	3977
3611	3978
3612	3979
"	3981
3613	3980
3614	3982
3615	3983
3616	3985
3617	3986
3618	3987
3619	3990
3620	3991
3621	3992
3622	3988
"	3993
3623	3994
3624	3995
3625	3996
3626	3997
3627	3998
3628	3989
"	3999
3629	4000
3630	4002
3631	4001
3632	4003
3633	4004
3634	4005
3635	10354
3636	4006
3637	4007
3638	4008
3639	4009
3640	4010
3641	4011
"	4012
3642	4014
3643	4016
"	4018
3644	4017
3645	4019
"	4020
3646	4021
3647	4022
3648	4023
3649	4024
3650	4025
3651	4026
"	4027
"	4028
"	4338
3652	10357
3653	4029
"	4030
3654	4031
"	4038
3655	4033
3656	4034
3657	4035
3658	4036
3659	4037
3660	10358
3661	
3662	4039
3663	4040
"	4041
"	4042
3664	4043
3665	4044
3666	4045
3667	4046
"	4047
3668	4049
3669	4048
"	4050
"	4051
3670	4052
3671	4053
3672	4054
"	4055
3673	10359
3674	4056
3675	10360
3676	4058
3677	4057
"	4060
3678	4058
"	4061
3679	10361
3680	4059
3681	4062
3682	4064
3683	4065
3684	4067
3685	4068
3686	4069
3687	4070
3688	4071
3689	4072
"	4073
3690	4074
3691	4075
3692	4077
3693	4076
3694	4063
3695	4078
3696	4079
3697	4080
3698	4081
3699	4082
3700	4083
3701	4084
3702	10362
3703	4085
3704	4086
3705	10363
3706	10364
"	10365
"	10563
3707	4087
3708	4088
"	4089
3709	4090
3710	4091
3711	4092
3712	4093
3713	4094
"	4095
3714	4096
3715	4097
"	4099
3716	4098
3717	4100
3718	4101
3719	4102
3720	4103
3721	4104
3722	4105
"	4106
3723	4107
3724	4108
"	4109
"	4110
"	4111
3725	4113
3726	2194
"	4112
"	6671
3727	4114
3728	4115
3729	10366
3730	4117
3731	4116
3732	4118
3733	4119
"	4120
"	4121
3734	4123
"	10367
3735	10369
3736	4124
3737	10368
3738	3928
"	4125
"	4127
"	4128
3739	4126
3740	4130
3741	4129
3742	4131
3743	4132
3744	10370
3745	10371
3746	4133
3747	4134
3748	4135
3749	4136
3750	4137
3751	4138
3752	4139
3753	4140
3754	4142
"	4148
3755	4141
"	4144
3756	4145
3757	4146
3758	4147
3759	4149
"	4152
3760	4150
"	4151
3761	4153
3762	4153
3763	4154
3764	10372
3765	4155
3766	4156
3767	4157
3768	4158
3769	4159
3770	4160
3771	4161
3772	4162
3773	4164
3774	4165
3775	4166
3776	4167
3777	4168
3778	4169
3779	10373
3780	4170
3781	4172
3782	4173
3783	4174
3784	4175
3785	4176
3786	4177
3787	4178
3788	4179
3789	4180
3790	10374
3791	4181
3792	10375
3793	4182
3794	4183
3795	4184
3796	4185
3797	10376
3798	4186
3799	4187
3800	4188
3801	4189
3802	4190
3803	4192
"	4193
"	4194
3804	4195
3805	4196
3806	4197
3807	4198
3808	2132
"	4202
"	4257
3809	10379
"	10384
3810	4203
"	4274
3811	4206
3812	4207
3813	4209
3814	4319
3815	4210
3816	4211
3817	4212
3818	4204
"	6652
3819	4205
"	8170
3820	4213
3821	10380
3822	4219
3823	4220
"	4221
3824	4222
3825	10381
3826	4226
3827	4225
3828	4227
"	4247
3829	4228
3830	4229
"	4230
3831	10382
3832	4231
3833	4216
"	4218
"	4232
"	4233
"	4234
3834	4223
3835	4235
"	4236
3836	4237
3837	4238
"	4239
3838	4241
"	4245
3839	4242
3840	4246
3841	4243
3842	4244
3843	4246
3844	4248
3845	4249
3846	4250
3847	4252
3848	10383
3849	4253
3850	4254
3851	4258
3852	4259
3853	4260
3854	4261
3855	4262
3856	3532
"	4263
"	4264
"	4271
3857	4265
"	4266
3858	4267
"	4268
3859	4269
3860	2176
3861	10385
"	10386
3862	4272
3863	4273
3864	4275
3865	4276
3866	4276
3867	4277
"	4278
3868	4279
3869	4280
3870	4281
3871	4283
3872	4284
"	4304
3873	2135
"	4285
3874	4286
3875	4287
3876	4288
3877	4289
3878	4290
"	4291
3879	10387
3880	4292
3881	4291
3882	4293
3883	4294
3884	4295
3885	4296
"	4328
"	4349
3886	4362
3887	4329
"	4370
"	4885
3888	4297
3889	4298
3890	10388
3891	4299
3892	4300
3893	4301
3894	4302
"	4303
3895	4305
3896	4306
3897	4308
3898	4309
"	4310
3899	4312
3900	10389
3901	4311
3902	4313
3903	4314
3904	10390
3905	4315
3906	4316
3907	4317
3908	4318
3909	4319
3910	4320
3911	4321
3912	4322
3913	4323
3914	4324
3915	4325
"	4326
3916	10391
3917	4327
3918	4330
3919	4298
"	4331
"	4332
"	4333
3920	4334
3921	4335
3922	4336
3923	4337
3924	4339
3925	4340
3926	4344
3927	4345
3928	4341
3929	4347
3930	4350
3931	4351
3932	4352
3933	4353
3934	4354
3935	4355
3936	4356
3937	4357
3938	4358
3939	4360
3940	4365
3941	4366
3942	7156
3943	4369
3944	4371
3945	4372
3946	4373
3947	3689
"	4374
"	7774
3948	4375
3949	4376
3950	4377
3951	4378
3952	4379
3953	4380
3954	4381
3955	4382
3956	4383
3957	4384
3958	4385
3959	4386
3960	4387
3961	10392
3962	4388
3963	4390
3964	10394
3965	4393
3966	4394
3967	4395
"	4405
3968	4396
3969	10395
3970	4397
3971	4398
"	4583
3972	4399
3973	4400
3974	4401
3975	4402
3976	4404
3977	10396
3978	4407
3979	4408
3980	4409
3981	4410
3982	4411
3983	10397
3984	10398
3985	4412
3986	4413
3987	4414
3988	4415
"	4416
"	5806
3989	4418
3990	4419
3991	4420
3992	4421
3993	4422
3994	4423
3995	4426

STRONG	G/K
3996	4427
3997	4427
3998	4428
3999	4429
4000	4430
4001	4431
4002	4432
4003	4433
4004	4435
4005	4436
4006	4437
4007	4438
4008	4439
4009	4440
4010	4443
4011	4445
4012	4446
4013	4448
"	4450
4014	4449
4015	4451
4016	4434
4017	4452
4018	4453
4019	4455
4020	4456
4021	4457
4022	4458
4023	4459
"	4461
4024	4460
"	4465
4025	4462
4026	4463
4027	4466
"	4464+446
4028	4467
4029	4468
4030	4469
"	4458
4031	4470
4032	4471
4033	4472
"	4473
4034	4475
4035	4476
4036	4474
"	4992
4037	4477
4038	4478
4039	4479
4040	10399
4041	4480
4042	4481
4043	4482
"	4483
"	4484
4044	4485
4045	4486
4046	4487
4047	4488
4048	4489
4049	10400
4050	4490
4051	4491
4052	4492
4053	4493
4054	4494
"	4495
4055	4496
4056	10401
4057	4497
"	4498
4058	4499
4059	4499
4060	4500
"	4501
"	4515
4061	10402
"	10429
4062	4502
"	5290
4063	4503
4064	4504
4065	4505
4066	4506
4067	1517
"	4528
4068	4507
4069	4508
4070	10403
4071	4509
4072	4510
4073	4511
4074	4512
4075	4513
4076	10404
4077	10404
4078	4537+1896
4079	4506
4080	4518
4081	4516
4082	4519
4083	10406
4084	4520
4085	4521
4086	4522
4087	4523
4088	4524
4089	4525
"	4526
4090	4506
4091	4527
4092	4520
4093	4529
4094	4532
4095	4533
4096	4534
4097	4535
4098	4536
4099	2158
4100	4342
"	4537
"	4768
"	8975
4101	10408
4102	4538
4103	4539
4104	4540
4105	4541
4106	4542
4107	4543
4108	4544
4109	4544
4110	4545
4111	4546
4112	4547
4113	4549
4114	4550
4115	4551
4116	4554
4117	4555
"	4556
4118	4557
4119	4558
4120	4559
4121	4560
4122	4561
4123	4562
4124	4565
"	4566
4125	4567
4126	4569
4127	4570
4128	4571
4129	4530
4130	4531
4131	4572
4132	4573
4133	4574
4134	4575
4135	4576
"	4577
4136	4346
"	4568
"	4578
4137	4579
4138	4580
4139	4581
4140	4582
4141	6015
4142	6015
4143	4586
4144	4587
4145	4588
4146	4589
4147	4591
"	4593
4148	4592
4149	4594
"	5035
4150	4595
4151	4596
4152	4597
4153	4598
4154	5048
4155	4599
4156	4600
4157	4601
4158	4602
"	4789
4139	4603
4160	5160
4161	4604
4162	4605
4163	4606
4164	4607
4165	4608
4166	4609
4167	4610
4168	4611
4169	4612
4170	4613
4171	4614
"	4615
4172	4616
"	4624
4173	4617
4174	4618
4175	4619
"	4620
"	4621
4176	4622
4177	4623
4178	5307
4179	5317
4180	4625
"	4626
4181	4627
4182	4628
4183	4629
4184	4630
4185	4631
4186	4632
4187	4633
4188	4634
4189	5436
4190	4636
4191	4637
4192	4637
4193	10409
4194	4638
4195	4639
4196	4640
4197	4641
4198	4642
4199	4645
4200	4646
4201	4647
4202	4648
4203	10410
4204	4650
4205	4649
4206	4651
"	4652
"	4653
4207	4656
"	4657
"	4658
4208	4655
4209	4659
4210	4660
4211	4661
4212	4662
4213	4663
4214	4665
4215	4668
4216	4666
4217	4667
4218	4669
4219	4670
4220	4671
4221	4672
4222	4673
4223	10411
4224	4675
"	4676
4225	4678
4226	4677
4227	4679
4228	4680
4229	4674
"	4681
"	4682
"	4683
4230	4684
4231	4685
4232	4686
"	4696
4233	4687
4234	4688
4235	4689
4236	4690
4237	4691
4238	4692
4239	4693
4240	4694
4241	4695
4242	4697
4243	4698
4244	4702
4245	4700
"	4701
4246	4703
4247	4704
4248	4705
4249	4706
4250	4707
4251	4708
4252	4709
4253	4710
4254	4711
4255	10412
4256	4713
4257	4714
4258	4715
4259	4716
4260	4717
4261	4718
4262	4719
4263	4720
4264	4722
4265	4723
4266	4724
4267	4725
4268	4726
4269	4727
4270	4728
4271	4729
4272	4730
4273	4731
4274	4732
4275	4733
4276	4734
4277	4735
4278	4736
4279	4737
4280	4738
4281	4739
4282	4739
4283	4740
4284	4742
4285	4743
4286	4741
4287	4744
4288	4745
4289	4746
4290	4747
4291	10413
4292	4748
4293	4749
4294	4751
4295	4752
4296	4753
4297	4754
4298	4755
4299	4757
4300	4758
4301	4759
4302	4760
4303	4761
4304	4762
4305	4763
4306	4764
4307	4766
4308	4765
4309	4767
4310	4769
4311	4772
4312	4773
4313	2126
"	3765
"	4770
4314	4771
4315	4774
4316	4775
4317	4776
4318	4777
4319	4778
4320	4779
4321	4781
4322	4780
4323	4782
4324	4783
4325	4784
4326	4785
4327	4786
4328	4588
4329	4590
"	4788
4330	4790
4331	4791
4332	4792
4333	10414
4334	4793
4335	4794
4336	10415
4337	4796
4338	4795
4339	4797
4340	4798
4341	4799
4342	3892
4343	4800
4344	4801
4345	4803
4346	4802
4347	4804
4348	4805
4349	4806
4350	1807
4351	4808
4352	4809
4353	4810
4354	4811
4355	4812
4356	4813
4357	4816
4358	4814
4359	4817
4360	4815
4361	4818
4362	4819
4363	4820
"	4825
4364	4821
4365	4822
"	4823
"	4824
4366	4826
4367	4827
4368	4828
4369	4807
4370	4829
4371	4830
4372	4832
4373	4831
4374	4833
4375	4834
4376	4835
4377	4836
4378	4837
4379	4838
4380	4839
4381	4840
4382	4841
4383	4842
4384	4843
4385	4844
4386	4845
4387	4846
4388	4847
4389	4847
4390	4848
"	4862
4391	10416
4392	4849
4393	4850
4394	4854
4395	4852
4396	4853
4397	4855
4398	10417
4399	4856
4400	4857
4401	4858
4402	4859
4403	4860
4404	4861
"	4905
4405	4863
4406	10418
4407	4851
"	4864
4408	4865
4409	4866
"	4868
"	4883
4410	4867
4411	4869
4412	4870
4413	4871
4414	4872
"	4873
4415	10419
4416	10420
4417	4875
4418	4874
4419	4876
4420	4877
4421	4878
4422	4880
"	4881
4423	4879
4424	4882
4425	4884
4426	4886
4427	4887
"	4888
4428	4889
"	4890
4429	4889
4430	10421
4431	10422
4432	4891
4433	10423
4434	4892
4435	4894
4436	4893
4437	10424
4438	4895
4439	4896
4440	4897
4441	4898
"	4899
4442	4900
4443	4901
4444	4902
4445	4903
"	4904
4446	4906
4447	2168
"	4907
4448	4910
"	4911
4449	10425
4450	4912
4451	4913
4452	4914
4453	4915
4454	4916
4455	4917
"	4918
4456	4919
4457	4920
4458	4921
4459	4922
4460	4923
4461	4924
4462	4584
"	4925
4463	4926
4464	4927
4465	4928
4466	4929
4467	4930
4468	4931
4469	4932
4470	4933
4471	4934
"	4935
4472	4936
4473	4937
4474	4938
4475	4939
4476	4940
4477	4941
4478	4942
"	4943
4479	10426
4480	4946
"	4974
4481	10427
4482	4944
"	4945
4483	10431
4484	10428
4485	4947
4486	10430
4487	4948
4488	4949
4489	4951
4490	4950
4491	4952
4492	4953
4493	4954
4494	4955
4495	4956
4496	4957
"	4967
4497	4959
4498	4960
4499	4961
4500	4962
4501	4963
4502	4964
4503	4966
4504	10432
4505	4968
4506	4969
"	4970
4507	4972
4508	4973
4509	4975
4510	10433
4511	4976
"	4977
4512	4978
4513	4979
4514	4980
4515	4981
4516	4982
4517	4983
4518	4984
4519	4985
4520	4986
4521	4987
4522	4989
4523	4988
4524	4990
"	4991
4525	4993
"	4994
4526	4995
4527	4996
4528	4997
4529	4998
4530	5002
4531	4999
"	5000
4532	5001
4533	5003
4534	5004
4535	5005
4536	5006
4537	5007
4538	5008
4539	5009
4540	5010
4541	5011
"	5012
"	5013
4542	5014
4543	5016
4544	5017
4545	5018
4546	5019
4547	5020
4548	5021
4549	5022
4550	5023
4551	5024
"	5025
4552	5026
4553	5027
4554	5028
4555	5029
4556	5030
4557	5031
4558	5032
4559	5033
4560	5034
4561	5036
4562	5037
4563	5039
4564	5040
4565	5041
4566	5042
4567	10434
4568	5043
4569	5044
"	5045
4570	5046
"	5047
4571	5048
4572	5049
4573	5050
4574	5052
4575	5051
4576	5053
4577	10435
4578	5055
4579	5054
4580	5056
4581	5057
"	5058
4582	5059
4583	5060
"	5061
"	5079
4584	5062
"	5063
4585	5104
4586	5064
4587	5065
4588	5066
4589	5067
4590	5068
"	5069
4591	5070
4592	5071
4593	6487
4594	5073
4595	5074
4596	5075
4597	5076
4598	5077
4599	5078
4600	5080
4601	5081
"	5082
"	5083
4602	5084
4603	5085
4604	5086
4605	5087
"	5093
4606	10436
4607	5089
4608	5090
4609	5091
"	5092
4610	5090+6832
4611	5094
"	5095
4612	5096
4613	5097
4614	5098
4615	5099
4616	4348
"	5100
4617	5101
"	5102
4618	5103
"	5105
4619	5106
4620	5107
4621	5108
4622	5109
4623	5110
4624	5111
4625	5112
4626	5113
4627	5114
4628	5115
4629	5116
4630	5120
4631	5117
4632	5118
"	6869
4633	5119
4634	5120
4635	5121
4636	5122
4637	5124
4638	5125
4639	5126
4640	5127
4641	5128
"	5129
4642	5131
4643	5130
4644	5132
4645	5133
4646	5134
4647	5135
4648	5136
4649	5137
4650	5138
4651	5139
4652	5140
4653	5141
4654	5142
"	5143
4655	5144
4656	5145
4657	5146
4658	5147
4659	5148
"	5149
4660	5150
4661	5151
4662	5152
4663	5152
4664	5153
4665	5154
4666	5155
4667	5156
4668	5158
4669	5157
4670	5159
4671	5161
4672	5162
4673	5163
4674	5164
4675	5165
"	5166
4676	5167
4677	5168
4678	5169
"	5170
4679	5171
4680	5172
4681	5173
4682	5174
4683	5175
4684	5177
4685	5178
"	5179
"	5182
"	5183
4686	5180
"	5181
"	5192
4687	5184
4688	5185
"	5198
4689	5186
4690	5187
4691	5188
4692	5189
"	5190
4693	5191
4694	5193
"	5211
4695	5194
4696	5195
4697	5196
4698	5197
4699	5185
4700	5199
4701	5200
4702	5201
4703	5202
4704	7582
4705	5203
4706	5204
4707	5205
4708	5206
4709	5207
4710	5208
4711	5209
4712	5210
4713	5212
4714	5213
4715	5214
4716	5215
4717	5216
4718	5216
"	5217
4719	5218
4720	5219
4721	5220
4722	5221
4723	5223
"	5224
"	7745
"	7750
4724	5225
4725	5226

STRONG	G/K
4726	5227
4727	5228
4728	5229
4729	5230
4730	5233
4731	5234
4732	5235
4733	5236
4734	5237
4735	5238
4736	5239
4737	5240
4738	5241
4739	5242
4740	5243
4741	5244
4742	7910
4743	5245
4744	5246
4745	5247
4746	5248
4747	5249
4748	5250
4749	5251
4750	5252
4751	5253
"	5287
4752	5254
4753	5255
4754	5256
"	5257
4755	5259
4756	10437
4757	5282
4758	5260
4759	5261
"	5262
4760	5263
4761	5265
4762	5358
"	5359
4763	5265
"	8039
4764	5266
4765	5267
4766	5269
4767	5268
4768	5270
4769	5271
4770	5272
4771	5273
4772	5274
4773	5275
4774	5276
4775	5277
4776	10438
4777	5278
4778	5279
4779	10439
4780	5280
4781	5281
4782	5283
4783	5284
4784	5286
4785	5288
4786	5289
4787	5285
4788	5291
4789	5292
4790	5293
4791	5294
4792	5295
4793	5296
4794	5297
4795	5299
4796	5300
4797	5301
4798	5301
4799	5302
4800	5303
4801	5305
4802	5306
4803	5307
4804	10440
4805	5308
4806	5258
"	5309
4807	5311
"	5314
4808	5312
4809	5313
4810	5311
4811	5316
4812	5318
4813	5319
4814	5320
4815	5321
4816	5322
4817	5323
4818	5324
4819	5326
4820	5327
4821	5328
4822	5329
4823	5330
4824	5331
4825	5332
4826	5333
4827	5334
4828	5335
4829	5337
4830	5338
4831	5339
4832	5340
"	5341
"	5342
4833	5343
4834	5344
4835	5298
4836	5345
4837	5346
4838	5347
4839	5348
4840	5349
4841	5350
4842	5351
4843	5352
4844	5353
4845	5354
4846	5355
4847	5356
4848	5357
4849	5360
4850	5361
4851	5390
4852	5392
4853	5362
"	5363
4854	5364
4855	5391
4856	5365
4857	5393
4858	5366
4859	5394
4860	5396
4861	5398
4862	5399
4863	5400
4864	5367
"	5368
4865	5401
4866	5402
4867	5403
4868	5404
4869	5369
"	5370
4870’	5405
4871	5406
4872	5407
4873	10441
4874	5408
4875	5409
4876	5397
"	5410
4877	5411
4878	5412
4879	5413
4880	5414
"	5415
4881	5372
"	5379
4882	5416
4883	5373
4884	5374
4885	5375
"	5376
4886	5417
4887	10442
4888	5418
"	5419
"	5420
"	5421
4889	5422
4890	5377
4891	5423
4892	5424
4893	5425
"	5426
4894	5427
4895	5378
4896	5428
4897	5429
4898	5430
4899	5431
4900	5432
4901	5433
4902	5434
4903	10444
4904	5435
4905	5380
4906	5381
4907	10445
4908	5438
4909	5382
4910	5440
4911	5439
"	5441
4912	5442
4913	5443
4914	5446
4915	5444
"	5445
4916	5447
"	5448
4917	5449
4918	5450
4919	5451
4920	5452
"	5453
4921	5454
4922	5455
4923	5457
4924	5458
"	5460
"	9044
4925	5459
4926	5461
4927	5462
4928	5463
4929	5464
"	5465
4930	5383
4931	5466
4932	5467
4933	5468
4934	5469
4935	5470
4936	5471
4937	5472
"	5473
4938	5474
"	5475
4939	5384
4940	5476
4941	5477
4942	5478
4943	5479
4944	5480
4945	5482
"	5483
4946	5484
4947	5485
4948	5486
4949	5487
4950	5488
4951	5385
4952	5489
4953	10446
4954	5490
4955	5386
4956	5387
4957	5388
4958	5389
4959	5491
4960	5492
4961	10447
4962	5493
"	5494
4963	5495
4964	5496
4965	566
"	2031
"	5497
4966	5498
4967	5499
4968	5500
4969	5501
4970	5503
4971	5504
4972	5505
4973	5506
4974	5507
4975	5516
4976	5508
4977	5509
4978	10448
4979	5510
4980	5511
4981	5512
4982	5513
4983	5514
"	5515
4984	5951
4985	5517
4986	5518
4987	5519
4988	5517
4989	5520
4990	5521
4991	5522
4992	5523
4993	5524
"	5525
4994	5528
4995	5529
4996	5530
4997	5532
4998	5533
4999	5661
5000	5534
5001	5535
5002	5536
5003	5537
5004	5539
5005	5538
5006	5540
5007	5541
"	5542
5008	5543
5009	5544
5010	5545
5011	5546
5012	5547
5013	10451
5014	5548
"	5554
5015	5549
"	5550
"	5551
5016	5553
5017	10452
5018	5555
5019	5556
"	5557
5020	10453
5021	5558
5022	5559
5023	10454
5024	5560
5025	5561
"	5562
5026	5563
5027	5564
5028	5565
5029	10455
5030	5566
5031	5567
5032	5568
5033	5569
5034	5570
"	5571
5035	5574
"	5575
5036	5572
5037	5573
5038	5577
5039	5576
5040	5578
5041	5579
5042	5580
5043	10456
5044	5581
5045	5582
5046	5583
5047	10457
5048	5584
5049	10458
5050	5585
5051	5586
5052	5587
5053	10459
5054	5588
5055	5590
5056	5591
5057	5592
5058	5593
5059	5594
5060	5595
5061	5596
5062	5597
5063	5598
5064	5599
"	5600
5065	5601
5066	5602
5067	5603
5068	5605
5069	10461
"	10219
5070	5606
5071	5607
5072	5608
5073	10462
5074	5610
5075	10463
5076	5611
5077	5604
"	5612
5078	5613
5079	5614
5080	5615
"	5616
5081	5618
5082	5619
5083	5621
5084	5620
5085	10464
5086	5622
5087	5623
5088	5624
5089	5625
5090	5627
"	5628
5091	5629
"	5630
5092	5631
5093	5632
5094	10466
"	10467
"	10465
5095	5633
5096	5634
"	5636
5097	5635
5098	5637
5099	5638
5100	5639
5101	5640
5102	5641
"	5642
5103	10468
5104	5643
5105	5644
5106	5648
5107	5649
5108	5650
"	5762
5109	5651
"	5763
5110	5653
5111	10469
5112	5617
"	5654
5113	5655
5114	5656
5115	5657
"	5658
5116	5659
"	5660
5117	5663
"	5664
"	5698
5118	5665
5119	5666
5120	5667
5121	5662
"	5668
"	5766
5122	10470
5123	5670
5124	5671
5125	5672
"	5768
5126	5673
5127	5674
5128	5675
5129	5676
5130	2185
"	5677
"	5678
5131	5679
5132	5680
5133	5681
"	5901
"	5902
5134	3567
5135	10471
5136	5683
5137	5684
"	5685
5138	5686
5139	5687
5140	5688
"	5689
5141	5690
5142	10472
5143	5691
5144	5692
"	5693
5145	5694
5146	5695
5147	5696
5148	5697
5149	5700
5150	5719
5151	5699
5152	5701
5153	5702
5154	5703
5155	5704
5156	5705
5157	5706
5158	5707
"	5708
"	5711
5159	5709
5160	5712
5161	5713
5162	5714
5163	5715
5164	5716
5165	5717
5166	5718
5167	5720
5168	5721
5169	5722
5170	5724
"	5725
5171	5726
5172	5727
5173	5728
5174	10473
5175	5729
5176	5731
5177	5732
5178	5733
"	5734
5179	5735
5180	5736
5181	5737
5182	10474
5183	5738
"	5739
5184	5740
5185	5741
5186	5742
5187	5744
5188	5755
5189	5746
5190	5747
5191	10475
5192	5748
5193	5749
5194	5750
5195	5745
5196	5751
5197	5752
5198	5753
"	5754
5199	5756
5200	5743
5201	5757
"	5758
5202	10476
5203	5759
5204	5760
5205	5764
5206	5765
5207	5767
5208	10478
5209	5769
5210	5770
5211	5771
5212	5772
5213	5773
5214	5774
5215	5776
5216	5775
"	5944
5217	5777
5218	5778
"	5779
5219	5780
5220	5781
5221	5782
5222	5784
5223	5783
5224	5786
"	5785
5225	5789
5226	5790
5227	5790
5228	5791
5229	5791
5230	5792
5231	5793
5232	10479
5233	5794
5234	5795
"	5796
5235	5798
5236	5797
5237	5799
5238	5800
5239	5801
5240	1022
5241	5803
5242	5804
5243	4908
"	4909
5244	5805
5245	10480
5246	5807
5247	5809
5248	5808
5249	5810
5250	5811
5251	5812
5252	5813
5253	8450
5254	5814
5255	5815
5256	10481
5257	5816
"	5817
5258	5818
"	5820
5259	5819
5260	10482
5261	10483
5262	5821
"	5822
5263	5823
5264	5824
5265	5825
5266	5826
5267	10513
5268	5827
5269	5828
5270	5829
5271	5830
"	5831
5272	5832
5273	5833
"	5834
5274	5835
"	5836
5275	5837
5276	5838
5277	5839
5278	5840
5279	5841
"	5842
5280	5844
5281	5843
5282	5846
5283	5845
5284	5847
5285	5848
5286	5849
5287	5850
"	5851
5288	5853
5289	5852
5290	5854
5291	5855
5292	5856
"	5857
5293	5858
5294	5859
5295	5860
5296	5861
5297	5862
5298	5863
5299	5864
"	5865
5300	5866
"	5867
"	5875
5301	5870
5302	5871
5303	5872
5304	5873
5305	5874
5306	5876
5307	5877
5308	10484
5309	5878
5310	5879
"	5880
5311	5881
5312	10485
5313	10486
5314	5882
5315	5883
5316	5868
"	5884
5317	5885
5318	5886
5319	5887
5320	5888
5321	5889
5322	5890
"	5891
5323	5892
5324	2205
"	5893
"	5894
"	5895
5325	5896
5326	10487
5327	5897
"	5898
5328	5900
5329	5904
5330	10488
5331	5905
5332	5906
5333	5907
5334	5908
5335	5909
5336	5910
5337	5911
5338	10489
5339	5912
5340	5913
5341	5903
"	5915
"	5917
5342	5916
5343	10490
5344	5918
"	5919
5345	5920
5346	2186
"	5921
5347	5922
5348	5923
5349	5924
5350	5926
5351	5925
5352	5927
5353	5928
5354	7752
5355	5929
"	5930
5356	5931
"	7734
5357	5932
5358	5933
5359	5934
5360	5935
5361	5936
5362	5937
"	5938
5363	5939
5364	5940
5365	5941
5366	5942
5367	5943
5368	10491
5369	5945
5370	5946
5371	5947
5372	8087
5373	5948
5374	5949
"	5950
5375	5951
5376	10492
5377	5958
5378	5957
"	5961
5379	5951
5380	5959
5381	5371
"	5952
5382	5960
5383	5957
5384	5962
5385	5953
5386	5963
5387	5954
"	5955
5388	5964
5389	10493
5390	5965
5391	5966
"	5967
5392	5968
5393	5969
5394	5970
5395	5971
5396	10494
5397	5972
5398	5973
5399	5974
5400	5956
5401	5975
"	5976
5402	5977
"	5978
5403	10495
5404	5979
5405	5980
5406	5981
5407	10496
5408	5983
5409	5984
5410	5985
"	5986
5411	5982
"	5987
5412	10497
5413	5988
5414	3851
"	3852
"	5989
5415	10498
5416	5990
5417	5991
5418	5992
"	5993
5419	5994
5420	5995
5421	5996
5422	5997
5423	5998
5424	5999
5425	6000
"	6001
"	6002
5426	10499
5427	6003
5428	6004
5429	6006
5430	6007
5431	6008
5432	6009
5433	6010
"	6012
5434	6013
5435	6011
5436	6014
5437	6015
5438	6016
5439	4585
"	6017
5440	6018
5441	6020

STRONG	G/K
5442	6019
5443	10501
"	10676
5444	6021
5445	6022
5446	10502
5447	6023
5448	6024
5449	6025
5450	6026
5451	6027
5452	10503
5453	6028
5454	6029
"	6030
5455	6031
5456	6032
5457	10504
5458	6033
5459	6035
5460	10505
5461	6036
5462	6034
"	6037
"	6038
5463	10506
5464	6039
5465	6040
5466	6041
5467	6042
5468	6043
5469	6044
5470	6045
5471	6046
5472	6047
5473	6048
5474	6050
5475	6051
5476	6052
5477	6053
5478	6054
5479	6055
5480	6057
5481	10507
5482	6059
5483	6061
"	6062
"	6101
5484	6063
5485	6064
5486	6066
5487	10508
5488	6068
5489	6069
5490	6067
5491	10509
5492	6070
"	6071
5493	6073
"	6233
"	8462
5494	6074
"	6076
5495	6075
5496	6077
5497	6078
5498	6079
5499	6080
5500	6081
5501	6082
5502	2900
"	6085
5503	6086
5504	6087
5505	6086
5506	6088
5507	6089
5508	6090
5509	6049
"	6092
"	6213
5510	6094
5511	6095
5512	6096
"	6097
5513	6098
5514	6099
5515	6060
"	6100
5516	6102
5517	6103
"	6104
5518	6105
"	6106
5519	6107
5520	6108
5521	6109
5522	6110
5523	6111
5524	6112
5525	6113
5526	6056
"	6058
"	6114
"	6115
"	6116
"	8503
5527	6117
5528	6118
5529	6120
5530	6119
5531	6121
"	8508
5532	6122
"	6125
5533	5015
"	6123
"	6124
5534	6126
"	6127
5535	6129
5536	6130
5537	6131
5538	6133
5539	6134
5540	6135
5541	6136
"	6137
5542	6138
5543	6132
"	6139
"	6140
"	6144
5544	6141
5545	6142
5546	6143
5547	6145
5548	6146
5549	6147
"	6148
5550	6149
5551	6150
5552	6151
5553	6152
5554	6153
5555	2165
"	4712
"	6154
5556	6155
5557	6156
5558	6157
5559	10513
5560	6159
5561	6160
5562	5552
"	6161
"	6162
5563	6163
5564	6164
5565	6165
5566	6166
5567	6168
5568	6169
5569	6170
5570	2189
"	2190
"	6171
5571	6172
5572	6174
5573	6175
5574	6176
5575	6177
5576	6178
5577	6180
5578	6179
5579	6181
5580	6182
5581	6183
5582	6184
5583	10514
5584	6185
5585	6186
"	6187
5586	6188
5587	6191
"	8546
5588	6189
5589	6190
5590	6192
5591	6193
"	6194
5592	6195
"	6196
"	6197
5593	6198
5594	6199
5595	6200
5596	6202
"	6203
"	8558
5597	6204
5598	6205
5599	6206
"	6207
5600	6208
5601	6209
5602	6210
5603	6201
"	6211
5604	6212
5605	6214
5606	6215
"	6216
5607	6217
"	8565
5608	6218
"	6221
5609	10515
5610	6222
5611	6223
5612	6219
"	6220
"	6225
5613	10516
5614	6224
5615	6228
5616	6227
5617	6226
5618	2191
"	6072
"	6230
5619	6232
5620	6234
5621	6235
5622	10517
5623	6236
5624	6237
5625	6238
5626	6241
5627	6239
"	6240
5628	6242
"	6243
"	6244
5629	6245
5630	6246
5631	6247
5632	10518
5633	6248
"	6249
5634	6250
5635	6251
5636	6252
5637	6253
5638	6255
"	6257
5639	6256
5640	6258
"	8608
5641	6259
5642	10519
"	10520
5643	6260
"	6261
5644	6262
5645	6265
"	6266
"	6267
5646	6264
5647	6268
5648	10522
5649	10523
5650	6269
5651	6270
5652	6271
5653	6272
5654	6273
5655	6274
5656	6275
5657	6276
5658	6277
"	6278
5659	6285
5660	6279
5661	6280
5662	6281
"	6282
5663	6283
5664	5589
"	6284
5665	10524
5666	6286
5667	6287
5668	6288
5669	6289
5670	6292
"	6293
5671	6294
5672	6295
5673	10525
5674	6296
"	6297
5675	10526
5676	6298
5677	6299
5678	6301
5679	6302
5680	6303
5681	6304
5682	6305
5683	2496
5684	6307
5685	6308
5686	6309
5687	6290
5688	6291
"	6310
5689	6311
5690	6313
5691	6312
5692	6314
5693	6315
5694	6316
5695	6319
5696	6318
5697	6320
5698	6321
5699	6317
"	6322
5700	6323
"	6324
5701	6327
5702	6328
5703	6329
5704	6330
5705	10527
5706	6331
5707	6332
5708	6340
5709	10528
5710	6334
"	6335
5711	6336
5712	6337
5713	6338
5714	6333
"	6341
"	6342
"	6345
"	10529
5715	6343
5716	6344
5717	6346
5718	6347
"	6348
5719	6349
5720	6350
5721	6351
5722	6352
5723	6353
5724	6354
5725	6355
5726	6356
5727	6357
5728	6362
"	6364
5729	6361
5730	6358
"	6366
5731	6359
"	6360
5732	10530
5733	6363
5734	6365
"	6367
5735	6368
"	6900
5736	6369
5737	6370
"	6371
"	6372
5738	6376
5739	6373
5740	6374
"	6375
5741	6377
5742	6378
5743	6380
5744	6381
5745	6382
5746	6383
5747	6384
5748	6385
5749	6386
"	6387
5750	6388
5751	10531
5752	6389
5753	6390
"	6391
5754	6392
5755	6379
"	6393
"	6394
5756	6395
5757	6398
5758	10532
5759	6396
5760	6397
5761	6398
"	6399
5762	6400
"	6511
5763	6402
5764	6403
5765	6401
5766	6404
"	6406
"	6593
"	6637
5767	6405
5768	6407
"	6408
5769	6409
5770	6523
5771	6411
5772	6703
5773	6413
5774	6414
"	6415
"	6545
"	6758
"	9507
5775	6416
5776	10533
5777	6769
5778	6417
"	6550
5779	6418
5780	6419
"	6420
5781	6421
5782	6424
"	6749
5783	6423
5784	10534
5785	6425
5786	6422
5787	6426
5788	6427
"	6428
5789	6429
5790	6431
5791	6430
5792	6432
5793	6433
5794	6434
"	6435
5795	6436
5796	10535
5797	6437
5798	6438
"	6446
5799	6439
5800	6440
"	6441
5801	6442
5802	6443
5803	6444
5804	6445
5805	6447
5806	6448
5807	6449
5808	6450
5809	6473
5810	6451
5811	6452
5812	6453
5813	6454
5814	6455
5815	6456
5816	6457
5817	6458
5818	6459
"	6460
5819	6461
5820	6462
"	6463
5821	6464
5822	6465
5823	6466
5824	10536
5825	6467
5826	6468
5827	6470
5828	6469
5829	6470
"	6472
5830	6474
5831	10537
5832	6475
5833	6476
5834	6477
5835	6478
5836	6479
5837	6480
5838	6481
"	6482
5839	10538
5840	6483
5841	6484
5842	6485
5843	10539
5844	6486
"	6487
5845	6489
5846	6490
5847	6491
5848	6488
"	6493
"	6494
5849	6496
"	6497
5850	6498
5851	6499
5852	6500
5853	6501
5854	6502
5855	6503
"	8794
5856	6505
5857	6504
"	6509
"	6569
5858	6506
"	6507
"	6508
5859	6510
5860	6512
"	6513
5861	6514
5862	6515
5863	2192
"	6300
"	6516
5864	6517
5865	6518
5866	6519
5867	6520
"	6521
5868	6522
5869	6412
"	6524
5870	10540
5871	6526
5872	6527
5872 to 5887	6525
5873	1712
"	6528
5874	6529
5875	2213
"	6530
5876	6532
5877	6533
5878	3008
"	6534
5879	6542
"	6543
5880	6535
5881	6544
5882	6325
"	6536
5883	6537
"	8080
5884	6538
5885	6539
5886	5624+9478
5887	6540
5888	6545
5889	6546
5890	6547
5891	6548
"	6549
5892	6551
"	6552
5893	6553
5894	10541
5895	6554
"	6555
5896	6562
5897	6563
5898	6558
5899	6559
5900	6564
5901	6565
5902	6566
5903	6567
5904	5730
"	6560
5905	6561
5906	6568
5907	6570
5908	6571
5909	6572
5910	6573
5911	6574
5912	6575
5913	6576
5914	6577
5915	6578
5916	6579
5917	6580
5918	6581
5919	6582
5920	6583
5921	6584
5922	10542
5923	6585
5924	10543
5925	6587
5926	6589
5927	6158
"	6590
5928	10545
5929	6591
5930	6592
5931	10544
5932	6594
5933	6595
"	6607
5934	6596
5935	6597
"	6615
5936	6598
5937	6600
5938	6601
5939	6602
5940	6605
5941	6603
5942	6604
"	6606
5943	10546
5944	6608
5945	6609
"	6610
5946	10548
5947	6611
5948	6612
5949	6613
5950	6614
5951	6617
5952	10547
5953	6618
"	6619
"	6620
"	6621
5954	10549
5955	6622
5956	6623
5957	10550
5958	6624
5959	6625
5960	6626
5961	6628
5962	10551
5963	6627
5964	6630
"	6631
5965	6632
5966	6633
5967	10552
5968	6634
5969	6635
5970	6636
5971	6638
"	6639
5972	10553
5973	6640
5974	10554
5975	6641
5976	5048
5977	6642
5978	6643
5979	6644
5980	6645
5981	6646
5982	6647
5983	6648
5984	6649
5985	6649
5986	6650
5987	6651
5988	6653
5989	6654
5990	6655
5991	6656
5992	6657
5993	5816+6639
5994	10555
5995	6658
5996	6659
5997	6660
5998	6661
5999	6662
6000	6663
6001	6664
"	6665
6002	6667
6003	6668
6004	6669
"	6670
6005	6672
6006	6673
6007	6674
6008	6675
6009	6676
6010	6677
6011	6679
6012	6680
6013	6678
6014	6682
"	6683
6015	10556
6016	6684
"	6685
6017	6686
6018	6687
6019	6688
6020	6689
6021	6690
6022	6691
6023	6692
6024	6693
6025	6694
6026	6695
6027	6696
6028	6697
6029	6698
6030	4361
"	6410
"	6699
"	6702
6031	6700
"	6701
6032	10558
6033	10559
6034	6704
6035	6705
"	6718
6036	6707
6037	6709
6038	6708
6039	6713
6040	6715
6041	6714
6042	6706
"	6716
6043	6717
6044	6719
6045	6721
6046	6722
6047	6723
6048	6724
6049	6725
"	6726
6050	10560
6051	6727
6052	6728
6053	6729
6054	6730
6055	6731
"	6732
6056	10561
6057	6733
6058	6734
6059	6735
6060	6736
6061	6710
6062	6737
6063	6738
"	6739
6064	6711
"	6740
6065	10562
6066	6741
6067	6742
6068	6743
"	6744
6069	6745
6070	6746
6071	6747
6072	6748
6073	6751
6074	10564
6075	6752
"	6753
6076	6754
6077	6755
6078	6756
6079	6757
6080	6759
6081	6761
6082	6762
6083	6760
6084	6763
"	6764
6085	6766
"	6767
"	6768
6086	6770
6087	6771
"	6772
6088	10565
6089	6775
"	6776
6090	6777
"	6778
6091	6773
6092	6774
6093	6779
6094	6780
6095	6781
6096	6782
6097	6785
6098	6783
"	6784
6099	6786
6100	6787
6101	6788
6102	6789
6103	6790
"	6792
6104	6791
6105	6793
"	6794
6106	6795
"	6799
6107	6796
6108	6797
"	6798

STRONG	G/K
6109	6800
6110	6802
6111	6801
6112	6804
6113	6806
6114	6807
6115	6808
6116	6809
6117	6810
6118	6813
6119	6811
6120	6812
6121	6814
"	6815
6122	6817
6123	6818
6124	6819
6125	6821
6126	6822
6127	6823
6128	6824
6129	6825
6130	6826
6131	6827
"	6828
6132	10566
6133	6830
6134	6831
6135	6829
6136	10567
6137	6832
6138	6833
6139	6834
6140	6835
6141	6836
6142	6837
6143	6838
6144	6840
6145	6839
6146	10568
6147	6841
6148	6842
"	6843
6149	6844
6150	6845
6151	10569
6152	6846
"	6851
"	6852
6153	6847
6154	6848
"	6849
"	6850
6155	6857
6156	6853
6157	6856
6158	6854
6159	6855
6160	6858
6161	6859
6162	6860
6163	6861
"	6862
6164	6863
6165	6864
6166	6865
"	6866
6167	10570
6168	6867
6169	6868
6170	6870
6171	6871
6172	6872
6173	10571
6174	6873
6175	6874
6176	6875
"	6898
6177	6876
6178	6877
6179	6878
6180	6879
6181	6880
6182	6881
6183	6882
6184	6883
6185	6884
6186	6885
6187	6886
6188	6887
6189	6888
6190	2197
"	6889
6191	6891
6192	6890
6193	6892
6194	6894
6195	6893
6196	6895
6197	6896
6198	6897
6199	6899
6200	6901
6201	6903
6202	6904

STRONG	G/K
6203	6902
6204	6905
6205	6906
6206	5123
"	6907
6207	6908
6208	6909
6209	6910
6210	6911
6211	6931
"	6932
"	6933
6211'	10572
6212	6912
6213	6913
"	6914
6214	6915
6215	6916
6216	6934
6217	6935
6218	6917
6219	6936
6220	6937
6221	6918
6222	6919
6223	6938
6224	6920
6225	6939
6226	6942
6227	6940
6228	6941
6229	6921
6230	6922
6231	6943
6232	6944
6233	6945
6234	6946
6235	6924
"	6927
6236	10573
6237	6923
6238	6947
6239	6948
6240	6925
"	6926
"	6930
6241	6928
6242	6929
6243	10574
6244	6949
6245	6950
"	6951
6246	10575
6247	6952
6248	6953
6249	6954
6250	6955
6251	6957
6252	6958
6253	6956
6254	6960
6255	6959
6256	6961
6257	6963
6258	6964
6259	6965
6260	6966
6261	6967
6262	6968
6263	10577
6264	6969
6265	6970
6266	6971
6267	6972
6268	10578
6269	6973
6270	6974
6271	6975
"	6976
6272	6977
6273	6978
6274	6979
6275	6980
6276	6982
6277	6981
6278	6962
6279	6983
6280	6984
6281	6987
6282	6985
"	6986
6283	6988
6284	6990
6285	6991
"	6992
"	6993
6286	6994
"	6995
6287	6996
6288	6997
"	6998
6289	6999
6290	7000
6291	7001
6292	7002

STRONG	G/K
6293	7003
6294	7004
6295	7005
6296	7006
6297	7007
6298	7008
6299	7009
6300	7010
6301	7011
6302	7012
6303	7013
6304	7014
"	7151
6305	7015
"	7016
6306	7017
"	7018
6307	7019
"	7020
6308	7021
6309	7022
6310	7023
6311	7024
6312	7025
"	7026
"	7030
6313	7028
6314	7029
6315	7031
"	7032
6316	7033
6317	7034
6318	7035
6319	7036
"	7280
6320	7037
6321	7038
6322	7039
"	7040
6323	687
"	7041
6324	7027
"	7043
6325	7044
6326	7045
6327	7046
"	7047
"	7207
6328	7048
6329	7048
"	7049
6330	7050
6331	7051
6332	7052
6333	7053
6334	7054
6335	7055
"	7056
6336	7057
6337	7058
6338	7059
6339	7060
6340	7061
6341	7062
"	7063
6342	7064
6343	7065
6344	7066
6345	7067
6346	7068
6347	10580
6348	7069
6349	7070
6350	7071
6351	7072
6352	7073
6353	10581
6354	7074
6355	7075
6356	7076
6357	7077
6358	7080
6359	7078
6360	7079
6361	10582
6362	7080
6363	7081
"	7082
6364	7083
6365	7085
6366	7023
6367	2112
"	2672
"	7084
6368	7086
6369	7087
6370	7108
6371	7089
6372	7090
6373	7091
6374	7092
6375	7211
6376	7093
6377	7094
6378	7095

STRONG	G/K
6379	7096
6380	2207
"	7097
6381	7098
6382	7099
6383	7100
6384	7101
6385	7103
6386	10583
6387	10584
6388	7104
6389	7105
6390	7106
6391	7107
6392	10585
6393	7110
6394	7109
6395	7111
6396	7112
6397	7113
6398	7114
6399	10586
6400	7115
6401	7116
6402	10587
6403	7117
6404	7118
6405	7119
6406	7120
6407	7121
6408	7122
6409	7123
6410	7124
"	7125
6411	7102
"	7126
6412	7127
"	7128
6413	7129
6414	7130
6415	7131
6416	7132
6417	7133
6418	7134
"	7135
6419	7136
"	7137
6420	7138
6421	7139
6422	7140
6423	7141
6424	7142
"	7143
6425	7144
6426	7145
6427	7146
6428	7147
6429	7148
6430	7149
6431	7150
6432	7152
6433	10588
6434	7157
6435	7153
6436	7154
6437	7042
"	7155
6438	7157
6439	7158
"	7159
"	7160
"	7161
6440	4367
"	4368
"	7156
6441	7163
6442	7164
6443	7162
"	7165
6444	7166
6445	7167
6446	7168
6447	10589
6448	7170
6449	7171
6450	7169
6451	7172
6452	7173
"	7174
6453	7175
6454	7176
6455	7177
6456	7178
6457	7179
6458	7180
6459	7181
6460	10590
6461	7182
6462	7183
6463	7184
6464	7185
"	7187
6465	7186
6466	7188
6467	7189

STRONG	G/K
6468	7190
6469	7191
6470	7192
6471	7193
6472	7194
6473	7196
6474	7197
6475	7198
6476	7199
"	7200
6477	7201
6478	7202
6479	7203
6480	7204
6481	7205
6482	7206
6483	2204
"	7209
6484	7210
6485	7212
"	7217
"	7227
6486	7213
6487	7214
6488	7215
6489	7216
6490	7218
6491	7219
6492	7220
6493	7221
6494	7222
6495	7223
"	7751
6496	7224
6497	7225
6498	7226
6499	7228
6500	7229
6501	7230
"	7241
6502	7231
6503	7232
"	7247
6504	7233
6505	7234
6506	7235
6507	7237
6508	7236
6509	7238
"	7311
6510	7239
6511	7240
6512	7051
6513	7242
6514	7243
"	7263
6515	7245
6516	7246
6517	7248
6518	7250
6519	7244
"	7252
6520	7251
6521	7253
6522	7254
6523	10591
6524	7255
"	7256
"	7257
6525	7258
6526	7259
6527	7260
6528	7261
6529	7262
6530	7264
"	7265
6531	7266
6532	7267
6533	7268
6534	7269
6535	7270
6536	7271
6537	10592
"	10593
6538	7272
6539	7273
6540	10594
6541	7274
6542	7275
6543	10595
6544	7276
"	7277
6545	7279
6546	7278
6547	7281
6548	2922
6549	7281+5785
6550	7282
6551	7283
6552	7284
6553	7285
6554	7286
6555	7287
6556	7288
6557	7289

STRONG	G/K
6558	7291
6559	7292
6560	7290
6561	7293
6562	10596
6563	7294
6564	7295
6565	7296
"	7297
6566	7298
6567	7300
"	7301
6568	10597
6569	7302
6570	7303
6571	7304
"	7305
6572	7306
"	7358
6573	10598
6574	7307
6575	7308
6576	7299
6577	7309
6578	7310
6579	7312
6580	7317
6581	7313
6582	7318
6583	7319
6584	7320
6585	7314
6586	7321
6587	7315
6588	7322
6589	7316
6590	10599
6591	10600
6592	7323
6593	7324
6594	7325
6595	7326
"	7336
6596	7327
6597	7328
6598	7329
6599	7330
6600	10601
6601	7331
"	7332
6602	7333
6603	7334
6604	7335
6605	7337
"	7338
6606	10602
6607	7339
6608	7340
6609	7347
6610	7341
6611	7342
6612	7343
"	7344
6613	10603
6614	7345
6615	7346
6616	7348
6617	7349
"	9520
6618	7350
6619	7351
6620	7352
6621	7353
6622	7354
6623	7355
6624	7356
6625	7357
6626	7359
6627	7362
6628	7365
6629	7366
6630	7367
6631	7368
6632	7369
"	7370
6633	7371
6634	10605
6635	7372
"	7378
6636	7375
"	7387
6637	2206
"	7376
6638	7377
6639	7379
6640	10606
6641	7380
6642	7381
6643	7373
"	7374
"	7382
"	7383
6644	7384
6645	7385
6646	7386

STRONG	G/K
6647	10607
6648	7389
6649	7390
6650	7391
6651	7392
6652	7393
6653	7395
6654	7396
"	7397
6655	10608
6656	10609
6657	7398
6658	7399
"	7400
6659	7401
6660	7402
6661	7403
6662	7404
6663	7405
6664	7406
6665	10610
6666	7407
6667	7408
"	7409
6668	5176
"	7410
6669	7411
6670	7412
"	7413
6671	7414
6672	7415
"	7416
6673	7417
6674	7364
6675	7363
6676	10611
6677	7418
"	7454
6678	7419
"	7420
6679	7421
"	7472
6680	7422
6681	7423
6682	7424
6683	7425
6684	7426
6685	7427
6686	7428
6687	7429
6688	7430
6689	7431
"	7433
"	7434
"	7487
6690	7432
6691	7436
6692	7437
"	7438
6693	7439
6694	7440
6695	7441
"	7442
6696	7443
"	7444
6697	7445
"	7446
"	7447
6698	7448
6699	7451
6700	7452
6701	7453
6702	7455
6703	7456
6704	7457
6705	7458
6706	7460
6707	7461
6708	7459
6709	7462
6710	7463
6711	7464
6712	7465
6713	7466
6714	7468
6715	7467
6716	7469
6717	7471
6718	7473
"	7474
6719	7475
6720	7476
6721	7477
6722	7479
6723	7480
6724	7481
6725	7483
6726	7482
6727	7484
6728	7470
6729	7485
6730	7486
6731	7488
"	7490
6732	7489

STRONG	G/K
6733	7491
6734	7492
6735	7493
"	7494
"	7495
"	7496
6736	7497
6737	7493
"	7494
"	7495
"	7496
6738	7498
6739	10612
6740	7499
6741	7500
6742	7501
"	7508
6743	7502
"	7503
6744	10613
6745	7505
6746	7504
6747	7505
"	7506
6748	7507
6749	7510
6750	7509
6751	7511
6752	7498
6753	2209
6754	7512
"	7513
6755	10614
6756	7514
"	7515
6757	7516
6758	7517
6759	7518
6760	7519
6761	7520
6762	7522
6763	7521
6764	7523
6765	7524
6766	7525
6767	7526
"	7527
"	7528
"	7529
6768	7530
6769	7531
6770	7532
6771	7534
6772	7533
6773	7535
6774	7536
6775	7537
6776	7538
6777	7539
6778	7540
6779	7541
6780	7542
6781	7543
"	7544
6782	7545
6783	7552
6784	7546
6785	7547
6786	7548
6787	7549
6788	7550
6789	7551
6790	7554
6791	7553
6792	7555
"	7556
6793	7557
"	7558
"	7559
6794	7562
6795	7563
6796	7564
6797	7561
"	7565
"	7566
6798	7567
"	7568
6799	7569
6800	7560
"	7570
6801	7571
6802	7572
6803	7573
6804	7574
6805	7575
6806	7576
6807	7577
"	7578
6808	7579
6809	7581
6810	7582
6811	7583
6812	7584
6813	7585
6814	7586

STRONG	G/K
6815	1300
"	7587
"	7588
6816	7589
6817	7590
6818	7591
6819	7592
6820	7580
"	7593
6821	7594
6822	7595
6823	7596
6824	7597
6825	7598
"	7609
6826	7599
6827	7602
6828	7600
6829	7601
6830	7603
6831	7604
"	7612
6832	7605
"	7616
6833	7606
6834	7607
6835	7608
6836	7610
6837	7611
6838	7613
6839	7614
6840	7615
6841	10615
6842	7618
6843	7619
6844	7620
6845	7621
"	7636
6846	7622
"	7623
6847	7195
"	7624
6848	7625
"	7626
6849	7617
6850	7627
6851	7628
6852	7629
6853	10616
6854	7630
6855	7631
6856	7632
6857	7634
6858	7633
6859	7635
6860	7637
6861	7638
6862	7639
"	7640
"	7641
6863	7643
6864	7644
6865	7450
"	7645
6866	7646
6867	7647
"	7648
6868	7649
6869	7650
"	7651
"	7659
"	7676
6870	7653
6871	7654
6872	7655
"	7656
"	7657
6873	7658
6874	7662
6875	7661
6876	7660
6877	7663
6878	7664
6879	7665
6880	7667
6881	7666
6882	7668
"	7670
6883	7669
6884	7671
6885	7672
6886	7673
6887	7674
"	7675
"	7677
6888	7678
6889	7679
6890	2241
"	7680
6891	7681
6892	7683
"	7795
6893	7684
6894	7685
6895	7686
6896	7687
6897	7687
6898	7688
6899	7689
6900	7690
6901	7691
6902	10618
6903	10619
6904	7692
6905	7692
6906	7693
6907	7694
6908	7695
6909	7696
6910	7697
6911	7698
6912	7699
6913	7700
6914	2246
"	7701
6915	7702
6916	7703
6917	7704
6918	7705
6919	7706
6920	7707
6921	7708
6922	10620
6923	7709
6924	7710
"	7711
"	7714
6925	10621
6926	7713
6927	7712
6928	10622
6929	7715
6930	7716
6931	7719
6932	7717
6933	10623
6934	7718
6935	7720
6936	7721
6937	7722
6938	7723
6939	7724
6940	7725
6941	7726
6942	7727
6943	7730
6944	7731
6945	7728
6946	7729
6947	1395
"	7732
6948	7728
6949	7733
6950	7735
6951	7736
6952	7737
6953	7738
6954	7739
6955	7740
6956	7741
6957	7742
"	7743
"	7744
6958	7794
"	7796
6959	7746
6960	7747
"	7748
6961	7749
6962	7752
"	7753
6963	7754
"	7825
"	7826
6964	7755
6965	7756
"	7856
"	9539
6966	10624
6967	7757
6968	7758
6969	7759
"	7801
6970	7760
6971	7761
6972	7763
6973	7762
6974	7763
"	7810
6975	7764
"	7765
6976	2212
"	7766
6977	7767
6978	7743+7743
6979	7769
"	7979
"	7981
"	7982
6980	7770
6981	7927
6982	7771
6983	7772
6984	7773
6985	7775
6986	7776
6987	7776
6988	7777
6989	7778
6990	3684
6991	7779
6992	10625
6993	7780
6994	7781
6995	7782
6996	7783
"	7785
6997	2214
"	7784
6998	7786
6999	5231
"	5232
"	7787
7000	7788
7001	10626
7002	7789
7003	7790
7004	7792
7005	7793
7006	7794
7007	10627
7008	7798
7009	7799
7010	10628
7011	10629
7012	7800
7013	7802
7014	7803
"	7804
"	7805
7015	7806
7016	7807
7017	7808
7018	7809
7019	7811
7020	7812
7021	7813
7022	7814
7023	7815
7024	7816
"	7817
7025	3085
"	3097
"	7818
"	7819
7026	7820
7027	7821
7028	7822
7029	7823
7030	10644
"	10630
7031	7824
7032	10631
7033	7828
7034	7829
7035	7827
7036	7830
7037	7831
7038	7832
7039	7833
7040	7834
7041	7835
7042	7836
7043	7837
7044	7838
7045	7839
7046	7840
7047	7841
7048	7842
7049	7843
"	7844
7050	7845
"	7846
7051	7847
7052	7848
7053	7849
7054	7850
7055	7851
7056	7852
7057	7853
7058	7854
7059	7855
7060	7857
7061	7858
7062	7859
7063	7853
7064	7860
7065	7861
7066	10632
7067	7862
7068	7863
7069	7864
"	7865
7070	7866
7071	7867
7072	7868
7073	7869
7074	7870
7075	7871
7076	7872
7077	7873
7078	7874
7079	7875
7080	7876
7081	7877
7082	7878
7083	7879
7084	7881
7085	7882
7086	7883
7087	7884
"	7885
7088	7886
7089	7888
7090	7887
7091	7889
7092	7890
7093	7891
7094	7892
7095	7893
7096	7894
7097	7895
"	7897
7098	7896
"	7901
7099	7898
7100	7902
7101	7903
7102	7904
7103	7905
7104	6681
"	7906
7105	7907
"	7908
7106	7909
"	7910
7107	7911
7108	10633
7109	10634
7110	7912
"	7913
7111	7914
7112	7899
"	7915
7113	10635
7114	7900
"	7917
"	7918
7115	7919
7116	7920
7117	7921
7118	10636
7119	7922
7120	7923
7121	7924
7122	7925
7123	10637
7124	7926
7125	7925
7126	7928
7127	10638
7128	7930
7129	10639
7130	7931
7131	7929
7132	7932
7133	7933
"	7934
7134	7935
7135	7938
7136	7936
"	7939
7137	7937
7138	7940
7139	7942
7140	7943
7141	7946
7142	7944
7143	7945
7144	7942
7145	7948
7146	7947
"	7949
7147	7950
7148	7951
7149	10640
7150	7952
7151	7953
"	7956
7152	7954
7153	7957
"	7959
7154	7958
7155	2941
"	7960
7156	7964
7157	7961
7158	6173
"	7962
"	7963
7159	7965
7160	7966
7161	7967
"	7969
7162	10641
7163	2199
"	7968
7164	7970
7165	7971
7166	7972
7167	7973
7168	7974
7169	7975
7170	10642
7171	7976
7172	7977
7173	7978
7174	7980
7175	7983
7176	7984
7177	7985
7178	7986
7179	7990
7180	7991
7181	7992
7182	7993
7183	7994
"	7995
7184	7987
7185	7996
7186	7997
7187	10643
7188	7998
7189	7999
"	8000
7190	8001
7191	8002
7192	7988
7193	7989
7194	8003
7195	8004
7196	8005
7197	8006
"	8007
7198	8008
7199	8009
7200	8011
"	8013
"	8021
7201	8012
7202	8011
7203	8014
"	8015
7204	2218
7205	8017
7206	8018
7207	8019
7208	8020
7209	8023
7210	8024
7211	8016
"	8025
7212	8026
7213	8027
7214	8028
7215	8029
7216	8030
7217	10646
7218	8031
"	8034
7219	8032
7220	8033
"	8396
7221	8035
7222	8036
7223	8037
7224	8038
7225	8040
7226	8031
7227	8041
"	8042
7228	8043
7229	10647
7230	8044
7231	8045
7232	8046
7233	8047
7234	8048
7235	2220
"	2221
"	8049
"	8050
7236	10648
7237	8051
7238	10650
7239	8052
7240	10649
7241	8053
7242	8054
7243	8055
"	8068
7244	10651
7245	8056
7246	8057
7247	8058
7248	4454
"	8059
7249	8060
"	8042+6247
7250	8061
7251	8062
7252	8061
7253	8063
7254	8061
"	8064
7255	8065
"	8066
7256	8067
7257	8069
7258	8070
7259	8071
7260	10647
7261	10652
7262	8072
7263	8073
7264	8074
7265	10653
7266	10654
7267	8075
7268	8076
7269	8077
7270	8078
7271	10655
7272	8079
7273	8081
7274	8082
7275	8083
7276	8084
7277	8086
7278	8085
7279	8087
7280	8088
"	8089
"	8090
7281	8092
7282	8091
7283	8093
7284	10656
7285	8094
"	8095
7286	8096
7287	8097
"	8098
7288	8099
7289	8100
7290	8101
7291	8103
7292	8104
7293	8105
7294	8105
7295	8107
7296	8106
7297	3724
"	8109
7298	8110
"	8111
7299	10657
7300	8113
7301	8115
7302	8116
7303	8108
"	8117
7304	8118
7305	8119
7306	8193
7307	8120
7308	10658
7309	8121
7310	8122
7311	3727
"	3753
"	8123
"	8225
"	8249
7312	8124
7313	10659
7314	10660
7315	8125
7316	8126
7317	8127
7318	8128
7319	8129
7320	6471
"	8251
7321	8131
7322	8344
7323	8132
"	8350
7324	8197
7325	8201
7326	8133
7327	8134
7328	10661
7329	8135
7330	8136
7331	8139
7332	8137
7333	8138
7334	8140
7335	8141
7336	8142
7337	8143
7338	8144
7339	8148
7340	8149
"	8150
7341	8145
7342	8146
7343	8147
7344	8151
7345	8152
"	8153
7346	8154
7347	8160
7348	8156
"	10662
7349	8157
7350	8158
7351	8112
"	8159
7352	10663
7353	8161
7354	8162
7355	8163
7356	8166
"	8171
7357	8165
7358	8167
7359	10664
7360	8164
"	8168
7361	8169
7362	8172
7363	8173
"	8174
7364	8175
7365	10665
7366	8176
7367	8177
7368	8178
7369	8179
7370	8180
7371	8181
7372	8182
7373	8183
7374	8185
7375	8186
7376	8187
7377	8188
7378	8189
7379	8190
"	8191
7380	8192
7381	8194
7382	10666
7383	8195
7384	1910
"	8196
7385	8198
7386	8199
7387	8200
7388	8202
7389	8203
7390	8205
7391	8204
7392	8206
7393	8207
7394	8209
"	8211
7395	8208
7396	8210
7397	8212
7398	8213
7399	8214
7400	8215
7401	8216
7402	8217
7403	8218
7404	8219
7405	8220
7406	8221
7407	8222
7408	8223
7409	8224
7410	8226
7411	8227
"	8228
7412	10667
7413	8229
7414	8230
"	8259
7415	8231
7416	8232
7417	8233
"	8234
"	8235
"	8237
7418	8238
"	8241
7419	8239
7420	8242
7421	811
7422	8243
7423	8244
"	8245
7424	8247
7425	8248
7426	8250
7427	8129
7428	8236
7429	8252
7430	8253
7431	8254
7432	8255
7433	8240
7434	2174
"	8256
7435	8258
7436	7435
7437	8257
7438	8260
7439	8261
7440	8262
7441	8263
7442	8130
"	8264
7443	8266
7444	8264
7445	8265
7446	8267
7447	8268
"	8269
7448	8270
7449	8271
7450	8272
7451	8273
"	8274
7452	8275
7453	8276
7454	8277
7455	8278
7456	8279
"	8281
7457	8280
7458	8280
7459	8282
7460	8283
7461	8284
"	8285
7462	8287
"	8289
7463	8291
7464	8292
"	8300
7465	8288
7466	8293
7467	8294
7468	8295
7469	8296
7470	10668
7471	8297
7472	8298
7473	8286
7474	8299
7475	8301
7476	10669
7477	8302
7478	8303
7479	8304
7480	8305
7481	8306
"	8307
7482	8308
7483	8309
"	8310
7484	8311
"	8312
7485	8313
7486	8314
7487	10670
7488	8315
"	8316
7489	5336
"	8317
"	8318
7490	10671
7491	8319
7492	8320
7493	8321
"	8322
7494	8323
7495	8324
7496	8327
7497	8328
"	8329
7498	8325
"	8334
7499	8337
7500	8326
7501	8330
7502	8331
7503	8332
7504	8333
7505	8336
7506	8338
7507	8339
7508	8340
7509	8341
7510	8335
"	8342

STRONG	G/K
7511	8346
7512	10672
7513	8343
7514	8345
7515	8346
7516	8347
7517	8348
7518	8349
7519	8351
7520	8353
7521	8352
"	8354
"	8355
7522	8356
7523	8357
7524	8358
7525	8359
7526	8360
7527	8361
7528	8362
7529	8363
7530	8364
7531	8365
"	8367
7532	8366
7533	8368
7534	8369
7535	8370
7536	8371
7537	8372
7538	8373
"	8374
7539	8375
7540	8376
7541	8377
7542	8378
7543	8379
7544	8380
7545	8381
7546	8382
7547	8383
7548	8384
7549	8385
7550	8386
7551	8387
7552	8388
"	8389
"	8390
7553	8391
7554	8392
7555	8393
7556	8394
7557	8395
7558	8397
7559	8398
7560	10673
7561	8399
7562	8400
7563	8401
7564	8402
7565	8404
7566	8405
7567	8406
7568	8407
7569	8408
7570	8409
7571	8410
7572	8411
7573	8412
7574	8413
7575	8414
7576	8415
7577	8416
7578	8417
7579	8612
7580	8613
7581	8614
7582	8615
"	8616
7583	8617
7584	8618
7585	8619
7586	8620
7587	8621
7588	8622
"	8623
7589	8624
7590	8764
7591	8625
7592	8626
"	8628
7593	10689
7594	8627
7595	10690
7596	8629
7597	8630
"	9003
7598	10691
7599	8631
7600	8633
7601	
7602	8634
"	8635
7603	8419
7604	8636

STRONG	G/K
7605	8637
7606	10692
7607	8638
7608	8640
7609	8641
7610	8639
7611	8642
7612	8643
7613	8420
"	8421
7614	8644
7615	8645
7616	8646
7617	8647
7618	8648
7619	8649
"	8742
7620	8651
"	8652
7621	8678
7622	8654
"	8669
7623	8655
"	8656
7624	10693
7625	10694
7626	8657
7627	8658
7628	8660
"	8665
7629	8661
7630	8662
7631	10695
7632	8663
7633	8664
7634	8499
7635	8666
7636	8667
7637	8668
7638	8422
7639	8422
7640	8670
7641	8672
"	8673
7642	8671
7643	8423
"	8424
7644	8674
"	8675
7645	8676
"	8677
7646	8425
7647	8426
7648	8427
7649	8428
7650	8678
7651	8679
7652	8680
"	8681
7653	8430
7654	8429
7655	10696
7656	8683
7657	8684
7658	8685
7659	8686
7660	8687
7661	8688
7662	10697
7663	8431
"	8432
7664	8433
7665	8653
"	8689
7666	8690
7667	8691
"	8694
7668	8692
7669	8693
7670	8695
7671	8696
7672	10698
7673	8697
"	8698
7674	8700
7675	8699
7676	8701
7677	8702
7678	8703
7679	8434
7680	10677
7681	8707
7682	8435
7683	1417
"	8704
7684	8705
7685	8436
7686	8706
7687	8437
"	8439
7688	8708
7689	8438
7690	10678
7691	8709
7692	8710

STRONG	G/K
7693	8711
7694	8712
7695	10699
7696	8713
7697	8714
7698	8715
7699	8716
"	8718
7700	8717
7701	8719
7702	8440
7703	8720
7704	8441
"	8442
7705	8721
7706	8724
7707	8725
7708	8443
7709	8727
7710	8728
7711	8729
"	8730
7712	10700
7713	8444
7714	8731
7715	10701
7716	8445
7717	8446
7718	8732
7719	8733
7720	8448
7721	5951
7722	8738
"	8739
7723	8736
7724	8737
7725	8740
7726	8743
7727	8744
7728	8745
7729	8746
7730	8449
7731	8747
7732	8748
7733	8749
7734	6047
7735	8451
7736	8720
7737	8750
"	8751
7738	9589
7739	10702
7740	8753
7741	8754
7742	8452
7743	8755
7744	8756
7745	8757
7746	8758
7747	8760
7748	8761
7749	8762
7750	6091
"	8454
7751	8763
7752	8765
"	8766
"	8867
7753	8455
7754	8456
"	8457
7755	8458
"	8459
7756	8460
7757	8767
7758	8768
"	8871
7759	8769
7760	8461
"	8492
7761	10682
7762	8770
7763	9071
7764	8771
7765	8772
7766	8773
7767	8774
7768	8775
7769	8780
"	8782
7770	8781
7771	8777
7772	8778
"	8779
7773	8776
7774	8783
7775	8784
7776	8785
7777	8786
"	8787
7778	8788
7779	8789
"	8790
7780	8791
7781	8793

STRONG	G/K
7782	8795
7783	8796
7784	8798
7785	8797
7786	8606
7787	8492
7788	8801
7789	8800
7790	8803
7791	8805
7792	10703
7793	8804
7794	8802
7795	8463
7796	8604
7797	8464
7798	8807
7799	8808
7800	8809
7801	10704
7802	8808+6343
7803	8811
7804	10706
7805	8812
7806	8813
7807	8814
7808	8465
7809	8815
7810	8816
7811	8466
7812	8817
7813	8467
7814	8468
7815	8818
7816	8819
7817	8820
"	8863
7818	8469
7819	8821
"	8822
"	8823
7820	8822
7821	8824
7822	8825
7823	6084
"	8826
7824	8470
7825	8827
7826	8828
7827	8829
7828	8830
7829	8831
7830	8832
7831	8833
"	8834
7832	8471
7833	8835
7834	8836
7835	8837
7836	8838
7837	8840
7838	8839
7839	8841
7840	8842
7841	8843
7842	8844
7843	8845
7844	10705
7845	8846
7846	8473
7847	8474
7848	8847
7849	8848
7850	8849
7851	8850
7852	8475
7853	8476
7854	8477
7855	8478
7856	8479
7857	8851
7858	8852
7859	10680
7860	8853
7861	8855
"	9231
7862	8856
7863	8480
7864	8857
7865	8481
7866	8858
7867	8482
7868	10681
"	10675
7869	8483
7870	8860
7871	8859
7872	8484
7873	8485
7874	8486
7875	6093
"	8487
7876	8861
7877	8862
7878	8488

STRONG	G/K
7879	8490
7880	8489
7881	8491
7882	8864
7883	8865
7884	4251
"	8866
7885	8868
7886	8869
7887	8870
"	8926
"	8931
7888	8872
7889	8873
7890	8875
7891	8876
7892	8877
"	8878
7893	8880
7894	8881
7895	8810
"	8882
7896	8883
7897	8884
7898	8885
7899	8493
7900	8494
7901	8886
7902	8887
7903	8888
7904	8889
7905	8496
7906	8497
7907	8498
7908	8890
7909	8891
"	8892
7910	8893
7911	4171
"	8894
7912	10708
7913	8895
7914	8500
7915	8501
7916	8502
7917	8502
7918	8896
7919	8505
"	8506
7920	10683
7921	5437
"	8897
7922	8507
7923	8898
7924	10684
7925	8899
7926	8900
7927	8901
"	8902
7928	8903
7929	8900
7930	8904
7931	8905
7932	10709
7933	8905
7934	8907
7935	8908
"	8909
7936	6128
7937	8509
"	8910
"	8912
7938	8512
7939	8510
7940	8511
7941	8911
7942	8914
7943	8913
7944	8915
7945	8611
7946	8916
7947	8917
7948	8918
7949	8919
7950	8920
"	8921
7951	8922
7952	8923
7953	8923
7954	10710
7955	10685
"	10711
7956	8924
"	8925
7957	8927
"	8928
7958	8513
7959	8930
7960	10712
7961	8929
7962	8932
7963	10713
7964	8933
7965	8934
7966	8936

STRONG	G/K
7967	8935
7968	8937
7969	5456
"	8993
7970	9001
7971	8938
7972	10714
7973	8939
"	8945
7974	8941
7975	8940
"	8942
7976	8943
7977	8944
7978	8946
7979	8947
7980	8948
7981	10715
7982	8949
7983	8950
7984	10716
7985	10717
7986	8951
7987	8952
7988	8953
7989	8954
7990	10718
7991	8955
"	8956
"	8957
"	8998
7992	8958
"	8999
7993	8959
7994	8960
7995	8961
7996	8962
7997	8963
"	8964
7998	8965
7999	8966
8000	10719
8001	10720
8002	8968
8003	8969
8004	8970
8005	8972
8006	8973
8007	8514
8008	8515
8009	8516
8010	8976
8011	8974
8012	8517
8013	8977
8014	8518
8015	8979
8016	8980
8017	8981
8018	8982
"	8983
8019	8984
"	8985
8020	8986
8021	8988
8022	8987
8023	8989
8024	8989
8025	8990
8026	8991
8027	8992
8028	8994
8029	9000
8030	8996
8031	8995
8032	8997
8033	9004
8034	9005
8035	9006
8036	10721
8037	9007
8038	9008
8039	9009
8040	8520
8041	8520
"	8521
8042	8522
8043	9010
8044	9011
8045	9012
8046	10722
8047	9014
8048	9015
8049	9016
8050	9017
8051	9018
8052	9019
8053	9020
8054	9021
8055	8523
8056	8524
8057	8525
8058	9023
8059	9024
8060	9025

STRONG	G/K
8061	9026
8062	9027
8063	8526
8064	9028
8065	10723
8066	9029
8067	9030
8068	9031
"	9032
8069	9033
"	9034
8070	9035
"	9082
8071	8529
8072	8528
8073	8530
"	8978
"	9036
8074	9037
8075	10724
8076	9038
8077	9039
"	9040
8078	9041
8079	8532
8080	9042
8081	9043
8082	9045
8083	9046
8084	9047
8085	9048
"	9049
8086	10725
8087	9050
8088	9051
8089	9053
8090	9054
8091	9052
8092	9055
8093	9056
8094	9057
8095	9058
8096	9059
8097	9060
8098	9061
"	9062
8099	9063
8100	9064
8101	9065
8102	9066
8103	9067
8104	9068
8105	9069
8106	9070
"	9013
8107	9081
8108	9072
8109	9073
8110	9074
"	9075
8111	9076
8112	5264
"	9077
8113	9078
8114	9079
"	9080
8115	10726
8116	9083
8117	9084
8118	9085
8119	9086
8120	10727
8121	9087
8122	10728
8123	9088
8124	10729
8125	9091
8126	9092
8127	9094
8128	10730
8129	9095
8130	8533
8131	10686
8132	9096
"	9101
8133	10731
8134	9098
8135	8534
8136	9099
8137	9100
8138	9101
8139	10733
8140	10732
8141	9102
8142	9097
"	9104
8143	2036
"	9105
8144	9106
8145	9108
8146	8535
8147	9109
8148	9110
8149	8536
8150	9111

STRONG	G/K
"	9112
8151	9113
8152	9114
8153	3822
8154	9115
8155	9116
8156	9117
8157	9118
8158	9119
8159	9120
8160	10734
8161	9121
8162	9122
8163	8537
"	8538
"	8539
8164	8540
8165	8541
"	8542
"	8543
8166	8544
8167	8545
8168	9123
8169	9124
"	9125
8170	9126
8171	9127
8172	9128
8173	9129
"	9130
8174	9131
8175	8547
"	8548
"	8549
8176	9132
8177	10687
8178	8550
"	8551
8179	9133
8180	9134
8181	8552
8182	9135
8183	8554
8184	8555
8185	8553
8186	9136
8187	9137
"	9138
8188	8556
8189	9139
8190	9140
8191	9141
8192	9142
8193	8557
8194	9147
8195	9143
"	9156
8196	9144
8197	8792
"	9145
"	9146
8198	9148
8199	9149
8200	10735
8201	9150
8202	9151
8203	9152
"	9153
8204	9154
8205	9155
8206	9157
"	9158
8207	9159
8208	9160
8209	10736
8210	8564
"	9161
8211	9162
8212	9163
8213	9164
8214	10737
8215	10738
8216	9165
8217	9166
8218	9168
8219	9169
8220	9170
8221	9172
8222	8559
8223	9171
8224	8560
8225	9175
8226	8561
8227	9176
"	9177
8228	9179
8229	9180
8230	9181
8231	9182
8232	10739
8233	9183
8234	9184
8235	9185
8236	9186
8237	9187

STRONG	G/K
"	9188
8238	10740
8239	9189
8240	9190
"	9191
8241	9192
8242	8566
8243	10741
8244	8567
8245	9193
"	9194
"	9195
8246	5481
8247	9196
8248	9197
8249	9198
8250	9198
8251	9199
8252	9200
8253	9201
8254	9202
8255	9203
8256	9204
8257	9205
8258	9206
8259	9207
8260	9208
8261	9209
8262	9210
8263	9211
8264	8799
"	9212
8265	8568
8266	9213
8267	9214
8268	9216
8269	6254
"	8569
8270	9218
"	9219
8271	10742
8272	8570
8273	9220
8274	9221
8275	9222
8276	8571
8277	8572
8278	8573
8279	8574
8280	8575
8281	9223
"	9224
8282	8576
8283	8577
8284	9224
8285	9217
"	9225
8286	8578
8287	9226
8288	8579
8289	4389
"	9227
8290	9228
8291	8602
"	8604
8292	9229
"	9241
8293	9230
8294	8580
8295	8581
8296	8582
"	8583
8297	8584
8298	9232
8299	8585
8300	8586
8301	8587
8302	9233
"	9234
8303	8590
8304	8588
"	8589
8305	8591
8306	9235
8307	9244
8308	8592
8309	9173
"	9236
8310	8593
8311	8594
8312	8595
8313	8596
8314	8597
8315	8598
8316	8599
8317	9237
8318	9238
8319	9239
8320	8601
8321	8603
8322	8605
"	9240
8323	8606
8324	8806
8325	9242
"	9243
8326	9247
8327	9245
8328	9247
8329	9246
8330	10743
8331	9249
8332	10744
"	10745
8333	9248
"	9249
8334	9250
8335	9251
8336	9253
"	9254
8337	9252
8338	9255
8339	9256
8340	10746
8341	9257
8342	8607
8343	9258
8344	9259
8345	9261
8346	9262
8347	9263
8348	9264
8349	9265
8350	9266
8351	9268
8352	9269
8353	10747
8354	9272
8355	10748
8356	9271
8357	9268
8358	9275
8359	9274
8360	9276
8361	10749
8362	9278
8363	9277
8364	9279
8365	9280
"	9281
8366	8874
"	9282
8367	9284
8368	8609
8369	9285
8370	10750
8371	9286
8372	9288
8373	9289
8374	9290
8375	9291
8376	9292
8377	9293
8378	9294
8379	9295
8380	9296
"	9339
8381	9297
8382	9298
8383	9303
8384	9300
8385	9299
"	9301
8386	9302
8387	9304
8388	9305
"	9306
8389	9307
8390	9308
8391	9309
8392	9310
8393	9311
8394	9312
"	9341
8395	9313
8396	9314
8397	9316
8398	9315
8399	9318
8400	9319
8401	9320
8402	9321
8403	9322
8404	9323
8405	9324
8406	10752
8407	9325
"	9433
8408	9326
8409	9327
8410	9329
8411	10753
8412	9330
8413	9331
8414	9332
8415	9333
8416	9335
8417	9334
8418	9336
8419	9337
8420	9338
8421	10754
8422	9317
8423	9340
8424	9342
8425	9328
8426	9343
8427	9344
8428	9345
8429	10755
8430	9346
8431	9347
8432	9348
8433	9349
"	9350
8434	9351
8435	9352
8436	9353
"	9400
8437	9354
8438	9355
"	9357
8439	9356
8440	9358
8441	9359
8442	9360
8443	9361
8444	9362
8445	9363
8446	9365
8447	9366
8448	9366
8449	9367
8450	10756
8451	9368
8452	9368
8453	9369
8454	9370
8455	9371
8456	9372
8457	9373
8458	9374
8459	9375
8460	10757
8461	9376
8462	9378
8463	9377
8464	9379
8465	9380
8466	9381
"	9385
"	9386
8467	9382
8468	9383
8469	9384
8470	9385
8471	9387
8472	9388
8473	9389
8474	3013
8475	9390
8476	9391
8477	9392
8478	5502
"	9393
8479	10757
8480	9394
"	9395
8481	9396
8482	9397
8483	2547
"	9398
8484	9399
8485	9401
8486	9402
8487	9403
8488	9405
8489	9404
8490	9406
8491	9407
8492	3770
"	9408
8493	9409
8494	9410
8495	9411
8496	9412
8497	9413
8498	9414
8499	9414
8500	9415
8501	9412
8502	9416
8503	9417
8504	9418
8505	9419
8506	9420
8507	9421
8508	9422
8509	9423
8510	9424
8511	9428
8512	9425
8513	9430
8514	9429
8515	9431
"	9445
8516	9432
8517	10758
8518	9434
8519	9442
8520	9436
8521	9426
8522	9437
8523	10759
8524	9435
8525	9439
8526	9440
8527	9441
8528	9427
8529	9443
8530	9444
8531	10760
8532	10761
8533	10762
8534	9446
8535	9447
8536	10764
8537	9448
8538	9450
8539	9449
8540	10763
8541	9451
8542	9452
8543	9453
8544	9454
8545	9455
8546	9456
8547	9457
8548	9458
8549	9459
8550	9460
8551	9461
8552	9462
8553	9463
8554	9464
8555	9465
8556	9466
"	9467
8557	9468
8558	9469
8559	9470
"	9471
8560	9472
"	9473
8561	9474
8562	9475
8563	9476
8564	9477
8565	9478
8566	9479
8567	9480
8568	9478
8569	9481
8570	9482
8571	9483
8572	9484
8573	9485
8574	9486
8575	9487
"	9488
8576	9489
8577	9490
8578	10765
8579	10766
8580	9491
"	9492
8581	9493
8582	9494
8583	9495
"	9497
8584	9496
8585	9498
"	9499
8586	9500
8587	9502
8588	9503
8589	9504
8590	9505
8591	9506
8592	9508
8593	9509
8594	9510
8595	9511
8596	4191
"	9512
"	9513
8597	9514
8598	9515
8599	9516
"	9517
8600	9518
8601	9519
8602	9521
"	9522
8603	9523
8604	9524
8605	9525
8606	9526
8607	9527
8608	9528
8609	9529
8610	9530
8611	9531
8612	9532
8613	9533
8614	10767
8615	9535
"	9536
8616	9534
"	9537
8617	9538
8618	9539
8619	9540
8620	9541
8621	9542
8622	9543
8623	9544
8624	10768
8625	10769
"	10770
8626	9545
8627	10771
8628	9364
"	9546
8629	9547
8630	9548
8631	10772
8632	10773
"	10774
8633	9549
8634	9550
8635	9551
8636	9552
8637	8078
8638	9553
8639	9554
8640	9555
8641	9556
8642	9557
8643	9558
8644	9559
8645	9560
8646	9561
"	9562
8647	9563
8648	10775
"	10778
8649	9564
"	9566
"	9567
"	9569
8650	9568
8651	10776
8652	10777
8653	9570
8654	9571
8655	9572
8656	9573
"	9574
8657	9575
8658	9577
8659	9576
"	9578
8660	9579
8661	9580
8662	9581
8663	9583
"	9589
8664	9585
"	9586
8665	9587
8666	9588
8667	9582
8668	9591
8669	9592
8670	9593
8671	9595
8672	9596
8673	9597
8674	10779

GREEK NEW TESTAMENT

STRONG	G/K
1	*1*
"	*270*
2	*2*
3	*3*
4	*4*
5	*5*
6	*6*
7	*7*
8	*8*
9	*9*
10	*10*
11	*11*
12	*12*
13	*13*
14	*14*
15	*16*
16	*17*
17	*18*
18	*19*
19	*20*
20	*21*
21	*22*
22	*23*
23	*24*
24	*25*
25	*26*
26	*27*
27	*28*
28	*29*
29	*30*
30	*31*
"	*35*
31	*32*
32	*34*
33	*72*
34	*36*
35	*37*
36	*38*
37	*39*
"	*420*
38	*40*
39	*41*
40	*41*
41	*42*
42	*43*
43	*44*
44	*45*
45	*46*
46	*47*
47	*48*
48	*49*
49	*50*
50	*51*
51	*52*
52	*53*
53	*54*
54	*55*
55	*56*
56	*57*
57	*58*
58	*59*
59	*60*
60	*61*
61	*62*
62	*63*
63	*64*
64	*65*
65	*66*
66	*67*
67	*68*
68	*69*
69	*70*
70	*71*
71	*72*
72	*73*
73	*74*
74	*75*
75	*76*
76	*77*
77	*78*
78	*79*
79	*80*
80	*81*
81	*82*
82	*83*
83	*84*
84	*85*
85	*194*
"	*86*
86	*87*
87	*88*
88	*89*
89	*90*
90	*91*
"	*916*
"	*917*
91	*92*
92	*93*
93	*94*
94	*96*
95	*97*
96	*99*
97	*100*
98	*101*
99	*102*
100	*103*
101	*104*
102	*105*
103	*106*
104	*107*
105	*108*
106	*109*
107	*110*
108	*111*
109	*113*
110	*114*
111	*116*
112	*117*
113	*118*
114	*119*
115	*120*
116	*121*
117	*122*
118	*123*
119	*124*
120	*126*
121	*127*
122	*128*
123	*129*
124	*130*
125	*131*
126	*132*
127	*133*
"	*1290*
128	*134*
129	*135*
130	*136*
131	*137*
132	*138*
133	*139*
134	*140*
135	*141*
136	*142*
137	*143*
138	*145*
139	*146*
140	*147*
141	*148*
142	*149*
143	*150*
144	*151*
145	*152*
146	*153*
147	*154*
148	*155*
149	*156*
150	*156*
151	*157*
152	*158*
153	*159*
154	*160*
155	*161*
156	*162*
157	*163*
"	*166*
158	*165*
159	*165*
160	*167*
161	*168*
162	*169*
163	*170*
164	*171*
165	*172*
166	*173*
167	*174*
168	*175*
169	*176*
170	*177*
171	*178*
172	*179*
173	*180*
174	*181*
175	*182*
176	*183*
177	*184*
178	*185*
179	*186*
180	*187*
"	*188*
181	*189*
182	*190*
183	*191*
184	*192*
185	*193*
186	*195*
187	*196*
188	*197*
189	*198*
190	*199*
191	*200*
"	*201*
192	*202*
193	*203*
194	*204*
195	*205*
196	*206*
197	*209*
198	*208*
199	*209*
200	*210*
201	*211*
202	*212*
203	*213*
204	*214*
205	*215*
206	*216*
207	*217*
208	*218*
209	*219*
210	*220*
211	*222*
"	*223*
212	*224*
213	*225*
214	*226*
215	*227*
216	*228*
217	*221*
"	*229*
218	*230*
219	*231*
220	*232*
221	*233*
222	*234*
223	*235*
224	*236*
225	*237*
226	*238*
227	*239*
228	*240*
229	*241*
230	*242*
231	*243*
232	*244*
233	*245*
234	*246*
235	*247*
236	*248*
237	*249*
238	*251*
239	*252*
240	*253*
241	*254*
242	*256*
"	*380*
243	*257*
244	*258*
245	*259*
246	*260*
247	*261*
248	*262*
249	*263*
250	*264*
251	*265*
252	*266*
253	*267*
254	*268*
255	*269*
256	*271*
257	*272*
258	*273*
259	*274*
260	*275*
261	*276*
262	*277*
263	*278*
264	*279*
265	*280*
266	*281*
267	*282*
268	*283*
269	*285*
270	*286*
271	*287*
272	*288*
273	*289*
274	*290*
275	*291*
276	*292*
277	*293*
278	*294*
279	*295*
280	*296*
281	*297*
282	*298*
283	*299*
284	*300*
285	*302*
286	*303*
287	*304*
288	*306*
289	*307*
290	*308*
291	*309*
292	*310*
293	*312*
294	*313*
"	*314*
295	*315*
296	*316*
297	*317*
298	*318*
299	*320*
300	*321*
301	*322*
302	*323*
303	*324*
304	*325*
305	*326*
306	*327*
307	*328*
308	*329*
309	*330*
310	*331*
311	*332*
312	*334*
313	*335*
314	*336*
315	*337*
316	*338*
317	*339*
318	*340*
319	*341*
320	*342*

STRONG	G/K
321	343
322	344
323	345
324	346
325	347
326	348
327	349
328	350
329	351
330	352
331	353
332	354
333	355
"	1461
334	356
335	357
336	358
337	359
338	360
339	361
340	362
341	363
342	364
343	365
344	366
345	367
346	368
347	369
348	370
349	371
350	373
351	374
352	376
353	377
354	378
355	379
"	384
356	381
357	382
358	383
359	385
360	386
361	387
362	388
363	389
364	390
365	391
366	392
367	393
368	394
369	395
370	396
371	397
372	398
373	399
374	400
375	402
376	401
377	404
378	405
379	406
380	408
381	409
382	410
383	411
384	412
385	413
386	414
387	415
388	416
389	417
390	418
391	419
392	421
393	422
394	423
395	424
396	426
397	427
398	428
399	429
400	430
401	431
402	432
403	433
404	434
405	435
406	436
407	437
408	438
409	439
410	441
411	442
412	443
413	444
414	445
415	446
416	448
417	449
418	450
419	451
420	452
421	453
422	454
423	455
424	456
425	457
426	458
427	459
428	460
429	461
430	462
431	463
432	464
433	465
434	466
435	467
436	468
437	469
438	470
439	471
440	472
441	473
442	474
443	475
444	476
445	477
446	478
447	479
448	447
"	480
449	481
450	403
"	482
451	483
452	484
453	485
"	493
454	486
455	487
"	1986
456	488
457	489
458	490
459	491
460	492
461	494
462	495
463	496
464	497
465	498
466	499
467	500
468	501
469	502
470	503
471	515
472	504
473	505
474	506
475	507
476	508
477	509
478	510
479	511
480	512
481	513
482	514
483	515
484	516
485	517
486	518
487	519
488	520
489	521
490	522
491	523
492	524
493	525
494	526
495	527
496	528
497	529
498	530
499	531
500	532
501	533
502	534
503	535
504	536
505	537
506	538
507	539
508	333
509	540
510	425
"	541
511	542
512	543
513	544
514	545
515	546
516	547
517	548
518	33
"	550
519	551
520	552
521	553
522	554
523	555
524	556
525	557
526	558
527	559
528	560
529	561
530	562
531	563
532	564
533	565
534	567
535	568
536	569
537	570
538	572
539	573
540	574
541	575
542	927
543	577
544	578
545	579
546	580
547	581
548	582
549	583
550	584
551	585
552	586
553	587
554	588
555	589
556	590
557	591
558	592
559	593
560	594
561	584
"	595
562	596
563	597
564	598
565	599
566	600
567	600
568	600
569	601
570	602
"	3898
571	603
572	605
573	604
"	606
574	607
575	608
576	609
577	610
578	611
579	612
580	613
581	614
582	615
583	616
584	617
585	618
586	619
"	620
587	621
588	622
589	623
590	624
591	625
592	626
593	627
594	628
595	629
596	630
597	631
598	632
599	633
600	634
"	635
601	636
602	637
603	638
"	2839
604	639
605	640
606	641
607	642
608	643
609	644
610	645
611	646
612	647
613	648
614	649
615	650
"	651
616	652
617	375
"	653
618	655
619	656
620	657
621	658
"	2143
"	3314
"	4336
622	660
623	661
624	662
625	663
626	664
627	665
628	666
629	667
630	668
631	669
632	671
633	672
634	674
635	675
636	676
637	677
638	678
639	679
640	680
641	681
642	682
643	683
"	2171
644	684
645	685
646	686
647	687
648	689
649	690
"	1852
650	691
"	935
651	692
652	693
653	694
654	695
655	696
656	697
657	698
658	699
659	700
660	701
661	702
662	703
663	704
664	705
665	706
666	707
667	708
668	709
669	710
670	711
671	712
672	713
673	714
674	715
675	716
676	717
677	718
678	719
679	720
680	721
681	721
"	4312
682	722
683	723
684	724
685	725
686	726
687	727
688	728
689	98
"	730
"	763
690	732
691	733
692	734
693	735
"	739
694	736
695	737
696	738
697	740
"	4076
698	741
699	742
700	743
701	744
702	745
703	746
704	748
705	749
706	750
707	751
708	752
709	753
710	754
711	755
712	756
713	757
714	758
715	759
"	760
716	761
717	762
"	3403
718	764
719	765
720	766
721	768
722	769
723	770
724	771
725	772
726	773
727	774
728	775
729	731
730	776
"	781
731	777
732	778
"	779
733	780
734	782
735	783
736	784
737	785
738	786
739	787
740	788
741	789
742	790
743	791
744	792
745	793
746	794
747	795
748	796
749	797
750	799
751	800
752	801
753	802
754	803
755	804
756	806
757	806
758	807
759	808
760	809
"	811
761	810
762	812
763	813
764	814
765	815
766	816
767	817
768	818
769	819
770	820
771	821
772	822
773	823
774	824
775	825
776	826
777	827
778	828
779	829
780	830
781	831
782	571
"	832
783	833
784	834
"	5646
785	835
786	836
787	837
788	839
789	840
790	841
791	842
792	843
793	844
794	845
795	846
796	847
797	848
798	849
799	850
800	851
801	852
802	853
803	854
804	855
805	856
806	857
807	858
"	2360
808	859
809	860
810	861
811	862
812	863
813	864
814	865
815	866
816	867
817	868
818	869
"	870
819	871
820	872
821	873
822	874
823	875
824	876
825	877
826	878
"	2964
827	879
828	880
829	881
830	882
831	883
832	884
833	885
834	886
835	887
836	888
837	889
"	891
"	3824
838	890
839	892
840	893
841	894
842	895
843	896
844	897
845	898
846	899
847	898
848	898
849	901
850	903
851	904
852	905
853	906
854	907
855	908
856	909
"	4060
857	910
858	911
859	912
860	913
861	914
862	915
863	918
"	1889
864	919
865	920
866	921
867	922
868	923
869	924
870	925
871	926
872	927
873	928
874	929
875	930
876	931
877	932
878	933
879	934
880	936
"	305
881	937
"	941
882	938
883	939
884	940
885	943
886	942
887	944
888	945
889	946
890	947
891	948
892	949
893	950
894	951
"	952
895	953
896	955
897	956
898	957
899	958
900	959
901	960
902	961
903	962
904	963
905	964
906	965
907	966
908	967
909	968
910	969
911	970
"	4817
912	972
913	973
914	974
915	975
916	976
917	977
918	978
919	979
920	971
"	980
"	981
921	982
922	983
923	984
924	985
925	986
"	2852
926	987
927	988
928	989
929	990
930	991
931	992
932	993
933	994
934	994
935	995
936	996
937	997
"	998
938	999
939	1000
940	1001
941	1002
942	1003
943	1004
"	2742
"	2744
944	1005
945	1006
946	1007
947	1008
948	1009
949	1010
950	1011
951	1012
952	1013
953	1014
954	1015
955	1016
956	1018
957	1019
958	1020
"	1021
959	1022
960	1023
961	1024
962	1028
"	1030
963	1029
964	1031
"	1032
965	1033
966	1034
"	1035
967	1036
968	1037
969	1039
970	1040
971	1041
972	1042
973	1043
974	1044
"	1045
975	1046
976	1047
977	1048
978	1049
979	1050
980	1051
981	1052
982	1053
983	1054
984	1055
985	1056
"	1057
986	1058
987	1059
"	1555
988	1060
989	1061
990	1062
991	1063
992	1064
993	1065
994	1066
995	1068
996	1069
997	1070
998	1071
999	1072
"	1073
1000	1074
1001	1075
1002	1076
1003	1067
"	1077
"	1078
1004	1079
1005	1080
1006	1081
1007	1026
"	1027
"	1082
1008	1083
1009	1084
1010	1085
1011	1086
1012	1087
1013	1088
1014	1089
1015	1090
1016	1091
1017	1092
1018	1093
1019	1094
1020	1095
1021	1096
1022	1097
1023	1098
1024	1099
1025	1100
1026	1101
1027	1103
1028	1104
1029	1105
1030	1106
1031	1107
1032	1108
1033	1109
1034	1110
1035	1111
1036	1112
1037	1113
1038	1114
1039	1115
"	3327
1040	1116
1041	1117
1042	1119
1043	1120
1044	1121
1045	1122
1046	1123
1047	1125
1048	1124
1049	1126
1050	1127
1051	1128
1052	1129
1053	1130
"	1135
1054	1131
1055	1132
1056	1133
1057	1134
1058	1136
1059	1137
1060	1138
1061	1139
"	1140
1062	1141
1063	1142
1064	1143
1065	1145
1066	1146
1067	1147
1068	1148
"	1149
1069	1150
1070	1151
1071	1152
1072	1153
1073	1154
1074	1155
1075	1156
1076	1157
1077	1158
"	1159
"	1160
1078	1161
1079	1162
1080	1164
1081	1163
"	1165
1082	1166
1083	1167
1084	1168
1085	1169
1086	1170
"	1171
1087	1172
1088	1173
1089	1174

STRONG	G/K
1090	1175
1091	1176
1092	1177
1093	1178
1094	1179
1095	1180
1096	1181
1097	1182
1098	1183
1099	1184
1100	1185
1101	1186
1102	1187
1103	1188
1104	1189
1105	1190
1106	1191
1107	1192
1108	1194
1109	1195
1110	1193
"	1196
1111	1197
1112	1198
1113	1199
1114	1200
1115	1201
1116	1202
1117	1203
1118	1204
1119	1205
1120	1206
1121	1207
1122	1208
1123	1209
1124	1210
1125	1211
"	2863
1126	1212
1127	1213
1128	1214
1129	1215
1130	1216
"	1217
1131	1218
1132	1219
1133	1220
1134	1221
1135	1222
1136	1223
1137	1224
1138	1226
"	1253
1139	1227
1140	1228
1141	1229
1142	1230
1143	1231
1144	1232
1145	1233
1146	1234
1147	1235
1148	1236
1149	1237
1150	1238
1151	1239
1152	1240
1153	1241
1154	1242
1155	1244
"	1247
1156	1245
"	1249
1157	1246
"	1250
1158	1248
1159	1251
1160	1252
1161	1254
1162	1255
1163	1256
1164	1257
1165	1258
1166	1259
"	1260
1167	1261
1168	1262
1169	1264
1170	1265
1171	1267
1172	1268
1173	1270
"	1271
1174	1273
1175	1272
1176	1274
1177	1275
1178	1278
1179	1279
1180	1280
1181	1281
1182	1281
1183	1282
1184	1283
1185	1284
1186	1285
1187	1286
"	1287
1188	1288
1189	1289
1190	1291
"	1523
1191	1292
1192	1293
1193	1294
1194	1296
1195	1297
1196	1298
1197	1299
1198	1300
1199	1301
1200	1302
1201	1303
1202	1304
1203	1305
1204	1306
1205	1307
1206	1308
1207	1310
1208	1309
"	1311
1209	1312
1210	1313
1211	1314
1212	1316
1213	1317
1214	1318
1215	1319
1216	1320
1217	1321
1218	1322
1219	1323
1220	1324
1221	1325
1222	1327
1223	1328
1224	1329
1225	1330
1226	1331
1227	1332
1228	1333
1229	1334
1230	1335
1231	1336
1232	1337
1233	1338
1234	1339
1235	1340
1236	1341
1237	1342
1238	1343
1239	1344
1240	1345
1241	1346
1242	1347
1243	1348
1244	1349
1245	1350
"	1351
1246	1352
1247	1354
1248	1355
"	1566
1249	1356
1250	1357
1251	1358
1252	1359
1253	1360
1254	1361
1255	1362
1256	1363
1257	1364
1258	1365
1259	1367
1260	1368
1261	1369
1262	1370
1263	1371
1264	1372
1265	1373
1266	1374
1267	1375
1268	1376
1269	1377
1270	1378
1271	1379
1272	1380
1273	1381
1274	1382
1275	1383
1276	1385
1277	1386
1278	1387
1279	1388
1280	1389
1281	1390
1282	1391
1283	1395
1284	1392
"	1393
"	1396
1285	1397
1286	1398
1287	1399
1288	1400
1289	1401
1290	1402
1291	1403
1292	1404
1293	1405
1294	1406
1295	1407
1296	1408
1297	1409
1298	1410
1299	1411
1300	1412
1301	1413
1302	1414
1303	1415
"	1416
1304	1417
1305	1418
1306	1419
1307	1420
"	1421
1308	1422
1309	1423
1310	1424
"	5775
1311	1425
1312	1426
1313	1427
1314	1428
1315	1429
1316	1431
1317	1434
1318	1435
1319	1436
1320	1437
1321	1438
1322	1439
1323	1440
1324	1441
1325	1442
"	1443
1326	1444
1327	1447
1328	1449
"	2256
1329	1450
1330	1451
1331	1452
1332	1453
1333	1454
1334	1455
1335	1456
1336	1457
1337	1458
1338	1459
1339	1460
1340	1462
1341	1464
1342	1465
1343	1466
1344	1467
1345	1468
1346	1469
1347	1470
1348	1471
1349	1472
"	2869
1350	1473
1351	1474
1352	1475
1353	1476
1354	1477
1355	1478
1356	1479
1357	1481
1358	1482
1359	1483
1360	1484
1361	1485
1362	1486
"	1487
1363	1488
1364	1489
1365	1491
1366	1492
1367	1493
1368	1494
1369	1495
1370	1496
1371	1497
1372	1498
1373	1499
1374	1500
1375	1501
1376	1502
1377	1503
1378	1504
1379	1505
1380	1506
1381	1507
"	1508
1382	1509
1383	1510
1384	1511
1385	1512
1386	1513
1387	1514
1388	1515
1389	1516
1390	1517
1391	1518
1392	1519
1393	1520
1394	1521
1395	1522
1396	1524
1397	1525
1398	1526
1399	1527
1400	1528
1401	1528
"	1529
1402	1530
1403	1531
1404	1532
1405	1533
1406	1534
1407	1535
1408	1536
1409	1537
1410	1538
1411	1539
1412	1540
1413	1541
1414	1542
1415	1543
1416	1544
1417	1545
1418	
1419	1546
1420	1547
"	1548
1421	1549
1422	1551
1423	1552
1424	1553
1425	1554
1426	1556
1427	1557
1428	1558
1429	1559
1430	1560
1431	1561
1432	1562
1433	1563
1434	1564
1435	1565
1436	1568
1437	1569
1438	1571
1439	1572
1440	1573
1441	1574
1442	1575
1443	1576
1444	1577
1445	1578
1446	1579
1447	1580
1448	1581
1449	1582
1450	1583
1451	1584
1452	1585
1453	1586
1454	1587
1455	1588
1456	1589
1457	1590
1458	1592
1459	1593
1460	1594
1461	1596
1462	1598
1463	1599
1464	1600
"	1715
1465	1601
1466	1602
1467	1603
1468	1604
1469	1605
1470	1606
1471	1607
1472	1608
1473	1609
1474	1610
1475	1611
1476	1612
1477	1613
1478	1614
1479	1615
1480	1616
1481	1617
1482	1618
1483	1619
1484	1620
1485	1621
1486	1622
"	1665
1487	1623
1488	1639
1489	1623+1145
1490	1623+1254 +3590+1145
1491	1626
1492	3857
1493	1627
1494	1628
"	2638
1495	1630
1496	1629
1497	1631
1498	1639
1499	1623+2779
1500	1632
1501	1633
1502	1634
1503	2036
1504	1635
1505	1636
1506	1637
1507	1813
1508	1623+3590
1509	1623 +3590+5516
1510	1639
1511	1639
1512	1642
1513	1643
1514	1644
1515	1645
1516	1646
1517	1647
1518	1648
1519	1650
1520	1651
1521	1652
1522	1653
1523	1654
1524	1655
1525	1656
1526	1639
1527	1651+2848
1528	1657
1529	1658
1530	1659
"	1737
1531	1660
1532	1661
1533	1662
1534	1663
1535	1664
1536	1623+5516
1537	1666
1538	1667
1539	1668
1540	1669
1541	1670
1542	1671
1543	1672
"	1673
1544	1675
1545	1676
1546	1678
1547	1679
1548	1680
1549	1681
1550	1682
1551	1683
1552	1684
1553	1685
1554	1686
1555	1687
1556	1688
1557	1689
1558	1690
1559	1691
1560	1692
1561	1693
1562	1694
1563	1695
1564	1696
1565	1697
1566	1698
1567	1699
1568	1701
1569	1702
1570	1704
1571	1705
1572	1706
1573	1591
"	1707
1574	1708
1575	1709
1576	1710
1577	1711
1578	1712
1579	1713
1580	1714
1581	1716
1582	1717
1583	1718
1584	1719
1585	1720
1586	1721
1587	1722
1588	1723
1589	1724
1590	1725
1591	1726
1592	1727
1593	1728
1594	1729
1595	1730
1596	1731
1597	1732
1598	1733
1599	1734
1600	1736
1601	1738
1602	1739
1603	1740
1604	1741
1605	1742
1606	1743
1607	1744
1608	1745
1609	1746
1610	1748
1611	1749
1612	1750
1613	1752
1614	1753
1615	1754
1616	1755
1617	1757
1618	1756
1619	1757
1620	1758
1621	1759
1622	1760
1623	1761
1624	1762
1625	1763
1626	1765
1627	1766
1628	1767
1629	1768
1630	1769
1631	1770
1632	1772
"	1773
1633	1774
1634	1775
1635	1776
1636	1777
1637	1778
1638	1779
1639	1780
1640	1781
"	1784
1641	1782
1642	1783
1643	1785
1644	1786
1645	1787
1646	1788
1647	1788
1648	1789
1649	1792
1650	1791
"	1793
1651	1794
1652	1795
1653	1790
"	1796
1654	1797
1655	1798
1656	1799
1657	1800
1658	1801
1659	1802
1660	1803
1661	1804
1662	1805
"	1806
1663	1808
1664	1809
1665	1810
1666	1811
"	1812
1667	1813
1668	1814
1669	1815
1670	1816
1671	1817
1672	1818
1673	1819
1674	1820
1675	1821
1676	1822
1677	1823
"	1824
1678	1825
"	1826
1679	1827
1680	1828
1681	1829
"	2287
1682	1830
1683	1831
1684	1832
1685	1833
1686	1834
"	1835
1687	1836
1688	1837
1689	1838
1690	1102
"	1839
1691	1609
1692	1840
1693	1841
1694	1842
1695	1843
"	4035
1696	1844
1697	1846
1698	1609
1699	1847
1700	1609
1701	1849
1702	1850
1703	1851
1704	1853
1705	1854
"	1855
"	1857
"	1858
1706	1860
1707	1861
1708	1862
"	4451
1709	1863
1710	1864
1711	1865
1712	1866
1713	1867
1714	1856
"	1859
"	1868
1715	1869
1716	1870
1717	1871
1718	1872
1719	1873
1720	1874
1721	1875
1722	1877
1723	1878
1724	1879
1725	1882
1726	1883
1727	1885
1728	1887
1729	1890
1730	1891
1731	1892
1732	1893
1733	1894
1734	1895
1735	1896
1736	1897
1737	1898
1738	1899
1739	1900
"	1908
1740	1901
1741	1902
1742	1903
1743	1904
1744	1905
1745	1906
1746	1907
1747	1909
1748	1910
1749	1911
1750	1912
1751	1913
1752	1641
"	1914
"	1915
1753	1918
1754	1919
1755	1920
1756	1886
"	1921
1757	1922
1758	1923
1759	1924
1760	1445
"	1926
1761	1927
1762	1928
1763	1929
1764	1931
1765	1932
1766	1888
1767	1933
1768	1916
1769	1917
"	1934
1770	1935
1771	1936
1772	1937
1773	1939
1774	1940
1775	1942
1776	1943
1777	1944
1778	1945
1779	1946
1780	1947
1781	1353
"	1948
1782	1925
"	1949
1783	1950
1784	1952
1785	1953
1786	1954
1787	1955
1788	1956
1789	1957
1790	1764
"	1958
1791	1959
1792	1960
1793	1961
1794	1962
1795	1963
1796	1964
1797	1965
1798	1966
1799	1967
1800	1968
1801	1969
1802	1970
1803	1971
1804	1972
1805	1973
1806	1974
1807	1975
1808	1976
1809	1977
1810	1978
"	2005
1811	1979
1812	1980
1813	1981
1814	1982
1815	1983
1816	1677
"	1984
1817	1985
1818	1987
1819	1988
1820	1989
1821	1990
1822	1992
1823	1993
1824	1994
1825	1995
1826	1996
1827	1998
1828	1999
1829	2000
1830	2001
1831	2002
"	1446
"	1674
1832	1997
"	2003
1833	2004
1834	2007
1835	2008
1836	2009
1837	2010
1838	2011
1839	2012
"	2013
"	2014
1840	2015
1841	2016
1842	2017
1843	2018
1844	2019
1845	2020
1846	2021
1847	2022
"	2023
1848	2024
"	2025
1849	2026
1850	2027
1851	2029
1852	2030
1853	2031
1854	2032
1855	2033
1856	2034
1857	2035
1858	2037
1859	2038

STRONG	G/K
1860	2039
1861	2040
1862	2041
1863	2042
1864	2043
1865	2044
1866	2045
1867	2046
1868	2047
1869	2048
1870	2049
1871	2050
1872	2051
1873	2052
1874	2053
1875	2054
1876	2055
1877	2056
1878	2057
1879	2058
1880	2059
1881	2060
1882	2061
1883	2062
1884	2064
1885	2065
"	2066
1886	2068
1887	2069
1888	900
"	2070
1889	2071
1890	576
"	2072
1891	2073
1892	2074
1893	2075
1894	2076
1895	2077
1896	2078
"	2393
1897	2080
1898	2081
1899	2083
1900	2084
1901	2085
1902	2086
1903	2087
1904	2082
"	2088
1905	2089
1906	2090
1907	2091
1908	2092
1909	2093
1910	2094
1911	2095
1912	2096
1913	2097
1914	2098
1915	2099
1916	2100
1917	2101
1918	2102
1919	2103
1920	2104
1921	2105
1922	2106
1923	2107
1924	2108
1925	2109
1926	2110
1927	2111
1928	2112
1929	2113
"	4658
1930	2114
1931	2115
1932	2116
1933	2117
1934	2118
1935	2119
1936	2120
1937	2121
1938	2122
1939	2123
1940	2125
1941	2126
1942	2127
1943	2128
1944	2063
"	2129
1945	2130
1946	2134
1947	2135
1948	2137
1949	2138
1950	2140
1951	2141
1952	2142
1953	2144
1954	2145
1955	2146
1956	2147
1957	2148
1958	2149
1959	2150
1960	2151
1961	2152
1962	2153
1963	2154
1964	2155
1965	2156
1966	2079
1967	2157
1968	2158
1969	2159
1970	
1971	2160
1972	2161
1973	2162
1974	2163
1975	2164
1976	2165
"	2193
1977	2166
1978	2168
1979	2169
1980	2170
1981	2172
1982	2173
1983	2174
1984	2175
1985	2176
1986	2177
1987	2179
1988	2181
1989	2182
1990	2184
1991	2185
1992	2186
1993	2187
1994	2188
1995	2189
1996	2190
1997	2191
1998	2192
1999	2180
"	2194
2000	2195
2001	2196
2002	2197
2003	2198
2004	2199
2005	2200
2006	2201
2007	2202
2008	2203
2009	2204
2010	2205
"	5181
2011	2207
2012	2208
2013	2209
2014	2210
2015	2211
2016	2212
2017	2213
"	2223
2018	2214
2019	2215
"	2971
2020	2216
2021	2217
2022	2219
2023	2220
2024	2221
2025	2222
2026	2224
2027	2131
"	2225
2028	2226
2029	2227
2030	2228
2031	2229
2032	2230
2033	2231
2034	2232
2035	2233
2036	3306
2037	2235
2038	2237
2039	2238
2040	2239
2041	2240
2042	2241
2043	2242
2044	2243
2045	2236
2046	3306
2047	2244
2048	2245
2049	2246
2050	2247
2051	2248
2052	2249
2053	2250
2054	2251
2055	2252
2056	144
"	2253
2057	2254
2058	1448
"	2255
2059	2257
2060	2258
2061	2259
2062	2260
2063	2261
2064	2262
2065	2263
2066	2264
2067	2265
2068	2266
"	2267
2069	2268
2070	1639
2071	1639
2072	2269
2073	2270
2074	2272
2075	1639
2076	1639
2077	1639
2078	2274
2079	2275
2080	2276
2081	2277
2082	2278
2083	2279
2084	2280
2085	2281
2086	2282
2087	255
"	2283
2088	2284
2089	2285
2090	2286
2091	2288
2092	2289
2093	2290
2094	2291
2095	2292
"	2301
2096	2293
2097	2294
2098	2295
2099	2296
2100	2297
2101	2298
2102	2299
2103	2300
2104	2302
2105	2304
2106	2305
2107	2306
2108	2307
2109	2308
2110	2309
2111	2310
2112	2311
2113	2312
2114	2313
2115	2314
"	2315
2116	2316
2117	2317
"	2318
2118	2319
2119	2320
2120	2321
2121	2322
2122	2323
2123	2324
2124	2325
2125	2326
2126	2327
2127	2328
"	2986
2128	2329
2129	2303
"	2330
2130	2331
2131	2332
2132	2333
2133	2334
2134	2335
2135	2336
2136	2337
2137	2338
2138	2340
2139	2341
"	2342
2140	2343
2141	2344
2142	2345
2143	2346
2144	2347
2145	2339
"	2348
2146	2349
2147	2351
2148	2350
"	2352
2149	2353
2150	2354
2151	2355
2152	2356
2153	2357
2154	2358
2155	2359
2156	2361
2157	2362
2158	2363
2159	2364
2160	2365
2161	2366
2162	2367
2163	2368
2164	2369
2165	2370
2166	2371
2167	2372
2168	2373
2169	2374
2170	2375
2171	2376
2172	2377
2173	2378
2174	2379
2175	2380
2176	2381
2177	1880
"	2383
2178	2384
2179	2385
2180	2386
2181	2387
2182	2388
2183	2389
2184	2390
2185	2391
2186	2392
2187	2394
2188	2395
2189	2397
2190	2398
2191	2399
2192	2400
2193	2401
2194	2404
2195	2405
2196	2406
2197	2408
2198	2409
2199	2411
2200	2412
2201	2414
2202	2415
2203	2416
2204	2417
2205	2419
2206	2418
"	2420
2207	2421
2208	2421
2209	2422
2210	2423
2211	2424
2212	2426
2213	2427
2214	1700
"	2428
2215	2429
2216	2431
2217	2432
2218	2433
2219	2434
2220	2435
2221	2436
2222	2437
2223	2438
2224	2439
"	2440
2225	2441
2226	2442
2227	2443
2228	2445
2229	2446
2230	2448
2231	2449
2232	2450
2233	2206
"	2451
2234	2452
2235	2453
2236	2452
2237	2454
2238	2455
2239	2456
2240	2457
2241	2458
2242	2459
2243	2460
2244	2461
2245	2462
2246	2463
2247	2464
2248	1609
2249	1609
2250	2465
2251	2466
2252	1639
2253	2467
2254	1609
2255	2468
2256	2469
"	2470
2257	1609
2258	1639
2259	2471
2260	2472
2261	2473
2262	2474
2263	2475
2264	2476
2265	2477
2266	2478
2267	2479
2268	2480
2269	2481
2270	2483
2271	2484
2272	2485
2273	2486
2274	2273
"	2487
2275	2488
2276	2482
"	2489
2277	1639
2278	2490
2279	2491
"	2492
"	2493
2280	2497
2281	2498
2282	2499
2283	2500
2284	2501
2285	2502
2286	2503
2287	2504
2288	2505
2289	2506
2290	2507
2291	2508
2292	2509
2293	2510
2294	2511
2295	2512
2296	1703
"	2513
2297	2514
2298	2515
2299	2516
2300	2517
2301	2518
2302	2519
2303	2520
2304	2521
2305	2522
2306	2523
2307	2525
2308	2526
2309	2527
2310	2528
"	2529
2311	2530
2312	2531
2312'	2532
2313	2533
2314	2534
2315	2535
2316	2536
2317	2537
2318	2538
2319	2539
2320	2540
2321	2541
2322	2542
"	3859
2323	2543
2324	2544
2325	2545
2326	2546
2327	2547
2328	2548
2329	2549
2330	2550
2331	2552
2332	2553
2333	2554
2334	2555
2335	2556
2336	2557
2337	2558
2338	2559
2339	2560
2340	2561
2341	2562
2342	2563
2343	2564
2344	2565
2345	2566
2346	2567
2347	2568
2348	2569
2349	2570
2350	2572
2351	2573
2352	2574
"	2575
2353	2576
2354	2577
2355	2578
2356	2579
2357	2580
2358	2581
2359	1295
"	2582
2360	2583
2361	2584
2362	2585
2363	2587
2364	2588
2365	2589
2366	2590
2367	2591
2368	2592
2369	2593
2370	2594
2371	2595
2372	2596
2373	2597
2374	2598
2375	2599
2376	2600
2377	2601
2378	2602
2379	2603
2380	2124
"	2604
2381	2605
2382	2606
2383	2608
2384	2609
2385	2610
2386	2611
2387	2612
2388	2613
2389	2614
2390	2615
2391	2616
2392	2617
2393	2618
2394	2619
2395	2620
2396	2623
2397	1624
"	2624
2398	2625
2399	2626
2400	2627
2401	2628
2402	2629
2403	2630
2404	2631
2405	2632
2406	2633
2407	2634
2408	2635
2409	2636
2410	2637
2411	2639
2412	2640
2413	2641
2414	2642
2415	2643
2416	2644
2417	2645
2418	2646
2419	2647
2420	2648
2421	2649
2422	2650
2423	2651
2424	2652
2425	2653
2426	2654
2427	2655
2428	2656
2429	2657
2430	2658
2431	2659
2432	2660
2433	2661
2434	2662
2435	2663
2436	2664
2437	2665
2438	2666
2439	2667
2440	2668
2441	2669
2442	2670
"	3916
2443	2671
2444	2672
2445	2673
2446	2674
2447	2675
2448	2676
2449	2677
2450	2678
2451	2679
2452	2680
2453	2681
2454	2682
2455	2683
"	2726
2456	549
"	2684
"	2686
2457	2685
2458	2687
2459	2688
"	5517
2460	2689
2461	2690
2462	2691
2463	2692
2464	2693
2465	2694
2466	2695
"	2704
2467	
2468	1639
2469	2696
"	2697
"	5000
"	5001
2470	2698
2471	2699
2472	2700
2473	2701
2474	2702
2475	2703
2476	2705
2477	2707
2478	2708
2479	2709
2480	2710
2481	2711
2482	2712
2483	2713
2484	2714
2485	2715
2486	2716
2487	2717
2488	2718
2489	2720
"	2721
2490	2722
2491	2722
"	2728
2492	2724
2493	2727
2494	2729
"	2730
2495	2731
2496	2732
2497	2733
2498	2734
2499	2735
2500	2736
2501	2737
"	2738
2502	2739
2503	2740
2504	2743
2505	2745
2506	2746
2507	2747
2508	2748
2509	2749
"	2778
2510	2750
2511	2751
"	2760
2512	2752
2513	2754
2514	2755
2515	2756
2516	2757
2517	2759
2518	2761
2519	2762
2520	2763
2521	2764
2522	2766
2523	2767
2524	2768
2525	2769
"	2770
2526	2771
2526'	2772
2527	2773
2528	2774
2529	2775
2530	2776
2531	2777
2532	2779
2533	2780
2534	2781
2535	2782
2536	2783
"	2784
2537	2785
2538	2786
2539	2788
2540	2789
2541	2790
2542	2791
2543	2792
2544	2793
2545	2794
2546	2795
2547	2796
2548	2797
2549	2798
2550	2799
2551	2800
2552	2801
"	2817
2553	2802
2554	2803
2555	2804
2556	2805
2557	2806
2558	2807
2559	2808
2560	2809
2561	2810
2562	2811
2563	2812
2564	2813
2565	2814
2566	2819
2567	2815
2568	2816
2569	2818
2570	2819
2571	2820
2572	2821
2573	2822
2574	2823
"	2824
2575	2825
2576	2826
2577	2827
2578	2828
2579	2829
2580	2830
2581	2831
"	2832
2582	2833
2583	2834
2584	2835
"	3019
2585	2836
2586	2837
2587	2838
2588	2840
2589	2841
2590	2843
2591	2842
2592	2844
2593	2845
2594	2846
2595	2847
2596	2848
2597	2849
2598	2850
2599	2851
2600	2853
2601	2854
2602	2856
2603	2857
2604	2858
2605	2859
2606	2860
2607	2861
2608	2862
2609	2864
2610	2865
2611	2866
2612	2867
2613	1463
"	2868
2614	2870
2615	2871
2616	2872
2617	2875
2618	2876
2619	2877
2620	1595
"	2878
2621	2879
2622	2880
2623	1597
"	2881
2624	2882
"	2883
2625	2884
2626	2885
2627	2886
2628	2887
2629	2888
2630	2889

STRONG	G/K
2631	2890
2632	2891
2633	2892
2634	2894
2635	2895
2636	2896
2637	2897
2638	2898
2639	2899
2640	2900
"	5698
2641	2901
2642	2902
2643	2903
2644	2904
2645	2905
2646	2906
2647	2907
2648	2908
2649	2909
2650	2910
2651	2911
2652	2873
"	2912
2653	2874
"	2913
2654	2914
2655	2915
2656	2916
2657	2917
2658	2918
2659	2919
2660	2920
2661	2921
2662	2922
2663	2923
2664	2924
2665	2925
2666	2927
2667	2928
2668	2929
2669	2930
2670	2931
2671	2932
2672	2933
2673	2934
2674	2935
2675	2936
2676	2937
2677	2938
2678	2939
2679	2940
2680	2941
2681	2942
2682	2943
2683	2944
2684	2945
2685	2946
2686	2947
2687	2948
2688	2949
2689	2950
2690	2951
2691	2952
2692	2953
2693	2954
2694	2955
2695	2956
"	2957
2696	2958
2697	2959
2698	2960
2699	2961
2700	2962
2701	2963
2702	2965
2703	2966
2704	2967
2705	2968
2706	2969
2707	2970
2708	2972
2709	2973
2710	2974
"	4201
2711	2976
2712	2977
2713	2978
2714	2979
2715	2980
2716	2981
[2717 Omitted by Strong]	
2718	2982
2719	2983
"	2984
2720	2985
2721	2987
2722	2988
2723	2989
2724	2990
2725	2991
"	2992
2726	2993
2727	2994
2728	2995
2729	2996
2730	2997
"	3001
2731	2998
2732	2999
2733	3000
2734	3002
2735	1480
"	3003
2736	3004
"	3006
2737	3005
2738	3008
2739	3009
"	3010
2740	3011
2741	3012
2742	3014
2743	3013
"	3015
2744	3016
2745	3017
2746	3018
2747	3020
2748	3021
"	3022
2749	3023
2750	3024
2751	3025
2752	3026
2753	3027
2754	3029
2755	3030
2756	3031
2757	2787
"	3032
2758	3033
2759	3034
2760	3035
2761	3036
2762	3037
2763	3038
2764	3039
2765	3040
2766	3041
2767	3042
2768	3043
2769	3044
2770	2132
"	3045
2771	3046
2772	3047
2773	3048
2774	3049
2775	3050
"	3052
2776	3051
2777	3053
2778	2133
"	3056
2779	3057
2780	3058
2781	3059
2782	3060
2783	3061
2784	3062
2785	3063
2786	3064
2787	3066
2788	3067
2789	3068
2790	3069
2791	3070
"	3071
2792	3072
"	3077
2793	3073
2794	3074
2795	3075
2796	3076
2797	3078
2798	3080
2799	3081
2800	3082
2801	3083
2802	1144
"	3007
"	3084
"	3085
2803	3086
2804	3087
2805	3088
2806	3089
2807	3090
2808	3091
2809	3092
2810	3093
2811	3094
2812	3095
2813	3096
2814	3097
2815	3098
2816	3099
2817	3100
2818	3101
2819	3102
2820	3103
2821	3104
2822	3105
2823	3106
2824	3107
2825	3108
"	3109
2826	3110
2827	3111
2828	3112
2829	3113
2830	3114
2831	3115
2832	3116
2833	3117
2834	3118
2835	3119
2836	3120
2837	3121
2838	3122
2839	3123
2840	3124
2841	3125
2842	3126
2843	3127
2844	3128
2845	3130
2846	3131
2847	3132
2848	3133
2849	3134
2850	3135
2851	3136
2852	3139
2853	3140
2854	3141
2855	3142
2856	3143
2857	3138
"	3145
2858	3137
"	3144
2859	3146
2860	3147
2861	3148
2862	3149
2863	3150
2864	3151
2865	3152
2866	3153
2867	3154
2868	3155
2869	3156
2870	3157
2871	3158
2872	3159
2873	3160
2874	3161
"	3162
"	3163
2875	3164
2876	3165
2877	3166
2878	3167
"	3168
2879	3169
2880	3170
2881	3171
2882	3172
2883	3173
2884	3174
2885	3175
2886	3176
2887	3177
"	3178
2888	3179
2889	3180
2890	3181
2891	3182
"	3183
2892	3184
2893	3185
2894	3186
2895	3187
"	3188
2896	3189
2897	3190
2898	3191
2899	3192
2900	3193
2901	3194
2902	3195
2903	3196
2904	3197
2905	3198
2906	3199
2907	3200
2908	3201
2909	3202
2910	3203
2911	3204
2912	3205
2913	3206
2914	3207
2915	3208
2916	3209
2917	3210
2918	3211
2919	3212
2920	3213
2921	3214
2922	3215
2923	3216
2924	3217
2925	3218
2926	3219
2927	3220
"	3224
"	3226
2928	3221
2929	3222
2930	3223
2931	3225
2932	3227
2933	3228
2934	3229
2935	3230
2936	3231
2937	3232
2938	3233
2939	3234
2940	3235
2941	3236
2942	3237
2943	3239
2944	3238
"	3240
2945	3241
2946	3242
"	3243
2947	3244
2948	3245
2949	3246
2950	3247
2951	3248
2952	3249
2953	3250
2954	3251
2955	3252
2956	3253
"	3254
2957	3255
2958	3256
"	3260
2959	3257
2960	3258
2961	3259
2962	3261
2963	3262
2964	3263
2965	3264
2966	3265
2967	3266
2968	3267
2969	3268
2970	3269
2971	3270
2972	3271
2973	3272
2974	3273
2975	3275
2976	3276
2977	3277
"	4996
2978	3278
2979	3280
2980	654
"	3281
2981	3282
2982	3283
"	3316
2983	3284
2984	3285
2985	3286
"	5697
2986	3287
2987	3288
2988	3289
2989	2139
"	3290
2990	3291
2991	3292
2992	3295
2993	3293
2994	3294
2995	3296
2996	3297
"	3298
2997	3279
"	3299
2998	3300
2999	3301
3000	3302
3001	3303
3002	3304
3003	3305
3004	1649
"	3306
3005	3307
3006	3308
3007	3309
3008	3310
3009	3311
3010	3312
3011	3313
3012	3317
3013	3318
3014	3319
3015	3320
3016	3321
3017	3322
3018	3323
3019	3324
3020	3325
3021	3326
3022	3328
3023	3329
3024	3330
3025	3332
3026	3333
3027	798
"	3334
3028	3331
"	3335
3029	3336
3030	3337
3031	3338
3032	3339
"	3341
3033	3340
3034	3342
3035	3343
3036	3344
3037	3345
3038	3346
3039	3347
3040	3348
3041	3349
3042	3350
3043	3351
3044	3352
3045	3353
3046	3354
3047	3355
3048	3356
3049	3357
3050	3358
3051	3359
3052	3360
3053	3361
3054	3362
3055	3363
3056	3364
3057	3365
3058	3366
3059	3367
3060	3368
3061	3369
3062	3370
3063	3370
3064	3370
3065	3371
3066	3372
3067	3373
3068	3374
3069	3375
3070	3376
3071	3377
3072	3378
3073	3379
3074	3380
3075	3381
3076	3382
3077	3383
3078	3384
3079	3385
3080	3386
3081	3387
3082	3388
3083	3389
3084	3390
3085	3391
3086	3392
3087	3393
3088	3394
3089	3395
3090	3396
3091	3397
3092	3399
3093	3400
"	3401
3094	3402
3095	3404
"	3406
3096	3405
3097	3407
3098	3408
3099	3409
3100	3411
3101	3412
3102	3413
3103	3417
3104	3418
"	3526
3105	3419
3106	3420
3107	3421
3108	3422
3109	3423
3110	3424
3111	3425
3112	3426
3113	3427
3114	3428
3115	3429
3116	3430
3117	3431
3118	3432
3119	3433
3120	3434
3121	3435
3122	3436
3123	3437
3124	3438
3125	3439
3126	3440
3127	3441
3128	3442
3129	3443
3130	3444
3131	3445
3132	3446
3133	3447
3134	2495
"	3448
3135	3449
3136	3450
3137	3451
"	3452
3138	3453
3139	3454
3140	3455
3141	3456
3142	3457
3143	3458
3144	3459
"	4753
3145	3460
"	3462
3146	3463
3147	3464
3148	3465
3149	3461
"	3461
"	3466
3150	3467
3151	3468
3152	3469
3153	3470
3154	3471
3155	3472
3156	3414
"	3473
3157	3474
3158	3415
"	3475
3159	3416
"	3476
3160	3477
3161	3478
3162	3479
3163	3480
3164	3481
3165	1609
3166	902
"	3482
3167	3483
3168	3484
3169	3485
3170	3486
3171	3487
3172	3488
3173	3489
3174	3490
3175	3491
3176	3492
3177	3493
3178	3494
3179	3495
"	3496
3180	3497
3181	3498
3182	3499
3183	3500
3184	3501
3185	3505
3186	3504
3187	3505
3188	3506
3189	3506
3190	3507
3191	3509
3192	3510
3193	3511
"	3512
"	3513
3194	3514
"	3515
3195	3516
3196	3517
3197	3518
3198	3519
3199	3508
"	3520
3200	3521
3201	3522
3202	3523
[3202 to 3304 Omitted by Strong]	
3303	3525
3304	3528
"	3529
3305	3530
3306	3531
3307	3532
3308	3533
3309	3534
3310	3535
3311	3536
3312	3537
3313	3538
3314	3540
3315	3541
3316	3542
3317	3543
3318	3544
3319	3545
3320	3546
3321	3547
3322	3539
"	3548
3323	3549
3324	3550
3325	3551
3326	3552
3327	3553
3328	3554
3329	3555
3330	3556
3331	3557
3332	3558
3333	3559
3334	3560
3335	3561
3336	3562
3337	3563
3338	3564
3339	3565
3340	3566
3341	3567
3342	3568
3343	3569
3344	3570
"	3573
3345	3571
3346	3572
3347	3575
3348	3576
3349	3577
3350	3578
3351	3579
3352	3580
3353	3581
3354	3582
3355	3583
3356	3584
3357	3585
3358	3586
3359	3587
3360	3588
"	3589
3361	3590
3362	1569+3590
3363	2671+3590
3364	4024+3590
3365	3592
"	3598
3366	3593
3367	3594
"	3599
3368	3595
3369	3596
3370	3597
3371	3600
3372	3601
3373	3602
3374	3603
3375	3604
3376	3605
3377	3606
3378	3590+4024
3379	3607
3380	3609
3381	3610
3382	3611
3383	3612
3384	3613
3385	3614
3386	3615
3387	3614
3388	3616
3389	3617
"	3618
3390	3619
3391	1651
3392	3620
3393	3621
3394	3622
3395	1807
"	3623
"	5041
"	5042
3396	3502
"	3503
"	3624
3397	3625
3398	3625
3399	3626
3400	3627
3401	3628
3402	3629
3403	3630
3404	3631
3405	3632
3406	3633
3407	3634
3408	3635
3409	3636
3410	3637
3411	3638
3412	3639
3413	3640
3414	3641
3415	3642
3416	3643
3417	3644
3418	3645
3419	3646
3420	3647
3421	3648
3422	3649
3423	3650
3424	3651
"	3652
3425	3653
3426	3654
3427	1609
3428	3655
3429	3656
3430	3657
3431	3658
3432	3659
3433	3660
3434	3661
3435	3662
3436	3663
3437	3524
"	3664
3438	3665
3439	3666
3440	3667
3441	3668
3442	3669
3443	3670
3444	3671
3445	3672
3446	3673
3447	3674
3448	3675
3449	3677
3450	1609
3451	3676
3452	3678
3453	3679
3454	3680
3455	3681
3456	3682
3457	3683
3458	3684
"	3685
3459	3686
3460	3688
"	3694
3461	3689
3462	3690
3463	3691
"	3692
3464	3693
3465	3695
3466	3696
3467	3697
3468	3698
3469	3699
3470	3700
3471	3701
3472	3702
3473	3703
3474	3704
3475	3705
"	3706
"	3707
3476	3709
3477	3710
3478	3711
"	3712
"	3713
"	3714
"	3715

STRONG	G/K
3479	3716
3480	3717
3481	3718
"	3719
3482	3720
3483	3721
3484	3723
3485	3724
3486	3725
3487	3726
3488	3727
3489	3728
3490	3729
3491	3730
3492	3731
3493	3732
3494	3733
3495	3734
3496	3735
"	3736
3497	3722
"	3737
3498	3738
3499	3739
3500	3740
3501	3742
3502	3743
"	3801
3503	3744
3504	3745
3505	3746
3506	3748
3507	3749
3508	3750
3509	3751
3510	3752
3511	3753
3512	3754
3513	3755
3514	3756
3515	3757
3516	3758
3517	3759
3518	3760
3519	3761
3520	3762
3521	3763
3522	3764
3523	3765
3524	3766
"	3767
3525	3768
3526	3769
3527	3770
3528	3771
3529	3772
3530	3773
3531	3774
3532	3775
3533	3776
3534	3777
3535	3778
"	3779
3536	3780
3537	3781
"	4469
3538	3782
3539	3783
3540	3784
3541	3785
3542	3786
3543	3787
3544	3788
3545	3789
3546	3790
3547	3791
3548	3792
3549	3793
3550	3794
3551	3795
3552	3796
3553	3797
3554	3798
3555	3799
3556	3800
3557	3802
3558	3803
3559	3804
3560	3805
3561	3741
"	3806
3562	3807
3563	3808
3564	3809
"	3810
3565	3811
3566	3812
3567	3813
3568	3814
3569	5422
3570	3815
3571	3816
3572	3817
3573	3818
3574	3819
3575	3820
3576	3821
3577	3822
3578	3825
3579	3826
3580	3827
3581	3828
3582	3829
3583	3830
3584	3831
3585	3832
3586	3833
3587	3834
3588	3836
3589	3837
3590	3838
3591	3839
3592	3840
3593	3841
3594	3842
3595	3843
3596	3844
3597	3845
3598	3847
3599	3848
3600	3849
3601	3850
3602	3851
3603	4005+1639
3604	3852
3605	3853
3606	3854
3607	3855
3608	3856
3609	3858
3610	3860
3611	3861
3612	3862
3613	3863
3614	3864
3615	3865
3616	3866
3617	3867
3618	3868
"	3871
3619	3869
3620	3870
3621	3872
3622	3873
3623	3874
3624	3875
3625	3876
3626	3877
"	3878
3627	3879
"	3882
3628	3880
3629	3881
3630	3884
3631	3885
3632	3886
3633	3883
"	3887
3634	3888
3635	3890
3636	3891
3637	3892
3638	3893
3639	3896
"	3897
3640	3899
3641	3900
3642	3901
3643	3902
3644	3894
"	3904
3645	3895
"	3905
3646	3906
3647	3907
3648	3908
3649	3909
3650	3910
3651	3911
3652	3912
3653	3913
3654	3914
3655	3915
3656	3917
3657	3918
3658	3919
3659	3921
3660	3922
"	3923
3661	3924
3662	3925
3663	3926
3664	3927
3665	3928
3666	3929
3667	3930
3668	3931
3669	3932
3670	3933
3671	3934
3672	3935
3673	3937
3674	3938
3675	3939
3676	3940
3677	3941
3678	3942
3679	3943
3680	3944
3681	3945
3682	3946
3683	3947
3684	3948
3685	3949
3686	3950
3687	3951
3688	3952
3689	3903
"	3953
3690	3954
3691	3955
3692	3956
3693	3957
3694	3958
"	5541
3695	3959
3696	3960
3697	3961
3698	3962
3699	3963
3700	3964
3701	3965
3702	3966
3703	3967
3704	3968
3705	3969
3706	3970
3707	3971
3708	1625
"	3972
3709	3973
3710	3974
3711	3975
3712	3976
3713	3977
3714	3978
3715	3979
3716	3980
3717	3981
3718	3982
3719	3983
3720	3984
3721	3985
3722	3986
3723	3987
3724	3988
3725	3990
3726	1941
"	3991
3727	3992
3728	3993
3729	3994
3730	3995
3731	3996
3732	3997
3733	3989
"	3998
3734	3999
3735	4001
3736	4002
3737	4003
3738	4004
3739	4005
3740	4006
3741	4008
3742	4009
3743	4010
3744	4011
3745	4012
3746	4013
3747	4014
"	4016
3748	4015
3749	4017
3750	4018
3751	4019
3752	4020
3753	4021
3754	4022
3755	4015
3756	4024
3757	4023
3758	4025
3759	4026
3760	4027
3761	4028
3762	4029
"	4032
3763	4030
3764	4031
3765	4033
3766	4034
3767	4036
3768	4037
3769	4038
3770	4039
3771	4040
3772	4041
3773	4042
3774	4043
3775	4044
3776	4045
3777	4046
3778	4047
3779	4048
3780	4049
3781	4050
3782	4051
3783	4052
3784	4053
3785	4054
3786	4055
3787	4056
3788	4057
3789	4058
3790	4059
3791	4061
3792	4062
3793	4063
3794	4065
3795	4066
3796	4067
3797	4069
3798	4068
"	4070
3799	4071
3800	4072
3801	3836+1639 +2779+2262
3802	4074
3803	4075
3804	4077
3805	4078
3806	4079
3807	4080
3808	4081
3809	4082
3810	4083
3811	4084
3812	4085
"	4088
3813	4086
3814	4087
3815	4089
3816	4090
3817	4091
3818	4092
3819	4093
3820	4094
3821	4095
3822	4096
3823	4097
3824	4098
"	4100
3825	4099
3826	4101
"	4113
3827	4102
3828	4103
3829	4104
"	4106
3830	4105
"	4107
3831	4108
3832	4109
3833	4110
3834	4111
3835	4112
3836	4115
3837	4114
"	4116
3838	4117
3839	4118
3840	4119
3841	4120
3842	4121
3843	4122
3844	4123
3845	4124
3846	4125
3847	4126
3848	688
"	4127
3849	4128
3850	4130
3851	4129
"	4131
3852	4132
3853	4133
3854	4134
3855	4135
3856	4136
3857	4137
3858	4138
3859	1384
"	4139
3860	4140
3861	4141
3862	4142
3863	4143
3864	4144
3865	4145
3866	4146
3867	4147
3868	4148
3869	4149
"	4150
3870	4151
3871	4152
3872	4153
3873	4154
3874	4155
3875	4156
3876	4157
3877	4158
3878	4159
3879	4160
3880	4161
3881	4162
3882	4163
3883	4164
3884	4165
3885	4166
"	4167
3886	4168
3887	4169
3888	4170
3889	4171
3890	4172
3891	4174
3892	4175
3893	4176
3894	4177
3895	4178
3896	4179
3897	4180
3898	4181
3899	4182
3900	4183
3901	4184
3902	4185
3903	4186
3904	4187
3905	4189
3906	4190
3907	4191
3908	4192
3909	4193
3910	4194
3911	4195
3912	4196
3913	4173
"	4197
"	4198
3914	4199
3915	4200
3916	4202
3917	4203
3918	4205
3919	4206
3920	4207
3921	4208
3922	4209
3923	4210
3924	4211
3925	4213
3926	4214
3927	4215
3928	4216
3929	4217
3930	4218
3931	4219
3932	4220
3933	4221
3934	4222
3935	4223
3936	4224
"	4225
3937	4226
3938	4227
3939	4228
3940	4229
3941	4230
3942	4231
3943	4232
3944	4233
3945	4234
3946	4235
3947	4236
3948	4237
3949	4239
3950	4240
3951	4241
3952	4242
3953	4243
3954	4244
3955	4245
3956	4246
3957	4247
3958	4248
3959	4249
3960	4250
3961	4251
3962	4635
"	4252
3963	4253
3964	4254
"	4260
3965	4255
3966	4256
3967	4257
3968	4258
3969	4259
3970	4261
3971	4262
3972	4263
3973	4264
3974	4265
3975	4266
3976	4267
3977	4268
3978	4269
3979	4270
"	4271
3980	4272
3981	4273
"	4274
"	4392
3982	2167
"	4275
3983	4277
3984	4278
3985	4279
3986	4280
3987	4281
3988	4282
3989	4283
3990	4284
3991	4286
3992	4287
3993	4288
3994	4289
3995	4290
3996	4291
3997	4292
3998	4293
3999	4294
4000	4295
4001	4296
4002	4297
4003	4298
4004	4299
4005	4300
4006	4301
4007	4302
4008	4305
4009	4306
4010	4307
4011	4308
4012	4309
4013	4310
4014	4311
4015	4313
4016	4212
"	4314
4017	4315
4018	4316
4019	4317
4020	4318
4021	4319
4022	4320
4023	4321
4024	4322
"	4323
4025	4324
4026	4325
4027	2753
"	4326
4028	4328
4029	4329
4030	4330
4031	4331
4032	4332
4033	4333
4034	4334
4035	4335
4036	4337
4037	4338
4038	4339
4039	4340
4040	4341
4041	4342
4042	4343
4043	4344
4044	4345
4045	4346
4046	4347
4047	4348
4048	4351
4049	4352
4050	4353
4051	4354
4052	4355
4053	4356
4054	4357
4055	4358
4056	4359
4057	4360
4058	4361
4059	4362
4060	4363
4061	4364
4062	4365
4063	4366
4064	4367
4065	4368
4066	4369
4067	4370
4068	4371
4069	4372
4070	4373
4071	4374
4072	4375
4073	4376
4074	4377
4075	4378
4076	4379
4077	4380
4078	4381
4079	4382
4080	4383
4081	4384
4082	4385
4083	4388
4084	4389
4085	4390
4086	4391
4087	4393
4088	4394
4089	4395
4090	4396
4091	4276
"	4397
4092	4399
4093	4400
"	4401
4094	4402
4095	4403
4096	4404
4097	4405
4098	4406
"	5229
4099	4407
"	4408
4100	4409
4101	4410
4102	4411
4103	4412
4104	4413
4105	4414
4106	4415
4107	4416
"	4417
4108	4418
4109	4419
4110	4420
4111	4421
4112	4422
4113	4423
4114	4424
4115	4425
4116	4426
4117	4427
4118	4498
4119	4498
4120	4428
4121	4429
4122	4430
4123	4431
4124	4432
4125	4433
4126	4434
4127	4435
4128	4436
4129	4437
4130	4398
4131	4438
4132	4439
4133	4440
4134	4441
4135	4442
4136	4443
4137	4444
4138	4445
4139	4446
4140	4447
4141	4448
4142	4449
4143	4450
4144	4452
"	4453
4145	4454
4146	4455
4147	4456
4148	4457
4149	4458
4150	4459
4151	4460
4152	4461
4153	4462
4154	4463
4155	4464
4156	4465
4157	4466
4158	4468
4159	4470
4160	4472
4161	4473
4162	4474
4163	4475
4164	4476
4165	4477
4166	4478
4167	4479
4168	4480
4169	4471
"	4481
4170	4482
4171	4483
4172	4484
4173	4485
4174	4486
4175	4487
4176	4488
4177	4489
4178	4490
"	1930
4179	2234
"	4491
4180	4494
4181	4495
4182	4497
4183	4498
4184	4492
"	4499
4185	4500
4186	4501
4187	4502
4188	4503
4189	4504
4190	4505
4191	4505
4192	4506
4193	4507
4194	4508
4195	4510
4196	4511
4197	4512
"	4515
4198	4513
4199	4514
4200	4516
4201	4517
4202	4518
4203	4519
4204	4520
4205	4521
4206	4522
4207	4523
4208	4524
4209	4525
4210	4526
"	4528
4211	4527
4212	4529
4213	4530
4214	4531
4215	4532
4216	4533
4217	4467
"	4534
4218	4537
4219	4536
4220	4538
4221	4539
4222	4540
4223	4541
4224	4542
4225	4543
4226	4544
4227	4545
4228	4546
4229	4547
4230	4548
4231	4549
4232	4550
4233	4551
4234	4552
4235	4553
4236	4554
"	4557
4237	4555
4238	407
"	4556
4239	4558
4240	4559
4241	4560
4242	4561
4243	4563
4244	4564
4245	4565
4246	4562
"	4566
4247	4567
4248	4568
4249	4569
"	4573
4250	4570
4251	4571
4252	4572

STRONG	G/K
4253	4574
4254	4575
4255	4576
4256	164
"	4577
4257	4578
4258	4579
4259	4580
4260	4581
4261	4582
4262	4583
4263	4584
"	4585
4264	4586
4265	4587
4266	4588
4267	4589
4268	4590
4269	4591
4270	4592
4271	4593
4272	4594
4273	4595
4274	4596
4275	4632
4276	4598
4277	4625
"	4597
4278	4599
4279	4600
4280	4625
"	4597
4281	4601
4282	4602
4283	4603
4284	4604
"	4617
4285	4605
4286	4606
"	4671
4287	4607
4288	4608
4289	4609
4290	4610
4291	4613
4292	4614
4293	4615
4294	4616
4295	4618
4296	4619
4297	4620
4298	4621
4299	4622
4300	4623
4301	4624
4302	4625
"	4597
4303	4626
4304	4627
4305	4628
4306	4629
4307	4630
4308	4631
"	4632
4309	4633
4310	4634
4311	4636
4312	4637
4313	4638
4314	4639
4315	4640
4316	4641
4317	4642
"	4652
"	4654
4318	4643
4319	4644
"	4645
4320	4646
4321	4648
"	4649
4322	4650
4323	4651
4324	4653
4325	4655
4326	4656
4327	4657
4328	4659
4329	4660
4330	4661
4331	4662
4332	4204
"	4663
4333	4664
4334	4665
4335	4666
4336	4667
4337	4668
4338	4669
4339	4670
4340	4672
4341	4673
4342	4674
4343	4675
4344	4676
4345	4677
4346	4678
"	4680
4347	4681
"	4679
4348	4682
4349	4683
4350	4684
4351	4685
4352	4686
4353	4687
4354	4688
4355	4647
"	4689
4356	4691
"	4692
4357	4693
4358	4694
4359	4695
4360	4696
4361	4698
4362	4699
4363	4700
4364	4701
4365	4702
4366	4703
"	4704
4367	4705
4368	4188
"	4706
4369	4707
4370	4708
"	4716
4371	4709
4372	4710
4373	4711
4374	4712
4375	4713
4376	4714
4377	4715
4378	4717
4379	4718
4380	4719
"	4722
4381	4720
"	4723
4382	4721
"	4724
4383	4725
4384	4726
4385	4727
4386	4728
4387	4728
4388	4729
4389	4730
4390	4731
4391	4732
4392	4733
4393	4734
4394	4735
4395	4736
4396	4737
4397	4738
4398	4739
4399	4740
4400	4741
4401	4742
4402	4743
4403	4744
4404	4745
4405	4746
4406	4611
"	4747
4407	4612
"	4748
4408	4749
4409	4750
4410	4751
4411	4752
4412	4754
"	4759
4413	4755
4414	4756
4415	4757
4416	4758
4417	4760
4418	4761
4419	4762
4420	4763
4421	4764
4422	4765
4423	4766
4424	4767
4425	4768
4426	4769
4427	4770
4428	4771
4429	4772
4430	4773
4431	4774
4432	4775
4433	4776
4434	4777
4435	4778
4436	4780
4437	4781
4438	4782
4439	4783
4440	4784
4441	4785
4442	4786
4443	4787
4444	4788
4445	4789
4446	4790
4447	4791
4448	4792
4449	4793
4450	4794
4451	4796
4452	4803
4453	4797
4454	4798
4455	4799
4456	4386
"	4800
4457	4387
"	4801
4458	4535
"	4803
4459	4802
4460	4805
4461	4806
4462	4807
"	4808
"	4809
4463	4810
4464	4811
4465	4812
4466	4814
4467	4815
4468	4816
4469	4819
"	4828
4470	4820
4471	4821
4472	4822
4473	4823
4474	4824
4475	4825
4476	1017
"	4827
4477	4829
4478	4830
4479	4831
4480	4832
4481	4818
"	4833
"	4834
"	4854
4482	4835
4483	3306
4484	4836
4485	4837
4486	4826
"	4838
"	4841
4487	4839
4488	4840
4489	4842
4490	4843
4491	4844
4492	4845
4493	4846
"	4856
4494	4847
4495	4848
4496	4849
4497	4850
4498	4851
4499	4852
4500	4853
4501	4855
4502	4857
4503	4858
4504	4859
4505	4860
4506	4861
4507	4864
4508	4865
4509	4866
4510	4862
"	4863
"	4867
4511	4868
4512	4869
4513	4870
4514	4871
4515	4872
4516	4873
4517	4874
4518	2407
"	4876
4519	4877
4520	4878
4521	4879
4522	4880
4523	4881
4524	4882
4525	4883
"	4966
4526	4884
4527	4885
4528	4886
4529	4887
4530	4890
4531	4888
4532	4889
4533	4891
4534	4892
4535	4893
4536	4894
4537	4895
4538	4896
4539	4897
4540	4899
"	4900
4541	4901
4542	4902
4543	4903
4544	4904
4545	4905
4546	4907
4547	4908
4548	4909
4549	4910
4550	4911
4551	4912
4552	4913
4553	4914
4554	4915
4555	4916
4556	4917
4557	4918
4558	4919
4559	4920
4560	4921
4561	4922
4562	4923
"	4951
"	4952
4563	4924
4564	4925
4565	838
"	4926
4566	4927
4567	4928
4568	4929
4569	4930
4570	2410
"	4931
4571	5148
4572	4932
4573	4933
4574	4934
4575	4935
4576	4936
4577	4937
"	4938
"	4987
4578	4939
4579	4940
4580	4941
4581	4942
4582	4943
4583	4944
4584	4945
"	4946
4585	4947
4586	4948
4587	4949
4588	4950
4589	4953
4590	4954
4591	4955
4592	4956
4593	4957
4594	4958
4595	4960
4596	4961
"	4986
4597	4962
4598	4963
4599	4964
4600	4965
4601	4967
4602	4968
4603	4969
"	4971
4604	4970
4605	4972
4606	4973
4607	4974
4608	4975
4609	4976
4610	4977
4611	4978
4612	4959
"	4980
4613	4981
4614	4982
4615	4983
4616	4984
4617	4985
4618	4988
4619	4990
4620	4991
4621	4989
"	4992
4622	4994
4623	4995
4624	4997
4625	4998
4626	4999
4627	5002
4628	5003
4629	5004
4630	5005
4631	5006
4632	5007
4633	5008
4634	5009
4635	5010
4636	5011
4637	5012
4638	5013
4639	5014
4640	5015
4641	5016
4642	5017
4643	5018
4644	5019
4645	5020
4646	5021
4647	5022
4648	5023
4649	5024
4650	5025
4651	5026
4652	5027
4653	5028
4654	5029
4655	5030
4656	5031
4657	5032
4658	5033
4659	5034
4660	5035
4661	5036
4662	5037
4663	5038
4664	5039
4665	5040
4666	5043
4667	2430
"	5044
4668	5045
4669	5046
4670	5047
4671	5148
4672	4898
"	5048
4673	5049
4674	5050
4675	5148
4676	5051
4677	5052
4678	5053
4679	5054
4680	5055
4681	5056
4682	5057
4683	5058
4684	5059
4685	5060
4686	5061
4687	2178
"	5062
4688	5063
4689	5064
4690	5065
4691	5066
4692	5067
4693	5068
4694	5069
4695	5071
4696	5070
4697	5072
4698	5073
4699	5074
4700	5075
4701	5076
4702	5077
4703	5078
4704	5079
4705	5080
4706	5080
4707	5080
4708	5081
4709	5081
4710	5082
4711	5083
4712	5084
4713	5085
4714	5087
4715	5088
4716	5089
4717	5090
4718	5091
4719	5092
4720	5093
4721	5094
4722	5095
4723	5096
4724	5097
4725	5098
4726	5099
4727	5100
4728	5101
4729	5102
4730	5103
4731	5104
4732	5105
4733	5106
4734	5107
4735	5109
4736	5108
4737	5110
4738	5111
4739	5112
4740	5113
4741	5114
4742	5116
4743	5117
4744	5118
4745	5119
4746	5115
"	5120
4747	5122
4748	5123
4749	5124
4750	5125
4751	5126
4752	5127
4753	5128
4754	5129
4755	5130
4756	5131
4757	5132
4758	5133
4759	5134
"	5135
4760	5136
4761	5137
4762	5138
4763	5139
4764	5140
4765	5141
4766	5142
"	5143
4767	5144
4768	5145
4769	5146
4770	5121
"	5147
4771	5148
4772	5149
4773	5150
"	5151
4774	5152
4775	5153
4776	4327
"	5154
4777	5155
4778	5156
4779	5157
4780	5158
4781	5159
4782	5160
4783	5161
4784	5163
4785	2975
"	5164
4786	5166
4787	5167
4788	5168
4789	5169
4790	5170
4791	5171
4792	5172
4793	5173
4794	5174
4795	5175
"	5346
4796	5176
4797	5177
"	5179
4798	5178
4799	5180
4800	5182
4801	2413
"	5183
4802	5184
4803	5185
4804	5186
4805	5187
4806	5188
4807	5189
4808	5190
4809	5191
4810	5192
4811	5193
4812	5194
4813	5195
4814	5196
4815	5197
4816	5198
4817	5199
4818	5200
4819	5201
4820	5202
4821	5203
4822	5204
4823	5205
4824	5206
4825	5207
4826	5208
4827	5209
4828	5210
4829	5211
4830	5212
4831	5213
4832	5215
4833	5214
"	5216
"	5240
4834	5217
4835	5218
4836	5219
4837	5220
4838	5221
4839	5222
4840	5223
4841	5224
4842	5225
4843	5227
4844	5228
4845	5230
4846	5231
4847	5232
4848	5233
4849	5234
"	5235
4850	5236
4851	5237
"	5239
4852	5238
4853	5241
4854	5242
4855	5243
4856	5244
4857	5245
4858	5246
4859	5247
4860	5248
4861	5249
4862	5250
4863	5251
4864	5252
4865	5253
4866	5254
4867	125
"	5255
4868	5256
4869	5257
4870	5258
4871	5259
"	5260
"	5276
4872	5262
4873	5263
"	5165
4874	5264
4875	5265
4876	5267
4877	5268
4878	5269
4879	5270
4880	5271
4881	5272
4882	5273
4883	5274
4884	5275
4885	5277
4886	5278
4887	5279
4888	5280
4889	5281
4890	5282
4891	5283
4892	5284
4893	5287
4894	5288
"	5323
"	5328
4895	5289
4896	5290
4897	5291
4898	5292
4899	5293
4900	5261
"	5295
4901	5296
4902	5299
4903	5300
4904	5301
4905	5302
4906	5303
4907	5304
4908	5305
4909	5306
4910	5307
4911	5308
4912	5309
4913	5310
4914	5311
4915	5312
4916	5313
4917	5314
4918	5315
4919	5316
4920	5317
"	5320
4921	5318
"	5319
4922	5321
4923	5322
4924	5324
4925	5325
4926	5326
4927	5327
4928	5330
4929	5332
4930	5333
4931	5334
4932	5335
4933	5337
4934	5298
"	5338
4935	5339
4936	5340
4937	5341
4938	5342
4939	5343
4940	5344
4941	5345
4942	5347
4943	5348
4944	5349
4945	5350
4946	5352
4947	5353
4948	5354
4949	5351
"	5355
"	5356
"	5835
4950	5358
4951	5359
4952	5331
"	5360
4953	5361
4954	5362
4955	5086
"	5363
4956	5364
4957	5365
4958	5366
4959	5367
4960	5368
4961	5369
4962	5370
4963	5371
4964	5372
4965	4993
"	5373
4966	5374
4967	5375
4968	5376
4969	5377
4970	5379
4971	5380
4972	5381
4973	5382
4974	5383
"	5384
4975	5385
4976	5386
4977	5387
4978	5388
4979	5389
4980	5390
4981	5391
4982	1751
"	5392
4983	5393
4984	5394
4985	5395
4986	5396
4987	5397
4988	5398
4989	5399
4990	5400
4991	5401
4992	5402
"	5403
4993	5404
4994	5405
4995	5406
4996	5407
4997	5408
4998	5409
4999	5411
5000	5412
5001	5413

STRONG	G/K
5002	5414
5003	5415
5004	5416
5005	5417
5006	5418
5007	5419
5008	2496
"	5420
5009	5421
5010	5423
5011	5424
5012	5425
5013	5427
5014	5428
5015	5429
5016	5430
5017	5431
5018	5432
5019	5433
5020	5434
5021	5435
5022	5436
5023	4047
5024	5437
5025	4047
5026	4047
5027	5438
5028	5439
5029	5440
5030	5441
5031	5442
5032	5441
5033	5441
5034	5443
5035	5444
5036	5444
5037	5445
5038	5446
5039	5447
5040	5448
5041	5449
5042	5450
5043	5451
5044	5452
5045	5454
5046	5455
5047	5456
5048	5457
5049	5458
5050	5459
5051	5460
5052	5461
5053	5462
5054	5463
5055	5464
5056	5465
5057	5467
5058	5466
"	5468
5059	5469
5060	5470
5061	5472
5062	5473
"	5477
5063	5474
"	5478
5064	5475
5065	5476
5066	5479
5067	5480
5068	5481
5069	5482
5070	5483
5071	5484
5072	5485
5073	5486
"	5487
5074	5488
5075	5489
5076	5490
5077	5491
5078	5492
5079	5493
5080	5494
5081	1315
"	5495
5082	5496
5083	5498
5084	5499
5085	5500
5086	5501
5087	5502
5088	5503
5089	5504
5090	5505
5091	5506
5092	5507
5093	5508
5094	5509
5095	5510
5096	5511
5097	5512
5098	5513
5099	5514
5100	5516
5101	5515
5102	5518
5103	5519
5104	5520
5105	5521
"	5522
5106	5523
5107	5524
5108	5525
5109	5526
5110	5527
5111	5528
5112	5529
"	5530
"	5531
5113	5532
5114	5533
5115	5534
5116	5535
5117	5536
"	4509
5118	5537
5119	5538
5120	3836
5121	5539
5122	5540
5123	5542
5124	4047
5125	4047
5126	4047
5127	4047
5128	4047
5129	4047
5130	4047
5131	5543
5132	5544
5133	5545
5134	5546
5135	5547
5136	5548
5137	5549
5138	5550
5139	5551
5140	5552
5141	5554
5142	5555
5143	5556
5144	5558
5145	5559
5146	5560
5147	5561
5148	5562
5149	5563
5150	5564
5151	5565
5152	5566
5153	5567
5154	5568
"	5569
5155	5570
5156	5571
5157	5572
5158	5573
5159	5574
"	5578
5160	5575
5161	5576
5162	5577
5163	5579
5164	5580
5165	5581
5166	5582
5167	5583
5168	5584
5169	5557
"	5585
5170	5586
5171	5587
5172	5588
5173	5589
5174	5590
5175	5591
5176	5592
5177	5593
5178	5594
5179	5595
"	5596
5180	5597
5181	5598
5182	2571
"	5600
5183	5601
5184	5602
5185	5603
5186	5604
5187	5605
5188	5606
5189	5607
5190	5608
5191	5610
5192	5611
5193	5612
5194	5613
5195	5614
5196	5615
5197	5616
5198	5617
5199	5618
5200	5619
5201	5620
5202	5621
5203	5622
5204	5623
5205	5624
5206	5625
5207	5626
5208	5627
5209	5148
5210	5148
5211	5628
5212	5629
5213	5148
5214	5630
5215	5631
5216	5148
5217	5632
5218	5633
5219	5634
5220	5635
5221	5636
5222	5637
5223	5638
5224	5639
5225	5639
5226	5640
5227	5641
5228	5642
5229	5643
5230	5644
5231	5645
5232	5647
5233	5648
5234	5649
5235	5650
5236	5651
5237	4238
"	5653
"	5666
5238	5654
5239	5657
5240	5655
"	5656
"	5658
5241	5659
5242	5660
5243	5661
5244	5662
"	5663
5245	5664
5246	5665
5247	5667
5248	5668
5249	5669
5250	5670
5251	5671
5252	5672
5253	5673
5254	5674
5255	5675
5256	5676
5257	5677
5258	5678
5259	5679
5260	5680
5261	5681
5262	5682
5263	5683
"	5684
5264	5685
5265	5686
5266	5687
5267	5688
5268	5689
5269	5690
5270	5691
5271	5693
5272	5694
5273	5695
5274	5696
5275	5699
5276	5700
5277	659
"	5701
5278	670
"	5702
5279	5703
5280	5704
5281	5705
5282	5706
5283	5707
5284	5709
5285	5710
5286	5711
5287	5712
5288	5713
5289	5714
5290	5715
5291	5716
5292	5717
5293	5718
5294	5719
5295	5720
5296	5721
5297	5722
5298	5723
5299	5708
"	5724
5300	5725
5301	5727
5302	5728
5303	5729
5304	5730
5305	5731
5306	5731
5307	5733
5308	5734
5309	5735
5310	5736
5311	5737
5312	5738
5313	5739
5314	5741
5315	2266
5316	5743
5317	5744
5318	5745
5319	5746
5320	5747
5321	5748
5322	5749
5323	5750
5324	5751
5325	5752
5326	5753
5327	5754
5328	5755
5329	5756
5330	5757
5331	5758
"	5760
5332	5759
5333	5761
5334	5762
5335	5763
5336	5764
5337	5765
5338	5766
5339	5767
5340	5768
5341	5742
"	5769
5342	5770
5343	5771
5344	5772
5345	5773
5346	5774
5347	5776
5348	5777
5349	5778
5350	5779
5351	5780
5352	5781
5353	5782
5354	5783
5355	5784
5356	5785
5357	5786
5358	5787
5359	5788
5360	5789
5361	5790
5362	5791
5363	5792
5364	5793
5365	5794
5366	5795
5367	5796
5368	5797
5369	5798
5370	5799
5371	5800
5372	5801
5373	5802
5374	5803
5375	5804
5376	5805
5377	5806
5378	5807
5379	5808
5380	5809
5381	5810
5382	5811
5383	5812
5384	5813
5385	5814
5386	5815
5387	5816
5388	5817
5389	5818
5390	5819
5391	5426
"	5820
5392	3055
"	5821
5393	5823
5394	5824
5395	5825
5396	5826
5397	5827
5398	5829
5399	5828
"	5830
5400	5831
5401	5832
5402	5833
5403	5834
5404	5836
5405	5837
5406	5838
5407	5839
5408	5840
5409	5841
5410	5842
5411	5843
5412	5844
5413	5845
5414	5846
5415	5847
5416	5848
5417	5849
"	5822
5418	5850
5419	5851
5420	5852
5421	5853
5422	5854
5423	5855
5424	5856
5425	5857
5426	5858
5427	5859
5428	5860
5429	5861
5430	5862
5431	5863
5432	5864
5433	5865
5434	5866
5435	5867
5436	5869
5437	5870
5438	5871
5439	5872
5440	5873
5441	5874
5442	5875
5443	5876
5444	5877
5445	5878
5446	5879
5447	5880
5448	5881
5449	5882
5450	5883
5451	5884
5452	5885
5453	5886
5454	5887
5455	1876
"	5888
5456	5889
5457	5890
5458	5891
5459	5892
5460	5893
5461	5894
5462	5895
5463	5897
5464	5898
5465	5899
5466	5900
5467	5901
5468	5902
"	5904
5469	5903
5470	5905
"	5911
5471	5906
5472	5907
5473	5908
5474	5909
5475	5910
5476	5912
5477	5913
5478	5914
5479	5915
5480	5916
5481	5917
5482	5918
5483	5919
5484	5920
5485	5921
5486	5922
5487	5923
5488	5924
5489	5925
5490	5926
5491	5927
5492	5928
5493	5929
5494	5930
5495	5931
5496	5932
5497	5933
5498	5934
5499	5935
5500	5936
5501	5937
5502	5938
5503	5939
5504	2396
"	5940
5505	5942
5506	5941
5507	5943
5508	5944
5509	5945
5510	5946
5511	5948
5512	1430
"	5949
5513	5950
5514	5951
5515	5952
5516	5947
"	5953
5517	5954
5518	5955
5519	5956
5520	5957
5521	5958
5522	5967
"	5959
5523	5960
"	6002
5524	5961
5525	5962
5526	5963
5527	5964
5528	5965
5529	5966
5530	5968
5531	3079
"	5969
5532	5970
5533	5971
"	5972
5534	5973
5535	5974
5536	5975
5537	5976
5538	5977
5539	5978
5540	5979
5541	5980
5542	5981
5543	5982
5544	5983
5545	5984
5546	5985
5547	5986
5548	5987
5549	5988
5550	5989
5551	5990
5552	5991
"	5997
5553	5992
5554	5993
5555	5994
5556	5995
5557	5996
5558	5998
5559	5999
5560	6000
5561	6001
5562	6003
5563	6004
5564	6005
5565	6006
5566	6008
5567	6010
5568	6011
5569	6012
5570	6013
5571	6014
5572	6015
5573	6016
5574	6017
5575	6020
5576	6018
5577	6019
5578	6021
5579	6022
5580	6023
5581	6024
5582	6025
5583	6026
5584	6027
5585	6028
5586	6029
5587	6030
5588	6031
5589	6032
"	6033
5590	6034
5591	6035
5592	6036
5593	6037
5594	6038
5595	6039
5596	6040
5597	6041
5598	6042
5599	6043
5600	1639
5601	2725
"	6044
5602	6045
5603	6046
5604	6047
5605	6048
5606	6049
5607	1639
5608	6050
5609	6051
5610	6052
5611	6053
5612	6054
5613	6055
5614	6057
5615	6058
5616	6059
5617	6060
5618	6061
5619	6062
5620	6063
5621	6064
"	6065
5622	6066
5623	6067
5624	6068

INDEX OF GOODRICK/KOHLENBERGER → STRONG NUMBERS

HEBREW OLD TESTAMENT

G/K	STRONG
1	
2	
3	1
4	3
5	5
6	6
7	8
8	9
9	10
10	11
11	11
12	12
13	13
14	14
15	16
16	17
17	18
18	19
19	20
20	15
21	
22	
23	21
24	22
25	23
26	24
27	
28	26
29	27
30	28
31	29
32	29
33	30
34	31
35	32
36	34
37	35
38	32
39	36
40	37
41	38
42	39
43	40
44	41
45	42
46	74
47	43
48	44
49	33
50	45
51	46
52	47
53	48
54	49
55	50
56	51
57	52
58	53
59	54
60	55
61	56
62	56
63	57
"	59
64	58
"	59
65	60
66	61

G/K	STRONG
67	180
68	62
69	63
70	64
71	65
72	66
73	67
74	68
75	72
76	71
77	73
78	70
79	74
80	75
81	76
82	77
83	78
84	79
85	80
86	81
87	82
88	83
89	84
90	85
91	86
92	87
93	52
94	53
95	88
96	89
97	90
98	91
99	92
100	93
101	94
102	95
103	96
104	97
105	
106	98
107	98
108	99
109	100
110	101
111	102
112	103
113	105
114	106
115	107
116	108
117	109
118	110
119	111
120	112
121	123
122	130
123	113
124	114
125	138
126	115
127	151
128	182
129	117
130	118
131	119
132	120
133	120
134	121
135	120
136	121
137	122
138	124
139	123

G/K	STRONG
140	125
141	127
142	128
143	127
144	126
145	132
"	726
146	129+5346
147	131
148	133
149	134
150	135
151	136
152	137
153	138
154	138
155	139
156	140
157	141
158	142
159	145
160	143
161	146
162	146
163	150
164	151
165	152
166	152
167	154
168	155
169	156
170	157
171	159
172	158
173	160
174	160
175	
176	161
177	162
178	163
179	164
180	165
181	1961
182	167
183	166
184	174
185	168
186	169
187	428
188	170
189	174
190	171
191	172
192	173
193	174
194	
195	175
196	176
197	176
198	177
199	178
200	178
201	179
202	181
203	183
204	184
205	185
206	186
207	187
208	188
209	189
210	190
211	191

G/K	STRONG
212	193
213	192
214	193
215	193
216	196
217	195
218	194
219	199
220	198
221	197
222	200
223	201
224	205
225	206
226	202
227	203
228	204
229	207
230	205
231	208
232	209
233	210
234	211
235	211
236	212
237	213
238	214
239	215
240	216
241	217
242	224
243	218
244	218
245	219
246	219
247	221
248	222
249	223
250	223
251	224
252	225
253	226
254	853
255	227
256	229
257	231
258	232
259	233
260	234
261	235
262	237
263	238
264	239
265	241
266	240
267	242
268	243
269	244
270	244
271	245
272	246
273	247
274	248
275	249
276	250
277	253
278	251
279	254
280	255
281	256
282	256
283	257
284	258

G/K	STRONG
285	259
286	260
287	261
288	264
289	262
290	270
291	265
292	266
293	267
294	268
295	269
296	270
297	270
298	271
299	272
300	273
301	274
302	274
303	275
304	276
305	278
306	277
307	279
308	281
309	281
310	282
311	283
312	284
313	285
314	286
315	287
316	288
317	289
318	290
319	291
320	292
321	293
322	294
323	295
324	296
325	297
326	298
327	299
328	300
329	301
330	302
331	303
332	305
333	304
334	306
335	308
336	309
337	312
338	313
339	310
340	314
341	315
342	316
343	310
344	319
345	322
346	323
347	325
348	325
349	326
350	327
351	328
352	
353	329
354	329
355	330
356	328
357	331

G/K	STRONG
358	332
359	333
360	334
361	335
362	339
363	338
364	336
365	337
366	340
367	341
368	342
369	343
370	344
371	345
372	346
373	347
374	348
375	349
376	350
377	349
378	351
379	349
380	352
381	352
382	352
383	352
384	353
385	354
386	364
387	355
"	365
388	337
389	357
390	356
391	356
392	358
393	359
394	360
395	361
396	362
397	359
398	366
399	367
400	368
401	369
402	370
403	371
404	372
405	373
406	374
407	375
408	376
409	376
410	378
411	382
412	379
413	380
414	3448
415	2978
416	863
417	384
418	385
419	386
420	387
421	389
422	390
423	391
424	392
425	393
426	394
427	395
428	396
429	397

G/K	STRONG
430	398
431	400
432	401
433	402
434	403
435	403
436	404
437	405
438	406
439	407
440	408
441	
442	352
443	352
444	352
445	410
446	410
447	411
448	413
449	415
450	416
451	1286
452	414
453	417
454	418
455	419
456	420
457	422
458	421
459	428
460	423
461	424
462	425
463	425
464	427
465	428
466	430
467	432
468	433
469	435
470	434
471	436
472	356
473	437
474	438
475	439
476	441
477	441
478	442
479	443
480	444
481	445
482	446
483	447
484	448
485	419
"	449
486	450
487	451
488	452
489	452
490	453
491	453
492	454
493	454
494	455
495	456
496	457
497	458
498	460
499	461
500	463
501	462

G/K	STRONG
502	464
503	465
504	466
505	467
506	468
507	469
508	470
509	471
510	472
511	473
512	474
513	475
514	476
515	477
516	478
517	448
518	480
519	481
520	481
521	482
522	483
523	484
524	485
525	486
526	487
527	488
528	488
529	489
530	490
531	491
532	492
533	440
534	493
535	494
536	495
537	496
538	497
539	498
540	499
541	500
542	500
543	501
544	502
545	503
546	504
547	505
548	505
549	507
550	467
551	508
552	509
553	469
554	510
555	511
556	512
557	513
558	514
559	514
560	515
561	518
562	517
563	519
564	520
565	522
566	4965
567	520
568	367
569	523
570	525
"	527
"	539
571	526
572	527

G/K	STRONG
"	528
573	529
574	529
575	530
576	531
577	532
578	550
579	533
580	534
581	535
582	535
583	536
584	537
585	538
586	539
587	539
"	541
588	542
589	543
590	544
591	548
592	549
593	546
594	545
595	547
596	550
597	551
598	552
599	553
600	554
601	555
602	556
603	557
604	558
605	558
606	559
607	559
608	562
609	561
610	561
611	561
612	564
613	564
614	565
615	565
616	567
617	566
618	568
619	568
620	569
621	570
622	571
623	572
624	573
625	575
626	577
627	578
628	579
629	577
630	580
631	605
632	582
633	583
634	584
635	585
636	587
637	588
638	589
639	590
640	592
641	591
642	593
643	594
644	595
645	596
646	597
647	599
648	
649	601
650	602
651	603
652	604
653	605
654	609
655	610
656	611
657	612
658	614
659	615
660	616
661	617
662	618
663	619
664	621
665	622
666	623
667	624
668	625
669	626
670	627
671	628
672	630
673	631
674	632
675	634

G/K	STRONG
676	635
677	637
678	639
679	640
680	646
681	641
682	642
683	643
684	644
685	644
686	645
687	6323
688	647
689	648
690	639
691	649
692	650
693	650
694	652
695	651
696	653
697	654
698	655
699	656
700	657
701	657
702	658
703	659
704	660
705	661
706	662
707	663
708	664
709	665
710	666
711	667
712	668
713	669
714	672
715	672
716	672
717	672
718	673
719	675
720	676
721	678
722	678
723	679
724	680
725	681
726	1018
727	682
728	682
729	683
730	684
731	685
732	686
733	687
734	688
735	689
736	690
737	691
738	739
739	692
740	692
741	693
742	694
743	695
744	696
745	1009
746	697
747	698
748	699
749	700
750	701
751	1835
"	3120
752	702
"	706
753	704
754	705
755	707
756	708
757	
758	709
759	709
760	710
761	712
762	3296
763	713
764	714
765	715
766	716
767	742
768	717
769	720
770	719
771	722
772	722
773	721
774	220
"	723
775	729
776	724
777	725

G/K	STRONG
778	727
779	728
780	730
781	731
782	732
783	733
784	734
785	736
786	737
787	738
788	221
789	741
790	740
791	740
792	743
793	744
794	745
795	723
796	746
797	224
798	747
799	748
800	750
801	752
802	753
803	750
804	751
805	757
806	758
807	758+4601
808	763
809	760
810	759
811	762
"	7421
812	761
813	764
814	765
815	766
816	767
817	768
818	769
819	728
820	770
821	771
822	774
823	775
824	776
825	777
826	779
827	780
828	2043
829	781
830	782
831	783
832	840
833	841
834	845
835	844
836	784
"	800
837	748
838	786
839	788
840	789
841	790
842	791
843	792
844	794
845	793
846	795
847	796
848	797
849	798
850	799
851	802
852	801
853	803
854	380
855	804
856	805
857	805
858	806
859	803
860	807
861	808
862	809
863	810
864	811
865	812
866	812
867	813
868	814
869	815
870	816
871	817
872	818
873	819
874	821
875	820
876	822
877	823
878	824
879	825
880	827

G/K	STRONG
881	828
882	829
883	830
884	831
885	832
886	833
887	833
888	836
889	834
890	835
891	837
892	838
893	838
894	838
895	842
896	843
897	835
898	843
899	377
900	847
901	848
902	850
903	851
904	851
905	859
906	853
907	854
908	855
909	856
910	857
911	859
912	860
913	862
914	859
915	863
916	862
917	859
918	864
919	865
920	859
921	866
922	867
923	388
924	869
925	868
926	871
927	
928	
929	872
930	874
931	875
932	876
933	884
934	877
935	879
936	883
937	884
938	878
939	880
940	881
941	882
942	885
943	886
944	887
945	889
946	891
947	890
948	834
949	892
950	893
951	894
952	897
953	898
954	899
955	899
956	900
957	901
958	902
959	1559
960	903
961	904
962	904
963	905
964	905
965	906
966	907
967	907
968	908
969	909
970	910
971	911
972	1767
973	912
974	913
975	913
976	914
977	915
978	916
979	917
980	918
981	919
982	920
983	922
984	931
985	923

G/K	STRONG
986	925
987	926
988	928
989	929
990	930
991	931
992	932
993	933
994	934
995	935
996	936
997	937
998	938
999	939
1000	940
1001	941
1002	942
1003	943
1004	945
1005	944
1006	944
1007	946
1008	947
1009	948
1010	949
1011	950
1012	951
1013	952
1014	953
1015	953+5626
1016	953+6228
1017	954
1018	954
1019	955
1020	957
1021	958
1022	959
"	960
"	5240
1023	961
1024	962
1025	963
1026	964
1027	965
1028	966
1029	967
1030	968
1031	969
1032	971
1033	970
1034	977
1035	979
1036	980
1037	970
1038	980
1039	971
1040	972
1041	973
1042	973
1043	974
1044	975
1045	
1046	976
1047	977
1048	977
1049	978
1050	
1051	981
1052	982
1053	982
1054	982
1055	983
1056	984
1057	985
1058	987
1059	986
1060	988
1061	990
1062	991
1063	992
1064	993
1065	994
1066	15
1067	995
1068	996
1069	998
1070	1000
1071	953
1072	1002
1073	1003
1074	1004
1075	996
1076	1006
1077	1007
1078	1008
1079	1009
1080	1004+791
1081	1010
1082	1011
1083	1012
1084	1013
1085	1014
1086	1015
1087	1016
1088	1017

G/K	STRONG
1089	1018
1090	1019
1091	1004+1588
1092	1023
1093	1020
1094	1021
1095	1022
1096	1024
1097	1025
1098	1026
1099	1027
1100	1028
1101	1029
1102	1031
1103	1032
1104	358
1105	1033
1106	1034
1107	1035
1108	1036
1109	1037
1110	1010
1111	1038
1112	1024
1113	1039
1114	1040
1115	1041
1116	1042
1117	1043
1118	1044
1119	1045
1120	1046
1121	1047
1122	1048
1123	1049
1124	1050
1125	1051
1126	1052
1127	1053
1128	1030
1129	1004+8425
1130	1054
1131	1055
1132	1057
1133	1056
1134	1058
1135	1059
1136	1063
"	1073
1137	1061
1138	1064
1139	439
1140	1065
1141	1066
1142	1067
1143	1068
1144	1069
1145	1070
1146	1071
1147	1060
1148	1062
1149	1072
1150	1074
1151	1076
1152	1075
1153	1077
1154	1077
1155	1078
1156	1081
1157	1112
1158	1082
1159	1083
1160	1084
1161	1085
1162	1086
1163	1088
1164	1089
1165	1087
1166	1091
1167	1090
1168	1090
1169	1092
1170	1094
1171	1095
1172	1097
1173	1098
1174	1099
1175	1100
1176	1101
1177	1101
1178	1102
1179	1103
1180	1104
1181	1104
1182	1104
1183	1105
1184	1105
1185	1106
1186	1106
1187	1107
1188	1108
1189	1109
1190	1109
1191	1110
1192	1111

G/K	STRONG
1193	1114
1194	1115
1195	1116
1196	1117
1197	1118
1198	1119
1199	1120
1200	1120
1201	1121
1202	1122
1203	1125
1204	1126
1205	1127
1206	1128
1207	1130
1208	2011
1209	1132
1210	1133
1211	1134
1212	1135
1213	1136
1214	1151
1215	1129
1216	
1217	1121
1218	1131
1219	
1220	1137
1221	1138
1222	1139
1223	1142
1224	1140
1225	1141
1226	1141
1227	1143
1228	1144
1229	1145
1230	1146
1231	1148
1232	1150
1233	1152
1234	1153
1235	1154
"	1155
1236	
1237	1157
1238	1157
1239	1158
1240	1158
1241	1166
1242	1160
1243	1161
1244	1162
1245	1162
1246	1163
1247	1164
1248	1165
1249	1166
1250	1167
1251	1167
1252	1168
1253	1170
1254	1171
1255	1174
1256	1176
1257	1177
1258	1178
1259	1179
1260	1186
1261	1187
1262	1188
1263	1189
1264	1190
1265	1193
1266	1172
"	1180
1267	1173
1268	1175
1269	1182
1270	1183
"	1184
1271	1185
1272	1191
1273	1192
1274	1194
1275	1195
1276	1196
1277	1197
1278	1197
1279	1197
1280	1198
1281	1199
1282	1200
1283	1202
1284	1201
1285	1203
1286	1204
1287	1205
1288	1206
1289	1207
1290	1208
1291	1209
1292	1210
1293	1210
1294	1211

G/K	STRONG
1295	1212
1296	1213
1297	1213
1298	1214
1299	1215
1300	6815
1301	1216
1302	1217
1303	
1304	1218
1305	1219
1306	1219
1307	1219
1308	
1309	1220
"	1222
1310	1221
1311	1221
1312	1223
1313	1224
1314	1226
1315	1225
1316	1226
1317	1227
1318	1228
1319	1229
1320	1230
1321	1231
1322	1232
1323	1233
1324	1234
1325	1235
1326	1237
1327	1238
1328	1238
1329	1239
1330	1241
1331	1242
1332	1242
1333	1243
1334	1244
1335	1245
1336	1246
1337	1248
1338	1249
1339	1250
1340	1250
1341	1252
1342	1253
1343	1254
1344	1254
1345	1254
1346	1262
1347	1255
1348	1011
1349	1256
1350	1257
1351	1258
1352	1259
1353	1261
1354	1260
1355	1260
1356	1262
"	1274
1357	1262
"	1274
1358	1263
1359	1305
1360	1265
1361	1266
1362	1267
1363	1268
1364	1269
1365	1269
1366	1270
1367	1271
1368	1272
1369	1272
1370	1272
1371	1281
1372	1273
1373	1275
1374	1277
1375	1278
1376	1279
1377	1282
1378	1280
1379	1276
1380	1283
1381	1284
1382	1285
1383	1287
1384	1288
1385	1288
1386	1290
1387	1292
1388	1293
1389	1294
1390	1294
1391	1295
1392	1296
1393	1296
1394	1264
1395	6947
1396	1298

G/K	STRONG
1397	1299
1398	1300
1399	1301
1400	1139
1401	1302
1402	1303
1403	1304
1404	1304
1405	1305
1406	1305
1407	1306
1408	1268
1409	1307
1410	1308
1411	1313
"	1314
1412	1315
1413	1319
1414	1320
1415	1309
1416	
1417	7683
1418	1310
1419	1311
1420	1312
1421	1316
1422	1316
1423	1317
1424	1318
1425	1322
1426	1323
1427	1324
1428	1004
1429	1326
1430	
1431	1327
1432	1328
1433	1328
1434	1329
1435	1330
1436	1331
1437	1332
1438	1333
1439	1334
1440	1335
1441	1336
1442	1337
1443	1338
1444	1339
1445	1340
1446	
1447	1341
1448	1342
1449	1344
1450	1343
1451	1345
1452	1346
1453	1350
1454	1347
1455	1348
1456	1349
1457	1350
1458	1351
1459	1352
1460	1353
1461	1354
1462	1354
1463	1356
1464	1356
1465	1360
1466	1357
1467	1361
1468	1362
"	1364
1469	1364
1470	1363
1471	1365
1472	1419
1473	1366
1474	1367
1475	1368
1476	1369
1477	1371
1478	1372
1479	1462
1480	1373
1481	1374
1482	1385
1483	1375
1484	1376
1485	1377
1486	1378
1487	1379
1488	1380
1489	1381
1490	1382
1491	1383
1492	1384
1493	1386
1494	1387
1495	1388
1496	1389
1497	1390
1498	1393
1499	1392
1500	1391
1501	1394
1502	1394
1503	1395
1504	1396
"	1399
1505	1397
1506	1398
1507	1402
1508	1403
1509	1404
1510	1405
1511	1406
1512	1407
1513	1408
"	1409
1514	1410
1515	2735
1516	1412
1517	1413
1518	1413
1519	1415
1520	2693
1521	1417
1522	1416
1523	1418
1524	1419
1525	1420
1526	1421
1527	1422
1528	1421
1529	1446
1530	1446
1531	1423
1532	1425
1533	1424
1534	1426
1535	1427
1536	1428
1537	1429
1538	1430
1539	1430
1540	1431
1541	1432
1542	1433
1543	1435
1544	1434
1545	1436
1546	1436
1547	1437
1548	1438
1549	1439
1550	1440
1551	1441
1552	1442
1553	1443
1554	1445
1555	1444
"	1447
1556	1448
1557	1449
1558	1450
1559	1451
1560	1448
1561	1452
1562	1453
1563	1454
1564	1455
1565	1456
1566	1457
1567	1458
1568	1460
1569	1460
1570	1359
1571	1462
1572	1461
1573	1463
1574	1464
1575	1467
1576	1465
"	1466
1577	1468
1578	1469
1579	1470
1580	1471
1581	1472
1582	1471
1583	1473
1584	1474
1585	1475
1586	1476
1587	1477
1588	1478
1589	1479
1590	1480
1591	1481
1592	1481
1593	1481
1594	1482
1595	1483
1596	1484
1597	1485
1598	1486
1599	1487
1600	1488
1601	1489
1602	1491
1603	1492
1604	1493
1605	1494
1606	1495
1607	1496
1608	1497
1609	1499
1610	1498
1611	1500
1612	1501
1613	1502
1614	1503
1615	1504
1616	1504
1617	1506
1618	1507
1619	1508
1620	1509
1621	1511
1622	1518
1623	1512
1624	1513
1625	1513
1626	1514
1627	1515
1628	1516
1629	2798
1630	1517
1631	1518
1632	1520
1633	1521
1634	1522
1635	1523
1636	1524
1637	1524
1638	1525
1639	1526
1640	1527
1641	1487
1642	1529
1643	1530
1644	1530
1645	1561
1646	1531
1647	1532
1648	1533
1649	1534
1650	1534
1651	1536
1652	1537
1653	1538
1654	1539
1655	1540
1656	1542
1657	1543
1658	1544
1659	1545
1660	
1661	1546
1662	1548
1663	1549
1664	1550
1665	1551
1666	1552
1667	1553
1668	1554
1669	1555
1670	1556
1671	1556
1672	1557
1673	1558
1674	1559
1675	1562
1676	1563
1677	1564
1678	1565
1679	1566
1680	1568
1681	1567
1682	1569
1683	1570
1684	1543
1685	1571
1686	1572
1687	1573
1688	1574
1689	1575
1690	1577
1691	1576
1692	1578
1693	1579
1694	1580
1695	1581
1696	1582
1697	1583
1698	1584
1699	1586
1700	1586
1701	1587
1702	1587
1703	1588
1704	1589
1705	1590
1706	1591
1707	1592
1708	1593
"	1594
1709	1595
1710	1595
1711	1597
1712	5873
1713	1598
1714	1599
1715	1599
1716	1600
1717	1601
1718	1602
1719	1604
1720	1603
1721	1605
1722	1606
1723	1607
1724	1608
1725	1609
1726	1610
1727	1610
1728	1612
1729	1613
1730	1614
1731	1616
1732	1615
1733	1617
1734	1618
1735	1619
1736	1619
1737	1620
1738	1621
1739	1622
1740	1623
1741	1624
1742	1625
1743	1626
1744	1627
1745	1628+3643
1746	1629
1747	1511
1748	1630
1749	1631
1750	1633
1751	1633
1752	1634
1753	1636
1754	1632
1755	1637
1756	1638
1757	1639
1758	1639
1759	1640
1760	1641
1761	1642
1762	1643
1763	1644
1764	1644
1765	1645
1766	1646
1767	1648
1768	1647
1769	1649
1770	1650
1771	1651
1772	1652
1773	1653
1774	1654
1775	1656
1776	1654
1777	1657
1778	1658
1779	1659
1780	1660
1781	1661
1782	1662
"	1667
1783	1662
1784	1667
1785	1663
1786	1664
1787	1665
1788	1666
1789	
1790	1669
1791	1670
1792	1671
1793	1672
1794	1709
1795	1673
1796	1674
1797	1675
1798	1676
1799	1756
1800	1677
1801	1679
1802	
1803	1680
1804	1681
1805	1682
1806	1683
1807	1686
1808	1687
1809	1688
1810	1688
1811	1690
1812	1689
1813	1691
1814	1015
1815	1692
1816	1695
1817	1694
1818	1696
1819	1696
1820	1696
1821	1697
1822	1698
1823	1698
1824	1699
1825	1699'
1826	1700
1827	1702
1828	1704
1829	1705
1830	1703
1831	1706
1832	1707
1833	1708
1834	1709
1835	1711
1836	1710
1837	1712
1838	1713
1839	1713
1840	1714
1841	1715
1842	1716
1843	1717
1844	1718
1845	1735
1846	1734
1847	1719
1848	1719
"	1720
1849	1721
1850	1724
1851	1725
1852	1726
1853	1727
1854	1728
1855	1729
1856	1730
1857	1731
1858	1732
1859	1736
1860	1733
1861	1734
1862	1737
1863	1736
1864	1738
1865	1739
1866	1740
1867	1741
1868	1742
1869	1673
1870	1743
1871	1744
1872	1745
1873	1746
1874	1746
1875	1747
1876	1748
1877	1834
1878	1777
1879	1777
1880	1749
1881	1750
1882	1751
1883	1752
1884	1752
1885	1754
1886	1755
1887	1755
1888	1756
1889	1758
1890	1760
1891	1760
1892	1762
1893	1764
1894	1765
1895	1766
1896	1767
1897	1769
1898	1769+1410
1899	1770
1900	1771
1901	1772
1902	1773
1903	1774
1904	1775
1905	1776
1906	1777
1907	1779
1908	1781
1909	1783
1910	7384
1911	1785
1912	1786
1913	1788
1914	1787
1915	1789
1916	1790
1917	1792
1918	1793
1919	1793
1920	1794
1921	1795
1922	1796
1923	1817
1924	1800
1925	1801
1926	1802
1927	1802
1928	1817
1929	1803
1930	1803
1931	1804
1932	1805
1933	1806
1934	1806
1935	1807
1936	1808
1937	1809
1938	1809
1939	1810
1940	1811
1941	1811
1942	1812
1943	1813
1944	1814
1945	1816
1946	1817
1947	1818
1948	1819
1949	1820
1950	1820
1951	1822
1952	1823
1953	1824
1954	1824
1955	1825
1956	658
"	6450
1957	1826
1958	1826
1959	1826
1960	1827
1961	1828
1962	1829
1963	1830
1964	1831
1965	1832
1966	1834
1967	1833
1968	1835
1969	1835
1970	1842
1971	1840
1972	1837
1973	1838
1974	1839
1975	1840
1976	1843
1977	3045
1978	1844
1979	1845
1980	1846
1981	1847
1982	1847
1983	1847
1984	1848
1985	1849
1986	1850
1987	1851
1988	1852
1989	1853
1990	1854
1991	1856
1992	1857
1993	1858
1994	1860
1995	1861
1996	1861
1997	1862
1998	1863
1999	1864
2000	1866
2001	1865
2002	1865
2003	1867
2004	1875
2005	1869
2006	1870
2007	1871
2008	1834
2009	1873
2010	1874
2011	1875
2012	1876
2013	1877
2014	1878
2015	1879
2016	1880
2017	1881
2018	1885
2019	1886
2020	
2021	
2022	
2023	
2024	
2025	
2026	1887
2027	1889
2028	326
2029	1017
2030	507
2031	4965
2032	1018
2033	7151+704
2034	2043
2035	3051
2036	8143
2037	1890
2038	1891
2039	1892
2040	1893
2041	1894
2042	1895
2043	1896
2044	2735
2045	1419
2046	2800+1471
2047	1897
2048	1898
2049	1899
2050	1900
2051	1896
2052	1901
2053	1902
2054	1903
2055	1537
2056	1588
2057	1904
2058	1905
2059	1906
2060	1908
2061	1909
2062	1910
2063	1911
2064	1912
2065	1921
2066	1913
2067	1913
2068	1914
2069	1939
2070	1915
2071	1916
2072	1918
2073	1919
2074	1920
2075	1921
2076	1924
2077	1926
2078	1925
2079	1927
2080	1928
2081	1929
2082	1930
2083	
2084	
2085	1931
2086	1935
2087	1936
2088	1937
2089	1938
2090	1939
2091	1940
"	1941
2092	1933
2093	1933
2094	1942
2095	1942
2096	1943
2097	1944
2098	1945
2099	1947
2100	1948
2101	1949
2102	1950
2103	1951
2104	1952
2105	2029
2106	1953
2107	1954
2108	1955
2109	2050
2110	1956
2111	1957
2112	6367
2113	1958
2114	
2115	1931
2116	1959
2117	1960
2118	1961
2119	1962
2120	1963
2121	1964
2122	1966
2123	1967
2124	1968
2125	1969
2126	4313
2127	1020
2128	1970
2129	1971
2130	1021
2131	1973
2132	3808
2133	1972
2134	1973
2135	3873
2136	1974
2137	1975
2138	1976
2139	1977
2140	1022
2141	1978
2142	1979
2143	1980
"	3212
2144	1982
2145	1984
2146	1984
2147	1984
2148	1985
2149	1984+3050
2150	1986
2151	1988
2152	1987
2153	1989
2154	1990
2155	1991
2156	1992
2157	
2158	4099
2159	1993
2160	1992
2161	1992
2162	1995
2163	1996
2164	1997
2165	5555
2166	1998
2167	1999
2168	4447
2169	2000
2170	2000
2171	1995
2172	2001
2173	2003
2174	7434
2175	1024
2176	2005
"	3860
2177	2004
2178	2008
2179	2007
2180	2009
2181	
2182	2010
2183	2011
2184	2012
2185	5130
2186	5346
2187	2013
2188	2013
2189	5570
2190	5570
2191	5618
2192	5863
2193	72
2194	3726
2195	1025
2196	1026
2197	6190
2198	2014
2199	7163
2200	2015
2201	2016
"	2017
2202	2018
2203	2019
2204	6483
2205	5324
2206	6637
2207	6380
2208	2020
2209	6753
2210	2021
2211	2521
2212	6976
2213	5875
2214	6997
2215	2022
"	2042
2216	2023
2217	2024
2218	7204
2219	2025
2220	7235
2221	7235

G/K	STRONG
2222	2026
2223	2027
2224	2028
2225	2029
2226	2030
2227	2037
2228	2032
2229	2033
2230	2030
2231	2032
2232	2034
2233	2035
2234	1027
2235	2036
2236	2038
2237	2039
2238	2040
2239	2041
2240	2043
2241	6890
2242	1029
2243	63
2244	2044
2245	2045
2246	6914
2247	2046
2248	2266
2249	3188
2250	2694
2251	2047
2252	2048
2253	2049
2254	2050
2255	
2256	
2257	
2258	2051
2259	2052
2260	2053
2261	2054
2262	2055
2263	2056
2264	2057
2265	2058
2266	2059
2267	2060
2268	
2269	2061
2270	2062
2271	2063
2272	2064
2273	2065
2274	2066
2275	2067
2276	2068
2277	2069
2278	2069
2279	2070
2280	2071
2281	2072
2282	2074
2283	2075
2284	2076
2285	2077
2286	2078
2287	2079
2288	2080
2289	2081
2290	2082
2291	2073
"	2083
2292	2073
2293	2085
2294	2086
2295	2087
2296	2088
2297	2090
2298	2091
2299	2092
2300	2093
2301	2094
2302	2094
2303	2096
2304	2099
2305	2097
2306	2098
2307	2100
2308	2101
2309	2104
2310	2118
2311	2105
2312	2106
2313	2107
2314	2108
2315	2109
2316	2111
2317	2113
2318	2115
"	2116
2319	2114
2320	2114
2321	2117
2322	2118
2323	2119
2324	2119
2325	2120
2326	2102
2327	2121
2328	2123
2329	2123
2330	2124
2331	2125
2332	2126
2333	2127
2334	2128
2335	2128
2336	2129
2337	2130
2338	2131
2339	2132
2340	2133
2341	2134
2342	2135
2343	2137
2344	2138
2345	2138
2346	2139
2347	2140
2348	2141
2349	2142
2350	2142
2351	2145
2352	2143
2353	2144
2354	2143
2355	2146
2356	2147
2357	2148
2358	2148
2359	2149
2360	2150
2361	2151
2362	2151
2363	2152
2364	2153
2365	2154
2366	2155
2367	2156
2368	2157
2369	2158
2370	2159
2371	2160
2372	2161
2373	2162
2374	2163
2375	2165
2376	2167
2377	2168
2378	2169
2379	2172
2380	2173
2381	2174
2382	2174
2383	2175
2384	2176
2385	2177
2386	2179
2387	2180
2388	2181
2389	2181
2390	2181
"	2185
2391	2182
2392	2182
2393	2183
2394	2184
2395	2186
2396	2186
2397	2187
2398	2111
2399	2188
2400	2189
2401	2190
2402	2191
2403	2193
2404	2194
2405	2195
2406	2196
2407	2196
2408	2197
2409	2198
2410	2199
2411	2201
2412	2202
2413	2203
2414	2131
2415	2131
2416	2204
2417	2206
2418	2205
2419	2207
2420	2209
2421	2208
2422	2210
2423	2212
2424	2214
2425	2213
2426	2214
2427	2215
2428	2216
2429	2218
2430	2219
2431	2219
2432	2220
2433	2221
2434	2222
2435	2223
2436	2224
2437	2225
2438	2226
2439	2227
2440	2228
2441	2229
2442	2229
2443	2230
2444	2231
2445	2232
2446	2233
2447	2235
2448	2235
2449	2222
2450	2236
2451	2236
2452	2237
2453	2237
2454	2238
2455	2239
2456	2240
2457	2241
2458	2242
2459	
2460	2243
2461	2244
2462	2245
2463	2246
2464	2247
2465	3160
2466	2249
2467	2250
2468	2251
2469	2252
2470	2253
2471	2254
2472	2254
2473	2254
2474	2256
2475	2256
2476	2256
2477	2256
2478	2258
2479	2260
2480	2259
2481	2258
2482	2256
2483	2261
2484	2262
2485	2263
2486	2264
2487	2265
2488	2266
2489	2266
2490	2267
2491	2268
2492	2270
2493	2271
2494	2272
2495	2274
2496	2275
"	5683
2497	2275
2498	2276
2499	2277
2500	2278
2501	2279
2502	2280
2503	2281
2504	2282
2505	2283
2506	2284
2507	2285
2508	2286
2509	2286
2510	2287
2511	2288
2512	2290
2513	2289
2514	2290
2515	2291
2516	2292
2517	2293
2518	2294
2519	2295
2520	2296
2521	2299
2522	2297
2523	2300
2524	2301
2525	2302
2526	2302
2527	2300
2528	
2529	2303
2530	2304
2531	2307
2532	2308
2533	2308
2534	2310
2535	2309
2536	2311
2537	2312
2538	2313
2539	2314
2540	2315
"	2316
2541	2317
2542	2318
2543	2319
2544	2320
2545	2321
2546	2322
2547	8483
2548	2675
2549	2325
2550	2326
2551	2327
2552	2328
2553	2329
2554	2330
2555	2331
2556	2331
2557	2333
2558	2332
2559	2335
2560	2336
2561	2337
2562	2339
2563	2340
2564	2341
2565	2342
2566	2343
2567	2344
2568	2344
2569	2345
2570	2346
2571	2347
2572	2348
2573	2349
2574	2350
2575	2351
2576	2436
2577	2712
2578	2357
2579	2787
2580	2353
2581	2354
2582	1032
2583	2355
2584	2360
2585	2359
2586	2361
2587	2361
2588	2362
2589	2773
2590	2363
"	2439
2591	2363
2592	2364
2593	2365
2594	2366
2595	2367
2596	2334
2597	2368
2598	2369
2599	2371
2600	2372
2601	2373
2602	2374
2603	2374
2604	2371
2605	2375
2606	2377
2607	2380
2608	2378
2609	2381
2610	2382
2611	2383
2612	2384
2613	2385
2614	2386
2615	2387
2616	2388
2617	2389
2618	2390
2619	2391
2620	2392
2621	2393
2622	2394
2623	2395
2624	2396
2625	2396
2626	2397
2627	2398
2628	2399
2629	2400
2630	2398
2631	2401
2632	2402
2633	2403
2634	2404
2635	2405
2636	2406
2637	2407
2638	2410
2639	2411
2640	2412
2641	2413
2642	2414
2643	2415
2644	2416
2645	2416
2646	2416
2647	2419
2648	2420
2649	2421
"	2425
2650	2422
2651	2416
2652	2416
2653	2416
2654	2424
2655	2342
2656	2342
2657	2428
2658	2426
"	2430
2659	2427
2660	2427
2661	2432
2662	2428
2663	2431
2664	2432
2665	2433
2666	2434
2667	2435
2668	2436
2669	2437
2670	2438
2671	2438
2672	6367
2673	2440
2674	2441
2675	2442
2676	2443
2677	2444
2678	2446
2679	2447
2680	2448
2681	2449
2682	2450
2683	2451
2684	2454
2685	2453
2686	1970
2687	2455
2688	2456
2689	2457
2690	2458
2691	2431
2692	2461
2693	2459
2694	2460
2695	2462
2696	2463
2697	2464
2698	2465
2699	2466
2700	2467
2701	2468
2702	2469
2703	2470
2704	2470
2705	2471
2706	2472
2707	2474
2708	2473
2709	2474
2710	2475
2711	2476
2712	2477
2713	2478
2714	2479
2715	2480
2716	2483
2717	2481
2718	2482
2719	2484
2720	2485
2721	2486
2722	2487
2723	2488
2724	2489
2725	2490
2726	2490
2727	2490
2728	2491
2729	2491
2730	2492
2731	2492
2732	2494
2733	2495
2734	2496
2735	2497
2736	2498
2737	2498
2738	2501
2739	2500
2740	2502
2741	2502
2742	2503
2743	2504
2744	2505
2745	2505
2746	2505
2747	2509
"	2511
2748	2510
2749	2506
2750	2506
2751	2507
2752	2512
2753	2513
2754	2513
2755	2515
2756	2514
2757	2516
2758	2517
2759	2518
2760	2518
2761	2519
2762	2520
2763	2521
2764	2522
2765	2522
2766	2523
2767	2524
2768	2525
2769	2526
2770	2527
2771	2534
2772	2529
2773	2530
2774	2531
2775	2532
2776	2530
2777	2533
2778	2534
2779	2534
2780	2535
2781	2536
2782	2537
2783	2538
2784	2539
2785	2540
2786	2556
2787	2541
2788	2542
2789	2543
2790	2543
2791	2544
2792	2545
2793	2546
2794	2547
2795	2537
2796	2548
2797	2549
2798	2550
"	2565
2799	2551
2800	2550
2801	2552
2802	2553
2803	2554
2804	2554
2805	2555
2806	2556
2807	2556
2808	2556
2809	2557
2810	2558
2811	2559
2812	2560
2813	2560
2814	2560
2815	2561
2816	2563
2817	2563
2818	2563
2819	2564
2820	2566
2821	2567
"	2571
2822	2568
2823	2569
2824	2570
2825	2572
2826	2572
2827	2573
2828	2574
2829	2575
2830	2575
2831	2576
2832	2578
2833	2577
2834	2580
2835	2581
2836	2582
2837	2583
2838	2589
2839	2584
2840	2585
2841	2585
2842	2586
2843	2587
2844	2588
2845	2590
2846	2590
2847	2590
2848	2592
2849	2593
2850	2594
2851	2595
2852	2596
2853	2598
2854	2599
2855	2600
2856	2601
2857	2602
2858	2603
2859	2603
2860	2605
2861	2606
2862	2607
2863	2608
2864	2608
2865	2609
2866	2610
2867	2611
2868	2611
2869	2612
2870	2613
2871	2614
2872	2615
2873	2616
2874	2616
2875	2617
2876	2617
2877	2618
2878	2619
2879	2620
2880	2621
2881	2621
2882	2622
2883	2623
2884	2624
2885	2625
2886	2626
2887	2628
2888	2629
2889	2630
2890	2633
2891	2634
2892	2636
2893	2637
2894	2638
2895	2639
2896	2640
2897	2641
2898	2642
2899	2643
2900	5502
2901	2644
2902	2645
2903	2646
2904	2647
2905	2648
2906	2649
2907	2650
2908	2651
2909	2652
2910	2653
2911	2654
2912	2654
2913	2655
2914	2656
2915	2657
2916	2658
2917	2659
2918	2660
2919	2660
2920	2662
2921	2663
2922	6548
2923	2661+6512
2924	2664
2925	2665
2926	2666
2927	2667
2928	2668
2929	2669
2930	2670
2931	2669
2932	2671
2933	2672
2934	2672
2935	2672
2936	2673
2937	2674
2938	2674
2939	2675
2940	2676
2941	7155
2942	2677
2943	2678
2944	2677
2945	2682
2946	2682
2947	2682
2948	2681
2949	2683
2950	2684
2951	2686
2952	2686
2953	2687
2954	2688
2955	2690
2956	2689
2957	2690
2958	2691
"	2699
2959	2694
2960	2692
2961	2693
2962	2694
2963	2701
2964	2702
2965	2703
2966	2704
2967	2705
2968	2695
2969	2696
2970	2696
2971	2697
2972	2698
2973	2691
2974	2695
2975	2700
2976	2706
2977	2707
2978	2708
2979	2709
2980	2710
2981	2711
2982	2712
2983	2713
2984	2714
2985	2715
2986	2356
2987	2352
2988	2735
2989	2716
2990	2717
2991	2717
2992	2720
2993	2717
2994	
2995	2719
2996	2721
2997	2721
2998	2722
2999	2723
3000	2724
3001	2725
3002	2726
3003	2726
3004	2727
3005	2728
3006	2729
3007	2730
3008	5878
3009	2733
3010	2731
3011	2732
3012	2733
3013	2734
"	8474
3014	2787
3015	2736
3016	2737
3017	2738
3018	2739
3019	2740
3020	2741
3021	2742
3022	2742
3023	2742
3024	2782
3025	2742
3026	2742
3027	2743
3028	2744
3029	2736
3030	2745
3031	2746
3032	2747
3033	2748
3034	2750
3035	2751
3036	2752
3037	2753
3038	2754
3039	2755
3040	2756
3041	
3042	2741
3043	2757
3044	2757
3045	2758
3046	2759
3047	2760
3048	2762

G/K	STRONG
3049	2763
3050	2763
3051	2764
3052	2764
3053	2766
3054	2765
3055	2767
3056	2768
3057	2769
3058	2770
3059	2771
3060	2771
3061	2772
3062	2774
3063	2775
3064	2775
3065	2776
3066	2775
3067	2777
3068	2777
3069	2778
3070	2778
3071	2778
3072	2778
3073	2780
3074	2779
3075	2781
3076	2782
3077	2782
3078	2784
3079	2785
3080	2786
3081	2787
3082	2787
3083	2788
3084	2789
3085	7025
3086	2790
"	2794
3087	2790
3088	2796
3089	2791
3090	2792
3091	2793
3092	2793
3093	2796
3094	2795
3095	2797
3096	2798
3097	7025
3098	2799
3099	2800+1471
3100	2801
3101	2802
3102	2817
3103	2834
3104	2820
3105	2835
3106	2834
3107	2834
3108	2803
3109	2805
3110	2803
3111	2806
3112	2807
3113	2808
3114	2809
3115	2810
3116	2811
3117	2811
3118	2812
3119	2813
3120	2814
3121	2815
3122	2838
3123	2366
3124	2821
3125	2822
3126	2823
3127	2821
3128	2824
"	2825
3129	2826
3130	2828
3131	2366
3132	2829
3133	2830
3134	2831
3135	2832
3136	2833
3137	2836
3138	2836
3139	2837
3140	2839
3141	2840
3142	2841
3143	2842
3144	2843
3145	2844
3146	2844
3147	2845
3148	2398
3149	2846
3150	2847
3151	2848
3152	2849
3153	2850
3154	2851
3155	2852
3156	2853
3157	2854
3158	2855
3159	2856
3160	2858
3161	2859
3162	2859
3163	2860
3164	2861
3165	2859
3166	2862
3167	2863
3168	2864
3169	2865
3170	2866
3171	2867
3172	
3173	2894
3174	2870
3175	2870
3176	2896
3177	2896
3178	2871
3179	2872
3180	2873
3181	2874
3182	2875
3183	2874
3184	2876
3185	2879
3186	2878
3187	2880
3188	2881
3189	2882
3190	2883
3191	2884
3192	2885
3193	2886
3194	2887
3195	2888
3196	2889
"	2890
3197	2891
3198	2892
3199	2892
3200	2893
3201	2896
3202	2896
3203	2897
3204	2897
3205	2896
3206	2898
3207	2899
3208	2896
3209	2900
3210	2900
3211	2901
3212	2902
3213	2903
3214	2904
3215	2905
3216	2907
3217	2909
3218	2911
3219	2910
3220	2902
3221	2912
3222	2913
3223	2912
3224	2914
3225	2915
3226	2916
3227	2918
3228	2919
3229	2921
3230	2923
3231	2922
"	2924
3232	2925
3233	2926
3234	2928
3235	2928
3236	2929
3237	2930
3238	2931
3239	2930
3240	2932
3241	2933
3242	2933
3243	2934
3244	2935
3245	2936
3246	2937
3247	2938
3248	2940
3249	2944
3250	2943
3251	2945
3252	2945
3253	2946
3254	2946
3255	2947
3256	2948
3257	2947
3258	2947
3259	2949
3260	2950
3261	2951
3262	2952
3263	2954
3264	2955
3265	2956
3266	2958
3267	2959
3268	2960
3269	2961
3270	2962
3271	2963
3272	2964
3273	2965
3274	2966
3275	
3276	
3277	2968
3278	2969
3279	2970
3280	2970
3281	2971
3282	2973
3283	2974
3284	2975
3285	2972
3286	2976
3287	2977
3288	2977
3289	2978
3290	2979
3291	2980
3292	2981
3293	2982
3294	2983
3295	2984
3296	2985
3297	2986
3298	2988
3299	2989
3300	2991
3301	2990
3302	2992
3303	2993
3304	2994
3305	2995
3306	2996
3307	2997
3308	2998
3309	2999
3310	3000
3311	3005
3312	3001
3313	3002
3314	3003
3315	3003
3316	3003
3317	3004
3318	3006
3319	3008
3320	3009
3321	3010
3322	3011
3323	3012
3324	3013
3325	3014
3326	3015
3327	3017
3328	3016
3329	3019
3330	3018
3331	3024
3332	3020
3333	3021
3334	3022
3335	3023
3336	3025
3337	3026
3338	3027
3339	3030
3340	3031
3341	3032
3342	3033
3343	3034
3344	3034
3345	3035
3346	3035
3347	3036
3348	3037
3349	3038
3350	3035
3351	3039
3352	3040
3353	3038
3354	3041
3355	3042
3356	3043
3357	3038
3358	3044
3359	3045
3360	3047
3361	3048
3362	3049
3363	3050
3364	3051
3365	3053
3366	3054
3367	3056
3368	3057
3369	3058
3370	3059
3371	3060
3372	3055
3373	3063
3374	3064
3375	3065
3376	3066
3377	3067
3378	3068
"	3069
3379	3075
3380	3076
3381	3077
3382	3078
3383	3079
3384	3080
3385	3081
3386	3082
3387	3083
3388	3084
3389	3085
3390	3086
3391	3086
3392	3087
3393	3088
3394	3089
3395	3090
3396	
3397	3091
3398	3092
3399	3092
3400	3093
3401	3094
3402	3095
3403	3096
3404	3096
3405	3097
3406	3098
3407	3099
3408	3100
3409	3101
3410	3102
3411	3103
3412	3103
3413	3104
3414	3105
3415	3106
3416	3107
3417	3108
3418	3109
3419	3110
3420	3194
3421	3111
3422	3112
3423	3113
3424	3114
3425	3115
3426	3116
3427	3117
3428	3117
3429	3119
3430	3120
3431	3121
3432	3122
3433	3123
3434	3124
3435	3238
3436	3125
3437	3126
3438	3127
3439	3128
3440	3129
3441	3130
3442	3131
3443	3132
3444	3133
3445	3134
3446	3289
3447	3135
3448	3318
3449	3136
3450	3335
3451	3079
"	3137
3452	3384
3453	3138
3454	3088
"	3139
3455	3140
3456	3141
3457	3142
3458	3143
3459	3144
3460	3145
3461	3146
3462	3147
3463	3148
3464	3149
3465	3149
3466	3150
3467	3151
3468	3152
3469	2109
3470	3153
3471	3153
3472	3154
3473	3155
3474	3156
3475	3157
3476	3157
3477	3158
"	3159
3478	3160
3479	3161
3480	3162
3481	3162
3482	3163
3483	
3484	3164
3485	3165
3486	3171
3487	3166
3488	3167
3489	3168
3490	3169
3491	3169
3492	3170
3493	3171
3494	3172
3495	3173
3496	3174
3497	3175
3498	3176
3499	3177
3500	3178
3501	3179
3502	3180
3503	3181
3504	3182
3505	3183
3506	3184
3507	3185
3508	3186
3509	3187
3510	3188
3511	3189
3512	2895
"	3190
3513	3192
3514	3193
3515	3195
3516	3196
3517	3197
3518	3204
3519	3198
3520	3199
3521	3199
3522	3200
3523	3201
3524	3203
3525	3203
3526	3204
3527	3204
3528	3205
3529	3206
3530	3207
3531	3208
3532	3856
3533	3209
3534	3210
3535	3211
3536	3213
3537	3214
3538	3215
3539	3217
3540	3218
3541	3219
3542	3220
3543	3223
3544	3224
3545	3225
3546	3226
3547	3228
3548	3233
3549	3227
3550	3229
3551	3229
3552	3230
3553	3222
3554	3231
3555	3232
3556	3233
3557	3234
3558	3235
3559	3236
3560	3237
3561	3238
3562	3239
3563	3239
3564	3241
3565	3241
3566	3242
3567	3243
"	5134
3568	3244
3569	3245
3570	3245
3571	3246
3572	3247
3573	3248
3574	3250
3575	3251
3576	3252
3577	3253
3578	3254
3579	3256
3580	3256
3581	3256
3582	3257
3583	3258
3584	3258
3585	3259
3586	3294
3587	3260
3588	3260
3589	3261
3590	3262
3591	3263
3592	3265
3593	3266
3594	3267
3595	3268
3596	3269
3597	3270
3598	3271
3599	3273
3600	3265
3601	3274
3602	3275
3603	3276
3604	3277
3605	3278
3606	3279
3607	3280
3608	3279
3609	3281
3610	3282
3611	
3612	3283
3613	3284
3614	3285
3615	3286
3616	3288
3617	3287
3618	3288
3619	3289
3620	3290
3621	3291
3622	3292
3623	3264
"	3293
3624	3293
3625	3293
3626	3295
3627	3295
3628	3294
3629	3296
3630	3297
3631	3298
3632	3299
3633	3299
3634	3300
3635	3301
3636	3302
3637	3303
3638	3304
3639	3305
3640	3306
3641	3307
3642	3308
3643	3309
3644	3309
3645	3304
3646	3310
3647	3311
3648	3312
3649	3313
3650	3314
3651	3315
3652	3316
3653	3316
3654	3317
3655	3318
3656	3320
3657	3322
3658	3323
3659	3324
3660	3325
3661	3326
3662	3326
3663	3327
3664	3328
3665	3329
3666	3326
3667	3331
3668	3332
3669	3333
3670	3335
3671	3336
3672	3337
"	3340
3673	3339
3674	3338
3675	3341
3676	3342
3677	3343
3678	3344
3679	3350
3680	3347
3681	3348
3682	3349
3683	3344
3684	2901
"	6990
3685	3351
3686	3352
3687	3353
3688	3354
3689	3947
3690	3355
3691	3356
3692	3357
3693	3359
3694	3360
3695	3361
3696	3362
3697	3363
3698	3368
3699	3364
3700	3365
3701	3368
3702	3366
3703	3368
3704	3369
3705	3370
3706	3371
3707	3372
3708	3372
3709	3384
3710	3373
3711	3374
3712	3375
3713	3376
3714	3377
3715	3378
3716	3379
3717	3380
3718	3381
3719	3382
3720	3383
3721	3384
3722	3384
3723	3384
3724	7297
3725	3385
3726	3386
3727	7311
3728	3387
3729	3388
3730	3388
3731	3389
3732	3391
3733	3392
3734	3394
3735	3405
3736	3395
3737	3396
3738	3397
3739	3398
3740	3399
3741	3400
3742	3401
3743	3402
3744	3403
3745	3404
3746	3404
3747	3405
3748	3406
3749	3407
3750	3408
3751	3409
3752	3411
3753	7311
3754	3412
3755	3406
3756	3406
3757	3413
3758	3414
3759	3414
3760	3415
3761	3416
3762	3417
3763	3419
3764	3418
3765	4313
3766	3420
3767	3421
3768	3422
3769	3423
3770	8492
3771	3424
3772	3425
3773	3446
3774	3450
3775	3455
3776	3478
3777	3480
3778	3481
"	3482
3779	3485
3780	3426
3781	
3782	3427
3783	3429
3784	3428
3785	3430
3786	3431
3787	3430
3788	3433
3789	
3790	3434
3791	3435
3792	3436
3793	3437
3794	3427
3795	3432
3796	3438
3797	3439
3798	3440
3799	3441
3800	3442
3801	3442
3802	3444
3803	3445
3804	3447
3805	3448
3806	3437
3807	3449
3808	3449
3809	3451
3810	3452
3811	1020
3812	3451
3813	3453
3814	3454
3815	3456
3816	3457
3817	3458
3818	3459
3819	3460
3820	3460
3821	3461
3822	3462
"	8153
3823	3462
3824	3465
3825	3463
3826	3464
3827	3466
3828	3467
3829	3468
3830	3467
3831	3469
3832	3470
3833	3470
3834	3472
3835	3471
3836	3473
3837	3474
3838	3477
3839	3477
3840	3475
3841	3476
3842	3483
3843	3484
3844	3486
3845	3489
3846	3490
3847	3491
3848	3492
3849	3494
3850	3495
3851	5414
3852	5414
3853	3496
3854	3497
3855	3498
3856	3499
3857	3499
3858	3500
3859	3501
3860	3502
3861	3503
3862	3504
3863	3505
3864	3506
3865	3507
3866	3508
3867	3509
3868	
3869	
3870	
3871	
3872	3510
3873	3511

G/K	STRONG
3874	3512
3875	2489
3876	834
3877	3513
3878	3515
3879	3516
3880	3514
3881	3517
3882	3518
3883	3519
3884	3520
3885	3520
3886	3521
3887	3522
3888	3524
3889	3523
3890	3525
3891	3526
3892	3527
"	4342
3893	3528
3894	3529
3895	3531
3896	3530
3897	3532
3898	3535
3899	3533
3900	3534
3901	3536
3902	3537
3903	1754
3904	1767
3905	3539
3906	3540
3907	3541
3908	3543
3909	3543
3910	3544
3911	3545
3912	3547
3913	3548
3914	3550
3915	3552
3916	3553
3917	3554
3918	3555
3919	3556
3920	3557
3921	3558
3922	3559
3923	3560
3924	3561
3925	3562
3926	3563
3927	3563
3928	3738
3929	3564
3930	3565
3931	3566
3932	3568
3933	3568
3934	3569
"	3571
3935	3570
3936	3572
3937	3573
3938	3574
3939	3575
3940	3575
3941	3576
3942	3577
3943	3578
3944	3579
3945	3580
3946	3581
3947	3581
3948	3582
3949	3583
3950	3584
3951	3585
3952	3586
3953	3587
3954	3588
3955	3588+518
3956	3588 +408+3651
3957	3589
3958	3590
3959	3591
3960	3593
3961	3592
3962	3594
3963	3595
3964	3596
3965	3597
3966	3598
3967	3599
3968	3600
3969	3601
3970	3602
3971	3603
3972	3605
3973	3607
3974	3607
3975	3608

G/K	STRONG
3976	3609
3977	3610
3978	3611
3979	3612
3980	3613
3981	3612
3982	3614
3983	3615
3984	3607
3985	3616
3986	3617
3987	3618
3988	3622
3989	3628
3990	3619
3991	3620
3992	3621
3993	3622
3994	3623
3995	3624
3996	3625
3997	3626
3998	3627
3999	3628
4000	3629
4001	3631
4002	3630
4003	3632
4004	3633
4005	3634
4006	3636
4007	3637
4008	3638
4009	3639
4010	3640
4011	3641
4012	3641
4013	
4014	3642
4015	3588+4100
4016	3643
4017	3644
4018	3643
4019	3645
4020	3645
4021	3646
4022	3647
4023	3648
4024	3649
4025	3650
4026	3651
4027	3651
4028	3651
4029	3653
4030	3653
4031	3654
4032	
4033	3655
4034	3656
4035	3657
4036	3658
4037	3659
4038	3654
4039	3662
4040	3663
4041	3663
4042	3663
4043	3664
4044	3665
4045	3666
4046	3667
4047	3667
4048	3669
4049	3668
4050	3669
4051	3669
4052	3670
4053	3671
4054	3672
4055	3672
4056	3674
4057	3677
4058	3676
"	3678
4059	3680
4060	3677
4061	3678
4062	3681
4063	3694
4064	3682
4065	3683
4066	3678+3050
4067	3684
4068	3685
4069	3686
4070	3687
4071	3688
4072	3689
4073	3689
4074	3690
4075	3691
4076	3693
4077	3692
4078	3695
4079	3696

G/K	STRONG
4080	3697
4081	3698
4082	3699
4083	3700
4084	3701
4085	3703
4086	3704
4087	3707
4088	3708
4089	3708
4090	3709
4091	3710
4092	3711
4093	3712
4094	3713
4095	3713
4096	3714
4097	3715
4098	3716
4099	3715
4100	3717
4101	3718
4102	3719
4103	3720
4104	3721
4105	3722
4106	3722
4107	3723
4108	3724
4109	3724
4110	3724
4111	3724
4112	3726
4113	3725
4114	3727
4115	3728
4116	3731
4117	3730
4118	3732
4119	3733
4120	3733
4121	3733
4122	1033
4123	3734
4124	3736
4125	3738
4126	3739
4127	3738
4128	3738
4129	3741
4130	3740
4131	3742
4132	3743
4133	3746
4134	3747
4135	3748
4136	3749
4137	3750
4138	3751
4139	3752
4140	3753
4141	3755
4142	3754
4143	
4144	3755
4145	3756
4146	3757
4147	3758
4148	3754
4149	3759
4150	3760
4151	3760
4152	3759
4153	3761
"	3762
4154	3763
4155	3765
4156	3766
4157	3767
4158	3768
4159	3769
4160	3770
4161	3771
4162	3772
4163	
4164	3773
4165	3774
4166	3775
4167	3776
4168	3777
4169	3778
4170	3780
4171	7911
4172	3781
4173	3782
4174	3783
4175	3784
4176	3785
4177	3786
4178	3787
4179	3788
4180	3789
4181	3791
4182	3793
4183	3794

G/K	STRONG
4184	3795
4185	3796
4186	3798
4187	3799
4188	3800
4189	3801
4190	3802
4191	8596
4192	3803
4193	3803
4194	3803
4195	3804
4196	3805
4197	3806
4198	3807
4199	
4200	
4201	
4202	3808
4203	3810
4204	3818
4205	3819
4206	3811
4207	3812
4208	1975
4209	3813
4210	3815
4211	3816
4212	3817
4213	3820
4214	3820+6965
4215	935
4216	3833
4217	2574
4218	3833
4219	3822
4220	3823
4221	3823
4222	3824
4223	3834
4224	905
4225	3827
4226	3826
4227	3828
4228	3829
4229	3830
4230	3830
4231	3832
4232	3833
4233	3833
4234	3833
4235	3835
4236	3835
4237	3836
4238	3837
4239	3837
4240	1121
4241	3838
4242	3839
4243	3841
4244	3842
4245	3838
4246	3840
"	3843
4247	3828
4248	3844
4249	3845
4250	3846
4251	7884
4252	3847
4253	3849
4254	3850
4255	1688
4256	3205
4257	3808
4258	3851
4259	3852
4260	3853
4261	3854
4262	3855
4263	3856
4264	3856
4265	3857
4266	3857
4267	3858
4268	3858
4269	3859
4270	
4271	3856
4272	3862
4273	3863
4274	3810
4275	3864
4276	3865
"	3866
4277	3867
4278	3867
4279	3868
4280	3869
4281	3870
4282	
4283	3871
4284	3872
4285	3873
4286	3874

G/K	STRONG
4287	3875
4288	3876
4289	3877
4290	3878
4291	3878
"	3881
4292	3880
4293	3882
4294	3883
4295	3884
4296	3885
4297	3888
4298	3889
"	3919
4299	3891
4300	3892
4301	3893
4302	3894
4303	3894
4304	3872
4305	3895
4306	3896
4307	883
4308	3897
4309	3898
4310	3898
4311	3901
4312	3899
4313	3902
4314	3903
4315	3905
4316	3906
4317	3907
4318	3908
4319	3814
"	3909
4320	3910
4321	3911
4322	3912
4323	3913
4324	3914
4325	3915
4326	3915
4327	3917
4328	3885
4329	3887
4330	3918
4331	3919
4332	3919
4333	3919
4334	3920
4335	3921
4336	3922
4337	3923
4338	3651
4339	3924
4340	3925
4341	3928
4342	4100
4343	
4344	3926
4345	3927
4346	4136
4347	3929
4348	4616
4349	3885
4350	3930
4351	3931
4352	3932
4353	3933
4354	3934
4355	3935
4356	3936
4357	3937
4358	3938
4359	
4360	3939
4361	6030
4362	3886
4363	3216
4364	1036
4365	3940
4366	3941
4367	6440
4368	6440
4369	3943
4370	3887
4371	3944
4372	3945
4373	3946
4374	3947
4375	3948
4376	3949
4377	3950
4378	3951
4379	3952
4380	3953
4381	3954
4382	3955
4383	3956
4384	3957
4385	3958
4386	3959
4387	3960
4388	3962

G/K	STRONG
4389	8289
4390	3963
4391	
4392	
4393	3965
4394	3966
4395	3967
4396	3968
4397	3970
4398	3971
4399	3972
4400	3973
4401	3974
4402	3975
4403	
4404	3976
4405	3967
4406	369
4407	3978
4408	3979
4409	3980
4410	3981
4411	3982
4412	3985
4413	3986
4414	3987
4415	3988
4416	3988
4417	622
4418	3989
4419	3990
4420	3991
4421	3992
4422	3993
4423	3994
4424	834
4425	854
4426	3995
4427	3996
"	3997
4428	3998
4429	3999
4430	4000
4431	4001
4432	4002
4433	4003
4434	4016
4435	4004
4436	4005
4437	4006
4438	4007
4439	4008
4440	4009
4441	
4442	1097
4443	4010
4444	1110
4445	4011
4446	4012
4447	
4448	4013
4449	4014
4450	4013
4451	4015
4452	4017
4453	4018
4454	7248
4455	4019
4456	4020
4457	4021
4458	4022
"	4030
4459	4023
4460	4024
4461	4023
4462	4025
4463	4026
4464	4027
"	4028
4465	4024
4466	4027
4467	4028
4468	4029
4469	4030
4470	4031
4471	4032
4472	4033
4473	4033
4474	4036
4475	4034
4476	4035
4477	4037
4478	4038
4479	4039
4480	4041
4481	4042
4482	4043
4483	4043
4484	4043
4485	4044
4486	4045
4487	4046
4488	4047
4489	4048
4490	4050

G/K	STRONG
4491	4051
4492	4052
4493	4053
4494	4054
4495	4054
4496	4055
4497	4057
4498	4057
4499	4058
"	4059
4500	4060
4501	4060
4502	4062
4503	4063
4504	4064
4505	4065
4506	4066
"	4079
"	4090
4507	4068
4508	4069
4509	4071
4510	4072
4511	4073
4512	4074
4513	4075
4514	1767
4515	4060
4516	4081
4517	4067
4518	4080
4519	4082
4520	4084
"	4092
4521	4085
4522	4086
4523	4087
4524	4088
4525	4089
4526	4089
4527	4091
4528	4067
4529	4093
4530	4129
4531	4130
4532	4094
4533	4095
4534	4096
4535	4097
4536	4098
4537	4100
4538	4102
4539	4103
4540	4104
4541	4105
4542	4106
4543	4107
4544	4108
"	4109
4545	4110
4546	4111
4547	4112
4548	
4549	4113
4550	4114
4551	4115
4552	65
4553	
4554	4116
4555	4117
4556	4117
4557	4118
4558	4119
4559	4120
4560	4121
4561	4122
4562	4123
4563	
4564	
4565	4124
4566	4124
4567	4125
4568	4136
4569	4126
4570	4127
4571	4128
4572	4131
4573	4132
4574	4133
4575	4134
4576	4135
4577	4135
4578	4136
4579	4137
4580	4138
4581	4139
4582	4140
4583	3971
4584	4462
4585	5439
4586	4143
4587	4144
4588	4145
"	4328
4589	4146

G/K	STRONG
4590	4329
4591	4147
4592	4148
4593	4147
4594	4149
4595	4150
4596	4151
4597	4152
4598	4153
4599	4155
4600	4156
4601	4157
4602	4158
4603	4159
4604	4161
4605	4162
4606	4163
4607	4164
4608	4165
4609	4166
4610	4167
4611	4168
4612	4169
4613	4170
4614	4171
4615	4171
4616	4172
4617	4173
4618	4174
4619	4175
4620	4175
4621	4175
4622	4176
4623	4177
4624	4172
4625	4180
4626	4180
4627	4181
4628	4182
4629	4183
4630	4184
4631	4185
4632	4186
4633	4187
4634	4188
4635	3467
4636	4190
4637	4191
"	4192
4638	4194
4639	4195
4640	4196
4641	4197
4642	4198
4643	4100+2088
4644	4100+2088
4645	4199
4646	4200
4647	4201
4648	4202
4649	4205
4650	4204
4651	4206
4652	4206
4653	4206
4654	2142
4655	4208
4656	4207
4657	4207
4658	4207
4659	4209
4660	4210
4661	4211
4662	4212
4663	4213
4664	2219
4665	4214
4666	4216
4667	4217
4668	2219
"	4215
4669	4218
4670	4219
4671	4220
4672	4221
4673	4222
4674	4229
4675	4224
4676	4224
4677	4226
4678	4225
4679	4227
4680	4228
4681	4229
4682	4229
4683	4229
4684	4230
4685	4231
4686	4232
4687	4233
4688	4234
4689	4235
4690	4236
4691	4237
4692	4238

G/K	STRONG
4693	4239
4694	4240
4695	4241
4696	4232
4697	4242
4698	4243
4699	2256+392
4700	4245
4701	4245
4702	4244
4703	4246
4704	4247
4705	4248
4706	4249
4707	4250
4708	4251
4709	4252
4710	4253
4711	4254
4712	5555
4713	4256
4714	4257
4715	4258
4716	4259
4717	4260
4718	4261
4719	4262
4720	4263
4721	2557
4722	4264
4723	4265
4724	4266
4725	4267
4726	4268
4727	4269
4728	4270
4729	4271
4730	4272
4731	4273
4732	4274
4733	4275
4734	4276
4735	4277
4736	4278
4737	4279
4738	4280
4739	4281
"	4282
4740	4283
4741	4286
4742	4284
4743	4285
4744	4287
4745	4288
4746	4289
4747	4290
4748	4292
4749	4293
4750	
4751	4294
4752	4295
4753	4296
4754	4297
4755	4298
4756	2892
4757	4299
4758	4300
4759	4301
4760	4302
4761	4303
4762	4304
4763	4305
4764	4306
4765	4308
4766	4307
4767	4309
4768	4100
4769	4310
4770	4313
4771	4314
4772	4311
4773	4312
4774	4315
4775	4316
4776	4317
4777	4318
4778	4319
4779	4320
4780	4322
4781	4321
4782	4323
4783	4324
4784	4325
4785	4326
4786	4327
4787	3243
4788	4329
4789	4158
4790	4330
4791	4331
4792	4332
4793	4334
4794	4335
4795	4338
4796	4337
4797	4339
4798	4340
4799	4341
4800	4343
4801	4344
4802	4346
4803	4345
4804	4347
4805	4348
4806	4349
4807	4350
"	4369
4808	4351
4809	4352
4810	4353
4811	4354
4812	4355
4813	4356
4814	4358
4815	4360
4816	4357
4817	4359
4818	4361
4819	4362
4820	4363
4821	4364
4822	4365
4823	4365
4824	4365
4825	4363
4826	4366
4827	4367
4828	4368
4829	4370
4830	4371
4831	4373
4832	4372
4833	4374
4834	4375
4835	4376
4836	4377
4837	4378
4838	4379
4839	4380
4840	4381
4841	4382
4842	4383
4843	4384
4844	4385
4845	4386
4846	4387
4847	4388
"	4389
4848	4390
4849	4392
4850	4393
4851	4407
4852	4395
4853	4396
4854	4394
4855	4397
4856	4399
4857	4400
4858	4401
4859	4402
4860	4403
4861	4404
4862	4390
4863	4405
4864	4407
4865	4408
4866	4409
4867	4410
4868	4409
4869	4411
4870	4412
4871	4413
4872	4414
4873	4414
4874	4418
4875	4417
4876	4419
4877	4420
4878	4421
4879	4423
4880	4422
4881	4422
4882	4424
4883	4409
4884	4425
4885	3887
"	3945
4886	4426
4887	4427
4888	4427
4889	4428
"	4429
4890	4428
4891	4432
4892	4434
4893	4436
4894	4435
4895	4438
4896	4439
4897	4440
4898	4441
4899	4441
4900	4442
4901	4443
4902	4444
4903	4445
4904	4445
4905	4404
4906	4446
4907	4447
4908	5243
4909	5243
4910	4448
4911	4448
4912	4450
4913	4451
4914	4452
4915	4453
4916	4454
4917	4455
4918	4455
4919	4456
4920	4457
4921	4458
4922	4459
4923	4460
4924	4461
4925	4462
4926	4463
4927	4464
4928	4465
4929	4466
4930	4467
4931	4468
4932	4469
4933	4470
4934	4471
4935	4471
4936	4472
4937	4473
4938	4474
4939	4475
4940	4476
4941	4477
4942	4478
4943	4478
4944	4482
4945	4482
4946	4480
4947	4485
4948	4487
4949	4488
4950	4490
4951	4489
4952	4491
4953	4492
4954	4493
4955	4494
4956	4495
4957	4496
4958	5186+4512
4959	4497
4960	4498
4961	4499
4962	4500
4963	4501
4964	4502
4965	3240
"	5117
4966	4503
4967	4496
4968	4505
4969	4506
4970	4506
4971	2679
"	2680
4972	4507
4973	4508
4974	4480
4975	4509
4976	4511
4977	4511
4978	4512
4979	4513
4980	4514
4981	4515
4982	4516
4983	4517
4984	4518
4985	4519
4986	4520
4987	4521
4988	4523
4989	4522
4990	4524
4991	4524
4992	4036
4993	4525
4994	4525
4995	4526
4996	4527
4997	4528
4998	4529
4999	4531
5000	4531
5001	4532
5002	4530
5003	4533
5004	4534
5005	4535
5006	4536
5007	4537
5008	4538
5009	4539
5010	4540
5011	4541
5012	4541
5013	4541
5014	4542
5015	5533
5016	4543
5017	4544
5018	4545
5019	4546
5020	4547
5021	4548
5022	4549
5023	4550
5024	4551
5025	4551
5026	4552
5027	4553
5028	4554
5029	4555
5030	4556
5031	4557
5032	4558
5033	4559
5034	4560
5035	4149
5036	4561
5037	4562
5038	
5039	4563
5040	4564
5041	4565
5042	4566
5043	4568
5044	4569
5045	4569
5046	4570
5047	4570
5048	4154
"	4571
"	5976
5049	4572
5050	4573
5051	4575
5052	4574
5053	4576
5054	4579
5055	4578
5056	4580
5057	4581
5058	4581
5059	4582
5060	4583
5061	4583
5062	4584
5063	4584
5064	4586
5065	4587
5066	4588
5067	4589
5068	4590
5069	4590
5070	4591
5071	4592
5072	
5073	4594
5074	4595
5075	4596
5076	4597
5077	4598
5078	4599
5079	4583
5080	4600
5081	4601
5082	4601
5083	4601
5084	4602
5085	4603
5086	4604
5087	4605
5088	4480+5921
5089	4607
5090	4608
5091	4609
5092	4609
5093	4605
5094	4611
5095	4611
5096	4612
5097	4613
5098	4614
5099	4615
5100	4616
5101	4617
5102	4617
5103	4618
5104	4585
5105	4618
5106	4619
5107	4620
5108	4621
5109	4622
5110	4623
5111	4624
5112	4625
5113	4626
5114	4627
5115	4628
5116	4629
5117	4631
5118	4632
5119	4633
5120	4630
"	4634
5121	4635
5122	4636
5123	6206
5124	4637
5125	4638
5126	4639
5127	4640
5128	4641
5129	4641
5130	4643
5131	4642
5132	4644
5133	4645
5134	4646
5135	4647
5136	4648
5137	4649
5138	4650
5139	4651
5140	4652
5141	4653
5142	4654
5143	4654
5144	4655
5145	4656
5146	4657
5147	4658
5148	4659
5149	4659
5150	4660
5151	4661
5152	4662
"	4663
5153	4664
5154	4665
5155	4666
5156	4667
5157	4669
5158	4668
5159	4670
5160	4160
5161	4671
5162	4672
5163	4673
5164	4674
5165	4675
5166	4675
5167	4676
5168	4677
5169	4678
5170	4678
5171	4679
5172	4680
5173	4681
5174	4682
5175	4683
5176	6668
5177	4684
5178	4685
5179	4685
5180	4686
5181	4686
5182	4685
5183	4685
5184	4687
5185	4688
"	4699
5186	4689
5187	4690
5188	4691
5189	4692
5190	4692
5191	4693
5192	4686
5193	4694
5194	4695
5195	4696
5196	4697
5197	4698
5198	4688
5199	4700
5200	4701
5201	4702
5202	4703
5203	4705
5204	4706
5205	4707
5206	4708
5207	4709
5208	4710
5209	4711
5210	4712
5211	4694
5212	4713
5213	4714
5214	4715
5215	4716
5216	4717
"	4718
5217	4718
5218	4719
5219	4720
5220	4721
5221	4722
5222	
5223	4723
5224	4723
5225	4724
5226	4725
5227	4726
5228	4727
5229	4728
5230	4729
5231	6999
5232	6999
5233	4730
5234	4731
5235	4732
5236	4733
5237	4734
5238	4735
5239	4736
5240	4737
5241	4738
5242	4739
5243	4740
5244	4741
5245	4743
5246	4744
5247	4745
5248	4746
5249	4747
5250	4748
5251	4749
5252	4750
5253	4751
5254	4752
5255	4753
5256	4754
5257	4754
5258	4806
5259	4755
5260	4758
5261	4759
5262	4759
5263	4760
5264	8112
5265	4761
"	4763
5266	4764
5267	4765
5268	4767
5269	4766
5270	4768
5271	4769
5272	4770
5273	4771
5274	4772
5275	4773
5276	4774
5277	4775
5278	4777
5279	4778
5280	4780
5281	4781
5282	4757
5283	4782
5284	4783
5285	4787
5286	4784
5287	4751
5288	4785
5289	4786
5290	4062
5291	4788
5292	4789
5293	4790
5294	4791
5295	4792
5296	4793
5297	4794
5298	4835
5299	4795
5300	4796
5301	4797
"	4798
5302	4799
5303	4800
5304	4800+3050
5305	4801
5306	4802
5307	4178
"	4803
5308	4805
5309	4806
5310	4807
"	4810
5311	4807
"	4810
5312	4808
5313	4809
5314	4807
5315	4809+6946
5316	4811
5317	4179
5318	4812
5319	4813
5320	4814
5321	4815
5322	4816
5323	4817
5324	4818
5325	
5326	4819
5327	4820
5328	4821
5329	4822
5330	4823
5331	4824
5332	4825
5333	4826
5334	4827
5335	4828
5336	7489
5337	4829
5338	4830
5339	4831
5340	4832
5341	4832
5342	4832
5343	4833
5344	4834
5345	4836
5346	4837
5347	4838
5348	4839
5349	4840
5350	4841
5351	4842
5352	4843
5353	4844
5354	4845
5355	4846
5356	4847
5357	4848
5358	4762
5359	4762
5360	4849
5361	4850
5362	4853
5363	4853
5364	4854
5365	4856
5366	1858
5367	4864
5368	4864
5369	4869
5370	4869
5371	5381
5372	4881
5373	4883
5374	4884
5375	4885
5376	4885
5377	4890
5378	4895
5379	4881
5380	4905
5381	4906
5382	4909
5383	4930
5384	4939
5385	4951
5386	4955
5387	4956
5388	4957
5389	4958
5390	4851
5391	4855
5392	4852
5393	4857
5394	4859
5395	
5396	4860
5397	4876
5398	4861
5399	4862
5400	4863
5401	4865
5402	4866
5403	4867
5404	4868
5405	4870'
5406	4871
5407	4872
5408	4874
5409	4875
5410	4876
5411	4877
5412	4878
5413	4879
5414	4880
5415	4880
5416	4882
5417	4886
5418	4888
5419	4888
5420	4888
5421	4888
5422	4889
5423	4891
5424	4892
5425	4893
5426	4893
5427	4894
5428	4896
5429	4897
5430	4898
5431	4899
5432	4900
5433	4901
5434	4902
5435	4904
5436	4189
5437	7921
5438	4908
5439	4911
5440	4910
5441	4911
5442	4912
5443	4913
5444	4915
5445	4915
5446	4914
5447	4916
5448	4916
5449	4917
5450	4918
5451	4919
5452	4920
5453	4920
5454	4921
5455	4922
5456	7969
5457	4923
5458	4924
5459	4925
5460	4924
5461	4926
5462	4927
5463	4928
5464	4929
5465	4929
5466	4931
5467	4932
5468	4933
5469	4934
5470	4935
5471	4936
5472	4937
5473	4937
5474	4938
5475	4938
5476	4940
5477	4941
5478	4942
5479	4943
5480	4944
5481	8246
5482	4945
5483	4945
5484	4946
5485	4947
5486	4948
5487	4949
5488	4950
5489	4952
5490	4954
5491	4959
5492	4960
5493	4962
5494	4962
5495	4963
5496	4964
5497	4965
5498	4966
5499	4967
5500	4968
5501	4969
5502	8478
5503	4970
5504	4971
5505	4972
5506	4973
5507	4974
5508	4976
5509	4977
5510	4979
5511	4980
5512	4981
5513	4982
5514	4983

G/K	STRONG
5515	4983
5516	4975
5517	4985
"	4988
5518	4986
5519	4987
5520	4989
5521	4990
5522	4991
5523	4992
5524	4993
5525	4993
5526	
5527	
5528	4994
5529	4995
5530	4996
5531	527+4996
5532	4997
5533	4998
5534	5000
5535	5001
5536	5002
5537	5003
5538	5005
5539	5004
5540	5006
5541	5007
5542	5007
5543	5008
5544	5009
5545	5010
5546	5011
5547	5012
5548	5014
5549	5015
5550	5015
5551	5015
5552	5562
5553	5016
5554	5014
5555	5018
5556	5019
5557	5019
5558	5021
5559	5022
5560	5024
5561	5025
5562	5025
5563	5026
5564	5027
5565	5028
5566	5030
5567	5031
5568	5032
5569	5033
5570	5034
5571	5034
5572	5036
5573	5037
5574	5035
5575	5035
5576	5039
5577	5038
5578	5040
5579	5041
5580	5042
5581	5044
5582	5045
5583	5046
5584	5048
5585	5050
5586	5051
5587	5052
5588	5054
5589	5664
5590	5055
5591	5056
5592	5057
5593	5058
5594	5059
5595	5060
5596	5061
5597	5062
5598	5063
5599	5064
5600	5064
5601	5065
5602	5066
5603	5067
5604	5077
5605	5068
5606	5070
5607	5071
5608	5072
5609	1713
5610	5074
5611	5076
5612	5077
5613	5078
5614	5079
5615	5080
5616	5080
5617	5112
5618	5081
5619	5082
5620	5084
5621	5083
5622	5086
5623	5087
5624	5088
5625	5089
5626	
5627	5090
5628	5090
5629	5091
5630	5091
5631	5092
5632	5093
5633	5095
5634	5096
5635	5097
5636	5096
5637	5098
5638	5099
5639	5100
5640	5101
5641	5102
5642	5102
5643	5104
5644	5105
5645	763
5646	
5647	
5648	5106
5649	5107
5650	5108
5651	5109
5652	3013
5653	5110
5654	5112
5655	5113
5656	5114
5657	5115
5658	5115
5659	5116
5660	5116
5661	4999
5662	5121
5663	5117
5664	5117
5665	5118
5666	5119
5667	5120
5668	5121
5669	
5670	5123
5671	5124
5672	5125
5673	5126
5674	5127
5675	5128
5676	5129
5677	5130
5678	5130
5679	5131
5680	5132
5681	5133
5682	3243
5683	5136
5684	5137
5685	5137
5686	5138
5687	5139
5688	5140
5689	5140
5690	5141
5691	5143
5692	5144
5693	5144
5694	5145
5695	5146
5696	5147
5697	5148
5698	5117
5699	5151
5700	5149
5701	5152
5702	5153
5703	5154
5704	5155
5705	5156
5706	5157
5707	5158
5708	5158
5709	5159
5710	
5711	5158
5712	5160
5713	5161
5714	5162
5715	5163
5716	5164
5717	5165
5718	5166
5719	5150
5720	5167
5721	5168
5722	5169
5723	2734
"	2787
5724	5170
5725	5170
5726	5171
5727	5172
5728	5173
5729	5175
5730	5904
5731	5176
5732	5177
5733	5178
5734	5178
5735	5179
5736	5180
5737	5181
5738	5183
5739	5183
5740	5184
5741	5185
5742	5186
5743	5200
5744	5187
5745	5195
5746	5189
5747	5190
5748	5192
5749	5193
5750	5194
5751	5196
5752	5197
5753	5198
5754	5198
5755	5188
5756	5199
5757	5201
5758	5201
5759	5203
5760	5204
5761	
5762	5108
5763	5109
5764	5205
5765	5206
5766	5121
5767	5207
5768	5125
5769	5209
5770	5210
5771	5211
5772	5212
5773	5213
5774	5214
5775	5216
5776	5215
5777	5217
5778	5218
5779	5218
5780	5219
5781	5220
5782	5221
5783	5223
5784	5222
5785	5224
"	6549
5786	5224
5787	3559
5788	3559
5789	5225
5790	5226
"	5227
5791	5228
"	5229
5792	5230
5793	5231
5794	5233
5795	5234
5796	5234
5797	5236
5798	5235
5799	5237
5800	5238
5801	5239
5802	959
5803	5241
5804	5242
5805	5244
5806	3988
5807	5246
5808	5248
5809	5247
5810	5249
5811	5250
5812	5251
5813	5252
5814	5254
5815	5255
5816	5257
5817	5257
5818	5258
5819	5259
5820	5258
5821	5262
5822	5262
5823	5263
5824	5264
5825	5265
5826	5266
5827	5268
5828	5269
5829	5270
5830	5271
5831	5271
5832	5272
5833	5273
5834	5273
5835	5274
5836	5274
5837	5275
5838	5276
5839	5277
5840	5278
5841	5279
5842	5279
5843	5281
5844	5280
5845	5283
5846	5282
5847	5284
5848	5285
5849	5286
5850	5287
5851	5287
5852	5289
5853	5288
5854	5290
5855	5291
5856	5292
5857	5292
5858	5293
5859	5294
5860	5295
5861	5296
5862	5297
5863	5298
5864	5299
5865	5299
5866	5300
5867	5300
5868	5316
5869	5299+1756
5870	5301
5871	5302
5872	5303
5873	5304
5874	5305
5875	5300
5876	5306
5877	5307
5878	5309
5879	5310
5880	5310
5881	5311
5882	5314
5883	5315
5884	5316
5885	5317
5886	5318
5887	5319
5888	5320
5889	5321
5890	5322
5891	5322
5892	5323
5893	5324
5894	5324
5895	5324
5896	5325
5897	5327
5898	5327
5899	
5900	5328
5901	5133
5902	5133
5903	5341
5904	5329
5905	5331
5906	5332
5907	5333
5908	5334
5909	5335
5910	5336
5911	5337
5912	5339
5913	5340
5914	5006
"	5132
5915	5341
5916	5342
5917	5341
5918	5344
5919	5344
5920	5345
5921	5346
5922	5347
5923	5348
5924	5349
5925	5351
5926	5350
5927	5352
5928	5353
5929	5355
5930	5355
5931	5356
5932	5357
5933	5358
5934	5359
5935	5360
5936	5361
5937	5362
5938	5362
5939	5363
5940	5364
5941	5365
5942	5366
5943	5367
5944	5216
5945	5369
5946	5370
5947	5371
5948	5373
5949	5374
5950	5374
5951	4984
"	5375
"	5379
"	7721
5952	5381
5953	5385
5954	5387
5955	5387
5956	5400
5957	5378
"	5383
5958	5377
5959	5380
5960	5382
5961	5378
5962	5384
5963	5386
5964	5388
5965	5390
5966	5391
5967	5391
5968	5392
5969	5393
5970	5394
5971	5395
5972	5397
5973	5398
5974	5399
5975	5401
5976	5401
5977	5402
5978	5402
5979	5404
5980	5405
5981	5406
5982	5411
5983	5408
5984	5409
5985	5410
5986	5410
5987	5411
5988	5413
5989	5414
5990	5416
5991	5417
5992	5418
5993	5418
5994	5419
5995	5420
5996	5421
5997	5422
5998	5423
5999	5424
6000	5425
6001	5425
6002	5425
6003	5427
6004	5428
6005	
6006	5429
6007	5430
6008	5431
6009	5432
6010	5433
6011	5435
6012	5433
6013	5434
6014	5436
6015	4141
"	4142
"	5437
6016	5438
6017	5439
6018	5440
6019	5442
6020	5441
6021	5444
6022	5445
6023	5447
6024	5448
6025	5449
6026	5450
6027	5451
6028	5453
6029	5454
6030	5454
6031	5455
6032	5456
6033	5458
6034	5462
6035	5459
6036	5461
6037	5462
6038	5462
6039	5464
6040	5465
6041	5466
6042	5467
6043	5468
6044	5469
6045	5470
6046	5471
6047	5472
"	7734
6048	5473
6049	5509
6050	5474
6051	5475
6052	5476
6053	5477
6054	5478
6055	5479
6056	5526
6057	5480
6058	5526
6059	5482
6060	5515
6061	5483
6062	5483
6063	5484
6064	5485
6065	2702
6066	5486
6067	5490
6068	5488
6069	5489
6070	5492
6071	5492
6072	5618
6073	3249
"	5493
6074	5494
6075	5495
6076	5494
6077	5496
6078	5497
6079	5498
6080	5499
6081	5500
6082	5501
6083	
6084	7823
6085	5502
6086	5503
"	5505
6087	5504
6088	5506
6089	5507
6090	5508
6091	7750
6092	5509
6093	7875
6094	5510
6095	5511
6096	5512
6097	5512
6098	5513
6099	5514
6100	5515
6101	5483
6102	5516
6103	5517
6104	5517
6105	5518
6106	5518
6107	5519
6108	5520
6109	5521
6110	5522
6111	5523
6112	5524
6113	5525
6114	5526
6115	5526
6116	5526
6117	5527
6118	5528
6119	5530
6120	5529
6121	5531
6122	5532
6123	5533
6124	5533
6125	5532
6126	5534
6127	5534
6128	7936
6129	5535
6130	5536
6131	5537
6132	5543
6133	5538
6134	5539
6135	5540
6136	5541
6137	5541
6138	5542
6139	5543
6140	5543
6141	5544
6142	5545
6143	5546
6144	5543
6145	5547
6146	5548
6147	5549
6148	5549
6149	5550
6150	5551
6151	5552
6152	5553
6153	5554
6154	5555
6155	5556
6156	5557
6157	5558
6158	5927
6159	5560
6160	5561
6161	5562
6162	5562
6163	5563
6164	5564
6165	5565
6166	5566
6167	
6168	5567
6169	5568
6170	5569
6171	5570
6172	5571
6173	7158
6174	5572
6175	5573
6176	5574
6177	5575
6178	5576
6179	5578
6180	5577
6181	5579
6182	5580
6183	5581
6184	5582
6185	5584
6186	5585
6187	5585
6188	5586
6189	5588
6190	5589
6191	5587
6192	5590
6193	5591
6194	5591
6195	5592
6196	5592
6197	5592
6198	5593
6199	5594
6200	5595
6201	5603
6202	5596
6203	5596
6204	5597
6205	5598
6206	5599
6207	5599
6208	5600
6209	5601
6210	5602
6211	5603
6212	5604
6213	5509
6214	5605
6215	5606
6216	5606
6217	5607
6218	5608
6219	5612
6220	5612
6221	5608
6222	5610
6223	5611
6224	5614
6225	5612
6226	5617
6227	5616
6228	5615
6229	
6230	5618
6231	3254
6232	5619
6233	5493
6234	5620
6235	5621
6236	5623
6237	5624
6238	5625
6239	5627
6240	5627
6241	5626
6242	5628
6243	5628
6244	5628
6245	5629
6246	5630
6247	5631
6248	5633
6249	5633
6250	5634
6251	5635
6252	5636
6253	5637
6254	8269
6255	5638
6256	5639
6257	5638
6258	5640
6259	5641
6260	5643
6261	5643
6262	5644
6263	
6264	5646
6265	5645
6266	5645
6267	5645
6268	5647
6269	5650
6270	5651
6271	5652
6272	5653
6273	5654
6274	5655
6275	5656
6276	5657
6277	5658
6278	5658
6279	5660
6280	5661
6281	5662
6282	5662
6283	5663
6284	5664
6285	5659
6286	5666
6287	5667
6288	5668
6289	5669
6290	5687
6291	5688
6292	5670
6293	5670
6294	5671
6295	5672
6296	5674
6297	5674
6298	5676
6299	5677
6300	5863
6301	5678
6302	5679
6303	5680
6304	5681
6305	5682
6306	2275
6307	5684
6308	5685
6309	5686
6310	5688
6311	5689
6312	5691
6313	5690
6314	5692
6315	5693
6316	5694
6317	5699
6318	5696
6319	5695
6320	5697
6321	5698
6322	5699
6323	5700
6324	5700
6325	5882
6326	5697+7992
6327	5701
6328	5702
6329	5703
6330	5704
6331	5706
6332	5707
6333	5714
6334	5710
6335	5710
6336	5711
6337	5712
6338	5713

G/K	STRONG
6339	
6340	5708
6341	5714
6342	5714
6343	5715
6344	5716
6345	5714
6346	5717
6347	5718
6348	5718
6349	5719
6350	5720
6351	5721
6352	5722
6353	5723
6354	5724
6355	5725
6356	5726
6357	5727
6358	5730
6359	5731
6360	5731
6361	5729
6362	5728
6363	5733
6364	5728
6365	5734
6366	5730
6367	5734
6368	5735
6369	5736
6370	5737
6371	5737
6372	5737
6373	5739
6374	5740
6375	5740
6376	5738
6377	5741
6378	5742
6379	5755
6380	5743
6381	5744
6382	5745
6383	5746
6384	5747
6385	5748
6386	5749
6387	5749
6388	5750
6389	5752
6390	5753
6391	5753
6392	5754
6393	5755
6394	5755
6395	5756
6396	5759
6397	5760
6398	5757
"	5761
6399	5761
6400	5762
6401	5765
6402	5763
6403	5764
6404	5766
6405	5767
6406	5766
6407	5768
6408	5768
6409	5769
6410	6030
6411	5771
6412	5869
6413	5773
6414	5774
6415	5774
6416	5775
6417	5778
6418	5779
6419	5780
6420	5780
6421	5781
6422	5786
6423	5783
6424	5782
6425	5785
6426	5787
6427	5788
6428	5788
6429	5789
6430	5791
6431	5790
6432	5792
6433	5793
6434	5794
6435	5794
6436	5795
6437	5797
6438	5798
6439	5799
6440	5800
6441	5800
6442	5801
6443	5802
6444	5803
6445	5804
6446	5798
6447	5805
6448	5806
6449	5807
6450	5808
6451	5810
6452	5811
6453	5812
6454	5813
6455	5814
6456	5815
6457	5816
6458	5817
6459	5818
6460	5818
6461	5819
6462	5820
6463	5820
6464	5821
6465	5822
6466	5823
6467	5825
6468	5826
6469	5828
6470	5827
"	5829
6471	7320
6472	5829
6473	5809
6474	5830
6475	5832
6476	5833
6477	5834
6478	5835
6479	5836
6480	5837
6481	5838
6482	5838
6483	5840
6484	5841
6485	5842
6486	5844
6487	4593
"	5844
6488	5848
6489	5845
6490	5846
6491	5847
6492	
6493	5848
6494	5848
6495	
6496	5849
6497	5849
6498	5850
6499	5851
6500	5852
6501	5853
6502	5854
6503	5855
6504	5857
6505	5856
6506	5858
6507	5858
6508	5858
6509	5857
6510	5859
6511	5762
6512	5860
6513	5860
6514	5861
6515	5862
6516	5863
6517	5864
6518	5865
6519	5866
6520	5867
6521	5867
6522	5868
6523	5770
6524	5869
6525	5872 to 5887
6526	5871
6527	5872
6528	5873
6529	5874
6530	5875
6531	
6532	5876
6533	5877
6534	5878
6535	5880
6536	5882
6537	5883
6538	5884
6539	5885
6540	5887
6541	2703
6542	5879
6543	5879
6544	5881
6545	5774
"	5888
6546	5889
6547	5890
6548	5891
6549	5891
6550	5778
6551	5892
6552	5892
6553	5893
6554	5895
6555	5895
6556	5892+2041
6557	
6558	5898
6559	5899
6560	5904
6561	5905
6562	5896
6563	5897
6564	5900
6565	5901
6566	5902
6567	5903
6568	5906
6569	5857
6570	5907
6571	5908
6572	5909
6573	5910
6574	5911
6575	5912
6576	5913
6577	5914
6578	5915
6579	5916
6580	5917
6581	5918
6582	5919
6583	5920
6584	5921
6585	5923
6586	5921+3651
6587	5925
6588	45
6589	5926
6590	5927
6591	5929
6592	5930
6593	5766
6594	5932
6595	5933
6596	5934
6597	5935
6598	5936
6599	1175
6600	5937
6601	5938
6602	5939
6603	5941
6604	5942
6605	5940
6606	5942
6607	5933
6608	5944
6609	5945
6610	5945
6611	5947
6612	5948
6613	5949
6614	5950
6615	5935
6616	
6617	5951
6618	5953
6619	5953
6620	5953
6621	5953
6622	5955
6623	5956
6624	5958
6625	5959
6626	5960
6627	5963
6628	5961
6629	5921+4192
6630	5964
6631	5964
6632	5965
6633	5966
6634	5968
6635	5969
6636	5970
6637	5766
6638	5971
6639	5971
6640	5973
6641	5975
6642	5977
6643	5978
6644	5979
6645	5980
6646	5981
6647	5982
6648	5983
6649	5984
"	5985
6650	5986
6651	5987
6652	3818
6653	5988
6654	5989
6655	5990
6656	5991
6657	5992
6658	5995
6659	5996
6660	5997
6661	5998
6662	5999
6663	6000
6664	6001
6665	6001
6666	
6667	6002
6668	6003
6669	6004
6670	6004
6671	3726
6672	6005
6673	6006
6674	6007
6675	6008
6676	6009
6677	6010
6678	6013
6679	6011
6680	6012
6681	7104
6682	6014
6683	6014
6684	6016
6685	6016
6686	6017
6687	6018
6688	6019
6689	6020
6690	6021
6691	6022
6692	6023
6693	6024
6694	6025
6695	6026
6696	6027
6697	6028
6698	6029
6699	6030
6700	6031
6701	6031
6702	6030
6703	5772
6704	6034
6705	6035
6706	6042
6707	6036
6708	6038
6709	6037
6710	6061
6711	6064
6712	1042
6713	6039
6714	6041
6715	6040
6716	6042
6717	6043
6718	6035
6719	6044
6720	3283
6721	6045
6722	6046
6723	6047
6724	6048
6725	6049
6726	6049
6727	6051
6728	6052
6729	6053
6730	6054
6731	6055
6732	6055
6733	6057
6734	6058
6735	6059
6736	6060
6737	6062
6738	6063
6739	6063
6740	6064
6741	6066
6742	6067
6743	6068
6744	6068
6745	6069
6746	6070
6747	6071
6748	6072
6749	5782
6750	
6751	6073
6752	6075
6753	6075
6754	6076
6755	6077
6756	6078
6757	6079
6758	5774
6759	6080
6760	6083
6761	6081
6762	6082
6763	6084
6764	6084
6765	1036
6766	6085
6767	6085
6768	6085
6769	5777
6770	6086
6771	6087
6772	6087
6773	6091
6774	6092
6775	6089
6776	6089
6777	6090
6778	6090
6779	6093
6780	6094
6781	6095
6782	6096
6783	6098
6784	6098
6785	6097
6786	6099
6787	6100
6788	6101
6789	6102
6790	6103
6791	6104
6792	6103
6793	6105
6794	6105
6795	6106
6796	6107
6797	6108
6798	6108
6799	6106
6800	6109
6801	6111
6802	6110
6803	
6804	6112
6805	3289
6806	6113
6807	6114
6808	6115
6809	6116
6810	6117
6811	6119
6812	6120
6813	6118
6814	6121
6815	6121
6816	
6817	6122
6818	6123
6819	6124
6820	1044
6821	6125
6822	6126
6823	6127
6824	6128
6825	6129
6826	6130
6827	6131
6828	6131
6829	6135
6830	6133
6831	6134
6832	6137
6833	6138
6834	6139
6835	6140
6836	6141
6837	6142
6838	6143
6839	6145
6840	6144
6841	6147
6842	6148
6843	6148
6844	6149
6845	6150
6846	6152
6847	6153
6848	6154
6849	6154
6850	6154
6851	6152
6852	6152
6853	6156
6854	6158
6855	6159
6856	6157
6857	6155
6858	6160
6859	6161
6860	6162
6861	6163
6862	6163
6863	6164
6864	6165
6865	6166
6866	6166
6867	6168
6868	6169
6869	4632
6870	6170
6871	6171
6872	6172
6873	6174
6874	6175
6875	6176
6876	6177
6877	6178
6878	6179
6879	6180
6880	6181
6881	6182
6882	6183
6883	6184
6884	6185
6885	6186
6886	6187
6887	6188
6888	6189
6889	6190
6890	6192
6891	6191
6892	6193
6893	6195
6894	6194
6895	6196
6896	6197
6897	6198
6898	6176
6899	6199
6900	5735
6901	6200
6902	6203
6903	6201
6904	6202
6905	6204
6906	6205
6907	6206
6908	6207
6909	6208
6910	6209
6911	6210
6912	6212
6913	6213
6914	6213
6915	6214
6916	6215
6917	6218
6918	6221
6919	6222
6920	6224
6921	6229
6922	6230
6923	6237
6924	6235
6925	6240
6926	6240
6927	6235
6928	6241
6929	6242
6930	6240
6931	6211
6932	6211
6933	6211
6934	6216
6935	6217
6936	6219
6937	6220
6938	6223
6939	6225
6940	6227
6941	6228
6942	6226
6943	6231
6944	6232
6945	6233
6946	6234
6947	6238
6948	6239
6949	6244
6950	6245
6951	6245
6952	6247
6953	6248
6954	6249
6955	6250
6956	6253
6957	6251
6958	6252
6959	6255
6960	6254
6961	6256
6962	6278
6963	6257
6964	6258
6965	6259
6966	6260
6967	6261
6968	6262
6969	6264
6970	6265
6971	6266
6972	6267
6973	6269
6974	6270
6975	6271
6976	6271
6977	6272
6978	6273
6979	6274
6980	6275
6981	6277
6982	6276
6983	6279
6984	6280
6985	6282
6986	6282
6987	6281
6988	6283
6989	
6990	6284
6991	6285
6992	6285
6993	6285
6994	6286
6995	6286
6996	6287
6997	6288
6998	6288
6999	6289
7000	6290
7001	6291
7002	6292
7003	6293
7004	6294
7005	6295
7006	6296
7007	6297
7008	6298
7009	6299
7010	6300
7011	6301
7012	6302
7013	6303
7014	6304
7015	6305
7016	6305
7017	6306
7018	6306
7019	6307
7020	6307
7021	6308
7022	6309
7023	6310
"	6366
7024	6311
7025	6312
7026	6312
7027	6324
7028	6313
7029	6314
7030	6312
7031	6315
7032	6315
7033	6316
7034	6317
7035	6318
7036	6319
7037	6320
7038	6321
7039	6322
7040	6322
7041	6323
7042	6437
7043	6324
7044	6325
7045	6326
7046	6327
7047	6327
7048	6328
"	6329
7049	6329
7050	6330
7051	6331
"	6512
7052	6332
7053	6333
7054	6334
7055	6335
7056	6335
7057	6336
7058	6337
7059	6338
7060	6339
7061	6340
7062	6341
7063	6341
7064	6342
7065	6343
7066	6344
7067	6345
7068	6346
7069	6348
7070	6349
7071	6350
7072	6351
7073	6352
7074	6354
7075	6355
7076	6356
7077	6357
7078	6359
7079	6360
7080	6358
"	6362
7081	6363
7082	6363
7083	6364
7084	6367
7085	6365
7086	6368
7087	6369
7088	
7089	6371
7090	6372
7091	6373
7092	6374
7093	6376
7094	6377
7095	6378
7096	6379
7097	6380
7098	6381
7099	6382
7100	6383
7101	6384
7102	6411
7103	6385
7104	6388
7105	6389
7106	6390
7107	6391
7108	6370
7109	6394
7110	6393
7111	6395
7112	6396
7113	6397
7114	6398
7115	6400
7116	6401
7117	6403
7118	6404
7119	6405
7120	6406
7121	6407
7122	6408
7123	6409
7124	6410
7125	6410
7126	6411
7127	6412
7128	6412
7129	6413
7130	6414
7131	6415
7132	6416
7133	6417
7134	6418
7135	6418
7136	6419
7137	6419
7138	6420
7139	6421
7140	6422
7141	6423
7142	6424
7143	6424
7144	6425
7145	6426
7146	6427
7147	6428
7148	6429
7149	6430
7150	6431
7151	6304
7152	6432
7153	6435
7154	6436
7155	6437
7156	3942
"	6440
7157	6434
"	6438
7158	6439
7159	6439
7160	6439
7161	6439
7162	6443
7163	6441
7164	6442
7165	6443
7166	6444
7167	6445

G/K	STRONG
7168	6446
7169	6450
7170	6448
7171	6449
7172	6451
7173	6452
7174	6452
7175	6453
7176	6454
7177	6455
7178	6456
7179	6457
7180	6458
7181	6459
7182	6461
7183	6462
7184	6463
7185	6464
7186	6465
7187	6464
7188	6466
7189	6467
7190	6468
7191	6469
7192	6470
7193	6471
7194	6472
7195	6847
7196	6473
7197	6474
7198	6475
7199	6476
7200	6476
7201	6477
7202	6478
7203	6479
7204	6480
7205	6481
7206	6482
7207	6327
7208	1048
7209	6483
7210	6484
7211	6375
7212	6485
7213	6486
7214	6487
7215	6488
7216	6489
7217	6485
7218	6490
7219	6491
7220	6492
7221	6493
7222	6494
7223	6495
7224	6496
7225	6497
7226	6498
7227	6485
7228	6499
7229	6500
7230	6501
7231	6502
7232	6503
7233	6504
7234	6505
7235	6506
7236	6508
7237	6507
7238	6509
7239	6510
7240	6511
7241	6501
7242	6513
7243	6514
7244	6519
7245	6515
7246	6516
7247	6503
7248	6517
7249	2661
7250	6518
7251	6520
7252	6519
7253	6521
7254	6522
7255	6524
7256	6524
7257	6524
7258	6525
7259	6526
7260	6527
7261	6528
7262	6529
7263	6514
7264	6530
7265	6530
7266	6531
7267	6532
7268	6533
7269	6534
7270	6535
7271	6536
7272	6538
7273	6539
7274	6541
7275	6542
7276	6544
7277	6544
7278	6546
7279	6545
7280	6319
7281	6547
7282	6550
7283	6551
7284	6552
7285	6553
7286	6554
7287	6555
7288	6556
7289	6557
7290	6560
7291	6558
7292	6559
7293	6561
7294	6563
7295	6564
7296	6565
7297	6565
7298	6566
7299	6576
7300	6567
7301	6567
7302	6569
7303	6570
7304	6571
7305	6571
7306	6572
7307	6574
7308	6575
7309	6577
7310	6578
7311	6509
7312	6579
7313	6581
7314	6585
7315	6587
7316	6589
7317	6580
7318	6582
7319	6583
7320	6584
7321	6586
7322	6588
7323	6592
7324	6593
7325	6594
7326	6595
7327	6596
7328	6597
7329	6598
7330	6599
7331	6601
7332	6601
7333	6602
7334	6603
7335	6604
7336	6595
7337	6605
7338	6605
7339	6607
7340	6608
7341	6610
7342	6611
7343	6612
7344	6612
7345	6614
7346	6615
7347	6609
7348	6616
7349	6617
7350	6618
7351	6619
7352	6620
7353	6621
7354	6622
7355	6623
7356	6624
7357	6625
7358	6572
7359	6626
7360	
7361	3318
7362	6627
7363	6675
7364	6674
7365	6628
7366	6629
7367	6630
7368	6631
7369	6632
7370	6632
7371	6633
7372	6635
7373	6643
7374	6643
7375	6636
7376	6637
7377	6638
7378	6635
7379	6639
7380	6641
7381	6642
7382	6643
7383	6643
7384	6644
7385	6645
7386	6646
7387	6636
7388	3320
7389	6648
7390	6649
7391	6650
7392	6651
7393	6652
7394	1225
7395	6653
7396	6654
7397	6654
7398	6657
7399	6658
7400	6658
7401	6659
7402	6660
7403	6661
7404	6662
7405	6663
7406	6664
7407	6666
7408	6667
7409	6667
7410	6668
7411	6669
7412	6670
7413	6670
7414	6671
7415	6672
7416	6672
7417	6673
7418	6677
7419	6678
7420	6678
7421	6679
7422	6680
7423	6681
7424	6682
7425	6683
7426	6684
7427	6685
7428	6686
7429	6687
7430	6688
7431	6689
7432	6690
7433	6689
7434	6689
7435	7436
7436	6691
7437	6692
7438	6692
7439	6693
7440	6694
7441	6695
7442	6695
7443	6696
7444	6696
7445	6697
7446	6697
7447	6697
7448	6698
7449	1049
7450	6865
7451	6699
7452	6700
7453	6701
7454	6677
7455	6702
7456	6703
7457	6704
7458	6705
7459	6708
7460	6706
7461	6707
7462	6709
7463	6710
7464	6711
7465	6712
7466	6713
7467	6715
7468	6714
7469	6716
7470	6728
7471	6717
7472	6679
7473	6718
7474	6718
7475	6719
7476	6720
7477	6721
7478	7227+6721
7479	6722
7480	6723
7481	6724
7482	6726
7483	6725
7484	6727
7485	6729
7486	6730
7487	6689
7488	6731
7489	6732
7490	6731
7491	6733
7492	6734
7493	6735
"	6737
7494	6735
"	6737
7495	6735
"	6737
7496	6735
"	6737
7497	6736
7498	6738
"	6752
7499	6740
7500	6741
7501	6742
7502	6743
7503	6743
7504	6746
7505	6745
"	6747
7506	6747
7507	6748
7508	6742
7509	6750
7510	6749
7511	6751
7512	6754
7513	6754
7514	6756
7515	6756
7516	6757
7517	6758
7518	6759
7519	6760
7520	6761
7521	6763
7522	6762
7523	6764
7524	6765
7525	6766
7526	6767
7527	6767
7528	6767
7529	6767
7530	6768
7531	6769
7532	6770
7533	6772
7534	6771
7535	6773
7536	6774
7537	6775
7538	6776
7539	6777
7540	6778
7541	6779
7542	6780
7543	6781
7544	6781
7545	6782
7546	6784
7547	6785
7548	6786
7549	6787
7550	6788
7551	6789
7552	6783
7553	6791
7554	6790
7555	6792
7556	6792
7557	6793
7558	6793
7559	6793
7560	6800
7561	6797
7562	6794
7563	6795
7564	6796
7565	6797
7566	6797
7567	6798
7568	6798
7569	6799
7570	6800
7571	6801
7572	6802
7573	6803
7574	6804
7575	6805
7576	6806
7577	6807
7578	6807
7579	6808
7580	6820
7581	6809
7582	4704
"	6810
7583	6811
7584	6812
7585	6813
7586	6814
7587	6815
7588	6815
7589	6816
7590	6817
7591	6818
7592	6819
7593	6820
7594	6821
7595	6822
7596	6823
7597	6824
7598	6825
7599	6826
7600	6828
7601	6829
7602	6827
7603	6830
7604	6831
7605	6832
7606	6833
7607	6834
7608	6835
7609	6825
7610	6836
7611	6837
7612	6831
7613	6838
7614	6839
7615	6840
7616	6832
7617	6849
7618	6842
7619	6843
7620	6844
7621	6845
7622	6846
7623	6846
7624	6847
7625	6848
7626	6848
7627	6850
7628	6851
7629	6852
7630	6854
7631	6855
7632	6856
7633	6858
7634	6857
7635	6859
7636	6845
7637	6860
7638	6861
7639	6862
7640	6862
7641	6862
7642	
7643	6863
7644	6864
7645	6865
7646	6866
7647	6867
7648	6867
7649	6868
7650	6869
7651	6869
7652	1224
7653	6870
7654	6871
7655	6872
7656	6872
7657	6872
7658	6873
7659	6869
7660	6876
7661	6875
7662	6874
7663	6877
7664	6878
7665	6879
7666	6881
7667	6880
7668	6882
7669	6883
7670	6882
7671	6884
7672	6885
7673	6886
7674	3334
"	6887
7675	6887
7676	6869
7677	6887
7678	6888
7679	6889
7680	6890
7681	6891
7682	
7683	6892
7684	6893
7685	6894
7686	6895
7687	6896
"	6897
7688	6898
7689	6899
7690	6900
7691	6901
7692	6904
"	6905
7693	6906
7694	6907
7695	6908
7696	6909
7697	6910
7698	6911
7699	6912
7700	6913
7701	6914
7702	6915
7703	6916
7704	6917
7705	6918
7706	6919
7707	6920
7708	6921
7709	6923
7710	6924
7711	6924
7712	6927
7713	6926
7714	6924
7715	6929
7716	6930
7717	6932
7718	6934
7719	6931
7720	6935
7721	6936
7722	6937
7723	6938
7724	6939
7725	6940
7726	6941
7727	6942
7728	6945
"	6948
7729	6946
7730	6943
7731	6944
7732	6947
7733	6949
7734	5356
7735	6950
7736	6951
7737	6952
7738	6953
7739	6954
7740	6955
7741	6956
7742	6957
7743	6957
7744	6957
7745	4723
7746	6959
7747	6960
7748	6960
7749	6961
7750	4723
7751	6495
7752	5354
"	6962
7753	6962
7754	6963
7755	6964
7756	6965
7757	6967
7758	6968
7759	6969
7760	6970
7761	6971
7762	6973
7763	6972
"	6974
7764	6975
7765	6975
7766	6976
7767	6977
7768	
7769	6979
7770	6980
7771	6982
7772	6983
7773	6984
7774	3947
7775	6985
7776	6986
"	6987
7777	6988
7778	6989
7779	6991
7780	6993
7781	6994
7782	6995
7783	6996
7784	6997
7785	6996
7786	6998
7787	6999
7788	7000
7789	7002
7790	7003
7791	
7792	7004
7793	7005
7794	6958
"	7006
7795	6892
7796	6958
7797	
7798	7008
7799	7009
7800	7012
7801	6969
7802	7013
7803	7014
7804	7014
7805	7014
7806	7015
7807	7016
7808	7017
7809	7018
7810	6974
7811	7019
7812	7020
7813	7021
7814	7022
7815	7023
7816	7024
7817	7024
7818	7025
7819	7025
7820	7026
7821	7027
7822	7028
7823	7029
7824	7031
7825	6963
7826	6963
7827	7035
7828	7033
7829	7034
7830	7036
7831	7037
7832	7038
7833	7039
7834	7040
7835	7041
7836	7042
7837	7043
7838	7044
7839	7045
7840	7046
7841	7047
7842	7048
7843	7049
7844	7049
7845	7050
7846	7050
7847	7051
7848	7052
7849	7053
7850	7054
7851	7055
7852	7056
7853	7057
"	7063
7854	7058
7855	7059
7856	6965
7857	7060
7858	7061
7859	7062
7860	7064
7861	7065
7862	7067
7863	7068
7864	7069
7865	7069
7866	7070
7867	7071
7868	7072
7869	7073
7870	7074
7871	7075
7872	7076
7873	7077
7874	7078
7875	7079
7876	7080
7877	7081
7878	7082
7879	7083
7880	
7881	7084
7882	7085
7883	7086
7884	7087
7885	7087
7886	7088
7887	7090
7888	7089
7889	7091
7890	7092
7891	7093
7892	7094
7893	7095
7894	7096
7895	7097
7896	7098
7897	7097
7898	7099
7899	7112
7900	7114
7901	7098
7902	7100
7903	7101
7904	7102
7905	7103
7906	7104
7907	7105
7908	7105
7909	7106
7910	4742
"	7106
7911	7107
7912	7110
7913	7110
7914	7111
7915	7112
7916	
7917	7114
7918	7114
7919	7115
7920	7116
7921	7117
7922	7119
7923	7120
7924	7121
7925	7122
"	7125
7926	7124
7927	6981
7928	7126
7929	7131
7930	7128
7931	7130
7932	7132
7933	7133
7934	7133
7935	7134
7936	7136
7937	7137
7938	7135
7939	7136
7940	7138
7941	3368
7942	7139
"	7144
7943	7140
7944	7142
7945	7143
7946	7141
7947	7146
7948	7145
7949	7146
7950	7147
7951	7148
7952	7150
7953	7151
7954	7152
7955	2696+7152
7956	7151
7957	7153
7958	7154
7959	7153
7960	7155
7961	7157
7962	7158
7963	7158
7964	7156
7965	7159
7966	7160
7967	7161
7968	7163
7969	7161
7970	7164
7971	7165
7972	7166
7973	7167
7974	7168
7975	7169
7976	7171
7977	7172
7978	7173
7979	6979
7980	7174
7981	6979
7982	6979
7983	7175
7984	7176
7985	7177
7986	7178
7987	7184
7988	7192

G/K	STRONG
7989	7193
7990	7179
7991	7180
7992	7181
7993	7182
7994	7183
7995	7183
7996	7185
7997	7186
7998	7188
7999	7189
8000	7189
8001	7190
8002	7191
8003	7194
8004	7195
8005	7196
8006	7197
8007	7197
8008	7198
8009	7199
8010	
8011	7200
"	7202
8012	7201
8013	7200
8014	7203
8015	7203
8016	7211
8017	7205
8018	7206
8019	7207
8020	7208
8021	7200
8022	883
8023	7209
8024	7210
8025	7211
8026	7212
8027	7213
8028	7214
8029	7215
8030	7216
8031	7218
"	7226
8032	7219
8033	7220
8034	7218
8035	7221
8036	7222
8037	7223
8038	7224
8039	4763
8040	7225
8041	7227
8042	7227
8043	7228
8044	7230
8045	7231
8046	7232
8047	7233
8048	7234
8049	7235
8050	7235
8051	7237
8052	7239
8053	7241
8054	7242
8055	7243
8056	7245
8057	7246
8058	7247
8059	7248
8060	7249
8061	7250
"	7252
"	7254
8062	7251
8063	7253
8064	7254
8065	7255
8066	7255
8067	7256
8068	7243
8069	7257
8070	7258
8071	7259
8072	7262
8073	7263
8074	7264
8075	7267
8076	7268
8077	7269
8078	7270
"	8637
8079	7272
8080	5883
8081	7273
8082	7274
8083	7275
8084	7276
8085	7278
8086	7277
8087	5372
"	7279
8088	7280
8089	7280
8090	7280
8091	7282
8092	7281
8093	7283
8094	7285
8095	7285
8096	7286
8097	7287
8098	7287
8099	7288
8100	7289
8101	7290
8102	1721
8103	7291
8104	7292
8105	7293
"	7294
8106	7296
8107	7295
8108	7303
8109	7297
8110	7298
8111	7298
8112	7351
8113	7300
8114	1721
8115	7301
8116	7302
8117	7303
8118	7304
8119	7305
8120	7307
8121	7309
8122	7310
8123	7311
8124	7312
8125	7315
8126	7316
8127	7317
8128	7318
8129	7319
"	7427
8130	7442
8131	7321
8132	7323
8133	7326
8134	7327
8135	7329
8136	7330
8137	7332
8138	7333
8139	7331
8140	7334
8141	7335
8142	7336
8143	7337
8144	7338
8145	7341
8146	7342
8147	7343
8148	7339
8149	7340
8150	7340
8151	7344
8152	7345
8153	7345
8154	7346
8155	7344+5892
8156	7348
8157	7349
8158	7350
8159	7351
8160	7347
8161	7353
8162	7354
8163	7355
8164	7360
8165	7357
8166	7356
8167	7358
8168	7360
8169	7361
8170	3819
8171	7356
8172	7362
8173	7363
8174	7363
8175	7364
8176	7366
8177	7367
8178	7368
8179	7369
8180	7370
8181	7371
8182	7372
8183	7373
8184	3399
8185	7374
8186	7375
8187	7376
8188	7377
8189	7378
8190	7379
8191	7379
8192	7380
8193	7306
8194	7381
8195	7383
8196	7384
8197	7324
8198	7385
8199	7386
8200	7387
8201	7325
8202	7388
8203	7389
8204	7391
8205	7390
8206	7392
8207	7393
8208	7395
8209	7394
8210	7396
8211	7394
8212	7397
8213	7398
8214	7399
8215	7400
8216	7401
8217	7402
8218	7403
8219	7404
8220	7405
8221	7406
8222	7407
8223	7408
8224	7409
8225	7311
8226	7410
8227	7411
8228	7411
8229	7413
8230	7414
8231	7415
8232	7416
8233	7417
8234	7417
8235	7417
8236	7428
8237	7417
8238	7418
8239	7419
8240	7433
8241	7418
8242	7420
8243	7422
8244	7423
8245	7423
8246	761
8247	7424
8248	7425
8249	7311
8250	7426
8251	7320
8252	7429
8253	7430
8254	7431
8255	7432
8256	7434
8257	7437
8258	7435
8259	7414
8260	7438
8261	7439
8262	7440
8263	7441
8264	7442
"	7444
8265	7445
8266	7443
8267	7446
8268	7447
8269	7447
8270	7448
8271	7449
8272	7450
8273	7451
8274	7451
8275	7452
8276	7453
8277	7454
8278	7455
8279	7456
8280	7457
"	7458
8281	7456
8282	7459
8283	7460
8284	7461
8285	7461
8286	7473
8287	7462
8288	7465
8289	7462
8290	
8291	7463
8292	7464
8293	7466
8294	7467
8295	7468
8296	7469
8297	7471
8298	7472
8299	7474
8300	7464
8301	7475
8302	7477
8303	7478
8304	7479
8305	7480
8306	7481
8307	7481
8308	7482
8309	7483
8310	7483
8311	7484
8312	7484
8313	7485
8314	7486
8315	7488
8316	7488
8317	7489
8318	7489
8319	7491
8320	7492
8321	7493
8322	7493
8323	7494
8324	7495
8325	7498
8326	7500
8327	7496
8328	7497
8329	7497
8330	7501
8331	7502
8332	7503
8333	7504
8334	7498
8335	7510
8336	7505
8337	7499
8338	7506
8339	7507
8340	7508
8341	7509
8342	7510
8343	7513
8344	7322
8345	7514
8346	7511
"	7515
8347	7516
8348	7517
8349	7518
8350	7323
8351	7519
8352	7521
8353	7520
8354	7521
8355	7521
8356	7522
8357	7523
8358	7524
8359	7525
8360	7526
8361	7527
8362	7528
8363	7529
8364	7530
8365	7531
8366	7532
8367	7531
8368	7533
8369	7534
8370	7535
8371	7536
8372	7537
8373	7538
8374	7538
8375	7539
8376	7540
8377	7541
8378	7542
8379	7543
8380	7544
8381	7545
8382	7546
8383	7547
8384	7548
8385	7549
8386	7550
8387	7551
8388	7552
8389	7552
8390	7552
8391	7553
8392	7554
8393	7555
8394	7556
8395	7557
8396	7220
8397	7558
8398	7559
8399	7561
8400	7562
8401	7563
8402	7564
8403	3573
8404	7565
8405	7566
8406	7567
8407	7568
8408	7569
8409	7570
8410	7571
8411	7572
8412	7573
8413	7574
8414	7575
8415	7576
8416	7577
8417	7578
8418	
8419	7603
8420	7613
8421	7613
8422	7638
"	7639
8423	7643
8424	7643
8425	7646
8426	7647
8427	7648
8428	7649
8429	7654
8430	7653
8431	7663
8432	7663
8433	7664
8434	7679
8435	7682
8436	7685
8437	7687
8438	7689
8439	7687
8440	7702
8441	7704
8442	7704
8443	7708
8444	7713
8445	2089
"	7716
8446	7717
8447	3026
8448	7720
8449	7730
8450	5253
8451	7735
8452	7742
8453	
8454	7750
8455	7753
8456	7754
8457	7754
8458	7755
8459	7755
8460	7756
8461	7760
8462	5493
8463	7795
8464	7797
8465	7808
8466	7811
8467	7813
8468	7814
8469	7818
8470	7824
8471	7832
8472	
8473	7846
8474	7847
8475	7852
8476	7853
8477	7854
8478	7855
8479	7856
8480	7863
8481	7865
8482	7867
8483	7869
8484	7872
8485	7873
8486	7874
8487	7875
8488	7878
8489	7880
8490	7879
8491	7881
8492	7760
"	7787
8493	7899
8494	7900
8495	
8496	7905
8497	7906
8498	7907
8499	7634
8500	7914
8501	7915
8502	7916
"	7917
8503	5526
8504	
8505	7919
8506	7919
8507	7922
8508	5531
8509	7937
8510	7939
8511	7940
8512	7938
8513	7958
8514	8007
8515	8008
8516	8009
8517	8012
8518	8014
8519	
8520	8040
"	8041
8521	8041
8522	8042
8523	8055
8524	8056
8525	8057
8526	8063
8527	
8528	8072
8529	8071
8530	8073
8531	
8532	8079
8533	8130
8534	8135
8535	8146
8536	8149
8537	8163
8538	8163
8539	8163
8540	8164
8541	8165
8542	8165
8543	8165
8544	8166
8545	8167
8546	5587
8547	8175
8548	8175
8549	8175
8550	8178
8551	8178
8552	8181
8553	8185
8554	8183
8555	8184
8556	8188
8557	8193
8558	5596
8559	8222
8560	8224
8561	8226
8562	5606
8563	5606
8564	8210
8565	5607
8566	8242
8567	8244
8568	8265
8569	8269
8570	8272
8571	8276
8572	8277
8573	8278
8574	8279
8575	8280
8576	8282
8577	8283
8578	8286
8579	8288
8580	8294
8581	8295
8582	8296
8583	8296
8584	8297
8585	8299
8586	8300
8587	8301
8588	8304
8589	8304
8590	8303
8591	8305
8592	8308
8593	8310
8594	8311
8595	8312
8596	8313
8597	8314
8598	8315
8599	8316
8600	
8601	8320
8602	8291
8603	8321
8604	7796
"	8291
8605	8322
8606	7786
"	8323
8607	8342
8608	5640
8609	8368
8610	
8611	7945
8612	7579
8613	7580
8614	7581
8615	7582
8616	7582
8617	7583
8618	7584
8619	7585
8620	7586
8621	7587
8622	7588
8623	7588
8624	7589
8625	7591
8626	7592
8627	7594
8628	7592
8629	7596
8630	7597
8631	7599
8632	1052
8633	7600
8634	7602
8635	7602
8636	7604
8637	7605
8638	7607
8639	7610
8640	7608
8641	7609
8642	7611
8643	7612
8644	7614
8645	7615
8646	7616
8647	7617
8648	7618
8649	7619
8650	
8651	7620
8652	7621
8653	7665
8654	7622
8655	7623
8656	7623
8657	7626
8658	7627
8659	
8660	7628
8661	7629
8662	7630
8663	7632
8664	7633
8665	7628
8666	7635
8667	7636
8668	7637
8669	7622
8670	7640
8671	7642
8672	7641
8673	7641
8674	7644
8675	7644
8676	7645
8677	7645
8678	7650
8679	7651
8680	7652
8681	7652
8682	884
8683	7656
8684	7657
8685	7658
8686	7659
8687	7660
8688	7661
8689	7665
8690	7666
8691	7667
8692	7668
8693	7669
8694	7667
8695	7670
8696	7671
8697	7673
8698	7673
8699	7675
8700	7674
8701	7676
8702	7677
8703	7678
8704	7683
8705	7684
8706	7686
8707	7681
8708	7688
8709	7691
8710	7692
8711	7693
8712	7694
8713	7696
8714	7697
8715	7698
8716	7699
8717	7700
8718	7699
8719	7701
8720	7703
"	7736
8721	7705
8722	
8723	1779
8724	7706
8725	7707
8726	1779
8727	7709
8728	7710
8729	7711
8730	7711
8731	7714
8732	7718
8733	7719
8734	
8735	
8736	7723
8737	7724
8738	7722
8739	7722
8740	7725
8741	
8742	7619
8743	7726
8744	7727
8745	7728
8746	7729
8747	7731
8748	7732
8749	7733
8750	7737
8751	7737
8752	
8753	7740
8754	7741
8755	7743
8756	7744
8757	7745
8758	7746
8759	
8760	7747
8761	7748
8762	7749
8763	7751
8764	7590
8765	7752
8766	7752
8767	7757
8768	7758
8769	7759
8770	7762
8771	7764
8772	7765
8773	7766
8774	7767
8775	7768
8776	7773
8777	7771
8778	7772
8779	7772
8780	7769
8781	7770
8782	7769
8783	7774
8784	7775
8785	7776
8786	7777
8787	7777
8788	7778
8789	7779
8790	7779
8791	7780
8792	8197
8793	7781
8794	5855
8795	7782
8796	7783
8797	7785
8798	7784
8799	8264
8800	7789
8801	7788
8802	7794
8803	7790
8804	7793
8805	7791
8806	8324
8807	7798
8808	7799
8809	7800

G/K	STRONG
8810	7895
8811	7803
8812	7805
8813	7806
8814	7807
8815	7809
8816	7810
8817	7812
8818	7815
8819	7816
8820	7817
8821	7819
8822	7819
"	7820
8823	7819
8824	7821
8825	7822
8826	7823
8827	7825
8828	7826
8829	7827
8830	7828
8831	7829
8832	7830
8833	7831
8834	7831
8835	7833
8836	7834
8837	7835
8838	7836
8839	7838
8840	7837
8841	7839
8842	7840
8843	7841
8844	7842
8845	516
"	7843
8846	7845
8847	7848
8848	7849
8849	7850
8850	7851
8851	7857
8852	7858
8853	7860
8854	
8855	7861
8856	7862
8857	7864
8858	7866
8859	7871
8860	7870
8861	7876
8862	7877
8863	7817
8864	7882
8865	7883
8866	7884
8867	7752
8868	7885
8869	7886
8870	7887
8871	7758
8872	7888
8873	7889
8874	8366
8875	7890
8876	7891
8877	7892
8878	7892
8879	
8880	7893
8881	7894
8882	7895
8883	7896
8884	7897
8885	7898
8886	7901
8887	7902
8888	7903
8889	7904
8890	7908
8891	7909
8892	7909
8893	7910
8894	7911
8895	7913
8896	7918
8897	7921
8898	7923
8899	7925
8900	7926
"	7929
8901	7927
8902	7927
8903	7928
8904	7930
8905	7931
"	7933
8906	
8907	7934
8908	7935
8909	7935
8910	7937
8911	7941
8912	7937
8913	7943
8914	7942
8915	7944
8916	7946
8917	7947
8918	7948
8919	7949
8920	7950
8921	7950
8922	7951
8923	7952
"	7953
8924	7956
8925	7956
8926	7887
8927	7957
8928	7957
8929	7961
8930	7959
8931	7887
8932	7962
8933	7964
8934	7965
8935	7967
8936	7966
8937	7968
8938	7971
8939	7973
8940	7975
8941	7974
8942	7975
8943	7976
8944	7977
8945	7973
8946	7978
8947	7979
8948	7980
8949	7982
8950	7983
8951	7986
8952	7987
8953	7988
8954	7989
8955	7991
8956	7991
8957	7991
8958	7992
8959	7993
8960	7994
8961	7995
8962	7996
8963	7997
8964	7997
8965	7998
8966	7999
8967	
8968	8002
8969	8003
8970	8004
8971	
8972	8005
8973	8006
8974	8011
8975	4100
8976	8010
8977	8013
8978	8073
8979	8015
8980	8016
8981	8017
8982	8018
8983	8018
8984	8019
8985	8019
8986	8020
8987	8022
8988	8021
8989	8023
"	8024
8990	8025
8991	8026
8992	8027
8993	7969
8994	8028
8995	8031
8996	8030
8997	8032
8998	7991
8999	7992
9000	8029
9001	7970
9002	
9003	7597
9004	8033
9005	8034
9006	8035
9007	8037
9008	8038
9009	8039
9010	8043
9011	8044
9012	8045
9013	8106
9014	8047
9015	8048
9016	8049
9017	8050
9018	8051
9019	8052
9020	8053
9021	8054
9022	
9023	8058
9024	8059
9025	8060
9026	8061
9027	8062
9028	8064
9029	8066
9030	8067
9031	8068
9032	8068
9033	8069
9034	8069
9035	8070
9036	8073
9037	8074
9038	8076
9039	8077
9040	8077
9041	8078
9042	8080
9043	8081
9044	4924
9045	8082
9046	8083
9047	8084
9048	8085
9049	8085
9050	8087
9051	8088
9052	8091
9053	8089
9054	8090
9055	8092
9056	8093
9057	8094
9058	8095
9059	8096
9060	8097
9061	8098
9062	8098
9063	8099
9064	8100
9065	8101
9066	8102
9067	8103
9068	8104
9069	8105
9070	8106
9071	7763
9072	8108
9073	8109
9074	8110
9075	8110
9076	8111
9077	8112
9078	8113
9079	8114
9080	8114
9081	8107
9082	8070
9083	8116
9084	8117
9085	8118
9086	8119
9087	8121
9088	8123
9089	8124
9090	1030
9091	8125
9092	8126
9093	1052
9094	8127
9095	8129
9096	8132
9097	8142
9098	8134
9099	8136
9100	8137
9101	8132
"	8138
9102	8141
9103	
9104	8142
9105	8143
9106	8144
9107	
9108	8145
9109	8147
9110	8148
9111	8150
9112	8150
9113	8151
9114	8152
9115	8154
9116	8155
9117	8156
9118	8157
9119	8158
9120	8159
9121	8161
9122	8162
9123	8168
9124	8169
9125	8169
9126	8170
9127	8171
9128	8172
9129	8173
9130	8173
9131	8174
9132	8176
9133	8179
9134	8180
9135	8182
9136	8186
9137	8187
9138	8187
9139	8189
9140	8190
9141	8191
9142	8192
9143	8195
9144	8196
9145	8197
9146	8197
9147	8194
9148	8198
9149	8199
9150	8201
9151	8202
9152	8203
9153	8203
9154	8204
9155	8205
9156	8195
9157	8206
9158	8206
9159	8207
9160	8208
9161	8210
9162	8211
9163	8212
9164	8213
9165	8216
9166	8217
9167	
9168	8218
9169	8219
9170	8220
9171	8223
9172	8221
9173	8309
9174	
9175	8225
9176	8227
9177	8227
9178	
9179	8228
9180	8229
9181	8230
9182	8231
9183	8233
9184	8234
9185	8235
9186	8236
9187	8237
9188	8237
9189	8239
9190	8240
9191	8240
9192	8241
9193	8245
9194	8245
9195	8245
9196	8247
9197	8248
9198	8249
"	8250
9199	8251
9200	8252
9201	8253
9202	8254
9203	8255
9204	8256
9205	8257
9206	8258
9207	8259
9208	8260
9209	8261
9210	8262
9211	8263
9212	8264
9213	8266
9214	8267
9215	
9216	8268
9217	8285
9218	8270
9219	8270
9220	8273
9221	8274
9222	8275
9223	3474
"	8281
9224	8281
"	8284
9225	8285
9226	8287
9227	8289
9228	8290
9229	8292
9230	8293
9231	7861
9232	8298
9233	8302
9234	8302
9235	8306
9236	8309
9237	8317
9238	8318
9239	8319
9240	8322
9241	8292
9242	8325
9243	8325
9244	8307
9245	8327
9246	8329
9247	8326
"	8328
9248	8333
9249	8333
9250	8334
9251	8335
9252	8337
9253	8336
9254	8336
9255	8338
9256	8339
9257	8341
9258	8343
9259	8344
9260	
9261	8345
9262	8346
9263	8347
9264	8348
9265	8349
9266	8350
9267	
9268	8351
"	8352
"	8357
9269	8352
9270	
9271	8356
9272	8354
9273	
9274	8359
9275	8358
9276	8360
9277	8363
9278	8362
9279	8364
9280	8365
9281	8365
9282	8366
9283	
9284	8367
9285	8369
9286	8371
9287	
9288	8372
9289	8373
9290	8374
9291	8375
9292	8376
9293	8377
9294	8378
9295	8379
9296	8380
9297	8381
9298	8382
9299	8385
9300	8384
9301	8385
9302	8386
9303	8383
9304	8387
9305	8388
9306	8388
9307	8389
9308	8390
9309	839
"	8391
9310	8392
9311	8393
9312	8394
9313	8395
9314	8396
9315	8398
9316	8397
9317	8422
9318	8399
9319	8400
9320	8401
9321	8402
9322	8403
9323	8404
9324	8405
9325	8407
9326	8408
9327	8409
9328	8425
9329	8410
9330	8412
9331	8413
9332	8414
9333	8415
9334	8417
9335	8416
9336	8418
9337	8419
9338	8420
9339	8380
9340	8423
9341	8394
9342	8424
9343	8426
9344	8427
9345	8428
9346	8430
9347	8431
9348	8432
9349	8433
9350	8433
9351	8434
9352	8435
9353	8436
9354	8437
9355	8438
9356	8439
9357	8438
9358	8440
9359	8441
9360	8442
9361	8443
9362	8444
9363	8445
9364	8628
9365	8446
9366	8447
"	8448
9367	8449
9368	8451
"	8452
9369	8453
9370	8454
9371	8455
9372	8456
9373	8457
9374	8458
9375	8459
9376	8461
9377	8463
9378	8462
9379	8464
9380	8465
9381	8466
9382	8467
9383	8468
9384	8469
9385	8466
"	8470
9386	8466
9387	8471
9388	8472
9389	8473
9390	8475
9391	8476
9392	8477
9393	8478
9394	8480
9395	8480
9396	8481
9397	8482
9398	8483
9399	8484
9400	8436
9401	8485
9402	8486
9403	8487
9404	8489
9405	8488
9406	8490
9407	8491
9408	8492
9409	8493
9410	8494
9411	8495
9412	8496
"	8501
9413	8497
9414	8498
"	8499
9415	8500
9416	8502
9417	8503
9418	8504
9419	8505
9420	8506
9421	8507
9422	8508
9423	8509
9424	8510
9425	8512
9426	8521
9427	8528
9428	8511
9429	8514
9430	8513
9431	8515
9432	8516
9433	8407
9434	8518
9435	8524
9436	8520
9437	8522
9438	2048
9439	8525
9440	8526
9441	8527
9442	8519
9443	8529
9444	8530
9445	8515
9446	8534
9447	8535
9448	8537
9449	8539
9450	8538
9451	8541
9452	8542
9453	8543
9454	8544
9455	8545
9456	8546
9457	8547
9458	8548
9459	8549
9460	8550
9461	8551
9462	8552
9463	8553
9464	8554
9465	8555
9466	8556
9467	8556
9468	8557
9469	8558
9470	8559
9471	8559
9472	8560
9473	8560
9474	8561
9475	8562
9476	8563
9477	8564
9478	8565
"	8568
9479	8566
9480	8567
9481	8569
9482	8570
9483	8571
9484	8572
9485	8573
9486	8574
9487	8575
9488	8575
9489	8576
9490	8577
9491	8580
9492	8580
9493	8581
9494	8582
9495	8583
9496	8584
9497	8583
9498	8585
9499	8585
9500	8586
9501	
9502	8587
9503	8588
9504	8589
9505	8590
9506	8591
9507	5774
9508	8592
9509	8593
9510	8594
9511	8595
9512	8596
9513	8596
9514	8597
9515	8598
9516	8599
9517	8599
9518	8600
9519	8601
9520	6617
9521	8602
9522	8602
9523	8603
9524	8604
9525	8605
9526	8606
9527	8607
9528	8608
9529	8609
9530	8610
9531	8611
9532	8612
9533	8613
9534	8616
9535	8615
9536	8615
9537	8616
9538	8617
9539	6965
"	8618
9540	8619
9541	8620
9542	8621
9543	8622
9544	8623
9545	8626
9546	8628
9547	8629
9548	8630
9549	8633
9550	8634
9551	8635
9552	8636
9553	8638
9554	8639
9555	8640
9556	8641
9557	8642
9558	8643
9559	8644
9560	8645
9561	8646
9562	8646
9563	8647
9564	8649
9565	
9566	8649
9567	8649
9568	8650
9569	8649
9570	8653
9571	8654
9572	8655
9573	8656
9574	8656
9575	8657
9576	8659
9577	8658
9578	8659
9579	8660
9580	8661
9581	8662
9582	8667
9583	8663
9584	
9585	8664
9586	8664
9587	8665
9588	8666
9589	7738
"	8663
9590	
9591	8668
9592	8669
9593	8670
9594	
9595	8671
9596	8672
9597	8673

ARAMAIC OLD TESTAMENT

G/K	STRONG
10001	
10002	
10003	2
10004	4
10005	7
10006	69
10007	104
10008	116
10009	144
10010	147
10011	148
10012	149
10013	153
10014	230
10015	228
10016	236
10017	252
10018	263
10019	280
10020	307
10021	311
10022	320
10023	317

G/K	STRONG
10024	318
10025	321
10026	324
10027	363
10028	574
10029	383
10030	399
10031	409
10032	412
10033	426
10034	429
10035	431
10036	459
10037	479
10038	506
10039	521
10040	524
10041	540
10042	560
10043	563
10044	576
10045	581
10046	582
10047	586
10048	598
10049	600
10050	606
10051	607
10052	607
10053	608
10054	613
10055	620
10056	629
10057	633
10058	636
10059	638
10060	670
10061	671
10062	671
10063	674
10064	677
10065	703
10066	711
10067	718
10068	735
10069	738
10070	746
10071	749
10072	755
10073	754
10074	756
10075	772
10076	773
10077	778
10078	783
10079	787
10080	785
10081	826
10082	846
10083	849
10084	852
10085	858
10086	861
10087	870
10088	
10089	
10090	873
10091	888
10092	870
10093	895
10094	896
10095	921
10096	924
10097	927
10098	989
10099	997
10100	999
10101	1001
10102	956
10103	1005
10104	1079
10105	1113
10106	1080
10107	1093
10108	1096
10109	1113
10110	1123
10111	1124
10112	1147
10113	1149
10114	1156
10115	1159
10116	1169
10117	1236
10118	1240
10119	1251
10120	1247
10121	1289
10122	1289
10123	1291
10124	1297
10125	1321
10126	1325
10127	
10128	1355
10129	1358
10130	1370
10131	1400
10132	1401
10133	1411
10134	1414
10135	1459
10136	1467
10137	1519
10138	
10139	1490
10140	1505
10141	1510
10142	1528
10143	1535
10144	1541
10145	1547
10146	1560
10147	1585
10148	1596
10149	1611
10150	1635
10151	1655
10152	
10153	
10154	1668
10155	1678
10156	1684
10157	1685
10158	1693
10159	1701
10160	1722
10161	1723
10162	1723
10163	1753
10164	1757
10165	1759
10166	1761
10167	1763
10168	1768
10169	1778
10170	1780
10171	1782
10172	1784
10173	1791
10174	1797
10175	1798
10176	1799
10177	1799
10178	1815
10179	1821
10180	1836
10181	1841
10182	1855
10183	1859
10184	1868
10185	1872
10186	1882
10187	1883
10188	1884
10189	
10190	
10191	
10192	
10193	
10194	1888
10195	1888
10196	1907
10197	1917
10198	1922
10199	1923
10200	1932
10201	1934
10202	1946
10203	
10204	
10205	1932
10206	1965
10207	1981
10208	1983
10209	
10210	1994
10211	2002
10212	2002
10213	2006
10214	
10215	
10216	
10217	2031
10218	927
10219	5069
10220	
10221	
10222	
10223	2084
10224	2095
10225	2103
10226	2110
10227	2112
10228	2122
10229	2136
10230	2148
10231	2164
10232	2166
10233	2170
10234	2171
10235	2178
10236	2192
10237	2200
10238	2211
10239	2217
10240	2234
10241	
10242	2248
10243	2255
10244	2257
10245	2269
10246	2273
10247	2292
10248	2298
10249	2306
10250	2305
10251	2323
10252	2324
10253	2338
10254	2358
10255	2370
10256	2376
10257	2379
10258	2402
10259	2408
10260	2409
10261	2417
10262	2418
10263	2423
10264	2429
10265	2445
10266	2452
10267	2493
10268	2499
10269	2508
10270	2528
10271	2562
10272	2591
10273	2597
10274	2604
10275	2608
10276	2627
10277	2631
10278	2632
10279	2635
10280	2685
10281	2718
10282	2749
10283	2761
10284	2783
10285	2804
10286	2816
10287	2818
10288	2818
10289	2819
10290	2827
10291	2857
10292	
10293	2868
10294	2869
10295	2877
10296	2906
10297	2908
10298	2917
10299	2920
10300	2927
10301	2939
10302	2942
10303	2953
10304	2957
10305	2967
10306	
10307	
10308	2987
10309	3007
10310	3026
10311	3028
10312	3029
10313	3046
10314	3052
10315	3061
10316	3062
10317	3118
10318	3136
10319	
10320	3191
10321	3202
10322	3221
10323	3255
10324	3272
10325	3272
10326	3321
10327	3330
10328	3345
10329	3346
10330	3358
10331	3367
10332	3390
10333	3393
10334	3410
10335	3479
10336	3443
10337	3487
10338	3488
10339	3493
10340	
10341	
10342	
10343	3538
10344	
10345	3542
10346	3546
10347	3549
10348	3551
10349	
10350	3567
10351	
10352	3604
10353	3606
10354	3635
10355	
10356	4101
10357	3652
10358	3660
10359	3673
10360	3675
10361	3679
10362	3702
10363	3705
10364	3706
10365	3706
10366	3729
10367	3734
10368	3737
10369	3735
10370	3744
10371	3745
10372	3764
10373	3779
10374	3790
10375	3792
10376	3797
10377	
10378	
10379	3809
10380	3821
10381	3825
10382	3831
10383	3848
10384	3809
10385	3861
10386	3861
10387	3879
10388	3890
10389	3900
10390	3904
10391	3916
10392	3961
10393	
10394	3964
10395	3969
10396	3977
10397	3983
10398	3984
10399	4040
10400	4049
10401	4056
10402	4061
10403	4070
10404	4076
"	4077
10405	4076
"	4077
10406	4083
10407	4070
10408	4101
10409	4193
10410	4203
10411	4223
10412	4255
10413	4291
10414	4333
10415	4336
10416	4391
10417	4398
10418	4406
10419	4415
10420	4416
10421	4430
10422	4431
10423	4433
10424	4437
10425	4449
10426	4479
10427	4481
10428	4484
10429	4061
10430	4486
10431	4483
10432	4504
10433	4510
10434	4567
10435	4577
10436	4606
10437	4756
10438	4776
10439	4779
10440	4804
10441	4873
10442	4887
10443	4887
10444	4903
10445	4907
10446	4953
10447	4961
10448	4978
10449	
10450	
10451	5013
10452	5017
10453	5020
10454	5023
10455	5029
10456	5043
10457	5047
10458	5049
10459	5053
10460	5665
10461	5069
10462	5073
10463	5075
10464	5085
10465	5094
10466	5094
10467	5094
10468	5103
10469	5111
10470	5122
10471	5135
10472	5142
10473	5174
10474	5182
10475	5191
10476	5202
10477	
10478	5208
10479	5232
10480	5245
10481	5256
10482	5260
10483	5261
10484	5308
10485	5312
10486	5313
10487	5326
10488	5330
10489	5338
10490	5343
10491	5368
10492	5376
10493	5389
10494	5396
10495	5403
10496	5407
10497	5412
10498	5415
10499	5426
10500	
10501	5443
10502	5446
10503	5452
10504	5457
10505	5460
10506	5463
10507	5481
10508	5487
10509	5491
10510	5481
10511	7859
10512	5481
10513	5559
"	5267
10514	5583
10515	5609
10516	5613
10517	5622
10518	5632
10519	5642
10520	5642
10521	
10522	5648
10523	5649
10524	5665
10525	5673
10526	5675
10527	5705
10528	5709
10529	5714
10530	5732
10531	5751
10532	5758
10533	5776
10534	5784
10535	5796
10536	5824
10537	5831
10538	5839
10539	5843
10540	5870
10541	5894
10542	5922
10543	5924
10544	5931
10545	5928
10546	5943
10547	5952
10548	5946
10549	5954
10550	5957
10551	5962
10552	5967
10553	5972
10554	5974
10555	5994
10556	6015
10557	3705
10558	6032
10559	6033
10560	6050
10561	6056
10562	6065
10563	3706
10564	6074
10565	6088
10566	6132
10567	6136
10568	6146
10569	6151
10570	6167
10571	6173
10572	6211
10573	6236
10574	6243
10575	6246
10576	3706
10577	6263
10578	6268
10579	
10580	6347
10581	6353
10582	6361
10583	6386
10584	6387
10585	6392
10586	6399
10587	6402
10588	6433
10589	6447
10590	6460
10591	6523
10592	6537
10593	6537
10594	6540
10595	6543
10596	6562
10597	6568
10598	6573
10599	6590
10600	6591
10601	6600
10602	6606
10603	6613
10604	
10605	6634
10606	6640
10607	6647
10608	6655
10609	6656
10610	6665
10611	6676
10612	6739
10613	6744
10614	6755
10615	6841
10616	6853
10617	
10618	6902
10619	6903
10620	6922
10621	6925
10622	6928
10623	6933
10624	6966
10625	6992
10626	7001
10627	7007
10628	7010
10629	7011
10630	7030
10631	7032
10632	7066
10633	7108
10634	7109
10635	7113
10636	7118
10637	7123
10638	7127
10639	7129
10640	7149
10641	7162
10642	7170
10643	7187
10644	7030
10645	
10646	7217
10647	7229
"	7260
10648	7236
10649	7240
10650	7238
10651	7244
10652	7261
10653	7265
10654	7266
10655	7271
10656	7284
10657	7299
10658	7308
10659	7313
10660	7314
10661	7328
10662	7348
10663	7352
10664	7359
10665	7365
10666	7382
10667	7412
10668	7470
10669	7476
10670	7487
10671	7490
10672	7512
10673	7560
10674	
10675	7868
10676	5443
10677	7680
10678	7690
10679	3026
10680	7859
10681	7868
10682	7761
10683	7920
10684	7924
10685	7955
10686	8131
10687	8177
10688	
10689	7593
10690	7595
10691	7598
10692	7606
10693	7624
10694	7625
10695	7631
10696	7655
10697	7662
10698	7672
10699	7695
10700	7712
10701	7715
10702	7739
10703	7792
10704	7801
10705	7844
10706	7804
10707	3319
10708	7912
10709	7932
10710	7954
10711	7955
10712	7960
10713	7963
10714	7972
10715	7981
10716	7984
10717	7985
10718	7990
10719	8000
10720	8001
10721	8036
10722	8046
10723	8065
10724	8075
10725	8086
10726	8115
10727	8120
10728	8122
10729	8124
10730	8128
10731	8133
10732	8140
10733	8139
10734	8160
10735	8200
10736	8209
10737	8214
10738	8215
10739	8232
10740	8238
10741	8243
10742	8271
10743	8330
10744	8332
10745	8332
10746	8340
10747	8353
10748	8355
10749	8361
10750	8370
10751	
10752	8406
10753	8411
10754	8421
10755	8429
10756	8450
10757	8460
"	8479
10758	8517
10759	8523
10760	8531
10761	8532
10762	8533
10763	8540
10764	8536
10765	8578
10766	8579
10767	8614
10768	8624
10769	8625
10770	8625
10771	8627
10772	8631
10773	8632
10774	8632
10775	8648
10776	8651
10777	8652
10778	8648
10779	8674

GREEK NEW TESTAMENT

G/K	STRONG
1	*1*
2	*2*
3	*3*
4	*4*
5	*5*
6	*6*
7	*7*
8	*8*
9	*9*
10	*10*
11	*11*
12	*12*
13	*13*
14	*14*
15	*18+2041*
16	*15*
17	*16*
18	*17*
19	*18*
20	*19*
21	*20*
22	*21*
23	*22*
24	*23*
25	*24*
26	*25*
27	*26*
28	*27*
29	*28*
30	*29*
31	*30*
32	*31*
33	*518*
34	*32*
35	*30*
36	*34*
37	*35*
38	*36*
39	*37*
40	*38*
41	*39*
"	*40*
42	*41*
43	*42*
44	*43*
45	*44*
46	*45*
47	*46*
48	*47*
49	*48*
50	*49*
51	*50*
52	*51*
53	*52*
54	*53*
55	*54*
56	*55*
57	*56*
58	*57*
59	*58*
60	*59*
61	*60*
62	*61*
63	*62*
64	*63*
65	*64*
66	*65*
67	*66*
68	*67*
69	*68*
70	*69*
71	*70*
72	*33*

G/K	STRONG
"	71
73	72
74	73
75	74
76	75
77	76
78	77
79	78
80	79
81	80
82	81
83	82
84	83
85	84
86	85
87	86
88	87
89	88
90	89
91	90
92	91
93	92
94	93
95	94+2923
96	94
97	95
98	689
99	96
100	97
101	98
102	99
103	100
104	101
105	102
106	103
107	104
108	105
109	106
110	107
111	108
112	
113	109
114	110
115	2288+1
116	111
117	112
118	113
119	114
120	115
121	116
122	117
123	118
124	119
125	4867
126	120
127	121
128	122
129	123
130	124
131	125
132	126
133	127
134	128
135	129
136	130
137	131
138	132
139	133
140	134
141	135
142	136
143	137
144	2056
145	138
146	139
147	140
148	141
149	142
150	143
151	144
152	145
153	146
154	147
155	148
156	149
"	150
157	151
158	152
159	153
160	154
161	155
162	156
163	157
164	4256
165	158
"	159
166	157
167	160
168	161
169	162
170	163
171	164
172	165
173	166
174	167

G/K	STRONG
175	168
176	169
177	170
178	171
179	172
180	173
181	174
182	175
183	176
184	177
185	178
186	179
187	180
188	180
189	181
190	182
191	183
192	184
193	185
194	85
195	186
196	187
197	188
198	189
199	190
200	191
201	191
202	192
203	193
204	194
205	195
206	196
207	
208	198
209	199
"	197
210	200
211	201
212	202
213	203
214	204
215	205
216	206
217	207
218	208
219	209
220	210
221	217
222	211
223	211
224	212
225	213
226	214
227	215
228	216
229	217
230	218
231	219
232	220
233	221
234	222
235	223
236	224
237	225
238	226
239	227
240	228
241	229
242	230
243	231
244	232
245	233
246	234
247	235
248	236
249	237
250	
251	238
252	239
253	240
254	241
255	2087
256	242
257	243
258	244
259	245
260	246
261	247
262	248
263	249
264	250
265	251
266	252
267	253
268	254
269	255
270	1
271	256
272	257
273	258
274	259
275	260
276	261
277	262
278	263

G/K	STRONG
279	264
280	265
281	266
282	267
283	268
284	
285	269
286	270
287	271
288	272
289	273
290	274
291	275
292	276
293	277
294	278
295	279
296	280
297	281
298	282
299	283
300	284
301	
302	285
303	286
304	287
305	880
306	288
307	289
308	290
309	291
310	292
311	906+293
312	293
313	294
314	294
315	295
316	296
317	297
318	298
319	
320	299
321	300
322	301
323	302
324	303
325	304
326	305
327	306
328	307
329	308
330	309
331	310
332	311
333	508
334	312
335	313
336	314
337	315
338	316
339	317
340	318
341	319
342	320
343	321
344	322
345	323
346	324
347	325
348	326
349	327
350	328
351	329
352	330
353	331
354	332
355	333
356	334
357	335
358	336
359	337
360	338
361	339
362	340
363	341
364	342
365	343
366	344
367	345
368	346
369	347
370	348
371	349
372	
373	350
374	351
375	617
376	352
377	353
378	354
379	355
380	242
381	356
382	357
383	358

G/K	STRONG
384	355
385	359
386	360
387	361
388	362
389	363
390	364
391	365
392	366
393	367
394	368
395	369
396	370
397	371
398	372
399	373
400	374
401	376
402	375
403	450
404	377
405	378
406	379
407	4238
408	380
409	381
410	382
411	383
412	384
413	385
414	386
415	387
416	388
417	389
418	390
419	391
420	37
421	392
422	393
423	394
424	395
425	510
426	396
427	397
428	398
429	399
430	400
431	401
432	402
433	403
434	404
435	405
436	406
437	407
438	408
439	409
440	507+2821
441	410
442	411
443	412
444	413
445	414
446	415
447	448
448	416
449	417
450	418
451	419
452	420
453	421
454	422
455	423
456	424
457	425
458	426
459	427
460	428
461	429
462	430
463	431
464	432
465	433
466	434
467	435
468	436
469	437
470	438
471	439
472	440
473	441
474	442
475	443
476	444
477	445
478	446
479	447
480	448
481	449
482	450
483	451
484	452
485	453
486	454
487	455
488	456

G/K	STRONG
489	457
490	458
491	459
492	460
493	453
494	461
495	462
496	463
497	464
498	465
499	466
500	467
501	468
502	469
503	470
504	472
505	473
506	474
507	475
508	476
509	477
510	478
511	479
512	480
513	481
514	482
515	471
"	483
516	484
517	485
518	486
519	487
520	488
521	489
522	490
523	491
524	492
525	493
526	494
527	495
528	496
529	497
530	498
531	499
532	500
533	501
534	502
535	503
536	504
537	505
538	506
539	507
540	509
541	510
542	511
543	512
544	513
545	514
546	515
547	516
548	517
549	2456
550	518
551	519
552	520
553	521
554	522
555	523
556	524
557	525
558	526
559	527
560	528
561	529
562	530
563	531
564	532
565	533
566	575+737
567	534
568	535
569	536
570	537
571	782
572	538
573	539
574	540
575	541
576	1890
577	543
578	544
579	545
580	546
581	547
582	548
583	549
584	550
"	561
585	551
586	552
587	553
588	554
589	555
590	556
591	557

G/K	STRONG
592	558
593	559
594	560
595	561
596	562
597	563
598	564
599	565
600	566
"	567
"	568
601	569
602	570
603	571
604	573
605	572
606	573
607	574
608	575
609	576
610	577
611	578
612	579
613	580
614	581
615	582
616	583
617	584
618	585
619	586
620	586
621	587
622	588
623	589
624	590
625	591
626	592
627	593
628	594
629	595
630	596
631	597
632	598
633	599
634	600
635	600
636	601
637	602
638	603
639	604
640	605
641	606
642	607
643	608
644	609
645	610
646	611
647	612
648	613
649	614
650	615
651	615
652	616
653	617
654	2980
655	618
656	619
657	620
658	621
659	5277
660	622
661	623
662	624
663	625
664	626
665	627
666	628
667	629
668	630
669	631
670	5278
671	632
672	633
673	575+3992
674	634
675	635
676	636
677	637
678	638
679	639
680	640
681	641
682	642
683	643
684	644
685	645
686	646
687	647
688	3848
689	648
690	649
691	650
692	651
693	652
694	653

G/K	STRONG
695	654
696	655
697	656
698	657
699	658
700	659
701	660
702	661
703	662
704	663
705	664
706	665
707	666
708	667
709	668
710	669
711	670
712	671
713	672
714	673
715	674
716	675
717	676
718	677
719	678
720	679
721	680
"	681
722	682
723	683
724	684
725	685
726	686
727	687
728	688
729	
730	689
731	729
732	690
733	691
734	692
735	693
736	694
737	695
738	696
739	693
740	697
741	698
742	699
743	700
744	701
745	702
746	703
747	
748	704
749	705
750	706
751	707
752	708
753	709
754	710
755	711
756	712
757	713
758	714
759	715
760	715
761	716
762	717
763	689
764	718
765	719
766	720
767	
768	721
769	722
770	723
771	724
772	725
773	726
774	727
775	728
776	730
777	731
778	732
779	732
780	733
781	730
782	734
783	735
784	736
785	737
786	738
787	739
788	740
789	741
790	742
791	743
792	744
793	745
794	746
795	747
796	748
797	749
798	3027

G/K	STRONG
799	750
800	751
801	752
802	753
803	754
804	755
805	
806	756
"	757
807	758
808	759
809	760
810	761
811	760
812	762
813	763
814	764
815	765
816	766
817	767
818	768
819	769
820	770
821	771
822	772
823	773
824	774
825	775
826	776
827	777
828	778
829	779
830	780
831	781
832	782
833	783
834	784
835	785
836	786
837	787
838	4565
839	788
840	789
841	790
842	791
843	792
844	793
845	794
846	795
847	796
848	797
849	798
850	799
851	800
852	801
853	802
854	803
855	804
856	805
857	806
858	807
859	808
860	809
861	810
862	811
863	812
864	813
865	814
866	815
867	816
868	817
869	818
870	818
871	819
872	820
873	821
874	822
875	823
876	824
877	825
878	826
879	827
880	828
881	829
882	830
883	831
884	832
885	833
886	834
887	835
888	836
889	837
890	838
891	837
892	839
893	840
894	841
895	842
896	843
897	844
898	845
899	846
"	847
"	848
900	1888

G/K	STRONG
901	849
902	3166
903	850
904	851
905	852
906	853
907	854
908	855
909	856
910	857
911	858
912	859
913	860
914	861
915	862
916	90
917	90
918	863
919	864
920	865
921	866
922	867
923	868
924	869
925	870
926	871
927	542
"	872
928	873
929	874
930	875
931	876
932	877
933	878
934	879
935	650
936	880
937	881
938	882
939	883
940	884
941	881
942	886
943	885
944	887
945	888
946	889
947	890
948	891
949	892
950	893
951	894
952	894
953	895
954	
955	896
956	897
957	898
958	899
959	900
960	901
961	902
962	903
963	904
964	905
965	906
966	907
967	908
968	909
969	910
970	911
971	920
972	912
973	913
974	914
975	915
976	916
977	917
978	918
979	919
980	920
981	920
982	921
983	922
984	923
985	924
986	925
987	926
988	927
989	928
990	929
991	930
992	931
993	932
994	933
"	934
995	935
996	936
997	937
998	937
999	938
1000	939
1001	940
1002	941
1003	942

G/K	STRONG
1004	943
1005	944
1006	945
1007	946
1008	947
1009	948
1010	949
1011	950
1012	951
1013	952
1014	953
1015	954
1016	955
1017	4476
1018	956
1019	957
1020	958
1021	958
1022	959
1023	960
1024	961
1025	
1026	1007
1027	1007
1028	962
1029	963
1030	962
1031	964
1032	964
1033	965
1034	966
1035	966
1036	967
1037	968
1038	
1039	969
1040	970
1041	971
1042	972
1043	973
1044	974
1045	974
1046	975
1047	976
1048	977
1049	978
1050	979
1051	980
1052	981
1053	982
1054	983
1055	984
1056	985
1057	985
1058	986
1059	987
1060	988
1061	989
1062	990
1063	991
1064	992
1065	993
1066	994
1067	1003
1068	995
1069	996
1070	997
1071	998
1072	999
1073	999
1074	1000
1075	1001
1076	1002
1077	1003
1078	1003
1079	1004
1080	1005
1081	1006
1082	1007
1083	1008
1084	1009
1085	1010
1086	1011
1087	1012
1088	1013
1089	1014
1090	1015
1091	1016
1092	1017
1093	1018
1094	1019
1095	1020
1096	1021
1097	1022
1098	1023
1099	1024
1100	1025
1101	1026
1102	1690
1103	1027
1104	1028
1105	1029
1106	1030
1107	1031
1108	1032

G/K	STRONG
1109	1033
1110	1034
1111	1035
1112	1036
1113	1037
1114	1038
1115	1039
1116	1040
1117	1041
1118	
1119	1042
1120	1043
1121	1044
1122	1045
1123	1046
1124	1048
1125	1047
1126	1049
1127	1050
1128	1051
1129	1052
1130	1053
1131	1054
1132	1055
1133	1056
1134	1057
1135	1053
1136	1058
1137	1059
1138	1060
1139	1061
1140	1061
1141	1062
1142	1063
1143	1064
1144	2802
1145	1065
1146	1066
1147	1067
1148	1068
1149	1068
1150	1069
1151	1070
1152	1071
1153	1072
1154	1073
1155	1074
1156	1075
1157	1076
1158	1077
1159	1077
1160	1077
1161	1078
1162	1079
1163	1081
1164	1080
1165	1081
1166	1082
1167	1083
1168	1084
1169	1085
1170	1086
1171	1086
1172	1087
1173	1088
1174	1089
1175	1090
1176	1091
1177	1092
1178	1093
1179	1094
1180	1095
1181	1096
1182	1097
1183	1098
1184	1099
1185	1100
1186	1101
1187	1102
1188	1103
1189	1104
1190	1105
1191	1106
1192	1107
1193	1110
1194	1108
1195	1109
1196	1110
1197	1111
1198	1112
1199	1113
1200	1114
1201	1115
1202	1116
1203	1117
1204	1118
1205	1119
1206	1120
1207	1121
1208	1122
1209	1123
1210	1124
1211	1125
1212	1126
1213	1127

G/K	STRONG
1214	1128
1215	1129
1216	1130
1217	1130
1218	1131
1219	1132
1220	1133
1221	1134
1222	1135
1223	1136
1224	1137
1225	
1226	1138
1227	1139
1228	1140
1229	1141
1230	1142
1231	1143
1232	1144
1233	1145
1234	1146
1235	1147
1236	1148
1237	1149
1238	1150
1239	1151
1240	1152
1241	1153
1242	1154
1243	
1244	1155
1245	1156
1246	1157
1247	1155
1248	1158
1249	1156
1250	1157
1251	1159
1252	1160
1253	1138
1254	1161
1255	1162
1256	1163
1257	1164
1258	1165
1259	1166
1260	1166
1261	1167
1262	1168
1263	
1264	1169
1265	1170
1266	
1267	1171
1268	1172
1269	
1270	1173
1271	1173
1272	1175
1273	1174
1274	1176
1275	1177
1276	1176+1803
1277	1176
	2532+3638
1278	1178
1279	1179
1280	1180
1281	1181
"	1182
1282	1183
1283	1184
1284	1185
1285	1186
1286	1187
1287	1187
1288	1188
1289	1189
1290	127
1291	1190
1292	1191
1293	1192
1294	1193
1295	2359
1296	1194
1297	1195
1298	1196
1299	1197
1300	1198
1301	1199
1302	1200
1303	1201
1304	1202
1305	1203
1306	1204
1307	1205
1308	1206
1309	1208
1310	1207
1311	1208
1312	1209
1313	1210
1314	1211
1315	5081
1316	1212

G/K	STRONG
1317	1213
1318	1214
1319	1215
1320	1216
1321	1217
1322	1218
1323	1219
1324	1220
1325	1221
1326	
1327	1222
1328	1223
1329	1224
1330	1225
1331	1226
1332	1227
1333	1228
1334	1229
1335	1230
1336	1231
1337	1232
1338	1233
1339	1234
1340	1235
1341	1236
1342	1237
1343	1238
1344	1239
1345	1240
1346	1241
1347	1242
1348	1243
1349	1244
1350	1245
1351	1245
1352	1246
1353	1781
1354	1247
1355	1248
1356	1249
1357	1250
1358	1251
1359	1252
1360	1253
1361	1254
1362	1255
1363	1256
1364	1257
1365	1258
1366	
1367	1259
1368	1260
1369	1261
1370	1262
1371	1263
1372	1264
1373	1265
1374	1266
1375	1267
1376	1268
1377	1269
1378	1270
1379	1271
1380	1272
1381	1273
1382	1274
1383	1275
1384	3859
1385	1276
1386	1277
1387	1278
1388	1279
1389	1280
1390	1281
1391	1282
1392	1284
1393	1284
1394	
1395	1283
1396	1284
1397	1285
1398	1286
1399	1287
1400	1288
1401	1289
1402	1290
1403	1291
1404	1292
1405	1293
1406	1294
1407	1295
1408	1296
1409	1297
1410	1298
1411	1299
1412	1300
1413	1301
1414	1302
1415	1303
1416	1303
1417	1304
1418	1305
1419	1306
1420	1307
1421	1307

G/K	STRONG
1422	1308
1423	1309
1424	1310
1425	1311
1426	1312
1427	1313
1428	1314
1429	1315
1430	5512
1431	1316
1432	
1433	
1434	1317
1435	1318
1436	1319
1437	1320
1438	1321
1439	1322
1440	1323
1441	1324
1442	1325
1443	1325
1444	1326
1445	1760
1446	1831
1447	1327
1448	2058
1449	1328
1450	1329
1451	1330
1452	1331
1453	1332
1454	1333
1455	1334
1456	1335
1457	1336
1458	1337
1459	1338
1460	1339
1461	333
1462	1340
1463	2613
1464	1341
1465	1342
1466	1343
1467	1344
1468	1345
1469	1346
1470	1347
1471	1348
1472	1349
1473	1350
1474	1351
1475	1352
1476	1353
1477	1354
1478	1355
1479	1356
1480	2735
1481	1357
1482	1358
1483	1359
1484	1360
1485	1361
1486	1362
1487	1362
1488	1363
1489	1364
1490	1417+3461
1491	1365
1492	1366
1493	1367
1494	1368
1495	1369
1496	1370
1497	1371
1498	1372
1499	1373
1500	1374
1501	1375
1502	1376
1503	1377
1504	1378
1505	1379
1506	1380
1507	1381
1508	1381
1509	1382
1510	1383
1511	1384
1512	1385
1513	1386
1514	1387
1515	1388
1516	1389
1517	1390
1518	1391
1519	1392
1520	1393
1521	1394
1522	1395
1523	1190
1524	1396
1525	1397
1526	1398

G/K	STRONG
1527	1399
1528	1400
"	1401
1529	1401
1530	1402
1531	1403
1532	1404
1533	1405
1534	1406
1535	1407
1536	1408
1537	1409
1538	1410
1539	1411
1540	1412
1541	1413
1542	1414
1543	1415
1544	1416
1545	1417
1546	1419
1547	1420
1548	1420
1549	1421
1550	
1551	1422
1552	1423
1553	1424
1554	1425
1555	987
1556	1426
1557	1427
1558	1428
1559	1429
1560	1430
1561	1431
1562	1432
1563	1433
1564	1434
1565	1435
1566	1248
1567	
1568	1436
1569	1437
1570	1437+4007
1571	1438
1572	1439
1573	1440
1574	1441
1575	1442
1576	1443
1577	1444
1578	1445
1579	1446
1580	1447
1581	1448
1582	1449
1583	1450
1584	1451
1585	1452
1586	1453
1587	1454
1588	1455
1589	1456
1590	1457
1591	1573
1592	1458
1593	1459
1594	1460
1595	2620
1596	1461
1597	2623
1598	1462
1599	1463
1600	1464
1601	1465
1602	1466
1603	1467
1604	1468
1605	1469
1606	1470
1607	1471
1608	1472
1609	1473
"	1691
"	1698
"	1700
"	2248
"	2249
"	2254
"	2257
"	3165
"	3427
"	3450
1610	1474
1611	1475
1612	1476
1613	1477
1614	1478
1615	1479
1616	1480
1617	1481
1618	1482
1619	1483
1620	1484

G/K	STRONG
1621	1485
1622	1486
1623	1487
1624	2397
1625	3708
1626	1491
1627	1493
1628	1494
1629	1496
1630	1495
1631	1497
1632	1500
1633	1501
1634	1502
1635	1504
1636	1505
1637	1506
1638	2229+3375
1639	1488
"	1498
"	1510
"	1511
"	1526
"	2070
"	2071
"	2252
"	2258
"	2277
"	2468
"	5600
"	5607
1640	
1641	1752
1642	1512
1643	1513
1644	1514
1645	1515
1646	1516
1647	1517
1648	1518
1649	3004
1650	1519
1651	1520
"	3391
1652	1521
1653	1522
1654	1523
1655	1524
1656	1525
1657	1528
1658	1529
1659	1530
1660	1531
1661	1532
1662	1533
1663	1534
1664	1535
1665	1486
1666	1537
1667	1538
1668	1539
1669	1540
1670	1541
1671	1542
1672	1543
1673	1543
1674	1831
1675	1544
1676	1545
1677	1816
1678	1546
1679	1547
1680	1548
1681	1549
1682	1550
1683	1551
1684	1552
1685	1553
1686	1554
1687	1555
1688	1556
1689	1557
1690	1558
1691	1559
1692	1560
1693	1561
1694	1562
1695	1563
1696	1564
1697	1565
1698	1566
1699	1567
1700	2214
1701	1568
1702	1569
1703	2296
1704	1570
1705	1571
1706	1572
1707	1573
1708	1574
1709	1575
1710	1576
1711	1577
1712	1578

G/K	STRONG
1713	1579
1714	1580
1715	1464
1716	1581
1717	1582
1718	1583
1719	1584
1720	1585
1721	1586
1722	1587
1723	1588
1724	1589
1725	1590
1726	1591
1727	1592
1728	1593
1729	1594
1730	1595
1731	1596
1732	1597
1733	1598
1734	1599
1735	1537+4053
1736	1600
1737	1530
1738	1601
1739	1602
1740	1603
1741	1604
1742	1605
1743	1606
1744	1607
1745	1608
1746	1609
1747	
1748	1610
1749	1611
1750	1612
1751	4982
1752	1613
1753	1614
1754	1615
1755	1616
1756	1618
1757	1617
"	1619
1758	1620
1759	1621
1760	1622
1761	1623
1762	1624
1763	1625
1764	1790
1765	1626
1766	1627
1767	1628
1768	1629
1769	1630
1770	1631
1771	1537+5455
1772	1632
1773	1632
1774	1633
1775	1634
1776	1635
1777	1636
1778	1637
1779	1638
1780	1639
1781	1640
1782	1641
1783	1642
1784	1640
1785	1643
1786	1644
1787	1645
1788	1646
"	1647
1789	1648
1790	1653
1791	1650
1792	1649
1793	1650
1794	1651
1795	1652
1796	1653
1797	1654
1798	1655
1799	1656
1800	1657
1801	1658
1802	1659
1803	1660
1804	1661
1805	1662
1806	1662
1807	3395
1808	1663
1809	1664
1810	1665
1811	1666
1812	1666
1813	1507
"	1667
1814	1668
1815	1669
1816	1670
1817	1671
1818	1672
1819	1673
1820	1674
1821	1675
1822	1676
1823	1677
1824	1677
1825	1678
1826	1678
1827	1679
1828	1680
1829	1681
1830	1682
1831	1683
1832	1684
1833	1685
1834	1686
1835	1686
1836	1687
1837	1688
1838	1689
1839	1690
1840	1692
1841	1693
1842	1694
1843	1695
1844	1696
1845	1722+3319
1846	1697
1847	1699
1848	
1849	1701
1850	1702
1851	1703
1852	649
1853	1704
1854	1705
1855	1705
1856	1714
1857	1705
1858	1705
1859	1714
1860	1706
1861	1707
1862	1708
1863	1709
1864	1710
1865	1711
1866	1712
1867	1713
1868	1714
1869	1715
1870	1716
1871	1717
1872	1718
1873	1719
1874	1720
1875	1721
1876	5455
1877	1722
1878	1723
1879	1724
1880	2177
1881	
1882	1725
1883	1726
1884	
1885	1727
1886	1756
1887	1728
1888	1766
1889	863
1890	1729
1891	1730
1892	1731
1893	1732
1894	1733
1895	1734
1896	1735
1897	1736
1898	1737
1899	1738
1900	1739
1901	1740
1902	1741
1903	1742
1904	1743
1905	1744
1906	1745
1907	1746
1908	1739
1909	1747
1910	1748
1911	1749
1912	1750
1913	1751
1914	1752
1915	1752
1916	1768
1917	1769
1918	1753
1919	1754
1920	1755
1921	1756
1922	1757
1923	1758
1924	1759
1925	1782
1926	1760
1927	1761
1928	1762
1929	1763
1930	4178
1931	1764
1932	1765
1933	1767
1934	1769
1935	1770
1936	1771
1937	1772
1938	1722+3551
1939	1773
1940	1774
1941	3726
1942	1775
1943	1776
1944	1777
1945	1778
1946	1779
1947	1780
1948	1781
1949	1782
1950	1783
1951	
1952	1784
1953	1785
1954	1786
1955	1787
1956	1788
1957	1789
1958	1790
1959	1791
1960	1792
1961	1793
1962	1794
1963	1795
1964	1796
1965	1797
1966	1798
1967	1799
1968	1800
1969	1801
1970	1802
1971	1803
1972	1804
1973	1805
1974	1806
1975	1807
1976	1808
1977	1809
1978	1810
1979	1811
1980	1812
1981	1813
1982	1814
1983	1815
1984	1816
1985	1817
1986	455
1987	1818
1988	1819
1989	1820
1990	1821
1991	
1992	1822
1993	1823
1994	1824
1995	1825
1996	1826
1997	1832
1998	1827
1999	1828
2000	1829
2001	1830
2002	1831
2003	1832
2004	1833
2005	1810
2006	
2007	1834
2008	1835
2009	1836
2010	1837
2011	1838
2012	1839
2013	1839
2014	1839
2015	1840
2016	1841
2017	1842
2018	1843
2019	1844
2020	1845
2021	1846
2022	1847
2023	1847
2024	1848
2025	1848
2026	1849
2027	1850
2028	
2029	1851
2030	1852
2031	1853
2032	1854
2033	1855
2034	1856
2035	1857
2036	1503
2037	1858
2038	1859
2039	1860
2040	1861
2041	1862
2042	1863
2043	1864
2044	1865
2045	1866
2046	1867
2047	1868
2048	1869
2049	1870
2050	1871
2051	1872
2052	1873
2053	1874
2054	1875
2055	1876
2056	1877
2057	1878
2058	1879
2059	1880
2060	1881
2061	1882
2062	1883
2063	1944
2064	1884
2065	1885
2066	1885
2067	
2068	1886
2069	1887
2070	1888
2071	1889
2072	1890
2073	1891
2074	1892
2075	1893
2076	1894
2077	1895
2078	1896
2079	1966
2080	1897
2081	1898
2082	1904
2083	1899
2084	1900
2085	1901
2086	1902
2087	1903
2088	1904
2089	1905
2090	1906
2091	1907
2092	1908
2093	1909
2094	1910
2095	1911
2096	1912
2097	1913
2098	1914
2099	1915
2100	1916
2101	1917
2102	1918
2103	1919
2104	1920
2105	1921
2106	1922
2107	1923
2108	1924
2109	1925
2110	1926
2111	1927
2112	1928
2113	1929
2114	1930
2115	1931
2116	1932
2117	1933
2118	1934
2119	1935
2120	1936
2121	1937
2122	1938
2123	1939
2124	2380
2125	1940
2126	1941
2127	1942
2128	1943
2129	1944
2130	1945
2131	2027
2132	2770
2133	2778
2134	1946
2135	1947
2136	
2137	1948
2138	1949
2139	2989
2140	1950
2141	1951
2142	1952
2143	621
2144	1953
2145	1954
2146	1955
2147	1956
2148	1957
2149	1958
2150	1959
2151	1960
2152	1961
2153	1962
2154	1963
2155	1964
2156	1965
2157	1967
2158	1968
2159	1969
2160	1971
2161	1972
2162	1973
2163	1974
2164	1975
2165	1976
2166	1977
2167	3982
2168	1978
2169	1979
2170	1980
2171	643
2172	1981
2173	1982
2174	1983
2175	1984
2176	1985
2177	1986
2178	4687
2179	1987
2180	1999
2181	1988
2182	1989
2183	
2184	1990
2185	1991
2186	1992
2187	1993
2188	1994
2189	1995
2190	1996
2191	1997
2192	1998
2193	1976
2194	1999
2195	2000
2196	2001
2197	2002
2198	2003
2199	2004
2200	2005
2201	2006
2202	2007
2203	2008
2204	2009
2205	2010
2206	2233
2207	2011
2208	2012
2209	2013
2210	2014
2211	2015
2212	2016
2213	2017
2214	2018
2215	2019
2216	2020
2217	2021
2218	
2219	2022
2220	2023
2221	2024
2222	2025
2223	2017
2224	2026
2225	2027
2226	2028
2227	2029
2228	2030
2229	2031
2230	2032
2231	2033
2232	2034
2233	2035
2234	4179
2235	2037
2236	2045
2237	2038
2238	2039
2239	2040
2240	2041
2241	2042
2242	2043
2243	2044
2244	2047
2245	2048
2246	2049
2247	2050
2248	2051
2249	2052
2250	2053
2251	2054
2252	2055
2253	2056
2254	2057
2255	2058
2256	1328
2257	2059
2258	2060
2259	2061
2260	2062
2261	2063
2262	2064
2263	2065
2264	2066
2265	2067
2266	2068
"	5315
2267	2068
2268	2069
2269	2072
2270	2073
2271	
2272	2074
2273	2274
2274	2078
2275	2079
2276	2080
2277	2081
2278	2082
2279	2083
2280	2084
2281	2085
2282	2086
2283	2087
2284	2088
2285	2089
2286	2090
2287	1681
2288	2091
2289	2092
2290	2093
2291	2094
2292	2095
2293	2096
2294	2097
2295	2098
2296	2099
2297	2100
2298	2101
2299	2102
2300	2103
2301	2095
2302	2104
2303	2129
2304	2105
2305	2106
2306	2107
2307	2108
2308	2109
2309	2110
2310	2111
2311	2112
2312	2113
2313	2114
2314	2115
2315	2115
2316	2116
2317	2117
2318	2117
2319	2118
2320	2119
2321	2120
2322	2121
2323	2122
2324	2123
2325	2124
2326	2125
2327	2126
2328	2127
2329	2128
2330	2129
2331	2130
2332	2131
2333	2132
2334	2133
2335	2134
2336	2135
2337	2136
2338	2137
2339	2145
2340	2138
2341	2139
2342	2139
2343	2140
2344	2141
2345	2142
2346	2143
2347	2144
2348	2145
2349	2146
2350	2148
2351	2147
2352	2148
2353	2149
2354	2150
2355	2151
2356	2152
2357	2153
2358	2154
2359	2155
2360	807
2361	2156
2362	2157
2363	2158
2364	2159
2365	2160
2366	2161
2367	2162
2368	2163
2369	2164
2370	2165
2371	2166
2372	2167
2373	2168
2374	2169
2375	2170
2376	2171
2377	2172
2378	2173
2379	2174
2380	2175
2381	2176
2382	
2383	2177
2384	2178
2385	2179
2386	2180
2387	2181
2388	2182
2389	2183
2390	2184
2391	2185
2392	2186
2393	1896
2394	2187
2395	2188
2396	5504
2397	2189
2398	2190
2399	2191
2400	2192
2401	2193
2402	
2403	
2404	2194
2405	2195
2406	2196
2407	4518
2408	2197
2409	2198
2410	4570
2411	2199
2412	2200
2413	4801
2414	2201
2415	2202
2416	2203
2417	2204
2418	2206
2419	2205
2420	2206
2421	2207
"	2208
2422	2209
2423	2210
2424	2211
2425	
2426	2212
2427	2213
2428	2214
2429	2215
2430	4667
2431	2216
2432	2217
2433	2218
2434	2219
2435	2220
2436	2221
2437	2222
2438	2223
2439	2224
2440	2224
2441	2225
2442	2226
2443	2227
2444	
2445	2228
2446	2229
2447	2229+3375
2448	2230
2449	2231
2450	2232
2451	2233
2452	2234
"	2236
2453	2235
2454	2237
2455	2238
2456	2239
2457	2240
2458	2241
2459	2242
2460	2243
2461	2244
2462	2245
2463	2246
2464	2247
2465	2250
2466	2251
2467	2253
2468	2255
2469	2256
2470	2256
2471	2259
2472	2260
2473	2261
2474	2262
2475	2263
2476	2264
2477	2265
2478	2266
2479	2267
2480	2268
2481	2269
2482	2276
2483	2270
2484	2271
2485	2272
2486	2273
2487	2274
2488	2275
2489	2276
2490	2278
2491	2279
2492	2279
2493	2279
2494	
2495	3134
2496	5008
2497	2280
2498	2281
2499	2282
2500	2283
2501	2284
2502	2285
2503	2286
2504	2287
2505	2288
2506	2289
2507	2290
2508	2291
2509	2292
2510	2293
2511	2294
2512	2295
2513	2296
2514	2297
2515	2298
2516	2299
2517	2300
2518	2301
2519	2302
2520	2303
2521	2304
2522	2305
2523	2306
2524	
2525	2307
2526	2308
2527	2309
2528	2310
2529	2310
2530	2311
2531	2312
2532	2312'
2533	2313
2534	2314
2535	2315
2536	2316
2537	2317
2538	2318
2539	2319
2540	2320
2541	2321
2542	2322
2543	2323
2544	2324
2545	2325
2546	2326

G/K	STRONG
2547	2327
2548	2328
2549	2329
2550	2330
2551	
2552	2331
2553	2332
2554	2333
2555	2334
2556	2335
2557	2336
2558	2337
2559	2338
2560	2339
2561	2340
2562	2341
2563	2342
2564	2343
2565	2344
2566	2345
2567	2346
2568	2347
2569	2348
2570	2349
2571	5182
2572	2350
2573	2351
2574	2352
2575	2352
2576	2353
2577	2354
2578	2355
2579	2356
2580	2357
2581	2358
2582	2359
2583	2360
2584	2361
2585	2362
2586	
2587	2363
2588	2364
2589	2365
2590	2366
2591	2367
2592	2368
2593	2369
2594	2370
2595	2371
2596	2372
2597	2373
2598	2374
2599	2375
2600	2376
2601	2377
2602	2378
2603	2379
2604	2380
2605	2381
2606	2382
2607	
2608	2383
2609	2384
2610	2385
2611	2386
2612	2387
2613	2388
2614	2389
2615	2390
2616	2391
2617	2392
2618	2393
2619	2394
2620	2395
2621	
2622	
2623	2396
2624	2397
2625	2398
2626	2399
2627	2400
2628	2401
2629	2402
2630	2403
2631	2404
2632	2405
2633	2406
2634	2407
2635	2408
2636	2409
2637	2410
2638	1494
2639	2411
2640	2412
2641	2413
2642	2414
2643	2415
2644	2416
2645	2417
2646	2418
2647	2419
2648	2420
2649	2421
2650	2422
2651	2423

G/K	STRONG
2652	2424
2653	2425
2654	2426
2655	2427
2656	2428
2657	2429
2658	2430
2659	2431
2660	2432
2661	2433
2662	2434
2663	2435
2664	2436
2665	2437
2666	2438
2667	2439
2668	2440
2669	2441
2670	2442
2671	2443
2672	2444
2673	2445
2674	2446
2675	2447
2676	2448
2677	2449
2678	2450
2679	2451
2680	2452
2681	2453
2682	2454
2683	2455
2684	2456
2685	2457
2686	2456
2687	2458
2688	2459
2689	2460
2690	2461
2691	2462
2692	2463
2693	2464
2694	2465
2695	2466
2696	2469
2697	2469
2698	2470
2699	2471
2700	2472
2701	2473
2702	2474
2703	2475
2704	2466
2705	2476
2706	
2707	2477
2708	2478
2709	2479
2710	2480
2711	2481
2712	2482
2713	2483
2714	2484
2715	2485
2716	2486
2717	2487
2718	2488
2719	
2720	2489
2721	2489
"	2490
2722	2491
2723	
2724	2492
2725	5601
2726	2455
2727	2493
2728	2491
2729	2494
2730	2494
2731	2495
2732	2496
2733	2497
2734	2498
2735	2499
2736	2500
2737	2501
2738	2501
2739	2502
2740	2503
2741	
2742	943
2743	2504
2744	943
2745	2505
2746	2506
2747	2507
2748	2508
2749	2509
2750	2510
2751	2511
2752	2512
2753	4027
2754	2513
2755	2514

G/K	STRONG
2756	2515
2757	2516
2758	2596+1520
2759	2517
2760	2511
2761	2518
2762	2519
2763	2520
2764	2521
2765	2596+2250
2766	2522
2767	2523
2768	2524
2769	2525
2770	2525
2771	2526
2772	2526'
2773	2527
2774	2528
2775	2529
2776	2530
2777	2531
2778	2509
2779	2532
2780	2533
2781	2534
2782	2535
2783	2536
2784	2536
2785	2537
2786	2538
2787	2757
2788	2539
2789	2540
2790	2541
2791	2542
2792	2543
2793	2544
2794	2545
2795	2546
2796	2547
2797	2548
2798	2549
2799	2550
2800	2551
2801	2552
2802	2553
2803	2554
2804	2555
2805	2556
2806	2557
2807	2558
2808	2559
2809	2560
2810	2561
2811	2562
2812	2563
2813	2564
2814	2565
2815	2567
2816	2568
2817	2552
2818	2569
2819	2566
"	2570
2820	2571
2821	2572
2822	2573
2823	2574
2824	2574
2825	2575
2826	2576
2827	2577
2828	2578
2829	2579
2830	2580
2831	2581
2832	2581
2833	2582
2834	2583
2835	2584
2836	2585
2837	2586
2838	2587
2839	603
2840	2588
2841	2589
2842	2591
2843	2590
2844	2592
2845	2593
2846	2594
2847	2595
2848	2596
2849	2597
2850	2598
2851	2599
2852	925
2853	2600
2854	2601
2855	
2856	2602
2857	2603
2858	2604
2859	2605

G/K	STRONG
2860	2606
2861	2607
2862	2608
2863	1125
2864	2609
2865	2610
2866	2611
2867	2612
2868	2613
2869	1349
2870	2614
2871	2615
2872	2616
2873	2652
2874	2653
2875	2617
2876	2618
2877	2619
2878	2620
2879	2621
2880	2622
2881	2623
2882	2624
2883	2624
2884	2625
2885	2626
2886	2627
2887	2628
2888	2629
2889	2630
2890	2631
2891	2632
2892	2633
2893	2596+2955
2894	2634
2895	2635
2896	2636
2897	2637
2898	2638
2899	2639
2900	2640
2901	2641
2902	2642
2903	2643
2904	2644
2905	2645
2906	2646
2907	2647
2908	2648
2909	2649
2910	2650
2911	2651
2912	2652
2913	2653
2914	2654
2915	2655
2916	2656
2917	2657
2918	2658
2919	2659
2920	2660
2921	2661
2922	2662
2923	2663
2924	2664
2925	2665
2926	
2927	2666
2928	2667
2929	2668
2930	2669
2931	2670
2932	2671
2933	2672
2934	2673
2935	2674
2936	2675
2937	2676
2938	2677
2939	2678
2940	2679
2941	2680
2942	2681
2943	2682
2944	2683
2945	2684
2946	2685
2947	2686
2948	2687
2949	2688
2950	2689
2951	2690
2952	2691
2953	2692
2954	2693
2955	2694
2956	2695
2957	2695
2958	2696
2959	2697
2960	2698
2961	2699
2962	2700
2963	2701
2964	826

G/K	STRONG
2965	2702
2966	2703
2967	2704
2968	2705
2969	2706
2970	2707
2971	2019
2972	2708
2973	2709
2974	2710
2975	4785
2976	2711
2977	2712
2978	2713
2979	2714
2980	2715
2981	2716
2982	2718
2983	2719
2984	2719
2985	2720
2986	2127
2987	2721
2988	2722
2989	2723
2990	2724
2991	2725
2992	2725
2993	2726
2994	2727
2995	2728
2996	2729
2997	2730
2998	2731
2999	2732
3000	2733
3001	2730
3002	2734
3003	2735
3004	2736
3005	2737
3006	2736
3007	2802
3008	2738
3009	2739
3010	2739
3011	2740
3012	2741
3013	2743
3014	2742
3015	2743
3016	2744
3017	2745
3018	2746
3019	2584
3020	2747
3021	2748
3022	2748
3023	2749
3024	2750
3025	2751
3026	2752
3027	2753
3028	
3029	2754
3030	2755
3031	2756
3032	2757
3033	2758
3034	2759
3035	2760
3036	2761
3037	2762
3038	2763
3039	2764
3040	2765
3041	2766
3042	2767
3043	2768
3044	2769
3045	2770
3046	2771
3047	2772
3048	2773
3049	2774
3050	2775
3051	2776
3052	2775
3053	2777
3054	
3055	5392
3056	2778
3057	2779
3058	2780
3059	2781
3060	2782
3061	2783
3062	2784
3063	2785
3064	2786
3065	
3066	2787
3067	2788
3068	2789
3069	2790

G/K	STRONG
3070	2791
3071	2791
3072	2792
3073	2793
3074	2794
3075	2795
3076	2796
3077	2792
3078	2797
3079	5531
3080	2798
3081	2799
3082	2800
3083	2801
3084	2802
3085	2802
3086	2803
3087	2804
3088	2805
3089	2806
3090	2807
3091	2808
3092	2809
3093	2810
3094	2811
3095	2812
3096	2813
3097	2814
3098	2815
3099	2816
3100	2817
3101	2818
3102	2819
3103	2820
3104	2821
3105	2822
3106	2823
3107	2824
3108	2825
3109	2825
3110	2826
3111	2827
3112	2828
3113	2829
3114	2830
3115	2831
3116	2832
3117	2833
3118	2834
3119	2835
3120	2836
3121	2837
3122	2838
3123	2839
3124	2840
3125	2841
3126	2842
3127	2843
3128	2844
3129	
3130	2845
3131	2846
3132	2847
3133	2848
3134	2849
3135	2850
3136	2851
3137	2858
3138	2857
3139	2852
3140	2853
3141	2854
3142	2855
3143	2856
3144	2858
3145	2857
3146	2859
3147	2860
3148	2861
3149	2862
3150	2863
3151	2864
3152	2865
3153	2866
3154	2867
3155	2868
3156	2869
3157	2870
3158	2871
3159	2872
3160	2873
3161	2874
3162	2874
3163	2874
3164	2875
3165	2876
3166	2877
3167	2878
3168	2878
3169	2879
3170	2880
3171	2881
3172	2882
3173	2883
3174	2884

G/K	STRONG
3175	2885
3176	2886
3177	2887
3178	2887
3179	2888
3180	2889
3181	2890
3182	2891
3183	2891
3184	2892
3185	2893
3186	2894
3187	2895
3188	2895
3189	2896
3190	2897
3191	2898
3192	2899
3193	2900
3194	2901
3195	2902
3196	2903
3197	2904
3198	2905
3199	2906
3200	2907
3201	2908
3202	2908
"	2909
3203	2910
3204	2911
3205	2912
3206	2913
3207	2914
3208	2915
3209	2916
3210	2917
3211	2918
3212	2919
3213	2920
3214	2921
3215	2922
3216	2923
3217	2924
3218	2925
3219	2926
3220	2927
3221	2928
3222	2929
3223	2930
3224	2927
3225	2931
3226	2927
3227	2932
3228	2933
3229	2934
3230	2935
3231	2936
3232	2937
3233	2938
3234	2939
3235	2940
3236	2941
3237	2942
3238	2944
3239	2943
3240	2944
3241	2945
3242	2946
3243	2946
3244	2947
3245	2948
3246	2949
3247	2950
3248	2951
3249	2952
3250	2953
3251	2954
3252	2955
3253	2956
3254	2956
3255	2957
3256	2958
3257	2959
3258	2960
3259	2961
3260	2958
3261	2962
3262	2963
3263	2964
3264	2965
3265	2966
3266	2967
3267	2968
3268	2969
3269	2970
3270	2971
3271	2972
3272	2973
3273	2974
3274	
3275	2975
3276	2976
3277	2977
3278	2978

G/K	STRONG
3279	2997
3280	2979
3281	2980
3282	2981
3283	2982
3284	2983
3285	2984
3286	2985
3287	2986
3288	2987
3289	2988
3290	2989
3291	2990
3292	2991
3293	2993
3294	2994
3295	2992
3296	2995
3297	2996
3298	2996
3299	2997
3300	2998
3301	2999
3302	3000
3303	3001
3304	3002
3305	3003
3306	2036
"	2046
"	3004
"	4483
3307	3005
3308	3006
3309	3007
3310	3008
3311	3009
3312	3010
3313	3011
3314	621
3315	
3316	2982
3317	3012
3318	3013
3319	3014
3320	3015
3321	3016
3322	3017
3323	3018
3324	3019
3325	3020
3326	3021
3327	1039
3328	3022
3329	3023
3330	3024
3331	3028
3332	3025
3333	3026
3334	3027
3335	3028
3336	3029
3337	3030
3338	3031
3339	3032
3340	3033
3341	3032
3342	3034
3343	3035
3344	3036
3345	3037
3346	3038
3347	3039
3348	3040
3349	3041
3350	3042
3351	3043
3352	3044
3353	3045
3354	3046
3355	3047
3356	3048
3357	3049
3358	3050
3359	3051
3360	3052
3361	3053
3362	3054
3363	3055
3364	3056
3365	3057
3366	3058
3367	3059
3368	3060
3369	3061
3370	3062
"	3063
"	3064
3371	3065
3372	3066
3373	3067
3374	3068
3375	3069
3376	3070
3377	3071
3378	3072

G/K	STRONG
3379	3073
3380	3074
3381	3075
3382	3076
3383	3077
3384	3078
3385	3079
3386	3080
3387	3081
3388	3082
3389	3083
3390	3084
3391	3085
3392	3086
3393	3087
3394	3088
3395	3089
3396	3090
3397	3091
3398	
3399	3092
3400	3093
3401	3093
3402	3094
3403	717
3404	3095
3405	3096
3406	3095
3407	3097
3408	3098
3409	3099
3410	3149
3411	3100
3412	3101
3413	3102
3414	3156
3415	3158
3416	3159
3417	3103
3418	3104
3419	3105
3420	3106
3421	3107
3422	3108
3423	3109
3424	3110
3425	3111
3426	3112
3427	3113
3428	3114
3429	3115
3430	3116
3431	3117
3432	3118
3433	3119
3434	3120
3435	3121
3436	3122
3437	3123
3438	3124
3439	3125
3440	3126
3441	3127
3442	3128
3443	3129
3444	3130
3445	3131
3446	3132
3447	3133
3448	3134
3449	3135
3450	3136
3451	3137
3452	3137
3453	3138
3454	3139
3455	3140
3456	3141
3457	3142
3458	3143
3459	3144
3460	3145
3461	3149
3462	3145
3463	3146
3464	3147
3465	3148
3466	3149
3467	3150
3468	3151
3469	3152
3470	3153
3471	3154
3472	3155
3473	3156
3474	3157
3475	3158
3476	3159
3477	3160
3478	3161
3479	3162
3480	3163
3481	3164
3482	3166
3483	3167
3484	3168
3485	3169
3486	3170
3487	3171
3488	3172
3489	3173
3490	3174
3491	3175
3492	3176
3493	3177
3494	3178
3495	3179
3496	3179
3497	3180
3498	3181
3499	3182
3500	3183
3501	3184
3502	3396
3503	3396
3504	3186
3505	3185
"	3187
3506	3188
"	3189
3507	3190
3508	3199
3509	3191
3510	3192
3511	3193
3512	3193
3513	3193
3514	3194
3515	3194
3516	3195
3517	3196
3518	3197
3519	3198
3520	3199
3521	3200
3522	3201
3523	3202
3524	3437
3525	3303
3526	3104
3527	
3528	3304
3529	3304
3530	3305
3531	3306
3532	3307
3533	3308
3534	3309
3535	3310
3536	3311
3537	3312
3538	3313
3539	3322
3540	3314
3541	3315
3542	3316
3543	3317
3544	3318
3545	3319
3546	3320
3547	3321
3548	3322
3549	3323
3550	3324
3551	3325
3552	3326
3553	3327
3554	3328
3555	3329
3556	3330
3557	3331
3558	3332
3559	3333
3560	3334
3561	3335
3562	3336
3563	3337
3564	3338
3565	3339
3566	3340
3567	3341
3568	3342
3569	3343
3570	3344
3571	3345
3572	3346
3573	3344
3574	
3575	3347
3576	3348
3577	3349
3578	3350
3579	3351
3580	3352
3581	3353
3582	3354
3583	3355
3584	3356
3585	3357
3586	3358
3587	3359
3588	3360
3589	3360
3590	3361
3591	3361+1065
3592	3365
3593	3366
3594	3367
3595	3368
3596	3369
3597	3370
3598	3365
3599	3367
3600	3371
3601	3372
3602	3373
3603	3374
3604	3375
3605	3376
3606	3377
3607	3379
3608	3361+4225
3609	3380
3610	3381
3611	3382
3612	3383
3613	3384
3614	3385
"	3387
3615	3386
3616	3388
3617	3389
3618	3389
3619	3390
3620	3392
3621	3393
3622	3394
3623	3395
3624	3396
3625	3397
"	3398
3626	3399
3627	3400
3628	3401
3629	3402
3630	3403
3631	3404
3632	3405
3633	3406
3634	3407
3635	3408
3636	3409
3637	3410
3638	3411
3639	3412
3640	3413
3641	3414
3642	3415
3643	3416
3644	3417
3645	3418
3646	3419
3647	3420
3648	3421
3649	3422
3650	3423
3651	3424
3652	3424
3653	3425
3654	3426
3655	3428
3656	3429
3657	3430
3658	3431
3659	3432
3660	3433
3661	3434
3662	3435
3663	3436
3664	3437
3665	3438
3666	3439
3667	3440
3668	3441
3669	3442
3670	3443
3671	3444
3672	3445
3673	3446
3674	3447
3675	3448
3676	3451
3677	3449
3678	3452
3679	3453
3680	3454
3681	3455
3682	3456
3683	3457
3684	3458
3685	3458
3686	3459
3687	
3688	3460
3689	3461
3690	3462
3691	3463
3692	3463
3693	3464
3694	3460
3695	3465
3696	3466
3697	3467
3698	3468
3699	3469
3700	3470
3701	3471
3702	3472
3703	3473
3704	3474
3705	3475
3706	3475
3707	3475
3708	
3709	3476
3710	3477
3711	3478
3712	3478
3713	3478
3714	3478
3715	3478
3716	3479
3717	3480
3718	3481
3719	3481
3720	3482
3721	3483
3722	3497
3723	3484
3724	3485
3725	3486
3726	3487
3727	3488
3728	3489
3729	3490
3730	3491
3731	3492
3732	3493
3733	3494
3734	3495
3735	3496
3736	3496
3737	3497
3738	3498
3739	3499
3740	3500
3741	3561
3742	3501
3743	3502
3744	3503
3745	3504
3746	3505
3747	
3748	3506
3749	3507
3750	3508
3751	3509
3752	3510
3753	3511
3754	3512
3755	3513
3756	3514
3757	3515
3758	3516
3759	3517
3760	3518
3761	3519
3762	3520
3763	3521
3764	3522
3765	3523
3766	3524
3767	3524
3768	3525
3769	3526
3770	3527
3771	3528
3772	3529
3773	3530
3774	3531
3775	3532
3776	3533
3777	3534
3778	3535
3779	3535
3780	3536
3781	3537
3782	3538
3783	3539
3784	3540
3785	3541
3786	3542
3787	3543
3788	3544
3789	3545
3790	3546
3791	3547
3792	3548
3793	3549
3794	3550
3795	3551
3796	3552
3797	3553
3798	3554
3799	3555
3800	3556
3801	3502
3802	3557
3803	3558
3804	3559
3805	3560
3806	3561
3807	3562
3808	3563
3809	3564
3810	3564
3811	3565
3812	3566
3813	3567
3814	3568
3815	3570
3816	3571
3817	3572
3818	3573
3819	3574
3820	3575
3821	3576
3822	3577
3823	
3824	837
3825	3578
3826	3579
3827	3580
3828	3581
3829	3582
3830	3583
3831	3584
3832	3585
3833	3586
3834	3587
3835	
3836	3588
"	5120
3837	3589
3838	3590
3839	3591
3840	3592
3841	3593
3842	3594
3843	3595
3844	3596
3845	3597
3846	3598+4160
3847	3598
3848	3599
3849	3600
3850	3601
3851	3602
3852	3604
3853	3605
3854	3606
3855	3607
3856	3608
3857	1492
3858	3609
3859	2322
3860	3610
3861	3611
3862	3612
3863	3613
3864	3614
3865	3615
3866	3616
3867	3617
3868	3618
3869	3619
3870	3620
3871	3618
3872	3621
3873	3622
3874	3623
3875	3624
3876	3625
3877	3626
3878	3626
3879	3627
3880	3628
3881	3629
3882	3627
3883	3633
3884	3630
3885	3631
3886	3632
3887	3633
3888	3634
3889	
3890	3635
3891	3636
3892	3637
3893	3638
3894	3644
3895	3645
3896	3639
3897	3639
3898	570
3899	3640
3900	3641
3901	3642
3902	3643
3903	3689
3904	3644
3905	3645
3906	3646
3907	3647
3908	3648
3909	3649
3910	3650
3911	3651
3912	3652
3913	3653
3914	3654
3915	3655
3916	2442
3917	3656
3918	3657
3919	3658
3920	
3921	3659
3922	3660
3923	3660
3924	3661
3925	3662
3926	3663
3927	3664
3928	3665
3929	3666
3930	3667
3931	3668
3932	3669
3933	3670
3934	3671
3935	3672
3936	
3937	3673
3938	3674
3939	3675
3940	3676
3941	3677
3942	3678
3943	3679
3944	3680
3945	3681
3946	3682
3947	3683
3948	3684
3949	3685
3950	3686
3951	3687
3952	3688
3953	3689
3954	3690
3955	3691
3956	3692
3957	3693
3958	3694
3959	3695
3960	3696
3961	3697
3962	3698
3963	3699
3964	3700
3965	3701
3966	3702
3967	3703
3968	3704
3969	3705
3970	3706
3971	3707
3972	3708
3973	3709
3974	3710
3975	3711
3976	3712
3977	3713
3978	3714
3979	3715
3980	3716
3981	3717
3982	3718
3983	3719
3984	3720
3985	3721
3986	3722
3987	3723
3988	3724
3989	3733
3990	3725
3991	3726
3992	3727
3993	3728
3994	3729
3995	3730
3996	3731
3997	3732
3998	3733
3999	3734
4000	
4001	3735
4002	3736
4003	3737
4004	3738
4005	3739
4006	3740
4007	3739+1065
4008	3741
4009	3742
4010	3743
4011	3744
4012	3745
4013	3746
4014	3747
4015	3748
"	3755
4016	3747
4017	3749
4018	3750
4019	3751
4020	3752
4021	3753
4022	3754
4023	3757
4024	3756
4025	3758
4026	3759
4027	3760
4028	3761
4029	3762
4030	3763
4031	3764
4032	3762
4033	3765
4034	3766
4035	1695
4036	3767
4037	3768
4038	3769
4039	3770
4040	3771
4041	3772
4042	3773
4043	3774
4044	3775
4045	3776
4046	3777
4047	3778
"	5023
"	5025
"	5026
"	5123
"	5124
"	5125
"	5126
"	5127
"	5128
"	5129
"	5130
4048	3779
4049	3780
4050	3781
4051	3782
4052	3783
4053	3784
4054	3785
4055	3786
4056	3787
4057	3788
4058	3789
4059	3790
4060	856
4061	3791
4062	3792
4063	3793
4064	
4065	3794
4066	3795
4067	3796
4068	3798
4069	3797
4070	3798
4071	3799
4072	3800
4073	
4074	3802
4075	3803
4076	697
4077	3804
4078	3805
4079	3806
4080	3807
4081	3808
4082	3809
4083	3810
4084	3811
4085	3812
4086	3813
4087	3814
4088	3812
4089	3815
4090	3816
4091	3817
4092	3818
4093	3819
4094	3820
4095	3821
4096	3822
4097	3823
4098	3824
4099	3825
4100	3824
4101	3826
4102	3827
4103	3828
4104	3829
4105	3830
4106	3829
4107	3830
4108	3831
4109	3832
4110	3833
4111	3834
4112	3835
4113	3826
4114	3837
4115	3836
4116	3837
4117	3838
4118	3839
4119	3840
4120	3841
4121	3842
4122	3843
4123	3844
4124	3845
4125	3846
4126	3847
4127	3848
4128	3849
4129	3851
4130	3850
4131	3851
4132	3852
4133	3853
4134	3854
4135	3855
4136	3856
4137	3857
4138	3858
4139	3859
4140	3860
4141	3861
4142	3862
4143	3863
4144	3864
4145	3865
4146	3866
4147	3867
4148	3868
4149	3869
4150	3869
4151	3870
4152	3871
4153	3872
4154	3873
4155	3874
4156	3875
4157	3876
4158	3877
4159	3878
4160	3879
4161	3880
4162	3881
4163	3882
4164	3883
4165	3884
4166	3885
4167	3885
4168	3886
4169	3887
4170	3888
4171	3889
4172	3890
4173	3913
4174	3891
4175	3892
4176	3893
4177	3894
4178	3895
4179	3896
4180	3897
4181	3898
4182	3899
4183	3900
4184	3901
4185	3902
4186	3903
4187	3904
4188	4368
4189	3905
4190	3906
4191	3907
4192	3908
4193	3909
4194	3910
4195	3911
4196	3912
4197	3913
4198	3913
4199	3914
4200	3915
4201	2710

G/K	STRONG
4202	3916
4203	3917
4204	4332
4205	3918
4206	3919
4207	3920
4208	3921
4209	3922
4210	3923
4211	3924
4212	4016
4213	3925
4214	3926
4215	3927
4216	3928
4217	3929
4218	3930
4219	3931
4220	3932
4221	3933
4222	3934
4223	3935
4224	3936
4225	3936
4226	3937
4227	3938
4228	3939
4229	3940
4230	3941
4231	3942
4232	3943
4233	3944
4234	3945
4235	3946
4236	3947
4237	3948
4238	5237
4239	3949
4240	3950
4241	3951
4242	3952
4243	3953
4244	3954
4245	3955
4246	3956
4247	3957
4248	3958
4249	3959
4250	3960
4251	3961
4252	3962
4253	3963
4254	3964
4255	3965
4256	3966
4257	3967
4258	3968
4259	3969
4260	3964
4261	3970
4262	3971
4263	3972
4264	3973
4265	3974
4266	3975
4267	3976
4268	3977
4269	3978
4270	3979
4271	3979
4272	3980
4273	3981
4274	3981
4275	3982
4276	4091
4277	3983
4278	3984
4279	3985
4280	3986
4281	3987
4282	3988
4283	3989
4284	3990
4285	
4286	3991
4287	3992
4288	3993
4289	3994
4290	3995
4291	3996
4292	3997
4293	3998
4294	3999
4295	4000
4296	4001
4297	4002
4298	4003
4299	4004
4300	4005
4301	4006
4302	4007
4303	
4304	4012+2087
4305	4008
4306	4009

G/K	STRONG
4307	4010
4308	4011
4309	4012
4310	4013
4311	4014
4312	681
4313	4015
4314	4016
4315	4017
4316	4018
4317	4019
4318	4020
4319	4021
4320	4022
4321	4023
4322	4024
4323	4024
4324	4025
4325	4026
4326	4027
4327	4776
4328	4028
4329	4029
4330	4030
4331	4031
4332	4032
4333	4033
4334	4034
4335	4035
4336	621
4337	4036
4338	4037
4339	4038
4340	4039
4341	4040
4342	4041
4343	4042
4344	4043
4345	4044
4346	4045
4347	4046
4348	4047
4349	
4350	
4351	4048
4352	4049
4353	4050
4354	4051
4355	4052
4356	4053
4357	4054
4358	4055
4359	4056
4360	4057
4361	4058
4362	4059
4363	4060
4364	4061
4365	4062
4366	4063
4367	4064
4368	4065
4369	4066
4370	4067
4371	4068
4372	4069
4373	4070
4374	4071
4375	4072
4376	4073
4377	4074
4378	4075
4379	4076
4380	4077
4381	4078
4382	4079
4383	4080
4384	4081
4385	4082
4386	4456
4387	4457
4388	4083
4389	4084
4390	4085
4391	4086
4392	3981
4393	4087
4394	4088
4395	4089
4396	4090
4397	4091
4398	4130
4399	4092
4400	4093
4401	4093
4402	4094
4403	4095
4404	4096
4405	4097
4406	4098
4407	4099
4408	4099
4409	4100
4410	4101
4411	4102

G/K	STRONG
4412	4103
4413	4104
4414	4105
4415	4106
4416	4107
4417	4107
4418	4108
4419	4109
4420	4110
4421	4111
4422	4112
4423	4113
4424	4114
4425	4115
4426	4116
4427	4117
4428	4120
4429	4121
4430	4122
4431	4123
4432	4124
4433	4125
4434	4126
4435	4127
4436	4128
4437	4129
4438	4131
4439	4132
4440	4133
4441	4134
4442	4135
4443	4136
4444	4137
4445	4138
4446	4139
4447	4140
4448	4141
4449	4142
4450	4143
4451	1708
4452	4144
4453	4144
4454	4145
4455	4146
4456	4147
4457	4148
4458	4149
4459	4150
4460	4151
4461	4152
4462	4153
4463	4154
4464	4155
4465	4156
4466	4157
4467	4217
4468	4158
4469	3537
4470	4159
4471	4169
4472	4160
4473	4161
4474	4162
4475	4163
4476	4164
4477	4165
4478	4166
4479	4167
4480	4168
4481	4169
4482	4170
4483	4171
4484	4172
4485	4173
4486	4174
4487	4175
4488	4176
4489	4177
4490	4178
4491	4179
4492	4184
4493	
4494	4180
4495	4181
4496	
4497	4182
4498	4118
"	4119
"	4183
4499	4184
4500	4185
4501	4186
4502	4187
4503	4188
4504	4189
4505	4190
"	4191
4506	4192
4507	4193
4508	4194
4509	5117
4510	4195
4511	4196
4512	4197
4513	4198

G/K	STRONG
4514	4199
4515	4197
4516	4200
4517	4201
4518	4202
4519	4203
4520	4204
4521	4205
4522	4206
4523	4207
4524	4208
4525	4209
4526	4210
4527	4211
4528	4210
4529	4212
4530	4213
4531	4214
4532	4215
4533	4216
4534	4217
4535	4458
4536	4219
4537	4218
4538	4220
4539	4221
4540	4222
4541	4223
4542	4224
4543	4225
4544	4226
4545	4227
4546	4228
4547	4229
4548	4230
4549	4231
4550	4232
4551	4233
4552	4234
4553	4235
4554	4236
4555	4237
4556	4238
4557	4236
4558	4239
4559	4240
4560	4241
4561	4242
4562	4246
4563	4243
4564	4244
4565	4245
4566	4246
4567	4247
4568	4248
4569	4249
4570	4250
4571	4251
4572	4252
4573	4249
4574	4253
4575	4254
4576	4255
4577	4256
4578	4257
4579	4258
4580	4259
4581	4260
4582	4261
4583	4262
4584	4263
4585	4263
4586	4264
4587	4265
4588	4266
4589	4267
4590	4268
4591	4269
4592	4270
4593	4271
4594	4272
4595	4273
4596	4274
4597	4302
4598	4276
4599	4278
4600	4279
4601	4281
4602	4282
4603	4283
4604	4284
4605	4285
4606	4286
4607	4287
4608	4288
4609	4289
4610	4290
4611	4406
4612	4407
4613	4291
4614	4292
4615	4293
4616	4294
4617	4284
4618	4295

G/K	STRONG
4619	4296
4620	4297
4621	4298
4622	4299
4623	4300
4624	4301
4625	4302
"	4277
"	4280
4626	4303
4627	4304
4628	4305
4629	4306
4630	4307
4631	4308
4632	4275
"	4308
4633	4309
4634	4310
4635	3962
4636	4311
4637	4312
4638	4313
4639	4314
4640	4315
4641	4316
4642	4317
4643	4318
4644	4319
4645	4319
4646	4320
4647	4355
4648	4321
4649	4321
4650	4322
4651	4323
4652	4317
4653	4324
4654	4317
4655	4325
4656	4326
4657	4327
4658	1929
4659	4328
4660	4329
4661	4330
4662	4331
4663	4332
4664	4333
4665	4334
4666	4335
4667	4336
4668	4337
4669	4338
4670	4339
4671	4286
4672	4340
4673	4341
4674	4342
4675	4343
4676	4344
4677	4345
4678	4346
4679	4347
4680	4346
4681	4347
4682	4348
4683	4349
4684	4350
4685	4351
4686	4352
4687	4353
4688	4354
4689	4355
4690	
4691	4356
4692	4356
4693	4357
4694	4358
4695	4359
4696	4360
4697	
4698	4361
4699	4362
4700	4363
4701	4364
4702	4365
4703	4366
4704	4366
4705	4367
4706	4368
4707	4369
4708	4370
4709	4371
4710	4372
4711	4373
4712	4374
4713	4375
4714	4376
4715	4377
4716	4370
4717	4378
4718	4379
4719	4380
4720	4381

G/K	STRONG
4721	4382
4722	4380
4723	4381
4724	4382
4725	4383
4726	4384
4727	4385
4728	4386
"	4387
4729	4388
4730	4389
4731	4390
4732	4391
4733	4392
4734	4393
4735	4394
4736	4395
4737	4396
4738	4397
4739	4398
4740	4399
4741	4400
4742	4401
4743	4402
4744	4403
4745	4404
4746	4405
4747	4406
4748	4407
4749	4408
4750	4409
4751	4410
4752	4411
4753	3144
4754	4412
4755	4413
4756	4414
4757	4415
4758	4416
4759	4412
4760	4417
4761	4418
4762	4419
4763	4420
4764	4421
4765	4422
4766	4423
4767	4424
4768	4425
4769	4426
4770	4427
4771	4428
4772	4429
4773	4430
4774	4431
4775	4432
4776	4433
4777	4434
4778	4435
4779	
4780	4436
4781	4437
4782	4438
4783	4439
4784	4440
4785	4441
4786	4442
4787	4443
4788	4444
4789	4445
4790	4446
4791	4447
4792	4448
4793	4449
4794	4450
4795	
4796	4451
4797	4453
4798	4454
4799	4455
4800	4456
4801	4457
4802	4459
4803	4452
"	4458
4804	
4805	4460
4806	4461
4807	4462
4808	4462
4809	4462
4810	4463
4811	4464
4812	4465
4813	
4814	4466
4815	4467
4816	4468
4817	911
4818	4481
4819	4469
4820	4470
4821	4471
4822	4472
4823	4473

G/K	STRONG
4824	4474
4825	4475
4826	4486
4827	4476
4828	4469
4829	4477
4830	4478
4831	4479
4832	4480
4833	4481
4834	4481
4835	4482
4836	4484
4837	4485
4838	4486
4839	4487
4840	4488
4841	4486
4842	4489
4843	4490
4844	4491
4845	4492
4846	4493
4847	4494
4848	4495
4849	4496
4850	4497
4851	4498
4852	4499
4853	4500
4854	4481
4855	4501
4856	4493
4857	4502
4858	4503
4859	4504
4860	4505
4861	4506
4862	4510
4863	4510
4864	4507
4865	4508
4866	4509
4867	4510
4868	4511
4869	4512
4870	4513
4871	4514
4872	4515
4873	4516
4874	4517
4875	
4876	4518
4877	4519
4878	4520
4879	4521
4880	4522
4881	4523
4882	4524
4883	4525
4884	4526
4885	4527
4886	4528
4887	4529
4888	4531
4889	4532
4890	4530
4891	4533
4892	4534
4893	4535
4894	4536
4895	4537
4896	4538
4897	4539
4898	4672
4899	4540
4900	4540
4901	4541
4902	4542
4903	4543
4904	4544
4905	4545
4906	
4907	4546
4908	4547
4909	4548
4910	4549
4911	4550
4912	4551
4913	4552
4914	4553
4915	4554
4916	4555
4917	4556
4918	4557
4919	4558
4920	4559
4921	4560
4922	4561
4923	4562
4924	4563
4925	4564
4926	4565
4927	4566
4928	4567

G/K	STRONG
4929	4568
4930	4569
4931	4570
4932	4572
4933	4573
4934	4574
4935	4575
4936	4576
4937	4577
4938	4577
4939	4578
4940	4579
4941	4580
4942	4581
4943	4582
4944	4583
4945	4584
4946	4584
4947	4585
4948	4586
4949	4587
4950	4588
4951	4562
4952	4562
4953	4589
4954	4590
4955	4591
4956	4592
4957	4593
4958	4594
4959	4612
4960	4595
4961	4596
4962	4597
4963	4598
4964	4599
4965	4600
4966	4525
4967	4601
4968	4602
4969	4603
4970	4604
4971	4603
4972	4605
4973	4606
4974	4607
4975	4608
4976	4609
4977	4610
4978	4611
4979	
4980	4612
4981	4613
4982	4614
4983	4615
4984	4616
4985	4617
4986	4596
4987	4577
4988	4618
4989	4621
4990	4619
4991	4620
4992	4621
4993	4965
4994	4622
4995	4623
4996	2977
4997	4624
4998	4625
4999	4626
5000	2469
5001	2469
5002	4627
5003	4628
5004	4629
5005	4630
5006	4631
5007	4632
5008	4633
5009	4634
5010	4635
5011	4636
5012	4637
5013	4638
5014	4639
5015	4640
5016	4641
5017	4642
5018	4643
5019	4644
5020	4645
5021	4646
5022	4647
5023	4648
5024	4649
5025	4650
5026	4651
5027	4652
5028	4653
5029	4654
5030	4655
5031	4656
5032	4657
5033	4658

G/K	STRONG
5034	4659
5035	4660
5036	4661
5037	4662
5038	4663
5039	4664
5040	4665
5041	3395
5042	3395
5043	4666
5044	4667
5045	4668
5046	4669
5047	4670
5048	4672
5049	4673
5050	4674
5051	4676
5052	4677
5053	4678
5054	4679
5055	4680
5056	4681
5057	4682
5058	4683
5059	4684
5060	4685
5061	4686
5062	4687
5063	4688
5064	4689
5065	4690
5066	4691
5067	4692
5068	4693
5069	4694
5070	4696
5071	4695
5072	4697
5073	4698
5074	4699
5075	4700
5076	4701
5077	4702
5078	4703
5079	4704
5080	4705
"	4706
"	4707
5081	4708
"	4709
5082	4710
5083	4711
5084	4712
5085	4713
5086	4955
5087	4714
5088	4715
5089	4716
5090	4717
5091	4718
5092	4719
5093	4720
5094	4721
5095	4722
5096	4723
5097	4724
5098	4725
5099	4726
5100	4727
5101	4728
5102	4729
5103	4730
5104	4731
5105	4732
5106	4733
5107	4734
5108	4736
5109	4735
5110	4737
5111	4738
5112	4739
5113	4740
5114	4741
5115	4746
5116	4742
5117	4743
5118	4744
5119	4745
5120	4746
5121	4770
5122	4747
5123	4748
5124	4749
5125	4750
5126	4751
5127	4752
5128	4753
5129	4754
5130	4755
5131	4756
5132	4757
5133	4758
5134	4759
5135	4759
5136	4760
5137	4761
5138	4762
5139	4763
5140	4764
5141	4765
5142	4766
5143	4766
5144	4767
5145	4768
5146	4769
5147	4770
5148	4571
"	4671
"	4675
"	4771
"	5209
"	5210
"	5213
"	5216
5149	4772
5150	4773
5151	4773
5152	4774
5153	4775
5154	4776
5155	4777
5156	4778
5157	4779
5158	4780
5159	4781
5160	4782
5161	4783
5162	
5163	4784
5164	4785
5165	4873
5166	4786
5167	4787
5168	4788
5169	4789
5170	4790
5171	4791
5172	4792
5173	4793
5174	4794
5175	4795
5176	4796
5177	4797
5178	4798
5179	4797
5180	4799
5181	2010
5182	4800
5183	4801
5184	4802
5185	4803
5186	4804
5187	4805
5188	4806
5189	4807
5190	4808
5191	4809
5192	4810
5193	4811
5194	4812
5195	4813
5196	4814
5197	4815
5198	4816
5199	4817
5200	4818
5201	4819
5202	4820
5203	4821
5204	4822
5205	4823
5206	4824
5207	4825
5208	4826
5209	4827
5210	4828
5211	4829
5212	4830
5213	4831
5214	4833
5215	4832
5216	4833
5217	4834
5218	4835
5219	4836
5220	4837
5221	4838
5222	4839
5223	4840
5224	4841
5225	4842
5226	
5227	4843
5228	4844
5229	4098
5230	4845
5231	4846
5232	4847
5233	4848
5234	4849
5235	4849
5236	4850
5237	4851
5238	4852
5239	4851
5240	4833
5241	4853
5242	4854
5243	4855
5244	4856
5245	4857
5246	4858
5247	4859
5248	4860
5249	4861
5250	4862
5251	4863
5252	4864
5253	4865
5254	4866
5255	4867
5256	4868
5257	4869
5258	4870
5259	4871
5260	4871
5261	4900
5262	4872
5263	4873
5264	4874
5265	4875
5266	
5267	4876
5268	4877
5269	4878
5270	4879
5271	4880
5272	4881
5273	4882
5274	4883
5275	4884
5276	4871
5277	4885
5278	4886
5279	4887
5280	4888
5281	4889
5282	4890
5283	4891
5284	4892
5285	
5286	
5287	4893
5288	4894
5289	4895
5290	4896
5291	4897
5292	4898
5293	4899
5294	
5295	4900
5296	4901
5297	4862+1985
5298	4934
5299	4902
5300	4903
5301	4904
5302	4905
5303	4906
5304	4907
5305	4908
5306	4909
5307	4910
5308	4911
5309	4912
5310	4913
5311	4914
5312	4915
5313	4916
5314	4917
5315	4918
5316	4919
5317	4920
5318	4921
5319	4921
5320	4920
5321	4922
5322	4923
5323	4894
5324	4924
5325	4925
5326	4926
5327	4927
5328	4894
5329	
5330	4928
5331	4952
5332	4929
5333	4930
5334	4931
5335	4932
5336	
5337	4933
5338	4934
5339	4935
5340	4936
5341	4937
5342	4938
5343	4939
5344	4940
5345	4941
5346	4795
5347	4942
5348	4943
5349	4944
5350	4945
5351	4949
5352	4946
5353	4947
5354	4948
5355	4949
5356	4949
5357	
5358	4950
5359	4951
5360	4952
5361	4953
5362	4954
5363	4955
5364	4956
5365	4957
5366	4958
5367	4959
5368	4960
5369	4961
5370	4962
5371	4963
5372	4964
5373	4965
5374	4966
5375	4967
5376	4968
5377	4969
5378	
5379	4970
5380	4971
5381	4972
5382	4973
5383	4974
5384	4974
5385	4975
5386	4976
5387	4977
5388	4978
5389	4979
5390	4980
5391	4981
5392	4982
5393	4983
5394	4984
5395	4985
5396	4986
5397	4987
5398	4988
5399	4989
5400	4990
5401	4991
5402	4992
5403	4992
5404	4993
5405	4994
5406	4995
5407	4996
5408	4997
5409	4998
5410	
5411	4999
5412	5000
5413	5001
5414	5002
5415	5003
5416	5004
5417	5005
5418	5006
5419	5007
5420	5008
5421	5009
5422	3569
5423	5010
5424	5011
5425	5012
5426	5391
5427	5013
5428	5014
5429	5015
5430	5016
5431	5017
5432	5018
5433	5019
5434	5020
5435	5021
5436	5022
5437	5024
5438	5027
5439	5028
5440	5029
5441	5030
"	5032
"	5033
5442	5031
5443	5034
5444	5035
"	5036
5445	5037
5446	5038
5447	5039
5448	5040
5449	5041
5450	5042
5451	5043
5452	5044
5453	
5454	5045
5455	5046
5456	5047
5457	5048
5458	5049
5459	5050
5460	5051
5461	5052
5462	5053
5463	5054
5464	5055
5465	5056
5466	5058
5467	5057
5468	5058
5469	5059
5470	5060
5471	
5472	5061
5473	5062
5474	5063
5475	5064
5476	5065
5477	5062
5478	5063
5479	5066
5480	5067
5481	5068
5482	5069
5483	5070
5484	5071
5485	5072
5486	5073
5487	5073
5488	5074
5489	5075
5490	5076
5491	5077
5492	5078
5493	5079
5494	5080
5495	5081
5496	5082
5497	
5498	5083
5499	5084
5500	5085
5501	5086
5502	5087
5503	5088
5504	5089
5505	5090
5506	5091
5507	5092
5508	5093
5509	5094
5510	5095
5511	5096
5512	5097
5513	5098
5514	5099
5515	5101
5516	5100
5517	2459
5518	5102
5519	5103
5520	5104
5521	5105
5522	5105
5523	5106
5524	5107
5525	5108
5526	5109
5527	5110
5528	5111
5529	5112
5530	5112
5531	5112
5532	5113
5533	5114
5534	5115
5535	5116
5536	5117
5537	5118
5538	5119
5539	5121
5540	5122
5541	3694
5542	5123
5543	5131
5544	5132
5545	5133
5546	5134
5547	5135
5548	5136
5549	5137
5550	5138
5551	5139
5552	5140
5553	5140+4999
5554	5141
5555	5142
5556	5143
5557	5169
5558	5144
5559	5145
5560	5146
5561	5147
5562	5148
5563	5149
5564	5150
5565	5151
5566	5152
5567	5153
5568	5154
5569	5154
5570	5155
5571	5156
5572	5157
5573	5158
5574	5159
5575	5160
5576	5161
5577	5162
5578	5159
5579	5163
5580	5164
5581	5165
5582	5166
5583	5167
5584	5168
5585	5169
5586	5170
5587	5171
5588	5172
5589	5173
5590	5174
5591	5175
5592	5176
5593	5177
5594	5178
5595	5179
5596	5179
5597	5180
5598	5181
5599	
5600	5182
5601	5183
5602	5184
5603	5185
5604	5186
5605	5187
5606	5188
5607	5189
5608	5190
5609	
5610	5191
5611	5192
5612	5193
5613	5194
5614	5195
5615	5196
5616	5197
5617	5198
5618	5199
5619	5200
5620	5201
5621	5202
5622	5203
5623	5204
5624	5205
5625	5206
5626	5207
5627	5208
5628	5211
5629	5212
5630	5214
5631	5215
5632	5217
5633	5218
5634	5219
5635	5220
5636	5221
5637	5222
5638	5223
5639	5224
"	5225
5640	5226
5641	5227
5642	5228
5643	5229
5644	5230
5645	5231
5646	784
5647	5232
5648	5233
5649	5234
5650	5235
5651	5236
5652	5228+1473
5653	5237
5654	5238
5655	5240
5656	5240
5657	5239
5658	5240
5659	5241
5660	5242
5661	5243
5662	5244
5663	5244
5664	5245
5665	5246
5666	5237
5667	5247
5668	5248
5669	5249
5670	5250
5671	5251
5672	5252
5673	5253
5674	5254
5675	5255
5676	5256
5677	5257
5678	5258
5679	5259
5680	5260
5681	5261
5682	5262
5683	5263
5684	5263
5685	5264
5686	5265
5687	5266
5688	5267
5689	5268
5690	5269
5691	5270
5692	
5693	5271
5694	5272
5695	5273
5696	5274
5697	2985
5698	2640
5699	5275
5700	5276
5701	5277
5702	5278
5703	5279
5704	5280
5705	5281
5706	5282
5707	5283
5708	5299
5709	5284
5710	5285
5711	5286
5712	5287
5713	5288
5714	5289
5715	5290
5716	5291
5717	5292
5718	5293
5719	5294
5720	5295
5721	5296
5722	5297
5723	5298
5724	5299
5725	5300
5726	
5727	5301
5728	5302
5729	5303
5730	5304
5731	5305
"	5306
5732	
5733	5307
5734	5308
5735	5309
5736	5310
5737	5311
5738	5312
5739	5313
5740	
5741	5314
5742	5341
5743	5316
5744	5317
5745	5318
5746	5319
5747	5320
5748	5321
5749	5322
5750	5323
5751	5324
5752	5325
5753	5326
5754	5327
5755	5328
5756	5329
5757	5330
5758	5331
5759	5332
5760	5331
5761	5333
5762	5334
5763	5335
5764	5336
5765	5337
5766	5338
5767	5339
5768	5340
5769	5341
5770	5342
5771	5343
5772	5344
5773	5345
5774	5346
5775	1310
5776	5347
5777	5348
5778	5349
5779	5350
5780	5351
5781	5352
5782	5353
5783	5354
5784	5355
5785	5356
5786	5357
5787	5358
5788	5359
5789	5360
5790	5361
5791	5362
5792	5363
5793	5364
5794	5365
5795	5366
5796	5367
5797	5368
5798	5369
5799	5370
5800	5371
5801	5372
5802	5373
5803	5374
5804	5375
5805	5376
5806	5377
5807	5378
5808	5379
5809	5380
5810	5381
5811	5382
5812	5383
5813	5384
5814	5385
5815	5386
5816	5387
5817	5388
5818	5389
5819	5390
5820	5391
5821	5392
5822	5417
5823	5393
5824	5394
5825	5395
5826	5396
5827	5397
5828	5399
5829	5398
5830	5399
5831	5400
5832	5401
5833	5402
5834	5403
5835	4949
5836	5404
5837	5405
5838	5406
5839	5407
5840	5408
5841	5409
5842	5410
5843	5411
5844	5412
5845	5413
5846	5414
5847	5415
5848	5416
5849	5417
5850	5418
5851	5419
5852	5420
5853	5421
5854	5422
5855	5423
5856	5424
5857	5425
5858	5426

G/K	STRONG
5859	5427
5860	5428
5861	5429
5862	5430
5863	5431
5864	5432
5865	5433
5866	5434
5867	5435
5868	
5869	5436
5870	5437
5871	5438
5872	5439
5873	5440
5874	5441
5875	5442
5876	5443
5877	5444
5878	5445
5879	5446
5880	5447
5881	5448
5882	5449
5883	5450
5884	5451
5885	5452
5886	5453
5887	5454
5888	5455
5889	5456
5890	5457
5891	5458
5892	5459
5893	5460
5894	5461
5895	5462
5896	
5897	5463
5898	5464
5899	5465
5900	5466
5901	5467
5902	5468
5903	5469
5904	5468
5905	5470
5906	5471
5907	5472
5908	5473
5909	5474
5910	5475
5911	5470
5912	5476
5913	5477
5914	5478
5915	5479
5916	5480
5917	5481
5918	5482
5919	5483
5920	5484
5921	5485
5922	5486
5923	5487
5924	5488
5925	5489
5926	5490
5927	5491
5928	5492
5929	5493
5930	5494
5931	5495
5932	5496
5933	5497
5934	5498
5935	5499
5936	5500
5937	5501
5938	5502
5939	5503
5940	5504
5941	5506
5942	5505
5943	5507
5944	5508
5945	5509
5946	5510
5947	5516
5948	5511
5949	5512
5950	5513
5951	5514
5952	5515
5953	5516
5954	5517
5955	5518
5956	5519
5957	5520
5958	5521
5959	5522
5960	5523
5961	5524
5962	5525
5963	5526
5964	5527
5965	5528
5966	5529
5967	5522
5968	5530
5969	5531
5970	5532
5971	5533
5972	5533
5973	5534
5974	5535
5975	5536
5976	5537
5977	5538
5978	5539
5979	5540
5980	5541
5981	5542
5982	5543
5983	5544
5984	5545
5985	5546
5986	5547
5987	5548
5988	5549
5989	5550
5990	5551
5991	5552
5992	5553
5993	5554
5994	5555
5995	5556
5996	5557
5997	5552
5998	5558
5999	5559
6000	5560
6001	5561
6002	5523
6003	5562
6004	5563
6005	5564
6006	5565
6007	
6008	5566
6009	
6010	5567
6011	5568
6012	5569
6013	5570
6014	5571
6015	5572
6016	5573
6017	5574
6018	5576
6019	5577
6020	5575
6021	5578
6022	5579
6023	5580
6024	5581
6025	5582
6026	5583
6027	5584
6028	5585
6029	5586
6030	5587
6031	5588
6032	5589
6033	5589
6034	5590
6035	5591
6036	5592
6037	5593
6038	5594
6039	5595
6040	5596
6041	5597
6042	5598
6043	5599
6044	5601
6045	5602
6046	5603
6047	5604
6048	5605
6049	5606
6050	5608
6051	5609
6052	5610
6053	5611
6054	5612
6055	5613
6056	5613+302
6057	5614
6058	5615
6059	5616
6060	5617
6061	5618
6062	5619
6063	5620
6064	5621
6065	5621
6066	5622
6067	5623
6068	5624

NOTES

NOTES

NOTES

NOTES

NOTES

NOTES

NOTES

NOTES

COLOPHON

The Portland Index database from which *The NIV Exhaustive Concordance* was extracted was produced by John R. Kohlenberger III and Edward W. Goodrick, using original software designed by Dennis Thomas and Barbara Perz for the Wang 2200 computer linked to a Control Data Plato terminal.

The database was edited and managed on AST Premium/286 and Premium/386 computers.

The Main Concordance was produced from the Portland Index with original software created by Dennis Thomas for the AT&T UnixPC. The Main Concordance was typeset by John R. Kohlenberger III, using Xerox Ventura Publisher 2.0 with the Professional Extension.

The Index of Articles Etc. was generated with WordCruncher 4.3 from the Electronic Text Corporation and was typeset by John R. Kohlenberger III, using WordPerfect 5.0 from the WordPerfect Corporation.

The Biblical-Language Index-Lexicons were produced from the Portland Index with original software created by Dennis Thomas for the AT&T UnixPC. These indexes were typeset by John R. Kohlenberger III, using WordPerfect 5.0. The Hebrew, Greek, and Aramaic fonts were generated with Scripture Fonts, a product of Zondervan Electronic Publishing.

Final camera-ready pages were produced on a Linotype Linotronic P200 at the facilities of Multnomah Graphics in Portland, Oregon.

The NIV Exhaustive Concordance was designed and edited by John R. Kohlenberger III, Ed M. van der Maas, Stanley N. Gundry, and Donald L. Potts.